W9-AMX-017

Lineberger Memorial
Library
Lutheran Theological Southern Seminary Columbia, S. C.

Encyclopedia of Appalachia

The Appalachian Region

Encyclopedia of Appalachia

Edited by
Rudy Abramson and Jean Haskell

Managing Editor
Jill Oxendine

Deputy Managing Editor
Troy Gowen

The University of Tennessee Press • Knoxville

First Edition.

Frontispiece: Map of Appalachia. Courtesy of the Appalachian Regional Commission.

This book is printed on acid-free paper.

Encyclopedia of Appalachia / edited by Rudy Abramson and Jean Haskell.— 1st ed.
p. cm.
Includes index.
ISBN 1-57233-456-8 (hardcover)
1. Appalachian Region—Encyclopedias.
I. Abramson, Rudy, 1937–
II. Haskell, Jean, 1947–
F106.E53 2006

To Students of Appalachia
Past, Present, Future

Major Sponsors

National Endowment for the Humanities

Appalachian Regional Commission
East Tennessee State University
(Center for Appalachian Studies and Services, College of Arts and Sciences,
Research and Sponsored Programs, Office of the Provost)

Tennessee Higher Education Commission

Mooneyhan Family Foundation, Inc.

State of Tennessee

State of Ohio

Tennessee Valley Authority

Humanities Tennessee

University of Tennessee Press

K-VA-T Food Stores, Inc.

Barnes & Noble College Bookstores, Inc.

Federal Express Corporation

ARAMARK

Arch Coal, Inc.

Knoxville News Sentinel

Lloyd E. Cotsen

Dr. and Mrs. Roy S. Nicks

Lee Smith

Jane B. Stephenson

Additional Supporters

Mr. and Mrs. James W. Deaton, Kathryn L. Greenspan, Barbara W. Hahn, Jean Haskell, Patricia G. Lane, Mr. and Mrs. John L. Lebert, Alice R. Manicur, Mary Jane Mattern, Jean Ritchie and George Pickow, Mr. and Mrs. Joseph C. Poore, Ronald V. Rash, Gayle E. Russell, Ben Sharfstein

Encyclopedia of Appalachia

Encyclopedia Staff

COEDITORS

Rudy Abramson and Jean Haskell

MANAGING EDITOR

Jill Oxendine

DEPUTY MANAGING EDITOR

Troy Gowen

ASSOCIATE EDITORS

Theresa Lloyd　　Ted Olson

STAFF

PHOTO EDITOR	Susan Grove-DeJarnett
ASSISTANT EDITORS	Nancy Fischman, Ajay Kalra, Charles Moore, and Emily Satterwhite
RESEARCHERS	Phyllis Crain, Clara Hasbrouck, and Ned L. Irwin
EDITORIAL ASSISTANTS	Lee Phillips, Roberta Hissey, and Adam Sanders
COPYEDITOR	Hugh Davis

SECTION EDITORS

The Landscape

GEOLOGY	Don W. Byerly, University of Tennessee John J. Renton, West Virginia University
ECOLOGY	George Constantz, Canaan Valley Institute
ENVIRONMENT	Donald E. Davis, Dalton State College Kevin E. O'Donnell, East Tennessee State University

The People

FAMILY AND COMMUNITY	Shirley L. Stewart Burns, West Virginia University Shaunna L. Scott, University of Kentucky Deborah J. Thompson, University of Kentucky
IMAGES AND ICONS	George Brosi, Berea Kentucky
RACE, ETHNICITY, AND IDENTITY	Roberta M. Campbell, University of Cincinnati
SETTLEMENT AND MIGRATION	Sheila R. Phipps, Appalachian State University
URBAN APPALACHIAN EXPERIENCE	Michael E. Maloney, Michael Maloney and Associates Phillip J. Obermiller, Cincinnati, Ohio

Work and the Economy

AGRICULTURE	Michael Best, Berea, Kentucky Curtis W. Wood, Western Carolina University

Contents

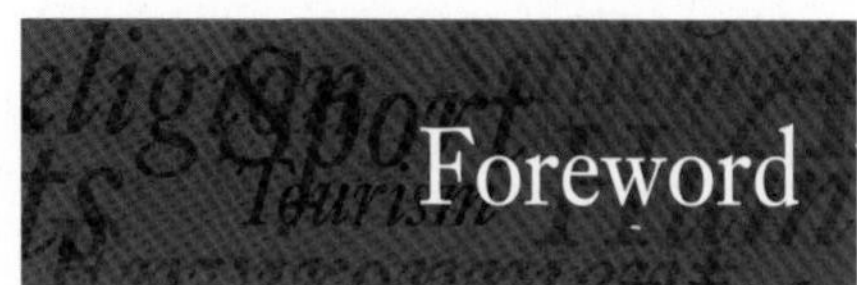

Foreword

The *Encyclopedia of Appalachia* is truly a feast of information about its region. This volume provides a remarkably detailed portrait of a landscape that runs from New York to Mississippi. Its diverse articles describe how Appalachia has shaped each generation of its people. The region has been home to bitter, sometimes violent labor disputes in places such as "bloody" Harlan County, Kentucky. Known for the fiercely independent spirit of its people, parts of southern Appalachia refused to join the Confederate cause and instead provided a haven for blacks who fled slavery and whites who fled the Civil War.

The *Encyclopedia* is a welcome resource for readers who seek a deeper understanding of our nation's rich history and culture. These readers can take comfort in the growing number of encyclopedias that treat American regions, states, and cities. This fine study of Appalachia joins ranks with other regional encyclopedias on the Great Plains, the Midwest, New England, the South, and the West. State encyclopedias are also being compiled throughout the nation, and those in the American South include Alabama, Georgia, Mississippi, North Carolina, South Carolina, and Texas. Still other encyclopedias feature American cities such as New York and Chicago.

As each generation seeks to understand what it means to be an American, place is a touchstone for its journey. These encyclopedias—both print and digital—are important links in a newly formed chain of resources on American history and culture that were developed with support from the National Endowment for the Humanities. Together they honor and celebrate American people through thoughtful portraits of their homes.

The novelist Lee Smith grew up in the "steep hills and dark hollers" of southwest Virginia, the Appalachian area in which she set her novel *Oral History*. Honoring her father's statement "I need a mountain to rest my eyes against," Smith grounds her fiction within these familiar mountains and stands among generations of writers, artists, musicians, and scholars who have chronicled their Appalachian worlds. The *Encyclopedia of Appalachia* is such a chronicle, intended to shine a beacon of understanding on its region.

In editing this encyclopedia, Rudy Abramson and Jean Haskell cast a wide net across Appalachian history and culture, and they did their work well, creating an essential resource about a people and a place that are at the heart of the American experience. This fine reference work will transform how future generations understand Appalachia. The region's singers, storytellers, and artists are now joined with its political, business, and educational leaders in a volume that tells a powerful tale about the enduring value of their worlds.

—William Ferris,
Joel R. Williamson Eminent Professor of History,
University of North Carolina, and *Coeditor, Encyclopedia of Southern Culture*

An Appreciation

People I know always seem surprised that I love West Virginia. I was born there in 1950, in Piedmont, a town with a population of 2,565 that was nestled against a wall of mountains on the banks of the Potomac River. It was beautiful, and still is, although time, the economy, and migration away from it by people like me have left it quaintly crumbling at best, starkly desolate at worst.

But I still love it. West Virginia nurtured me: this self-contained place taught me "how to be" in the wider world which I would go on to experience in my adult life. My friends' surprise comes, I think, from the fact that Piedmont is Appalachia and part of Appalachia is in the Deep South, and the Deep South of the 1950s has come to be known as not a very good place to be if you happened to be black (colored is what we called it then).

It's true: whites and blacks were slow to change in West Virginia, slow to move away from the comfortable, closed world we knew to the bigger world promised by integration. But we did change, and West Virginia changed, and the great stretch of the Appalachian land itself took on the character of this change. You can see it everywhere, in the stubborn mills that still stand in spite of decades of idleness, and in the vital commercial centers, college towns, and shiny new homes that have come to sustain a new generation.

The *Encyclopedia of Appalachia* lays out for everyone else what we who grew up there have always known. Appalachia is a rich and beautiful land steeped in tradition and open to change. It is home to countless storytellers and stories without end. Both its lushness and its rockiness teach us to make our way in the world, but Appalachia never leaves us.

—Henry Louis Gates Jr.,
W. E. B. Du Bois Professor of the Humanities and
Chair of the Department of African and African American Studies,
Harvard University

Acknowledgments

HAVING TAKEN TEN YEARS TO COMPLETE, THE *ENCYCLOPEDIA OF APPALACHIA* IS indebted to a host of individuals and organizations without whom the book would never have come to fruition. Some provided invaluable advice, encouragement, and copious amounts of time, wisdom, and insight, not to mention crucial funding, while others challenged, questioned, and debated. All were significant in making this a better piece of work.

John Stephenson, president of Berea College and one of the founders of the Appalachian studies movement, was an inspirational figure. As mentor and friend of the editors and one who was contemplating this work himself at the time of his death, John did much to shape thinking about the *Encyclopedia* and inspire resolve to get it done. Just two years before the project began, he gave a speech at Berea College titled "Appalachian Studies and the Third Millennium," in which he expressed pleasure that information and research about the region were making their way into mainstream thinking. "Our stuff is seeping out from under the woodwork," he said, "and beginning to make a noticeable mess on the floor." This seepage became a torrent of information in the *Encyclopedia*.

The editors wish to thank all of the agencies, foundations, companies, and individuals who provided funding for this project. The Appalachian Regional Commission (ARC) in Washington, D.C., not only funded the project at its most critical moments but also helped sustain it through the personal interest of its staff and their leadership. We especially thank Federal Co-Chair Jesse White and his successor, Anne Pope, Executive Director Tom Hunter, and Chief Economist Greg Bishak, who provided frequent support and advice. Numerous other members of the ARC staff assisted with information, guidance, and enthusiastic concern, including Guy Land, John Cartwright, Edward Terry, Duane Debruyne, Henry King, Summer Rutherford, Molly Curtin DeMarcellus, Jeffrey Schwartz, Pam Lautman, and Dan Neff.

The National Endowment for the Humanities (NEH) also provided major funding and helpful guidance for the endeavor. The organization's chairman, William Ferris, knew firsthand the challenges and pitfalls of producing a regional encyclopedia since he had been coeditor of the acclaimed *Encyclopedia of Southern Culture*. We are also grateful to NEH program officer Joseph Herring for his cheerful and unfailing assistance.

The project also received vital funding from the University of Tennessee Press, East Tennessee State University, Tennessee Valley Authority, Federal Express, Barnes and Noble, the State of Ohio, the State of Tennessee, K-VA-T Foods, the Mooneyhan Family Foundation, the Tennessee Humanities Council, and ARAMARK. Several individuals, including Lloyd Cotsen, Lee Smith, Jean Ritchie, Roy Nicks, Alice Manicur, Ben Sharfstein, and Jane Stephenson, made donations as well.

In the initial stages of the project, we brought together groups of interested persons in each Appalachian state to discuss what topics the *Encyclopedia* should contain. We are particularly grateful to the state coordinators—Fred Armstrong, Sandra Barney, Roger Dow, Ron Eller, Betty Fine, Bill Foster, John Inscoe, Gordon McKinney, Phillip Obermiller, and Kathleen Wilson—who organized these meetings and gathered hundreds of ideas that were later integrated into entry lists for the sections.

Our advisory and editorial boards, listed at the beginning of this volume, contributed both expertise and credibility. The advisory board, all either Appalachian by place of birth or residence, lent their good names to the reputation of the project and gave more tangible resources as well. Members of the editorial board provided advice on content, organization, and emphasis, and some also served as section editors and writers.

Of all the contributors to the project, the editors for the thirty sections accepted the heaviest responsibility. They helped conceptualize topics, selected writers, pushed and prodded to get work done, read manuscripts and proofs, and wrote overview essays, all while pursuing their full-time employment, most of them in academic institutions. Their work reflects commitment to the region that John Stephenson would have applauded.

East Tennessee State University (ETSU), taking its commitment to the Appalachian region as a special calling in teaching, research, and service, contributed to the project in innumerable ways. Supportive members of the faculty and staff are too numerous to mention, but special thanks must be extended to Paul Stanton, ETSU's president; Bert Bach, vice-president for academic affairs and provost; Michael Woodruff, assistant provost (and his staff); ETSU's offices of University Advancement and University Relations; the deans of the College of Arts and Sciences over the ten years (John Ostheimer, Don Johnson, Rebecca Pyles, and Gordon Anderson); and a host of faculty and staff colleagues.

From beginning to end, graduate and undergraduate student workers were involved in every phase of the work. Among those deserving special mention are Rebecca Adkins, Declan Fahy, Laura Tidwell, Colleen Carr, Curtis Light, Ryan Goodman, Abraham Spear, Jamee Roberts, Roy Andrade, Susan Mabe, Andre Pratt, Laura McNeese, John King, James Goodman, Ajay Kalra, Leslie Burrell, Benjamin Jenkinson, Daniel Boner, Brandon Lambert, Matthew Ball, Brittany Burke, Reese Stansberry, Sändra Henson, and Adam Sanders.

As publisher, the *Encyclopedia* is fortunate to have the University of Tennessee Press. Executive Director Jennifer Siler, Managing Editor Stan Ivester, designers Cheryl Carrington and Barbara Karwhite, and copyeditor Hugh Davis brought not only professional commitment and dedication but a wealth of patience and congeniality to the effort.

Other supporters ranged from political leaders such as U.S. Senators Robert C. Byrd and Lamar Alexander and Representative Bill Jenkins to community friends such as the First Tennessee Development District and the Birthplace of Country Music Alliance.

With technology rapidly changing as the book was written and edited, the editors were privileged to have daily assistance from East Tennessee State University's Office of Information Technology and computer consultants, including David King, Robb Clevenger, and David Cortner.

In times of special editing need, Fred Alsop, Jack Higgs, Jack Hurst, John Renton, Robert S. Turner, and others provided assistance. We also wish to thank Rebecca Tolley-Stokes, Marie Jones, Kathy Campbell, Cliff Boyd, Kim O'Connor,

Ed Speer, David Newhall, and others who accepted many writing assignments on short notice.

The *Encyclopedia of Appalachia* was undertaken as a project of the Center for Appalachian Studies and Services at East Tennessee State University, a Tennessee Center of Excellence. Many staff and faculty members at the center, which is composed of the Regional Resources Institute (with programs in Appalachian Studies; Appalachian, Scottish, and Irish Studies; and Bluegrass, Country, and Old Time Music), the B. Carroll Reece Museum, and the Archives of Appalachia, have contributed in ways large and small. For their many contributions, the editors especially thank Rebecca Grindstaff, Rachel Henry, Charles Moore, Jane Woodside, Nancy Fischman, Penelope Lane, Georgia Greer, Ned Irwin, Amy Barnum, Norma Myers, Blair White, Jack Tottle, Raymond McLain, Ted Olson, and Roberta Herrin.

Staff members of the *Encyclopedia of Appalachia* project, whose commitment, professionalism, and friendship held the project together, include associate editors Theresa Lloyd and Ted Olson; assistant editors Nancy Fischman, Ajay Kalra, Charles Moore, and Emily Satterwhite; photo editor Susan Grove-DeJarnett; fact-checkers Clara Hasbrouck, Phyllis Crain, and Ned Irwin; editorial assistants Lee Phillips, Roberta Hissey, and Adam Sanders; and indexer Alexa Selph.

The *Encyclopedia's* deputy managing editor, Troy Gowen, came on board later in the project but contributed immeasurably to helping us achieve the final product. We thank him not only for his writing and editing but also for his wit, wisdom, and leadership.

Finally, this work, in this form, would not exist without the competence, dedication, incomparable patience and diplomacy of Managing Editor Jill Oxendine. Her work fits perfectly Appalachian writer-humorist Loyal Jones's description of Appalachian scholars "chasing hats in high wind and getting them on the right heads." Jill chased hats in light breezes and howling gusts and still managed to get them on straight. Those who will use the *Encyclopedia of Appalachia* years hence should know that it is in significant measure Jill Oxendine's legacy to her native Appalachia.

—Rudy Abramson and Jean Haskell,
Coeditors

Guide for Readers

CONTENT FOR THE *ENCYCLOPEDIA OF APPALACHIA* IS ARRANGED UNDER FIVE MAJOR divisions: "The Landscape," "The People," "Work and the Economy," "Cultural Traditions," and "Institutions." Thirty sections are included under these divisions. An overview essay opens each section, followed by a series of alphabetically arranged entries. Readers are urged to consult the index, as well as the table of contents, in locating articles.

Articles contain cross-references to related articles within the same section and to articles in other sections. When the cross-reference is to an article or overview essay in the same section, only the article's title is listed. If the cross-reference is to an overview essay or to an article in a different section, the title of the article is shown followed by the section's name enclosed in parentheses. The following example is a cross-reference to an article in another section:

See also: COMBS, BERT (GOVERNMENT).

Every effort was made to update data as articles were compiled. However, some changes, such as contributors' affiliations or the updating of biographical information, could not be made after the book went to press.

Introduction

For as long as Appalachia has been thought of as a distinct part of the United States, it has been commonly perceived as a place with social and economic problems as great as the extraordinary natural wealth and diversity of the complex and weathered mountain system which gives the region its name. In the twenty-first century, as it has been for a hundred years, the region continues to be laden with mythology, subjected to recurring debate, and held up as one of America's enduring social and economic "problems." Beginning in the late nineteenth century, novelists, educators, and big-city journalists created a dominant image of the central Appalachians as a hinterland populated by a backward people left behind, more or less suspended in time as the rest of America modernized and prospered.

Over the years, the region has been periodically "rediscovered"—and its mythology reinforced—by home missionaries, charitable foundations, social workers, politicians, muckrakers, government officials, and other "outsiders" intent upon "helping" in one way or another.

In some instances, mountain folk were romanticized as thoroughly noble pioneers, in others ridiculed as inbred, violent, and barely civilized, but in any case socially and physically isolated from the rest of America and different from other Americans. In a dismissive commentary on the region, noted English historian Arnold J. Toynbee provided a toehold for those who would later attribute Appalachia's massively publicized economic and social deficits to a "culture of poverty" in which the inhabitants themselves were deemed to be substantially culpable. "The modern Appalachian has . . . failed to hold his ground and has gone downhill in a most disconcerting fashion," Toynbee wrote in a 1947 abridgment of his epic work *A Study of History*. "In fact," he continued, "the Appalachian 'mountain people' today are no better than barbarians. They have relapsed into illiteracy and witchcraft. They suffer from poverty, squalor and ill health. They are the American counterparts of the latter day White barbarians of the Old World—Rifis, Albanians, Kurds, Pathans and Hairy Ainus; but, whereas these latter are belated survivals of an ancient barbarism, the Appalachians present the melancholy spectacle of a people who have acquired civilization and then lost it." No wonder stalwart mountaineers' concern over stereotypes and negative images often borders on obsession even now.

Federal intervention in the Appalachian region, focusing on the economy, spanned most of the twentieth century, beginning with the creation of national forests after industrial logging had denuded vast areas of the mountains, leaving naked slopes cut by gullies and blackened by brush fires. This involvement grew and accelerated with a rush of 1930s New Deal initiatives, most conspicuously the Tennessee Valley Authority, and it expanded with the War on Poverty, creation of the Appalachian Regional Commission (ARC), and the rise of other programs during the 1960s and 1970s, when central Appalachia became nationally synonymous with rural poverty and all of its consequences.

Notwithstanding the more recent decline of social activism in government policy, special federal assistance continues to be provided to the region through numerous agencies, and the region still has its own dedicated federal-state bureaucracy in the ARC. The poverty stereotype persists. In the heart of the region, employment in the coal-mining industry has declined to a fraction of its heyday, and manufacturing languishes in urban centers. Now populated by some 23 million people, Appalachia still struggles to capitalize on its natural resources in a sustainable fashion.

The region remains a place of stunning natural and cultural extremes, though in the latter third of the twentieth century, it moved closer to the nation's social and economic mainstream. Like the rest of the country, Appalachia was transformed by modern technologies, albeit in ways that were often contradictory, and in certain ways painful, unwelcome, and even destructive. While rural mountain areas were swept out of isolation by modern roads and communications, once thriving coal-mining communities became ghost towns. Suburbs, retirement enclaves, and vacation retreats sprouted, but traditional farms were abandoned; local retailers failed and Main Streets declined as franchises and outsized chain stores sprang up along bypass roads and highway interchanges in county seats across rural Appalachia. And as smokestack industries declined, urban centers and manufacturing capitals such as Pittsburgh and Birmingham faced the imperative of reinventing themselves.

The pace and breadth of change has deepened interest in scholarly study of Appalachia's history and led to systematic deconstruction of the mythical mountain frontier, the forces that have changed it, and conflicting perceptions—harbored by both "insiders" and "outsiders"—of the past, present, and future. What has emerged in the light of continuing research is a more complex cultural tapestry incorporating images of a region historically engaged with the national economy.

In 1978, as the Appalachian studies movement came into its own, historian Henry D. Shapiro suggested that the Appalachia of the late nineteenth and early twentieth centuries was, rather than a distinctive region of the country, largely an idea created by writers from the urban North. In the academic community, Shapiro's landmark work *Appalachia on Our Mind: The Southern Mountains and Mountaineers in the American Consciousness, 1870–1920* resonated for years after its publication, inspiring continuing efforts to define the region and sort out the nuances of mythology and reality in its history.

The *Encyclopedia of Appalachia* embraces the notion of a region that, rather than an invention or a concept, is a real place with a distinctive history, people, and culture—though often redefined, frequently remapped, and exhaustively debated. The volume reflects a perspective expressed by David E. Whisnant, a keen observer of Appalachian mythology, culture, and institutions, who once remarked that the region "long characterized by a single stereotype is actually almost too diverse to generalize about at all."

Wherefore Appalachia?

Of all of America's distinctive regions, Appalachia has perhaps the most complex history, for as much as it is a geographical entity, it is indeed a cultural concept constantly evolving even as its borders' geographical boundaries are redrawn. In unconnected and changing political and historical frameworks, the region's maps have changed to suit myriad purposes. While all of the various efforts to define the region acknowledge the importance of the Appalachian Mountains, none of them adopt physiography or topography as the sole determinant of boundaries. In the case of other identifiable regions of the country, state lines help with geographical definitions, but in the instance of Appalachia, state boundaries are of no use in defining either the geographic or cultural outlines of the region. Thus the limits of Appalachia are a subject of recurring rumination, though in every conception the region stretches from the Deep South far beyond the Mason-Dixon Line into the North, assuring that both its political and cultural histories are as complex as its landscape.

The *Encyclopedia* broadly adopts the definition of Appalachia used by the federal government, more specifically the Appalachian Regional Commission. In 2005 the region encompassed 410 counties in portions of thirteen states. Amended several times over the years, the map was first codified in 1965 when Congress passed the Appalachian Regional Development Act, creating the ARC to work with eleven Appalachian states in promoting economic development. With economic need as the criterion, lawmakers fashioned an Appalachia composed of 360 upland counties, including the whole of West Virginia and areas more or less contiguous with the mountains in Alabama, Georgia, Kentucky, Maryland, Ohio, Pennsylvania, Tennessee, Virginia, and the Carolinas.

Before the end of the year, thirteen New York counties were added, and in 1967 twenty Mississippi counties were included, expanding Appalachia into a total of thirteen states. Further additions came in 1990, 1991, 1998, and 2002, bringing the total to 410 counties, spread as far west as the longitude of Louisville, Kentucky, southwest almost to the Mississippi River Delta, and south to the vicinity of Montgomery, Alabama. Further expansion appeared to be on the way, with preliminary congressional approval (in 2004) of legislation to add twelve more counties, further expanding Appalachian Tennessee, Virginia, Kentucky, and Ohio.

At the beginning, as ever since, the federal map reflected the exigencies of congressional politics as much as economic need, geography, or culture. Many inhabitants of Pennsylvania and New York were surprised to learn that the government in Washington considered them Appalachians, and some were opposed to the very idea. Newly elected New York Senator Robert F. Kennedy, who had taken up a deep interest in the region during his brother's 1960 presidential campaign, led the effort to make the southern tier counties of his adopted state part of the federal region. Similarly, Mississippi was included largely due to the influence of Representative Jamie Whitten, a powerful member of the House Appropriations Committee. On the other hand, a number of Virginia mountain counties that were Appalachian by any standard except political were left out because their representative, Richard H. Poff, was opposed to the 1965 bill.

While legend says that Hernando de Soto's 1539–40 expedition into the southern highlands gave the Appalachians a name the explorers had picked up from the Apalachee Indians in present day northern Florida, the first known map with the word *Apalachen* associated with a depiction of mountains appeared in 1562. It was not until after the Revolutionary War that *Appalachian* came to refer to the entire system of mountains in the eastern United States. The notion of the Appalachia as a distinct region developed only toward the end of the nineteenth century.

In the late 1890s, William Goodell Frost, president of Berea College in Kentucky, and geologist C. Willard Hayes outlined a region in parts of eight states. What Frost called "Appalachian America" included portions of the Piedmont Plateau, the Tennessee Valley, the Blue Ridge Mountains, and the Cumberland Plateau. Thereafter, several other Appalachias, based in varying degrees upon history, cultural artifacts, the economy, and physiography, were identified before Congress finally instituted its version heavily based upon economic need. In his 1913 book *Our Southern Highlanders*, Horace Kephart centered an Appalachian region in the Great Smoky and Unaka Mountains along the Tennessee–North Carolina border. In 1921 John C. Campbell's landmark *The Southern Highlander and His Homeland* outlined a far more expansive region of 254 counties in nine states. Fourteen years later, a study by the United States Department of Agriculture's Bureau of Agricultural Economics offered one concept of a 206-county region in six states and another reaching into three additional states.

Since 1938, continuing efforts to define the region have had the benefit of a remarkable description of the mountain system's physiography, confirmed in the Space Age by a variety of orbiting sensors. In his *Physiography of the Eastern United States* (1938), University of Cincinnati geologist Nevin M. Fenneman placed the Appalachians into four distinct provinces—from west to east, the Appalachian Plateau extending from western New York to northern Georgia; the Ridge and Valley running from New York to Georgia; the Blue Ridge, extending from Pennsylvania to northern Georgia; and the Piedmont, the low hills between the Blue Ridge and the coastal plain of the Atlantic seaboard.

To put the finest point on limits of the mountain system, some definitions have gone so far as to identify specific features as its beginning and/or end. Naturalist Scott Weidensaul and others have, for example, labeled the modest 2,407-foot Cheaha Mountain in northeastern Alabama as the southernmost peak of the Appalachians, and Belle Isle, a fifteen-square-mile granite island rising 700 feet above the North Atlantic between Newfoundland and Labrador as the northern terminus.

Still, even considering decades of work by historians, social scientists, natural scientists, writers, and government agencies, the perception of Appalachia perhaps best known to the world is the one associated with the Appalachian Trail, a 2,174-mile footpath extending through the highlands from Springer Mountain in north Georgia to Mount Katahdin in north-central Maine. Conceived in 1921 by naturalist and regional planner Benton MacKaye, the trail is used by as many as four million hikers each year.

The widely differing maps have encouraged efforts to incorporate earlier iterations into a distinctive region more clearly united by history, culture, economy, and topography. In 1984 University of Kentucky geographers Karl B. Raitz and Richard Ulack defined an Appalachia of 445 counties in thirteen states. While leaving out all of the Mississippi counties included in the federal definition, they added two counties in northwestern New Jersey and expanded the boundary to the south and east to include the urban areas around Columbia, South Carolina; Raleigh, North Carolina; Richmond, Virginia; and Atlanta, Georgia. Historian John Alexander Williams similarly drew upon six previous definitions to produce a "consensus" region and then a "core" region made up of counties found in all of the major maps previously drawn. The "core" region eliminated all counties in Alabama, Mississippi, South Carolina, Maryland, New York, and Pennsylvania, plus two in Georgia, six in Kentucky, four in North Carolina, five in Tennessee, nine in Virginia, and nine in West Virginia, leaving a core of only 164 highland counties in six states.

While the Appalachia created by Congress in 1965 was expanded southward by powerful southerners in Congress, it also recognized a northern Appalachia that had been excluded from the earlier more restrictive concepts. By including all of western Pennsylvania and angling across the state to its northeastern corner, the federal boundary embraced not only Pittsburgh, capital of the nineteenth-century industrial transformation fueled by Appalachian resources, but a "hearth place" of American culture and a wellspring of westward migration. As Williams noted in his widely read *Appalachia: A History* (2002), it was "from Pennsylvania that industrializing forces spread southward during the nineteenth century, and it was there that socioeconomic issues raised by de-industrialization emerged to make the entire region a focus of policy concern in the twentieth."

Accepting the broad, federally defined Appalachia as its universe, and sometimes looking beyond it, the *Encyclopedia of Appalachia* also reflects the reality of a "core" region where the affinity of history, culture, the economy, and the mountain land is strongest. Accordingly, the volume includes more entries concerning northern Georgia, eastern Kentucky, western North Carolina, east Tennessee, southwestern Virginia, and West Virginia. On the other hand, it recognizes the importance of natural history, natural resources, topography, and landscape, particularly in its "Geology," "Ecology," and "Environment" sections, which tend to look at the Appalachian Mountains rather than the Appalachian region enshrined in federal statutes or popular culture.

The Modern Place

All things considered, Appalachia changed more profoundly in the late twentieth century than in any comparable period in its history, although the statistical evidence is sometimes deceptive as well as revealing. In a span of thirty years following passage of the Appalachian Development Act and creation of the Appalachian Regional Commission, the poverty rate of the politically defined region was cut in half as the economy diversified, employment increased, educational attainment rose, transportation infrastructure modernized, and health care and housing improved. The "plumbing gap" and the famed Appalachian outhouse cauterized in the negative regional stereotype went the way of the one-room schoolhouse, replaced by "manufactured housing" as the new emblem of regional habitation.

Three decades after Washington set out to lift poverty from Appalachia, West Virginia economist Andrew M. Isserman found the region wholly different from the one the President's Appalachian Regional Commission in 1964 broadly described as rural and impoverished, with a declining population and deficits in education, income, and standards of living. In a report for the Appalachian Regional Commission based on findings of the 1990 census, Isserman concluded:

> The characterization of Appalachia promulgated by the Report of the President's Appalachian Regional Commission in 1964 is of limited validity today. At the time it reinforced the popular image of Appalachia—low income, high poverty, limited education, poor living standards, job deficits, high unemployment, outmigration, stagnation, and decline. Today those conditions do not characterize the region as a whole. Current data support neither the 1964 characterization of Appalachia as a region apart statistically nor the 1964 assertion that Appalachians lack fully active membership in the American society. Instead, the statistics show a region that has improved greatly, still lags the nation on some broad indicators, and still contains some of the worst off counties in the nation.

During the 1990s, the trends observed by Isserman continued. The region's population increased by 9 percent, urbanization accelerated, the population aged, and the service-oriented economy continued to grow as jobs in manufacturing, mining, forestry, and agriculture waned.

While revealing, regional economic statistics are also deceptive, for they obscure extremes of life in modern Appalachia, just as the political definition of the region muddies perceptions of a part of America unified by history, culture, ecology, and landscape.

Like the rest of the country, Appalachia has seen its prosperity concentrated in urban areas, not only within the region but within the suburbs stretching into the region from cities such as Atlanta, Birmingham, Winston-Salem, Lexington, Cincinnati, Columbus, Cleveland, and even Washington, D.C. Atlanta, as well as any city in America, exemplified the megalopolis of the late twentieth and early twenty-first centuries, its northern sprawl precipitating rapid development in Appalachian north Georgia, causing planners to contemplate a monorail rail link between Atlanta's Hartsfield International Airport and Chattanooga.

And also like the rest of America, Appalachia saw its rural areas continue to struggle; its neediest rural mountain counties, long exploited for their coal and timber, remained in some instances starkly poor.

Rather than regionwide, the economic dynamism of late-twentieth-century Appalachia was generally concentrated in the South, where the rate of growth exceeded that of the rest of the country. Not coincidentally, long before the Appalachian Development Act and late-twentieth-century regional initiatives, southern Appalachia had already been the beneficiary of the most audacious of all federally funded regional development projects—the Tennessee Valley Authority (TVA). But by the late twentieth century, TVA bore scant resemblance to the reform-minded agency of the New Deal years, and indeed its huge purchases of strip-mined coal in the 1950s had contributed to the conditions that made eastern Kentucky the face of poverty in the 1960s. Nevertheless, decades of cheap TVA power and a Tennessee River open to navigation had set the stage for the prosperity enjoyed in portions of southern Appalachia in the latter decades of the century, when the former farming region, with automobile, aluminum, and aerospace plants, became Appalachia's manufacturing area. Symbolic of the transformation of the rural South was Huntsville, Alabama, a cotton mill town that became one of the hubs of America's government and industry aerospace complex.

As the lingering impact of TVA illustrates, the distinctive twenty-first century faces of northern, central, and southern areas of Appalachia reflect distinctive histories. Even as the late twentieth century brought increasing prosperity to Appalachian portions of the New South, urban areas in the northern subregion, like the rest of the nation's Rust Belt, struggled to find themselves in the postindustrial economy. In 2004 Pittsburgh, the de facto capital of the American Industrial Revolution, was in danger of bankruptcy and officially designated as "financially distressed" by the State of Pennsylvania—even though surrounding Allegheny County was one of nine counties in all of Appalachia that equaled or exceeded national averages in per capita income, employment, and poverty levels.

While southern Appalachia's population grew by 18 percent in the 1990s, the northern subregion—New York, Pennsylvania, Maryland, Ohio, and fifty-five counties in northern West Virginia—barely grew at all. Ten of New York's fourteen Appalachian counties lost population.

The heart of the region, the "core" around the coalfields of eastern Kentucky, southern West Virginia, southwestern Virginia, and east Tennessee, while healthier in some instances and respects than it had been in the 1960s, 1970s, and 1980s, continued to lag behind the rest of the region and the country by nearly every measure of economic health at the beginning of the new century. Even though the Appalachian Regional Commission removed thirteen counties in the area from the officially "distressed" category in 2003, coal country still included sixty-seven of the ninety-one counties in that category—meaning they continued to have unemployment rates at least 150 percent of the national average, per capita income less than two-thirds the national average, and poverty rates at least double the national average.

With mining and forestry employment having declined and out-migration having continued, some of the distressed mountain counties were hardly any better off than they had been in 1960. Even though the area's population grew by 6 percent during the 1990s, many of the distressed counties' populations stood at under twenty-five thousand as the new century began, and some had fewer than ten thousand residents.

A Region Considered

Although popular awareness of Appalachia is a relatively recent phenomenon—its entry in the sixth edition of *The Columbia Encyclopedia* (2000) is only linked to articles on the Appalachian Mountains, Berea College, and the dulcimer—academic interest in the region has deep roots. From early conceptions of an entity unified by geography, history, and culture and from works such as such as John C. Campbell's *The Southern Highlander and His Homeland* (1921) and the 1922 reissue of Horace Kephart's *Our Southern Highlanders*, a nascent Appalachian studies movement developed about 1930. A New York conference, instigated by Campbell's widow, Olive Dame Campbell, and Berea College professor Helen Dingman and hosted by the Russell Sage Foundation in 1929, led to the landmark survey *Economic and Social Problems and Conditions of the Southern Appalachians*. Published by the U.S. Department of Agriculture in 1935, it covered a region of 205 mountain counties in six states.

Twenty-seven years passed before publication of another major regional analysis, *The Southern Appalachian Region: A Survey*, edited by Thomas R. Ford of the University of Kentucky and published by the University Press of Kentucky. During the interim, however, native-born sociologists and anthropologists were doing research that formed the underpinnings of the late-twentieth-century Appalachian studies movement. Among the seminal works were James S. Brown's epic, multigenerational study of families in an eastern Kentucky community he called Beech Creek; Cratis Williams's New York University doctoral dissertation, "The Southern Mountaineer in Fact and Fiction" (1961); and, later, John Stephenson's *Shiloh: A Mountain Community* (1968).

What greatly energized interest in regional study and helped to foster a community of Appalachian social science scholarship, however, were best-selling popular books and the characterization of Appalachia as the epitome of poverty at a moment when new federal government initiatives echoed the social activism of Franklin D. Roosevelt's New Deal. Appearing within a year of each other, just as the Kennedy administration contemplated a major economic-development program for the region, were Michael Harrington's *The Other America: Poverty in the United States* (1962), and Harry Caudill's *Night Comes to the Cumberlands: A Biography of a Depressed Area* (1963).

Widely read by government officials, politicians, and journalists in Washington, both works accepted and advanced the concept that a culture of poverty enveloped poor places in the country. Promoted by anthropologist Oscar Lewis, the culture of poverty social theory came into vogue in the 1960s and 1970s during the War on Poverty. It faded as historians and social scientists came to see that it perpetuated stereotypes and placed the blame for poor economic conditions at the feet of the poor themselves.

Night Comes to the Cumberlands, having done much to imprint economic conditions in the coalfields upon the national conscience, became a prime source of debate in what Berea College historian Richard B. Drake would later call the "Appalachian Conversation." Because of the power of its prose and the author's standing as a fifth-generation Kentuckian and former legislator, Caudill's book brought a flood of national and foreign journalists into central Appalachia and led to exposés of poverty, environmental destruction, and corruption. A generation after Caudill's death, *Night Comes to the Cumberlands* and subsequent works such as *Theirs Be the Power: The Moguls of Eastern Kentucky* (1983) continued to be controversial in academic circles, but his first book remained the most sweeping, best-known, and most influential text about the core region and its people.

From Caudill's era onward, negative imagery arising from print and broadcast journalism has been wildly embroidered by popular and profitable television sitcoms and movies. To outsiders with only a vague awareness of Appalachia, mass-media images blurred with reality. The extent of the region's consequent image problem is well illustrated by an entry in a 1991 *Encyclopedia of World Cultures*. It reported the following: "There are six or seven children in the average family, although families with ten or more children are not uncommon. Inbreeding is reported to be very common."

Although Appalachians' research and writing about their region blossomed in the 1970s, analysis, introspection, and reflection upon the people and place spanned the twentieth century. Early novelists and local color writers were joined by social workers, religious activists, teachers, and civic leaders in what Kentucky novelist Gurney Norman has styled as a perpetual dialogue.

Beginning in the late twentieth century, the region whose history was largely unwritten when Caudill published *Night Comes to the Cumberlands* saw an outpouring of traditional history, revisionism, cultural exploration, and social criticism. Becoming major regional study texts soon after publication were volumes such as Ronald D Eller's *Miners, Millhands, and Mountaineers: Industrialization of the Appalachian South, 1880–1930* (1982); Drake's *A History of Appalachia* (2001); John Alexander Williams' *Appalachia: A History* (2002); and *Appalachia Inside Out*, a two-volume collection edited by Robert J. Higgs, Ambrose N. Manning, and Jim Wayne Miller (1995).

Stirring long-running discussion of the region's elegant complexities and contradictions were works such as David E. Whisnant's *Modernizing the Mountaineer: People, Power, and Planning in Appalachia* (1981) and *All That Is Native and Fine: The Politics of Culture in an American Region* (1983); Deborah Vansau McCauley's *Appalachian Mountain Religion: A History* (1995); and Wilma A. Dunaway's *The First American Frontier: Transition to Capitalism in Southern Appalachia, 1700–1860* (1996).

The Volume

The *Encyclopedia of Appalachia* is a product of the historical, and the ongoing, Appalachian conversation. Like a number of other regional and state encyclopedia projects, this volume was to some extent inspired by the acclaimed *Encyclopedia of Southern Culture* (1989). Beginning with a general discussion at the 1995 annual conference of the Appalachian Studies Association at West Virginia University, it evolved through individual discussions, focus group meetings, editorial board conferences, and support from members of a national advisory board. Within its pages will be found the work of more than fifteen hundred individuals—writers, editors, photographers, cartographers, and others. The contributors include not only academic specialists from scores of educational institutions but also independent scholars, journalists, administrators, and professionals from far-flung public and private institutions.

Since there has been no general reference work on the Appalachian region, the volume is designed for a wide audience; accessibility has been made the hallmark of its presentation. Early in the project, a topical, rather than alphabetical, organization was selected in the belief that it would enhance readability and add a dimension of understanding and synergism. Thus the *Encyclopedia* is divided into thirty sections organized into five parts: "The Landscape," "The People," "Work and the Economy," "Cultural Traditions," and "Institutions." Each section is introduced by an essay intended to supplement the individual entries and provide further context for them.

In some instances, in sections such as "Visual Arts" and "Performing Arts," entries cover subjects on which published material is scarce and research largely remains to be done. In others, historical data is rich, but definitive contemporary information is difficult to find—such is the case with "Agriculture," due to the declining importance of farming in modern times. In still others—namely "Geology," "Ecology," and "Environment"—entries sometimes address the Appalachian Mountains as distinct from the cultural and political conceptions of the Appalachian region.

As might be expected, sections dealing with the region's signature subjects, those most clearly bespeaking Appalachian life, history, and identity, receive the most prominent treatment. Among these are "Food and Cooking," "Music," "Religion," and "Crafts."

Given the scope of the subject, the constraints of a single volume, the complexities of organization, the pace of change, and the inevitability of oversight, the *Encyclopedia* cannot presume to be all-inclusive. It was impossible, for instance, to include biographical entries on all of the Appalachians who have distinguished themselves (or achieved notoriety in less than admirable fashion). By their nature, some sections, such as "Literature" and "Sports and Recreation," are replete with biographical entries. Other sections incorporate biographical material throughout their texts, but nevertheless notable Appalachians are missing from these pages, often because their accomplishments lack a direct Appalachian association. Such individuals include Holmes Rolston III, the environmental and religious philosopher born in the mountains of Virginia, and Nobel Laureate John Nash, the West Virginian whose life and struggle with schizophrenia was the subject of the award-winning motion picture *A Beautiful Mind*.

The speed and power of communication technologies that have dramatically affected Appalachia have made the compilation of this volume a constantly evolving endeavor. Rather than a finished product, the editors look upon it as a beginning, a cornerstone of a regional reference that will be increasingly accessible, relevant, and useful.

—Rudy Abramson, *Reston, Virginia,*
and Jean Haskell, *East Tennessee State University*

Harry M. Caudill, *Night Comes to the Cumberlands: A Biography of a Depressed Area* (1963); Richard B. Drake, *A History of Appalachia* (2001); Wilma A. Dunaway, *The First American Frontier: Transition to Capitalism in Southern Appalachia, 1700–1860* (1996); Ronald D Eller, *Miners, Millhands, and Mountaineers: Industrialization of the Appalachian South, 1880–1930* (1982); William Goodell Frost, "Our Contemporary Ancestors in the Southern Mountains," *Atlantic Monthly* (March 1899); Andrew M. Isserman, "Appalachia Then and Now: An Update of 'The Realities of Deprivation' Reported to the President in 1964," Appalachian Regional Commission (1996); Deborah V. McCauley, *Appalachian Mountain Religion: A History* (1995); Kenneth M. Pollard, "Appalachia at the Millennium: An Overview of Results From Census 2000," Appalachian Regional Commission (2003); Henry D. Shapiro, *Appalachia on Our Mind: The Southern Mountains and Mountaineers in the American Consciousness, 1870–1920* (1978); David E. Whisnant, *Modernizing the Mountaineer: People, Power, and Planning in Appalachia* (1980); John Alexander Williams, *Appalachia: A History* (2002).

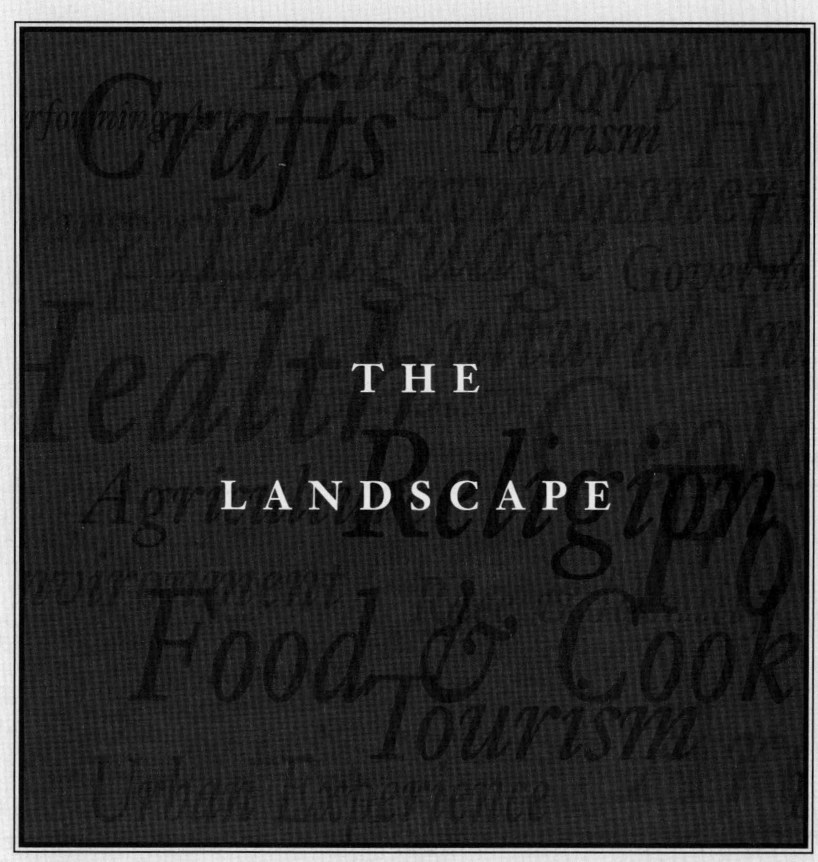

THE LANDSCAPE

Geology

Section Editors: Don W. Byerly and John J. Renton

Compared to Earth's tallest mountains, the Appalachians are hardly more than forest-covered hummocks that were rounded, weathered, and diminished by erosion long before the summits of the Alps, Andes, Himalayas, or Rockies were created. While the still-growing Himalayas exceed 25,000 feet at more than thirty places and Alaska's Mount McKinley rises to 20,300 feet, the loftiest point in the Appalachians—Mount Mitchell in North Carolina—stands at a modest 6,684 feet. Only in the southern Blue Ridge, the highest and easternmost subdivision of the ancient highlands, are there numerous peaks above 6,000 feet. The Allegheníes, extending from central Pennsylvania, across western Maryland, and down through eastern West Virginia, average only 2,000 feet in the north and 4,000 feet in the south. Nevertheless, the contrasts between the steep flanks of the mountains and the sprawling Great Valley extending from Pennsylvania to Alabama endow the entire region with marvelously scenic topography.

The complexity of the Appalachians' geology and physical geography is as impressive as their immensity and biological diversity. Rather than a chain, the Appalachians constitute a system encompassing no fewer than four distinct geological provinces: the Piedmont, the Blue Ridge, the Appalachian Plateaus, and the Ridge and Valley, each with a distinctive topography and geological history. South to north, they span several climate zones. Summers in Birmingham, Alabama, rival the tropics while winters on New Hampshire's 6,288-foot Mount Washington record temperatures that approach fifty degrees below zero and wind gusts far in excess of one hundred miles per hour.

Though muted beside snow-capped mountain chains of the world, the rugged, forested Appalachian landscape and its underlying geologic structures and resources have shaped life and culture in the region from the arrival of humankind. Fluted projectiles made from local stone have been found throughout the southern mountains, indicating that Paleo-Indians were living in the region about 10,000 B.C. Caves and rock shelters, common from north Alabama to eastern Kentucky, have yielded evidence of animal butchering. In the Great Smoky Mountains, the discovery of tools and projectiles made of stone from plateaus far to the west suggests that hunting parties traveled eastward into the highlands in search of game. Centuries before Christopher Columbus arrived on the shores of the New World, permanent villages

Facing page: Highly deformed sedimentary rock near Pinto, West Virginia, c. 2000. Although typically deposited in horizontal layers, sediment here was disrupted by the process of mountain building, resulting in a strikingly distorted rock formation.

existed in valleys where rich soil had accumulated from the inexorable erosion of the mountains and near rocky shoals where fish could be readily taken from major streams.

Just as the mountains framed the lives of native peoples for millennia before the arrival of the first Europeans, so did they influence the course of European exploration, migration, and displacement of Indian tribes. Early European settlers made use of Indian hunting trails and followed their leads in selecting settlement sites and places to farm. Until the rise of the salt, coal, and timber industries, mountain topography primarily determined where new arrivals put down roots on the frontier.

But after European colonists took up life on the coastal plain, a century and a half passed before settlers made a concerted push from the Tidewater and the Piedmont across the daunting Blue Ridge. (The Spanish explorer Hernando de Soto had led an expedition up from the southeast to the North Carolina Piedmont, crossing the Blue Ridge into present-day Tennessee in 1540. Though he failed to find the gold he sought, his men unleashed infectious diseases among the Cherokee people, and the expedition apparently led to the later appearance of "Appalachee" on sixteenth-century maps.) Crossing the Blue Ridge was particularly difficult, with the southern portion presenting the greatest challenge. In North Carolina, the near-vertical Blue Ridge Escarpment rose to more than six thousand feet, including the highest elevations in the eastern United States. Natural openings were few. Indeed, along the Blue Ridge from southern Pennsylvania to north Georgia, only three natural water gaps provided passageways through the mountains into the Great Valley. One was in northwestern North Carolina along the New River, another near Roanoke, Virginia, where the James River passed through the ridge on its way to the Chesapeake Bay, and a third in southern Pennsylvania. The last, in the area of the Susquehanna River, was a seventy-mile stretch where the "ridge" was nothing more than rolling, low-lying hills. Through the area, beginning around 1730, a stream of northern Europeans—Germans, Scots, Irish, and Quakers—poured into the Appalachian Valley from the east, establishing productive farms in the limestone soils and pressing ever southward in a wave of migration that reached all the way to the Tennessee Valley.

From the Great Valley, westward-bound settlers moved into the folded highlands of the parallel Ridge and Valley Province by following valleys that streams had carved from sandstone ridges and shale-bottomed lowlands. But travelers bound for the West found before them the imposing Allegheny Structural Front, a stone escarpment rising as high as 1,000 feet, separating the mountain ridges from the sprawling Appalachian Plateaus. There, even the passages opened by major streams were steep and narrow gorges. Historians would later consider the Allegheny Front second only to the Rocky Mountains as a natural obstacle to western migration in the United States. Except for broad interstate highways blasted through the rock, even modern-day roads take steep and winding courses across the escarpment. Beyond it, the topography again changes dramatically, though the contrast is far less striking than the demarcation between the Great Valley and the ridges on either side of it. In the Appalachian Plateaus Province, consisting basically of the Allegheny Plateau in the north and the Cumberland Plateau from Kentucky southward, the underlying rock has been less deformed and lies generally flat, its topographic features more random and its drainage patterns similar to the branches of a tree.

Far more than in the rolling Piedmont, the Great Valley, or the broad, rounded ridges of the Alleghenies in the northern Appalachians, topography has constrained and shaped human circumstance across both the Ridge and Valley and Appalachian Plateaus Provinces of the central and southern highlands.

There, early settlers, often taking their cue from the native peoples they displaced, gravitated to coves, hollows, and valleys that provided shelter from storms and offered arable soil, good water, and abundant timber. Mountain ridges and streams served as property lines, isolated developing communities, and sometimes marked political jurisdictions. The Virginia-Kentucky border follows the crest of Pine Mountain, for example, and the crest of the Blue Ridge separates North and South Carolina along a forty-mile stretch. More commonly, mountain ridges served as lines separating counties.

While early settlers settled in natural bowls with the best soil, those who came later established themselves in the heads of hollows, on mountainsides, and on remote ridges where survival was more problematic, thus beginning what would become enduring social hierarchies. As historian Ronald D Eller observed in his widely read study *Miners, Millhands, and Mountaineers*, the land shaped the culture and social patterns of Appalachia perhaps more profoundly than any other rural area of the country.

The rise of twentieth-century technology, construction of modern roads, and social intervention by state, local, and federal governments notwithstanding, the mountains remain an elemental force in the identity and self-perception of people who live in the highlands, in the organization of society, and in the evolution of the region's economic life. People who left the region in waves of migration, particularly from the coalfields of the Appalachian Plateaus, often expressed feelings of deep, persistent, and visceral longing, not only for friends and family but for the mountains themselves.

For geologists, the saga of the Appalachians' creation and the evolution of the region's topography are sources of endless fascination and continuing research. Some have contended for generations that the entire system is much older than the tallest mountains now on Earth and that far back in geologic time antecedents of the modern Appalachians towered as high as the present-day Rockies. But only in the 1960s did geologists settle on a satisfactory hypothesis for the origin and evolution of the major mountains chains of the world. Now generally accepted, the theory of plate tectonics was discussed for decades before research produced decisive new data. The last crucial piece of the explanation fell into place with confirmation that the floor of the Atlantic Ocean is spreading—America and Europe are drifting apart by a couple of inches a year. Moreover, since magnetite particles in molten rock line up with Earth's magnetic field as they cool, scientists were able to deduce that rocks, indeed continents, were formed far from their present location.

The world's great mountain chains, it is now accepted, formed when continental masses of Earth's outer crust, drifting on a molten or semi-molten mantle, collided and their margins buckled upward under millions of years of indescribable force.

The last of several mountain-building epochs in Appalachian prehistory, an event known as the Alleghenian Orogeny, came about 248 million years ago when the present North American continent came together with the landmass that is now western Africa. The eastern margin of North America was shoved about 160 miles to the west, and the grinding pressure raised the southern Appalachians to heights comparable to the tallest mountains on Earth today. The highlands of that event were leveled by erosion over the more than 150 million years that followed. About 65 million years ago, in an episode still not clearly understood, a general continental uplifting raised the entire eastern United States. The modern Appalachians appeared

TIME (MILLIONS OF YEARS AGO)	ERA	GEOLOGIC PERIOD	TECTONIC EVENT (Mountain Building)	RELATIVE SEA LEVEL CHANGE (Rising / Falling)	MAJOR EVENTS
.01 – 1.8	CENOZOIC	Quaternary			Ice ages end Northern Appalachia glaciated
1.8 – 65	CENOZOIC	Tertiary			Appalachia being eroded—modern mountains, ridges, valleys, and gorges taking shape
65 – 144	MESOZOIC	Cretaceous	Appalachia Uplifted	Present level	Fault-block mountains eroded
144 – 206	MESOZOIC	Jurassic			Fault-block mountains—Mt. Holyoke, Watchung Mountains, etc.
206 – 248	MESOZOIC	Triassic	Palisades Orogeny		Pangea breaks up—rifting begins to form present Atlantic Ocean Lava flows and sills of Newark Supergroup
248 – 290	PALEOZOIC	Permian	Alleghenian Orogeny		Africa and North America collide to form super continent of Pangea
290 – 323	PALEOZOIC	Pennsylvanian			Coal swamps prevalent
323 – 354	PALEOZOIC	Mississipian			Extensive deposits of limestone deposited in shallow seas
354 – 417	PALEOZOIC	Devonian	Acadian Orogeny		Chattanooga Black Shale deposited—a source rock for oil and gas in Appalachia
417 – 443	PALEOZOIC	Silurian			Iron and salt deposits—the iron formation in Red Mountain, Birmingham, Alabama
443 – 490	PALEOZOIC	Ordovician	Taconic Orogeny		Tennessee "marble" deposited as a reef in a shallow sea
490 – 543	PALEOZOIC	Cambrian			
543 – 1,100 – 1,600		Precambrian	Grenville Orogeny		Volcanic and glacial deposits in the Mt. Rogers region (Virginia, North Carolina, Tennessee) Oldest rocks in Appalachia

A generalized geologic time scale shows major geologic events and approximated sea-level fluctuations affecting Appalachia.

in that mighty uplift as rejuvenated streams sculpted the rising land. They are, therefore, remnants of earlier mountains and the product of episodic uplift, destruction, and rebirth. Estimates are that 50 million years from now, the Appalachians will have again worn down to an essentially featureless plain.

Confirming the mountains' most distant origins, geologists have found and dated rocks much older than the mountains themselves—billion-year-old "basement rocks" raised from the depths during Earth's first mountain-building episode back in deep time, long before life appeared on the planet. The saga of the Appalachian system itself began about 700 million years ago with the breakup of a supercontinent called Rodinia. Over a span of some 500 million years, collisions between five continental masses left from Rodinia's destruction produced three distinct periods of upheaval, the last the Alleghenian Orogeny. The "Tectonics" entry in the following section traces these events in more detail.

Besides creating a topographical template for human settlement and cultural evolution, the global wandering of the tectonic plates led to the formation of bituminous coal beds found beneath 63,000 square miles of the Appalachians from Pennsylvania to Alabama, as well as the famed anthracite beds in northeastern Pennsylvania. During the millions of years when the present-day Appalachian region lay near the equator, tree-sized ferns, horsetails, and mosses grew and died in steamy swamps. As the plants fell into oxygen-depleted water, they decayed into deepening beds of peat, which mounting temperature and pressure transformed into coal. Three hundred million years later, the Sun's energy thus stored by the plants' process of photosynthesis was released in burning coal, powering the steam engines and industries of the American Industrial Revolution.

While no match for the Rockies or other major mountain systems, the Appalachians have produced significant metallic deposits in times past and continue to be a source of nonmetallic minerals vital to a number of industries. Gold was first discovered in North America in North Carolina and later mined in the Piedmont Province in Virginia and Georgia as well as the Carolinas. Reminders of the gold-mining days remain in the names of communities such as Goldvein, Virginia. Iron, tungsten, copper, lead, and zinc have been profitably extracted from the region as well. Important from colonial times forward, Silurian Clinton iron ore combined with locally available limestone and coal to provide the basis for the steel industry of Birmingham, making the area a southern counterpart of Pittsburgh, the de facto capital of the Industrial Revolution in the United States. The fact that the Appalachians were once more than double their present height, however, has led to speculation that their chief mineral lodes were carried away during 200 million years of relentless erosion.

In spite of erosion and pulses of uplift, the strata of the modern Appalachians and the debris of the previous highlands record not only the tectonic history of the region but the evolution of life from shelled animals, vertebrates, amphibians, and reptiles as well. Evidence shows that Appalachia's first true forests, consisting of tree-sized ferns, appeared in the late Devonian period, a harbinger of the coal formation to come during the Pennsylvanian period.

Striking fossilized tracks of dinosaurs that walked the Appalachian Basin during the Triassic and Jurassic periods some 248 to 144 million years ago have been found in basins of the Piedmont Province. Outside the town of Stevensburg in Culpeper County, Virginia, for example, a six-acre area contains no fewer than two thousand dinosaur tracks, most of them left by a three-toed carnivore called Dilophosaurus. In the Ridge and Valley Province are two significant vertebrate sites: a sinkhole at Gray, Tennessee, that formed about five million years ago and contains fossils of many plants and animals, including tapirs, rhinoceroses, turtles, and mastodons; and Saltville, Virginia, notable for fossils of Pleistocene mastodons.

The Appalachians are undoubtedly the most thoroughly studied mountains on Earth. Early investigations of the structures from the Blue Ridge to the Ridge and Valley gave rise to modern concepts concerning the formation of folded mountains. Recognition of the extraordinary thickness of sedimentary rocks involved in the formation of the Appalachians led to the understanding of sediment accumulation in the geoclines that border opening oceans such as the Atlantic. But besides playing an important role in the evolving science of geology, the mountains have exerted profound influence on the spirit and the character of the people of the region, from the Native Americans who lived in harmony with the land, water, and forests to modern Americans whose technologies have brought accelerating and permanent change to the landscape.

—Don W. Byerly, *University of Tennessee*, and John J. Renton, *West Virginia University*

Nevin M. Fenneman, *Physiography of the Eastern United States* (1938); Clark Hubler, *America's Mountains: An Exploration of Their Origins* (1995); Karl B. Raitz and Richard Ulack, *Appalachia: A Regional Geography* (1984); William D. Thornbury, *Principles of Geomorphology* (1954); Scott Weidensaul, *Mountains of the Heart: A Natural History of the Appalachians* (1994).

Appalachian Plateaus Province

By definition, a province is a region characterized by a consistency of geologic structures and common weathering and erosion processes that have operated through its history. Based on these criteria, geologists have subdivided Appalachia into four provinces that are, from east to west, the Piedmont, the Blue Ridge, the Ridge and Valley, and the Appalachian Plateaus Provinces. It should be noted, however, that some geologists and geographers do not consider the Piedmont an Appalachian province. A major difference among the four provinces is the degree of deformation to which the rocks have been subjected, with the rocks of the Piedmont Province exhibiting the most intense deformation and those of the Appalachian Plateaus, extending from New York to north-central Alabama, the least.

There is no single Appalachian plateau, but several that are distinguished from each other by recognizable differences in topography. In contrast to the more highly deformed rocks in the provinces to the east, the rocks within the Appalachian Plateaus Province are essentially flat-lying or gently deformed into broad open folds. Throughout the Appalachian Plateaus, the topography is more the product of erosional and depositional processes than it is of subsurface structures.

In 1938 Nevin M. Fenneman, a professor at the University of Cincinnati, divided the vast Appalachian plateau region into seven distinct smaller plateaus. The northernmost, the Mohawk Section, is an elongated valley lying between the Adirondack Mountains and the Glaciated Allegheny Plateau. Consisting of the Mohawk lowland and Tug Hill cuesta (a ridge steep on one side and gently sloping on the other), the Mohawk Section bears a strong imprint of glaciation. South of the Mohawk Section is the Glaciated Allegheny Plateau, its ridges and hills formed by open folds modified by glaciation. East of the Glaciated Allegheny Pla-

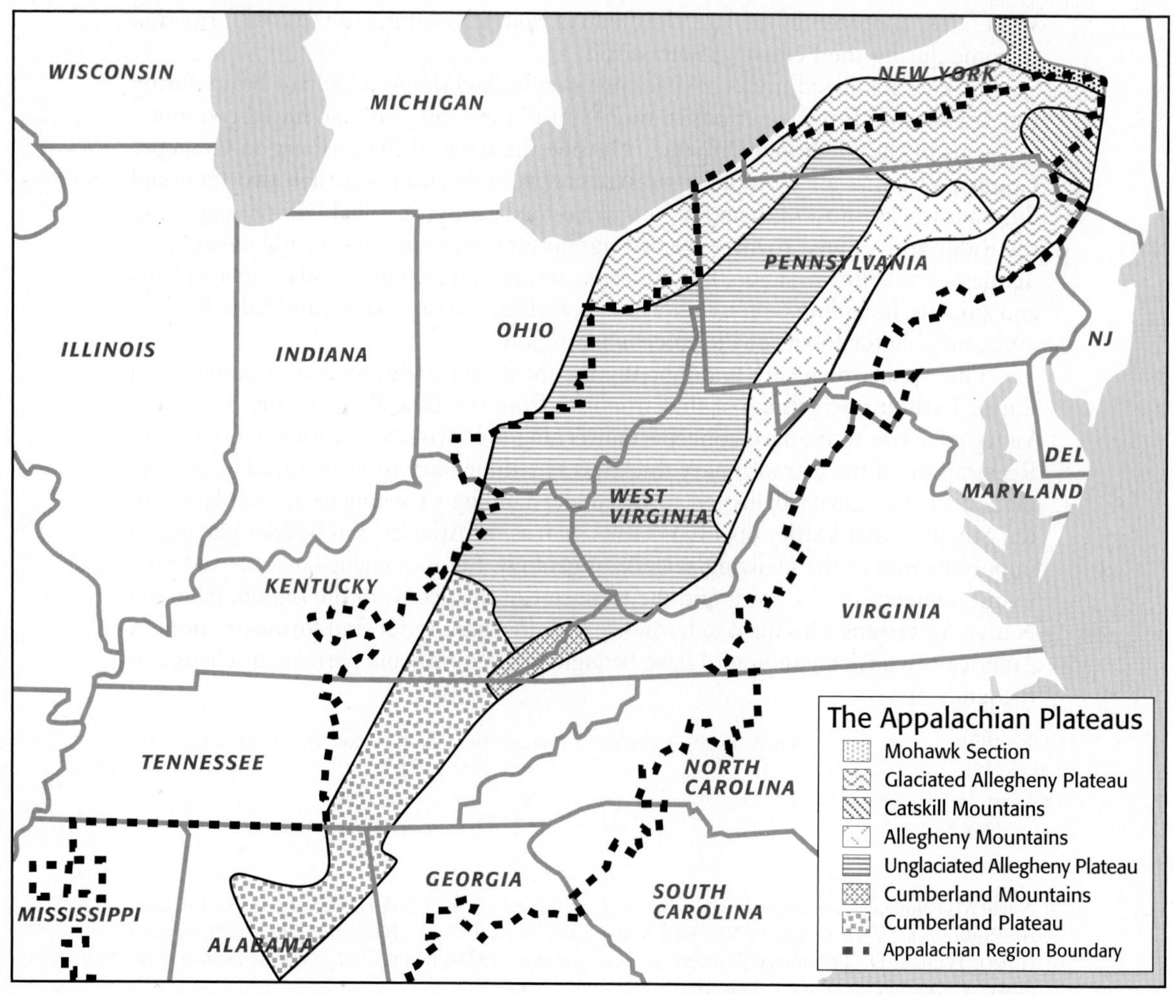

Recognizable differences in topography define seven distinctive plateaus within the Appalachian Plateaus Province.

teau is the Catskill Section. Long known as the Catskill Mountains, the Catskill Section is a small plateau dissected by stream erosion; it was glaciated but was not affected as profoundly by glacial erosion or deposition as was the Glaciated Allegheny Plateau to the north.

The Unglaciated Allegheny Plateau, the most extensive of the plateaus, extends from the New York–Pennsylvania border southward to eastern Kentucky. Its rocks are generally flat-lying and the topography consists of hills and valleys sculpted by dendritic streams. The portion along the eastern margin of the plateau extending from north-central Pennsylvania to Monroe County, West Virginia, is referred to by some geologists as the Allegheny Mountain Section and by others as the Appalachian High Plateau. It is characterized by linear ridges and valleys, reflecting the presence of maturely dissected, symmetrical folds sufficiently high as to affect the topography. Structurally, the Allegheny Mountain Section is a transitional segment of the plateau between the large-scale, asymmetric folds of the Ridge and Valley Province to the east and the essentially flat-lying rocks of the Unglaciated Allegheny Plateau to the west.

The Cumberland Plateau is considered by some to be the southern counterpart of the Unglaciated Allegheny Plateau, although it is not as dramatically dissected by erosion. The boundary between the two plateaus is rather arbitrary, but the major difference is that the Cumberland Plateau is marked by features that are the result of thrust faulting (a type of fault where ground on one side of the fault moves up and over adjacent ground). Surface exposures of these faults are best seen in the Cumberland Mountain Section, which is bounded by four faults. Two of these faults created elongated mountains, Pine Mountain and Cumberland Mountain, which extend from southeastern Kentucky into Tennessee. Although the numerous faults in the section are for the most part in the subsurface, the high elevations of the plateaus reflect the stacking of sediments as a result of vertical displacement along these faults.

Clastic rocks, composed of the fragments of older rocks, dominate formations throughout the Appalachian Plateaus with sandstones and shales being especially abundant. Conglomerates composed of rounded fragments of older rocks and siltstones composed of hardened silt are also present. Carbonate rocks (limestones) are exposed, but not to the same extent as the non-carbonate rocks.

All of the clastic rocks on the plateaus come from sediment accumulated following mountain-building episodes, or orogenies, that occurred during the span of some 500 million years when shifting tectonic plates brought continental landmasses into collisions, creating highlands that served as the source for the clastic material. For the most part, the sediments that accumulated following the Taconic Orogeny, about 450 million years ago, and the Acadian Orogeny, some 50 million years later, were deposited in basins that formed near the sediment source. These sediments are now found in the rocks exposed throughout the plateaus. Sediments shed from the mountains that were formed by the Alleghenian Orogeny about 248 million years ago have for the most part been removed from the region by erosion.

Most of the rocks within the Appalachian Plateaus Province are Mississippian and Pennsylvanian in age, meaning that they were formed from sediments that accumulated between 354 and 290 million years ago. Most of the rocks exposed throughout the plateaus are of Pennsylvanian age. Rocks originally identified as Permian (290 to 248 million years ago) on older maps have subsequently been identified on the basis of plant fossils to be late Pennsylvanian. No rocks of the more recent Mesozoic or Cenozoic eras are found within the province, though a veneer of unconsolidated Cenozoic deposits exists almost everywhere in the glaciated sections. Some of these deposits are unstratified glacial till while others are stratified, consisting of sands and gravels deposited from glacial meltwater. Beyond the margins of the glaciated regions are substantial deposits of lacustrine origin that resulted from glacial outwash or ice dams. In north-central West Virginia such deposits are found in the Monongahela and Cheat River basins, while in southern West Virginia and Ohio the deposits are found in the Teays River drainage system. Except for a number of small local streams, the Teays River drainage system is now abandoned. Many stream valleys are filled with debris from melting glaciers, and nearly everywhere a mantle of colluvium, or landslide debris, remains on valley slopes.

Elevations within the Appalachian Plateaus Province increase progressively from west to east with the eastern margins being generally higher than the westernmost highlands of the Ridge and Valley Province. As a result, the Eastern Continental Divide, where streams take a course either eastward to the Atlantic Ocean or southwestward to the Gulf of Mexico, is located within the easternmost portion of the Plateaus Province. For example, the northern portion of the province is drained by the Mohawk, Susquehanna, and Delaware Rivers, which flow to the Atlantic. Except for the Potomac River, which originates in the eastern portion of the Unglaciated Allegheny Plateau and drains eastward to the Atlantic, most of the central portion of the province is drained by the Monongahela, Allegheny, and Kanawha Rivers by way of the Ohio River to the Gulf of Mexico. The southern portion of the province is drained by the Tennessee and Cumberland Rivers to the Gulf of Mexico by way of the Ohio and Mississippi.

Throughout the province, rivers and their tributaries have dissected uplands into hills and ridges. In many places, pronounced escarpments have been formed where a resistant layer of rock such as sandstone or conglomerate overlies a weaker type of rock such as shale or limestone. In some cases, these escarpments form the boundary between adjacent provinces. The Allegheny Structural Front, for example, forms the boundary between the Allegheny Mountain Section of the Appalachian Plateaus Province and the Ridge and Valley Province in West Virginia, Maryland, and Pennsylvania. Rising one thousand feet above the valley floor at some places, the sandstone-capped front extends from Alabama to northern Pennsylvania and presents one of the country's more striking topographic boundaries. In Tennessee, pronounced coves are punctuated by the same resistant rock layer along the boundary between the Appalachian Plateaus and Ridge and Valley Provinces. These same basal Pennsylvanian sandstones cap topographic knobs of various sizes in the vicinity of Mammoth Cave, Kentucky, as well as the upper edge of the deep and steep-sided New River Gorge in West Virginia.

There are numerous examples of former stream channels in the unglaciated plateaus. Wierton, West Virginia, for example, was built in a prominent abandoned channel of the ancestral Ohio River. Indeed, the course of the modern Ohio River was influenced by a drainage change initiated by glaciers. The effect of glaciers on pre-glacial drainage channels is also striking in central New York, where glacial erosion deepened the valleys underlain by weak shales and siltstones, packing the resultant debris into the heads of the valleys to the south. The prominent valleys then filled with water to become the Finger Lakes. Similar valleys were also created in Pennsylvania but did not remain filled with naturally occurring lakes. Spectacular remnants of meltwater erosion in New York include the potholes at Herkimer, the dry falls near Syracuse, and the troughs between the Finger Lakes, the most prominent being the Cut at Syracuse. Such features reflect the profound effect of meltwater erosion following glaciation of the plateaus.

Geologists in the early twentieth century were convinced that numerous erosional surfaces were partially preserved as the region was uplifted during the Cenozoic and rivers began a new cycle of erosion. Called peneplains, these surfaces were foremost in the thoughts of early geologists who studied the Appalachian Plateaus. To them, the peneplains appeared to be bowed or arched, but in general the upland surfaces were considered by many to be at concordant elevations. The concept of the peneplain has not appeared in print in decades, but it did influence those who first considered the physiography of North America and of the Appalachian region. Although the original definition of *peneplain* as "an erosional surface at or near sea level" no longer applies, detailed studies of landscapes indicate that erosional surfaces controlled by lithology and structure do exist. As a result, the original concept of concordant erosional surfaces is now being resurrected, but they are no longer referred to as peneplains.

The geology of the Appalachian Plateaus has historically been a subject of more than academic interest because of the presence of sprawling bituminous coalfields. Formed from peat that accumulated in vast swamps during the Pennsylvanian period, coal consists largely of preserved wood of trees that dominated the Pennsylvanian landscape worldwide. Pennsylvanian coal beds vary in thickness, with some being too thin to be of economic importance, but those thick enough to mine have been a major force in Appalachia's social and economic history. Best known of the region's coal deposits is the famed Pittsburgh bed that underlies portions of Ohio, West Virginia, western Pennsylvania, and Maryland. Referred by some as the most valuable single layer of rock in the world, the Pittsburgh coal bed represents 25 percent of the total coal production of West Virginia.

Extraction of coal by underground and surface methods has created profound local effects on the landscape of the Appalachian Plateaus Province. Underground methods, both the older room-and-pillar method and the more recent longwall method of mining relatively thick and flat-lying coal beds, have resulted in sometimes dangerous and destructive local subsidence. Extensive surface mining, called "strip mining" because mines follow the contours of the terrain, evolved with development of giant earthmoving equipment. Late in the twentieth century, the practice of mountaintop removal emerged as a dominant form of surface mining, especially in the southern Appalachian coal basin, where coal beds were numerous but relatively thin. With the rise of environmental concerns in the 1970s, all methods of coal extraction became hotly debated. Acid mine drainage resulting from the exposure of sulfur-bearing rock during the mining process created lifeless streams and posed expensive reclamation issues.

Petroleum has also played an important role in the economy of the Appalachian Plateaus. Indeed, the first well drilled solely for the production of oil was the Drake Well at Titusville, Pennsylvania, in 1859. Folds in the unglaciated plateaus became of special interest to petroleum geologists after it was discovered that commercial deposits of oil and natural gas were sometimes found deep beneath them. A major event in the early history of the oil industry, and certainly an important one for the science of geology, was the successful testing of I. C. White's anticlinal theory along the Burning Springs Anticline in West Virginia. White, the founder and first director of the West Virginia Geological and Economic Survey, theorized that the most likely place for petroleum to accumulate was in the axial portion of arch-shaped anticlinal folds. Following initial discoveries, the oil and gas industry flourished for decades at the turn of the twentieth century. Today, however, there is only a shadow of the once enormous presence of drilling activity in West Virginia, Pennsylvania, Ohio, and New York.

See also: COAL; OIL AND GAS; SOILS.

—Robert Behling, *West Virginia University*

Nevin M. Fenneman, *Physiography of the Eastern United States* (1938).

Blue Ridge Province

Consisting of metamorphic and igneous rocks from the Precambrian eon and Paleozoic era, the Blue Ridge Province is a mountain range that extends from southern Pennsylvania to northern Georgia. A broad, low gap at Roanoke, Virginia, divides the province into two distinctive parts. The Northern Section is about 250 miles long and averages about 10 miles wide while the Southern Section is much larger, at 350 miles long and up to 75 miles wide. The Northern Section is entirely within the Atlantic drainage system, whereas the Southern Section drains almost completely to the Gulf of Mexico by way of the New, Tennessee, and Coosa Rivers. The northern Blue Ridge is essentially a long, low ridge that owes its existence to its composition of resistant rock that has withstood the forces of erosion. Elevations rarely exceed 4,000 feet. In comparison, the geology of the southern Blue Ridge, where distinctive subdivisions exist and the correlation between elevation and rock type is less clear than in the Northern Section, is more complex.

The southern Blue Ridge Province is by far the highest terrain in the eastern United States. Vast areas exceed 3,000 feet in elevation with more than forty peaks rising above 6,000 feet. The highest peak in the province is Mount Mitchell, North Carolina, at an elevation of 6,684 feet. Because temperature decreases on the average about three degrees Fahrenheit for every 1,000-foot increase in elevation, the highlands provide a haven from the sweltering summer heat that prevails elsewhere in the South while making ski resorts possible at unlikely latitudes during the winter. The high elevations also harbor plant and animal life typical of more northerly climates.

The most prominent topographic feature of the southern Blue Ridge is the long, steep Blue Ridge Escarpment along its southeastern margin. The main drainage divide between the Atlantic and the Gulf of Mexico occurs just northwest of the escarpment. A number of rivers, including the New River, originate near the escarpment and flow across the Blue Ridge to the Ridge and Valley Province. The height of the escarpment above the Piedmont ranges from 2,000 feet near Mount Mitchell to about 1,000 feet near Roanoke. The width of the escarpment averages nine to twelve miles.

The origin of the Blue Ridge Escarpment has been the subject of a great deal of discussion. One interpretation is that the feature is a fault scarp (a sharp declivity created by an offset of the land surface) with the southeastern side having moved down relative to the northwestern side. Although this explanation is compatible with the linear shape of the escarpment, detailed geologic mapping has shown little evidence of Cenozoic faulting. Whatever the original cause, many researchers have concluded that the scarp is gradually retreating to the northwest as a consequence of differences in the erosional energy of streams on the two sides of the escarpment. The streams on the southeast side flow directly to the Atlantic, whereas most of those on the northwest side flow to the Gulf of Mexico. Since average gradients of streams on the southeast side are much steeper, they erode headward at a faster rate than those on the northwest side, thereby pushing the divide to the northwest.

The northwest retreat of the Blue Ridge Escarpment has resulted in a number of stream captures. The term *stream capture* refers to the natural diversion of the headwaters of one stream into another stream having greater erosional activity and flowing at a lower level. Such captures may produce dramatic changes in drainage systems. For example, headwaters of the North Fork and South Fork of the Roanoke River are encroaching on tributaries of the New River, and millions of years in the future the New River itself may be diverted directly to the Atlantic.

In most parts of the Blue Ridge, the surface is covered with thin, loose deposits of late Cenozoic age. The most common of these deposits is colluvium, a mixture of angular rock fragments and soil that mantles most hilltops, having been emplaced by mass movements such as sliding, slope wash, and slow downhill creep due to frost action, tree roots, and burrowing organisms. Colluvium varies in thickness from a foot or less to as many as thirty feet at the base of some slopes and in steep streamless hollows on the flanks of many mountains. Most landslides in the Blue Ridge involve movement of colluvium. Debris slides, set off by heavy rainfalls of ten inches or more in a twenty-four-hour period, are extremely dangerous. Rain-saturated colluvium slides off steep hillslopes, particularly in hollows, where the material is thick and runoff tends to collect, turning the colluvium into viscous debris flows that can carry truck-sized boulders downstream at high velocities, wreaking great destruction. The most dramatic example in modern times took place in August 1969, when Hurricane Camille dropped up to twenty-eight inches of rain in eight hours on an area of central Virginia. More than one thousand landslides occurred, and the debris flows killed more than one hundred people. Autopsies showed that most victims were not drowned but rather crushed to death. Calculations of the amount of sediment transported by these slides and flows determined that the erosion they produced was equivalent to several thousand years of normal erosion. While such catastrophic events probably occur at a given location only once every several thousand years, the Blue Ridge Province experiences a potentially hazardous debris flow about once every three years.

See also: GEOMORPHOLOGY; SOILS; TECTONICS.

—Hugh H. Mills, *Tennessee Technological University*

Paula L. Gori and William C. Burton, *Debris-Flow Hazards in the Blue Ridge of Virginia,* U.S. Geological Survey Fact Sheet 159-96 (1996); J. T. Hack, *Physiographic Divisions and Differential Uplift in the Piedmont and Blue Ridge,* U.S. Geological Survey Professional Paper 1265 (1982); William D. Thornbury, *Regional Geomorphology of the United States* (1965).

Cenozoic Era

Long before the Cenozoic era began about 65 million years ago, rocks and geologic structures exposed throughout the modern Appalachian Mountains had already been created. These rocks record the sequence of events that occurred between the breakup of a supercontinent called Rodinia about 700 million years ago and the formation of another supercontinent called Pangea about 248 million years ago. It was during this final mountain-building episode at the end of the Paleozoic era that the structures seen in the modern Appalachian Mountains were created. At the time of maximum mountain building, the ancestral Appalachian Mountains were much higher than the modern Appalachians, with glaciers and jagged peaks perhaps comparable to those of the modern Alps.

Even if the highest peaks of the ancestral Appalachians were comparable to the peaks of today's Alps, they would have been worn away by the mid-Mesozoic era, about 200 million years ago, leaving behind a relatively flat, featureless surface, most likely not far above sea level. Studies show that the modern Appalachian Mountains are being lowered by erosion at the rate of about one hundred feet per million years. Assuming that this rate has prevailed since the rise of the ancestral Appalachian Mountains in the late Paleozoic era, it is estimated that at least thirty thousand feet of rock have been removed by erosion. The actual amount of erosion is probably much greater than that, however, for high mountains erode at a much faster rate than low mountains. Although the surface expression of the ancestral Appalachian Mountains has disappeared, the geologic structures created at the close of the Paleozoic era remain.

The modern Appalachian landscape owes its appearance almost entirely to the combined processes of weathering, mass wasting, and erosion that have operated from the beginning of the Cenozoic era to the present day, a period of about 65 million years. Unfortunately, the process of erosion during the Cenozoic left behind little evidence for scientists to use in reconstructing the events of the era. Ironically, geologists know more about events that occurred during the Paleozoic history of Appalachia from about 543 million years ago to 248 million years ago, when the ancestral Appalachian Mountains were being created.

There is, however, evidence that the topography of the region occupied by the modern Appalachian Mountains was much lower during early Cenozoic time than it is now. Clues lie in sediment eroded from the ancestral Appalachian Mountains and deposited on the Atlantic Coastal Plain and the continental shelf offshore. Study of these deposits has made it possible to compute the amount of sediment during different time intervals of the Cenozoic. The most important factor affecting the amount of sediment deposited appears to be rate of erosion in the uplands of the time. In turn, the rates and amount of erosion depend largely on the elevation and topography of the slopes. When elevations and topographic relief within the uplands are high and the slopes steep, there is more erosion, and thus more sediment is carried and deposited by streams. By plotting the volume of sediment deposited along the coastal plain and the continental shelf against time, an index of topographic relief can be created. The results show that during the first 50 million years of the Cenozoic very little sediment was deposited within the coastal plain or on the continental shelf, suggesting a low-relief landscape extending across the entire region. But beginning about 15 million years ago and continuing until the last million years, there was a twentyfold increase in sediment accumulation, indicating a significant increase in both uplift and relief throughout the region. Based on maximum elevations now seen within the southern Blue Ridge Mountains, the minimum amount of uplift experienced throughout the region must have been in excess of six thousand feet. It was during this period of time that streams were rejuvenated and subsequent erosion sculpted the landscape seen today. The cause of such uplift is a mystery. The most recent theory is that heat rising from deep within the planet caused expansion and increased buoyancy of underlying rock, resulting in an overall uplift and arching of the entire region. Experts have also suggested that climate change may have contributed to the increased erosion. Beginning in the late Cenozoic, a longterm drop in Earth's atmospheric temperature produced accelerated buildup of continental ice and subsequent glacial erosion. Combined with changes in annual precipitation, this may have contributed to an increase in sedimentation along portions of the continental margin.

In any case, structures of the modern Appalachian Mountains are the result of a mountain-building event that occurred about 248 million years ago at the close of the

Paleozoic era, and the topography is the result of Cenozoic uplift and combined processes of weathering, mass wasting, and erosion that have been sculpting the surface of the land for the past 15 million years.

See also: ICE AGES.

—Hugh H. Mills, *Tennessee Technological University*

Sandra H. B. Clark, *Birth of the Mountains: The Geologic Story of the Southern Appalachian Mountains* (2001); H. H. Mills and P. A. Delcourt, "Appalachian Highlands and Interior Low Plateaus," in *The Geology of North America, Vol. K-2: Quaternary Nonglacial Geology: Conterminous United States*, ed. R. B. Morrison (1991).

Coal

Coal is the preserved remains of land plants, including roots, bark, and wood. In the Appalachian coal basin, five major plant groups contributed to the formation of coal. These are lycopods, ferns, seed ferns, calamites, and cordaites. Appalachian coal was formed from vast deposits of peat derived from plant remains that accumulated in tropical to subtropical swamps during the Pennsylvanian period of the Paleozoic era from 323 to 290 million years ago. A number of natural physical changes were involved as the peat accumulated, was buried, and underwent a process called coalification that gradually turned it into a solid, highly combustible fuel.

A prime requirement for the transformation was a subtropical or tropical climate. As shifting tectonic plates rearranged Earth's continents during the late Paleozoic, the continent of Laurentia, consisting of what is now North America and Greenland, was located astride the equator. Thus what is now eastern North America experienced ever-warm, ever-wet subtropical to tropical conditions ideal for the abundant growth of plants such as tree-sized ferns.

At the same time peat was accumulating, the continents of Laurentia and Gondwana were converging, resulting in the uplift of the eastern margin of what is now North America. Simultaneously, the Appalachian Basin was being formed to the west of the highland. As this very large basin subsided, swamps, or mires, repeatedly formed and became buried by sediments derived from the eastern highland. Over a period of more than 20 million years, thousands of feet of sediments, including many layers of peat, were ultimately deposited in the Appalachian Basin.

The ultimate nature of the coal that formed was influenced by conditions that existed within the swamp during the formation of peat, including the mix of plant materials, the chemistry of swamp waters, and the drainage of the swamp where the plant debris accumulated. Once the peat was buried thousands of feet below the surface, temperature and pressure that existed at depth initiated the process of coalification. Of the two parameters, heat was the more important. Heat flows constantly from deep within Earth, a phenomenon called the geothermal gradient. The combination of depth of burial, duration of burial, and heat resulted in creation of different ranks of coal. Coal rank progresses from the lowest, lignite, a soft brown coal, to sub-bituminous and bituminous coal to the highest rank, anthracite. During the coalification process, volatile materials are driven off by heat, thereby concentrating carbon. The primary difference in various ranks of coal is the concentration of carbon. In general, as the rank increases, the heating value in British thermal units per pound increases. Within individual ranks, coals are further subdivided based on the amount of volatiles (gases) remaining into high, medium, and low. Most coal deposits of Appalachia, extending from Pennsylvania to Alabama, are bituminous with large anthracite deposits located in northeastern Pennsylvania. For Appalachian bituminous coals, the volatile matter ranges from about 25 percent to as much as 40 percent.

In addition to rank, coal is also classified by grade or quality, depending upon the content of ash, inorganic impurities (primarily mineral matter), and sulfur. Mineral matter consists largely of various clays and quartz with lesser amounts of carbonate minerals such as calcite and siderite and the iron disulfide minerals pyrite and marcasite. When coal is burned, the mineral matter becomes ash. Because the mineral matter is not a source of heat, it does not contribute to the energy potential of the coal and must be disposed of following combustion.

Most of the environmental problems associated with the utilization of coal as a fuel come from the sulfur content. In unweathered coal, sulfur is present in two basic forms: organic sulfur, an elemental component of the organic portion of the coal, and pyritic sulfur, the sulfur contained within the iron disulfide minerals, primarily pyrite (FeS_2). In general, organic sulfur is the major form of sulfur in coals containing less than 1 percent total sulfur. When the total sulfur content of coal exceeds 1 percent, it is because of the increasing content of the iron disulfide minerals. When coal is burned, the sulfur is oxidized to form various gases, usually designated SO_X. If allowed to enter the atmosphere, the sulfur oxides react with water to produce strong acids such as sulfurous and sulfuric acid (H_2SO_3 and H_2SO_4), which are major components of acid rain. Within the Appalachian Basin, coals from the central coal basin (southern West Virginia and eastern Kentucky) usually contain less than 1 percent total sulfur while many of the coals from the northern coal basin (northern West Virginia, western Pennsylvania, and Ohio) have total sulfur contents in excess of 1 percent.

For many years, power plants burning coal have been sources of acid rain. With the passage of amendments to the Clean Air Act in 1990, coal with low sulfur content became especially valued. Developments in combustion technology, including the use of scrubbers and fluidized bed combustors utilizing integrated gasification combined cycle units within

COAL PRODUCTION

State	1999 Production in Millions of Tons	Peak Production in Millions of Tons	Peak Year	Cumulative Production in Billions of Tons
West Virginia	158.0	173.7	1947	12.2
Kentucky	104.3	131.0	1990	5.6
Pennsylvania	76.4	276.7	1918	16.3
Virginia	32.3	46.4	1990	2.3
Ohio	22.5	55.2	1970	3.5
Alabama	19.5	28.1	1990	2.1
Maryland	4.1	5.5	1907	0.2
Tennessee	3.0	11.3	1972	NA
Basin Totals	420.1			42.2

the firebox, have significantly reduced the amount of atmospheric pollutants produced by coal-burning power plants.

The greater volume of coal consists of organic matter present as various kinds of macerals, coalified fragments of wood, leaves, roots, and other original plant materials that are observed under a microscope. Coal is ground to a fine powder, mixed with a binder and formed into pellets that are polished and viewed under high magnification. The rank of the coal is determined by the way that light is reflected from the polished surface: the higher the reflectance value, the higher the rank.

An important coal science is palynology, the study of the fossil spores and pollen contained within the coal. Palynological studies are accomplished by placing the powdered coal in a strong acid, which dissolves most of the coal, leaving a residue of spores. Analysis of spores makes it possible to identify types and ages of plants that lived within the swamps and contributed to the formation of the coal.

Appalachian coal is overwhelmingly of the banded type, which refers to the layering of bright and dull materials that are, in turn, a relic of the original peat deposit. Fires, droughts, floods, changing water chemistry, and changing peat communities within the swamp during accumulation of the plant debris create distinctive layers within the peat deposit that become the bright and dull banding in the coal bed.

Appalachian coal beds (formerly referred to as seams) range in thickness from a few inches to twenty feet with some beds extending as much as one hundred miles and reaching into as many as three states. Although coal beds of only a few inches can be mined at the surface, beds must be at least twenty-eight inches thick to be commercially mined underground. The average thickness of coal mined in both surface and deep mines in the Appalachian coal basin at the end of the twentieth century was about forty-two inches. Boreholes drilled within the Appalachian Basin sometimes penetrate dozens of different beds, depending on the geographic location of the hole. The geologic science of stratigraphy identifies the strata and coal beds within a basin. Fossils recovered from the boreholes are used to date and map individual coal beds. The first mapping of coal beds took place in the late 1800s in order to estimate coal resources and facilitate plans for mining.

According to production records kept by state and federal governments, as of 2000 the Appalachian region had produced 42.2 billion tons of coal since 1850. For comparison, in 2001 the United States produced and consumed a billion tons of coal, of which the Appalachian region produced about 42 percent.

Coal is mined in Appalachia by surface- and deep-mining techniques. Surface-mining methods include contour mining, area mining, and mountaintop removal. Deep-mining methods, either by shaft, slope, or drift, include room-and-pillar, longwall, and shortwall mining.

See also: APPALACHIAN PLATEAUS PROVINCE; COAL MINING (ENVIRONMENT); OIL AND GAS.

—James C. Cobb, *Kentucky Geological Survey*

James C. Cobb and C. Blaine Cecil, eds., *Modern and Ancient Coal-Forming Environments* (1993); James C. Cobb et al., eds., *Coal and Coal-Bearing Rocks of Eastern Kentucky* (1981); Claus F. K. Diessel, *Coal-Bearing Depositional Systems* (1992).

Geomorphology

Of all the scientific disciplines brought to bear upon the history, evolution, and characteristics of the Appalachian Mountains, geomorphology takes the most encompassing view. Geomorphic analysis can be organized in a variety of ways, but since the twentieth century geologists have divided Appalachia into four geomorphic provinces, each with a unity or consistency of geologic structures, a commonality of weathering and erosion processes, and a comparable interval of time during which those processes operated. The four geomorphic provinces of Appalachia are the Piedmont Province, the Blue Ridge Province, the Ridge and Valley Province, and the Appalachian Plateaus Province. The greater Appalachian region also includes the New England Province and the Adirondack Province, which are not included in the Appalachian Regional Commission's definition of the region. The provinces of Appalachia are bordered on the east and south by the Atlantic and Gulf Coastal Plains and on the west and north by the Interior Low Plateaus and the Central Lowlands of the United States and, to a limited extent, by the ancient rocks of the Canadian Shield north of the Great Lakes. Numerous sub-provinces or sections have also been defined. For example, in Appalachia the Ridge and Valley Province is subdivided into a Tennessee Section and a Middle Section. The plateau is also informally subdivided into glaciated and non-glaciated sections in recognition of the distinct geomorphic contrasts created when the northern portions of the Appalachians were repeatedly overrun by continental ice sheets.

The geomorphic (or physiographic) provinces of the United States were formalized by a committee of noted geologists and geographers chaired by Professor Nevin M. Fenneman of the University of Cincinnati in 1915. The eastern provinces are described in Fenneman's 1938 book *Physiography of the Eastern United States.* Boundaries chosen by the Fenneman committee of the Association of American Geographers have withstood every test with only minor

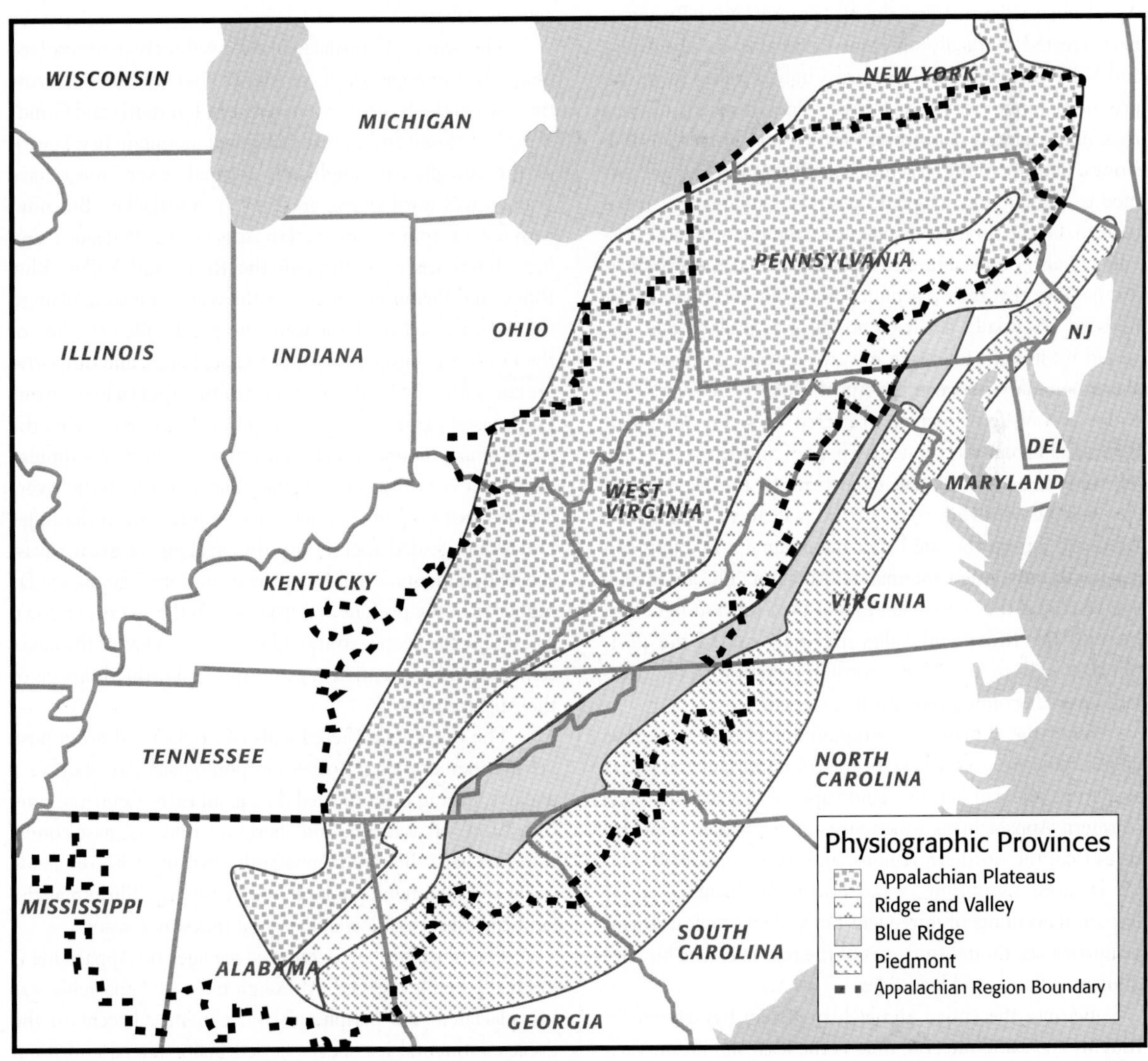

Geologists commonly divide Appalachia into four geomorphic provinces, each with a distinctive topography and geological history.

revisions, and its designations have been adopted as official terminology by the U.S. Geological Survey. Images from sensors in space and digitized shaded relief maps have provided striking confirmation of the Fenneman boundaries, emphasizing the remarkable achievement of their being defined when topographic maps were inferior and aerial photography was still a curiosity.

Of the three criteria used to define geomorphic provinces—structure, process, and time—geologic structure is the most obvious. Structure encompasses all rock properties, including mineral composition, crystallinity or particle size, and deformational features such as fractures and folds. Even to casual observers, it is evident that the granitic rocks of the Blue Ridge are different from those in the slate belt of the Piedmont or the "endless mountains" of folded sandstones, shales, and limestones of the Ridge and Valley Province. However, very similar rock types exposed in both the Appalachian Plateaus and the Ridge and Valley Provinces have created markedly different landscapes. In the Ridge and Valley Province, erosion across tightly folded strata has produced long, zigzag, repetitive ridges made of discrete rock units, namely Tuscarora, Pocono, and Pottsville sandstones. Because of the structures, the Ridge and Valley Province is drained and sculpted by streams following a trellis pattern. Of the three sandstone units, the Pocono and Pottsville are also exposed in the Appalachian Plateaus Province, but because this region is underlain by either broad, gentle folds or essentially flat-lying strata, it is drained and dissected by streams following mostly dendritic patterns. The sharp boundary between the Appalachian Plateaus and the Ridge and Valley Provinces, referred to as the Allegheny Structural Front, was created by beds of Silurian-age (417 to 443 million years old) salt deep beneath the plateau that allowed the overlying rocks of the plateau to slide northwestward during the late Paleozoic mountain-building episode with only minor internal deformation. The absence of salt beds, and the subsequent loss of their lubricating effect, beneath the Ridge and Valley Province caused the post-Silurian rocks to be folded accordion fashion with the resistant layers becoming repetitively exposed.

Since the climate of the region differs only in degree, geomorphic processes have been less important than rock structures in shaping the landscape of Appalachia. The southern Appalachians experience milder winter temperatures than the northern regions, and spring snowmelt runoff is more significant in the north. As documented by historical accounts of infrequent but violent tropical storms or hurricanes, though, any part of the region can be hit with disastrous floods and landslides.

Because the entire Appalachian system has existed for roughly the same interval, time is the least significant variable in defining the geomorphic provinces. The only exception to this generalization is the impact that the ice ages had on the northern Appalachians, where erosion by ice sheets and the intense tundra-like climate peripheral to the ice put a distinct and relatively young imprint over a much older landscape.

Of central importance to Appalachian geomorphology is the enormous amount of erosion that occurred during and since the late Paleozoic and early Mesozoic mountain building. Simple geometric reconstruction of the folded strata in the Ridge and Valley Province shows that at least five miles of rock have been eroded away to expose the present-day valley-floor-to-ridge-crest relief of only about one-half mile. The manner in which rivers, weathering, and soil creep accomplished such vast erosion has been the major theme of Appalachian geomorphic research for well over a century. Hypotheses developed to explain Appalachian landscapes have been applied to all other continents and continue to be actively debated.

The origin of Appalachian river valleys is an unresolved question. Geologic evidence shows that in late Paleozoic time, when the Iapetus Ocean between Laurentia and Gondwana had closed and a great collisional mountain belt known as the Alleghenian Highlands formed, rivers must have drained westward across present-day Appalachia. But now, with few exceptions, the eastern Appalachian Plateaus Province drains eastward through the Ridge and Valley, Blue Ridge, and Piedmont and across the younger coastal plain to the Atlantic Ocean. How were the great valley systems of the Delaware, Susquehanna, Potomac, James, and other rivers cut across the hard-rock ridges of the Appalachian chain? Did coastal plain rivers gnaw headward into and across the Appalachian mountain belt? Was there formerly a sedimentary cover over the entire Appalachians on which the rivers drained eastward in channels superimposed onto the older underlying folded rocks? Did the stacking of great thrust sheets by mountain building provide an initial landscape far higher than the present one from which the rivers cut down to exhume the deeper strata? These are but a few of the questions raised by scientists seeking to explain the drainage of the Appalachians.

The deeply weathered soils of unglaciated areas pose yet another challenge to geomorphologists. Are they very ancient, having been formed during an early Cenozoic time of subtropical warmth, and therefore relics of past conditions, or have they been constantly evolving with the landscape and maintaining a kind of dynamic equilibrium as the landscape has been lowered several miles by erosion?

The impact of late Cenozoic ice ages on Appalachia is gradually being clarified. Although most of Appalachia was not glaciated, the peripheral cold climate adjacent to the great continental ice sheets caused major faunal and floral dislocations, thereby changing the character of soil-forming processes and imposing a tundra-like climate on the Appalachian highlands. Specialists debate the origin of the great boulder fields and block streams that scar the upland slopes, but all agree that they are the result of severe cold climate.

The great issues of geomorphology have global implications and engage specialists from many nations, and Appalachia remains one of the world's special regions for geomorphic research.

See also: APPALACHIAN PLATEAUS PROVINCE; BLUE RIDGE PROVINCE; RIDGE AND VALLEY PROVINCE.

—Arthur L. Bloom, *Cornell University*

Nevin M. Fenneman, *Physiography of the Eastern United States* (1938).

Ice Ages

Recent research on glaciation has shown that the long-accepted chronology of four worldwide continental glaciations, or ice ages, during the last several million years separated by interglacial climates is in error. Hence, perception of their impact on the Appalachians has changed. The most recent glacial ages actually consisted of many more individual glaciations than had previously been thought. The ice ages probably began in Antarctica perhaps 10 to 20 million years ago during the Miocene epoch as Earth began to undergo a slow but progressive episode of global cooling. During many extreme cold phases that followed over the past 2.4 to 2.5 million years, great continental ice sheets waxed and waned over portions of North America, Scandinavia, Greenland, and Antarctica. All that remains of these great ice sheets are those on Greenland and Antarctica, both of which are in retreat. During these same periods of extreme cold, smaller ice caps developed in many other regions, including Baffin Island and Iceland, with valley glaciers becoming more extensive throughout many of the world's mountains.

During about the last 2 million years of the Cenozoic era, deepening snow recrystallized under great pressure and formed continental ice sheets several miles thick across northern and central Canada. These continental glaciers spread outward by a combination of flowage within the ice and basal sliding as they advanced over the land. In the Appalachians, thick ice sheets buried all of present-day New England and New York, northeastern and northwestern Pennsylvania, and much of Ohio. In the mountains, the topography was scoured and disrupted by ice movements, leaving behind intricate patterns of bedrock, exposed by glacial erosion in some places and covered by glacially derived debris in others. The size of rocks moved by the ice was unlimited. Glacially transported boulders can be found near the summits of New England's highest peaks such as Mount Washington in New Hampshire and Mount Katahdin in Maine. Despite occasional rumors, there is, as yet, no proof of any late Cenozoic glaciation within the Appalachians beyond these known glacial margins.

Within glaciated areas, direct effects of the ice were pervasive. Glacial erosion created basins for many bodies of water, including the five Great Lakes between United States and Canada and the Finger Lakes in New York. Another prominent effect of ice was the destruction or derangement of stream drainage patterns. Some streams that had originally flowed northward were switched to channels that now flow either away from or along the former ice margins. The present course of part of the Ohio River, for example, was largely determined by the combined effects of several ice sheets. The great mass of ice also depressed Earth's crust, further altering the flow of streams and the accumulation of water bodies.

In addition to the direct effects on drainage, glacial deposition affected stream flow by blanketing areas with extensive sheets of ice-deposited till and water-deposited stratified glacial drift. Vast amounts of glacial debris, entrained by meltwater streams issuing from the margins of melting glaciers, were carried away to be deposited downstream as outwash plains. The valleys of major rivers such as the Delaware, Susquehanna, Allegheny, and Ohio contain numerous river terraces composed of glacially derived sediments. Most soils in glaciated regions have formed from glacial parent materials and have developed since the melting and retreat of ice from the Appalachians during the last ten thousand to fifteen thousand years.

The effects of late Cenozoic ice-age climates on Appalachian landscapes and earth materials were both profound and regionally extensive. Compared to the present, climates were colder, drier, and windier. Cloud cover was more extensive, and much of the precipitation fell as snow. The wind eroded, transported, and deposited vast amounts of fine-grained sediment that either formed deposits of clay and silt called loess or became incorporated into other sediments and soils. Both deep seasonal ground frost and perennially frozen ground called permafrost formed in many areas. The resultant freezing and thawing disrupted and mobilized soil material. Frost wedging shattered bedrock and the combination of frost action and soil flowage moved great amounts of soil and rock downslope and deposited them in the valleys. The huge amount of water locked up in ice sheets lowered sea level, causing rivers near the coast to deepen their valleys. Massive dislocations and shifts in plant and animal communities took place. A wide belt of tundra vegetation with open subarctic woodland developed beyond the ice margins and extended southward into the Blue Ridge Mountains.

The causes of global climate change remain a subject of intense research. Cooling that was sufficient to cause continental glaciation in high latitudes also caused significant cooling in equatorial climates. Such episodes of extreme refrigeration are especially significant in light of the fact that throughout Earth's history worldwide climate has been more nearly subtropical and much warmer than the present-day global average. An eventual resolution of the causes of ice ages may include a number of complex groups of mechanisms that operate in harmony. Plausible mechanisms and explanations for major global cooling fall into four basic groups. Cosmic hypotheses include changes in solar radiation, comet or meteoroid impacts, and the possibility that our solar system passes through clouds of gas and dust. Planetary hypotheses incorporate periodic changes in Earth's orbit around the Sun, its rotation, and in the wobble of its axis of rotation, or notation. Although the combined effects of planetary motions acting alone are too small to cause ice ages, their periodicities coincide with times of glacial advances and retreats, causing them to be referred to as "pacemakers of the ice ages." Geophysical hypotheses include the many effects of plate tectonics and continental drift that affect global climates. These effects include: shifting of continental plates near to or under a pole; changes in heat input to the ocean floors along seafloor spreading centers (such as the Mid-Atlantic Oceanic Ridge); the opening and closing of seaways that alter global oceanic current patterns; building of great mountain chains and plateaus; the so-called "holes in the greenhouse"; and episodes of the outpouring of widespread plateau flood basalts and cataclysmic volcanic eruptions. Atmospheric hypotheses concentrate on possible effects of particulate matter and gases, either blocking incoming solar radiation or allowing terrestrial long-wavelength radiation (infrared radiation or heat) to escape Earth's atmosphere, a process called insolation. Atmospheric interactions are extremely complex and interact with other processes, such as volcanic eruptions and the rise in the Cenozoic era of great north-south-trending mountain chains, that affect atmospheric circulation patterns. The effects of global climatic changes in the atmosphere are even further complicated by the major human input of heat, gases, and particulate matter that began with the Industrial Revolution in the mid-1700s.

Although relatively rare throughout the great span of geologic time, ice ages are not unique to the late Cenozoic. Older continental glaciations are recorded in the geologic record by the presence of tillites (lithified glacial sediments) that overlie polished and striated billion-year-old basement rocks and by ancient glacial lake and marine sediments. A number of episodes of continental glaciation are known from Precambrian time, and more may be discovered.

A well-documented glaciation of at least ice-cap proportions occurred more than 443 million years ago during late Ordovician time in what is now the Saharan region of Africa, which at the time of glaciation was near the South Pole. The best preserved and most extensive record of pre-Cenozoic continental glaciation occurred on the supercontinent of Pangea when it traversed the South Pole at the end of the Paleozoic era more than 248 million years ago. Dismembered by the breakup of Pangea during the mid-Mesozoic era about 200 million years ago, Pangean sedimentary rocks of glacial origin are found today in southern South America, southern Africa, Madagascar, Saudi Arabia, India, and southern Australia. Several locations in the Appalachians also contain rocks of ancient glacial origin that record glaciations that occurred before the Cenozoic era. The most extensive and best known of these occurred during the late Precambrian time, about 700 to 650 million years ago; these rocks can now be found in the Mount Rogers–Whitetop Mountain area of the Blue Ridge of southwestern Virginia. Not all discoveries of pre-Cenozoic glaciations are easily resolved by references to present-day conditions. Some evidence of apparently large-scale glaciations occurs in rocks that were originally parts of continental plate fragments that lay in low latitudes. Much more than is known today remains to be learned about the driving forces behind Earth's ancient climatic changes, especially those that cause ice ages.

See also: CENOZOIC ERA.

—G. Michael Clark, *University of Tennessee*

William D. Thornbury, *Regional Geomorphology of the United States* (1965).

Industrial Mineral Deposits

See Nonmetallic, Nonfuel Deposits

Mesozoic Era

The Mesozoic era spans the time from approximately 248 million years ago to 65 million years ago, a period most widely known as the age of dinosaurs. It was also the time when sedimentary and igneous rocks of the Triassic and Jurassic periods (approximately 248 to 144 million years ago) were deposited in old fault-bounded valleys or basins in the Piedmont Province of Appalachia.

Triassic and Jurassic sedimentary rocks were formed at a time when the Alleghenian Highlands, created at the close of Paleozoic time, were much higher than the Appalachian Mountains are today. The Alleghenian Highlands were formed by the collision of Laurentia and Gondwana about 248 million years ago, an event that completed formation of the supercontinent Pangea (meaning "all lands").

During the Triassic period, Pangea began to break up, creating the continents that exist today. As Pangea began to split or rift apart, rift valleys bounded by faults formed within what is now the Piedmont Province of Appalachia.

These valleys were rapidly filled with thousands of feet of sediment derived from the adjacent Alleghenian Highlands.

Around the beginning of the Jurassic period (about 206 million years ago), as the continents were separating and the Atlantic Ocean was being created, basaltic lava erupted from cracks or faults in the valley floors and covered them. One crack (or set of cracks) became dominant and produced vast volumes of basaltic lava, which made up the first crust of the developing Atlantic Ocean. As forces deep beneath Earth's surface further separated the newly formed continents, more lava erupted along a central oceanic ridge to create the oceanic crust of the spreading Atlantic Ocean. This process continues today along the summit of the Atlantic Oceanic Ridge as the Atlantic continues to widen at a rate of a couple of inches per year, about equal to the speed at which human fingernails grow. As a result of this process of seafloor spreading, North America is moving westward away from the oceanic ridge while Europe and Africa move eastward.

Pangea did not split apart along the line where Laurentia and Gondwana collided during its formation. This old seam, or suture zone, now lies in the southern portion of Georgia. As Africa was pulled away by the widening Atlantic Ocean, a sliver of the African continent was left attached to the southeastern corner of North America.

Today, a chain of elongated basins filled with Triassic and Jurassic rocks stretches from South Carolina to Nova Scotia. Originally, the rocks within these basins were deposited in horizontal layers, but since their deposition, the rocks have been faulted, tilted, and eroded. Additional basins filled with Triassic and Jurassic rocks are now buried beneath Cretaceous and younger sediments of the coastal plain to the south and east of the Piedmont.

The Triassic and Jurassic sedimentary and igneous rocks in these basins are referred to as the Newark Supergroup. The sedimentary rocks of the Newark Supergroup were deposited in continental (non-marine) environments such as river channels, floodplains and deltas, lakes, alluvial fans, swamps, and deserts. Most are reddish brown conglomerates, sandstones, siltstones, mudstones, claystones, and shales, some of which contain bones and footprints of dinosaurs and other reptiles. Lake deposits consisting of gray to black siltstones, limestones, and shales commonly contain fossils of fish and freshwater clams. In Virginia and North Carolina, some of the basins contain coal that formed from peat that accumulated in swamps adjacent to freshwater lakes. In some cases, coals have been mined commercially.

All of the fossils in the sedimentary rocks of the Newark Supergroup are of continental or freshwater origin. Vertebrate fossils include several types of fish, amphibians, land-dwelling reptiles, swimming reptiles, winged gliding reptiles, dinosaurs, and the mammal-like reptiles that were the ancestors to mammals. Invertebrate fossils include clams, snails, shrimp, crayfish, ostracods, and insects. Plant fossils are also present, particularly in those basins that contain coal beds. Plant fossils include ferns, horsetails, conifers, petrified wood, pollen, and spores. Some rocks contain trace fossils, which are marks left by certain organisms in the sediment, including the burrows of crayfish and other organisms and the footprints of amphibians and reptiles.

The igneous rocks of the Newark Supergroup consist primarily of basaltic lava flows and diabase. Basalt is a very fine-grained, dark gray to black rock that cooled quickly on Earth's surface. Basalt also makes up the Hawaiian volcanoes and the oceanic crust. Diabase has the same composition as basalt but is slightly more coarsely grained, reflecting the fact that it cooled more slowly underground. The basalt flows and diabase are approximately the same age, between 206 and 248 million years old. Examples of basalt flows can be seen in roadcuts near West Orange, New Jersey, where they are about three hundred feet thick. One of the largest and best-known diabase sills (tabular igneous intrusions) in the Appalachian region is the Palisades Escarpment along the Hudson River near New York City, where the sill is about nine hundred feet thick.

Some of the rocks of the Newark Supergroup are economically valuable. Reddish-brown siltstones and shales have been quarried for brick making, and other shales have been quarried for lightweight aggregate. Conglomerates from the Culpeper Basin have been used as building stone, including for columns inside the U.S. Capitol. Other conglomerates have been used as millstones. Diabase and basalt have also been crushed and used as "road metal" and "riprap." As basaltic magma rose through the sediments to erupt as basaltic lava, heat from the magma thermally altered, or metamorphosed, the sedimentary rocks where they came in contact with it, oftentimes forming new suites of minerals that concentrated locally to form ore deposits containing iron, lead, and nickel.

See also: PIEDMONT PROVINCE; TECTONICS.

—Pamela J. W. Gore, *Georgia Perimeter College*

Gwendolyn L. W. Luttrell, *Stratigraphic Nomenclature of the Newark Supergroup of Eastern North America*, U.S. Geological Survey Bulletin 1572 (1989); Warren Manspeizer, ed., *Triassic-Jurassic Rifting: Continental Breakup and the Origin of the Atlantic Ocean and Passive Margins* (1988); Gilpin R. Robinson Jr. and Albert J. Forelich, eds., *Proceedings of the Second U.S. Geological Survey Workshop on the Early Mesozoic Basins of the Eastern United States* (1985).

Metallic Ore Deposits

Compared to the western United States or Canada, the Appalachian region has never been a major source of metals. Nevertheless, at certain times and at specific locales, mines have played an important role in local and regional economies. Concentrations of valuable metals are generally rare in the lithosphere (the outer layer of solid earth) unless they are concentrated by some geologic mechanism. To be economically viable, mineral concentrations must be near enough to the surface to allow both discovery and extraction. The process of concentration typically occurs when hydrothermal fluids (hot, metal-bearing water) that evolve during the final stages of magma cooling permeate host rock surrounding the magma. Because the intense heat needed to drive these processes is usually released during episodes of mountain building, mineral deposits are commonly associated with mountain systems. Typically, these mineral-concentration processes operate either in the upper few miles of rock associated with a growing mountain system or within the core of the newly formed mountain range at depths of ten to twenty miles. The Appalachians would thus seem to be a logical place for metallic mineral deposits; however, extensive deposits of metallic minerals have not been found. These deposits might have existed in the upper few miles of rock when the mountains were first created 248 million years ago, but near-surface deposits were probably removed by erosion during the first 100 million years. Although the near-surface deposits are gone, it is still possible that deposits of metallic minerals are concentrated deep within the core of the Appalachians and are yet to be exposed by erosion. Another plausible explanation for the scarcity of metallic mineral deposits in the Appalachian system is that metal deposits are often associated with certain periods of geologic time called metallogenic epochs, and the late Proterozoic episode of mountain building in Appalachia was not one of these times. Nevertheless, Appalachian metal mines have in instances been important in the region's economy, development, and ecology.

At Ducktown in Polk County, Tennessee, copper was mined for several decades from massive iron and copper sulfide ore bodies, producing environmental havoc as well as jobs. These mineral deposits occur in sedimentary rocks that have been hardened and compressed by heat and pressure since the late Precambrian. Once mined, the ores were processed by a technique called open-roasting, during which the copper was extracted as charcoal fires turned the ore into a molten state. Sulfurous gases released into the atmosphere as the ores roasted combined with water to form strong sulfurous (H_2SO_3) and sulfuric (H_2SO_4) acids that fell as acid rain. The intense acidity of the rain resulted in a complete deforestation of the area around Ducktown, followed by extreme soil erosion as the protective plant cover was destroyed. By the 1920s, in addition to the production of copper metal, sulfuric acid and iron sulfide concentrates were also produced from these same ore deposits. When mining ceased in the late 1970s, aggregate production had probably exceeded seven hundred thousand tons of copper.

Iron and copper sulfide deposits of a similar nature were also found near West Jefferson, North Carolina (the Ore Knob Mine), and Galax, Virginia (the Gossan Lead District). The Ore Knob deposit was much smaller than at Ducktown, while the deposit at the Gossan Lead District, although nearly as large as the one at Ducktown, contained far less copper.

In addition to the iron produced at Ducktown, major iron mines operated around Birmingham, Alabama, during the first half of the twentieth century. The thick Silurian Red Mountain Formation was first mined in 1864. Fortuitously, the three basic materials needed for the production of iron and steel—iron ore, coal to make coke, and limestone to use as a flux—were all located within the area. The large-scale production of these three basic materials began in 1899 and made Birmingham a major iron and steel center for the next fifty years. During this time, more than 300 million tons of low-grade iron ore were mined. Major resources of iron ore still remain in the Birmingham area, but the local iron ore industry cannot compete economically with the taconite (iron-bearing jasper and chert) deposits of the Great Lakes region.

The first significant gold discovery in North America occurred in 1799 with the retrieval of a seventeen-pound nugget in Cabarrus County, North Carolina. Since then, gold has been mined intermittently from Cambrian-aged metamorphic volcanic rocks within the Piedmont of Virginia, North and South Carolina, and Georgia. The first lode gold mine was opened in 1825 in Stanly County, North Carolina. Gold production figures for the region are scanty, especially in the nineteenth century, but perhaps two million ounces of gold have been extracted throughout the Piedmont from stream placer deposits, quartz veins, and disseminated gold in volcanic rocks. In the second quarter of the nineteenth century, federal mints operated in Charlotte, North Carolina, and Dahlonega, Georgia, making coins from local gold. As recently as late 1990s, gold was mined in the Piedmont of South Carolina and was processed by the open-air, cyanide heap-leaching technique.

Commercial lead mining was conducted in Appalachia as early as 1756, when operations began at Austinville, Wythe County, Virginia. Throughout the Civil War, the site produced significant amounts of lead, mostly for Confederate munitions. Following the Civil War, mining at the site recommenced with both lead and zinc being produced until the mine closed in 1982. As is commonly the case with lead sulfide minerals, the deposits were emplaced into carbonate host rocks, in this case in recrystallized Ordovician limestones in the Ridge and Valley Province northwest of the Blue Ridge Mountains. The ore minerals were galena (PbS) and sphalerite (ZnS), with varying amounts of pyrite (FeS_2), fluorite (CaF_2), and chalcopyrite ($(Cu,Fe)S_2$). The zinc deposits of the Mascot–Jefferson City District in eastern Tennessee have been mined continuously from 1854 to the present. Located about fifteen miles northeast of Knoxville in the Ridge and Valley Province west of the Great Smoky Mountains, these deposits are concentrated in fracture zones within Ordovician carbonates.

Perhaps one of the best-known Appalachian carbonate-hosted ore deposits is the zinc deposit of Franklin and Sterling Hill near Ogdensburg, New Jersey. Contained in the Franklin Marble of the Jersey Highlands, the geologic equivalent of the Blue Ridge in the southern Appalachians, this district is famous for the occurrence of more than two hundred minerals, about one hundred of which occur nowhere else in the world. The ores are spectacularly fluorescent, and collectors and museums prize them for their bold and bright colors when exposed to ultraviolet light.

Much of the lithium metal produced in the United States comes from granite pegmatites (coarse-grained granite) in the Kings Mountain belt near Gastonia, North Carolina. Although the area is called the tin-spodumene belt, no significant amount of tin has been produced in the region. Spodumene is a lithium-bearing silicate mineral ($LiAlSi_2O_6$). The pegmatites also contain cassiterite (SnO_2), beryl ($Be_2Al_2Si_6O_{13}$), and rare phosphate minerals. The lithium-bearing pegmatites were intruded into the host rock about 350 million years ago and are slightly younger than the feldspar-rich pegmatites of the Spruce Pine District, North Carolina. Lithium has a number of applications, including in pharmaceutical products such as lithia tablets, welding fluxes, and alloys with aluminum, magnesium, lead, and zinc to give them greater hardness.

Near Sanford Lake in the Adirondack Mountains of New York, ilmenite ($FeTiO_3$) occurs with magnetite (Fe_3O_4) in oxide-rich bands in certain Precambrian igneous rocks. Ilmenite is also found in the Blue Ridge in Virginia (Roseland District) and North Carolina (Cranberry Mine), though in amounts too small to be commercially exploited. Ilmenite has been used as a source of iron.

The most important domestic source of tungsten during both World War II and the Korean War was the Hamme District in Vance County, North Carolina. More than a million tons of tungsten oxide were produced in the Carolina Piedmont from quartz (SiO_2) and huebnerite ($MnWO_4$) veins along the contact between phyllites (metamorphic rocks) and a large Cambrian-age granite body. Mining ceased in 1971. The most important use of tungsten is as a steel-hardening additive. Because of its high melting point, tungsten is also used as a filament in incandescent electric lights.

In most cases, Appalachian ores were mined early in the nation's history when transportation of heavy commodities such as metals and ore concentrates was difficult. With the coming of the railroads and the opening of the mineral-rich West, the small, mineralogically and structurally complex deposits of the Appalachian region could no longer compete economically. An additional factor was that almost all of the land in Appalachia was privately held. In contrast, most of the land in the West was owned by the government, and federal legislation actually encouraged citizens to explore for and lay claim to minerals on public lands. Nevertheless, localized metal deposits often had deep and lasting influences on the cultural and economic history of specific areas within Appalachia.

See also: COAL; NONMETALLIC, NONFUEL DEPOSITS; OIL AND GAS.

—P. Geoffrey Feiss, *College of William and Mary*

P. G. Feiss and J. F. Slack, "Mineral Deposits of the U.S. Appalachians," in *The Geology of North America, Vol. F-2: The Appalachian-Ouachita Orogen in the United States*, ed. Robert D. Hatcher Jr., William A. Thomas, and George W. Viehle (1989); John. D. Ridge, ed., *Ore Deposits of the United States, 1933–1967* (1968); U.S. Geological Survey and U.S. Bureau of Mines, *Mineral Resources of the Appalachian Region*, U.S. Geological Survey Professional Paper 580 (1968).

Military and Cultural Geology

Two aspects of geology, landforms and mineral resources, profoundly affected the course of human history, including military events in three of the four physiographic provinces of Appalachia—the Blue Ridge, the Ridge and Valley, and the Appalachian Plateaus.

The Blue Ridge Mountains, underlain by resistant igneous and metamorphic rocks, host the highest elevations in the eastern United States. Because the slopes are generally steep and the soils are thin, local farms tended to be small, in sharp contrast to the plantations of the Tidewater and the Deep South. Geographically isolated in this difficult terrain, the inhabitants of the Blue Ridge developed a sense of social, political, and economic separation from the plantation culture. One example of this spirit of independence was strong Unionist sentiment that pervaded many of the Blue Ridge counties of Virginia, North Carolina, and Tennessee during the Civil War.

The eastern portion of the Ridge and Valley Province, known as the Great Valley, lies several hundred feet lower in elevation than the highlands of the Blue Ridge on the east and the ridges to the west. The Great Valley exists because of the predominance throughout the region of limestone, a soluble and therefore easily eroded rock. The western portion of the Ridge and Valley Province is topographically diversified with an intermittent series of parallel, even-crested ridges created by folded and thrust-faulted layers of resistant sandstone and conglomerate that stand high above the limestone, dolostone, and shales of the valley floors.

The Great Valley provides one of Appalachia's most striking connections between geology and human history. Within the valley, the weathering of pervasive limestone produced broad stretches of fertile bottomland and an easily accessible northeast-southwest-trending transportation corridor. The construction of the Virginia and Tennessee Railroad in the Great Valley of southwestern Virginia in the 1850s from Big Lick (Roanoke) to Bristol served to spur commercialization of the region and subsequently increased slaveholding, thus strengthening ties with the Tidewater and Piedmont sections. Unlike mountain people of southeast and northwest Appalachia, inhabitants of the Great Valley remained steadfastly loyal to the Confederate cause when war broke out in 1861.

The Appalachian Plateaus Province is underlain by thick, essentially flat-lying sedimentary rocks dissected by a dendritic network of streams into disconnected hills and valleys. The eastern portion of this region is the bold, forbidding escarpment of the Allegheny and Cumberland Plateaus, which served as the major barrier for westward migration in southern and central Appalachia during the early days of settlement, hence the importance of the Cumberland Gap. The Cumberland Gap is an example of a wind gap, which is a topographic saddle along a mountain ridge that was once occupied by a stream that has since disappeared. With an elevation of sixteen hundred feet, the Cumberland Gap provided the easiest opening along the entire plateau front for westward-bound travelers and, as a result, became the principal gateway to the frontier for migrants from Virginia and the Carolinas.

As was the case in the Blue Ridge, the steep slopes and thin soils of the Plateaus Province led to vastly different economic, social, and political views for its inhabitants relative to the slave-based agricultural systems of the low-relief areas of the southeastern and Gulf Coast states. Perhaps the most spectacular example of the impact of these conflicting cultural heritages occurred when a large portion of western Virginia's plateau counties joined with some of the counties within the Ridge and Valley and broke away from the rest of Virginia to form the Unionist state of West Virginia in 1863.

The mineral resources of Appalachia also have had a profound impact on the region's history and economic development. The Blue Ridge supplies a variety of valuable minerals typical of crystalline rocks, particularly those containing metals such as iron, copper, and gold. Among other minerals, the Ridge and Valley has rich deposits of gypsum, salt, and the ores of iron, lead, and manganese. Underlying the Appalachia Plateaus Province are copious amounts of coal, a resource intimately associated with the very fabric of life throughout the western part of the region.

Lead and salt deposits of the Ridge and Valley in southwestern Virginia figured prominently during the Civil War as battles raged around these strategic resources and the railroad that carried them. The lead mines of Austinville, Virginia, provided virtually all of the lead produced domestically in the South, eventually contributing at least one-third of the total amount of lead consumed by Confederate forces during the war. The saltworks of Saltville, Virginia, were an equally important strategic mineral operation, ultimately providing two-thirds of the total Southern salt supply.

Following the outbreak of hostilities in 1861, the mineral operations at Saltville and Austinville quickly attracted the attention of Federal strategists. A third major target soon emerged in southwestern Virginia when the Virginia and Tennessee Railroad established itself as the lifeline to the west for General Robert E. Lee and his Army of Northern Virginia. However, during most of the war, getting to these objectives was a formidable task for Northern commanders, who had to attack from bases in West Virginia and Kentucky. For the Federal forces, this meant moving through treacherous, deeply dissected plateaus and across the mountainous western portion of the Ridge and Valley. Steep ridges, narrow valleys, numerous streams, and poor roads made it virtually impossible to supply a sizeable army. The few large gaps through the ridges were especially dangerous in that a small force of defenders could use these narrow defiles to create death traps for the invaders. The Union commanders, therefore, had no option but to deploy small, fast-moving forces to get at critical mineral operations and the railroad.

In spite of daunting physiographic conditions, Federal forces staged a number of raids into southwestern Virginia. In July 1863, Union Colonel John Toland and about 1,000 mounted soldiers advanced from West Virginia toward the lead mines. Although they reached and burned part of nearby Wytheville, they returned home without damaging the lead works. Union General William Averell and his cavalry assaulted Wytheville again in May 1864 but were turned back. Averell's sortie was part of a larger campaign to incapacitate the Virginia and Tennessee Railroad that was launched from Charleston, West Virginia, and led by General George Crook. Crook and his 6,500 troopers crossed the Appalachian Plateaus and the western portion of the Ridge and Valley and defeated 2,500 Confederate troops along the western edge of the Great Valley at the battle of Cloyds Mountain. This fierce fight, resulting in more than 1,200 total casualties, was the largest battle in southwestern Virginia. Following his victory, Crook burned the railroad bridge over the New River at Central Depot (now Radford, Virginia) before retreating to his base in West Virginia.

In October 1864, a major battle erupted at Saltville when General Stephen Burbridge and 5,200 mounted Union soldiers came through the plateau country of southeastern Kentucky and southwestern Virginia. Once again, the rugged terrain had an impact on the campaign. Some men and animals fell to their deaths from precipitous trails while others had to be laboriously rescued by ropes. Burbridge eventually reached Saltville, only to be defeated by Confederate defenders entrenched along the heights guarding the northern approaches to the saltworks.

The mineral operations and the railroad were finally attacked successfully in December 1864, when Union General George Stoneman left his base in Knoxville, Tennessee, and followed the Great Valley northward into southwestern Virginia. Advancing along this natural highway, Stoneman drove the weak Confederate troops before him. Stoneman's forces burned railroad trestles, rolling stock, and depots from Bristol to ten miles north of Wytheville. On December 17, 1864, two regiments of Union cavalry attacked and destroyed much of the lead operations. Turning southward, Stoneman's forces arrived at Saltville three days later, overwhelmed its few defenders, and destroyed as much as possible before withdrawing back to Knoxville. Despite the damage caused by Stoneman, mineral operations continued. Within a few weeks, repair crews once again had salt production underway, and production at the lead works resumed in March 1865, near the war's end.

See also: APPALACHIAN PLATEAUS PROVINCE; CIVIL WAR (GOVERNMENT); RIDGE AND VALLEY PROVINCE.

—Robert C. Whisonant, *Radford University*

D. Evans, "Stoneman's Raids," in *Encyclopedia of the Confederacy*, ed. Richard N. Current (1993); Ella Lonn, *Salt as a Factor in the Confederacy* (1993); William Marvel, *The Battles of Saltville* (1992).

Mountain Building

See Tectonics

Nonmetallic, Nonfuel Deposits

Natural resources present in the nonmetallic, nonfuel deposits of the Appalachian region are an important source of raw materials for modern society. The construction industry, which depends heavily on nonmetallic materials, consumes enormous volumes of crushed rock, dimension stone, sand, and gravel. Crushed rock is produced by both open-pit quarries and deep mines and has a number of applications, from concrete aggregate, road base materials, and railroad ballast to various erosion-control applications such as the building of gabions, the wire-mesh boxes commonly seen stacked along stream banks. Although any type of rock is potentially a source for crushed rock, some rock types are more desirable than others, depending upon the application. Crushed rock intended as a road base material, for example, must pass the Los Angeles Abrasion Test, in which the rock is subjected to abrasion for a specified period of time in a ball mill. Rock materials that experience a specified minimum amount of physical degradation in the mill are considered acceptable. In general, rocks such as limestones and granites fare well, while many sandstones fail because they are either too brittle or poorly cemented. Soft rocks such as shale always fail such a test.

Dimension stone is extracted by cutting and wedging slabs or blocks from bedrock, mostly in open-pit quarries. These blocks or slabs may then be sawed, polished, or carved to meet individual job specifications. Dimension stone is used in building construction (foundations, walls, chimneys, sills, steps, trim), bridge abutments, paving, curbing, monuments, and statues. Within Appalachia, the types of stone available for dimension stone include sandstone, limestone, marble (metamorphosed limestone), granite, quartzite, gneiss, and slate. At the present time, most of the dimension stone produced in Appalachia is quarried in the Piedmont, Blue Ridge, and Ridge and Valley Provinces.

Two other nonmetallic materials produced in enormous quantities are sand and gravel. Most sand and gravel come from the excavation of fluvial (stream), glacial, or residual (weathering) deposits, although some sand is produced by the crushing of sandstones. Sand consists primarily of small grains of quartz, while gravels are mixtures of pebble-size and smaller particles of resistant rock materials such as sandstone, quartz, quartzite, and chert. Concrete, mortar, and plaster are made from sand. Glacial materials were transported into the northern Appalachian region by Pleistocene ice sheets and deposited in various forms of glacial till. Some of these materials were then picked up and carried further south by meltwater streams. As a result, some of these materials exist as surface accumulations while others are now associated with the floodplains and channels of major streams such as the Ohio River. Ohio River gravels are widely utilized in the northern plateaus for road base materials and as a source of aggregate in the manufacture of concrete and asphaltic mixes. Sands and gravels are produced in all of the Appalachian provinces although production in the Ridge and Valley is relatively low due to the lack of fluvial, glacial, and residual materials.

One particularly important rock type is limestone ($CaCO_3$). Limestone is produced in all of the Appalachian provinces but to a lesser degree in the Piedmont and Blue Ridge, where most of the rocks are igneous or metamorphic. In addition to serving as a dimension stone and being crushed to produce limestone aggregate, limestone is the raw material for a number of manufacturing processes. For example, limestone is heated in kilns to produce lime (CaO), which has a variety of chemical and metallurgical applications and is used in mine land reclamation, where high levels of alkalinity are needed. Limestone can also be ground to a fine powder and applied as agricultural lime, which neutralizes the acidic soils that characterize much of Appalachia. A new and increasingly important use for limestone is in controlling sulfur dioxide emissions from coal-fired power plants. Sulfur oxides from coal-burning plants contribute to the formation of acid rain. Powdered limestone is mixed with water to form a slurry that is sprayed into flue gases exiting from the plants. The limestone reacts with the sulfur oxide gases and forms gypsum. Some power plants recover this synthetic gypsum and use it to manufacture wallboard. Crushed limestone finds wide application in construction, from road bases to the erosion control of streams. Many homes throughout the Great Valley are constructed of locally quarried limestone.

High-purity quartz (SiO_2) is a valuable commodity that can be acquired from sand, high-purity sandstones, and quartzites (metamorphosed sandstones) as well as in high-purity quartz deposits found as veins in igneous and metamorphic rocks. Pure quartz is the raw material for molding sands, glass and refractories, and filter beds. Quartz crystals needed for the manufacture of electronic components such as silicon chips are grown from high-purity North Carolina quartz.

Because of its hardness, quartz also makes an excellent abrasive. Some higher-purity sandstones quarried in Ohio and West Virginia contribute to the manufacture of abrasive tools such as grindstones, pulpstones, oilstones, and whetstones. In the early days of settlement, several of the sandstone formations in the northern plateaus were found to be ideal for the manufacture of grinding stones for gristmills. Before the days of emery paper, quartz sand was sized and glued to paper to produce the various grades of sandpaper. Other natural materials used as abrasives include corundum, garnet, and feldspar. Corundum is mixed with magnetite or hematite for grinding wheels, abrasive powders, and emery cloth. Garnet paper and cloth are employed in the dressing of leather. Extremely fine-grained garnet powder can also sharpen razor blades and microtome blades. Feldspar is a common abrasive in household cleansers designed to scour, but not scratch, surfaces such as tile and porcelain.

Clay mineral deposits, especially high-kaolinite clays associated with certain coal beds, are components in the manufacture of paper, stoneware, and various ceramic products. Igneous and metamorphic rocks in the Blue Ridge and Piedmont Provinces have been sources of a number of silicate minerals used as raw materials in the manufacturing industry: feldspar for the manufacture of glass and other ceramic products; olivine in the production of refractories; and mica in a variety of products including joint compound, paint, roofing shingles, drilling mud, and rubber products. At present, most of these materials come from mining operations in North Carolina. The mineral barite ($BaSO_4$), the base of various barium chemical compounds, provides filler for paint and rubber and adds weight to the mud used in the drilling of deep oil and gas wells. Most of the barite produced in Appalachia comes from mines in Georgia.

The production of salt was a major industry throughout the Appalachian Plateaus Province dating back to the 1700s. In fact, even before the arrival of the Europeans, Native Americans boiled brines from salt springs to obtain salt. Originally, European settlers acquired salt by the same process as the Indians. In time, however, most of the brines were produced by drilling shallow wells into brine-producing rock formations. During the early years of migration after the Civil War, West Virginia was one of the major suppliers of salt to settlers heading west. During the drilling of many of these brine wells, it was not uncommon to encounter oil and gas, a discovery that eventually led to beginning of the modern oil industry. Modern Appalachian salt production primarily supports the chemical industry.

See also: COAL; METALLIC ORE DEPOSITS; OIL AND GAS.

—Garland R. Dever Jr., *Kentucky Geological Survey*

U.S. Geological Survey, *Mineral Commodity Summaries 2000* (2000); U.S. Geological Survey and U.S. Bureau of Mines, *Mineral Resources of the Appalachian Region,* U.S. Geological Survey Professional Paper 580 (1968) and *Minerals Yearbook, Area Reports: Domestic 1998* (2000).

Oil and Gas

The exploitation of petroleum in the Appalachians started in the early 1800s with drillers who were searching for salt brines. In 1859, with crude oil becoming widely recognized as a source of energy, a group of entrepreneurs drilled the Drake Well near Titusville, Pennsylvania. Although this is considered the beginning of the modern petroleum industry, the Appalachian Basin, stretching from eastern Tennessee to western New York, had already been producing oil for more than two centuries.

Long before Europeans arrived in the Appalachians, Native Americans used log structures to trap petroleum from seeps along the Allegheny River. In about 1625, French missionaries provided accounts of the use of oil by the Senecas of central and western New York and northwestern Pennsylvania. Native American recovery methods may have resembled those later employed by the Youngloves, two druggists from Bowling Green, Kentucky, who shortly before 1850 recovered a barrel of oil from a local seep by spreading a blanket over the seep and wringing out petroleum absorbed by the cloth.

In 1790, between Parkersburg and Charleston in what is now West Virginia, George Washington observed a burning spring, which he bought and willed to Virginia and which later became a major producer of oil and gas. In the early nineteenth century, it was well known in America and abroad that a substance called "rock oil" flowed from springs in parts of Pennsylvania and New York.

When the first significant oil discoveries were made, salt for food preservation and agriculture was far more valuable than petroleum. In 1802, for example, the U.S. Congress recognized the value of natural salt springs and seeps in the Northwest Territories (the Ohio River Valley) and declared those springs to be too valuable for private ownership. Inevitably, drilling for brines encountered some of the shallow petroleum reservoirs known today. As more discoveries of petroleum were made, the continuing quest for salt brines stimulated crucial advances in drilling technology. In 1806, determined to find a consistent source of brines, David and Joseph Ruffner of what is now Charleston, West Virginia, began drilling for salt brine in the Kanawha River Valley. They used a spring, or jack, pole with a drilling bit at one end and a rope anchor at the other. Because it required hard work to pound, or "kick," the bit through the rock, drillers experimented with a variety of contraptions that allowed them to jump up and down on the rig. In time, the Ruffners devised the rock drill, an iron rod with a steel tip. Using this new technology, they finished their 47-foot-deep well January 15, 1808, producing a satisfactory flow of strong brine. During this period, drillers in the Kanawha Valley, including the Ruffner brothers, invented additional drilling tools such as casing (steel pipes installed in a drill hole to prevent the walls from sloughing or caving) and jars (tools used to produce a jarring impact, especially in cable-tool drilling). Shortly after the Civil War, steam power supplanted human power. Replacing the human-powered jack pole with a reliable mechanical force was a significant improvement in drilling technology.

In the early nineteenth century, Pennsylvania became a major source of brine. The first salt wells were drilled before 1810 around Tarentum, a town located along the Allegheny River near Pittsburgh. By 1820, the area was the state's western center of salt production. Samuel Kier and his father owned and operated two brine wells. As was commonly the case, oil contaminated some of the brine. The younger Kier, convinced that there must be some use for the oil that was being flushed from the wells, employed salesmen who traveled the countryside in gaudy wagons selling the oil for medicinal purposes. Later, Kier probably purchased the Kentucky oil recovered by the Youngloves, who, after experimenting with the so-called Native American method of extraction, hand-dug shafts and cribs for collecting petroleum.

In the 1820s, S. P. Hildreth and others conducted a survey to identify both oil and gas in Ohio and western Virginia, publishing their findings between 1826 and 1836. In 1826 in the *American Journal of Science*, Hildreth documented a well drilled by a Mr. McKee in 1814 on Duck Creek, just north of Marietta, Ohio, that had hit oil while drilling for salt. In the same journal, Hildreth referred to oil and gas development in the Muskingum Valley and, based upon its use in the area, predicted that oil would be important in the future. With discoveries at Marietta and Burning Springs, southeastern Ohio and western Virginia (now West Virginia) were recognized as important oil-producing areas outside of Pennsylvania and New York. In 1818 Martin Beatty began a search for salt in southeastern Kentucky, where he acquired property on Oil Well Branch of the South Fork of the Cumberland River, not far from the main settlement routes through the Cumberland Gap. In the winter of 1818–19, his drillers found "rock oil" at an estimated initial flow of one hundred barrels per day. Nevertheless, Beatty became discouraged, moved to Texas, and died in 1859, shortly before the Drake Well was drilled in Pennsylvania. One of his drillers, however, built wooden casks, barreled the oil, and sold quantities in Kentucky, Tennessee, Virginia, North Carolina, and Georgia.

The Great American Well was drilled in 1829 near Burkesville in Cumberland County, Kentucky. Although not strictly located within the Appalachian Basin, the well had a far-reaching influence on the future development of the oil industry. Drilled to a depth of about 171 feet, it produced a gusher. The drill bit and rope shot out of the hole followed by a solid stream of oil that surged up to the treetops. Oil flowed from the well into the Cumberland River and covered the surface of the river downstream for fifty miles. From 1829 to 1860, the well produced an estimated fifty thousand barrels of oil. When the wife of oil distributor Samuel Kier developed tuberculosis and the doctor prescribed "American Medicinal Oil," the oil came from a well in Kentucky, probably the Great American Well.

The stage was set for the emerging oil industry. Petroleum was being found with increased frequency, mostly to the detriment of the salt-brine production. Oil had uses in medicine, as a lubricant, and as a substitute for increasingly expensive spermaceti (whale oil) for lighting. The problem with oil, however, was that its odor was offensive. Paraffin, discovered in 1830, could be distilled from coal and shale and used both as a lamp fuel and as a substitute for spermaceti in candle making. In 1848 a plant was started in Derbyshire, England, to extract paraffin from shales using a process patented by James Young in 1850. Abraham Gesner, a Canadian geologist, immigrated to the United States, where in 1848 he devised and patented a method to distill kerosene from petroleum. After witnessing the accidental burning of a local canal, Samuel Kier developed a lamp and an odorless fuel and by 1858 was distributing his "carbon oil" lamps in Pittsburgh. Kier, however, never patented either the distillation process or his lamp.

Kier's success in the oil business attracted the attention of Jonathan G. Eveleth and George H. Bissell, who came to New Haven, Connecticut, for the purpose of disposing of certain lands in western Pennsylvania. They collected a sample of oil and sent it to Professor Benjamin Silliman Jr. of Yale College, who in 1855 distilled the sample and reported its properties for illumination. Eveleth and Bissell formed the Pennsylvania Rock Oil Company to develop lands around Oil Creek near Titusville. After Eveleth and Bissell lost control of the company, it retained Edwin L. Drake to determine its holdings. Although a lease on the lands still controlled by Eveleth and Bissell was issued to the Pennsylvania Rock Oil Company, the New Haven stockholders formed a new company called the Seneca Oil Company before commencing drilling. In March 1858, Drake was appointed president of the Seneca Oil Company and in the spring of that year began his development of the property, which became the site of the famous Drake Well of 1859.

In 1875 John D. Rockefeller acquired the properties of the J. N. Camden Consolidated Oil Company, the key entity of the Standard Oil Company of Cleveland, Ohio. This purchase enabled him to control most of the production, transportation, and sales of petroleum in the latter part of the nineteenth century. The rise of Standard Oil during the following decades is well recorded. Rockefeller's methods and stupendous success caused the U.S. Congress to pass antitrust legislation that broke up the Rockefeller Standard Oil Trust and prevented future trusts from developing.

Many of the concepts used for oil exploration and development originated in the Appalachian Basin. Based on studies at Burning Springs, I. C. White, founder of the West Virginia Geological and Economic Survey, published his concepts in *Science* on June 26, 1885, in a paper entitled "The Geology of Natural Gas." While other geologists had previously discussed the theory, White's paper gave the first clear exposition of what was called the anticlinal theory of oil and gas accumulation. The anticlinal theory stated that if oil and gas were present, they would accumulate in the central regions of up-arched anticlines. The application of White's anticlinal theory was the first real use of science in the exploration for petroleum.

Beginning with the 1892 discovery of the Beaver Creek Field in Floyd County, Kentucky, and culminating with discovery of the Big Sinking Field in Estill and Lee Counties of Kentucky in 1918, the oil industry expanded far south within the Appalachian Basin. Big Sinking Field, still in production, has produced more than 120 million barrels of oil. Although that level of production is no longer considered major, it was very significant for the early part of the twentieth century.

The record of Appalachian Basin oil production begins with two thousand barrels produced in 1859 in Pennsylvania. Outstanding production occurred in 1891, 1896, 1897, and 1900, with more than 50 million barrels produced during each of these years. During this period, Pennsylvania, West Virginia, and Ohio dominated production of oil, with small amounts coming from New York. By 1901, with cumulative production exceeding a billion barrels, basin production began to decline. After 1900, peak production exceeded 30 million barrels yearly during World Wars I and II and in the 1960s, the latter peak a result of the discovery of oil in the (Ordovician) Knox Formation in the Morrow Fields of Ohio. Total cumulative production for the basin through 1999 exceeded 3.5 billion barrels.

The Appalachian Basin is a mature petroleum province. Its long history of drilling does not mean that its reserves have been exhausted, however. Although the basin has been thoroughly exploited at shallow depths, many of the deep Paleozoic strata remain undrilled. Given the basin's proximity to major industrial centers, the application of modern exploration ideas and technology to its reserves may well yield future entrepreneurs opportunities for both oil and gas production.

See also: NONMETALLIC, NONFUEL DEPOSITS; OIL INDUSTRY (BUSINESS, INDUSTRY, AND TECHNOLOGY).

—Donald C. Haney and Brandon Nuttall, *Kentucky Geological Survey*

Paul Henry Giddens, *Early Days of Oil: A Pictorial History of the Beginnings of the Industry in Pennsylvania* (1948); Willard R. Jillson, *The First Oil Well in Kentucky: Notes on the History, Geology, Production and Present Status of the Beatty Oil Well, Drilled in Wayne, Now McCreary County, Kentucky, in the Year 1818* (1952); Edgar W. Owen, *Trek of the Oil Finders: A History of Exploration for Petroleum* (1975).

Paleozoic Era

The Appalachian Basin contains one of the most complete records of the 300-million-year Paleozoic era, beginning with seas that spread nearly across the planet and ending with the uplifting of continents and mountain ranges such as the Appalachians and the Urals. During this period of time, the strata of Appalachia accumulated in nearly horizontal layers, with successively younger deposits forming on top of older ones, effectively creating a geological template that recorded movements of Earth's crust over the succeeding 265 million or so years.

At present, the Paleozoic rocks of the Appalachians are distributed in a broad rowboat-shaped manner with the youngest strata preserved in the center of the basin from the vicinity of Parkersburg, West Virginia, to the southwestern corner of Pennsylvania. From this center, older strata extend successively in all directions. The formation of the Appalachian Basin spanned the entire Paleozoic era. Created by flooding and uplift processes of the era, the Appalachian Basin constitutes the largest feature within the region. The Paleozoic, which means "ancient life," is now considered to have spanned the time interval from about 543 to 248 million years ago, when animal life was represented primarily by invertebrates. Only limited fossil remains of vertebrates such as fish, amphibians, and primitive reptiles are found within Paleozoic rocks.

The stratigraphic sequence method of dating is fundamental to understanding the Paleozoic era. At times of low sea level, continents are primarily emergent and undergoing erosion, leaving behind relatively few rocks deposited on the continents. The most extensive gaps in the record are called regional unconformities (buried erosional surfaces in the geologic record). The present land surface of the North American continent is a future regional unconformity in the making because today's sea level is lowered as a result of glacial ice. At times of high sea level, sediments carried to the sea are preserved widespread on the inundated continent with the thickest accumulations being along the continental margins. These sediments often accumulate with a content of age-defining marine fossils. The strata are arranged into natural successions called sequences, which are separated by unconformities. American geologist L. L. Sloss first developed the concept of sequences in the 1950s and 1960s. Each sequence may consist of many individual rock formations that are bounded by major unconformities. Sloss named the sequences for American Indian groups to make it clear that this arrangement of geologic time is distinct from the formal names of the geologic periods that occur on the geologic time scale. Because the sequence patterns are traceable worldwide, the concept of regional unconformities has been especially important to the oil industry, with application of the sequence concept to petroleum exploration being developed by Exxon in the 1970s.

Four major falls (lows) of global sea level mark the regional unconformities that form the boundaries of the Sauk, Tippecanoe, Kaskaskia, and Absaroka Sequences. The Sauk Sequence includes rock formations from the late Precambrian (Vendian) to early Ordovician time; the Tippecanoe Sequence from the middle Ordovician to the early Devonian; the Kaskaskia Sequence from the early Devonian to the late Mississippian; and the Absaroka Sequence from the early Pennsylvanian to the early Jurassic. Lesser sea-level fluctuations within sequences exerted an important influence on the strata deposited in Appalachia and are especially important in oil and gas exploration and in development of coal deposits.

The record left by events of the Paleozoic and subsequent times is revealed in folds, faults, and regional metamorphism of these sedimentary accumulations. Rock formation began with the deposit of unconsolidated muds, sands, and peats that were gradually transformed into sedimentary rock under increasing pressure and heat generated by the buildup of successive layers, a geologic process called lithification. In eastern Appalachia, some of the sedimentary rocks were transformed into metamorphic rocks.

Significant episodes of igneous activity in Appalachia during Paleozoic time involved transformation of rocks and deposit of new structures from molten material. For example, outpourings of basaltic and rhyolitic lava during the initial rifting of the supercontinent of Rodinia about 700 million years ago left some igneous deposits in Appalachia just beneath the oldest Paleozoic strata near Mount Rogers, Virginia, and Boone, North Carolina, and at the north end of the Blue Ridge in Maryland. During the Ordovician period, 490 to 443 million years ago, lava flows accumulated in thrust sheets in Pennsylvania and New York as the forces of the Taconic Orogeny raised mountain peaks and ridges. Ash from offshore island-arc volcanoes resulted in formation of extensive volcanic ash beds as volcanic dust fell over thousands of square miles and was preserved in quiet water on the sea bottom. The Tioga Ash, the only ash bed whose actual source is approximately known, came from a Devonian volcanic center near present-day Fredericksburg, Virginia. This ash fell over a vast area from Virginia to Kentucky, Ohio, and New York. Two prominent ash beds near the middle of the Ordovician probably covered the entire Appalachian region. These are thickest in southeastern Tennessee and northwestern Georgia, indicating a volcanic source in the present Piedmont of Georgia or South Carolina. Prominent igneous intrusions and lava flows occurred during the Devonian Acadian Orogeny in New England, and the two Devonian (about 400 million years ago) ash beds may have come from there, although the Center Hill Ash extends from Tennessee to New York.

Because the latest Precambrian and earliest Paleozoic strata are commonly metamorphosed, that is, they are not in their original states, fossils are difficult to find. Fossils of one-celled plants called acritarchs do occur within the Great Smoky Mountains in rocks of marine origin, and they range through the top of the Paleozoic. Trails and soft body impressions (trace fossils) that began to appear about 630 million years ago can be found in today's Great Smoky Mountains and Blue Ridge Mountains. Seashells and trilobites (marine arthropods) are apparent in the Cambrian marine strata. Shell life diversified throughout the Paleozoic of Appalachia with one of the era's most heralded marine organisms, the trilobite, diminishing in abundance to the point of near-extinction during Pennsylvanian time.

At certain times during the Paleozoic era, reefs grew in the warm tropical seas that flooded the Appalachian region. Reefs dominated by algae and an extinct animal group called stromatoporoids grew during Ordovician time in what is now Tennessee and Virginia. Coral and stromatoporoid reefs are found in the Silurian strata of present-day Virginia and New York, with small coral reefs being found in Devonian formations in West Virginia, Maryland, Pennsylvania, and New York. Algal limestone mounds contained within the Mississippian rocks of Kentucky and Tennessee contain important oil deposits.

At other times, when the climate of Appalachia became arid, gypsum ($CaSO_4 \cdot 2H_2O$) and salt (NaCl) deposits precipitated from evaporating seawater within the Appalachian Basin. These evaporite minerals are found in Silurian-aged rocks (443 to 417 million years ago) from Virginia to New York and Ohio and again in Mississippian-aged rocks (354 to 323 million years ago) in Virginia and West Virginia.

Fish first appeared during Ordovician time and are well represented in Appalachian strata, being found in Devonian and later ages of the Paleozoic. Amphibians appeared in the Devonian, followed by reptiles in warm and humid swamps of the Pennsylvanian period. Several amphibian and reptile tracks are known in Mississippian and Pennsylvanian strata. Whole skeletons are scarce, however, with teeth being more commonly preserved than bones. All of the Paleozoic strata within the Appalachian Basin accumulated before the appearance of dinosaurs, about 215 million years ago. Although devoid of dinosaur remains, Appalachian Basin rocks contain an important record of fossil plants. The most primitive plants are acritarchs (algae) from the late Precambrian of the Great Smoky Mountains. Thriving in marine waters, acritarchs remained common through the Devonian and Pennsylvanian periods, a total span of more than 200 million years.

The world's oldest land plants found in Appalachian bedrock are fossil liverworts, discovered at Massanutten Mountain, Virginia. Liverworts are soft-tissue plants that have not yet developed leaves; they are still present in modern flora. Early woody and leafy plants occur in Devonian strata from Appalachia, where they grew on riverbanks in the vast delta complexes that developed from New York to West Virginia. Driftwood fragments washed out to sea are found in sediments that accumulated in deltaic sands or in shales that formed from the muds that accumulated on a stagnant seafloor in what is now Tennessee and Virginia. Leafy plants with spores (ferns, sphenopsids, lycopods) appeared in the late Devonian and became the dominant flora in the peat swamps that developed during the period of time from the Mississippian through the Permian; these peats, which were composed of wood, leaves, and spores, were later transformed into the vast deposits of bituminous and anthracite coal for which Appalachia is known. Lycopod trees grew to heights of more than one hundred feet. The oldest known seed plants occur in Devonian coal near Elkins, West Virginia. Modern types of plants, including true woody trees such as pines, cycads, and deciduous trees, as well as flowering plants and grasses, did not develop until after the Paleozoic era came to an end. As a result, the flora of Paleozoic-age strata have a distinctive non-modern appearance.

The economic and cultural history of the Appalachian region is significantly linked to the geologic development that occurred during the Paleozoic. Rocks of great resistance to erosion are etched out to rise up as prominent mountains. These mountains are commonly sandstone or its metamorphic equivalent, quartzite. Shale, slate, dolomite, and limestone weather and erode more readily to produce valleys. Strata ranging in age from latest Precambrian to latest Pennsylvanian, folded and faulted by episodes of orogeny, have been brought to the surface in the form of a variety of rock types. The mining and quarrying of these rocks has provided a host of mineral products and coal while the penetration of these rocks by wells has allowed the extraction of oil and natural gas in many parts of Appalachia.

See also: CENOZOIC ERA; MESOZOIC ERA; PRECAMBRIAN EON.

—John M. Dennison, *University of North Carolina*

J. M. Dennison, *Geology of the Eastern Overthrust* (1984); Rodney M. Feldman and Merrianne Hackathorn, eds., *Fossils of Ohio* (1996); Donald M. Hoskins, Jon D. Inners, and John A. Harper, *Fossil Collecting in Pennsylvania* (1983); John Oleksyshyn, *Fossil Plants from the Anthracite Coal Fields of Eastern Pennsylvania* (1982).

Piedmont Province

The Piedmont Province is a broad, relatively flat plateau that serves as the eastern gateway to the Appalachians. From its western boundary adjacent to the Blue Ridge Mountains, it slopes gently southeastward toward the Fall Line Zone, which is the contact between the more resistant rocks underlying the Piedmont and the less resistant rocks and sediments of the Atlantic Coastal Plain. Because of the difference in resistance to erosion, streams flowing from the Piedmont to the Atlantic Coastal Plain typically flow over waterfalls at the point of contact. From this, the rocks of the Piedmont continue eastward under cover of the Atlantic and Gulf of Mexico Coastal Plain sediments. Barely 20 miles wide at its northern end in Pennsylvania, the Piedmont widens rapidly southward to a maximum width of more than 120 miles in North Carolina before coming to an end in eastern Alabama. The word *piedmont* is derived from the name of an Italian region and generally refers to an area lying or formed at the base of mountains. Although the Piedmont Province lacks the high elevations and steep relief that characterizes most of Appalachia, this land has nevertheless been intimately associated both geologically and culturally with the Appalachian Mountains.

Rocks and geologic structures of the Piedmont are much older than the landscape itself, but both have been major influences in the geologic development of the landforms that characterize the region today. More resistant rocks, such as granite and gneiss, stand stubbornly above the surrounding landscape, showing very little weathering or soil development. Less resistant schists and phyllites, by contrast, become highly weathered and often form layers of saprolitic soil (disintegrated rock lying in place where it formed). The degree of metamorphism in Piedmont rocks tends to increase toward the northwest, accentuating the impact of tectonic (mountain-building) influences in that area. Here, tectonic forces fractured and folded the rock in such a way to produce two major parallel sets of joints and faults that meet at nearly right angles. Such fracture points within the rock create linear zones of surface weakness that concentrate the flow of streams into straight channel stretches and tributaries punctuated by right-angle bends. Many Piedmont stream systems display such a rectangular drainage pattern, especially in the upper reaches closer to the mountains. The right-angle bends are particularly noticeable in several Piedmont reservoirs, including Lake Hartwell on the Georgia–South Carolina state border, Lake Norman on the Catawba River in North Carolina, and Smith Mountain Lake on the Roanoke River in Virginia.

In areas where fractures and faults are less dominant and the rock type is more homogenous, a dendritic drainage pattern is more common. This pattern resembles the branching of limbs on a tree or the veins in a leaf with the major stream channels showing no preferred orientation other than downhill. Stream erosion has been and continues to be the major geological force sculpting and modifying the landscape of the Piedmont Province. It is precisely this erosional process, generated by streams carrying sediment from mountains to the sea, that over time has created the gently undulating and relatively uniform land surface that now qualifies as a plateau. Only a few isolated hills, called monadnocks, remain to bear testimony to the high-relief, mountainous terrain that characterized the region at the time of the dinosaurs. Monadnocks are usually surrounded by relatively flat ground and can be seen from great distances across the plateau. Some of these hills owe their existence to outcroppings of very hard, resistant rock while others seem to have escaped erosion purely by chance. Stone Mountain, near Atlanta, is perhaps the best known of these erosional remnants, although many others exist, including Pilot Mountain near Mount Airy, North Carolina, and Sugar Loaf Mountain near Frederick, Maryland. Travelers descending the high peaks of the Blue Ridge are treated to spectacular views of the broad expanse of the Piedmont as they traverse the Blue Ridge Escarpment, a distinctive topographic feature characterized by a sharp drop in elevation and significant lowering of relief. Although the Piedmont Province is quite hilly near the escarpment, it levels off rather quickly to more uniform slopes toward the southeast. Actively eroding Piedmont rivers will sometimes cut deep channels into the land surface, producing steep-walled valleys and locally high relief. In general, however, the broad upland areas between river valleys are essentially flat.

There is some disagreement between geologists and geographers over the exact placement of the Blue Ridge–Piedmont boundary. Geologists usually consider the Brevard Fault Zone, stretching northeastward from Atlanta through northwestern South Carolina and Brevard, North Carolina, to be the western edge of the Piedmont Province, their argument being that this line separates rocks of the Inner Piedmont Terrane from those of the original North American continent. Most geographers, however, prefer to designate the highly visible Blue Ridge Escarpment, which they refer to as the Blue Ridge Structural Front, as the approved boundary line because it corresponds more closely to the observed regional differences in topographic landforms and land-use characteristics.

The Piedmont Province is more than just a geological gate to Appalachia, having long been an essential component to the settlement and economic development of the more mountainous portions of the region. The flatter Piedmont landscape permitted easier transportation along the early roads that brought large numbers of settlers southward. Most Piedmont rivers had rocky bottoms and occasional shoals that were shallow enough to allow them to be crossed easily by wagons and horses, especially at times of low water. Waterpower for textile mills was abundant and easily accessible, especially in the Fall Line Zone. Iron ore and other mineral deposits in Piedmont rocks enabled blacksmith forges and other colonial industries to flourish. Nevertheless, there is a continuing debate from a sociological perspective over just how much the Piedmont Province should be considered part of Appalachia. Some consider the Piedmont to be one of four major provinces that constitute Appalachia, while others exclude it. Regardless of which classification system is used, the landscape of the Piedmont Province has played a significant role in and remains inextricably linked to both the Appalachian Mountains and cultural Appalachia as defined by government agencies and social scientists.

See also: GEOMORPHOLOGY.

—John R. Wagner, *Clemson University*

Charles G. Kovacik and John J. Winberry, *South Carolina: The Making of a Landscape* (1989); Carolyn Hanna Murphy, *Carolina Rocks! The Geology of South Carolina* (1995); John R. Wagner, ed., *Southeast Maps and Aerial Photographic Systems* (2000).

Precambrian Eon

The Precambrian eon comprises the time from Earth's origin about 4.5 billion years ago to the beginning of the Paleozoic era about 543 million years ago. This 4-billion-year time span represents about seven-eighths of the entire history of the planet. During this vast period, the oldest rocks in Appalachia, commonly referred to as basement rocks, were formed. These Precambrian rocks are a combination of sedimentary rocks such as shales and quartzites, various carbonate sediments, volcanic rocks, and intrusive igneous rocks that were deformed and metamorphosed during a mountain-building episode known as the Grenville Orogeny. The Grenville Orogeny formed the supercontinent of Rodinia and created a towering mountain range that was the predecessor to the modern Appalachians. During the Grenville Orogeny, a large volume of magma (molten rock contained within Earth) was intruded into older crustal rocks and cooled to form an assemblage varying from quartz-rich granite to quartz-deficient diorite. These younger igneous rocks appear to have an average age of about 976 million years, allowing geologists to assign a date for the Grenville Orogeny of from 1 billion to 900 million years ago.

Continental crust began to form between 4.1 and 4.2 billion years ago, with the first material dated at about 3.8 to 4 billion years. Continental masses comparable in size to present-day continents were in place by 3 billion years ago. The oldest traces of life have been found in cherts from western Australia and South Africa dated at about 3.4 billion years; however, it is believed that the process of photosynthesis was established by 3.8 billion years ago in marine plants, leading to the oxygen saturation of ocean waters. Once oxygen became abundant in marine waters, it began to bleed off into the atmosphere, where atmospheric oxygen reached about 15 percent of modern levels by 2 billion years ago. Complex soft-bodied animals first appeared in rocks found in the Ediacara Hills of Australia dated at 700 million years ago.

The late Precambrian was a turbulent time in Earth's tectonic history. Approximately 700 million years ago, the supercontinent of Rodinia began to break up and form the new Iapetus Ocean along with several continents and microcontinents that would play important roles in the formation of Appalachia. The initial rifting created basins that became repositories of sediment eroded from the surrounding land. Examples of these early rift basins can be seen today in southwest Virginia, northwest North Carolina, and adjacent areas of Tennessee. The new continents created during the breakup of Rodinia and subsequently playing important roles in the geologic history of Appalachia included Laurentia and Gondwana. The former consisted of present day North America and Greenland, the latter the present southern continents of South America, Africa, Antarctica, Australia plus India, and the European continental mass east of the Urals. In addition, there were smaller microcontinents, including the Piedmont Microcontinents and Avalonia, a microcontinent that rifted from the northwest portion of Gondwana following the initial breakup of Rodinia. Subsequent mountain-building events occurred as the Iapetus Ocean closed and these continents and microcontinents collided to form the new supercontinent of Pangea at the close of the Paleozoic era, contributing to the development of the Appalachians.

See also: TECTONICS.

—Avery A. Drake Jr., *U.S. Geological Survey*

A. A. Drake Jr., L. M. Hall, and A. E. Nelson, *Basement and Basement-Cover Relation Map of the Appalachian Orogen* (1988); Allen H. Felter and Steven A. Goldberg, "Age and Geochemical Characteristics of Bimodal Magmatism in the Neoproterozoic Grandfather Mountain Rift Basin," *Journal of Geology* (May 1995); D. W. Rankin, A. A. Drake Jr., and N. M. Ratcliffe, "Proterozoic North American (Laurentian) Rocks of the Appalachian Orogen," in *The Geology of North America, Vol. C-2: Precambrian: Conterminous U.S.*, ed. John C. Reed Jr. et al. (1993).

Ridge and Valley Province

The Ridge and Valley Province extends nearly twelve hundred miles, stretching from the Gulf Coastal Plain near Tuscaloosa, Alabama, to the Saint Lawrence River. Characterized by long, high ridges and parallel valleys, the province is located between the Appalachian Plateaus Province to the west and the Blue Ridge Province to the east. First called the Ridge and Valley Province in a 1938 description by Nevin M. Fenneman, a professor of geology at the University of Cincinnati, the Ridge and Valley can be subdivided into three parts: the Hudson-Champlain Section, the Middle Section, and the Southern Section. The Hudson-Champlain Section is a relatively narrow twenty-five-mile-wide belt that extends along the Hudson River from the Saint Lawrence to the Delaware River. The section is primarily underlain by shales and shows the effects of glaciation. The Middle Section begins at the Delaware River, where it abruptly increases in width to approximately eighty miles, cuts across parts of New Jersey, Pennsylvania, Maryland, Virginia, and West Virginia, and terminates in southwestern Virginia at the divide between the Tennessee and New Rivers. The Southern Section extends from the Tennessee River–New River divide to the Gulf Coastal Plain in Alabama. Although the geologic structures within the Ridge and Valley are the result of the Alleghenian Orogeny that occurred towards the end of the Paleozoic era about 248 million years ago, the topography visible today is the product of combined efforts of weathering, mass wasting, and erosion that began at the close of the Alleghenian Orogeny and continues to the present.

Dominant structural features of the Ridge and Valley Province are parallel folds that have been sculpted by differential weathering into its parallel ridges and valleys. Differential erosion refers to the fact that the rate of erosion depends on exposed rock's resistance to physical and chemical attack. Softer rocks such as shales succumb relatively quickly to processes of physical weathering such as frost wedging. Limestone and other soluble rocks are attacked chemically and dissolved by water at relatively high rates. In contrast, quartz-rich rocks such as sandstones and conglomerates are resistant to both chemical and physical weathering. As a result, erosion of less resistant rocks culminates in the formation of valleys while more resistant rocks stubbornly resist attack and remain as ridges.

Of the three sections, the one that most typifies the Ridge and Valley Province is the Middle Section, which is divided into distinctly different regions, a western region of parallel ridges and valleys and the Great Valley in the east. Within the Middle Section, the most dominant ridge-forming rock units are the Pennsylvanian Pottsville Formation, the Mississippian Pocono Formation, and the Silurian Tuscarora Formation, all of which are composed of highly resistant sandstones and conglomerates. In some cases, the ridges are anticlinal, meaning that the resistant rock extends completely across the ridge. In most cases, however, erosion has removed the resistant rock along the axis of the anticline, a process called breaching, creating monoclinal ridges flanking a valley that has been carved into the less resistant rock below. In some cases the breaching of adjacent anticlinal structures has been so extreme that the intervening syncline has become a synclinal ridge. (Anticlinal ridges are those with rocks that dip away from the axis of the fold in opposite directions. In synclinal ridges, rocks dip toward the axis of the fold. Monoclinal ridges consist of rocks dipping in one direction only.) One well-known example of a synclinal ridge is Sideling Mountain, cut through by Interstate 68 in Maryland.

Throughout the province, individual folds vary in length with all folds eventually coming to an end by a process called plunging. Erosion of these plunging folds, especially in Pennsylvania, has resulted in formation of the intricate zigzag pattern of rock outcrops and ridgelines that is so distinctive on the geologic map of Pennsylvania. Some of the ridges can be followed for such long distances that the same ridge may have several different names.

The western boundary of the Middle Section is a prominent two-stepped escarpment. In central Pennsylvania, sandstones and conglomerates of the Mississippian Pocono Formation cap the upper escarpment, while the lower escarpment is capped by Devonian sandstones; the elevation of the upper escarpment is about 2,200 feet above sea level. From southern Pennsylvania and southward, the upper escarpment is capped by the Pottsville Formation at an elevation of about 2,800 feet with the lower escarpment held up by the Pocono Formation. South of the Potomac River in Virginia and West Virginia, the two-stepped escarpment is referred to as the Allegheny Structural Front with the narrow terrace formed by the lower escarpment known locally as the Fore Knobs. The upper escarpment of the Allegheny Structural Front reaches a maximum elevation of about 4,600 feet just west of Monterey, Virginia, after which the escarpment diminishes as a topographic feature southward.

Sideling Hill Cut on Interstate 68 near Hancock, Maryland, 1988. A superb example of inverted topography, this syncline became a synclinal ridge through the extreme erosion of the adjacent anticlinal structures.

South of about 39° latitude, the front disappears as elevations of the folds within the Ridge and Valley rise above the level of the plateau to the west.

In Pennsylvania the folds of the Middle Section are relatively symmetrical. However, as the structures are traced southward, the folds become increasingly asymmetric and overturned to the northwest. In addition to increased asymmetry of the folds, thrust faults begin to appear in southern Pennsylvania that break the steeper western limb of anticlinal folds. Southward, thrust faults increase in both frequency and displacement to the point where, in southern Virginia, nearly all of the folds are broken by eastward-dipping thrust faults.

In the eastern Great Valley portion of the Middle Section, Cambrian and Ordovician limestones have been brought to the surface along high-angle thrust faults with the valley being the result of dissolution of the limestones. The Great Valley has been eroded by the Shenandoah River and its tributaries southward from its confluence with the Potomac River at Harpers Ferry, West Virginia. The valley is noted for its many caves, caverns, and natural bridges, all common features associated with karst topography, the landform that results from the dissolution of soluble rocks such as limestone.

South of the James River, the character of the Ridge and Valley begins to change. The width of the province is reduced by half as increased thrusting continues to compress the rocks. Although the number of ridges remains the same, distance between adjacent fold axes decreases and dips on the limbs of the folds become steeper. Within this section, the eastern margin of the Great Valley is prominently marked by the presence of resistant rocks of the Blue Ridge that have been thrust westward.

The transition from the Middle Section to the Southern Section is placed at the divide between the Tennessee and New Rivers. One of the most conspicuous features of the Southern Section is the absence of the Great Valley, which is such a dominant feature to the north. Thrust faulting within the Southern Section has overturned all of the folds to the point where all of the beds essentially dip to the southeast. Within the Southern Section, valleys between the ridges begin to widen. One interesting aspect of valley development south of the Tennessee River–New River divide is reappearance of the escarpment along the western contact with the plateau with the Pottsville rocks capping the edge of the escarpment. In the Southern Section, one of the resistant ridge-formers is the Clinch Formation, which is the southern equivalent of the Tuscarora or Medina to the north. Another major ridge-former is the Silurian Clinton sandstone, called the Rockwood Formation in Tennessee and the Red Mountain Formation to the south. The Red Mountain Formation is of special economic importance since it contains the iron ore that made Birmingham, Alabama, a major steel-producing city until the 1970s, when ores from the Great Lakes region made it uneconomical to exploit. Another necessary resource that allowed Birmingham to flourish as a steel-producing center was the presence of coal. Because uplift in the Southern Section was significantly less than to the north, coal-bearing Pennsylvanian rocks that were removed by erosion from most of the Middle Section were preserved in the Southern Section.

Major rivers have cut their valleys across the northeast-southwest grain of the folded and faulted strata of the Ridge and Valley while their tributaries drain the valleys underlain by shales or limestone. The result is the formation of the trellis drainage pattern that characterizes the Ridge and Valley. Water gaps formed where the main west-to-east-flowing stream successfully carved downward through the structure while wind gaps (low swales or saddles on some ridges) represent locations where a stream failed to maintain its flow across the structure and abandoned its channel. Water gaps and wind gaps became avenues for the early pioneers crossing daunting mountainous barriers to the western frontier. One of the most famous wind gaps is the Cumberland Gap, discovered by Thomas Walker, near Harrogate, Tennessee. The Wilderness Road, used by Daniel Boone as he led pioneer parties into the frontier, passed through the Cumberland Gap.

See also: TECTONICS.

—Don W. Byerly, *University of Tennessee*

Nevin M. Fenneman, *Physiography of the Eastern United States* (1938).

Soils

Soil, both rich and poor, played a crucial role in the settlement and early development of Appalachia and remains a central consideration in modern land-use decisions. A soil consists of organized layers of minerals and organic matter. It supports and nourishes plants and animals, determines the kind of vegetation that grows on it, and furnishes a medium for the production of food, either directly or by way of animals. The nature of each soil depends upon material from which it forms, the topographic environment, and influences of plants, animals, and climate. With time, each soil develops layers, or horizons, that vary in texture, structure, color, and content of organic matter. The nature and thickness of the horizons determine the capacity of a soil to hold nutrients and water. They also serve as a basis for the classification and naming of the soil.

Though soils differ greatly, sometimes within short distances of each other, generally consistent rainfall, seasonal temperatures, and forest vegetation throughout Appalachia have resulted in development of similar soils across the region. A productive soil for farm crops, for example, may lie alongside large tracts of another soil suited mainly for forest.

Despite certain regional similarities, soil characteristics and patterns have distinct differences in the four physiographic provinces of the Appalachian system: the Blue Ridge, Ridge and Valley, Piedmont, and Appalachian Plateaus Provinces. The Blue Ridge Province is predominantly mountainous or hilly and is dissected by stream valleys. Where the slopes are gentle in stream valleys, soils formed from sediments that accumulated on modern floodplains and from older alluvial deposits that now reside on terraces above the floodplain. Many of these are deep, loamy soils that possess high available water capacity and are rich in minerals. In some places, these soils are poorly drained and remain wet during certain periods of the year. Some of the flattest soils on the stream terraces have compact, nearly impermeable layers beginning at depths of fifteen to twenty inches.

Footslopes, the gentle slopes at the base of a hill, are an important part of the Blue Ridge landscape, since colluvium (debris moved down from the slopes above) has produced thick, loamy soils that have few distinct layers and furnish an ideal environment for the growth of plant roots. On many north-facing slopes, the upper six to twelve inches of the soil may be dark-colored as a result of its high content of organic matter. Such soils are ideal for the growth of trees and, where the slopes are not too steep, for the growth of farm crops. The soils of the bottoms, second bottoms, and footslopes make up much of the farmland in the Blue Ridge.

On steep slopes, the nature of Blue Ridge soils has been affected by their geographic direction, or aspect. Soils that form on slopes facing north or east are generally thicker than those oriented toward the south and west. They also have fewer distinct layers and more favorable properties for the growth of many plants. Downhill creep of soil material can combine with the aspect to influence soil patterns. Creep robs soil from the upper slopes, but material moved downhill produces thick, productive soil where it accumulates. The resulting shallower soils, especially on south-facing slopes, have low available water capacity. Even with the high annual rainfall characteristic of the region, some seasons are so dry that plants exhaust the available water. Vegetation that survives is less vigorous and differs greatly in composition from that growing on deeper soils on the footslopes and northeastern-facing slopes. Within one square mile, the pattern of soil may include both extremely productive and shallow, unproductive soils.

At the highest elevations, above four thousand feet at the southern end of the province and somewhat lower in the north, the soil and vegetation pattern is different from that at lower elevations. Under beech gaps (areas occupied by growths of beech trees), soils have thick, dark-colored topsoils over brown, loamy subsoils. Under spruce-fir or rhododendron cover, a mucky or peaty organic layer is generally at the top of the soil, while the underlying layers may consist of a bleached, gray-colored, or sandy loam over a dark, loamy layer that may contain various oxides of iron and organic matter. These soils are more acid than those formed under hardwoods. Some of these soils are called spodosols (formerly called podzols) and resemble soils from New England.

Depending on geographic location, Blue Ridge soils can form from either igneous, metamorphic, or sedimentary parent materials. Compared to the sedimentary rocks of the Ridge and Valley or the Appalachian Plateaus Provinces, parent materials of the Blue Ridge soils are always richer mineralogically. However, in the days before widespread use of lime and fertilizer, crop yields were often low, causing many struggling settlers to abandon their farms. But with modern scientific knowledge of soil amendments such as lime and the use of adapted cultivars, these same soils now produce good yields of hay and pasture crops. On the best soils, vegetables, fruits, and other farm crops thrive.

Although numerous hills and mountains of the Blue Ridge have not been amenable to farming, their soils are deep enough for trees. Long-growing trees can endure the low level of nutrients through nutrient cycling. In their natural condition, most Blue Ridge soils contain enough phosphorus and potassium for the growth of forest vegetation. On deeper soils where water supply is adequate, especially on north- and east-facing slopes, hardwoods grow rapidly and produce good timber.

A contrasting pattern of soils is present in the Ridge and Valley Province, which lies between the Blue Ridge Province on the east and the Appalachian Plateaus Province to the west. The parallel ridges and valleys of the province critically affect soils, vegetation, and land use. Each ridge is the result of tilted or folded rocks, mainly sandstone, shale, or dolomite. The pattern of soils from ridge to footslope to valley floor differs for each of these rock types. Prominent sandstone ridges such as Clinch Mountain in Tennessee and Virginia usually have steep slopes with shallow sandy or loamy soils. On the less steep footslopes and terraces of sandstone ridges, soils are thicker with loam or clay loam subsoils. In the adjacent valleys, the more nearly level soils on floodplains are usually deep and loamy and, in some flatter spots, may remain wet during some seasons. All of these soils were originally acid and low in fertility, with soils on north- and east-facing slopes being more productive than those facing south and west. A high proportion of this association is still in forest.

Shale ridges may consist of either acidic or calcareous (calcium-rich and non-acidic) shale. On most steep slopes, soils are less than two feet thick with silt loam topsoils and shaley, silty, clay loam subsoils. Available water capacity is low or medium. On gentler slopes, soils range in depth from twenty to fifty inches and have silt loam topsoils and clay subsoils. Available water capacity is medium to high. Over acidic shales, soils are low in calcium, while over calcareous shales, the bases in the subsoil are high.

Soils on the floodplains and terraces of shale ridges are generally deep. Floodplain soils are usually silty throughout and high in available water capacity. Some are poorly drained and are wet in some seasons. Soils on terraces have more clay in the subsoil and range from well drained and productive to wet and swampy. On some flat locations, a compact layer at a depth of about two feet may restrict the flow of water and air within the soil.

About half of the soils of the Ridge and Valley are underlain by limestone or dolomitic limestone. By volume, chert fragments in these soils may range from nearly zero to about one-third. Hilltops are generally rounded and less prominent than those of the sandstone ridges. In places, sinkholes and karst topography are common. These dominant limestone Ridge and Valley soils are generally very deep with silt loam topsoils and very thick, yellowish red, clayey subsoils. The soils are strongly acid and low in fertility. Hardwood trees grow well, but except on steep slopes, these soils have been cleared and used for farming since early settlement. Depth to bedrock varies from zero where bedrock crops at the surface to many feet, with most of the soils being more than five feet thick. Where depth to limestone bedrock is less than five feet, soils are less acid and may be high in calcium in the lower subsoil. In places where the soils are shallow with depth to bedrock being less than two feet or even exposed as rock outcrop, available water capacity is low, forest growth is poor, and farming is difficult. Within this landscape, however, are some very deep soils with dark brown topsoils and reddish brown or dark red clayey subsoils. Where old alluvium is the parent material, the soils are naturally strongly acid, but with soil amendments they can be very productive. The lands containing these soils are nearly all cleared and since early human settlement have provided some of the best farmland in the Appalachians.

Soils of the Piedmont Province occupy the area, sometimes called the red clay hills, that lies between the foot of the Blue Ridge and the Atlantic Coastal Plain. Containing slopes that range from gently rolling to hilly, the entire region hosts numerous streams, generally running east and south. Elevation is four hundred to one thousand feet.

The soils of the Piedmont Province are naturally medium to strongly acid and low in organic matter. They are moderate in potassium content and low in phosphorus. Underlying rocks are igneous and metamorphic with occasional outcrops. Fragments of quartz are present in places on the surface.

Predominate soils have gray sandy loam or red clay loam surface soils and red clay subsoils. At thirty to forty inches, the material is more friable and lighter in color. Available water capacity is medium. Some of these soils have a higher content of mica, and some have gray surface soils and yellow clay or sandy clay subsoils. Several areas of soils found in the Piedmont formed from dark-colored basic rocks. These soils have red or grayish brown surface soils and dark red clay or brownish yellow clay subsoils. They are less acid and contain less potassium than the dominant soils.

Although thousands of acres of good farmland in the Piedmont have been lost to roads, homes, and industry, row crops can be successfully grown on large areas if well managed. In earlier days, clean cultivation of crops such as cotton and corn caused sheet and gully erosion of the sloping Piedmont soils. These exposed soils are now clay loam instead of sandy loam and have reduced available water capacity and slower infiltration. Many such soils are now pastures or pine forests. Steep and hilly soils are in either mixed hardwoods or pine forest. The modern practice of minimum tillage, which greatly reduces soil erosion, has led to the use of some marginal soils for row crops.

Soils of the Appalachian Plateaus Province are often derived from quartz-rich sandstone and shale parent rocks, resulting in soils that are mineralogically poor and extremely low in phosphorus. In combination with steep topography, these naturally poor soils presented an inhospitable environment for early agriculture. Adoption of fertilizer and lime in the latter half of the twentieth century overcame the handicap of poor soils, but the prominence of steep slopes assured that the main land use in the plateaus would remain forest vegetation.

Soils with gentle slopes on top of the plateau are underlain by either sandstone, siltstone, or shale. Soils over sandstone generally have loam or sandy loam topsoils over loam or sandy loam subsoils and are very strongly acid. Where the soils over sandstone are thinner than twenty inches, their available water capacity is low. As a result, farm crops and trees lack water during dry periods. Where the depth of soils is twenty to forty inches or greater, the available water capacity of the soils is favorable for both farm crops and trees.

Soils over siltstones or shales generally have silt loam topsoils and silty clay loam or clay subsoils. In most respects, they resemble plateau soils over sandstone in their acidity, fertility, and available water capacity. In a few of the flatter areas, soils over shales have compact layers called fragipans at a depth of about two feet. Fragipans restrict the downward movement of water so that during wet periods the surface soil becomes saturated, restricting the access of air to the roots of many plants.

Most plateau soils lie on the steep slopes of mountainsides and range in depth from zero where bedrock outcrops to very deep where material from the upper slopes has moved downslope and accumulated. As in other provinces of Appalachia, the geographic direction of the plateau slopes greatly affects the kinds of soil that form. Soils on south- and west-facing slopes are generally shallower and paler in color, have more distinct layers, and hold less water than those that form on north- and east-facing slopes. Also, annual soil temperatures are slightly higher, surface soil temperatures vary more between night and day, and seasonal water deficits are more common on the south- and west-facing slopes. Timber production is much greater on north- and east-facing slopes.

Throughout all regions of Appalachia, farming is concentrated on the soils of the floodplains and terraces associated with many streams. However, many of the formerly productive floodplains and terraces have been covered by reservoirs created for electrical power generation, flood control, and recreation.

Detailed surveys showing the location, characteristics, and classification of soils are available for most parts of Appalachia. From this information, the potential of a soil for farm crops, timber production, water disposal, roads, and recreation can be determined. Largely compiled by the National Cooperative Soil survey, these surveys are available at the Agricultural Extension Service or the Natural Resources Conservation Service in each county.

Early settlers, lacking such surveys, made land-use decisions by observing the slope and tree growth of the site. Generally, they made good decisions, but if a soil was too poor or too shallow for agriculture, a few years of crop failure would lead farmers to abandon the land, whereupon it would return to forest. Such choosing and sorting for several generations has influenced current land use for farm crops, pasture, and forest.

See also: GEOMORPHOLOGY.

—Maxwell Springer, *Knoxville, Tennessee*

S. W. Buol, ed., *Soils of the Southern States and Puerto Rico* (1973); R. L. Cunningham et al., *Soils of Pennsylvania: Characteristics, Interpretations, and Extent* (1977); M. E. Springer and J. A. Elder, *Soils of Tennessee* (1980).

Tectonics

The story of Appalachia begins about 1.1 billion years ago with the formation of a supercontinent called Rodinia. The formation of Rodinia involved the collision of a number of continents during a series of mountain-building episodes called orogenies. The last piece of the continent was added during an episode called the Grenville Orogeny, which created a lengthy mountain chain called the Grenville Mountains, the roots of which extend from Newfoundland in eastern Canada to Texas and underlie all of Appalachia. A sequence of tectonic events that eventually led to the formation of the Appalachians began about 700 million years ago when Rodinia began to break apart to form new continents. This separation eventually formed the Iapetus Ocean, which was surrounded by the continents of Laurentia, Gondwana, and Baltica and several smaller microcontinents called the Piedmont Microcontinents. Laurentia consisted of what is now North America and Greenland. Gondwana was composed of what is now South America, Africa, Antarctica, Australia, and India, and Baltica included the rocks of Europe west of the present Ural Mountains. Shortly after the breakup of Rodinia, a microcontinent called Avalonia broke away from the western margin of Gondwana. These continents and microcontinents were to play major roles in the formation of Appalachia. Other continents would eventually combine to form Asia.

During the initial breakup of Rodinia, a number of fault-bounded basins formed along the eastern margin of what would become Laurentia. Some of these basins were filled with sediment derived from the erosion of the Grenville Mountains. At first, the basins filled slowly, but later the rate of sediment input increased as the basins deepened and the sediments shed from the Grenville Highlands became coarser. Several of the faults that bounded the basins ruptured the entire crust and allowed the sea to flood into the basin as underlying rock began to melt. The resultant magma raced up along the faults and spread out to form the bottom of the new seafloor. In other instances the lava flows became interbedded with sediments as they continued to accumulate in the basins. Farther toward the interior of Laurentia, where the crust was thicker, the faults bounding basins did not penetrate the entire crust, and as a result, no volcanic rocks were introduced into these basins. The Ocoee Basin in eastern Tennessee, northern Georgia, and western North Carolina is a mostly volcanic-free basin (associated with thicker crust) that contains about nine miles of sedimentary rock, whereas the Mount Rogers and Grandfather Mountain basins in North Carolina, Virginia, and northeastern Tennessee, located nearer the margin of Laurentia, where the crust was thin, contain both sedimentary and volcanic rocks.

As the Iapetus Ocean opened and the eastern margin of Laurentia became more stable, the deep, sediment-filled, isolated basins coalesced to form a more extensive but shallower basin into which was deposited the cleaner (farther-transported) sediment that became the sandstones and shales of the early Paleozoic Chilhowee Group. These rocks form the backbone of Chilhowee, Holston, and Iron Mountains in eastern Tennessee and parts of Virginia as well as other prominent ridges along the Blue Ridge Structural Front from Maryland to Alabama.

Appalachia's first carbonate rocks were deposited on top of the Chilhowee Group as an extensive carbonate platform developed along the eastern margin of Laurentia, indicating that the new ocean was open and that a stable continental margin had been established. Following deposition of these carbonate rocks, an assemblage of intertidal shales and sandstones with only minor carbonates were deposited near sea level over much of the eastern margin of Laurentia. The presence of numerous tidal flat features such as mud cracks, rain imprints, salt casts, and ripple marks indicates quite clearly that these sediments were deposited in very shallow water.

Fossil evidence indicates that during Cambrian (early Paleozoic) time, a portion of the developing continental margin of Laurentia broke away, drifted across the Iapetus Ocean, and became part of Gondwana. This block of rock now resides in the Andes Mountains of northwestern Argentina and southern Bolivia.

About 400 million years ago, the entire carbonate platform along the eastern margin of Laurentia from what is now Texas to Labrador was lifted above sea level. Subsequent weathering and erosion converted most of the exposed surface to a karst terrain characterized by sinkholes and underground caves and caverns. At the beginning of the twenty-first century, this surface was recognized as a great unconformity, a surface or erosion and/or non-deposition representing the entire missed time interval. The amount of missing rock record varies from place to place, from parts of Pennsylvania, where none has been lost, to parts of Tennessee and Alabama, where hundreds of feet of the record are gone.

Following this period of erosion, carbonate (limestone and dolomite) deposition resumed as the platform subsided and a shallow sea returned to cover the eastern portion of Laurentia. This environment along the continental margin was, however, short-lived. Far to the east of Laurentia, the oceanic crust began to be drawn down, or subducted, beneath the western edge of the Piedmont Microcontinents, creating a chain of island-arc volcanoes. This event signaled the beginning of the first mountain-building episode to be recorded in the rocks of Appalachia, the Taconic Orogeny. During the later portion of Ordovician time, the entire ocean bottom between Laurentia and the Piedmont Microcontinents was subducted. At the close of Ordovician time, the microcontinents collided with and welded to the eastern margin of Laurentia. As a result of the collision, a large mass of oceanic crust, marine sediments, volcanic rocks, and continental crust were uplifted and thrust onto the eastern margin of Laurentia to become the Taconic Highlands. Concurrently with the collision, the carbonate margin of Laurentia was submerged as a depositional basin to the west of the Taconic Highlands. Erosion of the rising Taconic Highlands to the east generated sediments that were carried westward and deposited into the newly formed basin, first as black shale and then as mud and coarse sand as the highlands continued to rise. Because of the relative ages of the wedge-shaped masses of sediment that were shed into the basin from the eastern highlands, it is thought that the Taconic collision occurred first in North Carolina and Newfoundland and later in Pennsylvania.

Following the Taconic Orogeny, the interior of the southern and central Appalachians remained high above sea level for several tens of millions of years while a steadily deepening sea covered central New England. Then, about 400 million years ago, during early Devonian time, another mountain-building episode, the Acadian Orogeny, occurred as the microcontinent of Avalonia collided with Laurentia, forming another range of mountains along the eastern margin of Laurentia called the Acadian Highlands. In addition to the highlands, the Acadian Orogeny produced a number of intrusive igneous rock bodies called plutons as well as high-grade metamorphic rocks throughout much of the Appalachians.

As the Acadian Mountains were eroded, sediment was transported westward into the basin in the form of a delta complex called the Catskill Delta. Cenozoic erosion of some of these rocks was responsible for the formation of the Catskill Mountains in New York and northeastern Pennsylvania. Most of southern New England was affected by the Acadian Orogeny, as was what is now the Piedmont of the southern Appalachians. A lengthy fault zone in the southern Appalachians called the Brevard Fault may have originated during the Acadian Orogeny.

The final events leading to the formation of the Appalachian Mountains involved the closing of the Iapetus Ocean and the collision of Laurentia and Gondwana in a mountain-building episode known as the Alleghenian Orogeny. This final closure of the Iapetus Ocean resulted in the formation of another supercontinent, Pangea. The collisions that resulted in formation of Pangea produced the Appalachian Mountains in North America, the Ural Mountains in Russia, and the Variscan Mountains that extended from Poland, through Germany, France, and Spain to Morocco in northwestern Africa. Just before the collision of Gondwana and Laurentia, the collision of what would become South America with the southern margin of Laurentia created a narrow mountain chain, the Ouachita Mountains, extending from western Alabama to northern Mexico.

Evidence from the timing of faulting throughout the Appalachians indicates that the collision of Gondwana and Laurentia began in the north, first in Canada (Newfoundland, Nova Scotia, and New Brunswick), and migrated southward into New England and then into the southern Appalachians. The movement on the faults that formed first in the north was a slide-by or strike-slip motion, similar to that of the present-day San Andreas Fault in California. This form of slip faulting propagated southward throughout the entire mountain system during late Paleozoic time. The Brevard Fault in the southern Appalachians was reactivated at this time, forming the westernmost of a series of major slip faults. Near the end of the Paleozoic era, as the head-on collision of Gondwana and Laurentia began, thrust faults began developing, pushing rocks northwestward onto the continent from New England southward. During this process, a great slab of crust that had formed during the Taconic and Acadian Orogenies was sheared off and moved inland, shedding sediments onto the continental platform and pushing the sedimentary rocks that had formed in the Appalachian Basin into the folded and faulted structures of the Ridge and Valley Province—in much the same fashion that snow is pushed and deformed by a snow plow. This movement created the basic configuration of the crust that comprises the Appalachians, completing the Paleozoic tectonic cycle of the opening and closing of oceans. The final closure of the Iapetus Ocean can therefore be viewed as an initial oblique collision in the north that resulted in the rotation of one or both of the colliding continental masses before a later head-on collision concentrated in the southern portion of the Appalachians.

When the collision ended about 260 million years ago, a mountain range comparable in height and grandeur to today's Alps, Rockies, or Andes existed in what is now eastern North America. The supercontinent of Pangea that formed was comparable to the supercontinent of Rodinia that had formed during the late Precambrian time. Although there may have been, and most likely were, other supercontinents before Rodinia, Rodinia and Pangea are the best documented supercontinents in Earth's history.

During the early Mesozoic era, the Appalachians were rifted apart as Pangea began to break apart in a new tectonic cycle leading to the formation of the modern Atlantic Ocean. The highlands created by the late Paleozoic collision of Gondwana and Laurentia were rifted apart and rapidly eroded to fill the rift basins that formed along the eastern margin of North America as Africa and North America separated from each other. During the initial rifting, the eastern United States might have had the appearance of the present mountainous coasts of southeast China or the northern coast of Venezuela.

Rifting and extension terminated sometime during the late Mesozoic era, at which time stresses in the eastern United States once again became compressional, as they have remained until the present time. During the Cenozoic era, the remnant Appalachian highland experienced one or more episodes of uplift that elevated the land to considerable heights before another cycle of erosion began, which has lasted until the present. Modern stream drainage patterns and topography are thus a result of recent Cenozoic uplift and extensive stream and slope erosion with some modifications by glaciation in northerly regions.

See also: CENOZOIC ERA; MESOZOIC ERA; PRECAMBRIAN EON.

—Robert D. Hatcher Jr., *University of Tennessee*

R. D. Hatcher Jr., "Tectonics of the Southern and Central Appalachian Internides," *Annual Review of Earth and Planetary Sciences* (1987); R. D. Hatcher Jr. et al., "Characterization of Appalachian Faults," *Geology* (February 1988); Robert D. Hatcher Jr., William A. Thomas, and George W. Viele, eds., *The Geology of North America, Vol. F-2: The Appalachian-Ouachita Orogen in the United States* (1989).

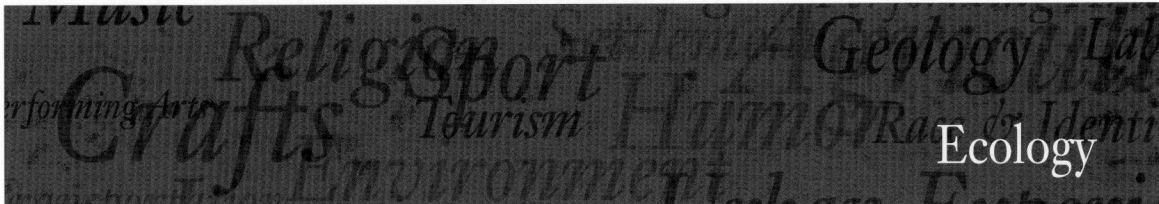

Ecology

Section Editor: George Constantz

APPALACHIAN FOLKS HAVE LONG BEEN KNOWN FOR THEIR STRONG SENSE OF place, a powerful attachment to the land. This affinity is manifest in numerous ways. For example, of all states in the nation, West Virginia has the highest percentage of home ownership, and Pennsylvania has the highest percentage of native-born residents. Across the entire region, the 2000 census showed that nearly three-fourths of Appalachians continue to live in the state where they were born. A significant feature of the Appalachian diaspora, in which sons and daughters left to work in places such as Detroit, Washington, D.C., and Atlanta, is that expatriates maintain connections to the homeplace and in great numbers return later in life.

While family and culture are the primary reasons for return, emotional attachments to the land also beckon displaced Appalachians, particularly those from small mountain communities whose heritage reflects the landscape and its natural resources. For centuries before Europeans' arrival, bonding with the natural Appalachian environment marked the cultures of native peoples, whose intricate understanding of plants, animals, weather patterns, and terrain preceded the modern science of ecology. European settlers moving into the Appalachians during the seventeenth century likewise depended on the forests, mountains, and streams for food, construction material, fuel, and other necessities.

The arrival of European technology and the growth of nineteenth- and twentieth-century extractive industries such as mining and logging doomed the sustainable traditions of Native Americans. Notwithstanding Europeans' social and economic dependence on the region's natural resources, it was not until some late-nineteenth-century conservationists decried the industrial logging of the forest that deeper appreciation of the Appalachians' natural wealth took hold. Since then, Appalachian citizens and institutions have been increasingly challenged by the often conflicting priorities of resource conservation and economic development. This tension is enhanced by the fact that Appalachia, particularly its southern highlands, constitutes one of the world's hot spots of biological diversity. Because this living diversity is inextricably bound with the region's culture and economy—as evidenced by the visceral bond between Appalachians and their landscape—this section of the *Encyclopedia of Appalachia* is devoted to the ecology of the Appalachian highlands.

Facing page: White-tailed deer *(Odocoileus virginianus)* near Boone Lake, Piney Flats, Tennessee, 2002. Appalachia, particularly its southern highlands, constitutes one of the world's hot spots of biological diversity—a living variety inextricably bound with the region's culture and economy.

The region is a center of Earth's salamander diversity. It also hosts more species of deciduous trees, darters, and shrews than any other region of North America. Spiders, moths, songbirds, mosses, ferns, insectivorous plants, sedges, heaths, wildflowers, and plants associated with rocky outcrops such as shale barrens also abound. A single Appalachian cove forest sometimes hosts thirty or more tree species. Streams and larger waterways host many species of mussels and crayfishes and more endemic fishes than any other region in North America. In the cave systems of Appalachia's karst landscapes, some invertebrates have evolved specialized adaptations. The Blue Ridge Mountains alone host more than one hundred species of native trees, two thousand species of other plants, and five hundred species of vertebrates. Because its temperate deciduous forest is now relatively undisturbed, the 520,000-acre Great Smoky Mountains National Park serves as the core of a biosphere reserve.

To understand the variety and origins of Earth's surface features, geographers classify the topography of land according to units called physiographic provinces. A physiographic province is a broad-scale region with a distinct topography shaped by common bedrock (ages, rock types) and climate (precipitation, weathering). Landscapes east of the Mississippi can be sorted into ten physiographic provinces, of which (from east to west) the Blue Ridge, Ridge and Valley, and Appalachian Plateaus Provinces form the core of the Appalachian Mountains.

A site's physiographic province hints at the types of organisms that live there. The relatively high elevations of the Blue Ridge and Appalachian Plateaus Provinces host the southernmost range extensions of several boreal species. For example, plants such as red spruce *(Picea rubens)*, Fraser fir *(Abies fraseri)*, and balsam fir *(A. balsamea)* and animals such as hermit thrush *(Catharus guttatus)*, snowshoe hare *(Lepus americanus)*, and northern flying squirrel *(Glaucomys sabrinus)* occur along the string of high Appalachian peaks. In the Ridge and Valley Province, the limestone of the valleys serves as the parent material for basic soils that buffer the effects of acid deposition, whereas the sandstones that cap ridges contribute to the formation of acidic soils that host a variety of heaths, including mountain laurel *(Kalmia latifolia)*. Thus, knowing a site's physiographic province is a start to understanding its potential plant and animal communities.

Appalachia's diverse ecological communities originated far back in geologic time. During the Paleozoic era (543 to 248 million years ago), collisions between the North American and African continental plates folded, faulted, and metamorphosed the terrain of eastern North America, raising the proto- and current Appalachians. Early in this process, the first fishes arose; about 200 million years later, terrestrial organisms occupied Appalachia. With the emergence of reptiles during the Mississippian and Pennsylvanian periods (354 to 290 million years ago), the continents began rifting apart, forming today's Atlantic Ocean. Since then, eastern North America has experienced relative tectonic calm.

Compared to ranges such as the Andes, Himalayas, and Alps, which are about 55 million years old, parts of the Appalachians have been uplifted for almost 600 million years, making the system one of the oldest continuously inhabitable terrestrial environments on Earth. This antiquity is important to understanding Appalachia's biological wealth, for older habitats have simply provided more time than younger ones for new species to evolve and diverse species to colonize. Further accounting for this living diversity is central and southern Appalachia's good fortune to have been south of the glaciers that scoured the northern United States in the last ice age.

The Pleistocene epoch, about 1.8 million to ten thousand years ago, brought heavy rains and erosion to warmer southern areas and continental glaciations to colder northern zones. The Pleistocene experienced eighteen to twenty glaciations, with each glacial cycle lasting about one hundred thousand years. The last glacial period, ending about ten thousand years ago, included the two-thousand-foot-thick Laurentide ice sheet, which leveled forests, excavated lake basins, and scraped away soils before grinding to a halt in northern Pennsylvania. As the ice retreated, boreal plants dispersed northward, reducing the boreal forest to one-third of its former size. Thereafter, deciduous plants recolonized the Appalachian highlands, delivering today's forest composition.

Another feature of Appalachian organisms is their remarkable similarity to those of a distant region. The forests of southeast China and southern Appalachia share many closely related plants and some animals. Referred to as a disjunction, this phenomenon involves more than fifty genera of plants such as hickories *(Carya)*, tulip poplar *(Liriodendron tulipifera)*, and sassafras *(Sassafras albidum)* that are common to the two regions but absent in between. These disjunct genera are descended from ancient plants that were once broadly distributed across the conjoined crustal plates of the Northern Hemisphere. Most likely, common ancestors, similar climates, and the lack of Pleistocene glaciations account for the continuing survival of disjunct organisms in both regions.

The convoluted topography of the Appalachian highlands has also contributed to the development of new species through an evolutionary process called allopatric speciation. New species generally arise when one population of interbreeding individuals becomes physically split into two groups, precluding interbreeding between the two groups. Over many generations, the separate populations accumulate observable differences, eventually reaching a point at which, should the two groups reestablish contact, interbreeding is impossible. It is believed that hundreds or thousands of generations must pass before divergence precludes interbreeding. Allopatric speciation is thought to be a primary process creating new species. Appalachia's mosaic of peaks and hollows has fractured populations, facilitating allopatric speciation.

Lungless salamanders (family Plethodontidae) illustrate the allopatric speciation process. Although sparse in northern Appalachia, salamanders appear to have evolved relatively undisturbed for millions of years south of the Pleistocene ice front. The landscape's antiquity and topographic diversity, coupled with salamanders' limited mobility, have allowed the formation of new salamander species. The landscape of central and southern Appalachia—numerous mountains and ridges separated by narrow, stream-filled valleys—has enforced genetic isolation among populations restricted to different mountains or headwaters, allowing divergence and leading to the modern variety of plethodontid species.

While allopatric speciation may lead to high biodiversity over a broad geographic area, ecological communities in the Appalachians are also notable for many species coexisting at each site. Recurrent continental cooling appears to have contributed to the overlapping ranges of several kinds of plants and animals. That is, cyclic cooling has induced species mixing. For example, the boreal coniferous forest, dominated by spruce and fir, extends southward from Canada along the crest of the Appalachians. The boreal islands in the Great Smoky Mountains are surrounded by a sea of deciduous trees. These boreal trees apparently dispersed southward into central and southern Appalachia during the Pleistocene and have persisted as isolated patches in high, cool sites. In this way, within a fairly small area, boreal and temperate species came to co-occur at local sites.

Appalachia's high biodiversity, facilitated by antiquity, topographic diversity, and species mixing, has been maintained in part by ecological disturbances such as

Black bears *(Ursus americanus)* on Grandfather Mountain, North Carolina, 2001. Once numerous in Appalachia, this large mammal was facing extinction at the beginning of the twentieth century through loss of forest habitat, encroaching civilization, and overhunting. Numbers have rebounded in recent years, and by the end of the century there were as many as thirty-three thousand black bears in the region.

wildfire. Important in conifer-dominated boreal and pine forests, fire also plays a role in drier parts of Appalachia's deciduous forest. Fire alters light intensity, microclimate at the soil's surface, water and nutrient contents of soil, and reseeding sources. Repeated fires favor species with fire-adaptive traits such as cones that release seeds when heated, resprouting by roots, and even high flammability of the whole plant. From an ecological view, fires truncate ecological succession at a site, restarting the succession process at an earlier stage. From a landscape perspective, small fires stimulate regrowth of a variety of plants, creating diverse habitats for animal species.

The coexistence of many species in small areas is a manifestation of both habitat and species diversity in Appalachia. On a single hillside, beside one stream, or under a single tree, one can often find numerous life forms adapted to specific local amounts and rhythms of light, temperature, and moisture, as well as to the presence of other species.

One of the more interesting microhabitats is the mound and pit. Created when a tree falls, a mound forms at the roots and attached soil, while a pit is left where the roots had grown. A mound differs from its pit in moisture, acidity, temperature, and litter depth. A mosaic of mounds, pits, and intervening flat areas contributes to diverse species of mosses, ferns, wildflowers, and other plants.

A mystery of the Appalachian forest is the southern mountain phenomenon known as a bald. A bald is a treeless area occupying a well-drained site in an otherwise forested area. Celebrated for their beauty and ranging in size from a few to hundreds of acres, balds take several forms (grass balds, shrub balds, and heath balds). Although the origins of balds are unknown, several hypotheses (including climate change, fire, and grazing) attempt to explain this absence of trees. Some balds may have natural origins; others are believed to have been created by repeated burning by native peoples.

Whether they are unnoticed microhabitats or popular attractions such as the azalea-covered balds of Roan Mountain on the Tennessee–North Carolina border, the Appalachians' plant communities are part of the vast eastern deciduous forest. The structure of this forest, both in terms of its composition of plant species and its three-dimensional architecture, changes as it develops. Over several years or a few plant generations, new plant assemblages replace old ones in a process called ecological succession. In central Appalachia, a simple succession may consist of stages in which species of lichens, mosses, grasses and ferns, blackberry *(Rubus)* and black locust *(Robinia pseudoacacia)*, pines *(Pinus)*, oaks *(Quercus)* and hickories, and hemlock *(Tsuga)* are dominant in turn.

In its natural state, a mature forest presents three distinct layers. At the top is a dense canopy of leaves put forth by the tallest trees. Beneath is an understory of shorter trees and woody shrubs, and at the foot of the trees grows a haphazard groundcover of green plants. The canopy, twenty to forty yards high, forms a continuous ceiling of leaves on trees such as oaks, hickories, tulip poplar, maples *(Acer)*, white ash *(Fraxinus americana)*, black walnut *(Junglans nigra)*, American beech *(Fagus grandifolia)*, basswood *(Tilia)*, and eastern hemlock *(Tsuga canadensis)*. Before the tragic spread of chestnut blight, the canopy also included the stately American chestnut *(Castanea dentata)*. Leaves of understory shrubs and trees, which may be six to fifteen feet tall, form a scattered, discontinuous layer that intercepts flecks of light penetrating the canopy. This understory consists of woody plants such as flowering dogwood *(Cornus florida)*, maple-leaf viburnum *(Viburnum acerifolium)*, common witch hazel *(Hamamelis virginiana)*, redbud *(Cercis canadensis)*, sassafras, and American hornbeam *(Ostrya virginiana)*. Short, shade-tolerant plants up to three feet tall make up the groundcover layer. Common groundcover plants include mosses, ferns, grasses, and herbaceous wildflowers.

Plantlike fungi are also common on the forest floor. Most of the forest's plants partner in a symbiotic relationship with fungi, an association called mycorrhiza, or "fungus root." The fungus colonizes either the outer or inner layer of young roots. This symbiotic "organ" facilitates the plant's uptake of water and certain nutrients such as phosphorus.

In the last three hundred years, Appalachia's forests have been changed by human actions. Today, four of the greatest environmental threats facing the region are forest fragmentation, inadequate land-use planning, acid deposition, and exotic species.

Before Europeans arrived, an almost unbroken forest blanketed the Appalachians. By 1920, most of the trees accessible by rail or river—more than 99 percent of the virgin forest—had been cut. Today's forest is an archipelago of second-growth woodlots scattered through a sea of human-cleared fields. Land development, road cutting, and other human activities continue fragmenting the forest. Habitat fragmentation raises the odds that native populations will become extinct, thereby decreasing native biodiversity.

Additionally, in many parts of the region there is still little, if any, systematic land-use planning. Consequently, homes are built in floodplains, septic drain fields are placed in soils that cannot assimilate sewage, and sprawling subdivisions displace soil-stabilizing trees.

Acid rain, snow, and fog, much of which result from coal-burning power plants in the Midwest, have reduced some high-elevation forests to expanses of grotesque skeletons. Acid deposition damages the waxy coverings of leaves, as well as leaching potassium, sugars, proteins, and amino acids from them, leaving damaged trees vulnerable to attack by fungi and bacteria. Excess acid also causes reproductive failure in fishes and amphibians.

Exotic, or non-native, species constitute the fourth major threat to Appalachian ecosystems. These newcomers can wipe out populations of native species in a few years through predation, parasitism, or competition. Among the damaging exotics found in Appalachia, some of which were intentionally introduced by humans, are honeysuckle *(Lonicera japonica)*, multiflora rose *(Rosa multiflora)*, kudzu *(Pueraria montana)*, tree of heaven *(Ailanthus altissma)*, gypsy moth *(Lymantria dispan)*, house sparrow *(Passer domesticus)*, European starling *(Sturnus vulgaris)*, and feral pigs *(Sus scrofa)*, dogs *(Canis familiaris)*, and cats *(Felis catus)*.

Although these and other human actions are changing the Appalachian highlands forever, Appalachians' strong sense of place can serve as a catalyst for natural resources conservation. This force is being expressed in various ways, including the organization of grassroots ecosystem-management initiatives in which people gather to prioritize issues and plan restoration of their local watersheds.

—George Constantz, *Canaan Valley Institute*

Chris Bolgiano, *The Appalachian Forest: A Search for Roots and Renewal* (1998); E. Lucy Braun, *Deciduous Forests of Eastern North America* (1950); Maurice Brooks, *The Appalachians* (1965); George Constantz, *Hollows, Peepers, and Highlanders: An Appalachian Mountain Ecology* (2nd edition, 2004); Peter Forbes, Ann Armbrecht Forbes, Helen Whybrow, eds., *Our Land, Ourselves: Readings on People and Place* (1999); Larry D. Harris, *The Fragmented Forest: Island Biogeography Theory and the Preservation of Biotic Diversity* (1984); Tim Palmer, *The Heart of America: Our Landscape, Our Future* (1999); Gary Snyder, *A Place in Space: Ethics, Aesthetics, and Watersheds* (1995); Bruce A. Stein, Lynn S. Kutner, and Jonathan S. Adams, eds., *Precious Heritage: The Status of Biodiversity in the United States* (2000); Scott Weidensaul, *Mountains of the Heart: A Natural History of the Appalachians* (1994).

Acorns

Dry fruits produced by oak trees, acorns are classified by botanists as nuts. The large number of oak species and their widespread distribution throughout Appalachia make acorns a familiar feature of forests, most conspicuous on the forest floor in autumn.

All oaks are classified in the genus *Quercus.* Within the genus, there is a primary division of species into two subgenera, white oaks and red oaks. Species in the white oak group are typically recognized by blunt, rounded tips of their leaves and production of sweet acorns that germinate in the first year after production. The many red oak species are recognized by the bristle tips of their leaves and their yield of bitter acorns that germinate in the second year after production.

The annual fruit production of oaks contributes to the forest's mast, which can vary substantially from year to year, leading to great variation in the successful production of seedlings. Acorns are an important food source for many animals including squirrels, white-tailed deer *(Odocoileus virginianus)*, and wild turkeys *(Meleagris gallopavo)*. Blue jays *(Cyanocitta cristata)* are a major seed-dispersal agent for oak trees, transporting and caching many thousands of acorns in the ground each fall as winter food stores. Many acorns germinate, having never been relocated by the birds. Squirrels also may fail to retrieve their harvest from hiding places in tree trunks or in the ground, leading to acorn germination and oak seedling establishment. Additionally, periodic production of vast numbers of acorns may lead to survival and eventual germination of acorns that are left unharvested by seed predators unable to exhaust the supply of nuts on the ground.

See also: FRUITS; MAST; SEED DISPERSAL.

—Christopher F. Sacchi, *Kutztown University of Pennsylvania*

Adaptive Radiation

Adaptive radiation is the branching of evolutionary lines in response to natural selection under different ecological conditions. The geologically ancient Appalachian Mountains provide ideal conditions for adaptive radiation. Mountain masses such as the Nantahalas, the Smokies, and the Blacks are well separated from one another, with major discontinuities provided by such great river valleys as the James and the French Broad. As climate changes over time, some connections between areas close while new ones are made. In addition, the great diversity of the flora and fauna of the region promotes competitive and cooperative relationships among species that interact with the topography over time to further increase species richness.

The term *adaptive radiation,* introduced by Henry Fairfield Osborn in 1899, denotes a process that lies at the heart of the modern theory of evolution. In *The Origin of Species,* Charles Darwin reasoned that variation and selection under slightly different conditions would lead inevitably to divergence among varieties and species as they became ever more closely adapted to their surroundings. One of the most celebrated examples of adaptive radiation, the finches of the Galapagos Islands provided Darwin with some of his strongest evidence for the theory of natural selection. As a result of studies by David Lack and Peter Grant, Darwin's finches remain the best-documented example of adaptive radiation. Other classic cases include the honeycreepers of the Hawaiian Islands and the cichlid fishes of the great African lakes. Almost any group of plants or animals can furnish additional cases.

Notable Appalachian adaptive radiations include the wood warblers (family Parulidae), oaks (genus *Quercus*), darters (family Percidae), and dusky salamanders (genus *Desmognathus*). The many species of *Desmognathus* have become adapted to a range of different habitats. The black-bellied salamander *(D. quadramaculatus)* is a large, fierce, almost completely aquatic predator. In contrast, the tiny pygmy salamander *(D. wrighti)* is completely terrestrial, even laying its eggs on land. Other species of *Desmognathus* occupy a series of intermediate habitats.

See also: BIODIVERSITY; CLINES; SUCCESSION.

—James Murray, *University of Virginia*

Allelopathy

Many gardeners throughout Appalachia have learned to avoid planting tomatoes near black walnut *(Junglans nigra)* trees because of the negative impact of walnut on these cultivated plants through a phenomenon known as allelopathy. Allelopathy is the release by a plant of chemicals that are harmful to nearby individuals of other plant species but not to the plant that has released them. In contrast to direct ecological interactions such as predation and parasitism, allelopathy is considered an indirect ecological interaction that benefits the releasing plant by reducing competition for resources. The relative scarcity of plants that grow successfully beneath black walnuts is attributed to the presence of juglone, a chemical produced by the tree and found in soils in the shade of a mature walnut's canopy.

Common Appalachian trees and shrubs that produce allelochemicals include rhododendron *(Rhododendron)*, sheep laurel *(Kalmia angustifolia)*, black cherry *(Prunus serotina)*, hackberry *(Celtis occidentalis)*, and eastern hemlock *(Tsuga canadensis)*. Some pines *(Pinus)* are also allelopathic. When their needles fall to the ground and begin to decompose, they release acids into the soil, inhibiting other plant species from growing. Thus, allelopathy may play an important role in influencing the germination, growth, and distribution of plants in Appalachian forests. Studies to document the importance of allelopathy in Appalachian forests and in plant communities around the world are still needed to document just how widespread this phenomenon is.

See also: INDUCED DEFENSES; SUCCESSION; SYMBIOSIS.

—Christopher F. Sacchi, *Kutztown University of Pennsylvania*

Amphibians

The Appalachian region supports a rich diversity of amphibians, hosting twenty-five species of frogs and toads and around sixty species of salamanders. Approximately 15 percent of the world's salamander species inhabit this region, which constitutes less than 1 percent of Earth's surface. Representatives of ten families occur in Appalachia, with lungless salamanders (Plethodontidae) being the most abundant. About one-half of the salamander species are found only in Appalachia, and many have restricted geographic ranges there. For example, the West Virginia spring salamander *(Gyrinophilus subterraneous)* lives naturally in only a single cave system in Greenbrier County, West Virginia. Sizes of Appalachian salamanders range from the midget, terrestrial, high-elevation pygmy salamander *(Desmognathus wrighti)* at 1.5-2 inches to the giant aquatic hellbender *(Cryptobranchus alleganiensis)* at over 29 inches. The two toad species *(Bufo americanus* and *B. woodhousei)* that live in Appalachia are characteristically squat and plump with warty skin. Both have a pair of large glands located dorsally on each side of their neck that secrete a sticky white poison that protects them from attack by many would-be predators.

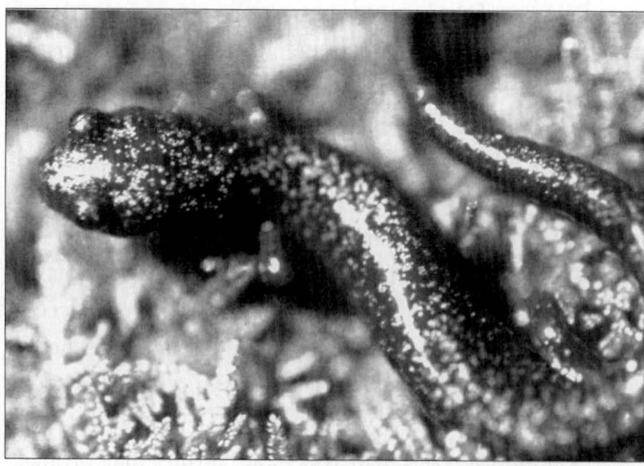

Cheat Mountain salamander *(Plethodon nettingi)*, Randolph County, West Virginia, c. 1997. The Appalachian region supports a rich diversity of amphibians, including twenty-five species of frogs and toads and around sixty species of salamanders. Approximately 15 percent of the world's salamander species exist in the region, with about one-half of those found only in Appalachia. The Cheat Mountain salamander, listed by the federal government as a threatened species, is found only on certain mountain peaks of West Virginia.

Most of the frogs, toads, and several species of salamanders native to the region depend on temporary springtime ponds or other shallow, fish-free habitats for breeding. Among these amphibians are the wood frog *(Rana sylvatica)*, spring peeper *(Hyla crucifer)*, and spotted salamander *(Ambystoma maculatum)*. Wetland habitats typically form during the winter and dry up during summer months, thus excluding predatory fishes. Many salamanders lay eggs in seepages and streams, and the larvae transform into juveniles after a few months to several years of growth. However, many lungless salamanders, such as the genus *Plethodon*, lack a larval stage and lay their eggs on land.

Frogs and salamanders feed on insects and other invertebrates and in turn constitute a food source for native vertebrates such as snakes and screech owls *(Otus asio)*. Salamanders can reach exceptionally high densities in Appalachian forests. For example, one study estimated the biomass (wet weight) of salamanders in a streamside community in western North Carolina to be greater than twenty times that of the site's birds. Because salamanders feed on forest-floor invertebrates that decompose leaf litter, they indirectly influence nutrient recycling within Appalachian forests.

Salamanders and frogs are indicators of the ongoing global decline in biodiversity associated with human population growth, though amphibians appear to be disappearing worldwide at rates that exceed those of other land vertebrates. Loss of amphibian populations from environmental degradation is well documented. More alarming is the fact that amphibian numbers are declining even in pristine areas that have not been conspicuously altered by human activity.

Amphibian populations in the Appalachian region have declined markedly since European colonization. Contributing factors include environmental alteration due to deforestation, habitat fragmentation, timbering, agriculture, destruction of wetlands, urban growth, stream pollution and siltation, and acid precipitation and deposition. As the region's human population continues to expand, urbanization and other forms of human disturbance will continue to adversely affect many native amphibians. Scientists constantly monitor amphibian populations throughout the Appalachians, and active measures are being taken to protect wetlands and find alternatives to forestry practices that threaten amphibian habitats.

See also: FOREST FRAGMENTATION; REPTILES; STREAMS.

—James W. Petranka, *University of North Carolina at Asheville*

Donald Edward Davis, *Where There Are Mountains: An Environmental History of the Southern Appalachians* (2000); Eugene P. Odum, *Ecology* (1963); Scott Weidensaul, *Mountains of the Heart: A Natural History of the Appalachians* (1994).

Aspect

Aspect, or slope exposure, is the compass direction a slope faces. In Appalachia, the sun is in the south during the warmest portion of the day; hence southern aspects receive the most sunlight and are hotter and drier than other aspects. Conversely, northern aspects are the coolest and moistest. East and west aspects exhibit intermediate conditions. Aspect indirectly affects plants and animals in a particular area by influencing environmental factors such as the amount of sunlight and wind the area receives. The types of plants that grow on a site and the animals that feed on them or that are associated with the community they support are directly related to the climate there.

The degree of slope on an aspect further affects conditions. Steeper slopes experience faster water runoff and more direct exposure to sunlight than gentler ones. Plants living on these aspects are more adapted to arid conditions. Soil moisture generally is greater at the bottom of a slope than at the top.

Plant communities often differ markedly on the extreme aspects of north and south. The cool, moist northern aspects may contain tulip poplar *(Liriodendron tulipifera)*, hemlock *(Tsuga canadensis)*, and other trees associated with high moisture, while scarlet oak *(Quercus coccinea)*, pines *(Pinus)*, and other trees associated with drier conditions are found on warm, dry southern aspects. Some animals, such as the Cheat Mountain salamander *(Plethodon nettingi)*, are found only on cool, moist northern and northeastern aspects. Hunters know that white-tailed deer *(Odocoileus virginianus)* and ruffed grouse *(Bonasa umbellus)* can be found on southern aspects during sunny winter days because of warmer temperatures and modest snowfall found there.

See also: CLIMATE; FOREST COMMUNITIES; SHALE BARRENS.

—James W. Rawson, *Canaan Valley Institute*

Balds

The mountains of southern Appalachia are not high enough to feature a climatic tree line, or alpine zone, which is the elevation above which trees do not naturally grow due to the combination of short growing season and low temperatures. Thus, the highest mountains, Mount Mitchell (6,684 feet) in North Carolina and Clingman's Dome (6,643 feet) along the Tennessee–North Carolina border, are forested to their summits. Despite this lack of a climatic tree line, some mountain ridges support treeless areas called balds.

Balds are treeless areas surrounded by forest on upper mountain slopes. While such treeless openings occur in the central and northern Appalachians for various reasons, including fire, agriculture, and soil erosion, the name for them originated in the southern Appalachians, where these communities are particularly distinctive.

There are three main kinds of balds: grass or grassy balds, shrub balds, and heath balds. Grassy balds host diverse communities dominated by grasses, particularly mountain oat grass *(Danthonia compressa)*, wildflowers, and other herbaceous plants. Shrubs such as blueberries and azaleas can also be prominent. Grassy balds tend to occur on broad upper

Rough Butt Bald as seen from the Blue Ridge Parkway, North Carolina, 1985. Balds are treeless areas surrounded by forest that occur on upper mountain slopes for various reasons, including fire, agricultural activity, and soil erosion. It is believed that some grassy balds were created by climatic warming during the Holocene epoch (10,000–5,000 years ago) and maintained by large native grazers such as elk and bison.

slopes and summits. Some grassy balds were created as upland summer grazing areas in the early to mid-1800s by settlers from nearby valleys, but most were already present when the first European explorers arrived, having most likely been created by climatic warming during the Holocene epoch (10,000 to 5,000 years ago) and maintained by large native grazers such as elk and bison. Controlled fires set by Native Americans may have also helped to maintain these balds.

All grassy balds, regardless of age and origin, were used as summer pastures beginning in the 1800s. With fewer cattle and sheep grazing on the balds starting in the early 1900s, trees and shrubs have reestablished themselves on many of them. The National Park Service and U.S. Forest Service have restored and are maintaining several grassy balds, including Andrews Bald and Gregory Bald in the Great Smoky Mountains National Park and Round Bald and Jane Bald on Roan Mountain on the border between Tennessee and North Carolina.

Shrub balds represent a stage in this succession process. They were previously grassy balds, but their dominance has shifted to shrubs such as azaleas, blueberries, blackberries, and rhododendrons.

In contrast to grassy and shrub balds, heath balds, also known as laurel slicks, are characterized by low-diversity evergreen shrub communities on convex upper-slope positions and narrow ridges. Although there have been no field experiments to directly test the mechanisms that may create or maintain heath balds, they are associated with sites that are steeply drained, exposed, and have acidic soils. Unlike grassy balds, heath balds are stable communities with little evidence of succession to forest. While heath balds do occur in undisturbed, old-growth watersheds, they also occur in second-growth areas, and in some cases they expanded following the large clear-cut logging of the late 1800s and early 1900s. Heath balds are common in Great Smoky Mountains National Park, where the June flowering of their characteristic dominant heath species, the purple rhododendron *(Rhododendron catawbiense)*, attracts many summer visitors.

See also: FOREST COMMUNITIES; HEATHS; SUCCESSION.

—Peter S. White, *University of North Carolina*

Peter S. White and Robert D. Sutter, "Southern Appalachian Grassy Balds: Lessons for Management and Regional Conservation," in *Ecosystem Management for Sustainability: Principles and Practices Illustrated by a Regional Biosphere Cooperative*, ed. John D. Peine (1999).

Biodiversity

The term *biodiversity* refers to the variety of living organisms at all levels, from genetics to species and even higher taxonomic classifications, such as genus and family, found in a given location. The term also takes into account the variety of habitats and ecosystems that organisms occupy. Thus, biodiversity is not just species richness (the number of species in an area) but a concept that also considers how organisms are arranged in space and time.

The Appalachian region is the cradle of biodiversity for North America. This is especially true of the southern Appalachians, where plant and animal diversities are high (there is a general northward decline in species richness for many groups throughout the region). For freshwater ecosystems in the Appalachians, the number of fish species ranges from 150 to 477, with about 300 upland fish species inhabiting the southern mountains. Crayfish biodiversity is also high, with species numbers ranging from 50 to 65 in the southern Appalachians, and 15 to 49 in the central portions. Mollusks, especially freshwater mussels, display high species richness, with more than 300 species found in the eastern United States, particularly in the Tennessee, Ohio, Cumberland, Mobile, and Mississippi Rivers. Additionally, the Appalachians have the greatest diversity of salamanders in the world and host more species of trees than are found in all of Europe.

Biodiversity is an especially complex issue, since it is subject to examination on many different levels. Furthermore, biodiversity is dynamic, constantly changing with evolution of the biosphere. Compositional, structural, and functional attributes of biodiversity have their basis in genes, genetic structure, and genetic processes—the basis for evolution.

Full appreciation of biodiversity requires examination at many spatial levels. At the global level, there are roughly 1.4 million species that have been described on Earth (estimates of the total species number range between 5 million and 30 million). On a finer scale, biodiversity may apply to a single small headwater Appalachian stream. A few species of fish, especially the native Appalachian brook trout *(Salvelinus fontinalis)*, and perhaps 25 to 45 species of aquatic invertebrates might be found there. Such a stream would not be as diverse as a larger one, as each habitat or ecosystem has its own natural limits.

On a global scale, the impact of human activity is causing the loss of species faster than they are being identified or their role in the biosphere is being understood. The once dominant American chestnut *(Castanea dentata)* is virtually extinct in Appalachia and other former major species such as the passenger pigeon *(Ectopistes migratorius)*, woodland bison *(Bison bison)*, mountain lion *(Felis concolor)*, and gray wolf *(Canis lupus)* are now missing components of the rich biodiversity of recent historic times in these mountains.

See also: ADAPTIVE RADIATION; CLINES; ENDEMISM.

—Ray Morgan, *University of Maryland Center for Environmental Science*

R. A. Abell et al., *Freshwater Ecoregions of North America: A Conservation Assessment* (2000); G. K. Meffe and C. R. Carroll, eds., *Principles of Conservation Biology* (1994); E. O. Wilson, ed., *Biodiversity* (1988).

Birds

The large variation in elevation and habitats over the more than 750-mile north-south span of Appalachia supports a wide variety of bird species. Many northern-breeding species such as Blackburnian *(Dendroica fusca)* and Canada *(Wilsonia canadensis)* warblers, blue-headed vireo *(Vireo solitarius)*, and winter wren *(Troglodytes troglodytes)* extend their range southward as far as Georgia through the high-elevation forests of Appalachia. Species such as Swainson's warbler *(Lymnothlypis swainsonii)* and blue grosbeak *(Guiraca caerulea)*, with breeding ranges primarily south of the region, also occur in the southern parts of the region. Because Appalachia is heavily forested, forest-nesting species such as Cooper's hawk *(Accipiter cooperii)*, ruffed grouse *(Bonasa umbellus)*, and black-throated green warbler *(D. virens)* attract much public interest, but Appalachian birds that nest in successional or scrub habitats also are of concern to conservationists. Unfortunately, since little information exists on bird populations before European settlement or even as late as the nineteenth century, it is difficult to document the impact of human environmental changes upon bird populations. Changes in forest extent and composition have undoubtedly influenced bird populations, however, and increases in forest cover over the twentieth century have contributed to increases in the populations of forest-nesting birds and declines in scrub-nesting populations.

In the latter part of the twentieth century, concern about population declines in North American birds led to two surveys that provide information on breeding bird populations in Appalachia. In the Breeding Bird Atlas projects, volunteers collect data over several years, and the information is summarized into distribution maps by state. The maps, historical references, and other summaries of bird data are usually published as books or Internet sites. Atlases have been published or are in preparation for almost all the states that comprise Appalachia. The North American Breeding Bird Survey is a roadside survey of birds conducted along fifty-stop survey routes throughout the continental United States, Alaska, and most of Canada. The survey has been conducted annually since 1966 and is a prime source of information on population change for breeding birds. Survey observers recorded 149 bird species in the Appalachian region from 1966 to 2000. As might be expected for a roadside survey, conspicuous birds that form flocks and/or prefer roadside habitats are most frequently encountered in the survey, and many species that inhabit large forest areas are less frequently detected.

The conservation initiative Partners in Flight designates thirty-four priority bird species breeding in Appalachia that are either rare or declining in populations. These priority species, which are the focus of conservation efforts, include Bewick's wren *(Thryomanes besickii)*, a species that has experienced extreme declines in the eastern United States in recent years. Other species known to be declining include the red-cockaded woodpecker *(Picoides borealis)*, brown creeper *(Certhia familiaris)*, golden-winged warbler *(Vermivora chrysoptera)*, cerulean warbler *(D. cerulea)*, prairie warbler *(D. discolor)*, field sparrow *(Sizella pusilla)*, Henslow's sparrow *(Ammodramus henslowii)*, and Bachman's sparrow *(Aimophila aestivalis)*. Species that are generally rare in the region include whippoorwill *(Caprimulgus vociferous)*, red crossbill *(Loxia curvirostra)*, Swainson's warbler, and Blackburnian warbler.

See also: HOLE NESTING; MIGRATIONS; SEED DISPERSAL.

—John R. Sauer, *U.S. Geological Survey, Patuxent Wildlife Research Center*

Albert R. Buckelew Jr. and George A. Hall, eds., *The West Virginia Breeding Bird Atlas* (1994); George A. Hall, *West Virginia Birds: Distribution and Ecology* (1983); Gerald M. McWilliams and Daniel W. Brauning, *The Birds of Pennsylvania* (2000).

Boreal Forest

A deep green mantle of spruce and spruce-fir forests is one of the characteristic features of the highest peaks in the Appalachians. This boreal (from the Latin word for "north") forest constitutes a distinct ecosystem dominated by needle-leaved evergreen species of the genera *Picea* (spruce) and *Abies* (fir).

Strictly speaking, boreal forest is limited to a broad arc from Nova Scotia to Alaska, but southward along the Appalachians a related ecosystem, the montane spruce-fir forest, reaches south to North Carolina and Tennessee. The characteristic spruce of this forest is red spruce *(P. rubens)*, a species absent from boreal Canada. The characteristic fir of the southern Appalachians is Fraser fir *(A. fraseri)*, a narrow endemic (a species found in a restricted geographical range) extending from North Carolina and Tennessee northward to southwest Virginia. Northward from central Virginia, the fir is balsam fir *(A. balsamea)*. Spruce, fir, and northern species also occur in cold air pockets and wetlands from West Virginia northward. Other important species in spruce-fir forests are yellow birch *(Betula alleghaniensis)*, American mountain ash *(Sorbus americana)*, and, after disturbance, pin cherry *(Prunus pensylvanica)*. The spruce-fir forest is the highest in elevation and coldest of the Appalachian forest ecosystems, existing where frequent cloud cover and high rainfall are characteristic.

Because precipitation increases with elevation and because spruce and fir needles are efficient scavengers of cloud moisture, spruce-fir forests are, despite their location on remote mountain slopes, victims of significant pollutant deposition, including acid rain. It is believed that pollutants are causing longterm soil changes in this ecosystem and mortality of red spruce. In addition, a pest organism inadvertently brought from Eurasia, the balsam woolly adelgid *(Adelges piceae)*, has been a severe threat to Fraser fir populations since 1960, causing the deaths of millions of mature firs.

See also: AIR QUALITY (ENVIRONMENT); FOREST COMMUNITIES; ICE AGE.

—Peter S. White, *University of North Carolina*

Box Huckleberry

Box huckleberry *(Gaylussacia brachycera)*, native to the eastern United States, is notable for its rarity and longevity. Approximately one hundred colonies of box huckleberry have been identified in scattered areas from Tennessee and Kentucky northward through West Virginia and parts of Virginia, Maryland, Delaware, New Jersey, and Pennsylvania. One Pennsylvania colony of this long-lived perennial is estimated to be thirteen thousand years old, making it one of the oldest known living plants. Some historical colonies have been lost through the activities of humans.

Box huckleberry grows low to the ground, ranging from only a few inches to two feet in height with small, oval, dark glossy green leatherlike leaves which are held yearround (all other huckleberry species in North America are deciduous). The plant has white or pinkish bell-shaped blossoms in May and early June. In late summer it bears edible blue berries that are hollow, seedless, and sweet tasting. Birds and mammals eat the fruit, and honeybees, which are probably the primary pollinating agents, are attracted to the flowers for nectar and pollen. This shrub is typically found on north-facing slopes over acidic shale bedrock and provides good groundcover for wildlife.

A colony of box huckleberry is derived from a single individual, which reproduces asexually through cloning. Because pollen from a different colony is required, only on very rare occasions will a box huckleberry have the opportunity to reproduce sexually. Box huckleberry is extremely rare in the wild and is considered a species of special concern throughout most of its range. Cross-pollination was accomplished artificially under laboratory conditions in the 1960s, though the germination rate was low and seedlings were weak and unable to grow. Box huckleberry grows runners or suckers (creeping horizontal stems called rhizomes), which produce new shoots outward from their centers, replacing older, dying branches. Each shoot will grow approximately six inches per year under optimal conditions. Thus, the age of a single colony of box huckleberry can be estimated by measuring the circumference of the colony.

French naturalist Andre Michaux first discovered box huckleberry in West Virginia in the 1790s. This single colony was the only recorded specimen until 1846, when Spencer Fullerton Baird, a professor at Dickinson College, discovered a box huckleberry in Perry County, Pennsylvania, near the town of New Bloomfield. This colony of box huckleberry is estimated to be approximately thirteen hundred years old and covers about ten acres of land preserved in the Hoverter and Sholl Box Huckleberry Natural Area within the Tuscarora State Forest.

In 1920 another box huckleberry colony was discovered outside Amity Hall, a small town also in Perry County, Pennsylvania. This colony is estimated to be approximately twelve thousand to thirteen thousand years old and it is thought to be the world's oldest box huckleberry, having established itself sometime after the last ice age. The colony, which is located about twenty miles from Baird's 1846 discovery, covers almost one hundred acres of ground.

In 1989 Blaine Miller accidentally discovered another patch of box huckleberry while surveying a piece of private property in Bedford County, Pennsylvania. Four years later, Miller read about the other box huckleberry discoveries in Pennsylvania and decided to write about his findings. In 1996 Charles Bier, an ecologist with the Western Pennsylvania Conservancy, read Miller's accounts. Bier and Steve Grund, a botanist with the conservancy, set out to locate and verify Miller's discovery. The conservancy is also working to establish protection for this thirteen-hundred-year-old colony, which covers nearly ten acres of Bedford County. Because both the New Bloomfield and Amity Hall plant colonies have been restricted in growth by roads, wildfires, farming, and other obstacles, the colonies could possibly be even older than their estimated ages. These patches of box huckleberry are by far the oldest and largest colonies of box huckleberry ever found.

See also: ENDEMISM; HEATHS; RARE PLANTS.

—Stacy Comer, *Canaan Valley Institute*

Katie J. Brown, "13,000-Year-Old Plant Thrives in Perry County," *Pennsylvania Magazine* (April 1993); Conrad Grove, "Ancient Huckleberry Is Wickedly Elusive," *Philadelphia Inquirer* (January 31, 1999).

Cactus

The two native Appalachian species of cactus are closely related. Both in the genus *Opuntia (O. humifusa* and *O. calcicola)*, they are commonly known as prickly pear cactus. In these species the fleshy, thickened plants have jointed, leafless stems. The large, showy yellow flowers occur singly. In the mountains, prickly pears are found on dry exposures with thin, rocky soils in low-rainfall areas. Shale barrens, common in the eastern parts of West Virginia and adjacent

Virginia, often support prickly pear cactus. These sites are underlain by Devonian shales with tilted bedding, which allows moisture to drain quickly from the surface.

The cactus family (Opuntiaceae) contains species uniquely adapted for life on dry, exposed sites. Most members of this family occur in Mexico and southwestern United States. A few species, however, thrive on dry, sandy soils of the southeastern states, including parts of Appalachia.

To restrict water loss, the leaves of cactus plants have evolved reduced sizes and numbers. The stems bear chlorophyll and have taken over the task of producing food. Many cactus plants are protected from predators by sharp spines that arise from small cushions called areoles. New branches and flowers also grow from these areoles.

The joints of the prickly pears are eaten, boiled or fried. The flowers can be made into salads, and the juicy fruits are eaten raw or cooked.

See also: ASPECT; SHALE BARRENS.

—Kenneth L. Carvell, *West Virginia University*

Carnivorous Plants

As elsewhere, green plants in the Appalachians serve as the base of food chains, but there are some Appalachian plants that feed on insects. Any plant species that has developed the physiology and structures for attracting, entrapping, and digesting insects is considered a carnivorous (or insectivorous) plant. All of the six hundred species of carnivorous plants found throughout the world produce flowers, leaves, and seeds, and all use photosynthesis for making sugars for building plant tissues.

In the Appalachians, most carnivorous plants live in nutrient-poor habitats such as bogs, swamps, or acidic waters. Nitrogen, essential for building proteins, is usually in low supply in such habitats, but plants with the ability to digest the protein of insects are able to assimilate amino acids and use them for synthesizing protein, especially for developing flowers, fruits, and seeds.

The bladderworts *(Utricularia)* are found commonly throughout the Appalachian Mountains. Though little known, these herbs grow submerged in shallow water, produce irregularly shaped, three-quarter-inch-wide flowers and alternate, finely dissected leaves that bear tiny bladders (small baglike traps). Usually, only the flowers grow above the water's surface. The egg-shaped bladders have an opening with a trap door near the narrow end that is surrounded by tiny trigger hairs. When an insect brushes against the hairs, the trap door opens quickly, sucking water and animal into the chamber. In less than a second, the door snaps shut. Protein-digesting enzymes released into the bladder reduce the insect's tissues to nutrients to be absorbed by the plant.

Common in Appalachian bogs, sundews *(Drosera)* are like ruby-colored jewels. Sometimes they form dense mats among sphagnum mosses. The main plant consists of a rosette of spoon-shaped leaves covered with bright red glandular hairs. The glands secrete a clear and sticky sweet-smelling digestive fluid that attracts and traps insects. In response to vibrations from the struggling insect, other hairs curl inward, dousing the victim with more digestive fluid. Within twenty-four hours, the plant assimilates the dissolved nutrients from its victim.

The pitcher plant *(Sarracenia)* uses a pitfall trap. Large leaves are fused together to form a goblet-shaped structure with a large hooded sheath rising along one side above the lip of the goblet. The inside of the goblet is filled with a protein-digesting fluid. The top half of the red-streaked hood is lined with downward pointing hairs and covered with nectar, which attracts insects. Below the hairs, the hood becomes a smooth slope with surface cells that slough off at the touch of an insect. Once attracted by nectar, an insect lands on the hair-covered surface and then slides down onto the smooth surface. The cells break free, the insect tumbles into the fluid, and it becomes plant food.

See also: INSECTS; RARE PLANTS; WETLANDS.

—Emily Grafton, *Canaan Valley Institute*

Caves

There are more than twenty thousand known caves in the Appalachians, and it is believed many more are yet to be discovered. Natural openings in the earth, caves come in many sizes and shapes, but of particular interest are those with zones of complete darkness large enough for humans to enter. They are formed when naturally occurring carbonic acid dissolves rock, typically limestone.

Because there is no light deep inside caves, there are no green plants, which provide the energy base of most ecosystems on Earth. Food is either carried in by water (in the form of leaf detritus, for instance) or left by animals that periodically visit caves. Nesting birds such as eastern phoebes *(Sayornis phoebe)* often nest on ledges around the mouths of caves in the Appalachians. Salamanders and frogs, including the cave salamander *(Eurycea lucifuga)*, the slimy salamander *(Plethodon glutinosus)*, and the pickerel frog *(Rana palustris)*, are common in the twilight zone near cave entrances and are sometimes found deep inside. The Allegheny wood rat *(Neotoma magister)* is also found in caves throughout the Appalachians. The best-known regular visitors to caves are bats, many of which use caves as maternity roosts, hibernacula, and day shelters. Three species of bats that make use of Appalachian caves are listed as endangered species by the U.S. Fish and Wildlife Service: the gray bat *(Myotis grisescens)*, the Indiana bat *(M. sodalis)*, and the Virginia big-eared bat

(Plecotus townsendii virginianus). The gray bat and the Indiana bat hibernate in groups of one hundred thousand or more in a few caves in the southern Appalachians. Other cave visitors of special importance to the ecosystem are cave crickets *(Hadenoecus subterraneus)*, which roost in the cave, often hundreds of yards inside, and periodically forage aboveground at night.

Guano (fecal droppings) and other organic material left by these periodic visitors to caves, together with the food brought in by flowing water, form the energy base for the inhabitants of caves—salamanders, fishes, and a wide variety of invertebrates (especially beetles, crustaceans, and arachnids). Nearly five hundred species of these cave dwellers are known to exist in the Appalachians.

The most biologically diverse single cave known to exist in the Appalachians is Shelta Cave near Huntsville, Alabama. Shelta Cave has twenty-four species of obligate cave animals (animals that complete their entire life-cycles underground), including three species of crayfish and one species of fish. Biodiversity is highest in the southern Appalachians, and northeast Alabama is a hot spot of terrestrial cave biodiversity—Jackson, Madison, and Marshall Counties rank first, second, and fourth, respectively, among all U.S. counties in number of obligate cave-dwelling terrestrial species. Other Appalachian counties with high terrestrial cave biodiversity are Greenbrier County, West Virginia, and Lee County, Virginia. Areas of high-level aquatic cave biodiversity include Greenbrier and Pocahontas Counties in West Virginia.

See also: CAVING (SPORTS AND RECREATION); ENDEMISM; KARST.

—David C. Culver, *American University*

Barry F. Beck, *An Introduction to Caves and Cave Exploring in Georgia: Georgia Department of Natural Resources, Geologic Survey, Geologic Guide 5* (1980); Patty Jo Watson, "Ridges, Rises, and Rocks; Caves, Coves, Terraces, and Hollows: Appalachian Archaeology at the Millennium," in *Archaeology of the Appalachian Highlands*, ed. Lynne P. Sullivan and Susan C. Prezzano (2001).

Climate

Diversity marks the climate of the Appalachians, just as it characterizes the landscape. This is partly due to the region's location within the midlatitudes of the Northern Hemisphere, a zone where a boundary occurs between cold, dry air masses originating from polar regions and warmer, moister air masses from the subtropics. This boundary, often called the polar front, can wander over most of the Appalachian area, although it retreats toward the northern reaches during the summer months. Because the Appalachian region lies in or near this transition zone, a wide range of weather phenomena affect the area, including blizzards, ice storms, tornados, hurricanes, and extremes in temperature and precipitation.

The various microclimates that exist in the Appalachian region also contribute to the great diversity in weather. Changes in elevation of thousands of feet over relatively short distances cause large differences in ambient temperatures (a change of approximately 3.5 degrees Fahrenheit for each one thousand feet). Steep ridges and deep hollows at various orientations to the sun produce strong differential daytime heating, which affects local air circulations and the production of cloud cover. Cloud formation induced by orographic uplift (air masses being pushed up over mountains) in turn alters solar input and local rainfall (making the southern Appalachians the second-wettest place in the lower forty-eight states). Complex topography can also channel airflow so as to cause high winds in localized areas. Further, the nighttime drainage of cooler air to valley floors can cause pools of cold air to collect, often making valley habitats much colder than ridge tops and cloaking the valleys in dense fogs. All of the above factors contribute to the diverse and often fast-changing climate of the region.

See also: ASPECT; ECOREGIONS; ICE AGE.

—Christoph A. Vogel, *Oak Ridge Associated Universities*

Clines

Those attributes of an organism that gradually and continuously vary across a defined area, usually the range of a species, constitute a cline. Generally, such gradual changes in traits and gene frequencies in populations of a species occur as the distance between populations increases. For example, many endothermic (warm-blooded) animals are larger and have shorter appendages in the northern, colder parts of their range.

Clines are found in many species throughout the world and represent an adaptation of populations to the local environment. In the Appalachians, black-capped *(Parus atricapillus)* and Carolina *(P. carolinensis)* chickadees display strong morphological and genetic clines in body size, song form, and habitat selection with black-capped chickadees residing in the higher elevations (above thirty-five hundred feet in the southern Appalachians) and Carolina chickadees occupying the lower slopes and valleys below. The wide-ranging and common dark-eyed junco *(Junco hyemalis)* is smaller, darker, and has a pinkish-colored bill in the northern Appalachians but is larger, paler gray, and sports a whitish bill in the southern part of the region. Flowering dogwood *(Cornus florida)*, a common tree in Appalachia, shows a tendency for fruit weights to decrease with decreasing latitude and increasing length of growing season.

Many plant species typically become shorter and more stunted in appearance with increasing elevation. Moreover, seeds collected from plants over the altitudinal cline maintain their height characteristics even when grown together in a "common garden" under the same environmental conditions. This characteristic is a genetically controlled adaptive feature that evolved over time in response to selection factors produced by variations in environments.

Clines are the product of many factors, including natural selection. Selection drives the organism to adapt to the local environment. If, by chance, gene flow among populations in a cline is terminated, then an opportunity exists for the formation of new species.

See also: BIODIVERSITY; ENDEMISM.

—Ray Morgan, *University of Maryland Center for Environmental Science*

Coal

Appalachia possesses vast coalfields located in three basins. The northern basin is located in Pennsylvania, Ohio, and West Virginia. The central basin includes southern West Virginia, Virginia, and Kentucky. Parts of Georgia, Alabama, Mississippi, and Tennessee comprise the southern basin. Coal was first discovered in the region in 1742 near the Coal River in Boone County, West Virginia.

Appalachian coals were formed during the Pennsylvanian period, 323 million to 290 million years ago, when the ecology and climate of the region were different from today. During this time, the Appalachians were located near Earth's equator in a hot and humid tropical climate, and sea levels were higher than they are today. Many swamps formed on the broad, flat coastal plain located alongside the Appalachian Mountains. It was in these swamps, similar to swamps in Louisiana and Mississippi along the Gulf of Mexico today, that the materials for coal were deposited. Many ancestors of modern-day animals, such as the dragonfly, thrived in the coal swamps, which were densely covered with plant species now extinct. Closely related to today's club moss, the giant *Lepidodendron* and *Sigillaria* attained heights of 125 and 100 feet, respectively.

The two key ingredients for making coal, which is composed almost entirely of carbon (77 to 90 percent), are found in swamps: abundant vegetation and acidic, fresh water. Acidic water is low in oxygen and bacteria and therefore retards the decomposition of organic matter such as dead vegetation. Organic matter called peat was buried by other sediments, thereby increasing pressure and temperature. This "cooking" (natural distillation) of peat increased its carbon content. Coal is classified into four categories according to its carbon content, listed in order of increasing carbon: lignite, sub-bituminous, bituminous, and anthracite.

See also: BITUMINOUS COAL INDUSTRY (BUSINESS, INDUSTRY, AND TECHNOLOGY); COAL (GEOLOGY); FERNS.

—Jocelyn M. Smith-Gaujot, *Canaan Valley Institute*

Cones

A cone, or strobilus, is a dense, rounded or elongated cluster of modified leaves or stems on a central axis that serves as the reproductive organ of a plant. Cones occur in the following five groups of Appalachian plants: cone-bearing trees (conifers or evergreen trees), club mosses, spike mosses, scouring rushes, and horsetails.

Conifers—pine *(Pinus)*, fir *(Abies)*, spruce *(Picea)*, hemlock *(Tsuga)*, tamarack *(Larix laricina)*, and northern white cedar *(Thuja occidentalis)*—possess two kinds of cones on the same tree. Pollen cones (male) have a spiral of very small, modified leaves that bear the pollen sacs. These small cones drop after the pollen is blown away by wind in the spring. Seed cones (female) are woody with a spiral of thin bracts and a thicker scale above each. Each scale bears two winged seeds that are dispersed by the wind.

In addition to various sizes and shapes, there are other conspicuous differences among seed cones of different Appalachian species. Eastern white pine *(P. strobus)* cones have smooth scales, whereas those of other Appalachian pines have a stout prickle. Spruce cones hang down while fir cones are erect. In Fraser fir *(Abies fraseri)*, an Appalachian endemic, the bracts protrude beyond the scales. In Virginia, the cones of shortleaf *(P. echinata)*, pitch *(P. rigida)*, and table mountain *(P. pungens)* pines persist on the tree for several years after the seeds are released. In these last two, the cones often persist unopened until heated by a forest fire; soon after the heat of the fire, many open, shedding their seeds. Suppression of natural fires as a forest-management practice has drastically reduced the numbers of seedlings of these pines in some areas of the Appalachians.

Eastern red cedar *(Juniperus virginiana)* differs from those previously mentioned by having the two kinds of cones on different trees and seed cones that are fleshy, fused, round, bluish, and berrylike; their seeds are dispersed by birds.

See also: SEED DISPERSAL; TREES.

—James W. Hardin, *North Carolina State University*

Coniferous Trees

See Trees

Cove Forests

Cove forests of Appalachia are found in protected bowl-shaped valleys, coves, and lower north slopes and constitute the most diverse forest type of North America. Part of the Central Hardwood Forest, the cove type is best developed in the Great Smoky Mountains of southern Appalachia, though it is also found throughout eastern Tennessee, eastern Kentucky, southeastern Ohio, West Virginia, and southwestern Virginia. For more than 300 million years this ancient landscape has been relatively free of major disturbances. Ample moisture (coves rarely experience even brief drought), deep soils with abundant nutrient supply, and the process of natural selection have resulted in high species diversity and complex ecological relationships.

Subjected to glaciation and the resultant plant and animal migrations, northern cove forests contain different species from those to the south. Farther north or at higher elevations, sites are more commonly clothed in beech, birch, maple, or northern hardwoods. Cove forests of southern Appalachia are more diverse since they developed in a warmer, moister climate and have had longer to recover from periods of northern glaciation. South-facing coves are protected from winter's cold air masses and provide shelter for both plants and animals.

High species richness is characteristic of cove forests, with six to eight dominant tree species in the canopy and twenty-five to thirty species frequently seen. A dozen other species are occasionally found. The mixture of species and relative abundance of the dominant trees varies greatly between sites, leading some to consider cove forests to be moist-site variations of the greater mixed hardwood forest.

Cove plant communities are made up of layers, and this stratification allows a variety of plants and animals to utilize sunlight and space efficiently. A mature cove forest may have tulip poplar *(Liriodendron tulipifera)* trees more than 120 feet high growing with basswood *(Tilia)*, cucumber magnolia, or cucumber tree *(Magnolia acuminata)*, sugar maple *(Acer saccharum)*, red maple *(A. rubrum)*, yellow buckeye *(Aesculus octandra)*, American beech *(Fagus grandifolia)*, white ash *(Fraxinus americana)*, bitternut hickory *(Carya cordiformis)*, and eastern hemlock *(Tsuga canadensis)*. The mid-canopy layers (20–75 feet) include redbud *(Cercis canadensis)*, sourwood *(Oxydendrum arboreum)*, mountain maple *(Acer spicatum)*, box elder *(A. negundo)*, sassafras *(Sassafras albidum)*, witch hazel *(Hamamelis virginiana)*, Fraser magnolia *(Magnolia fraseri)*, flowering dogwood *(Cornus florida)*, and, to the south, Carolina silverbell *(Halesia carolina)*. The understory is resplendent with great rhododendron *(Rhododendron maximum)*, mountain laurel *(Kalmia latifolia)*, flame azalea *(R. calendulaceum)*, ferns, vines, and numerous wildflowers.

In addition to plants, Appalachian cove forests feature one of the most diverse animal communities in North America, especially notable in the southern highlands. Forest birds reach their highest density there, and the diversity of salamanders (with at least sixty species and many more subspecies) is the highest in the world.

In the late 1800s and early 1900s, virgin cove forests fell to the axe and saw. Today's cove forests pale in comparison but are still dramatic examples of nature's diversity and a distinguishing feature of Appalachia's backwoods.

See also: BOREAL FOREST; FOREST COMMUNITIES; TREES.

—David A. Warner, *TimberLand Consulting*

Deciduous Trees

See Trees

Disjunction

Disjunction is the occurrence of a species outside of its main or contiguous range. Clusters of species occur in patches of favorable habitat surrounded by areas of otherwise inhospitable conditions. Although most disjuncts in the Appalachians are species that persist in pockets of favorable microclimates following a major climatic shift, some disjunctions have undoubtedly resulted from long-distance dispersal. For example, the slender lip fern *(Cheilanthes feei)* has been found in southwestern Virginia—far east of its main range in the western United States.

Disjunct species from the coastal plain can be found in two major Appalachian hot spots—wetlands in southeastern Kentucky and in western Virginia. Both locations may have served as refuges from glacial climates for plants from the Atlantic and Gulf Coastal Plains. Disjunctions from midwestern grasslands occasionally occur in natural forest openings such as the shale barrens of Virginia and the floodplains of rivers in the region.

In the southern Appalachians, many disjunct plants and animals are cold-adapted species associated with the high-elevation mountaintops that constitute an archipelago of Canadian zone climate. During the last glaciation (twenty thousand to ten thousand years ago), the southern mountains provided a refuge for northern species. As the climate warmed and the glaciers retreated, cold-adapted species migrated north, but they also found favorable habitat at higher elevations in the southern mountains. Consequently, the most noteworthy disjuncts in Appalachia are the plants and animals of the montane (cool, upland slopes) spruce-fir forests of the southern mountains. Many species of northern birds, such as juncos *(Junco hyemalis)*, brown creepers *(Carthia familiaris)*, pine siskins *(Carduelis pinus)*, and Blackburnian warblers *(Dendroica fusca)*, nest there in the southernmost extension of their breeding range.

Perhaps most famous is the eastern North American–eastern Asian disjunction. Many plant genera, including *Betula* (birch), *Cornus* (dogwood), *Ostrya* (hornbeam), and some animal genera, such as *Agkistrodon* (copperhead), *Cryptobranchus* (hellbender), and *Alligator* (alligator), are represented in both regions. The plants of Hubei Province, China, and the Carolinas in the United States are extremely similar, sharing 75 percent of their families. Collectively, all the disjunct, closely related living things give the forests of Appalachia and central China strikingly similar appearances.

See also: BOREAL FOREST; ICE AGE; PRE-COLUMBIAN ECOLOGY.

—Foster Levy, *East Tennessee State University*

G. Davidse, ed., *Biogeographical Relationships between Temperate Eastern Asia and Temperate Eastern North America* (1984).

Ecological Catastrophes

Native Americans in Appalachia routinely used fire to clear land for agriculture and to attract wild game for hunting. When Europeans began arriving in the region, human interference in Appalachian ecosystems increased dramatically. By the end of the nineteenth century, the landscape was largely devoid of forests due to agricultural activity, clear-cutting to produce charcoal to fire iron smelters, and timber harvest for lumber. Although reforestation throughout the eastern United States became an environmental priority during the twentieth century, burgeoning urbanization and the proliferation of chip mills in the southeastern United States, many of which can process up to ten thousand acres of clear-cut forest per year, threaten to reverse this reforestation trend.

In the late nineteenth and early twentieth centuries, coal mining, centered in eastern Kentucky and West Virginia, became highly mechanized, resulting in ecological destruction over thousands of square miles. Mountaintop removal, in which overburden is bulldozed into valleys and streams, is the mining technique used to extract smaller veins of coal economically. Though this type of mining is the most radical, surface mining of all types results in loss of biologically diverse terrestrial ecosystems and degrades water quality in rivers and streams.

Generally moving from north to south, waves of pests, pathogens, and exotic species also invaded the region during the twentieth century, significantly affecting the ecology of Appalachia. Many were introduced via commerce and trade in the northeast part of the region and migrated along the mountains to the southeast. The most ecologically devastating pathogen is American chestnut blight *(Endothia parasitica)*, which eliminated the most prolific nut-producing tree in the temperate forest, having significant impact on mammals and game bird species. Other pests, pathogens, and exotic species include balsam woolly adelgid *(Adelges piceae)*, hemlock woolly adelgid *(A. tsugae)*, beech bark disease complex (*Cryptococcus fagisuga* and *Nectria* spp.), southern pine beetle *(Dendroctonus frontalis)*, gypsy moth *(Lymantria dispar)*, butternut canker *(Sirococcus clavigignenti-juglandacearum)*, dogwood anthracnose *(Discula destructiva)*, oak diseases, European wild boar *(Sus scrofa)*, kudzu *(Pueraria montana)*, Japanese honeysuckle *(Lonicera japonica)*, oriental bittersweet *(Celastrus orbiculatus)*, and Japanese grass *(Microstegium vimineum)*.

Human pollution has also had a devastating effect on aquatic and terrestrial environments. For instance, pollution from the paper mill in Canton, North Carolina, is deemed responsible for killing most of the aquatic life of the nearby Pigeon River. After many years of litigation and delay, the mill's pollution was greatly reduced, and the river is now in recovery. Air pollution from coal-fired power plants has resulted in the acidification of lakes as far away as New England and stress on high-elevation forests. Red spruce *(Picea rubens)* trees have been adversely impacted by acid rain, while ozone pollution affects sensitive tree species such as black cherry *(Prunus serotina)* and tulip poplar *(Liriodendron tulipifera)*, as well as many other vascular plants.

Potentially, the most catastrophic ecological threat of all is climate change, which is predicted to change temperature regimens and bring more frequent and violent weather events. Extreme droughts, changes in the periodicity of rainfall, and frost-free days will likely dramatically influence ecosystem processes and species composition. Pests, pathogens, and exotic species are predicted to become more pervasive. The resulting increased stress on native trees, particularly climate-sensitive species such as the Fraser fir *(Abies fraseri)* and red spruce in high-elevation forests in the southern Appalachians, likely will be devastating over the long term.

See also: CHESTNUT BLIGHT (ENVIRONMENT); EXTINCT SPECIES; INDUSTRIAL POLLUTION (ENVIRONMENT).

—John D. Peine, *U.S. Geological Survey, University of Tennessee*

John D. Peine, ed., *Ecosystem Management for Sustainability: Principles and Practices Illustrated by a Regional Biosphere Cooperative* (1999).

Ecological Restoration

Ecological restoration is the return of an ecosystem to a close approximation of its condition prior to disturbance. As ecological damage to the natural resource is repaired, both the structure and the functions of the ecosystem are reestablished. Merely re-creating the form without the functions does not constitute restoration. The goal is to emulate a natural, functioning, self-regulating system that is integrated with its ecological landscape. The act of ecological restoration is not universally embraced, as some environmentalists consider it an unwarranted interference with natural processes and believe that nature should be left to take its course undirected. Other ecologists argue that restoration is an enlightened enhancement of natural processes.

Appalachia has many endangered and threatened species that may have been placed at risk when various ecosystems were damaged. Besides protecting damaged ecosystems, ecological restoration promotes ecotourism (tourism based on experiencing wild places or plant and animal species) and ecological services (such as atmospheric gas balance and improving water quality). Ecotourists are attracted to regions of high quality, rather than just a few isolated showplaces. Appalachia has tremendous potential for ecotourism with such drawing points as the Great Smoky Mountains National Park, the Appalachian Trail, the Blue Ridge Parkway, and millions of acres of national forests. Visitors from metropolitan areas may view these ecosystems as pristine, even though the region is fragmented by roads, power lines, shopping malls, and urban sprawl. One particularly important form of ecological restoration for Appalachia seeks to reestablish wildlife corridors so that forest fragments, however large, are connected in ways that enhance passage from one fragment to another. This restoration also benefits vegetation since animals are great transporters of seeds.

One question of concern is to what ends ecosystems should be restored. Natural capital (air, water, soil, forests, fisheries, and all other resources that collectively support human needs) is in serious decline. If natural capital is destroyed or impaired, these "ecosystem services" will be lost. Natural capital can be increased by ecological restoration.

Restoration depends on a harmonious relationship of human society to natural systems and requires both the understanding and support of the region's citizens. Restoration is futile if more damage occurs during recovery or after recovery has been completed. A longterm societal commitment is essential for protecting the restored area and preventing ecological damage from reoccurring.

Results of failed restoration projects are not generally published. However, more than a half-century of experience has revealed major problems that restoration projects may encounter: they may fail to outline specific goals (vague generalities may take the place of testable objectives); the proposed restoration of one area (as part of a mitigation agreement) may be used as justification for the destruction of another area; decisions are sometimes made hastily and without consultation; frequently no follow-up is planned to determine if the project was followed to completion of the stated goals; access may be denied when governmental agencies or citizens' groups seek permission to evaluate a restoration project on private property; reports are infrequently produced or are not subjected to peer review; the regulatory agency often lacks the personnel to enforce restoration requirements; and photographs of the vegetation growing at "restored" sites are presented at local, regional, or national meetings proclaiming the project a success without measurable criteria or data to support these claims.

Clean and healthy ecosystems are attractive to technical industries that offer high salaries and focus on products that are less polluting than heavy industries of the past. The new field of natural capitalism is based on environmentally sensitive industries that work profitably within communities in the long term. The Internet allows many businesses to locate anywhere in the world, and the most lucrative of these industries will choose the most attractive environments. However, care must be taken in locating these industries so that the very attributes that attracted them to Appalachia are not destroyed in the process. Regions that can attract industries that will not damage the area will prosper; those regions that do not will become ecological slums.

Skilled restoration can improve the quality of Appalachian life by producing healthy and clean ecosystems. Through successful restoration of ecosystems such as polluted rivers and clear-cut forests, the natural environment can stimulate economic development by attracting ecotourists and industry.

See also: FUTURE FORESTS; GRASSROOTS ENVIRONMENTAL ACTION (ENVIRONMENT); MINE LAND RECLAMATION (ENVIRONMENT).

—John Cairns Jr., *Virginia Polytechnic Institute and State University*

Donald Edward Davis, *Where There Are Mountains: An Environmental History of the Southern Appalachians* (2000); Denis A. Saunders, Richard J. Hobbs, and Paul R. Ehrlich, eds., *Nature Conservation 3: Reconstruction of Fragmented Ecosystems: Global and Regional Perspectives* (1993).

Ecoregions

The Appalachian Mountains encompass thirteen different ecoregions, or geographic areas with similar characteristics of climate, physiography, geology, soils, hydrology, potential natural vegetation, wildlife, and land use that affect or reflect differences in ecosystem quality and integrity.

Appalachia contains the most biologically diverse temperate deciduous forests in North America. Each ecoregion is distinguished by a unique assemblage of biological and physical characteristics. Mountainous and mountain plateau ecoregions make up 80 percent of Appalachia, while the remaining 20 percent falls within plains ecoregions. The relative importance of each characteristic varies from one ecoregion to another. For example, geology and topography are major factors distinguishing the Central Appalachian ecoregion from the neighboring Ridge and Valley ecoregion to the east and from the Western Allegheny Plateau to the west. The Central Appalachian ecoregion is a rugged plateau with steep slopes, infertile soils, and extensive deposits of bituminous coal. Because of these factors, coal mining and timber extraction are the dominant industries in the area, and agriculture is limited to the mountain valleys. In contrast, fertile valleys are plentiful in the Ridge and Valley ecoregion, contributing to the prevalence of agriculture and pastureland uses in those areas. The Western Allegheny Plateau is composed of horizontal layers of bedrock, has moderately fertile soils, and is less rugged than both the Central

Looking west from the Blue Ridge Parkway, Virginia, 1988. The region's remarkable biological diversity is due to many factors, among them numerous mountains and ridges separated by narrow, stream-filled valleys. This varied topography has led to the isolation of many species and facilitated genetic divergence.

Appalachian and Ridge and Valley ecoregions. Agriculture is traditionally more widespread and dominant in the Western Allegheny Plateau than in the Central Appalachian and Ridge and Valley ecoregions.

Both governmental and nongovernmental organizations have developed maps of ecoregions, which are subdivided into progressively smaller areas of uniform landscapes. Ecoregions are valuable units of analysis because they can be used to depict ecosystem patterns at various scales, identify appropriate reference sites for evaluating environmental change, and characterize patterns of human land use and disturbance that may pose specific risks to aquatic systems. Federal agencies are currently working together to develop a national hierarchical framework for defining ecoregions.

See also: BIODIVERSITY; CLIMATE.

—Randy Pomponio and Peter Claggett, *Canaan Valley Institute*

Endemism

Flora and fauna place most of Appalachia within the category of globally outstanding areas for biological distinctiveness, a rating based on species richness (the number of species present) and the degree of endemism (species found only within a specific geographic location). The Appalachians contain a large number of endemic species, both plant and animal. Many of the region's species of fishes, crayfishes, and mussels are found only in the Appalachians, especially throughout the southern range of the mountains. Endemic species number between 76 and 112 for parts of the Appalachians, with high degrees of endemism in the Tennessee-Cumberland and the Teays–Old Ohio River drainages. These same two drainages support large numbers of mussel species, 125 and 122, respectively. The New River (or Upper Kanawha) basin has 23 plant and animal species not found anywhere else. Most important, darters and minnows dominate Appalachian fish biodiversity. Crayfish constitute another important endemic species group.

The defined geographic area of any endemic species can vary in size. Some species may be endemic to a wide area—a classic example is black cherry *(Prunus serotina)*, found throughout the Americas. Alternatively, a species may be limited to a very small area such as a remote island, spring, old lake, or solitary mountain peak (especially on north-facing slopes). Considered one of the most important areas of plant endemism in the United States, the Appalachian Mountain region hosts 52 of the 100 genera endemic to eastern North America. Examples of rare plant endemics include spreading avens *(Geum)* and Heller's blazing star *(Liatris)*, found in very restricted habitats on mountaintops. At least 21 endemic species of salamanders are found in the southern Appalachians.

In part, these endemics occur widely throughout the Appalachians because of glaciation patterns. During the two million years of glaciations in North America, species moved up and down the Appalachian range as temperature patterns changed. Northern species dispersed south, and southern species moved north. Many species of both plants and animals became restricted to mountaintops, resulting in the formation of endemic populations.

Species that were once endemic to an area can become widespread. Human activity accounts for several exotics that have invaded the region. Among the most notorious are the house sparrow *(Passer domesticus)*, European starling *(Sturnus vulgaris)*, zebra mussel *(Dreissena polymorpha)*, colt's foot *(Tussilago farfara)*, round goby *(Neogobius melanostomus)*, and kudzu *(Pueraria montana)*. Whether introduced intentionally or accidentally, many exotic species have caused irreparable damage to ecosystems over the world and pose major threats as competitors to native endemic species.

See also: BIODIVERSITY; CLINES; EXOTIC SPECIES.

—Ray Morgan, *University of Maryland Center for Environmental Science*

R. A. Abell et al., *Freshwater Ecoregions of North America: A Conservation Assessment* (2000); G. K. Meffe and C. R. Carroll, eds., *Principles of Conservation Biology* (1994); R. B. Primack, *Essentials of Conservation Biology* (1993); E. O. Wilson, ed., *Biodiversity* (1988).

Energy Flow

The flow of energy through an Appalachian forest begins when plant leaves use the green pigment of chlorophyll to absorb energy from sunlight. The captured energy is involved in converting molecules of carbon dioxide and water into simple sugars, releasing oxygen as a by-product. These sugars form the building blocks of various plant parts such as leaves, twigs, and roots that serve as food sources for animal herbivores. Herbivores, such as the hundreds of species of moth caterpillars typical of Appalachian forests, are then consumed by predators such as the red-eyed vireo *(Vireo olivaceus)*, which, in turn, are eaten by larger predators such as the Cooper's hawk *(Accipiter cooperii)*. These plants and animals are parts of what is known collectively as the grazing food chain.

Plant parts not eaten by herbivores eventually die, contribute to forest soil's organic layer, and are decomposed by bacteria and fungi. These microbes and the organisms that consume them comprise the detrital food chain, degrading and returning nutrients stored in dead material such as oak leaves, downed limbs, or insect frass to the soil for recycling within the ecosystem.

The relative importance of the grazing and detrital food chains changes markedly as Appalachian forests are reestablished after farmland is abandoned or following disturbances such as fires or tornadoes. Grazing by herbivores on small plants such as goldenrod is often quite high, so detrital food chains are relatively unimportant early in the forest recovery process. However, as forest trees develop over time, herbivore consumption of leaves is generally reduced, and around 90 percent of the energy in leaves is added each fall to the forest floor, where they are slowly degraded by the detrital food chain.

See also: FOREST COMMUNITIES; NUTRIENT CYCLING; SAPROBES.

—Donald J. Shure, *Emory University*

Exotic Species

Also known as non-native, introduced, invasive, or nonindigenous species, exotics are accidentally or intentionally introduced into new habitats, where they sometimes establish populations that threaten native plants and animals. At least five thousand exotic species have become established in the United States since European colonization. In Appalachia, common exotics include the European starling *(Sturnus vulgaris)*, house sparrow *(Passer domesticus)*, gypsy moth *(Lymantria dispar)*, multifora rose *(Rosa multiflora)*, and kudzu *(Pueraria montana)*. The list is long and diverse, ranging from bacteria and protozoa to fungi, plants, and animals.

The starling and house sparrow, brought from Europe to New York City and other northeastern cities by bird fanciers in the late 1800s, compete with native birds for food and nesting space. Starlings nest in artificial and tree cavities also favored by the eastern bluebird *(Sialia sialis)* and many species of woodpeckers and may out-compete the native species for use of these limited nesting sites. The multiflora rose, a perennial shrub introduced from Southeast Asia in the 1800s, has become a common roadside and pasture hedge, crowding out native plants. In the mid-1900s, local state agricultural agencies recommended that farmers plant it for "living fences" that made excellent wildlife cover. The gypsy moth was accidentally introduced from Europe to trees around Boston in the late 1860s by naturalist E. Leopold Trouvelot, who was experimenting with ways to make silk and allowed some of his moths to escape. Within one hundred years, its colorful caterpillars could be found defoliating trees as far south as West Virginia, and its range continues to expand at rates of up to twenty miles per year. During major infestations, which can occur every few years, deciduous trees may lose all of their leaves and up to 20 percent may die.

The characteristics that make exotic species so successful—such as hardiness, competitiveness, and fecundity—make them difficult to control. Pesticides, herbicides, and mechanical methods such as uprooting and trapping have had limited success. Biological control, which involves releasing natural predators or pests from the target species' home range, is a promising approach. But some biological control agents, such as parasitic wasps and predatory mites, have themselves become threats to native species.

See also: ECOLOGICAL RESTORATION; ENDEMISM; FOREST FRAGMENTATION.

—David Malakoff, *Science Magazine*

Extinct Species

A wide variety of plant and animal species indigenous to Appalachia have become extinct over time. As elsewhere, many species disappeared as the ecosystems changed over geologic time, while others failed to adapt to pressures such as disease, hunting, pollution, and loss of habitat through competition or destruction by humans.

During the last ice age (ending approximately ten thousand years ago), woolly mammoths *(Mammuthus primigenius)*, mastodons *(Mammut americanum)*, and giant sloths *(Nothrotheriops shastensis)* all roamed the region; their fossilized remains have been found at sites such as Saltville, Virginia, and Big Bone Lick, Kentucky. There is some evidence that Neolithic hunters were a strong element in their demise.

Relatively recently, other large mammals were driven to regional extinction by modern man. The woodland bison *(Bison bison)* began declining with European settlement of the mountains, vanishing by the early nineteenth century. The eastern elk *(Cervus elephus)* had disappeared by the mid-nineteenth century. Both of these species were hunted to their extinction. Large predatory mammals such as the gray wolf *(Canis lupus)*, red wolf *(C. rufus)*, and mountain lion *(Felis concolor)* were extirpated from the Appalachians by the beginning of the twentieth century.

Some birds have also been hunted out of existence in Appalachia. The passenger pigeon *(Ectopistes migratorius)* is perhaps the best-known example of this type of extinction. Once the most common bird in Appalachia and the most numerous species in North America, with an estimated five billion when Europeans first arrived, the last pigeon died in captivity in 1914. The extinction of the passenger pigeon was primarily due to overhunting and the agricultural clearing of forests where they nested. The Carolina parakeet *(Conuropsis carolinensis)*, the region's only indigenous parrot species, also became extinct by the early twentieth century.

Other extinct animal species that once thrived in Appalachia include some salamanders and fishes and many invertebrates, including species of mussels and snails. Most of these disappeared after pollution or development significantly altered their habitats.

A number of Appalachian plants have become extinct as well. The American chestnut *(Castanea dentata)*, for example, was once the dominant hardwood tree in the Appalachian forests and, growing to circumferences exceeding twenty feet and to heights of more than one hundred feet, was considered queen of the eastern American forest. In 1904 the blight *Endothia parasitica* was accidentally introduced into New York City on nursery stock from the Orient planted in the New York Zoological Gardens. Chestnuts soon began to die, and by the 1920s the blight had reached the economically important American chestnuts in southern Appalachia. Despite all efforts at disease control, chestnut blight destroyed most of the chestnuts in the eastern United States within forty years of its introduction. Many species in modern Appalachia are increasingly at risk of extinction as human populations in the region continue to grow.

See also: CHESTNUT BLIGHT (ENVIRONMENT); ECOLOGICAL CATASTROPHES; RARE PLANTS.

—Elizabeth Hardy, *Caldwell Community College*

Ferns

Ferns have a lineage of more than 400 million years and are common throughout the Appalachians. About one hundred species can be found in rock crevices, on tree trunks, or in field borders, pastures, and waste areas in Appalachian forests and wetlands. Seldom are they found in cultivated fields or areas subject to frequent trampling. Ferns are rarely consumed by animals due to chemical compounds that are poisonous or distasteful to herbivores, and few seem to be parasitized by fungi and bacteria.

With a developed vascular system (veins with xylem- and phloem-conducting cells), ferns reproduce by scattering small one-celled spores into new habitats. These spores are produced on the sporophyte (the form of the fern usually seen) and in suitable habitat germinate to produce a separate living male or female gametophyte (the alternate generation which produces gametes). Ferns produce their food by photosynthesis as do other green plants. The sporophyte typically has a few to very many leaves borne on a horizontal fleshy stem (rhizome) at the ground surface. Most ferns have dissected leaves (*Asplenium rhizophyllum* is an exception), often delicately so, as in New York fern *(Thelypteris noveboracensis)*, with brown spots (sori with sporangia, the site of spore production) normally on the lower surfaces. Ferns of the Appalachians vary in size from the few-celled gametophytes *(Vittaria appalachiana)*, living independently of any sporophyte, to the large cinnamon ferns *(Osmunda cinnamomea)*, which may exceed five feet in height.

Appalachian ferns represent unique combinations of northern and southern or tropical disjunct species often living in the same habitat, such as tropical Tunbridge filmy fern *(Hymenophyllum tunbrigense)* and northern beech fern *(Phegopteris connectilis)*. Endemics represent other species unique to the flora, such as Taylor's filmy fern *(H. taylorae)* or Appalachian oak fern *(Gymnocarpium appalachianum)*.

While not closely related, several families of plants are considered fern allies. These include the horsetails (Equisetaceae), club mosses (Lycopodiaceae), and quillworts (Isoetaceae). These are separated from the ferns by either lack of leaf veins, presence of single leaf veins, or the presence of spores borne in leaf axils.

See also: ALLELOPATHY; DISJUNCTION; INDUCIBLE DEFENSES.

—J. Dan Pittillo, *Western Carolina University*

Fishes

Streams in Appalachia have long been noted for their high diversity of fish species. A key to this diversity is the abundance and variety of habitats. Cold, swift headwater streams starting high in the Appalachian Mountains and leading to large rivers in the valleys are home to more than three hundred fish species. Some streams drain west to the Mississippi River, others east to the Atlantic Ocean, and some south to the Gulf of Mexico. Some species are found only in specific drainages while others occur throughout the Appalachians. The boulder darter *(Etheostoma wapiti)* can be found only in the Elk River of Tennessee and Alabama, and the Smoky madtom catfish *(Noturus baileyi)* is endemic to a section of Citico Creek just a few miles long in Monroe County, Tennessee. Tennessee and Alabama have more species of freshwater fish than any other states.

The majority of Appalachian fishes are nongame species. Among these, darters and minnows (families Percidae and Cyprinidae, respectively) have more species than any other fish family. Darters, which lack swim bladders and so have low buoyancy, live on stream bottoms. Clear, cool streams are crawling with aquatic insect larvae, food for the bottom-dwelling darters. Banded *(Etheostoma zonale)*, greenside *(E. blennioides)*, arrow *(E. sagitta)*, and many other darters display breathtaking colors during breeding season (May to July) that rival those of tropical coral reef fishes. Some species hold their colors throughout most of the summer. At least sixty-eight species of darters are found in Appalachian streams, one of the most famous being the snail darter *(Percina tanasi)*. Discovery of this federally listed endangered species delayed completion of the Tellico Dam on the Little Tennessee River and led to protracted congressional debate over the federal Endangered Species Act. Although many people came to assume that all darter species are classified as endangered, the federal government protects only 16 percent of them.

The family Cyprinidae (minnows) contains at least ninety-five species in the Appalachian region. Many cyprinids swim in schools and include the warpaint shiner *(Nortropis coccogenis)*, saffron shiner *(N. rubricroceus)*, and blacknose dace *(Rhinichthys atratulus)*. Most are small, no more than three inches long, though some, such as central stonerollers *(Campostoma anomalum)*, often called "horny heads," can grow up to seven inches long and are caught by traditional hook and line. Many minnows take on beautiful breeding colors, as do darters. The redbelly dace *(Phoxinus oreas)*, for instance, turns a striking bright red, yellow, and silvery when spawning.

The family Ictaluridae (catfishes) includes well-known members such as the channel catfish *(Ictalurus punctatus)*, though others, such as madtoms, small catfishes in the genus *Noturus*, are not often seen. This genus includes many imperiled members, including the pygmy madtom *(N. stanauli)*. There has been some success in breeding these fish in captivity and releasing them in their native habitat.

Appalachia's game fishes are widely known. They provide food as well as recreation for anglers, who fish for bass, sunfish, and catfish, among others. The Appalachians are especially famous for their trout streams and their premier species, the native brook trout *(Salvelinus fontinalis)*. Smaller than the introduced rainbow *(Salmo gairdneri)* and brown *(S. trutta)* trout, brook trout can be found in waterways from New York to southern Georgia.

Many fishes in the Appalachians have interesting breeding behaviors. Male central stonerollers build nests in the gravel on the bottoms of streams by moving gravel one piece at a time. After a female lays eggs over the nest, a male then fertilizes and guards the clutch of eggs until they hatch. Tennessee dace *(P. tennesseensis)* and saffron shiners do not construct their own nest but lay their eggs in the nest of other species such as stonerollers.

During the last 125 years, the rich fish diversity that has characterized Appalachian streams for thousands of years has been increasingly threatened by exotic species, excessive siltation, dams, toxic chemicals, loss of riparian zones, and increasing demands for water. Several fishes have become extinct in the last century or so. The whiteline topminnow *(Fundulus albolineatus)*, last seen in 1889 in Huntsville, Alabama, was lost to channelization of Spring Creek. The harelip sucker *(Moxostoma lacerum)*, once found in Georgia, Alabama, Kentucky, and Virginia, is also now extinct. Because of threats to aquatic habitats, other species may soon follow this path of extinction. Appalachian aquatic life (especially fishes and mussels) represents one of the greatest potential losses of biodiversity in the country.

See also: HUNTING AND FISHING (SPORTS AND RECREATION); MOLLUSKS; STREAMS.

—Kevin Hamed, *Virginia Highlands Community College*

Tim M. Berra, *Freshwater Fish Distribution* (2001); William J. Matthews, *Patterns in Freshwater Fish Ecology* (1998).

Floodplain Forests

The floodplain forests of Appalachia are famous among nature lovers and biologists for their complex structure and high levels of species diversity. Eighteenth-century botanist William Bartram made some of the earliest descriptions of these forests during his explorations in southern Appalachia, and biologists today continue to make new discoveries. In southern Appalachia these forests are dominated by several tree species that can grow to immense size. These include the tulip poplar (*Liriodendron tulipifera*, 100–160 feet tall), several hickory species (*Carya* spp., 50–90 feet), oaks (*Quercus* spp., 50–80 feet), basswoods (*Tilia* spp., 60–80 feet), American beech (*Fagus grandifolia*, 60–80 feet), and sugar maple (*Acer saccharum*, 50–70 feet).

In addition to their large trees, floodplain forests are notable for the high levels of diversity among understory plants, including wildflowers, mosses, and ferns. The floodplain forests of the southern Appalachians have the greatest diversity of mosses found anywhere in the world. The forest diversity decreases as one moves northward, with tulip poplar, hickory, and basswoods becoming less common and beech, maple, and oak increasing. However, the floodplain forests of central Appalachia still contain levels of biological diversity comparable to that seen in certain tropical seasonal forests.

The diversity of animal taxa in floodplain forests is similar to that of plants, with a high diversity and density of nesting birds, particularly the colorful wood warblers, including the black-and-white warbler (*Mniotilta varia*), hooded warbler (*Wilsonia citrina*), Kentucky warbler (*Oporornis formosus*), worm-eating warbler (*Helmitheros vermivorus*), black-throated green warbler (*Dendroica virens*), and ovenbird (*Seiurus aurocapillus*). These forests are also rich in species of mammals, reptiles, and, most notably, amphibians—the number of salamander species is the highest in the world. The floodplain forests of southern Appalachia harbor a phenomenal number of endemic animal species (those found nowhere else), particularly among the salamanders. As with the plants of the floodplain forests, levels of animal diversity decline with increasing latitude, but certain groups, particularly birds, remain both diverse and abundant throughout.

Floodplain forests, because of their flat terrain, large trees, and ease of accessibility, were among the first to be logged by European settlers; few sites have not seen deforestation during the past two hundred years. Many sites that were logged, however, have recovered, and these forests are still beautiful examples of the eastern United States' most impressive forest ecosystem.

See also: BIODIVERSITY; COVE FORESTS; TREES.

—Manuel Lerdau, *State University of New York at Stony Brook*

Floods

Most flooding in the Appalachian region occurs in late spring or early summer as a result of convective storms associated with cold fronts or in late summer or fall as a result of tropical storms and hurricanes. Floods occur when rain and/or snowmelt exceed the capacity of a stream, river, or reservoir to contain or transport the water. In general, the timing, severity, and frequency of floods are controlled by regional climate patterns and characteristics of the local terrain, including geology, soils, and the shape and size of the drainage basin. The rugged, often steep terrain and sporadic, heavy rainfall over much of Appalachia create unstable flow patterns. As a result, the region's streams and rivers typically have greater runoff and more severe flooding than in most other parts of the country.

The environment created by the relatively high frequency and severity of flooding is stressful to aquatic and riparian (streamside) plants and animals. Large floods in the region frequently kill or displace a large fraction of fish and stream invertebrates, temporarily reducing biodiversity and productivity. However, despite the short-term impacts, biological communities in Appalachian ecosystems remain remarkably stable in the long term.

One reason for this persistence is that native species exhibit a wide range of morphological, behavioral, and life-history adaptations that allow them to survive and recolonize habitats denuded by floods. Some invertebrates, including many species of aquatic insects and freshwater mussels, migrate either into the substrate or to quieter backwaters. Some fish species migrate downstream where wider floodplains reduce scouring. Among many aquatic species in flood-prone environments, specialized life cycles have evolved, including high fecundity (number of offspring produced), exceptional mobility, and uneven age structure, all of which help ensure at least some individuals in each life stage survive floods and promote rapid repopulation following floods.

Floods also afford benefits to stream and riparian communities. In general, biological communities tend to be more diverse in ecosystems that are disturbed from time to time because disturbances prevent competitively superior species from driving other species to extinction—a process called competitive exclusion. Periodic flooding has been shown to prevent competitive exclusion in assemblages of riparian plants, algae, aquatic insects, and fish, thus allowing more species to coexist. In addition, floods rejuvenate streams and rivers by flushing pollutants, replenishing energy sources, and redistributing substrates.

This cleansing process has been shown to benefit aquatic species. For example, the redistribution of sediments associated with floods increases the suitable area for fish spawning, and many species of freshwater mussels exhibit significant increases in reproductive success in years following large floods. For these reasons, many scientists believe that periodic flooding contributes to the high levels of biological diversity and productivity commonly associated with streams and rivers in the Appalachian region. Proliferation of flood-control measures such as dams may cause irreparable harm to these stream ecosystems.

See also: FLOODPLAIN FORESTS; FLOODS (ENVIRONMENT); STREAMS.

—Craig D. Snyder, *U.S. Geological Survey*

Ted R. Angradi, "Hydrologic Context and Macroinvertebrate Community Response to Floods in an Appalachian Headwater Stream," *American Midland Naturalist* (October 1997); Luna B. Leopold, M. Gordon Wolman, and John P. Miller, *Fluvial Processes in Geomorphology* (1964).

Foliage Arthropods

Foliage arthropods are insects and their relatives that reside on the leaves of plants. Compared to many temperate zone localities, their abundance and diversity are especially high within Appalachian hardwood forests. Arthropods function as leaf chewers, sap suckers, predators, parasitoids, and scavengers.

Chewers, also called defoliators, include caterpillars, beetles, sawflies, and walkingsticks. These arthropods consume leaf tissue, while sap feeders such as aphids, adelgids, lace bugs, and spider mites puncture foliage to suck out the plant's fluids. These herbivores are typically kept in balance by predators, including ground beetles, lady beetles, lacewings, predatory stinkbugs, spiders, and predatory mites. After being laid as eggs or larvae on their living prey, parasitic flies and wasps kill other insects as they develop on or within their bodies. Scavenging arthropods feed on dead plant and animal material, feces, algae, lichens, and other materials; jumping bristletails, rove and fungus beetles, and many other insects occupy this niche.

In one study, 111 species of caterpillars from 13 selected moth and butterfly families and members of 212 other arthropod families were found on the foliage of Appalachian oaks, maples, black cherries, and black birches. A related study documented 91 species of caterpillars and a total of 200 families of arthropods on oak trees alone. Among the most abundant families are aphids, leafhoppers, plant bugs, weevils, sawfly larvae, inchworms, noctuid and gelechiid caterpillars, treehoppers, bark lice, ants, and foliage spiders such as theridiids, araneids, and linyphiids.

Diets of foliage feeders are varied; some feed on many types of leaves while others feed only on one specific type. During one outbreak of half-wing geometers *(Phigalia titea)*, a native inchworm, the larvae were found feeding on 41 different species of trees. Larvae fed on 35 additional species in the laboratory. In contrast, eastern tent caterpillars *(Malacosoma americanum)* are restricted to black cherry *(Prunus serotina)*, apple *(Pyrus malus)*, or related trees.

The impacts of herbivorous insects on trees vary with tree species, intensity of damage, and weather factors. If conifers are totally defoliated by herbivores such as sawflies, they generally die. Many hardwood trees are capable of surviving two or three consecutive years of defoliation by gypsy moths *(Lymantria dispar)*, but survival is reduced if the trees are stressed by drought, other insects, or diseases.

The most damaging species of defoliators take advantage of tree foliage when it is young, tender, high in water and nutrients, and lowest in defensive toxins. Native caterpillars such as fall *(Alsophilia pometaria)* and spring *(Paleacrita vermata)* cankerworms, linden loopers *(Erannis tilaria)*, elm spanworms *(Ennomos subsignaria)*, and half-wing geometers have one generation each year and feed only from bud break until late spring. Defoliation by these species may be damaging, whereas most caterpillar species later in the season occur in low to moderate numbers.

Native foliage feeders are usually kept in balance by predators, parasitoids, and diseases or by environmental conditions such as weather. In one study, 74 species of parasitic wasps and flies were reared from 46 species of foliage caterpillars, and at least 21 species of parasitoids use the half-wing geometer as a host. In the mountains of Virginia and West Virginia, 85 species of spiders that prey on foliage arthropods have been identified on the foliage of oaks, maples, and hickories.

Appalachian forests host several exotic insect species that have been introduced from elsewhere in the world. Balsam woolly adelgid *(Adelges piceae)* and hemlock woolly adelgid *(A. tsugae)* are small aphidlike sap feeders that kill entire stands of fir and hemlock. First detected in the eastern United States in the 1950s, the hemlock woolly adelgid rapidly spread from the southern Appalachians to Maine. By the early twenty-first century, 80 percent of the hemlocks in Shenandoah National Park were dead and hemlock stands in Pisgah and Nantahala National Forests and the Great Smoky Mountains National Park were infested. Gypsy moths, which cause severe damage to hardwood trees, especially oaks, have expanded their range throughout the Appalachians. To manage these exotic pests, insecticides and biological controls are used. Most insecticides used to control gypsy moths also affect other species of arthropods. Biological control also has drawbacks. For instance, a species of parasitic fly from Europe was introduced into New England in 1906 for control of gypsy moths. It spread southward and has subsequently been found to attack more than two hundred species of native caterpillars while having only a minor effect on gypsy moth populations. A more targeted biological control agent established in the Appalachians is a small lady beetle species introduced from Asia to control the hemlock woolly adelgid. Natural and human-caused factors such as logging, air pollution, insecticides, and the introduction of exotic insects influence the abundance and distribution of foliage arthropods.

See also: EXOTIC SPECIES; INSECTS; SPIDERS.

—Linda Butler, *West Virginia University*

Linda Butler, "The Community of Macrolepidopterous Larvae at Cooper's Rock State Forest, West Virginia: A Baseline Study," *Canadian Entomologist* (November–December 1992); Linda Butler et al., "Impact of Diflubenzuron on Non-Target Canopy Arthropods in Closed Deciduous Watersheds in a Central Appalachian Forest," *Journal of Economic Entomology* (June 1997).

Forest Canopy

The canopy, the upper layer of forest leaves where most photosynthesis takes place and most biodiversity lies, is a frontier for scientific discoveries. To access treetops, researchers employ ropes, towers, aircraft, cranes, and suspended walkways. In the eastern United States there are presently only eight walkways that allow scientists easy access into the canopy, which is sometimes as high as a seven-story building. With spreading deforestation and urban sprawl, these few study sites, along with other types of field stations, are an increasingly valuable scientific resource for understanding Appalachian forest dynamics.

Much of Appalachia is covered with deciduous forest, an ecologically young blend from the most recent ice age atop old geological formations. Canopies are studied from several perspectives, including plant community architecture (structure and stratification); community-atmosphere interface (including energy transfer, evaporation, and air pollutants); soil processes; and conservation issues (such as logging, habitat alterations, fire management, and pollution). A canopy consists of sessile organisms, which are immobile organisms such as sugar maples *(Acer saccharum)*, grape vines, and lichens, mobile organisms such as luna moths *(Actias luna)*, warblers, and opossums *(Didelphis virginiana)*, and canopy processes such as leaf fall and decomposition. Forest canopies are on the frontier of ecological research, with scientists continually discovering new species and processes, giving canopies a reputation as one of the most biologically diverse ecosystems on Earth.

Looking up through the forest canopy, Carter County, Tennessee, 2003. The canopy, the upper layer of forests where photosynthesis takes place, is the site of much biodiversity. With deforestation and urban sprawl on the rise, the canopy of Appalachia's deciduous forests is an increasingly valuable scientific resource for understanding forest dynamics.

See also: BIODIVERSITY; FOREST COMMUNITIES; TREES.

—H. Bruce Rinker, *Marie Selby Botanical Gardens*

Forest Communities

Renowned for their complexity and diversity, Appalachian forest communities support a rich array of plants and animals critical to downstream water quality and quantity. They supply harvested products such as wood, fiber, and medicinal plants and support tourism in the form of hiking, hunting and fishing, and nature study.

While forest composition changes to a certain degree with latitude, the most striking characteristic is the diversity of forest types within fairly small areas such as a single mountain slope or watershed. The factors that determine forest composition and structure at a particular location at this scale are elevation, soil moisture, geology, and disturbance history, which includes natural and/or human alterations to the forest community through processes such as floods, storms, fires, and logging.

Rivers and streams with wide floodplains support bottomland, riparian, and alluvial forests dominated by deciduous trees such as sycamore *(Platanus occidentalis)*, sweet gum *(Liquidambar styraciflua)*, willow *(Salix)*, elm *(Ulmus)*, alder *(Alnus)*, and ash *(Fraxinus)*. Coves and moist, or mesic, slopes are dominated by a rich mixed deciduous forest in which tulip poplar *(Liriodendron tulipifera)*, basswood *(Tilia)*, sugar maple *(Acer saccharum)*, beech *(Fagus)*, buckeye *(Aesculus)*, red oak *(Quercus rubra)*, white ash *(Fraxinus americana)*, cucumber magnolia, or cucumber tree *(Magnolia acuminata)*, and sweet birch *(Betula lenta)* are prominent. Hemlock *(Tsuga)* occurs on these sites and often dominates steeper slopes and ravines. Beech, sugar maple, buckeye, and yellow birch *(B. lutea)* thrive on moist sites to form patches of northern hardwood forest. The highest summits are cool and moist, supporting a spruce-fir, or boreal, evergreen needle-leaved forest above the northern hardwood forest.

Less moist submesic and subxeric sites at middle and lower elevations are dominated by red oak, white oak *(Q. alba)*, chestnut oak *(Q. prinus)*, pignut hickory *(Carya glabra)*, mockernut hickory *(C. tomentosa)*, red maple *(A. rubrum)*, and white pine *(Pinus strobus)*. Drier, or xeric, ridges support black oak *(Q. velutina)*, scarlet oak *(Q. coccinea)*, blackjack oak *(Q. marilandica)*, post oak *(Q. stellata)*, black gum *(Nyssa aquatica)*, sassafras *(Sassafras albidum)*, pitch pine *(P. rigida)*, table mountain pine *(P. pungens)*, Virginia pine *(P. virginiana)*, and shortleaf pine *(P. echinata)*. Although some pines occur on steep and rocky sites regardless of fire history, the widespread dominance of pine on other sites depends on fires, which open the canopy and remove organic matter from the mineral soil surface. For some pine species, fires also aid in opening seed-bearing cones. There has been a marked reduction in fire and a gradual decline of fire-dependent species across the region since about 1930, convincing some forest managers to reintroduce fire as an ecological-management tool.

Prior to the introduction of the Asian fungus known as chestnut blight *(Endothia parasitica)*, the American chestnut *(Castanea dentata)* was a widely distributed and important tree species in the region. Chestnut blight was first introduced into North America in New York City in 1904 and had caused widespread destruction of American chestnuts by the 1920s, with almost all specimens dead by 1950.

Although much of the region is dominated by second-growth forests (forests that have regenerated after the removal of the original forests by logging and farming activities), some of eastern North America's largest and oldest trees have been protected in sites such as the Great Smoky Mountains National Park and Joyce Kilmer National Forest. Many trees on these sites surpass 8 feet in diameter and 180 feet in height.

See also: BOREAL FOREST; OLD-GROWTH FOREST; PRE-COLUMBIAN ECOLOGY.

—Peter S. White, *University of North Carolina*

E. Lucy Braun, *Deciduous Forests of Eastern North America* (1950); R. H. Whittaker, *Vegetation of the Great Smoky Mountains* (1956).

Forest Fragmentation

Forest fragmentation is the process by which a once contiguous, mature forest landscape is reduced to smaller, separated areas. In Appalachia, this process is driven by two major forces: clearing of corridors of varying widths for paths, roads, and utility rights-of-way; and conversion of mature, structurally complex forests to simpler forests for various land uses. Short-lived conversions may arise from timber cutting or wind throw (zones of trees pushed over by strong winds), while more permanent changes occur from agriculture and urbanization.

Initially, the effects of fragmentation are confined to the local level, resulting in loss of habitat. Edge effects occur where different plant communities come together and are influenced by the shape and size of the fragment, as well as the landscape setting. Edge effects can be either beneficial or detrimental depending on the species or process in question, affecting plant community composition, wildlife use, and invasiveness by non-native species. Birds indigenous to certain types of edges may be more plentiful because of the abundance of nesting sites and food; however, as a result of their higher concentrations in narrow, shrubby forest edges, they run the risk of increased predation and of brood parasitism by brown-headed cowbirds *(Molothrus ater)*. Female cowbirds lay their eggs in the active nests of other birds, which then raise the cowbird chicks at the expense of their own nestlings. In wider shrub borders with more forest interior, where nests may be more dispersed and harder to find, these risks are lower.

As fragmentation increases, average stand size and age decrease, resulting in broader regional effects on species and processes. Harvesting of trees creates younger forests that are structurally simpler than the previous mature forests. Persistent conversion of forest to other land uses and the proliferation of roads eventually result in ever smaller, more isolated forest fragments, and smaller forests cannot support as many wildlife and plant species as larger forests. Additionally, species-area and edge effects act to reduce the quality of remaining fragments and lower overall biodiversity. Edge effects that extend a few feet to several hundred yards into a forest fragment can reduce the usable area of forest interior that many species require for survival with the resulting loss of some nesting birds such as the ovenbird *(Seiurus aurocapillus)*, wood thrush *(Hylocichla mustelina)*, and scarlet tanager *(Piranga olivacea)*. Elongated fragments have more edge and less interior habitat per unit area than round or square shapes.

As fragmentation continues and the habitat size threshold for various species is passed, losses of species occur with increasing rapidity. For example, some migratory bird species that need large mature forests or specialized habitats such as riparian areas are missing from small fragments. Many amphibians, reptiles, and mammals traverse stretches of open habitat with difficulty or not at all. The landscape changes from one dominated by forest species and processes to one characterized by human-adapted species and human-influenced processes. Despite the large forest cover in Appalachia compared to many other regions of the country, there has been a substantial loss of large tracts of forestland and, more significantly, of the quality of remaining forest habitats.

See also: FOREST COMMUNITIES; FOREST MANAGEMENT AND CONSERVATION (ENVIRONMENT); SPRAWL (ENVIRONMENT).

—J. Edward Gates, *University of Maryland Center for Environmental Science*

R. L. Burgess and D. M. Sharpe, eds., *Forest Island Dynamics in Man-Dominated Landscapes* (1981).

Frass

The dry, granular fecal pellets of herbivorous insects, especially leaf eaters such as caterpillars (order Lepidoptera), sawflies (order Hymenoptera, suborder Symphyta), and beetles (order Coleoptera), are known as frass. The term is thought to be derived from the German *frass voll* "gorged" or *fressen* "to eat."

Frass represents an important source of nutrient input in Appalachian ecosystems, notably in the form of nitrate-derived nitrogen. Although defoliation can remove nitrogen and other elements from forest ecosystems, microbial action in the soil can rapidly immobilize frass-derived nutrients, keeping them at the site. In this process, rapid microbial growth is stimulated in part by the usable carbon in frass, ultimately helping to retain nitrogen and other elements in the ecosystem by preventing them from being dissolved in water and carried away.

Chewing herbivory in Appalachian forests has been estimated at fifty-four to sixty-three pounds of foliage consumed per acre on average. Frass, greenfall (incompletely consumed or clipped green leaf tissue), and insect tissue resulting from herbivory return to the litter a significant percentage of the key elements of forest leaves, including nitrogen, potassium, calcium, magnesium, and sodium. Under herbivore outbreak conditions, especially the extensive defoliation by such cyclically eruptive species as gypsy moth *(Lymantria dispar)*, oakworms *(Anisota)*, spruce budworm *(Choristoneura fumiferana)*, and fall cankerworm *(Alsopyhila pometaria)*, the processing of nutrients is even greater.

See also: FOLIAGE ARTHROPODS; INSECTS; NUTRIENT CYCLING.

—James T. Costa, *Western Carolina University*

G. M. Lovett and A. E. Ruesink, "Carbon and Nitrogen Mineralization from Decomposing Gypsy Moth Frass," *Oecologia* (January 1995); B. C. Reynolds, M. D. Hunter, and D. A. Crossley Jr., "Effects of Canopy Herbivory on Nutrient Cycling in a Northern Hardwood Forest in Western North Carolina," *Selbyana* (December 2000); T. D. Schowalter, J. W. Webb, and D. A. Crossley Jr., "Community Structure and Nutrient Content of Canopy Arthropods in Clearcut and Uncut Forest Ecosystems," *Ecology* (August 1981).

Fruits

The great diversity of flowering plants, particularly in the southern Appalachians, rivals some tropical regions of the world. More than 4,000 species of flowering plants, including more than 130 tree species, have been identified in Great Smoky Mountains National Park alone—an area of only about eight hundred square miles. Fruits are unique to flowering plants, as they are derived in part or in whole from the ovary of the flower. All Appalachian flowering plants produce either fleshy or dry fruits. Fruits provide protection for the seeds they contain and in most instances provide a means by which seeds disperse. This dispersal provides a seed with better chances of finding conditions of soil, water, and sunlight that are free of plant competitors, including the parent and other seeds, and free of animals that tend to forage near the parent plant.

A fruit can be classified as simple if it is derived from a single ovary in one flower, typical of cherries and apples, or as aggregate when it is derived from many separate ovaries in a single flower, as in raspberries and strawberries. Fleshy fruits may contain one or many seeds. The three types of fleshy fruits are the single-seeded drupe of dogwoods *(Cornus)* and cherries *(Prunus)*; the multi-seeded berries such as blueberries *(Vaccinium)*, horse nettle *(Urtica)*, and tomatoes *(Lycopersicon esculentum)*; and a specialized fruit called a pome found in a subfamily of the rose, typified by serviceberries *(Amelanchier)*, apples *(Pyrus)*, and pears *(P. communis)*. Animals such as birds, mammals (including humans), and some fishes and turtles act as dispersal agents by ingesting the sweet, nutritious fruits and defecating the seeds away from the parent plant.

Dry fruits are classed based on whether they split along one or more sutures to release seeds or remain closed and disperse along with the seed. Dry fruits that split, or dehisce, include the legumes (pods) of pea family plants, such as redbud *(Cercis canadensis)* and black locust *(Robinia pseudoacacia)*, and the follicles containing plumed seeds of milkweeds *(Asclepias)*. Non-splitting, or indehiscent, fruits include the samaras of maples *(Acer)* and ashes *(Fraxinus)*, achenes found in sunflowers *(Helianthus)* and buttercups *(Ranumculus)*, and nuts such as acorns *(Quercus)* and hazelnuts *(Corylus)*. The seeds of dry fruits are dispersed through diverse mechanisms. The seeds of milkweeds and maples are dispersed by movement by wind; witch hazel *(Hamamelis virginiana)* and touch-me-not *(Impatiens)* through ejection from the fruit; poppies *(Papaver)* by dropping from pores in the tip; hickories *(Carya)* and oaks by being buried or hidden by scatter-hoarding animals such as squirrels and blue jays *(Cyanocitta cristata)*; and burdock *(Arctium)* by being carried on the coats of animals.

Familiar fruits are not always true to their popular names. Walnuts *(Juglans nigra)* and hickory nuts both may be technically considered drupes, while strawberries *(Fragaria)* are a special type of multiple fruit, not berries at all. The success of the flowering plants is in part related to the many adaptations in floral structure and in fruits that have allowed diverse means of protecting and dispersing seeds.

See also: MAST; SEED DISPERSAL; TREES.

—Christopher F. Sacchi, *Kutztown University of Pennsylvania*

Peter H. Raven, Susan E. Eichorn, and Ray F. Evert, *The Biology of Plants* (6th edition, 1999); Kingsley R. Stern, *Introductory Plant Biology* (8th edition, 2000).

Fungi

The fungi are a large and diverse group of organisms found everywhere in nature and are responsible, in part, for the health of the great forests that for many symbolize the

Mushroom of the *Boletus* genus, Carter County, Tennessee, 2003. Though casual observers often underestimate their significance, fungi play a vital role in forest ecosystems by breaking down organic matter, which is recycled, and, in some cases, by forming symbiotic relationships with plants. Most of the large and conspicuous fungi encountered in Appalachia, including almost all edible and poisonous mushrooms, are members of the phylum Basidiomycota.

Appalachian region. Despite their importance, fungi are often overlooked even by those attracted to the outdoors. Their sudden appearance and disappearance, their frequent association with decaying organic matter, their vivid colors and unusual shapes, and in some instances their poisonous properties often cause fungi to be regarded as objects of mystery and sometimes even to be associated with the supernatural.

Fungi are among the most important inhabitants of the natural world. Similar in some ways to plants (though they are not plants), they lack the green pigment chlorophyll. As a result, they cannot produce their own food through the process of photosynthesis. Instead, they obtain their food by breaking down dead organic matter or in some cases by attacking and living on or within living plants, animals, or even other fungi. Fungi that depend upon dead organic matter as their food source are called saprobes, whereas those that feed on living hosts are called parasites.

Some fungi form a symbiotic relationship with the roots of trees and other plants. This relationship, which is called mycorrhiza, is mutually beneficial to both the plant and the fungus. The fungus enables the plant to take up nutrients that would otherwise be unavailable, and the plant provides nutrition for the fungus. It is now known that the majority of plants—including such forest trees as oaks, maples, hickories, and pines—are involved in these associations. In some instances, the mycorrhizal association is so essential to the plant that the latter would not survive without its fungal partner.

Fungi also play an important role in maintaining forest functions. It has been estimated that in a year up to two tons of leaves fall to the ground per acre of Appalachian forest. These leaves do not continue to pile up year after year because various saprophytic fungi break them down. As a result, essential nutrients in the leaves are recycled to the soil. Fungi are also the major group of organisms responsible for wood decay. Although the vast majority of fungi are terrestrial, there are a number of aquatic forms, and some of these are of considerable ecological significance. In small, well-aerated streams, certain aquatic fungi play a key role, not only in the decomposition of organic matter introduced into streams but also as intermediates in food chains involving many aquatic insects and other invertebrates.

The vegetative body of a fungus consists of a system of very finely branched, microscopic, threadlike structures called hyphae. An entire mass of hyphae making up a particular fungus is known as a mycelium. The mycelium typically occurs in soil, leaf litter, or decaying wood, where the individual hyphae obtain the nutrients and water the fungus needs to grow. After a period of growth and under favorable conditions of temperature and moisture, the mycelium produces one or more fruiting bodies, within or upon which the spores (the seeds of the fungus) are produced. The plantlike structure known as a mushroom is an example of such a fruiting body, and it is somewhat analogous to an apple, since it is the fruit of the mycelium. Most fruiting bodies last for only a few days, but a mycelium may live for a number of years.

Most of the larger and more conspicuous fruiting bodies encountered in the region, including all the woody fungi and most of the large fleshy fungi (including almost all the edible and poisonous mushrooms), are produced by members of a single major taxonomic group—phylum Basidiomycota. In this group of fungi, the spores—usually four in number—develop on the outside of each special club-shaped cell called a basidium. Among the more familiar members of the Basidiomycota are the mushrooms, polypores, puffballs, boletes, and chanterelles. A few fungi with conspicuous fruiting bodies belong to a second major taxonomic group—the extraordinarily diverse Ascomycota. In the Ascomycota, the spores develop on the inside of an elongated cell called an ascus. Generally, there are eight spores per ascus, lined up like peas in a pod. Many of the larger members of this group have a fruiting body that is shaped like a cup or bowl, with the spore-producing cells forming a layer over the upper surface.

However, a few examples produce fruiting bodies with shapes more difficult to characterize. Such is the case for the morels *(Morchella)*, often called "sponge mushrooms," which are among the most highly prized edible fungi. Many people hunt them in the spring and prepare them by rolling the slices in cornmeal and browning them in butter in a saucepan. Many species of mushrooms are very poisonous, however, especially various species of genus *Amanita.* With such names as death cap *(A. phalloides)* and destroying angel

(A. virosa), they cause more than 90 percent of fatal mushroom poisonings. Also found throughout Appalachia are a broad range of minute fungi that cause plant and animal diseases—such as the introduced blight *(Endothia parasitica)* that destroyed one of the most abundant trees in the Appalachian forests, the American chestnut *(Castanea dentata)*.

See also: MUSHROOMS (FOOD AND COOKING); NUTRIENT CYCLING; SLIME MOLDS.

—Steven L. Stephenson, *Fairmont State College*

Constantine J. Alexopoulos, Charles W. Mims, and Meredith Blackwell, *Introductory Mycology* (4th edition, 1996); Gary H. Lincoff, *The Audubon Society Field Guide to North American Mushrooms* (1981).

Future Forests

Prior to the nineteenth century, the forests of the Appalachian Mountains were relatively undisturbed and continuous in their coverage of the entire fifteen-hundred-mile southwest-northeast-trending system. Between 1890 and 1910, however, more than 90 percent of these same forests were clear-cut—a result of technological advances in timber extraction, a belief that the vast forests could never be fully harvested, and the widespread perception that forest removal was synonymous with economic and cultural development. Fortunately, eastern landscapes proved to be highly resilient. By the year 2000, a secondary, mixed hardwood forest type covered more than 75 percent of the original range.

While modified from their pre-logging condition, Appalachian forests appear to be in good shape, though their soil-protection, production, and aesthetic futures are uncertain. The forests have again reached harvestable status. Most are privately owned and under contract to large timber companies, leaving them susceptible to clear-cutting when family economies dictate. Alternative harvesting methods are poorly understood. Community forestry is in its infancy, and little has been done to determine the economic potential of harvesting non-timber forest products such as ginseng *(Panax quinquefolius)*, mushrooms, and medicinal plants. Acid rain and air pollution are slowly killing thousands of acres of spruce *(Picea)* forest, and the balsam woolly adelgid *(Adelges piceae)*, an exotic insect first introduced in New England from Europe in 1908 that had spread to Great Smoky Mountains National Park by 1963, is destroying balsam fir *(Abies balsamea)* and hemlock *(Tsuga)* groves throughout the range.

Increasing public awareness of current problems and prospective solutions, support for applied, management-oriented research, and cooperation among universities, nongovernmental organizations, and the private sector are leading to practices that promote sustainability of forest resources, however. Examples of such cooperation include the 1999–2003 partnership between the Mountain Institute, John Dalen family, U.S. Fish and Wildlife Service, Nature Conservancy, and others to protect and restore fifty acres of high-elevation wetlands and balsam fir forest on private land in Pocahontas County, West Virginia.

Still lacking is a system of incentives to encourage private landowners to address crucial issues. Zoning to inhibit the subdivision of scenic mountaintop land and increasingly rapid construction of vacation homes could benefit watersheds as well as downstream populations. And while streams are often bulldozed in an effort to channel them and avoid periodic flooding, better governmental insurance and protection mechanisms could reward landowners' recognition of the biological and hydrological value of natural streams, contributing to the sustained health of Appalachian forest ecosystems.

See also: ALTERNATIVE CROPS (AGRICULTURE); FOREST COMMUNITIES; FOREST MANAGEMENT AND CONSERVATION (ENVIRONMENT).

—Alton C. Byers, *The Mountain Institute*

Galls

Galls are irregular tumorlike outgrowths of plant tissue caused primarily by certain specialized insects, though they are also caused by viruses, bacteria, fungi, nematode worms, mites, and parasitic plants such as mistletoe *(Phoradendron flavesceus)*. Galls are found on both herbaceous and woody plants in Appalachian ecosystems and come in a remarkable variety of forms, colors, and sizes. They may be smooth, spiny, or fuzzy. The plant species and plant part attacked, as well as the appearance of the gall, are determined by the identity of the gall-inducing agent.

Plants in Appalachian communities commonly found to possess galls include willows *(Salix)*, slippery elm *(Ulmus rubra)*, hackberries *(Celtis)*, oaks *(Quercus)*, witch hazel *(Hamamelis virginiana)*, maples *(Acer)*, dogwood *(Cornus)*, ash *(Fraxinus)*, and goldenrod *(Solidago)*. The simplest galls may be folds in leaves, while more complex forms consist of solid or hollow structures that develop on leaves, stems, roots, or buds. Mullein *(Verbascum)*, a common roadside weed in Appalachia, produces an enlarged, flattened, fan-shaped gall in its stem called a fasciation when attacked by a gall-forming insect. Large oaks often feature woody masses several feet in diameter caused by mistletoe.

While some galls are destructive to host plants, most are harmless, formed by the host as a defense mechanism to isolate an attacking invader. Insects that cause plants to form galls include particular species of flies, wasps, sawflies, aphids, and their relatives. Galls can be formed on all plant parts including roots, stems, leaves, buds, and flowers. For insects and mites that cause them, galls provide food and protection from predators. Some insects consume plant tissue contained in the gall, while others, such as aphids, obtain nutrition from fluids in the gall tissue. Insect larvae living inside plant galls are often eaten by birds and rodents.

Tiny wasps cause the oak apple galls found on several different species of oak. A typical oak apple may be a golf-ball-sized growth on an oak leaf with a central hard larval cell surrounded by a spongy substance. Aphids form the cockscomb elm gall. This gall's name reflects its resemblance to a rooster's comb. Familiar to Appalachians are reddish balls on junipers *(Juniperus)* called cedar apples, which are caused by a fungal rust that requires nearby apple *(Pyrus)*, crab apple *(Malus)*, or hawthorn *(Crataegus)* trees in order to complete its life cycle. For this reason, Appalachian farmers have learned not to plant junipers close to apple orchards if they want apples instead of cedar apples. Very small flies called gall midges may attack agricultural crops, as does the introduced Hessian fly *(Phytophaga destructor)*, which destroys wheat. This pest was thought to have been introduced by Hessian troops during the Revolutionary War and was so prevalent during the late eighteenth century that many American farmers stopped growing wheat.

See also: INDUCIBLE DEFENSES; INSECTS; TREES.

—Christopher F. Sacchi, *Kutztown University of Pennsylvania*

Grasses

Grasses are conspicuous in forest margins, meadows, and valleys of Appalachia and occur as dominant species on high-elevation mountaintops and ridges. High-elevation grass and heath balds in the central and southern Appalachians apparently were created when spruce-fir forests were displaced from mountaintops by climatic warming in the Holocene epoch (10,000 to 5,000 years ago). Shallow soils, animal grazing, and fires in these balds inhibit reinvasion of spruce and fir, favoring grassland vegetation. Grassy balds are popular scenic stopping points for mountain hikers, as they often provide open vistas of distant peaks and valleys. These high-elevation grasslands were used as summer pastures for cattle and sheep by local farmers from early settlement well into the twentieth century.

In the mountains of Appalachia, 42 percent of the grass species are in subfamily Pooideae and are adapted to cool seasons. Below the mountain crests 37 percent of the grass species are in subfamily Panicoideae with hot and humid requirements; 16 percent of the grass species are in subfamily Chloridoideae and well adapted to hot and dry conditions; and the remaining 5 percent are included in three other subfamilies (Aristidoideae, Danthonioideae, and Ehrhartoideae).

The grass family (Poaceae or Gramineae) is the fourth-largest flowering plant family and contains about eleven thousand species in eight hundred genera worldwide. The most important feature of this family is a one-seeded indehiscent fruit (a non-splitting fruit that contains the seed) known as a caryopsis, or grain. Grasses include barley, corn, oats, rice, sugarcane, and wheat; all are widely cultivated. The highly reduced floral structure and wind pollination in grasses has enabled the family to be extremely successful all over the planet. Grasses are well adapted to open, marginal, and frequently disturbed habitats and can be found on every continent.

See also: BALDS; HEATHS; SUCCESSION.

—Paul M. Peterson, *Smithsonian Institution*

Heaths

In the southern Appalachians, heaths dominate a distinctive shrub community locally called heath balds or laurel slicks. Heaths are small to large shrubs or small trees belonging to the heath family, Ericaceae. The group includes both evergreen and deciduous species. Heaths, which prefer acidic soils, are found in many habitats, including bogs, wetlands, rock outcrops, heath balds, and forests.

About twenty genera and fifty species of heaths are found in the Appalachian region. Prominent among these are twelve species of genus *Rhododendron* (rhododendrons and azaleas), three species of *Kalmia* (mountain laurel, sheep laurel, and bog laurel), four species of *Leucothoe* (doghobble), ten species of *Vaccinium* (blueberries and cranberries), and five species of *Gaylussacia* (huckleberry). Four other genera, while they each have just a single species, include several plants that are characteristic of the Appalachians: sourwood *(Oxydendrum arboreum)*, mountain fetterbush *(Pieris floribunda)*, the very fragrant trailing arbutus *(Epigaea repens)*, and minniebush *(Menziesia pilosa)*, a high-elevation, endemic species whose range is nearly exactly coincident with the Appalachian region.

Rhododendrons include the purple rhododendron *(R. catawbiense)*, which produces popular flowering displays at high elevations in late spring, and rosebay or great laurel *(R. maximum)*, which is often dominant along streams and on steep slopes. Azaleas include the orange-flowered flame azalea *(R. calendulaceum)* that grows in upland woods and pink *(R. periclymenoides* and *R. nudiflorum)* and white species *(R. viscosum)*, usually found along streams. Grassy balds in the southern Appalachians are famous for hybrid swarms of azaleas, with colors ranging from white to yellow, pink, deep red, and orange. *R. cumberlandense* is a deep-red species of these habitats. A rare endemic is the pinkshell azalea *(R. vaseyi)*, a pale pink-flowered species that blooms in early spring before the leaves emerge.

Mountain laurel *(K. latifolia)* is also a characteristic and popular species of the Appalachian region. Its flowers range from white to pale pink. Each stamen (the pollen-bearing structure) is held by a crease in the petals until a pollinator such as a honeybee causes it to spring forward.

Blueberries include tall-bush species such as *V. corymbosum*, as well as low-bush species such as *V. vacillans*. Blueberries grow in swamps and woods and along streams. Flowering and fruiting are often highest in open habitats or after disturbances such as fires. Closely related are the cranberries. The large cranberry *(V. macrocarpun)*, a trailing evergreen shrub, occurs in bogs and on high-elevation rock outcrops. The narrow endemic mountain cranberry *(V. erythrocarpon)* is a taller species found only at high elevations in the southern Appalachians.

See also: BALDS; BOX HUCKLEBERRY; FOREST COMMUNITIES.

—Peter S. White, *University of North Carolina*

Albert E. Radford, Harry E. Ahles, and C. Ritchie Bell, *Manual of the Vascular Flora of the Carolinas* (1968); P. D. Strausbaugh and Earl L. Cole, *Flora of West Virginia* (1977).

Hibernation

See Winter Adaptations

Hole Nesting

Hole nest sites include artificial nesting boxes or excavated, naturally formed, or man-made cavities in trees, earth, rock, buildings, or pipes. Birds such as woodpeckers and swallows, which excavate their own cavities by digging into trees or earthen banks, are called primary cavity nesters. In Appalachia, these include such tree excavators as pileated *(Dryocopus pileatus)*, red-bellied *(Melanerpas carolinus)*, red-headed *(M. erythrocephalus)*, red-cockaded *(Picoides borealis)*, hairy *(P. villosis)*, and downy *(P. pubescens)* woodpeckers; yellow-bellied sapsuckers *(Sphyrapicus varius)*; and northern flickers *(Colaptes auratus)*. Several small songbirds that also totally or partially dig their own tree cavities are black-capped chickadees *(Parus atricapillus)* and red-breasted *(Sitta canadensis)* and white-breasted *(S. carolinensis)* nuthatches. Other excavators include bank *(Riparia riparia)* and northern rough-winged *(Stelgidopteryx ruficollis)* swallows and the belted kingfisher *(Megaceryle alcyon)*, which burrow into earthen banks. Cliff swallows build rather than excavate elaborate vase-shaped mud-nesting cavities, which they place in colonies beneath concrete bridges and highway overpasses.

Other animals nest in available sites such as holes abandoned by excavators, natural cavities in rotted trees and fence posts, and in artificial nest boxes. Among these secondary cavity nesters are eastern bluebirds *(Sialia sialis)*; black-capped and Carolina *(P. carolinensis)* chickadees; tufted titmice *(P. bicolor)*; white-breasted, red-breasted, and brown-headed *(Sitta pusilla)* nuthatches; house *(Troglodytes aedon)*, Bewick's *(Thryomanes bewickii)*, and Carolina *(Thrythorus ludovicianus)* wrens; brown creepers *(Certhia familiaris)*; great-crested flycatchers *(Myriarchus crinitus)*; tree swallows *(Iridoprocne bicolor)*; purple martins *(Progne subis)*; American kestrels *(Falco sparverius)*; and barn *(Tyro alba)*, eastern screech *(Otus asio)*, northern saw-whet *(Aegolius acadicus)*, and barred *(Strix varia)* owls.

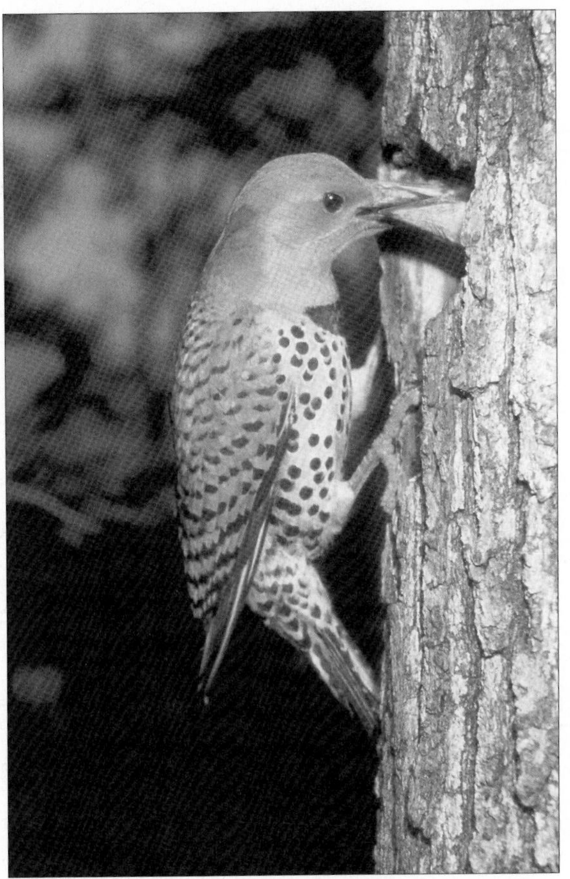

A yellow-shafted flicker *(Colaptes auratus)* feeding its young in a white oak tree *(Quercus alba)*, Virginia, 1996. Many hole nesters do not excavate their own sites but instead use naturally formed or man-made cavities in trees, earth, rock or in artificial nesting boxes, buildings, or pipes. Birds such as the flicker are primary cavity nesters, often excavating their own cavities by digging into trees or stumps. Other primary cavity nesters in Appalachia include pileated *(Dryocopus pileatus)*, red-bellied *(Melanerpes carolinus)*, red-headed *(M. erythrocephalus)*, red-cockaded *(Picoides borealis)*, hairy *(P. villosus)*, and downy *(P. pubescens)* woodpeckers and the yellow-bellied sapsucker *(Sphyrapicus varius)*.

Black *(Coragyps atratus)* and turkey *(Cathartes aura)* vultures often nest in small caves, hollow logs, or abandoned buildings, and chimney swifts *(Chaetura pelagia)* prefer chimneys. Most woodpeckers nest in both forests and forest edges using snags for foraging and nesting, while others use cavities near open habitat to forage on flying insects. Wood ducks *(Aix sponsa)* and prothonotary warblers *(Protonotaria citrea)*, both secondary cavity nesters, nest near or over water. Mature forests with big trees and dead snags large enough for nesting and denning sites are critical habitats for many species of birds and mammals. The loss of older southern pine forests with large diseased trees for nesting has led to the red-cockaded woodpecker's being placed on the federal endangered species list. Two non-native species, the house sparrow *(Passer domesticus)* and European starling *(Sturnus vulgaris)*, compete with native secondary cavity nesters.

Many species of mammals, including southern *(Glaucomus volans)* and northern *(G. sabrinus)* flying squirrels, are also hole nesters. Shrews, moles, rodents such as mice, rats, and groundhogs *(Marmota monax)*, bobcats *(Felis rufus)*, and foxes are Appalachian mammals that use holes, dens, or nesting chambers to hold and protect their young. Little brown *(Myotis lucifugus)*, big brown *(Eptesicus fuscus)*, and evening *(Nycticius humeralis)* bats all are known to establish breeding colonies in buildings, especially in attics, and some bats will use bat boxes, constructed just for them, as breeding and roosting sites. Many bats spend the winter in caves and mineshafts, and gray *(M. grisescens)* and Indiana *(M. sodalis)* bats use these locations for breeding colonies. Gray *(Sciurus carolinensis)* and fox *(S. niger)* squirrels often establish nests in hollow trees, as do opossums *(Didelphis virginiana)* and raccoons *(Procyon lotor)*.

See also: BIRDS; FOREST FRAGMENTATION; TREES.

—Patricia Adair Gowaty and Jason D. Lang, *University of Georgia*

Ice Age

An ice age can be defined as a block of time (likely lasting for several millions of years) during which global temperatures are cool and glaciers have covered large tracts of land on a continental or hemispheric scale. There have been many of these periods in the history of Earth, but when *Ice Age* is capitalized it refers to the last major glaciation in North America, which peaked about twenty thousand years ago and ended around ten thousand years later. The Ice Age featured polar ice caps more extensive and thicker than today and vast glaciers (as much as several thousand feet thick) covering much of northern Eurasia and North America. Sea levels were hundreds of feet lower than today, exposing a land bridge between Siberia and Alaska that created a migration corridor for plants and many animals, including humans, who used it to gain access to North America.

During the Ice Age, glaciers never covered the entire Appalachian Mountain system, but the northern region was extensively covered by ice on many occasions. Continental ice advancing from Canada moved as far south as northern and even central Pennsylvania, and a periglacial regime extended as far south as West Virginia on the higher montane areas. Animal and plant communities reflected these localized colder regions. A mixed cool-temperate forest belt extended across the region about thirty thousand to twenty-seven thousand years ago, shortly before the last glacial maximum. Spruce (genus *Picea*, including some extinct species) and jack pine *(Pinus banksiana)* forests could be found as far south as present-day Washington, D.C., and oak-hickory forests and southern pine forests extended from Maryland to northern Florida.

Appalachia's forests of twenty-one thousand to seventeen thousand years ago were drier and more open than today's. Spruce was common in dense stands that reached to the coastal plain of the Gulf of Mexico. Mixed with the dominant spruce were walnut *(Juglans)*, maple *(Acer)*, oak *(Quercus)*, and beech *(Fagus)* trees in low densities. These spruce-dominated forests were parklike, interspersed with lakes, marshes, and bogs frequented by ospreys and flocks of geese. Appalachia was home to some species of mammals easily recognized today, such as star-nosed moles *(Condylura cristata)*, hairy-tailed moles *(Parascalops breweri)*, porcupines *(Erethizon dorsatum)*, bog lemmings *(Synaptomys)*, snowshoe hares *(Lepus americanus)*, elk *(Cervus elaphus)*, and bison *(Bison bison)*. They shared these cool forests with now-extinct species, including the American mastodon *(Mammuthus primigenius)*, mammoth *(Mammut americanum)*, ground sloth *(Nothrotheriops shastensis)*, giant beaver *(Castoroides ohioensis)*, dire wolf *(Canis dirus)*, short-faced bear *(Arctodus simus)*, and saber-toothed cat *(Smilodon fatalis)*.

See also: COVE FORESTS; ICE AGES (GEOLOGY).

—Alan V. Morgan, *University of Waterloo, Ontario, Canada*

Induced Defenses

Since they cannot move to avoid being consumed, most plants produce physical and biochemical defenses that resist damage by herbivores. In some plant species, most typically woody plants, antiherbivore defenses are produced at high levels constantly, potentially inhibiting growth, regardless of whether herbivores are present. These defenses are mostly tannins and resins concentrated near surface tissues in leaves, bark, and seeds that protect the plant by lowering palatability and interfering with herbivore digestive systems. In many plant species, however, levels of induced defenses rise only after the plant has been attacked by herbivores.

Induced defenses range from increases in hair and thorn density on the leaves to increases in levels of toxic proteins and compounds in leaves and other tissues. Induced biochemical defenses can be produced quickly in tissues near the site of attack or are transported there from distant tissues. Some plant species even release volatile compounds into the air after herbivore damage.

Tobacco *(Nicotiana tabacum)*, common throughout south and central Appalachia, exhibits several types of inducible defenses. Nicotine is a commercially important compound that increases in tobacco leaves after herbivore damage, substantially deterring subsequent attacks. Tobacco plants also release volatile chemicals called terpenoids into the air when induced by herbivorous caterpillar damage, attracting predatory wasps that capture and consume the caterpillars. Red oaks *(Quercus rubra)* and sugar maples *(Acer saccharum)*, both native trees common to the Appalachian region, are induced by herbivore attack to raise levels of toxic and distasteful compounds called tannins in their leaves.

See also: INSECTS; TREE DISEASES; TREES.

—Don Cipollini, *Wright State University*

Insects

While the casual observer may value some Appalachian insects, such as colorful butterflies and moths, dragonflies, and iridescent beetles, for their beauty and others, such as praying mantises, luminous fireflies, or male dobsonflies, for their peculiar structure or behavior, all insects are vital to the functions of Appalachian ecosystems. They are the primary foods of many animals, including other insects. Additionally, insects perform early steps in the decomposition of dead plants and animals, returning vital nutrients to the soil, and they contribute to pollination, seed dispersal, and parasite control for plants of all types.

Most species of insects found in Appalachia are not restricted to the region but are widespread in eastern North America. Those found at higher elevations of Appalachia usually range into the northern United States and southern Canada. The geographical ranges of many insects found in the region, however, are still unknown. A specimen of an Appalachian cranefly *(Trichoceridae)* was collected in eastern Kansas—eight hundred miles to the west of its presumed range. One insect that has not been found outside of Appalachia, though it has been carefully sought, is the cockroach *Cryptocercus punctulatus*, a wood-eating inhabitant of decaying fallen logs (not to be confused with common household species).

Insects are the primary source of food for many kinds of birds and are equally important in the diets of many amphibians, reptiles, fish, and even some small mammals such as bats, shrews, moles, and mice. Bats, the only true flying mammals, are represented in Appalachia only by insect-eating species.

When a vertebrate animal dies and is not readily found by scavengers such as vultures or crows, soft parts of its body are soon consumed by carrion-feeding insects such as blowfly maggots; larvae of dermestid beetles later feed on skin or hair. Dead insects are discovered by ants and dismembered or carried intact to their nest as food. When a tree dies, termites, various beetle larvae (some of which may have killed the tree), and some larval flies devour the wood. Additionally, burrowing by these and other insects permits penetration of fungi into the wood, speeding its decomposition. Other species feed on fallen leaves and plant debris. Fly maggots and dung beetles are important agents in the removal of droppings from livestock and wild animals.

Honeybees *(Apis mellifera)* are important pollinators of garden, orchard, and field crops. Other species of bees, many flies, moths, and other insects also are involved in pollination of most kinds of flowering plants.

An important role of many insects in any ecosystem is control of other insect species. A few species are recognized as beneficial in controlling insects harmful to crops or forest trees. Lady beetles, which feed on aphids that attack plants important to humans, are an example. There are many other insects beneficial to man, such as the wasps that prey on the caterpillars that feed on tobacco leaves.

The leaves, stems, roots, or fruits of nearly every kind of plant in the Appalachian region are food for one or more species of insect. Plants are damaged mainly by chewing larvae, such as the caterpillars of numerous kinds of moths and butterflies, but insects such as aphids and scale bugs, which have piercing-sucking mouthparts, also do damage. Sometimes this damage is severely destructive to the ecosystem. Several species of beetles whose gnawing penetrated chestnut bark introduced spores of the fungus that causes chestnut blight, a disease that obliterated American chestnut *(Castanea dentata)* trees throughout the Appalachian forest. American elm trees *(Ulmus americana)* have been killed over a wide area by the fungus causing Dutch elm disease, carried by the introduced European elm bark beetle *(Scolytus multistriatus)*. Another pest from Europe is the balsam woolly adelgid *(Adelges piceae)*, which is destroying Fraser fir *(Abies fraseri)* in the southern Appalachian highlands by piercing thin bark to feed on the sap. Southern pine beetles *(Dendroctonus frontalis)* kill large tracts of pine in Appalachia during years of heavy infestation, and the introduced gypsy moth *(Lymantria dispar)* takes a heavy toll on deciduous trees.

See also: FOLIAGE ARTHROPODS; INDUCED DEFENSES; SPIDERS.

—George W. Byers, *University of Kansas*

Donald J. Borror, Charles A. Triplehorn, and Norman F. Johnson, *An Introduction to the Study of Insects* (1989).

Karst

A substantial portion of Appalachia is underlain by limestone, a hard rock that is nonetheless easily dissolved by water. This has had a significant impact on the topography of the region, creating a landscape known as karst, from the geographical name of part of Slovenia with similar features. In the limestone countryside, where streams disappear underground only to reemerge many miles away as large springs, rainfall creates large closed depressions called sinkholes, which dot the landscape, and the solvent action of underground waters carves out thousands of caves of many sizes and shapes. Such features make the Appalachians one of the most notable karst landscapes in the world and exert a significant influence on the ecosystems of the region.

The caves and sinkholes of Appalachia are home to many unusual species of bacteria, fungi, insects, crayfishes, fishes, salamanders, and bats, composing whole subterranean ecosystems that operate in the absence of direct solar energy. Some underground streams contain blind, non-pigmented crayfish, salamanders, and fish. Caves are also important sites for breeding colonies of bats or winter hibernating places (hibernacula), where they may number thousands of individuals. Many of these fragile communities are located on public lands such as parks and protected from disturbance by humans, but many more are on privately owned lands and are vulnerable to destruction.

One major karst province extends from central Alabama through east Tennessee and the Shenandoah Valley of Virginia and into Pennsylvania. Throughout this swath are numerous sinkholes, sinking streams, and small caves. A second major area is the sandstone-capped Cumberland Plateau of Alabama, Tennessee, and Kentucky, which is underlain by limestone that is exposed in the deep valleys at the margins of the plateau. Long underground rivers and caves mark this area.

Although karst provides some spectacular scenery and the caves provide habitat to unusual organisms, the landscape poses hazards to those who live on it. There are difficulties in obtaining stable water supplies due to the discontinuous nature of karst aquifers. Moreover, karst aquifers are very vulnerable to contamination by polluted surface water. Concentrated recharge from surface runoff can quickly travel great distances in underground streams, bringing urban and agricultural contaminants such as lead, chromium, oil, grease, bacteria from pet and livestock wastes, and septic tank effluents with high fecal coliform counts to wells and springs used as water sources. The dumping of toxic chemicals into sinkholes and seepage from underground storage tanks endanger cave ecosystems by polluting cave streams or filling cave atmospheres with poisonous fumes. Another danger arises from the undetected formation of sinkholes, which can unexpectedly cause the ground to collapse beneath buildings. Flooding of sinkhole complexes after heavy rains can also damage buildings and paved areas placed on sinkhole floodplains.

Of the thirteen longest caves in the United States and of the top forty-five in the world, four are located in the Appalachians: Friars Hole Cave System (44.15 miles) and Organ Cave (39.5 miles) in West Virginia and Blue Spring Cave (33 miles) and Cumberland Caverns (27.62 miles) in Tennessee. Dozens of tourist caves provide easy access across Appalachia.

See also: CAVES; CAVING (SPORTS AND RECREATION).

—William B. White, *Pennsylvania State University*

Leaf Litter

See Leaves

Leaves

One of the Appalachian region's most famous characteristics is its spectacular display of fall colors resulting from a diversity of leaf forms. The leaves of the sugar maple *(Acer saccharum)* turn bright yellow or orange; the tulip poplar *(Liriodendron tulipifera)* and hickory *(Carya)* yellow; the ash *(Fraxinus)*, sweet gum *(Liquidambar styraciflua)*, and black gum *(Nyssa aquatica)* purplish; and the red maple *(A. rubrum)*, scarlet oak *(Quercus coccinea)*, staghorn sumac *(Rhus typhina)*, poison ivy *(R. radicans)*, and Virginia creeper *(Parthenocissus quinquefolia)* brilliant red. Although most species have a characteristic fall color or range of colors, there is variation according to local rainfall, temperature, and light intensity.

The general function of leaves in green plants is the production of food (sugars) and the by-product oxygen from carbon dioxide, sunlight, and water through the process of photosynthesis. Leaves also form the reproductive structures such as flowers and most cones. Water is lost from leaves by evaporation (the process of transpiration).

In Appalachia, leaves are typically shed in the autumn by deciduous plants such as oak, maple, dogwood *(Cornus)*, and poplar or maintained for several years on evergreens such as holly *(Ilex)*, conifers, and rhododendron *(Rhododendron)*. Leaves of non-woody (herbaceous) plants, such as most ferns, trillium *(Trillium)*, and morning glory *(Ipomoea)*, die at the end of their growing season. Some of these, however, have a unique seasonal growth pattern. Trout lily *(Erythronium americanum)*, a spectacular spring flower in deciduous forests of the region, emerges early with one or two leaves and a single flower. It forms fruit quickly, disperses seeds, and dies back to the underground bulb before being shaded by newly growing tree leaves. The single leaf of the common cranefly orchid *(Tipularia discolor)* appears in the fall, remains green during winter, and withers in late spring. In summer, a leafless flowering stalk develops.

Flowers and cones are evolutionarily modified leaves and are divided into sepals, petals, or bracts. These may be rather inconspicuous, as with birch *(Betula)*, hickory, and ash, or very showy to attract insect pollinators, as with tulip poplar, trillium, silverbell *(Halesia carolina)*, and phlox *(Phlox)*. Stamens and pistils of a flower are modified leaves that hold the male and female reproductive structures. Most cones, such as those produced by pines *(Pinus)*, firs *(Abies)*, eastern red cedars *(Juniperus virginiana)*, and club mosses *(Lycopodium)*, are tight clusters of modified leaves containing the reproductive structures. In flowering dogwood *(C. florida)*, the four showy white bracts are expanded bud scales (modified leaves) surrounding the small yellow flowers in the center.

Carnivory is another leaf function found among several plants of the Appalachians. Sundews *(Drosera)*, pitcher plants *(Sarracenia)*, and bladderworts *(Utricularia)* have highly evolved leaves that trap and digest insects. This adaptation allows the plants to exist in habitats with a low availability of nitrogen, an essential element they obtain from the protein in their insect prey.

The obvious and tremendous diversities of leaf shapes, sizes, textures, colors, hairiness, and chemical constituents reflect the adaptations of various plants to their environment or to provide protection from insect or other animal predation. The evergreen conifers—spruce *(Picea)*, hemlock *(Tsuga)*, pine, fir, and eastern red cedar—have small, needle-like or scalelike leaves adapted to dry or winter conditions.

Nutrients that come from decaying leaves are a vital and constant value for the growth and death of Appalachian forests. Leaf litter is an important short-term nutrient pool, because it quickly decomposes and recycles. The build-up of leaves on the forest floor creates a layer of nutrients and life-filled (organic) litter on top of the soil. This layer acts as food for many bacteria and other microscopic organisms as well as larger decomposers such as millipedes. But more importantly, it provides a way of recycling nutrients back into the forest through the soil. As the leaves break apart, the nutrients are released and absorbed back into the ground, where they help feed the vegetation in the surrounding area. Without decaying leaves, it would be impossible for reforestation to take place.

Decomposition is one of the ways in which certain nutrients become available to plants for their survival and reproduction. Two important nutrients derived from the decomposition process are nitrogen and phosphorus. Nitrogen is a major component of proteins and nucleic acids, the building blocks of plant cells, and chlorophyll, essential for photosynthesis. Phosphorus is an important part of the biochemical reactions of all living things. These nutrients become available when organic matter in the leaf litter is decomposed.

The decomposers of leaves and other organic matter include bacteria, fungi, mites, nematodes, earthworms, millipedes, and herbivorous animals. Bacteria and fungi are the primary decomposers, but larger organisms also play an important role. The types of decomposers present depend on the type of forest. For instance, coniferous forests drop needles, which take longer to break down than deciduous leaves. Their acidic environments foster more activity from fungi than bacteria.

Not all leaves that fall in the forest end up on the forest floor. Many fall into streams, where they become just as vital to the aquatic ecosystem. In fact, the primary energy source for Appalachian Mountain headwater stream ecosystems is leaves. Bacteria begin leaf decomposition, making energy available to insect larvae, which in turn are eaten by small fish, which are eaten by larger organisms, and so on. Without leaves, a major food and energy source would no longer be available to support the diverse community of organisms that inhabit healthy stream ecosystems.

See also: CARNIVOROUS PLANTS; CONES; TREES.

—Michael A. Arcuri, *West Virginia Division of Environmental Protection*, and James W. Hardin, *North Carolina State University*

Kjell B. Sandved and Ghillean T. Prance, *Leaves: The Formation, Characteristics and Uses of Hundreds of Leaves Found in All Parts of the World* (1985).

Lichens

The Appalachians have an exceptionally rich diversity of lichens. An estimated seven hundred to one thousand species of lichen fungi, approximately one-fourth of all North American species, represent a mixing of northern and southern phytogeographic elements (species representing many geographical regions and habitats).

Often confused with mosses, lichens are common in Appalachia on tree trunks and branches (epiphytic), on rocks (saxicolous), and on soil (terricolous). More rarely, they are found on rhododendron leaves (epiphyllic) and even submerged in streams (aquatic).

Lichens are the symbiotic associations of fungi and algae. The fungal partner, an ascomycete or basidiomycete, derives its carbohydrate nutrition from the photosynthetic algal partner, either green algae or blue-green cyanobacteria. An estimated fifteen thousand species of fungi, almost 20 percent of all fungi, form lichen associations with about one hundred species of photosynthetic algae. Research suggests that the lichen habit has evolved independently and repeatedly in the fungi and algae. Lichens may reproduce sexually through the production of fungal spores or asexually through the production of vegetative structures containing both the fungi and algae.

The composite lichen structure, the thallus, is markedly different in appearance from fungal hyphae or algal colonies growing alone. Three growth forms of the thallus are recognized: crustose (the map lichen *Rhizocarpon geographicum*, which resembles paint), foliose (the leaflike shield lichen *Parmelia*), and fruticose (the shrublike British soldier *Cladonia cristatella* and reindeer lichen *Cladina rangiferina* or the grandfather's beard *Usnea*).

The slow growth and longevity of lichens allow them to be used to date natural and man-made rock surfaces such as rockslides and gravestones. Many lichen fungi produce antibiotic or antiherbivory (protection from plant eaters) compounds that traditionally were used as natural dyes and in litmus. Because many lichens are sensitive to air pollution, they are used as biomonitors of air quality and forest health in Appalachia. Ecologically, lichens are important as soil builders, eroding rock surfaces and trapping bits of organic matter in their bodies. In disturbed areas they are often pioneers that pave the way for many other organisms.

See also: FUNGI; MOSSES; SUCCESSION.

—Paula T. DePriest, *Smithsonian Institution*

Mammals

Mammals are found in every kind of Appalachian habitat: bats in the air; moles in the soil; beavers *(Castor canadensis)*, water shrews *(Sorex palustris)*, and river otters *(Lutra canadensis)* in streams; and squirrels in trees. Forest inhabitants such as opossum *(Didelphis virginia)*, black bear *(Ursus americanus)*, and white-tailed deer *(Odocoileus virginianus)* often extend their ranges into towns. Although the Appalachians, especially the southern portions, are notable for high diversities of plants, cave invertebrates, mussels, fishes, and salamanders, the area does not have a comparable richness of mammalian diversity. Contemporary Appalachia includes seven orders of mammals, seventeen families, and seventy-five species, of which twenty-six species are rodents and fourteen are bats.

The region's modern mammal fauna reflects mixed sources. Predominantly boreal in its make-up (star-nosed mole *[Condylura cristata]*, southern red-backed vole *[Clethrionomys gapperi]*, and snowshoe hare *[Lepus americanus]*), the region's mammals also include species from the western arid fauna (eastern harvest mouse *[Reithrodontomys humulis]* and eastern cottontail *[Sylvilagus floridanus]*) and southern tropical fauna (opossum and raccoon *[Procyon lotor]*). A few boreal species, such as water shrews and northern flying squirrels *(Glaucomys sabrinus)*, can also be found in isolated southern locations. There are more mammal species in southern Appalachia than in the north, primarily because of an increase in bat species as one moves southerly.

The opossum, the only marsupial native to North America, is fairly common throughout Appalachia. The animal has a strong resistance to venom of the copperhead *(Agkistrodon contortrix)*, which it eats. Some males mate with several females. After a short gestation of twelve to thirteen days, opossum joeys are born as mobile embryos with well-developed forelegs and clawed fingers. Young develop rapidly for sixty to seventy days in the pouch attached to a teat, mature quickly sexually (eight months), and are weaned in three months. Well-fed females produce litters with more males than females, in contrast to unbiased sex ratios produced by females of average condition. This is an example of adaptive sex-ratio manipulation.

Opossum *(Didelphis virginia)*, Limestone, Tennessee, 1989. The only marsupial native to North American, this nocturnal and solitary mid-sized mammal is common throughout Appalachia. Opossums have a strong resistance to copperhead *(Agkistrodon contortrix)* venom and include those snakes in their omnivorous diet, along with berries, insects, and small rodents.

In winter, the semifossorial short-tailed shrew *(Blarina brevicauda)* lives partly underground, existing mostly on insects. These shrews do not hibernate or become torpid during winter and usually eat their body weight in food each day to meet their high metabolic needs. They produce venom in salivary glands, with which they immobilize animal prey, storing it in comatose condition as a hedge against scarcity. Mammals that produce venom and store live prey in this manner are rare. Other Appalachian shrews include the masked shrew *(Sorex cinereus)*, which is one of the United States' most common mammals, southeastern shrew *(S. longirostris)*, smoky shrew *(S. fumeus)*, long-tailed shrew *(S. dispar)*, water shrew, pygmy shrew *(Microsorex hoyi)*, and least shrew *(Cryptotis parva)*. As little as three to five grams, shrews are some of the smallest mammals, comparable to hummingbirds in weight.

Another Appalachian insectivore, the star-nosed mole, is a small, semi-aquatic, burrowing mammal that dines on earthworms and insect larvae in muddy water, despite having poor eyesight. Its star-shaped snout tip is rich with nerves and blood vessels, and experiments have demonstrated that it functions as a tactile and electrosensory organ, detecting the electrical field emitted by prey animals. Two other moles live in Appalachia: the hairy-tailed mole *(Parascalops breweri)* and the eastern mole *(Scalopus aquaticus)*.

Like other bats around the world, the little brown bat *(Myotis lucifugus)* emits twenty to two hundred high-intensity ultrasonic pulses per second and hears the echoes to determine the direction, distance, size, and kind of flying insect prey. Some bats also listen for the echolocation calls of other members of the same species to locate promising feeding sites, a behavior called eavesdropping. Some insects (lacewings, katydids, moths) can detect bats' ultrasonic pulses and thereby avoid them. Some moths produce low-intensity ultrasonic clicks that serve to startle inexperienced bats (and thereby cause the bats to miss), warn bats of the moth's unpalatability due to noxious chemicals, or possibly even jam the bats' echolocation system. Appalachia is rich in bats: Keen's myotis *(Myotis keenii)*, Indiana bat *(M. sodalis)*, small-footed myotis *(M. leibii)*, northern long-eared bat *(M. septentrionalis)*, gray bat *(M. grisescens)*, silver-haired bat *(Lasionycteris noctivagans)*, eastern pipistrelle *(Pipistrellus subflavus)*, big brown bat *(Eptesicus fuscus)*, red bat *(Lasiurus borealis)*, hoary bat *(L. cinereus)*, Virginia big-eared bat *(Plecotus townsendii virginianus)*, Rafinesque's big-eared bat *(P. rafinesquii)*, and evening bat *(Nycticeius humeralis)*.

Snowshoe hares typically range to the north, but they extend through the higher elevations of the Appalachians as far south as West Virginia. Coniferous and regenerated northern hardwood stands are this hare's optimal habitats. Its furry hind feet and spreading toes allow it to move across deep soft snow, an advantage in escaping predators, as well as reaching foods growing above the snow. Winter foods include willows, poplars, birch, and alder. Snowshoe hares feed on these plants selectively, avoiding juvenile shoots of birch and aspen because of their defensive noxious compounds. The eastern cottontail, New England cottontail *(Sylvilagus transitionalis)*, and Appalachian cottontail *(S. obscurus)* also live in the region.

Gray squirrels *(Sciurus carolinensis)* eat oak and hickory nuts, maple samaras, mulberry fruits, fungi, other plants, and some animals such as nestling birds. Individual squirrels discriminate among food species, trees within a species, and even individual seeds within a tree based on the levels of fat and tannin (a poison that deters some herbivores), abundance, and ingestion times. Gray squirrels do not discriminate between acorns infested by beetles and uninfested ones.

The huge variety of other rodents inhabiting Appalachia includes the fox squirrel *(S. niger)*, groundhog *(Mamota monax)*, eastern chipmunk *(Tamias striatus)*, red squirrel *(Tamiasciurus hudsonicus)*, northern flying squirrel, southern flying squirrel *(G. volans)*, beaver, deer mouse *(Peromyscus maniculatus)*, oldfield mouse *(P. polionotus)*, white-footed mouse *(P. leucopus)*, golden mouse *(Ochrotomys nuttallii)*, hispid cotton rat *(Sigmodon hispidus)*, eastern wood rat *(Neotoma floridana)*, Allegheny wood rat *(N. magister)*, southern red-backed vole, rock vole *(Microtus chrotorrhinus)*, meadow vole *(M. pennsylvanicus)*, pine vole *(M. pinetorum)*, prairie vole *(M. ochrogaster)*, muskrat *(Ondatra zibethicus)*, southern bog lemming *(Synaptomys cooperi)*, eastern harvest mouse, Norway rat *(Rattus norvegicus)*, black rat *(R. rattus)*, house mouse *(Mus musculus)*, meadow jumping mouse *(Zapus hudsonius)*, woodland jumping mouse *(Napaeozapus insignis)*, and porcupine *(Erethizon dorsatum)*.

Once numerous throughout the mountains of Appalachia, by 1900 the black bear could be found only in remote areas of the region. Deforestation of bear habitat through logging and agricultural activities, along with extermination efforts in certain areas (a bounty for black bears was state law in Virginia as late as 1977), contributed to the animal's near extinction from most of the region by the early twentieth century. The establishment of state and federal parks such as the Great Smoky Mountains National Park helped preserve habitat for bears. Conservation efforts have further helped revive the bear population. The estimated black bear population in 2002 for Pennsylvania was as high as 18,995 bears, and West Virginia's was between 12,000 and 15,000. Counties in and around the Great Smoky Mountains National Park alone had an estimated 2002 population of nearly 2,000 bears.

Black bears are the largest land mammals in Appalachia, weighing between 125 and 400 pounds (though individual males sometimes reach 600 pounds or more). They have dark fur, usually black (sometimes cinnamon or brown, and occasionally white), with a lighter-colored muzzle and V-shaped blaze on their chests. Black bears are omnivorous and opportunistic; their diet includes berries, insects, small mammals, salamanders, and human garbage. Rarely, a black bear will kill a larger animal such as a wild hog or small deer as well.

Because of its expansive habitat needs, the black bear is threatened by habitat fragmentation. Roads, for example, have generally been considered to be obstacles to bears, presumably because bears associate roads with vehicles, dogs, and gunfire. In the Monongahela National Forest of West Virginia, male bears are more hesitant than females to venture within roadside corridors, though both sexes avoid intensively traveled areas. Male bears shy from and females are attracted to corridors within a half-mile of a road, and this sexual difference intensifies within one-quarter mile of roads. Therefore, the density and kinds of roads through an area are important considerations in sustaining bear populations.

Other Appalachian carnivores include the red fox *(Vulpes vulpes)*, gray fox *(Urocyon cinereoargenteus)*, coyote *(Canis latrans)*, red wolf *(C. rufus)*, domestic dog *(C. familiaris)*, raccoon, long-tailed weasel *(Mustela frenata)*, least weasel *(M. nivalis)*, mink *(M. vison)*, and short-tailed weasel, or ermine *(M. erminea)*, spotted skunk *(Spilogale putorius)*, striped skunk *(Mephitis mephitis)*, fisher *(Martes pennanti)* and marten *(M. americana)*, river otter, lynx *(Felis lynx)*, bobcat *(F. rufus)*, mountain lion *(F. concolor)*, and domestic cat *(F. catus)*.

Loud explosive snorts and flashing white tails are familiar signs of escaping white-tailed deer. For many years, biologists were uncertain about the function of tail flagging. Hypotheses included pursuit invitation (eliciting pursuit while the deer is still far enough away to escape easily), pursuit discouragement (signaling to the predator that it has been detected and the deer is ready to flee), and social cohesion (keeping individuals in a group, which benefits the signaling individual by increasing the number of deer fleeing with it). Several recent studies have shown that the third hypothesis best explains the deer's tail flagging. Snorting, on the other hand, functions as a signal to the predator that it has been detected, discouraging pursuit. Appalachia is also home to elk *(Cervus elaphus)* and wild pig *(Sus scrofa)*.

Although overpopulation and habitat disruption are often associated with exotic invasive species (Norway rat, feral cat, wild pig), some native mammal populations (eastern mole, groundhog, white-tailed deer) have exploded recently and are having a serious impact on crops and other valued resources. If recent population growth continues, the black bear could also become a problem species in certain areas of Appalachia.

Loss of habitat, caused most often by land conversion, agriculture, livestock grazing, outdoor recreation, and logging, is the most significant threat to mammals in the region. Forest fragmentation, which incorporates the effects of habitat loss and alien species, also threatens mammals. There is a well-known relationship: the larger the habitat area, the greater a species' population size and therefore its persistence. Conserving large contiguous blocks of forest is important for the longterm sustainability of many mammal species. Other threats to native Appalachian mammals include overexploitation, competition with alien species, pollution, and disease.

See also: DISJUNCTION; FOREST FRAGMENTATION; WINTER ADAPTATIONS.

—George Constantz, *Canaan Valley Institute*

C. O. Handley Jr., "Appalachian Mammalian Geography—Recent Epoch," in *The Distributional History of the Biota of the Southern Appalachians, Part 3: Vertebrates*, ed. P. C. Holt (1971); M. R. Pelton, "Mammals of the Spruce-Fir Forest in Great Smoky Mountains National Park," in *The Southern Appalachian Spruce-Fir Ecosystem: Its Biology and Threats*, ed. P. S. White (1984); Bruce A. Stein, Lynn S. Kutner, and Jonathan S. Adams, eds., *Precious Heritage: The Status of Biodiversity in the United States* (2000).

Mast

The fruits of woody plant species that are not disseminated by wind are collectively called mast. Prior to enactment in the mid-1890s of fence laws requiring that hogs and other livestock be confined, Appalachians most often released their animals to forage for mast and other food on the forest floor.

Mast is commonly described as either hard or soft. Hard mast is fruit with a hard exterior; soft mast is fruit with a fleshy exterior. Examples of hard mast are acorns, hickory nuts, walnuts, and beechnuts; hard mast generally ripens in late summer through early winter. Examples of soft mast are grapes, apples, blueberries, and blackberries, most of which ripen from late summer through early fall. In a forested environment, shrubs and small trees closer to the forest floor may produce mast more frequently, but large, dominant trees such as oaks and hickories produce greater quantities.

The most important group of mast-producing tree species in the Appalachians is the oaks. Oaks (genus *Quercus*) increased in importance early in the twentieth century as the previously dominant American chestnut *(Castanea dentata)* and American beech *(Fagus grandifolia)* were decimated by disease and parasites. Mostly produced on foliage exposed to full sunlight, acorn yields increase with tree size. In good seed years, annual acorn crops may exceed seven hundred pounds per acre. Acorns from oaks and other species are the most valuable and energy-rich plant food available in the dormant seasons of fall and winter. When oak forests reach seed-bearing age, mast may become the major food source for wildlife, exceeding that obtained by foraging on leaves, stems, and soft mast.

Mast production varies widely among species, location, and year, but weather is believed to be the most important factor affecting the quantity of mast. Various climatic factors, including frosts, freezes, rainfall, relative humidity, temperature, and wind, affect the dissemination of pollen and so influence flowering and mast yields. Some plants put energy into producing mast in one year and into growth and foliage the next, making wildlife food quantities vary annually.

Mast accessibility impacts wildlife populations directly and indirectly in the Appalachians. Mast comprises more than 75 percent of the fall, winter, and spring diet of gray *(Sciurus carolinensis)* and fox *(S. niger)* squirrels, so when mast is scarce, squirrel populations decline drastically. Tenfold declines in squirrel populations have been observed the year after a mast failure when there is little or no mast. White-tailed deer *(Odocoileus virginianus)* weights and antler development also reflect the availability of acorn mast. Mast failures may reduce harvest rates, delay sexual maturity, and reduce the birthrate of black bears *(Ursus americanus)*.

Mast is important for the regeneration of trees. While most animals that eat mast are simply consumers, a few, such as blue jays *(Cyanocitta cristata)* and squirrels, disperse mast over long distances to sites where the seeds' chances for germination and survival are enhanced.

Wildlife managers survey mast conditions to predict wildlife abundance and harvests. The establishment and maintenance of mast-bearing plants is a key to successful forest and wildlife management in Appalachia, and managers attempt to locate and protect individual trees or shrubs that are good mast producers.

See also: ACORNS; FRUITS; SEED DISPERSAL.

—James C. Pack, *West Virginia Division of Natural Resources*

Charles E. McGee, ed., *Proceedings of the Workshop: Southern Appalachian Mast Management* (1989).

Migrations

The Appalachian Mountains form one of the most important migratory corridors in North America—a natural skyway for travelers as small and delicate as monarch butterflies *(Danaus plexippus)* and as imposing as golden eagles *(Aquila chrysaetos)* with wings that span nearly eight feet. Migrations ebb and flow throughout the year, reaching a peak in spring and autumn, but never really ceasing, even in midsummer or the depths of winter. Migration routes that stretch across half the globe converge on the region—warblers and vireos that spend the winter in Amazonia or northern Central America and bobolinks *(Dolichonyx oryzivorus)* returning from Argentina cross paths in Appalachia with waterfowl bound for the Arctic or peregrine falcons *(Falco peregrinus)* that nest in Greenland.

Much of the migration takes place under the cover of darkness as most migratory birds, especially songbirds, travel at night, when the air is calmer, cooler, and denser. Although weather plays a major role in the day-to-day dynamics of migration, the timing of the phenomenon is remarkably consistent from year to year, triggered largely by photoperiod, the ever-changing seasonal ratio of daylight and darkness.

The central Appalachians are particularly important as a travel corridor for the autumn migration of raptors, which depend upon a subtle interaction of climate and topography to speed their journey. Prevailing northwesterly winds, which strike the ridges and are deflected upward, and rising air in thermals over cleared lands provide predictable lift to the migrants, which pass south through the mountains by the tens of thousands. Hawk watching has become a popular pastime in the region, with such overlooks as Hawk Mountain Sanctuary and Waggoner's Gap on the Kittatinny Ridge, both in Pennsylvania, and Rockfish Gap on the Blue Ridge in Virginia attracting thousands of visitors each year.

While birds are the most visible and diverse of Appalachian migrants, they are not the only ones. Though their numbers have been greatly reduced by dams, marine-dwelling American shad *(Alosa sapidissima)* still move long distances up some Appalachian rivers to breed, usually arriving when serviceberry *(Amelanchier)*, known in parts of Appalachia as shadbush, blooms in spring. American eels *(Anguilla rostrata)*, which grow to maturity in fresh water throughout the region, make the trip in reverse, descending to the ocean to spawn. At least two species of insects make long-distance journeys down the mountains each fall. Monarch butterflies form a colorful procession through the hills in August and September, the opening leg of a trip that will eventually take them to their traditional wintering grounds in the highlands of central Mexico. Green darner dragonflies *(Anax junius)* also sometimes move south through the Appalachians in vast swarms, though their movements are less well understood and do not appear to entail a return migration the following spring. Other notable Appalachian migrants include several species of bats, particularly tree-roosting bats such as red *(Lasiurus borealis)*, hoary *(Lasionycteris noctivagens)*, and silver-haired *(L. cinereus)* bats, which breed north into Canada and winter across the southern United States.

See also: BIRDS; FISHES; INSECTS.

—Scott Weidensaul, *Schuylkill Haven, Pennsylvania*

Maurice Brooks, *The Appalachians* (1965); Paul Kerlinger, *How Birds Migrate* (1995).

Mollusks

The most familiar members of the phylum Mollusca are gastropods (snails and slugs), bivalves (oysters, clams, and mussels), and cephalopods (squids and octopuses). Slugs, snails, mussels, and clams are found throughout Appalachia, and their species diversity is considered globally significant. Southeastern United States populations of aquatic snails, freshwater mussels (pearly mussels), and clams are the most diverse in the world, with particular richness in the Appalachian regions of Tennessee and Alabama. Appalachian terrestrial snail populations are the second most diverse in the United States.

The southeastern states, particularly the southern Appalachian regions, offer the largest assemblage of freshwater mollusk species in the world. The Tennessee-Cumberland River basin, which drains parts of Tennessee, Virginia, Kentucky, North Carolina, Alabama, Georgia, and Mississippi, is home to 100 species of freshwater mussels—one-third of the species found in the U.S. and one-sixth worldwide. Similarly, the rivers and streams of the Mobile River basin (draining Alabama, Georgia, eastern Mississippi, and southeast Tennessee) contain more than 120 species of freshwater snails. The state of Alabama alone boasts 43 percent of the aquatic snail and 60 percent of the freshwater mussel species in the nation, and many are endemic to the region (that is, they are found no where else in the world).

Freshwater mollusks are important indicators of aquatic ecosystem health. Of the more than 250 species of freshwater mussels in the Southeast, three-fourths are federally listed as threatened or endangered, with the majority of those species represented in, or endemic to, southern Appalachia. Eleven freshwater snail species in the Southeast are also listed. Major threats include loss of habitat and habitat deterioration from pollution. In southern Appalachia, the effect of dams may be the most significant. Beginning in the 1930s, the Tennessee Valley Authority began building dams for hydroelectric power and flood control, resulting in more than thirty dams on the Tennessee River and tributaries alone. For numerous species adapted to free-flowing waters, dams contributed to their decline by slowing or stopping the flow. An emerging threat to the southeastern freshwater mussel population is displacement by the non-native zebra mussel *(Dreissena polymorpha)*. The U.S. Fish and Wildlife Service has launched projects to protect freshwater mollusks, including programs for removing zebra mussels and for evaluating potential effluent limits for oxygen.

Freshwater mollusks are an important natural resource for a number of reasons. In the first half of the twentieth century, mussels were harvested for use in the manufacture of pearl buttons. In more recent times, the Japanese and domestic cultured pearl industries have produced seed pearls using pieces of mussel shell harvested primarily from southeastern rivers. In addition, freshwater mussel tissues are resistant to cancer and are consequently a subject of biomedical research. Freshwater shellfish remain an important source of food for numerous animal species.

Terrestrial snails and slugs, common throughout Appalachia, are a critical part of the food chain. The terrestrial mollusk fauna of Appalachia is second only to Hawaii's in species richness and endemism, with the greatest regional diversity in the few remaining old-growth forests of Appalachia. More than half of the 660 species of mainland terrestrial snails can be found in Appalachia; nationwide, 8 species are listed as endangered or threatened, half of which reside in the Southeast. Habitat loss and degradation are regarded as the primary factors threatening Appalachian terrestrial snails.

See also: FISHES; STREAMS; TENNESSEE VALLEY AUTHORITY (GOVERNMENT).

—Angela K Palau, *Oak Ridge, Tennessee*

M. Lynne Corn, "Freshwater Mussels," in *Congressional Research Service Report for Congress 94-560 ENR* (1994); Taylor H. Ricketts et al., *Terrestrial Ecoregions of North America: A Conservation Assessment* (1999); Bruce A. Stein, Lynn S. Kutner, Jonathan S. Adams, eds., *Precious Heritage: The Status of Biodiversity in the United States* (2000).

Mosses

Mosses grow abundantly on all types of materials: exposed and compact soil, old burns, decaying organic matter, rotting logs, rocks, and the bark of trees. They grow best in moist conditions. More than four hundred species of mosses are found in the Appalachians. Some can be identified by the naked eye or with a hand lens, but examination of most requires the use of a microscope.

Mosses are ancient terrestrial plants in a class in the division Bryophyta. The division is distinguished from more advanced plants (gymnosperms and angiosperms) in that bryophytes lack specialized transporting and supporting tissues. Thus, there are no tall, stately mosses, and they lack true roots, stems, and leaves. This division also includes liverworts and hornworts, although mosses are much more common, larger, and more conspicuous.

Due to a vast water-holding capacity, some Appalachian mosses, such as sphagnum, are widely used commercially as packing material around tree and shrub roots during shipping and transplanting operations.

In Appalachia mosses are often the first plants to invade denuded areas, thus stabilizing soil and restricting erosion. Carpet, cushion, bird wheat, and fern mosses facilitate invasion of other plants, paving the way for an eventual ground cover of woody plants. Some of the region's woody plants, such as rhododendrons, only survive when their seeds germinate on moss cover, where moisture conditions are ideal.

Mosses' absorption of water reduces surface runoff in hilly areas and thus helps to limit sheet erosion. Studies of Appalachian hardwoods show that the dense moss layer near the tree base absorbs most of the water after light rains; very little reaches the forest floor. Mosses do not resist dehydration in the way other land plants do. When their habitat becomes dry, mosses also dry out, and all their biochemical activities cease. The dry, brownish moss is not dead, however, and with the next rainfall or heavy dew will "come back to life."

Moss plants, sensitive to water and atmospheric pollution, can be used as early indicators of unnatural compounds in the environment. Such Appalachian species as carpet moss and water moss are particularly sensitive to pollution. Thus, when mosses become scarce or disappear, it is an indication that pollutants are having an impact.

See also: FOREST COMMUNITIES; LICHENS; SUCCESSION.

—Kenneth L. Carvell, *West Virginia University*

Mound and Pit Relief

Forested ecosystems in the Appalachians experience different types of disturbances, including fires, windstorms, ice storms, air pollution, acid rain, and pathogen-induced tree death. Fire and logging generally leave tree root systems intact and promote sprouting as a means of tree regeneration. In contrast, winds during severe storms, tornadoes, or hurricanes often uproot larger trees and produce varied sizes of canopy gaps within a forest. Fallen trees in these openings create mounds and pits where the root ball of each tree forms an elevated mound of soil adjacent to the pit where the roots had been growing. Mounds and pits often cover 20 to 50 percent of the forest floor in Appalachian landscapes and can persist for several centuries. The slight variation in elevation between adjacent mounds and pits offers an opportunity for colonization by different woodland herbs and tree seedlings. Soil conditions on mounds are drier, more acidic, poorer in nutrients, and lower in organic matter and litter accumulation than adjacent pits. Pits offer a more favorable location for the growth of seedlings that are able to tolerate water-saturated soils in the spring. These differences in soils facilitate the establishment of a variety of plant species associated with pits, mounds, or undisturbed areas of forest floor. This process contributes to the forest's overall plant diversity and to the mosaic of plant associations occurring across the forest landscape.

See also: BIODIVERSITY; OLD-GROWTH FOREST; SUCCESSION.

—Donald J. Shure, *Emory University*

Mycorrhiza

Mycorrhiza (which literally means "fungus root") is the symbiotic relationship of photosynthetic plants and various fungi that are unable to manufacture their own food. This relationship is mutually beneficial. The linkage is made underground on and in the roots of green plants with the mycelium or vegetative part of many fungi. Plants and fungi have been linking in this way for approximately 400 million years. With the Appalachian region hosting rich fungal flora and botanical diversity, mycorrhizal relationships abound.

Over 90 percent of terrestrial plants benefit from one or more fungus partners, including those in Appalachia. Many fungi will reproduce only in the presence of their plant partner. Conversely, the absence of the fungus results in slower growth of green plants, as fungi increase water absorption by the plant, making nutrient uptake more efficient. Seed germination may also be adversely affected. The implications of the importance of this symbiotic relationship in forestry and horticulture are well understood.

There are two general types of mycorrhiza. In endotrophic mycorrhiza, the fungus links inside the roots. This is an attachment only visible microscopically and is common to many trees, shrubs, and herbaceous plants. Some Appalachian trees with typical endotrophic mycorrhizal attachments are maples *(Acer)*, elms *(Ulmus)*, sycamores *(Platanus accidentalis)*, locusts *(Robinia)*, and cherries *(Prunus)*. The fungi involved usually do not produce fruiting bodies visible to the naked eye. When the fungus wraps itself around the outside of the plant roots, an arrangement that is visible without magnification, it is called ectotrophic mycorrhiza. Most Appalachian conifers benefit from this type of symbiosis, as do oaks *(Quercus)*, birches *(Betula)*, poplars *(Populus)*, and willows *(Salix)*. The fungus associates often produce visible mushrooms such as those in genera *Amanita* (such as destroying angel), *Lactarius* (milk caps), *Boletus*, and *Cortinarius*.

This relationship between plants and fungi has numerous benefits for both organisms. Green plants provide food to the fungus, primarily carbohydrates. Plants can only absorb small amounts of minerals, but fungi are recycling organisms and can absorb minerals and nutrients through their cell walls; these are shared with the host plant along with water. The root surface area of the plant is increased, often with an increase in water potential. The fungus helps to enhance the immune system of the plant. Some mycorrhizal fungi produce chemicals that inhibit nematodes, bacteria, and other organisms harmful to the green plant.

Mycologists continue to discover more about the complex interactions of fungi and plants. Recent studies show that the same mycelium may link with multiple trees, sometimes of different species, and may act as a conduit, moving materials from a tree with a surplus to one with a shortage.

While these interactions of plants and fungi are extremely important, mycorrhiza is not a relationship familiar to most Appalachians. On a basic level, the mushroom hunter in West Virginia knows to look for Bradleys *(L. volemus)* in oak woods while not fully understanding their relationship with oak trees. Of more general importance is the forester's knowledge that the dye-maker's false puffball *(Pisolithus tinctorius)* and other fungi can play an essential role in the reforestation of disturbed areas such as strip-mined lands. Tree seedlings, native shrubs, and grass species are sometimes inoculated with specific mycorrhizal fungi in nurseries before being introduced to denuded areas, where the fungi reduce overall plant stress through increased water and nutrient absorption, as well as decreased toxic materials absorption. Awareness of mycorrhiza's importance is increasing, as is knowledge of ways to utilize its applications in the Appalachian environment.

See also: FUNGI; SYMBIOSIS; TREES.

—Walter Sturgeon, *East Palestine, Ohio*

Nutrient Cycling

The greatest biodiversity in North America occurs in Appalachia in part because of the extensive and rapid cycling of nutrients through the region's ecosystems. Nutrient cycling is the movement of nutrient minerals between living organisms and their environment. Through the decomposition process, nutrients are either made available for reuse by organisms or enter the soil, water, or atmosphere. Some nutrients, such as nitrogen and sulfur, typically enter the atmosphere during part of their cycle, while others, such as phosphorus, remain within organisms, soil, or water. The warm temperatures and abundant precipitation of the southern Appalachians increase the rate of nutrient cycling.

In most ecosystems, nitrogen is the nutrient in shortest supply and a limiting factor in plant growth. The nitrogen cycle is highly dependent on soil microorganisms, both to capture nitrogen gas from the atmosphere and to release it back to the atmosphere during decomposition. Some bacteria associated with plant roots fix nitrogen in a form that makes it available to the plant. Acid deposition is the delivery of nitrates and ammonia (forms of nitrogen) and forms of sulfur in rain, snow, fog, or dry particles to the earth's surface. Acid deposition is increasing the acidity of Appalachian soils and streams, particularly at high elevations, which receive more precipitation than lower elevations, thereby depressing populations of some aquatic life, such as native brook trout *(Salvelinus fontinalis)* and salamanders. The spruce-fir forests in high elevations of the southern Appalachians are the region's most threatened ecosystem. Acid deposition on soil in spruce-fir forests may be leaching important nutrients such as calcium out of the soil and releasing aluminum into the soil solutions, further inhibiting uptake of vital nutrients by these trees. This nutrient inhibition, coupled with the stress caused by the balsam woolly adelgid *(Adelges piceae)*, is destroying the endemic Fraser fir *(Abies fraseri)* forests.

Phosphorus is another nutrient vital to plants. Its sedimentary cycle (so termed because the major source of phosphorus is found in sediments or rocks) occurs as rocks erode and phosphorus enters the soil and is taken up by plants. Animals, including many invertebrates in the soil, feed on the plants and their dead tissues, and the phosphorus is thus recycled back to the soil. As nitrogen becomes more available to plants due to acid deposition, phosphorus is replacing it as the limiting nutrient in forest soils of the southern Appalachians.

See also: ENERGY FLOW; FUNGI; SAPROBES.

—Barbara C. Reynolds, *University of North Carolina at Asheville*

Old-Growth Forest

Because industrial timber cutting removed nearly all of Appalachia's large old trees during the last century, the few remaining old-growth forests are found mostly in the region's national forests and parks. A study conducted by Rob Messick and the Western North Carolina Alliance from 1995 to 2000 estimated that 77,418 acres of old-growth forests existed in the Pisgah and Nantahala National Forests of North Carolina. *Old-growth* is not a scientific term but is applied generally to forests that have large trees and that do not exhibit recent timber removal. Most often, the term *virgin* is preferred for Appalachian forests where there is no evidence of historical alteration.

Appalachian old-growth stands are found mostly in more rugged regions where there was little opportunity for pioneers to establish homesteads. Very few areas of this type exist in the gentle sloping valleys because these were prime sites for settlement. A few valley old-growth stands do remain in the Great Smoky Mountains National Park. Most of these stands occur on the Tennessee side of the park at places such as Greenbrier Cove. Also, one significant valley of virgin forest remains in the Nantahala National Forest, North Carolina, as a memorial to the poet Joyce Kilmer. This area is now maintained as a part of the Joyce Kilmer–Slickrock and Citico Creek Wilderness Areas. While timber cutting has not taken place there, historical influences include the loss of the American chestnut *(Castanea dentata)* due to introduction of the chestnut blight *(Endothia parasitica)* that devastated these trees during the 1930s and somewhat lesser effects of human-caused fires.

Often unrecognized as old-growth forests because of their small stature are those that cap the highest peaks with weather-stunted trees. Rabun Bald in Georgia and Scaly and Little Scaly Mountains in North Carolina exhibit stunted scarlet *(Quercus coccinea)* and white *(Q. alba)* oaks. Some of these, such as white oaks of Little Scaly Mountain, are estimated to be up to four hundred years old, representing some of the oldest old-growth forests extant in the Appalachians. By comparison, tulip poplar *(Liriodendron tulipifera)* trees in the valleys are estimated to range from two hundred to three hundred years old.

See also: CHESTNUT BLIGHT (ENVIRONMENT); FOREST FRAGMENTATION; TREES.

—J. Dan Pittillo, *Western Carolina University*

Parasites, Faunal

To varying degrees, parasites (organisms that directly feed on other organisms, or hosts) affect most animal species in the Appalachians, influencing the occurrence, distribution, and robustness of host populations. It is possible for a single type of parasite to be responsible for the ultimate demise of a particular population within the Appalachians and, consequently, negatively impact other groups dependent on the host. Conversely, resistance to a specific parasite could lead to the population growth of a particular faunal group and those dependent on them.

Appalachian wildlife affected by parasites include mammals, insects, mollusks, amphibians, fishes, birds, and reptiles. External parasites are primarily arthropods and include numerous species of mites, lice, fleas, ticks, black flies, no-see-ums, and mosquitoes. These parasites flourish in the generally lush and wet ecosystems characteristic of the Appalachians and can pass on diseases and internal parasites through their bites.

Appalachian rodents host species-specific parasites that have been shown to be responsible for population crashes in some species of mice in the region. Black bears *(Ursus americanus)* harbor nematodes (which can cause trichinosis), and the southern bog lemming *(Synaptomys cooperi)* has been documented to harbor specific species of lice and mites. These examples indicate that intricate relationships exist between an animal host and its parasites and suggest that parasites may be a natural controller of animal populations in the Appalachians.

Parasites live on or within animals larger than themselves, feed only on small amounts of the host at a time, and release their metabolic wastes directly on or into the host's tissues. Detrimental effects on the host include mechanical damage (physical destruction of host tissue); nutritional damage (depletion of or competition with the host for essential nutrients); toxic damage (accumulation of the parasite's metabolic wastes in the host's tissue); and immune system damage (reduction of host immune system response due to the parasite). Parasite life-cycle stages can have specific effects on a host population; for example, only adult fleas are parasitic, whereas red bugs and screwworms are parasitic in the larval stages.

Internal parasites primarily consist of the trypanosomes and helminthes. Trypanosomes, which include protozoa of the order Coccidia and the genera *Giardia* and *Cryptosporidium*, affect the intestinal and respiratory tracts of affected fauna. Trypanosomes are introduced to their host through insect bites and/or ingestion of water populated with these organisms. The helminthes include a variety of parasites that typically thrive in the gastrointestinal tracts of their hosts. These include the nematodes (roundworms, hookworms, and pinworms), whose eggs are ingested by the host, hatch and mature inside the host, and are passed from the host back to the environment through their feces. They also include trematodes and cestodes (flukes and tapeworms) that require intermediate hosts (such as snails or earthworms), which are consumed by the eventual host.

See also: SYMBIOSIS; TREE DISEASES; ZOONOSES.

—Brian E. Caldwell, *EnSafe Inc.*

O. Wilford Olsen, *Animal Parasites: Their Life Cycles and Ecology* (1974); Carl Zimmer, *Parasite Rex: Inside the Bizarre World of Nature's Most Dangerous Creatures* (2001).

Pre-Columbian Ecology

Pre-Columbian Appalachia was a vast expanse of deciduous forest characterized by trees of immense height and girth, particularly in valleys and coves where soils and climate were most favorable. These forests had existed since the Pleistocene Ice Age (which peaked twenty thousand years ago), largely undisturbed by the first humans, who lived in them at least ten thousand years ago. They were home to many of the animal species present today, but some disappeared with European settlement. Animals such as the passenger pigeon *(Ectopistes migratorius)*, Carolina parakeet *(Conuropsis carolinensis)*, woodland bison *(Bison bison)*, mountain lion *(Felis concolor)*, and gray wolf *(Canis lupus)* are now either extinct or extirpated from Appalachia. The forests of the mountainous regions were still largely unlogged in the 1840s, when America's premier botanist at the time, Asa Gray, journeyed into the southern Appalachians "through regions which abound with the choicest botanical treasures which the country affords."

The Appalachian deciduous forest was (and is) a layered community comprised of canopy and subcanopy tree species above an understory of shade-tolerant shrubs and herbs. Openings in the forest occurred with the deaths of mature trees, windfalls, and natural or human-set fires. A highly diverse mixed mesophytic forest (deciduous-conifer mix with a well-balanced water supply) occurred where moisture was abundant and the climate mild, as in the Cumberland Mountains of eastern Kentucky, east Tennessee, and southwestern Virginia and the cove forests of the Blue Ridge of east Tennessee, western North Carolina, and western Virginia. With either increasing latitude or elevation, the deciduous forest transitions to a northern forest composed of sugar maple *(Acer saccharum)*, beech *(Fagus)*, yellow birch *(Betula lutea)*, and hemlock *(Tsuga)* and then to a spruce-fir coniferous forest.

Openings, or balds, characterize the high-elevation spruce-fir forest of the southern Appalachians. Balds support both locally endemic species (found nowhere else) and northern disjuncts (species found outside their typical northern latitudes). Whether balds originated from pre-Columbian human activity or formed as a result of natural processes stemming from the Ice Age climate is unclear. Rock outcroppings such as granitic intrusions and cliffs interrupt the forest canopy because tree roots are unable to penetrate the surface.

Several endemic plant species can be found on the granite outcrops of the Blue Ridge and Piedmont and the uplands of Alabama. Along the Virginia–West Virginia border, steep slopes and a highly erodible shale substrate have given rise to shale barrens that support several endemic plants. Noteworthy aquatic communities include the diverse fish and mussel assemblages endemic to the rivers of the Tennessee River drainage. These old and somewhat specialized ecosystems are little changed for thousands of years.

See also: FOREST COMMUNITIES; FUTURE FORESTS; OLD-GROWTH FOREST.

—Foster Levy, *East Tennessee State University*

Donald Edward Davis, *Where There Are Mountains: An Environmental History of the Southern Appalachians* (2000); Scott Weidensaul, *Mountains of the Heart: A Natural History of the Appalachians*

(1994); Susan L. Yarnell, *The Southern Appalachians: A History of the Landscape* (1998).

Rare Plants

Among the rich variety of plant species across the Appalachian Mountain system are a number of plants considered rare. Some of these are categorized as such because their populations are small, others because they exist in a restricted habitat, and still others because their geographical range is small. While the pink lady's slipper *(Cypripedium acaule)* is considered rare in many places, it is frequently encountered throughout the Appalachians. Conversely, some plants common elsewhere are considered rare in Appalachia. Highland rush *(Juncus trifidus)* is found only in isolated populations in Maryland, South Carolina, Tennessee, West Virginia, Virginia, and North Carolina, yet is common from New York northward.

In the 1970s, states began creating official lists of their most rare species, recognizing that many rare species of potentially great importance were being destroyed by land development. Such species not only add diversity to ecosystems, but they often have additional value to humans, especially for medicinal purposes. In 1973 the national Endangered Species Act established a procedure for listing the rarest plants and animals in the country, along with methods of recovery. Under the act, an endangered species (or larger taxonomic group) is "in danger of extinction throughout all or a significant portion of its range." A threatened species is one "likely to become an endangered species within the foreseeable future throughout all or a significant portion of its range."

Pink lady's slipper *(Cypripedium acaule)*, Virginia, 1981. While the pink lady's slipper is fairly common in some parts of Appalachia, it is rare in many places outside the region. The Appalachians support more than fifty species of native orchids.

Individual states define their own group of species and usually follow the same pattern designated by the U.S. Fish and Wildlife Service, especially for endangered and threatened categories. They often add others not federally designated, such as the peripheral species described above, but states cannot remove or downgrade those designated by the federal law. Because the Appalachians cross so many states, and make up only a portion of all but West Virginia (which is entirely within Appalachia), the listing of endangered and threatened species among states can be variable. Mountain golden heather *(Hudsonia montana)*, found only in Linville Gorge and surrounding counties of Burke and McDowell, North Carolina, is subject to trampling, providing for its endangered status. Small whorled pogonia *(Isotria verticillata)* is usually listed as threatened throughout Appalachia. On the other hand, starflower *(Trientalis borealis)* is classed as an endangered species in Georgia, while in North Carolina it is a candidate species, meaning that it is potentially threatened but not yet listed, and is quite common in northern portions of the region.

See also: BIODIVERSITY; COVE FORESTS; EXTINCT SPECIES.

—J. Dan Pittillo, *Western Carolina University*

Reptiles

Represented by sixty-two known species, including twenty species of turtles, nine species of lizards, and thirty-three species of snakes, reptiles are a major vertebrate component of Appalachian wildlife diversity. Reptiles vary in shape from the boxlike design of turtles to the elongated body style of lizards and snakes. All reptiles share the common characteristics of epidermal scales and an egg with embryonic membranes. Their skin and eggs allow them to live in more adverse (drier) habitats than their more evolutionarily primitive counterparts, the amphibians.

Some species of reptiles lay shelled eggs (oviparous), while others are live-bearers (viviparous). Eggs are deposited beneath a variety of cover objects or in loose soil, rotting logs and stumps, and sawdust. Clutch sizes generally depend on the size of the female; large females have more young than small females of the same species. Sex of the young of many species depends on the incubation temperature of the egg. Growth in young reptiles is rapid but slows significantly after maturity. All turtles are oviparous and are probably the longest-lived vertebrates, with life spans of more than one hundred years.

Freshwater turtles range in size from the 2- to 4.5-inch eastern musk turtle *(Sternotherus odoratus)*, which is found throughout most of Appalachia, to the 15- to 31-inch alligator snapping turtle *(Macroclemys temmincki)*, which occurs in parts of Mississippi and Alabama. Box turtles *(Terrapene)* are the most terrestrial turtle species in the region and are frequently seen along roads. The eastern box turtle *(T. carolina)* is the most widespread, ranging in Appalachia from Pennsylvania south to Mississippi, Alabama, and Georgia. The most common aquatic species are the common snapping *(Chelydra serpentina)*, eastern painted *(Chrysemys picta)*, and spiny softshell *(Trionyx spiniferus)* turtles. These three turtles occur in every state of the region. The ubiquitous snapping turtle occupies nearly every type of aquatic habitat and is often observed crossing highways during the spring en route to nesting sites. Least common are the flattened musk *(S. depressus)* and chicken *(Deirochelys reticularia)* turtles, both found in the Appalachian region of Alabama.

Lizards resemble salamanders, which are amphibians, but unlike salamanders have scales and claws on their toes. Lizards differ from snakes in possessing limbs, ear openings, and moveable eyelids. The legless eastern glass *(Ophisaurus ventralis)* and slender glass *(O. attenuatus)* lizards of the southern Appalachians are often mistaken for snakes, but they have moveable eyelids and external ear openings. Lizards range in size from the little brown skink *(Scincella lateralis)*, at 3 to 5.75 inches, to the legless glass lizard, 18 to 43 inches. The largest Appalachian lizard with legs is the broad-headed skink *(Eumeces laticeps)*, at 6.5 to 12.75 inches. The rough-scaled fence lizard *(Sceloporus undulatus)* and the smooth-scaled five-lined skink *(E. fasciatus)* are the most common Appalachian lizards. Country people often call young skinks with bright blue tails "scorpions" and erroneously claim they can use their tails to sting people. The coal skink *(E. anthracinus)* is found in all states in the region, but its distribution is patchy.

Copperhead *(Agkistrodon contortrix)*, Virginia, 1996. A major vertebrate component of Appalachian wildlife diversity is represented by reptiles through sixty-three known species, including twenty species of turtles, nine species of lizards, and thirty-three species of snakes. The copperhead is one of five venomous snakes (along with the cottonmouth and three species of rattlesnake) known to the region.

Of the thirty-three species of snakes known to occur in the region, five are venomous. These are all pit vipers: three rattlesnake species *(Crotalus)*, the copperhead *(Agkistrodon contortrix)*, and the cottonmouth *(A. piscivorus)*. Nonvenomous snakes include a variety of aquatic and terrestrial species. Ranges of ten species extend through all Appalachian states, and six species are represented in only one or two states. Garter snakes *(Thamnophis sirtalis)* and northern *(Nerodia sipedon)* and midland *(N. sipedon pleuralis)* water snakes have the largest distribution in Appalachia. These snakes and the black rat snake *(Elaphe obsoleta)*, which is commonly killed on highways, are frequently seen. Some nonvenomous snakes, such as the southern ring-necked snake *(Diadophis punctatus)*, worm snake *(Carphophis amoenus)*, earth snake *(Virginia valeriae)*, and red-bellied snake *(Storeria occipitomaculata)*, are small, usually less than 15 inches in length. Some snakes, such as rat snakes, are oviparous, while others, such as the pit vipers, are viviparous. Most snakes in Appalachia live less than twenty-five years, and many have their lives shortened prematurely by humans who believe that "the only good snake is a dead snake."

See also: AMPHIBIANS; BIODIVERSITY; WINTER ADAPTATIONS.

—Thomas K. Pauley, *Marshall University*

Roger Conant and Joseph T. Collins, *Reptiles and Amphibians in Eastern and Central North America* (1998).

River Cane

River cane (*Arundinaria gigantea* ssp.), an evergreen member of the bamboo family, once grew in profusion throughout the South and became an invaluable resource for Native Americans of the southern Appalachians. Also known as switch cane, swamp cane, giant cane, big cane, and southern cane, it could be found in widely varied habitats, including riverbanks, swamps and coastal bogs, alluvial valleys, pine barrens and flats, oak woods, loess and sandy bluffs, rocky cliffs, fields, hillsides, and mountain slopes up to an elevation of two thousand feet. Its geographic range extended from present-day northern Florida to New Jersey, and from the Atlantic Coast west to eastern Oklahoma and Texas. It grew in varying concentrations but often appeared in stands so dense that European settlers called them cane breaks (or canebrakes) as well as cane swamps, cane fields, cane meadows, and cane forests.

Cane's rapid regrowth contributed to the density of stands. During the growing season, the underground roots of each stalk extend laterally up to twenty feet. Each extension turns upward at regular intervals to form evenly spaced stalks. The new stalks grow as much as twelve inches per day, often completing growth in as little as six weeks and almost certainly by the end of the first season. At its full height, a cane stalk is from four to forty feet high and approximately one inch in diameter, with four to six lanceolate green leaves on each stem at the regularly-spaced growth nodes. Final height is determined by subspecies differences and conditions of climate, soil, and elevation.

Important in southeastern ecosystems, the presence of cane indicated rich soil for planting while its young shoots provided food for spring grazing animals. European settlers released livestock to forage in cane stands that sheltered various birds, reptiles, and mammals. Cane's densely matted roots also reduced soil erosion and floods.

Native Americans of the southern Appalachians found river cane an abundant and renewable resource for making everything from baskets to earplugs. Several properties of cane enhanced its usefulness for Native Americans. The relatively light stalks could be woven into large yet portable containers. They were also pliable enough to interweave with grass and saplings to create house walls and roofs. Their nearly hollow structure and upright growth made them suitable for arrow shafts, fishing poles, medicine tubes, and blowguns. High in silica content, cane stalks could be fashioned into sharp blades, pins, needles, or hooks. Silica also made cane objects resistant to water and heat damage and less likely to break or tear than goods created from other vegetable matter.

River cane is a disturbance-dependent plant that spreads primarily by extending its dense underground roots. Disturbances such as harvesting, fire, or flood may eliminate stalks, but the roots, containing stored nutrients, remain. Stands are thus enhanced by disturbances that clear out litter and competing vegetation, creating room for new stalks. Additionally, fires and floods replenish soil nutrients. Undisturbed stands thin out and die in about ten years.

Native Americans routinely burned forests and fields in the autumn to facilitate wild food gathering. This and the selective harvesting of stalks contributed to the vigor of stands. Since a Native American basket weaver could require fifty stalks to make a basket, a village of one hundred households might harvest as many as five thousand stalks for baskets, tools, and other household goods.

During the 1700s, the distribution and abundance of river cane diminished. In contrast to Native Americans, Europeans practiced spring burning to clear fields and woodlands, which killed cane's mature stalks and young shoots. Settlers also released horses and cattle to graze on river cane, and set hogs loose to root it up. Native Americans' adoption of livestock accelerated the destruction. By the end of the twentieth century, river cane could be found only sporadically in the southern Appalachians. Bachman's warbler *(Vermivora bachmanii)*, America's rarest bird species, is ecologically tied to cane stands for breeding purposes. It has disappeared along with the loss of its bottomland cane break habitat.

See also: CHEROKEE BASKETS (CRAFTS); FLOODPLAIN FORESTS; PRE-COLUMBIAN ECOLOGY.

—Sarah H. Hill, *Atlanta, Georgia*

Sarah H. Hill, *Weaving New Worlds: Southeastern Cherokee Women and Their Basketry* (1997); Daniel Lee Marsh, "The Taxonomy and Ecology of Cane, *Arundinaria gigantea* (Walter) Muhlenberg," Ph.D. dissertation, University of Arkansas (1977).

Saprobes

Life forms that obtain energy by eating dead organisms have historically been called saprophytes, but they are more properly referred to as saprobes, since not all of these organisms are plants. The former term comes from a time when bacteria and fungi, the principal saprobes, were classified as plants (*phyte* means "plant") by biologists. Saprobes break down, or reduce, the complex structures that make up the bodies of dead organisms in an action that is vital in recycling nutrients.

Of all ecosystems of the world, the Appalachians boast one of the richest biotas (total number of species). Plant life is especially diverse: more tree species are found in the Great Smoky Mountains than in all of Europe. When individuals die, their remains add to the natural detritus, which can include deer carcasses, large logs, thick layers of rotting leaves, and wet hay, as well as the many microorganisms that thrive on them. At this point the saprobes take over, reducing the detritus to humus and biochemically converting dead material for use in their own bodies.

Ecosystems with unusually high numbers of living species, such as those in Appalachia, provide nutrition for a wide array of saprobes. These saprobes eventually return organic material to the soil to be recycled as nutrition for photosynthetic plants. Thus, saprobe-reduced materials pass into green plants, and in turn some of their energy is transferred to herbivores that eat them, and so on to meat eaters who dine on the plant eaters. All eventually return to the menu of the saprobes.

The large and varied ecosystems that make up Appalachia contain unknown numbers of microscopic saprobe bacteria, including many undescribed forms, and thousands of species of fungi. The fungi are the familiar mushrooms, toadstools, and often colorful slime molds that dot the landscape.

See also: FUNGI; LEAVES; NUTRIENT CYCLING.

—Ron Petersen, *University of Tennessee*

Seasonal Rhythms

Seasonal rhythms that bring wide ranges of both moisture and temperature drive the ecological changes of Appalachia. In spring, increasing hours of daylight stimulate deciduous trees to grow new leaves, creating a closed canopy and a shady forest floor, where the light intensity is hundreds of times less than at the tops of the tallest trees. This determines the kinds of plants that grow in the forest, in contrast to those that require direct light and thrive on the forest edge or in clearings.

In deciduous forests, especially in their damp hollows, and on stream banks grow hundreds of kinds of wildflowers. Plants such as Virginia bluebell *(Mertensia virginica)*, twinleaf *(Jeffersonia diphylla)*, and bloodroot *(Sanguinaria canadensis)* sprout and bloom before the tree leaves emerge each spring while sunlight still reaches the forest floor. Other wildflowers, such as ginseng *(Panax quinquefolius)* and Solomon's seal *(Polygonatum)*, do not grow well in direct sunlight and consequently do not emerge and bloom until tree foliage is fully developed. Spring leaves also shade thousands of miles of Appalachian streams, providing cool, dark places for fish to hide from predators. In addition, they provide both food and shelter for birds and insects.

Although summer drought is a regular occurrence, severe episodes dry up water holes and streams, restricting many aquatic species and forcing other wildlife to travel in search of water. Wildfires, more common in summer, can be both destructive and important in cycling nutrients through the forest and in providing sunny, open habitat for new growth.

In autumn, vibrantly colored leaves on deciduous trees are more than a simple delight for tourists. Many bacterial and invertebrate decomposers feed on fallen leaves, releasing stored nutrients back into the ecosystem. This replenishes the forest soil, revitalizing it for spring growth. Once again, the forest canopy opens up, allowing full sunlight to reach the forest floor. Many leaves fall into bodies of water, where they change water chemistry as they decay.

To deal with frigid mountain winters, organisms migrate, hibernate, or adapt in other ways. The shedding of leaves by deciduous trees helps preserve their limbs by reducing the weight of snow and ice accumulation during winter storms, as well as their susceptibility to tissue destruction by freezing and thawing water. Trees also reduce the amount of water in their cells by storing the extra water between cells. The resulting concentration of nutrients in the cells further reduces damage from freezing.

Most trees are able to withstand temperatures close to their region's normal seasonal lows. Species that typically grow farther north or at higher elevations can withstand lower temperatures, although there is variability in cold tolerance within species. While eastern white pines *(Pinus strobus)* in Tennessee need only survive winter temperatures as low as five to ten degrees below freezing, those in Maine must commonly withstand lows of minus thirty to forty degrees Fahrenheit.

See also: LEAVES; MIGRATIONS; NUTRIENT CYCLING.

—Joy Drohan, *Eco-Write, Keedysville, Maryland*

Maurice Brooks, *The Appalachians* (1965); George Constantz, *Hollows, Peepers, and Highlanders: An Appalachian Mountain Ecology* (2nd edition, 2004); Scott Weidensaul, *Mountains of the Heart: A Natural History of the Appalachians* (1994).

Sedges

Appalachian sedges, like sedges around the world, tend to hide among other plants, obscuring their place in the ecosystem. Areas such as banks, seeps, springs, balds, and upland slopes—practically any area supporting vegetation—are likely sedge habitats. Some sedges, such as *Carex jamesii*, provide a flush of fresh greenery that deer heavily browse in spring, while others occupy disturbed habitats and wetlands.

Sedges are flowering plants, or angiosperms, and bear a superficial resemblance to grasses. However, most sedges have triangular stems, easily felt by rolling the stem between the fingers, while most grasses produce round stems ("sedges have edges and grasses are hollow and all round"). Additional sedge characteristics are: three-ranked leaves, closed sheaths that wrap the stem, flowers borne in the axils of single scales that overlap the scales of neighboring flowers, and achene (single-seeded nutlet) fruits.

Of the one hundred genera and five thousand species of sedges, roughly three hundred species in twenty-one genera thrive in Appalachia. Sedges are monocotyledons, or monocots, having only one seed leaf or cotyledon. *Carex* is the largest genus, including about half the sedge species in the Appalachian region.

Sedges are used as ornamentals, fiber and building materials, food and spice, and for making paper. They provide a highly significant structure and food base for many natural communities.

The correct identification of a sedge often requires study of its mature fruit. A hand lens provides adequate magnification in most cases. Since some species produce underground stems, or rhizomes, the entire plant may need to be examined.

Plant taxonomists still struggle with the identification of *Carex* and other sedge species, even in the United States, where their taxonomy is well studied. Several new species of sedges were discovered and described in the scientific literature in the last decade of the twentieth century. The grass-like sedges continue to provide fertile ground for scientific exploration.

See also: BALDS; GRASSES; WETLANDS.

—Philip E. Hyatt, *U.S. Department of Agriculture Forest Service*

Seed Dispersal

The function of seed dispersal by a parent plant is to get its seeds to a site favorable for seed establishment and far from competition with its sister seeds. Seeds of Appalachian plants have diverse adaptations that facilitate dispersal, either by self-propulsion or by using wind, water, and animals. Touch-me-not *(Impatiens)* has exploding fruits that throw seeds as far as ten feet. Goldenrod *(Solidago)* fruits have tufted fibers that act as parachutes, allowing them to drift on the wind. Similarly, cottonwood *(Populus deltoides)* seeds have fibers that allow them to float on the surface of streams and rivers. The small seeds of rushes ride on the feet of water birds such as ducks. The barbed fruits of tickseed sunflower *(Bidens)* latch onto fur, feathers, or clothing. Bloodroot *(Sanguinaria canadensis)* and wild ginger *(Asarum canadense)*, as with many spring wildflowers, are helped by ants, which carry the seeds underground, eat the attached fatty deposits (elaiosomes), and discard the seeds, effectively planting them in enriched soil.

Birds, mammals, and box turtles *(Terrapene carolina)* disperse sweet fruits; the seeds are spit out or transported in the digestive tract and eventually deposited in feces. Often, as in cherries *(Prunus)* and plums *(Prunus)*, the fruit is a drupe (also called stone fruit) and has a tough inner wall that protects the seed from digestion. Sassafras *(Sassafras albidum)* attracts migrating songbirds with fat-rich drupes, while bursting heart bush *(Euonymus americana)* offers edible outgrowths called arils that cloak the seeds. Poison ivy *(Rhus radicans)* and sumac *(R. vernix)* produce long-lasting, low-fat drupes that many birds eat throughout the winter.

Squirrels and blue jays *(Cyanocitta cristata)* disperse oaks *(Quercus)* and beech *(Fagus)* through scatter-hoarding behavior in which they bury the nutritious nuts in autumn for use at a later time. Since many of these nuts are never retrieved and eaten, they often sprout into new trees. The behavior is so beneficial to these trees that it is believed jays were significant in helping forests reclaim land after glaciers retreated from northern Appalachia during the last ice age.

Humans are also significant seed dispersers, both intentionally and accidentally. People can help maintain indigenous Appalachian biodiversity by planting native, noninvasive species such as pawpaw *(Asimina triloba)*, rather than invasive, exotic ones.

See also: FRUITS; TREES; WILDFLOWERS.

—Susan Moyle Studlar, *West Virginia University*

Shale Barrens

Initially described by E. S. Steele in 1911, the mid-Appalachian shale barrens can be found from south-central Pennsylvania to southwestern Virginia and adjacent West Virginia. A shale barren is an isolated area with a generally steep southern exposure, a surface of hard, weather-resistant shale and siltstone fragments, and a surface temperature ranging to more than 140 degrees Fahrenheit. These harsh landscapes contain little exposed soil or organic material, yet many of these shale barrens have a sparse community of native plant species occurring nowhere else, from lichens and herbs to scattered small shrubs. Seedlings of these plants can tolerate high surface temperatures, require direct sunlight for maximum growth, and need enough soil for their extensive root systems. This combination of physical conditions precludes competition from many possible invaders.

Eighteen species of plants are recognized as generally restricted to Appalachian shale barrens, but these endemic plants are not equally distributed throughout the region, presumably because of their unequal evolutionary age, unequal dissemination of seeds, and reproductive adaptations. Based on their evolutionary age and origin, five classes are recognized: two species with unknown close relatives; seven species with relatively restricted ranges and presumed recent origin; six species of relatively ancient origin with several species having their closest relatives in mid-central to western North America; two species ancestral to two or more species; and one species derived from two closely related species. Conservation of these endemics is needed, especially shale barren rockcress *(Arabis serotina)*, two species of clematis *(Clematis viticaulis* and *C. coactilis)*, and shale barren clover *(Trifolium virginicum)*, also known as Kates Mountain clover.

See also: ASPECT; ECOREGIONS; ENDEMISM.

—Carl S. Keener, *Pennsylvania State University*

Slime Molds

Slime molds are common inhabitants of soil, litter, and vegetation surfaces. Like mushrooms, slime molds form spore-bearing fruiting bodies and do not perform photosynthesis. Slime molds are mobile, and recent studies suggest that they are more closely related to protozoa (some scientists treat them as such). They consume large numbers of bacteria, influencing bacteria populations. Slime molds are in turn eaten by a variety of other creatures and are indicators of ecosystem health.

Two major types of slime molds occur in leaf litter and soils of Appalachian forest ecosystems. Many species of slime molds of the class Myxomycetes are common in the region, noticeable because their fruiting bodies may be quite large and colorful. Spores germinate into single amoebas that feed on bacteria and other soil microbes. Cells of compatible mating types fuse into zygotes, which continue to feed and enlarge as multinucleate, migrating, fan-shaped slimy masses called plasmodia, sluglike entities that continue to engulf bacteria. Eventually, one or more stalked fruiting bodies develop, each containing thousands of spores. A single plasmodium can grow large enough to cover an entire log on the forest floor.

Also common to the region's forests are species of cellular slime molds. They have entirely microscopic life stages and are unlikely to be noticed in nature. In the laboratory, they are cultured from soil and leaf litter. Each cellular slime mold spore germinates into a single amoeba that feeds on a variety of soil bacteria. When their food sources are depleted, the amoebas release a chemical signal that induces hundreds of slime mold cells to crawl together and clump into small, transparent, cigar-shaped masses that are called pseudoplasmodia, because the cells do not fuse with each other as do the myxomycetes, but instead remain as individuals and develop either into the stalk or spores of the fruiting bodies.

See also: FUNGI; LEAVES; SAPROBES.

—John C. Landolt, *Shepherd University*

Steven L. Stephenson and Henry Stempen, *Myxomycetes: A Handbook of Slime Molds* (1994).

Black-and-yellow argiope spider *(Argiope aurantia)*, Johnson City, Tennessee, 2003. As of 2002, nearly five hundred species of spiders had been identified in the Great Smoky Mountains National Park alone, and thirty-eight of those species were new to science. Currently, only one Appalachian spider, the spruce-fir moss spider *(Microhexura montivaga)*, is on the federal endangered list. The black-and-yellow argiope, also known as the "writing spider," is a species of orb-weaving spider commonly seen in the region.

Spiders

Spiders are abundant throughout the United States and are particularly diverse in the Blue Ridge and the mixed mesophytic forests of southern Appalachia. These ecoregions provide a variety of landforms, climate, soils, and geology, which support a broad range of species. Not subject to the Pleistocene glaciations, the area was a refuge for several species and communities. Consequently, southern Appalachia possesses a relatively high number of relict (apparently unchanged from ancient times) and endemic (found nowhere else) spider species, with a full complement of common and more rare species.

Spiders are members of the class Arachnida, order Araneae. They are closely related to, and commonly confused with, daddy longlegs (harvestmen), ticks, mites, and scorpions, which are also arachnids but are not spiders. Based on existing data, there are approximately thirty-five hundred spider species in the United States, with more than three hundred yet undescribed. A highly detailed species inventory project entitled the All Taxa Biodiversity Inventory is underway in the Great Smoky Mountains National Park of southern Appalachia. The project seeks to enumerate all of the species in the 815-square-mile park. As of 2002, nearly five hundred species of spiders had been identified, and thirty-eight of those species were new to science. Thus, the inventory of spider species in Appalachia, and indeed the entire country, is incomplete.

Many spider species are restricted to particular habitat types such as caves, old-growth forests, and bogs or other wetland habitats. Because of this specificity, they are highly threatened by loss or alteration of habitat. Currently, the federal endangered species list includes only one spider native to Appalachia (of four total species listed as of 2003): the spruce-fir moss spider *(Microhexura montivaga)*, which lives in moist but well-drained moss mat habitats in high-elevation spruce-fir forests of southern Appalachia. This habitat is being steadily degraded by the actions of the introduced balsam woolly adelgid *(Adelges piceae)*, acid precipitation, and air pollution.

Two of the more medically important and publicly familiar species of spiders in Appalachia are the black widow *(Latrodectus mactans)* and the brown recluse *(Loxosceles reclusa)*. Both types are distributed throughout Appalachia but are relatively uncommon, despite their notoriety. Black widows can be found throughout the region, including in northern portions, but brown recluse spiders are more sensitive to cold temperature and will not survive in northern climates unless they remain inside heated structures.

See also: BIODIVERSITY; FOLIAGE ARTHROPODS; INSECTS.

—Angela K Palau, *Oak Ridge, Tennessee*

Taylor H. Ricketts et al., *Terrestrial Ecoregions of North America: A Conservation Assessment* (1999); V. D. Roth, *Spider Genera of North America* (3rd edition, 1993); Kevin Skerl, "The Status of Spider Conservation in the United States," *Endangered Species Update* (March–April 1997).

Springs

See Streams

Streams

Appalachian streams vary in size from temporary rills inches across to those as wide as the Ohio River. Rain and snow falling on the high ridges and peaks along the Eastern Continental Divide flow to the ocean through numerous Appalachian streams. While most of these streams drain to the Gulf of Mexico, either directly or through the Mississippi-Ohio River system, many drain directly into the Atlantic Ocean and the Great Lakes.

These streams provide drinking water for the area's human population, livestock, and wildlife, cooling water for electric power generation, process water for industry, and irrigation water for agriculture. In addition, streams are used as transportation corridors for barges hauling coal, steel, and other products, as well as for recreational swimming, boating, and fishing. Increasingly, they have also become sinks for agricultural runoff, industrial pollutants, and sewage-treatment effluent.

Blackwater River, Tucker County, West Virginia, 1988. Rain and snow falling on the high ridges and peaks of the Appalachians flow to the ocean through the many streams of the region. While most eventually drain into the Gulf of Mexico through the Mississippi-Ohio River system, many drain directly into the Atlantic Ocean and the Great Lakes.

Streams closer to the ridge tops and peaks tend to be small, flow quickly, and have numerous riffles, cascades, and waterfalls. Some streams have carved broad valleys across the landscape. Typically, these are slower-flowing rivers, many of which have been controlled with locks and dams to allow commercial navigation, increase recreation, and promote flood control.

Much of Appalachia is a karst landscape, in which surface soils have been deposited upon limestone rock formed by the calcified remains of sea life while the region was part of the ocean floor 400 million years ago. Streams in these areas frequently flow under the surface for miles before resurfacing. Subterranean streams with names such as Lost

River, Sinking Creek, Spring Creek, and Sinks of Gandy are fairly common across Appalachia.

Some streams near ridge tops are low in natural alkalinity (pH of seven or lower) and have a limited ability to neutralize acids (low buffering capability). Hence, many of these streams support acid-loving vegetation such as evergreen trees, rhododendrons *(Rhododendron)*, and mountain laurels *(Kalmia latifolia)*. Acid precipitation adversely affects these streams by increasing the already naturally high acidity to the point at which fish and other aquatic life cannot survive.

Springs augment stream flow during dry spells and form the headwaters of some streams. They provide water for wildlife and a habitat for many living things. Salamanders, including several species of genus *Gyrinophilus*, are so often found in Appalachian springs and their cool, clear mountain streams that they are commonly called "spring lizards" in the region.

An Appalachian stream may be called a river, branch, fork, draft, rill, creek, kill, run, or other such name, usually depending on its size and the influences of the settlers who named it, not necessarily according to any standard definition. For example, Sang Kill in Mingo County, West Virginia, combines a corruption of the word *ginseng* with the Dutch word for a small stream.

Stream names often reflect the culture of the inhabitants. The Monongahela, Kanawha, Susquehanna, Great Miami, Chattahoochee, Guyandotte, and Potomac are Appalachian streams whose names reflect Native American tribes of the region. Holston River, Clinch River, Hughes River, Symmes Creek, James River, Jackson River, and many others take their names from historic people. The names of the French Broad, Big Sandy, Flint, and Bullpasture Rivers indicate natural or man-made features of the streams or the local area. Many streams are named for wildlife or vegetation once seen along their banks. Buffalo Creek, Wolf Creek, Elk River, and Chestnut Creek are common names for streams throughout Appalachia.

Before European settlers arrived in the Appalachian Mountains and for decades afterward, streams tended to be relatively pure. What pollution did exist was organic, quickly broken down and flushed from streams with minimal effects. As the human population in the Appalachians increased, more pollutants found their way into streams. Eventually the broad river valleys became industrialized, and pollutants became more complex, including many inorganic chemicals and metals along with increased quantities of organic wastes.

The U.S. Congress enacted the Clean Water Act of 1972 to restore the quality of the nation's waters. For more than twenty-five years, the act's National Pollutant Discharge Elimination System has reduced the quantity of pollutants piped to surface waters and significantly improved the quality of many Appalachian streams.

Sources of pollution with no specific point of origin continue to be a threat to water quality in Appalachian streams. This pollution originates from a variety of activities. Oil and grease washed from parking lots, fertilizers and pesticides running off golf courses or agricultural lands, and sediment lost from timbering operations or construction sites for highways, roads, buildings, and the infrastructure for oil and gas exploration and development are a few of the major types of non-point pollution.

Many Appalachian houses are built on narrow floodplain benches just above stream banks. These locations make installing new septic systems expensive and difficult. Even entire Appalachian communities find it an economic hardship to replace community sewage systems with up-to-date collection and wastewater-treatment plants. Failing sewage collection systems and septic tanks are major sources of fecal contamination in Appalachian streams.

Fecal coliform bacteria, an indicator of fecal pollution, also come from wild and domestic animals. Wildlife droppings are usually dispersed enough that it is not a problem, but concentrations of waterfowl can elevate fecal contamination to unsafe levels. More typically, pollution results from agricultural feedlots that concentrate many animals in small areas and allow rains to wash the manure into nearby streams. Giant hog farms in North Carolina, poultry operations in West Virginia, and cattle feedlots throughout Appalachia have all contributed fecal pollution to Appalachian streams.

A controversial method of mining, mountaintop removal, also threatens Appalachian streams. Literally removing the tops of mountains and hills to reveal the coal seams below, mine operators typically dispose of this overburden in hollows and valleys, effectively smothering streams at their source. The full effects of burying these headwater streams are not fully understood, and the complexity of the issue is reflected in the numerous changes and revisions to mining regulations. The 1977 Surface Mining Control and Reclamation Act prohibited mining within one hundred feet of streams, but waivers have been issued to companies that can show the activity does not degrade the stream. A 2002 relaxation of this prohibition allowed mining companies more discretion in respecting buffer zones, in effect undermining the intent of the act.

See also: COAL MINING (ENVIRONMENT); KARST; WATERSHEDS.

—Jim Hudson, *West Virginia Conservation Agency*

Donald Edward Davis, *Where There Are Mountains: An Environmental History of the Southern Appalachians* (2000); Eugene P. Odum, *Ecology* (1963).

Succession

The sequential change in the relative abundances of dominant species as one community replaces another over time is called succession. In analyzing the mixed mesophytic forest, E. Lucy Braun described the history and succession of the Appalachian forest, the most complex and oldest of the deciduous forest regions of eastern North America.

Logging, mining, agricultural land clearing, and fires have created massive ecological disturbances in the original forested landscapes of Appalachia. Abandoned croplands were a common sight in the 1930s in areas once covered with forest. When Appalachian farmlands are no longer tended, they first grow weedy with grasses and non-woody plants. These fields are then invaded by woody shrubs and scrub, which later give way to pioneer trees such as pines *(Pinus)*, black locust *(Robinia pseudoacacia)*, dogwood *(Cornus)*, and tulip poplar *(Liriodendron tulipifera)*. Thus, over a period of years one assemblage of plant species (called a community) gives way to other communities in the successional process (the sere) until, barring disturbance, a relatively stable forest (the climax) occupies the ground. In higher elevations where spruce *(Picea)* or spruce-fir forest is the climax, a disturbance such as fire or logging typically initiates a series in which stands of laurel *(Kalmia)* and rhododendron *(Rhododendron)* are produced on exposed windy ridges, while in more protected areas a succession of communities is dominated initially by fire cherry *(Prunus pensylvanica)* for about twenty to forty years. The fire cherry is succeeded by a yellow birch *(Betula lutea)* forest that in turn is occupied by a stable forest of spruce or spruce and fir *(Abies)*.

The concept of succession was adopted at the beginning of the twentieth century by pioneering American ecologists who sought to discover natural laws that govern these changes of ecological communities. Succession has been studied in terrestrial and aquatic plant and animal communities in tropical, temperate, arctic, alpine, and oceanic habitats. Although succession is universal, each biographic region, called a formation or biome, has its own idiosyncrasies, so general laws have proved elusive. Succession requires space with available resources, as well as migration and establishment of organisms, which modify the site and interact with other organisms to initiate a sere. Primary succession begins on a previously unoccupied site such as glacial debris, sandy beach, or volcanic material. Secondary succession begins after disturbance of a community where the site retains residual influences of organisms. Successional change in ecological systems is a series of complex interactions of physical conditions and organisms.

Knowledge of succession grew by increasing use of quantitative methods for sampling and analysis of communities and increasingly sophisticated methods of biogeochemical analysis to assess changes in chemical and physical conditions. Henry A. Gleason's "individualistic concept" held that succession did not follow fixed laws because its results were unpredictable, influenced by chance arrival of organisms and continuous change of the environment. In the 1950s, extended quantitative studies stimulated a revolution in ecology and widespread acceptance of Gleason's ideas.

In 1942 Raymond Lindeman developed the concept of trophic dynamics, emphasizing transfer of energy and materials from plants to animals and microorganisms during succession in lakes. Eugene Odum, in a 1953 textbook focused on the ecosystem concept, emphasized energy, nutrients, and productivity of organic material as criteria of succession. Empirical knowledge of succession is widely used to minimize human impacts on the environment. Reclamation, restoration, ecological engineering, and rehabilitation are approaches to supplement natural succession in restoring living communities to areas disturbed by erosion, mine and quarry spoils, dumping from myriad industries, and freshwater and marine pollution.

See also: BIODIVERSITY; ECOLOGICAL CATASTROPHES; TREE DISEASES.

—Robert P. McIntosh, *University of Notre Dame*

E. Lucy Braun, *Deciduous Forests of Eastern North America* (1950); Colin J. Burrows, *Processes of Vegetation Change* (1990); R. P. McIntosh, *The Background of Ecology: Concept and Theory* (1985); E. P. Odum, *Fundamentals of Ecology* (1953).

Symbiosis

Symbiosis is a biological relationship involving two or more species living together in close association. In one form of symbiosis, commensalism, one species is benefited while the other is not affected. A lichen growing on a tree trunk or limb has its fitness increased without affecting the tree. An ecologically more important association between species is mutualism, in which both partners benefit. Symbiosis provides a particularly intimate kind of mutual benefit in which individuals of different species associate closely for most, if not all, of their lives. A relationship essential for survival of both species is called obligatory mutualism; if it is nonessential, the relationship is facultative or nonobligatory. While a honeybee *(Apis mellifera)* and a flowering plant benefit one another, they are not considered obligatory symbionts because each bee interacts so briefly with any one plant. Many Appalachian plants benefit by having their heavy seeds dispersed by animals in nonobligatory mutualistic associations. Blue jays *(Cyanocitta cristata)* and squirrels scatter-hoard thousands of acorns, which they bury each autumn as a hedge against winter, thus aiding oaks *(Quercus)* in the dispersal of their large seeds far from the parent plants.

Two examples of obligatory mutualism are widespread and common in Appalachia. Lichens, among the best known of Appalachia's symbiotic organisms, arose through a union of fungi with algal cells, or cyanobacteria. The fungus provides nutrients, support, and a moist environment for the algae, which in turn provide photosynthesized sugars to the fungus. Mycorrhizae (literally "fungus roots") are also found throughout Appalachia. These are intergrowths between soil fungi and the roots of trees and other plants. The fungi absorb and pass scarce soil nutrients to the trees and obtain sugars in return.

The white-tailed deer *(Odocoileus virginianus)* browsing along a woodland edge depends on symbiotic microscopic organisms in its digestive track to break down the resistant cell walls of plants, allowing the deer to digest the sugars therein. Cattle grazing in Appalachian pastures have similar mutualistic organisms in their stomachs. Termites could not digest the wood of trees and homes without similar symbionts in their guts.

All multicellular beings, including humans, hold in their cells the presumed legacy of an ancient symbiotic partnership: hundreds of millions of years ago, the ancestral cells of modern-day plants and animals incorporated bacterial cells into their cytoplasm, or intracellular fluid. These bacteria evolved into mitochondria, the metabolic power stations found in all such cells, and chloroplasts, the light-capturing bodies found in plant and algal cells.

Symbioses as exemplified by the lichens and mycorrhizae were once considered mere oddities of nature but are now understood to support the growth of entire forests and have played dramatic roles in the evolution of life on Earth.

See also: MYCORRHIZA; PARASITES, FAUNAL.

—Eric J. Olson, *Earthwatch Institute*

Tree Diseases

Two significant native diseases of Appalachian trees are oak wilt and stem rot. Oak wilt, most serious in red oaks *(Quercus rubra)*, is a lethal disease caused by a fungus. White oaks *(Q. alba)* are more resistant to attack.

All tree species are subject to a wide variety of fungi that rot wood within the living tree. These fungi generally exploit an injury to the bark that exposes the wood. The most common injuries initiating stem rots are broken branches and tops, fire scars, and logging wounds. Rot in trees causes timber loss, but it also provides cavities for nesting wildlife. Natural cavities in rotting wood are important nesting and den sites for secondary cavity nesters such as chickadees *(Parus)*, titmice *(P. bicolor)*, great crested flycatchers *(Myriarchus crinitus)*, owls, squirrels, opossums *(Didelphis virginiana)*, and raccoons *(Procyon lotor)*.

Tree diseases play an important role in the development of Appalachian forest ecosystems by precluding dominance by a few species and opening holes in the canopy, thereby promoting growth of early successional species. Many tree diseases are caused by microorganisms, especially fungi, which infect the leaves, roots, or stems. Since native Appalachian trees seldom have natural defenses to them, the most damaging diseases are often those introduced from other parts of the world. By contrast, native tree diseases usually become a significant problem only in conjunction with some adverse environmental condition such as air pollution or drought that causes stress in the trees, lowering their resistance.

The most damaging disease introduced into Appalachian forests is chestnut blight *(Endothia parasitica)*, which was first seen in New York City in 1904. Within fifty years, it virtually eliminated the American chestnut *(Castanea dentata)*, a valuable tree that produced excellent timber, tannin, and nuts. Beech bark disease, first introduced to Nova Scotia from Europe in the late nineteenth century, was discovered in 1981 to have infested more than seventy thousand acres of forest in West Virginia. By the end of the century, the disease had spread to more than 3.5 million acres of Appalachian forest. The disease involves a scale insect and a fungus that initially kills some beech trees *(Fagus)* and deforms many others. Other new, introduced diseases include hemlock and dogwood blights.

See also: ECOLOGICAL CATASTROPHES; EXOTIC SPECIES; FUTURE FORESTS.

—Walter C. Shortle, *U.S. Department of Agriculture Forest Service Northeastern Forest Experiment Station*

Trees

Trees of the Appalachians are classified in two major groups: conifers and flowering plants. The conifers, which are softwoods, include pine *(Pinus)*, hemlock *(Tsuga)*, spruce *(Picea)*, fir *(Abies)*, tamarack *(Larix laricina)*, northern white cedar *(Thuja occidentalis)*, and eastern red cedar *(Juniperus virginiana)*. These are evergreens with needlelike or scalelike leaves. Conifers are wind pollinated, and their seeds are contained in cones.

The flowering trees are hardwoods and are the larger group. They include oaks *(Quercus)*, maples *(Acer)*, holly *(Ilex)*, beech *(Fagus)*, poplars *(Populus)*, and dogwood *(Cornus)*. Regardless of whether they are deciduous (maple), or evergreen (American holly *[I. opaca]*), their leaves are broad and net-veined. Oak, hickory *(Carya)*, birch *(Betula)*, and sweet gum *(Liquidambar styraciflua)* have flowers that are plain and wind pollinated; the flowers of dogwood, tulip poplar *(Liriodendron tulipifera)*, buckeye *(Aesculus)*, redbud *(Cercis canadensis)*, and serviceberry *(Amelanchier)* are showy and insect pollinated. Among flowering trees, the seeds of maple, elm *(Ulmus)*, and ash *(Fraxinus)* are enclosed in dry fruits; those of dogwood, cherry *(Prunus)*, sassafras *(Sassafras albidum)*, and mulberry *(Morus)* in fleshy fruits.

Pine, oak, hickory, and maple provide fuel and lumber; the barks of hemlock and oak produce tannin; pines and some hardwoods are sources of paper pulp; honey comes from sourwood *(Oxydendrum arboreum)*, basswood *(Tilia)*, and black locust *(Robinia pseudoacacia)*; and medicine may be obtained from the bark of white pine *(Pinus strobus)* and black cherry *(Prunus serotina)* and the buds of balm of Gilead *(Populus gileadensis)*. Balsam fir *(Abies balsamea)*, Fraser fir *(A. fraseri)*, and other evergreens are used as Christmas trees. The bark of several trees, including butternuts *(Juglans cinerea)* and walnuts *(J. nigra)*, are used as natural dyes. Acorns, hickory nuts, cherries, and numerous seeds provide food for wildlife, and trees provide shelter, nesting sites, and shade for many animals as well. Trees also reduce soil erosion and clean the air by absorbing carbon dioxide and some pollutants while supplying oxygen through photosynthesis.

Among the most beautiful and stately forms of nature, trees are a distinct aspect of the Appalachians, coming in an amazing diversity of forms, from the conspicuous spire-shaped conifers to rounded shapes of elms. Appalachian trees sport a variety of sizes, shapes, and textures of leaves, from the tiny needles of hemlocks to the thirty-inch leaves of bigleaf magnolias *(Magnolia macrophylla)*. The region's deciduous forests create a pallet of yellow, orange, purple, and crimson fall colors. Appalachian trees produce numerous varieties of flowers, fruits, and seeds, which have many different dispersal mechanisms, and the texture of their barks runs the gamut from shaggy to ridged to smooth. The Appalachian region harbors more tree species than all of continental Europe.

A tree is generally distinguished from a shrub in having a single erect trunk at least three inches in diameter at breast height (four and one-half feet), a more or less definitely formed crown of branches and leaves, and a height of at least thirteen feet at full growth. Several plants in Appalachia, including mountain laurel *(Kalmia latifolia)*, rhododendron *(Rhododendron)*, Chickasaw plum *(Prunus angustifolia)*, and hazel alder *(Alnus)*, usually grow as shrubs but occasionally reach tree size.

The mountains and valleys of Appalachia served as a refuge for many plant species when glaciers covered much of North America. There are more than 150 species of native and naturalized trees in the Appalachians. Some trees, such as Fraser fir, Carolina hemlock *(Tsuga caroliniana)*, Virginia roundleaf birch *(Betula uber)*, and table mountain pine *(Pinus pungens)*, grow naturally only in Appalachian areas, while most are more widespread throughout the eastern United States. The ranges of several native American trees, including red pine *(P. resinosa)*, tamarack, and gray birch *(B. populifolia)*, barely cross into the Appalachians in the north, while others, such as longleaf pine *(P. australis)*, barely encroach from the south. Naturalized trees, introduced to the region and established through cultivation, often become very common and may displace native trees. The empress tree *(Paulowinia tomentosa)*, tree of heaven *(Ailanthus altissima)*, mimosa *(Albizia julibrissin)*, and white poplar *(Populus alba)* were introduced from Eurasia. One of the rarest native trees of the Appalachians is yellowwood *(Cladrastis kentukea)*, a tree with elongated hanging clusters of pealike flowers and durable yellow to brown wood. Even more rare is the Virginia roundleaf birch.

Many of the highest peaks of the Appalachian Mountains are crowned with stands of conifer forests. Evergreens are often mixed with hardwoods on south-facing slopes, and hemlocks grow to large sizes in cove forests. Except for bald cypress *(Taxodium distichum)* and larch *(Larix)*, conifers are evergreen trees that, in general, produce seeds in scaled, woody cones. Conifers in Appalachian plant communities include pines, firs, spruces, hemlocks, arborvitae *(Thuja)*, and a juniper commonly called red cedar. In coniferous trees, pollen-bearing male structures and egg-bearing female structures are usually produced in the same tree. Abundant wind-dispersed pollen is produced by most species during late winter or spring. Seed-bearing cones vary in size from the tiny (one-third to one-half inch) cone produced by arborvitae to the large (four to eight inches) cone of the eastern white pine.

The diverse species of coniferous trees are valuable as protective cover and foods for wildlife. Animals, including insects, game birds, songbirds, and small and large mammals, consume seeds, needles, bark, and twigs on coniferous trees. Conifer species and their parts differ in their value as food sources. Junipers produce a berrylike fruit that is attractive to many birds, including cedar waxwings *(Bombycilla cedorum)* and yellow-rumped warblers *(Dendroica coronata)*, which act as dispersal agents when they defecate the seeds at some distance from the parent trees after eating them. Many conifers are killed by infestations of insects such as southern pine bark beetles *(Dendroctonus frontalis)* and balsam woolly adelgids *(Adelges piceae)*.

The various conifers have distinguishing characteristics. Pines produce needles in clusters of two to five, and hemlocks produce a small cone (less than one inch long) and single dark-green needles attached to the twig at angles of approximately sixty degrees. Spruces produce single pointed and angled needles attached around the entire twig, and their cones droop toward the ground. Firs produce single, flat needles attached around the entire twig; their cones point toward the sky. Arborvitae produce small cones and leaves that appear as overlapping scales on flattened twigs; junipers produce scale-shaped or awl-shaped needles on twigs that are not flat like arborvitae, while the fruit is slate blue and covered with a waxy bloom.

The rich variety of deciduous trees in Appalachia includes oaks, hickories, walnuts, magnolias, tulip poplars, maples, ashes, dogwoods, redbuds, and persimmons *(Diospyros virginiana)*. These trees can be recognized by differences in the size, shape, and position of attachment of leaves to stems and their flowers and fruits. Fruits include the winged fruits of maples and ashes to acorns of oaks, the nutritious bird-dispersed fruits of dogwood and serviceberry, and the dry legumes (pods) of redbud and black locust. Deciduous trees provide food in the form of twigs, leaves, and fruits for many animals, including insects, game birds, songbirds, small mammals, and deer. The vast majority of deciduous trees are flowering plants, as distinguished from nonflowering deciduous conifers such as bald cypress. Flowering trees attract many different pollinators, from insects to hummingbirds, to their flowers. They also provide holes for many cavity-nesting or denning species.

Deciduous trees produce a complete set of leaves during the growing season and shed them as temperatures and available sunlight decrease during autumn. A new set of leaves emerges at the beginning of the subsequent growing season. Throughout Appalachia, as winter approaches, trees become dormant through the loss of leaves. Leaf drop prevents plants from experiencing damage to tender tissues due to formation of ice crystals when water freezes within cells. Before leaves fall, the plant withdraws valuable nutrients such as nitrogen from them. Conserved nutrients are stored and support the growth of new leaves the next spring. Other preparations for winter dormancy include concentration of sugars in remaining plant tissues to act as antifreeze to prevent damage. Up to two tons of leaves per acre may be added each fall to the forest floor, where bacteria, fungi, and detritus-feeding animals break them down, thereby returning nutrients to the soil.

Among Appalachian hardwood trees, two are particularly noteworthy. One is the tulip poplar, or yellow poplar, which may reach over 5 feet in diameter, 175 feet in height, and 300 years of age. It is an attractive, fast-growing, and valuable hardwood tree. The wood of the tulip poplar is used for furniture, plywood, and lumber. Its seeds are a major source of food for wildlife, bees make honey from the nectar of its flowers, and deer and rabbits forage on its seedlings and saplings.

The other notable tree, the former queen of the Appalachian forests, is the American chestnut *(Castanea dentata)*. Prior to the accidental introduction of the chestnut blight *(Endothia parasitica)* from Asia into New York in 1904, this tree was one of the largest, most abundant, and most valuable hardwoods of the Appalachians. Blight had killed nearly every standing tree by the late 1930s. Sprouts continue to grow from old stumps, but they quickly succumb to the fungus. The trees reached 10 feet in diameter, 120 feet in height, and at least 205 years of age. Prior to its decimation, the chestnut was of huge importance. Its decay-resistant wood provided lumber, crossties, posts, and fences. The bark was used extensively to cure leather, and the large, sweet nuts were an important source of food for both humans and wildlife. Some forty years after the death of the large trees, the standing silver-gray snag remnants were cut and marketed as worm-eaten chestnut, a distinctive wood used for floors, paneling, and furniture.

Adversities to trees include fungus diseases, insect pests, forest fires, extreme weather (such as severe windstorms and ice storms), floods, air pollution, and loss of habitat—the latter two mainly due to human activities. The past few decades have seen the loss of the magnificent spruce and fir forests from the mountain peaks and ridges due to the destructive insect balsam woolly adelgid in combination with acid precipitation and increased ozone. More recently, the hemlock woolly adelgid *(A. tsugae)*, accidentally introduced in Richmond, Virginia, has spread into the southern Appalachians. This insect has the potential to destroy native hemlock stands. Flowering dogwood *(Cornus florida)* is threatened by dogwood anthracnose *(Discula destructiva)*, a fungus disease introduced from an unknown source in the 1970s. It has spread southward from the Northeast, causing a noticeable decline in southern Appalachian dogwoods.

See also: COVE FORESTS; FOREST COMMUNITIES; SEED DISPERSAL.

—James W. Hardin, *North Carolina State University*, and
Christopher F. Sacchi, *Kutztown University of Pennsylvania*

Thomas S. Elias, *Complete Trees of North America: Field Guide and Natural History* (1987); Wilbur H. and Marion B. Duncan, *Trees of the Southeastern United States* (1988); James W. Hardin, Donald J. Leopold, and Fred M. White, *Harlow and Harrar's Textbook of Dendrology* (9th edition, 2001).

Vines

More than thirty species of vines have been identified in the Appalachian region. They represent a successful adaptation to the challenge of reaching sunlight in a shaded forest. By evolving a twining habit of growth using various kinds of tendrils, holdfasts, and other forms of unusually positioned roots, vines cling to trees and other supports to ascend to the forest canopy without having to produce huge tree trunks. Vines in Appalachia are often prominent in forest edges and disturbed habitats such as cleared fields, strip-mine benches, and roadsides where plenty of sunlight is available.

The largest and most common vines of Appalachia belong to the grape family (Vitaceae) and produce fruits such as fox, possum, fall, and frost grapes, muscadines, and scuppernongs. All forms of grapes are prized as a food source by wildlife and by humans, who use them to make jelly, juice, and wine. Also in this family is the five-leafed Virginia creeper *(Parthenocissus quinquefolia)*, which is conspicuous in fall because of its bright red foliage and blue berries that are attractive to wildlife. Dutchman's pipe *(Aristolochia durior)* is another large vine that inhabits rich coves. This vine is also called smoke vine by many Appalachians, who use it in basketry and other crafts. The leaves provide food for the caterpillar of the pipevine swallowtail butterfly *(Battus philenor)*.

Poison ivy *(Rhus radicans)* can be identified by its "hairy" vine and characteristic three leaflets. The plant can cause severe dermatitis in sensitive individuals, blistering the skin. The greenbriers, or catbriers (several species in the genus *Smilax*), are thorny climbing vines. The widespread white-flowered honeysuckle *(Lonicera japonica)* and kudzu *(Pueraria montana)* vines are often troublesome and sometimes dominant introduced exotic species from Asia. Kudzu was purposely introduced and planted by state highway departments to control erosion on steep banks in road cuts, but it grows over surrounding vegetation and into trees so rapidly, sometimes killing the trees that support it, that it is considered a pest species.

See also: EXOTIC SPECIES; FOREST FRAGMENTATION; TREES.

—Douglas Elliott, *Union Mills, North Carolina*

Watersheds

A watershed is a geographic region bounded by ridgelines (or other physical divides) that drains water to a particular stream or body of water, thereby segregating the landscape into stream systems. Appalachian watersheds ultimately send their waters to the Atlantic Ocean or the Gulf of Mexico. In general, watersheds develop because precipitation forces the topography to maintain a balance between erosion and deposition of sediment, providing for stable stream structure and function.

Several structural components of a watershed allow for its proper function. Networks of streams and groundwater drain the watershed. Connections and interactions among the stream channel, floodplain, and groundwater dictate stream flow, sediment transport, and sediment deposition. A stream must be able to transport sediment within the channel and dissipate flood effects within a floodplain. A healthy floodplain not only reduces downstream erosion, but it also helps to maintain cool stream temperatures, stabilize stream banks, and provide cover for animals with its riparian, or streamside, vegetation. A healthy stream also maintains a zone beneath the stream channel called the hyporheos, where stream water and groundwater mix and exchange heat and chemicals.

Important physical, chemical, and biological linkages must be maintained to support a healthy river. Precipitation and temperature induce erosion and deposition of sediment and dictate chemical reactions and nutrient deposition in the water. During seasonal cycles, watersheds undergo many changes—stream channels change course, rocks are eroded, flows fluctuate with intensity and duration, and biological productivity is dispersed spatially and temporally.

Departures from natural conditions can cause watershed instability. Any human activity that affects water quality or quantity of water movement (such as logging, mining, agriculture, or fires) can change the characteristics of the stream at locations downstream. Instability can be induced by stream alterations in the channel and floodplain, causing bank erosion and unbalanced deposition, stream-flow depletion from floodplain wells, surface-water and groundwater contamination, surface development altering runoff, and infiltration characteristics of the hydrologic cycle. Watershed instability can inhibit critical physical, biological, and chemical relationships. Watershed assessments can help to identify unstable reaches and prioritize sites for remediation.

See also: SECTION OVERVIEW (GEOLOGY); STREAMS.

—Ryan Gaujot, *Canaan Valley Institute*

Elizabeth and M. Grant Gross, *Oceanography: A View of the Earth* (7th edition, 1996); Graham R. Thompson and Jonathan Turk, *Essentials of Modern Geology: An Environmental Approach* (1994).

Wetlands

Perhaps the most famous Appalachian wetlands are its cranberry *(Vaccinium)* bogs. Containing northern plant species that were pushed south when glaciers covered the Northern Hemisphere, these island ecosystems are acidic wetlands characterized by spongy layers of peat and inhabited by carnivorous plants and species in the heath family (Ericacea), including cranberries. Some animals are restricted to these unique habitats. An example is the bog copper butterfly *(Epidemia epizanthe)*, found only in acid bogs with cranberries and other Ericacea plants from Maine to northern West

Virginia. The only host food for its caterpillars are the leaves of shrubby cranberries, and the adults feed on nectar from cranberries and other heaths. The 750-acre bog in the Cranberry Glades Botanical Area in the Cranberry Wilderness of Monongahela National Forest in West Virginia is a well-known Appalachian wetland.

Although once considered wastelands, wetlands have achieved respected ecological and economic status. They provide breeding and feeding habitats for many species of wildlife, create habitats for rare and endangered species, reduce flooding by allowing floodwaters to spread out, reduce sediment runoff, recharge groundwater, and help maintain and improve water quality of rivers, lakes, and groundwater. However, more than half of the wetlands in the lower forty-eight states, including the Appalachian region, have been destroyed or degraded by human activities. Because of their ecological value, rapidly diminishing wetlands have been given special protection under state and federal laws.

To be classified as a wetland, an area must generally meet three principal criteria. It must first have conditions in which shallow standing water or waterlogged soil occurs sometime during the growing season and, secondly, must have hydric soils (soils formed in water) that develop due to saturated or flooded conditions. Thirdly, the area must also support plants adapted to live under the first two conditions. To exist in a wetland, a plant must be able to tolerate low levels of oxygen and nutrients. The presence of water for long periods of time leads to the depletion of soil oxygen and a reduction in the availability of nutrients. As a result, the vegetation of wetlands often appears different from that of surrounding uplands.

Wetlands generally include swamps, marshes, bogs, and seeps. Swamps in the Appalachians are characterized by woody vegetation dominated by such plants as alders *(Alnus)*, red maple *(Acer rubrum)*, and cranberries and other heaths; marshes by herbaceous plants, including cattails *(Typha)*, reeds, grasses, and sedges; and bogs by the presence of mosses, club mosses *(Lycopodium)*, and pitcher plants *(Sarracenia)* and the accumulation of partially decomposed organic matter or peat. Bogs generally develop in the high mountainous areas of the Appalachians; more than 80 percent of the wetlands in West Virginia are above two thousand feet in elevation.

The region's wetlands are considered inland freshwater wetlands, often appearing transitional between aquatic and upland habitats. Unlike many coastal wetlands, they are not influenced by salt water or tides. With few exceptions, wetlands in the Appalachians are smaller than those of low-lying coastal areas and more northern areas where the landscape has been heavily influenced by past glacial activity. The only areas of the Appalachian region to be directly affected by the most recent glaciers of the Pleistocene epoch are New York and the central and northern reaches of Pennsylvania.

Although each state in the Appalachians has protected wetland areas available for public use, the hilly to mountainous topography of the region is not conducive to the formation of large wetlands. Wetlands are generally restricted to level, low-lying areas on the floodplains of streams and rivers, in mountain valleys, and on flat landscapes on mountaintops. They therefore typically develop behind natural streamside levees that restrict the lateral flow of surface water and groundwater and where dense soil layers impede the infiltration of groundwater. Notable bogs can be found at Tannersville Cranberry Bog in Pennsylvania and Canaan Valley in West Virginia, which contains the largest wetland in the Appalachian Mountains. Wetland habitats can also be found in southern portions of the Appalachians, including Reed Branch Wet Meadow in Georgia, Schoolyard Springs in Tennessee, and Coosa Bog Preserve in Alabama.

See also: SEDGES; STREAMS; WATERSHEDS.

—Ronald H. Fortney, *West Virginia University*

Donald Edward Davis, *Where There Are Mountains: An Environmental History of the Southern Appalachians* (2000); Eugene P. Odum, *Ecology* (1963); Scott Weidensaul, *Mountains of the Heart: A Natural History of the Appalachians* (1994).

Wildflowers

Excluding woody plants, grasses, and other species that also flower, more than three hundred species of wildflowers grow in the Appalachian Mountain system, making the region famous for its colorful displays. Wildflowers occur in all habitats and bloom through a season from late February to November. The southern Appalachians contain a mixture of northern flowers in the higher elevations and southern species in the rich soils of the valleys. Many of the northern species took refuge there south of the glaciers during the Pleistocene Ice Age (twenty thousand to ten thousand years ago) and remain in the moist, cool highlands.

Spring wildflowers in moist deciduous woodlands show remarkable adaptation to the seasonal rhythm of the trees. The earliest blooming species open their leaves when the trees are still leafless, taking advantage of light reaching the forest floor. The species with the most remarkable adaptations are the spring ephemerals, plants that are only active for a four- to eight-week period in early spring. Their aboveground stems die back in late spring as the trees leaf out. These species are perennials that live for many years, lying dormant underground from summer until the following

Spring beauties *(Claytonia virginica)*, Virginia, 1982. The Appalachians contain a mixture of southern wildflower species in the rich soils of the valleys and northern flowers in the higher elevations, many of which took refuge there from the glaciers of the last ice age. Spring beauties, along with flowers such as trout lily *(Erythronium americanum)* and Dutchman's breeches *(Dicentra cucullata)*, are spring ephemerals, plants that are only active for a four- to eight-week period in early spring but live for many years, lying dormant underground from summer until the following spring.

spring. Examples include the trout lily *(Erythronium americanum)*, Dutchman's breeches *(Dicentra cucullata)*, squirrel corn *(D. canadensis)*, and spring beauty *(Claytonia caroliniana* and *C. virginica)*.

Other spring woodland wildflowers also take advantage of light in early spring but persist into the shady summer. Many spring wildflowers are in the lily family (Liliaceae), including trillium (*Trillium*, about fifteen species in Appalachia), Solomon's seal (*Polygonatum*, three species), false Solomon's seal (*Smilacina*, two species), Indian cucumber *(Medeola virginica)*, twisted stalk (*Streptopus*, two species), mandarin (*Disporum*, two species), bead lily (*Clintonia*, two species), wild lily of the valley *(Maianthemum canadense)*, devil's bit *(Chamaelirium luteum)*, colicroot *(Aletris farinosa)*, featherbells *(Stenanthium gramineum)*, false hellebore (*Veratrum*, two species), and bellwort (*Uvularia*, four species).

The largest genus of spring wildflowers is *Viola*, the violets, with thirty-one species in Appalachia. Also prominent in spring are hepatica (*Hepatica*, two species), buttercups (*Ranunculus*, fifteen species), toothwort (*Dentaria*, four species), bloodroot *(Sanguinaria canadensis)*, phlox (*Phlox*, ten species), foam flower *(Tiarella cordifolia)*, miterwort *(Mitella diphylla)*, mayapple *(Podophyllum peltatum)*, blue cohosh *(Caulophyllum thalictroides)*, and jack-in-the-pulpit *(Arisaema triphyllum)*.

The Appalachians support more than fifty species of native orchids. Unlike their tropical relatives, which primarily grow on trees, temperate orchids are terrestrial. Among the showy species are the lady's slipper (*Cypripedium*, three species), rein orchid (*Habenaria*, ten species), rose pogonia *(Pogonia ophioglossoides)*, grass-pink *(Calopogon pulchellus)*, lady's tresses (*Spiranthes*, five species), showy orchis *(Orchis spectabilis)*, and rattlesnake plantain (*Goodyera*, two species). Two orchids have distinctive lifestyles: the cranefly *(Tipularia discolor)* and adam-and-eve *(Aplectrum hyemale)* orchids put out their leaves in the fall and lose them in the spring, thus taking advantage of the winter sunlight in the leafless forest. Both flower in midsummer in a leafless condition.

Late spring and summer wildflowers include Bowman's root *(Gillenia trifoliata)*, bugbane (*Cimicifuga*, two species), goat's beard *(Aruncus dioicus)*, beebalm (*Monarda*, four species), butterfly weed *(Asclepias tuberosa)*, jewelweed (*Impatiens*, two species), lily (*Lilium*, six species), harebell *(Campanula divcaricata)*, and Joe-Pye-weed (*Eupatorium*, four species). The sunflowers, part of the Compositae family, are especially prominent in fall, and include aster (*Aster*, forty species), goldenrod (*Solidago*, thirty species), rattlesnake root (*Prenanthes*, five species), black-eyed Susan (*Rudbeckia*, ten species), and sunflower (*Helianthus*, ten species).

See also: BIODIVERSITY; FOLK MEDICINE (FOLKLORE AND FOLKLIFE); MEDICINAL PLANT USE (HEALTH).

—Peter S. White, *University of North Carolina*

Carlos C. Campbell, William Hutson, and Aaron J. Sharp, *Great Smoky Mountains Wildflowers: When and Where to Find Them* (1977); Roger Tory Peterson and Margaret McKenny, *A Field Guide to Wildflowers of Northeastern and North-Central North America* (1968); Harold William Rickett, *Wild Flowers of the United States, Vol. 2: The Southeastern States* (1967).

Winter Adaptations

Cold temperatures, the risk of freezing, and the scarcity of food all make winter a stressful time for animals in Appalachia. Although many birds migrate to warmer climates, other animals employ behavioral and physiological adaptations to survive.

Many warm-blooded (endothermic) animals can remain active during the winter, but small birds and mammals lose body heat too rapidly to do this for extended periods. Critical for winter survival are continuing access to adequate foods, large reserves of body fat that provide both fuel reserve and insulation, and extra insulation from thick undercoats of fur or down. Body design for cold climates also favors a more compact shape and shorter limbs, digits, ears, tails, and noses. Countercurrent heat exchangers minimize heat loss from extremities; arteries entering and veins leaving a limb branch into a fine network of capillaries, where heat shifts from warm arterial blood to cool venous blood. This reduces heat lost from limbs.

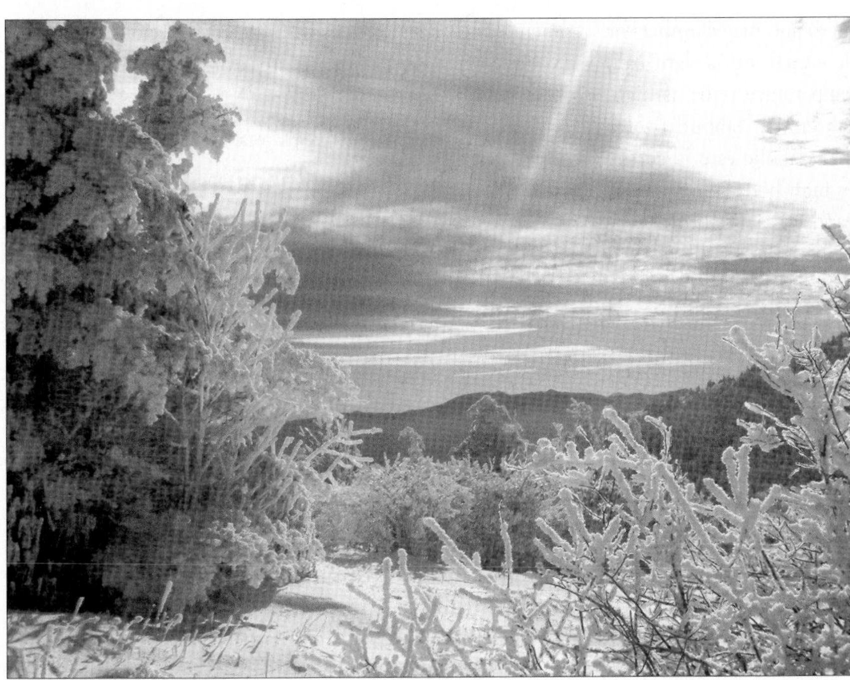

Winter in Roan Mountain State Park, Tennessee, 2003. Cold temperatures, the risk of freezing, and the scarcity of food all make winter a stressful time for animals in Appalachia. Although many birds migrate to warmer climates, other animals must adapt behaviorally and physiologically to survive.

Since the costs of maintaining a constant high body temperature all winter are too great, some birds and mammals have evolved energy-saving strategies. Some Appalachian species save energy by sinking into torpor while sleeping, allowing body temperature to drop by several degrees. For example, nightly torpor in chickadees *(Parus)* saves about 20 percent of the energy that would otherwise be needed to keep body temperature constant.

Some Appalachian mammals save even more energy by hibernating. By the classic definition, which requires a dramatic drop in body temperature, the only true hibernators in Appalachia are groundhogs *(Marmota monax)*, bats, and two species of jumping mice. Other animals that may enter an extended dormancy period during cold weather, but which are not true hibernators, include black bears *(Ursus ameicanus)*, chipmunks *(Tamias)*, reptiles, and amphibians. Raccoons *(Procyon lotor)* and opossums *(Didelphis virginiana)* also enter brief periods of torpor, but usually for no more than a few days at a time.

During true hibernation, metabolic rate may be reduced to less than 5 percent of normal, and body temperature falls almost to the surrounding environmental temperature. At intervals of one to three weeks, the bodies of hibernating animals re-warm, and they awaken for several hours. Stored brown fat is burned at high rates to generate the heat needed for reactivation. While awake, some animals eat from caches of food in their burrows, but most do not, so the reasons for periodic arousal remain unknown. Northern populations typically hibernate for longer than their southern counterparts, which may hibernate only briefly or not at all.

The groundhog, or woodchuck, is a true hibernator. During hibernation, its heart rate drops from one hundred to three or four beats per minute, respiration to one breath every five or six minutes, and body temperature from ninety-seven to about forty degrees Fahrenheit.

The woodland jumping mouse *(Napaeozapus insignis)* and meadow jumping mouse *(Zapus hudsonius)* are also hibernators, remaining dormant up to eight months per year. During this time, they exhibit extremely low body temperature and heart rate.

There are at least fourteen species of bats in Appalachia, and all are capable of hibernation, although some southern species prefer to migrate to overwintering grounds. During hibernation, body temperature matches ambient cave temperature, heart rate slows nearly a hundredfold, and breathing drops to approximately once every four minutes.

Eastern chipmunks *(Tamias striatus)* are not considered true hibernators because they become torpid inconsistently and briefly (rarely more than several days at a time). However, during dormant periods, respiration rates drop by 60 percent and body temperature drops to forty-five degrees Fahrenheit. Chipmunks do not develop a layer of brown fat and must wake frequently to eat and defecate.

Appalachian black bears enter wintering dens in burrows, rock crevices, caves, or hollowed-out trees (sometimes thirty or more feet above the ground) and may slumber for as long as one hundred days while curled into a tight ball. During this period, their body temperature remains high, around eighty-eight degrees Fahrenheit (about twelve degrees below normal), and their metabolic rate is cut by one-half. Because of the relatively high body temperature, sleeping bears can awaken quickly and are said to be in "winter lethargy" rather than in true hibernation. The denned bear does not eat, drink, urinate, defecate, or exercise. Pregnant females give birth to one to four cubs in January or February but remain denned all winter. Males and nonpregnant females may leave their winter dens and wander about from time to time.

For cold-blooded animals, winter is typically a time of inactivity. Many species spend the winter in simple early life stages (eggs, cysts) until temperatures rise in the spring. As the risk of body fluids' freezing is high, many Appalachian animals avoid exposure to freezing temperatures by hibernating underground or underwater. Toads *(Bufo)* dig down below the frost line; garter snakes may gather together by the hundreds in underground dens; and many insects such as dragonflies spend the winter as aquatic nymphs. Bullfrogs *(Rana catesbeiana)* and some other species spend winter on the bottom of ponds, breathing not with lungs but by exchanging gasses across their skin. Turtles also winter underwater; some can take up oxygen across the skin of their throat or cloaca (the body opening through which excretory and reproductive products exit the body), while others suppress their metabolic rate and live without oxygen for months at a time.

Other animals stay active but become resistant to cold temperatures in winter. Many insects, spiders, and other small creatures that winter in leaf litter or under the bark of trees add powerful antifreezes to their body fluids, which keep them liquid in temperatures as low as minus forty degrees Fahrenheit. These antifreezes are of two types: protein antifreezes bind to microscopic ice crystals to keep them from growing, and sugar-alcohol antifreezes (most commonly glycerol) lower the freezing point of body fluids as ethylene glycol does in an automobile radiator. Other kinds of insects, as well as a few species of woodland frogs, have developed the spectacular ability to freeze solid and survive. Wood frogs *(R. sylvatica)* can live for weeks with 65 percent of their body water frozen, with no breathing, heartbeat, or muscle movement. Yet within minutes of thawing, all their vital signs resume. Other adaptations for freezing survival include nucleating proteins that guide ice formation within the body, a tolerance for oxygen deprivation while frozen, and high concentrations of sugars or sugar alcohols inside cells that keep the cytoplasm in a liquid state. These sugars also stabilize large molecules and membranes, keeping cells from shrinking below a minimum volume when most of their water exits to join the ice masses that surround organs.

See also: MAMMALS; MIGRATIONS; SEASONAL RHYTHMS.

—Angela K Palau, *Oak Ridge, Tennessee*, and Kenneth B. Storey, *Carleton University*

James C. Halfpenny and Roy D. Ozanne, *Winter: An Ecological Handbook* (1989); Peter J. Marchand, *Life in the Cold: An Introduction to Winter Ecology* (2nd edition, 1991); Kenneth B. and Janet M. Storey, "Lifestyles of the Cold and Frozen," *The Sciences* (May–June 1999).

Zoonoses

Zoonoses are diseases of animals that can be transmitted to humans. There are many zoonoses in Appalachia, although none is unique to the region. Relatively familiar diseases of Appalachian people and wild animals include giardiasis, Rocky Mountain spotted fever, Lyme disease, rabies, hantavirus, histoplasmosis, and West Nile virus.

Giardiasis is a diarrheal infection caused by the protozoan *Giardia lamblia*. It is transmitted by ingesting fecal-contaminated material. Waterfowl and aquatic species of mammals are most frequently infected. During the past two decades, *Giardia* has become recognized as one of the most common causes of waterborne disease in humans in the United States. It affects many water sources and is a common concern of hikers.

Rocky Mountain spotted fever and Lyme disease are bacterial tick-borne diseases. Most cases occur in the summer when people are outdoors and more likely to encounter ticks. Rocky Mountain spotted fever is caused by *Rickettsia rickettsii*, which is hosted by rabbits, rodents, and canines and is transmitted by hard ticks (dog ticks). If untreated, the disease has 13 to 30 percent fatality in humans. It is most prevalent in the eastern United States, with the highest number of reported cases in North Carolina. Despite its greater health risk, Rocky Mountain spotted fever is generally overshadowed by the more publicized Lyme disease. Lyme disease is caused by *Borrelia burgdorferi* and is found in host deer, mice, and raccoons. Deer ticks (*Ixodes* spp.) act as the vector.

Rabies is a viral disease and can be contracted through the bite of any infected animal. Although raccoons, skunks, and bats are primary reservoirs of the virus, most human cases are caused by bats. Some animals, such as raccoons, are carriers and show no disease when infected. Symptoms of infection include excitability, paralysis, and death.

Hantavirus is a pulmonary infection caused by inhalation of feces or saliva from wild rats or mice. This uncommon disease has been contracted by hikers sleeping in wilderness shelters inhabited by infected rodents. If untreated, it can be fatal.

Histoplasmosis is a pulmonary infection caused by inhalation of the fungus *Histoplasma capsulatum,* which grows abundantly in soil and material contaminated with bat or bird droppings (particularly in roost areas). Most exposed people have only minor symptoms; however, the acute form of the disease, which resembles tuberculosis, can be fatal.

West Nile virus, a sometimes fatal encephalitis first detected in the United States in 1999, has been widely publicized in the media. The virus affects birds, particularly members of the Corvidae family (crows, blue jays, and ravens), and a variety of mammals, including humans.

See also: MAMMALS; PARASITES, FAUNAL; SECTION OVERVIEW (HEALTH).

—Angela K Palau, *Oak Ridge, Tennessee*

Guy Hodge, ed., *Pocket Guide to the Humane Control of Wildlife in Cities and Towns* (1990).

Environment

Section Editors: Donald E. Davis and Kevin E. O'Donnell

THE PHOTOGRAPH ON THE OPPOSITE PAGE FREEZES A MOMENT IN APPALACHIA'S environmental history. The scene is in West Virginia, around 1920. On a mountain slope beneath a rhododendron slick, a steam-powered loader dangles a section of poplar trunk over a rail car already loaded with logs, one of which appears perhaps six feet in diameter. Beneath the car, improvised crossties support steel rails over a makeshift bed consisting of a jumble of sticks and organic matter for the hastily constructed narrow-gauge railroad. The loggers in the picture affect nonchalant poses belying the dangerous and backbreaking nature of their work.

Though the image is both riveting and revealing, it gives no hint that the gaunt men on the West Virginia mountainside are participants in an environmental tragedy. By the time this photograph was taken, thousands of logging crews such as this one had leveled most of the virgin hardwood forest that covered the central and southern Appalachian highlands when European settlers arrived. The destruction was carried out with remarkable speed, most of it occurring between the time when railroads began penetrating the backcountry and the time the photograph was taken. During these years, the biggest, most diversified forest in eastern North America was sacrificed to the nation's voracious appetite for fuel, shelter, and building materials for infrastructure and innumerable necessities, public and private. Wood fueled trains, sawmills, steamboats, stoves, and fireplaces. It supported railroad tracks and formed ships, farm wagons, corncribs, water buckets, and milking stools. It was used for roadways, sidewalks, bridges, and fences. It sustained tanneries that made leather for plow harnesses, saddles, and boots. And it held up the roofs of countless coal mines. As flashing axes and crosscut saws felled ancient oaks, yellow poplars, chestnuts, walnuts, and hickories, new technologies sped the clearing process. Overhead cables snaked massive logs off of previously inaccessible ridges toward steam-powered loaders, which delivered them to waiting trains with strings of flatcars. At mills, new band saws reduced tree trunks to lumber with breathtaking dispatch. Axe and steam, it was said, conquered the Appalachian frontier.

By the late nineteenth century, coal was rapidly replacing wood as fuel, but the logging of Appalachia nonetheless accelerated, and sawmills proliferated to meet the demand for lumber required to house America's booming population. In West Virginia, half of the old-growth forest that still covered more than 10 million acres at

Facing page: Loading yellow poplar logs, West Virginia, c. 1910. Millions of acres of forestland throughout Appalachia have contributed to both the beauty and the livelihood of the region, giving rise to contentious issues regarding resource management and conservation.

the end of the Civil War was gone by 1900. By 1910, 80 percent of it had been cut. The story was much the same throughout the southern and central Appalachians. On Mount Mitchell in North Carolina and Mount Rogers in Virginia, loggers continued to advance up the slopes after they had felled the last hardwoods. At the highest elevations, they leveled great stands of spruce. In scarcely more than a generation, millions of acres, as much as 90 percent of the mature forests in the southeastern United States, had been replaced by expanses of brush, weeds, scrub, and dead treetops susceptible to raging fires set by lightning and vulnerable to winter and spring rains that cut deep gullies, leeched nutrients from the old forest floor, and exposed naked rock to bake in the sun. Mount Mitchell, the tallest mountain in the eastern United States, was swept by wildfires even before the clearing was finished.

With the industrial clearing of its forests, rural Appalachia became what the historian C. Vann Woodward would later call a "colonial economy," its natural and human resources exploited by outside capital, its wealth expropriated by distant corporations and industrial combinations. Growing numbers of conservationists and mountain people watched the destruction with horror, as did some industrialists, but the clearing proceeded apace. In 1910 an article in the *Manufacturers' Record*, a newspaper for industrialists, reported that lumber companies gave "no thought . . . to the effect which the cutting of timber may have on the mountain regions."

As the timber boom and forest clearing waned, the market for Appalachia's coal surged. Across the region many of the same land and lumber companies that had denuded the mountains reaped new profits from mineral rights they had acquired from mountaineers for a pittance. Compared to timber, Appalachia's coal deposits seemed to be nearly inexhaustible, and on the surface the effects of mining appeared less catastrophic than the razing of the forests. Indeed, for decades the environmental impact of the coal industry was overshadowed by the social conditions it created.

Coal came to prominence in the 1820s and 1830s as huge mines in the rich anthracite fields of northeastern Pennsylvania shipped shiny hard coal to markets in Philadelphia and New York. By mid-century, bituminous coal from the vast Pittsburgh seam was being heavily mined in western Pennsylvania, and the industry was spreading across the Allegheny Plateau and southward. Appalachian coal mines fueled the American Industrial Revolution and made Pittsburgh its capital. During the 1890s, production from mines in the region tripled. Between 1890 and 1910, southern West Virginia saw its population soar by 400 percent as mountain hollows became sites of thriving company towns and coal camps, often inhabited by newly arrived immigrants. The story in eastern Kentucky, western Maryland, southwestern Virginia, and east Tennessee was similar. By 1930, the Appalachian region accounted for 80 percent of the nation's output of coal.

These extraordinary times exacted a huge environmental toll. Even though trees again grew where the virgin timber had been removed, a number of plant and animal species were nearly wiped out, and the forest was permanently fragmented. Silt and mud from naked slopes, acid runoff from mines and coal-waste piles, and human waste from coal and timber camps poured into streams, disrupting fish and plant populations. Small farms, previously supported and protected by surrounding forests, declined under the effects of erosion and periodic flooding. In both conspicuous and insidious ways, the machine age changed the natural environment across large swaths of the Appalachians more than it had it had been altered in the more than ten thousand years of previous human occupation.

More important, the timber boom and the dramatic growth of the Appalachian coal industry established social and economic patterns that would persist for decades.

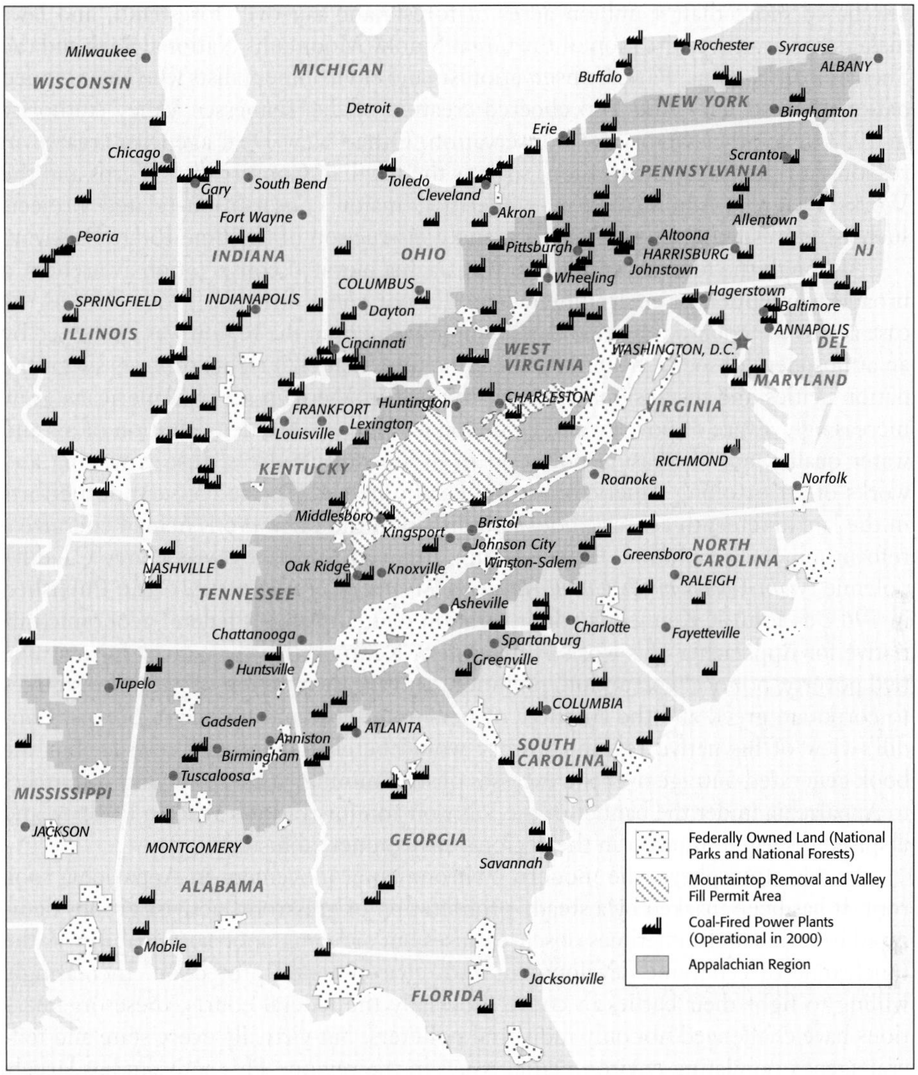

Map showing the location of coal-fired power plants, areas permitting mountaintop removal, and federally owned land, 2003.

In good times and bad, succeeding generations continued to witness the arrival of increasingly efficient technologies, continued export of the region's wealth, industry domination of local politics and community life—and the deterioration of environmental quality.

But the excesses during the years of the Industrial Revolution also stirred concern for the future of the region's natural resources, and from that concern eventually came far-reaching conservation initiatives. In the 1880s, conservationists began advocating the establishment of forest reserves in the southern Appalachians, but the idea gained little traction until the continuing destruction caused by industrial logging provoked growing revulsion. By then, even the lumber lobby came to support the idea, and in 1911, after a campaign led by the American Forestry Association, Congress passed the Weeks Act authorizing the federal government to create national forests. By 1930, the U.S. Department of Agriculture Forest Service had purchased more than 4 million acres of forests and cut-over forestland, and lawmakers had approved creation of the Great Smoky Mountains National Park and the Shenandoah National Park. Conservationists and environmentalists who championed national forests and parks also cheered creation of the Tennessee Valley Authority in 1933 as another victory for conservation. Other New Deal agencies created in response to the Great Depression, such as the Civilian Conservation Corps and the Works Progress Administration, undertook major conservation-related projects such as reforestation, erosion control, and construction of the Blue Ridge Parkway.

Although the federal presence in Appalachia elevated conservation awareness, a broader perception of environmentalism did not come until the 1960s. As was the case across the country, the environmental movement in the region was energized by an atmosphere of social protest. At the same time that civil rights protests swept the nation's cities and disillusionment over the war in Vietnam set in, Americans grew increasingly aware of poverty amidst national affluence, the deterioration of air and water quality, and increasing pollution from a host of sources. Just as writing and works of art extolling America's natural beauty helped inspire conservation efforts in the late nineteenth century, books published in the early 1960s helped energize a reform-minded generation. Especially important to Appalachia was Harry Caudill's polemic *Night Comes to the Cumberlands: A Biography of a Depressed Area.* Published in 1963, as John F. Kennedy's administration contemplated a federal economic initiative for Appalachia, this work by an eastern Kentucky lawyer-activist inextricably tied poverty, political corruption, pollution, and the destruction of natural resources to corporate greed and the absentee ownership of coal and timber resources. Caudill's view of his native region's history would be challenged and revised, but the book generated outrage over the excesses of strip mining, attracted young volunteers to Appalachia under the banner of the Johnson administration's War on Poverty, and inspired resurgent interest in the region's environmental history.

In this atmosphere, the modern environmental movement in Appalachia took root. It has been marked by a steady proliferation of grassroots activist groups dedicated to varied and sometimes obscure causes but agreeing upon sustainability as the touchstone of economic development and environmental protection. Increasingly willing to fight their battles in court, especially the federal courts, these organizations have challenged not only industrial polluters, but virtually every state and federal agency regulating environmental issues in the region. This activism has largely obliterated the perception of Appalachian people as passive victims. As Caudill himself recorded, there were instances of extraordinary commitment and courage by mountain people in the face of corporate hegemony. The coal industry was perhaps most famously challenged in 1965, when Ollie Combs, a sixty-one-year-old widow, sat down in front of a coal company bulldozer near Hindman, Kentucky, in a dramatic attempt to pressure the governor and the legislature to enact laws regulating strip mining.

Inspired by lonely figures such as "Widow" Combs, activist groups have become state and regional fixtures with continuing influence. Kentuckians for the Commonwealth, for instance, led a successful 1980s campaign to get rid of the state's notorious broad form deed, which had permitted strip miners to destroy landowners' property at will in order to reach coal beneath the ground. In Tennessee, Save Our Cumberland Mountains grew from an organization opposed to strip mining to one with a broad agenda that includes environmental justice, forest protection, and oversight of toxic-waste disposal. In North Carolina, the Western North Carolina Alliance, founded to oppose oil and gas drilling in national forests, expanded to carry on a long-running struggle against clear-cutting forests. In West Virginia, the Ohio Valley Environmental Coalition, the West Virginia Highlands Conservancy, and Coal River Mountain Watch went to court and into the streets in efforts to stop mountaintop-removal projects. For her inspirational leadership of the latter, Julia Bonds, a native of the Coal River Valley, was awarded the $125,000 Goldman Prize, often called the "environmental Nobel Prize," in 2003.

In large measure due to federal laws, often including provisions mandating public participation in environmental decisions, Appalachia's natural environment fared better in the late twentieth century than it did in the late nineteenth. Cities such as Chattanooga, Tennessee, and Pittsburgh, for decades shrouded in chronic smog, again enjoyed relatively clean air. Fatalities in the coal mines, accepted as inevitable in the old days, have become relatively rare. Reclamation of strip mines, long ignored, has come to be taken seriously. On the other hand, residents in hollows and communities in valleys surrounded by heavily logged and strip-mined mountains continue to be devastated by flooding. Regional air quality suffers from pollution wafting from giant coal-burning power plants, not only within the region but far to the west. In the Great Smoky Mountains and Shenandoah National Parks, ozone levels often exceed those of cities such as Atlanta. In the upper elevations of the parks and elsewhere in the Blue Ridge, acid rain and ozone pollution have reduced stands of majestic spruce and fir to grotesque skeletons.

Lawmen removing Ollie Combs from her land, Honey Gap, Knott County, Kentucky, 1965. In an action that galvanized opposition to strip mining in Kentucky, "Widow" Combs was jailed for attempting to block bulldozers from stripping her land.

The War on Poverty and decades of work by the Appalachian Regional Commission and other federal agencies notwithstanding, much of the region continues to be economically distressed, and conflicts between representatives of environmental groups and extractive industries remain seemingly intractable. A century after industrial logging ravaged the slopes of the Appalachians, environmentalists and organizations such as Save Our Cumberland Mountains and the Asheville, North Carolina–based Dogwood Alliance fight against construction of mills that grind logs into chips used to make paper, particleboard, and other products. Forest watchdog groups warn that, just as the completion of forest clearing in Minnesota and Wisconsin preceded the timber industry's move into the central Appalachians in the late nineteenth century, so late-twentieth-century clearing of the Pacific Northwest portends a major relocation into Appalachia and the Southeast in the twenty-first. Between 1985 and 2003, one hundred new mills had already been constructed in the southeastern United States.

But the most controversial modern incarnation of an old regional issue was the late-twentieth-century spread of mountaintop removal, taking the mechanization of coal mining to a level unimagined when strip mining became controversial in the mid-twentieth century. Even though such mechanization drove coal industry employment down to a fraction of its level a century earlier, the range of environmental problems caused by waste products from mining operations remained as daunting as ever. Lawsuits brought by environmentalists in West Virginia and Kentucky twice led the U.S. District Court of Southern West Virginia to issue rulings that would have limited the environmental impact of mountaintop-removal projects. In both instances, the rulings were overturned on appeal. Meanwhile, the administration of George W. Bush moved to make regulatory changes to clear the way for mountaintop mining to continue. In early 2003 a formal environmental impact statement prepared by the federal Office of Surface Mining, Environmental Protection Agency, U.S. Army Corps of Engineers, and Fish and Wildlife Service in collaboration with the West Virginia Department of Environmental Protection outlined some of the specific consequences of the technology. Across a 12-million-acre area encompassing much of eastern Kentucky and southern West Virginia, plus parts of southwestern Virginia and east Tennessee, the study found that 724 miles of streams had been buried and another 500 miles affected by valley fills created when overburden removed to expose coal seams was pushed off mining sites into valleys. By the agencies' estimate, some 816,000 acres stand to be affected by mountaintop-removal projects.

More than most other areas of the country, Appalachia remains wedded to the industrial age that it so conspicuously helped to create, but the region has not been left out of the national transition to a service economy. By 1990 combined wholesale, retail, manufacturing, and service sector businesses accounted for more than two-thirds of the employment in the southern part of the region. With diversification has come increasing opportunity for highly skilled employees, for whom there was little place in the heyday of logging and underground mining.

As always in Appalachia, the tide of change is heavily influenced by the landscape itself. Though scarred in the coalfields and clear-cut timber tracts and polluted by power plants in faraway flatlands, the region's resilient natural beauty remains intact across large portions of vast stretches of the Appalachians, providing the foundation of a promising future for tourism.

The restive young Americans who helped environmentalism to rise in Appalachia during the 1960s and 1970s were also harbingers of a back-to-nature sentiment among urbanites. Within a day's drive of most population centers east of the Mississippi, Appalachian locales have become destinations for weekend visitors and second-home owners as well as vacationers. Of all the sectors of the "new economy," tourism has become the most robust. Tourism and recreation in 1990 provided more than $6 billion in revenue and more than one hundred thousand jobs in the region. Inevitably, this economic impact has caused the business establishment to consider environmental protection in a favorable new light.

But better than statistics, the landscape itself reveals the shift toward a new economy. In the Great Smoky Mountains National Park, visitors can still see the old skid roads used snake logs out of the virgin forest more than a century ago. And throughout central and southern Appalachia, many hiking trails, including much of the Appalachian Trail, follow the routes of old logging railroads. The same temporary railroad beds that once carried old-growth tree trunks now transport hikers and outdoors enthusiasts into recovering forests.

—Donald E. Davis, *Dalton State College*, and Kevin E. O'Donnell, *East Tennessee State University*

Harvard Ayers et al., eds., *An Appalachian Tragedy: Air Pollution and Tree Death in the Eastern Forests of North America* (1998); Harry M. Caudill, *Night Comes to the Cumberlands: A Biography of a Depressed Area* (1963); Suzanne Crowell, *Appalachian People's History Book* (1971); Donald Edward Davis, *Where There Are Mountains: An Environmental History of the Southern Appalachians* (2000); Ronald D Eller, *Miners, Millhands, and Mountaineers: Industrialization of the Appalachian South, 1880–1930* (1982); Stephen L. Fisher, ed., *Fighting Back in Appalachia: Traditions of Resistance and Change* (1993); Michael Frome, *Strangers in High Places: The Story of the Great Smoky Mountains* (1980); Timothy Silver, *Mount Mitchell and the Black Mountains: An Environmental History of the Highest Peaks in Eastern America* (2003); U.S. Department of Agriculture, *Message from the President of the United States Transmitting a Report of the Secretary of Agriculture in Relation to the Forests, Rivers, and Mountains of the Southern Appalachian Region*, Senate Document No. 84 (1902); Susan L. Yarnell, *The Southern Appalachians: A History of the Landscape* (1998).

Air Quality

Two of the best-known and most celebrated areas in all of Appalachia possess names derived from the blue, sometimes smoky haze that has hung naturally over the region's mountains for millennia. By the end of the twentieth century, however, the blue of the Blue Ridge and the smoke of the Great Smoky Mountains had been replaced by clouds of air pollution obstructing views of entire mountains, sometimes reducing visibility to less than a mile.

By most measures, the Appalachian Mountains are at the center of one of the most air-polluted regions in the country. National studies have found that the three most polluted national parks and the top ten cities in death rates from power-plant pollution are all located in the Appalachian region. According to the American Lung Association, three of Tennessee's major cities—Knoxville, Chattanooga, and Nashville—rank in the top twenty-five in the United States in ozone pollution, the major by-product of smog, which also produces excessive coughing, shortness of breath, and increased susceptibility to respiratory infections. Counties in western Pennsylvania also perennially score high in ozone pollution, having levels in the unhealthy range for several weeks each year. A 2001 study found that the Great Smoky Mountains National Park had higher cumulative levels of ozone exposure than did the city of Los Angeles for a five-year period. Park visitors are often surprised to learn that urban centers such as Atlanta, Knoxville, and Pittsburgh (among the most ozone-ridden cities in the eastern U.S.) had less than half the total ozone exposure of the Smokies during the same period.

Visibility impairment is only one of numerous negative consequences of widespread air pollution in Appalachia. Sulfur dioxides, nitrogen oxides, mercury, and carbon dioxide are the main chemicals in the air pollution blanketing much of the mountain region. Sulfur dioxides, particularly in the form of sulfuric acid, damage vegetation, streams, and lakes and are the source of small particles that contribute to illness and death when inhaled. Nitrogen oxides, especially in the form of nitric acid, harm vegetation and water bodies, and mercury particulates cause damage to human neurological systems, especially those of younger children, who are more susceptible to the dangerous toxin. Carbon dioxide emissions contribute to global climate change, and ground-level ozone not only harms native vegetation, but also poses hazards to human health. Near the Appalachian Trail in Palmerton, Pennsylvania, a zinc factory has for decades filled the air with lead, cadmium, and zinc emissions, destroying more than two thousand acres of forests atop Blue Mountain and causing numerous cases of illness and fatigue in the nearby community.

But fossil fuels—coal, oil, and natural gas, in that order—produce most of the Appalachian region's air pollution, primarily from smokestacks and motor vehicles. Coal-fired industrial plants, mainly electric utility facilities, are the dominant source. While the nearest coal-fired plants are the main sources for pollution in any given location, plants as far as 500 miles away also contribute to declines in regional air quality. Several coal-fired plants within 150 miles of the Great Smoky Mountains National Park contribute the bulk of its sulfur dioxide and nitrogen oxide pollution, but more distant plants contribute the remainder.

The main reason for the mobility of pollutants from smokestacks is that—due to regulations developed in the 1960s and 1970s—many power-plant stacks are required to be hundreds of feet tall, thus releasing their chemicals high into the air, where strong wind currents take most of the pollutants eastward. Major point sources of sulfur dioxide emissions are located in the Ohio Valley and the Allegheny Plateau sections of West Virginia and western Pennsylvania. Other smokestacks are located in northwest Alabama, northwest Georgia, and east Tennessee. The Appalachian Mountains are downwind from these utility plants and thus bear the brunt of the pollutants' effects.

Many of the coal-fired plants in and around the region have been allowed to pollute at much higher rates than plants with modern pollution controls because these plants were built before 1977, when the Clean Air Act was passed by Congress. At that time, it was assumed that older and dirtier plants would be phased out over several decades and replaced by newer and much cleaner facilities. Thus these "grandfathered" plants were given a regulatory break. But many were never phased out as originally planned. Cheaper to operate without modern pollution gear, numerous plants have illegally upgraded their productive capacity and consequently produce even more pollution than before. Proposed federal rule changes would allow the grandfathered plants to continue polluting at high levels, even if they are further expanded.

After coal-fired plants, automobiles, trucks, and off-road vehicles such as tractors and recreational vehicles are the other major air-quality culprits in the region. On-road vehicles alone produce as much as 32 percent of the nitrogen oxides and 27 percent of the volatile organic compounds released annually into the air. With the number of vehicle miles anticipated to increase in the region, nitrogen oxide emissions from automobile exhaust will continue to have a detrimental impact on Appalachia's air quality.

While difficult to measure precisely, the broader social consequences of acid rain, ozone pollution, volatile organic compounds, mercury, and gases contributing to global climate change can be estimated. Studies on the economic effects of air pollution in the Appalachian region have found measurable impacts on everything from tourism and agriculture to forest and human health.

Evidence for the detrimental effects of air pollution on human health in the region can be found in the report *Death, Disease and Dirty Power*, drafted in 2000 by Abt Associates, a private consultant to the U.S. Environmental Protection Agency. This report was the first to compare death rates from utility-plant pollution in Appalachia to those elsewhere in the United States. Its authors found that the ten cities in the United States with the highest rates of power-plant mortality were all in Appalachia and that premature mortality was due to the numerous small particles penetrating human lungs and causing a variety of heart- and lung-related diseases.

Among the most obvious environmental consequences of poor air quality in the region is excessive tree mortality, which some estimate to be three times the normal rate for central and southern Appalachia. Acid rain and ozone pollution are major stressors of trees, especially at higher elevations, where pollutants concentrate in clouds. These pollutants cause unprecedented rates of tree mortality and will continue to have a major negative influence on Appalachian forests, particularly on the ability of trees to reproduce at normal, ecologically sustainable rates.

More research documenting the precise relationship between air pollution and forest decline is needed, but reduction of industrial emissions is considered to be the most promising course of action for both Appalachia's forests and the human population of the region. A legal settlement between the Environmental Protection Agency and the Virginia Electric Power Company in April 2003 was an important first step toward achieving cleaner air in the Appalachians. In what was one of the largest Clean Air Act enforcement settlements in history, the power company agreed to spend $1.2 billion over a decade in order to eliminate 237,000 tons of sulfur dioxide and nitrogen oxide emissions annually from eight coal-fired generating plants in Virginia and West Virginia.

See also: COAL MINING; ENVIRONMENTAL JUSTICE; FOREST MANAGEMENT AND CONSERVATION.

—Harvard Ayers, *Appalachian State University*

Harvard Ayers et al., eds., *An Appalachian Tragedy: Air Pollution and Tree Death in the Eastern Forests of North America* (1998); Clean Air Task Force, *Death, Disease and Dirty Power: Mortality and Health Damage Due to Air Pollution from Power Plants* (2000); Southern Appalachian Man and the Biosphere Cooperative, *The Southern Appalachian Assessment* (1996).

Buffalo Creek Flood

One of the worst environmental disasters in modern Appalachian history occurred on February 26, 1972, when the Buffalo Creek Dam broke and sent more than 130 million gallons of water and sludge flooding through Logan County, West Virginia. By the end of the day, sixteen coal-mining communities had been destroyed, and at least 125 people were dead. Seven were never found. Of the survivors, 1,100 were injured, and 4,000 were left homeless.

Buffalo Creek Dam was built as a result of efforts in the early 1960s to clean up streams in coal-mining communities. Known as coal-waste dams, or impoundments, these constructions were tools for filtering solid waste from streams that flowed from mines into towns. Buffalo Creek Dam was constructed as a succession of three such impoundments. Early on February 26, after several days of rain, the dams began to collapse. At 6:00 a.m., Dam No. 3 (the farthest upstream) began to fail. Within two hours, all three dams had given away, and by 8:05 a.m., the first town was flooded.

Immediately following the disaster, the U.S. Department of the Interior began an investigation. Three separate reports by the Bureau of Mines, the Bureau of Reclamation, and a geological survey team headed by dam experts came to the same conclusion—Dam No. 3 had not been built to hold large quantities of water. Further investigation suggested negligence on the part of Pittston Coal Company, sole stockholder in the Buffalo Mining Company and owner and builder of Buffalo Creek Dam. At the time of the flood, Pittston had the second-lowest safety rating of any American coal company. By 1971, the company's record showed nine fatal accidents, 743 serious injuries, and five thousand federal safety violations, including three violations of the Coal Mine Health and Safety Act of 1969 during construction of the Buffalo Creek Dam. In 1967, more than four years before the disaster, the Department of the Interior had warned officials that the dam was unstable. According to Thomas N. Bethell, then research director of the United Mine Workers of America, Pittston also knew twenty-four hours in advance that the water was rising behind Dam No. 3 and that the forecast predicted no decrease in rainfall. Although the company failed to warn communities downstream, its officials disavowed responsibility for the disaster, stating that "the dam was simply incapable of holding the water God poured into it."

Convinced that Pittston was not going to take responsibility for the flood, the people of Logan County formed the Citizens Commission to Investigate the Buffalo Creek Disaster. A group of about thirty citizens traveled to the stockholders' meeting in Richmond, Virginia, to express anger and request compensation. People who lost their entire homes asked for $15,000, but Pittston reduced the amount to $3,000 to $5,000. Unwilling to accept the offer, nearly six hundred citizens sued Pittston for negligence and demanded restitution for property damages and "psychic impairment."

In 1974, more than two years after the flood, Pittston settled out of court for $13 million, although property damage was estimated at $50 million.

In the months following the disaster, federal, state, and local relief was offered to survivors. The Red Cross and Salvation Army set up shelters and provided food, and work was begun to rebuild railroads, bridges, and remove debris. In addition, new sewage, water, and transportation systems and permanent housing developments were promised. However, few of these plans came to fruition. By 1976, communities were still suffering, and nearly one hundred families were still displaced. Furthermore, rates of mental illness, depression, and domestic violence had grown tremendously.

Though the Buffalo Creek flood sparked environmental awareness and government reform, law enforcement still proved difficult. After the disaster, new regulations were added to the existing Coal Mine Health and Safety Act of 1969. In addition, Congress passed the National Dam Inspection Act of 1972 mandating the inspection of each dam in the United States; by 1977, however, not a single dam had been inspected and there had been several other collapses. In 1973 the West Virginia legislature passed the Dam Control Act to regulate all dams in the state, but adequate funding was never appropriated. The Buffalo Creek disaster did help lead to federal passage of the 1977 Surface Mining Control and Reclamation Act. Twenty years after the Buffalo Creek disaster, the West Virginia Division of Natural Resources estimated that there were still four hundred hazardous dams in the state.

See also: COAL MINING; COAL SLURRY IMPOUNDMENTS.

—Heather Rhea Gilreath, *East Tennessee State University*

Thomas N. Bethell and Davitt McAteer, *The Pittston Mentality: Manslaughter on Buffalo Creek* (1972); Kai T. Erikson, *Everything in Its Path: Destruction of Community in the Buffalo Creek Flood* (1976); Mimi Pickering, *The Buffalo Creek Flood: An Act of Man*, Appalshop videocassette (1975).

Chemical Weapons Disposal

The United States began to research, produce, and store chemical weapons during World War I. Mustard gas was the first and most important chemical weapon until the 1940s, when the development of other chemical agents began. During the 1950s and early 1960s, the production of chemical weapons greatly increased. The chemicals were, and continue to be, stockpiled at eight continental storage depots. In the 1980s, the United States Army planned to incinerate the weapons at all eight locations, including two sites in Appalachia: one in Richmond, Kentucky, and the other near Anniston, Alabama.

The Anniston Army Depot, the site of a now active incinerator, is 3.7 miles west of the city proper, close to the African American West Side. One small African American town, Hobson City, is near the depot. Pockets of poor whites and working-class people, many employed by Anniston Army Depot, also live in Bynum, Eastaboga, and other small communities near the depot. Anniston, founded as an iron and pipe company town, still exhibits many of the characteristics of southern cities born during the Jim Crow years. Clear demarcation lines separate the races in residential areas, social relations, and political participation. Anniston has a population of 24,276, of which 50 percent is African American.

Anniston and the surrounding area first encountered the military in 1917, when Camp McClellan was built north of the town. Anniston Army Depot was established in 1941 as a separate facility for ammunition storage. In 1963 the army began to maintain a store of chemical weapons at the depot. At that time, many citizens were unaware of the lethal weapons stored nearby. Later, it was disclosed that people in the area had been significantly and disproportionately affected by pollution from the depot, as well as from other local industrial sites. Preliminary information from the Toxic Release Inventory National Report conducted by the Department of Defense showed that Anniston Army Depot was second in the nation for toxic releases—548,073 pounds in 1994. However, information about pollution was never widely disseminated.

In 1992 Families Concerned About Nerve Gas Incineration formed in Anniston to advocate the use of safer technologies for destruction of chemical weapons. The group allied with the Chemical Weapons Working Group, and members and others founded Serving Alabama's Future Environment in 1994 as a nonprofit anti-incineration group. Burn Busters, a group of students and other environmentalists, formed in 1995 to perform direct action and street theater and to apply other political pressures to force the army to halt incineration and to adopt alternative technologies. Despite their efforts, the Alabama Department of Environmental Management approved the army's permit on June 19, 1997.

The following year, the Alabama Department of Energy Management denied the opposing groups' appeal, and construction of the incinerator proceeded. Alabama activists continued to push for alternatives for their community. Another grassroots group, Coosa River Basin Initiative of Rome, Georgia—located downwind of the proposed Anniston incinerator—also entered the fight and filed a lawsuit in September 1998 regarding the permit's cancer risk analysis for stack emissions and called for a revocation of the permit. In 2001 the public learned that federal and state emergency management agencies could not present viable evacuation plans, as had been promised over the preceding ten years. Activists, the public, and local and state officials demanded full protection of public health and safety before allowing the incinerator to operate. The groups Families Concerned About Nerve Gas Incineration and Serving Alabama's Future Environment argued that alternative technologies could solve the problem because they would not include stacks that emitted low-level nerve agent, dioxin, PCBs, heavy metals, and hundreds of other toxins. Nonetheless, the incinerator was completed and dedicated in 2001 and began operations August 9, 2003, with the destruction of a single missile containing sarin.

The Bluegrass Army Depot, near the foothills of the Appalachian Mountains in eastern Kentucky, was established as a storage facility during World War II. It began receiving chemical weapons in 1942, providing jobs that were badly needed in a region of chronic unemployment and underemployment. The population of Madison County is approximately 70,000, a large percentage of which lives within a 6.2-mile radius of the depot. Although Madison County as a whole has few non-white residents, Richmond is about 9 percent African American. The poverty rate of the county is nearly 20 percent, significantly higher than the national average and reflective of the historic poverty of Appalachia. Of Richmond's 27,000 residents, 30 percent live near or below poverty level.

In 1986 a grassroots anti-incineration group, Common Ground, formed in Berea, Kentucky, in anticipation of a U.S. Army decision about disposal. In 1988 the army issued its formal decision that on-site incineration at all stockpile locations would be the preferred destruction method. Common Ground then organized the Kentucky Environmental Foundation in 1990 to serve as a nonprofit organization with a full-time staff to work on the issue. A year later, the foundation organized the first citizens' summit on chemical weapons disposal in Richmond. People from all continental U.S. chemical weapons storage sites, as well as from Johnston Atoll (Kalama Island) in the Pacific and from Russia, joined to share concerns about chemical weapons. Out of this meeting, the Chemical Weapons Working Group, an international coalition of citizens living near chemical weapons storage sites, was formed to oppose incineration and to ensure the safe disposal of the munitions. A few years later, the group elected the Kentucky Environmental Foundation as its lead organization.

The late 1990s saw important national developments regarding alternative chemical weapons disposal methods. In 1996 President Bill Clinton made development of alternative technologies the "highest priority" in the army's disposal program, putting alternative development on a fast track. Also in 1996, the National Research Council endorsed the use of alternative technologies in Maryland and Indiana, and later that year the army abandoned its incineration program in those two states and opted for alternative disposal methods. At the same time, Congress placed a moratorium on incinerator construction in Kentucky and Colorado while the process of demonstrating the use of new disposal technologies continued. In July of 1998 the Assembled Chemical Weapons Assessment announced alternative technologies that would move to the demonstration phase of its program. In 2002 the Pentagon recommended that non-incineration technologies be used at the Bluegrass Army Depot.

See also: RADIOACTIVE WASTE; SOLID-WASTE MANAGEMENT.

—Suzanne Marshall, *College of New Jersey*

Robert D. Bullard, ed., *Unequal Protection: Environmental Justice and Communities of Color* (1994); Suzanne Marshall, "Chemical Weapons Disposal and Environmental Justice," Kentucky Environmental Foundation paper (1996); U.S. National Research Council, *Disposal of Chemical Munitions and Agents* (1984).

Chestnut Blight

The massive American chestnut *(Castanea dentata)* tree, which grew to more than one hundred feet in height and from four to eight feet in diameter, was considered the crowning glory of Appalachian hardwoods. In many areas of the Appalachians, chestnut trees made up more than half of the forest. In the early 1900s, a fungus arrived in North America with the introduction of Oriental chestnut trees and spread south through the Appalachian system. Since the American chestnut was without natural immunity to the blight, it was virtually wiped out within fifty years, surviving only as a few small saplings sprouting from the roots of rotting stumps. Occasionally a sapling matures enough to produce a crop of nuts but usually succumbs the following year. Before its demise, the tree was important in both the ecology and economy of the region. Though various efforts to restore the American chestnut are underway, the very nature of the Appalachian forest was changed by the blight.

Unlike other nut trees, the chestnut bloomed early in the summer. Since there was less chance of a late frost killing the blooms, its nut crop was more reliable than those of other species. The chestnut is believed to have been one of the black bear's richest sources of food, and researchers speculate that the loss of the tree may have been an important factor in the depopulation of the species. Squirrels and wild turkeys also fed on the nuts, and deer browsed on saplings. Free-roaming domestic livestock used the chestnut for food as well. Before the blight, hogs throughout region were turned out in the fall to forage on the nuts, and the meat of animals on a chestnut diet was thought to be leaner and healthier than other meat.

Archaeological evidence suggests that Native Americans may have cultivated the chestnut along with other nut trees. Chestnut meal was mixed with corn to make bread, and chestnuts were parched for a coffee-like beverage. By the 1700s, European settlers were using the chestnut as a food source, and Cherokee women began trading chestnuts for European goods. The Cherokees also believed that the chestnut had medicinal properties. Teas made from the leaves were used to treat heart conditions, and the sprouts were made into a tea for cold sores and mixed with honey for a cough syrup.

After the Cherokee removal, European Americans continued to use the chestnut as an important food source. The nuts could be stored for extended periods of time, even years, since the tannic acid that preserves the wood also deters insects. Nuts could be eaten plain but were more often roasted or boiled. Many families also gathered them for sale or trade in cities. During the fall, a single person could pick up several bushels of chestnuts in a day. In 1900 a bushel of chestnuts brought twelve dollars. Like the Native Americans, mountain families had medicinal uses for the plant, among them a cream extracted from boiled leaves for treatment of burns and relief of tired, sweaty feet.

In the nineteenth century, wood from the American chestnut played a major role in the society and economy of the Appalachian region. It was said that the chestnut tree gave a person shelter from the cradle to the coffin. Chestnut timber was good for building, especially barns and fences. With few knots in the wood, it was easy to split into rails. It is said that a lumberman needed only an oak maul and dogwood wedges to split up to a hundred fence rails per day. Since the wood's tannic acid that made it invulnerable to insects also made it resistant to rot, chestnut was prized for a host of purposes. In 1909 its value to the timber industry was estimated at $20 million a year. At 15 to 20 billion board feet, chestnut wood made up 25 percent of the timber harvest in the region. The one household use for which the wood was not suited was firewood, since it pops violently and can throw sparks away from the hearth. But since it burns hot for a long time and creates little smoke, it was a favorite wood of moonshiners, who used it to heat their stills.

In 1904 a forester at the New York Zoological Park discovered the blight. The fungus attacks the tree's bark and grows in a ring around the trunk, killing it in a girdling effect. The blight can kill a large tree in one season, or a small one in a few weeks. Moving at about fifty miles a year, the blight spread from New York all the way down the Appalachian system. By the 1940s, areas as far south as North Carolina had lost a majority of their chestnuts, and by the 1950s, the chestnut was no longer a fixture in the Appalachian forest.

The occasional chestnut sprouting from a stump has given hope that someday the species will revive in the forests of North America. The chances of it returning to its original state appear hopeful, as efforts to develop a genetic hybrid of the American and Oriental chestnut continue. The goal is a hybrid that will be resistant to the blight of the Oriental and retain the shape and qualities of the American tree. Unfortunately, early hybrids have taken the size and shape of the Oriental chestnut. Research proceeds at the Brooklyn Botanical Gardens in New York and at Biltmore Forest in Asheville, North Carolina. Other promising efforts are underway by the American Chestnut Foundation, based in Vermont, and by the American Chestnut Cooperators' Foundation, based in Virginia.

See also: FOREST MANAGEMENT AND CONSERVATION.

—Cory Joe Stewart, *Appalachian State University*

Chris Bolgiano, *The Appalachian Forest: A Search for Roots and Renewal* (1998); Georganna Rice et al., "Memories of the American Chestnut," in *Foxfire 6*, ed. Eliot Wigginton (1980); Scott Weidensaul, *Mountains of the Heart: A Natural History of the Appalachians* (1994).

Coal Mining

At least since the late nineteenth century, coal mining has played a significant role in shaping the lives of residents of Appalachia. It determined patterns of settlement and residence, transformed cultures and values, influenced local and state politics, and set the course of the region's economic development. Coal mining has also greatly affected the natural environment in the region, causing deforestation, acid mine drainage and siltation of streams, air pollution and acid rain, and degradation of soil. Since the 1930s, state and federal governments have attempted to control some of these environmental effects through regulatory legislation but with only moderate success. As a result of weak laws, poor enforcement, and increasingly destructive surface mining, many serious environmental consequences continued through the latter part of the twentieth century and into the twenty-first.

Coal is found in Appalachia in an area stretching from northern Alabama to northeastern Pennsylvania. The mineral formed more than 300 million years ago when spores, ferns, conifers, and ancient scale trees growing in tropical swamps fell into the bog and were carbonized. The position of the coal in rock layers was determined primarily by uplift, erosion, and subsidence, while its rank—whether it would become lignite, bituminous, or anthracite—was due to varying amounts of heat and pressure from structural deformation of the earth's crust. Around 230 million years ago, flexural activity in northeastern Pennsylvania hardened bituminous coal into anthracite. Pressure drove off gases and impurities, increased the proportion of carbon, and left an organic compound with a high heat output and low ash content. On the eastern edge of the Appalachian Plateaus Province, coal was similarly affected by folding and compression, but it was not subjected to enough pressure to cause metamorphosis into anthracite. To the west, beyond the defor-

Dragline operating on a Martiki Coal Company mine near Pikeville, Kentucky, 1988. The environmental impact of coal mining took a new turn in the late 1970s, when the development of massive equipment literally able to scoop the tops from mountains introduced the controversial form of surface mining known as mountaintop removal.

mation zone, bituminous coal retained much of its volatile gases and sulfur.

Mining for coal in what became the United States began as early as 1750 in the Richmond field around the James River in Virginia. Production of coal in Pennsylvania started a few years later in the bituminous Pittsburgh bed, and by the turn of the nineteenth century, anthracite mines had opened in the northeastern fields. In Ohio, commercial production began in the late eighteenth century at Pipe Creek in Belmont County and started in other eastern counties soon after. The earliest records of production for eastern Kentucky also date back to the post–Revolutionary War period, when coal was mined in Lee County. Coal production did not start in east Tennessee and what is now West Virginia until the first two decades of the nineteenth century.

Early mining in Appalachia included primitive forms of both underground and surface extraction. Miners often drove short tunnels into stream banks where currents had exposed coal beds. Using picks and shovels, they followed the outcropping until the bank began to collapse or until the roof was stabilized with timber props. By the mid-nineteenth century, miners also used horse-drawn steel scrapers, drills, and black powder to expose and dig into coal beds. For the most part, these methods were small-scale, fit easily within the patterns of daily life, and had only minimal impact on the physical and organic environment.

In the 1870s, however, markets began to expand beyond local users. Industrial investment in the region led to a proliferation of railroad lines and the beginning of large-scale coal mining in Appalachia. In order to increase production, coal-mine operators adopted sophisticated technologies, which continued to evolve over succeeding decades. By the mid-twentieth century, variants of surface extraction (area, contour, and auger) became more prevalent. Surface mining overtook underground mining as the dominant method during the second half of the twentieth century.

The environmental effects of large-scale coal mining have been vast. By the late nineteenth century, industrial underground mining required substantial amounts of timber for roof props, and cutting for these props destroyed animal habitats. Later, strip mining cleared large forest tracts and produced a similar impact on wildlife. Deforestation from underground and surface mining also has affected wildlife populations and contributed to erosion, sedimentation of streams, and flooding. Stripping the land of its vegetation increases surface runoff, clogs creeks and rivers with sediment and debris, and causes floods in areas where none have previously occurred. Often flooding leads to the permanent displacement of residents, especially in counties where coal and land companies own most of the land.

Another significant impact of coal mining on waterways is acid mine drainage, which reached critical levels in some areas of Appalachia as early as the 1920s. By the 1960s, acid polluted nearly six thousand miles of streams in the region, primarily in the Susquehanna, Allegheny, Monongahela, Potomac, and Delaware River basins in Pennsylvania, West Virginia, and Maryland. Most of this pollution, a result of the exposure of sulfur-containing pyrite and marcasite to air and water, came from abandoned deep mines. By the 1960s, surface operations also represented a significant source of water pollution, though surface mines, both active and abandoned, accounted for less than 30 percent of the acid drainage at the time. In a 1966 study by the U.S. Department of the Interior of strip mines throughout Appalachia, more than half of all water samples taken one to two miles downstream from mine sites were found to be acidic (with pH values of 5 or less). Surface operations continue to cause siltation of streams and disastrous floods while active and abandoned mines pollute waterways and groundwater with acid mine drainage.

In addition to the more familiar types of water pollution, inadequate oversight and failure of coal slurry impoundments have led to significant problems. One of the more devastating failures of an impoundment occurred in 1972, when a wall of water, mud, rock, and other coal wastes rushed through the valley of Buffalo Creek, West Virginia, killing 125 people and destroying sixteen communities. In October 2000, more than 250 million gallons of coal slurry broke through deep mine workings below a Martin County, Kentucky, impoundment, seriously fouling residential areas and polluting Coldwater and Wolf Creeks as well as the Tug Fork of the Big Sandy River.

Coal mining and consumption have also polluted the air, both in miners' work environments and in the general atmosphere. The danger faced by miners from inhaling carbonaceous particles was recognized by some doctors and scientists in the nineteenth century, but their claims were disputed by other health professionals, government officials, and coal operators until the late 1960s. Meanwhile, coal dust in deep mines became increasingly worse with the introduction of continuous and longwall mining machines. Pollution of the air by burning coal reached notable levels with the growth in the number and size of urban areas in the late nineteenth and early twentieth centuries and rose even higher with the increased number of coal-fired power plants in the mid-twentieth century. Emissions from these plants have caused acid deposition, a product of the mixing of sulfur and nitrogen oxides with rain or other forms of precipitation. Measurements of precipitation on Mount Mitchell in western North Carolina, for example, have recorded readings as low as 2.12 pH, about the same level of acidity as that of lemon juice.

The direct impact of deep mining on land has generally been restricted to isolated though serious cases of subsidence and erosion around haul roads. Surface extraction has caused degradation of both arable and nonarable soil on a large scale. By the mid-1960s, more than 740,000 acres of land in Appalachia had been directly affected by strip mining for bituminous coal, in addition to 59,000 acres in the anthracite region of Pennsylvania and 74,000 acres disturbed by mine-access roads. More than a third of this acreage was on steep slopes, and only one-fourth of the land was reclaimed. As a result, there were massive slides, some more than 600 feet wide, along 1,400 miles of strip-mine terrace benches. Even when operators attempted to reclaim sites, they often failed because mining reshuffled soil layers and exposed silt shales with much of the topsoil buried, and newly exposed soil was too acidic to sustain plant life. The consequent failure of revegetation compounded erosion problems, which had an impact not only on actual mine sites but also on surrounding areas. In cases where strip operators mined under broad form deeds—which separated surface and mineral rights and were interpreted by Kentucky courts as allowing for destruction of the surface without compensation to the owner—directly affected lands often included farms, gardens, orchards, and grazing areas.

More recently, mountaintop removal, a newer and more destructive form of strip mining, has become predominant in some regions of Appalachia. Under this method, giant power shovels and draglines are used to remove entire mountaintops. The removed material, or "overburden," is dumped into huge valley fills, often burying mountain streams. For a 2003 draft of a court-ordered environmental impact statement, state and federal agencies evaluated the effects of mountaintop-removal mining on a 12-million-acre study area including parts of eastern Kentucky, southern West Virginia, southwestern Virginia, and east Tennessee. The study concluded that 6.8 percent of the forested territory in that region "has been or may be affected by recent and future (1992–2012) mountaintop mining." Of the 59,000 miles of streams in the area, the draft reported that 724 miles had been covered by valley fills between 1985 and 2001, while a total of 1,200 miles had been affected. The study concludes, "Mountaintop mining operations in the Appalachian coalfields involve fundamental changes to the region's landscape and terrestrial wildlife habitats. With the increasing size of these operations, a single permit may involve changing thousands of acres of hardwood forest into grassland."

Attempts to rectify some of the environmental problems caused by deep and surface mining date back to the early twentieth century, but weak state and federal regulatory laws, poor enforcement, and the steady expansion of strip mining (which surpassed deep mining in production levels by 1973) have conspired to hamper the effectiveness of these efforts. At different times, in various parts of Appalachia, mountain residents have organized to demand stronger laws, stricter enforcement, and even abolition of surface coal mining altogether. At best, however, implementation and enforcement of these laws have been inconsistent.

Some of the consequences of strip mining on surface soil have been addressed by state legislation, beginning with West Virginia in 1939, and eventually by the federal Surface Mining Control and Reclamation Act of 1977. This federal law set up a partnership between the Department of the Interior and state agencies, leaving control of regulatory programs in the hands of the states as long as they met or surpassed standards outlined in the act, which banned dumping debris on steep slopes and established an abandoned-mines reclamation fund to restore "orphan" lands. However, even these regulations produced comparatively meager results. There are now at least one thousand abandoned coal-mining sites in eastern Kentucky and even more in Pennsylvania, despite a surplus of more than a billion dollars in the abandoned-mines reclamation fund and that program's imminent expiration. The Surface Mining Control and Reclamation Act also allowed variances to provisions requiring restoration of land to "approximate original contour" and placed only weak restrictions on mountaintop removal. Additionally, the law allowed stripping without the consent of surface owners if permitted under state law. Mining by broad form deeds was not outlawed in Kentucky until activists amended the state constitution by referendum in 1988.

See also: BUFFALO CREEK FLOOD; COAL (GEOLOGY); COAL SLURRY IMPOUNDMENTS.

—Chad Montrie, *University of Massachusetts at Lowell*

Harry M. Caudill, *My Land Is Dying* (1971); Alan Derickson, *Black Lung: Anatomy of a Public Health Disaster* (1998); Chad Montrie, *To Save the Land and People: A History of Opposition to Surface Coal Mining in Appalachia* (2003); Barbara Ellen Smith, *Digging Our Own Graves: Coal Miners and the Struggle over Black Lung Disease* (1987); Richard H. K. Vietor, *Environmental Politics and the Coal Coalition* (1980).

Coal Slurry Impoundments

After being taken from the ground, coal is washed to remove impurities, and the dirty water, laden with particulate matter and called slurry, is stored in large impoundments created by dams in mountain hollows near mine operations. In an impoundment the "fines," or finer coal residues, settle to the bottom as sludge, while water becomes clear enough at the top to be reused or discharged. Some impoundment dams are hundreds of feet high and hold billions of gallons of slurry. The Marfork Coal Company's 645-acre Brushy Fork impoundment above Whitesville, West Virginia, for example, is permitted to hold 3.5 billion gallons of slurry. If expanded to its final planned stage, it could hold 5 billion gallons. The dam would then stand 920 feet from toe to crest, 200 feet higher than Hoover Dam on the Colorado River and 50 feet higher than the New River Gorge Bridge in Fayette County, West Virginia.

Though the Brushy Fork impoundment would be the largest in the region, there are many smaller slurry impoundments throughout Appalachia. According to the West Virginia Department of Environmental Protection, there are 136 impoundments in that state alone. Coal slurry contains toxic heavy metals, and impoundments have been subject to leaks and overflows, resulting in significant and chronic environmental problems in Appalachia.

The region's deadliest twentieth-century impoundment failure occurred in 1972, when a large dam failed on Buffalo Creek in Logan County, West Virginia, killing 125 people. Responding in part to this disaster, the federal Mine Safety and Health Administration in 1975 began regulating the engineering, design, and maintenance of certain coal-waste dams. The Buffalo Creek disaster also helped lead to the passage of the 1977 Surface Mining Control and Reclamation Act. Today, the Mine Safety and Health Administration and state environmental agencies issue permits for coal slurry impoundments. In addition, both the federal Office of Surface Mining and the U.S. Environmental Protection Agency oversee state regulation of impoundments.

Since the Mine Safety and Health Administration started regulating them in 1975, no impoundment dam has broken, but basins have failed in other ways. In a number of incidents, coal slurry has broken into adjacent underground mines or caverns. From there, slurry has flooded into streams, spreading toxic sludge for miles. The largest such event occurred on October 11, 2000, at a mountaintop-removal mine operated by Martin County Coal Company (a subsidiary of Massey Energy Company) near Inez, Kentucky. At that site, a crack opened between the bottom of a 2.2-billion-gallon impoundment and an underlying mine. Before workers could get control of the spill, more than 250 million gallons of lava-like black sludge gushed into the mine. The sludge then poured out of two mine portals into Coldwater and Wolf Creeks, wiping out all aquatic life. Eventually the sludge traveled about seventy-five miles, flowing into the Tug Fork and the Big Sandy River bordering Kentucky and West Virginia. Communities along the waterways were forced to shut down their drinking water intakes temporarily. Trailers and houses were inundated with sludge. The Environmental Protection Agency called it one of the worst-ever environmental disasters in the southeastern United States.

After the Martin County break, impoundment practices and regulations in West Virginia and elsewhere received increased scrutiny. One problem is that maps used to issue permits are often inaccurate. Such maps are frequently provided by mining companies unwilling to fund new, high-tech surveys. In the case of the failed Martin County impoundment, for example, maps showed about seventy feet of rock between the bottom of the basin and the ceiling of the underlying mine. But subsequent tests showed that the actual rock barrier was only a few feet thick in several places. Inaccurate mapping can create threats to safety as well as hazards to the environment. An inaccurate map was blamed for a July 2002 mine accident in Quecreek, Pennsylvania, for instance, when new operations broke through to an old, water-filled mine, threatening the lives of dozens of miners, including nine who were trapped underground for three days before being rescued.

The Martin County break also raised questions about the quality of federal oversight. For example, the Mine Safety and Health Administration ranks impoundments at either low, moderate, or high risk for breakthrough. Before the Martin County breakthrough, the agency had rated the risk at that impoundment as only moderate.

The Martin County break led to responses beyond Kentucky. In West Virginia, the state's Department of Environmental Protection began a reevaluation and possible re-permitting of fifty-one impoundments. At the federal level, Congress approved $1.6 million for the National Research Council of the National Academies of Science to examine coal-waste impoundments. The investigating panel looked at engineering, mapping, and alternatives to impoundments. Its report, delivered to Congress in October 2001, recommended increased regulation. Specifically, it said that the Mine Safety and Health Administration and the Office of Surface Mining should study impoundment basins as well as embankment dams. The report also recommended that federal agencies oversee the design, construction, and operation of impoundment basins. Finally, the report recommended that federal agencies work with states to establish standards for mine surveying and mapping.

Slurry impoundments remain a source of concern in Appalachia. The Mine Safety and Health Administration lists West Virginia with sixty-six, Kentucky with sixty, and Pennsylvania with seventy-three impoundments that have potential to break through into an underground mine. (A few of these impoundments are listed as "fresh water" impoundments, not slurry impoundments.) The dangers from impoundment leaks and spills are compounded by toxicity. Companies use flocculants (which help solids drop out of suspension) and surfactants, or soaps, to wash coal of impurities. Other cleaning agents include natural and modified starches, caustic starch, and anhydrous ammonia, as well as lime, sulfuric acid, and aluminum sulfate to adjust the pH of the impoundments. Both sludge and slurry usually contain trace metals that occur in coal, including mercury, lead, chromium, cadmium, boron, selenium, and nickel. Data from the Martin County break showed that the slurry also contained copper, vanadium, manganese, barium, arsenic, and cobalt.

See also: BUFFALO CREEK FLOOD; COAL MINING.

—Vivian Stockman, *Ohio Valley Environmental Coalition*

U.S. National Research Council, *Coal Waste Impoundments: Risks, Responses, and Alternatives* (2002).

Environmental Education

Across the Appalachian region, environmental education is part of the curricula of universities, a focus in secondary and elementary schools, and a key component of workshops, outdoor programs, lectures, and community events. Many of the region's major universities, as well as its smaller colleges, offer degrees in environmental studies or have interdisciplinary programs that provide environmental offerings.

Slippery Rock University, in the mountains of western Pennsylvania, offers a master's program in environmental education, one of the few such programs in the entire United States. Liberal arts colleges in the region, several with a religious focus, also offer excellent programs of environmental study. Warren Wilson College near Asheville, North Carolina, has one of the more innovative approaches to environmental education, requiring students to blend academics with work and community service. At Berea College in Kentucky, students who pursue an independent studies major may also take courses in environmental studies, sustainable development, and natural resources management. Berea's Appalachian Center also works to stimulate scholarly interest in the many environmental problems of the region.

There are numerous outdoor education programs in Appalachia as well, most of them led by private, nonprofit institutions. One of the best known of these institutions is North Carolina Outward Bound in Asheville. Emphasizing environmental stewardship and expeditionary learning, North Carolina Outward Bound offers wilderness backpacking, whitewater canoeing, and rock climbing, as well as courses for prospective outdoor education instructors and for business professionals interested in increasing organizational effectiveness. Castle Rock Institute, located in Brevard, North Carolina, conducts a semester-long off-campus study program that allows undergraduate college students to live, study, and explore together for up to five months. Affiliated with Brevard College, the Castle Rock Institute is dedicated to developing links between the humanities and the practical dimensions of human life in the natural world.

At the Tennessee Wildlife Center in Chattanooga, grades K–12 can learn about the flora and fauna of the region, including seeing red wolves, an endangered species, and participating in hands-on programs to determine water quality in area streams and rivers. In Townsend, Tennessee, the Great Smoky Mountains Institute at Tremont provides numerous educational programs for school groups, teachers, adults, and families, each designed to nurture appreciation for the Great Smoky Mountains National Park. The National Wildlife Federation contributes to environmental education in Appalachia through its Campus Ecology Program, which organizes the students, faculty, and staff of major colleges and universities. The organization also conducts camping and outdoor opportunities for children and adults such as the Family Summit Program in West Virginia.

See also: AGRICULTURAL TOURISM (TOURISM); ECOTOURISM (TOURISM); SECTION OVERVIEW (EDUCATION).

—Elizabeth M. Williams, *Appalachian State University*

C. A. Bowers, *Educating for an Ecologically Sustainable Culture: Rethinking Moral Education, Creativity, Intelligence, and Other Modern Orthodoxies* (1995); David W. Orr, *Ecological Literacy: Education and the Transition to a Postmodern World* (1992); Joy Palmer and Philip Neal, *The Handbook of Environmental Education* (1994).

Environmental Justice

Environmental justice is a term widely used to convey the idea that all people—regardless of race, color, national origin, or income—should be protected from the negative impacts of industrial, commercial, or governmental programs and policies. Perhaps the most commonly identified form of environmental injustice is a form of racism, subjecting people of color to disproportionate exposure to pollution-related health hazards and environmental degradation. Though environmental justice as an ethical and legal concept was formulated only in the last two decades of the twentieth century, environmental injustice in Appalachia has been a longstanding phenomenon.

A well-known historical example is the 1930 Hawk's Nest incident at Gauley Mountain, West Virginia, where hundreds of men, most of them African Americans, contracted silicosis while working to dig the tunnel for a hydroelectric power plant. Some estimates put the number of deaths at more than 700, though no exact figure is known. Another example occurred when toxic chemicals were accidentally released into the air from a Union Carbide plant in Institute, West Virginia, in 1985. More than 130 people were sent to nearby hospitals after plant officials there delayed notifying the town's largely African American populace that a toxic release had occurred. In 1979 a stream flowing through the poor, predominantly black community of Triana, Alabama, was found to contain levels of the pesticide DDT that were forty times the federal limit. Investigation subsequently showed that an Olin Chemical Corporation facility on the U.S. Army's Redstone Arsenal had discharged DDT-contaminated wastewater into the stream for more than two decades and that up to four thousand tons had accumulated in a 2.3-mile segment of Huntsville Spring Branch near Triana. The ensuing effort to obtain restitution involved the U.S. Environmental Protection Agency, the Army Corps of Engineers, Olin, and the citizens of Triana and became an early case study in environmental justice. After a three-year struggle, the chemical company agreed to pay $24 million to the 1,178 residents of the community, with $5 million set aside for a health-care program. It also agreed to clean up the polluted stream banks at a cost expected to reach as much as $137 million. Another notable instance of environmental negligence concerns the contamination of Chattanooga Creek in Tennessee from nearby industrial waste sites with PCBs, heavy metals, and pesticides—pollutants now associated with elevated rates of cancer in the predominately African American neighborhoods of Alton Park and Piney Woods.

Action on environmental racism in Appalachia has been connected with national efforts to address the issue. In Warren County, North Carolina, for example, following a battle in 1982 over a toxic landfill in an African American community, the U.S. General Accounting Office and the Commission for Racial Justice of the United Church of Christ published two seminal studies, both of which showed correlations between environmental threats and the racial and ethnic composition of local populations. In 1991 the First National People of Color Environmental Leadership Summit in Washington released seventeen "Principles of Environmental Justice" intended to guide the work of governmental and nongovernmental organizations. In 1994 President Bill Clinton issued an executive order, "Federal Actions to Address Environmental Justice in Minority Populations and Low-Income Populations," to reinforce the nondiscriminatory provisions of the Civil Rights Act of 1964, as well as the goals of the National Environmental Policy Act of 1969, which was intended to ensure a safe and healthy environment for all Americans.

Environmental injustice occurs not only in African American communities but also in poor and rural white Appalachian communities. Well-documented cases include the fight against a toxic landfill by the residents of Bumpass Cove, Tennessee, an environmental battle featured in the award-winning documentary *You Got to Move* (1985). During the 1980s, white residents of Hartford, Tennessee, combined forces with others in the surrounding county to force Champion International to stop polluting the Pigeon River with cancer-causing dioxins. Hartford had become known locally as "Widowville" because hundreds of people—mostly men who had fished and swum in the river—died of cancer over a relatively short period. At roughly the same time, a grassroots group near Middlesboro, Kentucky, the Yellow Creek Concerned Citizens, gained national attention in their ongoing efforts to stop the pollution of Yellow Creek by a local tannery.

See also: CHEMICAL INDUSTRY (BUSINESS, INDUSTRY, AND TECHNOLOGY); CHEMICAL WEAPONS DISPOSAL; HAWK'S NEST TRAGEDY (LABOR).

—Guy Larry Osborne, *Carson-Newman College*

Robert D. Bullard, *Dumping in Dixie: Race, Class, and Environmental Quality* (3rd edition, 2000); Mike Hollis, "The Persistence of Poison: Effects of Chemical Plant Spill Still Plague Alabama Town," *Washington Post* (June 15, 1980).

Environmental Legislation

The Appalachian region has been a focal point in America for important environmental and land-management legislation since the 1960s. Social change beginning in that period forced national and state policymakers to enact legislation protecting the environment and rural communities of Appalachia for the first time. In many cases, when such legislation has gone unenforced or proved inadequate, grassroots organizations have pressured a new generation of legislators to pass new laws or to require better enforcement. The resulting web of federal, state, and local environmental protection laws and regulations is far-reaching and complex. The histories of some particularly significant laws and legal actions reflect the critical intersection of political action, legislation, implementation, and enforcement.

Years in the making, the Weeks Act of 1911 stands as one of the most significant federal environmental laws affecting Appalachia. By the early 1880s, excessive soil erosion and flooding in the East, particularly in Appalachia, had created concern among conservationists, politicians, and timbermen regarding the role of standing timber in preventing excessive water runoff and the widespread loss of topsoil. Public testimony and debate left little doubt that injudicious lumbering and forest fires were causing excessive erosion, flooding, and topsoil loss in the mountain region. Not until tragic floods in West Virginia and Kentucky in 1907, however, was federal legislation proposed for protection of mountain forests.

Four years later, the Weeks Act authorized the federal purchase of "forested, cut-over, or denuded lands within the watersheds of navigable streams." The act was named after its chief sponsor, Massachusetts Congressman John W. Weeks. At the time of the law's passage, the federal government owned much of the land in the American West, while virtually all land in the East was privately owned. The act authorized the federal government to purchase private lands and incorporate them into the National Forest System under the U.S. Department of Agriculture. Eventually, the measure led to creation of millions of acres of national forests, including seven million acres in the Appalachian region, from Mississippi to New York.

Though one of the prime motives of the Weeks Act was to preserve watersheds by conserving forest cover, it did not stop the destruction of mountain forests. Over the first part of the twentieth century, forests grew back, and the U.S. Forest Service came to perceive national forestlands primarily as timber reserves. As lumber demands rose after World War II, the forests were once again logged. In fact, nearly unrestricted logging in Appalachia's national forests continued progressively for several decades, resulting in efforts by environmental and conservation groups to curtail the practice.

In 1975 a West Virginia citizens' group filed a lawsuit in U.S. District Court to enjoin the Forest Service from permitting the clear-cutting of timber, which was at that time the primary technique for timber harvesting on public lands. The lawsuit halted all logging in the mountain region for many months and became the incentive for new legislation, the National Forest Management Act, which was passed by Congress in 1976. The act required that the national forests be managed for "multiple use," considering not only the extraction of natural resources but conservation, recreation, and other values as well. The legislation also mandated development of formal management plans for all national forests.

Yet the effectiveness of the National Forest Management Act—like the effectiveness of the original Weeks Act and other environmental legislation—depended upon implementation and enforcement. Mandated management plans were begun in most of the region's national forests in the 1980s, but almost immediately the plans were appealed by environmental and citizens' groups. Actions by such groups resulted in further negotiations, administrative review, and federal lawsuits. Subsequent forest plans have also been affected by both environmental and industry groups. While slowing the rate of logging that developed in the 1950s through the 1980s, the plans remained unsatisfactory in the view of many conservationists, who believed they placed too much emphasis on timber harvesting and road construction.

Another significant federal law affecting the management of national forests in Appalachia is the Eastern Wilderness Areas Act of 1975. The act, a follow-up to the Wilderness Act of 1964, was passed by Congress in response to pressure by conservation groups and a growing environmental political lobby. The initial act of 1964 set aside large tracts of public land as "wilderness" areas that would be forever off-limits to private extractive industries. Such lands were to be managed primarily for conservation and recreational values. The government's interpretation of criteria for what constituted wilderness under the 1964 act, however, prevented all lands in the East, except for a few small tracts, from being considered for the designation. To rectify the problem, the Eastern Wilderness Areas Act was passed, and a total of nearly five hundred thousand acres of wilderness have subsequently been established in national forests in Appalachia.

Environmental legislation regarding the protection of privately held lands has been much less uniform than federal measures protecting public lands. In the coalfields, where individual states have historically been responsible for regulating mining practices, regulatory agencies and their statutes have often been ineffective. Although the earliest laws in Appalachia regarding coal-mining practices were enacted in West Virginia in the late 1930s, most states did not begin systematically enforcing their statutes and regulations until the threat of federal intervention in the early 1970s.

In 1972 representatives from several national environmental organizations testified in congressional hearings, detailing the abuses caused by surface mining. By 1974, the activities of these groups were coordinated by the Coalition Against Strip Mining, a national organization comprised of local citizens' groups, farmers, ranchers, Native Americans, sportsmen, and environmentalists. The coalition's political work eventually led to more federal legislation: the Surface Mining Control and Reclamation Act of 1977, which finally brought all surface-mining activities in Appalachia under federal regulatory statutes and enforcement.

During the last three decades of the twentieth century, however, new technologies—gigantic dump trucks, bulldozers, drilling machines, and draglines—increased the scale of surface coal mining tenfold. The dominant surface-mining technique in parts of central Appalachia was mountaintop removal, which involves the razing of entire mountaintops to provide access to underlying coal seams. When a mountain is leveled, the resulting debris, or overburden, is often dumped into surrounding streambeds. In October 1999, U.S. District Judge Charles Haden ordered West Virginia to enforce the provisions of the Clean Water Act of 1972, which required coal companies to establish buffer zones around free-flowing streams at all mining sites. In April 2001, however, a federal appeals court panel overturned the ruling, stating that coal companies had constitutional immunity from the lawsuit, which, the three-judge panel claimed, should have originally been filed in state court. Subsequent actions by the courts, as well as administrative rulings by the executive branch of the federal government, made the future scope and effectiveness of the Clean Water Act and Surface Mining Control and Reclamation Act uncertain.

The history of the implementation of coal-mining legislation shows the conflicting relationships that often exist among federal and state laws, the courts, and lobbying groups. Such complex relationships have influenced legislation and enforcement regarding hazardous-waste disposal as well as mining in the region. During the early 1980s, Appalachia became the target of large solid- and hazardous-waste conglomerates, absentee firms that saw the region as a potential dumping ground for garbage produced elsewhere in the United States. Residents reacted by fighting the permitting of landfills and hazardous-waste incinerators in their communities. One of the major legal tools in these battles was the Resource Conservation and Recovery Act of 1976, a federal law created specifically to regulate hazardous and toxic waste and set standards for state and regional waste management. In Roane County, Tennessee, Diversified Scientific Services, the first mixed-waste (hazardous and radioactive) processing facility permitted in the United States, began entering contracts with the U.S. Department of Energy in the early 1990s to treat hazardous and radioactive wastes from weapons production sites. While reviewing the company's files in the Tennessee Department of Environment and Conservation office, a member of Save Our Cumberland Mountains, a citizens' action group, found that the facility had misrepresented its operations on its Resource Conservation and Recovery Act permit application, stating that the terrain within a ten-mile area of the site was flat, even though all of east Tennessee is mountainous. The claim of flat terrain would have allowed emission levels ten times higher than provisions allowed. After Diversified Scientific Services was fined as a result of the misrepresentation, local residents continued to mobilize, increasing public scrutiny of the hazardous-waste industry and stopping several proposed facilities.

Since the 1990s, a number of grassroots groups in Appalachia have facilitated the passing and enforcement of local, state, and federal environmental laws. As it becomes increasingly obvious that protecting the environment improves the health and well-being of mountain communities, legislative efforts like those outlined above will continue to play an important role in the political dynamic of the Appalachian region.

See also: FOREST MANAGEMENT AND CONSERVATION; GRASSROOTS ENVIRONMENTAL ACTION; WEEKS ACT (GOVERNMENT).

—Andrew Kimbrell, *International Center for Technology Assessment*

Shelley Smith Mastran and Nan Lowerre, *Mountaineers and Rangers: A History of Federal Forest Management in the Southern Appalachians, 1900–81* (1983); Olga L. Moya and Andrew L. Fono, *Federal Environmental Law: The User's Guide* (2nd edition, 2001); Neal Shover, Donald A. Clelland, and John Lynxwiler, *Enforcement or Negotiation: Constructing a Regulatory Bureaucracy* (1986).

Erosion

Modern Appalachia is particularly susceptible to erosion because much of the land consists of steep mountains and hills. In the nineteenth and twentieth centuries, erosion became a severe problem in the region, due to the destruction of the mountains' protective forest cover by agriculture, mining, logging, and fire.

Long before white settlers migrated into the Appalachians, native peoples used fire to clear land for agriculture and grazing, beginning erosion processes that eventually led to horrific destruction. Their efforts were localized and caused little permanent damage to soils. Early white settlers in Appalachia also used fire for subsistence purposes without creating large-scale damage. But as population pressures increased in the mid-nineteenth century, farmers turned increasingly to a practice of girdling trees on hillsides and then planting and plowing, often with disastrous results. In many cases, sloping mountain farms lasted only a decade or less. When the land was worn out, farmers would simply move on to another area and begin the same cycle of girdling, plowing, and planting, until that land too was washed away. The longterm damage was recognized by the dawn of the twentieth century. In a 1902 report, Secretary of Agriculture James Wilson concluded that "more good soil is now washed from these cleared mountainside fields during a single heavy rain than during centuries of forest cover."

Land erosion near Marion, North Carolina, c. 1902. Reduction or destruction of forest cover can rapidly increase the normal rate of erosion.

Damage to Appalachian soils further increased with the arrival of industrial logging. Clear-cutting of trees directly destroys the network of roots and organic material that holds water and soil. Industrial logging caused more damage to terrain as crude logging roads, draglines, and rail tracks arrived in the mountains. Large trees were rolled down from embankment tops, and eventually steam engines equipped with cable skidders replaced mules, dragging tons of timber out of the forest. The massive clearing created deep gullies and ditches that were transformed by rain into mud-filled creeks. Industrial logging also caused erosion by promoting unnatural wildfires as fields of dried wood caught fire and burned uncontrollably, sometimes for months, destroying organic soils down to the bedrock. The 1902 report from the secretary of agriculture described logging practices that made uncontrolled burns "impracticable" and noted that fires had destroyed entire forests in some regions. After destruction of the humus of the forest floor, the remaining soil soon washed away, leaving trees to die on a bare surface of rock. In the wake of industrial logging and the resulting fires, wind and rain created furrows and gullies on the exposed earth almost immediately. Thus logging and repeated fires caused many acres of mountain land to be stripped of soil and left virtually lifeless.

Erosion problems continued to be severe in the twentieth century. During the 1930s, the Civilian Conservation Corps was put to work on erosion-control projects such as tree plantings and brush dam construction. In the 1940s the U.S. Soil Conservation Service promoted widespread planting of exotic invasive plants such as Japanese honeysuckle and kudzu to combat soil erosion. This practice was changed in the 1960s when fast-growing natives such as black locust were used in lieu of exotics.

Erosion continues from the slopes of Appalachia. Perhaps the greatest continuing enemy to Appalachian soils is surface mining. Modern surface mining involves cutting down mountains, layer by layer, to retrieve coal deposits. Surface mines remove a mountain's infrastructure, leaving barren crags prone to landslides and earth failures. Flooding and water contamination are thus greatly increased around surface mines. In 1977 Congress passed the Surface Mining Control and Reclamation Act requiring mining companies to replant mined areas with native plants and to restore a mountain's approximate original contour. Although the act has helped to temper the damage done by mining, millions of tons of soil are still eroded and lost due to surface mining every year.

See also: COAL MINING; FLOODS; FOREST MANAGEMENT AND CONSERVATION.

—Scott Honeycutt, *Georgia State University*

Steve Nash, *Blue Ridge 2020: An Owner's Manual* (1999); Tennessee Valley Authority Department of Regional Planning Studies, *The Scenic Resources of the Tennessee Valley: A Descriptive and Pictorial Inventory* (1938); U.S. Department of Agriculture, *Message from the President of the United States Transmitting a Report of the Secretary of Agriculture in Relation to the Forests, Rivers, and Mountains of the Southern Appalachian Region,* Senate Document No. 84 (1902).

Fire

In the western United States, fire is one of the most important of all natural disturbances, affecting both species composition and the overall forest regeneration process. In Appalachia, however, upland forests do not commonly regenerate as a result of fire. Because the region averages between forty-five and fifty inches of rain per year, soils remain relatively moist, and fuel loads do not readily accumulate in the Appalachian forest. Consequently, fire is not a significant element of natural forest succession.

Despite the relative rarity of naturally occurring forest fires, Appalachia is a geographic center for lightning strikes. Annually, an average of six lightning fires per million acres occurs in the southern Appalachians, a frequency greater than that recorded for the Great Plains, Mississippi Basin, or the northeastern United States. Lightning-generated fires contribute to the overall composition of forest species, especially in the southern end of the region, where fire-dependent species such as table mountain and longleaf pine are sometimes found.

Though naturally occurring fire has historically had a minor impact in shaping the forests of the Appalachians, human-caused fire, or anthropogenic burning, has played an important role in the region. Native Americans exploited the resources of the Appalachians for at least ten thousand years and affected the forest ecosystem through occasional programs of forest burning. Anthropogenic burning of the forest landscape is confirmed by the prehistoric presence of ragweed, a fire-dependent species that paleobotanists say became increasingly prevalent in the region during the sixteenth and seventeenth centuries.

Indians undoubtedly used fire in areas of permanent habitation. However, their settlements were limited in number and generally located near the rich alluvial soils of the region's largest rivers. The earliest historical documentation of anthropogenic burning in the region was recorded in 1756 by engineer and surveyor John William Gerard de Brahm, who remarked that the Cherokees replenished the soil by "phlogiston," or the annual burning of cultivated fields. In November 1799, Moravian missionaries Abraham Steiner and Christian de Schweinitz witnessed fire use along the level floodplains of the Tellico River in southeastern Tennessee, noting that Cherokee women and children set fire to the grass in the woods. The pair also observed the existence of a large open meadow, a beautiful plain entirely clear of woods that they believed was the result of past burnings by Cherokees or perhaps their "cultural ancestors" of the Mississippian period.

Even though Native Americans were responsible for making some discernible changes in the upland landscape, Europeans and the more intensive agricultural subsistence economy they practiced had a much more profound effect on the forest ecosystem. With the arrival of the first pioneers, the Appalachian Mountains became, in effect, an enormous grazing commons in which livestock could grow fat by browsing among mountaintop pastures, woodland glades, and river-bottom canebrakes. In addition, many of the first European settlers practiced "transhumance," an old-world agricultural practice requiring annual burning of the forest floor. In late fall or early spring, Appalachian herdsmen burned mountaintop pastures to encourage new growth for free-ranging cattle and sheep. Open-range grazing and seasonal burning had significant effects on the forest canopy, including slowing understory growth and the favoring of some tree species over others. The interruption of natural forest reproduction also resulted in severe erosion and the excessive drying of soils, particularly along the upper slopes and ridges of the region's highest mountains.

Commercial logging of nearly all of the Appalachians in the period from 1880 to 1930 greatly magnified the detrimental environmental effects of fire. Whereas earlier nineteenth-century practices of cyclical burning had merely suppressed natural forest growth, commercial logging changed the Appalachian forest even more dramatically by essentially clearing entire areas of standing trees. The unprecedented fuel loads produced by commercial logging enterprises also caused an explosion of devastating forest wildfires in the region and a dramatic increase in both the size and frequency of calamitous floods.

Many of the fires were caused by careless lumbermen, who routinely left behind large piles of brush and downed treetops at logging sites. During the hottest summer months, these materials became tinderboxes, ignitable by campfires, lightning, or carelessly tossed matches. William W. Ashe, the first secretary of the National Forest Reservation Commission—the federal agency that would later become the U.S. Department of Agriculture Forest Service—estimated that in 1891 alone between 800,000 and 1.2 million acres of woodlands burned in North Carolina due to unchecked forest fires. Though the fact was seldom admitted by industry spokesmen, many of the fires were caused by sparks from the coal- and wood-fired locomotives used to haul out harvested timber. John H. Finney, secretary and treasurer of the Appalachian Forest Association during the early 1900s, estimated the value of timber destroyed annually by forest fires started by railroad locomotives at $50 million. At a convention speech reported in the *Southern Lumberman*, the industry's trade magazine, Finney advised timber-holding companies to "clear up almost immediately all the downed timber on their land" so that the destructive fires "may be at least to some extent prevented."

The widespread adverse effects of logging resulted in the creation of national forests in the Appalachians, acquisitions for which started after the passage of the Weeks Act in 1911. Although the federal agency's original programs focused on restoring the original forest and reviving major streams and watersheds, after World War II the Forest Service began to adopt sustained-yield and even-age management practices that favored the regeneration of pine species over native hardwoods. Because these tree species benefit from the use of prescribed burning, the agency later adopted the use of intentional fire as a management tool throughout select areas of the Appalachians, annually burning thousands of acres in highly controlled conditions, not to replicate natural forest succession but to increase timber harvest. Wildfires started by arsonists are also a problem on both public and private lands in the region. One government study found that in a single five-year period, thirty-two thousand arson-related fires consumed more than 450,000 acres of land in the southern Appalachians alone.

See also: EROSION; FLOODS; FOREST MANAGEMENT AND CONSERVATION.

—Donald E. Davis, *Dalton State College*

Donald Edward Davis, *Where There Are Mountains: An Environmental History of the Southern Appalachians* (2000); Shelley Smith Mastran and Nan Lowerre, *Mountaineers and Rangers: A History of Federal Forest Management in the Southern Appalachians 1900–81* (1983); Southern Appalachian Man and the Biosphere Cooperative, *The Southern Appalachian Assessment* (1996).

Floods

Floods are among the most destructive natural disasters in Appalachia. Both natural topography and land-use practices have historically affected flood patterns in the region, where streams and rivers drain the highest peaks in the eastern United States. By the early twentieth century, flood problems were so severe in the southern Appalachians and the Tennessee Valley that the Tennessee Valley Authority (TVA) was created in 1933 largely as a flood-control measure.

Southern Appalachia has the highest rainfall on the North American continent outside of the Pacific Northwest. In the high mountains of western North Carolina and east Tennessee, precipitation averages eighty inches per year. In other parts of the region, it can be as much as seventy inches annually. Heavy downpours in short periods of time are common, and mountains create funnels for torrents of water. To compound the problem, southern Appalachia, which was never overridden by glaciers, has few natural lakes and ponds to help store water. Resulting floods can be extremely fast and destructive. In 1951, for example, four inches of rain and hail fell on Mount LeConte in the Tennessee Smokies in one hour. Landslides capped off the torrents by destroying bridges and roads and scooping out two-hundred-year-old trees.

Though forested mountains are sometimes subject to natural floods, the clearing of trees greatly increases flooding. A forest acts as a natural reservoir, maintaining a level of saturation that enables water to dissipate gradually. After forest cover has been cleared, streams rise rapidly. Floodwater moves over the cleared land like water over a dinner plate rather than being absorbed and stored. By the mid-nineteenth century, agricultural clearing was already causing flooding in Appalachia. In 1867 the Tennessee River crested at 57.9 feet at Chattanooga, well above flood stage, and flooding increased even more in the period of industrial logging that began around 1880 and continued to 1920. Severe flooding along the Ohio and Monongahela Rivers in 1907 helped to convince Congress of the importance of forest regulation in controlling water runoff. The Weeks Act, passed in 1911, authorized the federal purchase of forests to protect the headwaters of navigable streams. West Virginia was the first state to approve federal purchase of private forests as a way to control flooding in the mountains.

As the twentieth century progressed, flooding continued to be a problem throughout Appalachia. In 1930 a congressionally mandated report by the U.S. Army Corps of Engineers addressed three major problems: flooding, power production, and navigational obstacles. Responding in part

Flooding in McDowell County, West Virginia, 2001. Affected by both its mountainous topography and its patterns of land use, the county was hit by the "flood of the century" in 2001, only to be struck by even more destructive flooding the following year.

to the report, Congress authorized the Tennessee Valley Authority. With little oversight from Congress, TVA had the power to build high dams. At the time, it was assumed that flood control would take precedence over power production and that reservoirs would be low during the winter to guard against heavy rainfall, though nany of these policies would later change. TVA was awarded $36 million in 1935 for its construction program. After work began, continued flooding helped to accelerate dam building. Flooding in 1940 in Johnson County, Tennessee, for example, washed out the railroad and doomed the town of Butler.

A number of large floods occurred later in the twentieth century. In June 1995, five days of continual rain caused destruction throughout the eastern half of central and southern Appalachia. At that time, one area east of the Shenandoah National Park received twenty-four inches of rain in a twenty-four-hour period. During the same storm, up to twelve inches of water fell in two hours in some places. In January 1998 in upper east Tennessee, the Doe River and other waterways roared down into Carter County from the Roan Highlands, resulting in the area's being declared a federal natural disaster area. In 2001 and 2002, McDowell County, West Virginia, in the southwest part of the state, experienced a so-called one-hundred-year flood two years in a row.

See also: FOREST MANAGEMENT AND CONSERVATION; TENNESSEE VALLEY AUTHORITY (GOVERNMENT); WEEKS ACT (GOVERNMENT).

—Kathy H. Hallenbeck, *East Tennessee State University*

Chris Bolgiano, *The Appalachian Forest: A Search for Roots and Renewal* (1998); Donald Davidson, *The Tennessee* (1946–48); U.S. Department of Agriculture, *Message from the President of the United States Transmitting a Report of the Secretary of Agriculture in Relation to the Forests, Rivers, and Mountains of the Southern Appalachian Region*, Senate Document No. 84 (1902).

Forest Fragmentation

See Forest Fragmentation (Ecology)

Forest Management and Conservation

The Appalachian region, encompassing more than 128 million acres, is home to some of the most consolidated and unfragmented public lands in the eastern United States. More than 5.6 million acres lie in national forests, with a million more in national parks and national recreation areas. In addition, smaller but significant forestlands are under various state, federal, or other conservation management regimes. The roots of forest management, conservation, and restoration efforts in the region reach back more than one hundred years. The history of these efforts is a story of conservation proposals proceeding in complex ways through interactions of federal and state governments, business interests, and a wide range of citizen and conservation groups.

Barren landscape resulting from logging and fires, Mount Mitchell, North Carolina, 1923. Logging without environmental safeguards led to rapid destruction of Appalachian forests throughout the early decades of the twentieth century.

By the end of the nineteenth century, destructive agricultural and other practices in Appalachia had led to large-scale erosion and soil depletion across the region. More devastating, widespread industrial logging, including clear-cutting, caused severe wildfires and floods, further contributing to soil degradation. By the turn of the twentieth century, observers had begun raising alarms, both locally and nationally. A 1902 study authored by Secretary of Agriculture James Wilson in collaboration with some of the leading conservationists of the day and endorsed by President Theodore Roosevelt warned that unbridled exploitation of Appalachian forests, while creating wealth for a few, was leaving a barren economic and ecological landscape. Documenting the wanton forest destruction of the period, the report helped initiate a political process that resulted in the creation of national forests in the East under the Weeks Act of 1911. Great Smoky Mountains National Park was established in 1934, and Shenandoah National Park followed a year later.

Even after these management efforts had begun, however, forest destruction continued at an alarming rate for an additional thirty years in Appalachia. Major logging operations persisted in the Smokies, for example, up until the year the national park was established. In the first decades of the twentieth century, as investors foresaw an end to available timber in the South, land speculation became rampant. Logging operations during this period continued without environmental safeguards, perpetuating the devastating fires, erosion, and other destructive processes documented in the 1902 report. By the 1930s, most forested areas had either been acquired as public lands or logged—often both, since many areas were acquired only after they were stripped of trees.

Following the 1930s, Appalachian forests recovered. The lack of mature timber, combined with a U.S. Forest Service mandate, led to a period of regeneration. However, in the 1950s, the postwar boom, along with the maturing of trees in national forests, led to a dramatic increase in logging. This increase in turn led to growing opposition by environmental and conservation groups.

Initially, the emerging conservation movement had its most immediate impact through national legislation requiring protection of specific tracts of federal lands. The Wilderness Act, for example, which established the nation's National Wilderness Preservation System, was passed in 1964. Because of the way the Forest Service interpreted the act's criteria, only three areas in the Appalachians—Linville Gorge and Shining Rock in North Carolina and Great Gulf in New Hampshire—were initially considered for wilderness designation. This imbalance was addressed, however, in the Eastern Wilderness Areas Act of 1975, which validated existing criteria for wilderness in the East and designated several wilderness areas within Appalachia. Additional wilderness areas have since been added, and there were more than a half-million acres officially designated wilderness in Appalachia at the turn of the twenty-first century. Other legislative designations include national recreation areas and national scenic areas. The Mount Rogers National Recreation Area, managed by the Forest Service, and the Big South Fork National River and Recreation Area, managed by the Department of the Interior, are examples.

National forests in the United States are managed by the Forest Service, which is a division of the Department of Agriculture. Policies and procedures established under the executive branch have thus had an enormous influence on management of federal lands, as well as on the way protection and conservation legislation is implemented. For example, in 1977 the Carter administration established a formal procedure for identifying areas in the East that could be considered for wilderness designation. The process was called "RARE II" (the second Roadless Area Review and Evaluation, distinguished from a previous review that had been conducted only in the West). RARE II led to significant wilderness designations in Appalachia. Another example of an influential federal administrative initiative is the "Roadless Initiative," which the Clinton administration finalized in 2000. Under this initiative, a plan was developed for management of lands officially considered roadless in Forest Service inventories. The resulting plan was devised after the most extensive public-input process ever held in the nation up to that time. It established a ban on building roads in most roadless areas except under certain conditions, affecting hundreds of thousands of acres of Appalachian forests. The initiative stalled under the second President Bush, in part due to pressure of lawsuits by various groups and lack of support within the administration. Members of Congress planned to introduce legislation codifying the proposed administrative rule changes.

Management of federal lands is not determined by executive branch administrative decisions alone, however. Sometimes, Congress establishes guidelines that the executive branch must follow in administering the lands. For example, the National Forest Management Act of 1976 mandated development of management plans for all national forests. The act set guidelines under which the plans were to be developed, and it required input from the public. As a result, public participation in making decisions has been greatly increased. The Forest Service began to develop the mandated plans in the early 1980s, and most were finalized in the mid-1980s. In the process, most plans were influenced by citizen conservation groups, as well as by timber, mining, and other interest groups through negotiations, administrative review, and lawsuits. By influencing Forest Service management plans, conservationists have affected timber harvest levels, designation of administrative protection areas, wilderness recommendations, and a variety of other management improvements. While slowing rates of logging that had accelerated from the 1950s through the 1980s, however, the plans finalized in the mid-1980s were still unsatisfactory in the view of many conservationists because numerous roadless areas and sites of important biological and recreational value remained available for road construction and timber harvest.

Conservation efforts by state governments throughout Appalachia have also been significant. State acquisitions have added conservation and game lands in recent years. Planning and management efforts on state lands have also paralleled federal efforts, with many of the same issues and compromises affecting policies.

Southern Appalachian Man and the Biosphere is an interagency cooperative program that includes all federal land-management agencies in the region, as well as several state agencies. In the mid-1990s, this program produced *The Southern Appalachian Assessment*, a comprehensive regional appraisal that examined biological, aquatic, social, and atmospheric conditions and issues. This was the first comprehensive regional assessment since the 1902 report. It has been put to use as a basis for planning revisions to national forests and other efforts.

In recent decades, the number of significant private conservation groups in the Southeast has increased. These include regional groups such as the Southern Appalachian

Forest Coalition, Southern Environmental Law Center, Dogwood Alliance, Appalachian Voices, Heartwood, and Wildlaw, as well as forest watchdog groups that monitor activities on national forests throughout the region. The Southern Appalachian Forest Coalition has produced a document entitled *Return the Great Forest: A Conservation Vision for the Southern Appalachian Region*, which proposes a conservation network for the southern Appalachians. Addressing conservation issues on private lands is difficult because most federal environmental laws address only public lands. However, the Dogwood Alliance has carried out a campaign to protect private forestlands through campaigns to stop construction or expansion of wood-chipping facilities, to pass strong forest-protection policies in southern states, and to reduce the demand for virgin wood fiber and encourage the use of recycled and tree-free alternatives. National conservation groups have also been active in the region. The Wilderness Society has performed several studies in the Appalachians, including a series of "mountain treasure" books identifying remaining wildland areas in national forests in the region.

Forest-product industry groups, as well as other private corporate groups, also influence conservation activities and policies in Appalachia. The Southern Appalachian Multiple-Use Council and the Southern Timber Purchasers Council participated along with conservation groups in *The Southern Appalachian Assessment* and in Forest Service plan revisions. The timber industry has a high stake in the region. With timber production dropping in the Pacific Northwest, industry operations are moving to the East, particularly to the Southeast. According to the Forest Service's *Southern Forest Resource Assessment*, if the Southeast were a separate country, it would be the largest producer of forest products in the world on its own. Lands owned by utilities, lumber companies, and private citizens can often be managed for conservation purposes and wildlife habitat. Changes in land values and business strategies have prompted corporations, including Champion International and Duke Energy, to place large tracts on the market. These areas often retain great conservation values and have served as de facto components of broader landscape conservation areas. Many of these lands continue to be used for traditional uses such as hunting and fishing. Keeping these lands in their natural state and securing them under conservation management is one of the critical challenges of the early twenty-first century. Congress makes money available each year from the Land and Water Conservation Fund to buy such lands, but it has never received full funding. This shortfall hampers public agencies when acquisition opportunities occur; full funding is, therefore, a high priority for conservation groups.

Another significant conservation development at the turn of the twenty-first century was the emergence of private land trusts. In 1950 only fifty-three local and regional land trusts existed in the United States. By the year 2000, there were more than twelve hundred. In eight southeastern states alone, private land trusts expanded by 268 percent during the 1990s, from 107,861 acres protected to about 397,000 acres in 2000, with a significant portion of that acreage in Appalachia. Of the Appalachian states, Pennsylvania and New York have the highest numbers of land trusts. Though still constituting a comparatively small portion of protected areas, private land trusts are expected to play a significant role in Appalachia's conservation future.

See also: ENVIRONMENTAL LEGISLATION; EROSION.

—Hugh Irwin, *Southern Appalachian Forest Coalition*

Hugh Irwin, Susan Andrew, and Trent Bouts, *Return the Great Forest: A Conservation Vision for the Southern Appalachian Region* (2002); Southern Appalachian Man and the Biosphere Cooperative, *The Southern Appalachian Assessment* (1996); U.S. Department of Agriculture, *Message from the President of the United States Transmitting a Report of the Secretary of Agriculture in Relation to the Forests, Rivers, and Mountains of the Southern Appalachian Region*, Senate Document No. 84 (1902); David N. Wear and John G. Greis, U.S. Department of Agriculture Forest Service Southern Research Station, *Southern Forest Resource Assessment: Summary Report* (2002).

Grassroots Environmental Action

Many of Appalachia's local cultural traditions are closely tied to the natural environment. Yet since the late nineteenth century, Appalachia's economic history has been characterized by development of extractive industries that have often caused political and economic marginalization of citizens in addition to extensive environmental damage. Consequently, citizen efforts to preserve the environment have historically been connected with broader efforts to preserve local culture and independence and to ameliorate the ways in which modernization affects the region.

Historians such as Ronald D Eller and Ronald L. Lewis have documented Appalachia's transition from family-farm-based subsistence agriculture to an economy based on industrial-capitalist resource extraction in the latter half of the nineteenth century. In central Appalachia, the impact of industrialization has been especially profound due to the region's large reserves of timber, coal, and natural gas. As industrialization rose in economic importance, local groups often reacted against it. As early as the 1870s, West Virginia farmers opposed railroads because they feared that locomotives would damage their land and kill their livestock. A local newspaper in southern West Virginia, the *Greenbrier Independent*, reported that local farmers were concerned about hogs and cows being run over by trains. The paper ran articles in 1872 opposing the construction of the Chesapeake and Ohio Railway because it "carried whisky, killed chickens and cows, and scared the horses." Likewise, the residents of Tyler County, West Virginia, believed that construction of the Baltimore and Ohio Railroad would ultimately scare away the game upon which many local people depended for survival. Scattered early incidents of local resistance to industrialization such as these occurred even as the political and judicial systems increasingly favored and promoted industrial development, particularly the legal rights of railroad companies over the legal rights of farmers.

Full-fledged grassroots organization against environmental degradation did not emerge until the late 1960s and early 1970s, when groups such as Save Our Cumberland Mountains (SOCM—pronounced *sock 'em*) and Kentuckians for the Commonwealth (KFTC) were organized in response to damage caused by strip mining. By the early 1970s, flooding and silting of streams in the underdeveloped, coal-dominated regions of the Cumberland Mountains had led local people to question the longterm sustainability of strip mining. Within two years of its formation, SOCM had four hundred members working in a six-county region. Kentuckians for the Commonwealth, since its founding in 1981, has focused attention on problems associated with the uneven ownership and control of land and natural resources that have caused environmental degradation and social injustice within Appalachian Kentucky. The group has blocked unwanted incinerators, prevented industrial water pollution, acquired funds for community water systems, and led a historical campaign to ban the broad form deed, which permitted coal companies with subsurface mineral rights to destroy landowners' property. Such organizations typically address broader social justice issues, in addition to environmental issues. For example, neither SOCM nor KFTC can be simply labeled an environmental organization. SOCM defines itself as a citizens' organization working for social, environmental, and economic justice to improve quality of life within local communities. Similarly, KFTC defines itself as a citizens' social justice group that uses direct-action community organizing to improve the quality of life for all Kentuckians.

In the last three decades of the twentieth century, other groups in Appalachia coalesced around specific environmental issues. In 1972 the White Deer Valley Citizens Committee formed to stop a proposed landfill in Lycoming County, Pennsylvania; it later became the Organizations United for the Environment. The practice of coal mining through mountaintop removal prompted the formation of such organizations as the Citizens Coal Council, a coalition of forty-eight grassroots groups and individuals opposed to mountaintop removal in Kentucky, Tennessee, Virginia, and West Virginia. The increasing rate of timber extraction in the region has prompted the formation of groups such as the Southern Appalachian Forest Coalition, Appalachian Voices, and Cherokee Forest Voices. These organizations, based in east Tennessee and western North Carolina, share a common goal of promoting sustainable forest practices through citizen involvement. The decade of the 1990s saw the formation of numerous environmental groups in the coalfields of Pennsylvania, including the Shamokin Creek Restoration Alliance, the Mountain Watershed Alliance, and the Tri-State Citizens Mining Network. These organizations work largely on acid mine drainage remediation efforts in order to improve water supplies still threatened from decades of coal-mining abuses. Other grassroots environmental organizations that have been effective in Appalachia since the 1990s include the Ohio Valley Environmental Coalition, based in Huntington, West Virginia, and Coal River Mountain Watch, based in Whitesville, West Virginia.

The future of environmental advocacy within Appalachia is sure to become increasingly complex. Unlike environmental struggles at the end of the nineteenth century primarily between farmers and industrialists, contemporary struggles over the environment involve many groups, with overlapping and often conflicting opinions over how the environment should be preserved. Environmental organizations sometimes differ with local farmers over policy issues, for example. One such issue is the Wild and Scenic Rivers Act, which aims to limit the agricultural use of land adjacent to designated rivers in order to preserve rivers in a free-flowing condition and to protect them from pollution. Environmental groups have promoted the act, particularly within West Virginia, as a way to increase tourism and as a sustainable means of economic development. In Pendleton County, West Virginia, however, local farmers have opposed the act because they view it as a threat to their ability to use their land in a way that is agriculturally most productive. Such conflicts have resulted in the formation of a local citizen-based organization called the Ecological Policy Institute, spearheaded by the local landowning and farming population as a direct result of the perceived infringement on property rights by ecologically driven tourism groups. The institute and other such organizations hold the view that local environmental decisions are disproportionately influenced by recent immigrants to Appalachia from urban areas who are not sympathetic to local economic needs.

Negotiations between such overlapping groups will most likely characterize citizen environmental action in the Appalachian region in the twenty-first century. Because the natural environment is fundamental to the way in which Appalachians make a living and define themselves culturally, citizen groups will continue to play an important role in determining how nature is owned, accessed, and ultimately utilized by people living both within and outside of the mountain region.

See also: COMMUNITY ACTION GROUPS (FAMILY AND COMMUNITY); ENVIRONMENTAL LEGISLATION.

—J. Todd Nesbitt, *Lock Haven University of Pennsylvania*

Ronald D Eller, *Miners, Millhands, and Mountaineers: Industrialization of the Appalachian South, 1880–1930* (1982); Stephen L. Fisher, ed., *Fighting Back in Appalachia: Traditions of Resistance and Change* (1993); Ronald L. Lewis, *Transforming the Appalachian Countryside: Railroads, Deforestation, and Social Change in West Virginia, 1880–1920* (1998).

Industrial Pollution

Economic and industrial expansion following the Civil War created a strong demand for the rich natural resources of Appalachia. These resources were initially developed with little concern for environmental impacts. Coal and mineral mining, the growth of the related iron and steel industries, and massive timber cutting presented, and continue to present, longterm threats to land quality. Although mining and coal industries are now required to reclaim land after operations have been completed, these and other industries have left a long legacy of air, water, and soil contamination that was not addressed until the late twentieth century.

During the early days of coal mining, little thought was given to the environment. Early mining processes created severe environmental degradation, including acid mine drainage that contaminates surface water and groundwater. Other environmental contamination resulted from fuel spills and storage tank discharges, explosives, and nitrate fertilizers used for large fragmentation charges. Kentucky, West Virginia, Tennessee, Pennsylvania, and Ohio were most severely affected by past coal-mining practices.

Environmental contaminants associated with steel and iron production include heavy metals such as lead, zinc, arsenic, and cadmium and groundwater pollutants such as benzene, toluene, xylene, ammonia, cyanide, and phenolics. Other sources of contamination include leaking wastewater treatment ponds and lagoons; scrap yards; disposal piles; pits and ponds containing coal tars; sludges; and underground storage tanks used for fuel and chemicals. Many areas of Appalachia—especially Birmingham, Pittsburgh, and parts of Tennessee—bear the brunt of the environmental impact of iron and steel industries. Gold, copper, and lead mines also operated in the 1800s in southern Appalachia. The extraction and smelting processes often left behind heavy metal contamination from lead, copper, and arsenic.

The oil and gas industry, particularly in West Virginia, Pennsylvania, and Kentucky, causes significant environmental degradation in the form of soil, surface water, and groundwater contamination from seeps, spills, and mishandled extracted products. Oil and gas storage facilities also contribute to soil and water contamination by leaking and spilling fuel oils, motor oil, and oil sludges. Waste streams associated with oil and gas operations include petroleum hydrocarbons, metals such as zinc and lead, and polychlorinated biphenyls, or PCBs.

Coal-fired electric plant, Midland, Pennsylvania, 1982. The cooling towers of this plant represent a thermal pollution issue for fish and plant life in the adjacent river. A nearby steel mill in the town center, now closed, was a further source of pollution in this industrial region.

A wide variety of industries that produce products from Appalachian forests—shingles, lumber, furniture, and crossties, for example—also generate pollution in the form of creosote, waste paints, stains, petroleum products, and heavy metals. Paper mills pollute streams with wastewater and sometimes introduce spent pulping liquors into groundwater. Common contaminants include chlorinated organic compounds, dioxins, furans, chloroform, acetic acid, benzoic acid, formaldehyde, and hydrogen sulfide.

At the beginning of the twentieth century, the textile industry began to flourish in Georgia, South Carolina, Alabama, and North Carolina. Mills that handled dyes threatened both surface water and groundwater with aromatic compounds such as benzene and naphthalene; inorganic chemicals such as sulfuric acid, nitric acid, chlorine, and caustic soda; and heavy metals such as copper, chromium, mercury, and zinc. These constituents were stored in tanks, drums, or containers located on-site.

In the glass-manufacturing industry, heavy metals often provide pigment for glass and may include cobalt, zinc, thorium, and uranium. Organic dyes are also used. Surface soil and groundwater may be polluted from solid and liquid waste streams. Fluoride in waste streams (primarily from hydrogen fluoride used in etching the glass) is particularly hazardous to humans.

Among Appalachia's most polluted sites are abandoned chemical facilities concentrated in Tennessee, Kentucky, and West Virginia. Underground and aboveground bulk storage tanks for toxic chemicals used in formulating products are often seriously contaminated. Waste ponds, waste piles, and disposal pits add to contamination at these sites. Chemical facilities have also contributed to contamination of soil and groundwater by copper, lead, zinc, arsenic, mercury, chromium, and other elements.

See also: COAL MINING; COAL SLURRY IMPOUNDMENTS; POLLUTION CLEANUP PROGRAMS; SOLID-WASTE MANAGEMENT.

—Robert D. Schimtter, *Georgia Institute of Technology*

Ronald D Eller, *Miners, Millhands, and Mountaineers: Industrialization of the Appalachian South, 1880–1930* (1982); Robert A. Simons, *Turning Brownfields into Greenbacks* (1998).

Invasive Species

Invasive species include exotic (non-native) plants, animals, insects, fungi, and diseases that enter a region and expand aggressively, significantly altering native species and ecologies. The vast majority of exotic species brought into Appalachia do not become invasive, but the few that do threaten the region's special ecology and rich biodiversity.

Since the mid-1800s, the region has been increasingly vulnerable to this threat, and each year the federal government spends tens of millions of dollars on rapid response to invasive species in national forests and national parks alone. In addition, much more is spent on attempts at prevention of invasions, as well as detection, control, research, information management, and public education. Non-federal expenditures likely bring the total yearly cost of invasive species control to hundreds of millions of dollars for the region.

Exotic invasions come from every direction and affect all types of habitats. For example, the zebra mussel has worked its way into Appalachia from the Midwest and established itself across the region, clogging water pipes and endangering native mussels. The gypsy moth and chestnut blight started in northeastern cities before spreading southward. Kudzu, first introduced in Philadelphia in 1876, spread across the entire South after being heavily promoted by the Department of Agriculture to prevent and control soil erosion during the 1930s. Exotic animals that have become invasive include European wild boars, the progenitors of which escaped from a North Carolina game preserve in the early 1900s. The boars' extensive rooting interferes with native plants and wildlife. Efforts to control the boar population in the Great Smoky Mountains National Park have been ongoing in various forms since the late 1950s.

Grasses were among the first exotic plants introduced to the mountains by Europeans, as early settlers coming to America were often instructed to bring grass seed as part of their provisions. In fact, prior to 1800, the adjective *English* was often used to distinguish introduced grass species from indigenous vegetation. The first settlers also brought with them such herbaceous species as chicory, Japanese stilt grass, Japanese knotweed, garlic mustard, spotted knapweed, mile-a-minute vine, privet, oriental bittersweet, and Japanese honeysuckle. All of these plants continue to expand their ranges and increase their impact on the mountain environment.

Human activity often encourages exotic invasions. Land disturbance and development provide a convenient stepping-stone for exotic species to enter forests and woodlands. People also unknowingly plant or transport seeds or parts of plants that can grow, multiply, and invade natural areas. This process has accelerated in recent decades with increased trade, travel, and outdoor recreation. In the lower elevations of Appalachia, invasive plants are spreading deeper into the mountains, especially where roads, streams, development, railroads, and other rights-of-way converge. In mid-elevation forests, pest plants are appearing more frequently at locations exposed by fire, landslides, flooding, harvesting, and development. At high elevations, forests are increasingly vulnerable to invasive species because of the environmental stresses from air pollution and acid precipitation.

With increasing awareness of the threat, many state agencies, regional organizations, and interest groups in the region have begun developing their own lists of exotic invasive species. The species are often grouped by their degree of invasiveness or by the habitats they affect. New, potential, and expanding invaders include West Nile virus (causing death among many songbirds), tree-of-heaven, purple loosestrife, the princess tree (also called royal paulownia), the Asian long-horned beetle, fire ants, cogon grass, two woolly adelgids (affecting balsam firs and hemlocks), and sudden oak death. Aquatic habitats are also being increasingly overrun by hydrilla, Eurasian water milfoil, Asian clam, and grass carp. Since aquatic, wetland, and streamside habitats are especially diverse, invasions of these areas are of special concern to Appalachian ecologists and environmentalists.

See also: EXOTIC SPECIES (ECOLOGY).

—J. Warren Ranney, *University of Tennessee*

Andrew M. Liebhold et al., *Invasion by Exotic Forest Pests: A Threat to Forest Ecosystems* (1995); Mark H. Williamson, *Biological Invasions* (1996).

Johnstown Flood

On May 31, 1889, the small industrial city of Johnstown, Pennsylvania, suffered one of the worst man-made disasters in the history of the United States. With the failure of the South Fork Dam to contain Lake Conemaugh on the South Fork of the Little Conemaugh River in Cambria County, a wall of 20 million tons of water more than thirty-five feet high came crashing into Johnstown. The force, rivaling that of Niagara Falls, leveled commercial buildings, swept away homes, and killed more than twenty-two hundred people.

The earthen dam at South Fork had been constructed between 1838 and 1853 as part of a transportation canal project that was never completed. Members of the prestigious South Fork Fishing and Hunting Club (among them Henry Clay Frick and Andrew Carnegie) subsequently bought the lake and surrounding property. The dam was poorly maintained, however, and each spring there was talk—and even joking—among the townspeople about how the dam might not hold.

In the years before the disaster, the problem of yearly flooding was a routine hazard to the people of Johnstown. The town is nestled in a valley between the Little Conemaugh River and Stony Creek, and the confluence of the two streams forms the Conemaugh River at the western end of town. At least once a year, the melting of winter snows or seasonal heavy rains sent water out of its banks. During such floods, townspeople would scamper to save what they could of their belongings and homes, moving to the second stories of their dwellings to wait out the worst of the weather.

Heavy rains marked the end of May 1889, and the people of the city were in the midst of the usual flood preparation. However, unlike previous rains, this deluge proved catastrophic to the South Fork Dam. Despite efforts of the South Fork Fishing and Hunting Club officials and other town laborers, the structure gave way. The resulting wave of water, including debris such as buildings, animals, and people, living and dead, crashed into Johnstown, fourteen miles below the dam, at an estimated speed of forty miles per hour. The Pennsylvania Railroad Company's Stone Bridge, located in Johnstown, served as a barrier for much of the debris, which piled up at the structure and eventually caught fire. Some people were rescued at the bridge, but many died in the fire. Others were swept down Conemaugh River and were rescued at communities downstream. Many more, however, perished in the incident. In the aftermath of the disaster, the dead were collected in makeshift morgues at points throughout the city, including the Presbyterian Church on Main Street. In addition to the remnants of buildings and homes, coffins constructed to collect the dead lined the wreckage as townspeople began the process of cleaning up. Organizations such as the American Red Cross and individuals throughout the nation responded to the tragedy. Aid workers erected prefabricated buildings to house the homeless during the rebuilding effort and raised more than \$3.7 million in relief funds within the United States and from eighteen foreign countries.

Despite the immensity of the tragedy, survivors received no financial compensation, and the event led to no legislation or regulation. Efforts to control routine flooding were sporadic after 1889, until work teams under the federal government Works Progress Administration built masonry and concrete floodwalls in the 1930s.

See also: BUFFALO CREEK FLOOD; EROSION; FLOODS.

—Devon Koren Asdell, *East Tennessee State University*

David Beale, *Through the Johnstown Flood* (1890); David G. McCullough, *The Johnstown Flood* (1968); Richard O'Connor, *Johnstown: The Day the Dam Broke* (1957).

Land Trusts and Conservancies

Established to protect land that has natural, scenic, historic, cultural, recreational, or agricultural value, land trusts and conservancies have become important instruments of conservation in Appalachia, taking advantage of their nonprofit status to become directly involved in land transactions. Throughout the United States, the activity of such organizations has steadily increased in recent decades. In Appalachia, many types of land trusts have emerged.

At the beginning of the twentieth century, very few land trusts existed in the United States. The Trustees of Reservations, established in Massachusetts in 1891, was the first private statewide land trust. Most land trusts were established much later. In 1950 only fifty-three local and regional land trusts existed in the United States, but by the year 2000 there were more than twelve hundred. The proliferation of the trusts was aided by the Land Trust Alliance, established in 1982 to provide resource programs to the growing number of such organizations across the country. According to the alliance's 2000 census, local and regional land trusts helped protect more than 6.2 million acres of open space in the United States. In eight southeastern states alone, private land in trusts expanded by 268 percent during the 1990s, from 107,861 protected acres to about 397,000 acres in 2000. The alliance began a Southeast program in 2001 because of the burgeoning number of conservancies in the area. Of the Appalachian states, Pennsylvania and New York have the highest numbers of land trusts.

Trusts protect land in several ways. Some directly purchase land or accept donations of land. They may also assist other private or governmental organizations in acquiring land for conservation. Another method by which a land trust may protect property is by accepting a conservation easement, a legal agreement between the landowner and the land trust that permanently restricts the use and development of land. In this arrangement, the landowner may continue to own the property. The land trust helps monitor and enforce the terms of the easement. The property can be sold at a later date or passed on to heirs, but any future landowners are also bound by the terms of the easement. In return for giving up some rights to use or sell the land for future development, the landowner often obtains substantial tax benefits. In some cases, conservation easements thus help families to continue owning land that they might otherwise be forced to sell because of increased tax burdens that result when residential or commercial development encroaches on previously rural land.

Land trust and conservancy organizations in Appalachia are too numerous to list, but some have noteworthy achievements. The West Virginia Highlands Conservancy was founded in 1967. In addition to acquiring land, this group has worked to promote designation of federal wilderness areas and has campaigned against mountaintop-removal mining and for stronger timber regulations. The Southern Appalachian Highlands Conservancy has protected 21,000 acres in western North Carolina and east Tennessee since its inception in 1974. One of its conservation projects is the preservation of the Roan Highlands on the Tennessee–North Carolina border. In North Carolina, the conservancy also protects areas in the Black Mountains and at Cataloochee Ranch, which borders the Great Smoky Mountains. Another important land trust in southern Appalachia is the Chattooga Conservancy. Established in 1991, the trust protects the 180,000-acre watershed of the Chattooga River, which forms the boundary between northeast Georgia and northwest South Carolina and lies in three adjoining national forests in Georgia, North Carolina, and South Carolina. Intensive logging previously threatened the ecosystem in this area, and the conservancy monitors U.S. Forest Service activities in the watershed to ensure proper management. The Appalachian Trail Conference Land Trust was established in 1982 to help the federal government acquire land for a one-thousand-foot-wide corridor along the Appalachian Trail, which runs from Georgia to Maine. This conservancy buys land and accepts both donations of land and conservation easements adjoining the land on which the trail is located. Near the Great Smoky Mountains National Park, the Foothills Land Conservancy has acquired land to create a buffer zone against residential and commercial development along the Tennessee park boundary and to provide feeding grounds for black bears and other native wildlife. The Foothills Land Conservancy has protected more than 14,000 acres in east Tennessee since its inception in 1985. Another group, the Southeastern Cave Conservancy, was formed in 1991 to preserve and manage caves and their ecosystems. Caves provide the habitat for many native species, including the endangered gray bat and the Tennessee cave salamander. Land trusts can also protect land with historic value. For example, the Civil War Preservation Trust has protected more than 16,000 acres of Civil War battlefields, many of which are in the Appalachian region.

The U.S. Department of Agriculture's National Resources Inventory in 1997 showed that the country's privately owned open spaces were being developed at a rate of more than 2 million acres a year. The ten states with the highest rate of development included several in the Appalachian region, including Georgia, North Carolina, Tennessee, and South Carolina. It remains to be seen if the increasing numbers of Appalachian land trusts will reverse this trend.

See also: SPRAWL.

—Rhonda H. Rucker, *Maryville, Tennessee*

Eve Endicott, ed., *Land Conservation through Public/Private Partnerships* (1993); Julie Ann Gustanski and Roderick H. Squires, eds., *Protecting the Land: Conservation Easements Past, Present, and Future* (2000); Stephen J. Small, *Preserving Family Lands: Essential Tax Strategies for the Landowner* (1992).

Land Use

Appalachia can be divided into four main physiographic provinces. Proceeding generally east to west (perpendicular to the line of direction of the Appalachian Mountains), these provinces are the Piedmont, the Blue Ridge, the Ridge and Valley, and the Appalachian Plateaus. Each province possesses a distinct biophysical character and supports distinct settlement patterns and land uses. Although the Piedmont Province has important cultural and historical connections to the region, it is not discussed in this entry, which concerns land use in the more representative highlands of Appalachia.

The term *Blue Ridge* is often used to refer to the first high eastern rampart of Appalachian Mountain system. In their broadest sense, the Blue Ridge Mountains encompass all of the highlands on the eastern edge of the Appalachian region, including such ranges as the Unakas and the Smokies, which parallel the Blue Ridge proper, and concurrent or transverse ranges such as the Blacks and the Nantahalas. During colonial times, the Blue Ridge Mountains posed a topographic barrier to migration from the Atlantic Coastal Plain and Piedmont. Though the steep, forested slopes of granite and basalt do not suggest an agrarian landscape, the region did support farms in the hollows and on the gentler slopes. In recent times, the number of farms in the region has declined, and the Blue Ridge remains largely covered by second-growth forest. The region has experienced increased recreational development, but it has no major urban centers, and it has the lowest population density of the three physiographic provinces discussed here.

West of the Blue Ridge, the limestones, sandstones, and shales that form the Ridge and Valley are products of Cambrian seas that once submerged the interior of North America. Folding and selective erosion of these strata left steep, parallel ridges of resistant sandstone and rounded shale knobs, alternating with limestone and shale valleys. Today the ridges, with steep slopes and thin, infertile soils, remain forested, but the level, arable valleys experience intensive farm use and growing urban and industrial pressures. The anthracite region in the northeastern Ridge and Valley has been producing coal since 1790 and played a major role in the early industrialization of the eastern United States.

Farther west, above the Ridge and Valley, the Appalachian Plateaus Province includes what are now called the Allegheny Mountains in the north and the Cumberland Mountains and Greenbriar Karst to the south. Though the geology is similar to that of the Ridge and Valley, the strata of sandstone, shale, and conglomerate, rather than being folded, lie relatively flat and undeformed except for some gentle folding in the Allegheny Mountains. However, the high dissection of the plateau gives the impression of a rugged mountainous terrain. Strata of bituminous coal are a major element of the layered geology. Arable limestone areas, on the other hand, are not as widely distributed in this province as in the Ridge and Valley to the east. As a result, coal mining and silviculture (the development and care of forests), rather than commercial agriculture, are the major land uses in this province.

The same factors that determine the boundaries of the major physiographic provinces play a large role in determining land use. For example, constraints on human activities in the Blue Ridge, particularly in the middle highlands around eastern Pennsylvania, were evident during early European settlement, when topography, soil capability, and mineral availability greatly influenced migration patterns, farming practices, and the growth of industry. Beginning in the late eighteenth century, eastern Pennsylvania became the focal point for waves of immigrants following the axes of parallel valleys and mountain passes. In the agrarian society of the late 1700s, most of the settlers arriving in the central Appalachians expected to make a living through farming. Settlers unable to afford the rich farmland in the limestone valleys of the Ridge and Valley adopted frontier farming methods either on the forested Blue Ridge or on the Appalachian Plateaus. Farming on thin, sloping woodland soils proved to be futile in the long run. Over a period of 150 years, soil and nutrient loss made even subsistence farming too difficult and unproductive, and by the 1930s the trend toward farmland abandonment had begun. Limestone valley farms, on the other hand, located on fertile soils characteristic of the Ridge and Valley, have maintained high productivity despite land division among succeeding generations and economic pressures to expand production.

Other patterns have been influenced by the evolution of particular technologies as well as characteristics of the biophysical regions. The extraction of timber and coal, for example, was delayed by inaccessibility and isolation from eastern markets until railroads began penetrating both the Blue Ridge and the Appalachian Plateaus in the 1870s. A cycle of timber removal ensued, with virtually complete clearing of these regions by the 1920s, followed by erosion of the deforested hillsides, frequent fires in the regenerating brush fields, and eventual reforestation. The land-use pattern of coal mining has similarly followed economic cycles and advances in extraction technology. Underground mines of the nineteenth and early twentieth centuries were outnumbered by strip mines in the 1950s. By the 1990s, mountaintop-removal operations were increasing on the Appalachian Plateaus.

Within the major physiographic provinces, aerial photographs demonstrate the accumulated patterns of land use. On the Appalachian Plateaus, most of the remaining farmland, as well as urban and industrial development, is confined to narrow alluvial lands near streams. Upland forested areas show the pattern of strip mining. On the ridges of the Ridge and Valley, both clear-cut and selective-cut logging occur where steep slopes and infertile soil have discouraged agricultural clearing. The shale and limestone valleys, on the other hand, have level topography and a soil capability to support farming, as well as urban and industrial development.

The presence or absence of particular resources among regions determines, in turn, the types of regional disturbance and their ecological effects. Agriculture, a major human activity in the Ridge and Valley, is a minor pursuit in the forested Blue Ridge and Appalachian Plateaus. Mining is limited to the northeastern portion of the Ridge and Valley but widely distributed across the entire Appalachian Plateaus Province. The types of stressors or ecological effects on aquatic ecosystems likewise vary by region.

Future land-use trends across Appalachia may include increasing development of areas in the Blue Ridge and Appalachian Plateaus that were formally regarded as uneconomical. Though high mountains and rugged terrain were long considered barren, these areas have gained value from their scenery and natural beauty and from the moderating influence that elevation has on climate. These areas have thus become increasingly attractive to tourists and second-home and retirement-home owners. In addition, continued road construction in these areas has provided access to automobile travel, which will probably lead to increased land use and development in the twenty-first century. At the same time, these regions are expected to be subject to increasing pressures for energy extraction and refuse disposal.

See also: SECTION OVERVIEW (GEOLOGY); SPRAWL; VIEWSHED PROTECTION.

—John Fittipaldi, *Army Environmental Policy Institute*

R. G. Bailey, *Descriptions of the Ecoregions of the United States* (2nd edition, 1995); Karl B. Raitz and Richard Ulack, *Appalachia: A Regional Geography* (1984).

Mine Land Reclamation

Mine lands, or more accurately, abandoned mine lands, are a legacy of generations of both surface and underground coal-mining practices in the Appalachians. Large areas of abandoned mine lands exist in the Appalachian areas of Alabama, Kentucky, Maryland, Ohio, Pennsylvania, Tennessee, Virginia, and West Virginia. Of these eight states, the highest numbers of sites are in Pennsylvania and West Virginia. Such sites are characterized by public health and safety hazards and by degradation of land, water, and air. Specifically, they are marked by unstable and erodable outslopes; open portals and unmarked ventilation shafts; subsidence beneath homes and structures; burning coal-refuse piles that emit sulfur dioxide; exposed mine and mine-processing waste ("gob" piles) that can produce toxic or acid drainage; coal-waste impoundment dams prone to collapse; and miles of streams choked with sediment, making them subject to flooding.

Beginning with large-scale development of the coal industry in the region after the Civil War and until the 1930s, few efforts were made at mine land reclamation. In the 1930s and 1940s, reclamation largely consisted of moving enough earth to level the tops of spoil piles left behind by shovels or draglines. By the late 1940s, some states had begun to require surface mines to grade and level spoil and to place nontoxic material on the surface of completed mine sites.

Such regulation was minimal, however, until the tragic Buffalo Creek flood of 1972, when a large coal-waste impoundment dam failed in Logan County, West Virginia, killing 125 people. Spurred in part by that disaster and also by citizens demanding change for many years, Congress finally passed the Surface Mining Control and Reclamation Act of 1977. The act provides formal recognition of the adverse effects resulting from years of neglecting abandoned mine lands, declaring that "unreclaimed lands impose social and economic costs on residents in nearby and adjoining areas as well as continuing to impair environmental quality."

The Surface Mining Control and Reclamation Act established the Office of Surface Mining Reclamation and Enforcement under the U.S. Department of the Interior. The act also created an Abandoned Mine Reclamation Fund, made up of fees assessed against coal producers, to restore lands abandoned or left inadequately reclaimed prior to 1977. Regulation of land reclamation is now the responsibility of a combination of federal and state agencies, including the Office of Surface Mining Reclamation and Enforcement and state authorities such as the Abandoned Mine Lands Section of the Tennessee Division of Water Pollution Control. Current regulations require concurrent (while mining) reclamation, segregation of topsoils and subsoils with replacement in sequence after completion of mining, and strict controls on water quantity and quality.

Implementation of new regulations has been erratic, however. Success in reclaiming sites is determined not only by the adequacy of regulations, but also by consistency of enforcement. The patchwork nature of state and federal regulations often leads to inconsistent policing of sites. Another problem is that the cumulative effects of abandoned sites are often ignored. Federal and state regulators tend to focus attention only on single permits, while ignoring the overall impact of numerous sites on a watershed or region.

A number of citizens' groups work to promote enforcement of reclamation standards and act as regulatory watchdogs in Appalachian communities. Such groups include Save Our Cumberland Mountains (or SOCM—pronounced *sock 'em*) of Lake City, Tennessee, and the West Virginia Highlands Conservancy of Charleston, West Virginia. Such groups also promote reclamation regulations and standards. Save Our Cumberland Mountains, for example, was one of the first organizations to advocate state and federal laws to address issues relating to abandoned mine lands in the region. The group has also worked to develop comprehensive reclamation standards and secure funds to restore more than 280 known legacy sites in Tennessee.

Numerous institutions engage in continuing research on reclamation strategies and techniques. Work on revegetation of mine lands probably began in midwestern states such as Illinois in the 1940s and 1950s and was later expanded to studies more suitable for terrain of the eastern coalfields. During the 1950s and 1960s, university research in Pennsylvania, West Virginia, Kentucky, and Ohio, as well as U.S. Forest Service experiment stations, examined methods for amending mine soils with lime, organic matter, and fertilizers to allow more rapid establishment of trees, shrubs, and non-woody plants. While some investigators took care to promote native species for revegetation, many early researchers did not. One result has been the proliferation of invasive, non-native plant species on and near former mine sites in Appalachia.

The success of reclamation efforts has been mixed, especially at mountaintop-removal sites. Some industry-funded research groups, such as the Powell River Project of southwest Virginia, maintain that the use of advanced methods can lead to forests that are more productive than the native forests that stood on mined sites. In practice, such advanced reclamation methods are rarely implemented and cannot remedy the destruction of landscapes nor the burial of streams beneath valley fills. The destruction of streambeds results in excessive siltation and flooding and leads to damage of water resources historically used by households and agriculture.

See also: BUFFALO CREEK FLOOD; COAL MINING; POLLUTION CLEANUP PROGRAMS.

—Landon Medley and Annetta Watson, *Save Our Cumberland Mountains, Inc.*

James M. McElfish and Ann E. Beier, *Environmental Regulation of Coal Mining* (1990); *Surface Mining Control and Reclamation Act of 1977*, PL 95-87, 95th Congress (August 3, 1977); U.S. Department of Interior Office of Surface Mining, *Final Petition Evaluation Document/Environmental Impact Statement on Fall Creek Falls, Tennessee* (2000).

Pollution Cleanup Programs

Since the late 1800s, industrial development has profoundly modified both the cultural and environmental landscapes of Appalachia. During the first half of the twentieth century, the growth and expansion of the coal, chemical, and steel industries within Appalachia transformed parts of the region into some of the most industrialized areas in the world. The coalfields of southern West Virginia, for example, were among the most heavily industrialized and culturally diverse parts of the United States by the 1920s. Beginning in the mid-1950s, however, many plants and coal mines were closed due to mechanization and increased international competition. Particularly within central and northern Appalachia, the decline of industry left toxic environmental waste abandoned and untreated. Because of this history, local communities within Appalachia continue to be faced with often overwhelming environmental cleanup tasks. Although the responsibility for cleaning up fell largely to communities, the federal government initiated a number of programs to facilitate environmental remediation and economic redevelopment.

Within coal-dominated regions of central and southern Appalachia, the federal Office of Surface Mining has coordinated numerous cleanup programs. One such program is the Appalachian Clean Streams Initiative, a broad-based collaboration striving to eliminate acid mine drainage from abandoned coal mines. The U.S. Department of the Interior, which oversees the Office of Surface Mining, has determined that acid mine drainage from abandoned coal mines is the primary water-quality problem within Appalachia. The problem is extensive throughout coal regions in central and southern Appalachia; thousands of miles of streams are so badly polluted with acid mine drainage that all plant and animal life has been destroyed. The Clean Streams Initiative has responded to the problem by using a combination of government and private resources to facilitate cooperation among citizens' groups, university researchers, the coal industry, corporations, the environmental community, and local, state, and federal agencies involved in cleaning up streams polluted by acid mine drainage.

One of the most successful remediation projects undertaken by the Clean Streams Initiative is the cleanup of Sovern Run, a tributary of Big Sandy Creek located in northern West Virginia. Since the Environmental Protection Agency (EPA) began monitoring water quality in the stream in the early 1990s, it has found dramatic improvements in watershed quality. Collaboration among the National Mine Land Reclamation Center at West Virginia University, the West Virginia Division of Environmental Protection, a local engineering firm, and local community organizations has resulted in structural improvements to the watershed and has thus reduced acid mine drainage into Big Sandy Creek and the Cheat River.

Sovern Run represents but one example of how a government agency can involve Appalachian citizens in environmental remediation. Other examples include the Monday Creek Restoration Project in southeastern Ohio and the Conemaugh River Improvement Project in southwestern Pennsylvania. Like the Sovern Run Acid Mine Drainage Project, these projects involve a multitude of public and private agencies and organizations cooperating to improve environmental quality.

Other programs have been established to clean up pollution from abandoned industrial plants and factories in the region. Especially in northern Appalachia, industrial restructuring in the 1970s and 1980s led to plant closings on a massive scale. Manufacturing companies relocated to underdeveloped countries to gain access to cheap labor, leaving behind massive unemployment as well as many abandoned industrial sites, particularly in the Pittsburgh metropolitan region. Numerous government agencies have been involved in the cleanup of abandoned sites. One of their primary goals has been to involve the public in decisions regarding environmental quality.

The EPA's Brownfields Redevelopment Program is probably the most far-reaching of such initiatives. Also known as the Brownfields Economic Redevelopment Initiative, this program is designed to empower states and local communities to clean up and reuse brownfields. The EPA defines a brownfield as an abandoned industrial site that has actual or perceived contamination and an active potential for economic redevelopment. Since 1995, the EPA has funded more than 150 Brownfield Assessment Demonstration Pilots at up to two hundred thousand dollars each to support community-based, two-year explorations and demonstrations of brownfield solutions. Although not exclusive to Appalachia, many of the pilot projects have been carried out within the region, successfully remediating toxic waste and redeveloping abandoned industrial districts. Wheeling, West Virginia, and Johnstown, Pennsylvania, provide two of the best examples of cities within northern Appalachia that have been selected for Brownfield Assessment Demonstration Pilot Projects.

Such government-sponsored programs have succeeded in involving citizens in environmental policy in some parts of Appalachia. In other areas, however—especially within extremely underdeveloped Appalachian communities—citizens' interests remain grossly underrepresented. Local governing bodies are often made up of small groups of local elites who simultaneously serve as government leaders and major employers. Environmentally destructive policies that benefit the local elites while harming local majorities are often the result. Environmentalist Janice Morrissey's case study of landfill development in southern West Virginia and east Tennessee, for example, revealed that local government officials almost unanimously supported the creation of landfills without regard for longterm damage to communities' natural resources. Morrissey suggested that local elites, though often a product of local cultures, become tied to elites outside of Appalachia who invest in and control development projects within the region. Thus, in many of the most impoverished Appalachian communities, citizen participation programs, when they do exist, have limited impact on final decisions regarding environmental policy.

The success of governmental programs seeking to involve and empower the public in environmental cleanup within Appalachia depends upon a number of complex, interrelated factors. Experience has shown that government programs must be coordinated and administered by grassroots organizations in order to reach a majority of the local population. Furthermore, the success of government-led environmental programs depends on local governments' abilities to balance the interests of industry and local populations.

See also: MINE LAND RECLAMATION; STRIP MINE WORKERS (LABOR).

—J. Todd Nesbitt, *Lock Haven University of Pennsylvania*

Denise Giardina, *Storming Heaven* (1987); Janice C. Morrissey, "Citizen Participation in Environmental Policy: A Study of Landfill Siting in Two Appalachian Communities," Ph.D. dissertation, University of Tennessee (1996); U.S. Environmental Protection Agency, *Sites for Our Solid Waste: A Guidebook for Effective Public Involvement* (1990).

Radioactive Waste

Surrounded by extraordinary military secrecy, workers at Oak Ridge, Tennessee, enriched uranium for the world's first atomic bomb during World War II and quietly introduced the seemingly intransigent environmental issue of radioactive-waste management to Appalachia. In the early twenty-first century, the retired gaseous diffusion plant that completed separation of weapons-grade uranium from naturally occurring ore was yet to be fully decontaminated. By then, the region and the nation faced a variety of additional radioactive-waste issues spawned by nuclear technologies.

Sixty years after Oak Ridge played its crucial role in the Manhattan Project, ten nuclear reactors were generating electricity at five power plants in Appalachia, placing radioactive spent fuel in temporary storage, where it awaited permanent disposal. Across the region, hospitals, research laboratories, and government installations produced waste tainted with low-level radiation as policymakers continued to seek environmentally acceptable and politically palatable disposal arrangements. Permanent disposition of spent reactor fuel continued to be the most difficult problem in the host of "radwaste" issues.

Most of the nuclear plants in the region began operating in the 1970s. The Tennessee Valley Authority continues to operate two reactors at its Browns Ferry plant in north Alabama, two at its Sequoyah facility near Chattanooga, Tennessee, and one at Watts Bar, not far from Knoxville, Tennessee. In 2003 preparations began to restart a third Browns Ferry unit, which had been shut down since 1985. Duke Power Company operates three units at its Oconee generating plant near Greenville, South Carolina, and a consortium of electrical utilities runs two at the Beaver Valley Power Station in southwestern Pennsylvania.

In the course of twelve to eighteen months, one-fourth to one-third of the uranium fuel elements are removed from each of these reactors, and the spent fuel, still intensely radioactive, is stored in deep pools of water within the reactors' containment buildings. In many nuclear plants across the country, storage pools have been filled to capacity, forcing utilities to turn to heavy, permanently sealed metal casks for backup storage. At South Carolina's Oconee plant, storage pools reached their capacity in 1990; at Tennessee's Sequoyah station, pools reached their capacity in 2003.

After two decades of testing and analysis, the U.S. Department of Energy announced in 2002 that it would make Yucca Mountain, Nevada, the permanent repository for spent fuel waste accumulating at 131 sites in thirty-nine states. The federal conclusion that the material could be safely sequestered in the mountain one hundred miles northwest of Las Vegas for thousands of years did not end the issue, however. Environmental groups such as the Blue Ridge Environmental Defense League in North Carolina immediately launched campaigns to prevent reactor waste from being transported through their states on the way to Nevada.

Efforts to arrange for permanent disposal of low-level nuclear waste have been contentious and largely unsuccessful. In the 1980 Low-Level Radioactive Waste Policy Act, Congress declared states responsible for low-level waste produced within their borders. States were to organize compacts to collaborate in establishing and operating burial sites for waste such as contaminated clothing, mops, rags, and laboratory equipment. By the early 1990s, all of the Appalachian states except New York had joined a compact. Alabama, Georgia, Mississippi, North Carolina, South Carolina, Tennessee, and Virginia belonged to a Southeastern Compact, and Maryland, Pennsylvania, and West Virginia to an Appalachian Compact. Kentucky paired with Illinois in a Central Midwestern Compact, and Ohio belonged to a Midwestern Compact with Indiana, Iowa, Missouri, and Wisconsin.

Cooperation proved problematic. North Carolina left the Southeastern Compact in 1999 after environmentalists bitterly opposed location of a low-level waste dump in Wake County. South Carolina, one of three states that had accepted much of the country's low-level nuclear waste before 1980, also withdrew and created a new compact with New Jersey and Connecticut. After 2008, South Carolina officials announced, the state would accept no imported waste except from its new compact partners.

One of Appalachia's most notable problems with low-level radioactive waste surfaced in 1977, when Kentucky closed a contractor-operated burial site at Maxey Flats, near Hillsboro in Fleming County. Over a period of fourteen years, more than 186,000 cubic yards of radiation-contaminated refuse from military facilities, research laboratories, utilities, medical centers, and manufacturing operations had been buried in long, thirty-foot-deep trenches. In the area around the dump, individual wells provided residential water, and streams draining the area flowed directly into the Licking River. When both groundwater and runoff were found to be contaminated with radiation, the state canceled the lease of U.S. Ecology, Inc., and closed the facility. It was subsequently declared a federal Superfund site. In the late 1990s, cleanup operations pumped nearly a million gallons of water from the landfill, but estimates were that full environmental restoration of the forty-five-acre disposal area would take years and eventually cost as much as $60 million.

Environmental issues posed by radioactive waste from civilian sources are dwarfed in some ways by the problems of decontaminating nuclear weapons plants, including the Oak Ridge site, which became Oak Ridge National Laboratory after the end of World War II. In 1991 the U.S. Department of Energy listed five hundred contaminated facilities to be decommissioned and decontaminated. At the same time, the federal Office of Technology Assessment concluded that air, water, soil, vegetation, and wildlife had been contaminated at most, if not all, of the weapons sites.

Among the many lawsuits growing out of environmental contamination from radiation was a 1984 suit filed against the Department of Energy by the Legal Environmental Assistance Foundation in Knoxville and the Natural Resources Defense Council. The court found that the Energy Department was violating the federal Clean Water Act in operations at Oak Ridge's Y-12 plant, which conducted magnetic separation of uranium in World War II and thereafter continued to be involved in developing nuclear weapons. As a result of the suit, the federal government acknowledged that federal environmental laws applied to nuclear weapons production. Environmental groups thus gained access to previously secret details concerning radioactive contamination by military activities.

See also: GRASSROOTS ENVIRONMENTAL ACTION; NUCLEAR FUEL SERVICES (BUSINESS, INDUSTRY, AND TECHNOLOGY); OAK RIDGE NATIONAL LABORATORY (BUSINESS, INDUSTRY, AND TECHNOLOGY).

—Stevan Jackson, *Radford University*

Luther Carter, *Nuclear Imperatives and Public Trust: Dealing with Radioactive Waste* (1987); League of Women Voters, *Nuclear Waste Primer: A Handbook for Citizens* (1993); Nicholas Lenssen, *Nuclear Waste: The Problem That Won't Go Away* (1991).

Recreation and the Environment

More than 115 million people live within a day's driving distance of the Appalachian Mountains, and thousands regularly drive from metropolitan areas such as New York, Washington, D.C., and Atlanta to get away from the noise and stress of city life. In 1995 alone, more than 100 million outdoor recreational trips were taken to the southern Appalachian region. While travelers bring numerous economic benefits to the region's vibrant tourism industry, they also contribute to pollution and environmental degradation. As the population of the eastern United States continues to grow and as undeveloped areas consequently shrink, recreation is expected to have an even greater effect on the region's economy and ecology.

In addition to population growth, a number of other factors have caused dramatic increases in outdoor recreation in Appalachia. Increased leisure time has enabled more people to participate in outdoor recreation. At the same time, improved roads have made the region more accessible. More comfortable backpacks and hiking boots, lighter tents, and easier-to-use snow skis have resulted in larger numbers of people participating in outdoor activities.

The growth of recreation has produced profound effects on the regional economy. In Appalachia—as in most predominantly rural regions in the United States—the economy began shifting away from extractive industries, including timber and coal mining, in the early second half of the twentieth century. In recent decades, local economies have continued to diversify, expanding wholesale and retail commerce as well as professional and related services. In 1990 combined wholesale, retail, manufacturing, and service sector businesses accounted for more than 67 percent of the employment in the southern Appalachians. By 1990, the service sector alone accounted for an average of 27 percent of jobs across the region and for as much as 57 percent in some counties. A decade earlier the service sector had accounted for only 20 percent of jobs in the region. This means that 77 percent of the job growth in the southern Appalachian region in the 1980s was in the service sector.

The growth of the service economy largely reflects the development of tourism and outdoor recreation. In 1990 recreation in the Appalachians provided more than $6 billion in income and more than one hundred thousand jobs. Though jobs that directly serve the recreation industry make up less than 2 percent of the total job market, this figure varies significantly from locale to locale and does not include the related service and tourist industry jobs that benefit indirectly. When all related businesses are included, the recreation and tourism industry is among the region's largest employers.

In many parts of Appalachia, the tourism and outdoor recreation industry is thus recognized as an important economic base. Local, regional, and state governments often work to develop tourist and recreational resources as part of their economic strategies. In addition, municipalities are investing more in travel services, parks, and recreation facilities to attract tourist dollars. Regional officials and business people are also beginning to recognize that tourism provides financial incentive for higher levels of protection of public lands.

Along with the economic changes, there have been significant population and demographic changes, especially as more retirees become interested in the Appalachian region and outdoor recreation. Retirees and residents who do not work in the region, as well as those who work in the tourism and recreation industries, tend to be more devoted to preserving natural lands for recreation than to using them for more destructive purposes such as logging and mining.

Residents of Appalachia do not always view economic development through tourism positively, however. Studies have documented local residents' concerns that increased tourism and recreation may increase crime, cost of living, and pollution and detract from overall quality of life. In some instances, residents may not understand management policies, such as the establishment of different levels of protection for public lands. They also may worry about the policies' effects on their own personal recreation habits or access to private lands. However, longterm residents and private landowners report a desire to balance public-lands management between the extremes of clear-cutting for timber, on the one hand, and protecting areas for wilderness, on the other. Longterm residents also express concerns that their voices may be drowned out by those of special interest groups, including both industrial and environmental lobbies.

Of the top twenty national forest recreation uses, only two are motorized: off-road driving and motor boating. These uses create the heaviest environmental impacts, however, and conflicts have arisen between proponents of motorized and non-motorized recreation. For example, in Appalachian Pennsylvania the use of all-terrain vehicles caused a statewide debate, leading to a 2000 moratorium on motorized activity for all new trails on state recreational lands. Major points of concern were the destruction of streambeds and habitat disruption, which can affect fishing, hiking, and other forms of recreation.

Both motorized and non-motorized recreation can cause soil degradation—which also affects water systems—and disturb vegetation and wildlife. Ecological damage can in turn affect the recreational value of land. The largest ecological impacts occur in the most popular and accessible areas. Roads next to streams and rivers, roadside camping areas, multiuse interconnected trails, and sites of high popularity in the southern Appalachians are meeting or exceeding desirable levels of use. In general, however, despite high levels of crowding in "front-country" areas, the backcountry is not being used to capacity and thus continues to be a place of solitude.

Almost three-quarters of the Appalachian region are privately owned; about two-thirds of those privately owned lands have some sort of forest cover. Despite the huge increase in development over the last two decades, the main non-commodity usage of these private lands is outdoor recreation. According to one major study, 74 percent of private landowners in the southern Appalachians cited personal recreation as an important reason for owning land. However, only 23 percent stated that they allowed people other than family members to use their land, and this percentage is expected to decrease as the general demand for outdoor recreation opportunities increases. The trend will place a growing strain on public lands available for recreation in the region.

See also: LAND USE; SECTION OVERVIEW (TOURISM); SPRAWL.

—Christopher J. Paul, *The Wilderness Society*

Samuel V. Lankford and Al Williams, "Perceptions of Outdoor Recreation Opportunities and Support for Tourism Development," *Journal of Travel Research* (Winter 1997); Peter A. Morton, *Charting a New Course: National Forests in the Southern Appalachians* (1994); Southern Appalachian Man and the Biosphere Cooperative, *The Southern Appalachian Assessment* (1996).

Research Institutions

The many organizations conducting environmental research in Appalachia include government agencies, industrial entities, universities, and conservation groups. Beginning in the early twentieth century, the federal government played a central role in cooperation with many other interested parties. In the twenty-first century, research on Appalachia's forests and ecosystems has become increasingly collaborative, with major research projects conducted through the cooperation of federal and state agencies, academic institutions, and private groups.

Carl Alwin Schenck, a German forester, opened the Biltmore Forest School, the first scientifically conducted forestry school in the United States, in 1898 near Asheville, North Carolina, to provide training in practical forest management. Before the turn of the twentieth century, scientific forestry research was limited, occurring primarily in the Northeast. The research that did take place in the Southeast focused mainly on forestry on privately owned land.

In 1921 the federal government's role in environmental research in Appalachia assumed major importance with the creation of the Appalachian Forest Experiment Station by the U.S. Department of Agriculture Forest Service. Located in Asheville, the station's territory initially included the entire states of Maryland, Virginia, West Virginia, and North Carolina and portions of Kentucky, Tennessee, Alabama, Georgia, and South Carolina. This territory included more than 120 million acres, more than half of which were covered by widely divergent forests. Notable Appalachian Station accomplishments during its first two decades were its demonstration that other hardwoods could successfully replace stands of American chestnut devastated by blight and that softwood pines could replace cut-over stands that were difficult to reforest with hardwoods. A hopeful start was also made in developing control practices for the southern pine beetle.

At the same time that the Appalachian Station was established, the Forest Service was creating other research stations throughout the country. These stations were established to cooperate with private landowners and loggers, as well as state foresters, with the objective of increasing timber production. The stations also had a broader mission, however—including research related to forest protection, wildlife, recreation, and the full range of elements that influence forested ecosystems.

Under the auspices of the Forest Service research stations, a number of historically important sites were created in Appalachia. Two of the most significant are the Bent Creek Experimental Forest and the Coweeta Hydrologic Laboratory. Scientists at both of these sites conduct research in the Appalachians that draws worldwide recognition. Bent Creek Forest, established near Asheville in 1927, was the first federal experimental forest in the East. Its first few projects provide a snapshot of early forest research in the Appalachians: installation of a reservoir and water system for fire control; building and staffing an insectary; laying the groundwork for a regional fire warning system; surveying and mapping; and establishing plots for research on a variety of topics ranging from reforestation to the effects of prescribed burning. One of Bent Creek's distinctions during the 1930s was to be the workplace of Margaret S. Abell, the only woman employed by the Forest Service as a professional forester at that time. In 1934 the Coweeta Hydrologic Laboratory was established near Franklin, North Carolina. Knowledge gained from the longterm data sets from Coweeta has contributed to major advances in the stewardship of water, soil, and air resources for regional, national, and international programs.

The administrative organization of Forest Service research stations in the East has evolved over the years. In 1951 the Appalachian Station merged into the Southeastern Forest Experiment Station, which was later combined with the former Southern Forest Experiment Station to become the Southern Research Station, with headquarters in Asheville. The Southern Research Station's jurisdiction includes thirteen southern states. The Northeastern Research Station, headquartered in Newtown Square, Pennsylvania, was established in 1923 and covers the northern Appalachians, from West Virginia to Maine.

In addition to the Department of Agriculture, the U.S. Department of the Interior has played a significant research role in the region. In 1975 the National Park Service, under the Department of the Interior, established the Uplands Field Laboratory in the Great Smoky Mountains National Park near Gatlinburg, Tennessee. Laboratory personnel did research throughout the park and in other upland units on exotic and rare species, spruce-fir forest decline, visitor impacts, aquatics, and other issues. In 1993 most research responsibilities of this laboratory were transferred to the Department of the Interior's Geological Survey. At the same time, new funding provided by the National Park Service to establish an inventory and monitoring program made the Uplands Laboratory an administrative unit of Great Smoky Mountains National Park. The laboratory was renamed Twin Creeks Natural Resources Center, and it took on a more intensive role in natural-resources inventories and longterm ecological monitoring.

Research at various federal sites in Appalachia has often been coordinated with investigation by academics. For example, the Hubbard Brook Experimental Forest was established in 1955 by the Forest Service near North Woodstock,

New Hampshire, in the White Mountains, for study of forest and associated aquatic ecosystems. There, scientists from the Northeastern Research Station conduct studies in affiliation with researchers from university and private groups including Yale, Cornell, and Syracuse Universities and the Institute of Ecosystem Studies, Millbrook, New York. In addition, many universities have established their own research sites. The University of Maryland's Appalachian Laboratory, for example, is a research facility of the University of Maryland Center for Environmental Science. Founded in 1962, the Appalachian Laboratory is located on the campus of Frostburg State University in the mountains of western Maryland. Its faculty members conduct research in landscape and watershed ecology, conservation biology and restoration ecology, and behavioral and evolutionary ecology.

Private industry groups also continue to play an important role in environmental research in the region, both on their own and through affiliation with academic and government researchers. The National Council for Air and Stream Improvement conducts research into environmental and forest-management issues associated with the manufacture of wood products. Headquartered near Raleigh, North Carolina, the council was formed in 1943 to assist the pulp and paper industry in addressing wastewater treatment issues, but its mission was broadened in the 1970s. The council's research is used extensively within the wood-products industry, as well as by academic researchers and regulatory agencies. The Forest History Society is another example of cooperation between industry and academe. Based in Durham, North Carolina, the society was established as an industry group in 1946 but became a nonprofit organization in 1955. It is now affiliated with Duke University, though its funding comes primarily from forest-products industry groups. The organization promotes a wide range of research and publications regarding forest ecosystems in Appalachia and elsewhere.

Conservation groups have also played an increasing role in coordinating and disseminating environmental research in Appalachia. The Southern Appalachian Forest Coalition, for example, brings together a number of regional conservation groups. In 2002 the coalition released a major publication of ecosystem research, including new data along with summaries and reviews of previous work. The document is intended to provide a blueprint for legislative action to promote conservation. Another regional conservation group, Appalachian Voices, based in Boone, North Carolina, has sponsored and disseminated research about air pollution, the environmental costs of coal, and other issues.

As research into ecosystems has become more complex, coordination among federal, state, academic, industry, and conservation groups has increased. One example is *The Southern Appalachian Assessment*, published in 1996 and coordinated through the Southern Appalachian Man and the Biosphere, a cooperative entity whose members include a wide array of federal and state agencies. This document compiled the best available data about the land, air, water, and people of southern Appalachia, covering 17.4 million acres from northern Virginia and eastern West Virginia to northwestern South Carolina, northern Georgia, and northern Alabama. The assessment gave decision makers information for balancing issues related to biological diversity, economic uses, and cultural values.

Another example of cooperative research is the All Taxa Biodiversity Inventory of Great Smoky Mountains National Park, one of the largest and most comprehensive biodiversity inventories in the world. This project is coordinated by the National Park Service at Twin Creeks Natural Resources Center. The inventory consists of about 150 scientific activities each year, conducted by collaborating scientists from many institutions, states, and foreign countries.

See also: BILTMORE FOREST SCHOOL (ARCHITECTURE).

—Melissa Carlson, *U.S. Department of Agriculture Forest Service*

Earle H. Clapp and the Society of American Foresters, *A National Program of Forest Research* (1926); U.S. Department of Agriculture Forest Service Southern Research Station, *Scientific Forestry for Informed Choices* (1995).

Solid-Waste Management

Municipal solid waste, or common household garbage or trash, includes all the things people regularly throw away, including food scraps, furniture, grass clippings, paint, batteries, bottles, clothing, paper, and cleaning fluids. According to statistics from the U.S. Environmental Protection Agency, in 1999 each person in the United States produced an average of 4.6 pounds of solid waste per day, up from 2.7 pounds per day in 1960. Reduction, reuse, recycling, and composting helped to divert some 28 percent of materials from the waste stream, but the remaining 72 percent required disposal, either through landfilling (57 percent) or combustion (15 percent).

Rural, distressed communities of the Appalachian region tend to be disproportionately affected by waste disposal. More often than not, waste-disposal facilities are sited in lower-income areas, and landfills in particular tend to affect rural communities, where large tracts of land can be purchased cheaply. Grassroots opponents charge that waste-facility developers also target communities that offer the least resistance. To support this claim, opponents frequently cite a profile of communities developed by Cerrell Associates, a solid-waste industry consultant. According to the Cerrell report, less resistant communities are apt to be rural, in economic decline, low in educational levels, dependent on resource-extraction industries, low in per capita income, and populated by longtime residents.

Communities of Appalachia came into focus as potential landfill sites in the late 1980s, when the Environmental Protection Agency proposed new federal regulations governing solid-waste landfills. The final regulations issued in 1991 under the Resource Conservation and Recovery Act were intended to make solid-waste disposal safer, setting criteria for landfill design, operation, and monitoring; corrective action; closure and post-closure; and financial responsibility. The act set requirements for sophisticated, expensive liners and systems to collect and monitor leachate, a "toxic tea" that seeps from the bottom of landfills and contaminates groundwater.

The projected costs of building and operating landfills that meet the new requirements are prohibitive for many rural local governments, although some research suggests that those costs have been exaggerated by the waste industry. Many local governments have opted to turn their waste management over to large private waste haulers. Government leaders, developers, waste-industry representatives, and some environmentalists promote large regional landfills (two hundred to five hundred tons per day) as a means of meeting the increased costs of complying with the new regulations. Critics of this approach argue that the volume requirements of large regional landfills hurt recycling businesses by giving landfill operators an incentive to increase tonnage. Big waste haulers are not motivated to cooperate with local recycling efforts, critics argue, and federal tax subsidies further undermine recycling efforts.

Commercial development of larger landfills has grown rapidly in Appalachia as waste firms seek economies of scale to maximize profits. The political environment of the Appalachian region has played a critical role in determining the pattern of solid-waste impacts since the mid-1990s. In many parts of the region, developers can acquire land easily, waste haulers pay smaller tipping fees, and environmental regulations tend to be more lenient. The combination of such factors makes it cost-effective for large firms to haul waste long distances—particularly from major northeastern cities—into distressed rural communities of Appalachia. In West Virginia, for example, about one-third of the waste disposed is from out of state.

Waste companies frequently take advantage of land and existing infrastructure available from earlier resource extraction industries. Those who control the way land is used generally have power and influence with community officials. For example, a large Philadelphia-based landholding corporation offered to help McDowell County, West Virginia, solve its financial problems by developing a huge landfill in a hollow where coal had been exhausted and mines closed. Similarly, in Oliver Springs, near Oak Ridge in east Tennessee, a private waste firm proposed a large regional landfill in a former strip mine on land held by an absentee coal company. In both of these communities, the local political structures were dominated by individuals and groups whose business and public roles were interlocked and tied to the landfill development.

Landfill site selection is in many ways similar to "smokestack chasing," as local officials may see a landfill as a source of economic stimulus. Officials may then cut deals with landfill developers without citizen input, signing agreements with the developer that bargain away public accountability. Developers themselves are aware that local compensation is an effective strategy to gain crucial early approval and/or rezoning. In such cases, local residents are often not informed about plans until critical alternatives have been eliminated. Landfill opponents point to this strategy as a form of environmental blackmail, in which corporations rely on economic disparity and distress in a community to gain access.

Grassroots environmental activists have lobbied for stronger laws requiring early notification and provision of local approval or veto authority. However, state and local efforts to pass laws to increase local control and restrict waste imports have been overturned consistently in federal courts on grounds that such laws unconstitutionally interfere with interstate commerce. For example, Virginia, which is the nation's second-largest trash importer behind Pennsylvania, passed a law in 1999 to limit importation. The law was overturned in U.S. District Court in February 2000 after a conglomerate of waste haulers led by Waste Management, Inc., and Charles City County (which leases land to Waste Management for a large landfill) sued Virginia, challenging key provisions. In December 2002, Waste Management and state officials settled the lawsuit, and the company agreed to pay a controversial one-dollar-per-ton fee for transporting the trash.

Nevertheless, numerous grassroots groups have organized effectively in local communities throughout Appalachia to protest siting plans by large landfill developers. Examples include local chapters of Save Our Cumberland Mountains and the Blue Ridge Environmental Defense League. Such groups form building blocks in the more broadly based environmental justice movement, drawing attention to patterns of economic and environmental exploitation throughout Appalachia. Grassroots groups frequently are able to significantly alter the outcome of landfill development, if not the permit decision itself. In both the McDowell County and Oliver Springs cases, for example, citizen groups succeeded in mobilizing opposition. Both states issued permits to the developers, but opposition forced restrictions that reduced the volume of trash originally proposed, thus reducing profitability and compelling developers to put their plans on hold, perhaps indefinitely.

See also: ENVIRONMENTAL JUSTICE; GRASSROOTS ENVIRONMENTAL ACTION; SPRAWL.

—Janice Morrissey, *Grassroots Empowerment Alliance of Rome (Georgia)*

Janice C. Morrissey, "Citizen Participation in Environmental Policy: A Study of Landfill Siting in Two Appalachian Communities," Ph.D. dissertation, University of Tennessee (1996); William Sheehan, *Economics of Smaller Landfills* (1993).

Sprawl

Sprawl is a general term for uncoordinated, low-density residential and commercial development. Appalachia contains only a few metropolitan areas of the size usually associated with sprawl, but open space is steadily overrun by haphazard growth in urban and rural areas alike. Though often related to population growth, sprawl also occurs where population is steady or even declining. It presents the region with significant economic, social, and environmental challenges in the twenty-first century.

The phenomenon of urban sprawl in the United States dates to the mid-twentieth century. After World War II, economic expansion and federal highway programs promoted automobile use. At the same time, mortgage and loan policies and efficient new construction techniques encouraged single-family-home subdivisions. Middle- and upper-income families began fleeing from polluted and racially and ethnically mixed cities, seeking lower taxes, newer homes and schools, and safer streets. Through the 1950s and into the 1960s, white Americans' negative reactions to school desegregation magnified the trend. By 1970 the number of Americans living in suburbs surpassed the number in cities.

During the same era, increasing numbers of retail stores and restaurants relocated, first to shopping centers along commuter routes outside urban centers and later to malls at interstate access ramps. Industries and businesses likewise moved outside city limits, attracted by suburban governments' offers of tax breaks, subsidized roads, and cheap land and utility rates. Without income from their former tax bases, municipalities struggled to maintain adequate infrastructure, provide city services, and combat social problems. At the same time, certain city residents were unable to move out due to financial constraints or federally sanctioned housing discrimination against non-whites. Central cities thus became increasingly composed of black, poor white, and elderly citizens. The resulting economic and racial segregation further accelerated the decline of core cities and contributed to outward sprawl.

Compared to older cities in the Northeast, most Appalachian cities had little time to develop compact urban cores before the mid-twentieth century. Appalachian cities expanded mostly after World War II during an era of single-use zoning, when separate housing, shopping, and working districts were created. Separate zones require car travel, which in turn promotes strip growth, or narrow development spread out along thoroughfares and set back from roads by parking lots. Thus urban growth in late-twentieth- and early-twenty-first-century Appalachia has typically included the construction of shopping malls and industrial parks at the outskirts of towns, strip developments of gas stations and retail and restaurant chain stores along thoroughfares, and "big box" discount chain stores. In larger cities, office parks and hotels have also sprung up, often at the junctions of major thoroughfares and interstates. Low-density development has continued at the edges of metropolitan areas, despite population stagnation or decline. For example, the metropolitan population of Charleston, West Virginia, remained steady between 1990 and 2000, yet population shifted westward along Interstate 64, causing metropolitan Putnam County's population to grow by 20.4 percent. Even though Pittsburgh had one of the highest rates of land consumption per person in the United States, the city's population declined dramatically during the late twentieth century.

Sprawl in southern Appalachia has been accelerated by migration from the Northeast and Midwest. In the 1990s, southern Appalachian city populations grew anywhere from 9.6 percent (Chattanooga, Tennessee) to between 17 and 18 percent (Knoxville, Tennessee, and Asheville, North Carolina). The Greensboro–Winston-Salem–High Point metropolitan area, which falls partly within the region, grew by 19.2 percent in the 1990s. Knoxville, where the population center moved ten miles west of downtown in the 1970s, continues to expand west despite controversy over retail development in wetlands areas. In 2001 *USA Today* ranked Knoxville as the sixth most sprawling city in its size category and the seventeenth most sprawling metropolitan area in the nation.

Sprawl in Appalachia often results from the incursion of non-Appalachian metropolitan areas such as Cincinnati, Washington, D.C., Roanoke, Virginia, and Lexington, Kentucky, into Appalachian counties. If current growth rates continue, Nashville, Tennessee, and Charlotte, North Carolina, may join the list. Perhaps the most striking metropolitan expansion into Appalachia has been the northward suburban growth of Atlanta, which has overlapped with second-home development in the north Georgia mountains, threatening to meld there with the southward-sprawling subdivisions of Chattanooga. In 1990 federal redefinitions of metropolitan areas increased the number of Appalachian counties officially within the Atlanta metropolitan area from two to the following nine: Barrow, Bartow, Carroll, Cherokee, Douglas, Forsyth, Gwinnett, Pickens, and Paulding. Some of those counties have experienced astonishing growth. For example, Forsyth County, home to the popular vacation site Lake Lanier, increased its population by 123 percent between 1990 and 2000, making it the fastest-growing county in Georgia. Atlanta's sprawl has also affected Appalachian counties lying farther north, including Dawson, Hall, and Jackson.

Despite its association with cities, sprawl—usually in the form of commercial corridors rather than residential areas—has in recent decades occurred in parts of Appalachia otherwise considered rural. In West Virginia, Pennsylvania, and Kentucky, development of land per person grew 77 percent, 53 percent, and 48 percent, respectively. A significant portion of this increase is associated with rural sprawl. Rural sprawl often results from the growth of tourism and second-home development. Parts of northeastern West Virginia, east Tennessee, southwestern Virginia, north Georgia, and, most dramatically, western North Carolina, have witnessed such sprawl. In the 1990s, Boone, North Carolina, and surrounding counties were especially affected by sharp increases in both residential and retail development due to tourism-related growth. In Tennessee, one of the most remarkable tourism-related expansions in Appalachia has occurred along twenty-five miles of Highway 66 from Interstate 40 through Sevierville, Pigeon Forge, and Gatlinburg along the approach to the Great Smoky Mountains National Park. In addition to the national park, attractions include Dollywood and other theme parks and entertainment venues, hotels and restaurants, outlet malls, retail stores, and wedding chapels. Tourism is increasingly a year-round industry in the area, with the city of Gatlinburg alone hosting from thirty-five thousand to forty-five thousand visitors on any given day.

Sprawl in both urban and rural areas continues to cause negative economic and social repercussions in Appalachia. Retail strips tend to create few jobs that pay living wages. In addition, sprawl undermines the agricultural sector of the economy as farmland is converted to housing. The phenomenon also helps to maintain racial and class segregation in Appalachian cities when it traps the poor, the elderly, and minorities in deteriorating urban centers. It promotes the neglect or demolition of historic buildings and city centers. At the same time that it destroys scenic open spaces, farmland, and natural areas on the outskirts of cities, it causes traffic congestion, longer commutes, and higher taxes for new infrastructure and services within them.

Environmental consequences of sprawl range from the local to the global. Increased dependence on gasoline leads to more carbon emissions and related problems. Deforestation associated with sprawl causes a host of problems, including disruptions of native species, degradation of outdoor recreation areas, and increased energy consumption for cooling homes and businesses. Extensive paving associated with sprawl leads to flash flooding, falling water tables, rising levels of water contamination, and a phenomenon known as the urban heat island effect, whereby dark roofs, roads, and parking lots act as giant solar panels that store energy during the day and raise nighttime temperatures.

Nationwide, actions to address problems associated with sprawl date back to the 1970s and 1980s, when states such as Oregon, California, Washington, and Florida passed the first growth-management laws in the country. In 2000 the Livable Communities Initiative, a national program, focused federal attention on problems associated with sprawl. In 2000 voters nationwide approved 400 of 553 local measures proposed to manage urban growth. Likewise, national

Sprawl near the Great Smoky Mountains National Park, Tennessee, c. 1990s. Communities adjacent to Appalachia's natural attractions frequently face development pressures that lead to sprawl.

environmental groups have increasingly turned their attention to the issue. In 2000 the Sierra Club identified sprawl as the most pressing concern on its legislative agenda.

In Appalachia, local civic leaders often have little public support for limiting sprawl. In areas where poverty rates are high, the short-term benefits from low-paying jobs created by retail-strip growth often outweigh longer-term considerations. A number of recent attempts to control sprawl in the region have met with mixed results. In Tennessee, a 1998 "smart growth" law required cities to adopt growth plans by 2001 or risk losing state subsidies for highways, community development, and tourism, but the law's implementation was hindered by subsequent lawsuits. Also in 1998, a Pennsylvania environmental commission identified sprawl as the single greatest environmental problem in that state, and proposed potential solutions. In 1999 Georgia established a regional transportation authority to control funding for roads and to structure future growth patterns, though so far the authority has been reluctant to curb development. Relatively successful tactics for managing sprawl have included local zoning ordinances, legal mechanisms for protecting farms and open spaces, and the revitalization of central cities. Grassroots citizens' and environmental organizations in western North Carolina and western Pennsylvania have undertaken notable efforts at education, providing grants for smart growth. In the last two decades of the twentieth century, many Appalachian cities, including Birmingham, Alabama, Asheville and Hickory, North Carolina, and Chattanooga, Knoxville, and the Tri-Cities in Tennessee, undertook large-scale city- or regionwide planning projects to address sprawl-related issues.

See also: SECTION OVERVIEW (AGRICULTURE); SECTION OVERVIEW (URBAN APPALACHIAN EXPERIENCE).

—Emily Satterwhite, *Emory University*

Michael J. McDonald and William Bruce Wheeler, *Knoxville, Tennessee: Continuity and Change in an Appalachian City* (1983); Donald C. Williams, *Urban Sprawl* (2000).

Superfund

In 1980 Congress passed the Comprehensive Environmental Response, Compensation, and Liability Act. Also known as the Superfund Act, it created a broad and stringent liability system to hold persons linked to hazardous-substance contamination responsible for cleanup costs. It also established a Hazardous Substance Superfund to pay cleanup costs not allocable to a solvent, responsible party. There are hundreds of Superfund sites in Appalachia—including the notorious "Valley of the Drums," a waste-disposal site in northern Bullitt County, Kentucky, which by the 1970s had become so clearly hazardous and destructive that reports of the site helped convince members of Congress to pass the Superfund Act in the first place.

The Environmental Protection Agency has primary responsibility for managing cleanup and enforcement under the act. However, Superfund's administrative machinery is highly decentralized, with implementation occurring primarily in the agency's ten regional offices. Specific decisions are made in each region, where hundreds of remedial project managers and their supervisors are directly responsible for more than twelve hundred federal Superfund sites.

In addition, states dictate which locations can be listed as Superfund sites. Litigation is often used to identify liable parties and bring an end to environmental dangers, but states can either help or hinder investigations and prosecutions in particular cases. Conservation groups such as Save Our Cumberland Mountains have been involved in such litigation. Other considerations can also affect which sites are designated as Superfund sites. For example, although coal mining has ravaged the Appalachian landscape, coal mines are not usually in the domain of the Superfund Act and often answer to their own governing environmental agencies.

See also: COAL MINING; GRASSROOTS ENVIRONMENTAL ACTION; POLLUTION CLEANUP PROGRAMS.

—Ima J. Stephens, *Auburn University*

Viewshed Protection

The Appalachian Mountains are home to some of the most spectacular views on the North American continent. Each year millions of tourists are drawn to the region, largely to enjoy the unspoiled character of mountain vistas and scenic overlooks. Many of these sites have become increasingly threatened, however, as utility lines, microwave towers, and home-development sites spread indiscriminately across the mountain landscape. Numerous efforts have been launched to help remedy the problem; these range from local ordinances establishing greenways and the creation of protocols for scenic management on public lands to nongovernmental and citizen action on behalf of the region's scenery.

The U.S. Forest Service has established a system for providing for the integration of landscape aesthetics with other biological, physical, and cultural resources in the forest planning process. The system is designed to address concerns of both users and local residents who perceive the visual landscape as a resource that should be managed as an essential part of the forest experience. Accordingly, many Forest Service lands in the Appalachians have been given scenic attractiveness rankings that offer greater protection to those that qualify as "distinctive" under Forest Service criteria.

A similar management system has been created for the 469-mile Blue Ridge Parkway. Established by Congress in the 1930s, this first national rural parkway provides a connecting scenic roadway between the Shenandoah National Park in Virginia and the Great Smoky Mountains National Park in North Carolina. Traversing twenty-nine counties in two states, the parkway was deliberately located along ridge tops and mountainsides to showcase Appalachian scenery. From 266 overlooks, more than 850 managed vistas, and hundreds of open agricultural views, more than 20 million visitors a year look out across miles of scenery they have come to associate with the Appalachian region. As a result, the Blue Ridge Parkway's visual landscape has helped to define how all Americans view Appalachia.

Since 1994, the National Park Service has undertaken numerous steps to develop and institutionalize a comprehensive scenic management system for the Blue Ridge Parkway. Surveys have shown that nearly 95 percent of parkway visitors come to see views of multiple mountain ridges fading away into a distant blue haze, rocky outcrops, spectacular waterfalls, and rolling farmland contained by old wooden fences or edged by surrounding forest. Surveys have also found that visitors, who spend some $2.2 billion a year in the twenty-nine counties, say they will visit the parkway less often if the quality of the view diminishes, thus potentially costing counties millions of dollars in lost tourism revenues.

The Blue Ridge Parkway, with an average right-of-way width of eight hundred feet, is unusual in that most of the views visitors come to see lie beyond the parkway's boundary. Because it has no direct control over the scenic quality of these views, the management system allows parkway staff to gather and share information about these views, particularly when local landowners or county and city planners propose land-use changes. This allows managers to anticipate threats to the viewshed and to help preserve the visual heritage of the mountain region.

Of the many nongovernmental efforts to protect viewsheds in Appalachia, one of the most notable is the Appalachian Trail Conference. A private, mostly volunteer organization that maintains and promotes the Appalachian Trail, this group has worked with the federal government to acquire and protect viewshed lands in the trail corridor. It also helps to coordinate citizen awareness regarding development activity within the corridor that threatens the region's scenic value.

See also: BLUE RIDGE PARKWAY (TOURISM); LAND USE; SECTION OVERVIEW (TOURISM).

—Gary W. Johnson, *Blue Ridge Parkway*

R. Burton Litton Jr., *Forest Landscape Description and Inventories* (1968); Francis P. Noe and William E. Hammitt, *Visual Preferences of Travelers along the Blue Ridge Parkway* (1988); U.S. Department of Agriculture Forest Service, *Landscape Aesthetics: A Handbook for Scenery Management* (1995).

Water Resources

The Appalachian region is widely known not only for its mountains, but also for its many streams and rivers, which support a stunning concentration of aquatic life-forms. The remarkable aquatic systems of the highlands can be primarily attributed to the geologic history and climatic conditions that have influenced the evolution of species and historical development of biological communities. Since around 250 million years ago, the Appalachian region has been largely above sea level. Precipitation falling on the highlands has since drained into thousands of miles of freshwater streams and rivers. The great timescales over which flora and fauna developed, a relatively mild climate, and the great variety of landscapes and habitats all combined to produce a unique ecology within a temperate aquatic setting. The region is therefore a global center of biological diversity for many groups of organisms, including fishes, mussels, crayfishes, and aquatic insects.

Aquatic systems integrate the landscape through hydrological processes, so the freshwater ecosystem also comprises the terrestrial characteristics of watersheds as well as underwater features. Many of Appalachia's streams drain ancient landscapes. Most of the region south of the Ohio River has been uninterrupted by glaciation. For this reason, the region hosts a rich and distinctive native flora and fauna. The aquatic biodiversity in Appalachia is widely recognized as the highest of any temperate region in the world, rivaling tropical systems. The diversity of aquatic invertebrate species appears to be greater than in any other region in North America, with up to 50 percent of some groups still undescribed. Out of 297 mussel species occurring in the United States, 269 are found in the Southeast, largely in southern Appalachian rivers, which also host an estimated 350 species of fish, some 18 percent of which are imperiled.

This diverse fauna and its setting within a rapidly changing landscape present ongoing challenges to aquatic resource managers, especially regarding conservation of individual species, aquatic communities, and flowing-water habitats. The primary threats to the biological integrity of the region are habitat alteration and loss and introduced species.

Over the past century, a large body of knowledge has accumulated on the zoogeography, distribution, and biology of Appalachian fish species and to a lesser extent other aquatic organisms whose diversity is also greatly threatened.

All aquatic ecosystems in the region are sustained and perpetuated by the hydrologic cycle. Precipitation falling on land may evaporate or be transpired by plants back into the atmosphere, soak through to the groundwater, or drain toward stream and river channels. The interaction of climate with geology through erosion has created large and recognizable topographic features within the Appalachians. Most areas of high elevation and relief have been formed on resistant rocks, and the major drainage systems of the region have become closely adjusted to these various rock types. The process of infiltration and runoff of precipitation drives streamflow, and the interaction of this flow with geology and landforms creates these major drainages.

Waters draining from the western side of the southern Appalachians carry sediment to the Gulf of Mexico, while drainages to the north and on the eastern side flow to the Atlantic Ocean. Major Gulf drainages of the region flow to the Ohio River (New-Kanawha, Tennessee, and Cumberland River drainages) or to the Alabama-Apalachicola River system (Coosa-Tallapoosa and Chattahoochee River drainages). Atlantic drainages from north to south include the Saint Lawrence, the Hudson, the Chesapeake Bay (Susquehanna, Potomac, Rapidan-Rappahannock, and James River drainages) and those draining the Carolinas (Roanoke, Pee Dee, Santee-Cooper, and Savannah Rivers).

High-gradient, crystalline streams of the Blue Ridge Mountains typically have dendritic drainage patterns, which means the patterns resemble the trunk and branches of a tree. In the Ridge and Valley, or sedimentary Appalachians, streams may also be dendritic but downstream tend to follow a more trellised pattern. Historically, the Appalachian region has enjoyed abundant rainfall and a vast network of streams and rivers.

Special conditions occur along the margins of most waterways in the region, controlling and influencing the transfer of energy, nutrients, and sediments between terrestrial and aquatic systems. The unique stream margin habitats are called riparian zones. These zones receive special attention from regional land-use planners, who maintain that loss of aquatic habitat can be mitigated by carefully maintaining riparian buffers. Serving as natural sponges and filters, these buffers reduce bank erosion; trap and process contaminants such as pesticides; provide habitat for amphibious and terrestrial organisms; and afford recreational opportunities. While no national standard exists for establishment and maintenance of riparian buffers, several Appalachian states have considered legislation requiring farmers and private landowners to protect these fragile ecosystems.

Preservation of water quality is vital to the future of the Appalachian region. According to hydrologists, the dissolved and suspended material transported by stream water is determined by factors such as the geology and land cover of the drainage basin, as well as human activity within it. Materials are concentrated by evaporation and transformed by chemical and biological interactions within each stream. Mountain rivers and streams in the Appalachians can be quite pure, with very low concentrations of dissolved materials. However, land-use practices and effects—clearcutting, surface mining, acid mine drainage, industrial and municipal waste disposal, riparian zone disturbances, agricultural practices, sludge impoundments, and acid precipitation—pose profound threats.

Appalachia's rivers and lakes provide drinking water for mountain and foothill communities, as well as for major cities of the eastern and southeastern United States. Droughts and reports of water pollution in the late twentieth and early twenty-first centuries heightened concern over the quality and quantity of available water. The management of water resources in the region is slowly evolving from one of water-supply development to that of water-demand management and conservation. Although water supplies have historically been abundant, they face increasing demands for cities such as Atlanta, where dramatic urban and commercial development has proceeded unchecked for decades. Dams, urban and suburban development, and mining have among the largest impacts on hydrology in the Appalachians, substantially affecting river geomorphology and aquatic ecosystems. Population growth in Appalachian cities is certain to place increasing pressure on regional water resources. Conservationists, developers, and public officials agree that water issues will be among the most significant environmental concerns for decades to come.

Native aquatic species have adapted to prevailing conditions in Appalachian rivers and streams. Forests have historically been the natural cover of the region's various landscapes. Consequently, impacts to forest habitats directly affect aquatic organisms by altering their habitat. The most harmful impacts can even render the aquatic habitat unlivable for sensitive aquatic species. Habitat alteration may include any combination of the following: modification of natural flow regimes by dams, water diversions, and watershed land uses; changes in water quality due to point (source from a pipe) and nonpoint (source from land runoff) pollution; and deforestation along waterways, which reduces woody debris inputs (important in mountain stream hydrology and nutrient dynamics, as well as providing food and shelter for organisms) and contributes to nonpoint source pollution.

The combined, possibly synergistic, effects of poor resource management can modify the habitat for native aquatic species by altering the flow of water, warming temperatures, increasing the concentrations of nutrients and other dissolved material in stream water, and increasing the amount of sediment in the stream channel. Species tolerant of environmental change dominate biological communities where these changes occur, while less adaptive species decline.

Endemic species (those occurring in a very restricted area) appear to be particularly sensitive to the changes, disappearing where habitats have been altered extensively. Endemics are disproportionately listed as threatened or endangered by state and federal governments in the region. Loss of endemic Appalachian species erodes regional distinctiveness. Genetically unique and often with specialized ecologies, these evolutionary and biologically significant units disappear from human-dominated places across landscapes and continents, leaving a common suite of generalized, tolerant species, a process known as biotic homogenization. As land in Appalachia is converted under socioeconomic pressures from indigenous vegetation to various human uses, threats continue to mount to the well-being of both native organisms and ecosystems.

See also: EROSION; FLOODS; INVASIVE SPECIES.

—Mark C. Scott, *South Carolina Department of Natural Resources*

Eugene P. Odum, *Ecology* (1963); Karl B. Raitz and Richard Ulack, *Appalachia: A Regional Geography* (1984).

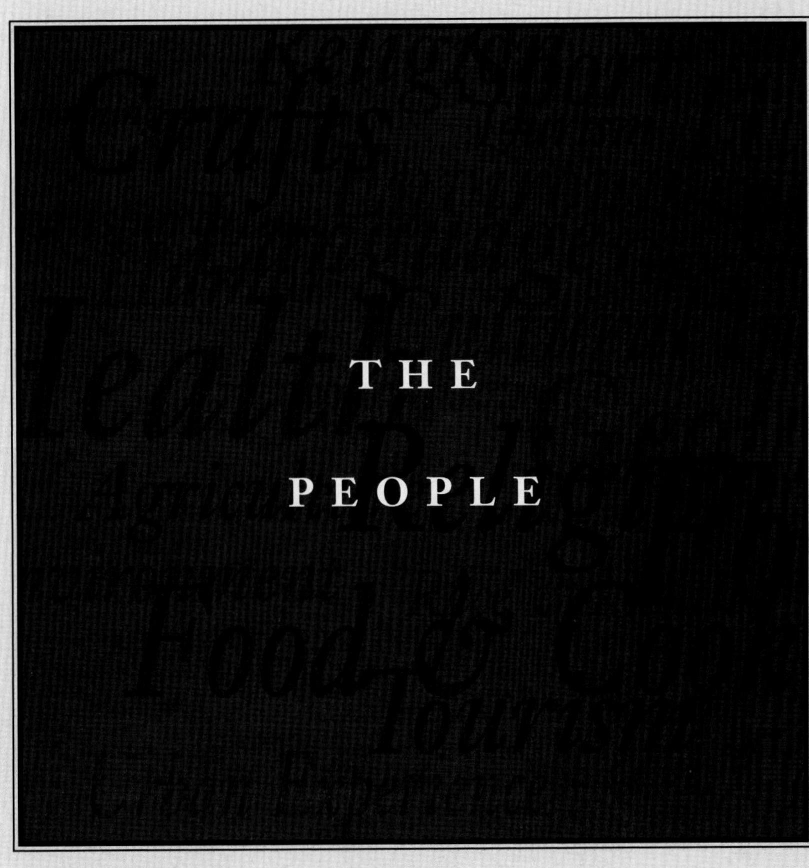

THE PEOPLE

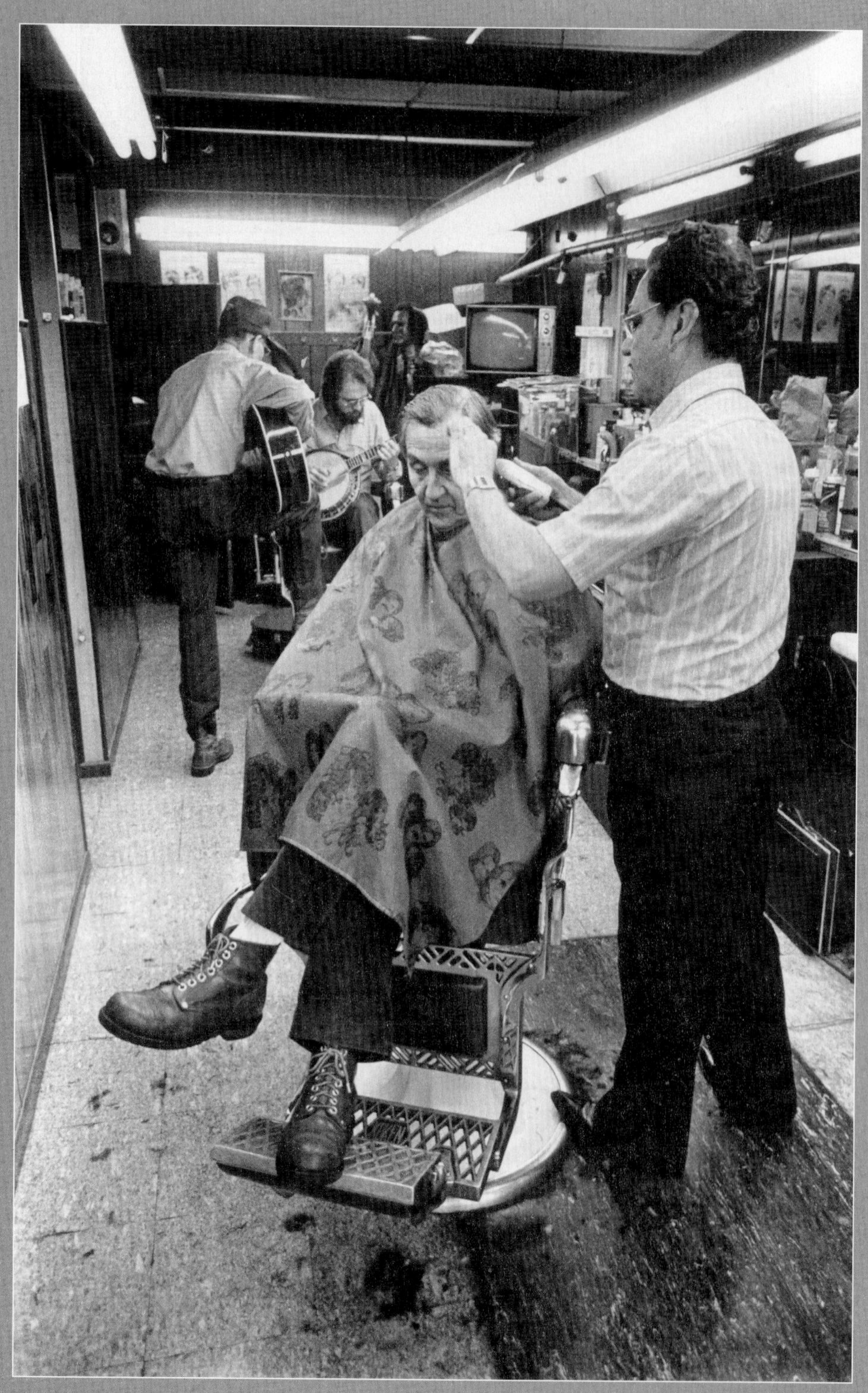

Family and Community

Section Editors: Shirley L. Stewart Burns, Shaunna L. Scott, and Deborah J. Thompson

FAMILY AND KINSHIP HAVE FORMED THE BACKBONE OF RURAL AND SMALL-TOWN America since colonial times, but in few places does the family remain as essential a component of culture and society as in Appalachia. As social institutions and networks of economic and emotional support, as political alliances, as indicators of social status, and as bases of personal and collective identity, family and kinship groups form the cornerstone of social and community life in the region. Although generalizations about this large, diverse area are doomed to oversimplification, it is reasonable to say that most Appalachians place great stock in the value of strong, close-knit families and community networks.

As testament to this deeply held conviction, Appalachians point to the prevalence of family reunions, the maintenance of family grave plots, return migration, family care of children and senior citizens, and numerous ways of family-based sharing as positive aspects of their lives. Kinship ties may also lead to detrimental effects in political, economic, and civic affairs of communities, however. In particular, members of county governments, school boards, and other local institutions have long been accused of nepotism, and not infrequently both community disagreements and civic aspirations can be seen to spring from family interests and alliances. Some observers have posited connections between pervasive kin-based influence and the persistence of poverty, episodes of corruption, and the stifling of democratic processes, particularly in communities of central Appalachia. In short, residents and scholars of Appalachia have come to see the entrenched social, political, and personal influence of family as a dominant thread in the region's cultural fabric, as well as a feature that distinguishes Appalachia from much of the United States.

Although Appalachia's population has become increasingly concentrated in urban areas, the region's small towns and communities continue to be inhabited by related families who have sometimes lived there for hundreds of years and have personal connections to local history. In a 1982 *American Ethnologist* article entitled "Mosbys and Broomsedge: The Semantics of Class in an Appalachian Kinship System," anthropologist Allen W. Batteau used the term *kin set* to describe cohesive, extended, and geographically connected families familiar in communities of all sizes throughout Appalachia. Members of these current-day kin sets, like their relatives

Facing page: Shop owner Gene Boyd cuts hair as a jam session gets underway at the Star Barber Shop in Bristol, Virginia, 1982. For decades, local musicians have gathered weekly at this local business for musical exchanges and fellowship.

A group of women attend an association meeting at Redmond Creek Baptist Church, Galax, Virginia, 1978. Appalachians point to the prevalence of family reunions, the maintenance of family grave plots, return migration, family care of children and senior citizens, and numerous ways of family-based sharing as positive aspects of their lives.

in preceding generations, support each other in both subtle and conspicuous ways. While some extend their interest and influence into the social, economic, and religious affairs of the community, others largely confine themselves to mutual support of the family group itself. If the patriarch or matriarch of such a kin set owns enough land, house lots may be deeded to children and grandchildren as they reach adulthood, marry, and establish their own households.

With adult children and grandchildren nearby to provide care, meals, and transport for shopping and medical appointments, some Appalachian seniors are able to remain in their own homes rather than take up residence in a care facility in their final years. Strong emphasis is traditionally placed on care of elderly family members and children, as well as the ill and disabled. To be sure, not all kin groups contribute to community stability or enhance family life in such an idealized fashion. Indeed, the Appalachian stereotype includes the clannish, inbred, antisocial family, united by blood in relentless self-destructive impulses. For novelists, journalists, and filmmakers, not to mention social scientists, both positive and negative family kin groups have served as vehicles for exploration of the region.

While communities can be well understood through their families and kin groups, their economic and cultural personalities are also shaped by recurrent pulses of immigration, by the evolution of technology, and by the landscape and natural environment. Before the industrial transition (1880–1920) that witnessed the region's becoming the main fuel source and a principal foundry of the American Industrial Revolution, Appalachians had largely depended upon agriculture and local enterprises such as logging and salt production. Communities developed along waterways, in mountain gaps, and in protected valleys, prospering where there was productive soil, where major streams provided access to markets, and where the terrain channeled immigration to the South and West. Exploitation of coal and timber required mines, mills, and company towns to be located near water sources and the resources themselves, but often the towns were further planned for corporate goals, which sometimes included dividing racial and ethnic groups or creating a paternalistic atmosphere.

Intentional communities, on the other hand, consist of groups of people who have committed to live together to pursue some ideology, whether spiritual, economic, environmental, and/or social. While Appalachia is not the hub of communes and experimental living that New England was in the eighteenth century or that California was in the twentieth, many groups have settled in the region throughout its history, and there are significant concentrations of these communities today near Asheville, North Carolina; Athens, Ohio; and Blacksburg, Virginia. Utopian experiments often look to the mountains for refuge and isolation, a place to separate themselves from the wider world. In addition to this ideological motivation is the very practical availability of inexpensive land far from metropolitan areas. Back-to-the-landers of the last thirty years are also attracted by their perception of the region as one awash in practitioners of traditional skills.

Intentional communities are as diverse as the region itself, from the Kingdom of Paradise, begun in 1736 by philosopher Christian Gottlieb Priber to improve life for the Cherokee, to the Susan B. Anthony Memorial UnRest Home, a community for women in contemporary Ohio. Himlerville, Kentucky, an ethnically Hungarian experiment in communal ownership of a mining company and town, shares a commitment to economic improvement for its residents with Rugby, Tennessee, an experiment for second sons of the English middle class. Many Anabaptist groups, from George Rapp's early-nineteenth-century Harmonists to the Mennonites, Amish, and Bruderhof of today, have sought to practice their religion both in Appalachia and other places in America. Abbeys, convents, monasteries, community land trusts, Krishna societies, racially integrated antebellum towns, utopian societies of the nineteenth century, and New Age communes of the late twentieth century share the view that social relationships and economic systems must be reordered in order to create a better world. These communities may appear to turn inward, but they often have a great impact on the world around them by providing a different social model from the mainstream, producing services and commodities for the larger community, and contributing to the environmental health of the region.

Some of these communities include a reordering of the idea of family, such as requiring celibacy in Catholic monasteries and convents, or the early-nineteenth-century Zoar Separatists' practice of separating children from the families at the age of three. Lesbian and gay communities allow for same-sex couples to live together, sometimes raising children, with greater freedom and acceptance than in the larger society. Some temporary communities are formed and re-formed through the coming together of communities of interest, such as Appalachian Trail thru-hikers or the Rainbow Family of Living Light, which has been holding large noncommercial gatherings in national forests (often in Appalachia) to pray for world peace and demonstrate the viability of a cooperative utopian community living in harmony with the earth. Retirement and gated communities carve out space for other types of homogenous populations.

Private groups are not the only ones creating alternative community models. The federal government created its version of model subsistence communities as part of the New Deal during the Great Depression of the 1930s. Arthurdale, a village near Morgantown, West Virginia, created to provide gardening and crafts work for former miners, opened in 1933–34 and was dedicated by First Lady Eleanor

Roosevelt in 1937. Another, called Cumberland Homesteads, was built on the Cumberland Plateau near Crossville, Tennessee.

The Great Depression, coal booms, and the dramatic rise of new technologies notwithstanding, the industrialization of America in the late nineteenth and early twentieth centuries remains the defining period for Appalachian communities. Although the agricultural southern area languished in the late nineteenth and early twentieth centuries, the steel mills and factories of Pittsburgh (and later Birmingham, Alabama) exemplified the United States' emergence as an industrial nation. The coal for its boilers and the lumber for its buildings were provided from the mountains of West Virginia, eastern Kentucky, southwest Virginia, and east Tennessee. While communities in the more urban and industrialized North were supported by a relatively diverse economic base, there emerged in the mountains of central Appalachia an economy dominated by coal and controlled by distant corporations.

Little manufacturing developed in this part of Appalachia, and where it did, few wage-earning opportunities were available to women. The system reinforced patriarchal control of both family and community life, leaving them vulnerable to the whims of single companies and the exigencies of extractive industries. Steadily, the entire region became increasingly embedded in a worldwide system of industrial production and commerce. With labor imported to work in the mines as well as manufacturing and industrial enterprises, the population of the region boomed during the early decades of the twentieth century, becoming ethnically, racially, and culturally more diverse in the process.

Although loosely associated by geography and landscape, communities in northern, central, and southern Appalachia evolved with their own histories and economies and with few apparent similarities. What continued to be a hallmark of steel towns, mining communities, and agrarian villages alike, however, was an enduring respect, even reverence, for family and kinship relationships and reciprocity. But while kin networks continued to underpin family security and survival, important new bonds gained prominence as the impact of industrialization advanced. Employers' organizations, labor unions, civic clubs, fraternal organizations, government offices, and sports teams became community fixtures. Religious life, though always important, became more institutionalized, diversified, and conspicuous, thanks in part to the efforts of missionaries and the construction of churches in company towns. Meanwhile public schooling became generally mandatory. With the arrival of professional medical care and the construction of hospitals, public health improved and birth rates declined dramatically as contraception became more widely available. From the early twentieth century, extrafamilial institutions—schools, hospitals, corporate employers, and the government—became increasingly important to the maintenance of Appalachian families. Both the complexity and the pressures of family life and community affairs accelerated with the passing decades as the mining industry mechanized and replaced jobs with machinery, women entered the workforce, life span increased, and the speed of travel and communication soared.

Even though scores of the region's counties, the majority of them in eastern Kentucky and West Virginia, continue to be federally designated as economically "distressed," Appalachian families and communities became generally more like their counterparts elsewhere in America as the twenty-first century began. Single-parent households became commonplace, divorce routine, and domestic violence frequent. Issues generated by homelessness, drug abuse, sexually transmitted diseases, and more open homosexuality became part of community dialogue.

The changing economy became increasingly based upon businesses and occupations in the service sector, while resource extraction and manufacturing jobs declined. Organized labor declined from its mid-century high. Women found jobs in virtually every sector and made inroads into management, although more and more were employed in low-income and part-time work. As in the rest of America, lifetime employment by a single company became less possible but was still part of normative expectations. Such developments produced new challenges for both communities and families. Family tensions often arose when increasing employment of women and decreasing opportunities deemed suitable for men propelled women into the role of breadwinner for the family. Child-care facilities failed to keep pace with increasing employment of women, although many families continued to rely on relatives, especially their parents, to take care of children while they worked. Though women's growing participation in the workplace led to problems in some families, it became vital to their financial security. It also extracted public as well as private tolls as a shortage of day-care facilities and child-care services, for example, became an endemic problem.

Although divorce rates rose through the 1980s and 1990s along with the number of single-parent households, available statistics showed Appalachia changing less rapidly in this regard than other regions or the United States in general—a fact perhaps attributable to the region's religious conservatism and relatively slower urbanization. In some specific instances, however, Appalachia experienced family problems perhaps more acutely than other areas. Research conducted in 1994 by Peggy J. Cantrell, a psychology professor at East Tennessee State University, for example, found rates of familial violence and abuse in southwestern Virginia to be significantly higher than in the United States overall. Teenagers and college students surveyed by Cantrell reported that mother to child abuse was most common, followed by father to child, mother to father, and father to mother. (Reported mother to father abuse was only slightly higher than father to mother abuse. In the study, abuse was defined as any behavior intended to hurt another and may account for acts of violent self-defense qualifying as abuse under these terms.)

While abuse and violence were most likely to occur in families where the parents' educational level was low, Cantrell's work also suggested that highly educated couples also experienced and engaged in domestic violence, contrary to national patterns. Unanswered is the question of whether domestic violence has actually increased or if public agencies, more attuned to family economic stresses and changing gender roles, are only recently recognizing a long-existing social problem. In any case, law enforcement, health, and social service agencies have begun to offer employee training on domestic abuse, and while advocacy groups have organized around the issue and hotlines and shelters have begun to appear, Appalachia, particularly in rural areas, lags behind the rest of the United States in the provision of such services.

As important as biologically based kinship is in the region, the evolution of family and community life in recent decades emphasizes that such ties are changeable and ultimately negotiable socially constructed relationships. Most obviously, divorce, remarriage, and adoption have come to play a more important role in forming and re-forming kin groups, as has acknowledgment of same-sex couples and other unmarried persons living together. Still, in their contemporary form, such groups strongly reflect their traditional roots in various ways, among them the continuing use of honorific, fictive kin titles such as *uncle* and *aunt* for respected elders, *cousin* for revered relatives or non-kin peers, and less frequently *mammaw*, *pappaw*, or *granny*. In addition to their traditional kin groups, many Appalachian communities have come to include "chosen families" made up of biologically unrelated individuals or couples united by political beliefs, sexual orientation, professional commitment, or some other flexible, negotiable social bond and organized to function as a family unit. To the mix, sociologists Harry Schwarzweller, James S. Brown, and J. J. Mangalam have added the concept of the Appalachian "stem family" to describe families with members who work and live in distant places while keeping their essential ties in place with their kin at home.

As for rural Americans everywhere, the future holds special challenges for rural Appalachians. The historic problems of families and communities endure even as the economy is transformed and public policy increasingly focuses on the issues of urban America. But with a history marked by government intervention, corporate exploitation, and environmental debacles, community activism blossomed in the late twentieth century. In important instances, neighbors joined forces to fight what often appeared to be insurmountable odds in efforts to save both themselves and their communities. Groups such as the Appalachian Group to Save the Land and People, Ohio Valley Environmental Coalition, Coal River Mountain Watch, Kentuckians for the Commonwealth, and Save Our Cumberland Mountains became important voices in environmental and economic debates.

Increasingly fading was the national perception of Appalachia as a place of special needs, continued efforts of the Appalachian Regional Commission and other federal and state government agencies notwithstanding. The Appalachia thought of as a national problem had by the beginning of the new century blended with images of communities and families facing the same trials across the country.

—Shirley L. Stewart Burns, *West Virginia University*, and
Shaunna L. Scott and Deborah J. Thompson, *University of Kentucky*

Allen W. Batteau, "Mosbys and Broomsedge: The Semantics of Class in an Appalachian Kinship System," *American Ethnologist* (August 1982); Patricia D. Beaver, *Rural Community in the Appalachian South* (1986); Dwight B. Billings and Kathleen M. Blee, *The Road to Poverty: The Making of Wealth and Hardship in Appalachia* (2000); Kate Black and Marc A. Rhorer, "Out in the Mountains: Exploring Lesbian and Gay Lives," in *Out in the South*, ed. Carlos L. Dews and Carolyn Leste Law (2001); James S. Brown, *Beech Creek: A Study of a Kentucky Neighborhood* (1988); F. Carlene Bryant, *We're All Kin: A Cultural Study of a Mountain Neighborhood* (1981); Peggy J. Cantrell, "Family Violence and Incest in Appalachia," in *Appalachia Inside Out, Vol. 1: Conflict and Change*, ed. Robert J. Higgs, Ambrose N. Manning, and Jim Wayne Miller (1995); Samuel R. Cook, *Monacans and Miners: Native American and Coal Mining Communities in Appalachia* (2000); Fellowship for Intentional Community, *Communities Directory* (2000); Ken Fones-Wolf and Ronald L. Lewis, eds., *Transnational West Virginia: Ethnic Communities and Economic Change, 1840–1940* (2002); Patricia L. Gagné, "Appalachian Women: Violence and Social Control," *Journal of Contemporary Ethnography* (January 1992); John C. Inscoe, ed., *Appalachians and Race: The Mountain South from Slavery to Segregation* (2001); Chad Montrie, *To Save the Land and People: A History of Opposition to Surface Coal Mining in Appalachia* (2003); Shaunna L. Scott, *Two Sides to Everything: The Cultural Construction of Class Consciousness in Harlan County, Kentucky* (1995); Stephen E. White and Stanley D. Brunn, "The Persistence of Social Isolation in Eastern Kentucky: An Examination of Marriage-Mate Selection Distances," *Southeastern Geographer* (May 1994).

Abundant Dawn Community

See Back-to-the-Land Movement (Settlement and Migration)

African American Families and Communities

Partially because of the stereotype that Appalachians are virtually all white, African Americans have been called an invisible minority in the region. In 2000 African Americans constituted about 8 percent of the population in federally defined Appalachia. Before the Civil War the region was racially more diverse than in modern times because of the widespread existence of African American slavery in the region. (One estimate is that as many as one-third of the region's landowning farmers owned slaves.) Opportunities created by railroad building, timbering, and coal mining also drew many African American families into the region, although many left when employment declined in those industries. At the turn of the twenty-first century the proportion of African Americans in Appalachia ranged from a low of around 2 percent in northern and central Appalachia to 13 percent in southern Appalachia, including northern Mississippi, where they constituted almost one-third of the population.

African Americans' relative invisibility is also heightened by the perception that the region is almost entirely rural. In fact, the vast majority of African Americans, perhaps as many as 85 percent, live in the small towns and cities of the region. Important exceptions, however, include a few coal-mining counties in southern West Virginia, where there is a significant concentration of African Americans. In the coal-rich counties of Fayette, McDowell, Mercer, and Raleigh, African American families comprise between 6 and 16 percent of all families, in sharp contrast to their relative absence in other parts of central Appalachia.

The longterm effects of slavery, economic exploitation, segregation, discrimination, racial violence, poverty, and the lack of public welfare programs in Appalachia have created special hardships and constraints for African American families. Generally speaking, levels of African American poverty throughout the region exceed the regional average. In Appalachian Mississippi, very high levels of African American poverty exist alongside low levels of white poverty. Less than 3 percent of whites in Noxubee County, Mississippi, for example, were poor in 1990, but 38 percent of African Americans there were impoverished. Throughout Appalachian Mississippi, low incomes influence the way African American households are organized. High levels of female workforce participation, female-headed households, and poverty are correlated. Female-headed households are also two to three times more prevalent among African Americans concentrated in West Virginia's coal-mining counties than among white households there.

African American families in Appalachia have received less scholarly attention than rural white families in the region, but several historical studies provide insight into the impact of exploitation and discrimination on African American household formation as well as the role of kinship in economic survival and community life. Some historians argue that in the nineteenth century Appalachian slaves generally faced less harsh treatment than did those on southern plantations, largely because the lower proportion of slaves in the mountain population made them seem less a threat to the security of whites. But other scholars contend that Appalachian whites not only exploited slaves' labor on farms but also profited from their biological reproduction by selling surplus laborers and children to buyers in the nonmountain South. Such slave sales had devastating effects on many African American households and families as men and women, parents and children, and more distant kin and friends were ruthlessly separated from one another by force.

A comparative study of African American and white households and families over six decades during the nineteenth and early twentieth centuries in Appalachian Kentucky's Clay County affirms the effects of exploitation, economic hardship, and discrimination on African American family life during both slavery and freedom. These effects were visible in racial differences in resource accumulation, migration and persistence, and household and family structure. Race influenced both wealth and opportunity in nineteenth-century Clay County, where landownership was the key to life chances and the acquisition of land by African Americans was exceedingly uncommon. Consequently, after slavery was abolished, most African American males were locked into such occupations as farm laborer and tenant farmer. African American women were more likely to be in the paid workforce than white women but were largely confined to service jobs as cooks and servants as well as farm laborers. While whites also performed such jobs, many did so at early stages of life before women married and while males waited to inherit land from parents. Their servitude was not a lifelong status. Later, when the economy became more extensively commercialized, education and occupation (rather than land) conveyed wealth and status, but segregation and racial discrimination blocked opportunities for African Americans. With little access to resources, African Americans either left the county or remained among its impoverished population.

Kinship networks and household arrangements can either ameliorate economic hardship by providing strategic resources or augment economic distress by burdening members with obligation and dependency. Slavery profoundly undermined family life in Clay County. Enslaved males were disproportionately employed in making salt, and most lived in large groups. Few slaves lived with family members. Most enslaved children lived with only one parent, almost always their mother. Free antebellum African American households, too, were much more likely to be headed by females than were those of whites. After emancipation, African Americans were far more likely than whites to live with nonrelatives, usually whites, who employed them as servants. African American children were subject to arbitrary seizure and forced apprenticeships. Reflecting the extreme economic marginality of most households headed by African Americans, substantial numbers of Clay County's African American elderly, especially women, were forced to live apart from kin, usually as lifelong servants in white households.

Although slavery and living conditions in rural Appalachian farm communities provided great obstacles to African American family life, kinship and friendship networks often contributed positively to the lives of African Americans in the segregated mining communities of central Appalachia. African American households in West Virginia's coal camps were significantly smaller than those of European immigrants and native whites. Effective networks of kin and friends facilitated African American migration into the area and aided the sharing of knowledge and skills necessary for occupational success there. Furthermore, important allegiances between working-class and middle-class African American families in coal-mining communities promoted solidarity and political assertiveness in the context of racial segregation.

See also: COAL TOWNS; FREE BLACKS, ANTEBELLUM (RACE, ETHNICITY, AND IDENTITY); FREED BLACKS, POSTBELLUM (RACE, ETHNICITY, AND IDENTITY).

—Dwight B. Billings, *University of Kentucky*, and Kathleen M. Blee, *University of Pittsburgh*

Dwight B. Billings and Kathleen M. Blee, *The Road to Poverty: The Making of Wealth and Hardship in Appalachia* (2000); Richard A. Couto, *An American Challenge: A Report on Economic Trends and Social Issues in Appalachia* (1994); Joe William Trotter Jr., *Coal, Class, and Color: Blacks in Southern West Virginia, 1915–32* (1990).

Aging

Although older adults make up the fastest-growing segment of the American population, research on aging in Appalachia is limited and outdated, and studies have tended to be limited to specific areas or small samples from individual states. Although useful, such studies do not provide a broad understanding of the elderly across the region.

Historically, work and retirement have different meanings in Appalachia than in the United States at large. Especially in central Appalachia, employment opportunity has been less consistent, more physically demanding, and lower paying than in most other areas of the country. In the early and mid-twentieth century, most workers labored for companies based outside the region in industries such as lumbering and mining. Generally, absentee owners improved local economic conditions only temporarily, and few offered retirement plans or benefits. Employment opportunities for Appalachian women were few, and elderly women usually relied on their husbands for income during both working years and retirement, as most have continued to do until the present time. Thus, the elderly in central Appalachia have historically been poorer than those in other Appalachian subregions, as well as other parts of the country.

Although it is widely assumed that the elderly in Appalachia generally remain in one place as age advances, there is no clear evidence to prove this. Whether or not older individuals age in place or migrate depends on factors such as their state of health, the location of family members, and the availability of community resources. Historically, Appalachian elders have been strongly attached to their homes and communities and have considered moving a difficult decision. Out-migration, especially for individuals over age seventy-five, was often made necessary in order to obtain support. Although health considerations could necessitate a move, elders' physical environments and social needs also contributed to the decision. While individual circumstances, such as a leaky roof or the death of a neighbor, might prompt an elder to leave Appalachia abruptly to live with family elsewhere, out-migration also occurs in phases. For example, an older individual might begin the transition by spending winter months with family and gradually take up a new residence. Although family ties suggest that support systems exist for older adults in the region, forces such as out-migration of younger generations also encourage migration of the elderly.

In Appalachia, more than half the population lives in a rural environment, compared to less than a quarter in the rest of the country. The rural nature of the region, low incomes, lack of health insurance, and cultural reluctance to use formal services all tend to complicate the circumstances of older adults. In areas that have become popular retirement destinations, in-migration of more affluent elders sometimes results in the availability of services not affordable to typical Appalachian elders.

Close examination shows that aging in Appalachia is particularly difficult for many elders because of their race, class, and gender. Although the region's population is older than the rest of the United States, this gap narrows with increasing age. A greater proportion of individuals are over the age of sixty-five in Appalachia than in the rest of the United States, but the proportion of individuals is nearly equal among those over the age of eighty-five. This suggests that environmental and cultural conditions have a negative impact on longevity in the region. Life appears to be relatively harder on women than men. In Appalachia, as in the rest of the United States, women tend to outlive men, but the proportion of women living to be very old (over age eighty-five) is smaller than elsewhere in the country. Of interest to scientists and others seeking to understand regional longevity are factors such as racial composition of the population and poverty, which tends to be more pronounced among older Appalachians than among older persons in other areas.

See also: DEATH LORE (FOLKLORE AND FOLKLIFE); ELDER CARE; FAMILIES AND HEALTH (HEALTH).

—Tammy Cook and Adam Davey, *University of Georgia*

B. Jan McCulloch, "Gender and Race: An Interaction Affecting the Replicability of Well-Being Across Groups," *Women and Health* (1992).

Arthurdale, West Virginia

See Arthurdale, West Virginia (Architecture); New Deal Communities

Back-to-the-Land Movement

See Back-to-the-Land Movement (Settlement and Migration)

Catholic Communities

From large Catholic religious orders such as the Benedictines, Franciscans, and Dominicans to smaller groups and volunteer programs, communities of Catholics have played a significant role in Appalachia. Strongly encouraged by church leaders to directly serve Appalachians in both religious and secular areas, members of planned Catholic communities have worked alongside secular groups on issues of poverty, education, health, the environment, and other social concerns in the region.

Catholic communities vary in size from large monasteries to smaller outreach programs and missions consisting of only a few members living as a family. Members of monastic communities take vows of a particular Catholic order and center their daily life on prayer. Chores and activities necessary to the success of the community are shared among the members and performed around a strict schedule of prayer and religious services. Non-monastic Catholic communities may include lay people and generally concentrate on providing to the community at large specific services such as nursing, elder care, or aiding recovery from substance abuse.

Saint Vincent Archabbey, located near Latrobe, Pennsylvania, was the first Benedictine monastery in the United States. Founded by Boniface Wimmer in 1846, the monastery includes a seminary and college with a faculty of both Benedictines and laypersons serving a student body of about fifteen hundred.

Cullman, Alabama, is the location of two notable Appalachian monasteries—Saint Bernard Abbey, established in 1891, and Sacred Heart Monastery, founded in 1902. The approximately twenty-four Benedictine monks of Saint Bernard devote their lives to daily worship, prayer, and meditation, as well as other kinds of spiritual labor. This includes caring for the abbey's more than eight hundred acres of property, operating a college preparatory school (grades 9–12), and running a retreat center. Saint Bernard Abbey is also the location of the Ave Maria Grotto, a four-acre park featuring 125 miniature reproductions of famous buildings and shrines of the world. The sisters of Sacred Heart Monastery originally went to Appalachia to teach the children of farmers, immigrant workers, and miners near Birmingham but have diversified their mission to provide ministerial, hospital chaplain, legal, medical, social, and educational services. On the monastery grounds, Sacred Heart operates Benedictine Manor, a retirement home, and the Benedictine Spirituality and Conference Center for retreats and workshops.

Other examples of Catholic communities in Appalachia, both permanent and temporary, include Nazareth Farm in Doddridge County, West Virginia; Glenmary Farm (sponsored by Glenmary Home Missioners) in Vanceburg, Kentucky; Young People Who Care, based in Frenchville, Pennsylvania; and the Benedictine Sisters of Pittsburgh. Smaller Catholic orders of Salesians, Carmelites, Passionists, and the Sisters of Saint Joseph also live in planned communities throughout the region.

See also: CATHOLICISM (RELIGION); GLENMARY HOME MISSIONERS (RELIGION); GLENMARY SISTERS (RELIGION).

—Mary Ruth Coffman, *Sacred Heart Monastery, Cullman, Alabama;* Jessica Hoey, *Jefferson City, Missouri;* and Deborah J. Thompson, *University of Kentucky*

Cherokee Families and Communities

Kinship and family relations were most important for the traditional Cherokees of the southern Appalachians and affected many aspects of their lives, including marriage,

Children at a Native American powwow conducted during the Trade Days Festival in Trade, Tennessee, 1991. Powwows, which generally combine open social dances with specialty dance competitions, were first held in the early 1970s on the Qualla Boundary in western North Carolina, home of the Eastern Band of Cherokee Indians.

social relations, economic activities, and political organization. Like many Native Americans of the southeastern United States, the Cherokee had a matrilineal kinship and descent system, wherein an individual's "kin" were defined by links through his or her mother. Thus, a man's mother, his mother's siblings, and their children were part of his kin group, but his father, his father's siblings, and their children were not.

The Cherokees used a system of kinship terminology first defined by anthropologists for the Crow Indians of the Great Plains. In this system, Ego (the individual who is the reference point for naming) called his mother's brother's children by the same names he used for his own children. Thus Ego would call his maternal cousins "son" and "daughter." These individuals were, of course, members of Ego's matrilineage and this naming emphasized that relationship. Ego called his father's sisters' children the same names he called his father and father's sister; these individuals were members of Ego's father's matrilineage.

The matrilineage included all kinsmen who could trace descent from a known female ancestor. In addition to one's mother's lineage, three other lineages were most important to an individual Cherokee. These included his father's lineage, his mother's father's lineage, and his father's father's lineage. Ego treated his parents, his mother's brother, and his father's sister with respect. His mother's brother was especially important as a lineage member who could both aid and discipline Ego.

Lineages and their members were also members of a larger kinship unit—the clan. The Cherokees recognized seven matrilineal clans—Wolf, Deer, Bird, Red Paint, Blue, Twister (also called Long Hair), and Wild Potato. Following the matrilineal system, each Cherokee was a member of his mother's clan. Clan membership was therefore determined at birth and was permanent. Lineage and clan membership were important factors regulating marriage. The Cherokees practiced clan exogamy, wherein it was considered incestuous (and therefore forbidden) to marry someone from your same clan or your father's clan. Preferred mates came from the father's father or mother's father's clans (hence their importance). After marriage, the Cherokees preferred matrilocal residence, resulting in a household comprised (ideally) of a senior couple, their unmarried children, their daughters and sons-in-law, and their daughter's children.

This extended matrilocal family household was the basic economic unit for the traditional Cherokees. Major activities were divided along gender lines. Men did heavy labor such as clearing the fields by the slash-and-burn method for agriculture and constructing houses and dugout canoes. Men also hunted and engaged in warfare. Women cared for children, planted and tended the gardens, and made items for domestic use, such as woven baskets and clay pottery.

Politically, traditional Cherokees were organized into "towns," which represented sometimes widely scattered households linked together by their association with the same council ceremonial center. Each town council was politically autonomous and independent but linked together by the kinship system. Because of clan exogamy, each village or town contained members of all seven matrilineal clans. Cherokee individuals traveling between towns could always find fellow clan members who could provide food and shelter. Kin ties thus took the place of a centralized political organization.

Beyond lineage and clan, traditional Cherokees saw each other as members of a broader community whose interpersonal relationships should be guided by a behavioral code called the Harmony Ethic. The Cherokee Harmony Ethic defines a good Cherokee as one who avoids arguments and conflict with his fellow Cherokees, who gives both time and material possessions to others in need, and who emphasizes the well-being of the group or community over any individual achievement or comfort. Thus, attitudes and behaviors required in familial relations were extended as ideal norms for the treatment of all Cherokees and illustrated the egalitarian nature of traditional Cherokee life.

By the mid-eighteenth century, traditional Cherokee lifeways began to change due to the Cherokees' dependence on English trade; these changes accelerated during and after the American Revolution. By the early nineteenth century, social and political factionalism and economic disparity had replaced the traditional egalitarian way of life.

By the mid-twentieth century, the Eastern Band of Cherokee Indians (who remained in the mountains of North Carolina after the removal of the Cherokee Nation) had modified kinship terminology to a more bilateral form, comparable to that of the broader American culture. A reduction in the importance of clan membership in regulating marriage and a greater frequency of nuclear family households were also consequences of modernization. However, kinship and descent are still important in defining tribal membership in the Eastern Band. Enrollment is limited to direct lineal descendants of Cherokees listed on the 1924 Baker tribal roll. Enrollees must also possess at least one-sixteenth Eastern Cherokee "blood quantum."

See also: CHEROKEE (RACE, ETHNICITY, AND IDENTITY); CHEROKEE RELIGIOUS TRADITIONS (RELIGION); CHEROKEE TRADITIONAL DANCE (PERFORMING ARTS).

—Cliff Boyd, *Radford University*

Charles M. Hudson, *The Southeastern Indians* (1976); Wendell H. Oswalt, *This Land Was Theirs: A Study of Native Americans* (7th edition, 2001); Theda Perdue, *The Cherokee* (1989).

Christian Service Groups

Since the late nineteenth century, Appalachia has been a special interest of Christian service groups seeking to better the region through evangelism, education, and social service. These organizations arrived in response to a variety of perceived needs. To many religious groups, the region seemed economically, socially, and religiously deprived and isolated from other parts of the country. Accordingly, the goal of many of the first Christian service groups establishing missions in the area was to convert Appalachian residents away from their "backward" ways through evangelism and education. Throughout the twentieth century, however, most organizations increasingly tended to concern themselves with services rather than conversion. Among the first of the service-oriented Christian groups in the region were the Salvation Army and the Council of the Southern Mountains.

The Salvation Army, founded in London in 1865 by William and Catherine Booth, began as an organization to help poor and working-class families and individuals. Entering Appalachia in the 1880s, the Salvation Army focused primarily on the urban steel cities of the northern part of the region and the coalfields of West Virginia and Kentucky. For several reasons, the organization's first few years in Appalachia were difficult. Areas most in need of help were unable to support Salvation Army offices financially. Moreover, especially in the southern mountains, many residents approved neither of the group's no-tobacco morality, its efforts to help blacks, nor its employment of women preachers in military uniforms.

The Salvation Army for many years did little else but evangelize. Throughout the highlands of Kentucky, Tennessee, and West Virginia, the group held large tent revivals addressing spiritual needs of the communities while helping to fund further endeavors for the organization. During the first decade of the twentieth century, one of the most famous of the group's revival preachers, Colonel Richard E. Holz, took a five-year circuit-riding campaign through the region holding open-air meetings at courthouses, jails, and on mountainsides.

The Salvation Army also began to attend to the physical needs, as well as the spiritual needs, of Appalachians. Cecil Brown, a native of the region, worked in the 1930s, preaching, teaching, and advising people in the Great Smoky Mountains of North Carolina. In 1945, another Appalachian native, Major Mary Peacock, became corps director at Athens, Georgia, and opened missions in the mountains of the northern part of the state. Currently, the Salvation Army maintains locations in most large towns and in some rural areas in Appalachia. Its services include disaster relief, boys' and girls' clubs, youth programs, summer camps, adult education classes and clubs, transient shelters, thrift stores, food pantries, and worship opportunities.

The Council of the Southern Mountains (originally the Conference of Southern Mountain Workers) was first convened ecumenically under the guidance of John C. and Olive Dame Campbell in 1913. The organization, which disbanded in 1989, generally approached the Appalachian region from a missionary vantage point, though its Christian rhetoric had

Members of the Appalachian Volunteers, a service group established by the Council of the Southern Mountains, present a puppet show in southern Appalachia, c. mid-1960s. The Council of the Southern Mountains, which existed from 1912 to 1989, assisted Appalachian communities by providing such services as health programs, settlement schools, and an Appalachian migrant program in Chicago.

diminished somewhat by the 1960s. At various times, the council offered such services as health programs, settlement schools, and an Appalachian migrant program in Chicago. In addition, the council established the service group Appalachian Volunteers, a Community Action Program, and made attempts to organize dairy, agricultural, and craft cooperatives.

Many other Christian service groups established themselves in Appalachia in the early 1900s. Among the most effective of these has been Catholic Charities USA. Established nationally in 1910, the organization has provided adoption services, child care, community-development resources, elderly services, emergency shelters, family support, job training, parenting education, pregnancy counseling, prison ministry, refugee and immigration services, services to persons with HIV/AIDS, soup kitchens and food pantries, treatment for alcohol and drug abuse, youth services, and Hispanic services. Some regional offices, such as those in Lexington, Kentucky, and Wheeling, West Virginia, provide care in rural as well as urban areas.

Each Catholic Charities office is run by a regional diocese. Since 1996, emergency grants for flood relief have been allocated to the Dioceses of Knoxville, Tennessee; Steubenville, Ohio; Wheeling, West Virginia; and Harrisburg, Pennsylvania.

Marie Cirillo, with forty-three other Glenmary Sisters, has led another notably effective Christian service group in Appalachia, the Federation of Communities in Service (FOCIS). Since its inception in 1967, the federation has been recognized throughout the Appalachian areas of Virginia, Tennessee, and North Carolina as an innovative force. It primarily administers grants for appropriate programs. Projects created by members and collaborators include community-development organizations, community arts programs, college extension offices, a workers' cooperative, emergency shelters, special education and art classes in the public schools, community water systems, health clinics, land trusts, a pallet factory, health fairs, paralegal services, and a mixed-income ecumenical retirement community. Cirillo, working within the Catholic Diocese of Tennessee in Clearfork Valley, has helped local groups launch health clinics, community-development corporations, and environmental and arts organizations. She also helps residents acquire corporate-owned land and has developed Woodland Community Land Trust, a cooperative community.

The ecumenical Commission on Religion in Appalachia has also been an innovative force in developing communities since its beginnings in 1965. With a mission to build communities and to fight injustice, the commission has helped striking miners in Harlan, Kentucky, and other places; supported striking J. P. Stevens textile workers; started a volunteer organization in Zanesville, Ohio; helped to revitalize a community in Cleveland, Tennessee; and has continually advocated for environmental, social, and economic justice. The Commission on Religion in Appalachia continues to encourage church congregations and communities to examine issues in their lives critically, promoting integral changes in life and society through a communal study of scripture.

Another Christian service group, Appalachian Outreach, concentrates most of its efforts on home repair for low-income families. This ministry from Carson-Newman College, started in 1984, has helped about eighty-five families a year in east Tennessee. Appalachian Outreach also operates a clothing and furniture ministry and a food pantry and offers high school equivalency and computer training.

Other Christian service groups include the Christian Appalachian Project of Lancaster, Kentucky; the Appalachia Service Project of Johnson City, Tennessee; and Grandfather Home for Children of Banner Elk, North Carolina.

See also: CATHOLIC COMMUNITIES; COMMISSION ON RELIGION IN APPALACHIA (RELIGION); GLENMARY HOME MISSIONERS (RELIGION).

—Kathy A. Campbell, *East Tennessee State University;* Helen M. Lewis, *Morganton, Georgia;* Joe Moore, *Appalachian Revival Ministries;* Connie Park Rice, *West Virginia University;* and Catherine Rumschlag, *Federation of Communities in Service*

Allan Atterlee, *Sweeping through the Land: The History of the Salvation Army in the Southern United States* (1989); Patricia D. Beaver and Burton L. Purrington, eds., *Cultural Adaptation to Mountain Environments* (1984); Deborah V. McCauley, *Appalachian Mountain Religion: A History* (1995).

Coal Towns

Families in coal towns were a mix of white Appalachian natives, African Americans from the Deep South, and immigrants who were mostly Italians and eastern Europeans, especially Hungarians, Poles, and Slavs. This mix of cultures created a rich but sometimes dissonant life in the small towns of the Appalachian coalfields.

Initially, coal companies hired single men to work the mines as the coalfields were settled from the 1880s through the early 1900s. However, turnover was commonplace, and coal companies began to recruit more workers with families because they believed they would stay longer.

Most coal-mining families lived in a coal camp built by the company. These camps differed greatly depending on the company and the amount of difficulty the company had finding employees. Mining families lived in segregated camps, with the best housing going to the native Appalachians, while the worst housing became the "colored camp" for African Americans. Housing standards for immigrants fell somewhere in between. While the three groups worked almost daily together underground, they did not mix socially. Immigrant families frequently spent the weekends visiting other immigrant families. Churches were generally segregated, with African Americans and native whites each having separate places of worship, while Europeans built Roman Catholic and Greek Orthodox churches. Most families did not want their children to marry "foreigners."

Mining families, like most families during the period, had numerous children. Since their homes were small, many families lived in overcrowded conditions. It was common for immigrant families to also take in several single men as boarders. In the early coal camps, most houses had electricity but usually lacked plumbing and running water. This made life difficult for the woman of the house. Her major role was to serve as housekeeper, cook, and mother. Because the men worked such long hours at difficult jobs, women tried to make life for their husbands as free from stress and burdens as possible.

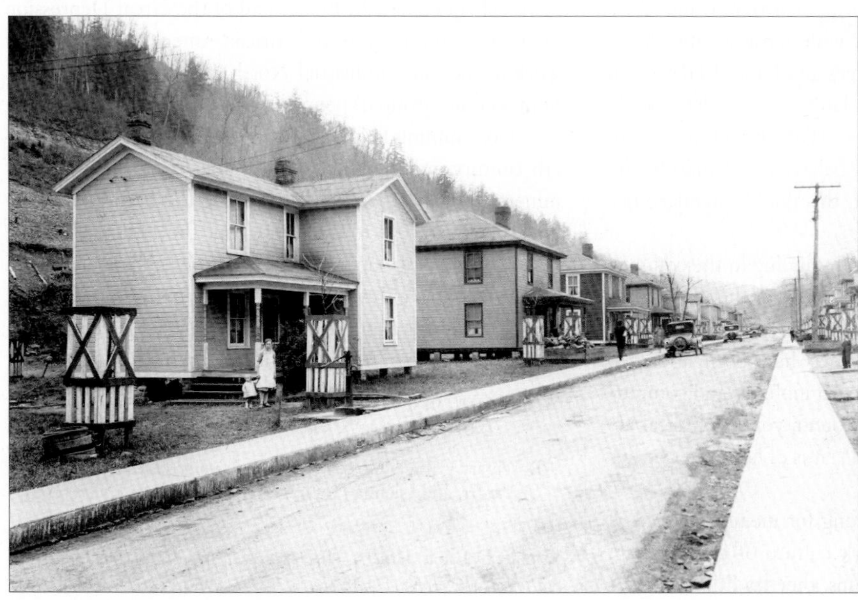

Company housing for the Amonate Mine of the Pocahontas Fuel Company, Tazewell County, Virginia, 1920. Coal camps were usually racially segregated, with the highest-quality housing reserved for native whites and inferior housing for immigrants and African Americans.

Few coal-camp women worked for wages, and independent financial opportunities were limited to services such as doing laundry, taking in boarders, sewing, and sitting with the sick. A few women worked as clerks in the company store, and with the passage of time some worked in retail stores in the nearest independent towns. The small number of professional women who were part of a coal-camp community included a few teachers and perhaps a nurse and a bookkeeper. There is indirect evidence of some coal-camp prostitution. Not until the 1970s were women allowed to actually work for wages in the mines; however, they never became a significant portion of the mining force.

A coal-camp family's economic well-being depended on the shifting fortunes of the coal industry, over which mining families had no control. What men could do to affect the family's economic situation was to go to work "under the hill" and work hard. Women sought to improve the family's economic position by carefully managing men's wages and through unpaid domestic work in the gardens and fields of the mining camp. They also endeavored to keep their husbands steadily at work.

Life in the coal camps was a different experience for men and women. The coal-camp wife, just as her husband, lived under the watchful eyes of the camp superintendent. Women were responsible for maintaining the family's reputation and their men's sobriety. Coal-company officials' perceptions of alcohol abuse by a miner or sexual impropriety on the part of a miner's wife or daughter could determine whether a man remained employed, whether a family was evicted from company housing, or whether a family was given credit at the company store.

Family life in the camps reflected the range of human nature, including many loving marriages and close families but also families filled with tension and abuse. However, there were few divorces until the 1940s. Men could smoke, play cards, use foul language, and drink while facing few community sanctions. Women did not share these privileges, and their sexual behavior was sharply circumscribed. After World War II, this double standard became less severe.

A woman's social mobility and standing in the community was linked to the occupational status of the men in her family, particularly her husband. A man's productivity, skill, or leadership ability might advance him occupationally, and, thus, socially. For women, social mobility and community status depended upon background, youth, physical attractiveness, and the occupational status of her father or her husband.

Community bonds were strong for men, employed as they were in the hazardous work culture of coal mining. Though women formed friendships, they traditionally kept close to their own mothers and sisters and were usually occupied by housekeeping and child care. A daily trip to the company store was routine, but there was no flurry of visiting, no women's clubs, no activities focusing on women's problems and concerns. African American women came closer to forging a sense of sisterhood. Their relationships with one another reflected the need to pull together in the context of African Americans' minority position in the coal camps.

While union sentiment, class awareness, and materialism differed to some degree between men and women, both usually supported unionization and strikes. Women's fears for their family's immediate economic situation sometimes precluded their support, however.

With the industrialization of Appalachia in the early twentieth century, men's wages became the determinant of women's economic security. Consequently, gender dynamics changed in men's and women's personal lives, in their families, and in their newly constructed communities. Women had been central figures in the economic and social sectors of a vital preindustrial society in the region. Late-nineteenth- and early-twentieth-century industrialization, brought about by the arrival of the railroads, large-scale timbering, and corporate mining operations, transformed the dynamics of gender and economics in mountain society. With mining jobs open to men only and with few other wage-earning opportunities available in coal camps, the economic role of mountain women withered. Their economic function became less direct and their social role more complex as they depended on the labor of fathers, brothers, husbands, and sons.

During World War I, many immigrant families left the Appalachian coalfields. By the end of the Great Depression many more immigrants and African Americans had left for work in the more industrial North, leaving behind a more homogenous group of people.

Coal-mining families existing at the end of the twentieth century and beyond usually came from a long line of miners. More women worked outside the home than they did from the 1900s to the 1960s, but they still carried the major burden of supporting the family and keeping the home. Life has always been hard for mining families, but from the early days of the coalfields they have used the family network as a source of emotional and financial support.

See also: COAL MINING (ENVIRONMENT); COMMUNITIES AND INDUSTRY; WOMEN'S ROLES.

—Rosemary Carucci Goss, *Virginia Polytechnic Institute and State University*, and Glenna H. Graves, *Morehead State University at West Liberty*

Ronald D Eller, *Miners, Millhands, and Mountaineers: Industrialization of the Appalachian South, 1880–1930* (1982); Carol A. B.

Giesen, *Coal Miners' Wives* (1995); Crandall A. Shifflett, *Coal Towns: Life, Work, and Culture in Company Towns of Southern Appalachia, 1880–1960* (1991).

Communities and Industry

Because of Appalachia's great natural wealth and resource-based economy, the region's communities and towns, particularly those in areas rich in coal and timber, have long found their quality of life, like their financial security, heavily influenced by local industrial operations. Increasingly efficient technology, cumulative environmental impacts, the loss of jobs, and a growing environmental justice movement have combined in many instances to create tensions between communities and their corporate neighbors. In modern times, lawsuits have become commonplace. Environmentalists have blamed coal and timber companies for a host of problems, including air and water pollution, flooding, structural damage to residences, and hazardous traffic. In some cases corporations have effectively eliminated communities by buying out residents and businesses one by one. Some confrontations, such as the struggle over mountaintop removal in West Virginia beginning in the late 1990s, have made headlines, as have disasters such as rupture of coal-waste dams on Buffalo Creek in West Virginia in 1972 and Martin County, Kentucky, in 2000. More often, modern conflicts between communities and corporate neighbors are chronic and involve not only contemporary issues such as overloaded trucks, clear-cutting of timber, and coal-waste disposal but legacy problems such as acid mine drainage, chemical pollution, and land subsidence in areas underlain by mines. In western Pennsylvania, particularly, subsidence remains an issue as it has been for decades, causing unpredictable damage to roads, streams, water supplies, and buildings when the ground's subsurface collapses into mines.

Such disputes are often joined and litigated by government regulators or environmental activists, but in notable confrontations entire communities may become involved. In February 2001, more than three-fourths of Sylvester, West Virginia's two hundred residents sued Elk Run Coal Company over the spread of coal dust by a nearby preparation plant. A jury subsequently ordered Elk Run, a subsidiary of Massey Energy Company, to pay residents $473,000 in damages. The plant was also required to construct a system to prevent dust from spreading across the community. In Pike County, Kentucky, the tiny community of Lick Creek, with about fifty homes, fought a two-year battle against a proposed coal mine in its midst. Residents finally prevailed in October 2002, when the Kentucky Environmental and Public Protection Cabinet ruled that the land where Clintwood Elkhorn Mining Company proposed to operate was unsuitable for mining. In Berea and Richmond, Kentucky, implacable community opposition throughout the 1990s caused the U.S. Army to abandon plans to incinerate stockpiles of nerve gas stored in bunkers at nearby Bluegrass Arsenal. Protests against incineration of similar stocks near Anniston, Alabama, brought additional safety precautions, though the incineration of the material went ahead.

More often, communities find themselves unified only in the wake of catastrophic events, such as the Buffalo Creek disaster, which claimed 125 lives and destroyed four thousand homes, and the Martin County Coal Company waste spill, which polluted streams and spread toxic sludge for miles. During the 1980s, Triana, Alabama, a predominantly African American community near Redstone Arsenal, became a case study in the environmental justice movement when its residents sued the Olin Corporation for pollution from DDT. For twenty-two years, the company had manufactured the pesticide at an army facility at the arsenal and as much as four thousand tons of it had escaped into a stream flowing through Triana. In 1983, four years after discovery of the contamination, the company reached a $24-million out-of-court settlement with residents. Federally mandated cleanup efforts continued into the mid-1990s.

As in the case of Buffalo Creek, Martin County, and Triana, water is often involved in the major issues between communities and industrial operations, particularly in the flood-prone hollows below the steep slopes of central Appalachia. Blasting associated with surface mining often destroys private wells, and acid from long-abandoned mines renders streams lifeless, but flooding that regularly follows torrential rain has come to be viewed as something more than natural disaster. With the use of modern mining equipment in gigantic mountaintop-removal operations, residents of coal-mining areas of central Appalachia have increasingly blamed surface mining and timbering for devastating floods. After floods in southern West Virginia in May and July 2001 destroyed thousands of homes and wiped out businesses across eight counties, a Flood Analysis Technical Team established by the governor concluded that surface mining and timbering had in fact increased surface-water runoff during the deluge, which saw more than five inches of rain in some places. The following year, floods struck southern West Virginia and eastern Kentucky again, taking several lives, destroying hundreds of more homes, and inflicting new damage on communities such as Keystone and Welch, West Virginia, which had been heavily damaged the previous year. In communities near coal slurry impoundments, the floods renewed public concern over the safety of dams. As with the Buffalo Creek disaster and the Martin County impoundment rupture, flooding from the torrential rains led to massive litigation. More than two thousand property owners and residents in southern West Virginia filed suit against some 175 coal, timber, and railroad companies after the July 2001 floods, claiming environmental damage by company operations had been responsible for the damage.

In times past, communities most affected by mines, mills, and timbering operations across Appalachia were company owned and maintained. When mines closed and timber operations ceased, such towns often ceased to exist. In the modern economy, communities of privately owned property and public institutions introduced new complexities for nearby industrial activities. In a few cases, corporate management has adopted a strategy of eliminating communities where serious tensions persisted. Best known is Blair, West Virginia, a historic community at the foot of a ridge where Arch Coal and its predecessor, Ashland Coal Company, operated a huge mountaintop-removal project in the 1990s. As mining operations proceeded twenty-four hours a day, the community was rocked by blasts that damaged houses, ruined wells, and coated buildings with dust drifting down from the Dal-Tex mine. Planning to operate in the immediate area for years to come, the company bought out businesses and residents one by one, requiring sellers to pledge that they would not buy property within a twenty-five-square-mile area around the mining complex. Between 1993 and 1998, Arch and its local subsidiary, Hobet Mining Company, bought out about two hundred residents. In October 1997, *U.S. News and World Report* reported that many of the houses promptly burned after they were vacated. By the turn of the century, only a fraction of Blair's former residents and none of its businesses remained.

See also: BUFFALO CREEK FLOOD (ENVIRONMENT); COAL SLURRY IMPOUNDMENTS (ENVIRONMENT); ENVIRONMENTAL JUSTICE (ENVIRONMENT).

—Rudy Abramson, *Reston, Virginia*, and Adam Sanders, *East Tennessee State University*

Frank Ahrens, "Thunder in the Valley: A Flood's Grim Wake," *Washington Post* (July 13, 2001); Roger Alford, "Town Wins Fight to Keep Out Coal Mine," *Lexington Herald-Leader* (October 29, 2002); Chad Montrie, *To Save the Land and People: A History of Opposition to Surface Coal Mining in Appalachia* (2003); Ken Ward Jr., "Buying Blair," *Charleston Gazette-Mail* (November 22, 1998).

Community Action Groups

Unlike large grassroots movements and activist organizations with shared beliefs and similar mission statements, Appalachia's community-based action groups generally pursue specific and sharply limited objectives, frequently collaborating through loose, informal affiliations. Such groups affect communities in two fundamental ways: they adopt goals shared by a broader community, and they foster social consciousness, which often leads to broader civic activism and reform efforts. In many cases, such local groups have empowered communities and joined large alliances that address broad political, social, and economic issues.

Modern community activism occupies an important niche in regional history, rising to prominence during coal strikes in the 1920s and 1930s, reemerging with growing environmental concerns in the 1960s, and continuing into the twenty-first century as issues have grown in both number and complexity. Groups making important marks on local and regional life have ranged from short-lived single-issue organizations such as the Appalachian Group to Save the Land and the People, which fought against strip mining in Knott County in the 1960s, to the Highlander Research and Education Center, which began as Highlander Folk School in 1932 and continues to serve as an incubator of community action initiatives. Among major achievements claimed by community-based groups in the late twentieth century were tighter restrictions on strip mining, the exposé of mountaintop removal as a major environmental issue, strengthened protection of natural resources, restrictions on U.S. Army plans for the destruction of chemical weapons, measures to improve trucking safety in coal-mining areas, and a rising awareness of environmental justice.

Constrained by limited funds, community action groups have nevertheless become increasingly inclined to join coalitions, expand their agendas, and to take their battles into court—often with the help of pro bono environmental lawyers and organizations such as the Kentucky Resources Council; the Lewisburg, West Virginia–based Appalachian Center for the Economy and the Environment; and the national firm Trial Lawyers for Public Justice. On occasions, local activism in the region has attracted national attention, as it did during conflicts over strip mining, beginning in the 1960s, and mountaintop removal, beginning in the 1990s. While the roles of small community-based organizations and local workers are often obscured by coalitions, their work underpins civic activism. In 2003, for example, Julia Bonds, leader of the tiny Coal River Mountain Watch in Whitesville, West Virginia, was awarded the $125,000 Goldman Environmental Prize, sometimes referred to as the Nobel Prize of environmentalism, for her crusading against mountaintop removal, overweight trucks, coal dust, and potentially dangerous waste impoundments in the Coal River Valley. Like many leaders of community-based action groups, Bonds, who is descended from generations of coal miners, has spent her entire life in the area where she pursues her agenda.

Although modern community activism is seen most conspicuously in organizations dedicated to environmental causes, community groups in varying degrees dedicate themselves to causes across the spectrum of civic life, especially in vital areas such as health and education. Reform-minded leaders of such organizations in many instances have received inspiration and training from the Highlander Center, which, beginning in the 1960s, focused its efforts upon community empowerment, working with groups such as the Appalachian Economic and Political Action Conference, the Federation of Communities in Service, the Marrowbone Folk School, and the Congress for Appalachian Development, among many others.

Appalachia's most successful community action groups have histories as varied as their objectives. Some originated with single-issue protests, others with broader agendas that spawned proliferating initiatives, making them established institutions. Notable among the former has been Berea, Kentucky–based Common Ground, which led, and prevailed in, a prolonged battle to prevent incineration of aging chemical weapons stockpiled at the nearby Bluegrass Arsenal. Collaborating with Concerned Citizens of Madison County, the leaders of Common Ground spearheaded a national Chemical Weapons Working Group, formed in the 1990s to challenge the U.S. Army's plans to incinerate such weapons at a number of storage sites across the country. While incineration went ahead at other sites, including one at Anniston, Alabama, the army abandoned the plan in Kentucky, and announced in November 2002 that it would use a chemical neutralization process to destroy the nerve and mustard gas munitions at the Kentucky arsenal.

Like the defunct Appalachian Group to Save the Land and the People, Save Our Cumberland Mountains began as a local protest against strip mining in Tennessee. From a door-to-door organizing campaign in 1972, it has expanded to address issues such as toxic and hazardous wastes, clear-cutting of forests, and environmental justice, developing a reputation extending beyond Appalachia. Over the years, its accomplishments included a prominent role in passage of several pieces of mining legislation, including a coal severance tax in Tennessee, and leadership of a successful campaign to secure federal protection for a sixty-one-thousand-acre watershed around Fall Creek Falls State Park. By contrast, Kentuckians for the Commonwealth, founded in 1981, was created with the idea of addressing multiple coalfield issues. As its agenda and membership expanded, the organization established a powerful reputation by leading the adoption of a 1988 constitutional amendment banning the broad form deed in Kentucky. Having grown to a membership of more than two thousand across the entire state, it has become Kentucky's foremost environmental advocate.

Other organizations, including the Ohio Valley Environmental Coalition, the Citizens Coal Council, the Appalachian Alliance, the Tri-State Citizens Mining Network, and the Pennsylvania Environmental Network, emerged as umbrella groups for scores of community-based groups, from Appalachian Voices in North Carolina to the Slippery Rock Stream Keepers in Pennsylvania. Stressing education as the foundation of environmental protection, Huntington, West Virginia–based Ohio Valley Environmental Coalition became one of the region's most visible activist organizations, staging street demonstrations at corporate board meetings, protesting mountaintop-removal projects, and challenging plans for expanded coal-waste impoundments.

See also: CHEMICAL WEAPONS DISPOSAL (ENVIRONMENT); ENVIRONMENTAL JUSTICE (ENVIRONMENT); GRASSROOTS ENVIRONMENTAL ACTION (ENVIRONMENT).

—Adam Sanders, *East Tennessee State University*

Bruce Ergood and Bruce E. Kuhre, eds., *Appalachia: Social Context Past and Present* (3rd edition, 1991); Stephen L. Fisher, ed., *Fighting Back in Appalachia: Traditions of Resistance and Change* (1993); Chad Montrie, *To Save the Land and People: A History of Opposition to Surface Coal Mining in Appalachia* (2003).

Community Centers and Settlement Houses

Neighborhood and community centers generally are educational, recreational, social service, and/or social action establishments operating out of buildings strategically located in urban neighborhoods or rural communities. The term *community center* is a generic one and may refer to a settlement house, religious mission, youth or senior activity center, multiservice center or clinic, or other similar facility. While the term may refer to a building, an entire neighborhood (as with the phrase *central business district*), or the middle of the community, a large body of scholarship places emphasis on centers as focal points, gathering places, points of interest, or embarkation points for community action.

Many intentional communities in Appalachia, from Arthurdale, West Virginia (founded 1933–34), and Rugby, Tennessee (1880), to contemporary middle-class housing subdivisions, feature buildings called community centers. However, community centers were originally outside imports into an Appalachian culture that generally placed greater emphasis on individuality and family than upon community. The community-center model has been repeatedly introduced by successive generations of "do-gooders" coming to Appalachia. In at least one major case, however, Appalachian thought and practice in this area led the entire world in new directions. Public policy analyst Robert Putnam credits L. J. Hanifan, superintendent of rural instruction in West Virginia, with the first use of the term *social capital* in a 1916 publication—seven decades before that concept became more widely known. Social capital generally refers to the potential for creating economic value embedded in social relationships such as trust. In a subsequent book, Hanifan developed the concept in a chapter on social capital in support of his argument for schools as the community centers of rural communities. His book was distributed to educators nationally and had a significant impact on pre–Great Depression thinking about the place of rural schools in their communities.

There is also a direct link between Appalachia and the international settlement-house movement in the person of Myles Horton and the Highlander Research and Education Center. The settlement-house movement began in London, England, in the late nineteenth century when a group of Oxford students under the influence of Canon Barnett moved to the East End to a residence they named Toynbee House in memory of one of their number. As a young woman, Jane Addams visited Toynbee House and applied its philosophy in the Halsted Street neighborhood of Chicago ("back of the yards") in 1895. Addams eventually became the leader of a national movement. Larger cities in or near the Appalachian region, including Atlanta, Pittsburgh, and Knoxville, Tennessee, were all active in the settlement-house movement, which at one time included more than six hundred settlements in the U.S. in smaller cities, including Charleston, Clarksburg, and Fairmont, West Virginia. Morgantown, West Virginia, also established community centers called settlement houses, but usually without the resident reformer population. Thus, most of these are more accurately termed neighborhood and community centers or missions.

In his autobiography, *The Long Haul* (1990), Horton recounts how he visited Addams in Chicago and came away determined to create a rural social settlement in Tennessee. Horton achieved regional notoriety in the 1950s when Highlander became the first white institution in segregated Tennessee to open its doors and racially integrate its staff and participants, a move entirely consistent with settlement-house principles.

In general, settlement houses were characterized predominantly by their pattern of being founded and staffed by educated and idealistic young, upper-middle-class men and women who came to live among the poor for a time as neighbors. Religious missions are characterized both by their denominational affiliations and their evangelical outlook. Following World War II, settlement houses in this original sense largely died out. Most settlement houses abandoned their residential programs and became neighborhood or community centers, whether or not they continued to be called settlement houses.

Beginning in the late 1960s, many communities in the Appalachian region created senior citizens' clubs, and public funds available through the Older Americans Act were used to initiate Senior Citizens Centers. Following passage of the Older Americans Act in 1965 and several crucial amendments in the early 1970s, these centers began to spring up in all of the larger and many of the smaller communities in Appalachia. In fact, the senior center may be the single most pervasive type of community center in Appalachia and the United States today.

One of the long-standing ideals of various community-center movements has been concentration of a broad array of coordinated services operating out of a single location. Such multiservice centers have been created in Appalachia in conjunction with religious missions, senior centers, family resource networks, and a number of other auspices.

See also: HIGHLANDER RESEARCH AND EDUCATION CENTER (EDUCATION); INTENTIONAL COMMUNITIES; SETTLEMENT, MISSION, AND SPONSORED SCHOOLS (EDUCATION).

—Roger A. Lohmann, *West Virginia University*

L. J. Hanifan, *The Community Center* (1920); Myles Horton, with Judith and Herbert Kohl, *The Long Haul: An Autobiography* (1990); Robert D. Putnam, *Bowling Alone: The Collapse and Revival of American Community* (2000).

Community Gatherings

Communities in Appalachia, large and small, gather both informally and in structured events for communal work and play. At various recognized community gathering sites, local folk may make music, dance, play games, eat, visit, or engage in a host of other community activities. The talk at such gatherings ranges from small talk and gossip to jokes and longer stories of personal and family experiences that give a sense of shared community and culture. As Patricia D. Beaver of Appalachian State University documented in *Rural Community in the Appalachian South*, community interactions take place "in daily visiting at the local store, in the daily telephone conversations of older women to each other, in the Saturday afternoon trading of gossip in someone's garage over an engine needing repair, or in the Sunday morning discussions in Sunday school and after services on the front yard of the church."

Many of the gathering places in contemporary Appalachia are much the same as those in the rest of the country. Retirees congregate at shopping malls, groups meet over coffee at fast-food restaurants, and people convene at community centers, churches, volunteer firehouses, and local performance venues.

In much of Appalachia, however, there remain more traditional gathering spots such as the country store, with traditional pot-bellied stoves inside and "liars' benches" outside on the porch for telling good stories. The popular image of local folks gathered around a stove or on the porch at a rural store remains a reality in numerous small, rural Appalachian communities. Some of them, such as Weaver's Self-Service Store in Stoney Creek, Tennessee, are known only in their local area. Others, such as the Original Mast Store in Valle Crucis, North Carolina, have become regional and national icons for community life in Appalachia. The Mast Store, established in 1883, provided all the items needed by its mountain neighbors, from "cradles to caskets," which led customers to say, "If you can't find it here, you don't need it." The Mast Store at one time housed a local doctor, the post office, and offered wildcrafters a place to bring roots and herbs for store credit. Most important, the store was the community gathering place for visiting with neighbors and playing a friendly game of checkers. Listed on the National Register of Historic Places as an excellent example of an old country store, the Mast Store remains in operation, bringing hundreds of tourists to its mountain valley location. It has also expanded to open locations in Waynesville, Hendersonville, Boone, and Asheville, North Carolina, and Greenville, South Carolina. The urge for a general store in which to gather has even led to more recent incarnations of the tradition, including Fred's General Mercantile on the top of Beech Mountain, North Carolina, the hub of activity and a daily gathering place in the ski resort community.

Other stores are known as sites for making mountain music. Cockram's Store in Floyd, Virginia, and the Rheatown Store in Greene County, Tennessee, host weekly music sessions in which tourists mingle with local folks who play music and dance. Similarly, the Star Barber Shop in Bristol, Virginia, is widely known for its Thursday-night gatherings of musicians, bringing together already famous mountain musicians with newcomers to traditional music. Sometimes workers will gather round the loading docks of factories or maintenance areas and "pick a little" together on breaks or after work.

Certain communal gatherings have become symbolic of the Appalachian region. Quiltmaking, for example, while often done as solitary work, has had a more publicly recognized communal form. As quilt scholar Laurel Horton notes, some communities develop quiltmaking traditions that may include finishing quilts for members of a community group, contributing to cooperative economic efforts, or making quilts for charity. She adds, "quilting groups offer opportunities for social interaction and the exchange of news and opinions, and they provide a means by which women can derive satisfaction and self-worth by contributing to a larger purpose."

Some community gatherings reflect less conventional traditions. The womanless wedding, for instance, is a humorous folk drama performed by an all-male cast that parodies the Protestant wedding ceremony; such performances take place throughout Appalachia and elsewhere in the country. According to Beaver's study of this event, "womanless weddings are staged for entertainment and fundraising purposes by community groups, voluntary associations, churches, and volunteer fire departments. The humor is derived from the appearance of men who are familiar to the audience in exaggerated roles and costumes." Describing the event as a ritual of inversion, Beaver notes that they "reveal, mock, and relieve social tensions concerning rural stereotypes, romantic love, idealized marriage, sexuality and premarital sex, male dominance and male authority, family relations, and class relations."

Community gatherings in Appalachia serve both social and economic functions. They help maintain bonds among community members, perpetuate community cultural traditions, and often provide a mechanism for incorporating newcomers into the community. At the same time, community gatherings are often fundraisers within the community for pressing needs such as school supplies, fire trucks, and ambulances. Because such gatherings frequently offer local traditions in music, dance, food, craft, and custom, they have become important attractions for tourists throughout Appalachia, adding tourist dollars to the local economy and increasing appreciation for local culture.

See also: COMMUNITY ACTION GROUPS; COMMUNITY CENTERS AND SETTLEMENT HOUSES.

—Jean Haskell, *East Tennessee State University*

Patricia D. Beaver, *Rural Community in the Appalachian South* (1986); Laurel Horton, "In Search of the Appalachian Quilt," *Now and Then* (Fall 1989); Jane Woodside, "The Womanless Wedding: An American Folk Drama," M.A. thesis, University of North Carolina (1987).

Company Stores

See Labor and the New Deal (Labor); Scrip (Labor)

Council of the Southern Mountains

See Christian Service Groups

Cumberland Homesteads

See Cumberland Homesteads (Architecture); New Deal Communities

Domestic Violence

Studies conducted over more than a decade address questions relating to family violence in Appalachia and whether or not Appalachian families are more violent than families in other American locations. Collectively, statistics parallel those on crime rates: family violence in Appalachia occurs at rates that do not significantly vary from national rates. In any given year, approximately 28 to 29 percent of married couples engage in violent behavior, and 80 to 85 percent of parents behave violently towards their children. These percentages reflect all behavior intended to hurt someone but may not be considered serious, as with slapping or pushing. Behavior that causes injury or is likely to cause injury is considered abuse and includes kicking, punching, choking, or use of a weapon. It is in this latter category where the regional samples differ from national data. Nationally, physically abusive behavior occurs in about 3 to 4 percent of married couples. In the regional samples, physically abusive behavior is reported in 12 to 13 percent of couples, or about three times as often. Similarly, 6 to 7 percent of children are subjected to abusive behavior by parents nationally, while the regional rates are about 20 percent.

Why partner violence occurs with some couples yet not with others is not entirely clear, although family violence researchers have identified risk factors inherent to couples or their environments that increase the probability of partner violence. Three risk factors especially common to Appalachia are lower economic and educational attainment, geographic isolation, and cultural values and practices. These risk factors vary through time and may not be present in all Appalachian communities.

Despite significant gains in recent decades, average employment opportunities, wage earnings, and educational attainment within Appalachia remain below rates for the United States as a whole. Since lower income and educational attainment represent risk factors for partner violence, it is possible that areas of Appalachia with high poverty rates and low educational attainment may experience higher rates of partner violence than more prosperous parts of the region and nation. This connection between lower socioeconomic status and partner violence is related to fewer resources for coping with family stressors, males' frustrations in trying to fulfill the role of provider, and females' economic dependency as a barrier to leaving abusive relationships. Also, in economically depressed regions lower levels of public funding are used for social services such as domestic violence shelters, family counseling programs, and drug and alcohol treatment centers.

Geographic isolation characterizes many areas of Appalachia, particularly in central Appalachia. Remote areas tend to have higher rates of poverty, lower rates of educational attainment, and fewer social services. Social services that do extend into rural Appalachia are usually more difficult to access. Victims and batterers alike may have more difficulty getting to social services or relatives who could otherwise serve as buffers between the feuding partners. This may be especially true for victims whose batterers or economic constraints limit transportation resources. Remote geography may also impede the timely delivery of protective services by law enforcement and social service agencies. For example, police responses to domestic violence calls may take more than an hour of travel time. In some cases, batterers may use geographical isolation as one means to control victims further or to hide the abuse from the surrounding community.

Family and community values can also foster a wider social acceptance of and consequently greater risk for partner violence. For example, the cultural practice of patriarchy, or male dominance, has been associated with partner violence. Researchers generally find cultures that have more egalitarian male-female relationships to have less severe or less frequent partner violence. Patriarchal values and practices can include: family and community pressures on women to give up employment careers for family responsibilities; beliefs that men should head families, churches, businesses, and political organizations; differential treatment of male and female employees with regard to pay or family leave policies; and differential treatment of women and men with regard to the structure and enforcement of governmental policies and laws. In Appalachian culture, patriarchal values may further be seen through social norms promoting women's deference to men, and through humor or music that portrays women as "property"—for example, jokes or musical ballads that suggest men value their hunting dogs more than their wives. The consequences of patriarchal practices often leave women with fewer social, economic, and political resources to extricate themselves from abusive relationships. Further, the steering of women from positions of economic and political power serves to minimize women's needs and complaints.

Another characteristic of Appalachian culture that appears to be relevant to partner violence is familialism, or loyalty to one's family. This cultural value may pose risks for partner violence when victims stay in abusive relationships due to strong social pressures to remain with one's family. In essence, it may be taboo to leave a family relationship, especially for women, regardless of the reasons. Another effect of familialism may arise when norms of family loyalty and privacy are so strong that they prevent victims or other family members from seeking help or, conversely, deter other kin or neighbors from aiding victims for fear of prying. Family tolerance of partner violence may be further reinforced by a normative distrust towards outsiders, especially representatives of governmental or social service agencies.

Finally, researchers have found some evidence that abused children tend to perpetuate partner (or child) abuse as adults. Consequently, families, churches, and communities that affirm corporal punishment may inadvertently be fostering family violence.

See also: FAMILY RELATIONSHIPS AND GENDER ROLES; VIOLENCE AND VENGEANCE (IMAGES AND ICONS); WELFARE AND POVERTY (IMAGES AND ICONS).

—Peggy Cantrell, *East Tennessee State University*, and Roy Fish, *Ohio State University*

Pat Arnow and Norma Myers, "Crime in Appalachia: The Search for Evidence," *Now and Then* (Summer 1991); Peggy J. Cantrell, "Rates of Family Violence and Incest in Southern Appalachia," in *Appalachia Inside Out, Vol. 1: Conflict and Change*, ed. Robert J. Higgs, Ambrose N. Manning, and Jim Wayne Miller (1995); Murray A. Straus and Richard J. Gelles, *Physical Violence in American Families* (1990).

Elder Care

As with the nation overall, the proportion of older adults in Appalachia is expected to accelerate dramatically over the next twenty years. For example, in 1995 adults over age sixty-five constituted 15.3 percent of the total population in West Virginia. According to the U.S. Census Bureau, by 2025 this number is expected to grow to 24.9 percent. In North Carolina, the percentage of adults over age sixty-five, at 12.5 percent in 1995, is expected to increase to 21.4 percent by 2025. Across Appalachia, the need for elder care will place increasing burdens on local resources as communities encounter these demographic changes. Elder care includes formal and informal care and services. Informal care comprises assistance and social support from members of the elder's social network. Formal care and services include home and community-based services such as senior centers, nutrition services, in-home and personal care, rural hospitals, physician services, and longterm care.

In keeping with an overall ethic of self-reliance and family loyalty, caregiving within Appalachian culture has historically been a family affair. Elders receive care from family members if possible, reflecting both the culture of care and the dearth of services provided to families. During recent decades, out-migration from certain areas has left many elders without sufficient informal support resources. Poverty, disabling chronic health conditions, and often the added burdens of isolation and lack of mobility have exacerbated the situation for some elders in Appalachia. In these cases, formal services would ideally fill the gap. However, a variety of barriers still impede service delivery in Appalachia. Challenges include limited services, inadequate transportation, distance from residences to county growth centers, and lack of comprehensive health and social programs.

Wide differences in the array of formal services, means of delivery, and ways citizens are informed of services exist among states, subregions, and counties. Some Area Agencies on Aging serving Appalachian counties maintain Web sites informing elders of services, but the degree to which elders have access to computers and the Internet varies. Some communities still rely on word of mouth and local resources such as churches to inform potential clients.

While out-migration can negatively affect elder care in rural communities, in-migration can positively affect the spectrum of services available. Communities that are favored destinations for retirement migration, such as Henderson County, North Carolina, and Washington County, Maryland, typically offer a more complete selection of formal care. As their numbers increase, elders who migrate to such communities make up a politically influential group of local constituents. They are often economically more affluent than existing resident groups and through lobbying and voting have power to affect local policy on allocation of funds and development of services in the area. Despite additional formal services provided, some elders must relocate to be near their families as they gradually require more support.

Although elder care needs in Appalachia will become more challenging as the elderly population grows, new technology and program developments may ease difficulty of service delivery and provide more complete care. For example, telemedicine may bring the expertise of physicians and specialists to remote communities and ease the problem of physician retention in rural areas. Establishment of rural health-care consortia such as Appalachian Regional Healthcare in central Appalachia has enabled resource sharing and improved management of rural hospitals, clinics, and longterm-care facilities. The development of caregiver support systems and training must tap into indigenous resources associated with family strength and tradition that will enable elders to remain in their homes as long as possible.

See also: AGING; COMMUNITY-INITIATED HEALTH EFFORTS (HEALTH); FAMILIES AND HEALTH (HEALTH).

—Debra J. Kleesattel and Hege Ravdal, *University of Kentucky*

Raymond T. Coward and John A. Krout, eds., *Aging in Rural Settings: Life Circumstances and Distinctive Features* (1998); Susan Garrett, *Miles to Go: Aging in Rural Virginia* (1998); B. Jan McCulloch, "Aging and Kinship in Rural Context," in *Handbook of Aging and the Family*, ed. Rosemary Blieszner and Victoria Hikevitch Bedford (1995).

Eugenics Programs

Although eugenics (from the Greek, meaning "well born"), a controversial movement broadly supported throughout the Unites States from the 1880s to the 1940s, did not occur to a great extent in Appalachia, eugenicist discourse of that day was replete with references to and studies of poor white mountain folk. Noted criminologist Nicole Hahn Rafter has since argued that the central image of the eugenics movement was "that of the degenerate hillbilly family, dwelling in filthy shacks, and spawning endless generations of paupers, criminals, and imbeciles." The portrayal simultaneously drew upon, reconfirmed, and expanded preexisting stereotypes of Appalachians and poor rural whites in general.

Most often associated with the racism and Nazi medicine of the 1930s and 1940s, eugenics programs focused on the belief that through "selective breeding" practices whites could ensure the mental, physical, and moral health and fitness of their children and future generations. In practice, eugenics offered two strategies for improving the hereditary characteristics of the race. "Positive" eugenics emphasized correct moral living, great care in the choosing of one's mate, and strict adherence to regimens of sanitation and hygiene. "Negative" strategies included institutionalization of individuals diagnosed as "feebleminded" and sterilization of both men and women to ensure that cacogenic ("bad seed") influences such as laziness, alcoholism, sexual degeneracy, and "hereditary pauperism" would not be passed on.

One of the more influential sociological studies conducted in the Appalachian Region was Mandel Sherman and Thomas R. Henry's *Hollow Folk*, published in 1933. A comparative ethnographic study of five Blue Ridge communities, *Hollow Folk* supported and popularized the eugenicist notion that cultural and social isolation result in racial degradation and decay. The inhabitants of one of these settlements, Colvin Hollow, were characterized by the authors as lazy, illiterate, dirty, incestuous, feebleminded, and immoral. Unlike more strictly hereditarian eugenicists, Sherman and Henry concluded that environment was an important factor in the "backwardness" they observed. Yet their study, couched in the language of scientific objectivity and truth, gave new power and authority to the idea that poor mountain whites were genetically inferior.

Influential polemicist Harry Caudill articulated eugenicist views as late as the 1960s in his numerous books, including *Night Comes to the Cumberlands*. Though largely responsible for the "internal-colony" theory to describe the exploitation of the region, Caudill blamed Appalachians for some of their lack of education and for stubbornness in the face of economic change, which resulted partially from poor genes. The isolation of the hollows and the close proximity of numerous family relations narrowed the gene pool, creating degeneration among residents. Caudill sometimes suggested that the government establish a military base in eastern Kentucky to introduce new genes into the population.

As a discourse about racial purity and racial hierarchy, eugenics especially focused on interracial marriage as a potential threat to white, Anglo-Saxon supremacy. Leaders of the eugenics movement lobbied for the passage and strengthening of antimiscegenation laws. One such law, the Virginia Racial Integrity Act of 1924, was passed in order to prevent the sort of interracial unions described in another (now notorious) eugenics study entitled *Mongrel Virginians: The WIN Tribe*. This purportedly objective study described a small group of "mixed bloods" descended from white, Indian, and Negro (thus *WIN*) ancestry found in the Appalachian counties of Virginia. Despite their scientific objectives, the authors barely concealed their ideological agenda, which was to demonstrate that mixing of the races results in lowered intellectual, social, and physical abilities for the offspring. While the scientific study of eugenics in the early twentieth century have been widely discredited, the stereotypes they perpetuated still linger.

See also: CAUDILL, HARRY (HUMOR); MOUNTAIN WHITES (IMAGES AND ICONS); WELFARE AND POVERTY (IMAGES AND ICONS).

—Matt Wray, *Smithsonian Institution*

Stephen Jay Gould, *The Mismeasure of Man* (1981); Edward J. Larson, *Sex, Race, and Science: Eugenics in the Deep South* (1995); Richard B. Sherman, "'The Last Stand': The Fight for Racial Integrity in Virginia in the 1920s," *Journal of Southern History* (February 1988).

Family Relationships and Gender Roles

The nuclear family is the fundamental unit of social organization in Appalachia, but rather than being independent, as is the norm for nuclear families in the larger U.S. culture, nuclear families in Appalachia frequently are connected to a larger social organization that includes the parents and siblings of the nuclear family's parents. These family-group households tend to reside geographically close to one another. Even if Appalachians migrate to urban areas, new arrivals typically choose places where kin have already located. In both rural and urban settings the larger group exerts significant influence on the nuclear family, particularly in regard to parenting and socialization.

Appalachian families generally follow traditional gender roles. Typically they consist of a provider father, a caregiving mother, and the couple's dependent children. Following this model, Appalachian households have been historically patriarchal with men serving as heads of households—owning land, directing production, controlling income use, and making decisions—while women act as loving nurturers to their husbands and children. In regard to paid and unpaid work, however, the roles of men and women have not always followed this traditional pattern.

Many areas of Appalachia were historically engaged in farming until the late nineteenth and early twentieth centuries, although most parts of the region had been industrialized. On the farm, the husband and wife worked as a team because the labor of both was needed to support the family. The day-to-day work was divided spatially. Mothers and daughters were primarily responsible for work done in the house and yard area; fathers and sons were responsible for crops and other chores beyond the house. As children shared in the work of the family, they learned culturally appropriate gender behavior from parental modeling. Thus, somewhat traditional expectations with regard to gender roles were incorporated into the child's sense of identity.

The division of labor began to shift as subsistence agriculture gave way to coal mining, logging, textiles, and other industries that came to parts of Appalachia from 1880 to 1920. Fathers and sons began to work for wages, and mothers and daughters managed the farm while continuing to work within the family and, at times, also provided home-based services such as keeping boarders who had migrated into the region to meet growing labor demands. The work of both men and women was usually necessary to ensure economic survival of the family. However, Appalachian women who worked in either provider or coprovider roles have been generally overlooked by larger society, which tends to maintain more traditional views related to gender roles in the region.

Of necessity, gender roles within Appalachian families began departing somewhat from traditional patterns in the first half of the twentieth century. Appalachian women became increasingly engaged in wage-earning work away from the family home, notably during World War II and during the 1970s and 1980s, when global economic restructuring produced declining employment in male-dominated manufacturing enterprises and an increase in female-dominated service and retail jobs. Many more mothers, regardless of marital status, began to work outside the home while retaining primary responsibility for child rearing and household management. As men and women began to incorporate less traditional gender roles into their families, extended family networks often stepped in to provide support. For example, while parents worked, extended family members of both genders often helped with child care and the supervision of older children.

In the final years of the twentieth century, many Appalachian women were providing nontraditional gender models for their daughters. The strength of this modeling may be partially responsible for the broader aspirations among Appalachian girls, who increasingly prefer nontraditional roles.

The expectations, attitudes, and behaviors associated with gender roles in Appalachian families have been influenced by views of gender in the broader community and in its economic system. For example, gender segregation in the workplace has traditionally provided higher-paying jobs for men and few opportunities for women beyond jobs in the service sector. Yet generations of Appalachian families have marshaled flexibility and perseverance, moving beyond traditional gender roles to meet changing demands and to ensure the family's survival.

See also: COAL TOWNS; FARM FAMILIES; WOMEN'S ROLES.

—Kevin Ray Bush and Sheryl Beaty Lash, *University of Georgia*

Susan Abbott, "Gender, Status, and Values among Kikuyu and Appalachian Adolescents," in *African Families and the Crisis of Social Change*, ed. Thomas S. Weisner, Candice Bradley, and Philip L. Kilbride (1997); Shaunna L. Scott, "Drudges, Helpers and Team Players: Oral Historical Accounts of Farm Work in Appalachian Kentucky," *Rural Sociology* (Summer 1996).

Farm Families

Throughout the nineteenth century, when the family farm was the backbone of the rural Appalachian economy, farm families constituted the majority of the region's population, but since then the number of such families has declined rapidly. In West Virginia, for instance, 90 percent of the employed population worked on farms around the time of the Civil War, but only 50 percent of the population was similarly employed in 1920. By the early twenty-first century, less than 2 percent of that state's employed population worked in agriculture. Across the entire region, the majority of farm families had become dependent upon nonfarm employment for income.

Although the farming practices of northern Appalachia have received less attention, a rich and consistent picture of farm families in central and southern Appalachia is contained in the numerous social histories, oral histories, ethnographies, and autobiographies of those sections of the region. Among them, James S. Brown's studies, made in the 1940s of a farming community in Appalachian Kentucky that he called "Beech Creek," offer one of the most comprehensive views. Beech Creek families practiced subsistence-first agriculture, in which family members grew food and livestock primarily to feed themselves, selling or bartering whatever remained after their household needs were met. Their farms were small, and most farm products were consumed at home. Farm families spent little money on consumer goods, and their incomes were low. Such practices were common throughout much of rural Appalachia in that era, especially on the Allegheny and Cumberland Plateaus. The 1930 federal census showed that the Cumberland Plateau contained the highest proportions of self-sufficient and low-income farms in the United States at that time. Another study found that subsistence practices still dominated throughout the entire region of central and southern Appalachia in the 1950s, when three-fourths of the region's farms reported gross sales below the federal government's criterion for commercial agriculture.

Appalachian farm families were constructed upon patriarchal social relations. As was common throughout rural America, male farmers attempted to exercise control over the labor and products of wives, children, and other household members (including other kinship relations and tenants) but frequently encountered resistance from the latter.

For the most part, though, women (except for widows) were effectively excluded from independent labor in agriculture, while sons' places in the economy were dictated largely by the life span and inheritance decisions of their fathers. Wider circles of kin, rather than impersonal markets, provided additional sources of labor. In zones of commercial agriculture, farm families typically limited fertility out of fear of failing to provide subsistence, land, and capital for offspring. But subsistence agriculture in central and southern Appalachia encouraged large families because it positioned fathers to use and benefit from the labor of all family members. Family size declined throughout the early twentieth century as the region moved from a predominately agrarian society and family-planning resources became more readily available. However, the level of fertility in central and southern Appalachia remained high in comparison with other rural American regions.

Ethnographies show that decision making in farm families was the result of patriarchal family strategies rather than individual choice alone. Control of land was generally reserved for males, but divorce records and court actions granting women independent rights to hold property suggest that patriarchal authority was not absolute. Male control over property transfer and cooperative labor among adult males also shaped economic decisions. Sons were more likely to remain on family land than daughters. Networks of farm families played important roles in economic exchange and in the redistribution of food and resources among households, especially in times of crisis. These family relationships also provided crucial resources when some family members migrated from Appalachia to find work outside the region.

Study of the Beech Creek farming community suggests that subsistence farms in central Appalachia were capable of providing an abundant living during the antebellum period. However, the combination of population increase, family farm subdivision, cultivation of increasingly marginal steep land, and alternative uses of land such as coal mining and timber harvesting resulted in economic decline in the late nineteenth century. The social composition of farming households changed as a consequence. The proportion of nuclear households declined rapidly with the onset of economic crisis, while the number of extended and multiple households expanded. Only with the out-migration in the twentieth century did the nuclear family form of household organization again predominate. Before that, landownership enabled some families to support dependent kin during times of economic hardship. White households formed around a landowning male were more likely to take in grandparents or grandchildren (extended family), brothers or cousins and their families (multiple family), or, less commonly, nonkin than were tenant-farming households. Because many of their families were headed by landless farm laborers or tenants, African American families were less able than whites to expand or contract during periods of crisis, and proportionately more African Americans were forced to live in non-kin households as domestic and agricultural laborers than were whites. The ability of farm families to respond to economic crises and opportunities thus varied widely depending on the race, age, gender, and landowning status of household heads.

Oral histories suggest that the patriarchal forms of family farm life captured in the social histories and ethnographies of central and southern Appalachia remain throughout the region and the rest of rural America. One such study in 1996 of farm families in the Kentucky coalfields documents a gendered division of labor allocating house and yard work, cooking, cleaning, sewing, child care, laundry, food preparation, gardening, poultry care, and dairying to women and girls, while males controlled machinery and worked in the fields. Women sometimes performed "male" tasks such as plowing and harvesting, and children of either gender were called upon to help with whatever needed to be done, though adult males rarely helped with domestic work. In describing their lives, men tended to minimize the contributions of women's labor. Women tended to express greater ambivalence about farm life and were more favorable than males to reducing or abandoning farming activities.

See also: AGRICULTURAL FRONTIERS (AGRICULTURE); SUBSISTENCE FARMING (AGRICULTURE).

—Dwight B. Billings, *University of Kentucky*, and Kathleen M. Blee, *University of Pittsburgh*

Dwight B. Billings and Kathleen M. Blee, *The Road to Poverty: The Making of Wealth and Hardship in Appalachia* (2000); James S. Brown, *Beech Creek: A Study of a Kentucky Mountain Neighborhood* (1988); Shaunna L. Scott, "Drudges, Helpers, and Team Players: Oral Historical Accounts of Farm Work in Appalachian Kentucky," *Rural Sociology* (Summer 1996).

Federation of Communities in Service

See Christian Service Groups

Feuds

See Feuds (Government)

Gay and Lesbian Life

Although havens of relative tolerance and even celebration of gay and lesbian life exist in Appalachia, large parts of the region regard homosexuality as criminal or immoral behavior. Research on gay and lesbian life and its complexities in Appalachia is scant.

The U.S. Census does not enumerate people by sexual orientation, making it difficult to estimate the extent of the region's gay and lesbian population, but estimates based upon sampling find that nationally 3 to 10 percent of Americans are exclusively homosexual. Another 30 percent or so report more than incidental bisexual experiences. Statistics on gay and lesbian people are by necessity based upon samples that may not be representative.

One common thread that provides a backdrop against which gay and lesbian lives can be viewed is legal status. As laws regarding homosexuality, specifically same-sex marriage, became nationally controversial, statutes varied considerably within Appalachian states. Five states with Appalachian regions outlaw sexual acts between members of the same sex even when these occur in the privacy of the couple's home. These particular states' laws also prohibit oral and other sexual acts deemed deviant among heterosexuals, but they are rarely enforced against heterosexuals. Such sodomy laws are primarily enforced in cases involving child custody disputes, public sex, or as rationale against extending civil rights.

Most states in the Appalachian region neither criminalize homosexuality nor offer legal protection. Early in the twenty-first century, it remained legal to fire an individual for being gay or lesbian, except in ten municipalities. Maryland, New York, and Pennsylvania had executive orders protecting homosexual state employees from employment discrimination, and New York granted homosexual state workers and their families limited domestic partnership benefits. A number of Appalachian unions, universities, and private employers also had policies outlawing discrimination based on sexual orientation. Only Kentucky had a hate crimes law that specifically covered sexual orientation.

Although a number of Appalachian gays and lesbians stay in the region and are fairly open about their sexual orientation, some Appalachian homosexuals flee to urban areas within and outside the mountains so they can blend into a more organized, visible gay community. This migratory pattern emulates that noted by other social researchers who believe that lesbians' sense of self often involves relocating to a social arena involving other gays and lesbians, that is, a discernible reference group situated outside rural communities.

A groundbreaking study of Appalachian homosexuals by sociologists Kate Black and Marc A. Rhorer found individuals moving to cities and college towns seeking tolerance. Gay Appalachians also are drawn to visible gay and lesbian communities with their social support networks for individuals and couples. Isolation, conservative socio-religious values, and even outright violence are factors behind this rural-to-urban migration within Appalachia and a similar flow of some gay and lesbian individuals out of the region altogether.

The stigma on homosexuality produces an impact early in life of some gay and lesbian persons in Appalachia. Three percent of more than three thousand students in grades six through twelve surveyed in four mountain counties by the 1999 Kentucky Youth Survey reported being teased for being homosexual. The students reported shoving and physical attacks at school as well as their belief that school rules were not equally enforced. *Through Their Eyes: Stories of Gays and Lesbians in the Mountains* (1999), a short film on gay and lesbian teens in Appalachia, also documents family beatings, attacks, forced Christian rituals to "cast out the demon of homosexuality," and death threats.

Well-publicized hate crimes have included attacks on lesbian tourists on the Appalachian Trail and the killings of gay men in western North Carolina. Black and Rhorer's interviewees repeatedly mentioned themes of isolation, fear, violence, and the exodus to safer havens. The two sociologists concluded, however, that homosexuals in Appalachia face the same challenges as gay and lesbian people living anywhere in rural America.

Interviewers have also found Appalachians with positive experiences including supportive families, happy relationships, close friendships, humor, and the empowerment of "coming out." Even in more conservative communities, gay and lesbian members of prominent families are often accepted because their kinship ties outweigh their stigmatized sexuality.

Increased visibility highlights the rapid changes affecting gay and lesbian Appalachians. With the prevalence of conservative Christianity in the region, many areas continue to suppress homosexuality. Fear of violence, ostracism, and discrimination have led gay and lesbian people and supportive heterosexuals to form advocacy organizations such as North Carolina's Southern Appalachian Lesbian and Gay Alliance, the West Virginia Lesbian and Gay Coalition, and the Kentucky Fairness Alliance. Three states with Appalachian counties (Kentucky, Tennessee, and Georgia) have abolished their sodomy laws. Even the isolation felt by many rural gay and lesbian Appalachians has begun to lighten through the safety and connectivity of the Internet.

See also: HIV/AIDS (HEALTH); VERGHESE, ABRAHAM (HEALTH).

—Lonnie R. Helton, *Cleveland State University*, and Jeff A. Jones, *University of Kentucky*

Appalachian Media Institute, *Through Their Eyes: Stories of Gays and Lesbians in the Mountains*, Appalshop videocassette (1999); Kate Black and Marc A. Rhorer, "Out in the Mountains: Exploring Lesbian and Gay Lives," in *Out in the South*, ed. Carlos L. Dews and Carolyn Leste Law (2001).

Hindu Families and Communities

Hindu communities in Appalachia, as throughout North America, are comprised of diaspora Hindus and western followers. The Hindu diaspora is comprised of immigrants and their descendants from India, Nepal, Sri Lanka, and the South Pacific. Western followers, who began to coalesce in the late 1960s, constituted the earliest manifestations of organized Hindu religion in Appalachia. Unlike diaspora Hindus, many Western converts and followers live in monastic communities called ashrams, while others either live in or visit lavish resort communities for a mix of Eastern spirituality and Western luxury.

A continuous Hindu presence has existed in the United States since the 1890s, when Swami Vivekananda, a proponent of Hindu universalism, toured the country as a missionary. Restrictions on immigration from South and Southeast Asian countries kept the number of diaspora Hindus in America small until the late twentieth century. The diaspora community within Appalachia has been based around large population centers that draw immigrants because of employment opportunities and the increasing size and relative stability of the ethnic communities in those centers and in rural retreat centers. While many diaspora Hindus are physicians, engineers, and educators, their ranks also include shopkeepers, restaurateurs, and other small-scale entrepreneurs. Temples and cultural centers serving Appalachian residents exist in Pittsburgh and Zelienople, Pennsylvania; Moundsville and Charleston, West Virginia; Lexington and Louisville, Kentucky; Charlotte, North Carolina; Birmingham, Alabama; Atlanta; and other population centers within or near the Appalachians. Although temples often serve as cultural hubs for Asian immigrants with Hindu backgrounds, a significant number of these immigrants are not active practitioners of the religion.

Two of the three major Hindu communes in Appalachia—Gita Nagari in Port Royal, Pennsylvania, and New Vrindaban in Moundsville, West Virginia—are operated by the International Society for Krishna Consciousness (ISKCON, popularly known as the Hare Krishna movement), which has maintained a presence in Appalachia since 1968. While the society's ashrams are large farming communities, smaller centers are located in various population centers throughout Appalachia including Pittsburgh; Morgantown, West Virginia; and Mulberry, Tennessee. The sect was brought westward in 1966 by A. C. Bhaktivedanta Swami Prabhupada, who planned to retire to New Vrindaban. ISKCON advocates agrarian simplicity to commemorate the mythological life of its deity, Sri Krishna, who is believed to have lived more than three thousand years ago as a cow herder in the town of Vrindaban in what is now northern India. Society members attempt to revive and perpetuate earlier farming practices that place a heavy reliance on dairy cattle, nonmechanized plowing, and the use of cow dung as fertilizer and fuel. Protection of cows is a central tenet of the sect, as it is of Hinduism, and the farms sustain large herds on extensive acreage. Prabhupada had hoped that cheap, rural farmland would enable each member to maintain four acres and a cow, as well as provide temples and places of pilgrimage for Hindus in the West. In the mid-1980s, Kirtananda Swami Bhaktipada, the leader of New Vrindaban community, began to dissociate his commune from ISKCON and Americanized its rituals and theology. The community was scandalized when Bhaktipada and other New Vrindaban community leaders were indicted on charges of racketeering; the leader was incarcerated in 1996. The community subsequently sought to reaffiliate with the society. Meanwhile, the remaining New Vrindaban residents provisionally abandoned the model of agrarian self-sufficiency and found employment in the surrounding Appalachian community.

The third large Appalachian community guided by an Indian spiritual leader—the Heavenly Mountain—was founded in 1993 by the followers of Maharishi Mahesh Yogi, famous for his association in the 1960s with British rock group the Beatles and the Woodstock generation. The residential resort in the Blue Ridge Mountains near Boone, North Carolina, is designed to attract well-heeled Westerners, who mostly come from other parts of America as well as from other continents. The Heavenly Mountain is a gated residential community and resort and is located adjacent to the Maharishi Spiritual Center of America—where men and women are trained in Transcendental Meditation, "yogic flying," and other spiritual principles—and the campuses of the Maharishi's Purusha and Mother Divine programs, the latter including the Heavenly Mountain Ideal Girls' School for grades seven to twelve. The resort covers more than seven thousand acres and features single-family dwellings with a minimum of two thousand square feet and an average value of six hundred thousand dollars; condominiums; boutiques; a hotel, golf course, and swimming pool; tennis courts; and other recreational facilities. Buildings are constructed in accordance with the ancient architectural science of Sthapatya-Veda. The Maharishi Open University, the world's first satellite-television university, also moved to the Heavenly Mountain in 1999 and broadcasts live to all continents twenty-four hours a day in fifteen languages from three studios. Like other Hindu spiritual sects that have found success in the West, Mahesh Yogi's programs do not emphasize conversion, and in that sense the Heavenly Mountain is not a Hindu community but a "spiritual" one.

See also: SECTION OVERVIEW (RELIGION).

—Christopher B. Stewart, *West Virginia University*, and Deborah J. Thompson, *University of Kentucky*

Surinder M. Bhardwaj and Madhusudana N. Rao, "The Temple as a Symbol of Hindu Identity in America?" *Journal of Cultural Geography* (Spring–Summer 1998); Gurinder Singh Mann, Paul David Numrich, and Raymond B. Williams, *Buddhists, Hindus, and Sikhs in America* (2001); Thomas Tweed and Stephen Prothero, eds., *Asian Religions in America: A Documentary History* (1999).

Incest

The assumption that the rate of incest in Appalachia is higher than elsewhere in the United States has always loomed large in the stereotyping of the region and its inhabitants. In contemporary popular culture, "hillbillies" and "white trash" are imagined to be especially prone to having incestuous relations, a notion perpetuated by jokes and anecdotes about the inbred nature of mountain people. Stereotypes of incest and inbreeding have also been promoted and promulgated by scientists, doctors, and educators as explanations for the supposed "backwardness" and "genetic inferiority" of the residents of Appalachia.

While the origins of the myth of the incestuous Appalachian are unclear, the image is closely associated with another popular, long-lasting myth—that of the cultural, social, and geographical isolation of mountain folk. Both myths grew in popularity in the late nineteenth and early twentieth centuries, when it was common for outside observers of Appalachia to report that, because of a lack of modern transportation and communication, the mountain hollows and settlements teemed with families and communities whose social isolation from surrounding areas was extreme. This extreme isolation, it was frequently suggested, caused residents of the hollows to turn to their own family members for sexual mates and marriage partners. By the 1930s and 1940s, community studies carried out by social scientists with interests in eugenics largely confirmed these early reports of frequent incest and intermarriage, thus lending the aura of scientific authority to anecdotes and nonscientific observations.

Although contemporary historians and social scientists have found the old image of extreme isolation to be misleading and inaccurate, the iconic incestuous hillbilly has not been subjected to the same sort of rigorous critical analysis. Therefore, in the absence of credible scientific evidence, the stereotype remains. The little scientific evidence that does exist suggests that rates of consanguineous union (sexual relations and/or intermarriage between family members) and isonymy (marriage between persons sharing the same last name) are slightly higher in some parts of Appalachia than they are in the general population. The evidence is not sufficient to justify singling out Appalachians, though, since higher rates can be found among some ethnic immigrant groups and many religious groups.

See also: FAMILY RELATIONSHIPS AND GENDER ROLES; HILLBILLY (IMAGES AND ICONS); VIOLENCE AND VENGEANCE (IMAGES AND ICONS).

—Matt Wray, *Smithsonian Institution*

James Stephen Brown, "Social Class, Intermarriage, and Church Membership in a Kentucky Community," *American Journal of Sociology* (November 1951); Harry M. Caudill, *Night Comes to the Cumberlands: A Biography of a Depressed Area* (1963); Robert B. Tincher, "Night Comes to the Chromosomes: Inbreeding and Population Genetics in Southern Appalachia," *Central Issues in Anthropology* (1980).

Intentional Communities

Appalachia has long been considered an ideal territory for those attracted to experimental lifestyles. Whether motivated by religious expression, utopian ideals, ecological concerns, or New Age philosophies, the region's relative remoteness and rich natural resources—and especially the availability of inexpensive land—have inspired diverse groups to create communities and settlement movements. Intentional communities are formed when these groups commit to live together to pursue a particular purpose. They may have a socially diverse population, as in the case of racially integrated Berea, Kentucky, or they may have a fairly homogeneous one, as in retirement communities or gated communities, and some have been founded by a single family. Communitarians may experiment with notions of income sharing, property co-ownership, spirituality, work, marriage, sex roles, and family, challenging the status quo and the greater public's ideas of what it means to be a community. The fates of various intentional communities have been as varied as their inspiration. Some thrive across generations while some founder within years or months. Not all of these communities disappear entirely; some long-established cities in Appalachia began as planned communities.

While they often sought to separate themselves from the larger society, these communities were also shaped by social movements and norms of their day, even if that meant working to counteract them. The earliest wave coincided with waves of religious revivalism and the energy and creativity spurred by revolutionary thought around the turn of the nineteenth century. Abolition, labor reform, women's rights, and other reform movements of the 1840s also gave rise to a number of intentional communities. Industrialization and the uneven business climate of the last quarter of the nineteenth century caused some communities to try alternative economic schemes. Allardt and Rugby, both in east Tennessee, exemplified this approach. The Progressive Era and the country life movement spawned a new wave of idealistic rural settlement in the first half of the twentieth century, as did the New Deal of the 1930s. The 1960s and 1970s witnessed perhaps the most active and widespread establishment of intentional communities. The back-to-the-land movement consisted mostly of young, white, middle-class suburbanites coming together to form communes and cooperative farms. At the turn of the twenty-first century, environmental awareness and sustainable development were often intertwined with spirituality and alternative economies.

Some areas emerged as gathering places for communes and other alternative communities. Athens, Ohio, Floyd, Virginia, and Asheville, North Carolina, became countercultural havens because of the presence of a nearby university as well as attractive scenery and available, inexpensive land. Located in rural foothills of the Appalachians, approximately seventy-five miles southeast of Columbus, Athens County is home to a number of communities, including Currents, Sunflower Farms, and the Susan B. Anthony Memorial UnRest Home, as well as Ohio University's twenty thousand students. Most of these communities were established in the late 1970s and early 1980s; the earliest of these, Sunflower Farms, began in 1974. Locating the communities near the university reduced the residents' sense of isolation in the rural setting and provided community members with diverse cultural activities. Moreover, the university's history and tradition of social activism appealed to people who shared an interest in communal experimentation.

Most of the intentional communities in the county are located on former small farms of 100 to 200 acres with fewer than a dozen dwellings. They tend to be small, with fewer than a dozen or so residents, and in most cases members supplement their community's income by working in the conventional communities around them. Residents include a wide variety of professions—lawyers, doctors, teachers, ministers, artists, and government and social service employees.

The ideals of these communities vary, but generally they include cooperative living, consensus-based governance, nonviolent conflict resolution, and feminism. Some have a history of social and political activism with the goal of promoting progressive change in society. Many also attempt to develop ecologically sound principles such as wind and solar power, energy efficient homes, alternative agriculture, organic foods, and other sustainable economic and environmental initiatives to guide the planning and development of community activities and resources.

Another thriving community that is much older but still possesses an educational institution at its heart is Berea, Kentucky. With an early-twenty-first century population of nearly 10,000, the town is located fourteen miles southeast of Richmond, the county seat of Madison County, where the Bluegrass region meets the foothills of the Cumberland Plateau. Abolitionist and Christian minister John G. Fee founded the community in the mid-1850s, choosing the name Berea from the New Testament (Acts 17:10–11). At the core of Fee's community were an antislavery church and a school that eventually became Berea College.

As the public struggle with the issue of slavery and secession became more intense, pro-slavery residents forced Fee and the abolitionists from Madison County on December 29, 1859. At the end of the Civil War, Fee returned to Berea and recruited black war veterans to settle in Berea with their families and attend school. Hundreds of African Americans moved into the community, forming interracial neighborhoods surrounding the church and the college. Fee asserted that faith in God, readily available land, and education (as existed in Berea) helped to create the extraordinary atmosphere, alleviating racial prejudices and demonstrating that the races could live, study, and work together in harmony. To some extent this was true, though racial tension still existed in Berea.

Berea had more than 500 residents when it was incorporated in 1890, one-quarter of whom were African American, and Berea College was one of the few integrated colleges in the South. The interracial life of the institution and town continued until 1904, when the Kentucky legislature passed the Day Law, a measure requiring segregation. In compliance with the statute, college administrators decided that the school would maintain its white rather than its African American students and faculty. A new school, the Lincoln Institute, was created for blacks near Louisville. African Americans did not reenter Berea College until 1950, when the state began loosening segregation laws.

On the Cumberland Plateau in east Tennessee, the small town of Allardt began as a planned commercial enterprise intended to capitalize on the area's natural resources. In 1879 German immigrants G. Bruno Gernt and M. H. Allardt recognized the economic potential for land, agriculture, timber, and mineral development in the area. Collaborating with the family of Cyrus Clarke, which held land titles on the Cumberland Plateau, Gernt moved from Michigan to Tennessee and began to build a model town with an economic base of agriculture and natural resources. Allardt died before the project came to fruition, and Gernt named the business (Allardt Land Association) and the town after his deceased business associate.

The company promoted the settlement with easy financing and sold 9,000 acres its first year. Farmers and skilled craftsmen, primarily from Germany, purchased 25-, 50-, and 200-acre lots at four dollars an acre. Gernt remained active in the business until his death in 1932. Volatility in the demand for natural resources coupled with transportation difficulties limited the town's development. By the end of the twentieth century, only a few original structures still stood in modern Allardt, which had a population of between 600 and 700 residents.

As elsewhere in the country, many intentional communities in Appalachia were short-lived experiments that disappeared, sometimes because the focus of the community was too narrow to be sustained and sometimes because of economic reasons, as was the case of Himlerville, Kentucky. A cooperative coal-mining town established by Hungarian immigrants in Martin County in 1919, Himlerville was named after its founder, Martin Himler. It was America's only experiment with cooperative capitalism in the coal industry. At Himlerville all workers were stockholders in the Himler Coal Company, and not even Himler himself owned more than 3 percent of the company's outstanding shares. Workers received one-third of company profits as wages, one-third was paid as dividend on stock, and the remainder was used to retire debt the company had incurred during construction.

Conceiving the idea in 1916, Himler organized the Himler Coal Company and advertised stock for sale in *Magyar Banyaszlap*, a Hungarian-language newspaper he published in New York before moving it to Kentucky in 1919. Investment in the company was slow at first because selling stock through foreign-language newspapers was a popular way for swindlers to cheat immigrants. Eventually, Himler raised $50,000 through stock subscriptions and used the money to purchase a mine at Ajax, West Virginia. When the Ajax mine proved to be too small, the Hungarians sold the property in 1917 for $150,000. They then increased the Himler Coal Company's capital to $500,000 through sale of a second stock issue and purchased property across the Tug Fork in Kentucky (near present-day Kermit, West Virginia), where they established Himlerville.

Modeled after Consolidation Coal Company's town at Jenkins, Kentucky, Himlerville included houses for workers, a company store, bathhouse, cooperative-owned bank, library, pool hall, school, and company offices. The community differed from other coal camps in southern Appalachia in that residents owned the houses they lived in and could modify them any way they wished. Many workers constructed their own houses, which meant that Himlerville did not contain identical houses and looked distinctly different from other coal camps. Private merchants were allowed to sell their wares in Himlerville, and workers were not required to shop at the company store.

At work and home, residents spoke Hungarian, wore traditional clothes, worshipped in the Catholic Church, and viewed plays performed in their native language. The town's bakery produced Hungarian breads and pastries, while the library contained books written in both English and Hungarian. After work, residents enjoyed reading *Magyar Banyaszlap*, which was published in Himlerville until 1929.

Unfortunately, the experiment with cooperative capitalism failed due to a slump in the coal industry during the 1920s. The Himler Coal Company was placed into receivership in 1925 and sold at public auction in 1929. Most of the immigrants moved away from eastern Kentucky, and shortly after the auction, a flood washed away the town. Today, only a few buildings remain.

Across Appalachia, there are several former communities that have been restored or preserved, allowing visitors to tour historic buildings and sample the lifestyle of these early idealists. The Hensley Settlement of southeastern Kentucky; Rugby, Tennessee, on the Cumberland Plateau; and the Harmonist colony of Old Economy in Pennsylvania are all planned communities open to the public.

The National Park Service operates the restored Hensley Settlement, a community established in 1903 by members of the Hensley and Gibbons families. Intending to escape the increasingly mechanized world of the early twentieth century, the families cleared land on a mountaintop near Middlesboro, Kentucky, built log cabins, farmed, and accomplished their daily tasks without electricity or modern conveniences. Although the community of approximately 100 residents had reached its peak by 1930, the settlement existed until 1951, when founder Sherman Hensley was the last to abandon the land.

Residents of Hensley Settlement sought to live in a self-sufficient fashion. The community included farms and pastures, a cemetery, a blacksmith and carpentry shop, and a one-room schoolhouse, which also served as a church on weekends, when itinerant preachers rode up the mountain for services. Restoration of the settlement (now part of the Cumberland Gap National Historical Park) began in the early 1960s and includes nearly thirty original buildings on about sixty acres.

In Morgan County, Tennessee, not far south of the Hensley Settlement, the restored historic town of Rugby is also open to visitors. Built in the early 1880s, Rugby was a socioeconomic experiment and the dream of English judge Thomas Hughes, author of *Tom Brown's School Days*, a thinly disguised recounting of Hughes' experience as a student at Rugby School in England. The popular novel brought the author fame and fortune, and he used his wealth to purchase 75,000 acres in east Tennessee. There, Hughes founded a utopian colony named for his old school and organized it to serve the well-educated and underemployed younger sons of England's wealthy classes. Under the inheritance system of the day, these younger sons ordinarily were not provided financial security, and few had socially acceptable careers available to them.

Rugby initially attracted about 200 persons and grew to a peak population of approximately 400 in 1884, half of whom were English and half American. Although his mother and his niece were residents, Hughes never lived in the colony but visited once a year through the 1880s until his mother's death in 1887. An agricultural village of approximately sixty-five buildings, Rugby included two hotels, two general stores, a drug store, a schoolhouse, a Gothic Revival church, and a stylish library with seven thousand volumes of Victorian era literature. Tourists were an early source of income for the colony, and *Harper's Weekly* featured Rugby in an 1880 issue. The community advertised itself as a health resort, and the Tabard Inn provided comfortable accommodations for visitors.

Problems plagued Rugby from the beginning. Hughes's absence and the long distance to the colony headquarters, a Board of Aid in London, created misunderstandings and unexpected difficulties. Rugby's agricultural goals failed due to inexperience of the residents and the poor land upon which the community was built. In 1881 a typhoid epidemic claimed seven residents, and in 1884 the Tabard burned, eliminating a major source of income for the town. In all, Hughes lost about $250,000 in the experiment. In 1899 the Rugby Land Company, an American enterprise, bought the land, and the English connection was severed. The village continued to exist with limited economic opportunities and a steadily declining population.

The 1960s restoration of Rugby began under the leadership of Brian Stagg, resident of a nearby village. Buildings from the original colony were restored or rebuilt, and Rugby became a popular historic attraction for visitors from all over the United States as well as England and Europe.

Situated on the banks of the Ohio River at present-day Ambridge, Pennsylvania, Old Economy was the third and final colony of the Harmony Society, a Protestant Separatist organization. Established in 1825 by Protestants from Iptengen, Germany, under the leadership of George Rapp, Old Economy was intended to be a model of Christian communism and a source of financial support for other utopian groups. Having first settled at Harmony, Pennsylvania, in 1804, the sect went on to develop New Harmony, Indiana, from 1814 to 1824, before selling the entire town to Scottish industrialist and philanthropist Robert Owen. Returning to Pennsylvania, the Harmonists established Old Economy, where they continued their communal lifestyle with temperance in all things, including strict celibacy, and awaited what they believed to be the imminent ending of the world. Harmonists invested in the fledgling oil and coal industries of northwestern Pennsylvania and developed the town of Beaver Falls as an industrial center on the Ohio River.

By the latter nineteenth century, the Harmony Society had lost much of its prosperity to lawsuits by some heirs of early Harmonists (who vied for ownership claims to the community's property), and the society declined in membership until it dissolved in 1905. The American Bridge Company bought most of the society's holdings and transformed the village of Old Economy into the industrial town of Ambridge, though the grounds and buildings of Old Economy have been preserved and opened to the public by the Pennsylvania State Historical and Museum Commission.

Spiritual beliefs such as those of the Harmonists have been a common inspiration for communities in Appalachia. Opportunities for self-sufficiency along with the freedom to practice religion unmolested have attracted religious groups from around the world to this region of America.

In 1817, Joseph Bäumler (sometimes Bimeler) led about 225 Protestant Separatists from Germany to Tuscarawas County in the Ohio wilderness about twelve miles from New Philadelphia, where they established Zoar. Although they did not intend to live communally, economic hardship led them to draw up articles of agreement, pool their resources, and work on neighboring farms for money. Construction of the Ohio-Erie Canal through their land in 1827 provided them enough income to pay off their debts and remain solvent.

Initially endorsing celibacy, they began tolerating intracommunity marriages by 1830, though until 1845 children older than three years lived in separate houses for boys and girls. On probation for one year, new members were allowed to keep property but gave up all cash to the society. Probationers and children had fewer rights than the full members. The Zoar Separatists led a sober, orderly, and nonintellectual lifestyle and displayed no outward religious signs or rituals. They addressed all others as equals, using the familiar *thou*. Zoarites did not use tobacco but allowed beer and cider.

Zoar was incorporated as a town in 1832 and expanded to encompass economic enterprises such as woolen factories, tanneries, flour mills, and machine shops. By 1874, the town had a population of about 500, and Zoarites owned 70,000 acres of land worth $3 million. Despite their prosperity, the Society of Separatists voted in 1898 to dissolve the society and fairly divide the land and other assets among the members. Many historic buildings remain in the village of Zoar, home to about 200 permanent residents at the beginning of the twenty-first century.

In 1851 spiritualist Thomas Lake Harris, with Reverend J. L. Scott and approximately a hundred followers from upstate New York, founded the Mountain Cove Community in Fayette County, Virginia (now West Virginia). Harris and Scott claimed to have received divine instructions written in the sky directing them to establish a cooperative agricultural colony and await the coming of the Messiah. They asserted that the land they chose was the original Garden of Eden, unchanged since the expulsion of Adam and Eve and since inhabited only by angels.

After two years, the faith of the followers faltered, and a letter published in the periodical *Spiritual Telegraph* accused Harris and Scott of creating mistrust, disbelief, and discord with their dictatorial, arbitrary rules. The two were also accused of bilking their followers of all possessions and property. Though Scott submitted a counterstatement to the periodical defending Harris and claiming innocence of the charges, the quarrels over property were a factor in the colony's demise in 1853.

Lily Dale Spiritualist Camp, an extant spiritualist community established in Chautauqua County, New York, in 1879, was organized around a religious philosophy first popularized in America and England during the late nineteenth and early twentieth centuries. In 1855 sisters Margaret and Catherine Fox claimed to have communicated with spirits at their farm near Hydesville in southwestern New York. Inspired by these incidents, Spiritualists in the area formed the First Spiritualist Society of Laona, an organization that practiced spiritual healing and held séances to communicate with the dead. In 1879 they purchased and developed 20 acres of land for a camp that, by the early 1900s, boasted a hotel, classroom buildings, a library stocked with books on Spiritualism, and an auditorium. Lily Dale accommodates approximately 250 permanent residents, increasing to about 500 in summer, when the camp features speakers, medium-guided meditation, healing services, and other activities.

The mountains of southwestern Virginia are the home of Light Morning, a small community founded in 1974 on the teachings of Edgar Cayce, known as the Sleeping Prophet. The community's philosophy has since been adapted to include works of similar prophets. Members' families work together full-time to create a simple, healthy, spirituality-centered lifestyle. The physical environs consist of rustic family dwellings, guest quarters for short- and longterm visitors, and a large common building for leisure, prayer, community gatherings, reading, meditation, and shared meals. Food is primarily vegetarian and grown in the community's own gardens, while meals serve as a vehicle for sharing experiences and addressing community issues.

The members of Light Morning have published two books. *Season of Changes: Ways of Response* is focused on dream work, meditation, prayer, and harmony with the earth. *Wax Statues, Cotton Candy and the Second Coming* grew out of the group's dream work and daily life together, reflecting their focus on consensus, bridge building, and reconciliation of the complexities of the self and human community.

Originating in Appalachian New York in 1942, Shiloh Community is a nondenominational Christian, self-sustaining community founded on a 500-acre farm by E. Crosby Monroe, a retired U.S. Navy veteran and nautical interior designer. It was intended to provide a Christian communal experience for members living, working, and worshipping with a singular purpose. From its earliest days the community was self-sustaining through such enterprises as farming, milling, and meat production. By the late 1960s, Shiloh bakeries were producing and selling a line of organic breads nationwide. The need for a more centralized setting for distribution of its baked goods sparked the community's relocation to the Ozark town of Sulphur Springs, Arkansas, in 1968.

In a rustic compound of more than 40 acres in the Appalachian foothills of High View, West Virginia, Buddhist nuns and monks dedicate their lives to teaching and meditation. The Bhavana Society Forest Monastery and Meditation Center opened in the 1980s, a few years after Bhante Henepola Gunaratana started the society in Washington, D.C. Gunaratana, a meditation teacher, scholar, and Sri Lankan Buddhist monk, had hoped to open a retreat near Washington but found the setting to be more peaceful—and cheaper—in rural Hampshire County, seventy-seven miles away.

Following conservative Theravada Buddhism, about a dozen of the center's 3,000 members live year-round at the site, which features a wooden prayer hall, library, small dormitory, and outlying cabins, or kutis. The center offers meditative retreats throughout the year, and the largest crowds visit in spring and fall for the major full-moon holidays, Vesak and Kathina. People come from all over the world to study at the center, though most often they reside in major cities along the East Coast. Proselytizing is not a part of the religion, and the center has a low profile in the community. Monks have slowly elevated the center's profile, attending the occasional blood drive or fire station open house.

Groups interested in promoting social change by example, and at times activism, have also sought Appalachia as a place to experiment with alternative communities. Many of these also espouse a spirituality-based lifestyle as the inspiration for their activism.

A sister organization to Habitat for Humanity and New Hope House in Griffin, Georgia, Jubilee Partners emerged from Koinonia Farms, a south Georgia racially integrated Christian community founded by Clarence and Florence Jordan along with Mabel and Martin England in 1942. Organized in 1979 by the Mosley, Karis, and Weir families, the Jubilee Partners are Christian pacifists. Situated on 258 acres of land in Comer, Georgia, just northeast of Athens, the community operates as a ministry to political refugees. Approximately 35 adults and children work toward the community's mission, though half of this number are resident partners and the other half are volunteers who are applying for admittance to the community. Finances and automobiles are shared, and food is grown on-site for residents.

Committed to its vision of social justice, the community resettles refugees from other countries, protests nuclear proliferation and militarization, works to improve race relations, and advocates the abolition of the death penalty. At the local level, members have cared for prisoners on death row in Georgia and provided burial plots on Jubilee Partners land for executed inmates.

The community's early international efforts were focused in El Salvador and Nicaragua, where they promoted peace and provided medical aid such as the establishment in Nicaragua of a prosthetics clinic for victims of land mines. Jubilee Partners have welcomed refugees from over fifteen countries, including Laos, Cambodia, Cuba, Thailand, Vietnam, and Bosnia. Members lead lives that they hope emphasize biblical values rather than materialistic ones. They have taught language and cultural skills to more than 2,200 refugees and helped them find homes and jobs in the United States.

The community of Raven Rocks estimates that nearly 80 percent of Monroe County, Ohio, has been leased or sold to strip-mining operations. In order to preserve Raven Rocks, a system of ravines, streams, woodlands, and rock formations in the county, a privately financed preservation effort was initiated. Located near the town of Beallsville in southeastern Ohio, the community has expanded its core mission of preservation to include exploration of sustainable environmental practices, alternative energy sources, and nontraditional education.

Nineteen former students from a local Quaker school were instrumental in the formation of the community, which originally consisted of 843 acres purchased for preservation in 1970. Christmas tree farms have generated funds for additional land purchase, allowing the community to expand and preserve the local watershed. Members live in six homes located on more than a thousand acres of land and support themselves through a variety of occupations while volunteering their time to do the work required to maintain the corporation. Raven Rocks also provides demonstrations of aesthetics, construction materials, alternative energy sources, and conservation techniques.

Situated in Yancey County, North Carolina, is Celo Community, a successful land-trust enterprise launched as a not-for-profit corporation in 1937. The original board of directors included Arthur E. Morgan, a former President of Antioch College in Ohio and first chairman of the Tennessee Valley Authority. Also on the board were Henry Regnery, a wealthy Chicago businessman who purchased 1,200 acres of land along the Toe River for the community, and Clarence Pickett, executive secretary of the Quaker-run American Friends Service Committee.

Converted into a land trust early in its creation, the corporation of Celo Community holds title to the land, and members purchase "holdings" that carry most of the privileges of ownership with restrictions on development. Celo members' activities include the larger community as well. Celo Health Center provides health care and education to people throughout Yancey County. Camp Celo offers a full range of camp activities to boys and girls ages seven to ten. Members operate a cooperative food store that does 80 percent of its business with people from outside the community. The Arthur Morgan School is a small boarding school that serves junior high school students, and in 1981 teachers there formed Rural Southern Voice for Peace, an organization promoting grassroots efforts for justice, peace, and environmental protection. Celo Community supported thirty-four families at the beginning of the twenty-first century, accepting two trial member families each year.

The Spiral Wimmin's Community and Land Trust, begun in 1981 by twenty women on approximately 300 acres in the Appalachian foothills of south-central Kentucky, is a community founded on communal and feminist ideals. The members strive to create a culture free of gender struggles and exploitation and intend to demonstrate the capacity for women to sustain a self-sufficient, interdependent, and ecologically harmonious community. The community supports several small businesses, operating an organic market garden called Blue Skink Farm and a primitive campground, selling Appalachian crafts, and providing labor for hire. With two houses, two barns, and six cabins, members share ownership of land, buildings, and equipment.

Many of Appalachia's intentional communities incorporate various ideas of ecology and communal living. Though they may emphasize different approaches to achieving their goals, the members of these communities tend to share an Earth-centered spirituality. Zendik Farm Arts Foundation near Asheville, North Carolina, promotes an arts-based communal system that encourages personal creativity. Union Acres in Whittier, North Carolina; Rosy Branch Farm of Black Mountain, North Carolina; and High Flowing of Floyd, Virginia, also combine ecological and spiritual interests. In addition to their observance of Native American traditions, residents at Union Acres recognize and celebrate seasonal passages such as the equinoxes and solstices. High Flowing is specifically based on the Mayan calendar of galactic synchronization. The Hermitage at Mahantongo Spirit Garden in Pitman, Pennsylvania, is a self-described queer community open to men and women of diverse sexuality who seek a spiritual life based on stewardship of the planet.

Eastern religious tradition is evident in the communities of Nature's Spirit in Salem, South Carolina, and New Vrindaban in Moundsville, West Virginia. Nature's Spirit has a central spiritual focus and values the diversity of life. New Vrindaban, also known as the City of God, is the oldest and largest Hare Krishna community in the West. Spiritual practices are based on the principles of the Bhagavad Gita and the practice of Bhakti-yoga, as well as devotion to Krishna. The community offers workshops including mantra meditation, yoga, and healing arts.

See also: BACK-TO-THE-LAND MOVEMENT (SETTLEMENT AND MIGRATION); PLANNED COMMUNITIES; PLANNED INDUSTRIAL TOWNS (ARCHITECTURE).

—Doug Cantrell, *Elizabethtown Community College;* W. Calvin Dickinson, *Tennessee Technological University;* Troy Gowen and Rebecca Tolley-Stokes, *East Tennessee State University;* Richard W. Greenlee, *Ohio University;* Gene Hyde, *Lyon College;* George W. Loveland and Susan Virginia Mead, *Ferrum College;* Arthur McDade, *National Park Service;* Ernest Morgan, *Burnsville, North Carolina;* Madelyn Rosenberg, *Roanoke Times;* Dana L. Stuchul and Shannon H. Wilson, *Berea College;* Deborah J. Thompson, *University of Kentucky;* and Gilson A. C. Waldkoenig, *Lutheran Theological Seminary at Gettysburg*

Karl J. R. Arndt, *George Rapp's Harmony Society, 1785–1847* (1965); Corrine McLaughlin and Gordon Davidson, *Builders of the Dawn: Community Lifestyles in a Changing World* (1985); Cris and Oliver Popenoe, *Seeds of Tomorrow: New Age Communities That Work* (1984).

Jehovah's Witness Families and Communities

See Adventist Denominational Family (Religion)

Land Trusts

See Land Trusts and Conservancies (Environment)

Marriage Customs

Courtship, marriage, and divorce in Appalachia have generally involved fewer customary behaviors than such other rites of passage as birth, death, and spiritual salvation. Indeed, in rural sections of the region through the World War I era, the establishment of formal social unions through the institution of marriage was frequently an unromantic, utilitarian process.

In rural Appalachia, a young person would often meet his or her love interest in a church, which was usually the social as well as the religious center of a community. The first stage of courtship, which people sometimes referred to as "talking," began shortly after boys and girls reached their adolescence. It might occur following Sunday service, at which time a young man would walk a young woman home from church after obtaining permission from her parents. In the second stage of courtship, often referred to as "sparking," the young man would escort the young woman to church on subsequent Sundays and bring her gifts at her parents' house, where his visits were under supervision. In preparation for seeing her boyfriend, the young woman would don her finest clothes and would occasionally apply some kind of makeup, but Appalachian society's behavioral codes expected a young single woman to act coyly toward her suitor. In some parts of the region, especially in eastern Kentucky, a young couple might be allowed to visit without parental supervision if they jointly played the "courting dulcimer," an Appalachian instrument possessing two fretboards. As long as the nearby parents could hear both sets of strings being strummed, they could leave the couple unobserved, knowing that the young man and woman were properly preoccupied.

The third stage of courtship, premarital sexual activity, was, of course, problematic. Despite religious strictures against such behavior, premarital and extramarital sexual activity was historically rather common in Appalachia, and many people within the region were forgiving of the consequences. A pregnancy out of wedlock generally led to a hastily arranged wedding. If held under such circumstances, a wedding was seldom an elaborate ceremony and most likely occurred away from the bride and groom's community—perhaps administered by an unfamiliar preacher or justice of the peace in another county. Once the homefolk had adjusted to the new social relationship, a celebration featuring music and dancing, as well as food and liquor, might be offered in honor of the newly married couple. If social pressure or legal action failed to coerce into marriage the man responsible for a woman's pregnancy, the woman would remain single, and sometimes her own parents would help raise the child.

If a marriage proved unworkable, a couple might separate, though such action might not lead to a legally mandated divorce. Historically in rural Appalachia, many people could not afford a lawyer, and courthouses were often inconvenient to divorcing couples. Some people, therefore, ignored the formality of filing for official divorce and simply remarried, undaunted by the fact that they were, according to civil laws, committing bigamy. Circumstances in rural Appalachia demanded flexibility in interpersonal relationships because, in an environment of geographical and social isolation, all adults were in principle equally important. Thus, forgiveness, acceptance, and interdependence were essential social values.

These customs were common but far from universal in Appalachia. The diversity of races, ethnicities, classes, religious affiliations, and geographical circumstances of the people living within the region ensured a variety of such customs. Since World War II, however, influenced heavily by American mainstream culture, attitudes toward courtship, marriage, and divorce have become increasingly homogeneous. One mass-culture phenomenon to appear in Appalachia in the late twentieth century was the commercial wedding chapel. Couples from both within and outside the region traveled considerable distances to marry in generally standardized ceremonies offered by wedding chapels in Appalachian tourist towns such as Gatlinburg and Pigeon Forge, Tennessee—often to avoid the waiting period for marriage licenses required in other states.

See also: SECTION OVERVIEW.

—Ted Olson, *East Tennessee State University*

John C. Campbell, *The Southern Highlander and His Homeland* (1921); Ted Olson, *Blue Ridge Folklife* (1998); Muriel Earley Sheppard, *Cabins in the Laurel* (1935).

Melungeon Families and Communities

Although the history and heritage of Appalachia's dark-skinned Melungeon people have been sources of deep and continuing controversy, there has been relatively little research on Melungeon communities or family life. This lack of scholarship indicates how little Melungeon life differed from that of their white neighbors even in the era before assimilation.

By the end of the twentieth century Melungeons, like other minority groups, had seen their lives and identity become largely embedded in the broader local and regional culture. To be sure, their predecessors who settled in the mountains of North Carolina, Tennessee, Virginia, and Kentucky faced hardships similar to those of other ethnic minorities in the region. For years, the term *Melungeon* was almost always used by whites in reference to the dark-complexioned, mixed-race people, but Melungeons have very rarely referred to themselves as such except in a pejorative sense. Only since the 1960s, as their social stigma faded and as exotic cultures began intriguing mainstream America, have some Melungeons accepted the nomenclature as an adequate, nonpejorative descriptor of their group.

The first written record of the term *Melungeon* is in the 1813 minutes of southwestern Virginia's Stony Creek Baptist Church. The term appeared in the context of an accusation by one church member that another harbored a "Melungin." Throughout the previous twelve years in the same church, many members bearing traditionally Melungeon surnames were excommunicated, demonstrating the stigma then attached to the ethnicity. It was perhaps in reaction to such discrimination that many Melungeons moved southward, a significant number of them settling on Newman's Ridge in present-day Hancock County, Tennessee.

Still they were not free from discrimination. Generally defined for census and tax purposes as "free persons of color," Melungeons saw their rights nullified along with those of mulattos, blacks, Native Americans, and mestizos as the governments of Virginia, North Carolina, and Tennessee passed laws in the 1830s revoking voting rights or threatening enslavement of non-white residents of the states. Until the 1850s, such institutional discrimination influenced the lives of many Melungeons. Some scholars argue that, in response to such societal biases, many Melungeons claimed Portuguese ancestry to avoid being numbered among the disenfranchised, perhaps giving rise to the popular myth that Melungeons descended from that country.

Between 1790 (roughly the date that the first Melungeons entered southwestern Virginia) and the 1830s, Melungeon life differed little from that of their white neighbors. Records show that many Melungeons owned their own farms, worked as laborers on nearby farms, and sometimes worked in the lumber industry. But there is reason to believe that during this period Melungeon life differed in at least one important way. Probably due to racial discrimination like that at Stony Creek, Melungeons many times settled in communities with other Melungeons. Vardy, in Hancock County, is one of the best examples. Melungeons, most likely in order to cope with the effects of ethnic discrimination, chose to live among others of their kind.

Though few accounts exist, one can surmise that from the 1830s until the Civil War life for Melungeons changed as they attempted to carry on their livelihoods amidst patterns of increased racial discrimination. In one Melungeon autobiography, Mattie Ruth Johnson recounts her childhood from 1940 to 1957 on Newman's Ridge near Sneedville, a community with historically one of the highest concentrations of Melungeons in southern Appalachia. Like that of many other Appalachians, her family's way of life revolved around physical labor in the field and home, where there was a distinct division of labor among males and females, and spiritual enlightenment at Church and other religious events. According to Johnson's account, Melungeon life by the mid-twentieth century differed little from that of other Appalachians, and other observers have noted that both groups depend on strong familial ties and social networks. Some have claimed that their permissive child-rearing practices strongly resemble those of Native Americans. Still others have noted a strong affinity among Melungeon communities toward Primitive Baptist worship, such as in the church in Stony Creek. After the Civil Rights movement, Melungeons shed the stigma attached to their dark complexion, many times even embracing the formerly disparaging term, as demonstrated by Johnson's autobiography and by several theater productions that have celebrated the people.

Because of the Civil Rights movement, a growing awareness of diversity across the country and in Appalachia, intermarriage with whites, and a fusion of Melungeon culture with Appalachian culture, most scholars now agree that Melungeons face little, if any, social ostracism because of their color or culture. Many value their ethnicity and heritage while realizing that they are first and foremost Appalachians and that their complexions or high cheekbones do not significantly distinguish them from others in the region.

See also: MELUNGEON (LANGUAGE); MELUNGEONS (RACE, ETHNICITY, AND IDENTITY).

—Heather Rhea Gilreath, *East Tennessee State University*

Pat Spurlock Elder, *Melungeons: Examining an Appalachian Legend* (1999); C. S. Everett, "Melungeon History and Myth," *Appalachian Journal* (Summer 1999); Mattie Ruth Johnson, *My Melungeon Heritage: A Story of Life on Newman's Ridge* (1997).

Mennonite and Amish Communities

Although not a major feature of the region, Mennonite and Amish communities are scattered throughout Appalachia, with the largest concentrations in Ohio and Pennsylvania and other groups in New York, Kentucky, Tennessee, and North Carolina. Mennonites arrived in Pennsylvania as early as the late seventeenth century, and Amish groups began immigrating to Pennsylvania in the early eighteenth century. However, these traditional groups did not remain rooted to William Penn's colony.

Mennonite and Amish traditions trace their origins to the sixteenth-century Anabaptist reformation that was part of the left wing of the Protestant Reformation. The Anabaptist movement stressed a radical biblicism and was known for its distinctive beliefs including a strong religious community orientation marked by adult baptism, pacifism, and separation of church and state. Many of the more progressive groups within these traditions extend their pacifism to a more general social concern and sponsor progressive mission activities. While Mennonite and Amish groups share a general tendency to separate the worldly sphere from the sacred, more traditional Amish groups take the general principle of separation from the world to the greatest length, eschewing "worldly" conveniences and associations. This tendency to separate from secular society results in a commitment to simple lifestyles, often oriented to rural and farming communities. Thus, the most traditional groups are community and family oriented, staunchly maintaining traditional cultures and sometimes separate societies while endeavoring to live to varying degrees apart from secular culture. Accordingly, Amish and Mennonite communities have sought out geographical areas conducive to rural ways of life.

The Mennonite tradition traces its roots to Menno Simons, a Dutch Anabaptist of the sixteenth century, while the Amish tradition springs from a splinter group led by Jakob Ammann and the Swiss Mennonites in the late seventeenth century. Mennonite and Amish groups tend to be rejectionist in their stance toward contemporary and secular culture. Old Order groups in both traditions observe the most stringent requirements for maintaining tradition and remaining separate from popular culture. For example, Old Order Amish groups distinguish themselves by their dress and hairstyles, by rejecting electricity, cars, and modern farming implements such as tractors, and by maintaining private community schools that provide education through the eighth grade. More progressive groups, some called New Order, are more accommodating to contemporary and secular culture, making use of contemporary farming techniques, automobiles, electricity, and public education. In general, the separation principle leads to varying degrees of social isolation and therefore greater dependence on strong social structures within the group. The more traditional the religious orientation, the more socially isolated the group tends to be. In the most traditional cases, marriage outside of the religious group is forbidden. The resulting social isolation creates stronger needs for communal support. As a result, extended family and community life is the backbone for many Mennonite and Amish communities. The more traditional of these groups tend to have large families and some even live together in multigenerational homes, excellent examples of which can be seen in Lancaster County, Pennsylvania.

Because of this strong family orientation, the home is the center of Amish and Mennonite life, education, work, and religion. The most traditional groups have historically tended to run family farms or small family businesses. In many traditional groups, after children complete the eighth grade, they continue their education by learning the trades of the family. The home is the center of religious life, as families reinforce religious observance through prayer and home devotion or through holding worship services in homes rather than in churches. Every function of life, even recreation, is centered on the family and the home as part of the effort to create a separation between the community and secular society. The typical traditional family is regulated in both gender roles and family power structures. Adherence to the Bible and submission to the community are prime virtues, and expressions of individual will are seen as suspect. Such reliance on traditional ways of structuring the family helps to reinforce the Mennonite and Amish approaches to life.

As Mennonites and Amish find themselves in closer and closer proximity to contemporary culture, their communities find it more difficult to maintain ways of life that separate them from popular culture and society. Many adopt more modern ways of living, while others seek new areas to live where their traditional ways can be preserved. In many respects, the traditional ways of Mennonites and Amish groups have resembled the lifestyle of other rural

Appalachians, especially in the importance of self-sufficiency and independence. While many of these fading attributes in Mennonite, Amish, and traditional Appalachian life have been romanticized, they still illustrate an affinity between Mennonite and Amish enclaves and traditional rural Appalachian communities, though the Anabaptist theology and teachings continue to set the Mennonites and Amish apart.

Through the Mennonite Central Committee the group, like many other Protestant denominations, sponsors missions to fight poverty in Appalachia. The Mennonite presence in Appalachia comes as a result of earlier missionary activity, as evidenced by the fact that Mennonite Brethren Churches in the mountains of North Carolina (where the Amish continue to establish new communities in places such as Yadkin and Iredell Counties) are predominantly African American.

See also: MENNONITES (RELIGION).

—Conrad Ostwalt, *Appalachian State University*

John A. Hostetler, *Amish Society* (1993); John A. Hostetler, Gertrude E. Huntington, and Louise S. Spindler, eds., *Amish Children: Education in the Family, School, and Community* (1992); Paul Toews, *Mennonites in American Society, 1930–1970: Modernity and Persistence of Religious Community* (1997).

Mill Towns

With post–Civil War modernization in the South, mill towns were among a number of different kinds of villages that replaced rural communities built around subsistence farming. Large textile mills in the Virginia, Carolina, and Georgia Piedmont drew many workers from the nearby mountains, though mill towns also developed in such Appalachian communities as Dalton, Georgia; Marion, North Carolina; Elizabethton, Tennessee; and Galax and Fries, Virginia. Unlike timbering and coal-mining communities, textile mill villages included large numbers of female workers and were almost exclusively white.

Mill owners claimed they were performing a social service to poor, rural whites, but their operations changed the nature of communities. The same economic conditions and monetary pressures that encouraged railway expansion, timbering, coal mining, and textiles rendered subsistence farming intolerable, increased poverty, and forced many rural and mountain people off their land. In the 1870s and early 1880s, mills attracted widows, female heads of households, and single women considered expendable on farms. In the late 1880s through the 1890s, tightening credit, cash-crop farming, and falling crop prices pushed increasing numbers of landowning and tenant farmers into the mills.

Mill villages typically provided workers and their families with four-room houses, a store, a school, churches, organized activities, and dependable (if small) paychecks. While the store was a convenience to families, the company profited by circulating payroll outlays back to itself and by holding power over workers through credit. Paved streets and electric lights came slowly, but not as slowly as sewer systems, which were common in most other municipalities by 1916. Toilets drained into vaults, which had to be emptied by company conveyances known euphemistically as "honey wagons."

Often, all family members, including children, worked long, monotonous hours for small wages. Twelve-hour workdays and six-day workweeks were common in the late 1800s. The eight-hour workday was not established until 1933 under the National Industrial Recovery Act, and child labor was not prohibited until 1938 with the passage of the Fair Labor Standards Act. Men and women both worked in the mills but usually at different jobs. Spinning was primarily the women's domain, whereas carding and machine repair were done mainly by men, with the weaving room being the one place the two sexes often worked together. A few African American men were sometimes hired for heavy lifting and honey wagon duty, well away from places where white women worked. Health and safety hazards associated with cotton dust, dangerous machinery, and high levels of noise were not effectively addressed until the 1970s.

Since the company built and maintained churches and schools, ministers in the pulpit tended to avoid controversial social issues such as fair labor practices, and teachers encouraged children to continue working. Thus, until automobile ownership became common and the radio a popular voice from the outer world, companies exerted a dominant influence upon village culture.

Before the Great Depression of the 1930s, companies attempted to use welfare workers to socialize families into industry-friendly patterns of living. Management organized social clubs, yard beautification contests, cooking classes, and the like, all with the end of bringing company influence into leisure as well as work time. They also arranged for different operations of the mill to compete against each other in baseball and other recreational activities, leading some observers to assert that the company was trying to undermine worker solidarity efforts or labor unions.

Workers tended to feel free, however, to complain about unjust supervisors, and mill owners would sometimes mediate in their favor. Middle-level supervisors often became so involved in the mill village life that worker-management distinctions blurred. Mill families, moreover, never completely lost the independence they had enjoyed in the mountains or countryside. They raised farm animals and grew gardens to minimize store needs. Women in particular were helpful with sickness or death in a neighboring family, just as they had supported each other on the farm.

Life outside of work revolved around family ties, especially in the earlier years. After several generations of marrying among themselves, most members of a mill town were kin. On Saturdays, mills normally shut down at noon. The men might go hunting or play baseball, and in the evening the more socially inclined families would organize house parties. Sunday revolved around church and church functions such as box dinners. Before automobiles, when newlywed couples spent their first night at home, they were traditionally serenaded by neighbors beating tin cans and hollering.

Chances for romance among the young were actually improved, as villages provided more potential mates and less parental control over choices than did farms. Cars, radios, and movie theaters of the 1920s and 1930s freed young people from the confines of the mill town itself. Once married, however, women took on the traditional roles of homemaking and child rearing while continuing long shifts as wage earners.

By the 1940s and 1950s, rising costs of maintaining mill housing combined with lessening company influence over residents spelled the end of mill towns. Yet even as mills were selling their housing, company social activities continued. There were still company baseball games and school Christmas parties with gifts for mill workers' children. What many mill families remembered most fondly was the company picnic, perhaps the last vestige of paternalism lost to the 1960s. Sometimes such affairs lasted as long as a week and included a traveling carnival, contests, and a covered-dish picnic. A precursor to modern outdoor concerts, the grand finale on Saturday night often involved appearances by *Grand Ole Opry* stars or bluegrass bands.

See also: MILL SETTLEMENTS (SETTLEMENT AND MIGRATION); TEXTILE WORKERS (LABOR).

—Peter Crow, *Ferrum College*

Douglas Flamming, *Creating the Modern South: Millhands and Managers in Dalton, Georgia, 1884–1984* (1992); Jacquelyn Dowd Hall et al., *Like a Family: The Making of a Southern Cotton Mill World* (1987).

Muslim Families and Communities

The majority of Muslims who reside in Appalachia do so for professional and economic opportunities. In Appalachia, Muslims often gain employment in such professions as medicine, engineering, and education, and the typical Islamic family in Appalachia is generally very stable. The value of the family unit within Islam itself serves to strengthen the bonds of commitment and affection holding the family together. This stability of the Islamic family is further enhanced by the region's own traditional and religious emphasis upon family values.

The Muslim family's cohesion in Appalachia is nurtured by the reality of being "other" or "different" in a Christian, predominantly Protestant culture. Muslims in the region report that a sense of "faith in exile" inspires careful attention to those obligations and lifestyle issues that set them apart from the surrounding culture. Attendance to the five daily cycles of prayer, attentiveness to an Islamic diet, and observance of other obligatory aspects such as dress serve to both strengthen the faith of the Islamic family and nurture the vitality and affirmation of family bonds. To this end, the family unit has been a source of spiritual vitality, personal security, and affirmation of the tradition as a whole.

Muslim families in the region strongly emphasize the rearing of children within the parameters of Islam as well as achievement of excellence in education. This can create an ironic conflict for families, since youthful accomplishments call attention to their Muslim identity, contrasting with the desire of many in the Islamic community in Appalachia to maintain a low profile.

The sacred rites of marriage and death illustrate the central importance of family and community of Muslims in the region. In most Islamic nations, marriages are arranged through familial negotiation and contractual agreement, but this is not always the practice among Appalachia's Muslims. While young people are strongly encouraged to marry within the Islamic community, individuals choose their partners in the same manner as non-Muslims in the United States. Once a couple has expressed a desire to marry, however, their families meet to conclude a marriage contract. Thus, consent of the families as commanded in the Qur'an is still essential. Family units are unusually stable in comparison with most families in the region, and divorce and spousal abuse are rare.

Death and the associated rituals pose more challenges for Muslims in the region. Islamic tradition requires that the body be washed and buried as soon as possible and forbids embalming. The stress upon the family as a result of a death is exacerbated by the separation of Muslims across the region, as well as the distance between mosques. The larger Islamic community performs a pivotal supportive role during these times of crisis. Muslims in larger cities, such as Charleston, West Virginia, Knoxville, Tennessee, and Pittsburgh, as well as some smaller ones, such as Johnson City, Tennessee, and Richmond, Kentucky, where there are significant Muslim populations, have established mosques and forged religious communities. Some have also established Islamic schools.

Holidays also underscore the importance of family and community networks among Appalachian Muslims. Ramadan is a sacred time during which the family comes together on a daily basis, especially in breaking the daily fast at evening. The community meets for a meal and prayer as required at Ramadan. These obligations emphasize the importance of family as well as the bonds between family and mosque.

As is the case with the whole of the United States, the cultural and social fabric of Appalachia is being changed by the influence of secularism. Muslim families in the region tend to share the religious, cultural, and social conservatism of Appalachia as a whole. Islamic families strive to frustrate encroaching secularism upon children and youth in the same manner as do Christian families. Islamic families in the region are especially concerned over increasingly overt sexuality in American culture. This concern is important given the distinct regulations relative to sexuality found in the Qur'an. To this end, Muslim families in Appalachia share an often invisible, uneasy, but genuine alliance with conservative Protestant Christians in the region. However, Christian communities in the region often fail to appreciate the extraordinary emphasis upon the family and related values found among Muslims.

See also: SECTION OVERVIEW (RELIGION).

—Yousif Elhindi and Michael Pinner, *East Tennessee State University*

Steven D. Martin, *Muslims in Appalachia: Islam in Exile*, Films for the Humanities and Sciences videocassette (2001).

Eleanor Roosevelt at Arthurdale, West Virginia, c. 1930s. Arthurdale became the first experimental community in Appalachia developed under President Franklin D. Roosevelt's New Deal.

New Deal Communities

Between 1933 and 1943, the United States government under the leadership of President Franklin D. Roosevelt developed ninety-nine back-to-the-land subsistence communities designed to improve the lives of those hardest hit by the Great Depression. Seventeen of these New Deal communities were built in the Appalachian region at a cost of approximately $22 million. As a result of new federal policies and swift executive action, 2,099 Appalachian families resettled into self-help, subsistence homesteads.

The first and most controversial publicly funded New Deal community in the Appalachian region was Arthurdale, near Morgantown, West Virginia. Because of its notoriety, Arthurdale, encompassing 165 homesteads specifically developed for economically dislocated or stranded coal miners, was the most extensively documented of the New Deal communities in the region. Four similar communities developed in Appalachia were Cumberland Homesteads, with 262 homesteads near Crossville, Tennessee; Tygart Valley Homesteads, with 195 homesteads near Elkins, West Virginia; Westmoreland (Norvelt) Homesteads, with 255 homesteads near Greensburg, Pennsylvania; and Red House Homesteads, with 150 homesteads in Red House (now Eleanor), West Virginia.

Throughout the 1920s, Appalachia was plagued by the closing of coal mines, and during the late 1920s and early 1930s the United States slipped into the most severe economic downturn in its history. The Great Depression increased the suffering of the region's families and resulted in some of the worst poverty seen by relief organizations. Appalachian communities threatened to spiral into chaos.

The federal government's action in Appalachia dates to 1931, when President Herbert Hoover requested the Children's Bureau to conduct a study of the living conditions in coal communities. The extreme poverty and despair revealed by the study provided the impetus for President Hoover to request assistance from the American Friends Service Committee, the service wing of the Quakers. The executive director of the organization was Clarence Pickett, later instrumental in the development of Arthurdale. This organization's rehabilitation of poverty-stricken coal communities began with child-feeding programs. By the winter of 1931–32, the American Friends Service Committee was providing food to forty thousand children a day. In Monongalia County in northern West Virginia alone, the group fed three thousand children.

When President Roosevelt took office in 1933, the federal government promised an immediate and comprehensive response to the crippling poverty affecting coal communities. The New Deal communities program was put forth as a self-help, subsistence strategy focused on alleviating the absolute poverty of communities, families, and individuals in the Appalachian region. A precedent for publicly funded back-to-the-land subsistence homesteading existed in Europe, but no such effort had ever been attempted in the United States. According to Canadian researcher Richard Harris, the first national programs sponsoring self-help, subsistence community building had been implemented more than a decade earlier in Austria and Germany. Back-to-the-land homesteading was described as a safety net for those most in need who could not access the free-enterprise system.

One influential school of thought during the inception of the publicly funded homesteading programs promoted economic and social welfare programs targeted at geographically unified regions. The Regional Planning Association of America, organized in the 1920s, advocated planning techniques developed by Britain's Garden City movement, which extended beyond buildings and streets into the ways in which people interact socially and economically. The movement was specifically oriented to combining the best elements of both rural and urban environments.

With modern transportation and decentralized industry, planned communities could be organized around the needs of people and could draw city dwellers away from the unhealthy urban environment. In a more rural setting, residents could enjoy the economic and health benefits of raising fruits, vegetables, and livestock from personal plots and yet be close to functionally designed community services and employment. The resettling of people from impoverished and often unsanitary urban conditions into rural planned communities with plentiful services became a natural extension of the Regional Planning Association of America's creed.

Relocation of people into planned communities also appealed to those who would move into the new subsistence homesteads. Rural industrial workers often supplemented their family income by producing fruits and vegetables from the family garden. Thus, resettlement from a company-owned coal camp plot to a self-owned homestead was viewed by low-income families as an opportunity to attain the "American dream" and fit neatly into the American self-help ethic of rugged individualism.

By the early 1930s, a number of factors converged into a national homestead movement. The depression and its resulting deprivation; the knowledge of the international, publicly aided community-development experimentation; the influence that new domestic organizations interested in city and regional planning had on public policy; and the American tradition of self-help all coalesced to form this movement. The convergence of these factors almost ensured the establishment of subsistence homestead communities programs. The most influential factor in the establishment of the program, however, was the support of President Roosevelt and First Lady Eleanor Roosevelt.

With the election of Roosevelt, progressives swept into the U.S. government, envisioning a larger role for the federal government in the lives of Americans. A few of these progressives were utopian and saw the depression as proof of capitalism's demise. However, most were simply looking for an alternative, more cooperative, and humane capitalist model for urban and rural communities. With vision and aggressive action, the Roosevelts sought to supplant the piecemeal and chaotic private development so prevalent in the industrial urban environment with a modern, publicly planned model of cooperative community development.

The cooperative communities envisioned by the Roosevelts would be developed into subsistence homesteads where low-income families farmed their land while working part-time in a cooperative community enterprise or industry. The back-to-the-land subsistence homesteading programs thus became one of the rural housing and employment programs of the New Deal. Although legislation specifically written to fund such New Deal communities was not popular enough to receive congressional support, the subsistence-homesteading program was made part of the National Industrial Recovery Act. In 1933 the act was passed, and Section 208, Title II provided $25 million for the movement of industrial workers back to the land.

Secretary of the Interior Harold L. Ickes was responsible for implementing the New Deal subsistence-homesteading community program. Ickes chose agricultural economist M. L. Wilson to lead the new program, and on August 23, 1933, the Division of Subsistence Homesteads was established. Little precedent existed for a government-funded, planned community with mixed community and private enterprise. Thus, the true experimentation had begun. The resulting communities would embrace some of the most idealistic, if not utopian, principles.

The principles espoused by the Roosevelts, Wilson, land-use planners, sociologists, and economists held much promise. Families left economically stranded by the depression could choose to move onto a subsistence plot, where they would live a more dignified life based in farming, crafts, and industrial enterprise and in doing so create a more cooperative and civic-minded community.

In contrast, Republican congressional conservatives rejected many aspects of the Division of Subsistence Homestead's New Deal community-development efforts. The Republicans were fervently against publicly funded, centrally planned communities; they were particularly opposed to government-sponsored decentralization of industry. In reference to the first homesteading experiment initiated by Roosevelt's Division of Subsistence Homesteads (the Jersey Homesteads), historian Paul K. Conkin recounts the words of a *Philadelphia Inquirer* editorial: "The American taxpayer is putting up $1.8 million to erect a model of a Russian Soviet commune half way between New York and Philadelphia." Conservatives loudly complained that features of the publicly funded New Deal communities were Communist at worst and socialistic at best.

Arthurdale, the second project approved for development by the Division of Subsistence Homesteads, became the first of Appalachia's experimental communities. Although controversy surrounded all the New Deal communities, few received as much attention as Arthurdale. The West Virginia experiment in cooperative community development served as a lightning rod for conservatives, who perceived much of the New Deal as subversive and anti-American. With the enthusiastic support of Eleanor Roosevelt, however, Arthurdale became a reality.

From the beginning, Arthurdale was plagued by many problems, not least of which were cost overruns. Each homestead was to cost $2,500, but eventually the cost mounted to more than $8,000. Many attributed the inflated cost to a lack of planning. In his diary, Ickes maintained that federal action in the development of Arthurdale occurred too quickly for sufficient planning to have been conducted. The first well-publicized problem resulted from the purchase of prefabricated cottages that did not fit the prepared foundations. The houses also lacked the sturdy construction needed for the cold weather of the area.

While some of the problems were confined to Arthurdale, the challenge of attracting industry and creating jobs plagued all the New Deal communities. Although the problem seemed simple, it proved to be insurmountable, despite the efforts of Wilson, Eleanor Roosevelt, and others. Many industries contacted found such a move to be economically infeasible. Eleanor Roosevelt worked to move government-supported industry to Arthurdale, but opposition in Congress prevented it. Numerous attempts at industry within the community failed. The problem involving the decentralization of existing industry was the most experimental and controversial aspect of the Arthurdale community and assured steady criticism from antagonistic Republicans and industry leaders. Neither of these groups believed in the value of decentralizing industry or publicly funded subsistence homesteading.

The American Friends Service Committee had recognized the problem of providing longterm employment to those who had been stranded without work in Appalachia in the early days of the depression. The group's experiment in community cooperative craft enterprising led to the formation of the Mountain Craftsmen Cooperative Association. By embracing local craftsmen's products and by training other people in weaving, furniture making, shoe repair, and other trades, the American Friends Service Committee worked to create at least a partial solution to the problems of unemployment. The association also recognized the need to diversify the local economy to protect the community from extreme economic decline resulting from the failure of a single industry. Eleanor Roosevelt was particularly supportive of the American Friends Service Committee's effort to create a craft industry.

Part-time employment in craft enterprising offered a way for families to supplement their incomes and proved to meet loftier goals as well. A cooperative craft industry in Arthurdale provided the way for communities working together to strengthen their social fabric. A craft industry also promised to revive handmade crafts and in doing so revived some of the workmanship that had been lost to factory-produced products. These lessons from the Arthurdale experiment later assisted the American Friends Service Committee in the development of Penn-Craft, Pennsylvania, the first privately funded New Deal–era self-help subsistence community.

By the mid-1930s, American Friends Service Committee leaders who had served in the New Deal's Resettlement Administration decided to create a more efficient, bottom-up approach to community building in the Appalachian region. In 1936 a two-hundred-acre farm in southwestern Pennsylvania was purchased with private grants from various sources including the United Mine Workers of America and the U.S. Steel Corporation. The Penn-Craft experiment in self-help, subsistence homesteading proved to be successful. This model for community building has been replicated throughout the world.

Depending upon one's perspective, Arthurdale, similar to the other New Deal communities, may be viewed as either a success or a failure in publicly funded community development. The economist may believe its failure was in its very cost; the conservative thinker may contend that the government had no responsibility developing communities and that philanthropic organizations are better equipped to provide relief programs; the progressive may believe that the best efforts of the New Deal enthusiasts could have been much more successful if opponents had not refused to accept the experimental nature of the program; and the homesteader may believe that the failure lay in the government's inability to create swift, effective action.

No matter how the effort is viewed, life improved for many who participated in the New Deal experiment. As detailed in the 1941 *Yearbook of the National Association of Housing Officials*, a survey of 1,106 families within nineteen New Deal communities suggested that family living conditions, possessions, and income had improved. In the end, the homesteading communities provided a home, a small plot on which to raise vegetables, fruit, and small animals, and a more cooperative community where families could live with increased dignity.

By 1943, the New Deal community-development movement had expired. Congress voted to end public support and ordered the sale of the homesteads and community properties. The federal Public Housing Authority, which remained the creditor for the homesteads, quickly began transferring deeds to individual homeowners who paid off their loans early. Any real government interest in the communities ended by 1948, when the selling of the subsistence homesteads was complete.

Conkin wrote that paramount to the New Deal were the idealistic people drawn into government service. In his view, they were "the glory of the New Deal . . . molded more in the humane image of Eleanor Roosevelt than that of her political husband. . . . [They were] the dreamers . . . [who] designed homesteads in Appalachia."

See also: ARTHURDALE, WEST VIRGINIA (ARCHITECTURE); CUMBERLAND HOMESTEADS (ARCHITECTURE); PLANNED COMMUNITIES.

—Louis E. Orslene, *West Virginia University*

Paul K. Conkin, *Tomorrow a New World: The New Deal Community Program* (1959); Stephen Edward Haid, "Arthurdale: An Experiment in Community Planning, 1933–1947," Ph.D. dissertation, West Virginia University (1975); Richard S. and Margaret Little, *Arthurdale: Its History, Its Lesson for Today* (1976).

Norris, Tennessee

See Norris Dam and Village (Architecture); Planned Communities

Oak Ridge, Tennessee

See Oak Ridge National Laboratory (Business, Industry, and Technology)

Parents' Days

The idea for special days to honor parents and grandparents originated in West Virginia. Mother's Day was inspired by Ann Marie Reeves Jarvis, the mother of twelve children. In 1907, two years after her death, one of her daughters, Anna Jarvis, held a memorial service for her. That first service was followed with a more public recognition. Mother's Day became a West Virginia holiday in 1910 and was observed nationally in 1914. Jarvis incorporated the Mother's Day International Association and turned her efforts overseas, hoping to inaugurate simple, worldwide celebrations.

Five of Ann Marie Jarvis's children died of epidemic diseases, and only four lived to adulthood. She learned how diseases spread and visited towns in what was then a united Virginia, educating women and forming Mother's Day Work Clubs, which focused on nursing care. She also worked for reconciliation among families split between the Union and the Confederacy when the western part of Virginia aligned itself with the North. After the Civil War, she used honoring motherhood as a healing salve, sponsoring Mother's Friendship Days.

In America, people used the celebration of motherhood as a political tool; both opponents and proponents of women's right to vote worked it into speeches. As the day became commercialized, Anna Jarvis fought florists and bakers who capitalized on sentiment, and she threatened to sue organizers of a festival because of the fear of commercial exploitation. She battled against preprinted greeting cards and protested carnation sales by the American War Mothers in the 1930s. Near the end of her life, she told a reporter she was sorry she had started the observance at all. But by then it was well established and is celebrated in more than forty countries.

From Washington State, Sonora Smart Dodd witnessed what she saw as success with Mother's Day and in 1910 petitioned for a day to honor fathers. It caught on, though it took until 1972 for President Richard Nixon to permanently establish the June holiday.

Marian H. McQuade of Oak Hill, West Virginia, founded Grandparents' Day. McQuade grew up on a farm with her grandmother, whose habit was to visit the community's sick and elderly. McQuade, a mother of fifteen, adopted the habit. She worked with senior citizens, serving on committees such as the West Virginia Commission on Aging. While organizing the state's Past Eighty Party, she came in contact with lonely nursing home residents and began campaigning for a day to honor shut-ins. A day honoring the elderly, and grandparents in particular, carried more public appeal, passing the West Virginia legislature in 1973. In 1978 President Jimmy Carter declared the first Sunday after Labor Day to be National Grandparents' Day. McQuade and her husband, Joe, funded much of the promotion for the holiday themselves, suggesting it should be celebrated by studying the family tree, talking to grandparents about their talents, and visiting nursing homes.

See also: CALENDAR CUSTOMS (FOLKLORE AND FOLKLIFE).

—Madelyn Rosenberg, *Roanoke Times*

James P. Johnson, "Death, Grief and Motherhood: The Woman Who Inspired Mother's Day," *West Virginia History* (January–April 1978); Marie Tyler-McGraw, "'But After All Was She Not a Masterpiece as a Mother and a Gentlewoman . . . ,'" *Goldenseal Magazine* (October–November 1977); Donald W. Wyatt, "National Grandparents' Day Originated in W.Va.," *Wonderful West Virginia* (September 1995).

Planned Communities

As the name implies, planned communities are neighborhoods that a private developer or government entity plans prior to the construction of the infrastructure and buildings. Such developments are generally classified by function and design and include: company towns (also known as natural resources towns); new towns (on urban planner Ebenezer Howard's Garden City model); single-product towns; energy towns; project construction towns; military towns; resort towns; development towns; satellite towns; land subdivisions; and gated communities. Theoretically, community planning optimizes the use of land resources and promotes conservation of green spaces; however, this ideal has been the exception throughout the history of urban development in the United States. Most towns develop haphazardly as populations grow and industry waxes or wanes. Appalachian experience in community planning follows this nationwide trend, yet examples of the various types of planned communities exist within its boundaries, including some of the most famous planned communities in the United States.

The first colonial towns were laid out in grid patterns, but in the Appalachians the rugged terrain made this type of layout impractical. The closest approximation occurred when a land speculator acquired a large parcel of land. After setting aside a few lots for community buildings such as a school, church, or store that the speculator owned and operated, the rest of the land was sold as small farms to settlers entering the region.

Many of the earliest planned communities were company towns established to provide housing for the labor force that companies needed to conduct their operations. As the name suggests, a company town was developed to accommodate the needs of a single industrial firm. Traditionally, the company owned the factory or mine that provided employment to the town's residents, the houses in which the workers and their families lived, and the stores where the inhabitants acquired the goods they needed. Due to the geographic isolation of company towns, inhabitants were completely dependent on the company for all commercial, medical, educational, and recreational needs. The company often reinforced this dependency by paying its workers in scrip, which was accepted only in the company store. The company profited from the exploitation of both human and natural resources. The profit motive and general disregard for longterm consequences frequently led to extreme environmental pollution in these communities, with detrimental effects on the health of residents. The numerous coal towns in central Appalachia provide excellent examples of this type of community.

At the beginning of the twentieth century, English town planner Ebenezer Howard consolidated many of the historical principles of community planning into the "new town" concept, in which local, state, or federal governments usually own (or subsidize) and control development. The dominant characteristic of new towns is a greenbelt (farmland or undeveloped forest) that completely encircles the hamlet. Maintaining the greenbelt prevents expansion and limits the population. The area within the greenbelt is zoned by purpose: residential, commercial, and light industrial. Farming and light industry provide employment for the residents, theoretically making new towns self-contained and self-sufficient.

Howard's theories were not used for community development in America until the Great Depression and Franklin D. Roosevelt's New Deal programs provided an economic incentive to establish subsistence homestead communities. The governing concept behind the subsistence homestead communities was to combine cottage industries with subsistence farming to provide economic support for stranded communities, typically company towns abandoned when the company closed during the depression.

To obtain housing through the homestead program, potential tenants were required to demonstrate some kind of income, a moderate net worth, good moral character, and the potential to be a successful farmer. In exchange for the opportunity to purchase a home and land for a low price at a low interest rate, the tenants had to submit to inspection, obtain permission to alter the property in any way, and submit monthly reports through the homeowners' association.

Construction of Arthurdale, near Reedsville, West Virginia, the first and most famous of the depression-era subsistence homesteads, began in 1933. The development became a pet project of Eleanor Roosevelt in her quest to teach people "how to live." To this end, the planners implemented a consumer and producer cooperative, health and education initiatives, and a handicrafts program. Further south, in Cumberland Homesteads near Crossville, Tennessee, all citizens, adults as well as children, attended school.

The houses at Arthurdale and Cumberland were typical of all houses constructed as part of the various homestead projects. Each was situated in the middle of one- to three-acre lots, providing room for gardens, a chicken coop, a pigsty, and a barn, while preventing subdivision of the lots. The houses boasted all the modern conveniences: paneled walls, hardwood floors, copper plumbing, brass fixtures, and a bathroom, and the lots included a well and septic tank.

The original goal of the Greenbelt Project, also initiated during the depression, was the construction of twenty-five communities using Howard's principles. Only three of these cities were actually completed: Greenbelt, Maryland; Greenhills, Ohio; and Greendale, Wisconsin. Although none of these communities fall within Appalachia, many of the same principles were used in the planning of Norris, Tennessee, an excellent example of the project construction town.

Tracy B. Augur, branch chief of regional and town planning in the Tennessee Valley Authority's Division of Land Planning and Housing, coordinated the planning and construction of Norris. The primary function of the town was to provide housing for workers of the Norris Dam project and their families. The common occupation of the original residents promoted a sense of community among the residents that was rare in the homestead towns.

Of the 4,200 acres in the town proper, only 1,000 acres were used for housing, community buildings, and commercial facilities. A school, shopping center, post office, and library met the various needs of the residents. Town planners designated a portion of the town for use by small industry. The goal was to create a light industrial and agricultural base that would sustain the community after the completion of the dam project. Although this plan was no more successful financially than other homestead communities, the construction of the Norris Freeway, connecting Norris to Knoxville, enabled residents of the small community to seek employment in the city. In this manner, Norris evolved into a residential suburb of Knoxville.

Most suburbs are haphazardly planned as real estate developers purchase land adjacent to cities and construct subdivisions and the support infrastructure to earn profit. The Levittowns constructed during the 1950s exemplify this most common type of planned community in the United States. Levitt and Sons, primarily house builders, purchased large quantities of land in areas where there was a high demand for housing. They then constructed houses using the principles of mass production: specialized labor, strict time schedule, precut lumber, and prepackaged materials. They increased the market appeal of their houses by constructing them in neighborhoods on dead-end streets and by providing a village green, school, shopping center, playground, swimming pool, and other amenities for the community. Although the goal of the Levitts was to earn a profit by building houses in attractive neighborhoods, they set the standard for community development throughout the United States during the last half of the twentieth century.

During the 1980s, Appalachian developers took advantage of the increasing concern about the safety of urban environments to create exclusive gated communities. For the most part, these communities followed the Levitts' principles but added a fence or wall to segregate the community from the larger urban environment and to prevent anyone but residents from entering the community.

As life expectancy increases, another type of planned community is gaining popularity in the mountains: retirement communities. These communities are also exclusive, often limiting residency to senior citizens. Services such as laundry, on-site nurses, and transportation help to increase the length of time that seniors can retain their independence. These communities are often expensive and therefore limited to the upper middle class.

See also: NEW DEAL COMMUNITIES; NORRIS DAM AND VILLAGE (ARCHITECTURE); PLANNED INDUSTRIAL TOWNS (ARCHITECTURE).

—Annette McGrew, *Winchester, Kentucky*

Diane Ghirardo, *Building New Communities: New Deal America and Fascist Italy* (1989); Gideon Golany, *New Town Planning: Principles and Practice* (1976); Michael J. McDonald and John Muldowny, *TVA and the Dispossessed* (1982).

Planned Industrial Towns

See Planned Industrial Towns (Architecture)

Pregnancy and Childbirth

In the eighteenth and nineteenth centuries, rural Appalachian women had little contact with formally trained, typically male physicians. Instead, granny midwives and female family members generally assisted in the delivery of babies and guided younger, less experienced women through pregnancy. By the early twentieth century, however, Appalachian women, like other females across the United States and the Western world, were increasingly reliant on formally educated physicians.

Although trained medical doctors dominated the scientific journals and the state departments of health that guided maternal and infant care in the first decades of the twentieth century, Appalachian women continued to play a role in pregnancy and delivery. With the help of state programs aimed at providing essential education, doctors used lay midwives, also called granny midwives, to help reduce maternal and infant mortality and morbidity rates. By promoting antiseptic and aseptic practices and urging midwives to refer problem cases to physicians, medical practitioners relied upon granny midwives to carry a modern message. At the same time, the formally educated nurse-midwives of the Frontier Nursing Service, established by Mary Breckinridge in Leslie County, Kentucky, in 1925, set a national standard for nurse-midwifery education and services.

Throughout the twentieth century, Appalachian governments and community groups, embarrassed by maternal and infant mortality statistics, provided more facilities, personnel, and resources to health departments and hospitals for prenatal and perinatal services. Through the local affiliates of such national projects as the Women, Infants, and Children nutrition program and the March of Dimes, public and private reformers struggled to increase knowledge, to further the reliance of Appalachian women on contemporary methods of medical care, and, by default, to weaken reliance on traditional cultural beliefs and practices. Access to modern prenatal care, increased literacy, and the improved economic status of many women have undermined cultural mountain influences and belief systems related to pregnancy. While nurse-midwives still oversee some home deliveries, most Appalachian women of the twenty-first century prefer delivering in hospitals. Those who prefer home deliveries tend to be individuals following an alternative lifestyle.

Although women still listen to their mothers and mothers-in-law regarding pregnancy and childbirth, they are less likely to follow the advice of the older generation, nonrelatives, or men. At the close of the twentieth century, most Appalachian women ignored such old prenatal warnings as "don't eat popcorn or you will cut the baby" or "don't bathe or you will drown the baby," and the practice of putting an axe or knife under the mattress of a birthing woman "to cut the pain" had become almost extinct. However, milder admonitions not to lift anything heavy, attend funerals, or laugh at another's misfortune while pregnant were still given some consideration.

Ironically, old-fashioned breast-feeding came to be promoted more enthusiastically by contemporary health professionals than by family members, perhaps because bottle-feeding is viewed by modern Appalachian women as an essential convenience. In the area of baby care, the placing of a flannel bellyband with a coin over the navel to prevent umbilical hernia is still recommended by some grandmothers in the region.

One of the longest-standing traditions about pregnancy relates to predicting a baby's sex. Expectant mothers may suspend a wedding ring or other object on a hair or string over the mother's abdomen or waist and watch how it swings—either in a circle or back and forth. Even with ultrasound imaging to reveal a fetus's gender, some women in the region may still rely on other means to verify the baby's sex.

See also: FRONTIER NURSING SERVICE (HEALTH); GRANNIES, MIDWIVES, AND HEALERS (IMAGES AND ICONS); MATERNAL AND INFANT HEALTH OUTREACH WORKER PROGRAM (HEALTH).

—Sharon L. Jacques, *Western Carolina University*

Alexander D. Allaire, Merry K. Moos, and Stephen R. Wells, "Complementary and Alternative Medicine in Pregnancy: A Survey of North Carolina Certified Nurse-Midwives," *Obstetrics and Gynecology* (January 2000); Patricia D. Beaver, *Rural Community in the Appalachian South* (1986).

Urban Out-Migration Families

See Appalachian Social Issues outside the Region (Urban Appalachian Experience)

Volunteer Fire Departments

Arising from the need to reduce the response time to fires in rural areas, volunteer fire departments in Appalachia are grassroots institutions founded on participatory democracy and community spirit. Volunteer fire departments are largely self-sustaining. With no tax base for support, entire Appalachian counties lack paid fire departments. Some departments receive funding through a fire tax if registered voters within the fire district consent. Despite money from occasional county and state grant allocations, members of volunteer departments spend most of their time raising funds, not fighting fires. Site development and firehouse construction are achieved through voluntary labor and pooled resources. Stations are centrally located where possible; fire districts lie within a five-mile radius. Leadership is formed of elected officers, and membership is limited by an individual's ability to donate time as well as state requirements. Though members of an independent organization, volunteer firefighters must comply with state regulations on age and education. Certification classes and proper documentation of fire responses are mandatory.

The founding of the first organized volunteer fire department by Benjamin Franklin in Philadelphia in 1736, almost one hundred years after the establishment of paid firefighters in cities such as New Amsterdam (New York City) and Boston, began a trend that inspired the creation of the first volunteer fire departments in Appalachia toward the end of the eighteenth century. Though urban areas, including those in Appalachia (such as Pittsburgh in 1869), began to hire career firefighters in the last half of the nineteenth century, rural areas remained dependent on volunteer services. Recent studies, though, demonstrate that between 1983 and 1999, the number of volunteer firefighters in Appalachia as well as the rest of the country declined while the number of paid firefighters increased. Researchers cite stringent state and federal training policies, lack of free time due to employment, lack of funding for training and equipment, and lack of community pride as reasons for the decline in volunteer participation.

When the terrorist attacks against America perpetrated by Islamic fundamentalists led by Osama bin Laden occurred on September 11, 2001, the Shanksville Volunteer Fire Company in Pennsylvania was called to the wreckage of

United Flight 93, which crashed into their service area. The department subsequently received donations that allowed them to purchase a new engine that could carry twice as much water as their previous one. Awareness of the importance of volunteer firefighters must increase as it did in Shanksville, or many volunteer departments will fold.

Special challenges in Appalachia include lack of consistent water sources. Because many areas have few or no hydrants, firefighting strategies require special equipment to transport water long distances. Cooperation among neighboring departments is not unusual. Volunteer fire departments further community development. Often in exchange for a donation, they may provide a secular location for social events. Homeowners' insurance rates are lower for residents within the fire district. As firefighters are usually first on the scene in emergencies, creation of medical response units within volunteer fire departments is a growing trend.

See also: SECTION OVERVIEW.

—Caroline E. Knight, *Appalachian State University*

Women's Groups

In the years following the American Revolution, a spirit of republicanism elevated women as keepers of public virtue and guardians of the moral climate of the nation. Translating the vision into practical reality, women organized societies through which they could begin to influence their communities without renouncing their commitment to domestic responsibilities. Organized by both whites and free blacks throughout the nation as well as in Appalachia, the earliest groups were benevolent societies designed to help the deserving poor. The changes and disruptions of social and economic patterns came amidst rapid expansion of the new nation. Growing poverty, as well as wealth, increased immigration, escalating crime, and immorality spawned another spiritual revival as the nineteenth century began. During the Great Western Revival, also known as the Second Great Awakening, the numbers and kinds of women's auxiliaries proliferated. Post–Civil War turmoil provided yet another impetus for the growth and development of women's organizations. In addition to the traditional benevolence societies and church-based groups, auxiliaries were organized around community needs, political issues, and cultural and socioeconomic bonds.

In the first half of the nineteenth century, these auxiliary groups, most often rooted in the church, became vehicles through which women offered aid to their congregations and communities. By providing food, education, counseling, money, medicine, and prayer, Appalachian women were able to set aside solely domestic roles for a limited place in the male-monopolized public sphere. Although it had been long considered unseemly for women to act in a businesslike manner, nineteenth-century organizations universally adopted written constitutions, a means of collecting money through dues, and rules for membership. Women used the money they raised (often of their own donations) to help allay church debt, fund missionary work, and provide for the needs of their congregations and communities. Though women were initially chastised by both husbands and church officials for crossing gender lines, over time these services came to be accepted as within the scope of women's work.

In Appalachia, the temperance movement grew out of women's crusades in the post–Civil War years. By 1874, the Woman's Christian Temperance Union had become the first mass women's movement, promoting Christian living, temperance, abstinence, and prohibition. Frances E. Willard, who served as president from 1879 to 1898, broadened the organization's moral and social agenda under what she called the "Do Everything" policy. This included Americanization efforts, public health and welfare, woman suffrage, substance abuse prevention, opposition to prostitution and pornography, and domestic violence prevention.

During the Woman's Christian Temperance Union's "grandest days," from the 1900s to 1930s, forty-three states had active state and local chapters, including all states in the Appalachian region. West Virginia's chapter was notable because of its high state membership and its socialization and Americanization efforts in the 1920s. In Morgantown, the group built a Community Building in 1922 as a place for conducting organizational affairs and as a location where women could gather or wait while their husbands did business around town. The building also contained sleeping rooms for single women, an auditorium, and a gymnasium. While chapters in other Appalachian communities provided humanitarian efforts, the Morgantown Community Building provided a central location for the Woman's Christian Temperance Union's social services. One of its projects specifically targeted the large Italian population in northern West Virginia by providing baby clinics, vaccination programs, mother's clubs, English classes, and American cooking classes. Though the union began as an organization for women, membership often included men and children. Still in existence at the start of the twenty-first century, the national platform promotes total abstinence from drugs, alcohol, and premarital sex.

Various sororal associations appearing in the mid-nineteenth century also encouraged women's domestic and traditional interests. Racially segregated and linked to male fraternal associations, these groups served to unite women by giving them a sense of sisterhood through secret rituals grounded in Christianity, mutual goals, and social activities. They provided leadership opportunities for women and used membership dues to establish homes for orphans and the elderly, as well as to develop programs that offered health care and death benefits for members' families before company pensions and government programs provided such assistance.

Sororal activities in West Virginia are typical of those found elsewhere in Appalachia. In Fairmont, West Virginia, members of the Order of Pythian Sisters, organized in 1888 as the auxiliary of the Knights of Pythias, sent financial aid, food, and other assistance to their sisters in Mononagah after the 1907 mine disaster. In 1910 the Daughters of Rebekah, organized in 1851 as the auxiliary for the Independent Order of Odd Fellows, dedicated a home in Elkins for the widows and orphans of Odd Fellows and their elderly members. In 1912 the Pythian Sisters supported ratification of the prohibition amendment to West Virginia's state constitution, and in 1927 the Daughters of Rebekah endorsed the "National Kindergarten Movement."

In the nineteenth century, Appalachian coal miners and railroad workers participated in the growing labor movement. Unions did not welcome women members, who consequently formed auxiliaries that were perceived as extensions of their conventional domestic roles. The members, wives, daughters, and mothers of union men, used their loosely organized groups to support their men and participate in the labor movement. Although they remained under the authority of male union members, the women's activities often extended beyond the workplace and into the community, especially where companies provided housing, health services, stores, and resources for community living. In the 1920s these auxiliaries were effective in working for government creation of local health departments and maternal and child health programs.

In 1929 women led a major textile mill strike in Elizabethton, Tennessee, protesting low wages, petty rules, and high-handed attitudes. They demanded equal treatment with male workers. Coal miners' wives also played important roles in strikes. When the miners in Harlan County, Kentucky, were faced with cuts in hours and pay in 1931–32, they demanded a strike that the United Mine Workers of America declined to support. Many of the miners responded by joining the National Miners Union, which supported the strike and assisted the miners by setting up more local chapters, women's auxiliaries, and soup kitchens.

In West Virginia, Ruth Voithofer Newell, a daughter and sister of union coal miners, returned to the coalfields after graduating from the College of Wooster in Ohio and set up educational programs for miners and their families in the late 1930s. The classes covered labor history, health, education, legislation, and consumer issues. The West Virginia Council of Women's Auxiliaries was an outgrowth of this program.

Appalachian women fought for and eventually gained union membership as they became wage earners in the mills and mines. In the 1940s, their numbers increased steadily, and by the 1950s an estimated three million were union members while another million women belonged to labor auxiliaries and through them participated in the union movement.

Auxiliary women became political advocates in 1973 as economic vulnerability and dependent household status pushed them to action in Brookside, Kentucky. The Brookside Women's Club operated its own strike actions that were often separate from the union-planned strategy. Their primary activity was to maintain a picket line twenty-four hours a day. Many union members disapproved of the auxiliary's activities, but the women organized so that they could meet their traditional responsibilities and participate on the picket line. The active role of the Brookside Women's Club resonated beyond the community, attracting national media attention.

In the 1970s, a window opened for women who wanted to be hired in traditionally male jobs that paid more and had better benefits, and three different women's organizations helped women seize the opportunity. The Coal Employment Project targeted coal mines, the Southeast Women's Employment Coalition focused on highway jobs, and Women and Employment took on the building trades in West Virginia. Each of these organizations sought to empower women by helping them obtain jobs and to support them as they faced obstacles created by men who expected passivity and acquiescence from women. These nontraditional advocacy groups used the various civil and employment rights laws passed during Jimmy Carter's presidency in their efforts to fight discrimination and create new organizational models of resistance. For example, during the Pittston coal strike of 1989–90, women of the United Mine Workers of America auxiliaries set up picket lines, got arrested, organized meals for supporters, conducted jail vigils, informed the public, and staged a peaceful occupation of the company's Virginia headquarters. Calling themselves the Daughters of Mother Jones in honor of the labor advocate who had fought against company owners for more than fifty years, they gave women a new sense of power. Many of the members remained politically active in the years that followed.

The evolution of women's auxiliaries from the close of the eighteenth century to the beginning of the twenty-first century reflects broad changes in the role and status of women in Appalachia. The benevolent societies that appeared in the 1790s shaped the future of women's organizations as they grew more complex and diverse. In the nineteenth century, poverty spread while local governments lagged behind in providing the means for obtaining food, clothing, and medical care. Women's church groups, sororal associations, and labor auxiliaries created community institutions: orphanages, schools, employment services, and homes for wayward girls and the aged. In time, women gained greater self-awareness and a collective voice that called the government to account for social welfare and reform. Women's groups such as the labor auxiliaries provided career opportunities and ways for members to acquire the skills and experience needed to exert political power. Twenty-first-century women in Appalachia, whether rural or urban, still make use of voluntary auxiliaries to achieve political and social change through their collective power.

In 1993 the Appalachian Women's Alliance was formed to network women and girls in several states, including West Virginia, Virginia, Kentucky, Tennessee, Ohio, and North Carolina. By empowering members individually and collectively, the alliance attempts to change institutions that foster economic, physical, and cultural violence towards women. The organization sets up "local circles" in communities through which members can build self-esteem and leadership skills. Besides publishing the *Appalachian Women's Journal*, the group sponsors an annual Sister Gathering and since 1994 has led a Women's Caravan through the mountains, advocating nonviolence against women and raising awareness of women's issues. The group's Ironweed Festival is held annually to bring together artists and activists to exchange visions and build solidarity for social change.

See also: COAL TOWNS; FAMILY RELATIONSHIPS AND GENDER ROLES; WOMEN'S ROLES.

—Meredith Dean, *Floyd, Virginia;* Suzanne R. Gosden and Barbara J. Howe, *West Virginia University;* Clara Hasbrouck and Sändra Henson, *East Tennessee State University;* and Lori Riverstone, *University of Tennessee*

Marat Moore, *Women in the Mines: Stories of Life and Work* (1996); Anne Firor Scott, *Natural Allies: Women's Associations in American History* (1991); Barbara Ellen Smith, ed., *Neither Separate nor Equal: Women, Race, and Class in the South* (1999).

Women's Roles

Absentee owners of timber and mineral rights dominated the economy of the Appalachian coalfields for more than one hundred years. Within this economic system, work in coal miners' homes was highly segregated. As men gave their lives to the mines, women gave theirs to the family. But life in the coalfields changed in the last decades of the twentieth century as technological advances reduced the labor force necessary to operate the mines. Since the 1970s, economic restructuring has brought a decline in manufacturing and mining employment and a rise in the service sector, including health care, food service, and tourism, transforming the social and economic landscape of Appalachian families.

Coupled with the simultaneous dismantling of federal social support programs for poor single women such as Aid to Families with Dependent Children, these trends have significantly affected the region's economic security and the gender division of labor in the region. One of the most important changes resulting from the economic transformation has been an increase in the number of women in the

Women at the first annual Ironweed Festival sponsored by the Appalachian Women's Alliance, Pipestem, West Virginia, 1997. The organization, founded in 1993, networks women and girls in West Virginia, Virginia, Kentucky, Tennessee, Ohio, and North Carolina.

Anxious families of miners during the Knox Mine disaster, Port Griffith, Pennsylvania, 1959. With the advent of industrialization, especially in coal communities, the economic role of women in mountain society became less direct and their social role more complex as they were forced into dependency on the earned wages of men.

labor force. The growing service economy offered more opportunities for women to work outside the home, particularly in places once dominated by coal mining. At the same time, declining wages and job security have made dual income households necessary for family economic security. According to political scientist Richard A. Couto, the number of Appalachian women who joined the labor force increased from approximately 36 percent in 1970 to 44 percent in 1990. The percentage increased less drastically from 1990 to 2000, while male participation in the workforce declined. This rise in female employment altered gender roles within households, family groups, and communities.

The importance of coal mining within the region meant that as late as 1970 the central and northern Appalachian economy was less diversified in terms of labor than the rest of the nation and that female employment was below the national average. During the 1980s, however, employment in resource extraction fell significantly, and between 1990 and 2000 it declined 38 percent. This decline of employment in the male-dominated coal industry provided both the opportunity and necessity for women to enter the wage labor market as low-wage, more flexible, and often part-time workers in the service sector. In southern Appalachia, where textile mills and other light manufacturing provided more jobs for women and where workforce participation by females has been historically higher, the number of women in the labor force increased from 38 percent in 1970 to 45 percent in 1990. But the economic evolution in the region also saw heavy losses of manufacturing jobs to other parts of the world. This factor, coupled with a rise in the service economy through the end of the century, led to more women working for wages but fewer earning wages sufficient to support a family.

Across the region, the increased number of women working outside the home has transformed gender roles. For example, until the late 1970s women were prohibited from participating in men's work such as mining, while men tended to avoid household work. Sociologist Shaunna L. Scott found that, as women in Harlan County, Kentucky, began taking jobs outside the household in the late 1980s, they also questioned traditional gender ideologies in which housework was solely the domain of women. This altered women's performance of their traditional roles in the family and the wider community and resulted in new social cleavages along the lines of class and gender.

In parts of southern Appalachia where farming remains an important economic activity, women's involvement in wage labor has also altered gender roles. Anthropologist Mary K. Anglin observed that women who earn wages assert more autonomy within the family. While women's unpaid work within the household is crucial to the maintenance of the family and larger network of kin, it is often devalued because it does not produce wages. As women work outside the home, Anglin suggests, both class and gender relations have been altered and, in turn, so have women's responsibilities and family ties.

By the last decades of the twentieth century, the majority of Appalachian women—unlike their mothers and grandmothers—were seeking both meaningful work and financial independence. They were attending college in unprecedented numbers. However, many of these women felt their actions conflicted with long-standing traditional roles of women in the region and with the lives of other family members, especially their mothers. Daughters of coal miners sometimes feared they were "getting above their raising," particularly if they adopted the behaviors of academic professionals and peers. Such feelings relate to gender identity and loyalty to family and place, which are strong Appalachian values.

Another conflict emerged as women contemplated leaving the coalfields to pursue graduate school or employment. Realizing they had to leave the mountains (at least temporarily) to achieve their goals, many were apprehensive about not belonging upon their return. However, some women who completed academic degrees have successfully returned and chosen to work in their local communities. Some have started social work, accounting, law, or counseling agencies. Others have planned after-school programs for children. One notable group established a transition center for victims of domestic violence and women who lost benefits due to welfare-to-work programs. The ideas and energies of such women represent a significant departure from the past. Instead of depending on outside financiers, they have come to envision participation in the economy. Such aspirations suggest a feminization of the economy as well as a shift from a patriarchal culture to one in which women have a strong voice in the community at large as well as the home.

See also: COAL TOWNS; FAMILY RELATIONSHIPS AND GENDER ROLES; WOMEN'S GROUPS.

—Christiana E. Miewald, *Ohio University*, and Mary O'Quinn, *University of Virginia at Wise*

Mary K. Anglin, "Redefining the Family and Women's Status within the Family: The Case of Southern Appalachia," in *Feminist Visions: Toward a Transformation of the Liberal Art Curriculum*, ed. Diane L. Fowlkes and Charlotte S. McClure (1984); Richard A. Couto, *An American Challenge: A Report on Economic Trends and Social Issues in Appalachia* (1994); Mary O'Quinn, *A Psychological Analysis of Abused Women of the Appalachian Coalfields* (2002); Mary O'Quinn and Shelby Roberts, "Using Modeling Theory to Increase the Technological Efficacy of Appalachian Women," in *Down Home, Downtown: Urban Appalachians Today*, ed. Phillip J. Obermiller (1996).

Images and Icons

Section Editor: George Brosi

Appalachian images and stereotypes, often overdrawn, frequently larger than life, and seemingly indestructible, have steadily become more entrenched in American culture with some, such as the venerable hillbilly, achieving the status of national icons. Robert Schenkkan, whose play *The Kentucky Cycle* won a Pulitzer Prize, gave a cogent analysis of the phenomenon in an interview with Bobbie Ann Mason for a 1993 *New Yorker* article, "Recycling Kentucky." "America *needs* hillbillies," Schenkkan said. "Mountain people are the last group in America it is acceptable to ridicule. No one would stand for it for a minute if you took any other group—Native Americans, African-Americans, Hispanics, women—and held it up as an example of everything that is low and brutal and mean. But somehow it's O.K. to do that with hillbillies." In other words, when people feel they can no longer look down upon groups that have traditionally been demeaned, they still may find that mountaineers serve that need. On the other hand, those seeking to idealize groups and individuals have transformed mountaineers into some of America's sturdiest iconic figures.

Public images from the region appeared long before Appalachia was considered to be a distinct place, yet in hindsight many of them coincide with later renderings of regional perceptions. In the eighteenth century, literate families began to settle the region, and travelers began to recount their impressions of not just the land but the people as well. William Byrd II's expeditions in the 1720s and 1730s to establish the boundary between Virginia and North Carolina resulted in the publication of *The History of the Dividing Line*, setting the tone for much of the travel writings about the "back country," the "up-country," or the "frontier." He portrayed a region where the people were lazy, dirty, and primitive in their lifestyles. Travel writers reinforced these negative frontier images of lawlessness and sloth for generations. Significantly, Henry Timberlake's writings about the Cherokee in 1765 and those of subsequent observers conveyed complex and conflicting images of the Indians, most of which paralleled observations of the white Europeans who settled in the mountains near them. Both Cherokee and mountaineers, for example, were viewed as lax in child rearing and rigid in their spiritual life.

Two of the most important Appalachian icons of the nineteenth century, David Crockett, born in Greene County, Tennessee, and Daniel Boone, who opened

Facing page: Newt Hylton hauls sassafras roots, Laurel Fork Creek, Virginia, c. 1953. The social construction of Appalachia as a distinct, homogenous, and culturally isolated folk society set the stage for the perception of the region as home to a "culture of poverty" in the mid-twentieth century.

Kentucky to settlement, exemplify the way that Appalachian images diverged from fact in the public imagination. In reality, Crockett and Boone both moved westward out of Appalachia and died west of the Mississippi River—in Crockett's case famously. Likewise, Crockett and Boone are depicted as mountain frontiersmen in much the same mold, though their lives were often diametrically opposed. For example, Boone worked for the eighteenth century's leading Appalachian land speculator, Richard Henderson, and was involved in land speculation throughout his life. In contrast, Crockett introduced legislation into the House of Representatives to curb the abuses of land speculators and to allow squatters a legitimate claim to occupied land. Furthermore, Crockett was a consistent advocate for Indians while Boone was sometimes antagonistic toward them.

Although Crockett and Boone both became icons of the intrepid backwoodsman, Crockett also became perhaps the earliest hillbilly icon as a result of his association with backwoods humor. Publication of Crockett's autobiography and the subsequent Crockett Almanacs, which transformed the historical David into the mythical Davy, provided the first widely circulated written images of the Appalachian region. Shortly after their publication, a distinct genre of writing called Old Southwestern humor arose in the foothills of the southern Appalachians featuring humorous, low-class characters who tended to be blatantly disrespectful of elite authority figures and proud of it. This writing came from a region that overlapped Appalachia but was not identical with the mountain region as a whole. *Georgia Scenes* (1835) by Augustus B. Longstreet provided caricatures of both Deep South blacks and upcountry whites, a juxtaposition that has vexed both groups ever since. The cultural heritage of plantation blacks could hardly be more different from that of Scots-Irish highland farmers, yet the stereotypes of the two groups—and even the renderings of their dialect—have often been exactly the same.

The Civil War changed the way Americans perceived regional realities, with Appalachia emerging as a region distinct from the Deep South and an area with its own cultural norms and problems. Regional scholarship has established that Union loyalty in the Appalachians was far from universal even though the "Mountain State" of West Virginia was created when the highland counties of Virginia withdrew from the bastion of the Confederacy. Nevertheless, both a perception of mountain fidelity to the Union and the relative strength of Union and Republican sentiment have persisted in many mountain areas and continue to influence politics and culture to the present day. Kentucky's racially integrated and coeducational Berea College, which had been founded by abolitionists before the war, was actively engaged in raising money throughout the North, thus strengthening the contrast between the Deep South and the mountains in the public mind.

Although southern Appalachia became a distinct region in the national consciousness after the Civil War, confusion about its inhabitants continued. White southerners have been stereotyped generally into three basic categories—mountaineers, poor whites, and rednecks—but the distinctions among them have often been blurred. Poor whites can be found anywhere, but "po' white trash" are generally associated with the Deep South. Rednecks are universal in American culture and defined by working-class status and cultural preferences in food, music, clothing, humor, religion, and other tastes. Mountaineers or hillbillies are defined both by geography and cultural traits, but hillbillies are always from the mountains, either the Appalachians or the Ozarks.

What is generally considered as Appalachian culture in popular opinion is in reality southern Appalachian culture, that of the area settled primarily by the Scots-Irish. It exists in sharp contrast to that of the mountains north of the Mason-Dixon Line, which were settled primarily by Germans, Slavic peoples, and other Europeans.

Perhaps the most prominent manifestation of the newfound recognition of Appalachia as a distinct region after the Civil War came in the popular local color writing of the late nineteenth century. Under the pen name "Charles Egbert Craddock," Mary Noailles Murfree, the leading Appalachian local colorist, portrayed mountain folk as childlike but charming and victimized by a backward culture that generally thwarted their ambition and civility. This dual image of the mountaineer as prone to violence yet basically harmless abetted the economic-development atmosphere that existed in the mountains at the end of the nineteenth century. The mountaineer was not so forbidding as to scare off investment or to deter prospective managers from coming to the region yet was too backward to be trusted to develop the region's resources. Consequently, mountaineers invited economic exploitation.

In 1888 southern Democrats effectively ended Reconstruction and began to divert the region's meager resources away from mountain districts that had supported the Republican Party. The ten-year-old feud between the Hatfields and the McCoys burst into the nation's headlines in 1888 as well, creating an enduring image of the violent and vengeful mountaineer. In this same year, Thomas William Humes published a book entitled *The Loyal Mountaineers of Tennessee*, providing the first written nonfiction testament to a distinct mountain culture while reinforcing positive images of the region. This combination of both positive and negative images has followed the region into the present day.

The tone for the early twentieth century was set by an article published in 1899 by William Goodell Frost, the president of Berea College, entitled "Our Contemporary Ancestors in the Southern Mountains." The word *ancestors* established a strong sympathetic tie between the reader and the mountaineer while setting up hill folk as backward and behind the times. The first two best-selling books set in the mountains, *The Little Shepherd of Kingdom Come* (1903) and *The Trail of the Lonesome Pine* (1908), both by John Fox Jr., further reinforced the prevailing images of this era by contrasting the natural world of the mountains with the technological world of "progressive" America.

The spirit of both nonfiction and fiction of the era before World War I resonated with a time when the profession of social work had begun to emerge nationally. The region attracted many outsiders seeking to uplift the area, especially through settlement and mission schools and colleges. In 1905 the first systematic study of mountain culture as a distinct sociological phenomenon was published, but *The Spirit of the Mountains* by Emma Bell Miles was hardly noticed at the time. In 1913 Horace Kephart's *Our Southern Highlanders* became the first study of the region as a distinct area to sell widely and attract considerable notice. The Conference of Southern Mountain Workers (later the Council of the Southern Mountains) was also created in 1913 for the community of service workers who had arrived in the region to serve the local people. Although this organization was never a major factor in regional history, its founding reflected not only a change in the image of the region but also the expansion of the service sector, an important development in the regional economy.

Janette Carter plays an autoharp, Scott County, Virginia, 1975. In the 1920s, the Carter Family of southwest Virginia became the pioneers of recorded mountain music, a phenomenon that created many icons and cemented friendly images of mountain folk in the minds of the public.

World War I brought thousands of Americans into direct contact with Appalachian servicemen and cemented the region's reputation as a deep pool of good soldiers. Nobody epitomized this more than Alvin York, a Tennessee mountaineer who was awarded the Medal of Honor and became the war's most celebrated soldier by almost single-handedly capturing more than one hundred enemy troops. He returned to his home community in Fentress County, where he attracted attention for the rest of his life, inspiring several biographies and a classic motion picture. Seldom has a "war hero" fit the image so poorly. A gentle soul who entered the army only after his application for exemption as a conscientious objector was denied, York devoted his life to expanding the educational opportunities of the people in his area, founding one of the region's best schools.

The relatively positive image of the Appalachian region that had emerged in the decade before the First World War and was reinforced by Sergeant York during the war continued into the 1920s. However, with the 1921 Battle of Blair Mountain, which pitted miners in West Virginia against not only the mine operators and their private police but also the new U.S. Army Air Corps, the image of the mountaineer as a hapless victim of mainstream oppression was even more powerful than the image of violence portrayed.

The image of mountain violence was reemphasized in the 1930s by mine wars in Harlan County, Kentucky, that gave the county its nickname, "Bloody Harlan." This conflict was etched into the consciousness of union stalwarts and their sympathizers by the powerful song, "Which Side Are You On?" by Florence Reece, the wife of a miner and one of many icons of protest to emerge from the struggles, as well as by the writing of nationally prominent authors such as Theodore Dreiser and John Dos Passos. The power of the militant miners and other workers and their allies was demonstrated not only by the actions of those they galvanized to their causes but also by those who were offended by the activism of the time. In 1934, perhaps encouraged by an atmosphere of fear of militant mountaineers, *L'il Abner* appeared on the scene, Snuffy Smith was introduced to the *Barney Google* comic strip, and Paul Webb's cartoon feature *The Mountain Boys* began its almost thirty-year run in *Esquire* magazine. All of these created images of mountain men as childlike and irresponsible, more pitiful than a threat. In October of 1940, the celebrated national newspaper columnist Ernie Pyle wrote a series of articles about moonshine making in Cocke County, Tennessee. The era between the world wars, which began with more mellow images that encouraged missionary work, ended with negative stereotypes of mountaineers as violent miners and moonshiners.

Despite the negative tone of the region's image during the decade, the 1930s also fostered some sympathetic, though stereotypical, treatments. In 1935 the U.S. Department of Agriculture published a survey of regional life revealing government consciousness of the region as a distinct "problem" area. The 1936 film version of *The Trail of the Lonesome Pine*, starring Henry Fonda, portrayed mountaineers as a distinct population and cultural group that lagged behind the times of a progressive America, while the 1941 movie *Sergeant York* reinforced images of regional innocence and patriotism.

After World War II, mainstream Americans came into increasing contact with the mountain subculture as recreational opportunities became affordable to the masses and the media took renewed interest in the region. Across the country, the 1954 novel *The Dollmaker* by Appalachian native Harriette Simpson Arnow gave thousands of readers their first appreciation of the region through a sympathetic portrayal of mountain folk who moved to midwestern industrial centers to find work. Overall, however, the post–World War II era emphasized American homogeneity, so images depicting the differences of Appalachia tended to be negative.

The most dramatic rediscovery of the region began with the West Virginia Democratic presidential primary election in 1960. Newspaper reporters and television commentators captured compelling images of West Virginia for an attentive national audience during the primary election between John F. Kennedy and Hubert H. Humphrey. In 1964 President Lyndon Johnson launched the government's War on Poverty from Tommy Fletcher's front porch in Martin County, Kentucky. The following year the Appalachian Regional Commission was created, the VISTA (Volunteers in Service to America) program began, and the Office of Economic Opportunity came into being. The Council of the Southern Mountains thrived in the 1960s, creating the Appalachian Volunteers in 1963, which eventually engaged hundreds of youths galvanized into social action by the spirit of the decade. In 1968 seventy-eight coal miners were killed in a mine explosion in Farmington, West Virginia, leading to extensive news coverage. Then on New Year's Eve in 1969, supporters of United Mine Workers of America President W. A. "Tony" Boyle from east Tennessee's District 19 entered the home of Joseph A. "Jock" Yablonski, Boyle's opponent for the union's presidency, and murdered Yablonski and his wife and children. The tumultuous decade reinforced the image of Appalachians as mired in poverty and doomed by frustration to seek violent solutions to their problems.

The realities of regional life in the 1960s were strongly reflected not only in the news media but also through images presented in books. These included *The Southern Appalachian Region: A Survey*, edited by Thomas R. Ford (1962), Harry Caudill's *Night Comes to the Cumberlands: A Biography of a Depressed Area* (1963), and Jack Weller's *Yesterday's People: Life in Contemporary Appalachia* (1965). Contrasting the ways of the mainstream middle class with those of mountain folk, Catherine Marshall's 1967 novel *Christy* became a best-seller, inspiring legions of do-gooders with its uplifting portrait of a schoolteacher from outside the region in a poor community in the Smoky Mountains of Tennessee.

The 1970s reinforced the negative images of the region carried over from the previous decade. In 1971 James Branscome described CBS's Tuesday-night line-up of *The Beverly Hillbillies*, *Green Acres*, and *Hee Haw* as "the most intensive effort ever exerted by a nation to belittle, demean, and otherwise destroy a minority people within its boundaries." None of these programs were explicitly Appalachian; they instead confused negative stereotypes of rural people in general with images from both the Ozarks and the Appalachians. The helplessness associated with the region was reinforced this same year by the Buffalo Creek flood, which caused the deaths of more than one hundred West Virginians and destroyed an entire community when a coal-waste impoundment dam burst. In 1972 the movie *Deliverance*, with its severely handicapped little banjo player and sexually deviant mountaineers, was released, inspiring fear and loathing for hillbillies in the public imagination. Headlines from the Brookside strike in Harlan County in 1973–74 and the movie *Harlan County, USA*, which won the Oscar for best documentary of 1976, emphasized violent images of mountaineers, though it also portrayed them as victims of a system of exploitation.

After the negative images of the 1960s, the remainder of the century witnessed a dramatic mellowing of the region's image. Thousands of back-to-the-land hippies moved into the region. In 1972 *The Waltons* began a nine-year run on television portraying a loving family with a strong sense of place, and the *Foxfire* books became best-sellers. Perhaps the greatest icon of this decade was Aunt Arie Carpenter, the charismatic bearer of old-fashioned values, skills, and ways of life who charmed the high school students who created the *Foxfire* books and their readers alike. The Museum of Appalachia in Norris, Tennessee, with its collection of mountain vernacular architecture, launched its Tennessee Fall Homecoming celebrations and scores of mountain music and craft festivals sprang up all over the region. Jean Ritchie of the Singing Family of the Cumberlands was in demand at national folk festivals, where she and her dulcimer became regional icons. Coal miners won black lung compensation and Arnold Miller's reform movement made him president of the United Mine Workers. Perhaps fittingly, as these new images emerged, the comic strip *Li'l Abner* ended its forty-three year run in 1977.

During the remainder of the twentieth century, with the region much less prominent in national consciousness, images of Appalachia have become more realistic. However, as American mass culture seemed to swallow up the region's distinctiveness, treatments of it have become increasingly nostalgic. The 1980 film *Coal Miner's Daughter* set the tone with its frank depiction of gender inequity and violence counterbalanced by genuinely loving feelings among mountain families. From 1978 to 1985, *The Dukes of Hazzard* television show portrayed fun-loving though imperfect characters who obviously lived in the hills but did not identify themselves primarily as mountaineers. Country music star Dolly Parton played a prominent role in reinforcing the nostalgia with songs of her mountain childhood, as did movies such as *October Sky*, which portrayed coal-camp high schoolers launching rockets and winning the National Science Fair in 1960.

Nevertheless, in the early twenty-first century the region continued to be viewed in a negative light by many Americans—as a place of widespread illegal substance abuse, for example. Moonshine was still being produced in the mountains, marijuana was a major cash crop, and the prescription drug OxyContin was known as "hillbilly heroin." However, in this same time period, films such as *Songcatcher, October Sky, Cold Mountain,* and *O Brother, Where Art Thou?* and celebration of the region at the 2003 Smithsonian Folklife Festival on the National Mall in Washington, D.C., galvanized interest and appreciation for regional music and other cultural traditions.

But Appalachian images continue to evolve, with negative stereotypes as removed from reality as the icons beloved by regional chauvinists. Although interest in the region appeared to have been diminished by concerns over terrorism and economic security, history suggests that Appalachia will remain a place of special interest in American culture, its images rekindled by movies, books, and songs as well as by social and political events.

—George Brosi, *Berea, Kentucky*

Allen W. Batteau, *The Invention of Appalachia* (1990); Dwight B. Billings, Gurney Norman, and Katherine Ledford, eds., *Confronting Appalachian Stereotypes: Back Talk from an American Region* (1999); David C. Hsiung, *Two Worlds in the Tennessee Mountains: Exploring the Origins of Appalachian Stereotypes* (1997); W. K. McNeil, ed., *Appalachian Images in Folk and Popular Culture* (1989); Marjorie Hope Nicolson, *Mountain Gloom and Mountain Glory: The Development of the Aesthetics of the Infinite* (1959); Henry D. Shapiro, *Appalachia on Our Mind: The Southern Mountains and Mountaineers in the American Consciousness, 1870–1920* (1978); J. W. Williamson, *Hillbillyland: What the Movies Did to the Mountains and What the Mountains Did to the Movies* (1995).

Anglo-Saxon Ancestors

Despite various ethnic and racial pride movements beginning in the early 1960s and the more recent advent of political correctness, American regional prejudices and stereotypes remained alive at the turn of the twenty-first century. Marginal, low-status southern whites labeled hillbillies, rednecks, and crackers remained the butts of demeaning jokes and slurs. But while white mountain people in Appalachia continued stereotypically to be regarded as backward, violent, incestuous, and shiftless, they were considered potentially capable of improvement because they descended from good Anglo-Saxon stock. Such a belief brought waves of reformers to Appalachia in various time periods. This ambivalence about Appalachians and the mixed messages it has produced about the culture has roots in a more distant history.

Ultimately, American interregional stereotypes are rooted in the ethnic strife of ancient Europe. Greek and Roman historians recounted protracted struggles between advancing Germanic-speaking Teutons and retreating indigenous Celtic speakers. Chronicles of conflicts between Israelites and Philistines, Athenians and Spartans, Teutons and Celts were part of the cultural baggage European explorers and settlers carried with them into the southern backcountry of the pre–Revolutionary War American colonial frontier. Images of Appalachia's frontier folk, who declared themselves to be "half horse, half alligator," not only obscured the boundaries between Native American and European cultures, but also between nature and culture, animal and human.

Simplistic fuzzy dichotomies pervade the writings of romantic commentators on racial and national character from the late eighteenth through the twentieth century. Though at first the terms *Teutonic* and *Celtic* specifically denoted branches of the greater Indo-European linguistic family, they quickly became associated with differences between races and nations that were assumed to be genetic in origin. Nineteenth-century proponents of racism, including Joseph-Arthur de Gobineau and Houston Stewart Chamberlain, claimed that language, race, and physiology were interconnected. Adopting the Darwinian doctrine of the survival of the fittest, they argued that long-headed Teutons, the purest type of Aryan stock, were inherently superior to round-headed Celts, naturally destined to dominate and displace their racial inferiors. In Great Britain and other western European countries, the dichotomy between Celts and Teutons served to explain and justify inequities between social classes and regions. In his study of Celtic literature, Matthew Arnold depicts the British national character as a salubrious mixture of the best of Teuton and Celt, leavening dull, phlegmatic, "masculine" Teutonic rationalism with sanguine, "feminine" Celtic imagination and ebullience. Equating Teutons with Anglo-Saxons, late-nineteenth- and early-twentieth-century American racists proposed that, since non-Teutons were congenitally incapable of appreciating and respecting America's Teutonic cultural values, only immigrants of pure Teuton ancestry should be permitted to become citizens of the United States.

Nonetheless, the image of the romantic Celt superseded that of the stolid Teuton in early discussions of Appalachia, popularly identified as an exclusively Caucasian agrarian stronghold in the midst of a rapidly changing urban industrial America. This legacy of ambivalent images about the culture remained potent at the beginning of the twenty-first century. Beginning with William Goodell Frost's 1899 article "Our Contemporary Ancestors in the Southern Mountains," early commentators on Appalachia tended to accentuate the British and particularly the Celtic element in Appalachia's population while discounting and negating the region's German settlers.

Horace Kephart explained Appalachian poverty and backwardness in *Our Southern Highlanders* (1913; revised 1922) by summoning stereotypes of Celtic irrationality and disorganization that continue to shape interpretations of southern backcountry life by modern American historians. Kephart invoked nineteenth-century British historian Thomas Babington Macaulay regarding English antipathy to Celtic culture: "In the south of our island scarcely anything was known about the Celtic part of Scotland; and what was known excited no feeling but contempt and loathing." Building on Macaulay's elaborations upon the barbarism, laziness, illiteracy, and superstitious paganism of the Scottish Highlanders, most of whom lived in abysmal primitive squalor, Kephart concluded that the southern highlanders of Appalachian America possessed the same virtues and flaws as the Gaels of the Scottish Highlands and their Celtic ancestors (although most of Appalachia's Scottish settlers were, in fact, Lowland Scots).

Popular historical studies published in the 1980s positing survivals of British regional subcultures in the United States resurrected these hoary stereotypes of Celtic superstition and disorganization. In *Cracker Culture* (1988), historian Grady McWhiney asserted that no fewer than 75 percent of the settlers of the hinterlands of the southern colonies were transplanted Celts, whose cultural heritage included traditions of shiftless pastoralism, laziness, intemperance, sensuality, violence, and anarchic individualism. In *Apples on the Flood* (1988) Appalachian scholar Rodger Cunningham noted that sentimental Celtophiles are fond of saying that the Celts, in their battles against the Germanic tribes, were hampered by "Celtic traits" such as "individualism" and "lack of organizing spirit," which have become iconically Appalachian in the popular imagination.

According to Cunningham, a dichotomy between "civilized" Lowland Scots and "wild" Highlanders emerged in Scotland by the fourteenth century. The Highlander is the unruly child, the ignoble savage that the Lowlander must suppress to become more like the superior, civilized, rational, and paternal Englishman. In this reading, the imposition of Teutonic Anglo-Norman culture in Lowland Scotland and suppression of Celtic traditions still reverberate in the divided Appalachian psyche to this day, but the dichotomy between Celt and Teuton ultimately reflects political and economic inequities, rather than race or national character.

See also: MOUNTAIN WHITES; SECTION OVERVIEW (RACE, ETHNICITY, AND IDENTITY).

—Richard Blaustein, *East Tennessee State University*

Rodger Cunningham, *Apples on the Flood: Minority Discourse and Appalachia* (1988); Horace Kephart, *Our Southern Highlanders* (1913; revised 1922); Grady McWhiney, *Cracker Culture: Celtic Ways in the Old South* (1988).

Ballads, Folk Songs, and Collectors

See Ballads (Music); Folk Music Collections (Music); Folk Music Revivals (Music); Folk Songs (Music)

Brier, Brierhopper

Brierhopper is a common, often derogatory term used in the United States to characterize Appalachian people. Usually shortened to *brier*, the term came into widespread use to refer to women and men from the uplands of Tennessee, West Virginia, and Kentucky who left the mountains looking for work during the Great Depression. Use of the epithet intensified during World War II, when mountaineers in large numbers joined the military or took factory jobs outside the region to assist with the war effort. Easily identified by their accents, these workers were negatively stereotyped as either impoverished dirt farmers or unsophisticated rural laborers. The term continued in vogue throughout the Great Migration decades of the 1950s and 1960s, but it is now heard less frequently than *redneck* or *hillbilly*.

Labels such as *brier* arise from contact among different social groups, usually as a result of migration. In cities outside of the region, Appalachians are largely nameless until they are perceived as a problem or a threat to the established order, whereupon they are stigmatized. Negative labels are a simple but powerful means of establishing and maintaining control of valuable social resources such as jobs, schooling, shelter, and ultimately group identity. Urbanites stigmatize Appalachians as brierhoppers because the newcomers' values and beliefs appear to threaten urban norms and customs. Moreover, the brier stereotype is often used to discriminate against Appalachians, in effect denying them access to housing, education, or employment. In his classic 1971 essay "Annihilating the Hillbilly: The Appalachians' Struggle with America's Institutions," James Branscome forcefully makes this point when he says that in the city "there is one thing more unacceptable than a black man—a hillbilly, a ridgerunner, a brierhopper."

While the use of the brier stereotype is an attempt to legitimize domination by elites or to give an advantage to competing social groups, it also leads to resistance among Appalachians. Hence, the term may also be used as an emblem of pride among Appalachian people themselves. For example, Jim Wayne Miller's poem "Brier Sermon," published in *The Mountains Have Come Closer* (1980), provides an extended metaphor for the interaction between Appalachian people and American mass culture. In a later volume, *Brier, His Book* (1988), Miller's Brier becomes an archetype for Appalachians who are aware of their history and have an astute understanding of their place in American society.

Because labeling is fundamentally an exercise in power, the Appalachian use of the word *brier* is neither hypocritical nor disingenuous. Rather, it represents an effort by Appalachians to rebel against the vocabulary of domination and regain control of their own identity, in this case by rehabilitating the term in a way that diminishes its usefulness to degrade.

See also: HILLBILLY; *HILLBILLY* (RACE, ETHNICITY, AND IDENTITY); SECTION OVERVIEW (RACE, ETHNICITY, AND IDENTITY).

—Phillip J. Obermiller, *University of Kentucky*

James Branscome, "Annihilating the Hillbilly: The Appalachians' Struggle with America's Institutions," *Katallagete* (Winter 1971); Frederic G. Cassidy et al., ed., *Dictionary of American Regional English* (1985–); Robert Hendrickson, *Mountain Range: A Dictionary of Expressions from Appalachia to the Ozarks* (1997).

Coal Images

John L. Lewis, Mother Jones, violent picket-line protestors, larger-than-life brawny miners, willing helpless victims, corporate paternalism, sinister coal operators, landscapes scarred by strip mines, totalitarian coal camps, economic enslavement, scrip, and black lung are among the many archetypes, images, and icons of the Appalachian coal industry.

Some of the strongest images and icons of Appalachian coal camps and communities are mythical or legendary creations, produced by various forms of media and/or perpetuated by distorted personal accounts. Others have basis in truth.

The images and icons of Appalachian coal are vested in landscape, people, industrial development, social phenomena, historical events, and political landmarks. Numerous aspects of culture drive public perception of a place, including music, still and motion picture film, a variety of visual art forms, journalism, creative writing, and a plethora of other elements.

Most Appalachian scholars agree that the images and icons of Appalachian coal mining fit on either end of two extremes. On one hand, Appalachian miners are portrayed as class-conscious militants who are interested in pursuing solidarity through unions and socialist politics. On the other, they are independent, complacent mountaineers with little interest in the betterment of anyone but themselves.

Many of the images of Appalachian coal arise from the destructive aspects of the Industrial Revolution. Among the first vehicles promulgating this image were songs about poor, distressed, enslaved coal miners who worked under dangerous circumstances. Robert Donelly and Will Geddes's "Don't Go Down in the Mine, Dad," Blind Alfred Reed's "Explosion in the Fairmount Mines," John Wallace Crawford's "Only a Miner Killed," Merle Travis's "Dark as a Dungeon," and Tennessee Ernie Ford's recording of "Sixteen Tons" are all examples. More recent songs such as Billy Edd Wheeler's "Coal Tattoo" continue the same themes. Jean Ritchie's "The L&N Don't Stop Here Anymore" creates the image of the small coal camp's being pillaged and then cast aside by voracious industrial moguls. In the 1960s, this image was brought to the national spotlight by Harry Caudill's book *Night Comes to the Cumberlands*, which depicts a region stripped of its physical and mental health.

The icon of the coal miner as rabble-rouser emerged as United Mine Workers of America President John L. Lewis became the quintessential union organizer and representative of oppressed coal miners in the 1920s and 1930s. Many Appalachian coal miners displayed pictures of the Last Supper and Lewis side by side on their camp-house walls. This image was also perpetuated in songs such as Florence Reece's "Which Side Are You On?" and George Davis's "When Kentucky Had No Union Men." Motion picture documentaries such as Barbara Kopple's Academy Award–winning *Harlan County, USA* also contributed to this concept. More contemporary images of rabble-rousers in coal communities have arisen out of grassroots protest movements against broad form deeds and environmental pollution, particularly strip mining.

The politics of coal camps added a new element to rural Appalachian life. The introduction of coal corporations into the culture changed the way power and position were used to influence labor issues and determine the outcome of elections. Many times political disagreements erupted into violence, which was then covered in the national news media. The image of the sinister coal operator as well as the violent coal miner became a part of national consciousness. As a result, pejorative geographic nicknames such as "Bloody Harlan" became common. The mythical coal miner "giant" was also generated in music and perpetuated by mainstream culture. Although the song "John Henry" is a railroad song, many believe that it was written with coal mining as its focus. This "steel-drivin' man" became one of the larger-than-life figures in American folklore.

The old icons and images of the coal region of Appalachia continue to be promoted by contemporary motion picture film and print media. Warner Brothers' 1997 *Fire Down Below* stars Steven Segal and promotes the sinister coal operator theme by portraying the coal company in concert with toxic-waste disposal outlaws. Showtime Network's 2000 *Harlan County War* stars Holly Hunter and is filled with numerous clichés of both coal operators and rank-and-file miners. Again, the sinister coal company is portrayed as an entity that denies the poor coal miner safe working conditions and critical benefits. On the other hand, the coal miner is depicted as a sometimes violent picket-line participant who is forced to live in abject poverty. He is formally uneducated but occasionally projects flashes of brilliance through innate common sense. Robert Schenkkan's Pulitzer Prize–winning drama *The Kentucky Cycle* also perpetuates the stereotype of greedy coal operators who have no regard for the environ-

Royale Theater marquee on Broadway in New York City advertises Robert Schenkkan's Pulitzer Prize–winning drama *The Kentucky Cycle,* 1993. The play perpetuated the stereotype of greedy coal operators and banal, slothful mountaineers.

ment or for the plight of coal miners. Schenkkan portrays mountain people as relatively passive victims of fate who are banal, avaricious, and slothful.

Some representations of Appalachia are transient, but others have remained constant and have become part of the folklore of the region. Many of the more permanent images have been formed by a variety of material culture forms such as political cartoons, sculpture, photography, and paintings. National news coverage of union struggles inspired political cartoons solidifying well-defined images of both the coal operator and rank-and-file miner. A process that allowed coal to be ground, mixed with a glue compound, and placed into molds produced a variety of sculptures of coal miners and their traditional tools, which helped establish iconic ideas among mainstream America. Photographers such as Earl Dotter have gone into coal mines and have played a major role in creating iconic images. Because of Appalachia's relative isolation, much of the culture has been spun out of the mainstream and will probably continue to be reduced to simplistic images by outsiders.

See also: ANTHRACITE COAL INDUSTRY (BUSINESS, INDUSTRY, AND TECHNOLOGY); BITUMINOUS COAL INDUSTRY (BUSINESS, INDUSTRY, AND TECHNOLOGY); HARLAN COUNTY MINE WAR (LABOR).

—James B. Goode, *Lexington Community College*

Alan Banks, "Miners Talk Back: Labor Activism in Southeastern Kentucky in 1992," in *Confronting Appalachian Stereotypes: Back Talk from an American Region*, ed. Dwight B. Billings, Gurney Norman, and Katherine Ledford (1999); Gurney Norman, "Notes on *The Kentucky Cycle*," in *Confronting Appalachian Stereotypes: Back Talk from an American Region*, ed. Dwight B. Billings, Gurney Norman, and Katherine Ledford (1999); Henry D. Shapiro, *Appalachia on Our Mind: The Southern Mountains and Mountaineers in the American Consciousness, 1870–1920* (1978).

Electioneering and Politics

The popular association of Appalachian politics with corruption, liquor, and election-related violence, though overstated, is not without historical foundation. Some variation of the saying that "two dollars and two swallers will get you a vote" is almost universally known, but successful political marketing, in Appalachia as elsewhere, is no longer predicated exclusively on such negative shenanigans. It continues to depend on how well candidates manipulate the language and images of family, God and country, and community—regardless of their ideology or party.

Family has historically played both organizational and symbolic functions in Appalachian politics. The invocation of "family values" by politicians has deep historical roots and has arguably been used more than any other tactic in Appalachian political culture. The centrality of family to the region's politics is well documented and has endured despite the transition from traditional to corporate political control and from personal to electronic communication. The basic unit of political organization in nineteenth-century Appalachian mountain communities was the kin group. Traditional leaders generally emerged from wealthy landed families. Their political success derived from their ability to mobilize kinship groups in the community through personal contact, attention to local issues, entertaining oratory, and banjo or fiddle playing.

As control of mountain resources was transferred to a new industrial elite in the four decades surrounding the turn of the twentieth century, legal and political authority shifted from traditional leadership to a corporate representative who significantly altered the methods of political communication but only subtly changed the messages. The new methods still proclaimed the power elite's commitment to family and community. However the political spokesmen of the new corporate order equated the well-being of one's family with the balance sheet of the local employer. Corporate devotion to family, country, and community was transmitted less often by stump speeches than through company magazines and company-owned or -influenced newspapers. The omnipresent rhetoric of "progress" and "modernization" instructed employees to promote and protect the financial health of corporate "families," thereby insuring the security of one's own family. Corporate manipulation of the imagery of kin is recreated periodically, as evidenced by slogans lauding the "Ford Family of Fine Cars" or the "Ashland Family of Companies."

Success in electoral politics at local, state, and national levels has historically depended on thorough organization and the symbolic linkage of a candidate or cause to the self-perceived best interests of the constituents. Candidates courting Appalachian voters seek to align themselves with the common man, a practice dating back at least to the presidential election of 1840, when Whig strategists successfully portrayed the aristocratic William Henry Harrison as a humble man who favored the simple life in a log cabin and enjoyed hard cider. Candidates for local office often distance themselves from their national party if they sense that the party's ideology or national agenda runs against the grain of local sentiment. For example, while Republicans often identify themselves with "the party of Lincoln," mountain Republicans in the late nineteenth and early twentieth centuries avoided their party's identification with black civil rights. Instead, they praised their party as the protector of the Union and provider of government largesse to local farmers and businesses.

Modern politicians, including those dependent on the good graces of the corporate forces that radically transformed the mountains, have continued to employ the images of traditional politics and traditional values. In 1948 Tennessee Democrat Estes Kefauver campaigned for the

United States Senate wearing a coonskin cap, linking himself to Tennessee icons David Crockett and Sam Houston. Few realized it was given to him as the symbol of Chattanooga's Pioneer Bank. Kefauver's famous retort, "I may be a pet coon, but I'm not Boss Crump's pet coon," reinforced his rural image. For decades, Democratic Senator Robert C. Byrd of West Virginia broke out his fiddle at campaign rallies, as did Senator Albert Gore Sr. of Tennessee. Tennessee's Lamar Alexander, a longtime Republican insider with international corporate and political connections, campaigned for the presidential nomination in 1992 wearing the same lumberjack shirt he had worn in a walk across the state that won him the governor's mansion in 1978. In the summer of 2002, Appalachian politicians rushed to attack a U.S. Circuit Court of Appeals ruling that the words *under God* in the Pledge of Allegiance violated the First Amendment's separation of church and state and could not be recited in schools. "I am stunned by the ruling," an eastern Kentucky congressman reported on his Web site. "We can't have a bunch of liberal judges out in California thwarting the will of the people like this."

John F. Kennedy's 1960 victory in the West Virginia Democratic primary, which propelled him to the presidential nomination, exemplified the integration of organization with the images of patriotism, family, and popular memory. Kennedy's campaign established extensive contacts with the state's courthouse and statehouse party regulars, capitalizing on their relationship to key kin-based voting constituencies. The Kennedy forces appealed to the common man idea by referring to tea and coffee receptions as "ox roasts" and "weenie roasts." They stirred up West Virginians' patriotism and sense of fair play by suggesting a vote against Kennedy, a Roman Catholic, was a vote for intolerance and against a World War II hero who had lost a brother in that conflict. Kennedy strategists also brought in Franklin D. Roosevelt Jr., whose father was revered in the Appalachian coalfields as a defender of the rights of labor. The symbolic connection of the younger Kennedy to the New Deal icon, for whom many West Virginians harbored paternal or filial sentiments, struck a responsive chord among voters.

Every Appalachian political faction or movement claims the symbolic ground of tradition, family, and community. This imperative is not limited to formal parties but also drives citizens' organizations that, unlike the major parties, resist corporate domination of the region. Organizations such as Kentuckians for the Commonwealth, Save Our Cumberland Mountains, Kentucky's Community Farm Alliance, and the Ohio Valley Environmental Coalition utilize tradition, cultural memory, values, religion, and family to mobilize citizens around environmental and social justice issues.

Putting a positive spin on traditional politics, West Virginia political boss Raymond Chafin spoke of old-fashioned candidates who "found you in your cornfield and told you what they stood for." The negative side of regional political life was emphasized in the elections of 2002 in eastern Kentucky, during which two candidates were shot to death by supporters of their opponents.

See also: POLITICAL HUMOR (HUMOR); SECTION OVERVIEW (HUMOR).

—John C. Hennen, *Morehead State University*

Raymond Chafin and Topper Sherwood, *Just Good Politics: The Life of Raymond Chafin, Appalachian Boss* (1994); Ronald D Eller, *Miners, Millhands, and Mountaineers: The Industrialization of the Appalachian South, 1880–1930* (1982); Stephen L. Fisher, ed., *Fighting Back in Appalachia: Traditions of Resistance and Change* (1993).

Entertainment Icons

As in other parts of the United States, frontier settlers and historical heroes provide much of Appalachia's most enduring imagery. But in the mountains of central Appalachia and the foothills of the rural South, music has produced modern-day entertainment icons revered not only in their region but in the country at large. Appalachian roots—real or concocted—remain central to the image and identity of many performers, even though pop culture and commercial recordings have blurred their musical heritage. Far beyond Appalachia, even casual listeners of music associated with the region know Bill Monroe as the "Father of Bluegrass" and Loretta Lynn and Roy Acuff as the "Coal Miner's Daughter" and the "King of Country Music."

The late "Father of Bluegrass" was not, in fact, Appalachian, nor was he from the Bluegrass region of central Kentucky, which gave the genre its name. However, the high-energy, acoustic string music employs instruments so profoundly identified with the mountains that both Monroe and bluegrass became icons of the region—perhaps better known than even Virginia's Carter Family, whose historic recordings marked the dawn of the country music industry. Adoption was unnecessary in the case of the "King of Country Music" and the "Coal Miner's Daughter." Both Acuff, born in Maynardville, Tennessee, and Lynn, of Butcher Hollow, Kentucky, were quintessentially Appalachian by birth, circumstance, and musical style.

Lynn's iconic label came from the title of her biographical hit song, and her life, perhaps better than any other, includes images popularly associated with Appalachian music. The daughter of a Johnson County, Kentucky, coal miner, she was wed to a twenty-five-year-old mountaineer at the age of thirteen. She saw her first recording become a hit when she was still a teenager—and used the money to buy her first pair of high-heeled shoes.

Images of similarly deprived circumstances and success against great odds are found in the biographies of other music stars who have achieved the status of regional

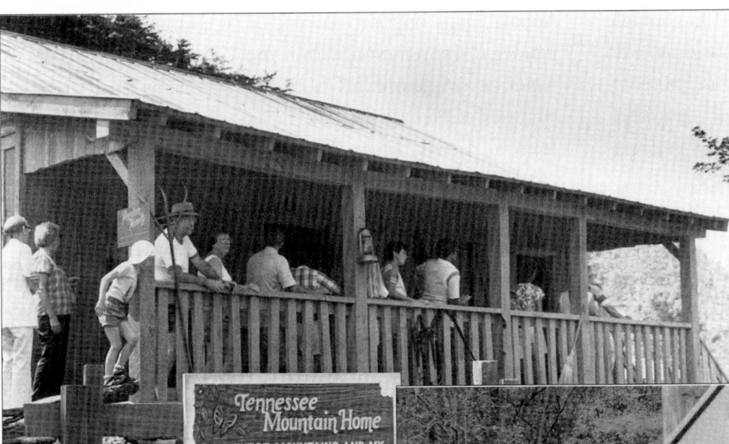

At the Dollywood theme park in Pigeon Forge, Tennessee, tourists line up to visit a replica of Dolly Parton's homeplace, c. 1991. Legendary in country music, Parton began performing at age ten on a Knoxville television show and made her first appearance on the *Grand Ole Opry* at age thirteen.

A primitive sign directs tourists to the homeplace of country singer Loretta Lynn, Butcher Hollow, Kentucky, 1999. Lynn's life, perhaps better than any other, includes images popularly associated with Appalachian music. The daughter of a Johnson County, Kentucky, coal miner, she was wed to a twenty-five-year-old mountaineer when she was only thirteen years old.

and even national icons, among them Patsy Cline, Dolly Parton, Tammy Wynette, and Elvis Presley. Such images resonate powerfully with music fans, who often come from comparable backgrounds. These stars' lyrics often deal with poverty and attendant social conflicts common to rural Appalachia. Among Lynn's hits, for example, are songs entitled "Don't Come Home A-Drinkin' (With Lovin' on Your Mind)," "You Ain't Woman Enough to Take My Man," and "The Pill," a saucy consideration of the liberating benefits of the birth-control pill.

Wynette, a five-times-married former waitress and beauty parlor operator born in poverty in northern Mississippi, evoked the pathos of dysfunctional families and relationships so effectively that she became known as the "Heroine of Heartbreak." Her songs, including "D-I-V-O-R-C-E" and "Stand By Your Man," which was voted the best country music song of all time in one poll of fans, made Wynette an iconic "wronged woman." Movies, a theme park, songwriting, and recording made Parton a national entertainment icon, but she maintained her mountain roots and even romanticized the modest circumstances of her Sevier County, Tennessee, family with songs such as "Coat of Many Colors."

Although mountain and country music have produced most of Appalachia's iconic figures in modern times, numerous others born in the region have become historical fixtures in American entertainment. Among them are jazz pioneer Bessie Smith, comedienne Lucille Ball, and actors Clark Gable and George C. Scott. These celebrities are not popularly associated with the region since their careers were not linked with romantic or stereotypical notions of Appalachia such as rurality, poverty, or dialect speech. Television comics Andy Griffith and Don Knotts and the singer-comedian Tennessee Ernie Ford made lucrative use of their regional roots, however.

In sports, the Appalachian region is amply represented in the record books of both collegiate and professional achievement, but in relatively few instances does regional identity attach itself to iconic status in athletics. One notable exception is Jerry West of Cabin Creek, West Virginia, who maintained his ties with his home community in the coalfields after literally becoming a professional basketball icon—his silhouette graces the Nation Basketball Association's logo—playing for the Los Angeles Lakers.

See also: SECTION OVERVIEW (MEDIA); SECTION OVERVIEW (MUSIC).

—Tina Rae Collins, *Berea College*

Jack Hurst, *Nashville's Grand Ole Opry* (1975); Loretta Lynn, with George Vecsey, *Coal Miner's Daughter* (1976); Dolly Parton, *Dolly: My Life and Other Unfinished Business* (1994).

Feuds

See Feuds (Government)

Fighting Mountaineers

Appalachians often exist in the national consciousness as quiescent people who are complicit in their own oppression. At the same time, these submissive mountaineers are seen as some of the most violent people in the United States. The bloody mine wars and skirmishes between miners and the coal industry are responsible, in large part, for this latter image. As contradictory as these images may appear, they are related. For most of the nation, coal miners are uninformed workers blindly following corrupt and manipulative union leaders. In the end, the verdict is the same: mountain people are gun-happy, unintelligent bumpkins culturally incapable of rational resistance to unjust conditions.

The prevailing positive images of collective resistance in Appalachia come from the coalfields as well. Films such as *Justice in the Coalfields*, *Matewan*, and *Harlan County, USA*, novels such as Denise Giardina's *Storming Heaven*, and photographs by Earl Dotter offer the most positive images of miners' efforts to gain union recognition, just wages, safe working conditions, black lung benefits, union reform, and job security. The campaign against strip mining calls forth images of blown-up mining equipment, heroic stands by Uncle Dan Gibson and "Widow" Combs, and sit-ins on mountaintop-removal sites. Songs growing out of these coal-related struggles—the most notable of which is Florence Reece's "Which Side Are You On?"—give voice to the participants' motivations, anger, and hopes. Many of these songs are found in Guy and Candie Carawan's *Voices from the Mountains* and on records such as *Come All You Coal Miners*, *Coal Mining Women*, and *They Can't Put It Back*.

Some supporters of democratic dissent actually reinforce the stereotype of mountain people's complacency. By focusing on economic exploitation of the region and the obstacles to dissent, they tend to reinforce notions of Appalachian people as victims. Painting romanticized pictures of resistance in the region by claiming, for example, that most Appalachians opposed slavery or by minimizing racial and gender discrimination within the United Mine Workers of America oversimplifies both the problems and the possibilities. Celebrating folk heroes such as Mother Jones, John L. Lewis, Myles Horton, Don West, and Joseph A. "Jock" Yablonski as evidence of a politics of resistance may leave the impression that most dissent in the mountains results from individual rather than collective action.

Grassroots resistance in Appalachia frequently occurs in struggles to preserve traditional values and ways of life against the forces of modernization. The most obvious examples are the countless efforts by local residents to prevent the destruction of their land and homes by strip miners, dam and highway builders, the Tennessee Valley Authority and the U.S. Forest Service, toxic-waste dumpers, the timber industry, and recreation and second-home developers. Less obvious are the ways in which mountain families and churches defend members from some of the harmful impacts of modernization and the attitudes and practices of workers who resist the capitalist separation of work and control. Indeed, the fact that so many of the protests in Appalachia are a result of defensive behavior has led some observers to refer to Appalachians as "reactionary radicals."

An outburst of grassroots community organizing began in Appalachia in the late 1960s. Media images erroneously imply that outsiders were crucial to these efforts. In fact, native mountaineers more often "radicalized" visiting students activists than vice versa. In addition to the defensive efforts discussed above, Appalachians organized to reform the United Mine Workers, secure black lung and welfare benefits, enact tax reform, build rural community centers and health clinics, and fight for better schools. Community groups pursued a wide variety of alternative economic-development strategies that resulted in agricultural and craft cooperatives, worker-owned factories, and new job opportunities for women. Most of the organizing arose in response to single issues, but there were also attempts to build and maintain regional coalitions (Congress for Appalachian Development; Appalachian Alliance), institutions (Appalshop; Southern Empowerment Project), publications *(The Plow; Appalachian Reader)*, and funding organizations (Appalachian Community Fund). One of the most common images from this period is that of citizens from across the region sitting in rocking chairs at Highlander Research and Education Center workshops sharing ideas and discussing ways to work together. Much of the spirit of these workshops is captured in the film *You Got to Move*.

Single-issue groups have won occasional victories. Two impressive examples are the Brumley Gap Concerned Citizens' defeat in the late 1970s of the Appalachian Power Company's plans to build a pumped storage dam that would have flooded their southwest Virginia community and the Yellow

Folksinger and labor activist Nimrod Workman conducting a workshop, Highlander Research and Education Center, New Market, Tennessee, 1972. Possessing qualities ascribed to the "fighting mountaineer," Workman labored in the coal mines for forty-two years and emerged a staunch labor union supporter who campaigned for compensation to miners suffering from black lung disease.

Creek Concerned Citizens' successful challenge to the poisoning of their eastern Kentucky community by corporate polluters. But these groups often lack a larger transformative social and political vision and disappear from the scene after their issue is resolved. One of the most exciting and hopeful developments in community organizing in Appalachia is the establishment and success of multi-issue membership-driven organizations such as Save Our Cumberland Mountains in east Tennessee and Kentuckians for the Commonwealth, the Western North Carolina Alliance, and the Virginia Organizing Project. These groups' primary concern is to empower their members for the long haul through a self-conscious leadership-training process designed to develop democratic skills, build a sense of ownership and community, and underscore the links between local issues and regional, national, and global patterns and concerns.

Dissent in Appalachia assumes other forms much less visible than picket lines and civil disobedience. These include such behavior as back talk (impudent or insolent replies), holding on to one's dialect, moonshining, and fashioning what anthropologist Rhoda H. Halperin has described as "multiple livelihood strategies," which enable people to resist becoming dependent upon a capitalist economy. Contrary to popular images of Appalachians as passive victims, there exists throughout the region a tradition of individual and organized efforts to establish community services and jobs, win and maintain safe workplaces, and preserve homeplace and community values.

See also: FEUDS AND VIOLENCE (MEDIA); NOBLE MOUNTAINEERS; VIOLENCE AND VENGEANCE.

—Stephen L. Fisher, *Emory and Henry College*

Guy and Candie Carawan, eds., *Voices from the Mountains* (1975); Richard Couto, *Making Democracy Work Better* (1999); Stephen L. Fisher, ed., *Fighting Back in Appalachia: Traditions of Resistance and Change* (1993).

Grannies, Midwives, and Healers

The popular image of the Appalachian healer is a complex and contradictory one, including the imputation of power and beneficence to individuals who are also seen as quacks and manifestations of ignorance. The figure of the male healer, usually a quasi-professional specialist often styled a "yarb" (herb) or "power" doctor, emerged early in literature devoted to Appalachian local color. Mary Noailles Murfree, writing under the pen name "Charles Egbert Craddock," created the character of Caleb Hoxie, perhaps the first of such fictional portraits, in the tale "Over on T'other Mounting" in her influential short story collection *In the Tennessee Mountains* (1884). In the story, Hoxie vainly attempts to cure the wife of Tony Britt, but her death among other misfortunes marks Hoxie for Britt's revenge. When Hoxie survives Britt's attempted murder and subsequently appears to him, Britt mistakes him for a supernatural being and loses his reason. In this convoluted plot, Murfree portrays Hoxie as ineffectual in actual healing skill but potent in his emotional and spiritual effect and respected in his role in the community—

a theme that recurs in the treatment of male mountain healers as late as folklorist Vance Randolph's work in the Ozarks, a related region, in the 1940s. The iconic picture of a man who manages to persuade a credulous community of his abilities despite the crudity of his knowledge and skills resembles the popular outsider image of the Appalachian "man of God," and early observers enjoyed ironically noting that preachers often served both as herb doctors and supernatural healers for their followers.

While the popularly perceived role of male Appalachian healers has traditionally been given a professional aura, implying a clientele and a practice paralleling (and threatening) that of regular medical doctors, the role of women healers has been represented as domestic and personal, based in the garden and hearth. In nineteenth- and early-twentieth-century works shaping the popular image of healers in Appalachia, writers paid scant attention to the role of women. During this period, the fictional treatment of Appalachian women in popular literature tended to identify them not as expert practitioners of plant-based healing but as wildflowers themselves—youthful blossoms too fragile to long survive the harsh forces at large in the mountains or lissome nature girls too direct and innocent to be at home amidst the artifice of "civilization." Nonfiction accounts such as Horace Kephart's *Our Southern Highlanders* focused not on their power but on their lack of it, suggesting utter domination by their menfolk. Older women—"grannies"—were marginalized by both age and gender, often depicted as slightly demented in the eccentricities of their healing practice. The exception to this early trivialization of the role of women as healers was the attitude toward midwives, a fixture of obstetric practice almost universal in the United States throughout the nineteenth century and surviving in importance in rural and immigrant communities well into the twentieth, despite vigorous institutional opposition.

Midwives loomed early and ominously in activist writings addressing medical conditions in Appalachia. In 1806 Kentucky physician Benjamin Dudley attributed high rates of infant mortality and female ills to the influence of midwives, whom he depicted as "ignorant old women" administering vile "whiskey stews and other nostrums." (Making use of the property of distilled alcohol in extracting medicinal properties from herbs—a perfectly valid technique—was frequently characterized as yet another example of regional degeneracy.) The activist spirit that stigmatized rural midwifery, which in actual practice ranged from poor to highly competent, paralleled in many ways the interventionist strategies applied to education, involving introduction of specialists and institutions from outside the region. The midwife, derided by the professional medical establishment throughout the nineteenth century as ignorant, venal, and steeped in dangerous superstitious practice, remained a symbol of the backward status of the mountain communities in which she practiced.

The early 1930s saw the introduction of several new entities reinforcing popular imagery concerning Appalachia. Notable were the first appearance of Paul Webb's *Mountain Boys* cartoons in *Esquire* magazine, the debut of Al Capp's *Li'l Abner* comic strip, and the introduction of Snuffy Smith and his mountain milieu to Billy DeBeck's *Barney Google* comic strip. The latter two works included strong female characters representing a kind of ethical and practical anchor in a maelstrom of male shiftlessness: the redoubtable Mammy Yokum and the more tentative but equally dependable Loweezy. Both of these figures habitually administered remedies to physical as well as social ills, offering tonics for the former and, in Mammy's case, her famed "good night Irene punch" for the latter. Their curative forcefulness, though comic in intent, suggested the emergence of a popular image concerning power of the mountain woman to create order in a disordered world through direct engagement with nature and a natural moral order. Irene Ryan reprised this comic construction in her role as Daisy Moses on the 1960s television show *The Beverly Hillbillies*, in which the matriarch's skills as an herbal practitioner were celebrated in episodes such as "Granny's Spring Tonic" and "Granny's Garden." Despite their coarse humor, these episodes remain in demand on DVD more than thirty-five years after their first airing.

The 1970s saw yet another significant shift in the portrayal of Appalachian healers. Widespread social malaise attributed to over-industrialization and over-institutionalization of mainstream American existence resulted in a renewed romantic fascination with rural and traditional lifestyle. To borrow a phrase from Eliot Wigginton's enormously successful *Foxfire* publications concerning Appalachian folklife, "matters of plain living" acquired a glamour that appealed even to those who hesitated to engage personally in the back-to-the-land movement. Interest grew in traditional herbal medical practice, not merely as a "window on the past," but as a more satisfactory means of addressing medical problems of the present. Healers who still engaged in such practice were regarded not as backward "contemporary ancestors" but as valued teachers. Individuals such as *Foxfire*'s Aunt Arie Carpenter and the exhaustively studied herbalist A. L. "Tommie" Bass have been elevated to the status of icons—not only among outsiders to the Appalachian region, but often among its inhabitants. They represent the latest in a series of symbolic representations of Appalachian healers. It remains to be seen what unexpected forms this malleable and contradictory set of themes may take in the future.

See also: GRANNY MIDWIVES (HEALTH).

—Erika Brady, *Western Kentucky University*

Allen W. Batteau, *The Invention of Appalachia* (1990); Anthony Cavender, *Folk Medicine in Southern Appalachia* (2003); John K. Crellin and Jane Philpott, *Herbal Medicine Past and Present, Vol. 2: A Reference Guide to Medicinal Plants* (1990).

Handmade Crafts

Before the turn of the twentieth century, most people living in the mountains of Appalachia created many items by hand. The Cherokee made all of their tools and implements, from baskets to arrows, by themselves. Virtually no specialization existed. Specialization was rare also among the earliest white settlers and their black slaves. Some large plantations in the wide valleys had separate blacksmith shops or barrel-making operations where individuals worked full-time on one craft, and a few communities supported a handful of craftspeople, but farmers who did not specialize in any one craft made most of the items created in the region. The few craft items that were sold were bought for their utility, not for their aesthetic value.

In 1896 President William Goodell Frost of Berea College, who had been studying mountain crafts since a summerlong horseback tour of the region in 1893, initiated a Homespun Fair in connection with the college commencement. This is the first known promotion and market for Appalachian crafts. In 1895 Frances Goodrich, working for the Presbyterian Church's Women's Board of Home Missions, began encouraging mountain women in Madison County, North Carolina, to weave. She established Allanstand Cottage Industries shortly thereafter and opened a retail outlet in Asheville in 1908 that continues to operate, since 1931 under the auspices of the Southern Highland Handicraft Guild (now the Southern Highland Craft Guild). Besides Frost and Goodrich, other early-twentieth-century icons of craft promotion included Mrs. George W. Vanderbilt, who started Biltmore Industries; Clementine Douglas, who opened the Spinning Wheel craft shop; Mary Sloop of the Crossnore School; Lucy Morgan of the Penland School of Crafts; and Olive Dame Campbell of the John C. Campbell Folk School, all in North Carolina. O. J. Mattil of the Pi Beta Phi Settlement School near Gatlinburg, Tennessee, and the leaders of Pine Mountain and Hindman Settlement Schools in Kentucky were also icons of this craft revival. They or their institutional representatives, along with Allen H. Eaton, the author of the 1937 book *Handicrafts of the Southern Highlands*, were present at a meeting at Penland, North Carolina, in 1928. From this gathering grew the Southern Highland Handicraft Guild, endorsed at the 1929 annual meeting of the Conference of Southern Mountain Workers. The guild has been at the center of Appalachian crafts promotion ever since, sponsoring annual fairs since 1948, first in Gatlinburg and later in Knoxville. The administrative offices have been in Asheville since 1955. During the first half of the twentieth century, the spotlight was on the craft promoters, and virtually no regional craft creators became well known.

Public perceptions of regional crafts solidified in the first half of the twentieth century. The dust jacket of Garry Barker's book *The Handcraft Revival in Southern Appalachia, 1930–1990* (1991) features a picture showing a dulcimer, a coverlet, a basket, a spinning wheel, a chair, and a dresser—all craft objects commonly associated with the region. The mountain dulcimer is the only item made primarily in the Appalachian region, though. The fact that it was never a common instrument among local people has not prevented it from becoming a regional icon. Handwoven coverlets had been fairly commonly made by women in the Appalachian Mountains and beyond and were among the very first items popularized by the promoters of regional handicrafts. The standard practice was for promoters to ask the women working under them, either at home or in shops such as Churchill Weavers in Berea, Kentucky, to follow designs created by professionals from northern urban centers. However, after the Second World War, mechanized looms became readily available and weaving by hand was recognized as being so time-consuming that this handicraft has almost died, although Churchill Weavers and a few other outlets still produce machine-made coverlets. Quilts have been made by many American geographical and ethnic groups and by Appalachian women, as well as a few men, continuously since European settlement. Baskets are commonly associated with the Cherokee as well as other Appalachian crafts workers. Spinning, once an integral part of a mountain housewife's routine, is mostly done by hand by artisans producing works intended for display. Chairs and other pieces of furniture have been made in the region continuously.

Many crafts made in the region never became icons. Pottery has been made in the mountains for generations, for example, yet it is so common all over the country that it is seldom associated with Appalachia. Nevertheless, Charles Counts, who grew up in Kentucky and Tennessee in the 1950s and settled in north Georgia, promoted the work of traditional potters and became well known as an artistic potter himself. Dick Schnacke's West Virginia wooden toys became popular late in the twentieth century. Both Counts and Schnacke wrote books promoting their crafts.

In contrast to Schnacke and Counts, most of the mountain artisans who became iconic figures were promoted by particular craft fairs or other institutions and worked with the crafts that are most commonly associated with the region. Sherman Wooten, a traditional chair maker from Leslie County, Kentucky, has become a symbol of the Appalachian Festival in Cincinnati. The spinner Granny Toothman enjoyed similar status at the Appalachian Celebration in Morehead, Kentucky, during the 1970s and 1980s. Alex

Stewart, a cooper, became a fixture of John Rice Irwin's Tennessee Fall Homecoming at the Museum of Appalachia near Norris, Tennessee, during this same period. Some icons of craft production came from other institutions that promoted crafts in the region, notably Verna Mae Slone, whose quilts have become synonymous with the Hindman Settlement School, and the cornhusk dolls of Sara Bailey, associated with the Pine Mountain Settlement School.

The best-known contemporary dulcimer maker in the region is Warren A. May of Berea, though most of his work today is in furniture. Homer Ledford, who grew up in Tennessee, learned woodworking at the John C. Campbell Folk School in North Carolina, and settled in Kentucky, makes and plays dulcimers and most other kinds of musical instruments common in the region. Terry Ratliff of Floyd County, Kentucky, is perhaps the best-known contemporary chair maker with deep roots in the traditional life of Appalachia. However, Chester Cornett of Letcher County was the best-known traditional chair maker in the first half of the twentieth century.

Among the most prominent craft promoters in the region in the late twentieth century were Sharon Percy Rockefeller, who created a quilting co-op in West Virginia, and Phyllis George Brown, a Kentucky first lady. Both authored books on regional crafts and represented consumers. Their political connections resulted in the allocation of considerable state resources to encourage crafts. Tamarack, in Beckley, West Virginia, and the Kentucky Artisan Center at Berea are state-sponsored craft outlets that draw hundreds of tourists and local people every day.

For many reasons, production of traditional mountain crafts has faded in the face of two contradictory trends. On the one hand, the crafts found at the fairs and festivals held in practically every county seat in the region have come to feature glue-gun "art" and crafts made on other continents. On the other hand, more expensive and artistic craft creations barely distinguishable from artwork have gained prominence. Most of the latter are produced by craftspeople without roots in the region. The beauty of the mountains and accessible markets have drawn craft workers from all over the country to tourist centers such as Berea, Asheville, and Gatlinburg. These crafts are also sold at major craft fairs in those cities, as well as in Elkins, West Virginia, and Norris, Tennessee, and at the guild shops on the Blue Ridge Parkway in North Carolina. Significantly, handlooms purchased by the crafts co-op in Norris are used almost exclusively by craftswomen who have immigrated to the area from Central and South America.

See also: SECTION OVERVIEW (CRAFTS).

—George Brosi, *Berea, Kentucky*

Garry G. Barker, *The Handcraft Revival in Southern Appalachia, 1930–1990* (1991); Allen H. Eaton, *Handicrafts of the Southern Highlands* (1937); Edward L. DuPuy and Emma Weaver, *Artisans of the Appalachians* (1967).

Hillbilly

The hillbilly is the dominant icon of Appalachia. Asked to list images related to Appalachia, those with limited knowledge of the region inevitably cite the hillbilly. Worldwide, the hillbilly image is consistently a lanky, black-bearded, white male who lives in a cabin in the mountains with an outhouse out back. He wears a battered slouch hat, totes a shotgun and a jug of moonshine, and holds little regard for the law, work, cleanliness, or book learning. He has loose morals and is decidedly dangerous.

The word *hillbilly* is believed to have first appeared in print in the United States in 1900 in a *New York Journal* article describing the "hill-billie" as "a free and untrammelled white citizen of Alabama, who lives in the hills, has no means to speak of, dresses as he can, talks as he pleases, drinks whiskey when he gets it, and fires off his revolver as the fancy takes him." By 1915, the term *hillbilly* began to appear in magazine articles and early movies, but the first media image of the hillbilly matching the icon still known today appeared in a 1926 film called *Rainbow Riley*. In the film, a reporter sent to cover a feud in eastern Kentucky finds men in dark beards wearing ill-fitting clothes and hats and sporting shotguns. In the 1930s, the icon was solidified through the hillbilly characters of Paul Webb's *Mountain Boys* cartoons in *Esquire* magazine, Al Capp's *Li'l Abner*, and Billy DeBeck's *Barney Google and Snuffy Smith*. These characters and their cartoon-world antics forever etched the hillbilly caricature into popular culture.

Although the visual hillbilly icon was established in the 1930s, the concept has antecedents stretching back for centuries. Mountain dwellers may have admirable qualities, but the idea that they are strange, peculiar, and potentially dangerous is an old one in Western culture and in other parts of the world. Many civilizations have mythologized mountain dwellers. Ancient Roman shepherds who spent their summers in mountain pastures returned to towns with fantastic stories of highland spirits and malevolent forces. By the second century, Christian missionaries began crossing European mountains but only with great trepidation and sometimes literally blindfolded against the terrors they felt lurked in high places. They told stories of hairy mountain women who traveled naked with tamed lions in tow. Medieval travelers told stories of outlaws, bandits, and ruffians who inhabited mountains and described monsters who were, in reality, mountain people who suffered the deformed necks and bulging eyes brought on by goiters (caused by lack of iodine in the water supply).

In subsequent centuries, even after the mountains came to be cherished for their awe-inspiring beauty and

"NAW HE KAINT READ HE'S JEST PUTTIN' ON AIRS"
XXX
GHB608
© MWM
WRITE ME SOON - I CAN READ

Hillbilly cartoon on a postcard, c. 1960s. The dominant icon of Appalachia, the hillbilly is consistently portrayed as a lanky, gun-toting, hard-drinking white male with little regard for the law, work, cleanliness, or education.

appreciated as places for inspiration and recreation, mountain dwellers themselves never fared as well as the scenery. Eighteenth-century writers found mountain folk to be a mixture of what one called "the terrible and the agreeable," the savage and the civilized. Nineteenth-century romanticism, developing just as Appalachia was being defined as a distinct cultural area, found much to admire in the free and noble mountaineer but also much to despise and pity in the ignoble hillbilly, perceived to live in squalor, ignorance, violence, and incestuousness.

In the New World, the mountains were initially a wilderness barrier to the settlement of areas populated by native "savages." White settlers who ventured into and beyond the mountains were often regarded with skepticism by coastal urbanites, who felt that the hills themselves led one to lose civilized manners, embrace lawlessness, and backslide from progress into vulgarity. Near the end of the Revolutionary War, British Major Patrick Ferguson described the men of the mountains, whom he called "Back Water men," as "barbarians," "dregs of mankind," and "mongrels"—before the self-described Overmountain Men defeated him soundly at the battle of Kings Mountain. Writers of the late eighteenth and early nineteenth centuries clearly delineated the split between the cultivated Tidewater elite and rough mountain backwoodsmen. In 1867 George Washington Harris created the character of Sut Lovingood (in *Sut Lovingood: Yarns Spun by a Nat'ral Born Durn'd Fool*), an east Tennessee mountaineer who epitomizes the crude, rude, dirty, and irreverent hillbilly trickster who uses his wits to give the smug and sanctimonious their comeuppance. David Crockett, backwoodsman and congressman, brought the ambivalences of the mountain character together in a real person who then became Davy, the subject of mythology.

By the late nineteenth and early twentieth centuries, the idea that mountain folk were "strange and peculiar" was entrenched in American popular culture. Local color writers, illustrators, early photographers, and filmmakers used various attributes of the hillbilly icon to depict people of Appalachia. During this time, music from the mountains made its way into popular culture with the advent of sound recording, and the genre of "hillbilly music" launched the American country music industry. Record promoters thought it would help sell records and boost the careers of radio and early television recording artists from the mountains if they dressed and acted according to the image of the hillbilly fool. Bands from the mountains from the 1920s to the time of the popular television show *Hee Haw* have used hillbilly trappings for laughs and as a kind of immediate regional identity. Contemporary country musician Dwight Yoakam, from eastern Kentucky, styles himself as "the hillbilly deluxe" and uses the irony of the icon in his music and presentation style, which pay homage to hillbilly heritage while appealing to sophisticated fans.

Although *hillbilly* has been used as a derogatory term in mass media, popular jokes, and mass marketing, it has also been embraced by many in the region as a term of regional pride and solidarity. The Internet hosts numerous hillbilly Web sites from the region, including some that play *The Beverly Hillbillies* theme song and display hillbilly icons.

The Appalachian hillbilly has equivalents worldwide. In Germany, Bavarians are often characterized in cartoons as country bumpkins and manglers of the German language. The Hmong hill tribes of Laos have been characterized as mountain goats (equivalent to hill-billies) and made the butt of jokes. The people of the Japanese Alps are called "people of the backwoods." The Kurds of northern Iraq and Turkey are seen as clannish, violent, and crude, which led historian Arnold Toynbee in the 1930s to compare them to the people of Appalachia, whom he considered uncivilized.

Notwithstanding his inferiority, the hillbilly is imbued with distinct powers. He can flatter, frighten, and humiliate. As a rugged frontiersman, he flatters the American self-image. As a savage, embodied in the mountain men of the movie *Deliverance,* he frightens and humiliates. The hillbilly both attracts and repels, representing both the complexity of Appalachia and the ambivalence about the region in the public mind.

See also: HILLBILLY (RACE, ETHNICITY, AND IDENTITY).

—Jean Haskell, *East Tennessee State University*

Dwight B. Billings, Katherine Ledford, and Gurney Norman, eds., *Confronting Appalachian Stereotypes: Back Talk from an American Region* (1999); Marjorie Hope Nicholson, *Mountain Gloom and Mountain Glory: The Development of the Aesthetics of the Infinite* (1959); J. W. Williamson, *Hillbillyland: What the Movies Did to the Mountains and What the Mountains Did to the Movies* (1995).

Historical Heroes

The history of Appalachia lends itself to the kind of larger-than-life figures who have come to be considered heroes or icons. Intrepid explorers ventured forth into the unknown; valiant soldiers risked their lives in combat; selfless volunteers placed the good of the whole above their personal interests; and gritty underdogs battled long odds and powerful opponents to improve the lives of their fellow Appalachians. Their names have achieved legendary status. Some, such as Daniel Boone, are rooted in the colonial period, while others, such as Mother Jones and Alvin York, lived only a few generations ago.

Heroes are people who have given their lives to something bigger than themselves. All of the best-known heroes in Appalachian history fit this pattern. Boone's physical deeds as a hunter, woodsman, frontier settler, and Indian fighter are matched by York's experience during the Meuse-Argonne offensive in France during World War I, where he killed twenty Germans and, with seven other men, captured 132 prisoners. In 1880, at age fifty, former teacher and dressmaker Mary Harris "Mother" Jones put herself in physical danger time and again fighting for powerless industrial workers throughout the region.

Historical conditions in Appalachia help explain why certain individuals have attained the status of heroes. During the colonial and revolutionary periods, whites who moved into the mountains faced indigenous populations that often resisted their presence; John Sevier's success as an Indian fighter and treaty negotiator made him a hero to many and provided the basis for his election as governor of the independent State of Franklin, as congressional representative, and as Tennessee's first governor. During the second half of the nineteenth century, many Appalachians held strong antislavery feelings and saw large portions of their economy transformed by industrialization, often for the worse. In John Henry they found a free African American in West Virginia fighting to his death a steam-powered machine that was threatening laborers, black and white alike, throughout the mountains. Coal mining, the harshest embodiment of industrialization in vast stretches of Appalachia, had impoverished workers and their families since the Reconstruction period. People demanded change and enthusiastically supported reformers such as Jones, who risked their lives to improve working and living conditions.

National attention has often focused on Appalachian heroes. John Mack Faragher wrote a biography of Boone that was a twentieth-century best-seller, and Mother Jones's name is associated with a national magazine and an international fund for documentary photography. By these measures, people living outside of the region care about heroes who have lived in and around the mountains. In general these heroes serve to reinforce traditional images of Appalachia. Many Americans ascribe distinctive characteristics to mountain residents, whether negative ones such as clannishness, inbreeding, and illiteracy, or positive ones such as independence, loyalty, and patriotism. The heroes seem to personify these stereotypes and have the ability to transform the negative images into positive ones. American moviegoers expect Appalachians to shoot accurately, and they criticize this skill when the Hatfields and McCoys fire upon one another but praise it when Sergeant York picks off German soldiers with precision. Many Americans expect Appalachians to suffer from poverty and poor working conditions, so they honor someone such as Jones, who fought such circumstances (while also reinforcing outsiders' misperceptions).

Outsiders often hold stereotypical images so strongly that their pantheon of Appalachian heroes includes individuals who arguably do not belong there. People see Andrew Jackson, "Old Hickory," as a hero of the frontier generally and they associate the frontier with Appalachia, but Jackson had relatively few connections with the region. Born in South Carolina, Jackson moved to North Carolina and as a young lawyer passed through east Tennessee. As a judge and congressional representative he worked within the region but never to the degree to which he involved himself with middle Tennessee and the Old Southwest during times of war and peace. One can see David Crockett in a similar light. His heroism, not only at the Alamo but also as a champion of the common man, is rooted in middle and west Tennessee and in Texas rather than in his mountain birthplace of Greene County in east Tennessee. Given examples such as these, the way nonresidents think about the Appalachian region and its heroes may operate counterintuitively—they do not use the heroes to understand the mountains, but may use images and stereotypes of the region to select their heroes even if, like Jackson and Crockett, those individuals have only tangential connections with Appalachia.

While heroes may provide one means by which outsiders come to think about Appalachia, heroes may serve a different function for the inhabitants themselves. The heroes may stand as symbols for the Appalachian experience, the touchstones that create a common identity. Association with these heroes may also enable inhabitants to feel proud about their past and hopeful about a better future. If they see Mother Jones and Sergeant York as a dressmaker and a church leader who acted heroically under trying circumstances, then the possibility exists that other ordinary Appalachians can meet the challenges to come. Heroes, in short, can foster optimism about the future that belies the stereotypical image of Appalachian fatalism. In this sense, understanding these historical heroes means understanding the heroism to which all can aspire.

See also: BOONE, DANIEL (SETTLEMENT AND MIGRATION); CROCKETT, DAVID (HUMOR); *SERGEANT YORK* (MEDIA).

—David C. Hsiung, *Juniata College*

John Mack Faragher, *Daniel Boone: The Life and Legend of an American Pioneer* (1992); Mary Harris Jones, *The Autobiography of Mother Jones* (1925); Thomas J. Skeyhill, ed., *Sergeant York: His Own Life Story and War Diary* (1928).

Homeplace

Appalachians typically use and understand the term *homeplace* to mean the piece of property where an individual grew up or spent the most significant portion of his or her childhood. The term may also refer to the ancestral home of a particular family. In either case it is understood to mean the entire parcel of land and all its features, both natural and man-made, and not solely or even primarily the house in which the family lived. The term *homeplace* is most often used by an adult in reference to his or her own childhood home or to that of a parent or other relative, and the generally positive memories associated with its use reflect strong attachments to place and family that characterize Appalachian culture.

In traditional usage, a homeplace includes the hills, streams, fields, forests, roads, paths, fences, garden plots, orchards, and outbuildings with which family members came into regular and intimate contact in both work and leisure activities. Although the degree of economic dependence on the land may vary widely and has in most cases decreased significantly since the mid-twentieth century, life on the homeplace implies farming, gardening, harvesting wild plants, fruits, and nuts, and hunting and fishing as means of providing or supplementing the family's living. Leisure activities as well take place out of doors, especially for the children. As the provider of food and shelter and as the remembered scene of labor and leisure, both communal and solitary, the homeplace is both a source and a symbol of physical and emotional security. Even after these functions have been altered or ended by the passage of time and changes in circumstance and the land sold, divided, or rendered unrecognizable by subsequent owners, the homeplace continues to serve as a touchstone of family and community memory for several succeeding generations. As a spot on a map or place in the heart, it may embody what many people in and outside the region find most attractive in the rural, rooted lifestyle traditionally associated with much of Appalachia.

The significance of the homeplace in Appalachian culture is, like the word itself, both clarified and complicated by joining the abstract with the concrete. As a regional icon, it first evokes the positive associations most people have for home as a concept, then puts that concept into tangible form by lending to it a physical shape as well as an exact location, which ideally adjoins or is very near to grandparents, cousins, aunts, and uncles.

The archetypical homeplace, with separate fields, a patch of woods, a running stream, and a spring or well, is small enough to be intimately known and remembered and to belong within a larger community yet large and complex enough to be more or less self-sufficient and self-contained. Particularly in retrospect, the homeplace is a safe world of manageable scale, distinct boundaries, and clear if arbitrary rules. The multigenerational household and farm of television's *The Waltons* provides a romanticized yet appropriate example of the ideal homeplace, one that simultaneously comforts and confines the young as they explore a wider world under the watchful eyes of grandparents who, at the other end of life's cycle, may depend at least upon the comfort of familiarity as they are drawn steadily toward the confinement of infirmity. More poignant examples of the homeplace as haven are central to the plots of classic Appalachian novels such as *River of Earth* by James Still and *The Dollmaker* by Harriette Simpson Arnow. Still's female protagonist, Alpha Baldridge, and Arnow's Gertie Nevels are repeatedly and ultimately thwarted, both by economic circumstance and by their husbands' conflicting dreams, in their attempts to create for their children permanent refuges from, in Alpha's case, the hand-to-mouth, rootless existence of itinerant coal mining, and, in Gertie's, the merciless anonymity and pseudo-prosperity of World War II Detroit.

In a widely read essay entitled "Appalachian Values," Loyal Jones, a longtime director of the Appalachian Center at Berea College, places fond regard for the homeplace among Appalachian natives' strongest values: "We are oriented around places. We never forget our native places, and we go back as often as possible. Our place is always close on our minds. It is one of the unifying values of mountain people, the attachment to one's place." As long as either parent is still living at the homeplace, it is a regular weekend gathering place for the immediate family, some of whom may drive long distances to be with familiar people in a familiar setting. The third generation may be especially fond of a homeplace because its members experience the attention of loving grandparents and acquaintance with cousins without the tedium of daily life and work or the tensions of constant close contact with siblings or confrontations with tired parents.

A family's homeplace is the preferred site of family reunions and in some cases is kept up specifically for that purpose even after family members have died or moved away. Sentimental descendants with careers and homes hundreds of miles away sometimes purchase and maintain a family homeplace as a second home or hunting preserve. Others may be drawn back in memory or fact by the particular taste of spring or well water, a reminder of the quality of soil and what grew best in it, or the smell or taste of a particular fruit or flower. Visits are sometimes made with the purpose of retrieving samples to taste, graft, or transplant as living reminders of a still important past.

Jones notes that "Appalachian people are family centered. As Jack Weller has pointed out in *Yesterday's People*, the mountain person wants to please his family, and he is more truly himself when he is within the family circle. Loyalty runs deep between family members, and a sense of responsibility for one another may extend to cousins, nephews, nieces, uncles and aunts, and in-laws." At homeplace gatherings, a family's oral history is passed down and shared, and it is here that a sense of belonging and responsibility to a group larger than the immediate family but still within the bounds of kinship is first formed.

As large families and small farms evoked by the traditional definition of *homeplace* have grown less common, so has the word's use in daily conversation. Its meaning may evolve along with the region's demographics to include a house on a subdivision lot or other land that is merely property rather than a homeplace and is incidental rather than integral to the lives of the people living upon it. Or it may gradually be relegated to the specialized vocabularies of the aged, the nostalgic family historian, or the entrepreneur, who recognizes the emotional appeal of a label that offers both an allusion to the ideal of home as understood by all cultures and an idealized embodiment of it as found in Appalachia and other traditionally rural, agrarian, place-oriented cultures.

See also: SECTION OVERVIEW (FAMILY AND COMMUNITY); SENSE OF PLACE.

—Ricky Cox, *Radford University*

Harriette Simpson Arnow, *The Dollmaker* (1954); Loyal Jones, "Appalachian Values," in *Voices from the Hills: Selected Readings of Southern Appalachia*, ed. Robert J. Higgs and Ambrose N. Manning (1975); James Still, *River of Earth* (1940).

Jack Tales, Tricksters, and Mountain Folklore

Many Appalachian folktales depict trickster figures that triumph over stronger adversaries by use of their wits, and the trickster Jack, who is the hero of a cycle of such stories, has become an icon of the region. Tricksters appear most often in Jack tales or wonder tales, stories of marvel and fantasy brought to Appalachia by German immigrants. Although any fictional hero can appear in a wonder tale—Wicked John, Whitebear Whittington, or Muncimeg—most recount the exploits of the adolescent boy named Jack who goes out into the world alone, surmounting difficult obstacles along the way.

In Jack tales, the hero is always a well-rounded, self-reliant character who eventually wins material wealth, symbolizing the rewards of a strong work ethic and uncompromising individuality. In one tale, a mountain man called Ol' Greasy Beard steals food from Jack. In the subsequent chase scene, Jack and his brothers rescue Sally, a girl that Ol' Greasy Beard has kept prisoner in his cave. By story's end, Jack and Sally marry, have seven intelligent sons, and live happily ever after. In another version, the old mountain man is a giant who turns into a fire-breathing dragon when underground. In order to win Jenny (yet another heroine), Jack must successfully slay the dragon and rescue her enslaved sisters. These two variants, as with most Jack tales, echo such earlier European epics as *Le Morte d'Arthur*, with its knight quests and damsels in distress, and *Beowulf*, with its hero who fights a dragon that lives underground. The main difference between Jack tales and these European epics, however, comes in the form of social leveling. A distinct product of American democracy and Appalachian identity formation, Jack interacts with kings, knights, and princesses as easily as he does with mountain men, animals, and monsters. Unlike his European counterparts, Jack is also a self-sufficient hero in charge of his own destiny, fulfilling the American myth of the self-made man. Thus, Jack tales are stories of initiation whereby the protagonist learns about himself and the world through a series of trials. Although feminists take issue with the static views of female characters and their subsequent objectification in most Jack tales, this genre of folktale preserves traditional views of marriage and social roles brought to Appalachia by Scots-Irish immigrants, whose culture influenced Appalachian notions of self-sufficiency and taking care of one's own.

Probably the best-known Appalachian tall-tale hero, who may also be considered a benevolent trickster, is Davy

David Crockett by William Henry Huddle, 1889. Oil on canvas. Crockett is the preeminent symbol of the Appalachian as rugged individual, a brazen, brutal, and boisterous frontiersman who helped open up the country west of the Appalachian Mountains.

Crockett, "king of the wild frontier," who was partially created through the historical David Crockett's self-aggrandizement, making it difficult to separate fact from fiction. Since the early nineteenth century, Crockett has become the preeminent symbol of Appalachia's rugged individual, a brazen, brutal, and boisterous frontiersman who helped open up the country west of the Appalachian Mountains. Many of the tales about Crockett appeared during his tenure in politics, during which he served first as justice of the peace and then as state senator and U.S. representative. He often won votes by telling tales in which he painted himself as a frontier hero with a pioneer spirit, good horse sense, and a hillbilly sense of humor; this image is now attached to most rural grassroots politicians who preach antiestablishment politics to plebian constituents. Early on, Whig journalists latched on to Crockett's tall talk, helping to make him an icon of backwoods democracy. In one story, Crockett bushwhacks a local bartender by purchasing ten rounds of drinks for his constituents with the same recently shot coonskin. In another, he bare-handedly kills a bear through a night of rough fighting aided only by his hunting dogs. In yet another, Crockett saves the world from destruction in 1835 by standing atop the Allegheny Mountains to tear the tail off of Halley's Comet as it passes. By the twenty-first century, Crockett had become a type of backwoods superman who could do the impossible with only a rifle, a pistol, and a hunting knife, emblems of the courage, fortitude, and braggadocio of the Appalachian character.

Another famous tall-tale hero is John Henry, the African American "steel-drivin' man" who helped build Big Bend Tunnel for the Chesapeake and Ohio Railway in southern West Virginia during the 1870s. He is one of many blue-collar workers whose pride in his work became legendary, symbolizing the superiority of man over machine during the early stages of the Industrial Revolution. As his tale recounts, Henry is the railroad's best "hammer swinger." He is challenged to duel with a new steam drill to see which is better, man or machine. Although Henry wins the contest, he collapses and dies at the finish line, the machine being the ultimate winner. As Henry's legend grew, so did his stature. Some tales have him born eight feet tall and working for the railroad at three weeks old. Others transplant him to a riverboat, where he loses in a competition with a steam winch loading cotton. All versions, however, are morality tales that comment negatively on the growing dangers of industrialization, celebrating the strength of the human condition in the face of problematic technological progress. Today, Henry is especially celebrated in his home state of West Virginia, where his defeat of the steam drill personifies the state's motto, *Montani Semper Liberi* ("Mountaineers Are Always Free"). Resisting the imposition of the values, beliefs, and practices of others is a hallmark of all Appalachian heroes.

Lumberjack Tony Beaver, another West Virginian, is Appalachia's forerunner to Paul Bunyan, whose better-known exploits closely mirror those of Beaver. According to legend, Beaver gets his start in the lumber business by beating Big Bill Simpson in a wood-chopping contest, the latter offering a share of his business to anyone able to out-chop him. Through time, Beaver becomes so strong that he can bring down hickory trees with one lick, making them look like matchsticks when falling. Bored by such repetitive hard work, Beaver finally reverts to tearing trees out by their roots instead of swinging an axe. So successful is he as a lumberjack that Beaver starts his own lumber business on the Eel River, a stream he named and claims to own, aided by his two faithful oxen, Hannibal and Goliath, becoming a symbol of upward mobility and Appalachian self-sufficiency. The values celebrated by lumberjacks—strength, ingenuity, humor, and independence—are characteristics equally shared by most Appalachian folk heroes, representing a hearty and resolute people to most of the outside world.

Other elements of folklore include proverbs, sayings, and colloquialisms that a community shares. Appalachian speech and culture have been so replete with such folkloric elements that Appalachia has become synonymous with folk culture. Some mountain proverbs deal with weather forecasts *(Frost will occur six weeks after hearing the first katydids)*, while others share medicinal wisdom *(Rub warts with a dishtowel and bury it; when the dish towel begins to rot, the warts will disappear)*. These illustrate the varied superstitions, medicinal knowledge, and weather prophesying used by early Appalachians to survive in an isolated and rugged landscape used largely for farming and, later, mining. Some sayings, however, are more didactic than pragmatic, disseminating universal truths or encouraging common sense. *When the horse falls in love with the grass, he dies of hunger* and *Life to the lamb is death to the wolf* are such examples. For many people in other regions of the country in which speech is not so colorful or metaphoric, this penchant for folk speech has made people in Appalachia appear quaint.

Appalachian folktales, tall tales, and folklore have helped form an image of the region for outsiders and insiders alike. They both entertain and reinforce regional values such as individualism, making do, and egalitarianism.

See also: STORYTELLING, HISTORY OF (PERFORMING ARTS); STORYTELLING IN THE TWENTIETH CENTURY, RENAISSANCE OF (PERFORMING ARTS).

—Shawn Holliday, *Alice Lloyd College*

Richard Chase, *The Jack Tales* (1943); David Leeming and Jake Page, eds., *Myths, Legends, and Folktales of America: An Anthology* (1999); Jane Polley, ed., *Reader's Digest American Folklore and Legend: The Saga of Heroes and Heroines, Our Braggers, Boosters and Bad Men, Our Beliefs and Superstitions* (1978).

Kinfolks

Stereotypically, the Appalachian mountain family has a large number of children mothered by a young and uneducated woman. They huddle in a small and crude log cabin near an extensive network of cousins, aunts, and uncles who live up the holler. Beyond this, the image of the family portrayed in popular media diverges. Sometimes Appalachian kin systems are romanticized in an image of a tightly knit and loving unit doing anything possible for neighbors or needy strangers and sacrificing for loved ones; at other points, these same families have been portrayed as clannish, inbred, and backward.

The Appalachian family was brought to the attention of the American public in the late 1800s with the notoriously violent family feud between the Hatfields of West Virginia and the McCoys of Kentucky. The Romeo-and-Juliet affair between a young Hatfield woman and a McCoy young man received much coverage in the newspapers of the time, beginning a tradition of portraying Appalachians as reactionary, family-centered, and trigger-happy hillbillies. Family feuds were only one way that family networks made for volatile politics in the mountains, however. Indeed, Elmon Middleton, a Harlan County historian, felt compelled to address the violent image as early as 1934, when he commented that, contrary to popular belief, the old-time mountaineer "prefers his peaceful simple life to that of shooting at his neighbor." Harry Caudill, in his widely read 1963 polemic *Night Comes to the Cumberlands*, asserted that nepotism and ancient conflicts had long dictated the developmental trajectory of Appalachian communities.

The late 1800s also saw the rise of public awareness of inbreeding in Appalachia. Though later scientific studies have demonstrated that inbreeding is no more common in Appalachia than in other parts of the country, the inbred hillbilly is a regional stereotype. Recessive genetic traits have, however, become notable at times in a small number of Appalachian families due to intermarriage. The most famous example is the "Kentucky Blue People," or "Blue People of Troublesome Creek," a Knott County family host to a rare disease known as methemoglobinemia, which causes blood to be a dark color, giving a purplish-blue tint to the skin of the afflicted. Although there were probably never more than a dozen people living with the disease at any given time—it began to appear in the 1800s and had nearly vanished by the mid-1970s—it became a public curiosity, cementing the perception that marriages between cousins and other close kin were accepted, perhaps desired, by mountaineers. Sensational photographs of the region have often featured retarded and filthy men and women, inviting further speculation about inbreeding. For example, the work of Shelby Lee Adams, who published three books of photographs of the region around the turn of the twenty-first century, may well leave the viewer to wonder if the very stock of people living in Appalachia is, at best, poor. A city character in the 1972 movie *Deliverance* makes a comment about "pitiful" genetic deficiencies when he first sees the mute, retarded mountain boy who plays the famous "Dueling Banjos" theme.

Despite the prevalence of negative stereotypes, positive images of Appalachian families are also powerful and durable. Books such as Wilma Dykeman's *The Tall Woman* (1962), Silas House's *Clay's Quilt* (2001), and Harriette Simpson Arnow's *The Dollmaker* (1954) include scenes where relatives prevent starvation, help build homes, birth babies, and give happiness—if only fleetingly—to mountaineer life. Other media present their own positive portrayals of mountain kin systems. Dolly Parton sings wistfully and lovingly of her Tennessee mountain home and family. Loretta Lynn particularly inspires fondness when she proclaims her pride in being the daughter of a coal miner. *Coal Miner's Daughter*, the 1980 movie based on her autobiography, depicts Lynn's marriage at the age of thirteen and domestic troubles such as abuse, infidelity, and unplanned pregnancies, but the basic upbeat theme is reflected in the lyrics of the title song: "We were poor, but we had love." The resilient and loving mountain family was the core of the television drama *The Waltons*, which aired from 1972 to 1981. In the show, the members of a large family surviving the hard times of the 1930s and 1940s enjoy affectionate relationships and supportive associations with their neighbors.

Familism, the extreme cultural importance given to family units, has been a major theme in less nostalgic portrayals of the region. The characters of the television show *The Dukes of Hazzard*, which aired from 1978 to 1985, embody family closeness, even as they evade the law in various struggles against the corruption of the local legal and political structure. Preserving family in spite of the law is also a theme in Vera and Bill Cleaver's 1969 children's book *Where the Lilies Bloom*. Continuous migration out of the region has meant that families are often the anchor that prevents individuals from moving up—and necessarily out. For example, NASA aerospace engineer Homer Hickam, born and reared in a West Virginia coal camp, had to convince his father, a miner, that college was a reasonable goal. His struggle to raise his horizons, told in his memoir, *Rocket Boys*, was dramatized in a 1999 film, *October Sky*. As Hickam's story illustrates, values such as upward mobility have often been perceived as secondary to preserving family in the mountains.

Family and kin continue to be an important part of life, and many youth still aspire to remain close to their family homes. Intense loyalty and love of family are values that make Appalachia distinct in popular opinion and set it as a region apart.

See also: FEUDS AND VIOLENCE (MEDIA); HOMEPLACE; SECTION OVERVIEW (FAMILY AND COMMUNITY).

—Sky Brosi, *Western New Mexico University*

Patricia D. Beaver, *Rural Community in the Appalachian South* (1986); F. Carlene Bryant, *We're All Kin: A Cultural Study of a Mountain Neighborhood* (1981); George L. Hicks, *Appalachian Valley* (1976).

Log Cabins

Since the mid-nineteenth century, the log cabin has served as a symbol of supposed independence, self-sufficiency, and wholesomeness in American frontier life, and to the extent that Appalachia has become a sign for the same qualities, the log cabin has come to be closely associated with mountain life. Because log dwellings continued to be built in the area somewhat longer than in most other parts of the country, log construction is particularly identified with Appalachia, even though other building materials were also historically employed throughout the region.

The antecedents of the log cabin myth lie outside Appalachia and can be traced as far back as the presidential election of 1840, when opponents tried to discredit presidential candidate William Henry Harrison by claiming he had been raised in a log cabin. Although this allegation was false, Harrison cleverly co-opted it and associated himself with the popular idea of the log cabin as a sign of pioneer virtues, a connection later made explicit in a nineteenth-century series of young people's "log cabin" biographies of presidents.

During the late nineteenth and early twentieth centuries, at the same time that Appalachia was being brought to national attention by travel writers, teachers, missionaries, and entrepreneurs, the Colonial Revival style predominated in architecture, furniture, and other crafts in the United States, which, influenced by the transatlantic Arts and Crafts movement, suggested that handicrafts were representative of the colonial era. Americans were thus provided with a tangible link to the patriotism of the Revolutionary War. Educators and social workers such as William Goodell Frost, Allen H. Eaton, and Frances Goodrich extolled the region's crafts tradition as evidence of Appalachia's role as a latter-day seedbed of democratic virtue. These advocates frequently used log structures to house craft industries and promote sales. At Chicago's 1933 Century of Progress celebration, for example, the Penland Weavers and Potters mounted an exhibit in a small log cabin (dubbed a "Travel-log") hauled from North Carolina on a truck. The Penland cabin was located near a display of five log cabins representing phases of Abraham Lincoln's life, thus strengthening the links between Appalachia, the log dwelling, and an idealized American history.

The romantic connection of Appalachia with log construction shaped architectural preservation in the region. When developing sites such as Cades Cove in the Great Smoky Mountains National Park in the 1930s, the National Park Service demolished frame houses on park property while preserving log structures, even though frame construction was characteristic of mountain architecture at that time. More recently, private collector and entrepreneur John Rice Irwin built a mecca for aficionados of log construction at his Museum of Appalachia in Norris, Tennessee, to which he relocated more than a dozen examples of log cabins and barns. As with Cades Cove, the Irwin museum has few examples of traditional frame houses.

The back-to-the-land movement of the 1970s, which brought numerous counterculturalists to Appalachia searching for a supposedly simple, wholesome, self-sufficient agrarian life, also stimulated romantic interest in log construction. Basic build-it-yourself log cabin kits appeared, and by the 1990s prefabricated log homes of opulent proportions were available, including a line marketed by the popular southern artist and designer Bob Timberlake. Mobile homes with simulated log siding became available as well.

The nostalgia for log cabins belies the fact that historically many people who grew up or kept house in these cramped, dark, and dusty dwellings were eager to move out. Furthermore, not all observers have viewed log cabins or the frontier as positive. Nineteenth-century architect Andrew Jackson Downing, for example, associated log "huts" with frontier lawlessness in *The Architecture of Country Houses*. Desirous of shedding connotations of backwardness, log cabin owners sometimes disguised the log siding with weatherboards when sawn lumber became available. In modern times, however, the popular imagination both within and outside of Appalachia continues to celebrate the log cabin as a symbol of a romanticized mountain culture resting on a bedrock foundation of pioneer virtue.

See also: LOG CONSTRUCTION TECHNIQUES (ARCHITECTURE); LOG DWELLING TYPES (ARCHITECTURE); MUSEUM OF APPALACHIA (CULTURAL INSTITUTIONS).

—Theresa Lloyd, *East Tennessee State University*

Mac E. Barrick, "The Log House as a Cultural Symbol," *Material Culture* (Spring 1986); Jane S. Becker, *Selling Tradition: Appalachia and the Construction of an American Folk, 1930–1940* (1998); John Morgan, *The Log House in East Tennessee* (1990).

Making Do

Throughout the United States, the poor are often admonished to "make do" or "do without" even as media and social pressures encourage consumption. Due to economic necessities, many people of limited incomes find themselves desperately trying to "make do." The results of these attempts to manage despite inadequate resources have become sources of jokes and stereotyping. Blacks often bear the brunt of jokes about making do with pieced-together work being referred to as "Afro-engineered" or worse. However, people who value simple living and conserving resources regard making do as a panacea for the environmental problems caused by overconsumption. Nowhere is this dichotomy more apparent than in Appalachia, where the topography of the region often means that homesteads where the inhabitants make do are close to the road and easily viewed by those passing by. Images of resourceful Appalachians making do in picturesque ways—such as by using pieces of hollow logs for bee gums—contrast with the images of yards filled with junk cars used for parts. Appalachia has become a focal point for both the negative and positive images of making do.

The ability of Appalachians to make do has been extensively portrayed by the media. The *Foxfire* books, created by high school students in north Georgia beginning in the 1970s, established a high standard for such media depiction. Appalachia—Science in the Public Interest, a group devoted to subsistence and sustainable living, chose to locate in eastern Kentucky, where its members could not only blend with the population but learn from the natives. Each year the organization publishes a calendar that features ways of sustainable living drawn from both local lore and published ideas from around the world. Rhoda H. Halperin, in her book *The Livelihood of Kin: Making Ends Meet "The Kentucky Way,"* delineates the roles of extended family members in making do. She illuminates many ways Appalachians remain self-reliant in spite of limited cash resources. Traditional skills such as gardening, auto repair, construction work, sewing, hunting, and other "hands-on" work are valued, Halperin found, but mountain folk

An enterprising Appalachian attempts to "make do" with a creative display of hubcaps and tires near Alma, Ohio, 1995. To outsiders, efforts to manage despite inadequate resources are often sources of jokes and stereotyping.

who do not adapt to mainstream standards are viewed as lacking in industriousness and/or competence. Li'l Abner puts a bucket under his roof when it is raining, rather than repair it when he can. There is also the image of Granny in *The Beverly Hillbillies* television series, who has access to a great deal of money but is unwilling to purchase what is easily available and insists on making her own "concoctions." Viewers of this television series are left with the impression that making do is a "hillbilly value" even when it is not a necessity.

Mountain people have been able, as have Native Americans, to live with limited currency by using abundant natural resources. A powerful example of this ability to live off the land is the Hensley Settlement near Cumberland Gap, Kentucky, an isolated mountaintop community that has never been accessible even by an ordinary automobile road. From 1903 until 1951, several families lived there, subsisting on what they could grow and make. They made do, and images of their lifestyle have been preserved by the Cumberland Gap National Historical Park. The buildings and other community infrastructure are open to visitor tours, and pamphlets and photographs depict the community as a positive example of ingenuity and skill.

Some of modern Appalachia's most negative images and stereotypes have arisen from the region's poorest residents making do in the face of daunting circumstances. Scenic mountain roads and creek banks become repositories for junked cars. Stripped of the engines, wheels, and axles, abandoned buses, vans, and trucks become shelters for farm animals. In the absence of septic tanks, outdoor privies are built over creeks. Derelict bathtubs and oil drums become watering troughs for animals. Discarded tires hold flowerbeds and cast-off television satellite dishes become holders for various plants in many yards. These images often leave deep negative impressions on visitors and reinforce regional stereotypes. Though various economic-development initiatives have reduced the number of Appalachians making do in the early twentieth-first century, the dichotomies between rich and poor, urban and rural, continue to be more stark in Appalachia than in other regions of the United States.

See also: CULTURE OF POVERTY (FOLKLORE AND FOLKLIFE); WAR ON POVERTY (GOVERNMENT); WELFARE AND POVERTY.

—Connie Brosi, *Berea, Kentucky*

Rhoda H. Halperin, *The Livelihood of Kin: Making Ends Meet "The Kentucky Way"* (1990); Eliot Wigginton, ed., *The Foxfire Book* (1972).

Moonshine

See Distilleries (Business, Industry, and Technology); Moonshine (Food and Cooking)

Mountain Whites

Because European Americans have been the dominant political group in the United States in modern times, most of the journalistic, scholarly, and creative focus on Appalachia has been on whites, who do outnumber other groups in the region—but not in the proportion suggested by media coverage. Prior to the late twentieth century, little was known about other racial or ethnic groups in Appalachia, and nearly all depictions of Appalachian life featured white mountaineers. The hillbilly caricature is always white, never Native American, African American, or of other ethnicity, even though the population of the mountains has always been diverse.

As representatives of this mountainous region, Appalachians of European descent who populate the uplands, particularly the Scots-Irish, are often depicted in imagery that exaggerates both their strengths and their weaknesses. This imagery derives from historical relationships between mountaineers and lowlanders, between rural and urban communities, and between the poor and the wealthy.

Though images of mountain whites are influenced by ancient cultural traditions that both revere and fear mountains and their inhabitants, such romantic images are mitigated by equally unrealistic images based on the tradition that rural regions in the United States are the province of poor, ignorant eccentrics of western European descent. Only in the past half-century or so have more realistic images of mountain whites, and to a lesser extent, other mountain groups, gained popularity.

Stereotypical images of mountain whites derive some of their potency from myths that mountains are places of mystical power, where supernatural creatures dwell and where others enter at great peril. One of the nation's early works of mountain literature exemplifies this tradition. Set in the Catskills, Washington Irving's "Rip Van Winkle" includes merry ghosts drinking a magical brew that causes Rip, who intrudes on their world, to sleep for twenty years upon sipping it. Many contemporary stories maintain this association of mountains with awesome powers for evil and good, whether embodied in the malevolent mountain men in James Dickey's *Deliverance* or the beneficent clairvoyant Nora Bonesteel in Sharyn McCrumb's *The Hangman's Beautiful Daughter*.

The association of power with mountains is unable, however, to negate influences that inspire ridicule of rural people. The economic relationship between rural and urban communities plays into stereotypical images of Appalachia, often demeaning all racial and ethnic groups in the region. Progress, as defined by wealthy urban interests, requires that rural people subscribe to values underpinning capitalist enterprise. Among the ways to justify these values and to undermine alternative lifestyles is to make rural people appear ridiculous.

Li'l Abner, hero of Al Capp's cartoon strip, and Jethro on *The Beverly Hillbillies* television series exemplify the dichotomous representation of young white men from the mountains. While their physical power is acknowledged, even exaggerated, so is their gullibility. Their good-natured guilelessness, in a sense, "un-mans" them by rendering them incompetent to adapt to modern life. Like caricatures of American Indians, such as Capp's Lonesome Polecat and the Cleveland Indians baseball team's Chief Wahoo, these representations make potentially threatening figures laughable. Even when the hillbilly image is made appealing, the untenable nature of his implied lifestyle is read by audiences as evidence of ignorance, inability to adapt, or lack of common sense. An implicit message is that mountain whites deserve to be poor.

Mountain women, also conceived of as white, have been spared neither the romance nor the ridicule allocated to men. They have often been portrayed as innocent naïfs, as with June Tolliver in John Fox Jr.'s influential novel *The Little Shepherd of Kingdom Come*, or as slatterns such as Moonbeam McSwine, cartoonist Capp's lazy, black-haired beauty. Sometimes, mountain women are represented as smarter, more ambitious, and harder working than their dim-witted, shiftless husbands. Capp's pipe-smoking Mammy Yokum epitomizes the comic version of the mountain matriarch, unswervingly—and inexplicably, as a symbolic means of ridiculing her judgment—devoted to her ne'er-do-well spouse.

Stereotypical images are commissioned primarily by money outside the mountains; mountain whites themselves often find the stereotypes appealing and/or commercially useful, however. Music jamborees hyping the hillbilly musician, towns celebrating hillbilly days, and craftspeople making hillbilly souvenirs for tourists are among the many events and artifacts acknowledging the nostalgic charm these images possess for Appalachian insiders and outsiders alike.

In many serious representations, the prevalent dichotomy governing images of mountain whites is that of hero versus victim. Mountain whites are sometimes portrayed as fearlessly heroic: for example, pilot Chuck Yeager in Tom Wolfe's *The Right Stuff*. The media, however, have also produced the stereotype of mountain whites as victims of an industrial and postindustrial economy. Particularly since the automation of mining and loss of jobs for miners, images of ill-kept yards and houses, old cars, out-of-work coal miners, and undernourished families abound. As West Virginia writer Maggie Anderson notes in poems about relatives depicted by photographer Walker Evans, this imagery often oversimplifies and thus misrepresents the lives of the people involved. Like other minority groups, mountain whites have been stigmatized by such images and incorporated into an iconography of defeat.

Although contemporary imagery of mountain whites continues to exaggerate the romance and comedy of mountain life, there is now a greater element of reality, thanks to the growing body of scholarship and literature from inside Appalachia. In addition, because of the Civil Rights movement and subsequent efforts to recover the histories of marginalized groups, mountain whites do not dominate Appalachian imagery to the extent they once did. Coverage in the media, particularly public television and radio, is more balanced. Movies such as John Sayles's *Matewan*, fiction such as Denise Giardina's *Storming Heaven*, and nonfiction such as the autobiography of African American educator Memphis Tennessee Garrison create broader perspectives on Appalachia by featuring African Americans and members of various immigrant groups who came to Appalachia to find work and diversified the regional culture. Regional scholarship has discovered many ethnic influences in a culture that the media long represented as homogeneous and white. Celebrating this change, the Center for Study of Ethnicity and Gender in Appalachia at Marshall University in West Virginia adopted an image of a quilt as its logo. This image, which readily lends itself as a symbol of community, is intended to call attention to the diversity of people living in the mountains and to the connections among these diverse groups.

See also: CULTURE OF POVERTY (FOLKLORE AND FOLKLIFE); SECTION OVERVIEW (MEDIA); SECTION OVERVIEW (RACE, ETHNICITY, AND IDENTITY).

—Edwina Pendarvis, *Marshall University*

Dwight B. Billings, Gurney Norman, and Katherine Ledford, eds., *Confronting Appalachian Stereotypes: Back Talk from an American Region* (1999); Richard B. Drake, *A History of Appalachia* (2001); John Alexander Williams, *Appalachia: A History* (2002).

Noble Mountaineers

The icon of the "noble mountaineer" comes from European roots that took hold just as the Appalachian region began to appear on maps and is a variant of the "noble savage" concept developed after European exploration of distant lands in the sixteenth century. As explorers encountered civilizations that challenged their ideas about non-Europeans, philosophers transformed the notion of a singular Civilization to plural civilizations, and views of distant peoples as barbarians were replaced by perceptions of them as noble savages. The concept of the noble savage rejected an older belief in a monolithic culture that the rest of the world had to follow.

In the eighteenth century in Europe, Enlightenment interest in science and an increase in mountain tourism brought increasing numbers of learned and wealthy persons into contact with mountains and mountain dwellers. While writers such as Horace Walpole called mountain folk "uncomely" and even "savages," many felt the purity and sacredness of mountains produced persons of greater innocence and virtue. They fretted that these noble mountaineers would lose their primitive purity through too much contact with civilization. French philosopher Montesquieu thought the lack of fertility of mountain soil made people "diligent, sober, tough at work." The Swiss writer Albrecht von Haller described mountain people as simple farm folk who were proud and virtuous by nature, poor but jealous of their liberty. Switzerland's legendary figure William Tell, who shot the apple off his son's head, became an icon of the tough, skilled mountaineer and an emblem of freedom and liberty.

By the end of the eighteenth and into the nineteenth century, alpine landscape painting in Europe and America and the move toward romanticism created a virtual cult of mountains in which the rugged, isolated, yet admirable mountain terrain was thought to produce folk who were compatible with such a landscape, reflecting a belief in environmental determinism. Anthropologist Benita J. Howell found in a cross-cultural study of the mountain man stereotype that backwoods hunters and foragers were viewed positively in early-nineteenth-century America and their rugged lifestyle was seen as adventurous and ennobling, a powerful symbol of the American experience. Nowhere did that symbol take on more importance than on the Appalachian frontier, with its iconic folk heroes such as Daniel Boone and David Crockett.

Many people continue to feel that noble mountaineers exemplify old-fashioned mountain virtue and values. The lifestyle of Ray Hicks, the legendary teller of Jack tales who lived on Beech Mountain in North Carolina, was portrayed as primitive, but he was admired for his native intelligence, wit, and wisdom, seen as intimately tied to his mountain home. Within the region, often the most powerful icons are those who not only live in an old-fashioned manner but also resist the forces of modernity when they encroach upon traditional ways. Good examples of these fighters are two eastern Kentuckians, Granny Hager, a United Mine Workers of America activist who supported union coal miners during the middle of the twentieth century, and Sarah Ogan Gunning, a singer of protest songs who emerged from the coalfield struggles to unionize the mines in the 1930s. Hazel Dickens and Nimrod Workman, two West Virginians who participated in labor struggles in the mountains through their music, are considered noble by many people inside and outside the region because of their deep-seated sense of right and wrong and a willingness to take a stand against exploitation of their land and their people. People see them as models for the way responsible mountain citizens can deal with powerful opponents. As the twenty-first century unfolds, a figure such as Private Jessica Lynch, who was wounded and captured in the 2003 war with Iraq and returned to her West Virginia home after a dramatic rescue, may become a new icon of the noble mountaineer, similar to yet more complex than Sergeant Alvin York of World War I fame.

In the face of negative portrayals, mountain people have been able to find a safe haven in the idea and image of the noble mountaineer. One great irony, however, is that mountain people tend to be self-deprecating and unpretentious and often make jokes about people who take themselves too seriously. Anyone who would use the word *noble* in self-description or in describing neighbors would surely be the object of ridicule. Thus, those considered by many to be "noble mountaineers" would never consider themselves worthy of the sobriquet.

See also: FIGHTING MOUNTAINEERS; MOUNTAIN WHITES.

—Herb E. Smith, *Appalshop*

Guy and Candie Carawan, eds., *Voices from the Mountains* (1975); Benita J. Howell, "Mountain Foragers in Southeast Asia and Appalachia: Cross-cultural Perspectives on the 'Mountain Man' Stereotype," in *Appalachia in an International Context: Cross-National Comparisons of Developing Regions*, ed. Phillip J. Obermiller and William W. Philliber (1994); Michael Tobias, ed., *Mountain People* (1986).

Old-Time Religion

Religion in Appalachia evokes images from tent revivals and serpent handlers to fire-and-brimstone preachers, from living water baptisms to "the little chapel in the pines." Popular recording artists such as Elvis Presley, Dolly Parton, Ralph Stanley, and Loretta Lynn started with and often returned to mountain gospel music, making modern America aware of faith in the mountains. In Dollywood in Pigeon Forge, Tennessee, Parton has placed at the center of her Appalachian theme park a restored one-room mountain church.

Stereotypes of mountain religion that came to the fore during the 1960s had been created over a century and a half through outside observations of religious practices in Appalachia, mostly by home missionaries or people seeking exotic experiences or local color. These stereotypes are epitomized by snake handling, the best-known and most notorious and sensational image of religion in Appalachia since the 1940s, even though serpent-handling churches and communities are rare.

Appalachia's regional religious tradition is made up of many church traditions and religious cultures. It bears the common image of being an old-time religion that remains unchanging and frozen in the past. It is stereotyped as hyper-Calvinist, trapped in a fatalism and passivity that strips Appalachia's people of power over their own destinies.

Mountain people are perceived by outsiders as embracing a Bible-thumping, literal fundamentalism: Christianity at its worst. Their religion is deemed the product of illiteracy, anti-intellectualism, and ignorance. It is called a "hillbilly religion," clannishly sectarian and individualistic, prone to internal conflicts in an endless epidemic of split congregations that create even more small, peculiar, and uncooperative churches.

Most recently, religion in Appalachia has been characterized as "the religion of the poor." It is hyped as the religion of an oppressed people who are voiceless victims in need of others more powerful than they to speak and act on their behalf in a struggle for justice that they are unable to wage for themselves. This label is based on the efforts of present-day social activists whose motivations are little different from those of home missionaries to Appalachia over the past two centuries who came to the region to "evangelize and uplift." Under the mantle of liberation theology, both modern mainline Protestants and Roman Catholics have since the 1970s embraced the romantic view of Appalachia as a Third World enclave in the United States. They declare Appalachia's "voiceless victims" to be disempowered by defeatist attitudes promoted by the pie-in-the-sky theology of their do-nothing religion that keeps them locked in oppression and poverty.

Religion is targeted for censure and condemnation more than any of Appalachia's other cultural realities. Its stereotyping has usually come out of the struggle for religious and secular power in the region. As a result, Appalachia's religious faithful are not seen as peers to be treated with mutual respect and may be willfully ignored as inconsequential.

Images often focus on the quaint, thus trivializing religion in Appalachia. Religious practice is portrayed as retrograde and devolving, not viable. Its demise is assumed to be not only inevitable but also imminent. Home missionaries first sounded the death knell for Appalachian religion in the mid-1850s, as many others do today.

Throughout history, mountain preachers have been identified as the crux of "the mountain problem." Mountain people commonly reject seminary education for credentialing and equipping their preachers and pastors. They know it is no substitute for spiritual inspiration and insight. They also reject a paid ministry and always have. Preachers and pastors must make their own way in the world and do not expect their churches to support them. As a result, another common image portrays the people of Appalachia as "unwilling to support the Gospel." Historically, mountain people looked to ministers hired by coal camps and mill towns as an example of "whoever pays you, owns you," and this has reinforced suspicion of paid preachers.

The fire-and-brimstone image represents mountain preachers as condemning the innate sinfulness of humanity and harping on immorality. Such preaching is not prevalent in the mountains. The preachers so labeled are usually independent or loosely affiliated Holiness-Pentecostals and Baptists, especially Old-Time Baptists. Together they represent the churches distinctive to Appalachia as a regional religious tradition. Their preaching is inspired by the Holy Spirit and lively. Appalachia's social fabric is very delicate, especially in small rural communities. It does not mend quickly or well when damaged. There is much tolerance for personal needs and quirks in the preaching and worship life of mountain church communities. Apart from uncommon exceptions, the images of clannish sectarianism and divisive individualism do not represent these churches' actual conduct with each other.

Fatalism and passivity are not compatible with religion in Appalachia, either. It is true that mountain preachers rarely use their pulpits to incite social change or political action; that is not the calling they understand for themselves. They may encourage people outside the church-house doors to vote or run for elected office, as even preachers themselves may do. People in Appalachia often use a church house for union meetings and political organizing and other purposes related to matters of social justice and quality of life. But church meetings themselves are not for politics. Appalachia's faith communities are formed by people who want to meet together as often as possible for renewal of the Holy Spirit: to preach, pray, sing, testify, and praise God. This reality stands in stark contrast and is a sign of radical contradiction to the works-righteousness orientation of direct, programmatic social action that has defined most of church life for American Protestant denominations and American Catholicism since the early nineteenth century.

Appalachia's people make a clear distinction between religion and faith. They have always understood that theology, words about God, is controlled and manipulated by human institutions far more easily than is Spirit-led faith. Inevitably, most mountain church communities operate almost entirely outside of denominational frameworks. They are largely self-determining and without denominational allegiances or agendas, believing that "each church holds the key to its own door." These churches are prevalent and widespread yet remain unnoted and uncounted in any census of church life in the United States. As a result, Appalachia has a prominent and false image of a region that is largely "unchurched." This image serves some denominations' justifications for maintaining mission work in Appalachia.

Many of the city and town dwellers in Appalachia have chosen to disdain as "hillbilly religion" the region's distinctive religious tradition that makes it a national treasure. Because many have handed over to others the power to determine and name what is "real religion," their fear of being outside the national norm has caused them to reject the richness and integrity of mountain religious life that flourishes in their midst.

See also: GREAT WESTERN REVIVAL AND CAMP-MEETING MOVEMENT (RELIGION); SECTION OVERVIEW (RELIGION); SERPENT HANDLING (RELIGION).

—Deborah Vansau McCauley, *East Orange, New Jersey*

Loyal Jones, *Faith and Meaning in the Southern Uplands* (1999); Bill J. Leonard, ed., *Christianity in Appalachia: Profiles in Regional Pluralism* (1999); Deborah V. McCauley, *Appalachian Mountain Religion: A History* (1995).

Outsiders and Summer People

In the Appalachian vernacular, the term *furriner* (for "foreigner") denotes not just a person from a foreign country, but also one from another state, county, or any place not local and well known. Even if a furriner arrives in a mountain area when young and stays a lifetime, his or her status as an outsider is never entirely forgotten, though it may become the subject of good-natured humor.

The actual usage of *furriner* faded as better roads and communication reduced the isolation of mountain residents in the twentieth century, but its meaning and synonyms were still acknowledged and occasionally used by the elderly even to the century's end. While *furriner* is contemporarily used with humor, it has been replaced in a more serious vein by terms such as *outlander* and *outsider.* More recent terms have been invented for specific groups of furriners and find usage in either joking or serious connotation. In western North Carolina, where furriners in increasing numbers retire, vacation, or construct summer houses, the terms *floridiot* and *half back* came into usage in the late twentieth century. *Half back* applies to New Yorkers or other northeasterners who moved to Florida before resettling to North Carolina, where they were "half back" to where they started.

In the nineteenth and early twentieth centuries, various furriners moved into mountain areas with the purpose of "fixing," or uplifting, mountain dwellers and their ways of life. Politicians and political organizers often visited remote areas in hopes of converting mountain dwellers to agendas that were often in themselves foreign since they met primarily the wants and needs of constituents in outside regions. The Presbyterian, Quaker, and Methodist denominations and other outland churches sent pastors and missionaries to Christianize mountain people, who were described as being fiercely independent, savage, and violent yet whose heritage was primarily Christian in the first place.

Some missionaries introduced alternatives to healthcare practices and customs, while others encouraged mountain talents, crafts, and skills at institutions such as the Hindman Settlement School in Kentucky. The more ambitious strived to systematically turn mountain people into mainstream middle-class people like themselves. When furrin women such as Katherine Pettit and May Stone from the Bluegrass area of Kentucky approached some areas of the southern Appalachian mountains, residents welcomed their

Left to right: Thomas Edison, Harvey Firestone Jr., R. J. H. Deloach, John Burroughs, Henry Ford, and Harvey Firestone Sr. at Old Evans Mill, Bolar Springs, Virginia, 1918. Prominent individuals and businessmen often vacationed in Appalachia in the late nineteenth and early twentieth centuries. These visitors differed from the "furriners" who took up residence for the purpose of "fixing," or uplifting, mountain dwellers and their ways of life.

offers to establish settlement schools. These women became known as "fotched-on" women, or women who were "fetched" from a distance to establish educational institutions. In their most blatant forms, outsiders' efforts to remake mountaineers into mainstream middle-class citizens have been considered "cultural imperialism," a concept examined closely by David E. Whisnant in his 1983 book *All That Is Native and Fine*.

Perhaps affecting the central Appalachians most profoundly were furriners who arrived to develop mineral (primarily coal) and lumber companies and eventually other industries and services. International Harvester, Consolidation Coal, and Champion Fibre are only a few of the companies that utilized, and ultimately exploited, the mountains' natural resources and influenced the religious, political, and educational lives of mountain dwellers. Such corporate absentee land and mineral resource owners have come to symbolize the most menacing of outsiders in political talk, scholarly writing, and community activism in the region. Some scholars in more recent times have argued that the insider-outsider dichotomy has limited clear understanding of regional history, in which local residents have also played an important role.

By the beginning of the twenty-first century, the arrival of individuals and families from outside the region had become almost as common in Appalachia as elsewhere in America except, perhaps, for the most rural sections of the region. In the parts of Appalachia closest to metropolitan areas and in places of special natural beauty, outsiders began to purchase vacation homes in the late twentieth century and eventually became full-time residents of areas they had first visited on vacation. The pattern has been particularly evident in western North Carolina and northeastern West Virginia.

Newcomers have sometimes contributed significantly to communities, changing local politics and energizing public life. Inevitably, some have failed to understand local politics and community norms, creating unintentional conflicts. Gradually, distinctions between locals and outsiders have become increasingly ambiguous with intermarriage and deepening ties between furriners and locals. Adding to the texture of communities in popular retirement areas is the return of natives who have pursued careers elsewhere.

In rural mountain areas, outsiders and locals often exaggerate images of each other. Ironically, locals often imitate outsiders as they strive for mainstream acceptance while outsiders consciously "go native," even taking courses at local colleges and folk schools to help with the transition.

See also: FOTCHED-ON WOMEN (EDUCATION); SECTION OVERVIEW (LABOR); SETTLEMENT, MISSION, AND SPONSORED SCHOOLS (EDUCATION).

—Jeannie Reed, *Cherokee, North Carolina*

Wilma A. Dunaway, *The First American Frontier: Transition to Capitalism in Southern Appalachia, 1700–1860* (1996); Horace Kephart, *Our Southern Highlanders* (1913; revised 1922); David E. Whisnant, *All That Is Native and Fine: The Politics of Culture in an American Region* (1983).

Recreation

Recreation in the Appalachian South conjures up many different kinds of images in the minds of Americans. People from outside the region see Appalachia as a place replete with opportunities for recreation that have become symbols of revitalization through contact with the natural world and with "authentic" mountain people. They also often have misconceptions of how locals enjoy themselves. Insiders are not always enthusiastic that they and their land serve as icons for the recreational value of others and often have their own ideas about what recreation means in the region.

For both insiders and outsiders, perhaps the greatest recreational icon of the region is the Appalachian Trail. Thru-hiking the trail—walking all the way from Georgia to Maine along the highest ridges of the mountains—is a lifetime aspiration for many people, including those who have never even seen it. Thru-hiking the Appalachian Trail is widely seen as a culminating achievement for the most seasoned hikers and campers. For drivers of motorcycles, cars, or pickup trucks, the Blue Ridge Parkway, which follows the tops of the mountains from the Great Smoky Mountains National Park to the Shenandoah National Park, where it continues as Skyline Drive, offers a similarly climactic recreational experience. Kayaking the Chattooga, the river forming the Georgia–South Carolina border, is often viewed as an ultimate feat for the river runner. The Chattooga was made famous and appealing by *Deliverance*, even though the novel and movie also created famously negative stereotypes about Appalachia. The lakes of the region are icons for fishermen throughout the nation. Most notable perhaps is Dale Hollow Lake, a Tennessee Valley Authority–created reservoir straddling the Kentucky-Tennessee border and home to world-record smallmouth bass. Lakes of the region also provide limitless opportunities for skiers, tubers, scuba divers, swimmers, and boaters. Snow skiers frequent resorts such as Snowshoe Mountain and Canaan Valley in West Virginia, Ober Gatlinburg in Tennessee, Bryce Resort and Massanutten in Virginia, and slopes throughout western North Carolina. The rock formations of places such as the Big South Fork in Tennessee and Kentucky's Red River Gorge offer abundant opportunities for hikers, rappellers, hang gliders, and spelunkers.

For the less adventurous, many localities within the region have historic luxury recreation sites, such as Asheville's Grove Park Inn, that have become icons of sumptuousness in a mountain paradise. Near the Grove Park Inn, millions of visitors flock to the Biltmore Estate, the Vanderbilts' grand American chateau, to see the way the rich relaxed in the mountains in the past. Perhaps the most significant icon for the wealthy and those who aspire to be is the Greenbrier Resort in White Sulphur Springs, West Virginia, one of America's most beautiful and luxurious resorts since the main building was erected in 1910. Three of the region's most prominent golf courses are also located there. Dollywood, in Pigeon Forge, Tennessee, is an icon among amusement parks and is near the entrance to the Great Smoky Mountains, the nation's most visited national park. Appalachia offers a wealth of national and state parks that are used by local residents and tourists from outside the region. These parks utilize the unique beauty and terrain for camping, hiking, and many other activities.

Residents of the region enjoy all of these recreational sites, often outnumbering tourists from far away. Yet locals also have plenty of places to go where they are unlikely to encounter out-of-state travelers, and many local, less commercial sites are sacred to their home communities. Along the back roads of modern Appalachia can be found old men fishing from stone bridges, children swimming in quarries, and people gathered for parties in their yards. Trail riding on four-wheeled all-terrain vehicles became a favorite pastime in the late twentieth century. Saturday nights often find people drag racing, attending a church singing, or taking moonlight cruises on the local lake. Sports play a major role in Appalachian culture, and communities proudly rally around their local football or basketball teams. Stock car racing is widely considered the first truly Appalachian sport to capture the attention of the entire world, and several prominent racetracks are located within the region, most notably the Bristol Motor Speedway in Bristol, Tennessee. Along interstate highways and back roads, a traveler can see cars and pickup trucks parked alongside the roadways as hunting season gets underway. Whether boar hunting near Tellico Plains, Tennessee, or stalking bear, deer, turkey, or other game in the mountains, many Appalachian families continue the long tradition of taking game with firearms or more primitive means.

Negative stereotypes of recreational activities in Appalachia emphasize cockfighting, illegal poker games, wild parties featuring alcohol and drugs, and Tough Man competitions, where amateur boxers gather to duke it out. These do exist, but mountain cockfighters go to Oklahoma for championships, and the region cannot claim these activities to be any more prominent in the mountains than in other rural areas across the nation. Some evidence does exist that recreational abuse of OxyContin, a prescription painkiller, was more widespread and intense in Appalachia than elsewhere in the first few years of the twenty-first century.

People outside the region tend to see Appalachia in a nostalgic light and think of regional recreation as it might have been more than one hundred years ago. In the nineteenth century, many activities revolved around the church, where dinners on the grounds, tent revivals, and camp meetings were held. Most recreation was interwoven with work, however. Communities came together for such events as corn shuckings, which were often made more enjoyable by the red-ear hunt: the boy who came to the first ear of red corn got to kiss the girl of his choice. Often a jar of liquor would be buried beneath a pile of corn, thus assuring that the whole pile would have to be shucked before the alcohol could be opened. Quilting parties became gatherings for meals, with the hostess preparing dinner and/or supper for friends who helped her do the quilting of already pieced fabric. Quiltings sometimes took place at the same time that a group of men banded together for a barn raising or to "run off" sorghum molasses. Although machinery now shucks the corn, women still gather, sometimes in senior centers, to quilt, and occasionally farmers converge to help each other, especially to harvest the crops of someone who has died. Dinners on the grounds at churches and for family reunions continue to figure in regional recreation, as do other church and family events. Icons of family and religion continue to figure prominently in recreation as in other aspects of mountain life.

In modern-day Appalachia, both rural people and urban dwellers pass their time much as do their counterparts elsewhere. The topography of Appalachia presents special recreational opportunities, however, for those who want to jump off a cliff into a river or slide down the moss-covered banks of a mountain creek.

See also: APPALACHIAN TRAIL (TOURISM); SECTION OVERVIEW (SPORTS AND RECREATION); SECTION OVERVIEW (TOURISM).

—Silas House, *Lily, Kentucky*

Barbara R. Duncan and Brett H. Riggs, *Cherokee Heritage Trails Guidebook* (2003); Fred C. Fussell, *Blue Ridge Music Trails: Finding a Place in the Circle* (2003); Tennessee Valley Authority, Department of Regional Planning Studies, *The Scenic Resources of the Tennessee Valley: A Descriptive and Pictorial Inventory* (1938).

Sense of Place

The images associated with Appalachia's landscape and identity are almost as varied as the place itself and function in multiple, sometimes contradictory ways. Depending upon one's perspective, the region can serve as anything from a frontier wilderness treasured by tourists and nature lovers to a scarred symbol of industrial exploitation and a place to be avoided. Collectively, these images and icons encompass much of the region's historical and cultural experience as well as the basis for its continued marginalization.

References to subregions or the entire mountain South as "the High Country" evoke labyrinths of hills, hollers, and wilderness, bringing to mind tall and timeworn mountains with craggy outcrops and cliff lines of limestone and sandstone. Mount Mitchell in western North Carolina and Pine Mountain in the Cumberland Mountains of Kentucky, Virginia, and Tennessee are the epitome of high country imagery and are local, regional, and national icons. Appalachia's picturesque waterways make their own contributions to the region's natural identity. In places such as the New River Gorge in West Virginia, the Linville Gorge in North Carolina, and the Pine Mountain Gorge at the Breaks of the Russell Fork of the Big Sandy River on the border of Kentucky and Virginia, the landscape constantly reinvents itself as rolling, fast-running streams cut through deep ravines and valleys. Associated modern images are those of whitewater rafters, kayakers, and trout anglers with fly rods and lure-adorned hats. Broader valley waterways such as the French Broad, Tennessee, Kanawha, and Ohio Rivers conjure up their own indelible images of chugging towboats pushing heavily laden barges past grazing cows and sheep and alongside tobacco farms and cornfields in lush river bottoms.

In terms of historical or traditional iconography, preindustrial Appalachia was a place of secluded hollers and coves with log cabins tucked away in primeval forest. This wilderness—one of the richest and most productive in the temperate zone of the Northern Hemisphere—was covered with trees and wildflowers and inhabited by all manner of wildlife, including deer, turkey, black bear, fox, wildcats, and the shadowy panther. Though exploited by humankind and scarred by natural and man-made disasters, the mountains continue to inspire the reverence of locals and outsiders alike for their pristine beauty and abundant wildlife.

Throughout the seasons, the landscape invites nature lovers and offers psychological respite. In springtime, the bright colors of redbud, sarvis (serviceberry), and dogwood glow against the green hillsides. In June, rhododendrons stand in full bloom—most beautifully perhaps on more than six-hundred acres atop Tennessee's Roan Mountain and in smaller patches on Virginia's Mount Rogers—their colors rivaled only by the hues of oaks, poplars, maples, ash, and chestnuts in autumn. Winter brings its own kind of beauty, be it that of a heavy snowfall hanging on the pines or of a gnarled, weather-beaten old tree standing alone against a windblown horizon.

Beside the natural splendor of the Appalachian region, the images and icons of industry and commerce pale. Visitors seeking authentic arts and crafts find themselves surrounded by mass-produced trinkets that stereotype the culture they ostensibly illuminate. In many renowned tourist destinations, hillbilly kitsch has supplanted genuine mountain craft. Perhaps the most heavily advertised single tourist attraction in Appalachia is Rock City, located on top of Lookout Mountain near Chattanooga, Tennessee. While the ubiquitous "See Rock City" signs came to be regarded as an endearing image on the region's twentieth-century landscape, the transformation of entire localities into commercial attractions—Boone, Blowing Rock, and Cherokee in North Carolina, Gatlinburg and Pigeon Forge in Tennessee, and Dahlonega and Helen in Georgia—has often led to a decline in quality of life for local inhabitants and an obscuring of natural beauty.

Industrialism has played its own distinct and important role in figuratively and literally creating an Appalachian sense of place. Innumerable images of underground mine openings and dirt-poor coal camps with skeletal tipples looming over the miners' board-and-batten houses are indelible in the memories of generations of both native Appalachians and visitors to the region. Even though employment has shrunk, the deep-mining industry continues to leave its mark on the landscape of the coalfields. Heaps of conveyer belts and piles of timbers once used to support mine roofs lie scattered about deserted supply and machine shops, while the lifeless hulks of heavy equipment stand frozen in their tracks, left to decay and rust along with the rail line and tipple.

Images of modern surface mining are no less stark. In the iconography of mining, the pickax, company store, and mine mouth have been replaced by dump trucks, power shovels, and naked high walls on mountainsides. Hundreds of miles of unreclaimed walls scar steep slopes, giving them the appearance of peeled apples with thin strips of skin left between cuts. Entire mountain hollows and waterways lie beneath overburden dumped from leveled mountaintops, and mountain roads crack and collapse under the weight of overloaded coal trucks.

Rock City advertisement on a barn, Bull's Gap, Tennessee, 1988. Painted by Garnet Carter as an advertising gimmick in the 1950s and 1960s, "See Rock City" signs, which direct motorists to Lookout Mountain near Chattanooga, became an endearing image on the region's twentieth-century landscape.

Even better known than strip-mine scars are the innumerable images of poverty, a staple of representation of the region since the early days of photojournalism. In modern times they are exemplified by beat-up trailers, roadsides littered with discarded appliances and junked cars, road signs shot through with bullet holes, and hand-painted signs exhorting passersby to "Get Right with Jesus" or warning that "The End Is Near." Country churches, some professing their faith with flashing signs, welcome believers to humble sanctuaries in makeshift structures. Only dimly understood by outsiders and embarrassing to many insiders, such images have been an important contributor to the tendency of the broader national culture to marginalize Appalachians as a peculiar people inhabiting a strange, wild landscape.

Recognizing the power of landscape to affect perception of an area's inhabitants, various agencies and communities in the Appalachian region have addressed the issue of visual blight. Statewide Adopt-a-Highway programs, legislation against roadside litter and dumping, and numerous community-action programs have sought to improve the appearance of the environment. In the 1970s, a program in West Virginia partially funded by the Appalachian Regional Commission removed junked automobiles from roadsides and ravines. The state also launched the Make It Shine Program, which was designed to promote volunteerism in dealing with roadside litter. Scenic Kentucky, allied with the national organization Scenic America, helped develop a scenic byways program and fought to reduce the number of highway billboards. In 1989 two families in Westmoreland County, Pennsylvania, organized Pennsylvania CleanWays with nine other counties to clean up rural roads and illegal dumping sites.

By their very nature, icons represent alternative meanings to those inside and outside a culture. In many instances, those who view with an outside perspective see quirks or peculiarities that make a people odd or dissimilar, while natives find value, significance, and cultural affirmation in the same images.

See also: HOMEPLACE; SECTION OVERVIEW (FAMILY AND COMMUNITY).

—Stephen D. Mooney, *Virginia Polytechnic Institute and State University*

Gaston Bachelard, *The Poetics of Space* (1969); W. K. McNeil, ed., *Appalachian Images in Folk and Popular Culture* (1989); Kathleen Stewart, *A Space on the Side of the Road: Cultural Poetics in an "Other" America* (1996).

Sorriness

Traditionally, when southern mountain people call a person "sorry," they mean he or she is lazy or, as elaborated by the *Oxford English Dictionary*, "mean, poor, or paltry (trashy, worthless, and despicable)." The origin of Appalachian application of this term is unknown, but, as the story goes, often when lazy people were asked why they had failed to perform a task, they replied that they were "sorry." Therefore, somebody who was habitually sorry was clearly habitually lazy and worthless.

The term was widely used in the first half of the twentieth century and is still often employed by local people and longterm residents. From the beginning, sorry people have been a minority, but outsiders have sometimes coupled sorriness with other stereotypes and characterized the region as a whole as lazy, trashy, worthless, and at times contemptible. Horace Kephart in his 1913 book *Our Southern Highlanders* observed mountain women doing hard physical labor and concluded it was because mountain men were "shiftless" and afflicted with an "acute disinclination to work."

Sorry people are typically described as illiterate, unemployed, living in trailers, and relying on welfare of one sort or another, but these attributes are often more the result of economics and geography than of less-than-acceptable effort. The mobile home is a workable and increasingly popular alternative for substandard housing and can be as well or poorly kept as a conventional dwelling. Some "welfare," such as black lung compensation, is actually the result of working hard for years in underground mines, and disability payments are available to people whose work in hazardous occupations has impaired their health. Illiteracy and low educational achievement may not be so much a function of unwillingness to try as of other factors, including inadequate schools, a lack of opportunities for those who do receive an education, and family awareness that most educated people leave the region, which results in lack of family encouragement for educational attainment. Unemployment is endemic in parts of the mountains where few job opportunities exist.

True sorriness can be related to fatalism, a feeling that comes from exerting effort many times only to experience failure and then an adaptation that involves no longer making an effort. It can also be related to the lack of means to make a credible effort. Many mountain residents, to the surprise of those who consider them lazy, simply prefer to live in relative isolation and to hold on to old ways in a manner that seems unusual to those looking in from the outside.

The opposite of sorriness and the central measure of an individual in most Appalachian communities is based on the concept of worth. According to Patricia D. Beaver in *Rural Community in the Appalachian South*, worth is assumed to exist in people who are responsible for their actions, rational in their decisions, and have common sense. Worth is associated with willingness to work. While worth is assumed, worthlessness, or sorriness, is more frequently expressed. Mountain speakers may opine, "He ain't worth the bullet it'd take to kill him, or he'd been dead years ago," or refer to "that worthless old woman." Sorriness is most

Hatfield family at a logging camp, Devon, Mingo County, West Virginia, 1897. The violent feud between the Hatfield and McCoy families in late-nineteenth-century Kentucky and West Virginia fueled the image of Appalachians as trigger-happy hillbillies.

associated with lack of desire to work, but the quality may also be ascribed to those who are considered troublemakers in the community or who lack common sense.

The use of the term *sorriness* can be as much an expression of the region's dry, self-deprecating humor as of any reality. *Sorry* can be an affectionate term when applied to in-laws, hound dogs, and old drinking buddies, partly as a manifestation of regional humility. Sometimes people are called sorry with the unspoken understanding that they are wise not to compete or to work feverishly for futile goals. Laughing at outsiders who denigrate mountain ways is an established form of humor in the mountains, and much of the perception of sorriness comes from telling people from other regions what they want to hear and watching them believe exaggerated nonsense.

The category of sorriness seems to exist in all cultures. In any region, greater respect is generally given to those who make an effort to live a better life, no matter how difficult the circumstances. So it is in Appalachia. Perceived sorriness may be more colorful and better publicized in Appalachia than in other regions, perhaps because of the stubborn delight many Appalachians take in pretending to live up or down to outside expectations. Sorriness is nevertheless, in Appalachia as anywhere else, the exception rather than the rule.

See also: CULTURE OF POVERTY (FOLKLORE AND FOLKLIFE); KEPHART, HORACE (LANGUAGE); WELFARE AND POVERTY.

—Garry Barker, *Morehead State University*

Patricia D. Beaver, *Rural Community in the Appalachian South* (1986); Dwight B. Billings, Gurney Norman, and Katherine Ledford, eds., *Confronting Appalachian Stereotypes: Back Talk from an American Region* (1999); Horace Kephart, *Our Southern Highlanders* (1913; revised 1922).

Sports Icons

See Section Overview (Sports and Recreation)

Violence and Vengeance

Violence as an Appalachian cultural trait has been so deeply ingrained in the popular mindset through a century's worth of popular fiction, films, plays, and documentaries that it has become almost a truism. The violent hillbilly, like his close cousin the violent southern redneck, is nearly as much a fictive icon as the hard-boiled detective or the strong and silent cowboy. Ironically, these character types share many of the same traits—fierce independence and loyalty, strongly defined codes, and an almost compulsive disdain for social constraints. The difference is that in the cowboy and detective these characteristics stand as heroic attributes, while in the hillbilly they are the driving force of depravity. As a villain, the hillbilly's role is that of cultural pariah who both threatens the foundations of civilized society and provides a convenient contrast against which the cultured mainstream may hold itself in high regard. In his best light, he is the product of a stagnant and backward social order; at his worst, he is the offspring of an incestuous gene pool.

The image has its seeds in the late-nineteenth-century fascination with southern Appalachian feuds. It was nurtured through the sensationalist journalism of the time and in the popular fiction of such writers as Mary Noailles Murfree and John Fox Jr. It was perhaps Fox, whose novels combine local color realism, dramatic plotting, romanticism, and specious sociological theory, who best defined the image of the violent, suspicious, and socially backward mountaineer that remains essentially unchanged even today.

In such novels as *The Trail of the Lonesome Pine* and *The Little Shepherd of Kingdom Come*, Fox portrays a benighted mountain people. The women are locked in drudging servitude to the men, even the best of whom are lowbrowed and brutish while the worst are degenerate to the point of being sociopaths. All are bound by clan loyalty and hindered by suspicion, the men given to violence and feuding as a first, last, and possibly only response to the world at large. In one moment of inspired literary zeal, Fox compares a male mountaineer character to Shakespeare's misanthropic Caliban.

Paradoxically, Fox does not view mountaineers as intrinsically degenerate. They are of good stock. It is their pathological culture that propagates the baseness of their character. The heroine of *The Trail of the Lonesome Pine*, June Tolliver, is an innocent and alluring backwoods primitive. She is benighted yet intelligent. When John Hale, the Bluegrass-born mineral hunter, enters her world, she immediately senses the limitations of her culture.

Possessing the best attributes both of rugged individualism and cultured sophistication, John embodies the romantic ideal of manhood at the turn of the twentieth century. He provides June with her first experience of civilized life and introduces her to genteel society. June undergoes a Pygmalion-like transformation, and by the novel's end she has developed in all the necessary ways to make her a suitable companion for her mentor become suitor.

John shoulders the burden not only of perfecting June but of reforming the mountain people of their brutal and lawless behavior. Central to the novel's plot is the ongoing family feud between the Tollivers and the Falins. To end the feud and bring law and order to the mountains, John organizes a militia of upstanding citizens, none of whom are native mountaineers. As force is the only thing a mountaineer will respond to, this "Volunteer Guard" imposes a system of martial law upon the region. By this means, the feud is brought finally to an end, and the mountaineers' barbaric instincts are subdued. Despite its condescension, however, Fox's depiction of the mountaineer character may be seen as kind, even positive, in light of many subsequent renderings.

What better example of hillbilly villainy run amok than in such a film as *Cape Fear?* The character of Max Cady (as portrayed by Robert Mitchum in the first version and Robert DeNiro in the second) is the embodiment of a classist nightmare vision of hillbilly monstrousness. Cady is intelligent and in his own manner educated, but his is a perverse intelligence. His self-achieved education, instead of ennobling him, renders him even more sinister, enhancing rather than diminishing his degenerate lusts and bloody-minded drive for revenge.

Imprisoned for rape, Cady believes (rightly) that his attorney, Sam Bowden, withheld evidence that would have maligned the character of Cady's victim and likely led to his acquittal. Cady, though unquestionably guilty of the crime for which he is convicted, nonetheless feels wronged by Bowden. At the end of his sentence, Cady sets out to terrorize and destroy Bowden and his family.

In the second version of the film, DeNiro's Cady commits a brutal sexual attack upon Bowden's mistress, stalks Bowden's daughter, and then murders the private investigator Bowden hires for protection. He even poisons the family dog. Though the plot allows for the consideration of some interesting questions concerning the ambiguity of guilt and innocence as well as the murkiness of heroism and villainy, ultimately good and evil are clearly delineated by the characters of Bowden and Cady. Despite his faults, Bowden is good, and Cady, of course, is evil.

Cady is, in fact, the embodiment of evil, a true descendant of Cain, and a sociopath no more governed by the rules of civilized society than a rampaging barbarian. Indeed, his assault on Bowden's family represents an assault on civilized society. His apocalyptic defeat by Bowden represents civilization's defeat of barbarity.

Yet another work that offers the pageant of civilized man contending with the mountain savage is the notorious *Deliverance*, the film version of which irrevocably couples banjo music with inbreeding and homosexual rape. Max Cady of *Cape Fear* is a cultured sophisticate compared to the skulking, subhuman predators who inhabit director John Boorman's backwoods milieu. The basic plot line of James Dickey's novel is adhered to in the film, though Dickey's theme of "deliverance" from a life of insignificance to one of meaning through extreme experience is maintained only vaguely. Lost also are the novel's irony, its complex portraiture of humanity, and, of course, its elevating poetic language.

Though Boorman's film is ambitious, even complex, by Hollywood standards, it fails to render Dickey's novel as much more than a sensationalistic adventure story—a cautionary tale of what happens when civilized man ventures foolishly into the wilderness and there encounters his own bestial nature, the personification of which is provided by the violent hillbilly icon.

The Kentucky Cycle, Robert Schenkkan's Pulitzer Prize–winning play, perpetrates an equally atrocious assault upon the character of southern Appalachian people. Loosely based upon such controversial social histories as Harry Caudill's *Night Comes to the Cumberlands* and blatantly derivative of Fox's work, *The Kentucky Cycle*, which premiered in 1991, has received much criticism for both its historic and artistic shortcomings. Perhaps the play's most objectionable offense lies in its extreme and unrelenting portrayal of southern Appalachian culture as inherently depraved. In his zeal, Schenkkan makes of the southern Appalachian a metaphoric scapegoat for outrages committed by white Anglo-Saxon Protestant society throughout the history of the United States.

Through two hundred years of settlement, Appalachians deceive and savagely murder every Native American they encounter. In one scene, Schenkkan has pioneers making use of blankets infested with smallpox as a method of genocide, a practice that has not been accepted as unquestioned historic fact even in isolated incidents.

Appalachians abuse, rape, and otherwise victimize black slaves. (That relatively few mountain settlers participated in or encountered slavery is yet another fact of history missed by Schenkkan.) Appalachians practice incest. They despoil the land and ultimately are called solely to blame for the poverty and other social ills extant within the region.

All of the authors and directors heretofore discussed share an outsider's perspective of the Appalachian region. Fox was a Bluegrass social climber, Dickey an Atlanta urbanite, and Schenkkan a Californian. None has at the heart of his experience what might be considered a true southern Appalachian heritage, Fox's career as a turn-of-the-century coal developer notwithstanding. One might assume then that the perpetuation of the violent hillbilly as a fictive icon is at least in part attributable to cultural and regional biases.

Consider, though, the writing of Pinckney Benedict, Chris Offut, and even that of the late Breece D'J Pancake, three authors who are among the most nationally recognized representatives of contemporary Appalachian literature. Each is native to the southern Appalachian region, and each has depicted in his writing the familiar character of the violent, sociopathic hillbilly.

Benedict's fiction relies heavily upon portrayals of sensational and often grotesque regional lifestyles—"The Wrecking Yard," for example, with its carnage-obsessed protagonists, or "Pit," a story of murder and retribution set in the world of dog fighting.

Offut writes convincingly and sympathetically of Appalachia's working-class poor yet still portrays the region as near pathological. In "Target Practice," a son achieves a moment of catharsis with his father by shooting him; in "Melungeons," an old man returns home after many years' absence to fall victim to a clan vendetta.

Pancake, who might well be considered the father of the gothic style of contemporary Appalachian literature, has almost no character who is not drawn to violence as a primary response to daily life. One may rightly argue that Pancake's stories ("Hollow," for example, or "The Scrapper") are concerned with characters who feel themselves trapped in extreme conditions. They are economically and culturally deprived and have little means of resolving their difficulties. To a great extent they are simply lashing out against the hopelessness of their situations. And yet the violence they exhibit seems more a result of character than circumstances. It seems a basic self-destructive need.

Ultimately the framework these contemporary authors share is not far removed from that of the turn-of-the-century local color writers. Despite having greater depth and complexity, their writing still reinforces many of the same attributes of poverty, cultural stagnation, and violence first depicted by the local colorists. The characters they portray have been received popularly in much the same way as those of Fox and Murfree—broadly representative of the region as a whole.

It seems clear that as a fictive as well as a cultural icon the violent hillbilly will remain as firmly fixed in the popular mindset of the twenty-first century as in that of the twentieth. He is at least as vigorous a figure in the writing of many contemporary authors (Appalachian included) as he was in the work of those who first rendered him. Even in the age of political correctness, where broad cross-cultural sensitivity is proclaimed the hallmark of the enlightened individual, the veracity of his portrayal is neither objected to nor questioned by any voice outside the region. He will persist.

See also: FEUDS (GOVERNMENT); FEUDS AND VIOLENCE (MEDIA).

—Chris Holbrook, *Morehead State University*

Pinckney Benedict, *The Wrecking Yard: Stories* (1992); James Dickey, *Deliverance* (1970); John Fox Jr., *The Trail of the Lonesome Pine* (1908).

Welfare and Poverty

One of the most pervasive images of Appalachia is that it is a region of poverty or, more specifically, a subculture of poverty. In the 1960s, national attention turned to Appalachia when it was disclosed that more than 50 percent of the population in many central Appalachian counties was poor. This discovery of poverty in the midst of presumed national affluence was prompted by a number of factors, including publication of Michael Harrington's *The Other America;* John F. Kennedy's widely televised battle for the Democratic presidential nomination, which was fought in impoverished coal communities of West Virginia; Kennedy's subsequent appointment of a presidential commission on Appalachian poverty; and the Lyndon Johnson administration's War on Poverty, which waged numerous much-publicized battles in the mountains. Indelible images of Appalachian poverty were created in the flood of national media attention that followed these events. Readers of the *Saturday Evening Post*, for instance, found unforgettable photographic images of Appalachian poverty in articles such as Roul Tunley's "The Strange Case of West Virginia" (February 1960) and Richard Armstrong's "The Tragedy of Appalachia" (August 1964), as did television viewers of the CBS network's 1964 broadcast "Christmas in Appalachia."

For many social scientists, policymakers, and popular writers, the theory of the culture or subculture of poverty best explained Appalachia's economic depravity. The notion of a subculture of poverty was first conceptualized by the anthropologist Oscar Lewis, who claimed that poor people in capitalist societies throughout the world share similar psychological and cultural traits that, while buffering them from the anguish of marginalization and impoverishment, nonetheless trap them and their children in poverty. In applying Lewis's model to Appalachia, one social scientist claimed in the 1960s that Appalachia's poor inhabited an "analgesic subculture," and in the 1990s another wrote that the culture of the entire region was shaped by post-traumatic stress syndrome. By far, however, the most influential book promoting the culture of poverty theory in Appalachia was Jack Weller's *Yesterday's People: Life in Contemporary Appalachia* (1966). Weller claimed that "independence-turned-individualism" had become "a great stumbling block for [mountaineers] finding a place in our complex and cooperative society." Their traditionalism, he argued, was "stubborn, sullen, and perverse," and where fatalism had become a way of life in Appalachia, "there [was] no rebellion, little questioning, little complaining." In Weller's bleakly pessimistic view, "The greatest challenge of Appalachia, and the most difficult, [was] its people." Such people simply did not want to change in order to improve their lives. In a preface to *Yesterday's People*, the distinguished sociologist Rupert Vance summed up the policy implications of the culture of poverty theory: "to change the mountains [was] to change the mountain personality."

During the War on Poverty, local projects designed to encourage "maximum feasible participation" of the poor in community development were inspired by the culture of poverty theory as were the initial efforts of VISTA (Volunteers in Service to America) workers and the Appalachian Volunteers, who, like their Peace Corps counterparts in the Third World, enlisted the poor in projects designed to overcome fatalism and alienation. However, they came up against major obstacles to participation by the poor, including the political and economic powerlessness of those who had been trapped in poverty for generations and the reality of entrenched local power structures that served the interests of absentee corporate owners who monopolized land, mineral, and political resources. Influenced by writings of Third World scholars, community organizers began to forge a more radical image of the region, depicting Appalachia as an "internal colony." According to this contrasting image of the region, Appalachia was poor because of the nature of its connection with—not isolation from—the United States corporate economy. Thus, some writers explored how blaming the victim and the denigration of Appalachian culture in culture of poverty theory helped to legitimate the exploitation of the region's land, resources, and people. Others interpreted indigenous cultural patterns as forms of resistance to colonization rather than the expression of a culture of poverty.

Appalachian scholars now contend that there is little evidence for the existence of a culture of poverty in Appalachia. They view its plausibility as stemming from longstanding traditions of stereotyping the region. Especially in the last third of the nineteenth century, Appalachia came to be described as a "strange land and peculiar people" that, because of isolation, was out of step culturally and economically with the progressive trends of American industrial and urban growth. Popular representations by local color writers, missionaries, educators, and reformers stressed sameness and identity in Appalachia to the neglect of geographical differences and population diversity. The social construction of Appalachia as a distinct, homogenous, and culturally isolated folk society thus set the stage for viewing Appalachia as a regionwide culture of poverty. So too did the depiction of Appalachians as lazy, shiftless, and perpetually poor "hillbillies" that gained great popularity in the national media during the Great Depression, especially in comic strips such as *Li'l Abner* and *Barney Google and Snuffy Smith*. It is here, in the discourses of past eras rather than in actual Appalachian communities, that the prototypes for "yesterday's people" and its "analgesic subculture" are best found.

See also: "CHRISTMAS IN APPALACHIA" (MEDIA); CULTURE OF POVERTY (FOLKLORE AND FOLKLIFE); WAR ON POVERTY (GOVERNMENT).

—Dwight B. Billings, *University of Kentucky*

Dwight B. Billings and Kathleen M. Blee, *The Road to Poverty: The Making of Wealth and Hardship in Appalachia* (2000); Stephen L. Fisher, "Victim-Blaming in Appalachia: Cultural Theories and the Southern Mountaineer," in *Appalachia: Social Context Past and Present*, ed. Bruce Ergood and Bruce E. Kuhre (3rd edition, 1991); Walter Precourt, "The Image of Appalachian Poverty," in *Appalachia: Social Context Past and Present*, ed. Bruce Ergood and Bruce E. Kuhre (3rd edition, 1991).

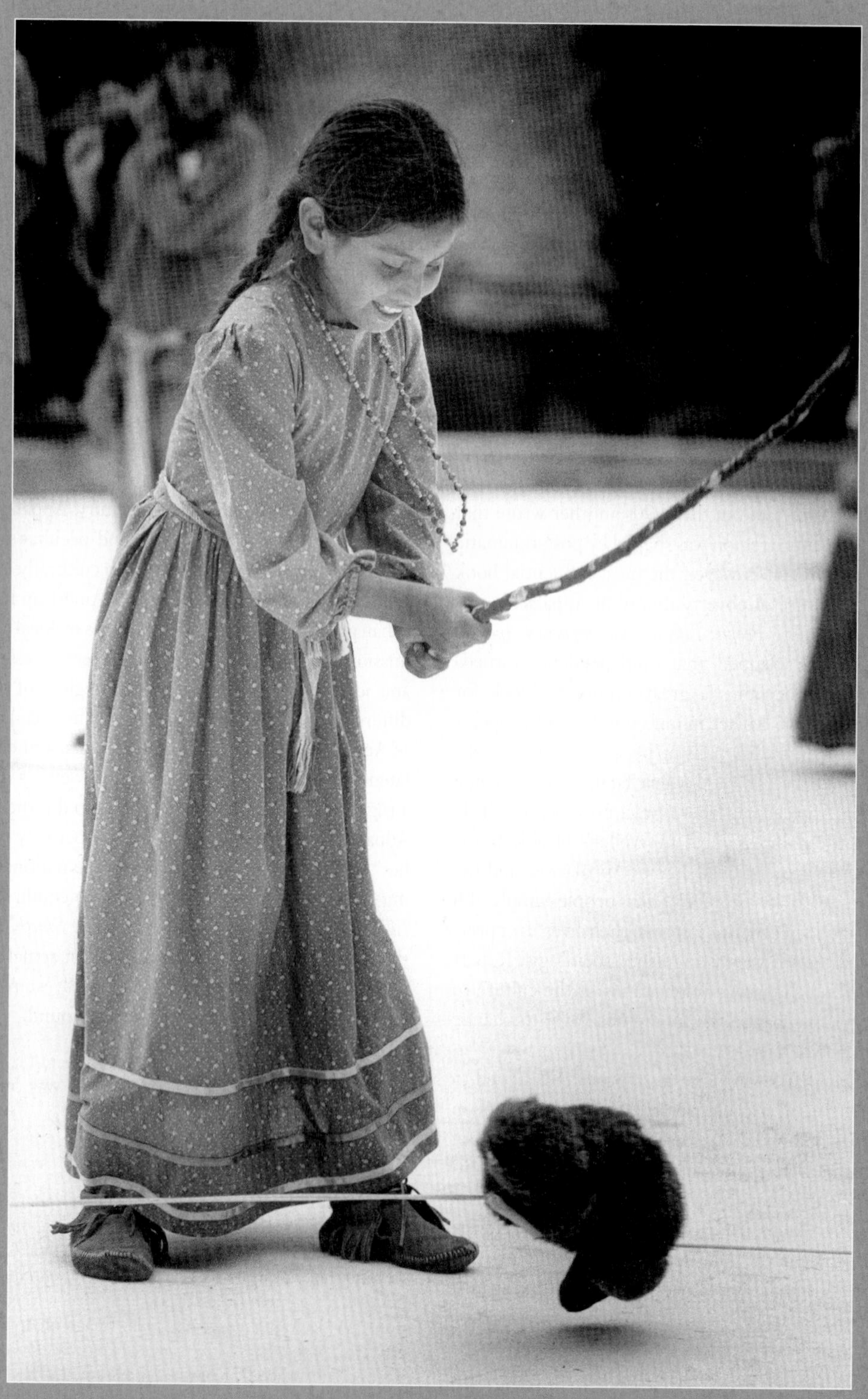

Race, Ethnicity, and Identity

Section Editor: Roberta M. Campbell

LONG BEFORE APPALACHIA WAS THOUGHT OF AS A DISTINCT PLACE OR ONE particular conception of it was codified by the federal government, inhabitants of the mountain region began to acquire an identity based on sweeping negative concepts that have persisted into modern times. Urbanization, cultural assimilation, technological revolution, racial integration, and ethnic diversification notwithstanding, these hoary images still frame an overarching regional stereotype, and to many Americans the very word *Appalachia* connotes isolation, poverty, backwardness, and peculiarity. Flawed from the beginning and long outdated, this durable construct presents Appalachia as an isolated internal colony predominantly inhabited by clannish, violence-prone Anglo-Saxon poor relations of the American family who were left behind as the rest of the nation marched on to prosperity and greatness.

In truth, racial, ethnic, and cultural assimilation began before European dominance, or even settlement, of the Appalachian Mountains. White fur traders who traveled into the mountains took Indian wives, and early settlers brought slaves from the Tidewater. By 1860 blacks made up as much as 15 percent of the region's population, and even as writers fashioned the mythical Anglo-Saxon Appalachia in the late nineteenth and early twentieth centuries, Italians, Poles, Hungarians, and other ethnic workers made up as much as 40 percent of the workforce in the coalfields, not to mention their presence in urban shops and factories of the nascent Industrial Revolution.

The forgotten-colony construct of Appalachia was not without room for worthy figures, heroic acts, and a romanticism to equal that of Margaret Mitchell's Old South or the cowboy West of Zane Grey. Within the colony dwelled a noble mountaineer of extraordinary personal bravery, patriotism, self-sufficiency, and spirituality. In this Appalachia, loyalty to the Union was staunch, and its limited tolerance of slavery fostered a form of human bondage claimed to be benign in comparison to that of the plantation South. But constructions such as these still supported the stereotype's essential notion that Appalachia was fundamentally different from the rest of America: a remote, socially and economically handicapped place with a homogeneous population more or less suspended in time. This view of Appalachia as a region apart survives into the twenty-first century in spite of modernized imagery and chronic tinkering with its definition (as Congress adds new counties as it sees fit). Ironically,

Facing page: A young Cherokee girl performs the traditional Beaver Dance at a festival at Beech Mountain Resort, Banner Elk, North Carolina, 1984. Participants dance with sticks and pretend to hunt a beaver that is manipulated on a cord by two other Cherokee.

Coal miners of European ancestry hold a sit-down strike, Coaldale, Pennsylvania, 1937. Many thousands of "new immigrants" came to Appalachia from southern and eastern Europe from the late nineteenth to the first quarter of the twentieth century to work in Appalachian coal-producing areas. Italians were the single largest group, followed by Hungarians, Poles, Austrians, and Russians.

this identity has been sustained and embroidered by the same tools of modern mass communications that helped foment massive twentieth-century changes that rendered essentialist images obsolete.

Since the 1950s, television networks in particular have exploited both negative and positive mountain stereotypes, solidifying the perception of Appalachia's peculiarity. The long-running CBS program *The Beverly Hillbillies* drew as many as 60 million viewers to watch the weekly misadventures of bumpkins (actually from the Ozarks) showered with accidental riches and cast into the bedroom community of Hollywood. Similarly successful were *The Dukes of Hazzard*, featuring vacuous hillbillies in a cultural milieu of wrecked cars, hound dogs, moonshine, and courthouse corruption, and *Hee Haw*, a long-running hoedown beloved by many Appalachians for both its mountain music and the self-parody of its stars. Perhaps more popular, though neither tacky nor musical, was the warm and fuzzy saga of *The Waltons*, a Blue Ridge Mountain family in Virginia between the beginning of the Great Depression and World War II. For nine years, between 1972 and 1981, episodes drawn from the life of producer Earl Hamner Jr. unfolded on CBS in prime time, evoking nostalgia for an innocent, uncomplicated world where the desperate need that enveloped the mountains and the rest of rural America in the 1930s was overshadowed by family bonds and the inevitable triumph of decency and old-fashioned values. The television standard for romanticizing the mountain man was set in 1954, however, when Walt Disney cast the prototypically handsome Fess Parker, turned out in coonskin cap and fringed buckskin, as Davy Crockett, creating a hit song and making "the king of the wild frontier" a national fad. Parker later played Daniel Boone as well.

Documentaries and motion pictures have even more effectively reinforced Appalachian stereotypes—the former because of their presumed truthfulness, the latter through an ability to create their own vivid giant-screen reality. Notable documentaries include broadcasts such as CBS's "Christmas in Appalachia" (1964) and a *48 Hours* episode on "Muddy Gut Creek" (1988) and the independently produced *American Hollow* (1999) by Rory Kennedy, daughter of Senator Robert F. Kennedy. "Christmas in Appalachia" brought fifty tons of donated food, clothing, and toys pouring into Whitesburg, Kentucky, from across the country. "Muddy Gut Creek" and *American Hollow* stirred resentment for their fostering of stereotypes but earned resigned admiration for their unblinking examination of the culture of poverty. Equally stereotypical, motion pictures have created folk icons of vastly differing Appalachian characters, ranging from Hollywood's *Sergeant York* (1941), based on the life of the World War I hero from Tennessee's Cumberland Mountains, to the mountain moonshine runner of *Thunder Road* (1958) to the half-witted, inbred backwoods sadists who terrorize whitewater canoeists in the adaptation of James Dickey's novel *Deliverance* (1972).

In the last half of the twentieth century, heightened racial and ethnic sensitivity, a surge of political concern over poverty, and increased interest in regional studies made the origins, evolution, and fallacies of Appalachian identity the subjects of enlivened scholarly research. Helping set the stage was Cratis Williams's three-volume doctoral dissertation, "The Southern Mountaineer in Fact and Fiction." Completed in 1961, Williams's tome accepted elements of the stereotypical identity, but he found mountain society to be structured in a hierarchy of city dwellers, valley farmers, and backcountry mountaineers. Massively researched, Williams's analysis helped to inspire a whole new Appalachian studies "industry."

As social scientists began to deconstruct and aggressively debate the popular identity—heavily based upon images from the coalfields and timber country of West Virginia, eastern Kentucky, eastern Tennessee, and southern West Virginia—many inhabitants of Appalachia and the Appalachians ceased to think of themselves, if they ever had, as part of the region. What emerged, especially from the 1970s onward, was a more complex construction that debunked much of the mythology about isolation, violence, "whiteness," and imperviousness to change. Far from resolved, however, were debates over the forces, within and without the region, that shaped its history and guided the evolution of its image.

In spite of its simplicity, the regional stereotype that had taken shape by World War I was the product of many contributors—missionaries, generations of lowland elites, capitalists, novelists, and journalists. Most important were the so-called local colorists, accomplished writers dispatched by New York's booming mass-circulation magazines to find titillating material for urban readers who were quite prepared to accept reports that backwoodsmen were less than their equal. Color writers who visited the Appalachians in the last three decades of the nineteenth century found the mountains a rich source of oddities: isolated people, extreme hardship, and cultural practices wholly mysterious to urban readers. Best known of these writers was Will Wallace Harney, whose landmark article "A Strange Land and a Peculiar People" was published in *Lippincott's Magazine* in 1873. Harney's exploration of Appalachia was followed by many more local colorists from the North as well as others with closer ties to the region. Notable among the latter were Mary Noailles Murfree, John Fox Jr., and William Goodell Frost, all of whom made full use of the southern mountain stereotype crafted by earlier local colorists. Although Murfree, a middle Tennessean who wrote under the pen name "Charles Egbert Craddock," had scant firsthand knowledge of the highlands, her short story collection *In the Tennessee Mountains* (1884) quickly became the foremost text on Appalachia. Seventeen editions were published in the first two years after it was issued, and seven more followed by 1922.

A product of the Kentucky Bluegrass region, John Fox Jr., like Murfree, became obsessed with the mountains and skillfully—and to great personal profit—romanticized his sturdy mountaineers and their remote ridges and hollows. His best-selling novel *The Little Shepherd of Kingdom Come* (1903) portrayed mountain folk as Union loyalists widely opposed to slavery, and the novel remained popular for decades. More pragmatically, Berea College President William Goodell Frost examined the mountains as part of his effort to extend the outreach of Berea College, an institution rooted in the abolitionist movement and located in an area where the mountains converge with the Kentucky Bluegrass region. Just as the missionaries who went into the Appalachians to spread salvation and enlighten the unchurched found it advantageous to emphasize the isolation and hard frontier conditions for the benefit of sponsoring churches and parishes, Frost appealed to Berea's donors in the urban North. Because of his standing as an educator, his perspective, aptly summarized in the title of his 1899 *Atlantic* article "Our Contemporary Ancestors in the Southern Mountains," authenticated the handiwork of the less credible and sensation-prone local colorists.

To be sure, some early writers and analysts aspired to insight and understanding. Frederick Law Olmsted visited southern Appalachia as a young journalist in 1854, years before he achieved fame as a landscape architect, and carefully recorded his observations of mountain slavery. African American historian Carter G. Woodson, in the very first issue of his *Journal of Negro History*, also addressed the subject of black slavery and freedom in Appalachia. But neither Olmsted nor Woodson was able to elude the regional stereotype. Olmsted, even as he systematically studied mountain slavery, generalized about the ignorance and backwardness of the mountain whites, and his book, *A Journey in the Back Country* (1860), provided a preface for the local colorists two decades later. Woodson, a West Virginian, accepted the since discredited picture of Appalachia as thoroughly abolitionist.

In succeeding generations, stereotypes have been further cemented by dismissive pronouncements by observers accorded credibility because of their fame rather than knowledge. For example, the English historian Arnold Toynbee, who never visited the backcountry of the Appalachians, famously declared inhabitants of the region to be "barbarians" who, in their isolation, had regressed and lost the civilization brought to the mountains by their antecedents. In a similar vein, the celebrated critic and iconoclast H. L. Mencken visited Dayton, Tennessee, "the bright, shining buckle of the Bible belt," in 1925 to cover John Scopes's notorious trial for teaching evolution. He pronounced Appalachians to be ignorant yokels, displaying a "peasant-like suspicion of all book learning that a plow hand cannot grasp."

Although the stereotype of isolation, poverty, and backwardness bloomed around the turn of the twentieth century, negative images of Appalachia's inhabitants go back to frontier days. In 1728 William Byrd II, the Tidewater Virginia aristocrat who helped survey the Virginia–North Carolina border, denigrated backwoodsmen as "lubbers." In the fall of 1780, just before mountain men played a crucial role in defeating him at the battle of Kings Mountain, the commander of the British army in South Carolina referred to frontier revolutionaries who had marched across the mountains from present-day east Tennessee as "barbarians" and "the dregs of mankind."

Regardless of their vintage, negative stereotypes remain in the fabric of the region's larger modern identity, reinforced not only by outsiders, but by Appalachians themselves. Two years after Cratis Williams's dissertation energized social science research in the region, Harry Caudill, a lawyer and former state legislator, brought his native eastern Kentucky to national attention with *Night Comes to the Cumberlands: A Biography of a Depressed Area* (1963). The book was a plea for government intercession in a mountain economy being devastated by strip mining and mechanization in the coalfields. But Caudill was unsparing in his use of jarring and evocative stereotypes as he sounded the alarm against the environmental destruction, political corruption, and economic hegemony of the mining industry. Compared immediately to *Silent Spring*, the environmental blockbuster by Rachel Carson, and *The Other America*, a landmark exposition on poverty by Michael Harrington, both published the previous year, *Night Comes to the Cumberlands* found a receptive audience in Washington and introduced national political powers, along with shocked readers across the country, to Appalachia. Caudill's polemic also brought scores of journalists and television crews into the region and to the author's hometown of Whitesburg, Kentucky. More often than not their reportage was not only compliant to the regional stereotype, but circumscribed by it—a not surprising outcome since much investigation was done at Caudill's dinner table. Appearing at a moment when poverty was gaining attention as a political issue, Caudill's book and incessant drumbeating helped prepare the ground for congressional passage of the 1965 Appalachian Regional Development Act, creation of the Appalachian Regional Commission, and implementation of the War on Poverty. But while he brought strip mining and mountaineers' economic plight into the consciousness of Americans far from Appalachia, Caudill also attracted sharp criticism from social scientists who found his scholarship inadequate and his perspective elitist. A lightning rod for academic critics was his assertion that white settlers of the Kentucky mountains had come from inferior European stock. This "gene theory," as it came to be called, was sketched in the dramatic summation of mountain settlement in his opening chapter. Using descriptions such as "human refuse," "social outcasts," and "raggle-taggle of humanity," Caudill went far beyond Toynbee and the local colorists in explaining both the peculiarities and the lamentable state of mountain folk. Though also criticized for his thin documentation, Caudill, a fifth-generation eastern Kentuckian, could not be dismissed. Indeed, *Night Comes to the Cumberlands* provided additional impetus and a framework for the incipient Appalachian studies movement.

Indicting distant corporations and other absentee owners for plundering natural resources and impoverishing mountain people, Caudill embellished and gave substance to the local colorists' picture of central Appalachia as America's internal colony. But in advocating government intercession on behalf of a people he found incapable of resisting the forces arrayed against them, he also provided an opening for deconstruction of the stereotype and for encouraging debate on the region's future in a larger theoretical and geographic context.

Nearly three decades after its publication and a little more than a year after Caudill's death, *Night Comes to the Cumberlands* provided the underpinning for an angry renewal of debate over perceived denigration of the region. The occasion was the opening of *The Kentucky Cycle*, a nine-part epic awarded the 1992 Pulitzer Prize for Drama. Although playwright Robert Schenkkan, who publicly thanked Caudill, insisted that eastern Kentucky and the play's mountain families were metaphors for America at large, the controversial drama rested on the element of Caudill's work that had so aroused his social scientist critics. Appalachians saw *The Kentucky Cycle*'s unstinting portrayals of depravity, violence, and greed as rank exploitation of the stereotype. But while some writers and scholars still blamed Caudill for having consecrated the negative identity resurrected by the play, others recalled that he had provided context omitted from *The Kentucky Cycle* and that the ultimate objective of *Night Comes to the Cumberlands* had been reform.

Reaction to *The Kentucky Cycle*, which played in Seattle and Los Angeles before moving to Broadway, continued long after its final curtain. Eight years after the West Coast opening, the University Press of Kentucky published a collection of relentlessly critical essays, *Confronting Appalachian Stereotypes: Back Talk from an American Region* (1999). The collection's title as well as its contents reflected growing militancy in Appalachians' reaction to portrayals perceived as exploitative or condescending.

In 2003 debate over image and identity spread beyond academic circles once again when the CBS television network announced plans to lavish a large, carefully selected mountain family with money and use it in a new *Beverly Hillbillies*–inspired "reality" show. Activists at the Center for Rural Strategies in Whitesburg retaliated with a national advertising campaign denouncing the planned show as demeaning, and protests poured in to CBS headquarters in Los Angeles not only from Appalachia, but across rural America.

Although negative imagery (and what Kentucky novelist Gurney Norman called willful omission of relevant positive images) has continued to be the most debated facet of Appalachian identity, portrayals of the region have been flawed in other important respects. Generally shortchanged are ethnic diversity and the place and identity of both African Americans and native peoples.

Two and a half centuries after European dominance spread across the region, descendants of Native Americans who had inhabited Appalachia for at least a millennium still preserve remnants of tribal heritage. In the Appalachian foothills of eastern Ohio, Shawnee rituals, including weddings officially recognized by the state, continue to be performed. In Mississippi, the Choctaw Band, with members in several Appalachian counties, is one of the largest employers in the state. In western North Carolina, descendants of some fourteen hundred Cherokees who remained in the mountains after the forced removal of eastern tribes to Indian Territory in 1838 prosper in native craft enterprises and the tourist industry. These and other pockets of enduring tribal and ethnic integrity only hint at the ultimate importance of Native Americans, who survived warfare, forced removal, and voluntary exile.

Native Americans can be viewed as the first of many immigrants who continue to shape the region's identity, contemporary stereotypes notwithstanding. Unknowable are the effects of their inexorable, eventually near-total assimilation under the waves of immigration that swept over the region. Colonial times brought English, Scots-Irish, and German farmers to the Appalachian frontier, but the region's most substantial influx of diverse ethnic groups came in the century between 1820 and 1920. With the Industrial Revolution, tens of thousands of immigrants from northern and western Europe poured into western Pennsylvania coal mines, foundries, mills, and glassworks. They were followed, in the late nineteenth and early twentieth centuries, by Italians, Poles, Hungarians, Austrians, Jews, Romanians, and Russians, who moved south into the coalfields and timber camps of southwestern Virginia, West Virginia, eastern Kentucky, and east Tennessee.

While these earlier immigrants have found their way into the portrait of Appalachia, the regional identity has been slower to accommodate more recent arrivals from Asia, Latin America, and the Middle East. During the 1990s, West Virginia welcomed new citizens from thirty-one countries, most of them representing new nationalities for the state. The story was similar elsewhere across the region.

By the end of the twentieth century, the identity consciousness encouraged by the Appalachian studies movement was manifest in organizations such as Marshall University's Center for the Study of Ethnicity and Gender in Appalachia, and the Affrilachians, a group of African American writers steadily gaining recognition by giving voice to the black perspective in the region. West Virginia–born Henry Louis Gates Jr., director of the Afro-American Studies Program at Harvard University, was among the nation's most distinguished African American scholars, and Cherokee writer-storyteller Marilou Awiakta was nationally recognized as important in preserving Native American identity.

But African American, Native American, and ethnic involvement in Appalachian studies and regional activism remained relatively meager, perhaps a reflection of how deep-seated the old identity and some of its odious truth remain. Nevertheless, research continued to clarify the historical experience of non-Anglo-Saxons and thus reveal a modern identity superseding the well-worn stereotype. Along with the negative images of hillbillies, violence, and depravity, some of the romanticists' cherished images of the region's past faded as well—among them the picture of the Appalachians as a main artery of the Underground Railroad, a solid bastion of Union loyalty, and a region where slavery was benign.

More than forty years after Cratis Williams's path-breaking dissertation and Harry Caudill's jarring portrayal of central Appalachia, the region is increasingly seen in a light revealing more subtle hues. Its emerging new identity takes stronger account of complexities in racial relations and ethnic diversity. It reconsiders class relations, moves beyond the notion of Appalachians as victims of outsiders, and invites more searching appraisal of its history.

—Rudy Abramson, *Reston, Virginia,* and Roberta M. Campbell, *University of Cincinnati*

Dwight B. Billings, Gurney Norman, Katherine Ledford, eds., *Confronting Appalachian Stereotypes: Back Talk from an American Region* (1999); Harry M. Caudill, *Night Comes to the Cumberlands: A Biography of a Depressed Area* (1963); Richard B. Drake, *A History of Appalachia* (2001); David C. Hsiung, *Two Worlds in the Tennessee Mountains: Exploring the Origins of Appalachian Stereotypes* (1997); John C. Inscoe, ed., *Appalachians and Race: The Mountain South from Slavery to Segregation* (2001); John Alexander Williams, *Appalachia: A History* (2002).

Abolition

See Slavery and Abolition (Government)

Affrilachians

The term *Affrilachian* refers to a person of African descent residing in or originating from a multiracial community within the Appalachian region. By creating and using this term in his 1991 poem "Affrilachia," poet Frank X Walker challenged the common definition of an Appalachian—a white resident of the mountains—by making visible the black and multiracial individuals of Appalachia and their contributions to the region, as well as their communities of origin. The term combines the words *African* and *Appalachian*, thus rebuking the idea that one cannot claim both an African American and an Appalachian identity.

Shortly after the word debuted in Walker's poem, the writing group Walker cofounded at the University of Kentucky began to call themselves the Affrilachian poets. In adopting a previously nonexistent term, the group celebrated its members' diverse origins, from Africa to Puerto Rico, and established a distinctive identity on the region's cultural landscape.

A reference to Affrilachians first appeared in the mainstream media in November of 1993 in *ACE Magazine*, Lexington, Kentucky's weekly newspaper. This signified the term's transcendence into popular culture and marked an expanding application of the word. As *Affrilachian* weaves through literary, academic, media, and Internet circles, communities from Birmingham, Alabama, and Knoxville, Tennessee, to Roanoke, Virginia, and Pittsburgh are embracing the word. The term draws attention to the relationship between African American and Appalachian culture, establishing a regional identity that is inclusive and heterogeneous. *Affrilachian*, in Walker's words, "existed to make visible / to create a sense of place / that had not existed / for us / any unwealthy common / people of color / now claiming the dirt they were born in."

See also: WALKER, FRANK X (LITERATURE).

—Elizabeth R. Newberry, *Kentucky Governor's School for the Arts*

Coal Black Voices: A PBS Documentary Film on the Affrilachian Poets, Media Working Group (2001); Frank X Walker, *Affrilachia* (2000).

African Americans

See African American Families and Communities (Family and Community)

Amish

See Mennonites (Religion)

Appalachian Identity Center

In the 1960s, several programmatic responses to the influx of hundreds of thousands of Appalachian migrants into metropolitan centers of the Midwest emerged. One of the first and most enduring programs was the Appalachian Identity Center in Cincinnati, Ohio. In the late 1960s, the city's Over-the-Rhine neighborhood, once a German American neighborhood across a canal from downtown, had an extremely high population density—thirty thousand residents filled an area where fewer than ten thousand live in the early twenty-first century. Appalachian immigrants were so common in this and other parts of Cincinnati that they were termed an "invisible minority." First- and second-generation Appalachian youth comprised a high percentage of the Over-the-Rhine population, and they often felt unwelcome at established recreation centers in the neighborhood. Conflicts between youth from different areas occurred daily. In response to this crisis, community organizers led by longtime activist Ernie Mynatt began to establish storefront youth centers in each section of Over-the-Rhine. A grant from the Appalachian Fund provided money for an Over-the-Rhine community center through an Appalachian-based sponsor, the Council of the Southern Mountains.

The Appalachian Identity Center opened in the spring of 1970 under the directorship of Robert Snyder, who later headed the Antioch Appalachian Center and contributed to Appalachian studies as a professor at Harvard University. Larry Redden, a Vietnam veteran and one of Mynatt's protégés, became the second director later the same year and was succeeded by William Chandler, another young Vietnam veteran from Over-the-Rhine, who served from 1971 to 1983. During its early years, the center occupied the former Walnut Bar location at Fourteenth and Walnut Streets.

From the beginning, center organizers encouraged youngsters' sense of Appalachian identity as a means of fostering pride and self-esteem. Youths' awareness of their Appalachian roots was encouraged by the organization of field trips to the mountains and by provision of posters and reading materials. Efforts to educate young people about ethnic diversity within the Appalachian community helped diminish racist attitudes. Young people who coalesced around Mynatt and center director Chandler later formed the Sons of Appalachia and the Daughters of Appalachia, fraternal organizations that engaged in neighborhood service activities such as helping maintain sanitary conditions and assisting families forced out of their homes by evictions or other circumstances.

The center played a crucial role in the emergence of what became known as the Appalachian movement in Cincinnati, in which first- and second-generation Appalachian immigrants organized in order to secure social services, improve living conditions, challenge stereotypes, and gain recognition as a cultural group. Its board became the model for the board of the Urban Appalachian Council in that it included both working-class Appalachians and allies from the broader Cincinnati community. In 1974 the center merged with the Appalachian Committee, a group of Appalachian advocates organized by the Cincinnati Human Relations Commission, to form the Urban Appalachian Council. The Appalachian Identity Center continued as a distinct and honored program within the council's structure. In 1976 the center moved to a renovated two-story building on Walnut Street, where it remains in operation. Some of the early youth participants became staff members of the Urban Appalachian Council. One of these, Phyllis Shelton, helped found the General Educational Development (GED) program in the late 1980s. Former center director Redden became program coordinator for the council.

The Urban Appalachian Council has satellite and independent affiliated programs in several Appalachian neighborhoods. The Appalachian Identity Center is the central office for the council's citywide education, employment, and training programs for all residents. It also operates GED programs and remains involved in other education and social service issues affecting residents of Over-the-Rhine, now a primarily African American neighborhood.

See also: CINCINNATI, OHIO (URBAN APPALACHIAN EXPERIENCE).

—Michael E. Maloney, *Michael Maloney and Associates*

Mountain Life and Work Special Issue: Urban Appalachians (August 1976); Phillip J. Obermiller, Thomas E. Wagner, and E. Bruce Tucker, eds., *Appalachian Odyssey: Historical Perspectives on the Great Migration* (2000).

Appalachian Tribe

Native Americans in West Virginia trace their ancestry to specific groups such as the Cherokee, Delaware, Shawnee, Wyandot, and others. However, the indigenous people in the state today also affiliate with an overarching group known as the Ani (meaning "all one people"), or the Appalachian Tribe. Chartered in 1989 as the Appalachian American Indian Society, the Appalachian Tribe is formally known as Appalachian American Indians of West Virginia, Inc., a state-recognized intertribal group and the largest Native American organization in the state. It gained state recognition in 1996 and 1998 with the passage of resolutions by the West Virginia Senate and House of Delegates, respectively. Members provide free educational programs about Native American culture in West Virginia and counseling to schools and civic groups and offer a sense of community to those with Native American ancestry.

The group's membership of more than four thousand members represents fifty-nine different indigenous groups, although the majority are descendants of Cherokee or Shawnee ancestors. Appalachian American Indians of West Virginia is governed by an elected tribal council consisting of a principal chief, chief, tribal officer, secretary, treasurer, and fourteen elected tribal councilors and is supported solely by the contributions of its members.

See also: NATIVE AMERICANS; WHITE CONQUEST (SETTLEMENT AND MIGRATION).

—Ima J. Stephens, *Auburn University*

Belgians

For the most part, Belgians who settled in Appalachia came to work in the window-glass industry. Many came from the glass-making region in Belgium near Charleroi, where a French Walloon dialect was spoken. Between 1880 and 1900, the glass industry in Belgium witnessed many conflicts, including violent strikes, as the result of technological innovations, corporate strategies, and the lack of universal male suffrage in the country. Consequently, many skilled craftsmen sought jobs in America, where workers had political rights and better working conditions.

During the peak years of Belgian immigration, window manufacture expanded into areas where natural gas was available. Belgians moved into new factories in southwestern Pennsylvania, New York, eastern Ohio, and West Virginia. In 1920 there were more than thirteen hundred Belgian-born citizens in these four states. They comprised a significant portion of the skilled craftsmen in the industry, even as it moved toward mass production. To offset changes, the Belgian immigrant workers utilized strong craft unions as well as traditions emphasizing worker-owned factories and cooperative stores. The Belgian enclave in the small town of Salem, West Virginia, supported three cooperative factories, a newspaper, and a cooperative store by 1915.

As large corporations gained dominance in the window-glass industry, Belgians were forced into semiskilled operative positions. Nevertheless, they remained a significant presence in window-glass towns such as Point Marion, Jeannette, and Charleroi, Pennsylvania, and in Clarksburg and South Charleston, West Virginia. Belgian communities were famous for their social clubs, orchestras, summer fairs, and New Year's rituals. Even today, elements of Belgian culture persist in the architecture, cooking, and entertainments of those communities.

See also: GLASS INDUSTRY (BUSINESS, INDUSTRY, AND TECHNOLOGY); GLASSWORKERS (LABOR).

—Ken Fones-Wolf, *West Virginia University*

Black Dutch

The American term *Black Dutch* is used to refer to a particular dark-complexioned people in southern Appalachia whose ancestors were of uncertain origin. Its use may have originated in Appalachian Pennsylvania as a corruption of *Plattdeutsch*, one of the principal divisions of the Low German language commonly spoken by early German settlers. Some historians connect the Black Dutch to Gypsies and Jews who migrated to North America. Even less likely is the explanation that the Black Dutch are the products of intermixing between the Spaniards and Dutch who warred in Europe during the sixteenth and seventeenth centuries. In southern Appalachia, *Black Dutch* often refers to a mixed race people of European and Native American ancestry.

During the first centuries of North American and European contact, some individuals claimed to be Black Dutch to escape discrimination and to ease their assimilation into white culture. But the Black Dutch did not escape scorn. The term came to be considered derogatory and was sometimes used as an insult. Genealogist and writer James Plyant conducted a survey of individuals with Black Dutch ancestry. The predominant characteristics included: a dark or very dark complexion (68 percent); brown, dark brown, black, or dark hair (60 percent); brown, dark brown, black, dark, or very dark eyes (41 percent); and fairly short, short, or very short stature (32 percent).

Sometimes the terms are used interchangeably, but *Black Dutch* and *Melungeon* are normally considered to refer to two distinct groups. Both terms usually refer to the descendants of Native American and white ancestors, but the latter often includes African ancestry. The Black Dutch were usually inhabitants of eastern central Tennessee and the surrounding area, while Melungeons inhabit much of northeastern Tennessee, southeastern Kentucky, and southwestern Virginia.

See also: MELUNGEON FAMILIES AND COMMUNITIES (FAMILY AND COMMUNITY); MELUNGEONS.

—Ima J. Stephens, *Auburn University*

Friedrich Lowlon Mucke, "A History of the German Element at French and Neubert's, Tennessee (Lutheran Valley)," *Tennessee Ancestors* (December 1990); James Plyant, "In Search of the Black Dutch," *American Genealogy Magazine* (March 1997).

Blue Creek Band

The Shawnee Indians have lived intermittently in parts of Appalachia for more than a thousand years. Historians place the Chalahgawtha and Makujay Septs (or groups) at the confluence of the Scioto and Ohio Rivers in the area of what is now Portsmouth, Ohio, as late as 1745. Flooding and encroachment by Europeans resulted in the Shawnees' emigration from the area, but a group of the inhabitants remained in the Upper Ohio River Valley in present-day Ohio, Kentucky, and West Virginia, where they secluded themselves in remote valleys and mountains. Intermarriage and assimilation with Europeans enabled this group of Shawnee (now known as the Blue Creek Band) to avoid being dislocated by the Indian Removal Act of 1830. By 1870, the Shawnee were the only Native American tribe in Ohio.

While outwardly appearing to have assimilated into European culture by the late twentieth century, the band maintained much of its language and many ceremonies and traditions. In 1992 the tribe publicly reassembled under the leadership of Principal Chief Cora Tula Watters, a direct descendant of the Chalahgawtha Sept and a member of the seventh generation of the Watters family to live in Adams County, Ohio. The traditional political structure of the tribe is administered by the principal chief, second chief, head man, and head woman, plus the clan chief and clan mother, who are equal in power to each other, from each of the twelve clans. Leadership is elected every three years. Grand Council meetings, open to all members from all twelve clans, are held monthly. At the meetings, tribal history, language, traditions, and ancient crafts are studied and practiced. Closed Council, which consists of the principal chief, second chief, clan heads, and elders, meets four times each year to conduct tribal business. Emergency sessions are called as needed. The tribe interacts on a continuing basis with the greater community in an effort to promote interracial relations and multiculturalism and to provide education about American Indians to outsiders.

The tribe of approximately two hundred members performs traditional ceremonies, including the Spring and Fall Bread Dance, Feast of Green Corn, Feast of the Dead, and naming and adoption ceremonies. Shawnee wedding ceremonies are recognized by the State of Ohio.

See also: SHAWNEE.

—Cora Tula Watters, *Antioch University, McGregor School*

R. David Edmunds, *The Shawnee Prophet* (1993); Helen Hornbeck Tanner, ed., *Atlas of Great Lakes Indian History* (1987); Jim Great Elk Waters, *View from the Medicine Lodge* (1999).

Catholics

See Catholicism (Religion)

Center for the Study of Ethnicity and Gender in Appalachia

See Center for the Study of Ethnicity and Gender in Appalachia (Cultural Institutions)

Cherokee

From the late seventeenth to the early nineteenth century, Native American culture in the southern Appalachians was predominantly that of the Cherokee. But trade with the British, which began in earnest after the founding of Charles Town (Charleston), South Carolina, in 1670, initiated changes in the Cherokees' traditional political organization toward a more centralized form of government. This evolutionary process culminated in the formation of the Cherokee Nation in 1828.

Traditionally, the Cherokee of the late seventeenth through the mid-eighteenth century were members of autonomous political units called towns. A town was not delineated spatially but was composed of all the individuals who used a specific ceremonial center. Each town had a council that made decisions on relations with other towns and with non-Cherokees. In special circumstances, the council resolved internal disputes. When a decision to go to war was made, a town war organization directed all activities related to conflict. All members of a town were also members of the council, and anyone could speak during council meetings, though procedures were dominated by elder males, with the town priest-chief and his assistants being the most important. Since all council decisions had to be unanimous, these leaders, as well as members of the seven-member inner advisory council of clan representatives, became skilled in oratory and persuasion. There was no central political authority unifying the towns.

English traders and soldiers, failing to understand the Cherokees' decentralized political system and their leaders' lack of coercive power, began to recognize certain influential Cherokees as "kings" or "emperors." This imposed English governmental terminology upon individuals such as Moytoy of Tellico and Old Hop of Chota. Additional factors forcing the Cherokees toward a more centralized government were their increasing dependence on English trade and recognition that the actions of single individuals or towns would be interpreted by the English and, later, the United States government as the actions of all Cherokees. Thus, the killing of an English trader or the massacre of a family of settlers by a few Cherokees could lead to war and hardship for all. A central tribal council was formed by the mid-eighteenth century to oversee relations with non-Cherokees, but it was too weak to prevent young warriors from continuing to raid white settlements. This division between young warriors and elders favoring peace was exacerbated by the American Revolution and the burning of many Cherokee towns by colonial militias. By the end of the eighteenth century, the tribal council had incorporated both elders and younger warriors into the inner council as an attempt at reunification. The tribal council as a whole consisted of influential men selected as representatives of their towns.

By the early nineteenth century, the National Council, as the Cherokee tribal council was called, began to pass laws regulating the internal affairs of all Cherokees, including matters that would previously have been resolved at the town level. In 1817 a thirteen-member committee, which became known as the National Committee, was established to serve as an executive board within the larger National Council. By 1823 both the National Committee and the National Council had oversight responsibilities regarding each other's decisions. District courts of law to adjudicate Cherokee legal issues were also in operation by this time.

Finally, the Cherokee Constitution, which was drafted in 1827 and adopted in 1828, so strengthened the power of the principal chief that he became the Cherokee equivalent of the president of the United States. Thus, the Cherokee Nation, a constitutional government, had clearly defined executive, legislative, and judicial branches and centralized political control over Cherokee towns. While town councils could still resolve local issues, the Cherokee Nation had become the entity that spoke for all Cherokees.

The chief spokesperson for the Cherokee Nation from 1828 until his death in 1866 was John Ross, who was repeatedly elected principal chief. Although only one-eighth Cherokee, Ross fought bitterly against the State of Georgia's appropriation of Cherokee lands and the federal push for the removal of the Cherokee Nation spurred by the Indian Removal Act of 1830. Ross also argued against those Cherokee who favored another treaty with the United States and removal to the West. However, members of the Treaty Party signed the Treaty of New Echota in 1835, which ceded all lands of the Cherokee Nation to the United States government for five million dollars with the stipulation that members of the nation move west to Indian Territory two years after treaty ratification. The treaty was ratified by the United States Senate in 1836 by a single vote.

Although estimates vary, approximately sixteen thousand members of the Cherokee Nation were removed from their homes (mostly in North Carolina) between 1838 and 1839 by the United States Army and were sent on the Trail of Tears to present-day Oklahoma. John Ross accompanied his people west; along the way, nearly one-fourth of the Cherokees died, including Ross's first wife. The Cherokee Nation thus ceased to exist in the southern Appalachians by the fall of 1838.

However, approximately fourteen hundred Cherokee remained in the mountains of western North Carolina. Some of these were fugitives from the removal but many were "Citizen Cherokee" who, by virtue of a previous treaty, were not considered members of the Cherokee Nation. These individuals and their descendants continued to reside in North Carolina and formed the core of what is now the Eastern Band of Cherokee Indians.

Throughout the rest of the nineteenth century, the Eastern Band faced many political and economic problems such as the potential loss of their lands and anomalous legal status. It was unclear whether they should be considered citizens of North Carolina or a federal tribe under U.S. government protection. Most Cherokees were subsistence farmers with few economic resources.

By 1900, some Cherokees were earning wages in the lumber industry, but by the 1930s tourism had developed as an important avenue for economic enrichment of the Eastern Band. By the 1960s, tourism was the major economic resource through attractions such as the Museum of the Cherokee Indian, Oconaluftee Indian Village, and the outdoor drama *Unto These Hills*. Most recently, proceeds from Cherokee Bingo and Harrah's Cherokee Smoky Mountain Casino have fueled rapid growth and development on the reservation of the Eastern Band in North Carolina.

See also: NATIVE AMERICANS; ROSS, JOHN; SEQUOYAH.

—Cliff Boyd, *Radford University*

John R. Finger, *The Eastern Band of Cherokees, 1819–1900* (1984); Duane H. King, ed., *The Cherokee Indian Nation: A Troubled History* (1979).

Cherokee Slavery

Prior to the nineteenth century, slavery as practiced by the Cherokee permitted capture of other Native Americans during war. The captives did not serve as laborers, and the Cherokee attached no economic value to them. Instead, the captives replaced lost family members and were eventually adopted into the Cherokee band.

But learning that Europeans considered slaves chattel, Native Americans learned to sell prisoners of war to traders, who also took indigenous people by force. During the early eighteenth century, traders in the Carolina Colony sent members of the Yamasee tribe to capture slaves, prompting raids of Tuscarora, Creek, and Cherokee settlements. Governor James Moore of Carolina Colony, who had taken hundreds of southeastern Native Americans captive as early as 1702, encouraged indigenous slavery.

Although the British House of Commons created an Indian Commission in 1707 that outlawed Native American enslavement, the British continued to send Cherokee slaves to the West Indies until at least 1715. Native Americans protested the enslavement of their people by sending emissaries to speak with white leaders in Charles Town (later Charleston, South Carolina). With increased importation of additional Africans for human bondage, slavery of indigenous North Americans diminished. By 1708 the number of Native American slaves in the Carolinas was only half that of African slaves. The Cherokee often assisted African slaves who escaped their white masters.

By the end of the eighteenth century, some Cherokee had modified their traditional patterns of slavery to accommodate the European capitalist practice of owning African slaves. Although few full-blooded Cherokee owned slaves, slavery was officially recognized and protected by the Cherokee Nation. Many of the indigenous slave owners were of mixed Native American and white ancestry who acquired slaves as a means to better their economic and social status in southern white society. During the Cherokee removal during the latter 1830s, some black slaves, many of whom served as English translators, accompanied the Cherokee to Indian Territory in present-day Oklahoma. In 1842 about twenty-five African slaves who had settled with their Cherokee masters in Indian Territory near Webber's Falls on the Arkansas River revolted and escaped. Attempting to make it to Mexico, where human bondage was illegal, the slaves passed through Creek lands and ten more Africans joined the escapees. Thirty-one of the slaves were eventually recaptured.

The Cherokee National Council believed that free blacks from other areas had enticed their slaves to revolt and on December 2, 1842, passed legislation directing that all free blacks leave Cherokee territory, except those whom Cherokees had freed. By 1851 about three hundred African slaves had tried to escape their Cherokee masters.

Although Chief John Ross attempted to remain neutral before the Civil War, the Cherokees' location between slave states and free states caused many Native Americans to join the Southern cause. Proslavery Cherokee formed a Southern Rights political party to fight abolition. In 1855, they passed a bill in which they referred to themselves as a "slave-holding people," although only about 10 percent actually owned slaves. On February 20, 1863, the Royal Council of the Cherokee Nation issued an emancipation of all slaves within their territory. This official act freed only a small number of slaves, however, because most were owned by mixed-ancestry Cherokee who were allied with the Confederacy.

See also: CHEROKEE; *CHEROKEE PHOENIX* (MEDIA); SLAVERY AND ABOLITION (GOVERNMENT).

—Ima J. Stephens, *Auburn University*

Almon Wheeler Lauber, *Indian Slavery in Colonial Times within the Present Limits of the United States* (1970); Henry Thompson Malone, *Cherokees of the Old South* (1956); Theda Perdue, *Slavery and the Evolution of Cherokee Society, 1540–1866* (1979).

Choctaw

The Mississippi Band of Choctaw Indians lives in eight communities scattered across central Mississippi. The tribe's northeastern lands fall within the Appalachian region.

Choctaw oral history describes the group's arrival in the area with two distinct myths: one of migration from the west and another of emergence from an earthen mound. Written records first recognized the Choctaw as a coherent group at the end of the seventeenth century, at a time when the effects of intertribal warring and European contact resulted in a dynamic reconfiguration of political and social organizations. Eventually, contact with these new settlers resulted in the 1830 Treaty of Dancing Rabbit Creek, in which Choctaw leaders ceded their land to the American government for land in Oklahoma.

The Choctaw men and women who moved west formed the Choctaw Nation of Oklahoma. Those who refused to leave Mississippi were forced to eke out a living as squatters and then sharecroppers on land they once owned. The rigid racial boundaries of the rural South encouraged the Choctaw to remain isolated from white and black alike. This situation has been slow to change, with race remaining an important part of Choctaw identity.

The Mississippi Band of Choctaw Indians gained federal recognition in 1945. It has one of the strictest membership requirements of any of the North American Indian tribes, accepting only those who are at least one-half Choctaw. At the end of the twentieth century, the tribe owned successful business, industry, and tourism enterprises, including a large casino, making it one of the largest employers in the state. Many tribal members continued to speak their native language while balancing traditional culture with modern convenience.

See also: CHOCTAW MUSEUM OF THE SOUTHERN INDIAN (CULTURAL INSTITUTIONS); NATIVE AMERICANS.

—Tom Mould, *Elon University*

Civil Rights Movement

Although the Deep South was the decisive battleground in the Civil Rights movement of the 1950s and 1960s, communities throughout Appalachia were profoundly and permanently changed by African Americans' demands for an end to racial segregation in public accommodations and institutions. Communities—and neighborhoods within communities—responded to the movement in dramatically different ways, depending upon their history, economy, racial composition, and local and state political leadership. To a significant degree, the course of the movement in Appalachia reflected the racial schisms and politics of the nation at large. In Pittsburgh, for example, the struggle against official discrimination began in earnest soon after World War II, nearly a decade before school segregation was outlawed by the U.S. Supreme Court. While the Montgomery, Alabama, bus boycott of 1955–56 marked the opening of the sustained struggle, the Civil Rights movement came to the southern Appalachians with lunch counter sit-ins by college students in 1960.

Although segregation prevailed throughout the region when the Civil Rights movement began, communities in the northern and central sections of Appalachia generally responded without the politically unified opposition and violent episodes that characterized the period in the South. By the 1950s, Pittsburgh, long past legally segregated schools, had already moved to desegregation of restaurants, housing, and swimming pools. In the wake the Supreme Court's 1954 school desegregation mandate in *Brown v. Board of Education*, Maryland, Kentucky, and West Virginia moved toward voluntary compliance, while Alabama, the Carolinas, Georgia, Mississippi, Tennessee, and Virginia adopted varying strategies of delay or outright defiance. States experiencing the most rancorous strife were led by politicians who exploited white racism to gain office and hold power. Notable among them were Governors John Patterson and George Wallace of Alabama, Ross Barnett of Mississippi, and Lester Maddox of Georgia.

But even in states where resistance to civil rights was official policy, some communities, usually in upland counties, desegregated without upheaval and bloodshed. On the other hand, de facto segregation often persisted in jurisdictions that officially espoused equal access. Clashes occurred in areas of large black populations where whites perceived threats to their control and in all-white neighborhoods where barriers were challenged. Henry Louis Gates Jr., director of the Afro-American Studies Program at Harvard University, recalled his hometown of Piedmont, West Virginia, in the 1950s as a place where black and white communities were "clearly demarcated, as if by ropes or turnstiles." Whites angrily drove Gates from the premises when he led a youthful attempt to desegregate a local drinking and dancing spot, but in some instances the demarcation between blacks and whites in mountain communities simply dissolved. In Whitesburg, Kentucky, two African American truck drivers walked into a white Main Street restaurant at the height of a noon rush in August 1963, took a table, and received service without objection. Thus ended segregation in eating places while the color line in schools of the town and county remained inviolate.

Particularly at the secondary level, schools proved to be the most problematic institutions to integrate. In Greenbrier County, West Virginia, public schools promptly integrated in the fall of 1954, but African Americans were removed after a week of white protest. In the coal-mining county of McDowell, West Virginia, only a small number of African American students chose to attend formerly white schools, for residents of black neighborhoods had long considered their schools sources of community pride. In Clinton, Tennessee, two years later, local whites and outsiders terrorized black children seeking school admission, requiring deployment of the National Guard to enforce the desegregation. Facing opposition of such varying intensity, school boards chose numerous strategies for removing color barriers. In Knoxville, Chattanooga, and elsewhere in east Tennessee, schools adopted the so-called Nashville plan, which mandated the desegregation of one grade each year.

The integration of central Appalachian colleges and universities generally proceeded without violence or confrontation, but in the southernmost states of the region there was bitter and sometimes violent opposition to integration of institutions of higher learning as well as desegregation of secondary schools. In 1956 the admission of a young black woman named Autherine Lucy to the University of Alabama was greeted by riots on the Tuscaloosa campus and her prompt dismissal for her own safety. The university did not undergo even token integration until 1963, and then only after Governor Wallace staged a symbolic stand in the schoolhouse door against federal authorities escorting two black students to registration. In Kentucky, by contrast, the legislature had in 1950 overturned the state's forty-six-year-old Day Law, which prohibited blacks and whites from attending the same school.

Although the issue was less complex and more quickly resolved than school integration, the opening of such places as lunch counters, cafeterias, and rest rooms produced explosive confrontations. In 1961 Freedom Riders seeking to desegregate interstate transportation facilities in the South had their bus firebombed outside Anniston, Alabama, and were jailed in Birmingham—where a church bombing and the use of police dogs and fire hoses later epitomized racial antipathy.

Tensions rose in Birmingham in the 1950s as a result of overcrowding in segregated black schools and official resistance to federal court orders against segregated housing. When Alabama Attorney General John Patterson obtained a state court order banning most activities of the state branch of the National Association for the Advancement of Colored People in 1956, Birmingham ministers Fred Shuttlesworth and Vernon Johns organized the Alabama Christian Movement for Human Rights in 1956 to carry on the struggle for civil rights in the city. This preceded the Southern Christian Leadership Conference, led by the Reverend Martin Luther King Jr., which became the best-known force against segregation in the nation and the keeper of the Civil Rights movement's philosophy of nonviolence. Less known but more confrontational, and in ways more effective, was the Student Non-Violent Coordinating Committee, founded in Nashville in 1960.

In larger towns, local ministerial organizations, including both black and white pastors, served to enhance communications and reduce tensions in divided communities. At times, these and other moderate civic organizations created unjustified illusions of racial harmony. Huntsville, Alabama, one of the centers of the growing aerospace industry and government space and missile development in the 1950s and 1960s, prided itself for racial tolerance, but when black students sought service at lunch counters in 1962, they were jailed, just as elsewhere in the South.

While activists from northern Appalachian communities such as Pittsburgh and college students from across northern and central Appalachia went south to join the Mississippi voting rights battle and other civil rights campaigns, southern Appalachia was not without indigenous white allies and institutional support.

Most prominent were the Highlander Folk School at Monteagle, Tennessee, and Berea College in Kentucky, the latter founded by abolitionists before the Civil War and still committed to interracial comity and education. Highlander, established by Myles Horton in 1932 to address labor issues, turned to civil rights after World War II. As the civil rights struggle loomed in the 1950s, the school trained several community leaders who later became national figures in the campaign, among them King, Rosa Parks, the inspirational figure in the Montgomery bus boycott, and John Lewis, a young leader of the Student Non-Violent Coordinating Committee and later a member of Congress. Highlander's notoriety led to its property being confiscated by the State of Tennessee and its eventual rebirth in Knoxville and New Market as the Highlander Research and Education Center.

Ironically, the court orders that ultimately ended segregation of public transportation and other facilities were issued by U.S. District Judge Frank M. Johnson, an Alabaman. A law school classmate of Wallace, Johnson was born and reared in the Appalachian foothills of Winston County, an area with traditions rooted in abolitionist sentiments and Union loyalty in the Civil War.

See also: BEREA COLLEGE (EDUCATION); HIGHLANDER RESEARCH AND EDUCATION CENTER (EDUCATION); KENTUCKY DAY LAW AND THE BEREA COLLEGE CASE (GOVERNMENT); KU KLUX KLAN (GOVERNMENT).

—Rudy Abramson, *Reston, Virginia,* and Mary A. Waalkes, *Lee University*

Paul H. Bergeron, Stephen V. Ash, and Jeanette Keith, *Tennesseans and Their History* (1999); Glenn T. Eskew, *But for Birmingham: The Local and National Movements in the Civil Rights Struggle* (1997); Robert Weisbrot, *Freedom Bound: A History of America's Civil Rights Movement* (1990).

Creek

At the time of European contact in the sixteenth century, the Creek lived in two groups, the Upper Creek and the Lower Creek, who resided in modern-day northern Alabama and northern Georgia, respectively, although some moved to Florida Territory after being displaced by war and adopted the name *Seminole*, meaning "runaway." The Creek spoke a language of the Muskogean variety.

In 1540, when Spanish explorer Hernando de Soto visited the Creek, he found that they had built huge ceremonial mounds out of earth, some up to fifty feet high. Although

Creek legend told of their warriors hiding in a mound to surprise the Cherokee in battle, the main purpose of the mounds was to provide a place for religious rituals. The Creek used tobacco for sacred purposes, as the smoke was thought to ward off ghosts.

By the eighteenth century, as many as thirty thousand Creek lived in Appalachia. After meeting the English, they began trading with them and grew dependent upon European goods, including guns. Although the goods provided an easier life, increasing dependence on the merchandise led to indebtedness to traders, who often asked for Creek land in payment.

During the War of 1812, Andrew Jackson led attacks against the Creek. Creek leader William McIntosh rode beside Jackson and was later killed by his people for this betrayal. The more militant Creek, known as "Red Sticks," fought Jackson famously and futilely. The Indian Removal Act of 1830, passed while Jackson was president, resulted in the forced relocation of the Creek, along with the Cherokee, Chickasaw, Choctaw, and Seminole, to Indian Territory in present-day Oklahoma. Known as the Trail of Tears, the removal of the southeastern Indians had a devastating effect, resulting in the estimated death of more than thirty-five hundred Creek. Descendants of the surviving Creek continue to live in Oklahoma.

See also: NATIVE AMERICANS; SOUTHERN NATIVE AMERICANS (SETTLEMENT AND MIGRATION); WHITE CONQUEST (SETTLEMENT AND MIGRATION).

—Ima J. Stephens, *Auburn University*

Kathryn E. Holland Braund, *Deerskins and Duffels: The Creek Indian Trade with Anglo-America, 1685–1815* (1993); Michael D. Green, *The Creeks* (1979); Claudio Saunt, *A New Order of Things: Property, Power, and the Transformation of the Creek Indians, 1733–1816* (1999).

Eastern Kentucky Social Club

The formation of social clubs by ethnic groups is a well-established feature of the American cultural landscape, and most urban areas host at least a few groups organized to celebrate their geographic or cultural heritage. Among these urban Appalachian groups is the Eastern Kentucky Social Club, formed by African American migrants who wanted to maintain long-standing friendships and celebrate a heritage rooted in the coalfields of southeastern Kentucky.

Benham and Lynch, coal towns built by Wisconsin Steel Company and U.S. Coal and Coke Company, lie along Looney Creek at the base of Black Mountain in Harlan County, Kentucky. The town of Poor Fork, later renamed Cumberland, became the commercial and rail center for the two enterprises. Both companies actively recruited local residents, foreign-born immigrants, and blacks from Alabama and other southern states to work in the mines and live in the towns. But the same push-pull economic factors that sent thousands of Appalachians streaming to the North after World War II dispersed black miners and their families living in Benham and Lynch.

The Eastern Kentucky Social Club was formed in 1967, when seven friends in Cleveland, Ohio, began talking about the possibility of a reunion of the migrants from Benham, Lynch, and Cumberland. The first reunion was held in 1970 in Cleveland, and so many came—driving in from Lynch, Benham, Cumberland, Atlanta, Detroit, and Chicago—that not everyone could get inside the building. By 1971 local branches of the organization had been formed in Lynch, Chicago, and Detroit to host future gatherings. The second reunion was held in Detroit in 1971 and the third in Chicago. Ultimately, fourteen chapters of the club were formed; ten were still active in 2001, including locals in Indianapolis, Detroit, Milwaukee, Chicago, Cleveland, Dayton, Atlanta, and Lynch, as well as in Connecticut and California. The club's annual Labor Day weekend reunion typically draws up to three thousand people. Between Labor Day and Memorial Day, local chapters of the club hold monthly meetings and fund-raisers to prepare for the next year's events. The California chapter's Web site and the *Eastern Kentucky Social Clubs Biography*, prepared by Andrea Massey, detail these activities.

See also: IMMIGRANT AND AFRICAN AMERICAN LABOR IN THE COALFIELDS (LABOR).

—Thomas E. Wagner, *University of Cincinnati*

Edward J. Cabbell and William H. Turner, eds., *Blacks in Appalachia* (1985); Ronald L. Lewis, *Black Coal Miners in America: Race, Class, and Community Conflict, 1780–1980* (1987); Phillip Obermiller, Thomas E. Wagner, and E. Bruce Tucker, eds., *Appalachian Odyssey: Historical Perspectives on the Great Migration* (2000); Joe William Trotter Jr., *Coal, Class, and Color: Blacks in Southern West Virginia, 1915–32* (1990).

English

Arriving in the seventeenth century, the first white explorers of Appalachia were Englishmen seeking furs and trade with the Indians. Persons of English descent—distinguished here from Welsh, Scottish, Anglo-Irish, and Scots-Irish—also comprised nearly a third of the region's earliest settlers. Because of their language, Protestant religious background, and familiarity with legal norms, the English assimilated into colonial American culture and married outside their ethnic boundaries more readily than did any other ethnic group. They supplied the bulk of leadership in Appalachia in politics, law, commerce, and literature. At present, English ancestry is probably present to some degree in a substantial majority of Appalachia's population, especially south of

Pennsylvania and New York, where there are more people of German and eastern European descent.

By 1790, 90 percent of the population of Appalachia had origins in England, Scotland, and Ireland, well over half of them "borderers" from the English-Scottish borderland and northeastern Ireland (Ulster). The English borderers emigrated from Cumberland, Westmoreland, Northumberland, Durham, Lancashire, and Yorkshire. Their motives were overwhelmingly economic: escape from enclosures (which further shrank already small farms), high rents, low wages, heavy taxes, crop failures, creditors, and distress in the linen industry. A majority were farmers or farm hands, a large minority craftsmen and petty traders. Toughened by seven hundred years of border warfare and brutal oppression by transient rulers, the 250,000 borderers who migrated between 1718 and 1775 were shunned by the long-settled coastal population. The best lands having been taken already, they migrated to the backcountries of Pennsylvania, Virginia, and North Carolina, which became their bases for expansion into the mountains. Their numbers gave to Appalachia a distinctly borderer cast which has lasted to the present.

Unlike the Presbyterian Scots, English borderers were Anglicans (Episcopalians). They scorned the "hireling" clergy imposed by southern England, however, and had become more evangelical (New Light Christianity) by the end of the eighteenth century. This tradition continued in America. Amid fierce sectarian disputes with Presbyterians, a majority of the English gradually drifted to the Methodists, Baptists, and small denominations or independent churches. Religion aside, those from English counties shared a common culture with other borderers. A prickly, stubborn pride distinguished them from fellow English Americans. Unlike most immigrants in the eighteenth century, borderers generally came in families, not as individuals or indentured servants. Harsh experience had led them to rely more on kinship ties than on governments for order and survival. Historian David Hackett Fischer, author of *Albion's Seed*, holds that disputes were often settled outside the formal court system by personal confrontation or vigilante justice. Personal qualities, not office, conferred authority; disloyalty to the leader was the gravest political sin. Borderers cherished natural liberty, which implies minimal government, low taxes, and a right of resistance. Liberty did not necessarily mean tolerance, however, and the suspicious, socially conservative borderers readily regarded opponents as enemies. To groups with less turbulent pasts, such characteristics betokened a lack of proper civilization. These traits, however, had long assured the borderers' survival in a pitiless environment and helped them to cope with the rugged terrain and hostile Indians of the Appalachian frontier.

Language, architecture, and the rural landscape in Appalachia show significant English influence. The conferring of colorful place names (alongside staid Cumberlands and Durhams) continued an English tradition and includes such locations as Bugtussle, Thousandsticks, and Head of Grassy. Slang terms likewise crossed the sea; in northern Britain *redneck* denoted a religious dissenter, *boozier* an unusually big and tough man, and *cracker* a low-class braggart. In architecture, a "cabin" was an impermanent borderland hut of earth and stones. (Log construction came to Appalachia from Scandinavia and Germany.) An English "pen" was a single room. There were (and still are) in Appalachia houses of single and double I-house design—two stories, two pens wide, one deep or larger, with four pens over four pens. The dogtrot cabin (with an open-air passageway between two pens, a common roof, and outside chimney) perhaps originated in the English-settled Tidewater country. Outside chimneys are typical of England. As for the landscape, surveys followed the English "mates and bounds" system, resulting in a crazy-quilt pattern. Landownership replicated the border norm: a tiny group of large owners, a modest number of small owners, and a crowd of tenants and squatters.

During the nineteenth century, English immigrants in Appalachia were mainly managers, engineers, and miners, bringing experience to the rising coal, iron, and steel industries and to railroad construction. Welsh miners dominated the anthracite coalfields, and Cornishmen were the backbone of copper, tin, and iron operations.

Generally speaking, the English moved more rapidly into better-paying jobs than did other immigrants. The most notable clusterings of English occurred around the steelworks of Birmingham, Alabama, and Pittsburgh and in the Pennsylvania coalfields. Two attempts to establish communities failed. Middlesborough (now Middlesboro), Kentucky, was an English-financed project (1890–94) to build iron- and steelworks, but after fueling eastern Kentucky's first boom, it collapsed. Rugby, Tennessee, was founded in 1880 by wealthy young Englishmen and Boston capitalists as an agricultural colony. Although the community partly recovered from an 1881 typhoid epidemic, it had completely failed by the next decade.

Because they assimilated rapidly and felt less threatened than other groups, the English did not develop strong ethnic organizations. They did establish American chapters of the Independent Order of Odd Fellows and the Ancient Order of Foresters, however, and became leading founders and managers of labor unions, continuing a tradition begun in England.

From the 1830s to World War II, the English (in America and Britain) were significantly involved in Appalachia through investment, primarily in coal and metal mining, iron and steel manufacture, and especially railroads. Almost always foreign owners contented themselves with investing and did not seek to run enterprises from London. The heaviest investing occurred between 1865 and 1914, notably in Kanawha coal in West Virginia and coal and iron operations in Tennessee and Alabama. As for railroads, the English were major investors, although seldom majority stockholders, in the main lines through Appalachia now included in the giant CSX and Norfolk Southern systems—among them the Reading; Erie; Baltimore and Ohio; Pennsylvania; Louisville and Nashville; Norfolk and Western; and future components of the Southern Railway, such as the Cincinnati, New Orleans and Texas Pacific and the Alabama Great Southern. Into the twentieth century, the Norfolk and Western and the Alabama Great Southern were exceptional cases, the former having a majority of its stock held by British investors and the latter not only built and owned but also operated by London interests.

See also: SCOTS; SCOTS-IRISH; SPECULATORS AND ABSENTEE LANDLORDS (SETTLEMENT AND MIGRATION).

—David S. Newhall, *Centre College*

Rowland T. Berthoff, *British Immigrants in Industrial America, 1790–1950* (1953); David Hackett Fischer, *Albion's Seed: Four British Folkways in America* (1989); Allen G. Noble, ed., *To Build in a New Land: Ethnic Landscapes in North America* (1992).

Finns

During the high tide of Finnish immigration to the United States in the late nineteenth and early twentieth centuries, small communities and neighborhoods of Finlanders were established in western Pennsylvania, the northern panhandle of West Virginia, eastern Ohio, and northern Alabama. Many of the new arrivals were single men with minimal skills who came to work in Appalachian coal mines, logging camps, and railroad construction sites. Once they gained a measure of security, they often moved on to urban communities and to other areas of the country.

As early as the 1870s, recent Finnish immigrants were working in railroad construction gangs around Titusville, Pennsylvania. In the years that followed, newly arrived Finns labored in the mines at Nanty Glo, Allenport, Canonsburg, Charleroi, Coal Center, and Twilight and lived in larger communities at Pittsburgh, McKeesport, and Glassport. In West Virginia, Finns worked in axe manufacturing in Charleston and labored in the steel and tin mills around Weirton. In the Appalachian foothills of Athens County, Ohio, they worked in coal mines at Jacksonville, San Toy, Redtown, and Poston.

Because of their relatively small numbers, eagerness to assimilate, and western and urban migration, the region's Finns usually saw their communities fade away within a few decades. In Cloverdale, Alabama, a dozen Finnish families who took up farming in the early twentieth century were the only recent immigrants in the area. Though set apart by their language and Lutheran religion, they quickly assimilated. A few members of the second generation married within the community, but by the 1950s their Finnish culture was largely a memory except for a few saunas and family recipes. A more recent study has indicated a post-1970 secondary migration of Finnish Americans to Appalachian Virginia from other U.S. states. Most have assimilated into American society and exhibit no particular interest in associating with others based on Finnish origin. Nevertheless, there are Finnish families and organizations in such places as Pittsburgh and Weirton that continue to preserve traditions from the old country during the twenty-first century.

See also: LUTHERANS (RELIGION).

—Rudy Abramson, *Reston, Virginia*

Hilda Hakola Gray, "A History of the Finnish Colony at Cloverdale, Alabama," unpublished manuscript, Florence State Teachers College (c. 1945); John I. Kolehmainen, *A History of the Finns in Ohio, Western Pennsylvania, and West Virginia* (1977); Mika Roinila, "Finnish Ethnicity in the State of Virginia," *Siirtolaisuus-Migration* (2001).

Free Blacks, Antebellum

Appalachia's free black population during the antebellum period was extremely small in both the southern and northern parts of the region. Federal census data suggests two basic reasons.

First, the number of slaves in southern Appalachia was low compared to those in the Deep South, seldom exceeding 10 percent of the local population and often much lower. With owners having little fear that slaves would abscond or rebel, bondage was generally less oppressive than in other parts of the antebellum South. Travelers through the region often remarked upon the contrast and also reported encountering ambivalent local feeling about slavery. In state politics, Appalachian counties tended to adopt an antislavery stance, but this was likely a reflection of interregional difference and competition with more densely populated coastal parts of the state rather than a genuine interest in ending slavery. Little evidence has been found to indicate that white Appalachians were less racist than whites in other parts of the antebellum South, and slaves were rarely freed.

The other major factor that kept the Appalachian free black population small was the low rate of migration into the region. Although employment opportunities and living conditions for people of color were probably better than in other parts of the rural South, prospects in northern states or southern cities tended to be more compelling. State laws also limited Appalachia's ability to attract free blacks from elsewhere. Virginia, for example, prohibited free blacks from other states from taking up residence. Slaves manumitted after 1806 were required to leave within twelve months.

Although these and similar restrictions were not always enforced, they remained available for selective application.

Studies of slavery in the region combined with studies of free blacks elsewhere in the rural South allow some inferences about the daily life of Appalachian free blacks. The majority of free blacks in the region lived in towns, where there were more wage-earning opportunities for the unskilled. Although a few free blacks attained property ownership, the overwhelming majority remained in poverty. The small size of both the free black and slave populations probably made it difficult to form and maintain families. Most Appalachian free blacks probably had enslaved kin and these ties no doubt kept free blacks from moving to places where they might achieve greater material comfort. Some free blacks also intermarried with Native Americans and whites.

The small size of the African American population probably made white Appalachians less susceptible to racial panic or fear of slave insurrection, and free blacks, who were often targeted in these incidents elsewhere, enjoyed greater safety from vigilante activity in Appalachia. Nevertheless, daily life for all blacks living in Appalachia was generally difficult and offered few opportunities for improvement.

See also: SLAVERY AND ABOLITION (GOVERNMENT); SLAVE TRADE; SLAVE WOMEN.

—Ellen Eslinger, *DePaul University*

Freed Blacks, Postbellum

The fate of Appalachian freed blacks at the close of slavery was similar to that of freed blacks across the South. Fewer numbers of slaves, a lower ratio of blacks to whites, and a higher proportion of non-planter slave owners in Appalachia did, however, produce several important differences between the experiences of Appalachian freed blacks and those former slaves in other parts of the South.

Many freed blacks in Appalachia earned a living through the sale of homegrown or handmade products and services or through tenant farming or sharecropping. Those freed from non-plantation yeomen farms faced fewer barriers in adjusting to the new order since many of them had previously been entrusted with more responsibilities than plantation slaves, acquiring specialized skills and somewhat more independence. Their closer associations with whites and with various societal institutions made them better prepared to function in white society after they were freed.

The transition for blacks freed from plantations was more difficult. Since the Bureau of Refugees, Freedmen, and Abandoned Lands (known as the Freedmen's Bureau) located its offices in southern cities and border states, it was difficult for former slaves from rural plantation areas to gain access to federal support. White individuals or families that had owned more than five slaves were generally unable to hire all of their former slaves as wageworkers. While smaller numbers of plantations in Appalachia meant that the freed blacks were absorbed more readily into the existing labor pool, they were also perceived as a threat to white laborers and faced strong competition for the few agricultural jobs found on the larger farms in the region. Freed plantation slaves were frequently victims of the predatory practices of their former owners or white gangs and were often jailed and forced to work as convict laborers in mining, forestry, and construction. White men, who had little access to wage jobs during slavery, displaced former slaves in the labor-intensive jobs of mining, forestry, and agriculture.

Freed blacks who remained in rural areas and small towns formed close-knit black rural settlements. Their small numbers led Appalachian rural freed blacks to have more ties to the larger white community, but in most encounters with whites, they were still viewed and treated as inferior.

Harper's Weekly depiction of freedmen registering to vote in Asheville, North Carolina, 1867. Although newly freed Appalachian blacks were optimistic after the demise of slavery, they were often held back by whites who supported segregationist Black Codes or used other intimidation tactics to relegate them to second-class citizenship.

Freed blacks who were not hired by former owners as wageworkers or absorbed into local rural economies frequently moved to the region's cities and towns. There, segregated black neighborhoods provided a somewhat secure environment and enabled the creation of various segregated institutions, including social circles, churches, cemeteries, schools, and economic associations. Despite the internal freedom nurtured in black enclaves, whites continued to prohibit their full social, economic, and political participation citywide.

From 1865 to 1900, freed blacks looked to the future with hope. However, with the end of Reconstruction and the withdrawal of federal troops, the white population in Appalachia and the South dismantled opportunities for black citizens. The short-lived gains of freed blacks, made with the aid of northern volunteers, Radical Republicans, and carpetbaggers in other parts of the South were less evident in the mountains. The white mountain population supported Black Codes, state laws enforced after the Civil War to restrict rights for blacks. Generally, they also supported other legal actions, social pressures, acts of violence, and intimidation tactics that pushed newly freed Appalachian blacks into a second-class citizenry. While contributions of freed blacks were subtly integrated into Appalachian culture, blacks themselves were rendered all but invisible in the region.

See also: FREE BLACKS, ANTEBELLUM; SLAVERY.

—Wilburn Hayden Jr., *California University of Pennsylvania*

Thomas R. Frazier, ed., *Afro-American History: Primary Sources* (1970); Ronald L. Lewis, *Black Coal Miners in America: Race, Class, and Community Conflict, 1780–1980* (1987); Mary Beth Pudup, Dwight B. Billings, and Altina L. Waller, eds., *Appalachia in the Making: The Mountain South in the Nineteenth Century* (1995).

French

During the seventeenth and eighteenth centuries, French immigrants settled in the Mississippi Valley and along the eastern seaboard, especially in Pennsylvania and South Carolina. Only a few, often with Anglicized names, drifted into Appalachia.

In 1749, to counter English incursions into the Mississippi and Ohio Valley regions, French soldiers journeyed via French Creek in northwest Pennsylvania and the Allegheny River to the Ohio River, where they buried claims plates at key locations. France also built several forts in the Appalachians, including Presqu'île (now Erie, Pennsylvania) and Duquesne (Pittsburgh). The French Broad River's name reflects these Ohio claims.

Two early French colonies in Appalachia failed. The Scioto Land Company attracted refugees from the French Revolution to a tract of land along the Ohio River. When their titles proved invalid, the United States Congress compensated the survivors with 25,200 acres (the French Grant) opposite the Little Sandy Creek. Asylum (formerly Asile or Azyl), a colony founded by emigré royalists on the Susquehanna River near Wilkes-Barre, Pennsylvania, disappeared after a decade, its residents unwilling to adapt to the rigors of frontier farming.

Evidence of French settlement in Appalachia includes the persistence of a number of French-influenced town and county names, as well as a variety of French and Anglicized French surnames. Most numerous are counties in Pennsylvania, West Virginia, Tennessee, Alabama, and Mississippi named for the Marquis de Lafayette, a French soldier and statesman, and Francis Marion, an American Revolutionary War general of French descent. Eleven Appalachian counties from Pennsylvania to Alabama bear French names, including Clermont County, Ohio, and Sevier County, Tennessee. Towns with French names appear throughout the region, including Dunkirk, New York; Latrobe, Pennsylvania; and Brevard, North Carolina. In addition to a variety of French family names, many English names in Appalachia may signal French antecedents, including Boyd/Boyard, Cheney/Chenais, Faulkner/Faconnier, Lawson/Loison, Rogers/Rozier, and scores of others.

See also: ERIE, PENNSYLVANIA (URBAN APPALACHIAN EXPERIENCE); PITTSBURGH, PENNSYLVANIA (URBAN APPALACHIAN EXPERIENCE).

—David S. Newhall, *Centre College*

Garrison, Memphis Tennessee

(1890–1988) Educator and civil rights activist.

Memphis Tennessee Garrison aided in the early work of the National Association for the Advancement of Colored People (NAACP) and was a tireless educator and worker for racial equality and civil rights in Appalachia. Garrison's career is remarkable because she was a public figure at a time when women, especially black women in the region, were seldom in the limelight. She particularly focused on protecting and educating African Americans in the coal-mining community of Gary, West Virginia, where she was known to mediate labor, community, and race issues on behalf of the coal owners and the community.

Born March 4, 1890, in Hollins, Virginia, Garrison later moved with her family to McDowell County, West Virginia, where her father worked as a coal miner. After high school, Garrison passed the examination required for public school teachers in West Virginia and began teaching in 1908 in McDowell County, though she did not complete her bachelor's degree at Bluefield State College until 1939. As a young woman, Garrison also became involved with the NAACP. In 1921, at the age of thirty-one, she organized a branch of the organization in Gary, the third in West Virginia. She started several other branches in the southern part of the state and eventually began traveling nationally as an NAACP recruiter. Garrison was also politically active as chairperson of the Colored Republican Women's Club and the National and State Advisory Committee for Colored Voters. Her loyalty remained with the Republicans until the John F. Kennedy administration.

Although Garrison was both a welfare worker with U.S. Steel from 1931 to 1946 and a civil rights advocate, she considered herself an educator first. She served as the first woman president of the West Virginia State Teachers' Association from 1929 to 1930 and was named vice-president of the American Teachers Association in 1931. After retiring from the classroom in the 1950s, Garrison moved to Huntington, West Virginia, and continued her work with the NAACP, becoming the first woman to serve as the organization's national vice-president, from 1963 to 1966. She was also part of the first Human Rights Commission in West Virginia during this period.

Garrison received numerous awards during her lifetime, including the NAACP's Madam C. J. Walker Gold Medal Award in 1929, the T. G. Nutter Award for outstanding achievement and service in the field of civil rights in 1959, and the Governor's "Living the Dream" Award in 1988 for service that exemplifies the principles and goals of Martin Luther King Jr. She died July 25, 1988, in Huntington at the age of ninety-eight.

See also: CIVIL RIGHTS MOVEMENT.

—Harriette C. Buchanan, *Appalachian State University*

Gates, Henry Louis, Jr.

See Gates, Henry Louis, Jr. (Literature)

Germans

Persons of German ancestry make up nearly 13 percent of the population in the Appalachian region. In the 2000 census, more than a million and a half residents in the Appalachian counties of Pennsylvania reported that they were of German ancestry. In addition, 43,139 identified themselves as being "Pennsylvania German," and another 3,296 listed their heritage as Russian German. In all, 1,618,694 persons living in the Appalachian counties of Pennsylvania (27.8 percent) were of German descent.

In the Appalachian counties of Maryland, 62,253 residents in 2000 claimed German heritage, as did 20 percent of the population in the Appalachian counties of New York. Appalachian Ohio reported 271,317 residents (18.6 percent) with German ancestry and West Virginia 14 percent. Other states in the region reported smaller percentages of the residents in their Appalachian counties with German ancestry.

The first permanent German settlement in America was in 1683 at Germantown, Pennsylvania, now part of the city of Philadelphia. By the time of the American Revolution, German immigrants had settled in areas now making up the following counties of the Appalachian Region: Monroe County, Pennsylvania; Washington County, Maryland; Jefferson, Berkeley, Morgan, Hampshire, Mineral, Hardy, Grant, and Pendleton Counties, West Virginia; and Rockbridge, Bath, Botetourt, Montgomery, and Wythe Counties, Virginia. With the great southern migration of the mid-1700s, German settlers moved down the Great Valley into the western Carolinas. Others entered the Appalachian region via the port of Charleston, South Carolina. Swiss and German immigrants who arrived in 1710 settled New Bern, North Carolina, named for Bern, Switzerland.

German immigrants also settled in Ohio, founding towns with names such as Berlin, Winesburg, Saxon, and Hanover. Zoar Village, near New Philadelphia, was founded by German immigrants in 1817 and has been preserved as a state memorial. German immigrants seeking religious freedom settled Amish and Mennonite farming communities, still in existence in eastern Ohio.

During World War I, an internment camp for German civilians was located on the grounds of a resort hotel at Hot Springs, North Carolina. In the late 1920s, the town of Elizabethton in upper east Tennessee saw an influx of German residents when the German corporation Vereinigte Glanzstoff Fabriken opened the American Bemberg rayon plant there.

Today German Americans in Appalachia celebrate their heritage in many ways, including Oktoberfests, held throughout the region, and the Sonnenwendefest, a celebration of the longest day of the year.

See also: EARLY WHITE SETTLEMENT OF WESTERN PENNSYLVANIA (SETTLEMENT AND MIGRATION); SYNTHETIC FIBERS INDUSTRY (BUSINESS, INDUSTRY, AND TECHNOLOGY).

—Linda Behrend, *University of Tennessee*

Greeks

Between 1880 and 1920, immigrants from Greece settled in coal-mining regions throughout Appalachia as part of a mass movement into the United States known as the New Immigration. Motivated by economics, religion, and politics, Greeks moved primarily to northern American cities such as New York, Boston, and Philadelphia. There, padrones, or labor agents hired by coal operators, recruited them for jobs in Appalachia, promising, often deceitfully, steady employment and coverage of transportation costs. Most Greeks worked in coal mines, on railroad construction crews, or around coal tipples as common laborers.

Greeks were present in virtually all coal-producing regions of Appalachia. Census records for 1920 indicate that

1,189 Greeks resided in the coalfields of West Virginia, southwestern Virginia, and eastern Kentucky. Like other immigrants, they created communal institutions to deal with life in Appalachian coal camps. They formed mutual benefit societies, imported the Greek Orthodox Church, lived in segregated housing, and faced prejudice. Most Greeks left Appalachia during the 1920s and 1930s due to the economic difficulties in the coal industry. The few immigrants who remained assimilated into Appalachian society so well that today it is impossible to identify them except by family.

See also: NEW IMMIGRANTS.

—Doug Cantrell, *Elizabethtown Community College*

Gypsies and Travelers

Gypsy is a generic term for a member of any number of groups believed to have a common origin in India but who now exist as separate ethnic entities, each with a distinct history, language, and culture. Unspecified "Gypsies" were noted in the Appalachian region by 1855 and those who can be identified with a specific group had arrived by 1859. Until the second half of the twentieth century, these groups generally relied on peripatetic occupations, providing goods and services that might not be permanently supported by any single community and valuing independent entrepreneurship and economic flexibility. Other groups referred to as Gypsies by outsiders include the Irish Travelers, who have also lived in and traveled through Appalachia since the middle of the nineteenth century, and the Scottish Travelers, who arrived in the area in the 1890s. Neither group shares the Indic origins of Gypsies nor identifies itself as such.

Romnichels, the first Gypsy group to settle in America, began migrating from England in 1850. Through the first quarter of the twentieth century some Romnichel families maintained travel routes through New York, Pennsylvania, West Virginia, and Virginia, combining fortune-telling at resort areas with horse trading, basket manufacture and sales, and tinsmithing. As livestock traders, they found a lucrative niche in the expanding horse and mule market until agriculture became largely mechanized. Romnichel religious preference has been conventionally Protestant, and the last part of the twentieth century saw an increase in Pentecostal congregations led by Romnichel pastors. The traditional form of marriage was elopement, a public wedding celebration being a recent addition to cultural practice. Social control within the group is informal.

The Rom, emigrating primarily from Serbia and Russia, reached America and Appalachia in the late nineteenth century. In the early part of the twentieth century, Birmingham, Alabama, was a center for traveling Rom coppersmiths, and West Virginia county seats became legal residences for some families. Rom specialized in retinning of industrial copper vessels, trading horses, and developing the urban fortune-telling business. Formal juridical institutions, a belief system regulating behavior, and arranged marriage with the payment

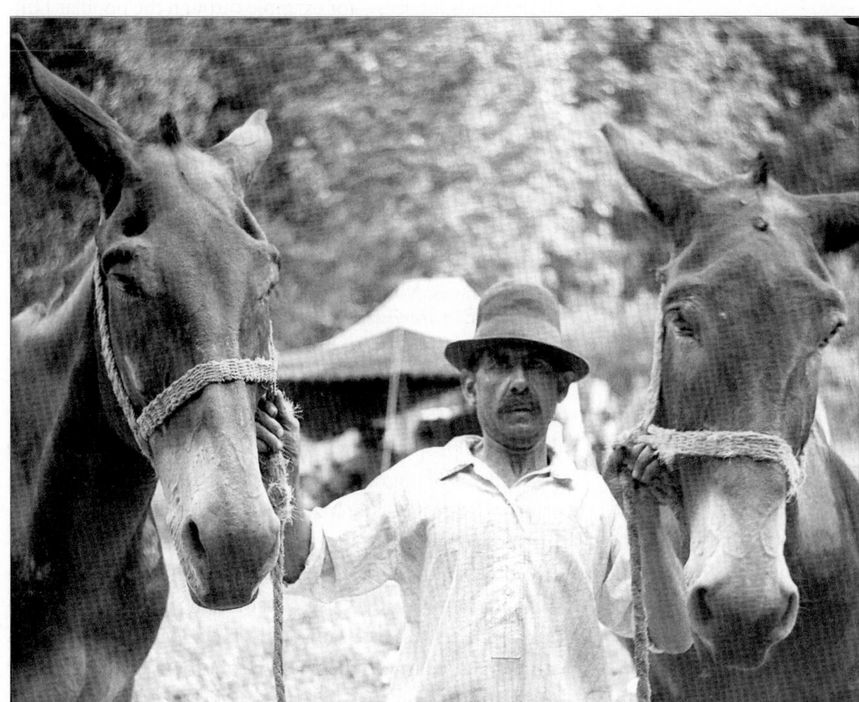

Romnichel mule trader, West Virginia, c. 1940. The Romnichels were the first Gypsy group to arrive in America, coming from England in 1850.

of bride price support a culturally cohesive, though geographically scattered, community. Rom traditionally have considered themselves Roman Catholic or Eastern Orthodox, and communal ritual echoes that of Serbian Orthodox practice. The past thirty years have seen the founding of Pentecostal churches led by Rom pastors.

The Ludar, who originated in Bosnia, began arriving in America and Appalachia in the 1880s. Animal exhibitors who immigrated with their trained bears and monkeys, the Ludar also traded horses and, in the twentieth century, operated carnival concessions. The off-season found many Ludar in industrial work, including at West Virginia pottery works and Pittsburgh steel mills.

Slovak Gypsies, historically sedentary, also came to America in the 1880s through 1914, primarily from Saros County in Austria-Hungary, now in eastern Slovakia. These Gypsies established settlements at the turn of the twentieth century in Appalachian industrial and mining areas, including Braddock, Homestead, Uniontown, Greensburg, Windber, and Lyndora, Pennsylvania, as well as Youngstown, Ohio, all of which remained viable communities until the 1940s. The economic life and ethnic ideology of the Slovak Gypsies have been defined by musical performance.

—Matt T. and Sheila Salo, *Cheverly, Maryland*

William G. Lockwood and Sheila Salo, *Gypsies and Travelers in North America: An Annotated Bibliography* (1994); Sheila Salo, *Register of the Carlos de Wendler-Funaro Gypsy Research Collection, c. 1920–1975* (1986).

Hillbilly

The term *hillbilly* historically referred to mountain dwellers, primarily those of Scots-Irish descent who lived in the southern part of the Appalachian Mountains. *Hillbilly* and similar terms, such as *white trash, redneck, hick, ridgerunner,* and *stump jumper,* are usually used in a pejorative sense, conjuring up a stereotype of backward, uneducated people existing on the bottom rungs of American society. One typical hillbilly depiction is that of a shiftless white man who lives only to drink corn liquor and go hunting with his dogs.

More recently, however, *hillbilly* has been claimed by many Appalachian natives to designate themselves as a distinct social group. To them, *hillbilly* connotes their origin or ancestry in a mountainous or rural area. In this light, *hillbilly* can also mean an independent-minded person who values family ties and the sense of neighborliness in mountain communities. Some of the other common hillbilly traits are a belief in tradition and religion and, in contemporary times, a reliance on the tourism and service businesses that have grown to replace the Appalachian economy's dependence on coal and lumber. A new term that points to a sense of identity formation around mountain life is *Hillbilly Nation*.

Still, many Appalachian natives reject the word *hillbilly* because it continues to evoke the image of the squalid and lazy mountaineer—an idea propagated at least since the Revolutionary War. The hillbilly stereotype was further perpetuated during the railroad and coal company land grabs of the early twentieth century, when government worked with big business to disfranchise individual landowners in both northern and southern Appalachia. Government and companies justified their actions by promoting the idea that mountain dwellers were too ignorant, drunk, and degraded to work their own land.

Other observers and commentators reject the word *hillbilly* on the grounds that no social group should be so openly stereotyped and derided in the mainstream media; they suggest the word should be shelved and left to die from disuse along with other exclusionary terms. In 2003 Appalachian advocacy groups such as the Center for Rural Strategies, an organization based in Whitesburg, Kentucky, protested strongly when the CBS television network proposed airing a "reality" series called *The Real Beverly Hillbillies* that would feature the adventures of a poor Appalachian family living in a Beverly Hills mansion.

In at least one instance, the term *hillbilly* has been appropriated for a humanitarian cause. In 1970 the Shrine of North America, an international service organization started by members of the Masonic Order, created a suborder called the Hillbilly Degree, making it possible for members to organize Hillbilly Clans or branch clans known as Outhouses. Shriners generally belong to several subgroups, or degrees, within the Shrine. The Hillbilly Degree donates all the funds it raises—for example through the popular Hillbilly Days Festival held each spring since 1977 in Pikeville, Kentucky—to Shriners Hospitals for Children. Such organizations and events, while exploiting regional caricatures, may actually diminish their negative impact by outrageously exaggerating hillbilly stereotypes and therefore clearly separating them from reality.

See also: HILLBILLY (IMAGES AND ICONS); *HILLBILLYLAND* (MEDIA); IDENTITY, CENTRAL AND SOUTHERN APPALACHIAN.

—Audra Himes, *Northern Cambria, Pennsylvania*, and Charles F. Moore, *East Tennessee State University*

Hispanics

Hispanic, as the term is used by the federal government, denotes all people living in the United States who hail or are descendants of migrants from countries where Spanish is the primary language. The majority of Hispanics in Appalachia are individuals with ancestry or origins in Latin American countries, particularly Mexico, though immigrants from Cuba and Puerto Rico also constitute a significant proportion. Scholars disagree on whom to include as Latin American but generally exclude people from the English-speaking islands of the Bahamas, Grenada, and Jamaica. In any case,

Latin Americans are a growing minority throughout the Appalachians, playing a considerable role in local economies and constituting a significant cultural presence.

According to the 2000 census, more than 465,000 Hispanics lived within the 410-county, federally defined Appalachian region. Though the fastest growth has occurred in southern Appalachia, the Hispanic population of the northern part of the region also increased. In Erie County, Pennsylvania, for instance, a greater than 60 percent rise in the Hispanic population (more than 6,000 individuals) accounted for almost all of that county's population growth during the 1990s.

There have been three main waves of Hispanic migration into Appalachia, with the most recent being the largest and most widespread. The majority of Appalachian Hispanics are either first-generation immigrants from Mexico and Central America or their children. However, populations of Latin American descent have lived in parts of northern Appalachia since the early twentieth century, when the industrialization and growth of cities such as Pittsburgh and Cincinnati attracted immigrants from all over the world. Several references to Pennsylvania have appeared in the folk songs, or *corridos*, of Mexican migrants of that era.

Only a small proportion of the Spanish-speaking immigrant population of Appalachia came directly from Spain, and for the most part they settled in northern Appalachia. By 1920, 1,500 Spaniards had settled in West Virginia, 1,015 of them in Harrison County (Clarksburg). One of the larger Spanish enclaves in the county was in Spelter, where the Spanish-speaking population was large enough that Spanish was for a time the common language spoken at the local factory and at the town's few businesses. Although Spanish immigration dwindled in the 1930s, Spanish monolingualism among adult women continued into the 1970s, reflecting older women's relative isolation.

Latin American–descent populations are small in most of urban Appalachia, with the suburban, fast-developing edges of Atlanta an important exception. In most rural areas, a Hispanic presence has been nearly invisible except during the growing and harvesting seasons. Migrant agricultural workers in Appalachia, as elsewhere, are predominantly Hispanic. Following traditional Appalachian patterns, migration trends respond to economic forces inside and outside of the region. Migrant-worker populations peak during the crop-growing seasons from May through October, when migrant workers perform the labor-intensive fieldwork of cultivating row crops early in the summer and harvesting tobacco, fruits, vegetables, and Christmas trees later in the season.

Most Hispanics in Appalachia are not agricultural workers, however. Many fill low-paying jobs in factories, poultry-processing facilities, and in the landscaping and garment industries. Others find employment in day labor and construction work. Some "settled-out" Latin Americans become business owners, restaurateurs, tradesmen, supervisors, and sales clerks in the tradition of immigrants working their way into the economic mainstream. International companies and universities for many years have added to the diversity in Appalachia by hiring Hispanic professionals. In specific locations, immigrant professionals may have become a part of Appalachian communities long before the more conspicuous recent growth. Hispanic students and younger children also compose a fast-growing population segment.

Hispanic population growth in Appalachia at the end of the twentieth century resulted from several factors. The region had a greater reliance on manufacturing than many other parts of the United States, and the economic boom in several Sun Belt cities on the margins of Appalachia such as Atlanta and Winston-Salem, North Carolina, created huge demands for low-wage labor. Large numbers of Hispanics in Appalachia have gravitated to jobs in the poultry-processing and carpet-manufacturing industries. Beginning in the 1980s, the carpet industry in Dalton, Georgia, attracted increasing numbers of Latin American immigrants, primarily from Mexico. Official figures show that, from 1990 to 2000 alone, the Latin American population of surrounding Whitfield County rose from less than 5 to 22 percent.

Once established, immigrant workers are usually joined by spouses, extended families, and friends. In 2000 Dalton became the first school district in Appalachia with more than 50 percent Hispanic enrollment, though the district's 1989 Hispanic enrollment had been less than 4 percent. Gainesville, Georgia, the "Poultry Capital of the World," was not far behind Dalton with a more than 40 percent Hispanic enrollment in 2000, and Gwinnett County public schools in suburban Atlanta enrolled more Hispanic students (11,273) than any other school district in Appalachia.

In these communities and similar ones in the Carolinas, Alabama, Tennessee, Pennsylvania, and New York, the slow but steady penetration of Hispanics into lower management positions, the emergence of Spanish-language newspapers, the growth of religious services available in Spanish, and the rising number of homes purchased by Hispanics increasingly suggested a permanent presence of Hispanics in Appalachia. However, given the vulnerability to economic swings of many jobs held by Hispanics, it is also true that many Hispanics in Appalachia were not securely anchored in their new locales.

Despite their importance to the region's economy, Hispanics faced instances of discrimination. But they continued to make inroads into the region's neighborhoods and culture while retaining their own traditions. Mexican Catholics, for example, celebrated specific holidays such as Dia de los Muertos and Cinco de Mayo. Cuban Americans celebrated Christmas in the traditional manner of their homeland with pig roasts. Where Latin American–descent and dominant populations collided, the meeting was sometimes violent and resentful on both sides. An indication of positive integration, however, could be found in the growing number of health-support groups, migrant Head Start programs, English as a Second Language classes offered in elementary and high schools throughout the region, church support systems, and bilingual signs in public areas. Spanish language newspapers such as *Mundo Hispano* in Knoxville, Tennessee, and *La Noticia* in Charlotte, North Carolina, were being published and distributed throughout Appalachia, and Spanish radio and television programs were commonplace.

The 2000 census showed that Hispanics constituted 1.7 percent of the Appalachian population, but that obscured substantial intraregional variation. Whitfield County, Georgia, population 83,525, counted a Hispanic population of 18,419 (22.1 percent); Allegheny County (Pittsburgh), Pennsylvania, population 1,281,666, had a Hispanic population of 11,166 (0.9 percent); and Van Buren County, Tennessee, population 5,508, had a Hispanic population of 18 (0.3 percent). Census figures may, however, underrepresent Appalachia's Latin American population because new immigrant populations (a category into which many Appalachian Hispanics fall) are exceptionally difficult to count.

See also: RECENT IMMIGRANTS.

—Edmund Hamann, *Brown University;* Rosemarie Mincey, *University of Tennessee;* and Charles F. Moore and Elena Pedroso Sausman, *East Tennessee State University*

Jim Minick, "Latino Hillbilly: An Interview with Marcos McPeak Villatoro," *Appalachian Journal* (Winter 2001); Barbara Ellen Smith, ed., *Neither Separate nor Equal: Women, Race, and Class in the South* (1999).

Hmong

The Hmong people, defined through common Sino-Tibetan languages, cultural practices, and religious beliefs, originated near the southern provinces of China and migrated to northern Vietnam, Laos, and Thailand several hundred years ago. Between 1976 and the early 1990s, approximately one hundred thousand Hmong people immigrated to the United States. The majority of these aided the United States in Laos during the Vietnam War and fled following the American withdrawal from the conflict. Approximately two thousand Hmong now live in the Carolina Piedmont, the western part of which falls within the Appalachian region. A small number of Hmong also live in the Appalachian foothills north of Atlanta.

Initially, most Hmong came to the Carolinas in the late 1980s via government-sponsored secondary resettlement programs from California, Minnesota, and Wisconsin, although some families came independently from Rhode Island, Massachusetts, and other states. While secondary resettlement ended in 1991, the Hmong population continues to grow, in some areas by approximately 10 percent each year, due to in-migration of kin.

The beliefs and religious practices of Hmong immigrants vary according to age, colonial experiences in Southeast Asia, and individual preference. Some elders practice animism—the belief that a soul or spirit exists in every object in nature—while a few have adopted Buddhism. Large numbers of Hmong converted to Christianity in Laos during the Vietnam War and upon immigration to the United States, where they formed independent Hmong-led churches.

Hmong contribute to the diversity and definition of local economies, and many have achieved relative social and economic independence by founding small businesses and cultural organizations. Hmong men frequently work as machinists and managers for textile and other local industries, while women often serve as operatives and clerical workers. Some men and women own and manage small businesses or hold professional positions in community colleges and government agencies. Continuing an independent way of life through landownership, agriculture, and outdoor activities is important for many Hmong in the Carolinas.

See also: RECENT IMMIGRANTS.

—Elizabeth Sheehan, *Bridgton, Maine*

Hungarians

Hungarians, or Magyars, as they were sometimes known, were the second most numerous ethnic group that came to southern Appalachia as part of the mass movement known as the New Immigration. Small numbers of Hungarians appeared in parts of Appalachia about 1880. They became more numerous between 1900 and 1920 as the coal industry expanded and more mines were opened. According to census records, West Virginia, southwest Virginia, and eastern Kentucky mining regions were home to 6,637 Hungarian immigrants in 1920. After the coal slump of the 1920s, many Hungarians left Appalachia for jobs in northern cities.

Most Hungarians who came to Appalachia did not come directly from Hungary, having lived for several years in northern cities. They were attracted to Appalachia by the promise of good jobs and steady work. Labor agents, or padrones, were employed by coal companies to recruit Hungarian immigrants. Padrones were paid by companies to secure labor and often cheated immigrants by charging a fee for finding them employment.

Two principal centers of Hungarian culture developed in the Appalachian coalfields—the town of Pocahontas in Tazewell County, Virginia, and the cooperative mining town of Himlerville (later renamed Beauty) in Martin County, Kentucky. Hungarian traditions such as the grape dance, in which fruit was suspended from the ceiling and women tried to get dancing partners to steal the hanging fruit so that a fine could be levied for charity, were performed in these localities.

See also: NEW IMMIGRANTS.

—Doug Cantrell, *Elizabethtown Community College*

Identity, Central and Southern Appalachian

Appalachian residents lack the church organizations, distinct language, or racial characteristics that usually define an ethnic group, one form of group identity to which Appalachian regional identity is often compared. Any group consciousness that Appalachians may have is forged from such factors as their shared understandings of kinship, religious beliefs, dialects, music, geography, sense of place, heritage, and historical experiences. The group's identity is thus only partial, but Appalachian people are often perceived as a unified group by people outside the region. Uncomplimentary stereotypes of Appalachians cause many people in or from the region to disavow their regional heritage, although stereotypes also sometimes function to evoke a sense of identity among those who react against them. Regional stereotypes are thus inseparable from identity issues in central and southern Appalachia.

Most scholars believe that Appalachia came to be defined as a distinct region of the United States in the late nineteenth century, when national publications portrayed the mountain South as void of the urban and industrial development occurring in other parts of the nation. Local color fiction and travel writers, educators, benevolent workers, missionaries, and spokespersons for commerce depicted Americans living in central and southern Appalachia as a distinct and culturally homogeneous group despite the great diversity of people living there. John Fox Jr., a popular novelist who played a major role in the creation and dissemination of Appalachian stereotypes, portrayed mountaineers as "proud, sensitive, kindly, obliging in an unreckoning way that is almost pathetic, honest, loyal, in spite of their common ignorance, poverty and isolation"; he also insisted upon their "shiftlessness" and "awful disregard for human life."

During the early twentieth century, national audiences were fascinated and repulsed by highly exaggerated stories and films portraying feuding and moonshine. In the Great Depression, images of violent mountaineers were somewhat displaced by images of poor, ignorant, lazy hillbillies popularized in nationally syndicated cartoons such as *Li'l Abner* and *Barney Google and Snuffy Smith*. During the second half of the twentieth century, the War on Poverty and the exodus of millions of people from the Appalachian region in search of jobs brought national attention to the Appalachians once again. Media images such as those in the television show *The Beverly Hillbillies* revived and reinforced earlier stereotypes.

Appalachians react in a number of ways both to the often unfavorable images disseminated by mass media and to outsiders who hold negative stereotypes. Some choose to disavow an Appalachian identity, while others embrace it. Several studies have shown that some residents do not think of themselves as being Appalachian but report knowing others who are and identify members of their communities who match negative stereotypes. Even among those who embrace an Appalachian identity, however, its meaning is not clear. For example, although contributors to the "Appalachian Voices" column in the *Lexington (Ky.) Herald-Leader* write as if there were common agreement about what being an Appalachian means, the diversity of their viewpoints demonstrates that Appalachian identity is anything but monolithic.

A number of social movements and organizations have struggled to foster a positive sense of regional identity among people in and from Appalachia. The 1970s witnessed creative efforts among Appalachian writers, scholars, musicians, and cultural workers to confront and refute stereotypes, while activist organizations and regional college campuses began to promote positive images of Appalachian identity. In some cases, residents and officials of counties included in the federally defined region served by the Appalachian Regional Commission have experienced a strengthened regional identity.

Appalachian identity may be strongest among mountain people living outside the region who frequently encounter negative Appalachian stereotypes in the communities to which they migrate. Appalachian social service and identity centers have been especially effective in responding to stereotypes and discrimination in cities such as Cincinnati, Dayton, and Akron, Ohio, and major metropolitan areas such as Chicago and Detroit. Also, the stereotypical "whiteness" of Appalachians has been challenged. The Eastern Kentucky Social Club promotes a sense of group identity among African American out-migrants from Appalachia and their descendants living throughout the United States. Since the 1990s, a literary movement led by a group known as the Affrilachian poets has heightened a sense of Appalachian identity among some African American writers in the region.

See also: AFFRILACHIANS; EASTERN KENTUCKY SOCIAL CLUB; IDENTITY, NORTHERN APPALACHIAN.

—Dwight B. Billings, *University of Kentucky*

Dwight B. Billings, Gurney Norman, and Katherine Ledford, eds., *Confronting Appalachian Stereotypes: Back Talk from an American Region* (1999); Roberta M. Campbell, "Appalachian Experience and Appalachian Self-Concept: Toward a Critical Theory of Regional Identity," Ph.D. dissertation, University of Kentucky (1994); Henry D. Shapiro, *Appalachia on Our Mind: The*

Southern Mountains and Mountaineers in the American Consciousness, 1870–1920 (1978).

Identity, Northern Appalachian

For a variety of reasons, including the tendency of scholars and government agencies to focus on the upland South, residents of northern Appalachia often do not consider themselves Appalachians. People in southern Appalachia tend not to claim them, either. However, residents of the non-Appalachian portions of Ohio, Pennsylvania, and New York sometimes try to distance themselves from the people and conditions in the hilly and mountainous sections of their states, as do the Piedmont and flatland residents of other states with Appalachian counties.

The Appalachian Regional Commission places all of its designated counties of Maryland, New York, Ohio, and Pennsylvania as well as central and northern West Virginia in the northern Appalachian subregion. However, at least part of the Ohio section and most if not all of West Virginia may be more related, culturally and socioeconomically, to central Appalachia. The predominantly rural countryside, small towns, and cities in much of the subregion, once dependent on a natural-resource-based economy, now struggle for sustainable development. Northern Appalachia can also be divided, not unlike its southern and central counterparts, into areas where mining has had a significant impact and those areas where its influence has been negligible to nonexistent. Still another distinction can be made among those areas where Anglo-Celtic-German ethnic influences have retained dominance and those portions that have been heavily affected by southern and eastern European cultures, particularly in western Pennsylvania and portions of eastern Ohio and West Virginia's northern panhandle. Native Americans indigenous to the subregion have retained little lasting presence outside of the southern tier of counties in New York, once in the heartland of the Iroquois Confederacy. Although northern Appalachia is predominately white, African Americans and a growing number of Hispanics and other racial and ethnic groups live in the area, especially in urban areas and near universities.

As in the central and southern areas of the region, associations of Appalachia with distressed economic conditions persist in the northern subregion. A number of news stories have focused on the economically depressed aspect of the region. When a newspaper poll asked residents of poorer counties of Appalachian Ohio to describe Appalachia, many alluded to the prevailing stereotypes of poverty and low intelligence. A majority of the poll's respondents believed that outsiders also viewed Appalachians in a negative light, although many held more positive views of their own region and mentioned hardworking people, good family values, and close-knit families. The proliferation in recent years of the word *Appalachia* in names of businesses, agencies, and initiatives and projects perhaps indicates a growing sense of Appalachian identity in northern Appalachia.

See also: IDENTITY, CENTRAL AND SOUTHERN APPALACHIAN.

—Deanna L. Tribe, *Ohio State University South Centers*

Identity, Political

The Appalachian political ethos has two main strands, relating respectively to physical topography and to political geography, which have combined and evolved to produce a distinct regional political identity.

For more than a century, the Appalachian Mountains have led aspiring politicians to adopt personal styles reflective of the rural highland culture. Running for governor of Tennessee in the 1880s, Bob Taylor sought votes in the eastern counties of the state with a fiddle as his chief prop; he would open a campaign appearance by serenading his audience with old-time tunes. Some seventy years later, long-serving Senator Robert C. Byrd presented himself as an authentic mountaineer by employing the same fiddle-playing technique in his campaigns in West Virginia. Because campaign speeches and rallies served as popular entertainment well into the twentieth century, a command of mountain lore and humor has been essential to political success.

The Appalachian South differs markedly from the Deep South, a truth most strongly evident during the century from the end of the Civil War to the creation of the Republican "Southern Strategy" at the beginning of the 1970s. During all those years the region was known as the Solid South, with the presidential electoral votes of its states always going to the Democratic candidate and all the lesser offices being filled by Democrats. In contrast to this overall lingering Civil War legacy in the lowlands, many of the mountain counties that had sent men to the Union army remained Republican in sentiment. Thus hundreds of thousands of Appalachian people found themselves politically not at home in their own states. Beyond that, as the political writer Neil Peirce noted, "Republican political cliques of the mountain counties were as prone to corruption as their Democratic counterparts and gradually lost any progressive hue they might once have had."

Whatever their views and their personal standards, mountain politicians in their campaigns for office traditionally had to follow a set of unofficial but stringent ground rules. For many years—and sometimes, perhaps, still—a rookie (male) candidate had to learn that he must never go into a house unless the man of the household was at home and invited him to come in. As reporter Rex Bailey observed some years ago, a mountain politician would never shake hands with a woman first, regardless of the circumstances.

He would first seize the husband's hand and give it a good squeeze; then, if the wife seemed willing, the campaigner could "press her flesh," too.

In his search for votes in mountain areas, a candidate for statewide office would soon realize that he could never risk saying anything bad about anybody, because everybody seemed kin to everybody else. As a corollary, if a candidate for office in a mountain county bore a popular family name, he had a strong edge in a race even if he personally was not particularly well known or liked.

These ground rules demonstrate that many of the norms governing personal conduct in traditional societies continued to operate in Appalachia long after they had lost most of their force not only in urban contexts but even in the rural lowland portions of the respective states. School board politics offers one of the clearest and most important examples. Since in most mountain counties the school system has long been the largest employer—often with no rivals for this status—the school superintendent has had enormous power through his control of jobs and general spending. With an array of jobs at their disposal and with numerous relatives eager to fill these posts, superintendents (and school boards) have tended in recent years to find themselves in ongoing conflicts with state antinepotism laws.

From another angle, it was easy to pick out counties in which school superintendents and board members had allowed politics to rule, commented Bailey, writing in the early days of consolidation. Because board members feared the wrath of the voters, they did their best to keep one- and two-room schools open; such a school often represented the last symbol of a community's identity. But the forces of consolidation soon proved irresistible, as rural communities lost not only their classrooms but also their beloved basketball teams.

Though generally defining themselves by county and sometimes by state, mountain people found themselves in the 1960s undergoing definition by other people. Definition by outsiders had occurred previously in history, of course, but this time it came with federal ideas and federal funds behind it, though many a mountain resident expressed surprise at the idea of being classed as "Appalachian," a member of a multistate entity. The Appalachian Regional Commission, doing the will of Congress, would ultimately take in a much larger area than that covered by the Appalachian Mountains; it grew to include 410 counties (as of 2004) in thirteen states from New York to Mississippi.

Despite the work of the Appalachian Regional Commission and all other governmental and private agencies, however, the mountain region continued to face the problem that, with the exception of West Virginia, it is made up of what one scholar has called the backyards of its states. The Appalachian region thus has always been cut through by lines of political division. But if it were in fact a state, it could indeed exert considerable political muscle in national politics.

See also: ELECTIONEERING AND POLITICS (IMAGES AND ICONS); POLITICAL HUMOR (HUMOR).

—Thomas Parrish, *Berea, Kentucky*

David C. Hsiung, *Two Worlds in the Tennessee Mountains: Exploring the Origins of Appalachian Stereotypes* (1997); Neil R. Peirce, *The Border South States* (1975).

Identity, Urban Appalachian

See Urban Appalachian Identity (Urban Appalachian Experience)

Indian Remnant Groups

In addition to the better-known Melungeons along the Tennessee and Virginia border and the West Hill Indians of West Virginia, at least twelve small Indian remnant groups have been identified in southern Appalachia. Though some of these groups may be traced to recognized tribes, others have vaguely defined Indian ancestry. Several of these groups have dispersed and are no longer in existence and, with few exceptions, have not been studied in detail. In general, they may be divided into three distinct clusters based upon their historic origins: those that are Cherokee related, those linked to historically known tribes, and those of unknown Indian ancestry.

The five Cherokee-related groups confined to Tennessee and Kentucky are the Coe Colony, the Upper Cumberland River Cherokee, the Sale Creek Indians, the Etowah Cherokee Nation, and the Indian Mound Cherokees. Of black, white, and Cherokee ancestry, the Coe Colony—established in 1866 and effectively dissolved in the 1950s—resided on an isolated ridge in Cumberland County, Kentucky, and relied heavily upon subsistence farming and moonshining. Little is known of the nearby Upper Cumberland River Cherokee in McCreary County, Kentucky, and Scott County, Tennessee. Residing in Hamilton County, Tennessee, since the early nineteenth century, the landowning Sale Creek Indians are a mixture of Cherokee and African American ancestry. As late as the 1970s, some members of the group retained examples of beadwork made by their Cherokee ancestors.

Named for the Stewart County, Tennessee, community where they lived after about 1830, the Indian Mound group was of Cherokee, white, and black origin. It no longer exists. The Etowah Cherokee Nation, a small group centered in Cleveland, Tennessee, has sought formal federal recognition as an Indian tribe, but little is known of its origins.

Three groups originated among other historically known tribes. Established in Ohio as early as 1850, the

Saponi Nation of Ohio resides in Gallia County. The United Remnant Band of Shawnee in portions of southern Ohio and nearby Indiana is the only vestige of the aboriginal occupants of the upper Ohio Valley. Both the Saponi and United Remnant Band of Shawnee sought formal federal recognition early in the twenty-first century. Centered in Amherst County, Virginia, the Monacan Indians have their origins in the historic Piedmont tribe of the same name. Many work as coal miners in Wyoming County, West Virginia. Beginning at the end of the twentieth century, this group increasingly reasserted its Indian identity.

Residing in Ohio since at least 1840, the Vinton County Indians are a mixture of Indian and black ancestry. Named for their residency as early as 1864 near Carmel, Highland County, Ohio, the now disbanded Carmel Indians represented the northernmost enclave of Melungeons. Originating in Floyd and Magoffin Counties, Kentucky, this small and now largely disbanded settlement once subsisted predominately on farm labor, foraging, and sporadic seasonal employment. Residing along Brown's Branch of the Middle Fork of Stinking Creek in Knox County, Kentucky, the Brown Family is a small enclave of Indian, African American, and white ancestry. The Graysville settlement in Rhea County, Tennessee, is a stable Melungeon-derived community based on small-scale farming, pulpwood cutting, mining, and some factory work.

See also: MELUNGEONS; NATIVE AMERICANS; WEST HILL INDIANS.

—Donald B. Ball, *U.S. Army Corps of Engineers, Louisville, Kentucky*

Samuel R. Cook, *Monacans and Miners: Native Americans and Coal Mining Communities in Appalachia* (2000); John S. Kessler and Donald B. Ball, *North from the Mountains: A Folk History of the Carmel Melungeon Settlement, Highland County, Ohio* (2001); William Lynwood Montell, *The Saga of Coe Ridge: A Study in Oral History* (1970).

Invisible Minority

See Appalachian Social Issues outside the Region (Urban Appalachian Experience)

Irish

The steady flow of Irish to North America increased dramatically after 1845 as the potato famine in Ireland forced more than a million Gaelic Irish, predominately Catholic, to emigrate. Many arrived in Appalachia to build the infrastructure and provide the necessary labor for essential industries. The canals, roads, and railroads they constructed opened the region for development. Irish immigrants helped build the National Road, stretching from Cumberland, Maryland, to Wheeling, (West) Virginia, by 1818, as well as the Baltimore and Ohio Railroad across present-day West Virginia. Other Irish laborers constructed public buildings throughout the region or worked in the iron and steel industries in Pennsylvania, Ohio, and western Virginia. They were equally involved in the extractive industries. From southern New York to northern Alabama, Irish immigrants mined coal and worked in the oil and gas fields.

These Irish laborers brought their religion and culture to Appalachia. By the second half of the nineteenth century, dioceses were established in every state in the region, often headed by Irish-born bishops. The Ancient Order of Hibernians also took root across Appalachia and, on occasion, provided a locus for labor organization and agitation, especially in the coalfields of Pennsylvania, West Virginia, and eastern Kentucky.

Scholars continue to research the Irish political, economic, and cultural contributions to Appalachia. *The Encyclopedia of the Irish in America* (1999) includes details on Irish immigrants in states that encompass the Appalachian region.

See also: MOLLY MAGUIRES (LABOR); OLD IMMIGRANTS; SCOTS-IRISH.

—Joyce E. East, *Marshall University*

Iroquois

The Mohawks, Oneidas, Onondagas, Cayugas, Senecas, and Tuscaroras comprise the Six Nations of the Iroquois Confederacy. While Iroquois people and clans still reside in the United States and Canada, their primary significance to the history of Appalachia stems from their status as the most powerful native confederacy in eastern North America during the colonial period. Iroquois diplomacy with Anglo-Americans made the settlement of the trans-Appalachian region possible.

In the fifteenth century, the Mohawks, Oneidas, Onondagas, Cayugas, and Senecas united and became the Haudenosaunee, or People of the Longhouse. A sixth nation, the Tuscaroras, joined the league in 1722. The confederacy's five original nations were arranged from east to west in a metaphorical Longhouse that sheltered clans from foreign invasion and provided a forum in which they adjudicated disputes peacefully among themselves. Spiritual ceremonies known as "mourning wars" were employed by league chiefs to mourn the dead, assuage the grief of bereaved relatives, preserve peace within the Longhouse, and ensure cultural continuity.

The cultural imperative to mourn the dead spurred the seventeenth-century conquests of several native groups on both sides of the Appalachians. During their mourning war, Iroquois warriors defeated native enemies from Lake Huron to the Appalachians. By the seventeenth century, warfare required annual infusions of European military aid to augment Iroquois capabilities, and Iroquois diplomats negotiated a series of alliances with English governors to secure needed military and economic assistance. They not only received weapons from their English allies, but also had their "right of conquest" recognized by colonial governors. Equipped with English arms, Iroquois warriors prosecuted wars against their western and southern enemies for the remainder of the seventeenth century.

In 1701 Iroquois diplomats negotiated neutrality treaties with the French at Montreal and the English at Albany, effectively ending the western wars, since their Algonquian-speaking enemies were all French allies. The Iroquois then directed their ferocity down the southern Warriors' Path to Piedmont Catawba villages and the Smoky Mountain Cherokee towns. As European settlers penetrated the Appalachians, they were attacked by Iroquois warriors who resented both interference with their wars against the Catawbas and the invasion of lands that had been guaranteed to them by right of conquest in their alliance with the British. In 1722, eager to end the Iroquois southern war and to promote settlement across the Appalachians, Lieutenant Governor Alexander Spotswood of Virginia negotiated with league chiefs at Albany a boundary line at the crest of the Appalachians across which neither European settlers nor Iroquois warriors could pass.

Spotswood's successors seized upon the previously neglected Iroquois right of conquest to wring further land cessions over the next half century. In a 1744 treaty council with the Six Nations at Lancaster, Pennsylvania, Virginia officials parlayed the Indians' position as "owners" of western lands into a large deed that awarded to the Old Dominion control over much of what is now West Virginia. In October 1768, the Iroquois ceded the Ohio Valley to the British. Their accession to the British land grab destroyed their prestige among the Shawnees, Delawares, and other native inhabitants of the Ohio Valley.

See also: SHAWNEE; SPOTSWOOD, ALEXANDER (SETTLEMENT AND MIGRATION).

—Matthew L. Rhoades, *West Virginia University at Parkersburg*

Francis Jennings, *The Ambiguous Iroquois Empire: The Covenant Chain Confederation of Indian Tribes with English Colonies from Its Beginning to the Lancaster Treaty of 1744* (1984); Daniel K. Richter, *The Ordeal of the Longhouse: The Peoples of the Iroquois League in the Era of European Colonization* (1992).

Italians

Of the ethnic groups that came to southern Appalachia as part of the mass movement known as the New Immigration, Italians were the most numerous. Small numbers of Italians first appeared in parts of Appalachia about 1880. They came into the region as laborers, constructing railroads to haul coal and timber from West Virginia, Kentucky, and Virginia. Italian immigrants were especially valuable to railroads because many had the stone-masonry skills needed to build bridge foundations, culverts, and offices throughout the mountains. After railroads were completed, many Italian laborers remained in Appalachia to work in coal mines. Mine owners often used these immigrants to build stone structures in company towns. Between 1880 and 1950, Italian masons built most of the cut-stone structures in southern Appalachia.

According to census records, coal-producing regions in West Virginia, southwestern Virginia, and eastern Kentucky

Italians and blacks working on the Clinchfield Railroad, McDowell County, North Carolina, 1906. A large number of railroad laborers in Appalachia in the early twentieth century were Italian immigrants, but construction gangs also included African Americans, Germans, and others.

had 14,754 Italian immigrants in 1910. Many were enticed to Appalachia by labor recruiters called padrones, who were sent to northern cities by coal operators and promised steady work and high wages. Any newcomer who signed a labor contract was put on a railroad car bound for a coal camp operated by the mine owner who employed the padrone. Padrones, who were paid a set fee by operators for each employee recruited, often cheated Italian laborers by charging a fee for securing work. Coal operators paid railroad fare only temporarily, for transportation costs were later deducted from the immigrant's pay. Operators called this system "on transportation," using it to bring large numbers of Italians to southern coal camps and sometimes to keep them in debt peonage.

Italians created a distinctive form of community in Appalachian coal camps, relying on European traditions to help them adjust to life in an industrial world. Institutions and activities such as the Catholic Church, the padrone system, ethnic dances, wine making, bread baking, and mutual benefit societies were brought to the southern Appalachians by Italian immigrants, who used and modified them in America.

Italians faced prejudice and discrimination by native-born whites, who called them derogatory names such as "tally," "wop," and "dago." When Italians died they were buried in segregated cemeteries along with African Americans and other immigrants. Housing arrangements in coal camps were also segregated according to ethnicity. Italians, as well as other foreigners and blacks, were given houses near creeks that flooded during heavy rains while coal operators assigned native whites houses higher on the hill to protect them from high water. Discrimination was also present in the workplace. The least difficult and most skilled jobs were reserved for native whites while Italians and other ethnic groups performed less-skilled jobs such as hand-loading coal buggies.

Most Italians left southern Appalachia during the coal slump of the 1920s and the Great Depression of the 1930s, migrating to northern cities to find employment. Only a few immigrants and their descendants remain in the Appalachian South today.

See also: NEW IMMIGRANTS; TALLY WAR (LABOR).

—Doug Cantrell, *Elizabethtown Community College*

Kenneth R. Bailey, "The Judicious Mixture: Negroes and Immigrants in the West Virginia Coal Mines, 1880–1917," *West Virginia History* (January 1973); Doug Cantrell, "Immigrants and Community in Harlan County, 1910–1930," *Register of the Kentucky Historical Society* (Spring 1988); Margaret Ripley Wolfe, "Aliens in Southern Appalachia, 1900–1920: The Italian Experience in Wise County, Virginia," in *Appalachia Inside Out, Vol. 1: Conflict and Change*, ed. Robert J. Higgs, Ambrose N. Manning, and Jim Wayne Miller (1995).

Jews

Appalachia has been home to thriving Jewish communities since the mid-nineteenth century. Although in recent decades the region's Jewish population has concentrated in metropolitan areas and university towns, merchant-based Jewish communities flourished in small towns throughout Appalachia until the late twentieth century, and some of these communities still exist.

Jewish migration into the region followed the pattern of Jewish migration to the United States. In the early to mid-nineteenth century, economic and social upheaval in Germany caused hundreds of thousands of Jews to journey to America. Many gravitated to small cities and towns in the nation's interior, including the growing river, rail, and resort towns in Appalachia. By the late nineteenth century, German Jews lived in most of the region's developed areas. At that time, deteriorating conditions in eastern Europe led to economic distress and severe persecution of the Jewish population. Millions responded by coming to America between 1880 and 1920. Although the vast majority settled in major U.S. cities, some trickled into Appalachia, joining their German predecessors in already established towns and forging new Jewish communities in recently opened timber camps and coalfields.

Jews found opportunity in Appalachia by recreating their traditional old-country role as traders in a rural economy. Many started out by traveling mountain routes with packs on their backs, bringing the merchandise from town into the countryside, much as they had done in Europe. They soon opened stores in the region's commercial centers, from booming coal and lumber towns to larger regional trading hubs. While Jews rarely became involved in Appalachia's dominant industries, their retail niche enabled them to find a place in the economy. Family businesses benefited from the combined efforts of husbands, wives, and children, as well as from connections to Jewish wholesalers in cities such as Baltimore, Cincinnati, and New York. Although the volatile economic conditions that plagued the region's industries took a toll on the commercial sector, causing periods of hardship and out-migration for the small Jewish population, many Jewish-owned businesses grew and prospered. Through the years, Jews became the developers and mainstays of numerous downtown business districts.

Jewish congregations have existed in the region at least since the 1840s. All three major branches of American Judaism (Reform, Conservative, and Orthodox) are represented. Communal life centers around local synagogues, where Jews worship, celebrate religious holidays and life-cycle events, and provide a religious education for their children. In addition, Jewish service clubs offer opportunities to socialize and to engage in local, national, and international Jewish causes. While establishing close-knit communities, Appalachian Jews also participate in the civic, social, political, and cultural life of their cities and towns. They have found few barriers to this participation since anti-Semitism has never been a major problem in the region.

During the last half of the twentieth century, the transformation of the Appalachian economy merged with the changing aspirations of American Jewry to cause a shift in the geographic and economic character of the region's Jewish communities. Factors such as the decline of the coalfields and the rise of the shopping mall debilitated small-town business districts. Meanwhile, post–World War II American Jews began to pursue professional rather than commercial careers. Small-town Jewry is dying out in Appalachia, as throughout the nation. By the turn of the century, Jews in the region lived primarily in larger towns and cities and were more likely to be lawyers, doctors, and professors than merchants. However, they continued to maintain their communal and religious traditions, with the local synagogue continuing to provide a vital center for Jewish life.

See also: JUDAISM (RELIGION).

—Deborah R. Weiner, *West Virginia University*

Wendy Lowe Besmann, *A Separate Circle: Jewish Life in Knoxville, Tennessee* (2001); Deborah R. Weiner, "Middlemen of the Coalfields: The Role of Jews in the Economy of Southern West Virginia Coal Towns, 1890–1950," *Journal of Appalachian Studies* (Spring 1998); Lee Shai Weissbach, "Small Town Jewish Life and the Pennsylvania Pattern," *Western Pennsylvania History* (Spring 2000).

Ku Klux Klan

See Ku Klux Klan (Government)

Lynching

See Lynching (Government)

Melungeons

When anthropologists became aware of Melungeons in the late 1880s, their origins were already shrouded in myth. Since then there has been a great deal of debate concerning the history and heritage of the people called Melungeons. Even the origin of the word is unclear, with suggestions ranging from the African-Portuguese *melungo*, meaning "shipmate," to the Turkish *melun can*, meaning "cursed soul."

During the mid-eighteenth century, Melungeons apparently moved from northern and central Virginia to northern North Carolina and then gradually westward into southwestern Virginia, coalescing in a small community on Newman's Ridge in Hawkins County, later Hancock County, Tennessee. This community was called Vardy, after one of the most prominent Melungeon patriarchs, Vardemon Collins. Melungeon landowners around Vardy purchased their property or obtained deeds and titles to legitimate land grants and established and maintained community institutions. Within a generation, founders and descendants of founders were moving into other areas of Appalachia. Many were small farmers and sharecroppers while others earned a livelihood by selling their labor, performing domestic work, fishing, or trading. Also, as with other racial groups migrating into Appalachia, some Melungeons remained behind when relatives moved on, thus leaving small family groups and individuals scattered across much of Tennessee, southwestern Virginia, and western North Carolina.

A Melungeon woman and children, Hancock County, Tennessee, c. 1971. Their origins still shrouded in mystery, the Melungeon people were first recognized as a distinct group in the late nineteenth century and are believed to have migrated from northern and central Virginia around 1750, with many eventually settling on Newman's Ridge in present-day Hancock County.

Through these migrations, Melungeons created a far-flung kinship network. The mixed racial background of Melungeons prevented wholesale absorption into white society. Yet some Melungeons were able to pass as whites, often by claiming a southern European background. This strategy was especially effective in the courtroom, where some Melungeons found themselves in the nineteenth century for violating laws enacted in Tennessee and North Carolina restricting gun ownership, suffrage, and interracial unions. Some Melungeons successfully merged into white families, and for all intents and purposes, their children became white. Such passing was facilitated by economic situations, and well-to-do mixed marriages were more likely to lead to "white" progeny.

Evidence strongly suggests that Melungeons probably developed through a conglomeration of African Americans, Anglo-Americans, Native Americans, and probably others—including East Indians, Portuguese, and Turks—in colonial Virginia. Many Melungeon ancestors were enumerated as *mulattoes* or *mustees*, terms used in reference to persons of mixed racial ancestry. Some Melungeons still typically describe themselves as Indians, usually Cherokee, or sometimes Portuguese-Indians. So far, historians have not verified Portuguese ancestry, though a number of scholars continue to research and debate this possibility. In particular, the 1997 book *The Melungeons: Resurrection of a Proud People: An Untold Story of Ethnic Cleansing in America* served as a catalyst for much investigation into the people's heritage and history. Where presumably Melungeon family names and relations were recognized, they often held to folk customs, including the "one drop" rule, whereby anyone suspected of even one drop of African blood was held to be "Negro" or "mulatto." When race relations and ideologies hardened in the 1820s and 1830s, Melungeons remained within their own family communities, intermarrying among kin.

Melungeons first appeared in newspaper and literary accounts in 1849. By the late nineteenth century, Melungeons were depicted in newspapers from Louisville to New York City and were featured in several magazine articles in the Boston-based *Arena* and in a short story by mountain writer John Fox Jr. In nearly all cases, writers focused on the mixed-blood heritage of Melungeons, posited various theories of their reputedly mysterious origins, and generally held them to be representative of the region as a whole—unclean, ignorant, and isolated. While direct connections are not entirely clear, the derogatory depiction of Melungeons by writers—many of whom were from outside the area—probably contributed in some measure to the negative image of Appalachia held by non-Appalachians.

DNA and blood group studies conducted in the late twentieth century and first years of the twenty-first century hint at the fascinating genetic background of Melungeons. At the same time, however, the studies reveal that the modern descendants of Melungeons are by and large indistinguishable from other Appalachians. This seems to indicate that the mixing and merging of peoples in Appalachia is more widespread and complex than generally realized, since Melungeons now appear to be just like other Appalachians, and Appalachians like Melungeons. Whatever the ultimate derivation of Melungeons, and regardless of whether they are defined as a social or racial caste, their historical existence points to the diverse roots of Appalachia in general.

See also: MELUNGEON FAMILIES AND COMMUNITIES (FAMILY AND COMMUNITY).

—C. S. Everett, *Vanderbilt University*

Pat Spurlock Elder, *Melungeons: Examining an Appalachian Legend* (1999); C. S. Everett, "Melungeon History and Myth," *Appalachian Journal* (Summer 1999); N. Brent Kennedy and Robyn Vaughan Kennedy, *The Melungeons: The Resurrection of a Proud People: An Untold Story of Ethnic Cleansing in America* (1997).

Mennonites

See Mennonites (Religion)

Mexicans

See Hispanics

Native Americans

The human population of the Appalachian Mountains includes a diverse indigenous heritage. Early Native American cultures in the northeast of the region included such groups as the Abenaki, Cayuga, Delaware, Iroquois, Maliseet, Micmac, Mohawk, Mohican, Oneida, Onondaga, Passamaquoddy, Pennacook, Penobscot, Pocumtuk, Seneca, Susquehanna, Wampanoag, and Wappinger. These groups used timber to build multifamily shelters called longhouses, and the Iroquois also built wigwams made of pliable young trees to form a round shape for the top, overlapped with tree bark and topped with thatch or dried grass. Hunting, fishing, farming, and gathering allowed indigenous groups to use abundant natural resources to feed their families. Many groups relocated seasonally, moving inland to hunt in the winter and to the seacoast to fish during the summer. The Abenaki lived in farming communities during planting and harvesting seasons. Competition among groups became fierce, so to prevent further wars the Cayuga, Mohawk, Oneida, Onondaga, and Seneca formed the Iroquois Confederacy in the later part of the sixteenth century, allowing the Tuscarora to join them in 1722.

Southeastern Appalachian bands, including the Catawba, Cherokee, Cheraw, Chickasaw, Choctaw, Creek, Koosati, Powhatan, Shawnee, Tuskegee, Tutelo, and Yuchi, lived in a mix of mountains, lowlands, and forests. These groups also engaged in seasonal activities. The Cherokee traveled, planted, harvested, and warred during the warm season, called *gogi*, and gathered and hunted in the cold season, known as *gola*. In more southerly areas, groups built flat-topped and conical ceremonial earth mounds. Homes, usually made of wattle (woven twigs, branches, and stalks) and daub (sticky mud or clay), looked like upside-down baskets.

When European settlers arrived in North America, some indigenous groups welcomed them, while others viewed them with suspicion. The European worldview and presumption of supremacy challenged the Native American self-image, causing them to become more materialistic and doubtful of their own self-worth. In time, it became difficult to differentiate one European nation's objectives from another's. Likewise, Europeans found it hard to understand the differences among and within indigenous groups. Despite colonial proclamations and treaties, white settlers encroached on indigenous land. This brought even more discontent among Indians already warring with each other when new foes appeared. European nations used Native Americans to their advantage, making them slaves and trading partners, as well as both pawns and allies in struggles to establish domination of North America. Threatened with genocide and forced onto reservations, countless Indians struggled with poverty, alcoholism, and unemployment. But most Native Americans, despite all the injustices and massive odds against them, contributed positively to American culture while continuing to honor their native heritage.

See also: *CHEROKEE PHOENIX* (MEDIA); WHITE CONQUEST (SETTLEMENT AND MIGRATION).

—Ima J. Stephens, *Auburn University*

Colin G. Calloway, *First Peoples: A Documentary Survey of American Indian History* (1999); Frederick E. Hoxie, ed., *Encyclopedia of North American Indians* (1996); Jill Maynard, ed., *Through Indian Eyes: The Untold Story of Native American Peoples* (1996).

New Immigrants

The thousands of people who immigrated to the United States from southern and eastern Europe between 1880 and 1920 were called "new immigrants" to distinguish them from pre-1880 settlers from northern and western European countries known as "old immigrants." A number of new immigrants from Italy, Hungary, Russia, Serbia, and territories in the Austro-Hungarian Empire that became Czechoslovakia, Yugoslavia, Hungary, Austria, and Poland settled in Appalachia. Census data indicate that more than sixty thousand new immigrants resided in southern Appalachian coal-producing regions in 1920. Italians were the single largest group, followed by Hungarians, Poles, Austrians, and Russians. Found in smaller numbers were individuals from Czechoslovakia, Albania, Greece, Turkey, Syria, Macedonia, Serbia, Romania, and other countries. Coal-producing regions in Pennsylvania and northern Appalachia also attracted a substantial number of new immigrants.

Coal operators recruited new arrivals by placing advertisements in ethnic newspapers, including the Hungarian paper *Magyar Banyaszlap* published at Himlerville (later renamed Beauty), Kentucky, and by sending labor agents called padrones to recruit in the port cities of New York, Boston, and Philadelphia. Often, coal operators and labor agents victimized immigrants by claiming that the coalfields were nearby and that the operator would pay all transportation costs. Upon arrival in the coal camp, immigrants found that they were farther from the city than they had anticipated and that coal operators had deducted transportation costs from their wages.

In Appalachian coal camps, new immigrants created a communal culture comparable to that fashioned by similar ethnic groups in northern cities, forming ethnic lodges, living in ethnic enclaves, speaking native languages, creating mutual benefit societies, and worshipping in the Roman Catholic and Eastern Orthodox traditions. In an attempt to re-create the extended families that they had known in Europe, newcomers participated in what was known as the "boarding boss" system. Married immigrants in large coal camps such as Lynch, Kentucky, operated boardinghouses and rented rooms to single males of their own nationality. An Italian couple, for example, rented rooms to Italian workers while a Russian couple rented rooms to Russians. The head of the house was called the boarding boss. His wife and daughters cooked and cleaned for the immigrants, who might number twenty or more.

New immigrants faced prejudice and discrimination from native-born Americans, who frequently called them "wops" and "Polacks." Immigrants were usually buried in a cemetery separated from those containing the remains of native white Americans.

Many new immigrants left Appalachia for northern industrial areas after the coal slump of the 1920s and the Great Depression of the 1930s caused layoffs in the industry. Those who remained after 1940 generally assimilated into mainstream Appalachian society, marrying into native families and adopting mountain values and culture.

See also: OLD IMMIGRANTS; RECENT IMMIGRANTS.

—Doug Cantrell, *Elizabethtown Community College*

Old Immigrants

Old immigrant is a term used to designate immigrants who came to the United States from 1820 to 1880. Approximately nine million people came to the United States during that period. Although individuals from across the world were represented, old immigrants largely came from northern and western European countries, including England, Germany, Ireland, Norway, Sweden, France, and the Netherlands. They left their homelands for a variety of reasons—the Irish to escape the potato famine during the 1840s,

Germans because of revolutions and political unrest, others in search of better financial prospects in America.

Appalachia received tens of thousands of old immigrants. Many came to work in the coal industry that flourished during the American Industrial Revolution. Mountainous regions in western Pennsylvania received the largest numbers of old immigrants, as Irish, German, and other nationalities migrated to the area to work in anthracite mines. Many of these immigrants came to Pennsylvania because they had worked in the coal mines of England, Germany, or other European countries and were highly valued by coal operators for their mining experience. Coal-producing counties in southern Appalachia did not receive as many old immigrants as did Pennsylvania. At the height of the Old Immigration, West Virginia coal-producing regions counted only about eight thousand residents from northern and western European countries, and Virginia, Kentucky, Tennessee, and other regions in southern Appalachia had even fewer.

Although the immigrant population in southern Appalachia was smaller than elsewhere, old immigrants played an important role in the development of the coal industry in the area. Many of the earliest coal mines in West Virginia, Virginia, and Kentucky were operated by old immigrants. After gaining valuable experience in underground mining techniques in Pennsylvania, they moved to southern coalfields and became pioneer operators there. Immigrants who developed mines in southern Appalachian fields included Englishmen John Lawton Beury, John Cooper, Jenkin Jones, John Freeman, Robert Goodwill, and brothers John and Lawrence Tierney and Scotsmen James and John Laing. Perhaps the most ambitious old immigrant coal operator was Alexander Alan Arthur. A Scottish-born Canadian, Arthur secured the backing of English capitalists, formed the American Association, Ltd., established the town of Middlesborough (now Middlesboro), Kentucky, and began to develop a coal- and iron-producing enterprise. Unfortunately, Arthur's grand plan to make Middlesborough the Pittsburgh of the South failed as a result of general economic decline during the early 1890s.

Old immigrants in Appalachia, as in the rest of the United States, faced prejudice engendered by nativism. They were blamed for taking jobs from Americans and, since Germans and Irish were overwhelmingly Roman Catholic, subjected to religion-based discrimination. Protestant Americans formed Native American Clubs that worked to increase the period of naturalization from five to twenty-one years, restrict the holding of public office to American-born persons, and allow only the Protestant Bible to be read in public schools.

See also: ENGLISH; GERMANS; IRISH.

—Doug Cantrell, *Elizabethtown Community College*, and Ima J. Stephens, *Auburn University*

Harry M. Caudill, *Theirs Be the Power: The Moguls of Eastern Kentucky* (1983); Maldwyn Allen Jones, *American Immigration* (1960).

Poles

Poles were one of the most prominent and widely represented ethnic groups that came to coal-mining areas in central and northern Appalachia between 1880 and 1920. The first documented arrival of Polish immigrants into central Appalachia was in Pocahontas, Virginia, in 1895, though Poles had worked in mines in Pennsylvania and other northern states much earlier. The majority of Polish immigrants came to Appalachian mining towns from northern cities after being recruited by coal companies desperate for labor. A few came directly from Poland. Census data indicate that 3,916 Polish immigrants lived in coal-mining counties in West Virginia, Virginia, and Kentucky in 1920. Generally, they were single males intent upon sending money back to relatives in the old country.

For the most part, Polish immigrants worked as general labor in and around the coal mines. They dug coal, loaded it into buggies, picked slate and other impurities out of the mineral, and worked around coal tipples and railroad loading docks. Poles experienced discrimination in Appalachian coal camps, where they generally lived in segregated sections and weathered insults. Following the coal slump of the 1920s and the Great Depression of the 1930s, most Polish immigrants left Appalachia to seek industrial employment in northern cities.

See also: NEW IMMIGRANTS.

—Doug Cantrell, *Elizabethtown Community College*

Race Riots

See Race Riots (Government)

Racism

There are two general and contrasting images of race relations in Appalachia, and while each has historical evidence to support it, neither accurately portrays the region as a whole. The more common of these beliefs is that Appalachia was overwhelmingly abolitionist before the Civil War, a haven for runaway slaves and freed blacks during and after the war, and an area of racial tolerance extending into the segregated South during the Civil Rights movement. The conflicting view is that Appalachians, through their supposed homogeneity, isolation, and class resentment of wealthy slave owners, were ignorant of and hostile towards blacks. Until recently, there has been very little serious study of racial attitudes in Appalachia to provide empirical data, and overly simple generalizations have rested upon preconceptions and myths of mountain character. Research has begun to reveal a much different and more complex history.

While there is abundant evidence of racial antagonism between whites and other racial and ethnic groups throughout the region, most infamously the racial antipathy accompanying constant early battles with Native Americans, recent study has focused on whites' racist attitudes and policies towards African Americans. Also, the perceptions applied to Appalachia in general are largely drawn from the central section of the region.

Contradictions are inevitable, given the region's sweep, economic diversity, historical complexity, and politics. Nineteenth-century travelers through Appalachia perpetuated the idea that the region was virtually devoid of blacks and that independent-minded mountaineers displayed an innocence of racial intolerance and a moral contempt for slavery. Yet in 1860 slavery existed in virtually every county of Appalachia, and the black population in the region totaled more than 170,000—nearly 275,000 by the century's end. Slave markets existed in Abingdon, Virginia, Knoxville, Tennessee, and Pikeville, Kentucky. Appalachian east Tennessee is conspicuous for supporting the Union during the Civil War, presumably from abolitionist leanings, yet many historians point to other motivating factors, including social stability. Prominent highland opponents of secession such as future President Andrew Johnson and North Carolina Governor Zebulon Vance were both slaveholders and argued that the institution would have a more secure future under Union control.

Journalist Frederick Law Olmsted traveled through the mountains of Virginia, Tennessee, North Carolina, and Georgia in 1854 and reported an overwhelming attitude of white superiority among the people there and a general acceptance of the institution of slavery. Appalachian-born African American historian Carter G. Woodson, however, insisted during the early decades of the twentieth century that racial tolerance was an identifying characteristic of highlanders in contrast to lowland southerners.

In the late nineteenth and early twentieth centuries, racial violence appears to have been proportionally as frequent in central and southern Appalachia as in the general South, where lynching, rioting, and terrorism were used to intimidate blacks into accommodating white social dominance. Although whites and immigrants were at times also the victims of mob violence, blacks were disproportionately targeted, not only in numbers, but also in the severity of the violence and the relatively minor nature of the offenses used as justification. A particularly revealing event occurred in Alleghany County, Virginia, in 1891, when four black miners were brutally and publicly executed by a white mob after a string of events sparked by boisterous behavior on the part of the miners in town to "blow off steam." The black men apparently committed no offense other than intimidating white residents of Clifton Forge and refusing arrest for their behavior.

There are also many examples of positive racial attitudes in Appalachia. By the middle of the twentieth century, the Highlander Folk School in Monteagle, Tennessee, was sponsoring workshops and conferences addressing race relations and training some of the most prominent national leaders of the Civil Rights movement including Martin Luther King Jr., Rosa Parks, and Andrew Young. Now known as the Highlander Research and Education Center, the nonprofit organization continues to address a wide range of social issues, including racism. In 1956 two Tennesseans, Albert Gore Sr. and Estes Kefauver, were two of only three southern senators (along with Texan Lyndon Johnson) and a handful of representatives who refused to sign a "Southern Manifesto" advocating resistance to racial integration of public education. Civil rights organizations such as the National Association for the Advancement of Colored People and Western North Carolina Citizens for an End to Institutional Bigotry support minority rights throughout the region.

Research undertaken in the wake of the Civil Rights movement began to draw a picture of race relations and racial attitudes in Appalachia that proved as complex as those in any region of the United States. Contemporary racial attitudes in Appalachia appear to reflect attitudes in the larger regions surrounding them. Underlying racial prejudices continue to influence access to jobs, housing, and education in Appalachia, as elsewhere in America, slightly more so in southern and rural communities than in western, northern, and urban settings.

See also: CIVIL RIGHTS MOVEMENT; HIGHLANDER RESEARCH AND EDUCATION CENTER (EDUCATION); TRAIL OF TEARS (SETTLEMENT AND MIGRATION).

—Troy Gowen, *East Tennessee State University*, and Mary A. Waalkes, *Lee University*

Paul H. Bergeron, Stephen V. Ash, and Jeanette Keith, *Tennesseans and Their History* (1999); John C. Inscoe, ed., *Appalachians and Race: The Mountain South from Slavery to Segregation* (2001).

Recent Immigrants

Recent immigrants is a term referring to individuals who have arrived in the United States since 1970 from Asia, Latin America, the Middle East, Africa, or eastern Europe. Although the United States Census Bureau does not compile figures on recent immigrants in Appalachian counties, records indicate that several thousand migrants from Asian and Latin American countries have settled throughout the region. West Virginia, the only state wholly in Appalachia, for example, received a total of 5,719 legal immigrants between 1991 and 2000. Immigrants to the Mountain State came from a total of thirty-one foreign countries, including

Iran, Pakistan, Korea, Japan, India, the Philippines, Vietnam, Laos, China, Mexico, the Dominican Republic, Ecuador, El Salvador, Guatemala, Haiti, Honduras, Jamaica, Russia, Nigeria, Poland, and Yugoslavia. Other Appalachian areas experienced immigration similar to that of West Virginia, though certain communities, such as Dalton, Georgia, saw an influx sufficient to alter their demographic profile.

Recent immigrants, like preceding generations of immigrants, moved to Appalachia for a variety of reasons. While some came for religious freedom, to escape political persecution, or to join relatives already in the United States, most sought economic opportunity and escape from poverty in their native lands. Recent immigrants have found job opportunities ranging from manual labor to professional pursuits. The shortage of doctors in the late twentieth and early twenty-first centuries would likely have been more acute in Appalachian counties without recent immigrants with medical degrees willing to practice in rural areas. Recent immigrants have also opened businesses, notably ethnic restaurants in mountain communities where they were previously rare or nonexistent.

Like preceding generations of immigrants to Appalachia, recent immigrants have encountered prejudice and stereotyping. Often, recent immigrants faced suspicion and unfounded charges of being involved in the illegal drug trade in Appalachia. In some instances, conservative organizations worked to restrict or stop the arrival of newcomers from certain areas. For example, the Federation for American Immigration Reform, headquartered in Charleston, West Virginia, published articles, lobbied Congress and state legislatures, and publicized negative news about recent immigrants in an attempt to lessen or eliminate immigration to Appalachia and the United States. Such groups blamed recent immigrants for a variety of problems and social ills such as poor schools. In reality, recent immigrants have merely followed the American tradition of seeking economic opportunity.

See also: HISPANICS; HMONG.

—Doug Cantrell, *Elizabethtown Community College*

Roanoke Race Riot of 1893

See Race Riots (Government)

Ross, John

(1790–1866) Cherokee chief.

Chief John Ross of the Cherokee was born October 3, 1790, in present-day Cherokee County, Alabama, the son of Daniel Ross, a native of Scotland, and Mollie McDonald, who was one-quarter Cherokee. Though only one-eighth Cherokee, John Ross was destined to become the foremost defender of Cherokee rights.

During the War of 1812, Ross and his brother formed a business to furnish supplies to the U.S. government and the Cherokee. The settlement that developed around their warehouse and ferry at Ross's Landing on the Tennessee River later became the town of Chattanooga. In the 1820s, Ross moved to a plantation in northern Georgia.

In 1817 Ross became a member of the National Council of the Cherokee and served as president from 1819 until 1826. The next year, in 1827, the Cherokee Nation drafted a written constitution, which provided for a government similar to that of the United States. Ross was elected principal chief of the eastern Cherokee in 1828.

In 1830 the State of Georgia assumed jurisdiction over Cherokee land in that state. Ross was forced to move to tribal lands in Tennessee. That same year, the U.S. Congress passed legislation that made Indian removal the official policy of the federal government. Like the majority of his nation, Ross opposed the removal of the Cherokee to territory west of the Mississippi. But in late 1835, the minority Treaty Party faction of the Cherokee Nation approved a treaty of removal at New Echota, Georgia, and in 1838–39 Ross and his associates oversaw the removal of the Cherokee to Indian Territory along the infamous Trail of Tears. In 1839 Ross became chief of the united Cherokee tribe, a position he held until his death on August 1, 1866, in Washington, D.C.

See also: CHEROKEE; TRAIL OF TEARS (SETTLEMENT AND MIGRATION); *UNTO THESE HILLS* (PERFORMING ARTS).

—Ed Speer, *Elizabethton, Tennessee*

Patrice Hobbs Glass, "Ross, John," in *The Tennessee Encyclopedia of History and Culture*, ed. Carroll Van West (1998); Gary E. Moulton, ed., *The Papers of Chief John Ross, 1807–1839* (1985).

Scots

Most Appalachian settlers with Scottish backgrounds were Scots-Irish from Ulster in Northern Ireland. Scots who immigrated directly to North America during the peak years of Scottish migration (the mid-eighteenth century) were equally divided between Highland and Lowland populations, and most settled close to the Atlantic coasts of Canada and the United States. Only a relatively small number of these people later migrated into Appalachia.

Most Scots-Irish settlers in Appalachia were of Lowland Scots background, their ancestors having moved to Ulster during the seventeenth century as part of a social project in Ireland sponsored by the English government. In the eighteenth century, Scots-Irish settlers—many traveling into southern Appalachia from Pennsylvania by way of the Great Valley of Virginia—transported Lowland Scots traditions to Appalachia, significantly influencing the region's evolving culture, particularly its verbal folklore. For instance, one-third of the approximately one hundred traditional British ballads sung historically in Appalachia—including such widely disseminated ballads as "Gypsy Laddie" and "Lord Randal"—originated in (or were most common in) the Scottish Lowlands rather than in England.

Among the Lowland Scots who migrated directly from Scotland to Appalachia, many were merchants. Some Highland Scots—having left Scotland following the 1746 conquest of the Scottish Jacobites by the English—journeyed from the stronghold of Highland settlement along North Carolina's Cape Fear River to southern Appalachia, where they intermarried with Scots-Irish settlers as well as with people of other ethnicities, including Native Americans. Although Highland Scots in Appalachia did not retain such characteristic aspects of their traditional folklife as bagpipes and kilts, Highland culture has in recent decades been revived within the region at such events as the Grandfather Mountain Highland Games and Gathering of Scottish Clans near Linville, North Carolina. While providing a forum for expression of ethnic identity among descendants of settlers from Scotland, such revivalist events in Appalachia also attract countless people not of Scottish ancestry who identify with their representations of Scotland's culture.

See also: HIGHLAND GAMES (SPORTS AND RECREATION); SCOTS-IRISH; SCOTTISH HERITAGE REVIVAL.

—Ted Olson, *East Tennessee State University*

Scots-Irish

The term *Scotch-Irish* has been widely used in America since colonial times to describe immigrants from the Irish province of Ulster to North America; today, *Scots-Irish* is preferred. (In Ireland this population is referred to as Ulster Scots.) The Scots-Irish were so influential in shaping Appalachia's settlement process that they have become an essential part of regional stereotypes. They have been characterized as independent, resourceful, family-oriented, deeply religious, and skilled in woodcraft, as well as indolent, belligerent, violent, and unduly bound by tradition. The Appalachian feud is mistakenly regarded as a lingering remnant of their border heritage. Regardless of their relevance, these stereotypes continue to shape the image of Appalachia.

The heaviest concentrations of Scots-Irish settlement in the first phase of migration occurred along passages such as the Great Valley Road and routes inland from southern ports such as Charleston, South Carolina. Estimates of population are difficult to verify, but in areas of significant Scots-Irish settlement such as western North Carolina it has been estimated that 30 to 35 percent of settlers before 1840 were Scots-Irish. While it is unlikely that they comprised a majority of settlers in most places, they exerted a powerful influence in shaping the development of Appalachian culture.

The history of the Scots-Irish dates from the late sixteenth century, when England's Queen Elizabeth I and her successor, King James I, attempted to pacify the unruly realm of Ireland by "planting" it with English-speaking Protestants. Though some of the settlers came from southeastern England, the great majority crossed over from the border region of Lowland Scotland and northwestern England. Those colonists, who hoped migration would improve their standard of living, found themselves living on an often violent frontier subject to attack by the Gaelic-speaking Catholic natives. Not until William III's crushing victory over the Catholic Irish at the battle of the Boyne in 1690 did the Ulster Scots feel secure in Ireland.

Most of the Ulster Scots were tenant farmers. As their population grew, competition for land increased, leading to dramatic rent increases. Early industrial development offered farm families the opportunity to supplement their incomes by linen production, but the linen industry experienced periodic slumps in the eighteenth century. In addition, the majority of Ulster Scots were Presbyterians, who suffered religious discrimination from the established Episcopal Church of Ireland. For all of these reasons, by the early eighteenth century many of them began to think of emigrating.

The Ulster Scots knew a great deal about America. Regular trade routes linked Irish ports with the ports of British North America. Land promoters such as the Ulster-born governor of North Carolina, Arthur Dobbs, recruited heavily in Ireland for immigrants. Ship captains, seeking profitable cargoes, promoted the advantages of life in America. From the 1690s a growing stream of Ulster Scots embarked for America.

Most sailed to Philadelphia, although lesser numbers entered Atlantic ports from Canada to Georgia. Entire families tended to migrate, though many individuals financed their way by indenturing themselves to an American master for several years of service. Most were farmers who hoped to own their own land. Colonial conditions in the mid-eighteenth century, including availability of land, land policies, and high population densities along much of the East Coast, quickly thrust new arrivals onto the Appalachian frontier. Some of Pennsylvania's large immigrant population moved west into the Allegheny Mountains and on to Ohio, but most turned southwest into Virginia's Shenandoah Valley. From there they took up lands along the Great Valley Road to the Piedmont Carolinas and Georgia and further westward into the Appalachian regions of Tennessee, Kentucky, and Alabama.

The strong Scots-Irish presence in Appalachia was not based on an ethnic preference for rough mountain land or on any lack of ambition to improve their lives. Rather, the decision of many Scots-Irish to settle and stay in the mountain region is explained by the availability of abundant cheap land and by their success in achieving a satisfactory level of comfort and prosperity there. In the nineteenth century, population pressure encouraged some Scots-Irish to move across the Mississippi into the Ozarks. By the twentieth century the Scots-Irish had spread across the country, but their greatest concentration remained in Appalachia and the South.

Scots-Irish immigrants were great adapters. They modified elements of other cultures easily, adopting agricultural crops (corn and beans) and techniques (slash-and-burn) from the Indians and construction techniques (the log cabin) from central and northern Europeans. Thanks to this willingness to borrow, and also to their English native tongue and their Protestantism, they quickly blended in with their new ethnic neighbors, becoming in some ways culturally invisible.

The Scots-Irish made several important contributions to the culture that developed in the Appalachian backcountry. Among these were their attachment to mixed agriculture, settlement patterns, and religion. From both their Scottish and Ulster backgrounds, the Scots-Irish brought a preference for a distinctive combination of livestock and crops in which livestock, especially hogs and cattle, predominated. They cultivated grain crops on land that they periodically allowed to recover by returning it to nature. They exploited unfenced forestland for grazing. The success of this land-use strategy made livestock a primary cash crop for mountain farmers. These practices reinforced another Scots-Irish characteristic, a settlement pattern of dispersed family farms. In the mountains, this settlement pattern resulted in single-family farms strung out along rivers and creeks. Scots-Irish practices were well suited to conditions of land and labor in the Appalachian region and account for the significant role these immigrants played in early community formation and development.

Scots-Irish Presbyterianism deeply influenced Appalachian religious traditions. They carried their church with them into western Pennsylvania, Virginia, and the Carolinas, where a strong Presbyterian presence survived well into the nineteenth century. Beliefs and practices rooted in Calvinist theology such as predestination, contentiousness regarding theology, and emotional evangelicalism had a widespread impact on Appalachian religious practice and culture. Eventually Presbyterians' insistence on a seminary-trained clergy proved untenable in a frontier environment, pushing most Scots-Irish into the arms of Baptists and Methodists.

Other Scots-Irish contributions included storytelling and music. Immigrants brought Jack tales and many of the ballads so popular in the Appalachian backcountry from their Irish and Scottish homes. Their version of English influenced mountain dialect, contributing such constructions as *you all*, *you'uns*, *might should*, *they's*, and *wait on*.

Disagreement continues over the role of Scots-Irish ethnicity in shaping Appalachia. Some recent scholarship argues strongly for a decisive Scots-Irish role in shaping an essentially Celtic Appalachian culture. Whatever interpretation prevails, there can be little doubt that the Scots-Irish were a resourceful and highly adaptable people who contributed to a diverse Appalachian culture.

See also: IRISH; SCOTS; SCOTTISH HERITAGE REVIVAL.

—H. Tyler Blethen and Curtis W. Wood, *Western Carolina University*

H. Tyler Blethen and Curtis W. Wood, eds., *Ulster and North America: Transatlantic Perspectives on the Scotch-Irish* (1997); David Hackett Fischer, *Albion's Seed: Four British Folkways in America* (1989); James G. Leyburn, *The Scotch-Irish: A Social History* (1962).

Scottish Heritage Revival

The Scottish heritage revival in southern Appalachia draws upon national and southern themes and popular American perceptions of Scottish culture, making many such heritage events in the mountains more "in" Appalachia than "of" Appalachia. Scottish Americans from across the country, of Highland, Lowland, and Scots-Irish ancestry alike, celebrate their ethnic identity with the imagery and material culture of Highland Scots. The form of heritage events and the traditions celebrated are largely creations of "Highlandism," a type of romanticism peculiar to nineteenth-century Scotland developed long after the ancestors of today's Scottish Americans left Scotland.

The term *Scots-Irish* distinguishes the group from the immigrant Highlanders and the latter's Loyalist reputation; later the name served to distinguish them from the Celtic, or native Catholic, Irish who came to America during the mid-nineteenth-century potato famines. The Scots-Irish were Lowland Scots Presbyterians who, in the early seventeenth century, began settling the province of Ulster, the area of Ireland most problematic for British rule and where they are known as Ulster Scots. Sometimes unwillingly induced to play a part in James I's "plantation" scheme, they maintained a frontier mentality for a century and a half before repressive trade laws, famine, and a decline in the linen industry encouraged emigration from Ireland to the colonies. Once in America, they remained distinct from both Highland and Lowland Scots and received government land grants to live on the frontier as a buffer between what were considered civilized, government-protected areas and hostile territory. The Scots-Irish composed a significant proportion of the first European settlers in Appalachia.

Despite the history of self-segregation among the various Scottish immigrants to America, Americans involved in the Scottish heritage revival of the last four decades have generally embraced Highland clan tartans and bagpiping in

The Virginia Highlands Pipes and Drums parade down East Main Street in Radford, Virginia, as part of the Radford Highlanders Festival, 2000. The Highlanders Festival is one of several events to come out of the Scottish heritage revival that emerged in southern Appalachia in the final decades of the twentieth century.

celebrations of "the auld country." While academics have encouraged a continuing awareness of Scots-Irish dialect elements and musical and storytelling motifs in Appalachia, commemorations of Scottish roots often generalize disparate Scottish traditions. For example, in 1996 Radford University in Virginia adopted the MacFarlane as its official tartan, began a Highlanders Festival, and adopted a new mascot, the Highlander, in celebration of its Scots-Irish roots.

The majority of Scottish Highlanders arriving in America during the colonial period settled in North Carolina's Cape Fear Valley. However, the major sites of ritual gatherings in North Carolina are those more evocative of Highland images of the homeland. Hence, the Scottish Tartans Museum and Heritage Center and the Grandfather Mountain Highland Games and Gathering of Scottish Clans are situated, not in the original Highlander settlement area, but in the Scots-Irish-settled Blue Ridge Mountains.

See also: GRANDFATHER MOUNTAIN (TOURISM); HIGHLAND GAMES (SPORTS AND RECREATION).

—Celeste Ray, *University of the South*

H. Tyler Blethen and Curtis W. Wood, eds., *Ulster and North America: Transatlantic Perspectives on the Scotch-Irish* (1997); James G. Leyburn, *The Scotch-Irish: A Social History* (1962); Celeste Ray, *Highland Heritage: Scottish Americans in the American South* (2001).

Seneca

The early Seneca lived in reinforced villages in present-day Canada and Appalachian New York. They spoke an Iroquoian language and fought with other related tribes such as the Cayuga, Mohawk, Oneida, and Onondaga, with whom they were collectively known as the Five Nations of the Iroquois Confederacy. They became the Six Nations after the Tuscarora joined them in the early eighteenth century. After many wars, these groups formed a league to establish peace and a Grand Council to debate troubling issues. Seneca warriors were considered to be protectors of the western portion of the Six Nations.

Family lineage was matriarchal, and husbands usually moved into their wives' households. The children belonged to their mother's clan. Women had a great deal of influence at Grand Council meetings.

During the Revolutionary War, the Seneca sided with the British, and George Washington ordered his soldiers to "lay waste all their settlements." General John Sullivan destroyed at least forty Seneca communities, razing homes and burning corn. After the war, the United States government gave away portions of Seneca land to American veterans. Because of their support of the British, there was little the people could do to prevent the loss of much of their territory.

Among the most prominent Seneca leaders was Otetiani, also known as Sagoyewatha or Red Jacket. Disapproving of Christian missionaries' influence among his people, Otetiani clashed with a Christian faction of the Seneca led by his half-brother Handsome Lake and was charged with witchcraft in 1801. Otetiani is credited with clearing himself of the charge with an eloquent self-defense.

See also: NATIVE AMERICANS; WHITE CONQUEST (SETTLEMENT AND MIGRATION).

—Ima J. Stephens, *Auburn University*

Sequoyah

(c. 1770–1843) Cherokee leader and inventor of the Cherokee syllabary.

Born in the Cherokee village of Tuskegee on the Little Tennessee River in what was then western North Carolina (near Fort Loudon in present-day Tennessee), Sequoyah singlehandedly invented a written language, the Cherokee syllabary. While written languages generally evolve over centuries, Sequoyah achieved his feat independently within a period of twelve years. He also served as a statesman and leader for the Cherokee in Arkansas and Oklahoma during the last two decades of his life.

Sequoyah was reportedly the son of a Virginia fur trader named Nathaniel Gist and a Cherokee mother, Wut-teh, who gave him the name George Gist. His Cherokee name, Sequoyah, which means "pig-foot," has led some to surmise that he was crippled, either from birth or from an injury sustained in a hunting accident or during military service. Sequoyah acquired the skills of a trapper, fur trader, blacksmith, and silversmith, but he learned little English and no writing while growing up. His earliest attempt to write came after he moved to Cherokee County in Appalachian Georgia, where, with assistance from local farmer Charles Hicks, he inscribed his name on jewelry he crafted in 1809. Sequoyah's interest in devising a script for the Cherokee language was further fueled when he served alongside white soldiers in the United States Army in the War of 1812 and in the Creek War. Fascinated with how the white soldiers could write letters, follow military communication, and keep records of the war, Sequoyah became convinced that literacy would empower his people.

As the idea grew in Sequoyah's mind, he attempted a cumbersome pictographic script, using individual symbols for each word. However, he soon rejected this approach in favor of a phonetic script that required fewer symbols (only eighty-six) for the individual sounds or syllables that make up essential units in the Cherokee language. Sequoyah presented the impressive syllabary before the tribal council in 1821; it was immediately accepted, and within months Sequoyah had managed to teach the written language to a majority of the Cherokee in his vicinity. He next traveled to Arkansas to teach his alphabet there. Within a short period, most Cherokee became literate, and the Cherokee National Council honored Sequoyah with a silver medal in 1825. Sequoyah's alphabet inspired publication of the *Cherokee Phoenix*, the first Native American newspaper, published in English and Cherokee in New Echota in northern Georgia starting in 1828. The same year, Sequoyah was part of a delegation sent to Washington, D.C., to negotiate with the U.S. government regarding the removal of Cherokee to Oklahoma. Sequoyah, along with a group of Cherokee later referred to as "old settlers," relocated to Oklahoma in 1829, a decade before the forced exodus of the Cherokee Nation along the Trail of Tears.

In 1843 Sequoyah embarked upon his last major campaign, setting out toward Mexico in search of a group of Cherokee who had moved there before the Trail of Tears, hoping to reunite them with the northern groups. This final effort for his people ended in Sequoyah's death in August 1843, probably near present-day Tyler, Texas; his grave was never found. Besides the establishment of a Sequoyah Birthplace Museum in Vonore, Tennessee, Sequoyah has been commemorated on a U.S. postal stamp, with a statue in the Statuary Hall at the U.S. Capitol, and through the naming of two species of the giant California redwood tree in his honor.

See also: CHEROKEE; ROSS, JOHN.

—Ajay Kalra, *East Tennessee State University*

Grant Foreman, *Sequoyah* (1938); Kevin E. Smith, "Sequoyah," in *The Tennessee Encyclopedia of History and Culture*, ed. Carroll Van West (1998).

Shawnee

Shawnee Indians, the most migratory of all North American tribes, have been present in all Appalachian states. Prior to European contact, the tribe included five septs, or groups, each with a specific function. The Chalahgawtha and Hathawagila Septs served as the administrative segment and selected the nation's principal chief from their members. The Piquas were responsible for religion and ceremonies, the Makujays dealt with medicine and health, and the Kispokos were warriors. With European encroachment, the distinctive roles of the septs became blurred, leading to their eventual dispersal. Clans were, and are, represented by a clan chief and clan mother, each having an equal vote. Up until cessation of military conflict between the American settlers and the Shawnee, clan mothers exercised the final decision about waging war.

The ancestors of the Chalahgawtha Sept are believed to have crossed the land bridge of the Bering Strait tens of thousands of years ago. Oral tradition holds that ancestors of the Makujay and Kispoko Septs, and perhaps a portion of the Piqua Sept, migrated from Lake Chapala, Mexico, during the tenth century A.D. Members of these groups divided into two bands, which later encountered each other near Etowah, Georgia, where they constructed the Stone Eagle Mound in the temple fashion of the Mayas. Around 1100, the Kispoko and Chalahgawtha Septs combined forces to repel the Iroquois from Ohio. The Piqua Sept of the Shawnee immigrated northwest into Tennessee, West Virginia, and Ohio. Some of these septs intermarried and became the group known as the Fort Ancients.

Throughout the 1600s and 1700s, a large number of combined septs occupied areas of Appalachia. Warring at times with the French and then the British, some Shawnee eventually allied with the latter. One group, choosing to remain neutral, returned to the Scioto River homeland. In the 1760s, the Shawnee combined armies with Virginia colonists to fight the Cherokee, expecting to remain on the eastern side of the Appalachians in return.

In 1789 approximately one thousand Shawnee septs (about a third of the total) voluntarily relocated to Missouri, then to Kansas, in hopes of protecting their people from further decimation. In spite of treaties and promises, the Indian Removal Act of 1830 ordered all Native Americans to lands reserved in present-day Kansas and Oklahoma. Thousands of Shawnee and other Appalachian Indians, most of them on foot, were driven from their homelands under arduous conditions over mountains and plains in the dead of winter to Oklahoma, where many Shawnee still reside.

There have been no Shawnee reservations since the mid-1800s, when Andrew Jackson dismantled the Ohio Reserves. Numerous bands of Shawnee are scattered throughout the Appalachian region, as are thousands of descendants not identified with an organized group. Of the five original septs, at least two have organized factions. The Blue Creek Band, primarily Chalahgawtha descendants, inhabits tribal grounds in ancient Shawnee lands in Adams County, Ohio. The Piqua Band of Ohio has a branch in Alabama. The United Remnant Band, primarily Kispoko Sept, is not based in Appalachia but has numerous members who reside in the region. There is also a large Indian alliance that includes Shawnee members in West Virginia and a small band of Shawnee in Kentucky.

Although many Shawnee have embraced Protestantism, many traditionalists still practice the religion of their ancestors.

See also: BLUE CREEK BAND; NATIVE AMERICANS.

—Cora Tula Watters, *Antioch University, McGregor School*

John R. Swanton, *The Indian Tribes of North America* (1952; reprint 1990); Dark Rain Thom, *Kohkumthena's Grandchildren: The Shawnee* (2001).

Slavery

Slavery, as an economic system and as a system of social control and white supremacy, existed throughout southern Appalachia from the early 1700s until the close of the Civil War. Although various statutes had restricted the rights of blacks and defined their status as slaves prior to this, the first comprehensive legal code defining slaves as property was adopted in Virginia in 1705. Other colonies swiftly followed this example. As in the South as a whole, slaves were forced to labor on yeoman farms where a single slave toiled in the fields alongside his or her master, on large plantations of twenty or more slaves, and in commercial and industrial ventures such as mines and saltworks.

Large plantations of twenty or more slaves were not widespread, but at least one such plantation could be found in each county throughout the southern Appalachian region. The Appalachian counties of Alabama and Mississippi harbored the heaviest concentration of large plantations in the region. Slavery in these counties resulted primarily from the relocation of whole plantations from the eastern seaboard to what was then the southwestern frontier during the first two decades of the nineteenth century. Planters moved in search of better farmland and opportunities and duplicated the plantation system of slavery in these new locales.

The plantation system was not as profitable an economic option for the remaining and more numerous Appalachian counties, where the dominant pattern was for one family to own one to four slaves. As was true throughout the South, greater numbers of slaves worked on plantations, but only a small minority of white slaveholders owned enough slaves to be considered planters. For the non-plantation slaveholders, particularly members of the prosperous entrepreneurial and professional classes, purchasing a slave was an economically feasible means of supplementing family members' labor in performance of routine tasks such as daily household chores or work on small farms. Often slaves with specialized skills were hired out or, in a few cases, allowed to work independently away from the owner's direct supervision. Unskilled slaves also were hired out for labor-intensive jobs in mining, forestry, or on larger farms or to assist merchants in towns. Slaves were also brought to the region as servants to the low-country planters who spent their summer months in the cool temperatures of the mountains.

Most slaves working and living apart from the plantations had more choice about their daily lives and social arrangements, but many suffered abuse and inhumane treatment. Southern Appalachian whites—slaveholders and nonslaveholders alike—generally supported the institution of slavery out of a desire to control the black population and to uphold the commonly held belief of black inferiority.

See also: CIVIL WAR (GOVERNMENT); SLAVERY AND ABOLITION (GOVERNMENT); SLAVE TRADE.

—Wilburn Hayden Jr., *California University of Pennsylvania*

Wilburn Hayden Jr., "The South Asheville Colored Cemetery, 1840–1943," *Appalachian Heritage* (Fall 1991); John C. Inscoe, *Mountain Masters: Slavery and the Sectional Crisis in Western North Carolina* (1989); James Oakes, *The Ruling Race: A History of American Slaveholders* (1982).

Slave Trade

Slaves in antebellum Appalachia did industrial, commercial, domestic, and agricultural work and often were acquired for investment purposes, but slave auctions were rare in the mountains. Few whites owned slaves because most people could not afford them. In nearly every case, the buying and selling of slaves was accomplished by private exchanges between individuals, smaller sales at courthouses on court days, or, rarely, at a regional broker's slave pen. Prices for slaves generally rose throughout the nineteenth century. Steady demand kept prices high because the supply of slaves was scarce, and owners usually were unwilling to sell their slaves.

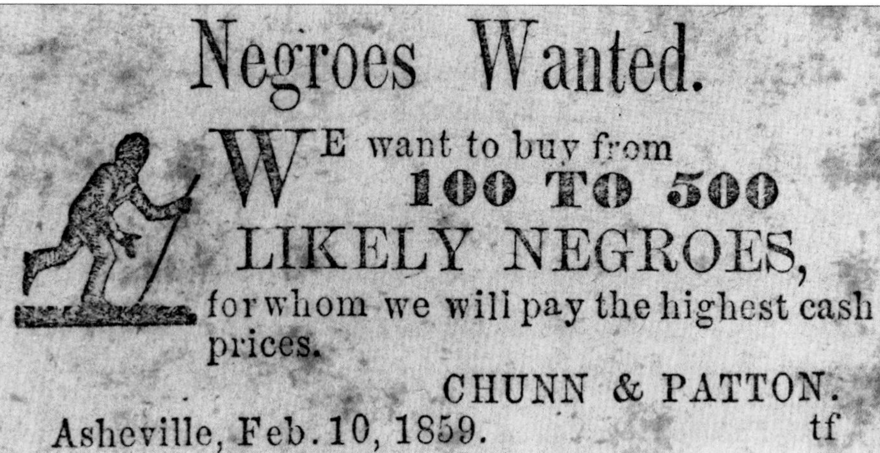
Negroes Wanted.

WE want to buy from
100 TO 500
LIKELY NEGROES,
for whom we will pay the highest cash prices.

CHUNN & PATTON.

Asheville, Feb. 10, 1859. tf

Asheville News advertisement soliciting slaves for railroad construction in Asheville, North Carolina, 1859. While the slave trade in Appalachia varied widely from place to place, slaves did industrial, commercial, domestic, and agricultural work and often were acquired for investment purposes.

The tax structure of the southern states encouraged many persons to shelter their cash in slave property. In western Virginia, some whites purchased very young slave children and raised them for a longterm investment. A slave child could be purchased for a modest sum that would return a substantial profit when the child was sold at the age of fifteen or sixteen.

Slave brokers advertised relentlessly for purchase of slaves, and their transactions often resulted in separation of family members. Testimony of former slaves from western North Carolina suggests that a few owners sold slaves to outside traders in transactions that the slaves found particularly difficult. The demand for slave labor and the operations of brokers added stress to the lives of free blacks as well, for they were constantly at risk of being kidnapped and sold into slavery.

Census reports for rural areas of the upcountry South show that in many areas the slave populations shifted from an equal distribution of the sexes and ages in the 1840s to mostly younger women and children by the time of the Civil War. This trend, probably caused by rising prices for field hands in the low country, exacerbated the harshness of bondage with the loss of fathers and husbands. Mountain slavery is often seen as somewhat less cruel than in plantation regions, but women and children enslaved in remote areas of the mountain South often faced lives of isolation and loneliness.

See also: SLAVERY; SLAVERY AND ABOLITION (GOVERNMENT); SLAVE WOMEN.

—Barbara Rasmussen, *Fairmont State College*

Slave Women

Although little research has been done on gender and slavery in the region, slave women were a significant population in antebellum Appalachia, working in nonagricultural jobs as well as on farms. Nonagricultural labor included domestic service, household manufacturing, work in mercantile stores, and gardening. Slave women also made candles, soap, textiles, and other items for their own use as well as that of their owners.

A primary concern of slave women in Appalachia was for their families. Not only did families face the possibility of being separated by sales to traveling slave traders, but they also found themselves subject to separation by the practice of leasing. Slaves were leased to farmers or merchants and sometimes to coal miners and industrialists for twelve-month terms, and their new workplaces were sometimes miles away from home and family. Slave families were also separated through inheritance, as heirs divided slaves along with other property or sold them to pay debts. As a consequence of family disruptions, the majority of slave women and children in Appalachia lived in female-headed households.

In Appalachia, slaves generally lived close to their owner's house and in some cases lived with the owner's family. This close proximity supposedly made slaves more like members of the family, but it also subjected them to closer supervision and increased the chances that slave women would be sexually assaulted. Estimates are that 10 percent of Appalachian slave families included children of white men.

The sexuality of slave women was exploited by the owners in other ways as well. Appalachian masters influenced the choice of spouse in about one-third of slave marriages. Slave marriages were important to owners because children of the union were the property of the mother's owner and could increase the wealth of the owner's family. Slave women in Appalachia were encouraged to marry and start bearing children earlier than in the plantation South, and the first child was usually born by the time the mother reached eighteen. She continued to have children at regular intervals (usually every two years or less) the rest of her reproductive years. Slave women were generally forced to wean their children in less than one year. Many slave mothers worked as wet nurses for white children in the owner's family, where children were breast-fed for two years. The cycle of births, weaning, and high child mortality, together with malnutrition and an unhealthy environment, led to a shorter lifespan for slave women than men. Appalachian death rates for slave women were 1.5 times higher than the national average and 1.8 times higher than white Appalachian women.

See also: SLAVERY; SLAVE TRADE.

—Tamara Jo Levi, *Asheville, North Carolina*

Wilma A. Dunaway, "Diaspora, Death, and Sexual Exploitation: Slave Families at Risk in the Mountain South," *Appalachian Journal* (Winter 1999); John C. Inscoe, *Mountain Masters: Slavery and the Sectional Crisis in Western North Carolina* (1989); Edward W. Phifer, "Slavery in Microcosm: Burke County, North Carolina," *Journal of Southern History* (May 1962).

Spanish

See Hispanics

Sullivan, Leon H.

(1922–2001) Minister and civil rights activist.

Born in Charleston, West Virginia, in 1922, the Reverend Leon Howard Sullivan led some of the most significant efforts in the latter half of the twentieth century toward ensuring civil rights for minorities. His "Sullivan Principles" influenced racially equitable corporate policy worldwide, and he is widely acknowledged for his significant contribution toward the dismantling of apartheid in South Africa. Sullivan traced the roots of his faith in the human ability to effect positive change to his spiritual upbringing in Charleston's Washington Court community.

Following his first confrontation with discrimination at the age of eight in a Charleston drugstore, Sullivan resolved to make fighting bigotry his life's goal. At six feet, five inches, he won a basketball scholarship to Garnett High School and the all-black West Virginia State College. After losing his college scholarship due to injury, Sullivan decided to become a minister and served at the First Baptist Church of Montgomery, West Virginia, while completing his college degree. Sullivan's motivational skills and leadership promise were conspicuous, and upon graduation in 1943 he was awarded a scholarship to the prestigious Union Theological Seminary in New York City. He took his first active role in the Civil Rights movement by helping to organize a march on Washington, D.C., in the early 1940s. In 1950 he moved to Philadelphia to serve as minister at Zion Baptist Church, where he became known as the "Lion of Zion" and gradually increased the six-hundred-member congregation tenfold, making it the largest black church in the city.

Sullivan recognized early the persuasive power of consumer boycotts in compelling corporations and even governments to abide by essential human rights principles in their employment and workplace policies and was able to convince many organizations to improve job opportunities and working conditions for blacks and ethnic minorities. In 1964 he founded the Opportunities Industrialization Centers of America. Stressing self-help, these centers became the nation's largest organization assisting individuals from minority groups in the development of self-esteem and professional skills.

In 1971 Sullivan joined the board of directors of General Motors, becoming the first African American on the panel of a major American multinational corporation. In 1975 he visited South Africa to inspect the company's operations in that country. Appalled at the country's apartheid policy, he drafted a set of six basic egalitarian principles in 1977 as corporate guidelines for U.S. firms in South Africa. As a result of his work through church and civic groups, other multinational corporations were persuaded to adopt the "Sullivan Principles." Sullivan's campaigning was a major factor in the denunciation of apartheid by the U.S. Congress in 1986 and in the imposition of a trade embargo against South Africa in 1987. In part because of this urging, more than seventy U.S. corporations pulled out of South Africa, and the resulting economic losses suffered by the South African government proved a major impetus to the demise of apartheid. Sullivan's contributions to a new era of equitable race relations in that country were recognized by South African President Nelson Mandela, among others.

In 1992 Sullivan was awarded the Presidential Medal of Freedom, America's highest civilian award. In 1999 the United Nations adopted the "Global Sullivan Principles of Corporate Policy." Sullivan died of leukemia on April 24, 2001.

See also: CIVIL RIGHTS MOVEMENT.

—Ajay Kalra, *East Tennessee State University*

A Principled Man: Rev. Leon Sullivan, MotionMasters videocassette (2000).

Swiss

Towns named Helvetia and Swiss in West Virginia, Bernstadt in Kentucky, and Gruetli in Tennessee indicate a legacy of significant Swiss influence in Appalachia. By 1890 more than thirty-five hundred Swiss settlers had established at least fifteen settlements in West Virginia, Kentucky, and Tennessee.

During the 1800s, land speculators advertised in the United States and Europe to attract settlers to Appalachia, and these advertisements appealed to Swiss suffering economic hardships in the wake of the Industrial Revolution and a series of crop failures in Europe. Most Swiss settlements in Appalachia began with a handful of settlers desiring to live near each other because of a common language. Switzerland's four language groups (German, French, Italian, and Romansch) were represented in these settlements, with German speakers by far the majority. These fledgling communities attracted Swiss, German, and Austrian settlers from nearby states. Settlers wrote letters home to Europe, attracting even more immigrants to their towns.

These communities lost most of their Swiss culture in the early 1900s, when two world wars made use of the German language dangerous. Availability of German-speaking preachers and teachers dwindled while modern transportation and communication made use of English a necessity. The tiny village of Helvetia, West Virginia, held on to much of its singing, yodeling, folk dancing, and cuisine due to near isolation in the Allegheny Mountains, but all that remains of most Swiss settlements in Appalachia are the names of towns and the last names of families.

See also: NEW IMMIGRANTS; SWISS DANCE IN HELVETIA, WEST VIRGINIA (PERFORMING ARTS).

—Bruce Betler, *Helvetia, West Virginia*

Syrians

Syrians who settled in Appalachia in the late nineteenth and early twentieth centuries comprised less than 1 percent of the region's booming immigrant population. Most Syrians were actually from present-day Lebanon, especially from the vicinity of Beirut. Many were Christians who were motivated by Muslim oppression and decline of the Lebanese silk industry to join the tide of immigration to the United States. By 1920, the census counted only 784 Syrians in the coal country of Appalachia.

While some Syrians worked in coal mines, most became pack peddlers. Syrians walked mountain roads carrying cookware, shoes, clothes, and other merchandise to Appalachian homes. During the early years of the nineteenth century, for example, Francis Abraham Modi is reported to have carried a pack of merchandise that weighed more than two hundred pounds from his home in Manington, West Virginia, to towns throughout the state. The Dawahare family of Kentucky, which now owns a statewide chain of clothing stores, traces its origins to pack peddling. Peddlers' packs were so heavy that the straps rubbed calluses onto their shoulders. Most Syrian peddlers additionally carried hand valises containing personal care products such as razors, shaving soap, facial powder, combs, and sewing implements.

See also: NEW IMMIGRANTS.

—Doug Cantrell, *Elizabethtown Community College*

Tally War

See Tally War (Labor)

Urban Appalachian Council

See Cincinnati, Ohio (Urban Appalachian Experience)

Washington, Booker T.

See Washington, Booker T. (Literature)

Welsh

Immigrants from Wales played a crucial role in the development of extractive and heavy industries in northern Appalachia from the mid-nineteenth through the early twentieth century. The first Welsh immigrants were among the colonial settlers of southern Appalachia, and they also established a successful rural enclave based on agriculture and iron production in Jackson and Gallia Counties in southeastern Ohio in the 1830s. However, it was after 1850 that Welsh immigration to Appalachia became most significant. Grounded in the mining and metallurgical industries of Wales, these immigrants provided much of the knowledge and experience necessary to the development of the coal, slate, iron, and steel industries of Pennsylvania. Skilled Welsh workers enjoyed a privileged position, often acting as supervisors, managers, and even owner-operators.

The 1900 census records 100,143 Welsh immigrants and their American-born children residing in Pennsylvania; concentrated in Luzerne, Lackawanna, Allegheny and Schuylkill Counties, their largest urban enclave was in the Hyde Park area of Scranton. The Welsh were different from other British immigrants in terms of their common use of a Celtic language and their distinctive brand of Protestant nonconformity (sects that did not conform to the established, state-sponsored Church of England), including the distinctly Welsh denomination of Calvinistic Methodism. Welsh-language poetry and choral music were important artistic traditions. Annual highlights in Welsh American communities included the *gymanfa ganu*, a hymn-singing festival; the *gymanfa pregethu*, a preaching festival; and the *eisteddfod*, a musical and literary competition and festival. Although much of their population has dispersed over time, Welsh Americans in southeastern Ohio and the Pennsylvania coalfields continue to celebrate their ethnic identity through the activities of Welsh churches and ethnic-fraternal organizations often named after Saint David, the patron saint of Wales.

See also: ANTHRACITE COAL INDUSTRY (BUSINESS, INDUSTRY, AND TECHNOLOGY); OLD IMMIGRANTS.

—John S. Ellis, *University of Michigan at Flint*

West Hill Indians

Numbering in the thousands, the West Hill Indians form a distinct ethnic enclave in north-central West Virginia. One of approximately two hundred recorded Indian remnant groups in the eastern United States, the West Hill Indians are actually several communities tied together through a network of kinship bound to specific racial identity. Some scholars attribute the origins of the group to a mixture of white, African American, and Native American ancestry. The West Hill community itself has historically claimed descent from Cherokee and Delaware Indians who intermarried with settlers along Virginia's mountain frontier. Commonly referred to as Guineas, considered highly offensive by members of the group, the West Hill Indians are also known as Maileys and Cecil Indians.

The earliest mention of ancestors of the West Hill Indians is found in regional records dating from 1784. Members of the group gradually migrated into the Tygart Valley from Hampshire County. By 1810, they were living in Hampshire, Monongalia, Harrison, and Randolph Counties. The group's principal and best-known settlement area is situated on Chestnut Ridge overlooking Philippi, Barbour County, West Virginia.

Due to the topographic constraints of their mountainous homeland, West Hill Indians practiced subsistence farming supplemented by moonshining. Many families remain on welfare, and chronic unemployment has prompted extensive migration out of the area since well before World War II. Considered by authorities to be a "colored" population, the West Hill Indians were segregated from white institutions throughout much of the nineteenth and twentieth centuries, a situation that created considerable resentment within the group. West Hill Indian social life at the start of the twenty-first century generally resembled that of other rural populations. Religion, primarily Methodism, is very important to the community. Other Protestant denominations are also represented, including the Pentecostal Church, the African Methodist Church, and the Church of God. Commonly encountered surnames within the group include Collins, Kennedy (Canaday), Male (Mail, Mahle, and Mayle), Minard (Miner), and Pritchard.

See also: INDIAN REMNANT GROUPS; MELUNGEONS.

—Donald B. Ball, *U.S. Army Corps of Engineers, Louisville, Kentucky*, and C. S. Everett, *Vanderbilt University*

Woodson, Carter G.

(1875–1950) Historian, educator, editor, and publisher.

Carter Godwin Woodson, one of the most influential African American intellectuals of the twentieth century, spent his early years in Appalachia. Born to former slaves in New Canton, Virginia, on December 19, 1875, Woodson moved to Fayette County, West Virginia, in the early 1890s. There he worked as a coal miner before beginning his formal education in 1895 at Frederick Douglass High School in Huntington, West Virginia. He earned a bachelor's degree from Berea College in Kentucky in 1903, a second bachelor's and a master's degree from the University of Chicago in 1908, and a doctorate in history from Harvard University in 1912, with a dissertation on the creation of the state of West Virginia. In 1915 Woodson published his first major book on African American history, *The Education of the Negro Prior to 1861: A History of the Education of the Colored People of the United States from the Beginning of Slavery to the Civil War*, and helped found the Association for the Study of Negro Life and History. The association published the *Journal of Negro History*, which Woodson edited until his death on April 3, 1950. Woodson was instrumental in establishing Negro History Week in 1926, and in 1937 he inaugurated the *Negro History Bulletin* as a resource for schoolchildren, teachers, and other nonspecialists.

In his landmark article "Freedom and Slavery in Appalachian America," published in the *Journal of Negro History* in 1916, Woodson argued that the geography and economy of the southern highlands combined with the religious and ethnic background of its populace to make the region largely antislavery. Although subsequent scholarship has challenged a number of Woodson's claims, his essay influenced the understanding of race in Appalachia for nearly a century.

See also: FREED BLACKS, POSTBELLUM; SLAVERY AND ABOLITION (GOVERNMENT).

—Steve Gowler, *Berea College*

Settlement and Migration

Section Editor: Sheila R. Phipps

IN 1893 HISTORIAN FREDERICK JACKSON TURNER PRESENTED A PAPER TO THE American Historical Association arguing that the frontier had played a significant role in both American history and development of the nation's democratic institutions. Formally titled "The Significance of the Frontier in American History" but best remembered as the "Turner thesis" or the "frontier thesis," the sweeping theory provided a touchstone for generations of historians, social geographers, and ethnographers researching the rise of the modern nation.

Turner's assertion that the frontier helped shape American character has been a subject of long scholarly debate. Though reluctant to agree with Turner that the frontier made Americans especially innovative, inquisitive, strong, and independent, some scholars accept the notion that the frontier did appeal to Americans' migratory impulses. In this view, the Americans who headed west from the Atlantic seaboard had already demonstrated an affinity for challenge and change by making the daunting crossing of the Atlantic. Their movement, then, was a continuation of that initial migration. The vast expanse of land and natural resources provided that migratory impulse with a goal and an outlet for its driving energy.

Archaeological and ethnographic evidence supports the idea that human beings are innately restless and have from the beginning wandered continuously, usually for environmental and economic reasons such as the desire for more favorable climate or reliable food supplies. Modern migrants still move in quest of more comfortable living conditions and in an effort to improve their financial lot. In other words, the usual reason for horizontal migration is vertical improvement.

The first migrants into Appalachia came from the west. Ancient Native American people at first followed their food sources in seasonal hunts and then established settled villages and ceremonial sites. Again, the earliest human migrations into the region can be viewed as simply a continuation of the migration impulse that brought humans to the Western Hemisphere in the first place. Genetic and linguistic evidence suggests that Asians began wandering into North America between 25,000 and 30,000 years ago when the final ice age lowered water levels, leaving the two continents joined at the Bering Strait.

Facing page: Detail from an 1851–52 painting of Daniel Boone escorting settlers through the Cumberland Gap. Led by men such as Boone, early settlers overcame many challenges in the mountains and forests of the region. A long-held romantic notion of Appalachian settlement is that of pioneers entering a pristine wilderness to cultivate civilization, but most migrants to Appalachia found that many institutions and individuals, from trading posts, taverns, and outfitters to speculators' agents and government officials, had preceded them.

Archaeological evidence of hunting camps suggests that the first humans arrived in the Appalachians approximately 14,000 years ago. Trade networks that exploited regional resources began between 3,500 and 5,000 years ago, and settlement started more than 3,000 years ago. With the development of agriculture and a sedentary culture, Native Americans began settling longer into one space. By the time of contact with whites, the Eastern Woodland nations of mostly Algonquian or Iroquoian language groups had begun living in single-family wigwams or multifamily longhouses of villages with large populations, making them even more susceptible to European diseases, to which they had no genetic resistance. They also began to surround their villages with fortifications of one type or another, indicating that tribal relations were often less than peaceful.

Sometimes conflicts arose between inhabitants of these villages and hunting parties from other areas in search of game or salt. The Shawnee of the Ohio Valley, for instance, regularly crossed the Greenbrier Valley of present-day West Virginia and moved south through the Appalachian Valley into western North Carolina or eastern Kentucky, hunting and processing salt at saline springs before returning to their village beside the Scioto River at modern-day Chillicothe, Ohio. After white settlement gained a solid foothold in the Appalachians, Ohio Shawnee occasionally carried out attacks on whites in the region and sometimes traveled even farther to forge alliances with southern native groups such as the Cherokee against white encroachment on hunting lands. Native American migratory and hunting practices indicate that distance did not deter them in their economic and diplomatic endeavors. Without jurisdictional traditions or belief in private ownership of property, Native Americans traveled the region freely, usually encountering resistance only when their travels brought them into competition with other tribes for limited game.

The pattern of initial white migrations into the Appalachian region mirrors that of the Native Americans, beginning with exploration and continuing with increasing exploitation of resources. Hernando de Soto, on an *entrada* for Spain in the mid-sixteenth century, is believed to have been the first European to investigate the mountains. Thomas Batts and Robert Fallam entered the region first for Britain, following the New River into southwestern Virginia in 1671. European interest in the area was driven by demands for the natural resources of the region, with furs being the primary object of widespread and violent competition. French and British agents first tapped into Native American trade networks, but independent operations by European trappers soon followed. Although furs provided the magnet for trappers and traders, the ensuing exploration and eventual settlement of the Appalachians were driven not only by economic opportunism but also by insatiable curiosity and the impulse to seek new opportunities.

The first white migrants into the Appalachians occupied both a physical and a cultural frontier. Any frontier includes at least two distinct cultures, with the new intruding upon a previously established culture until one is subdued or assimilated into the other. The process begins when the first few intruders arrive and generally involves both intercultural conflict and intracultural cooperation. The Appalachian frontier experienced these trends, but there were some notable exceptions.

International competition in North America, especially between the French and British, led colonial officials to incite Native Americans to make war on colonists of the other nation. At the same time, in order to ensure safety for their own settlers, administrators also promoted warfare between Native American groups, keeping them too busy warring against each other to be concerned with white incursion. For example, one method sometimes used by Europeans was to manipulate the deerskin trade in order to create strife between highly competitive tribes.

After the French and Indian War, however, with the issue of territorial control east of the Mississippi River resolved, the British moved to ensure the safety of their subjects by separating them from Native American groups. A figurative dividing line was established along the crest of the Appalachians with white settlement west of the line prohibited and economic contact between the two cultures regulated by colonial authorities.

This Proclamation Line of 1763 was widely ignored by white settlers. Some leased land from the Cherokee in eastern Tennessee, while others purchased property outright in violation of the law. Flouting the restriction most famously was Daniel Boone, who crossed through the Cumberland Gap in 1769. Steadily, the British government, then the fledgling American government under the Articles of Confederation, and finally the U.S. federal government negotiated large swaths of land in the region away from the Native Americans. In the 1795 Treaty of Greenville, Native Americans ceded the mountain region north of Kentucky and portions of Indiana and Illinois, creating stability for trans-Appalachian white settlement. The treaty provides revealing insight into the clash between the two cultures. When the federal government offered to compensate some of the tribes with payments of five hundred to one thousand dollars a year, Native American leaders, who felt mass migration only took place when necessary, misread the offer as an indication that whites in the East were starving and therefore being forced to migrate. They suggested that the payments be made to the struggling whites and that the Native Americans keep their hunting grounds. In the end, however, realizing that westward migration was inevitable and would cause them less harm than continued warfare, tribal leaders signed the treaty ceding their people's lands.

Migration usually has two driving forces, a push from the area already settled and a pull to the new region. In other words, people do not usually move away from an area as long as it meets their needs. The push for most of the first Appalachian settlers was economic scarcity. For the earliest migrants into Appalachia, it was most often scarcity of land in their previous location.

Settlement of colonial North America began on the Atlantic Coastal Plain, moved to the Piedmont by the eighteenth century, and then flowed into the mountains. Stable settlement in the East had grown through both immigration and natural increase. Although there was still plenty of arable land, there was a growing perception of shortage. As fathers divided their holdings among their sons, farms became ever smaller. In truth, land scarcity meant simply that succeeding generations of families could no longer work farms next to each other and that sons were increasingly moving west to settle their own families where property was readily available. In Appalachia, families hoped to begin their own stem families on property that was large enough to divide into contiguous family holdings.

Some of the Appalachian region's migrants came directly from Europe. From 1718 to 1775, approximately five thousand immigrants arrived in North America each year from the British Isles. Many of these newcomers had been literally pushed off their lands by high rents in their homelands. Scots who had been "planted" in Ulster by the British government in hopes of taming the Irish had never been truly assimilated into Irish culture, so when absentee landlords began to demand higher rents, they moved on to America to find better opportunities. Most of the Scots-Irish arrived in the port of Philadelphia, but they were often strongly encouraged by the Quakers to settle in the backcountry. Migrating first into the frontier regions of Pennsylvania and finding most of the best land already taken, they pushed south through the Valley of Virginia, often called the migration "funnel." Some settled in

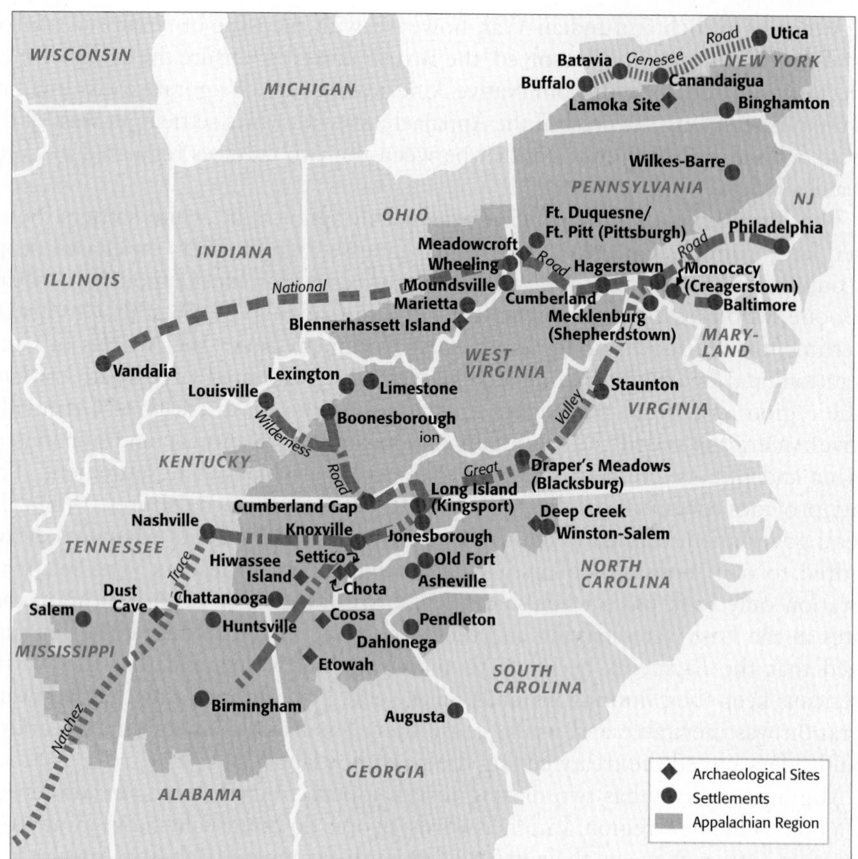

A map showing the boundaries of modern Appalachia also displays major migratory routes and early settlements in the region. The earliest archaeological site is Meadowcroft in Pennsylvania (dating to about 12,000 B.C.) while most of the settlements and roads date to the mid- to late 1700s. The terrain of the mountainous region influenced European settlement patterns, and migratory routes often followed existing Native American trails through valleys and passes. Many of these early trails and roads later became primary railroad and highway routes through the region. For instance, parts of the National Road are now U.S. Route 40 and Interstate 70.

the valley itself, while many continued into the Blue Ridge Mountains of North Carolina, where they settled in neighborhoods of extended families.

Across the nineteenth century, factors such as land scarcity, the potato blight, political turmoil, and religious intolerance pushed a tide of various Europeans to America—from the British Isles, France, and Germany in the early years and then from Italy and Greece toward the end of the century. Most of these migrants crossed the ocean in hopes of better economic opportunity and greater political and religious freedom, their optimism founded upon family letters, advertisements, and newspapers.

Migration decisions of new Americans, then as now, generally had two components: whether and where to move. For those who decided to leave a place, the only question was one of destination. Information gathering was usually the first step, and much of that came from family and friends already in the new region. The frontier was a common topic, especially in areas that were becoming crowded. There was sometimes so much contradictory information that prospective migrants had difficulty sorting through the sources.

When migrants decided to move into the Appalachians, they first considered the distance to the new locale, measuring it in both financial and psychological terms, taking into account family and friends who would be left behind. Other special considerations were land, water supply, and the cost, both in time and money, of necessities that could not be obtained through self-sufficiency. Potential migrants also had to think about the additional temporal and financial costs of transportation.

Not all migrants arrived in the Appalachians willingly. Although slaves in the mountains were fewer than in the plantation South, they arrived with owners relocating to the region or were rented from owners in the East and South. In any case, they did not make migration decisions. Others who did not have the luxury of choice were Native Americans forced out of the mountains, either unofficially, such as when white settlement reduced hunting lands, or officially, as with the forced westward march of southeastern peoples in what has become known as the Trail of Tears during the 1830s. In addition, maroon settlements in the mountains were created by runaway slaves whose only real choice was escape. The mountains seemed to offer the best location in which to hide, but the areas chosen by maroons offered few resources since they wanted to avoid discovery by whites attracted to arable land and abundant natural resources. Few maroon settlements lasted very long; one of the most successful was located in the mountains near present-day Lexington, Virginia.

Migrants who arrived in the Appalachian region by choice were generally attracted by economic opportunity, especially the chance to own land and provide for their families. Governments announced terms for newly opened areas of settlement, land companies advertised to attract settlers, and individuals already in the area encouraged family members to follow. In any event, early migrants rarely wandered into the region aimlessly.

In his landmark 1893 paper, Turner described a frontier where pioneers escaped the settled region, making their way into a pristine wilderness where they refreshed their spirit and cultivated democratic institutions in settlements hacked from the forests. According to Turner, "settlement from the sea to the mountains kept connection with the rear [England and then colonial administration] and had a certain solidarity. But the over-mountain men grew more and more independent." Although Turner's images are romantic and intriguing, modern scholarship has established that most migrants entering Appalachia found many of the same institutions they had left behind, from trading posts to speculators' agents and government offices. In fact, government officials initiated settlement of the region.

In order to assess settlement possibilities, Alexander Spotswood, the lieutenant governor of colonial Virginia, crossed the Blue Ridge into the Shenandoah Valley in 1716 with compatriots he called his Knights of the Golden Horseshoe. Other colonial governors also commissioned traders and Indian agents such as the eighteenth-century "King of Traders," George Croghan, to ease the way for white settlement by negotiating deals with Native Americans and establishing trading posts. Colonial legislatures granted large tracts of land to individuals who would settle on the frontier and help create buffers between established settlement and Native American populations. Such grants enabled settlers to work through land agents and secure property rights without traveling long distances to colonial capitals to record their titles. After the American Revolution, states offered grants such as the Virginia Military District between the Scioto and Miami Rivers in Ohio and the Military Tract in central New York east of Seneca Lake as compensation to war veterans. The "federal frontier" also included government funding of better roads into the region and settlement plans such as the Land Ordinance of 1785, which provided orderly patterns on the landscape by surveying and numbering ranges and platting townships into lots of one square mile and numbering the lots one through thirty-six.

Added to the settlement incentives offered by public agencies and officials were the efforts of speculators and developers. The combined influence of public and private promoters meant that most settlement of the Appalachian frontier resulted not from freedom-loving individuals creating new lives but from the machinations of land companies and speculators who bought vast tracts and reaped huge profits. Much like joint-stock ventures, these groups were financed and run by eastern elites or on capital borrowed from eastern merchants, banks, and even from foreign investors. For instance, a group of Massachusetts investors purchased a large portion of southeastern Ohio through the Ohio Company of Associates, affecting settlement along the Ohio River. Dutch banking interests speculated in the Holland Purchase that settled southwestern New York. By 1810, investment capitalists owned more than 5.5 million acres of land in the southern Appalachians. Both speculators and developers attempted to increase their profits not only by marketing land to prospective migrants, but also by laying out town designs, promising stable government, and building roads. Although some of the developers were certainly bold, these details refute Turner's picture of individuals wandering into the region and settling haphazardly on the landscape.

Besides land and freedom offered by governments and private speculators, abundant natural resources exerted a powerful attraction. Popular perceptions of Appalachia's economic history include the notion that world markets and industrial capitalists were uninterested in the region until the late nineteenth century. In this view, the region held modernity at bay for so long that it appeared to have been frozen in time. In fact, the world market brought some of the first whites into the region, where they traded for furs to satisfy the high demand in Europe. It is often forgotten that initial European settlement of North America was part of the economic competition between France, England, and Spain under early modern mercantilism. Economic competition was joined in the Appalachian Mountains even before the first permanent white settlements were established there. Indeed, world demand for natural resources such as furs led to some of the first permanent settlements in the region.

Industrialists quickly looked beyond the trade in fur and animal skins. Salt-processing operations were followed by logging, mining, and other extractive enterprises. The first gold rush in the United States began in Appalachia in the 1820s; the region supplied most of the copper used in the nation by the 1840s; and coal began leaving the region in the 1880s, much of it headed for both national and international markets. Each extractive industry spawned settlement, first to house the large labor corps necessary for the industry, then to supply services for the laboring population. Salt, for instance, helped foster settlement of Boonesborough in Kentucky, the Kanawha River Valley in present-day West Virginia, and towns in Ohio, Tennessee, Pennsylvania, and New York. Mill settlements appeared throughout the region, usually where travel routes intersected, to provide lumber or to process grain. Iron, copper, and coal pulled migrants into ten Appalachian states, creating high population centers in some cases. In effect, rather than a region protected from world markets, much of Appalachia grew in population because of national and international demand for these commodities.

Migrants flowed into Appalachia following waterways such as the Mohawk, Susquehanna, Chenango, and Delaware Rivers into New York, the Kanawha River into Ohio, and the Ohio-Mississippi River system into the lower South. They also followed routes that seemed to have been formed naturally from the landscape. In Tennessee and Kentucky, for instance, salt had drawn great herds of buffalo, and the bulky animals cut wide traces through the wilderness to salt licks. The buffalo-created traces thus provided first the Indians and then Anglo-Americans ready-made trails across the unsettled terrain. Many of these routes were adopted by state and federal agencies, which transformed them into roads, facilitating movement of populations and goods and influencing patterns of modern growth and development.

Along the way migrants found assistance in their travels from trading posts, inns (sometimes called "ordinaries"), and outfitters, which provided supplies and information as well as food and shelter. Many of these supply stations began as part of a trade network that serviced fur traders and long hunters. Situated at crossroads or river crossings, they later profited and grew as the trickle of hunters, explorers, and adventurers became a stream of settlers. Travelers found these outposts to be links to the world they had left behind, receiving from them reassurance that they were not alone in the wilderness.

The frontier experience for whites who settled the region was reflected in forts, or stations, created for protection and temporary structures erected for shelter. But the unsettled state lasted for a relatively short period of time. Most settlers immediately began cutting their farms out of the wilderness, establishing public institutions such as churches and schools and organizing in ways designed to recreate the stable environment they had left behind. They were aided in the process of closing the frontier by government and by the people with whom they had migrated.

Social geographers see the way people space themselves on the landscape as part of their communication process. Location decisions reveal much about the way people viewed the places they left and the places to which they migrated, including the areas' economic opportunities and geography, as well as their abilities to adapt to new environments. Those who moved into areas controlled by developers found many of their decisions made for them, but in other places migrants were left to create order out of chaos. Because they carried their own cultural traditions to the frontier with them, they rebuilt their visions of "civilization." If their area was too distant from government centers, they sought to organize new counties to bring jurisdictional authority closer to them. Absent that, they formed their own organizations, such as the five-member Boards of Police organized in northeastern Mississippi or the Watauga Association in east Tennessee. Churches were usually the first cooperatively constructed buildings in a settlement, replicating the moral authority of settlers' former environments. As they established rudimentary social institutions, most settlers also turned their attention to building more permanent shelter, gradually moving from log construction to framed houses of sawed timber. Town incorporation completed the transformation from a region where explorers, fur traders, and long hunters mixed and mingled with Native Americans who had no cultural traditions of private property into an area of permanent white settlement. Anglo-American hegemony was complete.

From the first permanent white settlements in Appalachia in the 1720s to the present, migration in and out of the region has continued for many of the same reasons that initially brought settlers to the region. Most of the coming and going, then and now, arises from a desire for economic opportunity. Over time, however, as travel has been made increasingly easy by modern transportation, both migration and location decisions have become less driven by consideration of distance.

Although both in- and out-migration have continued for more than two centuries, the twentieth century was noted for surges of out-migration. About a million Appalachians moved away in each decade of the 1940s, 1950s, and 1960s, most of them for economic reasons. Poverty rates in the region ranged much higher than the national average—almost 35 percent in central Appalachia compared to about 14 percent for the nation—and residents, especially those just gaining the age of majority, left the region for a better economic future. But Appalachia seems to endow its population with a keen sense of place, and many of those who left resettled in the nearest urban center to home so that they could return often for visits. For example, during a slump in the coal industry during the 1950s and 1960s, there was a saying in Dickenson County, Virginia, situated in the southwestern corner of the state, that the "three Rs" taught in school were "reading, 'riting, and the road to Washington." In fact, the suburbs of Washington, D.C., gained so many Dickenson County residents that they held an annual Dickenson County Reunion. The high number of Dickenson County migrants to Washington points to another link to the past: the high probability that migrants' destinations are determined by family and friends who have gone to that location before. Kin already situated at the other end of the move ease the transition for migrants, helping them adjust to new surroundings.

Since 1990, with the exception of Pennsylvania and New York, the region has once again experienced a net gain from in-migration. One reason for the increase is returning migrants who have retired and who want to live once again near home. Another migration flow has come from people pursuing a simpler existence, perceiving that life is slower and less stressful in the mountains. Development within the region has also attracted population. Retirement hubs increasingly entice the elderly to locate in the temperate climate of the mountains rather than Florida or the Southwest. The beauty of the mountains and widely varied recreational opportunities have become intensely promoted themes for state economic development agencies, facilitating the movement of people and industries into the region while changing the perception of distance to and from urban centers. Thus, both public and private interests continue to pull migrants into the Appalachian region. By the end of the twentieth century, the region had become home to almost 23 million residents, a diverse ethnic mix representative of those who through the centuries explored, exploited, and transformed the mountains to meet their settlement and economic needs.

—Sheila R. Phipps, *Appalachian State University*

Ray Allen Billington, ed., *The Frontier Thesis: Valid Interpretation of American History?* (1967); Alan Vance Briceland, *Westward from Virginia: The Exploration of the Virginia-Carolina Frontier, 1650–1710* (1987); Wilma A. Dunaway, *The First American Frontier: Transition to Capitalism in Southern Appalachia, 1700–1860* (1996); David Hackett Fischer, *Albion's Seed: Four British Folkways in America* (1989); G. S. George and Arnold Zellner, "Sequential Growth, the Labor-Safety-Valve Doctrine and the Development of American Unionism," *Journal of Economic History* (September 1959); Richard Hofstadter, *The Progressive Historians: Turner, Beard, Parrington* (1968); John A. Jakle, "Salt and the Initial Settlement of the Ohio Valley," Ph.D. dissertation, Indiana University (1967); John A. Jakle, Stanley Brunn, and Curtis C. Roseman, *Human Spatial Behavior: A Social Geography* (1976); Jack Temple Kirby, *Rural Worlds Lost: The American South, 1920–1960* (1987); Arthur Raymond Mangus, *Subsequent Movement of Kentucky Hill Families Relocated as Farm Laborers in Ohio* (1943); Fulmer Mood, "The Rise of Official Statistical Cartography in Austria, Prussia and the United States, 1855–1872," *Agricultural History* (October 1946) and "Studies in the History of American Settled Areas and Frontier Lines: Settled Areas and Frontier Lines, 1625–1790," *Agricultural History* (January 1952); George W. Pierson, "The M-Factor in American History," *American Quarterly* (Summer 1962); Barbara Rasmussen, *Absentee Landowning and Exploitation in West Virginia, 1760–1920* (1994); Malcolm J. Rohrbough, *The Trans-Appalachian Frontier: People, Societies, and Institutions, 1775–1850* (1978); Harry K. Schwarzweller, James S. Brown, and J. J. Mangalam, *Mountain Families in Transition: A Case Study of Appalachian Migration* (1971); Leonard Thompson and Howard Lamar, "Comparative Frontier History," in *The Frontier in History: North America and Southern Africa Compared*, ed. Howard Lamar and Leonard Thompson (1981); Frederick Jackson Turner, "The Significance of the Frontier in American History," in *The Turner Thesis Concerning the Role of the Frontier in American History*, ed. George Rogers Taylor (1956); Kenneth J. Winkle, *The Politics of Community: Migration and Politics in Antebellum Ohio* (1988); William Wyckoff, *The Developer's Frontier: The Making of the Western New York Landscape* (1988).

African American Industrial Migration

In the period between the turn of the century and 1930, African American migration to Appalachian mining camps and industrial towns increased greatly as part of a larger population shift of blacks generally called the Great Migration. Unlike moves to northern, southern, and western U.S. cities, migration to the Appalachian coal-mining camps and towns of Kentucky, Tennessee, Virginia, and most notably West Virginia constituted an aspect of African American migration that was not necessarily rural to urban, but rural to rural-industrial. Great urban metropolises rarely sprang up around southern coalfields. In some cases, towns and cities were slow to form or did not form at all, and both black and white miners were forced to live in largely inhospitable camps.

Due to the perilous nature of the work, and unlike other less dangerous industries that excluded African Americans, coal companies heavily recruited blacks to perform labor that many whites could afford to avoid. Thus, African American migration to mining camps and industrial towns for job opportunities was substantial. In West Virginia, blacks from the lower South were able to attain a better quality of life because they retained the franchise in that state.

Blacks also came to the region for reasons other than finding work in the coal-mining industry. The first large wave of African American migration to what would become the important industrial towns of southern Appalachia occurred between 1890 and 1900 when railroad construction, most notably by the Chesapeake and Ohio, employed black workers.

See also: AFRICAN AMERICAN TWENTIETH-CENTURY MIGRATION; COAL SETTLEMENTS; FREED BLACKS, POSTBELLUM (RACE, ETHNICITY, AND IDENTITY).

—Kolby W. Bilal, *College of William and Mary*

African American Twentieth-Century Migration

Twentieth-century African American migration and the subsequent settlement patterns that developed were a dynamic process resulting in one of the largest population shifts in the history of the United States. Although the majority of African American migrants left the rural South and traveled to northern industrial capitals in search of better opportunities, some ventured to nearer southern cities, and a sizeable portion settled in smaller cities, particularly Appalachian coal-mining towns. Thriving black communities sprouted in the Appalachian areas of Tennessee, Kentucky, Virginia, West Virginia, Maryland, Georgia, and Alabama.

Between 1900 and 1930, the black population in the central Appalachian region nearly tripled, from fewer than 40,000 to more than 108,000. During and immediately after World War II, however, African Americans left the southern Appalachian region in large numbers to pursue opportunities elsewhere. Although this out-migration trend reversed in the 1970s, large numbers of blacks, particularly from Kentucky, Virginia, and West Virginia, still left the area. By the end of the twentieth century, about 330,000 African Americans lived in southern Appalachia.

Throughout the twentieth century, the proportion of blacks living in southern Appalachia decreased. At the beginning of the century, the Appalachian sections of Georgia and Virginia had the highest ratios of black residents. African Americans became more urbanized in southern Appalachia as the century progressed. When the twentieth century began, about 7 percent lived in urban areas; by its close, this figure had jumped to 74.5 percent. In time, other black Appalachian communities became more densely populated as well.

See also: AFRICAN AMERICAN INDUSTRIAL MIGRATION; TWENTIETH-CENTURY IN-MIGRATION; TWENTIETH-CENTURY OUT-MIGRATION.

—Kolby W. Bilal, *College of William and Mary*

American Emigrant Company

Chartered in June 1863, the American Emigrant Company served as a recruiting agent for industrial companies in the United States. Working on behalf of American manufacturers and bankers, the company profited by recruiting, transporting, and settling tens of thousands of laborers in United States industrial centers, including in the Appalachian region. It specialized in recruiting skilled laborers from northern and western Europe.

The company was supported by the 1864 congressional Act to Encourage Immigration, which was designed to alleviate the American labor shortage by validating contracts made by foreign workers prior to their move to the United States. Contracts negotiated by agents of the American Emigrant Company benefited both manufacturers and migrants by allowing the two groups to set fixed wages and terms of service. The contracts also guaranteed manufacturers reimbursement for the cost of transporting and settling immigrant workers. Scholars have noted the similarities between this recruitment system and the indentured servitude system of the colonial era.

The American Emigrant Company was based in New York but maintained agencies or branches in many U.S. states and foreign nations. Overseas agents worked closely with foreign governments, industrialists, and labor unions to secure workers for manufacturing jobs in the United States. Company agents accompanied migrants on their voyage and facilitated their entry into the country. Agents in the United States maintained correspondence with industrialists and state government officials and arranged the transportation of immigrants to areas most in need of laborers. Throughout the Gilded Age, from roughly the end of the Civil War until the beginning of World War I, the company earned significant profits and praise.

As part of its efforts, the company published a monthly newspaper entitled the *American Reporter and Intending Emigrant's Guide*, which addressed a variety of concerns expressed by potential migrants. Distributed liberally in foreign nations where the company operated, the guide contained information about travel to and within the United States and official immigration policies. More importantly, it noted regions within the United States that most needed laborers.

In the Appalachian region, the American Emigrant Company especially provided labor for the rapidly growing extractive industries, enabling companies to develop railroad, coal, and timber claims. In January 1867, company agent John Williams wrote Arthur I. Boreman, the first governor of West Virginia, seeking information about the best locations in West Virginia for immigrants and the special advantages that West Virginia could offer laborers. The following year, perhaps in response to Williams's letter, the state legislature incorporated the State Immigration and Improvement Company of West Virginia. It was chartered to introduce immigration into West Virginia, to develop the transportation networks needed to encourage immigration, and to manage the purchase and sale of land. Based in Parkersburg, the company listed Governor Boreman as one of its incorporators. Shortly thereafter, West Virginia appointed an immigration agent, Joseph H. Diss Debar, to promote immigration into the state for industrial purposes. As part of his campaign, Debar dubbed West Virginia "The Switzerland of America." In the late 1860s, the state government adopted other measures to promote and aid European immigrants living in West Virginia.

The American Emigrant Company took part in other profit-making ventures as well, transferring money from immigrants in the United States to relatives in Europe for a fee and speculating in land, buying and selling thousands of acres in the Midwest and Far West. In 1865 the company's original charter was amended to allow it to purchase and operate transportation networks of its own. By extending its control over most aspects of the immigration process, the company came to resemble the vertically integrated industries of the time.

See also: OLD IMMIGRANTS (RACE, ETHNICITY, AND IDENTITY); RAILROAD PROMOTION AND IN-MIGRATION.

—Brian J. Daugherity, *College of William and Mary*

Barbara Rasmussen, *Absentee Landowning and Exploitation in West Virginia, 1760–1920* (1994); John Alexander Williams, *West Virginia and the Captains of Industry* (1976).

Archaeological Sites

Archaeological sites in Appalachia range from small prehistoric camps and historic mines to large Native American towns and historic battlefields. Stone artifacts and hearths at Meadowcroft Rockshelter in western Pennsylvania indicate a human presence in the region by 12,000 B.C. There is additional proof of late Pleistocene human activity in the Saltville Valley in southwestern Virginia. These seasonal camps provide evidence of migratory settlement and subsistence upon wild foods, possibly including fauna such as musk oxen, caribou, and mastodon.

Two stratified sites in the region—St. Albans (West Virginia) and Icehouse Bottom (eastern Tennessee)—chronicle human occupation in the early and middle Holocene epoch. Likewise, research at Dust Cave in northern Alabama has revealed extensive use of the region by hunter-gatherer societies from 8000 to 1500 B.C. In the middle Holocene (3000–1500 B.C.), the region's inhabitants developed an industry and trade network involving soapstone vessels. This soft rock, abundant throughout the Blue Ridge, was quarried at sites such as the Blue Rock Soapstone Quarry in western North Carolina and the Tallapoosa Quarry in northern Alabama. The Lamoka site in Schuyler County, New York, shows the beginnings of village life at approximately 1200 B.C. Ceramic technology was also introduced to the region at about that time.

Horticultural villages abounded in the lower elevations of the region by A.D. 200, when maize was introduced. The Garden Creek and the Biltmore Mound sites in western North Carolina reveal elaborate mortuary ceremony and ties through trade or other alliances with Hopewell sites of Ohio and Illinois. By A.D. 900 (early Mississippian period), human population of the region had expanded considerably. Mississippian chiefdom-level societies relying on maize agriculture and benefited by the adoption of bow-and-arrow technology are manifested at large mound centers such as Etowah in northern Georgia. Moundville, located in Tuscaloosa County, Alabama, is one of the largest Mississippian ceremonial centers in the region.

Large Mississippian villages such as Coosa in northern Georgia and the Berry site in western North Carolina were visited by Spanish explorers in the early to mid-sixteenth century. The region also boasts large historic Cherokee towns such as Quannassee in Hayesville, North Carolina, and Chota-Tanasee in Monroe County, Tennessee.

Understanding of the rich Euro-American history of the Appalachian region has been deepened by archaeological research at sites such as Fort Ligonier, a French and Indian War–era site in western Pennsylvania, and Arbuckle's Fort, a Revolutionary War–era frontier fort in eastern West Virginia. Research at sites such as Harpers Ferry in eastern

West Virginia and Antietam in western Maryland has elucidated the horrors and hardships of the American Civil War.

See also: MOUNDBUILDERS; MOUNDVILLE ARCHAEOLOGICAL PARK (CULTURAL INSTITUTIONS); NATIVE AMERICANS (RACE, ETHNICITY, AND IDENTITY).

—Thomas R. Whyte, *Appalachian State University*

Jefferson Chapman, *Tellico Archaeology: Twelve Thousand Years of Native American History* (1985); Lynne P. Sullivan and Susan C. Prezzano, eds., *Archaeology of the Appalachian Highlands* (2001); H. Trawick Ward and R. P. Stephen Davis Jr., *Time Before History: The Archaeology of North Carolina* (1999).

Back-to-the-Land Movement

Originating in the 1960s, the back-to-the-land movement stresses self-sufficiency and living close to nature. Rejecting both the stresses and security of the late capitalist economy, adherents of the social movement embrace an independent lifestyle. The movement is best characterized as the resettlement of "urban émigrés" seeking to live on small plots of land in rural areas. Members of the movement attempt to live in a subsistence or semi-subsistence manner, making the majority of their living from the land in cottage industries such as cultivation of fruit and other trees, truck farming, woodworking, small-equipment operation, and providing public accommodations. Some, however, must work part-time or full-time away from their landholdings.

While the movement did not originate in Appalachia, the availability of relatively inexpensive, undeveloped land close to major East Coast cities makes the region a prime destination for these "neopioneers." This proximity of the region to urban centers has made it particularly attractive because it allows people to sample the lifestyle while maintaining residences in the city. Many eventually move permanently to small rural holdings (typically fewer than seventy acres), where they often establish communities of like-thinking families and pursue their goal of living entirely from the land.

Floyd County, Virginia, is an example of an area where several of these intentional communities are located. The county is home to the Institute for Sustainable Living, a nonprofit organization involved in research and educational programming on topics such as organic agriculture, land stewardship, and the healing arts. The institute is associated with the Abundant Dawn community, located on a ninety-acre site in the county. The philosophy of this community includes enhancement of trust, group communication, and conflict resolution.

The Abundant Dawn community includes two subgroups known as pods. Members of the Tekiah pod, founded in 1990, share incomes and make decisions in a consensus manner. Activities of the group include organic gardening, research and consulting, and the manufacture and marketing of hemp hammocks and handbags. In the Dayspring Circle pod, created in 1994, members live in separate residences and do not share incomes. The membership includes computer programmers, building and construction professionals, and health and wellness practitioners.

Though details may vary among communities, in general the movement is driven by a desire to slow down the pace of modern life, thereby becoming physically and spiritually closer to other people and the cycles of nature. Members often build their homes from scratch or occupy existing, unmodernized farmhouses, grow organic food, and in some instances homeschool their children. Back-to-the-landers most often avoid modern technology in favor of animal- or hand-powered equipment and tools.

Traditional communities generally have been receptive to the infusion of money, professional skills, and respect that the back-to-the-land movement brings to local areas, though there are occasionally clashes between native Appalachians and newly arrived homesteaders over issues such as land development.

See also: ALTERNATIVE FARMING (AGRICULTURE); SECTION OVERVIEW (FAMILY AND COMMUNITY); TWENTIETH-CENTURY IN-MIGRATION.

—Connie Ann Kirk, *Mansfield University*, and Dana L. Stuchul, *Berea College*

Batts, Thomas

(d. 1698) Explorer.

In the fall of 1671, Thomas Batts and Robert Fallam led the first British expedition to travel overland to the New River in the Appalachian region of southwest Virginia. The expedition also included Thomas Woods, Jack Nesan, and Perecute, an Appomattox Indian of eastern Virginia. Except for the loss of Woods, the expedition was considered a successful exploration of the rivers west of Virginia's Blue Ridge Mountains.

The group set out September 1, 1671, from Fort Henry (present-day Petersburg), Virginia, and traveled west. After four days, they reached a Saponi Indian town located on what is known today as the Staunton River. From there they followed a trail that roughly paralleled the river to a town called Hanohaski, where they were forced to leave Woods due to an illness that claimed his life before the group returned from their explorations. On September 9, the party arrived at a village of the Totero tribe, located near modern Salem, Virginia. They reached the New River on September 14 and followed its course for four days to a point near the modern town of Pearisburg, Virginia, marking their farthest progress on trees and claiming the land for Britain. The party returned to Fort Henry on October 1, 1671.

See also: EARLY WHITE SETTLEMENT OF SOUTHWESTERN VIRGINIA; EXPLORERS AND SURVEYORS.

—John Hairr, *Lillington, North Carolina*

Blennerhassett Archaeological Site

Well known as the site of one of the earliest cases of alleged treason in the United States, Blennerhassett Island was a center of activity for both settlers and Native Americans. Located in the middle of the Ohio River southwest of Marietta, Ohio, near present-day Parkersburg, West Virginia, the island is one of the richest archaeological sites of the Old Northwest. Native Americans inhabited the island as early as 9000 B.C.

In the 1760s, the island, then known as Belpre Island, was home to Nemacolin, a Delaware chief, but is now named for Harmon Blennerhassett (1764–1831), an immigrant Irish aristocrat who came to the New World to escape social, political, and financial problems. He and his wife settled on the island in 1798, building a fine, lavishly furnished mansion and creating a regional cultural center. The Blennerhassetts entertained local friends as well as prominent figures from the new country. One such guest was Aaron Burr, who convinced Blennerhassett to finance Burr's scheme of setting up an independent state in the Southwest. After their plot was exposed, Blennerhassett fled the island in 1806 and was later arrested. Tried and acquitted of treason, he never recovered his social standing or financial security. Blennerhassett died in 1831 in England.

The mansion survived until 1811, when it burned to the ground. Archaeologists discovered the foundation in 1973; subsequently, the mansion was rebuilt from 1984 to 1991 by the State of West Virginia to what research suggests was its original appearance.

See also: ARCHAEOLOGICAL SITES; BURR, AARON (GOVERNMENT); NORTHERN NATIVE AMERICANS.

—Jenny L. Presnell, *Miami University*

Boone, Daniel

(1734–1820) Frontiersman.

Daniel Boone is perhaps best known as the builder of the Wilderness Road, the route through the southern Appalachians that opened up Tennessee and Kentucky to settlers from North Carolina. Boone blazed other trails, established communities and forts, served as an officer in the Virginia militia during the Revolutionary War, and scouted land in hostile Indian territories for early settlers. His reputation as an independent frontiersman, fierce Indian fighter, and legendary hunter contributed much to the westward expansion of America, luring many who identified with his pioneering image to cross the Appalachians.

Born to Squire and Sarah Boone in south-central Pennsylvania, Boone moved with his family to the western frontier of North Carolina in 1751. The family's homestead in the Yadkin Valley offered Boone the opportunity to explore the mountains. A crack shot and good hunter from the age of thirteen, Boone always had contributed fresh game to the family larder, and on the North Carolina frontier his hunting trips took him increasingly farther afield.

In early 1755, Boone joined General Edward Braddock's expedition to assault Fort Duquesne, situated at the site of present-day Pittsburgh. There he barely escaped an ambush by combined French and Native American forces in which Braddock was killed. A year after he returned to North Carolina, he married Rebecca Bryan, with whom he eventually had ten children. During spring and summer months, Boone farmed his land at Holman's Ford, near present-day Boone, North Carolina, but he spent the fall and winter hunting and blazing trails.

In 1767 Boone entered Kentucky for the first time. Upon returning home, he and a friend began guiding hunting parties into Kentucky. In the summer of 1769, Boone and his party passed through the Cumberland Gap and into Kentucky, where they stayed for two years before returning to North Carolina.

Published in 1878, a drawing depicts Fort Boonesborough as it appeared around 1778. The fort, situated along the Wilderness Road and named for Daniel Boone, offered protection to settlers moving through the Cumberland Gap into eastern Kentucky.

In 1773 Boone, by then a seasoned frontiersman, organized another expedition with the goal of establishing a permanent settlement in Kentucky. The expedition was abandoned, however, when Native Americans hostile to colonization of their land killed several members, including Boone's eldest son, in an attack on the party. Boone accepted a commission in the Virginia militia not long after returning home and commanded a small post during Lord Dunmore's War against the Shawnee in 1774. The following year Boone worked with the Transylvania Company, a land-speculation concern, establishing a road through the Cumberland Gap to the present location of Boonesborough on the Kentucky River. The Wilderness Road, as the route was called, quickly became the main route to the West.

During the American Revolution, while serving as an officer in the local militia, Boone was captured by the Shawnee, allies of the British at the time. By gaining the trust of the chief, Boone was able to escape and warn Boonesborough of an impending British and Shawnee attack, giving the townspeople time to prepare a successful defense.

During his lifetime, Boone acquired large tracts of land in Kentucky, but he lost all of them due to disputed land claims. Ever the pioneer, Boone moved on to the Spanish territory of Missouri in 1799, where he spent the remainder of his life. Boone died in 1820 and was buried alongside his wife in Defiance, Missouri. In 1835 his remains, along with those of Rebecca, were removed to the Frankfort Cemetery in Frankfort, Kentucky, the capital of the state where his most famous exploits occurred.

See also: EARLY WHITE SETTLEMENT OF EASTERN KENTUCKY; EXPLORERS AND SURVEYORS; WILDERNESS ROAD.

—Brian D. McKnight, *University of Virginia at Wise*

Bowman, Joseph

(1752–1779) Frontiersman and Revolutionary War soldier.

A grandson of Jost Hite, the first settler in Virginia's Shenandoah Valley in central Appalachia, Joseph Bowman and three of his brothers served in the American Revolution. Captain Bowman was second in command to George Rogers Clark in the white conquest of the Northwest Territory. Bowman recorded events surrounding the capture of Fort Sackville in Vincennes, Indiana, in his journal, which first appeared in print November 24, 1840, in a Louisville, Kentucky, newspaper.

One of Clark's most trusted associates, Bowman was commissioned major of a battalion of volunteers in December 1778 and rendered notable service to Clark at Kaskaskia, Cahokia, and Vincennes. Bowman raised a company in Frederick County, Virginia, for an expedition to the Falls of the Ohio River, now Louisville, Kentucky. Later, he established a garrison at Cahokia, where Clark appointed him superintendent of Indian affairs. In February 1779, Bowman was severely burned by a premature explosion of cartridges, part of a thirteen-gun jubilation, in one of the batteries at Vincennes. Bowman remained on active duty until August, when he succumbed to his injuries and died in Indiana near Fort Sackville, later renamed George Rogers Clark National Historical Park.

Bowman was a principal officer in the reduction of British posts and the only one who died in service in the conquered territory. Bowman received a total of 4,312 acres in Clarks Grant (also known as the Illinois Land Grant) for services under Clark. The land was inherited by his nephew Jacob Bowman Jr.

See also: CLARK, GEORGE ROGERS; EXPLORERS AND SURVEYORS; LAND GRANTS.

—Rebecca Tolley-Stokes, *East Tennessee State University*

Bullitt, Thomas

(1730–1778) Surveyor.

Born in Prince William County, Virginia, in 1730, Thomas Bullitt is credited with leading the first surveying party into Kentucky. Bullitt also is noted for surveying Virginia while serving as an officer in the militia.

In 1756 George Washington placed Lieutenant Bullitt in command of Fort Dinwiddie (near Bacova, Virginia), where he was soon promoted to captain. For his services in the French and Indian War (1754–63), Bullitt received a grant of 3,000 acres in central Appalachia in 1764. Bullitt led settlement and development there, convincing militia members to homestead in the area, which included seven mineral springs. In 1773 Bullitt led a party of surveyors down the Ohio River and through the Kanawha Valley. The party camped on the site that is now Louisville, Kentucky, in July and August of 1773 while lots were laid out along the shore. His plat for Louisville has never been found, but it has never been disputed that some of the city's present-day streets were those he staked off that summer.

Bullitt noted a salt lick near the Salt River in central Kentucky on his surveys, and later the salt lick, stream, and county were named for him. In 1774 he was deeded 1,240 acres of land on the Great Kanawha River by the mouth of the Elk River at the site of present-day Charleston, West Virginia, also for his service during the French and Indian War. Bullitt returned home to Fauquier County, Virginia, where he died in February of 1778. Kentucky's first commercial saltworks was erected in 1779 and named for Bullitt. It was the only saltworks west of the Alleghenies during the last years of the American Revolution.

See also: EXPLORERS AND SURVEYORS; FRENCH AND INDIAN WAR (GOVERNMENT); WASHINGTON, GEORGE.

—Rebecca Tolley-Stokes, *East Tennessee State University*

Citico Archaeological Sites

Citico, a word with no meaning in the Cherokee language, is the Cherokee derivative of the Muskogean place name Satapo. It is the name used to identify two different archaeological sites in Tennessee that contain artifacts associated with Muskogean-speaking peoples of the late Mississippian cultural period (A.D. 1300–1550, known as the Dallas phase) of east Tennessee.

One Citico site is a largely destroyed mound center located in Hamilton County near Chattanooga. Salvage excavation was conducted at this site between 1957 and 1958, after which the remains of both the mound and village site fell victim to development.

The other Citico, or Settico, is located in Monroe County on the south bank of the Little Tennessee River near its confluence with Citico Creek. Settico was the location of a mound center with eight mounds. Among the items excavated at the site were Clarksdale bells, which are associated with Spanish explorers. According to documentation from Spanish explorer Juan Pardo's 1567–68 excursion into the Little Tennessee Valley, it is believed the expedition visited Citico, then known as Satapo. Pardo probably interacted with people who spoke a Muskogean tongue, though some scholars argue that he encountered the ancestors of the Cherokee. By the eighteenth century, the region fell under control of the Overhill Cherokee. Citico, or "Settacoo," according to Lieutenant Henry Timberlake's 1762 map *A Draught of the Cherokee Country,* was one of the larger Overhill Cherokee towns in the upper Tennessee River Valley.

See also: CHEROKEE (RACE, ETHNICITY, AND IDENTITY); EARLY WHITE SETTLEMENT OF EAST TENNESSEE; SOUTHERN NATIVE AMERICANS.

—John R. Burch Jr., *Campbellsville University*

Clark, George Rogers

(1752–1818) Frontier leader.

George Rogers Clark's military expeditions helped secure portions of Appalachia for white settlement. He was born in Albemarle County, Virginia, to planters John and Ann Rogers Clark. Four of his brothers served as army officers during the American Revolution. His youngest brother, William, joined Meriwether Lewis in leading the historic Lewis and Clark expedition to the Pacific Ocean.

Clark learned surveying and explored along the Ohio River. In his first military experience, he served as a captain in Lord Dunmore's War in 1774 against Native Americans in Ohio, after which he surveyed for the Ohio Company along the Kentucky River.

During the Revolutionary War, Clark saw the importance of protecting Virginia's settlements in Kentucky and preventing British and Native American attacks from the west. He persuaded the Virginia legislature to recognize Kentucky as a county and acquired gunpowder for protecting the settlements. Commissioned a major in the militia, he secured Governor Patrick Henry's permission to defend the western regions and was promoted to lieutenant colonel.

Working with limited forces and equipment, Clark used surprise as his chief strategy in capturing Kaskaskia, Cahokia, and Vincennes. His greatest achievement involved leading a small force on an exceptionally rigorous winter march to recapture Vincennes. After achieving the rank of brigadier general, he led a final successful expedition against the Shawnee.

Although not intended for publication, Clark's writings were published some years later. His *Memoir* and his lengthy letter to George Mason include vivid descriptions of his campaigns.

See also: BOWMAN, JOSEPH; NORTHERN NATIVE AMERICANS.

—Marie Garrett, *University of Tennessee*

Coal Settlements

The rapid late-nineteenth-century industrialization of the United States required dramatically increased amounts of fuel for the steam-powered engines driving both manufacturing and transportation. As early as the 1880s, industrialists began developing unmined coal deposits in Appalachia, from western Pennsylvania through the mountains down into the Birmingham, Alabama, area. Eager to attract labor to the often remote mine locations, these developers designed and built entire settlements. Beginning as rough frontier towns, many evolved into small urban centers featuring schools, medical and police services, decent housing, and plumbing, which rural farm communities often lacked. These towns, and the employment they offered, were very attractive to people unable to make even a subsistence living from the land. In addition to attracting a cheap labor force, mining companies used their complete ownership of coal towns to help keep production costs low.

Mining companies practiced what they called "contentment sociology," the belief that relatively good living and working conditions would attract and keep hardworking and skilled labor. However, they often combined this strategy with manipulative practices such as paying workers in scrip (redeemable only at the company store at inflated prices) rather than cash. Further solidifying their control of workers were threats of blacklisting, which prevented miners from working other mines in the area, and eviction of entire families of troublemakers from company-owned lands. Miners were not ignorant of the trade-offs of the system. While their freedom was hampered, they benefited from the paternalistic attitudes of the companies, which sought at least to provide basic needs.

No. 11 Mine, New River and Pocahontas Consolidated Coal Company, Capels, West Virginia, c. 1935. Workers and their families often lived in close proximity to the mine operations around which their communities and lives revolved.

A significant number of black and immigrant miners lived and worked in coal towns, though usually in racially segregated neighborhoods. Aside from mining, there was no other work for men, and families lived on very little income. Gardens and small livestock such as chickens and pigs provided supplemental food. Some miners hunted the nearby forests for meat or furs to use or sell for additional income.

Community culture revolved around the company store, where managers and workers shopped and exchanged news. Life in and near the mines was harsh, yet there was time for leisure and recreation. Women created craft items for the home, children played simple games, and men played sports such as baseball or immigrant games such as bocce (similar to lawn bowling). McIntyre, Pennsylvania, like many other mining towns, featured a dance hall, movie theater, and even tennis courts.

The 1930s saw a decline in both living and working conditions in the settlements. During the subsequent decades, unionization made gains for worker safety while mine mechanization brought unemployment. In the 1940s and 1950s, the automobile not only further depressed the coal market but also gave the miner mobility, and he no longer required a central community. By the end of the 1950s, coal settlements were virtually extinct. Some company coal towns, such as Elkhorn, West Virginia, continued to thrive, but most have long since disappeared.

See also: COAL-CAMP ARCHITECTURE (ARCHITECTURE); COAL COMPANY SCHOOLS (EDUCATION); SPECULATORS AND ABSENTEE LANDLORDS.

—Jenny L. Presnell, *Miami University*

Ronald D Eller, *Miners, Millhands, and Mountaineers: Industrialization of the Appalachian South, 1880–1930* (1982); Bill Peterson, *Coal Town Revisited* (1972).

Copper Mining Settlements

Spanish and British exploration for mineral ores, including copper, began in the southern Appalachians before the 1700s. By the 1840s, most copper used in the United States came from Appalachian counties. The richest and purest copper reserve lay in the Ducktown Basin (also known as Ducktown District, Copper Basin), a hundred-square-mile geologic feature located mainly in mountainous southeastern Polk County, Tennessee, and adjacent portions of North Carolina and Georgia. For nearly 150 years, from 1843 to 1987, the Ducktown Basin was the site of the largest metal-mining operation in the southeastern United States.

Deep mining and smelting were in place in the Ducktown Basin by 1855, with about one thousand people employed in the local copper industry by 1860. In the twentieth century, as many as twenty-five hundred people were employed in the mines or aboveground in various processing or chemical by-product plants. By the time the local mines closed in 1987, the Ducktown Basin copper deposits had yielded more than 90 million tons of ore, much of it exported to Europe.

Originally, each mining company had a small, self-maintained settlement for miners near its active mines (fourteen in the first decade). Three communities, Isabella, Ducktown, and Copperhill, came to dominate local society and business beginning in the 1890s. The community of Isabella, which was never incorporated, no longer exists, though a small number of people still lived in the area at the end of the twentieth century.

Owners and investors in New England and Great Britain controlled most mining companies, and their managers were usually drawn from these places or from Great Lakes copper mines. Some managers were recruited from Sweden and, only much later, locally. In the 1850s, local white men and seasoned Welsh and Cornish miners recovered the ore. Day laborers in the smelters and related timber and charcoal industries were white men and boys from surrounding counties, aided in the first decades by a number of white girls and a few Cherokee men, women, and children. Around 1900, following national labor and immigration trends, Mediterranean and central European men were recruited from East Coast immigration ports and abroad. These miners, as well as temporarily imported African American railroad laborers (both usually unaccompanied by families), lived in segregated camps or settlements, separated from each other and from white miners, their families, and other area residents.

Everything in the social world and lifestyles of Ducktown Basin communities, from the mundane to the highly significant, was heavily influenced by the copper industry. Town or settlement locations and layouts, house type and placement on the barren hillsides, the company store where one shopped, children's playmates, club memberships, and church affiliation all reflected the particular company for which a man worked, his job in a company's hierarchy, and the loyalties owed by the man and his family. The legacy of company loyalties remains strong in the memories of many Ducktown Basin residents, who recall comparatively high wages and job security, punctuated by a few major downturns in national and international markets and labor disputes.

Recovery and exportation of the Ducktown Basin copper reserves came at a high cost to the environment. Before 1900, processing of copper ore led to the stripping of forests for fuel, air thickly clouded with sulfur dioxide fumes, and more than forty-eight thousand acres degraded through erosion and run-off. Reclamation efforts begun in 1930 yielded results decades later, as only about one thousand acres were still denuded in 2000. After the copper mines closed in 1987, residents, proud of their own or their ancestors' association with the industry, acquired some buildings, machinery, artifacts, and archives from the last mining company and established a museum on-site. Preserved nearby as testimony to the industrial landscape that was home to a major regional employer of generations of Ducktown Basin inhabitants are a barren, eroded cliff face and watery pit these residents call their "beloved scar."

See also: COPPER AND LEAD (BUSINESS, INDUSTRY, AND TECHNOLOGY); METALLIC ORE DEPOSITS (GEOLOGY).

—Betty J. Duggan, *Peabody Museum of Archaeology and Ethnology, Harvard University*

R. E. Barclay, *Ducktown Back in Raht's Time* (1946); Betty J. Duggan, *Being Cherokee in a White World: The Ethnic Persistence of a Post-Removal American Indian Enclave* (1998) and *From Furs to Factories: The Industrial Revolution in the Tennessee Overhill* (1997).

Crockett, David

(1786–1836) Frontiersman and folk hero.

Born on August 17, 1786, in Greene County, Tennessee, the son of John and Rebecca Hawkins Crockett, David Crockett was emblematic of the backwoodsman and the migration to the West. His exploits, both real and invented, established the Old Southwest, as southern and central Appalachia was known at the time, as fundamental to the idea of the American frontier. Crockett eventually lived in all three grand divisions of the state of Tennessee and became the best known of those who made the journey farther west to Texas.

By 1818, Crockett had been elected a lieutenant in the Thirty-second Militia and had served as a justice of the peace, town commissioner of Lawrenceburg, Tennessee, and colonel of the Fifty-seventh Militia Regiment of Lawrence County. However, he still was a relatively unknown backwoods hunter with a talent for storytelling until his election to the Tennessee legislature in 1821 and to the U.S. House of Representatives in 1827. Reelected in 1829, he split with President Andrew Jackson on land reform issues and was one of the strongest opponents to Jackson's Indian Removal Act, which led to the forced migration known as the Trail of Tears. Crockett was defeated in 1831 when he openly and vehemently opposed Jackson's popular policies on these issues, but he was reelected in 1833.

Crockett's image had a life of its own. In 1831 he became the model for Nimrod Wildfire, the backwoods hero of James Kirke Paulding's play *The Lion of the West.* Crockett said he had to publish his autobiography, *A Narrative of the Life of David Crockett of the State of Tennessee* (1834), written with the help of Thomas Chilton, to counteract outlandish stories printed in 1833. These accounts, published under Crockett's name as the *Sketches and Eccentricities of Colonel David Crockett of West Tennessee,* helped to initiate the literary genre now known as Old Southwestern humor. The more outrageous stories were expanded by anonymous eastern writers who spun out tall tales for the Crockett Almanacs (1835–56). In their hands, the fictional Davy became a backwoods screamer. Despite the death of the historical David at the Alamo in 1836, the mythical Davy continued in such exploits as saving the world by unfreezing the sun and the earth from their axes, riding his pet alligator up Niagara Falls, and wringing the tail off Halley's Comet.

Three works published under Crockett's name, together with his heroic last stand at the Alamo, completed the union of history and legend. *An Account of Col. Crockett's Tour to the North and Down East* (1835) and *The Life of Martin Van Buren* (1835) were overtly political, and *Col. Crockett's Exploits and Adventures in Texas* (1836) came out after his death. From his 1831 characterization as Nimrod Wildfire to the play *Davy Crockett; or, Be Sure You're Right Then Go Ahead* (1872–96), the heritage of Davy as the hero of romantic melodrama was passed on through a series of films. This was the Davy played by Fess Parker during the Crockett craze of the mid-1950s, by John Wayne in the movie *The Alamo* (1960), and found in the 1990s fiction of Cameron Judd and David Thompson. All build upon Crockett's Appalachian heritage to ensure that he remains both a hero and a preeminent representative of freedom and frontier individualism in the American mind.

See also: CROCKETT, DAVID (HUMOR); CROCKETT ALMANACS (MEDIA).

—Michael A. Lofaro, *University of Tennessee*

Michael A. Lofaro and Joe Cummings, eds., *Crockett at Two Hundred: New Perspectives on the Man and the Myth* (1989); James A. Shackford, *David Crockett: The Man and the Legend* (1956; revised 1986).

Croghan, George

(c. 1720–1782) Indian agent.

George Croghan's ventures as a trader and the most prominent Indian agent of the mid-eighteenth century helped open the land west of the Alleghenies for English settlement. Croghan played a major role in negotiating agreements between the British and the Indians, and his journals and correspondence help document America's pre-Revolution history. Born in Ireland, he settled near Carlisle, Pennsylvania, around 1741. Little is known about his early life.

In the late 1740s, Croghan established a series of trading posts in the upper Ohio Valley. As the "King of Traders," he became well versed in Indian languages and customs. After the advent of the French and Indian War ruined his trade, he became a scout for General Edward Braddock. In 1756 Sir William Johnson appointed him deputy superintendent of Indian affairs. He helped the British capture Fort Duquesne and then made the renamed Fort Pitt his headquarters.

In the 1760s, Croghan sought to occupy what the French called Illinois. Indians took him prisoner but soon released him. Not long thereafter, he negotiated peace with Pontiac, the Ottawa chief who organized a rebellion against western British outposts. In 1766 Croghan embarked on his most famous mission, the Grand Illinois Venture, then the largest western trade expedition. In 1768 he helped broker the first Treaty of Fort Stanwix, which restricted white settlement in the Appalachians. He resigned from the Indian Department in 1772, sold his vast land acquisitions, and moved to the area surrounding Fort Pitt in Pennsylvania (which became the city of Pittsburgh in 1816). There he engaged primarily in land speculation, taking part in the Indiana, Illinois, and Grand Ohio Companies until the American Revolution ended these ventures.

See also: OUTFITTERS, SUPPLIERS, TAVERNS, AND INNS; SPECULATORS AND ABSENTEE LANDLORDS; TREATIES OF FORT STANWIX.

—Marie Garrett, *University of Tennessee*

Cumberland Road

See National Road

de Soto, Hernando

(c. 1497–1542) Spanish conquistador and explorer.

Hernando de Soto gained wealth participating in the conquests of Panama, Nicaragua, and Peru between 1514 and 1535. Seeking fame, he obtained a contract to explore the southeastern portion of North America, including the southern Appalachian Mountains, which were rumored to contain gems and precious metals. De Soto built an army of approximately six hundred men and 240 horses for his expedition and sailed from Cuba for Florida in 1539.

While the specifics of de Soto's route are disputed, there is agreement on its general track. After landing in May 1539 at Tampa Bay, he marched his troops into present-day north-central Florida and wintered among the Apalachee. During 1540, they passed through present-day Georgia and South Carolina before beginning the Appalachian leg of their journey, which included the western portion of North Carolina, east Tennessee, northern Georgia, and Alabama. After wintering in the town of Chicaza in Mississippi, de Soto crossed the Mississippi River and spent most of 1541 exploring Arkansas. In May 1542, de Soto died of a fever. The expedition's survivors reached Mexico by boat in 1543.

De Soto's expedition marked the first European exploration of the Southeast, and written accounts from it give valuable information about Native American culture during that period. The expedition's success was achieved in part through harsh treatment and enslavement of native peoples and the use of superior military weaponry, horses, and dogs to brutalize them and instill fear. De Soto and his men brought European diseases that decimated the chiefdoms he encountered and ultimately depopulated much of the region he explored.

See also: ETOWAH MOUNDS ARCHAEOLOGICAL SITE; SOUTHERN NATIVE AMERICANS; WHITE CONQUEST.

—John R. Burch Jr., *Campbellsville University*

Early Historians

Appalachia's early historical writing focused on its role as America's "First West." This frontier concept of geographical remoteness and cultural uniqueness underpinned much of the later study of the region. Appalachia's historical consciousness, ignited by the accounts of early travelers, was promoted and dominated until late in the nineteenth century by antiquarian collectors and historians.

Explorer John Lederer, trader James Adair, soldier Henry Timberlake, naturalist Andre Michaux, Methodist bishop and circuit rider Francis Asbury, land speculator John Filson, traveler Francis Baily, and others like them gave the public some of the earliest accounts of the natural features and native cultures found in the region. These writers established many of the later conceptions and misconceptions held about Appalachia. Filson's *The Discovery, Settlement, and Present State of Kentucke* (1784) provided the facts about Daniel Boone from which later writers such as James Fenimore Cooper and Lord Byron devised the mythic image of the American frontier hero. Adair's *History of the American Indians* (1775) captured the unrecorded story of Appalachia's Native Americans even as others laid claim to their unrecorded lands. These early accounts often inspired others to explore in person, or in words, this new frontier. While most books of this type were contemporary with the times, occasional historical accounts were included in such works as Thomas Jefferson's *Notes on the State of Virginia* (1787).

Documenting the movement of America westward into Appalachia began even as events unfolded. In 1780 William Tatham and John Todd wrote what is likely the first history of the trans-Appalachian frontier in a now lost manuscript. Inspired by the patriotic and tradition-loving spirit permeating the early American republic, antiquarians and amateur historians soon began collecting historical materials and writing accounts of the region's history. These early historians were often doctors, lawyers, or ministers and included Humphrey Marshall, Mann Butler, and Lewis Collins of Kentucky; John Haywood, J. G. M. Ramsey, and Albigence W. Putnam of Tennessee; Ben Grosscup and Wilbur Zeigler of North Carolina; Joseph Doddridge, Alexander Scott Withers, Wills De Hass, and Noah Zane of West Virginia; Massachusetts native Timothy Flint; and Virginia's Samuel Kercheval.

Typically, these early historians had no formal training in historical scholarship. Such gentlemen historians were the norm in American letters prior to the early twentieth century. Their emphasis was on gathering facts, not on interpreting them. In an era dominated by oral rather than written documentation, the region boasted little in the way of printing presses, libraries, archives, museums, historical societies, or other means of preserving historical documents and information. Being nearer the people and events of which they wrote, these early historians were concerned with preserving information about frontier settlement that would otherwise be lost. Their published works were essential in saving the region's recorded history and remain their most important contribution to Appalachia.

Such historians were engaged in gathering accounts from available sources rather than examining in a critical and reflective way the individuals and events that were their subjects. Generally, their writings were narratives rather than interpretive histories. The actions of prominent political, military, and business figures who left written records or verbal accounts were emphasized over the efforts of the anonymous common man, who often did not record events. This focus is also partly explained by the influence of the romantic emphasis on the heroic "great man" over the common and ordinary one.

To an extent, ordinary life was ignored by antiquarians, who found it too familiar for detailed explanation. Therefore, the social, cultural, ethnic, and economic aspects of historical study that became prominent with later historians went largely unrecorded by these early predecessors, who espoused no general philosophy of history but rather displayed a respect for the past and a veneration of their pioneering forefathers.

Historians later in the nineteenth century used these early histories as a basis for their own studies, which sought to popularize the Appalachian frontier for a mass audience. Works such as Charles McKnight's *Our Western Border* (1876) and Theodore Roosevelt's *The Winning of the West* (1889) treated the region's early history with the same seriousness and epic scope that historians such as Francis Parkman had done with America's colonial frontier. Roosevelt's multi-volume study particularly served as a bridge between early efforts of antiquarian historians and the later analytical work of modern historians. Though they produced little historical writing themselves, John D. Shane, Lyman C. Draper, and Reuben T. Durrett, among others, supplemented the works of the early historians and stimulated the work of later ones. This was accomplished by gathering important manuscript collections that served as source material for the study of the early frontier period in Appalachia and the trans-Appalachian West.

One of the first important historians to make significant use of these primary materials was Frederick Jackson Turner. Near the end of the nineteenth century, his analysis of American sectionalism and its "frontier thesis" treated the frontier not merely as a place but also a social process by which the American character was formed. Turner's work gave an intellectual depth and context to all that had gone before. It provided Appalachia's history a national scope and initiated the modern era of historical scholarship about the region and the other "Wests" that were once, but no longer, the frontier. This emphasis on the social and cultural aspects of history would lead to a rewriting of both national and regional history, including that of Appalachia.

See also: HISTORICAL SOCIETIES (CULTURAL INSTITUTIONS); TRAVEL WRITING (LITERATURE).

—Ned L. Irwin, *East Tennessee State University*

Ray Allen Billington, *The Genesis of the Frontier Thesis: A Study in Historical Creativity* (1971); George H. Callcott, *History in the United States, 1800–1860: Its Practice and Purpose* (1970); Ned L. Irwin, "Collecting Memory: Antiquarians and the Preservation of the Early History of the Trans-Appalachian Frontier," *Journal of East Tennessee History* (2000).

Early Settlement Shelters and Forts

Settlement structures in eastern North America included a wide range of functional types and designs, with variations occurring due to local conditions, ethnic influences, and natural resources. As early settlers moved inland, they sheltered in tents and under wagons and occasionally used ledges, caves, and canebrakes. Numerous travel accounts of settlers, who often encamped with no more protection than a blanket and fire, reveal a common lack of preparation for harsh conditions. Some modern Appalachian cities began as frontier forts. Most notable of these is Pittsburgh, which began as an English trader's outpost and was built into Fort Duquesne by the French, renamed Fort Pitt by the English after the French and Indian War, and inherited by the Americans who flocked to the area in the early 1800s.

At destination, primary shelters included brush arbors and pole and canvas and bark- or hide-roofed lean-tos. Such structures were soon followed by hewn-log structures that sometimes sheltered both people and animals. In a week of hard work, two able men could construct a single-pen log house with space for animals below and sleeping loft above. When more substantial cabins could be built for the settlers' homes, the original primitive settlement structures became animal shelters. Frame construction using sawed timber generally denotes a post-pioneer phase of settlement, though early settlers sometimes fashioned planking from flatboats used in trans-Appalachian river journeys. Clues to the ethnicity of early settlers were left in the corner notching, floor plan, door and chimney placement, materials, and roof pitch used in cabin construction. Construction techniques are often as revealing as religion, dress, or language as indicators of ethnic influence.

Protective structures ranged from quickly prepared trenches and earthworks to the tactical use of terrain: swamps, river ledges, cliffs, and the frequently mentioned declivity (ravine or ditch) and eminence (hill or rise). Thickets and canebrakes served scouts and troops in small actions. Permanent fortifications ranged from single-tier star-shaped forts of elaborate geometric design constructed to defeat conventional frontal assaults to enormous multi-tier strategic forts consisting of several lines of defense covering hundreds of acres. Some fortifications consisted of large earthworks at strategic locations reinforced with masonry or stone, but most inland fortifications, such as at Fort Loudon and the Tellico Blockhouse, both in present-day Tennessee, typically utilized earthworks and timber. Large fortifications served obvious geopolitical military purposes, but they functioned also in the fur-trade system and provided support and refuge for settlers and merchants. Of particular significance in Appalachian settlement was the convergence of domestic and military construction in the palisaded small fort. This type of defensive structure consisted of log houses anchoring four corners of a rectangular site with the intervals between the corners closed by a strong palisade of partly buried logs and timbers. A variation of this design anchored the corners with cantilevered blockhouses or warehouses. At some distance from the fortification, earthworks and vegetative defenses—the limbs and branches of trees used in the palisade—were sometimes created. Some forts utilized thorny or densely growing plants such as greenbrier and honey locust for additional barriers. Fortified houses in the early settlement period often were built by men of military background and were frequently called "stations." Martin's Station, for instance, was located along the Wilderness Road near the border of Kentucky and Virginia.

See also: BOONE, DANIEL; EXPLORERS AND SURVEYORS; FRENCH AND INDIAN WAR (GOVERNMENT).

—Gerald L. Smith, *University of the South*

Jeremy Black, *War and the World: Military Power and the Fate of Continents, 1450–2000* (1998); Terry G. Jordan, *American Log Buildings: An Old World Heritage* (1985); Dell Upton and John Michal Vlach, eds., *Common Places: Readings in American Vernacular Architecture* (1986).

Early Westward Migration

Beginning in the 1730s and continuing until the American Revolution, thousands of families migrated from eastern Pennsylvania, New Jersey, and the Chesapeake area to the Piedmont and mountain regions of Virginia and North Carolina. Later in the century, this migration continued into eastern Tennessee and Kentucky. The migration to these areas comprised the first leg of the greater westward movement that continued throughout the nineteenth century.

When families embarked on the journey to their new homes, they had to find their way with only vague directions to a place they had never been. Only families with ample resources could send someone in advance to arrange for the family's settlement.

Of the roads to the west, the most prominent was the wagon road from Philadelphia, often called the Great Valley

Road or the Great Wagon Road. Following the course of the Great Valley, which had long provided a natural avenue for Native Americans traveling roughly northeast to southwest through the mountains, the road was actually a network of trails and paths from the Schuylkill River across southern Pennsylvania to Lancaster, where it hooked south through Maryland and western Virginia. Branching off from the primary paths of the Great Valley Road were several roads built into far western Maryland, Pennsylvania, and present-day West Virginia during the French and Indian War (1754–63). By the late eighteenth century, the road had spokes extending into upcountry South Carolina and west toward Tennessee. These roads were often poorly maintained and confusing, making travel complicated even during the mild-weather months of the year.

Finding suitable lodging and sustenance were the most difficult challenges migrant families faced on their journey. When a family or group of families had sufficient resources, they took advantage of ordinaries or taverns, which offered accommodations and some sort of food or drink. The quality of ordinaries throughout Pennsylvania, Maryland, Virginia, and North Carolina, especially in the backcountry and Appalachian frontier regions, was inconsistent. While some colonial travelers noted good conditions at establishments on primary roads, most remembered cramped sleeping arrangements, flea-infested bedding, and mediocre food and drink. In areas where ordinaries were sparse, frontier settlers often sought lodging in private homes. Numerous writers of travel accounts mention staying with total strangers. Some readily accepted guests, while others provided shelter only grudgingly. Migrants also purchased provender for their horses and any other livestock that they brought along on the journey.

For settlers who could not afford lodging at an ordinary or in a private home, the only remaining option was to camp out by the roadside, even though sleeping in the woods could be uncomfortable and dangerous. While travelers throughout the colonies resorted to this form of lodging from time to time, settlers in the sparsely settled areas of Appalachia camped out on a regular basis. Families often used their wagons, covered by canvas tarps or even branches from trees, as a shelter.

In some cases, individuals migrated to the mountain backcountry on their own, but for the most part the migration experience was a family undertaking. Evidence from marriage and land records suggests that multigeneration families consisting of infants and children as well as aging grandparents routinely made the overland trek. Additionally, it was common for several families to migrate in groups for security and to preserve a semblance of community both on the journey and on the frontier. Once at their destinations, they often took up land adjacent to or near the claims of other family members or friends from their former communities. These same traveling communities often remained together on subsequent moves farther west.

For many families, migration to the Piedmont and Appalachian regions signified only a partial detachment from friends or family who remained behind. Because travel between the frontier and the eastern regions was frequent, some frontier families sent news to their relatives on a regular basis. In letters home, western settlers asked relatives to send specific items, reported on the health of the family, and often encouraged those who had stayed behind to follow their route and settle on western lands.

See also: EXPLORERS AND SURVEYORS; GREAT VALLEY ROAD; OUTFITTERS, SUPPLIERS, TAVERNS, AND INNS.

—Creston Long, *Salisbury University*

David Hackett Fischer and James C. Kelly, *Away I'm Bound Away: Virginia and the Westward Movement* (2000); Robert D. Mitchell, *Commercialism and Frontier: Perspectives on the Early Shenandoah Valley* (1977); Robert W. Ramsey, *Carolina Cradle: Settlement on the Northwest Carolina Frontier, 1747–1762* (1964).

Early White Settlement of Eastern Kentucky

White settlement of present-day eastern Kentucky began in the 1760s with the arrival of long hunters. Sixty years later, a traveler from one of the early settlements would not have recognized the new society that had supplanted its predecessor.

It was only after the end of the French and Indian War in 1763, when the Ohio Valley became relatively secure, that the first whites arrived from the thirteen colonies. Though forbidden to do so by the British Crown, they traversed the Cumberland Gap from Virginia through the mountains to settle in Indian Territory. A mixed society existed in the early years of settlement. Young white male hunters and Indian tribes shared many cultural and social patterns and lived together in spite of their differences. In the 1770s, speculators arrived. Daniel Boone, one of the most famous Kentucky long hunters, worked for the Transylvania Company of Richard Henderson and founded Boonesborough in 1775. Soon after, other small towns appeared: Lexington in 1779 and Limestone (present-day Maysville) in 1784.

After independence was declared in the colonies, a new period began for the territory. American homesteaders, their families, and planters arrived. The population grew quickly, and the gender ratio became more even. The previous tolerance between whites and Indians in the territory deteriorated into years of bloody struggles. As the Native American population steadily declined, the planter society flourished. From the Virginia Piedmont migrants brought social order, aristocratic values, and black slaves. Many crossed the gaps and settled in the western part of the territory, but hunters either stayed in the eastern part, where the mountains became their last refuge, or traveled farther west, searching for new unoccupied lands. When Kentucky became a state in 1792, the state constitution supported slavery, and an 1808 law forbade free black settlement. By 1820, slaves represented one-third of Kentucky's population, though they were located almost exclusively in the western parts of the state. Eastern Kentucky, whose identity lay in its mountains, hunters' traditions, and pioneers' memories, became a marginalized part of the state with little political influence.

The period of pioneer settlement in Kentucky was actually very short. In spite of its brevity, this period was one of the most important in American history. Some historians consider it the paradigm for later western development. What occurred in the early years of Kentucky settlement became the pattern for the new frontier of the West in the nineteenth century.

See also: BOONE, DANIEL; LONG HUNTERS; SLAVERY (RACE, ETHNICITY, AND IDENTITY).

—Tangi Villerbu, *Lycée Emile Littré, Avranches,* and *Centre d'études nord-américains, École des hautes études en sciences socials, Paris, France*

Stephen Aron, *How the West Was Lost: The Transformation of Kentucky from Daniel Boone to Henry Clay* (1996); John Mack Faragher, *Daniel Boone: The Life and Legend of an American Pioneer* (1992).

Early White Settlement of East Tennessee

Although the Proclamation of 1763 prohibited European settlement west of the Appalachian Mountains and designated the transmontane region as a reservation for Native Americans, settlement of western Virginia continued, and by the end of the decade settlers had moved into present-day Tennessee.

The first permanent settlements in the Tennessee country were located west of the Proclamation Line in the valleys of the Holston, Watauga, and Nolichucky Rivers. The Treaty of Lochaber (1770), which established a boundary between the colony of Virginia and the Cherokee Nation, legitimized the settlement located between the South Fork of the Holston River and the present Tennessee-Virginia boundary. That area fell under the administration of the Virginia counties of Botetourt (formed 1769), Fincastle (formed 1772), and Washington (formed 1776), respectively, before a survey of the Virginia–North Carolina boundary in 1779 revealed that the settlement was actually located in North Carolina. Thus, the settlers were living on land rightfully claimed by the Cherokee Nation.

Realizing that they were outside the effective jurisdiction of either Virginia or North Carolina, the Watauga settlers in 1772 organized the Watauga Association to provide de facto local government and leased a tract of land for ten years from the Cherokees. Jacob Brown, who lived on the Nolichucky River, also leased a tract along that river from the Cherokees. In March 1775, when the Transylvania Company purchased a large tract in Kentucky and Tennessee from the Cherokees, the Wataugans and Brown (illegally) purchased their leased lands from the Cherokee.

After the beginning of the American Revolution, the settlers living in the vicinity of Long Island of the Holston River (present-day Kingsport, Tennessee) and those living in Carter's Valley (west of the main Holston River) organized the Pendleton District. In early 1776, these settlers petitioned the Virginia convention for formal recognition. The Watauga settlers likewise formed the Washington District; they petitioned the North Carolina Provincial Council for formal recognition in July 1776.

The Overhill Cherokees, who lived in present-day lower east Tennessee, attacked the settlements in July 1776. One group besieged a fort on the Watauga River while another moved up Carter's Valley. After a third group was defeated in a battle with settlers near Long Island, the Cherokees abandoned their attacks. In October, troops from Virginia and North Carolina invaded the Overhill Towns. The Cherokees agreed to observe a preliminary truce and to meet with commissioners the next year at Long Island. In July 1777, at Fort Patrick Henry, near Long Island, the Overhill Cherokees ceded territory in present-day northeast Tennessee to Virginia and North Carolina.

North Carolina formally recognized the Washington District in late 1776, and the next year the North Carolina General Assembly created Washington County, the first county in the Tennessee country, and later established Sullivan County (1779) and Greene County (1783) in present-day northeast Tennessee.

See also: CHEROKEE (RACE, ETHNICITY, AND IDENTITY); SEVIER, JOHN; STATE OF FRANKLIN (GOVERNMENT).

—Ed Speer, *Elizabethton, Tennessee*

Early White Settlement of Northeastern Mississippi

The first white settlers moved into the Appalachian region of northeastern Mississippi in the late 1820s and early 1830s in anticipation of land cessions by the Choctaw and Chickasaw. Before the 1830 Choctaw Treaty of Dancing Rabbit Creek and the 1832 Chickasaw Treaty of Pontotoc, most white settlers in the area were traders and land speculators. As soon as the Native Americans began moving west, settlers poured into northeastern Mississippi, primarily by way of two old Indian trails. One began in Georgia and continued through Alabama south of the Tennessee River into Mississippi; the other started near the border of Virginia and

Tennessee and followed rivers through Tennessee and down into Mississippi. Both of these trails were small footpaths along most of their lengths.

Except for small areas cleared by the Chickasaw, northeastern Mississippi in the 1830s was mostly covered in timber, and rivers such as the Tombigbee, Tallahatchie, and Yocona had many unnavigable stretches. Though the rivers offered advantages for town and mill sites, their banks were choked with wild peas and canebrakes; moreover, there were few roads, bridges, or ferries to provide access. These circumstances combined to keep the area an isolated frontier until the end of the Civil War and the coming of railroads.

Despite these obstacles, immigration gradually increased with the formation of counties in 1836. Early settlements established rudimentary governments, usually consisting of a five-member Board of Police that regulated inns and taverns and assigned workdays for roads in the community. Churches and schools were among the first buildings constructed in new towns. Most early settlers were Anglo-Saxon Protestants, and the 1840 census shows that Methodists were the largest group, followed by Presbyterians and Baptists. Each of these groups usually constructed a church upon arrival. By 1840, most towns in the region had at least one schoolhouse as well. The town of Salem, founded in 1837, boasted two schools—one for boys and one for girls—and College Hill established a small college within five years of its incorporation as a town. Most incorporated towns in northeastern Mississippi supported a local newspaper by 1840.

Early work by land speculators and settlers provided relatively quick development of northeastern Mississippi. Settlers created societies in the hills of Mississippi based upon the lives they left behind, including the introduction of slavery into the area. But since land in northeast Mississippi is hilly and suitable only for small, subsistence-type farms, the slave population in the area remained lower than in the rest of the state.

See also: NATCHEZ TRACE; SOUTHERN NATIVE AMERICANS.

—Melanie N. Gilpin, *University of Georgia*

William Hamilton, *Holly Springs, Mississippi, to the Year 1878* (1984); Robert Lowry, *A History of Mississippi* (1978); Forrest Reed, *Itawamba: A History* (1966).

Early White Settlement of Northern Alabama

In northern Alabama, the southern extremities of the Appalachian Mountains were witness to efforts by the French, British, and the fledgling United States governments first to win over powerful Native American tribes such as the Creek and Cherokee and later to remove them to make way for white settlers.

By the latter half of the seventeenth century, the Indian population of present-day Alabama was well acquainted with Europeans. In 1682 the French began to extend their presence from Canada to the Gulf of Mexico, and British traders reached the Alabama region from South Carolina sometime before 1690. In 1702 the French established Mobile, a fortified trading outpost, on the Gulf Coast and later extended their trading influence northward with the construction of Fort Toulouse in 1717 at the forks of the Coosa and Tallapoosa Rivers.

The rivalry between British and French traders for the lucrative Indian trade continued until British victory over the French in 1763 at the end of the French and Indian War. As compensation for their support of the British, the Creeks and Cherokees demanded an end to the encroachment of white settlers onto their lands. When the British issued the Proclamation of 1763 prohibiting settlement west of the Appalachian Mountains, all of northern Alabama became restricted land, causing great resentment among the colonists.

During the American Revolution, the Creek and Cherokee continued their alliance with the British against the colonists. Nevertheless, the region became part of the United States after the American victory, and white settlers pushed south and west from Georgia, Virginia, Tennessee, and the Carolinas. Many of them were Scots-Irish settlers from the mountainous regions of those states. The U.S. government built the Federal Road after the Louisiana Purchase in 1803 with the purpose of connecting the new territory with the national capital at Washington, D.C. It ran through Creek territory from Milledgeville, Georgia, to Fort Stoddert, north of Mobile.

The new road and the availability of cheap land caused thousands of settlers to move west. Cotton agriculture expanded quickly, with planters taking advantage of the fertile land and ease of transportation provided by several navigable rivers, including the Tennessee River in the north. In this area, the largest new settlement formed around Huntsville, founded in 1805 by John Hunt, who migrated from Virginia with his family in search of cheap land. The growing number of white settlers, however, caused increasing conflict with the Creeks, the largest and most powerful group native to the region.

Until the War of 1812, most of northern Alabama remained Indian Territory. With the outbreak of hostilities between British and American forces, the Creeks struck at the American colonists in Alabama, attacking Fort Mims, an outpost located north of Mobile, in 1813. In response, General Andrew Jackson assembled a contingent of Tennessee militia and "friendly" Indians and marched south from Huntsville. Jackson's force crushed Creek resistance, fighting the decisive battle at Horseshoe Bend on the Tallapoosa

River on March 27, 1814, and compelling the Creek to sign the Treaty of Fort Jackson, which ceded two-thirds of their land, including most of Alabama, to the United States.

The defeat of the Creeks opened the way for unimpeded white settlement in Alabama, and by 1819 the population had grown sufficiently to petition Congress for admission into the Union as the twenty-second state. The early years of the state's history were marked by regional tensions between the northern and southern regions. While the economic focus of southern Alabama centered on Mobile due to the easy transportation provided by the Tombigbee and Alabama Rivers, the northern region used the Tennessee River to transport its crops to New Orleans, thereby causing an inherent rivalry between the two regions.

See also: GOLD SETTLEMENTS; IRON AND STEEL INDUSTRY (BUSINESS, INDUSTRY, AND TECHNOLOGY); TRAIL OF TEARS.

—Timothy P. Grady, *College of William and Mary*

Kathryn E. Holland Braund, *Deerskins and Duffels: The Creek Indian Trade with Anglo-America, 1685–1815* (1993); Richard B. Drake, *A History of Appalachia* (2001); Virginia Van der Veer Hamilton, *Alabama: A Bicentennial History* (1977).

Early White Settlement of Northern Georgia

Much of the history of settlement in the Appalachian region of northern Georgia reflects the intertwining interests of the English and Native Americans. Winning the loyalties of Indians who resided in the contested area was critical to early European rivalries. Although trade with the Creek and Cherokee factored heavily in the early colonial economy, the growth of the colony put increasing pressure on the westward expansion. Finally, a succession of treaties with the Indians culminated in their removal westward and opened northern Georgia to white settlement.

Spain was the first European power in present-day Georgia and by the middle of the sixteenth century had established fortified missions among the Guale Indians along the Atlantic Coast and into the interior. When England founded Charleston, South Carolina, in 1670, the boundary with Spanish Florida became the focus of almost constant warfare. The Guale missions were subjected to assaults by Indians acting at the instigation of Charleston traders. At the beginning of the 1700s, the Spanish were forced to abandon their missions because of the resulting depopulation and destruction.

With Spanish influence in the region reduced, English trade with Carolina Indians expanded greatly. Charleston merchants regulated trade with the Creek and Cherokee, which was carried out by traders who often lived and intermarried with the native population. These economic activities served also as a means to combat Spanish and French efforts to influence the Indians, leading England's King George II to grant a license to James Oglethorpe and a group of investors to found Georgia as a buffer colony in 1733. That year Oglethorpe founded the town of Savannah on a defensible bluff above the river and near a friendly group of Creek Indians called the Yamacraw.

The importance of Indian relations led Oglethorpe to establish the trading outpost of Augusta in 1736, two hundred miles up the Savannah River at the fall line on the edge of the Piedmont Plateau. From this strategic location, traders could easily trade with the Creek and Cherokee Indians in the west and north of the colony and transport the goods by river to Savannah. Despite early peace along the frontier, the expanding population of white settlers caused increasing tension throughout the rest of the eighteenth century. After a series of skirmishes in the 1750s and 1760s, the Creeks were forced to sign the Treaty of Augusta in 1763, relinquishing a large section of territory west of the Savannah River. Various religious and ethnic groups took advantage of these new opportunities for land, among them a prominent group of Indian traders led by Lachlan McGillivray and John Rea, who received permission in 1765 to begin settling large groups of Scots-Irish immigrants west and north of Augusta.

After the American Revolution, a large wave of settlers moved from the Carolinas and Virginia through Georgia and into Alabama. As late as the War of 1812, though, most of northern Georgia was still controlled by the Cherokee, while the Creek controlled the westernmost borders of the state into northwestern Alabama. During the war, the British-allied Creek were defeated by troops under the command of General Andrew Jackson and forced to cede most of their lands in Georgia. Over the next decade, continued threats by the Georgia state government led the Creek to relinquish their claims to Georgia lands and move westward by 1827.

With the Creek gone, the State of Georgia grew increasingly hostile to the Cherokee. When gold was discovered in 1828 in north Georgia, a flood of prospectors descended upon Cherokee lands. The state government extended its authority over Cherokee territory and petitioned the federal government for help in removing the Indians. In 1835 the Jackson administration produced the Treaty of New Echota, signed by a handful of pliant Cherokee but contested by many others. The Cherokee were forced by federal troops in 1838 to leave their lands and move westward in a mass migration known as the Trail of Tears, on which some four thousand of an estimated total of eighteen thousand Cherokees died. With the Cherokee gone, all of northern Georgia was open to white settlement.

See also: GOLD RUSH OF 1829 (BUSINESS, INDUSTRY, AND TECHNOLOGY); TRAIL OF TEARS; TREATY OF AUGUSTA.

—Timothy P. Grady, *College of William and Mary*

Kathryn E. Holland Braund, *Deerskins and Duffels: The Creek Indian Trade with Anglo-America, 1685–1815* (1993); Brooke Coleman, *The Colony of Georgia* (2000); David Williams, *The Georgia Gold Rush: Twenty-Niners, Cherokees, and Gold Fever* (1993).

Early White Settlement of Northwestern South Carolina

The settlement of northwestern South Carolina occurred in two overlapping phases. Maintenance of the Indian trade dominated the early policy of South Carolina's government, but with the defeat of the Indians in the Yamasee War in 1717 the western frontier opened for a flood of land-hungry white settlers. From the 1720s on, a steady migration of European settlers followed in the footsteps of the numerous traders who had developed lucrative deals with the Yamasee, Cherokee, and Catawba Indians.

After establishment of Charleston in 1670, the governing authorities demonstrated a keen interest in exploring the interior of the colony by commissioning numerous expeditions at the turn of the eighteenth century. Among these early explorers was Henry Woodward, who, beginning in 1670, was sent on a series of explorations through the Carolina Blue Ridge. Others included James Moore and Cornelius Doherty, who were among the first traders to go into the Indian backcountry, establishing a regular trade with the Cherokee by 1690.

By the early eighteenth century, hundreds of traders were operating throughout the South Carolina backcountry and west through Cherokee and Creek territories. They maintained a trade in deerskins that averaged about fifty-four thousand skins annually. In addition, Indian slaves captured in the frequent wars between rival tribes were routinely traded before 1715. Working on behalf of Charleston merchants, traders often adopted cultural ways of the Indians with whom they dealt, some marrying native women and living among the tribes. However, most did not hold the Indians in such high esteem. Many traders routinely plied their Indian customers with alcohol before negotiations, reneged on transactions, and misused the Indians despite the efforts of the Charleston authorities to prevent this abuse.

Trader mistreatment and increased settlement westward resulted in a violent outbreak of hostilities between the English and the Indians as early as 1713. The Yamasee War involved not only the Yamasee, but also the Cherokee, Choctaw, and Creek, with the primary fighting occurring from 1715 to 1717. Encouraged by both the Spanish and the French, the Yamasee rebelled against British control, killing many of the English traders and laying siege to Charleston. The threat subsided when the English won the Cherokee's support, forcing the Yamasee to surrender. The terms imposed by the British forced the Yamasee to relinquish much of their lands and caused most to migrate to territory outside of English control. Those who remained merged into the Catawba tribe, who maintained friendly relations with the English.

By the 1730s, settlers were moving westward into the Piedmont in increasing numbers. Some came directly from Europe to the uplands of South Carolina. While many were German, Welsh, or Swiss, the majority of early settlers in the region claimed Scots-Irish ancestry, contributing greatly to the distinct language patterns, religion, and folk music that characterized the people of northeastern South Carolina. A significant proportion of the early settlers included African slaves who accompanied their owners and aided in the establishment of the small farms and subsistence lifestyle that dominated the backcountry of South Carolina throughout the eighteenth century.

See also: CHEROKEE (RACE, ETHNICITY, AND IDENTITY); OVERMOUNTAIN MEN (GOVERNMENT).

—Timothy P. Grady, *College of William and Mary*

Richard B. Drake, *A History of Appalachia* (2001); James H. Merrell, *The Indians' New World* (1989); Robert M. Weir, *Colonial South Carolina: A History* (1983).

Early White Settlement of Southeastern Ohio

Southeastern Ohio, east of the Scioto River and south of the National Road, was an area contested between the French and the English until French presence ended in 1763 with the termination of the French and Indian War. By the Proclamation of 1763, the English reserved the area for the Indians and halted westward white settlement east of the Appalachians. Pressure to settle the area farther west was considerable, however, and movement soon resumed, following overland paths to the Ohio River and its tributaries into the interior.

The region, part of the British Northwest Territory, passed into American control when George Rogers Clark defeated the British at the battle of Vincennes in 1779. Thomas Jefferson headed the committee appointed to plan for land disposal. The legal basis for land division, disposal, and settlement was the Northwest Ordinance, adopted by the Confederated Congress in 1787; that document established procedures for governance, guaranteed rights (including outlawing slavery and funding schools with land sales), and addressed the issue of landownership.

At the end of the Revolutionary War, squatters, purchasers, and others streamed into the district along a number of important paths. One prominent flow came down the Ohio River from Pittsburgh and then moved overland onto the westward animal path that would become the National

Road. Some of the earliest settlers followed that path and then moved south along natural corridors from the National Road. Others followed the Ohio River southward and then used the mouth of the Muskingum River at Marietta for an entry corridor into the southeastern interior. From the Muskingum River, access to the interior was extensive, with a common pathway moving westward along an Indian trail into Chillicothe. Another flow connected Baltimore, Maryland, with Clarksburg, (West) Virginia, and then with Marietta on an overland path that later became the Baltimore and Ohio Railroad. Flows from Virginia also followed the Kanawha River to the Ohio and into the western areas or up the Scioto River. Ultimately, each of these migration flows contributed to the diverse cultural pattern of the area.

The first layer of settlement followed a fortify-and-hold pattern, beginning with Fort Gower (1774) on the Hocking River and Fort Harmar (1785) on the Muskingum River. As Indians ceded their lands, surveyors came in to assert new control for the postcolonial government. Organization of space by the victorious Americans primarily formed a grid of townships, a variation on the Jeffersonian plan and reinforced by the Northwest Ordinance.

Three land division systems emerged. The Seven Ranges area, flanking the western side of the Ohio River almost to Marietta, was surveyed for sale in large parcels. Initial efforts in the federal rectangular survey system included some support for schools and local government but limited purchase of the subdivided land to those able to meet the minimum price of $640 to $1,280.

The second was a purchase of government securities by a group of Massachusetts investors who formed the Ohio Company of Associates to settle lands along the Ohio River downstream from the Seven Ranges to the southernmost point of the river. The 1.5-million-acre tract was surveyed in a township form with the addition of internal lots of approximately 232 acres. Each investor held a 1,000-acre share including tracts of 640 and 232 acres. The Land Ordinance of 1785, passed by Congress to regulate the disposal of lands in the western territories, ensured that certain sections of every township be reserved for government use. In particular, lot number sixteen of each was to be used for the maintenance of public schools. Additionally, two townships were divided into lots dedicated to support an early land-grant institution, Ohio University, established in 1804 in Athens. The eventual sale of these Ohio Company acres yielded less than ten cents per acre to the treasury. Earliest settlement of this purchase began in 1788 near the Campus Martius settlement across from Fort Harmar. North of the Ohio Company lands was a Donation Tract, a buffer of free land divided into 100-acre plots for males eighteen years of age who were willing to settle on the land and protect the southern lands from the Indians.

The third area, Congress Lands, was surveyed, sold, and settled shortly after the first two regions. The area was accessed via the paths mentioned above and Zane's Trace, an early path connecting the crossing at Maysville, Kentucky, to Chillicothe and on to the National Road. Settlement here lagged behind the others because of access and competition from the Scioto Salt Licks. As settlement began, a small but noteworthy group of Welsh settlers moved into Jackson County and started the early iron furnaces in the Hanging Rock Iron District, an important charcoal-iron-producing area of the nineteenth century.

West of these three regions was the Virginia Military District. More than 4 million acres of land satisfied relinquished claims and provided Revolutionary War veterans with land awards of 100 to 15,000 acres. The establishment of this region also created a place to relocate freed slaves. Overall this section of Ohio differs from the rest of the state in that it received major cultural infusions from the New England, Middle Atlantic, and South Atlantic regions. From the beginning, laws prohibited slavery, and free blacks found homes in the area. The Underground Railroad to Canada traversed this country.

See also: LAND GRANTS; LAND ORDINANCE OF 1785; NORTHERN NATIVE AMERICANS.

—Nancy R. Bain, *Ohio University*

William D. Pattison, *Beginnings of the American Rectangular Land Survey System, 1784–1800* (1957); William E. Peters, *Ohio Lands and Their History* (1930).

Early White Settlement of Southwestern New York

The Appalachian upland region of New York includes the fourteen counties bordering on northern Pennsylvania. This region of rolling hills was glaciated except for a small area where the Allegheny River loops through New York and contains the headwaters of southward-draining rivers such as the Susquehanna, Delaware, and Allegheny. Prior to white settlement, agricultural-based Native American tribes were thinly settled in villages located along watercourses. The Appalachian uplands were the southern boundary of the Iroquois Confederacy.

By 1775, only a few white settlers had moved beyond the coastal region and the Hudson-Mohawk River corridor into central and western New York. Following the American Revolution, increasing numbers of white settlers moved west along the Mohawk River and filtered into the Appalachian highlands from the north. Migrants also penetrated into the highlands from Pennsylvania along the upper reaches of the Susquehanna, Chenango, and Delaware Rivers and their tributaries, settling in fertile valleys.

After 1785, a combination of forces cleared the way for white settlement in central and western New York, including the Appalachian highlands. First, virtually all Native

American claims were settled by treaty between 1784 and 1789, allowing New York to issue clear title for lands in western New York. Second, Massachusetts and New York agreed in 1786 to settle rival claims to western New York. Massachusetts won the right to sell six million acres of land west of a "pre-emption line" drawn south of Sodus Bay on Lake Ontario with New York retaining title and political sovereignty to the region. Massachusetts sold its acreage to land jobbers as quickly as possible to provide revenue to retire its Revolutionary War debt.

Third, New York disposed of large units of land by granting land or selling to developers. New Englanders were invited to settle the Boston Ten Towns land unit near Binghamton and the Chenango Twenty Towns in present-day Chenango County. The Clinton Township area on the upper Susquehanna was reserved for the "Vermont Sufferers," who had been displaced in competing land claims with Vermont. Similarly, New York established a "new" Military Tract in central New York east of Seneca Lake in 1782 because it was the only way the state could pay former soldiers for service in the Revolutionary War. But clear title to the land could not be conveyed until 1789, when land claims were settled with Native Americans. Few veterans actually occupied the land reserved for them because they usually sold their warrants to speculators.

West of the Military Tract, developers obtained large land units comprising most of western New York from the Appalachian foothills to Lake Ontario on the north. A syndicate headed by Zerah Phelps and Nathaniel Gorham obtained the entire six-million-acre tract from Massachusetts for one million dollars and began the process of establishing instant "city towns," but it was forced to return two-thirds of the land two years later when it was unable to pay. Ultimately, portions of the land were acquired by an English syndicate (the Pulteney Purchase) and Dutch bankers (the Holland Purchase). The Holland Purchase was surveyed by Joseph Ellicott, who then served as the resident land agent for the parcel. Ellicott developed comprehensive plans, platted villages, and built roads, mills, and buildings prior to sale as an incentive for buyers. He was also given authority to modify the plans to fit local conditions. By this method, Ellicott and other private land agents established a "developer's frontier" in western New York.

New York grew in population from fifth among the states in 1790 to first in 1830. Unlike in the rest of western New York, however, immigration from Europe was not the primary reason. Rather, migration from surrounding states—particularly group migration from New England—was the principal factor in the settlement of the Appalachian upland section of New York.

See also: ELLICOTT, JOSEPH; IROQUOIS (RACE, ETHNICITY, AND IDENTITY); NORTHERN LAND AND DEVELOPMENT COMPANIES.

—John E. Damron, *Newport News, Virginia*

Milton M. Klein, ed., *The Empire State: A History of New York* (2001); D. W. Meinig, "Geography of Expansion, 1785–1855," in *Geography of New York State*, ed. John H. Thompson (1977); William Wyckoff, *The Developer's Frontier: The Making of the Western New York Landscape* (1988).

Early White Settlement of Southwestern Virginia

The first explorers to southwestern Virginia, Thomas Batts and Robert Fallam, left Fort Henry (present-day Petersburg, Virginia) in September of 1671 and traveled by the New River to Giles County, near today's West Virginia border. In the early eighteenth century, the first settlers moved into southwestern Virginia through the Holston Valley using a Native American trail that later became part of the Wilderness Road, continuing through Tennessee and into Kentucky.

The colonial government encouraged settlement west of the Blue Ridge Mountains as a buffer against western Indian nations by providing large grants of western land with the understanding that the grantees would then partition the grants to settlers. To accommodate the number of settlers expected west of the Blue Ridge Mountains, the governor appointed Jost Hite, Morgan Morgan, John Smith, Benjamin Borden, and George Hobson the first magistrates in 1734. Borden, a wealthy investor, recruited Scots-Irish families into the valley to comply with the conditions of a five-hundred-thousand-acre grant that he settle one hundred families there within ten years. Polly Mulhollin, an Irish indentured recruit on Borden's land, built cabins in return for 100 acres per finished cabin, resulting in a deed to three thousand acres. Irish immigrant John Lewis received one hundred thousand acres in current Augusta County in 1730, settling near present-day Staunton. Colonel James Patton, a dealer in western lands, staked William Ingles and John Draper in 1748, resulting in one of the most successful settlements, Draper's Meadows, site of present-day Blacksburg. About 1746, Jacob Castle bought land on the Clinch River from the Indians for a butcher knife and a rusty musket, naming it Castle's Woods, today's Saltville. After 1769, squatters moved onto Castle's land. This was a common occurrence in the vast western landholdings of the Loyal Land Company, which had been organized in 1750 to fix the boundary for eight hundred thousand acres of the most western Virginian lands for settlement. By 1770, more than eighty families of English, Scots-Irish, and German descent plus a few African slaves resided in Castle's Woods. Martin's Station, an important way station along the Wilderness Road, was established near the Cumberland Gap in 1775, encouraging more settlers to migrate in and through the area. Many of these were veterans of the French and

Indian War who received land grants from the Loyal Land Company.

Small forts were built in Scott County and elsewhere along the Wilderness Road to protect travelers moving west. Settlers built Snoddy's Fort, named after William Snoddy, around 1770. Moore's Fort was built a mile from Snoddy's Fort for the increasing population. In 1773 the new county of Fincastle, with its seat near Fort Chiswell and the Great Valley Road, was established with fifteen justices of the peace for the enormous territory. A store and tavern were erected, and a militia company was stationed at Fort Chiswell during the French and Indian War. The Virginia legislature chartered William Ingles to operate a ferry across the New River in lower Augusta County (modern-day Radford) at three pence per person. Ingles later added a general store and stables to attend to draft animals pulling wagons through the valley.

Beginning in the 1750s, the French and Indian War halted settlement in the Appalachian divide and through the valley. Then, after the capture of Fort Duquesne and in violation of the Proclamation of 1763, southwestern Virginia began to develop more permanent settlements. In 1777 Captain John Anderson built the Block House in Carter's Valley, six miles east of Moccasin Gap, to be the preparatory point for migrant companies entering the wilderness beyond Virginia. As land values plummeted from overuse in early-nineteenth-century Virginia, millions left the state, traveling through southwestern Virginia by way of the Great Valley Road and then the Wilderness Road. By the early nineteenth century, travel also was moving eastward through southwestern Virginia, and a tollgate was erected in 1805 in the saddle of the Cumberland Gap.

See also: EXPLORERS AND SURVEYORS; GREAT VALLEY ROAD; SALT SETTLEMENTS.

—Michelle M. Mormul, *California State University at Fullerton*

David Hackett Fischer and James C. Kelley, *Away I'm Bound Away: Virginia and the Westward Movement* (2000); Robert L. Kincaid, *The Wilderness Road* (1947); Parke Rouse Jr., *The Great Wagon Road: From Philadelphia to the South* (1973).

Early White Settlement of Western Maryland

Colonial Maryland was founded in 1634, and though its eastern shore was quickly populated, westward migration and settlement of the future state's Appalachian region proceeded slowly. The western reaches of Maryland were not settled permanently until German immigrants from Pennsylvania established the village of Monocacy, near present-day Creagerstown, in the late 1720s. Formerly the area had served as a route for hunters, traders, and immigrants passing from Pennsylvania to Virginia along the Great Valley Road (also known as the Great Wagon Road). In the early 1730s, sixteen families moved from Pennsylvania into the region.

These earliest settlers did not have to pay for the land but only needed to settle on and work their claims. They marked their land by what was known as a "tomahawk right," which involved notching trees to mark the boundaries of one's land and trusting that the claim would be respected. As the region became more settled and structured government moved in, these early settlers officially registered their land claims. In 1732 Charles Calvert, the fifth Lord Baltimore, officially proclaimed western Maryland to be open for settlement. To facilitate settlement of his Province of Maryland, Lord Baltimore offered the following terms: families could settle two hundred acres and defer payment for three years, at which time they were required to pay four shillings for every one hundred acres; and single persons could receive one hundred acres under the same terms.

In an effort to organize the region and exercise control over settlement, the colony appointed three commissioners to issue certificates of ownership and oversee land claims in the region. A few wealthy citizens quickly obtained large sections of the region. Although the majority of these wealthy landowners spoke English, most of the actual settlers were of German origin.

The Monocacy River Valley was one of the richest areas for both settlers and speculators. The main route followed by settlers became known as the Monocacy Road, along which towns such as Frederick-Town (present-day Frederick, Maryland) sprang up. Settlement was encouraged not only by the government but welcomed by the early settlers as well, since new settlers coming into the area brought protection, trade, skills, and connections to well-established settlements. Many Germans who moved into the region were skilled laborers who contributed greatly to the advancement of the growing region.

At the time of early settlement the borders separating Maryland from Pennsylvania were often violently disputed between the two colonies. Before the completion and acceptance of the Mason-Dixon Line in 1786, these disputes drove off many already living in the region and deterred future settlers leery of moving into the hotly contested territory. In addition, the Earl of Shelburne, president of the governor's Board of Trade, recommended that the region be closed to settlement until hostilities were resolved. Two Englishmen, Charles Mason and Jeremiah Dixon, were commissioned to survey and establish the official boundaries between Maryland, Pennsylvania, Delaware, and parts of Virginia.

During this time, the French and Indian War brought additional bloodshed to the region, further deterring settlement. Communities were abandoned or destroyed, and after the war many had to be rebuilt. Although progress into the region was slowed, it was not stopped. During the war new forts had been constructed, offering protection and drawing settlers. One of these was Fort Cumberland, constructed in 1755 to stabilize the extreme reaches of western Maryland after the defeat of Virginia militia commanded by George Washington at Fort Necessity. Both the French and Indian War and long-running border disputes delayed the settlement of western Maryland. By the time of the American Revolution, however, western Maryland had become a stable area for settlement, with decent roads, thriving towns, and protective forts.

See also: FRENCH AND INDIAN WAR (GOVERNMENT); GERMANS (RACE, ETHNICITY, AND IDENTITY); PROCLAMATION OF 1763.

—Cory Joe Stewart, *Appalachian State University*

Jack P. Greene, *Pursuits of Happiness: The Social Development of Early Modern British Colonies and the Formation of American Culture* (1988); Aubrey C. Land, *Colonial Maryland: A History* (1981); Thomas J. C. Williams, *History of Frederick County, Maryland* (1967).

Early White Settlement of Western North Carolina

Because settlers often patented their land only after they had established households, it is difficult to determine when early settlers arrived in the mountains of western North Carolina. By 1749, however, enough families and individuals had moved into the backcountry that Governor Gabriel Johnston called for the establishment of Anson County out of the western portion of Bladen County.

The first residents of Anson County (and, by 1753, of Rowan County) appear to have migrated from the vicinity of Cecil County, Maryland, and Chester County, Pennsylvania, often by way of the Valley of Virginia. About a half-dozen families settled on the Yadkin River near the area of Deep Creek, approximately twelve miles west of the future Moravian settlement that in time became the city of Winston-Salem. The most prominent of these settlers was Morgan Bryan, an immigrant and land speculator from Augusta County in the Valley of Virginia. Farther to the southwest, more than twenty families settled along the tributaries of the South Yadkin River and Second Creek between 1747 and 1749. The third area of concentrated settlement was along the Catawba River and its tributary, Davidson's Creek, where about two dozen families settled by 1751. Although some of the first residents were English, Scots-Irish Presbyterians predominated as settlement increased over the next two decades.

In each of these three settlements, families appear to have migrated with or closely after one another. Many families along the Yadkin and Catawba Rivers had known each other in Pennsylvania, Maryland, or Virginia before they migrated south. That such associations survived the migration process indicates that the early settlers in western North Carolina wanted to maintain a sense of community rather than build strictly individualistic lives.

The settlement of the western part of the province increased rapidly from the 1750s through the early 1770s. In 1754 Governor Arthur Dobbs, who owned more than two hundred thousand acres in the colony, reported to the English Board of Trade that hundreds of wagons were bringing more settlers into the western counties. During the French and Indian War (1754–63), hundreds of refugees from western Virginia fled south to the North Carolina backcountry, adding to its growing population. During the American Revolution, however, migration to western North Carolina dwindled. When westward immigration picked up again after the war, the flow of immigrants drifted increasingly west into Appalachian Tennessee and Kentucky.

See also: BOONE, DANIEL; OVERMOUNTAIN MEN (GOVERNMENT); STATE OF FRANKLIN (GOVERNMENT).

—Creston Long, *Salisbury University*

Johanna Miller Lewis, *Artisans in the North Carolina Backcountry* (1995); Harry Roy Merrens, *Colonial North Carolina in the Eighteenth Century* (1964); Robert W. Ramsey, *Carolina Cradle: Settlement of the Northwest Carolina Frontier, 1747–1762* (1964).

Early White Settlement of Western Pennsylvania

Located north and west of Pennsylvania's agriculturally rich Great Valley, the Blue, Jacks, and Tuscarora sedimentary rock ridges of the Appalachian Mountains stretch from southwest to northeast Pennsylvania to form the Allegheny Plateau. After William Penn's acquisition of Pennsylvania in 1681 from King Charles II of England, initial agreements prohibited white settlements on this plateau, reserving the area for the numerous Native American tribes living in the colony. However, British and French troops built outposts in the western region, and white missionaries, traders, and trappers interacted with Native Americans living there. During the eighteenth century, white settlers migrated into the Allegheny Plateau and the adjacent valleys running parallel to the mountain ridges of northeastern and southwestern Pennsylvania. These frontier areas were more isolated and less populated than the urban centers of the southeastern part of the colony surrounding Philadelphia, which had been settled at the end of the seventeenth century.

Early settlements were established in the Wyoming Valley of the Appalachian Mountains along the Susquehanna and Lackawanna Rivers in northeastern Pennsylvania by people primarily from nearby New York and Connecticut, which both claimed the northeastern section of Pennsylvania. One significant colonial northeastern Pennsylvania community was Wilkes-Barre, originally settled in 1769. In July 1778, settlers sought refuge in a fort near Wilkes-Barre from hundreds of British soldiers and Native Americans, who slaughtered almost two-thirds of the colonists during the Wyoming Valley massacre. Despite this setback, survivors rebuilt Wilkes-Barre. Nearby Scranton was settled in the 1780s.

In western Pennsylvania, both the French and the British were attracted by the Ohio, Allegheny, and Monongahela Rivers' potential for trade and industrial development. French soldiers erected Fort Duquesne in 1754. Four years later, the British built Fort Pitt, and the surrounding community was named Pittsburgh. To supply military needs, settlers received permits to erect buildings and plant crops at Pittsburgh, Redstone, and Stewart's Crossing.

Conflicts between English settlers and the French and their Native American allies escalated into the outbreak of the French and Indian War in western Pennsylvania in 1754. After the British victory, the Proclamation of 1763 declared that whites could not settle lands west of the Appalachians. An Indian uprising resulted in the first Treaty of Fort Stanwix in 1768, securing the southwestern part of Pennsylvania for white settlement.

Two waves of settlers had already migrated to western Pennsylvania. At Dunkard's Creek in the early 1750s, brothers Israel, Samuel, and Gabriel Eckerlin established what historians believe was the region's first agricultural settlement. Between 1760 and 1790, migrants settled in the southwestern counties of Westmoreland, Greene, Fayette, Washington, Allegheny, and Somerset. The Land Law of 1792 recognized squatters' rights to land they had settled. The town of Washington, established in 1781, was strategically located on the trading road between Wheeling in northwestern Virginia (modern West Virginia) and Brownsville in southwestern Pennsylvania.

After the American Revolution, large groups of settlers moved to western Pennsylvania in wagon caravans from the east. Many settlers arrived from Maryland and Virginia, which both claimed some of the Pennsylvania lands. Settlement of northwestern communities such as Erie began in 1790. Ethnically, the majority of white settlers were English, then Scottish, Irish, and German. According to the 1790 federal census, seventy-five thousand people lived in southwestern Pennsylvania, but no towns had populations exceeding four hundred people.

See also: ANTHRACITE MINERS, NINETEENTH-CENTURY (LABOR); FRENCH AND INDIAN WAR (GOVERNMENT); TREATIES OF FORT STANWIX.

—Elizabeth D. Schafer, *Loachapoka, Alabama*

Solon J. and Elizabeth Hawthorn Buck, *The Planting of Civilization in Western Pennsylvania* (1967); Richard K. MacMaster, *Land, Piety, Peoplehood: The Establishment of Mennonite Communities in America, 1683–1790* (1985); J. E. Wright and Doris S. Corbett, *Pioneer Life in Western Pennsylvania* (1940).

Early White Settlement of West Virginia

Early white settlement in present-day West Virginia was the result of three forces: competition by European powers for dominance in the eastern Ohio Valley, prior land occupation east of the Alleghenies, and removal of Native Americans from their traditional hunting grounds.

Exploration of the region that would become West Virginia began in the latter half of the seventeenth century. France and Britain both claimed the entire Ohio River Valley during the late seventeenth century. France based its claim on explorations by René-Robert Cavelier La Salle in 1669, while Britain's claim derived from a 1671 expedition into southwestern Virginia led by explorers Thomas Batts and Robert Fallam. After numerous skirmishes and organized campaigns, including the French and Indian War, Britain succeeded in removing France from all land east of the Mississippi by 1763.

In 1730, to encourage settlement, Virginia granted one thousand acres to speculators for every family to settle west of the Blue Ridge Mountains, launching the first major settlement of present-day West Virginia. By 1768, the British government had modified its policy of restricting settlement behind the Proclamation Line of 1763 in order to provide more land for speculators and to provide land warrants for veterans of the French and Indian War. Between 1769 and 1771, more than ten thousand families had settled in the upper Ohio Valley, largely in present-day West Virginia.

By the time of contact with whites, the Shawnee had succeeded the Iroquois as the dominant Native American group in western Virginia. Increasing conflict with white settlers led to the battle of Point Pleasant along the Ohio River, after which the Shawnee agreed to cede all claims to traditional hunting grounds in western Virginia and Kentucky.

The earliest region of white settlement in present-day West Virginia was by German settlers at Mecklenburg (later Shepherdstown) in 1727 on the western edge of the Valley of Virginia. By the end of the Revolutionary War, established towns and farms characterized the entire eastern panhandle region. Among them was the town of Romney beside the upper Potomac River. Much farther south along the Allegheny Front, settlement began in the Greenbrier and New River Valleys in the second half of the eighteenth century.

Settlers moving into the northern portions of present-day West Virginia formed a pattern of small settlements on the Ohio River between Pittsburgh and the mouth of the Kanawha River. Wheeling arose from Fort Fincastle (later Fort Henry) and became a major center on the frontier since it was on the most direct route from the Ohio to Braddock's Road (later included in the National Road) and at the upstream limit of low-water navigation on the Ohio River. Growing rapidly as an industrial and regional service center, it had become second in population only to Richmond by 1860.

Settlement in southwestern Virginia (present-day southern West Virginia) began along the Tug Fork following Lord Dunmore's War in 1774. Settlers moved into this region upstream from the Ohio River or filtered in from the east across formidable mountain barriers.

See also: FRENCH AND INDIAN WAR (GOVERNMENT); NATIONAL ROAD; PROCLAMATION OF 1763.

—John E. Damron, *Newport News, Virginia*, and John W. Damron, *Newport News, Virginia*

Robert D. Mitchell and Paul A. Graves, eds., *North America: The Historical Geography of a Changing Continent* (1987); Otis K. Rice and Stephen W. Brown, *West Virginia: A History* (1993); John Alexander Williams, *West Virginia: A History* (1976).

Economic Crises

Appalachia's economic relationship with the rest of the nation has often been troublesome, but it has never been static. National economic crises outside Appalachia have had varying effects upon the regional economy, including shifts in population. The largely barter- and trade-based economy of the early settlement period in Appalachia was relatively resistant to national economic fluctuations. However, during the mid- to late nineteenth century, the region's economy became increasingly dependent upon natural resources, which were sold in markets outside of Appalachia. Coal, lumber, and large-scale agriculture brought new wealth into the region but also made its residents susceptible to national fluctuations in markets.

The despair of the Great Depression hit Appalachia just as hard as any other region of the country. In the years immediately following World War II, Appalachia found prosperity by feeding the nation's demand for coal. By the mid 1950s, however, the national coal industry had shifted its focus to mechanization, leaving more than half of Appalachia's miners unemployed. A mild coal boom in the early 1970s once again caused an upswing in the economy of the region, but the energy crisis of the mid-1970s shifted the coal market to a reliance on western lignite coals, ending another brief period of prosperity for Appalachia's workers.

Changes in the economy of the region were accompanied by changes in personal mobility. Between 1900 and 1930, Appalachia's farming population grew by only about 5 percent; during the same time period, the number of people not actively engaged in farming as a primary source of income grew by about 75 percent, dramatically demonstrating the demographic shift away from agriculture as a foundation of the region's economy. The shift from a subsistence-based agrarian economy to an economy based upon industry and export also exacted a toll upon the region in terms of out-migration. Prior to about 1942, rural Appalachia had consistently retained a far higher percentage of its young adults than other rural areas of the United States. However, between 1940 and 1960, out-migration from Appalachia slowed the region's population growth rate to almost a tenth of the national average. From 1950 to 1960, some 2.2 million "displaced Appalachians" left the region, migrating to cities such as Detroit, Cincinnati, Gary, Indiana, and Wilmington, Delaware. Migration patterns naturally tended to follow destinations of perceived economic advantage, usually in areas where the availability of wage jobs followed an industrial boom. Coal mines outside of the region were a natural draw for experienced miners, but many more individuals followed job prospects to mills and factories in Ohio, Indiana, Illinois, and Pennsylvania. By the 1970s, emigration from the region began to slow as the nation's overall economy entered a recession, and migration patterns spread outward to western states, especially California.

Unemployment in Appalachia after 1980 was substantially higher than the national average, with the result that any downswing in the national economy was severely felt throughout the region. By the close of the twentieth century, Appalachia's uncertain economic future was inextricably reliant upon the economic well-being of the rest of the nation.

See also: SECTION OVERVIEW (LABOR); SECTION OVERVIEW (URBAN APPALACHIAN EXPERIENCE); TWENTIETH-CENTURY OUT-MIGRATION.

—Elijah Scott, *Chattanooga State Technical Community College*

Ellicott, Joseph

(1760–1826) Land agent.

Pennsylvania surveyor Joseph Ellicott helped shape the economic and political development of western New York, including portions of northern Appalachia, from 1800 to 1821. He was given the task of surveying and then selling the more than 3.3 million acres held by the Holland Land Company.

In 1800, eight years after Dutch banking houses formed the Holland Land Company, Elliott was hired as the company's sales agent in New York. His task initially was to live on and manage Holland Land Company holdings in western New York. Although the company had planned a quick disposal of its lands by selling the property in a few large holdings, most sales were in small lots.

When the plan of rapid sales failed, Ellicott adopted the English tradition of longer range, smaller plot settlements in the hope of attracting large numbers of buyers from landless families. Settlers placed a down payment of 5 percent on a lot and then paid the remaining debt over time. But without adequate transportation facilities, farmers could not hope to get their produce to the market and thereby make money to pay their debt to the company. To speed development of the area, Ellicott channeled his energies into the political arena in 1803, holding the position of Genesee County treasurer until 1809. Using his political influence, he promoted the construction of new roads, planned the western sector of the Erie Canal, and influenced the redrawing of county lines.

Ellicott resigned from the Dutch-owned Holland Land Company in 1821, possibly because of increased American hostility to foreigners and their agents after the War of 1812. There is some indication that he was forced to resign by his employers because of his increasingly abrasive personality.

See also: EXPLORERS AND SURVEYORS; NORTHERN LAND AND DEVELOPMENT COMPANIES; SOUTHERN LAND AND DEVELOPMENT COMPANIES.

—Caryn E. Neumann, *Ohio State University*

Etowah Mounds Archaeological Site

Etowah, a Mississippian-period mound center located near Cartersville, Georgia, had an economy based on maize and bean agriculture and was ruled by an elite caste whose residences were built on large, flat-topped platform mounds. Located on a bank of the Etowah River, the complex contains six mounds surrounded by a large defensive ditch. Besides the physical features, Etowah is known for the artifacts excavated there, which include carved shell gorgets, embossed copper plates, and two statues made of Georgia marble.

First occupied by Mississippian peoples approximately A.D. 950, Etowah reached its peak between 1200 and 1350, when the town covered more than fifty acres and was the capital of a paramount chiefdom. This paramount chiefdom, in which Etowah's chief lorded over chiefs from allied lesser chiefdoms, controlled a large part of present-day northern Georgia, and its influence extended into northeastern Alabama, eastern Tennessee, and western portions of the Carolinas. Soon after 1350, the site was abandoned for unknown reasons and remained uninhabited until the early sixteenth century. Etowah, then known as Itaba, reemerged as a small community in the paramount chiefdom of Coosa. In 1540 Hernando de Soto and his Spanish troops spent six days in Itaba, where they traded knives and mirrors for some women. By the beginning of the seventeenth century, Etowah was once again abandoned and remained so until the Cherokee arrived during the eighteenth century.

See also: CHEROKEE (RACE, ETHNICITY, AND IDENTITY); DE SOTO, HERNANDO; SOUTHERN NATIVE AMERICANS.

—John R. Burch Jr., *Campbellsville University*

Explorers and Surveyors

British-American colonists moving west encountered many barriers: the falls of rivers, dense forests, and Indians defending their lands. The greatest barrier was the Appalachian Mountains, which awed settlers and Indians alike. The latter referred to them as the "endless mountains." American colonists, however, always wanted to know what was on the other side. Early maps revealed the ignorance of seventeenth-century geographers. John Farrer's 1651 *Mapp of Virginia*, for example, showed the western side of the Appalachians sloping into the Pacific Ocean. Knowledge came slowly, awaiting explorations of French voyageurs descending the Mississippi River, which revealed the reality of trans-Appalachian America.

With hunger for land growing during the seventeenth century, explorers and scientists made halting advances toward the eastern slope of the Appalachians. In 1670 John Lederer was the first European to reach the Blue Ridge of Virginia, marking traces to guide other explorers. Exploration was sporadic for the next sixty or seventy years. The few westward wanderers undaunted by the mountain wilderness and French and Indian activity on the other side in the

A nineteenth-century engraving depicting young George Washington as a surveyor. Beginning at age fifteen, Washington worked for several years as a surveyor in areas of western Virginia, Pennsylvania, and Maryland. Surveyors explored and mapped often unseen land holdings for wealthy owners, making possible the partitioning and selling of much of Appalachia to land speculators and settlers.

Ohio, Tennessee, Cumberland, and Mississippi River Valleys included Alexander Spotswood, the lieutenant governor of Virginia, who led an expedition into the Blue Ridge Mountains in 1716.

Future President of the United States George Washington spent his early years as a surveyor and later a land speculator. At the age of fifteen, Washington was hired by Lord Fairfax to survey his extensive land holdings in the Shenandoah Valley. Two years later, the College of William and Mary appointed Washington official surveyor for Culpeper County, Virginia.

The maturation of British America during the eighteenth-century resulted in new westward explorations. The increase of population along the eastern seaboard and rivers forced hardy frontiersmen into the interior in search of land. After Thomas Walker discovered the Cumberland Gap in 1750, opening to view the fertile land of Kentucky, hunters and settlers followed in his wake. Daniel Boone, the most famous hunter and guide, forged a path through the wilderness despite lacking surveying skills. Boone led settlers through the Cumberland Gap in 1769, disobeying the British restriction to trans-Appalachian settlement enacted in 1763. After the initial penetration, surveyors and axe-men followed to discover the best course through the mountains, avoiding swampy land while seeking the lowest elevation with dry, sandy, or rocky soil.

Also journeying west to the Appalachians and beyond were scientists. Perhaps the most famous was John Bartram, who earned a living collecting seeds and selling them to European patrons who were planting American (even Appalachian) gardens on their estates. Bartram traveled thousands of miles collecting seeds, cataloging new species, and recording data and his experiences. He journeyed into the Blue Ridge Mountains in 1738, then up the Susquehanna River and across the Allegheny Mountains in 1742. Many others followed in his wake: Bartram's son William, the English botanist Thomas Nuttall, and John Filson. Filson published *The Discovery, Settlement, and Present State of Kentucke* in 1784, making such lands across the Appalachians the dream of many for years to come.

See also: BOONE, DANIEL; SPOTSWOOD, ALEXANDER.

—Russell M. Lawson, *Bacone College*

John Mack Faragher, *Daniel Boone: The Life and Legend of an American Pioneer* (1992); John Filson, *The Discovery, Settlement, and Present State of Kentucke* (1784); Russell M. Lawson, "Science and Medicine," in *American Eras: 1600–1754: The Colonial Era*, ed. Jessica Kross et al. (1998).

Fallam, Robert

See Batts, Thomas

Forced Migration of Slaves

After Congress curtailed participation in the international slave trade in 1808, virtually eliminating an outside supply of slaves, internal trade accelerated. This catapulted Appalachia into the role of gateway between the eastern and upper South and the slaveholding areas farther west for the more than half a million slaves forced to leave the eastern seaboard between the American Revolution and the Civil War. While most of these slaves merely passed through the mountains to markets in the Deep South, some remained in Appalachia.

Men chained together in caravan trains called "coffles," with women and children walking alongside, were a common sight in the region. Some of these individuals were purchased to work in the stores, mines, or homes of local residents. Others were purchased as investments, to be resold when prices were high. Relocating owners brought some slaves to the area, and still others arrived in the mountains after being loaned or hired out to residents there.

James A. Mitchell, a slave trader from Pittsylvania County, Virginia, participated in this "great migration." Leaving home in 1834 with fifty-one slaves, Mitchell arrived in Mississippi seven weeks later. He and the coffle had walked approximately seventeen miles per day, passing through Appalachia.

Slaves such as Adaline and her son Thomas, who belonged to John McKee, were sent to Asheville, North Carolina, to help McKee's recently widowed sister-in-law, Polly. During her stay Adaline came to prefer the mountains, and while she and her son were passed around to various mountain relatives, they never returned to the McKees' to live. This type of consideration for the enslaved was not uncommon among mountain masters, who lived by an ethical code that allowed for community censure of those who mistreated their slaves.

In addition to those brought into the region by their relocating owners, slaves were also sold into the region as part of the slave trade. One in 154 Appalachian households earned a portion of its income from the slave trade. This group included those who considered themselves primarily craftsmen and farmers, as well as merchants who specialized in the trafficking of human beings. The appearance of coffles in an area meant that slave families might be torn apart as members were sold and forced to migrate to distant locations, leaving loved ones behind.

See also: MAROON SETTLEMENTS; SLAVERY (RACE, ETHNICITY, AND IDENTITY).

—Jody L. Allen, *College of William and Mary*

John C. Inscoe, *Mountain Masters: Slavery and the Sectional Crisis in Western North Carolina* (1989) and ed., *Appalachians and Race: The Mountain South from Slavery to Segregation* (2001).

Fur Trappers

European fur trappers pioneered the interior settlement of North America. These trappers entered the backcountry to acquire pelts, hides, skins, and fur, but they also established the routes that later settlers would follow. Appalachian pelt production was predominantly oriented to deer hides, though trade also included some wildcat pelts and even hummingbird skins, which were used in European ladies' fashions during the eighteenth and nineteenth centuries. Trappers were part of an exchange system that predated European colonization of North America. The original Appalachian fur trappers were Native Americans who utilized the animal products themselves and in an interregional trade network. Native American trapping employed corrals, pits, drops, traps, snares, and fires. As prohibitions relaxed on guns as articles of the Indian trade, firearms became the dominant means of taking large mammals—deer, elk, bear, large wildcats—while traps were used for beaver, mink, muskrat, and other small animals. Firearms boosted hide counts but led to massive waste of food resources.

While both Native Americans and Europeans trapped locally for food and clothing needs, fur trapping was part of an extensive international trading and industrial production system. It was highly competitive and, despite rivalry and warfare, effectively organized. This commercial trapping system involved a network that reached from England, France, Germany, and Spain to America and utilized a series of ports, upriver depots, inland forts and trading posts, and trapping camps. Trappers proceeded upriver to trap and then floated their hides downriver. Before being shipped from ports such as Charleston, South Carolina, or Mobile, Alabama, pelts were processed at a series of locations to separate fur from the hides, cure or tan the hides, or begin preliminary dressing of hides for clothing manufacture. Fur trapping involved a twofold system of exchange—of furs to the European market and of European trade goods to the Native Americans. Most trappers in the settlement period were also traders. Beginning in the 1690s, this trapping system flourished. By 1750, though, large commercial expeditions and overland pack trains largely had replaced river transport. Such operations sometimes employed dozens of workers, and a season's production could require a hundred or more horses to transport it.

Because animal populations were dispersed, fur trappers also dispersed, furthering exploration and settlement of the upper Piedmont, the mountains, and, by the beginning of the eighteenth century, the plateaus and basins beyond the Appalachians. Vigorous competition for animal pelts produced patterns of ethnic mixing and increased knowledge of Native American life and details of the physical geography of North America. Appalachian trappers were successful producers. By 1750, hide production throughout Appalachia exceeded perhaps a million pelts per year.

See also: LONG HUNTERS; MAMMALS (ECOLOGY); SOUTHERN NATIVE AMERICANS.

—Gerald L. Smith, *University of the South*

Kathryn E. Holland Braund, *Deerskins and Duffels: The Creek Indian Trade with Anglo-America, 1685–1815* (1993); Verner W. Crane, *The Southern Frontier: 1670–1732* (1928); Paul Chrisler Phillips, *The Fur Trade* (1961).

Garden Creek Archaeological Site

Including all of western North Carolina and part of eastern Tennessee, the Appalachian Summit possesses the highest peaks and most rugged terrain in the Appalachian Mountains. This region, containing numerous microenvironments with distinctive ecologies that support diverse fauna and flora not generally found in the South, is the setting for Garden Creek archaeological site.

Garden Creek, a mound and village complex, is found in the Pigeon River Valley of Haywood County, North Carolina. The site consists of three mounds and two villages associated with the mounds. Two mounds and one village have been excavated to illuminate the area's prehistory. Pottery and other artifacts bearing distinct cultural affiliations were discovered, providing stratigraphic evidence of the cultural sequence of Garden Creek's former inhabitants. These stratified artifacts contribute significantly to the overall understanding of the prehistory of the Cherokee in the area and prove the existence of intercultural contact during the middle Woodland Connestee phase.

These cultural phases have been defined by the characteristics of their ceramics and put into a chronological framework. The earliest ceramic tradition dates to the Swannanoa phase, about 600–700 B.C. By 200 B.C., the Pigeon phase had emerged. Swannanoa pottery is heavy, thick, and generally cord-marked, while Pigeon ceramics are mostly stamped with a carved wooden paddle. The latter style appears throughout the Southeast around 500 B.C. In contrast, Connestee ceramics, appearing about A.D. 200, are relatively thin and finely crafted and include simple-stamped, cord-marked, brushed, or plain decorations, similar to ceramics from northern Georgia and eastern Tennessee. By about A.D. 600, the Connestee phase began to give way to the Pisgah phase (A.D. 1000), marked by ceramics often decorated with complicated stamps and thick rims decorated with incised patterns, or punctations.

See also: CHEROKEE (RACE, ETHNICITY, AND IDENTITY); MOUNDBUILDERS; SOUTHERN NATIVE AMERICANS.

—Jane L. Brown, *Western Carolina University*

Genesee Road

Also known as the Great Genesee Road or Main Genesee Road, this thoroughfare connected central and western New York by linking Utica, Batavia, and Buffalo. At the close of the American Revolution, the interior of New York was an unexplored wilderness with only one land route, the Iroquois Trail, connecting the Mohawk Valley with the western sector. The trail proved incapable of carrying the thousands of pioneers who deluged western New York with the opening of the Genesee country by land companies.

Recognizing the inadequacy of the trail, the state legislature passed a law in 1794 mandating the construction of a road from Utica to the Genesee River. The road remained little more than a well-worn path until the legislature voted to secure funds for the route's improvement from sales of Native American lands (1796) and statewide lotteries (1797). In 1797, after workmen widened the highway and laid down a gravel surface, stagecoach travel began between Utica and Geneva.

In 1798 the legislature provided for extension of the road to the western extremity of the state. Two years later, the section from Utica to Canandaigua became a toll road controlled by the Seneca Road Company. Subsequent to the Erie Canal's completion in 1825, stage and boat travel complemented one another, even though toll collections on the Genesee dropped off sharply. By 1850, competition from railroads diverted traffic from the road, and it fell into disrepair. In 1852 the Seneca Company ceased to exist and abandoned the road. New York State Route 5 from Utica to Buffalo follows the Genesee and is the main thoroughfare through Utica.

See also: EARLY WHITE SETTLEMENT OF SOUTHWESTERN NEW YORK; ELLICOTT, JOSEPH; NATIONAL ROAD.

—Marie Tedesco, *East Tennessee State University*

Gist, Christopher

(c. 1706–1759) Explorer.

Eighteen years before Daniel Boone's famous crossing of the Cumberland Gap, Christopher Gist fostered frontier expansion by exploring the Ohio Valley. His meticulously penned journals of three separate expeditions provide accurate, detailed records not only of the geography, but also of life in uncharted regions during the 1750s.

Born in Baltimore County, Maryland, between 1705 and 1708, he was the eldest son of Richard and Zipporah Murray Gist. As a surveyor and commissioner, Richard Gist helped lay out the plan for Baltimore. Little is known about Christopher's early life.

Gist married Sarah Howard in 1728. One of their sons, Nathaniel, eventually married a Cherokee woman named Wut-teh and fathered Sequoyah, inventor of the Cherokee syllabary. By 1750, the family was settled on a farm along North Carolina's Yadkin River. Gist traded with the Indians and also became well known as a surveyor. That year, the Ohio Company of Virginia commissioned him to explore the upper Ohio Valley. His instructions were to chart mountain passes and river courses, survey and describe land suitable for settlement, and note the strength, numbers, and trading habits of the Indians. Gist returned from this arduous journey to find that Indian raids had forced his family to flee to Roanoke, North Carolina.

The next winter (1751–52), the Ohio Company employed his services to explore south of the Ohio River. His goals included finding good land and the shortest route from the company's storehouse at Wills' Creek, Maryland, to the Monongahela; describing and surveying both good and bad land; documenting the streams that flowed into the Ohio; and locating suitable sites for storehouses and trading centers. Gist's journals of these expeditions, along with an account of his adventures with George Washington, show him to be a well-educated man and a thorough and accomplished writer. His precise surveys indicate a strong understanding of surveying and geography. Gist even returned from the second trip with an archaeological discovery: a four-pound tooth of a large beast found at Salt Lick. He also brought samples of stones and coal and a good collection of skins.

After this journey, Gist established a settlement near present-day Brownsville, Pennsylvania, and "Gist's Plantation" became a center of activity. In November 1753, he set out from his home as a guide for young Major George Washington on a mission to Fort Duquesne. The party delivered Governor Robert Dinwiddie's message urging the French to leave the Ohio Valley. Gist saved Washington's life twice on that journey, events well covered in Washington's journal, but hardly mentioned in Gist's. In 1754 Gist experienced with Washington the surrender of Fort Necessity. He also served as scout for General Edward Braddock's campaign against the French at Fort Duquesne in 1755. Two years later, he was appointed deputy agent of Indian affairs. "Father" Gist, as the Indians called him, died of smallpox on a mission to the Cherokee in 1759.

See also: EARLY WHITE SETTLEMENT OF SOUTHEASTERN OHIO; EXPLORERS AND SURVEYORS; SEQUOYAH (RACE, ETHNICITY, AND IDENTITY).

—Marie Garrett, *University of Tennessee*

Kenneth P. Bailey, *Christopher Gist: Colonial Frontiersman, Explorer, and Indian Agent* (1976) and *The Ohio Company of Virginia and the Westward Movement, 1748–1792: A Chapter in the History of the Colonial Frontier* (1939); William Darlington, ed., *Christopher Gist's Journals, with Historical, Geographical and Ethnological Notes and Biographies of His Contemporaries* (1893).

Gold Settlements

Although gold had been discovered and mined in Appalachia as early as 1799, the first American gold rush began around 1828 in North Carolina and Virginia after prospec-

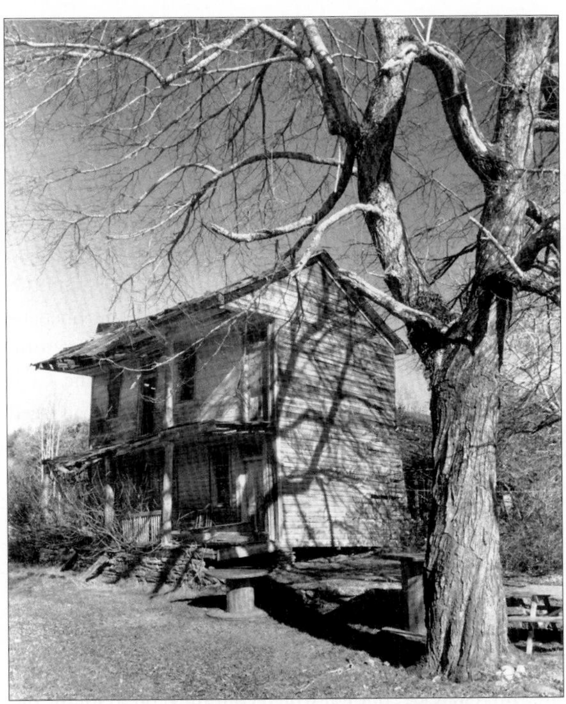

The Graham Hotel in Auraria, Georgia, 1991. The Graham is one of the very few structures built during the gold rush still standing in this boomtown. From a single-family cabin built in 1832, Auraria swelled in less than a year to boast a hundred houses, twenty stores, a newspaper, law offices, hotels, taverns, and a population of ten thousand.

tors found gold in veins running parallel to the eastern slope of the Appalachian Mountains. Significant gold rush settlements were located near the Culpeper, Vaucluse, and Woodville mines in Virginia; Albemarle and Charlotte, North Carolina; and the Brewer and Haile mines in South Carolina. As news about gold discoveries traveled south, there were more gold rushes beginning in 1829 and throughout the early 1830s in several eastern Alabama counties and in Georgia, where Dahlonega, derived from the Cherokee word meaning "yellow metal," became the center of gold-mining activity. Some settlers forced Cherokees off lands where gold was found in violation of federal treaties.

Because gold prospecting did not require money or special skill, only work and luck, people of various ages, social classes, ethnicities, and occupations participated in the Appalachian gold rush. Local residents gathered gold nuggets and dust to supplement agricultural earnings. Prospectors migrated to areas where gold strikes had been reported, and many lived in tents near gold sites.

Thousands of men and women, hoping to get rich quickly, established and settled gold-mining communities, either seeking or buying gold or selling goods and services to miners. These gold boomtowns usually consisted of dwellings and stores. Some gold settlements were considered lawless places where miners drank and gambled excessively. Other settlements were more orderly, although residents approved of vigilante punishments for crimes.

By 1830, twenty thousand people worked in the Appalachian gold fields, finding deposits worth up to five million dollars annually. An 1835 federal law established branch mints at Charlotte and Dahlonega, as well as New Orleans. When gold was discovered in California in 1848, many Appalachian gold miners rushed west. However, some southern communities' names, such as Gold Hill, Alabama, remind modern residents of the Appalachian gold rush, and local legends preserve stories about eccentric miners and gold hidden in caves. Gold mining continues in Appalachia but has been in steady decline since 1915.

See also: EARLY WHITE SETTLEMENT OF NORTHERN GEORGIA; GOLD RUSH OF 1829 (BUSINESS, INDUSTRY, AND TECHNOLOGY); TRAIL OF TEARS.

—Elizabeth D. Schafer, *Loachapoka, Alabama*

David Williams, *The Georgia Gold Rush: Twenty-Niners, Cherokees, and Gold Fever* (1993).

Grave Creek Mound

The Grave Creek Mound, located in Moundsville, West Virginia, is a product of the Adena culture, which existed from approximately 800 B.C. to A.D. 100 and extended from West Virginia to Kentucky, including portions of present-day Ohio and Indiana. The Adena, who were among the earliest migrants to the Appalachian region, built mortuary mounds that grew slowly, as individuals were buried on top of earlier burials. Grave Creek Mound exceeds all other Adena mortuary mounds in size and is the largest conical mound in North America. Built in successive stages between 250 and 150 B.C., Grave Creek once rose to an estimated seventy feet in height and had a base diameter of approximately three hundred feet. At one time it was also surrounded by a forty-foot-wide moat that had a depth of five feet.

The first known excavation of the mound, conducted in 1838, revealed two burials. Found in the upper burial was an oval sandstone tablet that was inscribed with what appeared to be hieroglyphic characters. This famous and controversial artifact, known as the Grave Creek Tablet, was never authenticated and is believed by many archaeologists to be a fake. The original has been lost, but facsimiles of the stone exist, including one in the Delf Norona Museum at the site of Grave Creek Mound.

See also: GARDEN CREEK ARCHAEOLOGICAL SITE; MOUNDBUILDERS.

—John R. Burch Jr., *Campbellsville University*

Great Valley Road

Across its history, the Great Valley Road, running from Philadelphia to coastal Georgia with an extension into

Kentucky, has been known by a number of different names, among them the Great Warrior's Path, the Great Wagon Road, and the Philadelphia Wagon Road. Long before whites came to the Valleys of Virginia and Tennessee, the Iroquois and Cherokee traveled down the path to trade with southeastern tribes, while other indigenous peoples migrated along the route from the Ohio Valley and Pennsylvania to the Southeast.

The Great Valley Road used by whites in the early eighteenth century began on the western bank of the Schuylkill River in Pennsylvania; by the 1720s the road reached only as far as Lancaster County. More than likely, whites built this segment. Near Lancaster, at the Susquehanna River, the road followed an Indian path that proceeded southwestward through York and Gettysburg, Pennsylvania, through Hagerstown to Watkins' Ferry, Maryland, on the Potomac River. From the ferry, the road progressed south into the Shenandoah Valley, across the North Branch of the Shenandoah River and the North Fork of the James River, and then via Looney's Ferry at modern-day Buchanan, Virginia, across the James River. The road dipped down to Roanoke and turned eastward through the Blue Ridge to cross the hill country into North Carolina. After crossing the Yadkin, the road followed open country between the Yadkin and Catawba Rivers, traversed the Catawba Valley to Pine Tree (Camden), South Carolina, crossed the Congaree River, and dropped down to Augusta, Georgia, and the Savannah River. An extension of the road connected it to the wilderness trail that cut through the Cumberland Gap to the Kentucky country. Along its route the wagon road utilized Native American trails that diverged at key points to follow other trails.

The segment that led from Philadelphia down the Shenandoah saw the first wave of Scots-Irish from Ulster and Germans from the Rhineland Palatinate settle the Valley of Virginia during the third and fourth decades of the eighteenth century. Both groups had entered America through Philadelphia but found the best frontier lands in Lancaster County occupied. Influenced by a generous land policy instituted by Virginia Governor William Gooch, the migrants moved south. Migration of the Scots-Irish and the Palatinate Germans continued through the 1740s and early 1750s, when they pushed south to settle on the Piedmont lands of the Carolinas.

By 1775, the Great Valley Road was the most heavily traveled route in America. Tens of thousands of vehicles used it yearly, carrying people, goods, and livestock. The road and its extensions connected the Shenandoah, the Carolina Piedmont, and the Valley of Tennessee to the great market of Philadelphia. Towns that sprang up on the road, among them Winchester, Staunton, and Roanoke in Virginia and Salisbury and Charlotteburgh (Charlotte) in North Carolina, became centers of commerce that tied backcountry settlers to markets.

During the early national period (1783–1815), the road carried thousands of conveyances loaded with passengers, goods, and U.S. mail, while herders drove cattle and swine north. From 1830 to 1860, the road continued to be a vital thoroughfare, even if its condition varied, with some segments planked and others left in dirt. The ninety-two-mile stretch from Winchester to Staunton was surfaced with macadam in 1840. Called the Shenandoah Valley Turnpike, it was an object of contention between Union and Confederate troops during the Civil War. From 1865 until the turn of the century, the road faced severe competition from the railroad for the business of transporting goods, people, and mail. Travel declined on the formerly great highway; many of the once ubiquitous inns and taverns closed their doors. The invention of the automobile, however, breathed new life into the old road. Concrete spans replaced ferries, and paved surfaces replaced roadbeds of planks and logs. Through the Shenandoah Valley, the route of the Great Valley Road became U.S. 11 and later Interstate 81, both of which continued on to follow the extension of the road through southwestern Virginia and east Tennessee. South of Roanoke in Virginia and the Carolinas, U.S. Routes 220, 52, 29, and 21 follow portions of the road.

See also: EARLY WESTWARD MIGRATION; SECTION OVERVIEW (TRANSPORTATION); WILDERNESS ROAD.

—Marie Tedesco, *East Tennessee State University*

James G. Leyburn, *The Scotch-Irish: A Social History* (1962); William E. Myer, *Indian Trails of the Southeast* (1971); Rouse Parke Jr., *The Great Wagon Road: From Philadelphia to the South* (1973).

Great Wagon Road

See Great Valley Road

Hite, Jost

(1685–1760) Frontier pioneer.

Jost Hite (also known as Hans Jost Heyte and Joost Hyte) was instrumental in the early German settlement in northern Virginia. Hite migrated from Germany to Kingston, New York, in 1710; five years later, he and his family migrated to Germantown, Pennsylvania, and later settled in the Monocacy River Valley. In 1731 Hite purchased a patent for forty thousand acres and obtained another for one hundred thousand acres in the northern Valley of Virginia. The patent required that Hite and his partner, Robert McKay, settle one family on each one thousand acres within two years. The next year, Hite, along with his sons and sixteen other families, moved to the vicinity of present-day Winchester, Virginia, establishing the first settlement west of the Blue Ridge Mountains.

In order to fulfill the grant's settlement requirements, Hite took an active role in recruiting mostly German families from Pennsylvania to settle in the valley. He and McKay conveyed tracts directly to settlers who preferred to purchase surveyed and patented land rather than arrange a survey and obtain a patent in the distant Virginia capital of Williamsburg. Hite's process of granting land, however, led to a series of protracted disputes with Lord Fairfax, the proprietor of the Northern Neck land grant, who accused Hite of establishing illegally shaped land plats and failing to conduct proper surveys. While several historians have surmised that the Hite-Fairfax lawsuits hindered settlement in the Valley of Virginia, there is no clear evidence that these disputes discouraged immigration to the region.

See also: EARLY WHITE SETTLEMENT OF SOUTHWESTERN VIRGINIA; GERMANS (RACE, ETHNICITY, AND IDENTITY); LORD FAIRFAX.

—Creston Long, *Salisbury University*

Hiwassee Island Archaeological Site

Located at the confluence of the Tennessee and Hiwassee Rivers in Meigs County, Tennessee, Hiwassee Island has been extremely influential in interpretations of the prehistory of the southeastern United States. Its 780 acres produced evidence from approximately one thousand years of history, including five late Woodland period (A.D. 600–900) burial mounds that have been completely excavated. The island was also once the site of a Mississippian village surrounded by a defensive palisade. This village included a large platform mound built in successive stages, the initial four phases attributed to early Mississippian Hiwassee Island culture (A.D. 1000–1300) and the remaining phases to late Mississippian Dallas culture (A.D. 1300–1550).

While archaeologists have been interested in the site since the nineteenth century, much of what is known about it comes from archaeological studies conducted by the federal Works Progress Administration from April 1937 to March 1939. The project, under the direction of Thomas M. N. Lewis and Madeline Kneberg, was conducted in conjunction with the construction of the Chickamauga Reservoir. The characteristics of the two Mississippian occupations of Hiwassee Island are still used, in part, to define the prehistory of present-day east Tennessee.

See also: CITICO ARCHAEOLOGICAL SITES; MOUNDBUILDERS.

—John R. Burch Jr., *Campbellsville University*

Iron Settlements

Deposits of iron, whether in bog or mineral form, can be found in every section of Appalachia. Where ore was locally accessible, early iron-mining operations sprang up in various sections of Appalachia and generated settlements of workers to mine, smelt, and forge the ore into tools and hardware supplies such as nails, screws, barrel hoops, and hinges. The first iron furnace was built in the Pittsburgh area in 1792, and by 1860 the city was producing half of the nation's steel. Birmingham, Alabama, also became a center of iron and steel production during the nineteenth century, and the industry continued to be significant in both urban areas into the twenty-first century.

Both mining and smelting are labor-intensive processes and were especially so before mechanization eased some of the work. Since smelting was inefficient and required massive supplies of wood for fuel, ironworks employed many laborers whose sole task was cutting trees. Some iron furnaces required two or more weeks of burning to reach the high temperature needed to separate the iron. Eventually, coal replaced wood as the fuel for iron production. The Fiery Gizzard settlement in Grundy County, Tennessee, developed to utilize local coal in a blast furnace.

An ironworks inevitably generated a settlement community because of the labor and multiple processes involved in producing the pig iron and forging and producing useable metal stock. Each process was reflected in additional members of the iron settlement. Although a few early ironworks were small family-based operations, economic and labor requirements meant that most ironworks became small communities of interdependent workers. Labor varied by region. Forces in northern regions of Appalachia were mostly free-wage laborers, while a mixture of slave and free labor could be found in the central region. Slave labor dominated in the South. These settlements were economically important because they stimulated construction of transportation networks and supplied materials for other industries.

The availability of both coal and iron ore was significant in the settlement of central and northeastern Alabama (particularly Birmingham), northwestern Georgia, eastern Tennessee, the Kanawha River Valley of (West) Virginia, and the western regions of the Carolinas, Virginia, Pennsylvania, Maryland, and New York.

See also: IRON AND STEEL INDUSTRY (BUSINESS, INDUSTRY, AND TECHNOLOGY); IRON AND STEEL MILL WORKERS (LABOR).

—Gerald L. Smith, *University of the South*, and Solomon K. Smith, *University of Georgia*

Land Grants

Grants of federally owned lands to states, individuals, and corporations were instrumental in the early development of the Appalachian region. Land grants to states for use by public schools and colleges and to private corporations for the construction of railroads had a lasting impact on the region, but even more significant were grants made to individuals, which encouraged organized settlement in the Appalachians after the American Revolution.

The British government routinely granted land to colonial Americans as gifts, rewards for loyalty, compensation for military service, and encouragement to settle unpopulated areas for strategic purposes. The nascent United States continued this tradition, in 1780 adopting a resolution recommending that individual states give their unappropriated lands to the federal government to help pay the public debt incurred during the Revolutionary War. The Land Ordinance of 1785 allowed the cash-poor federal government to compensate Revolutionary War veterans for their service by granting large blocks of this land in remote backcountry areas. For instance, a minimum of 160 acres went to those with the lowest rank of private. This created an influx of settlers and speculators into newly created states, resulting in the development of these states along largely private lines with very little government oversight of the exploitation of resources, planning of towns and settlements, and displacement of native peoples.

Although many veterans settled on granted land soon after the war's end, others failed to occupy the land for various reasons but retained their claims or sold them to land speculators. Nevertheless, Revolutionary War land grants exerted an immediate influence upon the social and economic organization of the Appalachian region, providing opportunities for numerous veterans and their families, many of whom were previously landless, to establish themselves as landed yeoman farmers possessing a great deal of autonomy and influence. Yet the prevalence of land-grant claims in many parts of Appalachia also restricted opportunities for landless migrants to the region as landed settlers came to occupy much of the prime river valley farmland in these areas, leaving the landless to subsist as renters or squatters on less desirable unclaimed land in mountainous and outlying areas. These divisions were most apparent during the Civil War, when owners of large valley farms were more likely to own slaves and to identify with the planter culture than were their neighbors in the mountains.

Land grants once again played a part in shaping socioeconomic structure in the Appalachians after the Civil War. Land speculators sought to exploit newly discovered coal deposits on granted land never claimed by Revolutionary War veterans. After acquiring the rights to these lands, speculators proceeded to evict squatters from land occupied by their families for generations. During the subsequent coal boom, many of these squatters were forced to make the transition from subsistence farming to wage labor in coal mines and other related industries.

See also: OCCUPYING CLAIMANT'S LAW; PROCLAMATION OF 1763; SPECULATORS AND ABSENTEE LANDLORDS.

—Michael H. Burchett, *Limestone College*

Edward Ayers and John Willis, eds., *The Edge of the South* (1991); Paul W. Gates, *History of Public Land Law Development* (1979).

Land Ordinance of 1785

The Land Ordinance of 1785 was one of three ordinances developed by the Confederation government to address the settlement of the territory northwest of the Ohio River, a region that includes Appalachian southeastern Ohio. Enacted May 20, 1785, the ordinance dispensed with the long-held practice of laying out property boundaries using natural features such as trees, creeks, and rocks. Instead, the ordinance called for a more systematic approach to surveying, including the careful maintenance of recording titles. The ordinance required surveyors to lay out towns based on meridians and parallels of longitude and latitude in a rectangular pattern. Towns were developed in six-square-mile grids and further divided into thirty-six one-square-mile lots of 640 acres. These lots were sold at auction for at least a dollar an acre. The sale of the land became a much-needed source of revenue for the government of the new nation. Few people could afford to buy or maintain such a large plot of land, however, and most of the parcels fell into the hands of absentee owners and speculators. Importantly, Congress required that one lot from each township be reserved for public schools. Later, Congress sold smaller plots for less money.

See also: EARLY WHITE SETTLEMENT OF SOUTHEASTERN OHIO; NORTHERN LAND AND DEVELOPMENT COMPANIES; SPECULATORS AND ABSENTEE LANDLORDS.

—Lisa A. Ennis, *Georgia College and State University*

Lenoir, William

(1751–1839) Land speculator.

William F. Lenoir was a Revolutionary War soldier, politician, and major land speculator in western North Carolina. Born to French Huguenots Thomas and Mourning Lenoir in Burnswick County, Virginia, he moved with his family to Edgecombe County, North Carolina, when he was eight years old. At twenty-one, he married Anne Ballard and took up an apprenticeship in surveying.

In March 1775, Lenoir moved his family west to the Fishers Creek area of the Yadkin Valley to take advantage of surveying opportunities. The Revolutionary War interrupted his plans, and that same year Lenoir joined the Patriot forces as a lieutenant. He participated in a number of forays, including attacks on villages of the Overhill Cherokee in 1776, the 1780 battle of Kings Mountain in South Carolina, where he was wounded, and the defeat of Tories near Hillsborough, North Carolina, in 1781.

Lenoir's Revolutionary War activities made him a local hero and gave him the opportunity to participate in local and state politics. First serving as clerk of the county court, he eventually became Speaker of the state senate in North Carolina in 1787. Although opportunities to rise politically ceased because Lenoir did not take criticism well and felt campaigning was undignified, he did serve as one of the first trustees of the newly founded University of North Carolina, a position he held until 1804.

Land speculation was the basis of Lenoir's prosperity. In 1775 he and several other Wilkes County residents formed a land company with 700,000 acres of land divided into tracts of 640 acres. Two years later, in partnership with Benjamin Cleveland, he bought six tracts of Wilkes County land totaling 11,000 acres. By 1784 Lenoir was one of the largest landowners in Wilkes County, controlling slightly more than 14,000 acres. Lenoir purchased property for speculation with money received from his military service, public office holdings, and the sale of farm produce. Lenoir farmed very little of the land he purchased. What land he did not sell, he rented out to local inhabitants or devoted to his lucrative enterprises, which included breeding racehorses and operating grist- and sawmills and a distillery.

Despite controversy arising from some of his land speculation, Lenoir's name has remained alive in the southern Appalachian region. A county and a city in North Carolina are named in his honor, and Lenoir City, Tennessee, is named for his son, who settled 5,000 acres of Lenoir's land there. Like other Appalachian leaders, he fought for the rights of the mountain people in the state legislature against their more wealthy lowland neighbors.

Lenoir opposed ratification of the U.S. Constitution on grounds that it contained no Bill of Rights and was too general to safeguard people's liberties. After ratification, Lenoir opposed many federal programs, believing the measures would benefit eastern merchants at the expense of western farmers.

See also: SPECULATORS AND ABSENTEE LANDLORDS.

—Jewel Tabor, *Roane State Community College*

William B. Lenoir, *History of Sweetwater Valley, Tennessee* (1976).

Long Hunters

Besides hunting locally for sustenance, early woodsmen such as Daniel Boone ventured deep into the wilderness on months-long hunting trips. These long hunters of the seventeenth and eighteenth centuries ranged across the Appalachians, establishing many of the routes later followed by settlers into southern Appalachia and the Ohio Valley. Precursors of long hunters were the logistical support parties of Hernando de Soto in the mid-1500s.

The economic and cultural setting of long hunting is the American fur-trade system from the early sixteenth century forward. Long-distance hunting began in the Southeast before 1650, and by 1690 European trader-hunters were working west of the Blue Ridge. While most of this trade-hunting was conducted along the Mississippi tributaries, some of the trade reflected English interests at Jamestown, Virginia, and eventually Charleston, South Carolina. Although barter of store goods dominated the fur economy, both companies and private parties of hunters ventured from settlement depots, forts, and central-place stores to acquire hides directly rather than engage the Native Americans in exchange.

Trade and hunting expeditions required significant capital investment in equipment and pack animals to support the hunters. American folklore idealizes the long hunters working in small kinship groups, but long-distance hunting trips to the Cumberland River or from Charleston to the French Broad required substantial planning and support. Most hunting expeditions were venture capital operations intended to bypass either the Native American trade system or the later colonial "factory" trade system. Long hunters who lacked corporate capital pooled their labor—in part to avoid the investment in trade goods necessary to purchase hides from the Native Americans and also to avoid the loss of profit to brokers and factors.

Long hunters entered hunting areas in groups, transporting the provisions necessary for protracted encampments ranging from temporary brush shelters to semipermanent log structures. Base camps included corrals for pack animals, as theft of horses was frequent. Frames for drying hides were constructed of poles lashed between trees or assembled as portable frames. Long hunters seldom preserved meat. Hides were the primary interest, and much meat was wasted. Typical prey included deer, bear, buffalo, elk, panther, and bobcat.

In the seventeenth- and eighteenth-century fur economy, the means of production was of far less importance than the quantity of production. Under normal conditions, firearms were the most efficient tools, but lead and powder were sometimes hoarded for defensive purposes and animals were taken by snares or traps instead. While one popular characterization of long hunters was their use of "long" rifles, firearms varied. Many came from notable manufactories around Lancaster, Pennsylvania, but firearms were also produced at Charleston, in central North Carolina, and in Tennessee. Long hunting faded rapidly after 1790 as large numbers of settlers entered Ohio, Kentucky, and Tennessee. Settlement caused fundamental changes in forest composition and animal habitat, and fabric preferences shifted quickly from leather to wool and then cotton. Buckskin clothing became associated with the primitive conditions of the frontier while wool, cotton, and silk symbolized settled, civilized life.

See also: BOONE, DANIEL; EXPLORERS AND SURVEYORS; FUR TRAPPERS.

—Gerald L. Smith, *University of the South*

Cecil B. Hartley, *Life of Daniel Boone* (1865); Newton D. Mereness, ed., *Travels in the American Colonies* (1916); Samuel Cole Williams, ed., *Early Travels in the Tennessee Country: 1540–1800* (1928).

Long Island of the Holston River

Long Island lies in the South Fork of the Holston River at Kingsport, Tennessee. Long regarded as a sacred site by the Cherokees, the island is located on what was the Great Indian Warrior Path and was also known as Great Island and Peace Island. During the Cherokee war with the British (1759–61), Virginia troops constructed Fort Robinson opposite the eastern end of the island. After the Transylvania Purchase (March 1775), Daniel Boone and a party of axe-men cut a road from the island through the Cumberland Gap and into Kentucky. The next year, Cherokees led by Dragging Canoe attacked the settlement in the upper Holston River Valley but were defeated at the battle of Long Island Flats (July 20, 1776). Invasions by four expeditions forced the Cherokees to make peace with Virginia and North Carolina in a treaty signed near Long Island at Fort Patrick Henry in 1777.

Following the 1777 treaty, Joseph Martin, newly appointed Indian agent for Virginia, moved to Long Island with his Cherokee wife. After the Cherokees finally relinquished claim to the island in 1806, Richard Netherland established a plantation on the island, based on a claim his wife's father purchased in 1776.

During the twentieth century, a residential area was established on the eastern end of the island. The area is now dominated by industry. In 1976 the Mead Corporation transferred the eastern end of the island to the city of Kingsport, and on July 16 of that year, the city deeded a portion of Long Island to the Eastern Band of Cherokee Indians.

See also: CHEROKEE (RACE, ETHNICITY, AND IDENTITY); PROCLAMATION OF 1763; TREATY OF LONG ISLAND OF THE HOLSTON RIVER.

—Ed Speer, *Elizabethton, Tennessee*

Lord Fairfax

In 1719 Thomas, the sixth Lord Fairfax, inherited rights to the Northern Neck, a vast tract of land extending from the Chesapeake Bay to the Allegheny Mountains. Because the grant's western boundary had never been surveyed, there were many uncertainties regarding legal land ownership in the Piedmont and Appalachian sections of the tract. In the 1720s, as settlers arrived from Pennsylvania, Maryland, and eastern Virginia, legal disputes mounted between people who had patented tracts from Virginia land agents and those who had secured their title from Fairfax. In 1729 Robert Carter, Fairfax's agent in Virginia, initiated a suit over contested land for which Virginia had issued grants. Seventeen years later, a commission comprised of agents from both parties in the suit confirmed Fairfax's right to collect property taxes, called quitrents, from nearly six million acres in the Northern Neck Proprietary.

Carter had the land formally surveyed by a group including fifteen-year-old George Washington and supervised settlement by granting land to immigrants and squatters who had already settled there. Carter also transferred almost half a million acres to family members and close friends of Fairfax from Virginia's Tidewater. Several authors have suggested that the significant ownership of land by eastern Virginia elites helped establish Tidewater economic and cultural patterns in the Northern Valley. Lord Fairfax returned to Virginia in 1747. A few years later, he built and settled into Greenway Court, an estate about twelve miles southeast of Winchester.

See also: EARLY WHITE SETTLEMENT OF SOUTHWESTERN VIRGINIA; SPECULATORS AND ABSENTEE LANDLORDS; WASHINGTON, GEORGE.

—Creston Long, *Salisbury University*

Lumber Settlements

During the eighteenth and early nineteenth centuries, timber removal in Appalachia was localized, supplying settlers with forest products and building material while clearing land for agriculture close to their settlement sites. Population growth ultimately created a wider demand for timber, inexorably leading to massive exploitation of the virgin resource by outside investors and speculators. Mountain streams and river systems provided transportation of forest products to distant markets.

Appalachian lumber settlements developed in response to specific needs. The forts and stations of the late eighteenth century were largely built with locally available trees for palisades and hewn logs. The building of the Tellico Blockhouse site around 1794 required sawed planking ordered from Knoxville. By 1800, specialized hamlets developed around shake factories, where oak logs were split to produce commercial quantities of roof shingles. Other lumber settlements developed to produce spokes and axles for wagon manufacturing. With railroads, the number of specialized lumber settlements increased. The community of Orme, Tennessee, developed around a rail station and produced crossties and oak bark for tanning. In contrast to the relatively localized tree cutting of the settlement period, large-scale timber harvesting began in Appalachia around 1860, coinciding with the industrial expansion of the Ohio Valley and the eastern portion of the Corn Belt.

Lumber camps could be raucous and disorderly due to the mostly male population and the danger of the work. Springing up in isolated locations, camps usually generated mercantile operations and service industries such as lodging houses and saloons. Mill sites became the basis of a small settlement of family members, sometimes slaves, and other workers who cut and handled logs or who operated the mill. Lumber settlements ranged in size from extended family sites to organized commercial communities of hundreds of people.

See also: LOGGING TERMINOLOGY (LANGUAGE); SPECULATORS AND ABSENTEE LANDLORDS; TIMBER AND LUMBER WORKERS (LABOR).

—Gerald L. Smith, *University of the South*, and Solomon K. Smith, *University of Georgia*

Maroon Settlements

During the antebellum period, slaves engaged in collective resistance to slavery ran away and formed communities known as maroon settlements. The term *maroon* referred to a runaway who remained in an isolated area where slavery was still in existence. These settlements cropped up in swampy, wooded, or mountainous areas, including the remote terrain of the Appalachian Mountains.

Some maroon settlements survived undetected for years, and a few lasted for generations. More often they were communities in flux. When a settlement was found or was in danger of being discovered, remaining members moved on to different hard-to-reach territories in both northern and southern Appalachia. Besides the danger of discovery, these settlements were difficult to maintain because the hilly and rocky soil in the region was not conducive to subsistence farming. Places suitable for crops and gardens were populated and thus not appropriate hideaways for runaway slaves. As a result, maroons were forced to make dangerous incursions into populated farming areas for food, clothing, livestock, and trading items. In order to obtain these provisions, maroons also often traded with free blacks and non-slaveholding whites.

Maroon communities were relatively small; the largest numbered around a few hundred persons. Despite their small size, these settlements were often found and stamped out after a short period of existence. Still, they created panic among whites, particularly the slaveholding class, disproportionate to these settlements' actual strength and numbers.

See also: AFRICAN AMERICAN INDUSTRIAL MIGRATION; FORCED MIGRATION OF SLAVES; FREE BLACKS, ANTEBELLUM (RACE, ETHNICITY, AND IDENTITY).

—Kolby W. Bilal, *College of William and Mary*

Mill Settlements

Along with homesteads, forts, stores, courthouses, schools, and churches, mills were significant Appalachian settlement institutions. Early mills included sawmills, gristmills, and turning mills; later mills also included textile and machining mills. Proliferation of roads and wagons led to wagon shops and spoke mills. Settlement mills were powered by water, animals, or humans. By 1870, most water-powered mills were upgraded to make use of large dams and wheels; industrial and commercial mills used steam power, then electricity. Mills supplied essential services and attracted both users and settlers at topographic boundaries such as falls, rapids, stream forks, and river mouths. These strategic locations intersected primary travel routes and supported the growth of villages and towns. Steep Appalachian stream gradients often allowed several mills to be built close together without interference, which further increased population growth in the area.

Because grinding in bulk was economical, mills quickly progressed from family enterprises to larger operations, utilizing hired help or slave labor. Large mill sites included the mill, the owner's residence (sometimes located over the mill in the manner of the country store), sheds, a warehouse, workers' quarters, a blacksmith shop, and other buildings. The many skills required for mill construction and operation encouraged a diversity of small industries around the primary mill. Mills also served as gathering places for many social functions. By 1875, powered textile mills spawned textile villages across the Appalachian Piedmont. Such villages matured into incorporated towns or into suburbs of adjacent towns.

See also: EARLY WHITE SETTLEMENT OF NORTHWESTERN SOUTH CAROLINA; TEXTILE WORKERS (LABOR).

—Gerald L. Smith, *University of the South*

Paul Salstrom, *Appalachia's Path to Dependency: Rethinking a Region's Economic History, 1730–1940* (1994); David E. Whisnant, *Modernizing the Mountaineer: People, Power, and Planning in Appalachia* (1980).

Moundbuilders

Thousands of mounds scattered throughout Appalachia were initially thought to be evidence of a vanished civilization or a lost tribe of Israel, but archaeologists now believe the people known as moundbuilders were descendants of Paleo-Siberians who arrived across the Bering Strait around 10,000 B.C. Three primary groups (Eastern, Western, and Archaic) are known to have built earthen mounds as part of their burial practices as early as 500 B.C.

It is believed that all moundbuilders shared similar ways of life. They subsisted on diets dictated by availability, lived in pole-constructed circular dwellings covered with woven fiber mats or daub and wattle, and wore clothing woven from fibers or made with fur and hide sewn together using bone needles and sinew or vegetable fibers. All moundbuilding groups used similar techniques to fashion tools for hunting and work, as well as burial artifacts. Art forms developed according to intellectual and skill growth, but burial artifacts indicate there existed widespread trade among groups.

Moundbuilders covered tombs with earth, and additional layers of tombs over time created mounds of varying size. Crematory mounds usually contained only one corpse, and effigy mounds were shaped like animals. The Great Serpent Mound in Adams County in southern Ohio is a notable example of an effigy mound, winding for nearly a quarter of a mile with an average height of three feet. Log-lined tombs were constructed for the deceased of particular prominence.

Burial rituals varied for different groups and changed over time. It is believed that religious ceremonies were held in circular ridges built around some of the mounds. Bodies were coated with red ocher or graphite. Shell necklaces were placed with the corpses, with the number of necklaces reflecting the prestige of the deceased.

The Adena culture, dating approximately from 800 B.C. to A.D. 100, was present primarily in Indiana, Kentucky, Ohio, West Virginia, and parts of New York and Pennsylvania. The largest remaining mound of this group is located near Dayton at Miamisburg, Ohio.

The Hopewell culture (200 B.C.–A.D. 500) initially lived in Ohio and Illinois and later spread to Michigan and throughout the East. Contemporaries of the Romans and possessing astronomical knowledge equal to that of the Mayas, they built their spectacular geometric solar and lunar calendar mounds along streams and high on wooded hills. The burial customs of the Hopewell often included cremation of the deceased, and the crematory mounds contain artifacts more highly refined than those of their predecessors, the Adena. One of the most exceptional of these is an octagonal mound located near Columbus, Ohio, now on a golf course.

Overlapping the Hopewell era were another people known as the Fort Ancients. Predecessors of the Shawnee, the Fort Ancients were so named when one of their remaining earthworks near Cincinnati was mistaken for a fortification. The Fort Ancients are credited with constructing the Great Serpent Mound, the largest known animal effigy in the world.

Three broad categories of moundbuilders have been identified for the period spanning A.D. 1400 to 1600: Woodland Indians of the Atlantic seaboard and northern Midwest; the Upper Mississippian cultures of the upper Ohio and upper Mississippi River Valley; and the Mississippian, part of which extended into the southern Appalachian part of the Tennessee Valley. Of these the Woodland culture of the Great Lakes area was dominant.

See also: GARDEN CREEK ARCHAEOLOGICAL SITE; MOUNDVILLE ARCHAEOLOGICAL PARK (CULTURAL INSTITUTIONS).

—Cora Tula Watters, *Antioch University, McGregor School*

Diana C. Gleasner, "The Native Americans: Moundbuilders of the Midwest and South," *Touring America* (February 1994); William N. Morgan, *Precolumbian Architecture in Eastern North America* (1999).

Natchez Trace

In 1801 the U.S. Army was directed to build a road from Nashville, Tennessee, to Natchez, in the newly acquired Mississippi Territory. Following a trail long used by Native Americans, the Natchez Trace cut nearly 450 miles through tribal lands of the Choctaw and Chickasaw. Congress authorized Postmaster General Gideon Granger Jr. to issue contracts for improvements along the road's entire length in 1808.

The Natchez Trace greatly benefited many southern Appalachian settlers by providing an accessible land route to the Old Southwest Territory. Of more immediate importance, however, settlers and business people who moved goods on flatboats down the Ohio-Mississippi River system to Natchez or New Orleans used the route to return home on foot or horseback. Highwaymen often made the road dangerous by robbing unsuspecting travelers, but it continued to be a vital commercial link to the Deep South until steam-powered riverboats revolutionized transportation and supplanted much of the need in the South for long, national roads.

The Natchez Trace became part of the National Park System in 1938, when Congress authorized the construction of the Natchez Trace Parkway. It eventually became part of the National Scenic Byways Program and was designated an All-American Road in 1995 for its scenic beauty and historic importance. The park includes and marks many historic and natural history sites along the route, including Emerald Mound, the gravesite of explorer Meriwether Lewis, and Tupelo National Battlefield. Parts of the Old Trace remain accessible to hikers along the Natchez Trace National Scenic Trail.

See also: OHIO RIVER (TRANSPORTATION); SOUTHERN NATIVE AMERICANS; WILDERNESS ROAD.

—Roger C. Adams, *Kansas State University*

National Road

The National Road, also known as the National Pike and, by statute, as the Cumberland Road, was one of the first federally funded highways built in the United States. Designated as U.S. 40 in the 1920s, the road extends from Cum-

Addison Toll House (also known as the Petersburg Toll House) along the National Road, Somerset County, Pennsylvania, 2002. Constructed of hand-cut native stone in 1835, the tollhouse was one of six built in Pennsylvania after responsibility for maintenance of the road shifted in 1831 from the federal government to the states through which the road passed.

berland, Maryland, to Vandalia, Illinois. The origins of the pike go back to a bargain struck in 1803 between the U.S. Congress and the legislature of the State of Ohio soon after its admission to the Union. Congress agreed to use 2 percent of the funds it received from the sale of public lands in Ohio to finance roads that crossed the state. Subsequent federal appropriations did not draw from this largely inadequate fund but from monies raised from other sources, most notably tariffs.

At the time federal and state officials agreed to the compact, construction of public roads was a crucial issue facing the new nation and the rapidly expanding western territories. Many political and commercial leaders realized that it was important for the young republic to connect the old mercantile centers of the East Coast to the newly emerging markets of the interior via overland roads. The trade between Ohio and the East had increased to such an extent that shipping via navigable rivers to Baltimore and Philadelphia was no longer adequate. An extension of the newly constructed Baltimore–Fort Cumberland Highway westward to southern Ohio seemed to offer a feasible overland route.

Under pressure from western mercantile interests concerned about the high costs of shipping goods to the East, the U.S. Senate in 1805 appointed a committee to investigate the status of the 2-percent fund. The same committee recommended a route from Cumberland through Pennsylvania and to the Ohio River at a point between Wheeling, (West) Virginia, and Steubenville, Ohio. The route through Pennsylvania was to follow a substantial portion of Braddock's Road, a deteriorating byway opened in 1755 by troops under British General Edward Braddock during the French and Indian War.

Congress passed the act to build the National Road in March 1806. Controversy in Pennsylvania over the course of the highway caused the state legislature to withhold approval for the road until 1807. As a result of the dispute, President Thomas Jefferson agreed to slight alterations of the route in Pennsylvania. Through the lobbying efforts of Senator Henry Clay of Kentucky, Wheeling became the terminus on the Ohio River rather than Steubenville.

Construction of the National Road took place over a thirty-five-year period beginning in 1806 and ending in 1841. Although the first construction contract for the pike was not let until 1811, workers already had cleared a right-of-way one-half the road's width to Brownsville, Pennsylvania, by 1808. The road was opened to traffic as far as Wheeling in 1818, and in that year torrents of traffic poured over the mountains to western Virginia.

By 1818, both Indiana (admitted to the Union in 1816) and Illinois (admitted in 1818) had entered into road-building compacts similar to Ohio's agreement with the federal government to extend the National Road. Congress appropriated funds in 1820 to continue the highway to the Mississippi River, but the road reached Vandalia, then the Illinois state capital, in 1839 and progressed no farther. Alton, Illinois, and St. Louis, Missouri, had already become engaged in an eighteen-year struggle to see which locale was to be the site for the crossing of the Mississippi. In 1848 the struggle officially came to an end, as the federal government decided to abandon plans to continue the road to the great river.

In Appalachia, the National Road covered 130 miles from Cumberland to Wheeling and carried passengers, freight, and the U.S. mail. The road was sixty feet wide with a gravel-covered surface and a ditch on either side. Tollhouses with heavy iron gates stood fifteen miles apart. Wheeling became the site of the busiest commission houses in the young nation. A noted historian of the National Road, Archer B. Hulbert, wrote that in 1822 one Wheeling commission house alone unloaded 1,081 wagons (averaging 3,500 pounds each) and paid ninety thousand dollars for freightage of goods.

Over the years, portions of the National Road have fallen into disrepair and disuse and have become obsolete.

Although U.S. 40 is still viable for hundreds of miles, interstate highways to a great extent have replaced the route. Nevertheless, there are many reminders of the old pike. Preservation societies such as the nonprofit National Road Heritage Corridor in Pennsylvania work to restore and protect historic structures, post informative mile markers, and engage in other activities designed to keep alive the memory of the old road.

See also: GREAT VALLEY ROAD; OUTFITTERS, SUPPLIERS, TAVERNS, AND INNS; WILDERNESS ROAD.

—Marie Tedesco, *East Tennessee State University*

Philip D. Jordan, *The National Road* (1948); Norris F. Schneider, *The National Road: Main Street of America* (1975).

Northern Land and Development Companies

In the eighteenth and nineteenth centuries, land and development companies accumulated large, profitable landholdings and were instrumental in settling the North American frontiers, including Appalachia, by surveying, developing, promoting, and ultimately selling parcels of land to settlers. These companies were usually financed by wealthy citizens who entrusted much of the work to job speculators and surveyors.

In New York and Pennsylvania, the Holland Land Company focused on the acquisition of western New York land that had originally belonged to the Seneca Indians and to the colony of Pennsylvania. Also operating on New York's Seneca (and other) lands was the Ogden Company. In 1792 the areas of Pennsylvania controlled by the Holland Land Company and the Pennsylvania Population Company were opened for settlement.

Three companies operated in Ohio. The first, the Ohio Company of Virginia, was formed in 1747 and consisted of a group of London merchants and wealthy Virginians. They were granted two hundred thousand acres west of the Allegheny Mountains, extending down both sides of the Ohio River. This company went out of business in 1792. The Ohio Company of Associates was organized in 1786 in Boston and received title grants for southeastern Ohio land to be sold to holders of army warrants, with some acreage free to settlers. The company reserved sections of each township for education, religion, and future congressional disposal. Ohio University, founded in 1804, was part of this agreement. The Ohio Company of Associates also founded the first capital of the Northwest Territory at Marietta. Although the company completed expansion efforts in Ohio and western Virginia in 1797, it did not dissolve until the early 1830s. The third Ohio business, the Scioto Company, secured the option to purchase five million acres in 1790, setting aside three million acres for sale to Europeans. Financial difficulties forced Scioto to close within a few months before any actual purchase, though not before founding the city of Gallipolis on the banks of the Ohio River.

Several of these companies were criticized for their methods of procuring Indian lands and transferring land to settlers. The Ogden Land Company was accused of using bribery, alcohol, and forgery to acquire Indian lands; such practices prompted Tonawanda women to petition President John Tyler to intervene. Several companies were criticized for selling acreage before they officially had title to it, thus causing hardship for migrating settlers, who arrived only to find that they did not own the land they intended to settle.

See also: EARLY WESTWARD MIGRATION; ELLICOTT, JOSEPH; SPECULATORS AND ABSENTEE LANDLORDS.

—Linda J. Trollinger, *University of Kentucky*

Ray Allen Billington, *Westward Expansion: A History of the American Frontier* (1960); Wilma A. Dunaway, *The First American Frontier: Transition to Capitalism in Southern Appalachia, 1700–1860* (1996); R. Douglas Hurt, *The Ohio Frontier: Crucible of the Old Northwest, 1720–1830* (1996).

Northern Native Americans

Prior to European contact, northern Appalachia was the homeland of a number of Native American nations. The Northeast Cultural Area is a geographic region whose native inhabitants shared similar characteristics. The region extended outside modern-day Appalachia to include other tribal groups exhibiting many of the same cultural traits. Native Americans most likely came to North America from Asia via the Bering Strait land bridge and eventually migrated across the continent. By 8000 B.C., humans were established in nearly every part of the continent, and archaeologists have found human remains in North America that may be more than fourteen thousand years old. According to oral histories and creation stories, Native Americans have been here since the beginning of time and are descended from the great moundbuilders. Several mounds, both ceremonial and burial, are located within the Appalachian region.

Important similarities among these tribes include the cultivation of maize, beans, and squash; hunting and fishing; division by a clan system (a clan is loosely equivalent to an extended family descended from an assumed common ancestor, often with a spiritual or symbolic association with a particular animal); hide and fur clothing; and either an Algonquian or Iroquoian language family. Each nation had distinct practices and beliefs, however. Woodland kinship patterns included both patrilineal (in which males and their male descendants are heads of household) and matrilineal (in which women and their female descendants are the family heads) systems and family dwellings varying from dome-shaped wigwams to multifamily longhouses. Tribes of the

Algonquian language family include the Delaware, Ottawa, and Shawnee, while the Iroquoian language family encompasses the Cayuga, Mohawk, Oneida, Onondaga, Seneca, Susquehannock, and Tuscarora nations.

The Delaware, who once inhabited the area from Virginia to Massachusetts, refer to themselves as Lenape or Lenni-Lenape, which means "real or original men." It is not known when they first arrived along the central Atlantic Coast, but from there they migrated westward into Ohio, Pennsylvania, and Indiana. Delaware families belonged to one of three clan systems: Turtle, Wolf, or Turkey. They lived in bark-covered wigwams, with each village retaining individual authority.

The Miami, whose name means "people who live along the peninsula," migrated southward into the Ohio, Indiana, and Illinois regions from an area near the Fox River in present-day Wisconsin. Divided into six bands, they lived in dome-shaped wigwams covered with elm bark or woven plant material. The Miami fought with the British in the American Revolution and were forced to cede Appalachian Ohio to the United States by the Treaty of Greenville in 1795.

The Ottawa, whose name translates as "to barter or trade with," lived along the Ottawa River in eastern Ontario and western Quebec, then migrated into northern Ohio around 1740. In their clan-based culture, labor was divided according to gender with males hunting, trapping, and trading while the females planted and harvested. They, too, were forced from the area by the Treaty of Greenville.

The Shawnee, whose historic homelands included parts of what is now Ohio, Pennsylvania, Kentucky, and West Virginia, migrated southward into Tennessee and South Carolina, then returned to the Ohio-Kentucky region. Large villages were located at Chillicothe, Ohio, and Lower Shawnee Town (now Portsmouth, Ohio). The nation, which held a strong tribal identity, consisted of five divisions, or septs: the Chalahgawtha, Hathawagila, Piqua, Makujay, and Kispoko; tribal leaders were determined according to the clan to which they belonged. Although Shawnee division of labor was based on gender, there was a high degree of equality between men and women. Shawnee means "people from the south" or "southerner."

The Susquehannock, or "people of the muddy river," lived near the Chesapeake Bay in Maryland, and migrated into Appalachian areas of New York, Pennsylvania, and Ohio. Although they were aggressive and fought bitterly with the Delaware and the Iroquois Confederacy, they were one of the least-known tribes of the northeastern area. A matrilineal society, the tribe lived in large fortified villages.

The Erie Indians, short for Erielhonan, occupied lands from Ohio to New York. They lived in traditional longhouses in scattered villages, used poison-tipped arrows, and traded with the Susquehannock. They were nearly destroyed by the Iroquois Confederacy.

The Lakota, Dakota, and Nakota (commonly referred to as Sioux) originally inhabited the upper Mississippi region extending into Ohio, Indiana, and Illinois. They migrated westward to the northern plains in the late eighteenth century.

The Iroquois Confederacy is also known as the Haudenosaunee, or the People of the Longhouse. Highly organized with a strong government and military, they were matriarchal and matrilineal, with women voting, holding property, and making governing decisions. They lived in large multifamily dwellings known as longhouses; individual longhouses housed six to ten related families, and villages consisted of thirty to fifty dwellings. The Iroquois Confederacy consisted of the Cayuga, Mohawk, Onondaga, Oneida, Seneca, and, after 1722, the Tuscarora. The Cayuga were the least warlike of the tribes and engaged in farming and growing orchards. Their principal village was Goioguen. The Mohawks' main villages were centered near Lake Mohawk, New York, making Mohawks the eastern-most tribe of the confederacy. They called themselves the "people of flint." The Onondaga, whose name means "on the top of," were considered the most traditional of the Iroquois nations and were Keepers of the Council Fire for two centuries. Living in what is now New York, they were known for salt making. The Seneca were the most western and largest tribe of the confederacy; their name is translated "people of the stone." The Mingoes of the Scioto River Valley in Ohio were members of the Seneca tribe who allied with the French, rather than the English, in imperial struggles over territory and trade. The Oneida, also matrilineal, consisted of three clans—Turtle, Bear, and Wolf—and women nominated clan leaders. The Tuscarora built ceremonial and burial mounds in their homelands of central North Carolina and later migrated to the area surrounding present-day Binghamton in western New York. Initially thought to be a confederacy of three tribes, the tribe consisted of seven female-led clans—Bear, Wolf, Turtle, Beaver, Deer, Eel, and Snipe—with the Turtle and Wolf clans each having two subdivisions. The Tuscarora were matrilineal and allowed marriage outside their own clan.

See also: IROQUOIS (RACE, ETHNICITY, AND IDENTITY); SOUTHERN NATIVE AMERICANS; TREATY OF GREENVILLE.

—Linda J. Trollinger, *University of Kentucky*

James H. Howard, *Shawnee* (1981); John L. Stoutenburgh Jr., *Dictionary of the American Indian* (1960); Carl Waldman, *Encyclopedia of Native American Tribes* (1988).

Occupying Claimant's Law

An "Act concerning occupying claimants of Land," passed by the Kentucky state legislature on February 27, 1797, provided compensation for the accidental improvement of land by a settler who earnestly but mistakenly believed that he was living upon a rightful claim.

The need for the new act arose because eighteenth-century surveying methods often led to squatters occupying property as if it were their own. While the Occupying Claimant's Law entitled lawful landowners to reclaim their land, it also provided that "lasting and valuable improvements" be considered by the courts for reimbursement from the property owner to the evicted settler. In addition, "damages the land may have sustained by the commission of any kind of waste, or by the reduction of soil by cultivation" made by a settler could be taken into consideration for reimbursement to the rightful property owner. Evaluations were made by a court-appointed commission, and by 1809 six cases had been brought to the Kentucky Court of Appeals for review.

The act of 1797 was repealed by act of the legislature passed on January 31, 1812. This law was an amended version of the 1797 act and was passed despite objections from Governor Charles Scott. Settlers in the Appalachian Mountains of Kentucky frequently lacked the resources to acquire land, and "free land" in the mountains simply did not exist. The two acts were, in some minor way, beneficial to those who had made lasting and valuable improvements to the land. The courts rarely decided in their favor, however, and poor Appalachian settlers were forced from the land by absentee owners.

See also: LAND GRANTS; PROCLAMATION OF 1763; SPECULATORS AND ABSENTEE LANDLORDS.

—Roger C. Adams, *Kansas State University*

Outfitters, Suppliers, Taverns, and Inns

Appalachian settlement adapted European social institutions to distinctive North American conditions. Establishments such as taverns, inns, "victualaries," draughts, and ordinaries reflected the European model of pubs and hotels as well as the peculiar conditions and opportunities of North America. By 1650, explorers from Virginia had entered the Blue Ridge Mountains and by 1690 may have reached the area around Memphis, Tennessee. By 1700, a system of forts, depots, and stores had developed along the fall line, protecting fur traders and their harvests of skins. These military and mercantile structures also distributed trade goods and provided bases for the advance of merchants and pioneers into the wilderness.

The needs of travelers—soldiers, explorers, traders, missionaries, naturalists, writers, peddlers, merchants, and settlers—were supported by an interconnected system of outfitters, suppliers, taverns, and inns. In the southern Piedmont, the Appalachian Mountains, and the plateau country to the west, these facilities were arrayed in an irregular grid defined by the natural features of the land and by the paths, trails, and roads imposed upon these natural features. There were several routes of passage and trade that ran roughly north to south, paralleling the Atlantic Coast, and several major west-tending routes that intersected the north-south lines. These westerly routes included Braddock's Road across Pennsylvania, the famous Wilderness Road into the Kentucky and Ohio country, and local routes such as "Three-Chopt Road," which reached westward from Richmond, Virginia. This European network was partly imposed upon prehistoric Native American routes that, in turn, had been laid over animal pathways.

Resources and people concentrated at the intersection of roads and topographic features. Every river crossing required a bridge, ford, or ferry. A ferry included a boat and a house for the ferryman's family and shelter for travelers. Nearby there might be a store or small inn. In the heart of the Appalachians, the intersection of routes provided the setting for stores and depots and for a network of backcountry stations and forts. Traders returning from Native American lands stopped at these combination forts-stores-warehouses-inns on their way eastward. Travelers following the trade routes westward also stopped at these places to rest, stock up on provisions, join with other travelers to form safer traveling parties, and gather essential information about the country ahead. As roads progressed from footpaths and horse trails to cleared wagon roads, stagecoaches became an important mode of travel. With stagecoaches came livery stables, blacksmith shops, and substantial inns for passengers. Many inns were elaborations of dogtrot log structures, but some were two-story structures that offered private accommodations and a dining room. John Wood's early-nineteenth-century inn, located in Appalachian Alabama, was constructed of massive stone walls and contained private rooms with fireplaces, a post office, a granary, and a nearby blacksmith shop.

The existing supply system for the fur trade also supported the needs of westward travelers: firearms, powder and shot, and food—salted meat, flour, sugar, salt, bacon, crackers, and dried beans—in addition to wilderness necessities such as tents, tools (especially axes, knives, hatchets, augers, wedges, mauls, and saws), tack and harness, and domestic supplies such as medicines, shoes, cloth, thread, needles, pots, and wooden barrels. Each category of supplies represented not only a line of merchandise in the stores but increasingly an assemblage of craftsmen—potters, blacksmiths, millers, carpenters, tanners, and weavers—who established their workplaces at or near the earlier settlement structures. A traveler could purchase an elaborate "kit" of essential items from these suppliers and could usually find someone within a few days' journey to make or repair a broken musket stock or wagon wheel.

The relationship among suppliers, travelers, and lodging is evident in the general stores along the drovers' routes from Appalachia to distant markets such as New York, Philadelphia, Savannah, Pensacola, and New Orleans. Stores serviced the grain and tack needs of drovers and were lodging points along the way. Most stores had a nearby corncrib where local corn taken in trade for store goods was sold to drovers for livestock. Sheds or bunkhouses were constructed to shelter the men who tended cattle, hogs, sheep, and turkeys driven to market from deep within the valleys and coves of Appalachia. This system of stores and suppliers became an auxiliary economic system that supported a mechanism of credit, banking, and wholesaling. The Moravian stores of western North Carolina, for example, served an essential brokerage function by receiving furs that were reshipped in wagon trains to warehouses in Savannah or Charleston. Virginia stores not only received hogsheads of tobacco rolled along the tobacco roads but also were the distribution points for shiploads of European goods destined for both military and domestic markets in the Piedmont and in the mountains.

Accommodations mentioned in narratives, journals, and letters illustrate the range of comforts found by travelers. Shelter varied from hollow trees and canebrakes to Native American dwellings and from barns, cribs, and sheds to hospitable family cabins. With the advance of settlement, resources such as sawed planking became more common, and a traveler might find lodging in a framed house with a bed or perhaps in some cases even a semiprivate room and the provision of an evening and morning meal. One group of travelers in Virginia in the 1720s was amazed to find lodging in a detached house containing a bath with running, albeit cold, water.

More common were conditions of filth and general uncleanliness. The most common complaint of travelers centered on infestations of insects—roaches, bedbugs, and lice. Other complaints included the high cost of goods and services, the raucous behavior of gamblers and drinkers, the absence of privacy, and unwashed servants. Many travelers reported having items and baggage pilfered from carriages or wagons. Experienced travelers learned to sleep with their essential luggage or to post watches through the night. Conditions in commercial lodging varied as widely as in domestic lodging.

The practical limits of daily travel for drovers and families dictated a stopover interval not greatly above ten miles. This interval, projected along the various routes, generated dozens of small settlements. The effects of this distribution of outfitters and lodging places continue to be visible in the hamlet and village pattern along the settlement routes. Between 1650 and 1850, America's population expanded from less than a hundred thousand to more than 23 million, pushing settlement as it grew. The needs of this mobile population were supplied by thousands of taverns, inns, and stores that provided supplies and lodging. In the fragmented terrain of the Appalachians, depots, stores, taverns, and inns were the critical interface between the economic and social networks that were the foundation of common life.

See also: GREAT VALLEY ROAD; NATIONAL ROAD.

—Gerald L. Smith, *University of the South*

Clarence Walworth Alvord and Lee Bidgood, *The First Explorations of the Trans-Allegheny Region by the Virginians, 1650–1674* (1912); Charles Lyell, *Travels in North America, in the Years 1841–2; with Geological Observations on the United States, Canada, and Nova Scotia* (1845); Newton D. Mereness, ed., *Travels in the American Colonies* (1916).

Proclamation of 1763

The British government issued the Proclamation of 1763 (October 7) following the signing of the Treaty of Paris (February 10, 1763), which ended the French and Indian War in North America. The proclamation regulated the settlement of land in North America and, more importantly, attempted to conciliate the American Indians in the territory acquired from France. In short, the proclamation was an attempt to stop the westward migration of settlers before obtaining the consent of American Indian tribes for the establishment of transmontane settlements. Unfortunately, it was issued too late to prevent the outbreak of Pontiac's War (1763–64).

The Proclamation of 1763 reserved the territory west of the Appalachian Mountains and north of the thirty-first parallel for American Indians. European settlement in the region was prohibited, and those who had already settled there were ordered to vacate their homes. Those trading with American Indians were to be licensed. Private land purchases from American Indians were forbidden; future acquisitions of land in the reserved territory were to be negotiated by the royal governors. The proclamation also created three provinces in the newly acquired territory: Quebec, East Florida, and West Florida.

The boundary established by the proclamation was subsequently modified in the Treaties of Hard Labor (1768), Fort Stanwix (1768), and Lochaber (1770), which were negotiated by the two colonial superintendents of Indian affairs. In 1768 the Board of Trade instructed John Stuart, southern superintendent of Indian affairs, to establish the Kanawha River as the boundary between the Cherokee Nation and the colony of Virginia. The previous year the Cherokee had agreed that their boundary with the colony of North Carolina would begin at the western terminus of the North Carolina–South Carolina border on Reedy River, then north to Tryon Mountain in North Carolina, and then in a direct line to Chiswell's Mine in Virginia. In October 1768, at Hard Labor, South Carolina, the Cherokee agreed to relinquish their claim to the territory east of a line drawn directly from Chiswell's Mine northwesterly to the confluence of the Kanawha and Ohio Rivers.

Sir William Johnson, northern superintendent of Indian affairs, negotiated a treaty with the Iroquois at Fort Stanwix, New York, in November 1768. In the Treaty of Fort Stanwix, the Iroquois ceded land east and south of the treaty line in western New York and Pennsylvania. The Iroquois also gave up their claim to the territory south of the Ohio River as far downstream as the mouth of the Tennessee River, a region also claimed by the Cherokee.

In October 1770, a Cherokee delegation met with John Stuart, his deputy, Alexander Cameron, and John Donelson (representing the colony of Virginia) at Lochaber, South Carolina, to negotiate a modification of the boundary established at Hard Labor. In the Treaty of Lochaber, the Cherokee agreed to cede the territory north and east of a line beginning where the Hard Labor line crossed the North Carolina–Virginia boundary (the 36° 30′ parallel). This line extended westward to a point in the South Fork of the Holston River six miles east of Long Island (present-day Kingsport, Tennessee), then to the North Fork of the Holston River six miles above Long Island, and northward to the junction of the Kanawha and Ohio Rivers. The Cherokee were opposed to ceding Long Island, fearing a fort would be constructed on the island.

During the survey of the treaty line in 1771, the Cherokee representatives agreed to two changes. When the survey party reached the South Fork of the Holston River, the Cherokee agreed to allow the line to follow that river downstream to a point six miles from Long Island, then north to the North Fork of the Holston River. More importantly, the Cherokee agreed to allow the line to extend from the North Fork of the Holston River across the mountains to the head of the Kentucky River and down that river to its confluence with the Ohio River. The latter change greatly increased the acreage ceded by the Cherokee.

See also: EARLY WESTWARD MIGRATION; TREATIES OF FORT STANWIX.

—Ed Speer, *Elizabethton, Tennessee*

Railroad Promotion and In-Migration

After the War of 1812, the federal government began to concentrate efforts to expand U.S. territory. Opening new territories to settlement required improved transportation such as transcontinental railroads. Private railroad companies, however, were at first unwilling to finance the costly venture into unsettled frontier lands.

In order to encourage railroad companies to expand, the government passed a number of land-grant bills giving railroads public domain lands at no cost. With this incentive, the railroads set out to attract settlers, working with the government to develop land committees and immigration boards to encourage migration. Representatives from various railroads often traveled overseas to recruit and organize immigrant groups for travel to America. The railroad companies produced maps and pamphlets in a variety of languages, extolling the quality of life in America as well as the excellent climate and conditions for farming, and distributed them overseas in places such as England, Germany, and Scandinavia.

People were recruited either to settle on the railroads' lands, work in rail construction gangs, or both. In their recruitment efforts, railroads worked with the U.S. and foreign governments and with state and private immigration agencies. Most foreign immigrants tended to work on railroads in the West, while black workers were a plurality in the South. For instance, in 1908 black workers made up about half of a five-thousand-strong workforce in West Virginia, east Tennessee, Virginia, and the Carolinas, while about 40 percent of the workers were immigrants from Italy and only 10 percent were native white laborers. As the railways were completed, many immigrants settled in the towns and industrial areas that developed along rail lines.

See also: AMERICAN EMIGRANT COMPANY; OLD IMMIGRANTS (RACE, ETHNICITY, AND IDENTITY); RAILROADS (TRANSPORTATION).

—Lisa A. Ennis, *Georgia College and State University*

Recreation and Immigration

See Twentieth-Century In-Migration

Retirees

See Twentieth-Century In-Migration

Salt Settlements

Deposits of salt, located throughout Appalachia, heavily influenced the location of human settlements by attracting industrialists, mercantilists, and agriculturalists to areas where the mineral could be found in either rock or saline form. Its preservative qualities significantly aided exploration and settlement of remote regions. Generally, Europeans exploited salt sources either by following animal herds or by driving Native American communities away from the sources. Salt makers normally preceded farmers into frontier regions, and salt production remained the primary occupation of inhabitants long after the arrival of agricultural activities. Salt sources had a threefold value: they supplied salt for food preservation and seasoning, served medicinal purposes, and attracted wild game.

Salt extraction varied by the source. Rock salt could be mined inexpensively, but salt springs differed in brine strength, and manufacturing costs were highest where brine

Store, with owner Ben Allison standing in the doorway, Allison Gap, near Saltville, Virginia, c. 1900. The Saltville Valley in southwestern Virginia has been a commercial source of salt and salt-related products since 1782. During the Civil War, every Confederate state maintained a furnace for salt production in the area.

was weak. Early production methods were primitive—saltwater was evaporated in large kettles, drained, and stored. Production required large labor forces to supply fire fuels, to raise saltwater, and to package the finished product. Salt settlements stimulated the construction of transportation networks and other industries, particularly meatpacking.

Salt was key to the settlement of Bullitt, Jefferson, Nicholas, Mason, Lewis, Henry, Boone, and Carter Counties in Kentucky; Muskingum, Jackson, Scioto, and Jefferson Counties in Ohio; the fifteen contiguous counties east of Knoxville in the upper east Tennessee River Valley; the Kanawha River Valley in Virginia (now West Virginia); the five counties adjoining Saltville in southwestern Virginia; Allegheny, Westmoreland, and Indiana Counties in Pennsylvania; and the region surrounding Syracuse in New York.

See also: EARLY WHITE SETTLEMENT OF SOUTHWESTERN VIRGINIA; NONMETALLIC, NONFUEL DEPOSITS (GEOLOGY).

—Solomon K. Smith, *University of Georgia*

Sevier, John

(1745–1815) Land speculator and first governor of Tennessee.

Few individuals equaled the distinction of John Sevier in the settlement of the southern Appalachian region. His importance is reflected in the presence of his statue in National Statuary Hall in the United States Capitol. During the Revolutionary War, Sevier, already noted as a fearless Indian fighter, served heroically in the decisive battle of Kings Mountain (1780). By the early nineteenth century, he had served in North Carolina's legislature and as district judge, brigadier general, United States congressman, governor of the short-lived State of Franklin, and the first governor of Tennessee. He was also a land speculator, investing in schemes to profit from the acquisition of territorial land.

In 1773 Sevier, a Virginian by birth, settled in western North Carolina, an area that became east Tennessee in 1796. He lived chiefly along the Nolichucky River and later established his Marble Springs plantation near present-day Knoxville.

In 1782 North Carolina's legislature voted to compensate the state's Revolutionary War veterans with land grants in the Tennessee wilderness. Although unscrupulous speculators had already illegally bought millions of choice acres, Sevier's honesty, generosity, and vibrant personality earned him great admiration from his Appalachian peers as a well-trusted land speculator. Besides trading warrants for money, Sevier sometimes placed other tracts of land in trust against future profits on speculative lands. In addition, successful political maneuvering guaranteed that absentee landowners paid no higher taxes on their lands than owners of improved properties.

In 1789 Sevier joined William Blount in acquiring great amounts of Tennessee land, becoming deeply involved in an enterprise called the Yazoo Land Company, which expected to make fortunes buying and selling Indian land at the "Bend of the Tennessee River" in current northern Alabama. Previously, Sevier, serving as governor of the State of Franklin, had considered aligning the state with Spain to obtain Indian lands. (The self-proclaimed State of Franklin existed in the western reaches of North Carolina, present-day Tennessee, from 1784 to 1788.) Although pressure from the federal government to uphold previous treaties with Native Americans in the area caused the Yazoo plan to be unsuccessful, Blount and Sevier continued to speculate together on Indian lands. Blount, who was appointed territorial governor in 1790, was aggressive in negotiating treaties that favored his ambitions to open more land to speculation and settlement, notwithstanding federal instructions to respect Cherokee boundaries. His unwavering pursuit of land wealth, coupled with numerous accusations of fraud and a plan to conspire with Britain in conquering Florida, eventually destroyed his national reputation and political career. Sevier, despite his relationship with Blount, escaped with his reputation intact, partly due to his popularity with Tennesseans.

By 1795, Sevier had used his own North Carolina military warrants to accumulate 70,000 acres of land. East Tennessee holdings included Greene, Jefferson, Knox, and Sullivan Counties, and Cumberland area tracts were in Roane, Sumner, Overton, and Smith Counties. He also co-owned 128,000 acres with speculator Landon Carter in Washington County. At that time, entries were listed at fifty shillings per 100 acres.

In 1801 Sevier and Andrew Jackson feuded for the major-general post in Tennessee's militia, and Jackson convinced Governor Archibald Roane that Sevier had fraudulently speculated in North Carolina. Although Sevier was cleared of the charges, Jackson received the office. Sevier died a poor man, but his heirs later received 5,000 acres of land promised by Georgia to Sevier as a commissioner and surveyor of land in the Tennessee River's Big Bend.

See also: SPECULATORS AND ABSENTEE LANDLORDS; STATE OF FRANKLIN (GOVERNMENT).

—Patricia Shirley, *Knoxville, Tennessee*

Alfred N. Chandler, *Land Title Origins: A Tale of Force and Fraud* (1945); Daniel M. Friedenberg, *Life, Liberty, and the Pursuit of Land: The Plunder of Early America* (1992); William H. Masterton, *William Blount* (1954).

Southern Land and Development Companies

Southern land companies during the colonial period operated in much the same manner as joint-stock companies. Members purchased shares, and each entity had to seek a charter for a specific area of land from the colonial governor and the British Crown. The terms of the charter might specify that a certain number of families had to be settled on the land in a given period of time or that grantees meet other conditions. Investors typically included members of the colonial planter aristocracy, but English and Scottish merchants frequently purchased shares and helped to coordinate companies' overseas administrative negotiations. Although individual settlers ventured forth to unofficially populate the Appalachian frontier, settlement legally recognized by colonial governments and the Crown occurred through land companies. Corporations purchased large tracts of land and then either rented or resold smaller parcels to individual settlers and families. Companies recruited settlers through promotional literature both within the colonies and in Europe, sometimes providing the opportunity for property ownership to groups such as Moravians and Scots-Irish.

Speculation west of the Appalachian Mountains became increasingly complicated beginning in the late 1740s. France and England had engaged in three imperial wars since the late seventeenth century, each of which had a colonial component. A climate of Franco-British tension persisted, especially over the Ohio Valley region. Southern elites, comprised of the landed gentry, began to pursue western lands under imperial auspices. They expressed fears that the British colonial population would be limited by the threatening presence of the French west of the Appalachians unless British settlements were quickly secured in the region. The 1748 Ohio Company of Virginia became the principal contender for this territory. Its actions heightened preexisting imperial tensions, aggravated intercolonial rivalries, and precipitated disputes among competing land companies and Ohio Valley Indians. The conflict erupted in the French and Indian War (1754–63).

The southern gentlemen who formed and invested in these companies rarely saw their territorial purchases in person. They relied heavily on a variety of working people to carry out the labor and logistics necessary to pursue their claims. Surveyors assessed and demarcated the parameters of a grant, staking out the most favorable areas for settlement. Agents of these privately owned companies, including men such as Christopher Gist and George Washington, had the complicated task of negotiating with the Native Americans who occupied the desired lands and were divided in their allegiances between the British and French. Company representatives in effect became colonial or Crown diplomats, while Native American representatives sometimes "sold" territory over which they had no formal jurisdiction.

After Britain's victory in the French and Indian War, King George III issued the Proclamation of 1763 in an attempt to pacify Native Americans. The French agreed to abandon their North American territory, causing great concern among the Indians, who feared aggressive British encroachments in the region between the Appalachian Mountains and the Mississippi River. The Proclamation Line forbade British colonial land acquisition west of the Appalachians. Southern developers vehemently resisted and ignored the policy, pursuing their claims despite both British administrative barriers and Indian treaties. In addition to the Ohio Company of Virginia, other important southern land companies were the Greenbrier Company, the Mississippi Company, and the Transylvania Company.

See also: GIST, CHRISTOPHER; PROCLAMATION OF 1763; WASHINGTON, GEORGE.

—Tania Boster, *University of Pittsburgh*

Kenneth P. Bailey, *The Ohio Company of Virginia and the Westward Movement, 1748–1792: A Chapter in the History of the Colonial Frontier* (1939); Daniel M. Friedenberg, *Life, Liberty, and the Pursuit of Land: The Plunder of Early America* (1992); James H. Merrell, *Into the American Woods: Negotiators on the Pennsylvania Frontier* (1999).

Southern Native Americans

The first inhabitants of southern Appalachia were nomadic hunters and foragers known as Paleo-Indians who arrived approximately 12,000 B.C. While little is known about these people and their culture, a significant number of Paleo-Indian artifacts—specifically, stone projectile points—have been found in both the Cumberland and Tennessee River basins.

By 8500 B.C., recognizable Archaic cultures had developed. While still hunters and gatherers, early Appalachians adapted to a post-Pleistocene environment marked by a warming climate and emergent modern forests. During this era, many large mammals previously hunted for food became extinct. Consequently, native peoples became more efficient in exploiting local resources and adapted their stone technology, including projectile points and woodworking tools, to local conditions. Evidence exists that some native plants were cultivated during this period in the southeastern portion of present-day United States.

Towards the end of the Archaic period, which lasted approximately 7,000 years, fiber-tempered pottery was invented. A new period, known as the Woodland, succeeded it and lasted from about 3,200 to 1,100 years ago. Archaeologists have studied the evolution of pottery in the Southeast from this time and have discovered a cultural continuity known as the South Appalachian Tradition. Centered in present-day Georgia and South Carolina and extending into contiguous areas of Tennessee, North Carolina, and Alabama, this pottery tradition dates from approximately 1000 B.C. to the decline of the Mississippian chiefdoms around the time of European contact in the mid-sixteenth century. Continuity in ceramic manufacturing was evident in the stamping used to decorate the pottery. This cultural thread also has been identified in the construction of projectile points. Although other stone and pottery technologies are evident in the same geographical areas, it implies a specific cultural area in southern Appalachia.

By 1000 B.C., the hunter-gatherer lifestyle was gradually replaced by a sedentary culture that constructed earthworks and mounds accompanied by mortuary rituals. While these people were not agriculturalists, there is evidence that they cultivated gourds, sumpweed, and sunflowers.

A 2000 painting depicts village gardeners of the middle Woodland period, c. A.D. 300. This period of Native American history is characterized by the rise of pottery making, elaborate burial customs, and a sophisticated and far-ranging trade system.

Hopewellian societies, which consisted of small, dispersed settlements associated with centralized ceremonial centers, arose by 200 B.C. Mortuary ritual, along with its associated symbol system, was a primary focus of their culture. An extensive trade network developed in exotic goods such as obsidian from the Rocky Mountains, copper from the Great Lakes, and mica from the mountains of present-day North Carolina. These trade goods were often interred with the social elite in burial mounds. By A.D. 450, the trade networks had disappeared, along with much of the mortuary ritual. Burial mounds were still being constructed, but on a much smaller scale.

By A.D. 800, people began consolidating in agricultural lands in river valleys. Maize, a highly productive and storable crop, became an important staple in these communities. Bean agriculture also arose during this period. Within two hundred years, these communities emerged as Mississippian chiefdoms. (The term *Mississippian*, as with *Archaic* and *Hopewellian*, refers to cultures that differed in languages and social customs, rather than individual groups of people.)

The Mississippian ancestors of the Cherokee spoke an Iroquoian language, while the predecessors of the Creek, Choctaw, and Chickasaw all spoke Muskogean languages.

These agricultural communities built large, flat-topped platform mounds that served both as residences for the ruling elite caste and as boundaries for a central public plaza. Mound centers were often protected with fortifications that included bastions.

The communities were chiefdoms, the leader of which inherited his position through his mother. The chief's close blood relatives comprised the elite caste that ruled over commoners. When members of the elite caste died, they were buried in mortuary mounds with the accoutrements of their position, including flint swords and carved conch shells. Many of the elite status symbols were acquired through long-distance trade networks that echoed the earlier Hopewellian matrix.

Chiefdoms were often parts of paramount chiefdoms, in which the chief of the dominant chiefdom lorded over the chiefs of the lesser chiefdoms. Status and power over chiefdoms was gained through warfare; thus, the fortunes of specific chiefdoms were in constant flux. For example, from approximately A.D. 1200 to 1350, Etowah was the center of a paramount chiefdom that controlled a large part of present-day northern Georgia and whose influence extended into present-day northeastern Alabama, eastern Tennessee, and western portions of North and South Carolina. By the time of Hernando de Soto's arrival in the sixteenth century, however, Etowah was a small community in the paramount chiefdom of Coosa.

By consolidating large populations into fortified communities such as Etowah, Citico, and Hiwassee Island, Mississippian communities rendered their inhabitants especially susceptible to biological agents introduced into their midst by the Spanish expeditions of the sixteenth century. The combination of disease and increased warfare led to the collapse of Mississippian sociopolitical society soon after European contact, and the major mound centers were abandoned. The collapse of Mississippian culture affected Native American groups differently. The ancestors of the Cherokee, who inhabited present-day northwestern Georgia and the western mountainous region of the Carolinas, stopped building mounds but remained a cohesive entity. They even expanded their territory into eastern Tennessee, filling the void left by the Muskogean peoples who vacated the area. The remnants of the Muskogean chiefdoms re-formed as the Creek, Chickasaw, and Choctaw.

See also: CHEROKEE (RACE, ETHNICITY, AND IDENTITY); MOUNDBUILDERS; NORTHERN NATIVE AMERICANS.

—John R. Burch Jr., *Campbellsville University*

Charles Hudson, *Knights of Spain, Warriors of the Sun: Hernando de Soto and the South's Ancient Chiefdoms* (1997); Charles Hudson and Carmen Chaves Tesser, eds., *The Forgotten Centuries: Indians and Europeans in the American South, 1521–1704* (1994); Bruce G. Trigger and Wilcomb E. Washburn, eds., *The Cambridge History of the Native Peoples of the Americas, Vol. 1: North America* (1996).

Speculators and Absentee Landlords

Land speculation, the practice of acquiring inexpensive, undeveloped land in anticipation of an increase in value over time, is intricately tied to the settlement and development of Appalachia. Colonial governors and aristocrats, eastern merchants, foreign and domestic land companies, southern planters, and individuals with investment wealth (and often political connections) were all early speculators in Appalachian lands. These investors rarely visited their vast holdings, instead buying and trading individual land claims and shares of land companies through brokerage houses. Since positive return on their investment—rather than the welfare of their tenants or lands—was their first concern, speculators acquired a reputation for price gouging, unfair competition, exploitation of people and resources, and fraudulent dealings in order to maximize profits. However, speculators also commissioned accurate land surveys, funded roads, established towns, extended credit to settlers, and facilitated the settlement of Appalachia in many ways.

Although the territory west of the British Proclamation Line of 1763 was reserved for Native American tribes, land speculators and squatters already were active in the area despite active resistance by the natives. After the American Revolution, Native American groups were pushed farther west, and Euro-American expansion began in earnest. Each new state was quick to make decisions about the dispossession of territory, and much land was privatized before federal and public domain laws could be created. States allowed war veterans, private speculators, and land companies to purchase huge tracts of choice land cheaply, forcing small homesteaders and squatters onto the least desirable land.

Most Appalachian land quickly came to be controlled by a few powerful individuals. In 1792 Virginia sold more than 2 million acres to only fourteen speculators. When lands were opened in Tennessee, 4 million acres sold in less than a year. By 1810, absentee speculators controlled more than 75 percent of southern Appalachia, and northern Appalachia experienced similar trends. Speculators often let their property lie unused, passed the deeds to heirs, or sold large tracts to other speculators, tying up useable land for generations. Land rarely found its way into the hands of individual farmers, creating a large population of tenant farmers in the region.

The speculation process during the 1700s was a boon to a number of different professions on the frontier. Surveyors were used to investigate new lands and make recommendations for investment. Absentee owners also used the services of local attorneys and courthouse officials to handle legal and tax issues for them. The landlord's most important employee, however, was the land jobber. Hired on commission, the land jobber managed the absentee owner's holding by supervising surveyors, buying and selling land, paying taxes, bribing officials when necessary, and managing tenant contracts, collecting rents, and enforcing evictions.

From the late seventeenth century through the nineteenth century, speculators engaged in a variety of commercial ventures. In rich, lush valleys, boomtowns were built from scratch to entice settlers into a certain region to enhance its value or to provide labor for industries such as textile milling or coal mining. Speculators advertised for settlers of these company towns, often appealing to foreign immigrants such as Germans and Scots-Irish. These settlers, now tenants, worked to improve the owners' investments, clearing land, cutting roads, planting crops, and building structures while simultaneously paying rent, usually a third of their crop, to the speculator. Tenants also kept the land free of squatters and Indians.

Another practice of speculators was to develop resorts catering to wealthy vacationers. The scenic beauty of the mountains, with their rivers, streams, game-filled forests, and hot springs, made Appalachian lands popular vacation spots. Large plantations were another option for investors, who sometimes owned a number of plantations all managed by employees.

The vast natural resources of Appalachia also offered substantial profits to speculators in the region. By 1820, every Appalachian state had conducted a geological survey, and by 1850 the mining industry was well established. Speculators began setting aside land rich with coal, zinc, copper, and gold, as well as timber and other resources, instead of opening it to settlement, which served to retard development of many portions of the region. Since the absentee owners viewed the region as a profit source, there was little concern for the people or the land. Production was geared toward extraction and export of natural resources, creating an economic dependence on outside markets, while the region itself received very little lasting benefit from its own industries. This concentration on extractive exports also encouraged exploitation and destruction of the environment.

The early pattern of speculation and absentee landownership in eighteenth-century Appalachia had a powerful effect on the region's economic development well into the twentieth century. Appalachia's wealth was typically drawn away from the region, and the heavy emphasis on extractive resources left the economy vulnerable to market fluctuations and stagnation. Small subsistence farmers were pushed onto unproductive land where growing enough food to care for a family was difficult, if not impossible, creating a need for additional income that the companies exploited. Most Appalachians were forced to depend on the very industries and speculators that had created their difficulties. Competition became fierce for low-paying mining, quarrying, smelting, timbering, and other industrial jobs, further eroding economic diversity in the region.

Absentee owners worked to keep wages low and sometimes designed and built entire towns in order to control costs of production. Workers lived in company houses and shopped at company stores, where all payments were deducted from their salary. Wages were issued in company scrip that was only redeemable in trade at the company store. At the end of a workweek, employees sometimes found themselves actually in debt to the company, creating a cycle difficult to break. Education and health care in these company towns were often far below national standards. Companies used political clout to maintain control over the region and ensure high profits.

In late 1970s, the Appalachian Regional Commission organized a task force to survey landownership patterns in the region and analyze and document their effects on Appalachian communities. Focusing on eighty counties in six states (Alabama, Kentucky, North Carolina, Tennessee, Virginia, and West Virginia) covering nearly 20 million acres, the study concluded that absentee landlords owned 72 percent of the acreage in the region. The study also listed the top fifty owners of surface and mineral businesses. The largest surface owner, the J. M. Huber Corporation, involved with timber and wood products and based out of Rumson, New Jersey, controlled 226,805 surface acres. The top mineral owner was the Columbia Gas Company of Wilmington, Delaware, owning the rights to 342,236 mineral acres.

See also: NORTHERN LAND AND DEVELOPMENT COMPANIES; OCCUPYING CLAIMANT'S LAW; PROCLAMATION OF 1763.

—Lisa A. Ennis, *Georgia College and State University*

Richard B. Drake, *A History of Appalachia* (2001); Wilma A. Dunaway, *The First American Frontier: Transition to Capitalism in Southern Appalachia, 1700–1860* (1996); John Gaventa et al., eds., *Who Owns Appalachia? Landownership and Its Impact* (1983).

Spotswood, Alexander

(1676–1740) Colonial governor and explorer.

As the deputy of George, Earl of Orkney, Alexander Spotswood served as Virginia's lieutenant governor from 1710 to 1722. Though many of his predecessors interested themselves in the expansion of British North America, Spotswood was the first viceroy in Virginia's colonial history to make the exploration and settlement of the trans-Appalachian region the focal point of his administration.

Spotswood scouted the Virginia backcountry frequently during his administration, but the 1716 "Knights of the Golden Horseshoe" junket was his most famous exploit. Comprised of selected members of the Virginia elite interested in land speculation and Indian trade, Spotswood's "Knights" sought new lands and native customers beyond the Appalachians. During their trek, the Knights reconnoitered the Blue Ridge Mountains, forded the Shenandoah River, and at journey's end toasted heartily their governor and their monarch, King George I. On their September return to Williamsburg, a grateful Spotswood presented each Knight with a golden horseshoe that bore the inscription *Sic juvat trancedere montes*, or "How delightful it is to cross the mountains." Though the Knights' expedition became the stuff of southern lore, their discoveries spurred provincial and imperial interest in the settlement of the trans-Appalachian West.

Enthralled by the bountiful land that he explored, Spotswood tirelessly promoted the settlement of the Appalachian backcountry. In 1720, in order to foster backcountry expansion, he created two new frontier counties, Spotsylvania and Brunswick, which encompassed Swift Run Gap to the north and Rockfish Gap to the south in the Blue Ridge Mountains. The new counties opened Virginia's Appalachian backcountry to land speculation and settlement for the first time. With civil government thus extended to the frontier, Spotsylvania County rapidly filled with settlers, initiating the eighteenth-century rush for trans-Appalachian land. Future Virginia governors such as Sir William Gooch enlarged on Spotswood's idea of county development to extend Virginia's western boundary across the Appalachians.

As a necessary adjunct to his land policy, Spotswood established a pattern of native diplomacy that his successors adopted to ease Euro-American settlement in Appalachia. In 1722 he traveled to Albany, New York, to renew Virginia's decades-long alliance with the Six Nations of the Iroquois Confederacy, the presumptive native proprietors of the Shenandoah Valley. Spotswood and the Six Nations' leaders, or *sachems*, negotiated an ambiguous mountain boundary line across which neither Virginians nor Iroquois could pass. The treaty held until the 1730s, when a new round of land speculation opened the Shenandoah Valley to settlement and invited clashes between Virginia settlers and Iroquois warriors who passed through the region to fight their southern enemies.

Ultimately, Spotswood's success hastened his own demise as a royal official. During his tenure in Virginia, Spotswood illicitly acquired as much as 85,000 acres of land in what became Spotsylvania County. Since Spotswood's royal instructions prohibited land speculation by crown viceroys, King George's Privy Council dismissed him in 1722. After a brief return to England, Spotswood retired to Virginia and enjoyed the use of the land that he had amassed as lieutenant governor. In 1740, he died in Annapolis, Maryland, where he had organized an American regiment for the British army.

See also: EARLY WHITE SETTLEMENT OF SOUTHWESTERN VIRGINIA; EXPLORERS AND SURVEYORS; IROQUOIS (RACE, ETHNICITY, AND IDENTITY).

—Matthew L. Rhoades, *West Virginia University at Parkersburg*

David Hackett Fischer and James C. Kelly, *Away I'm Bound Away: Virginia and the Westward Movement* (2000).

Trail of Tears

Trail of Tears refers to the 500- to 750-mile journey southeastern Indians were forced to make from their homelands in southern Appalachia to reservation land in present-day Oklahoma between 1831 and 1839 as a consequence of the federal government's Indian Removal Act of 1830. As many as 25 percent of the migrants died because of the harshness of the removal, over the course of which they battled weather, disease, exhaustion, and starvation.

The name of this infamous episode comes from the Cherokee *Nunna daul Tsuny*, or "the trail where we cried," and is used to describe the removal of all five of the major southeastern tribes. For Choctaw, Creek, Chickasaw, Cherokee, and Seminole alike, removal resulted in death, loss, and sorrow. To varying degrees, the same can be said of all Indian removal efforts, such as the "Trail of Death," the path of the Potawatomi removal from Indiana to Kansas in 1838.

The idea of removing Indians from their homeland in order to clear space for white settlers was not new. Colonists of the first permanent British settlement at Jamestown took less than four decades to lay permanent claim to the area by defeating the Powhatan and proportioning specific land for their use—a precursor to reservations. Not until the beginning of the nineteenth century, however, did removal of Indians from the Southeast become federal policy.

Initially, white public opinion about Native Americans was mixed. On one side stood colonialists and missionaries who believed that Indians could be "civilized," or enculturated, and that the most appropriate place to do so was in their traditional homelands. On the other stood an odd combination of nationalists, opportunists, and advocates for Indians. Among the nationalists, Presidents Thomas Jefferson, James Monroe, and Andrew Jackson all believed strongly in removal as part of a necessary and natural expansion of white settlers in a newly formed country. Opportunists saw land speculation as a quick way to make money. Even those advocating for Indian rights believed removal to be a positive compromise, one that would provide the necessary land out west to allow Indians to maintain their traditional lifestyles. Caught in the middle were the American Indians.

A 1942 painting depicts the Trail of Tears, the most notorious forced migration in American history. A fervor for national expansion and land speculation led to the Indian Removal Act of 1830, forcing thousands of Cherokee, Choctaw, Creek, and Chickasaw from their ancestral lands in southern Appalachia.

Within this context, Andrew Jackson emerged as the architect and staunchest supporter of removal. Between 1814 and 1820, while serving as major general of the army, Jackson was able to remove substantial populations of Chickasaw, Creek, Cherokee, and Choctaw from eastern lands, reducing their territory by half. Many of these treaties, sales, and agreements depended, as Jackson readily admitted, upon bribery and, it was claimed, forgery.

As the efforts to remove the Indians from east of the Mississippi gained national approval, state governments were making it seem increasingly appealing to native peoples to leave for the West. Georgia's extension of jurisdiction over the Cherokee was particularly oppressive after gold was discovered on tribal lands. The Cherokee were prohibited from mining, while white prospectors were given free trespass. When the Cherokee sued and won, Jackson is reported to have derided the chief justice of the Supreme Court, saying, "John Marshall has made his decision, now let him enforce it."

Once the Removal Act was passed, treaty negotiations in southeastern Appalachia progressed most rapidly in central and northeastern Mississippi with the Choctaw, who were the first to be removed beginning in 1831. The Creek in western Georgia and eastern Alabama, followed by the Chickasaw in southern Tennessee and northern Mississippi, were removed the next year. Most tribal members opposed removal but were resigned to move voluntarily once treaties had been signed. In many cases, the treaties were signed by a small group of men whose authority to enter into such treaties was debatable. Intratribal conflict exploded. For example, only a few hundred Cherokee signed the 1835 Treaty of New Echota, outraging the nearly seventeen thousand Cherokees who promptly petitioned against it.

Actual removal proved far more complicated—and deadly. Hunger, exposure, and outbreaks of cholera plagued virtually all of the removals, beginning with the Choctaw. Attempts by the U.S. government to more closely regulate and thereby improve removal benefited the Chickasaw, who migrated with relatively few casualties, but such success was short-lived. The Creek removal was even more deadly than that of the Choctaw. Of all these tragedies, however, the Cherokee removal stands starkly as the most brutal. U.S. soldiers rounded up the reluctant Cherokee at bayonet and gunpoint and forced them into concentration camps, where three thousand died from disease and starvation while waiting to be removed. At least one thousand more died on the journey to Oklahoma. Whether voluntary or forced, the removal of Native Americans from Appalachia was devastating to tribal communities.

See also: CHEROKEE (RACE, ETHNICITY, AND IDENTITY); SOUTHERN NATIVE AMERICANS; TREATY OF AUGUSTA.

—Tom Mould, *Elon University*

Grant Foreman, *The Last Trek of the Indians* (1946); William G. McLoughlin, *After the Trail of Tears: The Cherokees' Struggle for Sovereignty, 1839–1880* (1993); Ronald N. Satz, *American Indian Policy in the Jacksonian Era* (1975).

Treaties of Fort Stanwix

There were two Treaties of Fort Stanwix, the first signed on November 5, 1768, and the second on October 22, 1784. Representatives of the Six Nations of the Iroquois Confederacy entered into the 1768 agreement with Sir William Johnson, the British Crown's superintendent of Indian affairs for the Northern Department. The 1768 settlement modified the Proclamation Line of 1763, which the Crown devised after the defeat of the French in the French and Indian War.

Until the victory over the French, Britain had no western land policy concerning the conflicting interests of Native American tribes and white settlers. The Crown intended the 1763 line to keep white settlements on the eastern side of the Appalachian Mountains and to secure lands west of the mountains for the native tribes, at least until policymakers could fashion a comprehensive land program. The 1768 Treaty of Fort Stanwix aimed to confirm British policy and to settle new problems of white encroachment by establishing a definite boundary between Indian and white lands. By terms of the treaty, the Six Nations surrendered to the Crown much of western New York, the region between the branches of the Susquehanna River in Pennsylvania, and an area west of the Big Kanawha River. On November 3, land purchases by the Indiana Company from the Iroquois added 1.8 million acres southeast of the Ohio from the southern boundary of Pennsylvania to the Little Kanawha River. Tribes that were dependencies of the Iroquois, among them the Wyandots and Shawnees, already occupied ceded lands and protested the treaty terms. Protests were of no avail, however, as white settlers and land speculators poured into the lands, especially in the Kentucky country. Whites' violation of the treaty, together with their murder of a number of Indians, led to Lord Dunmore's War (1774). In that conflict, Virginia militia defeated a confederation of Indian forces led by the Shawnee chief Cornstalk at Point Pleasant in western Virginia. After the defeat, the Shawnee and their allies yielded hunting rights in Kentucky and agreed to allow unmolested transport on the Ohio by whites.

The 1784 Treaty of Fort Stanwix, signed by representatives of the American government under the Articles of Confederation and representatives of the Six Nations, stipulated the return of prisoners taken by a number of Iroquois tribes during the Revolutionary War, as well as cession of additional lands in western New York and western Pennsylvania. The treaties evidenced both whites' continued claims against Native American tribal lands and their refusal to respect the boundaries.

See also: FRENCH AND INDIAN WAR (GOVERNMENT); IROQUOIS (RACE, ETHNICITY, AND IDENTITY); PROCLAMATION OF 1763.

—Marie Tedesco, *East Tennessee State University*

Dale Van Every, *Ark of Empire: The American Frontier, 1784–1802* (1963).

Treaty of Augusta

Through the 1783 Treaty of Augusta, the Creek Nation ceded eight hundred square miles of prime territory to the State of Georgia, allowing for expansion of white settlers into the central part of the state.

In the wake of the American Revolution, Georgia officials invited pro-British and pro-American Creek leaders to convene at the site of old Fort Augusta. The Treaty of Augusta, which was signed at this meeting, centered around two major issues: land and trade. Georgia officials promised to forgive old trade debts and wartime depredations committed by pro-British Creeks against Georgians. The Georgians also offered to reestablish the old trading system, thus bringing much needed or desired manufactured goods back into the Creek Nation.

Many Creeks opposed the treaty, and they denounced the decision of some of their leaders to sign the treaty and abide by its provisions. The anti-treaty Creeks claimed the treaty was signed under the duress of force, thus negating the validity of the land cession. A three-year legal struggle ensued, with Georgia claiming ultimate victory. The state managed to obtain additional parcels of land and secure confirmation of the 1783 boundary.

The treaty created deep divisions within the Creek Nation and affected subsequent Creek political history. The occupation of former Creek lands by settlers also brought the Creeks into increased conflict with Georgians, a condition that ultimately led to the removal of Creeks from the South.

See also: CREEK (RACE, ETHNICITY, AND IDENTITY); NATIVE AMERICANS (RACE, ETHNICITY, AND IDENTITY).

—C. S. Everett, *Vanderbilt University*

Treaty of Greenville

Following their defeat by General Anthony Wayne and his combined force of federal army units and Kentucky militia at the battle of Fallen Timbers in August 1794, a confederation of Native American tribes from the Ohio Valley found themselves starving and abandoned by their British allies. Weary from decades of conflict and lacking British support, twelve tribes negotiated with Wayne the Treaty of Greenville, which was signed on August 3, 1795.

Under the treaty, tribes were forced to cede sixteen squares of land for the establishment of posts, which guaranteed control of key transportation and trade sites. The ceded land comprised portions of present-day Indiana and Illinois, as well as most of Ohio except for the northwestern corner, which was reserved for the tribes. The Native Americans received a guarantee that settlers would not encroach on their land and twenty thousand dollars in trade goods, plus annual payments. The Wyandot, Shawnee, Ojibwa, Miami, Potawatomi, Delaware, and Ottawa were to receive one thousand dollars annually, while the Wea, Eel River, Piankashaw, Kickapoo, and Kaskaskia were to receive five hundred dollars.

This treaty opened for settlement a large territory in Appalachia, ranging from the site of present-day Cleveland, to the land opposite the mouth of the Kentucky River. Unfortunately for the Native Americans, settlers did not honor the treaty terms; as a result, many of these tribes fought the United States a generation later as part of the confederacy led by Tecumseh and Tenskwatawa.

See also: EARLY WHITE SETTLEMENT OF SOUTHEASTERN OHIO; NORTHERN NATIVE AMERICANS; TRAIL OF TEARS.

—John R. Burch Jr., *Campbellsville University*

Treaty of Hard Labor

See Proclamation of 1763

Treaty of Lochaber

See Proclamation of 1763

Treaty of Long Island of the Holston River

The Proclamation of 1763 prohibited European settlement west of the Appalachian Mountains, reserving that region for Native Americans. Nevertheless, in the late 1760s, settlers began moving to present-day Tennessee. Though the boundary established by the proclamation was modified in the Treaties of Hard Labor (1768) and Lochaber (1770), the settlers illegally occupied land rightfully claimed by the Cherokees.

By the beginning of the American Revolution, white settlements were firmly established on the Watauga, Nolichucky, and Holston Rivers in the Tennessee country. In July 1776, the Cherokees invaded those settlements in a three-pronged assault. One group besieged a fort on the Watauga River, while another moved up Carter's Valley. After a third group was defeated in a battle with settlers near Long Island of the Holston River, the Cherokees abandoned their attacks.

That same summer, troops from Georgia, South Carolina, and North Carolina attacked the Lower, Middle, and Valley Towns of the Cherokee. In October, a force of Virginians, North Carolinians, and Wataugans invaded the Cherokee Overhill Towns. In response to an ultimatum from the whites, the Cherokees agreed to observe a preliminary truce and to meet with commissioners the next year at Long Island.

In July 1777, near Long Island at Fort Patrick Henry, the Overhill Cherokees agreed to a permanent peace with North Carolina and Virginia and ceded territory in present-day northeast Tennessee to the two states.

See also: EARLY WHITE SETTLEMENT OF EAST TENNESSEE; LONG ISLAND OF THE HOLSTON RIVER; PROCLAMATION OF 1763.

—Ed Speer, *Elizabethton, Tennessee*

Treaty of Sycamore Shoals

Judge Richard Henderson of the Transylvania Company negotiated the Treaty of Sycamore Shoals, also known as the Transylvania Purchase or Henderson Purchase, with the Cherokee in March 1775 at Sycamore Shoals on the Watauga River near present-day Elizabethton, Tennessee.

The Cherokees were sharply divided, with one faction, led by Attakullakulla, Oconostota, and the Raven of Chota, favoring a treaty and another faction, led by Dragging Canoe, favoring war over land concessions. Dragging Canoe and his warriors left after negotiations began, vowing that the settlement of the area would be "dark and bloody." The remaining Cherokees ultimately ceded approximately 20 million acres between the Cumberland and Kentucky Rivers, an area that today comprises most of Kentucky, central Tennessee, and a small portion of Virginia. In exchange, the Cherokees received approximately ten thousand British pounds' worth of trade goods.

Since it violated the Proclamation of 1763, which forbade white settlement west of the crest of the Appalachians, the land cession was illegal according to British law. Nevertheless, the Cherokees lost all claims to the land, despite their contention that Henderson had duped them. In December 1776, the Virginia legislature annexed the Transylvania settlements, which comprised most of present-day Kentucky, and compensated Henderson with a considerable amount of land. North Carolina also compensated Henderson when the state annexed the remainder of the land in 1783.

See also: BOONE, DANIEL; CHEROKEE (RACE, ETHNICITY, AND IDENTITY); EARLY WHITE SETTLEMENT OF EAST TENNESSEE.

—John R. Burch Jr., *Campbellsville University*

Twentieth-Century In-Migration

During the twentieth century, Appalachia's population fluctuated between periods of relatively high in-migration and periods of massive out-migration, resulting in a more socially and culturally heterogeneous population than traditionally believed. For instance, in a single five-year period from 1985 to 1990, in- and out-migrations accounted for a turnover of more than 25 percent of the region's population. The 2000 census established Appalachia's population at nearly 23 million, an increase of 9.1 percent from 1990, with the southern region growing rapidly and the northern and central regions experiencing net losses.

The twentieth century began with positive in-migration. Workers were attracted to expanding Appalachian labor markets in lumber (North Carolina, Tennessee, and Georgia), coal (primarily West Virginia and Kentucky), and steel (Pennsylvania and Alabama). These immigrants came from the eastern cities, the rural South, and southern and central Europe.

Because of a lack of economic diversity, the decline of both the lumber and coal industries between 1920 and 1968 reversed the migration trend to primarily an outward one. High rates of unemployment and poverty in the mountains coupled with higher wages and more job opportunities in urban factories contributed to this out-migration. Companies in areas such as Cincinnati actively recruited Appalachian workers, sending buses to transport them from counties in Kentucky. At the time, many studies emerged documenting the poverty and economic decline of the region. By the early 1960s, the Appalachian region had emerged as a "pocket of poverty" in the United States.

From about 1968 to 2000, rates of in-migration into Appalachia were generally positive. A surge in the rate of in-migration occurred between 1968 and 1982 as the region began attracting retirees, people looking for recreational opportunities, and return migrants.

Retiree migration to the Appalachian region takes two forms. The first consists of persons who previously left Appalachia for work and spent their working lives outside of the region. After inheriting land from their families, they returned to their home communities when they retired.

Retirement migration also includes elderly migrants from places outside of the region. Many of these migrants originally moved to Florida but found the climate uncomfortable and relocated farther north, seeking rural Appalachian areas that offer amenities such as golf and other leisure pursuits, low crime rates, and a moderate climate. Some rural Appalachian communities have begun to grow as a direct result of this migration pattern, but most older migrants into the region have located in suburban Appalachian counties near Cincinnati, Atlanta, and Pittsburgh. Henderson County, North Carolina, close to Asheville, is an example of a more rural retiree destination, with recreation areas, hospitals, and care facilities aimed specifically at older residents. Between 1985 and 1990, 134 migrants sixty-five years or older, all of them from the Chicago area, relocated to Henderson County.

During the nineteenth and early twentieth centuries, the relatively small numbers of immigrants attracted to the area for recreation and leisure activities came for the healing springs and natural amenities that the mountains provided. Population transfer into Appalachia due to recreation and leisure is a late-twentieth- and early-twenty-first-century phenomenon, aided by improved highways and the national interstate system, which offer easier access to formerly remote areas. Northern, central, and southern Appalachian communities have experienced growth as people are drawn by outdoor activities that include hiking, backpacking, whitewater rafting, golfing, and skiing. Economic growth for Appalachian communities has been spurred on by the introduction of ski resorts, golf courses, hiking trails, and other tourist activities.

During the 1970s and 1980s, the recreational and leisure appeal of the mountains did much to counter Appalachia's out-migration population losses. The proximity of the region's rural recreation areas to eastern and southern cities drew thousands of urban short-term visitors, some of whom decided to stay. Among the fastest-growing counties in the United States are those surrounding cites such as Chattanooga, Asheville, and Atlanta.

See also: SECTION OVERVIEW (URBAN APPALACHIAN EXPERIENCE); TWENTIETH-CENTURY OUT-MIGRATION.

—Marvin Pippert, *North Georgia College and State University*

Bruce Ergood and Bruce E. Kuhre, eds., *Appalachia: Social Context Past and Present* (2nd edition, 1983); William W. Philliber, *Appalachian Migrants in Urban America: Cultural Conflict or Ethnic Group Formation?* (1981); Harry K. Schwarzweller, James S. Brown, and J. J. Mangalam, *Mountain Families in Transition: A Case Study of Appalachian Migration* (1971).

Twentieth-Century Out-Migration

Like most primarily rural areas, the Appalachian region experienced high levels of out-migration during the twentieth century. The bulk of this migration occurred between the early 1940s and the late 1960s, as the region's economy shifted from resource extraction and manufacturing to a service economy. In particular, traditional Appalachian sources of employment such as coal mining generally declined during this period, encouraging laborers to seek work outside the region. Estimates of out-migration during this time period indicate that Appalachia lost approximately three million out-migrants during those three decades alone. The majority of these migrants left for urban areas close to the region such as Chicago, Cleveland, Cincinnati, Louisville, and Atlanta. These places offered not only higher-paying jobs, but easy travel back home on weekends or at holidays.

Migrants generally followed kin to the cities, creating Appalachian enclaves. A study published in 1977 showed that people who migrated from Beech Creek, Kentucky, tended to follow in the path of earlier family members. Urban relatives functioned as information centers about available jobs and also provided temporary living quarters for later migrants. As a result, ties remained between those left in Beech Creek and those who had moved. These ties made it easier for additional members of the family to move out of the area later.

Contemporary Appalachian out-migrants are most likely to be young, better educated, and single. Their primary reason for leaving the area is to find employment. Persons who are least likely to migrate are those who are older, have less education, and have families. Because of this tendency, the kind of mass out-migration experienced by Appalachian counties during the 1940s, 1950s, and 1960s decimated many Appalachian communities. Not only did populations of these communities become older and see their average education level drop, but out-migration also caused economic conditions to stagnate. As family members who had relocated sent word of new opportunities to relatives living in these economically depressed areas, further incentive for out-migration arose. Thus, the potential for a cycle of continued economic and population decline fell into place. Some have referred to this process as an Appalachian "brain drain," as communities lost many of their educated young people. This trend showed signs of reversing near the end of the twentieth century. In 1990 Appalachia gained about one hundred thousand more college students than it lost, and southern Appalachia's total population grew 4.6 percent that year. Northern and central Appalachia, however, lost 1 and 2.5 percent of their population, respectively, to out-migration in 1990, illustrating the variations that occur in the region's migration patterns. Much of the work of the Appalachian Regional Commission has been to fund projects aimed at building economic infrastructure and social capital (medical services and education) to retain persons who would otherwise leave the community, as well as to attract newcomers to the area.

The mass exodus from Appalachia slowed and then reversed in the late 1960s and throughout the 1970s as the trend in rural to urban migration across the United States also reversed. Out-migration approximately equaled in-migration to the region during the last decades of the twentieth century, with a net gain of about a half-million new residents between 1975 and 1990.

See also: SECTION OVERVIEW (URBAN APPALACHIAN EXPERIENCE); TWENTIETH-CENTURY IN-MIGRATION.

—Marvin Pippert, *North Georgia College and State University*

Bruce Ergood and Bruce E. Kuhre, eds., *Appalachia: Social Context Past and Present* (2nd edition, 1983); William W. Philliber, *Appalachian Migrants in Urban America: Cultural Conflict or Ethnic Group Formation?* (1981); Harry K. Schwarzweller, James S. Brown, and J. J. Mangalam, *Mountain Families in Transition: A Case Study of Appalachian Migration* (1971).

Washington, George

(1732–1799) Surveyor, land speculator, and first U.S. president.

Though a lifelong resident of northern Virginia, George Washington developed extensive ties to Appalachia, where he was involved in land speculation, military engagements, and the development of America's first water canal system.

Washington's first contact with Appalachia came during his years as a surveyor. At the age of fifteen, he was hired as one of a small group to survey the extensive Virginia holdings of Lord Fairfax and by seventeen was the official surveyor for Culpeper County, Virginia. In this capacity, the youthful Washington traveled west of the Blue Ridge Mountains, inspecting and appraising land grants. Through these experiences, he gained a deep knowledge of land value and soon began a corollary career in speculation. Throughout the remainder of his life, Washington held vast tracts in present-day western Pennsylvania, West Virginia, and Ohio. Most notably, he owned land in Frederick County, Virginia, which sits at the base of the Appalachians. Though not a resident, as a landowner he took advantage of a rule that allowed him to represent that county in the House of Burgesses for fifteen years, beginning in 1759.

Militarily, Washington fully understood the importance of Appalachia. As a young militia officer, he spent the mid-1750s trying to secure the upper Ohio River from the French threat, fighting there in the early battles of the French and Indian War. Through his wartime experiences and with his surveyor's eye, Washington quickly realized the potential of these western lands and spent much of his later life speculating in them.

Washington's next military activity in the region came nearly forty years after his service in the French and Indian War. The Whiskey Rebellion (1794) in the western counties of Pennsylvania forced President Washington to draft a nearly thirteen-thousand-man army and dispatch it to the rebellious region to keep order. While much of the strife can be credited to the tax on whiskey, the "Whiskey Boys" were also protesting absentee landlords such as Washington, who held the best farmland for speculative purposes while local residents worked comparatively marginal holdings.

The mountains were never far from Washington's mind. Throughout his later years, he gave much thought to the improvement of transportation in the region for the dual benefit of inhabitants and investors alike. In 1774 Washington introduced a plan to build canals around the five worst obstacles along the Potomac River, and in 1785 he became the first president of the Patowmack Canal Company, which completed the proposed canals three years after his death and operated until 1828. Washington's ideas led to the creation of the Chesapeake and Ohio Canal, which reached Cumberland, Maryland, in 1850, although by that time rail travel had made the need for the canal obsolete, and it never reached the Ohio Valley.

See also: EXPLORERS AND SURVEYORS; LORD FAIRFAX; SPECULATORS AND ABSENTEE LANDLORDS.

—Brian D. McKnight, *University of Virginia at Wise*

Washington Irving, *The Life of George Washington* (1855–59); Norris F. Schneider, *The National Road: Main Street of America* (1975).

White Conquest

Hernando de Soto is credited with being one of the first Europeans to establish contact with indigenous populations of North America. De Soto and his men journeyed through much of southern Appalachia in 1540, often lodging with native inhabitants. Near the present-day towns of Cartersville and Rome, Georgia, the Spanish battled the local Indians, took slaves and hostages, and claimed their harvest. Some Indian survivors took their own lives rather than be captured. Although Native Americans outnumbered them, the Spanish possessed superior weapons, and their appearance marked the beginning the white conquest of Appalachia.

Further contact among cultures, amplified through trade, gave increasing advantage to white settlers over native inhabitants. Not only did Indians begin to value European goods such as weapons to the exclusion of their own, but they also fell prey to such diseases as smallpox, bubonic plague, measles, and influenza. Since the indigenous people were without resistance to many diseases and infections carried by Europeans, entire villages were wiped out or abandoned.

Alcohol, a popular trade item virtually unknown to Indians prior to contact with Europeans, also served as a tool of conquest. Drinking spawned brawls and left natives vulnerable to exploitation and manipulation, as evidenced by the selling of a season's worth of animal hides or crops for a few jugs of whiskey. A Seneca from northern Appalachia named Otetiani, called Sagoyewatha when he became chief and Red Jacket after he began wearing a British army coat, suffered from the effects of alcohol use, negatively influencing dealings with his own people as well as European settlers. Later Sagoyewatha condemned the use of alcohol.

Sagoyewatha did not welcome missionaries and was accused of sorcery by Handsome Lake (who may have been Sagoyewatha's brother) for preferring traditional Seneca spirituality rather than Christianity. Seneca Christians were his principal foes. Before Sagoyewatha died in 1830, he asked that his funeral be according to the customs of the Seneca and that his grave marker not be made by a white man. Nevertheless, the Seneca Christian faction appropriated his corpse and gave him a Christian burial. Sagoyewatha, deprived of the religion of his ancestors, became a notable example of the cultural as well as geographic nature of white conquest.

Moravians, who were the first missionaries to the Cherokee and who were followed by Baptists, Methodists, and Presbyterians, found themselves ostracized by some chiefs. At first loyal to the Cherokee, some missionaries were intimidated by the government of Georgia into swearing allegiance to the state, thereby becoming traitors to the Cherokee they had come to serve. One missionary who remained devoted to the Cherokee was Samuel Worcester, who served sixteen months of hard labor at the Georgia Penitentiary at Milledgeville for his challenge to Georgia's law. Released in 1832, Worcester moved with the Cherokee during their forced removal to the West.

Indians suffered not only from conflicts with white explorers, settlers, and white institutions, but also from conflicts between rival colonial powers. In northern Appalachia, during Governor Kieft's War (1643–45), many Wappinger and Delaware died at the hands of the Dutch. English and French settlers vied for the allegiance of Indians, who were considered buffers among competing European interests. Whites often exploited rival indigenous groups during war by promising collaborators continued possession of their land. Under pressure, many Indian bands split into factions and entered into conflicting alliances. During the Revolutionary War, many Oneida and Tuscarora chose the American cause, while the Mohawk, Cayuga, and Onondaga fought for Britain, splitting the Iroquois Confederacy. The Cherokee, Creek, and Choctaw also sided with the British. Many allied with Europeans and fought their Indian enemies. Some Native Americans claimed neutrality during battles, choosing to avoid a war not of their making.

The Creek War, coinciding with the War of 1812, resulted from the constant incursion of white settlers into Creek territory. In 1813 the Red Sticks, a radical element among the Creek, attacked Fort Mims in Alabama, killing many of its inhabitants. To avenge the deaths at Fort Mims, Andrew Jackson attacked the Red Sticks at Horseshoe Bend (1814) in Alabama in one of the bloodiest battles fought between North American settlers and indigenous populations. After Chief Menewa's surrender, the Creek gave up approximately 23 million acres of land.

Presidential attitudes toward native populations varied. George Washington and Thomas Jefferson expected Native Americans to accept white ways and adopt white laws and customs. As settlers increased in number and continued to move south and west, though, Jackson, who was elected president in 1828, deemed it necessary to permanently remove members of nations such as the Five Civilized Tribes—the Cherokee, Creek, Choctaw, Chickasaw, and Seminole—so that more land would be available for white settlers. In defiance of a Supreme Court decision allowing the Indians to remain on their land, Jackson advocated this policy despite the fact that many Cherokee had fought beside him in past wars. Rationalizations for removal included the past union of Indians with the British and the establishment of the Cherokee Constitution, considered a threat to American policy. The most notable removal of Native Americans involved the Cherokee in 1838–39, but members of the all the Five Civilized Tribes, as well as others, were moved west to present-day Oklahoma during the 1830s along the Trail of Tears, with thousands dying along the way.

See also: CHEROKEE (RACE, ETHNICITY, AND IDENTITY); CREEK (RACE, ETHNICITY AND IDENTITY); TRAIL OF TEARS.

—Ima J. Stephens, *Auburn University*

James J. Cassidy et al., eds., *Through Indian Eyes: The Untold Story of Native American Peoples* (1995); Frederick E. Hoxie, ed., *Encyclopedia of North American Indians* (1996); Theda Perdue, *Slavery and the Evolution of Cherokee Society, 1540–1866* (1979).

Wilderness Road

The Wilderness Road was one of southern Appalachia's earliest and most traveled trails. Originating as a path following buffalo traces and Native American trails, the Wilderness Road covered a distance of more than two hundred miles through the Holston Valley of southwestern Virginia and northeastern Tennessee. Long Island of the Holston, near present-day Kingsport, Tennessee, was centrally located on the Great Indian Warrior Path initially traveled by Cherokees, white settlers, and traders and later traversed by wagons and stagecoaches. Following the Treaty of Sycamore Shoals in 1775, frontiersman Daniel Boone cleared and marked the road from Long Island of the Holston through the Cumberland Gap into Kentucky territory and on to the Bluegrass region. After 1796, the road was widened to permit the travel of Conestoga wagons. Officially named the Wilderness Road, it became one of the most important routes of migration in the nation's history.

A century before Daniel Boone marked the road west, early explorers such as James Needham (1670s), Gabriel Arthur (1670s), and Thomas Walker (1750s) traveled the Native American trails that later became known as the Wilderness Road. Before white settlement advanced in southern Appalachia, several Native American groups were depopulated and displaced, most notably the Cherokee. Even before negotiations for cessation of tribal lands were complete, Virginia, North Carolina, and Georgia began granting title of tracts to speculators and war veterans. Affecting the lives of the Native Americans in a more critical way were the activities of land companies, whose acquisition efforts accelerated with travel beyond the barrier of the Appalachian Mountains. The land companies organized their own treaty meetings to secure land illegally. Foremost among the companies engaging in this practice was the Transylvania Land Company, which arranged to lease-purchase more than 20 million acres of Cherokee lands in present-day Tennessee and Kentucky. To manage their extensive holdings, these distant speculators and financiers employed land jobbers such as Daniel Boone, who traveled in the Cumberland Gap area in 1769 and returned in 1775 with thirty woodsmen to mark out a road for the Transylvania Company.

After the American Revolution, large numbers of settlers crossed the mountains into the southern Appalachian region, many by way of the Wilderness Road. In 1783 only twelve thousand white settlers lived west of the mountains and south of the Ohio River, but by 1790 the census documented more than one hundred thousand residents of the future states of Tennessee and Kentucky. It is estimated that by 1800 approximately two hundred thousand migrants had traveled the road. After the building of the National Road in the 1840s, the Wilderness Road experienced neglect and was abandoned.

See also: BOONE, DANIEL; CHEROKEE (RACE, ETHNICITY, AND IDENTITY); SOUTHERN LAND AND DEVELOPMENT COMPANIES.

—Martha Avaleen Egan, *Kingsport, Tennessee*

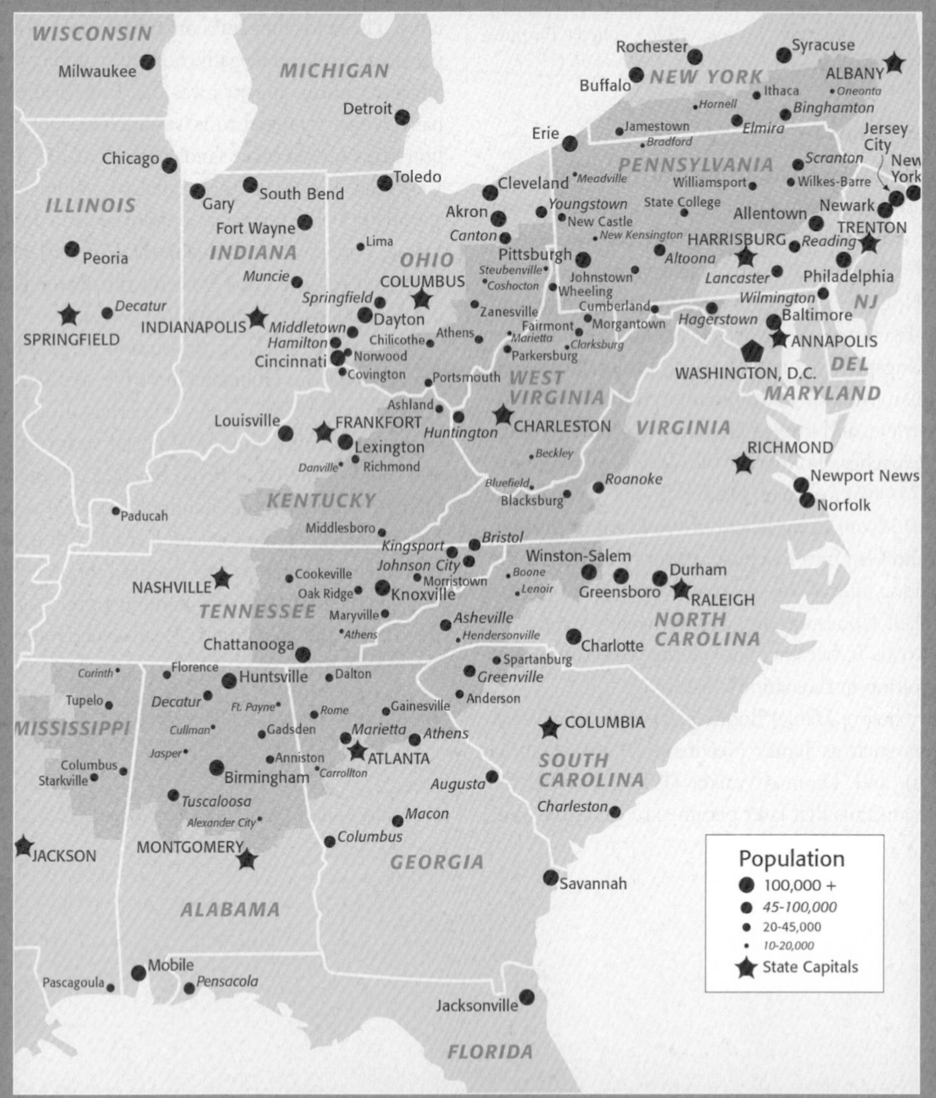

WISCONSIN
Milwaukee
MICHIGAN
Detroit
Rochester
Syracuse
ALBANY
Buffalo
NEW YORK
Ithaca
Oneonta
Hornell
Binghamton
Jamestown
Elmira
Bradford
Erie
Jersey City
Chicago
PENNSYLVANIA
Scranton
New York
Toledo
Meadville
Williamsport
Wilkes-Barre
ILLINOIS
Gary
South Bend
Cleveland
Youngstown
State College
Allentown
Newark
Akron
New Castle
TRENTON
Fort Wayne
Canton
New Kensington
HARRISBURG
Reading
Lima
Peoria
INDIANA
OHIO
Pittsburgh
Altoona
Steubenville
Johnstown
Lancaster
Philadelphia
Muncie
COLUMBUS
Coshocton
Wheeling
Springfield
Wilmington
NJ
Decatur
Zanesville
Cumberland
Baltimore
INDIANAPOLIS
Middletown
Dayton
Fairmont
Morgantown
Hagerstown
SPRINGFIELD
Hamilton
Chilicothe
Athens
Marietta
Clarksburg
ANNAPOLIS
Cincinnati
Norwood
Parkersburg
WASHINGTON, D.C.
DEL
Covington
Portsmouth
WEST VIRGINIA
MARYLAND
Ashland
Louisville
FRANKFORT
CHARLESTON
VIRGINIA
Huntington
Lexington
Beckley
RICHMOND
Danville
Richmond
Newport News
Bluefield
Roanoke
Blacksburg
KENTUCKY
Norfolk
Paducah
Middlesboro
Bristol
Kingsport
Winston-Salem
Johnson City
Durham
Cookeville
Morristown
Boone
NASHVILLE
Oak Ridge
Knoxville
Lenoir
Greensboro
RALEIGH
TENNESSEE
Maryville
Asheville
NORTH CAROLINA
Athens
Hendersonville
Chattanooga
Charlotte
Spartanburg
Corinth
Florence
Huntsville
Dalton
Greenville
Tupelo
Decatur
Ft. Payne
Rome
Gainesville
Anderson
MISSISSIPPI
Cullman
Gadsden
Marietta
Athens
COLUMBIA
Jasper
Anniston
ATLANTA
SOUTH CAROLINA
Columbus
Starkville
Birmingham
Carrollton
Augusta
Tuscaloosa
Charleston
Alexander City
Macon
Columbus
JACKSON
MONTGOMERY
GEORGIA
Savannah
ALABAMA
Mobile
Pascagoula
Pensacola
Jacksonville
FLORIDA
Population
100,000 +
45-100,000
20-45,000
10-20,000
State Capitals

Urban Appalachian Experience

Section Editors: Michael E. Maloney and Phillip J. Obermiller

THE NOTION THAT APPALACHIA IS A MONOLITHICALLY RURAL, SOUTHERN REGION is one of the overarching myths behind John C. Campbell's famous observation that there is more known about the region that is not true than about any other part of the country. In fact, Appalachia is located in one of the most densely populated areas of the country, and about half of the region's population now lives in urbanized areas. In addition to large cities such as Pittsburgh, Knoxville, and Birmingham, many medium-sized cities including Greenville, South Carolina, Charleston, West Virginia, and Johnstown and Scranton, Pennsylvania, are located throughout the region. Moreover, there are numerous "edge-of-Appalachia" cities—notably, Albany and Buffalo, New York; Charlotte and Greensboro, North Carolina; Columbus and Cincinnati, Ohio; Harrisburg and Reading, Pennsylvania; Montgomery, Alabama; Atlanta, Georgia; Nashville, Tennessee; and Roanoke, Virginia. Among all of these cities, and between them and rural Appalachia, high levels of social and economic interaction are inevitable and extensive. Many residents of Appalachia, for example, commute to cities outside the region for work, shopping, and recreation and rely on newspapers or radio and television programming originating in and focused on these urban cores. Demographic trends indicate that Appalachians will become even more urbanized in the future.

The historically rural ethos of the region is enduring, but it is no longer Appalachia's primary characteristic. Many observers have remarked upon the heterogeneous nature of the region, and its varying levels of urbanization are a case in point. The central Appalachian coalfields are a good example of the region's rural aspect—there are no major cities in central Appalachia—but this reality should not be used iconically to characterize the region as a whole.

Indeed, to understand Appalachia, it is important to consider the distribution of its urban populations. Close to half of Appalachia's population is located in the northern subregion, with well over a quarter of it located in Pennsylvania alone. Although the northern tier has a sizeable population, the majority of population growth is occurring in and near cities in the southern subregion. The city of Atlanta, for instance, is outside of but directly adjacent to the region and was responsible for much of the population increase in southern Appalachia during the late twentieth century.

Facing page: A map of cities in and near Appalachia as of 2002 gives an indication of the population distribution of the region. Increasingly urbanized, nearly one-half of all Appalachians live in cities, primarily in the northern and boundary areas of the region.

Appalachians moving to cities have a history quite similar to other immigrant and rural-to-urban migrant groups who brought along hopes and fears to their new locations and realized many of both. Mountaineers who left their homes and farms for the cities in the twentieth century did so under the influence of large-scale social and economic processes. Prior to World War II the urbanization of Appalachians was slow but steady. This movement toward urbanization was interrupted by the Great Depression but intensified during the war years. Following the war, the number of Appalachian people living in cities and suburbs grew dramatically, beginning a demographic trend that, with only minor fluctuations, has yet to end.

Thus "urban" Appalachians living both inside and outside of the region can be more accurately thought of as suburban Appalachians. Relatively few Appalachian migrants, for instance, are to be found in city centers or in the old port-of-entry neighborhoods. Most of these families have made their way to stable, working-class neighborhoods away from the old inner city or to suburban communities surrounding the central city or in some cases even to surrounding counties in the metropolitan area that have commuter access to the urban core. Here, the term *urban Appalachians* refers to Appalachian people in and near cities, whether those cities are inside or outside of the region.

Twenty-six Appalachian cities are presented in the following section. They were selected on the basis of several criteria: first, to ensure that cities of different population sizes are represented; secondly, to include at least one city from each of the thirteen states that have Appalachian counties; and finally, Roanoke, just outside the federally defined region, represents the many edge-of-Appalachia cities that have a strong effect on the region.

For the most part, Appalachian cities are not large. Those covered here have an average population of 85,329 and a median population of 52,651. Their combined populations comprise about 10 percent of the region's total inhabitants, although these census counts do not include the surrounding urban population. Pittsburgh, for instance, had 334,563 residents in 2000, but the Pittsburgh metropolitan area had 2,394,811 residents—more than the total population of all twenty-six Appalachian cities discussed in this section. This also underscores the northern and urban character of Appalachia's population.

Appalachia's rich heterogeneity is powerfully illustrated in its urban communities. Many have roots in the sites of Native American villages or along well-established pre-Columbian trails. Some were situated at the confluence of rivers (Asheville, Huntington, Knoxville, Pittsburgh, Rome), others along overland frontier routes such as the Buncombe Pike, the Great Valley Road, the Overmountain Trail, and the Natchez Trace (Cumberland, the Tri-Cities, Tupelo, Winston-Salem). Some owe their existence to canals (Portsmouth) while others grew from railroad stops (Altoona, Johnson City). Some can trace their founding to the late 1700s (Pittsburgh, Cumberland, Charleston, Knoxville, Asheville, Erie, Richmond) while others originated with the early-twentieth-century planned-city movement (Kingsport).

These cities belie the all-Caucasian stereotype of Appalachia. Slavery was readily found in southern Appalachian cities such as Asheville, and by 1830 Chattanooga was one-third black. African Americans constituted a large minority in urban Appalachia into the twenty-first century. In 2000 the African American populations of Roanoke and Birmingham were 27 and 74 percent, respectively. Cities in the Appalachian region are also home to some descendants of the original Native American population and increasingly to people from all over the world. Most early white settlers in Appalachian cities were of Scots-Irish, English, Irish, Welsh, and

German descent. More recently Hispanics have become the most rapidly growing ethnic group.

Early urban economies in Appalachia revolved around farming (especially tobacco and cotton), textile manufacturing, mining, and lumber milling. Eventually many larger cities grew into financial, commercial, legal, and political centers serving surrounding areas.

Much of the Civil War was contested on Appalachian soil, and its cities, especially in the southern tier, took the brunt of wartime devastation. Chattanooga, Knoxville, and Tuscaloosa, for example, all had a difficult time recovering from the effects of the conflict. During the wars of the first half of the twentieth century, the establishment of military camps and arsenals near Appalachian cities such as Greenville (Camp Sevier), Richmond (Blue Grass Army Depot), and Spartanburg (Camp Wadsworth, Camp Croft) reaped economic benefits. World War II gave rise to the Oak Ridge National Laboratory, located just northwest of Knoxville, which remains a key site for work on nuclear technology. The Cold War of the late twentieth century turned Huntsville's military arsenals into the home of the U. S. Army's ballistic missile development and eventually the National Aeronautics and Space Administration's Marshall Space Flight Center. Missile and rocket technology quickly became the driving force for a sprawling new urban community. A 2002 Appalachian Regional Commission study listed the Tri-Cities, Binghamton, Greenville-Spartanburg, Huntsville, and Pittsburgh as the five leading technology-based metropolitan areas. Technology also constitutes a crucial sector of the economy in Knoxville, Oak Ridge, and Asheville, as well as other urban communities in the region.

Tourism (Asheville, Chattanooga), health care (Johnson City, Roanoke, Tupelo, Winston-Salem), and manufacturing (Erie, Greenville, Huntsville, Kingsport, Spartanburg) have come to the fore in some Appalachian cities. Higher education is an important part of the economies of many Appalachian cities and towns, including Greenville (Furman University, Bob Jones University), Morgantown (West Virginia University), Pittsburgh (University of Pittsburgh, Carnegie Mellon University), Tuscaloosa (University of Alabama), Johnson City (East Tennessee State University), Knoxville (University of Tennessee), and Wheeling (Wheeling Jesuit College). One of the earliest opportunities for African Americans to obtain a college education was at the former Slater Industrial Academy, now Winston-Salem State College.

In addition to the major league sports teams in Pittsburgh, Appalachian cities host many minor league, college, high school, and civic sports teams. Asheville supported an early baseball team; Portsmouth was the first home of the Spartans, the team that later became professional football's Detroit Lions.

Despite the progress Appalachian cities have made, many continue to struggle. Huntington, Knoxville, and others have experienced serious decline of central business districts, in part because of business relocation to suburbs and highway bypasses. Cities in the northern tier of Appalachia, Pittsburgh in particular, posted significant losses of both jobs and population over the last decades of the twentieth century. Deindustrialization came early to the cities in the upper Ohio River Valley. In Ohio, Portsmouth and Steubenville lost half of their populations in the mid-twentieth century. In the 1980s declines in the coal and steel industries brought population loss and economic distress to other northern Appalachian cities as well. Pittsburgh lost eighty thousand steel-related jobs in a short period. Communities in the Monongahela Valley and in central Pennsylvania were similarly distressed. Singer Billy Joel, in his song "Allentown," and movies such as *The Deer Hunter* brought the plight of Appalachian communities in Pennsylvania to national attention.

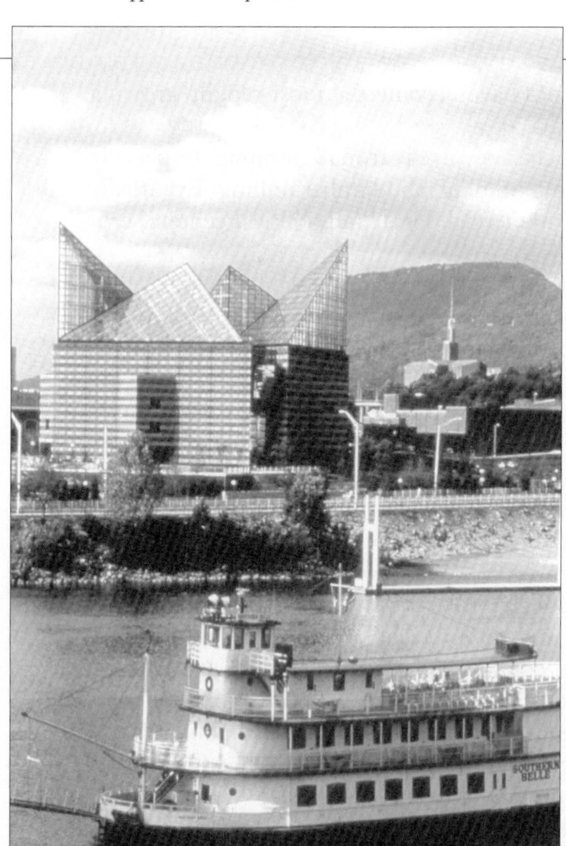

The *Southern Belle* cruises on the Tennessee River past the Tennessee Aquarium in downtown Chattanooga, 2001. The rapid urbanization of Appalachia has contributed to problems such as urban sprawl, inadequate infrastructure, traffic congestion, and environmental pollution. Chattanooga has successfully confronted these challenges, changing its reputation as one of the most polluted cities to one of the most livable in the nation.

In the period after 1980, the southern tier faced a different set of problems—those associated with rapid growth, urban sprawl, inadequate infrastructure, traffic congestion, loss of greenspace, and environmental pollution—as Sun Belt cities such as Spartanburg and Birmingham became destinations for Appalachians displaced from the economically depressed urban areas of West Virginia and Pennsylvania.

While not as pronounced as the Appalachian identity movements in cities bordering the region, there are nonetheless signs that cities within the region have come to see opportunity in their Appalachian heritage. Asheville, for example, has a museum that features Appalachian artifacts, and bluegrass music and other artistic expressions of mountain culture are popular in Pittsburgh and Birmingham. In West Virginia, Charleston is home to the public radio program *Mountain Stage* as well as the Commission on Religion in Appalachia. The state capitol building houses a mountain crafts store, and the offices of the Appalachian Studies Association are located in Huntington.

Appalachian migrants' strong tendency to relocate near family and friends who preceded them to the city has resulted in well-defined urban enclaves of formerly rural people. Some of the better-known such communities are Chicago's Uptown, Cincinnati's Over-the-Rhine, Atlanta's Cabbagetown, Dayton's Fifth and Wayne, Detroit's Cass Corridor, and large sections of Baltimore, Cleveland, and other major cities. Because many of the early residents of these Appalachian neighborhoods were young families just starting out, their incomes were inevitably low. In time, however, many of these poor but hardworking new urbanites moved on from their ghettos to achieve the blue-collar and middle-class lives they sought. The less fortunate among them fell into chronic poverty. Although the movement of people out of Appalachia into the cities of the upper Midwest has never stopped, the pace has slowed, and families of Appalachians who have lived in the cities for decades now outnumber newcomers. The Appalachian child in the Dayton or Cincinnati public schools of the early twenty-first century was typically a third- or fourth-generation urban dweller. Still, migration from the coalfields, declining farming areas, and small Appalachian communities continues, especially to southern cities that fringe the region.

Among many misconceptions about Appalachians living outside the region is a notion that Appalachian migrants only began moving out of the region with the Great Migration of 1940 to 1970. To be sure, the preponderance of Appalachians did arrive in the cities after World War II, but mountaineers have a long history of moving to urban areas. Historian Carter G. Woodson noted that between 1826 and 1840 Cincinnati received streams of poor whites flowing into the city from the highlands of Virginia and Kentucky.

Another mistaken assumption is that urban Appalachians were generally disorganized. Certainly, their churches did not provide the conspicuous levels of political and organizational leverage as did the churches of African American or European newcomers to the city, but Appalachian organizations formed in Chicago and Detroit, as well as in Cincinnati, Dayton, and Hamilton, Ohio. Equally erroneous is an impression that migrants from the mountains are exclusively white. The creation and growth of the Eastern Kentucky Social Club, comprised of African Americans with roots in the eastern Kentucky coalfields who now live in cities from New York to Los Angeles, are an unequivocal demonstration to the contrary.

In one way or another, organized labor has been a continuing part of Appalachian migration and urbanization. Automotive, energy and chemical, electrical, rubber, steel, and transportation unions and their locals frequently provided economic security and gave Appalachian workers a political voice, necessary for them to survive and later to thrive in cities. In metropolitan areas outside the region where unions were strong, urban Appalachians formed mostly social and cultural associations; in cities where labor federations were not as dominant, Appalachians tended to form advocacy and service organizations.

In terms of social class, Appalachians living outside of the region are as heterogeneous as their kinfolk in the region. Some are professionals or business owners; others have established middle-class, suburban lives, often with the help of their labor unions. A large portion are still blue-collar workers vulnerable to boom-and-bust cycles in the national economy, thriving in the good times and struggling to make ends meet during periods of economic decline, just as coal miners have historically been buffeted by booms and busts in the coalfields. A significant portion of the urban Appalachian population is still "poor, white, and out of sight." In many instances they are their cities' "invisible minority": invisible because they fall through the cracks of ethnically and racially targeted social welfare programs, and minority because of their powerlessness in cities where other social and cultural groups outweigh them economically or politically. Various entries in this section address social problems faced by impoverished urban Appalachians, as well as the institutions they have formed to confront these problems.

The issue of Appalachian stereotypes was still quite current at the turn of the twenty-first century, especially for Appalachians living outside of the region. Because they are in a minority position in their host communities, these groups of urban Appalachians are especially vulnerable to the effects of stereotyping. They feel these effects not from "outsiders," as do their kinfolk in the region, but as the actions of neighbors, coworkers, and public institutions.

Appalachians in communities outside the region have actively responded to stereotyping through the same means used by Appalachians within the region. Their organizations have initiated both academic and community-based research that has been published in books, journals, news releases, and newsletters. Urban Appalachian artists, photographers, poets, dramatists, and musicians counter stereotypes by openly celebrating Appalachian culture in their work.

Urban Appalachians outside the region derive cultural refreshment and preserve tradition from frequent trips and sometimes retirement "down home." But the myth of large numbers of urban Appalachians returning to their home counties is misleading. According to census data, few people over the age of fifty-five are entering the region. Older urban Appalachians appear reluctant to stray very far from the urban communities where their families, friends, neighbors, and coworkers have settled.

In cities outside of the region, community-based organizations foster pride in their members' Appalachian heritage through dances, cultural festivals, plays, concerts, arts and crafts fairs, murals, exhibits, parades, award ceremonies, anniversary celebrations, reunions, and homecomings. The existence of multiple generations of urban Appalachians makes social, economic, and even cultural assimilation a reality for many of the descendants of the original migrants. On the other hand, urban Appalachian cultural and advocacy organizations in the Midwest are both an indicator of and a support system for a communal sense of Appalachian identity. As personal identification with an Appalachian heritage among the descendants of the original migrants replaces being born in the region as the primary indicator of who is an urban Appalachian, Appalachian communities in America's cities may grow stronger even as their populations decrease.

—Michael E. Maloney, *Michael Maloney and Associates*, and Phillip J. Obermiller, *Cincinnati, Ohio*

J. Trent Alexander, "Great Migrations: Race and Community in the Southern Exodus, 1917–1970," Ph.D. dissertation, Carnegie Mellon University (2001); Chad Berry, *Southern Migrants, Northern Exiles* (2000); Kathryn M. Borman and Phillip J. Obermiller, eds., *From Mountain to Metropolis: Appalachian Migrants in American Cities* (1994); Carl E. Feather, *Mountain People in a Flat Land: A Popular History of Appalachian Migration to Northern Ohio, 1940–1965* (1998); Roger S. Guy, "From Diversity to Unity: Uptown's Southern Migrants, 1950–1970," Ph.D. dissertation, University of Wisconsin at Milwaukee (1996); Rhoda H. Halperin, *Practicing Community: Class, Culture, and Power in an Urban Neighborhood* (1998); Phillip J. Obermiller and Steven R. Howe, "New Paths and Patterns of Appalachian Migration, 1975–1990," *Journal of Appalachian Studies* (Fall 2001); Phillip J. Obermiller and Michael E. Maloney, "Looking for Appalachians in Pittsburgh: Seeking *Deliverance*, Finding *The Deer Hunter*," *Pittsburgh History* (Winter 1990); Phillip J. Obermiller and Michael E. Maloney, "'We Ain't Agoin' Back': A Retrospective Look at Urban Appalachians in Cincinnati," in *Appalachia: Social Context Past and Present*, ed. Obermiller and Maloney (4th edition, 2002); Phillip J. Obermiller, Thomas E. Wagner, and E. Bruce Tucker, eds., *Appalachian Odyssey: Historical Perspectives on the Great Migration* (2000); Thomas E. Wagner and Phillip J. Obermiller, *African American Miners and Migrants: The Eastern Kentucky Social Club* (2004).

Akron, Ohio

First attracted to the city by abundant job opportunities in the rubber tire industry, Appalachians have had a strong presence in Akron, Ohio, for nearly a century. Indeed, by the 1920s, Akron was being referred to as the "Capital of West Virginia." This first wave of migration from the mountains was so heavy that by 1920 approximately thirty-five thousand West Virginians lived in Akron and composed fully 17 percent of the city's population. Many of the early arrivals came as a result of job advertisements in their hometown newspapers and enticement by labor recruiters sent out by tire manufacturers. Appalachian migrants continued to arrive throughout the 1920s. By 1930, the city was home to forty thousand Kentuckians and Tennesseans, in addition to an equal number of West Virginians. In some rubber factories, natives of central Appalachia constituted one-third of all employees.

World War II initiated another wave of migration to Akron as government contracts reinvigorated the local economy. Between 1940 and 1970, Akron received as many as twenty-six thousand Appalachian migrants, the majority from West Virginia, but natives of Tennessee and Kentucky continued to arrive as well. In the decades after 1970, migration to Akron dwindled as factories closed and the city entered a lengthy period of severe economic malaise and population decline. Still, Appalachians and their descendants were believed to compose as much as 40 percent of the city's population at the turn of the twenty-first century.

Inevitably, Appalachians have had a profound impact on Akron. Compared to Appalachians in other Ohio cities, they have fared well both economically and educationally. Much of their success may be attributed to their early arrival and their important role in the local labor force from an early date. Early Appalachian newcomers created social and religious organizations. The West Virginia Society of Akron dates back to 1917, when it was established as a social club dedicated to promoting better relations between West Virginians and Ohioans. The organization hosted large annual summer picnics through the late 1970s, after which its membership dwindled. The heyday of these picnics was in the late 1930s, when they attracted crowds of thirty thousand or more; highlights of the annual event included the crowning of a Miss West Virginia and guest speeches given by West Virginia politicians. Natives of Appalachia have also been notably active in local churches, including the Akron Baptist Temple, which *Life* magazine once pronounced the largest Baptist church in the nation. In addition, native West Virginians were at the forefront of labor organizing in the 1930s and subsequently played important roles in the leadership of the United Rubber Workers of America.

See also: CLEVELAND, OHIO; TWENTIETH-CENTURY OUT-MIGRATION (SETTLEMENT AND MIGRATION); URBAN APPALACHIAN ENCLAVES.

—Susan Allyn Johnson, *Ohio State University*

Carl E. Feather, *Mountain People in a Flat Land: A Popular History of Appalachian Migration to Northern Ohio, 1940–1965* (1998); Steve Love and David Giffels, *Wheels of Fortune: The Story of Rubber in Akron* (1999); Phillip J. Obermiller, Thomas E. Wagner, and E. Bruce Turner, eds., *Appalachian Odyssey: Historical Perspectives on the Great Migration* (2000).

Altoona, Pennsylvania

Nestled at the base of the Allegheny Mountains, Altoona is one of the largest cities in Appalachian Pennsylvania. The city was created in 1849 by the Pennsylvania Railroad as a base camp for servicing locomotives heading west. During the 1860s, the company expanded its Altoona shops to include the fabrication of railroad cars and locomotives as well as their repair and servicing. At its peak in the 1920s, the various machine shops, testing laboratories, and iron foundries that comprised the Altoona Works of the Pennsylvania Railroad spread across seven miles of valley floor and employed 16,500 workers.

Owing to the sheer variety of the railroad's operations, Altoona attracted an occupationally diverse workforce that ranged from unskilled foundry laborers to highly trained mechanical engineers and scientists. Compared to the other steel and coal towns in west-central Pennsylvania, however, Altoona remained conspicuously Protestant and homogenous. In 1920 immigrants comprised less than 9 percent of its population, a rate less than half that of comparable western Pennsylvania communities. Part of the reason was that railroads offered fewer opportunities for unskilled workers than did the coal and steel industries. There was also a conscious effort to maintain social homogeneity: as late as 1912, city fathers boasted that "the almost entire absence of foreigners of the laboring class . . . adds greatly to the desirability of the city as a place of residence or a business location." Slavic and especially Italian immigrants had established communities by the 1920s, but citizens were frequently less than hospitable. In 1925 Altoona had the largest Ku Klux Klan membership in Pennsylvania.

After World War II, the Pennsylvania Railroad's transition from steam to diesel engines, along with increased competition from other forms of transportation, derailed Altoona's economic security. By 1952 local unemployment had climbed to 22 percent, and employment at the Altoona Works had fallen by 50 percent. While the city strove to attract other employers, its fate continued to rise and fall with that of the railroad industry. In 1968 the once mighty Pennsylvania merged with the New York Central before finally being absorbed into the Conrail system in 1976. The federally subsidized railroad continued to maintain a presence in Altoona and actually expanded some facilities there, but the city never came close to its former glory. In 1990 Altoona's population had fallen to fifty-two thousand from a prewar high of eighty-two thousand in 1930.

Culturally Altoona exhibits quintessentially rural, if not Appalachian, folkways. Hunting is a popular pastime, and in deference to local tradition public schools are closed on the first day of deer season. Country music also has a strong following in this and other central and western Pennsylvania counties. But Altoona's historical legacy of even prosperity and highly skilled labor contradicts the pattern of rural poverty in other parts of Appalachia.

See also: PENNSYLVANIA RAILROAD (TRANSPORTATION); SECTION OVERVIEW (RACE, ETHNICITY, AND IDENTITY).

—Curtis Miner, *Pennsylvania Historical and Museum Commission*

Robert L. Emerson, *Allegheny Passage: An Illustrated History of Blair County* (1984); Philip Jenkins, *Hoods and Shirts: The Extreme Right in Pennsylvania, 1925–1950* (1997); Kim E. Wallace, comp., *Railroad City: Four Historic Neighborhoods in Altoona, Pennsylvania* (1990).

Appalachian Social Issues outside the Region

As with other expatriate minority groups, Appalachians moving to cities outside the region have been confronted with police harassment, substandard education, housing and job shortages, and lack of health care, but they have often found ways not only to persevere but also to celebrate their Appalachian identity.

In the 1960s, urban Appalachians in the Uptown neighborhood on the North Side of Chicago organized community groups such as the Peoples' Uptown Center and the Young Patriots (the latter modeled on the Black Panthers) in their struggle to obtain education, housing, and jobs and to address problems of poverty and police harassment. Most of these groups dissolved after a time as residents of the neighborhood moved back to the mountains or dispersed to other areas of the city. In other cities, however, most notably in Cincinnati, Cleveland, Columbus, and Dayton, Ohio, groups of urban Appalachians and their supporters similarly sought to rectify discrimination by participating in movements for change.

Persistent institutional misconceptions about Appalachians have made adjustment to urban life difficult. Contrary to historical evidence, urban school officials sometimes concluded that Appalachian migrants had little interest in formal education. In fact, many early migrants to the cities felt they had been shortchanged in their educations in the mountains and hoped that their children would fare better in the city. Often they did indeed do better, and urban Appalachians can point to many success stories of individuals who grew up in urban poverty and went on to successful careers. Some of the migrants were teachers themselves and served as leaders and mentors in their new communities. For example, Ernie Mynatt, who moved from Harlan County, Kentucky, to work in the Cincinnati public schools, became an early advocate for migrants from the mountains and a founder of the Urban Appalachian Council, as well as an activist in the areas of civil rights, poverty, and education.

Often, however, urban Appalachians found city school systems ill equipped to meet the needs of migrant youth. In many cases, second-generation migrants faced even greater difficulty than the first, leading urban Appalachians to join efforts to revitalize schools, oppose school closings, and promote alternative educational programs. The Southern School in Uptown, for example, was established in the 1960s to meet the needs of Appalachian youth who were not succeeding in the Chicago schools. In the 1970s, the Peoples' Uptown Center, a branch of Northeastern Illinois University, united white Appalachians, Puerto Ricans, African Americans, and others around the theme of urban in-migration, helping students earn college credits through community service. In Dayton, Sinclair Community College offered an outreach program designed for the urban Appalachian community.

In Cincinnati, urban Appalachians fought school closings in Over-the-Rhine and other neighborhoods. At one point in the late 1970s, Appalachians in Over-the-Rhine went to court along with their African American neighbors to claim discrimination in the closing of Peaslee School. Although they lost their case, they were the first to make a legal claim to recognition of urban Appalachians as a minority.

Appalachians in Cincinnati have also set up a network of community-based schools for General Educational Development to prepare students for high school equivalency examinations. The Lower Price Hill Community School, one of the oldest of these programs, has established a relationship with a local community college to provide introductory college classes in the neighborhood. In the East End, another heavily Appalachian neighborhood, the community has established the East End Community Heritage School, a charter school emphasizing strong academics and Appalachian and African American culture.

In the 1960s and 1970s, urban Appalachians became involved in nearly every aspect of the War on Poverty. In Chicago, one of the bases for Martin Luther King Jr.'s Poor People's Campaign was in the heavily Appalachian neighborhood of Uptown. In other cities, urban Appalachians joined organizing efforts to create opportunities and eliminate barriers for low-income people through community councils and block clubs and through federal efforts such as the Model Cities program. Long after these initiatives lost federal support, urban Appalachians continued to voice concerns about urban poverty and to advocate for poor and marginalized people.

The effects of environmental pollution have also been a concern for urban Appalachians. In Cincinnati's industrialized neighborhood of Lower Price Hill, Appalachians, concerned about the health of local children, attempted to associate health problems with industrial pollution, but resistant city officials and local companies branded them with Appalachian stereotypes, blaming the problems on their supposed propensity towards violence, incest, and alcoholism. The community persisted and eventually forced implementation of environmental nuisance laws, reducing industrial pollution in Appalachian neighborhoods. Continuing the battle, the Lower Price Hill Environmental Leadership Group in 1998 completed a community survey documenting the health status of neighborhood children and describing high rates of asthma and lead poisoning, among other problems. The group continues to monitor pollution, keep pressure on polluters, and maintain community awareness. Other health initiatives have included struggles to establish health clinics in low-income neighborhoods and to improve access to medical benefits.

Urban Appalachians have been in the forefront of the labor movement in many midwestern cities, including Akron, Ohio, sometimes referred to as the "Capital of West Virginia" because of its many migrants from the Mountaineer State. Many were veterans of struggles to form the United Mine Workers of America, and they carried their experience with them to Ohio. There they organized with others to demand better wages and working conditions in Akron's rubber factories. Appalachian migrants also helped establish the United Automobile Workers in cities such as Detroit and Flint, Michigan, during the 1930s, taking part in the 1937 sit-down strike that gained the union recognition at General Motors. World War II brought many more mountain people to the urban north and swelled the ranks of unionized Appalachian workers. Unionization often involved many sacrifices and difficulties for the workers and their families. Harriette Simpson Arnow's novel *The Dollmaker* tells the story of one such family during World War II.

In the 1950s, layoffs due to mechanization in the coalfields and a decline in family farms in the mountains set many more mountain families on the road north. Postwar industrial expansion meant that many of these migrants were able to find jobs in union shops and industries. In many places, urban Appalachians formed the majority of the membership of locals. Urban Appalachians also supported union members in the mountains during the 1974 Brookside strike in Harlan County, Kentucky, by the United Mine Workers. Unions with large Appalachian memberships, such as the United Automobile Workers, also provided important support for the Civil Rights movement.

In northern cities, some early civil rights activists were African Americans transplanted from Appalachia. The shape of the urban Appalachian movement itself was strongly influenced by the Civil Rights movement and its leaders. For instance, the Reverend Fred Shuttlesworth brought his leadership north from Birmingham to Cincinnati, and Virginia Coffey, originally of West Virginia, became a founder of the Cincinnati Human Relations Commission and was an early supporter of the Urban Appalachian Council.

Coffey was one of many Appalachian leaders who moved back and forth between civil rights and Appalachian issues. Michael Maloney and Ernie Mynatt in Cincinnati and Iberus Hacker in Chicago were also urban Appalachian leaders with roots in the Civil Rights movement. In the late 1960s, black activists such as Stokely Carmichael and Dick Gregory challenged whites in the Civil Rights movement to turn their attention to the problems in poor white communities, and many activists did just that. They soon found that urban Appalachian communities also faced discrimination, inadequate housing, joblessness, and a school system that left many on the sidelines. Not surprisingly, many activists came to see the successful struggles of African Americans as a model for what urban Appalachians could accomplish.

Among other things, urban Appalachian activists followed African Americans' lead in placing an increased emphasis on cultural identity and cultural recognition. Many local governments, they found, were unwilling to recognize the existence of urban Appalachians as a distinct group, making it difficult to gain recognition for their social needs or cultural strengths. However, urban Appalachians and their allies have used a variety of means to demonstrate that they constitute an "invisible minority" with distinct needs. With the help of researchers from local universities, Appalachian groups have confronted local governments, social service agencies, and educational institutions with facts about urban Appalachian communities. The Urban Appalachian Council, for example, publishes a series of working papers and fosters further research on the urban Appalachian population. In 1993 advocates in Cincinnati, perhaps uniquely, persuaded the city council to include "persons of Appalachian origin" alongside categories relating to race, gender, religion, disability, marital status, sexual orientation, and HIV status in an ordinance that makes it illegal to discriminate.

Along with drawing attention to the problems of poor and working-class Appalachian communities, urban Appalachians have also sought to celebrate the strengths, values, and resources of Appalachian culture as a whole. Our Common Heritage in Dayton sponsors an annual Mountain Days Festival. The Appalachian community in Greater Cincinnati and northern Kentucky hosts a variety of

Appalachian events, from neighborhood affairs to the annual three-day Appalachian Festival. Urban Appalachian activists consider these cultural events as essential to the community building that goes hand in hand with efforts to address basic needs.

See also: TWENTIETH-CENTURY OUT-MIGRATION (SETTLEMENT AND MIGRATION); URBAN APPALACHIAN ENCLAVES.

—Michael Henson, *Urban Appalachian Council*

Kathryn M. Borman and Phillip J. Obermiller, eds., *From Mountain to Metropolis: Appalachian Migrants in American Cities* (1994); Stokely Carmichael and Charles V. Hamilton, *Black Power: The Politics of Liberation in America* (1992); Todd Gitlin and Nanci Hollander, *Uptown: Poor Whites in Chicago* (1970).

Asheville, North Carolina

Since its founding in 1794, Asheville has been an urban hub of western North Carolina and southern Appalachia. Its position at the intersection of the French Broad and Swannanoa Rivers made it the location for trade and travel west of the Blue Ridge Mountains, and in the nineteenth century, the community became a small crossroads for mountain farmers and drovers traveling the Buncombe Turnpike. Known first as Buncombe Courthouse and then as Morristown, the town was named Asheville in 1797 in honor of the state's governor, Samuel Ashe. The settlement's growth was slow until the mid-1880s, though civic leaders and outside investors joined to develop tourism as the foundation of the regional economy after the Civil War. The 1880 arrival of the railroad resulted in an increase in visitor traffic sufficient to make Asheville an Appalachian commercial center. By the beginning of the twentieth century, the city was emerging as a seat of mountain political power as well. It was, one historian remarked, an island of civilization in the southern highlands.

Although slavery played a smaller role in the Appalachians than elsewhere in the South, in 1860 slaves constituted 15.4 percent of Buncombe County's population, and during the Civil War Asheville became a Confederate stronghold. It was home to the Buncombe Rifles, the first company organized west of the Blue Ridge Mountains, and the Rough and Ready Guards, one of ten companies of the Sixtieth North Carolina Regiment.

Local writer Francis Tiernan, from Salisbury, North Carolina, established the popular landmark description for Asheville in 1878. Writing under the name "Christian Reid," Tiernan emphasized the city's clean air, temperate climate, and majestic highland landscape by referring to it as "The Land of the Sky." By the turn of the twentieth century, this image was being used to promote tourism in the area. Set amidst the natural beauty of the Appalachians' highest peaks, the city has long impressed visitors with both its picturesque setting and urban development. As tourism became more important to the community's economy, women began to open inns and boardinghouses, where they performed the majority of management functions.

With the rise of tourism came a decline in agriculture and changes in traditional patterns of regional life. Adver-

Armistice Day parade through downtown Asheville, North Carolina, 1923. The 1920s marked the city's greatest building boom with the construction of residential subdivisions, new hotels, civic buildings, and the town's first skyscraper.

tised as an ideal representation of the New South, Asheville was also home to industries such as textile and lumber mills. In 1888 the city's streets were illuminated with electricity, and in 1889 its electric streetcars became the first to run in North Carolina, providing an instant attraction for people from across the region. During the next decade, town leaders such as George Willis Pack helped to beautify the city. Pack provided much of the financial support for improvements in education, the creation of parks, and the construction of a library and a new courthouse.

In 1890 George W. Vanderbilt, one of Asheville's most prominent citizens, began construction of his soon-to-be famous home, Biltmore. Completed in 1895, the mansion became one of the town's leading tourist attractions and made Asheville a fashionable destination for northern elites. Because of the house's grandiosity and the publicity surrounding its construction, the region witnessed a population boom, and real estate values soared. Elaborate hotels such as the Grove Park Inn (1913) were built to accommodate the influx of tourists. Due to increased visitor traffic, the Good Roads Association of Asheville, created in 1899, became the first such southern organization to campaign for governmental highway development.

The twentieth century brought many changes to Asheville. With the construction of residential subdivisions, new hotels, civic buildings, and the town's first skyscraper, the 1920s proved a boom time. The city's baseball team, the Asheville Skylanders, which would eventually change its name to the Tourists, attracted thousands of fans. In 1929 Asheville's most famous resident, Thomas Wolfe, published *Look Homeward, Angel*, a novel based on the lives of Asheville's citizens. With the Great Depression, Asheville, like cities throughout Appalachia, faced fiscal calamity. But despite the collapse of the real estate market and the closing of industries during the 1930s, Asheville played an important role in the creation of two natural attractions. The formation of the Great Smoky Mountains National Park and the Blue Ridge Parkway set the stage for better times, making western North Carolina one of the most visited recreational areas of the country.

Finding that industry did not fully support the postwar economy, city leaders renewed Asheville's commitment to tourism as the best hope for urban prosperity. Sports became an important draw for the town as local athletes such as all-star football player Charlie "Choo Choo" Justice and Henry Logan rose to prominence. Logan enrolled at Western Carolina University in 1964, becoming North Carolina's first African American collegiate athlete and the first to play basketball for a traditionally white public institution.

Asheville remains the largest city in western North Carolina, but much has changed from the turn-of-the-century town made famous across the country by Vanderbilt and Wolfe. Current promoters of the city cite its growing gay and lesbian community, expanding art guilds, and religious tolerance as evidence to the claim that Asheville welcomes a broad range of ideas and lifestyles and generally embraces cultural diversity. Connections to Appalachian roots abide, however, as craft guilds and folk festivals celebrating regional heritage remain among its foremost tourist attractions.

See also: BILTMORE ESTATE (TOURISM); EARLY WHITE SETTLEMENT OF WESTERN NORTH CAROLINA (SETTLEMENT AND MIGRATION); SECTION OVERVIEW (TOURISM).

—Heather Murray, *Western Carolina University*

John C. Inscoe, *Mountain Masters: Slavery and the Sectional Crisis in Western Carolina* (1989); William Howard Plemmons, *The City Asheville: Historical and Institutional* (1935); Richard D. Starnes, *Creating the Land of the Sky: Tourism and Society in Western North Carolina* (1999).

Baltimore, Maryland

Baltimore is not generally recognized as a major destination for Appalachian migrants, but the city has long been a magnet for mountain workers and families seeking job opportunities. Although the migration stream to Baltimore began in the early 1930s, it was the economic pull of World War II defense industries that drew thousands of migrants to Baltimore from the Appalachian regions of Maryland, North Carolina, Virginia, and, especially, West Virginia.

As the demand for laborers grew during the war years, the federal government's Work Manpower Office and Baltimore's defense industries actively recruited workers from the Appalachian region by providing bus tickets and building dormitories for women migrants. In a study of mountain migrants to Baltimore during World War II, Thaddeus M. Smith found that the problems confronting the newcomers were similar to those facing Appalachian migrants to urban areas in the Midwest: isolation, lack of housing, rural-urban cultural conflicts, stereotyping, and discrimination.

Large numbers of migrants returned to the mountains at the end of the war, but many probably became migrants again due to the push-pull postwar economy in the region. Some undoubtedly returned to Baltimore in the 1950s and 1960s and rejoined those who had stayed following the war. In the 1960s the migrants were "discovered" and classified as a "problem group" by the city's residents and leaders. A June 1960 series of six articles in the *Baltimore Sun* by J. Anthony Lukas described the plight of "southern mountain migrants" and problems created by their influx. The following year the Baltimore Section of the National Council of Jewish Women published a comprehensive report about the migrants entitled *The Unaccepted Baltimoreans: A Report on the White Southern Rural Migrants.* The council's study committee, chaired by Ferne Kolodner, identified several "cultural islands" of migrants throughout Baltimore. The neighborhoods mentioned include Linden Avenue below North Avenue, Eutaw Place, Bolton Street, Park Avenue, and the Mount Royal–Fremont Urban Renewal Area, as well as several smaller "secondary cultural islands."

Lukas and Kolodner painted a familiar but stereotypical picture in describing the migrants as transient people with strong family values, peculiar ways, and little regard for education. Although Kolodner's report and the *Sun* articles provided balanced information about the status of migrants, there is little evidence that city leaders and agencies made significant efforts to aid them. Nor are there signs of efforts by the migrants themselves to form grassroots advocacy or social organizations such as those in Cincinnati and Dayton, Ohio, and other cities. Of the Appalachians who migrated to Baltimore, those who settled and stayed for the long term have become a part of the city's diverse background.

See also: APPALACHIAN SOCIAL ISSUES OUTSIDE THE REGION; TWENTIETH-CENTURY OUT-MIGRATION (SETTLEMENT AND MIGRATION); URBAN APPALACHIAN ENCLAVES.

—Thomas E. Wagner, *University of Cincinnati*

Ferne Kolodner, *The Unaccepted Baltimoreans: A Report on the White Southern Rural Migrants* (1961); Phillip J. Obermiller, Thomas E. Wagner, and E. Bruce Tucker, eds., *Appalachian Odyssey: Historical Perspectives on the Great Migration* (2000); Thaddeus Mondy Smith, "Where There Are No Mountains: Appalachian Culture and Migration to Baltimore," M.A. thesis, Brown University (1987).

Binghamton, New York

Binghamton, the seat of Broome County, is located in south-central New York near the Pennsylvania border. The town began as Chenango Point, founded by settlers from New England on the site of an Iroquois village in 1787 and soon renamed for its primary landowner and promoter, William Bingham. Conflicting crown titles and the predominance of settlers from New England led to a land dispute over the area between New York and Massachusetts that was finally resolved in the 1790s. Binghamton Village was incorporated in 1834. Through its location at the confluence of the Chenango and Susquehanna Rivers, the conjoining of the Erie and Chenango Canals in 1837, and the birth of the Erie Railroad in 1848, Binghamton became a key linking point between the anthracite coalfields of northeastern Pennsylvania and national markets and ports. Early industries included shoemaking, textiles, and cigar manufacturing.

While the early inhabitants of Binghamton came from New England, England, Germany, and Ireland, immigrants of eastern European descent began arriving directly from Europe and from the anthracite region of northeastern Pennsylvania after 1865. Among the most prominent of these new immigrants were Lithuanians who came to Binghamton to escape the dangers of the mines and gain factory employment while remaining close to relatives in Pennsylvania.

A major draw for these new immigrants was the shoe industry, most notably the Endicott-Johnson Shoe Company, an innovative concern established in 1899. The company invested in new technologies and factories in and around Binghamton and fostered a paternalistic system in which medical care, housing, subsidized food, and education were offered to workers. The plan, which encouraged the hiring of entire families, attracted many immigrants, and the company quickly became the largest employer in the region. Binghamton is also the home of International Business Machines (IBM), one of the area's largest employers at the beginning of the twenty-first century.

With the decline of industrial and manufacturing sectors, education has provided a major social and economic focus for Binghamton. The State University of New York at Binghamton, founded in 1946, was originally called Triple Cities College. Initially part of the private Syracuse University, it was absorbed into the state university system in 1950. In 1965 it formally became one of four doctoral-degree-granting University Centers in the State University of New York system.

See also: SCRANTON/WILKES-BARRE, PENNSYLVANIA; SECTION OVERVIEW (TRANSPORTATION).

—J. E. Steenshorne, *New York City Department of Environmental Protection Archives*

Aleksandras Gedmintas, "The Cultural Components of Ethnic Identity Retention among Binghamton, New York, Lithuanians," *Lituanus* (1982); Dennis P. Kelly, "The Contrasting Industrial Structures of Johnstown, Pa., and Binghamton, N.Y., 1850–1880," Ph.D. dissertation, University of Pittsburgh (1977); Gerald Zahavi, *Workers, Managers, and Welfare Capitalism: The Shoemakers and Tanners of Endicott Johnson, 1890–1950* (1988).

Birmingham, Alabama

The largest city in Alabama and long the industrial center of southern Appalachia, Birmingham is located at the southern end of the Appalachian Mountains. Covering an area of about 163 square miles in the Jones Valley of north-central Alabama, it is the seat of Jefferson County, home of the University of Alabama at Birmingham, and the site of some of the most tumultuous and memorable events of the American Civil Rights movement.

The area in and around Birmingham was first settled by Native Americans, particularly Cherokee, Choctaw, and Creek. Some Native American groups built permanent settlements in Alabama while nomadic tribes moved annually or biannually through the area. Descendants of many of these indigenous people still reside in and around Birmingham.

Europeans settled the site on which Birmingham now stands in 1813 as the town of Elyton. Rich iron ore deposits were mined during the Civil War, and deposits of coal, limestone, bauxite, and sand have also been exploited. Although the Confederacy was formed in Montgomery, Alabamians were not united in their support of the Civil War. From 1861 to 1865 much of the state, including Birmingham, was embroiled in angry disputes among citizens. Many Birmingham residents fought in the war, but no major conflicts occurred in the area or on Alabama soil.

In 1870 the intersection of two newly constructed railroads prompted the founding of the modern city, which was named by a local land company after Birmingham, England. It was incorporated in 1871. By the turn of the century, Birmingham had become a major iron- and steel-producing center and was known as the "Pittsburgh of the South." Northern Alabama's predominance in coal and steel was made possible by the entrepreneurship of such men as Henry DeBardeleben and Daniel Pratt. The development of the iron, coal, steel, and related by-products industries made certain that this area of the Alabama hill country would become one of America's major rail centers, as well. In 1886 DeBardeleben founded a city thirteen miles from Birmingham as a steel center for the nation, and named it Bessemer in honor of the British scientist Sir Henry Bessemer, inventor of the open-hearth method of producing steel. The growth of the Birmingham district, including Bessemer, was an important chapter in the development of the New South and in the growing urbanization of Appalachia.

In the 1960s, Birmingham was one of the most rigidly segregated cities in the American South, and its racial integration became a high priority of the Civil Rights movement. Birmingham residents and civil rights leaders, including the Reverends Fred Shuttlesworth and Martin Luther King Jr., participated in marches, boycotts, lunch counter sit-ins, and large demonstrations to protest racial segregation and discrimination in the city. Brutal police responses to these peaceful demonstrations were often televised to a shocked American public, and footage shot in the spring of 1963 was used to illustrate difficulties of the Civil Rights movement for decades.

In early 1963, King visited Birmingham to participate in a citywide boycott, was jailed for "parading without a permit," and wrote his "Letter from Birmingham Jail," one of the central documents of the Civil Rights movement. On September 15 of the same year, a bomb exploded at the Sixteenth Street Baptist Church in Birmingham during a Sunday morning worship service. The explosion killed four young black girls: Addie Mae Collins, Denise McNair, Carole Robertson, and Cynthia Wesley. Four Ku Klux Klan members were accused of the crime, and three were ultimately convicted—one in 1977, a second in 2001, and the last in 2002. Most historians conclude that the events in Birmingham were pivotal in gaining passage of the Civil Rights Act of 1964, which outlawed racial segregation and other discriminatory practices in the United States.

Birmingham accomplished gradual healing after the events of the 1960s. By the mid-1970s, construction of skyscrapers changed the city's skyline. Iron and steel mills were gradually replaced by an economy whose foundation includes multiple colleges and universities and medical, engineering, manufacturing, and service industries. City leaders opened the Birmingham Civil Rights Institute, a center for education and discussion about civil and human rights as well as a museum documenting the people and events of this struggle, in 1993. Mercedes-Benz opened its first American plant in nearby Vance in 1997. Other contemporary additions to the city include an outstanding science museum, an immense theme park, and the expansion of the world-class medical community. A highly industrialized city, Birmingham exports a wide variety of products, including railroad and airplane accessories, chemicals, automotive parts and equipment, plastics, and mineral deposits.

In 2000, the total population of Birmingham was 242,820 (74.1 percent claimed black, and 24.3 claimed white as their racial group). This was a slight decline from the city's 1990 population of 265,968.

See also: BIRMINGHAM CIVIL RIGHTS INSTITUTE (CULTURAL INSTITUTIONS); CIVIL RIGHTS MOVEMENT (RACE, ETHNICITY, AND IDENTITY); IRON AND STEEL INDUSTRY (BUSINESS, INDUSTRY, AND TECHNOLOGY).

—Steven Boyd and Julie Kate Howard, *Hickory, North Carolina*

Bristol, Tennessee/Virginia

See Tri-Cities, Tennessee/Virginia

Charleston, West Virginia

Located in the foothills of the Allegheny Mountains, Charleston, the capital of West Virginia, is situated midway along the length of the Kanawha River about fifty miles from the Ohio. The name *Kanawha* is derived from an obscure Indian tribe, the Conawees. With about two hundred thousand inhabitants in 2000, Kanawha County, of which Charleston is the seat, is the most populous in the state.

The earliest inhabitants of the site of Charleston were known as moundbuilders for their distinctive gravesites. The first white people to see the present site of Charleston (in 1755) are thought to have been captives of the Shawnee, the dominant tribe in the area. In the mid-1770s, more than one thousand acres were surveyed for much of what is now Charleston. The first European settlers arrived in 1788 and built Fort Lee for protection against the Native Americans. Their leader, George Clendenin, named the city after his father, Charles. In 1794 the Virginia General Assembly designated Clendenin's land a town. Originally known as Charlestown, over the years it became Charleston. Daniel Boone, who lived in a log cabin by the river in what later became Kanawha City, went west in 1799, perhaps marking the end of the pioneer period in this part of the Kanawha Valley.

Charleston was the site of rich deposits of the "red salt of Kanawha," which was characterized by high iron content resulting in deep coloration when boiled. Elisha Brooks is credited with building the first salt furnace, as the works were known in 1797. By simply sinking hollow logs into shallow wells and boiling the brine thus recovered, workers produced about 150 pounds of salt a day from two dozen kettles. The salt furnaces were labor-intensive, and unlike most western Virginians, owners became large slaveholders. The year 1812 was a crucial one for the town, as the war with England ended the importation of salt from the British West Indies and made Kanawha County's vast salt resources suddenly valuable.

The first steamboat to navigate up the Kanawha arrived in Charleston in 1820, and thereafter steamboats linking Charleston with Pittsburgh and Cincinnati became relatively routine and dominated travel between the urban centers until the coming of the Chesapeake and Ohio Railway in 1873.

The road linking Charleston with the Tidewater region of Virginia was the James River and Kanawha Turnpike, completed in the 1820s. A trip from Richmond to Charleston over the turnpike was perilous, as the stagecoach lurched over narrow mountain passes. Charleston's separation from Richmond by long distances and high mountains was a factor in West Virginia's secession from the Old Dominion in 1863. The northern part of present-day West Virginia was culturally and economically close to Ohio; thus, pro-Union sentiment ran stronger there than in the southern part. This north-south division was clearly reflected in the voting results on secession.

When the Civil War erupted in 1861, the ease of access to Ohio and the difficulty of traveling to Old Virginia spelled doom for the Confederacy's efforts to hold the Kanawha Valley and its saltworks. Federal units, with their ample supplies and manpower, sailed up the broad Kanawha aboard steamboats unmolested. On September 13, 1862, the last attempt by Confederate forces to return Charleston to the South resulted in a hard-fought battle followed by a Federal retreat. But the Confederates could not hold the town and withdrew.

After the war, West Virginia's first capital was located in Wheeling, but Charleston politicians succeeded in having the state capital moved to their city on March 28, 1870. In 1875 political rivalry between Charleston and Wheeling resulted in another move of the capital back to Wheeling. There, the seat of government remained until 1877, when a statewide referendum returned it to Charleston permanently.

A beautiful Victorian building was constructed on the block bounded by Capitol, Lee, Washington, and Dickinson Streets. The structure went up in flames in 1921, but its existence had sparked the development of the historic district of the old downtown, especially Capitol Street. The classic gold dome of the 1932 capitol, designed by architect Cass Gilbert, can be seen for miles; the building is hailed as one of America's most beautiful state capitols.

The twentieth century heralded an era of growth and wealth for Charleston, as numerous industries located near

State Capitol Complex on the Kanawha River at Charleston, West Virginia, 1995. The classic 1932 capitol building, designed by architect Cass Gilbert, stands five feet taller than the U.S. Capitol and features a gold-covered dome.

the city's resources and transportation. Charleston became known as the "COG City" for its coal, oil, and gas. World War I brought the Naval Ordnance Plant to South Charleston. By the end of World War II, the city was the "Chemical Center of the World." Charleston's prosperity reached its zenith in the 1950s, but, as with many other industrial communities, manufacturing employment declined thereafter.

Charleston has become a quintessential Appalachian city. It is centrally located in the region and has been associated with many historic regional events. Social movements, especially those relating to the coal industry, are often focused there, and the people associated with them, including Mother Jones and Senators Robert C. Byrd and John "Jay" Rockefeller, have helped keep Charleston in the public eye. As the state capital and a strong financial center, it remains the state's largest city.

See also: CHEMICAL INDUSTRY (BUSINESS, INDUSTRY, AND TECHNOLOGY); SECTION OVERVIEW (TRANSPORTATION).

—Richard A. Andre, *Kanawha Valley Historical and Preservation Society*

Julius de Gruyter, *The Kanawha Spectator* (1976); J. T. Hale, *History of the Great Kanawha Valley* (1891); William S. Laidley, *History of Charleston and Kanawha County* (1911).

Chattanooga, Tennessee

Chattanooga is located at an opening in the Appalachians once called the "Gateway to the South." The seat of Hamilton County and Tennessee's fourth-largest city, Chattanooga, with about 150,000 residents in the year 2000, is a rapidly developing urban center boasting commercial, natural, and historical attractions. Since its founding in 1838, Chattanooga has evolved from a river port and railroad village to a war-ravaged military camp to one of southern Appalachia's principal industrial and distribution centers to a diverse, modern city.

Immediately after the Cherokee removal in 1838, settlers marked off a town at Ross's Landing, the Tennessee River site of Chief John Ross's ferry. The founders soon changed the town's name from Ross's Landing to Chattanooga, a Creek word meaning "rock that comes to a point" and an old name for Lookout Mountain, which overlooks the city.

Among the pioneer settlers and speculators who succeeded the Native Americans were men of Scots-Irish, English, and German descent from Tennessee, Georgia, and neighboring southern states. The river port community endured, and in 1850 the Western and Atlantic Railroad was extended into Chattanooga. The railroad's celebrated arrival ensured economic growth, while the depot's placement at nine blocks from the river almost doubled the length of the town's main street. When the Civil War began in 1861, Chattanooga was a vital rail link, connecting Atlanta and the South, Nashville and the Midwest, and Knoxville and the Northeast.

The majority of the community sided with the Confederacy and was thus governed until 1863. Federal forces gained the strategically important town after a tremendous battle at Chickamauga Creek, followed by battles at Lookout Mountain and Missionary Ridge. Holding Chattanooga under occupation until war's end, the Army of the Cumberland suspended civil government for martial law and quickly transformed the fledgling town into a large military camp. The war and its aftermath wrought overwhelming change upon Chattanooga.

Amid the wreckage and with a displaced population, Chattanooga coped with dire poverty in the postwar years. Northern and midwestern carpetbaggers, many of them war veterans, controlled the government and the economy. For a time the municipality issued its own scrip for currency. It also faced widespread bankruptcy caused by one carpetbagger's fraudulent railroad schemes. By the late 1880s, however, such troubles vanished as the city boomed. Promoted as a "Pittsburgh of the South," industrialized Chattanooga once again had been transformed. Manufacturing brought improvements and expansion to the city, wealth and jobs to the citizens, heavy pollutants to the environment, and spoilage to the scenic landscape. This led, eighty years later, to Chattanooga's being ranked as one of the most polluted cities in America.

Racial and governmental changes affected the urban center. Near the close of the Civil War, the number of blacks in Chattanooga significantly increased, as freedmen gathered around Union camps. By 1870 African Americans accounted for one-third of the population and for nearly half by the turn of the century. Just three years after the war, blacks held office as aldermen and patronage jobs as policemen. For these and subsequent gains, the Republican Party dominated the black vote.

In the 1890s shifting attitudes, locally and throughout the South, manifested themselves in legislated segregation, beginning with streetcars. Black Chattanoogans subsequently lost all held offices in 1911, when the municipality turned to citywide elections and a commission form of government. The old system (a board of mayor and aldermen), in place except for the war years since 1840, was criticized for political rings, boss rule, disregard for law or public will, and petty politics. The new government brought little change along those lines. In 1990 Chattanooga again sought reform, adopting a representative form of government to ensure the inclusion of minorities. Blacks were afterwards elected or appointed to an increasing percentage of top positions. Race relations remained tolerant, though ambiguous. A recent phenomenon has been the influx of immigrants to the city from Mexico, promising a sharp rise in the Hispanic population.

Having long called itself the "Scenic City," a reference to its bold vistas formed by river, mountains, and ridges, Chattanooga has enjoyed a history of tourism. In antebellum days visitors came to see the natural attractions of Lookout Mountain. Additionally, by the 1880s, many came to see the sites made famous by battle. The dedication of the Chickamauga and Chattanooga National Military Park in 1895 drew the attention of the nation; the park was the first national military park and remains one of the largest reservations of its kind.

In 1950 Chattanooga had the highest number of manufacturing employees per capita in the country. The high level of industry in the area, relying mostly on soft coal for fuel, contributed to Chattanooga's being designated by the federal government in 1969 as one of the nation's worst air polluters. Furthermore, the exodus from downtown common to many cities was worsened in Chattanooga by this pollution, which drove people out of the city's center. Through self-imposed controls, which later served as a model for the Federal Clean Air Act, Chattanooga had become one of the nation's cleanest cities by 1972.

Applying the same community strategies used to clean up the air, Chattanooga began working to revitalize its dying downtown. In 1973 the city, along with business leaders and private citizens, began a series of projects that culminated in the transformation of Chattanooga into one of the South's most popular cities for tourists. Rather than dying, the old center along the river enjoyed a renaissance that included new parks, museums, theaters, the largest freshwater aquarium in the Southeast, an IMAX theater, a children's museum, riverboat rides, the world's longest pedestrian bridge, restaurants, and art galleries.

See also: CHATTANOOGA, TENNESSEE (TOURISM); RAILROADS (TRANSPORTATION).

—Gary C. Jenkins, *Chattanooga, Tennessee*

Gilbert E. Govan and James W. Livingood, *The Chattanooga Country, 1540–1976: From Tomahawks to TVA* (1977); James W. Livingood, *A History of Hamilton County, Tennessee* (1981); John Wilson, *Chattanooga's Story* (1980).

Chicago, Illinois

Throughout the 1950s and 1960s, thousands of Appalachian migrants settled in the Chicago communities of Uptown and Lakeview. At the height of the migration, more than 40 percent (and more than 80 percent in certain census tracts) of the newcomers to Uptown, known locally as Hillbilly Heaven, were from the mountain South. During 1963, more than 50 percent of the migrants to Uptown came from Kentucky and West Virginia. In 1960 official sources in Chicago estimated that there were between twenty thousand and fifty thousand Appalachians in the city. The Uptown neighborhood reached its zenith in the 1970s, before a series of arson-related fires and gentrification, the process of replacing low-income and working-class housing with market-rate housing, displaced most of the Appalachians to other neighborhoods. Some also returned to the South.

The migration of Appalachian whites was a symptom of the larger economic changes affecting the entire country during the 1950s and 1960s. While many left central and southern Appalachia as a result of technological and economic changes in mining and farming, others relocated to satisfy their curiosity or to join friends and family already in Uptown, and most sought to improve their economic circumstances.

Often the adjustment to urban life proved difficult as migrants confronted stereotyping and outright hostility. As their neighborhoods expanded, so did negative media accounts and community opposition rising from mountaineer images created by northern writers in the nineteenth century. These stereotypes resulted in exaggerated fears of Appalachians as criminals, drunkards, and malcontents.

To introduce new arrivals to urban life and to confront such stereotyping, the Council of the Southern Mountains opened the Chicago Southern Center to provide the migrants a sense of pride and identity in their mountain heritage. The center campaigned for positive treatment of southerners by the media and worked to show that migrants were capable workers and compatible residents. In various ways, the center made important inroads as a migrant representative and advocate. It also created a conduit that other social service agencies used to reach migrants.

The Students for a Democratic Society's Jobs or Income Now project marked the beginning of an era of community activism and social protest. In response to landlords' neglect and slack code enforcement that left many apartments in Uptown uninhabitable, activists helped organize Appalachians to fight for better housing and resist gentrification. Appalachians engaged in rent strikes, marches, and direct confrontations with city officials to pressure landlords to repair buildings. Police were held accountable for mistreatment of Appalachians, who took badge numbers and picketed police precincts. Through this struggle a sense of ownership of community and solidarity developed among the migrants.

In 1976 the opening of Harry S Truman College marked the beginning of the end of the Appalachian presence in Uptown. In spite of community opposition, entire blocks of large apartments containing thousands of Appalachian families were razed to make room for the college. Similarly, the construction in the 1980s of Pensacola Place, a huge commercial and residential complex, displaced another large group of Appalachians.

In the aftermath, there was little agreement among community representatives or even the remaining southerners as to what had become of the displaced Appalachians. Some local observers maintained that they had moved to the suburbs. Others argued that they had returned to the South after receiving settlements for black lung claims. Hard evidence was sketchy and sometimes contradictory. In any case, the few Appalachians left in Uptown gradually became inconspicuous among surges of new immigrants from Asia, Africa, and Central America.

Gentrification was an additional force that caused Appalachians to move out of Uptown. Unscrupulous developers sometimes used the ploy of moving mentally unstable people into buildings and at times resorted to arson to clear the way for their projects.

A few buildings on Magnolia and Racine Streets continued to be occupied by Appalachians early in the twenty-first century. Some remained by choice, others because they lacked the resources to relocate. Many had spouses buried nearby or grandchildren in Chicago. The migrants who remained in Uptown were often women who had acquired a feeling of neighborhood identity in the course of battles over housing.

See also: APPALACHIAN SOCIAL ISSUES OUTSIDE THE REGION; TWENTIETH-CENTURY OUT-MIGRATION (SETTLEMENT AND MIGRATION); URBAN APPALACHIAN ENCLAVES.

—Roger Guy, *Texas Lutheran University*

Todd Gitlin and Nanci Hollander, *Uptown: Poor Whites in Chicago* (1970); Roger Guy, "The Media, the Police and Southern White Migrant Identity in Chicago, 1955–1970," *Journal of Urban History* (March 2000); Karen Zaccor, "Uptown's 15 Year Battle in the Gentrification War," *Keep Strong* (September–October 1987).

Cincinnati, Ohio

Though west of the Appalachians and beyond the boundary of the federally defined Appalachian region, Cincinnati, Ohio, has been home to a significant population of mountain natives for decades. Even though the Queen City became a favorite destination of Appalachian migrants nearly a century ago, adaptation was difficult, and a positive identity for new migrants has not been easily forged. In recent years, effective leadership organizations have emerged to serve the growing Appalachian community, and the word *Appalachian* has gradually replaced derogatory terms such as *hillbilly*, *brier*, and *cracker*. Appalachians are now formally recognized as a minority group by the City of Cincinnati, which in 1992 adopted a human rights ordinance that includes protection for "persons of Appalachian origin."

Separated from Kentucky by the Ohio River, Cincinnati served as a natural jumping-off point for eastern Kentucky mountaineers migrating from rural communities in search of employment. Factories in Cincinnati and nearby Middletown and Hamilton were magnets because of the many available unskilled and semiskilled blue-collar jobs. A steady trickle of migrants from the Kentucky and Tennessee mountains to Cincinnati began in the early 1800s, but World War II, with its great demand for workers in war-related industries, triggered a huge influx from Appalachia. This migration continued in even greater numbers in the 1950s and 1960s, stimulated by a postwar urban boom, widespread unemployment in the coalfields, and the decline of the timber industry and farming in the mountains. During the 1950s, special bus runs were established to transport laid-off miners and their families to Cincinnati from eastern Kentucky coalfield communities.

The Great Migration between 1940 and 1970 transformed entire Cincinnati neighborhoods into Appalachian enclaves. During this period, new immigrants concentrated in the Lower Price Hill, Fairview, Camp Washington, Northside, Mount Adams, River Road, South Fairmont, East End, and Over-the-Rhine neighborhoods that had once housed German, Irish, and Italian immigrants. Previously a haven for German immigrants, Over-the-Rhine, on the northern outskirts of the downtown area, became home to a large number of Cincinnati's Appalachians in the 1950s. Norwood and Elmwood Place, smaller industrial cities surrounded by Cincinnati, also became popular migrant destinations, as did Covington and Newport, Kentucky, municipalities directly across the Ohio River.

Although factory jobs were the primary draw for migrants, plant layoffs were frequent, and periods of unemployment left many urban Appalachian families in poverty. Discrimination in hiring practices, housing, and bank financing added to the daily challenges of adjustment to urban life. Cincinnati's close proximity to eastern Kentucky, however, provided a safety valve for many new immigrants, who created traffic jams on the bridges leading to Kentucky as they journeyed home on weekends and holidays.

Despite social and economic obstacles, urban Appalachians began to build communities within their new neighborhoods. Informal networks of family and friends provided support systems for the newest arrivals from the mountains and for those left unemployed. Mainline churches organized to serve the spiritual, social, and sometimes material needs of numerous families. Stores, restaurants, bars, and social clubs also sprang up as part of this emerging community. Bluegrass and country music thrived, and Cincinnati became a center for recording Appalachian music in the 1950s and 1960s.

Some of the existing social service personnel in these neighborhoods recognized the need to adjust their programs to serve the new residents. Emanuel Community Center in

Over-the-Rhine decided in 1960 to recruit Appalachian outreach workers; this initiative led to the hiring of Ernie Mynatt, a native of Harlan County, Kentucky, to work with boys and adolescent males who roamed the streets of the neighborhood. Although the community center allocated space for his program, Mynatt spent most of his time on the street making connections and building relationships with Appalachian youth. He proved to be so skilled at keeping street kids out of trouble that the local courts remanded many youthful offenders to his care instead of incarcerating them. Mynatt became the most visible of a group of leaders who emerged in the 1960s and 1970s to serve the Appalachian community. Others included Stuart Faber, a businessman who supported various urban Appalachian causes with the Appalachian Fund, which was started by his father; Virginia Coffey, a respected social services administrator from Wheeling, West Virginia; Louise Spiegel, an outspoken and able civic leader; and Michael Maloney, a young community organizer with family roots in Breathitt County, Kentucky.

Poverty among white urban Appalachians was overshadowed by the national and local focus on the plight of African Americans. Although they gradually won a place for Appalachian residents in several federal and local programs designed to aid the urban poor, Mynatt and Maloney also recognized the need for freestanding organizations to speak for this growing community. An initial organization, United Appalachian Cincinnati, was launched in 1968 to advocate for civil rights and the social and economic needs of urban Appalachians. In 1970 Mynatt received support from the Appalachian Fund to establish the Appalachian Identity Center in Over-the-Rhine. Loosely structured with few formal programs, the center provided a place for young people to gather and learn about their heritage.

Events that buttressed the positive emergence of the urban Appalachian community included a series of conferences at Xavier University on "Southern Appalachians" and an annual Appalachian cultural and crafts festival sponsored by the Junior League of Cincinnati. The Xavier conferences stimulated a cadre of scholars and researchers to write reports, articles, and books depicting various aspects of urban Appalachian life. Meanwhile, the Appalachian Festival became such a success that a separate organization with a board fully representative of the city's Appalachian community was established in 1974. The culmination of this initial organizing was the creation of the Urban Appalachian Council in 1974. The council represented a merger of Mynatt's Appalachian Identity Center with the Appalachian Committee, a group organized under the auspices of the city Human Relations Commission. Led during its first decade by Maloney, the council has experienced a number of problems over its twenty-five year history, but strong leadership from both its Appalachian and non-Appalachian board members has steered it through financial and organizational difficulties. Despite the broad gains, however, the urban Appalachian community continued to see a high dropout rate from Cincinnati public schools.

While Cincinnati neighborhoods such as Lower Price Hill and Camp Washington remain Appalachian enclaves, residents with mountain roots now live throughout the metropolitan area. The Urban Appalachian Council continues to advocate issues and to promote and operate programs and services; AppalPAC, a political action committee, exerts its influence in local campaigns. Alternative community schools with General Educational Development classes have been established in many Appalachian neighborhoods, and an Appalachian Charter School approved by the Cincinnati Board of Education opened its doors in September 2000. The Appalachian Festival remains a popular annual event that draws thousands of visitors from all over Greater Cincinnati.

In addition to the development of Appalachian-specific organizations and programs, leaders reflecting the ethnic heritage and diversity of the Appalachian region have emerged in every area of Cincinnati's political, civic, religious, cultural, and economic life. These leaders include writers, teachers, school administrators, elected representatives, and corporate executives.

See also: APPALACHIAN SOCIAL ISSUES OUTSIDE THE REGION; TWENTIETH-CENTURY OUT-MIGRATION (SETTLEMENT AND MIGRATION); URBAN APPALACHIAN ENCLAVES.

—William K. Woods, *Applied Information Resources*

Don Corathers, Pauletta Hansel, and Malcolm J. Wilson, eds., *Perceptions of Home: The Urban Appalachian Spirit* (1996); Phillip J. Obermiller, Thomas E. Wagner, and E. Bruce Tucker, eds., *Appalachian Odyssey: Historical Perspectives on the Great Migration* (2000); Thomas E. Wagner and Phillip J. Obermiller, *Valuing Our Past, Creating Our Future: The Founding of the Urban Appalachian Council* (1999).

Cleveland, Ohio

Cleveland, Ohio, has an intense and diversified cultural life. Prior to World War I, the city attracted immigrants from Germany, Hungary, Italy, Poland, and the former Yugoslavia and Czechoslovakia. During the Great Depression and World War II, many African Americans relocated to Cleveland from the South. In the 1950s and 1960s, the principal migration flow came from a different part of the country—the Appalachian highlands.

A series of articles published by the *Cleveland Press* in 1958 reported that as much as 45 percent of Cleveland's Appalachian population came from West Virginia. Another 20 percent came from Tennessee; 8 percent from Kentucky; 7 percent from Alabama; 5 percent from Virginia; and 15 percent from various other mountain states. The importance of mountain migrants in Cleveland was indicated by a later

Press editorial that observed that Appalachians had been key to the city's postwar industrial growth and that the city owed Appalachians a debt of gratitude for what they had accomplished.

As coal mining declined and family farms failed in these states, mountain people moved to urban areas in search of factory employment. In Cleveland, they found entry-level jobs in automotive plants, steel mills, machine tool factories, aircraft engine plants, and household appliance factories. But they found it harder to deal with education, housing, and social issues than to find places in the workforce.

Misinformed Cleveland public school officials often believed Appalachian students were intellectually or developmentally deficient and placed them in grades behind their age group. Only later did teachers report that urban Appalachian students did as well scholastically as native-born Clevelanders.

As in other urban areas, migrant Appalachian families clustered in neighborhoods where they were able to retain customs and pursue shared interests. In some cases, they gradually rehabilitated the decaying neighborhoods where they settled. But while Appalachian migrants to cities such as Dayton, Ohio, began moving to the suburbs in the 1950s and 1960s, their movement to the suburbs of Cleveland did not start until the 1990s.

Most urban Appalachians in Cleveland remained in inner-city neighborhoods such as Tremont, Ohio City, Detroit Shoreway, and the Stockyards unless they were forced out by gentrification. Traditional community organizations such as the Ohio City Near West Development Corporation, Detroit Shoreway Community Development Association, Stockyards Area Development Association, and Tremont West Development Corporation continue to support housing rehabilitation, social justice, and community-development initiatives for all neighborhood residents, including Appalachians.

See also: TWENTIETH-CENTURY OUT-MIGRATION (SETTLEMENT AND MIGRATION); URBAN APPALACHIAN ENCLAVES.

—Carol Baugh, *Miami University* and *Sinclair Community College*

Julian Krawcheck, "Smile When You Say Hillbilly," *Cleveland Press* (January 29, 1958); Gene B. Peterson, Laure M. Sharp, and Thomas F. Drury, *Southern Newcomers to Northern Cities: Work and Social Adjustment in Cleveland* (1977); John D. Photiadis, *Selected Social and Sociopsychological Characteristics of West Virginians in Their Own State and in Cleveland, Ohio* (1970).

Columbus, Ohio

Columbus, Ohio, has been a major destination for Appalachian migrants since the early 1900s, but the majority arrived from eastern Kentucky and southern West Virginia during the Great Migration of 1940 to 1970. During those years, word spread through declining communities of central Appalachia that Route 23 was the avenue to well-paying jobs in Columbus factories.

First-generation migrants entered urban life in three major Columbus enclaves: the South Side (Southside), the Near North Side (formerly Flytown, later Victorian Village), and the Near West Side (known as the Bottoms or Franklinton). These neighborhoods provided proximity to relatives who had arrived earlier, to factory jobs, and to low-income rental housing. From these neighborhoods migrants frequently journeyed back down Route 23 to see their friends and families, creating Friday and Sunday traffic jams on bridges connecting Ohio with West Virginia and Kentucky.

Migration into Columbus declined during the 1980s and 1990s, but there were signs of resurgence due to welfare reform at the end of the century, when some states provided incentives such as cash payments or bus tickets for Appalachians to move to high-employment areas such as Columbus. Estimates of the percentage of first- and second-generation Appalachians residing in Columbus have ranged from 25 to 40 percent of the city's population. Adding to the weekday Appalachian population in Columbus are thousands of workers who commute daily to jobs in Columbus from the Appalachian area of southeastern Ohio.

Sporadic and short-lived efforts to organize Columbus's urban Appalachians began in the 1970s. Developments such as court-ordered busing for racial desegregation did away with Appalachian heritage programs in neighborhood-based schools and made it difficult for teachers to meet students' families. Rigid public school policies on tardiness and absenteeism, the high mobility of inner-city migrants, and a systemwide misunderstanding of Appalachian culture continue to create high dropout rates among Appalachian teenagers.

Initiatives such as the Harper Valley Mothers Club and Hilltop Festivals sponsored by Godman Guild Settlement House on the Near North Side ended as the neighborhood became gentrified and Appalachians were forced to move to more affordable housing. The Central Ohio Appalachian Council foundered after a few years, and no leader emerged to call attention to Appalachian issues. Unlike Cincinnati, Columbus has not designated its Appalachian residents a minority population. With the exception of a new Franklinton floodwall, few public projects help migrant neighborhoods.

At the beginning of the twenty-first century, many Appalachians were prospering in Columbus, having moved out of economically depressed neighborhoods and into better housing in the city and suburbs. As they approached retirement, some were planning to return to Appalachia, but more chose to remain in Columbus, a place their children and grandchildren considered home. However, the Near West and South Sides of Columbus were still heavily Appalachian and economically depressed, with high crime rates, environmental pollution, and deteriorating housing. For thousands of Appalachians, the dream of a better life in Columbus remained just that.

See also: APPALACHIAN SOCIAL ISSUES OUTSIDE THE REGION; TWENTIETH-CENTURY OUT-MIGRATION (SETTLEMENT AND MIGRATION); URBAN APPALACHIAN ENCLAVES.

—Peggy Calestro, *Columbus State Community College*

Roger Alford, "A New Appalachian Migration?" *Columbus Dispatch* (August 31, 1997); Peggy Calestro and Ann Hill, *Appalachian Culture: A Guide for Students and Teachers* (1976); Ohio Urban Appalachian Awareness Project, *A Report on Appalachians in Columbus, Ohio* (1978).

Cumberland, Maryland

Even before its incorporation in 1787, the town of Cumberland owed its significance and prosperity to its geographical assets. Established in western Maryland around the junction of Wills Creek and the Potomac River, Cumberland became an important stop along the east-west trade and migration routes that connected the frontier to the urban centers of the eastern seaboard. The mountains that surrounded the town—and provided it with an abundance of coal, wood, and sand—set Cumberland apart from its lowland Maryland neighbors.

What began in 1749 as the site of a trading company warehouse became Fort Cumberland, which served during the French and Indian War as the launching point for General Edward Braddock's ill-fated attack on Fort Duquesne in 1755. When colonial wars with France and, later, with England finally subsided, Fort Cumberland caught the eye of land speculators, including Thomas Beall, who purchased and subdivided lots in 1785, transforming the fort into a bustling town. Investors such as George Washington speculated on land in the Potomac River Valley, envisioning a canal and road network that would connect the East to expanding settlements in the Ohio River Valley.

By 1818, the National Road, also known as the Cumberland Road, linked Cumberland to Wheeling, (West) Virginia, and in 1842 the track of the Baltimore and Ohio Railroad connected Cumberland to Baltimore. Barge traffic to Washington, D.C., began with the opening of the Chesapeake and Ohio Canal in 1850. These new travel routes enabled Cumberland's population to quadruple, and in 1880 Cumberland was the second-largest city in Maryland. Local coal, timber, and fire clay were shipped eastward by barge and rail, as immigrants from England, Scotland, Ireland, and Wales poured in to work for one of the thirty iron and coal companies chartered between 1828 and 1850. When the Civil War began in 1861, Federal strategists moved quickly to protect the vital supply lines of the two railroads, maintaining Cumberland as a garrison for the duration of the war.

Cumberland's expansion continued in the years after the war, with coal mines in neighboring George's Creek reigning over an industrial sector that included timber companies, tanneries, breweries, glassworks, and dye works. This prosperity helped to fund the construction of schools, libraries, and theaters. In 1906, when mining employment in western Maryland peaked at 6,400, Cumberland boasted eight newspapers, seventeen churches, and a trolley system. Bitterly contested labor strikes and competition between companies marked the decline of the coal industry in the early 1920s, an economic blow that amplified the effects of the Great Depression and the severe flooding that devastated Cumberland in 1936. New industries such as the

View of downtown Cumberland, Maryland, 2000. Situated in the Maryland highlands near the confluence of Wills Creek and the Potomac River, Cumberland was an important water and rail link between the eastern seaboard and the Ohio Valley during the nineteenth century.

Kelly-Springfield Tire Company and the Celanese Corporation helped the city to rebuild, especially during the production boom years of World War II. In the postwar period, Cumberland continued to struggle, as did many other Appalachian cities, to find a new economic role that might rival or replace two centuries of development built upon the exploitation of natural resources. In 2000 Cumberland, which is listed on the National Register of Historic Places, had a population of 21,518.

See also: SECTION OVERVIEW (SETTLEMENT AND MIGRATION).

—Katie Scharf, *Yale University*

Harry I. Stegmaier Jr., *Allegany County: A History* (1976).

Dayton, Ohio

Most white Appalachian migrants who settled in Dayton, Ohio, during the 1950s and 1960s came from the mountains of Kentucky, West Virginia, and Tennessee and took up residence on the East Side. While some African Americans migrated to Dayton, their numbers were small in comparison to the white migrants.

During the mid-century manufacturing boom, jobs were plentiful in and around Dayton. Neither male nor female migrants had difficulty finding factory jobs. In addition to those at large manufacturing plants such as General Motors, Delco, National Cash Register, Standard Register, Frigidaire, and McCall's Publishing, jobs were readily available in the hundreds of smaller factories that dotted the region. Many newcomers also obtained positions at Wright-Patterson Air Force Base. For most Appalachians, working in the factories and bringing home a weekly paycheck was attractive and easy compared to working in the coal mines or on rapidly eroding mountain farms. The assimilation process was more difficult, however.

As they moved from their enclave in east Dayton into suburbs and smaller communities, Appalachians often found themselves subject to ridicule. Local people mocked their speech, dress, and mannerisms and called them hillbillies, ridgerunners, and brierhoppers. Appalachians were guided to specific areas of these suburbs and small towns away from the already established neighborhoods. As a result of this suburban segregation, numerous urban Appalachian neighborhoods remained half a century later. East Dayton remained the largest urban Appalachian neighborhood, with migrants and their descendants comprising perhaps 40 percent of the area's 2000 population. With growing awareness of cultural diversity, much of the ridicule that greeted arrivals during the Great Migration gradually faded away in the late twentieth century.

Programs and festivals celebrating Appalachian culture have become important civic occasions. Each summer Our Common Heritage, an organization that supports Dayton's urban Appalachian neighborhoods, sponsors the Mountain Days Festival, one of the largest festivals in the country highlighting Appalachian culture. Sinclair Community College in downtown Dayton works to increase college enrollment from Appalachian neighborhoods, fostering an appreciation for lifelong learning and providing cultural programs for the public.

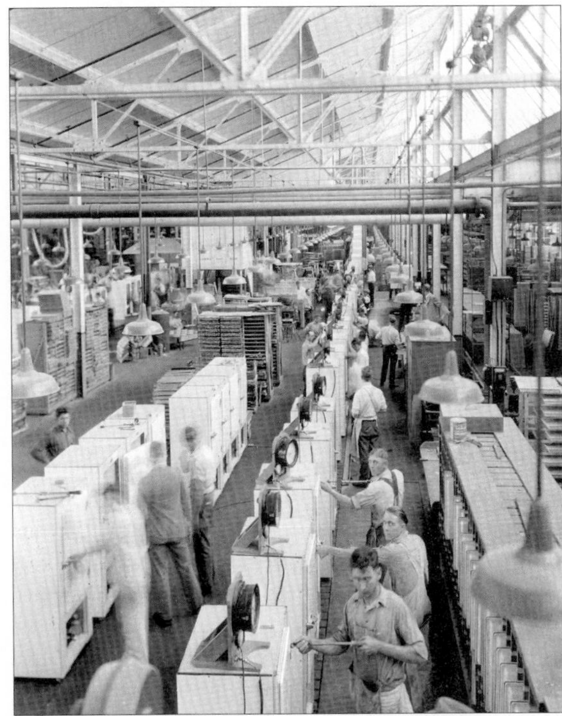

Workers at a Frigidaire factory in Dayton, Ohio, 1948. A mid-twentieth-century manufacturing boom drew Appalachian workers by the thousands to Midwest industrial centers. An estimated 40 percent of Dayton's residents claim Appalachian origins.

Dayton's urban Appalachians, like migrants to other metropolitan areas, passed through several stages in the process of settling into the city, from the difficulties of relocation to the strains of adjustment and discrimination and finally to the celebration of their culture.

See also: APPALACHIAN SOCIAL ISSUES OUTSIDE THE REGION; TWENTIETH-CENTURY OUT-MIGRATION (SETTLEMENT AND MIGRATION); URBAN APPALACHIAN ENCLAVES.

—Carol Baugh, *Miami University* and *Sinclair Community College*

Kathryn M. Borman and Phillip J. Obermiller, eds., *From Mountain to Metropolis: Appalachian Migrants in American Cities* (1994); Nicholas Lemann, *The Promised Land: The Great Black Migration and How It Changed America* (1991).

Detroit, Michigan

Of all the midwestern cities that lured Appalachians from the hills, Detroit best embodies the forces that shaped the northern migration. The city has long symbolized the emotionally harrowing experiences that characterized Appalachian urban migration. It also represents the disparate outcomes of the broad movement from rural to city life. While a large majority of Appalachians lived out the "American dream" by eventually finding homes in the suburbs, a core population of impoverished whites still resides in the heart of Detroit's inner city and in its Southwest Side neighborhoods.

Appalachians joined a stream of migrants from the Deep South and immigrants from Europe seeking work in the automobile factories of Ford, Chrysler, and General Motors. As early as 1920, Appalachians were moving to Detroit, lured by Henry Ford's five-dollars-a-day wage. During the Great Depression, major auto companies sent labor agents to Kentucky, West Virginia, and Tennessee to recruit factory workers. When Detroit boomed with wartime production during World War II, Appalachian migration to the city surged. Migration continued through the late 1950s and early 1960s, even as Detroit began rapidly to lose factory jobs. By the 1970s, some of the families that had relocated to Detroit were on the move again, heading for cities such as Houston where jobs were plentiful. Various writers and singers have given voice to this narrative in emotional detail. Harriette Simpson Arnow, author of the novel *The Dollmaker*, drew on personal experience in relating the terrible toll of life in Detroit. Others, including singer-songwriter Steve Earle, seized upon the city as a symbol of the experience of urban migration. In Earle's ballad "Hillbilly Highway," a coal miner heads for Detroit to make a better life for his family, but things do not work out as he had planned.

Appalachians reacted in numerous ways to the various shocks of life in Detroit. Some returned directly to the hills; others stayed only until they had saved enough money to raise their standard of living back home. Others commuted frequently between Appalachia and Detroit. License plates from West Virginia, Kentucky, and Tennessee are still frequently seen on neighborhood streets of the city's Southwest Side. Appalachians have remained distinct from other migrants to the city because they usually insist on being able to return home easily. This has caused many to remain ambivalent about city life and nostalgic for rural ways left behind.

Prior to World War II, Appalachians faced wide discrimination from native Detroiters—some landlords refused to rent to them, and sometimes Appalachians were denied entrance to bars. But at the height of Detroit's prosperity, Appalachians organized a vibrant social life near the city's downtown. Neighborhood bars with names like Hillbilly Heaven and Hillbilly Highway resounded with country and western tunes played by local bands and bright jukeboxes late into the night. These bars—featuring more interracial socializing than they had known in their rural, often "dry," home counties—provided a reason for some Appalachians to remain in Detroit for life.

See also: APPALACHIAN SOCIAL ISSUES OUTSIDE THE REGION; TWENTIETH-CENTURY OUT-MIGRATION (SETTLEMENT AND MIGRATION); URBAN APPALACHIAN ENCLAVES.

—John Hartigan Jr., *University of Texas*

Robert Coles, *Children of Crisis, Vol. 3: The South Goes North* (1971); Neil Fligstein, *Going North: Migration of Blacks and Whites from the South, 1900–1950* (1981); John Hartigan Jr., *Racial Situations: Class Predicaments of Whiteness in Detroit* (1999).

Erie, Pennsylvania

Because of its direct access to the Great Lakes, Erie, Pennsylvania, is seldom thought of as a part of Appalachia, but it is an important entrepôt for commerce between the region and the upper Midwest and Canada. Erie was also a focal point for mountaineers who worked as crew on ore carriers during the shipping season, returning home when frozen lakes suspended maritime traffic.

The city of Erie is located in the upper northwest corner of the Appalachian region, situated on Lake Erie between Cleveland, Ohio, and Buffalo, New York. The most distinguishing and enduring characteristic of the city is its magnificent harbor and peninsula, Presque Isle.

The harbor first caught the attention of the French, who built a fort in 1753 and named it Presque Isle (Presqu'île). The fort became the property of the English after the French and Indian War and was transferred to the new American government after the Revolutionary War. In 1795, after the Erie Triangle became part of Pennsylvania, a town was built at Presque Isle, with the new name Erie.

During the War of 1812, the Erie harbor was important to American forces because of its proximity to Canada and because it offered a safe refuge in which to build a fleet to gain control of Lake Erie. On September 10, 1813, Commodore Oliver Hazard Perry won an important victory at the battle of Lake Erie. Perry's flagship, the USS *Niagara*, has been rebuilt several times since 1813 and remains an important tourist attraction.

Erie's first white settlers, mostly English, Scots-Irish, and Pennsylvania German, arrived from the eastern United States in the late 1700s. After 1812, more immigrants came through the Erie Canal system on their way to Pittsburgh, and some of them remained in Erie. By 1851 the borough was large enough to become a formally incorporated city. After the Civil War, the growth of the city was once again fostered by immigration. Germans and Irish entered the city in large numbers and spurred development of its manufacturing and industrial economy.

By 1895, a hundred years after its birth, Erie's port was at its peak, with ships entering and leaving daily. Rapidly growing industry brought another wave of immigrants, many from southern and eastern Europe. Among the new arrivals were also people from the British Isles and Germany. After World War II, Erie's black community multiplied with the arrival of migrants from the rural South seeking factory jobs. Toward the end of the century, the area's Hispanic population boomed for similar reasons.

Since the 1920s, Erie's politics have been shaped by coalitions of its varied ethnic groups. The most prominent influence has come from the Italian-Polish alliance headed by Louis J. Tullio that gained power in the 1960s. Mayor Tullio, of Italian descent, held office from 1965 until 1989. In 2000 this same coalition continued to maintain control of City Hall. As with many other northern industrial cities, Erie's population and its socioeconomic characteristics have changed over the years. The city's population reached its peak of 138,000 in 1960; as of 2000, it was reported to be 108,718, much of the decline a result of movement to nearby suburbs.

From its rise as a harbor town, Erie has undergone several economic transformations. In the late 1700s, the salt trade was Erie's first business, with boats stopping in the small port to transfer cargoes of salt for shipment west on the Great Lakes or south to Pittsburgh. In the 1840s some of Erie's first factories, including foundries making molded metal objects, went into operation. The development of railroads in the mid-1850s hastened the city's development into a manufacturing center for the northern Appalachians. In 1898 the Hammermill Paper Company was founded, and in 1911 General Electric Company opened its doors. In addition, many other products were made in Erie by some five hundred manufacturing establishments. In the 1920s, Erie's Presque Isle Bay and the peninsula were promoted for summer and vacation use. In the second half of the twentieth century, new kinds of factories began operating with the most recent additions in the plastics industry.

Erie's educational system is a reflection of its ethnic heritage of Catholic immigrants (Italians, Poles, Irish, and Hispanics) with a large percentage of students attending Catholic schools. This has led to high levels of integration within the school system. However, because of this large percentage of lower-income minority groups, the school system finds it necessary to deal with the dual effects of poverty and dysfunctional families.

The 1993 Rand McNally report of best places to live ranked Erie as 84th out of 343 communities because of its affordable housing costs, low crime rate, good public transportation, and moderate climate. There was also increasing pride within the community and an optimism that the new millennium would bring to Erie a full share of American prosperity and happiness.

See also: SECTION OVERVIEW (BUSINESS, INDUSTRY, AND TECHNOLOGY).

—Joyce Miller Iutcovich, *Keystone University Research Corporation*

Rick Boyer and David Savageau, *Places Rated Almanac: Your Guide to Finding the Best Places to Live in America* (1993); Mary M. Muller, *The Town at Presque Isle: A Short History of Erie, Pennsylvania to 1980* (1991).

Gadsden, Alabama

Situated in the Appalachian foothills of northeastern Alabama, the city of Gadsden was founded in 1846 on the banks of the Coosa River. Major employers are Goodyear Tire and Rubber Company and a Honda manufacturing plant in nearby Lincoln. Gadsden is situated near several larger cities—one hour by car to Birmingham, an hour and a half to Chattanooga, and two hours to Atlanta—and outdoor attractions such as Noccalula Falls Park and Lookout Mountain. Gadsden boasts a symphony orchestra and a youth symphony, an amphitheater, and a functioning riverboat, the *Alabama Princess*. The city's cultural arts center, opened in 1990, attracts more than one hundred thousand visitors annually to exhibits, performances, and other functions. The 2000 census put Gadsden's population at 38,978.

Toward the end of the nineteenth century, Appalachian Alabama became the South's center of industrial coal and steel production. As they grew, the cities of Birmingham, Bessemer, and Gadsden became magnets for laborers out of the surrounding hill country.

Located in what is now Etowah County, Gadsden covers an area originally belonging to the Cherokee. The first white man to settle there was John Riley, who built a log cabin on the banks of the river with his Cherokee wife in 1825. After the forced removal of Cherokee from the area in the late 1830s, more white settlers began moving into the area, and the first white child was born there in 1842. In 1846 a 120-acre site was surveyed as the location for the town.

Prominent citizens in Gadsden's history include William Patrick Lay, the founder of the world's first hydroelectric plant in 1905; Robert Benjamin Kyle, a lumber baron who made Gadsden into a rail and steamboat center; and John Wisdom, known as the "Paul Revere of the South" for his prompt warning of Union troops marching on Rome, Georgia, enabling Confederate General Nathan Bedford Forrest to capture them. Ola Mize of Gadsden was awarded the Medal of Honor in 1953 for heroism during the Korean War.

John McMichael became Gadsden's first schoolteacher in 1843, and the first local board of education was appointed in 1895. In 1870 the first church for freed African Americans began holding services in town. The *Gadsden Times*, still published daily, first saw print in 1867.

Gadsden was initially a textile-manufacturing town, then one of northern Alabama's steel-producing cities, but both industries fell into decline in the city, as elsewhere. Dwight Manufacturing, a textile mill, operated from 1895 to

1959, and Gulf States Steel, which opened in 1904, closed in 2000 because of longterm financial problems related to the steel industry nationwide. The closing of the steel plant cost the city more than six thousand jobs, both at the plant and in related businesses, forcing many people to seek work outside of Gadsden.

See also: SECTION OVERVIEW (BUSINESS, INDUSTRY, AND TECHNOLOGY).

—Sarah L. Ashley, *Gadsden Public Library*

Deirdre Coakley, *Portrait of a City: An Informal History of Gadsden, Alabama, 1846–1996* (1996).

Greenville, South Carolina

The area around Greenville, South Carolina, in the Appalachian foothills, was a Cherokee hunting ground before the arrival of Europeans. About 1770 its first legal white settler, Indian trader Richard Pearis, acquired fifty thousand acres and established Great Plains plantation at the falls of the Reedy River. In the early days of the Revolutionary War, Pearis organized Cherokees to fight the patriots, and in 1776 they retaliated, destroying his property and imprisoning him in Charleston. He eventually settled in the Bahamas, but Paris Mountain (a corruption of *Pearis*), near the modern city of Greenville, was named for him.

Settlement began as early as 1776, and in 1786 Greeneville County was chartered and named for General Nathanael Greene, hero of the Revolution's Southern Campaign. The city of Greenville (population approximately sixty thousand in 2000) is situated on the Reedy River at the center of the county's 795 square miles.

About 1794 the state established a court near the falls of the Reedy River. The settlement around it was called Greenville Courthouse. The largest landowner was Lemuel Alston, who acquired eleven thousand acres and in 1797 laid out a plat for a village he called Pleasantburg. That name did not endure, and within a decade Greenville Courthouse returned. In 1816 Alston sold his land to Vardry McBee of Lincolnton, North Carolina, and moved to Alabama.

McBee is considered the founding father of Greenville. He established a corn mill and a gristmill, started making brick and quarrying stone, and opened a general store. He also donated land for the Greenville Male and Female Academies and for the first four churches. In 1836 he moved to Greenville, and by the time of his death in 1864, he also owned a cotton factory and a paper mill on the Reedy River.

Greenville grew in the antebellum period because of its location and climate. Swine, cattle, and wild turkeys fattened in the Appalachian valleys of Tennessee and North Carolina were driven down the Buncombe Road to Augusta, Georgia, where they were shipped to market. Drovers rested in Greenville before fording the shallow Reedy River at Main Street. Its "salubrious" climate made the foothills village a resort for summer visitors from low-country South Carolina.

A community of about six hundred when it was chartered in 1831, Greenville grew to almost two thousand

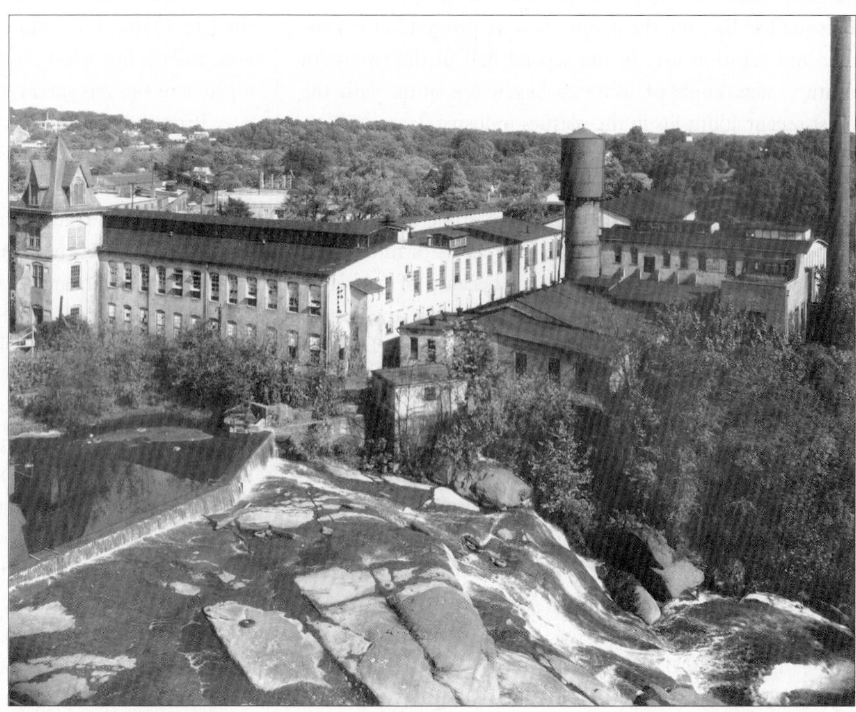

Camperdown Mill on the Reedy River in Greenville, South Carolina, c. 1950. Opened in 1875, Camperdown was the first textile mill in Greenville, starting the city on the road to becoming a national textile center by the 1930s. Camperdown closed in 1956.

people by 1860, thanks to the establishment of Furman University, located on a bluff above the Reedy River, and the arrival of the Greenville and Columbia Railroad. The period's major industry was the Gower, Cox, and Markley Coach Factory, by 1858 the largest farm cart and coach manufacturer south of the Potomac.

Greenville was solidly Unionist until just before the Civil War, when many residents were persuaded to change their views by the Reverend James Clement Furman, university president and a fervent secessionist, who preached orthodox religion and states' rights in local Baptist churches. During the Civil War, refugees flocked into the town, but Greenville was not in the path of William T. Sherman's march through South Carolina and was spared devastation.

In the 1870s, three Bostonians built Camperdown Mill on the Reedy River at Main Street, beginning Greenville's textile industry. At the turn of the twentieth century, several more mills opened, forming a textile crescent along the western edge of the city. Intense competition for mill operatives led to heavy in-migration in 1905, when recruiters scoured the isolated glens of the Appalachians and brought thousands of workers to Greenville mills. The first Southern Textile Exposition opened in Greenville in 1915; by 1930 there were 467 mills within a hundred miles, making Greenville the textile center of the South.

During World War I, the U.S. Army established Camp Sevier on the outskirts of the city; one hundred thousand men trained there. Afterwards, a building boom transformed Greenville's business district. Progressive leaders began a library system, expanded medical facilities, and raised funds to build social service centers for black residents, who accounted for 30 percent of the city's population. Mill owners opened the $125,000 Parker High School in 1924, establishing a national model of applied and vocational education.

The boom ended in 1926. Textile profits fell, and mill owners instituted the "stretch-out," a euphemism for increasing workloads, lowering salaries, and firing older workers. Strikes, labor unrest, unemployment, bank failures, and personal bankruptcies followed.

During the Great Depression, the Works Progress Administration funded Reedy River improvements, a new high school, and a post office. Mills operated on a limited basis. During a major textile strike in 1934–35, most Greenville workers stayed on the job when "flying squadrons" of union organizers tried to close mills. The strike failed, and Greenville became one of the least unionized cities in the nation.

During World War II, an army air base brought thousands of airmen to Greenville. After the war, national companies acquired many local textile mills and sold off their villages. Bob Jones University moved to town, and Furman University relocated to a new coeducational campus north of Greenville.

Industrial development led by Charles Daniel brought prosperity to postwar Greenville. Civil rights tensions in the 1960s led biracial committees to work together to ensure that racial unrest would not hinder growth. In 1970 Greenville schools integrated.

In the 1970s, the textile industry, employing nearly fifty thousand workers, was hurt by foreign imports. Mills cut production and then closed. The textile crescent died. But Greenville began to attract international investment, including U.S. headquarters for Michelin, Bowater, and BMW, and its economy diversified.

Main Street, hurt by the construction of shopping malls, was revitalized in the 1980s and 1990s through public-private partnerships, which also brought about construction of the Peace Center for the Performing Arts, the Bi-Lo Center, the Governor's School for Arts and Humanities, and restoration of the historic West End district. By the end of the twentieth century, Greenville was a vibrant and thriving international community.

Famous Greenvillians include Charles H. Townes, a Nobel laureate in physics; civil rights leader Reverend Jesse Jackson; and former Governor and U.S. Secretary of Education Richard W. Riley.

See also: SPARTANBURG, SOUTH CAROLINA; TEXTILE WORKERS (LABOR); UPLAND SOUTH CAROLINA INSTITUTIONS (CULTURAL INSTITUTIONS).

—Judith T. Bainbridge, *Furman University*

A. V. Huff Jr., *Greenville: A History of the City and County in the South Carolina Piedmont* (1995).

Hamilton, Ohio

Migrants from Appalachia began arriving in Hamilton and other cities in southwestern Ohio's industrial Miami River Valley as early as 1900. Between 1920 and 1930, Hamilton companies such as Champion Paper and Mosler Safe actively recruited the migrants, especially from eastern Kentucky, because of their strong work ethic. In 1924 the *Hamilton Evening Journal* reported that 138 families had arrived from Kentucky seeking jobs in one two-week period. Many companies recruited from specific counties in eastern Kentucky through family networks, and it was common to find most of the workers in one department of a plant to be from the same mountain county.

Raymond Paul Hutchens, in *Kentuckians in Hamilton: A Study of Southborn Migrants in an Industrial City*, found that 22.8 percent of Hamilton's residents in 1930 were born in Kentucky, with the vast majority coming from fourteen counties in eastern Kentucky. Hutchens characterized four "brier-like" neighborhoods—Peck's Addition, Gobbler's Knob, Happy Top, and Armondale—as easily identifiable by any native of Hamilton. His description of dilapidated houses, cars resting on blocks in junk-laden yards, and peculiar behavior of the residents in the four neighborhoods is consistent with the stereotypical images that haunted Appalachian migrants in cities throughout the Midwest.

While Appalachian migration provided a reliable supply of labor for Hamilton companies, it also led to the organization of county clubs and reunions. In 1959 Stanley Dezarn, an elementary school principal in Hamilton, founded an organization called the O'Tucks (derived from "Ohioans from Kentucky") to hold annual homecomings for Kentucky migrants. A year earlier Dezarn had led a successful effort to secure state bonuses for southwestern Ohio's Kentucky-born migrants who were World War I and II veterans. At first the O'Tucks were organized around common laborers, but later Dezarn created a board of directors and recruited prominent business leaders to join the board.

For the first several years, the O'Tucks held an annual Sunday picnic that attracted as many as sixteen hundred people. In the early 1970s, at the request of the sponsors of the annual Fort Hamilton Days, the O'Tucks' picnic became a part of the weekend event. At the end of the 1970s, the O'Tucks started holding an annual dinner at the Hamiltonian Hotel to celebrate their mountain heritage. At the beginning of the twenty-first century, it was estimated that more than one-half of Hamilton's residents were descended from Appalachian migrants. To paraphrase one migrant's comment in a 1983 *Hamilton Evening Journal* feature on the Appalachian origins of residents, Kentuckians took Hamilton without firing a shot.

See also: TWENTIETH-CENTURY OUT-MIGRATION (SETTLEMENT AND MIGRATION); URBAN APPALACHIAN ENCLAVES.

—Thomas E. Wagner, *University of Cincinnati*

Raymond Paul Hutchens, *Kentuckians in Hamilton: A Study of Southborn Migrants in an Industrial City* (1942); Phillip J. Obermiller, Thomas E. Wagner, and E. Bruce Tucker, eds., *Appalachian Odyssey: Historical Perspectives on the Great Migration* (2000); John L. Thompson, *Industrialization in the Miami Valley: A Case Study of Interregional Labor Migration* (1956).

Huntington, West Virginia

West Virginia's second-largest city, Huntington had a population of 51,475 in 2000. Charleston, the state's capital and largest city, is only fifty miles to the east on Interstate 64, and this juxtaposition assures a spirited civic rivalry.

Stretching along the Ohio River at its confluence with the Guyandotte River, Huntington is named for railroad mogul Collis P. Huntington, who founded it in 1871 as the western terminus of his Chesapeake and Ohio Railway. A Connecticut native who started his business life as a Yankee peddler, Huntington made a fortune during the California gold rush by selling supplies to the miners. Later, he joined forces with three other California businessmen—Charles Crocker, Mark Hopkins, and Leland Stanford—to build the Central Pacific, the western link in the long-dreamed-of transcontinental railroad. When Huntington bought a controlling interest in the Chesapeake and Ohio in 1869, many scoffed at his purchase of a railroad that was little more than a few miles of Virginia track and a rag-tag collection of rolling stock. But Huntington knew that a priceless strategic connection could be made with Ohio River ports if Chesapeake and Ohio tracks could be laid across the mountainous new state of West Virginia.

Traveling across the state to the banks of the Ohio, Huntington rejected the overtures of several small communities eager to welcome the railroad. Instead, he picked out a stretch of farmland on the Ohio just downstream from the mouth of the Guyandotte and there commenced building a new town that, with the purchase of twenty-one farms, totaled five thousand acres. Much of the property was reserved for the railroad—for right-of-way, repair shops, a depot, and other necessary buildings. The remaining land was sold off in lots. At Huntington's direction, Boston civil engineer Rufus Cook designed a town plan with a perfect geometric gridwork of broad avenues and intersecting streets, all consecutively numbered so that any address might be easy to find.

The city of Huntington grew and prospered as a gateway to and from the coalfields of southern West Virginia. Coal was transported from mines to market via the new town, and manufactured goods flowed in the other direction, the two-way traffic spawning thousands of jobs. The city's crucial location attracted manufacturers, who produced products ranging from railroad cars, steel, and brick to glassware, furniture, and church pews.

Over the years, Huntington came to be called the "City of Churches." Home to more than 130 congregations representing virtually every major faith, it boasts seven congregations within one six-block stretch of Fifth Avenue in the city's downtown. The First Congregational Church, organized in June 1872, is believed to be the city's oldest.

Huntington is the seat of Cabell County, but a small western portion of the city lies in neighboring Wayne County. The handsome Cabell County Courthouse, erected in 1901, is listed on the National Register of Historic Places. The city is the center of a tri-state area that includes the communities of Barboursville and Milton in Cabell County and Kenova, Ceredo, and Wayne in Wayne County. Many who work in Huntington live in these smaller communities or in their counterparts in neighboring Ohio and Kentucky. The metropolitan statistical area, which includes Ashland, Kentucky, and Ironton, Ohio, in addition to Huntington, had a population in 2000 of more than 315,000. Education, health care, transportation, and manufacturing were the area's major employers.

Marshall University is older than the city, having started as a one-room school in 1837. A state-supported school, Marshall grew steadily, especially after it became a university in 1961. At the beginning of the twenty-first century, it enrolled more than fifteen thousand undergraduate and graduate students. Marshall's Thundering Herd football team often attracts national attention and regularly draws capacity crowds to its thirty-eight-thousand-seat stadium. The Marshall Artists Series brings touring Broadway shows and other world-class entertainment to the stage of the city's Keith-Albee Theater, a grand 1920s-era movie palace. The university also hosts the Center for the Study of Ethnicity and Gender in Appalachia, as well as headquartering the Appalachian Studies Association.

Marshall's School of Medicine, founded in 1924, provided a catalyst for the city's development as a health-care center. Saint Mary's Hospital, with 440 beds, is the city's largest private employer. Cabell Huntington Hospital houses the region's only neonatal intensive care unit and the only burn unit in West Virginia. A U.S. Department of Veterans Affairs medical center is located in Spring Valley, just outside Huntington.

Like many Appalachian cities, Huntington has seen the center of retailing shift from the downtown to the suburbs. Despite its name, the Huntington Mall is located in Barboursville. With 130 stores and a million square feet of space, it is West Virginia's largest shopping mall. Huntington's Central City neighborhood is home to many antique shops that attract buyers from across the nation. Also popular with out-of-town visitors are Blenko Glass in Milton and the nearby Heritage Farm Museum and Village.

True to Collis P. Huntington's vision of tying together river and rail, the city remains a center of transportation. It is the busiest inland port in the nation. The old Chesapeake and Ohio Railway is now part of CSX Transportation, a major employer in the city. Tri-State Airport at Ceredo offers flights to regional airline hubs.

In recent years, Huntington's manufacturing base has eroded, as many of its old-line factories have closed, victims of the same Rust Belt problems found in many communities of the northern subregion. The newest and fastest-growing segments of the economy are in telemarketing and information technology.

Huntington points of interest include Ritter Park, built in 1913 on land originally intended for use as a city incinerator; Heritage Village, a shopping complex fashioned from the old Baltimore and Ohio Railroad Depot; and the Huntington Museum of Art, the largest museum in West Virginia.

See also: CHESAPEAKE AND OHIO RAILWAY (TRANSPORTATION); GLASS INDUSTRY (BUSINESS, INDUSTRY, AND TECHNOLOGY).

—James E. Casto, *Huntington, West Virginia*

James E. Casto, *Huntington: An Illustrated History* (1985); Doris C. Miller, *A Centennial History of Huntington, West Virginia, 1871–1971* (1971); George Selden Wallace, *Cabell County Annals and Families* (1935).

Huntsville, Alabama

Located in the foothills of the Cumberland Plateau in north Alabama, Huntsville was transformed from an ordinary farm town into a thriving center of technology in the last half of the twentieth century, its growth providing sharp contrast to the course of most urban communities in Appalachia. As Birmingham, Chattanooga, Knoxville, and Pittsburgh, along with Appalachian fringe cities such as Cleveland and Cincinnati, saw smokestack industries and coal economies decline, Huntsville's population soared from a mere 16,000 inhabitants in 1950 to more than 72,000 in 1960 to 178,000 at the turn of the century, when the metropolitan-area population reached 250,000. The expansion was driven by the U.S. Army's Redstone Arsenal and the National Aeronautics and Space Administration's Marshall Space Flight Center, both located on a 33,000-acre reservation acquired by the federal government in 1941.

Because many of Huntsville's new residents were scientists, engineers, and other white-collar professionals who came from all corners of the United States and around the world, the community took on a cosmopolitan flavor unusual for a town of its size. Jokingly called "Huntspatch" by some of its early aerospace immigrants, it became home to a professional symphony orchestra, a 112-acre botanical garden, a system of urban greenways, an art museum, and professional sports teams. At the same time, however, it retained a cultural personality reflecting both its location in a Deep South state and its place on the edge of the Appalachians. In its "old town" section, families continued to occupy some of Alabama's oldest residences.

While Birmingham, just one hundred miles to the south, became a battleground in the Civil Rights movement of the 1960s, Huntsville ended racial segregation with relative calm and promoted itself as "Rocket City" and the "Space Capital of the Universe."

For years after the beginning of the aerospace boom, the city's heavy dependence upon military weapons development and the civilian space program made its economy vulnerable to changes in government policy. It suffered the loss of seventeen thousand jobs when the Apollo lunar exploration program wound to an end in December 1972. Thereafter, planners made economic diversity their credo, and the community avoided the boom-and-bust cycles that continued to visit much of the Appalachian region. To proponents of federal activism in economic development, the Alabama city remains not only a regional but a national example. By the mid-1980s, only California's Silicon Valley had a higher concentration of high-tech employees.

For nearly a century and a half after its incorporation, though, Huntsville was a typical, if somewhat more prosperous, southern county seat. Its settlement began early in the nineteenth century. Called Twickenham by the developer who acquired large land holdings and promoted the town, it shortly took the name Huntsville for John Hunt, who had built the community's first cabin next to a huge spring about 1805. The spring and rich land on the floodplain of the nearby Tennessee River soon attracted a stream of settlers, who bought tracts in the new town and established farms across the area previously inhabited by the Chickasaws. Huntsville was incorporated in 1811 and became the first state capital when Alabama was admitted to the union in 1819. By then it was a community of more than 250 homes, some of them splendid three-story structures.

Since the hill country of northern Alabama did not offer the Deep South's best cotton land, most farms were small. Wealthy planters held the rich bottoms toward the river, prospered with the use of slave labor, and dominated the region's social and economic system. Huntsville was not without pro-Union sentiment, however, as evidenced by a vigorous Republican newspaper. During the Civil War, when the city's location on the Memphis and Charleston Railroad made it strategically important, the presence of loyalists helped save it from destruction by occupying Union forces.

Like other towns of the Confederacy, Huntsville languished for years after the conflict ended, but it gradually recovered and began to thrive as textile mills and timber operations opened and nurseries were established. For half a century, it was Alabama's leading mill town, with as many as nine mills operating at one time.

The foundation for the rise of modern Huntsville was created during the Great Depression, just as its aging cotton mills floundered and the oft-flooded Tennessee River Valley became known as the epicenter of rural poverty in America. Construction of giant hydroelectric dams by the new Tennessee Valley Authority (TVA), two of them near Huntsville, created an employment boom across north Alabama. Besides transforming the region with its cheap electricity, TVA created a navigable waterway linking the southern Appalachians and river towns such as Huntsville to the port of New Orleans on the Gulf of Mexico. Inexpensive power and the navigable river became magnets for industrial development, beginning with the Redstone and Huntsville Arsenals, established on federal property purchased in 1941. During the war, as many as eleven thousand workers were employed in production of munitions at the two installations, but during peacetime both were mothballed.

Led by U.S. Senator John Sparkman, a Huntsville resident, Alabama officials persuaded the army to reopen Redstone in 1950. It became the home base of German scientists and engineers who had surrendered to American forces after Hitler's defeat in 1945 and later migrated to the United States. Using the Germans' experience in developing rockets, the reopened arsenal at Huntsville led U.S. research in ballistic missile technology and provided early impetus for the exploration of space. The community, which had begun styling itself as the nation's "watercress capital," embraced a wholly new image and future on January 31, 1958. Receiving news that a Redstone Arsenal team led by German-born rocket designer Wernher von Braun had launched the United States' first artificial satellite, Huntsvillians danced in the streets around the courthouse.

During the years of its most rapid growth, cotton fields around the Redstone complex were rapidly replaced by housing developments inhabited by army and National Aeronautics and Space Administration personnel. But the dramatic slowdown at the civilian space agency gave urgent priority to economic diversification. Cooperating with leaders of the technical community, political officials pressed development of an infrastructure for longterm growth. Land was set aside for a research park, and the local branch of the University of Alabama became a research-oriented autonomous institution, with a campus located within the park. Appropriately, the park was named for Milton Cummings, who quit his successful cotton business and helped found one of Huntsville's first homegrown aerospace corporations in 1953.

By the turn of the century, interests of research facilities in the park ranged far beyond aerospace to include biomedical engineering, information technology, and health-care delivery. In a quest for manufacturing jobs, officials also established industrial parks, and late in the twentieth century occupants included manufacturers of tires and automotive parts as well as electronics and telecommunications equipment. While the town still promoted its "Rocket City" image, its medical center had become the community's third-largest employer and its Alabama Space and Rocket Center the state's most visited tourist attraction.

See also: AEROSPACE INDUSTRY (BUSINESS, INDUSTRY, AND TECHNOLOGY); AVIATION (TRANSPORTATION); MARSHALL SPACE FLIGHT CENTER (BUSINESS, INDUSTRY, AND TECHNOLOGY).

—Rudy Abramson, *Reston, Virginia*

Erik Bergaust, *Rocket City, U.S.A.: From Huntsville, Alabama, to the Moon* (1963); William Warren Rogers et al., *Alabama: The History of a Deep South State* (1994).

Johnson City, Tennessee

See Tri-Cities, Tennessee/Virginia

Kingsport, Tennessee

See Tri-Cities, Tennessee/Virginia

Knoxville, Tennessee

Located in the Great Valley of East Tennessee where the French Broad and Holston combine to form the Tennessee River, Knoxville was founded as White's Fort in 1786 and became the capital of the Southwest Territory as well as the early capital of Tennessee. By the turn of the twenty-first century, it was a major commercial, industrial, and educational center and one of the largest cities in southern Appalachia, with a population of about 170,000.

In 1786 James White, the city's principal founder and a captain in the North Carolina militia during the American Revolution, built a fort on a one-thousand-acre tract of land overlooking the Tennessee River and in 1791 auctioned off sixty-four half-acre lots for home sites. Two lots were set aside for a church and cemetery, and four lots were reserved for Blount College, the town's first school and the parent of the present University of Tennessee. In the same year, William Blount, the governor of the Southwest Territory, chose the fledgling settlement as the territory's capital and renamed it Knoxville in honor of George Washington's secretary of war, Henry Knox. The next year the town's name became official, and Blount built his residence there, a structure that served as the territory's capitol and which still survives as Blount Mansion. In 1793 the United States Army built a fort on the site of the present City-County Building, which in that same year came under attack by a confederation of Creeks and Cherokees.

From its founding until the Civil War, Knoxville grew slowly. With only 2,076 residents as late as 1850, the town with a reputation for having more saloons than churches and more prostitutes than preachers served primarily as a way station for travelers heading west. The Tennessee River, navigable during only parts of the year, never served as an important commercial artery.

By the late 1850s, the East Tennessee and Georgia Railroad finally connected Knoxville to Atlanta, Charleston, Savannah, and Richmond. Commercial ties with southern states help explain Knoxville's secessionist vote in the June 1861 statewide referendum on withdrawal from the Union, thus putting the city at odds with the Unionist majority of east Tennessee. The railroad's importance in supplying General Robert E. Lee's Army of Northern Virginia prompted Confederates to station troops in Knoxville to keep the rail lines open. East Tennessee Unionists burned bridges and harassed Confederate troops, activities that brought forth severe retaliation and repression by Confederate General Felix Zollicoffer.

By 1863, however, the South's hold on Knoxville could no longer be maintained, and Union troops under General Ambrose Burnside rushed in to occupy the city and cut the lifeline of the railroad. Two divisions of Confederates under General James Longstreet tried desperately to retake the city but were repulsed on November 29, 1863, at Fort Sanders. Longstreet's forces suffered more than eight hundred casualties in a battle that lasted less than thirty minutes.

After the Civil War, the railroad that had made Knoxville an important prize in that conflict transformed the town into a major commercial and industrial center. A bold cadre of businessmen, most of them from outside the South, flowed into Knoxville to take advantage of the area's natural resources, its potentially sizable and pliant labor pool, and its good rail connections. These carpetbaggers, as they were called, rebuilt much of the city, founding enterprises such as the Knoxville Iron Company; Sanford, Chamberlain, and Albers Drug Company; Knoxville Woolen Mills; Woodruff's Furniture Company; Dixie Cement Company; and the Knoxville, Sevierville, and Eastern Railway. Between 1880 and 1887, ninety-seven new factories were founded that produced textiles, clothing, shoes, processed food products, and iron goods.

Because of the railroad there were more than fifty wholesaling houses in Knoxville after the Civil War. By 1896 the city had become the South's third-largest wholesaling center in volume, eclipsed only by New Orleans and Atlanta. Goods were brought in by rail and distributed to the small towns and general stores of east Tennessee. Knoxville became a key commercial center for southern Appalachia, and the city's Market House hummed with activity as east Tennessee farmers brought their products to sell and left with wagons laden with manufactured goods.

By 1900, Knoxville's population had risen to 32,637, about one-third of which was under the age of fifteen. House construction boomed—between 1895 and 1904 more than five hundred new homes were built annually. An 1897 fire that destroyed a number of businesses on the city's main thoroughfare, Gay Street, was boastfully dubbed "The Million Dollar Fire" because city residents were proud that they had a million dollars worth of buildings to burn down. The separate town of West Knoxville, which possessed some of Tennessee's most magnificent and stately homes, was annexed to the city in 1897. Now known as the Fort Sanders neighborhood, it was the setting for Knoxvillian James Agee's Pulitzer Prize–winning novel, *A Death in the Family*.

Rapid growth brought major problems. Widespread burning of coal gave the city a grimy appearance and an unhealthy reputation. A reliable supply of safe drinking water was not available until the 1890s. What had been a comparatively progressive and peaceful racial environment turned ugly. African Americans and rural whites, both of whom streamed into the city looking for work after the Civil War, clashed with each other almost continuously. In 1919 Knoxville witnessed a serious race riot; a local Ku Klux Klan chapter was a major force in Knoxville politics until late 1923;

and in the Great Depression of the 1930s, many African Americans were turned out of their jobs to make room for unemployed whites.

In the midst of the depression, the federal government played a large role in the city's economic life. The Tennessee Valley Authority, created in 1933, established its headquarters in Knoxville and brought much-needed money and jobs to the region. As part of Roosevelt's New Deal, the federal Works Progress Administration undertook significant projects in the city, the McGhee-Tyson Airport and the University of Tennessee's Neyland Stadium being two of the most visible examples. By the 1950s, about 25 percent of all people employed in Knoxville worked for the government at some level.

Not long after World War II, author John Gunther described Knoxville as the "ugliest city" in America. Yet postwar problems existed that were deeper than the city's physical appearance. For one thing, the industries upon which Knoxville depended (textiles, clothing, shoes, processed food products, iron goods) fell victim to foreign competition at a time when the city's shortsighted business elite, fearing competition for labor, fought to keep other businesses from moving into the city. After 1956, the railroad that had been the city's commercial lifeline went into decline, a victim of interstate highways that were, ironically, slow in coming to east Tennessee. Knoxville's interstate highway linkages were not completed until 1984.

By the time of Knoxville's bicentennial celebration in 1992, the local economy had diversified and no longer was dependent on low-wage industries. Once again newcomers were welcomed, as much for their dynamism and ideas as for their money, and by the early 1990s large proportions of the city's business and professional communities were not native to the city. The University of Tennessee had grown from 2,477 students in 1945 to 30,000 by 1975, becoming a major force in the area's economy. Knoxville tourism relied heavily on the city's proximity to the Great Smoky Mountains National Park, and it served as the "Gateway to the Smokies" for many of the 10 million annual park visitors. In 1982 Knoxville hosted a World's Fair.

Nevertheless, the central business district struggled against increasing competition from suburban malls, and relations between Knoxville and surrounding Knox County became combative as the city tried to recapture tax dollars through annexations. Several attempts to create a single countywide government failed, and local politics often became personal and vicious. More recently, Knoxville has sought to avoid the problems of its past.

See also: KNOXVILLE, TENNESSEE (TOURISM); TENNESSEE VALLEY AUTHORITY (GOVERNMENT).

—William Bruce Wheeler, *University of Tennessee*

Lucile Deaderick, ed., *Heart of the Valley: A History of Knoxville, Tennessee* (1976); William J. MacArthur Jr., *Knoxville, Crossroads of the New South* (1982); Michael J. McDonald and William Bruce Wheeler, *Knoxville, Tennessee: Continuity and Change in an Appalachian City* (1983).

Pittsburgh, Pennsylvania

With 334,563 residents in 2000, Pittsburgh is by far the largest city in Appalachia and has held this distinction ever since being incorporated in the late eighteenth century. Yet Pittsburgh experienced a more severe loss of population than any other major Appalachian city in the twentieth century, particularly in the period from 1950 to 2000, when its population was reduced by half. In this way, the story of Pittsburgh has been one of both enormous expansion and precipitous decline.

Originally occupied by Native Americans, including the Delaware and the Shawnee, the area that is now Pittsburgh sits where the Allegheny and Monongahela Rivers join to form the Ohio. In the mid-eighteenth century, the area was hotly contested among the British, French, and local Indian tribes. General John Forbes finally seized the fur-trading post known as Fort Duquesne on behalf of the British in 1758. From that time forward, the post was known as Fort Pitt and the area Pittsburgh, in honor of contemporary British Prime Minister William Pitt. After this tumultuous beginning, Pittsburgh was incorporated as a borough of Pennsylvania in 1794 and as an official city in 1816.

As was the case in most of Appalachia, Pittsburgh's first settlers were primarily frontier-bound Scots and Englishmen from the East. The city soon rose to prominence by exploiting the rich and widespread coal, iron ore, and petroleum deposits in the region. Located at a prime transportation center, by 1860 it was one of the great industrial cities in America, producing a third of the nation's glass and half of its steel.

The area's coal mines, steel mills, and glass factories needed workers, and the city drew much more than its share of the mid- to late nineteenth century's "new immigrants," mainly Poles, Hungarians, Italians, and eastern European Jews. During World War I, as international immigration slowed, African Americans came north in large numbers—more than fifty thousand blacks made up about 8 percent of the city's population by 1930. Between 1860 and 1920 the city's population grew more than twelvefold, giving it an enduring personality as an international city characterized by tight, ethnically oriented neighborhoods. Even in modern-day Pittsburgh one can enjoy a walk through Squirrel Hill (Jewish), Shadyside (old elite), Bloomfield (Italian), Polish Hill (Polish), and the Hill District (African American) on the way to downtown.

Inevitably, relations among working-class groups and especially dealings between workers and employers were

Downtown Pittsburgh, 1999. Built in 1877, the Duquesne Incline is one of two cable-powered inclines still in operation in Pittsburgh, providing public transportation up and down the steep ridges and hills in this largest of Appalachian cities.

often far from harmonious. Pittsburgh was the site of several major railroad and steel strikes in the late nineteenth century. One of the most violent labor conflicts in American history took place at the Homestead Works of Carnegie Steel on July 6, 1892. The "Battle for Homestead," as it came to be known, was a brutal affair, with locked-out workers fighting against Pinkerton detectives and eight thousand members of the state militia. The failed strike ultimately crushed the local Amalgamated Association of Iron and Steel Workers and initiated a forty-year nonunion era in the heart of Appalachian Pennsylvania. Ironically, the Homestead mills were only a few miles from the Pittsburgh site where the American Federation of Labor had been formed eleven years earlier, in 1881.

World Wars I and II provided continued business for Pittsburgh's industrial base, but beginning as early as the 1950s and continuing through the 1980s, competition from abroad proved too much for the city's steel industry. The most devastating loss of jobs and population took place in the 1970s and 1980s, when the city lost more than 100,000 steel-related jobs and saw an out-migration of more than 150,000 people. Falling from a peak of 676,000 in 1950, Pittsburgh's population declined through 1998 to 341,000, only a few thousand more than had lived in the city a hundred years earlier.

Around the turn of the twenty-first century, these staggering losses showed signs of abating, as Pittsburghers rallied on several fronts. Significant numbers of new jobs were created in the health-care, technology, education, and service industries. The growth of these fields was facilitated in part by radical changes in the city's infrastructure. In the 1950s, Mayor David Lawrence's Renaissance project engineered a significant public-private partnership to rebuild much of downtown Pittsburgh, transforming the street layout, the skyline, and most notably the Point, where the three rivers meet. Formerly a warehouse district and railroad interchange, the Point became a beautiful riverside park. In the 1980s, Mayor Richard Caliguiri commenced Renaissance II, making way for a large-scale convention center and a lively downtown cultural district.

Modern Pittsburgh has emerged as the capital of northern Appalachia, thanks in considerable measure to the wealth accumulated during the city's industrial heyday. Local philanthropists were notably generous in their contributions to Pittsburgh's cultural scene. Major research universities, including the University of Pittsburgh (established in 1787) and Carnegie Mellon University (established in 1900), are near the grand Carnegie Museum and Library, founded by Andrew Carnegie in 1895. The new downtown cultural district boasts a world-class symphony, live theater, and the Andy Warhol Museum. Since the early 1900s, Pittsburgh's Hill District has also been a major locus of African American culture. Home of the nationally known *Pittsburgh Courier* (later the *New Pittsburgh Courier*), the Hill also gave birth to the fabled Negro League's two greatest teams—the Pittsburgh Crawfords and the Homestead Grays. Modern-day Pittsburghers support their beloved professional sports teams—the Pirates (baseball), Steelers (football), and Penguins (hockey)—year-round.

Over the years, Pittsburgh has taken on various nicknames reflecting its economic identity. Known as the strategic "Forks of the Ohio" in early colonial days, the city was referred to by frontier-bound Americans of the early 1800s as the "Gateway to the West." In the late nineteenth century, an *Atlantic Monthly* journalist termed the booming city "Hell with the Lid Off," referring to the pollution and overcrowding of the time. Fortunately for locals, the more neutral "Iron City" and ultimately "Steel City" were the monikers that stuck in the early twentieth century. By the 1970s, Pittsburghers rebelled against the image of a battered and declining Rust Belt metropolis by cheering on their "City of Champions" and rallying around successful baseball, football, and hockey teams. At the turn of the century, Pittsburgh was on its way to a new identity, entering the twenty-first century as an increasingly friendly place to live and work.

See also: IRON AND STEEL INDUSTRY (BUSINESS, INDUSTRY, AND TECHNOLOGY); SECTION OVERVIEW (BUSINESS, INDUSTRY, AND TECHNOLOGY); SECTION OVERVIEW (CULTURAL INSTITUTIONS).

—J. Trent Alexander, *Carnegie Mellon University*

John Bodnar, Roger Simon, and Michael P. Weber, *Lives of Their Own: Blacks, Italians, and Poles in Pittsburgh, 1900–1960* (1982); Samuel P. Hays, ed., *City at the Point: Essays on the Social History of Pittsburgh* (1989); Roy Lubove, *Twentieth-Century Pittsburgh: Government, Business, and Environmental Change* (1969).

Portsmouth, Ohio

Founded by Major Henry Massie in 1803, Portsmouth, Ohio, lies on the northern bank of the Ohio River, opposite Kentucky. First settled by Scots-Irish and German families, the city was incorporated in 1815, and five years later had a population of 527. Rapid growth began when the Ohio-Erie Canal, stretching 306 miles from Portsmouth to Cleveland, opened in 1832. By 1870, the population of Portsmouth had grown to 10,592, making Portsmouth, in distribution, the largest port between Pittsburgh and Cincinnati. The first railroad reached the city in 1853, signaling the end of the canal era, as canal boats could not compete with the railroad as cost-effective transportation.

During the Civil War, Portsmouth sent more than four thousand men to fight for the Union. Due to its strategic location along the Ohio River between free and slave states, Portsmouth became a center for the distribution of war supplies. Possessing close economic and cultural ties with eastern Kentucky, the city also served as a receiving center for migrants from that part of Appalachia.

Abundant supplies of stone and clay in the area led to the early establishment of stone quarries and brick foundries. Shoe manufacturing also became prominent in the late 1800s. The Vulcan Company produced heels, the Patterson Paper Box Company made boxes for shoes, and Mitchellace produced shoelaces. Foreign competition eventually began to dominate the shoe market, and no shoes are manufactured in Portsmouth today.

Portsmouth was home to one of the first teams in the National Football League, the Portsmouth Spartans. From 1930 to 1932, the team compiled a 23-10-4 record. The

Floodwall mural, Portsmouth, Ohio, 2002. Events from Portsmouth's history are illustrated along a two-thousand-foot section of the floodwall that protects the city from the Ohio River.

franchise was less successful financially, and in 1934 it was sold to owners in Detroit, who renamed the team the Lions.

In 2000 Portsmouth's population stood at 20,909. The city continues to be an industrial center for iron casting, chemical plants, and service industries. Shawnee State University, the newest public university in Ohio, is also a major employer in the community.

In 1993 artist Robert Dafford was hired to paint murals on two thousand feet of the floodwall that protects Portsmouth from the waters of the Ohio River. The purpose of the murals is to create an outdoor art gallery that depicts the history of Portsmouth and the surrounding area.

Some famous former residents of Portsmouth and the surrounding area include Cincinnati-born Roy Rogers, the cowboy matinee star, and Branch Rickey, who signed Jackie Robinson to the 1947 Brooklyn Dodger contract that broke the color barrier in major league baseball. Another notable resident was Vernal G. Riffe Jr., who was a member of the Ohio House of Representatives for thirty-six years, consecutively serving as Speaker for twenty of them.

See also: OHIO RIVER (TRANSPORTATION); SOUTHERN OHIO MUSEUM (CULTURAL INSTITUTIONS).

—Richard W. Greenlee, *Ohio University*

Henry Bannon, *Scioto Sketches: An Account of Discovery and Settlement of Scioto County, Ohio* (1920); Portsmouth Area Recognition Society, *History of Scioto County* (1986); Elmer Sword, *The Story of Portsmouth* (1965).

Richmond, Kentucky

The seat of Madison County, Richmond is located approximately twenty-five miles southeast of Lexington in the foothills of the Appalachian Mountains on the eastern edge of the Kentucky Bluegrass region. Although pioneers settled the area in the mid-1770s, Colonel John Miller, a Revolutionary War veteran, donated two acres of his farm to the county court in 1798 when the magistrates decided to move from the uninhabitable Milford precinct to a location between Boonesborough and Paint Lick, the largest population centers. The new town was named after the Virginia capital. Trustees erected a courthouse soon after, and the present Greek Revival structure was built in 1849.

By 1810, a population of more than three hundred made Richmond one of the fifteen largest cities of the state. A hotel and bank opened in the next decade, and Baptists, Methodists, and Presbyterians built the city's first churches in 1828. Thirteen newspapers failed during the nineteenth century, and the few schools that operated were private. Madison Female Institute, begun in 1858, provided a classical education for young ladies until shortly after World War I.

Many Madison Countians enlisted in the Confederate army, and a decisive Union defeat in the battle of Richmond, August 30, 1862, constituted the greatest Confederate victory in the Western Theater. Richmond expanded after the Civil War as freedmen and railroad workers moved into the county seat. During Reconstruction, James B. McCreary, a Confederate veteran, returned home and helped establish the Democratic machine that dominated local politics for a century. Elected governor twice, 1875 and 1911, he was Richmond's most successful political leader. In 1939 Keen Johnson, editor of the *Richmond Daily Register*, became the second Richmondite to be elected chief executive of the state. Despite smallpox epidemics and major fires, Richmond quadrupled in size after the Civil War and became a crucial railroad terminus for the Central Kentucky (later Louisville and Nashville) Railroad. Prospering from its tobacco warehouses, stockyards, flour mills, mercantile shops, hotels, and taverns, the city added streetlamps, a gasworks, and a telephone system by 1878 and by the turn of the century had a water plant, electric power, and a public school system.

Presbyterians opened Central University in 1874, but its transformation into Eastern Kentucky State Normal

Madison County Courthouse, Richmond, Kentucky, 1997. The Greek Revival–style courthouse building in Richmond, completed in 1850, displays a boulder featuring the 1770 signature of Squire Boone, younger brother of pioneer Daniel Boone.

School in 1906 was more significant. The school had three thousand students by 1960, when state education superintendent Robert R. Martin assumed the presidency and converted it into a regional university that grew to an enrollment of thirteen thousand students. With the expansion of the university, education surpassed agriculture and industry as the economic linchpin of the community. Renamed Eastern Kentucky University in 1966, the school attracts more than 60 percent of its students from the state's Appalachian counties. The university offers a minor in Appalachian studies through its Center for Appalachian Studies, which opened in 2000.

Although an industrial push commenced with the completion of Interstate 75 in the 1960s, the city's greatest boom occurred in the 1990s during the administration of Ann Durham, its first woman mayor, who established a recreational park at Lake Reba and reinforced the chamber of commerce's drive to attract new industries and further diversify the traditional agrarian economy. A population of more than twenty-seven thousand in 2000 secured Richmond's reputation as the fastest-growing city in the state. Richmond continues to be an important goods and services distribution center for Appalachian Kentucky and the eastern rim of the Bluegrass region.

—H. E. Everman, *Eastern Kentucky University*

William Ellis, H. E. Everman, and Richard Sears, *Madison County: Two Hundred Years in Retrospect* (1985).

Roanoke, Virginia

Roanoke, Virginia, with a city population of nearly 95,000 at the turn of the twenty-first century, lies at the center of a metropolitan area of some 236,000 in Roanoke County in the Great Valley of Appalachia. Its site offers extraordinary views of the nearby Allegheny Mountains to the west and the Blue Ridge to the east, where the Roanoke River cuts through Roanoke Gap at an elevation of 785 feet. Roanoke has been an important regional crossroads since before European settlement: the Great Warriors Path, running north-south through the Great Valley, crossed the east-west Petersburg-Saponi Trail at Roanoke Gap. These trails evolved today into railroad corridors and then into Interstate 81 and U.S. Route 460, respectively. The Totera Indians, a Siouan group, are believed to have inhabited a village named Totero on the riverbanks near the present-day site of the Thirteenth Street Bridge. Archaeological evidence, including fish weirs in the Roanoke River, dates Indian activity in the region to as early as 8000 to 9000 B.C. The name of the river is derived from the Indian word *rawanoke*, meaning "white shells," which were used by the Indians as currency.

An expedition led by Abraham Wood arrived in the area in 1671, and the first European settlers came shortly thereafter. Large numbers of settlers of German, Irish, and Scots-Irish ancestry migrated south through the Great Valley from central Pennsylvania and the Shenandoah Valley of Virginia. These early pioneers named the site Big Lick for salt marshes in the area. Later, they were joined by English settlers who migrated up the river from the Tidewater region of Virginia.

The first railroad, an east-west line running east from Richmond, Virginia, through the Roanoke Gap, reached the area in 1852. A north-south valley railroad line made Big Lick a railroad junction in 1882, and the city was chartered in 1884 and renamed Roanoke for the river. The community's early growth was due to its role as a railroad junction and agricultural center for the Roanoke Valley. The rich limestone valley region still produces hay and corn for silage for its dairy and cattle industry. Cattle graze and peaches grow on the surrounding hillsides. The area is also a major poultry- and egg-producing section of Virginia.

The forty-three-square-mile city serves as the hub of a metropolitan area that also includes neighboring Salem City (population 24,747), Roanoke County (85,778), and Botetourt County (30,496). Although the economy, physiography, and culture of Roanoke make it a decidedly Appalachian city, it does not lie physically within Appalachia as the region is defined by the amended Appalachian Development Act in 1965. But its influence reaches into federally defined Appalachia in various ways. For example, the *Roanoke Times and World News* is the dominant newspaper for most of the Appalachian area of southwest Virginia (although Roanoke is not considered part of the colloquially defined region of southwest Virginia, either). The city has been an urban magnet for generations of Appalachian migrants from nearby Virginia counties. Roanoke television and radio stations and the Valley View Mall, the largest in southwestern Virginia, extend the city's regional influence. Roanoke draws consumers from a two-hour-driving radius, giving it relatively high retail sales per capita. Rand McNally marketing statistics define Roanoke's trading area as a region of 615,000 people. Plans call for eventual construction of a new interstate highway (I-73) that will connect Roanoke with Charleston, South Carolina, and Detroit. Symbolic of the city's regional role, Roanoke's Mill Mountain Star, a five-pointed star of neon lights, is visible for a radius of sixty miles.

In Roanoke County, 24 percent of the population reports German as their first ancestry, followed by English (20 percent), Irish (16 percent), and Scottish or Scots-Irish (8 percent). There is also a substantial black population of 25,341 (27 percent) in Roanoke City and 30,496 in the metropolitan area (about 13 percent). Less than 4 percent of the population of the city and metropolitan region are of Hispanic, Asian, or other ancestry. Although the metropolitan area has seen continuous growth in recent decades through natural increase and in-migration, overall population growth is not strong because the region also has a high death rate, reflecting its substantial elderly population. The older population is particularly concentrated in the central cities of Roanoke and Salem, which have lost population over recent decades. Between 1990 and 2000, Roanoke City's population declined by 1.6 percent. Its percentage of population of persons over age sixty-five (16.4 percent) remains substantially higher than that of Virginia as a whole (11.2 percent).

The economic base of the area is diversified. Third-quarter business statistics for 2001 in the Roanoke metropolitan area showed about 30 percent of the population employed in services, 24 percent in retail, 9 percent in manufacturing, 10 percent in government, 6 percent in wholesale, 6 percent in construction, 7 percent in finance, insurance, and real estate, and 7 percent in transportation, communications, and public utilities. Major employers in the service sector include two large local hospitals and a Veterans Affairs hospital. Roanoke has a substantial legal community, which provides services for Virginia's coalfield area. Colleges in the area include National College of Business and Technology and Virginia Western Community College in Roanoke; Hollins College in Roanoke County; and Roanoke College in Salem City. Roanoke's excellent rail and highway accessibility has led to its important regional and national role as a distribution hub for two national package delivery firms and several large mail-order companies. Roanoke also has a large number of finance, insurance, and real estate businesses. The city lost its last Fortune 500 firm, the Norfolk and Western Railway, when that Virginia corporation became part of the Norfolk-based Norfolk Southern Corporation.

Roanoke has a substantial and broad-based manufacturing sector. Besides furniture making, food processing, metal fabrication, and chemical production, local enterprises are engaged in the manufacture of specialized products such as contact lenses, night vision goggles for the military, and telecommunications equipment. Roanoke is a center for the manufacture of industrial equipment such as wheeled scaffolding, assembly-line conveyors, coal-mining equipment, and other digging and lifting machinery. As is true of much of the rest of the Virginia Valley, there are a number of automobile-related manufactures, including firms that make tires and components for driveshafts, power-steering systems, and automatic transmissions. Regional businesses also make parts for air conditioners, electrical components, locks, and cosmetics, as well as high-tech materials such as fiber-optic products, cable wire, and some software. Local industry will be given a boost by the five-mile "smart" highway under construction in 2005 that will link Interstate 81 directly to Blacksburg, thus cutting fifteen minutes off of the drive time separating the city and access to the Virginia Polytechnic Institute and State University and its corporate research park. Another asset to industry is Roanoke Regional Airport, which connects Atlanta, Pittsburgh, and Chicago to Roanoke with more than forty flights per day on small jets and turboprop planes.

Roanoke offers a wide variety of recreational and tourist activities in the city and in the surrounding area. The Center-in-the-Square downtown complex houses a theater, a planetarium, and science, history, and art museums. Other attractions are Mill Mountain Zoo, the Virginia Museum of Transportation, the Harrison Museum of African-American Culture, and the nearby Salem Museum. The Hotel Roanoke, a late-1800s Tudor-style railroad hotel in the heart of the city, has been refurbished as a conference center. Outdoor recreational opportunities include those in nearby Washington and Jefferson National Forests, the Blue Ridge Parkway, the Appalachian Trail, and the Bikecentennial Trail. There are numerous hiking, fishing, canoeing, kayaking, biking, and mountain biking opportunities. The 22,000-acre Smith Mountain Lake lies just twelve miles to the east. Within an hour's drive of the city are the Booker T. Washington National Monument, Dixie Caverns, Natural Bridge, Peaks of Otter, and Mabry Mill on the Blue Ridge Parkway. Explore Park, a 1,450-acre outdoor living history museum located seven miles from downtown Roanoke, houses re-creations of Indian lodgings from the seventeenth century and villages and farmsteads from the eighteenth and nineteenth centuries.

See also: GREAT VALLEY ROAD (SETTLEMENT AND MIGRATION); VIRGINIA'S SMART ROAD (TRANSPORTATION).

—James W. Fonseca, *Ohio University*

Deedie Dent Kagey, *When Past Is Prologue: A History of Roanoke County* (1988); Dan Smith, Christian Moody, and Christina Koomen Smith, *Roanoke County and the Roanoke Valley: Turning the Century* (2001).

Rome, Georgia

Known as the "enchanted land where the rivers meet and the mountains begin," Rome, Georgia, is situated in hills about fifty miles from Lookout Mountain, one of the most distinctive peaks in the southern Appalachians. First called Chiaha (meaning "a meeting of the rivers") by the Cherokee, Rome is located where the Etowah and Oostanaula Rivers converge to form the Coosa River in northwest Georgia's Floyd County.

The city was founded in 1834 shortly after the discovery of gold in 1828 brought white settlers and traders to the area. Incorporated in 1847, it prospered as a trading center in its early years, while textile mills played an important part in the area's industrialization later in the century. The town was officially named by five founding fathers who put suggestions into a hat and drew a name. Colonel Daniel R.

Mitchell suggested "Rome" because, like its ancient counterpart, the town was built on seven hills. One of these, Tower Hill, features a one-hundred-foot clock tower that was built in 1871 as a water tower; a four-faced clock was added a year later. The timepiece still works and can be seen from almost any location within the city. Rome's six other hills are Old Shorter Hill with its castle-like spires; Lumpkin Hill; Blossom Hill; Jackson Hill; Mount Aventine, after one of the hills in Ancient Rome; and Myrtle Hill, a cemetery listed on the National Register of Historic Places. Among those buried there are Homer Virgil Milton Miller, the first senator elected from the South after the Civil War; Julia Omberg, the first woman to have an oophorectomy (surgical removal of an ovary); and Mary T. Banks, an African American teacher who educated two generations of students. Ellen Louise Axson Wilson, first wife of President Woodrow Wilson, lived in Rome from the age of six and is also buried on Myrtle Hill. The Washington Oak, planted by members of the Masons organization in honor of George Washington, is in the Veterans' Memorial area of the cemetery.

Famous visitors include President Calvin Coolidge, who used a mansion in Rome for his summer residence, and Margaret Mitchell, author of *Gone with the Wind*, who visited often with her longtime friend Agnes Fahy.

Rome landmarks and places of interest include thirty-four magnolia trees planted in honor of the men from Floyd County who died in World War I and the Nathan Bedford Forrest Monument, which honors the Civil War general who captured a federal raiding party and saved Rome from an attack. The Women of the Confederacy Monument honors the role of women in war. A statue of mythical founders Romulus and Remus was a gift from ancient Rome to modern Rome by order of dictator Benito Mussolini on July 20, 1929. Following a brief disappearance during World War II, the statue is now located at the entrance of Rome's Municipal Building.

In the late twentieth century, the city attracted a large number of industrial plants, increasing its manufacturing employment to about one-third of the workforce. At the start of the twenty-first century, Rome had a population of more than 32,000 and boasted three colleges—Berry, Shorter, and Floyd—and the Georgia School for the Deaf.

See also: BERRY SCHOOLS (CRAFTS); EARLY WHITE SETTLEMENT OF NORTHERN GEORGIA (SETTLEMENT AND MIGRATION).

—Teresa H. Kessinger, *Catholic Social Services*

Roger Aycock, *All Roads Lead to Rome* (1998); Bobby McElwee, *Floyd County* (1998).

Scranton/Wilkes-Barre, Pennsylvania

Scranton, the county seat of Lackawanna County, and Wilkes-Barre, the seat of Luzerne County, make up a single metropolitan area in the heart of Pennsylvania's anthracite region. Wilkes-Barre was founded in 1769 on the site of the Delaware Indian village of Wyoming. The settlers, primarily from New England, were almost immediately caught up in a dispute between Connecticut and Pennsylvania over claims to the Wyoming Valley. Two armed conflicts resulted: the First Pennamite War of 1769–71 and the Second Pennamite War of 1784. In 1778 a force of English loyalists and Iroquois led by John Butler attacked the primarily patriot settlement around Fort Wyoming, killing approximately four hundred settlers. After the Revolutionary War, the settlement was named after John Wilkes and Isaac Barre, English politicians who supported the American cause.

Although surface mining on the banks of the Susquehanna River commenced soon after anthracite coal was discovered in the Wilkes-Barre area in 1769, full exploitation did not occur until the early nineteenth century. The iron industry developed concurrently. Beginning in 1840, the year that George and Selden Scranton founded the Lackawanna Iron and Coal Company, the Scranton name came to dominate the local economy. Scranton companies also included the Delaware, Lackawanna, and Western Railroad, the First National Bank of Scranton, and the Scranton Gas and Water Company. The community of Scranton, which was formally laid out in 1841, was incorporated as a borough in 1851 and chartered as a city in 1866.

The mines and ironworks demanded cheap labor, and the social upheavals of Europe provided it. At first, Irish, English, Welsh, and German immigrants came from mining regions of Europe then, beginning in the 1880s, were supplanted by eastern Europeans, particularly Lithuanians, Poles, Hungarians, and Slovaks. Friction existed between old and new immigrants, a situation often exploited by mine owners to retard labor organization.

Communities surrounding the mines were built upon the "company town" model, in which housing was provided for workers by mine owners who also controlled the town's transportation, stores, politics, and police. Women and children of miners and railroad workers were employed in the emerging silk mills.

The industries of Scranton and Wilkes-Barre contributed much to the growing labor movement in the nation. Mining engendered many fatal disasters, usually from the explosion of mine gases. The most significant of these was the 1919 Baltimore Tunnel No. 2 explosion, which left ninety-two dead. Unsafe conditions, coupled with low wages and economic problems, fueled unrest in the area. The Molly Maguires were among the first to organize in the area. This secret outlawed society, active between 1865 and 1875, was broken by infiltration of Pinkerton agents in the pay of Franklin B. Gowen, president of the Reading Railroad. Two years later, in 1877, approximately eleven thousand rail workers from the Scranton/Wilkes-Barre area participated in the nationwide Great Rail Strike. The area also saw strikes in 1900, 1902, and 1925–26. Women silk workers struck in 1900 and 1901.

During the heyday of coal production, profits from railroads and coal mining enabled Scranton to electrify its streets in 1887, and it became known as "The Electric City." Scranton and Wilkes-Barre had two of the earliest scheduled electric trolley systems in the nation. Both towns became important stops on the vaudeville circuit, with their Poli Theaters attracting such acts as Harry Houdini and the Marx Brothers.

Despite a brief boost from wartime production, manufacturing and mining declined in the Scranton/Wilkes-Barre area after World War II. Mining was effectively finished on January 22, 1959, when the Susquehanna River flooded the Knox Coal Company's underground seams, killing twelve miners and rendering the mines useless. In the face of these setbacks, the chamber of commerce developed the Scranton Plan for economic development, which would become a model for other communities facing similar challenges. The plan, still in modified operation, also encompasses the community of Wilkes-Barre. The primary employers in this area have switched from industry and manufacturing to the service, medical, educational, tourism (focusing on its coal-mining past), and financial sectors.

Scranton is home to the University of Scranton (1888) and Marywood College (1915), and Wilkes-Barre is the location of Wilkes University (1933), King's College (1946), and a satellite campus of Pennsylvania State University specializing in engineering.

See also: ANTHRACITE COAL INDUSTRY (BUSINESS, INDUSTRY, AND TECHNOLOGY); EARLY WHITE SETTLEMENT OF WESTERN PENNSYLVANIA (SETTLEMENT AND MIGRATION).

—J. E. Steenshorne, *New York City Department of Environmental Protection Archives*

Edward J. Davies II, *The Anthracite Aristocracy: Leadership and Social Change in the Hard Coal Regions of Northeastern Pennsylvania, 1800–1930* (1985); Michael J. O'Malley, "Lackawanna County: The Last Shall Not Be Least," *Pennsylvania Heritage* (Winter 1991); Robert H. Wiebe, "The Anthracite Strike of 1902: A Record of Confusion," *Mississippi Valley Historical Review* (September 1961).

Spartanburg, South Carolina

Spartanburg County is located about 860 feet above sea level in upland South Carolina in the foothills of the Blue Ridge Mountains. British settlement of the former Native American hunting ground began after James Glen, colonial governor of South Carolina, signed a treaty with the Cherokee in 1755.

Up to that time, western Pennsylvania had offered opportunities for land grants to newly arriving settlers, many of whom were descendants of Scots who had settled in Northern Ireland in the seventeenth century. As land became scarce in Pennsylvania, these Scots-Irish immigrants were attracted to the newly opened lands in western Carolina. They traveled the Great Valley Road that extended in rude fashion from Pennsylvania down to western South Carolina. The first settlements were along the Tyger River in what would become the western region of Spartanburg County. The county's earliest church, Nazareth Presbyterian, was founded by these settlers in 1772. During the colonial period, the economy of the area was based upon subsistence farming.

Following the American Revolution, Spartanburg County was created in 1785 by the new state legislature. The name probably was derived from the Spartan Regiment, a patriot militia organized during the conflict with the British. The establishment of a courthouse and county jail several years later sparked the development of a small village that grew slowly and was incorporated as the town of Spartanburg in 1831. The opening of Wofford College in 1854 and the coming of the railroad to Spartanburg in 1859 greatly stimulated the local economy. Rapid growth in agriculture, manufacturing, and population did not come until after the Civil War. In the decades after the war, cotton production became the focus of agriculture, and the establishment of numerous textile mills made Spartanburg a major center for textile manufacturing. In 1889 higher education for women was established by the founding of Converse College. In 1911 Spartanburg Junior College opened; it later became Spartanburg Methodist College.

During World War I, Spartanburg benefited from the location of an infantry training center at Camp Wadsworth, just to the west of the city. After the war, cotton declined as a crop because of changing market demands, land exhaustion, and the boll weevil. In time, peaches replaced cotton as the major crop. During World War II, Spartanburg was home to another army training base, Camp Croft. The textile industry was stimulated to new growth during World War II but began a gradual decline in the second half of the twentieth century. This decline was offset by industrial diversification, beginning with the establishment of the Kohler Company and the Milliken Company in the 1950s. The arrival of several German and Swiss industries soon gave Spartanburg a significant international community. This trend continued in 1994 with the construction of a large BMW plant in the county. The founding of Spartanburg Technical College in 1961 and the University of South Carolina at Spartanburg in 1967 further contributed to the community's economic progress.

Spartanburg has produced a number of residents who achieved national prominence. Among these are U.S.

Secretary of State James F. Byrnes; Army Chief of Staff General William C. Westmoreland, who commanded American troops at the height of the war in Vietnam; and NASCAR driver David Pearson. Both the Marshall Tucker Band and jazz musician Pink Anderson claim Spartanburg as their home.

See also: GREENVILLE, SOUTH CAROLINA; SECTION OVERVIEW (BUSINESS, INDUSTRY, AND TECHNOLOGY); UPLAND SOUTH CAROLINA INSTITUTIONS (CULTURAL INSTITUTIONS).

—Jeffrey R. Willis, *Converse College*

J. B. O. Landrum, *History of Spartanburg County* (1900); Philip N. Racine, *Seeing Spartanburg: A History in Images* (1999); Jeffrey R. Willis, *Spartanburg, South Carolina* (1999).

Tri-Cities, Tennessee/Virginia

The Tri-Cities are Bristol, Tennessee/Virginia; Johnson City, Tennessee; and Kingsport, Tennessee. The Johnson City–Kingsport–Bristol metropolitan statistical area, created in 1970, includes seven counties and had a population of 480,091 in 2000. Each of the cities owes its founding to railway construction and related speculative interest in Appalachian timber and coal. The Tri-Cities area is a center of manufacturing, health care, social services, higher education, shopping, commercial entertainment, and arts and culture for much of northeastern Tennessee and southwestern Virginia.

The immigration of European settlers to the area increased following the Treaty of Long Island of the Holston River in 1777, which forced the Cherokee to cede all colonist-occupied land. Later immigrants from Tidewater Virginia brought slaves to the area, but non-whites (primarily African Americans) comprised a small fraction of the population through the twentieth century. In the late twentieth century, racial diversity in the Tri-Cities increased with recruitment outside of the region for managerial and medical positions and increased reliance on Hispanic agricultural laborers; only in Johnson City, however, did the non-white population approach 10 percent.

Early industry in the area included ironworks, textile mills, and tanneries, though farming dominated the economy. During the late nineteenth and twentieth centuries, the proximity of major river, railroad, and interstate routes spurred economic development. The establishment of the Tennessee Valley Authority in the 1930s stimulated tremendous growth through its development of dams, recreational lakes, and cheap electrical power. In the 1990s, tobacco, beef, and dairy farming persisted in outlying counties of the Tri-Cities, but employment was concentrated in the service and manufacturing industries. Post–World War II development and dependence upon automobiles introduced the myriad problems of urban sprawl, including annexation battles, inadequate public transportation, strip development, and struggling downtowns.

The Tennessee-Virginia state line bisects downtown Bristol. Although they share a central business district, Bristol, Tennessee (population 24,821), and Bristol, Virginia (population 17,367), are separate municipalities chartered independently in 1856. Present-day Bristol stands on land Cherokee leaders sold to the Loyal Land Company in the mid-eighteenth century. One hundred years later, news that the state line would be the terminus for two railroads originating in the respective states prompted real estate speculation and resulted in the founding of the city. Although a majority of Bristol's white citizens supported the Confederacy, divided allegiances resulted in bitterness and violence during and for years following the Civil War. In the late nineteenth century, the presence of coal deposits in southwestern Virginia triggered foreign and domestic investment in mines, furnaces, and railroads, and the development of the Clinchfield Railroad spurred a tourism and land-speculation boom. Timber companies prospered until forests were exhausted. In the 1990s, after a century of economic diversification, manufacturing accounted for almost 25 percent of employment, and the service industry was the city's fastest-growing sector.

Bristol is the birthplace of radio announcer and gospel singer Tennessee Ernie Ford and in 1927 was the site of recording sessions that launched the musical careers of Jimmie Rodgers and the Carter Family. These "Bristol sessions" produced the first commercially successful "hillbilly" music, and in 1998 Congress designated Bristol the "Birthplace of Country Music." The 147,000-seat Bristol Motor Speedway is one of the most popular tracks on the NASCAR circuit.

Johnson City (population 55,469) was established in 1856 as a water-refill point along the East Tennessee and Virginia Railroad. North Carolinian Henry Johnson built a depot, general store, and post office at the junction of the railroad and stagecoach road. Damage to the railroads and Confederate occupation stunted the growth of the pro-Union, pro-industrial town, whose African American population more than doubled after the Confederate defeat as freed slaves sought nonagricultural employment. Johnson City (chartered 1869 and 1885) was established as an industrial and trade center around 1900, when northern investors built additional railways to export iron ore, timber, and coal.

In the early twentieth century, Johnson City grew with the addition of a National Home for Disabled Soldiers (now the James H. Quillen Veterans Affairs Medical Center) and the opening of the East Tennessee State Normal School, which in 1963 became East Tennessee State University. The university's James H. Quillen College of Medicine was created by the Tennessee legislature in 1974. Throughout the twentieth century, consumer activity generated by hospital patients, students, and medical professionals stimulated demand for local foodstuffs and sustained city businesses. During the late twentieth century, Johnson City's economy diversified through the development of industry, retail, entertainment, health-care, and educational sectors. A retail boom brought more than eight thousand new jobs and an 82 percent increase in retail sales between 1980 and 1990 alone. The university city serves as a regional entertainment center whose restaurants, live music venues, and dance clubs attract visitors from the entire metropolitan area and surrounding counties.

Kingsport (population 44,905) was built near Long Island of the Holston River, an important Cherokee trading and treaty site. Beginning at Long Island, woodsmen led by Daniel Boone and funded by speculator Richard Henderson widened the Great Indian Warrior Path into the Wilderness Road. During the nineteenth century, the port on the Holston River was a shipping point for William King's salt and James King's iron ore. George Lafayette Carter, known as the "Empire Builder of the Appalachians," and outside investors built the Carolina, Clinchfield, and Ohio Railroad to link Carter's coal mines and iron furnaces in Kentucky and Virginia with his iron ore interests in the Carolinas. To ensure the railway's success, Carter promoted growth along it, particularly in Kingsport (incorporated 1917). Later, city leaders enlisted John Nolen's design firm, as well as architects, public-health professionals, and educational specialists, to create a planned industrial city. Boosters attracted industrialists by promising cheap electricity and nonunion Anglo-American labor and in 1920 convinced Eastman Kodak Company to build a large chemical factory there. The city benefited from war-related industries during World War I and from 1930 to 1945.

At the turn of the twenty-first century, air- and water-pollution levels in Sullivan County (home to Kingsport and Bristol) were among the worst in Tennessee, and Kingsport experienced controversy over proposed chip mills for processing timber. Though still the city's largest employer, Eastman (now the independent Eastman Chemical Company) expanded globally and laid off thousands of local workers. Kingsport attempted to reduce its reliance on manufacturing through development of service, technology, and tourism sectors. The city subsidized the Meadowview Resort and Convention Center and boasts a downtown Heritage Trail, Bays Mountain Park (the largest municipal park in the country), and the Netherland Inn and Exchange Place historical sites.

See also: BRISTOL SESSIONS (MUSIC); RAILROADS (TRANSPORTATION); STATE OF FRANKLIN (GOVERNMENT).

—Emily Satterwhite, *Emory University*

Carroll Van West, *Tennessee's Historic Landscapes: A Traveler's Guide* (1995); Margaret Ripley Wolfe, *Kingsport, Tennessee: A Planned American City* (1987).

Tupelo, Mississippi

Tupelo, a city of some thirty-five thousand residents in northeastern Mississippi, is thirty miles from Woodall Mountain, the highest point in the state. Tupelo lies about midway along the Natchez Trace, an old Indian extension of the Great Trading Path and Mississippi's first historic road. The Natchez Trace facilitated both trade and the migration of Appalachians and others into Mississippi and on to the Gulf Coast.

Tupelo was first settled by Chickasaw Indians migrating from the west. The Native American word *tupelo* may mean "place of lodging," "loud noise," or "long pole," depending upon which definition one chooses to accept. European Americans named the town in the mid-nineteenth century for the tupelo gum trees prevalent in the area. Located in Lee County, Tupelo is part of Mississippi's Black Belt—prairie land so named for its dark, fertile soil.

The Chickasaw remained the area's main residents until the 1832 Treaty of Pontotoc. A Chickasaw exodus was followed by land sales during which Appalachians and others established themselves as settlers and farmers. In 1859 tracks of the Mobile and Ohio Railroad were laid two miles to the east, and the village grew into a town with a store, two saloons, and a temporary railroad station.

During the Civil War, the Tupelo area was important because of the railroad, and General Nathan Bedford Forrest made his headquarters there, achieving a victory for the Confederates in the battle of Brice's Crossroads. In 1866 Lee County was formed. Tupelo was selected as the county seat, and in 1870 the town was incorporated.

Until the 1886 issuance of drainage bonds, much of Tupelo was boggy swampland thick with gum trees. The bonds initiated the reclamation of thousands of acres of bottomland, and in 1887 the Memphis and Birmingham Railroad crossed the Mobile and Ohio tracks at Tupelo, giving the town rail transportation in four directions. By 1900, the area was producing and selling cotton, as well as manufacturing bricks, fertilizer, and textiles. In 1916, when the boll weevil destroyed cotton fields and much of the textile industry, local bankers arranged to take the five thousand dollars spent annually for calendars and underwrite a livestock program. In 1926 the first Carnation Milk Company plant in the South was located in Tupelo, and in 1927 Tupelo farmers imported the South's first Jersey heifer. In 1933 Tupelo became the first city in the United States to purchase power from the Tennessee Valley Authority.

Tupelo has continued to grow, drawing immigrants from the Appalachians and elsewhere. Major items of manufacture in the area include furniture, lawn mowers, tires, light fixtures, refrigeration compressors, industrial buildings, and folding metal chairs. Tupelo's North Mississippi Medical Center is one of the largest nonmetropolitan health-care facilities in the United States, and the city generates a substantial tourist industry, fueled primarily by visitors to the small shotgun house in which legendary singer Elvis Presley was born.

See also: NATCHEZ TRACE (SETTLEMENT AND MIGRATION); PRESLEY, ELVIS (MUSIC).

—Julie Kate Howard and Jessica Siciliano, *Hickory, North Carolina.*

Tuscaloosa, Alabama

Tuscaloosa, Alabama, county seat of Tuscaloosa County, is located nearly sixty miles southwest of Birmingham beyond the foothills of the Appalachians. Situated at the fall line of the Black Warrior River, it was the upper limit of navigation until the river above the city was opened to navigation in the late nineteenth century. It is thus tied both to the southern Appalachian region and to the Gulf of Mexico. The city's 2000 population was 77,906.

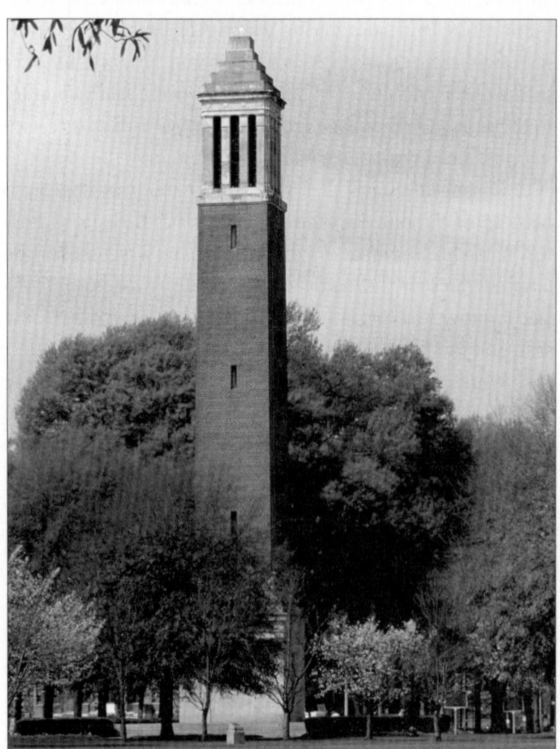

Denny Chimes on the University of Alabama campus in Tuscaloosa, 2002. The chimes were dedicated in 1929 and named for a former president of the university who helped build the former Alabama capital into a bustling commercial and educational center.

Originally settled in the early nineteenth century, the town was incorporated in 1819, underwent a period of rapid growth after it became the state capital in 1826, and developed into a bustling commercial and educational center with the opening of the University of Alabama in 1831. When the state capital was moved to Montgomery in 1846, however, both the city's population and its prosperity declined dramatically.

Isolated from the military actions of the Civil War, the city remained untouched by the conflict until April 4, 1865, when it was captured and briefly occupied by Federal troops. Part of the business district, several factories, and the University of Alabama were burned to the ground.

The city's postwar recovery was slow. Its population continued to decline, and by 1870 the city had fewer residents than twenty years before. Its economy had become wholly dependent on cotton grown on the surrounding farmland. Increased public spending and real estate development during the period from 1880 to 1890 marked a returning prosperity. A public school system was established in 1885, and by 1890 the population finally exceeded its prewar high.

A shift in the economic base from agriculture to industry was well under way by the early 1900s, and coal, iron, and timber were all important industries, joined in the next few decades by paper and chemicals. All these industries, as well as business in general, were hit hard by the Great Depression, and it was only with the coming of World War II that local industries recovered.

During the 1950s and 1960s, Tuscaloosa became a focus in the African American struggle for civil rights. In 1956 Autherine Lucy enrolled briefly at the University of Alabama, the first African American to do so, but was driven from campus by angry segregationists. Seven years later, the university was the site of Governor George Wallace's notorious stand in the schoolhouse door, his attempt to block the federally ordered admission of two African American students to the university.

During these same years, the city experienced a slow but steady expansion that laid the foundation for development in the 1980s and 1990s, when it became a regional center for health services, banking, transportation, and manufacturing. As the twenty-first century began, Tuscaloosa continued to attract new industry and enjoyed sustained growth.

See also: BIRMINGHAM, ALABAMA; CIVIL RIGHTS MOVEMENT (RACE, ETHNICITY, AND IDENTITY).

—Clark E. Center Jr., *University of Alabama*

Matthew William Clinton, *Tuscaloosa, Alabama: Its Early Days, 1816–1865* (1958); Ben Green, *A History of Tuscaloosa, Alabama,*

1816–1949 (1980); Guy Ward Hubbs, *Tuscaloosa: Portrait of an Alabama County* (1987).

Urban Appalachian Council

See Cincinnati, Ohio

Urban Appalachian Enclaves

Because they serve social, economic, and psychological needs of mountain migrants separated from their roots, Appalachian enclaves have become enduring fixtures in numerous cities of industrial America. Just as European, Asian, and Hispanic immigrants made their initial moves into port-of-entry areas in many American cities, so did Appalachians migrating from the mountains. These neighborhoods are the traditional destinations for newcomers seeking affordable housing, access to transportation, social services, and jobs. Many Appalachian newcomers used areas occupied by earlier immigrants from Europe, seeking bases from which they could make the transition to urban life during the exodus from the Appalachians in the 1940s, 1950s, and 1960s.

Migrants' moves into neighborhoods such as Chicago's Uptown, Cincinnati's Over-the-Rhine, Dayton's East Side, and Detroit's Cass Corridor came with mixed blessings. On the one hand, migrants soon found corner grocery stores where they could run a tab, storefront churches where worship was meaningful, and neighborhood bars where the jukeboxes offered familiar songs. More important, they were often surrounded by relatives, neighbors, and acquaintances from "down home" who helped with information about jobs and housing, tips on getting around the city, and advice on handling problems. In these neighborhoods, the local Appalachian community played the role that churches had often filled for other ethnic groups, helping migrants understand how things worked and how to survive in their new surroundings. Invariably, low-cost housing and ready access to transportation and jobs characterized neighborhoods of mountaineers.

On the other hand, these staging areas were the scenes of constant exploitation. Crowded tenements were generally substandard, overpriced, and unsafe. Temporary labor agencies blacklisted employers who offered migrant workers steady jobs, thereby creating a permanent pool of casual laborers. Port-of-entry areas typically had high rates of crime, substance abuse, and disease. Local banks discouraged newcomers as customers, leaving them to storefront check-cashing operations and pawnshops that charged extortionate fees. Slumlords, rent-to-own furniture stores, and pay-on-the-lot used car dealers also preyed on migrants. Overcrowded schools struggled to meet the special needs of migrant children and often failed.

Sociologist Herbert Gans describes these port-of-entry communities as "urban villages," places of convenience where new residents can find refuge from the turmoil of moving, sort out their options, and make decisions about returning to their place of origin or staying to put down roots in the new area. Appalachians often considered their new addresses to be temporary, and in many cases they were. With jobs secured, they left port-of-entry areas and settled into solid working-class neighborhoods with many of the same amenities but fewer drawbacks. Some moved from cities into mushrooming suburban communities being built near transportation corridors. Others moved into surrounding counties and bought homes or small farms in adjacent rural areas. The focal points of their new neighborhoods often were the religious communities provided by the large Protestant churches that grew up nearby.

In some urban areas, however, as many as a quarter of the Appalachian newcomers never made it much past the port-of-entry neighborhoods or other low-income areas in receiving cities. They increasingly shared these neighborhoods with African Americans and Hispanics, united with them in a common experience of poverty. Discrimination affected both groups, although for different reasons.

Urban social service agencies, advocacy organizations, and groups promoting Appalachian culture have grown up to serve Appalachians living in all types of neighborhoods. Appalachian celebrations, festivals, dances, and picnics now draw citywide participation from Dayton, Hamilton, and Cincinnati, Ohio, to Detroit. Many Appalachian newcomers thought they would, in time, leave the "concrete hollers" and return home. Now, living in urban and suburban neighborhoods surrounded by their children, grandchildren, and coworkers, they are much more likely to agree with one Appalachian resident who commented, "Just bury me under a sidewalk."

See also: APPALACHIAN SOCIAL ISSUES OUTSIDE THE REGION; TWENTIETH-CENTURY OUT-MIGRATION (SETTLEMENT AND MIGRATION).

—Maureen Sullivan, *Urban Appalachian Council*

Phillip J. Obermiller, ed., *Down Home, Downtown: Urban Appalachians Today* (1996); Phillip J. Obermiller, Thomas E. Wagner, and E. Bruce Tucker, eds., *Appalachian Odyssey: Historical Perspectives on the Great Migration* (2000); William W. Philliber and Clyde B. McCoy, eds., *The Invisible Minority: Urban Appalachians* (1981).

Urban Appalachian Identity

The term *Appalachian* is used broadly to classify those whose family roots lie within the political boundary of Appalachia as defined by the Appalachian Regional Commission, which has been in existence since 1965. This label, however, was imposed from outside the group rather than emerging as a self-description and, in the minds of most people, is limited to describing those from the central mountains.

Persons of Appalachian origin, both within and outside the region, are diverse in terms of race, historical experiences, religion, family practices, values, beliefs, language, and other markers of ethnicity. They may be of English, Scots-Irish, Welsh, French, German, Native American, African American, or other extractions or combinations of these groups.

Despite this diversity, *Appalachian* is sometimes used narrowly to imply homogeneity within the group. Values commonly ascribed to Appalachians include religiosity, individualism, pride in self-reliance, neighborliness and hospitality, family solidarity, a love of place, modesty, a sense of beauty, a sense of humor, and patriotism. Nevertheless, neither Appalachians nor non-Appalachians have reached a consensus on whether Appalachians, particularly those residing in urban areas in or outside the region, collectively constitute a distinct group.

In 1974 a major task of the first national conference on urban Appalachians was the selection of an appropriate analytic framework for viewing urban Appalachians outside the region. A number of questions were raised. Do Appalachians constitute a true ethnic group? Is class or culture more important in shaping their experiences?

Three competing views on urban Appalachian identity were presented. One view is that urban Appalachians do possess a distinct culture that sets them apart from other Americans. As such, they meet the criterion of an ethnic group. Some who hold this view also assert that they not only meet the definition of an ethnic group, but that of an ethnic minority as well. Ethnic minority status is generally ascribed to those groups that are singled out from others for differential and unequal treatment.

An alternative view, thought to be more widespread, holds that urban Appalachians are a distinctive group rather than an ethnic group. Proponents doubt whether urban Appalachians possess a culture that is significantly different from that of non-Appalachian whites. Other arguments are that they lack distinguishing or visible racial or physical features, language, and religion recognized in other ethnic groups. The contention is that Appalachians' development as a distinct group can be attributed more to regional and political identity than to ethnicity or culture.

A third perspective rejects the notion of ethnicity altogether. This perspective portrays apparent Appalachian group characteristics as being rooted primarily in common class experiences. Despite competing viewpoints, adherents of all three perspectives agree that urban Appalachians constitute a special case due to cultural, class, or other differences.

Conclusions on urban Appalachian identity are limited by a scarcity of empirical evidence from which to generalize and by differences in understanding or accepting the term *Appalachian*. Some scholars assert that there is little evidence indicating that Appalachians moving from the region thought of themselves as a group. Family and community appear to be more relevant to the migrants than their region of origin, and they are more apt to identify themselves as Americans than as Appalachians.

The recognition and treatment of Appalachians as a group in urban areas came initially from journalists, service providers, and social scientists. This movement was especially pronounced during the 1970s, when cultural diversity was embraced more than assimilation.

The notion that *Appalachian* is an external label is supported by a 1976 Norwood, Ohio, study that found others' identification of Appalachians as a distinct group tended to be stronger than Appalachian self-identification. Nonetheless, more than one-third of those of Appalachian descent felt that Appalachians did constitute an ethnic group. Lower-income group members tended to have stronger ethnic identification than those of middle-income status. At issue may be the reluctance to identify with a stigmatized group. Urban Appalachians' actual or perceived overrepresentation among those of lower socioeconomic status may lead some to generalize the experiences and often stereotyped characteristics of those at lower income levels to the group as a whole.

The question of urban Appalachian identity reemerged at a 1995 conference entitled "Down Home, Downtown—Urban Appalachians Today." Most participants felt that the culture was more urban than Appalachian. Others saw no difference between rural and urban Appalachian culture. Some of the characteristics that participants continued to view as distinctive to Appalachians included emphases placed on family life, religion, basic values, and sense of place. On the other hand, some scholars maintain that while urban Appalachians may possess attributes of an ethnic group such as marrying within the group, common geographic origin, a feeling of group belonging, and institutions separate from the dominant culture, identifying a unique culture remains elusive.

Appalachian identity for those outside the region may need to be reframed in terms of Appalachian subcultures to account for the variation within this population. As with any broad grouping, such as Native American or African American, clusters of subgroups exist within the larger group. These subcultures may share a similar history, common core values, behaviors, and/or relationship patterns. However, cultural differences may emerge across subgroups due to recency of migration, homeland ties, place of residency, race, religion, and socioeconomic status. Thus, while Appalachians outside the region may share some common cultural identifiers, they also exhibit the diversity recognized among those remaining within Appalachia.

See also: APPALACHIAN SOCIAL ISSUES OUTSIDE THE REGION; SECTION OVERVIEW (RACE, ETHNICITY, AND IDENTITY).

—Theresa I. Myadze, *Wright State University*

Theresa I. Myadze, "Revisiting Urban Appalachian Ethnicity," in *Appalachian Odyssey: Historical Perspectives on the Great Migration*, ed. Phillip J. Obermiller, Thomas E. Wagner, and E. Bruce Tucker (2000); Phillip J. Obermiller, ed., *Down Home, Downtown: Urban Appalachians Today* (1996); Phillip J. Obermiller and William W. Philliber, eds., *Too Few Tomorrows: Urban Appalachians in the 1980s* (1987).

Urban Appalachian Stereotypes

See Section Overview (Images and Icons)

Wheeling, West Virginia

Wheeling sits on the eastern side of the Ohio River between Ohio and Pennsylvania in West Virginia's northern panhandle. Known as the "Gateway to the West" in the 1800s, it was first settled by Ebenezer Zane and his brothers, Jonathan and Silas, in 1769. Fort Fincastle was built at the site in 1774 and subsequently renamed Fort Henry in honor of Patrick Henry, the first governor of Virginia. Fort Henry was the scene of one of the last battles of the American Revolution in 1782. The following year, Colonel Ebenezer Zane mapped out what is now the city of Wheeling.

Coal mining and iron and steel manufacturing emerged as the major industries in Wheeling in the early 1800s, along with the production of chemicals, glass, clothing, and tobacco products. The National Road was completed from the east to Wheeling in 1818 and the city chartered in 1836. A suspension bridge was completed from Wheeling to Wheeling Island in 1849. At the time, it was the longest bridge between two landmasses in the United States. During the Civil War, the city was the site of conventions in 1861 and 1862 that led to the formation of West Virginia as a state. Wheeling served as the capital of West Virginia from 1863 to 1870 and again from 1875 to 1885.

The city continued to grow in the 1900s, with the population peaking at more than 61,000 in 1930. Local cultural and recreational opportunities expanded at this time with the establishment of Oglebay Park, a 1,650-acre resort that was willed to the city of Wheeling in 1926 by philanthropist Colonel Earl W. Oglebay, a leader in the iron industry. Nearly a million people annually come to enjoy one of America's largest Christmas light displays at the Oglebay Winter Festival of Lights. The Capitol Music Hall was built in 1928 and is West Virginia's oldest and largest theater, seating twenty-five hundred. It is home to the *WWVA Jamboree*, the second-oldest broadcast country music program in the country next to the *Grand Ole Opry*. The theater also houses the Wheeling Symphony Orchestra, which was established in 1929 by Eleanor Caldwell, making Wheeling one of the smallest American cities with a metropolitan-class symphony.

Since 1930, the population has steadily declined—to 31,419 in 2000—due to the loss of coal mining and manufacturing employment. Despite its population loss, Wheeling continues to be a regional center for commercial, industrial, health-care, and educational opportunities.

In 1977 the city council passed an ordinance that established a board to nominate citizens or former residents for induction into the Wheeling Hall of Fame. As of 1998, seventy-two individuals had been selected for this honor. Among current members are Leon "Chu" Berry, the tenor saxophonist; Jesse Burkett, member of the National Baseball Hall of Fame; Rebecca Harding Davis, author; Simon P. Hullihen, pioneer oral surgeon; and Mifflin M. Marsh, cigar manufacturer.

See also: EARLY WHITE SETTLEMENT OF WEST VIRGINIA (SETTLEMENT AND MIGRATION); WEST VIRGINIA GLASSWARE (CRAFTS).

—Richard W. Greenlee, *Ohio University*

Charles J. Milton, *Landmarks of Old Wheeling and Surrounding Country: A Record of Post-Colonial Wheeling* (1943); Kenneth Robert Nodyne, *A Vignette of Wheeling during the Early Republic, 1783–1840* (1978).

Winston-Salem, North Carolina

A Piedmont city located in northwest North Carolina, Winston-Salem began life as two separate towns. German members of the pre-Reformation Moravian Church established Salem in 1766 as a religious and trading community. Winston was founded on Salem's northern border in 1849 as the county seat for newly created Forsyth County and quickly grew into an important manufacturing center. The two cities merged in 1913. In the ensuing years, Winston-Salem was not considered a part of Appalachia either geographically or culturally; however, in 1965 North Carolina politicians worked successfully to have that part of the state included in the federally designated Appalachian region. From its founding, Winston-Salem has served as a shipping way station into Appalachia, providing educational, medical, transportation, banking, and commercial services for the region.

In 1752 a survey party led by Bishop August Gottlieb Spangenburg chose a nearly one-hundred-thousand-acre tract of land on the three forks of Muddy Creek. They named the property Wachovia after a private estate in Austria that in the eighteenth century was the center of activity for members of the Unitas Fratrum, familiarly known as the Moravian Church. The Moravians had been invited to settle on the land by John Carteret, the Earl of Granville and the last of Carolina's eight Lord Proprietors (the men originally granted the land by Charles II of England). Fifteen men, with six horses and a wagon, arrived the next year. They traveled down the Great Valley Road through the Shenandoah Valley from Moravian settlements in Pennsylvania. Although construction of Wachovia's central town was delayed by the French and Indian War (1754–63), the Moravians of Wachovia quickly gained a reputation for the quality of their crafts, particularly pottery. Settlers from all over the backcountry sought out Moravian goods and services. They began construction of Salem in 1766, and when the majority of the population relocated to the new town five years later, the reputation of the Moravians continued to spread, even attracting a visit from President George Washington during his southern tour in 1791. He admired the "small but neat village" with its craftsmen, waterworks, fire-fighting equipment, schools, musical performances, and "society whose governing principles are industry and the love of order."

The residents of Salem produced flour, beer, whiskey, pottery, paper, lumber, and a variety of other products and crafts. In the nineteenth century, Francis and Henry W. Fries became leaders in the production of cotton and woolen textiles. Another important industry was wagon making, led by the Spach and Nissen families. A church board originally regulated banking in Wachovia, but in the early 1800s a branch of the Cape Fear Bank of Wilmington opened in Salem, providing western North Carolina with greater financial independence.

The Wachovia tract was included in Forsyth County when it was created in 1849, and Salem was the logical choice for the new county seat. Since the Moravians were hesitant to have their congregation town used for police and court activities, they sold the land on Salem's northern edge to the state. Once established, the new town of Winston quickly grew into a manufacturing hub as the production of cloth, wagons, tobacco products, and other goods continued to draw people to the community. Winston also became an important center for people from the western regions to sell their agricultural products, particularly tobacco and dried berries, which were used in cordials and medicines in the nineteenth century. Tobacco became increasingly important as P. H. Hanes and R. J. Reynolds established plants to process plug tobacco; they later produced cigarette brands including Camel, Winston, and Salem. After the Hanes family sold its tobacco holdings in favor of expanding its textile interests, the Hanes Company became one of the world's largest producers of hosiery. The Wachovia National Bank was founded in Winston in 1879, growing by the end of the twentieth century to be one of the ten largest banks in the nation. As the nineteenth century progressed, the towns of Winston and Salem became indistinguishable, and in 1913 the two merged and continued to prosper. In 1920 Winston-Salem boasted a population of nearly fifty thousand and was briefly North Carolina's largest city.

Part of the financial success of Winston-Salem was made possible by its access to transportation. Wagons manufactured in Winston-Salem plied the roads west into the Appalachians before the advent of other forms of transportation. After its completion in 1849, the 129-mile Fayetteville and Western Plank Road, terminating near Winston-Salem, provided citizens of western North Carolina with a wooden paved turnpike to the coast. The Roanoke and Southern Railroad, completed in 1892, gave easy access to shipping facilities. Major highways, U.S. 421, U.S. 52, and particularly Interstate 40, built through Winston-Salem in 1961, provided easy access into Appalachia. Piedmont Airlines, founded in Winston-Salem in 1948, was the first North Carolina–owned and –operated airline and specialized in regional and statewide service before growing into a national carrier and merging with other airlines. It provided many Appalachian communities with their first (and often only) air service.

Almost from its founding, Winston-Salem has been an important center for education in western North Carolina. In 1772 the Moravians established schools for both boys and girls that attracted the interest of parents outside of the community. Salem Female Academy, now Salem Academy and College, began accepting boarding students in 1802, training them in reading, grammar, writing, mathematics, history, geography, and needlework. Courses were also available in German, music, and drawing. The school was chartered to offer college coursework, although degrees were not awarded until the 1890s. The Moravians began offering classes for African American students in 1827. Higher education for African Americans began in 1892, with the founding of Slater Industrial Academy, which quickly developed into the center of black learning and culture in western North Carolina. Three years later it became part of the state school system and in 1925 was made into a four-year college, becoming Winston-Salem State College in 1969. The medical school of Wake Forest College moved to Winston-Salem in 1941, followed by the rest of the institution in 1956. It offers a variety of degree programs and is the only school in western North Carolina to train lawyers. In 1965 the North Carolina School of the Arts opened its doors, becoming the premier facility in the state for students in the performing arts.

Winston-Salem has also emerged as an important center for medicine. One of Wachovia's original settlers, Hans Kalberlahn, began his practice in 1754, traveling to see patients as far as one hundred miles away. Other doctors practiced in Salem through the rest of the eighteenth century, pioneering a variety of medical procedures, including cancer surgery and the use of opium as an anesthetic. A number of hospitals were built in Winston-Salem beginning in the nineteenth century. The most important of these, North Carolina Baptist Hospital, opened its doors in 1923. With the addition of the Wake Forest's medical school in 1941, Baptist Hospital became a nationally renowned center for medical research and treatment. By the late twentieth century, Baptist Hospital was the largest employer in the county, and it continues to pioneer new programs, including helicopter medical flights and physician video consultation to hospitals across the region.

Because of its geographical position, Winston-Salem continues to influence the development of the Appalachian region through markets, access to transportation, and a variety of services.

See also: MORAVIANS (RELIGION); SECTION OVERVIEW (BUSINESS, INDUSTRY, AND TECHNOLOGY); SECTION OVERVIEW (SETTLEMENT AND MIGRATION).

—Christopher E. Hendricks, *Armstrong Atlantic State University*

Adelaide Fries, Stuart Thurman Wright, and J. Edwin Hendricks, *Forsyth: The History of a County on the March* (1976); Frank Tursi, *Winston-Salem: A History* (1994).

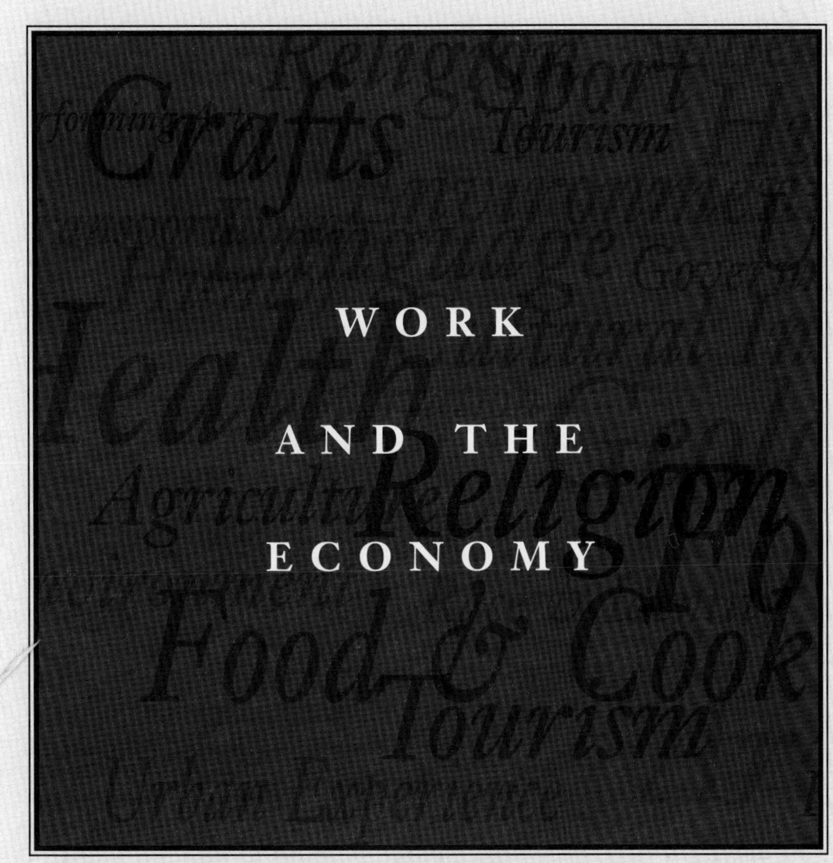

WORK AND THE ECONOMY

MECHANICAL TRANSPLANTER
MECHANICAL TRANSPLANTER

Agriculture

Section Editors: Michael Best and Curtis W. Wood

AGRICULTURE AND THE RURAL LIFE IT HAS SUPPORTED ARE AT THE CORE OF APPALACHIAN culture and history and have played a significant role in defining the region's changing relationship with the world. The physical environment of the region has shaped agricultural practices as much as the choices made by the peoples who have farmed its lands. A temperate climate, abundant rainfall, a network of rivers and streams, a landscape of valleys, coves, and hollows, and the great Appalachian forest have for millennia influenced land-use practices and agricultural possibilities. Far from imposing a static, uniform, easily defined agricultural heritage, this mountain landscape has promoted inventiveness and diversity. Regional agriculture has, at least in modern times, deviated from the dominant patterns of American agriculture and required adaptation of technique and rural lifestyle. For this reason, historic descriptions of mountain farming written by observers from outside the region have typically been negative, depicting land-use practices as wasteful, inefficient, and unscientific. Events of the late nineteenth and twentieth centuries give the appearance of fulfilling the negative stereotypes by marginalizing Appalachian agriculture and undermining its viability in a still largely rural region.

The origins of Native American agriculture in Appalachia are obscure, but the productive agriculture of the Mississippian culture in the seven-hundred-year period preceding European arrival was well established among the Cherokee and other Native American peoples by A.D. 900. Corn provided most of the food of native peoples and required considerable land clearance. Large fields of corn, beans, and squash, small garden plots, and foods gathered from the forest and uncultivated fields supported a well-organized village life along the major rivers of the region. Tobacco was cultivated for community use and as a trade item.

A defining characteristic of Mississippian agriculture was the use of slash-and-burn cultivation. Fire was used to clear patches of forestland, which were then planted for several years, until the soil fertility declined and new areas were put into production. Farming was considered women's work, and responsibility for planting and harvesting defined and supported women's status in the culture.

The arrival of Europeans in the Appalachians, beginning with the Spanish in the sixteenth century, produced immediate and continuing impact on farming and land use. With foreigners came communicable diseases so devastating that whole native settlements were wiped out. Much rich, cultivated land was abandoned. The

Facing page: Kyle and Rhonda Hurd riding a tobacco setter, Hancock County, Tennessee, 1988. In the still largely rural Appalachian region, agricultural practices have been shaped as much by a landscape of valleys, mountainsides, coves, and hollows as by the peoples who have farmed there.

Spanish also introduced new foods such as peaches and sweet potatoes, which became major subsistence crops during the period of transition from Native American to European control of the Atlantic seaboard from about 1500 to 1700. Other new foods—sorghum, field peas, melons, and okra among them—followed. By the eighteenth century, hogs, also introduced by the Spanish, were being raised for food by the Cherokee. Much of the ongoing cultural exchange took place beneficially and without disruption, but growing trade with coastal towns and the arrival of permanent white settlements had fundamentally altered traditional ways by the time of the American Revolution.

Indeed, a variety of Europeans had largely displaced Native Americans and settled most of present-day Appalachia by the end of the eighteenth century. These settlers included Scots-Irish, English, Scottish, German, Dutch, Welsh, and other immigrants. Each group brought its own agricultural practices and traditions. Some new arrivals, such as the Germans, were familiar with the forest environment and brought useful skills such as working with wood. However, they were accustomed to well-organized village life, intensive agriculture, and cultural practices that did not easily adapt to the challenging Appalachian environment. Others, such as the Scots-Irish, had little experience of forest life but brought a heritage of dispersed single-family farms and a tradition of land use more compatible with the slash-and-burn strategy of native farmers. The frontier environment of the Appalachians affected new settlers profoundly. On the great cultural meeting ground of the colonial American backcountry, they shared ideas and practices, adopted new crops, and acquired essential forest skills from Native Americans. Eventually, many of the traditional European practices were modified or abandoned, and a new synthesis of farming practices, dominated by corn, livestock, and forest products, emerged.

Appalachian farms of the late eighteenth and early nineteenth centuries varied greatly in size but typically consisted of less than 20 percent cleared land. Called "new ground" during their early use, fields were planted in corn (or wheat in some areas) and interspersed with crops such as beans, squash, and melons. Arable land was fenced to keep out open-range livestock. Forested land, the largest part of the farm, was a source of wild foods such as berries, chestnuts, and game plus marketable products such as ginseng, yellow root, and animal skins. Woodlands also served as pasture for hogs, which fed on the abundant mast, and for cattle and sheep, which were often driven to high mountain pastures to spend the summer months. The prevailing practice in new settlements was to hold uncleared forestland in common ownership by the community.

Though agricultural life began at the level of subsistence, new settlers seem to have been motivated more strongly by a desire for prosperity than the appeal of freedom and self-sufficiency. Consequently, western Pennsylvania and New York, the Appalachian Valley of Virginia and Tennessee, and the Blue Ridge and Smoky Mountain region of the Carolinas and Georgia had largely moved beyond subsistence agriculture by the time of the Civil War. In these areas, access to markets and production of surpluses drove a transition to more efficient agricultural practices and improved the conditions of farm life. Such advances were far from universal, however. Significant areas of the Cumberland and Allegheny Plateau regions remained at the frontier stage of economic and social life. Dispersed settlements continued to engage in subsistence agriculture rather than producing crops for market.

Small farm near the Great Smoky Mountains National Park, 1936. Subsistence farming was a significant aspect of Appalachian agriculture from frontier times to around the 1950s.

The prosperity of Appalachian farmers in the antebellum period depended upon their skill in managing abundant land with scarce labor, as well as their ability to produce goods that could be delivered to distant markets. Of particular importance were dried ginseng and other herbs, corn whiskey, and especially livestock that could be driven to coastal cities from Philadelphia to Savannah. Annual livestock drives offered small farmers not only the opportunity to market their stock, but also the chance to sell corn, meal, and other products to inns and taverns along their route. Coastal markets and the southern plantation economy both came to depend heavily upon Appalachian agriculture for certain goods. By the 1830s, more than 150,000 animals were annually driven from Kentucky, Tennessee, and North Carolina to South Carolina and Georgia markets along the Buncombe Turnpike. By the middle of the century, a network of railroads connected farmers in Pennsylvania, New York, and the Appalachian Valley of Tennessee and Virginia to growing urban markets. Farmers in fertile valleys and river bottoms had a natural advantage in this trade, and many augmented their operations with slave and tenant labor. Nonagricultural activity such as iron and salt production supplemented and strengthened the growing network of agricultural trade. Throughout the region, in an economy chronically short of currency, both goods and services were routinely bartered. Geographical differences and variations in economic development led to considerable social diversity. The egalitarian society of independent subsistence farmers perpetuated in regional mythology was not typical of antebellum Appalachia. Well-to-do valley farmers who frequently supplanted their agricultural income with land speculation, industrial activity, and commerce formed regional elites. They assumed political leadership and often intermarried with elites outside the region. Small farmers, tenants, and slaves completed the social hierarchy.

By 1860 agriculture was already in decline in much of Appalachia as population growth reduced farm sizes and forced farm families farther up coves and hollows and onto more marginal lands. The Civil War dealt Appalachian agriculture an overwhelming blow, especially in the central and southern mountains. Conscription took men away and left women to bear the burdens of farm management. Tax-in-kind, requiring families to give a percentage of their crops to Confederate or Union governments, and impressment, the practice by which armies took goods such as horses, wagons, and slaves for a price set by authorities, were deeply resented and produced economic distress and violent resistance. Divided loyalties within communities brought violence, hardship, and social disruption. Following the war, internal improvements, especially roads and schools, were neglected, and investments for railroads and economic development lagged for decades. The great livestock drives ended as railroads enabled midwestern livestock producers to capture national markets. In some areas new cash crops such as tobacco and apples brought profits, but a rapid resurgence of population growth put renewed pressure on the land and led to smaller farm sizes. Losing markets to larger and more productive flatland farms, Appalachian farmers retreated to traditional subsistence agriculture, relying upon corn and vegetable gardens, using simple tools, and looking to the forest common for raw materials and pasture. Even these traditional methods were made more difficult by the passage of state fence laws that required enclosure of livestock. Whiskey, long an important product of mountain farms, became subject to federal taxation, and government attempts to enforce the law produced violent confrontations between moonshiners and revenue agents. Not until the 1880s and 1890s did farmers become resigned to the law, after which direct opposition virtually disappeared.

The industrialization of Appalachia from about 1880 to 1930 remade the region's agricultural life. Purchases of timber and mineral rights transferred control of millions of acres of mountain land to absentee and corporate owners. Mining, logging, and railroad work took tens of thousands of mountaineers off their farms and into the "public work" of the mining and logging camps. Many supplemented their income by continuing subsistence farming on the side, and because their independent income from farming meant they could survive on smaller incomes from companies, they indirectly supplemented their employers. Others left the region to seek employment in the industrial cities of the South and Midwest.

No change was of greater import than the metamorphosis of the land itself. By the late 1920s the great Appalachian forest had been virtually destroyed. Departing logging companies left behind expanses of stumps, rocks, and gullies. Mountainsides littered with dry brush, treetops, and weeds were swept by wildfires. Heavy rains washed away the topsoil, compounding the destruction. No longer able to hold water, slopes baked under the sun and poured floods into valleys during thunderstorms and seasonal rains. Once steady perennial streams alternately became raging torrents and dry creek beds. This is being replayed in some areas of massive surface mining today.

For most of the nineteenth century, the defining problems of Appalachian agriculture were those of the subsistence farmer, most notably labor scarcity and isolation from markets. In the very different environment of the twentieth century, the central challenges were those of the small-scale commercial farmer: farm efficiency, loss of farmlands, farm sizes, out-migration, soil depletion, and the development of a sustainable and profitable agriculture.

The agricultural modernization that accompanied industrialization nationally did little for most of Appalachia. Organizations such as the Farmers' Alliance and the Grange in the 1880s and 1890s encouraged mountain farmers to work together to save themselves and preserve farming as a way of life in the region. Cooperative commodity organizations helped make small farmers more competitive by improving their buying and selling power, but mountain farmers were seldom able to effectively mechanize, and most found it difficult to shift to profitable staple crops. The mountainous topography, scarcity of capital, and small size of their farms conspired against them. Crops such as tobacco, apples, and cotton were adopted in some areas, but even farmers who turned to specialty crops remained at a disadvantage compared to their counterparts in other areas. The increasing distress of mountain agriculture and opposition to fence laws and hunting laws led to widespread sympathy for populist sentiments fostered by the Farmers' Alliance.

As the industrial boom waned in the 1920s, mountain families who went back to the land soon found there could be no return to traditional agricultural practices that had depended upon the forest as a central resource. Mountain farmers stood in dire need of education and assistance in dealing with problems such as adoption of staple crops and maintenance of soil fertility. The Morrill Act of 1862 had established land-grant colleges of agriculture, but in Appalachia the schools' research and teaching seldom addressed the special problems of agriculture in the region.

In the 1920s Appalachian farmers, like those across the country, suffered a catastrophic collapse of commodity prices. An extraordinary drought in 1930 and the Great Depression persisting throughout the decade multiplied their hardships. Farmers needed immediate disaster assistance as well as help in farm management, farm credit, and the creation of cooperative commodity organizations. Thousands of families lost their farms during this period despite increased federal intervention in rural problems. One of the most conspicuous government initiatives was the creation of the Cooperative Extension Service in 1915. By the late 1920s extension agents were at work in many of the counties of the region. The Cooperative Extension Service administered a program of emergency loans to farmers and in early 1931 promoted a "live at home" program that helped farm families produce, can, dry, cure, preserve, and store fruits, vegetables, and meats for home use.

Beginning in 1933, New Deal legislation massively expanded government's role in the rural economy, but the new programs had little relevance to the problems of the small farmers of Appalachia, and their effects in the region were marginal at best. The Agricultural Adjustment Act of 1933 created a program of acreage allotments, marketing quotas, and processing taxes. It was intended to regulate commodity prices through price supports and production quotas to a level of parity in order to provide farmers with stable purchasing power. Commodities primarily affected by parity calculations were wheat, cotton, corn, hogs, tobacco, and milk, but only the tobacco program had significant impact in Appalachia.

In 1938 a second Agricultural Adjustment Act tied price supports and production quotas to soil conservation practices. This gave larger mountain farmers an incentive to switch from crops that depleted the soil to those that conserved it, but once again few operators of ordinary family farms received any benefit. Other governmental programs spawned by the Great Depression include the Farm Security Administration, Civilian Conservation Corps, Soil Conservation Service, Tennessee Valley Authority, and Rural Electrification Administration. For the most part, these agencies also approached agricultural problems from a national rather than a regional perspective, stressing improvements in farm structure, efficiency, and competitiveness rather than seeking a sustainable agriculture addressing regional social and economic needs.

Many critics have long considered the small size of Appalachian farms an insurmountable problem for agriculture in the region, and the issue loomed even larger as technology advanced and transportation infrastructure improved. While large farms could readily adopt new technologies, family farmers in small valleys and hillside fields were sharply constrained by scale and topography. The first detailed study of agriculture in Appalachia was *Economic and Social Problems and Conditions of the Southern Appalachians*, edited by Lewis C. Gray and Claud F. Clayton for the U. S. Department of Agriculture and published in 1935. It recommended conversion of land to public ownership rather than the promotion of new crops and new techniques as a solution for region's economic and social problems.

Half a century later, strategists turned to sustainability as a guiding principle for the region's agriculture—and for natural resource policy and economic development in general. The term *sustainability*, though constantly refined, is generally understood to embrace economic, environmental, and cultural viability. Agricultural sustainability requires that crops and livestock be grown in a manner acceptable to community and environmental standards without soil depletion, loss of land, reductions in yields, or economic collapse. Rapidly evolving technologies and fluctuating costs influence the nuances of sustainability, but the essence of the concept is protection of both the land and the people who occupy it.

Observers of Appalachian agriculture see hopeful trends in niche farming and the practice of direct marketing. High-value crops such as field and greenhouse vegetables, nursery stock, Christmas trees, cut flowers, and ginseng, as well as value-added products such as salsa, apple butter, and jams processed by the farmer or by cooperative organizations, have a higher rate of return than traditional grain crops and livestock. Moreover, small farms lend themselves to such production.

Federal highways, including the interstate system and the Appalachian Development Highway System, have made transportation strikingly easier within the region in recent decades. But as a result, regional farmers have found themselves consistently undersold in their own markets, and many of them have found it financially irresistible to leave the land and work for a weekly paycheck. Some agriculturalists contend that small mountain farms no longer have a place in the modern agricultural system. Rather than sustain small operations with government intervention, their argument holds, government resources would be better spent on urbanization, human resource development, training for nonfarm employment, and even to assist out-migration. As a consequence of this changing perception of the economic future of the region, little research has been directed to agriculture in Appalachia by agencies such as the U. S. Department of Agriculture or the Appalachian Regional Commission since the 1960s. Agronomists seldom consider Appalachia as an agricultural region and focus instead on the county, state, and nation as units of study.

Defenders of mountain farming believe that the disappearance of the family farm would mean the loss of things more important than part-time jobs and mod-

In many areas of Appalachia, farmland continues to be lost to suburban development, as it is in rapidly growing Forsyth County, North Carolina, 2000.

est incomes. Small farmers have been the stewards of the woodland environment and the rural culture of the Appalachian region for more than two centuries. If the land of Appalachia passes into predominantly nonagricultural uses, a way of life will be lost.

The federal government began to move out of the national agriculture arena with the Freedom to Farm Act of 1995. The act proposed to phase out the federal program of annual farm subsidies that have shaped American agriculture since the 1930s. This change of course was based on the assumptions that the free market is the most efficient system for agriculture and that agricultural producers had become sophisticated enough to plan steps to remain economically viable in a bad year. Subsequent pressures from farm interests have actually increased farm subsidies, but since most payments go to large farmers and grain producers, the shifting subsidy policy has had little impact on mountain agriculture. Conditions on the farm and elsewhere in rural Appalachia have rapidly changed, but not for the better.

At the beginning of the new century some of the most productive farmland was being lost to various kinds of development. The average Appalachian farmer was older than the average American farmer, and his or her income level was lower. The number of full-time farmers continued to decline. In 1969, 47 million acres were being cultivated on 354,748 farms in the region. By 1997, the numbers had fallen to fewer than 35 million acres on 230,050 farms. In 1969, 37.8 percent of the land area of Appalachia was in farm use. By 1997, that figure had fallen to 28 percent. Over a somewhat longer time period, from 1959 to 1997, the average size of mountain farms in the region increased from 105 to 152 acres, and the real value of farm products increased from $18,000 to $45,000. For the nation as a whole, however, the average farm size in 1997 was 487 acres, and per-farm cash receipts averaged $103,000. The difficulty of farming in Appalachia is further indicated by the fact that in 1997 nearly 60 percent of farm operators reported some off-farm work and 42 percent reported 200 days or more of off-farm work.

The challenges to successful farming in the region are apt to increase in the future, requiring even more tenacity and inventiveness. Better strategies for sustainable production will be necessary, along with sharpened management skills, profitable new crops, strengthened marketing practices, and efficient new technologies.

—Michael Best, *Berea, Kentucky*, and Curtis W. Wood, *Western Carolina University*

Wendell Berry, *The Unsettling of America: Culture and Agriculture* (1977); Dale Colyer, "Changes in Appalachian Agriculture: 1965–2000," *Journal of Appalachian Studies* (Fall 2001); Donald Edward Davis, *Where There Are Mountains: An Environmental History of the Southern Appalachians* (2000); Lewis C. Gray, *History of Agriculture in the Southern United States to 1860* (1933); Steven Hahn, *The Roots of Southern Populism: Yeoman Farmers and the Transformation of the Georgia Upcountry, 1850–1890* (1983); Paul E. Lovingood and Robert E. Reiman, *Emerging Patterns in the Southern Highlands: A Reference Atlas, Vol. 3: Agriculture* (1982); John Solomon Otto, *The Southern Frontiers, 1607–1860: The Agricultural Evolution of the Colonial and Antebellum South* (1989); Paul Salstrom, *Appalachia's Path to Dependency: Rethinking a Region's Economic History, 1730–1940* (1994).

Agrarian Revival

See *Progressive Farmer*

Agricultural Cooperatives

Cooperatives are derived from the idea that individuals cooperating in a common purpose gain benefits for the entire group that the individuals alone would not enjoy. This is an attractive arrangement in an agricultural industry in which survival has been difficult for most small farmers, particularly in Appalachia. The United States Department of Agriculture reported 3,346 agricultural cooperatives in a 2000 survey, accounting for 3.1 million members nationwide. The thirteen Appalachian states in the same year headquartered approximately 630 agricultural cooperatives with a combined membership of nearly 1.1 million.

There has always been a tendency for larger buyers and sellers to exploit the relative weakness of individual farmers in the marketplace. However, if all the producers in a particular region join together and sell their product as one individual organization, they gain market power and stabilize or even increase prices. Farmers started organizing agricultural cooperatives shortly after the Civil War, although economic factors did not favor the expansion of cooperative forms of business until the early 1900s. Following World War I, agricultural commodity prices fell drastically, forcing individual farmers to accept the low market prices while farm suppliers made exorbitant profits and provided very little service. Serious attention was given to the organization of cooperative types of business between 1910 and 1930. In 1915 approximately 5,400 cooperatives existed in the United States, and that number had more than doubled, to 12,000, by 1930.

With the passage of the Capper-Volstead Act by Congress in 1922, agricultural cooperatives became legal entities. Three fundamental concepts distinguish them from other business entities. The first requirement is that ownership and control of the organization must be in the hands of the people who utilize its services; that is, it must be a patron-owned business. Secondly, the cooperative must be operated on an approximate-cost basis, and returns over cost must be refunded to the patron-owners. This requirement made agricultural cooperatives nonprofit organizations in the United States. The last concept differentiating cooperatives from other business entities is that the return on the owners' investment must be nominal to ensure focus on service rather than profit.

Early enthusiasm and growth gave way to consolidation from 1930 to 1950. As with most new concepts in business, fast growth produced some cooperatives that were unsound in their business structure. It also became clear that cooperatives could not solve the problems created by the Great Depression. Between 1925 and 1935 many small independent cooperatives consolidated into large regional associations.

Several kinds of cooperatives have developed in the Appalachian region over the last one hundred years, including marketing, purchasing, service, and processing associations. Marketing cooperatives derive most of their income from the sale of their members' farm products. Farm supply cooperatives make most of their revenue from the sale of farm production supplies, farmstead equipment, building materials, heating oil, and lawn and garden supplies. Service cooperatives specialize in business services relating to the agricultural operations of farmers, ranchers, and other agricultural producers; these include cotton ginning, trucking, storing, drying, and artificial insemination or other forms of value-added processing. That the Capper-Volstead Act provides a wide range of flexibility in choosing a structure leads to a variety of marketing cooperatives. The act does not require cooperatives to have either capital stock or a corporate form. In fact, associations that fall under the protection of Capper-Volstead may be structured as non-profit corporations, for-profit businesses, unincorporated associations, or stock or non-stock farmer cooperatives. Furthermore, several cooperatives may join together into a federation.

Southern States Cooperative, based in Richmond, Virginia, is a prime example of a supply cooperative. It was established in the early 1920s as the Virginia Seed Service to provide farmers in the state with high-quality seed. Later, the cooperative distributed feed and added a fertilizer service before changing its name in the 1930s to Southern States and expanding its service to Delaware, Maryland, West Virginia, Kentucky, and North Carolina. The Farmers Federation, founded in Asheville, North Carolina, to "help the mountain farmer help himself," was an example of an agricultural cooperative that organized markets for farmers as well as providing input supplies. Whereas Southern States continued to expand after the depression, the Farmers Federation disbanded, as did many other cooperatives in the 1950s and 1960s.

Even though the average size of the Appalachian farm increased slightly after 1960, the need for most agricultural cooperatives has not changed. The Capper-Volstead Act continues to benefit many small farmers in the Appalachian region by enabling them to purchase supplies and services and to market their commodities competitively.

See also: FARMERS FEDERATION; HOME DEMONSTRATION CLUBS.

—Michael Best, *Berea, Kentucky*

Dale Colyer, "Changes in Appalachian Agriculture: 1965–2000," *Journal of Appalachian Studies* (Fall 2001); U.S. Department of Agriculture, *Farmer Cooperative Statistics* (1995; 1997) and *Rural Cooperatives* (September–October 1997).

Agricultural Education

A century after its rise as an integral part of Appalachian students' high school experience, agricultural education has come to emphasize stewardship and conservation rather than vocational training and production. Especially in rural areas, it remains an important course of study, as it has been since the era of subsistence farming. It was through agricultural education in the secondary schools that up-to-date farming methods and potential avenues to improved living conditions were introduced to generations of rural families in the region. In some cases, the classes provided insights that warded off poverty.

Early agricultural education focused on introducing boys and men to modest advances in farming. Instruction was based on local agricultural experience and opportunities for better farm family life. The first instruction in the 1800s was in New York, Ohio, Pennsylvania, and Georgia. Usually it was offered in private schools such as the J. S. Green Institute in Habersham County, Georgia. Established in 1897 by northern Methodists to educate mountain children in northeast Georgia where there were no public secondary schools, the institute had a farm and forest that were used in teaching and to provide food for the students. Renamed Piedmont College, it remains in service as an affiliate of the National Association of Congregational Christian Churches.

In 1903 a public school in Carroll County, Georgia, was the first in Appalachia to have an agriculture teacher on staff. Interest spread to other schools in the region, but the absence of secondary schools was an impediment in many communities. Some students attended boarding schools with school farms, learning and working on the farm to help pay their school tuition and expenses. There was little coordination among these institutions, and teachers made use of whatever resources were available. An early textbook used in North Carolina, *Agriculture for Beginners* (1903), had chapters on soils, botany, zoology, insects and diseases, farm crops, meat and dairy animals, and mechanical tools and skills, including blacksmithing.

Industrial and agricultural expansion was rapid in the 1910s, as World War I generated critical needs for food, clothing, and other materials. The Smith-Hughes Act, signed by President Woodrow Wilson in 1917, provided funds for states to establish agricultural instruction in secondary schools for boys and men. States immediately began to implement in-school and adult farmer programs. Agriculture teachers trained at land-grant colleges were first known as Smith-Hughes teachers and later as vocational agriculture teachers.

After a few years of Smith-Hughes programs, teachers realized that boys needed motivation to remain in school. Corn clubs, poultry clubs, thrift clubs, and others were established throughout the 1920s to provide practical skills, but they lacked coordination. In 1925 four Virginia agricultural educators—Walter Newman, Harry Sanders, Edmund Magill, and Henry Groseclose—met at Virginia Polytechnic Institute and laid the groundwork for creation of the Future Farmers of Virginia.

Two years later, the Future Farmers of Tennessee was formed, and chapters throughout the state raised funds for a camp for agriculture students. Camp Clements opened in 1928 and for years provided farm youth their first opportunity to travel away from their rural homes. In 1928 national leaders in agricultural education adopted the basic concepts of the Virginia and Tennessee clubs as they founded the Future Farmers of America. The organization soon became a vital part of agricultural education, developing leadership and personal skills as well as recognizing achievement and instilling pride in farmwork.

Encouraged by state leaders, most rural public secondary schools in Appalachia made vocational agriculture part of their curricula by the mid-1900s. Schools were often quite small and had only one agriculture teacher, but farm projects added a practical dimension to classroom work. Students began by raising a pig or a small garden and advanced to larger projects. Teachers regularly visited homes and farms to check on progress, give individual advice, and reinforce classroom instruction at the family level.

Some schools also offered adult programs in agriculture, scheduling night meetings, field trips, and other activities. One of these included establishing school-community canneries. Operated under the direction of agriculture and home economics teachers, the initiatives were designed both to educate families and to improve rural nutrition. Agriculture teachers typically taught vegetable and animal production to men, while home economics teachers taught food preservation and nutrition to women. Citizens brought harvested foods for canning in industry-style retorts using steam boilers and semi-mechanized sealing machines. Although all but a few had been phased out by 2000, most areas of the Appalachian region had one or more schools with canneries.

The Smith-Hughes Act was renewed and amended several times, but these changes did not always meet needs. In the late 1940s, special programs conducted by vocational agriculture teachers were offered to returning World War II veterans who, having seen some the world outside Appalachia, sometimes found the instruction too concerned with "old-style" farming.

By the 1960s, larger-scale operations were rapidly replacing family farms in the nation, and educational needs were changing. A new federal law, the Vocational Education Act of 1963, redirected agricultural education, allowing the use of funds for instruction in areas other than farming. New subjects included ornamental horticulture, forestry and natural resources, agricultural supplies and services, and agricultural processing. Curriculum changes interested female students and teachers. In 1969 the Future Farmers of America voted to allow female members, and by 1988 the Future Farmers of America had formally changed its name to FFA in order to reflect its broader interests.

By the beginning of the twenty-first century, farming was no longer the predominant occupation in rural and small-town Appalachia. Former farmers worked in food processing, forestry, ornamental horticulture, and furniture manufacturing. Some jobs had no connection to farming; some involved processing rather than production.

Contemporary agriculture education includes complex and varied subjects—biotechnology, computer technology, wildlife management, small and companion animal husbandry, aquaculture, horticulture, and natural resource conservation and development. In some schools, students receive science credit for agriculture; classes once called FFA are often labeled agriscience, and former FFA teachers are designated agricultural or agriscience educators. The FFA and supervised activities continue to be used in most schools, but adult education has dwindled and teachers are less involved in community work.

See also: ENVIRONMENTAL EDUCATION (ENVIRONMENT).

—Jasper S. Lee, *Lee and Associates*

Charles W. Burkett, Frank L. Stevens, and Daniel H. Hill, *Agriculture for Beginners* (1903); Jasper S. Lee, *Program Planning Guide for AgriScience and Technology Education* (2000); Rufus W. Stimson and Frank W. Lathrop, *History of Agricultural Education of Less Than College Grade in the United States* (1942).

Agricultural Frontiers

Appalachian agriculture was developed in and shaped by a frontier environment. Various parts of the region experienced frontier conditions—inaccessibility to markets, abundant cheap land, scarcity of labor, and predominance of subsistence agriculture—at different times because the easiest farming areas were settled first and the most difficult last. Pennsylvania's backcountry began to receive European American settlers in the 1600s, and it became known as "the best poor man's country" that could be found anywhere in the British American colonies. By the 1720s, settlers of German stock began homesteading in Virginia's Shenandoah Valley, and Scots-Irish settlers followed closely on their heels. From that time until about 1900, frontier conditions could always be found somewhere in the region.

At the time of the American Revolution, frontier conditions were already ending in the Shenandoah Valley, having long since spread in both southerly and westerly directions. By then, most of far western Pennsylvania and the Monongahela Valley in northwestern Virginia had become a farming frontier, and that area would soon see the rise of the iron industry. Yet until the dawn of the twentieth century, there remained areas of the Appalachian Plateaus region, especially parts of eastern Kentucky, that were virtually uninhabited.

As the Appalachian region was settled, its agricultural economy took root and evolved in three vast subregions. In the Great Valley, including the Shenandoah and the rest of the Valley of Virginia as well as the Valley of East Tennessee, even the earliest settlers sent products north to market. Soon Winchester, Virginia, became an intermediary center of trade en route to the markets of Alexandria, Baltimore, and Philadelphia. Across the Ridge and Valley Province in western North Carolina, northern Georgia, and far eastern Tennessee, farmers worked fields at a somewhat higher average elevation, and, lacking easy access to markets, never enjoyed the prosperity of those in the Great Valley. In the Appalachian Plateaus Province, encompassing both the Allegheny and Cumberland Plateaus, obstacles to market access were even greater except for farmers close to rivers such as the Kanawha, the New, the Big Sandy, and the Kentucky.

As with the opening of Appalachia's farming frontiers, so did their closing proceed more or less sequentially through these three large subregions. By 1830 frontier conditions had basically ended throughout the entire Great Valley, and by 1870 the Ridge and Valley—except for a later timbering frontier in the upper elevations of the Smokies—had also made the transition. But the rugged Appalachian Plateaus Province still held several large frontier pockets as late as the 1890s, most notably in eastern Kentucky.

From the early days of European American settlement, sources of salt were exploited and the salt widely marketed. Iron ore deposits were also developed if they were located near both limestone and transportation, thereby making it profitable to build iron furnaces or forges. Back east, iron making was generally conducted on "iron plantations," where the workers were virtual serfs of the landowning ironmasters. But in western Pennsylvania and the rest of Appalachia, agricultural land was more widely available to industrial workers, and many early ironworkers became freeholders, owning homesteads and growing their own food. In fact, many of the region's ironworkers were independent subcontractors rather than employees of the local ironmaster.

In general, a frontier is a locale where more attractive opportunities are available (or at least are rumored to be available) than in the areas from which people are coming. It is often characterized by the kinds of opportunities that draw people to them. The historian Frederick Jackson Turner hypothesized that frontier opportunities adhered to the following sequence: Hunting and trapping opportunities drew people first, followed in turn by open-range livestock economies, followed by crop raising, timbering, and mining. Turner's sequence is more evident in the eastern United States than in the West. It applies well to Appalachia except for the early appearance of a salt-extraction industry and the beginning of iron making where conditions were favorable.

Appalachia's open-range livestock frontier and its crop-farming frontier followed the same subregional sequence. The Great Valley and the many smaller valleys parallel to it were excellent for both livestock raising and crop farming because their soils are underlain by limestone. Farming families settled there first, often trekking from Pennsylvania southwestward down the long valleys of Maryland and Virginia until they could claim or buy a substantial holding of good farmland. Such families filled the Great Valley with comfortable-sized farms, averaging just over 150 acres. In the 1780s, a foreign traveler reported, "[W]hen you see the Shenandoah you think you are still in Pennsylvania." Those early-arriving families resisted any temptation to subdivide their farms below their "comfort zone," since their children could usually acquire comfortable-sized farms not far away.

Of all the plants grown and harvested on the Appalachian frontier, none was more important than corn (maize). The cornshock, an upright stack of cut cornstalks left in a field to dry, came into use in the northwestern corner of the Great Valley in the mid- to late 1700s to preserve corn fodder in the field for winter livestock feeding. Probably originating along the South Branch of the Potomac River in today's Hardy County, West Virginia, the cornshock was taken west to Kentucky and Ohio and eventually became an emblem of the Corn Belt. In addition to the gradual spread of farming, some early salt extraction and iron making took place in the Great Valley, but it was small compared with later salt and iron output elsewhere in Appalachia.

Settlement of the Ridge and Valley Province was accelerated by gold rushes in the 1820s and 1830s in North Carolina and northern Georgia. Besides helping to attract more migrants, the search for gold contributed to the expulsion of the Cherokee. Due to the relatively high elevation, farm families of the Ridge and Valley continued to emphasize livestock raising even after the frontier era had passed, whereas the Great Valley's farmers had generally turned more toward crop farming (especially of wheat) following their own frontier era.

The Appalachian Plateaus filled up last. But settlement was not complete until railroads reached deep into the mountains and allowed timber and coal extraction to boom, beginning in the late 1800s. By then, significantly, comfortable-sized farms were no longer readily available anywhere in the continental United States. The economic pinch felt by many families is still evident in the tiny farms of the hollows. The difficulty of farming in the area prompted men to accept low wages at off-farm jobs, and the availability of cheap labor encouraged entrepreneurs to transform much of the plateau landscape into a timber and coal-mining frontier. Since they continued to carry on subsistence farming and extensive gardening, rural wageworkers effectively subsidized the low wages paid by the coal and timber companies that employed them. This enabled companies to undersell their northern competitors and thus prompted them to cut even more timber and mine even more coal in what today's economists would call "a race to the bottom."

Thus an irony accompanied the closing of Appalachia's last frontier. Earlier frontiers had closed while new frontiers were still opening and new opportunities still beckoning. Settlers of the 1700s had avoided exploitation by moving west into the mountain region, where they generally found more freedom and autonomy. But over time the paradigm of rugged familism, or family self-sufficiency, became elusive. By the late 1800s, thousands of families on the Appalachian Plateaus still lived under frontier conditions. However, they found themselves not on a farming frontier but on a coal frontier. Because of poor farming opportunities and the lack of any remaining farming frontiers elsewhere in the country, they became victims of labor exploitation, subsidizing overindustrialization by their willingness to accept low wages. Meanwhile they resorted to destructive hillside farming to make up the difference. Finally, when the Great Depression struck, they became dependent upon welfare assistance. During the New Deal, government officials began speaking of them as "stranded populations." In a sense, these were really stranded frontiersmen, and what had stranded them was the late closing of their frontier.

After World War II, with local autonomy undermined by government assistance, neighborhoods became targets for strip mining, clear-cutting, commercial garbage dumping, and radioactive-waste disposal. Yet this "Third World" subregion within a fabulously rich nation still retains its distinctive culture by refusing to abandon its hunting, its gathering of useful farm products, and its agriculture.

See also: SUBSISTENCE FARMING.

—Paul Salstrom, *Saint Mary-of-the-Woods College*

Dwight B. Billings and Kathleen M. Blee, *The Road to Poverty: The Making of Wealth and Hardship in Appalachia* (2000); R. Eugene Harper, *The Transformation of Western Pennsylvania, 1770–1800* (1991); Paul Salstrom, *Appalachia's Path to Dependency: Rethinking a Region's Economic History, 1730–1940* (1994).

Alternative Crops

Alternative crops and livestock are important elements of sustainable agriculture in the region, together with alternative cultivation and marketing techniques such as conservation tillage and the production of value-added items such as wine, molasses, and other specialty goods. As increased competition and production have driven down prices of more traditional crops, farmers have sought more efficient methods for cultivating and marketing in order to increase the productivity of their businesses. Often this has meant trying entirely new crops on their land. Alternative crops can be those that have a highly specialized, or niche, market. They also include crops that are regularly grown in other regions but have not been traditionally cultivated in Appalachia. While none of these cover a large acreage of Appalachian farmland, collectively they are increasingly significant enterprises on small mountain farms.

Alternative crops that are being grown to replace or supplement various types of traditional Appalachian crops include field crops (bird seed, flax, sunflowers, and canola, as well as foods such as buckwheat, popcorn, and soybeans); specialty and ethnic vegetables (asparagus, garlic, truffles, and wasabi); fruits and nuts (pawpaws, berries, and grapes); horticultural and nursery plants (annual flowers, herbs, and native plants and shrubs); agroforestry products (bamboo, Christmas trees, and firewood); and livestock (fish, poultry, game animals, and exotics such as emus and Angora rabbits).

Some crops, such as greenhouse flowers and vegetables, are practical alternatives in all of Appalachia and are grown throughout the region. Heirloom fruits and vegetables are also found throughout the region, as they can be grown anywhere the standard varieties they replace are grown. There is, however, more variation in crops than there is standardization. Factors such as climate and topography, demands of local markets, and grower preferences influence the distribution of alternative crops from state to state, sometimes from county to county. Farmers in New York's Chautauqua County harvested nearly 17,000 acres of grapes in 1997, while the two counties bordering it cultivated only 2,285 acres of vines combined. Christmas tree farming is ubiquitous throughout Appalachian North Carolina, though only sporadic in neighboring states that share similar growing conditions. Maple syrup production and fruit tree cultivation are readily found in New York and Pennsylvania, where thousands of trees are tapped each season, while cotton, soybeans, and sod are cash crops more often grown in Mississippi. Of Appalachian counties in Maryland, only Garrett County produces maple syrup commercially, though all have a large number of fruit trees; Washington County farmers harvested 26,009 peach trees in 1997. Western Maryland also produces large crops of barley, oats, and soybeans. Elephant garlic is an important specialty crop in Virginia, as is kenaf, a versatile crop that can be grown as a source of fiber and high-quality forage.

At the turn of the twenty-first century, many eastern Kentuckians who had formerly farmed tobacco began raising meat goats, primarily for increasing numbers of immigrants from Jamaica, northern Mexico, and the Middle East. Adapting to changing times, they recognized that the quadruple increase in the amount of imported goat meat (from 3 to 12 million pounds per year) from 1990 to 2001 represented a significant new market.

The declining tobacco market of the early twenty-first century had farmers seeking alternatives in Tennessee as well. Some farmers in Pickett County switched from burley tobacco to freshwater shrimp. A local company provides the juvenile shrimp to growers and offers to buy the mature crop back at the end of the four-month season; farmers also have the option of selling on the open market. In 2001 an acre of freshwater shrimp could sell for as much as twenty-five hundred dollars.

Pennsylvania has been a dominant eastern producer of mushrooms for many years, and in 2000 Virginia, with approximately 150 to 180 small-scale growers of gourmet mushrooms such as portobello, maitaki, and shiitake, also became competitive in the market. The nonprofit Lightstone Foundation, established in 1986 to promote sustainable agriculture in the region, operates a demonstration farm in West Virginia on which more than two hundred different species of mushrooms were discovered growing in 1999, abundantly indicating the suitability of the area for this crop. The foundation began testing four types, including the popular shiitake, on the farm at the beginning of the twenty-first century to determine the viability of this crop for mountain farmers. Among other alternative crops grown on Lightstone land are medicinal herbs such as goldenseal and black cohosh.

Native plants and herbs are grown as specialty crops throughout the mountainous region of Appalachia. The Smoky Mountains Native Plants Association promotes, among other things, the sustainable cultivation and marketing of plants native to this area of North Carolina and Tennessee. Herbs such as ginseng, ramps, bloodroot, and wild mushrooms and ornamentals such as boxwoods, rhododendrons, laurels, and azaleas are among the many plants native to the Smokies for which a market exists. The association, in cooperation with local agricultural extension services, provides education, test plots for research, and small loans for members interested in these crops. The association also operates a farmers' market in Graham County, North Carolina, as an outlet for native plants, as well as more traditional crops.

Alternative crops and the techniques needed to make them profitable are under research and development at universities, private organizations, and government agriculture stations throughout Appalachia. Pharmaceuticals and bioengineering are areas of research that offer additional alternatives to Appalachian farmers. For example, scientists at Virginia Polytechnic Institute and State University in Blacksburg hold a patent on a process to produce a human enzyme in tobacco plants and have developed the soybean cultivar Vanatto, which is grown in Virginia and exported to Asia for human consumption.

As Appalachian farmers move into the twenty-first century, the search for alternative crops, both old and new, will continue to play a significant role in establishing sustainable, competitive agriculture throughout the region.

See also: ALTERNATIVE FARMING; SUSTAINABLE AGRICULTURE.

—Troy Gowen, *East Tennessee State University*

James A. Duke, *Handbook of Alternative Cash Crops* (1993); James P. Shroyer, *Specialty and Non-Traditional Crops* (1987).

Alternative Farming

Because of Appalachia's geography, much of its agricultural economy throughout most of the twentieth century depended upon specialty products, niche crops, and nontraditional activities collectively known as alternative farming. The hilly terrain does not suit large-scale industrial farming, so countless farmers of the mountain region have had to discover unconventional ways to stay on their land, relying on creative alternatives such as aquaculture, organic growing, hydroponics, agroforestry, agritourism, and various ways of raising, processing, and direct-marketing crops. These alternatives are not unique to Appalachia, but many originated and have flourished in the region.

Though geography often imposes sharp limitations on agriculture, it also offers additional possibilities. Such is the case with aquaculture and agroforestry. Both techniques rely on using what is available. For aquaculture, the controlled growing of fish, mountain streams provide an ideal habitat, especially for trout but also for bass and catfish. All three of these species grow in channels or ponds throughout the region. Similarly, agroforestry takes advantage of mountain woodlands by cultivating crops normally found in the forest. These include many medicinal herbs, including ginseng, goldenseal, and black cohosh. Due to overharvesting of these wild medicinals, more and more pharmaceutical companies have sought farmers to grow them as crops. Other agroforestry crops include shiitake mushrooms (grown on shaded, inoculated oak logs), royal paulownia, and pawpaws.

A different approach is to create a controlled growing environment; such is the case with greenhouse and hydroponic production. Many farmers have created nurseries using greenhouses to provide seedling plants to customers. Others use their greenhouses to grow crops hydroponically (without soil). Tomatoes and strawberries, produced in the winter off-season, are two crops commonly grown this way.

As a result of heightened health consciousness and environmental awareness, organic agriculture has become the fastest-growing alternative farming technique in Appalachia and the nation. The practice excludes synthetic fertilizers, pesticides, and feed supplements. Instead, organic farmers use natural fertilizers such as manure and feathermeal, crop rotation, mulch, mechanical cultivation, and biological pest control (using beneficial plants and insects) to grow food in a way that harms the environment less than traditional farming. This method is currently used for products from blueberries to milk.

In addition to organic growing practices, many of the same farmers rely upon environmentally friendly marketing techniques, especially selling directly to consumers. Throughout Appalachia, the number of pick-your-own operations and farmers' markets has surged since 1980. Farmers have also found customers willing to buy food through mail order or on a subscription basis. For a set price, or "share," at the beginning of each season, such customers buy an agreed amount of produce, eggs, or meat. These "subscription" farms, falling under the rubric of community-supported agriculture, usually deliver their produce every week during the season. In the case of animals, customers order a specific number and the farmer raises and butchers them for a set fee.

One alternative farming technique that started in Appalachia is "pastured poultry." In the Shenandoah Valley of Virginia, Joel Salatin devised a different way of raising chickens and turkeys. The birds are kept in pens that are moved to fresh pasture every day. This saves the farmer about 30 percent in feed cost and improves the health of the animals. This method also fertilizes the pasture as the birds spread their own manure over it. The concept has been adapted to cattle, hog, and egg production. As in rotational grazing practiced in dairy and cattle operations, the animals are moved to different areas regularly to prevent overgrazing, thereby improving the overall health of the land.

In some Appalachian counties, nontraditional crops dominate the agricultural economy. Christmas trees, for example, thrive in the mountains and provide a major regional agricultural export. Other nontraditional crops include heirloom vegetable seeds for seed companies, exotic plants and animals such as emus, and rare species of domesticated animals.

To maintain their farms and lifestyle, some farmers rely on agritourism, marketing the farming "experience" as well as farm products. These farmers host tours or field days, often for schoolchildren, and charge admission. One of the most popular experiences is the fall festival, at which customers pick their own pumpkins, bob for apples, and go on a hayride. Agritourism can also involve the farm family's hosting guests in a style similar to a bed-and-breakfast, except that often the guests help with the daily chores.

To broaden their economic base, some farmers create value-added products. By doing so, the grower becomes both the producer as well as the processor of food. Usually after a large investment, farmers establish kitchens or similar facilities where they turn what they grow into a variety of ready-to-eat foods. Examples of these products include goat cheese, berry jams, and salsas.

All of these alternative farming techniques have allowed farmers to stay on their land and continue farming. As alternative agriculture continues to grow throughout Appalachia, it increasingly offers a model for standard practice.

See also: ALTERNATIVE CROPS; FISH FARMING; SUSTAINABLE AGRICULTURE.

—Jim Minick, *Radford University*

Robert Clark, ed., *Our Sustainable Table* (1990); U.S. Department of Agriculture, *Sustainable Agriculture: Definitions and Terms* (1994).

Appalachian Regional Office, U.S. Bureau of Agricultural Economics

The Appalachian Regional Office was a short-lived attempt by New Deal activists in the U.S. Bureau of Agricultural Economics (now defunct) to address a broad spectrum of related issues focused around small-scale farming in the mountain region. The office's most significant accomplishments were the Agriculture Department's 1935 survey of Appalachia and the heightening of region-specific discussion about land-use planning and the future of farming in Appalachia.

The U.S. Department of Agriculture created the Bureau of Agricultural Economics in 1922 and subsequently within that bureau the Appalachian Regional Office in 1929, although it was not formally named until 1934. One task of the Appalachian Regional Office was to coordinate research and writing for the first comprehensive social-science survey of Appalachia, which finally saw print in 1935 as *Economic and Social Problems and Conditions of the Southern Appalachians*.

The bureau's definition of Appalachia included 205 counties—15 more than were included in the next comprehensive social-science survey, *The Southern Appalachian Region: A Survey* (1962), edited by Thomas R. Ford of the University of Kentucky. Preparation of the 1935 volume was overseen by Lewis C. Gray, head of the bureau's Division of Land Economics and author of the authoritative two-volume *History of Agriculture in the Southern United States to 1860* (1933).

During the early 1930s, the Conference of Southern Mountain Workers, under the vigorous leadership of its executive secretary, Helen M. Dingham, kept tabs on preparatory work for the bureau's regional survey. Dingham tried to lure Gray and other officials to council meetings and tried to steer the bureau's survey toward a sociological perspective. Gray told Dingham, however, that he was "a hard-boiled economist" and was not a sociologist. The 1935 volume did encompass both viewpoints, but Gray's recommendations called for conversion of the land to public ownership and its utilization for public forests, parks, or game preserves. Gray concluded that economically rewarding jobs would remain scarce in the mountains even if the inhabitants were more educated; thus one way to depopulate the mountains was to educate their inhabitants, which would allow them to take advantage of opportunities outside the region.

The Appalachian Regional Office was headquartered in Washington, and it did little work in its own name until 1939. That year, the office conducted a major weeklong traveling conference designed to inform journalists, academics, state officials, and members of the general public about agricultural conditions in central Appalachia. With the help of a mile-by-mile, farm-by-farm guide, the 1939 traveling conference meticulously traversed more than two hundred miles through southeastern Kentucky and then entered east Tennessee for additional touring.

During World War II, the bureau provoked the ire of southern congressmen, partly because it was a hotbed of land-use planning, but also because it wanted wartime price controls to be set lower than many members of Congress desired. Federal land-use planning was totally prohibited by Congress by 1945, and this effectively abolished the Appalachian Regional Office.

In 1946 the chairman of the House Agricultural Appropriations Subcommittee, Congressman Malcolm C. Tarver of Georgia, alleged that a government report on the economic status of African American farmers in Mississippi written by a bureau employee had been inappropriately made public. Congress reacted by greatly reducing the bureau's operating budget and abolishing all of its regional offices, including the Appalachian one. The Bureau of Agricultural Economics ceased to exist in 1953 by order of Secretary of Agriculture Ezra Taft Benson. The sharply curtailed successor to the bureau is the Agricultural Marketing Service of the U.S. Department of Agriculture.

See also: AGRICULTURAL COOPERATIVES; APPALACHIAN REGIONAL COMMISSION (GOVERNMENT).

—Paul Salstrom, *Saint Mary-of-the-Woods College*

U.S. Department of Agriculture, Bureau of Agricultural Economics, *Economic and Social Problems and Conditions of the Southern Appalachians* (1935).

Apples

Appalachia is considered ideal for apple growing not only because of plentiful rainfall but also because of its thermal belts—areas on mountain slopes where temperature inversions ward off spring frosts. Apple growing has not always been widely practiced in the mountains, however, and is largely a twentieth-century horticultural undertaking for much of the region. In fact, by the early 1850s apple cultivation was so poor in many parts of Appalachia that one observer complained that mountaineers grew only one variety—the horse apple. Urban areas in southern Appalachia were supplied largely with apples from northern growers, who did not think that the fruit could be grown as a market crop in the South.

In the mid-1800s, Jarvis Van Buren founded the Georgia Pomological Society, an organization that sought to locate, name, and classify desirable apple varieties as well as seek new cultivation methods and promote apple growing in southern Appalachia. By the early 1860s, many areas in southern Appalachia had completely lost their dependence on the Northeast for apples, due largely to the efforts of Van Buren and others. By the late 1800s, commercial apple orchards could be found from northeast Alabama to New York. Orchard owners across the region expanded production, adding cold-storage houses and diversifying crops to ensure longer growing seasons.

By 1930 there were as many as five thousand fruit farms in the Appalachian region, with apples making up the greatest part of overall fruit production. According to a U.S. Department of Agriculture annual report, commercial orchards were both the largest farms in the region, leading in both total land area and crop acreage, and the most highly valued, exceeding the economic worth of all other farm types. The Shady Valley Apple Orchard in Shady Valley, Tennessee, near the southwest Virginia border, was one of the more prominent commercial orchards in the mountains, claiming more than 275 acres of trees.

By the end of the Great Depression, apples had become so central to the diet of the mountaineer that they were included in nearly every meal. Apples were baked, dried, made into juice, and consumed in the form of apple sauce, dessert pies, dumplings, jellies, jams, stack cakes, hard cider, and homemade vinegar.

The region's contemporary apple industry is a multimillion-dollar enterprise largely concentrated in select growing areas in New York, West Virginia, northern Georgia, western North Carolina, and southwest Virginia. Although many of the older apple varieties have been lost due to neglect or commercial monoculture, a few private growers across the region are attempting to bring back heirloom apple varieties. Because of these important efforts, heirloom apple trees are once again available in nursery catalogs.

See also: ALTERNATIVE CROPS; HEIRLOOM FRUITS AND VEGETABLES.

—Donald E. Davis, *Dalton State College*

Creighton Lee Calhoun, *Old Southern Apples* (1995); Donald Edward Davis, *Where There Are Mountains: An Environmental History of the Southern Appalachians* (2000); Samuel B. Hilliard, *Atlas of Antebellum Agriculture* (1986).

Bee Keeping

In the late eighteenth and early nineteenth centuries, when Appalachia was America's first western frontier, honey (along with sorghum molasses and maple syrup) was the most common sweetener in most households. Within the region, particularly in rural frontier areas, granulated sugar was often not available, and honey proved a convenient sweetener. Since honey does not spoil, it can be stored indefinitely in a sealed container. If the natural and harmless process of granulation does begin, honey is easily restored to a liquid state by slowly heating its container in hot water.

As recently as the mid-twentieth century, most family farms in the Appalachians kept active beehives. The honey they produced was consumed at home, given to friends and family, or sold, often at roadside stands. Even when it was no longer necessary as a source of food or income, bee keeping was a time-honored tradition and remained a widely practiced hobby throughout the region.

It was estimated that at the close of the twentieth century more than two hundred thousand people nationwide kept active beehives, which pollinated crops worth up to $10 billion and produced approximately $150 million in honey sales each year. Production was increasing during this period, with national output rising more than 8 percent from 1997 to 2000. According to National Honey Board data, the Appalachian region supplied 8 to 10 percent of the national total in 2000. However, while honey production was on the rise nationally (in the West and Midwest in particular), bee keeping throughout much of Appalachia declined.

Of the top ten honey-producing states in 2000 none were in Appalachia. In nearly all parts of the region, honey production declined throughout the 1980s and 1990s. One of the most notable declines occurred in West Virginia, where output dropped about 60 percent over the course of the 1990s. A number of factors contributed to the decline: the tradition is no longer routinely passed to succeeding generations; landowners are less inclined to consider bee keeping as "recreational farming"; small farms are being lost to urbanization; a federal honey subsidy was eliminated; tracheal mites (which infect air tubes), varroa mites (which destroy bee larvae), and other afflictions struck productive colonies; and publicity about aggressive African bees' arrival in the United States created fears, even though these bees have not been found in Appalachia.

Bee keeping plays a vital role in the pollination of crops. A typical hive consisting of twenty thousand to sixty thousand bees will visit a quarter of a million flowers in a single day during peak gathering season. Three different types of bees are found within a hive: a queen, drones, and workers. A single queen is responsible for laying all the eggs, which as many as several hundred male drones fertilize. The rest of the hive consists of thousands of female workers. Workers perform various duties, including defending against attack and tending the hive, but the primary function is gathering pollen, the raw material for making honey. Bees must visit some two million flowers to produce a single pound of honey.

The color, flavor, and texture of honey depend upon the type of flower worked by the bees as well as geographic and climatic factors. In Appalachia, clover honey is prevalent. Other common sources include sourwood trees in southern Appalachia, buckwheat in Pennsylvania, Ohio, and New York, and, to a lesser extent, basswood and tulip poplar. Bees also work a huge variety of other flowering trees and plants in addition to the varieties that may be prevalent in a given geographic area.

To provide consistency in color and taste, large-scale commercial honey producers often blend different varieties (clover and sourwood, for instance) together. Also, most honey found in retail outlets is commercially heat processed and either filtered (to remove pollen) or strained (which leaves the pollen and is sold as "raw honey"). Honey is usually not pasteurized, as it is naturally very low in bacteria and microbes. In fact, honey is such a strong inhibitor of microbial growth that it has been used to treat wounds.

See also: ALTERNATIVE FARMING; SUSTAINABLE AGRICULTURE; SWEETENERS (FOOD AND COOKING).

—Barry Donald Mowell, *Broward Community College*

Walter T. Kelley, *How to Keep Bees and Sell Honey* (1992); Roger A. Morse and Kim Flottum, *The ABC and XYZ of Bee Culture* (1990); Penn State Cooperative Extension, *Fundamentals of Beekeeping* (2000).

Cattle

The first settlers in Appalachia brought cattle with them, and America's first western frontier eventually became its first large-scale cattle-producing region. Pioneers and their herds paved the way for future settlers as they encroached on the foothills and valleys of the region, eager to utilize the abundant grasses and clover. By the early eighteenth century, herders had traversed the Blue Ridge Mountains and later continued moving westward into the Ohio Valley and beyond. Large herds of fattened cattle would be driven south and east to major coastal markets in Baltimore, New York City, Charleston, South Carolina, and Augusta, Georgia. Though Appalachia remained important, the focal point of the nation's cattle industry had permanently shifted westward by the time of the Civil War.

Until the mid-twentieth century, even small family farms in Appalachia were characterized by at least some dairy and beef cattle, and many people who inherit family farms still opt to keep some cattle on the property in order to "keep the pasture clean." This phenomenon of recreational, or "weekend," cattle farming is more prevalent in most parts of Appalachia than are larger-scale or full-time cattle operations. At the beginning of the twenty-first century, virtually all counties in the Appalachian region still included the cattle industry as a part of their economy. According to the U.S. Department of Agriculture, cattle and calves comprised between 15 and 50 percent of the value of all agricultural products sold throughout Appalachia, and nearly one-half of the region's farmland was devoted to pasturing.

But while cattle farming remains important within Appalachia, the region's role in beef and dairy production declined in the latter half of the twentieth century. The scale of cattle farms and the size of herds in Appalachia are typically smaller than the cattle operations of the western United States. According to data released by the National Agricultural Statistics Service, farms with two hundred or more cattle are concentrated mainly in the midwestern states, from the Dakotas south to Texas.

The U.S. beef cow inventory dropped from nearly 47 million head in 1975 to around 34 million head in 2000, and Appalachia followed this trend. A number of factors were responsible for the decline, including a significant decrease in beef consumption coupled with low market prices. Although the figures still represent an overall decline since 1975, the years between 1992 and 1997 were witness to a brief growth in beef cattle numbers with a national increase of about 1.5 million head. Most areas of the Appalachian region also experienced a corresponding increase in beef cattle inventories, with West Virginia, Pennsylvania, and New York being exceptions.

Preferred breeds of beef cattle in the Appalachian region are Herefords (first brought to the United States in 1817 by Kentuckian Henry Clay), Angus, and Charolais. Herefords are a popular breed due to their hardiness and their ability to put on weight rapidly, Angus due to their well-marbled meat, and Charolais because of the breed's lean beef.

Within the Appalachian region, beef cattle production is primarily concentrated in Kentucky, North Carolina, Tennessee, and Virginia. While beef cattle play some role in their agricultural economy, northern areas of Appalachia remain a focal point for the dairy industry. New York, Pennsylvania, and Maryland boast the major share of Appalachia's dairy cattle. All three states have historically served as leading suppliers of dairy products to the urban areas along the upper Atlantic seaboard, and as the population of this region has increased, so has dairy output.

Fraser firs on a Christmas tree farm in Alleghany County, North Carolina, 1995. Christmas trees are raised and harvested throughout Appalachia, but farms in western North Carolina are the leading producers in the industry.

The increase in beef cattle herds in recent years contrasts with a national and regional decline in the number of milk cows, which underwent a 9 percent drop from 1989 to 1998. In the last decade of the century, herd inventories declined, but milk output per cow increased some 20 percent, allowing dairy farmers to keep pace with growing populations. The only areas of Appalachia to have experienced an increase in net dairy cow inventory during that decade are certain localized areas in western New York and central Pennsylvania, with cattle operations in virtually all other locales of the region witnessing inventory decline.

The 1997 agricultural census revealed that of farms with a hundred or more milk cows, New York and Pennsylvania were the clear leaders, with the number and concentration of large-scale dairying operations declining dramatically farther south. The significance of dairy products to the overall agricultural economy is greater in northern Appalachia as well. From northern Virginia to Pennsylvania and New York, between 40 and 60 percent of all agricultural income is derived from the dairy industry.

See also: DAIRY FARMS; SUBSISTENCE FARMING.

—Barry Donald Mowell, *Broward Community College*

Jimmy M. Skaggs, *Prime Cut: Livestock Raising and Meatpacking in the United States, 1607–1983* (1986).

Christmas Tree Farming

About seven million Christmas trees are harvested from Appalachian farms from New York to Mississippi every fall and shipped to points throughout the United States and to markets overseas. This total represents almost 20 percent of the trees purchased by American households.

The production of Christmas trees in Appalachia, like many farm-based industries, developed gradually. At first, rural families harvested naturally occurring trees for their own use, selecting individual trees from such species as white pine, hemlock, balsam fir, red spruce, and Fraser fir. After World War II, many families in the region began to explore alternatives to traditional farm crops in an effort to provide sufficient and stable incomes. Soon, a small industry arose from the harvesting of trees from natural stands and selling those trees in the more populated cities of the region.

By the mid-1950s, a number of individuals began planting, managing, harvesting, and selling trees on a larger scale. As a result, about 90 percent of harvested trees are grown today on plantations established for that purpose. At the turn of the century, about fifty-five thousand acres of plantations were being managed by owners ranging from weekend farmers to commercial nurseries.

The major species in the southern Appalachians is the Fraser fir, named for Scottish naturalist John Fraser. Fraser firs are found in seven or eight (depending on classification) somewhat isolated, high-elevation stands from Mount Rogers in southwestern Virginia to Clingman's Dome in the Great Smoky Mountains. The balsam fir has historically been the most popular species grown in the northeastern United States. It has a wide geographic range across the eastern United States and Canada and includes a taxonomic variety known as the Canaan fir, found in West Virginia. Several other species, including white pine, hemlock, and even the non-native Douglas fir, are also planted for Christmas tree production, but Fraser and balsam firs are the most popular.

While Christmas trees are grown throughout the Appalachians, the major Christmas tree production area is the western region of North Carolina. This area of high-elevation mountainous terrain produces about 5.5 million trees each year. Significant numbers of wreaths are also produced, as are garlands, known locally as roping. Together, these value-added products account for 10 to 15 percent of the total evergreen sales of the region.

To many, Christmas trees may only be only important for two or three weeks of the year. But in the Appalachian Mountains, Christmas trees are a major part of the local economic structure and provide a stable, continuing income from the land.

See also: ALTERNATIVE CROPS; PART-TIME FARMING; SUSTAINABLE AGRICULTURE.

—Craig R. McKinley, *Oklahoma State University*

John Frampton, "Relationship among the Appalachian Firs," *Limbs and Needles* (Spring 1997); Craig R. McKinley, "Christmas Tree Species for the South," in *Forest Landowner Manual* (31st edition, 1997).

Conservation

See Sustainable Agriculture

Corn

Corn has been part of the landscape of the southern Appalachian region for centuries. Myths, legends, and ceremonies reflect the prominence of corn in Native American society, and the crop was a major food source for pioneer settlers and their livestock. Early settlers bartered corn as currency, crafted it into useful and decorative objects, and made it the basic ingredient for a potent drink called moonshine. In the nineteenth and twentieth centuries, its dominance as a major agricultural crop declined in the region, but corn refined by highly technical processes appears in a multitude of everyday products ranging from snack foods to paper and textile products to fuel additives.

Botanists and archaeologists believe corn, or maize, to be a variety of teosinte, a wild grass that grows in the foothills and highlands of Mexico and Guatemala. Corn was first successfully cultivated between four thousand and five thousand years ago by the Incan, Mayan, and Aztec civilizations of Central and South America and spread gradually throughout the Western Hemisphere, reaching Native American populations of the southeastern United States around A.D. 1300. Tribes such as the Cherokee cultivated the river bottoms that provided rich soil ideal for growing corn. Native Americans revered the corn plant. In addition to creating myths and legends to explain its origin, they celebrated the growing of corn through seasonal ceremonies. The annual Green Corn Ceremony of the Cherokee coincided with the ripening of late corn in the fall, and the rite served as an expression of thanksgiving for a successful crop.

During the eighteenth century, European settlers in the Appalachians readily adopted Native American practices for the cultivation of this indigenous plant. Corn rapidly became the mainstay of southern Appalachian farming, not only providing food for the pioneers and their livestock, but also serving as a standard by which to measure the exchange value of trade goods. One early-eighteenth-century exchange rate listed a pistol as being worth 120 bushels of corn. A calico petticoat was valued at 84 bushels, and a broad hoe could be purchased for 30.

Inadequate and rugged transportation routes forced frontier settlers to look for more efficient ways to transport the bulky harvested grain. One method was to feed corn to livestock, especially hogs. Fattened hogs could then be herded to distant markets over drover routes that had developed throughout the southern mountains. Farmers supplied corn for livestock feed to be sold to owners of stands along the roads. This corn-based livestock trade linked many mountain families to an outside economy, providing them a little cash for goods not produced on the farm.

Another method of reducing the bulky crop was to distill it into whiskey or moonshine. While Native Americans did not develop a distilling process, Europeans had distilled grains for centuries and found it easy to apply their techniques to corn. In the late 1700s, however, the federal government began to tax homemade whiskey in order to help cover the costs of the Revolutionary War. That decision initiated an ongoing struggle between federal revenuers, the agents assigned to collect the tax, and mountain farmers, who resisted the tax as a serious threat to the economic survival of their families. In 1794 President George Washington sent federal troops to put down riots against the tax during western Pennsylvania's Whiskey Rebellion.

Corn also provided the occasion for social community gatherings. Husking bees brought neighbors together to socialize while they helped each other with their labors. When work was completed, music and dancing commenced, accompanied by the occasional tasting of corn whiskey to cool parched throats.

During the nineteenth and twentieth centuries, several factors altered the dominant role of corn in the southern Appalachian region. Destruction of farmland and livestock during the Civil War, the subsequent arrival of railroads and extractive industries, and severe erosion caused by years of growing corn on steep hillsides removed large amounts of cropland from agricultural use. During the Great Depression, federal farm programs began to emphasize the growing of other cash crops such as tobacco and hay in the region. Finally, the development of insecticides and other chemicals, modern equipment, and hybrid corn varieties led to the growth of the Midwest as the major corn-producing region of the United States.

Nevertheless, corn remains an important and enduring part of southern mountain life. Every spring, cornfields sprout in newly plowed valleys, along river and creek bottoms, and in home gardens. Local mills continue to produce small quantities of stone-ground cornmeal, a much sought-after item for flavorful corn bread. Cherokee flour corn, a descendant strain of maize called Harinoso de Ocho that is native to northwestern Mexico, is grown each year by some members of the Eastern Band of Cherokee Indians. And each fall, the Green Corn Dance is again performed in communities on the Cherokee reservation to celebrate another successful season of corn.

See also: MOONSHINE (FOOD AND COOKING); NATIVE AMERICAN AGRICULTURE.

—Suzanne Hill McDowell, *Western Carolina University*

Jose Barreiro, ed., *Indian Corn of the Americas: Gift to the World* (1989); Betty Fussell, *The Story of Corn: The Myths and History, the Culture and Agriculture, the Art and Science of America's Quintessential Crop* (1992); Nicholas P. Hardeman, *Shucks, Shocks, and Hominy Blocks: Corn as a Way of Life in Pioneer America* (1981); Charles M. Hudson, *The Southeastern Indians* (1976).

Cotton

Cotton is produced across most of the southern United States but has never been a major crop for most of Appalachia. The region's steep terrain and cool climate are generally not suited for cotton production. As James Watt Raine wrote of Appalachia, "[P]arts of it are so steep that the only safe plan is to hoe the row from the bench up to the next cliff, then slither down and climb up the next row."

Unsuccessful attempts to grow cotton on marginal land in the late 1800s and early 1900s prompted farmers to try other crops. Appalachian farming families were not set up to produce crops that required a high acreage and large labor force, and the soils in the mountainous regions proved to be better suited for producing fruit. Shortly before the twentieth century began, cotton farmers in Jefferson County, Alabama, produced one bale of cotton lint for every fifty-six acres planted. For that reason, many families concentrated on making a living through smaller, home-based enterprises. Since row crops would not support most families, farmers moved to the newly formed jobs in mines and foundries.

While most farmers in the highlands of southern Appalachia have historically avoided cotton, many counties across northern Alabama and Mississippi and northwestern Georgia still successfully produce the crop. Cotton acreage reached a fairly high level in those counties during the 1950s but had decreased significantly by 1972. Higher cotton prices resulted in increased acreage again in the early 1990s. The best cotton fields in these counties are located in river bottoms and valleys and are characteristically productive and well drained. The warmer temperatures and later frost dates in those areas enable cotton to survive and produce profitable yields.

See also: ALTERNATIVE CROPS.

—C. Dale Monks, *Auburn University*

Emmett M. Essin III, *Appalachia: Family Traditions in Transition* (1975); James Watt Raine, *The Land of Saddle-Bags* (1924); William Sumner Rutledge, *An Economic and Social History of Ante-Bellum Jefferson County, Alabama* (1939).

Dairy Farms

Modern dairy farming in Appalachia evolved from subsistence agriculture to small commercial operations now threatened by giant producers and factory farms concentrated in states outside the region. Environmental restrictions, including curbs on agricultural wastewater, increased the financial burden on already struggling mountain dairy farms in the late twentieth century. But the history of Appalachian dairy farming has always been a story of survival.

Settlers in the region brought a legacy of dairy farming from Europe, and on the frontier dairy cows were an essential part of every subsistence farm. By the mid-seventeenth century, dairying along the East Coast was a flourishing farm industry. Cattle importation from Europe continued throughout the colonial period. Herds that arrived in Pennsylvania and surrounding areas were a mixture of breeds from Sweden and the Netherlands. Settlers brought their cattle with them as they pushed westward from the coast, and many times the movement to the frontier was for the purpose of finding more room for cattle. By the early eighteenth century, the influx of dairy herds into the Shenandoah Valley made cattle raising an important industry in the region. About 1795, the first cattle were taken from Virginia into the Ohio Valley.

The processing of most dairy products was done on the farm—in the kitchen in the case of families who owned one or two cows. Cows were milked by hand, and the milk was poured into pans or tubs to allow the cream to rise. Settlers cooled milk by placing it in a cellar or springhouse or lowering it into the family's well. As interest in livestock breeding increased, small farmers in Appalachia preferred to breed cattle for both milk and beef potential. Among cattle breeds, small farmers preferred Shorthorns, introduced from northeastern England in 1783, and Herefords, first imported from England in 1817 by Kentuckian Henry Clay. Although their milk did not match the richness of that from Jersey or Guernsey cows, a Shorthorn or Hereford could be milked, butchered, or sold.

Secondary milk products consisted primarily of butter churned for home use and barter. Cheese making became important in the valley region of central Appalachia, but it was uncommon in most of the southern Appalachians. The demand of rapidly growing eastern cities for fresh milk spurred the move of the butter and cheese industry to other parts of the country. Established butter and cheese regions of the East realized that greater profits lay in the production of fresh milk. As railroads made it possible to bring milk to the cities from an ever widening area, traditional butter and cheese makers converted to fluid milk production. New York dominated butter production from colonial days until about 1880.

Dairy cows caused significant health hazards for Appalachian farmers in the eighteenth and nineteenth centuries. Free-ranging cattle would sometimes consume toxic white snakeroot, which caused milk sickness in persons who consumed milk and dairy products from the contaminated animals. The malady appeared annually from July until the onset of winter. Symptoms began with weakness, nausea, and vomiting, and death could occur in two to ten days. In the worst cases, some communities lost one-quarter to one-half of their residents. Abraham Lincoln's mother is believed to have died of milk sickness in 1818, but it was not until 1906 that snakeroot and goldenrod were proven to be the sources of the illness.

In the 1930s, nearly all U.S. farms had one or more milk cows to provide milk for family consumption. Only about 14 percent of these farms were commercial dairy operations. But technological achievements drastically altered the nature of the American dairy industry and the future of small farms. Improvements in feed and milking processes have increased production efficiency and the minimum size of an economically feasible dairy farm. Genetic improvements have helped increase milk production per cow.

The number of dairy farms in the United States began declining after World War II. By 1987, only about 9.7 percent of all U.S. farms had milk cows, down from 76 percent in 1940. Several factors have caused a decline in Appalachian dairies. Increased demand for locally produced milk in areas of population expansion and cost incentives associated with milder climates encouraged the growth of very large specialized dairies in California, Arizona, New Mexico, Texas, and Florida. Moreover, the costs involved in meeting stricter environmental regulations made it impossible for many Appalachian dairy farmers to stay in business. Among the chief causes of higher environmental costs was a 1969 U.S. Department of Agriculture designation of waste from dairy operations as a major pollutant. The 1990 Farm Act, which created new water-quality programs, and additional state waste-management laws further increased pressure on mountain dairies. New facilities required for waste disposal, drainage, and shelter added more expense than many farmers could afford.

The new millennium began on a grim note for Appalachian dairy farmers. A precipitous drop in milk prices left some facing financial ruin. Rising production in the West lowered the minimum price of milk to $9.63 per one hundred pounds, a drop of more than $6.00 since September 1999. Prices had not been so low since 1978. In January 2000, the U.S. Department of Agriculture began distributing $125 million in direct cash payments to dairy farmers hurt by low prices. Farmers signed up for the Dairy Market Loss Assistance program, which provided payments based on a farm's milk production in 1997 and 1998. Additionally, many eastern farmers have favored federally authorized state compacts that set prices above the federal minimum.

See also: CATTLE; SUBSISTENCE FARMING.

—Karl Rohr, *Western Carolina University*

Paul Salstrom, *Appalachia's Path to Dependency: Rethinking a Region's Economic History, 1730–1940* (1994); John T. Schlebecker, *Whereby We Thrive: A History of American Farming, 1607 to 1972* (1975); Ralph Selitzer, *The Dairy Industry in America* (1976); U.S. Department of Agriculture, *Changing Structure of U.S. Dairy Farms* (1994).

Farmers Federation

The Farmers Federation was a Rochdale-style agricultural cooperative that organized markets, tested new farm products, and improved breeding stock for farmers in the Asheville area of western North Carolina during the first half of the twentieth century. The federation was founded in 1920 by James Gore King McClure Jr. (1884–1956), a Presbyterian minister from Illinois. Attracted to Asheville for reasons of health, he abandoned his ministry to work to improve the lot of struggling mountain farmers.

Farmers bought stock in the federation, which entitled them to vote on its affairs, buy from the cooperative store (earning an annual rebate based on the amount of their purchases), and sell their crops to its marketing arm. McClure won the support of influential patrons such as Mrs. George W. Vanderbilt and Edwin Wiley Grove for his 1927 Educational and Development Fund (later the James G. K. McClure Educational and Development Fund), established to "help the mountain farmer to help himself." The federation responded to the Great Depression by expanding into western North Carolina counties and creating a training school, a cannery, a dairy, poultry hatcheries, burley tobacco warehouses, and a Lord's Acre Plan, under which farmers planted an acre in crops for the benefit of rural churches.

Having survived the depression, the federation ironically collapsed during American postwar prosperity.

Dissident stockholders who accused federation leaders of negotiating a sweetheart deal for themselves blocked a 1959 merger with a larger North Carolina cooperative, and McClure's nephew and successor as president, James McClure Clarke, was forced to resign. After Clarke won a bitter court battle over ownership of the Education and Development Fund, the federation disbanded in 1963.

See also: AGRICULTURAL COOPERATIVES.

—H. Tyler Blethen, *Western Carolina University*

Farmers' Markets

Farmers' markets are an important outlet for small to medium-sized agricultural producers in Appalachia. While these farmers generally cannot compete with large industrial operations in selling to supermarkets, restaurant chains, and other national consumers, they can usually make a profit at local and regional farmers' markets. Because they have direct access to consumers, farmers can keep prices low and maintain a higher profit margin by eliminating middlemen. Additionally, farmers have more leeway to experiment with techniques such as organic farming and are free to develop heirloom fruits and vegetables. For many small-farm operators, farmers' markets are the primary source of farm income.

Farmers' markets are popular in local communities for many reasons. Since most produce at farmers' markets is harvested within twenty-four hours of sale, consumers have access to fresh food. Prices are on average lower than supermarket prices, and there is a wider variety of produce available. Personal contact with the grower may give consumers confidence in the quality and wholesomeness of the produce, and they may feel that their purchases are directly benefiting the local community rather than an impersonal corporation.

Historically, Appalachians have bartered with neighbors, often specializing in one type of domesticated animal or produce to trade for items not provided by subsistence farming. Early markets were primarily for livestock trade: cattle, both dairy and meat; hogs; goats and sheep; and poultry such as ducks, geese, and chickens. As regularly attended marketplaces became established, a wider variety of goods became available for purchase. Besides produce, merchants and craftsmen offered merchandise such as guns, knives, tools, hunting and working dogs, fighting birds, and crafted items not easily made on the farm.

As the population of Appalachia increased and communities grew into cities, more nonfarmers attended these markets. The addition of motorized trucks allowed farmers to haul larger amounts to more distant markets, thus increasing the significance of farmers' market income to individual farms. While the region has become more urbanized, markets have evolved from trading venues for farmers and supplemental resources for subsistence-based communities into markets catering mostly to nonfarming consumers.

The general trend toward organizing farmers' markets has been recognized and encouraged by governmental agencies, beginning in the early 1990s. As part of marketing strategies to support sustainable small farm operations, the U.S. Department of Agriculture has developed guidelines and procedures for establishing and operating farmers' markets and cooperates with state, local, and tribal governments, universities, farmers' groups, and private parties in coordinating these efforts. One example of this involvement is the requirement at department-sponsored farmers' markets that vendors participate in a food-gleaning program in lieu of entrance fees. At the close of each market day, vendors donate surplus produce to be distributed to nonprofit feeding and sheltering organizations.

With the exception of Virginia, all Appalachian states and the Mississippi Band of Choctaw Indians participate in the federal Farmers' Market Nutrition Program, in which low-income residents may qualify to purchase fresh produce from farmers' markets with food vouchers. Formally established in 1992, this nationwide program encourages the region's low-income families to eat nutritious foods while providing incidental economic aid to growers who sell through farmers' markets.

Among notable farmers' markets are the Western North Carolina Farmers' Market at Asheville, first opened in 1977, and the Lexington Farmers' Market in Kentucky, which has been operating since 1972. The Asheville market is a large, state-sponsored market attracting hundreds, at times thousands, of visitors daily. Farmers' markets operate in nearly a dozen locations throughout the city of Pittsburgh. Many of these urban farmers' markets offer much more than fruits and vegetables; patrons can find items such as meats, cheeses, baked goods, wines, honey, jams, jellies, and preserves. Some, such as the Asheville market, have associated nurseries where customers can buy plants, flowers, and gardening items, and markets throughout the region often host local musicians, performers, and handcrafting demonstrations.

After decades of increasing consolidation and industrialization of produce farming and marketing operations in the United States, consumers are showing a rapidly growing interest at the beginning of the twenty-first century in buying farm products directly from growers. The Department of Agriculture recognized more than eight hundred farmers' markets active in 2002 throughout Appalachia. This reflects the national trend in which the number of markets nationwide increased 63 percent during the years from 1994 to 2000 and supports the claim that farmers' markets are meeting the needs of consumers and small farmers alike.

See also: HEIRLOOM FRUITS AND VEGETABLES; SUSTAINABLE AGRICULTURE.

—Bill Best, *Berea College*

Vance Corum, *The New Farmers' Market: Farm-Fresh Ideas for Producers, Managers and Communities* (2001); Jeff W. Ishee, *Dynamic Farmers' Marketing: A Guide to Successfully Selling Your Farmers' Market Products* (1997); Deborah Madison, *Local Flavors: Cooking and Eating from American's Farmers' Markets* (2002).

Fence Laws

A common right to unenclosed land was an important foundation of Appalachian agriculture before the Civil War. The theory of common rights was drawn from English common law, which held that individuals had a right to graze their livestock, hunt, or fish on unfenced land regardless of ownership. This theory was transplanted to the southern colonial frontier and became an important component of the society and economy of the region.

By the late eighteenth century, common rights to unenclosed land dictated the methods of production in the mountains. Due to the rural nature of life in the region, farmers simply turned their hogs, sheep, and cattle out to forage rather than fencing them in a pasture. Following the English tradition, the fencing burden was placed on the landowner, not the stockowner. In order to collect damages from a stockowner, landowners had to build and maintain fences of specific dimensions around all cultivated fields. Fencing was expensive and time-consuming; as a result, most farmers did not fence their land.

Population growth and a transition from subsistence to market agriculture created tensions over common rights. As the population increased and new economic enterprises entered the region, more people began to call for an end to the open range, a phenomenon mirrored across rural America. Beginning shortly after the Civil War, state legislatures, particularly in the South, began to consider laws that would place the fencing burden on stockowners. Residents in valley towns favored such laws, while mountain farmers, faced with increasingly difficult economic times, did not. In Buncombe County, North Carolina, fence laws pitted rural farmers against tourism developers from Asheville. Developers hoped to eradicate what they saw as a primitive practice that damaged visitor perceptions of the region, while farmers sought to preserve the open range. Throughout Appalachia, the question of fence laws usually reflected tensions between rural and urban dwellers in a community. Such differences often led farmers to join the Populist Party, whose candidates promised to protect them from fence laws and other attacks on the farmer's way of life. This resistance proved futile. By the 1890s, all Appalachian states had passed some type of fence law, forever changing the nature of mountain agriculture.

See also: AGRICULTURAL FRONTIERS.

—Richard D. Starnes, *Western Carolina University*

Steven Hahn, *The Roots of Southern Populism: Yeoman Farmers and the Transformation of the Georgia Upcountry, 1850–1890* (1983); Shawn Everett Kantor, *Politics and Property Rights: The Closing of the Open Range in the Postbellum South* (1998).

Fish Farming

Fish farming, or aquaculture, emerged as an important industry in some areas of Appalachia during the latter decades of the twentieth century. Scientifically managed operations play a major role in sustaining fish populations in threatened and overfished streams and in providing nutritious and inexpensive food for increasingly health-conscious consumers. Because fish can be intensively raised in relatively small areas and yield a much higher percentage of marketable product than other crops, they are a particularly attractive alternative in Appalachia.

Trout and similar native cold-water fish are readily produced in the spring-fed mountain streams of New York, Pennsylvania, Virginia, West Virginia, Tennessee, North Carolina, and Georgia. According to the U.S. Department of Agriculture, these states accounted for more than $13 million in sales of food-sized trout in 2001. Native species such as the channel catfish thrive in pond environments of Tennessee, Alabama, and Mississippi, where they are harvested not only for southern consumers, but also for a vastly expanded national market. Ponds, streams, and lakes are stocked with cultivated bass, bream, and other native and improved species for sport fishing. A few non-native species are raised in closed tank systems in which conditions can be carefully regulated. Several species of tilapia, for

The Cantrell Creek Trout Farm and Hatchery, near Brevard, North Carolina, 1999. Cold-water native fish such as the rainbow trout raised at Cantrell Creek are frequently used to restock lakes, streams, and ponds in the region, providing farmers with an alternative cash crop on a year-round basis.

example, are being successfully grown in tank systems in order to supply restaurants and grocery stores because release of these non-native species into streams and lakes is prohibited in most states.

A few non-fish aquatic species are also farmed. Among these are crayfish, mussels, clams, and water plants such as cress. No saltwater fish are cultivated except for a few ornamental species raised on a small scale in carefully controlled environments. Aquatic species are sometimes grown in aquaponic systems together with terrestrial plants. Aquaponics is a method of raising two or more crops simultaneously, one of which is an aquatic animal. Cucumbers, tomatoes, and similar vegetables may be irrigated with the wastewater from fish farms.

Fish farming typically involves artificial hatching methods. Mated pairs of mature broodfish are placed in special pens or ponds equipped with spawning containers to promote egg laying and fertilization. The egg masses may be moved from the spawning area for artificial hatching in incubators, and the tiny fry reared to stocking size in tanks and small ponds free of predators. Young fish are stocked in water appropriate to the species and provided a complete nutritional diet. Several manufacturers market commercial feeds that meet the needs of fish at various stages of maturity. Disease can be a problem among fish, especially in densely populated systems, and some species of fish are sensitive to stress, which can also lead to physical ailments.

Early efforts at fish farming were at state-funded hatcheries established to enhance stocks of native fish being depleted through sport and commercial fishing in Appalachian streams and lakes. Stock enhancement is still one of the primary purposes of fish farming in the region, especially for trout, which are released annually into Appalachian waters to ensure perpetuation of the species.

Economic returns from fish farming focus on fish sold for food and those used for recreational purposes, while a few producers cultivate exotic and ornamental species often used in home aquaria. The channels through which food fish are marketed vary from large-scale operations that utilize automated processing plants to on-site farms that sell live fish. In some cases, small producers market ready-to-cook fish to local restaurants. Recreational marketing involves charging a fee for fishing in stocked lakes or ponds. These types of facilities are popular throughout Appalachia. Generally, for a per-pound fee, a sport fisher can catch quality trout in a pleasant setting without a state fishing license. Some of these facilities provide cleaning and icing services for customers.

Many Appalachian high schools offer educational programs in aquaculture, both for in-school and adult students. Instruction is provided in a variety of cultivation techniques involving tanks, ponds, and other types of facilities. Mineral County Vocational Center in Keyser, West Virginia, offers a program that provides hands-on experience with both native and introduced fish species. The purpose of these educational programs is to provide fish stock for release in local streams rather than for commercial resale.

See also: ALTERNATIVE CROPS; ALTERNATIVE FARMING; SUSTAINABLE AGRICULTURE.

—Jasper S. Lee, *Lee and Associates*

Jasper S. Lee and Michael E. Newman, *Aquaculture: An Introduction* (1997); B. L. Nerrie, *Aquaculture, Fishing, and Other Income Opportunities from Aquatic Systems* (1990); Robert R. Stickney, ed., *Encyclopedia of Aquaculture* (2000).

Forages

Forage crops grown for livestock feed fall into two distinct categories: grasses and legumes. Besides furnishing animal feed, forages play an important role in conserving the environment in Appalachia. Because most of the farmland in the region is sloping and highly erodible, forages, either in permanent pastures on the steepest land or in rotational meadows on gentler slopes, protect the land from erosion. Many forage species are also used for lawns and turf.

More than fifty species of forage grasses and legumes can be grown in the region. They include annuals (which live one year), biennials (which live two years), and perennials (which live more than two years). The annuals consist of summer crops such as sorghum-Sudan hybrids, Sudan grass, millet, and winter crops, including rye grass and hairy vetch. Of the perennial forages, two grasses (tall fescue and Kentucky bluegrass) and two clovers (white/ladino and red) occupy the majority of acreage in Appalachia. These are cool-season species; most of their growth occurs during spring and fall. Growth during summer, especially in July and August, is drastically reduced. Plants are usually dormant during winter months.

Tall fescue (*Festuca arundinacea* Schreb), the most important cool-season grass in the United States, provides the primary ground cover on approximately 35 million acres nationally. Commonly referred to simply as fescue, this widely adapted, persistent grass is easy to establish, tolerant of a wide range of management practices, and produces good forage yields. Nutritionally, tall fescue compares favorably with many other grasses.

Tall fescue was discovered and identified in 1931 in a hillside pasture on the W. M. Suiter farm in Menifee County, Kentucky, by E. N. Fergus of the University of Kentucky. Kentucky 31 tall fescue was released in 1943. Millions of acres were seeded in the 1940s and 1950s. Despite its wide acceptance, the new grass was not without problems. Palatability (acceptability to livestock) was sometimes low, and animal performance was often lower than expected based on quality analysis. Cattle grazing tall fescue occasionally developed lameness or lost portions of their feet and tails, an infrequent malady that came to be known as fescue foot. Cattle can also get "fat necrosis," an accumulation of hard fat deposits in the animal's abdominal cavity.

The most serious disorder is referred to as summer slump, summer syndrome, fescue toxicosis, or fescue toxicity. This ailment costs cattle producers in the Southeast approximately $600 million each year. It remained a mystery until the 1970s, when a fungus growing in tall fescue was positively linked to animal performance problems. The endophyte fungus affects neither the growth nor the appearance of the grass, and laboratory analysis is necessary to detect it. Since the fungus is apparently transmitted only through fescue seed, a number of strategies are available to cope with or eliminate it.

Kentucky bluegrass (*Poa pratenisis* L.) is a perennial that grows best in spring and fall, forming a dense sod with its spreading rhizomes. A high-quality grass, especially when grown with white clover, it is particularly well suited as food for grazing animals. Kentucky bluegrass tolerates close and frequent grazing better than most other grasses grown in Kentucky and is well adapted to mountain meadows and high-phosphate soils.

Clovers of numerous varieties are adaptable and can be grown successfully in much of the Appalachian region. These include annuals (crimson), biennials (sweetclover), and perennials (red, white, alsike). Other species are grown to some extent; however, red and white (ladino) clovers are the most common.

White clover (*Trifolium repens* L.) originated in the Mediterranean region. Introduced into North America by early colonists, it is the most widely grown clover in the Appalachian area. The very leafy plant grows eight to twelve inches tall and spreads by stolons (runners). White flowers are clustered into heads. Seeds are extremely small, with approximately 768,000 per pound. Three types of white clover are grown in Appalachia. Small white clover, generally called white Dutch, originated in Holland. The intermediate white clovers are larger than white Dutch. Most unnamed varieties of white clover sold in the United States are of the intermediate type and are often referred to as common white clover. Ladino is the most common white clover seeded by farmers. It is much larger and produces three to five times more forage by weight than white Dutch.

Red clover *(Trifolium pratense)*, the highest-yielding clover grown in Appalachia, is a short-lived perennial plant used for both pasture and hay. Stems develop from the crown and range in height from eighteen to thirty-six inches at maturity. Stems of most varieties are densely pubescent (hairy). Leaves are arranged alternately on the stems and are usually marked with a whitish V. Red clover seeds are mitten shaped with approximately 272,000 seeds per pound. Red clover is adapted to a wide range of climatic conditions, soil types, fertility levels, use patterns, and management. Being free from many diseases and insect pests, it is an excellent nitrogen fixer, easy to establish, and suitable for use in crop rotations.

Most red and white clovers are grown with cool-season grasses for a more efficient and sustainable forage production system. Adding clovers to grass usually results in higher yields, improved quality, and more summer growth. It also takes advantage of the clovers' ability to convert atmospheric nitrogen to a form that plants can use, reducing the need for commercial fertilizer.

See also: CATTLE; SUSTAINABLE AGRICULTURE.

—Garry D. Lacefield and Monroe Rasnake, *University of Kentucky*

D. M. Ball, C. S. Hoveland, and G. D. Lacefield, *Southern Forages* (1996).

Ginseng

Though it is probably the most valuable non-timber forest product in Appalachia (as it is in all of North America), American ginseng (*Panax quinquefolium* L.) is an ordinary-looking plant about twenty inches high that grows inconspicuously on the forest floor. A deciduous perennial, it produces a single new stalk with radiating leaflets each year, but its value lies buried in the slow-growing tuberous rootstock. Although American ginseng is a different species from the Asian ginseng *(Panax ginseng)*, a root the Chinese have treasured for at least five thousand years for its medicinal properties, it is very similar in appearance and is believed to possess similar beneficial properties. One other species of the *Panax* genus, *Panax trifolium*, or ground nut, is native to the Appalachian region, but it has little commercial value.

Ginseng grows best in the humus-rich hardwood coves of eastern North America, including the entire Appalachian region. Good ginseng sites have been passed on in families from generation to generation, and the oldest plants are harvested annually to provide supplemental income. In the southern Appalachians, this enjoyable foraging activity is called sanging or sang digging, and the plant is often referred to as green gold.

During the 1990s, approximately one hundred thousand pounds of wild American ginseng, worth about four hundred dollars per pound, were harvested annually in the United States, most of it coming from the Appalachians. Nevertheless, its relative economic importance to the region is less today than at almost any time in the last 250 years. As early as 1751, fur traders paid the Native Americans of New York (many of whom were familiar with the plant as an herbal remedy) to gather ginseng for twenty-five cents a pound. In London, the roots sold for five dollars per pound for shipment to China. After the Revolutionary War, the exchange of ginseng for Chinese tea became America's most important and consistently profitable foreign trade.

In the late 1700s and early 1800s, settlers moving into new areas were often able to obtain ready cash to finance their homesteading by digging and selling ginseng, usually to fur buyers. George Washington noted in his diary that he encountered pack trains crossing the mountains loaded down with ginseng. In Kentucky, Daniel Boone not only gathered ginseng for use by his own family but also in 1788 purchased twelve tons for export. By 1802, ginseng was one of the few products profitable enough to absorb the cost of overland transport from the Appalachians to Philadelphia for export overseas.

Overharvesting of wild plants led to rapidly declining ginseng markets by the mid-1800s, and enterprising individuals tried their hand at the difficult task of growing green gold. In the 1870s, after many before him had failed, Abraham Whisman of Boones Path, Virginia, became the first person known to have cultivated American ginseng successfully. A ginseng boom followed, spurred when the U.S. Department of Agriculture published a booklet on ginseng farming in 1895. Subsequently, except during times of war or trade embargoes, there has continued to be a market in China for both wild and cultivated American ginseng.

While ginseng farming originated, and continues, in the Appalachians, it has been far more successful in other locations, such as Wisconsin and southern Ontario. Mountain topography inhibits the use of mechanized equipment and encourages poaching, a form of thievery so common that few growers risk operation on a significant scale in the mountains. Thus, wild roots continue to constitute the bulk of ginseng produced in Appalachia.

Though no longer abundant, ginseng remains widely distributed and will remain a sustainable resource if foraged in the traditional manner—harvesting only older plants while planting the berries or seeds in the same location. However, during periods when both prices and unemployment are high, more harvesters take to the woods. In such times, younger plants are dug and poaching increases on public lands, serving to deplete the wild population over time. The Convention on International Trade in Endangered Species identifies ginseng as one of many species in need of protection. Since 1978, nations belonging to the convention have instituted a collecting season. In these countries, buyers are required to register and to record and report purchases and sales. The regulations have irritated many ginseng diggers and dealers, but they ensure the fall treasure hunt for green gold will continue for another 250 years.

Joe Williams "sanging" near Whitesville, West Virginia, 1995. Wild harvest continues to be the primary source of ginseng in the mountains of Appalachia.

See also: ALTERNATIVE CROPS; SUBSISTENCE FARMING.

—W. Scott Persons, *Tuckasegee, North Carolina*

Barbara R. Duncan, "American Ginseng in Western North Carolina: A Cross-Cultural Examination," *May We All Remember Well: A Journal of the History of Cultures of Western North Carolina*, ed. Robert S. Brunk (1997); W. Scott Persons, *American Ginseng: Green Gold* (1994).

Heirloom Fruits and Vegetables

Heirloom fruits and vegetables are those varieties grown from seed and plant materials collected from plants that have been open-pollinated and often have been passed down through generations of farmers within a family or a community. Growers of heirloom fruits and vegetables select and breed plants for qualities such as taste, texture, and aroma. By contrast, most modern commercial plants are prized for their size, durability, and ease of production, which makes for hardy but rather tasteless produce. Also, modern plants are often hybridized, rather than open-pollinated, produc-

Heirloom beans, Berea, Kentucky, 2002. The Big John cornfield bean, an heirloom variety collected by Bill Best, has quickly become a favorite at farmers' markets.

ing either sterile seeds or seeds that do not produce plants similar to the hybrid parent.

In Appalachia, cultivation of heirlooms has a long history, and many varieties of fruits and vegetables are still handed down in this manner. Families often enjoy the taste of the same tomatoes, beans, and other fruits and vegetables that their ancestors knew. Appalachian farmers have also discovered that this form of sustainable agriculture can provide specialty-crop income. Seeking alternatives to bland produce from large industrial farms, consumers often travel miles to farmers' markets and other outlets throughout Appalachia searching for these old-fashioned vegetables and fruits.

Immigrants to America usually carried seeds from their homelands to begin farms in the New World, and Europeans settling the Appalachians in the 1700s did so as well. In some cases the seeds they brought with them were seeds of indigenous North and South American plants that had been taken to Europe earlier. These seeds form the base of many of the heirloom vegetables and fruits found in Appalachia today. In addition to their own stock, settlers often traded seeds with Native Americans, who primarily grew corn, beans, and squash varieties. These exchanges, coupled with the steady migration of Europeans into the Appalachians, disseminated a wide variety of fruits and vegetables throughout the region.

The number of varieties of beans, in particular, flourished. Beans mutate relatively easily, and new varieties arise frequently. Not all mutations give rise to viable offspring, but if succeeding generations continue to exhibit a variation, a new variety is born. In traditional Appalachian farming, individual gardeners sometimes had several varieties of beans found nowhere else growing in their fields. If the bean proved to have a good flavor or some noteworthy characteristic, the farmer might trade or sell it to others, thereby establishing the new variety within the community or local region.

The naming of beans has been fairly consistent throughout the mountains. Typically, a bean is named for the person who discovered it or who is most associated with growing it. In many communities, most families had at least one variety of their own, and some claimed several. Traditionally, a bean of unknown origin was given the name of a community or locale where it flourished.

Beans were often a significant source of protein for Appalachian families, and the diversity of beans helped ease the monotony of their diet. In addition to being varied in flavor and appearance, the majority of these heirloom beans were tender right off the plant, unlike modern commercially grown beans that have been bred to withstand the rigors of mechanical harvesting.

Heirloom beans are described in terms of three general characteristics. Cut-shorts are beans packed so tightly in the hulls that the ends are squared off; that is, they cannot grow to full length inside the hull and are "cut short." Greasies do not have the fuzzy skins common to other beans but are shiny, or greasy, in appearance. One of the "three sisters" recognized by Native Americans, cornfield beans are climbing beans traditionally grown in corn along with pumpkins or squash, a technique that raises efficiency by fostering a symbiotic relationship among the plants. Beans can be any combination of these three types. For example, a particular bean might be described as a speckled long greasy cut-short cornfield bean.

In Appalachia, there have been several varieties of corn used for cornmeal, animal feed, and alcohol production, but the diversity is much less than that of beans. While most beans are self-pollinating, there is not much problem with cross-pollination with moderate separation between varieties. Corn, however, must be kept isolated in order not to cross-pollinate from the wind. Of the varieties available, Appalachians have generally preferred white corn for eating as corn bread, spoonbread, hominy, and other such dishes. Growers are increasingly aware of the importance of maintaining the purity and genetic diversity of this crop as well.

Squash and pumpkin also lack the diversity of beans and generally have been selected for their ability to keep fresh well into the winter months as a stored food source. Firmness and good flavor characterize these squashes, which are most often baked or used in pies. The candy roaster is an example of a popular heirloom squash. Another heirloom vegetable common to the region is okra, also known as cow's horn or longhorn, introduced to the region from Africa through the slave trade.

At the beginning of the twentieth century, it was estimated there were more than seven thousand varieties of apples in the United States; a century later only a few were commonly available in supermarkets. Alarmed by this decline in apple varieties, many growers and conservationists have brought back the art of grafting and actively search for apple and pear trees to resurrect. Some old-fashioned apple varieties such as northern spy, transparent, horse apple, June apple, and others are again finding favor among orchardists. While these apples may not have the shiny colors and uniform shapes of those found in supermarkets, they usually have excellent flavors and are good for eating raw or for drying or cooking. One individual taking the lead in this activity at the beginning of the twenty-first century was Harold Jerrell, an extension agent in Lee County, Virginia.

There are thousands of varieties of heirloom tomatoes in a surprising assortment of colors—black, white, brown, yellow, striped, green (when ripe), purple, pink, and red. These come in sizes ranging from the tiny "tommy toes" the size of cherries, to three- and four-pound German yellows. The Cherokee purple is credited to that tribe, while the Amish and Mennonites developed many varieties in Europe before transplanting them to North America. One of the best known of those originated in Appalachia is the "mortgage lifter," developed by West Virginian Charlie Byers, a radiator repairman by trade, to pay off his house note.

See also: ALTERNATIVE CROPS; FARMERS' MARKETS; SUSTAINABLE AGRICULTURE.

—Bill Best, *Berea College*

Bill Best, "Heirloom Beans," *Appalachian Heritage* (January 1998); Rosalind Creasy, *The Edible Heirloom Garden* (2000); William Woys Weaver, *Heirloom Vegetable Gardening: A Master Gardener's Guide to Planting, Seed Savings, and Cultural History* (1997).

Hemp

In the nineteenth century, hemp was one of the largest cash crops in Kentucky, creating an economic link between Appalachia and the Deep South through its reliance on slave labor and its importance to the cotton industry. In modern times, however, hemp has almost no commercial value due to competition from both natural and synthetic alternatives.

Hemp is the collective subspecies of *Cannabis sativa* L. containing less than 1 percent of the psychoactive element tetrahydracannibol (THC). The English introduced the non-native hemp plant to America, and by the late sixteenth century it was cultivated from Kentucky to Maine, including in Virginia, Pennsylvania, and Maryland. Beginning in the eighteenth century, many states subsidized hemp production by providing farmers free seed and immunity from tariffs in an effort to divert production away from the "precarious and immoral tobacco industry."

In the United States hemp quickly became a valued commodity. Hemp paper was used for the first two drafts of the Declaration of Independence and hemp cloth for the first American flag. While southern states were busy producing cotton, Kentucky and the Ohio Valley became leading producers of hemp. Early-nineteenth-century hemp production in Appalachia was labor-intensive and relied heavily on African slaves. On a good day, one man could harvest a quarter of an acre of hemp. Ropewalkers ran relays, passing hemp fibers along the line of workers to twist hemp twine.

The primary market for hemp in the nineteenth century was the South, where hemp was used for bagging and cordage for baling cotton. As cotton production grew, so did the hemp industry. Other markets for hemp included the maritime industry, the U.S. Navy, and farmers who used hemp for driving or plow lines.

In 1850 the United States boasted a $3.34-million hemp industry including 8,327 hemp plantations of 2,000 acres or more and 417 bagging and cordage factories. Kentucky alone produced more than a million dollars' worth of hemp and hemp products, with other Appalachian states accounting for only a negligible amount of U.S. hemp production.

Shortly after the mid-nineteenth century, hemp production in Appalachia and the United States reached its peak. But despite tariff protection, hemp production continued to be threatened by the uncertainties of the slave trade, the use of alternative bagging and cordage materials by the cotton industry, the failure to procure naval contracts, and increased competition from foreign-produced jute and coir. Eventually labor shortages contributed to declining hemp production in northern Appalachia. Kentucky, with a larger slave population, maintained hemp production until the Civil War, when slavery, along with the means to grow and harvest hemp effectively on a large scale, disappeared.

With the start of the Civil War in 1861, the cotton industry collapsed. Hemp prices tumbled and the U.S. government forbade the shipment of hemp to the South. After the war, the disintegration of the slave industry had dramatic consequences for both cotton and hemp production. Without access to cheap labor, both industries competed with imports of superior quality at a lower price. The cotton industry began using iron ties and bands and rope and hoops made from oak and hickory. In addition, the navy increasingly turned to foreign-produced alternatives.

By 1879, U.S. hemp production had fallen to 5,025 tons and about 30 factories, as sisal, jute, and Manila hemp replaced true hemp. In 1937 Congress passed the Marijuana Tax Act, effectively ending hemp production. During World

War II, the government permitted hemp production to aid the war effort, and Appalachian farmers once again planted the crop. But synthetic substitutes for hemp had been developed, and after the war commercial U.S. hemp production was once again outlawed. In the twenty-first century, hemp, known as ditchweed, continues to grow wild in much of Appalachia, particularly along fencerows, though its commercial value is negligible.

Despite optimism for future uses of hemp, increased competition from both natural and synthetic fibers and oils has reduced the use of hemp by various industries. Additionally, hemp fiber and oil processing are more costly than substitutes. Consequently, current demand for hemp is only from small, niche markets. It is illegal to produce hemp in the U.S. although it can be imported, exported, and sold. While many Appalachian states have talked of reviving their hemp industries, Kentucky is the only state that has passed legislation to research its market potential.

See also: ALTERNATIVE CROPS; SUSTAINABLE AGRICULTURE.

—Valerie L. Vantreese, *University of Kentucky*

Thomas D. Clark, "The Trade between Kentucky and the Cotton Kingdom in Livestock, Hemp, and Slaves," M.A. thesis, University of Kentucky (1929); James F. Hopkins, *A History of the Hemp Industry in Kentucky* (1998); Valerie L. Vantreese, *Industrial Hemp: Global Operations, Local Implications* (1998).

Hogs

Over the course of the last century, hog raising in Appalachia has changed from ubiquitous small-farm production for strictly local consumption to an industry dominated by large enterprises that utilize the latest advances in agricultural science to raise, slaughter, and process hogs for regional and national distribution. Many states that were not traditional hog-producing states have developed significant industries because of these advancements. States such as North Carolina have risen from obscurity to positions of prominence in the industry through advances in genetics, more efficient economies of size, and state-of-the-art facilities and management techniques. These new swine areas are usually dominated by large operations capable of processing more than five thousand hogs per day; some plants are capable of slaughtering more than thirty thousand hogs per day. Most large companies are vertically integrated—a structure that enables a facility to control several or all of the stages, from raising hogs to processing and packaging the meat. This has led to fewer but larger hog operations, which are more efficient than small farms and reduce the impact of hog production on the overall agricultural economy of Appalachia.

Hogs, introduced into the Appalachian region by Spanish explorers in the sixteenth century, have been important animals in the mountain region due to the fact they can be raised to slaughter weight quickly and easily. By the mid-1890s, fence laws, which require that hogs and other livestock be confined, had been enacted in all of Appalachia. Prior to these laws, hogs were often allowed to forage for mast and other food on the forest floor. Hogs also efficiently utilize human food wastes. As they are good scavengers, hogs are still often fed wastes from the kitchen, garden, orchard, and dairy.

During the nineteenth century much of the corn grown in the Appalachian region was fed to hogs. They were walked to markets in the Midwest and to eastern coastal cities in the great livestock drives of that era. Cincinnati became known as "Porkopolis," though by the mid-1860s, the center of activity had shifted to Chicago.

Hogs were also important to the local economy of Appalachia. Normally, hogs were butchered on farms for family consumption or sold at local markets. Those raised for butchering on the farm were fed to a weight of three hundred pounds or more so the family could have large hams and other cuts of meat. In addition, larger hogs made more lard. Animals raised to a weight of two hundred pounds were sold at the local market and normally brought a better price per pound.

In the hill country of Kentucky's eastern Pennyroyal, as in much of rural Appalachia, the ancient custom of hog slaughtering continues, though not to the extent of the pre–World War II era. "Hog killing time," as it was commonly called in much of Appalachia, occurred during the months of November, December, January, and February, when the temperature was usually below thirty-two degrees Fahrenheit. This made it ideal to safely preserve freshly dressed pork. Hog killing time also provided opportunities for families and neighbors to get together and share in this activity and fellowship as a community.

Modern refrigeration, which was made possible by the coming of Tennessee Valley Authority and rural electric cooperatives during the 1930s and 1940s, changed the way Appalachian families acquired their domestic meat supply. A farmer only needed to haul his hogs to the nearest combination butchery and frozen food locker plant, even during the heat of summer. During the 1940s farmers were still selling excess meat and lard to neighbors and local grocery stores. However, state and federal regulations regarding slaughtering and changing dietary habits have since caused a drastic decline in home butchering.

Production and marketing of hogs became decentralized during the period between World Wars I and II. Slaughter facilities were built near where the animals were raised, mainly in grain-producing areas. In the 1950s the swine industry underwent major changes. Improvements in genetics, crossbreeding systems, and nutrition improved efficiency and performance. New disease treatment and prevention strategies, sophisticated technologies in production, and improved management techniques have allowed more animals to be concentrated in smaller spaces. Though hog production in Appalachian states has a greater significance industry-wide than has been the case historically, fewer Appalachian farmers are directly involved.

See also: FENCE LAWS.

—Aaron Ashley, *Berea, Kentucky*

Charles S. Guthrie, "Hog Lore of the Cumberland Valley," *Kentucky Folklore Record* (September–October 1977); Lynwood Montell, "Hog Killing Time in the Kentucky Hill Country: The Initial Phases," *Kentucky Folklore Record* (July–September, 1972).

Home Demonstration Clubs

As with rural housewives for centuries, Appalachian women struggled to deal with loneliness and isolation. In the first decades of the twentieth century, organizations known variously as Farm Women's Clubs, Home Demonstration Clubs, or Extension Homemakers' Clubs were created to meet women's desires for knowledge and community.

Initiated in the 1910s and 1920s, these women's clubs often began as offshoots of farmers' days activities. While men met to learn new farming techniques, women gathered to learn ways to improve their families' lives. The staff of the Cooperative Extension Service of the U.S. Department of Agriculture provided resources and served as advisors to the groups. The clubs provided women with the opportunity to exchange information and to learn new ideas from experts. By the 1930s, state councils had been organized in most of the Appalachian states, providing women with the occasion to build social and civic ties with those from outside their local community. These state councils and the local clubs that support them continue to function today.

The club was often the only social outlet rural women had other than the local church. Clubs provided education, socialization, and community-development opportunities. Groups were usually organized in neighborhoods, and meetings were held in homes, schools, or churches. Study topics often included kitchen improvement, food preparation and preservation, stitching and repair of clothing, civic and citizenship issues, health concerns, personal development, money and time management, and family recreation. Homemakers' clubs have been instrumental in meeting community and national needs. They helped start school hot lunch programs, rural libraries, county public health services, and community recreation. They continue to support youth groups, especially 4-H Clubs.

Local groups joined together to form county and state councils and later a national council. Growth continues in states such as Tennessee, which has had local clubs since the 1920s but only organized a state council in 1982. State councils have since become affiliated with one of two national organizations and an international council. Through these organized clubs, rural Appalachian women can acquire new skills and work towards improving their homes and developing their communities. The growth evidenced in the members' family and social life extends into other spheres as well. Club experience leads many to continue their education, become wage earners, take leadership positions in the community, and seek volunteer opportunities. Some members claim their years of involvement in the organizations are equivalent to a college education.

See also: AGRICULTURAL COOPERATIVES; WOMEN IN AGRICULTURE.

—Shirley C. Eagan, *West Virginia University*

Horses and Mules

Horses and mules have played vital roles in Appalachian work and recreation since Spanish explorers, who reintroduced horses to the Western Hemisphere, traveled through the region in the 1500s. Appalachia's Native Americans acquired horses from colonial Europeans by the eighteenth century, but unlike nomadic Plains tribes, whose cultures were radically transformed when they acquired horses for buffalo hunting, groups such as the Cherokee integrated horses less fully into their woodland agricultural lifestyles.

Early white settlers brought their horses and mules into the mountains. For agricultural purposes, many Appalachian farmers favored the mule—the infertile offspring of a female horse (mare) and a male donkey (jack)—because of its legendary hardiness. Some southern Appalachian farmers raised mules off their mares; however, mules were also imported from middle Tennessee. Despite the popularity of mules, the relative coolness of mountain summers made farming with draft horses—typically Belgians and Percherons—more practical than in the hot lowland South. In addition, some Appalachian farmers, unable to afford specialized work breeds, employed saddle horses for farming.

For pre-automobile transportation and hauling in Appalachia's broader valleys, people used wagons and buggies pulled by horses or mules. In more rugged areas, sleds functioned better than wheeled vehicles for hauling, and in the most remote sections, that duty fell to saddle horses, causing James Watt Raine to dub the Kentucky mountains "the land of saddle-bags."

Ponies and mules were used extensively to haul coal out of mines. As with human workers, these animals' lives were difficult and dangerous; reports tell of the stench of dead pit ponies. With increasing mechanization, mines phased out ponies and mules.

Although draft animals have largely been relegated to recreational events such as plowing contests and wagon trains, horses and mules are essential to the agricultural economy and lifestyle of the Amish. Centered in Pennsylvania and Ohio but with small communities farther south, this groups eschews mechanized transportation and farm equipment.

Leisure-time horse usage marks class differentiation in Appalachia. From the 1790s until the 1830s, affluent Tidewater Virginians moving to the state's northern neck and the Shenandoah Valley found the lush grass and limestone soil conducive to the establishment of thoroughbred breeding farms. Estates stood stallions such as Sir Archie, whose brilliant offspring broke the hold of imported horses on American racing. In addition, Winchester, Virginia, and Charles Town and Martinsburg, now in West Virginia, boasted racetracks. After the Panic of 1837, the Virginia thoroughbred industry dwindled, with Kentucky's Bluegrass region and middle Tennessee gaining the ascendancy. Today, Charles Town has the region's only racetrack. Other thoroughbred-dominated equestrian sports in Appalachia, both historically and currently, are fox hunting, polo, and showing hunters and jumpers; these activities are still mainly found in the Valley of Virginia.

Probably the most prominent horse breeds in southern Appalachia are the "gaited" horses (so called because their intermediate gait is a very fast walk), particularly Tennessee Walkers and racking horses. Like thoroughbreds, gaited horses have a long history in the region. David Crockett, for example, wrote of his enthusiasm for racking horses. Their popularity in Appalachia is so great that even though the quarter horse had become the most numerous breed in the United States by the late twentieth century, gaited horses remained dominant in the southern mountains. They are used for trail riding and compete in many small local horse shows. Two gaited breeds developed in the mountains are the Rocky Mountain horse (initially bred in eastern Kentucky) and the Virginia Highlands pony.

The Morgan horse has also seen activity in Appalachia. In the late nineteenth century, West Virginia farmers touted the excellence of Green Mountain horses, which are thought to have descended from the Hale's Green Mountain line of Morgans. Currently, West Virginia has two important old-style Morgan horse-breeding farms, the Quietude Stud and Rohan.

An important stimulus to the horse industry in contemporary Appalachia has been the establishment of state horse facilities such as the Virginia Horse Center in Lexington and the Western North Carolina Horse Center near Asheville. These centers host a variety of shows, classes, and clinics.

See also: AGRICULTURAL FRONTIERS; MECHANIZATION.

—Theresa Lloyd, *East Tennessee State University*

Alexander Mackay-Smith, *The Thoroughbred in the Lower Shenandoah Valley* (1948); James Watt Raine, *The Land of Saddle-Bags* (1924).

Maple Syrup

Maple syrup, a thick sweet liquid derived from the sap of maple trees, was a common food product in the homes of Appalachian settlers. Syrup and other maple products, discovered by Native Americans centuries ago, are still produced throughout the region. Early Appalachians relied on maple products as sweeteners and sold or traded the products for other items.

Sugar maple season begins in late winter and lasts between four and eight weeks. A temperature-induced physiological process in maple trees causes the sap to flow during this time of cold nights and warm days. Early collection of maple sap was a destructive process of gashing the tree to release the sap, which was collected in wooden troughs placed on the ground. Both Native Americans and European settlers eventually began using augers to bore small tapholes, into which spouts were inserted to direct the sap into containers. These containers evolved from those made of birch bark to wooden and then metal buckets. The modern method is to use plastic tubing for collecting sap.

Once sap was collected, early settlers boiled it down in metal cauldrons or kettles over an open fire. The sap was boiled continuously, with more sap added as it boiled down, until a dark syrup of strong flavor resulted. Methods and equipment for processing sap into syrup improved with flat-bottom pans and the invention of evaporators in the mid-1800s. Cooks Sugar Evaporator (1858) was the first patented evaporator used in the industry. Evaporators reduce boiling time and produce a better quality product than does boiling alone. Modern maple syrup production increases efficiency through the use of tubing networks, vacuum pump and reverse osmosis systems, sap preheaters, pressure filtering, and canning machines.

Sugar maple trees exist throughout the Appalachian states from northern Alabama to New York; however, commercial production of syrup is limited to the central and northern Appalachians, including Virginia, West Virginia, Kentucky, Ohio, Pennsylvania, and New York (and, most famously, the mountains of New England).

Maple syrup production is a labor-intensive and time-consuming enterprise but very important for much of Appalachia in that it often provides supplemental income to farmers during the months when other farm products are not available. Communities in maple syrup–producing areas have organized festivals and fund-raisers focusing on maple syrup and other maple products. Such activities not only help market this specialty product, but also promote preservation of a cultural heritage and aid survival of the local maple sugar industry.

See also: ALTERNATIVE CROPS; PART-TIME FARMING; SUBSISTENCE FARMING.

—Rodney Leech, *Virginia Cooperative Extension, Highland*

Melvin R. Koelling and Randall B. Heiligmann, eds., *North American Maple Syrup Producers Manual* (1996); Tom McCrumm, *Maple History* (1991).

Mechanization

The earliest machines in Appalachia were little more than rudimentary adaptations of the wheel. Wagons and carts were used to haul crops, tools, and firewood. Foot-powered grindstones sharpened tools. Circular hand-sowers or seeders made the process of distributing small seeds faster and more economical. Huge water-driven wheels powered gristmills, producing meal and flour. Sawmills provided lumber for building.

Water-powered machinery was seldom used on small family farms of Appalachia, where animals or the farmers themselves supplied the necessary muscle. Farmers hand-cranked drill presses, corn shellers, cob crushers, and presses for making sausage, lard, and cider. Animals, usually mules, turned the sugar cane and sorghum presses.

A number of new farm machines were invented in the mid-nineteenth century, but acceptance and use in Appalachia came much later because of their expense and difficulty of application in steep mountainous regions. By the time much of this newer equipment came to the Appalachian region, it was outdated or impractical for the increasing sizes of farms in other parts of the country. Although these early machines eased the burden of human labor, mules and horses still provided most of the power for them.

No-till planting of corn into a cover crop of barley, Washington County, Virginia, 2002. The steep topography and small sizes of most Appalachian farms often make the use of smaller and older equipment more practical.

Some of this equipment was used for tilling the soil and some for planting crops such as corn and beans or for drilling holes for small seed grains such as wheat. The difference between drillers and planters involves the number of seeds required per square foot; drillers plant small seeds with close spacing, while planters place larger seeds at greater intervals. Mechanical mowers, reapers, and hay rakes were rare in Appalachia long after their wide acceptance and use in other parts of the country. Mowers had been in widespread use since the mid-nineteenth century, but according to county records, the first mower did not appear in Clay County, Kentucky, until 1942.

Farmers also benefited from machinery designed to aid in the harvesting and storage of crops. Grain must be separated from the plant, and in most of Appalachia this was done by hand until the advent of corn pickers and threshers. In the flatter areas of Appalachia such as Alabama, Georgia, Mississippi, New York, and Pennsylvania, grain combines revolutionized harvesting of crops such as wheat and oats. Some of the seed that was to be planted the next year was taken to a fanning mill, where the lighter dirt, chaff, and weed seeds were separated from the more desirable seeds. Hay was stored loose until mechanical baling methods became affordable. Baled hay was easier to handle and store, and some farmers used elevators or lifts to get the hay into the barn. Most grain and hay on Appalachian farms, however, continued to be stored manually.

Two developments, the internal combustion engine and electricity, dramatically changed farming in Appalachia, as they had across the country. The internal combustion engine was responsible for a host of new machines and equipment but, as with earlier mechanical equipment, came into use in Appalachia much later than in other farming areas. Late arrival did not lessen their importance. Cars and trucks transformed transportation and opened new markets. Tractors provided power for vastly more efficient designs of tilling, planting, and harvesting equipment, and small engines eliminated the need for hand-cranking machines and appliances. Similarly, electric motors pumped water to houses and livestock, while electric hand tools and household appliances such as sewing machines aided with crafts and repairs around the farm.

There were many reasons that the mechanization of Appalachia came at a snail's pace compared to most of the country. Larger farm machinery was not well suited for the steep hillside fields found in most of the region, and its cost put it beyond the reach of many small farmers. Often the older and more familiar low-cost technologies better suited Appalachian farming simply because of availability and ease of use and repair. Another factor may have been reluctance on the part of Appalachians, perceiving decades of exploitation at the hands of coal and timber companies, to accept change thrust upon them from outside the region.

See also: AGRICULTURAL FRONTIERS; SUSTAINABLE AGRICULTURE.

—Steve Tronc, *Somerset Community College*

Jerry Bushey, *Farming the Land: Modern Farmers and their Machines* (1987); Patrick W. Ertel, *The American Tractor: A Century of Legendary Machines* (2001); U.S. Department of Agriculture, *Power to Produce: The Yearbook of Agriculture* (1960).

Migrant Labor

An increasingly vital part of commercial agriculture in Appalachia, migrant labor has been an important feature of planting and harvesting since the early nineteenth century. The quest for a cheap source of seasonal labor emerged at the same time the region began a transition from subsistence farming to commercial agriculture in the years before the Civil War.

Each year the demand for hired hands to aid during planting and harvesting led to the development of a migrant labor market. Initially, these workers were drawn from within mountain communities, but when demand exceeded supply, large farmers recruited temporary workers from other states, particularly in the Deep South. When work ended in one area, these workers moved to another, migrating from place to place to take advantage of the changing seasons. These men were drawn largely from the ranks of tenant and sharecropper families. Such work was a way for sons to ease the household burden while at the same time earning money to help their families back home. Landowners became progressively more reliant on this labor system throughout the nineteenth century. Though black men were represented by 1900, whites were more likely to enter migrant ranks in the nineteenth century. This pattern continued until the demands of the military for these young men during World War II created a national shortage of inexpensive farm labor.

As agriculture diversified, the demand for migrant labor increased. The demand for cheap labor was exacerbated by an out-migration of native mountaineers who left the region to find higher-paying jobs in industry. Price fluctuations put pressure on farmers to keep their cost of production low. Migrant workers were a cheap solution to temporary labor shortages during peak periods of the growing season.

While the need continued, the face of migrant labor changed after 1945. Whites and blacks continued to work as migrants, but Appalachian migrant laborers increasingly came from Cuba, Mexico, and elsewhere in Latin America. As early as the 1950s, Hispanic laborers began the agricultural season in Florida, moving steadily northward as crops and work demanded. Upon reaching the mountains, these workers found work harvesting apples, peaches, pumpkins, tobacco, and other fall crops in western North Carolina, eastern Tennessee, northern Georgia, West Virginia, and other mountain communities. Usually, they returned south in the fall to find work in winter planting. Conditions for migrant workers remained poor. Wages hovered at or below subsistence level, and the work was hard and dangerous. Housing, which landowners often provided to supplement low wages, was usually in disrepair. Health care, unemployment insurance, and other benefits were nonexistent. Still, an increasing tide of immigration and persistent poverty within the region provided a steady supply of seasonal labor to mountain farmers.

During the 1970s, the ranks of migrant workers, once dominated by single males, began to include whole families moving from community to community in search of agricultural work. Since they are less mobile than individuals, the emergence of migrant families changed the nature of migrant labor. Families were more likely to locate semi-permanently within communities and enter other types of employment. Migrant men tended to remain in agricultural jobs, but by the 1980s they were traveling shorter distances from their homes to find work. At the same time, women entered service jobs to help their families' financial situation. In some Appalachian communities such as Asheville, North Carolina, and Gatlinburg, Tennessee, the tourism industry provided work for many migrant men and women as busboys, cooks, and housekeepers. As in agriculture, such work pays little, is arduous, and evaporates at the end of the season.

The persistence of a large, mobile, and landless class of agricultural workers has posed many different challenges for Appalachian communities. Federal and state officials have initiated programs to regulate the quality and safety of migrant housing. Several states made migrant workers eligible for public assistance and Medicaid, though changes in federal welfare rules in the early 1990s eroded such safety nets. Local school systems developed programs to better serve the needs of migrant children, who often remain in one school only a few months. Local churches, particularly evangelical Protestants, have led efforts to help migrant families. Church organizations in North Carolina, Tennessee, Georgia, West Virginia, and Kentucky have organized clothing drives, language classes, free medical clinics, and other programs aimed at helping improve the lives of migrant workers. Still, migrant families remain among the poorest residents of Appalachia.

The influx of migrant labor in some communities has sparked great tension between permanent residents and seasonal workers. In places with large numbers of migrant families, such as Henderson County, North Carolina, local residents blame migrants for myriad social ills ranging from rising crime rates to the loss of jobs. Natives resent paying for Spanish-speaking teachers, special educational programs designed for migrant children, and regulations that govern sanitary conditions in migrant housing areas. These criticisms often carry an anti-Hispanic bias, rarely grouping white or African American migrant workers with those from Latin America. Migrant workers often complain of social ostracization, police harassment, and discrimination, from which they have little protection.

Migrant labor has done more than fill a critical labor shortage for mountain farmers, though. It has also been an important social catalyst, injecting new languages, cultures, and tensions into Appalachian communities. It is no longer unusual to find migrant workers, many of them Hispanic, cutting tobacco and harvesting vegetables in the remotest of mountain communities. The emergence of migrant labor allowed mountain farmers to produce for larger markets, and later it became an important component of tourism and other service industries. Despite many attempts to ameliorate conditions, migrant labor continues to perpetuate poverty, landlessness, and abuse. It remains an important social and economic problem throughout the Appalachian region.

See also: HISPANICS (RACE, ETHNICITY, AND IDENTITY); TOBACCO.

—Richard D. Starnes, *Western Carolina University*

Wilma A. Dunaway, *The First American Frontier: Transition to Capitalism in Southern Appalachia, 1700–1860* (1996); Cindy Hahamovitch, *The Fruits of Their Labor: Atlantic Coast Farmworkers and the Making of Migrant Poverty, 1870–1945* (1997).

Native American Agriculture

By the time of Columbus's arrival in the New World, Native Americans, including those living in the Appalachians, were cultivating maize, beans, and squash as part of their subsistence base. Early European explorers and settlers repeatedly recorded the popularity of these plants as food crops. These records, however, do not indicate the long and gradual processes involved in domesticating plants over hundreds or thousands of years before the arrival of any Europeans to the region. Although there has been no detailed analysis or synthesis of the data and the archaeological record is incomplete, there is nonetheless sufficient information to draw a number of conclusions about plant domestication.

The origins of Native American agriculture in Appalachia closely parallel those in other world regions. By approximately 2700 B.C., Native American farmers began to supplement their gathered foods by deliberately planting seeds and tending wild stands of desirable indigenous plants. Though the reasons for the shift from foraging and hunting to agriculture have not yet been discovered, domesticated plants can be recognized in the archaeological record by several means. Typically, wild species have relatively thick seed coats that protect them from drying out. Measurements of the seed coats of domesticated seeds recovered from Native American archeological sites are larger and have thinner coats than their wild ancestors. The presence of storage containers and pits at archaeological sites provides additional evidence of the domestication of plants.

A number of wild plants were cultivated by Native Americans as a highly renewable resource, mostly for their starchy or oily seed. These included the sunflower *(Helianthus annus)* and marsh elder, or sumpweed *(Iva annua)*. Several species and subspecies of squash *(Cucurbita)*, goosefoot *(Chenopodium berlandieri)*, maygrass *(Phalaris caroliniana)*, little barley *(Hordeum pusillium)*, and knotweed *(Polygonum erectum)* produce seeds with high starch content. The seeds of the bottle gourd *(Lagenaria siceraria)* are edible, but native peoples probably used this species for containers. All of these plants were part of Appalachian Native American agricultural systems long before the nonindigenous species of squash, maize *(Zea)*, and the common bean *(Phaseolus vulgaris)* appeared about 4,700, 1,500, and 700 years ago, respectively, imported from Central America by early migrants.

By the Mississippian period (A.D. 900–1550), the largest group of indigenous people within southern Appalachia, the Cherokee, had become proficient in growing crops. A typical Cherokee agricultural site consisted of a walled village situated in the floodplain of a river or creek. Men cleared the land by cutting and burning small trees, shrubs, and other ground cover, both inside and outside the walls, though the women in the tribe controlled the use of the land in this matrilineal society.

Both men and women were involved in breaking the soil and readying the fields for planting with the aid of digging sticks, mattocks, and hoes made of stone or bone hafted to wooden shafts. However, Cherokee women did most of the planting and harvesting of crops. Cherokee division of labor by gender reflected roles in the legend of Kanati and Selu, in which men are associated with hunting and women with cultivation. Fields inside the walls were for family use and worked by clan members while those outside were for growing communal crops and worked by labor pools of women. Community storehouses held food for families whose crops had failed as well as provisions for visitors to the village.

Cherokee agriculture was much more tolerant of weeds than the European tradition. Many so-called weeds around the edges of cultivated plots were more than likely added to the harvest. Sunflower and goosefoot could be harvested about the same time as maize in late summer and early fall. Little barley provided the advantage of being harvestable in late spring and early summer—much earlier than other crops. This "starving time" was critical for Native Americans, as stored supplies were scarce while new plants, both wild and domesticated, were too young to harvest.

Cherokees supplemented their crops with gathered nuts, fruits, and berries. In this task, too, women served as the primary laborers. These gathered foods may have contributed as much as half of the Cherokee diet before European contact. The Cherokee adopted European food plants and livestock selectively, choosing those that fit their established agricultural practices. The sweet potato is one such example. Hogs and chickens also became common sources of meat after the second half of the eighteenth century, as game animals such as deer and bear declined in numbers.

From the earliest contact with Europeans, Native American farmers began to alter their agricultural customs and techniques in order to add new foods to their diets. Peaches and watermelons, introduced by the Spanish, were particularly popular, as were apples, with many orchards tended on Native American lands. As a result of treaties with various indigenous groups, the United States government provided tools and training in Western agricultural practices. These changes in agricultural practices altered traditional gender roles in Native American societies. The addition of domesticated livestock such as hogs and chickens reduced the importance of male hunters and placed women in the forefront of meat production, while the shift from subsistence farming to the labor-intensive agriculture of a market economy necessitated men with ox-, mule-, or horse-pulled plows to work the fields. Women began using cotton and flax, grown by men, to make their clothing.

It is not known whether Appalachian Native Americans domesticated plants independently or learned agriculture from other groups, but the archeological evidence suggests that agriculture has been practiced in Appalachia for almost five thousand years.

See also: AGRICULTURAL FRONTIERS; NATIVE AMERICAN FOODWAYS (FOOD AND COOKING).

—William L. Anderson and Jane L. Brown, *Western Carolina University*

Bruce Smith, "Seed Plant Domestication in Eastern North America," in *Last Hunters, First Farmers: New Perspectives on the Prehistoric Transition to Agriculture*, ed. T. Douglas Price and Anne Birgitte Gerbauer (1995); Samuel Cole Williams, ed., *Adair's History of the American Indians* (1986); Richard A. Yarnell, "Domestication of Sunflower and Sumpweed in Eastern North America," in *The Nature and Status of Ethnobotany*, ed. Richard I. Ford (1978).

Part-Time Farming

In most of Appalachia, the percentage of farmers classified as part-time has gradually increased since 1930. Part-time farmers are defined as those who earn more than half of their income from off-farm sources. Today, Appalachian people who continue the practice of part-time farming often see it as one way of preserving the rural lifestyle. Others see it as a means of holding on to family land while enjoying the more stable income levels of off-farm jobs.

The practice of part-time farming began in Appalachia with the arrival of extractive industries late in the nineteenth century and became widespread during the first three decades of the twentieth century. The availability of new jobs in lumbering, mining, railroads, and textiles drew many men into wage labor, which they called "public" work.

Up until the late nineteenth century, the typical Appalachian farm was a diversified subsistence operation. Using the labor of the entire family, farmers produced most of their food, clothing, and shelter on the land. They traded surplus products for a few necessities and luxuries. In 1880 the average size of Appalachian farms was 187 acres, generally ample to meet the subsistence needs of a large family.

Industrialization altered traditional subsistence patterns. Corporations purchased large tracts of Appalachian land, driving up farm values and property taxes. Tempted by high prices and squeezed by rising taxes, some farmers sold off portions of their farms to mining and timber interests. These sales gradually diminished the average farm size until parcels were sometimes too small to support a family. Partible inheritance practices (dividing land among several heirs) accelerated this trend. By 1930, the average southern Appalachian farm was only 76 acres, and in some counties the average was as small as 47 acres.

Pressured in part by small farm size, farmers were also lured into the labor force by cash wages. Initially, many worked on railroads or in lumber camps, mines, and factories. Wages helped pay taxes, purchase tools and livestock, and improve the family's living standard. Many farmers remained in the labor force for longer and longer periods, leaving their wives and older children to perform most routine farm labor. By 1930, 58 percent of all southern Appalachian farmers earned the bulk of their incomes off the farm.

As farmers stayed in the workforce year-round, they gave up some subsistence activities, preferring to purchase products they had once produced. Many began buying on installment plans, purchasing automobiles or other consumer goods on credit. Debt and the practice of purchasing necessities in turn forced many to remain in the paid workforce permanently.

Although many farmers with "public" jobs became more dependent on employers, some also saw part-time farming as a means to avoid total dependence on industrialists. Because most Appalachian industries depended on demand for goods from outside the region, local economies were vulnerable to even slight fluctuations. By maintaining at least a partial subsistence farm, families could survive economic downturns and labor disputes, as the farm provided food and shelter unavailable to laid-off or striking workers dependent on company housing and stores.

See also: SUBSISTENCE FARMING; WOMEN IN AGRICULTURE.

—Melissa Walker, *Converse College*

Ronald D Eller, *Miners, Millhands, and Mountaineers: Industrialization of the Appalachian South, 1880–1930* (1982); Paul Salstrom, *Appalachia's Path to Dependency: Rethinking a Region's Economic History, 1730–1940* (1994); U.S. Department of Agriculture, Bureau of Agricultural Economics, *Economic and Social Problems and Conditions of the Southern Appalachians* (1935).

Peaches

Despite the peach's reputation as a southeastern Piedmont crop, it is also grown in several Appalachian states. Only in South Carolina, however, which ranks second nationally in peach production, do Appalachian counties supply a significant proportion of the annual crop. The mountain areas of Georgia, Virginia, North Carolina, and Pennsylvania also produce peaches, though on a much smaller scale.

Peach trees need cold weather to allow the buds to develop properly but must also avoid spring frosts. Because peaches have a short shelf life and production season, multiple varieties are grown to provide fruit from April to September across different climates. Due to the region's early season temperature fluctuations, the search continues for a type of peach that can be produced consistently in Appalachia. Some tasty and high-yield varieties have been engineered and are popular with Appalachian growers. The Reliance peach has been used successfully, and the Legend and Contender varieties have become more popular because of their high yield. Contender has been one of the most reliable in the southern mountains where chilling time is adequate.

Spanish colonists first brought the peach to northern Florida and southern Georgia. A small, hard-textured variety commonly known to southern mountaineers as the Indian peach grew in upland pastures and was widely planted by Native Americans, who used the fruit for food and the leaves, bark, and seeds as remedies for skin diseases and intestinal disorders. By the early nineteenth century, peaches had spread as far north as (West) Virginia. Settlers grew peaches mostly for fresh fruit, brandy, and hog feed. Commercial peach production developed in Virginia and Maryland from 1800 to 1850 and expanded rapidly in Georgia and South Carolina in the early twentieth century.

Appalachian peach growers must contend with low prices, competition from other regions, and a lack of consistent production necessary for large-scale shipping. Most of the peaches grown in Appalachia are sold through roadside retail outlets, which provide the most dependable markets for small-scale growers.

Upstate South Carolina is protected from cold weather blasts by the Blue Ridge Mountains and produces nearly half the state's peach crop. Spartanburg County leads the state in production and contains 70 percent of the peach trees in the upstate area, with Redglobe a leading variety. The size of South Carolina peach farms has increased while the number of growers has decreased, and residential and commercial development has priced farmland at a premium, leaving about ten packing sheds statewide.

See also: ALTERNATIVE CROPS; APPLES.

—Karl Rohr, *Western Carolina University*

Poultry

Appalachian areas have been in the forefront of the growing poultry industry, particularly in the South. Broiler production nationwide was thirteen times larger in 1998 than in 1950, and most of the southern Appalachian states increased their relative market share during this period. Of particular note are Alabama, Georgia, Mississippi, and North Carolina, which together accounted for more than 44 percent of the nearly eight billion birds produced nationwide in 1998 and where a significant part of the broiler production remains in Appalachian areas of these states. The expansion of the broiler production in these areas has meant improved economic stability and off-farm jobs in hatcheries, feed mills, and processing plants.

Poultry has historically been an important source of food for the people of Appalachia. In the 1800s and early 1900s, poultry and eggs were produced mainly for home consumption, but around the middle of the twentieth century commercial poultry production rapidly developed. While the economics of production, particularly the cost of transportation, caused shifts away from some areas of the region, many other areas continue to support viable commercial poultry production.

A 1937 article in the *North Carolina Farm Forecaster* observed that although poultry was probably the most generally produced product in North Carolina, the average farmer gave little thought to his poultry's providing him with income, as that part of farming was "left to the womenfolk." Literature from the time shows that women, however, were quite aware of the value of these commodities and often sold or traded surplus eggs and chickens locally.

Eventually, Appalachian farmers organized to transport and sell their poultry products in the urban areas of the

Northeast. In 1980 T. B. Morris, a professor in poultry science at North Carolina State University, documented that as early as 1929 the Farmers Federation of Asheville, North Carolina, shipped fifteen thousand pounds of live turkeys to markets in the northeastern United States. A 1927 newspaper article headlined "Mountain Turkeys Headed to Markets for Thanksgiving" claimed that more than twenty-five thousand dollars' worth of birds had been shipped in rail cars to urban markets. Macon County, North Carolina, was shipping similar quantities of live poultry to the same markets during that time period. This type of poultry production and marketing continued to expand for the next two decades. Privately owned hatcheries, feed mills, and processing facilities were developed to keep up with the needs of farmers' increasing production.

During the 1940s and 1950s, integrated poultry businesses began to develop the concept of contract production, with farmers growing birds for businesses that had processing plants and service support segments. This vertically integrated practice is the predominant method of production today, as larger corporations contract individual farmers to raise chickens to established specifications. The corporations then slaughter, package, and market the birds. There is also a growing niche market for poultry raised by alternative methods, most of which involve pasture-raised birds housed in portable pens rather than the traditional houses, which hold twenty-five thousand or more birds.

See also: SUSTAINABLE AGRICULTURE; WOMEN IN AGRICULTURE.

—Thomas A. Carter, *North Carolina State University*

T. B. Morris, *Poultry Can Crow at NCSU: A History of Poultry at North Carolina State University, 1881–1976* (1980); U.S. Department of Agriculture, Bureau of Agricultural Economics, *Farm Production, Disposition and Gross Income: Chickens and Eggs, 1950–1951* (1952); U.S. Department of Agriculture, National Agricultural Statistics Service, *Poultry: Production and Value, 1999 Summary* (April 2000).

Progressive Farmer

Clarence Hamilton Poe (1881–1964) and the Raleigh, North Carolina–based *Progressive Farmer* magazine became synonymous throughout the first half of the twentieth century with the advocacy of modern agricultural practices for southern farmers. Poe, a neo-Jeffersonian, believed rural life superior to urban existence and championed the cause of the small, property-holding farmer, whom Poe wanted to remain the dominant force in southern life. He feared, however, that unless these farmers cast aside their antiquated practices, they were doomed to extinction.

Poe traveled extensively throughout the South during his years (1899–1954) as owner and editor of the best-selling farm journal in the region. He frequently visited southern Appalachia and delivered scores of speeches in such places as Asheville, North Carolina, Chattanooga, Tennessee, and Blacksburg, Virginia, urging farmers to adopt progressive agricultural methods to alleviate their depressed economic state. He established regional offices for his farm journal in Virginia and Tennessee to reach and serve farmers in those areas.

Developing his ideas from trips to other agricultural regions of the world and from extensive discussions with farm experts, Poe envisioned a metamorphosis for Appalachian farmers. Most importantly, he believed progressive Appalachian farmers would diversify their agricultural efforts to achieve the key goal of balancing animal and plant productivity. In addition, they would establish farm cooperatives to share profits and create financial resources for the agricultural revolution. These developments would enable Appalachian farmers to practice crop rotation, use better fertilizers, plant newly developed disease-resistant grains such as corn and soybean, and combat soil erosion by using humus and planting deeper to hold the rainfall. Fruit trees, such as peach and apple, would replace the cash crops of cotton and tobacco, while forest resources would be managed for longterm gains. Increased animal profitability would provide the farmer with a two-fisted economic arsenal. Only purebred hogs and cattle would be purchased and bred to produce larger, healthier animals and greater profits. Farm mechanization, a necessity for the agrarian revival, would enable farmers to compete better in the labor market with urban areas by allowing them to cut costs and offer laborers higher wages and shorter hours. Farm cooperatives would purchase such equipment. Finally, subscriptions to agricultural publications would keep farmers abreast of the latest agrarian developments.

Ironically, it was largely agricultural modernization that thwarted Poe's dream. In the twentieth century, as the nation increasingly urbanized, large commercial operations began to dominate rural areas, and family farms nearly disappeared from the landscape. Poe fought against this trend, but he could not stem the tide. After 1940 he accepted the economic reality that small farms could not compete against the agribusiness organizations. Farmers did modernize and become more prosperous, but large united enterprises forced out most of the small independent farms.

See also: AGRICULTURAL COOPERATIVES; SUSTAINABLE AGRICULTURE.

—Joseph A. Cote, *University of Georgia*

Clarence H. Poe, *How Farmers Co-operate and Double Profits* (1915) and *My First Eighty Years* (1963).

Sheep

Although their historical importance to mountain agriculture has been underestimated, sheep were second in importance only to hogs in the region and outranked all other livestock in actual numbers throughout the nineteenth century. The decline in the numbers of wolves and cougars along with the clearing of additional woodlands for pasture and grasslands made the mountain environs an ideal grazing area for sheep.

An English cultural tradition, sheep herding was practiced widely throughout the mountains by 1830. The primary purpose for raising sheep was the production of wool. Few mountain residents ate lamb and mutton, as sheep required high maintenance. Swine, on the other hand, multiplied across the landscape, and pork rapidly replaced mutton and beef on backcountry tables.

Prior to 1850, sheep raising had been far from scientific, with most herders showing only a modicum of interest in purebred varieties. No geographic province conspicuously dominated sheep production during the first three decades of the nineteenth century, though by 1840 east Tennessee clearly had the greatest number of sheep. In fact, in that year alone, Tennessee produced more wool than any other state except New York, an estimated three million dollars' worth.

By 1850 most sheep in Appalachia were of Merino or Saxony stock, common but improved breeds producing one to three pounds of wool per animal. Upper east Tennessee and southwest Virginia remained important sheep-raising areas, with most counties supporting populations of 5,000 sheep or more. Additionally, sheep raising became prominent on the Cumberland Plateau of Kentucky and Tennessee due partly to the proximity to Lexington and Nashville, hubs of the two most important sheep-raising areas in the region. Pulaski County, Kentucky, was by far the largest producer in Appalachia, with census records reporting 22,007 sheep for the year 1859. A few areas in the Blue Ridge Mountains of North Carolina, where mountaintop pastures were well suited to these grass-loving ruminants, also boasted herds of considerable size.

Throughout the nineteenth century, most wool remained on the mountain farmstead, where it was carded, spun, and dyed before being woven into blankets, coverlets, and clothing. In some areas, carding mills sprang up, giving those who could afford it the option of exchanging freshly sheared wool for finished and dyed yarn. Wool was "gold and silver" to many merchants, who often used it as currency when purchasing their own wares for the village store.

By 1900 sheep raising was in rapid decline across the mountains; just three decades later, only 46,000 farms in the entire region reported raising even one of the animals. Throughout most of America, cotton replaced wool as the fabric of choice, and sheep raising clearly declined as a result. Nonetheless, sheep raising continued throughout the Appalachians on a smaller scale, supplying lambs for meat and mountain wools for craft and specialty markets. By 1997 the number of farms raising sheep had fallen to 5,955, with the vast majority of these located in the northern half of the region.

See also: FENCE LAWS; FORAGES.

—Donald E. Davis, *Dalton State College*

Leonard W. Brinkman, "Home Manufactures as an Indication of an Emerging Appalachian Subculture, 1840–1870," *West Georgia College Studies in the Social Sciences* (June 1973); Allen H. Eaton, *Handicrafts of the Southern Highlands* (1937); Henry S. Randall, *Sheep Husbandry in the South* (1848).

Sorghum

Sorghum syrup, or molasses, has been made on farms in southern Appalachia since about 1870. Sorghum is a food source as old as recorded human history; the species *Andropogon sorghum* includes all groups of sorghum under cultivation, including sweet sorghums, grain sorghums, and broomcorns. Many varieties of sweet sorghum are grown in the United States today. Most of the modern varieties have been developed from seed stocks imported from China in 1853, though a few varieties were also later introduced from Africa.

Sweet sorghum syrup production was ideally suited to the subsistence farming culture that existed in the mountain hollows and valleys of the southern Appalachian region in 1870. The only sweeteners that the pioneers had were honey and, in some areas, maple syrup. Sorghum cane molasses was a welcome new addition to a diet that was often bland or salty. Farmers saved seeds from one year to the next, and regional varieties developed. A vertical press could be purchased to squeeze the juice out of the stalks. These mills could be powered by horses or mules, which were widely available. Many homesteaders owned a large copper kettle to cook down the juice from an acre of sorghum cane into a year's supply of sweet syrup. The cane was always cut in the fall and sorghum making was often a celebrated event.

Today, consumers pay four to five dollars per pint for sorghum syrup at festivals and gift shops throughout the South. Modern production techniques and improved varieties have brought yields up to two hundred gallons per acre, and sweet sorghum cane has become an important source of income for farmers looking for an alternative to burley tobacco.

See also: ALTERNATIVE CROPS; SUBSISTENCE FARMING; SWEETENERS (FOOD AND COOKING).

—Andy Hankins, *Virginia State University*

Subsistence Farming

Subsistence farming is a system in which families produce almost everything they need by living off the land. From the time the first settlers moved into Appalachia until about 1950, most farmers in the region practiced subsistence farming. They raised animals for food, grew vegetable gardens and orchards, and gathered from the nearby woodlands what they needed for clothing, shelter, and additional food.

The woodlands provided many kinds of wild game, and farmers used dogs to help find and capture them. Two examples of animals hunted with dogs are the opossum and groundhog. These animals furnished meat, and their skins were used for leather for such items as shoelaces and parts for repairing harnesses. The rendered fat from the animals was used in making many folk remedies for treating illnesses.

Dogs were also important for security against intruders, wild animals that posed risks to livestock and poultry, and venomous snakes. Dogs helped locate and retrieve livestock, which was allowed to range freely most of the time. Livestock was typically fenced out of crop fields, rather than being fenced in.

Farm families gathered wild fruits such as strawberry, blackberry, and raspberry and nuts such as chestnut, hickory, hazelnut, and black walnut. Acorns and beechnuts provided food for hogs, chickens, and turkeys. Trees provided wood for buildings, fences, and fuel. The wood of the American chestnut was a favorite because it was light, strong, durable, and easy to split. The "crooked rail" fence typical of Appalachia during that time was almost exclusively made from chestnut, as was the "paling," or picket fence used around yards and gardens to keep poultry out. Thick boards split from large chestnut logs were used for ceilings and floors in log homes. Wood shingles rived from chestnut logs provided roofing materials for homes, barns, and other farm buildings. The loss of the American chestnut by 1940 due to the chestnut blight was a major setback for Appalachian farmers.

Nearly every family had a vegetable garden and orchard. Corn, beans, tomatoes, Irish and sweet potatoes, turnips, squash, and pumpkin were some of the most important vegetables grown. Corn and beans were pickled for storage. Green beans were threaded on strings, hung from rafters, and dried to form shuck beans, or "leather britches." Irish potatoes were dug in the fall and "holed up" for storage in a soil pit, from which they could then be taken up anytime during the winter as needed. Sweet potatoes were also dug in the fall just before frost, packed in barrels or boxes with alternating layers of dry tree leaves, and stored where they would not freeze. Squash, pumpkins, and turnips could be stored for months when protected from freezing. Peaches, plums, apples, and other fruits were dried for storage. Some apples and pears were stored in cool places such as cellars or outside "dairies," which were rock-walled buildings partly submerged into the hillside.

Chickens, turkeys, ducks, geese, sheep, hogs, and cattle were grown on most farms for producing eggs, feathers, wool, milk, and meat. Poultry provided a variety of products, and the meat did not have to be preserved since the animal was kept alive until it was needed and all of it was used. Hogs were probably the most important large animal raised, since the meat could be cured by salting and smoking and stored for long periods of time. Lard rendered from hog fat was a favorite for cooking. Cattle and goats were primarily kept for milk production. Horses, mules, and cattle were used as work animals. Field crops such as corn were grown primarily to provide feed for livestock. Some corn—especially white corn—was taken to mills to be ground. In addition, tobacco was an important cash crop in some parts of the Appalachian region. Tobacco was also grown for personal use and made into "twist" for chewing and crumbled for pipe tobacco. Appalachian women often chewed tobacco or smoked a pipe.

Virtually no subsistence farms exist today in Appalachia. This is partially because the number of farms operating in the United States has decreased 50 percent since 1950. Some of the land in small farms in Appalachia has been incorporated into larger farms, but much of it has reverted back to woodland.

See also: AGRICULTURAL FRONTIERS; CHESTNUT BLIGHT (ENVIRONMENT); SUSTAINABLE AGRICULTURE.

—Garry D. Lacefield and Monroe Rasnake, *University of Kentucky*

L. E. Brown and W. Brannen, *Kentucky Agricultural Statistics* (2000); Janet Tietyen, *Kentucky Farms and Food*, University of Kentucky, College of Agriculture Cooperative Extension Publication FCS3-528 (2000); Richard Ulak et al., *Atlas of Kentucky* (1998).

Sustainable Agriculture

Sustainable agriculture is a farming approach that maintains viable productivity while at the same time preserving the ecosystem. In Appalachia sustainability is influenced by many of the same factors that affect the rest of the United States, including the availability of labor and capital. However, the primary restriction to sustainable agriculture development in the region continues to be the shortage of good farmland. In most of the region, the land is steep and the soil shallow and infertile, limiting farmers to permanent cover crops such as forages or trees for achieving longterm sustainability. In this environment, conservation of agricultural resources is vital to the continued survival of farming in the region, and several strategies have been employed over the years by public and private agencies, as well as farmers working independently, to develop sustainable farming practices.

In order for an agricultural system to be sustainable, available resources must maintain productivity, protect the resource base, and keep farms economically viable using methods acceptable to the community. The system must be adaptable to changes in available resources and social demands. Systems that are at one time sustainable may become non-sustainable. A prime example in the Appalachian area is the subsistence system of farming that required a plentiful supply of both land and labor. When these resources were lost and farmers found easier sources of off-farm income, subsistence farming virtually disappeared.

Conventional agriculture is designed to maximize yields through intensive use of energy. Since primary energy sources are nonrenewable oil and natural gas, the system cannot be sustained indefinitely. Unless new and renewable sources of energy can be developed, agriculture may be forced to revert to a less energy-intensive system. This could require that a much larger percentage of the population be directly involved in agriculture production as in the early twentieth century.

Soil conservation is particularly relevant to the mountainous areas of Appalachia, where erosion can quickly become disastrous to small fields situated on steep slopes. An increasingly popular method of control involves the management of crop residue through conservation tillage systems. Although there are variations on this type of tillage, they all involve leaving the plant residue (the nonharvested parts of the plants) to cover at least 30 percent of the soil surface from one year's harvest until the next season's planting. This system not only protects the soil against wind and water erosion but, as little or no tilling is involved, requires less time, labor, and energy resources, leaving farmers to attend to other facets of their operations. In 1995 an estimated 35 percent of crop acreage in Appalachia and the Northeast was planted using conservation techniques, with more than half of those planted using no-till practices.

Recognizing the necessity of conservation practices in creating sustainable agriculture, national legislation such as the Agriculture, Conservation and Rural Enhancement Act of 2001 has, among other farming concerns, provided conservation payment programs through which farmers are compensated for investments in sound conservation practices on working farmland. Agriculture extension offices and soil conservation districts provide encouragement in the form of education, low-priced equipment rentals, and the organizational ability to coordinate resources over large areas. There are also many nongovernmental agencies that promote conservation and sustainable farming practices. Organizations such as Core 4, the Appalachian Sustainable Agriculture Project, farmers' cooperatives, and universities throughout the region provide assistance with conservation tillage, pest and weed management, nutrient management, conservation buffers (vegetated areas separating cropland from surface water sources), and other problems.

Some conventional agricultural practices have become socially unacceptable, leading to increased awareness of sustainability issues. Public opposition to the overuse of chemical pesticides has resulted in the removal of some pesticides from use and prompted the expansion of organic farming in the United States. Large hog and poultry operations are facing increased opposition from the public because of the concentration of animal waste. The primary concerns are odor and the risk of water pollution from accidental spills and improper land application of the waste. Alternative methods of raising livestock, such as the use of portable poultry pens instead of large houses, are being explored throughout the region. The use of genetically modified plants and animals in agricultural production also raises concerns about risks to human health and the ecosystem. All of these things indicate that social acceptance may become a more important factor in directing agricultural sustainability in the future.

Consumer demands also influence the choices farmers make in attaining sustainability. Organic farming, a method that eschews synthetic fertilizers, herbicides, and pesticides, is an example of sustainable agriculture that could work well in the Appalachian region to help keep a limited number of farms in operation. It does not require large acreage of good farmland but does need to be near large population areas in order to provide a sufficient demand for organic produce. However, it is unlikely that a truly organic system can sustain adequate production of food and fiber to supply the needs of a large percentage of the population. Alternative agriculture is a middle-of-the-road system that, among such strategies as the cultivation of specialty and niche crops and other nontraditional activities, seeks to reduce the dependence on chemicals and other purchased inputs but does not advocate complete elimination of them, as does organic farming. Full utilization of natural processes such as biological nitrogen fixation, organic mulches for weed control, crop rotations, and intercropping for disease and insect control can replace some off-farm inputs and improve sustainability of the system.

Tree farming is perhaps best suited for most of Appalachia due to the abundance of steep, rough land. Sustainability of tree farming is simplified due to the crop's long growing period (usually four to sixteen years for Christmas trees, up to thirty years for softwoods, and as long as a century for quality hardwoods), low need for inputs during the growing cycle, and ability to protect the soil resource. Limitations to sustainability are the high-energy requirements for harvesting, the large land base needed to provide annual income for economic sustainability, and social resistance to some timber-harvesting practices. Alternative harvesting systems such as selective cutting rather than clear-cutting can be used—especially on a smaller scale—to help overcome those limitations to tree farming sustainability.

Resource conservation, alternative crops, and less intensive methods of cultivation that promote sustainable agriculture are rapidly gaining acceptance in Appalachia. Into the twenty-first century, farmers throughout the region are increasingly dedicated to the idea that land must be used, not consumed, if farming is to remain a way of life for generations to come.

See also: ALTERNATIVE CROPS; ALTERNATIVE FARMING; LAND TRUSTS AND CONSERVANCIES (ENVIRONMENT).

—Garry D. Lacefield and Monroe Rasnake, *University of Kentucky*

C. S. Edwards et al., eds., *Sustainable Agriculture Systems* (1990); John Pesek, *Alternative Agriculture* (1989); J. F. Tisdale, ed., *Highlights of a Sustainable Agriculture Workshop* (1993).

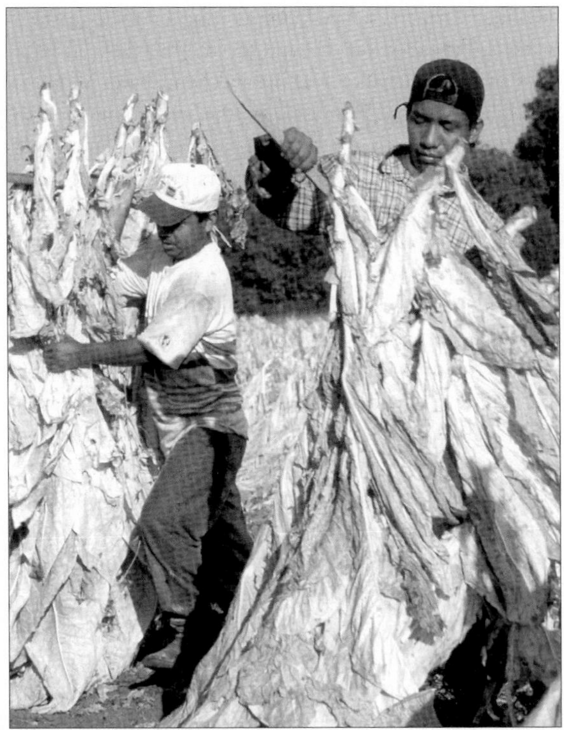

Tobacco harvest in east Tennessee, 1999. Growers of tobacco have relied on migrant workers to plant and harvest their crops each year since the early nineteenth century.

Tobacco

Tobacco cultivation is a defining aspect of community in many mountain areas. In the twenty-first century, children in some tobacco regions still are given time off from school in the fall to help their families cut, stake, and store the crop. Tobacco remains an important part of local culture, with many older farmers continuing to put in a crop simply to maintain their ties to the past. Some mountain farmers accuse tobacco companies of conspiring to keep prices low at auctions and boycott national retail chains that refuse to sell cigarettes. Mountain politicians regularly vote to protect tobacco subsidies. But demand for tobacco has declined, a fact that has rippled through the regional economy, affecting even those not directly involved in tobacco cultivation. As farmers make the transition to other crops, businesses that serve tobacco farmers are left without a clientele. For example, in the early twentieth century, Asheville, North Carolina, boasted a dozen tobacco warehouses. By 1999, all but two had closed.

For thousands of years, tobacco has shaped Appalachia's culture and economy. Though scholars are unsure when native peoples first cultivated tobacco, archaeologists have unearthed organic evidence and tobacco-related artifacts dating from 1500 B.C. Native Americans had numerous uses for tobacco, but it was most important for trade and ceremonial purposes.

Appalachian tribes such as the Cherokee cultivated tobacco, and European settlers soon recognized the importance of the golden leaf. Jamestown resident John Rolfe, though not a settler of Appalachia, helped make mountain tobacco cultivation possible by creating a market for North American tobacco in England. Introducing Caribbean seeds, Rolfe was able to produce a crop more marketable than native leaf. Through westward migration, Europeans had instituted profitable tobacco cultivation in the Appalachian sections of Virginia and North Carolina by the early eighteenth century. Tobacco was labor-intensive, and mountain farmers often used indentured servants or African slaves to work the crop.

Tobacco cultivation had spread into eastern Tennessee, northern Georgia, Kentucky, and eastern Ohio by the early nineteenth century. Though other tobacco-producing areas saw a decline in the number of farmers during the antebellum years, the number of mountain farmers remained fairly static. The crop represented a source of cash for individual farmers and continued to link Appalachia to the national and world economies. Tobacco was important in other ways as well, serving as a market crop and in more isolated communities as a direct form of currency. By the 1820s, mountain farmers stopped transporting crops to eastern markets, instead selling their tobacco at auctions in local hubs such as Asheville, Danville and Lynchburg, Virginia, and Johnson City, Tennessee. At the same time tobacco sales were changing, the varieties cultivated in Appalachia were as well. Originally, most farmers grew dark, course, air-dried burley tobacco, which was best suited for use as chewing tobacco. By the 1860s, flue-cured or bright leaf tobacco had replaced burley as a favored crop of farmers in some mountain areas of Virginia and North Carolina.

After the Civil War, tobacco continued to play a significant role in mountain agriculture. The mechanization of cigarette production in the 1880s by corporations such as the American Tobacco Company increased the demand for tobacco and introduced powerful new players into the tobacco market. Unfortunately, farmers reaped few benefits from the expansion of the cigarette industry. Tobacco companies controlled the auctions and often the government tobacco graders as well. Farmers believed that the giant corporations conspired to keep market prices low, creating tension that erupted in violence in the early twentieth century. Auction houses across Appalachia were burned, and buyers and graders were assaulted. Other mountain farmers took more direct action. In 1908 tobacco farmers in Kentucky and Tennessee, disappointed at the price offered at American Tobacco Company auctions, formed cooperatives to keep their leaf off the market until they were paid a decent price. By uniting, farmers forced cigarette company officials to meet a number of demands, setting an important example as a successful grassroots agrarian protest.

The Great Depression hit Appalachian tobacco farmers hard, and federal efforts to alleviate their suffering dramatically reshaped the economics and culture of mountain tobacco cultivation. The Agricultural Adjustment Act of 1933 provided for federal price supports of several commodities including tobacco, with the proviso that the government would institute an allotment system in the spring of 1934. Tobacco farmers who agreed to limit production by cultivating a certain percentage of their acreage would receive cash for taking land out of production. While regulating tobacco production, the allotment system was controversial. Many mountain farmers resisted the government's telling them how much tobacco to grow or what to do with their land. Others tried to bypass allotment regulations, only to be caught by federal agriculture officials or turned in by their neighbors. Also, the government paid the landowner for taking acreage out of production, not the person who actually farmed the land, a policy that displaced thousands of tenant families.

Mountain tobacco production after World War II continued to reap the mixed harvest of New Deal programs. The allotment system became a permanent fixture in tobacco economics, and though prices stabilized, smaller mountain farmers often sold their fields to larger producers. For the family farms that remained, profits were increasingly slim. Migrant labor replaced family members on larger farms, changing both the demographics and culture of Appalachia. Fewer and fewer mountain farmers relied on tobacco as their major cash crop.

Tobacco has helped define mountain culture, linked the region to the larger economy, and served as an important catalyst for change. Tobacco is a crop that, for better or worse, mirrors much of Appalachia's social and economic history and will potentially play a role in shaping the region's future.

See also: AGRICULTURAL COOPERATIVES; ALTERNATIVE CROPS; MIGRANT LABOR.

—Richard D. Starnes, *Western Carolina University*

Tracy Campbell, *The Politics of Despair: Power and Resistance in the Tobacco Wars* (1993); Pete Daniel, *Breaking the Land: The Transformation of Cotton, Tobacco, and Rice Cultures since 1880* (1985); Wilma A. Dunaway, *The First American Frontier: Transition to Capitalism in Southern Appalachia, 1700–1860* (1996).

Trees, Shrubs, and Native Plants

The early explorers of the Appalachian region entered an ecosystem unlike anything in Europe. Forest covered virtually the entire territory, and the diversity of trees, shrubs, and native plants astonished these adventurers. The mountains were rounded and generally heavily forested. Though explorers such as Hernando de Soto and Juan Pardo did not discover the gold they sought, they found a natural world teeming with game, timber, and botanicals that would soon attract later explorers and inspire poets and chroniclers.

The Appalachian Mountains stretch from Newfoundland to northern Alabama. The flora of the mountain range resulted from geologic and climatic changes that differed significantly from those in Europe. Northern and subalpine plant species were pushed southward during four glacier periods, adapting to the mountain climates alongside southern species. As the North American glaciers receded, hardwood forests followed them up the chain. In Europe the hardwood forests never reestablished. Of the two thousand species of Appalachian flora, more than two hundred are native and wholly confined to the southern Appalachians. Ferns, mosses, and mushrooms of many species also are part of the complex Appalachian plant life.

Reports by early explorers and later settlers of dense forests, plant diversity, and exotic species stirred the curiosity of landscape gardeners, plant collectors, physicians, textile dyers, and poets across Europe. Native plant materials became an early export for the American colonies and increased as settlement moved westward into the Appalachian system. The transfer of plants to Europe was managed at first through informal channels. Diplomats and missionaries, sea captains and travelers sent seeds and tubers home. Avid plant collectors such as Henry Compton, Peter Collinson, and Robert Ferber, who published a catalog of the plants and shrubs he handled, corresponded with like-minded collectors and gardeners throughout Europe. Physicians and herbalists also had great interest in the exotic plants of America and were soon funding expeditions to stock their pharmaceutical collections.

Often considered the father of American botany, John Bartram was a self-educated naturalist and explorer and the botanist for the American colonies to King George III. Bartram was the first American experimenter to hybridize flowering plants. In thirty years of collecting and exporting seeds and plants from the Alleghenies, the Carolinas, and other areas of North America, he sent some two hundred important plants to British gardens in sufficient quantity that they became widespread there. His son, William, continued his professional work.

William Bartram was commissioned by William Fothergill in 1773 to collect plants and seeds for his extensive garden. He departed alone for the Cherokee territory in April 1775. Along the way he both discovered new species and recorded the presence of known ones. His *Travels* (1791) lists many trees (dogwood, chestnut, stewardia, franklina, Carolina silverbell, sourwood, serviceberry, sugar maple, birch, walnut, cherry, red spruce, fir, hemlock, cucumber magnolia), shrubs (flame azalea, rhododendron, laurel, fothergilla, witchhazel, leucothoe, viburnum, yaupon holly, sassafras), and native herbaceous plants (ginseng, St. John's wort, strawberry, lady's slippers, trillium, Venus flytrap, mistletoe).

Botanist Andre Michaux established a nursery in New Jersey and shipped a significant quantity of plants to the gardens of Rambouillet and Versailles. In 1785 he followed the same route as Bartram, returning to the Appalachians in 1788, 1790, and 1794. He discovered the rare shortia, the object of more than a hundred years of later search. His son, Francois, taught the settlers near Grandfather Mountain how to dig and dry ginseng for Asian markets. John Fraser, for whom the Fraser fir and Fraser magnolia are named, had been the botanical collector for Catherine the Great of Russia and came to the Carolinas first in 1785. In 1799 he made another trip, discovering along the way the Catawba rhododendron, from which most hybrid rhododendrons are bred.

Early settlers quickly discovered uses for the abundant natural resources. Tulip poplars, sometimes eighty feet or more in height and eight to twelve feet in diameter, were used for cabin construction. Sugar maples were a source of sweetener. Chestnuts provided not only timber and tanning bark but also nuts for winter consumption and for sale. Walnut, cherry, apple, hickory, hazelnut, and other trees also provided both foodstuffs and valuable timber for special uses. Locust, oak, sassafras, dogwood, sourwood, ash, black gum, and basswood were harvested for barrel staves, pins, axe handles, axles, oxbows, bowls, furniture, and other uses. The timber industry later stripped much of the standing forests during the early part of the twentieth century. Logging and the harvest of hardwoods and pulpwood for furniture and paper continue but are much diminished industries today. Plantations of Christmas trees are rapidly overtaking traditional timber production.

By necessity, mountain settlers developed knowledge of herbal medicine, and this lore soon became a source of income. Families gathered goldenseal, bee balm, boneset, catnip, ginseng, New Jersey tea, blue cohosh, angelica, trillium, wintergreen, cardinal flower, bloodroot, sassafras, passionflower, pokeweed, Solomon's seal, echinacea, witchhazel, deertongue, various mints, yarrows, and other herbs for remedies. For most of the nineteenth century Shakers were the major traders in these products until companies such as Wilcox Drug of Boone, North Carolina, which collected and shipped more than a million pounds of these herbs in one year alone (1970), came to dominate. Trade in these plants can be quite lucrative with some varieties fetching very high prices; ginseng has commanded as much as $500 per pound of dried root, leading to the poaching of up to $5.3 million in green gold from the Great Smoky Mountains National Park in 2000.

The floral and nursery industries of Appalachia have developed into significant sources of income. The production of Christmas trees and greenery is a major agricultural industry. The floristry industry pays collectors to gather galax, break ivy (mountain laurel), break boxwood, holly, and mistletoe, as well as other greenery, and to harvest sheet moss. Nursery production of shrubs and native plants is a significant agricultural industry. The Cullowhee Native Plant Conference and regional agricultural universities have influenced the nursery industry to use native plants and encouraged Appalachian nurseries to grow species native to the region.

See also: AGRICULTURAL FRONTIERS; FOREST MANAGEMENT AND CONSERVATION (ENVIRONMENT); SUSTAINABLE AGRICULTURE.

—Newton Smith, *Western Carolina University*

William Bartram, *Travels through North and South Carolina, Georgia, East and West Florida, the Cherokee Country, the Extensive Territories of the Muscogulges or Creek Confederacy, and the Country of the Chactaws* (1791); Michael Frome, *Strangers in High Places: The Story of the Great Smoky Mountains* (1980); Arthur Stupka, *Trees, Shrubs, and Woody Vines of the Great Smoky Mountains National Park* (1964).

Mrs. Ed Hurst demonstrating culling to clubwomen, Franklin County, Alabama, 1927. Traditionally responsible for raising food-producing livestock, including chickens, cows, and hogs, Appalachian farmwomen often shared information through home demonstration clubs.

Women in Agriculture

In Appalachia, women were central to farming operations throughout most of the nineteenth and twentieth centuries. Although the quality of life and material conditions on the region's farms vary considerably, women historically have performed heavy work inside and outside the house and remain crucial to the success of farming.

Until the first quarter of the twentieth century, most Appalachian farms produced most of their own food, clothing, and shelter. In addition to bearing and rearing children and manufacturing clothing, Appalachian farmwomen were responsible for much of this subsistence production. They generally raised large gardens and preserved huge quantities of food for their families' winter diets. Women were also traditionally responsible for food-producing livestock, attending to chickens, cows, and hogs. Women participated in the butchering of hogs and preservation of pork and gathered berries and medicinal herbs in forests around their homes.

In addition to subsistence production, women frequently engaged in farm labor traditionally seen as "men's work." During the busiest times, they often worked in the fields alongside their husbands and children, planting or harvesting crops. Some women participated in farm management, sharing decision making with their husbands. Others kept the farm financial records.

On many Appalachian farms, women earned a substantial portion of the family's income by selling or bartering their surplus garden and livestock products. Women sold milk, butter, and cheese, eggs, garden produce, freshly gathered berries, medicinal plants, and other products to provide necessities and luxuries for their families. In lean years, women's milk and butter sales might provide the farm's only cash income.

Many black farmwomen, and some white women, took off-farm jobs to supplement the family income. Most often, they took jobs as domestic workers for more prosperous whites. White women sometimes clerked at crossroads stores or worked in canneries. Off-farm jobs proved more accessible to farmwomen who lived near towns. A few Appalachian women, mostly widows or single daughters who inherited land, operated their own farms. These women farmers depended on children, neighbors, and hired help in peak seasons and for heavy work, but they often performed much farm labor and management themselves.

With the arrival of industry in the late nineteenth and early twentieth centuries, many men took jobs in mines, lumber camps, and factories. Women replaced the labor of their absent husbands on the farms, continuing to provide much of the family's subsistence, thus reducing their dependence on wages from off-farm jobs. During economic downturns and prolonged strikes by unionized workers, women's subsistence production often secured the family's survival.

The role of women on Appalachia's contemporary commercial farms varies widely. Some continue to be full-time homemakers while others have off-farm jobs. Many continue to be partners in the farm's operation by sharing in farm management, keeping the books, or contributing farm labor.

See also: HOME DEMONSTRATION CLUBS; PART-TIME FARMING; SUBSISTENCE FARMING.

—Melissa Walker, *Converse College*

Oral History of Appalachia Collection, Archives of Appalachia, Marshall University (1970–76); Mary Beth Pudup, "Women's Work in the West Virginia Economy," *West Virginia History* (1990); Melissa Walker, *All We Knew Was to Farm: Rural Women in the Upcountry South, 1919–1941* (2000).

BLAST FU

Business, Industry, and Technology

Section Editors: Michael E. Birdwell and Jack Hurst

At the opening of the twenty-first century, Appalachia was still participating strongly in the national economy but continuing to struggle, as it had for years, in such traditionally important industries as coal, steel, textiles and apparel, and tobacco. Timber, by contrast, had rebounded—a century past the heyday of industrial logging. But broad technological advances that increased productivity and profits in several sectors had often multiplied negative effects of retrenchment and introduced new threats to the environment. Even though the region remained more dependent on manufacturing and other blue-collar jobs than the rest of the United States, it was becoming increasingly reliant on an expanding service economy to counterbalance the continuing decline of its heavy manufacturing, and thus a profusion of mini-industries appeared to be developing. In one service employment category alone, Eating and Drinking, the number of Appalachian employees rose from 186,000 in 1969 to 660,000 in 2003. Such tracking of the region's economic cycles and the ebb and flow of its individual business and industrial sectors is made possible by data provided by the Appalachian Regional Commission and collected and organized by Regional Economic Models, Inc., of Amherst, Massachusetts, since the 1980s.

In 2002 Appalachia continued to produce nearly 40 percent of the nation's coal, an amount sufficient to generate half of the electricity used in the United States. Still, 2002 Appalachian coal production, totaling more than 396 million tons, represented a drop of 8.1 percent from 2001 and was the industry's lowest in two decades. Over the same two decades, the number of Appalachian coal-mining jobs fell from 159,143 to 46,239. Yet total U.S. coal production from the beginning to the end of that time rose substantially, from 782.1 million tons extracted in 1983 to 1,093.8 million tons in 2002.

The 2002 Appalachian decrease was partly attributable to slowed demand at the coke plants of the U.S. steel industry, which, battered by cheaper overseas imports, used 9.3 percent less coal—just 23.7 million tons—during the same period. Appalachia's largest (and America's second largest) coal-producing state, West Virginia, decreased production by 7.6 percent. Eastern Kentucky decreased production by 12.4 percent and Pennsylvania by 7.8 percent, while Alabama, Ohio, Tennessee, and Virginia showed decreases ranging from 2.2 percent in Alabama to 16.7 percent in

Facing page: Blast furnace at Jones and Laughlin Steel Company's Aliquippa Works, Aliquippa, Pennsylvania, 1953. Booming Appalachian steel mills that once lit the night skies fell silent in the late twentieth century as the world economy exerted new pressures on American industry.

Miners of Paramont Mining Company operate a continuous mining machine at No. 1 Mine in Wise, Virginia, 1982. Picks and shovels became nearly obsolete with the development of machines capable of clawing through seams of coal faster than shuttle cars could haul it away. As of 2002, nearly 40 percent of the nation's coal was being mined in Appalachia.

Ohio. The only Appalachian state with an increase, Maryland, grew its production by 10.8 percent, but its total tonnage was just 5.1 million.

Pittsburgh, Appalachia's urban capital and the center of the American steel industry, had become both of those things in significant part because it also was headquarters to the internationally powerful Mellon Bank, which had long-standing business ties to a phalanx of some of America's best-known companies: Alcoa, Gulf Oil, United States Steel, Westinghouse, Pittsburgh Plate Glass, the Heinz Corporation, and Monsanto, among others. Finance burgeoned across the region over the final decades of the twentieth century. Jobs in banking, a service industry on both individual and corporate levels, doubled in the region, with 219,534 employees in that field in 2003 compared to 108,859 in 1969. Credit and finance employment during the same period almost tripled, from 41,046 in 1969 to 111,614 in 2003.

But Pittsburgh at the turn of the new century still contended with—and some of its corporate decision makers promoted—a general outflow and outsourcing of manufacturing and jobs to less expensive overseas workforces. The Steel City also endured a radical contraction of its signature industry, leading to the bankruptcy of some three dozen companies between 1998 and 2003 alone. By 2003, the failed firms were being acquired by an emerging Big Three that included venerable U.S. Steel. Pittsburgh's city government, however, remained financially distressed, having run annual budget deficits of 9 to 12 percent between 1998 and 2002.

Production of Appalachia's most profitable agricultural commodity, burley tobacco, had shrunk to less than a fourth of its former size as base quotas were cut, and from 1969 to 2003 the number of jobs in tobacco manufacturing dropped from 18,236 to 4,213. Increased governmental regulation of smoking and tobacco advertisement prompted U.S. tobacco companies to focus increasing efforts abroad. By 2003, Philip Morris, the nation's leading cigarette manufacturer, was selling more than two-thirds of its products overseas. In 2004 both the U.S. Senate and House of Representatives passed legislation providing for a government buyout of farmers' tobacco allotments in an effort to further discourage smoking and other tobacco uses without disproportionately affecting small farmers who have long depended on tobacco as a cash crop.

Likewise, textile and apparel manufacturers, industries associated with Appalachia for many decades, were steadily emigrating. From 1970 to 2001, apparel workers in the region decreased from almost a quarter-million to 83,000, while textile employees dropped from 275,000 to 193,000.

During the same general period, both the lumber industry and its workforce grew markedly. Between 1969 and 2003, the number of lumber jobs in the region grew from 74,269 to 131,340. An allied field, furniture making, also expanded its employment significantly, from 88,295 jobs to 116,121. Timber's dollar impact was most visible in the states of Tennessee, Kentucky, and West Virginia, where the wood industry employed a combined total of about 88,000 workers around the opening of the present century and produced a $6.3-billion impact on the economy.

Individually, many other Appalachian or Appalachia-rooted companies and entities had become nationally important in a wide variety of categories by the early twenty-first century. Pittsburgh-headquartered Alcoa was the world's largest manufacturer of sheet aluminum for drink cans, and in 2000 it acquired most of the facilities of Reynolds Metals, another prominent Appalachian aluminum manufacturer with major operations in north Alabama. The soft drink Mountain Dew, having originated, as did Reynolds, in east Tennessee, exchanged its original hillbilly image for a youthful aura to become one of the nation's better-known nonalcoholic commercial beverages.

The Heinz Corporation, which long since had expanded from condiments to acquire Del Monte Foods and StarKist Tuna, boasted number one or number two branded products in some fifty countries. North Carolina and Mississippi together produced one-fourth of the furniture manufactured in the United States, and Broyhill, now owned by the St. Louis–based worldwide conglomerate Furniture Brands International, claimed to be the furniture brand most recognized by 90 percent of buyers. Deer Park was the sixth-largest bottled water variety in the United States as of 1999, and Kentucky Fried Chicken had become the world's foremost restaurant retailer of chicken.

Little Debbie styled itself America's largest manufacturer of snack cakes. Tennessee marble was used in such edifices as the U.S. Capitol building in Washington, D.C., and the New York Public Library. General Nutrition Center was an international operation, promoting itself as the world's largest retailer of vitamin, mineral, and herbal supplements as well as sports nutrition and personal care products. Bush Brothers claimed 80 percent of the U.S. market for sugary baked beans, Appalachian Ohio annually ranked at or near the top nationally in the production of clay for the making of fire bricks, and Harris-Tarkett manufactured flooring sold across the United States and in Europe.

The economic story of Appalachia is that of a once insular and self-supporting region that over the course of a century and a half became inexorably dependent on business trends in the rest of the nation and the world and fought against long odds on many fronts to keep pace with better-capitalized exterior forces. This descent into dependence evolved in successive eras and resulted mostly from perceived progress rather than the opposite. The rise of industries connected with the extraction and distribution of coal, iron, timber, and commercial agriculture products in the late nineteenth century presented those goods to the world beyond, causing national and international boom-and-bust cycles to resonate increasingly in Appalachian hills and hollows from southwestern New York to northeastern Mississippi.

By the opening of the twentieth century, the coming of cash wages had lured many Appalachian residents away from subsistence agriculture into mines, mills, and logging camps. From 1900 to 1930 the number of the region's wage earners increased by 75 percent, fifteen times the increase in its number of farmers. Then the Great Depression diminished demand for and/or the capacity to buy natural resources and other regional products. World War II preceded a postwar manufacturing expansion that required coal for its fuel, and with the exception of burley tobacco, agriculture slipped farther and farther down the region's list of profitable occupations.

During the years between 1870 and 1950, Pittsburgh was Appalachia's unrivaled industrial capital and provided sharp contrast to the dependency stereotype of the region. The city was the seat not only of the steel industry but other nationally and regionally critical business blocs, most notably finance and coal. Decisions from corporate boardrooms directed much of the harvesting of the region's fossil fuels and funded large railroad and manufacturing firms that carried these mineral resources to markets around the globe. Over the final half of the 1900s, however, Pittsburgh declined in population and power, and its downslide coincided with the relocation of American heavy industry overseas and with the shift of the median Appalachian population southward toward more medium-sized and diverse municipalities.

Between 1950 and 1990, Pittsburgh's city population shrank from a peak of 676,806 to 369,879, and the reduction affected a broad surrounding area. In 1980 half of Appalachia's residents still lived in the 144 counties comprising the region's northern sector, but by 1996 the proportion had fallen to 46.2 percent. During the same period, the numbers in the 170-county southern sector rose from 39.4 to 44 percent. The central subregion, comprising eastern Kentucky, West Virginia, southwest Virginia, and part of northeast Tennessee, Appalachia's poorest and least accessible area, slipped from 2,143,052 residents to 2,125,095.

From 1979 to 1991 alone, Pittsburgh's manufacturing jobs fell by half. The 1992 passage of the North American Free Trade Agreement (NAFTA) precipitated another exodus of overseas-bound manufacturing, textile, and other industrial jobs from communities across the entire region. But the reverberations of the city's decline shook northern and central Appalachia particularly, because Pittsburgh controlled not only the steel industry, the best-paying of the region's urban blue-collar employers, but also much of the coal industry, which supplied many of the nonagricultural jobs in the region's more rural areas. Between 1980 and 1986, from 9,000 to 18,000 residents each were lost by Binghamton, New York, the Pennsylvania towns of Johnstown, Erie, and Wilkes-Barre, Chattanooga, Tennessee, and the South's primary steelmaking city, Birmingham, Alabama.

Pennsylvania's second-largest city sat atop part of one of the six major eastern coalfields of North America—the famed Pittsburgh seam of bituminous coal extending from central and western Pennsylvania into northern West Virginia, southeastern Ohio, and western Maryland. Three of the other five seams were also in Appalachia: the anthracite coal region of northeastern Pennsylvania; a cluster of semi-bituminous deposits in southwest Virginia, southern West Virginia, eastern Kentucky, and northeast Tennessee; and another seam stretching from southwest of Knoxville, Tennessee, across and down the Cumberland Plateau into northern Alabama. Of the other two, one was in eastern Canada and the other in the comparative flatlands of Indiana, Illinois, and western Kentucky.

Even before railroads snaked their way into Appalachia to haul out the "black gold," Pittsburgh was already connected—by 128 navigable miles of the Monongahela River—to a developing major mining center at Fairmont, West Virginia. The Ohio River meanwhile also linked the city, via the Mississippi River, to ocean traffic in the Gulf of Mexico. The first Pittsburgh-marketed West Virginia coal came from Fairmont in 1852, and the Pennsylvania city quickly became a major supervisor of Appalachian coal production.

Between 1840, when coal was beginning to fuel the onset of the American Industrial Revolution, and 1900, when that revolution started coming into its own, coal production in the United States increased from about a million tons to about 250 million tons. From the turn of the century to the mid-1920s, it increased by another 500 percent. By 1950, Appalachian production alone totaled 516.3 million tons, which grew to 628.8 million tons by 1980 and 693.2 million tons by 1990.

At the end of the twentieth century, the steel industry faced much the same kind of crisis it had encountered a century earlier, when with the assistance of Pittsburgh financier Andrew Mellon U.S. Steel was formed in 1901 by combining several struggling steelmakers. Four years after the United States had become the world's largest steel-manufacturing nation in 1897, U.S. Steel began operations as the world's largest steel company and the first firm in America to claim a billion-dollar market capitalization. After prolonged labor struggles during the late 1800s and early 1900s, U.S. Steel was unionized, and its workers became some of the best-compensated hourly employees in the country.

By the late 1900s, though, the industry strained under the burden of paying health-care benefits to its retirees, who at old-line companies outnumbered current workers by as many as eight to one. Firms declared bankruptcy to evade these responsibilities and moved more jobs overseas to avoid incurring new ones. Meanwhile, retirements and layoffs increased as the industry divested itself of 90 percent of its employees during the early and mid-1980s, helping to wipe out nearly 100,000 manufacturing jobs during that decade in Pittsburgh alone. While the nation as a whole lost 6 percent of its factory jobs from 1980 to 1986, Pittsburgh lost 44 percent.

By 2003, Appalachian jobs in primary metals stood at a total of 100,549, down another 45,000 from 1985, and the world picture looked challenging for the American steel industry. As the nonunion minimill Nucor Corporation, the newly formed International Steel Group, and U.S. Steel began buying up bankrupt competitors in an attempted resurrection, total global steel production stood at a billion tons annually, 200 million tons in excess of worldwide demand.

The year 1994, when NAFTA took effect, was another benchmark in the acceleration of job loss as American companies sought the least costly overhead in order to attract and retain stockholders. Effects on Appalachia were probably as marked as on the rest of the United States, although experts caution that many of the job losses in specific sectors—for instance, in the manufacturing of machinery and computing equipment, which fell from 175,327 in 1994 to 130,002 in 2003—were probably more attributable to automation and direct competition with lower-cost imported goods than the result of outsourcing of jobs overseas. However, all three factors are heavily influenced by the same dynamic: trade's inexorably increasing globalism. In chemical plants, the number of employees shrank from 104,307 to 81,939 during the same decade. As noted earlier, coal, steel, and tobacco agriculture had seen prolonged contraction, as had apparel and textiles.

In Blue Ridge, Georgia, a town of nearly 2,000, Levi Strauss and Company closed a jeans-making plant in 2002 in a move whose causes and effects illustrated the NAFTA phenomenon in the region. The company was decreasing its hands-on manufacturing everywhere, outsourcing that work to countries where wages were substantially less. Part of the goal was to produce jeans that could be sold for about $20.00 per pair in the U.S., whose residents buy more clothes than any other people in world history.

At the time, the average work rate per hour in Guatemala was $0.37, in China $0.28, in Nicaragua $0.23, and in Bangladesh as little as $0.13. The Blue Ridge Levi Strauss plant paid $10.79. The facility had employed about 400 people, and they tended to be unsuited for retraining for other jobs because they were older and unable to afford to take the time to go back to school. With little industry left, Blue Ridge fell to providing antique shops, retirement and convalescent homes, and summer residences for wealthy Atlantans.

Throughout Appalachia, protection of the environment has become an increasingly important consideration for the business community as well as public officials. In the late twentieth century the region faced the cumulative downside of operations by its traditional industries. Long ignored or flouted, environmental regulations came to be seriously enforced, and new ones were added by state governments, Congress, and federal agencies. Although conflicts over environmental regulations became a national phenomenon, many of the most conspicuous took place in central Appalachia. Strip mining, mountaintop removal, and the clear-cutting of timber placed mounting pressures on the environment and quality of life as improving technology increased the efficiency of production. As late as 1998, government officials in West Virginia, a state in which mountaintop removal was widespread, acknowledged that they did not know how many such projects were underway there. These operations dumped thousands of tons of rock and dirt into adjacent valleys, obliterating or polluting streambeds. Large coal-waste reservoirs also posed threats to miles of streams. Available figures showed that nearly 500 square miles of West Virginia had been strip mined between 1981 and 1998 and that the average size of acreage on new strip-mining permits had doubled, to about 450 acres, between 1993 and 1998.

Environmental issues were not limited to the mining industry, nor indeed to privately owned businesses and industries. For many decades, Tennessee residents along the Pigeon River downstream from the Champion Fibre plant in Canton, North Carolina, complained that the stream ran dark with Champion chemical waste that was carried all the way to Knoxville. Coal-fueled power plants of the Tennessee Valley Authority (TVA) were decried by environmental groups as prime polluters of the region's air, particularly in the Great Smoky Mountains and Shenandoah National Parks, and in 2000 the National Parks Conservation Association filed suit against TVA alleging that it had violated air standards for "visible emissions" at its Kingston and John Sevier plants in Tennessee thousands of times since 1995. A study of 14,095 workers hired at Oak Ridge National Laboratories between 1943 and 1972 linked low-level radiation exposure to shortened lives, with cancer mortality estimated to have increased by about 5 percent. Far better known, the effects of smoking came to threaten the continued existence of Appalachian tobacco fields.

Central Appalachia (including eastern Kentucky, West Virginia, southwest Virginia, and northeast Tennessee) remained the area with the weakest economy in the region throughout the final decades of the twentieth century. Between 1969 and 2003 the population in the northern subregion, undergoing drastic deindustrialization, remained almost level, increasing from 9.8 million to 9.9 million, while the number swelled in the southern subregion from 6.9 million to 11 million; in the central subregion, by contrast, it started from 1.8 million and grew to just 2.1 million.

Similarly, the central subregion had much less federal employment, both civilian and military, than the other two. In 2003 the southern claimed the most, with 75,000 civilian positions and 45,000 military ones, while the northern had 65,000 and 38,000; the central had just 12,500 and 11,200.

Yet wage rates, numbers of jobs, and disposable income in Appalachia as a whole continued to rise as its service economy expanded. Between 1969 and 2000, hospital jobs increased from about 147,500 to 385,000, while those in nursing homes and other personal-care facilities grew from 47,400 to 180,000. During the same period, positions in accounting and auditing increased from nearly 11,000 to more than 68,000, computer and data processing from 3,300 to almost 91,000, hotels and motels from about 70,000 to more than 113,000, and child day care from almost 28,000 to more than 80,000.

In 1969 the general sector designated Services was the largest single Appalachian employment category by a slight margin, with about 1,218,827 jobs compared to 1,180,604 in Durable Goods, 1,034,764 in Retail Trade, and 1,023,988 in Non-Durable Goods. In 2003 Services dwarfed the other categories, claiming nearly 3.4 million jobs compared to some 2.2 million in Retail Trade. The third-largest category had become State and Local Government, 1.3 million jobs, with Durable Goods shrinking to 987,000 and Non-Durable Goods to 793,000.

A statistic in a non-Service category, Construction, indicated new growth was proceeding—gradually. Between 1969 and 2003, the number of Appalachian construction workers rose from approximately 370,000 to more than 716,000.

—Jack Hurst, *Lancaster, Tennessee*

Rudy Abramson, "New Coal Isn't Old Coal," *Alicia Patterson Foundation Reporter* (Spring 2001); Michael Arndt, "Up from the Scrap Heap," *Business Week* (July 21, 2003); Harvard Ayers et al., eds., *An Appalachian Tragedy: Air Pollution and Tree Death in the Eastern Forests of North America* (1998); Christopher Davis, "Pittsburgh Region Sees Largest '00–'02 Population Drop," *Pittsburgh Business Times* (July 28, 2003); Fred Dickey, "Levi Strauss and the Price We Pay," *Los Angeles Times Magazine* (December 1, 2002); Dan Fitzpatrick, "Region Showed Net Loss of Nearly 58,000 from 1995 to 2000," *Pittsburgh Post-Gazette* (August 6, 2003); Dale A. Hathaway, *Can Workers Have a Voice? The Politics of Deindustrialization in Pittsburgh* (1993); David K. Nelson, "Timber Management Applications to Enhance Wildlife Habitat," *Alabama's Treasured Forests* (Spring 1999); David B. Richardson and Steve Wing, "Radiation and Mortality of Workers at Oak Ridge National Laboratory," *Environmental Health Perspectives* (August 1999); Paul Salstrom, *Appalachia's Path to Dependency: Rethinking a Region's Economic History, 1730–1940* (1994); U.S. Department of Energy, Energy Information Administration, *Annual Coal Report 2002* (2002); Ken Ward Jr., "Number of Mountaintop Mines in State Is Unknown," *Charleston Gazette-Mail* (August 9, 1998) and "Strip-Mining Battle Resurfaces in State," *Charleston Gazette-Mail* (March 22, 1998); John Alexander Williams, *Appalachia: A History* (2002).

AEI Resources

See Horizon Natural Resources Company

Aerospace Industry

The huge aerospace industry complex centered at Redstone Arsenal and Marshall Space Flight Center at Huntsville, Alabama, provides Appalachia's most powerful identification with space and aviation technology. In 2000, federal agencies employed more than seventeen thousand workers in the immediate Huntsville area, and payrolls of civilian contractors and high-tech corporations far exceeded those in the government workforce. At Cummings Research Park, only minutes from the military aerospace complex, more than twenty thousand employees worked for no fewer than 160 advanced technology companies.

But Appalachia has a long history of aircraft manufacturing predating the space program. At Hagerstown, Maryland, airplanes were first assembled in 1916, and for nearly seven subsequent decades aviation manufacturing was an important part of the area's economy. At Glen Dale, West Virginia, Fokker commercial passenger planes were built in the late 1920s and early 1930s. Elsewhere in the region, corporate antecedents, subsidiaries, and subcontractors for aerospace giants such as Lockheed-Martin Corporation and United Technologies produced components for airplanes and aerospace hardware across the last half of the twentieth century. After the mid-1990s, the industry included relative newcomers such as Montreal-based Bombardier Aerospace, which opened a regional airline, maintenance, and repair facility near Bridgeport, West Virginia. Located in a fast-growing Mid-Atlantic Aerospace Complex at Harrison/Marion Regional Airport (formerly Benendum Airport), Bombardier and its neighbors engaged twelve hundred employees in manufacturing, training, and aviation support activities.

During the 1950s, when employees of the Fairchild Industries plant at Hagerstown were assembling the famed C-119 "Flying Boxcar" for the United States Air Force, employment in the facility's shops, hangars, and warehouses exceeded ten thousand, and planes rolled out at the rate of one a day. From 1929 until 1983, enterprises founded by Sherman Fairchild, a pioneer of both aerial photography and aircraft manufacturing, built planes ranging from small trainers to massive transports to the A-10 Thunderbolt. The latter, a tank killer nicknamed the "Warthog" (famously deployed against Iraqi armored vehicles in 1991 and 2003), was the last plane assembled at Hagerstown before Fairchild closed the plant.

The first Hagerstown aircraft was built by Giuseppe Bellanca in 1916. After his test and demonstration program, Maryland Pressed Steel Company planned to put the tiny biplane into production, but the firm fell into bankruptcy in 1920. Aviation manufacturing was resurrected by Kreider-Reisner Aircraft Company, which built midget racers and biplanes before it was acquired by Fairchild in 1929.

Some of the Fairchild planes built in Hagerstown during the Great Depression were artistic successes but commercial failures. Notable were the Fairchild Model 91, a ten-passenger amphibian nicknamed the "Baby Clipper," and the Model 45, a small transport called the "Sedan of the Air." Pan American Airways canceled its orders for the Baby Clipper after delivery of the first two, and production of the Sedan of the Air was terminated after seventeen were built. Other planes designed by Fairchild and assembled at Hagerstown became workhorses for the American military in both war and peacetime. As World War II erupted in Europe, the company began manufacturing a two-seat trainer, the PT-19, later used by British and Canadian air forces as well as the U.S. Army Air Corps. Altogether, about six thousand PT-19s were built.

Production of Fairchild's C-123, successor to the Flying Boxcar, continued from the mid-1950s until the early 1970s. More than one thousand C-123s were built, and production of the A-10 reached about seven hundred. Aside from long production runs such as these, the plant at various times built small civilian passenger planes, helicopters, and components for other aircraft, including the Boeing 757 passenger plane and the B-52 strategic bomber.

About the time Fairchild Aviation Corporation arrived in Hagerstown, pioneer aircraft designer Anthony H. G. Fokker opened a $2-million plant south of Wheeling, West Virginia, and began assembling the F-10A, a "trimotor" passenger plane. Used by Pan American and a number of other early airlines as well as the American military, the all-wood F-10A, powered by Pratt and Whitney "Wasp" engines, could cruise at 120 miles per hour with a dozen passengers and a crew of two. Within a year of Fokker Aircraft's arrival in West Virginia, the company employed five hundred workers and rolled out two new "trimotors" a week, but the 1931 crash of an F-10A that killed eight people, including Notre Dame football coach Knute Rockne, caused temporary grounding of the plane and a loss of public confidence in it. Three years later, Fokker Aircraft sold its West Virginia plant, and production of the F-10A ended after fifty-nine had been built.

The aerospace industry's historic and enduring impact in southern Appalachia sprang from the U.S. Army's 1949 decision to make Redstone Arsenal in north Alabama the home of its guided missile research and development. Its rocket team, headed by Wernher von Braun, was built around German scientists and engineers who had developed the V-1 flying bomb and the V-2 rocket used by the Nazis in

World War II. Intermediate-range missiles developed at the arsenal—the Jupiter C and the Redstone—launched the first American Earth satellite in 1958 and sent the country's first two astronauts on brief suborbital test flights in 1961.

In 1960, with the United States and the Soviet Union entering a space race that would culminate with U.S. astronauts landing on the moon, the von Braun team was transferred to the National Aeronautics and Space Administration (NASA). Physically, however, the rocket experts remained in the same place. A portion of the arsenal was transferred to civilian control and designated as NASA's Marshall Space Flight Center. There, the team designed the Saturn super rockets used in the manned lunar exploration program. Von Braun died in 1977, having retired from NASA to become vice-president of Fairchild Industries.

More than half a century after its founding, with both the Cold War and the U.S.-Soviet space race fading memories, the federal complex in the hills of northern Alabama continued to flourish, as did high-tech private industry attracted by government contracts and an environment conducive to research and development activity. The Huntsville–Madison County Chamber of Commerce advertised the enclave as "the second largest research park in the nation." Further, it claimed that Huntsville was home to "the second highest concentration of technical workers in the U.S.," with more than eleven thousand professional engineers and eight hundred Ph.D.s. Redstone Arsenal, meanwhile, remained the center of the army's missile research, engineering, and development, directing the testing and deployment of tactical systems with combat forces, as well as the development of weapons for strategic defense—the latter sharply limited by the 1972 Strategic Arms Limitation Treaty between the United States and the Soviet Union.

At the beginning of the new century, the combined annual budgets of federal activities based in Huntsville stood at about $13.5 billion. Redstone was home to both the U.S. Army's Aviation and Missile Command and the Space and Missile Defense Command. There, officials managed more than half of the weapons-procurement budget, as well as more than half of foreign military sales, of the entire army. At Marshall Space Flight Center, meanwhile, NASA engineers and contractors were developing futuristic space transportation systems, having played a lead role in devising the propulsion system for the space shuttle, launching the Hubble Space Telescope, and designing the International Space Station.

From all of the federal activities in Huntsville, it was estimated that some $4 billion per year went into the Alabama economy, most of it spent in Huntsville and the surrounding area of southern Appalachia. More importantly, the complex served as a magnet for further regional development. In 1997 Boeing Company, the largest civilian employer in Huntsville, announced plans for a new facility to produce Delta rockets in nearby Morgan County. Projecting the eventual employment of two thousand workers, the company began producing the new two-hundred-foot-tall Delta IV (the first of which was launched in November of 2002) as well as earlier versions of the rocket used to orbit both military and commercial satellites. From the new plant located near the bank of the Tennessee River northwest of Decatur, Boeing planned to barge launch vehicles to Cape Canaveral, Florida, and to Vandenberg Air Force Base in California.

Access to transportation on the Tennessee River was a prime factor not only in Boeing's site selection but also in the choice of Redstone Arsenal as the home of army missile development in 1949. Before Redstone's selection, Alabama's political representatives in Washington had lobbied to get an air force wind tunnel testing center, but that complex had instead gone to Tullahoma, Tennessee, where it became the Arnold Engineering Development Center. First perceived as a consolation prize, Redstone transformed Huntsville from a cotton town into a technology center that eventually styled itself the "Space Capital of the Universe."

See also: ARNOLD ENGINEERING DEVELOPMENT CENTER; MARSHALL SPACE FLIGHT CENTER.

—Rudy Abramson, *Reston, Virginia*

Rudy Abramson, "Helping Small Business from Start to Finish," *Appalachia* (Summer–Fall 1995); Erik Bergaust, *Rocket City, U.S.A.: From Huntsville, Alabama, to the Moon* (1963); Frederick I. Ordway III and Mitchell R. Sharpe, *The Rocket Team* (1979).

Aluminum Industry

The American aluminum industry has its roots in Appalachia and is still strongly associated with the region. At the turn of the twenty-first century, the industry's dominant firm—Alcoa—continued to be headquartered in Pittsburgh and had recently absorbed Reynolds Metals, another Appalachian-rooted aluminum firm and its historic competitor. Near the beginning of the previous century, Alcoa had expanded into east Tennessee, where it built four hydroelectric dams and established a town that grew in size and significance. But by 2000, Alcoa faced maturity problems. Competition from other products as well as expensive energy and labor costs had had an adverse effect on its growth since the late 1970s. Nonetheless, following its acquisition of many of the Reynolds properties, Alcoa reigned as the world's largest manufacturer of sheet aluminum for beverage cans and continued to be a Fortune 500 company.

The aluminum industry in the United States began in northern Appalachia in 1886, when Charles Martin Hall of Oberlin, Ohio, discovered and patented an electrolytic process that could extract aluminum from ore. In 1888 Hall and a group of financial backers led by Alfred E. Hunt established an experimental shop in Pittsburgh called the Pittsburgh Reduction Company. There they determined that the Hall process was an economically feasible method of smelting aluminum ore. Shortly afterward, they opened a fabricating facility in nearby New Kensington, Pennsylvania. In 1907 they renamed the Pittsburgh Reduction Company the Aluminum Company of America, or Alcoa.

During the twentieth century, Alcoa and its competitors transformed aluminum from a semi-precious metal that had almost no market value into a major product in the building of modern America. Discovered in 1807 by British chemist Sir Humphry Davy, aluminum makes up 8 percent of the earth's crust—a larger proportion than any other metal or element except silicon and oxygen. Bauxite is the only ore containing enough aluminum to make the cost of extraction profitable, however, and because of aluminum's highly refractory nature the ore cannot be treated by a direct smelting process like those used for other metals. The Hall process solved this problem but required vast amounts of electricity.

The need for an economical source of electricity to power furnaces was the motivating force behind Alcoa's venture into the Tennessee Valley in southern Appalachia. In 1909, as a means of ensuring a source of hydroelectric power for a smelting facility it would complete in 1914, the company purchased the Knoxville Power Company and other utility firms and thereby obtained power and riparian rights to a forty-mile stretch along the Little Tennessee River near Knoxville, Tennessee. In 1919 an act of the Tennessee General Assembly officially gave the name Alcoa to the area surrounding the smelting plant. The firm took a paternalistic attitude toward the new town, designing parks, playgrounds, schools, and medical facilities for the benefit of the residents, many of whom made up its workforce. Until the mid-1950s, company management also managed the municipal affairs of the town, which still bears the name Alcoa. U.S. Highway 129 is still called Alcoa Highway, and Hunt and Hall Roads, state routes named after Alfred E. Hunt and Charles Martin Hall, still bear witness to the Aluminum Company of America's history in the area.

At the turn of the twenty-first century, Alcoa's wholly owned subsidiary Tapoco oversaw the waterpower resources of the Little Tennessee and Cheoah Rivers in Graham and Swain Counties of North Carolina and Blount and Monroe Counties in Tennessee. To provide electricity for Alcoa's Tennessee Operations division, Cheoah Dam was constructed by Alcoa in 1919 and Santeetlah (1928), Calderwood (1930), and Chilhowee (1955) Dams were built over the next thirty-six years. In 2001 the area Tapoco managed made up about 21,698 acres, including 5,898 acres of water and 15,800 acres of land.

Throughout its operations during the twentieth century, Alcoa's Tennessee Operations reflected the growth and development of the aluminum industry as a whole. During World War I, use of aluminum in the aviation industry helped change the metal's status from that of a viable substitute for brass, iron, zinc, and tin in cookware, machine parts, and other small products to that of a strategic industrial material. To capitalize on emerging markets, Alcoa began adding a sheet mill facility called the West Plant to its Tennessee site in 1920. At that time, Tennessee Operations had more than thirty-five hundred workers and an annual payroll of $3 million.

In 1940 Alcoa began construction of the North Plant, a five-million-pound-per-month-capacity sheet mill, to help accommodate an anticipated government demand for aluminum for World War II. Alcoa already produced 100 percent of the primary aluminum manufactured in the United States at the time, but it did not have the capacity to produce the quantity needed for the war. At the government's request, between 1941 and 1943 the company supervised the building and subsequent operation of more than twenty federally funded aluminum plants. Because of a Department of Justice antitrust action against Alcoa in 1945, however, the company was not allowed after the war to buy any of the federally funded facilities that it had helped to build and operate. The government sold these plants to other aluminum companies to try to establish competition and break Alcoa's monopoly in the aluminum market. As a result, Alcoa emerged from World War II as part of an oligopoly in which the Reynolds and Kaiser companies were its major domestic competitors.

Reynolds Metals was founded by Bristol, Tennessee, native R. S. Reynolds as the U.S. Foil Company in 1919. It initially began making aluminum powder, paste, and foil for packaging candy, chewing gum, and cigarettes. It bought the firm that manufactured the popular Eskimo Pie ice cream bar, which it wrapped in aluminum foil. Foreseeing the federal government's need for aluminum in World War II, Reynolds secured government loans in 1941 to locate an aluminum smelter and sheet mill near Sheffield, Alabama, in southern Appalachia. In 1947 he acquired the Sheffield sheet mill from the federal government.

Per-capita consumption of aluminum doubled in the postwar era. Competition spurred development in new and old applications, but Alcoa remained the largest producer of primary aluminum. In 1952 Alcoa erected a thirty-story aluminum building in downtown Pittsburgh to house its headquarters and showcase the potential for one of its most promising new applications, aluminum-intensive architecture.

Reynolds, with expertise in manufacturing and marketing, succeeded in developing new aluminum consumer products, with aluminum siding and Reynolds Wrap aluminum foil two of the more noteworthy. Reynolds Metals also pioneered aluminum scrap recycling, becoming the second-largest producer in the United States until that part of the firm was sold to Alcoa in May 2000. Alcoa's buyout included Reynolds's packaging and consumer business units, metals and construction products distribution businesses, and transportation business units. In 1998 Reynolds sold its Alabama facilities near Muscle Shoals and Sheffield to Wise Metals Group, the parent company of Wise Alloys and Wise Recycling.

Wise Alloys included the sheet mill facility built by Reynolds in 1941 and the Alabama Reclamation Facility, constructed in 1969. Wise Recycling was one of the largest direct-from-the-public collectors of aluminum beverage containers in the United States in 2002. Operating processing centers in several locations, including Bristol, Virginia, Wise is headquartered in Baltimore. In 2002 Wise was the third-leading U.S. producer of aluminum can stock for the beverage and food industries. About 75 percent of the material used to manufacture its can stock came from recycled aluminum.

In the last quarter of the twentieth century, in response to increasing competition from other products and high energy and labor costs, Alcoa began diversifying its product line and investing in non-aluminum manufacturing technologies. In the 1980s, in another move to remain competitive in the market, the company also increased its international operations. Two of the firm's largest domestic business units, the formerly Pittsburgh-headquartered Alcoa Rigid Packaging and Alcoa Primary Metals units, moved in 1990 to Knoxville. Alcoa's global energy division and its metal-purchasing activities were based there also. The Tennessee facility employed some eighteen hundred workers in 2001, putting $283 million into the local economy. To address public concerns about its environmental accountability as a major east Tennessee landowner, Alcoa's Tennessee Operations in 2001 formed an advisory board of representatives from business, education, and community organizations. It established a property management committee to seek input from key governmental agencies on land management and also substantially lowered its gaseous fluoride emissions after 1990.

At the turn of the century, the future of aluminum can sheet was uncertain because of competition from other materials such as plastic. The impact on Tennessee Operations, in particular, remained to be seen. In 2002 Alcoa built a new headquarters for its multinational organization on the North Shore in Pittsburgh.

See also: REYNOLDS, R. S.

—Janice Willis Barnett, *Unicoi, Tennessee*

Alcoa, *Tennessee Operations Report to the Community* (2001); George David Smith, *From Monopoly to Competition: The Transformations of Alcoa, 1888–1986* (1988).

Anthracite Coal Industry

After reaching peak production of more than 100 million tons per year and employment rolls exceeding 180,000 workers early in the twentieth century, America's anthracite coal industry fell into irreversible decline, leaving it a shadow of its former self even though huge reserves of anthracite remain in the ground. Nearly all United States deposits of the famed "hard coal" are located in an eight-county area of northeastern Pennsylvania between the Susquehanna and Delaware Rivers. For decades this region around Wilkes-Barre and Scranton was one of the cornerstones of the nation's thriving coal industry and styled itself the "Anthracite Capital of the World."

Development of huge heating and power-generating systems fueled by cheaper, more plentiful bituminous coal triggered anthracite's decline. By 1950, anthracite production had fallen to 46 million tons, 35 percent of which came from surface mines and from waste piles left by earlier operations. In 2001 the State of Pennsylvania reported anthracite production of only 3 million tons and total employment of 689. Just thirteen underground mines, with 99 employees, remained in operation. Activity in both deep and surface mining continued to diminish.

Marketed in six different sizes, or grades, anthracite continues to be employed in steelmaking, home heating, and as a filtration medium for public water systems and swimming pools. Reserves remaining in the anthracite region are estimated at as much as 7 billion tons, perhaps as much as one-third of the world's hard coal deposits.

Veins of the brittle, lustrous anthracite, sometimes referred to as black diamond, were discovered as early as 1762 and first used for heating in Pennsylvania about 1768. Distinguished by high carbon and low sulfur content, anthracite burns slowly and produces little smoke but yields exceptional amounts of heat. Consequently, it was an ideal fuel for both residential and industrial use.

For decades, anthracite was used primarily in the region where it was found, often in copious amounts at the earth's surface, where it could be readily dug with picks and shovels. The first significant shipments out of the region began about 1820, with heavily laden barges moving along canals and rivers on their way to market. Before the arrival of railroads, an industry began that fueled America's Industrial Revolution and played a major role in energy production for both World War I and World War II. Inevitably, the booming, largely unregulated enterprise was visited by mining tragedies. Brutal working conditions led to labor strife that made the anthracite region a birthplace of Appalachian unionism and a particularly rich source of American industrial and labor lore.

Because anthracite seams occur in folded layers of rock, underground mining in the area was more dangerous than in the mines of the bituminous coalfields to the west and south. Every year between 1870 and 1940 more than 200 miners were killed in explosions, fires, roof falls, and other accidents. The number of deaths exceeded 500 in many years, and in 1908 the fatality toll reached 708. The region's worst single accident occurred in 1869 when 108 miners died in a mine in the Avondale coalfield near Wilkes-Barre. Modern safety regulations and improved technology dramatically reduced deaths and injuries in the late twentieth century. In 1996 not a single fatality occurred in U.S. anthracite mines, but more than 31,000 workers had died since reliable record keeping began in 1870.

Safety hazards, coupled with low pay and generally odious conditions, led to historic strikes and some of the nation's earliest social, labor, and political reforms. In 1868 the Workingmen's Benevolent Association, the first union for American coal miners, and the Anthracite Board of Trade negotiated the industry's first wage agreement. In 1892 a strike against the Carnegie Steel Company at Homestead, Pennsylvania, led to deployment of the National Guard to keep the peace. President Benjamin Harrison considered the episode a factor in his loss to Grover Cleveland that fall. Eight years later President William McKinley, facing reelection, urged anthracite operators to settle a strike by granting workers' demands for a pay raise and an eight-hour workday. In 1902 President Theodore Roosevelt pressed for arbitration to end a long strike that made the United Mine Workers of America one of the most powerful unions in the country.

Facing sharpened competition and labor unrest, mining companies looked to new waves of immigrants to dig and haul the coal; consequently, the industry's social impact was as profound as its economic dominance. Between 1880 and 1914, Slovaks, Ukrainians, Russians, Serbs, Italians, Hungarians, and Greeks moved into the mines and Irish, English, and Welsh workers graduated into clerical jobs and other aboveground positions.

Social tensions and labor-management fights developed apace with the industry's growth. Exemplifying the bitter conflict was the hanging of twenty Irish immigrant miners suspected of belonging to a secret organization called the Molly Maguires. The men, who had protested against squalid working conditions and low wages, were convicted of nineteen murders, mostly of mine superintendents.

Ultimately, economic change rather than conflict between industry and labor killed the massive underground anthracite mining business, but its demise was hastened by an accident. In 1959 the Susquehanna River broke into underground works and swamped mines across a wide area near Wilkes-Barre and Scranton. Many never reopened.

To reduce labor costs, large anthracite coal operators had already taken the same course followed by companies in the bituminous coalfields after World War II, turning to surface mining operations. In the anthracite region, however, surface operations increasingly focused on re-mining of coal previously left behind. By processing and marketing this coal once considered waste, operators contributed to reduction of acid mine drainage and reclamation of thousands of acres of abandoned mine lands.

Following Arab oil embargoes and American concern over energy independence in the 1970s and 1980s, it appeared that a resuscitation of the anthracite coal industry might occur. Adopting an energy policy emphasizing the use of coal, the federal government promoted development of co-generation plants that would burn products such as lignite, a brown low-grade coal, and the anthracite mine wastes left in "culm piles." In the early 1990s, production from culm piles and the mixing of anthracite with lignite in new co-generation plants led to a 150 percent increase in production in the anthracite region. But before the century was over, decline resumed. In 2001 underground production was down another 43 percent from the previous year, surface production was down by 13 percent, and production from refuse processing was down 36 percent.

See also: ANTHRACITE MINERS, TWENTIETH-CENTURY (LABOR); MOLLY MAGUIRES (LABOR); UNITED MINE WORKERS OF AMERICA (LABOR).

—Rudy Abramson, *Reston, Virginia,* and Ima J. Stephens, *Auburn University*

Kevin Kenny, *Making Sense of the Molly Maguires* (1998); Donald L. Miller and Richard E. Sharpless, *The Kingdom of Coal: Work, Enterprise, and Ethnic Communities in the Mine Fields* (1985); Pennsylvania Department of Environmental Protection, *Annual Report 1999–2000* (2000).

Arch Coal

Arch Coal, Inc., the second-leading coal producer in the United States, was formed in 1997 by the merger of two coal giants, Ashland Coal Company and Arch Mineral Corporation. In 1999 the company and its subsidiaries produced approximately 115 million tons of coal, roughly 10 percent of the nation's output. In 2003 the company had major holdings and operations in West Virginia, Kentucky, Illinois, Wyoming, Colorado, and Utah. Its coal was sold principally to electric utilities operating 140 power plants in thirty-one states, and it generated about 6 percent of all electricity produced in the U.S.

Arch Coal's operations reflected patterns evident for the coal industry as a whole. More than 65 percent of its production was concentrated in the Rocky Mountains, as strip mining on leased federal lands outpaced older underground operations in Illinois and Appalachia. Arch's Black Thunder Mine in Wyoming produced 65 million tons of coal annually, more than 40 percent of the company's output. By 2003 it had shipped more than 750 million tons, making it the most productive coal mine in the nation and perhaps the world. Increasing demand for electricity and high prices for competing fuels led to a significant expansion of coal mining in the United States, with annual production growing by 29 percent between 1983 and 1998 and surpassing 1.1 billion tons by the latter date. Even as production soared, however, the number of working mines declined by almost half, and the number of mine workers declined by 54 percent to a current level of about 80,000.

A result of the merger of mining companies and the elimination of smaller mines, Arch Coal both reflected and contributed to these trends. In March 2002 it reported carrying 3,750 employees on its rolls, 600 of whom were members of the United Mine Workers of America. In the previous fifteen years the share of coal production controlled by the four largest operators had increased from 20 to 40 percent. Arch was prominently associated with mountaintop removal and other environmental controversies connected with coal in Appalachia. In 1998 the Environmental Protection Agency required Hobet Mining Company, an Arch subsidiary, to substantially scale back operations by as much as 41 percent at a Logan County, West Virginia, mine in connection with violations of the Clean Water Act, and Arch agreed to plant fifteen thousand hardwood trees, add perennial streams, and perform other land rehabilitation. At the end of the twentieth century, Arch operated nine mines and eight preparation plants in Kentucky, Virginia, and West Virginia.

Ashland Coal sold its part of Arch Coal in early 2001 after Ashland management was quoted as questioning whether the merger had been the most profitable place for its investment. But with the energy crisis deepening in California in 2003, the construction of coal-powered, electricity-generating plants seemed likely to increase and with it the demand for the kind of low-sulfur coal that Arch produced.

See also: CONSOLIDATION COAL COMPANY/CONSOL ENERGY; PEABODY COAL; UNITED MINE WORKERS OF AMERICA (LABOR).

—Thomas Dublin, *State University of New York at Binghamton*

Arnold Engineering Development Center

Arnold Engineering Development Center is the largest and most sophisticated aerospace testing facility in the world. The center provides technical support for developing and testing military and jet aircraft as well as major systems for the nation's space programs.

During World War II, General Henry H. "Hap" Arnold, commander of the U.S. Army Air Corps, spent much of his time dealing with the technology of air power. He appointed Theodore von Karmen, a Hungarian-born aeronautical engineer, as his special advisor, and during the course of the war German aerospace technology convinced Arnold and von Karmen that the United States lagged in this area. At the end of the war German facilities were dismantled and brought to the United States to provide a basis for a testing program.

In 1949 Congress authorized $100 million for construction of a testing facility. Tullahoma, Tennessee, was chosen as the location because the state owned more than forty thousand acres of land that had been the site of a former army training base, Camp Forrest. Also crucial was the availability of low-cost electrical power from the Tennessee Valley Authority, which was needed to operate the center's giant wind tunnels.

Construction of the center began in 1950. President Harry Truman dedicated the facility on June 25, 1951, and tests began in 1953. Since that time all major ballistic missiles, the space shuttle, military jets, and engines used in Boeing civilian aircraft have been tested at the center.

At the opening of the twenty-first century, the facility was one of the largest employers of engineers and other aerospace technical personnel in Appalachia. It has ensured that, in President Truman's words, "never again will the United States ride the coat tails of other countries in the progress and development of the aeronautical art."

See also: AEROSPACE INDUSTRY; MARSHALL SPACE FLIGHT CENTER; OAK RIDGE NATIONAL LABORATORY.

—Michael R. Bradley, *Motlow College*

Automotive Industry

Appalachia's economy has been significantly aided since the final quarter of the 1900s by the addition of numerous subsidiary plants and parts producers associated with automobile manufacturing—even though most of the new car-making facilities themselves have been built just outside the Appalachian region.

The automotive industry that began developing in the United States in the 1890s was first scattered among many small manufacturers competing to sell Americans cars, and at least a few of these were in Appalachia. Notably, around 1913 Henry Nyberg established a factory to manufacture automobiles in Chattanooga, Tennessee.

By the World War I era, however, the center of production had shifted to Detroit, with parts and accessory manufacturers scattered around its periphery, especially in northern Ohio, Indiana, and Illinois. Henry Ford's introduction of the Model T automobile accelerated the dominance of Detroit in the industry, as Ford's considerably lower price made cars more widely available and undercut the large profit margins that had allowed numerous manufacturers to prosper while producing a limited number of vehicles. This hastened company failures and industry consolidation as production became concentrated in a few companies within a narrow geographic radius around Detroit.

While attempts to produce cars in Appalachia such as Nyberg's proved ultimately unsuccessful, one niche product line for the industry was developed that proved sustainable: the automobile truck wrecker. Ernest Holmes invented the first wrecker in Chattanooga about 1916 to help handle the many accidents and breakdowns of automobiles in an era before good highways. The corporate descendant of the company Holmes founded, Miller Industries of Ooltewah, Tennessee, was described as the world's largest producer of this type of vehicle as of 2002.

The Appalachian economy did not benefit from the automotive industry until the transplanting of auto component and assembly plants in the surrounding region in the latter third of the twentieth century. The impact before that consisted of the shift of people out of Appalachia to work in the automotive factories of the Midwest or to travel by car to find better jobs away from their hometowns.

Although out-migration to urban centers was not limited to Appalachia, it did have a major impact on the region and on those who left it. Between 1940 and 1970, the Appalachian region had a net loss in population of more than three million people. The economic impact of the Great Depression began this cycle as the area's industries connected to timber, coal, and agriculture suffered. People looked for work where they could find it. Expansion of the home-front economy during World War II further attracted people from the region to better-paying jobs, and this pattern continued in the postwar period. Harriette Simpson Arnow's novel *The Dollmaker* deftly explores the cultural and economic conflicts the Appalachian migrants found during this era in the car factories of the industrial North.

Before the 1960s, the region's residents migrated to auto-industry plants in the Midwest, but then the process began to reverse itself. In the last decades of the twentieth century, development of important automotive manufacturing plants and parts producers came to Appalachia and its periphery. The auto industry repeated a pattern in industrial evolution found in the American textile industry about a century earlier. Just as New England's textile mill owners moved south to take advantage of a more favorable economic climate in the late nineteenth and early twentieth centuries, in the late twentieth century automotive manufacturers began moving south, including into Appalachia. Various factors encouraged expansion into the region: cheaper labor, less stringent environmental regulations, less expensive land, and numerous tax and other incentives offered by state and local governments in the region.

Much of the siting of major automotive manufacturing facilities occurred adjacent to the Appalachian region in middle Tennessee, central Kentucky, Alabama, and South Carolina. Ford established a car assembly plant in Louisville, Kentucky, in 1968. In the 1980s, assembly plants were established at Bowling Green, Kentucky, and at Spring Hill, Tennessee, by General Motors; Nissan built a plant at Smyrna, Tennessee; and Toyota opened an assembly plant at Georgetown, Kentucky. During the 1990s, expansion into the southeastern United States continued with the opening of a Mercedes plant near Tuscaloosa, Alabama, a BMW plant in Spartanburg, South Carolina, and a Honda all-terrain vehicle plant at Timmonsville, South Carolina. The Southeast as a region now produces about a third of all American-made cars and lightweight trucks.

The many subsidiary plants and parts producers needed to support these and other automobile assembly plants spread throughout Appalachia during this period. Such facilities brought increased employment and higher wages to many of the region's residents, as well as providing increased tax revenues and improved infrastructure to individual localities. At the opening of the twenty-first century the impact on just one state, Tennessee, provided a dramatic example. A quarter of its manufacturing jobs were linked to the automotive industry, with an annual payroll estimated at more than $5.8 billion.

The automobile changed twentieth-century America and Appalachia even more dramatically than the railroad had in the preceding century. Tractors revolutionized agricultural practice and production. Cars and trucks altered and expanded distribution channels. This led to massive road building, the decline of the rail industry, and the rise of drive-in theaters, air pollution, fast-food restaurants, stock car racing, gas stations, and drunk drivers. For Appalachia, such cultural and social impacts generally preceded any economic ones.

See also: INTERNATIONAL TOWING AND RECOVERY MUSEUM.

—Ned L. Irwin, *East Tennessee State University*

Sharyn Matthews, "Tennessee Grows as Center of the New Automotive South," *East Tennessee Business Journal* (February 2, 2001); Matthew N. Murray, with David T. Mayes and Kathleen Hoffman, *A Profile of the Automobile Sector in the U.S. and Southeastern States,* Report for the Tennessee Department of Economic and Community Development (1999); Philip Hillyer Smith, *Wheels within Wheels: A Short History of American Motor Manufacturing* (1968).

BAE Systems

BAE Systems North America, formerly British Aerospace, is a world-class systems, defense, and aerospace contractor headquartered in Rockville, Maryland. It combines key in-depth skills in naval platforms, military aircraft, intelligent electronic systems, information technology, and systems engineering for use in combat, reconnaissance, avionics, aeronautics, navigation, surveillance, and other related areas. BAE Systems serves customers in all branches of the armed forces, as well as commercial and civil aircraft markets.

In the early twenty-first century, the company employed more than one hundred thousand people worldwide. In the United States, BAE Systems employed twenty-five thousand people in facilities located in the District of Columbia and thirty states. Employees designed, developed, integrated, manufactured, and supported a wide range of advanced aerospace products and intelligent electronic systems for government and commercial customers, and the firm had annual sales of four billion dollars. Its Appalachian facilities were located in Johnson City, New York; Huntsville, Alabama; and Pittsburgh.

Ordnance Systems, Inc., is a wholly owned subsidiary of BAE Systems and is responsible for managing the Holston Army Ammunition Plant in Kingsport, Tennessee. The government-owned, company-operated facility of more than two hundred employees provides total management of all site activities involved in the production, handling, warehousing, transportation, supply, and data storage of high explosives to meet the requirements of the U.S. Department of Defense. Ordnance Systems, Inc., recently enlarged its market to include nonmilitary customers, supplying the demands for industries such as oil exploration.

See also: AEROSPACE INDUSTRY.

—Sandra Kay Heck, *Walters State Community College*

Banking

The most important banking institution headquartered in Appalachia is that established by the Mellon family, which in 2000 was the seventh-largest asset-management group in the United States and the fourteenth largest worldwide. Traditionally more than just a provider of checking and savings accounts, the Mellon National Bank and Trust Company of Pittsburgh in 1999 merged with the Dreyfus Corporation to become the largest bank manager of mutual funds, Dreyfus having had $180 billion in assets under its management and nearly two hundred mutual fund portfolios at that time. In 2002, by acquiring the human resources outsourcing and consulting businesses of the Unifi Network, Mellon became the fourth-largest provider of those services in the world. From its beginning the Mellon bank has been a driving force in the corporate and civic life of Pittsburgh, the industrial capital of Appalachia, as well as a primary catalyst in the creation and rise of some of Pittsburgh's—and America's—greatest companies.

There are other important banks in the region, as well. The first SunTrust Bank in Georgia, according to records of the Federal Deposit Insurance Corporation (FDIC), was opened in the Appalachian town of Rome in 1877. Now headquartered in Atlanta, the SunTrust chain of banks stretches from Maryland, Virginia, and the District of Columbia to Alabama and Florida, and in 2003 it claimed $81.2 billion in deposits and more than $125.4 billion in total assets.

The region's banks have had problems, also: high-profile failures built on wild growth, risky lending, and phantom assets were part of a trend of voracious consolidation in the industry during the 1980s and 1990s. Both failures and consolidation, however, appear to have occurred no more frequently in Appalachia than in other parts of America.

The first banks in colonial America were the Bank of North America, established in 1781, and the Bank of New York, founded in 1784. As Alexander Hamilton shaped the nation's financial system, banks formed in the Appalachian region, first in its northern states. The FDIC *Institution Directory* reports that five of these early financial institutions were operating in the region as of 1800. A hundred years later, 444 banks existed in Appalachian counties from Mississippi to New York. Of banks established prior to 1900, two-thirds no longer exist. While mergers and acquisitions contributed to the declining numbers, the banking industry also saw recurring financial fears in the United States during the late 1800s and early 1900s. Major nationwide banking panics occurred in 1873, 1884, 1893, and 1907. The last of these led to the creation of the Federal Reserve in 1913. Most disruptive of all, however, was the Great Depression. Nine thousand banks failed between 1930 and 1933.

Bankers fueled the growth of Appalachian businesses from the beginning, none more than the Mellons of Pittsburgh. Judge Thomas Mellon, an Irish immigrant, established the T. Mellon and Sons private banking firm in the Steel City in 1869 on retiring from the state bench. Before transferring the firm's ownership to his twenty-seven-year-old son Andrew in 1882, Thomas Mellon financially backed both Andrew Carnegie and Henry Clay Frick, who vied with Carnegie for leadership of the steel industry. The Mellons also invested strongly in railroads, coalfields, and other businesses that had great impact on the development of Appalachia. An example was their crucial investment in Charles Martin Hall in 1890 at a time when the chemist was having difficulty finding capital with which to use his 1889 patent for the electrolytic making of aluminum. The resultant company, in which Andrew Mellon bought large amounts of stock and even served as an executive, was Alcoa. Around the same time, Mellon became active in oil, including fields in western Pennsylvania, and he and a nephew, William Larimer Mellon, built a pipeline from Pittsburgh to Marcus

Hook, Pennsylvania, on the Delaware River in 1892. In 1889 Mellon and Frick organized the Union Trust Company with Mellon as its first president. The firm later merged with the Mellon Bank.

Another Andrew Mellon nephew, Richard K. Mellon, succeeded his uncle as leader of the firm and had great impact on the city of Pittsburgh and the profusion of large businesses with which Mellon banking had become involved. First an officer of the Mellons' small Ligonier Valley Railroad, Richard Mellon went on to become president of Mellon National Bank in 1934 and organizer of a community plan to revive Pittsburgh. After extensive War Department duties in World War II, he helped push through the Pennsylvania legislature a smoke-control law that cut Pittsburgh's smoke pollution by half in two years. One of the most influential businessmen in the United States, Mellon was also one of the wealthiest. Not counting his large holdings in the stock of Alcoa ($71 million), General Motors ($18 million), Gulf Oil ($200 million), and Pittsburgh Plate Glass ($10 million), his six hundred thousand shares of Mellon Bank alone were estimated to be worth $51 million in 1963. In 1946, under his leadership, the Mellon Bank had merged with Union Trust, and in 1955 it became one of the first banks in the U.S. to acquire and use its own computer. In 1958 it established the practice of overnight clearing of checks. In 2000 the Mellon Bank passed the $500-billion mark in managed assets.

No other Appalachian banking enterprise has been so successful, but a few have been spectacular failures. One of the most renowned collapses during the depression era involved the Tennessee-based empire of Rogers Caldwell. Known as the "J. P. Morgan of the South," Caldwell was a Nashville banker who specialized in bonds issued by southern companies. The failure of his Union Bank of Knoxville began a domino reaction in his banking empire, leading to the failure of nearly thirty banks and provoking a scandal over the loss of more than $6 million in state funds. Caldwell and his associates, including Governor Henry Horton, went to trial, but only Caldwell's associates received prison sentences. A second failure from that era was that of the Central Bank and Trust Company of Asheville, North Carolina. City and county leaders speculated in the land boom of the 1920s and were hit hard by the Great Depression. The Central Bank and Trust failed, taking city and county funds with it. One bank president received a prison term, and the mayor of Asheville committed suicide.

Other failures include that of the United American Bank and Southern Industrial Banking Corporation of Jake and C. H. Butcher Jr. in central southern Appalachia in the early 1980s. Together the brothers headed an interconnected chain of more than twenty financial institutions in Tennessee and Kentucky, and the Butchers had been primary forces in bringing the 1982 World's Fair to Knoxville. The FDIC conducted a surprise audit of all the Butcher banks the day after the World's Fair closed and found fraudulent and unsecured loans and debt-ridden paper corporations. The surprise audit foiled a system in which loans had been moved from one financial institution to the next in advance of bank examiners. Jake Butcher, a two-time Tennessee Democratic gubernatorial candidate, and his sibling both received prison sentences. C. H. Butcher's Southern Industrial Banking Corporation was an uninsured thrift. Its failure cost many account holders their life savings and made its chairman one of the most unpopular men in east Tennessee.

A more recent Appalachian bank scandal was that of the First National Bank of Keystone, West Virginia, which collapsed in one of the ten largest failures in U.S. banking history. Losses from its 1999 insolvency are estimated to have exceeded $800 million, resulting in one of the biggest payouts in FDIC history. This figure represents a 73 percent loss rate of the $1.1 billion in assets for Keystone, again one of the highest in banking history. Auditors and bank regulators were criticized for their role in allowing the failure, which began with an attempt to increase the size of the bank very quickly. To achieve rapid growth, Keystone paid exceptionally high interest rates to obtain deposits and then used the deposits to fund risky assets, particularly low-quality mortgages. Keystone executives then committed fraud by inflating the value of those assets in reports to auditors and bank regulators. Keystone was found to have destroyed documents to cover up the scheme and was reported to have posted armed guards to intimidate bank regulators. Several Keystone executives went to prison for their roles, and one was sentenced to a term of twenty-seven years.

An examination of financial institutions founded prior to 1900 has revealed that the proportion of banks no longer active in Appalachian counties is almost identical to the proportion of currently inactive banks in non-Appalachian counties around the major cities in each Appalachian state. The proportion of banks established prior to 1900 in Appalachia that subsequently needed regulatory assistance (and were in danger of failing or had failed) is again similar to their non-Appalachian counterparts. And the proportion of banks that have been merged or acquired is approximately the same for Appalachia (63 percent) as for the rest of the nation (59 percent). FDIC figures give no indication that Appalachian banks are better or worse managed than those in other areas. Neither do they indicate that they are more apt to be taken over by purchase or merger.

See also: FRICK, HENRY CLAY; MELLON, ANDREW.

—Steven A. Dennis, *East Tennessee State University*

Richard B. Drake, *A History of Appalachia* (2001); Richard G. Dreese, *Banks, Bankers, and Economic Growth in Appalachia* (1973);

Ann B. Matasar, *The Impact of Geographic Deregulation on the American Banking Industry* (2002).

Bituminous Coal Industry

From its ascendancy during the Industrial Revolution to its maturity as a technologically sophisticated and capital-intensive but fading giant in the regional economy, Appalachia's bituminous coal industry has been characterized by booms, busts, and domination by corporate interests outside the region. In recurring cycles, prosperity and booming production from increasingly mechanized mines have been followed by price collapses, waves of migration out of the coalfields, and flurries of ownership changes. Interspersed have been bitter, often violent strikes and, late in the twentieth century, mounting environmental damage from mining and processing.

Bituminous coal—soft, high in carbon content, and varying in volatility—is found in copious deposits in the Midwest, the Rockies, and the Far West, but nowhere has the coal industry equaled the economic, social, and political impact produced by mining and processing operations in Appalachia.

The very magnitude of high-quality deposits, reaching across 63,000 square miles between northern Pennsylvania and central Alabama, destined coal to play a powerful role in the life and economy of the entire region. The famed Pittsburgh seam, discovered in 1810 and first mined commercially in the early 1850s, reaches beyond western Pennsylvania into twenty-three counties of West Virginia and has been called the single most valuable mineral deposit on Earth. Significant bituminous deposits are found across twenty-one Pennsylvania counties, and geologists estimate that the Pittsburgh seam alone once contained more than 13 billion tons of coal.

In central and southern Appalachia, deposits underlie an estimated 50 million acres. West Virginia has sixty-two major bituminous coal seams and deposits across virtually the entire state. Eastern Kentucky coalfields spread across thirty-seven counties with no less than eighty mapped and named seams. Nearly two centuries after the first coal was floated from tiny mountain mines down the Kentucky River to market in Lexington, eastern Kentucky's reserves were still estimated at more than 33 billion tons.

Appalachian coal came into its own late in the nineteenth century. By 1900, two-thirds of the coal produced in the United States came from the Appalachian Mountains, and mining had replaced timber cutting as the region's leading industry.

Interlocking interests of coal and steel led the captains of American industry and banking to purchase mineral rights over vast stretches of the region for a pittance. Their investments established patterns of absentee landownership that would endure into the twenty-first century. Among the individual capitalists whose agents acquired fortunes in coal deposits from unsuspecting mountain families were J. P. Morgan, Henry Ford, and H. H. Rogers, a principal associate of John D. Rockefeller. Through such industrialists and Wall Street figures, the ownership of Appalachian coalfields fell under the control of corporate giants such as U.S. Steel, Bethlehem Steel, and the Pennsylvania Railroad. Oil and chemical companies and corporations abroad eventually became major Appalachian land and mineral owners as well.

For decades, coal owners and mine operators ruled local politics as firmly as they dominated the economy, their use of money and influence sometimes spawning notorious corruption. Their influence determined the outcomes of elections, created decisive voting blocs in state legislatures, and elected governors and members of the United States Senate and House of Representatives. Even with the industry's decline in relative economic importance, it continued to exert major influence upon politics and public policy in states such as Kentucky and West Virginia, where its influence was manifest in tax policies, environmental regulation, health programs, and safety issues. In the 2000 presidential campaign, Republican George W. Bush's crucial victory in West Virginia, a state long counted a Democratic stronghold, was widely attributed to support by the coal industry.

After years of robust expansion at the close of the nineteenth century, Appalachian coal production increased another fivefold between 1900 and 1923. Bituminous coal mines prospered in the Midwest and West as well. Nationwide, employment in twelve thousand bituminous coal mines soared to 700,000 in 1923. But demands generated by World War I evaporated, and European mines reopened, setting the stage for market collapse. Several years before the United States entered the Great Depression, mines closed, poverty spread, and labor conflict ensued. In a span of four years, 200,000 men left the nation's coal mines. The industry would recover as the United States prepared for and fought World War II, but mining employment never again reached the levels of the early 1920s. Technology developed during World War II was adapted for mining, and the coal industry's transition from a labor-intensive business into an increasingly capital-intensive one proceeded at a revolutionary pace in the last half of the century.

Strip mining, practiced as far back as the days when near-surface seams were exposed by scoops pulled by oxen and mules, exploded with the development of heavy earth-moving equipment. During World War I, steam shovels that had been used in the construction of the Panama Canal were deployed in a few surface mines, but strip mining became brutally efficient and controversial only after World War II.

In the early 1960s, a twenty-story machine owned by Peabody Coal Company was a tourist attraction in western

Mingo Logan Coal Company conducts blasting operations in Gilbert, West Virginia, 2002. With the use of explosives and giant earthmoving equipment, surface mining is considered an efficient, though highly controversial, method of coal removal in the Appalachian region.

Kentucky, and in 1965 Muhlenberg County produced more coal than any other county in the United States—17.6 million tons. Giant-sized equipment developed for strip mining in level areas was rapidly adapted to mountain use. Diesel-powered shovels, loaders, augers, and trucks opened the way for independent operators to strip mine in competition with corporate underground mines, speeding coal mining's conversion to a capital-intensive industry.

Underground mining became technically sophisticated as well. Continuous mining machines made men with picks and shovels obsolete, and conveyor belts took the place of the thousands who had loaded and hauled coal from mines to tipples. Longwall miners—rotating drums that hulled out entire seams as they advanced deep underground—rivaled the efficiency of power shovels and augers on the surface.

But as productivity soared, the demand for coal was tempered by the rise of oil and gas. In a transition of great symbolism as well as economic impact, coal-burning locomotives were driven off the nation's railroads by more powerful and efficient diesel engines. The demise of the "iron horse" in the 1950s was largely responsible for a price collapse that brought the bituminous coalfields of central Appalachia the worst times they had seen since the Great Depression.

Although better times would eventually return in the immutable cycle, mechanization continued to replace men by the thousands. In West Virginia, mining employment fell from a peak of more than 130,000 during the World War II boom to fewer than 15,000 in 1999. But the 14,000 or so workers in 1999 produced nearly 170 million tons of coal, 42 million tons more than the army of miners supplied in 1940.

Even after a century and a half of intense mining, large amounts of coal were still being extracted in about 120 counties of Appalachia. In the year 2000, West Virginia, Kentucky, and Pennsylvania ranked as the number two, three, and four coal-producing states in the nation, and Virginia ranked number eight. Smaller tonnage was mined in Alabama, Maryland, Ohio, and Tennessee, and a relatively minuscule amount was produced in Mississippi. Production centered in an area around the intersection of the Kentucky, Virginia, and West Virginia borders where three counties produced more than 10 million tons of coal per year from surface mines, and eight counties produced similar amounts from underground operations. Smaller pockets of huge productivity are found in Alabama and southwestern Pennsylvania.

Across the region, the coal mining industry, including the anthracite fields of Pennsylvania, accounted for 60,000 jobs and earnings of $4.03 billion in 1997, when production totaled 467 million tons. The industry's large employment rolls, vastly diminished since the mid-twentieth century, accounted for only 2 percent of the region's total workforce, and its earnings represented a little more than 3 percent of industrial output. Its impact was pervasive, however, in rural counties with rich seams.

The U.S. Department of Energy estimated that nearly 20 percent of industry earnings came from the coal-producing counties of southwest Virginia and eastern Kentucky. In West Virginia, the figure was nearly 10 percent. The overall economic impact from the principal coal counties was estimated at $6.9 billion in West Virginia, $4.4 billion in Kentucky, $2.9 billion in Pennsylvania, $1.5 billion in Alabama, and $1.5 billion in Virginia.

In spite of modern productivity and vast reserves, the industry's longterm future was uncertain as the new century began. Nationally, oil and natural gas reigned as the supreme U.S. energy sources. Air pollution, the bane of coal-burning power plants, remained a major national environmental issue, and within the region water pollution from coal mining and processing and potential hazards from waste storage produced continuing concern. Moreover, sharp competition from strip mines in the West mounted with each passing year. In Wyoming, the nation's top coal-producing state, bituminous coal seams sometimes exceeded sixty feet in thickness, compared to three to seven feet for seams in Appalachia. There, and elsewhere in the West, surface mines yielded low-sulfur tonnage at a fourth of the cost of mining in the mountains. Following the deregulation of railroads and subsequent reductions in transportation costs, western coal began moving into markets once monopolized by Appalachian fields. In the 1990s, utilities in Georgia, Alabama, and South Carolina, as well as the government-owned Tennessee Valley Authority, received coal trains from Wyoming and Colorado.

The boom-and-bust cycles that dogged the industry throughout the twentieth century in Appalachia resulted from an inability to achieve longterm balance between supply and demand. High prices generated by wars, expanded markets, or national prosperity inevitably led to overproduction, surplus supplies, and collapsing prices. Oversupply and weak markets consequently produced the shutdown of mines and migration from the coalfields to distant cities.

During the booming 1970s, the industry's nationwide productive capacity raced ahead of demand by an estimated 200 million to 250 million tons per year. With the productivity of an individual miner soaring by 200 percent and demands remaining stable, a coal glut resulted, and two decades of depressed prices followed. Three-fourths of Kentucky's two thousand mines, many of them "truck mines" opened by individuals attracted by high prices, closed during the 1980s and 1990s.

The boom of the 1970s, the last of twentieth century, came when oil-producing countries of the Middle East twice embargoed exports to the United States. During the resulting energy crisis, coal prices soared to as much as a hundred dollars per ton on the spot market. U.S. policymakers turned to coal as a cornerstone of a longterm strategy to reduce the nation's reliance upon foreign oil. In Appalachia, new mines were opened by the hundreds as both energy conglomerates and small entrepreneurs got into mining. By the thousands, young men who had left the region moved home and took jobs in the coalfields. But as the decade ended, the bubble burst. Surging capacity had gotten years ahead of the market. Compounding the problem of oversupply, the American steel industry went into sharp decline, devastating the market for metallurgical coal, and foreign producers competed with Appalachian coal for export sales.

During the 1980s and 1990s, the industry underwent profound change even as coal prices languished. Oil, steel, and chemical companies that had increased their stake in Appalachian coal during the 1970s began leaving the business in the 1990s, following independent operators who had failed or sold out. Big names long associated with Appalachian coal faded—Westmoreland, Island Creek, and Pittston among them. Ownership became increasingly concentrated in the hands of operators such as Arch Coal of St. Louis, Consol Energy of Pittsburgh, Massey Energy Company of Richmond, Virginia, and AEI Resources of Ashland, Kentucky, which entered bankruptcy in 2002 and emerged as Horizon Natural Resources Company. In former union strongholds such as the Coal River Valley of West Virginia, the once formidable United Mine Workers of America, in decline across the region for years, was a vestige of another era.

In West Virginia, where the mining industry had been historically geared to metallurgical coal, the overwhelming focus turned to production of steam coal. As a result of the 1970 federal Clear Air Act and its amendments of 1990, a premium was placed upon coal with low sulfur content. This led to a major shift of Appalachian mining into the low-sulfur fields of southern West Virginia and the rise of Wyoming as a coal producer in the 1990s.

Driven by competition from low-sulfur coal from western surface mines, major operators in Appalachia increasingly turned to mountaintop-removal mining. The practice actually took hold in eastern Kentucky in the 1960s, spurred by large coal purchases by the Tennessee Valley Authority. Rather than cut contours around mountainsides to expose individual seams, miners attacked from above, fracturing the overburden with explosives, then stripping away rock and dirt. Successive seams could be removed with near 100 percent efficiency, as compared to about 40 percent for conventional underground mines, where pillars of coal were left standing as roof supports. In southern West Virginia and eastern Kentucky, the spread of mountaintop removal and the growth of individual mountaintop mines to more than two thousand acres stirred passionate environmental opposition and complex litigation, beginning in the late 1990s.

Industry organizations maintained that mountaintop removal was necessary for Appalachian coal to successfully meet its western competition and argued that industrial and recreational developments would be attracted to new manmade plateaus. But environmentalists opposed the process as wantonly destructive. A major legal challenge attacked the practice of dumping millions of tons of rock and dirt from leveled mountaintops into adjacent valleys and drainage systems.

A quarter of a century after the peak of the 1970s boom and amid warnings of a new energy crisis, spot-market coal prices rose to levels not seen in years. On Wall Street, mining companies' stock prices moved up strongly, and newspapers in the coalfields carried ads offering employment for miners. But the circumstances were greatly changed from the 1970s, when coal production had exploded in response to surging prices. Tighter regulation precluded rapid reopening of shutdown mines, and the cost of modern equipment had become prohibitive for small operators and entrepreneurs. Major companies that had risen to dominance in the 1980s and 1990s faced delays in acquiring both new equipment and mining permits. In efforts to exploit coal resources, the administration of President George W. Bush began to ease environmental regulations to make both mining and coal use more profitable. With world oil prices reaching record levels in 2004, both coal production and prices saw robust gains, but the greatest growth in production came from mines in the West.

Whether another boom materialized or not, experts predicted a gradual, longterm decline for coal in Appalachia. A study by the University of Kentucky's Center for Business and Economic Research for the Appalachian Regional Commission concluded that the employment and earnings of the industry would probably decline 25 to 30 percent in the first decade of the century.

See also: ANTHRACITE COAL INDUSTRY; ARCH COAL; CONSOLIDATION COAL COMPANY/CONSOL ENERGY.

—Rudy Abramson, *Reston, Virginia*

Harry M. Caudill, *Night Comes to the Cumberlands: A Biography of a Depressed Area* (1963); Ronald D Eller, *Miners, Millhands, and Mountaineers: Industrialization of the Appalachian South, 1880–1930* (1982); John Gaventa, *Power and Powerlessness: Quiescence and Rebellion in an Appalachian Valley* (1980).

Books-A-Million

One of the nation's largest book retailers, Books-A-Million is based in Birmingham, Alabama, and traces its origins to a makeshift newsstand assembled from used piano crates in 1917. In 2003 the company reported net sales totaling $442.7 million and net income of $1.4 million from its 206 stores in eighteen states and the District of Columbia. This made it the number three bookseller in the country, behind Barnes and Noble and Borders.

Besides more than 160 "superstores" featuring discount books and coffee bars, the company operates Joe Muggs Newsstands and a string of traditional stores called Bookland. In Florence, Alabama, where the piano-crate newsstand was launched by entrepreneur Clyde W. Anderson, the Books-A-Million subsidiary American Wholesale Book Company provides wholesale and book distribution services to customers across the Southeast. NetCentral, an Internet development and services subsidiary, is headquartered in Nashville, Tennessee. An emphasis on superstores averaging twenty thousand square feet of floor space and located in major shopping malls reflected a company strategy of making its outlets destinations for leisurely shopping.

The firm's expansion from a local newsstand and bookseller in Florence to a major publicly owned retailer was led by the founder's son, Charles C. Anderson. The latter also expanded the family's interests in fireworks—which also began with the original Anderson Newsstand—and sporting goods retailing. Charles Anderson's son, Clyde B. Anderson, became Books-A-Million chairman and chief executive officer upon his father's retirement.

In 2001 Books-A-Million acquired the eighteen stores, leasing rights, and inventory of the defunct Crown Books Corporation. Besides Alabama, Books-A-Million stores operate in the Appalachian states of Georgia, Kentucky, Maryland, Mississippi, North Carolina, Ohio, Tennessee, and South Carolina.

See also: PRINTING/PUBLISHING PRESSES.

—Rudy Abramson, *Reston, Virginia*

Bowater Incorporated

Bowater Incorporated is a leading American producer of pulp and paper products. Listed on the New York Stock Exchange and headquartered in Greenville, South Carolina, it manufactures and sells products used by the newspaper, magazine, book publishing, construction, lumber, and paper products industries, including newsprint, coated and uncoated papers, and lumber. It is a principal supplier of newsprint to newspapers throughout the world and one of the largest consumers of recycled newspapers, magazines, and directories. It operates pulp mills and other manufacturing plants throughout the United States and Canada, as well as in South Korea, and controls timberland and cutting rights to millions of forested acres in North America.

Originally organized by the British paper company Bowater Corporation as a subsidiary to manage the firm's North American operations, Bowater Inc. became a separate company in 1984. British Bowater had begun in 1882 as a paper merchandising firm. In 1924 Sir Eric Bowater changed the direction of the company, making it a paper producer. The company's operations in North America began in 1938, when it acquired a newsprint production facility in Canada. As the American market for newsprint grew after World War II, Bowater expanded into the United States to meet demand. After careful study and cooperation with the Tennessee Valley Authority, Bowater in 1954 established North America's largest newsprint plant along the Hiwassee River at Calhoun, Tennessee. A subsidiary of the British company formed to manage these operations was known at the time as Bowaters Southern Paper Corporation and later as Bowater Inc. Over the next thirty years, the subsidiary grew to include sawmills and pulp and paper mills throughout the United States and Canada.

As part of the cyclical and competitive forest products industry, Bowater encountered several difficulties in the recessionary period of the late 1970s and early 1980s and opted to spin off its North American operations. The British Bowater Corporation concluded that such a move would ease tax disadvantages, make the company more competitive, reduce corporate debt, and allow the British firm to pay a higher stockholder dividend than was usual in the United States. The North American subsidiary, consisting of plant operations in both the United States and eventually Canada, became an independent corporation. It took the name of Bowater Inc., while the British corporate parent changed its name to Bowater Industries PLC. Despite the up-and-down nature of the pulp and paper business, the company invested more than two billion dollars to expand and modernize operations during the 1990s. This enhanced its position globally, making Bowater one of the leading companies in its field.

See also: LUMBER INDUSTRY; PRINTING/PUBLISHING PRESSES.

—Ned L. Irwin, *East Tennessee State University*

Roscoe C. Martin, *From Forest to Front Page: How a Paper Corporation Came to East Tennessee* (1956); Mergent, Inc., *Mergent Industrial Manual* (2001); W. J. Reader, *Bowater: A History* (1981).

Breweries

A backlash against nationally distributed beers and the massive advertising campaigns of the nation's largest brewers during the final quarter of the twentieth century prompted a market resurgence of Appalachian beer-making companies, old and new. In 2003 there were brewing jobs throughout Appalachia—1,800 of them in Alabama, 650 in Tennessee, 150 in Kentucky, 800 in West Virginia, 1,980 in Ohio, 1,580 in Pennsylvania, and 2,310 in New York. Additionally, there were many beer wholesaling and marketing jobs throughout the region, but the higher number of brewing jobs specifically signified the return of microbreweries and the resurrection of one of the earliest traditions of Appalachia. Many microbreweries combined their original beers with quality dining, often in the same buildings as former breweries.

But the region's breweries were not all micro or new. In addition to such Appalachian branding giants as Rolling Rock and Iron City, there was D. G. Yuengling and Son of Pottsville, Pennsylvania, America's oldest functioning brewery, which reputedly sold more than a million barrels a year. Having exceeded the capacity of its own facilities in 1997, Yuengling purchased a former Stroh Brewery in Tampa, Florida, in 1999 and began selling its beer in the Sunshine State as well. In 2001 the company built a new brewery just north of Pottsville that reconnected Yuengling with the New York market.

Some of the smaller brewers offered touches that national giants found difficult to match. For instance, Straub Brewery in St. Marys, Pennsylvania, was known as the home of the "Eternal Tap" because patrons could walk into the keg-washing room from the street and pour themselves a free beer; Straub also preceded Budweiser in putting a freshness date on its labels. Pennsylvania Brewing Company, located in Pittsburgh in part of the old Eberhardt and Ober Brewery building, was Pennsylvania's largest microbrewer and was known for its award-winning Penn lines: Penn Pilsner, Penn Gold, Penn Dark, and Penn Weizen. In southern Appalachia, Highland Brewing Company in Asheville, North Carolina, established in 1994 using adapted dairy equipment, in 2003 had an annual brewing capacity of about 6,500 barrels and was selling its products in the Carolinas and east Tennessee. Touting the mountain water used to make its products and focusing on Asheville's upscale tourist accommodations, Highland offered Gaelic Ale, Oatmeal Porter, Black Mocha Stout, and Cold Mountain Winter Ale. Across the Great Smoky Mountains, Rocky River Brewing in Sevierville, Tennessee, home of the Dollywood family theme park, had an annual capacity of 4,800 barrels and manufactured six year-round brands with names such as Bearbottom, Copperhead, Mad Wolf, and Highland Dew. The Appalachian area of Tennessee claimed at least eight different microbrewers as well as the Chattanooga corporate headquarters of Gordon Biersch Brewery Restaurant Group, an upscale chain of about twenty-five micropubs stretching across the United States and eastern Canada.

The history of brewing in the Appalachian region goes back to construction of a brewery by the British army at Fort Pitt (present-day Pittsburgh) in 1765. Ever since the first settlers had made the voyage to America, beer had been almost a necessity. In America, colonists were sometimes unsure of the quality of local water and depended on a steady supply of beer, and people forced to drink water were sometimes viewed as unfortunate.

Throughout the late eighteenth century, breweries were built in settled communities in the Appalachian region. Despite the positive views of beer at the time, it confronted the early Appalachian settlers with certain difficulties. Beer was troublesome to keep from going sour when shipped over long distances between settlements, so the small brewer's output was usually consumed in a very limited local area. Beer also had competition from other drinks. Spirits such as rum and whiskey were easier to distill, keep, and transport and thus easily surpassed beer in production and consumption throughout the colonies. Another preferred drink, especially in the Appalachian region, was apple cider.

By the time of the American Revolution, prominent Americans were planning ways to promote the newly independent country's beer industry for two major reasons. Before the war, England had a thriving beer-exporting industry that suppressed the colonies' marketing of beer. American leaders thought it was critical to promote beer as an alternative to liquor, which had begun to take a toll on citizens' health and morals. Spirits, though, remained prominent throughout the Appalachian region, and citizens rebelled against a federal government excise tax on the alcohol they produced. This revolt, known as the Whiskey Rebellion of 1794, resulted in the dispatch of militia to subversive areas of western Pennsylvania. The government's tax was only on liquors and, after suppression of the rebellion and enforcement of the tax, some Appalachian communities began to establish local breweries.

Breweries spread throughout the region, and the type of beer each produced usually reflected the kind that predominated in the individual brewer's home region of Europe. As settlements grew, competition between local breweries did also and promoted innovation, quality, and the closing of unsuccessful ventures. By 1810, out of 129 total breweries in the United States, there were 48 in Pennsylvania, producing 71,273 barrels that year, and 42 in New York, producing 44,521 barrels.

As Appalachian brewing continued to expand, a beer-brewing revolution took place in Europe. In 1842 Austrian brewers in the town of Pilsen, Bohemia, came up with a process for making a golden and clear beer later known as lager. Combined with the rising use of beer glasses instead of wooden, leather, or ceramic cups, the new golden liquid made drinking beer a more visually pleasing experience. Served cold, lagers also provided a more refreshing drink than traditional English ale, the dominant beer in America at the time. Following these innovations, brewing became a more commercial and profitable enterprise. Certain beers also came to be viewed as more luxurious and rivaling other alcoholic beverages in flavor. As the beer industry became more lucrative, in 1856 the Benedictine Society of Saint Vincent Archabbey near Latrobe, Pennsylvania, opened a brewery business to help fund its aims.

By the time of the Civil War, Pennsylvania and New York still dominated beer production, accounting for 85 percent of the country's overall beer output. Afterward, the discovery of pasteurization and advances in rail transportation, cold storage, and bottling led to the rise of massive breweries and resulted in a gradual decline of the country's many microbreweries. In 1900 there were still 2,400 different breweries in the United States, but by 1950 there were just 27. One of these was Pennsylvania's Yuengling, which survived prohibition by producing ice cream and near beer. When prohibition was repealed, Yuengling produced Winner Beer and in celebration shipped a truckload of it to President Franklin D. Roosevelt.

Consolidation—fueled by drive for profit, scientific innovation, World War I animosity against brewers of German descent, and prohibition's closure of many small breweries—destroyed diversity in types of beers and reduced quality. Although insulated from previous minor consolidations due to its geography, Appalachia suffered through the industry's centralization, losing most of its own microbreweries. After World War II, beer consumption rose dramatically, and massive beer companies began to focus on marketing and advertising, battling for market share. Branding became very important, and new niche beers were produced. As time went on, nationwide breweries and catchphrase marketing schemes provoked widespread adverse reaction. Nationwide breweries remain dominant, but microbreweries have returned in profusion to Appalachia and elsewhere.

See also: DISTILLERIES; LATROBE BREWING COMPANY; PITTSBURGH BREWING COMPANY AND IRON CITY BEER.

—Kristin L. Abramson, *Pittsburgh, Pennsylvania*, and Arthur Holst, *Philadelphia, Pennsylvania*

Ian Hornsey, *A History of Beer and Brewing* (2003); Max Rudin, "Beer and America," *American Heritage* (July 2002); Gregg Smith, *Beer in America: The Early Years, 1587–1840: Beer's Role in the Settling of America and the Birth of a Nation* (1998).

Brock Candy Company

The South's—and Appalachia's—largest candy maker, Brock Candy Company of Chattanooga, Tennessee, merged with the E. J. Brach Corporation of Chicago in 1994 to become the fourth-ranking candy manufacturer in the United States. But its growth was gradual, occurring over the course of nearly a century and illustrating changes in Appalachia itself.

The firm was founded in 1909, three years after salesman William E. Brock Sr. decided after years of traveling to take up a more settled life in Chattanooga. Borrowing money, he invested with some associates in the Trigg Candy Company and in 1909 bought his partners out and renamed the company for himself. Sugar rationing during World War I hampered the business, but in 1920 the company introduced a five-cent peanut stick that became a big seller. Using the experience and connections he had made as a traveling salesman, Brock focused on manufacturing penny candies sold primarily through former clients in small country stores. He also worked with the DuPont Company to develop and test the packaging of candy in cellophane bags, which influenced the entire candy industry.

In the late 1940s and 1950s, the rise of supermarket chains began eliminating the rural stores on which much of the company's business depended. Brock shifted its product line from penny candies to more expensive types of candy products, and the change probably saved the company. Candies such as Chocolate Covered Cherries, Starlight Mints, Old-Fashioned Creme Drops, and Gummi Bears proved popular and profitable.

The family-owned business became publicly owned following an issuance of stock in 1993. The following year, the company was acquired by Chicago's Brach and returned to the status of a privately held company. Under the merger agreement, the new company was renamed Brach and Brock Confections, Inc., and was headquartered at the Brock facility in Chattanooga. The merger placed the new company just below M&M/Mars, Hershey, and Nestlé in the American candy industry. In 2003 the firm's 1,600 employees, its $340 million in annual sales, and its prominent position in the North American market were acquired by Zurich-based Barry Callebaut AG, which claimed status as the world's leading maker of high-quality cocoa and chocolate products. In 2004 Barry Callebaut reported 9,500 employees and some thirty production facilities in seventeen countries.

See also: CHATTANOOGA, TENNESSEE (URBAN APPALACHIAN EXPERIENCE).

—Ned L. Irwin, *East Tennessee State University*

Buck Stoves

Wood-burning stoves enjoyed a revival during the energy crisis of the early 1970s. In 1976 the New Buck Stove Corporation of Spruce Pine, North Carolina, introduced a so-called triple woodstove that produced heat efficiently by burning wood, and by 1979 woodstove manufacturers numbered around two thousand. After the onset of the 1980s, however, except for a slight blip during the 1991 Persian Gulf War, woodstove sales declined markedly.

Buck stoves have a heritage that goes back to colonial America. The invention of the Franklin stove by Benjamin Franklin increased the warmth-generating efficiency of burning wood over the radiant heating of colonial fireplaces. By the early 1800s, foundries were making wood-fueled cookstoves.

Over time, many people began to call all types of wood-burning stoves "Buck" stoves. Hundreds of small manufacturers began to make stoves marketed under different names, some specific to the places where they were produced. By the mid-1800s, stove makers in the United States were considered among the best in the world. Their heating stoves and ranges became essential parts of everyday life. An abundance of wood for fuel made the Buck stove especially popular in the Appalachian region to the present day.

Cast-iron stoves came into vogue in the 1850s. By 1873 the Buck Stove and Range Company of St. Louis was making stoves with white porcelain enamel baked onto the inside of the oven door. In 1905 this company marketed the first completely enameled stove. Cylindrical models for heating were most popular in the 1880s, and their popularity continued into the 1920s.

At the turn of the twentieth century, stoves were usually freestanding heavy units made of cast iron. Some came with elaborate decorative designs. Units could weigh as much as half a ton and served the dual purposes of heating and cooking. By the 1920s, with the invention of indoor heating, such stoves became obsolete as a heating source in many places. From then on, sales of wood-burning stoves declined steadily.

The Arab oil embargo of 1973 suddenly, but temporarily, changed things. Users of woodstoves felt that heating homes with wood could keep petrodollars out of the coffers of foreign oil-producing companies. That prompted the innovations by the New Buck Stove Corporation of North Carolina (no relation to the Buck Stove Company of St. Louis), but to small avail. In 1990, at the time of implementation of Environmental Protection Agency regulations on individual stoves, the number of stove-manufacturing operations numbered near five hundred. As of 2003, however, just sixty manufacturers of federally certified woodstoves existed. Of these, only twenty manufactured more than a thousand stoves each. The others produce from five hundred to a thousand annually.

See also: CAST-IRON COOKWARE (FOOD AND COOKING); LODGE IRON WORKS.

—Arthur Holst, *Philadelphia, Pennsylvania*

Brennan Kearney, "Hot Stuff," *Country Living* (February 2003); Kara Kopplin, "Evolution of Cookstove Designs and Manufacturing Techniques," *Ceramic Engineering and Science Proceedings* (May 2000); John Vivian, "Mother's 1993 Wood and Coal Stove Advisory," *Mother Earth News* (December 1992).

Bush Brothers and Company

Bush Brothers and Company is a privately held and family-owned food corporation based in Knoxville, Tennessee. The firm achieved national distribution of its products in 1994, and the Bush brand became America's number one baked bean. At the opening of the twenty-first century, the firm produced more than forty canned food products but was best known for Bush's Baked Beans and Bush's Chili. The company claimed about 80 percent of the U.S. domestic market for sugary baked beans and 43 percent of the overall market for prepared beans.

A. J. (Andrew Jackson) Bush began the company as a tomato cannery with his oldest sons, Fred and Claude, in

1908 in Chestnut Hill, Tennessee, forty-five miles east of Knoxville. During World War I, Bush Brothers operated at capacity, with 85 percent of their tomatoes going toward the war effort. After its 1922 incorporation, the company acquired a second food processing plant in nearby Oak Grove. Fred Bush, eldest son of A. J., assumed the presidency of Bush Brothers in 1931. In the same deep depression year, the company opened a new plant in Clinton, Tennessee.

In a critical turn of events, in 1943 the Tennessee Valley Authority seized by eminent domain—and then flooded—all of the Bush farmland, as well as the Oak Grove plant, to create Douglas Lake. The company did not purchase new land, instead expanding their purchase of produce from farmers as far away as Michigan and southern Florida. Afterward Bush purchased the Blytheville Canning Company in Blytheville, Arkansas. In 1952 the company began canning dry edible beans and has continued to grow and add new products.

Significant company changes began in the 1990s when the Bush Brothers board of directors changed policy and included a majority of outside directors, and Condon Bush, grandson of A. J., became the board's chairman. The company moved its corporate headquarters from Chestnut Hill to Knoxville in 1992, and by 1994 all Bush products were available nationally. During this era, James Ethier became president and chief operating officer, and Condon Bush was named chief executive officer. The company won a prestigious Gold Effie award for television advertising in 1995.

Bush Brothers and Company has three plants in the United States, one in Chestnut Hill and the others in Shiocton and Augusta, Wisconsin. The Shiocton facility produces only sauerkraut. In February 2001 the company announced plans to build a $110-million dry edible bean processing facility in Chestnut Hill. The new plant was predicted to double the company's baked bean production capacity to more than 800 million pounds.

See also: SOUP BEANS (FOOD AND COOKING); STOKELY–VAN CAMP.

—Martha Avaleen Egan, *Kingsport, Tennessee*

Camden, Johnson N.

(1828–1908) Industrialist and U.S. senator.

Johnson Newlon Camden—with Henry Gassaway Davis, Stephen B. Elkins, and Nathan B. Scott—was one of the Big Four power brokers of West Virginia during the state's formative years. As a chief West Virginia agent of John D. Rockefeller, as well as a major figure in railroad construction, Camden was a prime example of the alliance in West Virginia of politics with big businesses based outside the state. Around 1900, he and the other members of the Big Four constituted four of the state's five millionaires.

Camden was born in Collins Settlement (now Jacksonville) in Lewis County, Virginia, on March 6, 1828. His parents were John S. Camden, a justice of the peace, and Nancy Newlon. After attending Northwestern Academy in Clarksburg, the younger Camden served as deputy clerk of Braxton County (1845–46) before enrolling at the United States Military Academy. Difficulties with mathematics caused him to return home in 1849, and he began to read law in nearby Sutton. He served as prosecuting attorney in Braxton and Nicholas Counties in 1851–52 and afterward practiced law in Weston. During the Panic of 1857 he speculated successfully in land and in 1858 married Anne Gaither Thompson. He then began speculating in cannel coal, a bright-burning variety that can be refined into oil and other products. In 1860 he became a partner in a pioneering oil-producing operation at Burning Springs in Wirt County.

During the Civil War, four of his brothers joined the Confederate army, but Camden supported the Union. Confederates razed his Burning Springs works on May 9, 1863, but he rebuilt and expanded into Ritchie and Wood Counties. He helped launch a bank at Parkersburg and after the war founded J. N. Camden Consolidated Oil Company, a refining operation, there. He then sold this business to Standard Oil, becoming in return Rockefeller's chief West Virginia agent until 1879. During the 1880s, he was a major figure in the Monongah Coal and Coke Company and in construction of the Ohio River Railroad and the West Virginia Central and Pittsburgh Railroad in central and northern West Virginia.

Camden influenced politics as well as industry. In 1868 he and Davis became allies and revitalized the Democratic Party by introducing modern methods of organization, communication (especially via newspapers), finance, and private and governmental patronage. Camden won election to the U.S. Senate in 1881. A moderate conservative, he defended business interests, notably Standard Oil, but walked a fine line on the burning issue of the day, protectionism. He supported a retreat from Republican protective tariffs, not to foster free trade, but to encourage more selective and moderate tariff rates. Factional in-fighting cost him renomination in 1887, but in 1893 the party elected him to fill the two-year unexpired term of Senator John E. Kenna.

By the early 1890s, the Republicans—rejuvenated by Scott and especially Elkins, Davis's son-in-law and business associate—were resuming congressional control, and Elkins's defeat of Camden in the 1894 senatorial election sealed their victory. In 1896, objecting to William Jennings Bryan's free-silver views, Camden supported the breakaway National ("Gold") Democrats, who lost badly. With Republican control unbreakable in West Virginia and Washington, Camden retired from politics after 1904. Around that time he also sold or leased his railroad and mining interests to the

Baltimore and Ohio Railroad and James Otis Watson's Fairmont Coal Company.

Self-made and generous, Camden lived unostentatiously. He died in Baltimore in 1908 at age eighty.

See also: DAVIS, HENRY GASSAWAY (GOVERNMENT); ELKINS, STEPHEN B. (GOVERNMENT); SCOTT, NATHAN B.

—David S. Newhall, *Centre College*

Festus P. Summers, *Johnson Newlon Camden: A Study in Individualism* (1937); John Alexander Williams, *West Virginia and the Captains of Industry* (1976).

Carnegie, Andrew

(1835–1919) Industrialist and philanthropist.

A Scottish immigrant who arrived in the Pittsburgh area of Pennsylvania at age twelve, Andrew Carnegie became legendary in his lifetime for amassing an immense fortune through investments and business innovation, but he achieved the status of an American icon by promoting and adhering to a "Philosophy of Wealth" that morally obligated the rich to be good stewards of their prosperity and to invest in mankind. True to his convictions, Carnegie gave away 90 percent of his wealth, more than $350 million by the time of his death. Some $44 million of that built 1,946 libraries across the United States.

Born in Dunfermline, Scotland, Carnegie was immersed early in the legends of Scottish heroes William Wallace and Robert the Bruce, whose influence inspired him into his adulthood. His father, William Carnegie, was a gifted linen weaver and political reformer, while his strong-spirited mother, born Margaret Morrison, ran a small grocery shop from the home and, like her ancestors, mended shoes. Prompted to leave Scotland in 1848 by a decline in handwoven linens, the family settled in Allegheny, Pennsylvania, now part of Pittsburgh. William Carnegie peddled woven tablecloths door-to-door while his wife stitched shoes for cobblers. Andrew Carnegie soon became the family's main support through a series of jobs that included work in a cotton textile mill, a bobbin factory, and a telegraph office.

At age seventeen, he was employed by the Pennsylvania Railroad Company, for which he eventually became general supervisor and then head of the Western Division. During this time, he began making keen investments, most notably in Woodruff Sleeping Car Company, a firm manufacturing an innovation that he introduced to the rail line. Carnegie worked to help the Union army keep railway and communication lines open during the Civil War. Afterward he invested in Columbia Oil and Pennsylvania Oil before shifting his interests to steel and bridge construction. He developed the Keystone Bridge Company, the Cyclops Iron Company (later Union Iron Mills), and the Freedom Iron Company. His consolidated holdings became known as the Carnegie Steel Company. In 1901 he sold the firm to J. P. Morgan for $480 million, and it went on to become United States Steel Corporation.

At fifty-one Carnegie married Louise Whitfield, and they had one daughter, Margaret. He devoted his retirement to philanthropic endeavors resulting in Carnegie Hall, the Carnegie Corporation of New York, Carnegie Foundation for the Advancement of Teaching, Carnegie Endowment for International Peace, Carnegie Hero Fund Commission, Carnegie Institute of Technology, and Carnegie Institution of Washington. He spent his final years writing articles and books, working for worldwide peace, and giving away money.

See also: IRON AND STEEL INDUSTRY; MORGAN, J. P.; RAILROADS (TRANSPORTATION).

—Sandra Kay Heck, *Walters State Community College*

Andrew Carnegie, *Autobiography of Andrew Carnegie* (1920); Joseph Wall Frazier, *Andrew Carnegie* (1970); Burton J. Hendrick, *The Life of Andrew Carnegie* (1932); Harold C. Livesay, *Andrew Carnegie and the Rise of Big Business* (1975).

Carter, George Lafayette

(1857–1936) Railroad builder, town developer, and entrepreneur.

George Lafayette Carter was one of the most influential figures in bringing the modern industrial age to the southern Appalachian region. He launched a major coal-producing enterprise and built a railroad connecting the Atlantic to the Ohio River, spawning urban development and other significant industry.

Born on a farm near Hillsville, Virginia, Carter began clerking there at age sixteen. Following an apprentice period with Wythe County iron entrepreneurs David Peirce Graham and John W. Robinson at Austinville, Carter became a partner in 1889 in organizing the Pulaski Development Company and the Dora Furnace at Pulaski, Virginia. He soon took over management of these enterprises. Throughout the 1890s, he was heavily engaged in acquiring and consolidating small iron, coke, and coal companies in southwest Virginia, Tennessee, and Kentucky. This effort culminated with his organizing the Virginia Iron, Coal and Coke Company in 1899, thereby creating the largest industrial enterprise in the region. Competition from the Mesabi iron ore range undermined the business, however, and forced Virginia Iron, Coal and Coke Company into bankruptcy in 1901.

Carter managed to salvage about $500,000 and a small railroad operation. He then proceeded to build what many before him had failed at building, a railroad across Appalachia. Securing funds from investors led by fellow Virginia native Thomas Fortune Ryan, Carter completed the initial line from the Virginia coalfields to Spartanburg, South

Carolina, in 1909, then in 1915 extended the line to Elkhorn City, Kentucky. A great engineering feat, the construction of the Carolina, Clinchfield, and Ohio Railway was one of the most expensive railroad-building projects in America. The city of Kingsport, Tennessee, was developed as a result of Carter's railroad, and many other communities were established or expanded as a result of its construction. Industry, commerce, and tourism followed its route and were heavily promoted. Largely through his efforts, the forerunner of East Tennessee State University opened in Johnson City in 1911.

Carter simultaneously built the railroad and developed coalfields in the Pocahontas field in McDowell County, West Virginia. At Coalwood, he sank the first deep shaft mine in the state, greatly influencing the development of the coal industry. His Carter Coal Company was at one time the largest private coal producer in America. It was sold to Consolidation Coal Company in 1922 for $17 million. He retired to develop extensive agricultural interests in Wythe and Carroll Counties, Virginia, dividing his time between Washington, D.C., and Hillsville.

He was not through with business, though. He reacquired his old coal operations in 1933 when Consolidation defaulted, and in 1935–36 Carter and his son, James Walter Carter, won a legal battle against the Roosevelt New Deal when the United States Supreme Court voided the Guffey Coal Act's attempt to control coal output and prices. Carter died soon afterward, and his son continued to operate the coal company until 1947, when he sold it at a substantial profit.

Carter married Mayetta Wilkinson in 1895. A private person, Carter was noted for his personal peculiarities as well as his business genius. He is buried in the family cemetery in Hillsville.

See also: CAROLINA, CLINCHFIELD, AND OHIO RAILWAY (TRANSPORTATION); TRI-CITIES, TENNESSEE/VIRGINIA (URBAN APPALACHIAN EXPERIENCE); VIRGINIA IRON, COAL AND COKE COMPANY.

—Ned L. Irwin, *East Tennessee State University*

Ray Stahl and Ned L. Irwin, *The Last Empire Builder: A Life of George L. Carter, 1857–1936* (forthcoming).

Champion Fibre Company

People in Haywood County, North Carolina, experienced industrialization differently from their Appalachian neighbors. Across much of Appalachia, industrialization wreaked economic and cultural destruction, but the record of Champion Fibre Company, located in Canton, North Carolina, illustrates a balance struck between employees and a company that resulted in prosperity for both. This prosperity came at substantial cost, however: controversies over environmental pollution that allegedly sickened some of the company's regional neighbors for most of a century dogged Champion into the 1990s and ultimately induced the firm to sell the Canton plant to focus on operations overseas.

Peter G. Thomson arrived in the area in 1906 with private capital seeking a facility to provide pulp for his burgeoning Ohio paper mill. After visiting Newport, the first town on the Tennessee side of the Pigeon River, he came to Haywood County, North Carolina, and toured Clyde, Waynesville, and finally Canton, which was then called Pigeon. He decided on Canton because of its railroad terminal, its potential as a flume destination, and its access to timber, water, and adequate waste-disposal facilities—including the Pigeon River, a stream flowing across the Tennessee border into the Tennessee River, which supplied water for the city of Knoxville.

Champion Fibre Company began operation in Canton on January 1, 1908. By December it employed more than 800 people in a town that now claimed two banks, a forty-acre mill village, several new stores and specialty shops, and a newspaper. As soon as production began, residents noticed the dense smoke, ash, and acrid smell coming from the mill's stacks. Many feared the discharge threatened the lives of trees, crops, and even people, but Canton residents soon rationalized the foul stench as "the smell of money." Within a year, Tennesseans downstream as far as Knoxville began to agitate against Champion over the black, foamy, odoriferous pollution that it was discharging into the Pigeon River. In 1910 the Tennessee legislature appropriated money to sue the company, but Governor Ben Hooper granted Champion a reprieve for cleanup.

Champion apparently made some adjustments, and the reprieves continued, but so did the problems. A fish kill in the 1920s, attributed to Champion's dumping of large amounts of acid into the river, produced an odor so strong that it was reported hundreds of yards beyond either bank. Meanwhile, Champion kept growing. In 1931 it announced a 75 percent increase in output. By 1940 Newport suffered a water shortage that necessitated its piping water from the distant French Broad River instead of the Pigeon on its doorstep. In the 1960s, with national environmental consciousness rising, Champion began undertaking a series of upgrades of its wastewater treatment. By the 1970s, the Environmental Protection Agency was targeting Champion with fines for pollution violations.

Haywood County enjoyed its prosperity. Its population doubled between 1900 and 1940, and its number of manufacturing employees rose from 149 to more than 2,100, nearly all of whom worked in what then was the largest pulp and paper mill in the world. The town and company prospered together. The average Champion worker earned about $1,000 per year in 1940, more than double the wage of the average southern textile worker and at a time when the average Kentucky coal miner earned just $57 per year.

Success continued unabated through the 1950s and into the 1960s. In 1950 the median Canton income of $3,750 led its state's 105 urban areas. In each decade the average annual manufacturing wage surpassed both state and national averages, while unemployment usually ran about half as high. Additionally, a geographical survey from 1954 reported that Haywood County produced more beef than any other county and the second-highest amount of burley tobacco. It was also among the five largest dairy counties, contained more concrete silos than any other southern county, enjoyed the largest farm-agent program in the state, and was home to the largest rubber factory. Haywood County had the highest farmland values in the South and the third highest in the nation.

But competition and technology engendered economic stagnation in the mid-1960s. Champion furloughed 300 employees in 1962 and eliminated time-service bonuses in 1963. By 1965 employment in the mill had fallen by 20 percent from its peak, and in 1966, after four tries, Champion employees voted in a union. By the mid-1980s the Pigeon emerged as a cause célèbre, with Tennesseans charging that dioxins and other toxins long discharged by Champion into the river were causing cancer and otherwise endangering life. Tennessee finally took legal action. The United States Supreme Court ruled that the Environmental Protection Agency (EPA) held jurisdiction and in 1985 rejected a North Carolina operations permit for the mill.

The next seven years witnessed contentious exchanges between Champion and Haywood County on one side and the EPA and Cocke County, Tennessee, on the other. In 1990 Champion announced a $250-million program to modernize its facilities and meet Tennessee water standards within three years. Champion finally received its EPA permit in February 1992. That same year a class-action lawsuit was filed by downstream east Tennessee property owners asking damages of $5 billion. It ended in 1993 with Champion's being required to pay $6.5 million to compensate the plaintiffs and their attorneys and endow environmental and educational projects in the area, but Champion did not remain long in the area after that. The profitability of overseas operations led the company to put the Canton mill up for sale in October 1997. On May 14, 1999, the union announced approval of an employee buyout plan creating Blue Ridge Paper Products, Inc. Blue Ridge continued in operation in 2003, employing more than 1,100 people and primarily manufacturing containers for products such as juice and ice cream.

Industrialization in Haywood County benefited the native population. A move to three shifts in the 1910s, a 1924 strike in which employees triumphed in such areas as wage and schedule issues, pay increases for service anniversaries, and innovative benefits programs all indicated Champion's interest over the years in ingratiating industry with its immediate population. The county's ability to build schools, hospitals, and libraries, some of the first in the region, resulted from the presence of Champion. While many mountaineers in other counties and states became consumers only to find themselves debtors to the company store or eviscerated by the Great Depression, Haywood Countians were able to enjoy the economic infusion of modern industry and the fruits of their labor. During the height of the depression, Champion sold the federal government more than ninety-three thousand acres of forest for the creation of the Great Smoky Mountains National Park (after initially opposing plans for the park) and used the $3-million compensation to expand its mill, installing the world's largest book-paper-making machine and hiring new workers.

The comparative financial independence of Haywood Countians differentiated them from the majority of other mountaineers, who often either found themselves beholden to the mine or mill or reliant on federal largesse. This independence resulted in community prosperity like no other in Appalachia and for many years like no other in the state or the South—to the inarguable detriment of its own environment and that of its neighbors.

See also: MILL SETTLEMENTS (SETTLEMENT AND MIGRATION); MILL TOWNS (FAMILY AND COMMUNITY).

—Daniel R. Varat, *Greenville, South Carolina*

W. C. Allen, *The Annals of Haywood County* (1977); Richard A. Bartlett, *Troubled Waters: Champion International and the Pigeon River Controversy* (1995); Ronald D Eller, *Miners, Millhands, and Mountaineers: Industrialization of the Appalachian South, 1880–1930* (1982); Daniel R. Varat, "The Champion Family: Mountaineers in the Modern World," Ph.D. dissertation, University of Mississippi (2002).

Chattanooga Medicine Company

Myriad cosmetic and personal comfort products made by a NASDAQ-traded firm in Chattanooga, Tennessee, have been endorsed by such celebrities as Priscilla Presley, Joe Namath, Larry King, Dolly Parton, and Porter Wagoner. The company's K rations and medicines for treatment of shock helped win World War II. But Chattem, Inc., began as Chattanooga Medicine Company, maker and marketer of patent remedies for constipation and the pains of menstruation and arthritis.

Chattanooga Medicine Company was created in 1879 by Zeboim Cartter "Zip" Patten, an Illinois Union soldier wounded in the battle of Chickamauga who stayed in Chattanooga to recuperate. With the help of investors including *Chattanooga Times* (and later *New York Times*) publisher

Adolph Ochs, who served an early three-year term as Chattanooga Medicine's second president, the company marketed its first patent product, a vegetable laxative originally called Simmons Liver Regulator but much better known by its second name, Black Draught. Containing senna, snakeroot, wild ginger, and mandrake, plants indigenous to the Chattanooga area, Black Draught found its way into many homes in the upland South. Among the people who came to endorse it was Mary York, mother of World War I hero Sergeant Alvin York of Fentress County, Tennessee.

The second product marketed by the company was Wine of Cardui, which the firm bought from its originator in 1882. Aimed at curing "women's ailments," Cardui was made primarily from combining the *Carduus benedictus* plant with generous portions of pure grain alcohol. It caused many women, including some who advocated the prohibition of alcohol, to swear by its curative powers. Inspired by the patent medicines of Lydia Pinkham, Zip Patten hired salespeople to take his products into remote areas and came up with an ingenius marketing ploy to make his medicine more attractive to mountain women. In addition to wall calendars and church fans, he began publishing the *Ladies Birthday Almanac*, which women could receive for free with the purchase of his elixir. Millions of these almanacs were distributed and can still be ordered. Patten also apparently began advertising his products on barn roofs decades before Rock City adopted the practice in 1935.

In 1916 the American Medical Association condemned Wine of Cardui as a temperance tipple, for by that time Tennessee had long been dry. In the 1930s, Chattanooga Medicine contracted with Irvine Grote, chair of the chemistry department at the University of Chattanooga, to create new products. Grote developed an analgesic balm, which the company eventually marketed as Soltice. The product caught on in Appalachia and elsewhere, and it continued to be successful for the company into the twenty-first century.

In the 1940s, Lupton Patten, grandnephew of the founder, chose to move the company in a more scientific direction. With Grote's aid, he formed a subsidiary, the Brayten Pharmaceutical Company, which made considerable profits producing ammonia for World War II combat shock victims. Chattanooga Medicine Company was also contracted to produce K rations for the army. It claimed to have turned out nearly 40 percent of all soldiers' three-a-day meal packages, some 34 million.

After the war, Chattanooga Medicine acquired the rights to manufacture dihydroxy aluminum aminoacetate, an ingredient used to mute the side effects of aspirin in Bufferin, and produced it into the 1960s. Further research led to the creation of dihydroxy aluminum sodium, the primary ingredient in the antacid Rolaids, which made the company millions of dollars. Chattanooga Medicine Company also developed Pamprin, an effective product for the relief of menstrual discomfort.

During the 1960s, a new president, Alex Guerry, expanded operations by buying up smaller pharmaceutical concerns such as National Toiletries Company, Prince Manufacturing Company, DePree Company, and Petrochemicals Company. As a result of the expansion and a desire to be a national company, Chattanooga Medicine changed its name to Chattem Drug and Chemical Company in 1966. It branched out to produce aluminum hydroxide and aluminum chlorohydrate, key ingredients in deodorants. In 1978 the company shortened its name to Chattem, Inc., and expanded its line to include Quencher Lip Stick and Nail Polish and the aloe analgesic Flexall, among other products.

In 2003 Chattem, Inc., continued to add new product lines and to be an important employer in Chattanooga.

See also: CHEMICAL INDUSTRY; OCHS, ADOLPH; PHARMACEUTICAL INDUSTRY.

—Michael E. Birdwell, *Tennessee Technological University*

Alexander Guerry, *Men and Vision: The Secret of Yesterday's Success, the Formula for Tomorrow's: A Brief History of the Chattanooga Medicine Company* (1963).

Chemical Industry

The rise of chemical manufacturing in some of the river valleys of Appalachia tended to parallel twentieth-century development of the region's chief cities and urban clusters. The availability of natural resources first attracted chemical companies to West Virginia, east Tennessee, and other locations in Appalachia when supplies from Europe were disrupted during World War I. The impact of both world wars was evident in the rapid growth of the region's chemical manufacturing plants during those eras. Following decades of sustained growth, a sharp decline in the Appalachian chemical industry in the late twentieth and early twenty-first centuries resulted from corporate globalization and U.S. economic and trade policies, exemplified by the North American Free Trade Agreement (NAFTA) and the General Agreement on Tariffs and Trade (GATT).

During the post World War II era, the Kanawha and Ohio River Valleys of West Virginia became known as the "Chemical Capital of the World." Union Carbide Corporation, now a part of Dow Chemical, made products in West Virginia for more than seventy-five years, and the chemical industry occupied thousands of acres in the Kanawha Valley and employed, by its peak in the mid-1970s, more than 25,000 workers in the Mountain State. Since then, a study by Marshall and West Virginia Universities reported that in 1980 the total employment of the chemical industry in the valley was 12,593 and that by 1995 the figure had declined to 5,879.

The world's first petrochemical plant was established by Union Carbide in 1920 in Clendenin, West Virginia. Five years later, another West Virginia plant was built at South Charleston to supply 3 million pounds of ethylene glycol, a chemical used to keep dynamite from freezing. This product brought Union Carbide international recognition and became the basis for antifreeze. The South Charleston Technical Center's first research laboratory was dedicated in 1949 and, at the opening of the twenty-first century, was a complex of more than six hundred acres and four hundred labs housing chemical pilot plants, computer and engineering operations, and other functions.

The Institute Plant, located near Charleston, was built in 1943 by the federal government to produce synthetic rubber for the war effort and was purchased by Union Carbide in 1947. Although the Institute Plant first manufactured commodity goods, it later changed to agricultural products and specialty chemicals and produced up to 500 million pounds of the latter annually. In 1986 the agricultural business was sold to Rhone-Poulenc, a French chemical manufacturer. Under agreements that the plant would share certain facilities, it was later purchased by Aventis CropScience, which in 2003 changed its name to Bayer CropScience. In 1990, the Polyois Unit of the plant was sold to ARCO Chemical. Dow acquired its West Virginia operations through a merger with Union Carbide in 2001 and could be termed a tenant at the plant. Today, Bayer Corporation owns the Institute site, the general facilities, and the agricultural production units.

The 1984 Union Carbide accident in Bhopal, India, involving a lethal pesticide chemical called MIC, resulted in the deaths of nearly four thousand people within hours (as of 2003 the number of attributable deaths had risen to more than fourteen thousand). A smaller MIC accident at Institute the next year prompted West Virginia residents in communities near the Union Carbide/Rhone Poulenc Company plant to voice concerns about health, safety, and employment. These debates and the community efforts to make the industry socially responsible for its actions were documented by filmmakers Mimi Pickering and Anne Lewis in *Chemical Valley* (1991). Interviews were done with residents of Institute and other towns around the Rhone Poulenc plant, which was ten times the size of the Union Carbide plant in Bhopal. Discussing the environmental impact of industries so vital to the economy of West Virginia made *Chemical Valley* a politically controversial film.

The industrial chemicals center at Nitro, West Virginia, also has an important history in the region. The town was established by the federal government during World War I as the home of the world's largest gunpowder plant. In eleven months, 90 percent of the town and the plant were constructed, but the war ended before gunpowder production began. Monsanto used the site as a herbicide plant that drew national attention after a 1949 explosion resulted in employee complaints of health problems resulting from exposure to a herbicide contaminated with dioxin. This herbicide was later the principal component of Agent Orange, a chemical defoliant used by the United States in Vietnam. In 1988 Monsanto agreed to a $1.5-million settlement in a chemical poisoning case filed by more than 170 former employees. In 1997 a settlement worth more than $130 million was reached for the Fike/Artel Chemical Superfund site

Chemical complex in Institute, West Virginia, 1999. Eight chemical companies have had operations on this site, which has been part of the Kanawha Valley chemical industry since it was built in 1942 to produce synthetic rubber for the war effort.

at Nitro. Deemed a "global" settlement involving fifty-four parties, including other federal agencies, the agreement was reported to reconcile all Superfund costs at the site and guarantee future cleanup efforts. The Fike/Artel Chemical Company was located on the site of the Nitro World War I munitions plant, and it operated as a specialty chemical concern before it was abandoned in 1988. In 1983 the Environmental Protection Agency designated the twelve-acre site as a priority for cleanup.

In an effort to combat changing international political and economic conditions negatively affecting the chemical industry in the United States, community leaders in the Kanawha Valley united to create the Chemical Alliance Zone, which included representatives from the chemical industry, as well as from education, labor, economic-development, state government, and local concerns. Established in 2000, the Chemical Alliance Zone aimed to attract at least $4 billion in chemical industry investment to West Virginia in the next decade.

Union Carbide and other chemical concerns have maintained a high profile in West Virginia by supporting various charities, public education initiatives, higher education programs, museums, and other community causes. According to company reports, the Kanawha Valley chemical industry during the late 1990s paid more than $21.5 million in taxes and gave another million dollars in charitable contributions. At the turn of the century, the average wage for a chemical industry employee in West Virginia was 133 percent higher than the state's average.

In 1920, after seeing World War I disrupt German supplies of chemicals needed in photographic processes, Eastman Kodak founder George Eastman of Rochester, New York, visited the planned new city of Kingsport, Tennessee. There he purchased thirty-five acres and the factory buildings of the U.S. government's American Wood Reduction Company and established the Tennessee Eastman Company. At the outset, Tennessee Eastman used wood to make methanol, a chemical needed in photographic film, but it soon marketed by-products of this process. By the mid-1920s, the company had laid the foundation for large-scale production of cellulose acetate yarn, Tenite cellulosic plastics, acetate dyestuffs, and cellulose acetate butyrate molding composition, which had uses in design and production in the automobile and communications industries. During World War II, Tennessee Eastman manufactured critical military chemicals, designed and operated Holston Ordnance Works in Kingsport, and from 1943 to 1947 managed the Y-12 plant (then known as Clinton Engineering Works) at Oak Ridge, Tennessee.

Soon the company became the largest private employer in the state. Kodak and Tennessee Eastman established plants in Texas (1952), South Carolina (1967), and Arkansas (1977). On January 1, 1994, Eastman Kodak and Eastman Chemical Company, formerly Tennessee Eastman Company, became separate firms, and in the mid-1990s Eastman Chemical Company became the tenth-largest chemical company in the U.S. As an advocate of NAFTA, Eastman Chemical Company committed to a globalization effort that resulted in the location of twenty-eight of its forty-eight manufacturing plants outside the United States. The strategy significantly reduced the company's earnings over the next several years and led to downsizing and layoffs. In March 2004, the firm announced plans to close a small co-polyester manufacturing plant in Hartlepool, England, and transfer most of its production to Kingsport.

The dangers in chemical manufacturing for employees and nearby residents were demonstrated to the entire region on October 4, 1960, when Tennessee Eastman Company suffered the most serious industrial accident in its history. An explosion at the company's aniline plant killed fifteen people and injured more than two hundred. In the late 1990s, Eastman Chemical's image as a responsible corporate citizen was damaged when the company pled guilty to participating in international price-fixing and when it was assessed civil penalties having to do with hazardous-waste disposal. The cost of these two actions totaled more than $35 million.

Problems also evolved out of longterm chemical manufacturing in Anniston, Alabama, in southern Appalachia, where the Southern Manganese Corporation began operations in 1917. Theodore Swann Company purchased the plant in 1930 and began producing polychlorinated biphenyls (PCBs), which were used as insulating materials in various electrical appliances. Monsanto purchased the Anniston firm in 1935 and continued manufacturing PCBs on the site until it suspended production of them in 1971. Health problems experienced by people living nearby were documented, but Monsanto denied any link with PCB production. Residents of the largely African American community filed a lawsuit. In *The People of Anniston, Alabama v. Monsanto*, an Alabama jury found in 2002 that the company had engaged in "outrageous" behavior by releasing tons of PCBs into the city of Anniston and concealing environmental violations for decades. In 2003 Solutia Inc., formed when Monsanto spun off its chemical division in 1997, spent $40 million in cleanup costs and $84 million to settle two other Anniston PCB cases.

Mercury contamination by Olin Chemical Company put Saltville, Virginia, on the federal Superfund list in 1983. Olin had operated from 1895 to 1972 along the North Fork of the Holston River and, according to the company's estimates, lost as much as a hundred pounds of mercury per day in the soil and the Holston River between 1951 and 1970. Hundreds of people lost jobs when changes in state law resulted in closure of the plant, which was soon demolished. Once Saltville's biggest employer, Olin agreed to pay for most of the cleanup.

The Appalachian chemical industry faced serious twenty-first-century challenges in attracting new investment by global chemical firms, providing employees with high-paying jobs, and assuring the public that revitalizing this economic sector can be consistent with community progress and quality of life.

See also: EASTMAN CHEMICAL COMPANY AND TENNESSEE EASTMAN COMPANY; MONSANTO CORPORATION; SUPERFUND (ENVIRONMENT).

—Martha Avaleen Egan, *Kingsport, Tennessee*

Charles Carpenter, "Coming of the Chemical Industry to Middle Appalachia," *West Virginia History* (April 1969); Michael Grunwald, "Monsanto Held Liable for PCB Dumping," *Washington Post* (February 23, 2002); Suzanne C. Hickerson, "Saltville Residents View Olin Cleanup Plans," *Bristol Herald-Courier* (April 17, 2001); William D. Wentz, *Nitro, the World War I Boom Town: An Illustrated History of Nitro, West Virginia and the Land It Stands On* (1983).

Clayton Homes

Clayton Homes, Inc., of Maryville, Tennessee, was one of the largest retailers of manufactured housing in the United States as of 2003. Founded in 1966, Clayton built, sold, leased, financed, and insured manufactured homes and commercial and educational buildings. The company operated in thirty-three states, employed 7,400 workers, and in 2000 had sales in excess of $1 billion. A homegrown Appalachian business, the firm also was influential across the region in promoting manufactured homes as a viable and affordable housing alternative. When it was bought by billionaire investor Warren Buffett's Berkshire Hathaway Inc. in April 2003 for approximately $1.7 billion in cash, the *Wall Street Journal* described Clayton as "a quality company" purchased "at a beaten-down price."

West Tennessee native James L. Clayton studied engineering at the University of Tennessee in Knoxville during the 1950s. While attending college he bought and sold cars, which led to his opening of a small used-car business and, later, automobile franchises in north Knoxville. As a law student at the university, Clayton sold mobile homes on behalf of classmates and, as he later reflected, "slid into the business." He launched Clayton Mobile Homes with a $25,000 loan in 1966. The first retail sales outlet was located across the street from Clayton's auto dealership. Clayton promoted his business ventures on *Startime*, a weekly television variety program that eventually made him a local celebrity.

The first manufacturing plant opened in 1969, and five years later the company began subsidizing mortgages. In 1983 Clayton Homes debuted on the New York Stock Exchange at $3.36 a share. Success came from high turnover, minimization of profit margins, vertical integration, survival of shifting industry trends, alertness to customer needs, focus on the major market region, and innovation in home construction. By 1989 Clayton Homes was one of *Forbes* magazine's "200 Best Small Companies in America." James Clayton received a Horatio Alger Award in 1991 in recognition of his journey from sharecropper's son to corporate founder and chief executive officer. Throughout the 1990s he appeared regularly on the *Forbes* list of wealthiest Americans, and Clayton Homes continued to receive peer industry awards in the twenty-first century. As of 2003, the company operated 20 manufacturing plants, 296 company-owned stores, 85 manufactured housing communities, and 611 independent retailers, along with a financial arm providing mortgage services to 168,000 customers and insurance protection for 105,000 families.

After 1999 the industry, in which Clayton ranked third with 10 percent of the market, suffered through fewer home purchases, tighter lending rules, and increased repossessions. The *Wall Street Journal* offered these as possible reasons why the Clayton board accepted the Buffett offer that amounted to perhaps half of what Clayton stock was worth per share at the time. The newspaper reported that in the final quarter of 2002 nearly three-fourths of the firm's income had been generated not by the manufacture of homes but by the company's financing and insurance operations.

—Lisa Roberts Jett, *California State University at Sacramento*

Coal Industry

See Anthracite Coal Industry; Bituminous Coal Industry

Coca-Cola Bottling

See Soft Drink Companies

Consolidation Coal Company/ Consol Energy

Consolidation Coal Company was a coalfield colossus that for well over a century played major roles in shaping the physical and cultural landscapes of southern Appalachia—as well as displaying some of the synergies of power at work in the relationships of railroads and the coal industry. Railroads were the nation's economic giants, and coal mines were their primary subsidiary business, particularly in the Appalachian states. The lives of unnumbered residents of remote hollows in such states as Maryland, Pennsylvania, Kentucky, and West Virginia, along with generations of their progeny, were ultimately controlled by the handful of capitalists directing American railroading from the 1850s until the ascendance of the superhighway. In recent years, Consolidation

Coal has only gotten larger. Through a complicated series of mergers and acquisitions, it had by 2002 become Consol Energy, claiming $2.2 billion in annual revenues and trading (as CNX) on the New York Stock Exchange. Consol is headquartered in Pittsburgh.

Created from the combined interests of several Maryland mining companies in 1860, the core company that became Consolidation Coal began operations during the Civil War; about a decade after Appomattox it came under the control of the Baltimore and Ohio Railroad. Like its competitors in the region, the Baltimore and Ohio was deeply interested in the coalfields, and it and Consolidation together controlled the extraction and sale of Maryland coal. At the turn of the twentieth century, both the Baltimore and Ohio Railroad and Consolidation were bought by the Pennsylvania Railroad, America's largest rail firm, at which point Consolidation began rapidly expanding into West Virginia and Pennsylvania. Most notably, it acquired a majority interest in the large Fairmont Coal Company of West Virginia.

By 1909 Consolidation had bought more West Virginia and Pennsylvania mining firms, as well as 100,000 coalfield acres in Kentucky. For another two decades, it continued to grow, and in 1915 the controlling interest of its securities was bought by the Rockefeller family. Some of its practices affected life in the mining camps positively. Two years after the Rockefeller acquisition, Consolidation opened an "employment relations department," and Consolidation and some other large companies sought to make the camps cleaner and more sanitary—partly because outbreaks of disease could be expensive. In 1919 Consolidation management allowed its employees to be organized by the United Mine Workers of America; however, after World War II the company withdrew from the agreement.

By 1927 Consolidation had emerged as the largest commercial producer of bituminous coal in the United States. At this time the company operated ninety-two mines and employed more than 12,000 workers representing forty-three nationalities. But the late 1920s and 1930s brought overexpansion, declining sales, depressed wages, labor unrest, financial ruin for the industry, and a 40 percent decline in production for Consolidation Coal. In 1932 the Great Depression pushed the firm into bankruptcy, but receivership and reorganization pushed it to the fore again.

After the Second World War, Consolidation acquired additional properties in West Virginia and Ohio. In 1945 Pittsburgh Coal and Consolidation Coal—then the two largest commercial coal companies in the country—combined to form the Pittsburgh Consolidation Coal Company. Consolidation's history since the merger with Pittsburgh Coal is reflective of changes that the coal industry has undergone over the last fifty years. It includes transition to highly mechanized surface mining, attempts at diversification, emphasis on providing feedstock for coal-fired power plants, expansion into western coalfields, and a series of new corporate associations. These included acquisition by the Continental Oil Company (Conoco) in 1966, 1981 affiliation with DuPont, and Conoco's merger with Phillips Petroleum in 2002. In 1991 DuPont and affiliates of the German firm Rheinbraum formed Consol Energy as a subsidiary. Seven years later the Rheinbraum companies purchased more Consol stock, advancing their ownership to 94 percent. Around this time, Consol was listed on the New York Stock Exchange.

Southwestern Virginia coal-bed methane reserves belonging to MCN Energy Group were bought by Consol in 2000, and the following year, Consol acquired from Conoco some coal-bed methane and gas production facilities in the area. Consol and Allegheny Energy announced plans to build a coal-bed methane-fueled power-generating facility there and completed construction in 2002. That year Consol reported having about 2,000 employees each in West Virginia and Pennsylvania, 675 in Virginia, 600 in Ohio, and about 425 in Kentucky. It owned some 440,000 acres of land spread across those states and Illinois.

See also: MORGAN, J. P.; PEABODY COAL; ROCKEFELLER, JOHN D. AND JOHN D., JR.

—Geoffrey L. Buckley, *Ohio University*

Copper and Lead

The last copper mine in Appalachia ceased production in 1987, giving way to other elements that originally were byproducts of the copper mines. Lead has not been produced in significant amounts in the region since 1880, other deposits having been found in the West. Before that, however, substantial Appalachian mining of both of these metals occurred until well after the Civil War.

The Appalachian copper region begins in Montgomery County, Virginia, and extends southwest into North Carolina between Iron Mountain and the Blue Ridge. It includes Floyd, Carroll, and Grayson Counties of Virginia and Ashe and Alleghany Counties of North Carolina. Copper was first discovered in Floyd County by an iron miner, but he did not attempt to develop the copper mine. Copper production began later, in 1832, at the Peach Bottom Mine in Ashe County. A second source of Appalachian copper was discovered in Polk County, Tennessee, in 1843. The industry developed during the mid-1850s with the opening of several Virginia mines near the original discovery site.

Copper's smelting process was similar to that used in iron furnaces. As with iron, early copper miners failed to see the need to smelt at the mine itself. Smelters were typically not located near the mines, so the ore had to be shipped to smelting companies located in the North. The copper veins in Tennessee and Virginia were not convenient to transportation, averaging thirty-six miles from the nearest railroad, and wagon transportation was expensive. Copper from the Virginia mines had to be shipped by wagon to Wytheville, Max Meadows, or Christiansburg, then to Richmond by train. Tennessee copper was transported by mule to Dalton, Georgia, or Cleveland, Tennessee, with either route requiring three days' travel. When Tennessee miners discovered that they could reduce costs by smelting their own ore, they constructed several smelters in Polk County. Virginia miners, however, continued to ship their ore to distant smelters. Miners were offered payment to ship the heavy, unsmelted ore, but they only earned money from the pure copper extracted from it. Smelting at the mine would have reduced the transportation cost, increasing the amount of pure ore shipped.

Just before the Civil War, twenty-five copper mines operated in the five Virginia counties, and prospects for production looked promising. More than 2,700 tons of ore, averaging 16 percent copper, were shipped. The Virginia mines were newer than those in Tennessee but less successful because of the high cost of shipping unsmelted ore. Virginia mine owners became discouraged because opening a mine offered little immediate payoff while at the same time involving a large initial investment and much labor.

Tennessee mines were more self-sufficient and the primary source of copper during the Civil War, but the Confederacy lost its copper works in Tennessee when Union troops occupied the state in 1863. Afterward the Confederate government reopened the mines in southwest Virginia and North Carolina, but it was too late to be of appreciable help.

The Commonwealth of Virginia operated lead mines in Wythe County throughout the 1700s and 1800s, supplying armies and militias in times of war. However, in spite of the importance of lead mines to the Continental Army and Virginia's militia, the state sold them in 1780 to a local family who operated them for twenty years, then abandoned them and moved away. The mines lay dormant until Virginia sold them to another family, who built a tower in 1807 to make lead shot. These businesses tended to wax and wane with wartime requirements, but civilian needs grew steadily.

The lead bullet was the primary product requested by the military. Production required a 150-foot shot tower, in which molten lead was dropped from the tower's top into a pool of water at the bottom. The tower's hollow center rose seventy-five feet above a shaft drilled another seventy-five feet into the ground. A water-filled kettle sat at the bottom of the shaft, and molten lead was poured through a sieve at the top. The liquefied lead fell through in small droplets, each of which formed a round ball as it descended through the air. Water in the kettle cooled the shot rapidly, causing it to retain its round shape. The Wytheville shot tower received extensive use during the War of 1812 and the Civil War, though lead was processed in the area earlier.

In August 1861, the Wythe County mines produced two tons of lead and 1,200 pounds of buckshot daily. During 1862 three Wytheville lead mines operated, along with the Silver Hill Mine in North Carolina and the Jackson Mine near Jonesborough, Tennessee. The Jonesborough facility reverted to iron production soon after opening, leaving the Wytheville mines as the Confederacy's primary source of lead throughout the Civil War. The mine produced only three to four tons per day, however, which was not enough to meet army demands.

Although the Wytheville mines could make shot at the nearby shot tower, getting it to an arsenal for the making of cartridges was difficult. Lack of reliable rail transportation crippled the industry. The Confederacy had several arsenals to supply arms and ammunition and needed a monthly total of 155,000 pounds of lead to meet its production requirements. Virginia produced approximately 60,000 pounds of lead monthly from 1861 to 1864 before a December 1864 Union raid destroyed the Wytheville mines.

The Confederacy's manufacturing capacity never matched that of the Union because of a lack of foundries and railroads, and during the war inadequate rail transportation and enemy interference prevented the Confederate lead industry from being fully effective. Even though Appalachia's lead-producing facilities were rebuilt after the surrender, transportation and legal arrangements remained difficult for several years.

See also: IRON AND STEEL INDUSTRY; IRON SETTLEMENTS (SETTLEMENT AND MIGRATION); SALTPETER MINING.

—Michael E. Lynch, *Carlisle, Pennsylvania*

Michael E. Lynch, "Confederate War Industry: The Niter and Mining Bureau," M.A. thesis, Virginia Commonwealth University (2001); Robert C. Whisonant, "Geology and History of the Civil War Iron Industry in the New River–Cripple Creek District of Southwestern Virginia," *Virginia Minerals* (November 1998) and "Geology and the Civil War in Southwest Virginia: The Wythe County Lead Mines," *Virginia Minerals* (May 1996).

Corning Glass

With a history spanning a century and a half, Corning Incorporated grew from a glass company located (after 1867) in northern Appalachia into a diversified global technology company that at the end of the twentieth century aggressively achieved world leadership in the manufacture of optical fiber and optical cable systems—and then suffered a downturn as the technology boom turned to bust between 2000 and 2003. As 2005 began, management still sought to regain corporate profitability following elimination of twenty thousand jobs, closing or idling some plants, and selling off parts of the company. By then professional observers were predicting that the business that invented the ovenproof glass Pyrex, optical fiber, and windows for manned spacecraft, among many other things, would avoid bankruptcy but that it might be damaged longterm by the reductions in research and production capacity that had to be made to survive. Ultimately, it was Corning's ongoing investments in research and development that led to its survival and waves of innovation.

The world corporate headquarters of Corning Incorporated—Corning, New York—is the primary industry of an Appalachian community with a population of approximately ten thousand. Amory Houghton Sr. and his son, Amory Jr., moved the Brooklyn Flint Glass Company to Corning in 1868 and changed its name to the Corning Flint Glass Works. The company went bankrupt in 1870 but secured new financing in 1871. It produced tableware and kitchenware.

Steuben Glass Works, a company founded in 1903, became part of Corning Glass Works in 1918. Steuben made a variety of lustrous lead glass in many styles and colors. Production of colored glass ended in 1933 when Corning scientists developed a new optical glass for lenses. The Steuben design team established a distinctive style virtually free of flaws. These lead crystal designs have been presented as gifts of state by every United States president since Harry Truman. Steuben glass artisans create molten glass designs at the Steuben Factory in Corning.

Corning Incorporated is a global high-technology company noted for its innovation and manufacture of glass and glass-related products. The name Corning has long been associated with Pyrex, CorningWare, Corelle, and Revere products, but in 1998 the company sold its consumer products business to what is now known as World Kitchen. The company's contributions to the aerospace industry, besides windows for all U.S. manned spacecraft, include the fabric used in astronauts' spacesuits. Corning invented low-loss optical fiber in 1970 and optical cable systems soon after and pioneered the technology in flat-panel screens for televisions and notebook and desktop computers. In 2000 it had facilities in Kentucky, North Carolina, New York, Ohio, Pennsylvania, Virginia, and West Virginia. The 2000 decision to invest heavily and expensively in optical fiber and optical cable production based on the high demand of the technology boom was made during one of the few times that a member of the Houghton family was not the firm's chief executive officer. James Houghton, who held that position during the 1980s and 1990s, took charge again in 2001 and led the dramatic restructuring that appears to have saved the firm. The restructuring focused on capitalizing on the appeal of flat-panel television and computer screens.

The Corning Museum of Glass is independent from but supported by Corning Incorporated. The museum follows the thirty-five-hundred-year history of glass from ancient Egyptian artifacts to fiber optics. It contains the world's greatest collection of glass, dating from 1400 B.C. into the twentieth-first century. More than four hundred thousand visitors annually watch skilled glassmakers shape products there. Guests also get a close-up view on overhead monitors inside the 2,350-degree furnaces at the Hall of Science and Technology. The facility offers an educational program at the Museum Studio, where glassmakers and novices come for instruction.

See also: GLASS INDUSTRY.

—Clara Hasbrouck, *East Tennessee State University*

Hoover's Master List of U.S. Companies (2003); Mark Pickvet, *The Encyclopedia of Glass* (2001); Chloe Zerwick, *A Short History of Glass* (1990).

Cottage Industries

Markets everywhere at the opening of the twenty-first century were becoming more and more global, so an increasing number of Appalachian home-based industries had to contend—directly or otherwise—with competitors from the Orient to Wal-Mart. Widely, they adapted.

The Appalachian image of backwoods businesses carried on by elderly people practicing eons-old crafts is a stereotype. Quilts are increasingly stitched by machine rather than by hand. The cultivation of produce bound for the roadside farm stand is done by garden tractor more often than by mule. Molasses can be cooked over propane rather than a wood fire. Homemade soap tends to be stirred electrically rather than by a muscle-driven paddle, and an electric lathe instead of a foot-powered one turns potters' wheels. Home-produced edible products frequently fall under the jurisdiction of state health and consumer regulatory agencies, and on the black market the most popular rural production facilities are no longer moonshine stills but marijuana plots and methamphetamine labs.

Also known as at-home, home-based, underground, or cash-and-carry businesses, cottage industries include legal (and if unhampered by law enforcement, illegal) small-scale agriculture as well as classic crafts production. The business model takes its name from limited, home-centered production requiring little capital, light tooling, native skill, local markets, and time. Cottage industry typically does not require a middleman, and production growth stems from do-it-yourself entrepreneurship, with low barriers to entry not limited by gender, ethnic background, religion, age, or production capacity. The Web site Experian BizInsight claims to list more than a million home-based businesses, which spend a total of more than $10 million on business-related goods and services.

Some home industries have county or state or even national associations to ensure consistent production and promote legislative agendas, and many cottage industrialists form localized clubs offering self-help and promotion. These are often very specialized. The Cottage Industry Miniature Trade Association, for example, is alliance of more than 230 professional handcrafters of dollhouse accessories.

Another example of a well-organized cottage business important in Appalachia is the bee-keeping industry. Honey production is an individual process (as opposed to corporate farming) at the hive level, but bee keepers form associations to keep up with current news and techniques. The American Beekeeping Federation was formed in Chicago in 1943 "to stop adulteration of honey." An American Beekeeping Federation director, Virginia Webb of Fannin County, Georgia, worked with local and regional associations for a dozen years—while producing honey that has won Georgia's annual Best of Show award two times. The government channels critical data to and from the associations, and at some level government regulation ensures consistent product and may also require fees. In Appalachia, one of the most common assistance programs for cottage industries is the county agricultural extension service, which is funded through land-grant universities.

Other common examples of cottage industries in the region include festival crafts, clothing alterations, housecleaning, and marketing of small-farm or surplus-garden produce. The roadside stand is a visible example of a cottage industry. The next level is city-located farmers' markets, followed by state-funded farmer's markets with larger sales areas and more produce. In the mountains, Christmas tree farming is an example of a cottage industry that has permanently matured into greater levels of sophistication. Entry into this industry has become prohibitive due to high capital costs, severe market competition, and slow profit realization.

Unique to Appalachia is the cottage industry of small-operations coal mining—which may have just one person digging coal from a rock face in his or her backyard, loading the dug coal onto a pickup truck, and selling it to a neighbor or on a local spot market to a school or small business. Even though the state has an interest in the industry and information is available about it, entry and exit are easy, because the labor comes from the efforts of one or two persons and capital requirement is minimal. Urban Appalachian cottage industries include the usual lawn-mowing services and flea markets. Perhaps the quintessential urban cottage industry in Appalachia as elsewhere is the lemonade stand.

Cottage industries are widespread throughout the region, but each still depends to a great extent on local resources and local economic health. Cottage industry ultimately relies on available cash markets. The poorest of poor communities may have no farmers' market on the town square not out of lack of available produce, personal transportation, or labor, but because of a shortage of discretionary income in the local economy. The ability of a seller to support credit in the form of checks and food stamps can sometimes override the local competitive market's perceived advantages. The Internet has vastly widened the reach of home-based businesses. In 2003 the Web site of Country Dolls Handcrafted by Patricia in Edwardsville, Pennsylvania, the cottage industry of a widow whose husband died of lung cancer, had logged 54,736 visitors since 2000.

Westward migration through Appalachia gave pioneers early opportunities to offer new services, establish baseline standards, and perhaps exemplify the "can-do" capitalist attitude. Settlers of the region became innkeepers, boat builders, and food suppliers to Appalachian through-migrants. That history of entrepreneurial cottage industriousness has continued even as resource materials changed from being based on farms to forests to coal and back again, depending on regional topography and changing markets. An example of the novel ways that history repeats, or almost repeats, itself is the rescuing of old barn and church timbers for reuse in nouveau chic homes.

One of the best-known examples of a cottage industry in Appalachia that developed into a major industry was homemade chenille or "tufted" bedspread production, which originated in Dalton, Georgia, in the late nineteenth century. Catherine Evans Whitener handcrafted the first such spread in her home, using embroidered candlewicking techniques from England and France. Evans produced one bedspread and then another, eventually launching a home business that was so successful that she solicited help from friends and neighbors. By the 1920s, however, demand for tufted bedspreads had outstripped the hand tufters' ability to supply the market. Machines were developed to do the work, and by 1941 ninety firms were producing tufted spreads in the Dalton area, totally displacing the cottage industry launched by Whitener. After World War II, when soldiers returned and housing construction increased, the need for floor coverings emerged, and the Dalton industries applied the tufting techniques to the production of carpet.

Cottage industries respond to global economics. Products and demand enter or exit the landscape easily. A cottage industry may require more time, effort, and expense, but it also gives the business owner freedom to decrease or stop production at will. In Appalachia, the homegrown cottage industry may continue over long periods suffering through worldwide or local booms and busts with limited effect on the actual operation of a particular small-scale business. For example, Hmong Vietnamese immigrants have incorporated their bead-sewing skills into creating a new product line of clothing for sale alongside wool, cotton, and leather goods.

Catherine Evans Whitener holds one of her handmade chenille bedspreads, Dalton, Georgia, c. 1950s. The popularity of tufted bedspreads initially made by Whitener in her home sparked a cottage industry that eventually evolved into the modern carpet industry.

Typically, illegal markets are of more concern to authorities than small at-home industries unless there are taxation or health issues. In rural Appalachia, the black market has stereotypically consisted of moonshine and marijuana production, while in large cities it may include other drugs. Trends indicate that lower-income persons with accessible forestlands migrate toward marijuana growing rather than crafts, although some states tout crafts programs as an economic alternative to marijuana production.

Crafts sold at festivals at the dawn of the twenty-first century often contained bulk-purchased parts, and the importance of the Internet in removing limitations on political and regional boundaries on the marketing of Appalachian products can hardly be overemphasized. Cities and counties in the region consolidated their local craft inventories and production into thriving industries marketed via the World Wide Web. Each producer could operate independently yet be part of an informal alliance. New tools opened up possibilities for new industries such as laser art, router-cut woodcrafts, or garage-band compact disc production. In 2003 artist John Warr of Scottsboro, Alabama, was selling his pen-and-ink-and-acrylic "Civil Warr" and wildlife paintings on the Internet for $25 to $136 each. Similarly, Susan Abramovitz of Athens County, Ohio, a former ceramics instructor at Case Western Reserve University, marketed her Rock Riffle Run Pottery on-line—keeping alive a three-thousand-year-old-art, she said, through the use of "modern equipment" and clay deposited 150 million years ago at the foot of the Appalachian Mountains.

The numbers of dollar sales or units produced do not determine at what point an activity qualifies as a cottage industry. A home-based business beginning as a one-person enterprise can grow from making baskets for collecting foodstuffs for the family to selling those same baskets for utilitarian purposes or as an art form, as in the Native American basket-making market. Other examples of businesses that originated as cottage industry to fit very local needs are the manufacture of glass and the bottling of drinking water. Such movement up the economic scale may create a problem of consistent production, which prompts the use of power tools and other shortcuts to meet demand.

The continued survival and evolution of Appalachian cottage industries depend on worldwide economic pressures, traffic, new entrepreneurs, and new generations of customers.

See also: BEE KEEPING (AGRICULTURE); MOONSHINE (FOOD AND COOKING); SECTION OVERVIEW (CRAFTS).

—Charles F. Moore, *East Tennessee State University*

Blair White, "Peacock Alley Revisited," *Now and Then* (Winter 1995); S. Mont Whitson, *Appalachian Business Heritage: The Surviving Craftsman Fulfilling the American Dream* (1982); Sam Venable, *Mountain Hands: A Portrait of Southern Appalachia* (2000).

Crab Orchard Stone

Crab Orchard stone is a colorful sandstone found only on the Cumberland Plateau of Tennessee. Known for its hardness and beautiful appearance, it has been used around the world in such diverse and prominent locations as the vice-presidential residence in Washington, D.C., Rockefeller Center in New York, the Cathedral of Saint Philip in Atlanta, the Nintendo office building in Honolulu, and Elvis Presley's swimming pool at Graceland in Memphis.

Early Appalachian settlers used the stone in fireplaces, and it has also been found in Native American burial grounds. It has an unusually high quantity of silica, which creates an uncommonly sturdy, weather-resistant variety of sandstone suitable for constructing buildings, walls, terracing, and fireplaces. Its shades of tan, buff, blue-gray, and pink were created by the minerals iron, titanium, and magnesium. Yellow and brown swirls and ripples have resulted from natural iron stains and weathering.

Charles H. Young started the Cumberland Stone Company in 1903 in Crab Orchard, Tennessee. Two years later, the stone was used in constructing the Cumberland County Courthouse. The demand for Crab Orchard stone has grown steadily. It was used in the hundreds of Homestead-style houses built during the Great Depression as part of the New Deal. Since that time, Crab Orchard stone has become a common building element for schools, churches, banks, and other government and commercial buildings in the area.

With modern technology and improved equipment, workers can reach many layers of rock that previously were inaccessible, and at the opening of the twenty-first century Crab Orchard stone was the basis of a multimillion-dollar industry in Cumberland County.

See also: TENNESSEE MARBLE INDUSTRY.

—Clara Hasbrouck, *East Tennessee State University*

Crown Mills

See Textile Workers (Labor)

Deindustrialization

See North American Free Trade Agreement (Labor)

Distilleries

Appalachia can still claim at least one notable legal whiskey distillery within the regional bounds delineated by Congress—George Dickel Distillery of Tullahoma, Tennessee—but probably the best-known such facility in the world and arguably the one most associated with the region is just a dozen miles down the road. This one, Jack Daniel's of Lynchburg, is legendary. Many familiar Kentucky bourbons, including Wild Turkey, Jim Beam, Old Fitzgerald, Maker's Mark, Early Times, and Heaven Hill, are also made in close proximity to the Appalachian section of the state. There is even at least one new one (as of 1999), Buffalo Trace, the former Ancient Age. Other Appalachian states also have distilleries, most of them located not far from Appalachian counties strongly identified with corn liquor. Although it is now history, there was long a thriving, and very national, distillery industry in western Pennsylvania.

As the twenty-first century opened, bourbon was selling well despite its advancing age (Jack Daniel's was first registered in 1866, for example, while George Dickel dates from 1870 and Kentucky's Jim Beam claims to have been founded in 1795). Bourbon sales in 2002 rose by 1 percent over the previous year, while the sale of premium bourbons—those costing fifteen dollars or more per fifth—rose by 10 percent. The latter hike was possibly driven by a mid-1990s martini-drinking trend that encouraged some participants to cross over from expensive vodkas to other premium brands of liquor. Actually, sales increases had been occurring since 1997 in all kinds of distilled spirits. The two Tennessee whiskeys together were reported by a trade publication to be selling nearly 4 million nine-liter cases per year. Almost 3.8 million of those cases were of Jack Daniel's; fewer than 200,000 were George Dickel.

Cascade Tennessee Whisky (the *e* eliminated from its spelling of *whiskey* in a bow to Scots-Irish heritage) was Dickel's earliest name, taken from the distillery's location in Cascade Hollow in Coffee County. The distillery formally opened in 1877, and its product was sold in the store of Nashville merchant George A. Dickel. A few years later Dickel and his brother bought controlling interest in the Cascade facility along with the sole right to bottle and sell its product. After Dickel's death in 1894, Cascade was eventually renamed George Dickel.

The roots of Jack Daniel's are even more distinctive. Jasper Newton "Jack" Daniel, one of thirteen children, learned whiskey making from a Lutheran minister to whom he was hired out at age seven. When Daniel was thirteen, the minister, apparently under some pressure from the community, sold the teenager his distillery. This was in 1863. In 1866 Daniel registered the distillery with the government and in 1904 won a gold medal against international competition with his whiskey at the St. Louis World's Fair. Subsequent to this triumph he turned the business over to a nephew, Lem Motlow, after injuring himself by kicking a locked safe to which he could not remember the combination. He died in 1911, but his charcoal-mellowing method of whiskey making continued to be followed in Lynchburg. In fact, Tennessee whiskey differs from Kentucky bourbon in its making by including an extra step, a filtering of the liquor through hard-maple charcoal to remove impurities before the aging process is begun.

The distillation procedures in Tennessee, Kentucky, and elsewhere, though, are all descended from a very Appalachian tradition to which the distillers of Jim Beam, Maker's Mark, and some other present-day bourbons claim lineal connection.

Backwoods whiskey making was an involved and arduous process. First a good site for the home distillery had to be found, usually in a forest mudhole lined with thick red clay that could be used to help construct a crude furnace beneath the cooking apparatus. It required a source of pure water, often a hillside spring. Then nine and a half bushels of a good white corn had to be chosen, after which a bushel and a half of it had to be sprouted, moistened in a sack in the sun in the summertime or in warm water beside a kitchen stove in winter. The corn would form roots and sprout to a height of two inches within four or five days. During that period, the furnace had to be built, usually with rocks and/or metal and clay, and the distillery parts installed within and atop it. The day before the sprouts were the desired size, the other eight bushels of corn had to be taken to a mill and ground finely, then hauled to the woods, added to the water to make mash, and boiled for about forty minutes in batches of about a gallon each. The next day the sprouted corn, or malt, had to be ground, too, and gradually added to the mash along with a double handful of raw rye to help the mixture begin working. The use of sugar dramatically increased yields, as much as quadrupling them, but the result could no longer be termed "pure corn whiskey." If sugar was used, ten pounds were added to each of the seven or so fifty-gallon barrels at this point in the process.

The mixture then had to be checked and stirred in each barrel every day or so to assure that it was working evenly. Without sugar, the mix was ready for cooking by the fifth day. With sugar, nine or ten days were required, and a lot more sugar, thirty-five to forty pounds per barrel, had to be added on the fourth day with another half-gallon of malt. When the malt had fully worked it was designated "beer" and poured into the distillery (or still) nearly to the top, leaving room for expansion under heat. Fire was then lit in the furnace beneath the metal still, which was connected to wooden barrels and to a tightly spiraled copper tube sixteen to twenty feet long called the worm. The ingredients were boiled in the furnace for ten to fifteen hours. The mash mix had to be stirred constantly to prevent scorching, which would affect the taste of the product. The boiling bubbles eventually released steam that was caught in a water-filled barrel containing cold beer; this barrel was called the thump because arrival of the steam inside it caused a loud thumping sound as the beer began to bubble. When the thumping stopped, the steam was condensed by being run through the worm, which was submerged in a water-cooled barrel called the flakestand. The result exited as a clear, crystal-like fluid that gave rise to the brew's most common name, white lightning. This process, a run, had to be repeated at least once to produce two or three gallons of usable whiskey. It also yielded seven or eight gallons of so-called backings, which in four or five more runs could become five to seven more gallons of pure corn whiskey. The proof of the alcohol content was established by adding gunpowder to the mix and igniting it. If the liquid burned, it was considered to be between one hundred and two hundred proof, meaning 50 to 100 percent pure alcohol. Collected in glass or crock jugs, it generally had to be diluted either with backings from the last run or with water. The final quantity produced for consumption or sale numbered about a dozen gallons.

For generations in the Appalachian region, farmers made whiskey—which was widely used as a medicine—for themselves and a few neighbors. Gradually but inevitably, some distilleries and sales totals grew, as did governmental restriction and taxation. Taxes easily paid by major distillers were beyond the means of small mountain still operators, and lines of legality and illegality began to be drawn. By the early 1800s there were full-fledged commercial distilleries, many of them in western Pennsylvania. Abraham Overholt, a Mennonite farmer whose father had been making rye (rather than bourbon) whiskey for home use on the homeplace in Bucks County, began commercially marketing rye in 1810 at Broad Ford in Westmoreland County. This whiskey was eventually labeled Old Overholt, and in 1880 the Overholt distillery was producing 3,450 gallons a day. By the next year its sole owner was industrialist Henry Clay Frick, an Overholt grandson, and in 1887 Frick sold one-third of the company to another industrial titan and Frick's sometime business associate, Andrew Mellon. Other prominent western Pennsylvania distilleries during the nineteenth century included Large Distillery near Broad Ford, which made nationally known Large Monongahela Rye, and Schenley, which in ensuing decades bought many other distilleries, including, for a while, the Cascade Distillery in Tennessee. George Dickel is so called, it is said, because Schenley already owned a different Cascade Whiskey when it bought the Tullahoma facility in 1937.

Rather than the large amount of corn used in bourbon, rye whiskey is manufactured from a small amount of corn and at least 51 percent rye. It is credited with having a more pronounced taste than bourbon and is thought to have fallen from favor during prohibition, when the diluted drinks of the abstinence era accustomed palates to less-obtrusive flavors. But rye's history is impressive. In 1799, after retiring from the nation's first presidency, George Washington is reported to have had a rye distillery that produced 11,000 gallons of whiskey and a then-handsome profit of $7,500.

Bourbon, with the misfortune of being produced in an area where roads and transportation facilities were ravaged by the Civil War, operated at a competitive disadvantage against the Pennsylvania whiskey industry until prohibition. Styling itself "The Bourbon Homeplace" and a designated national historic landmark, Woodford Reserve Distillery (formerly known as Labrot and Graham) in Versailles, Kentucky, was founded in 1812, but there were already other Kentucky bourbon distilleries by then. After beginning operations around 1780, the T. W. Samuels family later moved to establish the distillery at Loretto, where today it manufactures Maker's Mark. Jim Beam's distillers originated their efforts in 1795 before moving in 1854 to the Clear Spring Distillery at Clermont. In 1870 pharmaceuticals salesman George Garvin Brown in Louisville claimed to see a need for high-quality whiskey that met medicinal standards and started JTS Brown and Bro. with his half-sibling for $5,500. He began selling his products, the foremost of which was Old Forester, in sealed glass bottles instead of the usual barrels. In 1902, having formed Brown-Forman in a partnership with his accountant, he bought the Mattingly Distillery at St. Mary's and opened the Brown-Forman Distillery Company.

With the early twentieth century came hard times for the bourbon industry, beginning with the advent of prohibition in 1920. Restriction started early for George Dickel, which decamped to Kentucky when Tennessee decreed its own prohibition in 1910. Many legal distillers went bankrupt or took other employment during prohibition and the beginnings of the Great Depression. Some Appalachian farmers plied their old unlicensed craft on a larger scale. Old Forester was sold in its sealed bottles "For Medicinal Purposes," as its cardboard packaging proclaimed. With prohibition's repeal in 1933, though, there was a resurgence that has been followed by waves of consolidation into ever-larger conglomerates. Old Overholt was one of several brands in the American Medicinal Spirits Company during the national abstinence before being absorbed by National Distillers and then in 1987 by Fortune Brands of Lincolnshire, Illinois. In 1953 the Samuels family founded Maker's Mark, and it eventually was bought by Allied-Domecq, a British-rooted and Connecticut-headquartered firm traded on the New York Stock Exchange. In 1956 Jack Daniel's was bought by Brown-Forman, which is also traded on the stock exchange. Although still headquartered in Louisville at the opening of the twenty-first century, Brown-Forman was manufacturing Lenox china, Dansk giftware, and Hartmann luggage in addition to Old Forester, Early Times, and the new upscale Woodford Reserve. Wild Turkey at Lawrenceburg, Kentucky, became the property of French-owned Pernod-Ricard. Constellation Brands, headquartered in New York and billing itself "the largest multi-category supplier of beverage alcohol in the U.S." with more than two hundred brands, distilled its Barclay, Colonel Lee, Kentucky Gentleman, Kentucky Tavern, Ten High, Tom Moore, and Very Old Barton bourbons at Bardstown, Kentucky. At the turn of the twenty-first century, there were nine bourbon distilleries left in Kentucky.

Now a worldwide corporation, Brown-Forman reported in 2003 that it had total sales of $2.3 billion, including $1.7 billion from wine and spirits. It claimed that in 1998 it had sold a record 5.4 million cases of Jack Daniel's. Nearby, the George Dickel Distillery was operating again after a four-year layoff to give demand a chance to catch up with supply. The facility has had a varied ownership record. Acquired by Schenley in 1937, Dickel moved back to Cascade Hollow from Kentucky in 1958 and, following a number of mergers in the 1980s and 1990s, ended up the property of British-based Diageo PLC. Diageo owned such other liquors as Jose Cuervo tequila, Crown Royal, Seagram's V.O., Gordon's gin, Johnnie Walker scotch, and Captain Morgan Black Label rum. The management said Dickel continued to have its own niche consumer—men aged between thirty-five and fifty who liked such activities as fly-fishing and duck hunting—and sold best in North Carolina, followed by Tennessee and Virginia. In 2003 the company began working with Tennessee state tourism officials to create a "Whiskey Trail" from Tullahoma to Lynchburg.

See also: BREWERIES; MOONSHINE (FOOD AND COOKING); WINERIES.

—Jean Battlo, *Kimball, West Virginia*

Richard Lawson, "Dickel's Tullahoma Revival Stirs Spirits," *Nashville Tennessean* (September 14, 2003); Eliot Wigginton, ed., *The Foxfire Book* (1972).

Dow Chemical

See Chemical Industry

Duke Power Company

Duke Power, founded in 1904 and first known as Southern Power Company, played an important role through the twentieth century in lifting the Piedmont region of North and South Carolina out of poverty. Having begun with a single hydroelectric plant on the Catawba River, the company expanded to a series of dams providing electricity for the Carolina Piedmont, and in significant respects its progression from hydroelectric facilities to coal-fired steam plants and nuclear power stations paralleled the evolution of the government-owned Tennessee Valley Authority.

The principal figures launching the company that would become one of the nation's premier electrical utilities were W. Gill Wylie, a South Carolina–born physician; William States Lee, an engineer recruited by Wylie; and James Buchanan Duke, whose family had created one of America's great fortunes from its investments in tobacco and textiles. In 1997 a merger between Duke and PanEnergy Company of Houston created a new national enterprise, Duke Energy Corporation. Duke Power became one of its chief subsidiaries. Moving vigorously to expand after deregulation of the electric utility industry, Duke Energy recorded soaring profits and rose to number fourteen on the Fortune 500 list of corporations. But after the 2001 power crisis in California and the collapse of energy-trading giant Enron Corporation, Duke Energy was forced to retrench, selling off assets in the West in order to preserve the dividends paid to shareholders. After profits of $1.8 billion in 2001, the corporation recorded a loss of $1.3 billion in 2003. In 2004 it celebrated the centennial of Duke Power under new management and with improving prospects.

Duke's involvement in Appalachian coal mining in the 1970s marked another difficult chapter in its corporate history. By the end of the 1960s, the company had become one of the largest consumers of steam coal in the country, and with demands for electricity rapidly rising, it faced potentially critical shortages of fuel for its boilers. In 1970 it established Eastover Mining Company and purchased eastern Kentucky coal reserves, which officials hoped would fill 25 percent of the company's needs. Shortly, Eastover was struck by the United Mine Workers of America. Workers at Brookside Mine in Harlan County refused to sign a no-strike clause in a new contract, and the conflict dragged on from 1971 until 1974. There was sporadic violence in the coalfields, but the decisive fight took place in a union campaign of newspaper ads aimed at potential investors in Duke stock. In May 1974 an administrative law judge of the National Labor Relations Board ruled for the union on the no-strike clause issue. Three months later, after intense involvement by a federal mediator, the two sides reached an agreement to end the Brookside strike, but the impact of the dispute was deep. In 1983 Duke sold Eastover and its coal lands in Harlan and Pike County for a $30-million loss and got out of coal mining.

See also: ARCH COAL; BITUMINOUS COAL INDUSTRY.

—Rudy Abramson, *Reston, Virginia*

Eastman, George

See Eastman Chemical Company and Tennessee Eastman Company

Eastman Chemical Company and Tennessee Eastman Company

The Eastman companies together comprise one of Tennessee's largest employers. By the 1980s, Eastman was manufacturing not just film but polyester fibers and plastics for cars, beverage bottles, and huge sheets of weatherproof material for outdoor billboards, among many other products. In 1994 Tennessee Eastman's Chemicals Division was split off from Eastman Kodak to become publicly traded Eastman Chemical Company, the nation's tenth-largest chemical concern, and at the opening of the twenty-first century it manufactured and marketed more than twelve hundred chemicals, fibers, and plastics used in thousands of consumer products.

Eastman's establishment in Appalachia resulted from disruption of the supply of German photographic materials by World War I. The New York–based camera and film manufacturer Eastman Kodak wanted a way to control the sources of the raw materials it needed, and it was lured south in 1920 by promoters of a planned city—Kingsport, Tennessee—and executives of George Lafayette Carter's recently completed Carolina, Clinchfield, and Ohio Railway across the Appalachian Mountains. The Eastman Kodak Company had been founded more than thirty years earlier by George Eastman, a self-educated bank clerk, amateur photographer, and inventor born in 1854 in Waterville, New York. By 1880 Eastman had perfected a process for making photographic dry plates and a machine to produce large numbers of them. In 1884 he patented flexible-roll film, and in 1888, the year that he named his company Eastman Kodak, he also devised the first camera specifically designed for his film. The next year he invented flexible transparent film, which proved vital to the development of the motion picture industry. His eventual multinational corporation, based in Rochester, New York, dominated the global film market and led the way in the mass production of inexpensive and simple cameras.

After World War I interrupted his German supply of photographic paper, optical glass, gelatin, and an assortment of chemicals including methanol, acetic acid, and acetone, Eastman recognized that the forests of the Appalachian South offered a potential source of raw materials for the manufacture of methanol and acetone. In July 1920, he visited Kingsport and purchased thirty-five acres and the factory buildings of the U.S. government's American Wood Reduction Company, which had been erected for use during the war. Eastman's original purchase expanded to include an additional three hundred acres and a total investment of $1 million. The location of a subsidiary plant in the center of Appalachia appealed to Eastman for more than just supply reasons. It also offered a workforce that he believed would not interrupt production with labor unrest. To discourage unionization he instituted a profit share, or wage dividend, in which each employee received additional annual compensation in proportion to the yearly dividend on the company stock.

Tennessee Eastman was incorporated on July 17, 1920, and first manufactured methanol, a chemical needed in photographic film, along with methyl acetone and various by-products. With the demand for home-movie and X-ray film evolving in the 1920s, the production of cellulose acetate, the base for home-movie film, was transferred to Kingsport from Kodak Park in Rochester in 1929. Production of cellulose acetate yarn began at the Tennessee plant in 1931. Plastics, dyes, and molding compounds, with important applications for design and production methods in the automobile and communications industries, also began being produced there during this period. Tennessee Eastman's annual sales reached nearly $29 million by 1940.

In 1941 the National Defense Research Committee contacted Tennessee Eastman general manager James C. White and requested the building of a pilot plant for the manufacture of the powerful explosive RDX. Soon the company was manufacturing RDX in the large quantities needed to win the war in Europe. By June 1942, Tennessee Eastman had received official authorization from the U.S. Army Ordnance and the National Defense Research Committee to design and operate Holston Ordnance Works, which became the world's largest manufacturer of high explosives. In 1943 Eastman scientists and engineers were transferred from Kingsport to Oak Ridge, and Tennessee Eastman was directed to manage the operation of the Y-12 plant, a crucial facility in the Manhattan Project, the U.S. atomic weapon development program. They remained at Oak Ridge until 1947.

Large-scale expansion at Kingsport occurred during the late 1940s and 1950s. Located on the Holston River in Sullivan County, the plant covered hundreds of acres and became the largest private employer in Tennessee, with more than 9,500 workers by the early 1960s. With acetate yarn as its major product, Tennessee Eastman in the 1950s had annual sales of $130 million. Formation of the Eastman Chemicals Division of the company occurred in 1968, and the firm's sales climbed to $590 million during the 1970s. Kodapak polyester plastic, introduced for use in beverage bottles, gained worldwide success. In 1983 the firm created a coal gasification plant designed to make industrial chemicals from coal and reduce the company's dependence on oil, which earned it the twenty-eighth biennial Kirkpatrick Chemical Engineering Achievement Award.

In 1990 Eastman Chemicals Division was renamed Eastman Chemical Company (headquartered in Kingsport) and, on January 1, 1994, became an independent, publicly owned company. A supporter of the North American Free Trade Agreement, Eastman Chemical Company committed to a policy of globalization. In 1994, 95 percent of the firm's assets were inside the United States; by the fall of 2004, twenty-eight of the total forty-eight Eastman Chemical manufacturing sites were located outside the country.

Globalization affected the company's earnings. One of the largest manufacturing concerns in the southeastern United States, Eastman Chemical had once claimed 17,000 employees worldwide with 12,000 in Kingsport, but through retirements and layoffs the workforce had fallen to 15,800 worldwide and 7,800 in Kingsport by 2003. In 2004 Eastman announced plans to close its co-polyester manufacturing plant in Hartlepool, England, and relocate those operations to Kingsport.

See also: CARTER, GEORGE LAFAYETTE; CHEMICAL INDUSTRY; TRI-CITIES, TENNESSEE/VIRGINIA (URBAN APPALACHIAN EXPERIENCE).

—Martha Avaleen Egan, *Kingsport, Tennessee*

Elizabeth Brayer, *George Eastman: A Biography* (1996); Douglas Collins, *The Story of Kodak* (1990); Elery A. Lay, *An Industrial and Commercial History of the Tri-Cities in Tennessee-Virginia* (1982); Howard Long, *Kingsport: A Romance of Industry* (1928).

84 Lumber Company

Located twenty miles south of Pittsburgh in the town of Eighty Four, Pennsylvania, 84 Lumber Company was the largest privately held supplier of building materials in the United States at the turn of the twenty-first century. Styling itself the low-cost leader of its field, the company did business from no-frills stores that usually offered no heat or air-conditioning (which is perhaps why it had no outlets in most of the extreme northern states of the United States) and made 75 percent of its sales to professional contractors. In addition to lumber, it sold siding, drywall, windows, and kits for the making of decks, play sets, barns, and homes.

Although in 2002 the company operated 449 stores and eleven component plants in thirty-four states from coast to coast and reported sales of more than two billion dollars, it evolved from humble beginnings. Joseph Hardy Sr., its founder and long-time chief executive officer, initially sold vegetables door to door and worked in his family's jewelry business. On the advice of friend Jack Ryan, whose firm later evolved into the major homebuilder Ryan Homes, Hardy first entered the lumber business in 1952. Pooling his resources with his two younger brothers in 1956, he purchased a piece of farmland near the junction of Pennsylvania, West Virginia, and Ohio for five thousand dollars. As the company prospered, Hardy opened new stores in other states, but the business headquarters stayed in the small town of Eighty Four.

The number *84* continued to be significant for the company. In 1984 the U.S. Post Office provided 84 Lumber with its own zip code, 15384. The origins of the town's name are mysterious, and theories abound. It has been suggested that the name was chosen because it was once the location of mail drop 84 on the Railway Mail Service route. Other residents believe the name was simply chosen when a post office opened in the town in 1884. Because of 84 Lumber Company's great success, many younger residents of the area have come to assume mistakenly that the town was named for the firm.

In 1993 Hardy promoted his daughter, Maggie Hardy Magerko, to company president. Magerko, who in 2003 owned approximately 80 percent of 84 Lumber, was well trained for the position, having accompanied her father in the course of his business since the age of five. Under her guidance, the company achieved many more milestones, including being named the first-ranked supplier of building materials to professional contractors.

In addition to 84 Lumber, the Hardys also founded Nemacolin Woodlands Resort and Spa in 1987. The only five-star resort in Pennsylvania, it is located in the Laurel Highlands in Farmington, seventy miles southeast of

Pittsburgh. In 2002 the family and the Professional Golfers' Association concluded an agreement under which the company would sponsor the association's annual Pennsylvania event, to be called the 84 Lumber Classic, at the resort for four years beginning in 2003.

See also: BOWATER INCORPORATED; HARRIS-TARKETT CORPORATION; LUMBER INDUSTRY.

—Kristin L. Abramson, *Pittsburgh, Pennsylvania*

Feldspar Industry

The mining of feldspar—a group of related minerals (basically anhydrous aluminum silicates) used in glass bottles, glass fiber, tile, paint, plastics, and other products—has been centered in North Carolina. To a progressively lesser degree, feldspar is also mined in Connecticut, Georgia, California, Oklahoma, and South Dakota. The extent of United States reserves is not known, but there are estimated to be at least 200 million tons of feldspar around Spruce Pine, North Carolina, alone.

The Atlanta-based Feldspar Corporation, the largest producer in the U.S., is rooted in the Spruce Pine area and has an affiliated firm, Zemex Mica Corporation, that remains headquartered there. (Mica can be a by-product of feldspar operations.) Feldspar Corporation has plants in North Carolina, Georgia, Connecticut, and Texas and produces soda feldspar, high-potash feldspar, kaolin, talc, glass, and industrial sands for use domestically and abroad. A second Spruce Pine–based operation is K-T Feldspar Company, established by the Kentucky-Tennessee Clay Company.

American feldspar mining may predate the Revolutionary War. A shipment of the substance apparently obtained from Native Americans is said to have been sent to Europe in 1744 from the North Carolina mountains. Commercial production, however, began in 1825 in Connecticut, where feldspar was long broken into small pieces by hand, sorted, barreled, and shipped to Britain for use in pottery. Around 1850, a mill was built in Middletown to grind feldspar for the developing American pottery industry. Connecticut was the leading U.S. producer of feldspar until the early twentieth century, when that title passed to North Carolina.

Meanwhile, technological advances accelerated demand for the product. Its use in glass furnaces was found to facilitate the addition of alumina and some alkalis in the making of glass. Then glass to which alumina had been added was discovered to aid the automated manufacture of glass bottles, and rising demand for glass bottles made glassmakers primary users of feldspar. Around 1940 a froth flotation method was found to separate feldspar from mica, quartz, and certain iron minerals among which it tends to be found. This technique allowed feldspar to be mined more widely, reduced mining costs per ton, and enabled large-scale production.

The Feldspar Corporation, founded in 1929 as Feldspar Milling Company, began operation near Burnsville, North Carolina. In 1949 Feldspar Milling joined North Carolina Feldspar of Erwin, Tennessee, to build at Spruce Pine one of the first successful feldspar flotation plants. In 1954 the two companies teamed to build another flotation plant at Monticello, Georgia. The next year the Zemex Corporation, based now in Toronto, Ontario, bought Feldspar Milling and North Carolina Feldspar and their Georgia affiliate and built a second flotation plant at Spruce Pine in 1970.

K-T Feldspar Corporation of Spruce Pine had produced feldspar since 1955 and in 1994 had opened a subsidiary plant in Monterrey, Mexico. With its Mexican plant, K-T Feldspar became the first North American supplier of raw materials to also have its own complete line of materials for ceramics. That made the firm globally attractive. In 2001 it was acquired by the French-based worldwide mineral supplier Imerys, which gave Imerys access to the feldspar market and an abundant American source of raw material for its ceramics goods.

See also: MICA INDUSTRY.

—Jack Hurst, *Lancaster, Tennessee*

Michael J. Potter, "Feldspar," in *Mineral Facts and Problems*, U.S. Bureau of Mines Bulletin 675 (1985).

Fertilizer Industry

See Muscle Shoals Power; Tennessee Valley Authority (Government)

Florence Wagon Works

From 1889 to 1941, Florence Wagon Works of Florence, Alabama, was a major producer of wagons. Its annual production of fifteen thousand ranked it first in the United States and second in North America behind Canada's Studebaker Wagon Works. At its peak the company provided direct employment for 175 people and indirectly for hundreds more—tree cutters, timber haulers, and others—who worked in support capacities.

The company's story dates from the spring of 1889, when owners of the Atlanta Wagon Works of Georgia relocated their plant to Florence and renamed it for its new home. This placed it nearer to its major raw material, the plentiful hardwood timber in the foothills of the Appalachians.

In large part, the success of the Florence Wagon Works depended on the popularity of its Florence Light Runner wagon. The company also produced several other models, made plow handles, sold parts, and repaired wagons. World War I army wagons made in Florence were sent all over the United States and to France. Contributing to the company's success was the pride and loyalty of its employees. Long after the rise of motorized hauling forced the plant's closing at the outset of World War II, former employees met annually to celebrate their connections with the company.

See also: LUMBER INDUSTRY.

—William Lindsey McDonald, *Florence, Alabama*

Food Lion

Since opening its first store in Salisbury, North Carolina, in 1957 on the periphery of Appalachia, Food Lion has grown into one of the largest supermarket chains in the United States. Originally known as Food Town, the company was founded by three local grocers who started it with financial support from eighty-seven friends and neighbors. With its "every day low price" concept, Food Lion was by the early twenty-first century operating more than twelve hundred stores in Delaware, Florida, Georgia, Kentucky, Maryland, North Carolina, Pennsylvania, South Carolina, Tennessee, Virginia, and West Virginia. Distribution centers were located in Florida, North Carolina, Pennsylvania, South Carolina, Tennessee, and Virginia.

In 1974 the Belgian-based Delhaize Group bought 34.5 percent of Food Town, increasing its share to 52.5 percent two years later. In 1983 Food Town was renamed Food Lion after growing from 22 to 226 stores. Food Lion LLC became a member of a Delhaize America family of supermarket chains that came to include Hannaford stores in the Northeast and Kash n' Karry in the Southeast. In 1992 Food Lion sued the ABC television network after ABC's *PrimeTime Live* aired videotape appearing to show unsanitary food-handling practices in two Food Lion stores. Two undercover ABC reporters hired by the stores as regular employees were adjudged guilty of trespass but were absolved of fraud charges, and Food Lion was found not entitled to damage claims from broadcast of the story.

As of 2003, Food Lion had approximately seventy-three thousand workers and was one of the largest employers in both North Carolina and Virginia. It offered ongoing training programs and advancement opportunities for its employees and was also active in community and charitable causes such as the Children's Miracle Network, Easter Seals, American Red Cross, Food Industry Crusade Against Hunger, the Stay in School campaign, law enforcement agencies, churches, and youth programs.

See also: K-VA-T FOOD STORES; WALKER, CAS.

—Sandra Kay Heck, *Walters State Community College*

Frick, Henry Clay

(1849–1919) Industrialist.

Henry Clay Frick, a leading nineteenth-century coke and steel manufacturer based in Pittsburgh, played a crucial and ultimately controversial role in expanding Andrew Carnegie's steel operations, which he developed into the modern industrial model.

Frick was born in West Overton, Pennsylvania, where he received early business training working for his maternal grandfather, whiskey distiller Abraham Overholt, the wealthiest man in Westmoreland County. With little formal education, Frick became a reliable and hardworking businessman. In 1869 he joined in a partnership to acquire six hundred acres of bituminous coal land near Connellsville, Pennsylvania. His partners soon grew discouraged, and Frick bought them out. He realized that the new Bessemer process of steelmaking would provide a larger market for coke, a coal variety that burns with intense heat and little smoke.

On borrowed money, he acquired more coal land and in 1871 formed the Henry C. Frick Coke Company. When Carnegie established steel mill operations at Pittsburgh, Frick became his chief supplier of coke. Each company grew with the help of the other. The symbiotic relationship led to a personal partnership between the two men in the early 1880s, as each invested in the other's company. With Carnegie managing steel and Frick coke, America's largest steel and coke business soon developed. In 1889 Frick was named chairman of the Carnegie Steel Company with the purpose of reorganizing and expanding it as Carnegie lessened his daily involvement. It was Frick, over Carnegie's initial objections, who led the move to acquire the rich Mesabi iron ore range in Minnesota, a decision that proved to be immensely lucrative for the company. Under Frick's leadership, profits increased 600 percent.

In addition to business acumen, Frick was known for being a hard taskmaster and a union breaker. His actions during the Homestead Steel Strike of 1892 led to one of the most violent episodes in American labor history. The Homestead strike and various other business and personality differences broke the bond between Carnegie and Frick. After a long and acrimonious struggle, Frick was ousted from the Carnegie operations. Carnegie himself soon sold out to a syndicate headed by J. P. Morgan, which then created the United States Steel Corporation in 1901.

Frick divided the remainder of his life between business interests and development of one of the nation's most important art collections. He was involved in the formation of Union Steel and the Union Trust Company of Pittsburgh, the reorganization of the Equitable Life Assurance Society, and in Peruvian copper mining. In 1905 he moved his family to a New York City mansion specially designed to house his art collection. He died on December 2, 1919, and was buried in Pittsburgh. The mansion and art collection were left to the City of New York.

See also: CARNEGIE, ANDREW; DISTILLERIES; IRON AND STEEL INDUSTRY.

—Ned L. Irwin, *East Tennessee State University*

Martha Frick Symington Sanger, *Henry Clay Frick: An Intimate Portrait* (1998); Kenneth Warren, *Triumphant Capitalism: Henry Clay Frick and the Industrial Transformation of America* (1996).

Furniture Industry

North Carolina is the top producer of furniture in the United States, and the furniture industry is a high-profile component of the Appalachian economy despite its relatively small (2 percent from 1997 through 2001) share of the U.S. manufacturing market.

As of 1997, North Carolina and Mississippi ranked first and third in the nation in the production of household and institutional furniture and kitchen cabinets, with North Carolina accounting for 17 percent of all U.S. sales and Mississippi adding another 7 percent. Together, the two states claimed more than $8 billion in sales, nearly one-fourth of the entire American market, and in both states the bulk of the manufacturing was done in or near Appalachia. For example, the twenty-four Appalachian counties in Mississippi were responsible for 75 percent of that state's furniture industry jobs and revenue. In North Carolina the industry is similarly concentrated in Appalachian counties on the state's western end or the adjacent central Piedmont counties. In no other state is the industry so concentrated in and around Appalachia.

Abundant timber reserves in and adjacent to the Appalachian Mountains spawned numerous industries dependent on wood, including furniture. The Appalachian forest offered large reserves of poplar, walnut, oak, chestnut, cherry, spruce, hemlock, pine, and other valuable species, and the development of sawmill technology following the Civil War made timbering an important seasonal or second occupation for the region's farmers. By 1890, upon exhaustion of vast tree reserves in Michigan and Wisconsin, major timber interests began to look to Appalachia. Timber production there peaked between 1890 and 1920, although by 1909 the boom was beginning to wane. The timber industry subsequently stabilized, however, and at the turn of the twenty-first century it was still supplying the furniture business.

In the eighteenth and much of the nineteenth centuries, the furniture industry was concentrated in such large northeastern port cities as New York, Boston, and Philadelphia. But by the 1870s, as the nation's population and access to railroads expanded westward, Michigan and Illinois also became large producers, and Grand Rapids and Chicago became substantial production centers. As the Midwest began to offer significant competition, some northeastern producers moved southward to take advantage of Appalachia's timber, congenial climate, and eager workforce. During the first decade of the twentieth century, North Carolina—which in the 1880s had no substantial furniture industry—surged toward dominance on the strength of developments in and around the city of High Point.

Located in the midst of large hardwood forests along the tracks of the state's first east-west railroad, High Point appears to have offered a unique combination of transportation, raw materials, market, accessible labor, and willing investors. In the late 1880s, competitive sawmills already had been established nearby and were able to supply low-cost oak lumber, and an improving quality of life in the South created a ready market for furniture. Displaced tobacco farmers provided an especially ready pool of labor, because at that time the national taste had turned toward lighter eastern varieties of the leaf and farmers of the heavier types grown in the state's western end were left underemployed. Also, High Point's civic and business leaders were willing to invest money.

The histories of two North Carolina firms, one in Appalachia and another neighboring it, illustrate trends in the Appalachian furniture industry. Thomas H. Broyhill opened his first plant in Lenoir in 1905 and within fifteen years had bought a majority interest in Lenoir Furniture Corporation, a manufacturer of bedroom and dining room furniture. By 1924 Broyhill Furniture was manufacturing products under its own name, and at the close of the twentieth century its St. Louis–based parent company, Furniture Brands International, claimed that Broyhill was the most recognized furniture maker by 90 percent of clients.

By contrast, Thomasville Furniture in the High Point area, which includes Thomasville Cabinetry, opened a year earlier, in 1904, as the Thomasville Chair Company. In the 1960s, doing business as Thomasville Furniture Industries, it was bought by Armstrong World Industries and began providing furniture for hotels as well as government and military buildings. In 1995 it was sold again, this time to the same worldwide firm that bought Broyhill. Furniture Brands International claimed to have spent $7.4 million advertising Thomasville in 2002 and announced plans to spend more than that in 2004 in observation of Thomasville's centennial anniversary, but plants in Thomasville and Winston-Salem closed in 2002 and 2003, laying off more than eight hundred employees, and the parent company forecast more closings as production shifted overseas.

High Point is very close to Appalachia and owes much of its furniture-making history to the region's rich natural resources. Likewise, the prevalence of the furniture industry in southern Appalachia owes much to the growth of its development around High Point. In 2003, 60 percent of the furniture made in the U.S. was manufactured within a two-hundred-mile radius of the High Point area, a circle that includes parts of South Carolina, Tennessee, Kentucky, West Virginia, and Virginia. Much of that expanse is in Appalachia, and the rest is nearby.

See also: HARRIS-TARKETT CORPORATION; LUMBER INDUSTRY.

—Angela K Palau, *Oak Ridge, Tennessee*

Richard B. Drake, *A History of Appalachia* (2001); Oscar P. Fitzgerald, *Three Centuries of American Furniture* (1982); William S. Powell, *North Carolina: A Bicentennial History* (1977).

General Nutrition Center

Founded in 1935 in Pittsburgh, General Nutrition Center began as a small health-food store called Lackzoom. Its founder, David Shakarian, had longed to establish a health-food business. Shakarian sold foods such as honey and grains and specialized in yogurt, a food product that his father was instrumental in bringing to the United States. The name, too, originated in a somewhat similar Pittsburgh business that Shakarian's Armenian parents had operated for a while called Lackzoom Acidophilus. The word *lackzoom* may have referred to health problems that result from lactose intolerance, which are alleviated by acidophilus milk.

Although health food was considered merely a fad at the time, Lackzoom quickly gained popularity, and Shakarian opened a second store within six months of the first. During the next five years, he opened several more Pittsburgh area stores, in spite of a 1936 Saint Patrick's Day flood that destroyed his original two outlets and killed seventy people between Pittsburgh and Johnstown. During the following decades, Shakarian continued to introduce people to the benefits of health food.

By the 1960s, natural foods and good nutrition had become a leitmotif of the times, and Shakarian began to open stores in other states. He changed the name from Lackzoom to General Nutrition Center, since widely known as GNC, and began producing vitamin and mineral supplements in addition to health food, beverages, and cosmetic products.

In late 2003, GNC was a wholly owned subsidiary of the Dutch-based specialized nutrition conglomerate Royal Numico and was in the process of being sold by Numico to the New York investment firm Apollo Management. It had become a multinational business and styled itself the largest specialty retailer of vitamin, mineral, and herbal supplements, as well as sports nutrition and personal care products. More than fifty-seven hundred GNC retail stores with more than fifteen thousand employees operated throughout the United States and in twenty-nine other countries.

The firm's headquarters remain in Pittsburgh, two blocks from original storefront location established by Shakarian, who in 1983 was listed by *Forbes* magazine as Pittsburgh's richest resident. He died of cancer in 1984.

See also: CHATTANOOGA MEDICINE COMPANY; PHARMACEUTICAL INDUSTRY.

—Kristin L. Abramson, *Pittsburgh, Pennsylvania*

Georgia Power Company

Georgia Power is the largest subsidiary of Southern Company, one of the United States' major utility holding companies and generators of electricity. With almost half its power plants located in its Appalachian counties, Georgia Power serves more than two million customers in the state, offering rates about 15 percent below the national average. It has a workforce of almost 8,800 employees and has been a crucial recruiter of industry to the whole state, often teaming with local municipalities in the effort. President and Chief Executive Officer David Ratcliffe said in 2002 that Georgia Power's economic-development organization had been credited with helping harvest $924 million in new capital investment and 8,500 new jobs.

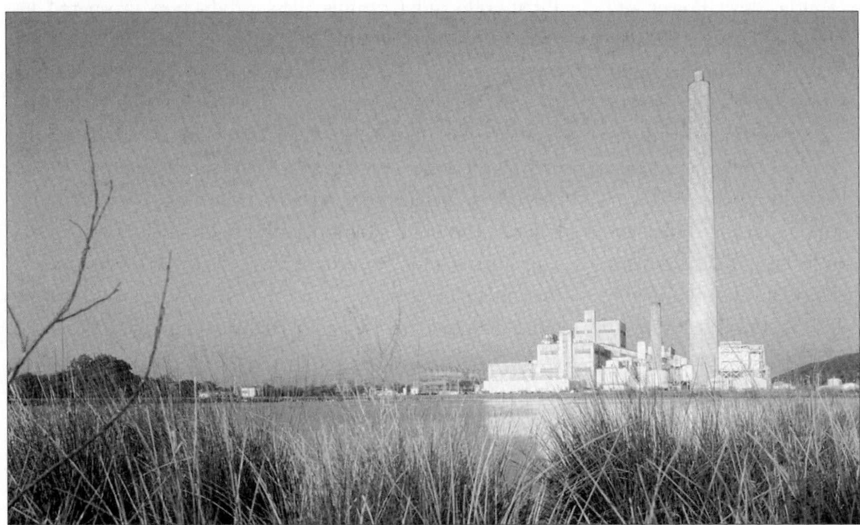

Georgia Power Company's Plant Hammond, Coosa, Georgia, c. 2000. One of eleven coal-fired units in the Georgia Power system, Plant Hammond has provided electricity for west Georgia since 1954.

The company dates back to 1883, when citizens of Atlanta raised $3,500 in an offering of stock and formed the Georgia Electric Light Company of Atlanta. By 1884 the new company had built a small generating plant that powered twenty-two streetlights. Five years later Atlanta boasted more than eight hundred streetlights and a system of electric streetcars. At about that time local banker Henry Atkinson acquired control through stock purchases, dropped the words *of Atlanta* from the company name, and began working to revolutionize and expand operations. He soon added eight hundred arc lights, two thousand incandescent lights, and a steam-generating plant capable of producing eleven thousand kilowatts.

Demand continued to grow. Atkinson hired a local lawyer, Preston S. Arkwright, to combine some of the streetcar lines and generating plants into a single firm, the Georgia Railway and Electric Company. The new firm made a series of acquisitions: the Atlanta Gas Light Company in 1903, the output of S. Morgan Smith's hydroelectric plant on the Chattahoochee River in 1904, the Atlanta Crackers baseball team in 1906, and Smith's entire Chattahoochee hydroelectric complex in 1912.

Atkinson agreed in 1911 to lease the Georgia Railway and Electric Company to the new Georgia Railway and Power Company, and in 1913 the first of six hydroelectric generators was on-line at Georgia Railway and Power's Tallulah Falls complex in Appalachian Georgia. Four other generators were added in 1914, and the final generating unit came on-line in 1919. When the Tallulah Falls complex was completed, it could generate seventy-two thousand kilowatts of power.

In 1925 a severe drought drastically reduced the generating capacity of the hydroelectric plants and forced Atkinson to move away from dependency on hydroelectric power. During another restructuring in 1926, many southern utilities were consolidated under the Southeastern Power and Lights Company, and Georgia Railway and Power became known as the Georgia Power Company, which at that point served more than half the state. Georgia Power continued to increase output to meet demand, and a dual coal-and-gas plant came on-line in 1930. By 1935 the company had sold its first billion kilowatt-hours of electricity.

In 1939 Atkinson died. Afterward, Georgia Power expanded and overcame financial difficulties. The Bartletts Ferry Dam was enlarged and Sinclair Dam finished in the years following World War II. In 1957 the company acquired the Georgia Power and Light Company. Coal plants were added in 1971 and 1974, as were nuclear facilities in 1974 and in 1989. During the late 1970s financial woes struck the company as a result of continued plant construction and rising power-generating costs, but the instability was overcome with the help of funding from rural electric cooperatives.

See also: DUKE POWER COMPANY; MUSCLE SHOALS POWER; NUCLEAR POWER.

—Arthur Holst, *Philadelphia, Pennsylvania*

Margaret Calhoon and Lynn Speno, *Tallulah Falls, Georgia* (1998).

Glass Industry

Glass production began in Appalachia in the late eighteenth century, making it one of the region's oldest industries after timber and salt. It is also one of the most diverse and durable. Artisans working in private studios and shops continue to produce masterworks of blown glass while industrial workers manufacture massive quantities of flat glass and glass fiber, the latter a principal component in the telecommunications revolution of the 1990s.

Historically, western North Carolina, northern West Virginia, western Pennsylvania, eastern Ohio, and western New York have been strongly identified with glass products. Throughout the nineteenth and into the twentieth century, Pittsburgh reigned as the American capital of the industry. From the city and its environs came important commercial products—bottles, canning jars, windowpanes, and globes for streetlights—that helped usher in the modern lifestyle. Corning, New York, emerged as the undisputed center of cut and engraved glass following the Civil War and in the early twenty-first century remained internationally known as the home of Corning Glass Company, the industry giant famous for CorningWare and fiber-optic cable. The city's reputation as a center of fine glasswork was secured when local shops provided glassware for Presidents Ulysses S. Grant, Grover Cleveland, Benjamin Harrison, William McKinley, Franklin D. Roosevelt, Harry Truman, and Dwight D. Eisenhower.

Far from the glass houses, craft shops, and factories of Pittsburgh and Corning, glass production prospered less visibly and spun off jobs and revenue in industries such as mining, natural gas, and transportation. The glass industry rose in Appalachia because of plentiful natural resources—coal, timber, limestone, silica, and natural gas—and the arrival of skilled immigrants. Pittsburgh and other early centers of production such as Wheeling, West Virginia, enjoyed the huge additional advantage of river transportation linking them to distant markets. By the beginning of the nineteenth century, western Pennsylvania was home to more than one hundred glass factories employing thousands of workers. Down the Ohio River from Pittsburgh, early-nineteenth-century glass factories became a cornerstone of Wheeling's development as the first industrial city in far western Virginia. Morgantown and other western Virginia communities developed a vibrant glassware industry and wide reputations for quality stemware and art glass.

Development of glass molds and the ability of individual glass factories to make their own molds opened the way to more rapid production, lower prices, and the mass use of glass for both decorative and utilitarian purposes. Shops and factories often faced shortages of both skilled and unskilled workers, and many of them resorted to the use of child labor. State governments, acknowledging the crucial importance of the industry, exempted glassblowers from military conscription in times of crisis. In the heyday of the business, some five hundred glass manufacturers operated in West Virginia alone, making fine pieces of leaded crystal, stained glass, and art objects as well as flat glass, containers, and stoneware. Besides gracing the White House, glass pieces from Appalachian communities adorned dining tables and drawing rooms of private mansions as well as the shelves of collectors and display cases of galleries and museums.

During the latter decades of the twentieth century, competition from new materials and increased prices for natural gas sent production of handmade glass into decline. By 2001, the number of companies in West Virginia had declined from more than five hundred to about twenty. In Morgantown, Corning, and elsewhere, tourists visit glass museums rather than factories, but the industry remains a significant part of area economies.

See also: CORNING GLASS; PITTSBURGH, PENNSYLVANIA (URBAN APPALACHIAN EXPERIENCE); WHEELING, WEST VIRGINIA (URBAN APPALACHIAN EXPERIENCE).

—Rudy Abramson, *Reston, Virginia*

David Levander, "West Virginia's Glass Industry Struggles to Survive," *Huntington Herald-Dispatch* (October 28, 2001); David Zuchowski, "West Virginia Glass Glitters at Oglebay Museum," *Wonderful West Virginia Magazine* (March 1999).

Gold Rush of 1829

The first gold rush in the United States occurred in southern Appalachia in 1829, two decades before the discovery of gold in California. White settlers were mining for gold illegally on Cherokee lands in north Georgia as early as 1819, and by 1828 at least two mines were in operation in what is now Polk County, Tennessee, and White County, Georgia. Although small quantities had been found periodically for some years, word of gold in the southern highlands spread rapidly after a three-ounce nugget was produced in Polk County in 1829 and would-be prospectors proclaimed, "There's gold in them thar hills." By 1830, thousands of people had flocked to work mines in north Georgia and southeastern Tennessee. They removed more than $250,000 in gold (three hundred ounces per day) by the end of the year.

Soon the focal point of mining activity shifted to the area just south of Dahlonega, Georgia, which became a boomtown overnight. The region had become so prominent as a gold production center that stamp mills were built in Georgia in 1833, and a federal mint was established in 1838. Gold worth more than $1.8 million was mined between 1830 and 1837. Production peaked in 1843 with a yearly total of $600,000. Eventually some ten thousand miners were working between the Etowah and Chestatee Rivers, so many that the United States military was brought in to maintain order and curtail illegal mining.

The fact that the land being mined belonged to the Cherokee by treaty was of little concern to the gold seekers. From the onset of the rush, the Georgia government endeavored to nullify Cherokee rights and bring them directly under Georgia law. Ignoring a ruling by the U.S. Supreme Court, the state proceeded with the "Land Lottery" in 1832. This resulted in the seizure and forfeiture of remaining Cherokee lands and ultimately resulted in the forced removal of the Cherokee to the West.

Today Georgia is the seventh-ranked state in the United States in terms of mineral production and the only Appalachian state in the top ten. However, its mineral wealth is based upon clays, stone, sand, gravel, and gemstones—not gold. Commercial gold-mining operations continued into the early twentieth century, but in modern times the only gold-mining activity in the area of the original rush is on the part of individual hobbyists, who find negligible quantities.

See also: CHEROKEE (RACE, ETHNICITY, AND IDENTITY); CHEROKEE REMOVAL (GOVERNMENT); GOLD SETTLEMENTS (SETTLEMENT AND MIGRATION).

—Barry Donald Mowell, *Broward Community College*

Goody's Family Clothing

Goody's Family Clothing, headquartered in Knoxville, Tennessee, retails moderately priced apparel for women, men, and children. The company in fiscal year 2003 realized $1.2 billion in annual sales from 335 stores located in eighteen states: Alabama, Arkansas, Florida, Georgia, Illinois, Indiana, Kentucky, Louisiana, Mississippi, Missouri, North Carolina, Ohio, Oklahoma, South Carolina, Tennessee, Texas, Virginia, and West Virginia.

A second-generation clothier, Mike Goodfriend started what was to become Goody's in 1953, opening a small discount store in Athens, Tennessee, that primarily sold close-out and irregular apparel. The success of that store led a year later to a small chain that has attained steady growth. Goodfriend's father, Morris, had entered the apparel business in 1913 in Athens operating Goodfriend's, a men's clothing store.

In 1972 Mike Goodfriend's son, Bob, joined his father's company. Bob's nickname from his college days became the twelve-store chain's new name, and a different market strategy developed. The company changed its merchandise from closeouts and irregulars to current-season, first-quality apparel, with plans calling for approximately 20 new stores per year. According to management, the new strategy initiated another growth surge that continued through the final decades of the twentieth century.

Bob Goodfriend was named president and chief executive officer in 1979. By 1991, Goody's had grown to 91 stores with $273 million in annual sales, and the family business was taken public. As of 2002, Goodfriend was the company's major stockholder with holdings of 42.1 percent.

See also: PROFFITT'S.

—C. E. Ford, *Berea, Kentucky*

Gould, Jay

(1836–1892) Industrialist.

Jay Gould, the quintessential American "robber baron," contributed to the nineteenth-century industrialization of Appalachia through his brief foray into leather tanning and as one of the nation's most avid railroad capitalists. In 1856, as a young surveyor, Gould built a tannery in the mountains of northeastern Pennsylvania to take advantage of abundant tanbark resources. However, this short-lived venture ended after a battle erupted between him and his New York backers that resulted in gunshots being fired in Gouldsboro, the tannery town that bore his name.

Afterward, Gould abandoned the forests and his native mountains of Delaware County, New York, for Wall Street. He spent the rest of his life in New York City, where he became a key player in the spread of railroads across the American West following the Civil War. Appalachian coalfields fueled his railroads, a vast network that stretched from New York to the Pacific. His son, George Jay Gould (1864–1923), followed him into business and became a major developer of railroads in West Virginia.

Jay Gould died in 1892 after battling physical infirmities his entire life. His legendary financial wizardry and uncommon wealth prompted incredible written and spoken accounts during his life and after his death. Portrayed as a devil in the press of his time, Gould left a legend that persisted into the 1930s in a hobo song titled "Jay Gould's Daughter."

See also: RAILROAD PROMOTION AND IN-MIGRATION (SETTLEMENT AND MIGRATION); RAILROADS (TRANSPORTATION); TANNING.

—David S. Rotenstein, *Bethesda, Maryland*

Granite Industry

The economic benefits of granite mining and processing are reaped by various communities from one end of Appalachia to the other, but the town that calls itself the "Granite Capital of the World" is Elberton, Georgia. Within a twenty five-mile radius of this town in the state's northeastern quadrant lie forty-five granite quarries supplying stone for scores of manufacturers of tombstones, countertops, signs, heroic monuments, and building facades.

Founded in 1889 with the opening of the first commercial quarry in Elbert County, the Georgia industry is one of the cornerstones of the area's economy. Extending for thirty-five miles, the Elberton Granite Deposit is approximately six miles wide and believed to be two to three miles deep. Much of its mining, however, occurs at a depth of 150 feet or less. In the mid-1990s, the U.S. Geological Survey listed McCannon Granite Company's quarry near Elberton as one of the ten most productive stone quarries in the United States and credited eleven other local quarries with production worth more than $500,000 each. With all the quarries in the area yielding a total of 495,000 metric tons in 1995, Georgia ranked third among the nation's granite-producing states. At the close of the twentieth century, about 280 separate companies were operating businesses in granite production or its allied services in the Elberton area, and employment in associated manufacturing operations stood at 2,300. The industry's annual payrolls totaled more than $50 million, and the Elberton Granite Association estimated the yearly economic impact at $220 million.

Although the industry's roots lie in the nineteenth century, its most rapid growth came during the last three decades of the twentieth, when local granite production doubled and producers in other states began shipping their stone to Elberton processing plants. The nation's largest single granite mine is located at Barre, Vermont, in the northern reaches of the Appalachian Mountains. The North Carolina Granite Company's quarry near Mount Airy, another of the most productive stone quarries in the United States, has an exposed face that extends for about a mile and is the largest open-face granite quarry in the country.

Granites are among the oldest rocks on Earth. Composed chiefly of quartz and feldspar, with small quantities of several other minerals, they were formed under pressure deep within the earth and were thrust upward in a molten state as forces beneath the surface caused the crust to buckle. The Elberton Deposit, younger than the granites of the northern Appalachians, is thought to have cooled and solidified from liquid rock rising from the depths more than 300 million years ago.

The age, distribution, and variety of Appalachian granites have linked the stone with the region's heritage and image as well as its economy. Both North Carolina and South Carolina have adopted it as the state stone. Granite quarries in the northern Appalachians led Massachusetts, New Hampshire, and Vermont similarly to adopt it as a state symbol. New Hampshire, where granite quarries were operating nearly a century before the Elberton Deposit was first mined, is known as the Granite State.

See also: NONMETALLIC, NONFUEL DEPOSITS (GEOLOGY).

—Rudy Abramson, *Reston, Virginia*

William R. Barton, *Dimension Stone* (1968); U.S. Geological Survey, *Mineral Industry Surveys* (1994–95).

Green Bank Observatory

The National Radio Astronomy Observatory facility in Green Bank, West Virginia, was created in 1956 for the study and observation of extraterrestrial electromagnetic signals. The Green Bank site was selected because of its remoteness and low level of industrialization, as well as the surrounding Appalachian Mountains, which offer a protective sound barrier around the site. Among the eight telescopes employed at the complex is the largest fully steerable radio telescope in the world. Named for U.S. Senator Robert C. Byrd, it was dedicated on August 25, 2000.

Radio telescopes collect faint emissions in radio frequencies of the spectrum produced by distant objects in space. When amplified, these signals provide astronomers a distinct view of the universe, just as do optical telescopes that gather visible light. Unfortunately, radio signals from man-made sources can interfere with radio astronomy observations, so it is necessary to locate radio telescopes in areas relatively free of such interference. The Green Bank telescopes are available for use by scientists and students, and tours of the facility and educational programs are offered to the public.

In 1958, a year after the observatory opened, the National Radio Quiet Zone was created, ensuring that the Green Bank area would always remain "quiet." This zone encompasses about thirteen thousand square miles surrounding the Green Bank site. Within this area, potential sources of radio frequency interference, such as industrial development and the use of electronic equipment, are restricted or forbidden. This quiet zone is a national treasure, one of only a few such locations in the world.

See also: LAND TRUSTS AND CONSERVANCIES (ENVIRONMENT); U.S. SPACE AND ROCKET CENTER (CULTURAL INSTITUTIONS).

—Rochelle Caviness, *Green Bank, West Virginia*

Harris-Tarkett Corporation

Harris-Tarkett of Johnson City, Tennessee, a flooring-manufacturing subsidiary of German and Swedish conglomerates, has seen its products distributed throughout America and the world in its more than a century of operation. In 2001 company executives counted 436 employees at the Johnson City plant, which also oversaw operations of two flooring facilities in southwest Virginia and one in Arkansas.

The firm originated in Johnson City in 1898 as Harris Manufacturing Company. It was founded by William Pond "W. P." Harris, a native of Worcester, Massachusetts, who moved to Johnson City in 1890 as a superintendent with the Charleston, Cincinnati, and Chicago Railroad. Harris's small business employed two other persons who, along with him, made such articles as golf club shafts. In 1899 the prospering new firm moved from its original location to a larger one alongside the Clinchfield Railway tracks and expanded its product line to include plow handles, trunk slats, and wagon wheel rims. Harris's son, Allen, entered the business in 1902 and added tabletops and oak flooring to the company's line. The following year, flooring became the company's main product, with virgin forests of east Tennessee and western North Carolina supplying its raw materials. Two subsidiary firms, French Broad Flooring in North Carolina and Doe River Flooring in Johnson City, supplied flooring planks to Harris.

Within two years of his company's 1910 incorporation in Tennessee, Harris secured funding to establish Harris Flooring Company, a New York City wholesale and distribution firm. At his death in 1915, he left the company in the hands of his son, who shepherded the business through the World War I era. During the war, Harris Manufacturing produced hardwood flooring, broom handles, and hickory wagon rims and ramrods.

From 1919 through 1935 Harris Manufacturing was highly successful financially and intent on expanding its operations. It increased its product line—adding different styles of strip and plank flooring, moldings, thresholds, and stair treads and risers—and extended its distribution network throughout the United States and to England and Europe. Two flooring manufacturers were added as subsidiaries: Harris Hardwood of Roanoke, Virginia, in 1919 and Cherokee Flooring of Burlington, North Carolina, in 1928.

The company flourished in the years immediately following the 1929 stock market crash, shipping more than a million feet of flooring per month during the early 1930s. By the middle of the decade, however, shipments had dropped approximately 90 percent. World War II's military demands then revived business. The companies' plants manufactured pre-finished flooring for military housing and such other products as tent pins.

The postwar boom years were profitable ones for Harris Manufacturing, now led by Allen Sr. and his son, Allen Jr. A Harvard business graduate who had joined Harris Flooring as a salesman in 1929, Allen Jr. returned from war service in the navy to work in the Johnson City office. The mid-1950s saw a shift in the flooring market, as asbestos tile and carpet became popular. In 1954 Harris Manufacturing introduced a specially designed parquet flooring called Bondwood for installation over concrete or wood. As Bondwood sales increased, strip flooring sales declined, and by 1972 management discontinued that product to concentrate on Bondwood, plank, and other specialty floor coverings.

From 1950 through 1970, Harris's principal stockholders—foremost among them Allen Sr. (as of 1968, chairman of the board) and his wife, Torrey S. Harris, and Allen Jr. (as of 1968, president)—invested in a number of other businesses. In addition to the Harris Hardwood, Harris Flooring, and Cherokee Flooring companies, the Harris holdings came to include Harris Properties, Bondwood Sales Corporation, Harris Corporation, Harris Appalachian Corporation, Citizens Loan Company, and Auto Sales Company. During the 1980s, though, a number of these were liquidated, including Harris Flooring and Bondwood Sales.

Allen Harris Sr. died in 1973. In 1983 Allen Jr., then chairman of the board, decided to merge his company with Tarkett AB International of Ronneby, Sweden. Becoming known as Harris-Tarkett, the Johnson City firm became part of Tarkett North America Holdings Inc., which was headquartered in Whitehall, Pennsylvania. At the time of the merger, the Tennessee company employed approximately 100 workers in the Harris Hardwood plant in Roanoke and 200 in the parent Johnson City plant. Throughout its history, workers at the Johnson City facility have never been unionized, although from the late 1940s until its closure in 2000, Harris Hardwood laborers in Roanoke were members of a United Woodworkers of America local.

Harris-Tarkett's parent organization in the early twenty-first century was the Domco Tarkett Group. Domco, a Canadian company, acquired Tarkett North America in 1999. Domco, in turn, was controlled by Tarkett Sommer, a conglomerate formed by the 1997 merger of Swedish Tarkett with the German flooring giant, Sommer Allibert. A joint venture agreement concluded in 2000 made the Domco group part of Tarkett Sommer and allowed Tarkett Sommer to market laminated flooring under different trade names, including Harris-Tarkett.

See also: LUMBER INDUSTRY.

—Marie Tedesco, *East Tennessee State University*

Harris Family Manufacturing Records and Harris Family Papers, Archives of Appalachia, East Tennessee State University.

Haydenville Brick Company

Haydenville, the last working company town in Ohio, was functional until 1964 and is best remembered for its manufacture and use of bricks and clay products.

The municipality was founded by Peter Hayden, who was born in 1806 in Massachusetts and moved as a young man to Columbus, Ohio. As a member of the board of directors of the Exchange Bank in Columbus, he ventured into coal mining around 1852, acquiring land along the Hocking Canal in Green Township in southeastern Ohio. Setting up an iron furnace, the entrepreneur started a township owned entirely by his company and employing every breadwinner in the community. In addition to coal mining and iron, Hayden's activities included sandstone quarrying. Proximity to the canal and the Hocking Valley Railroad, of which Hayden later became president, helped all of the enterprises prosper.

When competition made coal mining less profitable, Hayden started a kiln and clay products plant, renaming his company Haydenville Mining and Manufacturing Company. Incorporated in 1882, the firm earned a reputation for the quality of its bricks and tiles made from locally available clay capable of withstanding intense heat. All buildings in the township, including a Methodist church, houses, and the company store, used the company's products and served as a catalog and advertisement for them. As the popularity of brick and fireproof construction rose, the business flourished.

Hayden eventually moved to New York City, where he died in 1888. In 1900 his heirs sold Haydenville Mining and Manufacturing Company, and the company and township changed hands several times afterward. The National Fireproofing Company bought the township in 1906 and ran a plant there until 1964. Houses were sold to individual buyers when that company ceased operations.

In recent years, efforts have been directed toward celebrating the legacy of the company town, which was added to the National Register of Historic Places in 1973. During Ohio's bicentennial celebrations in 2003, the town was commemorated by a historical marker. To further preserve its history, residents have pursued support and funding to restore and renovate important buildings.

See also: OHIO CLAY INDUSTRY.

—Ajay Kalra, *East Tennessee State University*

Heinz Corporation

The worldwide, billion-dollar prominence of the Pittsburgh-based H. J. Heinz Corporation is rooted in the 1850s and a one-man door-to-door vegetable-selling enterprise. First-generation German American Henry John Heinz made his company famous boasting "57 Varieties" of condiments and vegetables, but the number of products marketed by the firm has long since proliferated. In the early 2000s the firm claimed the top one or two branded businesses in more than fifty world markets, with acquisitions that included Del Monte Foods and licensing agreements with such varied other brands as Weight Watchers, T.G.I. Friday's, and Jack Daniel's.

Heinz was born in Pittsburgh to German immigrant parents. When he was six they moved to nearby Sharpsburg, where he engaged in his first door-to-door vegetable selling. In 1859, as a fifteen-year-old, he completed a business college bookkeeping course and joined his father's brick-making business but continued selling vegetables as a sideline. He and a partner formed his first company, Heinz and Noble, in 1869 and began selling wholesale to Pittsburgh grocers. Their specialty was grated horseradish, which they touted as "pure and superior" and marketed in a clear glass bottle to show that, unlike the dark-bottled products of competitors, it contained no turnip leaves or other filler.

Heinz and his partner branched out to pickles, sauerkraut, and vinegar and grew their products on a hundred acres—thirty of them in horseradish—along the Allegheny River. They processed and packed their products in the company office, a Sharpsburg farmhouse, and drivers of two dozen horse-drawn wagons sold them to Pittsburgh's grocers. In 1875 a depression bankrupted Heinz and Noble, but Heinz restructured as a new business, H. J. Heinz, and in 1876 introduced a new product: Heinz ketchup. Marketing with visual images became a Heinz hallmark. The company brought out a "pickle pin" emblazoned with the word *Heinz* for the 1893 World's Fair in Chicago. By 1896, the original fifty-seven varieties had been surpassed by the growth of Heinz-manufactured products.

Heinz's marketing campaigns during the late nineteenth century quickly allowed the company to gain both a national and international market. Heinz goods have been sold in the United Kingdom since 1886, and the company has had factories operating there since the early twentieth century. It made its first acquisition of another company, a food processor in the Netherlands, in 1958. Five years later it acquired the StarKist firm and soon afterward began promoting Charlie the Tuna, one of the more famous food advertising media "personalities" of that era. The corporation eventually expanded into a public company with operations in more than two hundred countries.

Henry Heinz, who continually stressed the importance of product purity, lobbied for the Pure Food and Drug Act of 1906. In 1919, at age seventy-five, he died of pneumonia at his mansion on Pittsburgh's North Side, leaving an impressive legacy. He had been active in the Pittsburgh Chamber of Commerce, the Pittsburgh Flood Commission, and the Western Pennsylvania Exposition Society. He also founded a settlement house in memory of his wife and had traveled for the World Sunday School Association. His company's corporate headquarters remain in Pittsburgh, and the brand has become part of the city's identity in sports (Heinz Field), the arts (Heinz Hall), and architecture (Heinz Memorial Chapel).

Both the company and the family are prominently involved in community development. The H. J. Heinz Company Foundation, one of several Heinz philanthropic organizations, funds programs in southwestern Pennsylvania that focus on nutrition and quality of life to benefit youth and families. Interest in the public welfare and that of its own workers has been part of the Heinz corporate image since its early days. The founder's main plant in Allegheny City, now part of Pittsburgh, boasted employee facilities that included lunchrooms, roof gardens, a swimming pool, a gymnasium, a library, and an auditorium. In 1900, when the company moved its operation to Pittsburgh's Troy Hill, it began to employ many women and promoted reforms in wages, labor conditions, and working hours before most other employers addressed these issues.

See also: PITTSBURGH, PENNSYLVANIA (URBAN APPALACHIAN EXPERIENCE).

—Sarah Gibbard Cook, *DeForest, Wisconsin*, and Audra Himes, *Northern Cambria, Pennsylvania*

Robert C. Alberts, *The Good Provider: H. J. Heinz and His 57 Varieties* (1973); Eleanor Foa Dienstag, *In Good Company: 125 Years at the Heinz Table, 1869–1994* (1994); E. D. McCafferty, *Henry J. Heinz: A Biography* (1936).

Horizon Natural Resources Company

One of Appalachia's largest producers of steam coal, Horizon Natural Resources Company of Ashland, Kentucky, was created in 2002 from the bankruptcy reorganization of AEI Resources, Inc. Before that year was out, the new company also sought the protection of Chapter 11 bankruptcy law in order to reorganize its finances. In August 2004, Horizon's mining operations were sold at auction to a partnership led by billionaire New York investment banker W. L. Ross and then divided into two new entities—International Coal Group and Old Ben Coal Company. The sale of properties in four states brought $786 million, with Massey Energy Company gaining control of Horizon operations in central Appalachia. The acquisition by Ross's company, WL Ross & Co LLC, came up after other major purchases of bankrupt steel, coal, and textile companies had gained him the sobriquet of "Bankruptcy King." The sale of Horizon's operations followed a bankruptcy court ruling freeing Horizon from its obligation to provide lifetime medical benefits for its miners and retirees. The decision was appealed in U.S. District Court in Lexington, Kentucky; it also led to calls in Congress for bankruptcy law reform.

Horizon's history and that of its predecessor exemplify the complex and constantly changing ownership patterns in the region's modern coal-mining industry. Founded in 1970 as Addington Brothers Mining, AEI Resources was by the end of the twentieth century a conglomerate with about four thousand employees operating fifteen underground mines and twenty-nine surface mines. The latter included Starfire, a sixty-two-hundred-acre mountaintop-removal project in Knott County, Kentucky, and Princess Beverly, an oft-photographed mountaintop mine near Cabin Creek, West Virginia.

AEI sought bankruptcy protection in February 2002 when its longterm debts mounted to $1.3 billion following the financial collapse of Frontier Insurance Company, a New York firm that provided bonds covering AEI's mine reclamation and worker compensation programs. In the reorganization, AEI arranged new loans, renegotiated its debts, and severed formal ties with Larry Addington, the longtime chairman and principal owner, and his brother Stephen, the company president. In May, it emerged from bankruptcy, having been renamed Horizon Natural Resources Company—with mines in Illinois, Indiana, and Colorado as well as Kentucky and West Virginia. But in November the new company itself filed for bankruptcy protection, citing a weak economic environment, mounting customer inventories, and liabilities of $2.1 billion. As it proceeded with the new reorganization the following year, it announced the sale of various properties and the closing of the Princess Beverly Mine in West Virginia. It continued to operate thirty-eight mines in five states, selling steam coal to utilities in the eastern United States. It also continued to operate subsidiaries manufacturing mining equipment, providing trucking services, and rebuilding mining equipment.

During the years of operation by the Addington brothers—Robert, Larry, Bruce, and Stephen—AEI was as conspicuous for buying and selling companies and taking up new ventures as it was for mining coal. It sold mining operations to Ashland Oil Company and Pittston Minerals Group and entered the waste-management business. Shortly before AEI's financial crisis put it on the road to bankruptcy, EnviroPower, a Lexington, Kentucky, company headed by Bruce Addington, proposed to construct new coal-fired power plants in Illinois, Indiana, and Kentucky; one of these was at the Starfire mine, where it would burn coal waste known as "gob." Even as Horizon remained in bankruptcy reorganization, it continued to pursue necessary regulatory approvals and financial partners for the ventures in the face of opposition from Kentuckians for the Commonwealth and other environmental organizations.

As the national economy boomed in the 1990s and AEI acquired a dozen new mining operations, Larry Addington became known as one of Kentucky's major political contributors, donating more than $800,000 to political groups and candidates in the late 1990s, including about $500,000 to the National Republican Senatorial Committee.

See also: BITUMINOUS COAL INDUSTRY; COAL MINING (ENVIRONMENT).

—Rudy Abramson, *Reston, Virginia*

"AEI Bankruptcy Reorganization Plan Approved by Court, Bobby Brown Joins Board of Directors," *Coal Age* (May 1, 2002); "Horizon Natural Resources Files for Bankruptcy," *Coal Age* (January 1, 2003); Frank E. Lockwood, "Political Gifts of Coal Magnate Exceed $800,000," *Lexington Herald-Leader* (February 28, 2001).

International Towing and Recovery Museum

The roads of Appalachia probably spawned the first tow truck. The automobile towing industry is claimed to have been born in 1916 in Chattanooga, Tennessee, when an independent garage owner named Ernest Holmes and five helpers spent all of one night retrieving a Model T Ford from a local creek with only ropes and other equipment tied to trees. That was apparently the last straw for Holmes, who—the story goes—had been spending an increasing and increasingly dangerous amount of time trying to repair broken axles beside roads bad enough to break them. He is widely credited with building the first tow truck, equipping it with a reversible winch and then manufacturing twin-boom wreckers for transporting crippled cars. The Manley Manufacturing Company of York, Pennsylvania, claimed to have built and sold a similar device in the same year.

As cars multiplied, the Ernest Holmes Company grew. After its founder died in 1943, the firm was operated for thirty more years by Ernest Holmes Jr. After the second Holmes retired, the company was bought by the Dover Corporation, and a grandson of the founder opened Century Wreckers in neighboring Ooltewah, Tennessee. Under Gerald Holmes, Century used hydraulic power to become competitive with Dover. Both companies eventually were bought by Miller Industries, which, from its Ooltewah headquarters, claimed a position as world leader in the manufacture of towing equipment at the opening of the twenty-first century.

The Chattanooga area's eminence in this niche market was formalized in 1995 with the opening of the International Towing and Recovery Hall of Fame and Museum two blocks from where the first Ernest Holmes built his first garage. Its construction was the result of fundraising by the 350-member organization Friends of Towing, and the Hall of Fame includes honorees from twenty-one countries.

See also: AUTOMOTIVE INDUSTRY.

—Jack Hurst, *Lancaster, Tennessee*

John Gunnell, "Tow-tally Awesome," *Road King* (September–October 2003).

Iron and Steel Industry

Appalachia's iron and steel industry suffered from déjà vu at the outset of the twenty-first century. In a December 2000 article for a trade publication, the president of United States Steel, Paul J. Wilhelm, compared steel's situation to that facing it in 1901, when the problem of "cutthroat and chaotic" competition was solved by consolidating two-thirds of the nation's steel production and nearly a third of the world's.

A hundred years later, the industry once again was fragmented and fiercely competitive but far more global. U.S. Steel, once the world's largest steel company, generated more than a tenth of America's output and 3 percent worldwide. Imports flooded the market and helped force more than thirty-five domestic steel producers, including Appalachian companies such as Wheeling-Pittsburgh and Weirton, into bankruptcy. One-third of steelworkers in America, some 35,000, had lost their jobs in a world market in which the international capacity to manufacture the product outstripped demand by 200 million tons. In March of 2002 President George W. Bush—in answer to pleas from steel companies, the United Steelworkers of America, and such U.S. senators as West Virginia Democrats Robert C. Byrd and John "Jay" Rockefeller—approved three years of steel tariffs. Between August 2002 and August 2003, American steel imports decreased by almost one-fourth, and domestic steel prices improved, but in December 2003, the Bush administration lifted the tariffs to avert the threat of retaliatory European Union sanctions and a possible trade war.

U.S. Steel and such competitors as International Steel Group and Nucor Corporation led efforts toward consolidation and the kind of coordinated production that Wilhelm called for in 2000. But the bankruptcy filings endangered the pensions and health-care coverage of 230,000 steel mill retirees and dependents. International Steel's purchase of Weirton Steel in 2004 for a reported $255 million cut retiree health-care and life insurance payments affecting 8,000 people—workers and their family members—although union representatives claimed to have reached tentative agreement with the company to seed an employee health-care plan that would grow as Weirton's profitability returned. After decades of belt-tightening throughout the industry, there were eight times as many retired employees of the older steel companies, on average, than working ones.

Iron and steel production in the United States predates the American Revolution. It began in 1609 at Jamestown, Virginia, then ceased when Native Americans destroyed Virginia's only furnace. In 1664 Saugus Ironworks in Massachusetts became the first successful iron enterprise in America. Iron production expanded during the 1700s, when abundant mineral deposits were discovered in the Appalachian region of southwest Virginia near present-day Wythe County. Over the first few decades of the 1700s, industry in the region grew to meet civilian requirements for products made from iron ore. This demand encouraged many colonies to construct furnaces that by the onset of the American Revolution were producing tools and parts for weapons.

For the next several decades, the nation's iron industry was centered in Appalachia. Iron ore deposits were found across the region, although most abundantly in New York, Pennsylvania, and the areas that would become West Virginia and Ohio. Because of the vast mineral resources and plentiful water throughout the region, construction of iron forges and furnaces became common. Between 1716 and 1776, Pennsylvania took the lead in iron production. The colony had at least twenty-one blast furnaces along with forty-five forges, four bloomeries, six steel furnaces, and other various ironworks. Ironworks expansion in the colonies helped fuel conflicts with England and influence events leading to the Revolutionary War. To keep the colonies economically dependent, the British Parliament passed a law in 1750 that prohibited construction and operation of new ironworks in the colonies, but colonial iron masters ignored the law and continued to expand their industry. By 1775, colonial ironworks accounted for about one-seventh of the world's output of pig iron and castings.

From the 1840s to the 1980s, mills blazed in places such as Weirton, West Virginia; Youngstown, Ohio; Lackawanna, New York; Johnstown and the Monongahela Valley in Pennsylvania; and Birmingham, Alabama. The supply of iron ore expedited the construction of steel mills in northern Appalachia, an area widely considered the birthplace of industrial America. Pennsylvania, a leader in the iron industry since colonial times, also led in steel manufacturing, taking advantage of its river systems and its Great Lakes port on Lake Erie, which linked the Northeast to the Midwest. Individuals such as Andrew Carnegie and Henry Clay Frick built up the steel industry in Pittsburgh. However, the original "Big Steel" company was J. P. Morgan's United States Steel Corporation, also of Pittsburgh.

In the industry's early years, people from throughout the region embraced it for its apparent economic liberation, which induced an interregional migration to steel towns and cities. Many gravitated to jobs in steel out of feelings of disenfranchisement connected with the selling of their land to the railroad, coal, and timber industries. During the late 1800s and early 1900s, steel mills also attracted many European immigrants, who brought with them their own techniques for making tools and other machinery that improved steel production. Appalachian workers, too, brought innovations to the process. One such was the three-high rolling mill invented during the mid-1800s at the Cambria Iron Works in Johnstown. The device permitted iron to be taken from a blast furnace and rolled, strengthening it. In earlier methods of rail production, a bar of iron, called the pile, was reheated as workers passed it between the rolls and through grooves to shape it. The pile passed through the grooves twice to make a rail, and reheating was a problem because the metal often cracked as it cooled. The three-high rolling mill revolutionized rail making by adding a third roll, so the bar could be passed through one groove and then be sent back through a second. The process was continuous and quicker, keeping the metal from cooling, and it helped American steel achieve higher quality.

Serbs, Croats, Slovenes, Poles, Magyars and Slovaks from the Austro-Hungarian Empire, Ukrainians from north of the Carpathian Mountains and Ruthenians from the south, and Romanians were some of the eastern Europeans who came to Appalachia to work in steel mills in the early 1900s. Many of these immigrants had been peasants in European feudal societies, and this background was practically replicated for them by the steel companies. In addition, African Americans, many of them recruited during strikes, came from the South. Allegiances in the steel mills resulted in self-segregated communities. The various immigrants formed into work groups organized by ethnicity and often controlled by particular families. All of these workers found places for themselves in industrial cities in the company-planned employee lifestyle. The companies claimed that the institutions they established within the community met workers' everyday needs and that the workers did not need higher wages or outside interference by unions.

One factor in the steel companies' success was vertical integration. Commonly, a single firm owned the coal mines, had close partnerships with the railroads that moved the coal, and owned the towns as well. The company typically set up a welfare system that claimed to care for the employees from cradle to grave. Workers bought their necessities at the company store, where credit was always extended. They lived in company houses with the rents subtracted from their wages, sent their children to the company school, and went to the company hospital when they became ill. Quality of life in these company towns varied widely.

In the late 1800s, Appalachian steel manufacturing slackened. Iron ore discovered farther west yielded higher-quality metal than local sources, and the cost of transport made it difficult for Appalachian mills to compete with producers closer to the resources. Fewer furnaces were operated in the South than in the North. Virginia ore tended to be in pockets rather than veins, making the yield unpredictable. Ore fields in Alabama, however, were found to be more substantial. The size and abundance of their minerals, along with the application of new technology, made the Alabama fields successful competitors in the industry. By 1924 Alabama production ranked third nationally, reaching a record high in 1944.

Many of the new ironworks had begun by the 1830s to take the form of tall stone furnaces shaped like flattened pyramids. Furnaces were frequently constructed of large sandstone blocks weighing four hundred to six hundred pounds each. They were built twenty to forty feet high near mineral reserves such as coal, ore, water, and wood. When possible, they were located near railroads or river ports. Black, red, and brown ores—magnetite, hematite, and limonite—were found all along the Appalachian Mountains. Large supplies of other essential ingredients of iron making, including coal and limestone, were often in close proximity. Limestone was used as a fluxing agent in the blast process to promote the separation of impurities from the ore. Both anthracite and bituminous coal deposits covered about fifty thousand square miles in Alabama, Kentucky, Pennsylvania, Virginia, and West Virginia. At first, thousands of bushels of charcoal were used as fuel to fire the process, sometimes to twenty-five hundred degrees Fahrenheit or more. Later, coal and its coke by-product became the main fuel sources.

Air blasting expedited the reduction process, which separated the iron from other materials. Forced air was first provided by waterwheels and later by steam engines. As the process of iron making developed, hot blast stoves forced superheated air into the furnace chambers. Top-fed blast furnaces were connected to adjoining hillsides by covered bridges, which provided a means to convey raw materials. The charge, a combination of iron ore, limestone, and charcoal, was put into the furnace three times an hour. In a Civil War–era furnace, a typical charge included eight hundred pounds of iron ore, eighty pounds of limestone, and twenty bushels of charcoal. This produced up to four hundred pounds of pig iron, depending on the purity of the iron ore. Oxygen released from melting ore combined with limestone to form slag. As iron ore melted inside the furnace, limestone was converted into lime, which united with clay, sand, and other impurities. The slag was then removed from the furnace.

During the Civil War, furnaces were operated twenty-four hours a day and were tapped every six hours. Some large furnaces of this period employed more than five hundred workers. In the South, many were slaves. These furnace complexes could produce twenty to thirty tons of pig iron per day, while smaller furnaces produced six to ten tons. In large foundries and gun works, pig iron was recast into war materiel ranging from field cannon to ironclad boats. Two Civil War–era Appalachian facilities that now are well-preserved historical sites include Buckeye Furnace at Wellston, Ohio, and Tannehill Ironworks near Birmingham.

Refining iron ore was a simple process. After miners collected it from the mine, they moved it to a blast furnace to melt the ore. Molten iron was then poured into sand molds to cool, forming bars known as pigs. Nearly pure, pig iron was then ready to be treated or forged into iron products. Furnaces in the North differed from those in the South because Pennsylvania coalfields were discovered before those farther south. Southern furnaces for that reason were fueled more by charcoal than coal. Because they burned more effectively, coal-fired furnaces were preferred. Southern furnaces made quality iron but less efficiently; the weight of the ore tended to crush charcoal and snuff it out.

Pennsylvania coal burned better than Virginia coal. Northern furnaces used the "hot" blast method, in which air was heated before it was introduced to the furnace, melting the ore more quickly. Southern furnaces used the "cold" blast method, which employed unheated air and was less efficient. In addition to Virginia, Alabama, and West Virginia, iron deposits were present in Georgia, Tennessee, Mississippi, North Carolina, and South Carolina, but lack of infrastructure kept them from being much more than local suppliers. During the last two years of the Civil War, Alabama produced four times as much pig iron as Virginia, and Tennessee produced twice as much, but lack of adequate transportation prevented these states from becoming the sites of large-scale operations.

Advances in technology by the turn of the twentieth century resulted in the construction of giant coke-fired steel mills in a number of states, including the Appalachian areas of Pennsylvania, Ohio, and Alabama. Like their Civil War counterparts, some of the steel mills featuring the technology of the early 1900s have become major tourism sites. Sloss Furnaces, which closed operations in Birmingham in 1971, became a national historic landmark in 1981.

The American steel industry reached peak production during the 1960s, after which imported steel forced a decline. In the Appalachian states, some mills closed while a number modernized and survived. In the year 2000 nine steelworks were in operation in Ohio, two each in Pennsylvania, Alabama, and West Virginia, and one each in Kentucky and Maryland. In addition, six electric minimills using scrap were in blast in South Carolina, and there were five in Pennsylvania, four in Alabama and Ohio, three in Tennessee, Kentucky, and Virginia, two in West Virginia, and one each in North Carolina, New York, Georgia, and Mississippi. Minimills tend to be nonunion and for that reason are usually regarded as having a competitive advantage.

Some aspects of modern steelmaking resemble the earliest techniques. While portions of the process have been automated since the 1980s to make American steel competitive worldwide, parts of the job are done by hand. Hand-labor jobs in a mill include open-hearth foreman, first helper (who controls the furnace), second helper (who gets alloys and taps the furnace), and third helper (who assists the second helper and works closest to the heat). Overhead cranes deposit batches of scrap metal into furnaces, along with ladles full of molten iron. When liquid iron comes into contact with partially melted material in the furnace, the mixture boils violently. The first helper assesses progress through a peephole or opens the furnace door to extract samples with a long-handled spoon. The charge takes five hours to melt, with the first helper probing the furnace depths with a bar to monitor progress. When the mix fails to meet specialty steel requirements and needs ingredients such as silicon or nickel, helpers add material directly onto the furnace banks. The men line up at the hearth door, move forward, and throw their loads into the furnace, finishing with one arm and shoulder in front of their faces for protection from the heat.

Another process is rolling. A rolling mill is a long factory built around a series of tables placed end to end in a horseshoe shape. Glowing red steel bars, each about twenty feet long and weighing seven hundred pounds, move over the tables one at a time, powered by a five-hundred-horsepower drive. At each station along the horseshoe, a worker uses tongs to pick up the front of the bar and place it in a groove in the stand of rolls. The bar moves through the groove, which shapes it, and onto the table on the other side, where it continues toward the next station and next roller. The work is dangerous because the bar, heated to eighteen hundred degrees, can jam and fly back toward the person who put it in, who is known as the roller.

Industrialization provided badly needed jobs, but it also made the region a prime target for exploitation. Presently, coal is used primarily in the generation of electricity and in the production of coke for making iron and steel. In the 1970s, Appalachia held 27 percent of the nation's coal reserves and an estimated 81 percent of the land scarred by strip mining. Much of the land left over from years of coal and iron ore mining remains unclaimed, but federally mandated cleanup programs have improved some of the old fields. In some instances, the abandoned mills and coal mines of Appalachia have been given new life as tourist attractions that educate people about America's transformation during the industrial age.

Steel no longer employs many thousands, and those who do get its jobs have higher skills and are much likelier to be women. In 2003 the Appalachian counties that traditionally relied on the industry remained in economic malaise while the industry itself struggled on. In late 2003 Wheeling-Pittsburgh Steel Corporation emerged from bankruptcy, split from its parent WHX Corporation, and offered investors the chance to buy its stock on Wall Street for the first time in fifteen years. It also announced plans to build a new electric arc furnace to melt scrap iron at its plant in Mingo Junction, Ohio, by December 2004. The firm had about 3,500 employees.

In 1982 United States Steel acquired Marathon Oil Company and in 1986 acquired Texas Gas and Oil Corporation and changed its named to USX Corporation to reflect its broadened business base, which also featured a reduction of its domestic steelmaking. But in January 2002, to increase its appeal to stockholders, USX split its steel and energy divisions into two independent operations, U.S. Steel Corporation and Marathon Oil Corporation. In May 2003 U.S. Steel acquired virtually all of the steelmaking capabilities of

National Steel Corporation, which included several plants around the nation (but none in Appalachia).

Bankruptcies, which allowed failing companies to shed their pension and health-care obligations to former employees, made those firms more attractive to prospective mergers and takeovers, and industry leaders predicted further consolidation and more global operations (such as U.S. Steel's recent purchase of operations in the Slovak Republic and Serbia).

Before its 2004 move to acquire Weirton Steel, International Steel Group bought bankrupt Bethlehem, the nation's third-largest steelmaker, while North Carolina–based Nucor purchased two of its insolvent minimill competitors, Tricor and Birmingham Steel. In mid-2003, Nucor led the nation's steel companies in domestic capacity, and International Steel with its Bethlehem buy had jumped into second place; after International Steel Group's announced acquisition of Weirton, a representative of the Independent Steelworkers Union called International the nation's number one steel company. But U.S. Steel, which had lost $218 million in 2001, was vying strongly to buy another overseas steel mill, this time in Poland, and the 1901-style consolidation called for by U.S. Steel's Wilhelm in 2000 seemed to be coming to pass. Nucor, International, and U.S. Steel manufactured almost half the steel made in the nation.

See also: IRON AND STEEL MILL WORKERS (LABOR); IRON SETTLEMENTS (SETTLEMENT AND MIGRATION); MORGAN, J. P.

—James R. Bennett, *Montgomery, Alabama;* Audra Himes, *Northern Cambria, Pennsylvania;* and Michael E. Lynch, *Carlisle, Pennsylvania*

James R. Bennett, *Tannehill and the Growth of the Alabama Iron Industry* (1999); Michael E. Lynch, "Confederate War Industry: The Niter and Mining Bureau," M.A. thesis, Virginia Commonwealth University (2001); Paul J. Nyden, "Steel Tariff Repeal Could Hurt Industry, Credit Analysts Say," *Charleston Gazette* (October 13, 2003); John R. Park, *A Guidebook to Mining in America* (2000); Robert C. Whisonant, "Geology and History of the Civil War Iron Industry in the New River–Cripple Creek District of Southwestern Virginia," *Virginia Minerals* (November 1998).

J. M. Huber Corporation

The J. M. Huber Corporation, one of the largest family-held companies in the United States, owns vast acreage of primarily timberland in West Virginia, Kentucky, Tennessee, Alabama, and Virginia—as well as in Maine and New Jersey—and operates plants at sites that include Spring City and Etowah in Tennessee, Johnsonburg in Pennsylvania, Hawesville in Kentucky, and Commerce in Georgia. At Commerce it maintains the largest dedicated research facility in the engineered wood-derived products industry.

Having grown from a small New York ink and pigments firm launched in 1890, Huber at the opening of the twenty-first century was a globally diversified concern offering engineered wood and wood products, specialty minerals and chemicals for use in everything from tires to toothpaste, and financial services for the benefit of multinational companies in North America, Europe, and Asia. It has reported sales exceeding one billion dollars. Corporate headquarters are in Edison, New Jersey, with divisional headquarters in Atlanta, Houston, and Charlotte, North Carolina.

The firm was founded by Joseph Maria Huber, who visited New York on a sales trip from his native Bavaria in 1883 to develop new markets for his family's pigment-manufacturing business. By 1887 he had developed a client list sufficient to open a firm importing and distributing the firm's products, and in 1890 he bought out the American end of the enterprise and launched J. M. Huber Corporation. From the outset, the company prided itself on such attention to customer need that Huber himself hurried to print shops that developed difficulties with their inks. When fire razed his Brooklyn plant in 1913, he was in rented space and into production again within two days.

The company Huber founded now seeks out and produces oil and gas in Texas, Colorado, Wyoming, and Utah and pioneers and manufactures chemicals that affect the daily lives of people around the world. Huber specialty additives thicken toothpaste and improve its cleaning capability, spread nutrients throughout animal feeds and products, and help detergents flow more freely. The company's performance minerals can be found in such varied materials as PVC pipe, fiberglass showers, electrical and telecom wire and cable, and joint sealant for wallboard. Huber products improve the print quality of paper, reduce the rolling resistance of tires, and make carpets more resistant to fire.

Most directly affecting and depending on Appalachia are Huber operations in timber and engineered woods that manage forests and develop specialty wood products, including flooring and sheathing. Huber Engineered Woods is a leading producer of Oriented Strand Board, a pressed-board product that the firm manufactures in panels of custom sizes, tailoring thickness, length, strength, and water resistance to customer specifications. The company operates the first continuous Oriented Strand Board press in North America and offers fifty- and twenty-five-year warranties on the product. Huber Timber is one of the largest private landowners in the United States, managing a half-million acres in south-central Appalachia. In keeping with the firm's traditional focus on innovative techniques and solutions, Huber Timber uses computer models and technological assets to manage the land. The majority of the lumber extracted from Appalachia is hardwood, generally used for furniture and flooring. Softwoods in the area tend to be used for construction industries and paper processing, and the Huber Corporation specializes in a variety of coated and uncoated papers.

Huber Timber's technology is strongly focused on forest regeneration and sustained-yield harvesting, and Huber Engineered Woods has a lengthening history of demonstrated environmental concern. Meeting all environmental laws is a requirement of Huber Engineered Woods. Since 1976, the corporation as a whole has supported the Nature Conservancy and made large land donations to it in 1995. Huber's donation of twelve hundred acres made Fall Creek Falls State Park in east Tennessee that state's largest. The firm also supports the conservancy with financial gifts and by monetarily encouraging its employees to volunteer their services in preserves.

From its Appalachian land base, Huber continues to grow. In 2001 it acquired Noviant, a Finnish-rooted, Netherlands-headquartered company that has plants in Sweden, Finland, and the Netherlands and is the world's leading producer of carboxymethyl cellulose, a substance used in such diverse industries as paper, food, personal care, pharmaceuticals, and oil drilling. In 2003 Huber announced that it had reached an agreement with International Paper to build a plant in Svetogorsk, Russia. The facility was to manufacture precipitated calcium carbonate, which improves the print quality of paper. It is the twelfth such plant on which Huber and International Paper have collaborated, others including those in Hawesville and Johnsonburg.

See also: HARRIS-TARKETT CORPORATION; LUMBER INDUSTRY.

—Kate Smith, *East Tennessee State University*

Kanawha Salt Trust

The first trust in the United States was formed when salt producers along the Kanawha River in (West) Virginia banded together in an unsuccessful attempt to survive economic depression following the War of 1812.

In 1808 David and Joseph Ruffner began salt production along the Kanawha River. By 1815 there were fifty-two manufacturing furnaces along the river, making it the largest salt-producing area in the country. Growth of agriculture in the Ohio River basin, as well as of the pork packing industry in Kentucky and Ohio, was fueled by availability of Kanawha salt. As a result of the British blockade and uncertainty of overland routes, production boomed during the War of 1812. When wartime boom turned to postwar bust, many producers thought they would have to work with other producers in order to survive. On November 10, 1817, manufacturers agreed to form the Kanawha Salt Company, the first trust in the nation's history.

Taking effect on January 1, 1818, the trust was to expire on December 31, 1822. The directors and president were to receive all salt produced by the subscribers and inspect it for quality, regulate prices, arrange for its sale and transportation, negotiate contracts, and receive payment. The trust set a limit on the amount of salt to be produced and assigned quantities to each of the subscribers. Provisions were included to penalize subscribers who tried to circumvent the agreement. The depressed economic conditions continued in 1819, however, and effectively put an end to the trust before its expiration date.

See also: PORK (FOOD AND COOKING); SALT.

—Kathy A. Campbell, *East Tennessee State University*

Kelly Axe and Tool Manufacturing Company

From the 1920s to 1940s, Kelly Axe and Tool of Charleston, West Virginia, was the world's largest producer of axes, with its eleven hundred employees reportedly able to turn out forty-eight thousand a day. Besides axes, the company manufactured hammers, crowbars, sledgehammers, weed cutters, and garden tools. During World War I, it made mattocks for army field packs and, in World War II, pack shovels, bayonets, and machetes.

William C. Kelly (1849–1933), a native of Eddyville, Kentucky, began the business in Louisville in 1874 after inventing an axe that bit deeper and extracted more easily than existing models. In 1894 he moved to Alexandria, Indiana, because of supposedly ample natural gas there. The gas gave out, and Kelly moved to Charleston in 1904 because of the area's resources (notably gas and wood), water connections (the Kanawha, Ohio, and Mississippi Rivers), and rail service. In 1912 he bought out his main competitor, American Axe and Tool Company, and transferred operations of its seventeen plants to Charleston. In 1930 the company absorbed Shelton Shovel Works and merged with American Fork and Hoe Company, with Kelly chairing the new board.

Kelly Axe was a "family plant," employing whole families over several generations. Conditions were often harsh—employees worked in the alternately hot and cold and noisy plant for long hours with low pay—but acceptable by standards of the time. Kelly himself was strict but not heartless; during the Great Depression he guaranteed three days' work per week to all employees despite mounting unsold inventories. The company was nonunion until the United Steelworkers of America organized its workers after the merger with American Fork and Hoe.

In 1949 American Fork and Hoe changed its name to True Temper Corporation, and Kelly Axe slowly declined in competition with other companies specializing in the same line of tools. The recession of the early 1980s sounded the death knell, and in 1982 True Temper closed the erstwhile Kelly Axe works, which by then had fewer than a hundred employees. The following year, Allegheny International of Pittsburgh sold the site to Fred Haddad, a Charleston developer, who leveled it and built the Patrick Street Plaza.

Nothing remains of a complex which once included about forty acres and more than 140 buildings.

See also: IRON AND STEEL INDUSTRY; IRON AND STEEL MILL WORKERS (LABOR); LODGE IRON WORKS.

—David S. Newhall, *Centre College*

Kentucky Fried Chicken

Kentucky Fried Chicken Corporation (KFC) is owned by the world's largest restaurant system, Yum! Brands, Inc., which operates more than thirty thousand KFC, Pizza Hut, Taco Bell, Long John Silver, and A&W All-American Food restaurants in more than one hundred countries and territories. The origins of America's most famous fast-food fried chicken are, however, much humbler.

Armed with a sixth-grade education, Kentucky Fried Chicken founder Colonel Harland Sanders (born September 9, 1890, in Henryville, Indiana) began working full-time at age twelve. He spent the next twenty-five years in a variety of occupations, including soldier, railroad fireman, steamboat ferry operator, and insurance salesman. In 1930, in the Appalachian railroad town of Corbin, Kentucky, Sanders opened a gas station and small restaurant along U.S. 25, a major automobile route from Florida to the Midwest before the advent of the Interstate Highway System. Sanders's cooking, particularly of fried chicken, became so popular he closed the gas station to open a restaurant and motel, Sanders' Court and Café, across the street. A decade later, after the invention of the pressure cooker, he perfected a method of cooking chicken quickly and invented what he termed his secret "finger lickin' good" recipe from eleven herbs and spices.

When plans for new Interstate 75 called for bypassing Corbin, he sold his café and began franchising his business in 1956 by demonstrating his cooking method and secret recipe to restaurants all over the country. He eventually had six hundred restaurants paying him a nickel for each chicken they sold. In 1964 he sold his recipe and network of franchises to a group of investors for $2 million, choosing to take a $40,000 lifetime annual salary rather than stock options. After two more sales of the company, Kentucky Fried Chicken Corporation was bought from R. J. R. Nabisco by PepsiCo in 1986 for about $840 million. In the early twenty-first century KFC, which changed the original name to its initials in 1991 in an apparent move to distance itself from health connotations of the word *fried*, served more than 1.9 trillion pounds of chicken a year in its outlets worldwide.

Harland Sanders remained an active spokesperson for his product, appearing in television commercials and as a popular guest on television talk and variety shows. He died of leukemia in 1980 and was buried in Louisville, Kentucky, where the corporation he founded makes its headquarters. The original Sanders' Café in Corbin has been restored and placed on the National Register of Historic Places.

See also: CHICKEN AND BEEF (FOOD AND COOKING).

—Marianne Worthington, *Cumberland College*

Harland Sanders, *Life As I Have Known It Has Been Finger Lickin' Good* (1974).

Krystal Company

What became the largest privately held restaurant company in America began by offering a small, square hamburger to depression-era southerners for a nickel in Chattanooga, Tennessee.

Influenced by the rise of the White Castle hamburger chain in the Midwest a decade earlier, entrepreneurs Rodolph B. Davenport and J. Glenn Sherrill in 1932 opened a small restaurant with a clean, simple design incorporating white porcelain and stainless steel fixtures. Davenport's wife, Mary, named the business after noticing a decorative crystal ball in a neighbor's yard. A crystal ball became the company symbol, and the spelling of *crystal* was altered for trademark purposes. The small hamburger, covered in steamed chopped onions, quickly became popular, and a chain of hamburger restaurants on the Chattanooga model proliferated across the region.

Krystal was closely controlled by the founding families until the 1990s. Upon his death in 1943, Davenport was succeeded as company president by Sherrill, followed in 1961 by Davenport's son, R. B. III. In 1992 the company offered its stock to the public. Though initially successful as a public corporation, Krystal began experiencing legal and financial problems following a class-action suit by employees having to do with overtime pay. After seeking bankruptcy protection in 1995, the company was acquired in 1997 by former Coca-Cola executive Phil Sanford's Port Royal Holdings for some $108 million. It then became a privately held company again, and Sanford began rebuilding its business and reputation.

The Krystal menu expanded along with its stores over the years, but its initial specialty—that small, square hamburger—remained at the core of its success.

See also: CHATTANOOGA, TENNESSEE (URBAN APPALACHIAN EXPERIENCE).

—Ned L. Irwin, *East Tennessee State University*

K-VA-T Food Stores

One of the largest grocery chains in the Kentucky-Virginia-Tennessee region at the opening of the twenty-first century was K-VA-T Food Stores, Inc., consisting of eighty-six supermarkets primarily wearing the Food City banner. The company also had a warehousing and distribution center, Mid-Mountain Foods.

Jack C. Smith had just come home to Grundy, Virginia, after serving seven years as an officer in the U.S. Navy when he founded what eventually became K-VA-T Food Stores. He later recalled that he had not previously considered a career in retail, but after standing in a long line for forty-five minutes to be checked out by the single open cash register at a local grocery, he decided Grundy "needed a supermarket." He gave it one in 1955 with the opening of a single supermarket franchise in the Piggly Wiggly chain, which had been founded in Memphis in 1916. With the acquisition of a second store in Kentucky, Smith began operating as Williamson Piggly Wiggly. He continued expanding by purchasing a string of family-owned Piggly Wiggly stores in Kentucky and Virginia.

In 1984 Smith purchased Quality Foods, which operated nineteen Tennessee-based Food City stores, and merged the two companies into K-VA-T Food Stores. In 1986 K-VA-T bought the White Food Stores chain based in Knoxville, and during the 1980s Smith renamed all his Piggly Wiggly stores Food City. The Smith family still owns the majority of K-VA-T Food Stores. The rest of the company is owned by employees.

Headquartered in Abingdon, Virginia, the firm was ranked 44th among the nation's largest grocery chains—and 279th among the nation's top 500 privately held companies—by *Forbes* magazine in 2002.

See also: FOOD LION.

—Joel Davis, *Knoxville, Tennessee*

Latrobe Brewing Company

Best known for its Rolling Rock beer, one of the best-known specialty brands in not only its home Appalachian region but also America, Latrobe Brewing Company opened for business in 1893. Located thirty-five miles southeast of Pittsburgh in Westmoreland County, Pennsylvania, the town of Latrobe was a growing center of industry and trade. Its convenient location on the route of the Pennsylvania Railroad, combined with excellent natural resources, provided an ideal setting for a brewery.

Along with a number of other western Pennsylvania breweries of its time, Latrobe Brewing Company became a part of the Pittsburgh Brewing Company and, with the onset of prohibition in 1920, closed its doors. Thirteen years later, after repeal of the "noble experiment," Pittsburgh Brewing sold Latrobe Brewing Company to the Tito family. In 1939 the five Tito brothers brewed what they deemed a "perfect brand" and named it Rolling Rock for the mountain spring water that rolls from the Laurel Highlands into Latrobe-area reservoirs.

The marketing and research firm ACNielsen has named Rolling Rock the number two domestic specialty beer in the United States. In addition to its popularity, the Rolling Rock brand retains a bit of mystery. Ever since the first bottle was designed and produced, the label has included the brand's pledge of quality followed by the number *33*. Legions of Rolling Rock drinkers have speculated on meaning of the double digits ever since; theories include the year prohibition was repealed, the number of ingredients in the brew, and the number of words in the quality pledge.

The Tito family sold the business to Sundor Brands in 1985, and Sundor Brands then sold the brewery to John Labatt Ltd. of Canada in 1987, but the meaning of the mysterious number remained with Rolling Rock's creators. Since the 1987 sale, Latrobe Brewing has been part of Labatt USA, but the brewery remains in Latrobe and retains its western Pennsylvania cachet, which is considerable. Rolling Rock is a founding partner and the official beer of Heinz Field, home of the Pittsburgh Steelers.

See also: BREWERIES; PITTSBURGH BREWING COMPANY AND IRON CITY BEER.

—Kristin L. Abramson, *Pittsburgh, Pennsylvania*

Lew Bryson, *Pennsylvania Breweries* (1998); Donald Bull, Manfred Friedrich, and Robert Gottschalk, *American Breweries* (1984); Bill Yenne, *Beers of North America* (1986).

Limestone

Well over a century after it developed in Appalachia, the limestone industry continues quarrying operations to extract both dimension limestone, which can be carved and shaped, and crushed limestone, which is necessary for a wide variety of industrial, agricultural, and construction purposes.

Elmore and Lauderdale Counties in Alabama remain leading producers of dimension stone in Appalachia. (A third Alabama county bears the name of the rock, but it borrowed it from a local creek that flows through a bed of hard limestone.) Used for buildings, flagstone, monuments, and homes, dimension limestone is a significant product, but the crushed stone industry is much more prevalent and economically important.

Across Appalachia, limestone is quarried for crushed aggregate in at least one county of nearly every state. Pennsylvania, Georgia, Virginia, and North Carolina are among the top ten producers of crushed stone in the country, and many of their quarrying operations are located in Appalachian counties. Crushed stone is the leading nonfuel mineral commodity in West Virginia and Tennessee. Crushed aggregate has a multitude of uses, depending on its grade and size. Its physical properties make it useful in railroad beds, as sewage filter material, and in the construction of roads and highways. Crushed limestone is also a major component of portland cement (a cement that hardens underwater) and is used in a variety of home and commercial construction projects. It continues to be used as furnace flux in the iron and steel industries and as a soil sweetener for farm fields and suburban lawns.

A sedimentary rock widely distributed throughout the Appalachian region, limestone is a major natural resource formed from shells and organisms that lived in ancient seas that covered the region. Like coal and timber, limestone has been extensively exploited by large corporations and outside investors. Because so much of Appalachia—especially the southern mountain region—was geographically isolated from large mercantile centers, quarrying operations did not appear until after the Civil War, when railroads began to enter the area.

Even discounting its pure economic value, limestone is an integral part of Appalachia's physical geography and culture. The region's mountain coves were formed when streams cut their way down to limestone, forming hollows that washed out over millions of years. Limestone also preserves fossil records of the multitude of life forms that once inhabited prehistoric Appalachia. Deposits have formed such striking features as the Nantahala Gorge of North Carolina, which metamorphosed into marble, as well as numerous underground caverns winding beneath the mountain landscape. Some attribute the distinctive taste of moonshine to the quality of lime-enriched water used to make it.

Early settlers first took advantage of limestone resources by digging out small pits such as those found on Briery Mountain in Preston County, West Virginia. It was used for more than a rough building material. Calcium carbonate, the chief component of limestone, yields lime when burned, and farmers burned limestone in their own crude furnaces to produce lime for fertilizing crops. By 1900, large quarries moved into West Virginia to take advantage of its major limestone deposits, making Jefferson, Berkeley, and Monongalia Counties centers of production for lime, furnace flux, and aggregates of all types. Around the same time, limestone quarries in Henderson, Transylvania, and Madison Counties in North Carolina began production. After the coal and timber booms, New Deal programs of the 1930s led to the opening of more quarries in Appalachia to expand the area's economic growth. Extraction of Appalachia's limestone resources remains a significant contributor to the overall economy.

See also: IRON AND STEEL INDUSTRY; NONMETALLIC, NONFUEL DEPOSITS (GEOLOGY); SAND AND GRAVEL INDUSTRY.

—Selena Frye, *Louisville, Kentucky*

Ronald D Eller, *Miners, Millhands, and Mountaineers: Industrialization of the Appalachian South, 1880–1930* (1982); Paul Salstrom, *Appalachia's Path to Dependency: Rethinking a Region's Economic History, 1730–1940* (1994).

Little Debbie

Little Debbie, the best-known brand of goods manufactured by McKee Foods Corporation in southeastern Tennessee, claimed as of 2002 to be the leading line of snack cakes in the United States and the first to be sold individually wrapped in multi-pack cartons.

O. D. McKee of Collegedale, Tennessee, worked as a traveling snack cake salesman during the depression. A Seventh-Day Adventist who wanted to manufacture snack foods devoid of lard and other animal by-products, he purchased a Chattanooga cookie shop with his wife, Ruth, and her father in 1934 and converted it to a bakery. After opening and closing another plant in Charlotte, North Carolina, he founded McKee Baking Company in Chattanooga in the 1950s. The McKees moved the business from Chattanooga to Collegedale in 1957.

Little Debbie was named in honor of the McKees' four-year-old granddaughter. The line's logo was modeled after a photograph of the child wearing her play clothes and a straw hat. Ellsworth McKee and his wife, Sharon, were unaware of their daughter's impending rise in the public consciousness until they received their first carton of twelve individually wrapped Little Debbie Oatmeal Creme Pies in August 1960. When first introduced, a carton cost forty-nine cents, and within ten months 14 million Oatmeal Creme Pies had been sold. By 1964 the company had expanded its product line to include Nutty Bars, Wafer Bars, and Swiss Cake Rolls.

Headed by the McKees' sons since 1971, McKee Baking Company became McKee Foods Corporation in 1991. By 2002 the concern was manufacturing roughly seventy-five varieties of products, had sold more than 133 billion snack cakes, and was operating facilities at Stuarts Draft, Virginia, Gentry, Arkansas, and Kingman, Arizona, in addition to the plant at Collegedale.

See also: CAKES AND COOKIES (FOOD AND COOKING).

—Michael E. Birdwell, *Tennessee Technological University*

Lodge Iron Works

In 2003 Lodge Manufacturing Company in South Pittsburg, Tennessee, was the nation's only family-owned cookware company and its sole remaining manufacturer of cast-iron skillets, pots, and pans. The firm's nearly two hundred employees turned out ten thousand pieces of cast-iron cooking utensils a day, four days a week.

Lodge survived partly by celebrating the culinary arts of yesteryear and partly by adapting to times far removed from its pioneer beginnings. It partnered with Martha White Foods and Brown Stove Works in the National Cornbread Festival in South Pittsburg, sold serving ware to Ruby Tuesday and Hard Rock Café, and made the mold for the Cracker

Barrel Old Country Store signature skillets. In 2002 it introduced a slightly more expensive line of twenty-eight skillets, griddles, and Dutch ovens that were pre-seasoned for the benefit of modern kitchen keepers who knew little about cooking, let alone how to season iron cookware. The company's balance of present and past extended to Lodge's sales operation. Some of the firm's handiwork was to be found in housewares, hardware, camping, and department stores, but the entire line of more than 135 pieces was available only by mail or by visiting the Lodge outlet stores in South Pittsburg and Kodak, Tennessee.

Lodge was founded in 1896 by Joseph Lodge, a Pennsylvania native who was then forty-eight years old and had long indulged a prodigious wanderlust and appetite for foot travel. He walked many hundreds of miles across the midwestern and southern states and lived in Cuba and Peru before being lured back into Tennessee in the late 1870s by reports of a southern industrial revolution. On one of his typically lengthy "strolls," as company legend has it, he saw South Pittsburg and decided to stay. He became a superintendent for Tennessee Coal and Iron Company, and when the firm decided to relocate he stayed and built his own foundry, largely because of the iron in the area and the convenient access to river transportation. After his first facility burned and had to be rebuilt in 1909, the company incorporated under the name Lodge Manufacturing.

Cast iron has been used in cookware since the Middle Ages. Columbus is said to have brought cast-iron skillets to America and Paul Revere to have designed the venerable three-legged Dutch oven, a utensil that accompanied Lewis and Clark on their journey to the Northwest. The pig iron ingots that Lodge used at the beginning of the twenty-first century were imported from Brazil.

Ingots and scrap salvaged from previous molding processes are heated to twenty-eight hundred degrees Fahrenheit and melted, after which a computer-watched ladle apportions the fiery liquid iron into molds made of sand, clay, and water that have been fashioned into the desired pattern. After the metal has cooled considerably, the new ten-inch iron frying pan is pelted with steel BBs (like those shot by air rifles) to remove excess sand. Then it is swished for eight minutes in a stone wash drum full of Tennessee gravel to dull any sharp edges. After a subsequent rinse, the vessel—which will sell in stores for less than eleven dollars—is dipped in a food-grade wax and sent to packaging. The new pre-seasoned line of Dutch ovens, skillets, and griddles called Lodge Logic are also coated with vegetable oil and then heated to high temperatures to take on a deep black appearance.

Two of Lodge's great-grandsons—Bob Kellermann, chief executive officer, and Henry Lodge, president—had charge of the company's operations in 2003. Their last two American competitors (which included Griswold, an Appalachian company in Erie, Pennsylvania) closed their doors years ago, and now the Tennessee firm must compete with low-end goods from China and more expensive products from France. The backbone of Lodge's support, Kellermann has said, comes from southern, Amish, Mormon, and southwestern cooks. But the company's line of products has lengthened considerably from Joseph Lodge's day, when Lodge customers mostly wanted washing pots, rendering kettles, coal grates, tea kettles, and "sad" irons, nonelectrified appliances that had to be heated before being used to press clothes. Lodge's collection of historic memorabilia includes a letter from Booker T. Washington at Tuskegee Institute requesting sad irons for the school's laundry. The company also makes specialty pans in which breads can be cooked in the shapes of panfish or characters from Walt Disney and *Winnie-the-Pooh.*

In 1996, two years after being presented a Tennessee Governor's Award for Excellence in Hazardous Waste Management for switching from coke-fired to electric smelting, Lodge launched the most extensive upgrade in its history, investing six million dollars. With annual revenues reported at more than three times that, the company continued looking for new market possibilities, and it had to. Its products, as the management notes, never wear out.

See also: CAST-IRON COOKWARE (FOOD AND COOKING); IRON AND STEEL INDUSTRY.

—Jack Hurst, *Lancaster, Tennessee*

Nancy Bearden Henderson, "Iron Clad: The Fourth-Generation, Family-Owned Factory in South Pittsburg Is the Nation's Leading Maker of Cast-Iron Cookware," *Chattanooga Magazine* (Summer 1999); Walter Nicholls, "The All-American Pan," *Washington Post* (April 2, 2003).

Lumber Industry

Timber, one of Appalachia's most obviously rich natural resources since the first European ventured into the region's vast virgin forests, remained important at the end of the twentieth century. Lumber and wood-products industries were still providing jobs for thousands in Appalachian states. In West Virginia, the value of the wood industry was estimated at $500 million, with total employment at more than 12,000 people. In Tennessee, the comparative figures were $4 billion and about 50,000 jobs and in Kentucky, $1.8 billion and 26,000. After suffering a prolonged slowdown during the mid-1900s, timbering in the area again appeared to be on a longterm upswing, a trend that concerned some environmentalists even as it swelled state economies. During the 1980s, after focusing on the upper West Coast for decades, America's seven largest manufacturers of lumber and plywood decreased their operations in the Northwest by

34 percent while adding capacity in the South by well above 100 percent. It was predicted that lumbering jobs were safe for the short term, since only limits on old-growth timber cutting would cause the United States to increase overseas wood imports.

Appalachia's most important timber continues to be the hardwoods found throughout the southern reaches of the region. In 1991, in southern Appalachia alone, 12.3 million board feet of hardwood lumber were harvested. Part of the industry resurgence in the region in the 1980s was attributable to a rise in the manufacturing of particleboard, a relatively inexpensive lumber made from hardwood chips. The best timber was used in furniture manufacturing, and the hub of that industry remained in or near western North Carolina.

The expansion of the Appalachian timber industry from the local to regional and national levels was pioneered in the early 1900s by lumber entrepreneurs such as John C. Paty of Piney Flats, Tennessee. Paty's Piney Flats Lumber Company at its height operated seven lumber and building material centers in Tennessee and southwest Virginia. Its headquarters, as well as a component manufacturing and millwork assembly facility, were based in Piney Flats. An even more successful Appalachian lumber pioneer was William McClellan Ritter, who headquartered his W. M. Ritter Lumber Company in Welch, West Virginia, in the late 1890s before moving on to Columbus, Ohio. The Ritter company acquired several other lumber operations during its considerable history and became at one time the largest producer of hardwood timber in the United States. Then in 1960 it was acquired by Georgia-Pacific Corporation in a pattern that became familiar throughout the industry, with smaller lumbering firms selling out to larger, more diversified wood-products companies.

Georgia-Pacific, founded just outside the technical boundary lines of Appalachia, is perhaps the quintessential colossus among timbering enterprises rooted in the Appalachian area. Founded by Owen R. Cheatham in 1927 in Augusta, Georgia, the wholesaler was initially known as Georgia Hardwood Lumber Company. By 1938 Cheatham's firm was operating five southern sawmills, and during World War II it became the largest supplier of lumber to the U.S. armed forces. In 1947 it bought a West Coast plywood plant in Bellingham, Washington, and saw sales pass $24 million. The next year it changed its name to Georgia-Pacific and the year after was listed on the New York Stock Exchange. When it bought W. M. Ritter Lumber Company in 1960, the purchase included all of Ritter's timber, oil, coal, and other mineral rights. That brought Georgia-Pacific's total timberland ownership to a million acres. In 2000 the once obscure Georgia wholesaler acquired the Fort James Corporation and its Brawny, Quilted Northern, and Dixie brands to become the world's leading maker of tissue products. By then its holdings spanned the continent from Florida to Washington State.

Beginning in the 1980s the demand for choice lumber in Taiwan, Japan, and Europe was high. Propelling this market were environmental concerns, predominantly the impact that continued harvesting of tropical woods was having on Southeast Asian forests. White oak, ash, hard maple, and basswood grew in popularity abroad. By 1991 Appalachian companies were exporting hardwood to more than sixty nations, most notably Japan, Canada, and Germany. Appalachian hardwood filled the demand for furniture in Singapore, Germany, and elsewhere.

A study sponsored by the Appalachian Regional Commission showed that in 1987 about 135 firms of the 4,810 in the region exported $5,925,000 worth of lumber and related products such as veneered paneling and plywood. These firms offered, on the whole, more wages and benefits to their workers and had greater capital outlay than the non-exporting lumber companies. In comparison, a study of southern Appalachian exports showed that hardwood exports alone more than tripled from 1977 to 1991. Much of the increase in the industry's late-twentieth-century income generation and employment was directly attributed to the opening of Appalachian-area facilities in the early 1990s by Georgia-Pacific and such other large firms as Parson and Whittemore and MacMillan. In these corporate mills, billions of board feet of hardwoods were processed each year to make such items as beams, furniture, and casket bottoms. This represented a fundamental shift in industry practices to central processing facilities operated by large corporations—and away from the mountain communities' traditional mom-and-pop mills.

Since the arrival of Europeans in the United States, land has had to be cleared and the resultant lumber has been needed, in turn, to provide basic necessities. Chestnut and pine were among the woods that settlers found to their liking to build houses, erect fencing, and fashion home furnishings. Lumber was also required for commercial enterprises such as shipbuilding and railroad construction. The demand for lumber has rarely been slaked, as continual immigration and population growth have required ongoing construction.

The woodlot was a central part of early Appalachian life. Settlers initially cut timber to clear fields and construct life's necessities. The perceptive farmer typically set aside a plot of timberland and managed it in such a way that his family could continue to use it indefinitely. Forests were also used to graze livestock. Sawmills were typically located in the woods, as were related operations such as turpentine distilleries. The early timber industry had its epicenter in the Carolinas.

The lumber industry in Kentucky was started well before the Civil War and was centered in Frankfort. Stands of timber in the Kentucky River Valley included black walnut, wild cherry, river-bottom tulip, maple, and buckeye, which were used beginning in the 1830s. These were not exhausted until the end of the Civil War, and even after the war much of Appalachia was still covered with old-growth forest.

At that time self-sustaining southern farmers opted to log for much-needed extra income. Timber was cut selectively, and local mills, most located along major water tributaries, processed the wood. Transportation was by wagon, or else the felled trees were conveyed to mills by river. Reforestation naturally occurred with a method called forest fallowing, which allowed cleared fields time to grow back. The Appalachian industry eventually moved from the Carolinas into Georgia and grew more prominent on the national scene.

By the late 1880s the nation needed a new lumber source as supplies in the Northeast and Great Lakes regions dwindled. Corporate interests shifted their focus to Appalachia. Rampant railroad construction further fueled demand as main lines linked the eastern seaboard with the Midwest and beyond. Virgin forest was cleared to make way for the tracks and to build them. Smaller, independent railroads were timber hungry as well. Track mileage in West Virginia alone doubled every decade between the 1880s and 1917, making lumbering particularly big business in the state's Tucker, Randolph, and Pocahontas Counties. Lumber also became important in the Tellico Plains area in Tennessee.

Lumber operations changed significantly between 1890 and 1920, transformed by corporate interests and mechanization. To accommodate exponential demand, corporations purchased huge sections of the region's forests. People who had traditionally farmed the land and used the woods judiciously were uprooted as these companies—often from outside the state or region—sought to establish large parcels of land on which to open mills near supposedly inexhaustible lumber sources. Lumber companies had to become more efficient to meet demand, and in the mid-1880s railroads started carrying heavy equipment into remote forests to help with the ramped-up harvesting. The new machinery included rail equipment modified specifically for logging—the steam log loader, the steam skidder, and the Shay locomotive.

New towns anchored by sawmills grew from the furiously growing nation's voracious appetite for lumber. Timber towns became a source of new jobs, if only for relatively short periods. Thousands of small mills were located throughout Appalachia. Larger mills spawned larger towns to support the mill workers and the timber industry, but they also became important commercial centers in their own right. Peak lumber production in the Appalachians occurred soon after the turn of the century, the exact time varying somewhat from state to state. Historians estimated that West Virginia lumbering peaked in 1909, while in Kentucky 1907 was a record production year.

One of the most valuable Appalachian timber species was the American chestnut, which accounted for an estimated one in four trees in the region. The chestnut had been used in every manner of construction of buildings—exteriors, interiors, and furnishings. Its nuts were roasted and used in confections. Its bark was used in curing leather. So important was the tannin from chestnut that some major southern timber companies reportedly sought financial interests in leather companies because they could assure those companies a constant supply of the essential chemical. Once the tannin was extracted, the pulp was used in paper.

Because it could be grown in just about every soil type and had immense value to various industries, the chestnut remained the most economically important tree in the region until a fungus causing chestnut blight entered the United States in 1904. This killed the trees throughout the nation. Scientists in Pennsylvania and North Carolina attempted to control the blight by cutting isolation strips to divide stands of the trees, but containment of the disease was futile as the fungus continued to be spread by migrating birds. But the trees died slowly, borer infestations further decreasing the value of the timber. Lumber operations offered "sound wormy chestnut" for use in homes in decorative items such as picture frames. Lumber companies continued to slowly harvest the blighted stands well into the 1940s.

Another Appalachian tree highly prized for its hardwood is the American black walnut. It is said to grow best in Appalachian coves and is typically grown on lands once used as pasture. This tree and its products once had a host of uses, from nuts to gunpowder, but its greatest value has been as a wood used in crafting furniture and musical instruments. It often was exported to Europe and reportedly has been a favorite tree of poachers, for good reason. Reports show that a thousand board feet of black walnut lumber once sold for $25,000.

The regional and national economy changed drastically after World War I. Lumber and other industries attracted people who much preferred a steady wage to living from crop to crop, season to season. In some areas of Appalachia, agricultural land was abandoned by farmers tired of toiling with corn, tobacco, and other crops. Left fallow, the land reverted to forest, and some farmers eventually replanted with a new crop: stands of loblolly pine.

Forest management emerged as a scientific discipline during this era. The eastern white pine inspired some of the first studies in forestry in the Appalachian region. Gifford Pinchot, often called the father of American forestry, managed and studied a plantation of this species on the Biltmore Estate in Asheville, North Carolina, beginning in the 1890s. Meanwhile, frenzied clear-cutting by the lumber industry's capitalists began to take a toll throughout Appalachia. The boom resulted in fires, erosion, habitat destruction, pollution from sawmills and pulp mills, flooding and drought, and problems along navigable waterways. Some timber supplies only lasted until the boom, but stands in more remote regions, including some counties in Kentucky, were able to sustain the lumber industry until the 1930s. After the boom, much young hardwood lumber was of poor quality as a result of such logging practices as using fire to clear land.

In the latter twentieth century, numerous groups were created out of interest in timber production and related issues. These include private organizations as well as various special interest groups and quasi-governmental groups such as the Appalachian Regional Commission; the Mountain Association for Community Economic Development, concerned with eastern Kentucky timber practices; and the Appalachian Export Center for Hardwoods, developed to increase Appalachian hardwood exports.

In 1991 about twice as much hardwood was being grown throughout the region as was being cut, but environmental concerns about logging's regional impact were being voiced throughout the southeastern United States. Erosion and pollution resulting from corporate firms' clear-cutting of mountains were frequently equated by local residents with the ecological damage of strip mining by corporate coal.

The challenge for governmental bodies was and continues to be judiciously managing the natural resources throughout the region to prevent depletion and assure continued employment. Maintaining jobs is a priority, and some state governments court lumber corporations with tax credits. One company opening a mill in Hazard, Kentucky, was given $103 million in tax credits for a period of fifteen years. This spurred smaller family-run operations to explore other lumber-related processing such as kiln drying. Forestry officials have seemed unconcerned with the impact that financial incentives to corporations might have on smaller operations, according to some reports, but environmentalists contend that continued demand could potentially increase "renegade logging." This situation could be especially harmful in states with weak logging regulations, and many Appalachian states have either weak regulations or no laws at all governing timber-harvesting practices. This is particularly true in Kentucky, where there is little regulation, where 90 percent of the forests are in private ownership, and where more than a billion board feet are produced annually.

In the mid-1990s there was more interest in sustainable development and entrepreneurship in the region. Within wood manufacturing, small companies were created for various purposes. Some harvested local timber and lower-grade wood species for use as flooring, while others worked to earmark high-quality lumber for use by local craftsmen. Solar drying-kiln technology was explored in southwestern Virginia and eastern Tennessee. But nature continued to conspire against the lumber industry. Infestations of insects such as the southern pine beetle occurred every three decades or so and lasted about five years. After the 1999 outbreak the U.S. Army Corps of Engineers made plans to replenish pine forests with hardwoods, including oak and walnut.

National population increases undoubtedly will play a key role in timber's future. As Appalachian land, particularly that owned by private individuals, is cleared and developed for other uses, fewer timber stands will be available for harvest, and lumber production will suffer. Sustaining the industry well into the twenty-first century by balancing nature and progress is on a par with mining as an important political and economic concern.

See also: HARRIS-TARKETT CORPORATION; RAILROADS (TRANSPORTATION); TIMBER AND LUMBER WORKERS (LABOR).

—Linda Dailey Paulson, *Ventura, California*

Mary Beth Pudup, Dwight B. Billings, and Altina L. Waller, eds., *Appalachia in the Making: The Mountain South in the Nineteenth Century* (1995); U.S. Department of Agriculture, Foreign Agriculture Service, "Appalachia Aims to Be Apex of Rising Hardwood Exports," *AgExporter* (August 1991); Laurence C. Walker, *Forests: A Naturalist's Guide to Trees and Forest Ecology* (1990).

Marble Industry

Before the rise of the Appalachian Mountains, eastern North America lay beneath a shallow sea where marine organisms, mud, and layers of silt were gradually transformed into limestone. As the Appalachians formed, subterranean heat altered the limestone, resulting in the faint crystalline and translucent aspects of marble.

Marble quarrying was done to a significant degree in Appalachia by the late nineteenth century, and there are signs that it occurred earlier on a very small scale. Appalachian settlers first used native marble to make gravestones. As the United States began to grow and prosper, the country required government buildings, statues, historical monuments, banks, train stations, and grand hotels. Marble was expensive to ship, and the young nation turned to domestic supplies as they were discovered.

Human, horse, and mule power first extracted the stone from the earth. By the late nineteenth century, marble quarries were industrialized, having begun to utilize steam-powered shovels, derricks, and tractors. The greatest concentration of marble extraction took place in northeastern and eastern Tennessee, with less extensive quarries in Alabama and Georgia and extremely small operations in the other Appalachian states.

In Tennessee, Blount County and Hawkins County were early centers of marble production. The industry consolidated in Knoxville by the 1900s, taking advantage of rail lines and Tennessee River water transport for this heavy, durable material. In fact, Knoxville was known as the Marble City in the nineteenth century for its prominence in the industry. Several marble barons made their homes there and are buried beneath fine examples of their product.

The marble of Alabama and Georgia is of the highest quality. In Georgia, marble is quarried near Tate in Pickens County. Alabama marble is commercially exploited in Sylacauga in Talladega County. Reflecting a change in demand, most marble from Alabama is now ground and used for agricultural or industrial purposes. Sylacauga marble, however, is well suited to architectural, statuary, or monument work.

The marble industry fit into the historical pattern of Appalachia as a supplier of primary products for more industrialized economies outside the region. Most marble was exported in raw form. Skilled artisans, stonecutters, sculptors, and architects who purchased and used the marble generally resided outside Appalachia. The Appalachian industry usually employed unskilled or semiskilled labor. The industry also attracted a number of Italian immigrants, heirs to the great marble tradition of the Carrara region of their native country, who became sculptors, stonecutters, and marble entrepreneurs.

Marble is still quarried in Appalachia today, although perhaps the greatest American employment of the stone was in connection with the Neoclassical style that predominated in the nation from the nineteenth to the mid-twentieth century. Innumerable large business and government buildings throughout the southern, eastern, and midwestern United States are made in part with Appalachian marble. It graces the Tennessee State Capitol in Nashville and, among many other famous buildings, Grand Central Station in New York, the New York Stock Exchange, and, in Washington, D.C., the U.S. Capitol, the National Art Gallery, the U.S. Supreme Court, and the Lincoln Memorial.

See also: LIMESTONE; NONMETALLIC, NONFUEL DEPOSITS (GEOLOGY); TECTONICS (GEOLOGY).

—Charles Allan, *East Tennessee State University*

Ed Dodd, "A Brief History of the Marble Industry in Sylacauga," *Alabama Heritage* (Spring 1991); Stuart Maher and Joe P. Walters, *The Marble Industry of Tennessee* (1960); James M. Safford and J. B. Killebrew, *The Elementary Geology of Tennessee* (1876).

Marshall Space Flight Center

From its establishment by the National Aeronautics and Space Administration (NASA) in 1960 into the twenty-first century, George C. Marshall Space Flight Center at Huntsville, Alabama, has played a leading role in American exploration of the "new frontier" that opened during the Cold War with the Soviet Union. Saturn rockets developed at the center launched Apollo astronauts on six successful expeditions to the moon, and engines designed under the management of Marshall engineers powered NASA space shuttles. The Hubble Space Telescope, developed under the center's direction, opened a new era of astronomy, and Marshall-designed components formed a major portion of the International Space Station. In its fifth decade, Marshall remained NASA's primary center for development of new space transportation and propulsion systems.

Created two years after the formation of NASA, the center was named for General George C. Marshall, a Uniontown, Pennsylvania, native who served as World War II army chief of staff and postwar secretary of state and secretary of defense. The new center's technical leadership was heavily drawn from German-born engineers and scientists working for the U.S. Army at Huntsville's Redstone Arsenal who were reassigned to the civilian space agency. Sharing its

A Saturn V launch vehicle boosts Apollo 11 on its way to the Moon, Kennedy Space Center, Florida, 1969. Developed at the Marshall Space Flight Center in Huntsville, Alabama, the Saturn V sent U.S. astronauts on six successful moon expeditions. The Marshall Center also designed and tested propulsion systems for the space shuttle and played a leading role in designing the International Space Station.

forty-thousand-acre reservation with the army, Marshall was activated on July 1, 1960, and was dedicated by President Dwight D. Eisenhower on September 8 of that year.

The German rocket team that formed the nucleus of the new center, led by Wernher von Braun, had developed Nazi Germany's feared V-2 rocket late in World War II, as well as the V-1 "buzz bomb" earlier used to terrorize London. At war's end, these experts were objects of an army operation to capture and secretly bring German scientists to the United States. At White Sands Proving Ground in New Mexico, near Fort Bliss, Texas, they carried out guided missile research using captured V-2s.

In 1950 more than one hundred of the German scientists and engineers were transferred to Redstone Arsenal, which had been put into mothballs after producing artillery shells for the war. Reopened, Redstone took the lead in the army's frenetic effort to develop guided missiles.

Best known of the team's new weapons were a new intermediate-range ballistic missile, the Redstone, and later the more powerful Jupiter. On January 31, 1958, the von Braun team used a modified Redstone to launch Explorer I, the United States' first satellite. On May 5, 1961, another Redstone sent astronaut Alan B. Shepard to an altitude of 115.7 miles and a speed of more than 5,000 miles per hour, setting the stage for the first U.S. orbital space flights. But both Explorer I and the Shepard flight only echoed more impressive achievements by the Soviet Union. Nearly four months before Explorer I, the Soviets had launched Sputnik I, the world's first artificial satellite, and on April 12, 1961, three weeks before Shepard's brief flight to the fringe of space, cosmonaut Yuri Gagarin had orbited the earth. In a bid to regain the image of technical supremacy, President John F. Kennedy set a U.S. objective of a manned landing on the moon before 1970. With that goal established, the new Marshall Center was given the assignment of developing a rocket to carry out the mission.

Von Braun was by then a celebrity and considered a visionary by many, in part because of a series of articles he had written in the early 1950s for *Collier's* magazine forecasting landings on the moon and the development of a huge orbiting space station. Before Sputnik, he lobbied vigorously for the army to launch a satellite.

Along with the army's continued work on both offensive and defensive missiles, Marshall Space Flight Center's research and development brought Huntsville and its environs a booming economy. In 1950, when the German team arrived, Huntsville was a community of 16,000. By the time Apollo 11 astronauts Neil Armstrong and Edwin "Buzz" Aldrin made the first moon landing in July 1969, the population had soared to 140,000. The town that once had labeled itself the "watercress capital" now promoted itself as "Rocket City" and even the "Space Capital of the Universe."

Its evolution into a high-technology center was not entirely accidental. It emerged as a favorable site for development of huge booster rockets for space travel for the same reason that led the army to establish Redstone Arsenal early in 1941. The Tennessee Valley Authority provided cheap electric power, and the Tennessee River was a perfect transportation artery. The first Saturn boosters, fabricated in shops at Marshall, were barged down the Tennessee River to the Ohio, the Mississippi, and eventually to the launch site at Cape Canaveral, Florida.

German families who moved to Huntsville from Fort Bliss found the Appalachian foothills reminiscent of their homeland. Many settled in a subdivision at the summit of Monte Sano Mountain, the highest point in the area.

See also: AEROSPACE INDUSTRY; ARNOLD ENGINEERING DEVELOPMENT CENTER.

—Rudy Abramson, *Reston, Virginia*

Erik Bergaust, *Wernher von Braun* (1976); Frederick I. Ordway III and Mitchell R. Sharpe, *The Rocket Team* (1979); Loyd S. Swenson Jr., James M. Grimwood, and Charles C. Alexander, *This New Ocean: A History of Project Mercury* (1966).

Marsh Stogies

The oldest manufacturing enterprise in Wheeling, West Virginia, had declined from a high of six hundred employees in the 1940s to approximately fifty in 2003, but for more than a century its product—a particularly long, thin, inexpensive cigar—was an important commodity and helped to define the community's identity.

In 1840 Wheeling businessman Mifflin M. Marsh began rolling stogies, cigars of a style said to have been favored by the drivers of Conestoga wagons traveling west on the National Road. First producing them at his home, Marsh sold them to crews and passengers of steamboats traveling the Ohio River as well as to the Conestoga drivers. These mobile consumers soon took them all over the nation, and other local producers sprang up. Wheeling companies offered their product at half the price of the Boston cheroot, and easy access to the tobacco plantations of Kentucky and Ohio and high demand from a mobile customer base allowed Wheeling to become the nation's leader in the inexpensive cigar business. By the end of the nineteenth century, there were more than one hundred Wheeling cigar companies producing up to 30 million stogies a year. Testament to the product's popularity is the fact that in the 1920s the city's Middle Atlantic League baseball team was known as the Wheeling Stogies.

In 2001 Mifflin Marsh's company, M. Marsh and Son, sold all the Marsh Wheeling brands to National Cigar Corporation of Frankfort, Indiana.

See also: NATIONAL ROAD (SETTLEMENT AND MIGRATION); WHEELING, WEST VIRGINIA (URBAN APPALACHIAN EXPERIENCE).

—Hugh Davis, *University of Tennessee*

Martha White Foods

In 1899 Richard Lindsey founded the Royal Flour Mill in Nashville, Tennessee, and named his finest grade of flour for his three-year-old daughter, Martha White Lindsey. When Cohen E. Williams purchased Lindsey's mill in 1941, he changed the name of the company to that of its best-selling flour.

During the 1940s the Martha White Company began its advertising relationship with country and bluegrass music with a radio program called *Martha White Biscuit and Cornbread Time*. Airing at 5:45 a.m. on WSM in Nashville, it featured such artists as Marty Robbins, Chet Atkins, the Carter Family, and Lester Flatt and Earl Scruggs. After being hired by the company in 1953 to barnstorm the South promoting its products, Flatt and Scruggs became known as the "World's Greatest Flour Peddlers." Other Martha White spokespeople included Grandpa Jones and Tennessee Ernie Ford.

Martha White introduced the slogan *Goodness Gracious, It's Good* in 1945. In 1948, on an advertising budget of twenty-five dollars per week, Martha White first sponsored a segment of the *Grand Ole Opry*. Since then, the company has become the *Opry*'s longest-running continuous sponsor, having subsidized more than twenty-five hundred broadcasts of its Saturday-night radio show. In the 1950s Hot Rize, the company's "secret ingredient," established Martha White as a leading product in home baking, and in the early 1960s the company introduced Bix Mix, which allowed homemakers to create "the world's best biscuits" by just adding water. At the opening of the twenty-first century, Martha White continued offering "easy-to-bake foods with down home flavor."

See also: FLATT AND SCRUGGS (MUSIC); *GRAND OLE OPRY* (MEDIA).

—Hugh Davis, *University of Tennessee*

Massey Energy Company

One of the largest coal-mining companies in the United States in the early twenty-first century, Massey Energy operates in West Virginia, eastern Kentucky, and southwestern Virginia, providing fuel for electrical utilities whose power plants require low-sulfur coal to comply with federal clean-air regulations. In the 1990s, the company became West Virginia's biggest coal operator, increasing its production from 11 million tons in 1988 to almost 44 million tons in 2002. It also became one of the Appalachian region's most controversial industrial enterprises, the object of major environmental lawsuits and regulatory actions and the target of bitter animosity from environmental activists and organized labor.

During the 1980s, while it was a subsidiary of the California-based Fluor Corporation, Massey began aggressively to acquire deposits of low-sulfur and metallurgical coal in central Appalachia, purchasing mines from competing coal companies such as Consol, Island Creek, Pittston, and Peabody, as well as Bethlehem Steel. Its acquisition strategy anticipated increasing value for low-sulfur coal as a result of stricter federal clean-air regulations. It also took advantage of bargain prices for metallurgical coal as the U.S. steel industry declined in the face of foreign competition. At the same time it expanded, Massey moved to drive down its production costs. Pulling out of the Bituminous Coal Operators' Association and industry-wide labor negotiations, the company negotiated separately with workers at its individual subsidiaries. In the Coal River Valley of West Virginia, the United Mine Workers of America went on strike against the company, and violence ensued. After months of confrontation, Massey succeeded in converting nearly all of its subsidiaries into nonunion operations. On its marginal coal lands, it turned mining operations over to contractors, and critics charged that it used the tactic to avoid paying millions of dollars into the West Virginia Workers' Compensation Fund.

Such policies generated enduring hostility in communities near Massey operations as its subsidiaries expanded, imported workers, continued mine mechanization, and battled environmental activists over issues such as waste storage, overweight trucks, and dust. In October 2000, a seventy-two-acre coal-waste reservoir belonging to Martin County Coal Company, a Massey subsidiary in eastern Kentucky, ruptured and sent more than 250 million gallons of black sludge into two creeks flowing into the Tug Fork of the Big Sandy River, killing fish and plants for thirty-six miles and fouling water supplies for sixty miles downstream.

Massey Energy originated in 1916 as a coal brokerage firm in Richmond, Virginia, and until 1992 it was headed by descendants of its founder, A. T. Massey. A. T. Massey Coal Company did not begin mining operations until 1945, operating primarily in West Virginia. In 1974 it was acquired by a partnership of St. Joe Minerals and Royal Dutch Shell Corporation. The partnership was subsequently taken over by Fluor Corporation, a giant engineering and construction conglomerate. In 1987 A. T. Massey was reorganized as Fluor's wholly owned coal-mining subsidiary. E. Morgan Massey, the last member of the founding family to lead the company, retired in 1992 and was succeeded by Donald Blankenship, a West Virginian, who became the lightning rod for company critics.

Although Massey contributed significantly to Fluor's operating profits, mining metallurgical coal for the steel industry as well as steam coal for utilities, it was spun off as a separate, publicly traded corporation and renamed Massey Energy Company in November 2000. The reorganization was in process when the disastrous break occurred at the Martin County Coal Company waste impoundment near Inez, Kentucky.

A proxy statement filed with the Securities and Exchange Commission in early 2002 showed that Massey and its insurance companies had spent $41.5 million to clean up the mess. By 2003, the figure had risen to $58 million. The company also faced citizen lawsuits and agreed to pay a number of fines and cleanup bills, including $3.25 million from Kentucky, $600,000 from West Virginia, and $110,000 from the federal Mine Safety and Health Administration.

Other environmental problems dogged the firm before and after the Martin County episode. In 2001 Massey workers accidentally pumped thirty thousand gallons of sludge into a creek near Madison, West Virginia. In 2002 there were significant spills in Pike County, Kentucky, and Mingo County, West Virginia. In February 2003 a jury ordered Massey subsidiary Elk Run Company to pay $473,000 to citizens of Sylvester, West Virginia, for damages from dust spread over the community from a nearby coal preparation plant. In 2000 and 2001, West Virginia officials cited Massey operations for 501 violations of state regulations.

While oil and steel companies and conglomerates such as Fluor held large stakes in coal mining at times during the late twentieth century, Massey's largest stockholders are investment firms. Fidelity Management and Research Corporation, Merrill Lynch and Company, Wellington Management Company, and Boston Company owned about one-third of all the outstanding shares of Massey stock in 2002. Combined, institutional investors owned 90 percent of the company.

Included in Massey's 2.2 billion tons of coal reserves are the majority of U.S. deposits of metallurgical coal, used to create coke for steelmaking operations. While Massey is a major supplier of metallurgical coal, including exports to Europe and South America, its chief product is steam coal, most of it sold to about 125 utilities and industrial concerns in the eastern United States.

In 2003 Massey employed more than four thousand workers at twenty-nine underground mines, fourteen surface mines, nineteen processing and shipping centers, and other facilities in eastern Kentucky, southwestern Virginia, and West Virginia. Its corporate headquarters remained in Richmond, Virginia.

See also: BITUMINOUS COAL INDUSTRY; COAL MINING (ENVIRONMENT); COAL SLURRY IMPOUNDMENTS (ENVIRONMENT).

—Rudy Abramson, *Reston, Virginia*

Mike Boyer, "Massey Coal Co. Has Had Tumultuous Past," *Cincinnati Enquirer* (October 22, 2000); Bernard Condon, "Not King Coal," *Forbes* (May 26, 2003); Paul J. Nyden, "Massey Coal Keeps Growing, Report Shows," *Charleston Gazette* (March 3, 2002); U.S. Department of Energy, Energy Information Administration, *The Changing Structure of the U.S. Coal Industry: An Update* (July 1993).

Mellon, Andrew

(1855–1937) Statesman, financier, and art collector.

Pittsburgh native Andrew William Mellon became one of the leading financiers, statesmen, and art collectors of his day, amassing a two-billion-dollar fortune that rivaled any in America. Supplying capital to some of his era's most important entrepreneurs, he financed a significant portion of the growth of Appalachia and America.

Son of Thomas and Sarah Negley Mellon, he left college just short of graduation to make money. He started his career by borrowing from his banker father to establish a lumber business—which he sold at considerable profit just before a recession. The ability to foresee opportunity before others remained one of his most remarkable business traits. In 1874 he began working in the family bank in Pittsburgh. Soon recognized as the family business genius, he took over the institution's management in 1882.

Mellon quickly grasped the importance that industry held for both the country's prosperity and his own. He began supplying loans to men such as Andrew Carnegie and Henry Clay Frick as they developed iron and steel operations, and the bank's prosperity grew with theirs. From Frick, he acquired an interest in art collecting, and his judgment of art proved to be as astute as his knack for spotting new enterprises for investment. His investment in Charles Martin Hall's patent for the electrolytic manufacture of aluminum resulted in the Aluminum Company of America (Alcoa), of which Mellon became the principal stockholder. Similar support to other inventors and entrepreneurs led to the formation of Mellon-controlled enterprises such as the Carborundum Company, Koppers Company, Pittsburgh Plate Glass, and Gulf Oil Corporation. At one time he headed at least sixty major corporations. Mellon Bank became an important multinational entity through which Mellon was able to form several major American corporations outside the financial control of New York. This helped transform Pittsburgh into an industrial and monetary center and Mellon into one of the leading business figures of his era.

Mellon's appointment as U.S. secretary of the treasury in 1921 began the longest tenure of anyone in that position, as he served Presidents Warren Harding, Calvin Coolidge, and Herbert Hoover. He used the office to stimulate the nation's economy following the post–World War I recession through a mixture of tax reductions and reduction of the national debt. He also spearheaded efforts to settle war debts owed the United States by other countries. His policies led to the economic boom times of the 1920s, but they also are blamed for creating a climate of speculation and inflation that led to the 1929 stock market crash and the onset of the Great Depression. Appointed United States ambassador to Great Britain in 1932, Mellon served only until 1933.

Following retirement from government, Mellon devoted his last years to the far-flung family businesses and to his art acquisitions. The paintings and sculptures, gathered over many years, formed one of the world's great art collections when it was donated to the nation in 1937, becoming the core of the newly established National Gallery of Art. He also supplied the funds to construct the gallery's original building in Washington, D.C. This gift was Mellon's last great achievement. He died on August 26, 1937, and was buried in Allegheny Cemetery in Pittsburgh. Mellon married Nora McMullen and had two children, Ailsa and Paul.

See also: CARNEGIE, ANDREW; FRICK, HENRY CLAY; PITTSBURGH, PENNSYLVANIA (URBAN APPALACHIAN EXPERIENCE).

—Ned L. Irwin, *East Tennessee State University*

Burton Hersh, *The Mellon Family: A Fortune in History* (1978); Harvey O'Connor, *Mellon's Millions* (1933).

Mica Industry

Appalachia's mica industry has been small and erratic, but the United States is the world's largest producer and consumer of one of the mineral's two types, and North Carolina produces half of that. The two commercial varieties are sheet mica and scrap and flake mica, the latter produced in the United States. It is ground and used as an extender in wallboard joint cement, paints, and plastics. It is also used as a lubricant, as an ingredient in well-drilling muds, toothpaste, and cosmetics, and for other purposes. Sheet mica, which also can be produced synthetically, has long been used in the electronics and electrical industries and, although produced in the United States in the late nineteenth century, was imported during most of the twentieth—mostly from India, where high-quality deposits were discovered in 1885.

Employment in the U.S. industry has fluctuated wildly with demand. It has risen sharply in wartime, when sheet mica's use in sophisticated electronic equipment has been particularly important. In the early 1980s, only about four hundred people had jobs in the U.S. flake mica business. About 50 percent of flake mica came from North Carolina in 2002, with the rest being produced by Arizona, Georgia, New Mexico, South Carolina, and South Dakota.

Mica is formed when silica and aluminum melt into magma deep in the earth. This hot liquid rises up to the surface, cools, and then solidifies into mineral deposits that appear as small veins of varying size and quality. Far more than coal mining, mica extraction relies upon skilled labor, and the industry played a key role in creating a burgeoning wage economy while attracting northern capital to western North Carolina. Cyclical demand for mica also created difficult labor issues and doomed efforts to unionize the industry.

The Appalachian mica industry dates back to the aftermath of the Civil War. Merchants Elisha Clapp and John R. Heap of Knoxville, Tennessee, who dealt in stoves, saw a shipment of mica that had been collected in western North Carolina and sent to Knoxville by a prominent geology enthusiast. Clapp and Heap were familiar with mica's use in oven windows because of its heat-resistant properties, and they soon gave up their stove business for prospecting. By 1882, four hundred thousand pounds of the mineral had been mined in western North Carolina, most of it from lands Clapp and Heap acquired. The man whose Knoxville shipment had prompted them to get into the business in the first place, Congressman Thomas Lanier Clingman, had estimated that western North Carolina's mica deposits stretched across 150 miles to a depth of one thousand feet.

Demand for mica rose during World War I and World War II, as well as during the Korean and Vietnam conflicts, and during and after World War II the federal government subsidized domestic mica production and for a while bought it as a strategic mineral. With the end of all such programs in 1962, coupled with concurrent rising labor costs, Appalachian mica was almost entirely replaced by mica imported from India. U.S. consumption of Indian sheet mica, mostly driven by its use in spacers and insulators in vacuum tubes in the electronics industry, dropped precipitously between 1953 and 1983 (from 14.7 million pounds to 2.2 million pounds) because of the rapid development of solid-state electronics technology.

Environmental regulation in the late twentieth century increased the cost of mica pit mining, driving many operations out of business. Mica processing nevertheless continued in Appalachia, although on a much smaller scale than in years past.

See also: FELDSPAR INDUSTRY.

—Todd L. Cherry, *Appalachian State University*, and Nicholas G. Rupp, *East Carolina University*

Mary K. Anglin, *Women, Power, and Dissent in the Hills of Carolina* (2002); Lawrence L. Davis, "Mica," in *Mineral Facts and Problems*, U.S. Bureau of Mines Bulletin 675 (1985).

Mills

Mills played an important role in the lives of people in eighteenth- and nineteenth-century Appalachia, providing focal points for small communities as well as a vital service. People from the surrounding countryside brought their corn and wheat to the mill to have it ground into meal and flour, with the miller usually taking a small percentage of the grain in exchange for grinding. While at the mill, people socialized and caught up on the news. Shallow areas below the milldam provided travelers with fords for crossing streams, while millponds created fishing holes. Other businesses often followed mills—leading, in many cases, to the creation of communities and towns.

Most early mills were situated on streams where vertical drops in streambeds could turn large waterwheels. Made first of wood and subsequently of metal, the wheels converted the flowing water into usable power. Later mills often were equipped with more efficient turbines. Axles extending from waterwheels transmitted power into the mill structure, where gears engaged to turn shafts. A system of shafts and belts throughout the mill operated not only grindstones but also separators, sifters, and other equipment. Steam engines eventually replaced waterpower as a more reliable source of energy.

In early mills, millstones were frequently made from native stone from quarries in Powell County in Kentucky, Montgomery County in Virginia, and several Appalachian counties in Pennsylvania. Granite millstones were made in Alabama, North Carolina, South Carolina, and Tennessee. For grinding wheat, superior millstones were imported from France. Other equipment included separators for cleaning grain, bolters for sifting the ground meal into different products, and purifiers for the final cleaning of flour. Fans and dust collectors were used to remove the dust in the cleaning process. Elevators with metal buckets on moving belts moved grain throughout the mill.

Appalachian mills varied greatly in appearance. They included structures made from logs, timber clad with siding (usually horizontal or vertical, rarely diagonal), brick, and stone. Designs ranged from small, single-story buildings to large structures three and one-half to four stories tall. The styles of dams used to create millponds varied depending on the type of stream bottom and materials available. Many early milldams were nothing more than log cribs filled with rocks. More substantial dams were constructed from quarried stone. Water was moved from the millpond to the mill through a race or elevated wooden flume.

By the early twentieth century, gristmills were largely replaced by modern flour-making plants in larger cities. Many fell into disrepair and disappeared. Those located in the most rural areas operated longer due to poor transportation to the outside world. Some of the more magnificent structures have survived and still can be visited. Some are in public ownership in national and state parks, and a number are operated as tourist attractions. Mabry Mill, located in Floyd County, Virginia, is one of the most photographed sites on the Blue Ridge Parkway. Hagood Mill, near Pickens, South Carolina, is an example of an early gristmill. The refurbished facility at Mill Springs, Kentucky, near the Mill Springs Civil War battlefield, still operates seasonally and has the largest overshot metal waterwheel in Appalachia.

Equipped with more reliable power sources and steel rollers, new industrial mills produced more flour at cheaper prices, and customers became accustomed to established brand names for flour and cornmeal distributed through large grocery stores. There was no longer the need to make trips to a local mill.

See also: GRISTMILLS (FOOD AND COOKING); HAGOOD MILL (ARCHITECTURE); SECTION OVERVIEW (SETTLEMENT AND MIGRATION).

—Charles D. Hockensmith, *Kentucky Heritage Council*

B. W. Dedrick, *Practical Milling* (1924); Lynda Fralish, ed., *Historic Mills of America* (2000); David Larkin, *Mill: The History and Future of Naturally Powered Buildings* (2000).

Monsanto Corporation

Launched as a small chemical company in 1901, Monsanto has evolved into a multinational corporation that employed more than fourteen thousand workers worldwide and reported $4.7 billion in revenue for 2002. Its affiliated Appalachian industries over the years have included important rubber and insecticide-herbicide plants in Nitro, West Virginia, as well as a controversial acrylics manufacturer in Anniston, Alabama. Its many agricultural and other products have played significant roles in the lives of Appalachia's people.

In 1901 John Francis Queeny (1859–1933) opened Monsanto Chemical Works in St. Louis. Queeny named his company after his wife, Olga Mendez Monsanto. The firm operated in the red until 1905, and Queeny continued in a part-time job at another chemical company until 1908. In 1915 Monsanto's yearly sales topped a million dollars for the first time. Like other entrepreneurs, Queeny saw opportunities and wanted to capitalize on his vision. At the time, saccharin was being imported from Europe, as there was no American manufacturer. Saccharin became Monsanto's first product in 1902, and the following year Coca-Cola became a customer. Saccharin was then followed on Monsanto's menu of offerings by caffeine in 1904 and vanillin in 1905. In 1917, when Germany's Bayer Company's patent on acetylsalicylic acid expired, Monsanto added aspirin to its list of products, becoming the largest aspirin producer until the 1980s.

Using $3.5 million in stock, Monsanto in 1929 acquired properties that included a West Virginia factory, which became the foundation of its first business to be organized on a global basis. The Rubber Services Laboratories plant at Nitro had been bought seven years earlier as war surplus by four former employees of Goodyear Tire and Rubber Company. Their plan had been to offer technical help and supplies to a profusion of independent tire companies in the

Akron, Ohio, area. In those infant days of the automobile, tire blowouts constituted a continual and critical obstacle to quick growth in the automobile industry, and major tire manufacturers had found that chemicals could help produce longer-lasting tires. Queeny, realizing that rubber additives could be crucial items in the development of transportation, bought the Rubber Services Laboratories plants in both Akron and Nitro. Monsanto modernized the Nitro plant and used it to begin making accelerators, antioxidants, and other products aimed at the rubber industry. The company's rubber-allied business surged as such major tire brands as Goodyear, Firestone, and Michelin, as well as smaller companies, sought innovation in the making of, first, natural rubber tires and then synthetic ones to meet worldwide transportation needs.

Monsanto's ventures into multinationalism began in 1920, and eventually had sites in more than fifty locations—in Africa, Argentina, Australia, Brazil, Belgium, Canada, France, Germany, the United Kingdom, Guatemala, India, Japan, and Venezuela. In 1933 Monsanto Chemical Works became Monsanto Chemical Company. Yearly sales topped a billion dollars in 1962. In 1964 the name was changed again, this time to Monsanto Corporation, reflecting that Monsanto by then was producing much more than chemicals.

The firm's faith in chemicals as a large-scale solver of life's problems remained firm. When Rachel Carson's celebrated book *Silent Spring* warned of the dangers of chemical pesticides, Monsanto fired back with comments from a number of independent scientists saying that without pesticides and insecticides the world could not produce enough crops to feed itself. The defense was hardly surprising, coming from a company whose laboratories employed hundreds of scientists and had manufactured DDT and Agent Orange and for forty years was the exclusive U.S. manufacturer of polychlorinated biphenyls (PCBs).

While Monsanto branched out to other countries, it also expanded throughout the United States via joint ventures with some companies, purchases of others, and the opening of its own offices and factories. It sold a vast range of products over its first century of operation, including rubber chemicals, plastics, seeds, biotechnology crops, manmade fibers, petrochemical raw materials and intermediates, herbicides, feed supplements, fertilizer, insecticides, phosphates and detergents, packaging systems, electronic materials, and pharmaceuticals. The firm also became known for the invention of Acrilan and Astroturf, as well as Roundup and NewLeaf products, All detergent, a nonflammable hydraulic fluid for airplanes, Eskimo antifreeze, and the "wear-dated" apparel guarantee.

During World War II, Monsanto aided the war effort in several ways, researching uranium for the Manhattan Project, producing styrene monomer (used in the production of synthetic rubber), and afterwards operating Mound Laboratories in Miamisburg, Ohio—a nuclear facility under contract to the Atomic Energy Commission. Monsanto Research Corporation also designed and assembled a nuclear heating system used on Apollo moon missions as well as the plutonium capsule used on Apollo 12.

Controversy has also been a large part of Monsanto's history. In 1977 the Food and Drug Administration banned the first plastic soft drink bottle, thought to cause cancer, and it took Monsanto seven years to reformulate the bottle and obtain approval. Monsanto's production of DDT and Agent Orange (as well as other defoliants used in Vietnam) raised public anxiety. Environmentalists, consumer groups, and some farmers expressed concern about Monsanto's genetically engineered seeds as well as Posilac, or rBST, a bovine growth hormone that increases milk production in cows. In 2003 the company responded with a lawsuit against family-owned Oakhurst Dairy in Maine for advertising that its milk contains no rBST, on grounds that the label implied that rBST was unhealthy.

In 2003 Monsanto settled a major controversy over PCB contamination in Anniston, Alabama, involving Solutia Inc., a chemical business spun off from Monsanto in 1997. Solutia, the world's top producer of acrylic fiber, agreed to pay \$50 million of the settlement costs, while Monsanto agreed to pay another \$390 million. Plaintiffs alleged that large numbers of children had developed life-threatening diseases because of PCB exposure and that the former Monsanto firm had dumped millions of pounds of dangerous chemicals into the area's exposed landfills and streams while hiding the risks from the local population. Although it included no admission of wrongdoing, the settlement, along with lower sales of Roundup and selective herbicides, was cited as a reason for a Monsanto net loss approaching \$200 million in late 2003.

In 2000 Monsanto merged with Pharmacia and Upjohn, a subsidiary of Pfizer, to become Pharmacia Corporation. Its agricultural operations, still called Monsanto, remained based in St. Louis.

See also: CHEMICAL INDUSTRY; INDUSTRIAL POLLUTION (ENVIRONMENT).

—Paula K. Hinton, *Tennessee Technological University*

Allyce Bess, "Got Posilac?" *St. Louis Post-Dispatch* (August 10, 2003); Dan J. Forrestal, *Faith, Hope and Five Thousand Dollars: The Story of Monsanto: The Trials and Triumphs of the First Seventy-Five Years* (1977); "Monsanto Settles PCB Case in Alabama," *Reuters News Service* (August 21, 2003).

MoonPies

The MoonPie was originally a chocolate-covered graham cracker sandwich with marshmallow filling marketed by the Chattanooga Bakery in Chattanooga, Tennessee. MoonPies have since come in double-decker, mini, single-decker, low-fat, and seasonal mini-MoonPie versions, and in 2001 the bakery introduced FullMoons, which feature the addition of raspberry filling between two layers of marshmallow in a graham cracker sandwich frosted with vanilla icing. But some purists contend the later innovations just gild the lily.

The Chattanooga Bakery began as a means of using excess flour from the Mountain City Flour Mill, also located in Chattanooga. In 1910 the bakery started making the first of two hundred confectionery items, and the MoonPie came along in 1917. According to company legend, the MoonPie was invented by Earl Mitchell, a service representative whose territory included Kentucky, Tennessee, and West Virginia. Mitchell is said to have asked coal miners at a company store what they would enjoy as a snack, and they replied they wanted something solid and filling to put in their lunch pails. When asked how large the snacks should be, one miner indicated a size by framing the rising moon with his hands. Upon his return to the bakery, Mitchell saw workers dipping graham crackers in marshmallow and then putting them on a windowsill to harden. By adding another cracker and then coating both with chocolate, the company made the first MoonPies.

Initial samples proved popular, and the bakery added them to its line of confections. But the MoonPie's popularity was extreme. By the late 1950s, the bakery responded to public demand by discontinuing all its other products to make only MoonPies. Its prominence in southern Appalachia made it the subject of a 1951 song, "Give Me an RC Cola and a Moon Pie," recorded by *Grand Ole Opry* comedy duo Lonzo and Oscar.

See also: CAKES AND COOKIES (FOOD AND COOKING).

—Clara Hasbrouck, *East Tennessee State University*

Morgan, J. P.

(1837–1913) Financier.

The best-known and most powerful banker of his time, John Pierpont Morgan was involved in titanic economics from the 1870s into the early 1900s throughout America, Appalachia included. Morgan's continual financial reorganizations of failing railroads affected the region hugely through the capitalizing of rails to penetrate the region, exporting of coal and other natural resources, and bringing in business from outside. In addition, he was widely credited with settling a 1902 anthracite coal strike that for five months idled 150,000 Appalachian miners, all but paralyzed the industry, and stymied settlement efforts by President Theodore Roosevelt.

Morgan inherited much of his personal wealth from his father, Junius Spencer Morgan, a prominent London banker. The oldest of five children, Pierpont was born April 17, 1837, in Hartford, Connecticut. His mother, Juliet Pierpont Morgan, was the daughter of a Unitarian minister. The son studied at Boston's English High School, at Vevey in Switzerland, and at Germany's University of Gottingen. In 1861 he married Amelia Sturges, who died of tuberculosis a few months later. In 1865 he married Frances Louisa Tracy, with whom he had three daughters and a son.

In 1857 he joined Duncan, Sherman, and Company on Wall Street as a junior accountant. Four years later he established his own firm and in 1864 entered a partnership with Charles Dabney. After Dabney retired, Morgan joined forces with the prominent Drexel family of Philadelphia in 1871, and from then until the early 1890s Drexel, Morgan and Company increased in importance working on its own and in concert with J. S. Morgan and Company of London. After Anthony J. Drexel's death in 1893, Morgan headed the firm, changing its name to J. P. Morgan and Company in 1895. He prized order, stability, and efficiency, and, building on connections in Europe, developed a strong business in foreign exchange.

Following America's railroad boom after the Civil War, many major railroads neared collapse or went bankrupt during the 1880s and 1890s. Morgan strengthened faith in American securities by reorganizing many of them, including the Albany and Susquehanna; Baltimore and Ohio; Philadelphia and Reading; Southern; Chesapeake and Ohio; Northern Pacific; and Erie. His first major rail overhaul, in 1869, involved the Albany and Susquehanna, a transporter of coal to the East. A few years later, in revamping the major anthracite carrier Philadelphia and Reading and the management of its coal properties, he helped put together Consolidation Coal Company to stabilize prices among Pennsylvania producers. "Morganization" characteristically included naming the chief executives and placing a trusted associate on the board with the goals of more efficient operations and elimination of costly competition.

Morgan, who lent money only to people and organizations he trusted, also reorganized or financed major industrial corporations, notably General Electric, American Telephone and Telegraph, Western Union Telegraph, and International Harvester. In 1901 he purchased Andrew Carnegie's interests in the steel industry and through mergers formed United States Steel, America's first billion-dollar corporation.

During the depression of 1895, he and others lent $62 million to replenish federal gold reserves. In 1907 he helped avert a national financial panic and stabilize the stock market. When a congressional banking subcommittee investigating money trusts made him a prime target in 1912, he maintained his reputation, testifying that power becomes dangerous only in evil hands and assuring the committee that he sought no monopoly.

Morgan's philanthropies included educational, medical, and religious concerns, but he devoted his passion chiefly to collecting art, manuscripts, and rare books. These collections now belong to New York's Metropolitan Museum of Art and Pierpont Morgan Library and to Hartford's Wadsworth Atheneum.

On March 31, 1913, a few months after the conclusion of the congressional banking hearings, Morgan died in Rome. He is buried in Hartford.

See also: CARNEGIE, ANDREW; CONSOLIDATION COAL COMPANY/CONSOL ENERGY.

—Marie Garrett, *University of Tennessee*

Frederick Lewis Allen, *The Great Pierpont Morgan* (1949); Vincent P. Carosso, *The Morgans: Private International Bankers, 1854–1913* (1987); Jean Strouse, *Morgan: American Financier* (1999).

Muscle Shoals Power

From 1921 until 1933, Muscle Shoals, a turbulent, rock-choked barrier that blocked navigation on the Tennessee River in northern Alabama, was regularly in the headlines of newspapers across America. The river's steep descent through the shoals, climaxing with a drop of about 130 feet over a stretch of thirty-seven miles, made the site an ideal location to generate hydroelectric power, and during World War I the federal government had built two plants to produce nitrate for munitions and begun work on a massive dam with hydroelectric generators. At war's end, debate erupted over government versus private ownership of the nitrate works and arrangements for producing fertilizer critically needed by the nation's farmers.

Debate over the nitrate plants evolved into a political struggle over the dam, pitting southern utilities and other private interests against advocates of public power. In a sense, Muscle Shoals became a metaphor in a broader national debate over the ownership of natural resources. Presidents Calvin Coolidge and Herbert Hoover both vetoed legislation that would have established public ownership of the Muscle Shoals complex. In 1933, with Franklin D. Roosevelt in the White House, Congress created the Tennessee Valley Authority (TVA) and resolved the Muscle Shoals issue by making both the dam, named for President Woodrow Wilson, and the nitrate works a part of the new regional development agency. Muscle Shoals thus became a cornerstone of the TVA.

Industrial development of the site had been under discussion since early in the twentieth century, but it had never gone forward because of opposition from conservationists and others who considered it public property. National security concerns brought the debate to a head. As World War I broke out in Europe, the United States was heavily dependent upon nitrates imported from Chile for production of both munitions and fertilizer. Therefore, acting under the authority of the National Defense Act of 1916, President Wilson authorized federal construction of the nitrate production complex near Sheffield, Alabama, powered by electricity from the dam erected at Muscle Shoals. The second of two nitrate plants was completed a month before the armistice was signed on November 11, 1918, but construction of the dam had only begun. With the postwar future of the complex uncharted, the Wilson administration proposed creation of a government-owned corporation to sell both surplus power from the dam and fertilizer from the nitrate plant. Opponents of public power blocked passage in Congress, and twelve years of struggle ensued.

The future of the Shoals became an issue of national public interest when, in 1921, automobile magnate Henry Ford sought to buy the nitrate works and secure a hundred-year lease on the dam. His promise to make the Muscle Shoals area into another Detroit gained popular support in the area and triggered a real estate boom along the river. At the height of Ford's effort to gain control of the complex, Alabama Senator J. Thomas Heflin predicted that the industrialist would hire one hundred thousand men within ten days of approval of the bid. Ford held out the prospect of eventual employment of one million men. In March 1924 the U.S. House of Representatives voted 227 to 143 to approve the lease, and communities in north Alabama welcomed the news with bonfires and pealing church bells.

Standing in the controversial automobile manufacturer's way, however, were public-power advocates led by Senator George Norris, a Nebraska Republican who envisioned hydroelectric dams on the river as the engine of a government conservation and economic-development program to lift the entire Tennessee Valley out of poverty. Norris argued strongly that the dam should be put to public use, rather than be turned over to Ford for private gain in a deal that Norris maintained would benefit no one but the automobile tycoon. In the face of Senate opposition and a rising public perception that the deal was a give-away, Ford withdrew his bid in October 1924. Initiative in the debate shifted to the proponents of public power and public ownership of Muscle Shoals, but the impasse continued. In May 1928, three days before adjournment, Congress sent President Coolidge a public-ownership bill championed by Norris, but Coolidge exercised his "pocket veto," simply allowing the measure to die for lack of his signature. Two years later, in April 1930, another Norris bill was vetoed, with President Hoover declaring, "The power problem is not to be solved by the Federal Government going into the power business."

In February 1933, shortly after visiting Muscle Shoals, President-elect Roosevelt announced a Tennessee River development plan along the lines that Norris and other public-power supporters had advocated for a decade. On May 18, the Tennessee Valley Authority was created, becoming a showpiece of the New Deal.

See also: TENNESSEE VALLEY AUTHORITY (GOVERNMENT).

—Rudy Abramson, *Reston, Virginia*

Donald Davidson, *The Tennessee* (1946–48); Preston J. Hubbard, *Origins of the TVA: The Muscle Shoals Controversy, 1920–1932* (1961); John H. Kyle, *The Building of TVA: An Illustrated History* (1958).

Mussel Diving and the Freshwater Pearl Industry

Many of the nearly three hundred species of freshwater mussels found in the United States are indigenous to the streams and rivers of Appalachia. Archaeological sites show that Native Americans used mussels for food, their shells for tools and utensils, and the pearls for jewelry and decoration. Mussels continue to supply pearl buttons and support a cultured pearl industry.

In 1857 a large pearl was found near Paterson, New Jersey, and pearl fever spread throughout the nation. The discovery of another large pearl on the Caney Fork River in Tennessee nineteen years later brought searchers to other principal waterways in the state, including the Tennessee, Clinch, Cumberland, Calfkiller, Duck, Elk, Obey, Powell, and French Broad Rivers. The Clinch became a major source of pearls, and a historical marker in Clinton, Tennessee, identifies the town as a center of the pearling industry. Other notable stream sources were located in northern Alabama and French Creek, Pennsylvania.

The first factory to produce pearl buttons opened in Muscatine, Iowa, on the Mississippi River in the 1890s. In the early 1900s the Cumberland, Tennessee, and Ohio River drainage basins supplied mussel shells for button factories in Knoxville, Tennessee, and St. Marys, West Virginia. These buttons were cheaper than ocean-shell mother-of-pearl buttons, and the new industry flourished. In 1912 two hundred button plants existed, but after World War II, with the advent of plastic buttons and zippers, the industry declined.

Mussels are harvested by two basic methods: brailing and diving. Until about 1970, brailing, done from a johnboat, was the prevalent method. Harvesters used a brail pole to drag chain attachments and grapnel hooks along the bottom of a bed, gathering mussels that clamped onto the devices. The mussels were sorted by size, with small ones returned to the water. Brailing, though, has been largely supplanted by diving. Divers risk ear infections and injury due to poor underwater visibility, but they have the advantage of being selective. Working by touch, they take only the big shells, which they sell to exporters.

Pearls form when the mussel secretes nacre, a mixture of calcium carbonate and proteins, over an irritant. Most natural freshwater mussel pearls are baroque, or misshapen, and are traditionally used for costume jewelry. They are not easily matched, and very few are of gem quality. A cultured pearl is formed when the pearl grower introduces an irritant into the mussel. In the 1950s the Japanese discovered that beads made from freshwater mussel shell from the Mississippi, Tennessee, and Wabash Rivers make the best nuclei for cultured pearls. Japan then became the leading purchaser of mussel shell. Pearl farms in Tennessee have become the leading producers of cultured pearls in the United States.

Freshwater mussels are increasingly endangered by poaching, overharvesting of mussel beds, pollution, dams, and the introduction of the zebra mussel, a proliferating Eurasian variety that attaches itself to desirable mussels and weakens them. Since 1965 Kentucky, Tennessee, and Alabama have passed legislation to regulate mussel harvesting. Of the more than sixty species of freshwater mussels found in North Carolina, 50 percent are designated endangered, threatened, or of special concern. West Virginia has made possession of mussels illegal, and collecting them even for scientific purposes requires a permit.

See also: MOLLUSKS (ECOLOGY); STREAMS (ECOLOGY); WATER RESOURCES (ENVIRONMENT).

—Kathy A. Campbell, *East Tennessee State University*

Adele Conover, "To Reproduce, Mussels Go Fishing: The Evolution of This Freshwater Pearl-Maker Reaches Its Apex in Our Southern Rivers," *Smithsonian* (January 1998); Paul W. Parmalee and Arthur E. Bogan, *The Freshwater Mussels of Tennessee* (1998).

Natural Gas Industry

Natural gas is a fossil fuel found in underground reservoirs. It consists of mostly methane (CH_4) and often contains varying amounts of ethane, propane, butane, and other gases. When organic matter is trapped in rock, buried, and subjected to heat and pressure through time, it is converted to coal, oil, or natural gas depending on the type and amount of organic matter and other factors.

The natural gas industry consists of three sectors—production, transmission, and distribution companies—and a single firm may have separate divisions handling business in each of these areas. Production companies explore the subsurface for natural gas resources, acquiring mineral rights by lease or purchase, drilling and completing wells, and building gathering and compression facilities to deliver gas into pipelines. Columbia Natural Resources of Charleston, West Virginia, and Equitable Resources Exploration of Kingsport, Tennessee, are two of the biggest production companies in Appalachia. Companies such as Columbia Gas Transmission of Charleston operate pipelines that take the natural gas from the fields to the distribution companies. Local distribution companies deliver gas directly to consumers. There are large firms, such as Columbia Gas of Ohio, but many are much smaller, city-owned utilities.

Natural gas that occurs in coal, called coal-bed methane, is the fastest growing sector of the natural gas industry. Coal-bed methane includes methane that can be recovered from abandoned coal mines. A greenhouse gas that often was released into the atmosphere for safety, coal-bed methane is now produced in Alabama, Kentucky, Ohio, Pennsylvania, Virginia, and West Virginia. Producing coal-bed methane in conjunction with mining enhances mine safety, increases profits, decreases the cost of ventilation, and reduces the release of greenhouse gas into the atmosphere. In addition, coal-bed methane can be produced from thin or deep coals that are unlikely to be mined in the future. Most coal-bed methane is sold and delivered to consumers through pipelines. In West Virginia, one project converts coal-bed methane into liquefied natural gas to fuel heavy trucks and is processed and used locally.

In Appalachia natural gas was used as early as 1756, when survivors of the Sandy Creek expedition against the Shawnee stopped by Burning Spring, near the Tug Fork on what is now the border between West Virginia and Kentucky, and broiled their buffalo meat in the burning gas. The earliest recorded use of natural gas as a domestic fuel occurred in Fredonia, New York, where in 1821 William Hart drove a pipe into an outcrop of Devonian shale and used the gas to illuminate local streetlamps. In 1838 Daniel Foster of Findlay, Ohio, noted the amount of gas produced from water wells dug in the area. Foster inverted an iron kettle used in making salt over one of the wells and piped the trapped gas into his house, where he burned it in his fireplace using a perforated gun barrel. The government lighthouse at Barcelona, the lake port near Westfield, New York, used natural gas for illumination from around 1838 until it was abandoned in 1857. The first widespread industrial use of natural gas was in the production of salt; by 1841, gas was commonly employed as a fuel to evaporate brines in the Kanawha River Valley of (West) Virginia. Gas was first applied to making iron in October 1874 in Pennsylvania, where it was piped from the Harvey well, near Larden's Mill in Butler County, to the iron mill of Spang, Chalfant and Company at Etna, near Pittsburgh. This first natural gas pipeline was six inches in diameter and seventeen miles long. By the 1880s, natural gas was being used in glassmaking, the manufacture of carbon black, and in municipal and domestic heating and lighting.

At the opening of the twenty-first century, more than 56 million American homes were using natural gas. In 2001, 23 percent of the natural gas usage in the United States went to the residential market for home heating, hot water, cooking, clothes drying, and air conditioning. Thirty-six percent of consumption was by the industrial sector. Use of natural gas was increasing in the electric utility area, amounting to about 26 percent of the natural gas consumed. Most new power plants were smaller facilities designed to employ natural gas to generate electricity during periods of peak demand. Another 15 percent was used commercially for such purposes as the heating and cooling of office buildings, hotels, schools, and hospitals, and fuel for cooking in restaurants. Less than 0.1 percent of the natural gas used in the United States was used as a transportation fuel.

See also: GLASS INDUSTRY; OIL AND GAS (GEOLOGY).

—Brandon Nuttall, *Kentucky Geological Survey*, and Kate Smith, *East Tennessee State University*

Edward Orton, *Report on the Occurrence of Petroleum, Natural Gas and Asphalt Rock in Western Kentucky Based on Examinations Made in 1888 and 1889*, Kentucky Geological Survey, Series 2 (1891); U.S. Department of Energy, Energy Information Administration, *Natural Gas Annual* (2001); U.S. Environmental Protection Agency, Atmospheric Pollution Prevention Division, *White Paper: Coal Mine Methane in Today's Natural Gas Market* (1997); Carl Zipper, "The Bush Energy Policy and Appalachia: Back to the Coal Mines?" *Now and Then* (Winter 2001).

Nitro, West Virginia

See Chemical Industry

North American Free Trade Agreement

See North American Free Trade Agreement (Labor)

Nuclear Fuel Services

Nuclear Fuel Services, Inc., operates a manufacturing facility in Erwin, a Tennessee town about ninety miles east of Knoxville. At the end of the twentieth century, the company was the sole supplier of fuel for the United States Navy's nuclear-powered submarines and surface vessels.

Established in 1957, the company is licensed by the United States Nuclear Regulatory Commission. The firm's primary activities are production of fuel for the navy, decontamination and decommissioning operations, and down-blending highly enriched uranium from various weapons programs into a form usable in commercial nuclear power plants. Other functions of Nuclear Fuel Services include decontamination of mixed and medical waste, treatability studies, environmental remediation, transportation services, and facility support at U.S. Department of Energy sites as well as commercial businesses.

In addition to new processes for the manufacture of fuel for the navy, Nuclear Fuel Services has developed innovative technologies to eliminate mixed waste (which contains both radioactive and hazardous materials) and to decontaminate and decommission radioactively contaminated buildings and equipment. In 1993 the company constructed a treatment facility to process sludge contaminated with uranium, other radionuclides, and mixed and hazardous metals.

New dissolution and down-blending facilities are currently being designed.

Nuclear Fuel Services was purchased by Atlanta-based NFS Services, Ltd., in 1987. Previous corporate owners included W. R. Grace, Getty Oil, and Texaco. The company's production employees are represented by the Paper, Allied-Industrial, Chemical and Energy Workers International Union.

See also: NUCLEAR POWER; RADIOACTIVE WASTE (ENVIRONMENT).

—Ed Speer, *Elizabethton, Tennessee*

Nuclear Power

At the opening of the twenty-first century nearly half of the 103 commercial nuclear power plants in the United States, some 45, were located in the Appalachian states, and 19 were within or directly adjacent to the Appalachian region. The 45 included a plant or plants in every state except Kentucky and West Virginia. Their combined capacity was 42.9 gigawatts of electric power, which in 1998 produced 319.3 billion kilowatt hours of electricity. The total amount of electricity by state ranged from 10 percent in Ohio to 58 percent in South Carolina.

As of 2003, Appalachian or Appalachian-area nuclear power facilities were located at Beaver Valley (two plants) and Susquehanna (two plants), Pennsylvania; Sequoyah (two) and Watts Bar, Tennessee; McGuire (two), North Carolina; Oconee (three) and Catawba (two), South Carolina; and Browns Ferry (two), Alabama. Others at various times were planned for the area—at Phipps Bend near Surgoinsville, Tennessee, at Hartsville, Tennessee, and at Iuka, Mississippi, for example—but were never opened. Community concerns were raised in Hartsville as well as around the 1996 opening of Watts Bar regarding worries about accidental discharge of radiation or potential problems with the facilities' disposal of waste products.

Nuclear energy is generated in the form of the heat released from the splitting of uranium (U-235) atoms. The heat then generates steam that drives a turbine, which in turn drives an electric generator, the same process used in gas- or coal-burning power plants. Nuclear energy was first used for the generation of electricity in 1951, when four light bulbs were lit by the electricity generated by an experimental atom-splitting reactor. Designed by the U.S. Navy, the first commercial nuclear power plant became operational in 1957 at Shippingport, Pennsylvania. The Shippingport facility reached its full power of 60 megawatts of electricity twenty days after it was commissioned and continued in operation until it was decommissioned in 1967.

At the beginning of the new century commercial nuclear power plants in the United States generated a total capacity of almost 100 gigawatts. In 1998 they produced 673.7 billion kilowatt hours of electricity and contributed about 19 percent of the nation's electricity, second only to the 52 percent generated by coal-burning power plants. Because high-voltage transmission lines were interconnected throughout the United States, everybody in the lower forty-eight states got some electricity from nuclear energy.

The growth of the nuclear industry in the United States had resulted since 1973 in an estimated $65-billion reduction in the cost of oil imports necessary to meet the increasing demand for electricity, and the production cost of nuclear electricity was less than that generated by non-nuclear power plants. The average cost of nuclear-generated electricity in 1997 was 2.31 cents per kilowatt hour as compared to 3.87 cents for oil-generated electricity and 3.55 cents for natural gas-generated electricity. Although the production cost of electricity generated by coal-burning power plants was slightly less (2.12 cents in 1997), nuclear power plants do not produce air-polluting chemicals such as carbon dioxide, sulfur dioxide, and nitrogen dioxide. Each year, nuclear power plants in the United States avoid the emission of 5.3 million tons of sulfur oxides, 2.5 million tons of nitrogen oxides, and 155 million tons of carbon.

At the close of the twentieth century, the total of five facilities in South Carolina—two Catawba plants and three Oconee plants—produced 35.1 billion kilowatt hours of electricity. The two Sequoyah plants and the single Watts Bar plant in Tennessee produced 28.4 billion kilowatt hours; the two Beaver Valley and the two Susquehanna plants in Pennsylvania produced 20.9 billion; the two McGuire plants in North Carolina, 18.7 billion; and the two Browns Ferry plants in Alabama, 17.2 billion.

See also: RADIOACTIVE WASTE (ENVIRONMENT); TENNESSEE VALLEY AUTHORITY (GOVERNMENT).

—Kula C. Misra, *University of Tennessee*

Oak Ridge National Laboratory

Oak Ridge National Laboratory is an international center for scientific inquiry located in a once secret east Tennessee town between the older municipalities of Kingston and Clinton. It has contributed to the Appalachian region by providing opportunities for highly skilled and technical labor, stimulating the local economy, producing groundbreaking scientific discoveries, and bringing international attention to the area. Although its construction displaced about one thousand rural families, it soon provided urban-style salaries to the homes of some seventy-five thousand employees recruited from the Tennessee Valley for work so security-sensitive that most were prohibited from knowing its nature. Modern-day Oak Ridge research has yielded breakthroughs in cancer treatment, genetics, energy use, space exploration, and environmental progress. On the downside, it also has produced radioactive and toxic waste that began to be cleaned up only in the 1990s, a half-century after the site was established.

Oak Ridge National Laboratory was established as a component of the top-secret Manhattan Project, which was initiated by the United States in 1942 to develop an atomic weapon for use in World War II. In the fall of that year, about the time experiments at the University of Chicago were resulting in the first controlled nuclear reaction, the U.S. Army Corps of Engineers purchased nearly six thousand acres in rural east Tennessee near the Clinch River about twenty-five miles northwest of Knoxville. There scientists and engineers built a massive facility to produce enriched uranium and the world's first nuclear reactor to convert uranium into plutonium. Initially called the Kingston Demolition Range and then the Clinton Engineering Works, the secret community got its permanent designation from residents of the area, who named it Oak Ridge after the nearby Black Oak Ridge.

The facility's early program was directed by the deputy chief of the U.S. Army Corps of Engineers, Brigadier General Leslie Groves. The corps constructed three laboratories at Oak Ridge in 1943. The K-25 gaseous diffusion separated weapons-grade uranium isotopes from the heavier U-238. The enormous Y-12 plant employed electromagnetic equipment for U-235 separation. Finally, X-10 was a pilot plant for a larger plutonium-producing reactor built at Hanford, Washington. In 1944 plutonium-239 and the uranium-235 produced at Oak Ridge were sent to another secret facility at Los Alamos, New Mexico. There, under the leadership of J. Robert Oppenheimer, scientists used the material to build two atomic bombs nicknamed "Little Boy" and "Fat Man." "Little Boy," the bomb with a uranium core, was dropped on Hiroshima, Japan, on August 6, 1945; "Fat Man," with a plutonium core, was used on Nagasaki two days later.

During World War II, scientists and others from the University of Chicago, Columbia University, and the University of California at Berkeley had come to Oak Ridge, and afterward the town grew as a research center. In 1947 the Atomic Energy Commission took civilian control of the Manhattan Project and officially designated the reservation the Oak Ridge National Laboratory the following year. Private enterprises such as Lockheed Martin and Union Carbide were contracted to manage and expand the installation over the succeeding decades. To promote a new openness and an "atoms for peace" program, the government invited the rest of the world into the city of Oak Ridge in 1949. From then on, private and government researchers initiated programs to peacefully apply atomic energy to medicine, biology, and nuclear reactors.

National policy mandated that the facility share its technologies with American industry, and beginning in the 1950s and 1960s it did. Its scientists developed fission reactors as power sources, trained nuclear engineers, studied the effects of radiation exposure on humans, and produced radioactive and nonradioactive isotopes for use in medical diagnosis and treatment. In the late 1970s the Department of Energy took over its direction and launched research into the production, transmission, and conservation of energy. By the early 2000s, management responsibility had fallen to the University of Tennessee and the Battelle Memorial Institute, and together they began developing high-speed computing technology, conducting neutron research, and continuing to broaden the laboratory's scientific investigations.

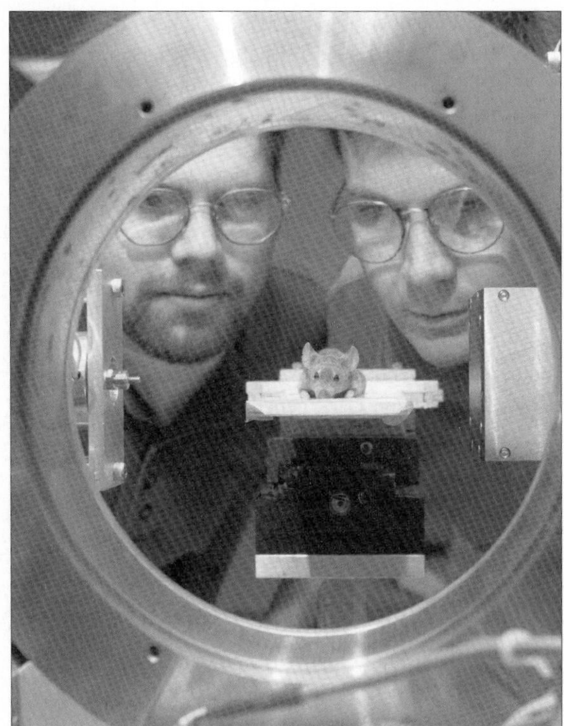

A small-animal X-ray computed tomography system (MicroCAT) developed by researcher Mike Paulus (pictured right) at Oak Ridge National Laboratory, Oak Ridge, Tennessee, 1998. The device is used to monitor internal changes, such as fat deposits and tumor growths, in experimental animals.

At the same time, Oak Ridge National Laboratory has remained involved in weapons activities but, especially in the final two decades of the twentieth century, with a significantly different focus. The Y-12 plant became a storage and management area for uranium components removed from retired thermonuclear weapons as limited nuclear disarmament got underway. Such weapons get most of their blast when plutonium squeezed into a critical mass sets off a hydrogen fusion reaction, but to aid the process these warheads also contain so-called secondary uranium that explodes as a second stage blast. These secondaries were sent to Y-12 as a number of warheads were taken out of service. By 1993, the Department of Energy and the contractors at Y-12 had begun redefining the mission of Y-12 "from weapons production to weapons dismantlement." Y-12 reduced its uranium weapons-casting facilities from a dozen to six and used these facilities to recast highly enriched uranium from the decommissioned warheads, placing them in new sealed containers, and storing them in a complex of seven concrete vaults in the highest-security zone of the plant.

Outstanding researchers at Oak Ridge have included radiation biologists Waldo Cohn and Alexander Hollaender, radioecologist Stanley Auerbach, radiation chemists Ellison Taylor and Sheldon Datz, geneticist Bill Russell, and neutron physicists Ernest Wollan and Clifford Shull. Their work has done much to modernize human existence. The facility's research established that radiation from diagnostic X-rays is harmful to human fetal development, and its scientists designed a moon rock scoop for Apollo lunar landing missions. Its energy conservation research resulted in national insulation standards and more energy-efficient refrigerators, heat pumps, ovens, and water heaters. In 1991 forensic experts even used neutron analysis developed at Oak Ridge to prove that President Zachary Taylor did not die by arsenic poisoning. The laboratories at Oak Ridge continue to contribute to the development of east Tennessee, Appalachia, and the larger scientific world.

See also: NUCLEAR POWER; RADIOACTIVE WASTE (ENVIRONMENT).

—Aaron D. Purcell, *University of Tennessee*

Charles W. Johnson and Charles O. Jackson, *City behind a Fence: Oak Ridge, Tennessee, 1942–1946* (1981); Leland Johnson and Daniel Schaffer, *Oak Ridge National Laboratory: The First Fifty Years* (1994); U.S. Congress, Office of Technology Assessment, *Dismantling the Bomb and Managing the Nuclear Materials* (1993).

Ochs, Adolph

(1858–1935) Publisher and philanthropist.

Adolph Simon Ochs is most often associated with the world of New York publishing, but he spent much of his early life and career in east Tennessee. Born in 1858 in Cincinnati, Ochs was the son of Bavarian immigrants who were outspoken and deeply divided on the issues of the day, and young Adolph learned early the importance of impartiality and objectivity. Forced from the North by his mother's Southern sympathies, the family eventually settled in Knoxville. There Ochs's father worked unsuccessfully as a merchant and later a minor local magistrate, and the son, in an effort to augment the family's precarious finances, took a job as a newsboy with William Rule's *Knoxville Chronicle*. Thus began his career in journalism.

Over the next few years, he improved his status at the *Chronicle*, eventually rising to the rank of journeyman printer. He perfected the skills of composition and typesetting and developed a lifelong appreciation for a page of well-crafted text. Soon in demand, he worked briefly at newspapers in Knoxville and Louisville, Kentucky, before taking a position in 1877 with the *Chattanooga Daily Dispatch*. That publication soon folded, leaving him penniless and stranded in the industrial town. Unable to return to his family in Knoxville, he performed assorted printing tasks and soon saved enough to purchase another failing paper, the *Chattanooga Times*. Starting with just $12.50 in working capital, he transformed the ragged daily into one of the South's most respected publications. A technical perfectionist and political moderate, Ochs produced a paper that was objective, attractive, and affordable. Under his direction, the *Times* encouraged economic diversification, sectional reconciliation, and racial cooperation. Such views made Ochs one of the town's leading citizens, and he emerged as an important spokesman for the New South movement.

By the 1890s, Ochs was one of Chattanooga's wealthiest and most recognizable citizens. Real estate losses and the Panic of 1893, however, brought his fledgling empire to the brink of collapse. Barely able to pay his mounting debts and desperate for a new source of income, Ochs pooled his remaining credit and purchased another failing publication, the *New York Times*, on July 1, 1896. Using lessons learned in Chattanooga, he transformed the *Times* into one of the world's most influential newspapers. In the process, he established a publishing dynasty, and his descendants continue to be a dominant force in American journalism.

Ochs was a devout Jew and a devoted philanthropist, contributing heavily to Jewish congregations and charitable causes in both New York and Chattanooga. He also led the effort to establish the Chickamauga and Chattanooga National Military Park and purchased much of the face of Chattanooga's Lookout Mountain to preserve it from development. He died on April 8, 1935, during a visit to Chattanooga, the city that launched his career.

See also: CHATTANOOGA, TENNESSEE (URBAN APPALACHIAN EXPERIENCE); PRINTING/PUBLISHING PRESSES.

—Tim Ezzell, *University of Tennessee*

Ohio Clay Industry

Southeastern Ohio boasts large deposits of distinctive clays necessary in the manufacture of a wide variety of products from sewer pipe to flue linings, and since World War II the Buckeye State has ranked between fifth and eighth nationally in overall clay production. Clays are classified as common-and-shale (or common), ball, bentonite, fire, fuller's earth, and kaolin. Ohio produces common and fire clay, usually ranking around fifth in the United States in the former and first or second (to Missouri) in the latter. Ohio's

Appalachian counties produce roughly four-fifths of the state's clay.

Tied closely to construction, the clay industry mirrors general economic trends, and employment, as in many Appalachian extractive industries, can be unsteady. Most clay mined in Appalachian Ohio is used locally for manufacturing. Common clay is used in bricks, portland cement, tiles, sewer pipe, flue linings, concrete blocks, terra cotta, pottery, and lightweight aggregate. Fire clay, which can retain a shape in intense heat, is used most notably in refractory mortar and cement for the steel, glass, and foundry industries but also for fire brick, flue linings, portland cement, glass, glazes, enamel, pottery, and other ceramics.

Prominent manufacturing locales have included plants for making brick in Tuscarawas, Jefferson, Hocking, and Jackson Counties; sewer pipe in Tuscarawas, Jefferson, Perry, and Lawrence Counties; tile in Tuscarawas, Harrison, Jefferson, and Hocking Counties; and pottery in Muskingum (notably Zanesville), Columbiana, and Perry Counties. Tuscarawas County leads production and contains the nation's only underground operation. Other significant producing counties have included Athens, Belmont, Carroll, Coshocton, Gallia, Highland, Holmes, Scioto, Vinton, and Washington, with Hocking and Jackson notable for fire clay.

Southeastern Ohio's clay was discovered by frontiersman Christopher Gist in the 1750s. In 1841 an industry was launched when A. Russell, taking advantage of the clay's characteristic of being able to be molded when wet, began making fire brick near East Liverpool. By 1900 the state's clay industry was thriving, perhaps most memorably led by artistic pottery making. This craft was centered in Zanesville, dubbed "The Clay City" during the art pottery industry's 1870–1920 heyday. At its zenith the area claimed approximately thirty pottery manufacturers. Local products were mostly handcrafted, and in the early twenty-first century they were in demand as collectibles. Most of the companies (Roseville, Rookwood, and S. A. Weller were three of the more prominent) went out of business between 1919 and 1940 because of unsuccessful attempts to adapt their mostly handmade, expensive products to more mundane and commercial mass production—as well as because of declining markets during the Great Depression. By 1967 all had ceased operation.

See also: COTTAGE INDUSTRIES; GLASS INDUSTRY.

—David S. Newhall, *Centre College*

Oil Industry

Small companies with fewer than twenty employees dominate oil drilling in Appalachia. They often drill only a few wells each year but may operate hundreds. Service companies provide them with pipe, cementing, equipment, well stimulation, environmental services, and logging. Large companies such as Halliburton, Schlumberger, and McJunkin provide many services, but there also are small independents that often specialize in one area. There are nineteen refineries in the Appalachian Basin. Some small independent companies—such as Somerset Oil in Somerset, Kentucky—refine locally produced crude oil and have a few service stations. Marathon-Ashland, Sunoco, Shell Chemical, and other huge companies have large refineries that process local and imported oil and market their gasoline at hundreds of stations.

Appalachia is probably more important for its historical role in the oil industry than for its current impact. No figures were available for Appalachia per se, but Appalachian states claimed less than 2 percent of total United States oil production in 2002. The largest were Mississippi, which had four refineries and produced 49,000 barrels per day; Alabama, with three refineries and 24,000 barrels per day; and Ohio, with four refineries and 16,000 barrels per day. The others were well behind: Kentucky, with two refineries and 7,000 barrels per day; Pennsylvania, five refineries and 6,000 barrels per day; West Virginia, one refinery and 4,000 barrels per day; Tennessee, one refinery and 1,000 barrels per day; New York, no refineries and 452 barrels per day; and Virginia, one refinery and 60 barrels per day. In 2002, Georgia had two refineries but no oil production, and Maryland, North Carolina, and South Carolina had neither refineries nor oil output.

Crude oil is a liquid to semisolid fossil fuel or hydrocarbon found in surface seeps and underground reservoirs. It is composed of varying amounts of many hydrocarbons from natural gasolines (C_5 to C_{10}) to tars and asphalt ($>C_{40}$). When organic matter is trapped in rock, buried, and subjected to heat and pressure through time, it is converted to coal, oil, or natural gas depending on type, amount, and other factors. In the presence of water and heat, the conversion (hydrous pyrolysis) of organic matter to oil increases the volume of the liquids. The resulting increase in pressure forces the oil to migrate. When oil encounters an underground rock unit that has sufficient spaces between its particles and a seal or trap, it will accumulate, forming a reservoir. Some of the migrating oil makes its way to Earth's surface, where it can form pools or springs. Many early oil discoveries, including the one found in 1859 and considered to be the first well in America, occurred near these kinds of springs.

Drilling for oil in Appalachia is usually done by using a bit at the bottom of a rotating string of pipe. Water or air is circulated down the pipe and out at the bit to remove crushed rock while drilling. Much like a jackhammer, many wells use high-pressure air to drive a bit. During drilling, strings of pipe called casing are installed in the hole to protect fresh water, prevent collapse of the hole, and stop unwanted fluids from entering the hole. Natural gas under pressure or dissolved in the oil can cause an uncontrolled fountain, or gusher, of oil to rise above the ground, although most gushers are now controlled by equipment called blowout preventers. After the hole has reached its deepest point, tools are lowered into it to measure rock properties and identify producing zones, called pays. These logging techniques commonly measure the electrical and radioactive properties of rock.

If required to increase production, a well may be stimulated by using acid, explosives, or high-pressure fluids. For most successful wells, tubing, a lift device called a pump jack, valves, and pipe are installed to deliver oil to a battery of storage tanks, where it is picked up and transported to refineries. Oil production decreases with time, and when it slows to an uneconomic rate, wells often are plugged and abandoned. After the primary production phase, as much as 60 percent to 70 percent of the original oil in the reservoir remains underground. Sometimes a company will pool many of these wells together, inject water, carbon dioxide, or other chemicals into the reservoir, and attempt what is known as secondary or enhanced recovery to produce the remaining resource.

In Appalachia, oil was first recovered from surface springs and used for lighting, sealing boats, waterproofing, lubrication, and other purposes. In the early 1800s oil was often found during searches for brines to use for salt making. During this era, crude oil was also commonly employed as a patent medicine. In 1859 Edwin L. Drake drilled the well at Titusville in northwestern Pennsylvania that launched the modern oil industry. The successful attempt to drill for and recover oil occurred at a critical moment when technology was becoming available to refine crude into inexpensive clean-burning kerosene and whale oil was too expensive to meet the demands for lamp fuel. By 1900 the oil-producing areas of the basin had yielded a billion barrels, with production in excess of 50 million barrels annually. Oil production in the basin has generally declined since, with production at the opening of the twenty-first century fewer than 25 million barrels annually.

A typical barrel of crude oil consists of 25 weight percent paraffins or waxes, 50 percent naphthenes, 17 percent aromatic hydrocarbons, and 8 percent asphalt. When refined, an average barrel of crude will produce about nineteen gallons of gasoline (45 percent), ten gallons of home heating oil and diesel fuel (24 percent), seven and a half gallons of bunker oil, asphalt, petrochemical feedstock, and other heavy tars (18 percent), five gallons of kerosene and jet fuel (12 percent), and one-half gallon of lubricating oil (1 percent). In addition to transportation fuels and motor oils, many other products are derived from refined crude oil. These include buttons, roofing shingles, vinyl, nylon, Dacron, rayon, tires, aspirin, antifreeze, food storage containers, soft drink bottles, Teflon, pesticides, herbicides, compact discs, heart valve replacements, PVC pipe, dyes, and road-paving material.

Edwin L. Drake (right foreground) in front of the engine house and derrick of Drake Well, Titusville, Pennsylvania, 1866. The Drake Well is known today as the birthplace of the modern oil industry.

One early oil company influenced all its competitors and other industries as well. In 1863, soon after the drilling of the Drake Well at Titusville, John D. Rockefeller became a partner in an oil-refining company being formed in Cleveland, Ohio, which was situated on two railroad lines that had access to the developing oil regions of Ohio and Pennsylvania. In 1865 Rockefeller bought out several of his partners and in 1866 brought his brother, William, into the partnership. The Standard Works refinery was built, and by 1868 Rockefeller, Andrews, and Flagler was the largest refining company in the world. On January 10, 1870, the Standard Oil Company of Ohio was created and organized as the first vertically integrated oil firm in the world. It owned all aspects of its business from the timber for its oil barrels to delivery wagons, railroads, and refineries. In 1882 Rockefeller created the Standard Oil Trust, using an idea suggested by attorney Samuel Dodd whereby a board of trustees was created to manage the assets of the company. By 1890 Standard's market dominance and policy of trying to force all grocery and hardware stores that sold kerosene and lubricants to sell only Standard products led to a general dislike of the firm by the American public. The Standard Oil Trust was dissolved in 1911 as the result of a suit brought by the attorney general of Ohio in 1892. While this effectively ended the monopoly of the petroleum industry held by Standard, its executives, including Rockefeller, still controlled the components of the former trust as majority stockholders of the severed companies.

At least one powerful benchmark of the pervasive influence of Standard Oil on the industry remains today. The company recognized that crude oil components could evaporate during shipment, and, to guarantee delivery of a full quantity of oil, Standard added two extra gallons to each barrel. To distinguish their barrels from those of others, Standard painted its barrels blue. The blue barrels came to be abbreviated *bbl*, and each contained forty-two gallons of oil. This remains the basic unit of measure for crude oil sold worldwide.

See also: OIL AND GAS (GEOLOGY); ROCKEFELLER, JOHN D. AND JOHN D., JR.

—Brandon Nuttall, *Kentucky Geological Survey*

A. I. Levorsen, *Geology of Petroleum* (2nd edition, 1967); U.S. Department of Energy, Energy Information Administration, *U.S. Petroleum States Data* (2003).

Peabody Coal

Based in St. Louis, Peabody Coal—more recently Peabody Energy—was the largest coal company in the world in 2003. Its coal generated 9 percent of the electricity used in the United States and about 2 percent of that consumed by the world. In 2003 the company produced 223.9 million tons of coal from thirty-three mining operations. One-third of that production still came from Appalachia, much of it from underground mines in Kentucky and West Virginia, despite the rising importance of the firm's coalfields in the West. Altogether, Peabody owned some 10 billion tons of proven or probable coal reserves.

Peabody Coal began in Chicago in 1883. Francis S. Peabody, then twenty-four years old, gathered a hundred dollars and used his family's business and political connections to start a retail coal company. By 1895 he had opened his first mine in Williamson County, Illinois, buying tens of thousands of acres of the Illinois basin. Coal contracts farther east were even easier to gain from Appalachian residents rich in acres but poor in capital. Their landscape held virgin timber, coal beds, natural gas, salt springs and licks, iron ore, and deposits of granite and marble. From farmers who were often illiterate, Peabody representatives bought thousands of acres of land and mineral rights for fifty cents or so an acre.

That put the company among the frontrunners during the golden age of the Appalachian coal industry from 1912 to 1927. Railroads were built into the roadless mountains to transport coal, and farmers left their land to work in mines and live in coal camps. Across Appalachia, Peabody and other outsider energy empires controlled the lives of miners. Companies built houses, stores, recreation centers, and hospitals in the coal towns, paying the miners in scrip that could be spent only in the company store.

Its long history notwithstanding, Peabody's name in contemporary Appalachia is probably known best because of John Prine's 1971 song "Paradise," which was inspired by the company's massive strip mining of Muhlenberg County in western Kentucky. During the late twentieth century, the gigantic equipment that became famous in the coalfields of western Kentucky and southern Illinois advanced into the Appalachians. In 1997 Peabody Coal received the Twentieth Anniversary Excellence in Surface Coal Mining Reclamation Award from the United States Department of the Interior, Office of Surface Mining, for work at its Gibraltar Mine in Muhlenberg County. In the western United States, however, Peabody has met with resistance to surface mining, with Native Americans battling Peabody Coal over mineral rights and the proceeds of mining.

While Native Americans saw mixed results in their mineral rights claims against the company, others have succeeded in requiring it to take additional financial responsibility for its actions. In 1991 Peabody agreed to pay $500,000 in fines for tampering with air samples from its mines in West Virginia, Kentucky, and Illinois. The company's actions defied a 1969 law requiring coal companies to take regular air samples to enforce limits on the amount of coal dust breathed by miners. Peabody was found to have taken samples at less dusty spots in the mine or outside the mine entirely, rather than at the face as required.

In 2003 the Supreme Court required Peabody to extend health-care coverage to approximately six hundred miners and their families who were assigned to Peabody after the workers' original employers could not be located. During the 1970s many major coal companies hired independent contractors to operate mines, particularly those with difficult working conditions. Through restructuring or bankruptcy, most of the contractors disappeared after their jobs were done, owing millions of dollars in wages and benefits, payments to mine supply companies, federal and state taxes, and workers' compensation premiums. In 2002 Peabody was ordered to pay $4,182,571 to the Workers' Compensation Division in West Virginia to cover unpaid premiums. The firm's fight against the assignment of health-care coverage for six hundred mining families coincided with its posting of a second-quarter 2002 profit of $24.5 million.

See also: BITUMINOUS COAL INDUSTRY; COAL MINING (ENVIRONMENT); MASSEY ENERGY COMPANY.

—Audra Himes, *Northern Cambria, Pennsylvania*

John R. Boxman, *Capitalist Collective Action: Competition, Cooperation and Conflict in the Coal Industry* (1989); Priscilla Long, *Where the Sun Never Shines: A History of America's Bloody Coal Industry* (1989); Crandall A. Shifflett, *Coal Towns: Life, Work, and Culture in Company Towns of Southern Appalachia, 1880–1960* (1991).

Pharmaceutical Industry

At least one Appalachian city—Bristol, Tennessee—has a lengthy pharmaceutical history that extends into the modern era. At the dawn of the twenty-first century, King Pharmaceuticals, a comparative newcomer, was traded on the New York Stock Exchange and listed in the Standard and Poor's 500 Index.

King Pharmaceuticals opened in the northeast Tennessee municipality in 1994 with ninety employees and a strategy of acquiring some drug brands and manufacturing others. It quickly acquired more than fifty brands and in less than a decade was operating manufacturing plants in not only Bristol but also in four well-scattered towns outside Appalachia. Its sales force had proliferated from twenty-four to eight hundred, and its revenues had multiplied from $13 million in 1994 to $872 million in 2001, a 41 percent increase from 2000. Brands owned by King included the well-known Neosporin, but its banner drug in 2003 was Altace, which had been shown to significantly reduce the chance of heart attack, stroke, and cardiovascular death in patients aged fifty-five and older.

King is rooted in a strong Bristol pharmaceutical tradition. The King company bought one of its earliest Bristol facilities, Beecham Laboratories, from a firm that had been absorbed by giant GlaxoSmithKline. Beecham had grown out of another highly notable Bristol concern, the S. E. Massengill Company, which Beecham bought in 1971. Massengill's history, mostly a distinguished one, went back to the end of the nineteenth century.

Before the nineteenth century, the majority of manufactured drugs came to America from Europe. Difficulties with importation during the Revolutionary War stimulated small-scale production in a few pharmacies. Most pharmaceutical manufacturing companies began by offering for sale a few galenicals, simple medicines whose ingredients had not been chemically changed. From galenicals they moved on to the preparation of a limited number of chemicals, progressing through research to a systematic production of certain groups of chemicals, medicines, antibiotics, and biologicals, which were made from living organisms. Between about 1820 and 1840 the beginnings of what would become large-scale drug manufacturing took shape. By the end of the nineteenth century, drug manufacturers had developed the machines and technologies that would eventually relieve community pharmacies of their age-old function of making drugs. Manufacturing the innovative compressed and coated tablet was beyond the range of production of the average pharmacy. Biological products and antibiotics discovered in the first half of the twentieth century were almost impossible for local pharmacies to process. With each innovation, the number of large-scale drug manufacturers grew. The Pure Food and Drug Act of 1906 and successive regulations made it increasingly difficult for small laboratories to meet all legal and scientific requirements.

Of the fifteen firms represented at the first meeting of the American Pharmaceutical Manufacturers' Association in Detroit in 1910, two were located in the Appalachian region. They were the Norwich Pharmacal Company of Norwich, New York, and the Zemmer Company of Pittsburgh. At the third annual meeting, which was held in Indianapolis, a representative from the Massengill Brothers Company in Bristol joined the group of representatives from twenty-seven firms.

The Zemmer Company had been incorporated in the District of Columbia in 1903 but was purchased by George C. Hall in 1904, moved to Pittsburgh, and appears to have survived into the 1950s. The more notable Norwich Pharmacal Company began as L. F. Moore, Pill Manufacturer, in an upstairs room above a carpenter shop in 1885. Its one-man staff, a minister named Lafayette Moore, ventured into business equipped with nothing more than a pill cutter and a gelatin pill coater, the latter of which is now on display at the Smithsonian Institution in Washington, D.C. In 1887 the minister left the Norwich business in the hands of a young partner and moved to Clinton, New York, where he was involved in the formation of Clinton Pharmaceutical Company, which later became Bristol-Myers. The company he founded in Norwich also prospered. In 1913 it began marketing its own invention, Pepto-Bismol, in a trademark three-sided bottle. After two mergers, it became Norwich Eaton Pharmaceuticals, which in the early twenty-first century was a wholly owned subsidiary of the Procter and Gamble Company. The Norwich facilities closed in 1993.

Another Appalachian firm, S. B. Penick and Company, was founded in 1914 in Marion, North Carolina, to sell medicinal plants gathered from nearby fields and woods. The company provided an improved source of supply for the line of botanical drugs and allied technical products required by manufacturing and the wholesale drug trade in the United States and abroad. Penick claimed to be the first company in the industry to hire botanical drug collectors. By 1936 the company had branch offices in several foreign countries and was one of the world's largest botanical drug houses, producing "a full line of solid and powdered concentrated Extracts, a number of Alkaloids, Glucosides and Resins to meet the demand of the manufacturer." Over the years, however, the firm was broken up, and its last remaining piece, Penick Pharmaceuticals, was sold to a private investor in 1988. At that time, Penick Pharmaceuticals was producing a variety of inorganic chemicals, especially bismuth salts, several products via chemical synthesis or fermentation, and a full range of opiate narcotics. Its main products were codeine and morphine. Penick is now a privately held company specializing in the manufacture of active-ingredient chemicals for the pharmaceutical, flavor, fragrance, and cosmetic industries. It specializes in the manufacture of controlled substances, especially medicinal narcotics derived from the opium poppy.

Samuel Evans Massengill, a native of Sullivan County, Tennessee, founded the S. E. Massengill Company. Massengill had been a salesman for a Boston wholesale drug house, and in his travels for that company he had noted that country doctors faced great difficulty in obtaining medicine for their patients because of poor roads in isolated communities. This observation led Massengill and his brother, Norman H. Massengill, to establish the Massengill Brothers pharmaceutical plant in Bristol in 1897. Later renamed the S. E. Massengill Company, the firm touted itself at one time as the largest manufacturer of pharmaceuticals in the South. A tragic event marred the history of the Massengill Company. In 1937 Massengill researchers were seeking a more palatable way to deliver the new miracle sulfa drugs, and they determined that diethylene glycol, the primary ingredient in some antifreezes, was a satisfactory solvent. They then began selling Elixir of Sulfanilamide without testing it. As a result, 107 people, most of them children, died from kidney and liver failure because the solvent was toxic. Under the Pure Food and Drug Act, Massengill could be prosecuted only for mislabeling the product as an elixir, since it contained no alcohol, and the public outcry pushed passage of the Food, Drug and Cosmetic Act of 1938. The last death resulting from the tragedy was that of the chemist who had developed the elixir. He committed suicide.

See also: CHATTANOOGA MEDICINE COMPANY.

—Martha Whaley, *East Tennessee State University*

Robert S. Loving, *Double Destiny: The Story of Bristol, Tennessee-Virginia* (1955); Birdsey L. Maltbie, *A Quarter Century of Progress in Manufacturing Pharmacy* (1937); V. N. Phillips, *Bristol, Tennessee-Virginia: A History, 1852–1900* (1992); Glenn Sonnedecker, rev., *Kremers and Urdang's History of Pharmacy* (4th edition, 1976).

Pittsburgh Brewing Company and Iron City Beer

Pittsburgh Brewing Company, with roots going back 140 years, is best known for its aptly named Iron City Beer, an icon of the city that reigned as the capital of America's Industrial Revolution. The firm survived not only prohibition but also the rise of national brands and the competition of giant corporate breweries to become the oldest brewing operation west of the Allegheny Mountains. It is the second-oldest beer producer in the nation and one of the ten largest.

Brewing began in Pittsburgh with the production of ale and porter soon after the city was founded in 1758, but the earliest record of a commercial brewery in the region dates from 1795. Other early brewing ventures included operations located near hillsides, where caves were dug to chill, store, and age the ale and porter. Notable brewing in Pittsburgh, though, began with the Iron City Brewery, which was created by Edward Frauenheim, a young German immigrant. Frauenheim's brewery, the first in America to produce a lager, created the Iron City brand in 1861.

The brewery outgrew its original facility in 1866 and moved to a four-story brick building on Liberty Avenue, where it continued to expand, adding a new three-story structure. It also acquired an additional owner when native Pittsburgh brewer Leopold Vilsak of Pittsburgh's Bennett Brewery joined the company. Frauenheim and Vilsak together built one of the most substantial breweries in the nation, which could claim a brewing capacity of fifty thousand barrels a year and a total value of some $150,000—an astonishing figure for a brewery of its time.

Its great success notwithstanding, Iron City joined eleven other Allegheny brewing companies as well as nine outside its local area and created a trust known as Pittsburgh Brewing Company. During this period, trusts were common in numerous industries. The establishment of Pittsburgh Brewing created the largest brewing operation in Pennsylvania and the third largest in the United States.

The robust operation was able to survive challenges to which other breweries succumbed, most notably prohibition. While thirteen ostensibly dry years forced many breweries, distillers, and taverns to close, Pittsburgh Brewing Company endured by producing soft drinks, ice cream, and near beer, as well as operating a cold storage business. When prohibition was repealed in 1933, the company was one of 725 breweries still operating. Innovation, too, sustained the firm in competition against national brands and larger breweries. In 1962, in collaboration with Alcoa, the Pittsburgh aluminum giant, Pittsburgh Brewing introduced the world's first snap-top can. Other notable creations of Pittsburgh Brewing include the first twist-off resealable cap and the first commemorative cans honoring sports teams. Iron City was the first draught beer available in a can, and in the 1970s the firm introduced a new light beer—I. C. Light—which increased Iron City sales. In 2004, again in conjunction with Alcoa, Pittsburgh Brewing introduced aluminum bottles, which were non-breakable and allowed beer to chill faster and stay cold longer.

In 1977 Pittsburgh Brewing Company was one of forty breweries left in the United States. It was acquired by

Pittsburgh native Joseph Piccirilli and his investment group, Keystone Brewing Company, in 1995.

See also: BREWERIES.

—Kristin L. Abramson, *Pittsburgh, Pennsylvania*

Lew Bryson, *Pennsylvania Breweries* (1998); Donald Bull, Manfred Friedrich, and Robert Gottschalk, *American Breweries* (1984); Bill Yenne, *Beers of North America* (1986).

Printing/Publishing Presses

Printing and publishing have been cultural keystones of the Appalachian scene for most of the twentieth century. Regional publishers and small presses, organizations and institutions, and a number of university presses located within and outside the region publish works about Appalachia, including fiction, nonfiction, poetry, and scholarship, or by Appalachian authors whose work might otherwise not see print. By the 1960s, Kingsport Press in Kingsport, Tennessee, had become a world leader in the printing of books. In 2003, as part of Montreal-based Quebecor World, its facilities were producing more than 100 million copies annually. Such national publications as *National Geographic* have been printed at Appalachian facilities. University presses have proliferated across the region, publishing books, scholarly journals, and other periodicals. Independent publishers and book dealers have contributed important reference works and other material and made the work of regional authors more widely available.

Small presses are common in the region, and many have a strong name association with their founding editor and sometimes operated out of that person's home. Although some were short-lived, others have become well established. In North Carolina, these include John F. Blair (Winston-Salem), a general trade publisher specializing in regional books, and McFarland and Company (Jefferson), which publishes a series entitled *Contributions to Southern Appalachian Studies.* Bright Mountain Books (Asheville), founded in 1983 by Eric V. Bright, publishes southern Appalachian regional books distributed through Bright Horizons Specialty Distributors. Puddingstone Press, affiliated with Lees-McRae College in Banner Elk, was founded in 1969 to make original manuscripts and reprints of Appalachian materials available. Parkway Publishers (Boone) publishes books on the history, culture, and tourism of western North Carolina.

The Foxfire Fund (Mountain City, Georgia) was founded in 1966 to publish southern Appalachian materials, both historical and contemporary. Its publications include the *Foxfire* books, *Foxfire Magazine*, *Active Learner* (a journal for teachers), *Foxfire News* (a newsletter), and Foxfire teaching materials. Foxfire grew out of an oral history project developed by Eliot Wigginton for students in his English class at Rabun County High School in the mountains of northeast Georgia. Students at Rabun County High still publish the magazine.

In Kentucky, Wind Publications, founded in 1971 by Quentin Howard of Pikeville, publishes *Wind* magazine, one or two chapbooks a year, and an occasional full-length poetry collection. The Jesse Stuart Foundation, founded in 1979 in Ashland, focuses on Kentucky and Appalachia, publishing books by Stuart and other regional authors. Gnomon Press, founded by Jonathan Greene in New York City in 1965, is now also located in Kentucky and publishes primarily Appalachian authors and titles.

Small presses in Tennessee include Overmountain Press (Johnson City), a family-owned business founded in 1970, which publishes southern Appalachian history, folklore, and nonfiction. Iris Press, founded in 1975 in Binghamton, New York, was acquired in 1996 by Robert B. Cumming of Oak Ridge. Primarily a literary publisher, it has published a number of southern Appalachian poets, including George Scarbrough, Ron Rash, and Jeff Daniel Marion.

In Virginia, small presses include Pocahontas Press (Blacksburg) founded in 1984, which publishes poetry, memoirs, and nonfiction books about Appalachia, as well as scientific, technical, and educational material. Rowan Mountain Press (also in Blacksburg) was founded in 1988 and publishes poetry and short stories relating to Appalachia. Among the Appalachian authors it has published are Jim Wayne Miller, Sharyn McCrumb, and Bennie Lee Sinclair. The Sow's Ear Press (Abingdon) was founded in 1989 by Larry Richman. It publishes the *Sow's Ear Poetry Review* and two to three books of southern Appalachian poetry a year.

In West Virginia, Trillium Press (Charleston), founded in 1992, publishes poetry, fiction, and autobiography by Appalachian and West Virginia writers. Butternut Publications (Martinsburg) was founded in 1991 and publishes only works by Appalachian authors or with Appalachian themes.

Although located in Big Timber, Montana, Seven Buffaloes Press has published a number of Appalachian writers, including Jim Wayne Miller, Patricia Shirley, and Rita Sims Quillen.

Perhaps the greatest advances in publishing in Appalachia stem from the efforts of universities. The University of the South (Sewanee, Tennessee) has published *Sewanee Review* since 1892. Other academic presses that publish or have published Appalachian authors and materials include University of Tennessee Press (Knoxville), Appalachian State University Press (Boone, North Carolina), the East Tennessee State University Research Council (Johnson City), and Morehead State University Press, founded by Albert Stewart while on the faculty at Morehead State College (now Morehead State University), in Morehead, Kentucky.

Mountain State Press, at the University of Charleston (West Virginia), publishes fiction, nonfiction, and poetry, specializing in Appalachian regional subjects and authors. West Virginia University Press in Morgantown publishes trade and scholarly materials with an emphasis on Appalachia, West Virginia, and the coal industry. Robert Munn, dean of West Virginia University Libraries, established the West Virginia University Press in the 1970s. Several of these academic presses publish periodicals focused solely on the Appalachian region, such as Berea College's *Appalachian Heritage* and Appalachian State University's *Appalachian Journal*.

University presses outside the region, such as the University of North Carolina Press, University of Georgia Press, University Press of Mississippi, and University of Illinois Press, also publish Appalachian authors and books about the region. Louisiana State University Press has published collections by Appalachian authors Fred Chappell, Lee Smith, Lou Crabtree, and Kathryn Stripling Byer. In 2000 Ohio University Press launched a new series, *Ethnicity and Gender in Appalachia*, designed to publish scholarly research related to both negative and overly positive stereotypical images of Appalachians.

Some regional publishers are functions of organizations or institutions other than universities and colleges. Foremost among these is the Appalachian Regional Commission, the federal agency that defines the contemporary Appalachian region. In addition to the journal *Appalachia*, the commission also publishes an annual report, research reports, policy documents, resource guides, and project summaries.

The Appalachian Trail Conference (Harpers Ferry, West Virginia), founded in 1925, publishes guidebooks and maps as well as *Appalachian Trailway News*, a membership magazine about the Appalachian Trail. The Regional Appalachian Center at the Children's Museum of Oak Ridge has published an Appalachian writers film series, the *Encyclopedia of East Tennessee*, and an *Appalachian Studies Teacher's Manual*. The Appalachian Studies Association, an organization of scholars and academics, publishes the *Journal of Appalachian Studies*, formerly titled *Journal of the Appalachian Studies Association*. It was originally issued as *Proceedings of the Appalachian Studies Association*.

Appalachian Consortium Press, headquartered in Boone, North Carolina, was a division of the Appalachian Consortium, a nonprofit educational organization comprised of institutions and agencies located in the southern highlands and dedicated to preserving and protecting the heritage of southern Appalachia. This press printed or distributed more than ninety books and recordings about southern Appalachia and its people before it stopped publishing in 2004.

Closely following the first settlers of the Appalachian Mountains, printing and publishing businesses played crucial roles in the development of cultural, political, and economic life in the region. Printing and publishing has informed Appalachian residents of local, regional, and national events, linking them to a broader community. Pittsburgh was the first Appalachian city to establish a printing press. Most of the earliest printers, such as John Scull and Joseph Hall, who started the *Pittsburgh Gazette* in 1786, specialized in newspaper publishing.

Soon after establishing a newspaper, many of the early printers proceeded to print and publish books. Some examples are *The Laws of the State of Tennessee*, printed by George Roulstone, founder of the *Knoxville Gazette*, in 1803; *Christian Panoply*, printed by West Virginia newspaper publishers Philip Rootes and Charles Blagrove in 1797; and *Ohio Navigator*, printed in Kentucky by William Hunter and William Beaumont in 1798. Most early books catered to regional interests—state laws, local education, and local history—although as early as 1800 Hunter and Beaumont printed Thomas Paine's *Age of Reason*.

In the early days of Appalachian printing, circulation rarely exceeded a few hundred copies, and printers performed the wide array of tasks that made production possible, including publishing, typesetting, bookbinding, and sometimes even distribution. As population increased, though, so did demand for higher yields. Technological advances such as offset printing, along with the need for increased productivity, led to a more specialized workforce. By the early and mid-1900s, workers had formed unions advocating for the needs of printers, stereotypers, electrotypers, platemakers, typographers, bookbinders, photo engravers, printers' assistants, booksellers, and publishers.

Unions for these professions commonly merged and divided throughout the 1900s. Oldest among printing and publishing unions was the International Typographical Union, formed in 1852 by journeymen printers. Pressmen separated themselves from the union in 1889 to found the International Printing Pressman's Union of North America. Other offshoots of the International Typographical Union included the International Brotherhood of Bookbinders, International Stereotypers and Electrotypers Union of North America, and the International Photo Engravers of North America. In 1896 the International Printing Pressman's Union of North America incorporated printers' assistants into its membership and became the International Printing Pressmen and Assistants' Union. In 1983 many of these unions merged into one, the Graphic Communication International Union.

The International Printing Pressmen and Assistants' Union exerted tremendous influence over the Appalachian region. In 1911 George L. Berry, president of the union, moved its headquarters to Pressmen's Home just outside Rogersville, Tennessee. Pressmen's Home offered the union's members a sanatorium, a technical school for training, and a hotel and other resort accommodations. In order to create jobs in the region, members staying at Pressmen's Home acquired the *Rogersville Review* newspaper and in 1926 opened the Card and Label Company, creating jobs that would remain even after the union withdrew its headquarters from the region in 1967.

Also contributing to the impact of printing in Appalachia was the founding in 1922 and development of J. J. Little and Company, later the Kingsport Press, which was designed to make use of the already functioning pulp mill in the town of Kingsport. Printing became the town's primary industry, employing thousands of people in the press, the paper and pulp mill, and a book-cloth furnishing plant. In the 1960s the press alone employed more than two thousand workers and produced more books than any other plant in the world. In 1963, because of a dispute between the company and the union, sixteen hundred workers began a four-year strike that was the International Printing Pressmen and Assistants' Union's longest, as well as one of the longest in American history.

The former Kingsport Press is now part of Canadian-based Quebecor World, one of the largest printing and publishing conglomerates on the international scene. At the dawn of the twenty-first century it still employed some three thousand people in Kingsport but in 2002 had begun to shift jobs overseas. Until the fall of 2002, Quebecor printed *National Geographic* at its plant in Corinth, Mississippi. The magazine then moved to Quad Graphics in Martinsburg, West Virginia. Wisconsin-headquartered Quad Graphics is the largest privately held printing firm in the world. It opened the Martinsburg plant in 1996.

Economically, the most immediate Appalachian impact of printing and publishing has been the creation of thousands of jobs in paper manufacturing, bookbinding, printing, and sales. The contributions of people such as Richwood, West Virginia, publisher and historian Jim Comstock, with his publication of the twenty-five volume *West Virginia Heritage Encyclopedia*, James S. Williams of the *Southwest Virginia Enterprise* in Wytheville, Virginia, and Jim Presgraves of the Wytheville book-dealing firm Bookworm and Silverfish have created a forum for writers that otherwise would remain inaccessible by making available works by regional authors and of regional interest.

See also: NEWSPAPERS (MEDIA).

—Linda Behrend, *University of Tennessee*, and Adam Sanders, *East Tennessee State University*

Leatha Kendrick, "Small Presses: Market Niches and Labors of Love," *Now and Then* (Summer 1998); Jack Mooney, *Printers in Appalachia: The International Printing Pressmen and Assistants' Union of North America* (1993); John William Tebbel, *A History of Book Publishing in the United States* (1972–81).

Proffitt's

A small Appalachian department store that rose to merge with Saks Fifth Avenue, Proffitt's was first established as the Ellis-Proffitt Company by David W. Proffitt and James N. Ellis in 1919 in Maryville, Tennessee. Two years later Ellis sold his share of the company to the cofounder. During the next several decades, Proffitt's slowly expanded in east Tennessee, opening a second store in Athens, then a warehouse and distribution facility in Maryville, two more stores in Knoxville, and another in Oak Ridge. In 1984 the firm was sold to RBM Venture Company, an investment concern led by R. Brad Martin of Memphis. Proffitt's offered one million shares of stock for public purchase on NASDAQ in 1987.

In 1988 the company began acquiring other retail outlets. It acquired five locations from Loveman's Department Stores in 1988 and eighteen more in Tennessee, Virginia, Kentucky, and Georgia from Hess Department Stores in 1992 and 1993. Beginning with McRae's in 1994, Proffitt's also acquired several other regional retailers: Parks-Belk (1995), Younkers (1996), Parisian (1996), Herberger's (1997), and Carson Pirie Scott (1998). These companies operated numerous outlets in the South, Midwest, and Great Plains.

Proffitt's transferred its shares from NASDAQ to the New York Stock Exchange in 1997. The next year, it merged with Saks Holdings, the holding company for Saks Fifth Avenue, and became Saks Incorporated. As of 2004, Proffitt's operated twenty-six department stores throughout the Southeast.

See also: GOODY'S FAMILY CLOTHING.

—Ed Speer, *Elizabethton, Tennessee*

Regal Cinemas

Regal Cinemas, headquartered in Knoxville, Tennessee, has locations throughout Appalachia. In early 2002, Regal was one of the youngest theater chains in the world and had risen to the top of the industry with nearly 4,000 screens in more than 300 midsized urban and suburban locations. The company also operated a handful of IMAX 3-D theaters in selected multiplexes.

The company was founded in 1989 by Mike Campbell, a grocery store manager, and his close friend and coworker Neal Melton. The two men leased their first theater in a suburb of Knoxville in 1982. That first venture into the theater business developed into an important regional exhibitor known for providing a high standard of customer service in attractive theater complexes. Regal Cinemas was one of the first to open a lobby café as an alternative to standard concessions in theaters. The company went public in 1993 and was bought by a joint venture of Kohlberg Kravis Roberts and Company of New York and Dallas-based Hicks, Muse, Tate and Furst, Inc., in 1998. Regal Cinemas became a subsidiary of Regal Entertainment Group, which includes United Artists Theatres and Edward Theatres. The combined venture operates 6,119 screens in 562 locations in thirty-nine states. *Forbes* magazine included Regal in its 1995, 1996, and 1997 list of the two hundred best small companies in America.

Regal Cinemas filed for bankruptcy in 2001 and was reorganized under Chapter 11 when Philip Anschutz, a Denver entrepreneur, acquired the debt to take controlling interest in the company. The combination of Regal with Edward and United Artists produced greater efficiency and substantial profits. The Regal Entertainment Corporation, described by financial analysts as the world's largest chain of movie theaters, claimed 2002 sales of $2.1 billion, $120 million in net income, and a net income growth from 2001 of some 2,300 percent.

See also: SECTION OVERVIEW (MEDIA).

—Clara Hasbrouck, *East Tennessee State University*

Reynolds, R. S.

(1881–1955) Metals manufacturer.

A pioneer Appalachian aluminum maker and marketer, Richard Samuel Reynolds Sr. founded Reynolds Metals, best known for its aluminum foil. He and his company were prime beneficiaries of a 1945 United States antitrust decision forbidding Alcoa from buying federally funded aluminum manufacturing facilities the government had commissioned it to build during World War II.

Born on August 15, 1881, in Bristol, Tennessee, Reynolds, the son and nephew of tobacco businessmen, studied at King College in Bristol, Columbia College in New York City, and the University of Virginia. While working in North Carolina for his uncle, R. J. Reynolds, he helped introduce Camel cigarettes and tin containers for pipe tobacco. In 1912 R. S. Reynolds started his own company in Bristol, making soap and then waterproof gunpowder containers for World War I. After the war he established the United States Foil Company in Louisville, Kentucky, which supplied wrapping materials made of lead, tin, and (eventually) aluminum to candy, cigarette, and chewing gum companies. The firm boomed in the 1920s and successfully entered the consumer market with its first acquisition, the Eskimo Pie Corporation, which sold foil-wrapped ice cream bars.

In 1928 Reynolds formed Reynolds Metals. Predicting that wartime demand for aluminum for military aircraft parts would outstrip Alcoa's monopoly production, he began mining bauxite in Arkansas in 1940. His first aluminum smelter soon opened near Sheffield, Alabama. Instead of closing plants after the war, Reynolds promoted an array of new aluminum products ranging from home siding to kitchen appliances.

In 1948 Reynolds became chairman of the Reynolds Metals board, with his oldest son succeeding him as president. The founder died in 1955.

See also: ALUMINUM INDUSTRY; R. J. REYNOLDS TOBACCO COMPANY.

—Sarah Gibbard Cook, *DeForest, Wisconsin*

R. J. Reynolds Tobacco Company

At the beginning of the twenty-first century, R. J. Reynolds Tobacco Company was the second-leading cigarette manufacturer in the United States, producing one in four cigarettes sold, and its best-selling brands included Doral, Camel, Winston, and Salem. In late 2003 it bought from British American Tobacco the American operations of Brown and Williamson, the third-leading U.S. seller, and became the manufacturer of about one in three cigarettes sold in the United States, gaining such additional name brands as Kent, Lucky Strike, and Kool. The merger, which formed Reynolds America Inc., was attributed to a management desire to gain Reynolds competitive leverage against America's top tobacco company, Philip Morris USA. Reynolds America is traded as RAI on the New York Stock Exchange.

R. J. Reynolds Tobacco was founded in 1875 in what was then Winston, North Carolina, by Richard Joshua Reynolds, son of a wealthy Virginia planter. The town, located on a rail line, was known for producing flue-cured tobacco. To further ensure the stability of Winston as the home of his budding company, Reynolds was instrumental in creating a savings bank there and building local roads. Winston later merged with a neighboring town and is known today as Winston-Salem. Reynolds not only built a successful company, but he also inaugurated a tradition of economic, educational, cultural, and medical philanthropy in North Carolina and Appalachia. This counterbalanced to some degree the negative publicity from the physical effects of smoking for many of the region's residents.

In 1929 R. J. Reynolds moved to new headquarters in the Reynolds Building in downtown Winston-Salem, and from there the company produced the first filter cigarette brand, Winston, in 1954. Following that, in 1956, the firm manufactured the first filtered menthol cigarette, Salem. The RJR Plaza Building was added as another office building in 1982, and the firm's largest plant, the Tobaccoville Manufacturing Center, was built in 1986.

In 2001 and 2002, *Fortune* magazine ranked R. J. Reynolds one of the top hundred companies for which to work. The rating was reported to be based on employee feedback as well as information obtained from the company's employee handbook on benefits and policies. But in 2003 the company announced that there would be twenty-six hundred fewer names on its payroll by year's end, a figure amounting to 40 percent of the workforce in place before the British

American Tobacco merger. The next day, in the face of decreasing domestic cigarette sales by all U.S. tobacco companies amid a climate of continual smoking-related litigation, R. J. Reynolds reported a net loss of $3.45 billion. Its sales total for the third quarter of 2003 was $1.38 billion, down 13 percent from the same quarter in 2002. Management said Reynolds expected its cost-cutting measures to save more than a billion dollars by 2005.

The company's voluntary employee turnover rate in 1999 was reported at just 3 percent in a workforce that was 33 percent female and 21 percent minority. Reynolds had a strong benefits package that allowed employees to invest in the local economy. The company and families directly associated with it contributed regularly to many educational, medical, and community facilities within North Carolina. Wake Forest University and the Bowman Gray School of Medicine attribute their beginnings to the tobacco company, and other recipients include North Carolina State University, the University of North Carolina, Slater Hospital, the Reynolds Temple Methodist Church, and the YMCA.

See also: TOBACCO (AGRICULTURE); TOBACCO AND HEALTH (HEALTH); TOBACCO INDUSTRY.

—Lucinda Barlow, *Tennessee Technological University*

Nannie Tilley, *The R. J. Reynolds Tobacco Company* (1985).

Rockefeller, John D. and John D., Jr.

Rockefeller, John Davison (1839–1937) Industrialist and philanthropist.

Rockefeller, John Davison, Jr. (1874–1960) Industrialist and philanthropist.

Appalachia provided much of the foundation of the Rockefeller fortune, one of the great accumulations of wealth in U.S. history, and received a sizeable portion of its benefits. A substantial part of the land for the Great Smoky Mountains and Shenandoah National Parks came from donations from Rockefeller funds or holdings, and this was by no means the extent of the Rockefellers' impact on the region.

From a small oil refinery in Cleveland, Ohio, John D. Rockefeller built one of the world's largest modern industries. He also established a family tradition of philanthropy, donating an estimated $550 million to many causes. Born on July 8, 1839, in Richford, New York, to William Avery Rockefeller, a small trader, and the former Eliza Davison, this second of six children was strongly influenced by his father's interest in business and his mother's Baptist faith. In 1864 Rockefeller married Laura Celestia Spelman, and they had four daughters and a son.

In 1855 Rockefeller worked as an accounting clerk for a firm in Cleveland. A series of partnerships beginning in 1859 led to the founding of Standard Oil Company in 1870. Rockefeller bought out rival refineries, monopolizing the industry. While critics attacked such practices as obtaining railroad rebates and using predatory pricing, he persisted toward his goal of bringing order to a chaotic industry. His management style included delegating authority, training workers, purchasing quality equipment, and keeping production costs down. In 1882 he established the Standard Oil Trust, which in addition to controlling most of the oil refining industry had large interests in a variety of other businesses from iron and lumber to manufacturing plants and transportation. The trust was later broken up under the Sherman Antitrust Act in 1911.

By then Rockefeller had retired and was spending most of his time giving away much of his wealth in association with his son, John D. Rockefeller Jr. A graduate of Brown University, the younger Rockefeller had gone to work for his father but soon found himself less interested in the oil business than in philanthropic and civic activities as well as conservation and historic preservation. By 1910 he was devoting most of his time to philanthropy. His father's first large gift, $35 million, helped establish the University of Chicago, and other Rockefeller beneficence followed. Father and son founded and expanded such notable foundations as the Rockefeller Institute for Medical Research in 1901, the General Education Board in 1902, the Rockefeller Foundation in 1913, and the Laura Spelman Rockefeller Memorial in 1918.

Some of these organizations have played important roles in Appalachia into the twenty-first century. The General Education Board helped shape the development of higher education and race relations in the South. By providing financing for many schools, including Spelman College, the board also fostered such by-products as the 4-H movement and federal farm and home extension programs. In addition, the Rockfeller Sanitary Commission, which operated between 1909 and 1915, worked with state officials to provide education and treatment toward the eradication of hookworm, fostering the 1910 launch of hookworm campaigns in Virginia, North Carolina, Georgia, South Carolina, Tennessee, Mississippi, and Alabama. The program was successful and led to other health-related initiatives. Through the Laura Spelman Rockefeller Memorial, the younger Rockefeller spent $5 million to purchase private land in the Great Smoky Mountains, which he donated to the federal government. He also donated land for Shenandoah National Park.

Rockefeller Sr.'s autobiography, *Random Reminiscences of Men and Events*, was published in 1909. He died at his home in Ormond Beach, Florida, on May 23, 1937. His son died in Tucson, Arizona, on May 11, 1960, having made philanthropic contributions of some $400 million.

See also: IRON AND STEEL INDUSTRY; LUMBER INDUSTRY; OIL INDUSTRY.

—Kathy A. Campbell, *East Tennessee State University*, and Marie Garrett, *University of Tennessee*

Ruby Tuesday

The Tennessee-based Ruby Tuesday restaurant chain has spread throughout Appalachia and across the nation since its 1972 founding. The chain takes its name from a song by the British rock group the Rolling Stones.

Sandy E. Beall III (1951–), the first chairman and chief executive officer of the company, leased property for his first restaurant in Knoxville, Tennessee, near the University of Tennessee campus. From its single Knoxville location, Ruby Tuesday rapidly became one of the fastest-growing chains in the food service industry. Within a year, a second restaurant opened in West Knoxville. A third restaurant opened in Chattanooga in March 1974. By 2002, there were more than 550 Ruby Tuesday restaurants, located primarily in the eastern United States.

Early success led to the chain's acquisition by cafeteria operator Morrison Restaurants Inc. in April 1982. Ruby Tuesday became part of the Specialty Restaurant Division of Morrison and moved its corporate offices to Mobile, Alabama. In 1992 Morrison renamed the Specialty Restaurant Division the Ruby Tuesday Group. At the time, the merger was thought to be mutually advantageous, providing Morrison with a wider customer base and Ruby Tuesday with additional financial support. Spurred by earnings losses, however, Beall, who had become chairman and chief executive officer of Morrison, led a successful effort to split up the company in 1996. The company's two smaller operating divisions were spun off. Ruby Tuesday Inc. became a separate, publicly held corporation with Beall its chairman and chief executive.

Corporate literature describes Ruby Tuesday as built on a casual dining restaurant concept and serving casual American food. In June 1998 Ruby Tuesday moved its corporate headquarters and training center to Maryville, Tennessee.

See also: KENTUCKY FRIED CHICKEN; SHONEY'S.

—Joel Davis, *Knoxville, Tennessee*

Salt

One of Appalachia's most notable gifts to world cuisine is salt-cured country ham. A more recent result of salt's presence in the region is a West Virginia–based firm that is the largest producer of chlorine in the world. Still another major contribution is a salt by-product called hydrazine from Saltville, Virginia, which has been used extensively in fuel for America's space vehicles. But in addition to its timeless roles in preserving and seasoning food and healing wounds, salt also has had a profound influence on Appalachian exploration, settlement, and conflict.

Many trails followed by explorers and pioneers such as Daniel Boone were created by buffalo and deer on their way to salt licks, areas in forests where mineral salts are commonly found on the ground surface. These licks are frequented by animals, which need salt for their digestive systems. Native American hunters, and then French and English traders, were also drawn to these salt licks. Pioneers followed the natural paths and built their settlements nearby, taking advantage of salt's attractiveness to the game they needed for food. French Lick on the Cumberland River began its evolution into the present-day city of Nashville, Tennessee, when James Robertson and John Donelson settled there in 1779–80—primarily because of the abundance of wildlife that depended on salt deposits.

Salt production was Kentucky's first industry. Boiled down from brackish springwater, the substance was shipped by flatboat and canoe throughout the Kentucky, Illinois, and Tennessee territories. From Bullitt's Lick seventeen miles south of Louisville, salt was transported in barrels down the Ohio and Mississippi Rivers to New Orleans. One of the most prolific salt-producing areas was a ten-mile section of the Kanawha River, which included the Great Buffalo Lick on the northern bank in what is now West Virginia. Long hunter Boone took Kanawha River salt with him in 1769 as he followed trails that animals created through the Cumberland Gap and across the Allegheny Mountains to the Ohio River Valley.

The first salt furnace in the Kanawha Valley was established by Elisha Brooks in 1797. He produced an average of 150 bushels of salt a day, selling it to settlers who bought it for use in curing butter and meats. Other entrepreneurs followed and found even richer brine at depths of some four hundred feet. By 1815, fifty-two furnaces were operating in the "Kanawha Salines." Salt makers there formed the nation's first trust to regulate price and quality and keep out foreign competition. At its most productive time, the cooperative sold more than 3 million bushels a year.

Early in the Civil War, Union General Jacob Dolson Cox took control of the Kanawha River Valley, including the saltworks, in one of the first major setbacks for the South. In the fall of 1862, however, a group of some five thousand Confederates recaptured the valley and pushed the Union troops back to the Ohio River. From then on, the Union army made every attempt to destroy saltworks immediately upon capture.

Although an 1861 flood and subsequent Civil War destruction created a general decline in salt production in the Kanawha Valley, World War I revived the industry by ushering in a demand for chemical products obtainable from salt brine such as chlorine and caustic acid. In 1914 the

Warner-Klipstein Chemical Company opened a plant in South Charleston, West Virginia, to make these products. It eventually became the Westvaco Chlorine Products Corporation, the world's foremost chlorine producer.

Saltville, Virginia, took its name from the existence of massive salt deposits. Saline springs were discovered in the Saltville area in 1748, and Colonel Arthur Campbell began commercial development of salt there in 1782. Before the coming of the railroads, Saltville salt was transported by boat down the Holston to the Tennessee River and then on as far south as Muscle Shoals, Alabama. This valley was the primary Confederate source of salt during the Civil War. In 1864 thirty-eight furnaces produced a peak of about 4 million bushels, at twenty-five dollars each.

Saltville was twice the scene of major Civil War fighting. In the fall of 1864 Union General Stephen G. Burbridge and his army attacked Confederates entrenched on ridges near the saltworks. After a daylong struggle, Union troops fled back into eastern Kentucky. The second battle of Saltville took place later that same year after Burbridge combined forces with General George Stoneman. Destroying railroad lines and advancing on Saltville on December 20, 1864, Union cavalry captured the town in thirty-six hours. Federal soldiers broke salt kettles, destroyed furnaces, and dropped cannon balls into wells where the brine had been drawn.

Mathieson Alkali Works bought the Saltville operations in 1892 and continued to manufacture salt until 1906. Afterward, a variety of salt by-products were made, from baking soda to rocket fuel. Saltville hydrazine was used extensively in fuel for U.S. space vehicles, including the Saturn rockets that sent Apollo missions to the moon in the 1960s and 1970s.

Kingsport, Tennessee, a planned city that is now the home of Eastman Chemical Company and a number of other industries, traces its origin to the salt trade. William King traveled from southwest Virginia to the banks of the Holston River, where he set up a distribution center for salt he produced back in Smyth County. Between 1802 and 1808 he constructed what became the Netherland Inn, with a boatyard from which salt was shipped downriver. This became a busy stop along the Great Stage Road, serving travelers bound for western Kentucky and middle Tennessee. Near that road during the Civil War, salt was rationed at Jonesborough, Tennessee's oldest town, and stored in a warehouse built in 1840.

Salt played a key role in the nation's settlement. Pork was America's first domesticated meat, and Appalachian settlers cured it with their region's salt. In a process still used today, salt removes the moisture and preserves the meat, and hams are aged in salt for at least six months. Salt was such a precious commodity during the Great Depression that a common practice was to sweep the floors of smokehouses to collect it for reuse.

See also: KANAWHA SALT TRUST; PORK (FOOD AND COOKING); SALT SETTLEMENTS (SETTLEMENT AND MIGRATION).

—Fred W. Sauceman, *East Tennessee State University*

John Egerton, *Southern Food: At Home, on the Road, in History* (1993); William B. Kent, *A History of Saltville, Virginia* (1955); Pamela D. Ripley, "Salt Was Kingsport Source," in *Home and Away: A University Brings Food to the Table*, ed. Fred W. Sauceman (2000).

Mathieson Alkali Works, Saltville, Virginia, c. 1900. Salt and salt by-products—including hydrazine fuel used on Apollo missions to the moon—have been manufactured on this site since 1895.

Saltpeter Mining

Appalachian saltpeter and nitrate mining for gunpowder production was especially important during the Civil War and the War of 1812 and of significance even during the American Revolution.

The extraction of rough nitrate from caves and rock shelters found throughout Appalachia was introduced in the mountains by European settlers who needed it for their firearms. Little was needed to mine saltpeter except a source of nitrate-rich soil or rock in caves or rock shelters, a small barrel or vat to put the soil in, water to leach out the nitrates, and a boiling kettle to distill and convert them from calcium nitrate into potassium nitrate. When mixed with sulfur and charcoal, potassium nitrate produces gunpowder. Potassium nitrate makes up about 75 percent of gunpowder, with the remainder comprised of equal amounts of sulfur and charcoal. One man with a nitre cave or rock shelter nearby could, with a little practice and a few tools, make enough gunpowder for his own use. In times of war, operations mushroomed to include hundreds of workers producing the large quantities of quality powder necessary for artillery.

A good example of a powder mine and mill was an operation run by a woman named Mary Patton during the Revolutionary War in what is now east Tennessee. She and her family had operated a mill in Carlisle, Pennsylvania, before selling it to move south. She apparently learned the trade in Scotland, where a cottage industry flourished in spite of its illegality under the laws of the English Crown. In the Watauga Settlement, pioneers obtained their nitrates from the Hyder and Gourley Caves. The nitrates were refined and turned into gunpowder at Patton's mill on Powder Branch, the same mill that supplied John Sevier and Isaac Shelby's soldiers with powder for their 1780 victory over Major Patrick Ferguson's British troops at the battle of Kings Mountain.

The British blockade of the United States during the War of 1812 created an increase in saltpeter mining throughout the Appalachians, with large-scale operations as far west as Mammoth Cave, Kentucky. Shares in the operation at Big Bone Cave in Van Buren County, Tennessee, sold for a combined price of sixty thousand dollars—a substantial sum in 1810—as speculators moved in on the valuable nitrate source. At times several hundred men labored in the cave, which was equipped with advanced waterworks sluicing the saltpeter containers, as well as a more sophisticated system for moving the nitre soils in and out of the vats. Records indicate that white miners leased nitre caves from the Cherokee during the war, paying them with a portion of the powder produced from the property.

Early in the Civil War, officials of the Confederacy started prospecting for nitrate sources throughout the region. The booklet *Notes on Making Saltpetre from the Earth of the Caves* by Confederate Major George W. Rains, printed in 1861, was widely distributed throughout the South. Major Rains asserted "that anyone residing in the neighborhood of a cave . . . can without any expense make at least a few pounds of the salt every day . . . and make it a very profitable business at the price which Government is now paying." Large operations such as the ones started at Big Bone Cave and Nickajack Cave in Appalachian Tennessee were productive during the first two years of the war. Manpower at these caves was often supplied by local farmers who were too old to serve in the army or who harbored divided loyalties. They were issued nitre certificates exempting them from military service. As the conflict lines moved southward, Union forces twice raided Nickajack Cave near Chattanooga, destroying the kettles, vats, and waterworks. Each time, the damage was repaired and Southerners resumed gunpowder production. Late in 1863, however, the area fell permanently under Union control, and operations at both caves were terminated.

As the war ground on and the South lost many of its richest nitre caves in the uplands, Southerners resorted to scraping out dirt beneath chicken coops, houses, and other farm buildings in search of nitrates. By the end of the Civil War, saltpeter operations in caves had been abandoned.

See also: CAVES (ECOLOGY); CIVIL WAR (GOVERNMENT).

—Stuart Carroll, *Fall Creek Falls State Park, Tennessee*

George Martin Crothers, "An Archaeological Survey of Big Bone Cave, Tennessee, and Diachronic Patterns of Cave Utilization in the Eastern Woodlands," M.A. thesis, University of Tennessee (1987); Robert A. Howard and E. Alvin Gerhardt Jr., *Mary Patton: Powder Maker of the Revolution* (1980); Marion Smith, *Saltpeter Mining in East Tennessee* (1990).

Sand and Gravel Industry

The quarrying of sand and gravel, common minerals that play important parts in industrialized society, occurs in many areas throughout the Appalachian region. Major quarries are located in Alabama, New York, North Carolina, Ohio, Pennsylvania, Tennessee, Virginia, and West Virginia.

Formed through the erosive power of wind, water, and ice, most deposits of sand and gravel are found by rivers and streambeds or in ridges and hills. Usually loose and easily handled, sand and gravel are easily compacted yet retain good drainage characteristics. Mixtures, or aggregates, constitute the material of choice for fills and as bases for pavements and other structures. Sand and gravel are also key ingredients in the production of concrete, asphalt, glass, ceramics, paints, plastics, soaps, and detergents. Because of the high cost of transporting this bulky, heavy product, most aggregates are commonly used within fifty miles of the quarry.

In the United States, the development of railroads in the 1850s and 1860s created a large demand for aggregates for use in roadbed construction and as ballast to support ties. A second boon to the industry came in the early 1900s with the advent of the automobile and drivers' demands for paved roads. Aggregate mining came into its own as an industry at this time. During the same period, the glass sand industry grew in West Virginia. The Hancock White Sand Company began to quarry Oriskany sandstone in Morgan County during the Civil War. In 1906, seven quarries were operating in the area. Because of the local availability of high-quality sandstone, West Virginia became a center for the production of fine glassware.

As a result of the aging infrastructure in the United States, demand for sand and gravel appeared at the beginning of the twenty-first century to be poised to increase, but two factors loomed as potential obstacles—bureaucratic red tape and land procurement. The sand and gravel industry has been regulated by a host of frequently vague local and state regulations that can require dual sets of permits. Since the only cost-effective way to produce sand and gravel aggregates is to locate operations close to consumers, operators must compete with other buyers for property with significant developmental possibilities.

The sand and gravel industry is a transitional one because of the limited life of quarries. Used quarries can be redeveloped for other economic or conservation uses, however. Unimin Corporation, which operates quarries in Alabama and Virginia and owns more than one hundred thousand acres of reserves around the world, has engaged in a number of conservation programs. Through the use of master plans, such sand and gravel operations can create attractive and economically useful landforms benefiting communities long after quarry operations have ended.

See also: GLASS INDUSTRY.

—Kathy A. Campbell, *East Tennessee State University*

U.S. Geological Survey, *Mineral Industry Surveys* (1994–95); West Virginia Geological and Economic Survey, *History of West Virginia Mineral Industries—Sandstone* (April 1997).

Scott, Nathan B.

(1842–1924) Industrialist and U.S. senator.

Nathan Bay Scott was one of the so-called Big Four (along with Henry Gassaway Davis, Stephen B. Elkins, and Johnson N. Camden) who played a dominant role during the formative years of West Virginia. An Appalachian Ohio native who maintained residences in Washington, Cleveland, and Denver as well as Wheeling, Scott exemplifies the rise of the power of big business, usually based out of state, in West Virginia's economy and politics. Around 1900, he and the others of the Big Four comprised four of the state's five millionaires.

Scott was born in Guernsey County, Ohio, on December 18, 1842. After attending the common schools there, he engaged in mining from 1859 to 1862 near Colorado Springs, Colorado. He then enlisted in the Union army and served in the Civil War until 1865, rising to regimental commissary sergeant. Afterward, he founded the Central Glass Company in Wheeling and became a major figure in the glass industry, amassing great wealth. He also engaged in banking and investing in Colorado. Reorganizing his business interests in the early 1890s to devote more time to politics, he sold Central Glass to the United States Glass Company in 1892 and retired from the company's board of directors two years later. The firm declined and left Wheeling, but Scott bought the factory back by 1900.

In politics, Scott was a member and president of the Wheeling city council (1881–83) before being elected to the state senate (1883–90). He was elected in 1888 to the Republican National Committee, on which he served six consecutive four-year terms. Becoming an ally of Elkins, who rebuilt the Republican Party in the latter 1880s, Scott by 1892 was Elkins's foremost lieutenant. More than Elkins, Davis, or Camden, he was willing to spend money on elections. Elkins was elected to the U.S. Senate in 1894 and helped Scott gain appointment as President William McKinley's commissioner of internal revenue following the 1896 election.

In 1898, again with Elkins's help, Scott was elected to the U.S. Senate by a margin of one vote in the state legislature. Senator Scott served two relatively undistinguished terms, notably chairing the Mines and Mining Committee, supporting business interests, and strongly backing protectionist trade policy. The Senate's foremost advocate of repealing the Pendleton (Civil Service) Act, Scott complained that the act restricted ability to meet constituents' reasonable requests.

Scott lost the senatorial nomination in 1911 to an insurgent, William P. Hubbard, who then lost to Democrat William E. Chilton. In 1912 Scott supported William Howard Taft against Theodore Roosevelt for the Republican presidential nomination, an unpopular stance in West Virginia that cost him his National Committee seat. He retired into banking in Washington, D.C., where he died on January 2, 1924. He is buried in the nation's capital.

See also: CAMDEN, JOHNSON N.; DAVIS, HENRY GASSAWAY (GOVERNMENT); ELKINS, STEPHEN B. (GOVERNMENT).

—David S. Newhall, *Centre College*

James Morton Callahan, *History of West Virginia, Old and New* (1923); John Alexander Williams, *West Virginia and the Captains of Industry* (1976).

Scott, Thomas A.

(1823–1881) Railroad magnate.

The major force that set the Pennsylvania Railroad on the track to national dominance of its industry in the late 1860s and early 1870s, Thomas A. Scott was an enterprising railroad baron who often used novel strategies to finance his expensive dreams of controlling and extending the business.

Thomas Alexander Scott started his career with the investor-owned Pennsylvania Railroad in 1851 as station agent in the Appalachian town of Duncansville, Pennsylvania. Rising through the ranks, he became one of the line's vice-presidents under J. Edgar Thomson in 1860. In 1861 he was summoned to war as a colonel and put in charge of transportation of Pennsylvania's troops. Extraordinary effectiveness and dispatch in this and later assignments elevated him to assistant secretary of war, but his biggest conquests came in the decade following the conflict.

From 1869 until 1873, Scott's ambitious and untiring expansionist policies changed the Pennsylvania Railroad from a state-based line into not only the largest railroad in America but also one of the largest corporations in the world. The major part of these additions to the company came not through construction of new railroads but through acquisition of controlling interests in existing ones. Under Scott, in addition to lines extending west from Pittsburgh and east to New York City, the Pennsylvania acquired control of three of the major southern routes from Washington, D.C., by 1871. To shield his acquisitions from public scrutiny, Scott developed new concepts such as the pure holding company with his Southern Railway Security Company.

The Pennsylvania Railroad was, however, only one vehicle for Scott's far-reaching ambition. Between 1869 and 1873, he also successively served as president of the Union Pacific, the Atlantic and Pacific, and later the Texas and Pacific Railroads. The latter under Scott became one of the main contenders for a southern transcontinental line along the thirty-second latitude. By 1873, however, Scott had financially overextended the Pennsylvania, and conservative stockholders were unwilling to bail him out when the Pennsylvania's southeastern subsidy roads suffered heavy losses. He offered to step down, but his resignation was not accepted, and in 1874, following Thompson's death, he became president of the Pennsylvania. His years in that office were spent in retrenchment, however, after an investigation by stockholders into the firm's unsustainable expansion resulted in severe curtailment of his power. The Pennsylvania's money was not available to Scott for his Texas and Pacific transcontinental venture, and by 1879 he had lost the transcontinental railroad race to Collis P. Huntington's Southern Pacific Railroad.

Scott was at the helm of the company when the Great Strike of 1877, spreading from the Baltimore and Ohio, reached the Pennsylvania on July 19, 1877. Scott avoided negotiations with and concessions to the striking workers and deflected to the Allegany County Sheriff's Department the blame for losses suffered by Pennsylvania's merchants and shippers. The sheriff was seen by the public as having sought help from the state militia, although he was following Scott's inducement in doing it. President Rutherford B. Hayes's dispatch of federal militia to quell the rebellion in Pittsburgh and other cities also reportedly came at the request of Scott, who had been instrumental in Hayes's election.

Scott suffered from complications arising from an old injury in his later years. He resigned from the presidency of the Pennsylvania Railroad in 1880 and died the next year.

See also: CARTER, GEORGE LAFAYETTE; MORGAN, J. P.; PENNSYLVANIA RAILROAD (TRANSPORTATION).

—Ajay Kalra, *East Tennessee State University*

Joseph G. E. Hopkins, ed., *Concise Dictionary of American Biography* (1964); S. R. Kamm, *The Civil War Career of Thomas A. Scott* (1940); Slason Thompson, *A Short History of American Railways, Covering Ten Decades* (1925).

Shoney's

The Shoney's restaurant chain, launched in West Virginia in the 1940s when the double-decker hamburger was a new national phenomenon, faced the twenty-first century in the tense company of a host of younger casual-dining, steakhouse, and family-style competitors. In the 1990s Shoney's downsized dramatically and invested most of the savings in its companion Captain D's seafood chain. In 2002 the company, traded publicly since 1969, was bought by a Dallas investment firm and taken private.

Shoney's restaurants were founded in 1947 in Charleston, West Virginia, by entrepreneur Alex Schoenbaum, who opened the Parkette Drive-In there. Four years later, he acquired southeastern franchise rights for the popular two-patty Big Boy hamburger. The chain grew under his leadership and in 1953 was renamed Shoney's after his nickname.

In 1959 Ray Danner of Nashville acquired Big Boy franchise rights for central Tennessee and incorporated Danner Foods nine years later to expand the Big Boy franchise across the South. By the end of 1971, the year Schoenbaum and Danner merged their companies to form Shoney's Big Boy Enterprises, more than 130 Shoney's restaurants were in operation. The company assumed its current name, Shoney's Inc., in 1976 and eventually saw the total number of Shoney's restaurants peak at more than 750 locations in thirty-three states.

The Big Boy sandwich and its caricature of a chubby boy in red suspenders were familiar sights for a while in most of Appalachia, but the original Big Boy sandwich had been introduced in 1936 in Glendale, California, by Bob Wian, who operated Bob's Pantry. A legal ruling forced Shoney's Inc. to stop using the character as its company logo in 1972. By 1986, the company logo had become the Shoney Bear.

Headquartered in Nashville, Shoney's Inc. owned and operated or franchised more than 360 Shoney's restaurants in twenty-two states, along with more than 560 Captain D's outlets in twenty-three states, as of the fall of 2003. Schoenbaum died in 1996, and his son, Raymond, was named chairman of the board in 1998. In 2001–2, the company experienced a major shakeup, and William M. Wilson was named chairman of the board and president of Shoney's Inc. before a merger with Lone Star U.S. Acquisitions, LLC, and U.S. Restaurant Properties.

See also: RUBY TUESDAY.

—Larry Sonis, *Arlington, Texas*

Stacey Hartmann, "Shoney's to Use Savings to Expand Captain D's," *Nashville Tennessean* (September 28, 1999); Shoney's Inc., "Shoney's, Inc. Reports Fiscal 2001 Third Quarter Results," *PR Newswire* (September 6, 2001).

Silk Industry

Silk manufacture and the raising of silkworms to supply it appeared in Appalachia early in the nineteenth century, but the venture failed because disease killed the silkworms. The industry later reappeared in the region as northern manufacturers sought a haven for cheap labor.

Popular in other parts of America during the colonial era, silkworm culture did not appear in Appalachia until the 1830s, when the discovery that the worms thrived on the mulberry tree led to a nationwide craze. In Tennessee, notably, farmers invested in silkworms, manufacturers set up small establishments to produce silk thread, and the legislature offered bounties for reeled silk and cocoons, the fibrous cases in which silkworm larvae are produced by caterpillars. In 1850 Tennessee led the nation in cocoon production, but during the ensuing decade disease swept the state and wiped out the cocoons. By 1860 domestic silkworm culture had declined.

Importation of raw silk from China, Japan, and Italy, however, allowed northern manufacturers to continue producing ribbons, trimmings, and silk for sewing. The imported raw material powered a growing manufacturing industry in which silk yarn reeled from the cocoon was twisted, or "thrown," into a form usable in weaving. By 1880 Paterson, New Jersey, had emerged as a leading production center of thrown silk yarn, but labor unrest in the 1880s led by skilled, unionized male weavers in the Paterson factories prompted many manufacturers to move their operations to the mountainous anthracite coal region of eastern Pennsylvania. There employers hired nonunion wives and children of the frequently laid-off male miners to tend power looms. Work in silk factories paid poorly, but the jobs offered young, single women with no economic prospects an opportunity for gainful employment.

The Pennsylvania manufacture of silk yarn was centered in Luzerne, Lackawanna, Carbon, Susquehanna, Schuylkill, and Northumberland Counties. By 1907, thirty-six mills were operating in Lackawanna and Luzerne Counties alone. Employees younger than age sixteen comprised 15 percent of the state's silk workforce as of 1910, causing progressive reformers to campaign for child labor laws, which the state enacted in the 1920s. Pennsylvania's silk industry peaked by the late 1920s, then declined as manufacturers moved south for still cheaper labor or shifted manufacture to synthetic fibers.

The quest for cheap, nonunion labor led a number of northern manufacturers to build facilities in eastern Tennessee. In 1916 a hosiery mill was incorporated in Johnson City, and A. P. Villa and Brothers of New York built a factory in Erwin. Other silk mills opened in McMinnville, Spring City, Cleveland, and Chattanooga. In the face of improved production of rayon and synthetic fibers, the demand for silk yarn and cloth diminished during the 1950s and 1960s, prompting some mills to close and others to switch to synthetic fibers or apparel. During the 1980s and 1990s, manufacture of silk and silk-synthetic blends took place on a limited scale in North Carolina, Pennsylvania, South Carolina, Georgia, and Virginia.

See also: SYNTHETIC FIBERS INDUSTRY; TEXTILE WORKERS (LABOR).

—Marie Tedesco, *East Tennessee State University*

Soft Drink Companies

Southern Appalachia—east Tennessee, in particular—has been a fertile ground for the development and innovation of soft drinks. Double Cola of Chattanooga was the first in the field to sell its product in a sixteen-ounce returnable bottle. Hartman Beverage of Knoxville launched the nationally prominent Mountain Dew brand. Tri-City Beverage of Johnson City, which developed Mountain Dew into a national product, also early embraced the idea of enriching nationally distributed soft drinks with healthful elements, one of the concepts on which the fledgling industry was founded.

During the late nineteenth and early twentieth centuries, it became fashionable to "take a cure" at one of the numerous mineral springs in the Appalachians and other mountains of the United States. Water found at these springs was bottled and sold. By the 1890s, demand for soft drinks was increasing, and new drinks were developed that used roots and herbs to provide or improve the curative qualities believed to be found in natural mineral water or manufactured carbonated water.

Bill Swartz, a Chicago chemist, developed a soft drink in 1949 that he named Dr. Enuf because the drink was enriched with vitamins and minerals. Charles Gordon, owner of Tri-City Beverage of Johnson City, bought the formula and marketed the drink as a tonic that banished "aches and pains" and "feelings of being run-down." Although it cost twenty cents more than other soft drinks, Dr. Enuf outsold competitors in northeastern Tennessee within a few months, and Tri-City Beverage continued to manufacture Dr. Enuf as well as Diet Dr. Enuf and Herbal Dr. Enuf into the twenty-first century.

In the 1940s brothers Barney and Ally Hartman, owners of Hartman Beverage of Knoxville, developed a lemon-lime soft drink to which they gave the name Mountain Dew. Charles Gordon met Barney Hartman on a train returning from the Tennessee Bottler's Convention in Nashville. Anxious to pick up new soft drinks, Gordon became interested in the Mountain Dew franchise. By 1954, Tri-City Beverage had become the first and only franchise for the Hartman brothers' Mountain Dew, which was sold in bottles featuring a hillbilly with a jug and the names of the bottle's makers. After Bill Bridgeforth became Tri-City Beverage's plant manager in 1958, he and Bill Jones of Marion, Virginia, developed a lemonade-flavored drink that became popular. Bridgeforth and Jones later changed the flavor of the Hartman brothers' Mountain Dew to the Tri-City lemonade flavor—first in the Tri-cities (Bristol, Johnson City, and Kingsport) area of northeast Tennessee. The new Mountain Dew flavor gained instant popularity, and North Carolina test markets replicated the northeast Tennessee success. In 1964 the franchise was sold to Pepsi Cola, which abandoned Mountain Dew's hillbilly image and restyled it as a drink for daring young people.

Chattanooga entrepreneurs Charles D. Little and Joe S. Foster first developed a product they called Good Grape Soda in 1922, and their Good Grape Company started marketing it. In 1924 they added Marvel Cola, which they soon renamed Jumbo Cola because it was sold in seven-and-a-half-ounce bottles. That year, the firm had changed its name to Seminole Flavor Company and developed Double-Cola—which got its name from its twelve-ounce bottle, twice the size of other cola products. In the 1950s the company renamed itself the Double-Cola Company, added a citrus soft drink, and began to offer its products in sixteen-ounce returnable bottles. In 1962 it was bought by Fairmont Foods, which introduced a sugar-free soft drink called Diet-Way Cola. Diet-Way's name changed to Sugar-Free Double-Cola in 1964. British-based KJ International bought Fairmont Foods in 1980 and changed the name to Double-Cola Co.-USA. Corporate headquarters are in Chattanooga.

Although produced in Columbus, Georgia, RC Cola is often associated with the life and lore of the Appalachian region. Following a dispute with a bottler from whom he purchased soft drinks, Claud Hatcher, a young pharmacist, created his own soft drink line to sell in his family's grocery store in Columbus. This enterprise grew into the Chero-Cola Company in 1912 and sixteen years later became Nehi Beverages. Sales dropped during the first years of the Great Depression, but following Hatcher's death in 1933, H. R. Mott, the company's vice-president, took over the firm and made it debt-free within a year. He gave the task of developing an improved cola product to company chemist Rufus Kamm, who took six months but came up with a new formula, which took the name Royal Crown from an earlier Hatcher ginger ale creation. It was an instant success, and the company soon was renamed Royal Crown Cola Company. By 1940 it was selling its products in forty-seven of the forty-eight states. It began distributing soft drinks in cans in 1954 and in sixteen-ounce bottles in 1958 and in 1962 offered its first diet soft drink. Bought by London-based Cadbury Schweppes in 2000, it became part of Dr. Pepper/Seven Up, Inc., the conglomerate's largest subsidiary.

See also: SMOKY MOUNTAIN SPAS AND RESORTS (TOURISM); VIRGINIA AND WEST VIRGINIA SPRINGS (TOURISM).

—Mary Grace Meador, *East Tennessee State University*

John Hart, "Dr. Enuf Is Still Here," *Now and Then* (Spring 1988); John J. Riley, *A History of the American Soft Drink Industry: Bottled Carbonated Beverages, 1807–1957* (1972).

Spring and Bottled Water Industry

The bottled water industry in Appalachia is fairly new, although individual family-owned companies have been in business for many years. Recent acquisitions in the region by international water companies suggest a desire to capitalize on the valuable reputations and goodwill of Appalachian firms to meet an increasingly chic market where looking healthy equates with being healthy. Executives of Perrier, the trend-setting French water bottler that has been importing to America since the advent of the twentieth century and is still the industry leader, told state officials in 2001 the company planned to buy a spring in the long-faded Tennessee resort hamlet of Red Boiling Springs—and to invest as much as $100 million there to build a five-hundred-thousand-square-foot plant.

Water companies crisscrossed Appalachia at the turn of the twenty-first century. Although some firms headquartered nowhere near the region used its name (including Royal Mountain in Canada, which touts its water as coming from "Appalachian rock"), many were actually located there. Appalachian Springs Water was advertised as coming from high on the Appalachian Trail at tiny Suches, Georgia, home of the state's smallest school. The Suches spring "has provided the purest drinking water for over fifteen families for over seventy-five years," the company claimed, adding that in addition to delivery service in northeast Georgia it would ship small bottles anywhere. Alpine Natural Springs in Appalachian Salineville, Ohio, made no Appalachian claim, describing its water as coming from a rock formation that had trapped the liquid between layers of sandstone.

Some of these brands expanded and marketed themselves to wide and densely populated areas. Alpine Springs was the eighth-largest bottled water variety in the United States in 1999, with a 2.9 percent share of the market and total sales of $151.4 million. The sixth largest, Deer Park, was one of several owned by Nestlé Waters North America. With $167.4 million in total sales and a market share percentage of 3.2 as of 1999, Deer Park reported that its first spring was located high in the Appalachians in Maryland and that this original source had been supplemented by water from "other natural springs" in Maryland, Pennsylvania, and Florida. 3 Springs Water of Laurel Run, Pennsylvania, had been bottling water from the Appalachian Penobscot Mountains since 1927 and in 2003 had a truck fleet servicing New York, Philadelphia, Baltimore, and Washington, D.C. Blue Ridge Mountain Waters of Blue Ridge, Georgia, in business since 1989, served Atlanta.

Labels tend to imply that springwater taken from the Appalachian Mountains is cleaner and better tasting because it is purified by the world's most ancient rock formations. Likewise, mountain water is marketed as mystically endowed, more natural, and therefore expressly better for the consumer, particularly when bottled by decades-old companies. Images of mountain ridges, crags, forests, laurels, or Native Americans are coupled with descriptive terms such as *pure*, *naturally refreshing*, and *oxygenated* in an attempt to promote an image of a rural and nostalgic uncorrupted Appalachian process and product. Any bottler may appropriate *Appalachia* for its label, and bottlers operate in all thirteen Appalachian states.

Consumers of bottled water should be careful in their selection of brands. Some bottled waters may in fact be derived from city water systems in the region, and water labeled as "springwater" could actually come from a well. Regulations regarding testing and labeling vary from state to state and may be stricter than federal guidelines. Some businesses also adopt voluntary guidelines. Federal regulation of such standards as sanitation, source protection, and storage requirements of bottled water are enforced by the Food and Drug Administration rather than the Environmental Protection Agency, which controls public water supplies (tap water).

Bottled water can come from any source, including municipal systems, surface water, artesian wells, deep wells (boreholes), and springs (hot or cold). Springwater is water from an unaltered, free-flowing spring. Bottled water includes the ubiquitous five-gallon water cooler. No brand name is required to use the same source for consecutive batches of product. Trade organizations and voluntary associations exist for both bottled water and bottled springwater. The terms are both specific and legally different, although vendors and the public tend to use them interchangeably.

See also: SOFT DRINK COMPANIES; STREAMS (ECOLOGY).

—Charles F. Moore, *East Tennessee State University*

Steel Industry

See Iron and Steel Industry

Stokely–Van Camp

Stokely–Van Camp is the largest and most successful canning company with roots in the Appalachian region. In 1898 Anna Rorex Stokely, her sons James R. and John M., and a neighbor, Colonel A. R. Swann, founded Stokely Brothers and Company in Cocke County, Tennessee. The next year, Swann sold his interest to another brother, William B., and in 1905 George Stokely became a partner in the company. The company constructed a warehouse and central office at Newport, the county seat, which enabled it to ship its products by railroad. The Stokely brothers managed the company. James served as president and chief financial officer, William managed the company's farm operations, John directed sales, George supervised production, and Jehu provided legal advice from his law offices in Birmingham, Alabama.

Following the deaths of three Stokely brothers (George in 1916, John in 1919, and James in 1922), William directed the company until 1928. That year Stokely purchased the Fame Canning Company, and soon afterward—early in the long tenure of William B. Stokely Jr., who served as president (1928–47) and chairman of the board (1947–66)—the company moved its general offices to Louisville, Kentucky. In 1933 the firm united with Indiana-based Van Camp canners and became Stokely–Van Camp Company of Indianapolis.

In 1967 Stokely–Van Camp acquired the rights to sell Gatorade, a sports drink developed by a University of Florida professor of medicine. The success of that product resulted in the acquisition of Stokely–Van Camp by Quaker Oats in 1983.

See also: BUSH BROTHERS AND COMPANY; HEINZ CORPORATION.

—Ed Speer, *Elizabethton, Tennessee*

Swift's Silver Mine

Legends of vast mineral wealth in Appalachia have circulated since the arrival of the earliest Europeans. One of the most enduring is that of Swift's Silver Mine, rumored to be located somewhere in southwestern Virginia, southern West Virginia, eastern Kentucky, or east Tennessee.

Swift himself is as mysterious as his mine. He may have been a sailor, British soldier, pirate, or surveyor who discovered vast treasure somewhere in southern Appalachia in the middle of the eighteenth century. In most versions of the legend, his fabulous mine was originally worked by Native Americans. According to tradition, he mined and coined silver, much of which is still buried somewhere in the mountains. Swift never returned for his treasure, and the reasons vary with versions of the tale. In some, he was blinded and could not see to find his way back. In others, he returned to where the mine was supposed to be but never could locate it again.

Dozens of counties and communities claim to be the true location, but the mine, like Swift himself, remains an enigma. Regardless of the legend's historical truth, it has become an important part of Appalachian lore, prompting generations of hopeful hunters to purchase counterfeit maps and journals that claim to reveal the mine's true site. There are those who still search for it, and the legend has become its own kind of treasure.

See also: ORAL NARRATIVE (FOLKLORE AND FOLKLIFE).

—Elizabeth Hardy, *Caldwell Community College*

Synfuels

Coal-based synthetic fuel, used effectively by the Nazis in World War II, received serious attention in American energy policy in the 1970s as a result of the Arab oil embargo against the United States. Calls for U.S. energy independence led planners to propose a massive new "synfuels" industry involving large-scale conversion of coal into gas and liquid fuels. Decline of world oil prices soon undermined political support for energy independence and expensive new initiatives. Crisis-inspired tax credits gave a boost to synfuel operations in the coal industry nearly twenty years later, however. Enacted by Congress in 1979, the credits provided twenty-six dollars per ton exemptions for coal-based synthetic fuels, but the incentives had little effect until 1996, when the Internal Revenue Service (IRS) ruled that the credits could be sold. The ruling enabled companies with low tax liabilities to purchase credits and profitably operate synfuel plants.

More than fifty plants went into production in the country in the next few years, nearly two dozen of them in the coal-mining areas of eastern Kentucky, West Virginia, and southwestern Virginia, with others in Pennsylvania, Ohio, and Alabama. Raleigh, North Carolina–based Progress Energy Company, the nation's largest producer of synfuels, was operating nine plants in central Appalachia by the end of 2001. Company officials estimated their total production would qualify for federal tax credits totaling $260 million to $390 million for the year. Rather than converting coal to gas or liquid fuel, the facilities treated unmarketable coal, coal dust, or waste from impoundments and gob piles by spraying them with materials such as organic resin from paper plants and compressing them into briquettes to be burned by power plants.

The IRS ruling was issued during a time of depressed coal prices, meaning that the twenty-six-dollar-per-ton credit for synfuel was worth more than a ton of coal. Critics of synfuel operations, including Kentucky Governor Paul Patton, branded the program a tax scam. Some operators were accused of spraying marketable coal and selling it as synfuel because the tax credit was more valuable than coal. In May 2001, the IRS issued new rules to curb abuses, but as approved by Congress, the federal tax credits remained available until 2007.

See also: BITUMINOUS COAL INDUSTRY.

—Rudy Abramson, *Reston, Virginia*

Rishawn Biddle, "The Ghost of Energy Crisis Past," *Reason* (April 2001); Paul J. Nyden, "Lucrative Synfuel Plants Expanding in West Virginia," *Charleston Gazette* (December 7, 2001) and "We Comply with Law, Synfuel Maker Says," *Charleston Gazette-Mail* (March 11, 2001).

Synthetic Fibers Industry

Attracted by nonunion labor and the availability of such natural resources as wood pulp, cotton linters (the short fuzzy fibers that remain stuck to cotton seeds after the ginning process), and large amounts of "pure" water, foreign companies began building synthetic fibers plants in the South six years after establishing the industry in America. The first southern plants were in Appalachia, and the very first, operated by British-owned Viscose Company in Roanoke, Virginia, became the largest viscose rayon factory in the world. By the end of the 1920s, Appalachian plants were crucial as the United States became the world's foremost manufacturer of rayon and acetate.

The Viscose Company (soon to be American Viscose) plant in Roanoke was built in 1917. It was followed by others in Lewistown and Meadville, Pennsylvania, in 1920 and 1929, and Parkersburg and Nitro, West Virginia, both in 1926. By the end of the 1920s the Roanoke plant employed around 5,600 workers and produced 20 million pounds of rayon-filament yarn a year.

Other companies also established Appalachian plants. American Celanese, a branch of British Celanese, built an acetate plant in 1924 near Cumberland, Maryland, that employed 2,000 workers. Industrial Rayon of Cleveland, Ohio, affiliated with the Italian company Snia Viscosa, opened a factory employing another 2,000 near Covington, Virginia. DuPont, with ties to Viscose Company's British parent corporation Courtaulds, as well as to Netherlands-based Enka and the German Vereinigte Glanzstoff Fabriken, established a cellulose acetate plant employing approximately 2,300 in Waynesboro, Virginia. American Bemberg, a subsidiary of leading German rayon producer J. P. Bemberg, began production of cuprammonium rayon in Elizabethton, Tennessee, in 1926. In 1927 American Glanzstoff, affiliated with Bemberg through Vereinigte Glanzstoff Fabriken, completed construction of a viscose rayon factory alongside the Bemberg plant in Elizabethton. Together the Elizabethton plants employed 3,200 workers by 1929. Other viscose rayon plants constructed in Appalachia included American Enka in Asheville, North Carolina, with 2,000 employees, and American Chatillon, a subsidiary of the Italian firm La Soie de Chatillon, in Rome, Georgia, employing roughly 1,500.

In the United States the synthetic fibers industry was associated with international cartels that controlled production worldwide. Synthetic fibers companies had emerged from chemical research and production, especially in the aniline dye and explosives industries, rather than from textile production. The first synthetic fibers were rayon and cellulose acetate, products of late-nineteenth-century and early-twentieth-century chemical experimentation, with nylon, polyester, and others being invented during World War II and the immediate postwar period.

The boom years of rayon and acetate occurred between 1916 and 1929. During those years foreign industrial giants formed American subsidiaries and built plants in the United States. The Viscose Company built the first United States plant in 1910 at Marcus Hook, Pennsylvania. Consumption of rayon increased steadily during the 1920s in items made purely of rayon or acetate or in blends with organic fibers. Women's dresses, undergarments, and hosiery, men's neckties and loungewear, and the linings of men's and women's coats were made of rayon. Knitted wear (hats, gloves, scarves, sweaters) and household items (bedspreads, draperies) were made either of blends of rayon and cotton or rayon and wool.

During the Great Depression, rayon and acetate production dipped but remained profitable as companies filled and shipped yarn orders and paid stock dividends to shareholders. Many of the Appalachian plants still had substantial workforces. American Bemberg and American Glanzstoff together employed 2,491 in 1932, and American Viscose in Parkersburg employed 4,300 in 1935. DuPont at Waynesboro expanded in 1935 and added 1,600 new jobs. In 1937 American Viscose also expanded, building a plant at Front Royal, Virginia.

World War II brought changes to production and ownership. A number of synthetics companies contributed to the war effort by producing war materials. American Bemberg in Elizabethton and American Viscose in Roanoke produced yarn used for parachute cloth, while the Front Royal plant began to concentrate on tire cord, as did the Asheville Enka facility. Companies with contractual ties to enemy countries (especially Germany and Italy) divested themselves of foreign investments, had their assets frozen, or came under the control of the Office of Alien Property. American Bemberg and North American Rayon—the latter the renamed American Glanzstoff—came under the control of the Office of Alien Property in 1943. American Viscose fell victim to wartime Lend-Lease Act politics, which forced the British government to sell it in 1941 to a purchasing syndicate led by Morgan Stanley.

World War II and the immediate postwar years were prosperous ones for the synthetics industry as employment at many of the Appalachian plants reached all-time highs. Celanese at Cumberland employed approximately 10,000 production workers in 1941, while its sister facility at Narrows, Virginia, began production in 1940 with another 1,400. In 1948 Celanese at Rome employed 2,400, while a new Enka rayon filament yarn plant that began production in 1948 at Lowlands, near Morristown, Tennessee, employed between 800 and 1,000. Combined, Bemberg and North American employed 6,250 in 1949.

Between 1950 and 1970, however, the synthetic fibers industry underwent dramatic changes. Freed from wartime demands, the industry began to realize the advantages of polymer research that produced myriad fibers. Nylon, polyester, acrylic fibers, and polypropylene, among other synthetics, challenged rayon and acetate's dominance. At the DuPont Waynesboro plant, production shifted in 1967 from acetate to lycra. The DuPont nylon plant at Martinsville, Virginia, established in 1941, expanded production and employed as many as 4,600 workers in the mid-1960s. Changes in fashion and a renewed interest in natural fibers during the 1960s and 1970s threatened the industry. In the 1960s rayon and polyester manufacturers engaged in cutthroat competition over production of tire cord. A number of companies, including North American and Bemberg (now controlled by Beaunit Mills, which had purchased the companies from the Office of Alien Property in 1948), entered into joint ventures with other companies to diversify production. Often, the joint ventures were financial disasters.

The 1970s proved to be a difficult decade for the industry. Economic recession, the Arab oil embargo, an acute crisis in the European man-made fiber industry, stiff competition among international fiber companies, and competition from cheaper imports from Asia and Latin America forced European companies to restructure and diversify to reduce reliance on the synthetic fibers market. Restructuring and diversification drove down profits of American companies and subsidiaries of the European giants. Beaunit sold American Bemberg to local interests in 1971, and in 1974 the company filed for bankruptcy. El Paso Natural Gas, Beaunit's parent, divested itself of its textiles and fibers division in 1976, with local interests purchasing the plant. American Viscose, purchased in 1963 by FMC Corporation, an agricultural chemicals and food machinery corporation, shut down its Roanoke facility in 1958. Its Parkersburg plant lasted into 1974. In 1969 Enka in Asheville became part of Akzo Nobel, an international corporation manufacturing chemicals, drugs, detergents, and cosmetics. The once-thriving Celanese plant in Cumberland, reduced to approximately 900 workers, shut down in the late 1970s.

Throughout the 1980s and 1990s, the synthetics industry continued to diversify and to see its companies merge. At the end of the century the most powerful firms were the conglomerates Hoescht of Germany, Akzo Nobel of the Netherlands (which controlled Acordis, of which Enka became a part), and Courtaulds Fibers of England. Production facilities were spread throughout the world, including Europe, Asia, and Latin America. Production in China increased in the 1990s, but production and demand in Europe declined.

Although a number of the Appalachian plants weathered shifting production trends (by the early 2000s in Virginia, the old Celanese Narrows plant was surviving as Celco, and the Waynesboro DuPont plant had added production of nylon flooring in 1997), others continued to decline. The Avtex Fibers Front Royal facility, formerly an American Viscose plant, prospered in the 1980s making carbonized rayon cloth used in the space shuttle, but it closed in 1989, leaving North American Rayon as the sole provider of the cloth. North American experienced a short-lived boom from the late 1980s to the early 1990s, but the plant, which had become an employee stock option plan company in 1985, was forced to lay off about 1,300 employees (most of its workforce) in 1997. The DuPont Martinsville facility shut down in 1998.

In the twenty-first century, changing world markets and the continued shift of production to Latin America and Asia likely will prevent synthetic fibers production in Appalachia from ever again becoming the powerful economic force it was for most of the twentieth century.

See also: APPAREL WORKERS (LABOR); TEXTILE WORKERS (LABOR).

—Marie Tedesco, *East Tennessee State University*

Janet Irons, *Testing the New Deal: The General Textile Strike of 1934 in the American South* (2000); Jeffrey Leiter, Michael Schulman, and Rhonda Zingraff, eds., *Hanging by a Thread: Social Change in Southern Textiles* (1991).

Tams, W. P.

(1883–1977) Coal baron.

An independent owner-operator, coal baron Major William Purviance Tams Jr. was the last survivor of the pioneers who opened the "smokeless" coalfields of southern West Virginia.

Born on May 19, 1883, to a prominent family in Staunton, Virginia, Tams was educated at public schools and Virginia Polytechnic Institute before joining Samuel Dixon, a major coal operator in Fayette County, West Virginia, as an engineer on October 1, 1904. With James O. Watts, he secured a lease in 1908 on the Winding Gulf in Raleigh County and began shipping coal on October 1, 1909. During his presidency—which lasted from 1912 to 1955, except for a stint as a major in World War I—the Gulf Smokeless Coal Company absorbed Gulf Coal, Wyoming Coal, and Covel Smokeless Coal. He acquired national prominence in the industry before selling out to Winding Gulf Coal Company at retirement.

Tams served not only as his firm's president but also as its chief mining engineer, structural designer, and sales manager. A dedicated paternalist, he built what he called "a decent place to live" for his workers. He electrified company houses when that was still a rarity and went on to provide the first bathhouse in his area of the coalfields in 1910, opened the first movie theater at any West Virginia mining camp in 1911, reduced working hours from ten to nine in 1911–12, paid better-than-union wages, and charged low prices in his company stores. At the same time, he ruled as an enlightened despot, expecting employees to "toe the line." Unionization became inevitable after 1929 because of wage cutting by his competitors and encouragement from Franklin Roosevelt's New Deal.

Answering a request, he published a short history, *The Smokeless Coal Fields of West Virginia* (1963; reprint 2001), an indispensable, engaging portrayal of the development and daily life of the fields. Never married, he lived and died—on August 3, 1977—in a bungalow in Tams, a mining town he built.

See also: WATSON, JAMES OTIS.

—David S. Newhall, *Centre College*

Tanning

Few tanners were plying this once widely practiced craft in Appalachia at the turn of the twenty-first century. Like many other Appalachian crafts, tanning, the process used to transform perishable hides and skins into durable leather, is all but extinct because cheap industrial replacement processes are readily available.

Most tanning operations were small. As Lycoming County, Pennsylvania, farmer and tanner Charles Kelchner replied to a query on Pennsylvania tanneries from the Commonwealth's Bureau of Industrial Statistics in 1876, "My tannery is a small concern, and is run in connection with a small farm. No workmen are employed." The small tanner differed from industrial tanners in several respects. Most notably, traditional Appalachian tanners produced leather from hides and skins derived from locally slaughtered meat animals and game, while industrialized operations relied upon large quantities of hides and skins procured from urban abattoirs and foreign ranches. The leather tanned by the farmer was used in his household or was exchanged or sold in the local community rather than on the emerging global leather market.

The tanning of animal hides and skins is one of the oldest documented technologies. Despite advances and specialization, the process of turning an organic and perishable hide into durable leather has remained little changed since prehistory and is documented through archaeological and historical research as far back as four thousand years. Known as vegetable tanning, the technique employs tannic acid leached from bark to turn hides into leather, a process that can take several weeks or months. Relying on abundant oak (and sometimes hemlock) bark from which tannic acid was leached, traditional Appalachian tanners transformed the dressed hides and skins from cattle, goats, sheep, and hogs, as well as horses, deer, and small mammals (including dogs), into leather for use in shoes, bellows, clothing, horse furniture, and a wide array of other domestic, agricultural, and industrial end-products. Family members and neighbors generally provided the labor.

Tanning was closely tied to the Appalachian logging industry. Denuded tree trunks were sent to sawmills while the bark fed the region's bark mills. Industrial tanners saw the virgin stands of oak and hemlock in the region as valuable commodities, and many farmers in West Virginia, Virginia, Pennsylvania, and New York supplemented their incomes by peeling bark and hauling it to nearby tanneries.

Small, traditional tanneries identified themselves as "country" tanneries. Most proprietors lived on farms; thus, minimal capital and facilities were required. A farmer needed only some pits excavated in the farmyard, a supply of tannin-rich bark, ashes for dehairing, lard or tallow, and hides or skins.

After an animal was butchered, the clean hide was immersed for as long as two weeks in a solution of water and ashes to loosen the hair. The hair was then scraped off for use in plaster or to be sold, while the clean hide was placed in a vat with ground tanbark and water.

Although vegetable tanning was the most common method used to make leather, other processes were often used on the hides of smaller animals. Brain tanning—treating a skin with a paste made from the animal's own pulverized brains—was widely practiced, as was alum "tawing." Although brain tanning and tawing helped stabilize skins, neither was as permanent or effective as vegetable tanning, the process immigrant Europeans brought with them to the New World.

Fully tanned and dried, new leather was trimmed and finished, usually with lard or oil to make it pliable. Most Appalachian cottage industry tanners used the leather they made, though some sold it in the local community or to distant manufacturers. By making their own leather, and tanning for neighbors and relatives on a barter system, farmers made full use of both domestic and wild animals, transforming hides into a diverse array of products.

Although leather tanning has nearly disappeared from the Appalachian craft repertoire, there remain some specialized tanners who continue to use craft products. One of the most prominent and best-documented examples is the use of groundhog skins to make banjo heads. From the mountains of Georgia to West Virginia, the groundhog—whose meat goes well in stews—was prized for its skin. Cats and calves also contributed their skins to banjo makers throughout Appalachia. Despite the widespread availability of inexpensive mass-produced leather, traditionally tanned skins still make the best banjo heads.

See also: COTTAGE INDUSTRIES.

—David S. Rotenstein, *Bethesda, Maryland*

Lucius F. Ellsworth, *Craft to National Industry in the Nineteenth Century: A Case Study of the Transformation of the New York State Tanning Industry* (1975); Peter Welsh, *Tanning in the United States to 1850: A Brief History* (1964); Eliot Wigginton, ed., *Foxfire 3* (1975).

Tennessee Electric Power Company

The Tennessee Valley Authority (TVA) gained national recognition as a federally created public utility to provide cheap hydroelectric power to residents of the Tennessee Valley to help relieve the Great Depression, but electricity already had been introduced to the area on a substantial scale by private power providers. Perhaps the most significant was Tennessee Electric Power Company (TEPCO), the largest electrical power monopoly in Tennessee during the early twentieth century.

Tennessee Electric Power Company was created with the merger of Chattanooga Railway and Light and the Chattanooga and Tennessee River Power Company on May 27, 1922. It continued to acquire lesser companies and stock and came to include the Blue Ridge Corporation, Lookout

Mountain Railroad Company, Lookout Incline Railway Company, Toccoa Electric Power Company, Nashville Railway and Light Company, and the Tennessee Transportation Company. At its zenith, the company combined the assets of forty-five different Tennessee companies, some dating to the nineteenth century.

Hydroelectric power was already a major source of electricity when the 1922 consolidation occurred. In 1905 the Chattanooga and Tennessee River Power Company had begun construction on a dam at Hales Bar on the Tennessee River. The Eastern Tennessee Power Company had built its hydroelectric facility at Great Falls on the Caney River, as well as Ocoee No. 1 and No. 2 in southeastern Tennessee, by 1916. A number of lesser plants in middle Tennessee built between 1901 and 1929 were owned by the municipalities of Cookeville and Lawrenceburg or controlled by the Southern Cities Power Company, which had been created in 1918. All were consolidated in 1929 under the Tennessee Electric Power Company, which in turn was absorbed by TVA in 1939 as a result of financial setbacks caused by the Great Depression and a U.S. Supreme Court decision, *Ashlander, et al. v. TVA*.

Tennessee Electric Power Company had a significant socioeconomic impact on the state. As a result of its formation, electrical power became an essential part of everyday life for many Tennesseans and residents of southeastern Appalachia. Because of Tennessee Electric Power Company and other private power companies, household life began to be characterized by a wide variety of labor-saving devices and such now-commonplace luxuries as refrigerators and radios. The workplace was suddenly transformed by electric lights, tools, mining gear, water pumps, dairy equipment, and other devices that increased productivity. The introduction of these tools and conveniences into everyday life was the result of hydroelectric development in Tennessee and the Appalachian region in the three decades from 1901 to 1933, and Tennessee Electric Power Company was a major contributor.

See also: GEORGIA POWER COMPANY; NUCLEAR POWER; TENNESSEE VALLEY AUTHORITY (GOVERNMENT).

—James B. Jones Jr., *Tennessee Historical Commission*

Tennessee Marble Industry

Historically one of the most prolific marble-quarrying areas of the United States, east Tennessee has produced majestic stone not only for tombstones and banks but also for some of the nation's most treasured memorials and admired public buildings.

Of particular note is its use in the Jefferson, Taft, and Lincoln Memorials, the United States Capitol Building, the Smithsonian Institution, the National Cathedral, and the National Gallery of Art—all located in Washington, D.C. In New York City, it appears in the interior of Grand Central Station, in the Pierpont Morgan Library, and in the huge lions guarding the entrance to the New York Public Library. It was also used in the General Motors Building in Detroit, the Federal Reserve Bank in Houston, and the state capitols of New York and Ohio. In Tennessee its distinctiveness can be seen in the state capitol and the Cordell Hull Building in Nashville as well as the Main Post Office in Knoxville.

A decline of public interest in marble-topped furniture during the World War I era caused some companies supplying the business to either stop operating or to find another market while awaiting a revival of interest in that style and color of marble, and construction slowdowns during the Great Depression and again in the 1980s seriously threatened the industry, but it substantially recovered. The Tennessee Marble Company at Friendsville in 2003 claimed a ninety-thousand-square-foot facility atop seventy-five acres of marble. Another Friendsville firm, Tennessee Valley Marble Company, also advertised a "modern plant" as well as shipping "throughout America." Some marble companies in east Tennessee have been periodically connected with others outside the region, and that tradition continued. The Tennessee Marble Company was affiliated with the Gawet Granite and Marble Company of Rutland, Vermont.

Holston marble—actually a hard, dense limestone—from east Tennessee was first used for Knoxville's tombstones in the eighteenth century, but the first quarry was not opened until 1838 in Hawkins County. The majority of marble quarried in the area comes from the Holston formation in the Ridge and Valley area of east Tennessee lying between the Great Smoky Mountains and the Cumberland Plateau. The Holston formation was created in the Ordovician period, some 490 to 443 million years ago. It varies in color from off-white to a dark red. Imperial black, one of just two black marbles quarried in the United States, is exclusive to Tennessee. Limestone is one of the two state rocks of Tennessee, and there has been debate as to whether its limestone deposits actually qualify as marble since they are not metamorphosed rock—meaning rock that has been heated, squeezed, and chemically altered, usually deep in the earth. Most geologists nonetheless declare that it is marble because of its quality, its hardness, and its ability to take a high polish.

See also: MARBLE INDUSTRY.

—Paula K. Hinton, *Tennessee Technological University*

Textile Industry

See Textile Workers (Labor)

Tobacco Industry

Tobacco agriculture, one of the largest cash crop industries in the United States, declined steadily in the late twentieth century, and its profit margins shrank, but tobacco production and marketing remained important to the economy of central and southern Appalachia. Of the six types of tobacco produced in the U.S., the most widely grown are flue-cured and burley, with flue-cured—better suited to wide and flat terrain where it can be harvested by machine—comprising more than half of annual U.S. tobacco production. Burley, better able to be grown on hilly land, accounted for most of the nation's remaining tobacco, and most burley was grown in Appalachia.

By the turn of the twenty-first century, Appalachian tobacco farmers battled global competition, which increasingly came from corporate relatives of the same companies for which they grew their own products. Philip Morris USA, whose corporate umbrella covered brands ranging from Marlboro and Virginia Slims to English Ovals and Basic, was the leading American cigarette manufacturer, claiming more than 48 percent of the market in the second quarter of 2003. At the same time its corporate sister, Philip Morris International, was the leading tobacco company in the world with a 14 percent market share thanks to its operation of or interest in fifty factories worldwide. It manufactured, sold, or distributed cigarettes in more than 160 countries and had seen its production volumes grow from 249 billion cigarettes in 1981 to almost 700 billion twenty years later.

The production of tobacco had long been an essential industry to many Appalachian communities, and often these communities did not have many economically viable alternatives. Per-acre profits from growing tobacco far exceeded those of other crops suitable to Appalachia's climate and topography. In Tennessee the average per-acre value of tobacco production in 1999 was $3,794, compared to $199 for corn and $86 for soybeans. But by the latter part of the twentieth century the industry was faced with adversity, leading to smaller and smaller profit margins for growers. The troubling factors, in addition to overseas competition, included evidence of health problems linked to tobacco use and the threat of additional federal legislation harmful to tobacco producers in the region. For individual farmers these hardships were compounded because many owned and operated small farms and produced only enough to support their families, and the difficulties made it more problematic for farmers to achieve even a level of subsistence for their labors. According to the U.S. Department of Agriculture, farmers nationwide received about 2 percent of tobacco's profits—as tobacco companies meanwhile profited greatly and federal and state governments reaped large revenues from cigarette and tobacco excise taxes.

There were several reasons why Appalachian tobacco farmers were only able to maintain subsistence profit levels. These included labor-intensive production methods and, more significantly, federal production quotas and price supports. Quotas for growing burley tobacco resulted in plots of land being assigned a certain amount of tobacco that could be grown. Farmers could only grow burley tobacco if they owned or leased land that had been assigned a quota, and debate raged annually over whether to continue the quota program. In July 2003, Mike Szymanczyk, chairman and chief executive officer of Philip Morris, urged the House Agriculture Committee to adopt a $15-billion buyout of the quota system, with the cost to be funded by cigarette manufacturers and importers. Many Appalachian farmers feared that ending the quota system would result in more volatile tobacco prices, consolidation of farms, and mechanization of production. They believed that Appalachian tobacco agriculture would not be competitive with that of flatland flue-

"Hands" of tobacco are packed for market, Johnson City, Tennessee, 1982. Tobacco production and marketing remained important to the central and southern Appalachian economy into the twenty-first century despite the decline of tobacco as a cash crop.

cured tobacco, resulting in a loss of jobs and livelihood throughout the region.

Farm jobs were not the only ones related to tobacco in Appalachia. There were others in product manufacturing and wholesaling, but these industries could not absorb individual farmers unable to maintain their small family farms without growing tobacco. The region's tobacco-related manufacturing jobs number in the thousands, but there are more than forty-four thousand tobacco farms in the state of Kentucky alone.

Despite external threats to tobacco agriculture—falling domestic demand, better public understanding of health risks associated with tobacco product use, and new federal legislation—the industry recovered from the initial effect of federal restrictions. Tobacco agriculture and production profited greatly from rising overseas demand, and increased marketing. Kentucky, the largest U.S. producer of burley tobacco and second-largest producer of all tobacco behind North Carolina, made more than $800 million annually throughout the 1990s, and its agricultural economy was very dependent on tobacco. Hard hit by volatile prices, Kentucky set up a compensation plan for tobacco farmers who suffered losses during the market's fluctuations. In addition to short-term relief, Kentucky Governor Paul Patton established the Governor's Tobacco Marketing and Export Advisory Council, which worked to implement an improved strategic plan to search for new foreign markets and to research and apply better marketing strategies.

Nationally, bans on smoking in bars, restaurants, and many public areas did not hurt the tobacco industry dramatically because international demand for U.S. tobacco products rose greatly during the same period. Federal legislation requiring U.S. tobacco companies to give money to various state health programs, admit the addictive nature of tobacco, and permit federal control over their products caused tobacco companies to shift their major marketing efforts overseas, particularly to eastern Europe and Russia. In 2003 Philip Morris sold more than two-thirds of its products outside the U.S.

Appalachia had another problem, along with the rest of America and the world. In addition to the external threats to tobacco agriculture, use of tobacco products severely injured the health of many people throughout Appalachia. It was detrimental to them monetarily as well, because coal-mining companies were able to dispute black lung compensation claims from former employees who smoked, claiming that their health problems were caused by tobacco products rather than working conditions in the mines.

Tobacco marketing budgets continued to increase as federal legislation placed a variety of restrictions on domestic tobacco advertising. The limitations included bans on the use of cartoons in advertisements or on packaging, bans on outdoor advertising, and bans on payment for product placement in media. But the tobacco companies found new ways to market the product, avoiding regulations through niche promotions at clubs and bars and direct-mail pitches to people over twenty-one. Despite the reduced outlets, the companies' marketing costs rose to $9.57 billion in 2000 from $8.24 billion in 1999.

In 2004 both the U.S. House of Representatives and Senate passed versions of legislation that would provide assistance to tobacco farmers. The Fair and Equitable Tobacco Reform Act mandated an overhaul of the New Deal–era tobacco quota system, which limited the amount of tobacco that farmers can grow. Designed to end the government's participation in the tobacco business, the legislation provides compensation to both quota owners and active farmers, as well as financial assistance, should they choose to discontinue farming the crop.

See also: R. J. REYNOLDS TOBACCO COMPANY.

—Arthur Holst, *Philadelphia, Pennsylvania*

John Reid Blackwell, "U.S. Tobacco Spent More on Advertising in 2000, despite Restrictions," *Knight Ridder Tribune Business News* (May 25, 2002); Martha A. Derthick, *Up in Smoke: From Legislation to Litigation in Tobacco Politics* (2002); John Van Willigen and Susan C. Eastwood, *Tobacco Culture: Farming Kentucky's Burley Belt* (1998); Lawrence E. Wood, *The Economic Impact of Tobacco Production in Appalachia*, Appalachian Regional Commission Report (November 1998).

Trucking

See Trucking (Transportation)

Union Carbide

See Chemical Industry

Vanderbilt, George W.

(1862–1914) Founder of the Biltmore Estate.

George Washington Vanderbilt was born in 1862 in New York City, but he built the largest private home in Appalachia and around it developed an estate that greatly influenced the modernizing of the region's farming and forestry.

Grandson of "Commodore" Cornelius Vanderbilt, a self-made shipping and railroad tycoon who was one of the wealthiest men in America, George W. Vanderbilt was preoccupied from youth through adulthood more with intellectual and cultural pursuits than the financial and social interests of his fellow family members. While traveling with his mother in 1888 to experience the southern Appalachian climate of Asheville, North Carolina, he fell in love with the mountains and was inspired to build a country home in the area. He named it Biltmore in honor of his family's original

Dutch hometown and bought 125,000 adjacent acres. He envisioned transforming the land surrounding the estate into gardens as spectacular as the mansion, and he hired Frederick Law Olmsted, the landscape architect of Central Park in New York as well as several college campuses, to bring it to pass. Olmstead was of the opinion, however, that the land should be farmed and the woods managed scientifically. Vanderbilt and Olmstead compromised on a plan for five aesthetic gardens along with a 250-acre wooded park and 100,000 acres of farm and forest.

Vanderbilt farmed Biltmore scientifically and memorably. His financially successful Biltmore Nursery was focused on the trees and plants of Appalachia. The first superintendent of his forests was Gifford Pinchot, who left Biltmore to become head of the U.S. Division of Forestry, and the Biltmore School of Forestry was founded on the estate and trained a significant number of young southern foresters in the scientific pursuit of their vocation. In agriculture as in forestry, Biltmore excellence pioneered and inspired the best in Appalachia. The ice cream from its dairies was sold widely, and one of its Jersey cattle broke milk production records. The journal *American Forestry* said that the inspirational effect of "his example towards improved agricultural methods in the south is beyond all estimate."

Construction of Biltmore Estate yielded many benefits to what was once a sleepy mountain community, including three miles of railroad track that had to be laid to haul in building materials for the great project. Vanderbilt purchased the small town of Best and renamed it Biltmore Village. It contained homes of Biltmore employees, along with a hospital, church, school, and several shops. Vanderbilt also was responsible for the founding of Biltmore Estate Industries, which instructed students in such traditional arts as woodworking, weaving, and other traditional arts.

Although he bought another residence in Washington, Vanderbilt spent most of his time in the Appalachian Mountains studying trees and wildlife. He remained active in the processes of the estate until complications of an emergency appendectomy resulted in his death in 1914.

See also: BILTMORE ESTATE (TOURISM); BILTMORE ESTATE COMPLEX (ARCHITECTURE).

—Elizabeth Rigg, *Wise, Virginia*

Virginia Iron, Coal and Coke Company

Virginia Iron, Coal and Coke Company, which has historically controlled extensive coal and other mineral lands in southern Appalachia, has been bought and sold repeatedly during its hundred-year history, exemplifying the continual changes in the mining business. In 2003 the firm was based in Roanoke, Virginia, and was part of a Texas-based corporation.

Founded by Appalachian entrepreneur George Lafayette Carter, Virginia Iron, Coal and Coke Company was incorporated at Pulaski, Virginia, on January 10, 1899, as a move toward consolidating many small iron manufacturing and mining operations scattered across the region. The intent mirrored a national trend. Consisting initially of properties transferred by Carter from his earlier Carter Coal and Iron Company, Virginia Iron, Coal and Coke used funds raised by the New York investment house of Moore and Schley to acquire furnaces, foundries, mines, coke ovens, quarries, railways, and land and mineral rights to hundreds of thousands of acres in southwest Virginia, east Tennessee, and southeastern Kentucky. Overcapitalization, overextension, and competition from the Mesabi iron ore range in Minnesota eventually pushed the firm into bankruptcy in 1901. At the time, it was the eighth-ranked iron producer in the United States and Virginia's largest industrial enterprise.

Two years later, Virginia Iron, Coal and Coke Company was reorganized. In its new incarnation, the business continued to struggle as an iron producer and mining concern. By the 1920s, all its furnaces had closed. Afterward, the firm operated primarily by leasing its coal and mineral properties, which encompassed more than 250,000 acres in Virginia, Tennessee, North Carolina, Kentucky, and Georgia. In 1969 Bates Manufacturing Company acquired Virginia Iron, Coal and Coke Company as a speculative investment and sold it in 1979 to American Natural Resources Company. Now based in Roanoke, the Virginia Iron, Coal and Coke Company operates as a unit of Coastal Corporation's Coastal Coal Company.

See also: BITUMINOUS COAL INDUSTRY; CARTER, GEORGE LAFAYETTE; IRON AND STEEL INDUSTRY.

—Ned L. Irwin, *East Tennessee State University*, and Ed Speer, *Elizabethton, Tennessee*

Ray Stahl and Ned L. Irwin, *The Last Empire Builder: A Life of George L. Carter, 1857–1936* (forthcoming).

Walker, Cas

(1902–1998) Entrepreneur, politician, media personality, and philanthropist.

One of the most prominent and colorful public figures to emerge from east Tennessee, Cas Walker made a fortune in the grocery business. He is perhaps best remembered, however, for the radio and television shows he hosted to promote both his business enterprises and his outspoken political views. The popular programs also launched the careers of several major bluegrass and country musicians of the mid-twentieth century.

Caswell Orton Walker was born on March 22, 1902, on English Mountain in Sevier County. Quitting school at age fourteen, he traveled around the country working at various jobs, including as a farmhand and coal miner. After returning to Knoxville, at age twenty-one he opened the first of twenty-seven Cas Walker Cash Stores. Three decades later, these stores produced annual revenues of some $60 million.

The young entrepreneur started the *Farm and Home Hour* on WROL-AM in 1929 to promote his grocery stores, which almost immediately experienced spectacular profits. Walker's subsequent shows included the *Cas Walker Show*, which aired on WROL-TV and later WBIR-TV from 1953 to 1983. These shows featured a mix of homegrown advertising jingles for Walker's grocery stores as well as country and bluegrass music by current and future stars—including Roy Acuff, Bill Monroe, Jimmy Martin, Carl Smith, a ten-year-old Dolly Parton, and the teenaged Everly Brothers—interspersed with Walker's raccoon hunting tales and uncompromising political observations.

Walker's political career was marked by his pugnacity and included an aborted one-year term as mayor of Knoxville in 1946, a stint as acting mayor in 1959, thirty years as a city councilman from 1941 through 1971, and a spot on the cover of *Life* magazine in 1954 following a fistfight with a political adversary in the council. His political harangues, which repeatedly landed Walker in litigious situations, also regularly surfaced in the *Watchdog*, a journal Walker published from 1964 to 1981.

A regular donor to charities in east Tennessee, Walker died on September 28, 1998, at the age of ninety-six.

See also: ACUFF, ROY (MUSIC); PARTON, DOLLY (MUSIC).

—Ajay Kalra, *East Tennessee State University*

Watson, James Otis

(1815–1902) Coal industry leader.

In 1852, at Fairmont in what would become West Virginia, James Otis Watson and a partner opened the first rail-shipping bituminous coal mine west of the Alleghenies. Watson, who has been called "father of the West Virginia coal industry," went on to dominate the Upper Monongahela fields and to sire ten children, three of whom—James Edwin, Sylvanus Lamb, and Clarence Wayland—became major figures in the industry.

Son of a civil engineer, Watson was born on May 17, 1815, near Benton's Ferry in what was then Virginia. Educated at home and in a private school in Morgantown, he became active in the Fairmont business community and completed a suspension bridge over the Monongahela in 1852, the year the Baltimore and Ohio Railroad reached the town. In 1853 the first carloads of coal left the American Coal Company owned by Watson and Francis H. Pierpont, who would later become West Virginia's first governor. Following the Civil War, having ended his alliance with Pierpont, Watson teamed with A. Brooks Fleming and James Boyce in numerous mining ventures and founded the Gaston Coal Company in 1874. He retired from mine management in 1885, but the next year, the coking qualities of Upper Monongahela coal having finally been recognized, he and nine associates founded the Montana Coal and Coke Company, named for a mine along the Monongahela. Montana built the first battery of beehive coke ovens in West Virginia. Watson's interests compromised Fairmont Coal Company, which was founded in 1901, and in 1903 Fairmont became part of Consolidation Coal Company, the world's largest bituminous operation.

In Watson's heyday, independent operators predominated. The Watsons ran a shrewdly paternalistic regime, paying above-average wages and providing low-cost housing, stores, and social services, so unionization held little appeal for the workers. Asked once by a representative of a Baltimore coal firm how he made money when the large firms were having difficulty, Watson replied: "I am my own president, my own secretary, my own mule boss and mine boss, and carry my office in my hat."

He died on June 12, 1902.

See also: BITUMINOUS COAL INDUSTRY; CONSOLIDATION COAL COMPANY/CONSOL ENERGY.

—David S. Newhall, *Centre College*

White, I. C.

(1848–1927) Geologist.

West Virginia geologist Israel Charles White was best known for his anticlinal theory, which explained where oil and gas were most likely to accumulate. His survey reports detailed the bituminous coalfields of Pennsylvania, West Virginia, and Ohio, and he helped make West Virginia a leading state in coal, oil, and gas production.

Born in rural Monongalia County in what is now West Virginia, White entered the new West Virginia University in 1867 and abandoned medical ambitions to study geology under John James Stevenson. White was graduated in 1872, completed his master's degree in 1875, and studied for a year at Columbia University. He earned his doctorate in 1880 from what is now the University of Arkansas.

In 1877 he became a professor in the geology department at West Virginia University while working on the Second Geological Survey of Pennsylvania (1875–84). He also helped with the United States Geological Survey (1884–88). After publishing his anticlinal theory in *Science* in 1885, he applied it to acquire profitable gas and oil leases. He resigned his faculty position in 1892 to concentrate on business.

White promoted establishment of the West Virginia Geological and Economic Survey in 1897 and headed it with vigor for the next thirty years as the state geologist. He consulted for various corporations, headed a coal survey in Brazil, and was a charter member of the Geological Society of America.

See also: BITUMINOUS COAL INDUSTRY; COAL (GEOLOGY); OIL AND GAS (GEOLOGY).

—Sarah Gibbard Cook, *DeForest, Wisconsin*

Wilder, John T.

(1830–1917) Industrialist.

With investors, John Thomas Wilder accumulated five hundred thousand acres of coal and iron fields in four Appalachian states of the central South. He built blast furnaces in two east Tennessee towns, opened a rail mill in Chattanooga, and, among many other business activities in the region, participated in building the Charleston, Cincinnati, and Chicago Railroad. He also became an urban mayor and postmaster in Tennessee and represented the Volunteer State as a foreign emissary.

Wilder was born in Greene County, New York, in January of 1830, the son of Reuben and Mary Merritt Wilder. As a teenager he worked in a foundry in Columbus, Ohio, where he learned the skills of a draftsman, patternmaker, and millwright. In 1850, after moving to Greensburg, Indiana, he established his own foundry, which, a decade later, he used to cast two cannon to form an artillery company and join the Seventeenth Indiana Artillery in the Civil War.

The war introduced Wilder to the Appalachian South. Within a short time he was promoted from captain to lieutenant colonel and eventually to brigadier general. In 1863 he and his brigade opened Hoover's Gap in middle Tennessee and pursued the rear guard of General Braxton Bragg's Confederate army to Chattanooga. When Bragg's soldiers evacuated the city, Wilder's were the first Union troops to enter. In the Union loss of the subsequent battle of Chickamauga in northern Georgia, Wilder's brigade opened the fight and was the only Federal force to remain on the field through the battle's second day. He and his unit were commended by General George Thomas for "occupying the attention of an entire corps of the rebel army while our army was getting around its flank."

Resigning from the military in October of 1864 after participating in General William T. Sherman's siege of Atlanta, Wilder explored the mineral resources of the Appalachian Cumberland Plateau and moved to Chattanooga in 1866. In 1867 he purchased land in Roane County, founding the blast furnace-equipped Roane Iron Works in the town of Rockwood. Eventually he and his investors acquired about a half-million acres of land rich in iron and coal in Tennessee, Kentucky, Virginia, and North Carolina. On Roan Mountain near the North Carolina–Tennessee border, he constructed the luxurious Cloudland Hotel for a wealthy clientele, and in Johnson City he built a Carnegie blast furnace. In 1870 he started a rail mill in Chattanooga and in the 1890s took part in the construction of the Charleston, Cincinnati, and Chicago Railroad. His other enterprises included the Wilder Machine Works and the Southern Car and Foundry Company in Chattanooga, the Dayton Coal and Iron Company, the Durham Coal Company, and the Fentress Coal Company.

In public service, General Wilder acted as Tennessee commissioner to the Vienna Exposition of 1873 and organized the Tennessee exhibit of minerals sent to the Philadelphia Centennial Exposition in 1876. In 1871 he was elected mayor of Chattanooga, and he went on to serve as postmaster between 1877 and 1882. President William McKinley appointed him in 1897 to supervise Tennessee's pension office for Civil War veterans, and he also served as president of the Chickamauga Memorial Association. He was even made an honorary member of the United Confederate Veterans.

Wilder owned houses in Chattanooga, Knoxville, Rockwood, and Monterey, Tennessee. His first wife, Martha Stewart, with whom he fathered six daughters and a son, died in 1892, and in 1904 he married Dora E. Lee. He died on October 20, 1917, in Jacksonville, Florida, and was buried at Forest Hills Cemetery in Chattanooga.

See also: CARNEGIE, ANDREW; IRON AND STEEL INDUSTRY.

—W. Calvin Dickinson, *Tennessee Technological University*

Wineries

Attempts at commercial wine production in the Appalachian region date back to the eighteenth century, when Thomas Jefferson and others imported grapevines from Europe. Blight and other problems made the ventures unsuccessful. Although home wine production on a small scale has existed throughout the region from the earliest days of settlement, it was not until the late twentieth century that wine production became a significant commercial enterprise in much of Appalachia.

The Bureau of Alcohol, Tobacco, Firearms, and Explosives has identified 145 viticultural areas in the United States, most of them in California. About 10 percent, or slightly more than a dozen of them, are located in the Appalachian region. These include such areas as the Lake Erie/ Chautauqua area of New York, the Cumberland Valley of Maryland and Pennsylvania, the Kanawha River Valley of West Virginia and Ohio, the Rocky Knob area of Virginia, and the Yadkin Valley of North Carolina. The winery at George W. Vanderbilt's Biltmore Estate near Asheville, North Carolina, is the nation's most visited. Wines produced at Biltmore since 1971 have won more than three hundred national and international medals.

A good example of the growth of the industry is Chateau Morrisette in Floyd County, Virginia, founded by the Morrisette family in 1978. By 1999, the company had constructed a four-million-dollar winery and retail sales building and developed an acclaimed restaurant. With eighty-five employees in a rural mountain county and a commitment to use local contractors for work and supplies, Chateau Morrisette constitutes a significant part of the county's sales tax base. Its wines have earned national recognition.

The importance of the wine industry in Appalachia is apparent in the support services created around it. The only two academic programs in the United States in viticulture (the growing of grapes) and enology (wine production) outside California are in the Appalachian region, one at Cornell University at its Agricultural Experiment Station in Geneva, New York, and one at Virginia Polytechnic Institute and State University in Blacksburg. The programs conduct research in viticulture, grape quality, grapevine breeding and genetics, and enology, and both programs offer many services to wine growers in their areas, including analytical laboratories.

Most of the wineries in the Appalachian region produce a variety of wines, but some are quite specialized. For example, the Little Hungary Farm Winery in Buckhannon, West Virginia, produces organic honey mead. In many parts of the region, wineries have become an important part of economic-development efforts through tourism as well as the sale of wine. In southeastern Ohio, the Appalachian Wine Heritage Trail invites visitors to tour vineyards and wineries, buy crafts, and celebrate the area's Swiss heritage. The Lake Erie/Chautauqua Wine Trail in New York encourages tourists to visit the largest grape-growing area in the United States outside of California, with more than twenty thousand acres of vineyards. The Blue Ridge Wine Trail of southwest Virginia and western North Carolina offers visitors wines and wine tours, restaurants, craft demonstrations and sales, scenic hikes, old-time mountain music, and pasta and Italian cooking demonstrations at the Villa Appalaccia Winery.

Some vineyards in the region are contributing to the ecological as well as the economic recovery of the coalfield areas of Appalachia. Experiments with growing grapes on land reclaimed from strip mining are proving complex but profitable. The Mountain Rose Vineyard in Wise County, Virginia, for example, has several acres of grapevines on strip-mined land. Problems have included a lack of organic matter and microorganisms in the soil and soil compaction that limits water absorption and root growth. However, the high mineral content of the soil as a result of mining can produce better-tasting wines. Most predictors suggest that wine production and its associated services will continue as a modest but vigorous part of the Appalachian economy and add to a perception of the region as more sophisticated in its tastes.

See also: WINE (FOOD AND COOKING).

—Jean Haskell, *East Tennessee State University*

Chris Kahn, "From Strip Mine to Fine Wine: Grapes Thrive in Land Left Behind," *Anniston Star* (September 1, 2003); North Carolina State University Cooperative Extension, *The Mid-Atlantic Winegrape Grower's Guide* (1995).

Wise Snacks and Moore's Potato Chips

As of 2002, the Wise Foods potato chip manufacturing complex in Berwick, Pennsylvania, covered 750,000 square feet and claimed to be the largest snack food plant in the world. Moore's Potato Chips of Bristol, Virginia, eventually merged with Wise but remained one of the strongest regional brands in the nation and continued to operate out of its Bristol facility.

The invention of the potato chip has been credited to Native American George Crum, who worked as a resort chef in Saratoga Springs, New York. After its introduction in 1853, the chip quickly gained popularity as a snack food. During the 1920s, two grocers—one at Wise Foods in Berwick and another at Moore's Quality Snack Foods in Bristol—began making the chips and selling them.

In 1921 Earl V. Wise Sr., a Berwick grocer, began using the well-liked snack as a solution for an overstock of potatoes. Wise prepared the chips in his mother's kitchen and sold them in paper bags. The success of his chips forced him to move into his remodeled garage, then into a separate concrete building. By 1942, he had expanded into a facility of more than 40 square feet of floor space. A fire in 1944 destroyed the plant but not the company. Within a few months of the fire, Wise built a small building and began producing potato chips as a larger plant grew around it. Between 1947 and 2002, the Wise Potato Chip Company's Berwick plant expanded from about 120 square feet to its present dimensions.

Similarly, Moore's Quality Snack Foods was started in 1924 by Bristol grocer J. W. Moore, who used a homemade chip fryer to make his potato chips and delivered them to customers in his truck. The flavor and quality of the snack enhanced the company's reputation.

Both businesses grew into large corporations, with Moore's Quality Snack Foods eventually merging with Wise during the 1980s. The 1960s had brought major changes to Wise. In 1964 Borden, a business famed for dairy products and snack foods, bought the company, and in 1969 Wise Potato Chips was renamed Wise Foods. When Palladium Equity Partners, a private investment firm, and its affiliate, PEP Snack Foods, bought Wise Foods in 2000, the company name was retained.

See also: POTATOES (FOOD AND COOKING).

—Mary Grace Meador, *East Tennessee State University*

Woolworth, Frank

(1852–1919) Retailer.

Frank Winfield Woolworth created America's first five-and-dime store, one of the more notable retail sales innovations of the twentieth century. His stores were embraced by virtually every class throughout America, and they played significant roles in small towns and in the social and business life of rural Appalachian communities.

Born on April 13, 1852, in Jefferson County, New York, Woolworth got his first job in a general store in Great Bend, New York, where he developed an affinity for retailing. He worked in several retail stores early in his career, and while with Moore and Smith in Great Bend in 1878 he introduced a five-cent counter. He also displayed goods so customers could help themselves to merchandise without the intervention of a clerk. Both ideas were considered revolutionary.

In 1879 the first Woolworth store opened in Utica, New York—and quickly closed because of poor location. In June of the same year, Woolworth's second store opened in Lancaster, Pennsylvania, with better results. Throughout the 1880s, 1890s, and the first decade following the turn of the century, Woolworth worked to expand his business. In December 1911, his purchase of five other retail chains located across America created F. W. Woolworth and Company and made it the first retail firm to operate in all forty-eight states.

Woolworth died in 1919, but his variety store chain prospered and remained a cultural icon through World War II and beyond. In small towns, these stores were places of Saturday afternoon socializing from the 1930s through the 1960s, and bargain prices on staple items made it a popular supplier for the demands of rural residents.

Woolworth's lunch counters were pivotal in the 1960s civil rights protests. African Americans staged sit-ins at the chain's lunch counters throughout the South, the first of which was in Greensboro, North Carolina, on February 1, 1960. A subsequent boycott resulted in losses for the company. Some Woolworth stores in larger cities integrated, but the Greensboro store remained segregated and the focus of protests until July 1960. The chain closed its last stores in the United States in 1998.

See also: CIVIL RIGHTS MOVEMENT (RACE, ETHNICITY, AND IDENTITY).

—Linda Dailey Paulson, *Ventura, California*

Karen Plunkett-Powell, *Remembering Woolworth's: A Nostalgic History of the World's Most Famous Five-and-Dime* (1999).

Zinc Industry

As recently as 1985, Tennessee accounted for 40 percent of America's production of zinc, but the economic downturn beginning in 2000 brought hardship to the zinc industry, especially in Tennessee. Declining world prices resulting from overproduction and excess capacity were critical. By 2002 the gigantic Red Dog Mine in northwest Alaska was producing 85 percent of the United States output, with Tennessee, Missouri, and New York combined contributing just 13 percent. Moreover, zinc was being challenged in most of its uses by steel, aluminum, magnesium, cadmium, and plastics. As a result of these pressures, the American Smelting and Refining Company and Zinc Corporation of America both ceased production in Tennessee in 2001, and Pasminco, Ltd., an Australian firm, announced plans to close or sell its Tennessee operations by mid-2004.

A bluish-white and relatively soft metal, zinc is used as galvanized coating in alloys and for appliances and automobile parts. It is also shaped into gutters, pipes, and flashing and is employed in various consumer products. The zinc industry in the United States began in the 1850s with the first zinc ingots produced at Friedensville, Pennsylvania, on the fringe of Appalachia near Allentown. Those ingots came from a mine that continued production until 1983. Other Pennsylvania zinc operations include a major smelting plant that opened in 1931 at Monaca in Beaver County and a plant that recovers zinc from the steelmaking process at Palmerton, north of Allentown.

A high-grade zinc ore has long been mined in southwestern Virginia around Austinville and Ivanhoe in Wythe County, and in West Virginia a slab zinc plant operated in Harrison County from 1911 to 1971. But the unquestioned center of Appalachia's zinc industry is located in east Tennessee. Just outside east Tennessee, on Appalachia's fringe in the state's central division, Rutherford, Cannon, Wilson, and Smith Counties also have housed significant zinc-mining operations since the mid-1970s. Tennessee surpassed New York as the nation's leading producer in 1958 and retained that status until 1990, a year after Alaska's Red Dog Mine went into operation and soon put that state in first place. The U.S. produces about 7 percent of the world's zinc, but it is also the world's largest user of the metal and still imports 70 percent of its supply.

Tennessee zinc was discovered by Gerald Troost in 1844. The first zinc mine in the Volunteer State opened ten years later at Mossy Creek, the present Jefferson City, but the first substantial mining was done by the Eades, Mixter and Heald Company at Mossy Creek beginning in 1883. The principal zinc-producing ore is sphalerite, a zinc-sulfide sometimes called blende. East Tennessee is rich in sphalerite deposits, nearly all of which are embedded in limestone or dolomite host rocks a half-million or more years old. Much Tennessee zinc ore, especially in the Mascot–Jefferson City and Copper Ridge Districts, is exceptionally free of contaminants and is often used to make zinc oxide for pigments.

Over many decades the east Tennessee industry developed in six districts. These are Mascot–Jefferson City in Knox and Jefferson Counties; Copper Ridge in Grainger and Hawkins Counties; Ducktown in Polk County, where zinc is a by-product of a copper operation; Embreeville and Bumpass Cove in Washington and Unicoi Counties; Fall Branch in Greene, Washington, and Sullivan Counties; and Powell River in Union and Claiborne Counties. Carter, Cook, and Bradley Counties contain old, abandoned mines.

Zinc mining, like most resource operations, has a history of economic ups and downs. The most prominent operators in Appalachia in the early twentieth century were the American, Tennessee, Holston, and Roseberry firms. Zinc Corporation of America, which since World War II has been one of the industry's major companies, claimed in 2003 to be the world's largest recycler of zinc and zinc-bearing metals.

Zinc can be completely recycled with no loss of physical or chemical properties, and more than one-third of world consumption is now of recycled zinc. That is fortunate, since zinc mining can be difficult on the environment. In Palmerton, Pennsylvania, the New Jersey Zinc Company mined and smelted for seventy years and left such an accumulation of zinc, lead, copper, cadmium, and arsenic on Blue Mountain, which runs through Palmerton, that no vegetation or wildlife inhabited its two thousand acres, leaving it populated only by dead trees. Rainwater carried some of the contaminants into nearby Aquashicola Creek and the Lehigh River. The federal Environmental Protection Agency stepped in and ordered a cleanup by Zinc Corporation of America, the corporate successor to New Jersey Zinc. The company, with help from the U.S. Army Corps of Engineers, had to apply sludge to the slopes of the mountain before they could be replanted with grass and tree seedlings. In 2002 another thousand acres remained to be replanted, but turkey, pheasant, fox, and deer were reported back on the mountain.

See also: AIR QUALITY (ENVIRONMENT); COPPER AND LEAD; INDUSTRIAL POLLUTION (ENVIRONMENT).

—David S. Newhall, *Centre College*

Stuart W. Maher, *The Zinc Industry of Tennessee* (1958); A. D. McMahon et al., *The U.S. Zinc Industry: A Historical Perspective* (1979); U.S. Geological Survey, *Minerals Yearbook* (1938–2003).

Labor

Section Editors: John C. Hennen and Ronald L. Lewis

To understand the complex and enduring importance of labor in Appalachia, one must look beyond the roles of unions, politics, ideology, and conflict in shaping a few dominant industries. Contrary to the notions of many outsiders, the region is not a place of cultural uniformity; consequently, the following section is shaped by two important principles: that labor has historically reflected the class and economic diversity of the region; and that work relations in Appalachia are best understood in light of the region's place in the world capitalist system.

The first of these principles is suggested by a description of Wheeling, (West) Virginia, in Joseph Martin's *Gazetteer of Virginia* in 1836. Strategically located at the juncture of the National Road and the Ohio River and serving both eastern and western markets, antebellum Wheeling was part of the national economy at an early date. Martin lauded Wheeling as "possessing unexampled facilities for manufacturing, in the abundance and low cost of all materials, and especially of fuel." The city's population had grown 800 percent over the previous fifteen years to eight thousand inhabitants, he noted, creating a dynamic network of professional, trade, and service occupations. A major ironworks formed the centerpiece of a thriving manufacturing and commercial district that included glass-cutting operations, a brewery, two distilleries, two cotton factories, woolen factories, shoe factories, paper mills, sawmills, tobacco factories, a glue factory, a brickyard, wagon makers, toolmakers, chair makers, tailors, silversmiths, blacksmiths, tanners, saddlers, painters, glaziers, carpenters, plasterers, and stone and brick masons. Other areas of the Appalachians could also boast of economic vitality, but Wheeling serves as a particularly vivid example of the diversity and dynamism that have characterized Appalachian labor from the earliest settlement period.

In addition to presenting the economic and class diversity of places such as Wheeling, the entries found here collectively explore the evolution of labor relations throughout the region. As labor relations have evolved, however, so have approaches to studying them, and this section reflects these changes within the field of labor history. Pioneering studies by labor economists John R. Commons, Selig Perlman, and Philip Taft focused on trade unions as organizations. Their work influenced three generations of scholarship on American workers, beginning in the early 1900s. They generally agreed that the best way to understand American workers was to study

Facing page: Miners and their spouses on the picket line in Wise County, Virginia, 1989. For nine months (until February 1990), the United Mine Workers of America waged a labor battle against Pittston Coal Company, one of the largest producers of coal in the nation.

A track gang works on the main line of the Chesapeake and Ohio Railroad near Thayer, West Virginia, 1944. Crew members hired for laying tracks in the rugged mountain terrain were often African Americans and Italian immigrants who worked long hours under perilous conditions.

their organizations and the collective bargaining agreements they negotiated with employers.

The problem with focusing the study of labor relations exclusively on unionization and contractual procedures is that labor unions have historically only been able to claim a small percentage of American workers. The number peaked in the mid- to late 1950s when about one-third of American workers had union contracts. Prompted by the democratization of higher education (speeded by the G.I. Bill), the Civil Rights movement, and other social developments, labor and the perception of labor history underwent dramatic change by the late 1960s. Within this broadened conceptual framework, labor scholars explored more fully how workers built and lived within their own communities.

This new approach to workers' history was inspired by the pioneering work of British historian E. P. Thompson and especially his American counterpart, cultural historian Herbert Gutman. Thompson and Gutman criticized the "old" institutional labor history's "narrow economic analysis," which separated workers not only from their own subculture but from society as well. "New" labor historians were guided by a conviction that the history of American workers should be integrated into community studies rather than restricted to the study of union bureaucracies. Contributors to this section are themselves participants in a continuing reevaluation of work and workers within the Appalachian region.

This section covers several broad topical areas: labor in theories of economic development; the antebellum era; extractive industries and the growth of industrial capitalism; non-extractive and service occupations; and recent and contemporary labor issues. With the exception of articles on slave and convict labor, only limited attention is given to unpaid labor. Labor relations in agriculture, informal economies, and professional and information-based occupations are not included because these topics appear in other sections of the *Encyclopedia of Appalachia.* While some background is provided on antebellum labor, the entries primarily emphasize the period from the late nineteenth through the end of the twentieth century.

Work entails more than the physical activities of producing and distributing goods or services; it also involves the social relations that result from production, distribution, and service activities. Thus, labor issues reach beyond mine, mill, and hospital ward into the homes and neighborhoods of workers, influencing their values, beliefs, traditions, and identities.

Not even work and community relations within highly similar industries can be assumed to operate under a set of universal practices. Compare, for example, the cultural, racial, and ethnic composition of coal and steel communities for the Monongahela Valley of Pennsylvania and West Virginia, with their high concentration of southern and eastern European immigrants and few blacks, with those communities in the Birmingham, Alabama, mineral district, where African Americans vastly outnumbered foreign-born workers. Therefore, this section does not presume to present a comprehensive analysis of working-class culture. It does cast light upon some fundamental aspects of individual identity and collective existence in such environments. Although the coal industry is not a powerful presence everywhere in Appalachia, it continues to have profound impact on life in large parts of the region through employment and tax revenues on the one hand and environmental destruction on the other.

The evolution of labor relations in Appalachia is part of the larger historical development of capitalism in America. The traditional view holds that, from colonial times to the Civil War, America was a strictly agrarian society made up of isolated subsistence farmers cut off from external markets. More recent scholarship suggests that a transportation revolution in the decades prior to the Civil War broke down isolation and linked rural Americans to national markets. Some revisionist historians have gone even further, rejecting the "agrarian myth" and arguing that farmers were engaged in the exchange of commercial goods and services from earliest colonial times.

A fourth perspective derives from the scholarship of eminent historical sociologist Immanuel Wallerstein. This view presents capitalism as an expansionist "world system" evolving over centuries. It sees capitalism as an economic system that has expanded unevenly, permitting coexistence of traditional agrarian life and the modern market system. According to the world systems theory, capitalism organizes the world into distinct economic spheres—a "core" of investment capital and commerce centers and "peripheral" regions that supply raw materials to support the more developed sphere. Within this model, peripheral regions such as Appalachia export their natural resources to support America's core industrial areas.

Recent Appalachian scholarship has greatly revised knowledge of the region. Traditional interpretations were grounded in fictional representations of Appalachia by late-nineteenth-century local color writers and by reformers seeking financial support for education from northern philanthropists. Improvements in education, the reformers argued, would rescue mountain people from the isolation that, while allowing them to retain their alleged Anglo-Saxon folk culture, had also insulated them from the forces of civilization. This representation of Appalachians was accepted uncritically by subsequent reporters, scholars, and policymakers. Revisionist scholars such as Henry D. Shapiro, in *Appalachia on Our Mind* (1978), and Allen W. Batteau, in *The Invention of Appalachia* (1990), have called this the "myth of Appalachia."

This view of Appalachia as a homogeneous regionwide folk society physically, culturally, and economically isolated from mainstream America has persisted in part because little formal history has been written about Appalachia, particularly in the preindustrial era. But more recent studies show that much of Appalachia was neither unusually secluded, nor were the people more homogeneous than those living in other sections of rural America. These studies reveal early commercial development in some sections of the region and document a wide variety of economic activities and labor relations far beyond the stereotypical subsistence farm.

The diversity of antebellum Appalachian labor relations is implicitly stated in this section's entries on slave labor, the salt industry, and iron and steel mill workers in Alabama. Existing on the South's periphery, Appalachian slavery complicated labor relations in the region even in the early days. Salt- and ironworks were among the first industries to develop in the mountains. Using coal-fired boilers for steam power, both contributed to the development of a nascent coal industry. Prior to refrigeration, salt was vital as a food preservative, and through the nineteenth century Appalachia was a major producer of the nation's supply. The most important centers of production were located in southwestern Virginia, eastern Kentucky, and the Kanawha Valley of present-day West Virginia. As John Stealey has shown in *The Antebellum Kanawha Salt Business and Western Markets* (1993), salt was a substantial industry. By the 1820s, the Kanawha Valley was already a major exporter of salt to cities on the Ohio River and downstream to St. Louis and New Orleans. Like its counterparts, the Kanawha industry relied partly on slave labor but attracted hundreds of free itinerant workers as well. In addition to those who were directly involved in the manufacture of salt, numerous other tradesmen were employed as coopers, carpenters, blacksmiths, and coal miners. After the Civil War, as the salt industry declined, a burgeoning coal industry gradually took its place as a major employer. Iron also was a basic necessity of America's coming industrial transformation, and blacksmiths throughout the mountains hammered it into practical implements. Charcoal furnaces were constructed wherever suitable ores were found. In urban industrial centers such as Pittsburgh, Birmingham, Wheeling, and Knoxville and Chattanooga, Tennessee, large iron-producing complexes arose in the late nineteenth century, supplying the coal and iron that forged America into an industrial power.

Like the dramatic growth of coal and iron, the history of the lumber industry in Appalachia is intimately connected to the nation's insatiable pursuit of natural resources for its phenomenal expansion between the Civil War and World War I. Lumber was one of America's first industries, but early-nineteenth-century logging operations in Appalachia were usually small family businesses characterized by selective cutting and river transport by independent raftsmen. This period was short-lived, however. By the 1880s the forests in Maine, New York, Pennsylvania, and the Great Lakes states had been depleted, and commercial timber operations turned their attention southward to the Appalachian Mountains. Access to the region's timber was facilitated by local and state lawmakers, financiers, and lawyers anxious to capitalize on the nation's voracious need for lumber to build growing cities and railroad crossties. Large companies acquired huge tracts of timberland, erected gigantic processing mills, and hired thousands of workers to cut, transport, and process timber into lumber. Corporate control rapidly evolved alongside the construction of railroads between the 1880s and 1920 as natural resource companies bought up land and timber and secured future rights to subsurface minerals and oil, gas, and coal. Corporations headquartered in distant financial capitals soon controlled millions of acres of mountain land.

Corporate logging encouraged technological innovation and production of heavy equipment, which in turn transformed work relations. Labor was the essential ingredient not only in the timbering process, but in the construction of railroads to transport equipment and lumber as well. As timbering became a large-scale enterprise, it also declined as a source of supplemental cash and off-season occupation for farmers. Companies recruited and managed large full-time crews housed in timber camps and logging towns. Crews hired for the brutal, labor-intensive work of laying tracks in the rugged mountain terrain were often comprised of African Americans and Italian immigrants who worked long hours under perilous conditions. Some of them were swept into a state of virtual debt peonage. Once the timber was gone, native Appalachian workers gravitated toward the coal mines, textile mills, iron mills, and railroads or left the region.

The history of thousands of communities in the Appalachians has been shaped by the coal industry. Early coal operators built their own towns and imported their own workforce. Central Appalachian districts dominated by the coal industry experienced the keenest demand for labor and consequently the greatest importation of workers. Tens of thousands of foreign immigrants representing nearly every European nation were transported directly from the eastern ports of entry to labor in the mines. The array of new languages and cultures produced a diversity hitherto unknown in the mountains. An influx of African Americans also altered the region's demographics. The preindustrial African American population of central Appalachia was relatively small, totaling only 14,360 in 1870, but that figure had quadrupled to 64,251 by 1910 and reached a peak of 108,872 in 1930, when the in-migration ended. Joe W. Trotter, in *Coal, Class, and Color: Blacks in Southern West Virginia, 1915–32* (1990), and Ronald L. Lewis, in *Black Coal Miners in America: Race, Class, and Community Conflict, 1780–1980* (1987), document the growth of African American population in the coalfields of Appalachia. In some Appalachian counties, particularly McDowell in West Virginia, African Americans and immigrants composed fully one-third of the mine workforce between 1880 and 1920 and in some locations represented an even higher proportion of total company employment.

Mine owners' control over daily life in early coal communities was manifested in many ways and was confirmed in 1917 by the U.S. Supreme Court's sweeping decision in the case of *Hitchman Coal and Coke Company v. Mitchell et al.* The *Hitchman* decision gave judicial sanction to two antiunion legal devices used by coal companies, the individual employment ("yellow dog") contract, which barred miners from joining a union, and injunctions restraining the union from approaching miners on company property. Owners' complete control over housing, the issuance of company scrip rather than legal tender, and the constant struggle of workers to survive in a highly competitive market all contributed to recurring tensions between miners and their bosses. Organizing efforts by the United Mine Workers of America occasionally flared into industrial warfare. Labor-management conflict and specific union struggles in the industry, beginning with an analysis of the Molly Maguires in the 1870s and resuming during the first decades of the twentieth century, are presented in several entries in this section. The Great Depression of the 1930s was a watershed era in American history, and its impact on the Appalachians is suggested in the entry on America's worst occupational health disaster, at Hawk's Nest Tunnel in West Virginia.

The depression prompted the federal government to grant additional protections to workers and, through the Wagner Act of 1935, the right to organize into unions. Although revisions of these protections, particularly the Taft-Hartley Act of 1947, somewhat curtailed the power of industrial unions, the New Deal system stabilized labor-management relations in basic industry. Collective bargaining for labor led to industry-wide agreements on wages, hours, and benefits for Appalachia's unionized coal miners. By the 1950s, however, United Mine Workers leader John L. Lewis's increasingly authoritarian control of the union alienated many rank-and-file miners. Moreover, Lewis and his heir, W. A. "Tony" Boyle, negotiated agreements with coal operators that increased the use of machinery and dramatically reduced the number of underground miners. Eventually, the perception of collusion between union officials and the operators led to a rebellion within the United Mine Workers and the rise of the Miners for Democracy movement in the early 1970s. In the 1980s and 1990s, reforms within the United Mine Workers led to closer relations between the leadership and the rank and file, thanks in part to the leadership of the organization's president, Richard Trumka. The major changes that swept over the industry and the United Mine Workers during the 1970s also opened the way for women to enter the mines for the first time in significant numbers.

While timber and coal have been the most researched of modern Appalachian industries, the importance of other Appalachian workers has begun to emerge in the recent deeper understanding of labor in the region. The scant attention given to workers in important industries such as glass, carpet, and chemical manufacturing belies their historic importance in the region's economy. Other workers whose history and culture is just beginning to emerge include textile employees, lock and dam operators, and hospital workers.

No longer isolated—if they ever truly were—Appalachians and their communities have, no less than other Americans, felt the impact of global economic integration. In the late twentieth century, the region suffered from the effects of the rapid mechanization of mining, corporate downsizing, outsourcing of production, and the flight of investment capital to offshore locations. Consequently, low-wage workers in Appalachia found themselves competing with even lower-wage labor in the Third World. The situation had been developing since the early 1970s, when technological innovation and plant relocation began the displacement of workers in mining and manufacturing. Many parts of Appalachia, particularly central Appalachia, have experienced excessively high levels of unemployment, collapsing community tax bases, and endemic out-migration. International trade agreements, notably the North American Free Trade Agreement (NAFTA), which opened the United States and Latin American borders for unrestricted trade, curtailed the economic options available to Appalachian workers even further.

A superheated economic expansion in the 1990s, which had cooled to the point of recession by 2001, masked troubling realities behind the facade of general prosperity. Appalachian wages continued to lag behind the rest of the nation, and poverty rates continued to be higher. At the turn of the century, only about 10 percent of private-sector workers had union representation despite a significant commitment by unions to organize the region's workers, especially in the booming service industries, including hospitals.

One consequence of the decline in union strength and the erosion of bargaining power was lagging wages for workers. Highly mobile firms dependent on low-wage labor offered no guarantee that they would either stay in a community or contribute to a significant increase in purchasing power for their workers. Even when plentiful, many of the jobs available to contemporary Appalachian workers offered pay and benefits too meager to provide even a moderately comfortable and secure standard of living. The unequal distribution of wealth and resources, a dominant historic theme in the Appalachian saga, threatened to continue well into the new millennium.

—John C. Hennen, *Morehead State University*, and Ronald L. Lewis, *West Virginia University*

Chad Berry, *Southern Migrants, Northern Exiles* (2000); Dwight B. Billings, Gurney Norman, and Katherine Ledford, eds., *Confronting Appalachian Stereotypes: Back Talk from an American Region* (1999); Paul F. Clark, *The Miners' Fight for Democracy: Arnold Miller and the Reform of the United Mine Workers* (1981); Wilma A. Dunaway, *The First American Frontier: Transition to Capitalism in Southern Appalachia, 1700–1860* (1996); Ronald D Eller, *Miners, Millhands, and Mountaineers: Industrialization of the Appalachian South, 1880–1930* (1982); Daniel J. Leab, ed., *The Labor History Reader* (1985); Ronald L. Lewis, *Transforming the Appalachian Countryside: Railroads, Deforestation, and Social Change in West Virginia, 1880–1920* (1998); Lawrence Mishel, Jared Bernstein, and John Schmitt, *The State of Working America, 2000–2001* (2001); Mary Beth Pudup, Dwight B. Billings, and Altina L. Waller, eds., *Appalachia in the Making: The Mountain South in the Nineteenth Century* (1995); Joe William Trotter Jr., *Coal, Class, and Color: Blacks in Southern West Virginia, 1915–32* (1990).

Anthracite Miners, Nineteenth-Century

Most of America's commercially exploitable anthracite coal is found in a 462-square-mile region of northeastern Pennsylvania. This small area lent itself early to industrial concentration. By the 1870s, seven railroad-mine operators controlled more than 90 percent of the industry's production and operated as a community of interests, or cartel. Anthracite was primarily a domestic fuel, and most of its consumers were on the eastern seaboard. The area's miners confronted the same issues faced by workers in the bituminous coalfields: low wages, threats to personal safety, and an exploitative paternal system that included company housing, stores, and doctors. However, capital concentration and a market heavily reliant upon individual consumers made the struggles of anthracite miners different from those in the bituminous fields.

The anthracite miners' initial effort to address poor wages was a spontaneous strike in July 1842, which was quickly broken by the arrival of a militia company. Six years later, miner John Bates organized a local union that enjoyed limited success until it fell apart amid rumors that Bates had absconded with the treasury. Collective activity remained dormant until the Civil War, when a number of local unions organized. Miners in the Pittston area received formal recognition in the form of a written contract in 1863. However, many operators took advantage of martial law imposed as a reaction to antidraft protests and used it to defeat strikes. By late 1865, most local unions had disappeared.

In 1868 postwar recession and a new law mandating an eight-hour day sparked a wave of strikes conducted by county rather than local organizations. The following year, the county organizations merged into an industry-wide union, the General Council of the Workingmen's Associations of the Anthracite Coal Fields of Pennsylvania (known as the Workingmen's Benevolent Association, or WBA). The new union sought to regulate the market by tying wages to the price of coal. Unfortunately for labor, the attempt to regulate the coal market coincided with a period of industrial consolidation. Railroad carriers defeated the union in the strike of 1871, and then forced its destruction during the "Long Strike" of 1875, a six-month lockout.

A wave of violence accompanying the Long Strike provided management with the opportunity to equate collective activity with terrorism. Rumors of a secret Irish-Catholic organization, the Molly Maguires, had circulated for years in Schuylkill County and gained credence during the antidraft protests in the Civil War. In 1871 Franklin B. Gowen, president of the Philadelphia and Reading Railroad Company, resurrected the rumor by insinuating that the Molly Maguires controlled the union. Two years later, he hired the Pinkerton Detective Agency to investigate the Molly Maguires. On the incriminating testimony of James McParlan, a Pinkerton undercover agent who had infiltrated the group, twenty Mollies were sent to prison and twenty more were hanged. Although no evidence emerged to link the accused with the union, the press, despite strong protests from labor, reasserted Gowen's innuendoes.

Only a few sporadic local strikes took place during the decade after the destruction of the WBA. In 1883 two unions, the Knights of Labor and the Miners' and Laborers' Amalgamated Association, began to organize the anthracite fields. Coordinating policy through a joint committee, the organizations called their first strike in September 1887. The strike generated a congressional investigation of the anthracite industry, but the probe did nothing to benefit the unions. By February 23, 1888, most miners had deserted their unions to return to work.

Although unsuccessful on the economic front, anthracite miners achieved some remarkable legislative gains. In 1870 they secured a comprehensive mine safety code and in 1889 a law requiring state certification of anthracite miners. To be certified, the candidate had to serve at least two years as an anthracite miner's laborer and pass an examination administered by a board of nine miners with at least five years' experience in the hard-coal mines. The certification act became an impregnable barrier against the use of strikebreakers when the United Mine Workers of America began organizing the hard-coal fields. The union had enjoyed little success when it first entered the anthracite fields, and organizers blamed its failure on the presence of a large numbers of Italian and Slavic immigrants in the mines. In an effort to eliminate these "unorganizables," the union successfully lobbied for the passage of an act that would tax alien mine workers in 1897. Demanding the repeal of the act, immigrants in the Hazleton area marched from colliery to colliery closing the mines. On September 10, one group of marchers confronted a sheriff's posse outside the village of Lattimer. Suddenly the posse opened fire, killing nineteen marchers, all of whom were shot in the back.

The United Mine Workers enjoyed only fleeting gains from the Lattimer Massacre; by 1900 it had enrolled less than 10 percent of the workforce. Nevertheless, local leaders pushed the hesitant national leadership into calling a strike. The response was overwhelming, as 146,000 men and boys walked off the job, closing down the entire industry. Realizing the political repercussion of a coal famine, the Republican Party's national committee pressured the operators into announcing a 10 percent wage increase.

Two years later, the United Mine Workers struck for recognition. Again, fear of a coal famine brought political intervention. President Theodore Roosevelt ended the strike by appointing a commission to investigate conditions. The commission granted a 10 percent increase on piece rates and created the Anthracite Board of Conciliation to rule on future grievances. Although operators refused to officially recognize the United Mine Workers of America until 1912, the commission's award established collective bargaining in the anthracite industry.

See also: ANTHRACITE COAL INDUSTRY (BUSINESS, INDUSTRY, AND TECHNOLOGY); ANTHRACITE MINERS, TWENTIETH-CENTURY; MOLLY MAGUIRES.

—Harold W. Aurand, *Drums, Pennsylvania*

Harold W. Aurand, *From the Molly Maguires to the United Mine Workers: The Social Ecology of an Industrial Union* (1971); Perry K. Blatz, *Democratic Miners: Work and Labor Relations in the Anthracite Coal Industry, 1875–1925* (1994); Kevin Kenny, *Making Sense of the Molly Maguires* (1998).

Anthracite Miners, Twentieth-Century

Stretching from Tower City to Carbondale, the Pennsylvania anthracite coal region includes small rural patch towns, so called because of the patchwork pattern created by the segregation of ethnic groups, and urban centers such as Wilkes-Barre and Scranton. For a century and a half, the region depended almost entirely on the mining of anthracite coal. Ninety-five percent of the nation's supply of anthracite coal lay below this triangular, five-county area, and at the peak of World War I, the mining and preparation of coal employed 175,000 men. By 1992 that figure had declined to 1,400.

Several currents intersect in the twentieth-century history of anthracite mining, including the assimilation of ethnic groups, the growth of industrial unionism, and the dramatic decline of coal mining. By the beginning of the century, recent central, eastern, and southern European immigrants had largely displaced English, Welsh, and Irish miners of an earlier generation, comprising more than 42 percent of mine workers. The workforce of the Lehigh Coal and Navigation Company in 1920 was probably typical. A bit more than half of the company's employees were born in America, while central and eastern Europeans comprised more than a third; immigrants from Italy, Great Britain, and Ireland constituted the remaining 11 percent. The English and Irish had the most experience of any group in the mines, having worked on average twenty-five years at the company, and they held the majority of supervisory jobs. The native-born were the youngest group but still averaged more than fourteen years of employment before 1920. Central and southern Europeans were the newcomers in the mines, averaging twelve and eight years respectively.

Beginning in the 1890s, the United Mine Workers of America sought to organize anthracite miners, with major strikes in 1897, 1900, and 1902. John Mitchell, the union's president, rose to prominence and with the 1902 strike succeeded in winning an arbitrated settlement through the intervention of President Theodore Roosevelt and the Anthracite Coal Strike Commission. As part of the settlement, the commission established a mechanism for addressing miners' grievances and for extending or renegotiating the initial settlement. Mine operators did not formally recognize the United Mine Workers but did bargain with the union. Not until 1936 did operators contractually recognize the union.

Anthracite production peaked in 1917 and 1918, but a severe postwar downturn followed and the industry never really recovered. A combination of strikes in the 1920s and the relatively cheaper price of bituminous coal undercut demand for anthracite. Production dropped from 100 million tons at its World War I peak to 84 million in 1926 and 69 million in 1929. The Great Depression reinforced this trend as unemployment surged throughout the nation's economy. By 1938 annual anthracite production was down to 46 million tons.

Miners responded collectively to slackening work during the 1930s. In the Panther Valley, they demanded equalization of working time across all mines of a given company. In the winter of 1933–34, the Lehigh Coal and Navigation Company acceded to miners' demands, dividing the work evenly among the company's collieries. In the southern field, miners operated abandoned mines, selling what came to be known as bootleg coal. Community groups fought pitched battles with the Coal and Iron Police, protecting their illegal operations and keeping strip-mining equipment from displacing underground miners.

With the upsurge in production during World War II, employment increased, and bootleg operations faded away. But the war period offered only brief respite. Beginning in 1946, decline set in again, and this time miners and members of mining families responded to mine closings with migration rather than collective action, leaving the region in growing numbers. In the postwar decade out-migration among adult residents topped 15 percent. Labor's collective efforts had no answer for declining demand for anthracite coal.

The region's population aged dramatically as younger men and women sought employment elsewhere. Increasingly, social security payments and compensation for black lung supported area residents. Except for limited stripping operations, anthracite mining lives on only as a vestige of an earlier era. In the new century, the industry is most conspicuous in mining museums, photographic exhibits, and oral histories.

See also: ANTHRACITE MINERS, NINETEENTH-CENTURY; UNITED MINE WORKERS OF AMERICA.

—Thomas Dublin, *Binghamton University*

Thomas Dublin, *When the Mines Closed: Stories of Struggle in Hard Times* (1998); Donald L. Miller and Richard E. Sharpless, *The Kingdom of Coal: Work, Enterprise, and Ethnic Communities in the Mine Fields* (1985).

Apparel Workers

Apparel workers, engaged in the manufacture of clothing, hosiery, hats, and caps, serve an industry with a rich history but a doubtful future in the Appalachian region. The industry's factory system emerged in the immediate post–Civil War period, replacing artisans and household manufacturers. From 1870 to 1900, new enterprises thrived in the urban Northeast and Midwest.

In southern Appalachia, hosiery manufacture became important in the early twentieth century, as local capitalists in east Tennessee started factories. Roane Iron Company entrepreneur James F. Tarwater founded Rockwood Mills in 1905, employing around 300 workers, and his son, Tom, bankrolled Harriman Hosiery Mills in 1912. With 100 workers, mostly women, Harriman began the manufacture of ladies' seamless cotton hose in 1913. In 1917 it added rayon and silk hosiery. A bitter strike in 1933–34 conducted by Local 1757 of the United Textile Workers of America involved 746 workers and centered on the company's violation of National Industrial Recovery Act guarantees of collective bargaining and National Recovery Administration wage and price codes. After losing the strike, Harriman's labor remained nonunion. Shortly after the end of World War II, Burlington Industries purchased Harriman, and it remained in business until 1985, when it closed due to competition from lower-priced foreign goods, costing approximately 1,200 workers their jobs.

In 1905 several leading citizens of Clinton, Tennessee, incorporated Magnet Knitting Mills, which became Magnet Mills, Inc., in 1929. The workers remained unorganized until a series of strikes in 1939–40 led to the 1942 election of the independent Anderson County Employees Association over the American Federation of Hosiery Workers, which was affiliated with the Congress of Industrial Organizations (CIO). But Anderson County Employees proved unable to deal with low and inconsistent piecework wages, poor maintenance and acceleration of machinery, and negligible work benefits. About 1950, the workers founded Branch 125 of the American Federation of Hosiery Workers, which merged with the Textile Workers Union of America in 1965. Cost-cutting measures inaugurated by New York–based owners, who had purchased the plant in 1962, contributed to further deterioration of working conditions. In January 1967, the union struck over issues relating to working conditions, wages, and benefits. When negotiators failed to reach agreement, owners shut down the plant, and another 1,750 apparel workers lost their jobs.

In northern Appalachia beginning in the 1920s, the Lackawanna Valley in Pennsylvania became home to scores of runaway apparel factories from New York City. Lackawanna workers overwhelmingly were women, many of them wives of disabled or unemployed coal miners. By 1970, approximately four hundred garment companies were operating in the region. But by the mid-1990s, only twenty or so remained, as competition from lower-paid foreign labor and changing consumer preferences drove the factories out of business.

During the 1920s and 1930s, as apparel companies began to move south to escape the cost of union labor, the Amalgamated Clothing Workers of America (men's clothing), and the International Ladies' Garment Workers' Union, stepped up efforts to unionize the industry. In La Follette, Tennessee, for instance, from 1936 to 1938, Amalgamated had to strike to organize both the 400-worker Atlas Shirts and the 600-worker Reade Shirts. A drive by the CIO's Textile Workers Organizing Committee beginning in 1937 was not overwhelmingly successful in the southern garment industry, but at the end of 1939 there were International Ladies' Garment Workers' and Amalgamated locals scattered throughout the South. The United Garment Workers, a men's clothing union affiliated with the American Federation of Labor, had made some inroads in the Appalachian South during the 1920s (Danville and Lynchburg, Virginia; Jefferson, Newport, and Covington, Kentucky), but lost members throughout the depression years.

The large-scale expansion of the garment industry to the South occurred during the post–World War II period. Cheap, nonunion labor, proximity to southern-produced textiles, and savings on transportation costs motivated manufacturers to head south. Garment unions sought to organize the new plants; the CIO's Operation Dixie (1946–53) tried to improve the wage scale of southern workers but had few successes in the garment factories.

In the Appalachian South apparel employment increased significantly from 1950 to 1985. In metropolitan Knoxville, Tennessee, for instance, from 1948 to 1960 the number of apparel workers increased from 2,900 to 4,100. Levi Strauss opened two plants in Knoxville and one in nearby Maryville. Levi also opened facilities in Blue Ridge, Georgia, and Elizabethton, Johnson City, and Mountain City, Tennessee. Tultex opened its Martinsville, Virginia, fleecewear factory in 1972.

Many of these plants employed large numbers (Tultex and the Levi Cherry Street plant in Knoxville both employed around 2,300 by the mid-1990s), but factories employing fewer workers found homes in the Appalachian region as well: Case Company in Olive Hill, Kentucky, employed 248; Honaker Mills in Honaker, Virginia, around 400; Holston Garment Manufacturing Company in Bristol, Tennessee, 50; Quality Apparel in Claiborne County, Tennessee, 125; and Banner Elk Glove Company in Banner Elk, North Carolina, 39.

While most apparel factories remained nonunion, employees at a number of plants organized in the years from 1960 to 1995. Levi Strauss workers in Maryville joined the United Garment Workers; Levi workers in Blue Ridge joined the International Ladies' Garment Workers' Union; the Martinsville Tultex workers joined the Amalgamated Clothing and Textile Workers Union; and the Cherry Street workers in Knoxville joined the Amalgamated Clothing Workers of America. But for many Appalachian apparel workers, voting for collective bargaining or striking for higher wages and decent working conditions meant risking one's job. At Honaker Mills and Russell Mills (Lebanon, Virginia) the 1978 vote in favor of the International Ladies' Garment Workers' Union led to a 1979 strike at both plants, as the common owner refused to abide by a National Labor Relations Board decision upholding the 1978 vote. The strike ended in failure in 1979 when the company refused to recognize the union. At Case Company in Olive Hill, the company's refusal to obey a 1978 National Labor Relations Board order recognizing the International Ladies' Garment Workers' Union as the workers' bargaining agent led to a 1979 strike, which in turn led to the company's decreasing employees' wages.

From the mid-1990s to the early part of the 2000s, partially in response to the passage of the North American Free Trade Agreement and the Caribbean Basin Initiative, apparel factories in Appalachia began to close down and move work to Latin America, the Caribbean, and Southeast Asia, where wages were extremely low and unions nonexistent. The 2,300 jobs lost at the Martinsville Tultex plant went to Latin America, as did more than 2,000 VF Imagewear jobs. From 1990 to 2002, Levi Strauss closed all of its east Tennessee plants, shifting the manufacturing work to Latin America and Asia. The Knoxville Cherry Street plant closed in 1998 with the loss of 2,300 jobs; Powell Street closed in 2002 with the loss of 900. The Elizabethton, Johnson City, and Mountain City plants shut down operations in 1990, 1998, 1999, respectively, with the loss of 250, 320, and 520 jobs. In the Muscle Shoals area in north Alabama and elsewhere in southern Appalachia, the story was the same.

The future is bleak for apparel workers in Appalachia—and in the nation as a whole—as companies such as Levi Strauss remake themselves into white-collar design businesses. Remaining in Appalachia early in the twenty-first century were mostly smaller, nonunion apparel manufacturers.

See also: TEXTILE WORKERS; WOMEN AND EMPLOYMENT.

—Marie Tedesco, *East Tennessee State University*

W. Calvin Dickinson and Patrick Reagan, "Business, Labor and the Blue Eagle: The Harriman Hosiery Mills Strike, 1933–1934," *Tennessee Historical Quarterly* (Fall 1996); Anne E. Sims, "Magnet Mills: A Study of the Textile Industry in Clinton, Tennessee," M.A. thesis, East Tennessee State University (1983).

Baldwin-Felts Detective Agency

The Baldwin-Felts Detective Agency was formed in 1900 when William G. Baldwin (1860–1936), head of Baldwin Railroad Detectives, elevated his employee Thomas L. Felts (1868–1937) to partner. Based in Roanoke, Virginia, and Bluefield, West Virginia, the agency investigated robberies, murders, and crimes against property (though it refused to take divorce cases). Baldwin helped introduce fingerprinting to the United States, and during World War I Baldwin-Felts detectives assisted federal agents in uncovering espionage plots.

The primary role of the agency was in the area of labor control, however. Often retained by the railroads and coal companies of southwestern Virginia and southern West Virginia to provide detectives, guards, and undercover men, the agency is best known for the antiunion activities of its employees in events at Ludlow, Colorado, in 1914 and in West Virginia during the Paint Creek–Cabin Creek strike of 1912–13 and the Matewan Massacre and Williamson-Thacker episodes of 1920–22. In each of these cases, Baldwin-Felts detectives spied on union organizers and strike leaders, protected strikebreakers, and engaged in armed conflict with union members. Because of their involvement in these infamous and violent labor incidents, Baldwin-Felts detectives became known as Baldwin "thugs." Although condemned by unions, political liberals, and several congressional committees, Baldwin and Felts insisted that their agency provided a vital service in the struggle to maintain law and order in communities that were unable or unwilling to provide security for themselves.

In the coalfields, however, the maintenance of law and order involved not only catching bootleggers, thieves, and murderers, but also denying miners their right to organize a union. The Baldwin-Felts Detective Agency became the bulwark of the coal operators' movement to resist and expel the United Mine Workers of America from southern West Virginia. Undercover or secret service men from the agency worked in and around the mines, even joining the union in order to apprise their employers of members' activities. At times, their cover was so deep that Baldwin-Felts men reported on each other.

The most controversial tasks undertaken by Baldwin-Felts agents were armed guard work and evicting miners and their families from company-owned housing. During the 1912–13 Paint Creek–Cabin Creek strike, Baldwin-Felts mine guards were so zealous in protecting company property and dispersing groups of miners that several violent confrontations broke out, including the Battle of Mucklow, which resulted in at least sixteen deaths. On May 19, 1920, the evictions of union miners from Stone Mountain Coal Corporation housing precipitated the Matewan Massacre, which left ten men dead, including five agents and two of Felts's younger brothers.

The Baldwin-Felts Detective Agency played an important if controversial role in the early industrial history of Appalachia. The agency disbanded in 1937 after the deaths of Baldwin and Felts and before its last chief, Estil Meadows, was called to testify before a congressional committee investigating strikebreaking and labor espionage.

See also: MATEWAN MASSACRE; PAINT CREEK–CABIN CREEK STRIKE; UNITED MINE WORKERS OF AMERICA.

—Rebecca J. Bailey, *State University of West Georgia*

David Alan Corbin, *Life, Work, and Rebellion in the Coal Fields: The Southern West Virginia Miners, 1880–1922* (1981); John A. Velke, *Baldwin-Felts Detectives, Inc.* (1997).

Battle of Blair Mountain

From August 24 to September 4, 1921, approximately seventy-five hundred (although some say as many as twenty thousand) West Virginia union miners and supporters led by Bill Blizzard, president of United Mine Workers of America, District 17, Sub-District 2, marched from union territory in Kanawha and northern Boone Counties to nonunion Logan County and fought a battle against a force of about twenty-five hundred men led by Logan County Sheriff Don Chafin. This conflict, known as the Miners' March and Battle of Blair Mountain, was broken up by the intervention of more than two thousand federal troops. It was America's largest armed insurrection since the Civil War and Appalachia's most significant mine war.

The main causes of this conflict were the United Mine Workers' repeated efforts to organize the southern West Virginia coalfields and the coal operators' equally powerful desire to keep the union out. Since 1898, when the organization completed its successful organization of the so-called Central Competitive Field (Illinois, Indiana, Ohio, and most of Pennsylvania's bituminous fields), a principal goal of the United Mine Workers had been to organize the highly productive West Virginia coalfields. The union sought to provide protection and higher wages for miners there and to prevent cheap, nonunion coal from stealing markets of higher-priced union operations in the North. Faced with higher transportation costs than northern producers, West Virginia coal operators sought to compensate by keeping wages lower than in the union fields. They also wanted to avoid strikes and maintain control over miners, so stopping the United Mine Workers was their principal goal.

From 1898 until 1918, the union made repeated attempts to organize West Virginia, but only one succeeded. The signal victory for the union was the organization of the Kanawha field (Kanawha, Putnam, Mason, northern Boone, and western Fayette Counties) during the 1902 strike. As a result, District 17, which encompassed all of West Virginia, was formed, and the United Mine Workers gained a foothold in the state. Surrounded by nonunion coalfields, Kanawha's miners and their District 17 leaders soon became militant adherents of the United Mine Workers, defending the organization during the 1912–13 Paint Creek–Cabin Creek strike and constantly seeking to increase membership and expand their territory.

A breakthrough for the United Mine Workers came during World War I. Following highly successful organizing campaigns, most of West Virginia had become union territory by 1919. Exceptions were the productive southern coalfields in Mingo, Logan, Wyoming, McDowell, and Mercer Counties. There, coal operators ruled through a system of repression known to miners as the "gun thug" system. While some companies hired private detectives from suppliers such as the Baldwin-Felts Detective Agency, Logan County companies paid Sheriff Chafin to maintain a force of three hundred deputies. With beatings and other forms of intimidation, Chafin's toughs kept union organizers out of the coalfields. On September 1, 1919, about five thousand union miners assembled at Marmet, near Charleston, and resolved to march into Logan and Mingo Counties. This first armed march was halted when Frank Keeney, president of District 17, and Governor John Cornwell persuaded miners to return home.

But nearly two years later, prompted by the August 1, 1921, murder of Matewan Police Chief Sid Hatfield, who had emerged as the miners' hero because of his role in the Matewan Massacre of 1920, preparations began for a second armed march. On August 7, five thousand miners and union supporters gathered on the capitol grounds in Charleston to hear Keeney and Mary Harris "Mother" Jones condemn Governor Ephraim F. Morgan for imposing martial law in Mingo County. Keeney ordered miners to arm themselves and await his call. On August 20, miners began to assemble at Marmet. Learning that the leaders of the march would be arrested and charged with treason, Mother Jones read a telegram to the group, allegedly from President Warren G. Harding, ordering miners to disband or face federal troops. Miners questioned the authenticity of the telegram and refused. The incident ended Jones's influence among the miners, and she soon left the state.

On the evening of August 24, the army left Marmet for the sixty-five-mile march to the county seat of Logan. Well armed and provisioned, the army included many veterans of World War I and a small corps of uniformed female nurses. Its organization mirrored that of the United Mine Workers, with Blizzard as commander and presidents of the locals as his officers. The avowed purpose of the march was to avenge Hatfield's death, overthrow martial law in Mingo County, unionize miners in Logan and Mingo Counties, and hang

Chafin "from a sour apple tree." On August 25, President Harding, responding to Governor Morgan's appeal for federal troops to suppress the revolt, sent General H. H. Bandholtz to Charleston to order Keeney to stop the march. Responding to Bandholtz's plea, Keeney and District 17 Vice-President Fred Mooney overtook the marchers at Danville in Boone County and on August 26 implored them to disband. Some did, returning home on special trains, but a contingent marched on. Animated by the shooting deaths of two miners at Monclo, on the border between Boone and Logan Counties, on August 27, and by stories that gun thugs were murdering women and children, miners commandeered trains, trucks, and buses to transport their comrades back to the battlefront near the communities of Blair, Clothier, and Jeffrey. Here they donned red bandanas to distinguish their army from Chafin's "whites," thereby becoming known as "red necks."

By August 28, the miners' army had grown to seventy-five hundred men. On the following day, the army deployed, with about half encamping in a grove near the Blair schoolhouse and the remainder assembled several miles north near the Sanders schoolhouse at the head of Hewitt Creek. The plan was to mount a two-pronged attack, with the Blair contingent advancing across Blair Mountain and the second group crossing Spruce Fork Ridge at Crooked Creek Gap. The two forces would meet at Logan.

Meanwhile, Sheriff Chafin deployed his forces along a fifteen-mile front on Spruce Fork Ridge. He also organized an air force of three biplanes and established headquarters at the Aracoma Hotel in Logan. On August 30, ignoring a dispersal order from President Harding, the miners mounted their first organized assault. A group led by Reverend John E. Wilburn advanced up Blair Mountain and engaged three deputies in a firefight that killed two of the lawmen and one miner. On August 31, fighting erupted all along the line. Miners mounted a frontal assault on Chafin's defensive positions and flanked them in small groups. On September 1, miners broke through at Crooked Creek Gap, prompting Chafin to mobilize reserves and order his air force, which had been flying reconnaissance missions, to drop black powder and poisonous gas bombs on the attackers. On the same day, General Bandholtz ordered federal troops into the battle zone. Most miners were disarmed by September 3, but fighting continued until September 4. Later, more than five hundred participants were indicted for treason and murder, although only one was convicted.

Casualties were light considering the number of shots fired. According to Lon Savage, sixteen men, including twelve from the miners' army, lost their lives. Even though the miners were forced to disband, they felt they had won the day by drawing the nation's attention to their desperate working conditions. Bandholtz and Chafin's forces had, however, stopped the invasion, preserving West Virginia's economic and political status quo and hastening the decline of the miners' union during the 1920s. The United Mine Workers of America was ejected from all of southern West Virginia, including the Kanawha field, during the 1920s and did not return until 1933.

See also: JONES, MOTHER; MATEWAN MASSACRE; UNITED MINE WORKERS OF AMERICA.

—Michael E. Workman, *West Virginia University*

David Alan Corbin, *Life, Work, and Rebellion in the Coal Fields: The Southern West Virginia Miners, 1880–1922* (1981); Lon Savage, *Thunder in the Mountains: The West Virginia Mine War, 1920–21* (1990); U.S. Senate, Committee on Education and Labor, *Hearings on Conditions in West Virginia Coalfields*, 67th Congress, 1st sess. (1921–22).

Black Lung Associations

See Black Lung Associations (Health)

Brophy, John

See Save the Union Movement

Carpet Industry Workers

The United States carpet industry is centered in the small southern Appalachian town of Dalton, Georgia, the self-proclaimed "carpet capital of the world." More than 70 percent of the carpet manufactured in the United States is produced in Georgia, primarily in Dalton and surrounding smaller communities such as Calhoun and Chatsworth. This industry is an important component of Georgia's economy, and Dalton's Shaw Industries is the largest single manufacturing employer in the state. While some American carpet is manufactured outside the area, this industry has become more localized over time.

Dalton became the nation's carpet capital in the 1950s, replacing New York's Mohawk Valley (home of Mohawk Carpet Company), Philadelphia, Pennsylvania (headquarters to several small firms), and Thomson, Connecticut (home of the Bigelow-Sanford Carpet Company and others). Though some of these older companies continued to exist, all relocated their headquarters to the Dalton area. More significantly, new firms adopted machine tufting, a locally developed technology that had grown out of a handcraft technique revived by Dalton-area native Catherine Evans Whitener. Though often associated with the southern highlands craft revival of the 1930s, the tufted bedspread industry was not a product of folk culture and had no deep roots in the region. It was a forgotten craft until Whitener and other local women revived it, sparking the creation of a cottage industry. In the 1920s and 1930s, merchants who specialized in employing rural women to tuft patterns onto cotton sheeting according to prestamped patterns began to search for ways to adapt sewing machines to the task. After sewing machines proved successful in making raised designs on bedspreads, small rugs followed. By 1950, manufacturers had begun using large machines to cover an entire piece of backing material with raised tufts of heavy yarn, thus duplicating a woven carpet. The new technology was more efficient than the old power loom process, and consumers who cared little for brand names gravitated toward the cheaper tufted products. Dalton was first acknowledged as the "tufted bedspread capital of the world" in the 1930s. By the end of the 1950s, tufted carpet sales far exceeded bedspread sales, and the tufted spread was a novelty item whose appeal was waning. Carpet, conversely, became a staple of American household furnishings, developing into an $11-billion industry by the end of the 1990s.

Though the concentration of carpet manufacturing in the Dalton area created jobs, nonunion textile mills in the South experienced recurrent labor shortages over the last half of the twentieth century. From the 1950s onward, mill owners in Dalton and Whitfield County regularly complained of worker shortages while assiduously resisting union organization efforts. During the 1980s and 1990s, immigrant workers arrived, mostly from Mexico, seeking jobs in carpet plants. In spite of the influx of foreign-born workers, the labor market remained tight because of resurgent demands for carpeting.

With the industry's increasing concentration in northwest Georgia, the United Textile Workers of America tried twice to organize workers in the Dalton area's tufted textile plants. A drive in the mid-1950s failed mainly because the Tufted Textile Manufacturers Association succeeded in associating union advocates with radicalism and Communism. When organizers launched another drive in the 1960s, mill owners prevailed with a campaign warning that unions would mean the end of growth and prosperity. With most of the industry's workforce remaining nonunion, new companies continued to form or move into the area. By the 1980s, the labor shortage had reached such proportions that company executives warned that mills might be forced to move elsewhere.

The 1980s brought a steady stream of Hispanic immigrants into the area. Although Whitfield County's white population grew only slightly in the 1980s and even declined somewhat in the 1990s, its total population grew a healthy 15 percent in the 1990s, a figure higher than the national average but less than Georgia's 26 percent. More specific statistics revealed important changes in the county and in the carpet business. Preliminary data from the 2000 census showed that Whitfield County's Hispanic population had increased from about two thousand in 1990 to more than sixteen thousand in 2000. The county's African American population grew very slightly in the 1990s and shrank as a proportion of the total population, from 4 percent to about 3.8 percent. Hispanic immigrants quickly outnumbered blacks as the county's largest minority group. At least one carpet capital resident in five was of Hispanic origin in 2000, and enrollment in Dalton city schools was more than 50 percent Hispanic. Around the community, increasing numbers of signs were posted in Spanish, and a local radio station began broadcasting in Spanish. Hispanic-owned businesses opened, and a forty-team soccer league was created.

Manufacturers welcomed the immigrants as at least a partial solution to the labor shortage. Other Dalton-area residents were less sanguine. Racial integration of the local workforce in the 1960s had apparently caused little tension, in large part because the African American population of the region was historically small. An anti-immigrant group, focusing on illegal immigration and undocumented workers, was created in the mid-1990s and helped convince the Immigration and Naturalization Service to open a local office in Dalton as a joint effort with the local police. A few highly publicized raids followed. But a boom in the industry in the late 1990s and new outreach efforts organized by local leaders had lessened tensions by the beginning of the twenty-first century.

Local efforts to deal with the cultural sea change were exemplified by an initiative called the Georgia Project. The idea originated with Erwin Mitchell, a Dalton attorney. Working with Robert E. Shaw, an industry executive experienced in joint ventures in Mexico, the city established an exchange program, bringing several Spanish-speaking teachers from Mexico to Dalton each year to help improve the educational prospects for Hispanic children. The project gained national attention. A writer for the *Nation* favorably compared Dalton to communities in California in its adjustment to rapid cultural change. This local phenomenon mirrored a larger regional trend toward the integration of hemispheric and global labor markets.

See also: HISPANICS (RACE, ETHNICITY, AND IDENTITY); KNOTTED BEDSPREADS/COLONIAL KNOTTING (CRAFTS); RUG MAKING (CRAFTS).

—Randall L. Patton, *Kennesaw State University*

Ruben Hernandez-Leon and Victor Zuniga, "'Making Carpet by the Mile': The Emergence of a Mexican Immigrant Community in an Industrial Region of the U.S. Historic South," *Social Science Quarterly* (March 2000); David Kirp, "The Old South's New Face," *Nation* (June 26, 2000); Randall L. Patton, *Carpet Capital: The Rise of a New South Industry* (1999).

Chemical Workers

Chemical manufacturing has been a major industry in sections of Appalachia since the early twentieth century. With their own company unions, excellent benefits, job security, and high wages, chemical workers did not see the need for labor organization for much of the twentieth century. Despite the efforts of employers to forge a bond with their employees, however, organized labor eventually succeeded in unionizing a number of Appalachian chemical plants when the shortcomings of welfare capitalism—the idea that corporations would shield workers from the strains of industrialism—prompted the desire for third-party representation among workers.

Employers often focused on the workers' families to inculcate a corporate identity among employees and engender loyalty. They generally hired local white males, preferring family members of former and current company employees. An employee family was often introduced to the benefits of a particular chemical company through picnics, newsletters, and recreational leagues. In this way, entire families were encouraged to be loyal to the company. Fair, and at times even generous, treatment of employees and their families decreased the possibility of labor activism and increased the likelihood of labor stability. Some large chemical manufacturing companies, such as Eastman Chemical Company in Tennessee, historically provided high wages and paternalistic programs and remained unorganized by national unions through the twentieth century.

Employees were further dissuaded from embracing organized labor by the presence of company or independent unions that were not affiliated with international unions. For example, management at the DuPont plant in Belle, West Virginia, established a company union, the Works Council, as part of an employee representation plan in 1933. The Works Council was funded by DuPont and included management representatives as members. By 1937, the Works Council had been replaced by the Association of Chemical Employees, which the company claimed was independent of management. For the next four years, the Association of Chemical Employees rebuffed all efforts to organize the workers at the plant.

Despite the presence of paternalistic programs and company unions, organized labor aggressively and successfully organized several Appalachian chemical manufacturing plants. From the late 1930s through the 1960s, the United Mine Workers District 50, the International Association of Machinists, and the Oil, Chemical and Atomic Workers competed with each other as well as with the companies' welfare capitalist programs to organize chemical workers. Facing heavy resistance from Union Carbide management, the International Association of Machinists organized the Union Carbide manufacturing plant in South Charleston, West Virginia. Unionization came as the company faced increasingly stiff competition from a growing number of companies and the expiration of exclusive patents. As its market share eroded, Union Carbide cut costs by laying off employees and moving operations to locations with cheaper natural resources. Hundreds of employees at the South Charleston plant lost their jobs, and those who remained saw their benefits decline. Thus, after several unsuccessful attempts to organize the South Charleston plant, the Machinists finally won a close election in 1965. The following year and under similar circumstances, the Machinists also organized the Union Carbide plant in Institute, West Virginia.

During the last third of the twentieth century, chemical workers who were members of labor unions belonged to the International Chemical Workers Union or the Oil, Chemical and Atomic Workers Union, both affiliates of the American Federation of Labor–Congress of Industrial Organizations (AFL-CIO).

See also: CHEMICAL INDUSTRY (BUSINESS, INDUSTRY, AND TECHNOLOGY); EASTMAN CHEMICAL COMPANY AND TENNESSEE EASTMAN COMPANY (BUSINESS, INDUSTRY, AND TECHNOLOGY).

—Jeffrey G. Blaydes, *Charleston, West Virginia*

Stuart Brandes, *American Welfare Capitalism, 1980–1940* (1976); Ray Davidson, *Challenging the Giants: A History of Oil, Chemical and Atomic Workers International Union* (1988); Sanford Jacoby, *Modern Manors: Welfare Capitalism since the New Deal* (1997).

Child Labor and the Coal Industry

During the American Industrial Revolution, coal was the major source of energy to power industries and trains and to heat homes. At its peak, the coal industry employed nearly eight million mine workers. In 1908 one out of every four mine workers was a boy between the ages of seven and sixteen. Girls were not employed, except in clerical positions in mine offices.

Boys worked in various positions at the colliery. Younger boys usually started out in the tipple (at a bituminous coal mine) or the breaker (at an anthracite coal mine). The tipple or breaker building stood on top of the mine shaft. Each coal car was brought to the top of the building along an inclined plane. The car was tipped and the coal spilled into revolving cylinders that crushed and screened the coal, separating it into various sizes. The coal was then fed through a series of chutes.

Boys sat in tiers on narrow planks astride the chutes. As the coal flowed past, each boy picked out the slate and other refuse. Clean coal was loaded into railroad cars for shipment, and the refuse was deposited at the culm bank. The breaker boy's workday averaged ten hours, six days a week. In the early 1900s, his daily wage was seventy-five cents.

Older boys worked underground as nippers, or door tenders, spraggers, and mule drivers. The door tender,

Young boys work in a South Pittston, Pennsylvania, coal mine, 1915. The two boys holding wood pieces are spraggers, workers who ran alongside coal cars and jabbed the wood pieces, or sprags, into the wheels to slow down the cars.

usually between eleven to thirteen years old, sat outside heavy wooden doors constructed across gangways or headings. The doors directed the flow of air through the mines. The door tender opened the doors to allow the cars to pass through. The fastest and most agile boys worked as spraggers. Spraggers controlled the speed of mine cars as they rolled down a slope by running alongside the cars and jabbing sharpened pieces of wood called sprags into the wheels. The mule driver, aged fourteen or older, traveled with his mule from chamber to chamber, coupling full cars together and leaving empty cars to be filled. Many boys were injured or killed from explosions, roof falls, or accidents with machinery.

In 1904 the National Child Labor Committee was formed with the objective of eradicating child labor in the United States. Not until 1916 and 1919 were the first federal child labor laws passed. The laws established fourteen as a minimum age to work in industries and limited the workday to eight hours for children ages fourteen to sixteen. By 1922, both laws had been declared unconstitutional. In 1938 the Fair Labor Standards Act established fourteen as the minimum age for employment and prohibited the employment of children under sixteen during the school session. This act also established eighteen as the minimum age to work at trades considered hazardous, including mining.

See also: ANTHRACITE COAL INDUSTRY (BUSINESS, INDUSTRY, AND TECHNOLOGY); BITUMINOUS COAL INDUSTRY (BUSINESS, INDUSTRY, AND TECHNOLOGY).

—Susan Campbell Bartoletti, *Binghamton University*

Susan Campbell Bartoletti, *Growing Up in Coal Country* (1996); Donald L. Miller and Richard E. Sharpless, *The Kingdom of Coal: Work, Enterprise, and Ethnic Communities in the Mine Fields* (1985); Alexander Trachtenberg, *The History of Legislation for the Protection of Coal Miners in Pennsylvania, 1824–1915* (1942).

Coal and Iron Police

Created in 1866, Pennsylvania's Coal and Iron Police was a state-commissioned but privately funded force used by employers in the coal and steel industries. Paid by the companies and used to protect corporate property, the forces had full, state-sanctioned law enforcement status on company property and in company towns. The role of these units quickly expanded from protecting property to maintaining order and enforcing the company's will against its employees. Noted for their brutality, they were conspicuously active in combating the Molly Maguires, a radical Irish labor organization, in the eastern Pennsylvania anthracite coalfields in the 1870s.

Use of the Coal and Iron Police was confined to eastern Pennsylvania throughout the nineteenth century, but as the twentieth century opened, they were increasingly a presence in the state's western coalfields. An example of their harsh tactics occurred during the 1909 strike against the Pressed Steel Car Company of McKees Rocks, Pennsylvania. The company, a subsidiary of United States Steel, used the force to fight striking workers, who were led by the radical Industrial Workers of the World. The Industrial Workers won the dispute, but the policemen's open use of naked force demonstrated how far major employers would go to retain dominance in the communities they controlled.

Economic desperation in the mining industry during the 1920s led operators to increase their reliance on the Coal and Iron Police. Although coal enjoyed a boom during World War I, worldwide demand had fallen sharply by 1922 due to overproduction. As a result, Pennsylvania coal operators who had once cooperated with the United Mine Workers of America broke their contracts and used the policemen to keep the union out.

Since many of the people who joined these forces were untrained, police brutality was rampant, and the forces were involved in myriad violent incidents. In one particularly vicious incident, a miner named John Barkoski was beaten to death by three policemen during a coal strike. The resulting outrage prompted a Pittsburgh assemblyman, Michael A. Musmanno, to introduce legislation outlawing all private police forces in the state.

Although Musmanno put up an impressive fight to win the bill's passage, he could not overcome the combined opposition of Pennsylvania Governor John S. Fisher and his pro-operator allies. The legislature did enact compromise legislation known as the Mansfield Bill, which required all such policemen be trained according to state guidelines.

Ironically, while coal operators hoped that the Mansfield Bill would end the controversy, it was the first step toward ending the system. In 1930 Gifford Pinchot, a liberal Republican, was elected governor. While failing to have such forces outlawed, Pinchot simply refused to issue any new private police commissions. The end of the Coal and Iron Police came when Pinchot's successor, George H. Earle, a liberal Democrat, finally managed to win the legislature's support in outlawing all such forces in the state.

See also: ANTHRACITE MINERS, NINETEENTH-CENTURY; ANTHRACITE MINERS, TWENTIETH-CENTURY; IRON AND STEEL MILL WORKERS.

—Richard P. Mulcahy, *University of Pittsburgh at Titusville*

Melvyn Dubofsky, *We Shall Be All: A History of the Industrial Workers of the World* (1969); Muriel Earley Sheppard, *Cloud by Day: The Story of Coal and Coke and People* (1947; reprint 1991); Anthony F. C. Wallace, *St. Clair: A Nineteenth-Century Coal Town's Experience with a Disaster-Prone Industry* (1987).

Coal Employment Project

See Women Coal Miners

Convict Labor

Historically, convict labor has been a staple of penal administration in Appalachia. Whether inside the walls of a prison, on public roads, in plantation fields, or in coal mines, Appalachian convicts have "earned their keep" for much of the region's history.

The idea that prison inmates should be compelled to work did not originate in Appalachia. European and American penal philosophers long argued that, without labor, convicts would only drain society's resources; moreover, the cleansing nature of work has often been seen as a valuable means of rehabilitation. A recurring criticism of convict labor, however, has been its potential for abuse and corruption. Reform advocate Julia Tutwiler expressed concern in 1913, for example, that Alabama's system of penal servitude earned the state unwelcome comparisons to Russia and Morocco.

Other issues surrounding convict labor included its questionable value as an instrument of reform, the danger that it might undercut the wages of free laborers, and the perception that any skills or crafts the convicts learned at work might actually serve to reward their illegal behavior. Forced labor of convicts also invited comparisons to slavery.

Convict labor came increasingly to be viewed as a cousin of chattel slavery after the profit motive began to supplant reformative zeal in the minds of Appalachian penal authorities. In 1825 Kentucky became the first state in Appalachia (and the United States) to lease the labor of state convicts to private citizens. Alabama followed suit in 1845, and Maryland, North Carolina, Virginia, and West Virginia embraced convict labor in various forms throughout the nineteenth century. After the Civil War, the potential for profit combined with virulent racism (African Americans often made up a disproportionately high percentage of postbellum convicts in much of Appalachia) to make convict labor little more than a state-sanctioned return of slavery. Georgia, Tennessee, and Alabama famously leased their prisoners to work in coal mines. This practice proved so remunerative that it took an uprising of free miners in 1891–92 in east Tennessee to bring down the system in that state. A corruption scandal ended Georgia's lease in 1908, and in 1928 Alabama became the last state to abandon convict leasing after pressure from the national media and decades of local agitation.

The decline of the private lease system was by no means the end of convict labor in Appalachia. Prisoners have long been employed by various government agencies in road maintenance, plantation agriculture, and light industry, including textile mills. One of the most important concepts linking the variations on penal labor is public opinion—the citizens of Appalachia (and of the United States in general) have repeatedly expressed the desire that prisoners should, in one way or another, earn their keep. Several Appalachian states continue to experiment with convict labor—Alabama reintroduced the chain gang for a brief period in the 1990s—and with the private management of prisons such as at the massive complex in Youngstown, Ohio.

See also: SLAVE LABOR.

—Gregory L. McDonald, *West Virginia University*

Edward L. Ayers, *Vengeance and Justice: Crime and Punishment in the Nineteenth-Century American South* (1984); Karin A. Shapiro, *A New South Rebellion: The Battle against Convict Labor in the Tennessee Coalfields, 1871–1896* (1998); Robert David Ward and William Warren Rogers, *Convicts, Coal, and the Banner Mine Tragedy* (1987).

Debt Peonage

Though the Thirteenth Amendment to the United States Constitution banned slavery, a form of involuntary servitude existed across the nation long after the Civil War through debt peonage. Debt peonage was particularly onerous in the South and the Appalachian Mountains in the late nineteenth and early twentieth centuries. There, rural areas with few officers of the law or where powerful interests could control the law enforcement process were especially susceptible to the practice. Blacks in the agricultural South and immigrants and blacks in the Appalachian coal, timber, and railroad industries were advanced money for food, lodging, transportation, or seed and then held in bondage until the debts were repaid.

In agricultural areas of the South, landowners used local civil government magistrates and sheriff's deputies to control those who owed them money. In the coal and timber industries of the Appalachian region, private armed guards (often provided by the Baldwin-Felts Detective Agency) would oversee the men at work and then lock them up at night to keep them from fleeing. The legal system lent legitimacy to the debt peonage practice. Laws such as the West Virginia "boarding house statute," for example, were intended to protect hotel operators from being defrauded of room and board. However, magistrates applied the law to immigrants and blacks who had been advanced transportation money, food, and lodging by coal, railroad, and timber companies. Immigrants and blacks who found working conditions intolerable were forcibly prevented from leaving a job before their advances had been paid. Magistrates frequently cooperated with employers by holding trials and binding the workers to the employers, who were allowed to use force to hold them until they had worked off the debts.

Complaints against the practice were made by such groups as the Society for the Protection of Italian Immigrants and the consulates of several foreign countries. It was difficult to get local and state officials to investigate, however, and complaints usually ended up in the hands of the United States attorney general. The federal government investigated the practice, prosecuted employers, and even got judgments against some of them, but the fines were minimal and the government imposed few jail sentences. U.S. Assistant Attorney General Charles Russell was particularly diligent in seeking prosecutions against violations of the law in the early 1900s, often appearing in court to argue for justice for blacks and immigrants who had been subjected to peonage. His success rate was low, however, and few federal court cases resulted in anything more than a slap on the wrist for the companies and company personnel involved. Frequently, federal judges and their assistants were former coal, timber, or rail company officers and often kept investments in those companies while serving in their federal offices. Such economic, social, and political connections between officials at the federal court level and those who ran coal, timber, and rail companies were too numerous for justice to be served.

While debt peonage was most common in the early part of the twentieth century, instances of the practice continued to be reported and prosecuted into the late 1970s and 1980s. In the later periods, debt peonage was imposed mainly upon Hispanic and Chinese immigrants in the urban areas of California and New York.

See also: BALDWIN-FELTS DETECTIVE AGENCY; SLAVE LABOR; SLAVERY (RACE, ETHNICITY, AND IDENTITY).

—Kenneth R. Bailey, *West Virginia University Institute of Technology*

Kenneth R. Bailey, "A Temptation to Lawlessness: Peonage in West Virginia, 1903–1908," *West Virginia History* (1991); Pete Daniel, *The Shadow of Slavery: Peonage in the South, 1901–1969* (1972).

Disabled Miners and Widows

See Miners for Democracy

Dreiser Investigation

Novelist Theodore Dreiser led a distinguished group of writers to investigate the bloody strike in Harlan County, Kentucky, in late 1931. The group, the National Committee for the Defense of Political Prisoners, was one of a number of Communist Party auxiliaries sent in support of the Communist-affiliated National Miners Union. Dreiser, who had previously investigated a National Miners Union strike in the northern coalfields at the request of party chairman William Z. Foster, favored the radical union in its opposition to the United Mine Workers of America. In addition to Dreiser, the investigators included John Dos Passos and several less famous writers and activists, as well as representatives of the *Daily Worker* newspaper and the International Labor Defense. Bruce Crawford, in 1931 the editor of a weekly newspaper in neighboring Wise County, Virginia, was the only mountaineer on Dreiser's committee. Crawford later became director of the Federal Writers' Project in West Virginia and edited the Work Projects Administration's *Guide to the Mountain State*.

Dreiser's committee entered eastern Kentucky in early November 1931, toured parts of Harlan and Bell Counties, and conducted formal hearings in the towns of Harlan and Pineville, the Bell County seat. Local officials refused to sanction the investigation by official participation, although Sheriff John Henry Blair and Prosecuting Attorney William E. Brock allowed themselves to be interviewed for the record. Governor Flem D. Sampson sent a military observer, who reported an unfavorable opinion of the committee. The writers carried on their investigation in the face of intimidation and petty harassment, including an adultery charge brought against Dreiser by an enterprising deputy who leaned a toothpick against Dreiser's door after a woman visitor entered his hotel room. Allegedly, the incriminating toothpick was still standing undisturbed the following morning.

The National Committee for the Defense of Political Prisoners published its report, *Harlan Miners Speak: Report on Terrorism in the Kentucky Coal Fields*, in 1932. Sherwood Anderson, a member of the committee but not present at the Kentucky hearings, contributed a chapter, which remains a standard source for the radical view of the Harlan-Bell strikes. Local midwife Aunt Molly Jackson provided testimony. The lyrics to her "Ragged Hungry Blues" were published in their entirety at the beginning of the book, helping to launch Jackson as a prominent singer of protest songs.

The National Miners Union strike in Harlan County concluded disastrously, as had the preceding effort by the United Mine Workers. Peace came to Harlan only several years later, following the reform of national labor laws. The Dreiser investigation, whose report offers glimpses of strike conditions and radical politics as practiced by the nation's intelligentsia, further aggravated a violently polarized situation and seems to have made no substantial difference to the situation in eastern Kentucky.

See also: HARLAN COUNTY MINE WAR; *HARLAN COUNTY, USA* (MEDIA); NATIONAL MINERS UNION.

—Ken Sullivan, *West Virginia Humanities Council*

John W. Hevener, *Which Side Are You On? The Harlan County Coal Miners, 1931–39* (1978); National Committee for the Defense of Political Prisoners, *Harlan Miners Speak: Report on Terrorism in the Kentucky Coal Fields* (1932).

Ethnic Labor

See Immigrant and African American Labor in the Coalfields

Farmington Mine Disaster

Occurring in Farmington, West Virginia, near the site of the 1907 Monongah mine explosion that killed nearly four hundred miners, the Farmington mine disaster of 1968 is known for riveting the attention of the nation, for prompting national coal-mine safety reform, and for helping to bring down a corrupt union leader.

Underlying an area approximately ten by six miles in 1968, the tunnels of Consolidation Coal Company's No. 9 mine at Farmington constituted one of the largest underground mines in the nation. Efficient production in such an extensive mine required several access portals and multiple fans to adequately ventilate the workings. The potential dangers associated with coal dust and methane in the Farmington complex had been emphasized in 1954 when a violent explosion necessitated sealing of the mine to bring fires and further explosions under control. Investigators at that time suggested that rock dust, spread to reduce the danger of a coal dust explosion, had been poorly applied. Despite this lesson, federal inspectors in early 1968 noted areas of insufficient rock dusting and dangerous accumulations of loose coal dust.

On November 20, 1968, at approximately 5:30 a.m., an explosion ripped through the west side of the mine containing nine production crews, each composed of six to eight miners. Violently surging to the surface, the blast destroyed ventilating fans, hoisting equipment, and a portion of a combination lamp, bath, and supply house, sending smoke bellowing into the sky. Workers in the 7 South section of the mine lost electrical power shortly before an onrush of air brought flying debris and a suspension of coal and rock dust. With visibility reduced, the workers stayed together by talking and crawling along the coal rib. Navigating their way to clear air, they reached a nearby shaft at 6:30 a.m. and soon felt the force of air movement from yet another explosion somewhere in the mine. After an anxious four-hour wait, the men gained the surface via a small bucket hoisted by a mobile crane. Twenty-one of the ninety-nine workers underground managed to reach safety, but the heavy volume of black, gray, and white-to-yellow smoke exiting from the portals signaled the probable futility of further rescue efforts.

That evening and early the following morning, flames shot from the Llewellyn portal, and on November 23, fires, hot coal, and debris were expelled. The release of smoke was continuous, and on November 29 another major explosion roared from the opening. This scenario was repeated at other shafts at various times, making it difficult to cap the openings to prevent oxygen from fueling the inferno. With no hope of reaching any of the entrapped miners, officials sealed the mine on November 30.

Recovery efforts resumed in September 1969. By April 1978, workers had recovered fifty-nine bodies, but officials decided that conditions made it impractical to continue and that the exact cause of the disaster could never be determined. Accordingly, the mine was permanently sealed in November 1978, entombing nineteen of the victims.

Before 1968, death and injury in Appalachia's coal mines occurred in an atmosphere of cultural and political acceptance, but events at Farmington came in an era when television could broadcast images of the community beyond local coal regions. While viewers witnessed the agony of affected families, many of them perceived a callousness in the public statements of state, company, and, most significantly, union officials, especially United Mine Workers of America President W. A. "Tony" Boyle. The reform atmosphere of the period encouraged union dissidents to reject Boyle's traditional justification based on the concept of inherent danger. Demands for political action led to the Federal Coal Mine Health and Safety Act of 1969, which provided statutory punishment for violation of safety standards and gave inspectors the legal right to halt production when conditions were unsafe. Boyle's unresponsiveness after Farmington added to the growing discontent with his leadership within the United Mine Workers and contributed to the success of the reformist Miners for Democracy movement within the union.

See also: MINE SAFETY AND HEALTH ADMINISTRATION; MONONGAH MINE DISASTER; UNITED MINE WORKERS OF AMERICA.

—Paul H. Rakes, *West Virginia University Institute of Technology*

John Braithwaite, *To Punish or Persuade: Enforcement of Coal Mine Safety* (1985); Brit Hume, *Death and the Mines: Rebellion and Murder in the UMW* (1971); Barbara Smith, "Miner's Widow: Sara Kaznoski, Fighter and Survivor," *Goldenseal Magazine* (Summer 1988).

Glassworkers

Skilled glassworkers have played a significant role in the social, cultural, and political development of Appalachia from the beginning of the nineteenth century. The availability of sand, easy transportation on the Ohio River, and cheap fuels—particularly coal and natural gas—made the Appalachian region of southwestern Pennsylvania, southeastern Ohio, and West Virginia a national center of all types of glass production. Combined, these three states contained more than half of all the glass plants in the country in the 1930s.

For centuries, glassworkers had been versatile, highly skilled artisans. During the mid-nineteenth century, however, factories began to specialize, making only bottles, window glass, or tableware. They also introduced new production methods that undercut the skills necessary to become a glass craftsman. The timing of these changes shaped the workforce's ethnic composition, wages, working conditions, organizational strategies, and political outlook in different ways. By the 1880s, three distinct unions organized craftsmen in the industry: the American Flint Glass Workers Union represented workers in tableware, the Glass Bottle Blowers Association controlled the bottle plants, and the Knights of Labor Local, Local Assembly 300, united the window-glass workers. In all three cases, the organizations were craft

Glassblower and mold boy in Grafton, West Virginia, c. 1930. The availability of sand, easy transportation on the Ohio River, and cheap fuels—coal and natural gas—collectively made West Virginia, southwestern Pennsylvania, and southeastern Ohio a national center for glass production.

unions representing a minority of skilled workers in the industry.

Membership in strong craft unions set glassworkers apart from most other workers. Glassworker neighborhoods in Pittsburgh and Wheeling, West Virginia, in the 1880s enjoyed more material comforts than other parts of town, and the craftsmen typically went to work in starched collars and ties. Long apprenticeships, family connections, and high dues and initiation fees enabled glassworkers to control labor markets and pass on their craft to their sons, brothers, and nephews. Many were immigrants or their children who came to an area willing to pay dearly for their skills. Indeed, reversing the pattern normally associated with immigrants and industry, the newcomers took the best jobs in the glass plants, and native-born workers filled the semiskilled and laborer positions.

The twentieth century brought new mass-production technologies that threatened the status of craftsmen. Bottle and window-glass manufacturers built large mechanized factories in small West Virginia, Ohio, and southwestern Pennsylvania towns to diminish skilled workers' control of production. The workers, including many French, Belgian, and German immigrants, fought back. Unions waged battles to maintain standards and jobs while introducing socialism into local politics. In the 1910s, glass communities such as Star City and Adamston in West Virginia elected Socialist Party mayors. By the 1920s, however, mechanization had reduced the influence of skilled workers in most branches of the industry.

Labor law changes enacted during Franklin Roosevelt's New Deal revived union influence in the glass industry. The Flint Glass Workers and the Glass Bottle Blowers more than tripled their memberships, and a new industrial union, the United Glass and Ceramic Workers, organized the window- and plate-glass workers. By the end of the 1930s, there were more than thirteen thousand glassworkers, most of whom were union members, in West Virginia alone. Through the 1970s unionized glassworkers continued to comprise an important portion of local communities in the north-central Appalachian region. In recent years, the closures of glass plants in Huntington, Clarksburg, and Moundsville, West Virginia, have devastated local communities and diminished the region's labor movement.

See also: GLASS INDUSTRY (BUSINESS, INDUSTRY, AND TECHNOLOGY).

—Ken Fones-Wolf, *West Virginia University*

Frederick A. Barkey, *Cinderheads in the Hills: The Belgian Window Glass Workers of West Virginia* (1988); Ken Fones-Wolf, "A Craftsman's Paradise in Appalachia," *Journal of Appalachian Studies* (Fall 1995).

Harlan County Mine War

The Harlan County Mine War, fought sporadically from 1931 until 1937 in Harlan County, Kentucky, pitted the Harlan County Coal Operators Association, dominated by the United States Coal and Coke Company (a subsidiary of United States Steel), against miners attempting to establish a labor union. Precipitating the trouble were impoverished conditions brought on by a coal industry slump in the late 1920s followed by the devastating effects of the Great Depression of the 1930s.

At different times, three unions were involved in the conflict: the National Miners Union (a Communist organization), the United Mine Workers of America, and the company-sponsored Progressive Mine Workers. Although the National Miners Union established soup kitchens and tent colonies to feed starving miners evicted from company housing for union activity, the United Mine Workers became the dominant union. As a result, the National Miners Union and the Progressive Mine Workers eventually halted activities in Harlan County.

The most spectacular event in the Harlan County Mine War was the Battle of Evarts, fought on May 5, 1931. The battle began when a group of angry miners met at the railroad depot in Evarts to prevent operators from transporting strikebreakers into the Black Mountain Coal Corporation's camp near Lynch. E. B. Childers, the superintendent of Black Mountain Mine, requested help from John Henry Blair, the Harlan County sheriff. Blair sent fifteen armed deputies, who joined ten mine guards to escort the strikebreakers to Black Mountain Coal Camp. Miners attacked the motor caravan carrying the mine guards. According to local lore, union men and "gun thugs," the name miners used to describe mine guards, exchanged more than one thousand shots, killing one miner and three guards. The rest of the operators' police force fled, and union miners temporarily controlled the situation. After the shootout, Kentucky Governor Flem D. Sampson, acting upon a request from the Harlan County Coal Operators Association, sent National Guard troops into Harlan County to restore order. Over the next several years, Harlan County resembled a war zone, as both guards and miners openly brandished firearms and occasionally shot at each other. Much of the violence occurred when miners attempted to shut down mines being worked by strikebreakers imported from outside the county. In 1937 Governor A. B. "Happy" Chandler sent troops into Harlan County to quell bloodshed once again.

The violence focused national attention on Harlan County, earning it the name "Bloody Harlan." Nationally known writers, including Theodore Dreiser and John Dos Passos, visited Harlan and published their observations in

Harlan Miners Speak: Report on Terrorism in the Kentucky Coal Fields (1932). Coal operators fought unionization by circulating blacklists containing names of miners who belonged to the union. Police, controlled by the Harlan County Coal Operators Association, denied access to the press, threatened, harassed, and assaulted reporters, and prohibited the circulation of pro-union newspapers such as the *Knoxville News-Sentinel*. Mine guards shot at and threw sticks of dynamite into union soup kitchens. In 1935 a car bomb killed County Attorney Elmon Middleton, evidently because he was sympathetic to union miners and organizers, who regarded him as a fair man. Overall, eleven men (six union and five company) were killed, and eighteen (thirteen union and five company) were wounded.

Conditions began to improve for union miners in 1935, when a state investigating committee concluded that coal operators had created a reign of terror in the county. Two years later the U.S. Senate's La Follette Civil Liberties Committee reached the same conclusion. These and other investigations, along with passage of the National Labor Relations Act, brought the Harlan County Mine War to an end. In 1937 the United Mine Workers filed charges against twenty-seven coal mines, causing the National Labor Relations Board to launch a nineteen-month investigation. The board ultimately ordered coal companies to pay back wages to employees unfairly fired for union activities. In September 1937, a federal grand jury in Frankfort indicted twenty-two coal companies, twenty-four operators, Sheriff Theodore Middleton, and twenty-two deputies for depriving Harlan miners of their civil rights. Even though the government failed to secure a conviction, the eleven-week trial cost Harlan County coal companies financially and put pressure on them to accept unionization. Shortly thereafter the Harlan County Coal Operators Association signed its first union contract. By 1938 local law enforcement officials had also been indicted for crimes committed against union miners, the mine guard system coal companies had employed to brutalize miners had been abolished, and state police officers patrolled coal company streets, protecting union miners against company violence. The union had won the Harlan County Mine War.

See also: DREISER INVESTIGATION; *HARLAN COUNTY, USA* (MEDIA).

—Doug Cantrell, *Elizabethtown Community College*

Jim Garland, *Welcome the Traveler Home* (1983); G. C. Jones, *Growin' Up Hard in Harlan County* (1985); Shaunna L. Scott, *Two Sides to Everything: The Cultural Construction of Class Consciousness in Harlan County, Kentucky* (1995).

Hawk's Nest Tragedy

On March 31, 1930, the Union Carbide Corporation began construction of a tunnel through Gauley Mountain in Fayette County, West Virginia. The tunnel was intended to divert part of the water from the New River to a Union Carbide hydroelectric generating station three miles downstream in Alloy. Shortly after construction began, newspapers referred to the tunnel as one of the greatest engineering conquests of the era. Later, it would be called America's greatest industrial disaster.

When the contractor, Rinehart and Dennis Construction Company, began the project, five thousand workers poured into Gauley Mountain from across the southeastern United States. Unskilled and nonunion, the majority of the workers came from areas in extreme economic distress, and they were willing to work for low wages under brutal conditions. African Americans migrating northward in search of jobs constituted a large portion of the workforce. Rinehart and Dennis found it easy to manipulate these workers since they were separated from their families and viewed as "undesirable" by locals.

As construction on the tunnel progressed, engineers realized that the excavation was cutting through vast deposits of nearly pure silica (assayed at 99.9 percent). Because silica of such quality was highly valuable in manufacturing, the company found itself with a windfall. Engineers therefore increased the diameter of the tunnel from thirty-three to forty-six feet on its lower end in order to mine the rich deposit. The decision greatly increased the workers' exposure to deadly silica dust. Although company officials and engineers were aware of the danger, they failed to inform the workers or provide them with protective gear. Soon workers were succumbing to a deadly form of acute silicosis. Although the disease was well known, company doctors diagnosed the silicosis as pneumonia, tuberculosis, or bronchitis. The miners called it tunnelitis.

In 1931 reports of the miners' deaths began to appear in local newspapers. Incidence of the disease was particularly high among the African American workers since they were overrepresented in the most susceptible tunnel jobs. Firsthand information on conditions at the construction site was unobtainable because of a gag rule instituted by executives of Rinehart and Dennis and the workers' fear of losing their jobs. As increasing numbers of workers died, Union Carbide continued to list the cause of the deaths as unknown or left the space blank on death certificates.

In 1933 reports of workers' lawsuits against the company began appearing in the press, and in March of that year, a case against Rinehart and Dennis was heard in Fayette County Circuit Court. The case, filed by a worker named Darrel Jones, reached the state supreme court and eventually led to ninety additional suits. Although silicosis was accepted as the legitimate diagnosis, company lawyers maintained that silicosis was a compensable disease and that benefits should be sought from the state compensation department. Lawyers collected most of the compensation awarded while the workers received meager settlements.

When construction was completed in 1935, Union Carbide evicted workers, burned camp housing to the ground, and impounded all records related to work in the tunnel. The state government of West Virginia joined in denying the public detailed information about the disaster. A thinly veiled novel on the disaster, *Hawk's Nest,* written in 1941 by Hubert Skidmore, was withdrawn when Union Carbide threatened to file a lawsuit. Governor Homer Holt suppressed a discussion of the incident in a state guide prepared by the Federal Writers' Project. These actions enabled Union Carbide to elude responsibility, but five hundred lawsuits were filed against Rinehart and Dennis. The firm never competed for a major project again, and its assets were liquidated five years after the tunnel project ended.

Profits generated at Hawk's Nest came at enormous human cost. Secretary of Labor Frances Perkins reported to the National Conference on Silicosis in 1936 that 476 tunnel workers had died, 1,500 more were dying, and 169 victims were buried in a mass grave with "cornstalks as the gravestones." In *The Hawk's Nest Incident,* Martin Cherniack maintains that at least 764 men died and thousands more suffered permanent damage effects from exposure to silica dust. The full count will probably never be known.

See also: IMMIGRANT AND AFRICAN AMERICAN LABOR IN THE COALFIELDS; MINE SAFETY AND HEALTH ADMINISTRATION.

—Connie Park Rice, *West Virginia University*

Martin Cherniack, *The Hawk's Nest Incident* (1986); Dennis Deitz, "'I Think We've Struck a Gold Mine': A Chemist's View of Hawk's Nest," *Goldenseal Magazine* (Fall 1990); Hubert Skidmore, *Hawk's Nest* (1941).

Highlander Center

See Highlander Research and Education Center (Education)

Hitchman Coal and Coke v. Mitchell et al.

As Appalachian coal mining boomed in the late nineteenth century, the rising production from nonunion mines in Kentucky and West Virginia threatened an uneasy peace between the United Mine Workers of America and the association of bituminous coal operators in western Pennsylvania, Ohio, Indiana, and Illinois known as the Central Competitive Field. These operators, who wanted Appalachian companies organized so they would lose the competitive advantage they maintained through paying lower wages, threatened to drop their union contracts if the union could not also organize the nonunion mines in Appalachia. Appalachian operators, including the Hitchman Coal and Coke Company, near Wheeling, West Virginia, responded to the subsequent organizing drive with "yellow dog" contracts, personal employment agreements in which the employee agreed not to join a union. In 1917 the U.S. Supreme Court upheld a lower court decision restraining the United Mine Workers from approaching employees on Hitchman property. A significant case in constitutional law as well as in the labor history of Appalachia, the *Hitchman* decision gave judicial endorsement to the combining of two powerful antiunion legal devices, the injunction and the yellow dog contract.

The court's decision not only denied miners at Hitchman the opportunity to join the union, but it also created an extremely adverse legal environment for labor organizations. Specifically, it encouraged antiunion employers to adopt yellow dog contracts. More than that, it cleared the way for judges to grant injunctions against union organizing at operations where yellow dog contracts were in force. In the 1920s, coal operators in Appalachia and beyond vigorously embraced the *Hitchman* formula, and the United Mine Workers of America fell into a precipitous decline. Not until the New Deal brought a more favorable legal atmosphere in the thirties did the organization recover and finally succeed in organizing Appalachia.

See also: LABOR AND THE NEW DEAL; UNITED MINE WORKERS OF AMERICA.

—Jerry Bruce Thomas, *Shepherd College*

Irving Bernstein, *Thse Lean Years: A History of the American Worker, 1920–1933* (1960); David Alan Corbin, *Life, Work, and Rebellion in the Coal Fields: The Southern West Virginia Miners, 1880–1922* (1981); Richard D. Lunt, *Law and Order vs. the Miners: West Virginia, 1907–1933* (1979).

Homestead Steel Strike of 1892

The Homestead Steel Strike of 1892 pitted one of the largest craft unions of the era against giants of industry in a bitter conflict that resulted in a forty-year setback for the labor movement in Appalachia and the nation. The Carnegie Steel Company's Homestead Works, near Pittsburgh, was one of the largest unionized steel factories in the late 1800s. In 1889 the Amalgamated Association of Iron, Steel, and Tin Workers struck the plant, successfully negotiating a sliding wage scale tied to plant profits. When the contract expired in 1892, however, technological advancements in steel production had weakened the position of skilled workers, leaving the union vulnerable. With owner Andrew Carnegie's approval, Henry Clay Frick, the company's general manager, slashed wages and refused collective bargaining. After lengthy attempts to negotiate failed, the union called for a strike. The action gained the support not only of union members but also of unskilled workers who, even though they were not eligible for membership in Amalgamated, had benefited from the sliding wage scale. Frick shut down production, ordered a lockout, erected a stockade around the

FRANK LESLIE'S ILLUSTRATED WEEKLY

HOMESTEAD TROUBLES.

NEW YORK, JULY 14, 1892. [PRICE, 10 CENTS.

THE LABOR TROUBLES AT HOMESTEAD, PENNSYLVANIA—ATTACK OF THE STRIKERS AND THEIR SYMPATHIZERS ON THE SURRENDERED PINKERTON MEN.—DRAWN BY MISS G. A. DAVIS, FROM A SKETCH BY C. UPHAM.—[SEE PAGE 47.]

The cover of a major newspaper during the Homestead Steel Strike shows citizens confronting Pinkerton guards, 1892. The strike's events were documented in newspapers by drawings that were sketched on-site and then printed in newspapers from woodblock engravings.

plant, and called in three hundred armed Pinkerton guards. When the Pinkertons approached by river barge, union supporters tried to halt their arrival. A daylong battle erupted, leaving at least ten dead and hundreds injured. The Pinkertons surrendered, and the union appeared victorious.

The tide turned when the governor of Pennsylvania ordered in the state militia. With this protection, Frick imported nonunion workers to resume production. Homestead workers, both union and nonunion, returned to work as well when all hope was lost. Wages were cut and working hours lengthened. Strikers were arrested, evicted from their homes, blacklisted, or otherwise harassed. The union was broken in the Homestead plant and weakened throughout the steel industry. Not until the New Deal would labor regain the strength it held before the Homestead strike.

See also: IRON AND STEEL INDUSTRY (BUSINESS, INDUSTRY, AND TECHNOLOGY); IRON AND STEEL MILL WORKERS.

—Susan Grove-DeJarnett, *East Tennessee State University*

Horton, Myles

See Horton, Myles (Education)

Immigrant and African American Labor in the Coalfields

Besides dominating the economy in broad areas of Appalachia, coal mining has played a central role in shaping the region's culture. When entrepreneurs moved into isolated areas to open coal operations, they first hired native white Appalachians who were glad to leave subsistence farms for a more stable income. It quickly became apparent, however, that large coal-producing operations needed more men than local areas could supply. Operators solved the labor problem by recruiting immigrant laborers from Europe and African American laborers from the agricultural South.

Hiring agents developed lucrative businesses around the port cities of Baltimore, Philadelphia, and New York City by contacting potential workers as soon as they left ships. Many immigrants were sent to the coalfields with only vague details about the location or the nature of the work they were being offered. Paid for each worker they recruited, agents thus had incentive to deliver as many men as possible using whatever approach they found successful. Some coal companies even sent recruiters to Europe in search of additional workers to supplement the numbers being supplied by labor agents. Although this latter process was outlawed when Congress adopted the Alien Contract Labor Act in 1885, some operators violated the law with impunity. Other companies sent recruiters to the agricultural areas of the South, where Jim Crow laws kept blacks in a state of poverty. The offer of good jobs in the coalfields and on railroad projects made it easy to recruit blacks, but the workers often found conditions in the coalfields far worse than represented.

Both African Americans and immigrants were subjected to discriminatory treatment; some were even held in a form of bondage called debt peonage to work off costs associated with transporting and equipping them for work. In some instances, coal operators and railroad builders used private guards to hold workers against their will until debts were repaid. Collusion with local magistrates and justices of the peace lent the practice an air of legitimacy. Thus it was left to the federal government to investigate and prosecute complaints of peonage.

Coal-town housing was segregated by race and, frequently, ethnic origin, as were educational, religious, and recreational facilities. Even baseball teams were segregated, though games frequently pitted white teams against black teams. Immigrants and blacks organized their own fraternal organizations, which thrived in company towns in the years before World War I. These organizations provided members with opportunities to purchase life and disability insurance and created settings for social gatherings based on race, nationality, and cultural traditions.

The United Mine Workers of America attempted to incorporate all races and nationalities into the union. Leaders were acutely aware that a united front against operators would be impossible otherwise. Any group excluded from membership would have no incentive to support strikes or union demands of any sort. Operators, on the other hand, attempted to use racial and ethnic differences to prevent solidarity among their workers. Segregated housing was but one device employed to this end.

See also: DEBT PEONAGE; SLAVE LABOR.

—Kenneth R. Bailey, *West Virginia University Institute of Technology*

Kenneth R. Bailey, "A Judicious Mixture: Negroes and Immigrants in the West Virginia Mines, 1880–1917," *West Virginia History* (January 1973); Crandall A. Shifflett, *Coal Towns: Life, Work, and Culture in Company Towns of Southern Appalachia, 1880–1960* (1991); Joe William Trotter Jr., *Coal, Class, and Color: Blacks in Southern West Virginia, 1915–32* (1990).

International Ladies' Garment Workers' Union

In the mid-1930s, the International Ladies' Garment Workers' Union estimated that 15,000 women were employed in nonunion garment factories in Pennsylvania's anthracite coal region. Many of these factories—"runaways" from New York in search of inexpensive labor—attracted the wives and daughters of unemployed or underemployed anthracite miners in the dismal days of the Great Depression. Drawn from the diverse ethnic groups that had characterized the coalfields, these women—Italians, eastern Europeans, Irish, and others—became the breadwinners for thousands of families struggling to survive.

In 1937, to counter the growth of the runaway garment factories, the International Ladies' Garment Workers' Union, which had been founded in New York City in 1900, chartered a number of locals to represent workers in the cloak- and dressmaking industry, including Locals 109 and 131 in Scranton, Local 249 in Wilkes-Barre, and others in Pottsville, Shamokin, and other towns in the anthracite region.

Successful organizing campaigns, effective community relations, growing political clout, and the impressive strength of women organizers resulted in remarkable growth of the union. In the Wyoming Valley/Wilkes-Barre area alone, where nearly two hundred garment factories had emerged by the early 1960s, the union organized almost 11,000 workers. Membership surged in other union districts as well: 5,000 in Scranton, 4,000 in Shamokin, and 3,000 each in Hazleton and Pottsville. Total membership rendered the anthracite region the largest union stronghold in the Keystone State, and by the mid-1960s the union was the largest and most active women's labor union in the history of the anthracite region.

By the 1990s, however, growing foreign imports and the flight of American garment manufacturers overseas dramatically affected the American apparel industry. Garment factories in Pennsylvania and across the United States closed by the score. Nationally, the union's membership plummeted from nearly 500,000 in the late 1960s to 120,000 in 1995. In Pennsylvania's anthracite region at the close of the twentieth century, only a few hundred union members remained at work in a handful of garment factories.

See also: MATHESON, MIN LURYE; TEXTILE WORKERS; WOMEN TEXTILE WORKERS.

—Kenneth C. Wolensky, *Pennsylvania Historical and Museum Commission*

Iron and Steel Mill Workers

The history of iron- and steelworkers in Appalachia has followed a course little different from workers elsewhere in the industrializing world. Small-scale production for local markets by highly skilled craftsmen in the first half of the nineteenth century rapidly gave way to highly centralized, large-scale steel production for national and world markets. During the period of craft-dominated production, most workers were part-time wage earners primarily devoted to farming. By the end of the nineteenth century, however, most workers had become full-time and permanent wage earners. This movement from temporary wage earning to permanent industrial labor was a transition fraught with social consequences. Many of the issues are exemplified in iron- and steelworkers' struggle to maintain control of their working lives in the face of technological change. Like other American workers swept along by industrialization, employees of the iron and steel industry rarely reached a consensus in the workplace or in their communities. On labor-related issues, as with most others, they divided along ethnic, racial, and occupational lines.

During the antebellum period, small-scale iron-making facilities requiring few workers could be found throughout the Appalachians from Virginia to Alabama. Generally located near known deposits of iron and coal, these furnaces produced pots, pans, and other iron implements for strictly local markets. Men involved in the iron business during these years often had prior experience in the more developed northern iron trade.

In larger companies, proprietors often limited their involvement to management duties, but the division of labor on the shop floor remained relatively simple, with skilled workers conducting discrete operations. Puddlers directed men who melted iron ore in furnaces until the ore reached a satisfactory level of purity. Patternmakers produced the molds used in the manufacture of some iron goods, while molders directed the molding process itself. Where rolling machines were used to manufacture rails, structural steel, and other products, rollers directed crews of men who passed heated sheets of iron back and forth.

These skilled workers did not receive conventional wages. Firmly controlling shop floors, they received a "price" for what they produced, based on costs. In most cases unskilled employees worked for the skilled ironworker, receiving what pay the skilled worker deemed fair. In the South, many skilled ironworkers bought slaves and included that cost in the calculation of their prices.

Particularly in the South, recruitment of both skilled and unskilled labor was a problem for the industry. Because of the need to be near raw materials, early iron furnaces were often distant from major slave populations. For unskilled labor, proprietors therefore relied upon part-time workers such as farmers. Men in rural Appalachia usually considered a permanent wage-earning status degrading, and as long as land was available, the majority of white males did not have to work for wages. But as land became less available in the later antebellum period, more turned to wage labor. About the same time, European immigrants began to enter the wage-labor market as well. Employers with sufficient means purchased or rented slaves to do a variety of jobs. According to sociologist Wilma A. Dunaway, most slaves in Appalachia were found on "industrial plantations." These communities served a number of purposes for the ironmaster, providing labor control and self-sufficiency. In addition to worker housing and gardens, such communities sometimes included facilities for the processing of agricultural products, extensive networks of roads, and enterprises linked to the core business.

Civil War demand for weapons, rails, and a range of other metal products brought expansion of Appalachian iron production in both the Union and the Confederacy. The most striking development was in the large portion of the Appalachians within the Confederacy. Soon after the outbreak of hostilities, the Confederate government began to subsidize iron manufacturers engaged in military production. Workers, particularly skilled workers, were exempted from the draft, and conscripts were detailed to manufacturing plants.

After the Civil War, the iron and steel industry boomed throughout the region, especially in the southern Appalachians. Boosters promoted development of new towns and cities built around extensive iron and coal deposits. But while historians have often portrayed the South as a land of plentiful cheap labor, iron and steel companies found the labor pool inadequate. Few southerners had the needed skills. Moreover, farmworkers, white and black, were still reluctant to work in manufacturing. Indeed, long-standing biases against what people at the time referred to as public work continued in rural Appalachia into the twentieth century. During the latter years of the nineteenth century, however, declining farm commodity prices and increasing personal debt began pushing families off farms and sending men into mines and iron and steel mills.

For a decade or so after the Civil War, labor relations continued to be similar, if not identical, to the antebellum pattern, but the arrival of new steelmaking technologies revolutionized shop floors throughout the region. In Birmingham, Alabama, open-hearth steelmaking eliminated the need for puddlers, heaters, and their helpers and sharply increased productivity. New machinery could produce items more accurately and rapidly than skilled machinists at their benches. Inevitably, the workforce's proportion of skilled workers fell. The new jobs required some skill but not the level of expertise possessed by traditional craftsmen. Managers therefore could tap a larger reservoir of labor and could more readily replace uncooperative and unproductive workers. Companies in the northern Appalachians recruited thousands of Europeans to meet the labor demands of their rapidly expanding plants. When skilled workers formed organizations such as the Amalgamated Association of Iron, Steel, and Tin Workers to preserve job security and independence, conflict erupted. During strikes and other protests, workers portrayed the transformation of the workplace as a conscious design to deprive them of the independence distinguishing them from slaves. Unions faced a daunting task in organizing workers because immigrants and, after World War I, southern blacks eagerly took available jobs. Performing semiskilled work or operating modern machinery, most immigrants and blacks enjoyed more economic security and respectability than they had ever known. Labor organizations worked to unionize new jobs created by advancing technology but met with only limited success. The majority of workers remained outside organized labor, satisfied with the many benefits American corporations offered them.

The iron and steel industry evolved differently in the southern Appalachians. There, technological change came later because of the poor quality of iron ore. Consequently, craftsmen who had become obsolete in more advanced sectors of the industry migrated to Knoxville and Chattanooga, Tennessee, and especially to Birmingham, where their skills were still in great demand. White-controlled labor organizations in the South insisted upon a racial division of work, vigorously resisting any managerial attempt to employ blacks in jobs they claimed for whites only. The insistence upon a racial division of work alienated blacks, many of whom willingly acted as strikebreakers. At times, organized labor attempted to bridge this racial divide by offering black workers the benefits of union membership, but such efforts stopped short of eliminating the racial division. Blacks were welcomed into most unions only as long as they were willing to accept second-class status.

Many historians have blamed racial and ethnic divisions on corporations, arguing that management fostered such divisions in order to dominate the entire labor force. But while managers did manipulate these schisms, they did not necessarily create them. More often, companies merely adapted to patterns of racial and ethnic relations that the larger community desired and that white workers demanded. Economic self-interest was only one component of a transcendent belief in white supremacy. If white native-born Americans were superior, workers reasoned, then they should not be placed on the same level as blacks or lesser Europeans in any area of their lives. To the extent that workers struggled with management over ethnic and race relations, they did so with the intent of ensuring the domination of the workplace by whites.

Divisions in the workplace extended into communities from Pittsburgh to Birmingham. Highly paid workers lived in better housing than unskilled laborers. Where workforces were divided along racial lines, community residential patterns reflected the racial division: black workers lived in the least desirable neighborhoods. When companies provided housing, they incorporated this pattern. In Fairfield, Alabama, for example, United States Steel built a community divided into zones, each zone defined by quality of houses within them. An entirely separate community was built for blacks.

Beginning in the 1930s, labor unions, led by the United Mine Workers of America, dramatically departed from past strategies when they embraced industrial organization. In many respects, industrial organization revolutionized labor-capital relations. Most of the old craft divisions, with their inherent jurisdictional disputes, were eliminated. In some places, unions associated with the Congress of Industrial Organizations (CIO), such as the United Steelworkers of America, addressed racial and other inequalities, though they brought very limited reform to racial patterns in the workplaces of the South. Indeed, under pressure from rank-and-file white members, they institutionalized seniority systems that discriminated against blacks. Only the intervention of the federal courts in the 1970s removed the barriers to black advancement that white workers had insisted upon as one of the terms of their employment. Nonetheless, labor organizations had established themselves as legitimate representatives of a significant minority of iron- and steelworkers by the 1970s and secured significant influence over working conditions for members. Even nonmembers benefited, since companies improved conditions, pay, and benefits to stave off threats of organization.

Old craft unions continued to flounder in adjusting to the industrial realities of the early twenty-first century, however. Workers' gains have paled in significance when compared to the losses Appalachian iron- and steelworkers incurred as heavy industry declined and the service economy arose. The abandoned hulks of iron and steel plants in Birmingham, Chattanooga, and Wheeling, West Virginia, as well as widespread unemployment or underemployment among the people who had worked in them, attest to this transformation. Some parts of Appalachia have adapted to the new economy. Birmingham, for example, has redefined itself as the home of a nationally recognized medical center. But much of Appalachia continues to grapple with the demise of the industrial economy.

See also: LEWIS, JOHN L.; UNITED MINE WORKERS OF AMERICA; WEIRTON STEEL STRIKE.

—Henry McKiven, *University of South Alabama*

David Brody, *Steelworkers in America: The Nonunion Era* (1960); Wilma A. Dunaway, *The First American Frontier: Transition to Capitalism in Southern Appalachia, 1700–1860* (1996); Henry McKiven Jr., *Iron and Steel: Class, Race, and Community in Birmingham, Alabama, 1875–1920* (1995).

Jackson, Aunt Molly

See Jackson, Aunt Molly (Music)

Jones, Mother

(c. 1836–1930) Labor advocate.

For more than fifty years, Mary Harris "Mother" Jones traveled the United States preaching the gospel of trade

Mary Harris "Mother" Jones, a notorious labor leader of the early twentieth century, c. 1912. Once called "the most dangerous woman in America," Jones was acknowledged as one of the most effective public speakers of an era that included Billy Sunday and William Jennings Bryan.

unionism. She inspired steelworkers and seamstresses, railroad men and textile workers, but she is best known for her association with the United Mine Workers of America, who in 1900 hired her as an organizer, a unique appointment then for a woman. She was acknowledged to be one of the most effective public speakers in an era that included Billy Sunday and William Jennings Bryan. She was also a bundle of contradictions: she was a Socialist lecturer who is never known to have uttered the name of Karl Marx; she extolled the role of women in society but had no use for the suffrage movement; she defied convention by drinking beer in miners' bars and occasionally using profanity publicly, but she dressed in the height of Victorian respectability.

Although in the public eye for nearly half a century, she seldom referred to her first fifty years, which remain obscure. The principal facts of her life, if not the details, are available from her autobiography, interviews with journalists, and occasionally public records or manuscripts. Born in Ireland, she grew up in Canada, where she attended parochial schools and a newly founded normal school. Her first teaching experience was in a convent school in Michigan, but by 1859 she had moved to Memphis, where she met and married George Jones, an iron molder. She bore him four children while they lived there during the Civil War. After her husband and children died of yellow fever in 1867, she moved to Chicago, where she established a successful seamstress enterprise until she lost home and business in the great fire of 1870.

Mother Jones's first known appearance in Appalachia was in the railroad strike that began in Martinsburg, West Virginia, in 1877. Between 1891 and 1902, she worked with striking coal miners in Pennsylvania, western Maryland, Virginia, and West Virginia. She was in Pittsburgh for the Homestead strike, and she lent her voice to the striking miners and steelworkers in the Pullman strike in Birmingham, Alabama. During the same decade, she worked with Thomas J. Morgan, Henry Demarest Lloyd, and other political reformers in Chicago, marched and raised funds for Coxey's Army, and attended the Populist Party convention of 1896. But she attracted the most attention for organizing brigades of women and children for demonstrations in strikes when miners were intimidated by the National Guard or company police.

In 1902 the United Mine Workers mounted an effort to organize the nonunion coal miners in West Virginia, and Jones worked for several months in the Kanawha and New River fields until silenced by multiple injunctions. She transferred to the Fairmont field to continue her work. Federal marshals arrested her and other union supporters at the Pinnikinnick mine near Clarksburg for violating an injunction by Judge John Jay Jackson. He sentenced her companions to brief jail terms but released Jones after lecturing her on her unwomanly behavior. She left immediately to join the continuing strike in the anthracite field in Pennsylvania. Shortly thereafter she led a march of children from Philadelphia to Sagamore Hill, President Theodore Roosevelt's home near Oyster Bay, New York, to emphasize the need for laws to protect child workers. Roosevelt was not at home, but the crusade attracted national notice.

Jones broke with John Mitchell, president of the United Mine Workers, after he failed to support her effort to have the coal miners of the southern Colorado field included in negotiations over contract terms. Thereafter, she occasionally appeared on the payroll of the radical Western Federation of Miners, and beginning in 1903 she lectured for the Socialist Party in the West and Southwest, where she became involved with Mexican revolutionists who were trying to overthrow the regime of Porfirio Diaz.

With the fall of Diaz, she advised the successor government on labor policy. In 1905 she was the only woman among the founders of the Industrial Workers of the World. She found time in 1910 to organize the women workers in the breweries of Milwaukee, one of her most successful campaigns, where she used the threat of a boycott of Milwaukee beer by her friends in the mines to bring the brewery owners to terms.

In 1911 she returned to the United Mine Workers, plunging into a lost-cause strike in western Pennsylvania, where she persuaded many women to violate an injunction and fill the jail with themselves and their crying children, but her efforts could not save the strike. The following year in southern West Virginia she was arrested and turned over to the National Guard for a court-martial. Convicted of conspiracy to murder, she was imprisoned for some five months, but a national wave of protest influenced Congress to establish a special subcommittee to investigate conditions in the West Virginia coalfields, the first use of such an inquiry in an industrial dispute. West Virginia's new governor, Henry D. Hatfield, freed Jones in time for her to witness from the capitol gallery the passage of the legislation authorizing an investigation. In 1914 her experience in Appalachia was matched in Colorado, where her militancy led to arrest by the Colorado National Guard and another brief imprisonment, but she was released shortly before a habeas corpus action was to be decided by the state supreme court. Federal troops and negotiators intervened in the Colorado strike.

During the First World War Jones was in and out of southern West Virginia, organizing that hitherto nonunion field but also participating in agitation elsewhere. In 1919–20 she devoted herself to an attempt led by Philip Murray to organize the steel industry, sometimes incurring arrest for speaking without a license in steel towns near Pittsburgh.

In 1921 Mother Jones reached the peak of her career as a labor advocate and also suffered her greatest defeat. Her

Mexican revolutionary friends of earlier years, now in power, invited her to Mexico City as a guest of the nation, and there she addressed the meeting of the Pan-American Federation of Labor. When she returned to West Virginia, she tried to restrain armed miners in Logan County who were mobilizing for a march into an unorganized field, telling them that she had assurances from President Warren G. Harding that he would intervene in the controversy, but the militants did not believe her. Broken in spirit and health, she retired to the room that Knights of Labor leader Terence V. Powderly had set aside for her use in his home in Washington.

Despite being crippled by rheumatism in her ninth decade, Jones still campaigned in person or by correspondence for the release of imprisoned labor leaders such as Tom Mooney. In her only known return to Appalachia, she went to Charleston, West Virginia, to plead successfully with Governor Ephraim F. Morgan for the release of men jailed after the march on Logan. Bedridden in her last year, she still summoned the energy to celebrate what she said was her hundredth birthday on May 1, making a brief prolabor speech to the newsreel cameramen, reporters, and union leaders who had come to honor her for her long and fearless fight for the workers of the world. Some six months later she died at the home of a friend in Silver Spring, Maryland, and was buried in the miners' cemetery in Mount Olive, Illinois.

See also: IRON AND STEEL INDUSTRY (BUSINESS, INDUSTRY, AND TECHNOLOGY); IRON AND STEEL MILL WORKERS; UNITED MINE WORKERS OF AMERICA.

—Edward M. Steel, *Morgantown, West Virginia*

Dale Fetherling, *Mother Jones, the Miners' Angel: A Portrait* (1974); Elliott J. Gorn, *Mother Jones: The Most Dangerous Woman in America* (2001); Mary Harris Jones, *The Autobiography of Mother Jones* (1925).

Keeney, Frank

See Battle of Blair Mountain

Labor and the New Deal

New Deal legislation such as the National Industrial Recovery Act in 1933, the National Labor Relations Act in 1935, and the Fair Labor Standards Act in 1938 reinvigorated the craft-oriented American Federation of Labor (AFL) and encouraged industrial unionists to form their own Congress of Industrial Organizations (CIO). In Appalachia the affiliates of the AFL and CIO faced determined resistance. Coal miners and steelworkers led the way in organizing antiunion strongholds, but textile workers found that the New Deal reforms did not adequately equip them to break through traditional regional barriers to labor organization.

The Appalachian coal and textile industries fell upon hard times in the 1920s, when most of the national economy enjoyed prosperity. Called "sick industries" by the economists of the day, the two shared certain characteristics, including the capacity to produce more than markets could absorb, paternalistic attitudes toward labor, and the conviction that union wages would destroy Appalachian companies' ability to compete with rivals outside the region. Both industries also drew heavily upon workers from subsistence mountain farms. The textile industry employed a high percentage of women but excluded African Americans and hired few foreigners. The coal industry excluded women as miners but generally welcomed African Americans and immigrants.

In the textile villages that stretched from the Piedmont of Virginia through the Carolinas and Tennessee and into Georgia and Alabama, the depression decade brought strikes, violence, and frustration. Neither the AFL-affiliated United Textile Workers during the early 1930s nor the CIO's Textile Workers Organizing Committee later in the decade had much success in using New Deal laws to break the antiunion tradition in textiles.

From the time the coal industry arose in southern Appalachia at the end of the nineteenth century until the New Deal, the United Mine Workers of America repeatedly tried to organize Appalachian coal miners. The rugged topography of the region kept miners isolated and almost totally dependent upon their employers. Miners and their families lived in company housing, traded at company stores, worshipped in churches built by the company, and received part or all of their pay in company scrip. In some coal camps, racial and ethnic differences divided the miners.

Political and judicial authorities and most of the daily press supported the notion that the struggle against the United Mine Workers was a struggle for regional economic survival. Coal operators organized to ward off the union threat and hired labor spies and heavily armed mine guards. Some of the guards—frequently employees of private agencies such as Baldwin-Felts—were also deputized agents of county governments. Operator associations often controlled county courts and other local jurisdictions in the coalfields and wielded substantial power at the state level as well. Federal courts approved the "yellow dog" contract, which prohibited union membership as a condition of employment. Moreover, in response to coal operator requests, judges issued highly restrictive injunctions against union activities.

In 1933 the United Mine Workers leadership lobbied heavily in Washington for Section 7(a) of the National Industrial Recovery Act, which granted labor the right to organize and bargain collectively. The union then sent organizers across the region from Pennsylvania to Alabama proclaiming, "The President wants you to join a union!" On September 21, 1933, union and industry representatives announced the signing of the Appalachian Agreement, which covered Pennsylvania, Ohio, West Virginia, Virginia, eastern Kentucky, and Tennessee. Besides establishing the eight-hour day and the forty-hour workweek, the agreement prohibited payment in scrip and abolished requirements that miners patronize company stores or live in company houses.

The most persistent resistance to the United Mine Workers in Appalachia came from the coal operators of Harlan, Bell, and Whitley Counties in eastern Kentucky. For nearly a decade, as they crushed organizing drives by both the United Mine Workers and the National Miners Union, the eastern Kentucky operators defied federal law, National Recovery Administration industrial codes, state pressures, and condemnation by the federal La Follette Civil Liberties Committee and the national press. But by 1941, even the operators of "Bloody Harlan" had accepted United Mine Workers contracts.

In northern Appalachia, another bastion of antiunionism fell in 1937, when the CIO's Steel Workers Organizing Committee persuaded thousands of steelworkers to abandon company unions and join their organization, which was soon to become the United Steelworkers of America. After the United States Steel Corporation surrendered, other companies followed suit. By 1941 the CIO had organized virtually the entire steel industry, including many steelworkers in Appalachian Pennsylvania and West Virginia.

In southern Appalachia, race was sometimes a factor in resistance to unions. The United Mine Workers met with determined resistance in northern Alabama, where its biracialism offended mining firms such as the Alabama Fuel and Iron Company. Similarly, in the red ore mining areas of northern Alabama and southeastern Tennessee, officers and members of the biracial International Union of Mine, Mill, and Smelter Workers faced recurrent violence, often at the hands of local authorities.

In 1937 organized labor appeared to win a big victory in Alabama when U.S. Steel's surrender to the Steel Workers Organizing Committee included a contract between twenty thousand steelworkers in the Birmingham area and U.S. Steel subsidiary Tennessee Coal and Iron. But few other firms followed Tennessee Coal's example, and Birmingham's business community quickly reaffirmed its antiunion sympathies.

The New Deal fell short of bringing full economic recovery either to the region or the nation and failed to break down the barriers to unionism in some areas of southern Appalachia. The changes in the legal atmosphere, beginning with the National Recovery Administration codes of 1933, however, helped to create a more receptive attitude toward labor reforms and to eliminate some of the worst abuses that Appalachian labor had suffered. Through federal child labor laws, minimum wages, maximum hours, and state reforms such as the ending of the mine guard system, New Deal reforms had brought about a less restrictive legal atmosphere and a higher standard of living in the region by 1941.

See also: ANTHRACITE COAL INDUSTRY (BUSINESS, INDUSTRY, AND TECHNOLOGY); BITUMINOUS COAL INDUSTRY (BUSINESS, INDUSTRY, AND TECHNOLOGY); IRON AND STEEL INDUSTRY (BUSINESS, INDUSTRY, AND TECHNOLOGY).

—Jerry Bruce Thomas, *Shepherd University*

Irving Bernstein, *The Turbulent Years: A History of the American Worker, 1933–1941* (1970); John W. Hevener, *Which Side Are You On? The Harlan County Coal Miners, 1931–39* (1978); James A. Hodges, *New Deal Labor Policy and the Southern Cotton Textile Industry, 1933–1941* (1986).

Lewis, John L.

(1880–1969) Labor leader and organizer.

A towering and enigmatic figure in the American labor movement, John L. Lewis had an enormous impact on the lives of Appalachian workers, particularly in the coal industry. Ruthless and dictatorial, Lewis had definite ideas about ways to achieve social equity for American workers. He strove to fulfill this goal as president of the United Mine Workers of America and as founder of the Congress of Industrial Organizations (CIO).

Born in Iowa of Welsh parentage, Lewis ended his formal education before he finished high school. After leaving home, he tried various jobs and eventually became a coal miner. Although he would often refer to his experience as an ordinary miner later in his career, he was anxious to leave the mines. Becoming a union official was his key to social mobility. Joining the United Mine Workers, Lewis became a functionary in the American Federation of Labor (AFL), eventually doing confidential work for AFL President Samuel Gompers.

During this period, Lewis cultivated the image of being a self-taught expert on the coal industry and succeeded in being elected United Mine Workers vice-president in 1918 under Frank Hayes. Although Hayes was a talented leader, he suffered from alcoholism and was forced to resign the union's presidency by 1919. While Lewis succeeded Hayes amid much stated goodwill, he was resented by a number of officials for having risen through the AFL rather than the United Mine Workers. This resentment eventually grew into open rebellion.

Lewis was excoriated by such United Mine Workers leaders as John Walker and John Brophy for his authoritarianism and apparent lack of militancy in dealing with management. Lewis worked hard to establish permanent

John L. Lewis speaks at the fiftieth anniversary of the founding of the Coaldale, Pennsylvania, local of the United Mine Workers of America, 1952. As president of the United Mine Workers of America and founder of the Congress of Industrial Organizations, Lewis had an enormous impact on the lives of Appalachian workers, particularly in the coal industry.

control over the union and achieved this goal by 1928. He persecuted his critics, abused power, and broke the authority of the union's district offices, which traditionally had been autonomous. This infighting contributed to membership losses, and by 1932 Lewis was generally viewed as discredited.

Lewis's policies were not the only source of the union's problems. Overproduction during the First World War had created a worldwide coal glut. With coal prices in a free fall, management sought to cut costs, which was tantamount to running the union out of the coal industry. These structural characteristics and conflicts in a highly competitive industry led to periods of industrial warfare in the Appalachian coalfields.

Lewis wanted to reduce coal production by consolidating mining operations into the hands of a few large firms. The majority of Appalachian coal companies were small and marginally profitable. Constantly cutting wages, many were also dangerous operations, as the annual toll of accidental deaths attested. Lewis understood that the industry's workforce was too large and needed to be reduced in order to strengthen the bargaining position of working miners. Once these changes were accomplished, he thought, coal production would proceed at a managed pace and offer secure high wage employment to those who remained in the industry. His views were outlined in *The Miners' Fight for American Standards*, a book ghostwritten under Lewis's name by United Mine Workers economist W. Jett Lauck.

Franklin Roosevelt's election in 1932 rescued Lewis from his tenuous position within the labor movement. The New Deal's early legislation included the National Industrial Recovery Act, which suspended portions of America's antitrust laws and allowed workers to join labor organizations of their own choosing for purposes of collective bargaining. Seeing an opportunity, Lewis initiated a massive organizing campaign under the exaggerated slogan *The President wants you to join a union!* Within one year, the union's membership rose from fewer than one hundred thousand back to its 1919 peak of more than four hundred thousand, signaling a nearly complete organization of the industry.

This marked the start of Lewis's glory years, highlighted by the first Appalachian Agreement, signed by the United Mine Workers and several Appalachian coal operators in 1933. Lewis founded the Committee for Industrial Organization within the AFL in 1935. Eventually separating from the AFL in 1938, this group became a rival labor federation, the Congress of Industrial Organizations. The goal of this group was to organize workers traditionally thought to have been beyond the labor movement's reach: unskilled workers in heavy industries such as steel, tire, and automobile manufacturing. Although several other unions joined with the United Mine Workers in forming the CIO, it was Lewis who brought the vision, leadership, and resources that made it work. Between 1935 and 1938, industrial giants that had successfully resisted all organizational efforts in the past fell one by one to CIO affiliates. Among them were General Motors and United States Steel.

A campaign to organize the so-called Little Steel companies in 1937 was bitterly resisted and brought a temporary halt to the CIO's success the following year. Roosevelt distanced himself from labor and management, which Lewis took as a betrayal, since the CIO unions had thrown their full support behind Roosevelt's reelection in 1936. Eventually, Lewis broke with Roosevelt, which in turn forced Lewis to resign the CIO's presidency in 1940.

Although no longer CIO president, Lewis remained an active national figure. He made headlines during World War II by defying a no-strike pledge. Yet Lewis's greatest accomplishment, second only to founding the CIO, came after the war's end when he succeeded in the creation of the United Mine Workers Welfare and Retirement Fund in 1946. Achieved with the federal government's help through the War Labor Disputes Act, the fund was under Lewis's control by 1950. The organization eventually became a leader in the area of industrial benefits and successfully established the right of a medical third party to monitor the quality of care rendered to its beneficiaries.

Operators agreed to Lewis's control of the fund, however, only if he acquiesced in the mechanization of the Appalachian coalfields. Rapid mechanization and the displacement of Appalachian coal by alternative fuels resulted in massive employment cutbacks throughout the region. Mechanization not only made tens of thousands of Appalachian miners expendable to the industry, but also radically increased the coal dust in the mines, which in turned increased the incidence of the coal workers' occupational disease pneumoconiosis, or black lung. Even though the Welfare and Retirement Fund lobbied for the recognition of black lung as a compensable disease, the United Mine Workers under Lewis's leadership did not aggressively encourage miners' claims for redress.

Lewis retired as union president in 1960 while remaining chairman of the Welfare and Retirement Fund's trustee board. He remained in this position until his death in June 1969. During the final phase of Lewis's career, the union hierarchy's seeming detachment from advocacy for miners' welfare combined with bureaucratic incompetence and corruption under the notorious W. A. "Tony" Boyle eventually caused an internal rebellion within the United Mine Workers.

Lewis brought Boyle to the union's headquarters in 1948 to represent the United Mine Workers' western districts. Although Boyle served Lewis faithfully, there is no credible evidence to substantiate the claim by some that Boyle was Lewis's hand-chosen successor as president. Rather, Boyle probably backed into the union's presidency due to the untimely death of Thomas E. Kennedy, Lewis's immediate successor, whom Lewis had in fact groomed to be his replacement.

There is little question that Lewis had numerous failings, many of which adversely affected the United Mine Workers of America and the coal industry. But it is also clear that he was one of the most successful, influential, and effective labor leaders of the twentieth century.

See also: MINE SAFETY AND HEALTH ADMINISTRATION; NATIONAL MINERS UNION; UNITED MINE WORKERS OF AMERICA.

—Richard P. Mulcahy, *University of Pittsburgh at Titusville*

Melvyn Dubofsky and Warren Van Tine, *John L. Lewis: A Biography* (1977); Maier B. Fox, *United We Stand: The United Mine Workers of America, 1890–1990* (1990); Richard P. Mulcahy, *A Social Contract for the Coal Fields: The Rise and Fall of the United Mine Workers of America Welfare and Retirement Fund* (2001).

Matewan Massacre

The Matewan Massacre was a violent encounter between pro-union citizens and private police on May 19, 1920, in Matewan, Mingo County, West Virginia. During an organization drive by the United Mine Workers of America, Matewan Police Chief Sid Hatfield, miners, and pro-union citizens confronted agents from the Baldwin-Felts Detective Agency who had come to Matewan to evict striking miners' families from housing owned by the Stone Mountain Coal Corporation. Though reports vary, at least ten men died in an ensuing shoot-out. Casualties included two innocent bystanders, Matewan Mayor C. C. Testerman, and seven detectives, among them Albert and Lee Felts, brothers of agency chief Thomas L. Felts. Hatfield and fifteen others were tried for the murder of Albert Felts. The surviving detectives were also tried for murder. All of the trials stemming from the massacre ended in acquittal, but the violence shortly led to the assassination of Hatfield, the Miners' March, and the Battle of Blair Mountain, the largest insurrection in the United States since the Civil War. It also precipitated a U.S. Senate investigation and the Williamson-Thacker coalfield strike of 1920–22.

Key elements of the story remain a mystery. The question of who fired the first shot remains unanswered. Since only three of the detectives were armed when the shooting began, Hatfield's claim of self-defense is also debatable. Hatfield's prompt marriage to the widow of Mayor Testerman further contributed to the historic controversy.

Interpretations of the massacre reveal biases among those who write about Appalachia. The United Mine Workers and pro-labor scholars and writers have often treated the perpetrators of the massacre as heroes for taking a defiant stand against the enforcers of antiunion oppression. Defenders of the legal and economic rights of the coal operators acknowledge the central issues of unionism while dismissing the killers of the Baldwin-Felts agents as a hillbilly mob. Moreover, because the massacre occurred in one of the principal locales of the legendary Hatfield-McCoy feud, analyses of the episode are often colored by preconceived notions about mountain justice and vengeance. The invocation of such events without correlation suggests that the people of Matewan were inherently violent and thus culturally inferior.

A pivotal event in West Virginia's early-twentieth-century mine wars, the Matewan Massacre violently underscored the divisions throughout Appalachia and the nation as a whole over labor's right to organize.

See also: BATTLE OF BLAIR MOUNTAIN; FEUDS (GOVERNMENT); *MATEWAN* (MEDIA); UNITED MINE WORKERS OF AMERICA.

—Rebecca J. Bailey, *State University of West Georgia*

David Alan Corbin, *Life, Work, and Rebellion in the Coal Fields: The Southern West Virginia Miners, 1880–1922* (1981); Roger Fagge, *Power, Culture, and Conflict: West Virginia and South Wales, 1900–1922* (1996); Lon Savage, *Thunder in the Mountains: The West Virginia Mine War, 1920–21* (1990).

Matheson, Min Lurye

(1909–1992) Labor organizer.

From 1944 to 1963, Min Lurye Matheson led the International Ladies' Garment Workers' Union in northeastern Pennsylvania's Wyoming Valley. Born in 1909, the second of eight children of immigrant Russian Jews in Chicago, Matheson was exposed to the labor movement at an early age through her father, Max Lurye, an organizer for the Chicago Cigar Makers' Union. In 1928, at the age of nineteen, she met Bill Matheson, a labor activist twelve years her senior. By the early 1930s, the couple had relocated to New York, where she worked as a dressmaker and befriended leaders of the International Ladies' Garment Workers' Union. In 1937 she was elected chair of the organization's 32,000-member Local 22.

In 1944 the union's president, David Dubinsky, asked Matheson to organize the growing number of garment factories that were "running away" from Manhattan to northern Appalachia's anthracite coalfields in Pennsylvania in search of cheap labor. She was appointed district manager and her husband educational director. The anthracite region had become an attractive location for garment factories because men, the traditional breadwinners, were experiencing unemployment or underemployment as the anthracite coal industry entered a long period of decline. Families were desperate, and the wives and daughters of miners were eager to sit down at a sewing machine to earn what they could. Women worked long hours for very low piece rates. Complicating matters was the underworld. The Pennsylvania Crime Commission confirmed that gangsters owned, controlled, or influenced numerous garment factories in the anthracite region, particularly in Pittston, a coal town along the Susquehanna River a few miles north of Wilkes-Barre. For organized crime syndicates, apparel making provided a legitimate front and a means to launder money from illegitimate activities.

Min Matheson found about 650 union members in 6 organized shops in 1944. By the time she departed in 1963, the Wyoming Valley District totaled nearly 11,000 members in 168 organized factories. As she organized factories, she developed the union's infrastructure to meet the needs of members. The Ladies' Garment Workers' Union built a health-care center in Wilkes-Barre to serve members throughout the anthracite region and established a popular chorus. The union also created a model workers' education program that included a partnership with local Wilkes College, giving garment workers the opportunity to attend evening college courses—something practically unheard of at the time. By the mid-1950s, the organization was recognized as an active political force that advocated for worker-friendly policies, legislation, and politicians. The union became an important lobbying influence in local politics and at the state capital of Harrisburg as well as in Washington, D.C. By the early 1960s, Matheson had transformed the union into the most powerful and influential labor organization in the anthracite region. As former Pennsylvania Governor George M. Leader (1955–59) explained, although the organization operated in other parts of Pennsylvania, only in the anthracite region was it really powerful, thanks to Matheson's courageous leadership.

In 1963 Matheson departed the Wyoming Valley for the union's headquarters in New York City. For much of the remainder of the twentieth century, the organization enjoyed wide recognition as an integral part of the community in the anthracite region, despite the fact that imported apparel resulted in staggering job losses, factory closings, and declining union rosters. She returned to the area in June 1972 and became active in efforts to assist local citizens recovering from the devastating impact of Tropical Storm Agnes.

Min Matheson passed away on December 8, 1992, in Wilkes-Barre General Hospital. She remains a legend in the annals of Pennsylvania labor history and in the history of the International Ladies' Garment Workers' Union. A state historical marker on Public Square in Wilkes-Barre commemorates her life and work.

See also: INTERNATIONAL LADIES' GARMENT WORKERS' UNION; TEXTILE WORKERS; WOMEN TEXTILE WORKERS.

—Kenneth C. Wolensky, *Pennsylvania Historical and Museum Commission*

Mica Workers

Although Appalachia is famed for coal deposits from Alabama to Pennsylvania, another mineral—mica, or isinglass—was once a crucial economic product of the southern

Appalachians, specifically western North Carolina, and a strategic element in America's economic expansion.

The mica business developed after the Civil War, when local developers and outside entrepreneurs focused their attention on the region's mineral wealth. For day laborers in the late nineteenth century, mica mining provided much needed employment in an economy slow to recover from the war. For farm families and merchants with access to the markets of Knoxville, Tennessee, Asheville, North Carolina, and beyond, mica deposits in the mountains became an important source of cash. But after Thomas Edison's invention of the electric motor in 1881, mica was transformed from its role as a source of supplemental income in the informal area economy into a vital industry. New technologies in electronics, transportation, communications, weapons, and biomedical devices would all use mica as an insulating material of unequalled quality.

The federal government deemed mica a strategic mineral and developed a variety of programs throughout the 1940s, 1950s, and into the 1960s to stimulate production. With three-quarters of American mica deposits located in western North Carolina, extensive new mining and production operations sprang up while established companies increased their production capacities through the aid of federal grants and other incentives. Small family operations, working up mica located on lands they either owned or leased, found a lucrative customer for their "crop" in the form of procurement agencies set up by the federal government.

While men prospected and mined mica, young girls and married women labored in informally organized mica processing operations, often referred to as mica houses. There, they split the translucent material into thin sheets, assisted in the process of sorting mica according to grade, and punched or cut the mineral into disks, washers, or other shapes. Smaller numbers of men also worked in mica houses and later in factories as machine operators, maintenance men, and supervisors. Young boys assisted women working punch presses, taking away sorted and processed mica and watching out for waste of the precious material.

Though mica processing involved both meticulous labor and individual judgment, it did not bring high wages, since the mineral never came in uniform shapes or quality. In the 1920s, women were paid one dollar for a ten-hour day. Federal concern in the 1930s led to shorter workdays, higher wages, and greater attention to occupational hazards. But because the value of western Carolina mica was tied to low costs of production as much as to the quality of its mineral resource, such reforms were limited. In the absence of a labor union, mica workers resorted to informal means—work slowdowns and personal confrontations with management—to secure better working conditions and labor agreements.

By the early 1960s, the federal government had stockpiled sufficient quantities of mica to meet its objectives. Thereafter, procurement programs ended, and most mining operations ceased. Nearly two thousand workers were laid off, and only a handful of companies remained in business. Once likened to gold for its importance to the economy of western North Carolina, mica saw its value disappear.

See also: MICA INDUSTRY (BUSINESS, INDUSTRY, AND TECHNOLOGY).

—Mary K. Anglin, *University of Kentucky*

Mary K. Anglin, *Women, Power, and Dissent in the Hills of Carolina* (2002); Milford L. Skow, *Mica: A Materials Survey*, U.S. Bureau of Mines Information Circular No. 8125 (1962); Jasper L. Stuckey, *North Carolina: Its Geology and Mineral Resources* (1965).

Migrant Labor

See Migrant Labor (Agriculture)

Miller, Arnold

See Miners for Democracy

Miners for Democracy

Miners for Democracy was a rank-and-file group within the United Mine Workers of America formed to return the leadership of the union to the miners, reinforce health and safety standards in the mines, and restore autonomy to union districts. The group opposed W. A. "Tony" Boyle, who had won the 1969 United Mine Workers presidential election over Joseph A. "Jock" Yablonski. Boyle was accused of collaborating with mine operators and of not supporting the interests of miners.

After the murder of Yablonski in December 1969, those who had supported him in the union election regrouped as the Miners for Democracy. Citing intimidation, fraud, improper use of the *United Mine Workers Journal* for campaign purposes, and irregularities in local union nominating processes, they filed suit to void Boyle's election. Mike Trbovich, a western Pennsylvania coal miner, was the first leader of the movement. The Black Lung Association and the Disabled Miners and Widows of Southern West Virginia joined in the efforts to reform the union. They were also assisted by a group of lawyers who used their legal skills to overturn the 1969 election of Boyle and to protest the way the Federal Coal Mine Health and Safety Act was being administered.

In May 1972, federal courts overturned the election, and later that month Miners for Democracy held a nominating convention in Wheeling, West Virginia. The meeting was open to all rank-and-file members, and nearly five hundred miners met to draft a platform and nominate candidates for leadership in the union. Arnold Miller was selected as candidate for president. He had served as a local president and president of the Black Lung Association. Trbovich was nominated for vice-president and Harry Patrick for secretary-treasurer. None of them had experience in union administration or politics, nor had any of the three dealt with the leaders of industry or participated in bargaining for coal miners nationally. The platform for reform included: restoration of district autonomy; overhaul of the union's administration in regard to salaries, nepotism, and pensions; provision of a bill of rights for members; and an emphasis on safety and health.

After a campaign and election closely monitored by the Department of Labor and guided by regulations outlined by a federal judge, Miller won over the incumbent Boyle by a margin of more than fourteen thousand votes. His victory was attributed to the large number of younger miners who were assumed to support the reform group and the fact that Boyle was facing several indictments, including one for the murder of Yablonski.

After Miller was elected, he chose not to use the influence of the Miners for Democracy to support reform candidates in the district elections of 1973. Some of his supporters said they believed he let the movement die in order to heal old wounds in the union. A number of the 1973 candidates ran under the banner of Miners for Democracy, but after the election, the winners devoted their efforts to working within the union.

Many of the reforms advocated by Miners for Democracy became reality. Improved safety in the mines was a top priority, and the safety division of the union was expanded and reorganized. Most of the reformed laws, practices, procedures, and policies could be changed only by vote of the membership.

See also: UNITED MINE WORKERS OF AMERICA; YABLONSKI, JOSEPH A.

—Clara Hasbrouck, *East Tennessee State University*

Paul F. Clark, *The Miners' Fight for Democracy: Arnold Miller and the Reform of the United Mine Workers* (1981); Joseph E. Finley, *The Corrupt Kingdom: The Rise and Fall of the United Mine Workers* (1972); George William Hopkins, *The Miners for Democracy: Insurgency in the United Mine Workers of America, 1970–1972* (1976).

Mine Safety and Health Administration

A government agency created in 1977 to enforce compliance with federal mine safety regulations, the Mine Safety and Health Administration replaced the Mining Enforcement and Safety Administration formed under the auspices of the Federal Coal Mine Safety Act of 1969. Operated through the Department of the Interior's Bureau of Mines, the Mining Enforcement and Safety Administration had an uneven enforcement record, which brought disapproval from the United Mine Workers of America and lobbying for further reform. The United Mine Workers sought the transferal of mine health and safety inspecting from the Department of the Interior to the Department of Labor, hoping that the latter would be more sympathetic to the union's concerns and less responsive to complaints by coal operators about regulatory costs.

After years of lobbying, the United Mine Workers managed to win passage of additional mine safety legislation in 1976 and 1977. This legislation not only created the Mine Safety and Health Administration, but it also improved mine inspection procedures and increased fines for companies found in violation. In the subsequent decades, the agency's record of improvement was notable. Between 1976 and 1999, the total average number of deaths in all mining industries (coal and non-coal) fell from 254 to 93 fatalities a year; in 1998 only 29 coal-mining fatalities were reported. For the same period, the average level of work-related injuries in all mining industries shrank from 41,220 to 21,351 injuries per year. Although these statistics also reflect a decline in employment in such areas as coal mining as well as an increase in safety, the Mine Safety and Health Administration had a significant impact on coal-mining safety in the closing decades of the twentieth century.

See also: UNITED MINE WORKERS OF AMERICA.

—Richard P. Mulcahy, *University of Pittsburgh at Titusville*

Molly Maguires

Twenty Irishmen identified as members of a secret society called the Molly Maguires were hanged in the anthracite region of northeast Pennsylvania in the late 1870s for a series of assassinations stretching back to the Civil War. The society was said to have been imported from the Irish countryside, where an organization of the same name was active in the 1840s. The Molly Maguires in Ireland were so named because their members (invariably young men) disguised themselves in women's clothing, used powder or burnt cork on their faces, and pledged their allegiance to a mythical woman who symbolized their struggle against injustice. The clothing and makeup were more than a disguise; they also served to invest the Molly with the authority of the symbolic figure on whose behalf he was fighting. In Pennsylvania the Molly Maguires were also linked to an Irish fraternal ethnic organization called the Ancient Order of Hibernians, founded in New York City in 1836 as a peaceful benevolent society. In the anthracite region, the society was used for violent as well as fraternal purposes, however, and most of the convicted Molly Maguires were also Hibernians.

There were two distinct waves of Molly Maguire activity in Pennsylvania, one in the 1860s and the other in the 1870s. The first wave, which included six assassinations, occurred during and directly after the Civil War. Nobody was convicted of these crimes at the time, though the mysterious group called the Molly Maguires was widely believed to be responsible. Only during the trials of the 1870s were the killings of the previous decade retrospectively traced to individual members of the Ancient Order of Hibernians. At the heart of the violence in the 1860s was a combination of resistance to the military draft with some form of rudimentary labor organizing by a shadowy group known variously as the Committee, the Buckshots, and the Molly Maguires. During the crisis of the Civil War, labor organizing and draft resistance were seen by the mine owners and their political allies as tantamount to treason. The second wave of violence did not occur until 1875, in part because of the introduction of a more efficient policing and judicial system but mainly because of the emergence of a powerful new trade union, the Workingmen's Benevolent Association, which united Irish, British, and American workers across lines of ethnicity and skill.

The labor movement of the anthracite region now took two distinct but overlapping forms. A powerful trade union movement, open to all workers, united the labor force. Half the leaders of the union were Irish born. The Molly Maguires represented a second, shadowy organization, composed only of Irishmen and favoring tactics of violence that the union always condemned as self-destructive. To gather information against both groups, but especially the Mollies, Franklin B. Gowen of the Reading Railroad hired America's foremost private detective, Allan Pinkerton. Pinkerton sent one of his best men, the Irish-born James McParlan, to work undercover in the anthracite region. It was largely on his evidence that the Molly Maguires were executed.

The defeat and collapse of the Workingmen's Benevolent Association during the "Long Strike" of 1875 led directly to the second wave of Molly Maguire assassinations. Temporarily assuming the unofficial leadership of the labor movement, or at least of its radical violent wing, the Mollies assassinated a policeman, a justice of the peace, a miner, two mine foremen, and a mine superintendent in the summer of 1875. In 1876 and 1877 more than fifty men, women, and children were indicted for Molly Maguire crimes. The trials, conducted in the midst of enormously hostile publicity, bordered on a travesty of justice. The defendants were arrested by private policemen and convicted on the evidence of an undercover detective who was accused of being an agent provocateur. A series of informers also turned state's evidence to save themselves. Irish Catholics were excluded from the juries as a matter of course, and most of the prosecuting attorneys worked for railroads and mining companies. The star prosecutor at the great showcase trials in Pottsville was none other than railroad president Gowen. Twenty Molly Maguires were sent to prison, and of the twenty who were hanged, ten died on a single day, June 21, 1877. To the people of the anthracite region, the day was known thereafter as Black Thursday.

See also: ANTHRACITE MINERS, NINETEENTH-CENTURY; ANTHRACITE MINERS, TWENTIETH-CENTURY.

—Kevin Kenny, *Boston College*

Wayne G. Broehl Jr., *The Molly Maguires* (1964); J. Walter Coleman, *The Molly Maguire Riots: Industrial Conflict in the Pennsylvania Coal Region* (1936); Kevin Kenny, *Making Sense of the Molly Maguires* (1998).

Monongah Mine Disaster

The worst coal-mining industry disaster in the history of the United States occurred on December 6, 1907, in Monongah, West Virginia. Nearly a century later, the exact death toll remains uncertain. According to the Mine Safety and Health Administration's official count, 362 men and boys were killed when explosions ripped through two mines owned by the Fairmont Coal Company. But the general manager of the two mines reported that 478 men had been checked off as entering the mines on that day, and a study of the Monongah cemeteries puts the estimated number of victims at more than five hundred. The discrepancies are attributed to the miners' practice of covertly recruiting relatives and friends to work in the mines and sharing their wages with them. The names of these unofficial workers did not appear on the company's roster. Most of the miners were Polish, Italian, Russian, Austro-Hungarian, and Irish immigrants. Eighty-five Native Americans were also listed in the death count.

About 10 a.m. on December 6, explosions erupted in mines No. 6 and No. 8, which were connected by underground tunnels. The explosions, which were felt eight miles away, shattered buildings, caused the pavement to heave, and derailed streetcars. A cave-in and wreckage from two strings of ore cars obstructed the entrance to No. 6. Ventilation was restricted when one of the fans was demolished, allowing the mine to fill with deadly gases, to which the miners who survived the explosions and cave-ins quickly succumbed. Fires in both mines created additional hazards and hampered the rescue attempts. The last survivor of the disaster, Peter Urban, was rescued late in the afternoon. By December 12, all work areas had been ventilated, and 337 bodies had been recovered. During cleanup operations an additional 25 bodies were found.

The Marion County coroner's investigation concluded that the explosion was due to an extra-heavy charge of black powder used for blasting that ignited the highly flammable coal dust found in all West Virginia bituminous coal mines or caused a pocket of gas to explode, setting the coal dust afire. What caused the blown-out shot is unknown though several theories emerged—carelessness with an open lamp worn by all workers, an extra-heavy charge of dynamite, a short circuit in electric lines. Other investigations were made by mine inspectors from West Virginia, Pennsylvania, and Ohio, representatives of the Fairmont Coal Company, the U.S. Geological Survey, and by a commission of European mine investigators who were in the United States at the time to study the problem of coal-mine explosions.

This and many other mining disasters, in which one thousand miners lost their lives between the years 1907 to 1909, increased the awareness of the industry's safety problems among the mine owners and the federal government. According to an official government report on mining accidents and deaths, these incidents were attributable to a lack of proper and enforceable mine regulations. The absence of information on the explosives used in mining and guidelines on how they should be used was another contributing factor. In 1908 the mine owners recognized that improving mine safety would increase profitability. At the same time the Progressive movement began to work toward government regulations to improve working conditions in the mines. Congress established the United States Bureau of Mines, an agency of the Department of the Interior, in 1910 to further research mine safety problems and conduct mine inspections.

See also: FARMINGTON MINE DISASTER; HAWK'S NEST TRAGEDY; MINE SAFETY AND HEALTH ADMINISTRATION.

—Clara Hasbrouck, *East Tennessee State University*

Hiram Brown Humphrey, *Historical Summary of Coal Mine Explosions in the United States 1810–1958,* U.S. Bureau of Mines Bulletin No. 586 (1960); Albert Rhone, "Monongah Mine Disaster," *POINTers* (Winter 1999).

National Miners Union

The National Miners Union was a Communist-supported union that competed with the United Mine Workers of America between 1928 and 1933. The National Miners Union attempted to organize nonunion and unemployed miners across northern and central Appalachia and led two strikes in the region during 1931. The strikes received substantial press coverage and brought national attention to the deplorable living and working conditions of Appalachia's coal miners.

Communists first made inroads in the coalfields as supporters of the United Mine Workers' Save the Union movement. But in 1928 the Communist Party changed its labor organizing strategy from working within established trade unions to creating new, revolutionary organizations that directly challenged them. The National Miners' radical program called for nationalization of the coal industry, organization of unorganized miners, equality for African Americans and women, and support for the Soviet Union.

Throughout its history, the National Miners Union could marshal neither sufficient funding nor an adequate number of field organizers. The organization also was handicapped by low membership. Most of its members were unemployed miners who had been expelled from the United Mine Workers or blacklisted by coal operators. Membership probably did not exceed five thousand members. The union's Marxist ideology further contributed to its recruiting difficulties. Most of the poverty-stricken miners of northern and central Appalachia were more concerned with feeding their families than building a revolutionary movement. Nevertheless, as the Great Depression intensified and more miners lost their jobs, the union saw an opportunity in Appalachia and organized strikes in western Pennsylvania and eastern Kentucky in 1931.

Between April and June of 1931, the National Miners Union led forty thousand miners in western Pennsylvania, eastern Ohio, and northern West Virginia in the largest strike ever conducted under the auspices of the Communist Party. The strike started because miners had received a wage cut. Alarmed at the appearance of the union and fearing that the strike would spread into other districts, coal companies evicted miners' families from company housing, hired strikebreakers, and utilized their own security forces to threaten miners and National Miners Union organizers. After twelve weeks, the organization, running short of money and organizers, called off the strike. The miners either returned to work under nonunion contracts or remained unemployed. However, the strike resuscitated the union's rival, and by the end of 1931 a number of coal companies in the Pittsburgh coalfield had signed contracts with the United Mine Workers.

Shortly after the Pittsburgh strike, the National Miners Union again tried to make inroads by leading a strike in eastern Kentucky's Harlan and Bell Counties. Initially, the United Mine Workers organized the Harlan strike in May after the miners received a wage reduction. But after a series of violent episodes and arrests, the organization pulled out of the strike and cut off aid to the miners. Abandoned and desperate, miners of eastern Kentucky turned to the National Miners Union. The Communists were no more successful than the United Mine Workers had been in securing union contracts for the Kentucky workers, however, and the miners eventually renounced the Communists for their atheism and their support for the Soviet Union. In reaction to the National Miners' strike, eastern Kentucky's powerful coal companies unleashed violence against the miners and rallied support of local and state police, governments, and courts. After one of its organizers was killed and a number of organizers and miners were arrested for criminal syndicalism, the union canceled the strike and left Kentucky in January 1932.

Although the strike failed, the National Miners Union was successful in bringing national focus to the plight of the eastern Kentucky miners, something the United Mine Workers had been unable to do. National journalists and a group of left-wing writers headed by Theodore Dreiser investigated and reported on the miners' situation. For the first time, the mainstream press focused attention on the economic problems connected with the coal industry rather than relying on Appalachian stereotypes to describe the miners' plight. Although conditions did not improve for the Harlan miners until the late 1930s, the nation became aware of the economic circumstances in Appalachia.

The loss of the Appalachian strikes seriously undermined the National Miners Union and the Communist Party's revolutionary movement. The organization disbanded in 1933, and the Communist Party returned to its earlier policy of working within established trade unions.

See also: DREISER INVESTIGATION; SAVE THE UNION MOVEMENT; UNITED MINE WORKERS OF AMERICA.

—Teresa Statler-Keener, *West Virginia University*

Maier B. Fox, *United We Stand: The United Mine Workers of America, 1890–1990* (1990); John W. Hevener, *Which Side Are You On? The Harlan County Coal Miners, 1931–39* (1978).

North American Free Trade Agreement

In the fall of 1993, Congress consented to ratification of the controversial North American Free Trade Agreement (NAFTA), producing longterm repercussions across Appalachia and elsewhere in the United States.

Although negotiations for free trade among Mexico, the United States, and Canada were completed during President Bill Clinton's administration, the pact traced its origins to the administration of his predecessor, George H. W. Bush. Indeed, Independent presidential candidate Ross Perot in 1992 adopted as one of his major themes criticism of the support both Bush and Clinton promised to NAFTA. From the beginning, the pact was staunchly opposed by the American Federation of Labor and Congress of Industrial Organizations (AFL-CIO), environmental organizations, and community groups. Each feared that free-trade rhetoric concealed a corporate agenda to move factories and union jobs to low-wage, largely unregulated Mexico.

NAFTA was promoted by corporations that stood to benefit from provisions of the treaty. Corporate leaders took responsibility for mobilizing political support for the agreement at the state level. Among those in the Appalachian region were officials of DuPont, IBM, Ashland Oil, AT&T, International Paper, and TRW, companies with records of eliminating jobs, polluting the environment, or both. NAFTA proponents promised that the treaty would expand markets for American companies, improve the balance of trade with Mexico and Canada, and create 200,000 new jobs in the United States. Labor and community groups in Appalachia and throughout the country viewed such projections as unduly optimistic. They worried because many of the pro-NAFTA companies already operated factories in the duty-free maquiladora region on the Mexican-U.S. border.

The first five years of trade relations under the agreement bore out the predictions of skeptics. The country's trade balance with Mexico grew from a $1.7-billion surplus to an almost $16-billion deficit. As corporations closed plants, the United States lost, by some estimates, more than 450,000 manufacturing and transportation jobs in less than a decade. By the end of 1998, the U.S. Department of Labor, which under the Transitional Adjustment Assistance Act can provide extended unemployment benefits to workers displaced by NAFTA-related plant closings, had certified 211,582 such workers.

Appalachian workers were hit hard by NAFTA, despite having generally lower wages than employees in other areas of the United States. Although statistics are compiled by state and thus do not directly correspond to the Appalachian region, seven states with numerous Appalachian counties (Kentucky, Alabama, North Carolina, Virginia, West Virginia, Tennessee, and Pennsylvania) experienced job losses totaling almost 74,000 through December 1996. Although workers in those states comprised 15.6 percent of the U.S. workforce, they accounted for 18.7 percent of the NAFTA-related job losses. Industries important to the region in recent years—automobile assembly, textiles, clothing, and glass—were among those most likely to move to new plants in Mexico.

NAFTA's negative impact was significantly offset by the long economic boom of the 1990s, however. Most states with Appalachian counties saw wage improvements relative to the rest of the country. West Virginia, Kentucky, North Carolina, and Tennessee all increased real median wages, while Pennsylvania, South Carolina, Georgia, and Ohio declined less than the national average. Only Alabama and Virginia fared worse than the nation as a whole. The image of generally improving wages relative to the U.S. average, though, is somewhat misleading, due in part to a generally lower starting point. In 1995 Appalachian wages were only 83.3 percent of the United States average, and poverty rates were almost 17 percent higher. In general, then, NAFTA produced a mixed record in the region.

More longterm implications for the region still appeared to be less than promising. Many U.S. exports to Mexico are capital goods, enabling American-owned plants operating in Mexico to produce goods for sale in the United States. Proponents of NAFTA predicted that U.S. firms would tap into an expanding Mexican consumer market, but peso devaluation and declining wages in Mexico prevented such an expansion, at least during NAFTA's first eight years. Early in the new century, conditions seemed to point toward continued flight of manufacturing jobs south of the border. In the economic boom of the 1990s, low U.S. unemployment and increasing wages helped soften the impact of the shift from manufacturing to service-sector jobs. But under less favorable economic conditions, a continuation of the early trend would have the potential for a far more jarring effect in Appalachia.

See also: CHEMICAL INDUSTRY (BUSINESS, INDUSTRY, AND TECHNOLOGY).

—Ken Fones-Wolf, *West Virginia University*

Robin Broad et al., "NAFTA's Corporate Cadre: An Analysis of the US-NAFTA State Captains," Institute for Policy Studies paper (July 1993); Public Citizen, *NAFTA's Broken Promises: The Border Betrayed* (1996).

Northern West Virginia Mine War

From 1924 to 1927 and from 1931 to 1933, the northern West Virginia coalfields were the scene of a violent mine war. With the support of United Mine Workers of America President John L. Lewis, miners fought to defeat the open-shop movement and eventually gained a collective bargaining agreement.

This war was centered in the Fairmont coalfield of Marion, Monongalia, Harrison, Preston, Taylor, and Barbour Counties. Other action occurred near Wheeling, in the northern panhandle field where miners had struck for union recognition several times since 1892 to no avail. The coal operators, led by the Fairmont Coal Company (after 1901 a part of Consolidation Coal Company) had successfully used injunctions, detectives, and other measures to keep the union out and to maintain a lower wage structure than that in coalfields north of the Ohio River. With backing from the Federal Fuel Administration, the United Mine Workers organized the miners of northern West Virginia during World War I.

The union protected its agreements until 1924, when a nationwide coal glut depressed prices and led many coal operators to demand an end to artificially high United Mine Workers wages. Some operators refused to sign the Jacksonville Agreement, a multicompany contract with the union in 1924, and others abrogated it as economic conditions worsened. Ten thousand miners responded to the union's call to strike to protest these violations. Fearful that the loss of a unionized northern West Virginia would lead to the loss of adjacent Pittsburgh and Southern Ohio districts, the organization opened its treasury and sent Van A. Bittner, one of its top organizers, to Fairmont. The result of this confrontation was a bloody mine war. Coal companies evicted union miners, obtained injunctions against demonstrations and rallies, and fortified their properties with guards armed with high-powered rifles to ward off attacks and sabotage. Militant union miners dynamited tipples and other mining facilities, shot up strikebreakers' coal camps, and threatened mining operations with marches and demonstrations. Responding to evictions, the United Mine Workers built barracks for miners and their families in forty-four mining centers throughout the Fairmont field. The strike continued through 1928, but by then most strikers had returned to work at nonunion mines. By 1929, there were no union mines in the entire Fairmont field.

As the fortunes of the United Mine Workers waned in the early 1930s, Bittner kept the union cause alive by focusing his efforts on Scotts Run, a densely populated coalfield near Morgantown. Here the railroads depressed the price of coal, and coal companies followed with wage reductions. In May 1931, hundreds of miners walked off their jobs to protest starvation wages. After the strike spread from Scotts Run to surrounding areas, Bittner negotiated a closed-shop contract with thirty-nine companies representing about one-half of the production of the Fairmont field. Confrontations and violence continued, however, as the remaining companies refused to recognize the United Mine Workers.

Settlement of the Scotts Run strike helped the national United Mine Workers of America survive in the early 1930s. The organization gained new life as several union contracts based on the Scotts Run settlement were signed in the Pittsburgh and Southeastern Ohio districts. Moreover, the union field in northern West Virginia provided a base for organizing efforts in southern West Virginia after the passage of the National Industrial Recovery Act in 1933.

See also: LEWIS, JOHN L.; UNITED MINE WORKERS OF AMERICA.

—Michael E. Workman, *West Virginia University*

Howard B. Lee, *Bloodletting in Appalachia: The Story of West Virginia's Four Major Mine Wars and Other Thrilling Incidents of Its Coal Fields* (1969); Michael E. Workman, "Political Culture and the Coal Economy in the Upper Monongahela Region: 1776–1933," Ph.D. dissertation, West Virginia University (1995).

Oil and Gas Workers

See Oil and Gas (Geology)

Paint Creek–Cabin Creek Strike

The coal miners' strike on Paint and Cabin Creeks, West Virginia, in 1912–13 was one of the longest industrial conflicts in the nation's history and arguably the bloodiest. The United Mine Workers of America organized coal mines on the two tributaries of the Kanawha River in 1902. However, coal operators on Cabin Creek shortly afterward refused to recognize the union. In 1912 the operators on Paint Creek decided to follow suit and refused to sign a new contract with the union. The miners went on strike in April 1912.

While the immediate cause of the strike was the lack of a contract, hostility between coal operators and workers had been steadily growing. Miners resented company ownership of everything—houses, stores, schools, and churches—in the coal towns and complained of brutal treatment from the coal company guards. Since the 1890s, coal companies had resisted the miners' demand for unionization and considered the union an unwanted and unwarranted challenge to their authority and an interference with business.

At the onset of the strike, the local population quickly polarized into opposing camps of coal operators and striking miners. The operators brought in additional guards hired from the Baldwin-Felts Detective Agency to evict the miners from company-owned homes and to protect company property from destruction. The union countered by creating tent camps, such as the one at Holly Grove on Paint Creek, to house the miners and by importing rifles and pistols with which to arm them.

Confrontations between the groups began almost immediately, as strikebreakers were brought in to work the mines and guards evicted strikers from their homes, but the real bloodshed began in July 1912. After suffering months of lost wages and frustration at the continued production of coal, miners attacked a detachment of guards on July 25 at Mucklow on Paint Creek, precipitating a battle in which about a dozen miners and four mine guards were killed. Finding that the local authorities were unable or unwilling to maintain order, Governor William E. Glasscock mobilized the West Virginia National Guard and sent it to Paint Creek, where it would remain on duty almost continuously until June 1913.

The strike zone, which extended for about ten miles, from Cabin Creek Junction eastward to Montgomery, was placed under martial law. As the National Guard solidified its control in the area, mine guards and miners were disarmed. Hundreds of rifles, bushels of pistols, and several machine guns were confiscated. Men and women accused of violating the law were tried before courts-martial and, if found guilty, were sentenced to varying terms in the local or state correctional facilities. The most famous prisoner brought before the court-martial was nationally known union organizer Mary Harris "Mother" Jones. While the imposition of martial law was criticized soundly by local and national leaders, Governor Glasscock used it three times during the strike. Three writs of habeas corpus were filed to challenge the right of military authorities to arrest and detain miners and/or their supporters. In all three, the use of martial law was upheld by the West Virginia Supreme Court of Appeals.

The strike ended in the early summer of 1913, when newly elected Governor Henry D. Hatfield issued an ultimatum to both the union and the coal companies to reach an agreement. The agreement awarded the miners many of their demands but not union recognition.

The long and bitter strike on Paint and Cabin Creeks was part of a larger struggle for the right to organize and bargain collectively in the southern West Virginia coalfields. In the 1890s, the United Mine Workers began efforts to organize southern West Virginia and had only meager success until the 1930s. The 1912–13 strike had far-reaching social, economic, and political implications. Coal miners and their families suffered severe economic and physical hardships; bewildered immigrants and southern blacks were brought into the area as strikebreakers; the lives of hundreds of National Guardsmen were disrupted during extended strike duty; and the strike cost the State of West Virginia hundreds of thousands of dollars and created a long-lasting negative public image. The United Mine Workers lost credibility when state and national union officials failed to support the strike as fully as the strikers had hoped. Finally, the strike and the use of the company guards and the National Guard in protecting company property created a climate of distrust between workers on the one hand and business and state government on the other that has colored labor relations in West Virginia to the present.

See also: JONES, MOTHER; UNITED MINE WORKERS OF AMERICA.

—Kenneth R. Bailey, *West Virginia University Institute of Technology*

Kenneth R. Bailey, *Mountaineers Are Free: A History of the West Virginia National Guard* (1978); David Alan Corbin, *Life, Work, and Rebellion in the Coal Fields: The Southern West Virginia Miners, 1880–1922* (1981); Edward M. Steel Jr., ed., *The Court-Martial of Mother Jones* (1995).

Roberts, Cecil

(1946–) Labor leader.

Cecil Edward Roberts, a sixth-generation coal miner, was elected president of the United Mine Workers of America on October 22, 1995. Recognized as one of the labor movement's most stirring speakers, he rallied union workers in 1998 to the highest percentage of votes to ratify a wage agreement in the union's history.

Born on October 31, 1946, Roberts grew up on Cabin Creek in Kanawha County, West Virginia. He was drafted in 1966 and served in Vietnam, where he became a sergeant and squad leader of a mortar platoon. Returning from Vietnam in 1968, Roberts completed two years of junior college before going to work in the coal mines. He worked in a variety of underground jobs including general inside laborer, shuttle car operator, greaser, beltman, and mechanic.

Recognizing that Roberts had strong leadership abilities, his fellow workers elected him to the Mine Safety and Political Action Committee in 1972. He became active in the Miners for Democracy movement, which restored the control of the United Mine Workers to its members after the election of W. A. "Tony" Boyle was overturned in court. Subsequently, Roberts was elected as a delegate to the District 17 convention, vice-president of District 17, vice-president of the United Mine Workers, negotiator in the Pittston Coal Company strike, and in 1995 to the presidency of the United Mine Workers. In 1997 he was reelected with support of 99 percent of the local units participating in the nominating process and elected again to a new five-year term in 2004.

Roberts graduated from West Virginia Technical College in 1987 and received an honorary doctorate in humanities from West Virginia University Institute of Technology in 1997. His other organizational memberships include the Committee for Employer Support of Veteran Employment; West Virginia Employment Opportunities and Economic Development Commission; National Council of the Holmes Safety Association; National Council of Senior Citizens; West Virginia University Institute for Labor Studies and Research Advisory Board; American Legion; and Veterans of Foreign Wars.

See also: MINERS FOR DEMOCRACY; UNITED MINE WORKERS OF AMERICA.

—Clara Hasbrouck, *East Tennessee State University*

Salt Workers

Salt was a vital food seasoning and preservative before the invention of chemical preservatives and refrigeration. It was one of the first natural resources exported from Appalachia, and the region led the nation in salt production until the 1840s, when it peaked and began a rapid decline.

The Appalachian salt industry was concentrated in southwest Virginia, eastern Kentucky, and the region that later became West Virginia. Saltworks in all three areas were established in the first decade of the nineteenth century, and although the works in Virginia and Kentucky were regionally significant, they paled in comparison with the scale and economic importance of the Kanawha industry. By far the most extensive salt-producing complex in Appalachia, the Kanawha saltworks were located along a ten-mile stretch of the Kanawha River near Charleston, (West) Virginia, where sixty-five salt wells and twenty furnaces were processing salt by 1828. Over the course of the 1840s, its most productive decade, the Kanawha industry produced approximately three million bushels of salt.

Like most industries in the Old South, Kanawha salt manufacturing relied heavily on slave labor. The industry's organization, capital, investors, and use of slaves reflected its outgrowth from the industry in eastern Virginia. More than 50 percent of the slaves employed at the Kanawha saltworks (totaling 1,497 in 1850) were leased annually from eastern Virginia planters. To oversee operations, a managerial hierarchy was maintained in positions such as general overseer, boss kettle tender, coal bank manager, and well manager, and managers who were also slaves were not uncommon. Slaves were employed in all phases of the production process, from the simplest jobs to those requiring the most skill. Saltworks operated around the clock six days a week, and the labor force was organized around the task system supplemented by monetary incentives to encourage slaves to produce beyond the required task.

Most occupations within the industry were dangerous. Mining the coal to fire the evaporation furnaces was most hazardous, but all who toiled near the furnaces were exposed to boiling water or the frequent explosions of steam boilers. Laboring so close to the Ohio River, slaves, particularly those from areas farther to the south or east, found freedom on the other side a constant allure, a temptation not unnoticed by wary saltworks operators.

By the start of the Civil War, the rapid growth of northern railroads, the development of a major salt deposit in Michigan, and a shift in the meatpacking industry further west to Chicago doomed the Appalachian salt industry. Nevertheless, it had stimulated large-scale industrial organization based on extraction, as well as the development of lumber, coal, and natural gas resources and smaller-scale industries such as boat building and coopering. Together, these enterprises paved the way for postbellum industrialization in the Kanawha Valley.

See also: KANAWHA SALT TRUST (BUSINESS, INDUSTRY, AND TECHNOLOGY); SALT (BUSINESS, INDUSTRY, AND TECHNOLOGY); SLAVE LABOR.

—Ronald L. Lewis, *West Virginia University*

Dwight B. Billings and Kathleen M. Blee, *The Road to Poverty: The Making of Wealth and Hardship in Appalachia* (2000); Wilma A. Dunaway, *The First American Frontier: Transition to Capitalism in Southern Appalachia, 1700–1860* (1996); John E. Stealey Jr., *The Antebellum Kanawha Salt Business and Western Markets* (1993).

Save the Union Movement

Save the Union was an insurgent rank-and-file coal miners' movement that operated within the United Mine Workers of America from 1926 to 1928. The movement challenged United Mine Workers President John L. Lewis and inspired miners to resist antiunion coal operators. During the 1920s, an antiunion drive by coal operators coupled with mechanization of coal production undermined the traditional "miners' freedom," a certain autonomy in the production process that miners historically viewed as their right. This resulted in a precipitous decline in United Mine Workers membership, a substantial loss of union jobs, and the deterioration of living and working conditions in coal-mining communities. Save the Union possessed a strong Appalachian component, and the region's miners fueled much of the movement's militant fervor.

Save the Union's efforts were supported not only by rank-and-file miners and union officials but also by the Communist Party and other left-wing organizations. The movement garnered the most support in eastern Ohio, central and western Pennsylvania, and northern West Virginia. In 1926 its members supported John Brophy, president of the United Mine Workers District 2 in central Pennsylvania, in his campaign to unseat John L. Lewis as the union's national president. Brophy campaigned on a program that called for nationalization of the coal industry, formation of a labor party, establishment of more democracy within the United Mine Workers, and the organization of nonunion miners. The primary elements of the Save the Union platform came from Brophy's 1921 pamphlet entitled *The Miners' Program*. It presented a progressive-left alternative to the conservative business unionism espoused by Lewis and his supporters.

Under Lewis's leadership, the United Mine Workers concentrated on improving wages, hours, and working conditions and advocated labor-management cooperation. Lewis defeated Brophy in a contested election, then declared Save the Union to be a dual union and expelled the movement's backers from the United Mine Workers organization. Defeat of the Save the Union movement ensured that Lewis and the business unionists retained control of a weakened organization. Although branded a dual union, the Save the Union movement continued efforts to rebuild the United Mine Workers by attempting to organize nonunion miners during the national coal strike of 1927. The strike lasted for more than a year but ended in defeat for the union as the majority of miners returned to work under nonunion contracts. After the loss of the 1927 strike, Save the Union's remaining supporters helped to organize the Communist-supported National Miners Union in 1928.

For Appalachia's miners, the success of the coal companies' antiunion drive along with mechanization and political infighting within the United Mine Workers of America resulted in the virtual collapse of the union in Alabama, Maryland, Kentucky, Tennessee, Virginia, and West Virginia. In parts of Ohio and Pennsylvania, it was no more than a skeletal organization. The majority of Appalachian coal miners would not be unionized until passage of the National Industrial Recovery Act in 1933.

See also: NATIONAL MINERS UNION; UNITED MINE WORKERS OF AMERICA.

—Teresa Statler-Keener, *West Virginia University*

John Brophy, *A Miner's Life* (1964); Maier B. Fox, *United We Stand: The United Mine Workers of America, 1890–1990* (1990); Elizabeth C. Ricketts, *Our Battle for Industrial Freedom: Radical Politics in the Coal Fields of Central Pennsylvania, 1916–1926* (1996).

Scrip

Appalachian coal companies issued scrip as a currency substitute at various mines from the late nineteenth century until the 1950s. Composed of metal, plastic, or paper tokens redeemable for products in company stores, it came in the same denominations as United States Treasury coins, as well as dollar bills. Most mining companies in the region issued scrip, and it is estimated that altogether about twenty thousand coal company stores in the United States, Canada, and Mexico issued and used it at various times. In many cases, miners' wages for work already performed were paid exclusively in scrip, while in others miners received scrip as a loan against future pay. Those who needed money before payday could simply go to the company office and request scrip.

The system victimized miners in a number of ways. Because scrip could only be used at company-owned stores, miners often accumulated more debt than they could reasonably pay, winding up in virtual peonage. Along with Tennessee Ernie Ford, many miners could sing, "I owe my soul to the company store," in the hit song "Sixteen Tons," written by Merle Travis. Miners using scrip were subjected to a form of price gouging since company stores charged more than independent retailers conducting business with government currency. Employees who tried to convert scrip into cash, a transaction called "discounting," sometimes took a loss as high as sixty cents on the dollar. Coal companies tried to prevent discounting by making the scrip they issued nontransferable and unredeemable by anyone other than the party to whom it was issued. Economic changes in the coal industry, coupled with the passage of state and federal laws strictly regulating the use of scrip, caused companies to stop issuing the currency in the late 1950s.

See also: COAL TOWNS (FAMILY AND COMMUNITY); DEBT PEONAGE.

—Doug Cantrell, *Elizabethtown Community College*

Harry M. Caudill, *Night Comes to the Cumberlands: A Biography of a Depressed Area* (1963); Ronald D Eller, *Miners, Millhands, and Mountaineers: Industrialization of the Appalachian South, 1880–1930* (1982); Crandall A. Shifflett, *Coal Towns: Life, Work, and Culture in Company Towns of Southern Appalachia, 1880–1960* (1991).

Service Employees International Union, District 1199

Formerly the National Union of Hospital and Health Care Employees, District 1199 WV/KY/OH of the Service Employees International Union represents doctors, registered nurses, licensed practical nurses, technicians, case managers, social workers, nurses' aides, maintenance workers, housekeepers, laundry workers, food service workers, and clerical workers in West Virginia, Kentucky, and Ohio.

From the beginnings of the national union in New York in 1932, 1199's leadership insisted that a union must emphasize not only wages and benefits but also social equality and community action beyond the workplace. Health-care workers desiring representation by 1199 had to set aside differences based on education, sex, race, or ethnic background. The union has historically projected a broader social agenda than the mainstream craft and industrial unions, including a consistent identification with militant civil rights campaigns. Its culture of social activism and rank-and-file participation led Martin Luther King Jr. to call the national 1199 his favorite union. The first union to speak out against the Vietnam War, 1199 laid a foundation for the internal organizing model that is now used in some form by most unions. Although health-care professionals are represented by 1199, its membership is largely comprised of women and minorities doing traditionally low-wage work in hospitals and nursing homes.

In 1970, 1199 organizer Larry Harless, a West Virginia native, returned to his home state from New York and opened an 1199 office in Huntington, convinced that hospital workers could be organized in private hospitals in the southern West Virginia coalfields. Victories in 1971 at Doctors' Memorial Hospital in Welch, West Virginia, in 1972 at Holden Hospital in Logan County, West Virginia, and in 1973 at Clinch Valley Clinic in Richlands, Virginia, soon made 1199 a force for health-care labor in the Appalachian region. Aided by the 1974 extension of federal labor law protections to workers in for-profit hospitals, 1199 began to organize larger facilities in Kentucky and West Virginia. In 1975 the union won a vigorous campaign against strong management resistance at Highlands Regional Medical Center in Prestonsburg, Kentucky. Management efforts to break 1199 at Highlands in 1981 and 1999 were unsuccessful.

Following the Highlands Regional Campaign, 1199 won bitter campaigns at Cabell Huntington Hospital in Huntington (1977), at Fairmont General in Fairmont, West Virginia, and at King's Daughters Hospital in Ashland, Kentucky (1980), resulting in one thousand members by 1980 in West Virginia and Kentucky. In 1982, 1199 workers in those states merged with Ohio members to form the WV/KY/OH district. This partnership required overcoming racial and cultural barriers between rural Appalachian whites and urban blacks. Some hospital administrators in West Virginia and eastern Kentucky sought to exploit these differences by portraying 1199 as a "communist union" and a "nigger union" to white workers. In spite of such tactics, the tri-state organization thrived, with membership growing to six thousand by 1986. In 1989, 1199 merged with the Service Employees International Union, creating a national union of service workers that, as of 2001, had more than 1.5 million members, including about fourteen thousand in the WV/KY/OH district.

Several factors have contributed to the survival and vitality of 1199 in the face of escalating corporate and political animosity towards unionism. The union's reputation for militant strikes, innovative mobilizing tactics, and internal democracy attracted a regional staff of civil rights, student, and antiwar activists with experience in the movements of the 1960s and 1970s. These organizers conveyed the union's commitment to grassroots organizing to health-care workers in the district, where election campaigns and collective bargaining relied largely on strategies devised and implemented by the workers themselves. The health-care union's decentralized structure minimized the bureaucratic "business unionism" practiced by the most powerful industrial unions, a top-down approach that often weakened rank-and-file support and left many unions vulnerable to the union-resistance strategies refined by corporations in the 1980s and 1990s. Philosophical commitment to rank-and-file participation in 1199 is augmented by practical training in media relations and the minutiae of contract oversight.

In recent years, most of the nation's industrial unions, wounded by the outsourcing of production and the out-migration of American-based multinationals, have begun to rediscover the militant tactics and community outreach strategies that 1199 has practiced since its beginning.

See also: APPALACHIAN HEALTH PROVIDERS (HEALTH); MINERS MEMORIAL HOSPITAL ASSOCIATION (HEALTH).

—John C. Hennen, *Morehead State University*

Leon Fink and Brian Greenberg, *Upheaval in the Quiet Zone: A History of Hospital Workers' Union 1199* (1989); John C. Hennen, "Putting the 'You' in Union: Danie Joe Stewart and the 1974–1975 Highlands Regional Campaign," *Journal of Appalachian Studies* (Fall 1999); Jill Kreisky, ed., *Working Together to Revitalize Labor in Our Communities* (1998).

Slave Labor

The first slaves came into southern Appalachia almost as early as the first white settlers. By 1860, almost every county in the mountain South had an enslaved populace, although proportionately their numbers were well below those in most other parts of the South due to the fact that the southern highlands did not lend themselves to large-scale plantation agriculture. In this region of small farms and farmers of modest means, agriculture alone could not support slave labor on a large scale. The presence of slaves—and the means of their utilization—points to an antebellum Appalachian economy more varied and complex than has often been recognized.

The vast majority of Appalachian slaves were part of modest holdings—fewer than five slaves—owned by small landholders who worked with their families and a few bondsmen or -women in fields or households. On these farms, slaves' duties often extended beyond fieldwork. They tended livestock, cleared timber, operated sawmills and gristmills, and engaged in various forms of home manufacture, from making shoes to weaving cloth. Census samplings of slaveholdings in both the North Carolina and Kentucky mountains show a disproportionate number of women and children owned by small farmers, suggesting that domestic and household duties were more of a priority than farmwork for many mountain families.

Far more significant for the region economically were those slaveholdings of masters engaged in nonagricultural enterprises. Recent studies of western North Carolina, southwest Virginia, and eastern Kentucky show that most slave owners were merchants or professional men who often used the capital they earned to purchase larger numbers of slaves. While they were landholders and sometimes used their slaves for farm labor, they also employed them in less traditional ways. Small-scale manufacturing, mercantile trade and transport, and, during the summer season, hotels and resorts all provided common outlets for slave labor. The diversity of this labor force led some outside observers to conclude that the "peculiar institution" in the highlands provided a more flexible, less restrictive range of activities that allowed slaves more freedom of movement and opportunities for advancement than was true of those tied to plantation systems in the lowland South.

A major part of this flexibility came from the hiring out of slaves. This provided cash income—on annual, monthly, or weekly bases—to slave owners who had more slaves than they could fully employ and allowed non-slaveholding whites access to slave labor on terms they could afford. Railroad construction in several areas of Appalachia in the late antebellum period provided an especially lucrative opportunity for owners to hire their slaves out to companies seeking local construction workers. The correlation between railroads and slavery was significant. The construction of the Virginia and Tennessee Railroad through southwestern Virginia in the mid-1850s was largely completed by slaves rented on an annual basis from local masters. By the end of the decade, North Carolina highlanders finally saw their hopes of a railroad materialize; with it came a flurry of slave trading and hiring negotiated between large owners from Morganton to Asheville and the Western North Carolina Railroad. So great was the anticipated demand for slaves that Asheville businessmen advertised statewide for "100 to 500 Likely Negroes Wanted" in 1859 and 1860.

Slave labor played an even more integral part in the various mining operations undertaken in antebellum Appalachia. The first gold rush in the region, in Burke and Rutherford Counties in North Carolina, brought hundreds of slaves into the area in the late 1820s, either with their masters or hired out from sources elsewhere in the state or beyond. The discovery of gold in the mountains of northern Georgia launched a much greater rush in 1829, with slaves a major part of the labor force brought into Auraria and Dahlonega either to pan for gold in creeks and streams or to undertake the far more risky work of digging in poorly supported tunnels or shafts. Many slaves purchased their freedom with gold they found on their own time or with negotiated percentages of what they mined for their masters.

Slaves were vital to coal-, iron-, copper-, and salt-mining operations as well, making up nearly half of the labor force in coal-mining operations in eastern Virginia as early as the mid-eighteenth century. More were brought west nearly a century later when coal deposits in the western mountains began to be mined. Most of the slaves engaged in underground coal mining in the Kanawha Valley were hired annually or seasonally from plantation areas to the east or purchased by coal companies. Coal mining was still in its infancy in northeastern Alabama before the Civil War, but the few companies already underway in the 1840s and 1850s also depended in large part on slave labor. The dangers of underground mining and the primitive hand-digging techniques still practiced in the mines made many slave owners reluctant to risk hiring their slaves out to highland mining companies. Therefore, slaves never made up a majority of the labor force in either western Virginia or Alabama, where they usually worked side by side with free workers, white and black.

Salt manufacturing, even more than coal, relied heavily on slave labor. In Kanawha County, (West) Virginia, alone, the slave population swelled to more than three thousand by 1850, with the saltworks employing more than half of that number. Slaves were employed in all parts of the process—drilling wells, tending furnaces, operating steam engines and pumps, building barrels, mining coal, and other tasks, both skilled and unskilled. A recent study of Clay County, Kentucky, indicates that slaves were just as integral to salt manufacturing there. But unlike the Kanawha operations, salt firms in Clay County split their slaves' time between salt making and farming. Slaves not only raised much of the food for the local labor force, but they also tended and slaughtered livestock, much of which was marketed for additional income.

Ironworks throughout Appalachia also employed slaves. The most extensive study of an individual operation, Charles Dew's book on Buffalo Forge in Rockbridge County, Virginia, focuses on the substantial slave community built up by owner William Weaver from the 1810s to the 1860s. By the beginning of the Civil War, he owned more than seventy slaves and leased nearly as many. Except for supervisory positions, they performed all functions of the furnace work at

Buffalo Forge and other nearby enterprises—as miners, ore pounders, fillers, and other technical positions within the blasting operation, as well as peripheral jobs as carpenters, blacksmiths, timber cutters, teamsters, and cooks. One slave, Sam Williams, stood out among Weaver's workers and rose to the position of master refiner, entrusted with the crucial task of refining the pig iron. Slaves also maintained Weaver's extensive farming operations in the Valley of Virginia.

In short, the variety of economic activity, both agricultural and industrial—from mining to railroad construction—made slavery viable and profitable in antebellum Appalachia. While the numbers of slaves in the region remained far fewer than in other areas, owners and entrepreneurs found they could profitably utilize their labor, both in the short and long term, in more diverse and flexible ways than did plantation owners of the lowland South.

See also: AFRICAN AMERICAN INDUSTRIAL MIGRATION (SETTLEMENT AND MIGRATION); SALT (BUSINESS, INDUSTRY, AND TECHNOLOGY); SLAVERY AND ABOLITION (GOVERNMENT).

—John C. Inscoe, *University of Georgia*

Charles B. Dew, *Bond of Iron: Master and Slave at Buffalo Forge* (1994); John C. Inscoe, ed., *Appalachians and Race: The Mountain South from Slavery to Segregation* (2001); William H. Turner and Edward J. Cabbell, eds., *Blacks in Appalachia* (1985).

Steel Mill Workers

See Iron and Steel Mill Workers

Strip Mine Workers

Rather than tunneling beneath the earth, strip miners dig coal directly from the land's surface. This mining method has transformed the type of work performed by mine workers and has brought the coal industry under increasing attacks from both environmentalists and mountain residents.

Strip mining, or surface mining, became possible with the advent of the steam shovel in the 1920s. However, it was not a significant source of coal until World War II. During the war years, coal was in great demand. Additionally, since the economy had shifted to a wartime mode, much domestic construction was halted. Idled construction companies found they could use their equipment to mine coal, thereby filling a supply niche and keeping their capital investments productive. Surface mining, which had produced a mere 1.5 percent of the nation's coal in 1920, accounted for roughly one-fifth of U.S. coal production by 1945.

At first, the United Mine Workers of America, which represented underground miners, attempted to organize the coal strippers. However, underground miners were angered when they discovered that strip workers were paid more than they per ton. Aboveground working conditions were better, the mining was safer and easier, and workers needed less training. Resentment of these differences led some within the United Mine Workers initially to oppose strip mining.

Other forces were also at work. Greater productivity at surface mines contributed to overproduction, threatening the jobs of underground miners. Plus, the same productivity that allowed strip operators to pay higher wages also helped them resist unionization more effectively than conventional mining companies.

In the 1960s and 1970s, a new generation of stripping equipment was introduced into the rugged terrain of Appalachia. Strip mining became a major form of coal extraction as operators started to strip on a large scale, especially in eastern Kentucky. The resulting environmental and labor problems brought growing opposition to the practice, which was still largely unregulated. Some environmental groups sought to ban strip mining altogether. Tensions over this movement eased somewhat in the 1970s, when United Mine Workers President Arnold Miller, whom many expected to oppose surface mining, instead led the union to support strip-mine reclamation laws. As Miller had probably anticipated, many of the reclamation jobs went to unemployed coal miners.

In the late 1990s, opposition emerged to a technique of surface mining called mountaintop removal. This form of mining, which falls into a loophole in reclamation laws, scalps entire hilltops to uncover coal seams. Leftover rubble is dumped into hollows, burying streams beneath enormous piles of rock and debris. This practice is employed in Virginia and Kentucky and is most widespread in the low-sulfur coalfields of southern West Virginia. By 1998, nearly a third of West Virginia's coal came from the removal of mountain and ridge tops by huge mining complexes.

A 1999 ruling by U.S. District Judge Charles H. Haden II limited the size of streams that mountaintop-removal operations could bury with valley fills. United Mine Workers President Cecil Roberts declared that the ruling would end all coal mining, and rank-and-file mine workers repeatedly protested outside the Charleston, West Virginia, federal courthouse.

Strip mining remains much different from digging coal underground. Strip mine workers are more like construction equipment operators, running huge bulldozers and shovels. Strip mining's much greater productivity played a major role in the continuing downward spiral in coal employment at the end of the twentieth century, as large surface mines yielded twice as much coal as all other types of mines in West Virginia combined.

See also: ANTHRACITE COAL INDUSTRY (BUSINESS, INDUSTRY, AND TECHNOLOGY); BITUMINOUS COAL INDUSTRY (BUSINESS, INDUSTRY, AND TECHNOLOGY); COAL MINING (ENVIRONMENT).

—Ken Ward Jr., *Charleston Gazette*

Harry M. Caudill, *My Land Is Dying* (1971) and *Night Comes to the Cumberlands: A Biography of a Depressed Area* (1963); Maier B. Fox, *United We Stand: The United Mine Workers of America, 1890–1990* (1990); U.S. Office of Surface Mining, *Report to Congress: Mountaintop Removal* (1999).

Tally War

The "Tally War" of April 14, 1906, was a confrontation within the community of North Cove, North Carolina, between local lawmen and Italian immigrant railroad construction laborers, pejoratively called "tallies" by locals. When laborers threatened to cease work until paid, their superintendent asked the McDowell County sheriff for assistance. Lawmen surrounded their camp, exchanged gunfire with the immigrants, and killed two laborers. The construction company was found guilty of peonage and fined minimally.

In 1905 Virginia businessman George Lafayette Carter spearheaded a plan to connect the coal mines of western Virginia with the Carolinas' Piedmont region. The South and Western Railroad Company contracted with the Carolina Construction Company to oversee the project. More than four thousand workers, including hundreds of Italian immigrants recruited by padrones in New York City, settled in camps along the route known as "the loops." North Cove residents looked down on the dark-skinned Italian immigrants, in part because they worked hard and willingly with African Americans. The immigrants were the subject of amusement and wonder. Locals shared stories of the Italians' broken English, bagpipes, bright clothes, and crusty bread.

Outsiders to North Cove, however, told darker stories of cultural hostility and violence. Oral accounts include tales about murders of "foreigners," about bodies of African American and Italian victims thrown into railroad fills, about locals' revenge on immigrant suitors of country girls, and about Anglo workers' execution of their own immigrant cook. Muriel Earley Sheppard, who moved to North Carolina from New York in 1928, attempted to give an objective version of such accounts in her book *Cabins in the Laurel* (1935), but the stories in it are largely undocumented or attributed to "Uncle Rube" Mosely, whose local color narratives are less than accurate. Little evidence exists to substantiate accounts of violent behavior between workers and locals or among railroad workers themselves. Such stories seem to have been fabricated long after the railroad was completed to serve as justification for local lawmen's violence against Italian immigrants during the labor dispute.

Local, regional, and railroad histories offer little information regarding the Tally War in North Cove, although oral narratives about the conflict are still told by present-day residents. Many of the Italian workers probably moved to coal-mining camps in Virginia. No connection has been maintained between their descendants and the families of North Cove.

See also: ITALIANS (RACE, ETHNICITY, AND IDENTITY).

—Joyce Compton Brown and Les M. Brown, *Gardner-Webb University*

Muriel Earley Sheppard, *Cabins in the Laurel* (1935); Rudolph J. Vecoli, "The Italian Immigrants in the United States Labor Movement from 1880 to 1929," in *Gli Italiani Fuori D'Italia*, ed. Bruno Bezza (1983); Margaret Ripley Wolfe, "Aliens in Appalachia: The Construction of the Clinchfield Railroad and the Italian Experience," in *Appalachia: Family Traditions in Transition*, ed. Emmett M. Essin III (1975).

Tannery Workers

Just as they looked to forests for a variety of building materials, early Appalachian settlers found it necessary to convert animal hides into leather for many uses. Consequently, tanneries became fixtures of scattered frontier communities throughout the region.

Using hides procured from local hunters and farmers, tanners scraped, cleaned, soaked, tanned, and pounded skins until they were chemically transformed and pliable enough to be made into shoes, boots, harnesses, and saddles. As the demand for leather increased along with the population throughout the nineteenth century, tanneries consolidated and expanded. The 6,686 tanneries that existed across the nation in 1850 had shrunk to 1,306 by 1900, but their capital value rose from $23 million to $174 million, and the number of employees increased from 26,000 to 55,000. By the 1930s, 40 to 50 tanning-related operations existed in the southern Appalachian region. The Catawba Tannery, built in Old Fort, North Carolina, in 1903, claimed to be the largest tannery in the world, processing 400 hides a day. The Virginia Oak Tannery in Luray, Virginia, which had operated under various names since 1840, was one of the 25 largest tanneries in the United States at 1,800 hides a day when it ceased tanning in 1980.

Tannery work was hard, malodorous, and increasingly dangerous as the industry adopted new technologies. Workers had to protect their limbs from the mechanical grinders that pulverized the tree bark used to make tanning agents, negotiate mazes of pipes carrying steam and long rows of vats of boiling bark leachate, and avoid the splashing of caustic solutions used to de-hair or bleach the hides. Yet the worst job was usually considered to be removing fat and flesh from raw hides by hand, a task that made "to smell like a tannery" an all too evocative description.

Tanneries' reliance upon tree bark for tannic acid made bark cutting and hauling important sources of seasonal employment and cash for farmers. For about six weeks in April and May when the tree sap began to flow and the bark was most pliable, men cut trees and peeled off the bark. The major species harvested were hemlocks in northern Appalachia and chestnut oaks in the South. The trunk was usually left in the forest to rot.

As tanneries grew larger, they required thousands of tons of bark every year, and spring bark-peeling camps of 50 or more men were common. Once rails and improved roads were available, large "ooze plants" were constructed to produce concentrated tannic acid for tanneries far from the region. As desirable bark became scarce, whole American chestnut trees were used for acid production. These were often salvaged after having died from the blight that struck in the early 1900s and eventually wiped out the species. By about 1950, tanneries had switched to chemically produced inorganic chromium for tanning, which ended the dependence on rural products and labor that once made them an important Appalachian industry.

See also: TANNING (BUSINESS, INDUSTRY, AND TECHNOLOGY).

—Chris Bolgiano, *James Madison University*

Lucius F. Ellsworth, *Craft to National Industry in the Nineteenth Century: A Case Study of the Transformation of the New York State Tanning Industry* (1975); E. H. Frothingham, *Timber Growing and Logging Practice in the Southern Appalachian Region* (1931); Peter Welsh, *Tanning in the United States to 1850: A Brief History* (1964).

Tennessee Industrial Renewal Network

The Tennessee Industrial Renewal Network is a coalition of labor, religious, and community groups as well as individuals in pursuit of economic justice. The Knoxville-based organization, formed in the summer of 1989, initially responded to the widespread industrial closings that occurred in Tennessee throughout the late 1980s. Originally focused on the social effects that closings of apparel, automotive, electronic, and textile factories had on the people of Tennessee, the organization assisted workers in part by bringing legal action, including one of the first actions ever filed under the Worker Adjustment and Retraining Notification Act of 1988. It also helped to organize financial and medical relief for displaced workers.

A worker exchange program began in 1991 with the exchange of female workers from Tennessee with female workers from the maquiladoras, or factories, of northern Mexico. The exchange program emerged as numerous factories moved from Tennessee in the late 1980s and early 1990s to other countries to reduce costs. As the years progressed, the Tennessee Industrial Renewal Network's vision expanded to include such issues as living wages, worker empowerment, and the local and global effects of the North American Free Trade Agreement (NAFTA), passed in 1993. The work around NAFTA stemmed from the concern of members regarding the increased transfer of jobs to other nations. The group's work concerning the global economy now includes public forums, workshops, and community organizing.

In 1997 the Tennessee Industrial Renewal Network, in conjunction with other local community groups and leaders, organized the Economic Democracy Project to target the wage gap as a main concern for workers and the community at large. This work led to the Knoxville Living Wage Campaign in 1999. A living wage is one that can sustain a family of four above the poverty level in a given community. A study conducted using economic data for Knoxville concluded that an hourly wage of $9.50 with benefits or $11.00 without benefits was necessary to sustain a family of four in the area. Hundreds of supporters from the Knoxville community came before the city council to support a city ordinance that would require all city employees as well as employees of contractors with the city and recipients of subsidies to be paid a living wage. Although the issue came to the forefront of several political races in the city, the living wage ordinance still had not passed several years after the campaign began. However, the advances of the Knoxville Living Wage Campaign led to the development of living wage campaigns in other Tennessee communities, including Nashville.

See also: NORTH AMERICAN FREE TRADE AGREEMENT.

—Carrie Ann Ancell, *University of New Mexico*

Barbara Ellen Smith, ed., *Neither Separate nor Equal: Women, Race, and Class in the South* (1999); Tennessee Industrial Renewal Network, *Responding to the Plant Closings in Tennessee* (1989); U.S. Department of Education, *School Community Renewal: A Cooperative Revitalization Strategy for Rural Schools, Students, and Communities: Full-Scale Version of Rural Renewal Strategies for Network Development* (1999).

Textile Workers

Textile workers have been employed in the manufacture of cotton yarn and thread, as well as in the manufacture of yarn, thread, and staple fiber in the rayon and synthetics industries, for many decades in southern Appalachia. Cotton textiles provided employment for thousands of Appalachian migrants to the Piedmont region from 1890 to 1960; rayon and synthetics plants in the Great Valley of Virginia, the Blue Ridge, and West Virginia likewise employed thousands from the 1920s through the 1960s, often in huge factories. From 1960 through 2000, the number of cotton, rayon, and synthetics workers declined drastically, as many textile companies moved production facilities to the Pacific Rim and Latin America.

Even during the antebellum period, when agricultural work predominated in Appalachia, small wool and cotton establishments in North Carolina, Georgia, Alabama, Virginia, and Tennessee employed laborers. By 1860, 299 textile manufacturers in Appalachian counties engaged in a variety of operations, carding wool, making staves and shooks for women's underwear, and producing finished cloth and clothing. According to the 1860 manufactures census, two-thirds

A female worker operates a carding machine at American Bemberg Corporation, a rayon factory in Elizabethton, Tennessee, 1952. Most rayon and synthetic yarn companies started in Appalachia during the first half of the twentieth century were tied to foreign cartels, dominated largely by the Big Three of Courtaulds (England), Snia Viscoa (Italy), and Glanzstoff (Germany).

of the firms were small artisan shops, while the remaining third employed fourteen or more workers. Twenty-two cotton mills in the region employed an average of thirty-one laborers, while a few large mills averaged seventy-one workers. Among the counties that boasted cotton mills were Coosa, Alabama; Chatooga, Georgia; Frederick, Maryland; and Washington, Tennessee.

After the Civil War, parts of the South turned to industry in order to bolster an economy severely weakened by war and by the decline in agricultural prices. The Piedmont South, in particular, heeded the call to industrialization. Beginning in the 1880s, local entrepreneurs raised the necessary capital to build mills, which attracted migrants from east Tennessee and western North Carolina. During the 1890s, growth, as measured by number of spindles, accelerated throughout the South, but especially so in the Piedmont. The period from 1890 to 1920 was one of continued growth in both number of mills built and spindles put into operation, as companies from the Northeast moved south to be closer to raw materials and cheaper, nonunion labor. Among the early mills were Crown Cotton in Dalton, Georgia (1885), Henrietta Mills in Rutherford County, North Carolina (1887), and Pearl Cotton Mill in Durham, North Carolina (1893). While many mills constructed mill villages for their workers, not all did so. Mills with villages (Crown Cotton in Dalton; Loray Mills in Gastonia, North Carolina) had housing, stores, and churches for the workers.

Nineteenth-century workers generally came to the mills from the nearby countryside, most often from failed farms of the upcountry. Workers tended to be younger than twenty-five years of age, many of them females who worked in the winding, spinning, and weaving rooms of the mills. Child labor was fairly common, with individuals as young as ten employed in the mills. Until the breakdown of segregation in the 1960s, workers in production jobs in cotton mills were white. In mills where blacks did work, such as Dan River at Danville, Virginia, males labored in the factory yard moving bales of cotton and loading boxcars and wagons with finished goods. Some mills also employed African American men to work in the picking and dye rooms or as sweepers and scourers, but black women were excluded except as occasional washing-room cleaners.

At the start of the twentieth century, cotton prices increased, and many of the Piedmont's industrial workers returned to their farms. The ensuing labor shortage convinced mill owners to seek white workers in the agriculturally depressed Appalachian Mountains. Many mills sent agents into mountain communities to lure residents with promises of a comfortable life in the mill villages. Labor shortages also convinced mill owners to institute paternalistic corporate welfare programs. Dan River and Crown became famous for programs that included domestic science classes for women and baseball teams for men. A number of mills also increased wages, but southern companies still paid poorly, often 50 percent less than their northern counterparts.

World War I proved a boon for cotton textile workers throughout the South: as demand for cotton products rose, so did the workers' wages. During and immediately after the war, the United Textile Workers made inroads in organizing mills in the Piedmont, particularly in the summer of 1919, when owners, facing declining demand, began to cut wages and hours. Mills in Charlotte, Kannapolis, Concord, Gastonia, and other North Carolina towns and cities formed United Textile locals. The success of the locals was short-lived, however. As the textile depression hit the South in 1920, many owners responded with wage and hour cutbacks, layoffs, and increases in employee workloads with little or no additional pay. Unsuccessful strikes in 1921 at Highland Park Mills in Charlotte, Cannon Mills in Concord and Kannapolis, and at other factories throughout the Piedmont soured workers on the United Textile Workers.

While cotton suffered during the 1920s, rayon and synthetic yarn production prospered. Rayon and synthetic yarn manufacture was under the control of foreign cartels, dominated largely by the Big Three of Courtaulds (England), Snia Viscosa (Italy), and Glanzstoff (Germany). Each of these corporations had ties to other firms, and each either had American subsidiaries or was tied to companies with American subsidiaries. The first rayon plant constructed in the Appalachians, and in the South, was at Roanoke, Virginia, in 1917 by the Viscose Company (soon to be known as American Viscose Company), the American subsidiary of Courtaulds. The Roanoke facility was a huge plant that employed six thousand workers making viscose rayon. By 1929, American Viscose also had large plants in Parkersburg and Nitro, West Virginia. Other rayon factories were built in Rome, Georgia (in 1929 by American Chatillon); Asheville, North Carolina (in 1929 by Enka, a Dutch-German company); and Elizabethton, Tennessee (in 1926 by American Bemberg and in 1928 by American Glanzstoff, a sister company). Celanese Corporation of America in the early 1920s completed a large acetate plant near Cumberland, Maryland. By 1930, rayon and acetate manufacture in the United States was concentrated in the South, with many of the largest plants located in the southern Appalachian region. The Appalachian region particularly attracted foreign manufacturers who needed large quantities of pure water and wanted white laborers who would work for relatively cheap wages. Mill owners also harbored a conviction that Appalachian workers were unlikely to join labor unions.

By the end of the 1920s, thousands of textile mill workers throughout the South, dissatisfied with low wages, petty workplace regulations, and increased hours without increased pay, began staging strikes. The first took place in Elizabethton, as approximately thirty-two hundred rayon plant workers walked out, first in March 1929 and again in April. Unorganized workers led the initial actions in March, but within a few days the United Textile Workers had sent organizers to Tennessee to lead the strike. A settlement in May ended the walkout, but dissatisfaction with the agreement led to lingering resentment and sporadic strike activity through March 1930. Other strikes of note took place throughout the Carolinas and also involved thousands of workers. Charlotte, Bessemer City, Pineville, Forest City, and Lexington, North Carolina, all experienced strikes, as did Honea Path, Ware Shoals, and Rock Hill, South Carolina. Millhands at the Loray Mills in Gastonia, North Carolina, walked out on April 1, 1930, under the leadership of the Communist National Textile Workers Union. Protesting longer hours, low pay, and a wage structure that discriminated against women and children, the Loray strikers stayed out for seven months, but they could not prevail over the combined power of capital, community, and state. In Marion, North Carolina, the United Textile Workers led employees at the Clinchfield Mill in a July 1930 strike, but as in Gastonia, they won few concessions from the mill owners.

That same year, the United Textile Workers launched its Southern Campaign to organize the mill workers of the region. The effort concentrated on cotton workers, largely ignoring the thousands of rayon and synthetics workers of the Appalachian region. In 1930 the campaign pinned its hopes on organizing the large Dan River and Riverside cotton mills in Danville, Virginia. Models for company welfarism and industrial democracy, Dan River and Riverside had nonetheless cut wages and increased hours. In September, the United Textile Workers local called a strike that—since the international union had neither the resources nor the willpower to support a prolonged struggle—had little chance to succeed. United Textile Vice-President Francis Gorman did not declare the strike over until January 29, 1931, but for all practical purposes the strike had ended in failure for the union in late November, when Dan River officially reopened the mills, prompting mass picketing by strikers and the calling of state militia to Danville. In the face of military power and an almost empty union treasury, approximately two thousand workers, both union and unorganized, returned to the mills. The Danville defeat signaled the end of United Textile's ill-fated Southern Campaign.

The Great Depression hit textiles hard, causing layoffs, wage cuts, and hour reductions in the cotton, rayon, and synthetics industries. Even though rayon and synthetics markets experienced peaks and valleys, many firms were able to remain profitable during the depression decade. Cotton fared less well. With the passage of the National Industrial Recovery Act in 1933, cotton and rayon came under the National Recovery Administration's code authority. Cotton was governed by one set of codes, while rayon and synthetics were governed by another.

Section 7(a) of the National Industrial Recovery Act provided workers with the right to bargain collectively, but textile operators, especially in cotton, became notorious for ignoring it. Incensed by the recalcitrance of the operators and with the failure of the National Recovery Administration's cotton board to support workers' demands, the United Textile Workers called a general strike to begin on September 1, 1934. In the South, including the Piedmont, thousands of cotton mill workers walked out, but the rayon and synthetics workers of the Appalachian region remained at work, as the United Textile Workers did not sanction a walkout for non-cotton workers. The textile union failed to recognize the depth of antiunion sentiment among southern textile operators and the immense resources it would take for the union to wait out the owners. A number of southern governors, among them North Carolina's J. C. B. Ehringhaus, South Carolina's Ibra Blackwood, and Georgia's Eugene Talmadge, called out the National Guard to control striking workers and protect scabs and strikebreakers. Facing insurmountable odds, the strike in the South ended in defeat within a month.

By the time the insurgent Committee for Industrial Organizations, precursor to the Congress of Industrial Organizations, was formed in 1935, the United Textile Workers was a weak union with little hold in the South. Two years later, at the beginning of its campaign to organize textile workers, the Committee for Industrial Organizations formed the Textile Workers Organizing Committee. Modeled after the successful Steel Workers Organizing Committee, the Textile Workers Organizing Committee focused on unionizing cotton mill workers of the South. It took over all locals of the United Textile Workers, including the relatively small number in the South. The slumbering local of the Elizabethton rayon plants, for instance, became Local 100 of the Textile Workers Organizing Committee. Conflict among old officials and the new group's leaders led to a rechartering of the United Textile Workers in 1939; in response, the Textile Workers Organizing Committee became the Textile Workers Union of America. For the next twenty-five years, the United Textile Workers and the Textile Workers Organizing Committee engaged in bitter internecine warfare over textile locals. The Textile Workers Union of America paid close attention to the rayon and synthetics factories by organizing the huge Celanese plant at Cumberland, Maryland, as well as rayon factories throughout the region. The Elizabethton workers remained with the Textile Workers Union until 1949, when they reaffiliated with the United Textile Workers. The former group also scored a major success in 1942, when it organized the thirteen thousand workers of the Dan River and Riverside mills.

Because of the organizing efforts of the Textile Workers Union and the production needs of World War II, Appalachian textile workers garnered higher wages and improved working conditions. But the 1950s textile recession saw many workers migrate from Appalachia to the industrial Midwest in search of jobs. As polyester cut into rayon markets and sent cotton into decline, Operation Dixie, the Textile Workers Union's postwar organizing campaign, ended with only limited success.

Throughout the South, the textile industry changed drastically in the 1960s. Black workers, who had first entered the mills in large numbers in the 1940s and 1950s, increased their presence in the 1960s. In an effort to cut labor costs, a variety of new industries moved from the unionized North to the nonunionized South. As a result, semi- and unskilled white labor moved out of the low-paying textile industry to such higher-paying industries as chemicals and electronics. Textile manufacturers were thus forced to hire those it had previously scorned. Some Appalachian textile towns with low black populations (Elizabethton and Morristown, Tennessee) were relatively unaffected by the textile labor shortage, but larger towns and cities (Roanoke, Virginia, and Parkersburg, West Virginia) with more significant minority populations saw black workers in textile factories for the first time. In the 1970s and 1980s, the dramatic rise of low-wage competition from Latin America and the Pacific Rim induced manufacturers of cotton, rayon, and synthetic yarns to leave Appalachia and other parts of the South. Among those closing their doors were American Bemberg in Elizabethton; Celanese in Rome and Crown Cotton Mill in Dalton, Georgia; and Ameri-can Celanese in Cumberland, Maryland. Some factories, including the Celanese plant in Narrows, Virginia, and the Dan River plant in Danville, remained in production; others were taken over by conglomerates such as Germany's Hoechst.

Textile unions inevitably felt the impact. In November 1995, the United Textile Workers became a council of the United Food and Commercial Workers, and the Textile Workers Union of America merged with the Amalgamated Clothing Workers in 1976 to become the Amalgamated Clothing and Textile Workers Union (which in turn merged with the International Ladies' Garment Workers' Union to form the Union of Needletrades, Industrial, and Textile Workers).

Although U.S. textile production remains concentrated in the Southeast, the industry is no longer the economic force that it was for nearly a century. Due to corporate restructuring and market trends of the late twentieth century, Appalachia suffered the permanent loss of thousands of jobs.

See also: SYNTHETIC FIBERS INDUSTRY (BUSINESS, INDUSTRY, AND TECHNOLOGY); WOMEN TEXTILE WORKERS.

—Marie Tedesco, *East Tennessee State University*

Janet Irons, *Testing the New Deal: The General Textile Strike of 1934 in the American South* (2000); Jeffrey Leiter, Michael Schulman, and Rhonda Zingraff, eds., *Hanging by a Thread: Social Change in Southern Textiles* (1991); Timothy Minchin, *What Do We Need a Union For? The TWUA in the South, 1945–1955* (1997).

Timber and Lumber Workers

Between 1890 and 1920, lumber barons bought and cut down huge tracts of Appalachian timber, devastating mountain forests in one of the biggest timber booms in history. For mountain residents, this boom meant the loss of valuable woodland and the coming of the first major form of nonfarm work.

Forests had always played a central role in the lives of mountaineers. Antebellum farmers cut timber to clear fields and to construct buildings, fences, furniture, and tools. After the Civil War, many farm families occasionally cut timber and sold it to local sawmills for extra cash. Timbering continued to be done by families rather than by logging crews.

Crew and team working at a log landing in Tucker County, West Virginia, 1903. At the end of the nineteenth century, large companies acquired huge tracts of timberland in Appalachia, erected gigantic processing mills, and hired thousands of workers to cut, transport, and process timber into lumber. Corporate control rapidly evolved alongside the construction of railroads between the 1880s and 1920 as companies bought up land and timber and secured future rights to subsurface mineral, oil, gas, and coal deposits.

By the late 1880s, as timber resources in the Northeast and Great Lakes states neared depletion, lumber barons turned to the Appalachians. Choice trees in easily accessible areas along rivers and streams were cut first. Completion of railroads brought larger companies that bought up huge tracts of forests and introduced new efficiency to logging. By 1890, southern Appalachia accounted for nearly a third of the hardwood cut in the United States. In the following decade, railroads pushed branch lines deep into the mountains, enabling lumber companies to establish their own mills close to the source of the timber supply. Logging railroads were connected to the branch lines, providing access to valuable trees in remote hollows.

Even with railroads and other technological innovations such as mechanized saws, labor remained the vital ingredient for logging the backcountry. Large crews were needed to lay rail tracks into the mountains. A large proportion of the unskilled track-laying workforce was made up of Italian immigrants, but construction gangs, which were segregated by race and ethnicity, also included African Americans, Germans, and others.

After rail lines were completed, "improvement" crews built temporary camps for the loggers, or "wood hicks." Typical camps included a bunkhouse that slept fifty to one hundred woodsmen, offices for the camp boss and the cook, a blacksmith shop, and a saw filer's shop. The buildings and often the furniture were rough-hewn from the trees on the site.

During the early years of the timber boom, skilled and experienced workers were in short supply. Companies imported men from northern states where timber supplies were dwindling. A large labor recruiting drive brought farmers out of their fields and into the timber industry, first for seasonal work and then as full-time employees. Loggers enjoyed the freedom to choose where they worked and consequently moved from camp to camp, making their way from one job to another either by foot or on the cars of log railroads. Life in the camps was rough, and the work was dangerous. Workers risked death or injury from falling limbs, rolling logs, and wrecked trains. Men worked six days a week, regardless of the weather, for $1.50 to $3.00 per ten-hour day.

Jobs within a lumber camp were determined by the type of operation. A cutting crew in the spruce woods of West Virginia, for example, usually included six men: the chopper, or fitter, notched the tree in the direction he wanted it to fall; two sawyers, using a six-foot crosscut saw, cut on the opposite side above the notch made by the fitter; and then three knot bumpers trimmed the limbs off the fallen trees and threw the brush aside.

Cut logs were skidded by horse from the timber camps down to landings, where they were arranged for transportation to mills in the lumber camps. Later, steam skidders powered cables that hauled logs to landings. At the landings, logs were loaded onto railcars headed out of the mountains to lumber mills.

Although some small mills used circular-blade saws, most mills used band saws. These were toothed loops of steel that traveled around heavy stationary wheels driven by stream power at seven to nine thousand feet per minute. The mill sawyer was among the most important and best-paid workers. Controlling the position and cut, he was responsible for getting the best lumber from each log.

By 1919, the logging boom had begun to take its toll. The forests had run out of trees, and the hillsides were scalped and barren. Sparks from locomotives set brush and dead wood left by loggers on fire, furthering the environmental damage. Jobs disappeared, too, as the industry pulled out of Appalachia to head for its next round of clear-cutting in the Pacific Northwest.

In the late twentieth century, the timber industry's boom-bust cycle appeared ready to repeat itself. Across the region, proposals popped up for new "chip mills" to grind Appalachian hardwoods into chips, which were glued back together as particleboard for inexpensive construction. In West Virginia alone, the annual timber cut doubled between 1987 and 1994. The wood-products business was the only state manufacturing sector where employment increased in the 1980s.

Mostly, however, the industry's growth remained confined to timbering and cheaper manufactured goods. The best wood was still hauled out of the central Appalachians, to be made into furniture in North Carolina. The best jobs went with it.

Loggers continued to be poorly paid in a job that remained dangerous. In West Virginia in the late 1990s, loggers were paid about $260 per week, compared to the state average income of $430 per week. Nationally, loggers were twice as likely to die on the job as miners.

See also: HARRIS-TARKETT CORPORATION (BUSINESS, INDUSTRY, AND TECHNOLOGY); LUMBER INDUSTRY (BUSINESS, INDUSTRY, AND TECHNOLOGY).

—Ken Ward Jr., *Charleston Gazette*

Roy B. Clarkson, *Tumult on the Mountains: Lumbering in West Virginia, 1770–1920* (1964); Ronald D Eller, *Miners, Millhands, and Mountaineers: Industrialization of the Appalachian South, 1880–1930* (1982); Ronald L. Lewis, *Transforming the Appalachian Countryside: Railroads, Deforestation, and Social Change in West Virginia, 1880–1920* (1998).

Trumka, Richard

(1949–) Labor leader.

One of the most important labor leaders to emerge from Appalachia, Richard L. Trumka served as the fourteenth president of the United Mine Workers of America, holding the office from 1982 through 1995. He is credited with returning stability to what had once been a leading American union. In 1995 he was elected secretary-treasurer of the American Federation of Labor and Congress of Industrial Organizations (AFL-CIO), a labor association comprised of more than sixty American unions.

The son and grandson of coal miners, Trumka was born in 1949 in the southwestern Pennsylvania coal town of Nemacolin. In a departure from the traditional career path, he went on to college and then law school rather than entering the mines. While earning a bachelor of science degree from Pennsylvania State University and a law degree from Villanova University, Trumka spent his summers and term breaks working as a coal miner.

Upon graduation from law school in 1974, Trumka joined the legal staff of the United Mine Workers during the turbulent presidency of Arnold Miller. Miller, a reformer, was leading an effort to rid the union of corruption and restore the democratic practices that had atrophied under the leadership of John L. Lewis and W. A. "Tony" Boyle. In 1977 Trumka left the union's staff to work as a miner in Pennsylvania, in part to finish accumulating the five years of coal industry work experience required to run for district or international office in the organization. After completing the required service time, Trumka successfully ran for president of United Mine Workers District 4 in June 1981.

The following November, he announced that he would challenge the organization's president, Sam Church, in the 1982 election. Focusing on Church's handling of the 1981 contract talks, Trumka castigated the incumbent for providing weak leadership. For his part, Church characterized Trumka as a militant with leftist associations. The final tally gave Trumka 68 percent of the vote to Church's 32 percent and made him the youngest president of a major union in North America.

The seeds for his election had been sown by the earlier democratic reform movement, which had included Joseph A. "Jock" Yablonski's 1968 challenge to Boyle as well as Miller's tenure as the union's president. Without the reforms adopted after Yablonski's murder in December 1969, Trumka would have been unlikely to unseat a sitting union president.

When Trumka and his slate of officers were sworn into office in December 1982, they faced a coal industry in the midst of fundamental change. Between 1970 and 1980, the unionized share of industry production had fallen from 424 million to 365 million tons. Union membership, which had peaked in the Lewis era at more than 400,000 members, was down to 160,000 active miners.

Recognizing the dire state of the organization, Trumka's administration implemented changes both in the union's internal operation and its dealings with the coal industry. As a result, the union emerged from debt and increased its efficiency in providing services to its members. New industry-wide contracts were concluded in 1984 and 1988, in each case without strikes, and in 1987 Trumka was reelected without opposition.

During Trumka's second term, the United Mine Workers engaged in a pitched battle with Pittston Coal Company, one of the largest producers of coal in the United States, with facilities in southern Virginia and West Virginia. Pittston had chosen to bargain separately from the rest of the Bituminous Coal Operators' Association, the first time that an individual operator had done so since the 1950s. Talks broke down in April 1989, and 1,700 Pittston workers walked off the job.

Over the next nine months, the United Mine Workers abandoned traditional strike tactics and employed mass civil disobedience. Hundreds of men and women, strikers and their spouses, blocked coal trucks from entering or exiting the Pittston facilities by sitting down on nearby roads. Virginia State Troopers arrested them, hauling their limp bodies away one by one as the television cameras rolled. The union combined this approach with a number of other creative and innovative tactics, including adopting camouflage clothing as a symbol of support for the strike. In February 1990, more than nine months after the strike had begun, Pittston miners overwhelmingly voted to accept the favorable contract negotiated by their union. In evaluating the Pittston struggle, many observers credited the victory equally to Trumka's leadership and the resolve of the strikers.

Besides negotiating new contracts without strikes and winning favorable terms to conclude the Pittston battle, Trumka's administration made significant advancements in employee-employer cooperation and in the enhancement of miners' job security, pensions, and benefits.

In the spring of 1995, Trumka joined the New Voice coalition challenging the incumbent leadership of the AFL-CIO. John Sweeney of the Services Employees ran for president, and Trumka was the ticket's candidate for secretary-treasurer, the second most powerful position in the AFL-CIO, and, thus, in the entire American labor movement. Linda Chavez-Thompson of the Communications Workers joined the ticket as a candidate for executive vice-president (a position the ticket planned to create).

The slate's unprecedented challenge to the sitting officers of the AFL-CIO resulted from what many union leaders and members perceived as a lack of dynamic leadership at the top of the labor hierarchy. The New Voice ticket was elected at the October 1995 convention, and Trumka became the youngest secretary-treasurer in the history of the AFL-CIO.

The new leadership quickly engaged in a program to reform and reenergize the labor movement. Much of their effort focused on organizing and political action. Many observers of the labor movement credit the Sweeney/Trumka/Chavez-Thompson administration as the catalyst for a revitalization of American labor.

Once viewed as the heir apparent to Sweeney, Trumka was hurt by his association with the 1996 Teamsters election scandal, which resulted in a federal investigation into financial transactions that laundered Teamster funds through the AFL-CIO. At the turn of the century, Trumka was still touted as one of several possible candidates to assume the AFL-CIO presidency after Sweeney.

See also: ANTHRACITE COAL INDUSTRY (BUSINESS, INDUSTRY, AND TECHNOLOGY); BITUMINOUS COAL INDUSTRY (BUSINESS, INDUSTRY, AND TECHNOLOGY); UNITED MINE WORKERS OF AMERICA.

—Paul F. Clark, *Pennsylvania State University*

Paul F. Clark, "The Legacy of Democratic Reform: The Trumka Administration and the Challenges of the Eighties," in *The United Mine Workers of America: A Model of Industrial Solidarity?* ed. John H. M. Laslett (1996); Maier B. Fox, *United We Stand: The United Mine Workers of America, 1890–1990* (1990); Ray Tillman and Michael S. Cummings, eds., *The Transformation of U.S. Unions: Voices, Visions, and Strategies from the Grassroots* (1999).

United Mine Workers of America

Founded in 1890, the United Mine Workers of America remains an important leader in America's labor movement, even as the coal industry has changed and evolved. There are many reasons for the union's strength. One of the most important historically has been mining's status as a skilled occupation requiring knowledge of geology and engineering. This caused coal miners to be among the first workers in America to organize along industrial lines. Sometimes these efforts took lawful forms such as mutual benefit associations. In other instances, especially during times of recession, miners resorted to violent methods to win their demands.

For the most part, however, miners have striven to win better pay and a safe workplace through legal means by the creation of labor organizations. Early efforts in this direction were frustrated because a number of local organizations had been formed. The founding of the United Mine Workers of America was an attempt to get around the problem by merging the nation's two largest miners' groups, the National Progressive Union of Miners and Mine Laborers and the National Trade Assembly 135 of the Knights of Labor.

Given a formal charter by the American Federation of Labor (AFL), the United Mine Workers differed from most other AFL affiliates in several important respects. First, the United Mine Workers was an industrial union and sought to include anyone who worked in the coal industry regardless of occupation. This was in stark contrast to most other AFL unions, which organized solely on a craft basis and refused to admit unskilled workers. Second, due to an industrial union philosophy, the United Mine Workers included in its ranks racial minorities and recent immigrants, groups usually barred from most other AFL affiliates.

In this regard, the policies of the United Mine Workers arose from a combination of solidarity and practicality. Coal mining was the single most dangerous occupation in basic industry. In an environment where extreme danger was a constant reality, a sense of mutual dependence and respect was a natural condition. In addition, since blacks and immigrants were usually recruited as strikebreakers, it made sense for the union to recruit them, denying management its source of replacement workers. This policy was a qualified success. On the one hand, the union used negative stereotypes in its literature, particularly about blacks, when the need arose. However, the union achieved a high level of solidarity in southern states such as Alabama despite attempts to break it through race baiting. The union was also sensitive to its multinational character and regularly published articles in its newspaper, the *United Mine Workers Journal*, in Polish, Italian, Slovak, and Russian.

Despite these strengths, between 1890 and 1902 the United Mine Workers had to focus on survival and building a stable membership. The union came of age with its first successful strike: a 1902 action by Pennsylvania's anthracite miners against the Reading Railroad for recognition and an eight-hour day. Led by John Mitchell, the union worked hard to present itself to the public as a responsible organization with reasonable demands.

The arrogance of the Reading's chairman, George F. Baer, in asserting an employers' divine right gave the union a legitimacy with the public that other labor organizations lacked. Moreover, President Theodore Roosevelt intervened in the dispute, creating a commission that eventually decided in the union's favor. Although the organization did not win official recognition as a bargaining agent, it did win the eight-hour day and a pay increase for its members. The 1902 strike, in addition to being a victory for the union, marked a watershed for the federal government relative to labor relations. Prior to this, if the government intervened at all, it was to break a strike.

The union's success in 1902 began a period of steady growth that lasted until 1921. During this time, the union organized a host of mines stretching from Pennsylvania and Maryland to Iowa. Part of this region became known as the Central Competitive Field, which set the industry's wage and price standards. But the union's efforts to organize growing coalfields in southern Appalachia were unsuccessful and punctuated by extended periods of industrial warfare between miners and their bosses. Failure to sustain organizational strength in the Appalachian coalfields was the union's single greatest weakness during these years.

With America's entry into World War I, the union enjoyed new heights of protection and influence with the federal government. Like the rest of the mainstream labor movement, the United Mine Workers benefited from an alliance that had been created with the Democratic Party under President Woodrow Wilson. It was during this time that the union came under the control of John L. Lewis. Unlike most of his colleagues, Lewis rose through the American Federation of Labor and not the United Mine Workers. Nominated as running mate to the popular Frank Hayes in 1918, Lewis assumed the union's presidency when Hayes was incapacitated by alcoholism.

Eventually the twentieth century's most successful and influential labor leader, Lewis spent his early tenure as the union's president wrestling with controversy, infighting, and failure. Critics complained about his authoritarianism and apparent conservatism, going so far as to create a rival organization, the Reorganized United Mine Workers of America, in an effort to unseat him. Lewis responded by creating a personal dictatorship and breaking district union autonomy. Though Lewis won these fights, he paid a huge price for his victories. The union's membership dropped from more than four hundred thousand in 1919 to less than one hundred thousand by 1932.

However, not all of the decline can be attributed to Lewis, as coal demand fell sharply due to overproduction during the war years. In a bid to cut costs, coal operators across the country made a concerted effort to drive the union out of the coal industry. Lewis's recommendation was for the industry to reduce coal production as well as the workforce so there would be steady employment at a good wage for those who remained. What ultimately saved the United Mine Workers and Lewis's career was President Franklin Roosevelt's election in 1932. Under the rules of Roosevelt's National Industrial Recovery Act, workers were given the right to bargain collectively through representatives of their choosing. Prompted by a series of organizing and contract victories in the West Virginia coalfields, the union's ranks filled to more than four hundred thousand members again in less than a year. With the union rejuvenated, Lewis founded the Committee of Industrial Organizations, precursor to the Congress of Industrial Organizations (CIO), in 1935. Even though other unions were involved in its creation, the United Mine Workers provided the leadership and financing that enabled the new federation to achieve its goals.

The United Mine Workers was most powerful in the labor movement between 1933 and 1949, reaching the height of its influence in 1946, when Lewis succeeded in creating the union's Welfare and Retirement Fund. Organized as a private version of the Social Security Administration, the program was a pioneer in industrial benefits, particularly health-care delivery. After 1949 the union went into a long-term decline. This was due primarily to coal's displacement by natural gas and petroleum as America's primary energy source. Also, as the coal industry mechanized between 1950 and 1960, a trend Lewis supported, the number of Appalachian working miners was cut in half. These events alone put the organization in an increasingly marginal position relative to the rest of the labor movement. This position was reinforced by a lack of effective leadership after Lewis retired in 1960.

In all likelihood, Lewis's chosen successor was Thomas E. Kennedy. A staunch Lewis ally and former Pennsylvania lieutenant governor, Kennedy had been Lewis's vice-president since 1941. Within two years of taking office, however, Kennedy died and was succeeded by W. A. "Tony" Boyle. Generally corrupt and willing to use brute force to remain in power, Boyle was also incompetent. His downfall resulted from his ordering the murder of his rival, Joseph A. "Jock" Yablonski, in 1969. Boyle was convicted and imprisoned after losing the United Mine Workers presidency to insurgent Arnold Miller of the organization's reform movement.

Backed by a coalition of anti-Boyle groups, primarily the Miners for Democracy, Miller began his administration amidst high hopes. These hopes were dashed, however, for even though Miller was more democratic, he proved no more effective a leader than Boyle. Particularly notable was his failure to prevent the destruction of the organization's Welfare and Retirement Fund's health-care program in 1977 and 1978 despite increasing coal production royalties. The National Bituminous Coal Wage Agreement of 1978 turned out to be organized labor's first giveback contract and showed corporate America that such a thing was possible. Although Miller was eventually forced to retire due to ill health, his replacement, Sam Church, fared little better.

These years were marked by the struggle of the United Mine Workers to maintain its position in the coal industry. Membership declined during this period, and leaders proved incapable of organizing new mines, particularly the large strip mines being opened in the American West. This situation changed with Richard Trumka's election to the union's presidency in the early 1980s.

Under Trumka, the union's decline slowed, while its leadership sought to reach out to other organizations. Most notable were its decisions to affiliate with the AFL-CIO (Lewis had periodically taken the United Mine Workers out of the parent AFL and, after the 1955 merger with the CIO, out of the joined labor federation) and to organize workers outside of the coal industry. These policies have been continued by Trumka's successor, Cecil Roberts. Trumka himself became the AFL-CIO's secretary-treasurer in 1995. For its part, the United Mine Workers of America not only recovered members but also part of its former standing in both the coal industry and the labor movement. Far from going into eclipse, the organization continues to play an important role in social policy and labor relations.

See also: LEWIS, JOHN L.; MINE SAFETY AND HEALTH ADMINISTRATION; YABLONSKI, JOSEPH A.

—Richard P. Mulcahy, *University of Pittsburgh at Titusville*

Paul F. Clark, *The Miners' Fight for Democracy: Arnold Miller and the Reform of the United Mine Workers* (1981); Joseph E. Finley, *The Corrupt Kingdom: The Rise and Fall of the United Mine Workers* (1972); Maier B. Fox, *United We Stand: The United Mine Workers of America, 1890–1990* (1990).

Weirton Steel Strike

The Weirton Steel Strike of September and October 1933 was a pivotal moment in early New Deal labor relations. The walkout of ten thousand steelworkers at the Ohio (Steubenville) and West Virginia (Weirton and Clarksburg) plants of the Weirton Steel Company, a subsidiary of the National Steel Corporation, constituted a major test of the National Industrial Recovery Act and the National Labor Board. During and after the strike, National Steel Chairman Ernest T. Weir won a battle of wills with the National Labor Board and intensified management control in his mills. The Weirton strike was a crushing defeat for organized labor and contributed to the disappointment many industrial workers experienced at the weaknesses of the Roosevelt administration's early labor law.

The strike began with a minor dispute in the tin plate department at the company's flagship plant at Weirton on September 28, 1933. The incident expanded into a full-scale strike for union recognition by the newly formed Weirton local of the Amalgamated Association of Iron, Steel, and Tin Workers. The Weirton local emerged from a rank-and-file movement prompted by the National Industrial Recovery Act's Section 7(a), which protected industrial workers' organizing rights. The strikers and local leaders William J. Long and Mel Moore counted on the National Labor Board to force Weir to negotiate with their union. That was not to be, however. Weir and his allies in the so-called Little Steel companies welcomed a showdown with the labor board, confident that its authority to intervene in labor relations was unenforceable and unconstitutional. Compounding the Weirton local's troubles was the fact that the conservative national leadership of the Amalgamated, unsettled by the growing militancy of steel's rank and file, disavowed the strike.

Weir refused to negotiate with the union, claiming that his workers were well represented by the company's new Employee Representation Plan. Employee representation plans, or company-created and dominated unions, were used widely by steel management to maintain strict control over labor relations while providing the facade of collective bargaining as instructed by Section 7(a). Weir defied a National Labor Board order to allow a board-supervised representation election at his plants and was later vindicated in federal court. The company broke the strike, the Amalgamated (locally and nationally) was thrown into disarray, and by early 1934 the National Labor Board had been proven ineffective. In this environment, many workers at Weirton Steel lost faith in the union movement and were unwilling to further challenge Weir.

The U.S. Supreme Court overturned the National Industrial Recovery Act in 1935, but the new National Labor Relations Act adopted Section 7(a), established a stronger labor board, and outlawed employee representation plans. When the Steel Workers Organizing Committee, capitalizing on labor's new legal and political strength, launched an aggressive steel campaign in 1936, organizers at Weirton faced Weir's effective antiunion strategies of relatively high wages, company welfare programs, and a goon squad called the Hatchet Gang. When the Steel Workers Organizing Committee struck Little Steel in 1937, Weirton Steel workers stayed on the job. Weirton established a new company-influenced union in spite of National Labor Relations Act proscriptions. The Steel Workers Organizing Committee and its successor, the United Steelworkers of America, eventually won contracts at other Little Steel companies but never organized Weirton Steel.

See also: IRON AND STEEL MILL WORKERS.

—John C. Hennen, *Morehead State University*

Alec Kirby, "Ernest Tener Weir," in *Encyclopedia of American Business History and Biography: Iron and Steel in the Twentieth Century*, ed. Bruce Seely (1994); Estelle Muraksen, "The Amalgamated Association of Iron, Steel, and Tin Workers: A Case Study in Unionism," M.A. thesis, New York University (1937); William Serrin, *Homestead: The Glory and Tragedy of an American Steel Town* (1992).

Women and Employment

Whether laboring for wages, bartering for farm goods and services, or bearing children who would become future members of the workforce, Appalachian women have always worked. The rural nature of the region, its dependence upon extractive industries, and the historical role of women have all shaped Appalachia's social and economic development.

Before industrialization, Appalachian women were confined to domestic work, taking care of the children, house, and garden. Goods not necessary for the family's subsistence were sold or bartered to neighbors or at the general store. But as the mountain economy made the transition to capitalism during the antebellum period and increased its dependence upon cash, women began looking for ways to increase their household income. Husbands without property occasionally contracted out their wives' labor to their landlords to work in the dairy or in the fields. A minority of women owned their own farms, however, and by 1860 women headed more than one-fifth of the truly subsistent farm households. In addition, women worked in coal mines alongside their husbands and fathers on a sharecropper basis or went to work in textile mills and glass factories.

As the number of coal mines increased at the end of the nineteenth century, men packed up their families and moved to the coalfields of Alabama, Kentucky, Pennsylvania, Tennessee, West Virginia, and Virginia. The move to the coal town or camp made women even more dependent upon their husbands' wages. Most women performed the less visible, unpaid tasks required for maintaining the family and household, but a few took in boarders or worked as servants, domestics, seamstresses, midwives, nurses, or teachers.

Especially in central Appalachia, dominance of the coal industry discouraged economic diversity, a factor that limited the region's ability to attract alternative industries where women might find employment. Women were usually legally excluded from better-paying employment in the mines, timber industry, steel mills, and railroads. Instead, they were confined to low-wage industries that mirrored traditional women's work such as sewing, weaving, canning produce, and making pottery.

In the early 1970s, the number of Appalachian women participating in the workforce began to increase as the number of coal mine and plant closures soared. Opportunities for female employment opened up in the rapidly growing service sector. Women found work in health services, retail sales, the clerical field, and tourism, areas characterized by low wages, erratic schedules, few benefits, and little job security. Options remained particularly limited for women living in rural areas where earning opportunities beyond housework, quilting, and sewing were few, though some operated day-care or preschool programs from their homes, baked cakes and pastries, and sold farm produce. These women contribute to a growing but undocumented workforce since, by working for cash or participating in the barter system, they are excluded from official databases.

See also: WOMEN COAL MINERS; WOMEN IN AGRICULTURE (AGRICULTURE); WOMEN TEXTILE WORKERS.

—Carletta Savage Bush, *West Virginia University*

Richard A. Couto, *An American Challenge: A Report on Economic Trends and Social Issues in Appalachia* (1994); Jacquelyn Dowd Hall et al., *Like a Family: The Making of a Southern Cotton Mill World* (1987); Barbara Ellen Smith, ed., *Neither Separate nor Equal: Women, Race, and Class in the South* (1999).

Women Coal Miners

Contemporary women coal miners come from a long line of women who have worked in American and European mines for centuries. Poor British women worked alongside their husbands and brothers hauling coal from the mine face to the surface, where other women, employed as boney pickers, sorted the coal and prepared it for transport. During the mid-nineteenth century, middle-class reformers clamored for legislation to prohibit women and children from working in British mines, finally succeeding in 1842 with the passage of the Mines and Collieries Act. This act banned all children under the age of ten and all females from working underground. Young girls known as pit brow lassies continued to work aboveground preparing the coal for market until 1972.

American women carried on the British tradition of working alongside their fathers and husbands in small, family operations in the new republic. By the close of the nineteenth century daughters and wives worked in family-owned or leased mines as Appalachian coal began to power the Industrial Revolution. A small number of women worked in larger operations during World War I and World War II, but once the war emergency was over, most women returned to traditional areas of female employment. A small, nearly invisible number of women continued to work in family operations throughout the 1950s.

Civil rights legislation passed during the 1960s opened the door for women to nontraditional occupations. Statutes such as Title VII of the Civil Rights Act of 1964, the Age Discrimination in Employment Act of 1967, and Executive Order 11246 required that coal operators hire women. The region's undiversified economy left women with few opportunities for jobs that provided good wages and benefits. As a result, many women, primarily divorced women with children, turned to the mines for the money. Though the first woman was hired to work in a West Virginia mine in 1973, operators resisted other attempts, forcing women to organize to benefit from the opportunity to work underground. The Coal Employment Project, headed by lawyer Betty Jean Hall, was formed in 1977 to help women find and retain jobs in the coal industry. Using existing law and the judicial system to force companies to hire them, women working underground increased their numbers. By 1989, more than four thousand women had been hired to work in Appalachian mines. Unfortunately, most women found that it was easier to obtain a job underground than keep it.

Male miners had worked the pits for centuries, creating a thoroughly masculine world underground and declaring it off limits to women. As a result, women endured verbal and physical harassment from coworkers and supervisors and were denied opportunities for training and advancement. Empowered by several years of mining experience and support and training by the Coal Employment Project, women turned to the courts for restitution for discrimination and harassment in the early 1980s. As the decade came to a close, women achieved a greater degree of acceptance underground and enjoyed increased opportunities for training and advancement. Females were trained to operate equipment used in every facet of the mine operation and became supervisors,

Charlene Griggs (bottom right) of Carbon Hill, Alabama, works alongside her male coworkers in an underground Alabama mine, 1983. By 1989, more than four thousand women had been hired to work in Appalachian mines.

safety inspectors, and union officials. However, the number of women working underground decreased as market conditions, mechanization, and environmental legislation sent the coal industry into a decline during the late 1980s. Women, who worked primarily in union mines organized under the United Mine Workers of America, were especially affected as coal companies cut back employment or closed operations. Under the seniority provisions of union contracts, women were usually the first to be laid off since they had typically been the last workers to be hired.

By the turn of the new century, few women remained in Appalachian mines. Although most of them had departed as a result of layoffs, many left by choice. In the short term, they had benefited from working underground because the jobs brought high wages and attractive benefit packages. But in the long run, the stress of hard labor under rugged conditions affected their health. Many former miners took advantage of funds established to retrain laid-off workers and went on to attend college or technical schools. Others used their skills to move into other nontraditional industries such as the building trades. The exact number of women continuing to mine coal in Appalachia is unknown.

See also: WOMEN AND EMPLOYMENT.

—Carletta Savage Bush, *West Virginia University*

John H. M. Laslett, ed., *The United Mine Workers of America: A Model of Industrial Solidarity?* (1996); Marat Moore, *Women in the Mines: Stories of Life and Work* (1996); Carletta Savage, "Regendering Coal: Female Miners and Male Supervisors," *Appalachian Journal* (Spring 2000).

Women Textile Workers

Women have been engaged in textile production as long as the industry has existed. Everywhere in early America and Appalachia, women spun, wove, and sewed in their homes. Consequently, the earliest settlers in Appalachia made textile production significant in the region long before factories moved in from the industrial North.

While early textile production was generally confined to the home, the situation began to change after 1880 with the arrival of railroads. By 1900, major railroad lines crossed the Appalachians, with smaller branches also being constructed. Cities that grew up along these lines included Asheville, North Carolina; Martinsburg and Charleston, West Virginia; and Knoxville, Tennessee. Although the majority of textile factories were located in the Piedmont, major textile centers opened in Elkin, Forest City, Marion, and Rutherfordton, North Carolina, and in Kingsport, Bristol, and Elizabethton, Tennessee. Textile factories offered steady employment, albeit with poor wages. In addition to the growing presence of textile factories within the Appalachian region, Piedmont mill owners sent representatives to recruit women from the mountains. Many relocated to the Piedmont mills for what they believed would be a better life.

Textile production in Appalachia would never be comparable to that in the Piedmont section of the South, but it did exist in practically every corner of the region. One of the first areas to see an increase in the presence of female textile workers was Wheeling, West Virginia. Scores of women worked in the city's fledgling textile industry. By the end of the nineteenth century, Martinsburg, West Virginia, also saw an expansion of textile manufacturing. Several northern investors helped establish woolen mills in the town to manufacture cloth; these mills provided jobs for women who had never worked outside the home. Berkeley Woolen and Dunn Woolen would remain in operation until 1949 and 1953, respectively. Twenty miles to the south, Winchester, Virginia, also benefited from the presence of woolen mills during the late nineteenth century and into the mid-twentieth century.

The women of Appalachia found work in the textile industry in eastern Tennessee at the Eureka Cotton Mills, later known as Englewood Manufacturing. The majority of workers at Eureka, like elsewhere in the industry, were women. Eureka preferred to employ married women or widows who were the primary earners in their families, but owners had to convince these families to leave the farm for the newly created mill villages. Those who did became dependent on the new textile industry. There was no male competition for spinning or spooling, and because of advanced technology, young girls were able to operate spinning frames as early as age ten or eleven. Children earned approximately $0.10 per day, while women in skilled jobs earned $1.90 per six-day week and their male counterparts $2.40. Eureka and Englewood were forced to close operations after the 1930s but would be replaced by newer, more advanced hosiery and garment factories.

Between 1900 and 1920, the number of people working in textile mills increased. Due to the development of rayon during the war period, European industrialists dominated the rayon industry, which was primarily situated in the southern Appalachian Mountains. In 1928 the American Enka Company in Asheville began to manufacture rayon and employed three thousand workers by 1940.

In 1927 female workers at the Harriet Mill in Henderson, North Carolina, walked out because the company had withdrawn bonuses and increased security at the plant. The local sheriff deputized the mill foremen, and the National Guard was called in to restore peace. Management threatened to evict the striking workers from their company-owned homes and the strike ended, but eight hundred workers had joined the United Textile Workers of America.

In 1925 German-owned J. P. Bemberg Company began building its first subsidiary in the United States in Elizabethton, Tennessee, where wood pulp was used in the production of rayon. Nearby, Vereinigte Glanzstoff Fabriken opened a plant in 1928 to manufacture viscose yarn. With hemlines growing shorter and women wanting sheer, smooth stockings, the production of high-quality yarns was in great demand. Elizabethton's population almost tripled, expanding from 2,749 in 1920 to 8,093 in 1930. The rayon factories employed 3,213 workers; women held 30 percent of the jobs at the Bemberg plant and 44 percent at Glanzstoff. Approximately 75 percent of the women were single and aged sixteen to twenty-one, while most of the male workers were older and married. Male workers dominated the chemical division, while women processed the finished yarn. In March 1929, female textile workers in Elizabethton initiated a three-month strike over poor wages and workers' safety issues, but the multinational corporation ultimately defeated the striking workers.

Over the next three decades, organized labor reform continued, and the lives of Appalachian women who worked in textile production significantly improved.

See also: TEXTILE WORKERS; WOMEN AND EMPLOYMENT.

—Jerra Jenrette, *Edinboro University of Pennsylvania*

Ronald D Eller, *Miners, Millhands, and Mountaineers: Industrialization of the Appalachian South, 1880–1930* (1982); Jacquelyn Dowd Hall, "Disorderly Women: Gender and Labor Militancy in the Appalachian South," *Journal of American History* (September 1986); Jerra Jenrette, "'There's No Damn Reason for It—It's Just Our Policy': Labor-Management Conflict in Martinsburg, West Virginia's Garment and Textile Industries," Ph.D. dissertation, West Virginia University (1996).

Yablonski, Joseph A.

(1910–1969) Labor leader and union reformer.

In the early morning of December 31, 1969, Joseph A. Yablonski, along with his wife and daughter, was brutally slain. The murders were a direct outgrowth of a dispute in the race for the presidency of the United Mine Workers of America, in which Yablonski was attempting to unseat incumbent W. A. "Tony" Boyle. A native of southwestern Pennsylvania, "Jock" Yablonski rose through the ranks of the United Mine Workers District 5, headquartered in Pittsburgh. He scored impressive organizing victories in his early days, especially at Jones and Laughlin Steel's Vesta Mine No. 6 in 1933. Popular with the membership, Yablonksi was elected to the union's International Executive Board in 1942 and the District 5 presidency in 1958. In his early days, the capable and well-respected Yablonski was seen as interested in self-enrichment and as enforcing without question the will of longtime union boss John L. Lewis in the field. Later, however, Yablonski's policies became more democratic.

Yablonski became embroiled in the United Mine Workers' leadership controversy after Lewis retired from the union's presidency in 1960. Initially the presidency passed to Thomas E. Kennedy, but his sudden death left the position to Boyle. A former district president from Montana, Boyle had been appointed to the union's headquarters in 1948 to represent the western section. Although Boyle was neither intellectually gifted nor a charismatic leader, he was, like Yablonski, a Lewis loyalist. While Boyle's supporters claimed he was Lewis's hand-chosen successor, there was no solid evidence to substantiate the claim.

Yablonksi publicly supported Boyle but was dissatisfied with Boyle's leadership and heavy-handed tactics such as the pro-Boyle squads' manhandling of anti-Boyle delegates during the union's 1964 convention. Disgusted, Yablonksi considered opposing Boyle in the union's 1964 presidential election but was dissuaded by a friend.

By 1969, however, Yablonksi was prepared to challenge Boyle. Boyle's failure to respond forcefully to the Farmington, West Virginia, disaster, which killed seventy-eight miners, galvanized anti-Boyle sentiment within the United Mine Workers. Supported by consumer advocate Ralph Nader, Yablonksi announced his candidacy for the union's presidency on May 29, 1969. He promised wide-ranging reform as well as aggressive pursuit of health and safety matters. Yablonksi hoped to receive Lewis's support, but Lewis died in early June without endorsing his candidacy.

The campaign was marked by fraud and intimidation. Boyle's supporters branded Yablonski as a traitor trying to destroy the union. Boyle also stressed his own dubious claim as Lewis's chosen heir. Despite Yablonski's repeated accusations of labor racketeering, Secretary of Labor George Shultz refused to intervene. Boyle won with an official count of 80,577 votes to Yablonski's 46,073.

Yablonksi planned to challenge the result in the courts, claiming that Boyle had stolen the election. The Yablonski slayings took place shortly thereafter. This tragedy was a disaster for the United Mine Workers, as Yablonski was one of the few effective leaders left in the union.

An intense investigation by special prosecutor Richard Sprague revealed that Boyle had ordered Yablonski's murder. In 1973, just before Boyle's arrest for this crime, he was defeated for the union's presidency by Arnold Miller in a new election ordered by the U.S. Department of Labor. Boyle was convicted of murder and died in prison.

See also: LEWIS, JOHN L.; MINERS FOR DEMOCRACY; UNITED MINE WORKERS OF AMERICA.

—Richard P. Mulcahy, *University of Pittsburgh at Titusville*

Stuart Brown, *A Man Named Tony: The True Story of the Yablonski Murders* (1976); Joseph E. Finley, *The Corrupt Kingdom: The Rise and Fall of the United Mine Workers* (1972); Maier B. Fox, *United We Stand: The United Mine Workers of America, 1890–1990* (1990).

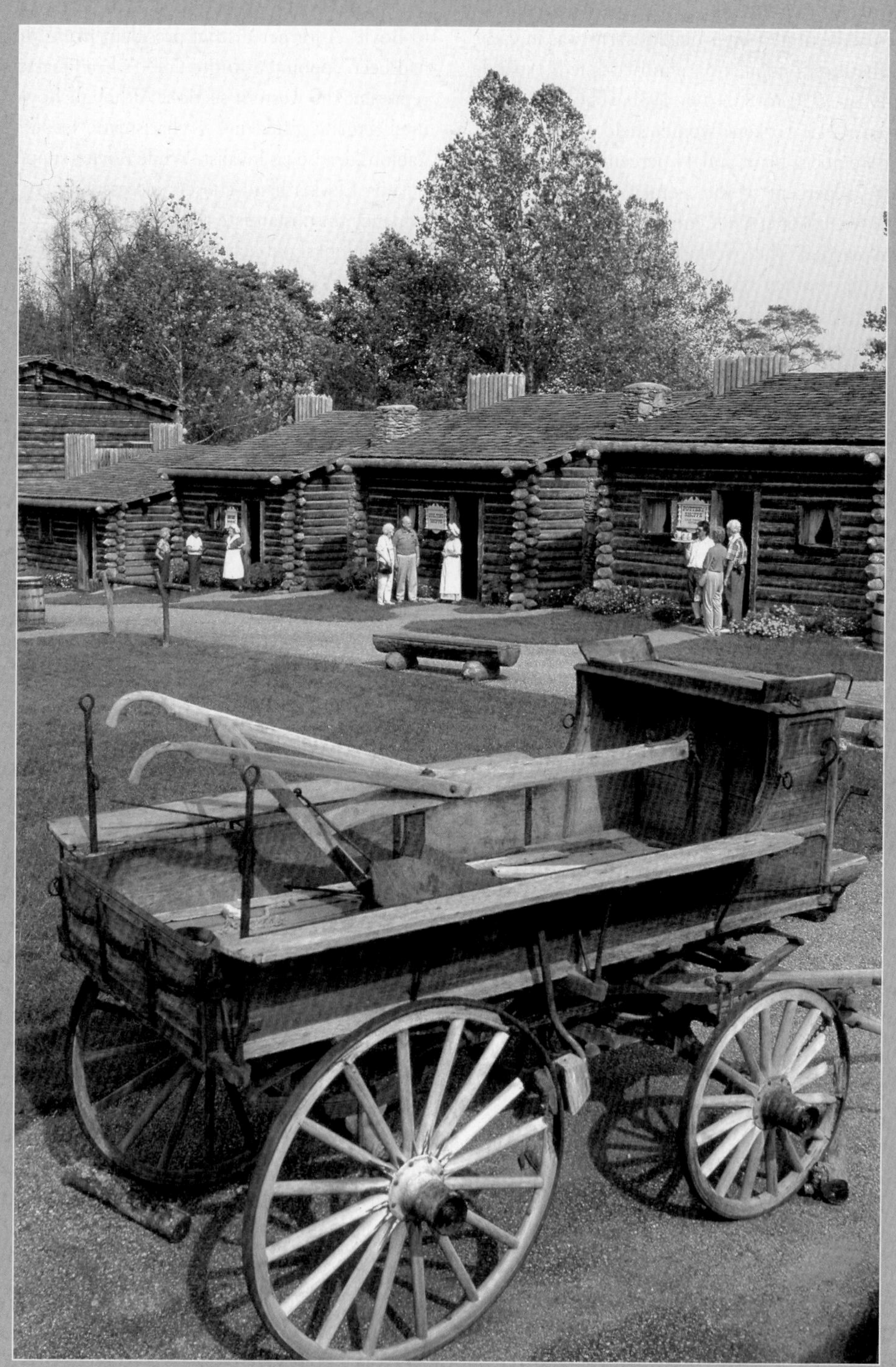

Tourism

Section Editor: Benita J. Howell

"TENNESSEE—SOUNDS GOOD TO ME." "WEST VIRGINIA—WILD AND WONDERful." "Virginia Is for Lovers." With such lively slogans, state travel and tourism agencies seek to develop brand recognition and to lure repeat visitors to increasing numbers of tourist destinations in Appalachia. However, the growing popularity of tourism as an economic-development strategy and the proliferation of destinations and attractions make for increasingly intense interstate competition to win visitors. Creative marketing has become key to success. The West Virginia Division of Tourism secured the rights to John Denver's "Take Me Home, Country Roads" and used the song in an award-winning television advertising campaign. The Mountain State, as West Virginia is known, also transformed its traditional media information kit into a photo-filled CD-ROM package designed to help travel and outdoor writers publicize attractions.

As it built tourism into the state's leading engine of growth, West Virginia began to compare itself to Pennsylvania, North Carolina, and Virginia in terms of traveler demographics, daily average expenditures, length of stay, and top activities. Potential visitors now enjoy convenient access to colorful multimedia tourism information and reservation services via the Internet. By bundling the attractions and activities of small regions into well-advertised vacation packages, state and private tourism organizations throughout the region seek to increase revenues by drawing more affluent visitors and increasing their length of stay. During the 1990s, many states started to look abroad to increase their visitor base; a Travel Appalachia Web site was launched to assist international travel agents marketing the region around the world, especially in Europe and Japan.

Without doubt, tourism looms large in Appalachia's postindustrial economy. This segment of the new service economy experienced sustained expansion during the last quarter of the twentieth century as employment in extractive industry and manufacturing declined. By the 1990s, state tourism bureaus throughout Appalachia not only provided visitor information, but also played key roles in developing longterm strategies for economic revitalization through job creation, tourist spending, and tax revenues gleaned from out-of-state visitors. In 1998, tourists to West Virginia spent more than $2.8 billion, an increase of 5.65 percent over the preceding year. But to put those figures in perspective, tourists already had spent $7.4 bil-

Facing page: Fort Boonesborough State Park, Richmond, Kentucky, c. 1995. Costumed artisans and interpreters recreate eighteenth-century life in the Fort Boonesborough settlement.

Rye harvest at the American Farm, Frontier Culture Museum, Staunton, Virginia, 2000. The American Farm, moved from its original site in Botetourt County, Virginia, is now a living museum showing farm life in Appalachia from the early nineteenth through the early twentieth century.

lion in Kentucky in 1997, and North Carolina reported $11.9 billion in tourist expenditures for 1998. Tourists visiting Virginia in 1999 spent $12.4 billion, but even that figure was dwarfed by the $20.5 billion that tourists had spent in Pennsylvania in 1995. Throughout the decade of the 1990s, revenues generated from travel and tourism in the Appalachian states increased by 5 to 6 percent most years. But what do these revenues and growth rates really mean for Appalachian counties?

In states such as North Carolina and Pennsylvania, far more tourist dollars are spent in cities outside the region than in the Appalachian counties. For example, 1999 tourist expenditures in Mecklenburg County (Charlotte) were $2.45 billion, while the top three western North Carolina counties of Buncombe (Asheville), Henderson (Hendersonville–Flat Rock), and Watauga (Boone and Blowing Rock) drew only $432.5 million, $144 million, and $143.6 million respectively. Governor Tom Ridge of Pennsylvania greatly increased state support for tourism promotion and made a well-publicized bicycle trip through the Poconos to meet workers in the industry. The state awarded $1.4 million in matching grant funds to the Pocono Mountains Vacation Bureau but awarded the Philadelphia Convention and Visitor's Bureau its largest grant of $1.43 million. Most grantees in the state's Appalachian counties received significantly less than $100,000 in state matching funds. Conventioneers who combine business with pleasure travel spend more dollars and visitor days in cities, and tourists in general spend less on entertainment than on food, transportation, or shopping (their number one activity). Nevertheless, Appalachian counties are well situated to take advantage of the growing popularity of outdoor recreation and sightseeing that includes visits to historical sites. Beaches are Americans' favorite vacation destination, but mountains are second, and many Appalachian resorts offer abundant water recreation opportunities along with mountain scenery and activities.

Although Appalachian state governments rediscovered tourism in the 1980s and 1990s, tourism is one of Appalachia's oldest industries. Intercultural encounters between rural Appalachian people and tourists from the growing urban leisure class helped to establish Appalachia in the nineteenth-century American consciousness as an exotic land that time had forgotten. Many of the century's stereotypical images and icons have proved to have remarkable staying power—in part because they still satisfy tourists' expectations and yearning for an old-timey, country Appalachia.

The mineral springs of western Virginia and mountain communities such as Flat Rock, North Carolina, attracted elite southerners beginning early in the nineteenth century. These visitors enjoyed the Appalachian climate and scenery but socialized chiefly among themselves. Resort tourists such as Mary Noailles Murfree, however, helped shape national awareness when their impressions based upon limited encounters with Appalachian people received wide circulation in popular local color literature.

Visitors who became residents often influenced the development of Appalachian communities, transforming their chosen destinations into havens with amenities attractive to elite newcomers and their guests. Blowing Rock, North Carolina, was a summer retreat from the low country as early as 1850. By 1890, the village boasted three hotels and three general stores although it was accessible only via stagecoach from Lenoir or Wilkesboro. When textile industrialist Moses H. Cone purchased thirty-five hundred acres near Blowing Rock and developed his Flat Top estate after the turn of the century, he introduced other influential visitors to Blowing Rock, which became a forerunner of contemporary second home and retirement communities. Foremost among wealthy "rusticators" was certainly George W. Vanderbilt, who created an entire town, Biltmore Village, near Asheville, North Carolina, to house and provide for the needs of his estate workers. Vanderbilt's private forest and hunting

Postcard of Wigwam Village, No. 1, Horse Cave, Kentucky, 1936. A variation on the motor courts popular in the pre-motel decades of the twentieth century, Wigwam Village substituted teepee-shaped structures for typical white clapboard cottages.

resort, Buck Spring Lodge, copied the European pattern of private hunting preserves for aristocrats and their guests. Ironically, his Cradle of Forestry in America became the nucleus of Pisgah National Forest, where public outdoor recreation became much more important than timber production.

The advent of rail passenger service not only brought more visitors to Appalachia, but also extended the experience of leisure travel to the middle class as well as the wealthy. Promotion of Asheville as "The Land of the Sky" brought teachers to modest boardinghouses such as Julia Wolfe's (mother of Thomas Wolfe) Old Kentucky Home and attracted presidents, captains of industry, and other luminaries to the world-renowned Grove Park Inn. Surveying tourism history in America, geographer John Jakle points out how technology and geopolitics came together to change the face of tourism in the early twentieth century. World War I curtailed the Grand Tour to Europe just as adventurous members of the upper classes were discovering automobiles and automobile touring as a recreational pursuit. But this was a time-consuming and challenging adventure that only the privileged few could afford until Henry Ford put automobile ownership in reach of ordinary people and a highway system began to take shape. In the 1920s, clubs of auto tourists became key advocates for highways. Their influence was conspicuous in an ambitious proposal for a highway that would connect most of the parks and key tourist destinations of the entire Appalachian region. This concept, reduced in scale, became reality when the Blue Ridge Parkway and Skyline Drive were constructed in the 1930s. States as well as the federal government established or expanded park and forest recreational facilities during the Great Depression. Most of the region's state park systems were authorized in the 1920s, but park development began in earnest only when Civilian Conservation Corps workers were available to build roads, bridges, trails, and facilities in Alabama, Georgia, Kentucky, Maryland, North Carolina, Pennsylvania, South Carolina, Tennessee, Virginia, and West Virginia state parks.

By the 1930s, campgrounds, tourist courts, and precursors of fast-food establishments were catering to middle- and working-class travelers. The Sanders' Court and Café in Corbin, Kentucky, was such an establishment. Roadside accommodations and attractions became more plentiful and more commercialized in the 1950s. For example, Stuckey's, the restaurant and souvenir shop known for pecan confections, expanded from its Florida base into Appalachia along the highway corridors that carried northern vacationers to Florida during the post–World War II boom in tourism. By the 1960s, interstate highways had again transformed vacation travel: Sanders' Café gave way to nationwide Kentucky Fried Chicken franchises, and many establishments along the old two-lane highways saw their business dwindle.

Entrepreneurs responded to the expansion and democratization of tourism with an array of roadside attractions and amusements to lure travelers off the new superhighways. Many tourist businesses, such as Gatlinburg's Christus Gardens or Ripley's Believe It or Not Wax Museum, had little intrinsic connection to their Appalachian surroundings. Mass tourism led entrepreneurs to create a galaxy of amusements and diversions embodied in places such as Pigeon Forge, Tennessee, where wedding chapels, theme parks, outlet malls, and music theaters sprang up alongside the older roadside attractions of Gatlinburg, the gateway to the Great Smoky Mountains National Park.

Show caverns became popular attractions, often combining geological education and local history with kitsch marketing of features such as the Looking Glass Lakes of Sequoyah Caverns near Birmingham, Alabama, or the Lost Sea, near Sweetwater, Tennessee, which claims to be America's largest underground lake. The additional attractions that show caverns use to lure more visitors are sometimes bizarre. Luray Caverns, open to the public since 1878, installed the world's largest pipe organ and added an antique car exhibit aboveground. Laurel Caverns, south of Pittsburgh, offered miniature golf in a simulated aboveground cave. Kentucky Caverns at Horse Cave collaborates with Kentucky Down Under, an educational nature park featuring animals and birds of Australia.

The 1970s brought developments that stimulated new thinking about tourism. The 1969 National Environmental Policy Act obliged planners of federally funded projects such as highways, dams, and national recreation areas to consider environmental impact and to weigh the potential costs and benefits of several possible development scenarios. Opportunities for public comment and participation in planning raised awareness of environmental issues and stimulated thinking about alternative, sustainable forms of tourism. Sustainable tourism requires preservation of host communities and their attractions rather than mere sustained growth in revenues. Sustainability entails principles widely ignored in poorly planned mass-tourism development, for example, appropriately scaled use of technology, protection of the environment so that visitation does not exceed an area's carrying capacity or degrade natural resources, and aesthetic harmony that preserves the destination's unique identity and character. Advocates of sustainable tourism also call for democratic participation of community members in decisions that affect them and consideration of social justice issues, so that investors do not reap great benefits at the expense of less powerful stakeholders who live in destination communities.

Agricultural tourism, cultural heritage tourism, and ecotourism are three potentially sustainable forms that many places in Appalachia have embraced, often involving neighboring communities. Each offers possible economic benefits while avoiding development that carries unacceptable sociocultural costs for communities or degrades the environment that visitors find attractive. Although each specialized form of alternative tourism by definition serves a niche market and has a narrower appeal than mass tourism, demographic trends suggest an expanding consumer base eager for these experiences. As baby boomers grew older, the core market for heritage tourism—well-educated, affluent, middle-aged professionals and retirees—expanded. At the same time, outdoor recreation grew in popularity, and the proportion of Appalachian visitors engaging in active outdoor pursuits rose dramatically. So many outdoor enthusiasts flocked to the Appalachian Mountains that overuse threatened wilderness areas. As resorts, vacation retreats, and retirement homes replaced farms and forests, the scenery and rural ambiance that had attracted newcomers became increasingly endangered. Conservationists, including recent newcomers, began to ask whether the tourism bandwagon had become overloaded and in danger of careening out of control.

Writing in a 1995 special issue of *Tennessee's Business*, Robert Cogswell, the Tennessee Arts Commission director of folk arts programs, wisely advised community leaders intent on pursuing tourism development to sell citizens in the host communities on tourism before attempting to market their attractions to visitors. Entire communities are rarely as enthusiastic as boosters and entrepreneurs who stand to gain the most from tourism. This is not surprising, for neither the economic benefits nor the sociocultural and environmental costs of tourism have been equitably distributed. By the 1990s, community-based alternative tourism projects had begun efforts to redress these imbalances. With professional assistance, local people began taking control of marketing decisions and strategies with the objective of keeping a larger share of the revenues at home.

Is Appalachia's late-twentieth- and early-twenty-first-century enchantment with tourism too much of a good thing? Worldwide, mountains are consistently popular tourist destinations; but the histories of once popular, now vanished resorts in Appalachia strike a cautionary note for those who see tourism as the answer to the boom-and-bust cycles of the region's extractive industries. Scores of spas that once flourished in the Great Smokies and once popular resorts such as Mountain Meadows Inn near Asheville, North Carolina, were out of business by World War II. After a very long decline, however, the spa at Hot Springs, North Carolina, experienced a revival, thanks to a vogue in hot tubs and relaxation therapies in the late twentieth century. Because tourism and leisure pursuits are subject to changes in fashion as well as economic cycles, any destination can expect a fickle clientele. For this reason, successful, far-sighted planners treat tourism as just one element in a comprehensive strategy for community revitalization. Several articles in the following section describe how entrepreneurs and multicounty coalitions of government and private organizations, encouraged and supported by state tourism initiatives, are cooperating to identify, develop, and market attractions as regional packages. Their experiences show that controlled tourism can conserve natural and cultural assets, enhance the quality of life in host communities, and help those communities build diverse, resilient economies.

Outdoor recreation and tourism experienced so much growth in the late twentieth century that an entire volume would be needed to catalog all of the region's tourist destinations and the organizations that market packages of attractions in cities or multicounty regions. This section makes no attempt to list every popular tourist destination or attraction. Many types of destinations that tourists frequent, such as historic homes, museums, arts venues, festivals, and other special events, are covered in other sections, as are activities that tourists pursue, such as outdoor recreation and sports. Articles on selected destinations are not intended to summarize or duplicate the promotional materials available through numerous Internet sites or in print publications. Regional travel guides, magazines such as *Blue Ridge Country*, and booklets and brochures distributed by state departments of tourism, chambers of commerce, and destination marketing organizations are readily available for travel planning. This section seeks to provide historical perspective on the development of tourism and resources for outdoor recreation in the region. Through articles on selected destinations and areas, it illustrates especially the alternative tourism programs that many communities initiated toward the end of the twentieth century in an effort to conserve as well as showcase and profit from their distinctive natural and cultural resources.

—Benita J. Howell, *University of Tennessee*

Erve Chambers, *Native Tours: The Anthropology of Travel and Tourism* (2000); Tim Hollis, *Dixie Before Disney* (1999); Benita J. Howell, "Appalachian Tourism and Cultural Conservation," in *Cultural Heritage Conservation in the American South*, ed. Howell (1990); John A. Jakle, *The Tourist* (1985); Steve Nash, *Blue Ridge 2020: An Owner's Manual* (1999); *Tennessee's Business Special Issue: Economic Revitalization through Tourism* (Winter 1997); *Tennessee's Business Special Issue: Preserving and Promoting Cultural Resources* (Winter 1995).

Agricultural Tourism

Agricultural tourism, or agritourism, has developed particular importance in Appalachia because it has both helped to shape tourist perceptions about the region's history and has opened new avenues of economic development. While examples of agritourism are found throughout Appalachia, it is most common to the southern subregion.

Early visitors to the region forged a link between Appalachia's agricultural history and the emerging tourism industry. By the late nineteenth century, pamphlets, travel books, and other promotional literature extolled Appalachia as a place where isolated, self-sufficient mountain farmers supported their families much as they had for more than a century. Though certainly not a completely accurate interpretation of Appalachian history, this view helped to shape visitor expectations and played an important role in the development of early tourist attractions. In resort areas such as Asheville, North Carolina, and White Sulphur Springs, West Virginia, visitors were encouraged to take scenic drives to view the mountain scenery and picturesque farms. The emphasis on land and agricultural heritage in early promotional literature and the resulting visitor interest created a demand for baskets, quilts, wood carvings, and other crafts. During the twentieth century, the early interest in agritourism increased exponentially.

By the 1930s, federal and state agencies had become leaders in promoting agritourism as a component of the Appalachian economy. New recreational areas such as Shenandoah National Park, the Great Smoky Mountains National Park, and the Blue Ridge Parkway all portrayed and interpreted the region's agricultural heritage for visitors. By preparing exhibits, preserving structures, and depicting regional history, government agencies detailed life in the region during the late nineteenth and early twentieth centuries, focusing on small family farms and isolated farming communities. As exemplified by National Park Service exhibits at Kentucky's Hensley Settlement (Cumberland Gap National Historic Park), Cades Cove (in the Great Smoky Mountains National Park), and Mabry Mill (on the Blue Ridge Parkway in Virginia), interpretations emphasized isolation, persistence of subsistence agriculture, and daily life on the farm. Such exhibits give visitors a realistic, often vivid, impression of agriculture in Appalachia during a particular period, but they often lag behind the latest scholarship and fail to educate tourists on Native American agricultural practices, the role of women, or the presence and place of other minority groups in Appalachian agriculture.

In northern Appalachia, one of the most notable examples of agritourism can be found in Otsego County, New York, where working farms offer bed-and-breakfast accommodations and where the Farmers' Museum in Cooperstown has established one of the country's oldest outdoor living history museums. Similar historic sites through the region, such as Virginia's Frontier Culture Museum and the National Park Service's Mountain Farm Museum near Cherokee, North Carolina, demonstrate traditional agricultural practices—such as molasses making, crop harvesting, and food preservation—and provide a much better educational experience than static exhibits. Other institutions, such as the Museum of the Cherokee Indian and Western Carolina University's Mountain Heritage Center, have developed exhibits on the evolution of Native and European American agricultural practices. In 2002 agriculture remained an important component of historic sites throughout Appalachia.

Another component of Appalachian agritourism is the marketing of local agricultural products to visitors. By establishing roadside fruit and vegetable stands, mountaineers have capitalized on the tourist expectation that agrarian lifeways still exist in rural Appalachia. Located along well-traveled highways, roadside stands vary considerably in size and quality but provide a ready outlet for locally grown produce and commodities much in demand by mountain visitors. The majority of businesses also market locally produced crafts, regional foods, and other items. Signs touting tomatoes, apples, and peaches also hawk quilts, handmade toys, cured hams, and boiled peanuts. Many tourists continue to believe that mountain residents earn their living entirely from the land. Although a few roadside stands market souvenirs that reinforce negative images of Appalachian people, the majority sell fruits, vegetables, and crafts.

In recent decades, state and local governments have developed farmers' markets to capitalize on the roadside stand concept, particularly in areas with a large, established tourist trade. In Asheville, the Western North Carolina Farmers' Market, built by the North Carolina Department of Agriculture in 1976, is an excellent example. Within sight of the Biltmore Estate and with easy access to two interstate highways, the market plays host to thousands of visitors each year. Tourists purchase not only fruits and vegetables, but also crafts, antiques, furniture, breads, cakes, jelly, fudge, and countless other items. Similar facilities in Tennessee, Georgia, Virginia, Kentucky, and West Virginia reinforce the link between agriculture and tourism.

Hoteliers and innkeepers have also recognized the importance of the region's agricultural history. Drawing on earlier successful experiments in the West and New England, some mountain resort operators have merged impressive accommodations with the setting of a working farm. Meals are usually served family style and often include fruits, vegetables, and meats grown on the farm. Guests can also try their hand at farm chores during their stay. Such businesses have been successful in Virginia, West Virginia, Tennessee, eastern Ohio, and Pennsylvania and have allowed farmers to keep their operations viable in an increasingly difficult agricultural market. Other attractions, including Asheville's Biltmore Estate, have created more exotic agricultural attractions such as vineyards and wineries to extend their appeal to visitors. Such uses of agricultural tourism represent important new directions in regional economic development.

See also: CULTURAL HERITAGE TOURISM; FARMERS' MARKETS (AGRICULTURE).

—Richard D. Starnes, *Western Carolina University*

Caneta Skelley Hankins, "Agritourism," *Tennessee's Business* (Winter 1997); Daniel S. Pierce, *The Great Smokies: From Natural Habitat to National Park* (2000).

Alabama and Mississippi State Parks

Alabama's state park system is one of the state's prime tourist attractions. Of the twenty-four state parks located throughout the state, eleven are found in northern Alabama and in the Appalachian region.

The system was developed in the late 1920s, and two major factors facilitated its early growth. Hundreds of depression-era Civilian Conservation Corps workers helped erect the infrastructure, and private citizens donated land for preservation within the parks. Nearly four thousand acres had been given to the state by the end of 1933.

Fluctuations in the number of state parks over the years were primarily due to budget restrictions and the transfer of their control between state agencies. Nonetheless, attendance grew steadily after World War II. At the close of the twentieth century, the twenty-four parks in the system were hosting millions of visitors every year.

One of the distinctive features of the state park system in Alabama is its maintenance of several recreational resort parks. A majority of these are located in Appalachian Alabama. Joe Wheeler, Cheaha, Lake Guntersville, and DeSoto State Parks all have convention facilities, restaurants, hotels, cabins, and lodges. These amenities, in addition to eighteen-hole championship golf courses, draw hundreds of thousands of tourists each year. Joe Wheeler, which hosted more than six hundred thousand visitors in 1997–98, is the premier resort park in the system. Its most popular attraction is the 69,700-acre Wheeler Lake.

All of the parks offer a variety of day-use recreational opportunities such as boating, hiking, fishing, mountain biking, and tennis. One of the most popular parks for day use is Oak Mountain, located near Birmingham. Its proximity to the largest city in the state provides approximately one-half million annual visitors the opportunity to enjoy the outdoors close to home.

The state parks in Appalachian Alabama boast rich natural attractions. Rickwood Caverns State Park boasts a 260-million-year-old underground limestone cave, and Cathedral Caverns, the newest park in the system, offers visitors the opportunity to learn about cave formation at its interpretive center. Hikes to waterfalls are popular in DeSoto and Oak Mountain State Parks. Cheaha Mountain, the only modern state park in continuous existence since 1933, is the site of the state's highest peak, at 2,407 feet.

Tourism is the number one industry in Alabama. The Alabama Bureau of Tourism and Travel and the Division of State Parks work to attract visitors to the state and its parks through television, radio, and national magazine advertisements. These agencies also reach potential visitors through brochures, guidebooks, and the Internet. Approximately 9 million people visited the state in 1998, generating 5.4 billion dollars in economic activity. The eleven parks in Appalachian Alabama alone saw 2.9 million visitors in 1997–98, making them vital components in the economies in which they are located.

Although not a part of the Alabama state park system, the Natchez Trace Parkway, maintained by the National Park Service, cuts across the northwest corner of the state. Forty miles of the parkway pass within an hour's drive of Joe Wheeler State Park. The trace likely began as several Native American foot trails that eventually evolved into a direct path from modern-day Natchez, Mississippi, to the Cumberland River Valley near Nashville, Tennessee. Trade by settlers along the Mississippi began to flourish in the late 1700s, and the trace then became one of the most important and heavily traveled wilderness roads. However, the advent of Mississippi River steamboats in the early nineteenth century diminished traffic on the trace substantially. Begun in 1938, construction of the parkway was nearing completion at the end of the twentieth century. The modern road, which closely follows the path of the original trace, is dotted with numerous historical sites, overlooks, and exhibits.

Along the Natchez Trace Parkway in Mississippi, visitors can camp and enjoy canoe float trips, geological features, and other natural attractions at rustic Tishomingo State Park. Tishomingo also boasts well-preserved examples of Civilian Conservation Corps architecture and a 45-acre lake. At Tupelo, two small state parks, Tombigbee and Trace, offer outdoor recreation, water sports, and meeting accommodations. On the Tennessee River in the northeast corner of Mississippi is J. P. Coleman State Park, located on Pickwick Lake, where visitors can enjoy a marina and water sports. Accommodations range from tent pads and cabins to condominium units and a hotel. Lake Lowndes State Park, near Columbus, offers facilities for indoor and outdoor tennis, basketball, volleyball, and softball as well as water sports. In north-central Mississippi, Wall Doxey State Park,

George P. Cossar State Park, Hugh White State Park, and John W. Kyle State Park all have developed the fishing, water sports, and nature study potential of reservoir lakes. The Bureau of Mississippi Outdoors/Media publicizes the state's nature study and outdoor recreation opportunities through a popular educational television program and a bimonthly magazine, both titled *Mississippi Outdoors*.

See also: CIVILIAN CONSERVATION CORPS (GOVERNMENT); NATCHEZ TRACE (SETTLEMENT AND MIGRATION).

—Sara Mace Kidd, *Suffolk, Virginia*

David Bertleson, *Alabama State Park System* (1975); National Park Service, *Natchez Trace Parkway: Official Map and Guide* (1988); Cathy and Vernon Summerlin, *Traveling the Trace* (1995).

Allegheny National Forest

Allegheny National Forest is the only national forest in Pennsylvania. It was established in 1923 through the 1911 Weeks Act, the federal government's first effort to purchase land for forest reserves east of the Mississippi River. The forest's 513,257 acres cover parts of Elk, Forest, McKean, and Warren Counties in the northwestern corner of the state.

Unregulated logging before 1923 had left much of northern Pennsylvania covered with brush and slash. With careful forest conservation, trees rapidly grew back on the once bare hillsides, with mature black cherry, ash, maple, oak, birch, beech, and hemlock in profusion at the end of the twentieth century. Most of the trees in the second-growth forest at the turn of the twenty-first century were the same age (seventy to one hundred years old). Much of the Allegheny National Forest is located on the Northern Unglaciated Allegheny Plateau, which is divided by three major waterways—the Allegheny River, the Clarion River, and Tionesta Creek—characterized by steep banks. Segments of the Allegheny and Clarion are designated as federal wild and scenic rivers.

Allegheny National Forest claims 312 wildlife species, including deer, bear, and turkey, and 71 fish species, including trout and walleye. River otters and fishers were reintroduced in the 1990s. Five federally endangered species are known to inhabit the area: the bald eagle, the Indiana bat, the small-whorled pogonia (an orchid), and two types of mussels.

Allegheny is a popular destination for outdoor enthusiasts, including those attracted by hunting and fishing. Sixteen campgrounds offer a range of amenities from more developed facilities with hot water and electricity to rustic settings that are accessible only by boat or foot. Six boat launches access the Allegheny Reservoir, and six canoe sites are located along the Allegheny River, the Clarion River, Tionesta Creek, and Beaver Meadow Lake. Eleven picnic areas and four beaches are scattered throughout the forest. Facilities such as campgrounds and fishing piers have been upgraded to be universally accessible.

Wildlife viewing, especially bird watching, is popular at Buzzard Swamp and the Little Drummer Historical Pathway. Hundreds of miles of trail offer opportunities for hiking, cross-country skiing, and riding all-terrain vehicles or snowmobiles. Equestrians and bicyclists also have areas to use.

Popular locations include the Hearts Content National Scenic Area, Tionesta National Scenic Area, Tionesta Research Natural Area, Hickory Creek Wilderness, Allegheny River Islands Wilderness, Allegheny National Recreation Area, Longhouse National Scenic Byway, Kane Experimental Forest, Tracy Ridge National Recreation Trail, Black Cherry National Interpretive Trail, and overlooks at Tidioute, Jake's Rock, and Rimrock.

In most years Allegheny is visited more than any national forest in the northeast quadrant of the country except the White Mountain National Forest in New Hampshire. Visitation has increased since the 1980s and is linked to weather conditions, with more recreationists enjoying the forest in years with warm, dry summers or cold, snowy winters. Nearly half of the recreation visitors enjoy motorized (including automobile) travel and viewing scenery.

See also: ECOTOURISM; LUMBER INDUSTRY (BUSINESS, INDUSTRY, AND TECHNOLOGY); MONONGAHELA NATIONAL FOREST; WEEKS ACT (GOVERNMENT).

—Katherine Frank, *Allegheny National Forest*

Tom Dwyer, *A Guide to the Allegheny National Forest* (1999); Stephen J. Ostrander, *Great Natural Areas in Western Pennsylvania* (2000).

Appalachian Trail

The Appalachian Trail, known officially as the Appalachian National Scenic Trail, is a 2,174-mile recreational footpath that stretches from Mount Katahdin in Maine to Springer Mountain in Georgia. Proposed in 1921 by forester and regional planner Benton MacKaye (rhymes with *sky*), the trail was first completed in 1937, though subsequent disruptions forced its reconstruction and relocation in the years surrounding World War II. In 1948 Earl Shaffer completed the first solo "thru-hike," or uninterrupted hike of the entire trail; in 1955 Emma Gatewood of Ohio became the first woman to accomplish the feat. By the turn of the century, approximately four thousand people had made the same journey. Today, the Appalachian Trail receives millions of visitors every year and is one of the defining features of the region.

When MacKaye (1879–1975) first offered his vision of "an Appalachian Trail" in a 1921 article in the *Journal of the*

American Institute of Architects, he had in mind much more than a recreational footpath. During his youth, MacKaye had been an avid hiker and explorer of the mountains of his native New England, and these experiences were crucial to his trail vision. Moreover, the decades around the turn of the century had seen the organization of various hiking clubs in the region and a growing interest in a grand system of "trunk" trails. The idea for such a grand trail, then, was not entirely unprecedented. But the way in which MacKaye presented his trail vision was novel, and it betrayed the formative influence of his early career as a resource conservationist.

MacKaye was among the first generation of trained foresters in the United States, and he spent his early career with the U.S. Forest Service pushing foresters to recognize the social problems that plagued the nation's timber industry. The Forest Service was not particularly receptive. During the late 1910s, MacKaye moved to the Labor Department, where he worked on plans to use the remaining public domain to settle unemployed workers—and in a later iteration, soldiers returning from World War I—in planned communities premised on sustainable resource development and social equity. He drew upon these efforts in his "Appalachian Trail" article, offering a grand regional plan for Appalachia that was to include a string of recreational and resource communities, publicly owned, guided by a communitarian ethos, and linked by the trail. His plan, which he referred to as a "project in housing and community architecture," was to mix meaningful work and leisure in close contact with nature and to provide what he called a "retreat from profit" at a time when America was becoming more mechanized, urbanized, and commercialized. Only a portion of MacKaye's grander vision was ever realized.

From its beginning, and true to MacKaye's vision, the trail has been in the hands of a series of local hiking clubs, some already in existence at the time of his 1921 proposal and others organized for the purpose of building and maintaining portions of the trail. In 1925 trail activists formed the Appalachian Trail Conference to coordinate the activities of these various clubs. One of the most active early leaders of the conference was Myron Avery, a Washington, D.C., attorney who headed the organization from 1931 until 1952. Avery, a tireless trailblazer and masterful organizer of volunteer labor, was responsible for overseeing the completion of the connected trail. The Appalachian Trail was finally completed in 1937, when Civilian Conservation Corps workers finished an isolated section of the trail in Maine. But the uninterrupted trail did not last long. The great hurricane of 1938 obstructed hundreds of miles of the trail in New England, and the construction of the Blue Ridge Parkway forced the relocation of more than 120 miles in Virginia. World War II interrupted reconstruction and relocation efforts, and the trail was not complete again until 1951.

In the mid-1930s, the Appalachian Trail Conference was rocked by a dispute between MacKaye and Avery over how the organization should respond to a series of New Deal–sponsored skyline roads being planned and built along the Appalachian ridgeline. The Skyline Drive through Shenandoah National Park and the Blue Ridge Parkway were the most famous of these, but proposed roads such as the Green Mountain Parkway in Vermont never materialized. Avery, who was bent upon the practical task of building trails and had little patience for MacKaye's philosophizing, was not overly concerned about these proposed roads. More important, he was reluctant to obstruct the efforts of the federal government, which had emerged as a major ally in the trail-building process. MacKaye, on the other hand, saw these roads and the automobiles that would use them as symbols of the very forces he was hoping to exclude from his planned Appalachian realm. In 1935, after a series of sharp exchanges with Avery and defeat of a resolution opposing these roads, MacKaye and a pair of close allies, Harold Anderson of the Potomac Appalachian Trail Club and Harvey Broome of the Smoky Mountains Hiking Club, split from the conference. Overwhelmingly concerned about the impacts that roads and automobiles were having on the nation's remaining wild lands, they helped to found the Wilderness Society, the first national organization dedicated solely to the preservation of wilderness. Early Appalachian Trail politics thus played a formative role in the modern wilderness movement.

After World War II, with the trail complete again, the Appalachian Trail Conference focused on securing a protected right-of-way—what the organization referred to as a "trailway"—for the Appalachian Trail. Where the trail passed through national parks and national forests, it was generally well protected from encroaching development; such protection was made more secure with a 1938 agreement between the conference, the Park Service, and the Forest Service to create a buffer free from roads and timber cutting along the 875 miles of trail that passed through federal lands. But the majority of the trail traversed privately owned land, and various developmental pressures, from road building and resource extraction to second homes, ski resorts, and sprawl, threatened large portions of the trail after World War II. In 1958, for instance, commercial development forced the relocation of the southern terminus of the Appalachian Trail from Mount Oglethorpe to Springer Mountain, which was surrounded by Georgia's Chattahoochee National Forest. Throughout the 1950s and 1960s, the trail was constantly being relocated. Some of these changes were aimed at adding peaks and other scenic views to the route, often to the dismay of thru-hikers who were not always eager to go out of their way to get yet another scenic view. Others addressed the continuing problem of

Battery Park Hotel, Asheville, North Carolina, c. 1910. Built in 1886, the hotel contributed to Asheville's reputation as one of the South's premier tourist destinations during the 1890s.

maintaining such a trail through a privately owned and constantly changing landscape.

With these problems in mind, trail activists turned their attention in the 1960s to the goal of ensuring that the entire path was publicly protected. Senator Gaylord Nelson of Wisconsin introduced a bill for the public protection of the Appalachian Trail in 1964, and over the next several years this effort expanded into a more comprehensive campaign to protect a national system of trails. This effort culminated in the 1968 passage of the National Trails System Act, which designated the trail—renamed the Appalachian National Scenic Trail—as the first piece in a growing system of long-distance trails overseen by the National Park Service. The act also provided various mechanisms for purchasing or otherwise protecting the trail's right-of-way. In the wake of the act, however, federal purchase of buffer lands occurred only slowly and sporadically. Not until the passage a decade later of the Appalachian Trail Bill, amending the 1968 act, did federal protection, largely through purchase and easements, become a reality. Today, more than 98 percent of the Appalachian Trail is publicly protected.

The Appalachian Trail remains a remarkable example of democracy and volunteerism at work. The model for greenway conservation throughout the country, it is at the core of a still-growing movement to protect and connect the recreational and ecological resources of the entire Appalachian region.

See also: HIKING (SPORTS AND RECREATION); STATEWIDE TRAIL SYSTEMS.

—Paul S. Sutter, *University of Georgia*

Ronald Foresta, "Transformation of the Appalachian Trail," *Geographical Review* (January 1987); Benton MacKaye, "An Appalachian Trail: A Project in Regional Planning," *Journal of the American Institute of Architects* (October 1921); Paul S. Sutter, *Driven Wild: How the Fight against Automobiles Launched the Modern Wilderness Movement* (2002).

Asheville, North Carolina

Tourism, one of the most important social and economic forces in Appalachia, emerged in Asheville, North Carolina, during the 1820s. Seasonal visitors from South Carolina, Georgia, and eastern North Carolina flocked to Asheville, drawn by the moderate climate and the breathtaking scenery. Some built elaborate mountain estates, while others stayed in local hotels built to serve visitors who could afford to flee summer heat and tropical fevers. These annual pilgrimages became increasingly important social and economic influences upon the city. Each summer, Asheville became something of a social mecca for the prominent families of the South. One of the area's earliest resorts, Sulphur Springs, touted the health benefits of its mineral springs and boasted a wide variety of activities, including tennis, scenic drives into the countryside, and an orchestra of black musicians brought in from Columbia, South Carolina. The social and economic significance of antebellum resorts heralded the rising importance of tourism in city life.

After the Civil War, tourism grew into the defining force in Asheville. Capitalizing on antebellum interest in health, Asheville became a popular destination for those suffering from respiratory diseases. Physicians from across the world, including Edwin Gatchell and Karl von Ruck, established sanitariums in and around the city and publicized the health benefits of Asheville's climate in national and international medical journals. By the 1880s, with the arrival of the railroad, city leaders recognized that tourism could be the cornerstone of Asheville's longterm prosperity, and they spared no expense in promoting the city to visitors. The construction of the Battery Park Hotel, one of the most modern resorts in the South, in 1886 marked an important shift from health tourism to leisure tourism in the city. By the 1890s, Asheville was one of the most important tourist destinations in the South, attracting nearly fifty thousand visitors annually, including a growing convention trade. Patent medicine magnate Edwin Wiley Grove added to the city's reputation in 1913 with the construction of the Grove Park Inn. In subsequent years, many prominent Americans vacationed in the city; some visitors, including humorist Bill Nye, writer William Sydney Porter ("O. Henry"), and F. Scott and Zelda Fitzgerald, enjoyed Asheville so much they became residents. The result was a cosmopolitan atmosphere that city leaders promoted at every opportunity. Thousands of African Americans came to Asheville during this period as well, drawn not by leisure, but by the service jobs tourism created.

By the 1920s, tourism had developed into a boom. New residents poured into the city, property values skyrocketed, and millions of dollars worth of municipal bonds were sold for capital improvements that would enhance its resort reputation. City leaders pushed for the establishment of the Great Smoky Mountains National Park and sponsored events such as the Rhododendron Festival to attract more visitors. The city supported craft fairs and the Mountain Dance and Folk Festival but distanced itself from stereotypically negative images of Appalachia. The stock market crash hit Asheville's tourist industry hard when failure of the Central Bank erased the city's assets and left it $50 million in debt and with a ruined credit rating.

Cornelia Vanderbilt Cecil, heir to the Biltmore Estate, agreed to open the estate to visitors in the 1930s, giving Asheville a prominent attraction for building future tourism. After World War II, the industry rebounded. Most visitors, however, came to enjoy mountain scenery in the Smokies or along the Blue Ridge Parkway and to spend a few days in Asheville on the way to somewhere else. During the 1950s and 1960s, when urban renewal was popular, Asheville managed to save many old buildings from the wrecking ball. Interstate highway construction made the city more accessible, but the local tourism-based economy was susceptible to the recessions of the 1970s and 1980s. By the late 1980s, however, the city's impressive architecture, resorts, and scenery and the promotion of mountain culture had fostered another tourism boom. Several national magazines named Asheville one of the best places in America to retire, and a New Age youth culture also developed in the city. Tourism remains the defining force in city life, a fact that shapes visitor perceptions, native attitudes, and the contours of the local economy.

See also: BILTMORE ESTATE; BILTMORE ESTATE COMPLEX (ARCHITECTURE); BLUE RIDGE PARKWAY; GROVE PARK INN (ARCHITECTURE).

—Richard D. Starnes, *Western Carolina University*

Mitzi Schaden Tessier, *Asheville: A Pictorial History* (1982).

Atlanta, Georgia

Although Atlanta, Georgia, lies outside of what is considered southern Appalachia, the city has played a significant role in the development of the region. As a railroad center, Atlanta began welcoming visitors soon after being founded in 1847, and throughout its history residents have been hospitable to visitors and businesses. In the pre–Civil War era, industrial fairs were held to bring farmers from north Georgia into the young town to sell their goods and to buy supplies. Hotel owners used slave labor to cook, clean, and carry bags. As the city rebuilt following the war, its hospitality businesses were quickly restored. Local leaders such as Henry Grady and hotel owner H. I. Kimball promoted tourism through a series of three expositions held in 1881, 1887, and 1895. The expositions showcased the city as a place for investment.

Early in the twentieth century, Atlanta's leaders built a municipal auditorium in order to host conventions and trade shows such as the 1909 meeting of the National Association of Automobile Manufacturers. These events took advantage of the city's transportation connections and promoted Atlanta as a place to do business. The Atlanta Convention and Visitor's Bureau was organized in 1912, making it among the oldest in the nation. In a city segregated first by custom and later by law, a separate African American convention business developed with its own set of hotels, restaurants, bars, and amusements for both visitors and local residents. Despite the fact that Atlanta served as the headquarters for the revived Ku Klux Klan, national and regional conventions for African Americans attracted crowds of tourists to the city. White business and political leaders welcomed these meetings and even desegregated city parks long enough to entertain visiting African American conventions. During the 1920s and 1930s, white supremacist organizations contributed to Atlanta's economic growth by hosting numerous Klanventions as well. The Civil Rights Act of 1964 ended segregation in the city's convention business and contributed to the decline of black-owned hotels, restaurants, and amusements.

During the 1960s Atlanta emerged as a city of increasingly national importance with new convention facilities, major league sports teams, and new hotels with innovative designs by local architect John Portman. The new Hartsfield-Atlanta International Airport opened in 1980 and quickly became one of the busiest in the country. Atlanta's leaders boasted of being the nation's third-largest convention city and dreamed of overtaking New York and Chicago with the construction of the Georgia World Congress Center. In seeking national recognition as a convention center, the city's promotional efforts downplayed the history and culture of the region. Older landmark buildings were destroyed as leaders focused on the sleek modern image of a city with a new skyline. Major events such as the 1988 Democratic National Convention and the 1994 Super Bowl showcased Atlanta as a major destination for both business and recreational tourists.

The 1996 Centennial Olympic Games climaxed efforts by city leaders to draw the attention of the world to Atlanta. More than 19 million tourists visited Atlanta during that year. Events such as the opening and closing ceremonies of the games featured the biracial culture of the region through music and dance. The inclusion of clogging and step dancing as well as gospel choirs and bluegrass music suggested that Atlanta had become more comfortable with its regional location and identity. The Olympics may be seen as the culmination of a series of historic efforts by business leaders and public officials to use tourism as a means of promoting the growth of Atlanta.

See also: AFRICAN AMERICAN TWENTIETH-CENTURY MIGRATION (SETTLEMENT AND MIGRATION); KU KLUX KLAN (GOVERNMENT); SECTION OVERVIEW (URBAN APPALACHIAN EXPERIENCE).

—Harvey K. Newman, *Georgia State University*

Harvey K. Newman, *Southern Hospitality: Tourism and the Growth of Atlanta* (1999).

Beckley Exhibition Coal Mine

The Beckley Exhibition Coal Mine, centerpiece of New River Park in Raleigh County, West Virginia, is a key attraction in Appalachia's growing coal heritage tourism industry. Located on the Coal Heritage Trail, a national scenic byway that routes visitors through the eleven-county National Coal Heritage Area, the Beckley show mine opened in 1962 when the municipality acquired the Phillips family mine.

Visitors ride empty coal cars—"man-trips" in the industry's vernacular—along fifteen hundred feet of the twelve-foot-wide-by-six-foot-high haulageway while veteran coal miners give interpretive talks at stops that take visitors back through the stages of mining technology to pick-and-shovel days. Next door to the exhibition mine is a coal museum housing artifacts and photographs that depict the culture and history of coal mining in the area. The museum complex includes a typical turn-of-the-twentieth-century three-room miner's home relocated from Sprague, West Virginia; Samuel Dixon's 1906 superintendent's house, relocated from Skelton, West Virginia; and the 1925 school from Helen, Georgia.

The exhibition mine attracts from fifty to sixty thousand visitors annually for a look inside the underground world of the miner and also sponsors seasonal events such as the Coal Town Christmas Lights Festival. New River Park also has additional historic exhibits and offers camping facilities.

See also: COAL HERITAGE TOURISM; COAL SETTLEMENTS (SETTLEMENT AND MIGRATION).

—Stuart McGehee, *West Virginia State College*

Big South Fork National River and Recreation Area

Formed by the merging of the Clear Fork River and the New River in Scott County, Tennessee, the Big South Fork of the Cumberland was designated a National River and Recreation Area in 1974 when the Water Resources Development Act authorized the U.S. Army Corps of Engineers to acquire up to 123,000 acres in McCreary County, Kentucky, and in Morgan, Scott, Fentress, and Pickett Counties, Tennessee, for the purposes of restoring water quality and protecting the natural, scenic, and cultural heritage assets of the river gorge while developing a multiuse recreation area on the surrounding plateau tableland.

A scenic region of river-carved gorges cutting through the sandstone and limestone of the Cumberland Plateau, the area thrived on timber cutting and mining from the 1880s through the 1920s but never recovered from the economic decline of the Great Depression. In the late 1960s environmentalists and outdoor enthusiasts began promoting conservation of the Big South Fork as a wild and scenic river. The National Park Service assumed full control of the recreation area in 1990, and by 1999 the area encompassed 119,000 acres that had belonged to the Stearns Coal and Lumber Company, other timber and coal companies, and private owners, many of whom were descendants of the original Euro-American settlers. Pickett Rustic Park and Forest lies adjacent to the western boundary in Tennessee, and Daniel Boone National Forest surrounds the Kentucky portion of the recreation area.

In addition to an extensive trail system for hikers and horseback riders, the recreation area offers equestrian camps, a fully equipped campground with visitor center and swimming pool at Bandy Creek, and rustic accommodations at Charit Creek Lodge, accessible only by foot or on horseback. The river and its tributaries offer Class I–II calm water for novice paddlers as well as Class III–IV whitewater rapids that challenge the most experienced rafters. Scenic attractions include Yahoo Falls, rock shelters, chimney rocks, and several natural arches, including Twin Arches in Tennessee and Split Bow Arch in Kentucky. The area supports numerous rare, threatened, or endangered species of flora and fauna. Nature photography, astronomy, cycling, and rock climbing have become popular pursuits.

Homesteads and cemeteries offer glimpses into the lives of settlers in the nineteenth century. Blue Heron, Kentucky, a former coal camp, is the site of a second fully equipped campground and a museum complex that interprets the history of the region's largest industrial employer, Stearns Coal and Lumber Company. During the summer and autumn tourist season, the Big South Fork Scenic Railway, a private enterprise, transports visitors from Stearns, Kentucky, to Blue Heron. While planned full-service lodges in the Kentucky and Tennessee sections of the recreation area await funding, chain motels and restaurants as well as local businesses in nearby towns offer visitor services and additional attractions for tourists. Big South Fork hosted 860,224 visitors in 1999.

See also: APPALACHIAN PLATEAUS PROVINCE (GEOLOGY).

—Benita J. Howell, *University of Tennessee*

Russ Manning, *Exploring the Big South Fork* (1994).

Biltmore Estate

In the 1890s, George W. Vanderbilt constructed the estate of his dreams, a luxuriously appointed and furnished 250-room French chateau designed by leading American architect Richard Morris Hunt. Nestled in the North Carolina mountains, Biltmore House was surrounded by gardens designed by Frederick Law Olmsted that rivaled those of European castles and featured an exceptional array of indigenous and imported plants. By the time Vanderbilt invited the first guests to his mountain estate in December 1895, it already had become something of a regional tourist attraction.

Vanderbilt came to Asheville during a formative period in the city's history. Following the Civil War and the subsequent arrival of the railroad in 1880, Asheville became an important tourist destination. The mountain scenery and mild climate attracted health and pleasure seekers from across the nation. The estate was an important component of the evolving cosmopolitan image of Asheville. Though no tours were allowed, even the construction of this landmark house drew locals, tourists, and travel writers from across the nation, all of whom marveled at the structure and hoped for a glimpse of the famous family and their visitors.

In 1914 Vanderbilt died, leaving Biltmore to his wife, Edith. Shortly after she deeded a vast tract of land to the U.S. Forest Service, Edith married Rhode Island Senator Peter G. Gerry and moved out of the house. The estate passed to the couple's only daughter, Cornelia Vanderbilt Cecil. In an effort to rebuild the city's economy following the stock market crash of 1929 and failure of the Central Bank, Asheville leaders approached Cecil about opening the estate to visitors. She agreed, and in 1930 Biltmore hosted its first tourists. Almost immediately, the estate drew thousands of visitors, boosting the region's resort reputation and creating a nationally recognized attraction.

Estate managers tried to preserve the Victorian elegance and ambiance enjoyed by George Vanderbilt and his guests, which was an expensive undertaking. Beginning in 1960, Cornelia Cecil's son, William Amherst Vanderbilt Cecil, oversaw the much needed historic preservation and undertook restoration projects that opened more of Biltmore House to tours. In the 1990s, William Cecil Jr. attempted to draw more visitors by offering seasonal attractions such as dazzling Christmas decorations and a spring Festival of Flowers, adding restaurants, and developing a winery. In 2001 a luxury hotel, Inn on Biltmore Estate, was completed, turning the estate into a multi-day destination. Other proposed revenue-generating enterprises include the sale of azalea nursery stock to complement sales of wine. In recent decades, Biltmore Estate has taken advantage of the popularity of heritage tourism and its proximity to the Blue Ridge Parkway to remain western North Carolina's single most important tourist destination. In 1999 Biltmore Estate attracted nine hundred thousand visitors, even with a thirty-dollar ticket price.

See also: ASHEVILLE, NORTH CAROLINA; BILTMORE ESTATE COMPLEX (ARCHITECTURE); CULTURAL HERITAGE TOURISM.

—Richard D. Starnes, *Western Carolina University*

Birmingham, Alabama

See Birmingham, Alabama (Urban Appalachian Experience)

Blue Ridge Parkway

A 469-mile ridge-top scenic highway stretching from Waynesboro, Virginia, to Cherokee, North Carolina, the Blue Ridge Parkway connects the Shenandoah National Park with the Great Smoky Mountains National Park. Although it was built under the direction of the National Park Service and federal Bureau of Public Roads, the parkway project originated in the minds of business-oriented leaders in the mountains of North Carolina, Virginia, and Tennessee who had long dreamed of a scenic road to connect their most beautiful spots. Serious planning began in 1933, when these leaders secured funding from the New Deal's Public Works Administration. In a contentious 1934 routing battle with supporters in Knoxville, Tennessee, Asheville-area tourism boosters and officials with the North Carolina State Highway and

Public Works Commission convinced federal officials to build the highway entirely in Virginia and North Carolina. Construction—by local contractors using workers initially hired from federal relief rolls—began in 1935; the road's final link (the Linn Cove Viaduct) was completed in 1987. Enormously popular from the 1930s on, the parkway by the late 1990s was the most visited site in the National Park System.

As a scenic highway, the parkway differed from the roads local citizens had become accustomed to in the 1920s, when state highway systems expanded across the South. To assure strict control over roadside views, the National Park Service required Virginia and North Carolina (who had acquired lands via eminent domain, then turned them over to federal officials) to provide a right-of-way that was much greater than the sixty feet usually taken for state roads. Parkway standards dictated rights-of-way of at least two hundred feet, but in practice, fee simple rights-of-way or scenic easements placed under Park Service control a swath of land more than eight hundred feet wide along most of the parkway.

National Park Service regulations allowed few adjoining landowners direct access to the parkway, prohibited commercial development along the roadside, and forbade commercial traffic. Combined with the large rights-of-way required, these restrictions ultimately created an uncluttered and pristine road, but they also generated disappointment among local landowners and tourist entrepreneurs who had hoped the new parkway would become either a means of transportation or a conduit for customers to their businesses. Instead, established tourist centers such as Asheville—whose newspaper and chamber of commerce leaders fought hardest to get the road—have been the greatest beneficiaries of the increased tourist travel the parkway eventually brought.

The Blue Ridge Parkway was a significant achievement that set a new standard for transportation and tourism development in the United States. It also resulted in a complex set of costs and benefits for people in various sectors of mountain society. Several conflicts over the parkway in the 1930s revealed the complex social, cultural, and economic issues raised by its construction. While the Eastern Band of Cherokee Indians, for example, successfully fought to keep the road from cutting through the heart of their western North Carolina farmlands, a North Carolina Supreme Court justice who owned the Little Switzerland resort near Spruce Pine persuaded state and federal officials to bring the parkway directly to that development's front door, violating the otherwise rigidly enforced right-of-way and access rules. Less powerful small landowners along the highway protested the parkway by writing letters, cutting timber along the right-of-way, and opening illegal accesses to the road from their property, but their actions usually failed to alter the course of parkway development.

See also: BLUE RIDGE PARKWAY (ARCHITECTURE); GREAT SMOKY MOUNTAINS NATIONAL PARK; SHENANDOAH NATIONAL PARK.

—Anne Mitchell Whisnant, *Duke University*

Harley Jolley, *The Blue Ridge Parkway* (1983); Anne V. Mitchell, "Parkway Politics: Class, Culture, and Tourism in the Blue Ridge," Ph.D. dissertation, University of North Carolina (1997); Phil Noblitt, "The Blue Ridge Parkway and the Myths of the Pioneer," *Appalachian Journal* (June 1994).

Bramwell, West Virginia

Incorporated in 1888, Bramwell, West Virginia, was once the richest town per capita in the United States. At one time, fourteen millionaires lived in Bramwell, located on the West Virginia–Virginia border eight miles northwest of Bluefield. The town, which was home of the Flat Top Coal Land Association and later the Pocahontas Land Corporation, was settled by wealthy coal barons, many of whom had moved from large cities such as Philadelphia.

Numerous stately mansions were built between the turn of the century and 1912. Features found in some of the homes include an indoor swimming pool, a grand ballroom, elaborate stained glass windows, a copper roof, and a carriage wash.

Bramwell flourished along with the coal boom. At one time as many as four thousand people lived in the town, and the Bank of Bramwell was so successful it even helped to finance the Burning Tree Country Club in Washington, D.C. The stock market crash of 1929 and the ensuing depression took their toll on both the bank and the town.

In 1983, 65 buildings in Bramwell were listed on the National Register of Historic Places. The National Register historic district was greatly expanded in 1995 to encompass 151 buildings. Bramwell homes have been well preserved and provide a glimpse of the daily lives of those who prospered most from the rich coalfields of central Appalachia. Many of the privately owned mansions are open to the public twice yearly for walking tours sponsored by the Bramwell Millionaire Garden Club. In 1996, with funds from an Intermodal Surface Transportation Efficiency Act grant intended to enhance tourism opportunities along transportation corridors, Bramwell began reconstruction of its railroad station. The station has become a primary interpretive center for West Virginia's eleven-county National Coal Heritage Area and for a self-guided auto tour along southern West Virginia's Coal Heritage Trail.

See also: BITUMINOUS COAL INDUSTRY (BUSINESS, INDUSTRY, AND TECHNOLOGY); COAL HERITAGE TOURISM.

—Rosemary Carucci Goss, *Virginia Polytechnic Institute and State University*

Cashiers-Highlands Area, North Carolina

The towns of Cashiers and Highlands, North Carolina, are located along the southern crest of the Blue Ridge Mountains some sixty-five miles from Asheville and are known as popular retirement and tourist communities. The area developed in the nineteenth century when an 1819 treaty with the Cherokee made the western North Carolina mountains available for pioneer settlement. During the 1820s, the first settlers appeared in the Cashiers Valley vicinity, and more followed in the early 1830s, attracted by the presence of gold. The nearby town of Highlands was established in 1875; its sole purpose was tourism.

Cashiers Valley, renamed Cashiers in 1881, was located on a route that opened the Waynesville, North Carolina, area to markets in upstate South Carolina. Drovers, traders, and travelers stopped overnight at boardinghouses in Cashiers, where they and their livestock were fed and bedded down for the night. The accommodations for travelers also attracted South Carolinians who hunted the area's plentiful game and fished its many streams. By the 1840s and 1850s, prominent South Carolina plantation gentry were hearing about the serenity and natural beauty of the mountains, far from the hot, humid South Carolina low country, and dignitaries such as John C. Calhoun and members of South Carolina Governor Wade Hampton's family visited Cashiers Valley.

Because of the Civil War and Reconstruction, there was little mountain tourism in the 1860s and early 1870s. But in 1875, two northern men, Clinton Carter Hutchinson and Samuel Truman Kelsey, investigated the possibilities of developing a summer tourist town on the beautiful Highlands Plateau wilderness. They purchased 839 acres and surveyed it with a pocket compass, carving Main Street through the dense virgin forest. They promoted the area in many states by distributing pamphlets advertising the high elevation of the area as a curative for certain diseases. David Norton, a descendant of original area settlers, started taking boarders at his Central House in 1878.

By 1883, Highlands had a population of three hundred. The Highlands House, a thirty-room inn built in 1880, advertised in the *Blue Ridge Enterprise* in 1884, promising good rooms, pleasant suites for families, and table fare supplied with the best the markets afforded, all for $1.25 per day. By 1887, the town boasted three hotels and several private boardinghouses. It was the highest incorporated town east of the Mississippi River, and it would soon become a haven for tourists and owners of summer homes.

The first real hotel to be built in Cashiers was the Fairfield Inn, located in nearby Sapphire Valley. Part of a chain of resorts erected in western North Carolina by a group of Pennsylvania entrepreneurs, Fairfield Inn opened its doors to guests in 1896. Visitors, who often stayed three months at a time, came by rail and then were transported the last few miles by horse-drawn surreys.

Advertised as the "Switzerland of America" at the turn of the twentieth century, the present day Cashiers-Highlands area remains a popular tourist destination.

See also: GOLD RUSH OF 1829 (BUSINESS, INDUSTRY, AND TECHNOLOGY); TOURISM ARCHITECTURE (ARCHITECTURE).

—Jane Gibson Nardy, *Atlanta, Georgia*

Cashiers Area Chamber of Commerce, *The Cashiers Area: Yesterday, Today, and Forever* (1994); Gert McIntosh, *Highlands, North Carolina . . . A Walk into the Past* (1983); Max R. Williams, ed., *The History of Jackson County* (1987).

Cass Scenic Railroad State Park

In the first quarter of the twentieth century, the Greenbrier, Cheat, and Elk Railroad was the lifeline for West Virginia Pulp and Paper Company operations at Cass, a town in Pocahontas County, West Virginia. Mower Lumber Company briefly revived the railroad in the 1940s, but in 1960 the company closed the lumber and planing mill at Cass and took steps to scrap the railroad. Railroad enthusiasts mobilized and by 1961 had persuaded the state legislature and governor to acquire eleven miles of track for creating a state park that would focus on the history of the logging railroad and the timber industry. Twenty-three thousand visitors came the first year. Since then, the nonprofit Mountain State Railroad and Logging Historical Association has collaborated with park representatives to work on historical projects and restoration and to fund public history internships for park interpreters and guides.

At the park, visitors can learn about and ride excursion trains pulled by restored steam engines—the Heisler, the Shay, and the Climax—to Whittaker Station, restored as a 1940s logging camp, to the ghost town Spruce, where the company once operated a bark-peeling mill, and through what was once the highest stretch of mainline railroad in the East to 4,842-foot Bald Knob, the second-highest peak in West Virginia. In the restored town of Cass, visitors can view a diorama exhibit and take guided walking tours through the town, the lumber mill ruins, and the locomotive shop. A country store, dining facilities, Saturday evening dinner trains, and company houses outfitted as rental cottages now attract overnight visitors.

See also: CULTURAL HERITAGE TOURISM; LUMBER INDUSTRY (BUSINESS, INDUSTRY, AND TECHNOLOGY); RAILROADS (TRANSPORTATION).

—Benita J. Howell, *University of Tennessee*

Caverns as Tourist Attractions

See Section Overview

Chattahoochee National Forest

The Chattahoochee National Forest stretches across north Georgia and includes parts of all four Appalachian physiographic provinces. Because of this geologic diversity, the forest has a rare mixture of flora and fauna from both north and south, mountain and plain.

The establishment of national forests in Appalachia was the result of concern about exploitative logging in the South. Shortly after passage of the Weeks Act in 1911, the federal government purchased thirty-one thousand acres of land in north Georgia and added it to North Carolina's Nantahala National Forest and Tennessee's Cherokee National Forest. Over the next two decades, the U.S. Forest Service bought much of the land at the top of the Blue Ridge, most of which had been logged. During the New Deal, in addition to replanting the land in oak and pine, Civilian Conservation Corps workers constructed roads and recreation areas. In 1936 the Chattahoochee National Forest became a separate entity located entirely within Georgia. Today the six ranger districts of Chattahoochee National Forest are managed in conjunction with Oconee National Forest in middle Georgia.

In the 1960s, following congressional directives to manage national forests for multiple uses in addition to timber production, the U.S. Forest Service with assistance from other government agencies built or improved several recreation areas. It paved a highway up Georgia's highest peak, Brasstown Bald (4,784 feet), and put a visitor center near the top. Timber contracts also were issued during the 1960s as the first stands of trees planted during the 1930s reached maturity. Renewed emphasis on logging, along with construction of the Richard B. Russell Highway through a previously remote area, prompted Georgians who were becoming environmentally aware to contest Forest Service policies and operations. Chattahoochee became one of the first Forest Service units in the country to solicit public involvement in its management planning. The public responded by asking for more land to be designated as wilderness and more areas to be made available for off-road vehicle use. About 15 percent of the 750,000 acres in the Chattahoochee National Forest presently are set aside in ten wilderness areas.

The Chattahoochee National Forest's beauty and variety make it especially attractive to hikers and campers. Beginning at Springer Mountain, the Appalachian Trail winds seventy-nine miles through Georgia, mostly along the Blue Ridge, before continuing another two thousand miles to Maine. The trail crosses the top of Blood and Tray Mountains, the state's third- and fourth-highest peaks, both of which are heath balds. Other long trails include the ninety-mile Benton MacKaye Trail that extends from Springer Mountain to U.S. Highways 64 and 74 near the Ocoee River in Tennessee and the thirty-seven-mile Bartram Memorial Trail, which cuts across the northeastern corner of Georgia and also traverses North and South Carolina.

These long trails are all in the Blue Ridge, but other parts of the forest are just as interesting. Thick loam covers the Rich Mountains and makes possible a lush covering of trees very different from the Blue Ridge's drier forests. In northwest Georgia, the Armuchee Ridges fold up on the floor of the Appalachian Valley, and the Cumberland Plateau rises even higher to the west. East of the valley are the Cohutta Mountains, which extend north from the Blue Ridge into Tennessee. In 1975 Congress designated this area the Cohutta Wilderness; with more than thirty-five thousand acres, it is the Chattahoochee's largest wilderness area. Rugged mountains and a lack of roads make it the forest's wildest, most remote area. Lake Chatuge and Lake Blue Ridge are popular destinations for camping and fishing, and the nearby towns of Young Harris, Hiawassee, and Blue Ridge offer additional attractions for tourists. The Chattahoochee River Recreation Area is located near Anna Ruby Falls and the Bavarian-styled town of Helen. On the southeastern rim of the Chattahoochee where the Blue Ridge borders the Piedmont, Lake Russell offers camping, fishing, swimming, hiking, and a nearby area for off-road vehicles. The Chattooga River, designated a National Wild and Scenic River, is one of the premier whitewater paddling rivers in America. Chattahoochee National Forest hosts more than 10 million visitors annually.

See also: APPALACHIAN TRAIL; BLUE RIDGE PROVINCE (GEOLOGY); WHITEWATER SPORTS (SPORTS AND RECREATION).

—Wallace H. Warren, *Cornelia–Habersham County Library*

Tim Homan, *The Hiking Trails of North Georgia* (1997); Harold K. Steen, ed., *The Origins of the National Forests* (1992).

Chattanooga, Tennessee

Chattanooga's commitment to attracting tourists is visible in the Tennessee Riverpark, a twenty-mile corridor featuring parks, trails, landmarks, cultural venues, and commercial areas along the Tennessee River. Its attractions include Coolidge Park, a fishing park, a private rowing center, Ross's Landing Park and Plaza, and the Walnut Street Bridge. The Bluff View Arts District contains an outdoor Sculpture Garden, the Hunter Museum of American Art, and the Houston Museum of Decorative Arts. The Tennessee Aquarium, billed as the world's largest aquarium dedicated to the study of freshwater ecosystems, has become the centerpiece of Chattanooga's downtown renaissance. Built in 1992, the aquarium attracted more than a million visitors in its first year of operation. This surge of visitation led to the development of more than 160 new businesses including restaurants, family-focused attractions, and lodgings.

Chattanooga's successful tourism economy is the result of a twenty-year process that began as an effort to shed its reputation as the city with the worst air quality in the United States and to redevelop more than six hundred acres of derelict industrial and commercial property along the riverfront. In 1982 Chattanooga citizens formed Landmarks Chattanooga to develop recommendations for the revitalization of the riverfront and downtown. Subsequently, a Moccasin Bend Task Force refined the plan and established four goals: "Build on Chattanooga's assets: natural beauty, fascinating history and industry; preserve and enhance these natural and historic treasures; carefully add private development sites along the river; and create new parks, trails, attractions and industry to replace run down and abandoned spaces." Planning, evaluation, and formation of specific development guidelines for the Tennessee Riverpark, Ross's Landing, the Riverwalk, and the Tennessee Aquarium followed.

In 1985 a nonprofit downtown development company called RiverCity (later renamed River Valley Partners) was formed to help Chattanooga and Hamilton County implement the Tennessee Riverpark master plan. A major accomplishment of River Valley Partners was acquisition and donation of the land on which the Tennessee Aquarium was built. In order to alleviate transportation problems and address air quality issues, Chattanooga developed a fleet of electric shuttles, free to riders, to link tourist destinations that are miles apart. The Tennessee Riverpark, the Tennessee Aquarium, and the revitalized downtown collaborated with long established tourism destinations such as Rock City Gardens and Ruby Falls to develop a regional hospitality industry. By the late 1990s, national magazines were featuring Chattanooga as a prime family vacation destination and a desirable place to live.

See also: DESTINATION MARKETING ORGANIZATIONS; TENNESSEE RIVER (TRANSPORTATION).

—Benita J. Howell, *University of Tennessee*

Nancy Bearden Henderson, "Chattanooga," *Blue Ridge Country* (November–December 1998); James Kennedy, "Chattanooga," *Tennessee's Business* (Winter 1997).

Chautauqua Institution

Long before educational study tours became popular, Americans flocked to Chautauqua Lake in southwestern New York State for educational vacations. In 1874 Methodist clergyman John Heyl Vincent and Ohio industrialist Lewis Miller organized a "summer school" for young people at Fair Point, a church camp on the lake. Chautauqua soon became an annual assembly offering a program of lectures on academic subjects, music, art, and physical education as well as informal recreational and social activities. The scenic, healthful setting, outings on the lake, and good but inexpensive food and lodging made Chautauqua the site of a pleasurable learning experience for families and individuals of all ages. The summer schools were so successful that multiple meeting halls and educational buildings were erected to accommodate humanities and arts education and performance as well as the Chautauqua Assembly lecture series on diverse topics. Family cottages, modest boardinghouses, and hotels accommodated thousands of visitors each summer.

A 1917 visitor called Chautauqua an "Institution for the Refinement of the Commonplace," but he favorably compared this thriving vacation community of middle-class Christians to the casinos, horse racing, and risqué cabaret acts he found at formerly fashionable Saratoga Springs. A product of the Victorian impulse toward self-improvement, Chautauqua continued to expand its offerings during the twentieth century, adding a symphony orchestra, an opera company, a theater season, and popular entertainers to its program. During the nine-week season in 2000, summer school programs enrolled more than 8,000 students, and more than 142,000 attended arts performances or lectures on public issues and international affairs, literature, religion, and science. The colony's well-preserved Victorian architecture and small-town ambiance have become attractions in their own right. Chautauqua's grandest hotel, the 1881 Athenaeum, was restored in 1983 to offer all the modern conveniences alongside Victorian décor and furnishings.

See also: CHAUTAUQUA VILLAGE, NEW YORK (ARCHITECTURE).

—Benita J. Howell, *University of Tennessee*

Cherokee National Forest

Tennessee's only national forest, Cherokee National Forest, was established in 1920, following passage of the Weeks Act in 1911 authorizing land purchase for forest reserves. Originally including land in north Georgia and southwestern North Carolina, Cherokee National Forest boundaries were redrawn in 1936 to coincide with Tennessee state boundaries. The new boundary encompassed the Tennessee portion of Unaka National Forest to the north of the Great Smoky Mountains National Park. By 2000, the forest had grown to 630,000 acres. Statistics from a 1998 management report showed that recreational use of the area had risen approximately 44 percent during the previous decade.

Selection of the Ocoee River Gorge as site of the 1996 Olympic slalom canoe and kayak events brought the Ocoee

Oconaluftee Indian Village, Cherokee, North Carolina, 1998. A member of the Eastern Band of Cherokee Indians demonstrates white oak basketmaking as the Cherokee practiced it in the 1750s.

district of Cherokee National Forest to the attention of thousands of whitewater and outdoor enthusiasts. In cooperation with the Tennessee Valley Authority, the U.S. Forest Service built a world-class whitewater course as the key attraction of the Ocoee Whitewater Center. The course is carefully engineered but natural in appearance. The visitor center provides tourist information and historic interpretation for the region as well as exhibits on the sport of paddling and the Olympic competition.

Visitors to the forest have access to numerous picnic areas. Camping facilities range from small primitive campgrounds to Indian Boundary, a large recreational vehicle campground near Tellico Plains. Less active visitors can enjoy forest scenery on three auto routes: U.S. Highway 64 along the Ocoee River, the Cherohala Scenic Byway that connects Cherokee National Forest to Nantahala National Forest in North Carolina, and the Unaka Mountain Auto Tour. In 1998, 60 percent of visitor demand was for dispersed recreation activities such as hiking and backpacking, horseback riding, mountain biking, off-road vehicle use, whitewater rafting and canoeing, fishing and hunting, and nature study. The forest offers more than 650 miles of trail, including more than 150 miles of the Appalachian Trail and segments of the John Muir and Warrior's Passage National Recreation Trails. Hikers and backpackers can enjoy the Big Laurel Branch Wilderness on Watauga Lake; the Unaka Wilderness and adjacent Unaka Scenic Areas; the Little Frog Wilderness bordering Georgia's Cohutta Wilderness; and the Citico Creek Wilderness that borders the Joyce Kilmer–Slickrock Wilderness in North Carolina. Since the late 1980s, approximately 10 percent of the forest has been designated federal wilderness, and an additional 66,000 are presently managed as scenic or primitive areas.

During the 1990s, planning and resource management policies for Cherokee National Forest have increasingly reflected the growing popularity of outdoor recreation and persistent efforts of environmentalists to ensure wilderness preservation. Forest managers also have collaborated effectively with the Tennessee Valley Authority and Tennessee Overhill, southeast Tennessee's heritage tourism organization.

See also: ECOTOURISM; HIKING (SPORTS AND RECREATION); WEEKS ACT (GOVERNMENT); WHITEWATER SPORTS (SPORTS AND RECREATION).

—Benita J. Howell, *University of Tennessee*

William H. Skelton, ed., *Wilderness Trails of Tennessee's Cherokee National Forest* (1992).

Cherokee Tourism

Tourism emerged as the primary economy for the Eastern Band of Cherokee Indians in the 1930s. Living in impoverished conditions and lacking other economic possibilities, Eastern Cherokees began encouraging tourism by improving accessibility, accommodations, and recreational and commercial activities. A convergence of federal policies, road development, the southern Appalachian arts and crafts revival, and the opening of the Great Smoky Mountains National Park created a matrix for subsequent development of Eastern Band tourism. By the end of the twentieth century, tourists comprised 80 percent of the more than three million annual visitors to the Qualla Boundary, the Cherokee reservation in western North Carolina.

During the late nineteenth and early twentieth centuries, small numbers of tourists arrived seasonally to enjoy the North Carolina mountains, observe Native Americans in their own setting, and purchase indigenous crafts. The state promoted the successful annual Cherokee Fair, which began in 1914 and attracted several thousand visitors each fall. Tourists stayed in Cherokee homes or roomed at the government boarding school and purchased crafts at the fair, directly from artisans, or at shops on the reservation. No systematic effort to develop tourism was made, however, until poor economic conditions among Cherokees worsened during the Great Depression. As lumber companies abandoned southern Appalachian forests, wage work declined, and crafts and agricultural products once again became the primary sources of income.

To address widespread Native American poverty, Commissioner of Indian Affairs John Collier (1933–45) instituted a policy of economic rehabilitation based, in part, on marketing Native American heritage, customs, and crafts. Although the reservation lacked tourist housing, restaurants, or recreation, the Cherokee tradition of handicrafts endured, offering tourists souvenirs such as small baskets, wood carvings, and pottery. Handicraft popularity and the number of artisans grew as Collier's new federal policies called for crafts instruction in schools and community clubs. Increasing numbers of men and women turned to craft work, contributing to a market supply that provided the impetus for attracting tourists.

The government established the Indian Arts and Crafts Board in 1935, drafted craft standards, and opened craft shops at federal sites such as national parks and dams. Such federal support for Cherokee handcrafts coincided with the southern Appalachian arts and crafts revival. The Southern Highland Handicraft Guild, founded in 1930 to preserve and promote southern Appalachian handicrafts, coordinated the initiatives of numerous craft revivalists and the work of more than twenty-five craft-producing centers. In 1932 the Cherokee Council authorized the expenditure of tribal funds to finance a guild chapter and set aside a craft salesroom in the Council House. By 1938, requests for Cherokee crafts exceeded the supply. Following World War II, the small salesroom was moved to its own facility and developed into the Qualla Arts and Crafts Mutual, the most successful Indian cooperative in the country. The Cherokee management, board, and membership set prices and benefits, and the cooperative became the first reservation shop to guarantee a year-round market for craft producers and buyers.

While promoting indigenous handwork, craft revivalists of the 1930s joined other promoters from Tennessee and North Carolina to support the government's most significant southern Appalachian tourism initiative, the Great Smoky Mountains National Park. The opening of the park in 1934, with entries through Gatlinburg, Tennessee, and Cherokee, North Carolina, virtually guaranteed tourism for both communities. By 1941, more than a million tourists had visited the park, a sevenfold increase over thirty years. By the end of the twentieth century, the Great Smoky Mountains National Park was the most visited park in America. Several million cars entered each year through the park's southern gateway on the Cherokee reservation.

Road construction was essential to the park's success and also facilitated tourism. By 1934, U.S. Highway 441 linked the north and south park entrances, and tourists could travel directly from Gatlinburg, across the mountains, to Cherokee. At the end of that decade, the Cherokees made land available for the terminus of the Blue Ridge Parkway, extending it from Soco Gap across the upper reservation to Highway 441. In exchange for the parkway right-of-way, the state paved Highway 19 from east to west through the heart of Cherokee. Completion of these three major arteries made trans-reservation travel easier for tourists and Cherokees alike.

Until the second half of the century, however, tourism generally remained limited to family groups interested in abbreviated visits, few meals, modest purchases, and overnight room rentals in the summer and fall seasons. Marketing cheap novelties more than indigenous crafts, local merchants attracted customers by erecting Plains Indian teepees in front of their shops. Cherokee men wearing western Indian regalia and polyester feathers posed for photographs beside the sheet-metal teepees to encourage visitation. Recreation in Cherokee was limited to seasonal shopping, camping, and fishing.

Tourism nearly ceased with the outbreak of World War II and the reduction of available fuels, but efforts to develop the industry accelerated dramatically. A postwar survey indicated the presence of only seven rooming houses, nine restaurants, and even fewer craft shops. Facilities for tourist meals, lodging, and recreation soon became top priorities for economic planners at the tribal, state, and federal levels.

To provide recreation, business leaders from western North Carolina met in 1946 and agreed to finance the annual production of an outdoor play on Cherokee history to be staged on the reservation as a tourist attraction. Incorporating as the Cherokee Historical Association, the group ultimately sponsored the popular outdoor drama *Unto These Hills*. From its first performance on July 1, 1950, to the end of the twentieth century, the drama attracted an average of two thousand persons per performance, totaling almost five million viewers in all. As an attempt to inform the public about Cherokee history up to the mid-nineteenth century, the play represents the commencement of heritage tourism on the reservation.

Heritage tourism was further stimulated by the 1948 founding of the Museum of the Cherokee Indian. Housed in the Oconaluftee Inn at the intersection of Highways 441 and 19, the museum initially consisted of a limited number of artifacts from a private collection. After more than two decades of promoting a new museum and interpretive center, the Cherokee Historical Association opened a large facility in 1976 with extensive collections, audiovisual exhibits, and mini-theaters. Visitation was sufficiently high for the museum to remain open all year, and at the end of the century, an expansion and renovation resulted in a state-of-the-art facility that attracted both tourists and awards. The year following its reopening in June of 1998, the museum hosted nearly 125,000 visitors.

In 1952 the Cherokee Historical Association developed the Oconaluftee Indian Village, a living history museum located adjacent to the amphitheater. Intended to represent an eighteenth-century Cherokee community, the village appealed to tourists by providing workstations where Cherokees demonstrated crafts and subsistence activities. Like the drama, the village was open only in summer and early fall months. Nonetheless, the number of tourist lodgings and eating facilities had more than tripled by the following year, indicating the successful marketing of heritage attractions.

While the drama, museum, and village concentrated on family tourism, reservation gaming developed a different market. High-stakes bingo, introduced in the early 1980s, brought in more than $600,000 annually. In 1990 a weekly lotto game produced even greater revenues, and in the mid-1990s video gaming arrived. After Harrah's Cherokee Casino opened in 1997, annual revenues from gaming tourism increased in annual increments of $10 million, reaching nearly $100 million in 2000.

At the end of the twentieth century, two separate tourist markets existed in Cherokee. Heritage tourism continued to attract family groups but was subject to adverse effects of gasoline prices, weather conditions, and competing family attractions in other communities. Gaming tourism appealed to single-purpose visitors who seldom ventured beyond the casinos and bingo halls. Along with consistent campground use, both heritage and gaming contributed to the community's middle-level economic growth that was reflected in the expansion of lodging and food service. Between 1996 and 2001, the number of motel rooms increased from 1,400 to 1,950. Restaurant growth was concentrated in fast-food franchises as alcohol prohibition persisted. Cherokees had met their historic goals of developing tourism by providing lodging, food, and recreation but remained uncertain about the long-range effects of gaming and the difficulty of merging divergent tourist markets.

See also: MUSEUM OF THE CHEROKEE INDIAN (CULTURAL INSTITUTIONS); QUALLA ARTS AND CRAFTS MUTUAL (CRAFTS); *UNTO THESE HILLS* (PERFORMING ARTS).

—Sarah H. Hill, *Atlanta, Georgia*

Margaret Lynn Brown, *The Wild East: A Biography of the Great Smoky Mountains* (2000); George Frizzell, "The Native American Experience," in *The History of Jackson County*, ed. Max R. Williams (1987); Sarah H. Hill, *Weaving New Worlds: Southeastern Cherokee Women and Their Basketry* (1997).

Chesapeake and Ohio Canal National Historical Park

In October 2000, a new museum and visitor center opened at the Maryland terminus of the famed Chesapeake and Ohio Canal, offering tourists opportunities to interactively experience the operation of the vital waterway in its heyday. Completed in 1850, the 184.5-mile canal linking the highlands of western Maryland and Washington, D.C., was for two decades the primary means of sending coal to market from the area's mines. Though doomed by the coming of the railroads, the canal remained in operation until 1924. It was sold to the federal government in 1938, becoming a national historical park in 1971. During the last decades of the twentieth century, the twelve-foot-wide towpath, once used by horses and mules pulling barges, attracted growing numbers of joggers, hikers, cyclists, campers, and history buffs. After establishment of the park, water was restored to the lower reaches of the canal, permitting canoeing and barge rides, but the park in the Washington area was devastated by floods on the Potomac in 1972 and 1976. Early in the twenty-first century, plans called for restoration of a portion of the canal in western Maryland as well.

The museum and visitor center at Cumberland, adjacent to Interstate 68, shares a building with the Western Maryland Scenic Railroad, which offers daily excursions between Cumberland and Frostburg from spring through the autumn foliage season. Other visitor centers along the canal are at Hancock, Williamsport, and Brunswick, Maryland.

See also: CHESAPEAKE AND OHIO CANAL (TRANSPORTATION).

—Rudy Abramson, *Reston, Virginia*

Chimney Rock

Chimney Rock Park, located twenty-five miles southeast of Asheville, is one of the longest-standing commercially successful tourist attractions in western North Carolina. As early as 1885, visitors came to admire the spectacular view of Hickory Nut Gorge from the impressive rock outcropping. Though earlier owners had promoted Chimney Rock, it was Lucius B. Morse who developed the area as a tourist destination. A native of Missouri, Morse purchased Chimney Rock and the surrounding land, including breathtaking Hickory Nut Falls, in 1902 in order to create a park and set about improving visitor amenities and access. Originally, visitors had to negotiate a narrow trail and climb several sets of stairs to reach the summit. In 1948 the Morse family built an elevator to take visitors to the top, an endeavor that required blasting more than 250 feet through the center of the mountain. Since the 1940s, promoters of Chimney Rock Park, which is still owned and managed by the Morse family, have marketed the local flora and fauna aggressively. By the 1980s, a nature center and several interpretive nature trails had been built, and the park employed a full-time naturalist.

The park's popularity resulted in a tourism boom in nearby Lake Lure, where visitors can find accommodations, craft shops, restaurants, and other attractions. Near the end of the twentieth century, several feature films, including *The Last of the Mohicans*, were shot at Chimney Rock, which promoted the park and the local area to an even larger market. The area remains one of the most popular attractions in the North Carolina mountains.

See also: BLUE RIDGE PROVINCE (GEOLOGY).

—Richard D. Starnes, *Western Carolina University*

Civilian Conservation Corps

See Civilian Conservation Corps (Government)

Civil War Tourism

Civil War tourism is a manifestation of the enduring fascination of Americans with the nation's great internal conflict of 1861 to 1865. Veterans and their families began the custom of touring Civil War sites, and the idea eventually became firmly entrenched in the nation's culture. Spurred by Shelby Foote's narrative history, Ken Burns's television documentary, a stream of books on the period, and a general boom in heritage tourism, millions visit Appalachian Civil War sites each year. Visitation far exceeds trips to battle sites associated with other conflicts on American soil, including the Revolutionary War.

Civil War tourist sites in Appalachia number at least seventy-five. Run by federal, state, and local governments, as well as corporations and nonprofit organizations, they are located from Gettysburg and Harrisburg in Pennsylvania to Stone Mountain, Georgia, and Huntsville, Alabama. Battlefields are the best-known sites, but the homes and graves of political and military leaders and museums such as Atlanta's Cyclorama (housing a painting of the battle of Atlanta and other exhibits) are also part of the picture. The terrain of Stonewall Jackson's campaigns in northern Virginia, the resting place of Robert E. Lee in Lexington, Virginia, the battlefields surrounding Chattanooga in Tennessee, and Abraham Lincoln's birthplace in Larue County, Kentucky, are among Appalachia's most popular Civil War–related destinations. Deeply divided between union and separation, Appalachia is especially rich in battlefield sites: Antietam, the Shenandoah Valley, Harpers Ferry, Chickamauga, and Kennesaw Mountain.

As the nation's two million Civil War veterans grew old in the late 1800s, many sought to establish their place in history by setting aside battlefields as memorials. Victorious and prosperous, the North took the lead in commemorative activity. Before the war ended, the federal government had already begun establishing national cemeteries at important battlefields, and many southern cities had set aside Confederate cemeteries. Nineteenth-century customs of grave decoration and remembrance of the dead made these cemeteries popular places to visit. After 1880, organized veterans' groups proliferated, with the Grand Army of the Republic and the United Confederate Veterans in the lead. Large battlefield reunions became a defining feature of the time. The 1888 encampment marking the twenty-fifth anniversary of the three-day battle of Gettysburg was widely reported in the press and served as a model for subsequent events. Railroad officials recognized a new market and began making stops at or near important battlefields and offered special rates for reunion groups. In the 1890s, the federal government furthered the trend by establishing four national military parks: Chickamauga and Chattanooga (Georgia and Tennessee), Shiloh (Tennessee), Gettysburg (Pennsylvania), and Vicksburg (Mississippi).

Before the automobile, visits to battlefields were unhurried affairs, involving train trips, carriage rides, and leisurely walks over the fields. In addition to major gatherings for reunions and patriotic holidays, the sites played host to low-key family visits and picnics. The opportunity to reinforce nationalistic and moral lessons at battlefields made them ideal free-time destinations for Americans ambivalent about leisure activities.

Widespread automobile ownership and increased free time made vacation trips possible for many more in the twentieth century, and Civil War tourism expanded. In 1933 the National Park Service took over the national military parks from the War Department. Although the parks continued to be used for military study and training, their primary audience became the general public. While encouraging encampments and living history at its sites, the Park Service prohibits battle reenactments as incompatible with the deep meaning of these places. Battle reenactments often take place on nearby private property.

The question of whose heritage is commemorated at Civil War tourist sites has provoked considerable controversy. The first national military parks are celebrated as symbols of the reconciliation of North and South. This reconciliation came at the heavy expense of African Americans' hopes and proceeded only because the North ended Reconstruction and did not challenge the subsequent disfranchisement and segregation of black Americans. Even in the heyday of veteran-led commemorative activity, America's 175,000 black Union veterans typically were forced to hold separate events on holidays such as Memorial Day.

The extensive presence of Confederate imagery at Civil War sites—imagery often used by racist groups through the years—has further complicated the reaction of many to the whole phenomenon of Civil War tourism. Sites such as

Stone Mountain near Atlanta have drawn criticism for glorifying the Confederacy and for an allegedly selective presentation of the past. The first promoters of the sculpture of Confederate leaders on the mountain had ties to the Ku Klux Klan, and for decades the mountain was the site of annual Klan cross burnings. None of this history is addressed in the exhibits at Stone Mountain. The Harpers Ferry National Historical Park in West Virginia marks the location of John Brown's abortive 1859 attempt to free southern slaves. A 1931 memorial erected there by the United Daughters of the Confederacy honoring African American Heyward Shepherd has drawn protests because it characterizes Shepherd as a symbol of faithfulness. In response to demands that the memorial be removed, the National Park Service has erected an additional marker, explaining the context of the original monument.

Visitors to Civil War sites reflect great diversity and variety of motives. They include students on field trips, descendants following an ancestor's footsteps, reenactors deeply identifying with the period's soldiers, and joggers unconcerned with historic significance. But with most of them feeling compelling connections to the bravery and endurance of soldiers and civilians and to the great enduring issues of nationalism, regional identity, and race relations, Appalachia's Civil War sites will remain popular tourist destinations.

See also: CULTURAL HERITAGE TOURISM; MONUMENTS (VISUAL ARTS); RECONSTRUCTION (GOVERNMENT).

—Robert W. Blythe, *National Park Service*

David W. Blight, *Race and Reunion: The Civil War in American Memory* (2001); Tony Horwitz, *Confederates in the Attic: Dispatches from the Unfinished Civil War* (1998).

Coal Heritage Tourism

Coal heritage tourism, seeking to attract recreational visitors to mining culture, has proceeded in three broad phases. The first such activities resulted from industry promotion and public relations efforts. The Chicago Museum of Science and Industry mounted a coal mine exhibit in 1933; the Pocahontas Operators Association opened the Pocahontas (Virginia) Exhibition Mine, the first show mine, in 1938; and the Coal House in Williamson, West Virginia, formed from sixty-five tons of locally mined coal, was built in 1933. The Tug Valley Chamber of Commerce operates the Coal House as a tourist attraction. One of the later and most successful coal heritage attractions in this phase was the Beckley Exhibition Coal Mine located in Raleigh County, West Virginia, which was a mine worked by the Phillips family during the nineteenth century and opened to the public for tours in 1962. Listed on the National Register of Historic Places, Beckley features a museum complex that includes several historic miners' homes as well as an underground tour of more than a quarter-mile of tunnel.

In the second phase, beginning in the 1970s, extant and interpretable cultural resources were preserved through government acquisition. Examples include sites such as the Blue Heron Historical Outdoor Museum west of Stearns, Kentucky, part of the Big South Fork National River and Recreation Area, and the Kay Moor property in the New River Gorge National River area. With community assistance in developing its interpretation, Blue Heron has become one of the most popular Big South Fork attractions. The Kay Moor properties are listed on the National Register of Historic Places. In 1992 a National Park Service–sponsored study of West Virginia's coal heritage resources recommended that the town of Kay Moor itself be developed as a tourist attraction. Stabilization and access to industrial sites on public lands varies, however, with the agencies' missions and access to resources for promoting heritage tourism.

At the close of the twentieth century, public and private agencies collaboratively embraced coal heritage tourism as a means of pursuing economic development in areas where the decline of mining had produced depressed conditions. Boone, Logan, McDowell, Mingo, and Wyoming Counties in West Virginia incorporated a marketing organization called Coal Country. Most significant, however, is the larger eleven-county National Coal Heritage Area of Boone, Cabel, Fayette, Logan, McDowell, Mercer, Mingo, Raleigh, Summers, Wayne, and Wyoming Counties. Within the area, the National Park Service and state, local, and private agencies protect and interpret cultural resources in a manner that stimulates economic revitalization through tourism. Established by Congress in 1996, the Coal Heritage Area emphasizes local involvement and control but receives substantial longterm federal funding. An important aspect of multicounty programs is coordination in promoting coal-related tourist attractions such as monuments, festivals, reunions, outdoor dramatic performances, small private museums, and traveling exhibits—even the Pete Dye mining-oriented golf course near Clarksburg, West Virginia. Among the West Virginia localities that have developed significant heritage tourism resources during the 1990s are Matewan, site of the bloody 1920 clash between union members and mine security; Bramwell, the "millionaire's town" in Mercer County, which sponsors walking tours of historic homes built by coal operators; and Coalwood, a company town in McDowell County made famous by the book *Rocket Boys* and its film adaptation, *October Sky.*

Other Appalachian states also have notable and established coal history attractions. In Kentucky, these include the Kentucky Coal Mining Museum in Benham and an

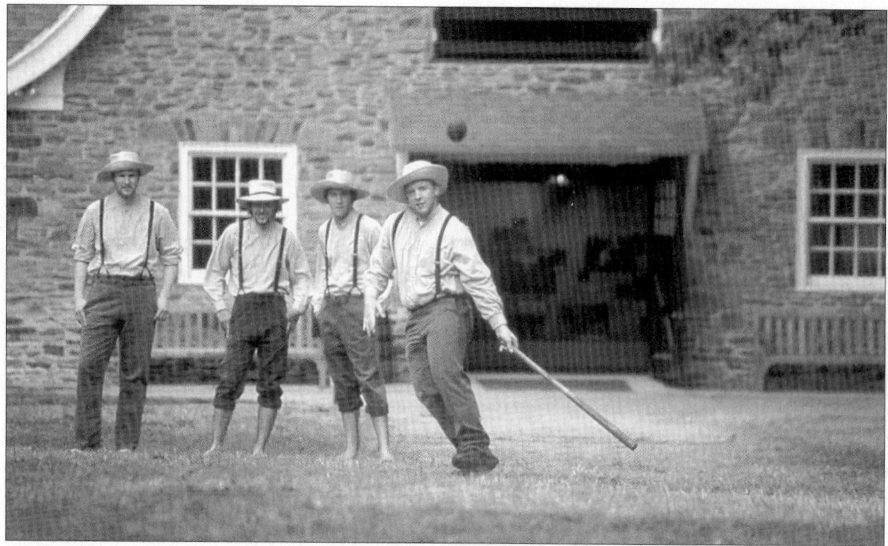

Townball at the Farmers' Museum, Cooperstown, New York, 2002. A nineteenth-century village, exhibition galleries, and a working farm comprise one of the oldest living history museums in the United States.

exhibition mine in Lynch, a coal town built by the U.S. Coal and Coke Company and operated by U.S. Steel until 1950. The state-sponsored Alabama Mining Museum in Dora interprets coal mining and social life in coal towns from 1890 to 1940. In Big Stone Gap, Virginia, the Westmoreland Coal Company owns and operates the Harry W. Meador Jr. Coal Museum, built from private collections of artifacts, photographs, and memorabilia. It is housed in a renovated building that was once author John Fox Jr.'s library. The Virginia Museum of Transportation in Roanoke also interprets coal-mining heritage.

Ashland, Pennsylvania, is the center for interpretation of anthracite coal mining. Opened in 1963 in an old drift-mouth mine, the Pioneer Tunnel Anthracite Coal Mine Tour, designated one of the top ten Pennsylvania tourist attractions, takes its forty thousand annual visitors a distance of eighteen hundred feet into Mahanoy Mountain for a tour conducted by veteran miners. Ashland also offers tourists a Museum of Anthracite Mining. Another exhibition mine, Lackawanna Coal Mine, is located in Scranton. As in West Virginia, Pennsylvania's anthracite region has built destination marketing around the theme of coal heritage. The trend continues. In the year 2000, citizens of Briceville, Tennessee, and neighboring communities embarked on a multifaceted project that combined environmental restoration with cultural heritage documentation. Ultimately tourists will be able to experience the heritage of the Coal Creek area and learn of the role Coal Creek miners played in national labor history.

See also: BECKLEY EXHIBITION COAL MINE; BRAMWELL, WEST VIRGINIA; MINING MUSEUMS (CULTURAL INSTITUTIONS).

—Stuart McGehee, *West Virginia State College*

National Park Service, *A Coal Mining Heritage Study: Southern West Virginia* (1992); Douglas Root, ed., *Compass America Guide: Pennsylvania* (2000); Lynn Seldon et al., *Country Roads of West Virginia* (1999); Zoe Ayn Strecker, *Kentucky: Off the Beaten Path* (4th edition, 1999).

Cooperstown, New York

Located in Otsego County, Cooperstown, which was founded by William Cooper, the father of writer James Fenimore Cooper, is considered one of the premier tourist sites of the Central Leatherstocking Country region of upstate New York. Many of the younger Cooper's novels were set in and around this area.

Originally settled in the late eighteenth century as an agricultural community, Cooperstown evolved into a summer retreat by the mid-1800s, drawing wealthy home and estate builders who set the foundation for Cooperstown's current economy. While agriculture remained an important component, both private and public sectors invested heavily in tourism during the twentieth century. The Otesaga Hotel, built in 1909 and overlooking Lake Otsego (called the "Glimmerglass" by Cooper), stands as the village's centerpiece. The town also has three nationally recognized museums: the National Baseball Hall of Fame, which draws some three hundred thousand visitors each year; the Farmers' Museum, one of the country's oldest outdoor living history museums; and the Fenimore House Museum, built on the site of a James Fenimore Cooper residence known as Fenimore Farm. Together, the two latter museums attract more than one hundred thousand visitors annually.

Thousands of tourists flock to Cooperstown each year for special events such as the annual canoe regatta, inductions of Baseball Hall of Famers, baseball games at Doubleday Field, and other seasonal happenings.

See also: COOPER, JAMES FENIMORE (LITERATURE); SPORTS HALLS OF FAME (SPORTS AND RECREATION).

—Jill Oxendine, *Johnson City, Tennessee*

Cradle of Forestry in America Historic Site

Located near the Blue Ridge Parkway on North Carolina Highway 276 outside Brevard, North Carolina, the Cradle of Forestry in America was the home of the first forestry school in America, the Biltmore Forest School (1898–1913). The site is located in a part of the Pisgah National Forest that was once owned by George W. Vanderbilt, who is noted for building the famed Biltmore House, promoting scientific forestry, and being a historical force in resource conservation.

Established as a historic site by Congress in 1968, the Cradle of Forestry's rustic buildings have been rebuilt or refurbished to commemorate the school and the beginnings of American forestry. In addition, visitors are shown various aspects of southern Appalachian culture and the principles of multiple-use forest management. Designed for persons of all ages and abilities, exhibits in the site's Forest Discovery Center focus on forest dynamics, natural resource careers, and forest management. Two of the more popular displays are a burrow through which visitors can crawl in order to observe the forest ecosystem from below ground level and a helicopter firefighting simulation.

Outdoor activities at the site include two trails that wind past historic cabins where crafters can be seen weaving, quilting, and making baskets and traditional toys. An antique sawmill and a 1915 logging locomotive symbolize the shift from Appalachian farms to industrial logging in the mountains. Other exhibits interpret the continuing history of forestry in America.

See also: CULTURAL HERITAGE TOURISM; FOREST MANAGEMENT AND CONSERVATION (ENVIRONMENT); LUMBER INDUSTRY (BUSINESS, INDUSTRY, AND TECHNOLOGY).

—Cindy N. Carpenter, *U.S. Department of Agriculture Forest Service*

Cultural Heritage Tourism

Historic sites, displays and performances of regional heritage, and expressions of ethnic identity form the core attractions of cultural heritage tourism. The most vigorously promoted and fastest growing sector of Appalachia's tourist economy at the end of the twentieth century, cultural heritage attractions include historical museums, occupational history centers, and outdoor dramas and festivals, as well as public and commercial attractions that present Appalachian music and dance, food, handicrafts, storytelling, and social customs. This form of tourism caters to an aging population's nostalgia and takes advantage of federal and state incentives for historic preservation. If well managed, this form of tourism can bolster local economies while avoiding many of the environmental and socioeconomic disadvantages of mass tourism.

Cultural heritage tourism is distinct from mass tourism in several respects. Rather than depending on generic attractions or stereotypical "local color," heritage tourism destinations work with cultural specialists to identify special heritage assets and develop high-quality interpretation and presentation based on historic and ethnographic research. Marketing is secondary to resource preservation. Because their visitors seek authentic experiences, heritage tourism destinations limit inappropriate or excessive development in order to maintain the character of their locality and operate in a sustainable manner. Effective participation of local stakeholders in planning and in representing their culture to visitors is critically important because cultural heritage tourists seek more than superficial interaction with the places they visit. Cultural heritage presentations appeal most strongly to people who are older, better educated, and more affluent than average. Small-scale and limited visitation helps provide the kind of experience that such visitors seek.

Historic preservation provided the impetus for these developments. Since 1980, the National Trust for Historic Preservation has worked with communities to save and rehabilitate downtown structures through its Main Street program. Economic revitalization in Main Street communities typically incorporates tourism, as arts organizations, restaurateurs, and merchants are encouraged to collaborate in making old downtown areas fun places to visit for entertainment and shopping. Many Appalachian towns and cities have developed award-winning Main Street programs. These include Saratoga Springs, New York; York, Pittsburgh, and Johnstown, Pennsylvania; Morgantown and Beckley, West Virginia; Cumberland, Maryland; and Gallipolis, Ohio.

During the 1990s, the Appalachian states experienced a proliferation of regional heritage tourism packages developed and marketed in collaboration with businesses, nonprofit organizations, and local, state, and federal agencies. Effective destination marketing organizations and Internet presence have become important tools as heritage tourism attractions compete with one another for tourists' attention and dollars. The idea of regional marketing is not of recent origin, however. It is at least as old as the Fingerlakes Association of western New York, founded in 1919.

Although the term *cultural heritage tourism* dates from the last quarter of the twentieth century, this form of tourism in Appalachia is as old as the historic preservation and Arts and Crafts movements. The Chickamauga and Chattanooga battlefield in Tennessee was designated the nation's first national historical park in 1890, while Fireside Industries at Berea College in Kentucky and Allanstand Cottage Industries in western North Carolina became turn-of-the-century harbingers of today's HandMade in America program and state promotion of craft heritage trails.

Private groups organized early efforts to preserve historic sites, primarily homes of former presidents of the United States and other places connected to important historical figures. For example, following abortive attempts of the owner to donate Monticello to the nation during the nineteenth century, the Thomas Jefferson Memorial Foundation purchased the former president's home near Charlottesville, Virginia, in 1923 and opened it for tours.

Individuals envisioned, organized, and promoted festivals of music and dance that were precursors of today's heritage tourism events. In Appalachia, the best known were Bascom Lamar Lunsford's Mountain Dance and Folk Festival, begun in Asheville, North Carolina, in 1928; the southwest Virginia White Top Folk Festival, begun by Annabel Morris Buchanan in 1931; and Jean Thomas's American Folk Song Festival begun in Ashland, Kentucky, in 1932. During the New Deal, Works Progress Administration folklife programs encouraged preservation and perpetuation of cultural arts, and the Historic American Building Survey and Historic Sites Act supported historic preservation. Perhaps most important for cultural heritage tourism was the Federal Writers' Project. State guidebooks written by government-supported authors included detailed itineraries and introduced the public to the history and cultural attractions of country towns and byways as well as urban areas. Published in 1940 or 1941, the state guides were ready for the surge of automobile tourism that followed World War II. Creation of the National Endowment for the Arts in 1964 and the National Endowment for the Humanities in 1965 provided federal encouragement and grant support to museums, historical societies, and arts organizations, either directly or through state councils. Such funds have helped heritage sites throughout Appalachia to develop strategies for interpretation, museums for mounting new exhibits, and arts organizations for developing performance pieces based on local heritage themes. The nation's bicentennial in 1976 presented an opportunity to package cultural heritage resources as tourist attractions. With continuing support from the National Trust for Historic Preservation's Main Street program and Heritage Tourism Initiative, state and multicounty offices of tourism development intensified their efforts to develop and promote regional packages of cultural heritage tourism attractions during the 1980s and 1990s.

See also: NATIONAL TRUST HERITAGE TOURISM INITIATIVE; SUSTAINABLE TOURISM.

—Benita J. Howell, *University of Tennessee*

American Folklife Center, *Cultural Conservation: The Protection of Cultural Heritage in the United States* (1983); Benita J. Howell, "Beyond Historic Preservation," *Now and Then* (Spring 1996); *Tennessee's Business Special Issue: Preserving and Promoting Cultural Resources* (Winter 1995).

Cumberland Falls

The Cumberland Falls are situated in southeastern Kentucky in Whitley County. The waterfall forms a 125-foot-wide curtain that, depending on the water level of the Cumberland River, plunges more than 65 feet into a boulder-strewn gorge. One of the largest waterfalls in the Southeast, the falls are nicknamed "Niagara of the South" and have been a major tourist attraction for the area since the nineteenth century. Particularly notable are the appearance of rainbows at the falls and occasionally a moonbow at night, caused by the large cloud of mist from the cascading water.

The Cumberland Falls were considered sacred by the Cherokee, Shawnee, and other Native Americans who inhabited or visited the area. White explorers and long hunters ventured into the region in the late 1700s, and settlers, primarily Scots-Irish, arrived in the 1850s. The first permanent settlers at the falls were Louis and Mary Renfro, who established a small rustic inn for visitors.

Samuel Garland from Virginia first claimed ownership of the falls. In 1928 Mr. and Mrs. T. Coleman DuPont of Kentucky offered to purchase Cumberland Falls and surrounding acreage for a state park. In 1930 the area was designated the Cumberland Falls State Resort Park. Current accommodations include a lodge named for the DuPonts, cottages, camping areas, and seventeen miles of hiking trails with connections to backpacking trails in the Daniel Boone National Forest.

See also: KENTUCKY STATE PARKS.

—Carol Jo Evans, *University of Kentucky*

Cumberland Gap National Historical Park

The first recorded discovery of the Cumberland Gap was by Virginia explorers led by Thomas Walker in 1750. He named it for the Duke of Cumberland, son of King George II. Daniel Boone blazed a trail through the gap in 1775; it later became the Wilderness Road.

When automobiles and paved roads were still rare, an "object lesson road" was constructed through the gap, initiating Kentucky's road-building program. Completed in October 1908, the macadam road improved transportation through the difficult mountain passage and became part of a tourism route that extended from Detroit to Miami.

As part of the park's efforts to restore the Wilderness Road and primarily for safety purposes, a tunnel with a four-lane highway was constructed beneath the gap and opened to traffic on October 18, 1996. The 3.8-mile-long Pinnacle Road leads to the top of the mountain above the gap and provides panoramic views.

The gap was an important military objective during the Civil War, and Civil War fortifications still exist along the road. About fifty miles of hiking trails allow visitors to reach attractions such as Sand Cave, Tri-State Peak, and White Rocks. The remains of an iron furnace are found within park boundaries at the town of Cumberland Gap. In 2000 the twenty-thousand-acre park received more than 1.5 million recreational visits. A campground is located in the Virginia section, and there are four others accessible only by foot along the hiking trails. The park interprets its cultural and natural history through campfire programs, hikes, walks, music, crafts, and tours to the Hensley Settlement. The Cumberland Gap's evolving role in American history as a route for exploration, western migration, commerce, and transportation is interpreted in the park's visitor center.

See also: BOONE, DANIEL (SETTLEMENT AND MIGRATION); CIVIL WAR TOURISM; WILDERNESS ROAD (SETTLEMENT AND MIGRATION).

—W. Eugene Cox, *Great Smoky Mountains National Park*

Dahlonega, Georgia

Dahlonega, Georgia, is located in the Blue Ridge Mountains about an hour north of Atlanta and near the southern end of the Appalachian Trail. Its name comes from the Cherokee word for yellow or gold, *talonega*. Although gold had been discovered in several locations in the United States prior to 1828, when Benjamin Parks stumbled on gold while hunting, rumors of his find drew thousands of prospectors to the area. Dahlonega became the site of the nation's first major gold rush. In 1835 Congress authorized construction of a United States Mint to coin the north Georgia gold. The Dahlonega Branch Mint only operated from 1838, at the beginning of the Cherokee removal on the Trail of Tears, until the start of the Civil War in 1861, but commercial gold mining continued well into the twentieth century.

Dahlonega's nineteenth-century prosperity is evident in the town's architectural heritage. The 1836 Lumpkin County Courthouse, now housing the Dahlonega Gold Museum, and other buildings on the public square constitute the Dahlonega Historic Commercial District, with fifteen buildings listed on the National Register of Historic Places. Another National Register district, Hawkins Street Neighborhood, preserves houses built from the 1840s through the early 1940s. Both are interpreted in walking tours. The Gold Museum displays coins minted at Dahlonega and interprets the technology of gold mining and lifestyles of prospectors and miners through a video. Mine tours are offered at Consolidated Mines, Gold Miners' Camp, and Crisson Mines, a family-owned enterprise that operated from 1847 until 1987.

Dahlonega hosts several annual festivals, nearly all associated with the gold rush that began in 1829. The primary fall festival is Gold Rush Days, the third weekend of October. It includes the largest arts and crafts fair in northeast Georgia with more than three hundred booths, liars' and hog callers' contests, pioneer competitions in crosscut sawing, and a variety of musical and buck dancing presentations. Other annual events include World Championship Gold Panning; Bear on the Square, which focuses on authentic mountain music and crafts; Wildflower Festival of the Arts; Buckskinners Frolic; Autumn Festival; Old Fashioned Christmas; and the largest July Fourth celebration in north Georgia.

There are ample and excellent lodging and dining facilities in the area. In fact, Dahlonega and Lumpkin County have a long tradition of tourism. A nineteenth-century resort, Porter Springs, attracted visitors to imbibe its chalybeate waters and enjoy its fine cuisine. The clubhouse of Dahlonega Consolidated Gold Mining Company was converted into a resort hotel, the Mountain Inn (now called the Mountain Lodge), when the company ceased operation in 1906. The Smith House Restaurant and Hotel, still world famous for its family-style meals, opened in 1922 and quickly attracted a following. Dahlonega draws visitors from Atlanta and elsewhere for its heritage tourism, festivals, and to enjoy the cool climate, scenery, and recreation opportunities of the Blue Ridge Mountains.

See also: BLUE RIDGE PROVINCE (GEOLOGY); GOLD RUSH OF 1829 (BUSINESS, INDUSTRY, AND TECHNOLOGY); GOLD SETTLEMENTS (SETTLEMENT AND MIGRATION).

—Ray Rensi, *North Georgia College and State University*

Anne Dismukes Amerson, *I Remember Dahlonega: Memories of Growing Up in Lumpkin County* (1992).

Daniel Boone National Forest

The Daniel Boone National Forest covers portions of twenty-one counties in eastern Kentucky. Originally designated the Cumberland National Forest in a 1937 proclamation by President Franklin D. Roosevelt, the area was renamed in 1966. As of September 1999, the forest encompassed more than 2.1 million acres, with nearly 700,000 acres in federal ownership.

Railroads brought large-scale commercial logging to the area, and coal-mining operations were begun during the 1870s and 1880s. By the 1930s, a majority of the timber and coal resources had been depleted, and the federal government acquired and began to restore large tracts that had been logged and mined by the Stearns Coal and Lumber Company (48,000 acres), the Castle Craig Coal

Company (27,000 acres), and the Warfork Land Company (22,000 acres).

Like Appalachia's other national forests, Boone is managed for multiple uses that include timber production, watershed management, and fish and wildlife conservation. In the forest are approximately thirty-two endangered, threatened, or rare species, including the red-cockaded woodpecker, the bald eagle, various species of mussels, and the Virginia big-eared bat. In recent decades, Boone has become one of the most popular outdoor recreation destinations among the southern national forests, attracting more than five million visitors annually to participate in a wide range of recreational activities, including hiking and backpacking, rock climbing and cave exploration, hunting and fishing, canoeing, whitewater rafting, swimming, mountain biking, and horseback riding. Redbird Crest Trail in the Redbird district is open to off-road vehicles.

The forest includes two wilderness areas and offers a system of more than five hundred miles of hiking and mountain-biking trails. Its backbone is the 254-mile Sheltowee Trace National Recreation Trail, which runs north-south through the length of the forest with links to popular visitor attractions in and adjacent to Boone: the Red River Gorge Geological Area, Natural Bridge State Resort Park, Cave Run Lake, Laurel River Lake, Cumberland Falls State Park, Lake Cumberland, and the Big South Fork National River and Recreation Area. Sheltowee (meaning "Big Turtle") was the Shawnee name given to Daniel Boone. The most visited area is the scenic Red River Gorge Geological Area, covering 25,663 acres and featuring Kentucky's first designated national wild and scenic river and more than eighty natural stone arches sculpted by wind and water. Sky Bridge is the most accessible and most visited of these arches. The Zilpo Scenic Byway and handicap-accessible campgrounds offer persons with disabilities opportunities to camp, picnic, engage in nature study, and enjoy the scenery of Daniel Boone National Forest.

See also: ECOTOURISM; FOREST MANAGEMENT AND CONSERVATION (ENVIRONMENT).

—Carol Jo Evans, *University of Kentucky*

U.S. Forest Service, *The Daniel Boone National Forest* (1996).

Destination Marketing Organizations

Many areas in Appalachia have established regional (i.e., multicounty) associations known as destination marketing organizations, which are partnership groups that have come together on the basis of a common history, image, geology, geography, or culture to market tourism in a specific area. These organizations promote existing tourism products and do not develop or build new ones. Generally funded with member dues, a destination marketing organization may also receive grants from federal or state agencies that support the area's economic development. In some cases, subgroup members may get funds from bed or occupancy taxes through local government agencies.

The tasks and responsibilities of these marketing groups include such activities as creating a destination vision; selecting strategic markets; positioning the product, then packaging and distributing information; operating a regional welcome center; managing a Web site and/or telephone center and faxing requested information on demand; advertising cooperatively via print, television, radio, or electronic media; producing guidebooks, maps, and targeted brochures; attending consumer and wholesale industry travel shows; sponsoring consumer or economic impact tourism research; providing local news to the tourism community; and providing visitors with information that interprets natural, cultural, historical, and other tourism resources.

A good example of a destination marketing organization in southern Appalachia is the North Carolina High Country Host. Established in 1980 as a grassroots membership organization, the group was the first regional cooperative marketing organization in the state, successfully promoting travel to the six northwestern North Carolina counties of Alleghany, Ashe, Avery, Mitchell, Watauga, and Wilkes. By year 2000, the economic impact of the tourism industry in these counties was about $300 million per year.

The High Country Host's mission is to attract new and repeat visitors to the region and then direct them to member businesses. The member businesses also belong to their town or county chambers of commerce. Advertising dollars are pooled among private businesses and the local chambers of commerce. The fundamental marketing concept is first to sell the consumer on the destination and then to let individual business firms intercept tourists while they are visiting.

This organization's major marketing tool is the *Vacation Guidebook*, a booklet that showcases the six counties and provides visitors with a foldout map. The organization also sponsors joint or co-op advertising for its members in leading magazines and newspapers to reduce advertising costs. The host group operates a regional visitor information center in Boone, North Carolina, the heart of the High Country. Each year thousands of visitors come through this center to obtain travel information and recommendations on where to stay and what to do.

For destination marketing organizations to be successful, the destination region should have a strong leadership group that builds a united team effort. This team needs to develop a tourism policy that outlines regulations, rules, guidelines, directives, objectives, and strategies to provide a common framework for the collective and individual decisions affecting tourism promotion and development.

See also: ECONOMIC DEPENDENCY AND TOURISM; SUSTAINABLE TOURISM.

—Michael R. Evans, *Appalachian State University*

C. Goeldner, J. R. Ritchie, and R. McIntosh, *Tourism: Principles, Practices, Philosophies* (2000); Norma P. Nickerson, *Foundations of Tourism* (1996).

Dollywood

Dollywood is a theme park created when its namesake, singer-songwriter Dolly Parton, entered into a partnership with owner Herschend Enterprises and invested several million dollars into revamping the existing Silver Dollar City theme park in Pigeon Forge, Tennessee. As its name implies, Dollywood embraces traditional mountain culture and the razzle-dazzle commercial appeal that Parton combined to create her own successful public persona.

Though easily the most successful, Dollywood was not the first commercial park on the site, nor even the first with a mountain life theme. Grover and Harry Robbins, who also owned Tweetsie Railroad in North Carolina, opened an amusement park called Rebel Railroad on the site in 1961. Rebel Railroad provided visitors with the experience of a simulated ride on a Confederate train attacked by hostile Union soldiers. After the Rebels drove back the Yankees in a staged skirmish, the train returned to a frontier village, where tourists could stop in the general store, watch a blacksmith at work, or eat a hamburger while catching the cancan act in the saloon. The park was a moderate success, but in the late 1960s, the Robbins brothers decided to sell the park to the most unlikely of investors, Art Modell and the Cleveland Browns.

Modell and the Browns quickly abandoned the Confederate motif, gave the place a multimillion-dollar facelift, and reopened in 1970 as an Old West theme park called Goldrush Junction. Tourists still rode the train, but Indians had replaced Yankees as the ambushing aggressors. However, the Cleveland investors soon realized that quaint images of mountain life were a stronger selling point than the Old West in the area, and in 1972 they gave the park another makeover and converted Goldrush Junction into a hillbilly theme park.

Modell and the Browns proved to be unsuccessful in the tourism business. Mired in debt, they sold Goldrush Junction in 1976 to Jack and Pete Herschend, who owned a thriving mountaineer theme park in Branson, Missouri. A year later, the Herschends renamed the park Silver Dollar City and gave tourists authentic hillbilly experiences that included bluegrass music, handcrafts, and a mock reenactment of the Hatfield-McCoy feud.

In 1985, the Herschends approached Parton, who wanted to invest in the booming tourist industry of her native Sevier County. After a year of negotiations, Parton bought in as a minority owner, and by the turn of the century the rechristened Dollywood had become one of the twenty-five most visited theme parks in America. Encompassing 125 acres, welcoming more than two million visitors each year, and at the center of tourist attractions, restaurants, and motels, Dollywood makes Pigeon Forge the most significant source of revenue in Sevier County.

Theme parks in general owe their success to the desire of a vacationing public to travel to a new place and encounter something of its distinctive character without fear that geographic and cultural dislocation will force them into threatening or disorienting situations. Dollywood is popular because it offers safe, controlled proximity to a southern hillbilly culture that has simultaneously intrigued and alienated Americans for over a century.

While it relates having fun with spending money as successfully as any profit-oriented American theme park, Dollywood has an unusual emotional core. The park has done much for local prosperity, and even the most urbane of its attractions are suffused with the Appalachian hillbilly's perspective. Glittering Dollywood Boulevard, a tribute to classic movies and film stars, touchingly reflects the appeal of the movie house to Appalachians. While the hillbilly mystique is present and even celebrated in amusements as diverse as old-time soap making and high-tech simulations of the white lightning chase in Thunder Road, depictions of the gullible hillbilly and his suspicious gun-toting cousin are emphatically excluded.

Parton's music and spirit pervade Dollywood, but she is explicitly present in three locations: the Rags to Riches Museum contains chronologically arranged memorabilia from different phases of her career; the replica of her two-room childhood home offers visitors an impossibly tidy and charming version of the Parton household on her native Locust Ridge; and the Heartsongs multimedia show romantically highlights the origins of her music in the natural beauty of the mountains. Parton is straightforward and cheerful about the artifice in these and many other park attractions, but her particular conviction about memory—that good ones should be treasured and bad ones forgotten—subtly justifies the relentlessly upbeat tone and commercial polish of a park where the diversions play off the traditional lifeways of people whose lot involved exhausting work and few material rewards. A similar resolution is implicit in the park's mission statement: "Create Memories Worth Repeating."

See also: PARTON, DOLLY (MUSIC); PIGEON FORGE, TENNESSEE.

—C. Brenden Martin, *Northwestern State University*, and Camille Wells, *University of Virginia*

Ray B. Browne and Michael T. Marsden, eds., *The Cultures of Celebration* (1994); Jack Neely, "Where Dali Meets Dolly," *Metro Pulse* (June 3–17, 1994); Dolly Parton, *Dolly: My Life and Other Unfinished Business* (1994); J. W. Williamson, *Hillbillyland:*

What the Movies Did to the Mountains and What the Mountains Did to the Movies (1995).

Economic Dependency and Tourism

Historically, the signs of economic dependency in Appalachia have been observable in the region's poverty and in its economic reliance on logging and coal mining, export industries for the industrial North. Popular dependency theory suggests that persistently poor, underdeveloped areas such as Appalachia depend on exports to pay for imports of capital and finished goods from industrial areas. Tourism is becoming another significant source of jobs and income for the region. In some communities, tourism is the primary component of the local economy, but one that still displays the characteristics of dependency. That is, it acts as an export industry with low wages and significant amounts of imported capital.

North Carolina economists estimated that in 1996 tourism accounted for 61 percent of gross retail sales in Swain County, North Carolina, home of the Qualla Boundary reservation and North Carolina gateway to the Smoky Mountains. Following two decades of modest growth, the pace of tourism development in the town of Cherokee accelerated after western North Carolina was "rediscovered" in the 1970s. Overall growth, however, was limited by property right restrictions on Cherokee tribal lands, federal ownership of most remaining adjacent lands, and its relatively remote location. Cherokee's tourist industry retained high levels of local ownership while also growing to dominate the small local economy. The economic impact of this development was that many of Cherokee's social welfare indicators were superior to those of some remote communities in the region with little or no tourism yet significantly lower than those of other economies with more diverse investments.

Analyses of tourism's economic impacts vary depending on the perspective of the researcher and the methods employed. The most common approach used by government and business emphasizes economic growth and focuses on first-order impacts, such factors as employment rates, income levels, tax revenues, investments, and profits. Using this perspective, tourism is viewed as an engine of economic development, with statistics showing to what degree it has been successful. Unfortunately, such aggregate-income studies fail to address two important aspects of tourism development: they give no indication of how the costs and benefits of development are distributed across stakeholders, and they do not recognize that tourism is an evolving force that can dramatically alter the economic landscape of a community. When these factors are considered, the emphasis shifts to second- and third-order impacts such as levels of poverty, unemployment, per capita income, public debt per capita, participation in government welfare programs, and labor force participation. This perspective acknowledges the evolutionary nature of the tourist industry.

An example of this evolutionary process can be found in the Smoky Mountain gateway communities of Gatlinburg and Pigeon Forge in east Tennessee. After creation of the Great Smoky Mountains National Park in 1934, Gatlinburg experienced a long period of slow tourism development characterized by strong local participation through ownership of tourist businesses and a handicraft industry. In 1969 the Pigeon Forge city council passed a zoning plan assigning the commercial strip through the heart of the community almost exclusively to tourism use. In such an environment, imported capital produces rapid development and supports entities such as chain motels.

In 1982, after the World's Fair in neighboring Knoxville, Pigeon Forge embarked on a concerted program of development that eventually consisted of several components not typical of tourism in the region: the creation of Dollywood theme park, country music theaters, and factory outlet malls. Five outlet malls had been built in Pigeon Forge by 1992, providing the community with 44 percent of its gross revenues. Subsequent to 1982, the area's tourism was characterized by rapid development, increased outside investment, and an economy dominated by the tourist industry. By 1999 Pigeon Forge and Gatlinburg had the following businesses committed to tourism: 386 lodging establishments, 624 specialty shops and factory outlets, 106 entertainment attractions, 26 wedding chapels, 21 galleries, 165 restaurants, and 76 craft shops.

Aggregate statistics measuring growth indicated increasing success. Gross tourist revenues increased from approximately $200 million in 1981 to $660 million in 1992. During the same period, however, social welfare indicators did not show similar improvement; the State of Tennessee officially designated the county "depressed." Dependency theory suggests an explanation for this apparent contradiction.

Chain motels, large music theaters, factory outlet malls, resort developments, and theme parks require considerable capital investment. Given the capital requirements for such large-scale tourism development, these businesses typically exist as corporations or investment pools. Of a sample of Appalachian resorts and theme parks whose ownership was identified, 61 percent were corporate owned, 11 percent were owned by investor groups from outside the region, 17 percent were publicly owned (by state or local governments), and only 11 percent were family-owned smaller resorts.

The low-wage nature of mass-tourism employment is another feature that conforms to dependency theory. No one claims that tourism suffers from declining terms of trade. Empirical evidence does suggest, however, that since the 1970s federal government policies, especially those of the Federal Reserve Board, have produced an environment in which earnings of low-wage service industry employees declined relative to earnings of upper income groups and technology industry employees. This trend indicates that tourism as an industry suffers from what might be considered "declining terms of labor."

What this means for employees in mass-tourism destinations is that in Sevier County, for instance, the annual unemployment rate has been cut virtually in half since the mid 1980s, yet the number of people in poverty also has risen (up approximately 27 percent between 1990 and 1995) and the county's average annual wages are consistently among the lowest in the state. Many of the jobs created by tourism are low paying, part-time, and seasonal, offering little or no opportunity for upward mobility on a career path. The service-sector jobs created by tourism often are gender-biased or considered to be "women's work" (making beds, cleaning, serving food). Such part-time work may be adequate to supplement household income, but underemployment is a serious problem because primary wage earners are trying to support their households on these wages. Effects of underemployment are exacerbated because the cost of housing continues to escalate as rural land is replaced by vacation homes and condominium developments. Would-be employees find that they cannot afford to live near the jobs generated by tourism development.

This profile of Sevier County's tourism development suggests that a more thorough approach to evaluation would consider the structure of the local economy, the way the tourist industry evolves over time, and corresponding changes in social welfare indicators during distinct stages of development. From this perspective, maximizing economic growth is not the principal objective. Instead, economic impacts on the local population and labor force are prime considerations.

Tourism development clearly provides underdeveloped areas with opportunities for increasing jobs and incomes. However, the combination of low and declining relative wages coupled with the withdrawal of profits to compensate imported capital suggests that tourism's benefits would be limited for stakeholders who have the greatest need for more and better jobs with higher wages. Thorough assessment of second- and third-order impacts will continue to demand attention as more communities in Appalachia turn to tourism as an economic development strategy.

See also: CHEROKEE TOURISM; GATLINBURG, TENNESSEE; PIGEON FORGE, TENNESSEE.

—Margaret D. Foraker, *University of Tennessee*, and L. Alex Tooman, *Sherwood, Oregon*

Charles P. Oman and Ganeshan Wignaraja, *The Postwar Evolution of Development Thinking* (1991); Paul Salstrom and Steve Hollenhorst, "Increasing Dependency and the Touristization Rag," *Appalachian Journal* (Summer 1994); Michal Smith, *Behind the Glitter: The Impact of Tourism on Rural Women in the Southeast* (1989); L. Alex Tooman, "Applications of the Life-Cycle Model in Tourism," *Annals of Tourism Research* (January 1997).

Ecotourism

The term *ecotourism* came into use in the 1980s as widespread societal concern for environmental issues escalated. On the most superficial level, the term means travel aimed at the enjoyment of a natural area. Deeper levels of meaning involve the responsibilities of travelers and tourism service providers to abide by certain environmental and ethical standards.

As of 2001, no international code of standards existed, but several basic principles were widely recognized. Ecotravelers should engage in nonconsumptive activities that have minimal or no impact on the environment they are visiting; native peoples should benefit economically so that tourism provides an incentive for conservation of natural areas; and ecotourism businesses should make significant efforts to operate in environmentally sustainable and culturally sensitive ways. The Ecotourism Society, an international organization founded in 1990, summarizes these principles in its definition of ecotourism as "responsible travel to natural areas that conserves the environment and sustains the well-being of local people."

Travel for the purpose of enjoying nature dates to the eighteenth century in Appalachia, but other tenets of ecotourism as defined above are new. Hot springs and mineral waters in the region attracted some of the earliest tourists. During the nineteenth century, wealthy people fled the malarial, cholera-ridden summers in lowland cities for clean air and pure water in the mountains. These two kinds of tourism usually led to the establishment of large hotels such as the Homestead in Hot Springs, Virginia, and resort communities such as Highlands, North Carolina, which were mostly developed by and catered to people from outside the region, benefited few local people, and had significant impacts on local environments.

Beginning in the early twentieth century, the federal government's purchase of some seven million acres for national forests in the Appalachians and the acquisition of about a million acres more for national parks provided a focus for nature-oriented tourism. With the increasing affluence and urbanization of society after World War II, the demand for recreation based on environmental amenities grew rapidly. Great Smoky Mountains National Park in North Carolina and Tennessee now receives more than 10 million people annually, the most of any national park. Visitation to Appalachian national forests increased by 72 percent from 1975 to 1990, raising tourism significantly above logging in terms of generating jobs and income. Visitation to undeveloped areas was expected to increase 150 percent over the 1990 level by 2005. More than half of national forest visitors are residents of mountain counties, an indication of the growing value of natural amenities to local populations.

Outdoor activities also have greatly expanded. Downhill skiing, for example, became popular in some high-elevation parts of Appalachia beginning in the 1960s, but its reliance on huge resorts and destruction of large swaths of mountain forest disqualifies it as ecotourism. Hiking, on the other hand, the growth of which is reflected in increasingly crowded conditions on the Appalachian Trail since the 1950s, has had relatively minor environmental impact while widely dispersing the economic benefits from hikers.

Since the 1970s, new types of outdoor activities, supported by access to many world-class natural features on the Appalachian public lands, have further stimulated a gradual trend toward smaller, dispersed facilities. Whitewater river running in rafts, canoes, and kayaks attracts tens of thousands to such rivers as the New in West Virginia, the Nantahala in North Carolina, and the Chattooga in Georgia and South Carolina. The Ocoee River Gorge in the Cherokee National Forest, Tennessee, was the venue for the 1996 Olympic slalom canoe and kayak events. Nordic (cross-country) skiing is well established in the Canaan Valley of West Virginia and elsewhere. Rock climbing, caving, and horseback riding draw smaller but still growing clienteles. In the late 1990s, mountain biking was probably the fastest-growing recreational activity in some areas, notably West Virginia, which was ranked by readers of *Mountain Bike* magazine among their top four destinations in the world. Both mountain biking and horseback riding are controversial as ecotourism because of their environmental impacts, however.

Many of these activities require guides and equipment, enhancing the opportunities for local economic involvement. Less vigorous ecotourism pastimes that have also become increasingly popular in recent years include bird watching, wildlife viewing, wildflower identification, autumn color appreciation, nature study, and car camping. Weekend naturalist meetings and nature-based retreats for businesses and other organizations have become common, but there are few tourism service suppliers who attempt to operate in environmentally sensitive ways by using solar power, for instance, or minimizing the use of vehicles, recycling, and purchasing locally produced food.

The most distinct segment of travel that can be defined as ecotourism is based on the system of congressionally designated wilderness areas. There are sixty wilderness and wilderness study areas on Appalachian public lands. Averaging less than ten thousand acres in area, they comprise less than 1 percent of the region's total land base, and it is estimated that demand for wilderness will soon exceed supply. In wilderness areas, motorized activities are prohibited, and day hikes and backpacking are the primary uses. Some areas, such as St. Mary's River in Virginia, have been overused for years, causing erosion along stream banks. Control of access to prevent environmental degradation in wilderness areas is a serious management issue and reflects an emerging problem with overuse of many scenic areas.

Disadvantages of ecotourism include some of those inherent in tourism in general, as jobs tend to be seasonal and often low-wage. In addition, ecotourism depends on the maintenance of scenic viewsheds and healthy wildlife populations, conditions that depend on careful land-use planning to avoid fragmentation of habitats, overdevelopment of ecologically fragile areas, and unattractive, pollution-inducing sprawl.

See also: FOREST MANAGEMENT AND CONSERVATION (ENVIRONMENT); LAND USE (ENVIRONMENT).

—Chris Bolgiano, *James Madison University*

Taylor Barnhill, *Our Green Is Our Gold: The Economic Benefits of National Forests for Southern Appalachian Communities* (1999); Southern Appalachian Man and the Biosphere Program, *Southern Appalachian Assessment Report* (1996); Pamela A. Wright, "Sustainable Ecotourism: Balancing Economic, Environmental and Social Goals within an Ethical Framework," *Journal of Tourism Studies* (December 1993).

Fallingwater

See Fallingwater (Architecture)

Flat Rock–Hendersonville Area, North Carolina

Tourism began in the early nineteenth century in the Flat Rock–Hendersonville area of North Carolina. Coastal Carolinians and others discovered these southern Blue Ridge Mountain slopes to be a summer respite from the low country's oppressive heat and diseases such as yellow fever and malaria. Listed on the National Register of Historic Places, downtown Hendersonville, located twenty-one miles southeast of Asheville, was settled in 1836. This county seat city, population 10,420, takes its name from Leonard Henderson (1772–1833), a chief justice of the North Carolina Supreme Court.

Modern highways leading to the area follow parts of Cherokee trading paths, used later by drovers who stopped to rest and trade as they took sheep, cattle, hogs, mules, and geese to eastern markets. The Henderson County Curb Market, with third- and fourth-generation vendors of handmade and locally grown items, has been in continuous operation since 1924. In the 1920s, heavyweight boxing world champion Jack Dempsey set up his training camp there, drawing thousands of visitors.

One-half mile west of Main Street in Oakdale Cemetery stands Wolfe's Angel, made famous by Thomas Wolfe in his first novel, *Look Homeward, Angel* (1929). The statue, which was purchased by an Asheville couple to mark their family plot, was among those actually sold by Wolfe's father from the porch of his tombstone shop.

Five miles away, the entire district of Flat Rock is included on the National Register of Historic Places. The village sits on an enormous granite dome, which according to legend was a sacred spot of power and prayer to the Cherokee. Affluent nineteenth-century Europeans and South Carolina low-country plantation owners, especially Charlestonians, built large English-style homes in Flat Rock. At an elevation of 2,130 feet, they spent pleasant summers in what became known as the Little Charleston of the Mountains. The Woodfield Inn, built in 1852 as the Farmers Hotel, served as the first stagecoach stop along the Old Indian Trail. Later, summer travelers rode on the Carolina Special to the Hendersonville Depot, which was built in 1879 and is now used as a museum. The Special ran between Charleston and Cincinnati from 1911 to 1968. The train required an extra rear engine to push it from Melrose up the Saluda Mountain Grade, the steepest mainline standard gauge section of railroad in the United States.

Many early settlers were the wealthy elite of southern aristocracy. In the cemetery of Flat Rock's Saint John in the Wilderness Episcopal Church, built as a private chapel by a local family in 1833 and deeded to the Episcopal diocese in 1936, lie such prominent people as family members of three signers of the Declaration of Independence. The Reverend John Drayton, an early 1800s South Carolina governor who conceived and laid out Charleston's world-famous Magnolia Gardens, rests in the cemetery, as does Christopher Memminger, first secretary of the Confederate treasury.

It was the Memminger home, Connemara, built as a summer home in 1838, that Carl and Paula Sandburg bought in 1945. Carl Sandburg—author, poet, biographer, socialist, lecturer, and musician—was born to Swedish immigrant parents in Galesburg, Illinois, in 1878. During his eighty-nine years, he produced forty books. Twenty years went into the research for his 1940 Pulitzer Prize–winning biography of Abraham Lincoln. His many awards included a second Pulitzer Prize for poetry. However, Sandburg made more money lecturing about Lincoln and poet Walt Whitman and singing ballads to his guitar accompaniment than he ever did from writing books. The 245 acres of secluded hillside with a stunning view of the Blue Ridge Mountains was perfect for the Sandburgs' simple lifestyle—Paula raised prize-winning goats, and Carl pursued his literary interests. The couple, with their daughters and grandchildren, lived at Connemara for the final twenty-two years of Sandburg's life.

Following Sandburg's death in 1967, his family removed only personal belongings, leaving the lived-in clutter that characterized the family's life there. The following year, Connemara became a national historic site, the country's first private home to be administered by the National Park Service. An estimated 125,000 visitors pay homage annually to the nationally acclaimed writer. Programs include making goat cheese in summer, poetry readings, and Christmas celebrations of music and storytelling.

See also: AGRICULTURAL TOURISM; BLUE RIDGE PROVINCE (GEOLOGY); CULTURAL HERITAGE TOURISM.

—Helen Barranger, *Blue Ridge Country*

Helen Barranger, "Connemara: The Spirit of Carl Sandburg Lives on in Flat Rock, N.C.," *Blue Ridge Country* (May–June 1999); Penelope Niven, *Carl Sandburg: A Biography* (1991).

Fort Necessity National Battlefield

Eleven miles east of Uniontown, Pennsylvania, Fort Necessity's reconstructed stockades and breastworks mark the site of the first major action in the military career of George Washington and the beginning of the French and Indian War. Commanding a regiment of Virginia militia and a detachment of regular British troops from South Carolina, the twenty-two-year-old Washington gave up the fortress in the wilderness and led his men back to Virginia after holding off a superior force of French troops and their Indian allies throughout the day of July 3, 1754. Washington's men were permitted to keep their personal weapons and withdraw under a negotiated end to the engagement, but the newly promoted colonel had, in effect, surrendered. It was the only time in his career that Washington surrendered to an enemy force.

Washington's Virginia regiment had constructed the rudimentary fortress at a place known as Great Meadows after a bloody skirmish with a party of French soldiers seven miles away on May 28. Ten Frenchmen, including Joseph Coulon de Villiers, Sieur de Jumonville, had been killed in a surprise attack by Washington's men, and as Washington expected, a large French force from Fort Duquesne (later Pittsburgh) arrived to retaliate. The ensuing clash became known as the battle of Great Meadows.

The fifty-three-foot circular log fortress that Washington named Fort Necessity was poorly located and still incomplete when it came under attack. Because the stockade was not finished, some of Washington's men were protected only by earthworks. Even those behind walls of the fort could be taken under fire from surrounding heights. Hostilities were interrupted by a downpour, but by evening a third of Washington's men had been killed or wounded. He quickly accepted a French offer to discuss terms. As Washington retreated toward Virginia on July 4, the French burned the evacuated outpost and headed back to Fort Duquesne.

The Fort Necessity National Battlefield was established in 1931. Besides the reconstructed fortress, it includes Jumonville Glen, the site of Washington's ambush of the Sieur de Jumonville; Mount Washington Tavern, an early-nineteenth-century stage stop; and the grave of British General Edward Braddock, who was mortally wounded in the battle of the Monongahela a year after the battle of Great Meadows. Within the battlefield are also traces of Braddock's Road, first blazed as an Indian trail about 1750, expanded by Washington before the battle at Fort Necessity, and improved by Braddock's forces the following year.

A number of related sites are in the general vicinity of Fort Necessity. They include Point State Park at Pittsburgh, the site of Fort Prince George, constructed by Virginia troops in 1754; Fort Ligonier and Bushy Run Battlefield, both in Westmoreland County, Pennsylvania; and Fort Bedford Park and Museum in Bedford County. In Fayette County, twenty miles west of Fort Necessity National Battlefield, is Friendship Hill National Historic Site, home of Albert Gallatin, who served as secretary of the Treasury under Presidents Thomas Jefferson and James Madison.

See also: BRADDOCK'S ROAD (TRANSPORTATION); FRENCH AND INDIAN WAR (GOVERNMENT); NATIONAL ROAD (SETTLEMENT AND MIGRATION); PENNSYLVANIA STATE PARKS.

—Rudy Abramson, *Reston, Virginia*

John R. Alden, *George Washington: A Biography* (1984); Jill MacNeice, *A Guide to National Monuments and Historic Sites* (1990).

Gatlinburg, Tennessee

The reputation of Gatlinburg as one of the most controversial tourist destinations in Appalachia has grown along with the increasing popularity of the Great Smoky Mountains National Park—usually attracting more visitors per year than any other park in the National Park System.

Gatlinburg, located in northeast Tennessee, was named after Radford Gatlin, whose store was designated an official post office in 1860. Although Gatlin left that same year, Gatlinburg remained the official name of the place formerly known as White Oak Flats, an agricultural community that included several businesses and churches. Martha Jane Huskey Ogle and her family were the first to settle the site (about 1806) near the confluence of Baskins Creek and the Little Pigeon River, at the center of modern-day downtown Gatlinburg.

The timber industry grew in the Smoky Mountains after the Civil War, and the dawn of the twentieth century brought with it a peaceful prosperity. A few families supplemented their incomes by providing lodging to people coming to Gatlinburg on lumber business or on hiking trips. During the 1920s, Gatlinburg's business community, supported by hikers from Knoxville and elsewhere, spearheaded a movement to create a national park in the Great Smoky Mountains. An equally important development for the community was the establishment in 1912 of the Pi Beta Phi Settlement School. The Pi Beta Phi Women's Fraternity provided primary education for Gatlinburg children and vocational courses that taught adults to produce and market traditional mountain crafts. Gatlinburg became widely known as a center for craft production and promotion, especially in weaving and woodcraft. Sales venues were provided through the fraternity's alumni network, but the Arrowcraft Shop, which opened in 1926, attracted tourists interested in crafts to Gatlinburg.

Better roads and the opening of the Great Smoky Mountains National Park in 1934 drastically changed Gatlinburg. Forty thousand visitors were believed to have passed through Gatlinburg the first year, but in 1935 the visitor count exceeded half a million. That number continued to increase steadily. By the 1950s, Americans had leisure time available, a car in the garage, and roads to get them where they were going. Gatlinburg became a city of hotels and motels, restaurants, and gift shops.

At the close of the twentieth century, tourism was the main industry in Gatlinburg. Although lucrative, such a high level of visitation places pressure on the area's natural environment and creates demands on the city's infrastructure, requiring constant planning and adaptation of resources. The area's air quality became a matter of continuing concern, as did demands on local families and working conditions in the industry. However, for most residents, pride in the small Appalachian town's accomplishments overshadows the negative aspects. Even as tourism developed impressively in other towns near the Great Smoky Mountains National Park, Gatlinburg retained its historical position as the "Gateway to the Smokies."

See also: ARROWMONT SCHOOL OF ARTS AND CRAFTS (CRAFTS); GREAT SMOKY MOUNTAINS NATIONAL PARK; PIGEON FORGE, TENNESSEE.

—Lisa N. Oakley, *East Tennessee Historical Society*

Ed Trout, *Gatlinburg: Cinderella City* (1984); Elena Irish Zimmerman, *Sevierville, Gatlinburg, and Maryville: A Postcard Tour* (1996).

George Washington National Forest

The George Washington National Forest in northwestern Virginia and eastern West Virginia was originally established as the Shenandoah National Forest in 1917, uniting the Potomac, Massanutten Mountain, and Shenandoah Purchase units formed immediately after the Weeks Act of 1911. The name was changed in 1933 to prevent confusion with the new Shenandoah National Park to the east. In the 1990s, the administrations of the George Washington and the Jefferson National Forests combined with headquarters in Roanoke, Virginia, and another office in Harrisonburg, Virginia.

It was the policy of the U.S. Forest Service to acquire lands for national forests only from willing sellers. Most tracts purchased for the George Washington had previously been extensively cut to supply charcoal for iron furnaces and bark for tanneries, as well as timber for domestic and commercial uses. In many sections, chronic fires continually destroyed regenerating growth. By the early 1920s, administrators in the (then) Shenandoah National Forest had developed a system of appointing local wardens to organize and dispatch firefighting crews that was soon adopted by other national forests. In 1933, during the Great Depression, the Civilian Conservation Corps, a federal jobs program, opened its first national camp on Massanutten Mountain in the George Washington.

The forest currently covers 1.1 million acres. Within its proclamation boundaries, the Forest Service owns 62 percent of the land, making it both the largest and the least fragmented of the Appalachian national forests. It is also the driest, being mostly on the east side of the Allegheny Front and subject to drought. Dominant tree species are oaks, especially chestnut and white oaks, red maple, and Virginia and pitch pines. The dominant forest product sold commercially is pulpwood. The forest has approximately 380 resident vertebrate wildlife species, with eleven species on or proposed for the federal list of endangered and threatened wildlife and plants.

The George Washington National Forest is within a two-hour drive of Washington, D.C., and Richmond, Virginia. The Forest Service estimates annual visitation by recreational users at approximately three million, including eighty thousand hunters of white-tailed deer, black bear, and wild turkey. There are more than nine hundred miles of trails, including fifty to sixty miles of the Appalachian Trail, some thirty campgrounds, four congressionally designated wilderness areas, and three hundred miles of stocked streams.

The forest's large recreational constituency stimulated perhaps the most extensive controversy over an Appalachian national forest land-use plan in the 1980s, as all national forests developed plans to comply with the National Forest Management Act of 1976. The George Washington's initial emphasis on logging and road building was challenged by hiking, horseback riding, rod and gun, hang gliding, and other associations; municipal, state, and federal agencies; and almost a thousand individuals. After eighteen appeals were filed, the chief of the Forest Service directed that a new plan be developed, which was eventually adopted. The revised plan significantly reduced logging and road building, but controversy continued, especially over road building. In October 1999, the forest's Reddish Knob served as the venue for President Bill Clinton's announcement of a new federal initiative to increase the protection of roadless areas in the national forests.

See also: ECOTOURISM; FOREST MANAGEMENT AND CONSERVATION (ENVIRONMENT); LUMBER INDUSTRY (BUSINESS, INDUSTRY, AND TECHNOLOGY).

—Chris Bolgiano, *James Madison University*

Chris Bolgiano, *The Appalachian Forest: A Search for Roots and Renewal* (1998); Charles Randall, "George Washington: Our History-Making Forest," *American Forests* (March 1969); Jean Satterthwaite, *George Washington National Forest: A History* (1991).

Georgia State Parks

The Appalachian region of Georgia, with its terrain spreading through the Ridge and Valley, Appalachian Plateaus, Blue Ridge, and Piedmont physiographic provinces, contains some twenty-five state parks and historic sites representing the broad diversity of the picturesque area. Besides taking advantage of the varied territory for recreational activities, the parks help preserve and interpret native cultures, wars, the mining industry, and small farms that have shaped the region's history.

Numerous name changes and organizational shifts in the state parks system reflect changing economic, political, and administrative conditions and priorities as the system evolved. The system traces its formal origins to 1925 with two parks, one of them the present Vogel State Park in the Appalachian region. Although the other, now Indian Springs State Park, is in central Georgia, south of the Appalachians, it is nevertheless significant because it is one of the oldest state parks in the nation. It is part of lands ceded to the State of Georgia in 1825 following a treaty between the Creek Indians and the federal government.

Georgia's state parks expanded during the 1930s and 1940s through the collaboration and contributions of state and federal governments and public and private interests. Projects of the Civilian Conservation Corps, which brought rapid progress to the state's park movement, are still evident at several parks, including Fort Mountain in northern Georgia. In 1937 management of the state parks was placed within a division of the Department of Natural Resources. A reorganization in 1943 abolished that department and established the Division of Conservation, of which one section was the Department of State Parks, Historic Sites, and Monuments. At that time a State Park Advisory Committee of citizens was created for each county containing a state park.

The 1950s saw many changes in the system. The Department of State Parks, Historic Sites, and Monuments was renamed the Department of State Parks. Still under the Division of Conservation, its powers and duties did not change. The Georgia General Assembly repealed the act authorizing the citizens' advisory committee and recommended discontinuing the cabin-building program, which had suffered financial losses. The U.S. Army Corps of Engineers, by leasing land on reservoirs, made possible several state parks. One that the corps leased in 1952 was at first designated for use "by Negroes."

As a part of then-Governor Jimmy Carter's massive state government reorganization in the early 1970s, a new Department of Natural Resources managed Georgia's parks under its Parks and Recreation Division, soon renamed the Parks, Recreation, and Historic Sites Division. Eighteen additional historic sites were transferred to the new department with the abolition of the Georgia Historical Commission. A state fiscal crisis in 1975 led to a substantial reduction in the number of parks and historic sites operated by the state. Of the twenty-eight closed or transferred to local or private operation, eight were in the Appalachian region. As conditions improved, some parks added lodges, and in the 1980s and 1990s, a number of additional parks entered the system. But in 1991, as Governor Zell Miller sought to downsize state government and privatize many programs, a number of park operations, including lodges, exhibit shops, and the historical marker program were transferred to private contractors. A membership group, the Friends of Georgia State Parks and Historic Sites, was organized to support the system. By staffing gift shops at state parks, the volunteer group helped restore several state positions to park management duties; the Friends also financed a new trading post shop at Amicalola Falls State Park, near Helen.

The state parks within Georgia's Appalachian region safeguard aspects of its rich history and provide public recreational opportunities. American Indian culture is preserved at the Etowah Indian Mounds, New Echota, and Chief Vann House Historic Sites. At Fort Mountain State Park may be seen along the brow of the mountain an ancient line of boulders variously attributed to American Indians, the Welsh Prince Madoc, Spanish explorers, or even a mysterious early native "moon-eyed" people. Fort Yargo State Park features a 1792 log fort built for defense against Creek and Cherokee Indians. Within this park is Will-A-Way Recreation Area, which is designed for populations with accessibility needs.

Civil War–related sites include Sweetwater Creek State Park and Pickett's Mill Battlefield State Historic Site. Traveler's Rest Historic Site is an example of an early inn. Cloudland Canyon, Amicalola Falls, Moccasin Creek, Black Rock Mountain, Vogel, and Unicoi State Parks, some with lodges, are mountain destinations popular with hikers, campers, and leaf viewers in the fall, as is rugged Tallulah Gorge. A trail at Amicalola Falls leads to Springer Mountain, the southern end of the Appalachian Trail. The Dahlonega Gold Museum commemorates the nation's first major gold rush and the site of an early U.S. mint.

In northern Georgia, water sports are popular attractions at Red Top Mountain Park and Lodge and at Tugaloo, Hart, Bobby Brown, Richard B. Russell, and John Tanner State Parks. James H. "Sloppy" Floyd State Park (named for a popular Georgia legislative leader) is known for its fishing and its large bluebird population. There is a nine-hole golf course at Victoria Bryant State Park. Watson Mill Bridge State Park contains the longest original-site covered bridge in Georgia.

See also: CIVIL WAR TOURISM; TALLULAH GORGE; TOURISM ARCHITECTURE (ARCHITECTURE).

—Jane Powers Weldon, *Calhoun, Georgia*

Georgia Humanities Council, *The New Georgia Guide* (1996); Thomas W. Hodler and Howard A. Schretter, *Atlas of Georgia* (1986).

Grandfather Mountain

Located in North Carolina's Avery County, Grandfather Mountain is perhaps the most distinctive peak in the Blue Ridge Mountains. Owned and managed by Hugh Morton, Grandfather Mountain is the only United Nations–designated International Biosphere Reserve to be privately owned. Deer, black bears, panthers, otters, and eagles are among the forty-seven rare and endangered species that make their homes in the reserve.

Morton's grandfather, Hugh MacRae, purchased the mountain around 1888. Since 1952, Morton's management has made the mountain the top tourist attraction in North Carolina, averaging a quarter of a million visitors each year. Morton built a road to the top, opened hiking trails, and constructed America's highest swinging footbridge one mile above sea level. Amenities also include a visitor center and nature museum.

Two annual events bring tens of thousands of visitors to the mountain's MacRae Meadows. Since 1924, a day of gospel music and preaching known as the Singing on the Mountain has come to the Meadows every June. Joe Hartley Sr., affectionately known as Uncle Joe and the Apostle of Grandfather Mountain, conceived the Singing as a celebration of the gospel in song and word. Hired by MacRae, who began the tourist resort at Linville, Hartley served as Grandfather Mountain's caretaker and fire warden for seventy-seven years and delivered the welcome at forty-one of the Singings. Originally, the gathered crowd sang along with local church quartets. Shape-note singing and spontaneous fiddle and guitar sessions throughout the crowd dominated the first decades. With inclusion of radio and recording artists such as Little Betty Johnson, Roy Acuff, the Carter Family, and Doc Watson, the Singing evolved into a concert with a central stage and set program. Speakers through the decades have included governors, athletes, and evangelists and ministers such as Billy Graham, Franklin Graham, Jerry Falwell, and Oral Roberts.

Founded in 1956 by Agnes MacRae Morton (daughter of Hugh MacRae) and journalist Donald F. MacDonald, the Grandfather Mountain Highland Games and Gathering of

The Grandfather Mountain Highland Games and Gathering of Scottish Clans at Grandfather Mountain, North Carolina, c. 1991. This annual event draws more than thirty thousand people to MacRae Meadows, at the base of the mountain, for a celebration of Scottish heritage.

Scottish Clans annually draws more than thirty thousand visitors to MacRae Meadows for four days of events. Organizers attribute the event's success to the Scotland-like setting and have adopted a Games tartan with a green, grey, and blue sett (pattern), symbolic of the Grandfather Mountain landscape. In lieu of the ultimate pilgrimage to physically experience ancestral lands in Scotland, Scottish Americans claim to visit the Grandfather Mountain Highland Games to see "a wee bit of the Scottish Highlands" in America. This feeling has been enhanced by the erection of memorial cairns with Scottish stones to honor the Scottish American community's dead and through annual rituals evoking the homeland. The events conclude with the annual visit of the bagpiping ghost of Alexander MacRae, the late-nineteenth-century Highland immigrant for whom the Meadows are named.

See also: BLUE RIDGE PARKWAY; HIGHLAND GAMES (SPORTS AND RECREATION); LINVILLE GORGE AREA, NORTH CAROLINA.

—Celeste Ray, *University of the South*

Shepherd M. Dugger, *The Balsam Groves of the Grandfather Mountain* (1934); Celeste Ray, *Highland Heritage: Scottish Americans in the American South* (2001); Bill Sharpe, *A New Geography of North Carolina* (1954).

Great Smoky Mountains National Park

By almost any measure, the Great Smoky Mountains National Park is the most significant tourist attraction in the southern Appalachian region. Its 521,000 acres of remarkable biodiversity, old-growth forests, spectacular views, and sites reflective of the pioneer history of the Smokies attract an estimated 11 million tourist visits and pump more than $600 million into local economies annually.

The Great Smoky Mountains National Park was the dream of regional boosters primarily located in urban areas of east Tennessee and western North Carolina. Although there had been earlier movements, revived interest and campaigning in the early 1920s—by members of local chambers of commerce, automobile clubs, newspaper editors, and clubwomen—strengthened efforts to make the Smokies into a national park. Advocates wanted not only to preserve the distinctive landscape and the flora and fauna of the mountains, but also to use these assets to bring good roads, tourists, and ultimately prosperity to the region. Knoxville park booster Russell Hanlon asserted that if the park became a reality, "millions will annually come through our gates and scatter the golden shekels in our midst."

Making this dream a reality, however, proved a challenging and lengthy process. Park boosters had to first convince the National Park Service that the Smokies were indeed worthy of designation as a national park. That done, they had to raise more than $10 million to purchase land in one of the most impoverished regions in the country. The U.S. Congress made the fund-raising process even more difficult by initially declaring that while the government would accept the park as a gift from the States of Tennessee and North Carolina, no federal funds could be used to purchase the land. Park boosters also faced concerted opposition from the timber and pulp companies that owned most of the land.

In spite of the odds, park boosters eventually collected nearly $10 million to purchase land for the park. An initial fund-raising and publicity campaign in east Tennessee and western North Carolina brought more than a million dollars in pledges from bankers, real estate agents, teachers, bellhops, and schoolchildren. The state legislatures of North Carolina and Tennessee each issued park bonds worth $2.5 million despite determined political opposition. But the movement received its greatest boost in 1928, when John D. Rockefeller Jr. donated $5 million in honor of his mother, Laura Spelman Rockefeller. In 1933 the U.S. government supplied $1.55 million to complete land purchases. Although park promoters considered the project virtually completed with the successful conclusion of the fund-raising campaign, the actual purchase of parkland also proved difficult. However, on September 2, 1940, the dream became a reality when Franklin D. Roosevelt stood on a native-stone platform at Newfound Gap to officially dedicate the park, six years after its establishment by Congress.

Years before the dedication, large numbers of visitors had begun visiting the Smokies. They were attracted by such natural wonders as the spectacular sunrises off Myrtle Point near Mount LeConte; the panoramic views from the Chimney Tops, Clingman's Dome, Newfound Gap, and Gregory Bald; and the old-growth hardwood forests of the Greenbriar section. They were also drawn by the possibility of sighting black bears, often seen rummaging through the garbage cans at picnic grounds, campgrounds, and scenic overlooks during the early years of the park.

The park also presented glimpses of frontier life in coves, hollows, and valleys once inhabited by an estimated 5,665 individuals. The Park Service sought to memorialize the lives of the former inhabitants by preserving structures and interpreting the human history of the region at popular sites such as Cades Cove and its Cable Mill, the Mingus Mill, the Mountain Farm Museum at the Oconaluftee Visitor Center, and the Cataloochee Valley. Although purporting to portray an accurate view of life lived in the Smokies at the time of removal (late 1920s to late 1930s), the Park Service made a conscious decision in the early days of park development to preserve only structures reflective of pioneer existence. As a result, most of the preserved structures were constructed before 1890, and the more modern frame and vertical-plank homes, schools, and churches that characterized life in the Smokies in the early twentieth century were dismantled or burned. In a 1995 book by Michael Ann Williams, former Cades Cove resident Bonnie Meyers commented, "We never noticed these cabins, growing up, paid them no mind. . . . All those [frame] houses were torn down. They left the cabins, you know, more pioneerish."

In recent years, the park faced a number of serious challenges. Throughout its history, the area had been known as a drive-in wilderness where visitors could cruise the Cades Cove Loop Road, the Roaring Fork Motor Nature Trail, the Little River Road, or U.S. Highway 441, rarely straying from their cars. Increasingly, however, as tourist attractions and accommodations multiplied at the park gateways, the Smokies threatened to become a drive-*through* wilderness: a scenic drive connecting the theme parks and outlet shopping malls in Pigeon Forge and Gatlinburg and the gambling casino in Cherokee.

Even visitors who got out of their cars, however, faced a different experience than those who came prior to 1960. Budget cuts coupled with increasing visitor use created a huge backlog of deferred maintenance, crumbling facilities, and heavily eroded trails in the park. Invasive species such as dogwood anthracnose, stem canker, and the balsam woolly adelgid *(Adelges picea)* caused extensive damage to plant life in the park. Increasing air pollution in the summer months reduced visibility in the southern Appalachians by 80 percent in the latter half of the twentieth century, and high ozone levels forced park officials to issue air quality advisories warning against strenuous activity, especially for those with respiratory problems. Such threats presented scientists and park management with challenges almost as daunting as those faced by the park's founders.

See also: BLUE RIDGE PARKWAY; CHEROKEE TOURISM; GATLINBURG, TENNESSEE.

—Daniel S. Pierce, *University of North Carolina at Asheville*

Margaret Lynn Brown, *The Wild East: A Biography of the Great Smoky Mountains* (2000); Daniel S. Pierce, *The Great Smokies: From Natural Habitat to National Park* (2000); Michael Ann Williams, *Great Smoky Mountains Folklife* (1995).

Harpers Ferry, West Virginia

Historic tourism in Appalachia is epitomized by Harpers Ferry, West Virginia, a picturesque community at the confluence of the Shenandoah and Potomac Rivers where John Brown's famous raid on a federal armory in 1859 foretold the coming of the American Civil War. Hoping to spark an insurrection by slaves, the fiery abolitionist and his band of twenty-two men held the armory and arsenal for thirty-six hours before U.S. Marines led by Colonel Robert E. Lee overpowered the guerrillas and captured Brown, who was later hanged.

First designated a national historical monument by President Franklin D. Roosevelt in 1944, much of the community became part of the 2,343-acre Harpers Ferry National Historical Park in 1963. With the Antietam National Battlefield, the Monocacy National Battlefield, and the Chesapeake and Ohio Canal national historical park only minutes away, Harpers Ferry is one of the country's favorite destinations for history buffs. As many as five hundred thousand tourists per year visit the park to see the firehouse where Brown was captured and the house where the federal armorer lived at the time of the raid. The community, with a population of about 350 at the turn of the twenty-first century compared to 3,000 at the outbreak of the Civil War, has been restored to its nineteenth-century appearance. Visitors' experience is enhanced by a number of living history exhibits.

Although the firehouse where Brown was captured, the John Brown Museum, and other structures associated with the famous raid are the centerpiece of the national historical park, the abortive attempt to foment a slave uprising was but one chapter in the community's extraordinary history.

The armory seized by Brown was established in 1794 during the administration of President George Washington. The town's location made it an early commercial center and transportation junction as well as a strategic military post during the Civil War, and it was under military occupation by one side or the other throughout the conflict. Confederate General Stonewall Jackson captured Harpers Ferry from Union control just before the battle of Antietam in September 1862. Union General Philip Sheridan later used it as a supply base in his campaign in Virginia's Shenandoah Valley.

Besides visiting Civil War sites, Harpers Ferry visitors can climb to Jefferson's Rock, Thomas Jefferson's vantage point for his famous description of the confluence of the Shenandoah and the Potomac Rivers as "one of the most stupendous scenes in nature" and one "worth a voyage across the Atlantic." Stone steps also lead to the house built between 1775 and 1782 by Robert Harper, who gave the town its name after the river crossing had been known for decades as the Hole. Numerous destructive floods have threatened the historic treasure that is Harpers Ferry; in 1996 alone, the town and the park recovered from two floods of a magnitude expected once in a century.

In addition to its historic sites, Harpers Ferry visitors are attracted to canoeing and whitewater rafting on both of the rivers, hiking and biking along the Chesapeake and Ohio Canal, and hiking on the Appalachian Trail, which passes through the national historical park. The park is open the year round.

See also: CHESAPEAKE AND OHIO CANAL NATIONAL HISTORICAL PARK.

—Rudy Abramson, *Reston, Virginia*

Helen, Georgia

Helen is a small community in the heart of Georgia's Blue Ridge Mountains. In the late 1960s, its residents transformed the dying town, long since abandoned by the timber industry that had created it, into a Bavarian village of shops and restaurants that is now the third most popular tourist destination in the state of Georgia. Only Atlanta and Savannah attract more visitors annually.

Located on the headwaters of the Chattahoochee River at the edge of the Nacoochee Valley in White County, Helen emerged in the early twentieth century in what had, a century earlier, been the heart of both Cherokee and gold-mining country. Attracted by the area's vast virgin forest of hardwood trees, the Matthews Timber Company established a major sawmill there around 1912. Shortly afterward, a railroad connector linked the new town—named Helen after the daughter of a railroad surveyor—to Gainesville in the foothills to the south. The operation thrived until the 1930s Great Depression, when most of the timber had been cut, and the company and most residents moved on to more promising forests elsewhere. By the 1950s and 1960s, the town was nothing more than a bleak row of concrete block structures and supported only about nine businesses.

In 1968 a group of local businessmen met for what soon became a legendary lunch. In seeking to intercept some of the considerable traffic that moved through Helen on the way to the mountains and waterfalls beyond, they came upon the idea of sprucing up their storefronts. They consulted John Kollock, a prominent regional artist in nearby Clarkesville. Inspired by his 1950s military service in southern Germany, he suggested that they transform their business district into a Bavarian village and presented them with a series of watercolors depicting what the town could become. Led by Pete Hodkinson, local merchants rallied, and by 1972 Kollock's paintings had taken tangible form, and a trickle of curious visitors soon became a flood.

Hodkinson, a fun-loving visionary as well as an entrepreneur, infused the enterprise with a lively spirit. He drew crowds to Helen throughout the year by staging hot air balloon races, motorcycle races, and what remains the biggest annual event, a seven-week-long Oktoberfest. Ironically, Hodkinson was killed in a balloon accident in 1976. Nearby

Anna Ruby Falls, Unicoi State Park, and other natural attractions contribute to Helen's appeal, as does the Chattahoochee, which flows through the middle of town, drawing tubers and fishermen.

Today, Helen's residents still number only about 300 people, yet the town supports more than 150 shops, 30 factory outlets, 24 restaurants, and nearly 1,200 hotel rooms. Most buildings still display chalet facades and red roofs, many sales clerks wear lederhosen and dirndls, and most restaurants serve German cuisine. Many question Helen's rampant commercialism and its failure to focus more attention on its own Appalachian history and culture, rather than that of the German Alps. Yet Helen's economic success is undeniable. In the last few years of the twentieth century, the village attracted 1.5 million tourists who spent more than $100 million annually in White County.

See also: BLUE RIDGE PROVINCE (GEOLOGY); LUMBER INDUSTRY (BUSINESS, INDUSTRY, AND TECHNOLOGY).

—John C. Inscoe, *University of Georgia*

Fred Brown and Neil Jones, *The Georgia Nature Conservancy's Guide to the North Georgia Mountains* (1991); Georgia Humanities Council, *The New Georgia Guide* (1996).

Hot Springs, North Carolina

The resort community of Hot Springs, North Carolina, initially was known as Warm Springs. Travelers began coming to the area as early as 1778, and in 1791 the first tavern was built at Warm Springs (in present day Madison County) by Dutch settler William Neilson. Prior to the 1820s, most of the visitors to Neilson's Tavern were stock drovers, migrant families, and various sojourners, but Bishop Francis Asbury, who stayed at Neilson's Tavern nine times between 1800 and 1810, noticed more and more health seekers coming to Warm Springs. Following the practice of hydrotherapy, they were "taking the cure" by purifying the body with salubrious mineral waters.

After the State of North Carolina completed the Buncombe Turnpike in 1828, accessibility to Warm Springs improved. Consequently, Asheville businessman James Patton built an elegant hotel on the site of the old tavern. With improved access and better accommodations, Warm Springs emerged as a popular spa for the planter elite of South Carolina and Georgia during summer. Seeking to escape the malarial lowlands, they were drawn to the Patton Hotel by the combined appeal of health and leisure. The existence of an elegant hotel amid the humble domiciles of nearby residents underscored the social, economic, and cultural gap between lowland visitors and local mountaineers. James Silk Buckingham, an English socialite who visited Warm Springs in 1841, found the scenery "nobly picturesque" and the waters "delightful," but the local people struck him as "very mean and dirty."

The Civil War wiped out most of the spa's antebellum clientele, but after the war, Warm Springs was one of the few resorts in the Blue Ridge Mountains still owned by a southerner, Colonel James H. Rumbough. Business at the old Patton Hotel boomed after Warm Springs got rail service in 1882, but two years later, the old hotel burned down. Lacking the means to rebuild, Rumbough sold the property to the Southern Improvement Company, a group of investors from New York. The Southern Improvement Company initiated many changes to draw more visitors from the North. They built the lavish Mountain Park Hotel, renamed the town Hot Springs for greater marketing appeal, and built North Carolina's first golf course. When the new investors went bankrupt, Rumbough bought back the property, which stayed in family hands until 1940.

Hot Springs struggled to adapt to the changed circumstances of twentieth century tourism as spas went out of fashion. Tourists bypassed Hot Springs, and the resort fell into decline until 1990, when Madison County native Gene Hicks opened Hot Springs Spa and Resort, offering cabins and campground facilities, jacuzzi tubs, and therapeutic massage. As in the 1890s, advertising and testimonials from a new generation of health seekers promoted Hot Springs waters for rheumatism, gout, and other ailments. The Bluff Mountain Music Festival added to the resort's appeal.

See also: APPALACHIAN TRAIL; SMOKY MOUNTAIN SPAS AND RESORTS; WHITEWATER SPORTS (SPORTS AND RECREATION).

—C. Brenden Martin, *Northwestern State University*

Ina W. and John J. Van Noppen, *Western North Carolina since the Civil War* (1973); Manly Wade Wellman, *The Kingdom of Madison: A Southern Mountain Fastness and Its People* (1973).

Ivy Green

The birthplace of Helen Keller (1880–1968), the famed author and lecturer who overcame the isolation of both blindness and deafness, Ivy Green was opened as a shrine and tourist attraction in 1954. Every year, visitors from around the United States and the world visit the white clapboard house in Tuscumbia, Alabama, and thousands attend an annual Helen Keller Festival in June. The week-long festival, begun in 1979, is highlighted by outdoor performances of William Gibson's play *The Miracle Worker*, dramatizing Keller's triumph over her dual handicap under the guidance of her teacher and companion, Anne Sullivan. Undisciplined and unable to communicate when she came under Sullivan's care at the age of six, Keller broke through her isolation by learning a fingertip alphabet, then progressing to Braille, which she mastered by the age of ten. Accompanied by Sullivan, she entered preparatory school at sixteen and later proceeded to Radcliffe College, where she was graduated cum laude in 1904. The author of several books, Keller became one of the world's most famous and admired women, traveling the globe, lecturing, writing, and raising funds for the blind and deaf. A documentary film about her life won the Academy Award in 1954, and a film adaptation of *The Miracle Worker* won Academy Awards for actresses Anne Bancroft and Patty Duke.

Built in 1820 by Keller's grandfather, Ivy Green's main house is a frame structure with four large downstairs rooms and three upstairs bedrooms. Adjacent to the house is a kitchen and a small two-room cottage, which was made into a bridal suite for her parents, Arthur and Kate Adams Keller. Keller was born in the cottage, and in the cottage she worked with Sullivan during her struggle to overcome darkness and silence.

The property, which survived the Civil War undamaged, remained in the ownership of the Keller family until it was purchased by the city of Tuscumbia. Surrounded by magnolias and English boxwoods planted in the mid-nineteenth century, the structures are furnished much as they were when Helen lived there with her parents. Listed on the National Register of Historic Places, Ivy Green is operated by the nonprofit Helen Keller Foundation.

See also: ALABAMA AND MISSISSIPPI STATE PARKS.

—Rudy Abramson, *Reston, Virginia*

Helen Keller, *The Story of My Life* (1903); Joseph Lash, *Helen and Teacher: The Story of Helen Keller and Anne Sullivan Macy* (1980).

Jefferson National Forest and Mount Rogers

The Jefferson National Forest was established in 1936 out of lands formerly contained in the Unaka and Natural Bridge National Forests and the Clinch and Mountain Lake Purchase Units. It covers 719,763 acres primarily in southwestern Virginia with boundary spillover into West Virginia and a small acreage in Kentucky. Like the other Appalachian national forests, much of the land that comprises the Jefferson was cut-over, burned, and eroding when purchased by the U.S. Forest Service. It was Forest Service policy to acquire land only from willing sellers, and many of the early acquisitions came in large tracts from coal, iron, and timber companies that no longer wanted to pay taxes on land from which they had extracted most of the salable resources. Smaller tracts were purchased as tax-delinquent lands during the depression of the 1930s. Administrated jointly with the George Washington National Forest, also in Virginia, the Jefferson's headquarters are in Roanoke, Virginia.

The eastern part of the forest lies within the Blue Ridge physiographic province and the western part is in the Ridge and Valley. Elevations range from 600 feet to 5,729 feet at Mount Rogers, the highest peak in Virginia. The forests are made up of Appalachian mixed hardwoods interspersed with conifers, with some isolated northern hardwood communities at the highest elevations, and there are several balds. Within the Jefferson's boundaries are seven biologically diverse watersheds: the James, Roanoke, New, Holston, Clinch, Big Sandy, and Cumberland Rivers. The forest contains the most concentrated area of woodland salamander biodiversity in the world, and more than 160 species of nesting or migrating birds have been identified within it. Twenty-nine species of plants and animals are on or proposed for the federal list of threatened and endangered species, with the largest category being mussels. Administrators of the purchase units that later became the Jefferson National Forest made some of the earliest efforts in any of the eastern national forests to restock native wildlife that had been nearly extirpated by overharvesting and habitat loss. Deer stocking began by 1927, beaver in 1938, and wild turkey in 1940.

Few people from outside the region visited the forest before World War II. The completion of Interstate 81 in the 1960s made the area accessible from many metropolitan areas and accelerated the demand for recreational amenities. Attractions in the forest include more than 1,000 miles of hiking and riding trails, including 282 miles of the Appalachian Trail; 28 campgrounds; 17 picnic areas; 11 congressionally designated wilderness areas; and 500 miles of stocked streams. The Forest Service estimates visits at more than two million annually, including many thousands of deer and turkey hunters.

Included in the Jefferson is the Mount Rogers National Recreation Area. A presidential advisory council conceived national recreation areas in the early 1960s in response to a 900 percent increase in recreational use of national forests between 1945 and 1960. Mount Rogers was deemed suitable for such designation because of its 360-degree vista from the top, its scenic stone outcrops and rhododendron thickets, its uncommon spruce-fir forest, and its large open bald (created by humans through grazing and burning) called the Crest Zone. Created by President Lyndon Johnson in 1966, the recreation area encompassed 154,000 acres, 85,000 of them owned by the Jefferson National Forest.

In a reversal of its long-standing acquisitions policy, the Forest Service initiated condemnation proceedings against a total of 6,500 acres in Mount Rogers National Recreation Area in the 1970s. It also formulated plans for highly concentrated development aimed at eventually attracting up to five million people annually—two large resorts, 900 camping units, a winter sports center, and a scenic highway. While some local business leaders supported these plans, other local citizens organized first to protest the condemnation proceedings, then the intensity of development. The Sierra Club and several other national environmental groups joined them. By 1980, the Forest Service had been forced to scale back its acquisition plans and to abandon many of its development proposals. Dispersed, lower-impact recreation, especially camping, hiking, backpacking, horse riding, and cross-country skiing, became the management principle. Mount Rogers includes two of the Jefferson National Forest's congressionally designated wilderness areas. The Crest Zone is maintained through prescribed burning and grazing by cattle and ponies. Grayson Highlands State Park, adjacent to the recreation area, offers additional recreational facilities as well as trail access to the Crest Zone.

See also: APPALACHIAN TRAIL; BALDS (ECOLOGY); CAMPING (SPORTS AND RECREATION).

—Chris Bolgiano, *James Madison University*

Chris Bolgiano, *The Appalachian Forest: A Search for Roots and Renewal* (1998); Lionel Melancon, "You're Missing the Best If You Haven't Discovered the Jefferson National Forest," *Virginia Wildlife* (July 1988); Will Sarvis, "An Appalachian Forest: Creation of the Jefferson National Forest and Its Effects on the Local Community," *Forest and Conservation History* (October 1993).

Kentucky State Parks

Promoted by geologist Willard Rouse Jillson, Kentucky's state park system dates to the 1924 establishment of the Kentucky State Park Commission. The commission was authorized to accept land for parks, and land was acquired to establish parks at Pine Mountain and Natural Bridge in eastern Kentucky. The system now numbers forty-nine parks, twenty-two of those in eastern Kentucky, plus Breaks Interstate Park on the Kentucky–West Virginia border. The commission also manages a number of historic sites. Resort parks provide visitors such conveniences as lodges with dining rooms, golf courses, and swimming pools, while less developed recreational parks offer few amenities other than campsites and picnic areas.

Pine Mountain State Resort Park, the state's first park, is located on Pine Mountain, a ridge that forms the northwest boundary of the Cumberland Overthrust block and extends 125 miles northeast from Jellico, Tennessee, to Elkhorn City, Kentucky. The park's 1,519 acres include virgin stands of eastern hemlock and offer visitors hiking trails, a nature center, and two natural bridges, as well as campsites and picnic areas, cottages, a lodge with dining room, an eighteen-hole golf course, miniature golf, a pool, and an amphitheater that seats two thousand during the Mountain Laurel Festival. The state's highest park is Kingdom Come, which includes the twenty-seven-hundred-foot crest of Pine Mountain.

Resort parks that offer facilities similar to Pine Mountain include Natural Bridge, located in the heart of the Daniel Boone National Forest in Powell County, and the 1,350-acre Carter Caves State Resort Park in Carter County, which features more than twenty caves. Visitors can take guided tours of the distinctive rock formations of X Cave. Cascade Caverns, which features dripstone cascade formations and an underground lake, was developed as a private tourist attraction in 1925 and acquired by the state in 1959. Carter Caves Bridge and other large limestone arches, some originally formed underground, also attract visitors to the Carter Caves Park. While the sandstone arch at Natural Bridge State Resort Park, more than seventy-five feet long and sixty-five feet high, is neither the largest nor the oldest natural arch in the area, it has long been one of the most popular. The Kentucky Union Lumber Company developed Natural Bridge as a tourist attraction in the late 1880s; the Louisville and Nashville Railroad donated it to the park system in 1926. The original 137 acres have expanded to 1,900 acres that include a 994-acre nature preserve and Millcreek Lake, which offers opportunities for canoeing and fishing.

Lake Cumberland State Resort Park, created with the construction of the Wolf Creek Dam by the U.S. Army Corps of Engineers in the 1950s, is considered one of the finest fishing and recreational lakes in the eastern United States. The 3,117-acre park is surrounded on three sides by Lake Cumberland, the biggest lake in Kentucky. Facilities include a lodge and dining room, cottages, campsites, a marina, rental boats, ski boats, canoes, fishing, a nine-hole golf course, miniature golf, nature trails, picnic areas, horseback riding, tennis, a nature center, a spa, and the only indoor pool in the state park system. In the upper reaches of Lake Cumberland on Chandler Island is General Burnside State Park, a 430-acre recreational park accessible by a causeway and equipped with a boat ramp, an eighteen-hole golf course, a public pool, a picnic shelter, a playground, and campsites. Cumberland Falls State Resort Park, one of the region's oldest tourist destinations, is located nearby. Other state resort parks featuring water-based outdoor recreation are Buckhorn Lake and Greenbo Lake. General Burnside, Carr Creek, Grayson Lake, Yatesville Lake, and Paintsville Lake lack lodges but offer beaches, marinas, and excellent sport fishing.

Kentucky history is the key attraction at some state parks as well as at historic sites. Jenny Wiley State Resort Park contains an eight-hundred-seat amphitheater where visitors view an outdoor drama based on Virginia Wiley's eleven-month captivity and escape from her Native American captors in 1789–90. Old Fort Harrod State Park commemorates Kentucky's first permanent settlement with an outdoor drama, *The Legend of Daniel Boone*, as well as offering extensive interpretation of pioneer lifeways and a Mansion Museum with Native American and Civil War artifacts and an Abraham Lincoln collection. Fort Boonesborough State Park, the site of the original settlement founded by Daniel Boone in 1775, offers many recreational opportunities but also interprets pioneer experience through the reconstructed fort. Its blockhouses and cabins display eighteenth-century furnishings and house demonstrations of crafts such as soap making, quilting, wood carving, and candle making. A film describes the struggle to settle Kentucky's wilderness. Levi Jackson Wilderness Road State Park offers visitors an opportunity to hike along sections of Boone's Trace and the Wilderness Road, the trails on which settlers entered Kentucky between 1774 and 1779. The Mountain Life Museum is a reconstruction of a pioneer settlement using seven original log structures. McHargue's Mill is a fully operational mill with one of the world's largest collections of millstones.

The Dr. Thomas Walker State Historic Site marks the location where the explorer built a small cabin in 1750 before returning to Virginia from his initial exploration of the Cumberland Gap and Cumberland River. Pioneer William Whitley's house, Sportsman's Hill, is Kentucky's oldest brick house and was also the site of the state's first circular horse racing track, completed in 1788. Sportsman's Hill became a state historic shrine in 1951. Another popular house museum managed by the state park system is White Hall, the former home of the famous Kentucky abolitionist and congressman Cassius Marcellus Clay. Guided tours include former slave quarters, a blacksmith shop, corncrib, gristmill, smokehouse, icehouse, and family cemetery, as well as the Italianate mansion.

The multiplier effect of tourism and travel employment is extremely important to Kentucky's economy. With about fourteen hundred full-time employees and 7.9 million visitors annually, the Kentucky State Park System accounted for $282 million in total economic impact in 1999.

See also: CULTURAL HERITAGE TOURISM; ECOTOURISM.

—Carol Jo Evans, *University of Kentucky*

William L. Bailey, Bill Bailey, and Mark A. Lovely, *Kentucky State Parks: A Guide* (1995); Kentucky Department of Parks, *Kentucky State Parks* (1998).

Knoxville, Tennessee

In the late 1790s, the road through Knoxville was well traveled by adventurers from around the world, "tourists" drawn to this edge of Western civilization. Among them were young French noblemen escaping revolution at home. The Chevalier du Chateaubriand allegedly stayed at White's Fort in 1791 shortly after the site was renamed Knoxville; the future Citizen King, Louis Philippe, visited in 1797. Knoxville was appealing to them partly because it was the territorial capital—some visitors were guests of Governor William Blount—and because it was the supply station nearest the settlements of the Cherokee, who interested Europeans. Chateaubriand later wrote popular novels romanticizing the Cherokee. Others, such as botanist Andre Michaux, came to study the area's diverse flora.

East Tennessee's topography presented difficulties to developing railroad and steamboat routes, and in 1818 the city lost its state-capital status. Railroads finally arrived in 1855. By then, Knoxville was a way station to area mineral water resorts such as Montvale, a popular resort hotel touted in national magazines. German tourists disembarking from trains in pre–Civil War Knoxville to ride carriages to the Montvale resort are described in Sidney Lanier's 1867 novel *Tiger Lilies*.

After the Civil War, a suburb known as the Fountainhead—later Fountain City—billed itself as a clean-living resort. Both Fountainhead and nearby Whittle Springs featured enormous hotels with formal dinners and events. By 1900 the Fountainhead Hotel had failed, but Whittle Springs, which advertised medicinal waters, remained busy into the twentieth century.

Knoxville proper touted its own attractions, such as the well-preserved Indian mound near the University of Tennessee and the remains of the Union's Fort Sanders. Civil War tourism, especially veteran reunions, accounted for some of Knoxville's large tourist events of the late nineteenth century. Ethnic festivals and major musical shows at Staub's Theater also attracted thousands, mostly from within the region.

A new era for tourism arrived in 1910 with the opening of the Appalachian Exposition at Knoxville's Chilhowee Park. Highly successful, it was repeated the following year. In 1913 came the National Conservation Exposition, which in only two months brought more than a million visitors. With its emphasis on conservation, it seemed a harbinger of a new era for the Great Smoky Mountains, located some forty miles from Knoxville.

The Smokies were little traveled until roads were built in the 1920s. About the same time, a group of Knoxvillians led the movement to establish the Great Smoky Mountains National Park. By 1930, Knoxville was positioning itself as the "Gateway to the Smokies." The new Andrew Johnson Hotel led the way in touting Knoxville as a mountain-related tourist destination. Knoxville enjoyed that status for more than thirty years as new motels served the tourist trade.

In 1933 the city became headquarters for the Tennessee Valley Authority, a huge experiment in regional planning that drew intellectual tourists as diverse as Jawaharlal Nehru, David Ben-Gurion, Ernie Pyle, Le Corbusier, and Jean-Paul Sartre.

In 1947 Knoxville tourism suffered a blow when John Gunther called Knoxville "the ugliest city" in America in his best-selling guidebook, *Inside U.S.A.* The description angered many but prompted beautification measures including, in the 1950s, Knoxville's first Dogwood Trails, automobile routes through tree-lined neighborhoods that highlight flowering plants. The idea was augmented in 1960 with a two-week Dogwood Arts Festival in April that was a critical and popular success.

Meanwhile, Gatlinburg, Pigeon Forge, Townsend, and other tourist communities closer to the mountains assumed

Knoxville's mantle as the Smokies' gateway. Consequently, several tourist-oriented businesses in Knoxville closed.

In the final quarter of the twentieth century, Knoxville enticed tourists with ambitious new events and building projects. The largest was the 1982 World's Fair, sited in a former industrial area between the University of Tennessee and downtown. Organized around an energy theme built on Knoxville's status as headquarters of the Tennessee Valley Authority and its proximity to Oak Ridge National Laboratories, the fair brought more than 11 million visitors in its six-month run, placing it among America's most popular World's Fairs.

Meanwhile, the enduring popularity of University of Tennessee football led to the expansion of Neyland Stadium to a capacity of 106,000, placing it among the nation's largest football stadiums and making the home of the Volunteers a tourist attraction in itself. At least half of each capacity crowd is estimated to come from outside the Knoxville area. The men's and women's basketball teams have likewise become attractions.

The Knoxville Museum of Art, built on the World's Fair site in 1990, mounted several popular exhibits and emerged as the most popular museum in the city's history. In 1996 the East Tennessee Historical Society established the Museum of East Tennessee History at the Custom House downtown. Two years later the society held its first Cradle of Country Music tour, featuring downtown sites identified with country music's history.

In 1999 Knoxville opened its Women's Basketball Hall of Fame as the anchor of a large riverfront development, much of it tourist related, including the Gateway Regional Visitor Center, an attempt to reestablish Knoxville's connection to the Smokies and other natural attractions. A planned convention center and extensive development on the former World's Fair site promised a major impact on tourism in the twenty-first century.

See also: CIVIL WAR TOURISM; GREAT SMOKY MOUNTAINS NATIONAL PARK; TENNESSEE VALLEY AUTHORITY (GOVERNMENT).

—Jack Neely, *Knoxville, Tennessee*

Lucile Deaderick, ed., *Heart of the Valley: A History of Knoxville, Tennessee* (1976); Michael J. McDonald and William Bruce Wheeler, *Knoxville, Tennessee: Continuity and Change in an Appalachian City* (1983).

Linville Gorge Area, North Carolina

In North Carolina's Blue Ridge Mountains, seventeen miles from Boone, the Linville River cascades a dramatic ninety feet into Linville Gorge. According to historical accounts, William Linville and his son John left their name to the area after a fatal encounter with the Cherokees while camping near the gorge in 1766. Known for its natural beauty, the gorge area encompasses the Avery County communities of Linville, Linville Falls, Pineola, and Crossnore along the Blue Ridge Parkway.

Although explorers and naturalists had visited the location for centuries, planned tourism did not begin until Donald MacRae's 1888 formation of the Linville Improvement Company. MacRae's son Hugh purchased sixteen thousand acres for development and built the sixteen-mile Yonahlossee Road to Blowing Rock. His July Fourth opening of the Eseeola Inn in 1892 launched Linville as a resort. A Donald Ross golf course and private club opened in 1928. Following a 1920s tourism boom, the Great Depression and World War II delayed further tourism development until the 1950s. With the demise of the American chestnut (Linville summer homes before the mid-1940s had chestnut-bark shingles) and the increasing demand for less expensive summer homes, many 1970s and later developments, such as the Linville Land Harbor, offered compact lots for permanent campsites and trailers.

At the beginning of the twenty-first century, seasonal tourism provides the main source of income. Ski resorts and the sale of Christmas trees fuel the winter economy. Summer tourists enjoy golf, tennis, trout fishing, hiking trails through rhododendron and mountain laurel, and excursions to nearby Pisgah National Forest. Other sites of natural interest include the Linville Falls, given to the Blue Ridge Parkway in 1952 by John D. Rockefeller Jr., and Linville Caverns, discovered within Humpback Mountain in the early 1800s and opened to the public in 1937. The area's major attraction, Grandfather Mountain, hosts two events that draw tens of thousands of visitors to the mountain annually. Since 1924, the Singing on the Mountain has offered a day of preaching and gospel music, and the internationally renowned Grandfather Mountain Highland Games and Gathering of Scottish Clans began there in 1956. A permanent cultural attraction is the Weaving Room of Crossnore School. Developed as a self-help project through a Presbyterian mission school, the weaving school has produced handwoven clothing and home furnishings since 1923 in patterns used by early European settlers in the Appalachian Mountains.

With the success of the games, Agnes MacRae Morton and her son Julian Morton, descendants of Donald MacRae, planned in 1964 to build a two-thousand-acre Scottish village at Linville. Inspired by the vernacular architecture of sixteenth-century Lowland Fife, they planned to market real estate and cottages among their friends of Scottish ancestry and create antique and Scottish import shops to appeal to tourists. Never completed, the village of Invershiel, renamed Tynecastle, reflects efforts to expand Linville's resort by presenting the landscape through a heritage lens.

See also: BLUE RIDGE PROVINCE (GEOLOGY); HIKING (SPORTS AND RECREATION); PISGAH NATIONAL FOREST.

—Celeste Ray, *University of the South*

Howard E. Covington, *Linville: A Mountain Home for One Hundred Years* (1992).

Little Switzerland, North Carolina

The resort community of Little Switzerland is located in western North Carolina's Blue Ridge Mountains between Asheville and Boone on the Eastern Continental Divide. Following Cherokee dispossession, the area was known as Grassy Mountain to the early Scots and Scots-Irish settlers, whose folklore and surnames, such as Buchanan, Burnett, and McKinney, are still prevalent.

North Carolina lawyer and local official Heriot Clarkson renamed the area in 1909 for its Alpine-like views and began development of a summer resort. However, a tollgate and a guard shack sealed off the top of the mountain from all but local traffic until 1921, when the state purchased the road. With the construction of the Blue Ridge Parkway in the 1930s, the community soon began to draw visitors. In the same decade, what is now known as Big Lynn Lodge was built beside a seventy-five-foot linden tree that was itself part of local legend. The Overmountain Men reportedly camped under the tree on their way to the 1780 battle of Kings Mountain in South Carolina, and locals sometimes married there since the tree stood on the county line and allowed local couples whose families did not approve of the match to escape legal jurisdiction of one county for the other. In 1965, fearing the ailing "Big Lynn" might fall, the lodge's owners cut the tree down.

The Great Depression stalled tourism in western North Carolina and ended novelist Thomas Dixon's plans for an artists' colony at Little Switzerland. Author of *The Clansman*, which inspired D. W. Griffith's film *Birth of a Nation*, Dixon completed construction of the Wildacres Hotel before going bankrupt. At the beginning of the twenty-first century, Wildacres was known as a popular retreat center.

Little Switzerland now consists of a post office, bookshop, café, general store, craft and gem shops, and six inns and motels, all distinguished by Swiss architectural details. Attractions include performances of bluegrass music, buck dancing and clogging at the century-old apple orchard in neighboring Altapass, and local gem mines that once supplied emeralds to Tiffany's in New York City.

See also: TOURISM ARCHITECTURE (ARCHITECTURE).

—Celeste Ray, *University of the South*

Mad River Valley, Vermont

Vermont's Mad River Valley prides itself on maintaining an authentic rural ambiance—despite the fact that innkeepers provide more than sixty-six hundred beds for visitors who ski Mad River Glen's General Stark Mountain and the six mountains of Sugarbush Resort. In 2001 investors associated with Mad River Valley purchased Sugarbush from its corporate owners, pledging to protect the environment and to collaborate with local businesses to develop the resort without impairing the integrity of the valley's scenic and heritage tourism assets. Since its beginning in the early 1950s, Sugarbush has expanded to encompass more than four thousand acres and more than fifty-four miles of trails served by eighteen lifts; it now includes two terrain parks and a regulation half-pipe for snowboarders.

Nearby Mad River Glen, begun in 1948, is unusual among American ski resorts. Founder Roland Palmedo intended it to be a community of enthusiasts for the sport rather than a commercially oriented tourist park. Successive owners maintained that vision until 1995, when the Mad River Glen Cooperative, formed by the skiers themselves, assumed ownership and began directing operations through an elected board of trustees. The cooperative's commitment to environmental protection is evident in its award-winning program of year-round environmental education activities and its forest management plan. Financial success permitted upgrading of facilities and services, but the goup resisted innovations and trends adopted by commercial resorts, such as high-speed, high-capacity lifts and snowboarding. The original single chairlift, now unique in the industry, recently was refurbished. Along with five other lifts, it serves forty-five trails for novice, intermediate, and experienced skiers. With an average 250 inches of snowfall annually, Mad River Glen offers expert skiers natural snow conditions and trails that challenge even Olympic athletes.

See also: ECOTOURISM; SKI RESORTS.

—Benita J. Howell, *University of Tennessee*

Maryland State Parks

The first national park, Yellowstone, had existed since 1872 and the National Park Service was established in 1916, but when the first National Conference of State Parks was held in 1921 in Des Moines, Iowa, twenty-nine states still had not established any state parks at all. As Stephen Mather, director of the National Park Service, noted at the time, Maryland was one of those states. However, the state already had acquired thousands of acres in forest reserves that often served a similar purpose though not officially designated as parks. A 1916 report by Fred W. Besley, Maryland's first state forester, described the forest reserves as serving multiple purposes from the outset: in addition to conserving forest resources, reserves were established to ensure that public benefits were protected from private monopolistic use and to meet the general public's demand for recreational space.

By the beginning of the twentieth century, much of Maryland's marketable timber had been removed, and what little remained was being consumed at a rapid rate. State officials, concerned businessmen, and others began to fear that Maryland was running out of timber and that the state's forests would soon be unable to meet the needs of important local industries. Efforts to set aside and hold lands in public trust were first initiated in the far western portion of the state—Maryland's mountainous Appalachian region. In 1906 Robert and John Garrett, grandsons of Baltimore and Ohio Railroad President John W. Garrett, donated 1,917 acres of land near the Youghiogheny River in Garrett County to the State of Maryland. The Garretts donated the land on the condition that the state develop a professional forestry management program. This led to the drafting of the Maryland Forestry Conservation Act, the establishment of the Office of the State Forester, and the creation of the Maryland State Board of Forestry.

This donation of land from the Garretts began Maryland's modern system of state forests, parks, wildlife areas, natural environmental areas, natural heritage sites, and fish management areas amounting to more than 338,000 acres. Currently, the state maintains forty-seven state parks, nineteen of which lie in the three Appalachian counties—Washington, Allegany, and Garrett.

Western Maryland's state parks offer the outdoor enthusiast a wide range of recreational opportunities, from boating and fishing on Deep Creek Lake to hiking, fishing, hunting, and rustic camping in the three hundred acres of Big Run surrounded by the Savage River State Forest. Situated in the Catoctin Mountains, another popular hiking and camping park is Cunningham Falls State Park, which hosts the Annual Maple Syrup Heritage Festival and features the seventy-eight-foot cascading Cunningham Falls. The 3,000-acre Rocky Gap State Park, named for the mile-long gorge that runs through it, contains a 243-acre lake and an eighteen-hole golf course. The Youghiogheny River, which runs north into Pennsylvania, provides a scenic mountain setting for whitewater rafting and kayaking. During the winter months, hiking trails in both New Germany and Herrington Manor State Parks become popular cross-country skiing tracks, with Herrington Manor holding races each year. State forests, wildlife management areas, and other public holdings also support important recreational and sporting activities.

While these public lands were set aside primarily to conserve forest resources and provide recreational space, other parks in the state system were established to protect distinct cultural and historical treasures. Falling into this category are Casselman River Bridge, Fort Frederick, Gathland, Tonoloway, and Washington Monument State Parks. The Appalachian Trail traverses western Maryland along South Mountain in Washington County, and the Chesapeake and Ohio Canal National Historical Park has its terminus at Cumberland, in Allegany County. Both the Appalachian Trail and the Chesapeake and Ohio towpath are commonly used for day hiking and backpacking and, in the case of the towpath, cycling.

The distinction between Maryland's state parks and its state forests has not always been clear. Many of the state parks were carved out of the forest reserve system. In 1964, for example, Big Run and New Germany State Parks were created from the Savage River State Forest. The same holds true for Herrington Manor and Swallow Falls State Parks, both of which were originally contained within Swallow Falls State Forest.

The Civilian Conservation Corps also played a significant role in developing Maryland's resources. Big Run, Herrington Manor, New Germany, and Washington Monument State Parks, among others, all bear the mark of the New Deal entity in some shape or form, whether it is a trail, shelter, road, cabin, or campsite. During the 1930s, the Civilian Conservation Corps restored both Fort Frederick, originally built by the colony in 1756 to protect the frontier, and Washington Monument, the first monument devoted to the memory of George Washington.

Brochures about Maryland distributed at the close of the twentieth century claimed that either a state park or forest is within a forty-minute drive of any location in the state. The parks and forests situated in Maryland's Appalachian region contain the most rugged terrain in the state and some of its most striking landscape features.

See also: CIVILIAN CONSERVATION CORPS (GOVERNMENT); FOREST MANAGEMENT AND CONSERVATION (ENVIRONMENT).

—Geoffrey L. Buckley, *Ohio University*

Geoffrey L. Buckley and J. Morgan Grove, "Sowing the Seeds of Forest Conservation: Fred Besley and the Maryland Story, 1906–1923," *Maryland Historical Magazine* (Fall 2001); Ross Kimmel, Offutt Johnson, and Dorna Cooper, *Three Centuries of Change: The History and Tradition of the Maryland Rangers* (1994); Freeman Tilden, *The State Parks: Their Meaning in American Life* (1970).

Matewan, West Virginia

Matewan is best known for the Hatfield-McCoy feud that raged on the Tug Fork of the Big Sandy River in Mingo County, West Virginia, during the 1880s. Forty years later, the town was the scene of a bloody conflict in the West Virginia coal mine wars. The area experienced a major transformation in the 1990s as coal mining reemerged as a major economic force and Congress directed the U.S. Army Corps of Engineers to address the periodic flooding that caused social havoc and stymied economic growth in the Tug Fork Valley.

Several developments in the early 1990s set the stage for tourism to become part of the town's economic revitalization plans. The Corps of Engineers constructed a floodwall to protect the town and completion of Appalachian Corridor

"G" linked Matewan to the federal interstate system. At the same time, the feature film *Matewan* and books such as Denise Giardina's *Storming Heaven*, Lon Savage's *Thunder in the Mountains*, and Altina Waller's *Feud* brought public attention to the town's colorful association with the Hatfield-McCoy feud and the 1920 Matewan Massacre, a battle that left seven Baldwin-Felts mine guards, two miners, and the town mayor dead on the street.

Community leaders, businesses, and individuals pledged funding over a five-year period to establish a nonprofit community economic-development corporation, the Matewan Development Center. With a professional director in place, the center sought private and public partnerships and grant support. Key to planning was a Memorandum of Understanding signed in 1989 by the governor of West Virginia, a Kentucky congressional representative, the town of Matewan, the National Park Service, the Army Corps of Engineers, Marshall University, and the Matewan Development Center. In it, these parties agreed to cooperate in developing strategies and building financial and other resources needed to pursue economic development and tourism while conserving Matewan's natural, cultural, and historic resources.

The $40-million floodwall was completed in 1997, the same year the downtown area was designated a historic district. By 1999, when Matewan was featured in the television documentary *Restore America*, the first two phases of a three-phase historical restoration were complete. In June 2000 Matewan hosted the Hatfield-McCoy Reunion, and in August 2000 the play *Terror on the Tug*, written by Jean Battlo, about Sid Hatfield and the Matewan Massacre, was performed at the outdoor Globe Theater in Landgraff, West Virginia. Another play, *The Matewan Massacre Reenactment*, was performed in September for the Matewan Homecoming, an annual event during which the town pauses to reflect on its history. A local community action team, the town council, and various civic organizations in Matewan and the surrounding area host the homecoming.

Additional tourist attractions include holiday events at Halloween and Christmas, new recreation facilities, a visitor center, and the Matewan Museum. Matewan's revitalization was not directed solely toward encouraging tourism, however. Accomplishments during the community revitalization of the 1990s included a new city hall building, elementary school, Little League baseball field, and a new residential area using a 1920s design motif.

See also: COAL HERITAGE TOURISM; CULTURAL HERITAGE TOURISM.

—Johnny Fullen, Sue Fullen, and Donna May, *Matewan Development Center*

David Alan Corbin, *Life, Work, and Rebellion in the Coal Fields* (1981); Lon Savage, *Thunder in the Mountains* (1990); Altina Waller, *Feud* (1988).

Mississippi State Parks

See Alabama and Mississippi State Parks

Monongahela National Forest

When President Woodrow Wilson established the Monongahela National Forest in West Virginia on April 28, 1920, providing for recreational opportunities was not a high priority. At the time, there were few facilities for visitors, not many trees, and no good roads.

One of the U.S. Forest Service's first attempts to spur tourism came in 1930, when it joined with the community of Elkins, West Virginia, to organize the Mountain State Forest Festival, an event designed to promote the Monongahela and to boost the Elkins economy. In the mid-1930s, the Civilian Conservation Corps, a federal agency established to conserve natural resources and provide jobs for the unemployed, worked in the Monongahela, stocking streams for fishing and building recreation facilities such as picnic tables, forest camps, and roads. By 1938, the corps had constructed the Horseshoe Forest Camp and the Blue Bend, Smoke Hole, Bickle Knob, Alpena Gap, and Stuart Recreation Areas. That same year, the Forest Service published the first information pamphlet about the Monongahela; entitled "Time to Relax at the Forest Camps," it helped to draw a record 122,882 visitors to the facilities.

In 1940 the Civilian Conservation Corps participated in developing the Horseshoe Organizational Camp to provide vacation experiences for children and adults. Two-thirds of the camp season was reserved for children receiving charity or for organizations such as the Young Men's Christian Association. Still, recreation was not a high priority.

Attention to tourism increased by 1959, when the Monongahela began to plan improvements to recreation facilities as part of a Forest Service program. The 1960 Multiple Use–Sustained Yield Act gave the Forest Service its first explicit authority to consider recreation as a forest product comparable to timber production and watershed protection. The 1964 Land and Water Conservation Fund Program focused more attention and funding on recreation facilities. On September 28, 1965, President Lyndon Johnson designated the Spruce Knob–Seneca Rocks area as the nation's first national recreation area in a national forest.

By the 1970s, the environmental movement began to have an impact on tourism in the forests. The 1975 Eastern Wilderness Areas Act designated the Dolly Sods Wilderness and Otter Creek Wilderness Areas in the forest. Both are open for activities such as hiking, backpacking, and bird watching. In June 1978, Senator Robert C. Byrd of West Virginia dedicated the first visitor center at Seneca Rocks. The 1984–85 Management Plan for the forest established new categories of land management for semiprimitive recreation and was highly influential in setting precedents for forest planning nationally.

During the 1990s, there were several major debates over recreational use of the forest versus logging and gas drilling. Officials estimated that more than 3.5 million visitors used the Monongahela National Forest in 1997 for camping, viewing scenery and exhibits, hiking, picnicking, hunting, and fishing. As of September 1999, the forest included 903,079 acres.

See also: CAMPING (SPORTS AND RECREATION); HIKING (SPORTS AND RECREATION); HUNTING AND FISHING (SPORTS AND RECREATION).

—Barbara J. Howe, *West Virginia University*

Allen de Hart and Bruce Sundquist, *Monongahela National Forest Hiking Guide* (1999); Barbara J. Howe, Gillian Mace Berman, and Melissa Conley-Spencer, *The Monongahela National Forest, 1915–1990* (1992).

Moses H. Cone Memorial Park

See Southern Highland Craft Guild (Crafts)

Mount Mitchell

Located in North Carolina's Black Mountains, Mount Mitchell, rising 6,684 feet, is the highest peak east of the Mississippi River and the site of the state's first state park, established in 1915. Originally part of Cherokee hunting grounds, Mount Mitchell has attracted botanists and geographers since the 1770s. Media promotion and improved transportation and public accommodations sparked a tourist boom in the 1850s. In 1858 the peak was named for University of North Carolina professor Elisha Mitchell, who fell to his death in 1857 while measuring its elevation.

The Civil War halted tourism and scientific study on the mountain for several decades, and after 1912 logging denuded the area. In 1915 North Carolina preservationists and tourism promoters convinced the state legislature to purchase 525 acres at the summit as a state park. Meanwhile, the Perley and Crockett Lumber Company sparked a new tourist influx by opening their logging railroad up the mountain to sightseers. When the railway closed in 1919, public outcry encouraged construction of private toll roads in 1922 and 1925.

In the 1930s, the Civilian Conservation Corps added facilities and better trails, preparing the park for increased visitorship brought by the Blue Ridge Parkway, which after 1940 provided the first toll-free route to the mountaintop. When the parkway was finished between Mount Mitchell and Asheville in 1950, yearly visitorship surged to more than two hundred thousand, and conflicts ensued between the state and neighboring citizens over further tourist development. A proposal for a national park at the site in the 1970s met local opposition and failed to materialize. Meanwhile, acid rain and the balsam woolly adelgid *(Adelges picea)* destroyed many of the mountain's trees in the 1980s and 1990s. Land acquisition boosted park acreage to 1,855 acres by 2001.

See also: BLUE RIDGE PARKWAY; CIVILIAN CONSERVATION CORPS (GOVERNMENT); NORTH CAROLINA STATE PARKS.

—Anne Mitchell Whisnant, *Duke University*

Mount Washington

Travelers began visiting New Hampshire's Presidential Range in the late 1790s, arriving via a new road through Crawford Notch and staying at inns and taverns built to accommodate them. In 1819 Abel Crawford blazed a trail to Mount Washington, making it possible for visitors such as Daniel Webster, Ralph Waldo Emerson, Nathaniel Hawthorne, and Henry David Thoreau to climb the 6,288-foot peak. The Mount Washington Cog Railway to the summit of the mountain was completed in 1869, but the heyday of Mount Washington tourism postdated the Gilded Age.

Joseph Stickney, a New Hampshire native whose investments in coal mining and the Pennsylvania Railroad made him wealthy, bought the Mount Pleasant House inn and ten thousand acres with a view of the mountain in 1881. In 1902 he opened the luxurious Mount Washington Hotel at Bretton Woods. It incorporated the latest technology, including electricity and central heating, and attracted many celebrities through the 1930s. When David Steele published accounts of his vacation travel across the country in 1918, he described the geologic and scenic attractions of the White Mountains in detail. He was equally enthusiastic about the imposing Mount Washington and the hotel at its foot, describing it as "probably the finest summer hotel in America . . . a haunt of city luxury in a mountain fastness." The hotel at Bretton Woods became world famous in 1944 as the site of the Bretton Woods International Monetary Conference.

Much of Stickney's original landholding was sold to White Mountain National Forest in 1975, but the Mount Washington Hotel continued to operate through several changes in ownership until 1990. It was placed on the National Register of Historic Places in 1978 and became a national historic landmark in 1986. The hotel was acquired by the Federal Deposit Insurance Corporation and sold at auction in 1991 to a group of New Hampshire natives, who acquired or developed facilities for the Mount Washington Hotel and Resort. This four-seasons destination now offers fine accommodations and dining, thirty-six holes of golf, tennis, swimming, bridle paths, mountain biking and hiking, and various special events. The Bretton Woods Ski Resort, originally part of the Mount Washington Hotel complex, has operated as a separate business since 1988.

After several expansions and upgrades to lift facilities, it now offers skiers convenient access to three mountains—Mount Rosebrook, West Mountain, and Mount Stickney—from one base. The Mount Washington Cog Railway still transports visitors to the summit from late spring through the fall color season.

See also: SKI RESORTS.

—Benita J. Howell, *University of Tennessee*

Gene Daniell and Jon Burroughs, *Hiking Guide to Mount Washington and the Presidential Range* (1998); David M. Steele, *Vacation Journeys East and West* (1918).

Nantahala National Forest

With 528,446 acres, the Nantahala National Forest, headquartered in Asheville, North Carolina, is the largest of four national forests in the state. Congress established Nantahala National Forest in 1920 under the authority of the 1911 Weeks Act to safeguard watersheds and provide the nation with a continuous supply of timber. While the forest continues to protect water quality and provide wood products, it also conserves diverse ecosystems, plant and animal habitat, and wilderness areas and offers outstanding recreational opportunities.

The Cherokee had long inhabited the forest region until their 1838–39 mass deportation on the Trail of Tears. Only after negotiations concluded in 1973 were they able to partly resettle in the area; a part of the Qualla Boundary reservation falls within the northern border of the forest. The area's rich Native American heritage is evident from names used throughout the forest. Even the name Nantahala *(Nundayeli)* is Cherokee, meaning "land of the noonday sun"—a fitting name for a place where the sun only penetrates to the valley floor when high overhead at midday.

The forest is noted for its hundreds of miles of trails. Two long-distance routes cross the forest—the Bartram Trail, which approximates the 1775 route of naturalist William Bartram, and the Appalachian Trail. A favorite place for mountain biking is at Tsali Recreation Area on Fontana Lake. For horseback riders, both Standing Indian Basin and Fires Creek Area offer primitive horse camps and a variety of trails. Upper Tellico and Wayehutta trail networks are for off-highway vehicles.

Scenic byways provide automobilists another popular way to enjoy the Forest. Mountain Waters National Scenic Byway, for example, runs sixty-one miles through forests, rural countryside, and two spectacular river gorges complete with waterfalls—the Cullasaja Gorge and the Nantahala Gorge, the latter famous for whitewater rafting. A side trip to the top of Wayah Bald provides a panoramic view of the surrounding mountains. Cherohala Skyway, which takes its name from the Cherokee and Nantahala National Forests, also figures on the list of national scenic byways designated by the Federal Highway Administration. The skyway winds across the crest of the Unicoi Mountains linking Robbinsville, North Carolina, to Tellico Plains, Tennessee.

Cherohala Skyway begins not far from Joyce Kilmer Memorial Forest, a magnificent remnant of Appalachian old growth. This 3,800-acre forest was dedicated to Joyce Kilmer, the World War I soldier and poet who penned the lines "I think that I shall never see / A poem lovely as a tree." The towering four-hundred-year-old trees can be enjoyed from an easy, figure-eight trail through the cathedral-like forest. The trail is only open to foot travel since the Memorial Forest is also part of the Joyce Kilmer–Slickrock Wilderness.

The Nantahala's lakes, rivers, and waterfalls also provide beauty and recreational opportunities. Several lakes—Fontana, Chatuge, Cherokee, Hiwassee, and Santeetlah—offer boating, swimming, camping, and fishing. At 411 feet, Whitewater Falls is considered the highest series of waterfalls in the East.

See also: APPALACHIAN TRAIL; WHITEWATER SPORTS (SPORTS AND RECREATION).

—Pat Momich, *National Forests in North Carolina*

Jack Coriell and Nancy Shofner, eds., *Appalachian Trail Guide to North Carolina–Georgia* (1994); Sara Pacher, *Insiders' Guide to North Carolina's Mountains* (4th edition, 1999); Sheila Turnage, *Fodor's North Carolina* (2000).

Natchez Trace Parkway

See Alabama and Mississippi State Parks; Natchez Trace (Settlement and Migration)

National Scenic Byways

Created by Congress in 1991, the National Scenic Byways Program recognizes outstanding roads as National Scenic Byways or All-American Roads based on their historic, cultural, scenic, natural, recreational, and archeological qualities. The U.S. secretary of transportation designates routes from nominations submitted by communities through the states or federal land-management agencies. There are currently seventy-two designations in thirty-three states. Eleven of these byways are located either completely or partially within the Appalachian region: the Natchez Trace, part of which lies in upper Mississippi and northern Alabama; Talladega in Alabama's Talladega National Forest; Russell-Brasstown in Georgia's Chattahoochee National Forest; Cherokee Foothills in South Carolina's Blue Ridge region; Cherohala Skyway in the Cherokee and Nantahala National Forests in Tennessee and North Carolina; Blue Ridge Parkway in North Carolina (an All-American Road); Canal Way Ohio Scenic Byway, following U.S. Highway 52 in Ohio; and four byways in West Virginia. The West Virginia byways are the

Coal Heritage Trail in Raleigh, Wyoming, McDowell and Mercer Counties; the Highland Scenic Highway in Monongahela National Forest; the Washington Heritage Trail in the eastern panhandle area; and the Midland Trail, following U.S. Highway 60 from Charleston to White Sulphur Springs. At the turn of the twenty-first century, Kentucky, Pennsylvania, and Maryland had no national byways. There were state-designated byways in these as well as the other Appalachian states, however.

The Intermodal Surface Transportation Efficiency Act of 1991 and, after 1998, the Transportation Equity Act for the Twenty-First Century provided funds for the program. By the year 2000, it had granted approximately $139 million to states and communities for planning, acquisition of conservation easements, and construction of trails, rest areas, turnouts and overlooks, and interpretive facilities. Byway efforts have forged new partnerships among conservation, recreation, transportation, and tourism interests. The National Scenic Byways Program helps the byway community create a memorable travel experience and enhance local quality of life through efforts to preserve, protect, interpret, and promote the intrinsic assets of designated byways. Many rural communities, in particular, view the program as an opportunity to bring traffic into their towns and boost local economies. National designation has stimulated the development of local leadership, new tourism-based businesses, Main Street programs, countywide planning, and, most importantly, local pride. Narrow, winding two-lane roads once viewed as barriers to economic development came to be celebrated as tourism assets.

Consumer demand and a feasibility study encouraged Congress to create the program. Automobile travel has consistently accounted for three-fourths of all travel in the United States and continues to be the most popular means of transportation for both business and pleasure travel. Between 1986 and 1996, weekend trips by Americans jumped by 70 percent and accounted for more than half of all U.S. travel late in the twentieth century. The Appalachian region is within reasonable driving distance from many urban population hubs, so its scenic byways are well positioned to attract weekend vacationers traveling by car.

See also: BLUE RIDGE PARKWAY; COAL HERITAGE TOURISM; SKYLINE DRIVE (ARCHITECTURE).

—Sharon Hurt Davidson, *National Scenic Byways Program*

National Geographic's Guide to Scenic Highways and Byways (1996).

National Trust Heritage Tourism Initiative

In 1989 the National Trust for Historic Preservation, with grants from the National Endowment for the Arts and American Express, launched a three-year pilot program, the Heritage Tourism Initiative. This project extended the National Trust's long-established Main Street program in ways that were particularly significant for Appalachia. By gaining national visibility, Appalachian pilot projects became models for emulation throughout America.

Main Street projects help medium-sized towns rehabilitate public buildings and revitalize cultural activities in order to lure visitors and enhance quality of life, but many Appalachian towns are too small, have too few potential attractions, and lack the combined expertise in historic preservation, arts management, planning, and tourism promotion to launch a successful Main Street program. The Heritage Tourism Initiative took a more comprehensive regional approach, encouraging collaboration among small town arts and preservation groups, cultural institutions, government agencies, and the tourism industry to protect the distinctive historical and cultural resources of multicounty areas. Working together, small towns in a multicounty area could develop and successfully market their cultural heritage attractions. By the end of the 1990s, these principles were at work throughout Appalachia, for example, in West Virginia's Coal Heritage Trail and Coal Heritage Area, the Rivers of Steel National and State Heritage Area in Pennsylvania, the Route 23 Corridor Project in Kentucky, the Birmingham Industrial Heritage District in Alabama, and the Forestry Heritage Trail Project of West Virginia and western Maryland.

In the original 1989 Heritage Tourism Initiative, Tennessee was one of four pilot states, along with Indiana, Wisconsin, and Texas. Two of Tennessee's four competitively chosen pilot areas were in Appalachian Tennessee. These included the vicinities known as Northeast Tennessee: America's First Frontier, which included Hancock, Hawkins, Greene, Washington, Unicoi, Sullivan, Carter, and Johnson Counties, and the Tennessee Overhill, named for the Cherokee Overhill Towns, which included the southeastern Tennessee counties of McMinn, Monroe, and Polk.

The initiative in Tennessee included resource inventory, investigation of opportunities, program design, training, marketing, and evaluation. Each pilot area agreed to provide staff and administrative funding and to commit to the National Trust's principles of heritage tourism: authenticity and quality, interpretation and education, preservation and protection, local capacity building, and partnership development.

The America's First Frontier project, led by the Northeast Tennessee Tourism Association, brought together the communities of Elizabethton, Greeneville, Johnson City, Jonesborough, Kingsport, and Rogersville to identify heritage tourism possibilities focused on the theme of early Euro-American settlement, address preservation issues, and create new marketing and training programs.

Several Overhill communities already were working with the Tennessee Humanities Council and Tennessee Arts Commission on heritage interpretation, but local organizers had little experience with tourism development. The newly established Tennessee Overhill organization sought to incorporate local history and culture into a tourism program previously based on outdoor recreation. Both regions incorporated large portions of the Cherokee National Forest and hoped to combine natural and cultural resources into one package. The U.S. Forest Service and other public land agencies became valuable partners along with the state arts, humanities, tourism, and conservation agencies.

Unlike some Appalachian tourism promotions that feature hillbillies resting on front porches of mountain cabins, these heritage tourism projects worked to interpret authentic stories of their respective regions. America's First Frontier highlighted Tennessee's oldest towns and their role in the early development of the state. The Tennessee Overhill, with its company towns and worker villages, presented the story of regional commerce and industry from the Cherokee fur and hide trade through copper mining, textiles, railroading, logging, and farming.

Upon completion of the Heritage Tourism Initiative, all four Tennessee areas established permanent heritage tourism programs. In the America's First Frontier area, Northeast Tennessee Tourism continues to work with communities on preservation issues and to ensure that preservation interests are represented on the regional tourism governing board. The Tennessee Overhill Heritage Association became a permanent nonprofit organization devoted exclusively to heritage tourism development in McMinn, Monroe, and Polk Counties.

Partly as a result of this initiative, heritage tourism is recognized as a viable economic-development strategy in Appalachia. Tennessee, North Carolina, Kentucky, and Virginia now have official heritage tourism divisions within their state tourism agencies.

See also: CULTURAL HERITAGE TOURISM.

—Linda Damron Caldwell, *Tennessee Overhill Heritage Association*

National Trust for Historic Preservation, *Getting Started: How to Succeed in Heritage Tourism* (1993; reprint 1999).

Natural Bridge

Natural Bridge in Rockbridge County, Virginia, has been a landmark for as long as there have been human travelers in central Appalachia. This natural rock formation bridges a canyon that is approximately 90 feet long and 150 feet wide at one end and 50 feet wide at the other. Some believe the bridge was formed when the roof of a limestone cavern collapsed, leaving the present formation, while others contend the shape was carved over many years by the waters of Cedar Creek. Estimated to be more than 100 million years old, the formation is listed among the seven natural wonders of the world and was designated a National Historic Landmark in 1998.

Legend holds that Monacan Indians fleeing from attacking Shawnees and Powhatans accidentally discovered the bridge when it loomed before them as an escape route. It remains sacred to the Monacans. In 1750 George Washington surveyed the bridge site, and on July 5, 1774, Thomas Jefferson purchased 157 acres of land in Virginia, including the bridge, from King George III of England for twenty shillings. In 1833 Jefferson's heirs sold the site, and the new owner erected the Forest Inn to accommodate the increasing number of visitors. During the following decade, under the ownership of Colonel Henry Parsons, Natural Bridge's reputation as a resort attraction became firmly established.

Many early settlers to the region traveled the area in their trek along the Great Valley Road from Philadelphia into the mountain backcountry of Virginia and the Carolinas. Natural Bridge and Niagara Falls were the two wonders of the new world that Europeans visited during the eighteenth and nineteenth centuries. Still popular, the site draws thousands of travelers annually to its attractions, which include the Cedar Creek Nature Trail, a living history Monacan Village complex, and a sound and light show. Visitors can also take a guided tour through the nearby caverns or visit a wax museum that features scenes from American and Shenandoah history.

See also: TECTONICS (GEOLOGY); WASHINGTON, GEORGE (SETTLEMENT AND MIGRATION).

—Shannon Young Brooks, *National D-Day Memorial, Bedford, Virginia*

New River Gorge and Gauley River

A fifty-three-mile stretch of the New River in southern West Virginia was designated a National River in 1978. The designation helps protect the stream, its deep canyonlike gorge, and the natural, historic, and recreational resources on more than seventy thousand acres lying between the towns of Hinton and Fayetteville. The gorge, almost nine hundred feet deep in some places, has long been called the "Grand Canyon of the East." Managed by the National Park Service, the New River Gorge National River attained the further designation of American heritage river in 1998. Although estimates of its age vary greatly, the New River is certainly one of the continent's oldest rivers. It still flows northward along part of the course that the extensive Teays River system followed before the Ohio and the Mississippi formed.

The New River Gorge has become a prime destination for outdoor recreation enthusiasts, offering excellent whitewater paddling, fishing, climbing, mountain biking, hiking, and backpacking. Several visitor centers offer a variety of interpretive programs, but the national area has only primitive camping facilities. With coordinated planning and encouragement from the state, however, the federal area draws visitors to nearby destinations such as the Bluestone and Pipestem State Parks. Local governments and private-sector organizations in many nearby towns have developed or expanded tourist accommodations, outdoor recreational opportunities, and attractions that recount the area's coal heritage and aspects of the region's cultural and industrial history.

The National Park Service reported more than 235,000 recreation visitor days in the federal area for the 1999–2000 fiscal year; but just outside the northern boundary, more than 200,000 visitors come on a single day for the annual Bridge Day festival during October leaf season. The steel-span New River Gorge Bridge, built in 1977, is 876 feet high. On Bridge Day, crowds cross on foot or watch as rock climbers rappel and parachutists jump from the bridge into the gorge.

Canyon Rim Visitor Center, near Fayetteville, is the primary location where visitors can get information year-round, purchase publications, view slide and video programs and special events in the auditorium, and see displays on cultural history, recreation, and natural history in the exhibit hall. Rangers at Canyon Rim provide guided bus tours and special educational programs.

Grandview, near Beckley and Lewisburg, was formerly a state park but was incorporated into the national area in 1990. In addition to hiking and picnicking, Grandview offers a summer season of outdoor drama presented by Theatre West Virginia. Another visitor center at Thurmond, near Glen Jean, is housed in the restored Chesapeake and Ohio Railway depot. The furnishings and exhibits reconstruct life in Thurmond in its heyday of the early twentieth century, when steam railroads brought coal from the surrounding mines to support a wealthy, vibrant boomtown. The visitor center near Hinton at the south end of the national river provides orientation and information about the upper stretch of the river where paddlers can tackle intermediate-level rapids. The lower stretch of the river near the bridge has the more challenging Class IV and V whitewater rapids. Local outfitters guide commercial raft trips through the gorge downstream from Thurmond.

Northeast of the New River area, twenty-five miles of the Gauley River and six miles of the Meadow River were designated the Gauley River National Recreation Area in 1988. This area protects another scenic gorge where whitewater enthusiasts kayak or participate in guided whitewater raft trips. Visitors spent the equivalent of more than eighty thousand days at Gauley River National Recreation Area in 1999. The National Park Service manages the Gauley and New River areas jointly from headquarters at Glen Jean.

Much of the land along the Gauley and Meadow Rivers remains in private hands because the National Park Service no longer takes the land of unwilling sellers through condemnation proceedings. However, the U.S. Army Corps of Engineers has developed a campground with electric hookups and recreation facilities at Summersville Lake. Additional river access mitigates the presence of Summersville Dam and hydropower facility adjacent to the recreational area. South of the New River, the Bluestone National Scenic River also was established in 1988. The National Park Service manages a wild and scenic stretch of the Bluestone, extending about eleven miles, that provides a corridor for paddling or hiking between Bluestone and Pipestem State Parks.

See also: COAL HERITAGE TOURISM; NEW RIVER GORGE BRIDGE (TRANSPORTATION); WHITEWATER SPORTS (SPORTS AND RECREATION).

—Benita J. Howell, *University of Tennessee*

Colleen Anderson, *The New West Virginia One-Day Trip Book* (1998); Allen de Hart, *West Virginia Hiking Trails* (1997).

New York State Parks

New York claims the nation's first state park, the Niagara Reservation, established to protect the popular tourist destination Niagara Falls. Seventeen of the 163 parks currently in the state system are located in Appalachian counties. Retreating glaciers of the Cenozoic ice ages left spectacular gorges, kettle ponds, amazing rock formations, moraines, and waterfalls. In addition to conserving the physical resources and wild beauty of the area, the parks provide facilities for all seasonal activities including camping, skiing, ice skating, snowshoeing, hiking, ice fishing, snowmobiling, bird watching, golfing, boating, fishing, swimming, and hunting.

Allegany State Park in the western part of the state is New York's largest four-season park with sixty-five thousand acres. Long Point on Lake Chautauqua State Park is situated on a peninsula in one of the highest navigable bodies of water in North America. Bird watchers especially enjoy Lake Erie State Park, where many birds stop on the protected shore before they fly across the lake.

The parks of the Finger Lakes region have some of the more spectacular scenery caused by glaciers. Taughannock Falls State Park, near Ithaca on Cayuga Lake, features one of the highest waterfalls in the East; a second park named Long Point is located on the eastern shore of Cayuga Lake. Watkins Glen State Park has nineteen waterfalls within two miles with trails that permit hikers to walk behind the falls. Swimming in natural pools or hiking through a wild gorge are activities available at Stony Brook, Buttermilk Falls, and

Robert H. Treman State Parks. The Allan H. Treman State Marine Park has the state's largest inland marina. Thousands of years ago, as glaciers retreated, they deposited hundreds of feet of sand, gravel, and silt and created depressions called kettle ponds. Today an eighteen-hole golf course at Mark Twain State Park near Horseheads makes the most of these geological features. Hunters, anglers, and golfers can enjoy their sports surrounded by the breathtaking views of Pinnacle State Park.

Chenango Valley State Park, near Binghamton, with its two kettle lakes, is another prime location for fishing, camping, and bird watching. Year-round lake activities such as swimming and camping in the summer and ice skating and ice fishing in the winter are available at Oquaga Creek State Park, which is just three hours from New York City. Bowman Lake, Gilbert Lake, and Hunt's Pond State Parks provide areas for serious camping enthusiasts. Glimmerglass State Park, whose name comes from James Fenimore Cooper's *Leatherstocking Tales*, is located on Otsego Lake near Cooperstown. Its picturesque trails provide views of Otsego Lake and a wide variety of wildflowers, shrubs, ferns, and mosses.

The Finger Lakes region also is home to Ganondagan State Historic Site, a seventeenth-century site with a replica bark longhouse, where visitors learn about Seneca history and culture from Native American interpreters.

In addition to state parks and historic sites, New York operates several centers that offer seasonal festivals as well as year-round programs of nature study and environmental education. In the state's Appalachian counties, Rogers Environmental Education Center in Sherburne in Chenango County encompasses 571 acres with varied habitats and opportunities for nature study.

See also: COOPER, JAMES FENIMORE (LITERATURE); COOPERSTOWN, NEW YORK; ECOTOURISM.

—Clara Hasbrouck, *East Tennessee State University*

Deborah Williams, *Natural Wonders of New York: Exploring Wild and Scenic Places* (1999).

North Carolina State Parks

The North Carolina State Parks System got its start in the western region of the state in 1915 with the dedication of Mount Mitchell State Park. Administered by the Division of Parks and Recreation of the North Carolina Department of Environment and Natural Resources, the system includes thirty-four parks, seven state lakes, four recreation areas, four state rivers, and ten natural areas. Eleven of these units contribute to the tourism attraction complex of the southern Appalachians by providing a backdrop of protected scenic areas with outdoor recreation opportunities.

Located on the Blue Ridge Parkway in Yancey County, Mount Mitchell State Park encompasses the highest peak east of the Mississippi at 6,684 feet. The park's original 795 acres have been expanded to 1,855 acres with hiking trails, picnic areas, campsites, and a restaurant. Hanging Rock State Park, dedicated in 1936, covers 6,921 acres of mountainous terrain, forest, and streams and is bordered by the Dan River. Located in Stokes County, the park offers hiking trails, a bridle trail, picnic areas, campsites, vacation cabins, swimming, fishing, rock climbing, and rowboat and canoe rentals.

Stone Mountain, added to the system in 1969, and Pilot Mountain, added in 1968, are located in Wilkes and Surry Counties, respectively. Both parks offer hiking and bridle trails, picnicking, and recreational vehicle, tent, and trailer camping. Pilot Mountain is a 3,703-acre park bordered by the Yadkin River and offers canoeists river access and two wilderness campsites on the larger Yadkin Island. Stone Mountain's 13,670 acres include day-hiking trails, and backpack camping sites. Hikers can fish in streams designated for single-hook lure angling. Pilot Mountain's two prominent pinnacles and Stone Mountain's cliffs offer climbing in designated areas.

South Mountains State Park in Burke County was added to the system in 1976 and includes 12,800 acres of woodlands with twelve miles of mountain trout streams. The eighty-foot High Shoals Falls and the view atop Chestnut Knob are major attractions. The park meets the needs of hikers with seventeen trails, group camps, and primitive campsites. There are nearly thirty miles of equestrian trails with a horse trailer camping area. Mountain bikers are free to use eighteen miles of bridle paths.

Located in Ashe and Alleghany Counties, New River State Park consists of a series of properties linked by the New River. This portion of the New was designated a national scenic river by Congress under the federal Wild and Scenic Rivers Act in 1976. The New (of North Carolina, Virginia, and West Virginia) was designated an American heritage river in 2000. The park allows canoeists to begin a trip at one of several public access points and travel downriver to three riverfront state park campgrounds. Parklands totaling 1,580 acres help ensure the natural quality of the experience and provide hiking and picnicking opportunities. The river is suitable for novice canoeists, and local outfitters offer canoe rentals, shuttles, and supplies. The New River is famous for smallmouth bass and trout fishing.

At Lake James State Park, located on 595 acres of shoreland in Burke and McDowell Counties, the focus is on aquatic recreation. The park has two boat ramps and offers canoe rentals. Picnic sites and shelters are available, and there are several trails and a backpack camping area for hikers.

Gorges State Park is the system's newest addition, dedicated in April 1999. Land for the park was acquired from Duke Energy Corporation in the Jocassee Gorges region of Transylvania County, on the state line with South Carolina.

The gorges constitute a unique environment with rapid changes in elevation, more than eighty inches of rainfall per year, and unusually warm temperatures for the region. At least fifty rare plant species are found in the area, along with diverse populations of mammals, birds, reptiles, and amphibians. Tentative plans call for the park to be managed in order to protect natural resources while allowing access to recreationists. Two access points are planned with parking areas, picnic sites, toilet facilities, and a hike-in campground.

Mount Jefferson is managed as a state natural area on land donated by the citizens of Ashe County. Two scenic trails provide vistas of the surrounding countryside, including the New River. The park includes picnic areas and picnicking shelters on a total of 489 acres.

All of the above parks offer natural and cultural history programs and environmental learning experiences for schoolchildren. The North Carolina Department of Health and Human Services publishes detailed information on accessible park facilities in *Access North Carolina*.

Several linear parks are located within the Appalachian region of North Carolina. The North Carolina Natural and Scenic Rivers System was established in 1971 to preserve free-flowing streams, including sections of the Horsepasture and Linville Rivers in the western part of the state. The North Carolina Trails System includes greenways, rails-to-trails, and river trails as well as park system trails. The Yadkin–Pee Dee River Trail starting in Wilkes County and the French Broad River Trail starting in Transylvania County offer canoeing, camping, wildlife viewing, and fishing. The Mountains-to-Sea Trail will cross the Appalachians in North Carolina starting in Great Smoky Mountains National Park and ending at Jockey's Ridge State Park on the coast.

In 1999 nearly three million people visited eight North Carolina state parks in the Appalachian region. According to the *1995 to 2000 North Carolina Outdoor Recreation Plan*, expenditures by out-of-state visitors to North Carolina state parks generated approximately $96 million in total gross output annually and helped provide jobs for 3,054 North Carolinians.

See also: ECOTOURISM; HIKING (SPORTS AND RECREATION); MOUNT MITCHELL.

—Wayne Williams, *Appalachian State University*

Paul Gaskill, ed., *Introduction to Leisure Services in North Carolina* (1997); North Carolina Department of Environment, Health, and Natural Resources, *1995 to 2000 North Carolina Outdoor Recreation Plan* (1995).

Ohio State Parks

The southern and eastern counties of Ohio occupy the edge of the Appalachian Plateaus Province and share many traits with the larger Appalachian region. They differ from the rest of Ohio by the concentration of forestry and extractive activities and the absence of major farming and urban developments. Resource-rich areas boomed in the nineteenth century. Other sections were never completely settled, and their population peaked after the Civil War. Recent growth has come with long-distance commuters and recreational users from nearby urban centers. Public lands, especially state parks, intertwine with the area's land-use history, remain relatively concentrated in the hill country, and complement the proposal for Ohio wildlands developed in the 1990s.

After 150 years of land use beginning with pioneer agriculture and continuing with industrial expansion that claimed the coal, iron, and forests of the area, Appalachian Ohio had large areas in public management by several state agencies. From 1900 to 1949, various state agencies created units to serve the recreation needs of the heavily populated, densely settled state. During this same time period, various environmental initiatives, including game limits and dredging rules, were also scattered among a number of state agencies. The fragmented and reactive structure of recreational public land management was frustrating to those seeking the consolidated, proactive approach needed for a modern state park system.

In 1949 Ohio created a separate agency, the Ohio Department of Natural Resources, to manage its 170,000 acres of land resources. Its charge was to plan and program for the wise use of natural resources and to increase available opportunities. At that time forestry management dominated, but the first state parks, including Hocking Hills and Lake Hope, were already established. By 1963, the public land area had doubled, and wildlife areas increased rapidly as extractive industries relinquished their lands. A recent report listed 462,000 acres divided among state forest, wildlife areas, and parks. These holdings are not evenly distributed statewide. The forested hill country (one-fourth of the counties) has 63 percent of the public land. A large share of federal landholding in Ohio also lies in the hills.

Both conservation and preservation were motivations in the emerging state park system. The hill country had the advantage of large parcels of land from iron furnace development or mineral exploitation available for acquisition and conservation. Such a conservation effort was applied to Lake Hope State Park in Vinton County, which began as Lake Hope State Forest Park in 1937. The park occupies a charcoal iron furnace site, the Hope Furnace, a feature typical of the abandoned furnaces and deforested hillsides of the Hanging Rock Iron District derelict since 1900 and under state forest management. It has second-growth forest covering the scars of past exploitation by both coal mining and woodcutting for iron furnace operations. It started with two thousand acres of forestland, to which one thousand additional acres were added to form the new park. Preser-

Schoolchildren visit United States Steel's Edgar Thomson Works on the Big Steel Journey bus tour sponsored by the Rivers of Steel National and State Heritage Area, Braddock, Pennsylvania, 2000. A network of industrial and cultural sites in and around the steel towns of southwest Pennsylvania, Rivers of Steel is helping to preserve the region's industrial legacy through development of its tourism potential.

vation motivated the founding of other parks occupying areas with especially significant natural features. The state purchased the first parcel, the canyon landscape carved by glacial melt water in Blackhand Sandstone, in 1924. Initially a state forest park, the Hocking Hills State Park (a complex of six unique parcels altogether) in Hocking County started with one thousand acres in 1949 and is now twice that size.

The definition of recreation has expanded since the state parks were organized. In determining what amenities to offer visitors, an Ohio recreation plan in 1983 emphasized facilities for day trips within the state. The earlier emphasis on developed camping and lake facilities has evolved to include more nature education and newer recreational activities. These activities are not confined to parks; the tally of recreation land also includes the state forests and wildlife areas. Forest lands and wildlife areas often lie adjacent to parks, and they offer primitive recreational opportunities. Additionally, private concerns (for example, the American Electric Power ReCreation Lands, simply known as the ReCreation Lands, are 49,000 acres of reclaimed coal lands in southern Ohio) and nonprofit organizations also provide recreational opportunities.

The growing interest in environment has sparked initiatives to provide wildlife habitat amid built-up areas. Linking public lands with recreation corridors can create important habitat options. A state wildlands proposal in 1996 envisioned such a connected network of public land and corridors. The Nature Conservancy and Cincinnati Museum of Natural History now own and manage the Richard and Lucile Durrell Edge of Appalachia Preserve System, which encompasses significant portions of Scioto and Lawrence Counties and follows the Little Miami, Brush Creek, Scioto, Hocking, Muskingum, and Cuyahoga Rivers.

See also: APPALACHIAN PLATEAUS PROVINCE (GEOLOGY); FOREST MANAGEMENT AND CONSERVATION (ENVIRONMENT); LAND USE (ENVIRONMENT).

—Nancy R. Bain, *Ohio University*

Directory of Ohio's State Nature Preserves (1996); Ohio Department of Natural Resources, *1997 Land Inventory* (1997); *Ohio Statewide Comprehensive Outdoor Recreation Plan* (1993).

Pennsylvania State Parks

Paralleling historical developments on the national level, the establishment of a system of state forests and parks in Pennsylvania came in response to America's shift to an urban industrialized society in the post–Civil War era. In the Appalachian region of Pennsylvania, extraction of anthracite and bituminous coal, massive timber clear-cutting, and production of coke, steel, glass, and aluminum degraded both regional watersheds and urban environments. Romantic writers and artists had long urged preservation of nature as a refuge from the ills of civilization. The first generation of conservationists believed that America's longterm economic health had been placed at risk by egregiously inefficient and reckless exploitation of resources as well as urban pollution that undermined the health and efficiency of workers.

In Pennsylvania, deforestation provided the strongest impetus for the conservation movement. By 1890, only seven of the state's sixty-seven counties still possessed one-half or more of their virgin timber. A broad swath of the Appalachian midstate came to be known as the "Pennsylvania Desert." The impact was felt far and wide. City officials feared that watershed degradation endangered water supply; farmers faced increased erosion, flooding, and drought; sportsmen and vacationers saw fewer recreational opportunities; and loggers witnessed increasing threat to their livelihoods. The situation prompted the formation in 1886 of the Pennsylvania Forestry Association, whose founding members would exert strong leadership in the establishment of the state forests and parks. Their efforts to have the state acquire surviving forest and replant deforested lands represented the genesis of the forested state parks of the future.

The first state park was actually a historic site. In 1893 Valley Forge, the site of George Washington's Revolutionary War winter encampment, established the precedent (it became a national park in 1977). This set the stage for the subsequent addition of other historically centered parks, a number of which held remnants of old iron furnaces, including Pine Grove Furnace (through which passes the Appalachian Trail) and Greenwood Furnace (in Huntingdon County). When such historical remains were established as parks, their boundaries were always extended to include large parcels of woodlands or deforested lands slated for replanting. When Civil War veteran and botanist Joseph Rothrock became the state's first commissioner of forestry in 1895, he persuaded the state to purchase and replant more than a half-million acres of clear-cut land. Believing strongly in the medicinal benefits of nature, Rothrock established the first of Pennsylvania's state forest parks.

The first significant era of growth for the state park system arrived in the 1920s, signaled by the acquisition of Presque Isle—a seven-mile-long strip of beach jutting out into Lake Erie that became the most popular park in the state. Further growth came under the leadership of Gifford Pinchot, who had risen to national prominence as America's first chief forester under President Theodore Roosevelt. Upon his return to Pennsylvania, he served as state commissioner of forestry and as governor from 1923 to 1927 and again from 1931 to 1935. Under Pinchot, other large forest parks were added, including Cook Forest in northwestern Pennsylvania, which features the state's largest stands of virgin pine and hemlock. In 1937 the state dedicated what remains the largest of the parks at more than thirty thousand acres—Pymatuning State Park, also in the northwest. During the Great Depression, young men of the Civilian Conservation Corps built roads, trails, picnic areas, fire towers, and cabins throughout the Pennsylvania park system.

After World War II, growth was vigorous, primarily due to Maurice K. Goddard, a trained forester and educator, whose tenure as a cabinet officer stretched over five gubernatorial administrations. Goddard set out to establish more parks closer to urban areas, believing that most existing parks were too far removed for many Pennsylvanians. That trend began in 1946 with the purchase of thirty-six acres of land at the confluence of the Allegheny, Monongahela, and Ohio Rivers in downtown Pittsburgh. What later became Point State Park embraces a French and Indian War–era blockhouse but, more importantly, symbolizes Pittsburgh's postindustrial renaissance. From the mid-1950s through the mid-1970s, the state established scores of new parks, expanded others, and professionalized their management. One of the most notable parks added during Goddard's tenure was the 19,053-acre Ohiopyle along the scenic Youghiogheny River Gorge.

Rooted in the industrial era, the Pennsylvania state park system achieved a remarkable first century of growth. Embracing nearly three hundred thousand acres in 116 parks, it is exceeded only by the state systems of Alaska and California. The state park system currently is divided into eight regions. Six of those regions and 89 of the individual parks lie within the Appalachian region. Situated in the north-central part of the state, the vast Allegheny National Forest Region is characterized by remote wilderness and features Cook Forest (the "Grand Canyon" of Pennsylvania) at Colton Point State Park and Kinzua Bridge State Park, where a coal bridge that was once the world's highest railroad viaduct stood 301 feet above a creek valley and stretched 2,053 feet. In the northeast, the Pocono and Endless Mountains Region has twenty-two named waterfalls and a number of scenic gorges. Forest-covered Allegheny Mountain ridges, scenic overlooks, and smallmouth bass and trout fishing characterize the midstate Valleys of the Susquehanna Region. Toward the west, the Laurel Highlands/Southern Alleghenies Region includes Mount Davis, which at 3,213 feet is the highest point in Pennsylvania, and nearby Ohiopyle, which has whitewater rafting. This region also includes Allegheny State Heritage Park, where the Path of Progress National Heritage Tour Route spotlights the area's industrial history. Similarly, in the adjacent Pittsburgh Region, there are natural parks as well as historical sites centered on the region's frontier history. Another state heritage park area, Rivers of Steel, explores the region's industrial and cultural legacy. The northwest Lake Erie Region features

Presque Isle State Park, Pymatuning State Park, Oil Creek State Park, and the National Oil Heritage Area.

See also: CULTURAL HERITAGE TOURISM; FOREST MANAGEMENT AND CONSERVATION (ENVIRONMENT).

—Chris J. Magoc, *Mercyhurst College*

Bill Bailey, *Pennsylvania State Parks: A Complete Outdoor Recreational Guide* (1995); Dan Cupper, *Our Priceless Heritage: Pennsylvania State Parks* (1993); William C. Forrey, *History of Pennsylvania's State Parks* (1984).

Pigeon Forge, Tennessee

Pigeon Forge, Tennessee, was a small, rural settlement in the foothills of the Smoky Mountains until the creation of the Great Smoky Mountains National Park and post–World War II prosperity brought an avalanche of tourists and commercial development. Although visitors had been coming to immerse themselves in the health-restoring waters of nearby Henderson Springs since the 1870s, tourism had a major economic impact on Pigeon Forge only after the national park was created in 1934. That year, a Tennessee Valley Authority report indicated that Pigeon Forge had no tourism-related structures or businesses.

In the first two decades following establishment of the Great Smoky Mountains National Park, Sevier County tourism developed mostly in the neighboring community of Gatlinburg. But after construction of U.S. Highway 441 in the 1950s, development spilled over from Gatlinburg into Pigeon Forge. Local landowning families such as the Ogles, the Householders, the Harmons, and the Whaleys dominated the flurry of development in the late 1950s and early 1960s. For the most part, these local developers undertook projects such as tourist cabins and campgrounds because they required little capital investment.

After 1960, outside entrepreneurs played a much greater role in developing Pigeon Forge. Because local families owned all of downtown Gatlinburg, outside investors who wanted to enter the local tourist trade turned to Pigeon Forge, where land was more readily available. Following incorporation in 1961, land values rose exponentially, exceeding four thousand dollars per square foot of frontage property by the mid-1980s. This rise in property values helped outside developers force out the remaining farmers who still cultivated fields along the highway. Many families tried to hold on to their land, but the mounting property taxes that accompanied rising land values compelled most to sell or lease their property to developers.

As developers swarmed into the community, motels, restaurants, theme parks, miniature golf courses, go-cart tracks, and assorted tourist amusements rose on former farmlands. Between 1980 and 1992, the community's gross business receipts shot up from $51 million to $379 million, due in large part to outlet malls. The mall phenomenon began with the opening of Factory Merchants in 1982. As shoppers flocked to its stores, three equally successful new outlet centers opened within a four-year period. Their success, combined with the popularity of Dollywood, led to the rampant growth of Pigeon Forge in the 1980s and 1990s. By the end of the 1990s, more than 12 million visitors a year shopped and patronized the eclectic array of tourist diversions along the strip. Beyond the strip, away from the tourists, life in Pigeon Forge remained essentially rural, in sharp contrast to the lights and bustle of the parkway.

See also: DOLLYWOOD; GATLINBURG, TENNESSEE; GREAT SMOKY MOUNTAINS NATIONAL PARK.

—C. Brenden Martin, *Northwestern State University*

C. Brenden Martin, "From Golden Cornfields to Golden Arches: The Economic and Cultural Evolution of Pigeon Forge, Tennessee," *Journal of the Appalachian Studies Association* (Spring 1994).

Pisgah National Forest

On October 17, 1916, Pisgah National Forest became the nation's first national forest composed of purchased lands. All national forests up to that time had been carved out of public domain land that no one had homesteaded, but in 1911 Congress authorized the federal government to purchase "forested, cut-over, or denuded" lands for the protection of watersheds. Thereafter, forests, wildlife, and water quality were restored to vast tracts of eroded fields and cutover, burned land.

As of 1999, Pisgah National Forest, one of four national forests in North Carolina, encompassed more than five hundred thousand acres of mountain lands in the state's Appalachian counties. Pisgah took its name from Mount Pisgah, a landmark along the Blue Ridge south of Asheville named for the biblical mountain from which Moses viewed the Promised Land. For millions of visitors each year, Pisgah National Forest offers hiking, biking, camping, fishing, hunting, rafting, sightseeing, and a host of other outdoor activities.

Forest history can be relived on the Forest Heritage National Scenic Byway. This 79-mile byway follows many old roads and logging railroad beds (now designated U.S. 276, North Carolina 215, and U.S. 64). The route passes through part of the Biltmore Estate owned by George W. Vanderbilt and past the Cradle of Forestry in America, where Vanderbilt's forester, Carl Alwin Schenck, established the country's first forestry school. Adjoining the Cradle of Forestry are the Pink Beds, named for summer displays of mountain laurel and other wildflowers. Other popular attractions along the byway include the beautiful Looking Glass Falls, Sliding Rock, three picnic areas, two campgrounds, and the Pisgah Center for Wildlife Education and

Fish Hatchery, operated by the North Carolina Wildlife Resources Commission.

Pisgah National Forest boasts nearly 800 miles of trails, including about 138 miles of the Appalachian Trail. While all the trails are open to hikers, some are also open to mountain bikes and horses. Harmon Den, with a by-reservation horse camp, is popular among horseback riders.

The forest's miles of cold, rushing streams offer excellent trout fishing, while the French Broad and Nolichucky Rivers are excellent venues for rafting. Most of the ten family campgrounds and seven group camps are located beside mountain streams—from the large Davidson River campground to primitive, tents-only Curtis Creek campground.

The Appalachian Trail connects several popular destinations along the North Carolina–Tennessee border: Max Patch, Rich Mountain, and Roan Mountain. These three mountaintops provide spectacular panoramic views of the surrounding Appalachians. Roan Mountain is especially famous for its acres of Catawba rhododendrons.

Linville Gorge, another extraordinary scenic attraction, is located just off the Blue Ridge Parkway. Wisemans View, east of the town of Linville Falls, also provides a magnificent view into this steep-walled gorge all the way to the river fifteen hundred feet below. The gorge is at the heart of the Linville Gorge Wilderness Area.

See also: BILTMORE ESTATE; CRADLE OF FORESTRY IN AMERICA HISTORIC SITE; CULTURAL HERITAGE TOURISM.

—Pat Momich, *National Forests in North Carolina*

Kevin Edgar, ed., *Appalachian Trail Guide to Tennessee–North Carolina* (1995); Harold K. Steen, *The U.S. Forest Service: A History* (1991); Sheila Turnage, *Fodor's North Carolina* (2000).

Planned Communities

See Planned Communities (Family and Community)

Rails-to-Trails

As Appalachia's coal and timber industries declined in the late nineteenth and early twentieth centuries, many rail lines that supported them reduced or ceased operations. The abandonment of railroad lines peaked in the 1960s and 1970s, but some two thousand miles of railroad were still being abandoned annually at the century's close. During the 1990s, many of the shut-down rail lines were converted into linear trails for recreational use by pedestrians, hikers, bicyclists, and rollerbladers. These rails-to-trails endeavors became an important ingredient in sustainable tourism for a growing number of Appalachian counties, towns, and cities.

When it adopted amendments to the National Trails System Act in 1983, Congress directed the Surface Transportation Board to set aside for possible reactivation any rail rights-of-way about to be abandoned. The amendments helped proponents of recreational trails who stood to be outbid by land developers seeking to acquire abandoned railways. The "rail banking" provision allowed rights-of-way to be used as trails until they might be needed at a later time. A trail developer's dream, the rail-trails provided an already-established linear corridor with a single owner, removing the need to reach a consensus among numerous landowners along a given route.

The Rails-to-Trails Conservancy, the primary national organization dedicated to creating rail-trails, was formed in 1985. Its mission is to preserve rail corridors, develop a national advocacy law to support rail banking, and assist with local rail-trail efforts. When the conservancy was begun, its officials knew of only 35 rail-trails nationally, with 90 in the planning stages. By 2001, the rails-to-trails system involved more than eleven thousand miles and included 1,109 trails. Bikers, hikers, bird watchers, anglers, campers, in-line skaters, equestrians, and other types of outdoor enthusiasts use the trails on average more than 100 million times annually. More than twelve hundred new rail-trail projects were under development in 2001. The conservancy's goal of establishing a national, interconnected network of trails paralleling the old railroad network was rapidly becoming a reality.

Examples of rail-trails in Appalachia are diverse. Several West Virginia rail-trails provide access to vast stands of timber, while the Greenbrier River Trail follows a river's course along an old Chesapeake and Ohio Railway (at one time the Baltimore and Ohio) line. Other notable trails in the state include the Limerock Trail, which descends rugged walls into the Blackwater Canyon, and the Gauley Mountain Trail, found in the center of black bear country. The Virginia Creeper Trail runs from Abingdon, Virginia, through Jefferson National Forest to the North Carolina state line.

Other rail-trails pass through farming areas and small towns, offering changing panoramas of farms and cultural heritage sites. West Virginia's North Bend Rail Trail follows a route filled with tunnels and rural scenery. The New River Trail State Park in southwest Virginia follows the North Carolina branch of the Norfolk Southern rail line for fifty-seven miles through the pastureland of Virginia from Pulaski to Galax. Trails in rural areas often pass through former railroad and mill towns that are capitalizing on the trails to compete for tourist dollars. Cliffside Heritage Trail, in Rutherford County, North Carolina, was planned to connect several textile mill towns. Trail users often discover that railroad and other heritage sites, bed-and-breakfasts, restaurants, and unusual shops make weekends on the trail more diverse than usual hikes.

Urban areas also form part of the rail-trail network. Examples include the Abingdon section of the Virginia Creeper Trail and the Deckers Creek Trail, which follows an old rail line from rural countryside to the center of Morgantown, the site of West Virginia University. Atlanta's Silver Comet Trail, named for the passenger train that once followed its route from Boston to Birmingham, permits Atlanta residents or visitors to walk, bike, or skate without traveling to a state park or recreation area. As the twenty-first century began, plans were in place to extend the trail from Atlanta to join Alabama's Chief Ladiga Trail. Officials in North Carolina planned a trail that would extend from downtown Brevard to Pisgah National Forest. Other rail-trail promoters include Pennsylvania's Allegheny Trail Alliance, a group with plans to establish a trail connecting Pittsburgh with Cumberland, Maryland, where users might pick up the Chesapeake and Ohio Canal towpath and continue on to Washington, D.C. The endeavor also integrated a plan to protect the Youghiogheny River environment and interpret cultural heritage, including the industrial sites of Pittsburgh's "valley of steel."

See also: HIKING (SPORTS AND RECREATION); RAILROADS (TRANSPORTATION); STATEWIDE TRAIL SYSTEMS.

—Keith Norman, *West Virginia Trails Coalition*

Bonnie Nevel and Peter Harnik, *Railroads Recycled: How Local Initiative and Federal Support Launched the Rails to Trails Movement* (1990); Barbara A. Noe, *The Official Rails-to-Trails Conservancy Guidebook: Maryland, Delaware, Virginia, West Virginia* (2000).

Recreation Lakes

Federal man-made lakes contribute to the recreation resources of all of the Appalachian states. The National Recreation Lakes Study Commission found that in 1998 lakes of more than a thousand surface acres accounted for more than a billion dollars of economic impact in each of six Appalachian states: Tennessee, Kentucky, Alabama, Georgia, North Carolina, and Mississippi. Employment directly related to recreation on these lakes ranged from 16,500 jobs in Mississippi to 96,800 jobs in Tennessee. Flood control, power generation, and watershed management were predominant purposes when the Tennessee Valley Authority and the U.S. Army Corps of Engineers constructed these lakes, but each year they attract increasing numbers of recreational users for fishing, camping, boating, swimming, and wildlife observation. Visitation, already more than 9.6 million in Mississippi and 56.4 million in Tennessee, is projected to increase by 2 percent annually over the first twenty years of the new century. Lakes anchor popular recreation areas in state parks and national forests. Examples include Smith Mountain Lake and Lake Moomaw in Virginia and Lake Chatuge along the North Carolina–Georgia border.

In 1996 Congress created a National Recreation Lakes Study Commission to consider awarding some lakes national designation and creating a National Recreation Lakes Demonstration Program. The commission's challenge was to determine how to provide for infrastructure improvements and additional attractions to satisfy public demand for water-based recreation without adversely affecting power generation, water management, wildlife protection, or sustainable development of nearby communities. Marinas, lodging, nature centers, golf courses, visitor centers, and similar amenities offered opportunities for additional private-sector investment.

See also: TENNESSEE VALLEY AUTHORITY (GOVERNMENT).

—Benita J. Howell, *University of Tennessee*

Roadside Signs and Attractions

See Section Overview

Roan Mountain

Roan Mountain (6,285 feet) is located on the boundary between North Carolina and Tennessee about thirty-five miles south of the Virginia border. The mountain became a haven for tourists after General John T. Wilder built a hotel on the summit in 1877. The hotel was located at Cloudland, which advertising described as "a region justly so-called, since it lies six thousand feet above the level of sea, supported upon the Atlas shoulders of Roan mountain." A larger structure, appropriately named the Cloudland Hotel, was constructed in 1885 but abandoned about 1910.

The U.S. Forest Service purchased seven thousand acres of the mountain in 1941, property now administered by the Pisgah (North Carolina) and Cherokee (Tennessee) National Forests. The Tennessee General Assembly created Roan Mountain State Park in 1959, but the park was not developed until the late 1970s. Park attractions include campgrounds and cabins, hiking trails, a swimming pool, cross-country skiing, and a mountain farmstead. The park is the site of several annual events, including the Carter County Wildflower Tour and Bird Walk in May, the Rhododendron Festival in June, and the Roan Mountain Naturalist Rally in September.

Roan Mountain's major attraction is the spectacular expanse of Catawba rhododendrons *(Rhododendron catawbiense)* usually in full bloom in late June or early July. The gardens cover portions of the grass balds located on the mountain. Another important attraction is the Appalachian Trail, which follows the state line along the top of the mountain.

See also: BALDS (ECOLOGY); HEATHS (ECOLOGY).

—Ed Speer, *Elizabethton, Tennessee*

Roanoke, Virginia

See Roanoke, Virginia (Urban Appalachian Experience)

Rock City Gardens

Rock City Gardens, fourteen acres of natural rock formations and gardens with more than four hundred different native species of wildflowers, plants, and shrubs, is located on Lookout Mountain, Georgia, approximately ten minutes from Chattanooga, Tennessee. The locale makes possible an unusual blend of geological wonders with man-made attractions.

Lookout Mountain, once submerged beneath an inland sea, developed over millions of years, rising today to 2,350 feet above sea level. The rock formations of Rock City Gardens were carved over time by the receding waters of that sea and other natural forces. The vision of Rock City Gardens took shape during the late 1920s with the help of Garnet and Frieda Carter. Garnet, an entrepreneur, invented miniature golf and developed Fairyland, a subdivision on Lookout Mountain. Frieda, a lover of beauty and folklore, created a nature garden called Rock City, which was to be part of Fairyland. Following the stock market crash of 1929, Garnet sold his miniature golf enterprise. Meanwhile, what had started out as Frieda's private garden grew to include trails through rock outcroppings, a swinging bridge, and statues of gnomes, in addition to indigenous wildflowers and shrubs. Interested in new ways to make money, Garnet turned it into a commercial enterprise and opened Rock City Gardens on May 21, 1932.

Looking for a way to attract more visitors, Garnet hired Clark Byers to paint "See Rock City" on the roofs of barns along the nation's highways. The advertising campaign was a huge success. Rock City Gardens attracted around half a million visitors annually, and the roadside barns became a fixture of popular tourist routes.

See also: CHATTANOOGA, TENNESSEE; TECTONICS (GEOLOGY).

—Traci Greenberg, *Geiger & Associates Public Relations*

Shenandoah National Park

Shenandoah National Park, created from parts of eight adjoining Virginia counties between 1924 and 1936, encompasses more than 197,000 acres along the crest of the Blue Ridge Mountains. About two million persons access the park annually by way of Skyline Drive, a scenic parkway built between 1931 and 1939 that bisects the 105-mile length of the park from its northern entrance in Front Royal to Rockfish Gap in the south.

Encouraged by National Park Service leadership in early 1924, Interior Secretary Hubert Work appointed a Southern Appalachian National Park Committee to examine suitable sites for an eastern park. A newly formed regional development organization, Shenandoah Valley Inc., lobbied for a park in the Massanutten Mountain area of Rockingham County. The rival Northern Virginia Park Association's spokesman, George Freeman Pollock, proposed his own Skyland resort, located on more than 5,000 acres acquired by his father and associates for copper speculation in the 1880s, as the park's centerpiece in the Blue Ridge Mountains.

After the Southern Appalachian National Park Committee chose the Skyland site in December 1924, the contending groups merged as the Shenandoah National Park Association and, with the State Chamber of Commerce in Richmond, began a public solicitation of funds and land donations for the future national park. The State of Virginia officially entered the park campaign only after Harry F. Byrd became governor in 1926. By March, Byrd established the Virginia Commission on Conservation and Development with the park its sole objective. Following President Calvin Coolidge's authorization of a 521,000-acre Shenandoah National Park on May 22, 1926, Governor Byrd quickly appointed the commission's first chairman: Shenandoah Valley businessman William E. Carson.

Carson shrewdly used Coolidge's interest in developing a presidential retreat and his successor's avid interest in fly-fishing to tout the excellent streams of the Blue Ridge and influence President Herbert Hoover's choice of a campsite. By April 1929, Hoover had taken the hook and agreed to build his retreat on the upper Rapidan River in an area of Madison County that would become part of the national park—a decision that provided incalculable publicity for Carson's mission. Later, Hoover's presence in the area led him to sponsor drought-relief funds for highway construction employing local men in the initial stages of work on Skyline Drive—the first section of which opened between Thornton Gap and Hawksbill Peak on October 22, 1932.

The federal act establishing the Shenandoah National Park required Virginia to acquire title to all the land for the proposed national park. Carson called upon his brother, Judge A. C. Carson, to resolve the dilemma of prosecuting thousands of condemnation cases against individual private landowners. The resulting 1928 Public Park Condemnation Act allowed blanket condemnation of all tracts in each of the eight counties by a single suit in each county court. The 1928 act (used only in Shenandoah National Park) was later repealed.

Carson then faced monumental economic problems: the state could condemn, but it could not afford to pay for all the land it was obliged to buy for the park. This challenge ultimately required separate acts of Congress in 1928 and 1932 to twice reduce the minimum acreage mandated for the park. In December 1935, the Department of the Interior finally accepted title to slightly more than 176,000 acres of land. On July 3, 1936, President Franklin D. Roosevelt formally dedicated Shenandoah National Park as a natural preserve and in his speech dismissed its prior occupancy as a wasteful use of the land by people whose ancestors, in many cases, had settled there in the mid- to late eighteenth century.

Mandel Sherman and Thomas R. Henry's *Hollow Folk* (1933), which stereotypically portrayed these people as isolated, unlettered, and uncivilized squatters, was employed to justify their displacement and promote the park's formation. The book's reliance on gross misrepresentations, lack of documentation, and use of suspect theories of evolution and behavior fit the assumptions and practice associated at that time with Virginia's pernicious eugenics laws. In that context, Sherman and Henry's work was persuasive in shaping social policy.

In February 1934, newly appointed Park Service Director Arno Cammerer announced that the government would accept no land from the state until all inhabitants had left the area. More than five hundred families (or three to four thousand people) were relocated or removed from their homes, some forcibly. If tenants and others who voluntarily moved in advance of condemnation or without compensation for their losses were included, the numbers of people actually dislocated by Shenandoah National Park would be substantially higher.

Under Roosevelt's New Deal programs, Civilian Conservation Corps camps were established in the park area in 1933. The first ranks of resident "CCC boys" executed the designs of landscape architects and engineers, planted or removed trees and vegetation, and built trails, rock walls, and other structures. They also helped remove people from their homes and assisted in razing their houses and outbuildings.

The Resettlement Administration built subsistence homestead projects to house a portion of the families removed, and Resettlement and Farm Security Administration photographers documented both the park and the homestead projects, visually representing the before and after displacement cases. Sherman and Henry's representations influenced those of the photographers and prevailed as the generally accepted view of the people removed. These representations began to be seriously questioned in the late 1970s, however.

A nonprofit group, the Children of Shenandoah, was organized in the 1990s by members of former park families to address general grievances enduring since removal and specific issues such as access to graveyards and family-related historical materials in park archival files. The park staff is working cooperatively with the Children of Shenandoah where possible and is trying to improve the park's public image. These efforts have corrected some of the more obvious misrepresentations of former park residents by replacing a factually flawed and offensive interpretive film, *The Gift*, and providing a more objective portrayal of their history and culture in signage and exhibits at visitor centers. Still, arguments continue, and Shenandoah's past history is not yet laid to rest in local people's memories.

All the counties surrounding Shenandoah National Park bear added tourism costs, including demands for better roads and services, but the benefits to each from park visitation are unevenly distributed. Albemarle County, which experienced less population displacement and tax base loss in the park development process, already had a number of tourist attractions but benefited further from the park. In contrast, Madison County lost substantial acreage and suffered one of the largest population dislocations but never gained the tourism advantage of a direct entrance into the park. In recent years, the park has been plagued increasingly by deteriorating infrastructure, staff shortages, and environmental degradation, generally attributable to pollution, budgetary crises, and, ironically, overuse.

See also: BLUE RIDGE PARKWAY; CIVILIAN CONSERVATION CORPS (GOVERNMENT); SKYLINE DRIVE (ARCHITECTURE).

—Nancy J. Martin-Perdue, *University of Virginia*

Darwin Lambert, *The Undying Past of Shenandoah National Park* (1989); Charles L. Perdue Jr. and Nancy J. Martin-Perdue, "Appalachian Fables and Facts: A Case Study of the Shenandoah National Park Removals," *Appalachian Journal* (Autumn–Winter 1979–80) and "To Build a Wall around These Mountains," *The Magazine of Albemarle County History* (1991).

Ski Resorts

Appalachian ski resorts lack the history and prestige of traditional skiing regions such as New England, the western Rocky Mountain states, or most European mountain areas, but the number of quality resorts in the region has increased steadily over the past decades. This is primarily due to the convenience of these resorts to those living in and around the Appalachians. Most Appalachian ski resorts cater to weekend skiers, offering convenient and inexpensive alternatives to more distant ski destinations. Although most of the downhill runs offered at these resorts are in the beginner and intermediate categories, advanced skiers appreciate the opportunity to keep in practice at local venues. Additionally, most Appalachian resorts readily welcome enthusiasts of other snow sports such as snowboarding, snowshoeing, tubing, and cross-country skiing. The resorts are typically small, owner-operated businesses that promote themselves as nonintimidating venues for novices, families, and groups.

Skiing at Blue Mountain Ski Area in the Pocono Mountains, near Palmerton, Pennsylvania, c. 1998. The development of ski resorts in both northern and southern Appalachia has made winter sports accessible to most residents of the region.

Many Appalachian ski resorts are located on the highest mountains in the eastern United States. Ski Beech in western North Carolina is the highest ski resort in eastern North America. Mountain snowfall and freezing temperatures are plentiful, even in the southern Appalachians, but winter weather is more variable and unreliable than in the mountains of New England, making ski conditions inconsistent. This significant difference initially placed limitations on skiing at most Appalachian locations. However, snowmaking machines, first patented in 1954, easily compensate, and the typical Appalachian skiing season now runs from Thanksgiving to late March.

Pennsylvania has long attracted avid skiers to Pocono Mountain resorts such as Jack Frost, Big Boulder, and Camelback. These resorts operate year-round, offering real estate for rent or purchase and sponsoring a variety of activities including music festivals, art exhibits, craft fairs, water park activities, biking, and motor sports. In the Blue Ridge Mountains of Virginia, Bryce Resort has operated since 1965, featuring ski instruction and special opportunities for children to ski its more gentle slopes; in the summer it becomes a golf resort. Virginia's Massanutten and Wintergreen resorts, like Bryce, attract tourists from the region to activities in all four seasons of the year. North Carolina's ski resorts include Wolf Laurel near Asheville and Appalachian Ski Mountain between Boone and Blowing Rock. Both cater to families, welcoming snowboarders and tubers as well as skiers. Cataloochee and Beech Mountain offer multiple slopes to challenge all skill levels. In Tennessee, the Ober Gatlinburg resort operates an amusement park served by a chairlift and tramway to attract visitors year round. On average, skiers in the eastern United States spend almost sixty-two dollars per visit to a ski area, with nearby communities enjoying the multiplier effect in the form of increased business revenues, employment, and development.

West Virginia offers several large ski areas within a day's drive of more than 75 million people. Rather than competing directly with each other, each West Virginia ski resort has developed its own niche and targets its marketing accordingly. These resorts cooperate to offer a wide variety of skiing experiences to maximize the total number of skiers who visit the state.

Snowshoe Mountain in eastern West Virginia draws visitors with exceptional off-slope activities in addition to its excellent skiing. Ranked in the top 5 percent of North American winter ski resorts, Snowshoe's fifty-seven slopes hosted 464,000 skiers in the 2000–2001 season. To achieve such success, Intrawest, the resort's owner, invested more than $72 million in improvements during the late 1990s. It was the largest expansion on record for a winter sports complex in the southern United States, and it transformed Snowshoe into a vacation resort village. Snowshoe's snowmaking operation is the largest in the region, providing skiers with a season lasting from November until April. Construction of additional lodging facilities has made it possible for 9,000 guests to stay at Snowshoe for extended periods, and high speed quad lifts capable of moving 2,400 skiers per hour assure visitors quick access to slopes.

Even in the southernmost Appalachians, where the winter months were for generations the "off season," skiing has become a popular sport. Georgia's Sky Valley advertises skiing just two hours from Atlanta, and Alabama draws skiers to Cloudmont Ski Area at Mentone.

The strategy of developing village-style resorts means that more activities are available after the ski day has ended. At Snowshoe, these include shops, a variety of restaurants, indoor pools, a Kid's World, and an aquatic center. With increasing numbers of visitors each year, the dollars spent and jobs generated at Snowshoe have boosted the economy of the surrounding area and the entire state.

Winterplace, another large West Virginia resort, has succeeded by offering its target market the most accessible ski resort with the longest ski day in the Southeast (fourteen hours); visitors enjoy free night skiing, using their day lift tickets. Ninety percent of the Winterplace's twenty-seven slopes and West Virginia's largest snow-tubing park are lit for exhilarating nighttime runs. This lengthy ski day and free night skiing make Winterplace a bargain for skiers, an economic boon to the surrounding community of Ghent, and a profitable enterprise for its owners. Winterplace also has developed a marketing niche catering to groups. Each ski day the parking lots of Winterplace are packed with tour buses, evidence that this resort's VIP group services are gaining a reputation throughout the East for providing group members with excellent services. Prearranged lift tickets and rental equipment ready to go the moment these groups step off the buses make access to the slopes fast and convenient. Groups may choose the Mountain House Sleepover Package, an indoor camping type experience for groups.

Though other resorts in West Virginia are smaller and have fewer ski trails, they have other means to attract tourists and tourist dollars. Timberline offers a backcountry experience for cross-country skiers and snowshoe enthusiasts with its ten miles of trails and the region's longest run. Canaan Valley Ski Area offers visitors sleigh rides, ice skating, children's programs, and scenic cross-country trails that provide exquisite views of the beautiful mountains of West Virginia and the glades along Blackwater River. These two resorts offer a combined ski ticket that enables skiers to visit both resorts and ski on all sixty-nine trails in the Canaan Valley area.

Construction of ski resorts in pristine mountain areas has engendered environmental controversy, causing owners and developers to pay increased attention to their impact. Steps have been taken to ensure that slopes do not erode and that streams are not damaged by runoff from spring melts. Timberline takes pride that it is home to the Cheat Mountain salamander, a creature listed as an endangered species and therefore accorded federal protection. Virginia's Wintergreen Resort is unusual because of its Nature Foundation, which since 1980 has preserved 6,000 undisturbed acres as a nature preserve where visitors can learn about regional flora and fauna.

Many skiers from the region regularly patronize the resorts of New England, as well. As in the southern mountains, snowmaking machines have enabled these resorts to ensure reliable skiing conditions for longer seasons than the natural weather might provide. Most of these resorts are larger than their counterparts in the central and southern Appalachians and offer more non-skiing activities to attract tourists year round. Swimming, fishing, boating, hiking, bicycling, water skiing, and golf are popular off-season activities, and many New England traditions such as autumn foliage viewing and maple syrup festivals are preludes to the upcoming winter season.

New Hampshire, billing itself as "America's Ski State," boasts fifteen alpine resorts and claims one of the oldest in the nation. Black Mountain, with its eleven-hundred-foot vertical drop, has been in continuous operation since 1935, when the first overhead cable lift in the country was installed there. Now four lifts service 143 acres of slopes, 98 percent of which are covered by snowmaking machines.

Cannon Mountain, in New Hampshire's Franconia Notch State Park, offers thirty-nine trails for skiers of all abilities on its 2,146-foot-high vertical slope, 97 percent of which is covered by snowmaking machines. There are seven lifts of varied types, including the famed Cannon Mountain Aerial Tramway, which uses 5,139 feet of cable to transport seventy passengers up the mountain. At the foot of the Tramway is the New England Ski Museum, dedicated to preserving the history of the sport and its technological developments, from skis and clothing to lift designs and snow machines. Mount Sunapee Ski Area is one of the largest and most elaborate resorts in the state. The resort's Mountain Dew Snowboard Zone includes a challenging terrain park and New Hampshire's longest half-pipe, both of which are surrounded by a music sound system. By 2000, skiing added more than half a billion dollars to New Hampshire's economy annually.

In Vermont, skiers were on the slopes even before the opening of the first overhead cable lift at Black Mountain. The state's first ski tow went into operation in 1932, and soon Suicide Six, near Woodstock, was a leading alpine resort. Stowe Mountain Resort, established in 1934 on Mount Mansfield, offers the East's first detachable quad chair, forty-seven trails a mile or more in length, and a gondola reputed to be the fastest in the world. Located near the state's highest peak—4,393 feet above sea level—Stowe averages more than 260 inches of snowfall a year, but it also has 73 percent snowmaking coverage. Across the mountain, Sugarbush, in the heart of Vermont's Green Mountain National Forest, offers 115 trails and eighteen lifts on a 2,650-foot vertical drop.

Among the newer attractions are two resorts in Maine—Sunday River and Sugarloaf. Although small resorts have existed since the early 1900s in Maine and more than fifteen are presently operating, only Sugarloaf and Sunday River compete with big regional complexes such as

Stowe and Sugarbush. Sugarloaf has a 4,327-foot peak, the state's second highest. With a 2,820-foot vertical descent, it boasts New England's steepest skiing terrain. In summer and fall, Sugarloaf's ski trails challenge mountain bikers, while other visitors turn to outdoor adventure camps, environmental education programs, and whitewater rafting. At the 660-acre Sunday River resort, ski slopes stretch across eight interconnected peaks with 127 ski trails, several terrain parks, and a superpipe for snowboarding. Sunday River advertises "the most dependable snow in New England."

See also: GATLINBURG, TENNESSEE; WEST VIRGINIA STATE PARKS.

—Betty Parker Duff, *University of Maine*, and Kathy Lewis-Payne, *Mountain State University*

Charles A. Leocha et al., *Ski America and Canada 2001* (2000); Laura Sutherland, *The Best Family Ski Vacations in North America* (1997); Jonathan Wiesel and Dianna Delling, *Cross-Country Ski Vacations* (1999).

Smoky Mountain Spas and Resorts

A century before creation of the Great Smoky Mountains National Park, visitors traveled to spas and resorts in the Smokies in search of health and leisure. Montvale Springs in present-day Blount County, Tennessee, was among the first. In 1832 Daniel Foute built a ten-bedroom log building for health seekers who came to partake of the salubrious mineral waters. Twenty-one years later, wealthy Mississippi planter Asa Watson built the famed Seven Gables Hotel, which catered to elite cotton planters of Georgia and cane growers of Louisiana. Advertised as the Saratoga of the South, Montvale Springs was renowned for its elegant ballroom, exotic plants, and splendid vistas.

Another antebellum Smoky Mountain spa was Henderson Springs in Sevier County near present-day Pigeon Forge. Henderson Springs had a reputation as a health spa as early as the 1830s, but its first hotel was erected in 1878. In the 1870s and 1880s, several new resorts opened in the Smokies, including Mount Nebo Springs (1877), Doyle Springs (c. 1878), Wildwood Springs (1886), and Alleghany Springs (1886). Although none of these spas had direct railroad access, their development reflected the entry of more northern proprietors into Appalachian tourism in the late nineteenth century. Whereas local people built the resorts at Mount Nebo Springs and Doyle Springs in the 1870s, northern entrepreneurs initiated the spas of the 1880s. In 1886, Nathan McCoy, a Civil War veteran from Indiana, opened the plush Alleghany Springs Hotel, which could accommodate up to four hundred guests. That same year, Reverend Claudius B. Lord of New York added on to his log house to build Wildwood Springs Hotel.

The coming of railroads and the decline of hydrotherapy in the late 1800s and early 1900s forever changed the nature and character of resorts in the Smoky Mountains. As lumber and railroad operations opened up the Smokies to greater numbers of people, more tourists came to mountain resorts for rest, recreation, and scenic beauty than for health reasons. When the Little River Railroad and Lumber Company penetrated the dense hardwood forests of Blount and Sevier Counties, Tennessee, the company learned to maximize its profits by offering scenic railroad tours to visitors from Knoxville. With direct rail access, the new resort at Kinzel Springs thrived as a popular tourist retreat. The company also converted one of its log camps into the Elkmont Club, a private group of wealthy Tennesseans who owned several cabins and operated a hotel. Elkmont's tourists immersed themselves in the scenic beauty of the Smokies but were stunned to see how large-scale lumber operations had scarred the land. One visitor warned that unless the Smokies were protected from lumber companies, the forests would be "wrecked, ruined, desecrated, turned into a thousand rubbish heaps." Indeed, members of the Elkmont Club were at the core of the movement to create the Great Smoky Mountains National Park.

Within a few years of the park's opening in 1934, new resort communities such as Gatlinburg and Pigeon Forge replaced the abandoned spas as major tourist destinations. Gone, but not forgotten, the early spas and resorts of the Smoky Mountains laid the foundation for tourism in the region.

See also: GATLINBURG, TENNESSEE; HOT SPRINGS, NORTH CAROLINA; PIGEON FORGE, TENNESSEE.

—C. Brenden Martin, *Northwestern State University*

Vic Weals, *Last Train to Elkmont: A Look Back at Life on Little River in the Great Smoky Mountains* (1993); W. Bruce Wheeler, ed., *The Gentle Winds of Change: A History of Sevier County, 1900–1930* (1986).

South Carolina State Parks

The first state parks in South Carolina were built in the 1930s by the Civilian Conservation Corps, a New Deal agency initiated by President Franklin D. Roosevelt to conserve natural resources and provide jobs for the unemployed. By the time Civilian Conservation Corps construction ended in 1941, sixteen parks had been opened to the public. Three of these, Oconee, Paris Mountain, and Table Rock, are in the northwest corner of South Carolina, now marketed to tourists as the Upcountry. Oconee, one of the system's most popular parks, preserves many structures that exemplify the rustic stone construction typical of Civilian Conservation Corps projects; the park museum uses photographs and artifacts to tell the story of the corps's involvement in park construction. Paris Mountain State Park was formerly a watershed for the city of Greenville. It now offers green space, lake swimming, a group camp, and a lodge with meeting facilities, all a short distance from the center of the city. The most mountainous and most visited of the upcountry parks is Table Rock, where visitors can enjoy scenic views from the lodge restaurant, visit the nature center, or hike on challenging mountain trails. This entire park is listed on the National Register of Historic Places.

The largest of the upcountry parks, 7,054-acre Croft State Natural Area, was an army training camp during World War II. The old army buildings and the cemeteries of early settlers add cultural interest to a park that has boating, hiking, camping, and nature study. Croft State Natural Area caters to horse lovers with a network of equestrian trails, stables, and a show ring. Lake Hartwell, completed by the U.S. Army Corps of Engineers in 1963 for hydroelectric power and flood control, has become the focal attraction for two state recreation areas, Sadlers Creek and Lake Hartwell, both known for fishing, boating, camping, and nature study.

Among the state's newer parks, Caesars Head State Park and the adjoining 3,346-acre Jones Gap State Park make up part of the 10,000-acre Mountain Bridge Wilderness Area. Attractions include Caesars Head, one of the state's highest mountain peaks; nearby Raven Cliff Falls, one of the highest waterfalls in the Southeast; and the Middle Saluda Scenic River, South Carolina's first designated scenic river. The Foothills Hiking Trail, which follows the North Carolina–South Carolina state line, links several of South Carolina's upcountry parks and gives hikers access to backcountry primitive camping and a wealth of flora and old-growth timber for nature study. Tourists seeking more amenities may choose Devils Fork State Park at Lake Jocassee, which was developed in cooperation with Duke Energy Corporation. It offers vacation villas, picturesque scenery, fishing, and proximity to the other Blue Ridge parks located along the Cherokee Foothills Scenic Parkway (State Route 11). Cultural heritage sites along this route include the Cowpens National Battlefield and state historic sites that explore Cherokee history, among them the Oconee Station State Historic Site. The stone "station" was used as a frontier fort and trading post in the eighteenth century. Cherokee history also is interpreted in the park museum at Keowee-Toxaway State Natural Area.

See also: CIVILIAN CONSERVATION CORPS (GOVERNMENT); CULTURAL HERITAGE TOURISM; ECOTOURISM.

—Benita J. Howell, *University of Tennessee*

Morrison Giffen, *South Carolina: A Guide to Backcountry Travel and Adventure* (1997).

Statewide Trail Systems

By the late twentieth century, the rugged topography that long hindered transportation development in Appalachia had become a valuable resource drawing increasing numbers of visitors to the region's expanding system of outdoor recreation trails. The development of trail systems became an important part of outdoor recreation planning in 1968, when Congress passed the National Trails System Act. The act tied federal money to the development of trails as part of each state's comprehensive planning and development efforts.

West Virginia's Statewide Trail Plan provides a good example of collaboration fostered by the act. Created to provide new income sources and encourage healthier lifestyles, the state's trail plan emerged from efforts by the nonprofit West Virginia Trails Coalition, state and federal governments, and the state's private sector. Many outfitters and nonprofit groups were among the nongovernment participants. Owners of outdoor recreation businesses saw expansion of the trail network and increased trail use as a potentially powerful way to increase tourist spending. Local businesses and groups also foresaw cooperation with the state Division of Tourism and state convention and visitors' bureaus in promotion efforts previously left to businesses and nonprofit organizations.

During the last twenty years of the twentieth century, tourism grew increasingly important to West Virginia's economy. In 1997 tourism became the leading source of revenue for the state. Many visitors to West Virginia are attracted by its excellent land and water trails. The statewide trail system was conceived to encompass all types of trails, from existing paths in state parks and national forests to urban greenways and water trails that carry visitors along West Virginia's many miles of navigable streams and rivers. The plan also envisioned collaboration with land trusts and private landowners to create trails on nonpublic lands.

In the Greenbrier River Trail and the North Bend Rail Trail, West Virginia boasts two of the country's finest rail-trails. These trails and their spurs cross the entire state in an east-west and north-south direction. The Statewide Trail Plan called for using these flagship trails as backbones for the development of more trail mileage.

See also: ECOTOURISM; RAILS-TO-TRAILS.

—Keith Norman, *West Virginia Trails Coalition*

Charles A. Flink, *Trails for the Twenty-First Century* (2000); Charles A. Flink and Robert M. Stearns, *Greenways: A Guide to Planning, Design, and Development* (1993).

Sustainable Tourism

Tourism expanded greatly in the Appalachian region in the last half of the twentieth century both because of improvements in transportation and hospitality services in destination areas and because consumers had more leisure time and disposable income for travel. Like the extractive industry of Appalachia's past, tourism depends upon a resource base—

mountain scenery and recreational opportunities, historical sites, and entertainment derived from traditional arts of the region. Tourism can provide a more sustainable economy than the region experienced in the early twentieth century but only if the resource base is properly managed, not destroyed or degraded through inappropriate development or overuse.

Cities and rural mountain areas have welcomed the economic growth generated by the tourist industry as a means to provide jobs, reduce unemployment, and alleviate poverty for their residents. In order to achieve these goals, sustainable tourism carefully manages the pace and nature of development. Otherwise, tourism can and does become unsustainable for host areas. Incompatible building adjacent to historic sites, traffic congestion and air pollution in scenic areas, and overuse of wilderness areas make tourist destinations less attractive to visitors. Other adverse effects can undermine the community's intention to revitalize itself. Growth can outpace local government's ability to provide clean water, sanitary sewerage, and solid-waste disposal; sharply rising property values and real estate developments can raise property taxes on rural land and make affordable housing less available to local residents; and corporate development can send profits out of the region and concentrate local workers in low-wage, part-time service jobs. Planning for sustainability matches growth to the community's capacity to absorb it and encourages local control and local entrepreneurship to avoid these undesirable consequences of tourism. Conservation of the tourism resource base, revitalization of local economies, and enhanced quality of life for local residents go hand in hand when tourism development is managed for sustainability.

Abingdon, Virginia, the oldest town west of the Blue Ridge Mountains, has a twenty-block historic district filled with outstanding examples of Federal and Victorian architecture lining shaded brick sidewalks. An "arts depot" housed in the 1870s restored railroad station features regional arts and crafts. Abingdon's major sustainable tourism products include the Barter Theater (the official state theater of Virginia) and the Martha Washington Inn, a four-star Historic Hotel of America built in 1832. The city cooperated with the U.S. Forest Service in developing the Virginia Creeper Trail, a world-class mountain-biking and hiking trail.

Beckley, West Virginia, a typical small U.S. city, is surrounded by excellent examples of successful sustainable tourism development. At Tamarack, visitors can experience the nation's first statewide collection of handmade crafts and cuisine prepared by the Greenbrier Resort—the "best of West Virginia"—in one major retail center. Opportunities for ecotourism and outdoor recreation are found nearby at Pipestem and other full-service state park facilities and along the Gauley River and the New River, which have become centers for outdoor activities and provide some of the best whitewater rafting opportunities in the eastern U.S. along with biking, hiking, and rock climbing.

Corning, New York, long famous for the Corning Glass Center and the National Soaring Museum, is developing a twelve-mile recreational trail on a former railroad property linking Mark Twain State Park with Watkins Glen State Park. It will be available for cross-country skiing and snowshoeing as well as hiking and biking. The area's winery tours are an example of sustainable agricultural tourism.

The Roscoe Village living history complex is the primary example of sustainable tourism in Coshocton County, Ohio. This restored 1800s canal town was built on the old Ohio and Erie Canal system. Today guests can climb aboard an authentic canal boat and float through a living history experience. The village has artisans and crafters demonstrating their skills and provides historic restaurants, lodging, and shopping. Theme festivals include Dulcimer Days, the Heritage Craft and Olde Time Music Festival, and Apple Butter Stirrin' in the fall.

As these examples illustrate, systematic strategic planning to protect and make the most of a community's unique tourism resources can also provide attractive amenities for local residents. Virtually every research project on consumer travel indicates that rest and recreation, the appeal of clean and scenic areas, and opportunities to learn about cultural heritage are top motivators. Sustainable tourism planning entails strategies to protect and make the most of a community's distinct resources so that visitors will stay longer, spend more money in the community, and leave feeling they have experienced a unique area.

In striving for sustainability, planners typically take steps to conserve the natural and cultural assets that are their unique tourism resource base and to design quality activities and interpretation around these resources. The community takes steps to manage growth, often considering some form of land-use management and transportation planning that also makes the journey to the destination a pleasant experience. Environment and aesthetics—factors such as clean air and water, architectural design for new construction that suits the locality, and good landscape design—also are key elements in planning for sustainability.

Community stakeholders (civic, business, educational, and government institutions) throughout Appalachia can take a leadership role in promoting community discussion and comprehensive planning policies that emphasize a sustainable tourism product. These initiatives will strengthen the local economy and quality of life of all residents by protecting and enhancing the community's natural, cultural, heritage, and scenic resources.

See also: AGRICULTURAL TOURISM; CULTURAL HERITAGE TOURISM; ECOTOURISM.

—Michael R. Evans, *Appalachian State University*

Michael R. Evans, "Newport, Rhode Island—America's First Resort: Lessons in Sustainable Tourism," *Journal of Travel Research* (November 1997); Michael R. Evans, J. Fox, and R. Johnson, "Identifying Competitive Strategies for Successful Tourism Destination Development," *Journal of Hospitality and Leisure Marketing* (Spring 1995); Edward Manning and David Dougherty, "Sustainable Tourism," *Cornell Hotel and Restaurant Administration Quarterly* (April 1995); Edward McMahon, "Tourism and the Environment," *Planning Commissioners Journal* (Fall 1997).

Tallulah Gorge

Tallulah Gorge is a six-hundred-foot-deep chasm a quarter-mile wide and two miles long in northeast Georgia. Formed by the Tallulah River, the gorge cuts through the Tallulah Dome, a mass of intermingled sandstone and rock (metagraywacke, quartzite, and schist) that geologists believe was pushed up by colliding continental plates. The gorge formed in the stretched and weakened crust at the spine of the dome.

For local Native Americans, as ethnologist James Mooney recorded in *Myths of the Cherokee*, Tallulah Gorge was a disquieting, dangerous place, where the underworld bordered this world. After northeast Georgia passed into the control of whites in 1819, Tallulah Gorge became a popular tourist destination.

The swift waters of the Tallulah River had a potential for electricity that the Georgia Railway and Power Company sought to exploit in 1912. Helen Dortsches Longstreet, the widow of Confederate General James Longstreet, led an unsuccessful crusade to designate the area a state park and stop the dam the company wanted to build. Longstreet's campaign was among the first in the nation aimed at protecting a place solely for its beauty. Georgia Railway and Power (later Georgia Power Company) quickly completed its dam, which, at the time, was the third largest in the United States. Much of the power went ninety miles south to run streetcars in Atlanta. After the dam was completed, most tourists passed by Tallulah Gorge.

In 1993 the State of Georgia created Tallulah Gorge State Park in partnership with the Georgia Power Company.

See also: GEORGIA STATE PARKS; TECTONICS (GEOLOGY).

—Wallace H. Warren, *Cornelia–Habersham County Library*

Tennessee State Parks

Federal programs and assistance strongly influenced the development of Tennessee's state park system. The birth of the National Park Service led to a far-ranging state parks movement, encouraged by an annual National Conference on State Parks, first held in 1921. In his annual report for 1919, Tennessee State Geologist Wilbur Nelson suggested the state "set aside for a full development of nature in her pristine condition, wild tracts which man has not yet altered (if any are still untouched) that can be dedicated to the generations yet to come as state parks." Six years later, a State Park and Forestry Commission was created with the authority to acquire such sites, but most legislative attention was diverted by a long battle to purchase land for the Great Smoky Mountains National Park.

Considerable progress was made during the New Deal years. The first board of directors of the Tennessee Valley Authority (TVA) considered recreation an important by-product of water projects and organized a recreation planning office in Knoxville. By 1938, TVA was managing four east Tennessee parks, all eventually deeded to Tennessee as state parks (Harrison Bay, Cove Lake, Big Ridge, and Norris Dam). The federal Resettlement Administration acquired tracts considered marginal for agricultural purposes, relocated residents, and arranged for the National Park Service to manage four "recreation demonstration areas," including Fall Creek Falls on the Cumberland Plateau. All but one received state park designation in the early 1940s. The Farm Security Administration developed Cumberland Mountain State Park, originally called Cumberland Homesteads Park, as a recreational area for some 250 families who had been selected to homestead "subsistence farms" in Cumberland County. The Civilian Conservation Corps and the Works Progress Administration provided the labor and technical skills to build the cabins, trails, and dams that remain in these parks.

Following proposals of the newly formed Tennessee State Planning Commission, Governor Gordon Browning signed legislation in 1937 that created a Department of Conservation and a Division of State Parks to preserve areas selected for their "natural and historic features, scenic beauty or location . . . [and] natural or potential physical, aesthetic, scientific, creative, social, or other recreational values." The first commissioner, Sam Brewster, had been a landscape architect and planner with TVA, and the first director, R. A. Livingston, was a former national park superintendent.

After 1965, the federal Land and Water Conservation Fund supported the purchase of several significant sites and encouraged development of resort facilities within the parks. Tennessee moved to the national forefront in state-sponsored conservation legislation, passing the Tennessee Scenic Rivers Act in 1968, the Tennessee Trails System Act in 1971, and the Natural Areas Preservation Act of 1971. As of 2001, the Tennessee Bureau of State Parks managed a system of fifty-four developed parks, sixteen state natural areas, and two state scenic rivers.

Because of extensive federal public lands along the eastern boundary of Tennessee, there are few state park sites in the Unaka Mountains physiographic region. Roan Mountain State Park, situated between the historic village of Roan Mountain and the famous Roan summit, includes a pristine section of the Doe River, a nineteenth-century iron mine, and the Miller Farm, an interpretive site presenting twentieth-century Appalachian architecture and agriculture. The unspoiled Hiwassee State Scenic River crashes through a magnificent gorge described by naturalist John Muir in his *A Thousand-Mile Walk to the Gulf* as "vine-draped and flowery as Eden!" The Ocoee Recreational River, Tennessee's most popular commercial rafting waterway and site for the 1996 Olympics whitewater competition, is managed in cooperation with the U.S. Forest Service and TVA.

Because of the close historical relationship with TVA, many east Tennessee parks are located in the Tennessee Valley. Warriors Path State Park and Panther Creek State Park were acquired from TVA to protect significant natural features adjacent to the population centers of Kingsport and Morristown, respectively. Their long ridges, river bluffs, and sinkholes typify Tennessee Valley topography. Norris Dam State Park offers limited access to Norris Lake, one of the cleanest reservoirs in the South, and to numerous trails, structures, and programs connected to TVA history. The Lenoir Museum, Rice Grist Mill, and the Crosby Threshing Barn present a broad view of life in the Tennessee Valley before TVA. Big Ridge State Park and Cove Lake State Park offer outstanding opportunities for wildlife viewing, fishing, and hiking. Harrison Bay State Park and Booker T. Washington State Park, both just north of Chattanooga, provide access to Chickamauga Lake, another TVA reservoir.

The Cumberland Plateau and Cumberland Mountains include some of Tennessee's most scenic parks. Pickett State Rustic Park in Jamestown, surrounded by the eighteen-thousand-acre Pickett State Forest, includes two remarkable sandstone arches and many voluminous rockhouses, cavelike incisions at the base of the sandstone bluffs. Cumberland Mountain State Park in Crossville features elaborate stonework of the Civilian Conservation Corps and quiet nature trails that follow lakeshore and streams. Located near Pikeville, Fall Creek Falls State Park, with twenty-two thousand acres, includes some of Tennessee's greatest natural wonders: steep waterfalls, massive caves, sheer bluffs above deep gorges, and a rare patch of old-growth timber. The South Cumberland Recreation Area is a collection of separate beauty spots and historic sites on the southern end of Tennessee's Cumberland Plateau. A 280-mile-long hiking trail, the Cumberland Trail State Park, traverses the eastern edge of the Cumberlands from Cumberland Gap to Signal Mountain.

Among the most significant of historic sites, Fort Loudoun State Historic Area includes an interpretive center and fort reconstruction based on the archeological excavation of one of the earliest British forts in Tennessee territory. Sycamore Shoals State Historic Area in Elizabethton includes the site of the Transylvania Purchase and the spot where the Overmountain Men mustered during the Revolutionary War before marching to the battle of Kings Mountain, South Carolina. Red Clay State Park, located near Cleveland, protects the historic council grounds of the Cherokee Nation. The Sergeant Alvin C. York Historic Park in Pall Mall preserves many aspects of the home life and career of World War I's most celebrated soldier. Davy Crockett Birthplace State Park in Limestone interprets the history, mythology, and legacy of one of Tennessee's most famous sons.

Tennessee's state parks also serve as important centers of community activity such as family reunions, dances, baptisms, and weddings. The State Parks Folklife Project (1979–86) documented and presented traditional arts and folklife, recognizing the role of state parks in conserving culture as well as protecting and managing scenic features, historic treasures, natural resources, and outdoor recreation opportunities that attract tourists.

See also: CIVILIAN CONSERVATION CORPS (GOVERNMENT); CULTURAL HERITAGE TOURISM; TENNESSEE VALLEY AUTHORITY (GOVERNMENT).

—Bob Fulcher, *Clinton, Tennessee*

Bevley R. Coleman, *A History of State Parks in Tennessee* (1968); Ney Landrum, ed., *Histories of the Southeastern State Park Systems* (1992).

Tweetsie Railroad

The narrow-gauge freight and passenger rail line that ran between Johnson City, Tennessee, and Boone, North Carolina, was nicknamed "Tweetsie," supposedly by children from summer camps near Linville Gorge and Grandfather Mountain mimicking the sound of the whistle. The Cranberry Iron and Coal Company built the East Tennessee and Western North Carolina Railroad in 1882, primarily to carry timber, coal, and iron between the Cranberry Mine and a forge in Johnson City. Its 33.4 miles of track included five rock tunnels, four of which were in the spectacular Doe River gorge. By the turn of the century, this line was referred to as the Stemwinder.

Excursion trains on the line became popular in the years before World War I. The Linville River Railway, built between 1896 and 1898 to transport virgin spruce and pine cut near Pineola, North Carolina, was acquired by Cranberry Iron and Coal Company in 1913 and extended to Boone in 1918. Following depletion of the iron and timber resources, tourist excursion trains between Johnson City and Boone enjoyed a revival in the 1930s and 1940s, but the line was finally abandoned following a farewell run on September 24, 1950. In 1957 a theme park was begun in Blowing Rock, North Carolina, using the last locomotive and cars from the East Tennessee and Western North Carolina. By the year 2000, Tweetsie Railroad was considered North Carolina's oldest continuously operating theme park.

See also: DOLLYWOOD; GRANDFATHER MOUNTAIN; RAILROADS (TRANSPORTATION).

—Kevin E. O'Donnell, *East Tennessee State University*

Mallory Hope Ferrell, *Tweetsie Country: The East Tennessee and Western North Carolina Railroad* (1976); Elmer G. Sulzer, *Ghost Railroads of Tennessee* (1975; reprint 1998).

Virginia and West Virginia Springs

The springs of Virginia became tourist attractions by virtue of nature, history, and fashion. After the restoration of Charles II to the British throne in 1660, royal patronage made newly fashionable the mineral hot springs at Bath, a town in southwest England built around the ruins of the extensive Roman baths at Aquae Sulis. During the eighteenth century, Bath became a showplace for wealth and fashion. Virginia's plantation gentry, always ready to emulate those Englishmen whom it regarded as peers, found the opportunity to do so as settlement broke through the Blue Ridge into the central Appalachians.

Bath in Virginia—now known by its postal designation of Berkeley Springs, West Virginia—was discovered in the 1730s in the domain of Lord Fairfax, the only resident British peer in the colony. In 1776 Fairfax donated the springs and surrounding acreage to the colony of Virginia. George Washington, whose first recorded visit to the springs occurred in 1748, later helped to retain Berkeley Springs in public ownership. Farther south, the Virginia Hot Springs and Warm Springs, both located in what in 1790 became Bath County, also remained state property, although private lessees developed the resorts that grew up around these waters. Private developers created the other spas. White Sulphur Springs, which became the most fashionable of all Virginia springs during antebellum times, was developed by the Bowyer and Calwell families, heirs of the original settlers; in 1857 a joint stock corporation succeeded these proprietors and in turn became a subsidiary of the Chesapeake and Ohio Railway in 1910. By the time of the Civil War, several dozen similar resorts were scattered throughout the mountain counties along the present West Virginia–Virginia border and in the nearby Valley of Virginia. Thanks to railroad accessibility and successful promotion during the automobile age, Berkeley Springs, Hot Springs, Warm Springs, and White Sulphur Springs survived as resorts into the twenty-first century.

Promoters advanced health claims, often backed up by reams of data from medical "experts," for nearly all of the resorts, claiming cures of diseases ranging from rheumatism

"Old White," White Sulphur Springs, West Virginia, c. 1880s. This grand old hotel served guests at the White Sulphur Springs resort beginning in the mid-1800s.

to cancer. Even at the close of the twentieth century, the Greenbrier, the grand hotel erected in 1913 at White Sulphur Springs, maintained a medical clinic for the use of its patrons. While these claims were often unfounded, it is easy to conclude why a stay at the waters improved visitors' health. The remote location of most of the springs encouraged at least a week (more commonly a month or two) of idleness and relaxation in pre-automobile times. Mountain air brought refreshment and a relative absence of disease-bearing insects. Soaking in the waters eased the aches and pains of men who spent a large part of their lives on horseback and also calmed the nerves of Victorian ladies. If the waters were bubbly as well as soothing and warm, they could also aid in what gentlemen called "rejuvenation," and the custom of visiting the springs in family groups facilitated courtship in a region where suitable marriage partners for the wealthy young were scattered among the predominantly rural locations of visitors' homes. The springs provided a venue for the display of wealth and for the exchange of views on fashion and politics. Historian Ulrich B. Phillips went so far as to claim that White Sulphur Springs constituted the summer capital of the Old South, since it provided a meeting place for the propagandists of southern independence each summer and an audience of influential planters among whom to propagate their views. Presidents from Jackson through Wilson regularly visited the springs; at White Sulphur Springs, the proprietors provided free accommodations to the Kentucky politician Henry Clay because of the patronage his presence attracted. During the twentieth century, the successor hotel extended this privilege to visiting British royalty and Hollywood stars.

Because their upper-class patronage was drawn mainly from southern plantations and cities, scholars have usually treated the mountain spas as places in but not of the Appalachian region. This approach ignores their importance as seeds of Appalachia's tourism industry. Both transient and residential tourism first appeared at the resorts: a South Carolina planter built the first private residence at White Sulphur Springs in 1825, a dozen years before the first Charlestonian built a summer home at Flat Rock, North Carolina.

There are at least two other points of connection of the spas with Appalachian history. As a meeting place, the springs helped to propagate the social values and political outlooks of the southern plantation-owning class among the Appalachian social elite, notwithstanding the differing economic interests of the two groups. Later they performed a similar function linking the metropolitan rich with coal operators and their retinues of small-town lawyers and bankers. John L. Lewis, the stormy and charismatic leader of the United Mine Workers of America, understood this when he summoned the operators to White Sulphur Springs to sign the 1941 Appalachian Agreement, reorganizing the industry's wage scales on a nationwide basis. Thereafter Lewis became a regular patron of the resort—symbolically taking possession of a place the operators had regarded as their own. He also successfully promoted unionization of hotel and maintenance workers at White Sulphur Springs.

The springs also provided points of connection between patrons and ordinary mountaineers. Local color writers such as David Hunter Strother, Mary Noailles Murfree, and Margaret Prescott Montague drew on such encounters to create characters—and caricatures—of mountain people. The resorts also provided seasonal work for locals: construction and maintenance work for men and housekeeping and service work for women, for while earlier patrons were often attended by slaves, a free labor force had become the norm even before the Civil War. For this reason, the towns of White Sulphur Springs, West Virginia, and Hot Springs, Virginia, each attracted significantly larger proportions of African American residents than their surrounding region. Local men also served as hunting and fishing guides for well-to-do sportsmen. One of Appalachia's greatest twentieth-century athletes, Sam Snead, Greenbrier's golf professional from 1936 to 1975, was a Bath County native who got his start in the sport as a caddy on the Hot Springs links.

Today, the Greenbrier and its Hot Springs counterpart, the Homestead, thrive as meeting places for conventions and trade shows. Families and weekend visitors from Washington, D.C., and other nearby cities still patronize both resorts and dominate the cozier and less luxurious accommodations at Berkeley Springs and Warm Springs. Second-home colonies have sprung up at these resorts in response to the growth of residential tourism; however, the spas no longer monopolize this trade but rather share it with numerous other properties, which are noted exclusively for their scenery and recreation. The Greenbrier acquired an attraction of a different sort in 1992, when it was revealed that an underground facility constructed during the 1950s was actually a fallout shelter designed to house the U.S. Congress in the event of nuclear attack. Tours of this Cold War artifact have become as popular as tours of the resort's historic properties. The hotel pressured the West Virginia legislature for authority to turn the shelter into a gambling casino but with little success.

See also: BLUE RIDGE PROVINCE (GEOLOGY); HOT SPRINGS, NORTH CAROLINA; SMOKY MOUNTAIN SPAS AND RESORTS.

—John Alexander Williams, *Appalachian State University*

Stan B. Cohen, *Historic Springs of the Virginias* (1981) and *The Homestead and Warm Springs Valley, Virginia* (1984); Robert Conte, *History of the Greenbrier* (1995).

Virginia State Parks

Virginia is home to forty-six state parks and natural areas, serving nearly five million residents and travelers annually. Seventeen of these parks and areas are located in Appalachian Virginia, providing approximately 40 percent of the annual visitation to state parks overall and including the second, third, and fourth most popular parks in the state. Managed by the Department of Conservation and Recreation, Appalachian Virginia's parks and natural areas represent a significant contribution to the local economy and provide distinctive educational and recreational opportunities for residents and tourists.

The Virginia state parks system opened in 1936, the result of a massive make-work effort under the New Deal. Civilian Conservation Corps members had begun construction of six state parks in 1933, three of which were to be located in Appalachian Virginia: Douthat State Park in Bath and Alleghany Counties, Fairy Stone State Park in Patrick and Henry Counties, and Hungry Mother State Park in Smyth County. These sites remain in operation, with the Douthat Park ranking as the third most popular park in the state. In the decades since the New Deal, Virginia's state parks have continued to grow in number, with lands being either purchased by the state or donated by businesses and individuals.

Appalachian Virginia's state parks are located primarily in the Blue Ridge Highlands, though several parks can be found among the foothills of the Blue Ridge in the Shenandoah Valley and central region of the state. The Blue Ridge Highlands parks include Claytor Lake, Grayson Highlands, Hungry Mother, Hemlock Haven, Natural Tunnel, Shot Tower and New River Trail, Southwest Virginia Museum, and Wilderness Road. Douthat State Park is located in the higher portions of the Shenandoah Valley. Fairy Stone State Park and Smith Mountain Lake State Park are located in the central portion of the state.

Programs and facilities at each park differ, but in general, all boast outdoor recreation and educational opportunities. A few parks include restaurants and lodges, while others offer only picnic shelters and hiking trails. Picnicking, camping in tents or trailers, fishing, hiking, and swimming are the leading outdoor activities, but some locales offer biking, canoeing, paddleboating, horseback trails, hunting, and other options. Some parks also offer courses in outdoor skills such as cross-country skiing, backpacking, and fly-fishing.

Virginia was the first state in the Southeast to offer historical and environmental programs at its parks, introducing them as early as the 1950s. Historic sites such as the Wilderness Road State Park offer glimpses into life along the Virginia frontier through interpretive programming. The Southwest Virginia Museum depicts the evolution of everyday life in western Virginia across the centuries, and Hungry Mother, Natural Tunnel, and Claytor Lake each have environmental education centers. Other parks have created hiking programs with environmental emphases, and a few have junior ranger programs for children during the summer months. Most parks include some regular natural science, historical, and cultural programming for their guests throughout the spring, summer, and fall.

The state's parks host special events celebrating everything from regional history, crafts, food, and music to the scenic beauty of the changing seasons. The annual Whitetop Mountain Ramp Festival at Grayson Highlands State Park pays homage to the potent wild plant so integral to mountain foodways; gospel music is celebrated with a festival at Fairy Stone State Park; and more than one hundred quilts are exhibited every spring at the Southwest Virginia Museum. Many parks also hold fall festivals as the changing foliage nears its peak of color. These events attract new visitors to parks and build traditions for area residents.

The Department of Conservation and Recreation also oversees six natural preserves in Appalachian Virginia. Natural area preserves in the Blue Ridge include Buffalo Mountain, Clinch Mountain Wildlife Management Area, Lick Creek, and Pinnacle. Goshen Pass Natural Area and Poor Mountain Natural Area Preserve are found in the Shenandoah Valley at the base of the Blue Ridge. These preserves are meant to protect biodiversity and to serve as observation areas for scientists, environmentalists, and visitors. Public access to these areas varies because construction of access routes must be consistent with preservation policies. Developed under the Natural Heritage Program of 1989 to protect the natural legacy of the state, the preserves represent another branch of environmental education and protection by the state.

Large numbers of people visit Virginia's parks each year, with millions of dollars generated directly and indirectly through the parks. User fees are the largest source of park revenue, but areas around the parks reap additional monies through sales of food and gas, as well as camping and fishing supplies. Thus communities and parks exist symbiotically. The proliferation of these locations in Virginia ensures that guests are never more than an hour's drive from a state park, and the modest usage fees make programming and facilities accessible.

See also: BLUE RIDGE PROVINCE (GEOLOGY); CIVILIAN CONSERVATION CORPS (GOVERNMENT); CULTURAL HERITAGE TOURISM.

—Shannon Young Brooks, *National D-Day Memorial, Bedford, Virginia*

Bill Bailey, William L. Bailey, and Joe Elton, *Virginia State Parks: A Complete Outdoor Recreation Guide* (1996); Garvey and Deane D. Winegar, *Highroad Guide to the Virginia Mountains* (1998).

Weeks Act

See Weeks Act (Government)

West Virginia State Parks

West Virginia state parks and forests comprise nearly two hundred thousand acres set aside to protect natural resources, showcase scenic beauty, and preserve sites of historical significance while providing places for outdoor recreational pursuits.

In the late 1800s and especially near the turn of the twentieth century, West Virginia was a booming industrial area, thanks to its immense resources of coal, natural gas, and timber. Clear-cutting of the forests and careless mining practices brought economic prosperity and thousands of jobs to the state, but these extractive industries ravaged the land, leaving bald mountaintops, smoky air, and murky streams. The idea of a state park system in West Virginia can be traced to 1925, when state leaders recognized the need for preservation and protection of the state's natural environment for future generations.

The site for West Virginia's first state park, Droop Mountain Battlefield in Pocahontas County, was acquired in 1928, and the park opened the following year at the place of the state's largest Civil War engagement. The state legislature in 1933 formed the State Park System, a division of the Conservation Commission of West Virginia, giving it the mandate "to promote conservation by preserving and protecting natural areas of unique or exceptional scenic, scientific, cultural, archaeological or historic significance, and to provide outdoor recreational opportunities for the citizens of this State and its visitors."

Aside from the establishment of Droop Mountain, little happened to the park system until the Great Depression. The Civilian Conservation Corps (CCC), one of President Franklin D. Roosevelt's first depression-relief programs, in the 1930s built the facilities and infrastructure that would become the core of the West Virginia State Park System.

Expert stone masons and carpenters led hundreds of members of the CCC, unmarried men between the ages of eighteen and twenty-five, in building vacation cabins, hiking trails, roads, and swimming pools at Watoga, Cacapon, Babcock, Lost River, Hawks Nest, and Grandview State Parks. Two other federal depression-era programs, the Works Progress Administration and the Resettlement Administration, built facilities at Tomlinson Run and Holly River. Initially, vacation cabins built of native hardwoods and locally quarried stone were the chief buildings in the parks. As more people visited, the demand for inns, lodges, restaurants, and gift shops followed.

The CCC development of state park infrastructure halted in 1942 as the manpower and resources of the historic conservation program were dedicated to the war effort. Despite the war and the end of the CCC program, the park system continued to grow with the addition of the Tygart Lake, Cathedral, and Audra State Parks. By the late 1940s, the parks struggled with a number of incomplete CCC projects and lack of maintenance during the war, even as postwar national prosperity in the early 1950s produced increasing demand for facilities.

The existing condition and plans for improvement of the state parks became campaign issues during the 1952 gubernatorial race. In 1953 West Virginia made history by selling revenue bonds to finance improvements and additions to the park system. The first state park campground opened at Watoga in 1953. In 1953 and 1954, the state built lodges at Blackwater Falls and Cacapon as well as cabins, roads, bridges, utilities, and infrastructure at other parks with bonds totaling $4.4 million. By 1958, nearly two million people were visiting West Virginia's state parks each year.

The 1950s also saw a change in the philosophy of the parks program. Rather than focusing strictly on preservation and recreation, the state recognized that parks offered significant economic benefits. Accordingly, the development plan for Blackwater Falls included the statement that the development of scenic natural resources could "awaken a dormant industry." For the first time, the parks began to organize recreation programs for guests.

In the early 1960s, state parks again benefited from federal programs. With the help of loans and grants of $28 million from the Area Redevelopment Administration, West Virginia added three resort parks—Pipestem, Canaan Valley, and Twin Falls. These parks offered the first golf courses in the system. Other parks underwent major improvements during that time.

The famous Cass Scenic Railroad was added in the summer of 1962 after the legislature approved the purchase of twelve miles of abandoned logging railroad on Cheat Mountain in Pocahontas County. This distinctive park draws thousands of visitors each year to experience incredible scenery and a hint of West Virginia's tumultuous industrial past.

In the early 1970s, the Canaan Valley ski area opened, making it the first major commercial alpine ski facility in West Virginia. Its development launched a winter tourism industry that drew more than 750,000 visitors annually by the turn of the century. Other privately owned ski areas developed after Canaan Valley opened.

From 1977 to 1980, the parks spent $20 million to upgrade roads, water and sewer systems and to build cottages and a Cass train depot, but in 1977 the legislature halted further expansion of the park system without its approval. Lawmakers feared limited state resources would not be able to handle a larger park system. Two new parks have been added since that time, however. Beech Fork and Stonewall Jackson Lake began as U.S. Army Corps of Engineers flood-control projects.

In 1996 the legislature approved the sale of $44 million in bonds for park system expansion and improvements—the most significant capital investment in decades. The money was used to build handicapped-accessible, deluxe vacation cabins and to expand conference facilities at Blackwater, Cacapon, and Pipestem. New swimming pools were built at Beech Fork and Moncove Lake, along with numerous other accessibility and infrastructure improvements at other parks. Beech Fork, previously a camping-only vacation park, received six new cabins to offer year-round vacations. Conference facilities were completed at Chief Logan State Park in 2001. Stonewall Jackson Lake, in an unusual public-private partnership, along with $10 million of the bond money, became a four-seasons resort with construction of a two-hundred-room lodge, golf course, and cabins.

With thirty-one state parks, four resort parks, nine state forests, four wildlife management areas, and two rail-trails, the West Virginia State Park System has become one of the finest in the country. Its facilities host more than 8.1 million visitors each year and provide a source of state pride as well as significant employment and financial contributions to the state's coffers. The parks employ 450 full-time workers and up to 1,000 additional temporary employees during the peak season and provide an estimated direct economic impact of $105 million. The parks continue to be about 65 percent self-supporting, a figure that ranks among the best of all fifty state park systems.

See also: CASS SCENIC RAILROAD STATE PARK; CIVILIAN CONSERVATION CORPS (GOVERNMENT); SKI RESORTS.

—Matthew R. Turner, *West Virginia Division of Tourism*

Darrell E. Holmes, ed., *West Virginia Blue Book* (1998); West Virginia State Parks History Committee, *Where People and Nature Meet: A History of the West Virginia State Parks* (1988).

Transportation

Section Editors: Mark L. Burton, Richard V. Hatcher, and Thomas Maraffa

Since the days when logs from virgin forests were floated out of the mountains on spring floods, transportation has been the most constant, expensive, and challenging issue of public policy in Appalachia. In the twenty-first century, with the mythic isolation of the region long faded, issues concerning highway safety, road construction, airports, railroads, and waterways still weigh heavily upon state, local, and federal budget makers. They continue to frame political debates and alter the future of communities. The same general transportation issues prevail in every corner of America, but in Appalachia the geographic, economic, and environmental considerations give such matters additional complexity, special urgency, and permanent priority.

Beginning with studies in Kentucky, West Virginia, and Pennsylvania in the 1950s, transportation came to be considered the linchpin for growth in a region hampered by isolation, rural poverty, and stunted economic development. "Development activity in Appalachia cannot proceed until the regional isolation has been overcome," the President's Appalachian Regional Commission declared in February 1964. "Its cities and towns, its areas of natural wealth, and its areas of recreation and industrial potential must be penetrated by a transportation network which provides access to and from the rest of the nation and within the region itself." While not original, this declaration of Appalachia's foremost need became the mantra for federal-state collaboration in regional development.

The Appalachian Regional Development Act, passed in 1965, mandated an ambitious regional highway system as a principal mission of the new Appalachian Regional Commission. Half a century later, transportation improvement projects still stand near the top of the agency's agenda.

Improved transportation has transformed the region, precipitating cultural change, altering the landscape, and remaking communities, as well as lifting the economy. Inevitably, local impacts have been profoundly mixed, and strategic decisions have been fraught with controversy. But the Interstate Highway System, the Appalachian Development Highway System, and improved local roads have shortened distances between rural Appalachia and urban centers of the East, South, and

Facing page: The East Tennessee and Western North Carolina Railroad (also known as the Tweetsie) on the line between Cranberry, North Carolina, and Johnson City, Tennessee, c. 1882. The narrow-gauge railroad began operations in the 1880s after fifty miles of track were laid through the rugged Blue Ridge Mountains. By the 1950s, passenger railway traffic for most of the region had ended due to the affordability of automobiles and improved feeder roads to the rapidly expanding Interstate Highway System.

Midwest and put once remote communities closer to courthouses and markets in their own counties. Modern roads have spawned suburbs around small towns as well as urban cores and made long-distance commuting a way of life. Bypasses, attracting shopping centers with ubiquitous chain stores, franchises, and warehouse retailers, have sometimes decimated the business districts of historic communities. In some instances, downtown restoration and preservation movements have arisen in reaction, occasionally featuring refurbished railway stations abandoned with the demise of the passenger train.

In modern-day Appalachia, urban-development plans speak of "intermodal" transportation needs, and modest communities that once prospered at railroad junctions look beyond highway access to airports as magnets for business and industrial growth. But for areas still struggling to share in Appalachia's improved economic prospects, the era of airline deregulation has made local service uncertain. Air travelers from southeastern Kentucky and southwestern Virginia, for example, find it necessary to travel to the Tri-Cities Airport in east Tennessee to board a flight. Venerable airports at such places as Muscle Shoals, Alabama, struggle to keep air service since travelers can reach metropolitan airports an hour's drive away via a four-lane freeway. While metropolitan airports in such cities as Atlanta and Cincinnati provide worldwide connections, Pittsburgh is the only major air-passenger hub within Appalachia. Huntsville, Alabama, is the region's burgeoning center for air freight. Just as extensive highway projects require years of planning and construction, so do important aviation complexes. In West Virginia, a major regional airport was briefly considered in the late 1960s and debated throughout the 1990s. In December 2001 the West Virginia Port Authority voted to proceed with a $350-million facility (about half of it federally funded) to be located midway between Charleston and Huntington in Lincoln County, but the project was again shelved.

While the challenges and costs of modernizing transportation in the region continue to be daunting, the accomplishments in opening the region during the last decades of the twentieth century were often spectacular. In Letcher County, Kentucky, for example, construction crews blasted and removed more than 9 million cubic yards of rock to widen U.S. Highway 23 through Pound Gap on Pine Mountain, turning a route once followed by Native American hunters and frontier settlers into an interstate-standard freeway. Exposing rock strata recording 150 million years of mountain-building history, the cut also created what the Kentucky Society of Professional Geologists designated as the state's first "official distinguished geological site." In western North Carolina, engineers excavated 37 million cubic yards of material, making cuts as deep as 600 feet and creating two 100-foot embankments to complete an interstate link between the Asheville area and eastern Tennessee. In West Virginia, the second-longest single-arch bridge in the world was built across the New River Gorge, cutting a winding forty-minute, up-and-down journey to one minute. Standing 876 feet above the whitewater streambed, the span, opened in 1977, soon became one of the state's leading tourist attractions. At the historic Cumberland Gap, a $280-million tunnel through the mountain was completed in 1996, eliminating a dangerous 2.3-mile winding journey along U.S. Highway 25-E to pass through the gap between Kentucky and Tennessee. Construction of the four-lane, 4,600-foot tube took seventeen years. In North Carolina, construction of the Linn Cove Viaduct around Grandfather Mountain completed the Blue Ridge Parkway in 1987. Long delayed by environmental concerns, the parkway's "missing link" was not completed until nearly half a century after ground was broken for the scenic route through the Blue Ridge Mountains between the Great Smoky Mountains and

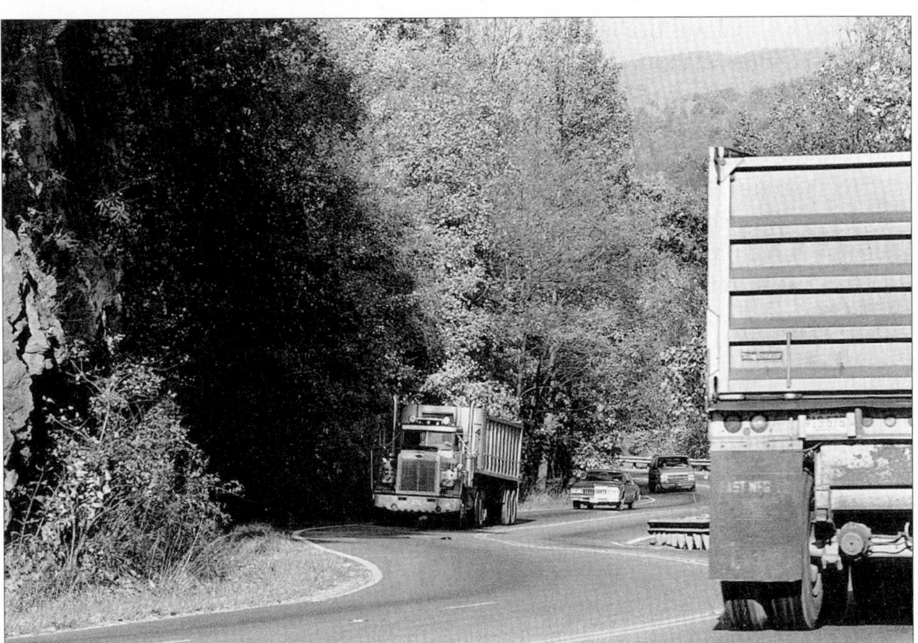

Trucks travel U.S. Highway 23 from Pound, Virginia, to Jenkins, Kentucky, 1994. In one of the highway construction feats of the late twentieth century, work crews had to blast and remove millions of cubic yards of rock to widen the highway through Pound Gap on Pine Mountain.

Shenandoah National Parks. To complete the passage around the mountain at an elevation of more than 4,000 feet without destruction of the landscape, architects and engineers fashioned the 1,243-foot viaduct from 153 pre-cast segments, all but one of them curved, weighing fifty tons each.

Promoted as an economic boon, the $2-billion Tennessee-Tombigbee Waterway was the most expensive and controversial transportation development in the region. The largest single project in the history of the U.S. Army Corps of Engineers, the 234-mile channel required cuts as deep as 175 feet and the excavation of more dirt than was moved in construction of the Panama Canal. Work was completed in December 1984 after twelve years, connecting the Tennessee River from a point in northeastern Mississippi with the Tombigbee River in southwestern Alabama and creating a barge route between ports on the upper Tennessee and the Gulf of Mexico about 800 miles shorter than the route to the Gulf via the lower Tennessee, the Ohio, and the Mississippi.

Landscape-altering technology for road construction and surface mining did not arrive until the latter half of the twentieth century, but even before nineteenth-century steam engines and potent explosives came into use, efforts to open the mountains to transportation were remarkable for their audacity.

In 1802 the Patowmack Canal, long championed by George Washington, opened for traffic from the highlands of Maryland and present-day West Virginia down to the Potomac ports of Georgetown and Alexandria. Until 1828, 75-foot flatboats carrying as much as twenty tons of cargo used locks of the canal to circumnavigate the rocky shallows and churning falls above Washington, D.C. During the peak year of 1811, no fewer than thirteen hundred boats were maneuvered through the locks. But there were years when river levels limited lock operations to as few as forty-five days, and by the 1820s, at the outset of an era when shipping canals were built by the hundreds, the

Patowmack Canal was deemed obsolete. In 1828 construction began on the Chesapeake and Ohio Canal, a waterway with an adjacent tow path for mules pulling barges parallel to the river. The canal eventually reached Cumberland, Maryland, but Washington's dream of a man-made waterway linking the Atlantic seaboard with the headwaters of the Ohio River was never realized.

To shorten the route to Cumberland by an estimated 6 miles, workers dynamited and shoveled a 3,118-foot tunnel through the Allegheny Mountains' Paw Paw Ridge near the present Maryland–West Virginia border. Tunnel construction took fourteen years, rather than the expected two, but its completion in 1850 created one of the canal era's most notable pieces of infrastructure. Twenty-four feet tall and lined with 6 million bricks, it helped inspire tunnels that became a hallmark of Appalachian highway routes opened after the development of power tools and more efficient explosives.

Until canals and railroads began to alter the landscape, Appalachian travel and mountain commerce adapted to the terrain, and even into modern times travel patterns reflect centuries of movement by animals and native peoples. Large mammals—bison and deer—wore paths to salt licks. Native Americans who lived and hunted in the region—Catawba, Cherokee, Chickasaw, Creek, Delaware, Iroquois—created routes to suit their needs, following streams and creating footpaths through mountain openings and around natural obstacles. Their trails, stream crossings, campsites, and villages formed rudimentary templates used by European explorers and long hunters, who were followed by growing numbers of settlers bringing domestic animals and wagons along with saws, axes, and farm implements. With European settlement, ancient walking paths became pack trails, and pack trails became wagon roads. Wagon roads, in time, became highways. The streams that transported logs from the Appalachians were the first export routes for other Appalachian products, providing natural avenues for flatboats, keelboats, tobacco canoes, and eventually steamboats.

Decades before railroads cut into the interior to reach the region's timber and coal, principal rivers draining the mountains connected Appalachia's developing antebellum economy to far-flung markets. Flatboats on the Clinch, Cumberland, Coosa, Holston, Kanawha, Monongahela, Ohio, Tennessee, and other rivers carried flour, salt, iron, whiskey, furs, and coal from Appalachian farms, furnaces, forests, and mines. In addition to Pittsburgh, river towns such as Knoxville, Tennessee, and Wheeling and Charleston, (West) Virginia, prospered as collection and transshipment centers. Wheeling, set where the National Road from Baltimore reached the Ohio, became a genuine early-nineteenth-century boomtown. A bustling river port and a supply center for westward-bound immigrants, it was also the home of a burgeoning boatbuilding industry.

The National Road from Baltimore to Wheeling and on to the Midwest was but one of several early overland routes connecting the region to the outside world and providing access for streams of settlers. Others included improved roads such as Braddock's Road and Forbes Road, opened across western Maryland and southern Pennsylvania when English troops marched on Fort Duquesne (Pittsburgh) during the French and Indian War. The most important artery, however, was the Great Valley Road (also known as the Great Wagon Road) from Philadelphia to Hagerstown, Maryland, where it turned south through the Appalachian Valley, eventually intersecting with the Wilderness Road leading through the Cumberland Gap into Kentucky and to routes into Tennessee.

By the time of the Civil War, Appalachia had few improved roads, and for the most part railroads were confined to the periphery of the region. Destructive as the conflict was, it provided stimulus for transportation development, including the expansion of railroads in the postwar era. In the South, the Southern Railway penetrated the Appalachians with several lines, and the Louisville and Nashville connected northern Alabama with the Ohio Valley. Into the coalfields and trackless forests of southwestern Virginia, West Virginia, and eastern Kentucky moved new rails of the Norfolk and Western and the Chesapeake and Ohio. In some instances, improved transportation links helped create vibrant local economies, even during the dark years of Reconstruction. Chattanooga, a town of only thirty-five hundred inhabitants at the time of the war, grew to twelve thousand by 1880. Birmingham, Alabama, an inconsequential community before the coming of the railroad, blossomed into a steelmaking "southern Pittsburgh."

Backcountry Appalachia, particularly the southern highlands, remained isolated into the twentieth century, the coming of the railroads notwithstanding. Away from the river towns, railroad junctions, and scattered industrial centers, the chief impact of the railroads was to open Appalachian forests to massive industrial logging and launch mining operations that provided the fuel for America's Industrial Revolution. After a visit to eastern Kentucky in 1899, Berea College President William Goodell Frost reported, "Its highways are the beds of streams; commerce and intercourse are conditioned by horseflesh and saddlebags."

As the timber and coal booms waned in the 1920s, railroad expansion slowed and ended, too. Periods of favorable coal prices and rising employment in mining would follow, but derelict railroad tracks and abandoned rail passenger terminals became commonplace as automobiles and trucks came to rule the twentieth century. Mergers and consolidations became the hallmark of the railroad industry, and when the twentieth century ended, only the Norfolk Southern and CSX remained.

Like the rest of the country, Appalachia found itself dependent upon trucks and automobiles, a situation clearly recognized by 1916 when Congress passed the Federal Aid Road Act, providing assistance to states' road improvement efforts. But as the region had been bypassed in the early years of railroad development, so it fell behind in the age of the automobile. In the highlands, road construction was dangerous, torturously slow, and astronomically expensive. Modern routes across the region or between population centers required tunnels or deep cuts through solid rock, massive excavation, landfills, bridges, and guardrails. In the era of four-lane roads, construction in mountainous terrain cost on average $8 million per mile more than the same road across level country. Thus, by the 1960s, when social and economic conditions in central Appalachia became a source of intense national media interest and fodder for political debate, the mountainous portions of Appalachia continued to be served by narrow winding roads with steep grades and switchbacks. Deep in hollows, roads remained unpaved, and some rural Appalachian homes still depended on streambeds for access. When the national Interstate Highway System was laid out, the most isolated portions of Appalachia were again bypassed by planners because of high construction costs.

In the thirty-five years after passage of the Appalachian Regional Development Act in 1965, the Appalachian Regional Commission spent about $2.3 billion on roads in West Virginia, $1.6 billion in eastern Kentucky, $1.5 billion in Pennsylvania, and $1 billion in Tennessee, with some segments costing as much as $18 million per mile. Still, creation of satisfactory links to national commerce and development of fully modern transportation infrastructures within the region remained works in progress. Yet to be completed were expensive segments of the Appalachian Development Highway System. At the end of 2003, the Appalachian Regional Commission projected that the final cost of the twenty-six corridors (tentatively to be completed around the end of the twenty-first century's second decade) would be some $8.5 billion. Still in various stages of conception and planning were new interstate routes in Mississippi, Alabama, Kentucky, and West Virginia, some with segments following Appalachian Regional Commission corridors.

For all the strides in opening traffic in, out, and within the region, transportation strategies continued to be subjects of disagreement. Some political conservatives viewed federal spending on regional roads with disdain. Others challenged analyses showing that economic growth more than offset the construction and maintenance of modern highway corridors. In some instances, they were joined by environmentalists, who argued that the destruction of natural resources had not been adequately factored into construction costs. Many of these same critics continued to advocate smaller highway projects to benefit needy counties still served by inadequate roads, some of them heavily traveled by coal trucks. In eastern Kentucky and southern West Virginia in particular, the weight of coal trucks was a source of chronic tension for decades. In 2002 a rash of accidents involving coal trucks in southern West Virginia led to a bitter fight over truck weights and changes in the law for the first time in many years. In the end, truck weight limits were increased—almost doubled in some instances—but in exchange, roads for hauling coal were officially designated.

Inevitably, given the political popularity of transportation projects, the Appalachian program has continued to be painted as the epitome of pork-barrel politics, wherein members of Congress build careers by capturing federal construction dollars for their states and governors benefit by manipulating allocations within their borders. Critics often point, in addition to highway projects, to the Tennessee-Tombigbee Waterway, pressed to completion by powerful southerners in Congress, including House Appropriations Committee Chairman Jamie Whitten, a Mississippi Democrat, even though President Jimmy Carter once put it on a "hit list" for cancellation. The project failed to live up to predictions that it would have a major impact on Tennessee River shipping costs. Rather than taking the shortcut between the Tennessee Valley and the Gulf of Mexico, barge operators found it more economical to take the long route via the Ohio and the Mississippi Rivers. Pushing as many as forty-five linked barges, they found it too time consuming to disconnect their tows and put them through several canal locks eight at a time.

Notwithstanding the experience of the great waterway and lesser controversies in the development of modern roads, airports, and other facilities, transportation projects continue to be favorites of state and federal lawmakers competing for pork-barrel dollars.

—Mark L. Burton and Richard V. Hatcher, *Marshall University*

Appalachian Regional Commission, *Appalachian Development Highways Economic Impact Study* (1998); Richard B. Drake, *A History of Appalachia* (2001); Ronald D Eller, *Miners, Millhands, and Mountaineers: Industrialization of the Appalachian South, 1880–1930* (1982); Ronald L. Lewis, *Transforming the Appalachian Countryside: Railroads, Deforestation, and Social Change in West Virginia, 1880–1920* (1998); Paul Salstrom, *Appalachia's Path to Dependency: Rethinking a Region's Economic History, 1730–1940* (1994); David E. Whisnant, *Modernizing the Mountaineer: People, Power, and Planning in Appalachia* (1980).

Appalachian Development Highway System

Since its creation in 1965, the Appalachian Regional Commission has spent about 85 percent of its budget on a system of modern highways conceived as a cornerstone of federal-state collaboration in fostering social and economic development in the region. By the turn of the twenty-first century, work in the twenty-six corridors of the Appalachian Development Highway System had cost $4.6 billion, and it was estimated that the final cost would reach $8.5 billion, with $4.5 billion of that the federal share. As initially designed, the system called for a total of 3,440 miles of roads to complement state highways and routes of the federal interstate system, enhancing transportation within the region and improving Appalachia's links to national commerce. By 2003, Congress had formally authorized construction of 3,025 miles of roads in the corridors, mostly four-lane highways with at least partial entry control. In some cases, the new roads involved modernization of existing routes and infrastructure; in others, the corridors opened entirely new highway alignments. Of the authorized total, more than 2,500 miles (85 percent) were open to traffic, and about 600 more were in various stages of planning, design, or construction.

Nearly four decades after it was first proposed, completion of the highway system, long controversial because of its sheer magnitude, complexity, and decentralized management, continued to be one of the Appalachian Regional Commission's foremost priorities. But while more than three-fourths of the mileage had been completed, major expenditures still lay ahead because of projects yet to be completed in rugged mountainous terrain, where construction costs would be among the highest in the entire system. Political skeptics continued to question the regional network's real economic impact, environmentalists opposed remaining segments slated for areas of special sensitivity and natural diversity, and state officials struggled with deepening budgetary crises. At the end of 2002, location, design, or construction projects were still underway in all thirteen states of the region.

The rationale for the Appalachian Development Highway System was formally put forth in 1964 when the President's Appalachian Regional Commission issued a landmark report creating the framework for the Appalachian Regional Development Act enacted the following year. First on the commission's list of recommendations was a system of highways to provide access to isolated areas. A modern transportation network, the report concluded, was a "double priority" and the first requisite for regional economic development. Included in the report to the White House was a rough map of what would eventually become the Appalachian Development Highway System, showing how regional

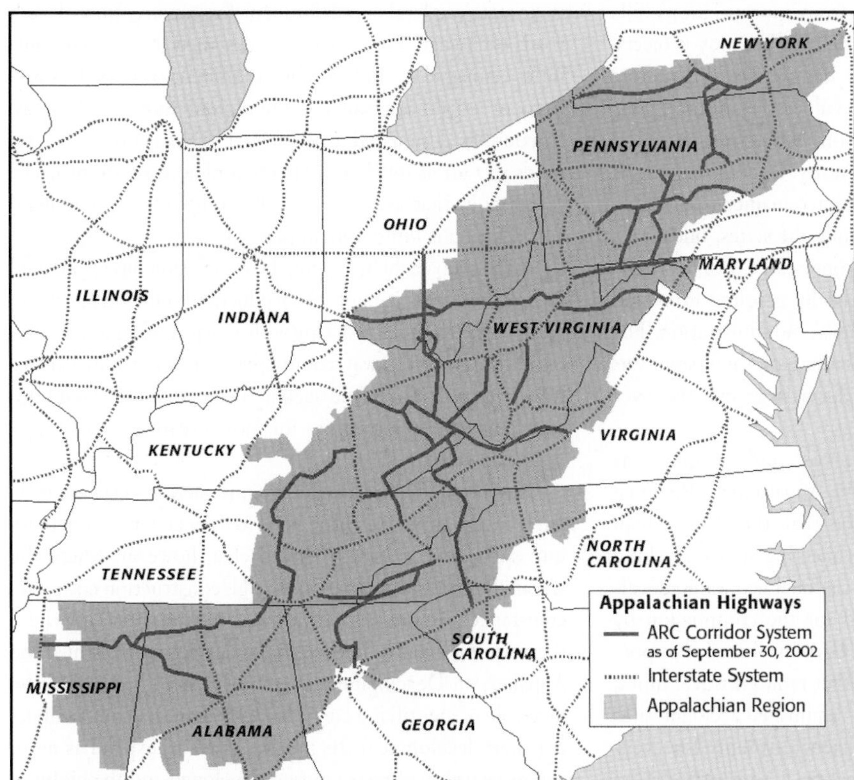

Map showing planned corridors of the Appalachian Development Highway System, 2002. Under development by the Appalachian Regional Commission since the 1960s, the system calls for a total of 3,440 miles of roads to complement state highways and federal interstates, enhancing transportation within the region and improving Appalachia's links to national commerce.

corridors would open up areas served by narrow mountain roads and connect rural Appalachia with the interstate system, which had purposely skirted the highlands to avoid prohibitive construction costs. The northernmost corridor connects Binghamton, New York, with Interstate 90 near Erie, Pennsylvania; the southernmost cuts across northern Mississippi and Alabama. But the network is most evident in the highlands of eastern Kentucky and Tennessee, Pennsylvania, southwestern Virginia, and West Virginia. At completion, Kentucky, Pennsylvania, and West Virginia will each have more than 400 miles of system roads.

While the Appalachian Regional Commission, with the approval of Congress, designed the corridor system and provided the federal portion of construction funds, individual state governments guided construction within their borders and appropriated funds to match federal contributions. At the outset, states were required to provide 50 percent of the construction funding, but their portion was subsequently reduced to 20 percent. With expensive mountain projects still on the drawing boards, consideration was given to reducing state portions to 10 percent in counties formally designated as "distressed" by the Appalachian Regional Commission.

Controversy over the Appalachian Development Highway System has persisted in part because the Appalachian Regional Commission and Congress have historically deemed it a broad economic-development initiative rather than simply a major transportation project. This distinction led to a funding process separate from appropriations bills that provided money for all other federal highway projects. Consideration as a separate budget item rendered the effort more visible and therefore more vulnerable to cuts. This approach ended after passage of the 1998 Transportation Equity Act for the Twenty-First Century. Under the new law, the Appalachian Regional Commission remained responsible for apportioning system funds among the states, but rather than a special appropriation, the money came from the Federal Highway Trust Fund, financed by gasoline taxes and administered by the Federal Highway Administration. For the years 1999 to 2003, federal spending on the system was authorized at $450 million per year, a large increase over annual outlays during the 1990s.

In response to criticism of cost and to questions concerning economic impact, the Appalachian Regional Commission has offered evidence that the Appalachian Development Highway System is meeting its overarching longterm objective of promoting regional economic development. A 1998 study conducted for the commission by Wilbur Smith Associates, a South Carolina–based transportation consulting firm, concluded that reduced travel times, lower vehicle operating costs, and diminished accident rates had produced $1.18 in travel efficiency benefits for every $1.00 invested in highway construction. Using information from 165 counties along twelve corridors substantially complete at the time, the analysis further concluded that each dollar invested in the system had yielded $1.32 in economic impact through population growth, an increased number of jobs, better wages, and other factors. Specifically, the study estimated that by 2015 the completed portions of the system will have led to a net increase of more than forty-two thousand jobs, nearly $3 billion in value added, and nearly $1.2 billion in wages.

Other research has suggested that the improved road network has led to growth and improvement of complementary infrastructure such as water, sewer, and electrical services that particularly benefit local economies. Studies at Marshall University have shown that small firms located near the highway corridors are relatively more productive than those that are farther away. Recognizing such interconnections, several West Virginia legislators in the 1990s proposed legislation that would have mandated that the state upgrade utilities in conjunction with any new highway construction.

While the Appalachian Development Highway System continued to be its centerpiece, the Appalachian Regional Commission has pursued a number of other highway and non-highway transportation initiatives. The commission's Access Road Program works to link regional commerce to system highways and other key components of the region's transportation network by providing funds for building access roads. Governors may direct $500,000 plus 5 percent of their state's federal apportionment for construction of such roads each year. The program is designed to assist communities damaged by unfavorable alignment of corridors and to focus federal assistance on the region's more needy areas. In counties designated as distressed or transitional, federal funds pay for as much as 80 percent of access road projects. In counties that are economically competitive, the federal contribution is limited to 30 percent.

The Appalachian Regional Commission has also joined in the national pursuit of productivity-enhancing intermodal opportunities, working with a variety of regional agencies in studying the way commodities are moved by various transportation modes and seeking better to understand both problems and opportunities for more creative use of transportation resources.

In a region where highway construction costs are relatively low, planners see little need to direct economic activity into specific corridors. In Appalachia, however, where the terrain limits options and causes high construction costs, circumstances require identification of specific corridors where there is opportunity for economic development. Thus, the Appalachian Development Highway System has played the dual role of identifying corridors with potential and facilitating their development. Its impact stands to expand as more extensive utility infrastructure is developed and the highway system is linked more effectively to commercial navigation, railroads, and commercial air carriers.

See also: APPALACHIAN REGIONAL COMMISSION (GOVERNMENT).

—Mark L. Burton, *Marshall University*

Appalachian Regional Commission, *Appalachian Development Highways Economic Impact Study* (1998); Robert S. Kirk, "Appalachian Development Highway Program (ADHP): An Overview," in *Congressional Research Service Report No. 98-973E* (December 7, 1998); West Virginia Department of Transportation Division of Highways, *As a Matter of Fact* (2001).

Aviation

By the centennial celebration of the Wright brothers' 1903 introduction of powered flight, aviation had become a powerful force in the business and human interests of Appalachia and in the region's prospects for the future. At the turn of the twenty-first century, more than 100 million travelers flew in and out of the region's 272 public-use airports, while businesses increasingly used air cargo services to link their high-value products with consumers and suppliers throughout the global marketplace. The growth of Appalachian aviation spans nearly a century of technological achievements in aircraft, communications, navigation, and airport design. It is a history filled with fledgling airline companies and strong-willed, visionary entrepreneurs.

Much of modern commercial airline service within the region has roots going back to homegrown innovators. In 1940 Thomas H. Davis founded Piedmont Airlines as a successful charter service. Eight years later an expanded Piedmont launched its first scheduled passenger service, flying propeller-driven planes developed during World War II. Rapid expansion of routes and steadily growing ticket sales continued through the 1950s and 1960s, and Piedmont emerged as one of America's most important regional air carriers.

With the Bristol/Kingsport/Johnson City airport serving as one of its major regional hub airports, the company flew propeller and jet-powered turboprop aircraft, generally serving short-haul routes because of the equipment's limited range. After the introduction of jet aircraft in 1967, however, the airline found it more profitable to concentrate on longer-haul air corridors and opened new routes to Chicago, New York City, Boston, and several Florida cities.

The transition from short-haul DC-3 and Convair propeller-driven aircraft to longer-haul Boeing 727 and 737 jets caused a number of smaller Appalachian communities, including London/Corbin, Kentucky, Hickory, North Carolina, and Princeton/Bluefield, West Virginia, to lose scheduled air service. Not until the late 1980s did airline manufacturers respond to the specific needs of such communities, for the first time offering twenty-five- to fifty-seat planes to air carriers. These commuter aircraft were specifically designed for short-haul services to and from small and medium-sized markets. As they became available, Piedmont and other major carriers established their own commuter affiliates linking smaller Appalachian airports with major hubs at cities such as Atlanta, Pittsburgh, and Cincinnati.

Elimination of government control over airline routes followed the deregulation of the U.S. airline industry in 1978. As change swept commercial aviation, Piedmont became both a target for acquisition and a purchaser of smaller airline properties. Its acquisition of Empire Airlines in 1986 gave it a strong presence in important northeastern markets as it endeavored to sustain its success through growth. In 1987 Norfolk Southern Corporation made an unsuccessful bid to take over Piedmont, but its offer was superseded by one from USAir. Although supporters of the Piedmont-USAir merger feared that overlapping route systems and concerns over higher fares and degraded service would be a fatal impediment to the alliance, it was approved by the U.S. Department of Transportation on October 30, 1987. When the two systems were finally assimilated two years later, the historic Piedmont Airlines name and logo disappeared from Appalachia and the aviation industry.

Piedmont's absorption was but one piece in the sweeping industry consolidation that eventually saw the disappearance of industry stalwarts such as Eastern Airlines and Pan American World Airways. USAir has subsequently become US Airways, a major carrier throughout the eastern United States, with routes reaching to the West Coast, the Caribbean, Canada, Mexico, and Europe. US Airways and its affiliate, US Airways Express, provide one of the most extensive networks of jet and commuter air carrier services to the Appalachian region. In 2003 the US Airways Group system flew more than three thousand daily flights to nearly 200 hundred airports. US Airways is the seventh-largest airline in the United States and the largest air carrier in the eastern U.S.

Like Piedmont, US Airways originated in Appalachia, beginning in 1939 as an airmail service in western Pennsylvania and the Ohio Valley. First known as All American Aviation, it changed its name to Allegheny Airlines in 1953. Fifteen years later, in 1968, Allegheny merged with Lake Central Airlines, based in Indianapolis, Indiana, and in 1972 it acquired Mohawk Airlines, based in Utica, New York. With these mergers, the Allegheny system linked Appalachian airports directly to key Midwest and New England markets. Following deregulation of the industry, Allegheny Airlines changed its name to USAir in 1979. In 1988 USAir acquired Pacific Southwest Airlines, and in 1989 Piedmont was integrated into USAir in the largest merger in airline history.

Aviation in Appalachia encompasses much more than airline companies and their aircraft. The industry's growth has led to the rise of airports as magnets for economic growth

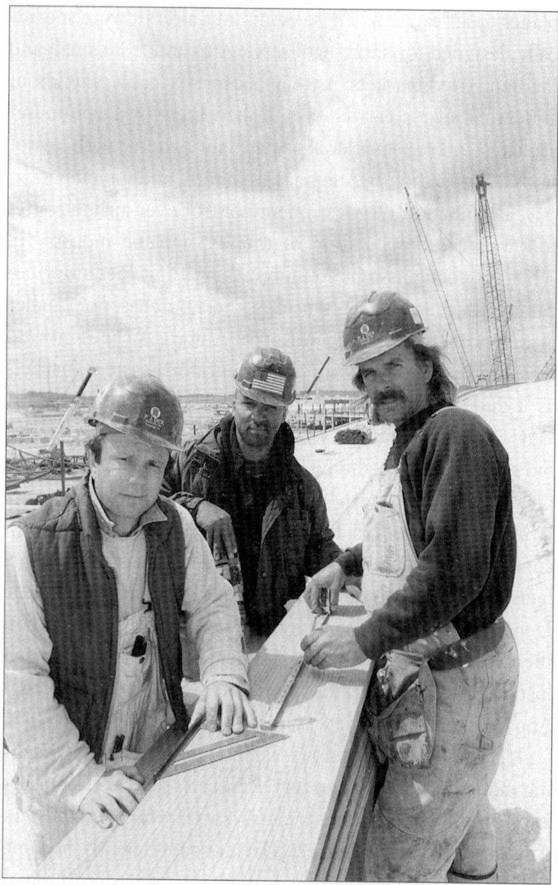

A work crew helps construct the Pittsburgh International Airport, 1991. Completed in 1992, the airport is the only major airline hub located in Appalachia. While airports were magnets for economic growth and community development in the last half of the twentieth century, the lack of competition among air carriers has left many smaller Appalachian cities underserved.

and community development. The 272 public-use airports in the region include 39 that offer scheduled service. In terms of scheduled airline service, the region's dominant facility by far is Pittsburgh International Airport.

Opened in October 1992, the complex is situated in Findley Township, sixteen miles northwest of downtown Pittsburgh. The three terminals that comprise the airport include landside (featuring parking areas, curbside pickup/drop-off, checked baggage, and ticketing facilities), airside (offering boarding concourses and gates for main line services), and commuter facilities, with a total of one hundred gates. Visually, the design evokes memories of great American train stations of the past, with sixty-foot ceilings and exposed steel trusses, as well as arched floodlights and skylights. Approximately 20 million passengers pass through the terminals each year. Served by half a million airline flights annually, Pittsburgh International is a major hub for US Airways and is used daily by twenty-four other airlines. It is the most recent of several air terminals to serve the area since Rogers Field opened as Pittsburgh's first municipal airport in the 1920s.

From 1931 to 1952, the Allegheny County Airport in South Hills, located approximately ten miles south of downtown Pittsburgh, was the primary aviation center in the area. With increasing congestion and mounting traffic making the facility obsolete, it was replaced in 1952 by the Greater Pittsburgh Airport, later renamed Greater Pittsburgh International Airport. The new $30-million airport was recognized as one of the finest in the United States. During its first full year of operation, the airport served 1.4 million passengers; by 1986, it was serving that many every month. But lacking room for expansion, it too became obsolete as air transportation witnessed explosive growth during the 1970s and 1980s.

The solution was the new Pittsburgh International Airport, two miles west of the former airport site and utilizing the runways of the old airport. Designed to accommodate up to 35 million passengers per year, the billion-dollar complex can be expanded to eventually serve as many as 50 million airline passengers annually. While it plays a key role in the regional transportation network, it has its greatest impact on Pittsburgh's economy. In 2000 the airport helped stimulate more than $5.4 billion of area spending and contributed to the creation of nearly ninety-five thousand jobs, generating $2.7 billion in wages and benefits. The "Airmall" inside the airport has more than one hundred thousand square feet of retail space, making it one of the largest and most successful airport shopping complexes in the United States. One reason for its success is that stores are required to offer the same prices as at their other locations, making airport shopping far more affordable and attractive.

While Pittsburgh International Airport leads Appalachia in passenger air service, Huntsville, Alabama, is home to the region's premier air cargo center. Conceived by J. E. "Ed" Mitchell in 1963, this state-of-the-art complex, operated by the Huntsville/Madison County Airport Authority, is comprised of Huntsville International Airport, the International Intermodal Center, Jetplex Industrial Park, and Foreign Trade Zone No. 83.

Besides meeting the area's air travel needs, the center is designed to serve the cargo needs of the entire Tennessee Valley region with one multimodal facility. The International Intermodal Center is recognized as one of the most innovative and comprehensive inland port facilities of its kind in the world. Its two one-hundred-thousand-square-foot warehouse buildings accommodate the air freight operations of six major all-cargo air carriers, using Boeing 747 air freighters to link Huntsville to Europe and Mexico.

The center also includes a rail yard, situated on eight acres of airport land immediately adjacent to the air cargo facility. The intermodal yard includes four parallel railroad tracks that can accommodate forty-four double-stacked container rail cars. At the heart of the intermodal container operation are two forty-five-ton gantry cranes that are used to transfer freight containers to and from both trucks and rail cars. Through partnerships with thirty different steamship lines, daily intermodal "stack trains" shuttle freight containers between Huntsville and major deep-water ports in Los Angeles/Long Beach, Oakland, Seattle, Charleston, Savannah, and Jacksonville.

Airport tenants and nearby businesses employ approximately fifteen thousand workers with a combined annual payroll of $600 million. These jobs and the spending associated with them contribute to a multiplied regional impact of more than twenty-eight thousand jobs and nearly $1 billion in total payroll.

While aviation has a colorful past in Appalachia, its best days may still lie ahead. High-value, time-sensitive cargo is expected increasingly to move by air freight. At the turn of the new century, international air freight centers such as Huntsville were preparing for a 15 percent increase in capacity with the introduction of giant Airbus A-380 cargo freighters.

See also: SECTION OVERVIEW.

—Scott Hercik, *Appalachian Regional Commission;* Marie F. Jones, *East Tennessee State University;* Don Kiel, *State College, Pennsylvania;* and Ed Speer, *Elizabethton, Tennessee*

Appalachian Regional Commission, *An Assessment of Intermodal Transportation Plans, Systems, and Activities in the Appalachian Region* (1999); Douglas W. Nelms, "X Marks the Brand-New Spot," *Air Transport World* (September 1992).

Baltimore and Ohio Railroad

The Baltimore and Ohio Railroad (B&O) was chartered in 1827 to link the port of Baltimore with the Ohio Valley. When passenger and freight operations began in May 1830, the B&O was the first common carrier railroad in the United States. The initial stretch of line to Ellicott's Mills in Maryland was also the site of the famous race in 1830 between the steam locomotive *Tom Thumb* and a horse-drawn carriage. But the real test of steam-powered locomotives did not come until the completion of the Parr's Spring Ridge inclined planes that took the B&O line into Frederick. These planes involved grades of more than 3 percent, considered impossible to climb without stationary engines to pull the trains upgrade. However, the early B&O steam locomotives proved capable of ascending such grades, thus demonstrating that steam locomotion was feasible. By late 1834, the main line had been completed to Harpers Ferry, (West) Virginia.

Since any route from Baltimore to the Ohio River had to pass through the lower part of northern Appalachia, the B&O railroad was destined to play a major role in the development of the region. From Harpers Ferry ninety-seven miles westward to Cumberland, Maryland, the B&O traveled through the Potomac River Valley. Still, it took more than twenty years before the railroad reached the Ohio River at Wheeling (1852) because its difficult route through Virginia included long grades, many bridges, and the first long tunnels constructed in America.

During the first two decades of the company's history, a substantial portion of its revenue came from passenger service. But when coal mines began opening around Cumberland and in the mountains west of the city, coal traffic to Baltimore became the railroad's major source of revenue. Efforts to secure additional coal traffic led to the extension of B&O branches or the purchase of small railroads throughout northern Appalachia and expansion as far south as Charleston, West Virginia. Coal traffic became the major source of revenue in the immediate post–Civil War era.

The B&O suffered significant damage during the war, but President John W. Garrett and his employees reopened the line quickly and operated the company at a profit, paying 8 percent dividends on common stock. By the time the war ended, it was in position to expand. This expansion began with construction of large wrought-iron bridges over the Ohio River at Wheeling and Parkersburg. Through a combination of leases and purchases, the B&O reached Columbus, Ohio, Lake Erie, and Pittsburgh (from Cumberland) in 1871. Other lines took the B&O to Philadelphia and to Chicago. At the end of the Civil War, the B&O operated 520 miles of railroad, and by the time Garrett died in 1884, it had expanded to 1,700 miles. Unfortunately, most of this expansion was financed by borrowed money. Furthermore, the B&O had engaged in a series of rate wars with the Pennsylvania, New York Central, and Erie Railroads that reduced profits.

In the decade after Garrett's death, only one of several presidents, Samuel Spencer, attempted to address the B&O's financial problems. Spencer received no support from the board of directors, though, and the quality of the railroad's maintenance and service began to decline rapidly, as did traffic. In 1889 the B&O hauled 31 percent of the nation's Tidewater-bound traffic in soft coal. By 1896 it hauled only 4 percent. The precipitous decline in traffic caused by the 1893 depression forced the B&O, along with many other railroads, into receivership.

The B&O recovered with the return of prosperity in the late 1890s, and it continued to expand, primarily by purchasing or by entering into operating agreements with other railroads. In 1900 it added the 922-mile Baltimore and Ohio Southwestern Railroad, providing a through line from southeastern Ohio to St. Louis, and the Monongahela River Railroad (Fairmont to Clarksburg, West Virginia). In 1901 it began the process of acquiring the Ohio River Railroad from

Wheeling through Parkersburg and Huntington to Kenova. In the 1920s, operating agreements were developed with the Morgantown and Kingwood Railroad and the Coal and Coke Railroad (Elkins to Charleston), essentially completing its routes in West Virginia. All of these railroads were eventually incorporated into the B&O.

After the Pennsylvania Railroad controlled it for a short period in the first decade of the twentieth century, Daniel Willard became president of the B&O in 1910 and held the position until 1941. Willard carried out a major modernization of the system that transformed the B&O into one of the premier American railroads. In the 1920s, the railroad averaged revenues of about $225 million a year with dividends of up to 6 percent. Willard became one of the best-known railroad executives of the century. His fairness to labor won the loyalty of employees, and his combination of conservatism in financial matters and innovation in service (such as air-conditioned passenger cars) endeared him to stockholders and travelers. His service on most of the major transportation boards and commissions of his era reflected the respect of his peers.

The Great Depression of the 1930s hit the B&O harder than most railroads. Barely surviving receivership, it recovered briefly between World War II and the early 1950s, but the decline of the coal industry and increasing competition from other railroads and highways placed the company in a weak financial position by 1960. In 1962, faced with mounting debt, the B&O accepted merger overtures from the Chesapeake and Ohio Railway. The absorption of the oldest common carrier proceeded slowly and was not finalized until 1973. At the start of the twenty-first century, the B&O was part of the vast CSX Transportation system.

See also: CHESAPEAKE AND OHIO RAILWAY; CSX TRANSPORTATION; RAILROADS.

—Robert L. Frey, *University of Charleston (West Virginia)*

Edward Hungerford, *The Story of the Baltimore and Ohio Railroad: 1827–1927* (1928); John F. Stover, *History of the Baltimore and Ohio Railroad* (1987).

Braddock's Road

Braddock's Road holds the distinction of being the first overland route across the Appalachian Mountains. The road stretched between the Potomac River near Cumberland in western Maryland to the Monongahela River at the site of present-day Pittsburgh along an early Native American trace called Nemacolin's Path. Edward Braddock, a British army general, gave the road his name in 1755 during the French and Indian War as a result of his ill-fated assault on Fort Duquesne.

In the spring of 1755, Braddock began his westward march toward Fort Duquesne with approximately twenty-four hundred British and colonial troops. The army progressed slowly, improving and widening the road (to twelve feet) along the way. There are conflicting accounts, however, as to whether Braddock and his men traveled wholly on Braddock's Road or also used the nearby Middle Turnpike. Regardless of how they arrived, Braddock's troops fared poorly against the enemy. On July 9, 1755, a Canadian and French Indian contingent all but eliminated Braddock's troops, and the general died four days later from a battle-inflicted wound. His remaining troops buried his body in the middle of Braddock's Road, where workmen found the remains in 1804. The remains were reinterred on a small knoll adjacent to the road, and in 1913 a marker was placed on the site.

After the war, Braddock's Road remained a major route through the area, and the first settlers to southwestern Pennsylvania used it to reach their destination. The road's prominent location, near the burgeoning town of Cumberland and the Potomac River, prompted the Maryland legislature to pass a series of road improvement acts between 1795 and 1802.

See also: FRENCH AND INDIAN WAR (GOVERNMENT).

—Charlene Howard McDonald, *Universiteit Utrecht, The Netherlands*

Carolina, Clinchfield, and Ohio Railway

Two economic forces brought about the construction of the Carolina, Clinchfield, and Ohio Railway—the desire to connect the southern Atlantic seacoast to the Midwest and the need to ship coal from the mines in southwestern Virginia and eastern Kentucky. The greatest challenge to completion of the rail route was the rugged terrain of the Cumberland and Blue Ridge Mountains. In 1915 the railway succeeded in connecting the southern Ohio River Valley to the Piedmont of South Carolina by completing a line from Elkhorn, Kentucky, to Spartanburg, South Carolina. The 277-mile route cut directly through the southern Appalachians, crossing four mountain ranges and five major watersheds.

The Carolina, Clinchfield, and Ohio built upon previous attempts to cross the mountains. The Louisville, Cincinnati, and Charleston Railroad (chartered in 1836) had attempted to build a line connecting Cincinnati and Charleston, South Carolina, but the venture failed after only 18 miles of track had been constructed. In 1886 the Charleston, Cincinnati, and Chicago Railroad, headed by General John T. Wilder, proposed building a 625-mile rail line from Ironton, Ohio, to Charleston with a connector to Cincinnati. The "3-C," as it is commonly known, began at its headquarters in Johnson City, Tennessee, and constructed the line both

Railroad crew on the Carolina, Clinchfield, and Ohio in Dante, Virginia, 1908. From 1865 to World War I, railroad construction increased rapidly in the region. One of the most expensive railroads ever built in America, the Carolina, Clinchfield, and Ohio passed through five states and ranged in elevation from 741 feet near Spartanburg, South Carolina, to 2,628 feet at Ridge Tunnel in the Blue Ridge Mountains.

north and south. The tracks reached Erwin, Tennessee, in 1890, and the grading for the line to Dante, Virginia, was nearly complete when the railroad failed in the economic depression of 1893.

In that year Charles E. Hellier purchased the assets of the 3-C and organized the Ohio River and Charleston Railway Company. The Ohio River and Charleston Railway extended the line through the Nolichucky Gorge (near the Tennessee–North Carolina border) to Boonford, North Carolina, and planned an extension to the Big Sandy River in Kentucky. By 1897, Hellier began selling segments of the road. George Lafayette Carter purchased the section from Johnson City to Boonford in 1902 and began the South and Western Railway.

Carter's primary objective was to construct a railroad that could connect the coalfields in southwestern Virginia and Kentucky and ship coal through the mountains to southern Atlantic ports. With financial backing from a syndicate of New York bankers, primarily Blair and Company, Carter extended the route south through Spruce Pine, North Carolina. In 1905 he began simultaneous construction north of Johnson City and south of Spruce Pine using the old roadbeds of the 3-C Railroad. The Carolina, Clinchfield, and Ohio Railway, chartered in 1908, consolidated the South and Western Railway with smaller lines including the Lick Creek and Lake Erie, the Clinchfield Northern, and the Elkhorn Southern. One year later, the railway connected Dante to Spartanburg and by 1915 finished a 35-mile extension to Elkhorn. The first Carolina, Clinchfield, and Ohio coal train pulled into Spartanburg on December 9, 1909, followed by the first passenger train two days later.

When completed, the five-state route passed through fifty-five tunnels totaling nearly 10 miles, crossed more than 17,000 feet of bridges, and ranged in elevation from 741 feet at the Pacolet River (near Spartanburg) to 2,628 feet at Ridge Tunnel in the Blue Ridge Mountains. M. J. Caples, chief engineer and general manager of the South and Western Railway in 1905, convinced Carter to build the railroad to much higher engineering standards than usual in anticipation of heavy loads of coal. The construction established a precedent of tunneling through mountains rather than building low-grade roadbeds skirting rugged terrain. Following the principle of maintaining the grade in spite of construction costs or engineering difficulties, the engineers constructed a road with a maximum grade of 1.7 percent for southbound traffic and 1.5 percent for northbound traffic. In most instances, curves on the road were limited to ten degrees or less, even though 43 percent of the track was curved. Tunnels and bridges were built to standards that have allowed them to remain in use.

On October 16, 1924, the Atlantic Coast Line Railroad and the Louisville and Nashville Railroad leased the properties of the Carolina, Clinchfield, and Ohio Railway for 999 years. The agreement gave Atlantic Coast Line direct connections to existing coal mines in Virginia and Kentucky and relieved the Louisville and Nashville's shortage of cars serving coal-mining areas. Through this agreement, the railway continued operation under the name of Clinchfield Railroad.

The Clinchfield Railroad is known for hauling coal, which for many years accounted for nearly half of its revenue. The first coal train to arrive in Spartanburg in 1909 consisted of seven cars, but with the introduction of diesel locomotives, trains grew to a standard of ninety cars carrying 1,100 tons of coal. In 1982 Clinchfield handled 21 million tons of coal. Merchandise accounted for most of the remaining revenue, with passenger and mail service accounting for less than 10 percent. Passenger train service declined during the 1930s and 1940s and ended in 1955. Clinchfield continued the Santa Claus Special service, however, sending a train from Elkhorn south to Kingsport, Tennessee, on the Friday after Thanksgiving. Along the way it distributes candy and small gifts to children gathered along the tracks.

On November 1, 1980, the Interstate Commerce Commission approved a merger between the Clinchfield Railroad Company and the Chessie System to become the Clinchfield Division of the Seaboard System Railroad. The Seaboard System was part of CSX Transportation, and in 1982 CSX purchased the outstanding Clinchfield Railroad stock. On January 1, 1983, the Clinchfield Railroad ceased to exist.

See also: CARTER, GEORGE LAFAYETTE (BUSINESS, INDUSTRY, AND TECHNOLOGY); CSX TRANSPORTATION; RAILROADS.

—Norma Myers, *East Tennessee State University*

James A. Goforth, *Building the Clinchfield: A Construction History of America's Most Unusual Railroad* (1983); Steve King, *Clinchfield Country* (1988); William Way Jr., *The Clinchfield Railroad: The Story of a Trade Route across the Blue Ridge Mountains* (1931).

Casselman River Bridge

Congress authorized the creation of the Cumberland Road in 1806 to connect the eastern United States to the Ohio River. Construction of the road began at Cumberland, Maryland, in 1811 and was completed to the Ohio River at Wheeling, (West) Virginia, by 1818. The National Road, as it became known, was the nation's first federally funded and designed "interstate" highway. In 1813 in what is today Garrett County, Maryland, an 80-foot single-span stone arch bridge was laid over the Casselman River, becoming an important link along the National Road. The largest of its type in America, the Casselman River Bridge stands at the location named "Little Crossings" by George Washington in 1755 while on his march to Fort Duquesne during the French and Indian War. Built with 3-foot-thick walls and locally quarried stone, the bridge's entire length measures 354 feet, and it has more than 30 feet of clearance, a 26-foot right-of-way, and 48-foot-wide entrances.

Some felt the arch would collapse once the supporting timbers were removed. According to legend, the road superintendent had the key timbers quietly removed the night before the public opening. The next day, he stood beneath the arch and proclaimed that, if the bridge fell, he might as well be dead. The bridge stood, and it served continuously from 1813 to 1933, when a new steel bridge was constructed along adjacent Route 40. In 1954 the bridge was closed to all vehicular traffic. It is now the focal point of a state park.

See also: NATIONAL ROAD (SETTLEMENT AND MIGRATION).

—Albert L. Feldstein, *LaVale, Maryland*

Chesapeake and Ohio Canal

In an effort to remain economically competitive with northern cities such as Philadelphia and New York during the 1820s, Marylanders pursued a variety of internal improvement schemes designed to connect the ports of the lower Potomac River with the natural resources and waterways of Appalachia and the Midwest. One such project involved constructing a canal connecting Georgetown in the east with Maryland's Appalachian region and, beyond that, the upper Ohio River—a distance of some 342 miles. The endeavor was an especially ambitious one given the number of locks that had to be built to negotiate the rise from the Tidewater to an elevation of approximately three thousand feet.

Prior to this undertaking, the Patowmack Company had sought to extend navigation to the upper Potomac River. While navigation on the lower portion of the river was improved, the project ultimately ended in failure, and efforts to find another transportation link were initiated. In 1825 the Patowmack Company—saddled with substantial debt—relinquished its charter to the Chesapeake and Ohio Canal Company, which in 1828 also obtained its properties as well. On July 4, 1828, construction of the Chesapeake and Ohio Canal began in earnest.

Labor unrest and a lack of adequate funding ensured that the canal would never make it all the way to the Ohio. In 1850 the canal reached its western terminus at Cumberland, Maryland, 185 miles upriver from Georgetown. Within a short while, the economic benefits of the canal were felt. Along with agricultural products and other assorted goods, the canal was a major carrier of western Maryland's renowned George's Creek coal. Aided by an improved canal boat capable of hauling double the quantity previously possible, coal shipments increased considerably during the post–Civil War era. Between 1865 and 1885, the Chesapeake and Ohio Canal never carried fewer than 300,000 tons of coal per year. A record 904,898 tons were transported in 1875, the greatest coal trade for a year in the history of the canal company.

In some ways, the canal was a success; in other ways, it was not. With regard to comparative costs, the canal provided what the National Road could not—economical long-distance transportation. Indeed, by the second half of the nineteenth century, shipment by canal was particularly cost-effective. In 1860 the cost of transporting goods on America's turnpikes was fifteen dollars per ton-mile. By contrast, the cost of transporting coal on the Chesapeake and Ohio Canal was twenty-five cents per ton-mile. In the end, however, the Chesapeake and Ohio Canal could not emulate the success of the Erie Canal. Nor could it compete favorably with an even newer form of transportation—the railroad. Ironically, groundbreaking ceremonies for the Baltimore and Ohio Railroad, America's first commercial line, took place on the very same day in 1828 that construction of the canal was inaugurated. With more solid financial backing and fewer engineering obstacles to overcome, the Baltimore and Ohio reached Cumberland in 1842, eight years ahead of the canal. In 1924 a powerful flood destroyed large sections of the old canal, forcing it to cease operation.

The story of the Chesapeake and Ohio Canal does not end in 1924, however. In 1938 the Baltimore and Ohio Railroad, which had acquired the canal while it was still in service, sold it to the federal government for two million dollars. Under National Park Service supervision, the Civilian Conservation Corps restored and re-watered the twenty-two-mile section between Georgetown and Seneca, Maryland, for recreational use. After an October 1942 flood ravaged the canal again, plans to restore additional sections of the canal were put on hold. In 1945 the U.S. Army Corps of Engineers proposed to construct a series of reservoirs along the Potomac River that would have flooded large portions of the canal. In 1950 the National Park Service, which opposed the project, threw its support behind an alternative plan that would have converted most of the canal into a scenic parkway. Although this plan was popular among residents in economically distressed western Maryland, the plan was ultimately defeated when, in 1954, Supreme Court Justice William O. Douglas, accompanied by a coterie of conservationists and journalists, led a well-publicized protest march along the canal's entire route from Cumberland to Washington, D.C. Both the Corps of Engineers and parkway proposals were eventually defeated, and in 1971 the canal was accorded national historical park status.

See also: BALTIMORE AND OHIO RAILROAD; CHESAPEAKE AND OHIO CANAL NATIONAL HISTORICAL PARK (TOURISM); OHIO RIVER.

—Geoffrey L. Buckley, *Ohio University*

Barry MacKintosh, *C & O Canal: The Making of a Park* (1991); James F. Simon, *Independent Journey: The Life of William O. Douglas* (1980); George Rogers Taylor, *The Transportation Revolution, 1815–1860* (1951).

Chesapeake and Ohio Railway

The Chesapeake and Ohio (C&O) Railway, created by an 1868 merger of the Virginia Central, the Blue Ridge, and the Covington and Ohio Railroads, was a major force in the development of coal transportation in northern and central Appalachia.

The intention of the C&O was to build a line linking Richmond, Virginia, with the Ohio River, but a lack of capital in the aftermath of the Civil War delayed completion of the railroad, and by 1869 the C&O had run out of money. The company needed to attract broad-based financial support to continue construction, and its officers approached Collis P. Huntington, nationally known for his leadership in completing the western section of the first transcontinental railroad. Huntington agreed to take over the construction of the C&O. His contacts with international financial interests expedited the sale of bonds necessary to continue expansion and led to his control of the company.

Huntington's motives in assuming the leadership of an underfinanced railroad of only local significance are obvious in historical hindsight, but they were probably not clear to many people of his day. Huntington believed the C&O could be the eastern link of a great transcontinental railroad empire, the Southern Pacific route from New Orleans to San Francisco being the western portion. Construction moved rapidly, and by January 29, 1873, the C&O was completed through the central Appalachians from Richmond to the confluence of the Big Sandy and Ohio Rivers. A line was also constructed into Lexington, Kentucky. Construction through the mountains of western Virginia and the new state of West Virginia was challenging. At some points the line ran through the New River Valley in areas so inaccessible that workers were lowered into the gorge in baskets to reach the area where the railroad was being constructed. The legendary John Henry of "steel-drivin'" fame reputedly labored on this stretch of line. But the cost of this construction and the rapid extension of the line drove the company into bankruptcy. It was reorganized in 1878 as the C&O Railway with Huntington still in control.

After reorganization Huntington spearheaded the creation of several railroads to link the C&O at Lexington with the Southern Pacific at New Orleans via Memphis. Other extensions continued as well. On the eastern end of the C&O, the main line was extended from Richmond to the seaport at Newport News, an extremely important extension for the C&O. In 1888 the C&O was constructed into Cincinnati, but by this time investors were turning to other more promising rail projects, and the C&O's expansion caused it to run out of money again. This time Huntington's empire collapsed, and his role in the C&O ended.

Financier J. P. Morgan picked up the pieces and sent one of his major railroad reorganization experts, Melville E. Ingalls, to rescue the company. His leadership provided much needed stability, and with the financial support of the Morgan interests the C&O regained its financial solvency and continued to expand—but in a more careful fashion. Ingalls finalized control of the Richmond and Allegheny, a railroad with a low-grade line running from Richmond via Lynchburg to Clifton Forge, Virginia, a few miles east of Covington. This line provided favorable grades for the C&O's heavy freight trains. Ingalls also gained access to Washington, D.C., by negotiating trackage rights over a predecessor of the Southern Railway. By 1900 the C&O had more than doubled the mileage it operated in 1888; new locomotives and rolling stock had been purchased; the line had been ballasted and relaid with heavier rails; and the company paid a one-dollar-per-share dividend annually.

After the turn of the century, the population growth of the Midwest made the region an attractive market for the coal mined along the C&O. To assure access to this area, the C&O gradually absorbed the Hocking Valley Railroad after 1905. Control of this railroad gave the C&O connections to Columbus and Toledo, Ohio. Organization of the Chesapeake and Ohio of Indiana and construction of the Chesapeake and Ohio Northern eventually gave the C&O access to Chicago and the Great Lakes. Temporary control of the Kanawha and Michigan (later a part of the New York Central) linked the Hocking Valley with the C&O main line in Charleston, West Virginia.

Unlike many American railroads, the C&O did not suffer extensive damage while operated by the United States Railroad Administration during World War I. After the war the C&O went through several leadership changes before ending up under the direction of brothers Oris P. and Mantis J. Van Sweringen, two colorful real estate developers in Cleveland. The Van Sweringens attempted to combine the C&O, the Erie, the Pere Marquette, and the Nickel Plate into one major railroad system. The headquarters of the C&O were moved from Richmond to Cleveland despite the fact that C&O rails did not enter Cleveland. The Interstate Commerce Commission refused to allow the merger and the Van Sweringen empire was eventually disbanded, but the C&O did acquire a controlling interest in the Pere Marquette Railroad, operating primarily in Michigan.

Because of coal traffic, the C&O survived the Great Depression better than most railroads. From 1937 to 1954, under the direction of Robert R. Young, the railroad grew to a 5,100-mile system with thirty-five thousand employees and an annual revenue of $319 million. In 1962, with Walter J. Tuohy as president, the C&O acquired the faltering Baltimore and Ohio Railroad in a contest with the New York Central, which had earlier wanted to merge with the C&O. It was not until 1973 that the C&O, the Baltimore and Ohio Railroad, and the Western Maryland Railroad were merged together into the Chessie System. In 1980 the current CSX Corporation was created by merging the Chessie System and the Seaboard Coast Line System, itself a merger of the Seaboard Air Line, the Atlantic Coast Line, and the Louisville and Nashville Railroads.

See also: BALTIMORE AND OHIO RAILROAD; CSX TRANSPORTATION; RAILROADS.

—Robert L. Frey, *University of Charleston (West Virginia)*

Charles W. Turner, *Chessie's Road* (1956).

Combs, Bert

See Combs, Bert (Government)

Covered Bridges

See Truss Bridges

CSX Transportation

CSX, one of two dominant Appalachian railroads operating at the beginning of the twenty-first century, is a successor to the Chessie System. A holding company developed by the Chesapeake and Ohio Railway in 1973, the Chessie System was composed of the Chesapeake and Ohio, the Baltimore and Ohio, and the Western Maryland Railroads. The acronym *CSX* stands for Chessie, Seaboard, and many times more.

Aware of the problems in acquiring a railroad with such an illustrious history, the Chesapeake and Ohio did not want to move too rapidly in eliminating the identity of the Baltimore and Ohio. Until 1972 the two railroads operated independently and maintained separate corporate identities. In 1973 the Chessie System was created to hold the stock of the Chesapeake and Ohio, the Baltimore and Ohio, and the Western Maryland Railroads. Efforts were made to develop a "family" of the three railroads, and it was not until 1976 that the corporate identity of the Baltimore and Ohio began to disappear.

Responding to continuing merger efforts on the part of the Norfolk and Western Railway, its most direct competitor, the Chessie System continued to look for other merger partners. With the Southern Railway System moving closer to a merger with the Norfolk and Western, the other major railroad system in Appalachia was the loose affiliation of lines known as the "Family Lines"—the Seaboard Coast Line (which had absorbed the Atlantic Coast Line) and the Louisville and Nashville Railroad (which had absorbed the Nashville, Chattanooga, and St. Louis Railroad).

On November 1, 1980, the Chessie System and the Seaboard Coast Line–Louisville and Nashville Railroad joined to create the CSX Corporation. This was a complex merger, and the two systems remained somewhat separate for a time. It was not until 1982 that the Louisville and Nashville was actually merged into the Seaboard Coast Line. By the late 1980s, the merger was complete. Little remained of the former railroads, including the Baltimore and Ohio. Rapid line abandonment took place, eliminating, for instance, most of the Western Maryland.

In retrospect, the combination of the Chesapeake and Ohio and Baltimore and Ohio Railroads, and later the Chessie System and the Seaboard Coast Line, was accomplished successfully. Because the individual companies were gradually combined, operations were generally efficient. By the mid-1990s, however, there was evidence that CSX had cut costs to the point that track and equipment were being inadequately maintained. Numerous accidents in Appalachia—in West Virginia, in particular—caused the Federal Railroad Administration to compile a report that led to a compliance agreement on April 20, 2000. CSX promised to improve repair and maintenance of its track and equipment.

By the time this agreement was signed, another merger had taken place. In the mid-1990s, Norfolk Southern, a corporation resulting from the merger of the Norfolk and Western and the Southern Railway System, attempted to acquire Conrail, a merger of Penn Central and several other eastern railroads. CSX protested vigorously, and the result was an arrangement that divided Conrail's lines between CSX and Norfolk Southern. In order to maintain competition, numerous special arrangements were made before the absorption of Conrail was complete, but in May 1999 the division took place and CSX acquired significant additional track mileage.

Initially, the CSX-Conrail merger was less successful than the two earlier ones. CSX proved incapable of keeping traffic moving. On-time performances dropped below 50 percent in early 2000, compared to more than 80 percent prior to the merger. The influx of Conrail managers to CSX that took place prior to the merger (in hopes that it would smooth the process) was reversed in early 2000 as many of the former Conrail executives were ousted. After mid-2000, however, the performance of the railroad improved.

Most Appalachian coal is hauled to the Tidewater for shipment abroad, although some of the highest-quality bituminous coal continues to be shipped to eastern and midwestern power plants. But CSX is no longer primarily a coal-hauling railroad. Manufactured goods, forest products, chemicals, and agricultural products comprise a large part of the freight tonnage shipped over the system. Heavy competition from strip-mined western coal makes dependence on more costly eastern coal uneconomical.

Although the U.S. Surface Transportation Board placed a fifteen-month moratorium on railroad mergers in 1999, one more round of mergers among the seven Class I North American railroads appeared likely. The most probable scenario seemed to be for Norfolk Southern and Burlington Northern Santa Fe to merge (also including Kansas City Southern and Canadian National), thus leaving CSX to merge with Union Pacific (also including Canadian Pacific). CSX and Union Pacific, while not in favor of further mergers, could be forced into a merger because of the more aggressive merger philosophy of the Burlington Northern Santa Fe.

The Chesapeake and Ohio Railway, the Chessie System, and CSX Transportation have been essential components of Appalachia for more than 150 years. CSX continues to transport items produced in Appalachia all over the nation and brings essential items into the region. Many families in Appalachia have been supported by jobs with these railroads. Although the number of workers has declined, the influence of this railroad system is still extremely significant.

See also: CHESAPEAKE AND OHIO RAILWAY; RAILROADS.

—Robert L. Frey, *University of Charleston (West Virginia)*

Charles W. Turner, *Chessie's Road* (1956).

Forbes Road

Forbes Road, stretching from Philadelphia across the Alleghenies to Fort Duquesne in present-day Pittsburgh, began as a Native American trade route and was initially known as the Old Trading Path. It later became a strategic military thoroughfare and eventually a prominent pioneer route between the East and the Ohio basin.

John Forbes, an English general, first utilized the path as a military supply line in April 1758 during the French and Indian War. The original wagon segment of Forbes Road ended at Fort Loudon, west of Chambersburg, Pennsylvania. There Forbes and his chief assistant, Henry Bouquet, enlisted Colonel George Washington to help construct a through road to the French-occupied Fort Duquesne. Washington and Bouquet disagreed on the new road's location, as Washington wanted to use the existing Braddock's Road and Forbes faced pressure from area settlers to build the new road through their territory. Ultimately, Forbes's choice of alignment prevailed. The road was completed in November 1758, when Forbes's weary army reached Fort Duquesne.

Later known as the Pennsylvania Road, Forbes Road became one of the most prominent westward routes between 1775 and 1815. Improvements such as grading and bridges helped increase road usage. By the turn of the nineteenth century, Forbes Road carried heavy volumes of both freight and passenger wagons. The section of Forbes Road between Philadelphia and Lancaster was one of the first roads paved with macadam, or layers of stone that have been compacted into a solid mass and sealed with tar or asphalt, in the United States.

See also: BRADDOCK'S ROAD; FRENCH AND INDIAN WAR (GOVERNMENT).

—Charlene Howard McDonald, *Universiteit Utrecht, The Netherlands*

Great Valley Road

See Great Valley Road (Settlement and Migration)

Hocking River and Canal

The Hocking River drains a 1,682-square-mile area of southeastern Ohio. Along its course, it passes through two of Appalachian Ohio's earliest settlements, Lancaster and Athens. Rising southeast of Columbus, it follows a meandering path for nearly a hundred miles before joining the Ohio River at Hockingport. Declared a navigable stream by the state legislature in 1808, the Hocking was easier to legislate than navigate. Because of erratic flow, rocks, and snags, early river traffic was limited to flatboats carrying agricultural products downstream to the Ohio River.

When Ohio's initial phase of canal construction bypassed the Hocking Valley, entrepreneurs from Lancaster underwrote a lateral connection to the Ohio and Erie Canal. The Lancaster Lateral Canal, completed in 1834, joined the Ohio and Erie Canal. Wheat, flour, and pork packed in barrels were the primary commodities moving on the canal. Mining interests and communities downstream from Lancaster persuaded the State of Ohio to extend the canal to Athens. Completed in 1843, at a cost of nearly a million dollars, the canal was fifty-six miles in length, required thirty-one locks, and included an eighty-foot aqueduct. Along its route, the Hocking Canal stimulated manufacturing activities such as flour milling and salt making. It played an important role in the development of coal mining in the Hocking Valley and in connecting this segment of Appalachian Ohio to national markets. Floods, poor management, and railroads spelled the end of the canal, however, and it was abandoned for navigation in 1894.

See also: OHIO RIVER.

—David T. Stephens, *Youngstown State University*

Huntington, Collis P.

(1821–1900) Railroad magnate.

Best known for his role in building the transcontinental railroad, Collis Potter Huntington also extended the Chesapeake and Ohio Railway across the Appalachian Mountains during the 1870s. The site he chose for its Ohio River terminus eventually became the city of Huntington, West Virginia.

Born October 22, 1821, the sixth child of a poor Connecticut farm couple, Huntington left school at thirteen, traveled about peddling watches, clocks, silverware, costume jewelry, and other easily transportable items, and became a partner in his brother's general store in Oneonta, New York. In 1849 he followed the gold rush to California to sell shovels to miners. Soon he had a thriving hardware store in Sacramento.

With three associates, Huntington organized the Central Pacific Railroad in 1861. He lobbied aggressively for coast-to-coast rail connections. This goal of a transcontinental railroad was finally achieved when the Central Pacific met the Union Pacific in Utah in 1869.

His other railroad investments included the former Virginia Central Railroad, renamed the Chesapeake and Ohio to reflect plans for expansion. Inspecting possible sites for its Ohio River terminus in 1870, Huntington chose a tract of West Virginia farmland called Holderby's Landing. The new city incorporated as Huntington in 1871, and the railroad arrived two years later. By 1884, the Chesapeake and Ohio's lines stretched from Newport News, Virginia, to the Mississippi River to connect with other Huntington lines to California.

Often accused of being unscrupulous, as well as financially shrewd, Huntington was condemned by journalists and investigated by Congress. He died August 13, 1900, at Raquette Lake, New York.

See also: CHESAPEAKE AND OHIO RAILWAY; HUNTINGTON, WEST VIRGINIA (URBAN APPALACHIAN EXPERIENCE); RAILROADS.

—Sarah Gibbard Cook, *DeForest, Wisconsin*

James River and Kanawha Canal

The James River and Kanawha Canal project was the Commonwealth of Virginia's bid to capture western trade by connecting the port of Norfolk and the Tidewater James River to the rivers of present-day West Virginia to the Ohio River. Construction began in 1836 under the leadership of Joseph Carrington Cabell. By 1840, 150 miles of canal had been completed between Richmond and Lynchburg, Virginia. Ten years later, the canal was extended another 50 miles to Buchanan, Virginia.

Although extensive engineering studies were developed to push the James River and Kanawha Canal system across the Allegheny Mountains to complete the connection with the Greenbrier, New, and Kanawha Rivers, Buchanan remained its westernmost terminus. The massive construction cost of Virginia's waterway west was too great a burden for the limited financial resources of the state. Although freight barges and passenger packets plied its waters for forty years, the James River and Kanawha Canal never generated a profit for its investors because the linkage to the rich agricultural and mineral resources of the western states was not realized.

The height of activity on the James River and Kanawha Canal occurred in the 1850s. However, railroads, not water transportation, were the wave of the future. Although the canal served as a vital transportation artery for the Confederacy during the Civil War, it could not compete with the extensive railroad system developed after hostilities ended in 1865. After a fifteen-year struggle to survive, the canal's assets were sold to the Richmond and Allegheny Railroad in 1880.

See also: KANAWHA RIVER; OHIO RIVER.

—Langherne Gibson, *Richmond, Virginia*

Kanawha River

The bustling Kanawha Waterway moves coal, aggregates, chemical, and other bulky items from the Kanawha Valley of West Virginia to the Ohio River navigation system. So successful has been this "canalization" of the river into slack water pools connected by locks and dams that a new 800-by-110-foot lock was opened in 1998 at Winfield, West Virginia, to handle increasing barge traffic. The lock has become one of the busiest locks in the entire U.S. Army Corps of Engineers inland waterway system. A similar large-scale lock at Marmet to improve the movement of barges in the upper reaches of the river was under consideration at the beginning of the twenty-first century.

Interest in the Kanawha River for navigational purposes dates to colonial times, when leading Virginians, most notably George Washington, sought to connect the Chesapeake Bay with the Ohio by means of a canal from the eastern-flowing James River to the westward-flowing Kanawha. Virginia interests were also intrigued with the possibility of a canal from Tidewater Virginia to Ohio utilizing the Potomac and the tributaries of rivers that formed the Ohio at Pittsburgh.

One of the essential characteristics of the early United States was a strong commitment to internal improvements. What developed was not a national system under the aegis of the federal government, however, but an intensely competitive scene with every East Coast port from Boston to Norfolk involved in schemes to establish connection with the Ohio River or the Great Lakes.

Among other projects, the clamor for internal improvements prompted the formation of the James River and Kanawha Canal Company in Virginia. After much struggle the James River and Kanawha Canal was made navigable to Cowpasture River near Clifton Forge, on the eastern slopes of the Appalachians. Limited improvements were also made below the falls of the Kanawha as far as its mouth at Point Pleasant. The missing link over the mountains was completed by a turnpike road, but the commonwealth remained committed to the canal project until the eve of the Civil War.

Following the Civil War, the vision of a state-supported waterway was expanded into a grand scheme of a central waterway stretching from Chesapeake Bay to the foothills of the Rocky Mountains by way of the Ohio and Missouri Rivers. Realizing that state-supported plan would never be sufficient, the federal government became involved in this national vision, and the U.S. Army Corps of Engineers reported favorably on the project's feasibility.

With the grand vision still alive, an essential link in the central waterway was undertaken to improve the Kanawha River by means of a series of locks and dams. The improvement would open the abundant natural resources of the valley to river traffic, serving both regional purposes and linking the Kanawha River to the Ohio navigation system.

River men wanted what seemed to be impossible: a system to move timber rafts and other large vessels during favorable river levels as well as one that would provide the benefits of a slack water system of dams during periods of low flow. In a significant example of technology transfer, the French movable dam system, developed by Jacques Chanoine of the French Corps of Engineers in 1852, was adopted. A series of wickets (panels) were placed side-by-side and mounted on a concrete base in a manner permitting them to be dropped flat on the base, allowing vessels to pass over the dam unimpeded. During times of low flows in the river, when wickets were up, locks would enable vessels to move from one slack water pool to the next.

The proposed system consisted of twelve dams and twin locks at each site. With little prospect for the Central Water Line developing, the first lock at the falls of the Kanawha was omitted. In an ingenious move, number twelve lock and dam was moved onto the Ohio River just below the confluence of the Kanawha and Ohio Rivers to form a slack water pool in both rivers. The remaining ten locks and dams were completed at the end of the nineteenth century, creating the first "canalized" river in America.

By the end of the 1920s, the dams on the earliest two locks and dams had deteriorated to such an extent that replacement was necessary. This situation led to the adoption of the German roller-gate system at four new high-level dam locations, replacing all ten of the original movable dams. The roller gates, while featuring movable roller gates to control the pool levels and pass floodwaters as necessary, did not permit open navigation, as had their predecessors. Thus, all traffic would pass through the lock at each of the dam sites. With the design ready for construction, proponents of the New Deal identified the roller-gate lock and dam project as a worthwhile project to fund, in part because the design would allow construction to begin quickly, providing numerous jobs for unemployed men in the area. The project comprised three locks and dams at London, Marmet, and Winfield on the Kanawha River together with a roller-gated dam at Gallipolis on the Ohio.

The Kanawha River waterway has proved to be a great asset to the economy of the Kanawha Valley and in a larger sense a vital link of the Ohio River system.

See also: JAMES RIVER AND KANAWHA CANAL; OHIO RIVER.

—Emory L. Kemp, *West Virginia University*

Wayland F. Dunaway, *History of the James River and Kanawha Company* (1922); Leland R. Johnson, *Men, Mountains, and Rivers: An Illustrated History of the Huntington District, U.S. Army Corps of Engineers, 1754–1974* (1977); Emory L. Kemp, *The Great Kanawha Navigation* (2000).

Linn Cove Viaduct

The Blue Ridge Parkway transverses the forests of Grandfather Mountain in North Carolina by way of the Linn Cove Viaduct, an elevated roadway spanning 1,243 feet and made up of 153 fifty-ton segments. Only one of the segments in the viaduct is straight; others curve in order to follow the contours of the mountain.

The section of the Blue Ridge Parkway that traverses Grandfather Mountain was the last section of the scenic highway to be built. The other sections were completed between 1935 and 1967. Environmental and private property concerns led to numerous delays in completing the final section, and it was not until 1979 that construction of the Linn Cove Viaduct commenced.

The structure's designer, Eugene Figg Jr., overcame numerous obstacles to complete the viaduct. In addition to negotiating the rugged terrain, Figg was required to construct his roadway in a way that would have the least impact on the sensitive environment of Grandfather Mountain. Accordingly, the bridge was placed into position one segment at a time from a gantry crane system extended from a previously completed segment. In this way, the construction crew avoided damaging trees, rocks, or other parts of the natural surroundings.

The Linn Cove Viaduct was completed in 1983, but it took nearly four more years for the final section of the parkway leading up to the structure to be finished. The viaduct was officially opened on September 11, 1987.

See also: BLUE RIDGE PARKWAY (TOURISM); GRANDFATHER MOUNTAIN (TOURISM).

—John Hairr, *Lillington, North Carolina*

Louisville and Nashville Railroad

The Louisville and Nashville Railroad (L&N), a major line running through central and southern Appalachia, was created to channel trade from the upper South into Louisville, Kentucky. Its original main lines—from Louisville south to Nashville and thence to Montgomery, Alabama, and New Orleans, as well as a branch west to Memphis—were located primarily to the west of the Appalachians. However, the later main line (from Cincinnati through Knoxville, Tennessee, down to north Georgia), as well as a connection with the Atlantic and Western Railroad to Atlanta, operated through much of central and southern Appalachia. Branches running east of Winchester, Kentucky, and Knoxville tapped coal resources in the region.

Begun in 1850, construction of the line was slow, and the entire 185-mile route between Louisville and Nashville did not begin operation until November 1859. The L&N prospered during the Civil War because it tied Kentucky, a border state, with Tennessee, a Confederate state. The military forces of both sides needed the railroad as they moved back and forth in combat through the area. If one side destroyed the railroad, the other side tended to rebuild it quickly. The crucial location of the line allowed the L&N to charge high rates. Consequently, the company paid dividends as high as 12 percent to stockholders in 1864. In addition, it managed to purchase more locomotives and rolling stock of the best quality. At the war's end, the company had a modern, well-maintained system that continued to make substantial profits.

The L&N escaped the worst financial problems of the Panic of 1873, although it ceased paying dividends for several years. This success attracted the interest of northern financiers, who took a more significant role in managing the company. Along with new capital came greater control from northern interests, and expansion continued. The pace of expansion could not be sustained, however, even with the infusion of northern capital. Faced with a huge debt, the L&N barely avoided receivership in 1884 by suspending dividends and reducing expansion for several years. But the most important event of 1884 was the succession of Milton H. Smith to the presidency of the railroad, a position he held for thirty-two of the next thirty-seven years (1884–86, 1891–1921). His leadership led to slower expansion and greater emphasis on financial stability.

In 1902 the L&N came under the control of J. P. Morgan's empire. Morgan, however, did not retain control of the railroad for long, selling his shares, which amounted to 51 percent of the L&N, to the Atlantic Coast Line. Under Smith's presidency the L&N maintained its independence, despite Atlantic Coast Line ownership. In the next decade, additional track was added east of the Cincinnati-Knoxville line, most of it in central Appalachia, where the L&N tapped coal reserves and linked up with the Norfolk and Western Railway in Norton, Virginia. By 1910 coal was L&N's major source of traffic, followed by agricultural, manufactured, and timber products. Most of the coal flowed on the excellent double-tracked main line from L&N branches in Harlan County to Corbin, Kentucky, and then north to Cincinnati.

President Smith was primarily interested in moving freight and disliked passenger service. Consequently, from 1880 to 1920 the L&N's passenger trains were poorly equipped and frequently sidetracked to keep more profitable freight trains moving. Public criticism meant little to Smith, who fought any form of government regulation at the state or federal level with unusual ferocity. Smith also believed that his railroad could produce steam locomotives less expensively than the major builders. Between 1905 and 1923, the South Louisville shops produced four hundred locomotives of the 2-8-0, 2-8-2, 4-6-2, and 0-8-0 types, using interchangeable parts as much as possible. (The numbers identify the type of locomotive and refer to the number of leading wheels starting at the front of the locomotive, followed by the number of driving wheels and trailing wheels.)

In 1931 the L&N reached its operational peak, with more than 5,200 miles in use. Although able to avoid some of the worst financial difficulties in earlier depressions, the L&N suffered extensively during the Great Depression of the 1930s. Traffic declined throughout the system, and improvements to the line and purchase of new equipment ceased for more than a decade. From 1930 to 1942, no new steam locomotives were acquired. But the obsolete steam fleet could not handle World War II traffic demands, and between 1942 and 1949 a fleet of forty-two 2-8-4 Berkshire-type steam locomotives were purchased to handle heavy freight trains, most of which carried coal. At the same time, the line began to purchase diesel-electric locomotives and in 1956 was one of the first major railroads to dieselize.

Because the Atlantic Coast Line and the Seaboard Air Line served much of the same territory, by the late 1950s plans for a merger were being devised. Although approved in 1967, these two railroads and the L&N continued to operate in a significantly separate manner and were known as the "Family Lines." Eventually the Family Lines merged with the Chessie System to form the CSX system in 1980, but it was not until 1982 that a complete merger of the lines was legally completed.

Prior to the 1960s, the L&N and the Southern Railway were the two key railroads of south-central and southern Appalachia. The L&N served the area from the west, while the Southern served the area from the east. The L&N depended heavily on Appalachian coal, while the Southern was more oriented towards passenger service. Both lines had a major affect on the economy and people of Appalachia.

See also: RAILROADS.

—Robert L. Frey, *University of Charleston (West Virginia)*

Kincaid A. Herr, *The Louisville and Nashville Railroad, 1850–1963* (1964); Maury Klein, *History of the Louisville and Nashville Railroad* (1972).

Morgantown Monorail

West Virginia University's Personal Rapid Transit, or Morgantown Monorail, is considered one of the more innovative recent transportation systems built in either the Appalachian region or the United States. Since its introduction, the system has received national recognition on several occasions. For example, in 1972 it was named one of the nation's ten best engineering achievements by the National Society of Professional Engineers. In July 2001, Samy E. G. Elias won the Henry Gantt Medallion Award from the Institute of Industrial Engineers for its design.

Powered by electricity and guided by computers, the Morgantown Monorail was designed to alleviate traffic congestion as well as pollution. Its design and implementation came during a time of increased concern among Americans about air quality and the nation's dependence upon foreign oil. The mass transit system gained federal approval in July 1969, and its first phase was dedicated on October 24, 1972. Tricia Nixon, daughter of then-President Richard Nixon, attended the dedication ceremony and rode in one of the monorail's cars during its first demonstration run.

The original grants to cover costs related to developing, studying, and constructing the Morgantown Monorail totaled $123.6 million, and the system has been upgraded several times since. In 1998 the monorail's main computer system was replaced, and other improvements were made for an additional $5.2 million. Also, on September 6, 2002, U.S. Senator Robert C. Byrd's office announced that the U.S. Department of Transportation had released an additional $3.97 million to replace the system's thirty-year-old heating system for melting ice and snow on its guideway.

By its thirtieth anniversary in October 2002, more than 57 million passengers had ridden the Morgantown Monorail. At that time, its seventy-one fully automated cars transported an average of fourteen thousand passengers a day on its 8.7-mile guideway. The system has five stations, two in downtown Morgantown and three on the West Virginia University campus.

The Morgantown Monorail is a landmark for both the city and the university. Its innovative design and contribution to efforts to find cleaner methods of transportation make it a source of pride to West Virginians, as well as one of Appalachia's more notable transportation projects.

See also: SECTION OVERVIEW.

—Richard V. Hatcher, *Marshall University*

Jim Bissett, "PRT Celebrates Thirty Years," *Dominion Post* (November 3, 2002).

Muskingum River and Canal

The confluence of the Tuscarawas and Walhounding Rivers at Coshocton, Ohio, creates the Muskingum River.

Draining one-fifth of the state, the Muskingum winds southward for 112 miles through the communities of Dresden, Zanesville, and McConnelsville before joining the Ohio River at Marietta. Changes in transportation modes on the Muskingum played an important role in developing this section of Appalachian Ohio.

Because of the river's shallowness, early navigation on the Muskingum was limited to flatboats. This downstream traffic included cargoes of flour, whiskey, and salt. In 1836 the Ohio legislature authorized the Muskingum Improvement, a series of locks and dams that allowed steamboat navigation from Marietta to Dresden. A connection to the Ohio and Erie Canal provided access to East Coast markets via Cleveland, Lake Erie, and the Erie Canal. These improvements stimulated agriculture and industry in the Muskingum Valley. The valley's farms provided cargoes of tobacco, wool, pork, lard, butter, and grains. The pottery, salt, glass, and iron industries, along with flour milling, flourished with improved access.

However, railroads siphoned away traffic, revenues declined, and the system fell into disrepair. This led Ohio to cede the Muskingum Improvement to the United States in 1887. Federal intervention brought improvements to the system, but traffic slowly waned. The last steamboat reached Zanesville in 1934. Though some barge traffic (mainly coal) continued, the eventual change of transportation modes spelled the end of commercial traffic on the Muskingum. In 1951 the federal government closed the locks, and title to the Muskingum Improvement passed back to the state in 1958. By the start of the twenty-first century, Muskingum's navigation system was used exclusively by pleasure craft.

See also: CHESAPEAKE AND OHIO CANAL; JAMES RIVER AND KANAWHA CANAL; PATOWMACK CANAL.

—David T. Stephens, *Youngstown State University*

Natchez Trace

See Natchez Trace (Settlement and Migration)

National Road

See National Road (Settlement and Migration)

New River Gorge Bridge

In 1889 an iron truss bridge was constructed deep in the New River Gorge at the small town of Fayette Station, West Virginia. There were numerous coal-mining operations and towns upstream from this bridge, and access across the river had always been a problem in the rugged terrain. This bridge served the area until increased highway traffic forced its replacement by the present-day New River Gorge Bridge.

Opened on October 22, 1977, the New River Gorge Bridge, located in Fayette County, is 3,030 feet, 6 inches long. Standing 876 feet above the New River, it is the second-longest single-arch bridge in the world and the second-highest bridge in the United States. Only the Royal Gorge Bridge in Colorado is higher. Made of unpainted weathering steel, it will not rust and does not require painting, which saves the West Virginia Department of Highways millions of dollars in upkeep.

The new bridge, crossed by U.S. Highway 19, has become one of the best-known man-made structures in Appa-

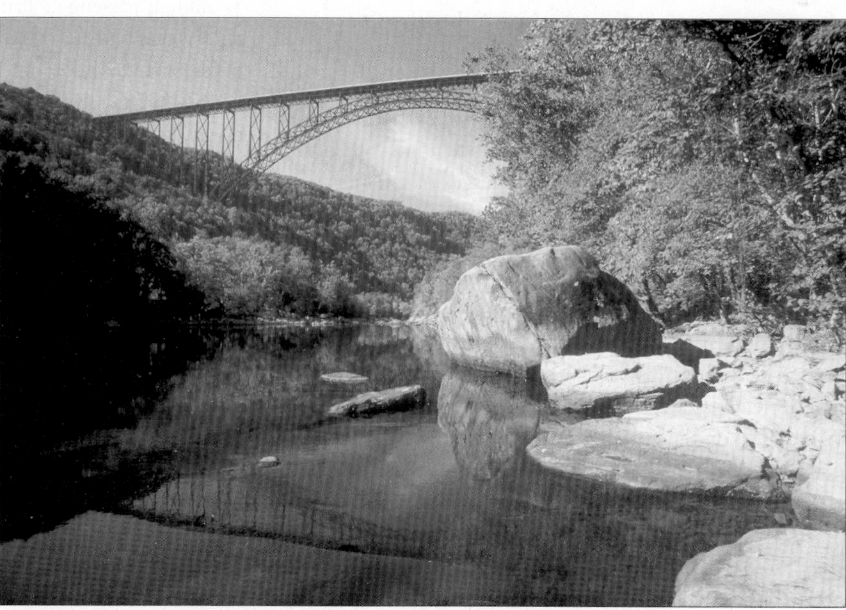

New River Gorge Bridge in Fayette County, West Virginia, c. 1998. Opened in 1977, the bridge has the second-longest single-arch steel span in the world and is the second-highest bridge in the United States. Only the Royal Gorge Bridge over the Arkansas River in Colorado is higher.

lachia. Since 1980, one side of bridge traffic has been closed on the third Saturday in October, and huge crowds converge for Bridge Day festivities. On this day visitors may walk the bridge to get a better view of this engineering marvel and enjoy the scenery at the height of the autumn foliage season. Other activities include parachuting and bungee jumping from the span, arts and crafts sales and demonstrations, and various other spectator and participatory activities. As many as a quarter of a million people attend this event.

See also: CASSELMAN RIVER BRIDGE; SILVER BRIDGE; WHEELING SUSPENSION BRIDGE.

—W. Eugene Cox, *Great Smoky Mountains National Park*

Norfolk and Western Railway

The Norfolk and Western (N&W) was one of the dominant railroads in opening the coalfields of central Appalachia. Formed in 1881, it was created by merger of the bankrupt Atlantic, Mississippi, and Ohio Railroad, which ran from Norfolk, Virginia, to Bristol, Tennessee, and the Shenandoah Valley Railroad running from Hagerstown, Maryland, through the Shenandoah Valley of Virginia. Owned primarily by the Philadelphia banking firm of E. W. Clark and Company, the N&W immediately interested Philadelphia financiers and merchants in the coal deposits of western Virginia and West Virginia. Under the direction of Frederick J. Kimball as vice-president and later president, the N&W acquired the New River Railroad, which owned about one hundred thousand acres of land, and built a 75-mile extension from the N&W main line near Radford, Virginia, to Pocahontas, West Virginia. The first load of coal was transported from the vast coalfield to the Virginia Tidewater on March 17, 1883.

The Southwest Virginia Improvement Company was organized to develop and manage the coal lands. Although many individuals held stock in both, the railroad itself was not a stockholder in the improvement company. But agreements between the company and the N&W gave the railroad exclusive right to ship coal from company land. Furthermore, since Pocahontas coal had to find a market on the East Coast, agreements were established for compensation between the N&W and the Southwest Virginia Improvement Company.

While the N&W built spurs to newly opened mines, expansion northwest toward the Ohio River had to wait until the completion of Elkhorn Tunnel through Flat Top Mountain (McDowell County, West Virginia) in 1888. Thereafter, the N&W expanded in two directions. The Clinch Valley Extension pushed the N&W west to open the coalfields of the Clinch Valley in southwest Virginia and to secure a western connection with the Louisville and Nashville Railroad at Norton, Virginia. Clark and Company also owned significant interest in the Louisville and Nashville, and several members of the board of the N&W also served on the Louisville and Nashville's board. In 1890 the N&W acquired the Scioto Valley Railway, an isolated 126-mile line that ran from a small town near Columbus to Coal Grove, Ohio, located across the river from Kenova, West Virginia. In slightly more than two and a half years, the 191-mile gap between the N&W at Elkhorn, West Virginia, and Coal Grove had been closed. During rail construction, the N&W found itself in the middle of the Hatfield-McCoy feud at the Hatfield Bend of the Tug Fork. President Kimball complained that lawlessness and shooting had made it almost impossible to get good men to work.

By the early 1890s, construction of the Clinch Valley and Ohio extensions, the development of Tidewater port facilities in Norfolk, major improvements in equipment and facilities, and the assumption of the $6.5-million debt of the Shenandoah Valley Railroad combined to create serious financial difficulties for the N&W. Along with many other railroads, the company went into receivership in 1895, and in 1896 it was reorganized as the Norfolk and Western Railway Company. In 1900, as the N&W was beginning to recover from its financial difficulties, the Pennsylvania Railroad began purchasing N&W stock. Although never able to gain more than 39 percent, the Pennsylvania Railroad remained the major stockholder in the N&W for the next sixty years.

In the early part of the twentieth century, the N&W regained its financial stability and expanded to two major Ohio cities. Acquisition of the Cincinnati, Portsmouth, and Virginia Railroad in 1901 gave the N&W access to Cincinnati. Shortly thereafter, the N&W connected with the Pennsylvania Railroad in Columbus and completed several new branch lines to tap additional coal resources. Prior to World War I, a number of significant main line improvements and relocations reduced bottlenecks and allowed higher train speeds.

Through World War I, the Great Depression, and World War II, the N&W remained one of the most successful railroads in the nation primarily by transporting coal. It developed a fleet of outstanding steam locomotives, most of them constructed in the company shops at Roanoke, Virginia. The J-class streamlined 4-8-4 passenger locomotives, the huge A-class 2-6-6-4 simple articulated locomotives, and the Y-6-class 2-8-8-2 compound freight locomotives operated well into the 1950s. (The numbers refer to the number and arrangement of the axles or wheels beginning from the front of the locomotive.) The N&W was the last major railroad to rely on coal power, and its modern steam locomotives could have lasted many additional years had the supply industry for steam engine parts not disappeared.

About the time diesel-electric locomotives appeared on the N&W, the corporation began to expand by acquiring other railroads. In 1959 it acquired the Virginian, essentially a redundant system. The Atlantic and Danville Railroad, running from Norfolk to Danville, Virginia, was purchased three years later. Challenged in part by the Chesapeake and Ohio Railway's acquisition of the Baltimore and Ohio Railroad, in 1964 the N&W acquired the Nickel Plate in a merger that included the Wabash Railroad; the Akron, Canton and Youngstown Railroad; and the Pittsburgh and West Virginia Railroad. As a condition of this merger, the N&W temporarily assumed control of the Erie Lackawanna, but it eventually became part of Conrail.

In 1982 the N&W and the Southern Railway System merged to become the Norfolk Southern Corporation. The combined railroad was a major force in central and southern Appalachia, with 15,000 route miles of track, 23,000 employees, and annual operating revenues in excess of four billion dollars. Over the next seventeen years, the Norfolk Southern developed a reputation as one of the United States' most successful and best-managed railroads. Norfolk Southern attempted to acquire the Conrail system in the mid-1990s. Because of opposition from the CSX system, a plan was developed to divide Conrail between the Norfolk Southern and CSX. This plan was implemented in 1999, and currently the Norfolk Southern serves all of Appalachia.

See also: NORFOLK SOUTHERN CORPORATION; RAILROADS.

—Robert L. Frey, *University of Charleston (West Virginia)*

Joseph T. Lambie, *From Mine to Market: The History of Coal Transportation on the Norfolk and Western Railway* (1954); E. F. Pat Striplin, *The Norfolk and Western: A History* (1997).

Norfolk Southern Corporation

The Norfolk Southern Corporation was created in 1982 as a holding company to facilitate the merger of the Norfolk and Western Railway and the Southern Railway System. Both major railroads in central and southern Appalachia, the Norfolk and Western was best known as a coal-hauling railroad, while the Southern had a reputation as a family railroad providing a variety of passenger and freight service for small towns and rural areas in the South.

The Norfolk and Western of 1982 had been created by mergers of several major railroads, including the Virginian, the Nickel Plate, the Wabash, and the Pittsburgh and West Virginia. These lines tapped many of central Appalachia's coal mines. The Southern Railway System was a conglomeration of many smaller lines that were organized into the dominant system of the South in the late nineteenth century by the J. P. Morgan interests. More recently, both railroads have been known for efficient operation and excellent safety records, although the nature of the Norfolk and Western's traffic has made it the more profitable of the two. The main lines of the merged Norfolk Southern ran from Washington, D.C., to Atlanta and New Orleans; from Cincinnati to Atlanta and New Orleans; and from Norfolk, Virginia, to Chicago and St. Louis.

The newly merged Norfolk Southern continued to develop a reputation as an innovative and efficient railroad. Judicious financial management allowed the company to invest in new locomotives and freight cars and to keep its roadbed in outstanding condition. Frequently ranked first in safety nationally, despite the operation of extremely heavy trains and high traffic density on some sections of the line, the Norfolk Southern demonstrated the success of a carefully planned and orchestrated merger. At the same time the company recognized the historic value of railroads by running an extensive steam locomotive excursion schedule.

Although the U.S. Department of Transportation tapped the Norfolk Southern as the railroad to purchase Conrail, when it attempted to do so in the mid-1990s, the CSX system protested the sale. After extensive negotiations, Conrail was divided between Norfolk Southern and CSX. In the months after the division of Conrail, Norfolk Southern proved better prepared for the event. Because of more effective management and better planning, Norfolk Southern experienced fewer problems than CSX.

No longer primarily a coal-hauling railroad, the Norfolk Southern transports cars, trucks, automobile parts, grains, chemicals, oil, lumber, pulpwood, agricultural produce, and a wide variety of manufactured goods. Some of these commodities are moved in high-speed container trains pioneered by the Norfolk Southern.

The Norfolk Southern and its predecessor lines are deeply entrenched in the economic and social fabric of Appalachia. Many Appalachians worked on these railroads, and even more are dependent on the products shipped on their rails. Norfolk Southern and CSX dominate rail transportation in Appalachia and in the eastern United States today. Railroad analysts predict that the Norfolk Southern will be part of a future merger (probably with the Burlington Northern Santa Fe) to create a true transcontinental railroad serving most of the states in the continental United States as well as Canada and Mexico.

See also: NORFOLK AND WESTERN RAILWAY; RAILROADS; SOUTHERN RAILWAY SYSTEM.

—Robert L. Frey, *University of Charleston (West Virginia)*

Ohio River

Formed by the juncture of the Monongahela and Allegheny Rivers at Pittsburgh, the Ohio is one of Appalachia's major streams. It meanders northwest then southwest through the Appalachian region on its thousand-mile journey. Its 204,000-square-mile basin touches parts of Indiana, Illinois, Ohio, Kentucky, Tennessee, West Virginia, Virginia, North Carolina, Maryland, Pennsylvania, and New York. Major tributaries include the Tennessee, Cumberland, Wabash, Kentucky, Kanawha, Big Sandy, Licking, Green, Muskingum, Miami, and Scioto Rivers. Commercial barge traffic plies the river's entire length, and floating palaces such as the *Delta Queen*, *Mississippi Queen*, and *American Queen* offer passengers a taste of yesteryear. Industrial corridors along certain stretches have brought comparison to the famous Ruhr Valley in Germany.

Before the arrival of Europeans, the Ohio sustained Native American existence, making possible migration, transportation, communication, and agriculture, in addition to providing food and water for the communities established along its reaches. Inhabitants of its watershed received cultural ideas from travelers who had visited ceremonial complexes such as that at Cahokia in present-day Illinois. Manufactured goods preceded the first Europeans in the form of an iron axe forged at Montreal in 1630. By 1700, the first French explorers had pushed southward, followed soon by trappers, speculators, diplomats, surveyors, and settlers.

Both Europeans and Native Americans recognized the river's strategic importance. During the American Revolution, Mohawk raiders led by Joseph Brant seized American supply vessels; decades later Tecumseh's Shawnees successfully destroyed settlers' flatboats. Easterners launching their flatboats westward from Pittsburgh also feared attacks by plunder-hungry bandits.

This broad migration route provided access to farmers seeking rich western lands. An overland journey to Pittsburgh late in the year, flatboat building in January and February, launching on winter's rain-swollen crest, and careful downstream steering allowed arrival in time to plant corn. Barring an unfortunate navigational accident, the pioneer family could ride the Ohio to their new home, built perhaps from their boat's timbers.

Loads of coal in a lock on the Ohio River, 2003. Bulk cargoes of coal, gasoline, oil, steel, petrochemicals, cement, sand, gravel, and other products are regularly carried on the Ohio through Appalachia's heartland, descending more than four hundred feet in elevation from Pittsburgh to Cairo, Illinois, through twenty U.S. Army Corps of Engineers dams. Congressional legislation in 1954 funded the modern dams, which have twelve-hundred-foot chambers for locking massive barge tows.

Ohio River travel changed dramatically in 1811 when the steam-powered *New Orleans* left Pittsburgh, ran the falls at Louisville, and reached New Orleans. By 1815 the *Enterprise* ventured upstream, opening western waters to shallow-draft steamboats carrying passengers and cargo. In 1830 navigation was improved when the Louisville-Portland Canal bypassed the falls.

Despite the steamboat's power, the cheapest transportation southward was the lowly flatboat. In 1815 about six hundred flatboats reached New Orleans; the numbers peaked in 1846–47 at nearly twenty-eight hundred. Similar in construction to the flatboat was the lumber raft, or drift, steered by hardy crews along the Ohio and its tributaries with logs or lumber for downstream markets.

Water levels and obstacles such as snags, rocks, and sandbars hindered navigation. As early as 1824, the U.S. Army Corps of Engineers attempted to clear the river. In 1885 a dam was built below Pittsburgh to keep that port open in low water; by 1911 dams were begun along the Ohio to establish an all-season navigational pool. Congressional legislation in 1954 funded modern dams with twelve-hundred-foot chambers to lock seventeen barge tows. Bulk cargoes of coal, gasoline, oil, steel, petrochemicals, cement, sand, gravel, and other products traverse Appalachia's heartland, descending more than four hundred feet in elevation from Pittsburgh to Cairo, Illinois, through twenty Corps of Engineers dams. In 2001 just more than 242 million short tons were transported down the Ohio.

While low water restricted navigation, high water destroyed lives and property in frequent flooding. In 1913 came the Great Ohio Flood. Precipitated by an extremely wet winter, the deluge began on March 23 with more than six inches of rain falling in many Ohio counties. When the Muskingum-Ohio confluence crested at fifty-seven feet, more than twenty-two feet above flood stage, every Muskingum River bridge was destroyed, and towns were inundated for miles. As a result of this flood and another in 1937, many cities in Appalachian Ohio's floodplain built protective floodwalls. Numerous conservancy districts began upstream flood-control projects to mitigate precipitous rainfall.

Although citizens of Appalachia's immediate Ohio River Valley (Pennsylvania, West Virginia, Ohio, and Kentucky) continue to use the river for commerce, recreation, and water supply, they also encounter the water-quality and pollution problems that have long plagued the waterway. In 1897, for instance, a fisherman near Parkersburg, West Virginia, complained that oil wells and iron slag killed the fish in the river. At the beginning of the twenty-first century, pollution, bank erosion, and silting threatened full use and enjoyment of the Ohio River.

See also: FLOODS (ENVIRONMENT); TENNESSEE RIVER.

—James H. O'Donnell, *Marietta College*

Edward J. Cleary, *The ORSANCO Story: Water Quality Management in the Ohio River Valley under an Interstate Compact* (1967); Samuel Cummings, *The Western Pilot* (1847; reprint 1978); Robert L. Reid, *Always a River: The Ohio River and the American Experience* (1991).

Patowmack Canal

In 1772 George Washington introduced a bill in the Virginia House of Burgesses for the improvement of the navigation of the Potomac River. His plan was an attempt to connect the eastern and western portions of the American colonies in an effort to stimulate trade and bind the country together. In order to do this, it was necessary to tame the Potomac River through a system of canals so it could be made into a common highway for navigation and commerce.

The Potomac had been virtually impassable north of Georgetown, and boatmen were forced to unload the produce they were carrying from the western portions of the colonies at places where the river became unmanageable and then to reload after bypassing them. These trips were expensive and often disastrous. The Patowmack Company, jointly chartered by Virginia and Maryland, was incorporated after the Revolutionary War to build the series of canals so commerce and trade could circumnavigate the House Falls, Shenandoah Falls, Seneca Falls, Great Falls, and Little Falls of the Potomac River. Construction of the Patowmack Canal began in the spring of 1785. Washington was chosen as the company's first president, and James Rumsey was named chief engineer.

The first tasks of removing loose rock and sandbars from the river bottom were left to the men (many of whom were indentured servants) who operated the flatboats. Passageways were blasted through solid rock formations to eradicate sharp turns and to provide additional river depth. Low dams were built across the water to raise its elevation and divert it into walled channels. The canals were cut into the riverbanks to bypass obstructions. Some of these canals were equipped with lock gates, the first to be built in America, to control the water flow and enable craft to be lowered and raised in lock chambers.

Despite labor troubles and Rumsey's resignation, the canal was finished and ready for navigation in 1802. The facilities were operational but crude. After the canal had operated for twenty-six years, the charter of the Patowmack Company was revoked when Maryland and Virginia decided against giving further financial aid. In 1828 the Chesapeake and Ohio Canal Company assumed all charter rights of the Patowmack Company but surrendered them shortly thereafter, eventually abandoning the canal in 1830 to focus on the Chesapeake and Ohio Canal, which would stretch from Georgetown to Cumberland on the Maryland side of the river.

See also: CHESAPEAKE AND OHIO CANAL; WASHINGTON, GEORGE (SETTLEMENT AND MIGRATION).

—Ima J. Stephens, *Auburn University*

Penn Central/Conrail

Plans for a merger of the Pennsylvania Railroad and the New York Central System were made public in 1957, but the new company, the Pennsylvania New York Central Transportation Company, was not officially created until February 1, 1968. Implementation of the merger was delayed because the Interstate Commerce Commission did not approve it until 1966 and then under conditions that required the merged railroad to take on other weak northeastern railroads, including the New York, New Haven, and Hartford Railroad. The resultant Penn Central Transportation Company was one of the least successful corporate mergers in American business history.

At the time of the merger, despite a variety of traffic and financial problems in the post–World War II era, both the Pennsylvania Railroad and the New York Central System were in the black. From many quarters came enthusiastic predictions for the success of the merged railroad. However, by the end of 1970 Penn Central had registered a deficit of more than $320 million, and on June 21, 1970, the company entered bankruptcy. Eventually, the court decided that Penn Central did not have a viable financial future. By that time, the Regional Rail Reorganization Act of 1973 had created a temporary government agency—the United States Railroad Administration—to combine the properties of seven major eastern railroads (Penn Central; Central of New Jersey; Erie-Lackawanna; Lehigh Valley; Reading; Lehigh and Hudson River; and the Pennsylvania-Reading Seashore Lines) to continue providing rail service to the Northeast.

The collapse of the Penn Central was an event of major significance in the worlds of business, finance, and railroading. Initially much was made of the cultural differences between the two railroads. The "green" team from the New York Central had many young, innovative, and impatient executives, while the "red" team of the Pennsylvania Railroad (known as the Pennsy) was composed of more experienced, cautious, and traditional individuals. The "red" team soon dominated management ranks as "green" team members left the company in frustration. In retrospect it was clear that the merger had not been well planned despite a decade of preparation. Personnel of the two railroads were inadequately trained. Paperwork was not coordinated, and trains with "no bills" (no one had any idea where the individual freight cars were supposed to go) were dispatched aimlessly over the system, producing chaos and confusion.

But even after the worst problems were corrected, the Penn Central continued to lose money. In hindsight, the problems were obvious—too much track, too much physical plant, too many aging locomotives and cars, too many employees—and all caused by a rapidly declining traffic base. In the 1950s and 1960s, many of the industries that had supplied traffic for the Pennsy and the New York Central became obsolete and the region became known as the Rust Belt. The construction of the Interstate Highway System and the expansion of the airline transportation system drained long-distance passengers off the railroads, leaving them with expensive, labor-intensive commuter service and almost empty long-distance passenger trains. These were problems that the most innovative managers could not have countered easily.

From 1974 to 1976, the United States Railway Administration, a nonprofit corporation under the jurisdiction of the U.S. Department of Transportation, operated the former Penn Central. Its managing board included representatives from all constituencies of the former Penn Central, and since the Railway Administration was a government agency, it could carry out the elimination of unprofitable lines and service without Interstate Commerce Commission delays. On April 1, 1976, the Consolidated Rail Corporation (Conrail), a for-profit corporation with credit guaranteed by the U.S. government, took over the ownership and management of the former Penn Central.

For five years Conrail appeared to handle traffic no better than Penn Central. Despite the abandonment of extensive track miles, it was often difficult to find an operable locomotive to move a train. Once a train was underway, the maintenance of the line was so poor that trains moved at slow speeds with frequent long stops. Because of the continued deterioration of industries along the line, traffic declined 18 percent from 1977 to 1984. In final settlements with creditors, the U.S. government acquired most of the stock of Conrail.

In 1981 the appointment of L. Stanley Crane of the Southern Railway as chief executive officer of Conrail began a revitalization of the system. Crane was aided by the passage of the Northeast Rail Reorganization Act of 1981, which allowed Conrail to rid itself of commuter passenger trains and gave it greater freedom in dealing with restrictive labor contracts. Crane continued to streamline the system by eliminating unprofitable service and trackage while developing a positive relationship with labor and infusing a sense of pride and confidence in management. The results began to show quickly as Conrail posted its first profitable quarter in 1981 and from then until 1999 yielded a profit annually—a remarkable turnaround for a system that appeared hopeless in the 1970s.

The Northeast Rail Reorganization Act had identified 1984 as the year to make Conrail a totally private corporation. Norfolk Southern Corporation was selected by the Department of Transportation to purchase Conrail for $1.9 billion. The decision produced so much opposition that Norfolk Southern withdrew its bid under threat of congressional investigation. On March 26, 1987, Conrail was sold to the public for twenty-eight dollars a share. However, Norfolk Southern did not give up its quest to control Conrail. When it developed merger arrangements with Conrail in the late 1990s, CSX Transportation led the opposition. Eventually, Norfolk Southern and CSX developed a plan to divide Conrail between themselves, and in 1999 Conrail ceased to exist as a separate entity. Norfolk Southern and CSX became the only major railroads in Appalachia.

See also: NORFOLK SOUTHERN CORPORATION; PENNSYLVANIA RAILROAD; RAILROADS.

—Robert L. Frey, *University of Charleston (West Virginia)*

Albro Martin, *Railroads Triumphant: The Growth, Rejection, and Rebirth of a Vital American Force* (1992).

Pennsylvania Main Line Canal

The Pennsylvania Main Line Canal was the 395-mile, trans-Appalachian spine to a statewide network of canals completed in the 1830s. This expansive system resulted from the 1824 creation of the state Canal Commission to direct the construction of canals across the Appalachian Mountains, along the Delaware River, beside both branches of the Susquehanna, and between Pittsburgh and Lake Erie.

Because it functioned as Pennsylvania's, and more specifically, Philadelphia's, primary link to the trans-Appalachian West, the Main Line Canal was the most important part of the system. Southern Pennsylvania was one of three trans-Appalachian transportation corridors that emerged to link the port cities of the northern Atlantic seaboard with the navigable waterways of the North American interior. To the north, the Hudson-Mohawk Lowland extended up the Hudson River from New York City to Albany, then west along the Mohawk Valley to the Lake Ontario Plain. To the south, the Potomac Valley funneled transportation links extending west toward the Ohio River from Baltimore and Washington, D.C. Between the two, the Southern Pennsylvania route to the Ohio River at Pittsburgh had few natural advantages, but it represented the political will of the state to keep Philadelphia competitive with its neighbors in the race to establish a western hinterland beyond the mountains.

Pennsylvania's Main Line of Public Works included 270 miles of canals, 120 miles of railroad, and a dozen inclined planes. Although cumbersome, this was Pennsylvania's answer to New York's Erie Canal, which opened in 1825 between the navigable Hudson River at Albany and Lake Erie in Buffalo, giving New York City an all-water route to the Great Lakes. The success of the Erie Canal stimulated a trans-Appalachian canal-building boom. On July 4, 1826, Governor John Andrew Shulze broke ground for the Main Line system at Harrisburg. Two years later, construction began on the Chesapeake and Ohio Canal outside Washington and the Baltimore and Ohio Railroad in Baltimore, both bound for the Ohio River by way of the Potomac Valley.

The best water route west from Philadelphia was a less-than-adequate course up the Schuylkill River to Reading and through the Lebanon Valley to the Susquehanna-bound Swatara Creek. This route had been opened by the Schuylkill Navigation and Union Canals in 1828. The course was tortuous, the canal small, and the water level in the Lebanon Valley section unreliable, causing the Canal Commission to avoid this pre-existing infrastructure in favor of building the Philadelphia-Columbia Railroad. From Philadelphia, the railroad climbed out of the Schuylkill Valley by way of the Belmont Inclined Plane. At the western end, the Columbia Plane lowered rail cars down to the Eastern Division Canal Basin along the banks of the Susquehanna River. Parts of the Philadelphia-Columbia Railroad were put into operation as early as 1832, carrying private horse-drawn rail-wagons, which paid tolls in the fashion of a turnpike. The entire line opened in 1834, and although state-owned steam locomotives pulled most of the traffic, private rail-wagons continued to be accommodated up until 1844. Railroad realignments bypassed the Columbia Plane in 1840 and the Belmont Plane ten years later.

North from Columbia, the Eastern and Juniata Divisions of the Main Line Canal followed the east bank of the Susquehanna River through Harrisburg and the Juniata River to Hollidaysburg. Natural water gaps, which cleaved through nine major ridges, afforded passage through the folded Appalachians. The packet boat *John Blair* made the first trip through the mountains in the spring of 1833. Beyond Hollidaysburg, the steep slopes of the Allegheny Mountains, rising more than twenty-three hundred feet, stood as a formidable rampart insurmountable by any canal. To connect its Juniata and Western Division Canals, the state built the Allegheny Portage Railroad, incorporating ten inclined planes and levels to carry rail cars over the mountains at Blair Gap Summit between Hollidaysburg and the Conemaugh Canal Basin in Johnstown. Opened in 1834, the Allegheny Portage Railroad was the Main Line's most ingenious section, as well as the most expensive to operate, requiring stationary steam engine houses at the top of all ten planes, locomotives for the levels, and, initially, time-consuming loading and unloading at both terminal canal basins. The Main Line built the nation's first railroad tunnel at Staple Bend and pioneered the use of steel hoisting cables in the place of hemp rope. By 1838, the railroad had developed sectional canal boats designed to be carried over the mountains by rail to save break-of-bulk costs. The inclined planes were abandoned in 1855 after the state rebuilt the line as the New Portage Railroad.

From Johnstown, the Western Division Canal followed the Conemaugh, Kiskiminetas, and Allegheny Rivers 105 miles to Pittsburgh, entering the city from the north shore over the system's longest aqueduct. The Western Division opened in 1830, three years before any other Main Line section. In 1832 it was extended through a tunnel beneath Grant's Hill to Pittsburgh's Monongahela Wharf. The Monongahela Canal Basin anticipated the arrival of and Main Line interface with the Chesapeake and Ohio Canal actively being constructed through the Potomac Valley, but the canal was destined never to go beyond Cumberland, Maryland.

The Pennsylvania Main Line Canal was critical to the development of central and western Pennsylvania and in maintaining Philadelphia's connection with the trans-Appalachian West. However, it was never profitable. During its peak year of 1845, 83,972 tons of freight moved on the Main Line; the Erie Canal moved more than a million tons. In 1857 the state sold the entire system at a loss to the paralleling Pennsylvania Railroad. The Pennsylvania Railroad began operations between Philadelphia and Pittsburgh in 1852, but only by using the state-owned Columbia and Allegheny Portage Railroads. Two years later, the Pennsylvania Railroad completed the Horseshoe Curve over the Alleghenies and discontinued its service with the Portage Railroad. Under Pennsylvania Railroad ownership, the New Portage Railroad was dismantled (only to be reconstructed in 1904 to relieve congestion on Horseshoe Curve), and the canals were allowed to die a slow death of dwindling traffic. The Western Division closed in 1864, followed by the Juniata Division in 1899 and the Eastern Division a year later.

See also: CHESAPEAKE AND OHIO CANAL; PENNSYLVANIA RAILROAD.

—Kevin J. Patrick, *Indiana University of Pennsylvania*

David Fritz and A. Berle Clemensen, *Pennsylvania Main Line Canal: Juniata and Western Divisions* (1992); Robert McCullough and Walter Leuba, *The Pennsylvania Main Line Canal* (1973); William H. Shank, *Three Hundred Years with the Pennsylvania Traveler* (1976).

Pennsylvania Railroad

The Pennsylvania Railroad (Pennsy) was chartered in 1846 to create an all-rail route from Philadelphia to the headwaters of the Ohio River at Pittsburgh. J. Edgar Thomson, chief engineer of the Georgia Railroad, was hired to build the Pennsylvania. He chose a route through northern Appalachia that made use of the Juniata River Valley to Altoona in constructing a line with favorable gradients. From Altoona west the assault upon the Allegheny Front required heavy grades (although not as heavy as required on the Baltimore and Ohio Railroad) and construction of the famous Horseshoe Curve. West of the mountains other river valleys were used to take the line to Pittsburgh with minimum grades. With the completion of a summit tunnel at Gallitzin in early 1854, the 245-mile line from Harrisburg to Pittsburgh was put into operation. At Harrisburg, the Pennsylvania connected with the state-owned Public Works railroad, including the New Portage Railroad, purchased by the Pennsylvania in 1857, to Philadelphia.

From 1860 to the early 1880s, the Pennsy grew primarily by leasing or purchasing already existing railroads. The Pittsburgh, Fort Wayne, and Chicago Railroad took the Pennsy to Chicago, and the Pittsburgh, Cincinnati, Chicago, and St. Louis Railroad extended it to Cincinnati and St. Louis. Both of these railroads resulted from mergers of many smaller railroads. In the East, the acquisition of the Philadelphia and Trenton Railroad and the Camden and Amboy Railroad gave the Pennsy critical access to the New York City area, thus eliminating the need to turn New York–bound traffic over to the Reading Railroad at Harrisburg. The Pennsy also acquired lines south of Philadelphia to Baltimore and Washington, D.C., and built additional lines into Reading territory.

In addition to Thomson, the Pennsylvania Railroad had a string of outstanding executive leaders. Thomas A. Scott, vice-president for many years and president from 1874 to 1880, was an expansionist who put together chains of railroads extending as far south as Atlanta. George Roberts (1880–97) was able to blunt the efforts of William H. Vanderbilt and the New York Central and Reading Railroads to build a competing line from Pittsburgh to Philadelphia known as the South Pennsylvania Railroad. Victory in this battle, eventually mediated by J. P. Morgan, went to the Pennsylvania. More than fifty years later, a significant part of the South Penn route was used for the Pennsylvania Turnpike—a much more effective competitor of the Pennsylvania Railroad than the New York Central. Other Pennsy presidents of note included Alexander J. Cassatt (1899–1906), Samuel Rhea (1913–25), and W. W. Atterbury (1925–35). Unlike the presidents of many other American railroads, most of the Pennsy chief executives in the first century of the company's history came from an engineering background.

By 1910 the Pennsylvania was the largest railroad in the United States and one of the largest corporations in the world. It was a leader in railroad innovations. Its construction of tunnels under the Hudson and East Rivers, bringing the railroad into the heart of New York City, was a major engineering feat. The electrification of main lines from New York to Washington and Harrisburg was the longest such installation in the country. An early advocate of the steel passenger car, the Pennsy owned more than half of such cars out of about ten thousand in the entire United States by 1918. Pennsy shops, along with those of the Baldwin and the American locomotive works, produced hundreds of locomotives of the same wheel arrangement using interchangeable parts. Locomotives were often identified by the number and arrangement of their axles or wheels beginning at the front of the locomotive, with the number of leading wheels (trucks) given first, followed by the number of driving wheels and trailing wheels. The major passenger locomotive was the famous K-4 4-6-2 Pacific-type, of which there were 425. The standard freight locomotives were the 579 L-1 Mikado (2-8-2) and the 598 Decapod (2-10-0). The Pennsylvania came to be known as the "Standard Railroad of the World," a title originally proclaimed by President Roberts that proved to be justified.

The Pennsylvania Railroad was fortunate to have major lines through Appalachia that carried heavy trains of iron, steel, coal, timber, agricultural products, manufactured goods, and millions of businessmen moving back and forth between the United States' major financial and industrial cities—New York, Philadelphia, Baltimore, Washington, Pittsburgh, Cincinnati, Columbus, Cleveland, Chicago, St. Louis, and Detroit. The urban, industrial northern Appalachian region through which the four-track main line of the Pennsylvania operated was quite different from rural central and southern Appalachia.

The high points of the Pennsy came in the late 1920s and during World War II. Not even the Great Depression of the 1930s was powerful enough to bring it to its knees or keep it from paying dividends. Although World War II put a great strain on the system, the railroad met the challenge by using every employee and every piece of equipment to the breaking point. When the war ended, the Pennsy was exhausted. Its locomotive fleet was worn out, its employees overworked, and its physical plant in need of refurbishing. Furthermore, many of the coal mines in its territory were exhausted and many steel mills obsolete. Automobiles began to divert people from passenger trains, and new manufacturing centers in areas not served by the Pennsy replaced older plants along its lines. The Pennsylvania's tradition of standardization and success became a weakness. Company leaders did not perceive the necessity for change, and instead of reducing redundant trackage, developing new marketing techniques, or modernizing technology, they waited passively for the good times to return.

Finally, company officials did take action, and an unexpected and surprising merger was announced with its traditional rival, the New York Central Railroad, in November 1957. Unlike the Pennsylvania, the New York Central had made an attempt to reduce redundant traffic and service, it had dieselized more efficiently, and it had developed more innovative marketing techniques. Since these systems were essentially parallel and not "end-to-end," it was hoped the merged system could eliminate duplicate trackage and service and return to prosperity. Because of opposition from other railroads, the Interstate Commerce Commission did not approve the merger until 1966. The merged railroad became known as the Penn Central.

See also: RAILROADS; SCOTT, THOMAS A. (BUSINESS, INDUSTRY, AND TECHNOLOGY).

—Robert L. Frey, *University of Charleston (West Virginia)*

George H. Burgess and Miles C. Kennedy, *Centennial History of the Pennsylvania Railroad Company: 1846–1946* (1949).

Pennsylvania Turnpike

The Pennsylvania Turnpike was the forerunner of the Interstate Highway System, and the first limited access road to completely traverse any state. Sometimes called "America's Dream Highway," the toll road was constructed in four main stages from the central portion in late 1938 to November 1954, when the Delaware River Extension was opened. Today, the Pennsylvania Turnpike comprises a 514-mile network of toll roads with 55 toll collection facilities, 500 tollbooths, and 22 service plazas operated by 2,407 employees.

The idea for the turnpike was rooted in a combination of Franklin D. Roosevelt's aspirations of New Deal employment and military functionality and Pennsylvania's need to link east and west more efficiently. Walter Adelbert Jones, a Pittsburgh industrialist, was selected to head the Pennsylvania Turnpike Commission in 1937. The Works Progress Administration funded original surveys, and the estimated $70 million for construction of the first stretch came from the Reconstruction Finance Corporation's purchase of $41 million in bonds and a $29-million grant from the Public Works Administration. Construction contracts were awarded to 155 companies in eighteen states.

Perhaps to show how quickly nature could be subdued, the Appalachian Mountain section was engineered first. This central 160-mile portion of the turnpike was constructed between October 1938 and October 1940 at an average of 1.5 miles of four-lane highway a week. By the spring of 1940, 15,000 workers were employed. This stretch ran from west of Harrisburg to just southeast of Pittsburgh and only contained eleven points of access and exit, then dubbed "interchanges." This section crossed the most rugged portions of the Pennsylvania Appalachians, starting in the Great Valley, passing through the Ridge and Valley system, then moving up onto the Allegheny Plateau. The original turnpike road varied from about 400 feet above sea level west of Harrisburg to a high of 2,456 feet at Laurel Hill.

Seven two-lane tunnels were constructed from the remnants of William H. Vanderbilt's South Pennsylvania Railroad, abandoned in 1885. These were the Laurel Hill, Allegheny, Ray's Hill, Sideling Hill, Tuscarora, Kittatinny, and Blue Mountain Tunnels. Mileage in tunnels alone took up nearly 7 total miles, but the ones at Laurel Hill, Ray's Hill (the shortest, at 2,532 feet), and Sideling Hill (the longest, at 6,782 feet) were later bypassed. All others were eventually widened, and additional tunnels were built parallel to accommodate four-lane traffic. Where tunnels were impractical, monumental cuts removed huge quantities of rock. Among the largest was at Clear Ridge west of the Breezewood interchange, where a tunnel had originally been planned. The cut is 150 feet deep and 2,600 feet long. Nearly 1.1 million cubic yards of earth and rock were removed from the site.

Since World War II halted domestic highway construction while national military capacity was expanded, the central section of the Pennsylvania Turnpike was the only section fully operational through the 1940s. Ironically, a primary reason for original turnpike funding was to ease military transport across the rugged Appalachians. Commercial use of the turnpike passed five million vehicles in 1955 after the Philadelphia, the Western, and the Delaware River Extensions were completed, adding 200 miles to the turnpike's length. With the completion of the Delaware River Bridge in 1956, the turnpike was fully connected to adjacent turnpikes in Ohio and New Jersey. The modern highway thus permanently breached the Appalachian barrier. In the late 1950s, a northwestern extension of 110 miles was completed between suburban Philadelphia and Scranton.

At this time, passenger cars were charged one cent per mile or about five dollars to cross the state. By 1991, charges had only increased to about four cents per mile or around twenty-one dollars. This modest increase has been made up for in total vehicle use. In its first full year of use (1941), 2.4 million vehicles traveled the new road. Today that number can be observed in six days. Tolls worth approximately $18 million were collected in 1941. In 2000, with more than 100 million passenger vehicles, 15 million additional commercial vehicles, and an average distance traveled per vehicle of 33 miles, revenues of more than $367 million were generated. Though 87 percent of turnpike traffic consists of passenger vehicles, about 47 percent of revenues comes from commercial traffic.

Turnpike maintenance costs are enormous, but they are more than made up in revenues. In 2000 estimated costs exceeded $39 million—over half of the expense to build the first section of tollway in 1940. The monthly maintenance cost is about $4,300 per mile. Still, revenues from interest income and plazas net up to $350 million yearly. Some of these revenues have gone into a new turnpike network circling to the west and south of metropolitan Pittsburgh. The route is planned to extend southward, focusing development along the Monongahela Valley toward Interstate 68 in West Virginia. Besides tunnels, eight bridges more than 1,200 feet long must also be maintained. The longest are the Delaware River Bridge, at 6,571 feet, and the Susquehanna River Bridge, at 4,526 feet.

Since 1940, turnpike images have greatly changed. No speed limits were enforced when the turnpike opened, many stretches contained few vehicles, and commercial traffic was scarce. The feeling of an ethereal "dream highway" pervaded, as new construction evoked conquest over nature and the beauty of the road for the road's sake. That view has changed drastically. Compared with newer interstate highways, the road seems narrow and congested. Commercial traffic abounds. In 1998 there were 1,940 crashes resulting in 1,506 injuries and 24 deaths. In 2000 more than 74,000 traffic citations were written, and 5.3 billion total miles were driven on the Pennsylvania Turnpike, the equivalent of eight-tenths of a mile for every person on Earth.

See also: RIDGE AND VALLEY PROVINCE (GEOLOGY); SECTION OVERVIEW.

—Craig S. Campbell, *Youngstown State University*

Dan Cupper, *The Pennsylvania Turnpike: A History* (1990); Penelope Redd Jones, *The Story of the Pennsylvania Turnpike* (1950); Tom Lewis, *Divided Highways: Building the Interstate Highways, Transforming American Life* (1997).

Railroads

Railroads were the first form of transportation that made it possible for large numbers of people to leave Appalachia, either temporarily or permanently. Railroads were also the first form of transportation that made it possible for large numbers of people to enter Appalachia. The exploitation of Appalachia's coal and timber resources that railroads made possible brought mixed blessings to the area. The movement of people out of and into Appalachia profoundly changed the nature and the culture of the area and made it a less distinctive part of the United States. In that respect, radio, television, and interstate highways have expanded the railroads' original impact on Appalachia.

North America's earliest railroads developed during the 1830s and 1840s from major port cities along the East Coast. As construction of these railroads moved west, the mountains, rivers, and valleys of the Appalachians posed significant challenges.

New York's Erie Railroad, a sometimes forgotten trans-Appalachian line, encountered five ridges on its original main route from Piermont, slightly north of New York City, to Dunkirk on Lake Erie. This railroad was remarkable for its careful planning, high-quality construction, and its "wide-gauge" of six feet between the rails (partially to avoid interchange with competing roads) rather than the standard gauge of four feet, eight and one-half inches. Benjamin Wright, the line's chief engineer, famous for his work on the Erie Canal, made excellent use of the headwaters of the Delaware, Susquehanna, Genesee, and Allegheny Rivers (flowing predominantly north-south) to create an east-west line with grades no greater than 1 percent. The route had no tunnels, and only a few major bridges, the most prominent being Starrucca Viaduct in northeastern Pennsylvania.

The railroad line across Pennsylvania, eventually known as the Pennsylvania Railroad, had to fend off canal interests to complete its line from Philadelphia to Pittsburgh. It used the river valleys of the Susquehanna, Juniata, and Little Juniata west of Harrisburg to avoid steep climbs over the Blue, Tuscarora, Shade, Jacks, Tussey, and Brush Mountains. About 132 miles from Harrisburg, however, the railroad encountered the Allegheny Front. Although the line had climbed gradually from 310 feet at Harrisburg to 1,174 feet at the new railroad town named Altoona, the next dozen miles rose almost 1,000 additional feet. Using curves (including the famous Horseshoe Curve) rather than steeper grades, the new railroad snaked up the Allegheny Front at a maximum grade of 1.72 percent. From the peak at Sugar Gap, the line dropped to Pittsburgh using the Conemaugh River, Brush Creek, and the Monongahela River. Unlike the Erie, the Pennsylvania required several tunnels.

The Baltimore and Ohio Railroad, the first common carrier railroad in the United States, initially began construction with the same emphasis on quality as the Erie. Massive stone viaducts and low grades marked early construction. However, inadequate financial resources forced the new railroad to make compromises, and the bridge over the Potomac at Harpers Ferry, (West) Virginia, was built of wood. The Baltimore and Ohio used the Patapsco and the Potomac River Valleys to reach the Allegheny Front at Cumberland, Maryland. Because Pennsylvania resisted construction of the Baltimore and Ohio into that state, the railroad had to lay tracks directly west over the Appalachian ridges encountered further north by the Pennsylvania Railroad. With no river valleys to follow, the Baltimore and Ohio encountered more difficult terrain than did the other railroads. After a 17-mile climb up the Allegheny Front to the highest point (2,626 feet), the line was built east-west across the plateau for 170 miles, where for the most part the drainage was northeast-southwest. Due to the need for grades of up to 2.2 percent, as well as several tunnels and numerous bridges, construction was expensive.

The southernmost early railroad project was the South Carolina Canal and Railroad Company. Built quickly over favorable terrain, the 136-mile railroad, which ran from Charleston to Hamburg, South Carolina, was finished by 1833. Utilizing the *Best Friend of Charleston,* the first steam locomotive in regularly scheduled service, the line was for a few years the longest railroad in the world. It did not reach the Appalachians, however, until after the Civil War, when a line was completed from Columbia through Spartanburg, South Carolina, and Asheville, North Carolina, to Knoxville, Tennessee, using the favorable grade provided by the French Broad River Valley. South of Asheville, the line climbed Saluda Hill on the steepest main line grade in the United States at 4.7 percent. This line eventually became part of the Southern Railway.

Two other early southern railroads, the Georgia Railroad and the Central of Georgia, combined to build from Macon to Terminus (eventually Atlanta) in northwest Georgia. The Western and Atlantic Railroad struck northwest through southern Appalachia to Ross's Landing (Chattanooga, Tennessee) on the Tennessee River using the favorable grades provided by Allatoona Pass. The entire line from Savannah to Chattanooga was opened in May 1851 and provided access from the coast into the southern Appalachians.

Most of the southern railroads were constructed to a gauge of five feet, probably initiated by Horatio Allen, chief engineer of the South Carolina Railroad. However, the Baltimore and Ohio and Pennsylvania Railroad lines were constructed to what is now standard gauge (four feet, eight and one-half inches). While the Erie's decision to build to a gauge of six feet was primarily motivated by the desire to eliminate interchange with other railroads, the choice of a gauge of five feet in the South appeared to be motivated by engineering considerations. In the 1880s, all lines were converted to standard gauge.

By the outbreak of the Civil War the Erie, the Pennsylvania, and the Baltimore and Ohio Railroads had gained access to northern Appalachia. Southern Appalachia had been entered by the Western and Atlantic and the Nashville and Chattanooga Railroads. Most of central Appalachia, as well as the Appalachian counties of Alabama and Mississippi, had no railroad access to the East or Gulf Coasts or to the Mississippi or Ohio Rivers. The one exception, the Virginia and Tennessee Railroad, was completed from Lynchburg, Virginia, to Bristol, Tennessee, in 1856 and provided rail connections to Norfolk, Virginia, after 1858. Since most of Appalachia had rural or locally based economic systems, there was neither urgency for rail connections nor capital to support such construction.

From 1865 to the World War I era, railroad construction in Appalachia developed rapidly and significantly changed the life and culture of the region in the process. In northern and central Appalachia, profits from coal mining led to the expansion of many railroads, including the Baltimore and Ohio Railroad, the Western Maryland, the Pennsylvania, the New York Central, the Chesapeake and Ohio, the Norfolk and Western, the Louisville and Nashville, and several predecessors of the Southern Railway System. Frequently, this expansion took the form of mergers with or purchase of smaller lines developing in the areas. In other cases, new lines were built. New railroads also developed to tap coal and timber resources, including the Virginian, the Atlantic Coast Line, the Seaboard Air Line, and the Carolina, Clinchfield, and Ohio Railway.

Many short lines developed throughout Appalachia. Several, such as the East Tennessee and Western North Carolina Railroad, were constructed to narrow-gauge standards (three feet, six inches) and were intended for local service only. Other short lines were built into logging areas or to tap mines several miles from one of the main line railroads. These lines were intended for short duration and were built as inexpensively as possible. Some of these colorful railroads still exist as "museum" lines. One of the best examples is West Virginia's Cass Scenic Railroad.

The shortage of capital experienced by the southern railroads prior to the Civil War was resolved by the injection of money from northern financiers after the conflict ended. J. P. Morgan, the financial force behind the Southern Railway System, Collis P. Huntington, who expanded the Chesapeake and Ohio into a major railroad, and the Pennsylvania Railroad system, which gained control of the Baltimore and Ohio and the Norfolk and Western, were responsible for the growth of the railroads in northern and central Appalachia. European financial investments in southern railroads were never as extensive as they were in eastern, midwestern, and western railroads. Northern capital alone could not provide all of the capital required by the railroads of Appalachia. Railroads based on coal hauling in northern Appalachia prospered, and they were able to maintain their physical plants, purchase the newest and best locomotives and rolling stock, and compete on a national level with any other railroad. But other lines, including the Louisville and Nashville and the Southern, were periodically strapped for cash and had to make do with older locomotives and equipment. One of the major reasons southern railroads were quick to adopt the diesel locomotive is that their steam locomotive fleets were obsolete by the end of World War II.

The years from World War I to World War II were not kind to America's railroads. Heavy wear caused by the traffic during World War I, increasing competition from the automobile and even the telephone, and the consistent unwillingness of the Interstate Commerce Commission to grant reasonable rate increases made investment in railroads an unwise choice from the perspective of many investors in the 1920s and 1930s. Only a few railroads, such as those hauling coal, were able to make profits during these years. Efforts to reduce service or to institute practical mergers were rejected by the Interstate Commerce Commission or by less amenable state regulatory commissions.

The traffic generated by World War II revived many railroads. However, even such railroads as the Baltimore and Ohio could not regain all the lost revenue they needed to emerge from the war as strong organizations. During the 1950s and 1960s, the construction of the Interstate Highway System and the expansion of air travel, along with the declining demand for coal, weakened many railroads serving Appalachia. The railroads responded by attempting to develop effective mergers. While the Pennsylvania–New York Central merger was an initial failure, other mergers involving Appalachian railroads were much more successful. The Norfolk and Western successfully absorbed the Virginian, and the Chesapeake and Ohio eventually created the CSX system in a merger with the Seaboard Coast Line, which had already absorbed the Atlantic Coast Line, the Louisville and Nashville, the Nashville, Chattanooga, and St. Louis, and the Clinchfield. Even the Penn Central eventually evolved into a successful railroad named Conrail. In 1982, with the merger of the Norfolk and Western and the Southern System into the Norfolk Southern, Appalachia had only three major railroads. In 1999 Conrail was divided between CSX Transportation and the Norfolk Southern, consolidating Appalachian railroading further. In the southern tip of Appalachia, the Burlington Northern Santa Fe has a line, and there are a handful of regional short lines scattered throughout Appalachia, but most of the railroad lines that once traversed Appalachia are gone.

Passenger traffic for most of Appalachia disappeared in the 1950s. During the ensuing decade, as traffic continued to decline, railroad management did little to reverse the trend. By 1970 the federal government, recognizing that American railroads had given up on passenger service, created Amtrak to provide intercity links throughout the nation. The Southern Railway System stayed out of Amtrak for a number of years and continued to provide limited passenger service to southern Appalachia. With people able to afford automobiles at a level not possible in Appalachia prior to the 1950s, with improved feeder roads to the rapidly expanding Interstate Highway System by 1970, and with the flexibility of auto transportation, passenger trains were not as essential to Appalachia as they were prior to World War II.

See also: SECTION OVERVIEW.

—Robert L. Frey, *University of Charleston (West Virginia)*

George H. Drury, *The Historical Guide to North American Railroads* (1985); Albro Martin, *Railroads Triumphant: The Growth, Rejection, and Rebirth of a Vital American Force* (1992); James E. Vance Jr., *The North American Railroad: Its Origin, Evolution, and Geography* (1995).

Sandy and Beaver Canal

Conceived by Philadelphia merchants as the shortest route to the markets of east-central Ohio and by locals as an outlet to the world for their agricultural and manufacturing production, the Sandy and Beaver Canal failed to live up to expectations. The Panic of 1837, an inadequate water supply, floods, competition from the Pennsylvania and Ohio Canal to the north, and the coming of railroads doomed this venture. The last of Ohio's canals to be completed, the Sandy and Beaver was short-lived. Construction began in 1834, but the first boat did not traverse the canal until 1848. Four years later the last boat made the journey. A six-mile section connecting to the Ohio Canal at Bolivar, Ohio, remained in operation until 1884.

Named for the two streams whose valleys it followed, the Sandy and Beaver Canal extended for seventy-three miles from Glasgow, Pennsylvania, on the Ohio River to Bolivar. Along this route the canal crossed over the Tuscarawas River on an aqueduct and passed through two tunnels and more than ninety locks. Ohio communities located on the canal included Lisbon, Hanoverton, Minerva, Malvern, and Magnolia. It was the stimulus for much speculation, since many towns were platted along its course. Few survived and fewer still prospered; yet significant portions of the canal remain because much of the region along its course has experienced little economic development. Another legacy is the region's strong Irish ethnic imprint, which reflects the workers who built the canal.

See also: CHESAPEAKE AND OHIO CANAL; JAMES RIVER AND KANAWHA CANAL; PATOWMACK CANAL.

—David T. Stephens, *Youngstown State University*

Silver Bridge

Before 1928, there was no direct route between Columbus, Ohio, and Charleston, West Virginia. Construction of the Silver Bridge across the Ohio River created a direct route and turned the road into a major artery for travel between these two state capitals.

Congress passed legislation authorizing construction of the bridge in 1926, and in May 1928 the $1.2-million span opened. It was the first two-way vehicular suspension bridge in the United States. Unlike other suspension bridges, the structure used heat-treated eyebar chains for suspension; it was also the first bridge painted aluminum, a feature that inspired the structure's name.

Nearly four decades after the Silver Bridge opened, tragedy struck. On December 15, 1967, malfunctioning traffic lights at both ends of the bridge caused a traffic jam. A cracked eyebar, unable to withstand the heavy traffic, snapped. Corrosion fatigue and the weight of cars and trucks contributed to the resulting bridge collapse, which claimed forty-six lives.

Recognizing the importance of the span across the Ohio, President Lyndon Johnson declared a national emergency in February 1968 and ordered a replacement bridge built immediately. In December 1969, the $14.5-million Silver Memorial Bridge opened, located about one mile downstream from the site of the original structure.

See also: OHIO RIVER.

—William E. Plants, *Gallipolis Career College*

Southern Railway System

Until the mergers of the 1970s and 1980s, the Southern Railway System was one of the two major railway systems of southern Appalachia. Extending from Washington, D.C., to Atlanta and New Orleans and from Cincinnati through Knoxville and Chattanooga, Tennessee, to New Orleans, the Southern served many of the cities, towns, and rural areas of the region. The trains of the Southern Railway carried people out of Appalachia to school, to war, to vacation spots, and to jobs when none were available in Appalachia. Its trains also carried cotton, coal, timber, and tobacco from Appalachia to markets all over the nation. It transported men back from war (sometimes in coffins), brought students home from school, returned former residents, introduced salesmen to the area, and delivered manufactured goods to Appalachia.

In the years after the Civil War, several financial groups attempted to merge various small southern railroads into a larger, more efficient system using the Richmond and Danville Railroad as the base. Initially, Thomas A. Scott, vice-president for many years and president of the Pennsylvania Railroad from 1874 to 1880, and Pennsylvania Railroad interests attempted to construct such a system. The Panic of 1873 derailed these efforts, however, and the Pennsylvania interests sold most of their holdings. In the 1880s, steamship magnate William P. Clyde led northern and southern capitalists in creating the Richmond and West Point Terminal Railway and Warehouse Company to build a large system of southern railroads. While the system eventually included more than eight thousand miles of track, it, too, encountered financial difficulties and was placed in receivership in 1892.

In February 1893, Drexel, Morgan and Company agreed to take over the Clyde properties and attempt to revitalize them. Reorganization was complete in 1894, and on July 1 the Southern Railway System began operations. The reorganization of the Richmond Terminal was probably one of the most important economic and financial events of the post–Civil War railroad business in the South. The major railroads in the 1894 merger creating Southern Railway System were the Richmond and Danville; the Atlanta and Charlotte Air Line; the Virginia Midland; the Alabama, Mississippi, and Kentucky; and the East Tennessee, Virginia, and Georgia. In the early twentieth century, the Cincinnati, New Orleans, and Texas Pacific (Queen and Crescent route) Railroad and the Virginia and Southwestern were added to the system. In 1963 the Central of Georgia was merged into the system.

Samuel Spencer was named president of the new system in 1894 and remained in this post until 1906, when he was killed in a train wreck south of Lynchburg, Virginia. During his presidency, the Southern System's mileage, net income, and quality of its rolling stock and physical plant increased tremendously, although dividends were paid infrequently to stockholders. Spencer was a strong proponent of using the railroad to improve the economic status of the area through which it passed. The company encouraged agricultural interests in the South to diversify rather than to rely on tobacco and cotton and took an active role in educating farmers on improved farming techniques, erosion control, and irrigation methods.

Development of the Southern System was slowed by United States Railroad Administration control during World War I, but in the 1920s a number of additional improvements—line relocations, the purchase of new steam locomotives, improved line signaling, and expanded passenger service—allowed the Southern to claim that it was one of the most forward-looking railroads in the nation. During this decade, the Southern Railway developed an attractive apple-green and gold color scheme to distinguish its passenger locomotives and cars. Powered by the famous Ps-4 Pacific-type locomotives, one of which is preserved at the Smithsonian Institution, Southern Railway passenger trains were among the best in the nation in terms of on-time performance and excellence of onboard service.

Few railroads were as hard hit by the Great Depression as the Southern, and many of the advances made during the 1920s were nullified by the loss of traffic and the financial difficulties of the 1930s. Much of the traffic on the Southern was agricultural in nature, including timber, and these commodities suffered significant declines in traffic during the depression. While the Southern did haul some coal, it was a relatively small part of the overall traffic mix. Only loans from the Reconstruction Finance Corporation allowed the company to avert bankruptcy.

World War II brought a resurgence of business traffic and allowed the railroad to enjoy a third stage of growth. Diesel locomotives replaced the obsolete steam fleet, new yard facilities improved freight handling, centralized traffic control speeded train movements, streamlined passenger trains on faster schedules pleased customers, and innovative marketing initiatives brought more business. Many advances in the reduction of the labor costs were pioneered by the Southern, including "helper" locomotives operated by radio control. By the late 1960s, the Southern was known widely as one of the best-managed and safest U.S. railroads. But the creation of the Family Lines (a merger of the Seaboard Air Line, the Atlantic Coast Line, and the Louisville and Nashville) forced the Southern to look for a partner. In 1980 it began negotiations with the Norfolk and Western Railway, another well-managed railroad with extensive coal traffic, and two years later they merged into the Norfolk Southern. Efforts in 1986 to purchase Conrail failed, but in 1999 Norfolk Southern and CSX divided Conrail between themselves. The Norfolk Southern Corporation continues to be a major railroad in southern and central Appalachia. With the addition of Conrail lines, the railroad now spreads throughout northern Appalachia as well.

See also: NORFOLK SOUTHERN CORPORATION; RAILROADS.

—Robert L. Frey, *University of Charleston (West Virginia)*

Burke Davis, *The Southern Railway: Road of the Innovators* (1985).

Tennessee River

The Tennessee River system is a vital component in the network of waterways linking communities and industry in southern Appalachia and the river valley with a nationwide system of waterways and ports. It is also an essential element of one of the world's greatest irrigation and hydropower systems and a world-famous example of multipurpose waterway development. Formed by the confluence of the Holston and French Broad Rivers, just east of Knoxville, Tennessee, it flows south-southwest to Chattanooga, turns west through the Cumberland Plateau into northeastern Alabama, and continues across northern Alabama before bending north through Tennessee and then Kentucky to join the Ohio River at Paducah, Kentucky. Its U-shaped course of 652 miles drains a basin covering about 40,910 square miles.

The river's name may have come from a Cherokee Indian village located on the Little Tennessee River and originally spelled *Tennassee*, *Tinasse*, or *Tanasi.* First used by early American Indians as a trade corridor, the Tennessee later provided a route for the French, Spanish, and English in their exploration and trade. During the period of rivalry for the territory west of the Appalachians, a few small forts and posts were established on the banks of the river. In later years, it became an important artery for settlers moving southwestward, though its role was minor compared to that of the Ohio River.

The upper course of the Tennessee, originally quite shallow and filled with short rapids, was only navigable by flatboats. Its middle course, through the Cumberlands, contained whirlpools and was interrupted by a series of rapids or shoals (now submerged by reservoirs) in northwest Alabama. Only its lower course was easily navigable, but the advent of railroads in the Tennessee River Valley after the 1840s kept river traffic from reaching the level of importance it had on other western and more easily navigated rivers. During the Civil War, the Tennessee's north-flowing lower course was strategically important, as its valley provided an invasion route into the western portion of the Confederacy.

The idea of making the Tennessee River navigable in its entirety was discussed as early as 1793, but its full development as a commercial waterway began only in 1933 with the establishment of the Tennessee Valley Authority. A system of locks and reservoirs controlled by multipurpose dams now harnesses the Tennessee for navigation, power, and flood control. The mainstream dams include Pickwick Landing (1938), Hales Bar (1913), Chickamauga (1940), Watts Bar (1942), and Fort Loudon (1943) in Tennessee; Wilson (1925), Wheeler (1936), and Guntersville (1939) in Alabama; and Kentucky Dam (1944) in Kentucky. Its chief tributaries, besides the Holston and French Broad, are the Little Tennessee, Hiwassee, Paint Rock, Duck, and Ocoee Rivers, all entering from the south, and the Clinch, Flint, Elk, and Sequatchie Rivers, entering from the north. Chief riparian cities are Chattanooga and Knoxville in Tennessee and Florence and Decatur in Alabama.

The Tennessee River is navigable along the 652-mile main channel from Knoxville to Paducah, as well as 150 miles of tributary channels. The inland waterway system connects terminals on the Tennessee River with river ports in twenty-one states and ocean ports in Mobile, Alabama, and New Orleans. For the most part, today's Tennessee River waterway is wide and deep with very little current. Locks where the channel was dredged through rock have a width of three hundred feet and a minimum depth of eleven feet, adequate for barges loaded to a nine-foot draft. Nine mainstream dams with locks, plus Melton Hill Lock and Dam on the Clinch River, provide navigation on the waterway. Canals above Kentucky and Fort Loudon Locks connect the Tennessee River with the Cumberland and Little Tennessee Rivers, respectively.

Coal comprises 50 percent of all cargo on the Tennessee River. Crude materials, including building products, iron, and steel, are the next most common items shipped on the system by barge, followed by petroleum chemicals and farm products. Barge transportation requires less energy than any other type of transportation. One gallon of fuel will move one ton of freight 500 miles by barge. In contrast, a train can move a ton of freight only 200 miles and a truck only 60. Inland waterways such as the Tennessee River are therefore ideal for low-cost shipping of raw materials, fuels, and other bulk items.

See also: OHIO RIVER; TENNESSEE VALLEY AUTHORITY (GOVERNMENT).

—Priscilla Holland and Angelia Mance, *University of North Alabama*

G. P. Palo and J. Porter Taylor, *The Tennessee River Navigation System: History, Development, and Operation* (1964).

Tennessee-Tombigbee Waterway

Creating an 800-mile shortcut for waterborne cargo moving between southern Appalachia and the Gulf of Mexico, the Tennessee-Tombigbee Waterway was completed in December 1984 and by the turn of the century had conveyed shipments totaling more than 100 million short tons through its navigation locks. The cargo ranged from the region's historical exports, such as coal, crushed rock, and wood products, to rockets on their way to their launch site at Cape Canaveral, Florida.

By providing a connection between the Tennessee River at a point near the conjunction of the Tennessee, Alabama, and Mississippi borders and the Tombigbee River in southwestern Alabama, the waterway makes it unnecessary for barges to travel the length of the Tennessee and continue to the Gulf of Mexico via the lower Ohio and Mississippi Rivers. Instead, shipments can take a direct course from the Tennessee Valley to the Tombigbee, continuing on to the Gulf of Mexico at Mobile Bay. During an extreme drought in 1988, when it became hazardous for barges to navigate the lower Mississippi, the Tennessee-Tombigbee provided the primary route to the Gulf of Mexico for shippers in the upper Mississippi and Ohio River Valleys.

The 234-mile-long canal is operated by the U.S. Army Corps of Engineers. Between the Tennessee and Tombigbee Rivers, vessels pass through ten navigation locks, lowering traffic a total of 341 feet. Tonnage shipped through the waterway gradually increased through the 1980s and 1990s, reaching a high of nearly 10 million tons in 1988, the year of the drought. A 1994 study commissioned by a trade association, the Tennessee-Tombigbee Waterway Development Council, estimated that some fifty thousand new jobs had been created as a result of the corridor. The canal also became an important recreational attraction, drawing increasing numbers of tourists and local outdoor enthusiasts to camping, fishing, hunting, and boating along the waterway and the forty-four thousand acres of lakes associated with it.

But despite avid promotion, the Tenn-Tom, as it came to be known, failed to produce the economic boom predicted by supporters, who worked for decades to see the two-billion-dollar project completed. Its critics continue to hold it up as a prime example of pork-barrel politics in federal water projects. Once removed from the lineup of congressionally authorized projects and later put on President Jimmy Carter's "hit list" of projects to be canceled, the Tenn-Tom was approved and constructed in the face of intense opposition from the environmental lobby and the railroad industry, among other detractors. Its chief supporters were powerful southerners in Congress, notably senior Democratic Representatives Jamie Whitten of Mississippi, long-time chairman of the House Appropriations Committee, and Tom Bevill of Alabama, who chaired the Subcommittee on Energy and Water Development, and Mississippi Senator John C. Stennis.

Initially considered when Ulysses S. Grant was president, the Tennessee-Tombigbee linkup was the subject of eleven major studies over the generations. It was first authorized by Congress in 1946, but work did not begin until December 1972. Although the concept was simple, the project became the largest and costliest federal navigation project in the history of the Corps of Engineers, requiring a third more excavation than the Panama Canal linking the Atlantic and Pacific Oceans. At one point in the high country, a cut 175 feet deep was required to open the way through a ridge. Another cut, 12 feet deep and 280 feet wide for a distance of 39 miles, required the excavation and moving of 307 million cubic yards of dirt and rock. Along the route, thirteen highway bridges and six rail bridges were built to carry traffic across the channel.

Each of the canal's navigation locks is 600 feet long by 110 feet wide, large enough to accommodate eight standard-sized barges at a time. The highest, a chamber holding 40 million gallons of water, vertically raises or lowers barges 84 feet.

In spite of the Tenn-Tom's impressive dimensions, many shippers continue to find it more economical to use the long route via the Mississippi River for shipments between the Tennessee Valley and the Gulf. Some tows link as many as forty-five barges, and the process of disconnecting and putting them through each of the locks in groups of eight is slow and laborious.

Still, the waterway's chief advocates—the Tennessee-Tombigbee Waterway Development Authority, led by the governors of Tennessee, Alabama, Mississippi, and Kentucky; the Tennessee-Tombigbee Waterway Development Council, a nonprofit support group with members in more than a dozen states; and the Tennessee-Tombigbee Tourist Association—maintain that its benefits will continue to accrue for years to come.

See also: TENNESSEE RIVER.

—Rudy Abramson, *Reston, Virginia*

Carolyn B. Patterson, "Bounty or Boondoggle: The Tennessee-Tombigbee Waterway," *National Geographic* (March 1986); Jeffrey K. Stine, *Mixing the Waters: Environment, Politics, and the Building of the Tennessee-Tombigbee Waterway* (1993); Tennessee-Tombigbee Waterway Development Authority, *Progress Report: A Bright Spot in the Sunbelt* (2000).

Trucking

Throughout Appalachia, motor carriage, or trucking, is the most common method of hauling freight. Not surprisingly, the region's distinct geographic, economic, and demographic characteristics have shaped the form and extent of truck transportation.

Truck transport within Appalachia can be divided into three categories: general commodity transport; transportation of natural resources; and pass-through traffic that both originates and terminates in other parts of the country. With regard to general commodity transport, significant differences exist between the urban and rural portions of the region. Truck transport to and from the urban centers reflects a healthy mix of intermediate manufactured products and final goods destined for business and households. Traffic volumes to and from Appalachia's urban centers are consistent with volumes observed elsewhere throughout the eastern United States, so that equipment availability and freight rates are generally competitive.

General commodity truck transportation to and from Appalachia's rural areas is more difficult. Lower traffic volumes often lead to traffic imbalances between inbound and outbound traffic. These imbalances, in turn, often produce equipment shortages, unfavorable truck rates, and inefficiencies. In many of the region's most rural areas, the lack of manufacturing means that the vast majority of truck activity is related to the delivery of consumer goods. In many such areas, there is very little truckload traffic. Instead, freight is moved in "less-than-truckload" shipments, where a single truck operating over a specified route provides service to multiple shippers.

Much of Appalachia abounds with natural resources. In many cases, raw resources are first moved by truck before being shipped by either rail or barge. This is particularly true in the case of coal mined in southern West Virginia and eastern Kentucky. The use of coal trucks coupled with the extremely competitive nature of fuel markets has led to inevitable conflicts between cost-sensitive coal-truck operators and regional residents who are concerned about safety and truck-related damage to local roadways. Throughout most of the region, coal trucks are restricted to a gross weight of eighty thousand pounds. However, it is common for trucks to operate illegally at weights that are nearly double the prescribed maximum. In 2003 West Virginia designated a system of coal haul roads in an effort to deal with problems caused by overloaded trucks.

The final form of trucking involves the accommodation of pass-through traffic. Interstate highways and other high-volume roadways came to Appalachia relatively late. As a consequence, historically nonregional traffic skirted Appalachia in favor of better highways. However, over the past three decades, new interstate segments and other high-capacity roads, including the Appalachian Development Highway System, have vastly improved the region's highway infrastructure. Not surprisingly, motor carriers moving shipments between the eastern seaboard and the Midwest have adopted new, shorter routings through Appalachia. On many of the region's high-capacity roadway segments, more than 90 percent of truck traffic is bound for areas outside the region.

See also: APPALACHIAN DEVELOPMENT HIGHWAY SYSTEM.

—Scott Hercik, *Appalachian Regional Commission*

Truss Bridges

Covered truss bridges are an American development, resulting from the land's extensive timber resources and a growing country's need to expand. Although the principles of wooden trusses had been understood for centuries, European builders did not erect wooden truss bridges in large numbers until the eighteenth century, and then most commonly in heavily wooded countries such as Switzerland. Beginning in the late 1700s, builders erected wooden truss bridges in the United States extensively, and by the mid-1800s this country led the world in wooden truss bridge design. This situation resulted from the need for better infrastructure to support the rapidly growing population and the availability of materials produced as forests were cleared.

A truss bridge is composed of a series of individual members acting in tension or compression and performing together as a unit. Tension members are subject to forces that pull outward at the ends. Even on a "wooden" truss bridge, these members are often individual metal pieces such as bars or rods. In comparison, compressive forces push or compress together and are heavier. Two long, usually straight members, known as chords, form the top and bottom. A web of vertical posts and diagonals connects the chords, creating a triangular pattern. The truss distributes stress through the structure, allowing the bridge to support its own weight, the weight of vehicles crossing it, and wind loads. The pattern formed by the truss members, combined with the stress (tension and compression) distribution, creates a specific truss type, such as a Warren or Pratt. Most truss types bear the name of the person or persons who developed the pattern. For example, the Pratt truss is named for Caleb and Thomas Pratt, who patented it in 1844.

Contrary to common perceptions, builders did not originally cover wooden truss bridges. In the early 1800s, Timothy Palmer was one of the first builders in the United States to promote covering the wooden truss, the structurally essential load-bearing portion of the bridge, with a barn-like structure as a means to protect the wood from weathering. The covering can provide a secondary function as well—lateral bracing that makes the entire structure more resistant to wind shear. By the early twentieth century, builders had found that chemical preservatives such as creosote applied to timber could also provide protection from weathering, which made wood coverings less essential.

Wooden truss bridges provided a means to span large crossings efficiently, and builders developed a variety of

Watson Mill Covered Bridge on the South Fork of the Broad River in Madison County, Georgia, 1994. Built in 1885 by Washington W. King, Watson Mill Bridge was constructed using the Town lattice truss system, which is typical of many covered bridges built during the nineteenth century.

truss types throughout the nineteenth century, the heyday of wooden truss design. At the same time, construction of wooden truss bridges led to experimentation with new variations in iron and later steel truss designs. Although builders erected wooden truss bridges from the mid-nineteenth century until World War II, subsequent designs in metal eventually rendered them virtually obsolete by the end of the nineteenth century.

Notable covered bridges in Appalachia include the Swann Bridge, a 1933 Town lattice truss over the Locust Fork of the Warrior River in Alabama; the Euharlee Creek Bridge, an 1886 Town lattice truss built by former slave and master bridge-builder Horace King in Barlow County, Georgia; the Bennett Mill Bridge, the only Wheeler truss bridge in the country, erected in 1855 over Tygart's Creek, South Shore, Kentucky; the Hune Bridge, a Long truss erected in 1879 over the Little Muskingum River, Lawrence, Ohio; the McConnell's Mill Bridge, a Howe truss erected in 1874 over the Slippery Rock Creek, New Castle, Pennsylvania; the Blenheim Bridge, the longest single-span covered bridge in the world, erected in 1855 over the Schoharie River, New York; the Bunker Hill Bridge, one of two Haupt trusses in the country, built in 1894 spanning Lyle Creek, Claremont, North Carolina; the Campbell Bridge, a 1909 Howe truss, spanning the Beaver Dam in Greenville County, South Carolina; the Elizabethton Bridge, a Howe truss erected in 1882 over the Doe River, Elizabethton, Tennessee; the Humpback Bridge, a multiple King Post truss erected in 1857 over Dunlap Creek, Covington, Virginia; and the Philippi Bridge, the only covered bridge that carries traffic on a U.S. highway, built in 1852 over the Tygart Valley River, Barbour County, West Virginia.

See also: CASSELMAN RIVER BRIDGE; SILVER BRIDGE.

—Martha Carver, *Tennessee Department of Transportation*

Martha Carver, "Historic Bridge Survey" (unpublished manuscript available through Tennessee Department of Transportation, Nashville); Brian J. McKee, *Historic American Covered Bridges* (1997); Henry G. Tyrrell, *History of Bridge Engineering* (1911).

Virginia's Smart Road

Virginia's Smart Road is the designation given to a highway intended to connect Blacksburg, Virginia, to Interstate 81. As of 2003, the road was a research test-bed 2.2 miles long managed by the Virginia Tech Transportation Institute. The strip includes a 170-foot-high bridge, the tallest in Virginia, which spans a valley with 2,000 feet of roadway. Researchers control the weather with seventy-five weather towers that can produce varieties of snow and rain, and they further control driving conditions through experimental lighting and pavement. The control and measurement of the transportation research is guided from a 30,000-square-foot control center. In-pavement sensors can transmit information through wireless and fiber-optic communications technologies to drivers on experimental signage and instruments installed in vehicles, all of which have inspired the "smart road" designation. Collaboration among Virginia Polytechnic Institute and State University, the Virginia Department of Transportation, and the Federal Highway Administration created the facility, and its support is augmented by sponsored research projects.

The road's origins lie in more ordinary desires for transportation connectivity and economic development—specifically, a desire to resolve the barrier of distance between

Virginia Tech and Roanoke, the largest metropolitan area in Virginia without a public university, about 45 miles away. When the northeast-southwest trending Interstate 81 was planned, it was routed approximately 10 miles south of Blacksburg, failing to provide the connection that later became desired.

In 1985 the Roanoke–Virginia Tech Advisory Council suggested that the two locations be linked more directly, and in 1986 Roanoke's mayor further promoted the idea. Proponents saw a shorter transportation path between the two nodes as facilitating economic development in both locations, shortening access to commercial aviation in Roanoke for Blacksburg residents, to the university for Roanoke residents, and to the university's research for Roanoke businesses. Opponents saw the highway as increasing urban sprawl, destroying views of scenic mountain forests, victimizing residents living in the path of the roadway, and wreaking environmental havoc. Environmental issues included concerns for an endangered species of coneflower, air quality, impact on karst landscapes, and the potential for flooding, as well as concerns for cemeteries that may need to be relocated. Meanwhile, urban sprawl on the existing road connecting Blacksburg to the interstate continued, increasing the travel time between Blacksburg and Roanoke.

In 1989 a member of the Roanoke County governing board proposed that a highway link employ smart technology. The high-tech roadway would build on the expertise of engineering, information technology, and materials sciences faculty at Virginia Tech, simultaneously increasing the funding opportunities for a direct-link highway.

Pro-growth coalitions in Blacksburg and Roanoke backed the newly dubbed "smart road." Interests in Christiansburg—the county seat at the junction of the interstate and the road to Blacksburg—were threatened by being bypassed and opposed it. Environmental groups argued in meetings and hearings that the road would destroy valuable ecological habitats and the scenic beauty of the proposed route.

Although federal and private research money augmented more conventional highway funds, as of 2003 the entire highway intended to connect with I-81 had not been funded. Ground was broken for the initial segment in the summer of 1997, and the first 1.7-mile stretch was completed in December 1999, with the high bridge and additional segment completed in 2001. When the road is completed by 2020, it will be 5.8 miles long with four lanes of traffic. There will also be provisions to continue testing while routing traffic around controlled test environments.

See also: ROANOKE, VIRGINIA (URBAN APPALACHIAN EXPERIENCE).

—Susan R. Brooker-Gross, *Virginia Polytechnic Institute and State University*, and Holly J. Myers-Jones, *Bowling Green State University*

Holly J. Myers-Jones and Susan R. Brooker-Gross, "Newspapers as Promotional Strategists for Regional Definition," in *Place Promotion: The Use of Publicity and Marketing to Sell Towns and Regions*, ed. John R. Gold and Stephen V. Ward (1994).

West Virginia Turnpike

The West Virginia Turnpike, an eighty-eight-mile toll highway that winds and cuts through the mountains from Princeton to Charleston, West Virginia, has been an arguable success since it was completed mid-twentieth century. Expensive to build and maintain and its status as a toll road resented by many residents who use it to reach the state capital, the highway nevertheless has been vital to transportation and commerce in the state. An impressive feat of highway engineering in the face of major challenges, the turnpike represents West Virginia, for better or worse, to the millions who travel it.

West Virginia seceded from Virginia in 1863, forming a frontier state dominated by mountains and hollows. Most travelers believed the state was easier to go around than through, and even residents found travel so difficult that many communities remained relatively isolated well into the twentieth century. Building and maintaining roads were the responsibilities of individual counties in nineteenth-century West Virginia, resulting in a patchwork of disconnected road systems; only two county seats were connected by paved road as late as 1909. These county road systems contributed greatly to the population's remaining fairly localized until the state government bought up the county roads in 1933.

At that time, and throughout the 1930s and 1940s, many other parts of the country were working to improve their state highway systems dramatically. The slow, hazardous mountain travel through West Virginia that kept the state's communities segregated also discouraged interstate commerce, especially tourism. A possible solution was presented when the four-lane Pennsylvania Turnpike opened nearby in 1940.

Within ten years, a four-lane "superhighway" was planned to run the length of West Virginia from Princeton in the south to Wheeling at the north end. Cost for this plan proved to be too great for the state treasury, however, and in 1951 it was revised to a two-lane highway reaching only from Princeton to Charleston. The $133-million price of the final plan was funded by bonds to be paid back eventually through toll revenues from the completed highway.

Construction of the roadway began in 1952 and was completed in 1954. Seventy million cubic yards of earth were moved in the creation of the turnpike, which climbs from an elevation of 600 feet above sea level to 3,400 feet at Flat Top Mountain. The Memorial Tunnel, connecting the towns of Paint Creek and Standard, was considered by many the crown jewel of the turnpike. By 1954 standards, the tunnel was state of the art, incorporating lights and automatic exhaust equipment.

Two years after the opening of the turnpike, the federal government authorized the creation of the Interstate Highway System (officially the Dwight D. Eisenhower System of Interstate and Defense Highways). This proved to be a commercial boon to the state, but it had a downside. As interstates around West Virginia were completed and connected to the state's own highway system, the already overburdened turnpike became a primary transportation route both from the East Coast to the Midwest and from the Great Lakes and Canada to the Southeast. In addition to structural degradation, accidents and fatalities reached a high level.

Upgrade of the turnpike began in 1976 and was not completed until 1989, when the Memorial Tunnel was bypassed to accommodate four lanes of traffic. The final cost of the improvements was $683 million, more than three times the original estimate, but safety improved greatly. By 1975, just before the upgrades began, there were 278 traffic deaths on the turnpike, contrasted with only 4 in 2002. Still, since the turnpike links Interstates 64, 77, and 79, traffic is consistently heavy, especially during peak travel holidays, and annual maintenance costs run more than $14 million.

The West Virginia Turnpike is a toll road operated by the West Virginia Parkways, Economic Development and Tourism Authority. In 2002 toll rates ranged from $1.25 for passenger cars to $6.00 for the largest commercial trailer trucks, generating about $54 million per year for the state. Additional revenues, from sources such as restaurants and crafts sales, increased overall revenue in 2002 to a little more than $63 million. However, operating expenses for the same year totaled more than $63.5 million, continuing a loss trend that began in 2000, despite the fact that in 2000 traffic on the turnpike increased by about 3 million vehicles. Turnpike revenue is spent on operation and maintenance, employee payroll, and numerous tourism projects, such as the building of Tamarack (located at Exit 45 near the town of Beckley), a $16-million multipurpose facility that serves as a rest stop, complete with restaurant and information services, and a gallery and gift shop featuring Appalachian crafts.

Since the majority of the 35 million vehicles on the toll road each year pass through West Virginia to other destinations, the turnpike is viewed as an integral part of the state's tourism and public relations system. An effort is made to give the best impression of the state possible to this captive audience. The mountain views from the turnpike are inspiring, especially during the fall. Attesting to the difficult terrain faced by early West Virginians, the winding route cuts through mountains and crosses 116 bridges. Three of the more prominent bridges are named for West Virginia military heroes: Medal of Honor winners Sergeant Cornelius Charlton and Sergeant Stanley Bender and Brigadier General Charles E. "Chuck" Yeager, the first pilot to break the sound barrier.

See also: PENNSYLVANIA TURNPIKE; TAMARACK (CULTURAL INSTITUTIONS).

—Troy Gowen, *East Tennessee State University*

Wheeling Suspension Bridge

When completed in 1849, the 1,010-foot Wheeling Suspension Bridge over the Ohio River near Wheeling, West Virginia, was the longest clear span bridge in the world. It ushered in America's century-long ascendancy in suspension bridge engineering. The mighty span symbolized not only American engineering prowess but the internal improvements movement, which sought to connect East Coast ports with the rich resources of the former Northwest Territory by a system of roads, canals, and, later, railways crossing the Appalachian Mountains. The suspension bridge was the most important and visible structure on the entire National Road, the nation's first federally funded highway.

After serving on several canal projects, engineer Charles Ellet Jr. sought to advance his career by studying in France, where he became a devotee of French suspension bridge engineering. Upon his return to America in 1831, he promoted French-style suspension bridges in America. His first success was the Fairmount Suspension Bridge over the Schuylkill River in Philadelphia (1842), but his great triumph was the Wheeling Bridge, which features numerous French design details. The bridge has been modified several times, resulting in changes to its appearance, but the essence of Ellet's design remains. In celebration of its sesquicentennial, the bridge was restored to its former glory, and new features were incorporated to ensure the safety of the traveling public and longterm durability of the structure.

See also: NEW RIVER GORGE BRIDGE; WHEELING, WEST VIRGINIA (URBAN APPALACHIAN EXPERIENCE).

—Emory L. Kemp, *West Virginia University*

Whisman, John D.

(1921–1995) Development theorist and administrator.

One of the architects of the Appalachian Regional Commission, John D. Whisman was born May 20, 1921, on a farm near Rochester, Indiana. When he was twelve, his parents returned to their native Kentucky. After service in the Eighth Air Force in World War II and graduation from the University of Kentucky in 1950, he became interested, while president of the Kentucky Junior Chamber of Commerce, in systematically developing Appalachian Kentucky. In 1957 he was named executive director of a new Eastern Kentucky Regional Planning Commission, and three years later Governor

Bert Combs persuaded the Conference of Appalachian Governors to adopt Whisman's approach to development.

Whisman became the most influential figure on the task force under Presidents Kennedy and Johnson that laid the groundwork for the creation of the Appalachian Regional Commission. He became the thirteen member states' representative on the commission in 1966 and served for a decade as one of the two officials empowered to review and recommend projects to it. In 1976 he decided to resign because powerful political figures in Washington regarded him as too independent and were circulating charges—later proved baseless—that he was double-billing for expenses. Thereafter, he served as a consultant to the Appalachian Regional Commission, though he also became executive secretary of the National Governors' Council on Regional Development.

"Instead of giving people welfare," Whisman observed, the Appalachian Regional Commission "gave them opportunities." He envisioned multistate development regions linked with the federal government to undertake comprehensive programs involving roads, water control, forestry, agriculture, mining, tourism, education, health, and social support. He also promoted intrastate development districts modeled on similar lines. In 1995 the Appalachian Regional Commission began naming a John D. Whisman Scholar; since 1997, the Development District Association of Appalachia has conferred the John D. Whisman Vision Award.

See also: APPALACHIAN REGIONAL COMMISSION (GOVERNMENT); COMBS, BERT (GOVERNMENT).

—David S. Newhall, *Centre College*

Wilderness Road

See Wilderness Road (Settlement and Migration)

Zane's Trace

Laid out by Ebenezer Zane and opened in 1797, Zane's Trace was the only significant early road in Appalachian Ohio. The trace began at Wheeling, (West) Virginia, and ended some 230 miles away at Aberdeen, Ohio, on the banks of the Ohio River opposite Limestone (Maysville), Kentucky. It ran westward from Wheeling to Zanesville, Ohio. At that point, it veered southwestward and continued on through Lancaster and Chillicothe before arriving at Aberdeen.

Zane's Trace was an important alternative to travel on the Ohio River. Westward travelers faced the river's vagaries of irregular flows, sandbars, snags, and seasonal closure due to ice. Eastward travelers faced a longer sinuous route and the unenviable prospect of pushing their craft upstream. Many opted for this more direct land route. Settlers from Pennsylvania and Maryland took up residence along the trace in southeast Ohio. Both the eastern and western termini of the road were utilized by Virginia veterans taking advantage of land warrants entitling them to property in the Virginia Military District in southern and southwestern Ohio. Artifacts found in the landscape along the trace reflect the lives of these travelers.

Land-hungry settlers were quick to settle along the route, which provided a connection to eastern markets. Early settlers found a ready market in supplying goods to those traversing Zane's Trace. Towns developed at important stream crossings, and Kentucky and Ohio livestock was driven to market over the trace. The early development of Appalachian Ohio was greatly influenced by this pioneer route.

See also: EARLY WHITE SETTLEMENT OF SOUTHEASTERN OHIO (SETTLEMENT AND MIGRATION); GREY, ZANE (LITERATURE).

—David T. Stephens, *Youngstown State University*

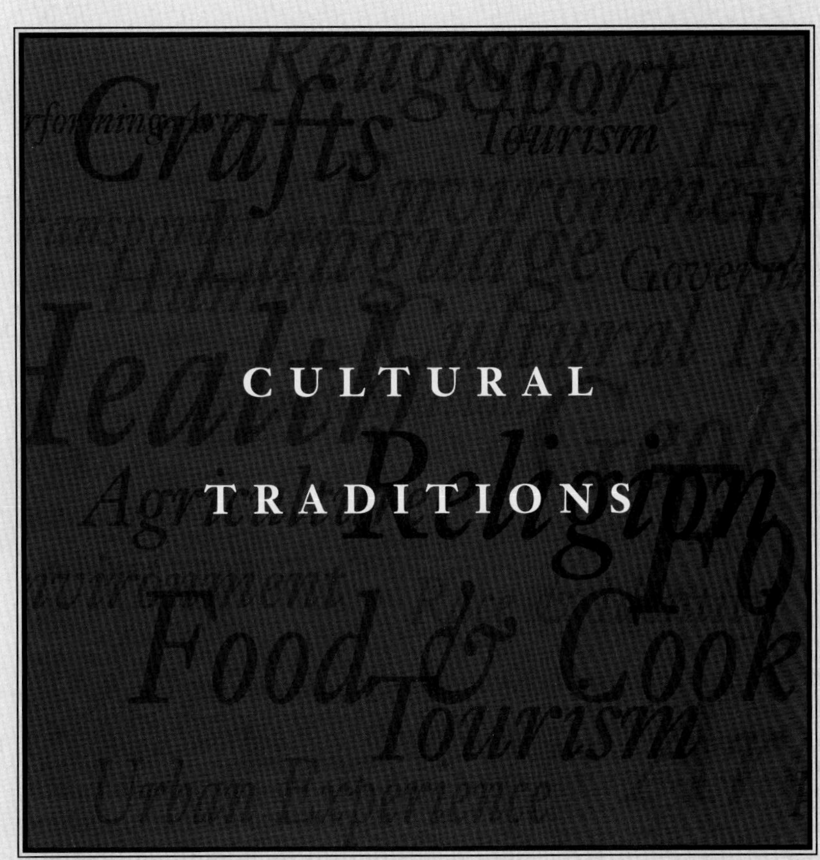

CULTURAL TRADITIONS

Architecture

Section Editor: Carroll Van West

Reaching from the prehistoric past to the present and embracing the contributions of hugely diverse peoples, the architectural legacy of Appalachia includes the most basic building blocks of architectural forms and the latest in faddish modern styles. Several important landmarks represent extensions of larger national architectural movements into the region, or what can be called architecture *in* Appalachia. Many other places illustrate ways that residents and architects took themes and materials from the rugged Appalachian landscape and translated them into three-dimensional spaces, or what can be described as architecture *of* Appalachia. Then, naturally, a few special places blend national architectural movements with local traditions and materials to create Appalachian buildings that speak not only to the region but to the nation at large. There is no better example of this third category than Frank Lloyd Wright's majestic design for Fallingwater, a house in Bear Run, Pennsylvania, considered by many to be the epitome of American domestic design.

The stereotype of architecture *of* Appalachia is the log building, typically a single-pen cabin with half-dovetail notching covered with a cedar-shake gable roof. When serious scholars of American architecture turned their attention to the region in the twentieth century, they considered log buildings the only ones worth preserving—witness the selective preservation of the historic rural landscapes at Cades Cove in the Great Smokies during the 1930s. Log construction fit into scholars' preconceived notions of frontier life, symbolizing the rugged individualism of an isolated Anglo-Saxon culture within the context of a preindustrial, preconsumer domestic environment. Log buildings were, after all, chopped out of nature itself, shaped by hands taught by old traditions, and raised in an event that celebrated unity, shared goals, and community values. The scholarly attention and preservation efforts directed at log buildings not only reflected a twentieth-century preoccupation with the folk, but also celebrated simple, direct dwellings, outbuildings, schools, and churches that served as expressions of craftsmanship thought to be lost in the pursuit of modern things.

Log buildings are not the sum of the architecture of Appalachia, however; thinking in those terms attempts to freeze the region's residents in some imagined golden age that never existed. But a discussion of log buildings is a good place to start since, if for no other reason, people will equate logs with the region's design traditions

Facing page: Civilian Conservation Corps gazebo, Cherokee National Forest, Tennessee, 1999. Many of the constructions in state recreation areas, national parks, and national forests exhibit Rustic-style "parkitecture."

for a long time to come. More importantly, log construction provides a good example of the way Appalachian residents used locally available materials to shape their own built environment.

Almost seven hundred years ago, Native Americans in northernmost Appalachia built various structures with logs and bark, most famously the longhouse, often a huge structure between twenty and thirty feet in width and hundreds of feet in length. A thousand years earlier than that, along the rolling valleys of present-day Ohio in the westernmost section of Appalachia, native peoples constructed log-braced effigy mounds and dwellings. Serpent Mound in Adams County is the most spectacular. Between A.D. 700 and 1000, groups in northern Georgia also constructed a great number of mounds, making the Appalachian region one of the most important areas to study these early architectural monuments.

After European settlers introduced the old-world technology of notched-log construction in the seventeenth century, native peoples incorporated it into their building practices as well. The longhouses of various tribes in southwestern New York and western Pennsylvania became rectangular log houses. The Cherokees of the Tennessee Valley learned techniques for log construction from fur traders venturing west from the markets of South Carolina.

During the eighteenth century, when settlers began to occupy Appalachia in significant numbers, their early built environment was one dominated by log construction. The region's most important contribution to the American tradition of log construction is the cantilever barn, a unique building tradition centered in an area where Tennessee, Virginia, and North Carolina meet.

Building with logs was rarely a matter of aesthetic preference; instead, it solved two practical problems. First, families needed to turn forested land into fields for cultivation and livestock grazing. Second, they needed to produce weather-worthy buildings from construction materials and designs that did not require skilled carpenters. Craftsmen were rare on the frontier, and imported building materials were scarce and expensive. Raising a dwelling and outbuildings with logs was not the only solution, just the most common. Throughout Appalachia settlers who knew how to build with stone or could find experienced masons in their communities often built their primary residence and major outbuildings with locally available stone. The Ramsey House, outside of Knoxville, Tennessee, is an excellent example of the type of skilled masonry of late-eighteenth-century Appalachia. Another impressive achievement of stone construction is the Casselman River Bridge, an eighty-foot-long stone structure built on the National Road in western Maryland in 1813. At the time of its construction it was the longest such stone bridge in the country.

Until settlement numbers reached the critical mass that would attract entrepreneurs with sawmills, exposed notched-log buildings were the dominant form in the regional built environment. The arrival of early sawmills led to the covering of log buildings with clapboards and the construction of heavy-braced frame structures. Not until the region's railroad network matured in the late nineteenth century and steam-powered sawmills became standard technology did the era of notched-log construction finally wane in Appalachia. As the research of geographer John Morgan and folklorist Charles Martin has emphasized, frame-and-box construction did not supplant building with logs until the beginning of the twentieth century in southern Appalachia.

As notched-log construction was leaving the vernacular of Appalachian life, a more formal architectural style rooted in the native materials of wood and stone was gaining popularity in mountain camps, resorts, and homes. In the northern reaches of the region, this modern architectural tradition is known as Adirondack Rustic style. In the southern highlands, it is typically identified as Appalachian Rustic. Scholars conclude that the style rose from the general Arts and Crafts movement of the late nineteenth and early twentieth centuries, and they locate its genesis in the summer resorts of New York State's Adirondacks. Designers of the early twentieth century asserted that Rustic was a true American style. It did not rely upon European precedents, and it reflected the natural harmony, purity, and impressive monumentality of North America's mountains. In a place such as Appalachia, the assumption was that Rustic style was a perfect fit since "nothing" was there but nature and the mountains. The most imposing landmark of this merging of the Arts and Crafts with the beauty and monumentality of log construction is the Grove Park Inn in Asheville, North Carolina, which displays many outstanding Arts and Crafts interior design elements as well as furnishings from the Roycrofters, a furniture manufacturer and design group in East Aurora, New York.

The Rustic style enjoyed a second life in the 1930s, when it became the preferred approach for the design of a distinctive "parkitecture" for many state recreation areas, national forests, and national parks developed by the National Park Service, the Civilian Conservation Corps, and various other New Deal agencies. At the many state parks throughout the region, travelers and residents alike will encounter this twentieth-century tradition of log construction which, in its own way, was a well-meaning attempt to celebrate building traditions of earlier Appalachian people and cultures. This celebration of the nineteenth-century vernacular was a design trait in various New Deal resettlement experiments in Appalachia, including Arthurdale in West Virginia and Cumberland Homesteads in Tennessee. At the latter, federal architects used colorful Crab Orchard stone (a type of sandstone found only in the Cumberland Plateau) to build Arts and Crafts–inspired cottages for the homesteaders.

The designs of New Deal resettlement communities fit an already established pattern of environmental determinism found in other model projects reshaping Appalachian life in the early twentieth century. Pine Mountain Settlement School in Kentucky, the Pittman Center in Tennessee, and the Kate Duncan Smith Daughters of the American Revolution School in Alabama all shared the basic assumption that better, more modern built environments would produce progressive, more modern citizens. Reformers across the region believed that redesigned communities and community buildings would uplift Appalachian attitudes and serve as models of progressive social planning.

Reform efforts during the 1930s transformed Appalachia in both small and large ways. As the Civilian Conservation Corps worked in the mountains of Pennsylvania, Maryland, and West Virginia, for instance, an international team of engineers and architects in the southern highlands executed plans for the largest and most fundamental transformation of the Appalachian landscape to date: the creation of the Tennessee Valley Authority (TVA). Although earlier dam projects dotted Appalachia, nothing had been attempted on the scale of TVA, whose impact stretched across the entire southern half of Appalachia, from Virginia to the northwest corner of Mississippi. In its wake, TVA inundated a number of old river villages, moved others to new locations overlooking lakes, and designed and created new communities to serve its employees. TVA erected marvels of engineering and design that architectural critics worldwide studied and praised, and it carved out a new infrastructure of roads, lakes, and rivers that, in turn, attracted new landmarks of roadside, resort, and commercial architecture. Where TVA did not build dams and reservoirs, the U.S. Army Corps of Engineers often did. By the 1960s, the engineered landscape of modern technology

Grove Park Inn overlooking (at far right) Asheville, North Carolina, 2001. A landmark of Rustic-style architecture, the inn is one of Appalachia's oldest and most popular resort hotels.

was a fundamental component of the Appalachian built environment. There is perhaps no place in all of Appalachia that is as architecturally incongruous as Norris, Tennessee. There, within a one-mile radius stand architect Roland Wank's modernist Norris Dam, the Civilian Conservation Corps's Rustic-style Norris Dam State Park, a vernacular Gothic frame church, and the many log buildings of John Rice Irwin's nostalgic park of memories, the Museum of Appalachia.

The engineered landscape of TVA is like other regional places where engineers and architects combined talents to produce structures that were modern solutions to the age-old difficulties of traversing Appalachia. The Wheeling Suspension Bridge and the New River Gorge Bridge of West Virginia (see "Transportation" section) are engineered solutions to the demands of the landscape, but the beauty of their design helps to soften their intrusion into the environment. Similar in effect are designed parkways such as the Blue Ridge Parkway, which winds along the spine of the southern Appalachians. Because TVA was viewed as a success, it encouraged the federal notion that only massive projects of transformation could make a difference in Appalachia. In the middle decades of the twentieth century, engineers more than architects shaped the regional built environment.

But the architects should have their due—the region is home to several nationally significant architectural landmarks. In the Great Depression decade, Frank Lloyd Wright designed Fallingwater, his acknowledged masterpiece of modernism, as a constructed extension of a waterfall in the southwestern Pennsylvania mountains. Fallingwater interprets International style through its incorporation of building, site, and materials. A breathtaking achievement, it is recognized as one of the country's most important landmarks, and due to its setting and materials, Fallingwater is both *in* and *of* Appalachia. To a lesser extent this is also true of Henry Hobson Richardson's Allegheny County Courthouse and Jail in Pittsburgh. Richardson's imposing sandstone edifice seemingly rises out of the soil. Before the advent of the modern office building, the courthouse and jail gave the body public in the Steel City its own civic place to counteract the deadening symbols of corporate power that dirtied the air with their ever-belching smokestacks. In a different vein, the PPG Place, a steel and glass skyscraper designed by Philip Johnson and John Burgee, created a new type of civic plaza for the city—one that embodies in the materials of its construction the contributions of established Pittsburgh industry even while reflecting in its glass walls the image of a city no longer solely dependent on heavy industry.

Still other landmarks powerfully represent architecture *in* Appalachia. The West Virginia Independence Hall in Wheeling, for example, is typical of the late antebellum classical designs of U.S. Treasury architect Ammi Young. West Virginians only made the building their own when it served as a center for secessionist activity from the Confederacy during the American Civil War. At the western entrance into Appalachia stands the Cincinnati Union Terminal, an Art Deco masterpiece that was, as both a gateway to the West and into Appalachia, an important transfer point between two cultural regions. The Queen Anne style of the Baltimore and Ohio Railroad passenger depot in Oakland, Maryland, is an intrusion of Victorian suburban architecture into the western Maryland mountains, a style designed to appeal to patrons who used the railroad to reach their mountain resort homes. The best known of all architectural landmarks in Appalachia—Biltmore House in Asheville—has little to do with the region except for the appropriation of its setting, and even that was manipulated to match the refined cosmopolitan tastes of landscape architect Frederick Law Olmstead, architect Richard Morris Hunt, and owner George W. Vanderbilt. Biltmore is a marvel of American domestic architecture, an attempt to replicate the estate of a Continental country gentleman complete with a village for its workers. It is also a chilling reminder of the impact of capital on the region and the way certain Americans viewed Appalachia, its natural resources, and its peoples as ripe for the taking.

A more direct reminder of that attitude can be found in Appalachia's many remaining, although often derelict, mining towns. The mark of capital on the landscape can be discerned in many forms. Industrial communities such as Kingsport, Tennessee, were progressive model communities, alleged demonstrations that capital and labor could coexist within the same environment. Some mining companies planned their coal towns in similar fashion, with progressive ideas expressed in well-designed schoolhouses or community halls. Others left it for the workers to choose how best to scratch out a place—and a sense of identity—in an environment dominated by work and company. Within these divisions of classes also existed divisions of color. Kingsport may well have been a model industrial town, but the lines of segregation were drawn tightly there, as they were in many Appalachian communities, north and south. Despite living in Jim Crow times, however, several African Americans made their own distinctive architectural marks. Next to the Great Smoky Mountains, for example, Fred McMahan built a Colonial Revival–style school and post office in addition to a modernist-styled home taken directly from ideas at the New York World's Fair of 1939.

Barriers of segregation and blocks of unadorned worker housing are just two reminders of how Appalachia became more like the rest of America (or is it that America became more like Appalachia?) during the twentieth century. Segregation was a prevailing feature of the American landscape—in the North, South, East, and West. Company towns were just as plentiful—and often very similar in appearance—in the western states as they were in Appalachia. The region has its share of manufactured homes, but those vaguely Ranch-style buildings are much the same no matter where they are found. Even the outhouse, celebrated partly in jest and partly in truth as Franklin D. Roosevelt's most important contribution to the region, was actually part of a New Deal effort to raise the public health of all rural Americans. As Americans took to the highways in increasing numbers, they demanded and got a commercial architecture that promoted brand names and consumer loyalty to corporate image at the cost of regional diversity and creativity. Appalachia began to blend into the sameness that afflicts most of modern America.

Does this modern homogenized landscape of America explain the seemingly unlimited popularity of Dollywood and other tourist destinations that flaunt the stereotypes of Appalachia? Does the region revel in the stereotypes of hillbilly heaven because what it has is otherwise so divorced from a sense of place and identity? The following entries on architecture, in addition to many others in this volume, reflect the reality and the stereotypes of the design arts in Appalachia. Even with the profound changes of the last fifty years, there are places that celebrate and recognize what has been achieved, that note what has been lost and forgotten, and that represent both the architecture *in* and *of* Appalachia.

—Carroll Van West, *Middle Tennessee State University*

John M. Bryan, *Biltmore Estate: The Most Distinguished Private Place* (1994); Henry Glassie, *Pattern in the Material Folk Culture of the Eastern United States* (1968); Charles Martin, *Hollybush: Folk Building and Social Change in an Appalachian Community* (1984); Linda Flint McClelland, *Presenting Nature: The Historic Landscape Design of the National Park Service, 1916–1942* (1993); Marian Moffett and Lawrence Wodehouse, *East Tennessee Cantilever Barns* (1993); John Morgan, *The Log House in East Tennessee* (1990); Lynda S. Waggoner, *Fallingwater: Frank Lloyd Wright's Romance with Nature* (1996); Michael Ann Williams, *Homeplace: The Social Use and Meaning of the Folk Dwelling in Southwestern North Carolina* (1991).

Adirondack Rustic Style

Adirondack Rustic is an architectural style commonly associated with lavish vacation homes, national park hunting lodges, and posh mountain resorts. Adirondack Rustic style takes its name from the rugged and spectacular Adirondack Mountains of northeastern New York State, where this unique American mode originated in the late nineteenth century. By the first decades of the twentieth century, this handsome architectural style was fashionable in mountainous regions throughout America, including the Appalachian Mountains. Historically, Adirondack Rustic architecture was most popular between approximately 1870 and 1940, but the straightforward, masculine style never disappeared entirely and witnessed a renaissance in the late twentieth century.

Renowned architects and landscape designers such as Andrew Jackson Downing, Henry Hobson Richardson, and Frederick Law Olmsted began pushing for a new American style of rustic and picturesque cottages as early as the 1850s. Rustic architecture, however, was most popularized by the Arts and Crafts movement, a worldwide architectural and decorative arts revolution initiated in the late nineteenth century in America as a reaction to increasing urbanization and industrialization. Although influenced by European and Japanese precedents, Adirondack Rustic is considered a uniquely American architectural style.

Constructed on a massive scale, Adirondack Rustic–style lodges are characterized by the use of indigenous building materials such as bark-covered logs and river rocks that blend harmoniously with the natural setting. They also exhibit rustic vernacular elements such as colossal stone fireplaces, battered stone foundations, crowned saddle notching with oversized logs, decorative half-timbers, steep roofs with wide overhangs and split wood shingles, and deep porches supported by rough log columns. Often surrounded by natural landscaping and situated with scenic views, Adirondack Rustic buildings are typically located in heavily wooded areas along creeks, lakes, or mountaintops.

The interiors of most Adirondack Rustic buildings feature vertical plank doors, exposed ceiling beams and roof trusses, walls made of peeled-bark logs, and wood floors. Owners typically furnished the interiors with unadorned Mission-style furniture. Other interiors were furnished with distinctive Adirondack Rustic–style "twig furniture" made of native wood and incorporating natural bark and twisted branches.

In the early twentieth century, contemporary magazines such as *House and Garden* and Gustav Stickley's *The Craftsman*, as well as architectural books such as William Phillips Comstock's *Bungalows, Camps and Mountain Houses* (1915), published numerous examples of Adirondack Rustic architecture. With increased publicity, Adirondack Rustic–style vacation homes and mountain resorts became fashionable across the country from Maine to California. Furthermore, the National Park Service adopted Adirondack Rustic as the architectural style for new park buildings in the western Rocky Mountains, and the style soon carried over to all national parks. During the Great Depression, federal New Deal programs, mainly the Civilian Conservation Corps, constructed hundreds of modest rustic park buildings throughout America, typified in the Appalachian Mountains by the "parkitecture" of the Shenandoah and Great Smoky Mountains National Parks as well as that of the connecting Blue Ridge Parkway.

In the Appalachian Mountains, numerous Adirondack Rustic–style summer resorts, vacation homes, rental cabins and chalets, roadside automobile motor camps and courts, first-class hotels, and public park buildings were constructed from New York to Alabama. In the early twentieth century, a wide range of mountain vacationers, mainly wealthy urban businessmen but also people of more moderate means, built Adirondack Rustic–style cabins and lakeside getaways in the Appalachian Mountains. Good examples include the Appalachian Clubhouse and Elkmont Cottages constructed in the 1910s in what is now the Great Smoky Mountains National Park; the Cascade Village, a group of creekside log vacation homes built in the late 1930s outside Gatlinburg, Tennessee; and the Penland School of Crafts, completed in 1935 and reportedly the largest log building in North Carolina. In recent years, busy, technology-oriented Americans have rediscovered the rugged aesthetics and simplicity of Adirondack Rustic–style furniture and architecture.

See also: PENLAND WEAVERS AND POTTERS (CRAFTS).

—Robbie D. Jones, *The Hermitage, Nashville, Tennessee*

Harvey H. Kaiser, *Great Camps of the Adirondacks* (1982); Linda Flint McClelland, *Presenting Nature: The Historic Landscape Design of the National Park Service, 1916–1942* (1993); Ann Stillman O'Leary, *Adirondack Style* (1998).

Allegheny County Courthouse and Jail

A landmark in the cityscape of Pittsburgh and in American public architecture, the Allegheny County Courthouse and Jail, designed by the celebrated American architect Henry Hobson Richardson, was built between 1884 and 1888. With its massive stone Richardsonian Romanesque arched entrances, impressive vaulted central staircase, well-lit and ventilated courtrooms, and stone clock tower soaring more than 250 feet skyward, the huge courthouse embodied the confidence and position of Pittsburgh's civic leaders during the city's age of industrial expansion and prosperity. The courthouse's vertical emphasis, heavy masonry aesthetic, and diverse but not overstated decorative detail soon became a model for other municipal buildings throughout the country, although none quite matched the balance between beauty

Details of pressed-tin ceiling and proscenium, Apollo Theatre, Martinsburg, West Virginia, 2001.

and function found in Richardson's design. The architect himself considered the courthouse and jail one of his best works, a judgment that continues to be endorsed by architecture critics more than a century later.

Richardson organized the courthouse in an open rectangular plan, with the 200-by-300-foot building creating a 70-by-145-foot interior courtyard. The great utility of the plan was that courtrooms faced both the street and courtyard, allowing for proper light and better air circulation. Richardson's focus on natural light and ventilation was compensation for the polluted environment of Pittsburgh; on an overcast day when the steel mills were in full production, the city could be quite dark.

Connected to the courthouse by a closed stone arched walkway is the county jail. Although characteristic touches of Richardsonian Romanesque style such as Syrian arches can be found in the jail, Richardson allowed function to override aesthetic concerns, leading some architectural scholars to label the jail a more Richardsonian than Romanesque building. The massiveness of the masonry creates a stern, almost overbearing, exterior which conveys well the building's function and shows that the residents therein were effectively walled off from society. Contemporaries accepted Richardson's elemental yet bold composition, but later twentieth-century commentators expressed a decided preference for the jail's functional aesthetic compared to the rich design legacies embodied in the courthouse. Dividing Richardson's design into two separate buildings, however, is an artificial and misguided distinction. Richardson's achievement lies in how the courthouse's decorative elements express the majesty and humanity of the law while the lack of these elements in the jail emphasize the harsh reality of final justice.

See also: PITTSBURGH, PENNSYLVANIA (URBAN APPALACHIAN EXPERIENCE).

—Carroll Van West, *Middle Tennessee State University*

Apollo Theatre

The Apollo Theatre of Martinsburg, West Virginia, presented early movie, vaudeville, and concert events. Designed in 1912–13 by Reginald Geare of Washington, D.C., in cooperation with local architect Chapman E. Kent, the one-thousand-seat theater accommodated the early movie industry yet reserved space for theatrical events by retaining a proscenium stage. The theater was expanded in 1920 to include a larger stage, an enlarged orchestra pit, and a fifty-foot fly loft over the stage.

The original facade of this three-story brick building, distinguished by segmental arched windows and doorways to the lobby space and side entries for the upper floors, blended well with the storefronts of Martinsburg. The pediment above a bracketed cornice notes the construction date and the name of the theater's developer, H. P. Thorn.

An elaborate pressed-tin ceiling is the highlight of the interior of the auditorium. The proscenium arch is heavily decorated with bands of detailed classical features, and pendants along the walls display dancing figures.

Early entertainers promoted their movies or performed live vaudeville at the Apollo. Will Rogers visited the theater to open his film *State Fair*. Country musician Tex Ritter and violinist David Rubinoff also performed there. The Apollo Theatre in addition served local theatrical groups and hosted public functions. The second floor, "Roseland," and the third floor, "Thornwood Hall," were used for receptions, cotillion dances, and grand balls. Since 1936 local groups have used and supported the Apollo. As of 2001, there was renewed interest in the theater house's revival and its continued use as a meeting place and performance venue.

See also: THEATER, HISTORY OF (PERFORMING ARTS).

—Susan M. Pierce, *West Virginia Division of Culture and History*

Arthurdale, West Virginia

Located in Preston County, West Virginia, Arthurdale was a subsistence homestead community created in 1933–34 as part of Franklin D. Roosevelt's New Deal. The community is notable because of its association with First Lady Eleanor Roosevelt. Administered by the Division of Subsistence Homesteads, Arthurdale was the nation's first homestead project developed specifically for unemployed coal miners. Two similar projects in West Virginia, also under the guidance of Eleanor Roosevelt, included Tygart Valley (Randolph County) and Red House Farms (renamed Eleanor and located in Putnam County). All three communities were created to relieve the state's unemployed coal and timber industry workers.

In April 1933, 63 percent of West Virginia's coal-camp workers were unemployed, including approximately twenty thousand individuals in Monongalia County. One area in particular, Scott's Run, was described in a 1935 *Atlantic Monthly* article as "the damnedest cesspool of human misery . . . in America." Lorena Hickok, an Associated Press reporter and friend of Eleanor Roosevelt, stated that it was the "worst place" she had ever seen. Accounts such as these inspired the federal government, with the assistance of West Virginia University farm extension staff, to support Arthurdale's rapid development. The site, along with several adjacent tracts, was purchased from a "gentleman farmer" named Richard M. Arthur for a sum of thirty-five thousand dollars. Arthurdale's first residents, assisted by the Civilian Conservation Corps, began construction in 1933. In June 1934, the first fifty families moved into their homes. Upon completion in 1937, Arthurdale consisted of 165 homes, all of which are standing today.

By October 1933, more than six hundred individuals had applied for residency at Arthurdale. A selection committee, with the assistance of Eleanor Roosevelt, set the criteria for the homesteaders. Applicants had to be native-born Caucasians, in good physical condition, and knowledgeable about farming. Approximately half of the first homesteaders were miners, one-quarter were sawmill workers, and the remainder were farmers. Most residents were native West Virginians, and many qualified because they had technical skills. West Virginia University's agricultural staff assisted in deciding which crops to raise, and approximately 440 acres were set aside for a cooperative that produced vegetables, poultry, and dairy cattle.

In addition to its individual farm units, Arthurdale supported six schools, a community center complex, a clinic, an inn, and three factory buildings. The educational system emphasized training in Appalachian heritage and promoted student production of pioneer crafts. The community also supported a shop for the Mountain Craftsmen Cooperative Association, which specialized in woodcraft, needlework, and weaving. As with similar homestead projects across the nation, Arthurdale's cooperative efforts proved unsuccessful, however. Several industrial attempts to support the community's factories failed within one to two years of their establishment. In 1941 the government began liquidating its interests in Arthurdale, converting the entire area to private ownership by 1947.

Listed in the National Register of Historic Places in 1989, Arthurdale retains all of its original housing units and many community buildings. Much of the site's road system, considered its most unusual landscape feature, is still covered with the original "red dog" surface material, a by-product of uncontrolled burning of coal.

See also: COAL-CAMP ARCHITECTURE; COAL SETTLEMENTS (SETTLEMENT AND MIGRATION).

—Ruth D. Nichols, *TRC Garrow Associates, Nashville, Tennessee*

Stephen E. Haid, "Arthurdale: An Experiment in Community Planning, 1933–1947," Ph.D. dissertation, West Virginia University (1975); Barbara J. Howe, Iris Allsopp, and Elizabeth Nolin, "Arthurdale Historic District," National Register of Historic Places Form (1988).

Bacon, Henry

(1866–1924) Architect.

Born in Illinois, Henry Bacon grew up in Wilmington, North Carolina, where he formed important friendships with the family of Donald MacRae, a businessman with varied real estate and industrial interests. The MacRaes were the principal developers of Linville, an exclusive resort community along the Blue Ridge in North Carolina that contains an impressive collection of architecturally distinct late-nineteenth- and early-twentieth-century summer cottages.

The MacRaes persuaded Bacon to design three of the earliest cottages in Linville between 1895 and 1910, and he responded by developing a regionally unique rustic style of architecture for the buildings. Bacon chose to cover the structures with chestnut bark shingles inside and out and to use rough logs both structurally and decoratively. The most visible of Bacon's designs in Linville is the All Saints Episcopal Church (1910–13), which cleverly renders high church motifs in rustic, natural materials. Until the 1930s, when the supply of chestnut trees ran out, these buildings set the style for all future construction in Linville and many of the surrounding resort areas. The informal rustic character of Bacon's resort structures contrasts with his better known Neoclassical works.

Early in his career, Bacon worked for McKim, Mead and White, the preeminent American architectural firm at the turn of the twentieth century. He died in 1924, less than a year after winning the American Institute of Architects Gold Medal for his design for the Lincoln Memorial in Washington, D.C.

See also: LINVILLE GORGE AREA, NORTH CAROLINA (TOURISM); RUSTIC ARCHITECTURE.

—Clay Griffith, *North Carolina State Historic Preservation Office*

(Top) Interior of All Saints Episcopal Church, Linville, North Carolina, 2001. An example of Rustic style by architect Henry Bacon.

(Above) Exterior of All Saints Episcopal Church.

Barber, George F.

(1854–1915) Architect and carpenter.

George Franklin Barber was one of the first mail-order catalog architects and probably the most renowned architect in Tennessee at the turn of the twentieth century. In 1891 he published *The Cottage Souvenir No. 2: A Repository of Artistic Cottage Architecture and Miscellaneous Designs*, an expanded version of his earlier catalogs. Offering plans for residences, which he encouraged prospective buyers to customize, the catalog began Barber's career as a nationally known designer.

Born in DeKalb, Illinois, Barber grew up in Kansas. He was not formally educated in architecture and was listed in tax records as a carpenter. He returned to Illinois in the 1880s. Ill health forced Barber to seek a better climate, and in 1888 he arrived in Knoxville, Tennessee, and set up practice as a builder and architect. He had already printed two catalogs of designs, and, possibly due to difficulties in establishing himself in Knoxville, Barber printed his third book in 1891. In this plan book and others he would later publish, the designs were principally Queen Anne, Romanesque, or very eclectic. His intent was not to provide cutting-edge styles but to get the reader to purchase Barber houses and materials. Barber also took advantage of Knoxville's extensive railroad connections and shipped construction materials throughout the country. George F. Barber and Company, Architects, was the largest architectural firm in Knoxville in 1900. Around 1908 the mail-order business ended, and in 1910 Barber's son Charles, schooled as an architect, began to change the direction of the firm's designs.

See also: KNOXVILLE, TENNESSEE (URBAN APPALACHIAN EXPERIENCE).

—Claudette Stager, *Tennessee Historical Commission*

Barns, Cantilever and Pennsylvania

Among the more distinctive buildings associated with Appalachian farmsteads are the cantilever barn and the Pennsylvania barn. The cantilever barn is found in southern Appalachia; most examples of the type are located in the east Tennessee counties of Blount and Sevier. This barn features a huge, cantilevered gable-roof loft which overhangs the lower level on either two or four sides and is supported by long, hand-hewn logs resting atop two (sometimes four) hand-hewn log cribs. These cribs, typically used for livestock, are rectangular in shape, measure roughly twelve feet by eighteen feet, and are separated by a large open space or driveway that measures between fourteen and sixteen feet in width. Depending on the pitch of the roof and the length of the cantilevered logs, the loft, which was used for grain and hay storage, can be quite large. According to the research of Marian Moffett and Lawrence Wodehouse, most of the existing cantilever barns were built by self-sufficient farmers between 1870 and 1915. The barns satisfied the dual needs for livestock protection and grain storage in southern Appalachia, where humid, rainy conditions prevailed.

Some scholars have suggested that the cantilever barn represents a post–Civil War adaptation of the earlier Pennsylvania barn (also called the forebay or bank barn), which has a gable-roof upper level that is cantilevered and extends over the ground level on one side, creating an overhang varying in length from four to twenty feet. Another side of the lower level is built into a hill or an embankment, allowing farmers direct access to the upper level. Like the cantilever barn, the ground level was meant for livestock and the upper level for hay and grain storage. On most Pennsylvania barns, the forebay of the upper level served as a granary. Pennsylvania German farmers originated this barn type in southeast Pennsylvania, but during the nineteenth century its use extended westward into Ohio and southward into Maryland and Virginia.

Cantilever barn, Museum of Appalachia, Norris, Tennessee, 1994. This distinctive style of barn is found primarily in east Tennessee.

See also: LOG CONSTRUCTION TECHNIQUES; LOG DWELLING TYPES.

—Carroll Van West, *Middle Tennessee State University*

Beth Salem Presbyterian Church

Beth Salem Presbyterian Church, built around 1920 in McMinn County, Tennessee, is an unadorned frame gable-front building that has changed little since its construction in 1920. Listed in the National Register of Historic Places, it is a rare survivor of an architectural type that was once commonplace across Appalachia. Built by African Americans as a church and community center, the building is a testament to the importance of spirituality and simplicity in an era of racial turmoil.

The church was built after a fire destroyed the circa 1866 log chapel of the congregation in 1920. Reflecting the spirit of the congregation and support of the local community, the new building took shape with lumber that was donated by a white neighbor, Ray Lessely, and hauled sixteen miles by horse-drawn wagon.

Set near a crossroads and opposite a historic cemetery, the church has a handwritten sign reading "Bethsalem Presbyterian Church" across its front entrance. A symmetrical two-panel door is the only bay of the facade while the west and east elevations contain three symmetrical bays, with original shutters flanking two-over-two double-hung windows. The building rests on brick piers, and metal covers its gable roof.

The understatement of the exterior is in keeping with the restraint in architecture typical of rural African American churches built during the Jim Crow era. Economics accounted for part of the restraint—rural black communities did not have enough resources for brick buildings—but potential white backlash was another cause. If rural African Americans were too showy in their goods, homes, and places of worship, white vigilantes sometimes struck them.

The interior of Beth Salem, however, exhibits the craftsmanship of the black community. The walls and ceiling are beaded board, and the original hardwood floor is intact. The altar maintains a prominent place in front of the pulpit.

Due to migration to the growing towns and cities of southern Appalachia, weekly church services ended during

Beth Salem Presbyterian Church, McMinn County, Tennessee, 1998. The building serves as a chapel and community center. The unpretentious exterior represents both a tribute to simplicity and an effort by the congregation to remain inconspicuous.

the 1950s. Every August, however, former county residents, congregation members, and their descendants continue to meet at Beth Salem for an annual homecoming celebration.

See also: AFRICAN AMERICAN RELIGIOUS TRADITIONS (RELIGION).

—Susan Besser, *Fort Worth, Texas*

Biltmore Estate Complex

Biltmore, the renowned estate of George W. Vanderbilt, originally spread across approximately 120,000 acres of Blue Ridge Mountain land in and around Asheville, North Carolina. This grand complex, named for Bildt, the Dutch town from which the Vanderbilt family originated, and *more*, an archaic English word for "rolling country," took shape between 1889 and 1895 and stands as a symbol of Gilded Age opulence. The result of Vanderbilt's vision and the accomplishment of prominent professionals, Biltmore remains a masterpiece of high-style architecture and a model of landscape planning.

George Washington Vanderbilt (1862–1914), the youngest son of railroad magnate William Henry Vanderbilt and grandson of "Commodore" Cornelius Vanderbilt, first bought land around Asheville in 1888 after visiting the city with his mother. Impressed with the spectacular views and favorable climate, he sought to establish a country estate in the southern Appalachians. In contrast to resort areas in the Northeast such as Bar Harbor and Newport, Vanderbilt found cheap land readily available in Asheville.

Once he had located a suitable house site on Lone Pine Mountain, Vanderbilt began purchasing land formerly occupied by squatters who had exhausted the soil. He called upon Frederick Law Olmsted (1822–1903) to create a landscape plan for the estate. Olmsted, leader of the American parks movement in the mid-nineteenth century, designed a masterwork landscape composed of natural areas interspersed with farmland and spectacular French gardens surrounding the manor house. It was Olmsted's vision that inspired Vanderbilt to turn Biltmore into a productive venture where farming, forestry, and landscape design became key components. Olmsted envisioned creating a 250-acre park surrounding the house, clearing and farming the bottomland along the French Broad River, and reforesting the remaining land. Olmsted placed great emphasis on the importance of forestry at Biltmore and assured Vanderbilt that his estate could include the finest forest in the country, one that would prove profitable as well as enjoyable to Vanderbilt and his visitors. Except for the arboretum, all of Olmsted's ideas for Biltmore were realized. Much of the credit for the execution and preservation of Olmsted's plan goes to Chauncey Delos Beadle, who started working for Olmsted in 1890 and held the position of superintendent of Biltmore Estate for sixty years.

While Olmstead worked on the design for the estate grounds, Vanderbilt asked Richard Morris Hunt (1827–1895) to design a grand house for the country retreat. Hunt, architect to the wealthy and exponent of the Beaux Arts style in the United States, had studied in Europe, becoming the first American student to attend the École des Beaux Arts in Paris. Throughout his career, Hunt returned to Europe over and over again, studying, sketching, and photographing its architecture and developing a knowledge and familiarity that influenced his own work in the United States. In the spring of 1889, Vanderbilt and Hunt traveled through England and France to view firsthand the newest French Renaissance–style estates that would provide the inspiration for Biltmore.

Hundreds of workers started construction of the house in the summer of 1890. In order to transport the building materials to the site, a three-mile-long railroad line was built from the rail station in Asheville. Artisans from the United States as well as Europe were employed to carve and fit the Indiana limestone used to build the exterior walls.

Biltmore Village—a community containing a church, a depot, shops, offices, and housing—developed as a vital part of the Biltmore complex, and like the manor house, it resulted from collaboration among master designers. Olmsted planned the street pattern; Hunt's firm designed the major buildings, including All Souls Episcopal Church; Vanderbilt named the streets; and Richard Sharp Smith, Hunt's on-site supervising architect for Biltmore, designed worker houses, the hospital, the post office, and commercial

Biltmore House shortly after construction, c. 1900.

buildings. As construction of the manor house was completed in 1895, Smith resigned from Hunt's firm and established his own architectural practice in Asheville. He went on to become one of western North Carolina's most prolific and influential architects.

More than 850,000 people visit Biltmore annually to admire the work of Olmsted and Hunt and the vision of George W. Vanderbilt. A priceless collection of art and furnishings appoint the 250-room house containing four acres of floor space.

See also: BILTMORE ESTATE (TOURISM); BILTMORE FOREST SCHOOL; VANDERBILT, GEORGE W. (BUSINESS, INDUSTRY, AND TECHNOLOGY).

—Jennifer F. Martin, *Edwards-Pitman Environmental Incorporated, Raleigh, North Carolina*

Catherine W. Bishir, Michael T. Southern, and Jennifer F. Martin, *A Guide to the Historic Architecture of Western North Carolina* (1999); John Morrill Bryan, *Biltmore Estate: The Most Distinguished Private Place* (1994); Pamela Lynn Messer, *Biltmore Estate: Frederick Law Olmsted's Landscape Masterpiece* (1993).

Biltmore Forest School

The Biltmore Forest School, the nation's first school of forestry, operated as part of George W. Vanderbilt's estate from 1898 to 1909 at Biltmore (present-day Asheville) and at its field school in the Pisgah Forest of Transylvania County, North Carolina.

Landscape architect Frederick Law Olmsted urged Vanderbilt to hire a trained forester to improve the estate's extensive holdings, much of which had been damaged by overforestation, resulting in a tract riddled with "old, crippled, and otherwise inferior trees." In 1898 German forester Carl Alwin Schenck succeeded Gifford Pinchot as Biltmore's forester and established the school to teach young men the principles and practical aspects of forest management. On the estate's approximately 120,000 acres, Schenck devised the country's first working forestry plan. Forestry at Biltmore focused on combining utility and natural beauty by improving native timber stock and implementing a program of planting. The scientific approach Schenck espoused and taught his students allowed Vanderbilt to profit from harvesting timber while sponsoring a conservation program that would serve as a model for the country's timber industry.

Vanderbilt closed Biltmore's forestry school site in 1909 after some financial difficulty, but Schenck maintained the school in North Carolina, Darmstadt, Germany, and elsewhere. When it closed in 1913, the school had educated more than three hundred men and made a lasting mark on the history of forestry in the United States. Several restored and reconstructed buildings that made up the Pisgah field school stand at the Cradle of Forestry in America exhibition center located in Pisgah National Forest near Brevard.

See also: BILTMORE ESTATE (TOURISM); BILTMORE ESTATE COMPLEX; VANDERBILT, GEORGE W. (BUSINESS, INDUSTRY, AND TECHNOLOGY).

—Jennifer F. Martin, *Edwards-Pitman Environmental Incorporated, Raleigh, North Carolina*

Blue Ridge Parkway

The Blue Ridge Parkway traverses the Blue Ridge Mountains for 469 miles from Rockfish Gap, Virginia, to Cherokee, North Carolina, at the Oconaluftee River. Allowing motorists to drive easily and safely over some of the highest peaks in the eastern United States, the world-famous road offers inspiring views and picturesque landscaping.

An earlier plan advanced by several businessmen to build a private motor road along the crest of the Blue Ridge had been aborted during World War I. The Blue Ridge Parkway, approved for construction in 1933 as a "public works" project, was intended to provide jobs for depression-era Blue Ridge residents, encourage economic growth through tourism, facilitate recreation for city-dwellers, and connect Shenandoah National Park and Great Smoky Mountains National Park. Rights-of-way for the parkway were obtained by Virginia and North Carolina after Secretary of the Interior Harold L. Ickes, in a 1934 decision, chose engineer R. Getty Browning's proposed ridge-top route through the latter state over a ridge-and-valley course through Tennessee. The federal government provided all subsequent support, allocating it through the Public Works Administration, a component of Roosevelt's New Deal. The Bureau of Public Roads initially oversaw the road's construction—a fifty-two-year process begun on September 11, 1935—as well as the construction of tunnels and bridges, some of which were built by Spanish and Italian stone masons. Personnel employed by the Works Progress Administration and Civilian Conservation Corps, utilizing Stanley Abbott's master plan, embellished the parkway with landscaping (most notably through strategic planting of native flowering shrubs), signage, overlooks, hiking trails, roadside parks, campgrounds, visitor centers, and museums. Continued maintenance and management of the Blue Ridge Parkway was assigned to the National Park Service on June 30, 1936.

See also: BLUE RIDGE PARKWAY (TOURISM); SKYLINE DRIVE.

—Ted Olson, *East Tennessee State University*

Boone Tavern

In Berea, Kentucky, Boone Tavern symbolizes efforts to promote economic development in Appalachia. Upon the suggestion of Eleanor Marsh Frost, wife of Berea College President William Goodell Frost, the institution built a two-story, twenty-five-room hotel in 1909 to lodge campus visitors. Consistent with the college's mission of providing meaningful training to the region's disadvantaged populace, the inn has given valuable experience to hundreds of Berea students who work there as bellhops, desk clerks, and waitresses.

Choosing the Neoclassical Revival style, New York architectural firm Cady and See designed the Boone Tavern as an impressive hotel. Apparently the business was so successful that the college added a third story to the building within a year of its opening. The hotel's reputation is largely due to the successful management of Richard T. Hougen, a noted chef and Cornell University graduate who also taught courses in Berea College's hotel management program. Many items on the Boone Tavern menu are Hougen creations, including his version of spoonbread, a corn bread soufflé that is a hotel specialty.

Beginning in the 1910s, automobile tourists traveling on the Dixie Highway helped to popularize the hotel and its restaurant. Following completion of Interstate 75 in the 1970s, Berea lost much of the through-town traffic. Remarkably, however, the hotel has maintained a respectable share of the tourist trade. Into the twenty-first century, Berea College continued to own and operate the historic inn, with Berea students holding most of the hotel staff positions.

See also: BEREA COLLEGE (EDUCATION); TOURISM ARCHITECTURE.

—Jeffrey L. Durbin, *URS Corporation, Gaithersburg, Maryland*

Chautauqua Village, New York

Chautauqua Village, New York, is known for its picturesque buildings, brick walkways, well-tended gardens, and restriction on vehicular traffic, all of which create a Victorian ambiance and the impression that the village is suspended in time. Started in 1874 as a summer retreat for Protestant Sunday school teachers, the village has become part of the Chautauqua Institution, a summer center for the arts, education, religion, and recreation. Although rented tents and cots were the earliest accommodations for retreat participants, eventually cottages were erected, and the small Victorian-era village took form. The cottages reflect Victorian domestic architecture, including Carpenter Gothic, Stick, and Shingle styles. Many of the early cottages drew from the styles popularized by Andrew Jackson Downing's catalogue *The Architecture of Country Houses* (1850), with board and batten siding, decorative scrollwork, and gingerbread trim. Originally, the summer homes were not made for winter use, though many have since been modernized to include heating and cooling systems. The Second Empire–style 160-room Athenaeum Hotel (1881) was one of the earliest buildings in the village to be electrified.

The architecture of the institution's buildings ranges from the open-air, Greek Revival–style Hall of Philosophy (1903–6) to the Craftsman-style amphitheater (1892) to the Miller Bell Tower (1911), built to represent an Italian campanile, or freestanding bell tower. The village also includes hotels and boardinghouses in the same styles as the picturesque cottages. Smith Memorial Library (1931), constructed in the Georgian Revival style, reflects the changing American tastes in architecture. Chautauqua Village's growth continued until World War II and included religious, housing, performance, rehearsal, and educational facilities.

See also: RUSTIC ARCHITECTURE; TOURISM ARCHITECTURE.

—Susan S. Goodsell, *Benton Harbor, Michigan*

Chief Vann House

The Chief Vann House was the home of Cherokee Indian leader Chief James Vann and his son, Joseph Vann. Located on the Old Federal Road in Spring Place, Murray County, Georgia, the Vann House is an imposing two-story brick I-house with Federal-style detailing. Chief Vann, who was half Scottish and half Cherokee, built the house in 1805 for his family. Chief Vann is best known for establishing a Moravian mission in Spring Hill. Joseph Vann inherited the house after his father's death in 1809. In 1835 William N. Bishop, leading a troop of Georgia guardsmen, forced Joseph Vann to forfeit his property as a part of the Cherokee removal. Joseph Vann joined the Trail of Tears and eventually settled in Oklahoma, where he built a replica of his Georgia home.

Few historic houses in the North Georgia region are as impressive as this "showplace of the Cherokee Nation." Architecturally, the Chief Vann House is significant as a rare and intact early-nineteenth-century brick I-house, a two-story dwelling with a central hallway and chimneys of either limestone or brick placed at the gable ends. The house is also notable for its elaborate Federal-style detailing with two-tiered front and rear porches, a cantilevered staircase, and the intricate woodwork found throughout the house. The Chief Vann House is listed on the National Register of Historic Places and is owned by the State of Georgia, which operates it as a historic house museum.

See also: CHEROKEE (RACE, ETHNICITY, AND IDENTITY); RAMSEY HOUSE; TRAIL OF TEARS (SETTLEMENT AND MIGRATION).

—Leslie N. Sharp, *Georgia Institute of Technology*

Chota Village

Located in the Little Tennessee River valley of east Tennessee, Chota Village was one of more than sixty eighteenth-century Cherokee towns. Regarded by many as the capital of the Cherokee Nation, Chota rose to political, military, and economic prominence in the 1750s. The British recognized the town's strategic position on the frontier, as did the French and their Native American allies. In return for supporting the British, Chota received economic and military support, and as a result, its strong leaders were able to exert economic and political influence over neighboring Cherokee towns. French influence was greatly diminished and eventually eliminated after they were defeated by the British and their Cherokee allies.

Chief Vann House, Chatsworth, Georgia, 2001. Former home of Cherokee leader Chief James Vann, the two-story house, built in 1805, is an example of an early-nineteenth-century brick I-house.

By 1760 Chota consisted of about sixty households and more than four hundred people. Households included a circular winter house with a conical roof, an adjacent rectangular summer house with a gable roof, and associated areas for domestic activities. Built 150 to 300 feet apart and surrounded by agricultural fields, households were scattered along the river for more than one and a quarter miles. Similar in architecture to domestic houses but much larger, the townhouse provided seating for nearly five hundred people and, along with the summer pavilion and village plaza, was a focal point for community religious, social, and political activities.

American militia attacked Chota during the Revolutionary War. By 1807 only thirty-four people remained in the town, and in 1819 Chota was ceded to the United States. The University of Tennessee conducted extensive archaeological work at the site before its inundation by the Tellico Reservoir in 1979. In the 1980s two memorials were dedicated to the Cherokee at Chota, and the Eastern Band of Cherokee Indians now administers a small area preserved at the site.

See also: CHEROKEE (RACE, ETHNICITY, AND IDENTITY); CHEROKEE REMOVAL (GOVERNMENT).

—Gerald F. Schroedl, *University of Tennessee*

Cincinnati Union Terminal

The cornerstone of the Cincinnati Union Terminal in Cincinnati, Ohio, was laid in 1931, and the terminal opened to the public in 1933. Alfred Fellheimer and Steward Wagner of New York collaborated with Paul Cret, a Philadelphia architect, and Winold Reiss, a German American artist, to create one of the last great municipal train stations. With its graceful streamlined design, the terminal is not only a remarkable example of the Art Deco style, but also houses the largest collection of secular mosaics in the United States. In its day, the terminal represented the best of the Art Deco movement while solving many of the transportation and passenger problems that plagued other municipal train stations. Servicing seven trunk lines with twenty-two buildings, 287 acres of railroad yards, and ninety-four miles of tracks, it quickly became the major north-south transfer point in the region, opening Appalachian markets both to commercial enterprises and passenger traffic.

Cincinnati Union Terminal represents the relationship of Art Deco to the Academic Classical Revival movement through Cret's use of stylized classical motifs, traditional limestone facing blends, and modern aluminum. Some critics of the terminal's architectural elements compared it to a giant table radio; however, most others recognized the importance of the twenty-thousand-square-foot rotunda encircled with mosaic murals depicting panoramic sweeps of local, state, and national history. The murals, divided into three sections, contain foreground figures, landscapes, and transportation timelines. The twelve-foot-tall common folk mosaics, the highlight of the murals, illustrate river pilots, stoic pioneer wives, brawny high-steel workers, and Revolutionary War heroes.

Automobile and air travel eventually made trains obsolete, and the last two passenger trains pulled out of the terminal in 1972. After many failed attempts, the terminal was finally preserved as the Cincinnati Museum Center in 1990 through the joint efforts of the Cincinnati Museum of Natural History and the Cincinnati Historical Society. As a multiuse facility, the terminal continued to buzz with activity at the turn of the twenty-first century, hearkening back to its former life as one of the greatest and last municipal train stations in the United States.

See also: CINCINNATI, OHIO (URBAN APPALACHIAN EXPERIENCE).

—Harrison Stamm Gowdy, *Cincinnati, Ohio*

Coal-Camp Architecture

The emergence of coal mining as an industry in Appalachia between the turn of the century and 1920 spurred the creation of communities where companies controlled the architectural styles and layout of the buildings. These coal camps and, later, towns were similar to other mining communities that developed throughout the United States. For the most part, coal-community architecture emphasized functional concerns over architectural style, designed most buildings to be impermanent, and utilized natural resources from the area for construction materials.

Scholars have identified four basic mining town patterns in field surveys of coal-mining communities in West Virginia. They are the block pattern, with a uniform system of closed blocks; the linear pattern, with a single street with houses on one or both sides; the cruciform pattern, with more open streets than closed blocks; and the fragmented pattern, with a divided area. The more uniform layouts came, in most cases, from formal designs by the mining company. Although this survey focuses on West Virginia, similar patterns appear in many Appalachian coal communities.

Almost every mining community town possessed a uniform style of company home. The eight primary styles include the one-story L-style; the pyramid cottage; the bungalow; the I-style; the two-story four-room; the two-story shotgun; the saltbox; and the two-story L-style. Some residents gave these homes distinctive vernacular names; the "duck-bill" house, for instance, was a two-story, four-room house with prominent overhanging porches on the first story. Superintendents' houses were larger and often had formal stylistic elements. Many Victorian-style superintendents' homes, usually blending Queen Anne and classical details, were built in the towns.

The companies also provided other buildings in the coal towns. Reflecting the company's power and prosperity through their central location, company stores varied in architectural styles but were usually housed in a three-story, brick or clapboard block-shaped building. Also located in the center of town was a community building. This building could contain an auditorium, billiard room, dining room, and lodge hall. Like the company store, the community building's architecture reflected the prosperity of the company. When African American workers were employed, the companies created segregated spaces in the community buildings as well as segregated, often substandard, housing for them.

Coal companies also built churches and schools that were architecturally unadorned and followed basic standardized plans. They were simple box-shaped buildings with front- and rear-facing gables with a cupola. White churches were located in the center of the town while African American churches were located on the outskirts in segregated neighborhoods.

See also: COAL IMAGES (IMAGES AND ICONS); COAL SETTLEMENTS (SETTLEMENT AND MIGRATION).

—Edward G. Salo, *Geo-Marine, Inc., Plano, Texas*

Richard V. Francaviglia, *Hard Places: Reading the Landscapes of America's Historic Mining Districts* (1994); Mack H. Gillenwater, *Cultural and Historical Geography of Mining Settlements in the Pocahontas Coal Field of Southern West Virginia, 1880–1930* (1972); Crandall A. Shifflett, *Coal Towns: Life, Work, and Culture in Company Towns of Southern Appalachia, 1880–1960* (1991).

Cumberland Homesteads

Cumberland Homesteads was a subsistence farm community in Cumberland County, Tennessee, created in 1933–34 under the Division of Subsistence Homesteads of the Department of Interior as part of Franklin D. Roosevelt's New Deal. It served as a prototype for similar communities across the nation.

Established in 1933, the Division of Subsistence Homesteads emerged following an experimental project of subsistence farms that had proved successful in New York. The agency's initial goal was to provide locally displaced miners and farmers with farms, paid for by the government, on which owners would clear the land, construct housing, and raise livestock and crops. Owners signed contracts with the government by which they were required to pay the money back after they became financially sound. Each homestead consisted of between 10 and 160 acres, with a single-family home, a barn, support buildings (such as poultry sheds, smokehouses, and privies), livestock, and farm equipment. Initial plans also called for the establishment of a cooperative dairy, mill, community center, and school.

Two hundred fifty homesteaders were selected from the thousands who applied to participate in the Cumberland Homesteads project. In December 1934, the first ten families moved into their new homes constructed of native Crab Orchard sandstone. The Civilian Works Administration cleared more than 10,000 acres for the initial project and constructed the original homes and support buildings. Also created from the original tract was Cumberland Mountain State Park, a heavily forested area of more than 1,400 acres developed for recreation in 1933 by the Civilian Conservation Corps. The original homestead site designated 8,903 acres as farm units and 1,245 acres as "common land." An additional 11,200 acres were set aside for future development. By 1938 the entire tract consisted of 27,802 acres. The community celebrated its completed efforts on July 28, 1938, at which time it supported 251 individual homesteads, 100 fewer than originally planned.

In addition to individual farmsteads, Cumberland Homesteads featured community facilities, also constructed of native sandstone. These included two schools, an eight-story water tower that housed administrative offices, a canning factory, a hosiery mill, a coal mine, a trading post, a sorghum plant, a poultry farm, and a credit union. Restrictions on what homesteaders were allowed to do with their property—limitations on the types of crops that could be raised, for example—resulted in the departure of many residents. Community dissent led to closure of the cooperative efforts as well. Deficient soils and limited farm sizes forced many residents to leave in search of other means of support. The project was shifted between government agencies until 1939, when owners were asked individually to purchase their homesteads. Approximately half of the community's residents consented, and the site was converted to private ownership.

In 1988 Cumberland Homesteads was listed on the National Register of Historic Places. The site comprises a total of 10,250 acres, including Cumberland Mountain State Park, which currently encompasses 1,720 acres. Located within the Cumberland Plateau near downtown Crossville, Tennessee, the Cumberland Homesteads/Cumberland Mountain State Park site is a feature of the nation's largest timbered plateau.

See also: ARTHURDALE, WEST VIRGINIA; CIVILIAN CONSERVATION CORPS (GOVERNMENT).

—Ruth D. Nichols, *TRC Garrow Associates, Nashville, Tennessee*

Jane Polansky, "Homesteading in the Cumberlands: Cumberland Homesteads Cumberland Mountain Park," *Tennessee Conservationist* (September–October 1999); Elizabeth A. Straw, "Cumberland Homesteads Historic District," National Register of Historic Places Registration Form (1988).

Ellington, Douglas D.

(1886–1960) Architect.

Born in eastern North Carolina, Douglas Dobell Ellington studied architecture at Drexel Institute and the University of Pennsylvania before winning the 1913 Paris Prize from the Society of Beaux Arts Architects, an award that provided for study at the École des Beaux Arts in Paris. In 1913 Ellington won the Prix de Rougevin, the top honor for decorative competitions at the École, becoming the first American ever to do so. He returned from Europe during World War I and served in the U.S. Navy's newly formed camouflage unit. After completing military service, he taught in the Beaux Arts–influenced architecture programs at Drexel, Columbia University, and Carnegie Institute of Technology. Ellington ran an office in Pittsburgh in the first half of the 1920s, and his work of these years shows a relatively rapid evolution from the classical vocabulary of the Beaux Arts to the modern aesthetic of Art Deco.

Ellington relocated his office to Asheville, North Carolina, in 1926, when he was awarded the commission for the city's First Baptist Church. Ellington created an architectural synthesis that brought together Beaux Arts classicism, modern functionalism, and fashionable Art Deco styling on several highly visible civic projects: the Asheville City Building (1927), Asheville High School (1929), and the S&W Cafeteria (1929). The church design, however, introduced a vocabulary of forms, material combinations, color motifs, and surface treatments that signaled the origin of an idiomatic style tailored to the environment of Asheville. Ellington wanted his buildings to reflect the colors and contours of the surrounding mountain landscape, to employ natural materials suited to the region, and to incorporate motifs relating to the Native American people who occupied the land before European settlement, all the while responding to the modernization of the city. From the geometric plan and rough stone exterior of Asheville High School to the exotic sophistication of the S&W Cafeteria, Ellington's buildings comprise a distinctive collection of Art Deco–style architecture in North Carolina. Even for lesser commissions such as the Merrimon Avenue Fire Station (1927), Lewis Memorial Park Office (1927), and Biltmore Hospital Extension (1930), the architect adapted his vocabulary of forms, materials, and motifs to a smaller, more utilitarian scale.

Asheville's real estate boom of the late 1920s ended suddenly with the Great Depression, and Ellington moved to Washington, D.C., to serve with Reginald Wadsworth as principal architect for the federally sponsored new town of Greenbelt, Maryland. In 1937 Ellington relocated to Charleston, South Carolina, to direct the reconstruction of the historic Dock Street Theater. He reestablished his office in Charleston and worked there almost exclusively during the years of World War II. Ellington continued to return regularly to western North Carolina, however, and from the late 1940s until his death in 1960 he worked on a number of residential projects in and around Asheville.

See also: ASHEVILLE, NORTH CAROLINA (URBAN APPALACHIAN EXPERIENCE).

—Clay Griffith, *North Carolina State Historic Preservation Office*

Catherine W. Bishir, *North Carolina Architecture* (1990); Douglas Swaim, ed., *Cabins and Castles* (1981).

Fallingwater

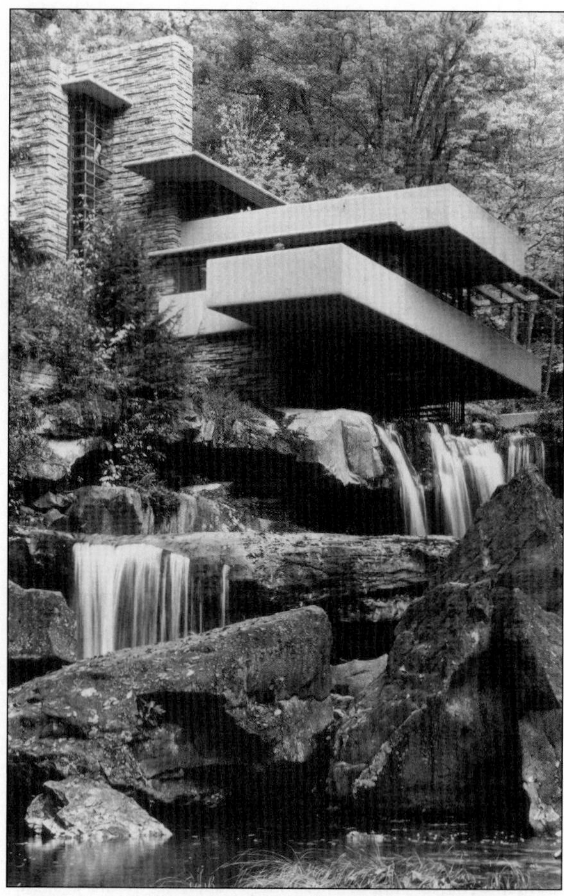

Fallingwater, Fayette County, Pennsylvania. Designed by Frank Lloyd Wright for Pittsburgh businessman Edgar J. Kaufmann Sr., this acclaimed piece of architecture, completed in 1939, fused native materials and Rustic motifs with the International style.

One of the most renowned monuments of twentieth-century American architecture is Fallingwater, a house located on Bear Run in Fayette County, Pennsylvania. Designed by Frank Lloyd Wright (1867–1959) for wealthy Pittsburgh department store owner Edgar J. Kaufmann Sr. and built between 1936 and 1939 on Kaufmann's foothills retreat, Fallingwater is more often discussed as a landmark of twentieth-century American architecture than as an Appalachian structure. Yet few structures owe so much of their status to the character, distinctive forms, and raw materials of their sites.

By the 1920s Wright had distinguished himself for the Prairie House, a horizontal dwelling often called organic for its incorporation of wood and masonry in unforced ways, emphasis on open plans in which various household activities naturally flowed together or floated apart, and sensitive fusion of building and site. In 1932, however, an exhibition at the Museum of Modern Art in New York downplayed Wright's importance to modernist architecture by portraying him as an outdated eccentric bystander to the heralded new International style, which emphasized planar forms and industrially produced materials such as glass, steel, and reinforced concrete. At about this time, Edgar and Liliane Kaufmann, motivated by their son's admiration for Wright's work, invited the architect to design a country house on their 1,543-acre estate southeast of Pittsburgh. Wright, confronting financial as well as professional stagnation, seized this opportunity, creating an audacious structure that famously resuscitated his career.

Wright began with the dramatically unexpected: instead of positioning the house so that it would command the tract's most arresting view—a steep rocky ledge over a waterfall—he boldly chose this promontory for the site of the house itself. He then assembled a multileveled structure of strong native-rock verticals and molded concrete horizontals. This complex design combines Wright's organic principles of design, which emphasize the inherent qualities of natural building materials, and the International style's insistence on severe-looking industrial-age materials.

Beneath the house, parallel concrete ribs both visually and literally anchor the house to the hill beside it. These members coalesce into slabs as they pass through the house, emerging to project over the waterfall as cantilevered, gravity-defying eaves, parapets, and terraces. The exterior walls are built from native stone, which is recessed in many places beneath the concrete horizontals and interspersed with glass. Wright also used rock indoors. The unadorned interior walls are constructed of deeply textured stone, and the polished stone floors suggest solid rock outcroppings in Appalachian streambeds. Overall, the interior of the house, with its many low-ceilinged views of the surrounding forest, resembles a mountain cave. A boulder that erupts through the stone floor near the principal hearth emphasizes Fallingwater's rootedness in place; the structure is a rock-solid, protective mountain home.

In some ways, Fallingwater owes its status as a landmark of Appalachian culture less to Wright's design than to the structure's distinctive materials and site. In fact, one of Wright's unexecuted ideas—concrete walls covered in gold leaf—would have rendered the house a visually worrisome intruder in the mountain landscape.

Donated to the Western Pennsylvania Conservancy by Edgar Kaufmann Jr. in 1963, Fallingwater is the earliest —and still the most famous—instance of International-style architecture in Appalachia. The house's popularity among visitors has supported the acquisition, protection, and public enjoyment of many surrounding acres of mountain woodland.

See also: RUSTIC ARCHITECTURE.

—Camille Wells, *University of Virginia*

Donald Hoffman, *Frank Lloyd Wright's Fallingwater: The House and Its History* (revised edition, 1993); Edgar Kaufmann Jr., *Fallingwater: A Frank Lloyd Wright Country House* (1986); John McAndrew, *A New House by Frank Lloyd Wright on Bear Run, Pennsylvania* (1938); Dell Upton, *Architecture in the United States* (1998).

Farmer's Society Hall

Located in South Carolina's upcountry, the Pendleton Farmer's Society Hall represents early efforts to make Appalachian farms more productive. The building is also significant for its association with several prominent South Carolinians. The society counted as members John C. Calhoun, Thomas Pickens, and the Pinckney brothers, Thomas and Charles.

One of the upcountry's oldest towns, Pendleton owes its existence to the fertile land which attracted settlement following a 1785 treaty with the Cherokees. Within five years the population was large enough to form a county government based at Pendleton. The Farmer's Society was formed in 1815 to promote local agriculture. Thirteen years later, the group began meeting in its present location after it bought and completed a building intended to serve as the county courthouse.

Tied to a select group of community leaders, the Farmer's Society Hall was an important gathering spot where members discussed agriculture, as well as debating thornier issues such as nullification of the Tariff of 1832. Calhoun's son-in-law, Thomas Green Clemson, gave an address in the hall calling for the establishment of an agricultural college in the state, which led to the eventual creation of nearby Clemson University. Surviving the Civil War, the Pendleton Farmer's Society Hall also outlasted larger agrarian groups, including the Farmer's Alliance and the Populist party. Today, the Greek Revival–style hall is the country's oldest farmer's society building in continuous use and an important destination for tourists visiting the area's many historic places.

See also: AGRICULTURAL EDUCATION (AGRICULTURE); FARMERS FEDERATION (AGRICULTURE).

—Jeffrey L. Durbin, *URS Corporation, Gaithersburg, Maryland*

Fort Stover

Built in the late eighteenth century, Fort Stover is a two-story stone dwelling that is representative of several existing historic homes associated with an earlier Swiss Mennonite settlement along the South Fork of the Shenandoah River east of Massanutten Mountain in Page County, Virginia. Research by Edward A. Chappell has found that several homes—Fort Egypt, Fort Philip Long, Fort Rodes, and Fort Stover, for instance—retained such Germanic architectural traits as the three-room plan of the *Flurkuchenhaus,* or hall-kitchen house, where the kitchen *(Kuche)* is an interior central room and an informal family space. Other Germanic traits included the use of the attic for grain storage and the placement of the house itself into an embankment or hillside, allowing for exterior access to the basement. The basement was typically large and sometimes vaulted, creating a cool cellar for the storage of perishable commodities. Due to the size and vaulted construction of the cellars, early observers thought that they were designed for defense against

Native American attacks and consequently described the homes as "forts." This incorrect assumption is reflected in the popular name for the dwellings.

Fort Stover also exhibits several characteristics of Anglo-American domestic architecture such as its gable-end chimneys, three-bay facade, and interior rooms heated by fireplaces rather than stoves. These architectural elements give the exterior of the dwelling a somewhat Anglo-American face, while the retention of the *Flurkuchenhaus* plan and the vaulted cellar suggest German influences. Fort Stover is significant as a material culture example of ethnic acculturation on the late-eighteenth-century western frontier.

See also: GERMANS (RACE, ETHNICITY, AND IDENTITY); SWISS (RACE, ETHNICITY, AND IDENTITY).

—Carroll Van West, *Middle Tennessee State University*

Friends Meeting House

Quakers in southeastern Ohio built the Friends Meeting House at Mount Pleasant, Jefferson County, in 1814–15 to accommodate the Ohio Yearly Meeting. It was the first yearly meetinghouse for Quakers west of the Alleghenies. The plain, well-proportioned, two-story brick building sits on a limestone foundation. A gable roof covers the massive structure, which is sixty feet wide by ninety-two feet long. With a seating capacity of two thousand, it nearly burst at the seams during the annual August meetings when the village bustled with festivities.

Grove Arcade, Asheville, North Carolina, c. 1930. Designed as a massive commercial mall by architect Charles N. Parker for Edwin Wiley Grove, this sophisticated Tudoresque arcade building was completed by Walter P. Taylor before construction was stopped by the 1929 stock market crash.

The last yearly meeting was held at Mount Pleasant in 1918. The Ohio Historical Society opened the Friends Meeting House in 1966 as a state memorial to recognize the role of Quakers in early Ohio. The Friends contributed significantly to social concerns such as education, temperance, and equal rights for men and women—regardless of race or creed. Many Quakers from the South migrated north of the Ohio River to avoid having to live in states which supported slavery. Located in Jefferson County, which borders along the Ohio, Mount Pleasant welcomed runaway slaves and became an important center for the Underground Railroad.

The Mount Pleasant Historical Society manages the Friends Meeting House and provides tours of the house and the historic district that include stops along the Underground Railroad and the Benjamin Lundy House and Free Labor Store, which is a National Historic Landmark.

See also: FREE BLACKS, ANTEBELLUM (RACE, ETHNICITY, AND IDENTITY); QUAKERS (RELIGION).

—Karen Lowe, *Chagrin Falls, Ohio*

Grove Arcade

Edwin Wiley Grove envisioned the Grove Arcade (1926–29), located in downtown Asheville, North Carolina, as a massive commercial mall with covered pedestrian thoroughfares and rooftop terraces surmounted by a skyscraper tower. Architect Charles N. Parker, who worked for the firm of Smith and Carrier in Asheville before setting up his own practice, designed the Grove Arcade, which occupies a site that Grove graded and cleared in front of the new Battery Park Hotel. Although construction paused after Grove's death in 1927, it resumed under Walter P. Taylor, who completed the arcade portion of the building. After the stock market crash in 1929, Taylor chose not to construct the intended tower. The arcade building was the most ambitious project conceived by Grove, a wealthy patent medicine manufacturer, real estate developer, and major benefactor of the city.

The elaborate Tudoresque building occupies a full city block; glazed terra cotta covers the reinforced concrete and steel structure. Deep barrel vaults form the major entrances, which are located at the center of each elevation, while a series of ramps to the roof terraces flank the main entrance at the north of the building. The two interior corridors intersect beneath the tower and form an open octagonal space. Wooden storefronts with similar Tudor Gothic Revival–style details and cantilevered bronze stairs finish the interior.

Occupied and modified by the federal government since 1942, the Grove Arcade is a rare example of the sophisticated arcade form in North Carolina.

See also: ASHEVILLE, NORTH CAROLINA (URBAN APPALACHIAN EXPERIENCE); BILTMORE ESTATE COMPLEX; GROVE PARK INN.

—Clay Griffith, *North Carolina State Historic Preservation Office*

Grove Park Inn

The Grove Park Inn is one of Appalachia's oldest and most renowned resort hotels and a landmark of Rustic-style architecture. Constructed of local granite boulders, it commands a breathtaking view from Sunset Mountain in Asheville, North Carolina. The hotel is listed on the National Register of Historic Places and boasts one of the country's largest collections of Arts and Crafts–style furnishings, many of which are original pieces created for its opening in July 1913.

Edwin Wiley Grove got his start as a clerk and pharmacist and soon made his fortune through patent medicine. Although he lived in St. Louis, he spent summers in Asheville. At the start of the twentieth century, Asheville was known for tuberculosis sanitariums, but Grove recognized the economic possibilities tourism held if the mountains were promoted as an escape for harried businessmen. In the fall of 1911, Grove announced plans to build a hotel. Numerous architectural firms came to view the site at their own expense, but none of their plans pleased him. Even Smith and Carrier, the leading Asheville firm and the only one formally invited to submit sketches, was unsuccessful. At this time Grove met architect Henry Ives Cobb of Boston. While Grove considered a new prospect, his son-in-law, Fred Seely, assumed a more active role in the project. In the spring of 1912, Seely took over negotiations with Cobb while working on a sketch of his own. Although he had no architectural training, Seely produced a plan that exactly suited Grove, one that was only minimally changed before the hotel's completion a year later. Cobb's plans were never located, though, and Seely's debt to him therefore remains unclear.

The finished structure demonstrates harmony with its environment. The building is sited on the side rather than the top of the mountain so that it enjoys the view while remaining sheltered from the elements. Grove was taken with the rustic quality of hotels such as the Grand Canyon Hotel and the Old Faithful Inn, and Seely translated this style to the Blue Ridge by using stone instead of logs. Massive granite columns and two thirty-six-foot-wide fireplaces, which concealed (and quieted) elevator shafts, distinguished the large lobby. Stone also had the advantage of being fireproof, as is the inn's characteristic undulating red tile roof, which covers continuously poured concrete.

Construction of the hotel was a feat involving about four hundred workers, including Italian stone masons who had worked on the Biltmore House. Their handiwork ensured that only the weathered, uncut sides of the boulders are visible.

Seely personally supervised every detail of the hotel's furnishing. He contacted the Roycroft Shops in East Aurora, New York, to design Arts and Crafts furniture and light fixtures. The job was too large for the Roycrofters alone, so Seely engaged a North Carolina company to make white oak beds, desks, and tables for guest rooms. The Roycrofters' copper and mica chandeliers for the lobby and dining room have been retained, as have other fixtures and many pieces of furniture. Seely followed Arts and Crafts fashion by inscribing mottoes and quotations on stones throughout the lobby.

The inn quickly became a popular resort for wealthy Americans and hosted a string of famous patrons. After Grove's death in 1927, the hotel changed hands, and a series of owners allowed the facilities to deteriorate. During World War II, it served as a confinement center for Axis diplomats and later as a naval rehabilitation center, and though it continued to welcome notable guests, the inn eventually began to decline. Its purchase by entrepreneur Charles Sammons and the Jack Tar Hotels Corporation in 1955 marked the first major renovation. Unfortunately, attempts at modernization resulted in the masking of the very elements that defined the hotel's rustic character, including much of the exposed granite in the lobby. This renovation also began the inn's transition to a modern resort and convention hotel through the addition of an outdoor pool, a cocktail lounge, meeting rooms, and a motor lodge. A second wave of renovation began in 1978 and continued through the 1980s. This massive expansion more than doubled the number of the original 156 rooms through the construction of two new wings. More Arts and Crafts antiques were added to the inn's collection, and sensitive restoration revealed the beauty of Seely's design for the main building while the wings echoed its historic character.

See also: BILTMORE ESTATE COMPLEX; GROVE ARCADE; RUSTIC ARCHITECTURE.

—Blythe Semmer, *Metropolitan Nashville Historical Commission*

Bruce E. Johnson, *Built for the Ages: A History of the Grove Park Inn* (1991) and "Built without an Architect: Architectural Inspirations for the Grove Park Inn," in *May We All Remember Well: A Journal of the History and Cultures of Western North Carolina*, ed. Robert S. Brunk (1997).

Hagood Mill

A symbol of permanent settlement and a physical reminder of how self-sufficient farmers converted their grain to flour and cornmeal, Hagood Mill is also an early example of an Appalachian industry. The mill is located on Twelve Mile River, three miles outside of Pickens, South Carolina. Like many such buildings, Hagood Mill is a simple but sturdy wood building constructed of hand-hewn parts that are sheathed by weatherboards. The mill rests upon a fieldstone foundation, and its grist stones are powered by an overshot waterwheel.

While it stands in the upcountry section of the state, the building has ties to a wealthy Charleston planter named Benjamin Hagood, who had the mill constructed sometime before 1830. Hagood initially came to the area to escape the humid low-country climate. Through the mill, he derived an important supplemental income to support his family during the times they stayed at their nearby summer home. In addition to being a center of commerce, Hagood Mill was also significant as a meeting place. Living in virtual isolation and with few outlets for socializing, local farmers often gathered at the mill to hear the latest news and to share agricultural techniques.

Once numbering in the hundreds and a common feature throughout Appalachia, relatively few gristmills remain standing. However, Hagood Mill is one of several extant mill buildings in Pickens County, and it continued to operate into the twenty-first century, though on a limited basis.

See also: AGRARIAN REVIVAL (AGRICULTURE); AGRICULTURAL TOURISM (TOURISM); GRISTMILLS (FOOD AND COOKING).

—Jeffrey L. Durbin, *URS Corporation Gaithersburg, Maryland*

Halltown Memorial Chapel

Built in 1901 as the Halltown Union Colored Sunday School to serve the religious and educational needs of African Americans in Jefferson County, West Virginia, the Halltown Memorial Chapel is an impressive symbol of identity, culture, and architectural achievement. The architect is not known, but local residents and artisans worked on weekends and after the workday to build the stone chapel in Gothic Revival fashion, complete with a gable entrance and short stone buttresses, in a manner reminiscent of the Arts and Crafts style then popular throughout the nation. The choice of locally available stone as the primary building material reflected not only an aesthetic principle of the Arts and Crafts movement, but also conveyed the community's desire to create a permanent landmark within the broader, mostly white cultural landscape of Jefferson County.

Daniel B. Lucas donated the land for the building, which stood adjacent to the community's public school. Community members constructed the building to serve not only as a Sunday school but also as a nondenominational church—thus "Union Colored Sunday School." They also used the building for weddings, funerals, social occasions, and community events.

Listed in the National Register of Historic Places in 1984, the Halltown Memorial Chapel is a significant architectural statement of the centrality of religion and community to the African American residents of Appalachia.

See also: AFRICAN AMERICAN EDUCATION (EDUCATION); AFRICAN AMERICAN RELIGIOUS TRADITIONS (RELIGION).

—Carroll Van West, *Middle Tennessee State University*

Hunt, Reuben H.

(1862–1937) Architect.

Reuben Harrison Hunt arrived in Chattanooga, Tennessee, from Georgia in 1882. While working as a builder and carpenter, Hunt studied architecture in his spare time. By 1886 he had begun his own firm, one that would dominate the architectural profession in Chattanooga for the next fifty years. Hunt's firm was one of the most prolific and widely known in the Southeast, undertaking projects throughout the region. In the early 1920s, Hunt started a second office in Dallas. Specializing in churches, educational buildings, and public buildings, his practice included designs in Gothic, Romanesque, Beaux Arts, Neoclassical, Georgian Revival, Greek Revival, and Art Deco styles. An active member and deacon in the Baptist Church, Hunt was also a Mason, a member of the Chattanooga Planning Commission, and a local civic leader. The architect produced and distributed his own pattern book of church designs, generously designing many church buildings across the South at no cost to the congregations. An indication of Hunt's prominence in Chattanooga is that he designed all the city's major government buildings between 1895 and 1935, as well as several of its major office buildings. Hunt's contributions to the early-twentieth-century development of the physical landscape of Chattanooga cannot be overestimated. Local editorials at his death in 1937 termed him the "master builder of Chattanooga" and "the outstanding architect in the entire South."

See also: CHATTANOOGA, TENNESSEE (URBAN APPALACHIAN EXPERIENCE).

—Martha Carver, *Tennessee Department of Transportation*

Kate Duncan Smith Daughters of the American Revolution School

Located on the edge of Gunter Mountain in the foothills of the Appalachians in Grant, Alabama, the Kate Duncan Smith Daughters of the American Revolution School was constructed in 1924 to improve educational opportunities for local children. The National Daughters of the American Revolution began its educational campaign in the early 1900s, targeting disadvantaged children, especially in mountain locations, who lacked easily accessible educational facilities. The Alabama chapter's efforts to bring a Daughters of the American Revolution school to its Appalachian region originated during its twelfth state conference in 1910; however, its monetary goal of ten thousand dollars was not reached until 1923.

The location of the school was selected over twenty-six other applicants, and construction began in October 1924. A local family deeded approximately one hundred acres for the site, and the rest of the community contributed as they could. Some gave money, but most donated time and labor by clearing the land and building the school. Plans and specifications for the building were supplied by the Alabama Department of Education for a school that could be easily enlarged. This first unit was constructed of local fieldstone and originally had four large classrooms along a corridor extending the length of the building, an office, a library, and a reception hall. Eventually an auditorium and twelve classrooms were added to the first unit, and numerous other buildings were added to the campus: the first teacher's cottage in 1928; a cobblestone vocational building in 1934; a home economics cottage and a log library in 1935; and a cobblestone water tower in 1937. The campus has since grown to include additional teachers' cottages, a chapel, recreational facilities, and a model farm for the vocational program. In 2001 more than 1,110 students attended grades K–12 on a 240-acre campus supporting more than thirty buildings and five recreational sites.

See also: SECTION OVERVIEW (EDUCATION).

—Trina L. Binkley, *Alabama Historical Commission*

Log Construction Techniques

Horizontal log construction was the earliest permanent building method utilized by European Americans in the Appalachian area. Its simplicity and utility suited the forested environment well. The technology was easy to learn, and the communal backwoods work ethic of the pioneers ensured enough help when it was needed. Although techniques have evolved during the three centuries that log construction has been practiced in America, the basic principles remain the same today.

The fundamental unit of log dwellings is the pen. (This unit is called a "crib" in reference to farm outbuildings.) The pen is usually a four-sided structure composed of horizontal logs held together by means of notches in the corners. The distinctive shape of the notch plus the weight of each log locks each individual timber in place. Consequently, the corner notch is the key element in horizontal log construction.

A number of different notch types are encountered within the Appalachian region. The inverted V and half-dovetail notch tend to predominate in permanent log dwellings and barns, while the saddle notch is commonly found on temporary cabins and farm buildings. Both the full dovetail and the square notch remain established minority types, each occurring contemporaneously with, though less frequently than, the former two notches. Some older and rarer forms of corner timbering such as the diamond or double notch are also occasionally encountered.

Settlers used similarly sized whole logs, either unbarked or peeled, for temporary shelters and smaller outbuildings, but the construction of permanent buildings usually required carefully hewn or cut logs. The sills and plates of houses were dressed by hand on all four sides, but after the eighteenth century, wall logs were commonly hewn only on the two wider sides to a thickness of five to six inches. The curved shape of the two sides that remained within the plane of the wall helped to retain the chinking and daubing between the logs.

The primary reason for hewing is to remove the bark and sapwood from the exterior surfaces of the log. This softer material is subject to attack from insects, fungi, and moisture, and once established, any or all of these can spread throughout the structure and destroy it. Hewing the timbers exposes the tougher, resistant heartwood and effectively planes the exposed faces. The resulting smoother surface considerably reduces the capacity of the wood to absorb water.

Almost all the extant log buildings in Appalachia rest on rock piers, and many of the older dwellings have small cellars with walls of roughly dressed stone. Huge oak, walnut, or cedar sill logs hewn to twelve inches by twelve inches or larger support the structures. The floors, whether puncheon or plank, are supported by log sleepers twelve inches in diameter. These supports are usually hewn flat on the top but otherwise left in the round with the bark on. Sometimes hewn logs or whipsawn joists are in evidence, but only rarely.

After the logs forming the walls had been stacked, the building could be covered with either a ridgepole and purlin roof or a raftered roof. The most commonly used early-nineteenth-century rafter system consisted of a group of five-inch-diameter poles (or four-by-five-inch whipsawn scantling) laid up in pairs, each pegged to the top plates at the lower end and joined at the peak with pegged half-lapped joints. Collar ties mortised to the sides of each pair of rafters completed the framing. As time went on, nailed joints replaced the earlier pegs and mortises.

The ridgepole and purlin roof featured two vertical forked posts, each centered over an end wall, which supported the ridgepole itself. The rest of the system consisted of a transverse series of medium-sized poles (ribs). These ribs were borne at each end by gable logs of decreasing size (trapping). Each rib ran the full length of the building in a series from plate to ridge at approximately four-foot intervals. Layers of boards were then placed on the ribs and held down by weight poles and large stones.

The use of this roofing system was not restricted to the cabins. Many early hewn-log houses originally featured this type of roof for economic or logistical reasons. Since a raftered roof required skilled carpenters and often a large quantity of nails and sawn lumber, the ridgepole and purlin roof often served as an intermediate step until additional building materials could be obtained. Some of these roofs were never converted, and a few of these hybrids have survived until the present time.

Until the end of the Great Depression, the most common roof covering consisted of wooden shingles or boards. Straight-splitting white oak was the first choice; other species such as chestnut and cedar were also used. After being rived from suitable tree sections with a cleaving tool known as a froe, the shingles were nailed to parallel lathing strips that had been fastened to the rafters.

Many frontier families found it difficult to remain confined to a one-room house and sought to expand their living quarters. Architectural historians have commented on the difficulty of adding one log pen to another, and some have even implied that this difficulty led to the development of the dogtrot design. This seems highly unlikely, however, since there were actually quite a number of ways to attach a three-walled log room to an existing single-pen log house. The most common method involved the construction of a cornerpost. Superficially resembling those in French-derived *piece-sur-piece* log construction, cornerposts were used to attach the newer log section of a building to a section already standing. In order to make a cornerpost, a deep groove was cut into one side of a squared timber. It was then set vertically and pegged to the side of the first pen. Tenons (projecting parts of a piece of wood) almost as thick as this groove were fashioned on one end of each of the logs to be added. Then these tenons were inserted into the groove and pegged in place. The other end of each log was notched in the prevailing manner and fitted into the standard corner.

Sometimes carpenters pegged an ungrooved post to the first pen, then cut out a corresponding rabbet or groove on the inside face of each log near the end and pegged them into place. At times the log ends were notched halfway into a thick vertical log that had been pegged to the first pen; other times the logs were just spiked or pegged into a hewn vertical plank on the interior. Another way was first to cut out half of each notch either vertically or horizontally and then cut out the corresponding half in each of the new logs and join the two together. The logs of the addition could also rest on the projections of the logs at the corners of the original house.

Log construction techniques have varied over time and space. The most time-consuming methods were gradually abandoned and others greatly simplified in response to changes wrought by the Industrial Revolution. Late in the nineteenth century, log buildings themselves began to fade from the cultural landscape. Partly due to the advent of the railroad and the portable sawmill and partly due to the trend away from neighborhood work projects and toward outside wage labor, the frame-and-box house built of lightweight sawn lumber gradually supplanted the log house in the Appalachian region.

See also: LOG DWELLING TYPES.

—Michael T. Gavin, *Middle Tennessee State University*

Fred Kniffen, "On Corner Timbering," *Pioneer America* (January 1969); Charles E. Martin, *Hollybush: Folk Building and Social Change in an Appalachian Community* (1984); Hermann Phleps, *The Craft of Log Building* (1982).

Log Dwelling Types

No American region is so identified with log dwellings as southern Appalachia, even though log houses were also common in other parts of the United States. In southern Appalachia, however, the period of horizontal log construction was particularly enduring, stretching from the mid-eighteenth to the mid-twentieth century.

The origins of American log construction have been much debated. A variety of Scandinavians and other Germanic peoples, Finns, and, later, eastern Europeans brought their techniques to North America. In the Valley of Virginia and parts of the Piedmont of North Carolina, a strong log construction tradition was especially associated with German Americans during the late eighteenth and early nineteenth centuries. However, the Cherokee may have been the first to build horizontal log homes in the southern mountains. Having apparently learned the technique from European Americans farther east, the Cherokee already had an established log building tradition by the time of European American settlement in many parts of Appalachia. People of English, Scottish, and Irish origin also quickly adopted log construction, even though the technique was not part of the cultural legacy these groups brought from Europe. Consequently, log construction in Appalachia did not have a strong affiliation with any one ethnic group.

If the construction techniques had their origins in Europe, the common house types built of logs were largely American in origin, although a variety of European antecedents do exist. While distinctly German house plans are found in log in Virginia and North Carolina, a modular system of expanding on a single log unit developed

Oliver Cabin, Cades Cove, Tennessee, 1992. This single-pen dwelling is typical of many built on the eastern frontier during the 1850s.

throughout most of the upland South. The most basic house plan was the single square or rectangular unit, which could be anywhere from one story to two and a half stories in height. Sometimes the main room on the first floor was partitioned, creating a plan somewhat similar to the asymmetrical hall-and-parlor plan without the second chimney. True hall-and-parlor houses, while found farther west in Kentucky and to the east, are relatively uncommon in the southern mountains.

The single-pen plan could be expanded to a double-pen plan in a variety of ways. The most common was to build two units of roughly equal size on either side of a double chimney, creating a "saddlebag." Alternately, two chimneys could be built on the exterior ends of the two rooms. This type of house plan, labeled "Cumberland" by some, is often simply referred to as a double-pen. Sometimes an open passageway was inserted between the two rooms, creating a dogtrot house. (Most of the terms now used to label house plans, with the possible exception of *dogtrot*, were invented by scholars and were not used by the people who built the houses.) All of these plans could also be built with frame or boxed construction, though frame single-pen houses are relatively rare in the mountains.

In some instances, single-pen houses were expanded incrementally. However, it was just as common for the various double-pen plans to be built all at once. Kitchens, built as a separate unit or attached to the rear of the house, were an option throughout most of the nineteenth century, but they became far more common at the turn of the century as more and more rural people acquired cookstoves. In the coal regions, stoves were often used for heat as well as cooking, but in other parts of the southern mountains, many families relegated the stove to the rear kitchen and continued to heat with an open hearth.

The various house plans are perhaps most meaningful in their representation of family life and the use of space. The small single-room house sustained a complex system of functions. Families cooked and ate, entertained, did a variety of chores, and slept within a single room. If space was available on the second floor or loft, it was commonly used as a sleeping space for older children. Parents, sometimes grandparents, and infants slept in the main room. The addition of a separate kitchen segregated cooking, although families often continued to congregate around an open hearth in "the room we lived in." In some parts of Appalachia, this plan was known as the "big house and kitchen."

While privacy would seem to be nonexistent in single-pen houses, many who grew up in these houses claim that privacy was maintained in other ways and that they did not feel crowded, even with several generations sleeping in the same room. Significantly, in the nineteenth century, the addition of another room in the double-pen plan added a parlor to the living space. That the extra room was so defined indicates the high value placed on social visiting. While privacy may have been increased, since beds were frequently placed in every room except the kitchen, the new room was ostensibly for entertaining and was defined as public, not private, space. After the turn of the twentieth century, larger spaces were often divided into smaller private rooms, and the parlor was frequently redefined as a bedroom.

For many, the log dwelling is still viewed as an unfortunate stereotype of southern Appalachia. Except for the earliest days of European American settlement, however, a variety of housing options always existed. It should also be noted that the widespread and persistent use of logs for building is not attributable solely to isolation or poverty. A major factor in the maintenance of the log building tradition was the cooperative work system that existed in many rural communities. Far from being the work of isolated individuals, most log homes were products of a cooperative building system. This system tended to have a conservative influence, since a family benefiting from the free labor of their neighbors was likely to conform to the community norm. In timber-rich areas, log houses could be built easily with little outlay of cash.

By the early decades of the twentieth century, more and more rural Appalachians were being drawn into paid employment away from home. Although the cooperative work traditions persisted in many communities, people simply had less time to spare. The cooperative construction of boxed houses—characterized by single-wall construction with vertical sawn boards—often replaced the more labor-intensive log building. Log homes that were built tended to be small in size. The construction of log outbuildings persisted a bit longer, and some cooperatively built log outbuildings date from as late as the 1940s.

As their numbers decreased, log homes, once commonly burned for firewood, came to be recognized as treasured historic sites. For more than a century they have been invested with symbolic meaning. Far from being artifacts of isolation, they are usually viewed now as products of rural communities that valued working cooperatively and social exchange.

See also: LOG CONSTRUCTION TECHNIQUES; RUSTIC ARCHITECTURE.

—Michael Ann Williams, *Western Kentucky University*

John Morgan, *The Log House in East Tennessee* (1990); Michael Ann Williams, *Homeplace: The Social Use and Meaning of the Log Dwelling in Southwestern North Carolina* (1991).

Mayo Mansion

The Mayo Mansion, located on Third Street in Paintsville, Kentucky, was built between 1907 and 1912. The imposing three-story, forty-room (including ten bathrooms) brick and native limestone structure was constructed in Classical Revival style by architect Herman Geisky of Ashland, Kentucky, for pioneer coal developer John Caldwell Calhoun Mayo. Mayo lived in the home for less than three years before his untimely death at age forty-nine in 1914.

The Mayo family moved to Ashland in 1917 and took much of the furnishings and ornate woodwork with them. For the next twenty years the mansion was used as part of the campus for John C. C. Mayo College and other educational programs. In 1936 the mansion and accompanying office building were sold to gas and oil developer E. J. Evans. Evans, in turn, sold the mansion to the Catholic Church that has operated an elementary school, Our Lady of the Mountains, in the building since 1945.

Mayo Mansion and the nearby Gothic-style Mayo Memorial United Methodist Church stand as significant symbols of the wealth that could be accumulated in the mineral-rich Appalachian region of eastern Kentucky at the turn of the century. The mansion has remained virtually unchanged since 1945. Our Lady of the Mountains permits the Paintsville Tourism Commission to conduct tours of the mansion.

See also: CHIEF VANN HOUSE.

—Carole Summers, *Kentucky Department of Travel*

McMahan, Fred

(1895–1980) Builder.

A native of Sevierville, Tennessee, Fred McMahan was a prosperous brick mason and builder who was one of numerous professional African American builders who made significant contributions to east Tennessee's constructed environment. McMahan learned the building trade from his grandfather, Isaac Dockery (1832–1910), a free black who established a brick kiln and masonry business at Sevierville in the late 1860s. A master brick mason who completed many landmark buildings in the region, including Sevierville's New Salem Baptist Church (1886), one of Tennessee's oldest African American churches, Dockery taught his craft to several generations of his male descendants.

In the 1910s McMahan earned advanced degrees from Knoxville College and the University of Illinois. Around 1920 McMahan returned to Sevierville and established the J, F & N McMahan Construction Company along with his brothers, James and Newt McMahan. In 1922, aided by the Julius Rosenwald Fund, a philanthropic organization that supported establishment of schools for blacks in the rural South, the company constructed the Pleasant View School, an African American elementary school, on land donated by McMahan. His wife, Mary McMahan (1896–1983), taught there for more than forty years. McMahan specialized in the construction of commercial, religious, and educational buildings. While white patrons commissioned most of his projects, McMahan also supervised the construction of many educational buildings at African American college campuses in Knoxville, Morristown, and Nashville.

In 1940 McMahan completed two of his most significant commissions: the Work Projects Administration–funded Sevierville Federal Post Office (now housing a museum for the Smoky Mountain Historical Society) and a distinctive dwelling for Dwight and Kate Wade. As newlyweds, the Wades had toured the futuristic Town of Tomorrow exhibit at the 1939 New York World's Fair. Upon returning to Sevierville, they ordered blueprints of the ultramodern Garden Home designed by Verna Cooke Salimonsky, a notable female architect from Scarsdale, New York. Due to his reputation as a superior brick mason, the Wades hired McMahan to complete the complicated brickwork. McMahan continued to hone his craft until the 1960s. His own elegant home still stands on a hill outside Sevierville.

See also: AFRICAN AMERICAN EDUCATION (EDUCATION).

—Robbie D. Jones, *The Hermitage, Nashville, Tennessee*

Robbie D. Jones, *The Historic Architecture of Sevier County, Tennessee* (1997).

Monteagle Assembly

The 1882 establishment of a "Sunday School Assembly in the South" at Monteagle, Tennessee, signified advances in several areas. In 1873 an assembly for training Sunday school teachers during the summer months had been initiated in Chautauqua, New York, in northern Appalachia. Emphasizing self-improvement through the attending of educational lectures, artistic performances, and daily devotionals in a wooded, outdoor setting, this assembly model appealed to Americans in other locations and was widely imitated. In the South, though, successful imitation depended as much upon the increased laying of railroad track—which made family travel easier and remote areas accessible—as it did upon locating an elevated setting with vistas and breezes away from yellow fever. That southern families could consider extended periods away from home also signaled the beginnings of economic recovery after the Civil War. Monteagle Assembly, listed in the National Register of Historic Places, was among the two hundred assemblies that formed nationwide in the nineteenth century and is one of a small number thriving today.

William Webster's design for Monteagle Assembly's ninety-six acres emphasized parkland, footpaths, and meandering roadways. Webster situated public buildings near the center of the grounds and surrounded them with tent sites. In the assembly's second summer, construction of private cottages commenced; some have passed down through families for generations. Since parkland composes 40 percent of the enclosure, the 162 residences form clusters. Porches are ubiquitous in the eclectic mix of late Victorian styles. Fire among the wooden buildings is justly feared. One conflagration in 1906 burned eleven buildings around the central Mall and resulted in Frank Butler's 1907 modifications to Webster's layout. The auditorium and nondenominational chapel, both important to the assembly's very identity, also burned but have been rebuilt.

While automobiles, radio, cinema, and television have transformed the pace and focus of modern life, for a particular segment of southerners, summers at Monteagle Assembly remain indispensable to the rejuvenation of mind, body, and spirit.

See also: CHAUTAUQUA VILLAGE, NEW YORK.

—Margaret D. Binnicker, *Tennessee Historical Society*

Norris Dam and Village

The Norris Dam project, almost from its inception, was the Tennessee Valley Authority's model venture, embodying TVA's own ideology and the promise of what it could bring to the people and landscape of the Tennessee Valley. It began in the 1920s as a proposed Bureau of Reclamation dam designed to complement and support its more important project at Muscle Shoals, Alabama. TVA officials changed that approach quickly in the summer and fall of 1933, however. Through redesign, new engineering, and comprehensive planning—all accomplished with breathtaking speed—TVA made Norris its signature project, the ultimate yardstick for all its future endeavors. All of the project's major components and design elements—Norris Freeway, Norris Village, the Norris parks, Norris Lake, and the Norris overlooks—remain much as they were during the 1930s, making the Norris landscape a tangible metaphor for TVA's hopes, image, and reality.

The Norris project was conceived on a large scale, much as if landscape architects had been given tens of thousands of acres to redesign as a nature reserve, as long as they placed a huge modern machine in the middle of it. That centerpiece is Norris Dam, a powerful statement of modernism. It is a concrete and steel gravity-type dam measuring 1,860 feet in length and 265 feet in height. When architecture critic Kenneth Frampton compiled his international survey, *Modern Architecture* (1980), the only example from Tennessee —and one of the few from the United States not designed by Frank Lloyd Wright—was Norris Dam. The Bureau of Reclamation developed the dam's initial design and construction plans, but scholars today credit Roland Wank (1898–1970), TVA's chief architect, with the structure's style, landscaping, and overall appearance. TVA engineers initially did not like Wank's design, and the respected industrial architect Albert Kahn, famous for his automobile plants for the Ford Motor Company, was brought into the project. Kahn strongly endorsed Wank's plans, and from that point on, all TVA dams in the New Deal era were designed in a modernist style. This legacy to American architecture is significant as an example of aesthetic cooperation among architecture, engineering, and landscape design.

Like the dam, Norris Village, with its emphasis on comfort and economy and its variety in house plans, building materials, and domestic architectural styles, became an architectural and planning model in its design. The town site, designed by TVA landscape architect Tracy B. Augur and his staff under the supervision of Earle Draper, included some 4,200 acres, though only about one-fourth of that area was used for homes and related community buildings. TVA strove to maintain a rustic setting for its modern village by maintaining greenbelt areas to the north and south, thus making the village one of the first towns in the nation to implement the progressive greenbelt principles developed by British reformer Ebenezer Howard. TVA also directed construction crews to conserve as many original trees as possible.

Central to the village plan was a two-story Colonial Revival–style school; it has proved to be one of the project's lasting institutions. The school, staffed by TVA personnel, also became a prototype, utilizing the latest in classroom technology. Other demonstration projects included dairy and poultry farms, a ceramics lab, and the Norris Creamery, considered to be the world's first all-electric milk plant. The town was the first in Tennessee to have a comprehensive telephone system.

The first houses in Norris Village expressed the contradiction of introducing modernity into the agrarian world of the Clinch River Valley. TVA director Arthur E. Morgan wanted the model village to reflect the local vernacular and for the houses to fit into, and not dominate, the landscape. Thus, the houses were placed along natural contours, and most were on small lots. The dwellings were small and had a central-hall floor plan similar to that of the common dogtrot house, but they were fully electrified and had modern appliances. Some cottages were covered in shingles or native stone to convey a rustic quality while another 130 dwellings were built from cinderblocks to reflect the technological experiment embodied in the Norris project.

Upon its completion in the spring of 1935, architects and planners proclaimed the many virtues of Norris Village, lauding its quaint, though modern, electrified dwellings, its varied community buildings, and its natural, rural setting shaped by the best ideas of Garden City (designed residential community) planning. But the village had cost twice what TVA had originally estimated. Worse, it pandered to southern racism by excluding African Americans, even though the racial groups in this region had previously often lived side by side. Eventually, it evolved into little more than a pricey TVA suburb for its employees. By 1948, with the Republican Party in control of Congress, the federal government finally balked at the annual subsidy given to Norris Village. TVA had little choice but to get out of the model town business, and on June 15, 1948, it sold the village to a private company, which, in turn, sold the housing units to private owners.

The Norris project represented a composite of what was perceived by some as America's best in architecture, engineering, and landscape architecture. But it proved to be a model that few other TVA projects ever emulated, perhaps because the idealism and hope of the initial New Deal years quickly dissolved into bureaucratic thinking that emphasized efficient power production over the ideas of reform and renewal which had initially propelled the authority into action.

See also: TENNESSEE VALLEY AUTHORITY (GOVERNMENT).

—Carroll Van West, *Middle Tennessee State University*

Carroll Van West, *Tennessee's New Deal Landscape: A Guidebook* (2001).

Old Mulkey Meeting House

Two miles from Tompkinsville, Kentucky, the Mill Creek Baptist Church, established about 1798 by Philip and John Mulkey, built a log meetinghouse on the banks of the creek from which it took its name. During this time, the population of this part of Kentucky was increasing rapidly, and church membership was growing due to the influence of the Cane Ridge revival movement, which had started three counties to the west in Logan County around 1799.

In 1804 the members of Mill Creek Baptist Church decided to build a new church about two hundred yards from the older one. A committee of church members planned the new structure and selected Jiles Thompson to build it. The gable-roof building, fifty feet long and thirty feet wide, was constructed of hewn logs with V notches; the longest logs in the walls were about thirty feet. Clapboard covered the gables, and shakes covered the roof, which was supported by reinforced trusses. The exterior wall structure had twelve corners, five windows, and three doors. The twelve corners, created by an extrusion on each long wall, supposedly represented either the twelve apostles or the twelve tribes of Israel. The doors, made of clapboard, represented the Trinity. Clapboard shutters covered the five windows, perhaps indicative of the five wounds of Christ. A puncheon floor completed the basic building.

A raised speaker's podium was built in front of the extrusion on the long wall, and although most church buildings seat the congregation in line with the two short walls, the Mill Creek congregation sat parallel with the long walls, facing the podium.

The building served as a church until about 1856. It was renovated in the 1870s, in the 1890s, and in the 1920s. The Kentucky Department of Parks identifies Old Mulkey Meeting House as the oldest wooden building of its type in the state.

See also: LOG CONSTRUCTION TECHNIQUES; LOG DWELLING TYPES.

—W. Calvin Dickinson, *Tennessee Technological University*

Pine Mountain Settlement School

In 1913 Katherine Pettit, cofounder of Hindman Settlement School, and Ethel DeLong (later Zande) began Pine Mountain Settlement School in Harlan County, Kentucky, on land donated by William Creech. Like other reformers who opened Appalachian settlement schools, Pettit and DeLong wanted to educate Pine Mountain children and through them to reach their families. The primary architect of the original campus was Mary Rockwell Hook, a Kansas native who had graduated from Wellesley College in 1900 and then undertaken architectural training from the Chicago Art Institute in 1903–4 and from the atelier of Marcel Aubeertin in 1905–6.

Hook's design reflected the school's curriculum of a work program that incorporated lessons related to the school farm, home management, and handicrafts. The historic campus buildings combined locally available materials such as log and stone into an interpretation of the Arts and Crafts style which was in keeping with the vernacular architecture of the community. Cecil Sharp visited Pine Mountain School in 1917; there he collected the Kentucky Running Set, a popular Appalachian dance, and taught English morris and other traditional dances. The school became known for folk dance performances. High school classes added in the 1920s expanded in the 1930s into an innovative program linking liberal and vocational arts, and the grade school curriculum ended. From 1949 to 1971, Pine Mountain cooperated with the county board of education to provide public education and pioneered early regional preschool and kindergarten programs.

In 1971 Harlan County officials consolidated the public schools and moved students away from Pine Mountain. The settlement school became an environmental education center. Since 1913 the campus has grown to eight hundred acres and serves academic, recreational, and community functions. Several of the most prominent historic buildings, including the chapel, Jubilee Cottage, and Big Log, the original log boarding school building, have been restored and serve as key architectural links between the site's past and present.

See also: HINDMAN SETTLEMENT SCHOOL (CRAFTS); PETTIT, KATHERINE (EDUCATION); SETTLEMENT, MISSION, AND SPONSORED SCHOOLS (EDUCATION).

—Margaret D. Binnicker, *Tennessee Historical Society*

Pittsburgh Plate Glass Place

Located on 5.5 acres in Pittsburgh's central business district, the Pittsburgh Plate Glass (PPG) corporate headquarters, designed by Philip Johnson and John Burgee, opened in 1984. The six-building complex surrounds a plaza and consists of a forty-story tower and five other buildings—one with fourteen stories and the other four with six stories each—that contain retail and office space. In materials, design, and scale, PPG Place typifies Johnson's postmodernist approach and is his outstanding work in Appalachia.

Architectural historian Alan Gowans has found the composition notably similar to the University of Pittsburgh's Cathedral of Learning designed by Charles Z. Klauder (1927). Johnson and Burgee also borrowed from modernism's glass curtain-wall construction, transforming this 1960s idea by giving it a pleated exterior. The faceted, mirrored surface reflects movement from a variety of angles, and the glass functions as a colossal advertisement for Pittsburgh Plate Glass products. The effect is memorable, but it has produced mixed reviews from both the architects' peers and from the public.

Within Pittsburgh's Point, so dubbed because the Monongahela and Allegheny Rivers join there to become the Ohio, industrialists, bankers, merchants, and government officials had earlier built equally impressive structures, including the Allegheny County Courthouse and Jail, designed by Henry Hobson Richardson, in the 1880s and a number of tall buildings around the turn of the twentieth century. Following flood- and smoke-control legislation in the 1940s, urban renewal efforts within the downtown Golden Triangle district initiated traffic control, slum removal, and building replacement. These efforts at a downtown renaissance failed to entice the city's population back to the Point beyond business hours, however. PPG Place represents a more recent attempt at revitalization.

See also: ALLEGHENY COUNTY COURTHOUSE AND JAIL.

—Margaret D. Binnicker, *Tennessee Historical Society*

Planned Industrial Towns

The American factory system, which originated in the late eighteenth century in the Northeast, soon spread south and west. As the increasing mechanization of local industry required more workers and created overcrowding, early mill village and company towns faced the problem of how to house an expanding labor force. Many company owners hired engineers who laid out worker housing along streets that stretched away from the factory in a regimented grid pattern. The monotonous repetition of lot size and house

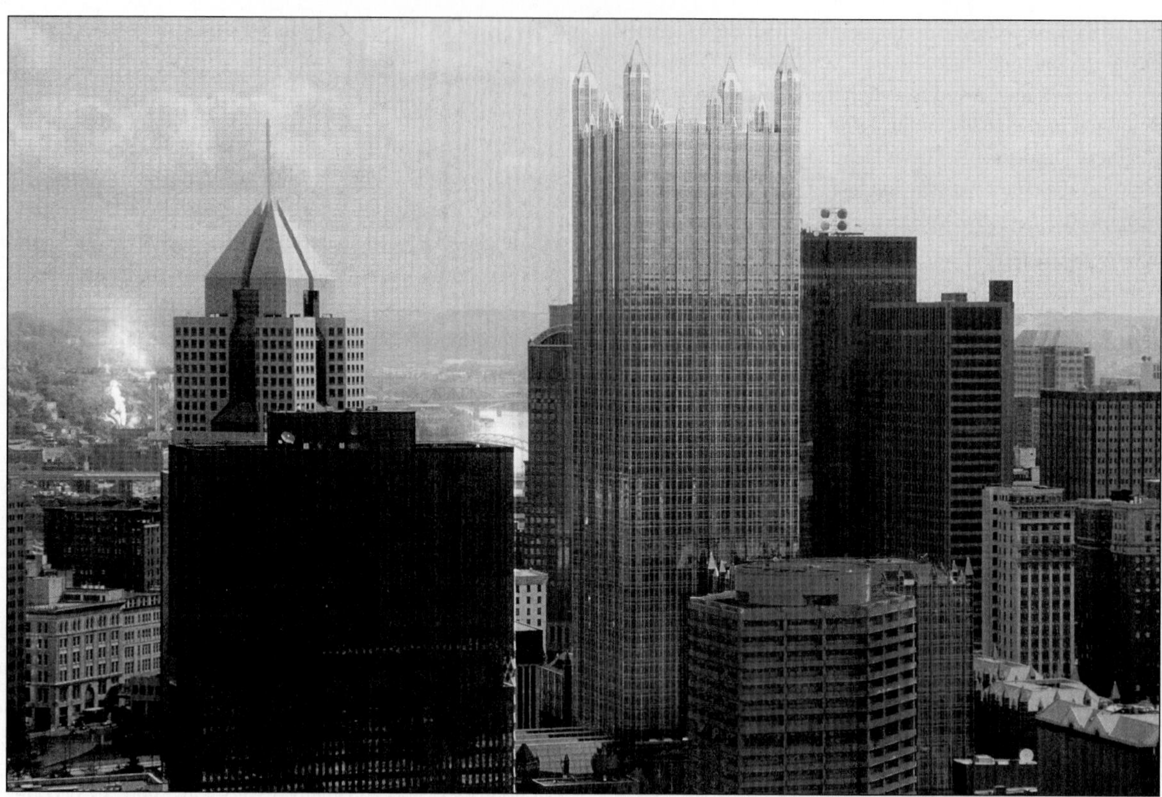

Pittsburgh Plate Glass Place in downtown Pittsburgh, 1999. Designed by architects Philip Johnson and John Burgee, PPG Place represents a bold statement of postmodernist architecture in urban Appalachia.

placement reinforced the idea of the factory owner's power to impose regulation from above, even upon his workers' free time. By the last quarter of the nineteenth century, criticism of industrialization's detrimental effect on workers and communities raged across the nation. Politicized by desperate circumstances, workers began to organize unions for protection.

Some capitalists sought to counter such developments, improve stability among their labor ranks, and soften the outward manifestation of their control by asking architects and urban planners to develop "model" planned industrial communities. At the same time, escalating demand for steel needed for train tracks and tall-building construction accelerated the industry's need for coal and timber. Construction of rail lines in the decades around the turn of the twentieth century opened up the entire Appalachian region, making its resources accessible to the rest of the nation. After 1880, while typical coal and timber company towns and mill villages were built throughout Appalachia, planners adapted and applied their solutions for urban slums to some of these nonurban settings as well. For roughly fifty years, America and Appalachia witnessed a small number of significant attempts to construct better housing for industrial workers.

Newly professionalized town designers had learned from the English Garden City movement to replace the ordinary grid arrangement of streets with roads that followed the terrain and allowed for variety in building placement. Instead of rows of identical house facades, architects introduced several residential designs. While skilled workers and managers traditionally had better and larger living quarters than those designed for unskilled laborers, in model towns builders used appropriate and quality materials and enhanced sites through adequate plantings to make each area more attractive. Company owners intended their towns to generate money through rents paid by workers for their housing, but the creation of a pleasant, stable environment often offset the drive for substantial rental profits in model towns. Improvements resulted from increased attention to common areas shared by town residents, namely, the post office, churches, schools, and community shops. Even in the most enlightened situations, though, discrimination based on ethnic and racial backgrounds persisted and could require that facilities be used by different groups at separate times. African American workers might be denied access to some public places. With clearly segregated residential sections, model communities aimed at providing better housing rather than addressing issues of equality.

The idea of constructing a well-designed working community evolved in stages and over years. Appalachia's early steel centers at Homestead and Duquesne, Pennsylvania, and at Steubenville, Ohio, followed the grid plan. The cotton mill area in Tupelo, Mississippi, did, too, but there choices between exterior trim of white paint on yellow walls or white walls with yellow details helped alter the appearance of sameness in the housing. Residences in the textile village begun in 1882 in Pelzer, South Carolina, rose along curving streets that climbed the hill above the mills. The arrival of railroads in the Appalachian counties of Maryland and Virginia introduced industrial districts and related housing adjacent to the established rural communities. Among the new towns built in the rush for coal, an occasional one such as Holden, West Virginia, or Stearns, later Lynch, Kentucky, displayed well-appointed central business and commercial areas. The development of prefabricated structures for sale and shipment shortly after the turn of the twentieth century provided industry owners another option for the look and atmosphere of their workers' complexes.

A small number of companies chose to construct industrial towns prepared by architects and planners, particularly in the period from the Progressive Era early in the twentieth century to the Great Depression. Apollo Iron and Steel Company set an example in 1895 at Vandergrift, Pennsylvania. John Charles Olmsted, stepson of Frederick Law Olmsted, designed the town site with features reminiscent of his stepfather's plan for the Chicago suburb of Riverside, Illinois. Other companies moving into Appalachian locations and bent on building wholesome communities followed suit and turned to urban planners from New York and Massachusetts for town plans. The Alabama steel and lumber towns of Fairfield (1910) and Kaulton (1912) resulted from designs commissioned by George Miller of Boston. In 1916 the Clinchfield Railroad hired Grosvenor Atterbury of Manhattan to create a residential area for both its employees and those of various industries the railroad intended to attract to Erwin, Tennessee.

Certain Appalachian endeavors that involved industries new to the region considered model town settings appropriate signals of their distinctiveness. John Nolen, the urban planner based in Cambridge, and Earle Draper, the assistant Nolen sent south and who later opened a practice of his own, had important roles in several such sites. The 1915–16 design for the town center and residential areas of Kingsport, Tennessee, which attracted the Tennessee Eastman chemical plant, came from Nolen's office, with Draper on site as supervisor. Nolen's office also prepared the plan for Mount Union Refractories' fire-brick industry in Kistler, Pennsylvania (1918). Almost a decade later, when the German company Vereinigte Glanzstoff Fabriken located its rayon facilities at Elizabethton, Tennessee, local officials turned to Nolen for the necessary worker housing. In 1927 Draper designed the workers' community at Chicopee, Georgia, for Johnson and Johnson's mill for producing sanitary gauze. Incorporating all of the elements of model planning, these communities represented industrial towns at their best.

Economic hardships in the depression decade put an end to such privately funded endeavors, but philanthropic and government agencies financed two projects of note before preparations for World War II diverted national attention. In 1932 the Buhl Foundation had Henry Wright and Clarence Stein create one more example of a Garden City residential community at Chatham Village, near Pittsburgh. In 1933–34 Draper worked with the Tennessee Valley Authority (TVA) to design and build Norris, Tennessee, in conjunction with TVA's initial dam construction on the Clinch River. Though Chatham Village and Norris proved to be superb examples of planned communities, interest in such undertakings did not revive after World War II. By the 1950s, automobiles had made nearby housing less an issue for industries, and most companies chose to divest themselves of rental housing by selling it to their employees. Also, Cold War antagonism towards the Union of Soviet Socialist Republics with its government-run housing made the idea of controlled workers' communities in the United States seem somewhat un-American.

Today, the National Register of Historic Places lists a sprinkling of Appalachian examples of model planned communities. Most residential areas of this type, however, are viewed by local citizens merely as interesting parts of the larger communities that now surround them. To be remembered as a company town is not an association everyone celebrates. The number of planned communities always remained small, perhaps because of a conflict they presented. The setting meant to make workers happier as individuals in their situations also supported the notion of community participation, and feelings of self-determination could run counter to the automatic responses required of good workers on the job. Though the results that company owners sought with these model communities served the workers, the overriding presence of paternalism could not be avoided. Improved living conditions and community activities still hinged on accepting management's position, creating a constant, if underlying, tension for workers and owners alike.

See also: PLANNED COMMUNITIES (FAMILY AND COMMUNITY).

—Margaret D. Binnicker, *Tennessee Historical Society*

Arthur C. Comey and Max S. Wehrly, "Planning Communities," in *Urban Planning and Land Policies: Volume Two of the Supplementary Report of the Urbanism Committee to the National Resources Committee* (1939); Margaret Crawford, *Building the Workingman's Paradise: The Design of American Company Towns* (1995); John W. Reps, *The Making of Urban America: A History of City Planning in the United States* (1965).

Prehistoric Public Architecture

Between 500 B.C. and A.D. 200, the Greeks built their majestic classical temples on the Acropolis, the Chinese erected the Great Wall, and the Romans designed the Pantheon and the Colosseum. From 500 B.C. to A.D. 1500, as scholar William Morgan has pointed out, the Adena and Hopewell cultures in central Appalachia (southeastern Ohio, West Virginia, and northwestern Kentucky) and the Mississippian people in the Tennessee Valley of southern Appalachia designed and constructed some of the greatest prehistoric structures of North America.

Beginning around 500 B.C., the Adena culture introduced such new ideas as agriculture, greater and wider use of ceramics, and the construction of large burial mounds and associated earthen structures. Long shrouded in myth, the achievements of Adena and the later Hopewell cultures were classified as those of the "moundbuilders" by nineteenth-century scholars who wondered, in some cases, if some lost tribe of Israel had not constructed the large mounds, truncated pyramids, and open plazas found along or near many river plateaus in the region. Archaeological study during the late twentieth century, however, eliminated much of the myth and restored the architectural reputation of the region's first designers and builders.

Adena builders generally constructed conical burial mounds, inside of which were log tombs, as part of larger circular enclosures containing smaller mounds and earthworks that were used for various social and cultural ceremonies. More expressive Adena structures took the shape of animals that were important within the culture and its understanding of the world. Serpent Mound, for instance, an impressive effigy mound in south-central Ohio, takes the shape of an uncoiling snake ready to strike. When measured in 1846, the snake was about 29 feet wide, 5 feet high, and more than 1,300 feet in length.

The architecture of the Hopewell culture shares some similarities with that of the Adena but also shows greater sophistication. Hopewell peoples established extended trade networks which introduced both new building ideas and materials into their culture. Like the Adena, Hopewell peoples built elaborately furnished tombs, basins, burial platforms, and pits for storage and burial within their mounds. But the mounds are larger, and rather than being only conical, they embrace additional geometrical shapes such as squares and octagons. Located in Chillicothe, Ohio, the Hopewell Culture National Historical Park, formerly known as Mound City, contains a range of circular, rectangular, and octagonal structures. Other representative Hopewell sites include a central square at Marietta, Ohio, and a portion of the prehistoric remains at the Portsmouth site in northeast Kentucky. The Hopewell phase of prehistoric architecture was largely over by A.D. 200.

The next set of new architectural ideas appeared in the Mississippian culture of A.D. 900 to 1550. The Tennessee Valley of southern Appalachia contained some of the nation's most significant prehistoric sites in the Hiwassee site (excavated before its destruction by a Tennessee Valley Authority reservoir) and the Etowah site in northern Georgia. Large temple mounds and ceremonial and recreational plazas, around which stood smaller burial and ceremonial mounds as well as habitations of various sizes and materials, were typical architectural traits of Mississippian peoples. The primary platform mound at Etowah, for example, contained almost 122,000 cubic meters of building material, making it the second-largest mound constructed in North America in the prehistoric period.

Native peoples constructed hundreds of mounds throughout Appalachia. Considering that the soil for mounds was dug and carried by hand, the achievements of the Adena, Hopewell, and Mississippian builders are truly impressive.

See also: ARCHAEOLOGICAL SITES (SETTLEMENT AND MIGRATION).

—Carroll Van West, *Middle Tennessee State University*

Ramsey House

Ramsey House, constructed between 1795 and 1797 near Knoxville, Tennessee, remains a distinctive example of the evolution of frontier architecture. Built for Colonel Francis Alexander Ramsey (1764–1820) by English-born master craftsman and cabinetmaker Thomas Hope (1769–1831), Ramsey House illustrates the synthesis of eastern architectural design with frontier craftsmanship and materials in late-eighteenth-century Appalachia.

The two-story Ramsey House exhibits a late Georgian I-house design. The main part of the house contains a central hall with two rooms on either side; behind this section is a two-story attached kitchen addition. One of the first stone structures built in the area, Ramsey House owes its distinctiveness to walls of pink marble, contrasting blue limestone stringcourse and quoins, and intricately carved corner consoles and interior woodwork. Other features include original interior wood shutters, chair railing, and baseboards, as well as furniture pieces by Hope. These features demonstrate a high level of craftsmanship rarely available in the unstable Appalachian backcountry.

Sold out of the family after the Civil War, Ramsey House passed through many owners before the Knoxville Chapter of the Association for the Preservation of Tennessee Antiquities purchased it in 1952 to preserve as a historic house museum. Ramsey House is open to the public and interprets the Ramsey family's and the property's historic role in westward expansion and the

Ramsey House, Knox County, Tennessee, 1997. Built by Thomas Hope for Colonel Alexander Ramsey between 1795 and 1797, this home represents a synthesis of eastern architectural design and frontier craftsmanship.

early settlement of the eighteenth-century Appalachian frontier.

See also: CHIEF VANN HOUSE.

—Stacey Leah Griffin, *Birmingham, Alabama*

Rustic Architecture

Rustic architecture—buildings and structures executed in rock, log, and bark—did not originate in the Appalachian Mountains but became an exceedingly popular idiom in the region, especially in tourist areas in the late nineteenth and early twentieth centuries. The appearance of the Rustic style in the nineteenth century coincided with a larger back-to-nature movement that was gaining momentum and encouraging Americans to return to a simple existence away from an increasingly industrialized world. Architects and builders picked up on the theme, which stressed that buildings should be part of a well-ordered natural system and that the outside world should be brought into the home. Exterior surfaces were finished in stone, shingles, and brown or green-tinged wood to give the building a textured appearance imitative of nature's diversity. The outside world was brought inside the house through the use of native wood in its natural form as a decorative element.

While the Rustic style seems to be a single expression carried out through several decades, in reality it developed over time and from many sources. In mid-nineteenth-century publications, landscape architect Andrew Jackson Downing espoused harmonization of buildings and their settings through the use of native materials in construction. Downing's vision inspired park designers, architects, and builders to use rock and native wood for building in order to create an organic aesthetic.

One of the oldest existing collections of Rustic architecture in southern Appalachia is found at Linville in Avery County, North Carolina. The character of the small resort community is defined by its outstanding bark-shingled and log buildings. Development of Linville began in the 1880s when Samuel Kelsey, a Kansas native and one of the founders of the town of Highlands in Macon County, North Carolina, enlisted his friend Donald MacRae of Wilmington and MacRae's son Hugh, an engineer, to develop the town as a resort settlement. The Eseeola Lodge was the first building erected; it was built in 1891–92 and was followed by the construction of several summerhouses. The original Eseeola was replaced in the 1920s by a two-and-one-half-story bark-covered building. What sets Linville apart are the many buildings designed by eminent architect Henry Bacon and constructed from the 1890s through about 1910. Bacon, who grew up in Wilmington, was also a friend of the MacRae family, and his work at Linville is important to the Rustic style in western North Carolina because he was the first builder or architect to use chestnut bark as an exterior sheathing. The centerpiece of Linville is Bacon's elaborate All Saints Episcopal Church, built in 1910. Overall, the gable-front church has a simple form common to rural churches of the period found in the region. But All Saints is covered inside and out with bark shingles. In the eaves are exposed log beams, and a log cross surmounts the square roof tower. The apse is separated from the nave by a screen of logs, and the baptismal font is on a log support entwined by dried laurel vines.

The Rustic style evolved in the new century. It still took inspiration from the Arts and Crafts movement, an idiom that had become particularly popular in the boomtown of Asheville, North Carolina, where English architects created Biltmore for George W. Vanderbilt. The Rustic style also showed characteristics of architect William West Durant's Adirondack camp style. The National Park Service, the United States Forest Service, and the Civilian Conservation Corps, all active in Appalachia, employed what is sometimes called "government rustic" style for their lodges, shelters, and bridges. Pattern books such as *Bungalows, Camps, and Mountain Homes*, published in 1915 by William Comstock, helped to propagate the ideals of naturalistic architecture suited to leisure. Also contributing to the style's vast appeal were easy access to building material—most importantly logs and stone—and the availability of regional craftsmen and builders who practiced traditions of stonework and building that had been passed down through generations.

The most visible hallmarks of the Rustic style in the early twentieth century were the inns and lodges constructed around the turn of the century. The region's most prominent hotel of the period exemplifying the genre is the Grove Park Inn in Asheville, a building that exhibits an unusual combination of grandeur and rusticity. Built in 1913 of uncut granite boulders laid over a reinforced concrete frame to form the walls and chimneys, the Grove Park Inn is a monument to the melding of the Rustic and the Arts and Crafts movements. Windows are crowned with huge boulder lintels, and a distinctive tile roof made from Tennessee red clay caps the building and shelters its undulating eaves. Edwin Wiley Grove, a St. Louis pharmaceutical manufacturer and real estate developer, began buying land in north Asheville around the turn of the twentieth century. He developed a residential neighborhood but held off construction of a hotel. From correspondence between Grove, William Randolph—the man Grove hired to oversee his residential development—and Grove's son-in-law, Fred Seely, it is obvious that Grove was looking for the most appropriate style for the building. Especially impressed by Old Faithful Inn in Yellowstone National Park, Grove felt that a Rustic-style building was most suitable for the hotel's site on the side of Sunset Mountain. When word of Grove's intention to build a grand hotel got out, architects from Asheville to Boston submitted plans, but in the end it was a sketch by Seely, who had no training in either architecture or construction, that served as the model for the inn. More than four hundred men built the hotel by hand in less than a year.

Rustic architecture was exceedingly popular for summer camps. Camp Merrie-Woode, located on Lake Fairfield in Jackson County, North Carolina, was established in 1919 as a boarding camp for girls. The camp flourished under its founder, Mabel "Dammie" Day. Day owned the property from 1922 to 1952, and it was under her directorship that most of the cabins and support features were built. Before coming to North Carolina, Day had worked at a camp at Bear Mountain in the Adirondacks of upstate New York and was likely inspired by the Great Camps of the region. Royal Morrow, a civil engineer from the town of Brevard, designed many of the camp's log and bark-shingled buildings and constructed his own Arts and Crafts–style stone cottage from plans appearing in Gustav Stickley's magazine, *The Craftsman*. Local builders, well versed in stone masonry and indigenous building materials, were responsible for the actual construction.

In the late 1920s, saddle-notched log buildings and structures emerged as the most common type of naturalistic architecture in the region. Their appearance, not only in resort communities, but also to some extent in small towns and suburban neighborhoods along the East Coast, coincided with a widespread movement in which America's pre–Civil War history was romanticized and commercialized. Throughout the country, while the immensely popular Colonial Revival style paid homage to the Revolutionary-era past, log buildings of the period were shrines to the hardy pioneers who had settled in the Appalachians a hundred years before.

The Rustic style provided the southern Appalachians with an architectural idiom particularly well suited to the mountains and to the leisurely pursuits associated with the area. In the twenty-first century, the sight of a log, stone, or shingled building continued to elicit romantic feelings about Appalachia's past.

See also: ADIRONDACK RUSTIC STYLE; GROVE PARK INN; LOG CONSTRUCTION TECHNIQUES.

—Jennifer F. Martin, *Edwards-Pitman Environmental Incorporated, Raleigh, North Carolina*

Catherine W. Bishir, Michael T. Southern, and Jennifer F. Martin, *A Guide to the Historic Architecture of Western North Carolina* (1999); Bruce E. Johnson, "Built without an Architect: Architectural Inspirations for the Grove Park Inn," in *May We All Remember Well: A Journal of the History and Cultures of Western North Carolina*, ed. Robert S. Brunk (1997); Linda Flint McClelland, *Building the National Parks* (1998).

Skyline Drive

Predating the Blue Ridge Parkway by several years, Skyline Drive was the first federally subsidized scenic motor road in Appalachia. First envisioned in 1924 by several proponents of the proposed Shenandoah National Park, the road was realized during Herbert Hoover's term in the White House. In fact, this president played such an active role in the road's development that it was nearly named "Hoover Highway." Skyline Drive was constructed by crews comprised of Blue Ridge residents supervised by engineer James Ralph Lassiter, who later became the first superintendent of Shenandoah National Park, and the road was built entirely on the crest of the Blue Ridge at the request of U.S. Secretary of the Interior Harold L. Ickes. Skyline Drive was not universally welcomed. The Potomac Appalachian Trail Club, hoping to preserve a roadless area for the Appalachian Trail in one section of Shenandoah National Park, unsuccessfully lobbied against the mountaintop placement of the road.

When Skyline Drive was ready for use by park visitors in late 1932, much of the northern Blue Ridge had been denuded by logging companies. Therefore, the road offered motorists many unimpeded vistas eastward toward the Virginia Piedmont and westward toward Shenandoah Valley and the Allegheny Mountains. President Hoover called these views "the greatest in the world."

In 1933 President Franklin D. Roosevelt placed the nation's first Civilian Conservation Corps camps along Skyline Drive, ensuring that Shenandoah National Park would receive extensive landscaping, including the planting of trees. By the late 1940s, when visitation to the park was increasing after a wartime lull, a regenerating forest had obscured views along many sections of Skyline Drive. Consequently, the park's superintendent, Edward Freeland, instigated a formal program of tree clearing, angering many conservationists.

Late in the twentieth century, despite markedly reduced views due to air pollution, the 105-mile Skyline Drive traversing the Blue Ridge between Front Royal and Rockfish Gap, Virginia, continued to draw approximately two million visitors each year to Shenandoah National Park.

See also: BLUE RIDGE PARKWAY; SHENANDOAH NATIONAL PARK (TOURISM).

—Ted Olson, *East Tennessee State University*

Smithfield Plantation

When constructed in 1773–74, Smithfield Plantation, located near Blacksburg, Virginia, was on the western edge of the Virginia frontier. The plantation was the residence of early settler, land speculator, and planter William Preston (1729–1783). The Irish-born Preston named the plantation in honor of his wife, Susannah Smith Preston. He later served with distinction in the Revolutionary War, where he helped plan the Kings Mountain campaign, and in the Virginia House of Burgesses. After his death in 1783, Susannah Preston managed the plantation for the next forty years.

Smithfield is an exceptional piece of domestic architecture and craftsmanship, rivaling the best frame houses found at that time in the Virginia Tidewater region. It is a one-and-one-half-story heavy-braced frame building with a five-bay symmetrical facade and a prominent ell wing. Four dormer windows, Flemish bond brick gable-end chimneys, and the pedimented double-entrance door with transom well reflect the Georgian principles of balance and symmetry. The interior retains many historical features, including paneled dadoes and molded chair rails in the primary public rooms, while the front stairway was constructed with a Chippendale-influenced Chinese lattice railing. Surrounding the house are various historic outbuildings, including a log smokehouse, kitchen, and two-story weaver's cabin.

The outbuildings and architectural sophistication of the dwelling conveyed the Preston family's prominence in the politics and society of Appalachian Virginia. Two future governors of Virginia, James P. Preston and John Buchanan Floyd, were born at Smithfield.

See also: CHIEF VANN HOUSE; RAMSEY HOUSE.

—Carroll Van West, *Middle Tennessee State University*

Stevenson Depot and Hotel

Representative of the distinctive railroad landscape that developed in southern Appalachia in the late nineteenth century, the Stevenson Depot and Hotel date to around

The Stevenson Depot, Stevenson, Alabama, c. 1990. Built around 1872, the building typifies railside development in southern Appalachia in the years following the Civil War.

1872. Stevenson, Alabama, was a key antebellum railroad junction of the Nashville and Chattanooga Railroad and the Memphis and Charleston Railroad. At the outbreak of the Civil War, the small town and its railroad facilities became a strategic focus for both Union and Confederate commanders. Union troops occupied the town, and heavy use of its tracks and buildings, especially during the Chickamauga campaign, damaged most of the railroad structures. During Reconstruction the Nashville, Chattanooga and St. Louis Railroad built the depot and hotel as part of its aggressive campaign to restore the company to its former prominence and to extend its service throughout the region.

As symbols of the railroad's commitment to Stevenson and the town's prospects for growth and prosperity, the two buildings complemented each other. The brick material and Victorian architecture of the depot reflected permanence and style; its short central tower not only provided additional interior light but also suggested the railroad's centrality in the local townscape. The adjoining two-story gable-roof brick hotel was comparatively plain in appearance, but its mere presence promoted business growth and opportunity in Stevenson. It served an increasing number of passengers who stayed overnight to either catch a train on the other line or to conduct business in the region. Drummers—traveling salesmen who drummed up business—were its primary patrons.

Although little but their survival distinguishes these two buildings arranged symmetrically along the track from hundreds of others built and similarly arranged in Appalachia in the decades after the Civil War, the Stevenson Depot and Hotel are important artifacts of the region's once dominant railroad landscape. They were listed in the National Register of Historic Places in 1976.

See also: CINCINNATI UNION TERMINAL; RAILROADS (TRANSPORTATION).

—Carroll Van West, *Middle Tennessee State University*

Tourism Architecture

Although Appalachia's popularity as a resort area increased in the late nineteenth century, automobile tourism in the twentieth century transformed the region into a favorite vacation destination for a broader range of visitors. Road-building campaigns in the 1920s and establishment of the Shenandoah and Great Smoky Mountains National Parks in the 1930s attracted visitors from throughout the eastern United States. Most came in their cars via interstate tourist routes such as the Dixie, Lee, and Lincoln Highways, and entrepreneurs along the way capitalized on the travelers' needs. Tourist courts, gift shops, and gas stations sprang up at the intersections of major and minor highways as well as at destinations such as Gatlinburg, Tennessee, the principal gateway community for the Great Smoky Mountains National Park. Though twentieth-century roadside architecture in Appalachia sometimes imitated traditional regional building styles, it ultimately brought nationally popular commercial styles and mainstream culture to the area.

Appalachian resort hotels were important forerunners of the region's roadside architecture. North Carolina's Grove Park Inn and High Hampton Inn, for instance, embodied the early-twentieth-century emphasis on outdoor recreation and mountain culture in their design and materials. The resort hotels' shingles, stone, and unpainted woodwork were design features intended to harmonize with nature. Pre–World War II tourism architecture demonstrated sensitivity to the fact that natural scenery drew tourists to the area. Builders repeated mountain themes such as the log cabin and shingled resort as they created an environment related to its natural surroundings.

The proliferation of tourist courts and motels in Appalachia was part of a larger national trend toward accommodations that were economical and efficient rather than luxurious. The first step in this transition was the cabin camp, often a group of cabins added to a tourist home. Tourist courts were more carefully and elaborately planned. A variety of cottage arrangements developed to fit differently shaped sites. Detached cottage courts preserved the distinction of individual buildings, while motor courts linked all units under a common roofline. Tuckaleechee Village in Blount County, Tennessee, built during the postwar tourism boom, is an intact row of double cottages that can easily be seen by travelers on U.S. 321.

Regional imagery frequently enlivened early-twentieth-century tourism architecture. Tourist courts in Appalachia drew heavily on stock images of log cabins as well as the mountain vernacular architecture of resort hotels through the use of local stone, native-wood paneling, and shingles. Rustic exteriors usually belied the creature comforts inside, but owners sometimes imparted mountain appeal to interior spaces through the use of furniture or coverlets handmade by locals. Domesticity met regional imagery in the form of the log cabin, the dwelling type that most symbolized the mountaineer lifestyle to visitors. Some tourist courts offered guests the opportunity to stay in an individual log cabin, occasionally built from disassembled log houses, thereby creating an idyllic vacation environment combining the picturesque associations of mountain life with modern conveniences. The Log Cabin Motor Court near Weaverville, North Carolina, still evokes this period.

Regional imagery also included Native American motifs meant to recall another side of the frontier story. Unfortunately, they usually referred to Plains Indian traditions rather than those of groups that populated Appalachia. Visitors to Cherokee, North Carolina, beguiled with the area's Native American heritage, could rent a cottage with a playfully inauthentic teepee entrance. The first Wigwam Village, opened in 1933 near Horse Cave, Kentucky, also offered guests the chance to stay and dine in a teepee.

Nationally, tourist courts began to follow design trends toward streamlining by the late 1930s, embracing the modern on the exterior as well as the interior. Amenities included steam heat, hot and cold running water, and modern bath fixtures. Owners enthusiastically advertised these conveniences. Roadside businesses also proclaimed their modernity through architecture when they displayed nationally popular styles such as Colonial Revival or streamlined Moderne.

Although a variety of revival styles graced the small houselike buildings of the 1920s and 1930s, gas stations showed the least sensitivity to regional architectural heritage as oil companies developed brand identity through the use of standardized building plans and styles. Gas stations also capitalized on the modern quality of automobile travel and incorporated streamlined, aerodynamic materials such as enamel panels and plate glass. The entire station developed into a sign emblazoned with the oil company's colors and logo. Gas stations exemplified how national commercial styles would overwhelm Appalachian architectural traditions on tourist routes.

The postwar years witnessed the transition from tourist court to motel. According to John Jakle, the new term accompanied the shift from detached or semidetached cottages to long, one-story buildings that maintained a single, unified roofline. Postwar motels were generally arranged on their sites in a manner similar to tourist courts. Neon lighting aided visibility as motels relied less on nostalgic or fantastic imagery to lure guests in for the night. Signage took on a more significant role relative to architecture, as in the case of Holiday Inn's instantly recognizable "Great Sign."

Motels offered more amenities than their tourist court predecessors, and the distinction between motels and hotels blurred with the addition of lobbies, restaurants, coffee shops, meeting rooms, and conference facilities. More rooms were added through the use of center-core construction, a wartime innovation that efficiently stacked blocks of rooms back to back with central plumbing units. Motels also instituted the swimming pool as a standard feature of roadside accommodation designed to appeal to families traveling with children. In most cases modern motels bear only a passing resemblance to the tourist courts from which they descended.

Other tourist-oriented businesses saluted postwar prosperity by updating their buildings in a more national commercial style that emphasized smooth surfaces and plate glass. Gas stations, which had pioneered the concept of using standardized architecture, were joined by fast food restaurants and new motel chains that began to build in trademark styles across all regions.

The architectural integrity of the roadside generally has a very short life span. Profit lies in continually adapting to travelers' needs, and communities that remain closely tied to automobile tourists for their livelihood evolve rapidly. Breezewood, Pennsylvania, the "town of motels" at the intersection of the old Lincoln Highway, Pennsylvania Turnpike, and Interstate 70, exemplifies ways that the active tourism landscape perpetually adapts. Bypassed highways hold reminders of travel before interstate standardization, though, and reveal the varied ways Appalachian tourist businesses marketed themselves to visitors. The surviving architecture illustrates the changing nature of tourism in Appalachia while showing how national culture has exerted its force on this once rural area.

See also: SECTION OVERVIEW (TOURISM).

—Blythe Semmer, *Metropolitan Nashville Historical Commission*

Warren J. Belasco, *Americans on the Road: From Autocamp to Motel, 1910–1945* (1979); John A. Jakle and Keith A. Sculle, *The Gas Station in America* (1994); Chester H. Liebs, *Main Street to Miracle Mile: American Roadside Architecture* (1985).

West Virginia Independence Hall

Constructed as a federal post office, customhouse, and courthouse in 1858–59, the sandstone building at the corner of Sixteenth and Market Streets served the city of Wheeling, West Virginia, until 1912. The Italianate Renaissance building was designed by federal architect Ammi B. Young and is unusual in its use of an interior cast iron support system. The design was used for other customhouses in varying degrees of grandeur, with extant examples in Norfolk, Virginia, and Charleston, South Carolina.

Wheeling was the scene of a series of conventions held in 1861 and 1862 to establish the Restored Government of Virginia, and Virginia's secession from the Union was denounced in the building's courtroom. Led by Governor Francis H. Pierpont, the new State of West Virginia was approved by Congress and with President Abraham Lincoln's signature became the thirty-fifth state of the Union in 1863.

Remaining in the customhouse for another year, the state offices under the leadership of the first governor of West Virginia, Arthur I. Boreman, moved to the former Linsley Institute building at Eoff and Fifteenth Streets. The customhouse continued to serve the city until replaced by a new federal building in 1912. Over the next fifty years, various businesses used the building, which led to several insensitive architectural changes.

The state purchased the building in 1964, and restorations in the 1970s and 1980s returned the customhouse to its original appearance. Using the documents and drawings at the National Archives, a restoration architect reconstructed the post office, custom offices, and historic courtroom. The office of Governor Pierpont has been furnished with family pieces and reflects the 1860s period. Gaslight illuminates the office and post office hallway. Administered by the Division of Culture and History, the museum offers exhibits interpreting the state's history.

See also: WEST VIRGINIA STATEHOOD (GOVERNMENT); WHEELING, WEST VIRGINIA (URBAN APPALACHIAN EXPERIENCE).

—Katherine M. Jourdan, *West Virginia Division of Culture and History*

West Virginia State Capitol Building

Located in the heart of Charleston, West Virginia, the State Capitol Building is the fifth edifice to house the state's legislative branch since West Virginia achieved statehood in 1863. The State Capitol Building stands as a distinctive example of twentieth-century Classical Revival architecture. Constructed in three stages between 1924 and 1932, the building is dominated by a 292-foot-high gilded dome and features porticos graced with Corinthian columns at the north and south entrances. Its design reflects the fact that classical Greek and Roman democratic and egalitarian ideals inspired America's Revolutionary generation. The building is not alone in attempting to embody physically the nation's founding principles; classical architectural motifs provided the template for countless public buildings in America until well into the twentieth century.

Noted architect Cass Gilbert (1859–1934) created the design for the state capitol. A native midwesterner, Gilbert began his career with the famous New York firm of McKim, Mead and White in 1880. Two years later, he established a practice in St. Paul, Minnesota, and it was his execution of that state's capitol building that elevated him to national prominence. Known for his mastery of Classical architecture, Gilbert went on to design such landmarks as the United States Supreme Court Building and the United States Treasury Annex, both in Washington, D.C. He received the commission to create West Virginia's State Capitol Building after the state's 1885 capitol was destroyed by fire in 1921. Gilbert's rendering is notable for its symmetry, classical detailing, and balanced proportions.

See also: CHARLESTON, WEST VIRGINIA (URBAN APPALACHIAN EXPERIENCE); WEST VIRGINIA STATEHOOD (GOVERNMENT).

—Lena L. Sweeten, *Cincinnati, Ohio*

Crafts

Section Editor: Kathleen Curtis Wilson

INSPIRED BY NECESSITY BUT LONG ADMIRED FOR ORIGINALITY, BEAUTY, AND SPIRITuality, Appalachian handcrafts, like mountain music and religious practices, tap the wellsprings of the region's culture and provide an unmatched perspective on its history. Though replicated, mass-produced, and commercialized through much of the twentieth century, original works continue to be fashioned by a far-flung community of artisans.

Handcrafted objects in Appalachia serve utilitarian, aesthetic, economic, and symbolic functions. A handmade quilt, for example, may be used as a bedcovering, a decorative wall hanging, an item for sale, or a symbol in a photographic scene to convey immediately a sense of "Appalachianness" to the viewer. The history of craft work in the region reveals much about Appalachia's changing economic and social climate over the last 250 years and how handcrafted items emerged as icons of the region.

Traditionally, craft work in Appalachia, as elsewhere, entailed creation of objects by hand from local materials and reflected community aesthetics and established techniques. Although handmade objects could be decorative, they were usually functional. People learned their crafts through informal channels such as word of mouth and demonstration rather than through formal education.

In general, the word *craft*, derived from the Old English word for strength and skill, implies both diligence and aptitude, but in Appalachia craft has most often been equated with poverty, utilitarianism, and an absence of sophistication. Material culture scholar Simon Bronner has observed that crafts have physical and intellectual effects: they give ideas and feelings a three-dimensional existence. For example, the fashioning of clothing by Native Americans and by European settlers in early Appalachia took quite different forms because clothing items reflected, and still reflect, wealth, social standing, cultural needs, and ideas important to each community. As the two groups increasingly intermingled, so did materials, techniques, and norms for making clothing, with white settlers adopting the use of buckskin construction and indigenous people adopting elements of European style. Throughout the region's history, such changes in craft production have embodied changes in social and economic life.

Facing page: Double Bowknot and Table overshot woven coverlet by Jane Davis Parks, Unicoi County, Tennessee, c. 1855. Coverlets were the pride of skilled hand weavers throughout Appalachia, and those woven in the four-harness overshot weave structure were especially admired. This type of weaving continued in southern Appalachia long after it had disappeared from the Northeast.

In the frontier period, both Native Americans and immigrant settlers made objects by hand out of necessity and as a means of cultural expression, using abundant natural resources and employing skills and knowledge handed down by forebears. Since manufactured products were scarce, distant, and costly, the growing Appalachian population of the preindustrial period depended upon handcrafted tools, structures, and gadgets to provide food, shelter, clothing, transportation, and even entertainment. Community traditions of pattern, process, and style combined to produce brightly colored woven bedcovers, intricately woven baskets for carrying berries, eggs, and wool, hollowed-out bowls for biscuit dough, brooms for sweeping, tools for farmwork, and musical instruments and toys for enjoyment. The process of craft production was sometimes a community event such as a quilting bee or barn raising; sometimes it demanded the solitary work of the wood-carver, weaver, or silversmith. Those with specialized skills such as blacksmithing or loom weaving often turned their work into an economic resource by providing products for others in the community. Products of the craftsperson's hands were judged by community aesthetics, and good work sometimes catapulted a craft artisan into local fame and some measure of prosperity.

Life on the mountain frontier demanded self-sufficiency, and the rise of new communities required creative adaptations embracing both tradition and innovation. The combination gave birth to an Appalachian craft tradition incorporating a mixture of cultural expressions and presenting opportunities for economic gain. Local materials often gave rise to specific and notable craft traditions, such as the making of hickory chairs and oak baskets, that remain dynamic and associated with modern Appalachian culture. Early-twentieth-century Kentucky basket maker Bird Owsley, for example, fashioned an egg basket designed to hold a dozen eggs without spilling as they were carried on horseback; at their destination, the baskets were customarily sold along with the eggs.

As the United States and Appalachia industrialized in the mid- to late nineteenth century, the need for handcrafted items declined. Manufactured goods, more readily available from traveling salesmen, stores, and mail-order catalogs, solved many of the mundane problems of domestic life. Ownership and use of commercially produced goods often became symbols of status while the use of handmade objects came to suggest poverty and lack of sophistication. In time, increasing urbanization and availability of mass-produced goods brought a wave of nostalgia for rural life and handmade artifacts, viewed in the new light as expressions of the idealism, clarity, and moral purity missing from modern, urban, industrialized life.

A renewed interest in crafts in Appalachia and in America in general was influenced by the Arts and Crafts movement that began in England around the mid-nineteenth century. John Ruskin in 1851 decried the sameness and tedious perfection of manufactured goods and argued for the essential humanity of handcrafted artifacts because they demanded creativity, displayed a wonderful irregularity, and possessed individuality instead of industrial perfection. Ruskin's work influenced William Morris, a young Oxford student, who ultimately established his own firm in England for the creation of craft and craft designs in decorative art in the 1860s.

Interest in Ruskin's and Morris's ideas of craft as a moral force in society surfaced in America in the 1870s, coinciding with the formation of patriotic societies to celebrate the American centennial in 1876. Unable to join all-male patriotic societies, women formed organizations such as the Daughters of the American Revolution, the United Daughters of the Confederacy, and the Colonial Dames. Concerned with issues of women's rights, education, and health care, these societies turned some of their attention to the Appalachian region, accepting popular opinion that the region was impoverished and culturally backward but populated by a worthy Anglo-Saxon people. Adding focus to their zeal to uplift the mountaineers, *The Craftsman*, a popular magazine devoted to the work of Morris, praised the art, work, and lives of preindustrial people and suggested that modern Americans could simplify their lives by owning native crafts and identifying with "the common people."

As college-educated men and women began to move to Appalachia at the turn of the twentieth century to serve the region as teachers and Christian missionaries, they soon discovered that locally made crafts could raise both the profile and income of their mountain schools and assist local families financially. William Goodell Frost became president of Berea College in Kentucky in 1892 and, after seeing some locally woven coverlets, began to espouse a connection between handmade objects and the good moral character and educational potential of mountain folk in what he called "Appalachian America." He quickly discovered that this was a successful strategy for fund-raising. By 1896, the year Morris died in England, Berea College held the first of its annual Homespun Fairs, and the making of crafts, or fireside industries, became a major part of the college's curriculum. A Berea woven coverlet won a medal at the Paris Exposition in 1900.

Throughout the mountain region, crafts became a focus for the work of teachers, settlement schools, and industrial schools. Frances Goodrich established her Allanstand shop in Asheville, North Carolina, in 1895 to market woven coverlets, hooked rugs, and baskets. In 1902 Katherine Pettit and May Stone left prominent Kentucky Bluegrass families to move to the mountains of Kentucky and establish the Hindman Settlement School, which taught handcrafts and brought local artisans to prominence. Pettit broke away in 1913 to establish her own Pine Mountain Settlement School in Kentucky but continued an emphasis on craft work. In that same year, two Appalachian women, Allie Josephine Mast and Elmeda McHargue Walker, wove rugs and upholstery fabric to decorate the White House bedroom, afterward called the Blue Mountain Room, of President Woodrow Wilson.

Many of these craft organizations were aware of one another through their common association with the Southern Industrial Educational Association, founded by Alabama native Martha Sawyer Gielow. Established in 1905 to provide financial aid to southern Appalachian schools that taught agriculture, horticulture, handicraft, and domestic science, this unique association was headquartered in Washington, D.C. By 1909, it sponsored an annual sale of mountain-made crafts called the Exchange for Mountain Handicrafts in Washington. The Exchange, as it was known, featured textiles from Allanstand Cottage Industries, baskets from Hindman Settlement School, brooms from Berea College, and crafts from other schools. Sales provided funds for educational supplies and improvements to facilities at industrial schools, as well as income to individual craft makers. The association's Washington base provided a place for Appalachian school directors to interact with each other, discuss fund-raising initiatives, meet political supporters, and explore new markets for craft sales.

Clementine Douglas, educated in Washington and New York, fell in love with Appalachia's weaving traditions during a 1919 summer sojourn in the mountains and by 1925 had opened her shop, the Spinning Wheel, in Asheville, North Carolina, to sell handmade objects from the mountains. In the early twentieth century, Olive Dame Campbell came to the mountains with her husband, John C. Campbell, to teach and to document mountain life, working with ballad collector Cecil Sharp and later establishing the John C. Campbell Folk School, which was patterned after

European folk schools. Her school had a broader focus than crafts but came to be widely known for its craft instruction programs, especially wood carving. Lucy Morgan, a native of the region, helped create the Penland School of Crafts at Penland, North Carolina, in the 1920s and ultimately brought Appalachian crafts to national attention at the Chicago World's Fair in 1933. Many of these women who came to live and work in Appalachia made profound changes across the region. For the rest of the century, strong-willed urban women used their educational backgrounds, influential friends, and political savvy to intertwine education and craft marketing for the benefit of both sellers and buyers.

Growing national interest in Appalachian crafts attracted the attention of Allen H. Eaton of the Russell Sage Foundation in New York in the 1920s. Eaton, long a supporter of the value and virtues of craft work, had promoted interest in crafts from all types of rural and ethnic groups throughout America through his association with the American Federation of Arts and the American Country Life Association. The country life movement began about 1900 in response to national surveys showing significant numbers of Americans leaving rural life for urban areas. Alarmed by what seemed a dissolution of the American ideal of rural life and the cultural traditions they spawned, social reformers encouraged national consideration of the values of rural life, appreciation for the making of crafts, and strategies for making rural life economically sound. President Theodore Roosevelt appointed a government Commission on Country Life in 1908. Spurred on by this national debate, Eaton began organizing various craft cooperatives in Appalachia to form in 1930 the Southern Mountain Handicraft Guild, which very quickly became the Southern Highland Handicraft Guild, the name by which it was known until the mid-1990s, when it became the Southern Highland Craft Guild. The purpose of the guild was to preserve mountain crafts and create national markets for them as a step to economic independence for mountain people. In 1933 Eaton organized a major Appalachian craft exhibition for the annual meeting of the American Country Life Association in Blacksburg, Virginia, and in 1937 published his comprehensive and still influential *Handicrafts of the Southern Highlands*.

Many other craft proponents played a role in the so-called craft revival in Appalachia, an interest in handcrafted objects that spread throughout America and extended to the work of Native Americans, Eskimos, African Americans, and new immigrants, as well as mountain artisans. The resurgent interest saved some Appalachian craft traditions, such as weaving, that were in decline and led to standards and marketing strategies that made Appalachian crafts economically viable. Still, the craft revival has been criticized as a cultural intervention in which forces outside Appalachian communities shaped the processes, design, production, and marketing of what had been traditional craft work into products tailored to widespread commercial consumption. Some scholars have argued that the idea of using crafts as an educational and moral force, as well as an economic opportunity, reflected the values of middle-class, mainstream America and not necessarily the values of mountain communities.

Interest in crafts declined during the World War II years as industrial production surged, raw materials became scarce, and tourism and personal spending faded. Even so, in 1948, the Southern Highland Handicraft Guild held its first craft fair (still held annually) in Gatlinburg, Tennessee. The event coincided with the beginnings of a postwar boom in tourist travel to the mountains. But with the new emphasis on science and technology in the 1950s, ordinary Americans became concerned over the possibility of atomic war and enchanted with innovations such as television. In such an environment, handcrafted work would have seemed to be wholly irrele-

Randy Shull works on a permanent display at Independence Center in Charlotte, North Carolina, 2000. New technologies and global markets for Appalachian craft work have blurred the lines between craft and fine art.

vant, but as Appalachian novelist Harriette Simpson Arnow aptly perceived, interest in mountain crafts moved out of the mountains and into urban areas with Appalachian migrants seeking work. In Arnow's highly praised novel *The Dollmaker* (1954), mountain woman Gertie Nevels makes her way, both emotionally and economically, in a bustling northern industrial city with her talent for wood carving.

In the postwar years, Appalachian craft work moved in two directions simultaneously. Some artisans continued to use traditional styles and materials of earlier generations while employing contemporary designs, new technologies, and skills learned at art schools such as the School for American Craftsmen at Alfred University in New York, Black Mountain College near Asheville, and Cranbrook Academy of Art in Bloomfield Hills, Michigan. Inspired by principles of cultural pluralism, ecological concerns, and supposed rural simplicity, many urban young people moved to rural Appalachia in the counterculture decades of the 1960s and 1970s and embraced rural customs and lifestyles, encouraging a rebirth of interest in crafts. In the mountains, newly arriving artists found plentiful natural resources, affordable land, and inspiration—the latter from both the natural beauty of the mountains and association with traditional mountain artists. They built homes and studios, taught skills learned outside the region in formal academic institutions, and marketed craft products to an increasingly broad-based tourist market.

While Appalachian handicrafts remain important into the twenty-first century, contemporary craft work with more tenuous connections to regional norms has made steady inroads into the region's craft economy. New craft artists from diverse backgrounds continue to move to the mountains because of the welcoming environment of a region steeped in craft history; they are also drawn by the abundant natural resources and a large tourist base to which they can market their work. Some Appalachian communities have developed substantial populations of full-time craft artisans who find expanding infrastructure and educational opportunities to support their work. Western North Carolina, for example, has such a concentration of craft artists that the organization HandMade in America was formed there in 1994 to present the area as the nation's center of handmade crafts. Some Appalachian towns and cities promote resident artisans as enthusiastically as mountain trekking and wild river rafting; still others create affordable studio space and offer banking and health insurance advice to emerging artists. Specialized craft centers such as the Qualla Arts and Crafts Mutual in Cherokee, North Carolina, offer showcases for Native American craft artists.

By effectively using the Internet, artisans and craft show organizers have vastly expanded the customer base, creating global as well as national marketing opportunities. But even before on-line sales and promotion, the popularity of mountain crafts and the complexity of modern marketing had already become evident. In 1992 a national controversy arose when the Smithsonian Institution made Appalachian and other American quilt designs in its historic collections available to a company in China. Mass-produced at lower standards of quality, the Chinese-made quilts were exported to the United States and marketed as authentic American reproductions. Quilters were outraged at this exploitation by an institution of such prestige, and their protests were echoed by historians and members of Congress. More than commercial exploitation, many critics felt the heart of the issue was proper control and protection over regional and national cultural traditions of great symbolic value.

Counterbalancing the Smithsonian controversy, the White House in 1993 showcased a wide variety of contemporary Appalachian crafts in a special exhibition and featured numerous Appalachian craft artisans in the 1995 book *White House Collection of American Crafts*, in which nearly one-fifth of the seventy-six artists featured had some connection to the Appalachian region. Some sixty years after Josie Mast and Elmeda Walker helped create the Blue Mountain Room in the White House, Appalachian crafts still adorn the nation's most famous residence. First ladies from Ellen Wilson and Grace Coolidge to Eleanor Roosevelt and Hillary Clinton have shown a great appreciation for the region's crafts and craft artists.

New technologies and global markets for Appalachian craft work have blurred lines between craft and fine art. Many craft artists would like for their work to be judged by the same criteria as fine art; some critics suggest the category of craft is no longer meaningful if it can embrace those who practice a traditional craft with utilitarian uses and artists who create craft for decorative purposes only. Still others suggest that craft must embrace both kinds of craft artists because both serve to counter mass commercialism and serve as visible reminders of individuals in places such as Appalachia where creative work originates. Even while the critical debates about the meaning and marketing of Appalachian craft work continue, the craft tradition itself remains culturally and economically viable and valuable throughout the Appalachian region.

Since the nearby Great Smoky Mountains National Park opened in 1934, Gatlinburg has become known as a place to purchase inexpensive Appalachian craft work reflecting "mountain" aesthetics. While craft stores and places such as the Arrowmont School of Arts and Crafts continue to make and sell contemporary as well as traditional Appalachian handmade crafts, many gift shops, especially during the 1980s and 1990s, increasingly sold mass-produced and internationally made goods alongside genuine Appalachian crafts. At times this phenomenon has prejudiced the public's perception of Appalachian crafts, since many buyers assume items purchased in the mountains are all authentic local products.

Craft traditions in Appalachia run deep and are not exclusive to professional craftspeople. Across the region, it is not uncommon to find creative objects such as whirligigs, painted figures on rocks or trees, and sculptures in the yards of ordinary people. Generally referred to as yard art, this mode of expression seems to have grown in popularity in recent decades. Whether a hedge sculpted into a replica of an eighteen-wheeler near Old Fort, North Carolina, or a guitar-shaped tree trunk advertising music lessons in east Tennessee, this type of art offers a creative outlet for the maker and a moment of delight to the passing viewer.

There is little scholarship regarding developments such as the Gatlinburg tourist trade and yard art, but because crafts have been so integral to the image of the region, it is important that serious study of these issues continue. For more than a hundred years handmade crafts have been used to promote Appalachian culture, to provide economic assistance, and to define a people marginalized from mainstream America. Twenty-first-century makers, consumers, and scholars who embrace contemporary craft work while maintaining a reverence for traditional styles of previous decades continue to document the history of Appalachian crafts at a time when craft work is evolving to meet the challenges of an increasingly sophisticated audience and competition in the global marketplace.

—Kathleen Curtis Wilson, *University of Ulster, Northern Ireland*

Garry G. Barker, *The Handcraft Revival in Southern Appalachia, 1930–1990* (1991); Jane S. Becker, *Selling Tradition: Appalachia and the Construction of an American Folk, 1930–1940* (1998); Simon J. Bronner, *Grasping Things: Folk Material Culture and Mass Society in America* (1986); Allen H. Eaton, *Handicrafts of the Southern Highlands* (1937); David E. Whisnant, *All That Is Native and Fine: The Politics of Culture in an American Region* (1983); Kathleen Curtis Wilson, *Textile Art from Southern Appalachia: The Quiet Work of Women* (2001).

Allanstand Craft Shop

See Southern Highland Craft Guild

Appalachian Center for Crafts

In the mid-1970s, the concept of a multifaceted craft center in Tennessee that would offer residential training in studio crafts, workshops, craft marketing, and exhibitions and serve as a focal point for craft symposia and events emerged from the craft division of the Tennessee Arts Commission. The commission staff garnered grassroots support and the help of Congressman Joe L. Evins to secure five million dollars in funding from the Appalachian Regional Commission. Construction began in late 1977 at a site on a 562-acre peninsula at Center Hill Lake near Smithville, and the Joe L. Evins Appalachian Center for Crafts opened on December 9, 1979, with a major exhibition of contemporary Appalachian crafts followed by a slate of workshops.

A national advisory committee worked with the Tennessee Arts Commission and Tennessee Technological University officials to design programs, culminating in the approval of bachelor of fine arts and bachelor of science programs in crafts, commencing in the fall of 1980. Despite persistent funding problems, the early 1980s produced numerous successful graduates and notable events such as the 1985 International Ceramics Symposium. During the 1985–86 fiscal year, management of the center was transferred from the Arts Council to Tennessee Tech. In 1989 the curriculum was streamlined to the bachelor of fine arts degree, eliminating the bachelor of science in crafts. At the same time, courses were reorganized under the university's Department of Music and Art, inaugurating a stable period for academic classes and workshops in the early 1990s.

Funding cuts to higher education in 1996 led the university to recommend closing the programs, but a partnership between Tennessee Tech and the nonprofit Friends of the Appalachian Center for Crafts of Tennessee provided access to general public funding. Since 1998, academic, workshop, and gallery programs have grown steadily. Stronger relationships with professional organizations such as the Tennessee Association of Craft Artists and improved community outreach have renewed important elements of the center's original mission. Students and alumni have become more visible nationally and internationally, participating in events such as the 1999 Furniture Society Conference.

See also: CONTEMPORARY CRAFTS; SOUTHERN HIGHLAND CRAFT GUILD.

—Ward Doubet, *Appalachian Center for Crafts*

Apple Carving

During the time when Appalachian children had only handmade toys, apple head dolls were one of their favorites. Costumed to reflect the regional culture, the dolls were often posed with props to demonstrate familiar activities such as quilting or farmwork. They were sometimes designed to resemble a very elderly person complete with wrinkled, leathery skin and a crooked smile.

The maker of an apple head doll uses a large, firm apple with light colored flesh. The peeled apple is first placed in a mixture of saltwater and distilled vinegar to prevent it from turning brown. A face is then outlined with a pointed stick and completed with the use of a knife to cut slits for eyes and a mouth. Once the face is complete, a small hole is made through the apple core and a string is threaded through the head and attached to a stick to keep it in place. A mixture of cloves, allspice, sulfur, and salt on the inside of the apple preserves it and keeps it free of insects. Finally, the apple is hung in a warm place where air can circulate around it. During the first three weeks of drying, the maker pinches the apple to shape the face, taking care not to break the surface. Black-eyed peas are often used for the eyes. As the apple dries it will shrink approximately 80 percent. Properly cared for, an apple head doll can last for many years.

See also: CORNHUSKS; DOLLS; HILLBILLY MOTIF CRAFTS.

—Janice S. Miracle, *Middlesboro, Kentucky*

Arrowcraft Shop

See Arrowmont School of Arts and Crafts

Arrowmont School of Arts and Crafts

Established in 1910 as a philanthropic project by the Pi Beta Phi Women's Fraternity to provide education in a community where no formal schooling existed, the Arrowmont School of Arts and Crafts has become an internationally respected visual arts complex that serves thousands of individuals each year. Located two miles from the entrance to the Great Smoky Mountains National Park in east Tennessee, Arrowmont strives to preserve the area's craft heritage while broadening appreciation of the role art plays in the creation of these crafts. The school achieves this by developing aesthetic appreciation and fostering self-expression through experiences provided to its students.

Designated by the then U.S. Bureau of Education as a district in need of schools, Gatlinburg was chosen as the site for the Pi Beta Phi Settlement School. The school held its first class in an unused church in 1912, with thirteen children in attendance. In 1914 the women's fraternity (as it was called) purchased land using its own resources and funds contributed by local citizens and built a new primary school. Later, the fraternity built and operated a second primary school and high school. A health clinic was opened in 1920 and served as the primary medical resource for the area.

From the beginning, fraternity members admired the workmanship of the local artisans. Realizing that handicrafts might become obsolete as store-bought goods became more readily available, they encouraged the local community to continue these craft traditions. Members who visited the school often purchased native crafts, and in 1926 the fraternity provided a constant market for the handmade crafts through alumnae club sales and by opening the Arrowcraft Shop on the Blue Ridge Parkway in Gatlinburg.

The original focus of the school's philanthropic mission changed with the times. While Sevier County gradually took control of basic education and health care, the school's directors focused on craft education. Attracting fifty students from nineteen states, Arrowmont held its first summer workshop in 1945. Original settlement school buildings were converted into studio spaces and Marian Heard, a University of Tennessee professor, helped establish the workshop curriculum. This was the beginning of the school's affiliation with the university's College of Home Economics's Craft Department.

In 1977 the affiliation shifted to the Department of Art as multidimensional courses were offered with a broader emphasis on blending conceptual aesthetics with a strong technical component. Upon Heard's retirement in the late 1970s, University of Tennessee ceramics professor Sandra Blain assumed the leadership of Arrowmont, a position she held until 2001, when David Willard became the director. Arrowmont is now a leading influence in contemporary art education, serving not only the local community but also artists and craftsmen throughout the nation and the world.

See also: BLUE RIDGE PARKWAY (TOURISM); CRAFT FAIRS; SETTLEMENT, MISSION, AND SPONSORED SCHOOLS (EDUCATION).

—Caroline Malone, *Arrowmont School of Arts and Crafts*

Art Pottery

Inspired by the English Arts and Crafts movement, handmade ceramic wares produced between 1875 and 1940 frequently are described as *art pottery*, though the term has evolved over time to include more modern pieces as well. As industrialization and urbanization spread throughout Appalachia, factory-produced porcelain, glass, or metal products replaced functional ceramic wares, effectively ending traditional pottery production in the central and northern parts of the region by the mid-nineteenth century. Southern Appalachia did not change as rapidly, and traditional ware persisted into the early twentieth century. Appalachian potters turned their talents to producing art pottery, and utilitarian items were replaced or supplemented by vases, tableware, and other decorative items that could be sold to tourists or shipped to other markets.

The Omar Khayyam Pottery at Candler, North Carolina, belonged to Oscar Louis Bachelder and was one of the earliest art potteries founded in the region (1916). Bachelder had been a production potter, but his lifelong goal was to make art pottery. His classic wood-fired shapes were glazed with Albany slip (a watery clay mixture used to decorate or cement pieces of pottery). Successive dippings and firings combined with wood ash in the kiln to produce many different and mostly successful results. His creations were exhibited in national exhibitions, and people such as the acclaimed American potter Paul St. Gaudens came to study with him.

Another important art pottery was Pisgah Forest Pottery, founded in the mid-1920s by Walter B. Stephen in Arden, North Carolina. Stephen had worked with his mother in Tennessee before moving to the Asheville area, where he opened his own shop to make deliberately decorative porcelain, stoneware, and earthenware. The earliest pieces are dated 1925. Large monochrome vases, elegant crystalline-glazed vases in many shapes, sizes, and colors, and cameo ware that mimicked Jasperware manufactured by the Wedgewood Company of England all sold well. Pisgah Forest Pottery is still a working establishment.

Some potters in the region continued to work in traditional styles and methods—hand turning and wood firing and utilizing a limited number of glazes and little decoration. The Penland Pottery in Buncombe County and Brown's Pottery in Arden are examples from North Carolina. Bybee Pottery in Kentucky produced plain useful ware but also made inexpensive colorfully glazed wares. The Gordy family of northern Georgia produced some art pottery along with traditional useful ware. Although art pottery enabled many makers to survive and sometimes prosper throughout the region, various attempts at creating and sustaining a new market for these products of the area were severely hampered by the Great Depression and World War II.

Art pottery as an early-twentieth-century art form was transformed by the evolution of American craft into expressions valued for their form and beauty as much as their functionality. Rising Fawn Pottery in northern Georgia exemplifies the kind of establishment whose wares are both useful and expressive. The explosion of craft in the latter half of the twentieth century has rendered the notion of art pottery obsolete. The term remains useful primarily to describe the evolution of indigenous, purely traditional wares into more elegant and decorative work. Art pottery was designed to replace utilitarian ware and to be sold beyond local and regional borders.

The identification of Appalachian art pottery has not been easy since some work is nearly indistinguishable from more traditional functional ware. The task is especially difficult since some potters did not sign or date consistently, makers did not advertise except locally, sales tended to follow tourist routes, and much work left the area. In the past few decades, however, a body of work has been assembled at

North Carolina State University's Gallery of Art and Design that enables serious attribution and comparison with better-known art potteries such as Grueby (Boston) and Newcomb (New Orleans).

See also: CONTEMPORARY CRAFTS; FACE JUGS; POTTERY.

—Charlotte V. Brown, *North Carolina State University*

John A. Burrison, *Brothers in Clay: The Story of Georgia Folk Pottery* (1983); H. E. Comstock, *The Pottery of the Shenandoah Valley Region* (1994); Charles G. Zug III, *Turners and Burners: The Folk Potters of North Carolina* (1986).

Atwater, Mary Meigs

(1878–1956) Weaver and author.

Mary Meigs Atwater devoted much of her life to teaching, researching, and writing about the technical elements and historical background of American hand weaving. In the early twentieth century, she started a hand-weaving project in Basin, Montana, that was modeled after the early Appalachian hand-weaving cottage industries in Kentucky, Tennessee, and North Carolina. She is widely credited with helping to revive the craft of weaving through a series of instructional correspondence bulletins that eventually became major publications.

One of six daughters born to Montgomery and Grace Lynde Meigs, Atwater spent her early life in Keokuk, Iowa. At thirteen, she left home to attend a boarding school in Providence, Rhode Island, where her love for art was nurtured through international travel. She later studied painting at the Art Institute of Chicago and the Chicago Art Academy.

She married Maxwell Wanton Atwater in 1903, and they traveled with their two children to his mining engineering jobs in the mountains of Colorado, Oregon, South America, Mexico, and Montana. Always curious, energetic, and strong-minded, Atwater found an outlet for her own artistic talents when she began the Shuttle-Craft Guild and Weaving Shop in Basin in the early 1920s. The guild and weaving shop were intended to provide a social service project for the women of the mining community by introducing them to the world of art.

When Atwater started her project in Montana, only a handful of similar projects existed in the United States, many located in the South. Atwater's Basin project closely resembled two of the early Appalachian hand-weaving programs: the Fireside Industries program at Berea, Kentucky, and Frances Goodrich's Allanstand Cottage Industries near Asheville, North Carolina. Atwater had knowledge of these cottage industries and greatly respected the legacy of southern mountain weavers and their handwoven coverlets. She featured several coverlet designs in her weaving publications, acknowledging that the mountain women of the South had been of primary importance in preserving old patterns.

Atwater, like other teachers and weavers of her era, was severely hampered by a lack of published weaving resources and patterns. Lucy Morgan of Penland, North Carolina, noted that the only book on the art of hand weaving available in the United States when she was learning to weave was Edward F. Worst's *Foot-Power Hand-Weaving*, published in 1924. Over the next several decades, Atwater addressed this problem by researching old coverlet patterns in museums, libraries, and private collections, unlocking the secrets of complex weave structures and sharing her discoveries through a series of blueprinted pattern drafts published for hand weavers. Atwater's influence on Appalachian hand weaving is reflected in the papers of Frances Goodrich, the pattern books of Penland School of Crafts, and the work of contemporary hand weavers.

Atwater authored numerous publications, including *Shuttle-Craft Guild Bulletin* (begun in 1924), *A Book of Designs from the John Landes Drawings in the Pennsylvania Museum* (1925), *Shuttle-Craft Book of American Hand-Weaving* (1928; reprint 1951), and *Byways in Hand-Weaving* (1954). These and other publications remain major reference works for weavers today.

See also: BEREA COLLEGE (EDUCATION); FIRESIDE INDUSTRIES; WEAVING.

—Suzanne Hill McDowell, *Western Carolina University*

Mary Meigs Atwater, *Shuttle-Craft Book of American Hand-Weaving* (1928; reprint 1951); Lucy Morgan and LeGette Blythe, *Gift from the Hills* (1958; reprint 1971); Mary Jo Reiter and Veronica Patterson, *Weaving a Life: The Story of Mary Meigs Atwater* (1992).

Baskets, Oak

The craft revival of the early twentieth century significantly affected basketmaking in Appalachia. People from outside the region, influenced by the Arts and Crafts movement and the social reform programs of the early urban settlement houses, moved to the southern mountains and created a renewed interest and market for old-time crafts. Numerous regional groups and organizations became active, and some founded their own fireside industries. Among these were the Allanstand Cottage Industries (which became associated with the Southern Highland Handicraft Guild) near Asheville, North Carolina, and the Hindman Settlement School and Berea College, both in eastern Kentucky. These fireside industries not only encouraged the making of regional basket styles, but they also introduced innovative styles leading to the creation of new forms. Many of the new basket styles became traditional forms for basket makers of later generations and are accepted today as traditional forms of Appalachia. The use of color, the introduction of new shapes, and a high level of workmanship are all encouraged by these groups.

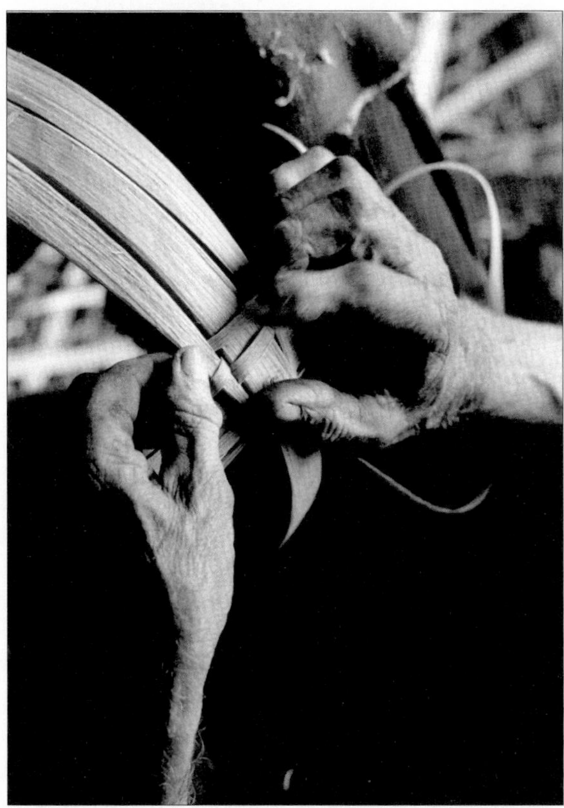

Hands of basket maker Jesse Jones, 1982. Baskets were a rural life necessity for generations of Appalachians and continue to be made today. Some traditional forms have evolved into new variants, and new kinds continue to emerge as part of a living tradition.

Used to contain, transport, and measure various products, as well as for specialized tasks such as sieving grain, trapping fish, and drying fruit, baskets constituted a rural life necessity for generations of Appalachians. Common names reflect the basket shape, use, or size: egg baskets, coal baskets, melon baskets, wall baskets, and bushel baskets. While some of these forms continue to be made today, others have evolved into new variants, and new kinds continue to emerge.

In the early twentieth century, basket forms became more decorative than utilitarian. Changes in agricultural methods, as well as the availability of alternative containers and cheaper baskets made from machine-veneered splits, reduced the demand for handcrafted utility baskets. The Arts and Crafts movement generated a market for ornamental baskets, and the creation of the Great Smoky Mountains and Shenandoah National Parks during the 1930s brought tourists and travelers to Appalachia looking for souvenirs. In response to changing demands, white oak basket makers produced a wide variety of baskets in many shapes, sizes, and colors. Many of these baskets were smaller than standard utilitarian sizes, more varied in shape, and often decorated with colored splits. *Fancy basket* and *novelty* were two terms applied to the new products, which included baskets, flower vases, trays, decorative wall pieces, and fans.

The extensive hardwood forests of Appalachia have proved a plentiful resource for many generations of basket makers. Among the numerous plant species available, oak emerged as the predominant basket material. Because of their ease of splitting, strength, flexibility, and versatility for making many types of baskets, two species of oak are favored: *Quercus alba* (white oak) in the central region and *Q. michauxii* (swamp chestnut oak) in southern Appalachia.

Split, rib, and rod baskets, named for the chief structural element of each form, are the three major categories of white oak baskets found in the Appalachian region. Most white oak basketmaking has been handed down through a family or community network. Each basket maker or basketmaking group develops an identifiable style through particular construction techniques. Detailed examination often makes it possible to link a basket to regional or family tradition or in some cases to a specific basket maker.

Throughout the region, males and females, young and old, European, Native, and African Americans all participated in white oak basketmaking. Often the work was specialized according to the ability or skill of the individual or segregated according to the traditions of the community. Regardless of region, gender, or culture, common knowledge that all white oak basket makers share encompasses finding timber, splitting wood, and making the basket.

The first and most important step in white oak work is finding a suitable tree. Although white oak is an abundant species in the Appalachian woodlands, locating a good tree can be a challenge, and many makers lament that good timber is hard to find. Generally, the best white oaks grow in rich bottomland soil in protected hollows. Basket timber is small: from four to eight inches in diameter at the base, with straight, smooth bark and no visible knots or blemishes up to the first branch. After felling a tree, the basket maker cuts the section of the trunk from the ground to the first knot or branch, called the butt log, for basket use.

Working the oak while still green and moist from sap, makers use a variety of tools, including axes, wedges, mauls, heavy hammers, froes, hatchets, shave horses, drawknives, and handheld knives, to shape basket materials from the butt log by splitting, whittling, and scraping the wood.

The wood of a white oak is comprised of two distinct sections: heartwood (the darker inner section) and sapwood (the light colored wood beneath the bark). In very good timber the sapwood and heartwood may split equally well and be used interchangeably for all materials. However, sapwood is usually more moist and flexible than heartwood, and is often the easiest section to split into thin weaving materials, leaving the heartwood for thicker materials such as handles, hoops, rims, and ribs.

Using axes, wedges, and mauls, makers employ the pith as a guide for centering the division and split the log in half radially, from the top down. The halves are split into quarters and the quarters into eighths. Once a piece of timber is reduced to an eighth, bark is removed and halving continues with the splitting now oriented in line with the growth rings until the wood is separated into single growth rings. These thin, flexible strips, called splits, are the basic elements of basketmaking.

Made in round, oval, square or rectangular shapes, split baskets are the simplest of all white oak baskets to construct. Because their weave structure is basic, split baskets are common in the Appalachians, with a strong ongoing tradition among members of some families in the Blue Ridge Mountains of Virginia.

A split basket is made of stakes interlaced with thin weaving splits. Beginning with the basket base, stakes are laid out to form a square, rectangular, or round shape and then interwoven to stabilize the base shape. The stakes are turned up and woven with the thinner splits to create the sides of the basket. Rims and handles are carved and secured to the basket with a lashing and feet may be added to protect the basket base.

Splitwork shows a wide range of craftsmanship and details such as skillfully carved handles and feet, decorative lashings, and lids. Weaves, which form the basis for splitwork, are plain weave (over one, under one) and twill weaves (over and under multiple counts), which are enhanced by the use of color.

A rib basket, with its graceful curves, is constructed by weaving thin splits through an armature of ribs, making an exceptionally strong and lightweight container. Ribwork is thought to have originated in Europe, where it has been made and used primarily in rural areas. In the Appalachians, rib baskets are found throughout the central region in areas heavily settled by Germans and Scots-Irish. Hart County, Kentucky, and Cannon County, Tennessee, are especially known for ongoing traditional rib basketmaking.

A rib basket begins with the construction of the framework composed of the handle and rim hoops and ribs. The size of the hoops and length of the ribs determine the size and shape of the basket. After the two hoops are joined with pegs or nails, they are wrapped at their intersection with a thin split. Wrappings vary from simple rings or crosses to intricately woven patterns. Round or flat ribs (whittled from thicker pieces of oak) are inserted into the wrapping, and weaving splits worked in plain weave (over one, under one) interlace with the ribs and hoops to create the body of the basket. There are several different techniques for adding the ribs into a framework; variations in techniques often reflect a community tradition or an individual's innovation. Additional details often include top ribs added above the rim of the basket, decorative braids woven over the rim and handle hoops, the addition of feet on the basket bottom, and lids.

Rod baskets are made with long slender rods, which are split from the tree and then whittled or pulled through a metal die to round them off. As a technique, rodwork is nearing extinction, as few makers continue the tradition. Oak rodwork appears to be a distinctively American adaptation of European willow basketwork. European willows were introduced and cultivated for basket use in some Appalachian regions, particularly German-settled areas where there was adequate open space and water for the plants' growth. In other mountainous regions, shoots were cut from native willows growing along river or creek banks. Exactly when and why basket makers turned to oak rodwork can only be guessed, but the extent of this tradition is quite widespread. Oak rod baskets are found from Pennsylvania to North Carolina and as far west as Indiana; however, they are often localized to areas settled by Germans such as the Shenandoah Valley of Virginia and Landis Valley of Pennsylvania.

The construction techniques of rod baskets are similar to those used in willow wickerwork. The oval or round basket base is made first. Side stakes are then inserted into the base and bent up to create the basket sides. Weaving rods interlace the side stakes to form the basket body. Several different weaving methods have been documented, including randing (over one/under one) and increasingly more complex weaves such as French randing, fitching, pairing, and waling. The weaves are both functional and decorative. Ends of side stakes are woven to create the top border of the basket. The basket may have a foot (woven like the top border) to elevate and protect the base. Handles on rod baskets are typically made of an arched foundation piece wrapped with smaller rods resulting in a roped handle. Of the three white oak basket types, rod baskets are the most complicated technically.

Two subgroups of rodwork are found in the Appalachian region. Rod/split baskets are known in North Carolina and Pennsylvania. These baskets are made with a foundation of flat splits over which rods are woven. The construction sequence is similar to that of splitwork; however, finishing details of handles, rims, and top lashings reflect various regional or individual styles. Rod/rib baskets are simply rib baskets woven with rods instead of flat splits.

Appalachian white oak basket forms and the distinguishing details of style or technique continue to evolve as the lives of both basket makers and consumers are influenced by changes in economic, ecological, and social conditions. White oak basketmaking remains dependent on the availability of good basket timber, the market for handmade baskets, and the basket maker's opportunity for better employment. It is a time-consuming craft that has never paid well in terms of the time invested but requires relatively few tools and produces an economic commodity.

Since the 1940s basketmaking generally has been in decline. Economic and social forces during and following World War II changed traditional work values and family structures. Industrialization brought better work opportunities, and many basket makers, especially younger ones, abandoned the craft. In the succeeding years, primarily the older generation carried on the tradition.

Although the number of white oak basket makers remains small, there is a renewed interest in the craft. In recent years, federal, state, and local groups have encouraged the practice, teaching, and sales of traditional crafts. Beginning in the 1960s, organizations and institutions interested in folklife have documented and bestowed honors upon traditional white oak basket makers and continue to encourage practice of the craft through apprenticeships and public demonstrations at festivals.

Widespread exchange of ideas through travel and information media continues to spark public interest and influence the white oak baskets that are made in Appalachia. Contemporary makers of traditional baskets embellish them with color and surface decorations, experimenting with new basket shapes and sizes. They are joined by revivalists who have learned the craft from books or formal workshops. Alongside the traditional functional forms are innovative approaches to traditional styles. The once necessary white oak basket has evolved from a purely functional item for a rural community into a decorative object at home in art galleries, museums, and private collections.

See also: CHEROKEE BASKETS; FIRESIDE INDUSTRIES; SOUTHERN HIGHLAND CRAFT GUILD.

—Rachel Nash Law, *Fayetteville, West Virginia*, and Cynthia W. Taylor, *Parkersburg, West Virginia*

Jeannette Lasansky, *Willow, Oak and Rye: Basket Traditions in Pennsylvania* (1979); Rachel Nash Law and Cynthia W. Taylor, *Appalachian White Oak Basketmaking: Handing Down the Basket* (1991); Rachel Nash Law and John Rice Irwin, *Baskets and Basket Makers in Southern Appalachia* (1982).

Berry Schools

The Berry School, located in Rome, Georgia, was founded at the beginning of the twentieth century with the mission to educate the "head, heart, and hands" of mountain children, many of whom would not otherwise have gone to school. From this simple beginning, the school, based on the ideology that hard work with one's hands builds moral character, grew into an independent coeducational college with fully accredited arts, sciences, and professional programs plus specialized graduate programs in education and business administration.

School founder Martha Berry (1866–1942) was born in northeast Georgia and grew up at her family's plantation, Oak Hill, in Rome. In the 1890s she inherited a sizable estate from her father, a wealthy cotton broker who had capitalized on the growing southern textile industry that was beginning to dominate the area due in part to the abundance of cheap labor. Berry, like many other wealthy, educated women at the time, began her career as a teacher and social reformer, and she focused on the large population of children living in the nearby mountain region, emphasizing craft production.

In 1902 Berry opened the Boys' Industrial School, where boys from the county worked six days a week on the sweeping Berry property for the opportunity to attend grammar school there. By 1917 the school's name changed to the Berry Schools, and both girls and boys were admitted to its residential campus. Work was divided into three main categories: agriculture, vocational mechanics, and home economics; crafts were produced in the latter two domains. Berry's work-study program resembled other settlement and missionary-based institutions that sprang up at the time in the South.

Craft production at the Berry Schools yielded income and reinforced Berry's traditional work ethic. Martha Berry set up craft displays for her many fund-raising campaigns, and donors were rewarded with student-made products such as handwoven ties and bookmarks. Woven goods, including coverlets and towels produced from traditional overshot patterns, especially the Whig Rose design, exemplified the Berry mission. Perfect metaphors for productive labor, they were pure reminders of the heritage of mountain people and stood in stark contrast to the industrialized products of the city, especially the nearby town of Rome, where just a few miles from campus three large textile plants pumped out rayon and cotton products.

Girls, some of whom sang traditional folk songs to zither accompaniment as members of the Ballad Singers, worked in the Sunshine Cottage under the supervision of a skilled craftsperson. Handicrafts were also produced in the neo-Gothic Ford Buildings, where one fireplace inscription reads, "she layeth her hands to the spindle," one of the phrases from Proverbs 31 that defines a virtuous woman. Besides producing woven goods from hand-spun and -carded wool, girls were assigned to make cane and pine-needle baskets, lavender sachets, dolls, feather fans, and corn-shuck mats and rugs, as well as to sew the Berry uniform. Boys worked in the printshop or woodshop producing practical crafts such as stationary, letter openers, brooms, looms, and furniture such as tables, chairs, stools, and bookshelves.

Located on twenty-eight thousand acres of land, Berry College now serves all of its students without regard to economic status. The junior college was established in 1926, the four-year college in 1930, and graduate programs in 1972. Of the handicrafts programs, the products of which are sold at the gift store on the Oak Hill grounds, weaving remains the strongest. Male and female students working the old looms continue to weave cloth from traditional patterns, and alumni continue to produce woodcrafts.

See also: SETTLEMENT, MISSION, AND SPONSORED SCHOOLS (EDUCATION); TEXTILE WORKERS (LABOR); WEAVING.

—Virginia Gardner Troy, *Berry College*

Janet Kardon, ed., *Revivals! Diverse Traditions, 1920–1945: The History of Twentieth-Century American Craft* (1994); W. D. Weatherford, ed., *Educational Opportunities in the Appalachian Mountains* (1955).

Biltmore Industries

In 1901 Eleanor Park Vance (1869–1954) and Charlotte Louise Yale (1870–1958), two recent graduates of the Moody Bible Institute of Chicago, arrived in Asheville, North Carolina, determined to use both their training as missionaries and their skills in the fields of wood carving and weaving to aid in the enrichment of the lives of the young people of southern Appalachia.

The two young women rented a small house in Biltmore Village, a quaint collection of cottages and shops constructed by George W. Vanderbilt for the hundreds of employees required for the construction and operation of his 250-room home, Biltmore House, and his 125,000-acre Biltmore Estate. Word of the arrival of the two young women spread quickly, as did the reputation of Vance, who had trained as a wood-carver under the watchful eye of master craftsman William Fry.

Vance and Yale were soon teaching informal wood-carving classes in their home for a growing group of young men. With the aid of the Reverend Rodney R. Swope, rector of Vanderbilt's newly constructed All Souls' Episcopal Church in Biltmore Village, the classes were moved to a nearby vacant building and the women were hired as parish workers and Sunday school teachers. By the end of 1901 they had formed the Boys' Club of All Souls' Church, where they combined religious instruction with the teaching of hand carving for boys between the ages of twelve and sixteen.

In 1905, with the financial support of Vanderbilt and the public endorsement of his wife, Edith, Yale and Vance founded Biltmore Estate Industries, providing young men and women in the area with the opportunity to utilize their skills in wood carving, woodworking, and the weaving of homespun fabric as a means of generating income for their families. The Vanderbilts provided the fledgling business with the necessary woodworking equipment to produce a growing line of mahogany and walnut bookends, candlesticks, picture frames, hearth brushes, bowls, benches, chairs, and chests. Each item featured finely detailed carving, often inspired by either classical or regional motifs, including the famous dogwood petal design.

Among the many talented young men and women trained by Vance and Yale was George Arthur, who rose to become their first shop foreman. Under his direction both the wood carving and weaving produced at Biltmore Estate Industries garnered national recognition, including medals at the Panama-Pacific International Exposition held in San Francisco in 1915.

Also in 1915, following the unexpected death of George Vanderbilt the year before, Vance and Yale left Biltmore Estate Industries to carry their missionary work to Tryon, North Carolina, where they formed the Tryon Toy-Makers and Wood-Carvers. In 1917, saddled with the enormous responsibility of managing the Biltmore Estate and raising her daughter, Edith Vanderbilt decided to sell Biltmore Estate Industries to Fred Seely, who in 1913 had played an instrumental role in the design and construction of the Grove Park Inn, owned by his father-in-law, Edwin Wiley Grove.

Seely constructed on land adjacent to the nationally known resort a series of workshops, weaving rooms, and showrooms intended to showcase the work of the newly named Biltmore Industries. Seely's emphasis on discipline and production led to the resignation in 1917 of George Arthur, who later opened his own woodworking business, the Artisans Shop, near Biltmore Village. Over the course of the next fifteen years, Seely gradually phased out the woodworking and wood-carving departments in favor of the weaving of homespun fabric. Up until his death in 1942 and for several years thereafter, the cloth of Biltmore Industries was renowned for its beautiful colors and quality weaving.

Though the term *homespun* originally referred to any fabric woven by hand on a loom, when Biltmore Industries began using larger industrial looms to weave high-quality fabric after 1917, much of the work still required a great deal of hand operation, and its cloth was still considered homespun. This fabric was sold by the yard to make men's and women's suits, which were worn by such notables as President and Mrs. Calvin Coolidge and Eleanor Roosevelt.

The wooden objects made at both Biltmore Estate Industries (1905–17) and at Biltmore Industries (1917–70) were marked with a brand burned into the wood. Earliest examples featured a ribbon encompassing the word *Forward* over *Biltmore, N.C.*, while those made later were branded with the phrase *Hand-Made and Hand-Carved/Biltmore Industries/Asheville, N.C.*

Biltmore Industries was purchased in 1955 by local businessman Harry Blomberg, who continued operations until 1980, when all production ceased.

See also: ASHEVILLE, NORTH CAROLINA (URBAN APPALACHIAN EXPERIENCE); COTTAGE INDUSTRIES (BUSINESS, INDUSTRY, AND TECHNOLOGY).

—Bruce E. Johnson, *Fairview, North Carolina*

Bruce Johnson, "Eleanor Vance, Charlotte Yale and the Origins of the Biltmore Estate Industries," in *May We All Remember Well:*

A Journal of the History and Cultures of Western North Carolina, ed. Robert S. Brunk (2001).

Bird Houses

See Gourd Art

Blacksmithing

As in other parts of America, blacksmithing in Appalachia began as a necessary and utilitarian trade. While metalworkers such as silversmiths, tinsmiths, and goldsmiths depended on larger populations to provide a demand for their work, blacksmiths, who worked with iron or steel, were more geographically dispersed, often serving isolated, sparsely populated mountain communities. Industrialization made many blacksmithing techniques, skills, and products obsolete. The resulting decline in the number of practicing blacksmiths was somewhat offset in Appalachia through the development of traditional crafts as a staple of regional tourist attractions.

Prior to the Civil War the blacksmith was an essential craftsman in any sizeable Appalachian community, making and repairing necessities such as horseshoes, tack, wagon hardware, farming implements, and nails. The industrial expansion of the late nineteenth century caused a sharp decline in the number of blacksmiths, as many items traditionally fashioned by hand were replaced by manufactured components. The need for skilled smiths was further reduced by the introduction of the automobile and the tractor. With utilitarian work no longer in demand, skilled smiths turned their experience to the production of more ornamental work.

Building construction was rampant in the American Northeast and Midwest during the early twentieth century, and smiths worked collaboratively with architects to create massive gates and chandeliers for public buildings and the elaborate private estates of American industrialists. The field developed differently in Appalachia, where a market system evolved to promote home-scale items such as pot racks, fire tools, and candleholders. During the Appalachian craft revival from the 1890s to the 1930s, handcrafted items were marketed to the American middle class outside the region by settlement schools, production centers, and, after 1930, by the Southern Highland Handicraft Guild (later the Southern Highland Craft Guild). Also in the 1930s, work began on the construction of the Blue Ridge Parkway and the Great Smoky Mountains National Park, providing increased opportunities for mountain craftsmen through sales to tourists.

Regardless of product or time period, techniques used by blacksmiths are the same, although the process varies somewhat depending upon the scale of the finished piece. A smith begins with a fire, traditionally fueled by coal, though the use of natural or propane gas became common in the late twentieth century. Heat is controlled by varying the air supplied to the fire. To increase heat, air can be supplied in a number of ways, from the most primitive animal-bladder bellows to the more modern hand-cranked or electric-powered blower. A forge, the smith's workstation, includes an air-fed fire that vents through an exhaust chimney. Always within an arm's reach is an anvil. The smith, armed with a variety of hammers, heats the steel in the forge and, once it is white hot, removes it to the anvil and begins forging the metal into shape. Skilled smiths can hammer metal into any shape, drawing out a bar to a fine point to make a knife, scrolling it to hold a candle, or flattening it into a hinge.

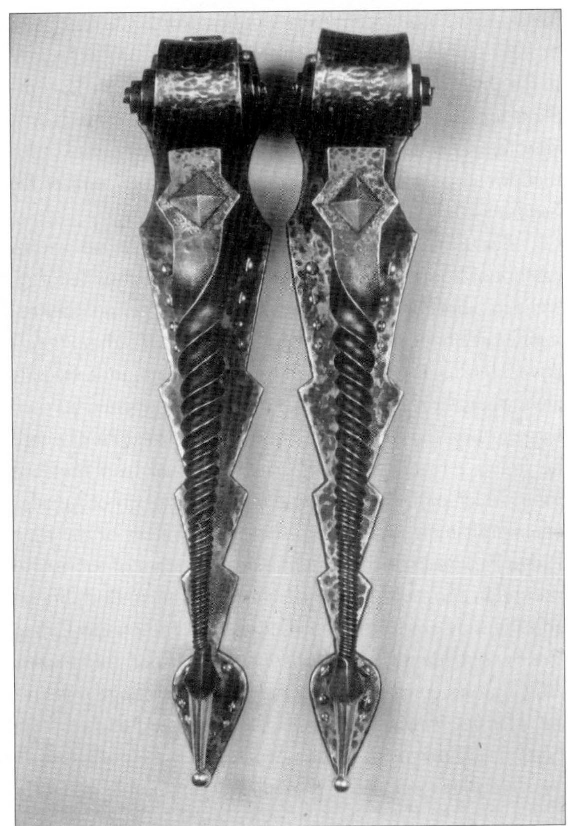

Matching forged-steel door pulls by blacksmith William S. Rogers, c. 1980. Blacksmithing in Appalachia began as a necessary and utilitarian trade but declined with the increase in manufactured pieces during the late nineteenth century. The craft did not disappear, however, as skilled smiths turned their experience to the production of more ornamental work. Contemporary Appalachian smiths such as Rogers combine tradition with innovative design.

The best-known blacksmiths to perpetuate the pioneer tradition in Appalachia were Daniel Boone VI and his brother Lawrence, descendents of the famous frontiersman. By the mid-1920s, the Boone brothers were supporting themselves making ornamental iron in North Carolina. While Lawrence worked at the Biltmore Estate in Asheville, Daniel had his own forge in Burnsville, several miles to the northeast. During the 1930s Daniel taught ironworking at

Lees-McRae College in Avery County, North Carolina, and in 1937 he received a contract from Colonial Williamsburg in Virginia to forge all their restoration ironwork. To complete the job, he built a new forge in Spruce Pine, North Carolina. Daniel, who died in 1970, was the only blacksmith mentioned by name in Allen H. Eaton's *Handicrafts of the Southern Highlands.*

Bea Ellis Hensley, a neighbor who grew up within earshot of Boone's anvil and frequented the Burnsville forge, went to work for Boone after finishing high school and remained at Boone's forge for eleven years. Although not a relative, Hensley learned the skill from Boone and inherited his anvil when the shop closed. In 1955 Hensley opened his own forge just off the Blue Ridge Parkway in Spruce Pine, where he found a ready market for his functional iron fireplace tools. Much of his success—and the success of other Appalachian craftsmen—was due to the establishment of the Blue Ridge Parkway, which brought a steady stream of tourists to the studio doors of rural Appalachian craftsmen. Both Boone and Hensley are featured in Edward L. DuPuy and Emma Weaver's *Artisans of the Appalachians,* published thirty years after Eaton's comprehensive study. In 1995, at age seventy-six, Hensley was named a National Heritage Fellow by the National Endowment for the Arts.

Hensley's son, Mike, grew up working beside his father in the forge. When he was only sixteen, Mike and his father took first place at the 1963 North Carolina State Fair in Raleigh. After completing college, Mike joined his father in business, and together they produced larger works such as entrance gates. In 1965 First Lady Lady Bird Johnson commissioned Bea Hensley to make a boot scraper for the president. He has also made objects for actress Elizabeth Taylor, evangelist Billy Graham, and cowboy star Gene Autry. The Hensleys were among the first craftsmen to demonstrate their work on the National Mall in Washington, taking part in the Smithsonian Institution's Folklife Festival in 1969.

Another notable Appalachian blacksmith, Oscar Cantrell, gained a wide reputation during seventy years with the John C. Campbell Folk School. A native of Brasstown, North Carolina, Cantrell set up the first blacksmith forge at the school and, in the mid-1930s, began to teach. After World War II, he taught blacksmithing to returning veterans receiving vocational training under the G.I. Bill. The Campbell Folk School's blacksmithing program has grown to include a forge with a dozen workstations.

Similarly well known as an Appalachian blacksmith was Phipps Bourne, who demonstrated his skills for the National Park Service at Mabry Mill in southwest Virginia from the 1970s into the 1990s. Bourne was known locally as Festus, in reference to the ancient Greek god and mythological smith Hephaestus. In keeping with the objective of the National Park Service to demonstrate local traditions, Bourne produced such items as traditional hardware for the mill during his demonstrations of the craft before thousands of visitors to the site.

Contemporary Appalachian smiths combine tradition with innovative design. Lee Sauder, who operates a forge in Lexington, Virginia, produces contemporary iron sculptures from ore he finds for himself in abandoned iron mines. William S. Rogers, who learned to braze and weld while growing up on an east Tennessee farm, specializes in *repoussé,* a technique in which a two-dimensional sheet of metal is hammered repeatedly into a three-dimensional form. Bill Brown, who grew up at the Penland School of Crafts near Spruce Pine, where his father was director for many years, makes massive steel sculptures.

While blacksmithing has traditionally been a male occupation, there are also a number of accomplished women smiths, including Elizabeth Brim, who became the resident smith at the Penland School in the late 1980s.

Contemporary blacksmiths have a national organization, the Artist-Blacksmith Association of North America, which publishes two quarterly magazines, the *Anvil's Ring* and *Hammer's Blow.* In Appalachia, blacksmithing classes are offered at John C. Campbell Folk School and Penland School in North Carolina, the Appalachian Center for Crafts in Smithville, Tennessee, and the Kentucky School of Craft in Hindman, Kentucky.

See also: CONTEMPORARY CRAFTS; CRAFT REVIVAL (FOLKLORE AND FOLKLIFE); JOHN C. CAMPBELL FOLK SCHOOL.

—M. Anna Fariello, *Virginia Polytechnic Institute and State University*

Edward L. DuPuy and Emma Weaver, *Artisans of the Appalachians* (1967); Allen H. Eaton, *Handicrafts of the Southern Highlands* (1937); Alexander G. Weygers, *The Modern Blacksmith* (1974).

Blue Mountain Room

When Woodrow Wilson took office as president of the United States in 1913, First Lady Ellen Wilson agreed to serve as honorary president of the Southern Industrial Educational Association, drawing national attention to the work of the association and the educational needs of Appalachian children. By way of showing her support, Wilson commissioned two mountain women to weave fabrics for the president's personal bedroom, creating the Blue Mountain Room at the White House.

In the spring of 1913, the association organized its annual display and sale of handmade mountain crafts in the Exhibition Hall of the Southern Commercial Congress Exhibit held in Washington's Southern Building. The Exchange for Mountain Handicrafts had a dual purpose: money from the sale of the crafts provided financial assistance to mountain women, and the display offered the association a chance to recruit new members. As honorary president and vice-president of the organization, Wilson and Lois Irene Marshall, wife of the U.S. vice-president, visited the craft exhibit frequently. Planning an extensive redecoration of the White House private quarters, Ellen Wilson decided to use Appalachian creations in the bedroom located on the south side of the second floor.

In her weave shed in Valle Crucis, North Carolina, Allie Josephine Mast wove two rugs in the Sun, Moon and, Stars overshot design for Wilson's bedroom. Mast used cotton and dark blue jute to weave six strips, stitched together to make the room-size rug measuring approximately seventeen square feet. A smaller rug was displayed under a writing table next to the fireplace.

Seventy-six-year-old Elmeda McHargue Walker of Flag Pond, Tennessee, wove sixty yards of upholstery fabric in blue wool and natural cotton in the Double Chariot Wheels pattern. The material was used to cover three slipper chairs, an armchair, and a chaise lounge, as well as to make curtains for the two large windows overlooking the lawn and fountain in the rear of the White House.

Wilson also purchased a cream-colored cotton coverlet for the Victorian Lincoln bed and three baskets from the Washington crafts exhibit. The total cost of these items was $292.16. Oil paintings by Wilson were displayed in the bedroom alongside the creations of the Appalachian women.

When the decoration was completed in late autumn 1913, the first lady allowed the association to use two photographs of the room as five-cent souvenir postcards. Referring to the predominant color of the furnishings, the caption on the postcard gave the room its lasting name—*The President's Blue Mountain-Room at the White House.*

A 1917 photograph of the Blue Mountain Room depicts an altered version of the space. In this later photograph the furniture is rearranged, a map of Alaska hangs across a doorway, and a different, ill-fitting coverlet is seen on the Lincoln bed.

See also: CRAFT REVIVAL (FOLKLORE AND FOLKLIFE); SOUTHERN HIGHLAND CRAFT GUILD; WEAVING.

—Kathleen Curtis Wilson, *University of Ulster, Northern Ireland*

Kathleen Curtis Wilson, "Allie Josephine Mast, 1861–1936," in *May We All Remember Well: A Journal of the History and Cultures of Western North Carolina*, ed. Robert S. Brunk (1997) and *Textile Art from Southern Appalachia: The Quiet Work of Women* (2001).

Blue Ridge Parkway Craft Centers

See Southern Highland Craft Guild

Blue Ridge Pottery

See Southern Potteries, Inc.

Brasstown Carvers

Olive Dame Campbell, who also founded the John C. Campbell Folk School, started the Brasstown Carvers in 1930. It is one of the country's oldest craft cooperatives. While seeking a way to bring income to depression-era farm families in the area surrounding Brasstown, North Carolina, Campbell observed men sitting on the "loafer's bench" at Fred O. Scoggs's store. As the men talked, they whittled on wood—some just "making shavings," but a few, such as W. J. Martin Jr., carving animals such as wild turkeys. This scene is said to have inspired Campbell to establish a program to encourage these native talents. The school helped them with the less creative parts of the process, cutting rough blocks on a band saw and sanding and finishing completed works, as well as buying and marketing the carvings.

In 1935 Murrial Galt (who later married carver Martin) came from Baltimore to teach carving and further develop the Brasstown program. "Murray" Martin, as she was known, led the cooperative from 1935 to 1973. Together, she and the carvers created patterns that drew national publicity, including a news column by Dale Carnegie and a Ford Motor Company travelogue.

Popular subjects included animals and mountain people, but perhaps the best known were the crèche figures carved for Christmas nativity scenes. After Martin's retirement, second-generation carver Jack Hall assumed the role of teacher. Helen Gibson, another second-generation carver, succeeded him in the mid-1980s. Carving in Brasstown has been concentrated in a few family groups, among them the Hall, Beaver, Anderson, McClure, Coffey, Brown, Morris, Reece, Massey, Dockery, and Fleming families.

See also: JOHN C. CAMPBELL FOLK SCHOOL; WHITTLING; WOOD CARVING.

—Jan Davidson, *John C. Campbell Folk School*

Brooms, Hearth

Historically, the hearth was both the literal and symbolic center of the home. Around this central hearth the family lived, worked, ate, and often slept. The broom used to sweep the hearth is traditionally made from materials locally available: sweet grass, guinea grass (an African species of grass cultivated in the southern United States to use as fodder), tree limbs, and broom sedge, or sage, that grows abundantly where the soil is poor and lacks lime. Appalachians chose river birch and hickory for the brush brooms used in heavier jobs such as sweeping barn lots, yards, walkways, and dirt floors.

Until relatively recent times, tree limbs were the most frequently used material for brooms. Stiff limbs were soaked and pounded until they splintered. The common Appalachian broom was made out of broomcorn tied in a circular arrangement around a central stick. Broomcorn, also called millet, is a type of sorghum *(Sorghum vulgare)* and has long been considered the best material for making a good broom. Plaiting the stalks of the broomcorn onto the handle adds beauty and makes a more secure and durable broom.

Wooten Fireside Industries, Berea College, John C. Campbell Folk School, Pleasant Hill Academy, and the Shenandoah Community Workers are only a few of the schools that have made and sold attractive and high-quality brooms, some with dyed sweeps and decorated handles.

See also: BEREA COLLEGE (EDUCATION); CRAFT REVIVAL (FOLKLORE AND FOLKLIFE); SETTLEMENT, MISSION, AND SPONSORED SCHOOLS (EDUCATION).

—Ann Stover Bell, *Knoxville, Tennessee*

Cabin Creek Quilts

Cabin Creek Quilts began in the spring of 1970 as a self-help project developed during the War on Poverty. Working with the wives and widows of coal miners in the Cabin Creek area of Kanawha County, West Virginia, the crafts cooperative was organized by Volunteers in Service to America (VISTA). Cabin Creek Quilts was governed by a board composed of quilters and operated by a paid staff.

Skilled workers, paid on an hourly basis, made quilts and other products using traditional patchwork designs and new fabrics. Cabin Creek Quilts quickly became an efficient cottage industry by choosing attractive designs, buying fabric and supplies, and making marketing and distribution decisions. Its patchwork quilts soon made their way from rural West Virginia to the White House and into shops in New York City and Beverly Hills. The organization received national attention when Sharon Percy Rockefeller, wife of Governor John "Jay" Rockefeller, promoted the cooperative. After First Lady Jacqueline Kennedy purchased a quilt made by Cabin Creek, its place in the history of crafts was assured.

As many as three hundred home patchwork makers and quilters worked for Cabin Creek Quilts at one time, but by the late 1980s imported Chinese quilts began cutting into the cooperative's market. Fire, flood, repeated thefts, and vandals failed to stop the group, and the cooperative fought and won trade-name infringements against Wal-Mart and the Orvis Company in the 1990s.

In 1991 the cooperative moved its headquarters, training, and community workshops into two restored nineteenth-century homes in the village of Malden, West Virginia. From 1970 to 2001 more than two thousand individual West Virginians produced seven million dollars in sales for Cabin Creek Quilts. Leading the way in support of the reconstruction of Booker T. Washington's boyhood home and the Women's Park in Malden, Cabin Creek Quilts continues to provide community service.

See also: COTTAGE INDUSTRIES (BUSINESS, INDUSTRY, AND TECHNOLOGY); QUILTS; WAR ON POVERTY (GOVERNMENT).

—James Thibeault, *Cabin Creek Quilts*

Canopy Tying

Fishnet canopies were not part of traditional bedroom decoration in the southern Appalachians, but they have been made in some Appalachian homes since the 1930s as a source of supplementary income. The craft's development is linked to the popularity of four-poster canopy beds in Colonial Revival furniture. The canopies drape over flat or arched wooden frames atop the bedposts and are made in pieces formed by tying rows of bleached white or greige (natural) cotton twine with mesh knots to form a field of diamond designs with tassel decorations added. Makers and craft outlets have developed names based on these tassel patterns, such as Lover's Knot, Double Diamond, and Single Diamond. Because the skills and tools in canopy tying are similar to those in tying fringe for knotted bedspreads, families of bedspread makers also made canopies; however, while spread making was mostly the work of women, canopy tying seems not to have been as gender-specific.

An area particularly noted for canopy tying is Ashe County, North Carolina, where it has been handed down by example in families. As with knotted bedspread making, middle marketers such as Blowing Rock Crafts in Blowing Rock, North Carolina, and Rosemont in Marion, Virginia, served as connections between rural makers and outside consumers. National mail-order companies such as Country Curtains and advertisements in magazines such as *Antiques* have kept the Colonial-style home furnishings in fashion across the United States for generations.

See also: KNOTTED BEDSPREADS/COLONIAL KNOTTING.

—Thomas McGowan, *Appalachian State University*

Chair Making

Chairs made in the Appalachian Mountains follow a tradition dating back to the twelfth century. Generally characterized by a post-and-rung frame and a woven seat, they have a number of variations, giving them colorful descriptive names such as ladder-back, stick, slat-back, common, straight, mule-eared, sittin', and crooked-back. Made in prolific numbers from the time of first settlement through the 1930s, and much later in a few places, they have come to symbolize rural Appalachia as vividly as the log cabin.

The quality of chairs ranged from crude, boxy constructions made by families for their own use to highly refined pieces made by well-known professionals. Creative stylization in the turnings and decorations created some individualization, but the four-post, ten- to twelve-rung construction was maintained.

Inspired by need and available materials, the creation of a country chair required a variety of skills. Chair makers participated in the entire process, from cutting the tree to splitting the log, whittling the parts, boring the holes by hand, and weaving a seat with bark stripped from a hickory tree in the spring. An individual working alone in the forest could accomplish the entire operation—in contrast to the modern industrial process, which involves heavy machinery, specialty mills, and shipment from place to place.

Traditionally, maple was selected for the post and hickory for the rungs, but choice of wood varied with function and availability. Ash, oak, and walnut were also used, but only when maple and hickory were not available or because of a rare request. The most common seat-weaving material was inner bark of the hickory tree, though white oak splits (or splints) and twisted cornhusks were also used.

Early chair makers used tools common to any farmstead—drawknife, brace and bit, froe, axe, chisel, wedge, and maul. Once their efforts produced sufficient income, some acquired additional tools such as a spring-pole lathe or a horse- or water-powered lathe. Freshly felled timber could be split and easily worked while green and soft, which eliminated the need for a sawmill. Parts were then finished and the chair pounded together. Pieces were fitted together so tightly that glue was unnecessary.

The traditional southern Appalachian chair had two or three slats and bent rear posts. The origin of the bend has been lost, but it is known that it did not exist prior to the mountain chair makers. Consequently, the bent post is one of the most reliable characteristics identifying an authentic southern Appalachian slat-back chair.

Once chair makers found wider markets, new buyers influenced their styles. A more formal dining chair with four or five slats and a straight post evolved, and cornhusks were used as seating, possibly to copy finer chairs with rush seats popular in the cities. These chairs were called ladder-backs and straight chairs. By whatever name, the design was not known for its comfort—notable chair maker Shadrack "Birdie" Mace of Buncombe County, North Carolina, called them "company chairs" because if a host wished his visitors' stay to be brief, he would give them ladder-backs to sit on.

As nineteenth-century industrialization spread, incomes increased, and markets grew more accessible, the American public began to choose more expensive factory furniture over its country counterpart. While the Northeast soon lost its handmade chair makers, craftsmen in the mountain areas of West Virginia, Virginia, North Carolina, Kentucky, Tennessee, Georgia, and South Carolina retained their chair-making skills. Because of isolation and self-reliance, mountain chair makers continued to prosper up until World War II. The last of these country chair makers had reached their eighties and nineties by the end of the century, and their long tradition was dying out. There has been a return to chair making by revivalists using the same tools and techniques as the early settlers, but this sometimes involves guesswork, as few records remain from early country chair makers. While urban makers of stylish furniture left detailed descriptions and drawings, country chair makers left only the unsigned product.

The history of a few chair-making families is known. The Mace family's migration to a settlement in North Carolina is documented in *May We All Remember Well*, edited by Robert S. Brunk. Jerry Israel, who contributed an article about the Mace family, traces the clan back to 1752, when a fifteen-year-old cabinetmaker's apprentice stowed away on an English ship bound for America. Two hundred years of family chair making continued until 1973, when Birdie Mace died.

Other chair-making families fell victim to industrialization and the higher wages provided by factory work. In 1930 the price of one dollar for a chair, though well below its worth, could compete with wages earned at a sawmill. By 1970, however, jobs were plentiful and the minimum wage was $1.60 for an hour of work. In Macon County, Tennessee, Dallas Newbery and his son Louis were earning only five dollars for a crooked-back chair, which led Louis to Nashville for work to support his wife and two sons. Fortunately, Louis returned three years later, keeping five generations of Newbery family chair making alive. Into the twenty-first century, he and his youngest son, Mark, continued the Newbery tradition of making chairs and raising tobacco.

Supplementing chair income by raising tobacco or operating a gristmill or grocery store attached to the shop was common practice among chair makers. Taking to dirt roads through the mountains, they carried tools to repair chairs and large balls of hickory bark to re-bottom them. There was also a demand for such services in cities from Birmingham to Philadelphia.

See also: COTTAGE INDUSTRIES (BUSINESS, INDUSTRY, AND TECHNOLOGY); FURNITURE INDUSTRY (BUSINESS, INDUSTRY, AND TECHNOLOGY); MACE CHAIRS.

—Curtis Buchanan, *Jonesborough, Tennessee*

Allen H. Eaton, *Handicrafts of the Southern Highlands* (1937); Jerry Israel, "The Mace Family of Chair Makers," in *May We All Remember Well: A Journal of the History and Cultures of Western North Carolina*, ed. Robert S. Brunk (1997).

Cherokee Baskets

For centuries, Cherokee women have excelled in making baskets of materials gathered from local environments. By the mid-twentieth century, they were specializing in four materials: river cane *(Arundinaria gigantea)*, white oak *(Quercus alba)*, Japanese honeysuckle *(Lonicera japonica)*, and red maple *(Acer rubrum)*. Cane weaving originated centuries ago and is the oldest surviving basket tradition. Red maple basketry is the newest, having originated in the early 1900s. The most common basket material is white oak, and Japanese honeysuckle remains the only nonindigenous vegetation used. Other materials sometimes used are shagbark hickory *(Carya ovata)* and commercial reed.

Weavers also make basket dyes from local vegetation, boiling roots or nut hulls of black walnut trees *(Juglans nigra)* for dark brown and distilling black from roots or nut hulls of butternut trees *(J. cinerea).* The boiled roots of bloodroot *(Sanguinaria canadensis)*, an early spring wildflower, produce an orange-red dye applied sparingly next to brown or black tints. Weavers have also experimented with yellow root (commonly known as goldenseal), pokeberries, red cedar bark, oak galls, blueberries, and angelica. Commercial dyes became popular in the 1880s, and some weavers continued to use them throughout the twentieth century. The inexpensive and fast commercial dyes produce a variety of colors, including gold, pink, purple, orange, and blue.

Initially, women were the principal makers and users of baskets, a custom held sacred in Cherokee mythology. The primeval account of the capture of fire features a female water spider who spins thread for a container to carry fire to the world's inhabitants. Until the 1800s, the myth was ceremonially reenacted when women collected embers from the new sacred fire to kindle household fires.

Utilitarian cane baskets were created in a variety of shapes and sizes to gather, process, serve, or store foods and to protect household and personal valuables. The common weaving technique for utility baskets was simple plaiting of splits. Women also fashioned cane trade baskets, often in the double-weave technique that made two separate, nested baskets joined with a common rim. They varied the twill weave and applied dyes for intricate double-woven patterns. Families or clans may have specialized in particular designs.

In the early 1800s, Cherokee men began to manufacture white oak utility baskets for farmwork, adopting European-style features such as carved wooden handles and rib construction. Women then fashioned utility and trade baskets of cane and white oak, gradually establishing exchange networks with white neighbors. Basket production probably reached its height in the early 1900s, as Cherokees continued subsistence farming that required numerous workbaskets and tourists sought ornamental baskets. As tourism became the primary economy in the 1950s, women again became the predominant weavers, producing decorative baskets of cane, oak, honeysuckle, and maple for the market.

See also: BASKETS, OAK; NATIVE AMERICAN ARTS AND CRAFTS; RIVER CANE (ECOLOGY).

—Sarah H. Hill, *Atlanta, Georgia*

Betty J. Duggan and Brett H. Riggs, *Studies in Cherokee Basketry* (1991); Marshall M. Gettys, ed., *Basketry of the Eastern United States* (1979); Sarah H. Hill, *Weaving New Worlds: Southeastern Cherokee Women and Their Basketry* (1997).

Cherokee Masks

Native masking traditions were once widespread in eastern North America. Most famous are the Society of Faces of the Iroquois Confederacy and the Booger Dance of the Cherokees. Masks made of shell, copper, and wood have been found in archaeological sites, and historical accounts describe masks made from wood, bark, gourds, pumpkins, melons, and even of hornets' nests, with some masks painted, stained, or trimmed with animal fur. Some prehistoric southeastern masks strongly resemble the "long-nosed god" of Mesoamerica, suggesting distant prehistoric cultural connections. Archaeological finds of paired, painted human and animal masks may indicate maskers shifted from one symbolic being to another during some performances. Storage of certain masks in prehistoric and early historic mound-top temples in the Southeast denotes their ritual power, as do the presence of fixed human, animal, and mythological masks or carvings on public structures.

Historic Cherokees had masking traditions for practical, social, and ceremonial purposes. Animal masks of buffalo, deer, bear, and wildcat (for stalking wild turkey), along with corresponding animal skins were suffused with ritual power. For instance, in the Hunting Dance a man wore the deer (or other) mask and deerskin; he would later don the same costume to stalk game and still later wear the symbolic clothing in another dance celebrating success. Masks, dancing, and related songs, myths, and rituals combined in this cycle of symbolic activities aimed at, as the Cherokees said, "using the magic of the mask." A mask for the Warrior or Brave Dance, decorated with a human face adorned by a carved rattlesnake on the forehead or top of the head, was used in like fashion.

The Cherokee Booger Dance occurred in fall or midwinter during an all-night dance held in a public building and later in a home. A sequence of animal and social dances was temporarily interrupted by arrival of the Boogers. These uninvited visitors spoke in a whispered gibberish that needed translation, looked odd, had obscene names, frightened children, and made suggestive advances to and then danced with the women during their amusing Booger or Mask Dance. Often misshapen, bent, and dressed in makeshift costumes—tattered clothes, long johns, quilts, and later, even cardboard masks—the Boogers appeared ridiculous and socially uncouth.

Drawing on certain mask features and oral traditions, anthropologists Frank Speck and Leonard Broom interpreted the Cherokee Booger Dance as a caricature of early Cherokee experiences with Europeans, blacks, and other eth-

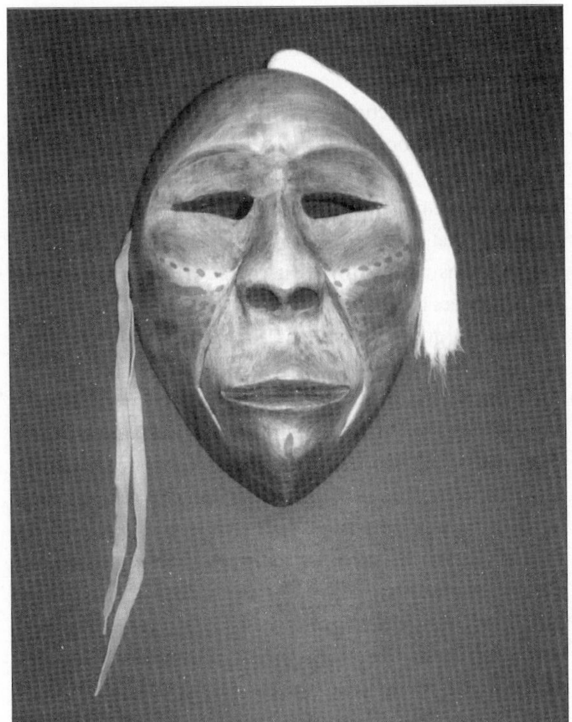

Cherokee Booger Mask made from buckeye wood by John Julius Wilnoty II, 2003. Appalachian Native Americans had masking traditions for practical, social, and ceremonial purposes. The Booger Dance, which occurred in fall or midwinter and featured cavorting dancers dressed in masks and grotesque costumes, may have reflected anxieties about disease, fertility, aging, and the unknown.

nic groups enacted to relieve anxiety and social disarray caused by the newcomers and to exorcise their diseases. The Booger Dance may also relate to older masking traditions. The War Dance of the historic Waxhaw Indians of North Carolina, in which young male dancers in gourd masks engage in mock battles and pursue girls, suggests features of the Booger Dance. Anthropologists Raymond Fogelson and Amelia B. Walker have skillfully argued that the Booger Dance reflects anxieties about and efforts to control disease, fertility, aging, and unknown worlds, paralleling in general purpose, some mask features, and body postures the historic Old Man's Dance of the Creeks and other groups, as well as the Iroquoian False Faces.

During the first two decades of the twentieth century, young Cherokees were discouraged from practicing Cherokee language and cultural traditions at federally run boarding schools they attended, and between the 1920s and 1940s masked dancing ceased. In recent decades, some traditionally unmasked social dances have been brought back into practice among the Eastern Cherokees in North Carolina, with aid from Western Cherokees from Oklahoma. Mask making as a crafts tradition, however, never ceased in the East. The Qualla Arts and Crafts Mutual, a tribal cooperative for the Eastern Band of Cherokee Indians, reports that in 2003 at least twelve Eastern Cherokee men were regularly carving wooden masks and about six were making gourd masks, with a few occasionally making masks from hornets' nests, primarily for purchase by collectors of fine native arts.

See also: CHEROKEE BASKETS; NATIVE AMERICAN ARTS AND CRAFTS; QUALLA ARTS AND CRAFTS MUTUAL.

—Betty J. Duggan, *Peabody Museum of Archaeology and Ethnology, Harvard University*

William N. Fenton, *The False Faces of the Iroquois* (1987); Raymond Fogelson and Amelia B. Walker, "Self and Other in Cherokee Booger Masks," *Journal of Cherokee Studies* (Fall 1980); Frank G. Speck and Leonard Bloom, with Will West Long, *Cherokee Dance and Drama* (1951).

Churchill Weavers

Located in Berea, Kentucky, Churchill Weavers was established in 1922 by Carroll and Eleanor Churchill as a business to market handwoven products while providing employment to local residents of Appalachian Kentucky. Although similar efforts already existed in the college town at the time, they were low-paying institutional programs. Churchill Weavers was the first attempt to run a for-profit weaving business in Berea.

As a young engineer and inventor, David Carroll Churchill was a missionary to India, where he designed and built hand looms in the years prior to World War I to help the country's impoverished people compete with new power looms. When war broke out, Churchill returned with his wife, Eleanor, to the United States to teach at Berea College. Churchill's plans for a new technology department at Berea College did not materialize, so the Churchills built a shed on the outskirts of Berea and opened Churchill Weavers. Carroll Churchill patented and built the looms, while Eleanor designed the patterns, trained the weavers, and aggressively marketed merchandise in urban centers such as Chicago and New York, where she obtained orders from large department stores. Baby blankets, shawls, scarves, and couch throws woven from wool and cotton were and are the mainstay of the product line, though in recent years a line of rayon chenille throws has been developed for the more contemporary marketplace.

The Churchills shared the management of Churchill Weavers until Carroll's death in 1968. Eleanor, who passed away in 1981, turned over management to Lila and Richard Bellando in 1973. Churchill Weavers operates as a division of Crown Crafts and offers self-guided tours of the production facilities in Berea, where eight to ten weavers operate Churchill's flyshuttle looms.

See also: BEREA COLLEGE (EDUCATION); LOOMS; WEAVING.

—Garry Barker, *Morehead State University*

Garry G. Barker, *The Handcraft Revival in Southern Appalachia, 1930–1990* (1991); Carol Strickler, *American Woven Coverlets* (1987); Kathleen Curtis Wilson, *Textile Art from Southern Appalachia: The Quiet Work of Women* (2001).

Clinch Valley Blanket Mills

A small weaving company in Cedar Bluff, Virginia, originally owned and operated by Charles Eugene "C. E." Goodwin and his four sons, the Clinch Valley Blanket Mills produced bedcovers, linens, and blankets during peace and wartime during the twentieth century, providing a valuable wool market for hundreds of farmers across the central region of Appalachia.

Goodwin followed the weaving trade learned from his English father, James, who came to the United States about 1837. Goodwin ran mills for absentee owners or rented buildings to set up his own businesses in Kentucky, Tennessee, and West Virginia before moving to southwest Virginia in the late 1880s to manage the Klondyke Cotton and Woolen Mill. He first installed power looms in 1892 and used the water of the Clinch River flowing nearby to turn carding machine cylinders, propel spinning machines, and activate the looms. Eventually, a combination of water, steam, and electric power increased production.

In 1916 Goodwin purchased both the Klondyke Cotton and Woolen Mill and the Cedar Bluff Woolen Mill, renaming his operation Clinch Valley Blanket Mills. At different times during the next sixty years the mill employed from 30 to 120 workers who processed huge quantities of wool from seven surrounding Virginia counties and nearby states.

Wool was gathered from farms in Virginia, West Virginia, Kentucky, and Tennessee by horse- or ox-drawn wagon in the early days; later trucks pulled the wagons across the region. Piled high with finished coverlets and blankets when they left the mill, the big wool wagons traded wool for goods or purchased the wool outright. When trading for wool, Goodwin exchanged two all-wool blankets for twenty-five pounds of wool. In the mill, the wool was scoured, cleaned, carded, spun, and dyed before weaving began.

The mill represented a valuable wool market for hundreds of farmers across the region. It was difficult and uneconomical for farmers to transport wool out of the mountains, so the wool wagon enabled them to get their wool to market in a manner that benefited both buyer and seller. When times were hard and wool prices low, farmers traded all their wool for coverlets and blankets to furnish bedding to the extended family or to put away for the next generation. Even in good times, many families used a little of their wool fleece in trade for finished goods. Woven coverlets were not only functional and warm, but beautiful as well. The trade made it possible for families to acquire luxurious bedcovers that they otherwise could not have afforded. Mill-woven items were prized as wedding gifts, baby presents, and household linens. These items were especially desirable, since the giver usually had some association with the weaver or worker at the mill involved in its production.

As C. E. Goodwin advanced in age, the mill's ownership passed on to his four sons: Jim, Jake, John, and Ras. Owners and employees worked long hours and side by side in a trade that was arduous and dirty, and strong chemical-dye solutions and cotton dust caused health problems for many workers and owners.

Under government contract, Clinch Valley Blanket Mills produced thousands of wool U.S. Army blankets during both world wars. They wove lining for army sleeping bags, puttees (gaiters) for World War I uniforms, maroon and navy afghans for the British Royal Air Force, and wool blankets for the Bundles for Britain shipments used in home-front air-raid shelters.

In peacetime, the mill produced overshot and double-weave coverlets, lap robes (for horse-drawn buggies and automobiles), table linens, baby blankets, tweeds, and portieres. Smaller items such as two-ply knitting yarn, yardage in each pattern, pillow covers, dresser scarves, luncheon sets, and tablemats were also available. Colors and sizes coincided with current fashion trends and popular demand. Coverlets came in full, twin, daybed, and crib sizes, depending on the pattern, and seven patterns were woven on a regular basis. Goodwin published a small catalog for direct mail-order sales and occasionally sent out flyers promoting new items. The volume of sales, diverse patterns, and style set a standard for unsurpassed quality and durability in woven bedcovers for more than sixty years.

To sell these household goods, the Goodwin brothers avoided revealing factory production capacity, which amounted to twelve thousand coverlets annually in 1941, and focused on selling a concept of tradition. While using mechanized equipment, Goodwin and other production weaving mills marketed craft revival nostalgia. Most of his advertising suggests that Goodwin created the first seamless coverlets, appealing to northern buyers who did not like the "unsightly" seam down the middle seen in nineteenth century handwoven coverlets. The buying public remains uncertain of the differences among handwoven, hand-loomed, and production weaving, and promotional materials in the twenty-first century do little to enlighten customers.

The production mill in Cedar Bluff closed a few years after World War II, and C. E.'s son John Owen Goodwin moved his family to Blowing Rock, North Carolina, in 1950 to establish Blowing Rock Crafts, Inc., Goodwin Guild. He continued to weave overshot coverlets and table linens in patterns and colors similar to those made in Cedar Bluff. Goodwin's daughters, Mary Goodwin and Edith Goodwin Harman, and his grandchildren worked with him and carried on the business after his death in 1974. By the 1980s the general public was less interested in quality and historical traditions and more concerned with price and production speed. The old looms used by John Goodwin and his descendents were stored, and in 1991 the company was sold to Crown Crafts, a large Georgia textile manufacturer.

In 1999 John Goodwin's grandson Mike Harman took the old production looms out of storage and started a new business, Buffalo Creek Weavers, in Ashe County, North Carolina. Mike and his wife, Dana, with occasional help from his brother continue to weave coverlets and throws in traditional patterns and colors made famous in southern Appalachia by the Goodwin family since the beginning of the twentieth century.

See also: ATWATER, MARY MEIGS; COVERLETS; WEAVING.

—Kathleen Curtis Wilson, *University of Ulster, Northern Ireland*

Garry G. Barker, *The Handcraft Revival in Southern Appalachia, 1930–1990* (1991); Carol Strickler, *American Woven Coverlets* (1987); Kathleen Curtis Wilson, *Textile Art from Southern Appalachia: The Quiet Work of Women* (2001).

Coal Art

In coal-producing areas of the Appalachian region such as West Virginia, eastern Kentucky, southwest Virginia, and western Pennsylvania, craftsmen use coal to fashion artifacts primarily as souvenirs for tourists or sale items for craft fairs and exhibitions. Such items include replicas of miners and mining implements, log cabins, animals, jewelry, and even delicately carved wall plaques of mountaineers that sometimes are painted. Many coal art items are made from powdered coal that is mixed with a bonding agent and cast in a mold. However, some artisans sculpt pieces from hard grades of lump coal. The carving, often done with hand-fashioned tools, ranges from the simple inscription of writing or letters into the coal to elaborately carved details of objects and faces. For example, James Stewart of Boone County, West Virginia, used his knowledge of coal from thirty years as a coal miner to carve busts of coal executives that grace many corporate boardrooms. The craft of making coal objects in Appalachia is part of a broader craft tradition of coal artisans in such places as Scotland, England, and Wales. In Scotland, for instance, it is part of the New Year's tradition of "first-footing" to bring a lump of coal to the first house visited after midnight, and gifts of coal there are often cast with the current year's date.

See also: HILLBILLY MOTIF CRAFTS; WHITTLING.

—Jean Haskell, *East Tennessee State University*

Contemporary Crafts

Although historical and traditional crafts remain an integral part of Appalachian identity, craftspeople and artists in the region have readily and successfully adapted their works to contemporary markets. In southern Appalachia, handcrafted objects described as contemporary are generally those crafts made since about 1925. Not all crafts created during this period are so considered "contemporary," however. For example, contemporary wood carving done in middle Tennessee in the 1930s typically featured everyday scenes of rural life in the style of artists such as Thomas Hart Benton, while wood carving in mountainous western North Carolina at the same time was more traditional in appearance, featuring non-stylized elements of nature such as animals and flowers. The two styles had a close relation, though, since it was the presence of the traditional craft that drew contemporary craftspersons to the southern mountains.

The focus on the southern mountain region's social issues during the late nineteenth and early twentieth centuries involved much discussion of the role of craft. Craft came to be viewed as an economic boon and marketing tool as well as family tradition, and its uses were successfully exploited through the marketing of Appalachia as a tourist destination and a source of fashionable home furnishings. This initiative resulted in institutions of higher learning for craft, such as Penland School of Crafts (Penland, North Carolina), John C. Campbell Folk School (Brasstown, North Carolina), Arrowmont School of Arts and Crafts (Gatlinburg, Tennessee), and Berea College's Student Crafts Program (Berea, Kentucky). These institutions were created by religious, fraternal, and social reformers to teach "local but dying" ways of weaving, carving, blacksmithing, basketmaking, and woodworking to the local population. Over a period of time, the student population changed, original school administrators gradually relocated, and the focus began to shift to teaching more mainstream art classes.

These institutions focused primarily on teaching and making local traditional crafts, but they frequently resorted to seeking well-known and expert artists from outside the region. Penland sponsored workshops by textile artist Anni Albers, who taught at Black Mountain College with her husband, Josef, and respected weaver Edward Worst was a regular guest teacher at Penland. It was considered important to expose students to the best minds and talents available, wherever they came from. Over time these schools changed to promote more innovative art instead of marketing and selling traditional craft work. This focus, which coincided with the years just after World War II and opportunities made available by the G.I. Bill, saw an explosion of university art and craft departments across the country. At this time a new, more professional group of directors began being hired to run the school craft programs.

Areas of eastern Kentucky, western North Carolina, southwest Virginia, eastern Tennessee, northeast Georgia, and northwest South Carolina became the focus of intensive federal and private (mostly religious) efforts on behalf of mountain people. Notable among this new influx of craft professionals was Bill Brown, who arrived at Penland School of Crafts in the early 1960s and brought significant changes to the school. Brown actively recruited nationally known instructors, started a residency program, and brought Harvey Littleton, considered the father of the contemporary studio glass movement, to live and work at Penland. The studio glass movement did not exist before about 1960; until then, glass companies had provided space for individuals to create one-of-a-kind pieces. Harvey Littleton and Dominic Labino developed the small-scale studio concept that allowed artists to create their own style and market unique designs blown in individual workspaces. As a result of Littleton's work, Penland became the leading studio glass center in America for many years. Brown's success as an administrator and visionary brought wide recognition to the region for excellence in craft and created an environment that encouraged craftspeople to move to southern Appalachia to live and work. The majority of these craftspeople were university trained and working in a nationally recognized contemporary style, not a traditionally Appalachian style.

In other parts of Appalachia, craft programs developed differently from those at Penland, Arrowmont, and Campbell Folk School. While many were founded around the turn of the twentieth century, only the schools in southern Appalachia survived or developed into centers known nationally for their excellence in craft education. Penland, in particular, has become an important part of the national craft psyche, acting as the model for Pilchuck Glass School in Seattle, Washington, and Haystack Mountain School of Crafts in Maine.

The Southern Highland Craft Guild, headquartered in Asheville, North Carolina, is another hub of activity for contemporary craft. The long-standing organization has built a reputation for both modern and traditional design, and its marketing program, retail shops, and craft fairs have drawn many new craft businesspeople to the region. It operates the oldest retail craft shop in the country and is nationally recognized for its excellence in traditional craft. Southern Appalachia is home to a growing number of contemporary craftspeople, and Asheville is considered one of the top contemporary art cities in the nation.

At the turn of the twenty-first century, educated and well-traveled collectors expected to see a full range of contemporary work as well as traditional favorites, and Appalachian regional galleries began representing more contemporary artists to satisfy them, as they could no longer survive catering exclusively to the traditional market. In addition, fewer traditional craftspeople worked for the wholesale market. Consequently, the entire region has slowly shifted from traditional Appalachian to more contemporary American work, a change driven by collectors looking not for regional work, but for contemporary work done by regional craftspeople with national reputations.

Places in Appalachia once considered the source of traditional craft work have become known for contemporary crafts. Inspired by the success of Berea College's craft program, nearly the entire town of Berea is focused on craft and its related marketing. Boone, North Carolina, a town located in a mountain setting, is home to a very large number of artists and craftspeople. Contemporary artisans working and teaching at Arrowmont in Gatlinburg, Tennessee, have sold their work locally and influenced the buying public's perception of Appalachian crafts.

Studio glass artist Stephen Powell provides an example of how personal vision can combine with location, education, and state support to change the landscape of contemporary crafts in southern Appalachia. Hired to teach studio art and design at Centre College in Danville, Kentucky, he created a small glass studio and offered classes in different areas of glass art. This small program has grown into a highly specialized undergraduate program respected throughout the country for producing excellent master of fine arts candidates in studio glass craftsmanship. Powell capitalized on Kentucky's ongoing efforts to support craft as well as the flexibility of a small liberal arts college to meet his needs as an instructor.

Among the most interesting aspects of the contemporary craft world are the businesses that have sprung up across southern Appalachia to support craftspeople and integrate their talent into local communities. Highwater Clays, a small, high-quality clay and ceramic supply house in Asheville, is owned by Brian and Gail McCarthy, who also operate a school and gallery adjacent to the supply house. The school, Odyssey Center for the Ceramic Arts, supports resident artists and employs a faculty of nationally recognized artists. The ceramics gallery is among the best in the Southeast. This blend of commercial and educational goals is something that Appalachians have done at least since the beginning of the twentieth century. Like the Odyssey Center, many other businesses supporting a wide range of craftspeople, schools, and galleries have sprung up across Appalachia.

Another enterprise important to the growth of contemporary craft in Appalachia is Tamarack in Beckley, West Virginia. This $16-million state-supported facility has given thousands of Americans their first exposure to a wide variety of traditional and contemporary regional crafts. Both high-quality crafts and less expensive tourist souvenirs are displayed and sold there. Located adjacent to a major interstate, Tamarack has marketed itself as a combination craft shop, restaurant, state souvenir shop, theater, and rest stop. The success of large retail galleries located in multipurpose facilities such as Tamarack and Asheville's Folk Art Center have vastly increased the visibility of contemporary craft in Appalachia.

The connection between craft and economic development has been strong and enduring in Appalachia. Consequently, objects offered for sale run the gamut from very fine contemporary craft to inexpensive tourist ware, without much effort to educate the public about craft work in general and contemporary workmanship in particular.

Methods used by founders of the craft revival movement of the early twentieth century are being employed anew one hundred years later with great success. Early revivalists took traditional crafts and, in short order, created contemporary designs based on a cultural heritage. This process has continued for more than one hundred years and appeared to be gaining momentum at the beginning of the twenty-first century. Appalachia, which has always been known for its traditional craft, is increasingly being recognized for its contemporary crafts as well.

See also: JOHN C. CAMPBELL FOLK SCHOOL; SOUTHERN HIGHLAND CRAFT GUILD; TAMARACK (CULTURAL INSTITUTIONS).

—Andrew Glasgow, *The Furniture Society*

Phyllis George, *Kentucky Crafts: Handmade and Heartfelt* (1989); Paul Greenhalgh, *The Persistence of Craft* (2003); Ramona and Millard Lampell, *O, Appalachia: Artists of the Southern Mountains* (1989).

Cornhusks

The outer leaves of an ear of corn, known as cornhusks or shucks, protect the silk and kernels of the corn plant. Historically, cornhusks provided the raw materials to create a host of useful and creative objects that have a long tradition among the people of the Appalachian region, Native Americans and settlers alike. Cherokees used braiding, twining, or weaving methods to shape cornhusks into useful cordage, baskets, shoes, wall mats, and ceremonial masks. Appalachian settlers used loose husks to stuff mattresses and wove husks into doormats, chair bottoms, and stool tops. They also fashioned hats, sandals, fans, trays, brooms, and baskets with husks. Farmers used braided husks for stout, durable horse collars.

Industrial school craft programs encouraged students and community artisans to make cornhusk dolls, brooms, and doormats for sale to tourists at craft fairs and locally. During the Great Depression of the 1930s, some Appalachian women supported their families by selling cornhusk dolls to craft stores in the area. While the making of cornhusk crafts remains popular, the older, more delicate pieces are most prized by collectors and museums.

While growing and saving homegrown cornhusks was a tradition in the past, modern-day artisans who make cornhusk items usually purchase materials at craft stores or grocery stores, where they are sold as tamale wrappers.

See also: DOLLS; FLOWER ART; SETTLEMENT, MISSION, AND SPONSORED SCHOOLS (EDUCATION).

—Suzanne Hill McDowell, *Western Carolina University*

Counterpanes

During the eighteenth and nineteenth centuries, handwoven counterpanes were popular as lightweight alternatives to wool blankets and quilts in southern Appalachia, where inexpensive cotton was readily available and the warm summer climate demanded lightweight fabrics for bedding and clothing. Parts of northern Appalachia, most notably Maryland, also produced counterpanes for summer use. Although older mountain people sometimes refer to any woven or decorated bedcover as a coverlet, counterpane, county-pin, kivver, or coverlid, at its simplest level an Appalachian counterpane is a white cotton bedcover. It can be made of two or three widths of handwoven cloth stitched together or a single piece of store-bought cloth, and it can be decorated with knots, embroidery, or cross-stitch. Some counterpanes hang off the bed all the way to the floor, while others barely cover the mattress.

Typical Appalachian counterpanes were woven in abundance, washed frequently, and often had a decorative fringe along three sides. After the cloth was woven and assembled, washing tightened the threads, which "puckered" the material, giving it depth and accentuating the intricacies of the white-on-white design. The thick and thin cotton threads used in counterpanes were usually purchased from a commercial source—only occasionally did Appalachian weavers grow small amounts of cotton to spin for home use. Typical counterpane patterns had descriptive names such as Huck and Dimity, M's and O's, Block and Dimity, and Honeycomb.

A type of counterpane commonly made in western North Carolina during the first half of the twentieth century was the knotted bedspread. These bedcovers were large pieces of unbleached or white sheeting decorated with designs formed by embroidery characterized by the dominant use of tight small pearl-like embroidery stitches called colonial knots, though also employing stitches such as French knots.

Some people in Appalachia also refer to mill-woven bedcovers, which began replacing handwoven pieces in the region in the late nineteenth century, as counterpanes. Eighteenth- and nineteenth-century handwoven counterpanes were worn threadbare from use and often discarded when factory-made bedcovers became available. Bedspreads such as the white Marseilles (named for the French port city) were fashionable in the late nineteenth century, and the mid-twentieth century saw the rise of chenille bedspreads with a cut pile design, such as the George and Martha Washington pattern manufactured by the Bates Company.

See also: CANOPY TYING; COVERLETS; KNOTTED BEDSPREADS/COLONIAL KNOTTING.

—Kathleen Curtis Wilson, *University of Ulster, Northern Ireland*

Country Life Movement

The country life movement in early-twentieth-century America brought national attention to Appalachian crafts and fostered efforts to market crafts from the region. The movement began around 1900, as the nation became alarmed by the accelerating pace of migration from farms to urban centers. The decline in farm population was caused by a transportation revolution, industrial expansion, and the growing efficiency of agriculture, which reduced the number of farmworkers.

Many advocates for stemming the tide of rural out-migration—state and federal agricultural officials, land-grant colleges, rural schools and churches, and urban social reformers—concluded that deficiencies in rural life were driving people to cities. Accordingly, they sought to increase the attractiveness and efficiency of country living.

By 1908, the need for rural reform seemed so great that President Theodore Roosevelt appointed a Commission on Country Life to study rural social and economic conditions in America. The report by this commission led to creation of the national extension service in agricultural colleges, new academic disciplines in rural economics and rural sociology, and numerous country life conferences and publications in succeeding years.

Hoping to "build in America a rural civilization finer than the world has ever seen," rural advocates formed the American Country Life Association in 1919. The primary person to connect the American Country Life Association with Appalachian crafts was Allen H. Eaton, who was working for the American Federation of Arts and the Russell Sage Foundation in New York in the 1920s, primarily on immigrant folklife. He planned a series of exhibits on arts and crafts of the European homelands that led to his book *Immigrant Gifts to American Life* in 1932.

In 1926 Olive Dame Campbell, who was working with a folk school and craft cooperative effort in the southern Appalachian Mountains, invited Eaton to speak to a meeting of the Conference of Southern Mountain Workers and to see a small display of handicrafts from mountain craft centers. Impressed by the crafts, Eaton helped organize what was to become the Southern Highland Handicraft Guild.

By 1930, Eaton had become a member of the Rural Arts Committee of the American Country Life Association, just as he was organizing a traveling exhibit for the Southern Highland Handicraft Guild and the American Federation of the Arts with backing from the Russell Sage Foundation. When Virginia Polytechnic Institute in Blacksburg, Virginia, was selected as the site for the association's 1933 annual meeting, Eaton used his connections with all these organizations to develop a major exhibition of Appalachian crafts.

Eaton believed the meeting would be an appropriate forum for reintroducing Appalachian crafts and folklife to a national audience and for promoting his philosophy of the inherent value in craft work. Since newly elected President Franklin D. Roosevelt supported the work of the association and sent some members of his cabinet to be featured speakers, Eaton wisely enlisted the sponsorship of Eleanor Roosevelt and former First Ladies Grace Coolidge and Lou Hoover for the mountain crafts exhibition.

The Blacksburg exhibition was composed of three parts: an exhibit of color prints depicting rural scenes and country life by such painters as Jean François Millet and Claude Monet; handicrafts from the southern highlands; and the photographs of Appalachian crafts and their makers by Doris Ulmann. A catalog accompanied the exhibit, detailing the 586 articles offered for sale. Among the items were chairs and stools, quilted and braided chair mats, wood-carved animals, handmade tables covered by hand-woven cloths, toys, quilts, hooked rugs, and Indian bows, arrows, baskets, and beadwork.

At the exhibition Eaton also gave a speech entitled "Woodpiles and Haystacks," in which he argued for the aesthetic value of folk arts and pointed to craft work as an important supplement to income. He argued that crafts would make it possible for mountaineers to stay in the mountains and farm families to stay on their farms.

Eaton continued his work on behalf of Appalachian crafts beyond his work with the American Country Life Association. In 1937 he published *Handicrafts of the Southern Highlands* and assembled a major exhibit on rural arts for the seventy-fifth anniversary of the U.S. Department of Agriculture.

The country life movement and the American Country Life Association provided context, forum, and advocates for appreciation and marketing of Appalachian crafts, particularly during the 1930s. With the onset of World War II, the movement waned, eventually ending in the postwar industrialization and modernization boom. Much of the philosophy and sentiment of the movement, however, continue to influence understanding of Appalachian crafts into the twenty-first century.

See also: CAMPBELL, JOHN C. AND OLIVE DAME (EDUCATION); EATON, ALLEN H. (FOLKLORE AND FOLKLIFE); SOUTHERN HIGHLAND CRAFT GUILD.

—Jean Haskell, *East Tennessee State University*

William L. Bowers, *The Country Life Movement in America, 1900–1920* (1974); Allen H. Eaton, "Woodpiles and Haystacks," *Mountain Life and Work* (October 1933); Jean Haskell Speer, "Woodpiles and Haystacks: Allen Eaton's Vision of Southern Highland Handicrafts," *Southern Folklore* (Winter 1989).

Coverlets

Older southern Appalachians continue to describe their handwoven bedding as a kivver, coverlid, counterpin, county pin, or counterpane, but the term *coverlet* is the preferred name for the handwoven wool and cotton covers. Although a coverlet can be any bedcover, including decorative quilts and counterpanes, for practical reasons a coverlet is usually identified as a bedcover woven on a hand-powered loom by individuals outside of a factory setting. Also, coverlets cover the top and sides of the bed, while bedspreads spread over the mattress to the floor at the sides and end of the bed. A coverlet is one thickness of fabric woven on a loom in one long piece, then cut in half or thirds and sewn together to make the width needed to cover the top of the bed. The width of the loom determines the maximum width of a finished coverlet.

Southern Appalachian hand weavers created fabrics to make towels, sheets, clothing, table linens, and blankets on family looms using affordable and easily obtained wool and flax (often raised on the family land); cotton was frequently purchased by the bale to spin at home until the last quarter of the nineteenth century. Fibers were colored with natural plant matter or purchased packaged dyes. Weavers also used extra bits of their home-woven fabric to piece quilts.

Coverlets were the pride of skilled hand weavers throughout Appalachia, and those woven in the four-harness overshot weave structure were especially admired. In overshot weave structure, some threads (usually the colored wool) lie loose or "float" to give the material a raised appearance. Each pattern is a geometric grouping of small square blocks that creates an illusion of circles. The addition of a second or third color can greatly alter the appearance of a pattern, offering more possibilities for variation.

Overshot coverlet weaving continued in southern Appalachia long after it had died out in other regions of the country and with greater diversity in color and pattern than coverlets typically seen in museum collections nationwide. These coverlets were rarely used on a daily basis; instead, they were carefully preserved and displayed only on special occasions. Families often slept under plain woolen blankets, saving their coverlets for the next generation to appreciate.

An overshot coverlet weaver begins with a pattern draft that determines how to thread the warp and treadle the pattern. Before drafts were organized in book form, weavers used long narrow pieces of paper marked with short lines determining how to group warp threads in series of repetitions to form squares and circles for the final pattern. Weavers altered threading and used color to change the appearance of a design to suit their personal aesthetic. In southern Appalachia, weaving drafts were passed between family members, sent to distant relatives, and shared with friends, resulting in regional favorites. Handwoven coverlets are labor-intensive and too warm for most centrally heated homes. The popularity of handwoven coverlets had declined by the beginning of the twenty-first century. Factory-made reproductions have mostly filled the market for country-style coverlets.

See also: COUNTERPANES; FIBERS; WEAVING.

—Kathleen Curtis Wilson, *University of Ulster, Northern Ireland*

Carol Strickler, *American Woven Coverlets* (1987); Kathleen Curtis Wilson, *Textile Art from Southern Appalachia: The Quiet Work of Women* (2001); Sadye Tune Wilson and Doris Finch Kennedy, *Of Coverlets: The Legacies, the Weavers* (1983).

Craft Cooperatives

When the Appalachian Mountains formed America's western frontier, the spindle, the loom, and hand-carved artifacts were as much a part of everyday life as were the hand-forged plow and the community meetinghouse. Handcrafts were everyday tools necessary for pioneer life. There was no distinction between beautiful hand-carved dough bowls as works of art and the everyday objects used in preparation of daily meals.

Only with the "rediscovery" of Appalachia and its people in the early 1900s did handcrafts become art objects sought after by people who recognized their utilitarian and intrinsic beauty. The John C. Campbell Folk School in North Carolina and other settlement schools brought recognition to pioneer artifacts. As crafts became fashionable in mainstream culture, mountain people began to see them as an extension of their subsistence-based economic system. Through the reproduction of traditional and modified artifacts, they could enhance their cash-poor economy.

As a result of the War on Poverty in the 1960s, Appalachian communities exploded with their own versions of cooperatives and cottage industries. Using culturally acquired talents, they began producing household items, apparel, and decorative products for local as well as national markets. In the late 1960s, three sisters from Sandy Hook Ridge in Wolfe County, Kentucky, received national attention when they traveled to Washington, D.C., and presented an eagle quilt they had made to President Lyndon Johnson. As the

Sandy Hook Ridge sisters began to sell their quilts, many other women became eager to use handcrafts to supplement family income. This interest led to the organization of the Grassroots Craftsmen of the Appalachian Mountains. Grassroots, as it was called, was organized as an agricultural marketing cooperative, since craft cooperatives were unheard of at that time. One of the main goals of Grassroots was to give women unprecedented opportunities to own and run their own businesses. Many other special needs of women, such as driving lessons and literacy classes, were subsequently recognized and met.

By the late 1970s, the cooperative began to experience a decline in markets, access to resources, and proper training. The idea of using the federated cooperative approach to address these needs took root. Federations added expertise and scale but still allowed control by local cooperatives. In 1974 Marketing Appalachia's Traditional Community Handcrafts (MATCH) was organized as a "cooperative of cooperatives." Its mission was to increase the social and economic value of the market interface between producers and consumers. MATCH began with thirty craft groups, representing two thousand crafters from seven states. It brought together grassroots organizers and established businesses. MATCH tried to sensitize consumers to the struggles of Appalachia as well as to the rich heritage of the region.

With innovations such as a warehouse to expedite orders from a catalog that showcased the cottage industry production, MATCH both strengthened local craft cooperatives and supplemented family income. Design, marketing, and production workshops were instituted, along with training in grant writing, financial management, business planning, board training, pricing, and other issues that affected the member cooperatives. MATCH was housed in a renovated train station in Berea, Kentucky, and the area around the station was dubbed "Old Town Berea" and became a thriving craft community.

After the catalog and the warehouse were established, MATCH opened retail shops in a Cincinnati suburb, in downtown Lexington, and in the Berea train depot. Profits from store sales were returned to respective member groups. But funds had been borrowed for this developmental stage of MATCH, and after ten years of operation, heavy debt load contributed to the demise of the cooperative effort.

Although MATCH had many successes, increasing competition for its members' products from the private sector, leadership transitions, and difficulty in maintaining grant funding finally overwhelmed it. Cheaper factory-produced imitations from Japan and other foreign countries also began to flood the national market. The primary goal of MATCH was to sell craft products at a price that could actually provide a living for the artisans. For most of the marketing world, however, supply and demand is the driving principle, not quality or concern for the issues of social marketing. Few of the surviving MATCH groups continue as cooperatives.

See also: ARROWMONT SCHOOL OF ARTS AND CRAFTS; CABIN CREEK QUILTS; QUALLA ARTS AND CRAFTS MUTUAL.

—Nina J. Poage, *Richmond, Kentucky*

Richard A. Couto, *Making Democracy Work Better* (1999); Phyllis George, *Kentucky Crafts: Handmade and Heartfelt* (1989); Ramona and Millard Lampell, *O, Appalachia: Artists of the Southern Mountains* (1989).

Craft Fairs

Craft fairs are a staple of community celebrations, homecomings, and holiday events across the length and breadth of Appalachia. Drawing together artisans to demonstrate, display, and sell their works to a relaxed audience, usually with food and music as part of the package, craft fairs are popular fixtures in Appalachian culture. It has not always been so.

The first Appalachian craft fair was probably held on Commencement Day at Berea College in 1896; the purpose of the Homespun Fair was to improve quality and design among the many hand weavers and other craftspeople working in the area. Small prizes were awarded in numerous categories, such as homespun coverlets, axe handles, and chairs, but the fair was discontinued after a few years when the same local craftspeople won all the prizes.

By 1909 the Southern Industrial Educational Association was sponsoring annual craft fairs in Washington, D.C., bringing together the craftsmanship of Appalachian workers who sold their handmade items through various settlement school craft programs. Until the association disbanded in 1926, these fairs provided an opportunity for selling crafts from states such as Tennessee, North Carolina, Virginia, and Georgia. Most of the early founders of Appalachian settlement schools with craft programs for raising money to support the school came to Washington seeking government funding. They viewed the Southern Industrial Educational Association craft show as an opportunity to promote their school as well as to raise national awareness about the beauty of mountain-made objects.

Berea continued its involvement with other schools and crafts production centers in southern Appalachia and annually displayed items in the association's Washington craft show. Berea worked closely with the Conference of Southern Mountain Workers and was part of a cooperative effort during the late 1920s that led to the formation of the Southern Highland Handicraft Guild (since the mid-1990s the Southern Highland Craft Guild), a nine-state confederation of craft centers that essentially created a marketplace for quality Appalachian craft work. During the 1930s, the Tennessee Valley Authority created Southern Highlanders, Inc., an economic-development program, to market the work of Appalachian craftspeople, and for nearly twenty years the two associations jointly operated in stores in Tennessee, New York, and Washington, D.C.

Among those who helped develop a broad-based market for mountain crafts, Allen H. Eaton, an Appalachian field-worker for the Russell Sage Foundation and author of *Handicrafts of the Southern Highlands*, stands out as the individual with the most influential role in the Appalachian craft revival. It is believed that Eaton suggested the first Craft Fair of the Southern Highlands after seeing a similar event in New Hampshire a few years earlier.

Along with Clementine Douglas, Marion Heard, a University of Tennessee crafts instructor and metalworker, completed an extensive survey of the crafts and craftspeople of southern Appalachia in the mid-1940s. Funded by a grant from the Rockefeller Foundation, Heard embraced the crafts fair concept and made a passionate plea to guild members to get approval for the first show.

In 1948 the first Craft Fair of the Southern Highlands was staged in Gatlinburg, Tennessee, on the grounds of what was then the Phi Beta Phi School, now the Arrowmont School of Arts and Crafts. Sponsored by the Southern Highland Handicraft Guild and Southern Highlanders, Inc., the fair was intended to bring together craftsmen and their best crafts, illustrating through demonstrations and exhibits the value of beautiful handwork and its influence on the lives of the people in the southern mountain area.

More than six thousand people came to the first fair, where craft demonstrations and sales were coordinated by the guild's education committee. The fair soon became an Appalachian fixture. Among the exhibitors at the first fair were Berea College, Bybee Pottery, Stuart Nye Hand Wrought Jewelry, and Churchill Weavers, still-familiar participants in guild-sponsored fairs.

No one except possibly Eaton and Heard suspected the market impact the fair and those who imitated it would have on the southern Appalachian states over the second half of the twentieth century. For about ten years the guild switched the fair location back and forth between Gatlinburg and Asheville, North Carolina. In 1960 the guild added a second fair, and a July and October schedule is still followed, though both fairs are now held in Asheville.

Other craft organizations in the southern mountains were slow to follow the guild's lead, but the first Mountain State Arts and Crafts Fair was held in 1963 at Cedar Lakes, near Ripley, West Virginia, and by 1965 attracted twenty-five thousand visitors. In 1967 the first Kentucky Guild of Artists and Craftsmen's Fair, held in Indian Fort Theater near Berea, attracted five thousand visitors. To the north, craft fairs flourished in the mountains of New Hampshire, Vermont, New York, Pennsylvania, Ohio, Maine, and Maryland, benefiting from larger and more affluent populations.

What might be termed the second twentieth-century Appalachian craft revival began during the late 1960s, when the federal War on Poverty drew massive media attention and federal funding to the region, bringing not only crafts-seeking customers but also crafts makers to the mountains. These young artisans were drawn to the rural setting almost as much by the lifestyle as by the growing ready market for craft work. The wave of volunteers who moved to Kentucky, West Virginia, Tennessee, and North Carolina organized local crafts fairs and crafts cooperatives such as Grassroots Craftsmen in Kentucky and Cabin Creek Quilts in West Virginia, plus many others that did not survive.

Numerous craft fairs, co-ops, and community centers sprang up, creating an incipient regional movement. When the federal funds disappeared after about twenty years, so did a number of fair organizers, though most transplanted craftspeople chose to remain in their adopted home.

Craft fairs tended to assume some of the personality of their sponsors and organizers, with varying degrees of emphasis upon regional music, dance, and food in addition to the crafts. In Kentucky and West Virginia, visual arts were an added feature of the shows. Major events such as the Central Pennsylvania Festival of the Arts, the Mountain Heritage Arts and Crafts Festival at Harpers Ferry, West Virginia, and the innovative American Crafts Council Fair in Rhinebeck, New York, added new exposure, sales, and professionalism to the crafts trade.

All these shows, as well as many more that followed, were operated by organizations with membership standards and/or jury requirements, ensuring the quality and authenticity of the art and crafts on display. By the late 1960s and throughout the 1970s, hordes of people who flocked to Gatlinburg, Berea, and Cedar Lakes attracted the attention of communities and promoters across America who quickly followed their lead, often without adequate planning or quality controls. Craftspeople with authentic, high-quality wares avoided sideshows at major events and concentrated on fairs requiring a jury process and charging for admission.

The craft fair is much more than a source of economic activity, though sales are the driving factor. The casual atmosphere of craft fairs has introduced thousands of visitors to art and craft, many of whom have never visited a formal museum or art gallery. Craft demonstrators at the events have also drawn young people to craft professions. By bringing the artist and the visitor together, the craft fair serves as a vital communications link between the producer and the marketplace.

From the beginning, Appalachian craft fairs have incorporated regional music and dance, giving exposure to performers who maintain mountain traditions and offering perspectives on Appalachian people and their lifestyles, often contradicting stereotypical images.

The craft fair continues to be a major factor in the Appalachian craft world; the Kentucky Guild added a Fall Fair in 1975, and the Berea Craft Festival started in 1982. Other craft fairs in Kentucky, Tennessee, West Virginia, North Carolina, Georgia, Virginia, and northern Appalachia focus on quality to keep their market alive, while other so-called craft fairs are either civic and ethnic events or flea markets. The sheer number of craft fairs has diluted the overall impact, and attendance at most events has declined over the past two decades.

The process of participating in a craft fair has also evolved as the making and selling of crafts as a profession became more widespread. The early guild fairs were major construction projects, with each booth built, complete with tables, shelves, and lighting, during a weeklong work session; the booth fee was a percentage of sales, with all income collected by the guild then paid back to the craftsperson. The exhibitor simply drove in, unloaded, set out his or her products, sold wares, and then left at the end of the week. Most exhibitors were, during those years, part-time professionals, and the only craft fairs available to them were guild events. As the craft fair developed into a year-round way of life, most craftspeople acquired portable tents, display units, lighting, and systems to process sales, and the guild ultimately charged a flat booth fee, a practice in widespread use at other events.

The face of Appalachian craft fairs has changed dramatically over the decades, reflecting the cultural and technlogical transformations and a new diversity among exhibitors. With the passing of venerable artists such as North Carolina chair maker Shadrack "Birdie" Mace and Kentucky folk artist Edgar Tolson, modern craftspeople are increasingly professional, college trained, and attuned to the artistic and economic value of their work.

Under contemporary circumstances, it has become difficult to distinguish an Appalachian craft fair from one held anywhere else in the United States. Large national wholesale craft shows, such as those sponsored by the American Crafts Council, the Rosen Agency, and George Little Management grew out of the local craft fairs, dating at least back to the 1960s, when buyers from urban stores descended upon regional craft fairs to purchase in quantity. In 1968 the Southern Highland Handicraft Guild responded to that movement by opening a wholesale craft warehouse in Asheville; others created large national markets in Baltimore, Philadelphia, New York, Chicago, and other major cities.

The Appalachian craft fair is a cornerstone of modern cultural heritage tourism—which is what Marian Heard had in mind when she envisioned the first guild fair in 1948. Scholarly debate in the late twentieth century centered on the question of whether the Appalachian craft culture is real or invented, but most craft fairs operate well outside academic argument. The Southern Highland Craft Guild's annual fairs, though not the largest or most successful of modern events, are still the regional benchmark, as befits the event and organization which spawned all other craft fairs. Guild fairs have survived decades with minimal change in the intent or the event. Folk crafts have transcended humble beginnings as functional crafts, though the early influences are still often reflected in the contemporary craft work of today's mountain artisans.

See also: ARROWMONT SCHOOL OF ARTS AND CRAFTS; SOUTHERN HIGHLAND CRAFT GUILD; SOUTHERN INDUSTRIAL EDUCATIONAL ASSOCIATION.

—Garry Barker, *Morehead State University*

Garry G. Barker, *The Handcraft Revival in Southern Appalachia, 1930–1990* (1991); Elisabeth S. Peck and Emily Ann Smith, *Berea's First 125 Years: 1855–1980* (1982).

Craft Revival

See Craft Revival (Folklore and Folklife)

Crossnore School

See Weaving Room of Crossnore School

Dolls

Cloth dolls, as a part of the region's cultural heritage, date back to the earliest families that settled in Appalachia. Similar to the patchwork quilt, dolls were stitched from rags and scraps of fabric such as feed or flour sacks. The body and extremities were stuffed with materials that were readily available in the maker's environment such as sawdust, bran, horsehair, feathers, bits of wool, and straw. Because Appalachian dolls were traditionally styled solely by the imagination of the maker, their individuality makes them a part of the American folk art tradition.

Faces were fashioned in the image of their maker, often resembling an adult woman rather than a child. Most often they wore a faint smile or a somber expression penciled on with charcoal or ashes. Noses were embroidered, painted, or applied with the tip of a twisted piece of cloth. Lips and cheeks were often stained with pokeberries. Short-necked dolls were babies, while dolls with longer necks represented women. Feet were rarely the same size and usually not proportioned to the doll bodies. Elbows and knee joints were stitched to allow flexibility of movement. "Mammy" dolls depicted African American stereotypes and were made with cloth or stocking heads with appliquéd, embroidered, or painted features. The stuffed bodies of some mammy dolls were used to decorate wooden spoons and brooms.

Due to a severe shortage of fabric during the Civil War, temporary dolls crafted from handkerchiefs silently entertained children during long church sermons. In the mid-1800s, German and French porcelain dolls became popular but were too expensive for most Appalachian families; resourceful mothers, therefore, used house and barn paint and varnish to harden the soft round cloth heads, hands, and feet to imitate the foreign dolls.

Fashioned by creative and ingenious mothers, dolls were by necessity made at little or no cost from functional domestic items. Stick horses combined a horse head fashioned with rags or socks like a doll and a broomstick as the body. Clothespins were among the first commercial American household objects to be turned into dolls. By 1910, whiskbrooms and feather dusters were used as doll bodies, and clothed whisk dolls with walnut heads were seen a decade later.

See also: APPLE CARVING; CORNHUSKS; FOLK TOYS.

—Ann Stover Bell, *Knoxville, Tennessee*

Dough Bowls

German, Italian, Swedish, and Swiss immigrants brought the oblong wooden dough bowl to the American colonies. In many areas of Appalachia, these bowls were routinely employed for bread making and were handed down from generation to generation. Although few contemporary cooks use dough bowls for mixing ingredients, preferring to display them as mementos of domestic life during an earlier era, some traditional craftspeople continue to fashion the handsome wooden vessels using the same techniques as their ancestors.

The tools needed to create a dough bowl are an axe, drawknife, bowl adze, spokeshave, and scorp. Though tulip poplar is sometimes used, buckeye and basswood are the woods of choice because they are lightweight and nonporous. Traditional craftspeople believe that cutting the trees used for dough bowls during the week of a full moon will cause the wood to dry at a slow pace, preventing cracks. After a tree is cut, a section of the tree, fifteen to twenty inches in diameter and containing no limbs or knots, is cut into thirty-inch lengths. The log is split with an axe lengthwise into two halves, each half making one dough bowl. After the outer bark is removed, the bottom of the bowl is flattened, and an axe, drawknife, and spokeshave are used to shape the rounded outside of the bowl. Because the wood is still green at this stage of construction, the maker stands the bowl on end, away from heat or wind, to hollow out the inside section with a bowl adze, then smooths it with a scorp. In about six weeks the dough bowl is dry enough to finish by sanding it to its finished smooth surface, inside and out.

See also: FOLK TOYS; WHITTLING.

—James K. Miracle, *Middlesboro, Kentucky*

Dyeing

See Fibers

Eaton, Allen H.

See Eaton, Allen H. (Folklore and Folklife)

Ernberg, Anna

See Fireside Industries

Face Jugs

Appalachian potters have made important contributions to the southern pottery tradition of jugs modeled with human faces. The origin of the tradition is uncertain, but this has not devalued face jugs, which today are considered an

Alkaline-glazed face jugs by potter Lanier Meaders of Mossy Creek, Georgia, c. 1978. Pottery jugs modeled with human faces are prized by museums and collectors. Although the origins of this tradition are unclear, by the late 1800s folk potters in Appalachia were making face jugs such as these from northern Georgia.

emblem of southern folk art and are prized by museums and collectors. In 1909 ceramics historian E. A. Barber was the first to suggest African roots for face vessels made in the early 1860s by Edgefield District, South Carolina, slave potters, although a white Edgefield potter, Thomas Chandler, made face jugs as early as 1850. Chandler had worked in New York State, where he may have met Remmey family potters. Johannes Remmey came to Manhattan from Germany's Rhineland, where there was a tradition of jugs with a bearded face molded onto the neck. The Remmeys were responsible for some of the earliest Euro-American face vessels.

Whatever the source, by the late 1800s folk potters in Appalachia were making face jugs. Salt-glazed examples from east Tennessee's Keystone Pottery reflect founder Charles Decker's earlier association with Richard Remmey, the great-great-grandson of Johannes, in Philadelphia. John Dollings, another potter with a Mid-Atlantic background, made Negroid face jugs glazed with brown Albany slip near Zanesville, Ohio. At Mossy Creek in the Georgia foothills, Cheever Meaders learned about face jugs from the Hewells and Browns, who owned potteries just south of the Appalachian region. Although Cheever made only a small number of face jugs, they became the specialty of his son, Lanier Meaders. The Browns made face jugs in Atlanta, and this tradition was brought to the North Carolina mountains when Davis and Javan Brown established the Brown Pottery at Arden in 1924.

See also: MEADERS POTTERY; POTTERY.

—John A. Burrison, *Georgia State University*

Feather Fans

Although weaving, basketmaking, and wood carving are better known as industrial school crafts, delicate and elegant fans made from soft, pale-colored down feathers were also products of these schools and were sold outside the region to raise money for education. Because they are fragile and easily destroyed, however, few Appalachian feather fans remain in existence.

The making of fans from the feathers of geese, turkeys, guinea fowls, and peacocks was an old-time home industry in Appalachia. The number of feathers in a fan corresponded to the length of the feathers. To make a fan, the feathers were held below the barbs by the quills. The quills were then bound or braided with twine, string, or yarn into a firm handle, and the feathers above the handle were spread out and arranged in an attractive manner. Several rows of string were woven in an over-and-under pattern from the handle up into the spread portion of the fan to hold the feathers in a permanent fan shape.

In addition to this decorative fan, a fly bush (or brush) of peacock feathers was made for use in other parts of the South. Fly bushes were used to shoo flies away from the dining table before the advent of mosquito netting and wire screens. The feathers, sometimes as many as one hundred, were held together by braiding the quills into a strong, firm, handsome handle. The completed fly bush, about three or four feet long, stirred the air in the same manner as a more traditional fan.

See also: SETTLEMENT, MISSION, AND SPONSORED SCHOOLS (EDUCATION).

—Patricia L. Fitzpatrick, *Asheville, North Carolina*

Fibers

Cultivation of plants and animals for the purpose of fiber production began in the mountains with early European settlers in the eighteenth century. Although Native American and many Euro-American craftpersons utilized fibers found naturally in the environment, the manufacture of textiles in particular has relied on the use of cultivated fibers. In Appalachia, the most common fibers spun into yarn and thread are wool, cotton, and flax.

Sheep adapted well to the mountain climate, and wool fleece spun into usable fiber was popular for its warmth and durability. All-wool blankets were common, but clothing often combined wool with cotton or linen.

Cotton grows well only in the more temperate zones of Appalachia, and although it was a desirable fiber for clothing, bedding, and other household goods, spinners in most areas purchased it by the bale to spin into thread. Eighteenth-century cotton was considered a luxury fabric in contrast to linen, which was a common fabric in Appalachia.

Linen is obtained from flax, a plant that grows well in most of Appalachia and was a cash crop for many farmers. Some home weavers cultivated a small flax bed for spinning linen yarn for personal use. Linen has many positive qualities, including texture and strength, but processing flax into linen thread is a tedious and complicated job and was more often done in factories than by hand.

Efforts were made to establish silk as a locally produced fiber in the nineteenth century. Frederick Ross built the Ross Silk Factory in the 1820s on the North Fork of the Holston River near Kingsport, Tennessee. There, he built a huge cocoonery, purchased French reels, planted white mulberry trees to feed the silk worms, and convinced neighboring farmers to plant additional trees. A reduction of the federal tariff on imported silk eventually made the Tennessee business unprofitable, but the mulberry trees continue to thrive more than 175 years later.

Sometimes, two or more types of fibers were combined. A popular cloth called "linsey woolsey" was once thought to refer exclusively to a combination of linen and wool woven together. However, textile historians now maintain that cotton was often substituted for linen or combined with the linen and wool fibers. Linsey woolsey was particularly desirable for pants, shirts, and skirts, offering the durability and warmth of wool while retaining the lightness and aesthetic qualities of cotton and linen fabrics.

A common step in the processing of fibers was to dye them with colors. Although dyeing was not necessary to produce cloth, many Appalachians took great pains to collect and process plants and other local materials into suitable dyes and use them to enhance the look of their weavings. Producing reliable dyes from natural ingredients and using them creatively required both skill and experience, and recipes for dyes were closely guarded and passed down within a family for generations.

Linen and cotton thread did not take natural dyes well, but wool was often dyed, either before it was carded (dyed in the wool) or after it was spun. Color was extracted from the plants by boiling, and the colors set by using mordants (metals that help pigments bind to the fiber molecules) such as aluminum, iron, or copper. Barks, roots, flowers, and berries furnished most of the coloring materials—pokeberries and sumac for reds; persimmon, oak bark, and chestnut for black; cedar berries for dove gray; smartweed, dock, and goldenrod for yellow; touch-me-not for orange; mulberries and larkspur for blue; and so on. Some colors and effects were a combination of dyes. Overdyeing yellow-dyed wool with indigo in a copper pot produced an olive or teal color. Skilled dyers were restricted only by their imaginations and the availability of materials.

Commercially packaged dyes were also available for purchase. Madder red and indigo blue were imported dyes used in Appalachia. Madder, which is a brick or dark rust color, is made from the root of the madder plant found in the Middle East. Indigo was imported from India in the form of dried cakes. Water-insoluble indigo was usually dissolved in fermented urine; the blue dye pot was most often simmered outdoors.

Synthetic dyes came into use after 1856, when English chemist William Perkin developed the first synthetic dye while searching for a cure for malaria. By the end of the nineteenth century, commercially produced synthetic dyes were inexpensive and widely available and began replacing vegetable dyes in Appalachia. Synthetic dyes made for brighter, sharper colors and decreased the amount of work and time involved in the dyeing process. Some traditional dyers, however, feel the uniformity of synthetics lessens the creative control and aesthetic quality of natural dyes.

Enthusiasts have kept the use of natural dyes alive. Around the beginning of the twentieth century, several enterprises began reviving and preserving southern Appalachian crafts, including dyeing. Industrial schools taught the skill of dyeing fibers to weavers for making overshot coverlets and household linens for sale. At Biltmore Estate Industries in Asheville, North Carolina, workers received training, also available to the public, in the use of traditional dyes. Organizations such as the John C. Campbell Folk School in Brasstown, North Carolina, still teach students dyeing techniques. Historic sites such as Rocky Mount Historical Association in Piney Flats, Tennessee, and the Museum of Appalachia in Norris, Tennessee, promote traditional dyeing techniques through demonstrations at festivals.

Although technology has changed, the steps in fiber processing remain the same. After cleaning, carding, and dyeing, if desired, all fibers are spun into thread or yarn on some type of spinning device (usually a wheel). The thread or yarn is then used in crocheting, knitting, quilting, sewing, tatting, or weaving. At times, especially in artistic creations, unspun fibers are woven into the textile for effect. The style of handwork and the combination of fibers produces a variety of results appropriate for both functional and decorative crafts. In addition to wool, cotton, and linen primarily used for clothing, other plant-based fibers such as hemp were used to make rope and twine and woven into sacks and other industrial textiles.

While traditional textile production focused on practicality, artisanship was also a factor, as spinners, dyers, and weavers worked to make the fibers beautiful as well as practical. Modern fiber production continues to reflect this duality.

Despite the availability of synthetics and commercially produced fabrics, amateur and professional craft workers in the twenty-first century continue to spin fibers into thread for artisans, demonstrators, and other consumers. Fiber producers in Appalachia seek to both preserve old techniques and create new ones. Farmers in the region have responded to a demand for the preservation and reintroduction of historic sheep breeds, as well as alpacas, llamas, and other fiber-producing animals. While many textile artists use synthetic fibers or imports such as silk, others still rely on regionally produced fibers. The region is home to many artists who grow, harvest, and process their own fibers for weaving in an effort to retain creative control, despite the availability of commercial alternatives. Fiber production and fiber art remain important sources of income and artistic outlets for many residents of the region.

See also: BASKETS, OAK; SPINNING; WEAVING.

—Elizabeth Hardy, *Caldwell Community College*, and Rebecca Tolley-Stokes, *East Tennessee State University*

Philis Alvic, *Weavers of the Southern Highlands* (2003); Allen H. Eaton, *Handicrafts of the Southern Highlands* (1937); Frances Louisa Goodrich, *Mountain Homespun* (1931).

Fireside Industries

For people in the Appalachian craft revival of the early twentieth century, the term *fireside industries* came to identify a type of cottage industry in which craft items were made at home for sale. Though other terms were used for these enterprises, *fireside industries* carried a romantic connotation that appealed to craftspeople and consumers alike. William Goodell Frost, the third president of Berea College in eastern Kentucky, is credited with coining the term for home-based crafts manufacture in an 1898 article in *Outlook*, a weekly magazine published in New York. As early as 1897, Berea College was buying woven items from women to help defray school expenses for their children. At first the college merely resold purchased items but soon began managing their production, and the operation became known as Berea's Fireside Industries by the early 1900s.

In 1911 Frost hired Swedish-born weaver Anna Ernberg to run Berea's Fireside Industries and coordinate weaving among community women and an increasing number of students under the college's labor, or work-study, program. Ernberg believed that after her students served apprenticeships with her, they would return to their mountain homes and establish small weaving businesses. Very few weavers, however, ever set up their own businesses, preferring instead to work through an institution that handled the details of production and marketing.

While Berea's Fireside Industries was developing, another craft program was taking shape on the eastern ridge of the Appalachian Mountains near Asheville, North Carolina, under the name of Allanstand Cottage Industries. Settlement schools throughout the region began modeling programs on those at Berea and Allanstand; most preferred the Berea designation. Both the Hindman and Pine Mountain Settlement Schools in Kentucky called their crafts programs "Fireside Industries," and Penland Weavers and Potters first began production in 1923 as the Department of Fireside Industries at the Appalachian Industrial School in Penland, North Carolina.

Fireside industries provided jobs for women with few opportunities for paid employment, and working at home allowed them to continue gardening, rearing children, and doing other household chores. While some centers marketed baskets, wood carvings, or other small craft items, weaving dominated fireside industries as a whole. Schools designed items, procured materials, managed the production, and paid women for completed pieces before selling them through outlets such as church groups, art organizations, civic clubs, and craft fairs.

See also: BEREA COLLEGE (EDUCATION); FROST, WILLIAM GOODELL AND ELEANOR MARSH (EDUCATION); SETTLEMENT, MISSION, AND SPONSORED SCHOOLS (EDUCATION).

—Philis Alvic, *Lexington, Kentucky*

Philis Alvic, *Weavers of the Southern Highlands* (2003); Allen H. Eaton, *Handicrafts of the Southern Highlands* (1937).

Flower Art

Appalachian craftspeople have created flowers from wood, paper, and cornhusks whenever these resources have been available. Various colors and shapes of flowers have been made from different types of wood. Black walnut makes a beautiful rich brown blossom, and maple creates a delicate soft white flower. Cedar can form a warm pink bloom, and sumac is used for a glowing yellow flower. Chrysanthemums are formed when the whittler carves row after row of small, delicate petals on a stick with a one-inch diameter. Larger flowers such as roses, dogwoods, daises, and black-eyed Susans are shaped from thin strips of wood cut into individual petal shapes. These variously shaped petals can be left the natural wood color or dyed the brilliant shades of fresh flowers. Each flower is assembled on a long stem using string, glue, and wire.

The thin, soft, inside layers of cornhusks make the best material for cornhusk flowers. Cornhusks are dampened to prevent splitting, and then cut into flower shapes and assembled with wire. Flower petals can be dyed, but traditionally the flowers are left the natural shade of tan. Crepe paper, flexible and available in a wide range of colors, is easily shaped into delicate roses, carnations, or violets. String is used to secure the paper flower on a stick or wire. Paper flowers are sometimes used on traditional decoration days to adorn family graves.

Sold at craft shops across the region, long-lasting flowers created out of natural materials are most often made by craftspeople in Appalachia who have passed down their skills from one generation to the next, keeping alive this whimsical art form.

See also: CORNHUSKS; WHITTLING.

—Janice S. Miracle, *Middlesboro, Kentucky*

Folk Art Center

See Southern Highland Craft Guild

Folk Toys

The making of American folk toys has a strong tradition in Appalachia. This is partly because of economic factors, but also because many early settlers in the region brought with them a wealth of toy-making knowledge and tradition from western Europe. Early toy makers incorporated Native

American toy designs and adapted the work of other makers to suit their own interests and skills, creating wooden toys with distinctive Appalachian flair. The original designer usually cannot be identified since folk toy patterns may have been modified many times through the generations. A great many individuals and organizations had an early influence in the production, rediscovery, and preservation of Appalachian toys. Individual craftsmen, as well as students working in the industrial school programs during the first quarter of the twentieth century, carved folk toys. The ingeniously made toys have been sold across the Appalachian region at craft fairs, festivals, and gift shops for over a century to tourists and collectors alike.

During the 1920s the average American's affluence and the growth of the manufactured toy industry caused folk toys almost to disappear, but handmade toys reemerged by necessity during the Great Depression, when there were few toy stores and no money for amusements. However, it was not until about 1960 that the general public rediscovered collecting and making traditional wooden toys.

Many of the known toys are made of readily available materials, including cloth, metal, corncobs, cornstalks, elder stalks, and leather, but most are wooden. Various native woods are used, but the most common is poplar because it is easily worked and does not require painting. Walnut and cherry woods are frequently used for trim pieces to enhance the toy's appearance.

In the early days, hand tools such as knives, saws, and chisels were generally used for woodworking, although some artisans built their own foot-powered tools, including spring-pole lathes and jigsaws. Whether powered by water or, later, electricity, factory shops for making toys were rare. Today, power tools fashion the shapes faster and more accurately than hand tools, although a few artisans prefer to use the traditional tools and methods.

The names of these toy creations are a part of the folklore. Whimmydiddle, flipperdinger, bullroarer, limber jack, jumping jack, and penny pincher are just a few of the hundreds of imaginatively named toys. Some toys are named to describe function, while other names seemingly have no relevance to the toy. Names are occasionally based on Bible stories and legends, but others are humorous or colloquial. There is often a sly humor in the action of or operation of a toy, and some designs become popular because they satirize stereotypes of Appalachian life, as do the "hound dog," "worn-out shoe," and "coal miner." Whatever the inspiration for each toy, the whimsical names evoke a nostalgic tradition that can be as important to collectors as the toy itself.

Folk toys made today are produced in quantity, carving techniques are taught at various craft schools, and designs and patterns are readily purchased for the amateur or expert to use. The majority of wooden toys are still for the amusement of children, but the work of some carvers is highly collectible and cherished for its craftsmanship.

See also: DOLLS; WHITTLING; WOOD CARVING.

—Dick Schnacke, *New Martinsville, West Virginia*

Jim F. Comstock, ed., *West Virginia Heritage Encyclopedia* (1974); Dick Schnacke, *American Folk Toys: Eighty-Five American Folk Toys and How to Make Them* (1973); Eliot Wigginton, ed., *Foxfire 6* (1980).

Foxfire Books

See Foxfire (Education)

Frost, William Goodell

See Frost, William Goodell and Eleanor Marsh (Education)

Goodrich, Frances

(1856–1944) Crafts advocate.

Frances Louisa Goodrich was an early advocate of combining social work and crafts in what became known as the craft revival. She founded two important crafts organizations, promoted cottage industries as an economic aid to Appalachian families, and was instrumental in establishing a national market for mountain crafts. Her Allanstand Cottage Industries still thrives as part of the Southern Highland Craft Guild, the second-oldest craft organization in the country.

Born in Binghamton, New York, reared in Cleveland, Ohio, and educated at the Yale School of Fine Arts, Goodrich moved to Buncombe County, North Carolina, in 1885 as a Presbyterian missionary. As part of her mission work, she organized "mother's meetings" in Brittain's Cove, a small community near Asheville, where she learned that local families continued to dye, spin, and weave beautiful coverlets of wool and cotton. This discovery inspired her work in crafts, and in 1895 she established a mission station in Madison County, North Carolina, at a small community known as Allanstand. Goodrich retained a few master weavers, such as Elmeda Walker of Flag Pond, Tennessee, to teach the younger women, and Allanstand Cottage Industries was born.

Goodrich sold the craft products on trips to northern cities, and in 1902 she converted a roadside cabin in Allanstand into a showroom and shop. In 1917 the Allanstand Craft Shop was moved to downtown Asheville. After helping to organize and found the Southern Mountain Handicraft Guild in 1928 (chartered in 1930 as the Southern Highland Handicraft Guild), Goodrich donated the Allanstand business to the new organization. Today, Allanstand is the oldest continuously operated craft shop in America.

Goodrich's approach to using crafts as a tool to improve socioeconomic conditions had a lasting influence on a younger generation of craft promoters, including Olive Dame Campbell (founder of the John C. Campbell Folk School) and Lucy Morgan (founder of the Penland School of Crafts). Goodrich is also a central figure in Allen H. Eaton's *Handicrafts of the Southern Highlands* (1937). She published her memoir, *Mountain Homespun*, in 1931.

See also: BLUE MOUNTAIN ROOM; SOUTHERN HIGHLAND CRAFT GUILD; WEAVING.

—Jan Davidson, *John C. Campbell Folk School*

Gourd Art

Gourds were among the first plants to be cultivated by humans and have continued to be used throughout the world for thousands of years in all aspects of daily life. Native Americans in Appalachia used gourds as birdhouses, storage containers, eating utensils, rattles, and whistles. The earliest European explorers in the region noted that even masks for ceremonial events were made from gourds. Occasionally Native Americans decorated gourds with crude linear designs burned in by spear point.

On frontier homesteads, settlers used gourds for water dippers, canteens, and containers for gunpowder. Very small gourds were placed in the nests of laying chickens as a substitute for eggs removed. This practice fooled a chicken into continuing to lay its eggs in the same place, believing that a particular spot was safe from predators. Slaves introduced many additional uses for gourds, including making musical instruments such as the guitar, banjo, thumb piano, and shekerie, a rattle in which the noisemakers (seeds, beads, pods, or even buttons) are woven into a netting surrounding the outside of the gourd.

In recent times craftspeople and artists have become attracted to the endless variety of shapes and sizes of this relative of pumpkins and squash. Once a mature gourd is completely dry, the woodlike exterior may be embellished with any tool or material that can be applied to wood, leather, or paper. Artists also use techniques such as painting, carving, etching, burning, basketry, and beading to transform simple gourds into works of art. Unadorned hollowed-out gourd birdhouses and dippers are familiar sights across Appalachia. Gourds can vary from functional and traditional to very decorative. Whether plain or fancy, gourds given proper care will last for many years.

See also: NATIVE AMERICAN ARTS AND CRAFTS; WOOD CARVING.

—Ginger Summit, *Los Altos Hills, California*

Hambidge Center for Creative Arts and Sciences

Founded in 1934 by Mary Crovatt (1885–1973) as an inspiring environment for artists and craftspersons, the Hambidge Center for Creative Arts and Sciences is a nonprofit organization located in Rabun County in northeastern Georgia. The center stresses a positive connection between the natural environment and creativity and maintains a working residency program for artists from all over the world in various fields to work in an unspoiled natural setting.

Crovatt, originally from coastal Brunswick, Georgia, was working as a model at the New York School of Fine and Applied Art when she met her future husband, Jay Hambidge, in 1915. Hambidge, an artist and teacher, was known for his theory of dynamic symmetry, which linked natural human and plant growth patterns to the harmonious proportions of classical Greek design. The center, with its focus on this theoretical connection, is named in honor of Hambidge, who died in 1924 at the age of fifty-eight.

After her husband's death, Crovatt continued to apply his theory to the arts, particularly weaving. She felt strongly that creativity was nurtured by working in close harmony with nature, and she publicly protested the encroachments of modern progress. In 1934 she acquired eight hundred acres of land near Rabun Gap, where she founded the center. Begun as a group of local spinners and weavers, which Crovatt called the Weavers of Rabun, the cooperative, one of many that grew during this era, was unique in that the woven products were not copies of traditional southern overshot patterns but were based on Crovatt's concepts of dynamic symmetry and incorporated more "natural" patterns. Products by the Weavers of Rabun were showcased for the next twenty years at Rabun Studios, a Madison Avenue boutique.

Artists who are accepted to the Hambidge Center stay for two to six weeks in private cottage/studios, gathering for evening meals during the March to December season. Time is otherwise unstructured, and the majority of all residency costs are underwritten by private donations. The Hambidge Center is funded in part by the Georgia Council for the Arts, the National Endowment for the Arts, and the Fulton County Arts Council (Atlanta), providing artists with time and space to pursue their work.

See also: CONTEMPORARY CRAFTS; JOHN C. CAMPBELL FOLK SCHOOL; WEAVING.

—Virginia Gardner Troy, *Berry College*

Philis Alvic, *Mary Hambidge, Weaver of Rabun* (1989); Frances Forbes Ison, "The Weavers of Rabun," *Georgia Review* (Fall 1950); Aspasia Voulis, ed., *Apprentice in Creation: The Way Is Beauty* (1975).

Haywood Community College Professional Craft Program

The Professional Craft Program of Haywood Community College is located on the college campus in Clyde, North Carolina, a few miles west of Asheville. It was founded in recognition of the strong heritage of craft in the region. The founders of the college wanted to create a place where each student could learn the basics of his or her craft's medium as well as learn how to transform that craft into a business. The pottery studio opened in 1974, and the entire program was fully operational by 1977, with comprehensive curricular programs in clay, jewelry, wood, and weaving. Instructors were invited to the college because of their professional experience and desire to teach.

Classes are small, with about sixty students in the consolidated program. Students enroll with or without experience in their chosen discipline. They come from the local community, from across the United States, and even from other countries, representing a broad range of ages and life experiences. Many of them pursue craft making as a second or third career. The program of study is challenging, and students spend the majority of their time concentrating on work in the studios. Comprehensive media courses stress development of skills and creativity. These are supplemented with classes in design, drawing, craft history, media electives, photography, business, and marketing. The program awards an associate degree in applied science to its graduates at the end of the two-year program.

Each student is provided a personal workspace in which to develop basic and advanced skills and to focus on design; every medium has its own curriculum. Forming, glazing, and firing functional pottery are the focuses of the clay program. Students get practical experience in design while refining their skills by creating simple objects. This applied experience gives them the ability to translate their own ideas into original objects.

The development of professional skills such as marketing, business, and photography has distinguished this program from similar ones for many years. Haywood Community College was one of the first craft programs in the nation to deal with these professional issues. The college has worked closely with a North Carolina agency called Rural Entrepreneurship through Action Learning in developing a hands-on approach to the business and marketing of crafts. This practical approach to entrepreneurial business skill development has proved far more successful than traditional academic approaches to business education.

Haywood Community College became an educational member of the Southern Highland Handicraft Guild (now the Southern Highland Craft Guild) in 1980 and maintains an active membership. Students have the opportunity and are encouraged to participate in the Craft Fair of the Southern Highlands each summer and fall, as well as an annual Graduate Show held at the guild's Folk Art Center on the Blue Ridge Parkway each spring. This Graduate Show has become one of the most popular and well-attended exhibitions at the Folk Art Center Gallery and has given high visibility to the program graduates. Many of these graduates go on to become active members of the guild.

The craft community in and around Haywood County has grown as a direct result of students who graduate and then stay in the area to run businesses and studios. Others settle in communities outside the region, enroll in four-year institutions, or work for established craftspeople.

See also: SOUTHERN HIGHLAND CRAFT GUILD.

—Catharine Ellis Muerdter, *Haywood Community College*

Hillbilly Motif Crafts

More appropriately termed hillbilly kitsch or hillbillyana, hillbilly motif crafts are souvenir items that caricature images of perceived hillbilly life. Sometimes crafted by hand, they are more often mass-produced in pseudo-handmade style. Stereotypical images include male hillbillies with moonshine jugs, hound dogs, and/or shotguns; female hillbillies who are barefoot, scraggly, and pregnant or buxom and scantily clad; gaunt, corncob-pipe-smoking, sun-bonneted granny women; and landscape images of ramshackle cabins, outhouses, and a general sense of bad taste and sloth. Created primarily for the tourist trade, these items range from coal and wood carvings to inexpensive ceramics, postcards, key chains, and T-shirts.

Hillbillyana began to appear in the late 1930s after the launch of Paul Webb's *Mountain Boys* cartoons in *Esquire* magazine, the appearance of Al Capp's *Li'l Abner* in newspapers, and the introduction of Snuffy Smith to Billy DeBeck's *Barney Google* comic strip, all in 1934. As tourist travel into the southern Appalachian Mountains increased after the establishment of the Great Smoky Mountains National Park and the Blue Ridge Parkway in the 1930s, a market developed for souvenirs of the mountains that matched both romanticized images of the Appalachian past and popular cartoon images. Shops throughout the mountains began to specialize in either high-end, high-quality, locally produced craft work or kitschy hillbilly items made locally, nationally, or even internationally in places such as Taiwan and China. A parallel development occurred with Cherokee crafts in the mountains. In sharp contrast to authentic Cherokee pottery and baskets, cheap, mass-produced tomahawks and headdresses, which had nothing to do with the Cherokee, were created to sell to tourists as icons of Indian culture.

In more recent years, there has been a trend to mass-produce wooden items that play on supposed traits of hillbilly culture. Some examples include an exploding hillbilly outhouse (the whole structure collapses when the unwitting victim opens the door), a hillbilly flashlight made from a box of matches attached to a wooden stick, and a hillbilly computer that is a wooden plank with five holes for the fingers of one hand. In addition to these widely available examples of hillbilly kitsch, there are exceedingly rare examples of obscene hillbilly items, such as the horny hillbilly, which sports an oversized phallus. Less broadly drawn stereotypes occur in wood carvings of lanky mountaineers and wood-carved scenes of bucolic mountain homesteads in which the quality of the carving deserves more attention than the caricatured image.

Some people in the region believe these hillbilly items are harmless, noting that their sales add to the region's economy. Others would prefer these items disappear from the consumer market, as they believe they perpetuate negative stereotypes of the Appalachian region.

See also: CHEROKEE (RACE, ETHNICITY, AND IDENTITY); HILLBILLY (IMAGES AND ICONS); *LI'L ABNER* (MEDIA).

—Jean Haskell, *East Tennessee State University*

Jean Haskell Speer, "Hillbilly Sold Here: Appalachian Folk Culture and Parkway Tourism," in *Parkways: Past, Present, and Future*, ed. Barry Buxton (1989); J. W. Williamson, *Hillbillyland: What the Movies Did to the Mountains and What the Mountains Did to the Movies* (1995).

Hindman Settlement School

Hindman Settlement School was the first rural social settlement school in the United States. Founding directors Katherine Pettit and May Stone viewed crafts as an important part of mountain life and the school's curriculum. Even before Hindman Settlement School opened in 1902 under the name Women's Christian Temperance Union Settlement School, Pettit and Stone endeavored to promote mountain crafts. They developed a fascination for the beauty of various items produced by local people while visiting homes in Knott County, Kentucky, during the summers of 1899, 1900, and 1901. During these three summers, Pettit and Stone held temporary settlement camps in the Hindman region. From then on, one of their objectives became the preservation of traditional mountain handicrafts.

Education of "the whole child" was the primary purpose of the Hindman Settlement School. This ideology was reflected in its core academic curriculum and extensive work programs, in which the teaching philosophy was comparable to modern-day vocational programs. Hindman's curriculum included classes from the elementary grades through high school. In addition to academic subjects, courses were taught in manual arts, home economics, agriculture, art, music, folk art, and crafts, especially weaving.

Craft production, known as fireside industries, began around the same time the school was created. Through producing and selling various crafts such as baskets, woven items, and small pieces of furniture, students could earn money to pay their tuition and board. Local residents were also able to earn small amounts of cash, which at that time was not always available, from their handwork. In addition, fireside industries provided the school with some small profits. Just as important was the recognition the school received from outside the region for its craft enterprises.

The school served not only as a local sales outlet for the crafts made by students and local craftspeople, but also marketed these products outside the region through brochures and flyers. In the actual production of crafts, Pettit and Stone emphasized mountain traditions and cultural identity, requiring the use of natural materials, including dyes. Local craftspeople were expected to demonstrate a superior quality of work that could be marketed successfully.

One of the earliest organizations founded to support Appalachian settlement school education was the Southern Industrial Educational Association, founded in 1905 by Martha Sawyer Gielow. Hindman received financial support from the Washington, D.C. association from 1907 to 1926, when it disbanded. Baskets and weaving made at Hindman or by local women and sold by Hindman were featured at association craft sales in Washington for more than fifteen years, raising additional money for the school.

Along with other settlement schools, handicraft centers, and individual crafters, Hindman was a founding member of the Southern Highland Handicraft Guild (now the Southern Highland Craft Guild), formed in 1930, and May Stone served on the first board of directors. One purpose for establishing such a guild was to create a central body that would oversee the standardization of design and workmanship. Among other things, it worked to improve the marketing of Appalachian crafts. Throughout the years, Hindman also participated in the yearly craft fairs sponsored by the guild and continues to be a Southern Highland Craft Guild member.

Currently, Hindman operates the Marie Stewart Craft Store. Opened in October 1995, this consignment shop provides local residents an outlet for their handwork and sponsors various crafting classes.

See also: PETTIT, KATHERINE (EDUCATION); SETTLEMENT, MISSION, AND SPONSORED SCHOOLS (EDUCATION); SOUTHERN INDUSTRIAL EDUCATIONAL ASSOCIATION.

—Carol Baugh, *Miami University* and *Sinclair Community College*

Allen H. Eaton, *Handicrafts of the Southern Highlands* (1937); Jess Stoddart, ed., *The Quare Women's Journals* (1997); David E. Whisnant, *All That Is Native and Fine: The Politics of Culture in an American Region* (1983).

Industrial School Crafts

See Settlement, Mission, and Sponsored Schools (Education)

John C. Campbell Folk School

Dedicating it to the memory of her late husband, Olive Dame Campbell established the John C. Campbell Folk

School in Brasstown, North Carolina, in 1925. With the enthusiastic support of the Brasstown community, students enrolled in the school to pursue an education that included courses in wood carving, basketry, weaving, pottery, music, dance, art, and other crafts of southern Appalachia. The goal was to educate the young people of the region while preserving Appalachian culture.

In 1908 Campbell obtained a Russell Sage Foundation grant that allowed him and his wife to travel and study conditions in the mountains of Appalachia. While John researched the region's geography and culture, Olive collected a variety of musical forms and in 1917, in collaboration with British ballad collector Cecil Sharp, published *English Folk Songs of the Southern Appalachians.* Following John's death in 1919, Olive completed the writing of his *The Southern Highlander and His Homeland* and then traveled in Europe, where she studied firsthand the Scandinavian folk schools on which the John C. Campbell Folk School would be modeled. In Denmark, the long tradition of folk schools, known as schools for life, transformed the Danish countryside into growing, creative communities. She hoped the John C. Campbell Folk School would have a similar impact by providing an alternative to the higher education facilities that drew young people away from family farms.

The result, according to some Appalachian scholars, was a hybrid view of culture driven by outsiders' perceptions. For example, the school initially stressed Danish folk school songs and dances while ignoring the mountain music Campbell had earlier explored and published. The dulcimer was promoted while the banjo was rejected, and the mountaineers' adaptations of jazz and their creation of songs about coal mining, labor troubles, and feuding were discouraged.

John C. Campbell Folk School offers programs in the performing arts, agriculture, and crafts rooted in the traditions of southern Appalachia and other regions of the world. The school's twenty-first-century goals remain loyal to its founding principles—to foster creativity in its students while promoting their social development as tolerant, caring members of a community.

See also: CAMPBELL, JOHN C. AND OLIVE DAME (EDUCATION); CRAFT REVIVAL (FOLKLORE AND FOLKLIFE); SETTLEMENT, MISSION, AND SPONSORED SCHOOLS (EDUCATION).

—Sändra Henson, *East Tennessee State University*

David E. Whisnant, *All That Is Native and Fine: The Politics of Culture in an American Region* (1983).

Kentucky Appalachian Artisan Center

In 1997, as part of the Kentucky Appalachian Community Development Initiative, the Knott County Art and Craft Foundation was created and funded by executive order of the governor of Kentucky with the purpose of providing training and market services to artisans working in eastern Kentucky. Specific funding was provided to create the Kentucky Appalachian Artisan Center in downtown Hindman as a combined gallery and showroom with space for workshops, demonstrations, performances, and marketing services, including a Web-based retail and wholesale program.

Two older commercial buildings were purchased in Hindman near the historic Hindman Settlement School, and the first was renovated to serve as the Kentucky Appalachian Artisan Center. A second facility functions as the artisans' business incubator, with working studios, sales areas, and some living quarters. Both facilities serve the artists and craftspeople now working in the region who want to develop their skills and expand their markets.

Part of Hazard Community College's Hindman Campus, the School of Craft is located in the old Hindman High School, which has been renovated into crafts teaching studios. The curriculum emphasizes skill and production, along with marketing and business training and respect for the region's cultural heritage. In 2003 the school began offering workshops in a variety of media, and two-year associate degrees in areas such as jewelry, metalsmithing, and ceramics became available in 2004.

Hindman's Community Development Initiative is based on building a sustainable economy derived from its own history and culture, using education and the arts to create a community and an economy rooted in the strong local traditions of art, craft, music, storytelling, writing, and other creative endeavors. It also hopes to develop the area into a tourism destination to draw new people and business to the area.

The center hosts rotating exhibitions, classes, and marketing programs, and the facility includes a computer center and library plus flexible space for a showroom and demonstration and performance areas.

See also: HINDMAN SETTLEMENT SCHOOL; SETTLEMENT, MISSION, AND SPONSORED SCHOOLS (EDUCATION); SOUTHERN HIGHLAND CRAFT GUILD.

—Garry Barker, *Morehead State University*

Kentucky Folk Art Center

The Kentucky Folk Art Center is a museum of expressive folk art established as a cultural and educational service of Morehead State University and developed from the university's collection of Kentucky folk art accumulated since 1985. The focus of the center is on visual art created by self-taught Kentucky artists rather than on traditional or contemporary crafts.

In 1997 the center was moved into a renovated turn-of-the-century warehouse building with two galleries, a museum store, and a non-lending library and archives.

A fifty-seat auditorium is located within the building in a brick-walled structure with a cantilevered brick arch ceiling that once served as the warehouse cooler.

Four new exhibitions are presented each year, usually developed in-house, and many later go on tour. The exhibition schedule offers a variety of subjects and themes selected and designed to expand the understanding of creative expression by self-taught artists. Educational programs place strong emphasis on providing children with arts and humanities exposure and cultural awareness through the museum experience. School tours are tailored to the needs of individual teachers. Presentations address issues such as understanding the creative process, the validity and importance of individual interpretation, and open-response writing. The center is operated by Kentucky Folk Art Center, Inc., a university-affiliated nonprofit corporation, in partnership with Morehead State University.

See also: ART MUSEUMS (CULTURAL INSTITUTIONS).

—Adrian Swain, *Morehead State University*

Knotted Bedspreads/Colonial Knotting

Influenced by the craft revival and handicraft marketing, knotted bedspread making, an important domestic craft form in the southern Appalachians, was popular in the first half of the twentieth century. A small number of women continue to make such spreads, but because of economic factors, the stitches and patterns have become more frequently used for smaller items such as pillows. Ashe and Watauga Counties in the North Carolina Blue Ridge region have been particularly active centers of this craft.

The positioning of beds in public spaces in southern Appalachian homes provided ample opportunity for the display of decorated bedspreads, woven coverlets, and quilts and fostered an appreciation of virtuosity in embroidery. Home use of such decoration beginning in the nineteenth century led to a tradition of passing down decorative craft traditions within families and fostered a meaningful process of communication and interaction among women. The teaching of embroidery stitches in schools also contributed to this craft.

Knotted bedspreads are large pieces of unbleached or white sheeting, often greige muslin, decorated with designs formed by embroidery stitches, including tufting, French knots, satin, and running stitches. They are often characterized by the dominant use of colonial knots, a tight small pearl-like embroidery style. In forming the knot, makers twist the needle to form two opposite coils, rather than loops in the same direction as in French knots. Although outside writers sometimes use the term *candlewicking* to incorporate colonial knotting into tufted work, southern Appalachian practitioners insist on the use of *colonial knotting, hand knotting*, or *knotted bedspreads* to describe the dominant use of the colonial knot in their patterns.

In the early twentieth century, colored tufted patterns known as turfing were popular in the southwestern North Carolina and Georgia Appalachians, and this local preference contributed to the development of the tufted carpet industry around Dalton, Georgia. The dominance of the colonial knot design and preference for white-on-white patterns characterize development in the northwestern North Carolina mountains. Although some home use of colonial knotting employed colored fiber, this tight beadlike stitch is especially associated with regional whitework, particularly knotted bedspreads.

Basic designs are formed by combinations of curving and straight lines of knots and larger patterns such as leaves, grapes, or small birds formed by clusters of knots. Designs often have local names that makers readily recognize and use to identify patterns; these include Bird in Tree, Grapevine, Cucumber Vine, Swinging Basket, and Bowknot and Thistle. Patterns for new spreads were often copied from an older spread by a process called stamping, using bluing to reproduce the placement of knots.

Finished spreads are trimmed with a fringe of string tied into rows of knotted loops. The practices used in forming this fringe have also contributed to the development of canopy tying as a craft in North Carolina. The Laura Riley Collection at Appalachian State University includes an excellent overview of the patterns and methods used in knotted bedspread making.

An important contribution to the continuation of knotted bedspread making was the emergence of a succession of outside entrepreneurs, often women, who owned small shops or mail-order businesses for marketing spreads. These relationships counter the stereotype of mountain isolation. Through contacts on vacation visits and the establishment of regular parcel post service, northern women with a mix of social conscience and commercial initiative carried on business by mail and established regular communication with rural spread makers seeking outside income. Rosemont in Marion, Virginia, and Alnwick Bedspreads, established by Laura Riley, wife of a philosophy professor at Vassar College, offer interesting instances of this development in knotted bedspread marketing in the first half of the twentieth century. The role of these female entrepreneurs also illustrates productive spheres of influence for middle-class women in defining a women's culture linking craft production and social reform. Connections with these mail-order businesses, gift shops, Colonial Revival museums, and antique businesses contributed to the marketing of colonial knotted pieces. The dominance of patterns made almost exclusively with colonial knots may have been a form of standardization influenced by the preferences of these outside entrepreneurs.

Knotted bedspread making often involved folk processes including learning by example in family or community settings, homemade tools such as needles and shunts for fringe tying, and narratives about learning the craft, exceptional makers, and humorous incidents in making spreads. The term *colonial* also connotes the traditions important to makers' presentation of their craft.

Three widely recognized practitioners of this craft were mother and daughter Cary Hodges and Bertha Hodges Cook of Watauga County, North Carolina, and Elsie Trivette of Avery County. Hodges and her daughter often demonstrated the craft at Southern Highland Handicraft Guild (later Southern Highland Craft Guild) events, including regular presentations on the porch of Moses H. Cone's Flat Top Manor on the Blue Ridge Parkway. The guild honored both by naming them life members, and in 1984 the National Endowment for the Arts named Bertha Cook a National Heritage Fellow. Elsie Trivette was a longtime demonstrator at the Village of Yesteryear of the North Carolina State Fair and other festivals, and in 1994 the North Carolina Arts Council presented her the North Carolina Folk Heritage Award.

See also: CANOPY TYING; CRAFT REVIVAL (FOLKLORE AND FOLKLIFE).

—Thomas McGowan, *Appalachian State University*

Annette Riley Fry, "Bedspreads from the Blue Ridge Mountains," *Americana* (May–June 1978).

Rigged looms in the weaving room at John C. Campbell Folk School, 1934. Blankets, coverlets, rugs, and other household linens have been woven on looms for more than two hundred years in Appalachia. Constructed with a timber frame, early looms took up significant space and were commonly found in small weaving sheds or other outbuildings.

Looms

Large, timber-framed traditional looms and the more technologically advanced, lightweight looms of the twentieth century represent two different eras of textile production. Examples of the first period reflect the typical horizontal looms of various European traditions, while the second are an outgrowth of the arts and craft revival in Appalachia.

The Irish, Scots, English, and German settlers of Appalachia built their looms using the basic technology and designs familiar to their ancestors. Massive in form and constructed of a mortise-and-tenon timber frame, these early looms took up significant space. They were commonly found in small weaving sheds or in other outbuildings. The common four-post loom, with a built-in seat, stood as high as seven feet and usually had a width and depth of six feet. The less common cantilevered loom, with only two tall posts and no seat, saved little room, as a weaver's stool or chair was still required. Looms of this period were most often built as one of a kind, and each loom reflected the range of abilities of the individual builder. Frequently identified by the untrained eye as crude or primitive, some looms have exquisite detail in terms of finishing techniques, decorative embellishments, and, at times, creative solutions to technological challenges. The metal gears needed to advance the cloth beam were commonly made by a local blacksmith. In addition to their size, the overhead batten, or swinging beater, is one of the characteristic features of the looms of this period.

While pockets of traditional weaving on the barn frame loom persisted into the second quarter of the twentieth century, another style of hand weaving began during the early years of the twentieth century, when the arts and crafts revival was occurring in Appalachia and other parts of the country. The perceived need for smaller and simpler looms, both aesthetically and technically, resulted in the development of lighter-weight, mass-produced looms. In many cases, the beater pivoted from the base of the loom, eliminating the need for the superstructure associated with the older looms and solving some of the space problems.

Following traditional designs similar to those of their Appalachian ancestors, many weavers now use the newer lightweight looms to produce textiles woven from natural and synthetic fibers. In general, an appreciation for the barn frame loom has been lost over the years, and the skills associated with its use have all but disappeared in the Appalachian region. Additionally, experienced hand weavers can use computers to improvise design patterns and complex weaves with greater ease, expediting the treadling process on the loom. With the adaptation of the mechanized loom, Appalachian hand weavers still create a wide variety of textiles with skill and efficiency—from the traditional overshot coverlets associated with the region to contemporary wall hangings incorporating found objects.

See also: CRAFT REVIVAL (FOLKLORE AND FOLKLIFE); WEAVING.

—Craig F. Evans, *Sanbornville, New Hampshire*

Mace Chairs

Starting around the time of the Civil War, the Mace family constructed tables, beds, coffins, billy clubs, and baseball bats, but it is best known for thousands of handcrafted chairs, many of which can still be found around the country. Jesse Mace began making chairs in the mid-1800s, primarily as a source of supplementary income. His succeeding family members made it their primary source of income, creating comfortable and durable "settin' cheers" for thousands of households.

The Mace family first arrived in western North Carolina in the early 1800s with the migration of Jonas Mace to the Toe River Valley, close to present-day Spruce Pine. Jesse Mace, born in 1840, was a grandson of Jonas and his wife, Elizabeth. In 1869 Copenny Mace was born to Jesse and Sallie Mace in McDowell County. Copenny married Lovada Ramsey and moved to Madison County, where the two bore a son, Shadrack Burdic "Birdie" Mace. Birdie and his wife, Sara, along with Copenny and Lovada, took out a sizable loan and moved down the mountain on East Fork. The move gave the family and the business more visibility, and chair making became their primary source of income. On East Fork, Birdie and Sara bore three daughters: Ella, Pauline, and Helen, all of whom, along with their mother and grandmother, participated in the construction of Mace chairs.

Though difficult to trace, there is evidence that Jesse Mace learned the art of woodworking from a man named Emanuel Rose. "Man" Rose, a resident of the same area as Jesse and referred to in the Mace family lore as Jesse's instructor, was a descendant of William Pendley, an English cabinetmaker's apprentice. Some believe that many techniques used by the Mace family craftspeople originated with Rose.

The Mace family's fame mostly derives from their construction of chairs. In contrast to the elegant New England ladder-back chairs that have straight backs and knob finials, the functional Mace chairs were created for use and comfort. Very few Mace chairs have decorations beyond those that make the chair more functional. The curved back of the Mace chairs, a common feature of Appalachian chairs, differentiates them most acutely from their New England counterparts. Mace chairs tended to have two or three curved slats in addition to the bent back, but the makers created a variety of styles, from children's chairs to arm and armless chairs to benches and rockers. The Mace family never thought the New England ladder-back chairs very comfortable, but because of demand, they began to make a limited number of straight-back chairs, though these should not be mistaken as having a traditional Mace design.

Early on, the Mace family began making chairs primarily out of ash and hickory on account of their durability. As these trees became scarcer, the family started using maple, cherry, oak, and walnut. The construction of the chairs included both manual and mechanized labor. By 1922, they had a one-lung gasoline-powered engine in their shop and obtained electrical power in the 1950s. The Mace family used no glue. They cured dry hardwood posts and slats and fit these preshrunk rounds into holes of wood that had not yet shrunk, creating durable, tight joints. The bent pieces, including the back and the back slats, required boiling in water and then bending on frames or presses. Very rarely did the family apply any finishes to their chairs.

The division of labor by gender in the Mace family was not strict. Everyone in the family worked on the chairs. Generally, the women of the family participated by weaving the seats of the chairs with oak splits or sea grass, but they would switch jobs for a while if another specific production task fell behind. Sometimes overlooked, the participation of women in the process was vital. Bottoming chairs was perhaps the most tedious and time-consuming step in the production process.

The Mace family opened their market initially by selling to people in the surrounding communities of Mars Hill, Weaverville, and Asheville. With the advent of the automobile and better roads in the area in the 1920s and 1930s, their market expanded. The national appreciation of traditional crafts during the same time period and the Mace family's participation in the Southern Highland Handicraft Guild further broadened their consumer base. Birdie Mace most likely sold his chairs through a guild "center," only later becoming an active participant in guild activities in the 1950s. Birdie Mace died in 1973, ending more than one hundred years of family chair making.

See also: CHAIR MAKING; COTTAGE INDUSTRIES (BUSINESS, INDUSTRY, AND TECHNOLOGY); SOUTHERN HIGHLAND CRAFT GUILD.

—Adam Sanders, *East Tennessee State University*

Allen H. Eaton, *Handicrafts of the Southern Highlands* (1937); Jerry Israel, "The Mace Family of Chair Makers," in *May We All Remember Well: A Journal of the History and Cultures of Western North Carolina*, ed. Robert S. Brunk (1997).

Meaders Pottery

John Milton Meaders established the family folk pottery operation in the Georgia foothills pottery center of Mossy Creek in 1892–93 for his sons Wiley, Caulder, Cleater, Casey, L. Q., and Cheever. He hired two members of local "clay clans" to work in the log shop and teach his older boys. Cheever, the youngest, learned from his brothers and took over the shop in 1920. With a declining demand for food-related farm wares and the increasing popularity of Allen H. Eaton's *Handicrafts of the Southern Highlands* (1937), which described the family potters, craft enthusiasts became Cheever's main customers. In the 1960s his wife, Arie, produced a line of ingenious and colorful decorative wares, including wheel-thrown birds and animals. Their sons, John, Lanier, Reggie, and Edwin, all learned the craft.

Stimulated by the 1967 visit of a Smithsonian Institution film crew, Lanier Meaders took over the shop upon the death of Cheever. Combining his father's stubborn adherence to the old ways and his mother's artistic vision, Lanier revitalized the tradition of face jugs on which his fame was largely based and was awarded a National Heritage Fellowship by the National Endowment for the Arts in 1983. Meaders has been recognized with many other awards, including the Georgia Governor's Award for the Arts in 1987. In carrying on and refining the craft of alkaline-glazed stoneware, he was a crucial link between the past and future of southern folk pottery, and his success encouraged others, including members of his own family, to keep this tradition alive.

See also: ART POTTERY; EATON, ALLEN H. (FOLKLORE AND FOLKLIFE); FACE JUGS.

—John A. Burrison, *Georgia State University*

Morgan, Lucy

See Penland Weavers and Potters

Mountain Craftsmen Cooperative Association

The Mountain Craftsmen Cooperative Association originated in 1932 as a possible solution to the increasing poverty of communities in the coal fields around Charleston and Morgantown, West Virginia. The Extension Department of the University of West Virginia agreed to teach a small number of underemployed miners the craft of woodworking after volunteers from the Quaker organization American Friends Service Committee contacted them.

The Elmhirst Fund soon rewarded the success of the program with a ten-thousand-dollar grant, allowing the association to set up three workshops around Morgantown. Recognizing the need for an experienced woodworking instructor, the association hired Bob Godlove, who taught the prospective craftsmen all steps in the production of tables, chairs, candlesticks, dinnerware, and other objects. Training soon relocated to a larger workshop in Morgantown before settling in 1935 in Arthurdale.

After selling well in New England and Philadelphia, in the 1930s Godlove chairs and tables made an appearance at the World's Fair in Chicago and were later displayed at the Paris Exposition. The association soon expanded its line of products to include pewter and iron pieces in addition to wood crafts—a replica of a sixteenth-century astronomy instrument, crafted by noted blacksmith James Londus Fullmer, is held by the Smithsonian Institution. Despite a high demand for their handcrafted products, however, the Mountain Craftsmen Cooperative Association never realized a profit and was forced to close the Arthurdale shop in 1941.

See also: CRAFT COOPERATIVES; CRAFT REVIVAL (FOLKLORE AND FOLKLIFE).

—Adam Sanders, *East Tennessee State University*

Native American Arts and Crafts

Native American arts and crafts in Appalachia span thousands of years and include works of the Cherokee and Iroquois, among others. These tribes have vital folk traditions in storytelling and music as well as folk arts passed down through the generations over millennia. The Eastern Band of Cherokee Indians is a federally recognized tribe of more than thirteen thousand and owns fifty-seven thousand acres of land held in federal trust in the mountains of western North Carolina, where members continue craft traditions into the twenty-first century. More than sixteen thousand members of tribes of the Iroquois Confederacy live in New York State on the Akwesasne, Oneida, Onondaga, Tonawanda, Tuscarora, Cattaraugus, and Allegany reservations. Their members also continue craft traditions, which differ from those of the Cherokee.

Native Americans created everything they needed—clothing, shelter, tools, weapons, jewelry, medicine—from the Appalachian environment in which they lived for more than ten thousand years. Archaeological evidence suggests that fiber twining and basketmaking occurred in present-day east Tennessee about 9,500 years ago, and pottery was being made in the southern Appalachians 2,900 years ago. During these millennia, Native Americans traded craft materials

Cherokee cloth dolls at Qualla Arts and Crafts Cooperative, Cherokee, North Carolina, 2002. An American folk art, the making of cloth dolls is part of the region's cultural heritage and is rooted in both European and Native American traditions. Cherokee women still make dolls from fabric, blankets, wood, and other natural materials, arranging them in elaborate tableaux.

such as minerals, shells, and stone throughout the region and beyond, from the Great Lakes and Atlantic Coast to the Gulf of Mexico.

During this early period, baskets were created for storage, carrying, sifting, cooking, and game playing. Mats were woven as floor and seat coverings and wall hangings. Plant fibers were twined to create shoe soles, as well as rope and fishnets. Smoking pipes used in ceremonies, weights for fishnets, soapstone bowls, and game pieces were all carved from stone, and ceremonial masks, canoes, corn pounders, tools, and weapons (such as the atlatl, or spearthrower, bows and arrows, and blowgun darts) were carved from wood. Spinning and weaving materials such as hemp and the inner bark of mulberry trees produced skirts, sashes, and shrouds. Essential tools such as points for spears and arrows, axes, scrapers, and grinders were products of flintknapping. Though early crafts were functional, they were often decorative as well. Even the earliest stone points have beautiful lines that must have appealed to the aesthetic vision of their creators.

The development of these crafts over time (as well as other material remains) helps archaeologists define changes in cultures from the early Paleo-Indian period (11,000–8000 B.C.) through the Archaic period (8000–1200 B.C.) and the Woodland period (1200 B.C.–A.D. 900). Today's Appalachian tribes can be traced through pottery and other material traditions to their ancestors who lived during the Mississippian period, about A.D. 900–1550.

The Cherokee and the tribes of the Iroquois Confederacy have been distinct groups for thousands of years, but their languages are considered to be part of the same language family. Linguists have determined that Cherokee began to separate from other Iroquoian languages about 3,500 years ago. The Six Nations of the Iroquois Confederacy consisted of the Cayuga, Mohawk, Oneida, Onondaga, Seneca, and Tuscarora, each possessing their own language and customs. As with language, Iroquois and Cherokee culture share some similarities: the equal status of women, the development of agriculture, and celebrations such as the Green Corn Festival. They also shared the stamped pottery tradition predominant in the southern Appalachian Mississippian period. In other ways the two groups differ: the Iroquois lived in communal longhouses, while the Cherokee lived in detached dwellings occupied by extended families. Today, the arts and crafts of the Cherokee and the Iroquois tribes are distinctly different, having evolved over time.

Traditionally, Cherokee arts and crafts have been passed down through oral tradition and imitation within families and community groups, a system that integrates craft techniques with cultural values. Among twenty-first-century Cherokee, crafts are still associated with particular families. These traditional crafts include basketmaking, pottery making, wood carving, stone carving, beadwork, finger weaving, and the creation of musical instruments, weapons, and clothing. However, natural materials used for these crafts such as river cane, white oak, local clay, various woods, and plants for dyes are becoming increasingly difficult to find.

Intricately woven baskets may be the best-known Cherokee craft. One double-weave river cane basket was sent from the governor of Charlestown (present-day Charleston, South Carolina) in the 1720s to England; it resides in the British Museum in London today. Several Cherokee women continue to weave the nearly waterproof double-weave river cane baskets with no visible seams. Baskets and mats made of river cane are the earliest Cherokee tradition, but as the Cherokees' territory changed, women began using white oak (1800–present), honeysuckle (1880s–present), and maple (1930s–present). Although not as strong a material as white oak, honeysuckle was used because baskets were being sold as decorative items to tourists who were not concerned about strength and functionality. An import from Japan, honeysuckle thrives in the mountain areas left bare from years of logging. Red maple is also abundant in logged areas, and about 1930 basket makers began using it in baskets intended for sale to tourists. They continue to dye these materials with walnut, bloodroot, and butternut.

Cherokee pottery is formed by hand, either through coiling or pinching, and is fired outdoors in an open wood fire. No glazes are used. Color is determined by the type of clay and by the way that the smoke is directed in firing. For centuries, Cherokee pottery has been distinguished by its stamped, textured exterior and burnished, double-fired waterproof interior. Carved wooden paddles are used to form the pot and to impress designs on the wet clay. Incising is also used for decoration, often on the shoulders of the pot. Some pots are decorated with impressions made by corncobs, peach pits, or paddles wrapped with cords. Exceptions to this tradition come from east Tennessee, where potters made smooth pots covered with clay slips of different colors to create pots with white, black, and red designs during the Mississippian period.

For most of the twentieth century, Eastern Cherokee potters departed from this ancient, functional tradition, influenced by Catawba women living among them and by an influx of visitors, who preferred to buy the small black pots with shiny exteriors more characteristic of Catawba pottery. In 2002 Cherokee potters began reviving their old tradition through a series of workshops at the Museum of the Cherokee Indian, finally forming the Cherokee Potters Guild to teach, create, and promote the authentic stamped pottery. Their work has appeared at the Smithsonian Folklife Festival as well as the Cherokee Fall Fair and is becoming part of the Cherokee pottery traditions of the twenty-first century. Other Cherokee potters still make the Catawba-influenced burnished pottery, recreating old forms such as effigy oil lamps and creating new forms by incising pots with the Cherokee syllabary. Other Cherokee potters make contemporary pottery influenced by the work of southwestern tribes.

Before European contact, the Cherokee frequently carved functional, ceremonial, and representational objects from wood—dugout canoes from poplar logs, bows from black locust, and corn pounders from the sweet gum tree. Masks were carved from buckeye and cucumber wood and used in ceremonial dances. Today people carve masks as well as representational figures of bears, dogs, and other animals. Stone is also carved into these figures and into pipes. Some Cherokee craftsmen have revived the thousand-year-old tradition of incising designs on shells, creating gorgets based on designs from the Mississippian period. These circular pendants, several inches in diameter, were originally carved from shell traded from the Gulf of Mexico and incised with spiral designs, crosses, and creatures from Cherokee myths: rattlesnakes, spiders, and birds. Flintknapping, one of the oldest crafts, is still practiced to create arrowheads. Blowguns are crafted from river cane, and the darts consist of thistledown around a shaft of locust. The carving tradition is preserved by people such as Cherokee High School teacher Amanda Crowe, an influence to a generation of woodcarvers who, in turn, are now teaching another generation.

Beadwork dates back to the use of shells to decorate clothing, the creation of clay beads, and the carving of shells into beads for wampum. Wampum belts were considered sacred and were sent as messages between tribes. Trade beads were introduced during the contact period and were worn as jewelry. With the introduction of small glass beads, the Cherokee began creating new designs on leather. Today's beadworkers use pony beads, seed beads, hex beads, and other new forms to decorate clothing, bags, moccasins, lamps, hats, and other items. Some recreate wampum belts with beads carved from shell from New England.

Several art and craft traditions are required to create traditional Cherokee clothing. Finger weaving is a tradition unique to the Cherokee in the Appalachians. Weaving sashes without a loom, women use as many as two hundred strands of yarn to create intricate patterns. Beaded belts are woven on a loom using large pony beads with leather ties. Cherokee moccasins were made originally with a center front seam, and these are being re-created today. Women's traditional clothing included skirts made of buckskin or woven mulberry bark, buckskin capes and leggings, and ceremonial feather capes. Men's clothing included leggings, breechcloth, and buckskin shirts. Linen shirts replaced the latter in the eighteenth century, as trade items such as blankets, cloth hunting coats, metal bells, and calico petticoats became part of Cherokee dress.

Today, when Cherokee men and women celebrate their cultural identity, they often wear ribbon shirts and tear dresses. Men's ribbon shirts are made of calico or plain colored lightweight cotton in a pattern much like the eighteenth-century trade shirts. They are decorated with three or four bands of quarter-inch satin ribbon sewn parallel across the chest and back, with several inches hanging loose down the sides. Cherokee women's tear dresses are made of calico. To cut out the dress, the maker just has to "tear" a length of cloth into square sections that become the body of the dress and the sleeves, gathered at the waist and wrists. These dresses are also decorated with appliquéd ribbon across the front and back and above the hem. Some Cherokee women also incorporate geometrical cloth appliqués as borders. A beaded belt or finger-woven sash, beaded rosette bolo, and front-seam moccasins complete the modern version of traditional dress.

The Cherokees also practiced metalworking. During the Mississippian period, Cherokee artists worked copper, cutting figures out of flattened sheets of the metal. Until the forced removal from their ancestral lands by the U.S. government in 1838, Cherokee silversmiths created earrings, armbands, and other jewelry. Sequoyah, inventor of the Cherokee syllabary, was well known as a silversmith in east Tennessee in the early 1800s. From about 1800 through the mid-1900s, Cherokee blacksmiths made guns, horseshoes, and metal objects for a variety of uses, including wagon building. Today some Cherokees continue the silversmithing tradition.

The beliefs, myths, and legends of the Cherokee and other Appalachian tribes are expressed in their arts and crafts. In addition, craftspeople created items that were essential for religious ceremonies. Pipes were carved from stone, often with effigies of birds, animals, and people, and were smoked in a sacred ceremony of prayer. Carved wooden masks were worn in ceremonies such as the Booger Dance. Arts and crafts also reflected beliefs: incised carvings on shell gorgets show animals and figures presumed to have sacred significance. Cherokee myths cast arts and crafts in central roles; one explains how the people got fire when a water spider wove a tiny basket to carry it to them. In an annual ceremony, Cherokee women carried fire in baskets from a central, sacred fire to rekindle the hearths in their own homes. Other Cherokee myths tell the origins of blowguns and pottery.

Many Native American artists also incorporate their tribal cultural values and images into fine art forms including painting, drawing, sculpture, jewelry, and fabric design, resulting in works influenced by a sense of place, tribal myths, and the individual artist's vision. Members of the Eastern Band of Cherokee Indians, painters Jenean Hornbuckle and William Taylor have worked in oil and canvas, and a new generation of fine art painters and mixed-media artists is emerging that includes Shan Goshorn, Luzene Hill, Nikki Nations, Paula Maney Nelson, Sean Ross, Margaret Shanusdi, and others. Stone carver John Julius Wilnoty has created sculptures internationally recognized as visionary fine art pieces. Among artists of the Cherokee Nation in Oklahoma are Donald Vann, Dorothy Sullivan, and Connie Jenkins, who create fine art paintings and prints with Cherokee themes and subjects. Their work is often exhibited among the Eastern Band as well.

The arts and crafts of the Cherokee and northern Iroquois tribes have not only incorporated forms and materials from European traditions, but have also taken up distinctly American folk art forms. The creation of patchwork quilts, for example, has been popular with Native American women for more than a hundred years. Their designs often reflect their cultural aesthetics, with the star design being the most popular among Native American quilters.

Influence has traveled in the other direction, as well. Numerous "Appalachian" arts and crafts actually derive from Cherokee and Iroquois traditions. Cornhusk dolls were originally made by Cherokee and Iroquois women; the faceless dolls illustrate an Iroquois legend with a moral about vanity. Contemporary Cherokee women make dolls from fabric, blankets, wood, and other natural materials, arranging them in elaborate tableaux. Purple martin birdhouses, made from gourds and erected on poles, were used by the Cherokee for centuries in their cornfields. Cherokee crafters today grow and decorate gourds as storage containers (their original use), as well as works of art, painted, incised, and decorated with leather and feathers.

Tribes throughout the Appalachian region participate in powwows, which have their own associated pan-Indian arts and crafts. These gatherings became an important feature of tribal life throughout the United States beginning in the mid-twentieth century. Originally weekend events featuring tribal dances, powwows expanded to include people of other tribes, and in some cases, the general public. Today, they celebrate and affirm Native American identity through dance, food, ceremony, and arts and crafts.

Powwows focus on dancing—both traditional dances originating from particular tribes and modern dances created at previous powwows. Dance events require elaborate costumes, usually crafted by the dancer or his or her family members, particular to that dance. These colorful and extremely intricate creations require skills in sewing, beadwork, silversmithing, leathercraft, and feather creations. For example, dresses worn by women and girls for jingle dance competitions are covered with hundreds of metal cones. Grass dancers wear costumes featuring butterfly-like headdresses and long fringes that sway like grass in the wind. Others, such as fancy dancers and hoop dancers, also wear particular costumes.

Powwow dances are accompanied by large, rawhide-covered, handmade wooden drums played by several men at one time. In Cherokee sacred dance traditions, other handcrafted instruments are used. Water drums are crafted from small hollow logs covered with skin. Rattles, used by individuals, are made from gourds, turtle shells, or leather and decorated with feathers and beadwork. Women wear turtle-shell rattles attached to leather backing just below their knees to provide rhythmic accompaniment as they dance. Traditional Cherokee flutes are made from lengths of river cane, although modern Cherokee flute makers also use cedar and walnut decorated with wood and stone carvings.

During the twentieth century, as the Cherokee and Iroquois people turned to tourism for economic development, crafts became more decorative and less functional. While some crafts, such as pipes, masks, drums, and rattles, are still used in sacred ceremonies, their forms have also been adapted to appeal to a popular market. For example, in Cherokee, North Carolina, sets of small masks representing the seven clans are very popular among tourists and are often displayed as well in local businesses as a sign of Cherokee identity.

Some arts and crafts that originated with particular tribes have become popular nationwide in response to market demand. Dream catchers, for example, originated with the Ojibway in Minnesota. About two inches in diameter and made of a strip of red willow bark bent into a circle with small strands of sinew woven across, dream catchers were attached to babies' cradleboards to "catch" bad dreams, whose power would dissipate with the rising sun. Over the course of the 1990s this tradition captured the popular imagination, and dream catchers are now crafted and sold by people of many Native American tribes including the Cherokee, Oneida, Seneca, and Mohawk, as well as by the general public. They have grown in size and are decorated with feathers, fur, beads, crystals, and other materials. Their design has been adapted for earrings, T-shirts, and logos. Dream catcher kits are available in craft stores and on the Internet.

Recognizing that for many tribes traditional arts and crafts have provided significant income, the U.S. Congress passed the American Indian Arts and Crafts Act and created the Indian Arts and Crafts Board in 1995. The Indian Arts and Crafts Act is a truth-in-advertising law that provides fines and penalties for anyone claiming to produce Indian arts and crafts who is not a member of a federally or state-recognized tribe.

In Cherokee, North Carolina, three nonprofit organizations present and preserve Cherokee arts and crafts. The Qualla Arts and Crafts Mutual, founded in 1946, is one of the most successful tribal cooperatives in the country. Its board, staff, and member artists are all enrolled members of the Eastern Band of Cherokee Indians. They set high standards for work in basketmaking, pottery, carving, beadwork, and all other traditional crafts. Qualla provides income for artists by purchasing crafts throughout the winter months—the off-season for tourism—and by distributing an annual share of the cooperative's profits to its more than three hundred members. At the Oconaluftee Indian Village and Living History Museum, operated by the Cherokee Historical Association, Cherokees demonstrate arts and crafts in a re-created 1750s village open to visitors. This organization has provided a place for informal apprenticeships between novice employees and master craft workers. The Museum of the Cherokee Indian, founded in 1948, sells the work of more than a hundred crafts people in its gift shop. It also sponsors festivals, art shows and exhibits, and classes on Cherokee traditions for Cherokee people wishing to learn arts and crafts.

See also: CHEROKEE (RACE, ETHNICITY, AND IDENTITY); CHEROKEE BASKETS; QUALLA ARTS AND CRAFTS MUTUAL.

—Barbara R. Duncan, *Museum of the Cherokee Indian*

Barbara Duncan, *Where It All Began: Cherokee Creation Stories in Art* (2000); Sarah H. Hill, *Weaving New Worlds: Southeastern Cherokee Women and Their Basketry* (1997); Rodney L. Leftwich, *Arts and Crafts of the Cherokee* (1970).

Needle Lace

Although spinning, weaving, and quilting are typically associated with Appalachia, lace making was also popular. Needle and bobbin lace are the two true laces, using western European techniques persisting since the 1500s. Needle lace is created with a single strand of yarn, usually linen, threaded through a needle. Stitches are looped row upon row, building upon a foundation of thick threads without a woven background. Following European trends in lace fashion, Americans exhibited a passion for lace from the eighteenth through the early twentieth century. Most lace was imported, but women also made lace at home by copying European patterns.

Lace was particularly popular in the South. Lace making and cutwork embroidery were skills often taught in girls' schools throughout the South, including much of Appalachia. When immigrants from eastern and southern Europe settled in Appalachia in the nineteenth and early twentieth centuries, many brought with them lace-making techniques particular to their heritages. The women of these groups found their expertise in demand and, with a little adaptation, an opportunity for income.

For instance, Anna Peluso, an Italian immigrant to West Virginia in 1913, originally made and sold cutwork lace for girls' trousseaux in her home country. Such items were not needed much in the coal camps and towns of West Virginia, so she put her skills to use making and selling popular crocheted corset covers and crocheted lace by the yard for bed linens instead.

See also: CANOPY TYING; SPINNING; WEAVING.

—Joan L. Saverino, *University of Pennsylvania*

Peacock Alley

From the 1920s through the 1950s, travelers along U.S. Highway 41—the main artery from the northeastern states to Florida—were often treated to a peculiar and arresting sight as they approached the Dalton, Georgia, area in southern Appalachia: hundreds of gaily patterned, tufted bedspreads flapping on clotheslines at roadside stands and small stores. This portion of the highway became known as "Peacock Alley" because of this display of spreads, many featuring the gaudy peacock design.

The spreads represented a radical concept for the time in what was then a largely agricultural area—the idea that women could earn money and help support their families with their crafts. From the women's tufting on display along Peacock Alley eventually came mechanized production and development of the carpet industry that became an economic powerhouse in the region.

Tufting is a variation of the early colonial craft of candlewicking, which involved creating a pattern on fabric with knotted running stitches. In tufting, the same running stitch is employed, but the stitches are clipped, not knotted, thus producing a fluff, or tuft, which adds texture, weight, and fullness to the finished piece. Both candlewicking and tufting borrow designs from traditional American quilt patterns, but the tufters also created original patterns, such as the peacock.

A young Dalton woman named Catherine Evans Whitener is generally credited with being the first to popularize tufting. Soon after making a tufted spread (c. 1895) using white thread on old flour sacks, she was inundated with requests for copies. Realizing the potential to earn money from her new craft, Whitener enlisted women in the Dalton area, many the wives of farmers, to work on the spreads. She hired others to haul supplies to the home workers and pick up the finished spreads. Thus, two separate types of workers came into being: tufters and haulers. Soon, a number of local competitors went into the tufted bedspread business as well.

The tools used were simple and included long needles adapted from candlewicking and embroidery; homemade thimbles of tough fabric, leather, or other pliable, sturdy material; a "stamping iron," which was often simply a tin pie plate, dish, or clothing iron; and marking material, such as soot or a greasy meat skin, that could be used to stamp a design on a piece of fabric. Unbleached muslin replaced the old flour sacks first used by Whitener. The thread was the same cotton floss used in candlewicking.

The method was as simple as the tools and easy to duplicate. Blank fabric was placed on top of a completed tufted item and the surface rubbed with a stamping tool and marking material, thus producing an outline of a dotted design on the top fabric. The tufter then used a running stitch to work the design. After the stitches were completed, the thread was clipped to form tufts. The completed item was then boiled in a large outdoor kettle or tub and hung to dry, causing the fabric to shrink around the tufts, which caused them to fluff up. If necessary, tufted items were beaten and shaken to "plump up" the texture of the tufted design. Variations, including the use of colored thread, were added.

From 1900 to 1920, the bedspread business grew from a few home workers into something approaching a bona fide industry. At first, the men of the region viewed the tufting business as women's work, and not until the early 1920s did they begin to participate seriously as haulers. As demand for tufted items grew, companies established hauler routes, often covering several hundred miles, throughout Georgia, Alabama, Tennessee, and South Carolina.

Mainly due to the flourishing tufting industry, the Great Depression did not affect the Dalton area as badly as it did other parts of the South. Men who had previously scoffed at their wives' "hobby" now found that tufting put food on the table and shoes on their children's feet. During this period, there was more family involvement in bedspread production, with children and men helping to tuft, boil, and fluff the spreads.

With the enactment of the Wage and Hour Law in 1933, women left their homes and went to work in factories, where they were paid by the hour instead of by the piece. Meanwhile, female entrepreneurs further promoted the tufting industry by contacting department stores in the South and across the nation, describing their bedspreads, wearable items, and small rugs. Even the smallest spread house flourished and had a ready-made form of advertising in the form of clotheslines spread with peacock-patterned bedspreads. The peacock design became a symbol of the bedspread industry, but its creation was essentially practical. Rendered in the richest and most striking color combinations imaginable, the design was simply a good way to use up leftover colors of yarn from other patterns. Other popular designs were the Wild Rose of Georgia, Black-eyed Susan, and Double Wedding Ring.

In 1936 another revolutionary change in the industry came about when Glen Looper adapted a commercial Singer sewing machine to do single-needle tufting. The design was quickly improved to include up to twenty-four rows of tufted stitches. With the advent of the tufting machine, the term *tufting* was replaced with the more cosmopolitan *chenille*, French for "caterpillar." The term was appropriate because the machine produced a uniform running stitch with a raised, fuzzy pile, much like a caterpillar's skin.

Further mechanical experimentation yielded machines that could tuft nearly any type of base fabric with nearly any type of thread. Bedspread production was eventually replaced with carpet manufacturing in the Dalton area, which continues to the present time.

See also: COTTAGE INDUSTRIES (BUSINESS, INDUSTRY, AND TECHNOLOGY); COVERLETS; QUILTS.

—Maria Neder Douglas, *Oglethorpe University*

Marguerite Ickis, *The Standard Book of Quilt Making and Collecting* (1949); John Rice Irwin, *A People and Their Quilts* (1984); Blair White, "Peacock Alley Revisited," *Now and Then* (Winter 1995).

Penland Weavers and Potters

From its inception in 1923 until it disbanded in 1967, Penland Weavers and Potters provided a place of community and a form of income for a number of women in the small Appalachian community of Penland, North Carolina. Throughout the years, the focus of their work changed, as did the various forms of funding that supplemented their work, but the heart of the program remained intact. Founder Lucy Morgan (1889–1981) cited the revival of weaving and the promise of income for women as the impetus for the program. The first weavers were new to the craft, welcoming the opportunity to make money.

In 1920 Morgan joined the Appalachian Episcopal Mission School in Penland to serve as a teacher. Raised in western North Carolina, she left to attend college at Central State Normal School (later Central Michigan Teacher's College), graduating in 1915. For the next five years she taught school in the Midwest, worked at the Children's Bureau in Chicago, and took summer classes at the University of Chicago. Aware of Jane Addams's work in Chicago, in 1920 Morgan arrived in the small community of Penland to work at the Appalachian Industrial School, teaching and filling in as acting director. In 1923 Amy Burt came to Penland as director of the school, allowing Morgan to pursue her interests in community programs. Morgan visited Berea College in Kentucky, where she learned to weave and had a chance to see community-based weaving programs in action. Returning to Penland, she brought with her three looms designed by Swedish-born Anna Ernberg and began her project.

Morgan paid cash for weavings, and soon a number of women were involved in production. The Episcopal Church offered Morgan support, and the program became known as Fireside Industries, a division of the Appalachian School. This endorsement helped spread the word about Morgan's work, and she began accepting consignments from various church bazaars throughout the country. The church provided Morgan with a truck, and she traveled widely to market the crafts of Penland. In 1924 she loaded a loom onto her truck and went to the North Carolina State Fair in Raleigh, where she learned of the federal Smith-Hughes fund, administered through the state. A requirement for this funding was that the recipients have a central location for member meetings. In 1926 Morgan organized the building of a log cabin structure that came to be known as the Weavers' Cabin. The people of Penland backed the Weavers' Cabin by donating their time and building supplies, making community support a cornerstone of Morgan's project.

Excellent at networking, Morgan welcomed visitors to the mountaintop. One of those visitors in 1928 suggested the name Penland Weavers and Potters. Morgan added pottery to the production but soon found that shipping pottery from the mountains was not feasible at the time. Even though pottery played only a small role in the production work, the name remained.

As the number of weavers increased, Morgan continued to shape the program and look for ways to expand. Realizing that the women needed more weaving techniques than she knew, Morgan sought an invitation to study with master weaver, Edward Worst. In 1926 Morgan traveled to Chicago, where Worst worked as the supervisor of manual arts for the Chicago school system. Worst was interested in the weaving project, and in 1928 he visited Penland Weavers and Potters. When Worst returned for a visit in 1929, several people asked whether they could come and learn from the master. This led to the creation of the Weaving Institute, sponsored by the Penland Weavers and Potters.

The weaving program gained momentum in the 1930s, and the Weaving Institute became ever more popular. The Great Depression shaped the direction of the programs Morgan had carefully nurtured. By the mid-1930s the church withdrew its support for the weaving cooperative, leaving Morgan with not only a deficit but also a number of items unsold. Morgan set out for the 1933–34 Century of Progress World's Fair in Chicago with a small log cabin constructed on the back of her truck. There she set up shop, selling weaving and advertising both Penland Weavers and Potters and the Weaving Institute as well.

When Morgan returned home, she needed to find a location for the growing Weaving Institute. Worst continued to come to Penland to teach and enjoyed working with the women of the community, who assisted him and became an important part of the Weaving Institute. In 1935 the Penland projects shifted with the construction of the Edward F. Worst Craft House. The school adopted the name Penland School of Crafts and incorporated in 1938; in 1939 the Penland Weavers and Potters officially became the crafts production department of the Penland School.

Throughout the years the number of workers fluctuated, as did the variety of their products. Items such as silk capes with coverlet designs appeared on their early list of goods. In 1926 there were seventeen weavers, thirty the next year, and sixty-three by the end of that decade. In 1941 there were fifty-six crafts workers. Their products included not only weaving but also such items as candles, nature print stationery, and children's sunsuits, pinafores, and bibs. In the early 1960s the craft world was changing, bringing new and exciting energy, but it was also the end of an era. Lucy Morgan retired in 1962 as the Penland School's director, and in 1967 the weaving cooperative disbanded. Penland's influence on the craft movement continues to be substantial.

See also: WEAVING; WEAVING ROOM OF CROSSNORE SCHOOL.

—Lynn Ennis, *North Carolina State University*

Philis Alvic, *Weavers of the Southern Highlands* (2003); Bonnie Willis Ford, *The Story of the Penland Weavers* (1934).

Pine Mountain Settlement School

Incorporated in 1913, Pine Mountain Settlement School was a boarding facility established for the industrial, intellectual, and moral training of students in the mountains of eastern Kentucky. Its first directors, Katherine Pettit and Ethel DeLong Zande, also saw to it that the school served as a social center for the community. Located in Harlan

County, Kentucky, Pine Mountain functioned as a boarding school until 1949. At that time, it became a consolidated public school under the direction of the Berea College Board of Trustees and the Harlan County Board of Education. From 1949 until 1972, Pine Mountain assisted the Harlan County Board of Education with public school activities. Since 1972, Pine Mountain has served as an environmental education center for schools, civic organizations, and older adult groups.

In addition to Pine Mountain's educational pursuits, craft production, or fireside industries, became an integral part of the school's activities. Teachers and local residents informally taught students the fundamentals of flax preparation, sheep shearing, carding, dyeing, and weaving. In 1921 the school established an official Department of Fireside Industries and hired a weaving teacher from outside the Pine Mountain region. Besides the Weaving Department, it also maintained an Industrial Arts Department, where students made a variety of items such as stools, chairs, brooms, and baskets. All these handmade items, including the handwoven articles, were advertised in fliers and sold to people who visited the school and craft stores throughout the country. Prices ranged from ten cents for a small wooden hook to thirty dollars for a three-yard-long coverlet.

Founding director Pettit recognized the importance of profits as an incentive for those producing the crafts. Pine Mountain listed fireside industries in its yearly financial reports as a separate line item from 1922 until 1947. During these years profits ranged from a low of $5.45 to a high of $442.16, with losses incurred in seven of these years. Some students and local residents did make a little money, but profits diminished rapidly during the 1940s, and craft production ended in 1949, when Pine Mountain ceased to function as a boarding school.

According to her personal notes, Pettit believed that the true value in craft production was preserving dying art forms, developing an understanding of work, and building character.

See also: HINDMAN SETTLEMENT SCHOOL; PETTIT, KATHERINE (EDUCATION); SETTLEMENT, MISSION, AND SPONSORED SCHOOLS (EDUCATION).

—Carol Baugh, *Miami University* and *Sinclair Community College*

Pisgah Forest Pottery

Pisgah Forest Pottery was the last of three pottery businesses established by Walter B. Stephen (1875–1961), who was the first Appalachian potter to develop crystalline glazes (c. 1930) and to produce art pottery using porcelain clays and oriental forms. Pisgah Forest wares can be described as both art pottery and folk pottery. While he produced extremely fine art forms and glazes, Stephen also created raised cameo designs that seemed the folksy representations of an untrained artist. These bas-relief decorations depicted American folklore scenes including covered wagons, buffalo hunts, fiddlers and cabins, and square dancers.

Stephen officially opened this pottery at Arden, North Carolina, in the mid-1920s, following five years of part-time experiments with clay bodies and glazes. Although crock makers had operated in western North Carolina since the early 1800s, Stephen's Nonconnah and Pisgah Forest Potteries were the first western North Carolina potteries dedicated to the production of decorative ware.

In 1904 Stephen opened the first Nonconnah Pottery in Capleville, Tennessee, but by 1913 had moved to Skyland, North Carolina, where he opened a second pottery, also named Nonconnah. Stephen used molded forms with multicolored cameo designs on matte green to blue-gray backgrounds, but strongly influenced by the Arts and Crafts movement, he also began to make decorated forms with raised shapes of ivy, grapes, or geometric designs, glazed white.

At Pisgah Forest, Stephen incorporated elements of Asian ceramic styles through changes in the shapes and glazes he had previously used at his two Nonconnah Potteries. Stephen preferred to mix his own solid white porcelain, feeling that local clay had too many impurities to use for art glazes. Both functional tableware and oriental-styled art pottery were produced in brightly colored monochrome and crystalline glazes. Most of these wares can be identified by the embossed figure of a potter at the wheel, the logos *Pisgah Forest Pottery* or *W. Stephen*, and the year of production.

Pisgah Forest Pottery is a well-preserved craft industry still in its original site with the original kiln and clay mixer in the buildings where Stephen worked. Several workers assisted Stephen at Pisgah Forest, the most important to the pottery's production being Billy Rhodes, Herman Case, Grady Ledbetter, and Stephen's step-grandson, Thomas Case, who continued to operate Pisgah Forest Pottery on a limited basis at the turn of the twenty-first century with his wife, Dorothy.

See also: ART POTTERY; POTTERY.

—Rodney Leftwich, *Asheville, North Carolina*

Pottery

Rather than developing a distinctive Appalachian style, the forefathers of traditional Appalachian pottery brought styles and techniques with them as they moved into the region. Hence, Appalachian pottery covers a diverse ceramic range, from lead-glazed, salt-glazed, and alkaline-glazed folk pottery to mass-produced wares and art pottery. There is no unified approach to pottery that can be considered uniquely Appalachian, though potters working in the region have created wares particular to their locales. In the past, most of these were folk potters who learned community-shared designs and handcrafting technology informally, usually in a family setting, and who sold their jugs, jars, churns, pitchers, and bowls to fellow farmers for storing, preparing, and serving food and drink. Although sometimes decorated, this folk pottery is inherently functional, in contrast to the self-consciously aesthetic work more typical of school-trained studio ceramists working in present-day Appalachia.

Early potters, who did not have the means to import their basic raw material, settled where their suspicions of usable clay could be confirmed. Pockets of high-quality clay were known in Appalachia even before 1767, when Josiah Wedgwood, "father" of Staffordshire's pottery industry, sent an agent into the North Carolina mountains near present-day Franklin to dig and ship back to England a load of kaolin, a pure white clay used in making porcelain or china.

But it was not china clay that Appalachia's earliest potters sought. Both Native Americans and whites used widely occurring, impure (typically red-firing) clay to produce earthenware, a relatively soft and porous ceramic product. Native American and Euro-American earthenware traditions differed dramatically, however. Native American women made pottery by hand building and pit firing clay; some Carolina Cherokees and Catawbas still use this aboriginal technology. The European tradition, in contrast, was male dominated and featured the potter's wheel, kiln, and lead-based glaze, which came to be recognized as hazardous by the late 1700s.

Partly for that reason, the tougher stoneware, using nontoxic glazes and purer alluvial clays that fire gray or tan, eventually became the South's chief ceramic product. The Germanic stoneware tradition, with its clear glaze created by throwing salt in the kiln at the height of firing, was introduced to the East Coast in the early 1700s; by the mid-1800s it was being embraced by potters of northern Appalachia. At the same time in the Deep South, stoneware with a glaze otherwise known only in the Far East had become the norm. Probably inspired by a published description of Chinese high-firing glazes that used wood ashes and lime to help melt glassy ingredients such as feldspar, these green or brown alkaline glazes may have been developed by Abner Landrum about 1815 in the old Edgefield District of west-central South Carolina and were soon carried westward. Two other stoneware glazes were adopted in the late 1800s: brown Albany slip, a natural clay glaze from near Albany, New York, and white Bristol glaze, formulated in England.

In northern Appalachia, a large stoneware center flourished in southwestern Pennsylvania's Monongahela Valley from the 1840s until about 1915. Much of this activity was focused in the towns of Greensboro in Greene County and New Geneva in Fayette County. The earliest stoneware differed little from the general Mid-Atlantic type, characterized often by cobalt-blue stylized floral designs brushed on before firing and salt glazing. By the 1860s, local features had emerged: straight and wavy horizontal zoning bands to set off the decoration and increasing use of stencils to apply designs—the most elaborate being an eagle with outstretched wings—and names of potters or their merchant customers. The stencils suggest a more industrial approach, and, indeed, operations such as Hamilton and Jones (active from southwestern Pennsylvania in the mid- to late 1800s) expanded to factory scale without abandoning their hand-thrown wares. "Tan ware" flowerpots and pitchers, unglazed outside except for freehand decoration in Albany slip, were a distinctive Monongahela Valley product.

The southeastern section of Ohio shares with neighboring eastern Kentucky and West Virginia a rugged terrain and coal-mining economy. Associated with the coal deposits are extensive deposits of clay, which attracted small-scale potters and later served a major industry. The first factories, which replaced skilled craftsmen with more cost-effective molds and machines, opened in the 1840s at East Liverpool in Columbiana County and Zanesville in Muskingum County. Firms such as Vodrey Brothers specialized in mottled-brown, Rockingham-style wares similar to those of Bennington, Vermont, as well as banded yellow wares for the kitchen.

The study of West Virginia and eastern Kentucky pottery is still in its infancy, but two individual operations stand out. In Morgantown in Monongalia County, (West) Virginia, Jacob Foulk Jr. opened an earthenware shop about 1805, selling it in 1817 to his apprentice, John W. Thompson. A lead-glazed, lug-handled molasses jar attributed to Thompson anticipates the common mid-1800s southern stoneware jar form. His son, Greenland Thompson, began making salt-glazed stoneware in the 1840s. Near Waco in Madison County, Kentucky, on a site used for potting as early as 1809, Webster Cornelison founded the Bybee Pottery in the 1840s. Five generations later, Cornelison's descendants were still running it. At first, salt-glazed stoneware was made, but in the twentieth century, in a reversal of the usual pattern, it was determined that the local clay was more suitable for earthenware than stoneware. Colored glazes were created to match this local clay, and these are applied to a line of utilitarian table and kitchen wares, some now formed with mold-based jigger machines, others still hand thrown.

The largest pottery center in Appalachia (nearly 350 potters) was in Virginia's Shenandoah Valley. The subject of three books, this is also the most researched Virginia pottery area, due partly to interest among collectors in its more decorative wares. The Great Valley Road (now U.S. Route 11) was a major access route into the mountains, bringing settlers of German, British, and Scots-Irish ancestry. The local pottery reflected this population mix and was personified by the Bell family of potters, whose patriarch, Peter Bell, started his career in Hagerstown, Washington County, Maryland. Bell likely apprenticed under German-born John George Weis, who was potting in Hagerstown by 1755. In 1824 Bell relocated to Winchester, Frederick County, Virginia. Two of his potter sons, Samuel and Solomon, moved to Strasburg, Shenandoah County, Virginia, while another, John B., settled in Waynesboro, Franklin County, Pennsylvania.

All contributed to an identifiable Shenandoah Valley style. Early pots were finely crafted earthenware, some with underglaze decoration in colored slip (liquid clay). Later earthenwares were decorated in manganese brown or copper green over a white slip wash. Remarkable among these are hand-modeled lion doorstops by Solomon and John Bell, with extruded "coleslaw" manes and whiskers and not very menacing "zipper" teeth. Inspired by English mantel ornaments, local potters used molds to make other animal figurines, especially dogs.

Among the earliest (1820s or 1830s) Shenandoah Valley stoneware potters were Manhattan-trained John Morgan, who worked in Rockbridge County, and John Miller of Strasburg, whose brushed cobalt floral designs were in the Pennsylvania style. By the 1850s, stoneware, typically dark gray in color, was being widely produced; among the more unusual items were cemetery headstone slabs with cobalt-blue inscriptions. A few factories, such as the Strasburg Steam Pottery, opened in 1891 but could not compete with more established industrial operations elsewhere. By World War I, pottery making in the Shenandoah Valley had all but come to an end.

Farther south, along a westward branch of the Great Valley Road, the Great Road pottery center of Wythe and Washington Counties, Virginia, and adjacent Sullivan County, Tennessee, was active from the late eighteenth to late nineteenth centuries. Potters such as the Cain family of Sullivan County (which operated until the early 1900s) made earthenware distinguished by bulbous forms and bold manganese daubing, the jars often having semidetached, arched handles like those on German stoneware.

In the Nolichucky Valley of Washington County, Tennessee, Charles Decker opened his Keystone Pottery in 1872. German-born Decker began his American career by working for Richard Remmey in Philadelphia, and his east Tennessee stonewares retained much of this Pennsylvania character. Among the specialized items made by Decker and his sons were wheel-thrown, salt-glazed grave markers. Samuel Smith, William Grindstaff, and the semi-industrial Weaver and Brothers Company also made stoneware in Knoxville, Knox County, Tennessee. Fully industrial east Tennessee pottery operations were the Herty Turpentine Cup Company of Soddy-Daisy, Hamilton County, where cups for collecting pine resin were machine-molded from 1905 to 1940, and Southern Potteries, Inc., of Erwin, Unicoi County, where hand-painted dinnerware, later marked *Blue Ridge*, was manufactured from 1917 to 1957.

North Carolina is a transitional state in the production of folk stoneware. The upper South's salt-glaze tradition is found in the center of the state, while the lower South's alkaline-glaze tradition prevailed in the western part, including mountainous Buncombe County. At Candler, William Penland operated Jugtown Pottery, not to be confused with the famous Seagrove shop of the same name. Edward Stone, who was trained in South Carolina's old Edgefield District in the alkaline-glaze tradition, began working at Jugtown Pottery in the mid-1840s. Three other potters from South Carolina joined Stone at this shop, which produced stoneware with a dark brown ash glaze that contained iron ore. At Weaverville, brothers David and George Donkel established Reems Creek Pottery in 1897. William Barnhill's 1917 photographs show a rustic operation that could be interpreted as stereotypically Appalachian but was in fact typical of the western Piedmont's Catawba Valley, where the Donkels were trained. In Arden, North Carolina, sixth-generation potters Davis and Javan Brown of Atlanta opened the Brown Pottery in about 1923 and added, in the 1930s, a line of machine-molded cookware to more traditional hand-thrown face jugs and churns, mostly glazed with Albany slip.

Oscar L. Bachelder and Walter B. Stephen were Buncombe County potters of a different stripe. A third-generation utilitarian potter from Wisconsin, Bachelder worked all over the country before settling at Luther to open Omar Khayyam Pottery in 1914. There, in his sixties, he realized his dream of making a more artistic product and became known for his refined shapes and mirror-black glaze. His friend Stephen was also a midwesterner, whose artist mother took up potting after the family moved to Tennessee. At Pisgah Forest Pottery, which he opened near Arden in 1920, Stephen perfected his mother's technique of building up designs in brushed layers of porcelain slip over a colored ground to create cameo wares with pioneer scenes such as an oxen-pulled covered wagons. The ceramic branch of the Arts and Crafts movement inspired Stephen and Bachelder. Studio pottery resulting from that movement is now taught at the Penland School of Crafts in Mitchell County, North Carolina, begun in 1923 as part of the craft revival.

South Carolina pottery research has emphasized the old Edgefield District, but there was also an upland center known as Jugtown, near Gowensville, on the border of Greenville and Spartanburg Counties. William Henson was an early potter in South Carolina's Jugtown, and in the late

1980s his great-grandson Billy Henson revived his family's tradition of alkaline-glazed stoneware there. African American potter Rich Williams opened a shop in this community in the late 1800s, at the same time the Whelchels, another local pottery family, were decorating their alkaline-glazed wares with dark brown stenciling.

In Georgia there were fewer than a dozen shops in true mountain terrain, but the state's largest pottery center was in the foothills, at Mossy Creek, below Cleveland in southern White County. Among the more localized alkaline-glazed forms made here were cylindrical kraut jars for pickling cabbage and multinecked flower jugs to display cut flowers. The Meaders family entered the craft late, becoming the best known of some eighty local potters by keeping the tradition alive long after others abandoned it. There were potters at Mossy Creek as early as the 1820s, including Frederick Davidson from Buncombe County, North Carolina. Abraham, one of Davidson's five potter sons, migrated to Sand Mountain in DeKalb County, Alabama, in the late 1850s. At about the same time, William Dorsey and William Pitchford, also from Mossy Creek, began potting in Itawamba County in northeastern Mississippi. Both destinations became stoneware centers.

Gillsville, Hall County, arose as another north Georgia center in the late 1800s as potters from Mossy Creek to the north and Barrow County to the south gravitated there. Among them were the Hewells, who came to specialize in unglazed, hand-thrown horticultural wares in the 1940s. In the 1980s, as a sideline to this garden pottery for which Gillsville is known, the Hewells revived the wood-fired, alkaline-glazed stoneware with which the family began six generations earlier.

In 1935 William J. Gordy opened his Georgia Art Pottery at Cartersville in the hills of Bartow County. Unfulfilled by the middle Georgia utilitarian tradition inherited from his father, Gordy worked as a journeyman to broaden his ceramic horizons and was introduced to glaze chemistry. At Cartersville, he built his reputation on refined stoneware echoing the shapes of his early folk training but with glazes such as his trademark Mountain Gold, with its variegated coloring in autumnal leaf shades of brown and tan, that went far beyond the limited palette of traditional wares. A life member of the Southern Highland Handicraft Guild, Gordy died in 1993; grandson Darrell Adams maintains his studio.

See also: ART POTTERY; CRAFT REVIVAL (FOLKLORE AND FOLKLIFE); FACE JUGS.

—John A. Burrison, *Georgia State University*

John A. Burrison, *Brothers in Clay: The Story of Georgia Folk Pottery* (1983); H. E. Comstock, *The Pottery of the Shenandoah Valley Region* (1994); Charles G. Zug III, *Turners and Burners: The Folk Potters of North Carolina* (1986).

Qualla Arts and Crafts Mutual

The Qualla Arts and Crafts Mutual is the oldest American Indian crafts cooperative in the United States. Organized in 1946 as the Cherokee Indian Crafts Co-op, this organization and several members became well known in ethnic and folk art circles. As an official tribal enterprise of the Eastern Band of Cherokee Indians, Qualla Arts has been a critical economic resource for tribal craftspeople for more than a half-century, especially when low-paying, seasonal tourism jobs were the primary source of local employment. Membership in Qualla Arts has brought income, as well as annual organizational dividends, to generations of Eastern Cherokee craftspeople and their families. As a tribally operated business responsible for encouraging and ensuring continuation of quality traditional and innovated Cherokee crafts, Qualla Arts has served as a singular example of self-determination and pride for Eastern Band members. From the 1960s to the 1980s, Qualla Arts, in cooperation with the U.S. Department of the Interior's Indian Arts and Crafts Board, also assisted with workshops for and promotion of the crafts of other southeastern Indian tribes.

The foundation for Qualla Arts was laid informally several decades before its official founding. The advent of automobiles in western North Carolina and the Cherokee Fall Festival, first held in 1914, marked the beginning of mass tourism into the heart of Cherokee, North Carolina. While the Great Depression temporarily slowed tourism, two key events during the era held great significance for the Eastern Band and for Qualla Arts. The Great Smoky Mountains National Park opened in 1934 with Cherokee as its eastern entry point. Then, in 1935, the Indian Arts and Crafts Board was created as part of the federal "Indian New Deal" to offer tribes technical and marketing assistance regarding their crafts. In Cherokee, these events prompted the Bureau of Indian Affairs, Department of Agriculture, and Eastern Band to initiate craft classes taught by Eastern Cherokee master craftspeople in the tribal high school. A small crafts shop was opened to market students' handiwork. A decade later, in 1946, fifty-three Cherokee craftspeople, some of them teachers and graduates of the school craft classes, and many others who learned their crafts at home in daily practice, came together to form the Cherokee Indian Crafts Co-op to obtain better prices for their crafts from visitors. Crafts represented in the early years included basket weaving, wood carving, pottery, beadwork, loom and finger weaving, rag doll making, and metalworking. In 1954 the cooperative incorporated as the nonprofit Qualla Arts and Crafts Mutual, Inc.

At the beginning of the twenty-first century, Qualla Arts consisted of more than three hundred members, each accepted through juried assessment of their craft products. The increased availability of year-round jobs coupled with annual payments from tribal gaming meant that increasing numbers of Eastern Cherokees no longer relied on Qualla Arts for income and marketing but made and sold crafts for personal fulfillment and a sense of ethnic pride. In 2002–3 Qualla Arts sponsored a series of workshops conducted by Eastern Cherokee river cane basket weavers to renew interests and skills in their traditional craft.

See also: ARROWMONT SCHOOL OF ARTS AND CRAFTS; CABIN CREEK QUILTS; CRAFT COOPERATIVES.

—Betty J. Duggan, *Peabody Museum of Archaeology and Ethnology, Harvard University*

Betty J. Duggan, "Tourism, Cultural Authenticity, and the Native Crafts Cooperative: The Eastern Cherokee Experience," in *Tourism and Culture: An Applied Perspective*, ed. Erve Chambers (1997); Rodney L. Leftwich, *Arts and Crafts of the Cherokee* (1970).

Quilts

Patchwork quilts are among the most desirable of the handcrafted items available in shops throughout the Appalachian region. Valued for their bright colors, appealing patterns, and delicate stitching, quilts are purchased as examples of American folk art and as colorful contributions to home decor.

Quilts on a clothesline near Berea, Kentucky, c. 1940. Valued for their bright colors, appealing patterns, and delicate stitching, quilts are among the most sought after of the handcrafted items available in shops throughout the Appalachian region. During the first half of the twentieth century, quilts, often perceived as a link with America's preindustrial past, were a means of financial support for many low-income families.

Technically, a quilt is a bedcover constructed of textile layers. Typically the top layer is made of patchwork, which may be pieced in a combination of individual fabric patches, or appliquéd, in which fabric motifs are cut out and sewn to a larger background. The completed quilt top is then joined to a filling and plain backing, using rows of hand or machine stitching. The lines of quilting stitches joining the layers together form an additional decorative element. The word *quilting* can refer specifically to the process of stitching the layers together or more generally to the entire quilt-making process.

Although it is commonly assumed that American quilting originated from the necessary converting of discarded fabric into much-needed warm bedcovers, research indicates that colonial and pioneer families actually had access to a variety of bedcovers, including purchased or home-woven blankets or coverlets, heavy woven bed rugs, and animal furs and skins. Throughout the eighteenth and early nineteenth centuries, textiles were valuable commodities, and any fabric scraps not repeatedly recycled for household use could be sold for making paper. Pioneer families, including those on the Appalachian frontier, traded forest and agricultural products for textiles they could not supply themselves.

Quilt patterns may be traditional or original. Among the hundreds of traditional patterns, the Log Cabin, Double Wedding Ring, and Eight-Pointed Star variations are among some of the most widely recognized. A few American quilt patterns developed in the late eighteenth and early nineteenth centuries, derived from the design traditions of European immigrants. A century later, the number, variety, and distribution of quilt patterns had increased dramatically due to the availability of print sources. Quilters who did not have access to published sources or who chose not to use them created their own designs, taking inspiration from the leaves and flowers in their gardens or from architectural, celestial, or imaginary shapes and images. Although it is often assumed that the rustic Log Cabin quilt pattern is of pioneer origin, research suggests that the pattern developed first in urban areas, perhaps even in Europe, sometime in the mid-nineteenth century. While there are no quilt patterns specific to the Appalachian region as a whole, subtle local designs and individual variations are found throughout the area.

Historically, the materials considered suitable for quilts consisted primarily of factory-made woven fabrics, usually cotton but occasionally wool or silk. Although there are examples of nineteenth-century quilts made from remnants of home-woven textiles, these fabrics were not finely woven enough to be cut into intricate shapes without raveling. Quilters purchased printed or plain cotton fabrics for both clothing and quilts. Some women purchased less expensive undyed fabric and dyed it at home using natural or synthetic dyes.

Unlike those needed for weaving, the basic tools and material required for quilting are simple. Historically, needles, thread, and scissors were found in virtually all households. When scissors were not available, fabric could be torn into strips or cut with a knife. Although many men developed sufficient skill to do simple mending, women were more actively encouraged to develop skills in both plain and fancy sewing. Plain sewing included the construction of simple pieced patchwork, while appliqué, embroidery, and fine hand quilting were considered fancy work. There is evidence that in many early American households children of both sexes were taught to sew.

The invention and wide adoption of the sewing machine in the second half of the nineteenth century changed the way American women sewed. Because the construction of clothing took less time, some women found more time for fancy work, including quilting. Well-to-do families, including those in the towns and larger farms throughout Appalachia, purchased sewing machines, while poorer families continued to sew by hand. During the late nineteenth century, machine-sewn clothing and quilts signified a family's favorable economic status. By about 1900, when sewing machines had become commonplace, fashionable women rediscovered the social value of hand sewing. The Colonial Revival movement encouraged a nostalgic return to early American values, and quilters throughout the twentieth century were encouraged by popular writers to sew their quilts by hand.

The Colonial Revival was responsible not only for encouraging women to make quilts like their grandmothers had, but also for creating a market for these quilts among urban families. Particularly during the 1920s, the 1960s, and the 1980s, cottage industries supplied finished quilts to shops and department stores in major cities, as well as to local and regional craft outlets catering to tourists. Purchasers valued the quilts as a perceived link with America's preindustrial past, and some may also have derived satisfaction from providing support for low-income families, including those in the Appalachian South.

Because of their size and complexity, quilts require a significant investment of time and expertise. Quilters who sell their work must balance the value of their time and the cost of the materials with the price a buyer is willing to pay for the finished quilt. Because Appalachia is widely viewed as having a preindustrial economy, buyers expect to be able to buy high-quality quilts at low cost. The history of the commerce in Appalachian quilts reflects the interplay between these two competing factors.

Rural Appalachian women historically have had relatively few opportunities for paid employment. Home-based work, including making quilts for sale, has provided one economic alternative. The participation of women in making quilts for sale includes individuals marketing their own work directly to consumers, small cooperative production and marketing efforts, and companies that contract with individual workers to produce parts of quilts.

The quilts offered for sale are generally different from those made for home use. In order to satisfy consumers, a quilter must produce aesthetically pleasing work, which often requires attention to current trends in home decorating. She must also be able to standardize her work to produce quilts of a predetermined size, pattern, and color combination, as well as achieve a degree of technical quality. In contrast, a quilter making a quilt for her own personal use may try a variety of patterns, experiment with unusual color combinations, and choose her own measure of technical skill. Quilts made for home use often depend on sewing leftovers or store remnants and include a variety of fabrics, while quilts made for sale more often are made from coordinated fabrics purchased especially for a particular quilt.

Pre–World War I economic-development efforts to help women earn money in the depressed rural Appalachian economy may have promoted quilting, as well as the better-known weaving and carving craft industries. Although craft cooperatives in the early twentieth century included some quilt-making activity, by the 1930s the market was dominated by commercial companies operating in Kentucky. A bulletin published by the Women's Bureau of the United States Department of Labor in 1935 identified twelve quilt companies headquartered in Breckinridge, Fayette, Hardin, Jefferson, Larue, and Meade Counties. These companies reported contacts with over a thousand workers, mostly women working at home. Companies typically supplied the women with materials and collected the finished works, sometimes by mail. More often, the women were required to pick up and deliver the goods themselves. The companies sold the quilts either through their own shops or at department stores in cities such as New York and Chicago. Retailers interviewed for the Women's Bureau survey reported that they could market Appalachian handcrafted textiles more readily if the items were available in related product lines, such as coordinated baby clothing and bedding, and if the products could be continually redesigned to stay ahead of less expensive imported imitations.

Some quilters were able to make higher wages than workers in other craft media, although they reported that in order to do so they had to work ten-hour days and require other family members to assume household responsibilities. In 1933 quilters reported earnings of one to five dollars per week, compared with factory weekly wages of twelve to seventeen dollars. Of course, many families lived in areas where factory jobs were not available. The survey indicated that home craft workers reported little control over the nature or availability of their work, the wages they received, or fluctuations in the market. The onset of World War II diverted fabric production to military purposes and provided additional employment options for women. During the 1950s, Americans generally preferred modern, factory-made bedding to quilts or woven coverlets.

In the 1960s, renewed economic-development efforts as part of the federal government's War on Poverty encouraged rural low-income people, particularly those in Appalachia, to develop marketable craft skills. A variety of commercial, cooperative, individual, and government-sponsored marketing efforts provided outlets for quilts and other crafts. Although the Southern Highland Handicraft Guild was formed in 1930 to facilitate the production and marketing of Appalachian crafts, apparently no quilters were accepted as individual members until the 1970s. This suggests quilting was seen by the guild and its affiliate centers as a production craft, as it had become in the 1930s, rather than as one of individual creativity. During the final three decades of the twentieth century, however, the guild admitted a number of quilters, including both production centers and individuals. A growing appreciation of quilting as an art form and recognition that quilters need adequate compensation for their work allows skilled quilters to charge higher prices for their work.

In the 1990s, in response to a desire among domestic consumers to buy affordable quilts, American companies began to contract with their counterparts in other countries, such as Haiti and China, to produce American-style quilts. These imported quilts are often the work of entire families working for low wages on projects over which they have no control. Their situation is very much like that of Kentucky craft industry quilters of the 1930s. The impact of imported quilts in America has been varied. Traditional American quilters attempting to sell their works have found they must cut their prices in order to be competitive. Quilters who do not depend on their craft for income have expressed fear that the perceived desirability of American-made quilts is devalued by the larger volume, lesser quality, and lower prices of look-alike imported quilts. Just as in the 1930s, the conditions affecting the sale of quilts in America at the turn of the twenty-first century depended upon larger economic and fashion trends.

As the Appalachian economy changed during the late twentieth century, fewer mountain women depended upon making quilts in order to support themselves and their families. In recent times, those who found the activity to be enjoyable continued to make quilts for their own use and for gifts to family and friends. The influx of population from other parts of the country in the late twentieth century brought new residents, some seeking to experience a simpler way of life by working with their hands in craft work such as quilting. Native-born and more recently arrived Appalachian quilters joined together to form guilds and clubs whose purposes are social and artistic rather than economic. Quilt guilds throughout the Appalachian region continued to hold regular meetings, sponsor exhibitions and quilt shows, provide educational classes and workshops for their own members or for others, and frequently make quilts for charity, either as direct donations or through fund-raising events.

Quilters practice a wide range of new techniques and skills, including various forms of surface design and embellishment. While many quilters enjoy making quilts by hand, the use of the sewing machine is recognized as a valid option for both making the quilt top and for the actual quilting.

In addition to the activities of local guilds and clubs, many states sponsor quilt documentation projects with the goal of recording data on quilts and quilters in each state. Although these state projects have not always succeeded in identifying commensurate numbers of quilts from mountain counties, they nonetheless have compiled a body of useful data for a more informed understanding of the scope, regional variety, and historical and functional contexts of Appalachian quilts.

See also: COTTAGE INDUSTRIES (BUSINESS, INDUSTRY, AND TECHNOLOGY); CRAFT REVIVAL (FOLKLORE AND FOLKLIFE); WAR ON POVERTY (GOVERNMENT).

—Laurel Horton, *Seneca, South Carolina*

Ellen Fickling Eanes, *North Carolina Quilts* (1988); Bets Ramsey and Merikay Waldvogel, *The Quilts of Tennessee* (1986); Fawn Valentine, *West Virginia Quilts and Quiltmakers: Echoes from the Hills* (2000).

Rug Making

In Appalachia, the craft of rug making primarily derived from English, Scottish, and Scandinavian traditions brought to the region by settlers of the eighteenth century who wove

Bruton Parish, Williamsburg, Virginia
(Originated by Us)

Wedgewood
(From an Old Design)

4

Historic Scenes
Made to be used either as wall hangings or as floor rugs.

The "Bruton Parish" Rug
(Originated by Us)

The Parish dates from 1632. The Church was built in 1710. Four Presidents of the United States, Washington, Jefferson, Monroe, and Tyler, have worshiped within its walls.

There is much shading in the soft brick red of the old Church and the greens of the vine over it. Although most of the old houses which have been restored in Williamsburg are white, our artist sees them in the rug in shades of soft lavenders, greys, browns, and tans.

The "Wedgewood" Rug
(Originated by Us)

This rug has been copied from a rare old plate and the colors used are similar to those used in the Bruton Parish rug.

The "Country Squire" Rug

(Originated by Us from an Old Hunting Scene)
A delightful rug for a Hunting Lodge, Den, Library or Living room.

5

Pages from a Rosemont catalog advertising hand-hooked rugs, 1932. Enterprises such as Rosemont ran advertisements in national home-decorating magazines, and thousands of hooked rugs were sold from the 1930s through the 1970s.

rag rugs from scraps of material. Rugs were made to be cheap and practical, covering cold wood or earthen floors and blocking drafts from under doors. Appalachian rug making as a craft known outside the region flourished during the craft revival in the early part of the twentieth century. The height of the Appalachian rug-making industry came during the first few decades of the twentieth century. Beginning with a gradual decline in the industry after the 1930s, most handcrafted rugs were foreign made by the end of the century, though there was a short-lived resurgence of the industry in the region during the 1980s. Hooked rugs in Appalachia provided opportunities for both financial gain and artistic expression.

The two types of rugs commonly associated with Appalachia are hooked rugs, which are hooked, or punched, through a stiff backing, and woven rag rugs, sometimes called loopers when loops of material are used (similar to the pot holders made by children as arts and crafts projects). A third common method of making rugs is braiding, which, in its simplest form, utilizes agricultural materials such as cornhusks, straw, rushes, cotton, or wool. Braiding is not characteristic of Appalachian rugs and remains primarily a northeastern style, though the craft did spread into the region, particularly with the arrival of mission schools in the first quarter of the twentieth century.

Rug hooking was not common in Appalachia prior to the twentieth century, but this style of rug quickly became associated with the region in the early 1900s. Recent scholarship suggests that the supposedly traditional craft probably arrived in the mountains with the mission schools movement (c. 1910 until the mid-1950s). The schools taught hooked rug making to local women as a means of generating income, and the rugs became very popular decorative items throughout the nation. In particular, rugs became a major source of income for western North Carolina women, who soon learned to gear their craft to a market economy. Nearly all hooked rugs made in twentieth-century Appalachia were created for sale in upscale department stores outside the region such as Neiman Marcus. Made to cover the floors of the rich and well-to-do, the rugs were rarely laid in the homes of the makers.

In an effort to maximize production, makers developed machines to punch rugs, as opposed to hooking them by hand. Sometimes called turfing machines, these labor-saving devices were handmade by local craftsmen or purchased from a company such as the northeastern-based Susan Burr Company. Machine punching massively increased rug production for commercial profit and contributed significantly to the escalation of the southern Appalachian rug-making industry.

The traditional nature of the punched variety of hooked rugs is questionable, as punched hooked rugs in Appalachia have been a commercial venture almost from their introduction into handicraft circles in western North Carolina, east Tennessee, and southwest Virginia. The hooked-rug industry in Madison, Buncombe, and Yancey Counties of North Carolina and Unicoi County, Tennessee, was spurred by consumer demands resulting from feature articles in the *Asheville Citizen-Times* newspaper during the 1890s, as well as out of various national women's magazines, rather than growing from a handed-down tradition.

One significant outlet for Appalachian hand-hooked rugs was Rosemont in Marion, Virginia. Established and operated by Laura Copenhaver, Rosemont offered a catalog of hand-hooked rugs along with canopies, coverlets, and other items. Patterns were designed and yarn dyed at Rosemont before being sent to local makers to hook into finished rugs and sold under the Rosemont label. Enterprises such as Rosemont ran advertisements in national home-decorating magazines, and thousands of hooked rugs were sold from the 1930s through the mid-1970s. In addition to individual customers, hooked rugs were also sold to northern department stores.

Any type of fabric can be used, including scraps, but hooked rugs for commercial sale are usually made of more expensive wool strips, or yarn, pulled through a tough backing such as burlap with a rug hook. These rugs were durable and featured intricate patterns, often landscapes or floral patterns, and were sometimes displayed on walls as tapestries. A smaller type of hooked rug made to cover chair seats was also very popular and commonly sold well through the 1980s, mostly through advertisements in magazines.

Though some rug makers worked from home in a cottage industry, many also worked under assembly-line conditions at the Madison County Rug Shop, in Mars Hill, North Carolina. Owned and operated by Jake Buckner, the shop at one time employed more than a hundred rug workers, who were paid to complete different steps in the rug-hooking process.

At a time when small-farm incomes were failing to adequately support rural families, the rug shops provided supplemental jobs. The industry allowed previously unemployed women to contribute to the family income, many for the first time, helping farmers to remain viable and even climb out of debt. The additional income of rug hooking eased families of southern Appalachia through non-crop-producing months and in some cases allowed tenant farmers to purchase the land they worked.

The manufacture of hooked rugs and its identification as a cottage industry depended on several factors. Not all of the rug makers within the industry worked at home, and many were not the sole proprietors of the revenue from the sale of their product. Many rug makers worked through a reseller, such as Rosemont in Virginia, or the Treasure Chest in Asheville, North Carolina, who in turn did business with department stores and other outlets. Rugs also were sold in roadside stands up and down the East Coast.

Some families, however, did work for themselves out of their homes and were more appropriately considered part of a cottage industry. Individual operations varied from family to family, but elder daughters were the main producers of hooked and punched rugs. Men of the families, usually uncles or fathers, helped sell the rugs and constructed the frames for punching them. Occasionally, men also helped punch rugs, but usually this was left to the women.

Elder family members and children cut rags and scraps left over from regional textile mills into long strips to be punched into rug backings. These strips were dyed with colors according to market demands. Because they were pliable, easily dyed, and abundant, by-products of hosiery mills were a common choice of the rug hands. Later, as commercial demand for hooked rugs increased, rug makers switched to strips of wool for the fabric's dye-holding qualities, aesthetic appeal, and durability.

Whether in a school program, a business such as Rosemont, or a family operation, decisions were made based on market demand. Popular colors and design motifs were used for the patterns, with themes such as flowers (the dogwood), leaves, animals, and idyllic scenes (mountains and cottages, winding paths, smoke curling out of chimneys). A combination of stove blacking and kerosene rubbed onto the back of the paper pattern transferred the pattern for the rug design to burlap. The strips, or wool yarn, were then threaded through the turfing machine to be punched into the burlap backing, which was stretched taut on a wooden frame. The turfing machine then did the actual punching and helped create a large quantity of rugs in a short amount of time.

More commonly associated with Appalachian tradition are rag rugs, made from a wide variety of scrap material and woven on a loom. Intended to cover drafty floors in bedrooms, halls, and kitchens, most are made of cotton or wool scraps from old blankets, housedresses, jackets, jeans, and other worn-out clothes. They are characteristically multicolored, inexpensive, and washable. When the "country look" was popularized in the 1970s and 1980s by national magazines such as *Country Living*, *Country Home*, and *Early American Life*, these simple rugs became a profitable business for entire families.

The mass production of cotton tube socks in textile mills such as those of South Carolina resulted in millions of stretchy machine knitted loops easy to dye and sold by the pound as factory scraps. Men and women around these mills in Spartanburg and Gaffney bought or built simple four-harness floor looms to weave small area rugs. The sock scraps, or loopers, were sold unsorted and varied from week to week, depending on what the mill was weaving. Family members old and young made long chains from the loopers, sorting through colors to find combinations that were the most marketable. The resulting chains of loopers were then woven into colorful rugs with a rustic appearance, no two of which were exactly alike.

Loopers were exceedingly popular for about a decade, providing work mostly for unemployed textile workers and their families, many of whom had no prior training or even a real interest in weaving as a craft. As opposed to the previous hooked-rug industry, most families sold their woven rag rugs themselves, either to shops or directly to the consumer. Makers and extended family members traveled across southern Appalachia selling stacks of looper rugs at flea markets, roadside stands, and wholesale to craft shops and country decorators. Fashion changed in the early 1990s, and the country look developed a Victorian flair. Cotton sock-top looper rugs all but disappeared.

The close of rug-hooking businesses and the dwindling of cottage industries in general may be attributed primarily to two factors. First, the wage law, created by Franklin D. Roosevelt's Fair Labor Standards Act of 1938 and the U.S. Department of Labor's Wage and Hour Division, set a standard wage for the mountain handicraft industry that smaller hooked-rug businesses had difficulty meeting. Secondly, the Great Depression ended, the national economy recovered, and the United States entered World War II, gearing up factories and industries across the nation. Many new jobs less tedious and better paying than hooking rugs were created. The combination of mandatory minimum wages and competition from other industries for workers proved too much for Appalachian rug makers. Eventually, the industry relocated mostly to Mexico, where reduced labor costs provided better profit margins for companies.

See also: CRAFT REVIVAL (FOLKLORE AND FOLKLIFE); FIRESIDE INDUSTRIES; PEACOCK ALLEY.

—Cassie Robinson, *Mars Hill College*

Jane S. Becker, *Selling Tradition: Appalachia and the Construction of an American Folk, 1930–1940* (1998); Pauline Cheek, *Hooking Past to Future by Hand* (1983); Allen H. Eaton, *Handicrafts of the Southern Highlands* (1937).

Sand Mountain Pottery

Scholars and collectors of southern folk pottery prize nineteenth-century Alabama stoneware manufactured in the Belcher's Gap/Rodenton area of Sand Mountain in DeKalb County. The pottery produced in this watershed between the Coosa and Tennessee River systems in northeast Alabama is made of fine clay with ash- or lime-based alkaline glazes often scored with a zoned wavy-line decoration. The most famous Sand Mountain pottery is double-dipped; that is, it displays both the light green lime glaze and the darker green ash glaze on the same piece of pottery.

Double-dipped "Alabama churn" made in late-nineteenth-century Sand Mountain, Alabama. The pottery produced in the watershed between the Coosa and Tennessee River systems in northeast Alabama is made of fine clay with ash- or lime-based alkaline glazes often scored with a zoned wavy-line decoration.

The members of the Davidson (or Davison) family, who came from White County, Georgia, in the late 1850s, were the first potters to work these smooth, uniformly textured clays. They made large storage jars and jugs with a runny brown-green alkaline glaze.

After the Civil War, the Davidsons left the area and another group of potters moved to Sand Mountain. Their work exhibited a greener, shinier type of alkaline glaze highly prized by collectors today and is the pottery most often referred to as Sand Mountain. The principal potters in Sand Mountain during this period were Edmond T. Belcher (1817–1897), his son, William T. Belcher (1846–1918), his sons-in-law Thomas Jefferson Henry (1837–1921) and Archibald McPherson (1838–1909), and his grandson E. E. McPherson (1860–1942).

The later Sand Mountain potters made churns with two strap handles on one side called Alabama churns, which were sometimes dipped into two different glazes to give a two-tone effect. Their pottery often features a combing decoration resembling a fork dragged around the body of the vessel. They also made a unique form of double-lipped homebrew crock and a squatty type of half-gallon canning jar.

Because these potters were related to each other and worked side by side for three generations, their pottery shares some characteristics. One identifying feature is an indentation placed on the lower end of vessel handles. The most common makers' marks from these families are *E. E. McPherson* and *T. J. Henry, D S. Ala.* Sometimes these wares are marked or signed with the names of the potters.

Pottery making ceased in this area just before World War I, when improved roads into remote Sand Mountain and better railroads permitted northern factories to deliver mass-produced, inexpensive pottery.

See also: ART POTTERY; POTTERY.

—Joey Brackner, *Alabama State Council on the Arts*

Joey Brackner, "Made of Alabama: Alabama Folk Pottery and Its Creators," in *Made in Alabama: A State Legacy*, ed. E. Bryding Adams (1995); Joey Brackner and Ron Countryman, *Pottery from the Mountains of Alabama* (1986); Henry Willett and Joey Brackner, *The Traditional Pottery of Alabama* (1983).

Southern Highland Craft Guild

The Southern Highland Craft Guild, headquartered in Asheville, North Carolina, is the second-oldest craft organization of its kind in the country. Chartered in 1930 as the Southern Highland Handicraft Guild, the organization has played a role of national importance in traditional and contemporary American craft movements. In 2002 the guild represented nearly eight hundred craftspeople in 293 counties of nine southeastern states.

The guild had its beginnings in the late-nineteenth-century missionary movement's focus on southern Appalachia. In 1885 Frances Goodrich, a Presbyterian missionary and Yale graduate, moved to the Asheville area from Cleveland, Ohio. There she established schools, health-care projects, and home-improvement programs for local families. Goodrich founded Allanstand Cottage Industries in 1895, which she relocated from Madison County, North Carolina, to downtown Asheville in 1917.

In 1928, at Penland, North Carolina, Goodrich met with other craft promoters of the day, including Lucy Morgan, the founder of Penland School, Olive Dame Campbell, founder of John C. Campbell Folk School, and Allen H. Eaton, the Appalachian field representative for the Russell Sage Foundation. These leaders discussed the possibility of creating an organization that could further what each was doing individually. The new organization would act as an umbrella organization without harming any of the smaller institutions doing similar work. This meeting led to the founding the Southern Mountain Handicraft Guild, later renamed the Southern Highland Handicraft Guild.

Shortly after the guild's founding, Goodrich donated Allanstand Cottage Industries to serve as the financial foundation from which the guild educated, marketed, and preserved craft work throughout the region. Initially, the guild was comprised only of institutional members, though craftspeople associated with these institutions were entitled to membership benefits. The first individuals were not juried into the membership until 1933.

These early members, both institutional and individual, enjoyed benefits that included an outstanding public relations machine as well as direct connections to high political offices: the guild's exhibition of Appalachian crafts, cosponsored by the wives of Presidents Herbert Hoover, Calvin Coolidge, and Franklin D. Roosevelt, was held at the Corcoran Gallery of Art in Washington, D.C., after its debut at Blacksburg, Virginia. This exhibition created the impression of the newly formed guild as the government-sanctioned authority on Appalachian crafts—an impression that proved to be useful in promoting the region's artisans.

The guild prospered during the Great Depression in spite of hard times. It was also during these years that the Works Progress Administration began the Blue Ridge Parkway, a scenic roadway from the Shenandoah National Park in Virginia to the Great Smoky Mountains National Park in North Carolina. Again utilizing political contacts in Washington, the guild forged a relationship with the Blue Ridge Parkway project organizers, a relationship that continues to be the guild's most important alliance. The parkway currently hosts two guild retail facilities.

During the 1940s, education became a priority for the guild, which hired professional staff to implement them. With the improving economy and a working relationship with the Blue Ridge Parkway, the guild was ready to organize its first major craft fair. In 1948 the Craft Fair of the Southern Highlands opened in Gatlinburg, Tennessee. Considered a great success, the fair featured demonstrations, exhibitions, mountain music, and the opportunity for fairgoers to interact with working Appalachian craftspeople. It quickly became an annual tradition that has continued into the twenty-first century for thousands of people. In the late 1940s and early 1950s the guild also opened several new retail shops at Blowing Rock, North Carolina, Norris, Tennessee, and New York City's Rockefeller Plaza.

The 1960s brought about great change, both in the southern mountains and in the guild. Robert Gray, of the

Worcester Craft Center in Massachusetts, was hired as director in 1961 and oversaw a move to new headquarters in Asheville, the opening of a large-scale wholesale business (1967–77), and the hiring of an expanded staff. Gray also began to work with the Blue Ridge Parkway on what would become the guild's current headquarters and flagship operation, the Blue Ridge Parkway's Folk Art Center. This $3.2-million facility, which opened in 1980, was a joint effort of the guild, the Appalachian Regional Commission, and the National Park Service. With more than twenty-eight thousand square feet of exhibition, library, auditorium, and retail space, the center quickly became the most visited attraction on the parkway.

The guild also operates a craft shop inside the historic home of textile merchant Moses H. Cone, located just north of Blowing Rock, North Carolina. Known as the "denim king," Cone, who was born of German immigrant parents in Jonesborough, Tennessee, built Flat Top Manor in the 1890s on thirty-five hundred acres as a grand country estate. In 1950 the estate was opened to the public as the Moses H. Cone Memorial Park. The Parkway Craft Center inside Flat Top Manor features contemporary and traditional mountain crafts as well as demonstrations by guild craftsmen during the summer months.

With four retail shops in three cities, active outreach programs of traveling exhibitions and membership meetings, and strong financial resources and support, the Southern Highland Craft Guild continues to operate under its original mission to meet the needs of regional and national craft communities.

See also: GOODRICH, FRANCES; JOHN C. CAMPBELL FOLK SCHOOL.

—Andrew Glasgow, *The Furniture Society*

Jane S. Becker, *Selling Tradition: Appalachia and the Construction of an American Folk, 1930–1940* (1998); Allen H. Eaton, *Handicrafts of the Southern Highlands* (1937); Frances Louisa Goodrich, *Mountain Homespun* (1931).

Southern Industrial Educational Association

After attending a missionary meeting in Chautauqua, New York, at the turn of the twentieth century, Martha Sawyer Gielow resolved to find a way to provide better educational opportunities for Appalachian children. In 1905 she founded the Southern Industrial Educational Association, Inc., and used her organization to promote the settlement school system of education with its curriculum of agriculture, horticulture, handicraft, and domestic science. The idea was to give children practical instruction in skills necessary to make a living from their rural communities. Headquarters were established in Washington, D.C., where the subject of education in rural America was under discussion by federal government officials.

Gielow, a native of Alabama, successfully convinced prominent and wealthy Americans to serve as officers and trustees of the association. Among them were Woodrow Wilson, then president of Princeton University; North Carolina Episcopal Bishop Joseph Blount Cheshire; Governor Edwin Warfield of Maryland; former U.S. Attorney General Charles Bonaparte; U.S. Senator John Sharp Williams of Mississippi; and former Ambassador to Italy Thomas Nelson Page. Seth Shephard, chief justice of the Court of Appeals in the District of Columbia, served as president for many years.

To raise money for her organization, Gielow traveled across the country giving ardent speeches at meetings of the Daughters of the American Revolution, the United Daughters of the Confederacy, and other patriotic societies. Auxiliary chapters were formed in New York, Maryland, California, Virginia, Alabama, and Pennsylvania. Each auxiliary had its own fund-raising events and membership drives and gave a report at the association's annual meeting in Washington. Due to the endeavors of President Mary Mildred Sullivan, the New York Auxiliary was the major financial contributor. For nineteen years, Sullivan was a member of the association's board of trustees, during which time she served as president of the New York Auxiliary, personally funded student scholarships, headed various subcommittees, and used her significant social and political contacts to raise money. Sullivan and her son George established the Algernon Sidney Sullivan Foundation before her death in 1933 to ensure the scholarships would continue long after their deaths.

The *Quarterly Magazine of the Southern Industrial Educational Association* was first printed in 1909. Initially a small booklet containing only association minutes, reports, and subscription blanks, it expanded over the years to include a variety of information related to Appalachia. Articles covered everything from speech patterns and outbreaks of typhoid and hookworm to weaving, yarn-dyeing, and basket-making. Field secretaries sent in reports of medical disasters, educational advances, building designs, and heartfelt stories of impoverished mountain life written to elicit more funds.

By 1909 members raised money by sponsoring an annual display and sale of handmade mountain crafts in the Exhibition Hall of the Southern Commercial Congress held in Washington's Southern Building. The event, called the Exchange for Mountain Handicrafts, had a dual purpose. Money from the sale of the crafts provided financial assistance to mountain women who had little opportunity to market their products, and the event raised money for student scholarships, educational supplies, and improvements to facilities at industrial schools. The well-attended display also offered the association a chance to publicize its mission and recruit new members. Individual auxiliaries also held mountain craft sales, as well as large gala social events and small recitals to raise money for the national association. In 1919 the New York Auxiliary established a permanent sales room for displaying and selling mountain handicrafts.

First Lady Ellen Wilson became honorary president of the association in 1913 and actively supported the Exchange by purchasing weaving and baskets to use in the White House. After Wilson's sudden death, her daughter Margaret served as honorary president from 1914 to 1920, followed by First Lady Florence Harding from 1921 to 1924.

Over the years, items sold included dresser scarves, a variety of woven coverlets, knotted and tufted cotton spreads, hearth brooms, rag rugs, towels, turkey tail-feather fans, carved tea trays, nut bowls, gourd art, and a large collection of baskets. In the first seven years of the craft show, mountain industrial workers collected nearly $40,000, and by June 1926 almost $100,000 had been paid to workers in nine schools and 833 mountain homes. Many craftsmen used the money to pay for their children's settlement school education; in 1906 a $50 scholarship provided one Appalachian student with room and board and a year's tuition at a settlement school.

The board of trustees, agreeing that the primary work had been accomplished and that unresolved issues could be addressed by other organizations established throughout Appalachia, voted to disband on June 30, 1926. From 1906 until its dissolution, the association paid out nearly $130,000 for student scholarships and teacher salaries.

See also: BLUE MOUNTAIN ROOM; HINDMAN SETTLEMENT SCHOOL; SETTLEMENT, MISSION, AND SPONSORED SCHOOLS (EDUCATION).

—Kathleen Curtis Wilson, *University of Ulster, Northern Ireland*

Kathleen Curtis Wilson, *A Legacy for Appalachia: Mary M. Sullivan, an Icon of Nineteenth-Century Philanthropy* (2005).

Southern Potteries, Inc.

Collectors of china dinnerware scour shops and malls for items marked *Blue Ridge Hand Painted Under Glaze*, the mark of Southern Potteries, Inc., a distinctive pottery that operated in Erwin, Tennessee, until the late 1950s. At its peak in the mid-1940s and early 1950s, Southern Potteries employed more than one thousand workers who produced more than 324,000 pieces of decorated ware each week. The plant included scores of potters' wheels for flatware and a casting department for hollow ware, finishing and stamping departments, five huge kilns, a barrel-making department, and a section where the frit or glaze was produced. There was a storage area, a shipping department, a warehouse, and a section that produced the basic raw material used to make the clay bodies. Inventory was sold through various means, from large national sales organizations to traveling salesmen in small trucks who served family-owned stores throughout the South and Midwest.

Seeking to promote industry along its lines, the Clinchfield and Ohio Railroad purchased land in Erwin from the railroad's Holston Corporation for the purpose of building a pottery works at the turn of the twentieth century. The site was chosen for the availability of white kaolin clay and feldspar. Along with housing for forty workers, the original pottery works consisted of one long building with seven beehive kilns: four for glaze and decorator firing and three for bisque firing. All of the kilns were coal-fired in the beginning. In 1917 several dozen skilled pottery tradesmen and their families arrived from the areas of East Liverpool and Sebring, Ohio, and Chester, Virginia, to make traditional decal and gold-trimmed dinnerware for Clinchfield Pottery, as it was then known.

The name was changed to Southern Potteries, Inc., on April 8, 1920. Over time, it was enlarged and its name changed repeatedly. Additional kilns were added in 1923, and eventually the coal-burning kilns were replaced with modern, oil-fired continuous tunnel kilns. In one highly successful modernization, pottery owner Charles W. Foreman of Ohio introduced the technique of hand painting under the glaze. Girls and women from the area were trained in freehand painting techniques, and the quality of workmanship improved continually. By 1938, Southern Potteries had evolved into a full hand-painting operation.

This fresh, uninhibited approach, combined with a spectrum of bright, clear colors, was a welcome innovation in the world of mainly decal-decorated dinnerware with its necessarily rigid and uniform styling and is still highly prized by collectors. Mainstays such as Sears, Roebuck and Company and Quaker Oats used Blue Ridge dinnerware in advertising and promotional giveaways. The dinnerware was produced in as many as four hundred different patterns, including some for children, and eleven shapes with names such as Pie Crust, Colonial, and Woodcrest.

By the mid-1950s, Southern Potteries, Inc., found itself fighting to stay afloat in a new world of postwar imports, rising salaries, and plastic dinnerware. Despite all efforts to keep it open, the plant was finally closed on January 31, 1957, and the remaining stockholders paid off.

See also: CAROLINA, CLINCHFIELD, AND OHIO RAILWAY (TRANSPORTATION); POTTERY.

—Betty Newbound, *Sanford, North Carolina*

Diane Larkin, "Southern Potteries—Erwin, Tennessee's Dinnerware Legacy," *Blue Ridge Country* (May–June 1994); Betty and Bill Newbound, *Southern Potteries Inc.—Blue Ridge Dinnerware* (1980).

Spinning

Spinning, the ancient art of compressing and twisting fibers into thread, has historically been an important part of survival and an outlet for artistic expression in Appalachia. Several fibers can be spun by hand, but the most commonly used in Appalachia were wool, flax, and cotton. Many early settlers throughout the region kept sheep and grew flax, the plant from which linen is obtained. Cotton, grown in the Deep South, was acquired through trade. In order to spin any of these fibers, the spinner must first clean and card the fibers, separating them and making them susceptible to spinning. Crude spinning can be done by simply pulling and twisting the fibers, but strong thread can be produced either by a spinning wheel or drop spindle.

While the spinning wheel is often viewed as symbolic of the art of spinning, the drop spindle was used for thousands of years. The drop spindle, though small and highly portable, is considerably slower than a wheel and consists of a weight attached to a long wooden spindle. As the spinner controls the spindle, the weight pulls and twists the fibers as it falls, producing thread.

A more sophisticated machine is the spinning wheel, which became popular in Europe during the late Middle Ages, and later traveled to Appalachia with European settlers. In the preindustrial period, both great wheels and low wheels were common. Later, only the great wheels, also called wool wheels or walking wheels, continued to be used. The term *walking wheel* refers to the fact that the spinner walks back and forth in the process of spinning the yarn.

All great wheels are simple pulley systems with the following design: a table rests on three legs, one leg at one end and a pair at the other. A wheel post at one end holds the drive wheel, which usually has a flat rim and can have from eight to twelve spokes. A spindle post at the other end holds the spindle head where the spinning actually takes place. The spindle head can be either a simple direct drive or an accelerating minor's head. A band connects the drive wheel to the spindle whorl or pulley. There may be a tensioning device on the spindle post.

Although structurally the same as great wheels found in other parts of the country, a variation with specific characteristics developed in Appalachia. There, great wheels usually have a very tall single leg under the spindle post, giving the table a steep slant. The drive wheel has ten spokes and a relatively narrow rim of one to two inches wide, and the spindle head is a simple, direct-drive type. To adjust the tension on the drive band, a large threaded screw passes through the spindle post into a block of wood set into the table.

Regardless of the type, all spinning wheels follow the same basic principle: the wheel's spin provides the pull and twist that creates thread from the fibers. The thread is collected onto a bobbin held by the spindle. The thread can then be wound into skeins, dyed, and woven into cloth.

Spinning was traditionally practiced by women who then provided thread for their kinship groups; however, with the advent of readily available and commercially produced threads and fabric, spinning, along with weaving, nearly became a lost art. Revived interest in spinning came with the Arts and Crafts movement and with settlement schools that taught spinning as a fireside industry. Spinning and weaving allowed Appalachian people to preserve a traditional practice while providing income through the sale of hand-spun and woven items.

Spinning continues to be an important Appalachian handcraft, supporting weaving. Modern Appalachian spinners use a variety of materials, spinning machines, and techniques, incorporating tradition with innovation to keep the art of spinning alive.

See also: FIBERS; WEAVING.

—Florence Feldman-Wood, *The Spinning Wheel Sleuth*, and Elizabeth Hardy, *Caldwell Community College*

Spinning Wheels

See Spinning

Spruce Pine Pottery

Spruce Pine Pottery, originally called Muscle Shoals Pottery, is one of several early-twentieth-century Alabama potteries that exemplify the market transition from traditional functional pieces to decorative art pottery. In 1913 George Glover, an Illinois potter, moved to northwest Alabama and opened a pottery business in Spruce Pine, in Franklin County.

Glover was the first potter in the South to use a beehive-shaped kiln, previously seen only in factories in northern states and Europe, rather than the common semisubterranean southern groundhog kiln. His wares, both utilitarian and decorative, were glazed with imported brown glazes such as Michigan and Albany slips, sometimes in a two-tone fashion with a white Bristol glaze. Each piece was marked *Spruce Pine Pottery* on the bottom. The use of store-bought glazes and the idea of decorative nonutilitarian ware were both new concepts in north Alabama in 1913. These innovations were later widely adopted by potters throughout the state seeking new markets, but Spruce Pine Pottery distinguished itself by being the first to employ northern factory traditions instead of the family folk methods that had been used in the Alabama countryside for generations.

In 1925 the pottery business was sold to Grady Rauschenberg, a local entrepreneur who was not a potter. Rauschenberg employed a number of Alabama potters from the Boggs and Miller families, whose family potteries were in decline, to make the traditional utilitarian forms of churns and canning jars. To further enhance his business, Rauschenberg also hired art potters such as Frank and Ola Long to make the swirled-ware decorative pieces they had made famous at Niloak Pottery in Arkansas. Spruce Pine Pottery remained in operation until 1941, when it closed due to the start of World War II.

See also: ART POTTERY; POTTERY.

—Joey Brackner, *Alabama State Council on the Arts*

Stone Masonry

The traditional building craft of stone masonry has been practiced in Appalachia from the arrival of the first settlers until the present day. The quality of stone masonry structures varies from the crude, unskilled work of frontier people who built out of necessity to the formal architecture of quarried and cut stone used in public buildings and historic homes. Building with stone is an ancient art, modified by individual groups to meet their own unique circumstances. The European settlers who came to America brought their folk building methods from abroad. These methods were then adapted to the new environment, to the availability of materials, and to individual needs. The abundance of timber in Appalachia and its relative cheapness has always made it a more popular building material, though stone is superior in strength, durability, and natural beauty.

Granite is found along the eastern edge of the Appalachians, with marble present to the west. The most widely distributed types of stone throughout the region are sandstone and limestone. The earliest quarries in America operated in New England and the East during the seventeenth and eighteenth centuries, but by the mid- to late nineteenth century, quarries for sandstone, limestone, granite, and marble were operating in southwestern Pennsylvania, Ohio, Kentucky, and Georgia.

Problems of transportation through the narrow passes and mountainous terrain, however, continued to limit the availability of quarried stone. Transportation expense added significantly to the price of quarried stone, making it prohibitive to most Appalachian builders. For these reasons, early masons used native stone lying close to the surface that could be removed easily with a pickax. Masons also used fieldstones and rock from streambeds or exposed ledges.

Although some of these stones could be shaped with hammer and chisel, most builders used them unshaped, in a style known as rubble, or random rubble. This is a familiar style of Appalachian masonry, which makes use of accessible rock and stone to construct chimneys, walls, foundations, springhouses, and numerous other structures. Well-laid rubble stone is sturdy, long lasting, and has a natural aesthetic beauty intrinsically linked to its environment. The mountain cabin with its indispensable rock chimney has become an Appalachian icon symbolizing the resilience and ingenuity of the region's inhabitants.

Generally, of the many European immigrants to settle in the Appalachians, the most skilled masons came from areas such as Ireland, Scotland, Holland, Switzerland, France, and parts of England and Germany that were not heavily forested. In the Catskill Mountains of New York, French Huguenots and Dutch settlers used the local blue sandstone to build rectangular houses of uniform size and appearance. In Pennsylvania, the Germans and Swiss are well known for fieldstone houses with steeply pitched roofs.

The strong stone-masonry tradition of Germanic settlers gradually spread from central Pennsylvania westward into the valleys and passes of Appalachia, where stone houses appeared along with the familiar log cabins. Seth Smith, a Quaker stone mason from Lancaster County, Pennsylvania, moved to Tennessee in the early 1790s and built several stone houses in and around Washington and Greene Counties. The Moravian settlement on the nearly one-hundred-thousand-acre Wachovia tract brought skilled masons into North Carolina. First established in Pittsburgh, the Moravians began to settle Salem (Winston-Salem) in 1766. The large community store was the first all-stone building in Salem. The Moravians strictly upheld the guild system, which required formal training of artisans and the system of apprenticeship to master craftsmen.

There are also many examples of Scots-Irish stone masonry in the Appalachian region. After the Thomas Walker and Daniel Boone expeditions opened up Kentucky for further western settlement in the mid- and late 1700s, settlers threaded the gaps into northern and central Kentucky. Surviving limestone rock houses in the area were laid up without mortar. The outside joints were later sealed with mortar and the inside walls chinked with mud. A survey of these houses built between the late 1780s and 1820 found that many of the owners had Scots-Irish surnames. One example is the Cyrus McCrackin cabin in Woodford County, Kentucky. Scots-Irish masons are also credited with many of the rock fences that bound the fields and roadsides in the Kentucky Bluegrass region to the west of the Appalachians. Irish stone masons immigrated to the area during the potato famine in the middle of the nineteenth century. The style of dry stone fencing (laid without mortar) goes back many hundreds of years and is common to Scotland, Ireland, and England. Irish fence masons directed the work of apprentices, including some slave labor. Black freedmen later went into the trade for themselves, and after the turn of the century black stone masons constructed much of the stone fencing in Kentucky.

Some of the wealthier settlers coming into Kentucky and Tennessee from other states such as Virginia, North Carolina, and Pennsylvania hired builders and stone masons to construct their houses. Thomas Hope, an English-trained builder who settled in the Knoxville, Tennessee, area, is credited with designing and building the first stone house in Knox County—the 1797 Ramsey House. Built for Colonel Francis Alexander Ramsey, the house is an example of Georgian architecture, using native blue limestone and pink marble. Its formal architectural elements include quoins (exterior corner stones), keystone arches over the windows, and carved consoles under the cornice.

Italian immigrants were responsible for much masonry work around the turn of the twentieth century, including large structures such as canals, railroad tunnels, bridges, and public buildings. Such work increased the demand for experienced quarry men, stonecutters, and masons, and Italian immigrants brought their skills to a vast range of projects. One pocket of this large group settled in the coalfields of West Virginia in Mercer and Fayette Counties. They contracted work on roads, railroads, and many municipal buildings, including those in downtown Bluefield. Italian masons are also credited with many public buildings in eastern Kentucky, tunnels and bridges along the Blue Ridge Parkway, and Rockville Bridge in Marysville, Pennsylvania. Completed by Italian masons and Irish laborers in 1902, the railroad bridge spanning the Susquehanna River is the longest stone masonry arch bridge in the world and is listed in the National Register of Historic Places.

One of the most successful public works projects in the Appalachians, the Blue Ridge Parkway, is also a showcase for artistic stone masonry. Planners of the route sought to create structures that blended with the natural environment. Both Italian and Spanish stone masons applied their talents to the tunnel facings, bridges, signs, and retaining walls that line the route. Even some of the gas stations and convenience stores on the parkway feature beautiful native stone in their construction.

Perhaps the grandest example of stone masonry in the Appalachians is George W. Vanderbilt's French-style chateau, Biltmore House, in Asheville, North Carolina—reputed to be the country's largest private residence. With his vast economic resources, Vanderbilt employed Vermont native Richard Morris Hunt as the architect, along with hundreds of masons and artisans from America and Europe, including the Austrian sculptor Karl Bitter. In addition, hundreds of local laborers helped build Biltmore House, which was completed in 1895. Constructed of native, hand-tooled limestone, the 250-room mansion includes a black marble fireplace in the library and numerous stone sculptures and fountains.

Stone masonry is still a valued skill in the Appalachian region, whether in new construction or restoration, large projects or small. Although formal training may be obtained at local vocational schools or through apprenticeship programs offered by local contractors' groups, most masons learn their craft informally. Many individuals learn on the job by working as labor assistants to experienced masons and by observing and practicing the basic techniques. Stone masonry is a traditional craft often passed down from generation to generation.

See also: ITALIANS (RACE, ETHNICITY, AND IDENTITY); SECTION OVERVIEW (ARCHITECTURE).

—Selena Frye, *Louisville, Kentucky*

Patrizia Audenino, "The Paths of the Trade: Italian Stonemasons in the United States," *International Migration Review* (Winter 1986); Harley J. McKee, *Introduction to Early American Masonry: Stone, Brick, Mortar and Plaster* (1973); Jessie Poesch, *The Art of the Old South: Painting, Sculpture, Architecture, and the Products of Craftsmen, 1560–1860* (1983).

Stuart Nye Silver

The dogwood bloom featured on Stuart Nye handwrought silver jewelry is a symbol of Appalachian artistry seen in craft stores throughout the region and across the country since the 1930s. Well made, attractive and affordable, the pins and earrings are sought by tourists who relate the designs to the beauty of the mountain hillsides and appreciate the handwrought simplicity.

Stuart Nye was born in Brooklyn, New York, and served in World War I, but he made Appalachia his home after an extended hospital stay at the Veterans Hospital near Asheville, North Carolina, while recovering from tuberculosis. When he was released from the hospital, he did a little wood carving and even won a prize for a walnut tray decorated with dogwood blossoms. The tray took a week to make and sold for twenty-two dollars, but Nye continued to work as manager of a local popcorn stand to earn a living.

In 1933 a silversmith friend sold Nye the tools of his small business for ninety-eight dollars. With only limited experience in silver work, Nye began to make bangle bracelets. When he made a silver dogwood bloom and showed it to a customer, she advised him to make it a pin. The Dogwood design was an instant success and soon the demand was too much for a single silversmith. Nye hired the wives of patients and workers at the Veterans Hospital in Oteen to increase production in the workshop located in a group of additions to Stuart's garage in east Asheville.

Owner and employees worked as a team to produce a quality product at a fair price, copying nature's designs to expand the jewelry selection. Successful designs such as the Pansy, Lily, Trillium, Galax, and Pinecone were added to the line, but Dogwood remained the favorite. During the metal shortages of World War II, Nye began to work in copper; brass was added in 1980 when silver prices rose sharply.

After World War II, Nye went into a partnership with Ralph D. Morris Sr., a merchandise manager at a local department store and a friend who made style and fashion suggestions over the years. Nye retired in 1947 but continued as an advisor to Morris until his death in 1962. In 1949 Ralph Morris Jr. joined his father, and a shop was built for visitors to watch the jewelry being made and see a display of the items produced. It was one of the first businesses to demonstrate crafts production to the public.

The shop's work methods remain much the same as those of the early days, and the jewelry continues to be entirely handcrafted. Stuart Nye Hand Wrought Jewelry is a member of the Southern Highland Craft Guild and has been represented at every guild fair since 1948. Joe Morris, the third generation of the Morris family, carries on the traditions begun by Nye.

See also: ART POTTERY; ASHEVILLE, NORTH CAROLINA (URBAN APPALACHIAN EXPERIENCE); WEST VIRGINIA GLASSWARE.

—Kathleen Curtis Wilson, *University of Ulster, Northern Ireland*

Weaving

Blankets, bedcovers, rugs, and other household linens have been woven on Appalachian looms for more than two hundred years. Until the mid-eighteenth century, weaving cloth by hand was a necessity of frontier life. As inexpensive, factory-produced cloth became readily available, the craft practically became a lost art until revived by industrial schools during the early twentieth century. Weaving was a core element of the craft revival sparked by these industrial schools, and handwoven pieces became icons of Appalachian crafts. Weaving is still the craft most associated with the region.

The weaving process involves intricate and repetitive movements, and it often attracts an audience. For most of its Appalachian history, hand weaving has been a women's craft, although factory production work is associated with men. Few non-weavers understand the process of producing cloth or the detailed preparation necessary to ready a loom for weaving, but this knowledge deepens appreciation for the finished product.

The process of weaving—the interlacing of warp yarn and weft yarn to produce fabric—is a basic one and requires in most cases the technology of a loom. Appalachian weavers follow several distinct steps to produce finished cloth. Once the fiber has been spun into yarn, the yarn is wound onto spools that are placed in a spool rack, commonly known as a skarne. Next, the weaver uses a warping frame to measure the yardage of the warp for the loom. The warp is all of the threads aligned on the loom before weaving begins. In Appalachia, pegs stuck into the outside walls of a house, shed, or barn sometimes were substituted for the usual large portable frame. This step also allows the weaver to lay the threads in sequence, crossing the yarns, one after the other, which is preparation for the threading-up process. When measurement is complete, the warp is securely tied in a very specific way. This first step in the weaving process, which is the foundation for the successful and skillful completion of the weaver's task, requires mathematics and careful planning.

Next, the weaver winds the warp onto the large cylindrical beam at the back of the loom. Because of its significant circumference—many looms have a warp beam that measures a full yard in circumference—this beam is often made from a tree trunk. It is important to maintain an even tension throughout the installation of the warp in order to weave an even piece of cloth. This step is more comfortably done with two people working to ensure the warp remains at a constant width as the threads are wound onto the beam. Old-time weavers, who needed to produce quantities of material for practical use, often put on warps that were dozens of yards long, and coverlet weavers were known to put on warps long enough to produce several coverlets from the same warp. Many weavers often wove only one coverlet pattern over and over.

Once the winding, or beaming, of the warp is complete, the weaver sits down within the four posters of the loom with the harnesses suspended on perpendicular sticks to begin the threading up or drawing through process. Two important skills are required at this stage: the ability to read a pattern draft and the technical skill to translate that pattern by placing certain warp threads or ends through the eyes of particular heddles (wires, strings, or flat steel rods) attached to one of four shafts. Most Appalachian looms had four shafts, raised and lowered by four foot treadles. Where embellishment or decoration was not required, as in simple blankets and sheets, weavers used only two shafts.

Fancy weaving, such as the well-known overshot patterns often identified with Appalachian weaving and lesser-known fine weave patterns learned from previous generations of women such as Bronson spot weave, Huck, or Ms and Os, was highly valued and displayed in the home where others could appreciate it. Many of these fine pieces, treasured as heirlooms, remain with the descendants of the weavers.

The drawing-in process can take many hours for a warp as wide as forty-eight inches with thirty or more ends to each inch. Hundreds of warp ends must be threaded through individual string heddles on specific shafts in a specific sequence in order to produce the desired pattern. Once the threading of the four harnesses has been completed, the threads then go through a comb called a reed with a certain number of slots per inch. Early on, reeds were likely handmade of split cane reeds that were strong and flexible. Many modern weavers use reeds made of metal, similar to those used in industrial weaving.

After the drawing-in process, the weaver is ready to tie up the warp ends to the cloth beam, creating an even tension across the warp and a ninety-degree angle where the yarn passes through the reed. The reed, which is placed in the batten or overhead beater, will pack the filler yarn, or weft, into the warp to create the woven cloth. Meanwhile, the shafts have been suspended with pulleys from an overhead bar and have been tied up to the foot treadles that the weaver tromps in order to control the shafts and subsequently the pattern.

Some experienced weavers wove their patterns without a draft, having committed them to memory. As cloth was woven, it was rolled onto the cloth beam from the front, and more unwoven warp was released from the warp beam; the weaver always maintained a uniform tension so as to produce an even fabric.

The final process of weaving the cloth involves pushing down one or more foot treadles, separating the warp to create an opening, or shed, through which the shuttle is thrown with one hand, while the batten is held back with the other. The batten, or beater, presses the weft thread into the warp, with the pressure controlled by the weaver. The beater is then pushed back, the feet push on the next set of treadles, the next set of warp threads is raised, and the shuttle is thrown once again through the shed. The design is built, one treadling at a time, with as many as forty or more treadlings to fill one inch on a fine piece of linen, or ten to twenty treadlings to complete an inch of woolen blanketing.

Perhaps because of the satisfaction of watching the pattern develop with each crossing of the shuttle or the sense of accomplishment when a piece comes off the loom, weaving has been said to stir the soul as much as any creative art. Craft or art, weaving continues to be very much a part of Appalachian culture into the twenty-first century.

See also: COVERLETS; FIBERS; SETTLEMENT, MISSION, AND SPONSORED SCHOOLS (EDUCATION).

—Craig F. Evans, *Sanbornville, New Hampshire*

Garry G. Barker, *The Handcraft Revival in Southern Appalachia, 1930–1990* (1991); Carol Strickler, *American Woven Coverlets* (1987); Kathleen Curtis Wilson, *Textile Art from Southern Appalachia: The Quiet Work of Women* (2001).

Weaving Room of Crossnore School

The Weaving Room of Crossnore School is the only weaving program remaining from the Appalachian craft revival still employing community women. Weaving at Crossnore School began in 1920 with funding from the Smith-Hughes Vocational Education Act passed by the United States Congress in 1917. Initially the Weaving Room was part of the school program with classes for children, but it was always open to community women for production weaving. In the early 1960s classes for children were disbanded.

Students and community women in front of the Weaving Room of Crossnore School, c. 1930. The Weaving Room of Crossnore School, the only weaving program remaining from the Appalachian craft revival, still employs community women. Lillie Clark Johnson (Aunt Newbie), manager of the school from 1926 until 1961, is pictured third from right.

Mary Martin Sloop instigated expansion of the small public school at Crossnore, North Carolina, in 1913. As the school grew to include an elementary school and high school with facilities for boarding students, Sloop financed the venture with a mixture of public and private funds, while the county paid the teachers. Most of the students boarded only during the week and returned home for weekends. The boarding facilities and special classes were funded by rummage sales, gifts from the Daughters of the American Revolution, and other private donors. Crossnore School provides a home and school for children in crisis, usually from abusive or negligent homes.

Lillie Clark Johnson, known as Aunt Newbie, managed the Weaving Room for more than three decades, from 1926 until her retirement in 1961. Her assistant and successor, Ossie Phillips, started weaving as a young girl and in 1998 was awarded a North Carolina Folk Heritage Award by the North Carolina Arts Council.

The Weaving Room program actually occupied several small spaces around campus until 1929, when two large log buildings were moved beside the main road through town to serve as a consolidated weaving room. In 1935 these log buildings were destroyed by fire, and children from Crossnore School helped collect rocks from the nearby Linville River to build a stone structure, which has housed the weavers to the present day.

The weavers produced coverlets, rugs, couch covers, dresser scarves, placemats, sofa cushions, bags, guest towels, and baby blankets. These handwoven goods and hooked rugs were sold to tourists who visited the Weaving Room and to members of church and civic clubs through mutual acquaintances. The Weaving Room of Crossnore School was a charter member of the Southern Highland Handicraft Guild (later the Southern Highland Craft Guild) established in 1930. Still located adjacent to the school, it employs community women to weave placemats, baby blankets, women's apparel, and other household items sold to tourists from their showroom in Crossnore and at Southern Highland Craft Guild Fairs.

See also: SOUTHERN HIGHLAND CRAFT GUILD; WEAVING.

—Philis Alvic, *Lexington, Kentucky*

Garry G. Barker, *The Handcraft Revival in Southern Appalachia, 1930–1990* (1991); Carol Strickler, *American Woven Coverlets* (1987); Kathleen Curtis Wilson, *Textile Art from Southern Appalachia: The Quiet Work of Women* (2001).

West Virginia Glassware

Glassmaking is an important industry in various parts of Appalachia. Places such as Pittsburgh and Corning, New York, have been significant world suppliers of glassware, but the glassware most closely identified with Appalachia is from West Virginia, where more than five hundred glass-manufacturing companies have operated throughout the state's history. Used widely in hotels, restaurants, cafés, homes, and church suppers, West Virginia glassware is avidly collected around the world.

Blenko decanters and bowl by Wayne Husted, 1963. More than five hundred glass-manufacturing companies have operated in West Virginia throughout the state's history. Of these, Blenko Glass Company, located in Milton, has been the source of some of the most colorful and innovative modern glass made in the United States.

West Virginia has been widely known for its glass companies since it attained statehood. The area was ideal for glass manufacture because of its proximity to natural resources and transportation corridors. Abundant supplies of coal and gas fueled the furnaces; native silica provided the main ingredient in the glass formulas; networks of rivers provided the means to transport other materials in and the finished products out of the region. The skilled labor force responsible for creating more than a century of glassware from sand and fuel was made up of both native and imported craftsmen. Throughout the nineteenth and twentieth centuries, West Virginia glasshouses satisfied the demand for both utilitarian and decorative objects in traditional styles.

Nineteenth-century Victorian styles and objects provided the foundation for the West Virginia glass industry. Hobbs, Brockunier and Company in Wheeling was in business as early as 1845 and a leading glasshouse from 1863 to 1891, with color and variety the keys to its success. Another Wheeling firm, Central Glass Company, also operated from 1863 to 1891 and specialized in pressed tableware with little color. Fenton Art Glass Company began making colorless glass in Williamstown in 1905, but their historic reproductions ensured success throughout the twentieth century.

Among the most visually remarkable West Virginia glass is the colorful modern ware designed by professional designers in the mid-twentieth century. While continuing to use traditional methods of blowing, glassmakers moved beyond traditional ware, producing glass that was not pressed or molded, nor made in familiar shapes or sizes. Off-hand or blown glass requires the skills of a team of artisans. Although following a prescribed design, each piece is unique. By its nature, blown glass includes subtle irregularities and variations, but these irregularities are precisely what give the glass its handmade charm.

As the first company to employ a full time staff designer, Blenko Glass Company, located in Milton, has been the source of some of the most colorful and innovative modern glass made in the United States. Founded by Englishman William John Blenko in 1893, the company began by making stained glass for windows. Better known for colorful oversized bottles and an assortment of decorative items, Blenko still rolls out flat glass from large cylinders and remains the major American producer of stained glass for architectural installations. Some of the many buildings with Blenko windows are Saint Patrick's Cathedral in New York City, Washington Cathedral, the United States Air Force Academy Chapel, Grant's Tomb, and Riyadh Airport in Saudi Arabia, as well as thousands of private residences.

Blenko's decorative wares have been sold in major department and specialty stores coast to coast. Since its methods were well suited to making antique reproductions, in 1936 Colonial Williamsburg contracted Blenko to make reproductions of early American glassware. Richard Deakin Blenko, great-grandson of the founder, currently heads the company, which makes both stained glass sheets from cylinders and decorative items by using old methods. Today, both new designs and some of modern classics are blown in vivid colors that have become synonymous with Blenko.

Another major West Virginia producer of primarily blown glass at the beginning of the twenty-first century was Pilgrim Glass Corporation of Ceredo. Trained as a ceramic engineer, founder Alfred E. Knobler entered the glass business via pottery sales in the 1930s. In 1949 Knobler purchased the failing Tri-State Glass Company in Huntington. Over the next seven years he added a successful new glass line and purchased land in Ceredo to build the present facility, renamed Pilgrim. Corning Museum of Glass featured one of Knobler's designs in its *Glass 1959* exhibit.

From inception Pilgrim specialized in free-blown crackle glass in vivid colors. The crackle comes from dipping the hot glass object in cold water, which causes it to crack in random patterns over the entire surface. The piece is then reheated to smooth the surface, but the fine crackle lines remain as part of the design. Like other companies in the area, Pilgrim made a range of decorative objects in both crackle and plain-colored glass. Pilgrim also produced a line of satin finished items that were given an acid bath to degloss the surface and give it a satiny feel.

Designers and brothers Allesandro and Roberto Moretti, who came from Italy in the 1950s, and their brother-in-law Mario Sandon, who arrived in 1963, were the creative force at Pilgrim. Roberto had worked in Italy for the famed association Fucina degli Angeli (Foundry of Angels) and executed designs by artists such as Pablo Picasso, Marc Chagall, and Jean Cocteau. His work attracted national attention at the 1965–66 New York World's Fair. The Moretti family's introduction of glass animals, figurines, and other Venetian-style items gave Pilgrim another desirable line. Since Venetian glass imports were becoming popular with American consumers, the Pilgrim Venetian style met with success.

Other Pilgrim innovations included an outstanding shade of pink (cranberry) introduced by plant manager Karel Konrad in 1968 and throughout the 1970s a line called Kitchen Chemistry that included canisters and jars with both utilitarian and aesthetic appeal. Also introduced about this time were Rock Crystal pitchers with a bumpy surface, salt and pepper shakers, paperweights, bells, plant hangers, and candleholders. In 1977–78 Pilgrim produced a series of signed studio pieces.

In addition to Blenko and Pilgrim, other companies, notably Kanawha, Rainbow, and Bischoff, specialized in colorful blown glass in the mid-twentieth century. When Dunbar Glass Company closed in 1953, production head D. P. Merritt and others joined to form the Kanawha Glass Specialties Company. Named after the nearby Kanawha River, the company opened in Dunbar in 1955 and made blown crystal in addition to cutting and decorating purchased glass. By 1960 they were producing colorful decorative wares, especially crackle glass. Soon Kanawha was making 350 production items in seven colors.

In 1969 Kanawha purchased Hamon Handcrafted Glass in Scott Depot. Hamon had begun in 1932, and their crackle glass production during the 1950s and 1960s coincided with that of other companies. The Hamon crackle glass that was added to the Kanawha line retained its identity, which explains why Kanawha catalogs often showed two different types of glass—molded and hand blown.

In the early 1970s, cased milk glass was introduced in which the outer (or sometimes inner) layer was made in bright solid colors. Peachblow, with gradations resembling nineteenth-century art glass by that name, was one of the most popular of these cased lines. In 1987 Kanawha was sold to Raymond Dereume Glass in Punxsutawney, Pennsylvania, which closed only two years later in 1989.

The Rainbow Art Glass Company in Huntington started in the 1940s as a glass-decorating business called the Rainbow Art Company. It turned to producing its own hand-blown glass in 1954, when it became the Rainbow Art Glass Company. Like other neighboring companies, it produced blown glass in vivid colors, often with a crackle finish. Rainbow made crackle through the 1970s, later than many of its competitors, which may account for the large number of Rainbow crackle items still on the market. In 1973 the company was purchased by Viking and continued to make crackle glass until 1979. The Rainbow factory burned down in 1983, and all operations ceased.

Rainbow mainstays were crackle and plain miniature vases and pitchers. Although many of the crackle miniatures and even larger decanters and bottles are similar to those of other companies, Rainbow made a number of distinctive forms. These can often be identified by large round or elongated teardrop-shaped stoppers, and the top of the bottle neck normally has a flat collar, which also helps to differentiate Rainbow pieces. Rainbow's contribution to mid-century culture may have been the countless ruffled miniatures, but its tall slender bottles or the decanters with oversized ball or flame stoppers are significant to the history of design.

A. F. Bischoff Glass Company in Culloden, founded in 1922, made items very similar to those of other West Virginia companies. In addition to using some unusual, even bizarre, original shapes, Bischoff copied designs from leaders such as Blenko. Lancaster Colony, of Columbus, Ohio, purchased Bischoff in 1963, keeping the Bischoff name and molds. Sloan Glass bought Bischoff in 1964 but closed in 1996.

Many of the Bischoff items bear a striking resemblance to Blenko designs. In some cases they are modified enough to prevent confusion. Of course, not all Bischoff designs are unoriginal. In fact, many can be recognized by a distinct style that these designs seem to share. Exaggerated forms, complicated ruffles, bumps, and baubles, crystal stoppers and handles, and a generally heavier look characterize the company's product. Novelty rather than modern design seems to have been the focus.

Other West Virginia glass companies made a variety of historic and modern, molded and blown, colored and colorless glass. Three giants were Fostoria, Viking, and Morgantown. Besides their West Virginia location, there is another reason for grouping these three distinctly different companies together. The last years of Morgantown's production (1965–71) took place under Fostoria ownership. Then, shortly after Fostoria closed in 1986, its president, Kenneth Dalzell, purchased the defunct Viking and revived it as Dalzell-Viking. Several of Fostoria's earlier items continued to be produced by Dalzell-Viking using original molds. There is some irony to Fostoria's bridging Viking and Morgantown: Fostoria did not focus on either the vibrant colors or modern forms of the period from 1950 to 1975, while Viking and Morgantown did both. All three companies, however, emphasized molding their wares rather than the off-hand method preferred by Blenko, Pilgrim, and others.

Fostoria took its name from Fostoria, Ohio, where the first factory was opened in 1887, making fruit jars, oil lamps, and colorless Victorian pattern glass. The company moved to Moundsville, West Virginia, in 1891, where it remained until closing in 1986. Through its century of serving the American table, most of which was under Dalzell family leadership, Fostoria made glassware in such a wide range of styles, colors, and techniques that it could appeal to most any taste. From the most traditional etched stemware to Art Deco vases, the product demonstrated Fostoria's versatility and adaptability in a fickle marketplace. The company's "American pattern" captivated consumers for more than seventy years and has been the most popular American glass pattern ever produced. The Corning Museum's *Glass 1959* exhibit featured two Fostoria pieces to represent the best of modern American glass design.

The New Martinsville Glass Manufacturing Company was incorporated in 1900. It began, like many other glass companies, by making utilitarian glass and soon expanded into more ornamental items. Financial problems plagued the glass industry as much as any other in the 1930s, and the company went into receivership in 1937. A group from Connecticut purchased it and reopened as the New Martinsville Glass Company. In 1944 former partner G. R. Cummings purchased all of the New Martinsville stock and changed the name to Viking Glass Company because of its reference to Scandinavia and its modern glass designs.

Under the new Viking name and ownership, color became a focus. Its subsidiary, Rainbow Art Glass of Huntington, established in 1939, also relied heavily on color for its identity and appeal. Both Rainbow and Viking were featured in *Glass 1959*.

Kenneth Dalzell, the fourth generation of an eighty-four-year family presidency of the Fostoria Glass Company, joined Lancaster Colony after it purchased Fostoria in 1983.

When Fostoria closed in 1986, Dalzell left Lancaster to head his own glass company again. He reopened Viking as Dalzell-Viking in 1987 and continued to make high-quality hand-pressed glass in both crystal and vibrant colors such as ruby red and cobalt blue. In addition to decorative giftware sold at department stores and specialty shops, Dalzell-Viking made reproductions of early glass for clients such as the Smithsonian Institution, the Metropolitan Museum of Art, Oneida, Coca-Cola, and the Heisey Collector Club. Dalzell-Viking fired its last furnace in 1998.

The Morgantown Glass Factory (1899–1971) operated under several names—Morgantown Glass Works, Economy Tumbler Company, Economy Glass Company, and Morgantown Glassware Guild. Particularly under the leadership of Joseph Haden and his sons, J. Richard and Samuel, Morgantown produced high-quality handmade lead glass in both traditional and modern designs with an emphasis on color. In 1965 Fostoria purchased Morgantown Glassware Guild but closed the Morgantown facility in 1971. The loss of this vibrant glassworks was indicative of a larger trend toward blandness in Fostoria's later and final years.

A vibrant and vital cultural institution in the mid-twentieth century, the West Virginia glass industry is being reduced to collections of historic artifacts and information in books. With Fostoria, Morgantown, Viking, and others gone, Blenko and Pilgrim are among the few survivors of a once booming American glass industry.

See also: GLASS INDUSTRY (BUSINESS, INDUSTRY, AND TECHNOLOGY); GLASS MUSEUMS (CULTURAL INSTITUTIONS).

—Leslie Piña, *Ursuline College*

Eason Eige, *A Century of Glassmaking in West Virginia* (1980); Leslie Piña, *Blenko: Cool '50s and '60s Glass* (2000).

Whittling

At one time, myriad whittled wooden objects were essential to running a farm or household. In the house, they included spoons, churn dashers, potato mashers, rolling pins, butter molds, and weaving shuttles, not to mention children's toys. On the farm, tools such as hayforks, rakes, axe and hoe handles, and ox yokes—even door hinges and latches—were whittled out of wood. Whittling was also a fundamental skill in basketmaking, chair making, and coopering.

Possibly because whittling appears easy and is frequently done idly, producing nothing other than wood shavings, little merit has been given to the craft. Stereotypes abound of old men sitting on slat-back chairs on porches, idly passing the time while whittling large pieces of wood into small ones. But as a craft, whittling is a form of sculpture in which handheld pieces of wood are carved with a knife, most often producing practical items for use around the home or farm but sometimes creating works of art. The image of whittling as a creative hobby grew once there was no longer need for hand-whittled items such as wooden spoons and axe handles.

Most mountain whittlers chose folding knives over fixed blades and prefered carbon steel to stainless for the single, versatile tool of their craft. The wood used by a whittler was not arbitrary, but chosen for specific characteristics. Basswood was the traditional choice for hunting decoys and detailed figures because its hardness held carved features well. Weaver's shuttles were most often made of dogwood, while the resilience of hickory lent strength to tool handles.

In contemporary Appalachia, most whittled objects are produced for the tourist trade as souvenirs, particularly children's toys such as whistles, cars and trucks, wooden knives, and animals.

See also: FOLK TOYS; WOOD CARVING.

—William T. Henry Jr., *Oak Ridge, Tennessee*

Wood Carving

At once a practical skill and an elegant art form, wood carving is a quintessentially Appalachian form of creativity. Surrounded by abundant and varied resources from the wooded hills and forested mountains, the region's wood-carvers have their choice of native materials, including pine, poplar, chestnut, oak, dogwood, cherry, walnut, cedar, and basswood. Both artisans and builders choose wood according to the way it splits, the color, the smoothness of the grain, and other purely aesthetic qualities, matching it to its intended purpose, ranging from spoons and axe handles to purely whimsical creations.

Appalachian wood-carvers, as woodworkers elsewhere, employ standard methods and techniques in their work. Three-dimensional figures are carved in the round and can be viewed from any angle; relief carvings are made by meticulously removing the background, allowing a raised design to emerge from the wood. In chip carving, small triangular pieces of wood are sliced away by knife blade or chisel to create a richly textured piece. Some artists use only traditional tools such as gouges, chisels, drawknives, and penknives. Others use electric band saws and even chainsaws to rough out their subject before finishing with hand tools. Dedicated carvers often modify or make tools to suit their own very specific needs.

Among earlier generations of Appalachian practitioners, wood carving as an art often sprang out of woodcrafting as a practical skill. Living on isolated farms and raising their own food, people rarely had money to spend on store-bought goods. Logs, planks, and stripped bark supplied the materials for their homes and provided the basics for fencing and furniture. They fashioned an endless array of everyday items from wood: handles for scythes, hammers, and axes; wagon tongues and yokes; plates and utensils for the kitchen; fishing rods and gunstocks. Men whittled as they talked, women gathered and chopped wood for the stove, and children made their own toys. Accustomed to handling wood as they acquired basic crafting skills, many wood-carvers often recount discovering their artistic interests gradually, carving designs into a fireplace mantle, for example, or turning a plain walking stick into a sinuously curved snake.

As a raw material for artistic expression, wood is cheap and easy to come by—many carvers use scrap pieces, oddly shaped roots, or fallen limbs that suggest a certain shape or idea. Appreciative of the beauty and unique qualities of species of wood, accomplished carvers sometimes confess to feeling that wood, in effect, "speaks" to them. They see with their artist's eye something in the wood waiting to be released. Carvers produce work for their own enjoyment and for the challenge it provides in their efforts to shape their own vision of the world in concrete forms. Although many talented wood-carvers eventually exhibit and sell their work, they usually begin by giving pieces away as gifts to family and friends. Wood-carvers tend to be as individual in their subject matter, skill levels, and techniques as other artists. One branch of the art is known as chain carving. Chain carvers take a single piece of wood and create interlocking links that present a picture puzzle to the eye. The links are "freed" by carefully shaving away the superfluous wood to create solid and unbroken chains. These artists often enhance their creation by adding a caged ball—another optical puzzle in which a solid wooden sphere is caged within a grilled box. Other additions to the chain may include spoons, swivels, and hinged joints.

Contemporary chain carvers tend to be older men, and often they have taken up the intricacies of chain carving as a pastime after retirement, physical or medical hardship, or death of a spouse. Chain carving requires patience, steady hands, mental sharpness, and steadfast attention to detail. Chains may be large enough to drape across a fireplace mantle or so tiny as to be carved from matchsticks. Carved chains combine artistic beauty with mathematical precision, and even a certain romance.

The origins of chain carving and the accompanying caged balls and spoons have been traced back as far as the Viking era (A.D. 793–1100). In Scandinavia, decorative wooden spoons and chains were given both as proofs of skill and as tokens of love. Likewise, examples of this particular art were common in fourteenth-century France, seventeenth-century Wales, and afterwards in England and in the American colonies. Variations of the caged ball very similar to those made by slaves in Georgia have been documented among the Tsonga, Venda, and Nguni tribes of Africa, suggesting a continuous African tradition, as well.

Other Appalachian wood-carvers draw inspiration from the past, and their work often has a nostalgic quality. Their art preserves and celebrates old ways of doing things and expresses appreciation for traditional values, even as the modern world encroaches upon the once isolated, rural landscape of the mountains. Wood carving as an art hearkens back to the days before mass production, when needed items were more often made or repaired than purchased. Artists' backgrounds as housewives, truck drivers, coal miners, farmers, and railroaders emerge frequently in the simple, down-to-earth quality of their art, reflecting individual interpretations of the world in which they live.

Common subjects of Appalachian wood carving are depictions of the natural world, traditional ways of life, everyday human figures, and religious themes. Representations of animals and birds abound; figures are large and small, painted and natural, realistic and fantastical. Carved, twining snakes are a familiar motif, as are horses and common hound dogs. Minnie Adkins, a native of Kentucky, is known for her carved foxes, opossums, and bears, often brightly painted with distinctive expressions on their faces. S. L. (Shields Landon) Jones of West Virginia drew on his memories of the past to create railroad men and horse-drawn wagons. He is perhaps best known, however, for carving massive, usually asymmetrical, human heads. His work is part of the permanent collection of the Smithsonian American Art Museum in Washington, D.C.

The late Edgar Tolson, among the most famous of Appalachian wood-carvers, was renowned for biblical scenes such as *The Fall of Man* series, which depicts Adam and Eve in the Garden of Eden through works such as *The Temptation, Expulsion,* and *Cain Going into the World.* Tolson, an eastern Kentuckian who died in 1984, also carved chains, walking canes, figures of oxen and unicorns, and reliefs. He won a National Endowment for the Arts Fellowship in 1981. His work has been sold at auction at Sotheby's, exhibited at the Whitney Museum in New York, and is part of the permanent collections of the Milwaukee Art Museum and the Smithsonian American Art Museum.

Although many artists turn to wood carving entirely on their own and are "discovered" by one means or another, outside interest has also encouraged many over the years. The craft revival in the southern mountains of Appalachia fueled interest in native crafts and folk art, beginning in the 1930s with schools and organizations such as the John C. Campbell Folk School in Brasstown, North Carolina, Berea College in Kentucky, and the Southern Highland Handicraft Guild. They promoted all types of traditional arts and crafts, including wood carving. Other Appalachian artists (especially the younger generation) have benefited by seeking formal training, either by apprenticeship to master carvers or enrolling in art schools and at universities.

Modern wood-carvers have ample opportunity to share their work with the public. Artists exhibit their work at fairs, flea markets, art galleries, folk art centers, museums, and on the Internet. Some important centers with collections of wood carvings and other folk art of Appalachia include the Huntington Museum of Art in West Virginia; the Cumberland Museum in Clintwood, Virginia; the Art Museum of Western Virginia in Roanoke; the Museum of Appalachia in Norris, Tennessee; and the Kentucky Folk Art Center in Morehead, Kentucky.

See also: BRASSTOWN CARVERS; DOUGH BOWLS; FOLK TOYS.

—Selena Frye, *Louisville, Kentucky*

Julia S. Ardery, *The Temptation: Edgar Tolson and the Genesis of Twentieth-Century Folk Art* (1998); Simon J. Bronner, *Chain Carvers: Old Men Crafting Meaning* (1985); Ramona and Millard Lampell, *O, Appalachia: Artists of the Southern Mountains* (1989).

Folklore and Folklife

Section Editor: Mary Hufford

Described by Richard Dorson as "folklore's natural habitat," the Appalachian region has been at the forefront of developments in the field of American folklore throughout the twentieth century. The first folk festival took place in Asheville in 1928; the first graduate folklore program focusing on Appalachian material was established in North Carolina; the Archive of Folk Culture at the Library of Congress was founded on Robert Winslow Gordon's Appalachian collections; and the first studies in occupational folklore took place in the Appalachian coalfields.

The idea of folklore is complicated; it may be cast as antiquarian, antimodern, communitarian, traditional, vernacular, or resistant. These concepts are all linked to the idea of progress but nevertheless exhibit a profound ambivalence toward it. This ambivalence reflects two perspectives on Appalachian culture: a rational perspective that idolizes progress on one hand and a romantic perspective that fears it on the other. Viewed through the romantic lens, Appalachia glimmers as a region uncontaminated by commerce and its excesses, a place where people know their neighbors, value their elders, live close to the land, and preserve old-time craft, music, and stories. Through a rational lens, these views give way to images of inbred, feuding, superstitious, welfare-dependent hillbillies. Both lenses serve to "distress" Appalachia as a region set backward not only in time but also in space (the "hinterlands," the "backcountry"), separated from the rest of America.

In modernizing countries, *folklore* is a term used to describe culture that is not modern. Because folklore is constantly changing and evolving in the face of modernity, each new technological revolution produces new forms of regional folklore and folklife. Since Appalachia was chronically transformed by the Industrial Revolution, the region has been and remains a good place to examine the dynamics of folklore. Paradoxically, this is not because Appalachia has remained unchanged, but because the pressures of modernization are continually engendering new forms of folklore and new frameworks within which to view the region.

Collection and study of folklore began in Europe in the late eighteenth century in tandem with romantic and nationalist movements sweeping the continent and transforming its politics, art, and culture. During that time, German philosopher Johann Gottfried von Herder proposed a central role for folklore in the building of nations. He argued that folklore, the language and culture attached to a geopoliti-

Facing page: A young girl wears a necklace of rhododendron leaves believed to ward off disease and ensure good health, Patrick County, Virginia, 1954. Reliance on folk medicine in Appalachia has diminished significantly since World War II due to economic development, improved access to public and private health-care services, and the increased presence of alternative and complementary medicine.

cally bounded territory, provided a common culture with which each nation could uniquely identify and that could aid in the formation of citizens for the nation-state.

In the United States, the use of regional culture to create a national identity, though based on European models, took a distinctly American turn. In the mid-nineteenth century, regional cultural difference provided a way to define an emerging urban middle class. Influenced by social evolutionist theories popular at the time, local color writers imagined Appalachia as a premodern "strange land" inhabited by "a peculiar people." There, one could learn about the past by studying and interacting with "our contemporary ancestors," as William Goodell Frost, president of Berea College, famously put it. At the same time, what seemed to some Americans an alarming influx of immigrants from Europe, drawn by the promise of work in factories, mills, and mines, triggered a search by writers and collectors for roots and attributes of "authentic" American identity. It was during this period, for instance, that Theodore Roosevelt and John Lomax saw the American West as a mythological realm for Americans enamored by the frontier. Discerning in cowboy balladry the remnants of Camelot, the Viking spirit, and Homeric poetry, Roosevelt proclaimed Lomax's cowboy collections to be a national literature based in "our own soil, mental and moral."

Over the past 150 years, folklore studies have reflected shifting cultural, economic, political, and international trends; therefore, ideas about the ways in which folklore shapes American and Appalachian identity have changed. During the first half of the twentieth century, Appalachian folklore figured prominently in debates over the importance of America's many ethnic cultures versus the romantic notion of a pure Anglo-Saxon culture as the source of American identity. The legacy of these debates lingers in archives, museums, national parks, and festivals that were created around Appalachian culture during the first half of the twentieth century. Late in the century, such places increasingly turned away from collection of folklore toward initiatives emphasizing cultural planning and cultural expression in contemporary communities. To examine the history of folklore and folklife in Appalachia is to track Appalachia's emergence as a recognized region in American culture.

From its connections to British culture and civilization, Appalachia offered an American identity with Anglo-Saxon roots, a domesticated counterpart to the untamed West. During the first two decades of the twentieth century, the collection of folk songs, ballads, and stories canonized classic forms of Appalachian folklore and defined a core region within which such folklore flourished. Folk song and ballad collections by Lomax, Cecil Sharp, and Maude Karpeles, and writings by Sharp and Olive Dame Campbell, John C. Campbell, Emma Bell Miles, and Horace Kephart helped fix the mountains of Tennessee, Kentucky, North Carolina, and Virginia in the national imagination as the setting for an authentic folk culture. Their work articulated four key ideas about Appalachian folklore as a resource for nation-building: that folklore harbors and conveys the spirit of a people; that the southern highlanders belong to the nation; that there is a generalized southern highlander; and that the southern mountains form a repository of culture from an earlier period in the history of civilization.

Underlying these principles is the idea that folklore from one region can fill in for culture lost in metropolitan areas to modernization, an idea that enabled Appalachian cultural expression to take on national significance. Sharp, for example, the noted collector of Appalachian folk songs, explained his decision to bypass Maryland by saying, "Owing to the disturbance of rural life by the big coal industry, [songs and ballads] did not lie so ready at hand as in the other states." Sharp's comment suggests that, in a time of rapid progress, the key role for folklorists is salvage collecting. In other words, the collection of culture lost or obscured by rapid modernization can help to redeem the nation's lost connections to nature and to those who live closest to it. Southern Appalachia is incorporated into national thought in both the romantic and rational guises of its folk culture. As Robert Winslow Gordon, first head of the Archive of American Folk Song (later Archive of Folk Song) at the Library of Congress, put it: "The government recognizes the hill-billy and the American Negro as the basis of American folk-song and music."

The contrast between modern (America) and premodern (Appalachia) helped to define cultural work at state levels as well as nationally. During what is considered the "golden age of collecting" in the Appalachians, local collectors and writers visited the mountain portions of their states and produced a number of collections and publications. Among them were Madeleine Vinton Dahlgren's *South-Mountain Magic* (1882), James Otis Watson's *Marion County in the Making* (1917), Henry W. Shoemaker's *The Music and Musical Instruments of the Pennsylvania Mountaineers* (1923), Arthur Kyle Davis's *Traditional Ballads of Virginia* (1929), Emelyn Elizabeth Gardner's *Folklore from the Schoharie Hills, New York* (1937), and Anne Grimes's *Ballads of Ohio* (1957). Such works led to the creation of folklore repositories at state agencies or academic institutions that later provided impetus for formal programs of folklore research and presentation. Early collecting work was often pursued under the aegis of state folklore societies formed to preserve material salvaged from the past.

Collectors and writers during this period established genres that came to epitomize in public opinion the most authentic Appalachian folklore: lyrics from the types of ballad identified by Francis James Child; märchen, or tales, celebrating the genius and uncanny good fortune of a trickster named Jack; and forms of dance and craft promoted in festivals and settlement schools. What made this lore seem "authentic" was the purity of a lineage uncontaminated by commercial sources. Lomax saw authentic American folklore as grounded in isolated rural communities that were being destroyed by "machine civilization." Folklore, in such a view, could only survive when isolated from modern life, as it was perceived to be in Appalachia.

Paradoxically, the antimodernist idea of Appalachia in the 1930s served the needs of industrial planners in the region, providing a rationale for redistributing Appalachian people and resources. The public could be compensated for destruction of mountains, forests, and rivers by creating state and national parks and forests; folklife museums and festivals at such places could substitute for culture sacrificed for the sake of progress. Reformers working to alleviate backwardness and poverty in Appalachia likewise saw traditional crafts as a means of affirming and preserving mountain ways, turning them into commodities for sale. During the 1930s, Allen H. Eaton argued that this remedial work could compensate for cultural losses created by modernization. American urbanites, detached from their cultural roots, could adopt Appalachian crafts as touchstones of American identity—and provide Appalachians with a means of making a living. By the same token, evicting Appalachians from what would become the Shenandoah and Great Smoky Mountains National Parks was justified as a way to improve the lives of mountain folk. Reformers reasoned that those displaced by the parks could make their living outside the parks by engaging in basketmaking and other crafts.

Contending visions of the role of folklore in national life have shaped the study and uses of Appalachian folklore throughout the twentieth century. In a politically conservative view, Appalachian craft and folklore are seen as resources for defining American tradition; from a more liberal perspective, folklore contains the seeds of political resistance to social and cultural inequity. During the New Deal years of the 1930s, a more progressive strain of nationalism arose, holding common people to be the font of civilization. In line with this philosophy, New Deal programs led to a modern reinvention of folklore not as a remnant of the Old World, but as an expression of the experiences of ordinary people of the New World. The experience of industrialization, which earlier collectors saw as contaminating folklore, was legitimized as a proper object of folklore study. Folklore collecting initiated during this period under Benjamin Botkin as part of the Federal Writers' Project reflected a move away from the high romanticism of earlier collectors toward a cultural pluralism more suited to the goals of a democratic nation. Repudiating narrowly circumscribed, romantic canons for "authentic" folklore, Botkin encouraged a new generation of collectors and writers to document American expressions crafted from the experience of working to build a nation on the path of progress.

Folklorist George Korson, who collected and published songs and stories from the coal miners of Pennsylvania and West Virginia, typified this shift toward modern folklore. Believing it was important for miners to present their own traditions to the public, Korson invited miners to perform at folk festivals. Their songs, hybrids of tradition and innovation, were not only documents conveying miners' experiences in their own voices, but also critiques of modernization, which replaced laborers with machinery. Transforming their experience into art, miners found a new niche for their culture as objects of scholarly study and public presentation. Korson's pioneering work in the coalfields anticipated the rise of the subfield of occupational folklore in the 1960s and 1970s, exemplified by *Only a Miner*, folklorist Archie Green's study of recorded coal-mining songs.

This kind of fieldwork represented a shift from building a national culture out of regional folklore to using performances of folklore to give a public presence to underrepresented cultural groups. This shift was most clearly realized in the 1960s with inauguration of the Smithsonian Folklife Festival on the National Mall and subsequent academic and community programs in public folklore. Drawing on the New Deal precedent, publicly supported folklife research and presentation was seen as a way to achieve "cultural equity," as ethnomusicologist Alan Lomax put it, by helping to "amplify voices in a democratic polity," a phrase used by Green when lobbying for the American Folklife Preservation Act of 1976 before Congress.

Between World War II and the 1960s, however, folklore scholars argued over the propriety of "popularizing" folklore, or of putting folklore research to any use other than building knowledge by those with academic credentials. As this scholarly debate unfolded, Appalachian migrants were pouring into Detroit, where some of the earliest public folklore efforts took place. As a professor at Wayne University (later Wayne State University) in the mid-1940s, Thelma James promoted folklore research and presentation as ways to resolve cultural conflicts related to the influx of immigrants from the southern states and to help the Appalachian community enhance its public visibility.

Indeed, a trend toward more applied uses of research in the social sciences coincided with the great migration of three million people out of Appalachia to cities in search of jobs, bringing displacement of workers and their culture into the purview of folklore study. During the 1960s and 1970s, Congress contributed to the revitalization of public folklore with a series of laws encouraging protection of cultural and natural resources. Laws creating the National Endowments for the Arts and Humanities, the National Trust for Historic Preservation in the United States, and the American Folklife Center institutionalized folklore programs in the Appalachian states, building upon earlier collecting efforts. With new financial and political support from the endowments, connections between folklore and public life were strengthened in succeeding decades, and Appalachian culture was consistently in the national spotlight. Appalachian musicians and artists came to be featured at the annual Smithsonian Folklife Festival, and the American Folklife Center at the Library of Congress conducted Appalachian projects. The National Endowment for the Arts provided seed money for professionally run folklife programs in every Appalachian

People stroll by a part of the *Appalachia: Heritage and Harmony* exhibition of the Smithsonian Folklife Festival held on the National Mall in Washington, D.C., 2003. The large picture in the background is a reproduction of a billboard-sized mural located on a building in Bristol, Tennessee. The mural's images commemorate the Bristol sessions of 1927, when record producer Ralph Peer of the Victor Talking Machine Company traveled to the mountains of Appalachia to record traditional music. The success of Peer's recordings marked the beginning of commercial country music.

state and has consistently recognized folk artists from the region through National Heritage Fellowships.

Numerous public events and programs during the last two decades of the twentieth century emphasized the Appalachian diaspora and the importance of mountain culture for communities of displaced Appalachians living well outside the region. A tour of traditional musicians, dancers, and storytellers produced by the National Council for Traditional Arts and called "Mountain Music Homecoming" visited such sites of Appalachian out-migration as Chicago, Cincinnati, and Detroit. The Great Lakes Arts Alliance in Ohio created an archive of materials from Appalachian communities in Ohio, Indiana, Illinois, and Michigan, and the Mid Atlantic Arts Foundation sponsored a traveling exhibition, *Appalachian Views*, that focused on historic commonalities of life throughout the Appalachian Mountains from New England to the Deep South.

At the same time, folklorists and anthropologists continued working to understand the dynamic between region and nation that makes Appalachian culture distinctive. In settings where health, education, welfare, and public lands are administered, informal systems and strategies for cultural survival have emerged in the face of widespread negative stereotyping. Anthropologist Rhoda H. Halperin, for example, examined support networks created by Appalachian migrants who share electricity, swap favors, and piece together livelihoods through subsistence hunting and gardening, wage labor, and welfare. Folklorists Michael Ann Williams, Charles Perdue, and Nancy Martin-Perdue studied culture created by descendants of families evicted from their homes for creation of the Shenandoah and Great Smoky Mountains National Parks. Anthropologist Allen W. Batteau analyzed the interaction between social workers and Appalachian clients as a ritual game of "eligibility," where one must denigrate oneself to prove qualification for government assistance. Historian David E. Whisnant scrutinized middle-class promoters of early folk festivals at White Top, Virginia, and in Asheville, North Carolina. Folklorist Mary Hufford studied

West Virginia activists' use of tradition, historic emblems, and songs in contemporary protests against the form of surface mining known as mountaintop removal.

From the mid-1970s through the end of the twentieth century, there was an explosion of interest in the study of place in Appalachia as a means of understanding cultural survival in the face of negative stereotyping. In the twenty-first century, research by folklorists and anthropologists continues to focus on place and on practices such as homecomings that continue to give people in Appalachia a sense of shared history and destiny.

The focus on place brings together categories of doing and thinking usually separated in ways that pit "nature against industry, and culture against commerce," to cite critic Raymond Williams. But while a legislative agenda geared to integrating nature and culture was created during the Great Society, cultural scholars and workers in Appalachia only began to exploit it in the last years of the twentieth century. For example, the National Environmental Policy Act of 1969 provided a basis for combining culture and nature with politics in urban and regional planning. The principle was also included in the 1977 Surface Mining Control and Reclamation Act, allowing communities to challenge surface-mining permits on grounds that such mining destroys aesthetic, historic, scientific, and recreational values. Scholarly studies in folklore in the 1980s and 1990s reinforced the legislation by pointing to the difference between bureaucratic categories such as "environment" and "cultural resources" and vernacular categories that resist the separation of culture from ecology.

Increasingly resisting the separation of culture from environment, mountain communities express their struggles against ecological and social crisis in cultural terms. Coal River Mountain Watch, in Whitesville, West Virginia, for example, is dedicated to "Remembering the past, working for the future." Even places for public folklore, which are often educational or festive, now tend to combine aesthetic, traditional, political, and ecological concerns.

In public spaces such as streets and in front of the facades of power such as government or corporate buildings, Appalachian groups transform folklore and tradition into acts of political purpose. Using spirituals as protest songs, ritually uncrowning and dethroning "King Coal" in demonstrations before state capitols, and holding annual reunions at sites of former community life in coal camps, churches, and schools, people continually gather, use, and change Appalachian traditions and keep them dynamic. Appalachian folklore and folklife are not fixed in time; they are evolving practices in which romantic nationalism, cultural pluralism, community and place-based development, and democratic ideas often vie for prominence and sometimes coalesce.

—Mary Hufford, *University of Pennsylvania*

James Abrams, "Lost Frames of Reference: Sitings of History and Memory in Pennsylvania's Documentary Landscapes," in *Conserving Culture: A New Discourse on Heritage*, ed. Mary Hufford (1994); Jane S. Becker, *Selling Tradition: Appalachia and the Construction of an American Folk, 1930–1940* (1998); Archie Green, *Only a Miner: Studies in Recorded Coal-Mining Songs* (1972); Mary Hufford, "Interrupting the Monologue: Folklore, Ethnography, and Critical Regionalism," *Journal of Appalachian Studies* (Spring 2002); Ellen J. Stekert, "Focus for Conflict: Southern Mountain Medical Beliefs in Detroit," in *The Urban Experience and Folk Tradition*, ed. Américo Paredes and Stekert (1971); Kathleen Stewart, *A Space on the Side of the Road: Cultural Poetics in an "Other" America* (1996); Jeff Todd Titon, *Powerhouse for God: Speech, Chant, and Song in an Appalachian Baptist Church* (1988); Allen Tullos, *Habits of Industry: White Culture and the Transformation of the Carolina Piedmont* (1989); David E. Whisnant, *All That Is Native and Fine: The Politics of Culture in an American Region* (1983); Michael Ann Williams, *Great Smoky Mountains Folklife* (1995).

Birth Lore

Appalachian lore about the reproductive cycle has been at its core an oral tradition held by women, and its overriding theme is the mortality of mother and child. Birth lore is an expansive category of folk belief and practice related to fertility, conception, abortion, pregnancy, birth, infancy, and the supernatural. Most of these beliefs cannot be tracked to an original source; rather, they are often a mixture of European tradition, Native American practices, and African slave culture. Beliefs vary regionally, reflecting concentrations of Scots-Irish, German, and Dutch settlements, though some themes are recurrent.

Kinship within Appalachia is strong and vividly represented by the community of women who come together during the birth of a child. Historically, and even at times in contemporary Appalachia, rural childbirth practices have included not only the presence of a midwife or attending doctor, but also women who tend to household needs before, during, and after the birth of the child. Men can also play important roles in this process, even in some communities in the past filling the role of the midwife, but most birth lore beliefs and practices are passed down through generations in the community of women.

Increased access to modern medical services has caused a decrease in the use of traditional folk medicine related to childbirth, yet some folk beliefs are still shared when women gather during folk rituals marking the life cycle. Though contemporary women widely deny that they accept these beliefs, some are still held, and mothers-to-be continue to be reminded of taboos.

Fertility and conception lore has included stories told to children about where babies come from, as well as practices rooted in old European fertility rituals. The widespread tale of the stork delivering babies was often adapted to regional animals such as the raccoon or buzzard. Superstition related to menstruation and phallic symbols is still observed by some women. The most common account says a woman should not tend cucumbers, okra, or squash in the garden, nor should she can (preserve) these vegetables while she is menstruating for fear plants will die or pickles ruin. Another act that echoed old fertility rituals was the throwing of peas, beans, or seeds by a husband onto a well-traveled dirt path or road to ensure his wife's fertility. Mandrake root or mayapple worn as a charm was another fertility practice that has been found in Appalachia.

Some beliefs concerning abortion and miscarriage involve native plant use and early Western medicinal products, as well as superstition. Natural abortifacients, or agents causing abortion, are common in most folk cultures. Native American tribes in the Appalachian region had broad knowledge of local plant use, and their beliefs filtered into European settlements. Baby berry, often called buck vine or partridge berry, and tea made from cotton roots, ginger, or mayapple were said to induce premature labor. Quinine and turpentine, common folk remedies for many ailments in Appalachia, were also purported to induce abortion. Eating or inhaling the odor of pungent or spicy foods was believed to induce labor, and some believed miscarriage would result if a pregnant woman carried or ingested a large quantity of salt.

Beliefs concerning confinement during pregnancy were related to either health concerns or the perception of a woman's "liminality," a betwixt and between state often marked by ritual. There are historical reports of socially isolating pregnant women during meals and, more recently in regions of the Blue Ridge Mountains, throughout her last days of pregnancy and several days after birth. One of the reasons given for this belief was that mother and child are, in essence, passing through a supernatural state and that any interference may cause harm.

Superstitions about the prenatal period were extensive in Appalachia and were associated to some extent with elevated infant mortality rates lasting into the twentieth century. These beliefs warn against anything that might injure, or "mark," the unborn child. Older women advised expectant mothers to avoid unusual or emotionally wrought situations and especially not to risk "a fright" or deny a food craving. Birthmarks resulting from such trauma often were reported to bear a shape related to the incident. Food cravings are also said to pass from mother to child. Being startled by animals or viewing a dead animal, it was often said, would result in an animal-shaped mark. It was believed that lancing boils, pulling teeth, or performing similar minor medical procedures on a pregnant woman could mark her child with deformity or illness rather than a simple blemish. Such beliefs were most likely related to the historically real risk of an ensuing infection affecting the fetus. Most instances of physical deformity and mental impairment fell into the general category of afflictions, believed to be caused in some instances by making light of the disabled or wishing harm on another while pregnant.

Birth customs have revolved around labor (sometimes called travail), afterbirth practices, and the physical recovery of the mother. A staple in Appalachian folklore has been practice of the signs, a system based on the Zodiac, in which the twelve signs are divided into body parts (head, neck, breast, bowels, loins, knees, feet, legs, thighs, kidneys, heart, and arms). When the sign is said to be "in loins," it is an unfavorable time for giving birth. Bad luck during labor could be caused by the mother raising her hands above her head, a dove mourning outside the window, or a member of the household sweeping the steps after sundown. One recurrent theme in childbirth lore is the placing of a knife or axe under the mattress to help cut the pain or bleeding.

Folk remedies used to hasten or ease childbirth include ingestion of quinine, turpentine, gunpowder, tansy tea, flaxseed, or slippery elm. A traditional practice of "quilling," blowing red pepper or gunpowder through a quill into the mother's nose, also hastened delivery by causing sneezing and contraction of the diaphragm. A snake skin placed around the thigh was also thought to ensure a quick delivery.

There were varied practices related to afterbirth. Some midwives and attending doctors had a woman blow with great force into her fist or clasped hands to help pass the placenta after birth. Folk practices called for disposal of the placenta in a hole deep enough to prevent it from being dug up by human or animal, which would bring bad luck, illness, or death to the mother or child. There were also reports of the placenta's being burned to prevent fever in the recovering mother.

Additional beliefs concerned both the health and disposition of a child after it was born. Cutting an infant's fingernails during the first few weeks of life was said both to result in death before six months of age or to cause it to be a thief. Some accounts of a mother's biting the child's nails rather than cutting them may be attributed to these beliefs. Cutting the hair of an infant induced bad luck. Stepping over a baby was reported to stunt growth. The day of the week on which a child was born was said to have great influence; babies born on Friday, for instance, were said to be unlucky.

The supernatural manifested itself in multiple ways in Appalachian birth lore, and divination came in various forms. Dreaming of death was frequently reported to foretell a birth. There were also numerous practices used to foretell the number or sex of children a woman would bear, including counting the remaining seeds after blowing the fluff off a dandelion. In a recent account from northeast Tennessee, a threaded needle stuck in the eraser of a pencil was used as a divining mechanism, the pendulum effect over a woman's wrist predicting the number of the children she would bear. A child born with the fetal membrane still covering its face, called the caul or veil, was said to have "the Sight," or the ability to see elements of the supernatural and predict the future. A baby with the Sight was often reported to be a quiet and well-behaved child, and there were accounts of crosses, amulets, and amber beads being used to protect these infants.

See also: GRANNIES, MIDWIVES, AND HEALERS (IMAGES AND ICONS); PREGNANCY AND CHILDBIRTH (FAMILY AND COMMUNITY); SIGNS.

—Shannon M. Smith, *University of Tennessee at Chattanooga*

B. A. Botkin, *A Treasury of American Folklore* (1944); Wayland D. Hand, ed., *The Frank C. Brown Collection of North Carolina Folklore, Vols. 6–7: Popular Beliefs and Superstitions from North Carolina* (1961–64); Benita J. Howell, *A Survey of Folklife along the Big South Fork of the Cumberland River* (1981).

Calendar Customs

In Appalachia, as elsewhere in America, the calendar year provides ample grist for celebrations. Appalachian calendar customs embody and celebrate the enduring and distinctive aspects of mountain life, integrating the life of region and nation through localized observances of national holidays.

During midwinter in contemporary Appalachia, Christmas, New Year's Eve, New Year's Day, and Hanukkah are observed in ways that resemble celebrations in other parts of the country. However, historically and in some places even today, regionally distinctive observances are rooted in vernacular tradition. For example, in the mountains of Pennsylvania, eastern West Virginia, and the Great Valley region of Virginia, where substantial numbers of Germans settled, some communities practice the old German custom of belsnickling. Over time, the belsnickle, from the German Pelz Nichol, or "Saint Nicholas in fur," evolved from a dark figure who threatened and admonished children to be good to a friendly character recognizable in the modern-day Santa Claus. In some Appalachian communities, belsnickles still visit neighbors at Christmas and, in much the same way as carolers, are rewarded by gifts or food.

As recently as the early twentieth century, many people in southern Appalachia observed Old Christmas, occurring on January 6 according to the Julian calendar, which was still followed in England at the time when many settlers came to the mountains. It coincides with the day of Epiphany, when the three Wise Men brought gifts to the Christ Child, though some feel the two observances are unrelated. After the custom of celebrating Christmas on December 25 in accordance with the Gregorian calendar became widespread, many families and small communities in Appalachia held celebrations for the twelve nights of Christmas, going to a different home each night for music and merrymaking. In the most rural parts of Appalachia, even until the mid-twentieth century, Christmas was often observed quietly, with church attendance, a family dinner, and sometimes the exchange of small gifts. Decorations were few. Sometimes children would hang stockings on the fireplace, and these would be filled with fruit, nuts, and perhaps some hard candy. In coal towns in parts of the region, there might be a central Christmas tree provided by the coal company. Old Christmas was associated with such miraculous events as the kneeling of livestock in prayer at the stroke of midnight on

Christmas Eve and the bursting forth of blooms on the elder tree on Christmas Day.

If Christmas in Appalachia was quiet, New Year's Eve and Day were more boisterous. At midnight on New Year's Eve, many rural Appalachian residents in years past shot guns into the air to welcome in the new year and drive away any bad spirits left from the departing year. In a few places in Appalachia, such as Lewisburg, West Virginia, communities still organize a Shanghai parade on New Year's Day, marching through town banging on pots and pans or using a variety of noisemakers and cross-dressing or wearing other masquerades in a traditional practice of inverting the normal social order. Although the origin of the name *Shanghai* is unclear, the traditions of noisemaking and guising harken back to the British Isles and Europe.

Some people in the mountains recall the New Year's shooting as a ceremonial practice wherein groups of men would go from farm to farm at midnight and fire off volleys of shots at places indicated by a man designated as the "captain." Cherryville, North Carolina, still maintains this practice, and the captain gives a recitation to bless the family, their farm, livestock, and crops for the new year. In contemporary Appalachia, New Year's Eve and Day are celebrated in much the same way as in the rest of America, with parties past the magical midnight hour, music, food, and often excessive drinking. By the beginning of the new millennium, many communities across the region, as in towns and cities elsewhere, were adopting community-sponsored First Night celebrations featuring family fun and abstinence from alcohol.

In some areas, special foods are still thought to bring good luck if eaten on New Year's Day. Black-eyed peas and hog jowls are traditionally eaten in southern Appalachia, while sauerkraut and pork highlight the menu in the more northerly parts of the region. Symbolically, pork rather than chicken is eaten because hogs root forward, but chickens scratch backward, portending the direction of luck for the new year.

Other winter celebrations in the region are related to religion and cultural heritage. Hanukkah, for example, the Jewish festival of lights, is celebrated by Appalachia's Jewish communities in mid-December and Kwanzaa, an African American tradition originating in 1966, extends from December 26 until January 1.

Between January 6 and the beginning of the Easter season with the fasting of Lent, some Appalachian communities with German and Swiss origins celebrate the winter carnival of Fastnacht. For example, Helvetia, West Virginia, a Swiss community, marks the transition from winter into spring by burning an effigy of winter, eating special foods, and playing music and dancing. Another such celebration, Groundhog Day on February 2, attracts national attention when Punxsutawney Phil, the Pennsylvania groundhog, makes his annual prediction on the arrival of spring. If he sees his shadow, additional weeks of winter can be expected; otherwise, spring is said to be at hand. This tradition derives from old-world celebrations of Candlemas Day, on which forecasts for spring could be made by observing bears, badgers, hedgehogs, or weather signs.

While both Easter and Passover are observed in contemporary Appalachia in ways found throughout the country, there are some special traditions such as the Peters Hollow egg fight in east Tennessee. Since the nineteenth century, neighbors and friends have gathered in Peters Hollow to compete in an egg-tapping contest. The person with the last unbroken egg is declared the winner.

Springtime in the mountains brings rituals associated with new growth, as wild greens are gathered for spring tonics and for flavoring food. Highly aromatic ramps *(Allium tricoccum)*, or wild leeks, are gathered in high elevations, cooked with beans, corn bread, and potatoes, and served at suppers and festivals organized as community fund-raising events. From Virginia into the more northern stretches of the region, maple trees are tapped for syrup making, and festivals celebrating maple trees, syrup, and candy take place at sugaring time.

Among the most distinctive and important celebrations in southern Appalachia are decoration days. Held in the summer, usually mid-June, families and communities gather to clean and decorate the family or church cemetery in anticipation of the decoration day event. (In northern Appalachia, similar observances take place on Memorial Day.) An entire Sunday is devoted to preaching, singing, a communal dinner on the grounds or gathering in local homes, a family reunion and church homecoming, and a time to honor the dead and to heal divisions among the living. As in the rest of America, the Fourth of July typically includes parades, picnics, fiddle contests, greased pig races, political speeches, and fireworks. Fiddle contests and other traditional music competitions and festivals, such as the famous Old Fiddlers' Convention in Galax, Virginia, occur all across Appalachia during the summer months.

In autumn, the mountains attract droves of so-called "leaf peepers" (tourists who come to see the glorious fall colors). Residents of the region decorate more during this season than at any other time of the year. Homes and businesses are adorned with corn shocks, gourds of many colors, pumpkins, and commercially produced seasonal decorations. Roadside produce stands offer honey, jellies and jams, pumpkins, gourds, sweet potatoes, apples, cabbages, and all manner of recently harvested produce. The fall months are filled with community festivals such as antique fairs and craft

Descendants of Jack and Ellen Stanley celebrate Independence Day at a park they established atop of Kayford Mountain, near Cabin Creek, West Virginia, 1996. The family hosts public gatherings annually on Memorial Day, Fourth of July, Labor Day, and Columbus Day. The Stanley heirs own both mineral and surface rights to this part of Kayford Mountain, which overlooks an eleven-thousand-acre mountaintop-removal site.

shows, apple butter and molasses festivals, and sausage and pancake breakfasts, all timed to take advantage of the influx of tourists, fall weather, and the wealth of the harvest. In the early twentieth century in coal towns with Hungarian workers, the community would be invited to grape harvest celebrations, with food, drink, and dancing surrounded by festoons of grapes.

Halloween, now celebrated in accordance with national custom, was once a time for distinctive youthful mischief in rural areas, where outhouses were overturned and wagons parked on rooftops. In rural areas, the first day of deer hunting season qualifies as another autumn holiday. Fresh venison adds to the fall fare, and in some places schools are closed for the day and workers take a day off. In Appalachia as elsewhere in the country, Thanksgiving Day is usually given over to family gatherings for the sharing of abundant food; in some places, it is a traditional hunting day. In earlier times in much of the region, Thanksgiving marked the beginning of hog-killing time, since the weather was cold enough to keep the meat from spoiling. Families and neighbors would gather to slaughter, clean, and prepare the meat for preservation.

As the demographics of the Appalachian region continue to change, new festivals and celebrations are added to the cultural mix. In numerous Appalachian communities in the twenty-first century, for example, Hispanic residents have introduced Cinco de Mayo (May 5), along with Latin music and traditional foods new to the mountains.

See also: FESTIVALS, FOLK; FESTIVALS, FOOD (FOOD AND COOKING); PARENTS' DAYS (FAMILY AND COMMUNITY).

—Jean Haskell, *East Tennessee State University*, and Gerald Milnes, *Davis and Elkins College*

Robert Chambers, ed., *The Book of Days* (1869); Jack Santino, *All Around the Year: Holidays and Celebrations in American Life* (1994); Chester Raymond Young, "The Observance of Old Christmas in Southern Appalachia," in *An Appalachian Symposium*, ed. J. W. Williamson (1977).

Chase, Richard

(1904–1988) Folklore collector and performer.

Richard Chase's family was from New England, but his father established a nursery in Huntsville, Alabama, where Chase grew up. At the age of twenty, he visited Pine Mountain Settlement School in Kentucky, where he heard students singing ballads and learned about the work of English folk song collector Cecil Sharp. Chase was particularly excited by Sharp's notion of giving children knowledge of their culture's past through the collecting and publishing of folklore. To Chase, the contemporary generation had moved away from what he saw as its traditional and racial inheritance. Although he eventually published several books, Chase followed up on Sharp's idea, seeing his own mission as teaching people about heritage through the performance of folk songs, dances, and tales.

By his twenty-first birthday, Chase was teaching songs from Sharp's collection to rural north Alabama schoolchildren. During the next ten years (1925–35), he worked periodically in the field of recreation and as a performer and teacher. He attended Harvard University and Antioch College, graduating from the latter in 1930 with a bachelor of science degree in botany. During the 1930s, he was also deeply involved in the White Top Folk Festival in southwest Virginia.

At a conference in North Carolina in the spring of 1935, Chase learned from Marshall Ward about Ward's family in Beech Creek, North Carolina, and their Jack tales. This was Chase's first awareness of the Jack tales, and he was intrigued by the prospect of uncovering an active tale-telling tradition in the North Carolina mountains. From then on, he focused much of his time and energy on the collection, publication, and performance of Jack tales.

Chase published six of the North Carolina Jack tales in the *Southern Folklore Quarterly* between 1937 and 1941. In late 1940, he learned through the Ward family's correspondence with collector James Taylor Adams that Jack tales could also be found in Wise County, Virginia. About a year later, he was employed by the Work Projects Administration's Virginia Writers' Project to compile a book on Wise County folklore; with the agreement of project officials and Adams, Chase changed the goal to focus primarily on folktales, instead of folklore in general. For various reasons—in part because the project ended—the Wise County book was never published, but thirty-four Wise County tales, fifteen of which were Jack tales, were included (in whole or part) in Chase's three books: *The Jack Tales* (1943), *Grandfather Tales* (1948), and *American Folk Tales and Songs* (1956).

Richard Chase contributed greatly to the general public's increased awareness of Jack tales and his books and performances led ultimately to the storytelling revival of the last two decades of the twentieth century. Chase's role in Appalachian folklore is best seen in his work as an editor and writer; he used his creativity and familiarity with published sources to put together as many as seven versions of each Jack tale when he told it or when he published it. For Chase, the tales were never final products, and he continued to alter them as long as he told them. Chase's altered and more literary versions of the tales tended to replace traditional oral versions, however, and his public performances came, in the view of many critics, to supplant those of traditional tale tellers of the southern mountains.

See also: JACK TALES, TRICKSTERS, AND MOUNTAIN FOLKLORE (IMAGES AND ICONS); SHARP, CECIL; STORYTELLING IN THE TWENTIETH CENTURY, RENAISSANCE OF (PERFORMING ARTS).

—Charles L. Perdue Jr., *University of Virginia*

Richard Chase, *Grandfather Tales* (1948) and *The Jack Tales* (1943); Charles L. Perdue Jr., "Old Jack and the New Deal: The Virginia Writers' Project and Jack Tale Collecting in Wise County, Virginia," in *Outwitting the Devil: Jack Tales From Wise County, Virginia*, ed. Perdue (1987).

Craft Revival

The revival of southern Appalachian crafts was rooted in the work of missionaries and other benevolent workers who arrived to provide relief and support to the poor in mountain communities in the late nineteenth century. Between 1880 and World War II, these social reformers launched a "revival" of southern Appalachian handicrafts that involved a complex network of craft producers, government officials, industries, museums, urban markets, and consumers, all of whom contributed to the redefinition of Appalachian craft production to serve a national cultural identity. Historically and in the popular imagination, the Appalachian craft revival has focused on the southern mountains of Tennessee, Kentucky, North Carolina, Georgia, Virginia, and West Virginia, largely because the craft revival emerged as part of a broader interest in the nation's folk heritage. Since the late nineteenth century, many Americans have looked to the Appalachian South as the locus of the nation's folk heritage. There, they imagined, was a "traditional" culture marked by a preindustrial economy, a set of social relations, and quaint remnants of an eighteenth-century Anglo-Saxon culture. Currents in regional and national culture, including the colonial revival, the Great Depression and attendant New Deal cultural and economic programs, and the industrial design profession, fueled this craft revival.

The reformers who worked to teach and revive the craft techniques of earlier days were influenced by the European-inspired Arts and Crafts movement. They believed that the methods, aesthetics, and community of preindustrial labor offered an antidote to the ills of industrial society, as well as a foundation for social and economic uplift for the mountaineers. The middle-class women who led such benevolent craft programs usually arrived from outside the mountain region. College educated and often professionally trained in crafts or art, craft leaders designed the products that they taught local people to make. At missions and schools such as Penland School of Crafts, Berea College, and Hindman Settlement School, the recovery and "revival" of local crafts served as a source of cultural pride and wholesome recreation and provided opportunities for social interaction, and cottage industries provided cash incomes. Settlement school and mission projects often led to the establishment of small craft industries by people sympathetic to the ideals of art and reform.

In 1930 craft leaders—mainly from the settlement schools—founded the Southern Highland Handicraft Guild, which quickly established itself as the arbiter of standards and workmanship of the region's craft products. The connection of arts and crafts to social reform lay at the very center of the guild's ideology and programs, but from its inception, leaders were interested in selling and pricing mountain crafts and understanding the marketplace. By the end of the decade, the guild had established itself as the recognized authority on matters relating to southern Appalachian handicrafts.

While the guild educated craft producers and craft industries in the mountains about consumer preferences and market trends, it was the idea of tradition and the notion that the past persisted in the present that sold mountain crafts and made them valuable. Advertising and public displays often used artifacts such as log cabins and spinning wheels to create quaint environments for craft work. Such publicity frequently relied upon romantic portraits of mountain craftspeople at work by photographer Doris Ulmann, who posed them with yesterday's tools, dressed in archaic costume. Allen H. Eaton's 1937 *Handicrafts of the Southern Highlands*, lavishly illustrated with Ulmann's photographs, supported the myth that southern Appalachian crafts were produced for use in traditional mountain homes.

Such images and the newly "revived" and "traditional" crafts helped preserve an imagined pioneer past for the entire nation. But these portrayals of southern Appalachian artisans obscured the larger social and economic contexts of poverty and labor surrounding the production of handmade goods in the 1930s. All mountain workers understood craft production as a form of disciplined labor. Despite the influence of the guild and benevolent craft industries, in 1933 more than 90 percent of all producers in the region did piecework for commercial companies—hand-tufting bedspreads, quilting clothing and home textiles, or weaving chair bottoms. Ninety-five percent of the workers were women, most laboring long hours in their own homes. Few mountain craft producers kept handmade goods for their own use. Some were ambivalent about the goods they made, and many disliked the physical demands of their work and worried about the longterm consequences for their health. The images created by craft leaders to sell the goods did not allow such contradictions or ambiguities, however.

The notions of "tradition" that served as the engine for the revival of southern Appalachian crafts obscured gender roles. Frequently the crafter was a woman, plying her trade in a domestic environment, but the images that sold the crafts concealed the Appalachian woman's role as breadwinner, businesswoman, and laborer, as well as the participation of the rest of her household in craft production. This complex relationship between craft as tradition and craft as labor was closely scrutinized in the 1930s as a result of the Women's Bureau of the Department of Labor's study of mountain craftswomen and as the Southern Highland Handicraft Guild and craft industries struggled to maintain their goals under the new wage and hour laws established by the Fair Labor Standards Act in 1938. Despite the meager earnings gleaned from craft work, New Dealers in the Tennessee Valley Authority, Subsistence Homesteads Division, and Resettlement Administration tried to establish craft production and craft cooperatives in the region to promote economic self-sufficiency.

Since World War II, the craft revival in the Appalachian South has traveled on two paths. Within the guild and in general, there has been a movement toward development of crafts as fine art. Schools such as Penland and Arrowmont, rooted in the early efforts of church and social settlement, have become international centers for training in fine crafts and attract renowned staff and students. A glance at the goods sold at the guild's shop at the Folk Art Center on the Blue Ridge Parkway in Asheville, North Carolina, provides a reminder that regional culture has become global and that artisans in southern Appalachia participate in a world with international standards and influences.

But the connection of southern Appalachian crafts to notions of tradition still prevails. From time to time, cultural and economic initiatives refer to those images and ideologies of the early-twentieth-century revival. During the War on Poverty programs in the 1960s, for example, organizing efforts by VISTA (Volunteers in Service to America) and the Appalachian Volunteers again brought local handicrafts into the national spotlight, and again a craft revival was promoted as an economic self-help strategy for distressed communities. The products brought to attention included the quilts and coverlets of yesterday, once again evoking the supposedly unique culture of a vague past.

Though the myth they embody continues to mask their relationship to the larger economy, both the earlier Appalachian craftspeople and contemporary craft artists in the region are part of complex networks of industry, commerce, labor, and culture.

See also: ARROWMONT SCHOOL OF ARTS AND CRAFTS (CRAFTS); HANDMADE CRAFTS (IMAGES AND ICONS); SOUTHERN HIGHLAND CRAFT GUILD (CRAFTS).

—Jane S. Becker, *Arlington, Massachusetts*

Jane S. Becker, *Selling Tradition: Appalachia and the Construction of an American Folk, 1930–1940* (1998); Eileen Boris, *Art and Labor: Ruskin, Morris, and the Craftsman Ideal in America* (1986); David E. Whisnant, *All That Is Native and Fine: The Politics of Culture in an American Region* (1983).

Crafts

See Section Overview (Crafts)

Culture of Poverty

In the 1960s and 1970s, public perceptions of folklore and folklife in Appalachia were colored by a dominant social model of the time called the culture of poverty theory. For some people, it has remained an enduring association. The culture of poverty theory was part of academic and popular discourse in those years, and its major adherents were anthropologist Oscar Lewis (1914–1970) and activist Michael Harrington (1928–1989). While both Lewis and Harrington were advocates for the poor and sought a deeper understanding of the condition of poverty, their writings clearly established the notion of poverty as a cultural rather than economic condition. The culture of poverty theory was not developed from anthropological studies or folklore studies of Appalachian culture and society, but it became associated with the region when analyses of American poverty focused on Appalachia as the quintessential example of a culture mired in intergenerational cycles of poverty.

Lewis popularized the idea that families who were impoverished from one generation to the next reproduced their conditions through specific cultural traditions. The poor were characterized as a subculture in Western society with ways of life handed down from generation to generation, accompanied by traits of fatalism, helplessness, dependence, and inferiority. Because Appalachia had long occupied a place in American imagination as a folk culture passing traditions from generation to generation, when the region was hit with economic decline in the mid-twentieth century, it was easy for scholars and the public to conflate folk tradition and poverty, suggesting that Appalachia was poor because it suffered from the tyranny of its own cultural traditions.

Not only did Lewis identify nearly seventy cultural traits of individuals from communities in a culture of poverty, but he also felt that individuals from these communities would demonstrate a strong present-time orientation and have little predilection to defer gratification or plan for the future. Not surprisingly, Lewis also characterized such people as having a provincial or local outlook with little or no sense of history. He believed the development of a culture of poverty involved a sudden transformation from traditional life to modern market society and noted that, in order to end the cycle of the culture of poverty in the United States, the government would need to raise the standard of living for the poor and gradually integrate them into the middle class.

Harrington, in *The Other America*, described the culture of poverty as one so dissimilar to mainstream America that the poor had a separate language, psychology, and worldview. In his view, the poor talked and thought differently from dominant society and were, in fact, "internal aliens." The effect on Appalachia of both Lewis's and Harrington's work was to reinforce a long-standing stereotype of Appalachians as unlike other Americans. It placed upon them the responsibility for their own poverty, identifying their speech patterns, religious practices, kinship relationships, music, and other traditions as markers of the culture that prevented their entering the economic mainstream. These views also led people to misunderstand the history and culture of Appalachia, which had a long and troubled relationship with the market economy. These ideas encouraged public policy for the region that focused on imposing middle-class values, often at the expense of the region's traditional culture.

Recovering the region's history and adopting new approaches to studying Appalachian folklore and folklife, including studying performances in context and understanding folklife as being more about the present and less about the past, provided a response to the culture of poverty theory and counteracted much of its negative effect on Appalachia. Nevertheless, some of the images and ideas that originated with the culture of poverty notion continue to influence some contemporary perceptions of Appalachia.

See also: WAR ON POVERTY (GOVERNMENT); WELFARE AND POVERTY (IMAGES AND ICONS).

—Debra Lattanzi Shutika, *George Mason University*

Michael Harrington, *The Other America: Poverty in the United States* (1962); Oscar Lewis, *The Children of Sanchez: Autobiography of a Mexican Family* (1961) and "The Culture of Poverty," *Scientific American* (October 1966).

Death Lore

For Appalachian pioneers, death was a constant companion. Disease and accidents were prevalent. There was a continuous threat of being killed by human or animal agent. Hospitals were nonexistent, and doctors were few. Children were often delivered by midwives, and many infants and mothers died in childbirth.

The first Appalachian settlers sought isolation. According to John Fetterman in *Stinking Creek* (1967), "a distant shot heard faintly across the misty mountains, was enough to cause a frontiersman to pack up his belongings and move on to less crowded quarters." With the Appalachian population increase, two major cultural traits emerged: familism (family cohesion) and neighborliness. These traits played a major role in the development of practices related to death and dying in the Appalachian Mountains.

When the physical condition of a mountaineer was considered life threatening, neighbors and friends performed what was called the "death watch." Someone would sit with the ailing person until he or she either recovered or died. A gurgling sound caused by excessive respiratory secretions known as the "death rattle" was an important sign that death was imminent.

As soon as death occurred, friends and relatives were contacted, the grave was dug, a coffin was constructed, and the corpse was prepared for burial. A messenger might walk or travel on horseback from residence to residence with a

A grave shelter in a family cemetery in east Tennessee, c. 1981. Such shelters are sometimes constructed over graves to protect them from rain and snow. Historically, death rituals in Appalachia may also include a wake—borrowed from the Scots-Irish practice of reviving, or "waking," the dead—in which neighbors and friends gather for several hours or days at the home of the deceased.

death notice. In some communities a bell was rung as a means of conveying a death message. A black badge or black wreath was occasionally hung on the door of a home. In a town or village, a funeral notice was posted in the window of certain businesses. Residents and visitors could go to the business, determine who had died, and respond accordingly. Until the early 1900s, a letter edged in black served to invite someone to a funeral. Later, telephones were used as a means of death notification.

Male neighbors would gather to dig the grave. Graves were dug six feet deep and in an east-west direction so the decedent would face the rising sun in preparation for "judgment day." It was the neighborly thing to do, so pay was never a consideration.

In rare instances, an individual had his or her coffin prepared prior to death. However, it was usually constructed after death by someone in the area who was adept at carpentry in one of a variety of woods, including walnut, oak, chestnut, poplar, and cherry. The most common was pine because it was plentiful and cheap. Originally, coffins were not lined. When lining was introduced, it was a quilt, black or white cotton, or a form of cotton called muslin. The mummy-shaped coffin was used until the introduction of metal, rectangular-shaped caskets.

While the grave was being dug and the coffin was being prepared, the body of the deceased was prepared for burial. The early mountaineers placed the body on what was called a "cooling board" or "laying out board." It was generally a door removed from the hinges for temporary use or a special piece of wood designed for the purpose of "laying out" the deceased. The corpse was thoroughly washed and clothed. Sometimes a shroud was used to cover the corpse, but most often it was dressed in regular clothing. Pennies or other coins were placed over the eyes to keep them closed.

In the days prior to embalming, burial had to take place within twenty-four hours, especially in the summer, because the body decayed rapidly and the odor was unbearable. On the night after death or the following night, a wake would be held. Neighbors would sit with the deceased through the night. Many wakes were festive affairs with lots of food, laughter, games, and, in a few instances, dancing. In more recent times, relatives or friends have taken this opportunity to photograph the corpse. Originally a Scots-Irish practice to revive, or "waken," the dead, the wake served several purposes: it prevented cats, rats, and insects from getting to the corpse; it was a social affair that brought family, friends, and acquaintances together to honor the deceased; it provided an opportunity to comfort survivors during their time of bereavement; and it provided those present with a realization that a fellow member of their society was actually dead. In some parts of the country, the wake also deterred grave robbers from stealing the corpse and selling it to a medical school to be used for teaching or experimentation.

In the early days of Appalachia, when no clergyman was present to perform a funeral service, mountain people practiced funeralization. The deceased would be buried, but the funeral would take place at a later date when a clergyman could be present to perform the service.

In contrast to modern practice, early funeral services were quite lengthy. They might last for hours or even more than a day. In comparison to the wake, funeral services were highly emotional. Because of the extensive familism and neighborliness, almost everyone attended the wake, funeral, and burial. Businesses would shut down, and farmers would leave their work to attend all services.

Services were generally followed by a solemn procession to the place of burial. The immediate family would be at the front of the procession with friends and neighbors following behind. At the burial site, prior to the placing of the deceased in the ground, there would be a dedication service. Friends carried the coffin to the cemetery and placed the remains in the grave. While a coffin usually served as a container for the corpse, there were instances in which the deceased was interred without a burial receptacle. In later years, burial vaults of wood, metal, or concrete were used as outer containers for the coffin.

In modern times, the rituals surrounding death and burial in Appalachia are generally like those elsewhere in rural and small-town America. While the early death watch took place in the home, in contemporary Appalachia if there is a death watch, it usually takes place in a hospital or nursing home. Often the person present at death is a stranger—perhaps a doctor or nurse. Few people in modern times know about the death rattle.

In addition to the telephone, modern means of death notification include daily radio broadcasts and the obituary published in the newspaper. If accidental death occurs, a police officer or clergyperson may deliver the news. A nurse, doctor, or member of the clergy may convey the news if a mountaineer dies in a hospital or nursing home. When someone dies in the service of his or her country, the news is usually delivered by a military chaplain or high-ranking military officer. In wartime, notification may be via registered mail.

Today in the mountains, the body is taken to a funeral home after death occurs. It is embalmed, cosmetics are applied, and the corpse is clothed by a licensed embalmer. The grave is seldom dug by friends and neighbors. Instead, it is prepared by the cemetery using modern equipment such as a backhoe.

Wakes today are also referred to as "visitation," "calling hours," or "viewing." The wake takes place at the funeral home and is no longer an all-night event. There are many types of funerals, including night funerals and private funerals. Graveside services and services in a chapel at the cemetery have become common. More and more mountaineers are choosing cremation. While early Appalachians were usually buried in a family cemetery, today interment is generally in a church or community cemetery. Fewer people attend wakes, funerals, and burial services.

Appalachians have selected to memorialize their dead in a variety of ways. In the early years, there was no memorialization. Later, sticks and rocks were used to mark the grave of the deceased. Some mountain people began to carve initials on a field rock to mark a grave. Later, stones such as marble, granite, and soapstone were employed as markers at the head and foot of a grave. Today, some forms of denoting a grave are architectural marvels. Some headstones even contain ceramic memorial portraits of the deceased. Many Appalachian families, past and present, observe a decoration day, a specific day of the year to memorialize their dead by performing various rituals, including religious ceremonies and cleaning of the cemetery and grave.

See also: FOLKLORE AND THE SUPERNATURAL; FUNERAL FOODS (FOOD AND COOKING).

—James K. Crissman, *Benedictine University*

James K. Crissman, *Death and Dying in Central Appalachia* (1994); John Fetterman, *Stinking Creek* (1967); Robert Kastenbaum et al., eds., *Encyclopedia of Death and Dying* (2003).

Eastern Kentucky Public Folklore

As with public folklore anywhere, the history of public folklore in Appalachian Kentucky is inseparable from popular ideas and images that outsiders harbor about the culture of the region. In the late nineteenth century, the coming of mines and railroads opened the area to educated outsiders looking for "authentic" mountain culture and to cultural dissenters seeking alternatives to industrial capitalism. Many of these newcomers perceived a purity of culture and tradition in the ballads, quilts, baskets, and fiddle tunes of eastern Kentucky, and some of them became collectors, interpreters, and promoters of mountain lore.

Kentucky's earliest examples of public folklore were associated with the settlement school movement, marked by Katherine Pettit's founding of Hindman Settlement School (1902) and Pine Mountain Settlement School (1913). Such institutions provided what they called a "superior basic education" for hundreds of children in eastern Kentucky while providing food, clothing, shelter, and medical care. They also attempted to preserve or revive a version of Appalachian culture palatable to middle-class America while teaching mountain people genteel values. In some cases, traditions that were "revived," such as morris dancing at the Hindman School, were not regional traditions at all.

Hindman and other settlement schools became important repositories of Appalachian traditions and materials, often collected by folklorists from outside the region. Following in the footsteps of Berea College, which had begun selling and popularizing craft items in the 1890s, they also became centers for marketing traditional crafts. Hindman's Fireside Industries, for example, operated for six decades. Crafts offered for sale were influenced by outside ideas, such as the decorative philosophy of Englishman William Morris and the Arts and Crafts movement, but the baskets, brooms, quilts, coverlets, chairs, and other items produced by the school formed a core repertoire which the public took to epitomize mountain tradition.

By the twentieth century, academic study of folklore was well established in Kentucky. The Kentucky Folklore Society, made up largely of academics and teachers, was founded in 1912 as a local branch of the American Folklore Society and held its annual meeting in conjunction with the Kentucky Education Association in Louisville from 1916 to 1950. Presidents of the society included nationally recognized folklorists Herbert Halpert, D. K. Wilgus, and Gordon Wilson. During the 1920s and 1930s, the society had two irregular publications, the *Bulletin of the Kentucky Folk-Lore Society* and the *Kentucky Folk-Lore and Poetry Magazine*, which published both scholarly articles and amateur pieces. In 1955 the *Kentucky Folklore Record* made its debut and gradually evolved into a more professional journal with a scope not limited to Kentucky, especially during the 1980s under the editorship of Camilla Collins. It nevertheless ceased to exist in 1986, as did the Kentucky Folklore Society.

During the Great Depression, the New Deal's Federal Writers' Project, directed in Kentucky by Urban R. Bell of Paducah, deployed approximately one hundred field workers to interview Kentuckians and photograph people, landscapes, and architecture. From their abundant documentation, approximately fifty researchers, writers, and editors, including Gordon Wilson, created *The WPA Guide to Kentucky*, published in 1939. The volume's chapter on "Folklore and Folk Music" deals primarily with Appalachia, describing mountain culture erroneously as a survival of Elizabethan England and the people as being "on the defensive" against encroachment of the modern world. Other sections on "Cities and Towns" and "Highways and Byways" describe numerous local traditions and cultural landscapes.

For more than three decades, Kentucky's Appalachian folklife was celebrated with the American Folk Song Festival, staged annually in the mountain town of Ashland. The event, organized by Jean Thomas, a local photojournalist who conducted extensive fieldwork in the area, collected folk songs, promoted the careers of selected artists, and published several books, ended in 1972.

Also famous in Kentucky public folklore is Louisville native John Jacob Niles, a lifelong collector, writer, performer, and promoter of folk music born in 1892. The songs Niles wrote were closely related to the songs he collected. His collecting included but was not limited to Kentucky or the Appalachians, and his books include collections of southern African American music and songs sung by soldiers, though his passion was for ballads. In 1936, after a brief stint as music director at the John C. Campbell Folk School in North Carolina, Niles settled in Kentucky, where he became a prolific recording artist and an important figure in the postwar folk song revival. He died in 1980.

Perhaps the most influential Kentucky folk music entrepreneur was John Lair. A native of Renfro Valley in Rockcastle County and a lifelong promoter of folk music, Lair was a pioneer in broadcasting folk and country music. While working on radio barn dance programs for WLS in Chicago and WLW in Cincinnati, Lair began to promote Kentucky performers. This led him back to Kentucky, where he became an avid collector of sheet music and gained a reputation as an authority on folk music. He published five books and became a prolific songwriter. While broadcasting the *Renfro Valley Barn Dance* show on WLS, Lair developed a country music tourist complex, which opened in Renfro Valley in 1939. Part of the complex was a large barn from which he broadcast the *Renfro Valley Barn Dance* live over the radio. Focusing on comedy, old English ballads, and string-band music among other offerings, Lair's shows were heard across the United States and had significant impact on the public image of Appalachian music. In the 1950s, Lair's show made it to television. Lair continued to promote Kentucky music until his death in 1985. The complex at Renfro Valley currently includes the nonprofit Kentucky Music Hall of Fame and Museum.

Appalshop, the well-known nonprofit film production enterprise founded in Whitesburg in 1969, has developed numerous programs and documentary films in addition to recordings of mountain music and theater projects exploring regional folklife, ethnography, and traditional arts, as well as political issues.

Other worthwhile initiatives have shown promise but proved not to have Appalshop's durability. Funded by the National Endowment for the Humanities, the Appalachian Oral History Project, based at Alice Lloyd College and Lees Junior College in Kentucky, Emory and Henry College in Virginia, and Appalachian State University in North Carolina, employed students to conduct tape-recorded interviews. Although it grew into an important educational initiative in the 1970s, the project faded out of existence in the 1980s.

The present-day Kentucky Folklife Program also began as a consortium. Supported by the Kentucky Oral History Commission, the Kentucky Humanities Council, the Tennessee Valley Authority, and Berea College, the program has seen some of its most notable achievements take place in the Appalachian area of the state—among them surveys of folklife along the Kentucky River and along the

Highway 23 "music corridor" in eastern Kentucky, an area that has been home to numerous famous country music performers. Since 1992, the program has been located in Frankfort as an interagency activity of the Kentucky Historical Society and the Kentucky Arts Council. Administering folklife grants, including project grants and apprenticeship grants with funds from the Kentucky Arts Council, the Kentucky Folklife Program also established a statewide Kentucky Folklife Festival, which has showcased music, crafts, dance, storytelling, and occupational traditions such as those relating to coal mining.

See also: APPALSHOP (MEDIA); HINDMAN SETTLEMENT SCHOOL (CRAFTS); NILES, JOHN JACOB (MUSIC).

—Timothy H. Evans, *Western Kentucky University*

F. Kevin Simon, ed., *The WPA Guide To Kentucky* (1996); David E. Whisnant, *All That Is Native and Fine: The Politics of Culture in an American Region* (1983).

East Tennessee Public Folklore

The mountains of east Tennessee have long been portrayed as a land that time forgot and a quaint, backward repository of Appalachian folk traditions. The development of east Tennessee's thriving tourism industry can be attributed at least in part to the early-twentieth-century emergence of the Appalachian folk arts and crafts movement, which was influenced by this perception of quaintness and contemporaneous with the beginning of industrial exploitation of the region.

Emma Bell Miles, a visionary teacher, artist, and poet who lived and worked near Chattanooga, celebrated east Tennessee's heritage of Appalachian folk arts and crafts in her evocative book *The Spirit of The Mountains* (1905). A self-taught folklorist and avid devotee of traditional crafts, Miles advocated cottage industries based on spinning and hand weaving as alternatives to factory work for mountain people.

Miles's call for the revival of Appalachian handicrafts, particularly weaving, did not fall upon deaf ears in east Tennessee. By 1912, the Pi Beta Phi Women's Fraternity established a weaving program in the tiny settlement of Gatlinburg in Sevier County. Like their counterparts elsewhere in Appalachia, the founders of the Arrowmont School of Arts and Crafts believed that weaving and other traditional crafts could be profitably marketed to tourists with a taste for folk art. Tourists were scarce in Tennessee's Great Smoky Mountains in 1912, but they would come.

The Appalachian settlement school movement played a key role in making the outside world aware of the region's folk heritage. Founded in 1913, the Conference of Southern Mountain Workers, a regional association of teachers and service workers, evolved into the Council of the Southern Mountains, the single most influential Appalachian organization from the 1920s through the 1960s. Two mainstays of this important regional association were John C. Campbell and his wife, Olive Dame Campbell, who invited the eminent English folk song scholars Cecil Sharp and Maud Karpeles to tour the southern mountains between 1916 and 1918 to collect the songs and tunes published in *English Folk Songs from the Southern Appalachians* (1917; revised 1932). Sharp and Karpeles collected several ballads in Sevier, Knox, and Unicoi Counties in east Tennessee.

The publication of the expanded *English Folk Songs from the Southern Appalachians* in 1932 inspired a generation of American folk song scholars to collect ballads in the field. Edwin C. Kirkland joined the English Department of the University of Tennessee in 1931. He and his wife, Mary, accumulated an extensive collection of field recordings of various genres of sacred and secular music collected in the vicinity of Knoxville making use of portable disk recording equipment. The Kirklands were early members of the Tennessee Folklore Society, established in 1934. From its inception, the society welcomed amateur folklore enthusiasts as well as professional scholars such as George Pullen Jackson, Mary Barnicle, and Tillman Cadle, who was Barnicle's husband and a labor organizer and folklorist.

Since the founders of the Tennessee Folklore Society came to folklore via English language and literature, they initially tended to concentrate upon spoken and sung traditions. There was no lack of interest, however, in handicrafts and other genres of material culture in east Tennessee during the 1930s. Allen H. Eaton's *Handicrafts of the Southern Highlands* (1937) notes several mountain crafts shops in addition to the original Arrowcraft shop located in Gatlinburg, the modest nucleus of what would become a sprawling tourist destination.

Great Smoky National Park planners had originally hoped to set up an outdoor folklife museum and crafts center. However, plans for this proposed folk arts museum were scuttled following the outbreak of World War II. Instead, as historian Durwood Dunn has documented, the National Park Service dispossessed the residents of the Cades Cove community, then removed modern improvements they had made to their homes to make the buildings appear antiquated. In *Great Smoky Mountains Folklife*, folklorist Michael Ann Williams describes these vacated homes as "empty shells," spurious nostalgia symbols evoking a falsified past. More recently, John Rice Irwin has continued this nostalgic view of Appalachian material culture at his Museum of Appalachia in Norris.

Throughout the United States, popular and academic interest in folklore burgeoned during the tumultuous 1960s. Thomas G. Burton and Ambrose N. Manning of the English Department at East Tennessee State University in Johnson

City began documenting the area's folk culture, especially traditional songs and music. Not only did they employ audiotape and hand-held 16mm sound film, but they also appear to be the first folklorists to have used portable videotape in their fieldwork. Like the Kirklands, they also encouraged students to collect folklore from their families and neighbors, creating the core of the Archives of Appalachia at East Tennessee State. From 1964 to 1972, Burton and Manning published a folk song column in the Johnson City newspaper that prompted contributions of texts of songs and ballads from readers in the region. They also organized successful folk festivals and folklore courses aimed at teachers. Both served as president of the Tennessee Folklore Society during the 1960s; both also served on the Folk Arts Panel of the Tennessee Arts Commission, established in 1967 as the first state folk arts program in America. The commission hired its first state folklorist, Linda White, in 1975. Robert Cogswell became Tennessee state folklorist in 1984 and maintained the position into the twenty-first century.

More community-oriented folklore projects followed during the 1970s at East Tennessee State University with the arrival of folklorist Richard Blaustein in the Department of Sociology and Anthropology in 1970. The establishment of Broadside Television, an experimental public-access video production center in Johnson City, inspired Blaustein to develop the Southern Appalachian Video Ethnography Series project, which recorded videotapes of local folk performers between 1973 and 1977. After Broadside Television ceased operation in 1977, its extensive videotape library was donated to the newly created Archives of Appalachia in 1978. With grants from National Endowment for the Arts Folk Arts Program and the Tennessee Arts Commission, Blaustein also developed Golden Days, a Folk Arts in the Schools program involving area performers, and the Old Time Country Radio Reunion, an annual gathering of veterans of live local country radio in east Tennessee first held in 1979.

That same year, the Tennessee Department of Parks initiated a statewide survey of folk performers and craftspeople under the direction of cultural conservationist Bobby Fulcher. Fulcher and his teams of young folklorists located and identified outstanding proponents of diverse folk traditions. In 1982 many of these individuals identified by the Tennessee State Parks Folklife Survey participated in the folklife festival at the World's Fair in Knoxville, as well as the 1986 Smithsonian Folklife Festival.

In 1983 the Tennessee General Assembly passed the Comprehensive Educational Reform Act, which led to the establishment of the Center for Appalachian Studies and Services at East Tennessee State. Since its inception in 1983, the center has produced records and radio and television programs and organized conferences, workshops, festivals, and special courses dealing with Appalachia's cultural heritage, particularly the region's links with Scotland and Ireland. East Tennessee State University also boasts the only program in bluegrass and country music at a four-year institution, and its master's degree in storytelling builds upon close connections with the International Storytelling Center and its acclaimed National Storytelling Festival in nearby Jonesborough.

Since 1994, the Center for Appalachian Studies and Services has strongly supported the efforts of the Birthplace of Country Music Alliance to promote the folk and country music heritage of the city of Bristol, which straddles the Tennessee-Virginia border. The alliance has sponsored successful concerts in the restored Paramount Center for the Arts in Bristol, Tennessee, put together a temporary country music history museum, and embarked upon an ambitious oral history project and the creation of a permanent museum, the Birthplace of Country Music Heritage Center in downtown Bristol.

Though much has changed, east Tennessee is still rich in living traditions of music and other Appalachian folk arts. Beginning with Emma Bell Miles nearly a century ago, devoted individuals in the public and private sectors have continuously worked to promote appreciation of this region's distinctive cultural heritage.

See also: BLUEGRASS (MUSIC); BROADSIDE TELEVISION (MEDIA); MUSEUM OF APPALACHIA (CULTURAL INSTITUTIONS).

—Richard Blaustein, *East Tennessee State University*

Allen H. Eaton, *Handicrafts of the Southern Highlands* (1937); Emma Bell Miles, *The Spirit of the Mountains* (1905); Michael Ann Williams, *Great Smoky Mountains Folklife* (1995).

Eaton, Allen H.

(1878–1962) Arts advocate and author.

Allen H. Eaton, a leader in the southern mountain craft revival, helped establish handicrafts as a defining feature of southern Appalachian culture. Trained in sociology, Eaton began his career in state politics and art education. In 1918 his commitments to cultural pluralism and the handcrafted arts drew him to New York, where he organized a series of exhibitions of immigrant crafts. He joined the Russell Sage Foundation in 1920, beginning a long career promoting the social benefits of art.

Through the Russell Sage Foundation, Eaton met leaders of several southern mountain craft enterprises and began his own study of the region's crafts and craft makers. An organizer of the Southern Highland Handicraft Guild in 1930, Eaton shaped guild programs ranging from craft exhibits to souvenir sales in the region's national parks. In 1937 Eaton published his research on mountain crafts and their makers in a volume entitled *Handicrafts of the Southern Highlands*. As a recognized authority on American arts and crafts and an advocate of rural life and culture, Eaton also served as an advisor to federal agencies during the New Deal and helped organize the Department of Agriculture's Rural Arts Exhibition in 1937.

In reviving crafts, Eaton hoped to create a "handicraft culture" in the southern mountains. Critics note that Eaton's romantic view of life in the Appalachian South as exclusively agrarian and essentially preindustrial prevented him from seeing that domestic, economic, and cultural life in the region had shifted and that craft production occupied a new place in this order.

See also: CRAFT REVIVAL; SOUTHERN HIGHLAND CRAFT GUILD (CRAFTS).

—Jane S. Becker, *Arlington, Massachusetts*

Festivals, Folk

The modern folk festival was born in Appalachia. Although the term *folk festival* had been used previously for a few cultural display events, it became fully established in the national consciousness when four prominent festivals were created between 1928 and 1934. The first three, the Mountain Dance and Folk Festival in Asheville, North Carolina, the American Folk Song Festival held near Ashland, Kentucky, and the White Top Folk Festival in southwest Virginia, all focused on Euro-American, Appalachian culture. Only the last, the National Folk Festival, was not held initially in Appalachia and was not monocultural in content.

America's fascination with certain regional cultures had earlier been quenched with literature. Just as the popularity of literature of the American West gave birth to the visual spectacle of the Wild West show, so popular presentation of the regional culture of Appalachia broadened from written to theatrical form. While the creation of four major folk festivals in six years indicates a response to national interests, it should be noted that all four were created independently and were informed by a variety of economic, personal, and political motives.

The Mountain Dance and Folk Festival, founded and directed by western North Carolina lawyer and folk song collector Bascom Lamar Lunsford, was created in direct response to growing promotion of tourism in the region. In 1928 the Asheville Chamber of Commerce invited Lunsford to present folk music and dance as part of its Rhododendron Festival. The following year the Mountain Dance and Folk Festival was established as a separate event, but it was always predicated in part on the popularity of Asheville as a tourist destination. Although his festival was largely monocultural, Lunsford generally avoided purist rhetoric, and a number of individuals of Cherokee descent participated. Lunsford accepted some change in tradition, and the festival was partially responsible for spawning the new dance form of team clogging.

In 1930 Jean Thomas, a native of eastern Kentucky and an avid self-promoter, created an informal festival in her own backyard. The successful event led to the establishment of the American Folk Song Festival in 1932. Thomas stressed that Appalachian culture was rooted in Elizabethan England and wrote that participation was limited to "mountain minstrels" who learned their songs through oral transmission. In the year between Thomas's backyard event and her first formal festival, Annabel Morris Buchanan established the White Top Folk Festival in uneasy alliance with John Blakemore, an attorney who wished to develop the area around White Top Mountain commercially, and Richmond composer John Powell, whose ideas about preserving Anglo-Saxon culture had a racist foundation. While the Mountain Dance and Folk Festival and the American Folk Song Festival survived for decades under the direction of their founders, White Top succumbed to both bad weather and bad feelings among its organizers and did not survive the decade.

The folk festival has often been tied to the earlier American enthusiasm for historical pageantry that flourished at the turn of the century. The connection can be seen most directly in the career of Sarah Gertrude Knott, founder of the National Folk Festival. While teaching drama at a small college in North Carolina, Knott fell under the spell of the Carolina Playmakers' Frederick Koch, one of the most influential dramatists to emerge from the pageantry movement. While pageantry, like the folk festival, could be fueled by reactionary agendas, Koch's students generally held progressive views, especially on race relations. Knott's festival from the outset was diverse in emphasis, and the first year included African American, Native American, Hispanic, and French traditions. After relocating to St. Louis and working with local theater groups, Knott developed the idea of staging a folk festival that was national in scope. Though she consulted with Lunsford, Buchanan, and Thomas, Knott always gave primary credit to Koch for the inspiration in creating her festival.

Although the National Folk Festival was adamantly multicultural, Knott considered Appalachia and the Ozarks to be important "seedbeds" of American culture. The first festival included a large contingent of performers from the Ozarks who had been identified at a series of small, regional festivals, as well as performers brought from western North Carolina by Lunsford. The second festival was held in Chattanooga and was preceded by several small festivals in east Tennessee. Lunsford's contingent once again performed, as did traditional Cherokee dancers. Although the National Folk Festival would not be held again in Appalachia until

1969, Appalachian culture was always well represented on the festival's program.

For some, the creation of the early folk festivals was a reaction against the commercialized representations of regional tradition, especially by radio and the recording industry. However, while Buchanan denounced the type of folk song heard on the radio as crude and degrading, other festival organizers worked with the radio industry. Despite her avowed purist sentiments, Thomas, who had previously worked in show business, was eager to promote herself on radio, and she used radio star Bradley Kincaid as a master of ceremonies for her festival. Lunsford worked on a number of collaborative projects with radio entrepreneur John Lair, creator of the *Renfro Valley Barn Dance*, and Lair himself served on the National Committee of the National Folk Festival. Many of the early radio stations, in turn, preferred to label the music they presented as "folk" rather than "hillbilly" and found common ground with the folk festivals.

Folk festivals continue to flourish in Appalachia. As with the earliest, the content and intent vary enormously. Many, such as Lunsford's, were created to promote a particular part of the region economically. Some focus largely on Anglo-Celtic traditions. Others celebrate diversity. All serve as vehicles to represent and interpret the culture of Appalachia to others.

See also: FESTIVALS, FOOD (FOOD AND COOKING); FESTIVALS, HUMOR AND STORYTELLING (HUMOR), FESTIVALS, MUSIC (MUSIC).

—Michael Ann Williams, *Western Kentucky University*

Loyal Jones, *Minstrel of the Appalachians: The Story of Bascom Lamar Lunsford* (1984); David E. Whisnant, *All That Is Native and Fine: The Politics of Culture in an American Region* (1983); Charles K. Wolfe, *Kentucky Country: Folk and Country Music of Kentucky* (1982).

Folk Healing

See Folk Medicine

Folk Ideas and Worldview

In the mountains of Appalachia, an Appalachian "folk" is often romantically associated with closeness to the land and to nature. In reality, Appalachian land-based concepts of creation and husbandry are far more complex and stand in marked contrast to modern, mainstream notions of nature. These concepts, which folklorists call folk ideas, serve as units of worldview, the philosophical and cultural frameworks that condition the ways in which people interact with their surroundings. In Appalachia, these frameworks represent some distinctly different ways of thinking about relationships between people and the environment.

In mainstream modern usage, the term *nature* represents something to be conquered. Nature is, as Katharine Hepburn informs Humphrey Bogart in *The African Queen*, "what we were put in this world to rise above." The impetus to tame the natural world pits nature against the higher (rational and supernatural) aspirations of civilization. Since the Middle Ages, a view of nature as civilization's nonhuman Other has yielded practices that have led to turning land and natural resources into commodities to be bought and sold and to exploitation and domination of people seen as living close to nature, such as the rural people of the Appalachian Mountains.

Throughout the Appalachian region, what mainstream Americans consider to be nature is subsumed along with people under a broader concept of creation, referred to in Appalachian parlance as "the land." The resulting relationship in Appalachia, often misrepresented in mainstream culture as submissive and misguided immersion in nature, is really a reciprocal relationship with the natural world and all of creation.

Attitudes about nature found throughout Appalachia have antecedents in Native American and Celtic worldviews, as well as in Calvinist religious teaching. John Calvin held that nonhuman creation was perfect and good, and that humanity's alienation from it was part of Adam's fall. For Calvin, the natural environment was a manifestation of God's grace. Since early modern times, some theologies of creation assigned a particularly important role to mountains. Calvinists who settled among mountains—and there were many in Appalachia—may have been expressing through their choice of location their belief in the goodness of nature. This traditional belief finds expression in contemporary Appalachia in community-based protests against strip mining, clear-cutting, and dumping of toxic waste in the mountains.

Such protests contradict mainstream notions of nature, which may lead to land-use policies that either convert land into property for development or resource extraction or else set it aside as wilderness apart from industrial or residential development. The Appalachian concept of creation, on the other hand, allows for longterm reciprocity between communities and their surroundings. Harvard psychiatrist Robert Coles, for example, witnessed a mountain woman placing her baby on the ground in a gesture to extend the child's feeling of trust from its mother's body to the body of the earth. This ritual was designed to foster a feeling of reciprocity with the land in mountain children from infancy. Coles also had an Appalachian resident say to him that "this land is as much a part of me as my arms and legs are." In another expression of the relationship with creation, Walter Franklin of MacDowell County, West Virginia, told a filmmaker that "if we lived in a country that loved the land, then we'd live in a country that loved people."

The folk idea of husbandry in Appalachia also expresses a worldview of reciprocity between people and the natural world. Husbandry describes a farmer's caring relationship with the domesticated worlds of farm and family, linking life in the natural world of the mountain farmstead with life in the human world of family and community. Appalachian farmers in the eighteenth and nineteenth centuries felt the power and mystery of the natural world; as they realized their limits to intervene and control nature, for example, they hedged their bets by engaging in diversified, rather than specialized, farm production. The concept of husbandry, appearing widely in Judeo-Christian tradition, connects people to land in a spiritual framework. Not all nineteenth-century Appalachian farmers were Christians, but most were familiar with the tradition of Bible stories, and they provided a framework within or against which they struggled to make their lives meaningful.

Rural life in early Appalachia largely demonstrated the close harmony between land and people, as farmers adapted to the local landscape. In Appalachian valleys, prosperous agricultural communities featured midsized farms, diverse crops, intensive cultivation, and ample livestock, with surplus crops sold in local and regional markets. Streams became sources of power for mills, tanneries, forges, foundries, and iron furnaces. Farmers in more mountainous parts of the region did not have the advantage of large, flat, fertile fields for intensive agriculture, so they adapted their farming operations to the mountain ecology. Rather than growing large quantities of corn to feed hogs, for example, for much of the year they let the hogs range in the woods, feeding themselves on products of the forest, especially chestnut mast. Hunting game, trapping for fur, and gathering mountain ginseng and other forest products (which could be sold) took advantage of the resources offered by the natural landscape. Such diversity led them to prize versatility, the ability to do many things well, which in turn led to self-reliance both individually and as small communities. Appalachian farmers daily had to rely on both the land and their immediate families and frequently on neighbors and kinfolk. This reliance fostered a set of relationships for which the term *husbandry* is appropriate. While the percentage of full-time farmers in the region has now decreased to below 10 percent, the folk idea and social patterns of husbandry still remain.

In both historical and contemporary Appalachia, life has been shaped by the interaction of opposing worldviews—the traditional worldview based on folk ideas such as creation and husbandry and what some call the technological worldview. The technological worldview drives global economic development and represents the dominant point of view in modern industrial and capitalist societies. Rather than the spiritually and naturally based traditional worldview in Appalachia, the technological worldview is rooted in pragmatic and mechanistic approaches to understanding the world.

The two worldviews have often come into conflict in Appalachia. The technological worldview is seen in Appalachia in the industrial projects of the Tennessee Valley Authority and the Appalachian Regional Commission, mills and factories of the Carolina Piedmont, the railroad system that girds the region, chemical and chip mills of the Kanawha River Valley, power plants and strip mines of the Cumberland and Allegheny Plateaus, and even in the network of state and federal forests and parks, heritage corridors, and pioneer villages where traditional culture, folklore, and folklife are set apart from normal life yet displayed as authentic regional culture. Appalachia's division into bucolic and industrialized spaces epitomizes the technological worldview, which makes it possible to expunge spiritual and cultural values from land that has resources to extract.

This technological worldview helps create the idea that new technologies inherently require a social design that protects managerial control. The company town in Appalachia is one historical example of technology as social design, as are contemporary efforts by legislators and industrial leaders to roll back clean air and water laws to accommodate giant mining machinery and associated methods of disposing of mine wastes. Both suggest that industrial economic development has priority over nature and local communities.

Kentucky farmer and writer Wendell Berry has articulated the inseparable relationship of land and culture and has criticized strip mining in Appalachia as the logical and disastrous outcome of attitudes that exploit land and people. Ben Turner, a coal miner from West Virginia, expressed the conflict of opposing worldviews in Appalachia, saying, "Here's a thought. It says in the Bible that if man don't cry out to God against injustice, the rocks and trees will. Satan knows that, and that's why he's using these companies to destroy everything. They don't know what they're doing, but Satan does." The conception of land as a "sacred mystery" finds expression in widespread grassroots efforts in Appalachia to resist destruction of place, habitat, and cultural memories and in ecological and sustainability movements in the region.

It is important to note that the Appalachian experience may reflect the technological worldview and a folk worldview simultaneously. In protests against destruction of mountain forests, for example, the paradox becomes clear. In such protests, Appalachian folk ideas about creation, land, and place come into conflict with mainstream concepts of nature and technology as Appalachian people variously resist or support commodification of land resources and enclosure of wilderness.

See also: COMMUNITY ACTION GROUPS (FAMILY AND COMMUNITY); SECTION OVERVIEW (IMAGES AND ICONS); SECTION OVERVIEW (MEDIA).

—Rodger Cunningham, *Alice Lloyd College;* Herbert G. Reid, *University of Kentucky;* and Jeff Todd Titon, *Brown University*

Robert Coles, *Children of Crisis, Vol. 2: Migrants, Sharecroppers and Mountaineers* (1967); Rodger Cunningham, *Apples on the Flood: Minority Discourse and Appalachia* (1988); Jeff Todd Titon, *Powerhouse for God: Speech, Chant, and Song in an Appalachian Baptist Church* (1988).

Folklore and Education

See Section Overview (Education)

Folklore and Social Protest

While it is true that much folklore embodies and ratifies majority values and perspectives, many elements of it arise out of disagreement and conflict with them. Both in the course of everyday life and at moments of overt conflict, folklore may be used as an instrument of social protest. Within Appalachia, it has been used to comment on historical processes; critique public officials, policy, and institutions; express collective will; and effect change.

Such uses—reaching across virtually all genres and forms of folklore—have focused on a wide spectrum of issues. Many of the aphorisms, tales, and legends that are a perennial part of everyday discourse contain elements of protest, as do the jokes that poke gentle and ironic fun at class distinctions, social pretense, and self-importance ("He's getting above his raising"). Examples are in evidence in every historical period. Opposition by men from around North Carolina's Grandfather Mountain to Civil War conscription produced "Deserter's Song," and the song "Coal Creek Troubles" emerged from the fight of east Tennessee miners against the convict-lease system in the early 1890s.

The 1930s produced a large volume of protest music framed within traditional musical idioms, much of it emanating from the coalfields of eastern Kentucky. Singer-composers Sarah Ogan Gunning, Aunt Molly Jackson, Jim Garland, and Florence Reece created an extensive corpus of songs, some of which wedded protest lyrics to traditional hymn tunes. Gunning, for example, used the tune of "As I Went Down in the Valley to Pray" for her union organizing song "Down on the Picket Line"; she also wrote "Dreadful Memories." Reece's "Which Side Are You On?" later spread into protest movements far beyond the mountains, and Garland and Jackson wrote "The Death of Harry Simms" about the assassination of a young labor organizer. Pinewood Tom's "Silicosis Is Killin' Me" of 1936 protested the brutal disregard for the health and lives of workers building the Hawk's Nest Tunnel in West Virginia. The economic and social distress of those who left the mountains for jobs in Piedmont cotton mills provided subjects for many songs by Dave McCarn ("Cotton Mill Colic"), Dorsey Dixon ("Babies in the Mill"), J. E. Mainer ("Hard Times in the Cotton Mill"), and others.

Other major links between social protest and several genres of folklore emerged in the 1960s and again were associated primarily with the coalfields. As early as 1960, the Wright Brothers took "Island Creek Mine Fire" into the bluegrass repertoire. Billy Edd Wheeler's "Ain't Goin' Home Soon" and Jean Ritchie's "Last Old Train's A-Leavin'" and "The L&N Don't Stop Here Anymore" commented on forced out-migration following mine mechanization and the conversion to strip mining. Uncle Dan Gibson and Warren Wright deployed the forms and language of traditional mountain preachers in the service of protesting strip mining. Numerous protest songs were produced by coalfield composers and singers such as Jean Ritchie ("West Virginia Mine Disaster," "Blue Diamond Mines," and "Black Waters"), Hazel Dickens ("Black Lung," "Clay County Miner," "Mannington Mine Disaster," and others), and former miners Nimrod Workman ("Don't You Want to Go to That Land?") and Mike Paxton ("Black Lung Blues"). In 1977 Rich Kirby and Michael Kline produced an album of anti-strip-mining songs entitled *They Can't Put It Back*. Michael Kline's 1969 "Talking Community Action Blues" used the traditional blues form to satirize the contradictions of the War on Poverty.

From the 1960s onward, the women's liberation movement used a number of folkloric materials and practices for purposes of protest, but such themes had been present for many decades. Child and broadside ballads from earlier centuries spoke of the emotional and physical pain women suffered at the hands of inconstant and abusive men. The traditional folk lyric "Single Girl" compared the autonomy and freedom of an unmarried woman to the burdens of a married one "with a baby on her knee." In the 1930s, Lily May Ledford and the Coon Creek Girls' "Banjo Pickin' Girl" celebrated the assertive autonomy of a woman who had "been all around this world" by herself. Several decades later, Hazel Dickens's hard-edged "Don't Put Her Down," "My Better Years," and "Custom Made Woman Blues" protested explicitly the hard lives of women "in a world made by men." More recently, Mary K. Anglin has documented how women mica workers in the North Carolina mountains "used the language of evangelical Protestantism to create arguments of opposition that criticized factory owners as sinful and corrupt."

For purposes of protest, folkloric forms and genres have more often than not been employed not singly (as a song, aphorism, or tale) but in synergistic combinations. Protracted protests by citizens of Ashe County, North Carolina, in the early 1970s over the proposed damming of the New River by an electric power company culminated in the New River Festival of 1975, which featured traditional music and topical songs written for the occasion, handcrafts, local foods, public testimony, and an epic drama about the county and its people. Taken together, these activities highlighted and validated the local history and culture that would be lost if the dam were built.

In the late 1980s, the southwest Virginia mining community of Ivanhoe also inventoried, revitalized, and presented many folkloric elements of its local history and culture in order to protest and respond to the grave social and economic crisis that followed the closing of the last local industrial employer. Many public events—preeminently the annual Jubilee Festival—included bluegrass and gospel music, communal meals, brief dramatic presentations, and (most spectacularly) giant puppets. As in the New River Festival, satire and protest blended seamlessly with cultural recovery and visions of possible futures.

Both on the New River and at Ivanhoe, protest was a dynamic process that continued over many months and involved a continually shifting array of folkloric elements. In contrast, the striking workers' takeover of Pittston Coal Company's Moss 3 plant in southwest Virginia in 1989 was brief and intense. Its major chroniclers called it "a giant cultural event, something like a cross between a bluegrass festival, a turkey shoot, and an oldtime revival." String musicians were scattered throughout the crowd, playing many types of traditional music to rally protesters' spirits and bind them together in their effort. Morning prayers and communal meals also figured in the elaborately developed protest event. Protest songs from the 1930s coalfield wars were sung again, together with newly composed ones. At one intense moment, a strike supporter used a bullhorn to lead workers occupying the plant and their supporters outside in a lined-out performance of "Amazing Grace." Situated in such a way, a gentle and sweet-spirited hymn functioned for the moment as a powerful unifying statement of protest, resistance, and solidarity.

The relationship of folklore to statements and movements of protest in Appalachia is inseparably linked to larger issues—passivity and resistance, political acquiescence and assertiveness—among Appalachian people. The force of tradition may limit social action at times, yet it can also be a powerful tool in social activism and community solidarity.

See also: COAL-MINING AND PROTEST MUSIC (MUSIC); MINE WARS AND THE TWENTIETH-CENTURY MEDIA (MEDIA); WORKMAN, NIMROD, AND PHYLLIS BOYENS (MUSIC).

—David E. Whisnant, *Chapel Hill, North Carolina*

Stephen L. Fisher, ed., *Fighting Back in Appalachia: Traditions of Resistance and Change* (1993); Stephen William Foster, *The Past Is Another Country: Representation, Historical Consciousness, and Resistance in the Blue Ridge* (1988); Archie Green, *Only a Miner: Studies in Recorded Coal-Mining Songs* (1972).

Folklore and the Supernatural

Many people who perpetuate stereotypes of Appalachian subcultures continue to link people in the region to beliefs in quaint superstitions. Supernatural beliefs, in Appalachia as elsewhere, represent attempts to describe and explain events that folklorists and anthropologists characterize as "liminal," that is, representing a threshold between the everyday world and a world where laws of nature do not apply.

Supernatural beliefs may involve entities such as ghosts and witches that perform physically impossible feats, or they may describe events unexplainable by science. *The Frank C. Brown Collection of North Carolina Folklore* (1952–64) and many similar collections of popular superstitions show that Appalachia is a rich area for beliefs and legends related to these areas of the supernatural. Three major factors may account for belief in supernatural folklore in the mountains: folk religion or beliefs that support and coexist with official religious doctrine; anomalous experiences or phenomena that cannot readily be explained rationally; and the mystery of death.

In many areas of Appalachia, religious experience involves personal contact with the divine—an encounter with one's Savior or a reliance on miraculous healing power. Such religious beliefs assume a world with a door constantly open to divine forces, and testimonies of miraculous events and signs are a part of the worship practices of many sects. However, the extent to which such divine power can be channeled and used by individuals is a matter for dispute among various religions and denominations. "Charming," a common tradition found in both Anglo-American and African American communities, involves folk healing. Charming (or "powwowing" as it is known north of the Mason-Dixon Line) is religious in intent, but many see it as potentially blasphemous. Hence cultures preserving belief in folk healing balance this belief with traditions about witchcraft or conjuring. Healers frequently blame illness on evil counterparts and offer to "turn the trick," causing evil to fall on the person responsible. Many such rituals mirror the evil spells supposedly being cast by witches or conjurers, and indeed some individuals, predominantly older single women, have adopted the role of evil charmer (or encouraged rumors to that effect) to give them a source of income or protect them against theft or harassment. Hence supernatural beliefs of faith healing and witchcraft tend to coexist, even in contemporary times.

Anomalous phenomena occur in Appalachia, as they do elsewhere, and folklore collections include many accounts of puzzling sights seen in remote areas of the region. These locations generate reputations as doorways to mysterious happenings, and they are visited especially by young people anxious to experience the paranormal. Most are little known outside nearby communities, but some have drawn attention from outside the region. The Brown Mountain Lights, unexplainable luminous balls that appear over a mountain ridge in western North Carolina, have become internationally known.

Scientific explanations of such phenomena vary widely, as do folk explanations. One common tradition attributes these strange events to otherworldly agencies. Mysterious lights are often described by names such as "Jack o' Lantern," and tales frequently attribute them to persons who for some reason were excluded from both heaven and hell and consequently forced to wander the earth eternally. Alternatively, the location may have been the site of some human tragedy: a suicide, execution, murder, or untimely death by accident. The Brown Mountain Lights are variously attributed to a battle between Native American tribes, the murder of a settler's family, or, in the words of a bluegrass song, "A faithful old slave, come back from the grave, / Searching for his master who is long, long gone." Many explanations are romantic rather than seriously held, but the phenomenon continues to inspire groups of psychic investigators who now use modern technology such as the Internet to share experiences and theories.

Many supernatural beliefs focus on the threshold between this life and the hereafter. Folklorist and oral historian William Lynwood Montell has noted the way in which such lore expects, perhaps demands, the return of the dead to the living. He suggests that the multiplicity of legends and beliefs reflects a long-standing tension between folk images of death, in which spirits remain close to those with whom they lived, and the orthodox Christian belief that the dead go to God and do not return. Death "tokens," or symbolic warnings of the passing of a loved one, are especially common in tradition and are often explained as the final farewell of the dead to survivors. Appalachian ghosts appear to be more socially motivated than those found in lore elsewhere. Many stories exist about haunts that are laid to rest when someone is bold enough to speak to them, allowing them to pass on a secret message to the living such as the location of a lost treasure. Overall, ghost lore implies that the dead remain much like the living or at least have promises to keep, spiritual or literal, before passing through the portal to the other world.

While most Appalachians have readily accepted new scientific and philosophical concepts alongside more traditional beliefs, people in Appalachia, like people elsewhere, likely will continue to maintain some level of folk belief about the supernatural.

See also: JACK TALES, TRICKSTERS, AND MOUNTAIN FOLKLORE (IMAGES AND ICONS); SERPENT HANDLING (RELIGION); SIGNS.

—Bill Ellis, *Pennsylvania State University at Hazleton*

Wayland D. Hand, ed., *The Frank C. Brown Collection of North Carolina Folklore, Vols. 6–7: Popular Beliefs and Superstitions from North Carolina* (1961; 1964); William Lynwood Montell, *Ghosts along the Cumberland: Deathlore in the Kentucky Foothills* (1975); Barbara L. Reimensnyder, *Powwowing in Union County: A Study of Pennsylvania German Folk Medicine in Context* (1982).

Folk Medicine

Appalachian folk medicine is an amalgam of traditional healing knowledge derived from various cultures, most notably English, German, Native American, Scottish, and Scots-Irish. Folk medicine is conventionally distinguished from popular medicine (chiropractic, reflexology) and official medicine (Western biomedicine) by an essentially informal, oral process of transmitting knowledge from one generation to the next. Folk, popular, and official health belief systems are interactive, however, and each influences the others.

Appalachians acquired considerable knowledge of health and illness from popular and official medicine through various printed sources, including almanacs, patent medicine company pamphlets and brochures, United States Department of Agriculture publications, and especially domestic medicine books produced in the nineteenth century such as John C. Gunn's *Domestic Medicine, or Poor Man's Friend in Hours of Affliction, Pain, and Sickness* (originally published in 1830). Much of the research on Appalachia's folk medical belief system from roughly 1870 to the present primarily emphasizes the south-central and southern areas of the region. It is important to note that Appalachian folk medicine is a regional manifestation of Euro-American folk medicine, which is to say that the folk medical beliefs and practices are not distinctive to Appalachia alone but are or were common among Euro-Americans residing outside the region.

Appalachian folk medicine was profoundly influenced by the prevailing theories of illness causation that dominated official medicine in the eighteenth and nineteenth centuries, most notably humoral and miasmatic pathology.

Humoral pathology, which originated with the ancient Greeks around the sixth century B.C., is based on the belief that health depends upon a balance in the volume of four body fluids, or humors: blood, phlegm, black bile, and yellow bile. Over time, humoral medicine evolved in Europe and America to a central concern with blood. It was thought that many illnesses were caused by the accumulation of morbific matter (poisonous substances) in the blood originating from various miasmata, that is, noxious air derived from decaying animal and plant materials. In the eighteenth and for much of the nineteenth centuries, physicians employed "heroic therapy," which consisted of bloodletting, blistering, purging, cupping, and sweating, to treat illness.

Appalachians widely believed that well-being depended upon equilibrium of two oppositional blood states: thick and thin, and high and low. Thick blood was thought to contain excessive morbific matter, whereas thin blood was thought lacking in vital properties. Laxatives and various blood purifiers were ingested to clean the blood, especially during the spring but also during episodes of sickness. Thin blood was treated through eating various foods (poke sallet, meat, eggs) or taking a "blood toner" or tonic. Sulfur and molasses constituted one of the more popular tonics. The high and low oppositional set concerned the volume of blood in the body; high blood was too much blood. Bleeding and ingesting various teas were used to lower blood volume. The treatments used for thin blood were also used for low blood. Appalachians believed that the state of one's blood was altered by various influences: season (blood is thicker in the winter and thinner in the summer, and blood volume rises during the spring, much like the sap in a tree); age (blood becomes thinner as one grows older); and geography (people in warmer climes tend to have thinner blood). Humoral pathology is also evident in the belief that a change in ambient temperature, especially from warm to cold, affects the blood system. Exposure to cold drafts of air was avoided, and seasonal transitions were thought to be occasions when one was especially vulnerable to illness. Many of these folk beliefs about blood and illness persist in the region today.

For many illnesses, Appalachians depended on so-called home remedies. Home remedy *materia medica* included an extensive and bewildering array of botanical, animal, and mineral substances. Whether due to the region's well-known botanical diversity or the fact that south-central Appalachia has been the major source of crude drugs in the United States since the Civil War, Appalachians have long been viewed as highly dependent on medicinal plants. More than one thousand plants in Appalachia have been reported to have medicinal properties, but of these only eighty to one hundred were widely known, and of this core group probably fewer than fifty were extensively used in the family. Reports indicate a close correspondence among types of use of medicinal plants throughout Appalachia, but individual, family, and community variation in the knowledge and use of medicinal plants was common. A few examples of some of the medicinal plants more frequently mentioned in Appalachia are boneset (for cold and flu), poke (for cleaning blood, scabies, and rheumatism), catnip (for colic and hives), goldenseal (for upset stomach and indigestion), mayapple (for constipation), slippery elm (for sore throat), jimsonweed (for asthma), sassafras (for cleaning blood), balm of Gilead (for dry skin and abrasions), and wild cherry (for coughs). Native Americans introduced many plants to European settlers: boneset, goldenseal, poke, sassafras, jimsonweed, Jerusalem oak, and rabbit tobacco, to mention a few. Europeans also brought many medicinal plants from the Old World, including peppermint, mullein, balm of Gilead, catnip, red clover, plantain, ground ivy, and coltsfoot. Of all the plants used by Appalachians in home remedies, cultigens such as onion, potato, and corn were prominent. The onion was, in fact, one of the great panaceas of Appalachian folk medicine, as was turpentine, a distillate of pine. From corn, Appalachians obtained sour mash whiskey, a key ingredient in many remedies.

Though Appalachians were dependent on medicinal plants in times of sickness, reports indicate that they resorted to animal (including human) and mineral substances just as often, if not more. Fat rendered from hog, sheep, bear, snake, and polecat (skunk) was used singularly or in combination with other substances for various salves but also ingested. Sheep dip (dung) tea was a popular remedy for breaking out measles and hives, and cow dung, preferably fresh, was widely used as a poultice for sprains. Blood from a black cat or chicken was a well-known cure for shingles. Warmed human urine was a popular remedy for an earache. Some of the more commonly used mineral substances were salt, soda, Epsom salts, borax, bluestone, sulfur, carbolic acid, copperas, alum, and coal oil (kerosene). These materials were purchased at stores, as were some other widely used commercial products, such as paregoric, calomel, sweet oil (olive oil), castor oil, Spanish fly, quinine, and asafetida. The displacement of folk *materia medica*, especially medicinal plants, in many families began in the mid-1800s, but the advent of the patent medicine era following the Civil War marked a time of dramatic change. The J. R. Watkins Company, founded in Plainview, Minnesota, in 1868, was remarkably successful in promoting its line of medicines in Appalachia, even in remote rural communities, through locally recruited sales representatives.

Sympathetic magic was a significant aspect of the magico-religious component of Appalachian folk medicine.

It was believed, for example, that one could "cut" (stop or diminish) the pain of a woman in labor by placing an axe or knife under her bed or cut a nosebleed by letting blood from the nose drip on a knife blade or by sliding a pair of scissors down the back. Two variant techniques of the sympathetic principle were "measuring" and "passing." Childhood asthma, for example, was often treated by cutting a stick, usually of sourwood, the exact length of the child and then placing the stick up the chimney or in the attic. As the child outgrew the length of the stick, he outgrew his asthma. Colic was treated by passing a child from mother to father, usually three times, under a horse or mule, through a horse collar, around a table leg, under a bush, or through a split sapling. The underlying notion was that the child would pass from a state of sickness to wellness. Another magical technique, "transference," was used to treat many illnesses, but was perhaps best known in wart remedies. One common wart cure involved placing stones equal to the number of warts one had into a poke (paper sack) and then placing it on the side of a road. When a curious person picked up the poke to see what was inside, he would "pick up" the warts as well.

Appalachians believed in the existence of some illnesses not recognized as real by official medicine, which anthropologists and folklorists refer to as "folk illnesses" or "culture-bound syndromes." "Bold hives," an infant-specific illness introduced by the Scots and Scots-Irish, is a good example. Many believed that all newborns have a mysterious entity within them known as the hives. Infants were administered a tea, often made of catnip or ground ivy, to induce the hives out of the body. If not treated, the hives would "turn inward," causing damage to the heart and lungs and ultimately death. Another infant-specific folk illness, "livergrown," was introduced by the Germans. According to tradition, an infant's liver sometimes formed a fibrous attachment to the ribs or spine, especially if an infant was left in a supine position for too long. Symptoms of livergrown were sensitivity to touch, irritability, and constriction of the lower abdomen. Treatment entailed holding the infant in the air by his ankles and shaking him vigorously up and down or through an exercise of pulling the infant's legs up beyond its head.

Appalachians relied on a variety of traditional medical practitioners. Though family members, usually mothers, were well informed about medicinal plants, there were people known as "yarb" (herb) doctors who possessed extraordinary knowledge. Some of these herbalists were known as "Indian doctors" because they claimed, often falsely, to have acquired their knowledge of medicinal plants while living with Native Americans. Most communities had a granny midwife, though they were not necessarily old or female as the tag *granny* suggests. Though many granny midwives obtained their training from other midwives, often their mothers, some were trained by physicians and later served as physician assistants. Seventh sons or daughters and people who had "never looked into the eyes of their father" (that is, their fathers died before they were born) were believed capable of curing thrush and other infant and childhood illnesses as well. Bloodstoppers were able to stop profuse bleeding by reciting Ezekiel 16:6 while passing a hand back and forth across and slightly above a wound. Another charm used by bloodstoppers was: "God made the ocean; God sent the flood. God calms the ocean; God stops the blood." Anyone could become a bloodstopper by being told the secret charm by a bloodstopper of the opposite sex. Burn doctors "talked the fire" out of burns and promoted quick healing by moving a hand across and slightly above the burn while reciting the following: "There came an angel from the east bringing fire and frost. In frost, out fire, in the name of the Father, the Son, and the Holy Ghost." Other traditional medical practitioners included bonesetters, goiter rubbers, and those skilled at pulling, or "jumping," teeth.

Recent research indicates that reliance on folk medicine in Appalachia has diminished significantly since World War II due to economic development, improved access to public and private health-care services, and the increased presence of alternative and complementary medicine. Furthermore, many Appalachians over time internalized the official medical establishment's position that folk medicine in general, despite specific evidence to the contrary, is not only primitive and backward but harmful. Though reliance on folk medicine has eroded considerably, various folk beliefs and practices persist. For example, folk beliefs about blood serve as impediments to effective communication between some Appalachian patients and health care providers. Traditional medical practitioners can still be found, but they are not as prevalent as in times past. Few Appalachians today believe in folk illnesses such as bold hives and livergrown, but a relatively new folk illness, "nerves" (an incapacitating nervous disorder), appeared sometime in the late 1950s and has become increasingly common over the years. Recent investigations on the use of folk medicine show that over-the-counter medications have displaced much of the folk *materia medica* used in home remedies, particularly medicinal plants, and that residents of the region are as likely to use official medicine as other Americans.

See also: GRANNY MIDWIVES (HEALTH); MEDICINAL AND HEALTH TERMINOLOGY (LANGUAGE); MEDICINAL PLANT USE (HEALTH).

—Anthony Cavender, *East Tennessee State University*

Anthony Cavender, "Folk Hematology in the Appalachian South," *Journal of Folklore Research* (January–April 1992) and *Folk Medicine in Southern Appalachia* (2003); Anthony P. Cavender and Scott H. Beck, "Generational Change, Folk Medicine, and Medical Self-Care in a Rural Appalachian Community," *Human Organization* (Summer 1995); John K. Crellin and Jane Philpott, *Herbal Medicine Past and Present, Vol. 1: Trying to Give Ease* (1990).

Folk Speech

See Section Overview (Language)

Foodways

See Section Overview (Food and Cooking)

Gainer, Patrick Ward

(1903–1981) Folklorist and professor.

Patrick Ward Gainer documented West Virginia's folk music and ballad traditions while battling the stereotype of the ignorant "Snuffy Smith" mountaineer. A professor of English, nineteenth-century literature, and folklore at West Virginia University, Gainer never forgot the folktales and shape-note singing he heard as a boy in his hometown of Tanner in Gilmer County. Schooled at home and at the Glenville Normal School, Gainer went on to West Virginia University, where he started collecting folklore with faculty member Carey Woofter, a boyhood friend.

In Gainer's day, lyrics and melody were "caught" by ear and transcribed by hand. Gainer was interested in everything from folk songs and church melodies to butter churning and witches. As a student, he worked with the acclaimed folklorist Louis Watson Chappell to document the John Henry legend in Talcott.

By 1928, Gainer had his master's degree and went to St. Louis University to earn his doctorate. He also sang on the radio and with the opera there but continued his West Virginia collecting trips during summers. During World War II, Gainer, who said he spoke French, German, Italian, Portuguese, Spanish, and Polish, served as director of USO operations in the South Atlantic and Caribbean. In 1946 he joined the English Department at West Virginia University.

One of his lasting contributions started modestly in 1949, when Gainer was a visiting professor at Glenville College. He was teaching a class in Appalachian culture and asked students to bring in local residents to demonstrate "folk arts." This classroom project became the West Virginia Folk Festival, which is still held each June. Gainer would travel through the region to transport the singers and fiddlers featured at the festival, which he ran for ten years and performed in as well.

Gainer was disdainful of radio and its dissemination of popular "hillbilly" music, which he felt diluted mountain traditions. He spread this message in every county of the state while teaching folklore for West Virginia University's extension service and speaking at garden and civic clubs, where he would sing while playing the dulcimer (an instrument that he believed descended from the rebec in the British Isles).

In 1963 Gainer assembled *The West Virginia Centennial Songbook of One Hundred Songs,* which was followed by *Witches, Ghosts and Signs: Folklore of the Southern Appalachians* and *Folk Songs from the West Virginia Hills* in 1975. In the 1960s, he also recorded two albums: *Patrick Gainer Singing Songs of the Allegheny Mountains* and *Folksongs of the Allegheny Mountains*. Gainer died on February 22, 1981.

See also: DULCIMER, FRETTED (MUSIC); FOLK MUSIC COLLECTIONS (MUSIC); JOHN HENRY.

—Paul Gartner, *Sod, West Virginia*

Ghost Lore

See Folklore and the Supernatural

Gordon, Robert Winslow

(1888–1961) Folklorist.

Robert Winslow Gordon, the founder of the Archive of American Folk Song at the Library of Congress, was a pioneering folklorist who left a safe academic career to devote himself to documenting American folk music. He planned to record folk songs all around the United States and began this journey by spending two months in the North Carolina mountains in 1925, using Asheville as a base for his fieldwork.

Gordon traveled to surrounding areas, attending fiddlers' contests and visiting people in their homes. He made nearly four hundred wax cylinder recordings, which constituted an important early collection of traditional Anglo-American ballads, folk songs, and dance music. Unusual for folklorists of the time, he also photographed some of his subjects as well as traditional house types, handmade banjos, and graveyards.

Gordon chose to publish his work exploring the roots of American music in popular publications. The *New York Times Magazine* printed his account of Appalachian folk song in 1927 and 1928, and the men's outdoor pulp magazine *Adventure* featured his ongoing column. In his widely read writings, Gordon romanticized yet valued Appalachian music and culture. By many accounts a difficult man, Gordon never accomplished the great job of collection he imagined, but his recordings, photographs, and manuscripts from the Appalachians became the foundation of an enduring collection, the Archive of Folk Culture, now part of the American Folklife Center at the Library of Congress.

See also: BALLADS (MUSIC); FOLK MUSIC COLLECTIONS (MUSIC); SHARP, CECIL.

—Debora Kodish, *Philadelphia Folklore Project*

Granny Women

See Granny Midwives (Health)

Heritage Areas

The observance of the United States' bicentennial in 1976 stimulated a movement to conserve sites and landscapes that tell the story of national economic and industrial growth. One result was the establishment of heritage areas. Sometimes called heritage corridors or heritage parks, heritage areas are regions recognized by federal, state, or local governments as touchstones for America's collective identity.

By 2003, Congress had designated twenty-four national heritage areas, nine of them wholly or in part in the Appalachian region, and a number of states, including New York and Pennsylvania, had also developed their own heritage area systems. Studies anticipating the creation of new national heritage areas were also underway in Kentucky.

Unlike conventional national or state parks, heritage areas are not tracts of land set aside by governments for protection from commercial development. Rather they are multi-community regions designated as eligible for special funds to encourage documentation and preservation efforts, interpretive and educational programming, and usually tourism promotion. While a few are managed by government commissions, most heritage areas are public-private partnerships supported by a combination of public funds, foundation or corporate assistance, and private donations.

The term *heritage* as used here embraces all aspects of a region that bear upon its residents' sense of identity: geography and topography; the built environment; significant historical events and issues; and ethnography, including early settlement, constantly changing networks of cultural connections, and ongoing traditions and attitudes. A heritage area focuses attention on the interaction of people in the region with each other and with their environment over time. Because of this broad scope, heritage areas are often staffed with professionals from diverse disciplines, which may include public folklore, public history, landscape architecture, historic preservation, economic development, regional planning, education, ecology, tourism, and communications.

Interpretive programming, especially in national heritage areas, builds upon such broad historical themes as the great migrations and immigrations, westward expansion, industrialization, the growth of ethnic and religious diversity, the issue of slavery, and racial segregation. In northern Appalachia predominant themes are industrial life and ethnic diversity, while in some of the southern Appalachian states the issue of slavery and the legacy of segregation take precedence.

In terms of physical landscape, heritage areas usually have one or several large topographical features that provide an armature for their interpretive plan: a major river or river system, a mountain chain, a stretch of arresting coastal geography. Mostly these unifying elements are aspects of the natural landscape, but some heritage areas are organized around man-made features such as navigational canals, railways, or roadways. The Rivers of Steel, National Coal Heritage, and Shenandoah Valley areas are all organized around rivers. The Delaware and Lehigh Canal and Erie Canal areas both feature man-made navigational canals, while the Path of Progress concentrates on the communities along Route 40, America's first federally built highway. Authorized in 2003, the Blue Ridge National Heritage Area in North Carolina emphasizes the mountain landscape.

Heritage areas encourage and support a variety of activities. Some, such as Shenandoah Valley in Virginia, emphasize interpretation of the natural environment in its historical context. Others focus on significant sites and properties in the built environment. Several have major industrial sites as interpretive focal points, including steelmaking facilities (Rivers of Steel, Path of Progress), coal mines and mining towns (Rivers of Steel, Path of Progress, and Lackawanna Valley in Pennsylvania and Coal Heritage in West Virginia), and oil wells (Oil Region). The homes of thematically significant historic personages, such as Henry Clay Frick's Clayton estate in Rivers of Steel, often serve as tourist destinations in heritage areas. Identifying and interpreting the living cultural traditions in communities have become increasingly important. Most of Pennsylvania's heritage areas have included folklife or ethnographic field research as part of their planning and programming, as have those in West Virginia. North Carolina's Blue Ridge National Heritage Area includes the showplace Highland Folk Arts Center. Ideally, heritage areas take a comprehensive approach that addresses all of these components—natural, historic, and cultural—from their particular thematic perspective.

The goals and audiences for heritage areas vary, depending on the stated wishes of their constituents. Many heritage areas in the industrial regions of New York, Pennsylvania, and West Virginia aim to spur economic revitalization in their communities. Others, such as Lancaster-York in Pennsylvania, with its large Amish population, and Blue Ridge in North Carolina, seek to slow externally prompted development so that their communities can maintain their identities and evolve at their own pace. Still others, such as Civil War National Heritage Area, Shenandoah Valley, and South Carolina's national heritage corridor, primarily seek wider recognition of the role their regions have played in the development of state and national identity. Similarly, some heritage areas focus inward, designing activities mostly for their own citizens' participation and benefit (Lackawanna Valley, Coal Heritage), while others have emphasized looking outward to develop activities that will attract newcomers (Path of Progress, Delaware and Lehigh, Wheeling, National Road, Shenandoah, and others). Several attempt to integrate and balance the needs and interests of both visitors and residents (Rivers of Steel, Lancaster-York, Blue Ridge).

Whatever their individual approaches, heritage areas provide an important vehicle for increasing and disseminating information about Appalachia. They encourage preservation of physical thresholds to the region's history and document and interpret living traditions through which Appalachian communities can share knowledge of themselves with people from across the region, the nation, and the globe.

See also: CULTURAL HERITAGE TOURISM (TOURISM); SECTION OVERVIEW (TOURISM).

—Doris J. Dyen, *Rivers of Steel National Heritage Area, Pittsburgh, Pennsylvania*

James Abrams, "Lost Frames of Reference: Sitings of History and Memory in Pennsylvania's Documentary Landscapes," in *Conserving Culture: A New Discourse on Heritage*, ed. Mary Hufford (1994); Shalom Staub, "Cultural Conservation and Economic Recovery Planning: The Pennsylvania Heritage Parks Program," in *Conserving Culture: A New Discourse on Heritage*, ed. Mary Hufford (1994).

Hunting and Fishing Lore

Fishing and hunting have offered food, recreation, and fodder for stories and other cultural traditions as long as humans have occupied Appalachia. The lore of hunting and fishing has been an integral part of mountain culture, woven into music, art, literature, and, of course, storytelling and customs. In addition to keeping specific skills alive, hunting and fishing traditions preserve history and ideas, memorialize individuals, offer inspiration, and serve as rites of passage, as well as simply providing humorous and entertaining tales.

Fishing and hunting lore permeates the folk beliefs, stories, songs, and even more recent written literature about the Appalachian region, attesting to the significance of these two activities in the mountains. Horace Kephart, in his book *Our Southern Highlanders* (1913; revised 1922), recounts a bear hunt to which he was invited. The local mountain men told him to "mark what you dream about, tonight: hit'll shore come true tomorrow," adding, "but you musn't tell whut yer dream was till the hunt's over, or it'll spile the charm." Kephart told his dream prior to the hunt, and the prophecy was fulfilled in that he was not the one to kill the bear.

The stories of mountain legend Davy Crockett abound with hunting tales that are wildly exaggerated, as is the story "I Bought Me a Dog," collected by Leonard Roberts in the 1950s in Kentucky. In the story, a man out hunting sees a snake just as 5,000 wild ducks and 5,000 wild geese fly overhead. Unsure which to shoot at first, the man shoots the snake, the barrel on the gun breaks, and half the gun debris kills 5,000 thousand wild ducks and the other half kills 4,999 wild geese. As he gathers up his catch and crosses the bridge over the river, the bridge gives way and he falls in, but emerges on the bank with 3,000 pounds of fish in his hip boots. The narrator concludes, "I went to the house and told my wife I thought I had purty good luck. And that was all of that."

The lore of hunting and fishing are also woven into the music of the region. Kephart documented one song that goes: "Call up your dog, O call up your dog! / Call up your dog! / Call up your dog! / Let's a-go huntin' to ketch a groundhog / Rang tang a-whaddle limky day!" Songs such as "Fox on the Run" and "Ole Slewfoot" are common in the repertoires of modern bluegrass bands. A contemporary band from the mountains of North Carolina called Cullowhee has these lines in a song called "Fishin'": "So, when my boys get old enough, and learn how to bait a hook and how to wade / I think I'll take 'em fishin' and show 'em where God stays / 'Cause they'll never feel more at peace, they'll never feel more whole / Than when the whitewater rushes round their legs and the mountains fill their souls."

Even written literature from the mountains often draws upon the lore of hunting and fishing for inspiration. In Harriette Simpson Arnow's 1949 novel *Hunter's Horn*, Nunn Ballew is obsessed with killing a fox known as "King Devil" that has raided local farms for years. As he lies shot, Ballew realizes that "it was the damned fox that was sending him now to eternal damnation." More recently, Harry Middleton philosophized in *On the Spine of Time* (1991) that "truth has a befuddling quality about it, even in the deep quiet of the mountains. It's like quantum physics. Sooner or later, you've got to let loose of certainty's hand and leap. Jump. Believe in something, like mountains and mountain streams, trout and mountain people."

The great diversity of aquatic habitats and fish species that exists throughout the mountain range has stimulated a broad variety of fishing lore, craft, and folk customs. Brook trout, a traditional symbol for Appalachia, served as trail fare for early Native American travelers. One traditional method for getting trout was to sprinkle a pool with poison made from local plants; after being stricken with the poison, the stunned fish floated to the surface and were easily gathered. Native Americans also caught fish with hook and line, shot them with bow and arrow, gigged, and speared them. They crafted fish traps and weirs (fencelike structures that corral the fish) in streams and rivers, sometimes on a large scale. Building and maintaining weirs were communal efforts that European settlers continued, with neighbors and families sharing the work. Families worked together to keep traps clean and divided the resulting catch, often at a community fish fry.

Native Americans caught spawning catfish with their hands, a practice that may be part of the origin of the sport of noodling. Also called hand grabbing, grabbling, hand fishing, or hogging, noodling is still a well-known activity in the larger rivers and reservoirs of Appalachia. Noodlers target most catfish species but their real prize is the flathead catfish, known in Appalachia as the mudcat. Noodling remains popular with some, but the method is only practical during the brief few weeks in which catfish spawn and noodlers can locate them in hollow logs and other cavities where they nest.

Since fishhooks were often unaffordable, early mountaineers used the fishing method known as "choking," which involved tying suitable bait to a length of string and dropping it into the water. If a trout took it, the angler attempted to jerk the fish onto the bank quickly before it had a chance to expel the bait. According to old-timers, many a meal of fresh trout came to the table as a result of choking fish.

By far the most common means of fishing is with hook and line. Native brook trout, or brookies, smallmouth and spotted bass, walleye, sauger, and introduced species such as rainbow and brown trout are the favored game of Appalachian fishermen. Gathering bait for these fish has traditions of its own—fishermen seine crayfish, minnows, and hellgrammites (larvae of the dobson fly, known in some mountain communities as grampus). Another glamorous fish that attracts outsiders to Appalachian fishing is the muskellunge, or muskie, a very large, usually solitary member of the pike family. Muskies can reach fifty pounds, though most run much smaller. Traditionally, anglers have used large live or dead bait fish on stout tackle to cast or troll for muskie. However, since the 1980s, lures made by traditional craftsmen have become popular.

Although species such as trout, bass, and muskies are the most popular game, lesser-known fish such as suckers also have a wide following. Some sixty-three species of suckers live in North America, and several, such as the buffalo and redhorse, are common in parts of Appalachia, where they are traditionally favored as food among rural folk. People harvest suckers by a number of methods, and many age-old local customs have been codified into state fishing regulations. Appalachians still catch them with dip nets, gig them, and in winter snare them through holes in the ice. For a season during spring, rifles are allowed for shooting suckers (except on Sundays and inside town limits) along the Clinch River in Scott County, Virginia.

Since the time of early settlement, hunting, like fishing, has been prominent in the mountains of Appalachia. Over the past three hundred years, it has evolved from a means of survival to an expression of cultural values. The first pioneers hunted deer, elk, buffalo, bear, and smaller animals such as turkeys, rabbits, squirrels, ducks, geese, and swans. Prior to the 1780s, men hunted in any season, and they often left unused parts of the deer or elk to rot in the woods. By 1780 big game of all kind was scarce in most of Kentucky, Virginia, and Tennessee due to unregulated hunting. Deer populations suffered so greatly that territorial assemblies passed game laws restricting the killing of deer solely for their skins.

At the same time as the legal system restricted some hunting practices in the mountains, it promoted slaughter of other animals. In Tennessee, squirrels were so damaging to corn crops that the state made squirrel scalps "legal tender." Usually armed with the .45 caliber Kentucky long rifle designed for large game, experienced riflemen would often "bark the squirrel." To do this, the hunger attempted to shoot the branch under a squirrel's feet, stunning the animal and knocking it to the ground. Because the Kentucky rifle could do great damage to the flesh of small mammals, "barking the squirrel" minimized waste.

Raccoons, another frequently hunted mammal, are today valued for their fur and as a food source. Because raccoons are nocturnal, capturing them generally requires the use of hunting dogs, which help isolate the elusive prey. Hounds are trained to "tree" the raccoon, holding the animal at bay in a tall tree until the hunter arrives.

Dogs in the southern mountains play an important role in the region's traditional lore. Stories abound about the abilities and exploits of legendary dogs. Mountaineers hunted black bears by using dogs to force them into trees or hold them at bay in rock houses or caves. The Plott hound is probably the best-known breed of bear dog in the southern Appalachians. Treeing feists, another breed, are now synonymous with squirrel hunting, while Brittany spaniels are the preferred dog for hunting ruffed grouse. Blue Ticks, Black and Tans, and Redbones have been popular coon dogs; bulldogs are used for boar, Treeing Walkers for fox, and beagles for rabbit. However, as one mountain man explained, when he got a new dog and took him out, "whatever he ran, why, that's what kind'a dog it's goin' to be." Traditional hunting stories often involve tales of the bravery, intelligence, loyalty, or quirkiness of dogs.

For the early mountaineers, hunting was a means of survival. In the twenty-first century, the annual rite seems no less important for many of the region's residents, who continue to practice traditions of reading animal signs, imitating animal sounds with the help of "callers" (homemade as well as commercially manufactured), and emulating habitat through elaborate means of camouflage. Nearly every rural mountain community maintains a hunting club that sponsors annual banquets and fund-raisers, which are usually accompanied by the telling of hunting tales. In some areas, schools and places of work are closed during the traditional "deer week" (first week of December). In many communities, hunting looms large in the socialization of young boys, whose first hunts function as rites of passage toward manhood and responsibility. Not surprisingly, hunting is often referred to as a "calling" that perpetuates important family traditions while strengthening bonds between generations. As a means of supplementing the family larder, hunting helps to sustain a shadow economy that anthropologist Rhoda H. Halperin terms "the livelihood of kin." Hunting practices are thus ensured a place in the cultural landscape of the Appalachians for generations to come.

See also: BIG GAME (FOOD AND COOKING); SMALL GAME (FOOD AND COOKING); HUNTING AND FISHING (SPORTS AND RECREATION).

—C. Doyle Bickers, *Auburn University;* Donald E. Davis, *Dalton State College;* and Wiley C. Prewitt Jr., *Kilmichael, Mississippi*

Donald E. Davis and Jeffrey Stotik, "Feist or Fiction?: The Squirrel Dog of the Southern Mountains," *Journal of Popular Culture* (Winter 1992), Stuart A. Marks, *Southern Hunting in Black and White: Nature, History, Ritual in a Carolina Community* (1991); Roy Edwin Thomas, *Southern Appalachia, 1885–1915: Oral Histories from Residents of the State Corner Area of North Carolina, Tennessee, and Virginia* (1991).

Jack Tales

See Oral Narrative

John Henry

One of the most widespread and most studied folk figures in Appalachia is John Henry. The legend of John Henry, often told in the form of a ballad, is based on an incident that reportedly occurred in the mountains of West Virginia (or possibly north Alabama). The story has hundreds of variations: film, sheet music, art, poetry, drama, and recordings in various media. It is so well known that in 1996 the United States Postal Service paid tribute to John Henry with a stamp.

It is generally believed that John Henry was a freed slave who worked for the Chesapeake and Ohio Railway as a steel-driver around 1870. Steel-drivers were also known as hammer men and drove holes into rocks by hitting thick steel drills or spikes to create openings for the explosive charges. Consequently, they were necessarily strong men. Some sources claim that John Henry was over seven feet tall and weighed more than three hundred pounds. However, there is no consensus on his reputed size or strength.

The most common versions of the story tell that when the railroad was extending its line from the Chesapeake Bay to the Ohio Valley, the workers came to Big Bend Mountain. The mountain was too vast to build around so it was decided to drill a tunnel through the mountain, and a mechanical steam drill was brought in. John Henry challenged the mechanical drill that was destined to take away his job and, according to a ballad, said, "A man ain't nothin' but a man, / fo' I let your steam drill beat me down, / I'll die with this hammer in my hand." He won the contest, driving fourteen feet to the machine drill's nine. He died from the effort, however, leaving behind a wife and a baby.

It is natural that the legend first appeared in song. Singing set a rhythm and pace for the men while they worked and made the hazardous, intensive labor in the tunnels more tolerable. Such an event as John Henry's death, along with the wretched working conditions, could be acceptably related in song without facing punishment or dismissal.

A two-line fragment of the John Henry song was first published in a 1909 collection of songs from western North Carolina. Versions of the song from Indiana, Tennessee, Mississippi, and Kentucky were published in 1913. In the 1920s, sociologist Guy Johnson and historian Louis Watson Chappell collected many alleged firsthand accounts of the contest from around the region, and although there were many contradictions, they concluded that the John Henry tradition is factually based.

There is also some confusion between the character of John Henry and another steel-driver named John Hardy. Many ballads have also been written about Hardy, a legendary desperado who was hanged for murder in West Virginia in 1894. Although some maintain they are one and the same, most folklore scholars believe they were two different men, each with his own legend.

See also: COAL IMAGES (IMAGES AND ICONS); HISTORICAL HEROES (IMAGES AND ICONS).

—Clara Hasbrouck, *East Tennessee State University*

Louis W. Chappell, *John Henry: A Folk-Lore Study* (1933); Guy B. Johnson, *John Henry: Tracking Down a Negro Legend* (1969); Brett Williams, *John Henry: A Bio-Bibliography* (1983).

Karpeles, Maud

(1885–1976) Folk song and dance collector.

Born in England in 1885, Maud Karpeles became associated with the Appalachian region primarily through her work in folk song, especially her collaboration with English ballad collector Cecil Sharp. Early in her life, Karpeles took up social work and began to use traditional dances collected by Sharp to teach at girls' clubs where she worked. She became a member of a demonstration team that illustrated Sharp's lectures and ultimately collaborated with Sharp and George Butterworth on *The Country Dance Book* (1918). Continuing to work with Sharp as collector and editor as he became more interested in folk songs and ballads, Karpeles developed into an authority on folk song in her own right. From 1916 until 1918, she accompanied Sharp on trips to the Appalachian Mountains to collect ballads and folk songs with British origins; there they found a great number of songs that came with immigrants to the mountains and seemed less changed by time than the same songs in Britain. Their work led to publication of the seminal work *English Folk Songs from the Southern Appalachians* (1917; revised 1932), for which Karpeles served as editor. Much later, in 1968, she published *Eighty Folk Songs from the Southern Appalachians*, which she and Sharp had collected between 1916 and 1918.

After Sharp's death in 1924, Karpeles continued fieldwork on folk dance and song. She spent part of 1929 and 1930 in Newfoundland, gathering material that led to *Folk Songs from Newfoundland*, a collection of ninety songs eventually published in 1971. She also wrote a biography of Sharp entitled *Cecil Sharp: His Life and Work* (1965) and *An Introduction to English Folk Song* (1973). An active promoter of folk song and dance throughout her life, Karpeles died in 1976.

See also: DANCE (PERFORMING ARTS); FOLK SONGS (MUSIC); SHARP, CECIL.

—Jean Haskell, *East Tennessee State University*

Korson, George

(1899–1967) Folklorist.

A collector of coal-mining folklore, George Korson did considerable fieldwork in the early 1940s in Virginia, West Virginia, Kentucky, Tennessee, and Alabama. Born into a working-class Jewish family in Ukraine, Korson grew up in Pennsylvania, where he became a newspaper reporter and, later, a folklorist.

Korson started collecting the songs and stories of anthracite coal miners in Pennsylvania in the 1930s. His successful work there brought him to the attention of John L. Lewis, president of the United Mine Workers of America. Lewis encouraged Korson to expand his folklore research to include the bituminous coal miners of Appalachia, which culminated with the publication in 1943 of *Coal Dust on the Fiddle*, a voluminous work documenting the way of life in the coal camps and the folklore of coal miners. Korson presented the union in song and story, with emphasis on famous strikes and violent confrontations with mine owners.

Over his lifetime, Korson wrote five books on coal-mining folklore, as well as many articles. His recordings of miners' songs and ballads are deposited with the American Folklife Center's Archive of Folk Culture at the Library of Congress, and the collection forms the basis for two albums: *Songs and Ballads of the Anthracite Miners* and *Songs and Ballads of the Bituminous Miners*. He was awarded a Guggenheim Fellowship in 1957 and a University of Chicago Folklore Prize in 1961 and was elected a Fellow of the American Folklore Society in 1960.

Korson was sympathetic to the problems of Appalachian coal miners in terms of wages and working conditions, but politically he was not a revolutionary but a liberal reformer, supporting the idea of strong labor unions as a corrective force against the excesses of capitalism.

See also: COAL-MINING AND PROTEST MUSIC (MUSIC); FOLKLORE AND SOCIAL PROTEST; UNITED MINE WORKERS OF AMERICA (LABOR).

—Angus Kress Gillespie, *Rutgers University*

Lomax, John and Alan

John Lomax (1867–1948) Folklorist.

Alan Lomax (1915–2002) Folklorist.

Although only a small portion of their collecting work occurred in Appalachia, John and Alan Lomax were responsible for many important Appalachian field recordings. Born in Holmes County, Mississippi, on September 23, 1867, but reared in Bosque County, Texas, John Lomax from an early age was fascinated with the cowboy culture he observed near his parents' hardscrabble Texas farm. In 1907, while a Texas A&M University professor on leave at Harvard, Lomax began to compile a collection of transcribed cowboy songs and ballads. That project was eventually published as *Cowboy Songs and Other Frontier Ballads* (1910), which, according to biographer Nolan Porterfield, was "the first important collection of American folk song." Although in his subsequent fieldwork he favored the folk songs and ballads of Texas cowboys and African Americans in the Deep South, Lomax made several important collecting forays into Appalachia between 1933 and 1936. Usually accompanied by his son Alan (b. January 31, 1915), John Lomax traveled and collected in mountainous sections of Kentucky, Virginia, and North Carolina. Their Appalachian field recordings are housed in the Archive of Folk Culture in the American Folklife Center at the Library of Congress. The Lomaxes included transcriptions of material they collected in Appalachia in three of their jointly edited books: *American Ballads and Folk Songs* (1934), *Our Singing Country* (1941), and *Folk Song U.S.A.* (1947).

After his father's passing on January 26, 1948, Alan Lomax made further collecting trips to Appalachia, where he recorded numerous traditional ballads, songs, instrumental tunes, and religious hymns. During the 1990s, many of the younger Lomax's Appalachian field recordings were released commercially in the compact disc format on the Rounder and the Atlantic labels. His 1990 commercial video production *Appalachian Journey* showcases contemporary musicians, storytellers, and dancers from the region. Alan Lomax died July 19, 2002.

See also: BALLADS (MUSIC); FOLK SONGS (MUSIC).

—Ted Olson, *East Tennessee State University*

Mississippi Foothills Region Public Folklore

Although not a mountainous area, Mississippi's Appalachian Foothills region supports cultural traditions that align it more closely with the upland South region in neighboring Tennessee and Alabama than the rest of the state. The Appalachian Regional Commission includes twenty-four northern and central Mississippi counties in its region of service, but the Foothills region as commonly understood by Mississippians consists of only the six most northeastern counties in the state: Alcorn, Itawamba, Lee, Monroe, Prentiss, and Tishomingo. Relatively little folklore fieldwork has been conducted in the Foothills region compared to other sections of Mississippi. This can be partially attributed to scholars' strong interest in blues music and its related culture, which are found primarily in the state's Delta region.

Research in the Foothills region began in the 1920s, influenced by ballad and folk song collecting efforts going on throughout the South during the early 1900s. Mississippi natives James Madison Carpenter and Arthur Palmer Hudson both collected song texts from the Foothills region during this period.

Carpenter was a native of the region, born in Booneville (Prentiss County) in 1888. He is best known for extensive folk song collection work in Great Britain. In addition to this work, he collected a number of song texts from neighbors and acquaintances in Prentiss County during the late 1920s, including blues songs, spirituals, nursery rhymes, and other folk song genres. Carpenter never formally published information about his work, but the materials are part of the Archive of Folk Culture Collections at the American Folklife Center of the Library of Congress in Washington, D.C.

Hudson, a native of Attala County in central Mississippi, became interested in collecting folk songs while teaching at the University of Mississippi, where he enlisted his folklore students in his collection efforts in the early 1920s. This enabled him to gather song texts from throughout the state, including more than sixty items from the Appalachian Foothills counties. His book, *Folksongs of Mississippi and Their Background* (1936), includes some of these texts and analyses of them.

Folklore collecting in Mississippi increased dramatically during the 1930s, when state-level managers of the Federal Writers' Project began to emphasize the importance of collecting folk songs to their county-level workers. Herbert Halpert, a New York–based folk song collector, utilized the information collected by the county workers on a 1939 recording trip to the state. Halpert was sent to Mississippi (and several other states in the South) by the Federal Music Project to record the traditional music of the region. Halpert traveled throughout the state with a mobile recording unit in May and June of 1939 and recorded more than three hundred songs and tunes, including the music of several musicians in the Appalachian Foothills region. Samples from some of the musicians he recorded from the region (including W. E. Claunch of Guntown and John Alexander Brown of Iuka) can be found on the recording *Great Big Yam Potatoes: Anglo-American Fiddle Music from Mississippi* (1985).

Over the next sixty years, several scholars documented aspects of traditional culture in the Foothills region, but no comprehensive projects focusing specifically on the area were initiated. Some of the projects touching on artists or traditions of the Foothills during this period include: documentation of craftspeople by teams from the Smithsonian Institution for the 1974 Festival of American Folklife; a study of African American shape-note singing in Mississippi and Alabama conducted by Chiquita Walls and the Center for the Study of Southern Culture during the early 1990s; and documentation done by fiddle music researcher Norman Mellin during 2001 on the history and traditions of the family of John Alexander Brown, a Tishomingo County fiddler who was recorded by Halpert during his 1939 trip.

As part of an effort to rectify the lack of recent documentation in the region, the Mississippi Arts Commission and the Center for the Study of Southern Culture cosponsored a fieldwork project from 2002 to 2003 documenting traditional musicians and music performance sites in northeastern Mississippi, including the Appalachian Foothills region. Veteran Mississippi fieldworker Wiley Prewitt interviewed more than sixty musicians working in the region. A significant number of those documented were residents of the Foothills. The original documentation from the project is now part of the commission's Folk Arts Archive. Databases of the musicians and sites documented are available to organizations within the region.

See also: FIDDLE (MUSIC); SECTION OVERVIEW.

—Larry Morrisey, *Mississippi Arts Commission, Jackson, Mississippi*

Arthur Palmer Hudson, *Folksongs of Mississippi and Their Background* (1936); Tom Rankin, liner notes, *Great Big Yam Potatoes: Anglo-American Fiddle Music from Mississippi* (1985); Chiquita Walls, *The African American Shape Note and Vocal Music Singing Convention Directory* (1994).

Musick, Ruth Ann

(1897–1974) Folklorist.

One of the primary folklore scholars to preserve and perpetuate the cultural heritage of West Virginia, Ruth Ann Musick was in fact an adopted West Virginian. Born in Kirksville, Missouri, on September 17, 1897, Musick grew up on a farm and her early experiences influenced her later support for animal rights, vegetarianism, and protection of land from strip mining, as well as her love of Scots-Irish traditions.

While earning a doctorate in creative writing from the State University of Iowa in 1943, Musick first became interested in folklore. She brought this interest to West Virginia in 1946, when she accepted a teaching position in mathematics and English at Fairmont State College, where she remained until her retirement in 1967. Recognizing that this part of Appalachia was virtually unknown in folklore scholarship, Musick started a folk literature class at the college. In 1950 she helped revive the West Virginia Folklore Society, and she organized the society's annual conferences and folk festival. She founded and served as editor for the society's quarterly publication, the *West Virginia Folklore Journal*, now published annually as *Traditions: A Journal of West Virginia Folk Culture and Educational Awareness*.

Musick became West Virginia's folklore ambassador, promoting appreciation for folklore through public programming, radio broadcasts, and television. In addition to writing two popular columns on folklore for West Virginia newspapers, she published four folktale collections: *Ballads, Folk Songs, and Folk Tales from West Virginia* (1960), *The Telltale Lilac Bush and Other West Virginia Ghost Tales* (1965), *Green Hills of Magic: West Virginia Folk Tales from Europe* (1970), and *Coffin Hollow and Other Ghost Tales* (1977).

When Musick died on July 2, 1974, she bequeathed her unpublished folklore collections and research to Fairmont State College to be used for programming and publications. The West Virginia Folklife Center was established at Fairmont State in 1998 to continue Musick's legacy.

See also: BALLADS (MUSIC); SCOTS-IRISH (RACE, ETHNICITY, AND IDENTITY); WEST VIRGINIA PUBLIC FOLKLORE.

—Judy Prozzillo Byers, *Fairmont State College*

National Heritage Fellows

The National Heritage Fellowship is an annual honor bestowed upon select masters of folk arts by the National Endowment for the Arts (NEA). Bess Lomax Hawes, former director of the NEA Folk and Traditional Arts Program, initiated the fellowship in 1982 as form of recognition for groups and artists who have contributed to the cultural heritage of the United States. The fellowship is the highest honor bestowed upon traditional and folk artists by the federal government. Since its inception, the fellowship has been awarded annually to artists representing traditions in music, dance, narrative, and crafts from throughout the United States. It is both a public honor and a monetary award; honorees are invited to Washington, D.C., in the fall of the year to receive a cash stipend in support of their work, greet members of Congress and other officials at a reception, and perform at a public concert.

The National Heritage Fellowship program selects recipients who represent a democratically chosen cross-section of the traditional arts currently practiced throughout the United States. Each year the NEA collects nominations for the award from private citizens; fellows are ultimately selected from these nominations by a rotating panel of specialists in arts and culture. Of the 272 fellowships awarded between 1982 and 2003, 33 were bestowed upon traditional artists residing within the Appalachian region. Eighteen fellows, including ballad singers, storytellers, musicians, and weavers, have been recognized for mastery of specifically Appalachian traditions. Artists who have received fellowships for Appalachian traditions include nationally known performers such as musician Arthel "Doc" Watson (1988), singer Lily May Ledford (1985), storytellers Ray and Stanley Hicks (both in 1983), and singer and songwriter Hazel Dickens (2001).

Other winners residing in Appalachia, who are not necessarily working in traditions classified by the NEA as Appalachian art forms, are work song singers John Henry Mealing and Cornelius Wright Jr. (both in 1996) and potter Jerry Brown (1992) from Alabama; potter Lanier Meaders (1983) and shape-note singer Hugh McGraw (1982) from Georgia; fiddler Clyde Davenport (1992) and banjo player Morgan Sexton (1991) from Kentucky; banjo player and singer Ola Belle Reed (1986) from Maryland; harmonica player Elder Roma Wilson (1994) from Mississippi; guitarist

Etta Baker (1991), Cherokee dancer Walker Calhoun (1992), knotted bedspread maker Bertha Cook (1984), blacksmith Bea Hensley (1995), fiddler Tommy Jarrell (1982), and ballad singer Douglas Wallin (1988) from North Carolina; musicians Ralph Blizard (2002), Will Keys (1996), and Earl Scruggs (1989) and cooper Alex Stewart (1983) from Tennessee; musicians Ralph Stanley (1984) and Wayne Henderson (1995) from Virginia; and weaver Dorothy Thompson (2000), fiddler Melvin Wine (1991), ballad singer Nimrod Workman (1986), and Trinidadian steel pan (or drum) builder and musician Elliott Manette (1999) from West Virginia.

The Bess Lomax Hawes Award, introduced in 2000, expands the reach of the National Heritage Fellowship program to honor and support artists, producers, teachers, and activists who have contributed significantly to the practice and appreciation of traditional arts through their own performing, mentorship, or cultural work. The award, which carries the same public recognition and stipend as those offered to National Heritage Fellows, was instituted by the NEA to acknowledge private citizens who support a diverse national cultural heritage in ways other than mastery of a traditional art form. Two of the first three Bess Lomax Hawes Awardees were cultural workers from the Appalachian region. Tennessee native and folklorist Joseph T. Wilson (2001) is the executive director of the National Council for the Traditional Arts, which produces the National Folk Festival as well as performances, exhibits, and other educational activities. Kentucky musician and activist Jean Ritchie (2002) advocates for Appalachian culture through her own songwriting and national performances of traditional music.

The idea of a national award to folk artists was first broached at the NEA in 1977, when then-director Nancy Hanks suggested that the endowment provide support to individual masters working in folk traditions. Central to the fellowship is the recognition of folk arts as the cultural property of communities rather than individual artists. The program is careful to honor the art form and the community from which the fellow comes, with the artist serving as a representative of the community tradition. As individual exemplars of the diversity of American folk arts, unique National Heritage Fellows embody a contradiction inherent in the award, manifesting individual excellence in the arts while also representing the nation's common cultural assets.

Appalachia and the West are distinguished in the National Heritage Fellowships program as the only two American regions used to describe a particular folk art form, as in the fellowship category specifically recognizing Appalachian storytelling. All other traditions honored through National Heritage Fellowships are identified by ethnic, occupational, linguistic, or religious origins.

In recognizing Appalachian folk arts, the program supports and lauds the range of artistic forms practiced throughout the region. However, fellowships awarded to artists as Appalachian folk masters also perpetuate a correlation between the physiographic and cultural boundaries of the region. When fellows residing in the Appalachian region are artists in Native American or immigrant traditions, they are recognized by their ethnic or tribal affiliation rather than as Appalachians. With the exception of Appalachian banjo picker Wade Mainer (1987) of Flint, Michigan, no National Heritage Fellowships have been awarded for mastery of Appalachian traditions by artists living in Cincinnati, Detroit, or other cities in the urban Appalachian diaspora. As a national honor, such recognition may reinforce a conception of the physical Appalachia as the reservoir of American folk culture documented by nineteenth-century ethnographers, while neglecting the reach of Appalachian culture beyond the region's physical bounds and the growing ethnic and cultural diversity within them.

See also: AUGUSTA HERITAGE CENTER (CULTURAL INSTITUTIONS); FEDERAL FUNDING (CULTURAL INSTITUTIONS).

—Michael L. Murray, *University of Pennsylvania*

Alan Govenar, ed., *Masters of Traditional Arts: Biographical Dictionary* (2001); National Endowment for the Arts, *National Heritage Fellowships, 1982–2002* (2002); Steve Siporin, *American Folk Masters: The National Heritage Fellows* (1992).

Neighboring

An informal or folk network of economic and social exchange among households, neighboring is grounded in a shared sense of place and enlivened and facilitated by particular kinds of speech. Appalachia is often seen as a place with strong traditions of neighboring and kinship relations.

This perception is inaccurate when based on a stereotyped picture of mountain people as premodern, self-reliant folks who live in homogeneous communities driven by custom and blind attachment to place and beyond the reach of formal institutional support systems or industrial development. In reality, the many forms of neighboring in Appalachia parallel national patterns. While modern institutions seem to displace reliance on neighbors and kin, they have transmuted these relationships into new forms. In Appalachia, as elsewhere, the role and importance of neighboring depend on how its informal webs of mutual aid and exchange fit in among dominant formal institutions. Economic markets, government safety nets and regulations, specialized professions, and schools have taken over many ancient functions of neighboring and kinship in distributing resources, healing, knowledge, and help, yet strong neighbor and kin ties remain in the region.

Neighboring can be categorized according to whether it is "thick" or "thin," anthropological descriptions for strength and depth versus weakness and superficiality and whether neighboring is central or peripheral to the culture's social structure. In political and economic systems that encourage constantly changing or unequal relations between people in everyday life, being a good neighbor becomes peripheral. Nationally, the weakest relationships between households are in upper-middle-class suburban communities where everyday domestic tasks are paid for, where social interactions are based on career rather than place, and where landscapes divide rather than link homes. Although this pattern also occurs in Appalachia, middle-class and elite communities in the region have been less studied than rural, less affluent communities. Appalachian studies have little to say about upper- and middle-class relations among neighbors or about life in urban and suburban, rather than rural, settings.

The richest descriptions of networks among neighbors and kin in Appalachia have emerged in community studies where neighboring is central to social structure—small-scale farming communities, coal camps, company towns, and other areas of postindustrial subsistence. In these settings, important social and economic resources flow along neighboring networks, making neighbors central to community, self-identity, and perceptions of the social good. Such communities and their neighborly ways, romanticized both positively and negatively, have become Appalachian icons in the imagination of wider America. Perhaps they stand out not because they are more prevalent, but because they have been looked for and looked at more than other types of mountain communities.

Neighboring and kinship are excellent vehicles for orchestrating survival strategies and managing the risks of life in a dependable manner. Without formal codes or contracts, these informal, traditional ways of relating to one another can produce a wide social network based on long-term trust, intimacy, and reciprocity that can be dormant but quickly mobilized in times of need. Small-scale mountain farming tends toward diversification, as people hedge their bets against the vagaries of weather, pests, and markets with ways to supplement income through foraging and hunting in forest commons, horticulture, subsistence gardening, odd jobs, craft specialties, and swapping and barter. The boom-and-bust or slow-decay cycles of mining, textiles, and chronic underemployment encourage similar diversification and improvisation. In such circumstances throughout the region (as in much of rural America), a social and cultural network based on reliance on neighbors and kin is widely distributed.

This network has several basic constituent elements: webs of interdependence among households aimed towards maintaining household independence; elaborate traditions of talk that can transmit tangled ecological, social, economic, political, psychological, and kinship information quickly over wide distances; and skills in indirect conflict management and personalized care. These traits produce a rich sense of place and history, a system of egalitarian relationships, and strong notions of who are insiders and outsiders in a community.

Neighbors in such a system are obliged to help one another. To be a neighbor is to accept another's needs as part of one's own daily life—the people for whom you need to

Women gather in Naoma, West Virginia, for their weekly quilting bee, 1995. The tradition of "neighboring," defined as an informal or folk network of economic and social exchange among households, still remains strong in many Appalachian communities.

care if you are to maintain your own sense of worth and identity. Neighbors watch for threats to the self-sufficiency of other households. They anticipate the needs of others, especially the elderly, vulnerable, or antisocial, in small ways such as looking for curtains undrawn, cars too frequently stopping, children unfed, or signs of physical danger. This unseen work provides a civic early warning system. Collective action in such communities can coalesce suddenly without formal organization, drawing on awareness and accumulated knowledge.

Neighboring is more than literal exchange of physical help. It also involves speech and performance. Appalachian life includes rich traditions of talk among neighbors and kin that carry strong elements of playfulness, narrative artistry, and the full range of human experience—moving back and forth among the scandalous, tragic, practical, intimate, mundane, political, comic, or sublime. In spite of their casual appearance, these networks create a durable social sphere in which daily interaction, moral obligation, and shared knowledge, identity, speechways, memories, and history produce a sense of place, a community where neighbors matter.

These feelings of a commonly shared life relate to an ethic of equality among neighbors and kin. Recent scholarship has shown that social inequality has been much greater in agrarian Appalachia than stereotypes suggest, yet talk among neighbors often gives the appearance of equal relationships and noninterference in the affairs of others. A neighborly offer of help might begin with "I was just going to town. . . ," "I don't mean to be nosy, but I saw your light was out," "Let's us fix this fence," or "Would you care if I mowed your lawn?" These non-intrusive speechways bind people to each other and to the community and allow people to make inquiries and offer help while maintaining a sense of relationship.

Communities based on kinship and neighborliness can create strong social prejudices against those who are not identified as part of a place. On the other hand, neighborly sharing of knowledge and resources can help newcomers with assimilation, as often happened with Appalachian settlement school workers in the late nineteenth century, new ethnic groups to the coal camps in the 1920s to 1930s, and back-to-the-land in-migrants in the 1960s.

Political rhetoric often uses images of neighborly, egalitarian "country" lifeways to obscure and manipulate inequalities based on race, ethnicity, gender, sexual orientation, or class, claiming everyone is neighbor and kin when, in fact, there are sometimes deep divisions.

Case studies in the region indicate that the kin/neighbor society can also provide powerful tools for resistance movements. Particularly striking has been the regional growth of place-based, multi-issue citizens' groups in response to local environmental threats such as mountaintop-removal mining. These organizations include local citizens, scientists, various religious organizations, and other seemingly disparate groups who use the traditions of neighbors and kin to come together to affect public policy in the region.

See also: COMMUNITY ACTION GROUPS (FAMILY AND COMMUNITY); KINFOLKS (IMAGES AND ICONS); TRADE AND BARTER.

—Betsy Taylor, *University of Kentucky*

Dwight Billings, Kathleen Blee, and Louis Swanson, "Culture, Family, and Community in Preindustrial Appalachia," *Appalachian Journal* (Winter 1986); Rhoda H. Halperin, *The Livelihood of Kin: Making Ends Meet "The Kentucky Way"* (1990).

New York Southern Tier Public Folklore

The fourteen counties making up the New York State portion of Appalachia have never had a strong regional identity, falling instead within other popularly accepted regional designations such as Chautauqua, the Finger Lakes, or the Catskills. *Southern tier*, a term encountered with varying frequency across the region, refers to seven counties, all within the Appalachian region, sharing the straight-line boundary with Pennsylvania. The lack of a coherent regional identity may explain why no folklorist has compiled a collection specific to the region as a whole and why since its inception in 1945 the *New York Folklore Quarterly* and successor organs of the New York Folklore Society have never referred to New York's mountains as "Appalachia."

At the same time, New York has long had an active cadre of professional and amateur folklorists, many of whom have touched on the region in the context of more wide-ranging projects. In the early twentieth century, upstate New York, in which the Appalachian counties lie, produced enthusiasts, often members of historical societies, devoted to the preservation of the state's folklore, artifacts, and architecture. Their activity was dominated by two professors, Harold W. Thompson of Cornell University and Louis C. Jones of Albany State College. Thompson produced a collection entitled *Body, Boots, and Britches* (1939), which defined for several decades the way New Yorkers saw their folk culture, and Jones established the Farmers' Museum in Cooperstown in Otsego County as a major showcase for upstate New York's early folklife. While both Thompson's collection and Jones's museum are sources of incidental material from the Appalachian counties, neither refers to them as a distinct region.

The region did yield one exemplary folklore collection, Emelyn Elizabeth Gardner's *Folklore from the Schoharie Hills, New York* (1937), devoted to material gleaned in Schoharie

County. The product of six summers' worth of interviews, Gardner's work is considered groundbreaking for its attention to the presentation of folktales and ballads without unnecessary adornment or reworking.

For the rest of New York's Appalachian Mountains, the most popular folkloric work is the two-volume *Southern Tier* (1953) by newspaper columnist Arch Merrill, who was born in the area. Best described as a travelogue, Merrill's work includes a substantial number of very localized histories, information on place names, and legends and anecdotes about famous personages. The most comprehensive treatment of folk music in the region can be found in Simon J. Bronner's *Old-Time Music Makers of New York State* (1987). While focusing on upstate New York as a whole, Bronner includes abundant material on music and musicians from the Appalachian counties. Until a general demise of old-time music after World War II, the region was home to an active old-time music tradition including groups such as Floyd Woodhull's Old-Tyme Masters and the Hornellsville Hillbillies, who achieved a measure of fame beyond their local areas. A complement to Bronner's book is ethnomusicologist James Kimball's article "Country Dancing in Central and Western New York State" published in *New York Folklore* in 1988.

The establishment of a folk arts program at the New York State Council on the Arts in the early 1980s spurred the development of long-standing public folklore programs around the region, most notably those developed at the Roberson Museum and Science Center in Binghamton and the Arts of the Southern Finger Lakes in Corning. In addition to producing exhibits on the region's folk culture, the Roberson Museum has acquired many examples of folk art for its permanent collection. In keeping with the museum's mission, material folk art dominates the Roberson program's archives. Archival holdings at the Arts of the Southern Finger Lakes are somewhat more eclectic, including a higher percentage of narrative and musical materials.

See also: CHAUTAUQUA INSTITUTION (TOURISM); COOPERSTOWN, NEW YORK (TOURISM); FOLK SONGS (MUSIC).

—Peter Voorheis, *Arts of the Southern Finger Lakes, Corning, New York*

Simon J. Bronner, *Old-Time Music Makers of New York State* (1987); Emelyn Elizabeth Gardner, *Folklore from the Schoharie Hills, New York* (1937); Arch Merrill, *Southern Tier* (1986).

North Alabama Public Folklore

Appalachian north Alabama is defined not only by physical geography but also by cultural traditions initially brought by settlers who came mostly from the upland South regions of the Carolinas, Georgia, Tennessee, and Virginia in the early nineteenth century. For this reason, the region shares many traits with adjacent areas of Tennessee, Georgia, and Mississippi.

While nineteenth-century writers such as Howard Weeden of Huntsville mined north Alabama folk traditions for material, very little academic folklore research was done in the area during the nineteenth and early twentieth centuries. Still, a few early items, such as a 1902 article in the *Journal of American Folklore* about a north Alabama folk remedy, can be found. In a map facing the title page of Olive Dame Campbell and Cecil Sharp's *English Folk Songs from the Appalachians* (1917; revised 1932), the southern Appalachians clearly include nearly one-third of the state of Alabama, yet the authors apparently chose not to collect songs within the borders of the state. The first systematic research of north Alabama folk traditions can be credited to George Pullen Jackson. Jackson analyzed the religious music of the South and was interested in the relationship between black and white spirituals. His research during the 1920s on the origins of shape-note singing provided a foundation for future ethnomusicologists and folklorists. In such books as *White Spirituals in the Southern Uplands* (1933), he documented north Alabama's rich hymn-singing traditions, especially those associated with various editions of *The Sacred Harp*, and placed them in a national context.

Even more than Jackson, writer Carl Carmer brought Alabama folk traditions to the attention of the nation. While his commercially successful *Stars Fell on Alabama* (1934) was a romanticized statewide survey, it included interesting observations on quilting patterns and folk customs from north Alabama. The first folklore research sponsored by a public agency in north Alabama was probably the 1939 project that included the recording of musicians from the resettlement camp at Skyline Farms in Jackson County. Herbert Halpert recorded the Skyline Farms Band and other musicians on his Southern Recording Expedition, a field trip sponsored by the Library of Congress and the Works Progress Administration.

George Korson researched the music of north Alabama miners during the 1930s. The results were included in *Minstrels of the Mine Patch* (1938) and *Coal Dust on the Fiddle* (1943). While not an employee of a government agency, Korson was publicly oriented and his recordings were later included in Library of Congress archives. From 1945 to 1947, University of Alabama music professor and folklorist Byron Arnold collected field recordings through a special university research grant. He later presented his research in the book *Folk Songs of Alabama* (1950), through public lectures, and on radio broadcasts.

Peter Brannon, an archivist and later director of the Alabama Department of Archives and History, may have been the first state officer to research and disseminate Alabama folklore. Brannon provided researchers with folk material such as the Shelby County version of the ballad "John Henry." He also wrote on Alabama folk traditions in his column "Through the Years" (1931–50) for the *Montgomery Advertiser*.

Public folklore activity increased dramatically in the 1970s. In 1975 cultural geographer Eugene Wilson authored a report called *Alabama Folk Houses* published by the Alabama Historical Commission. In 1976 a group of Samford students headed by Mark Gooch and Cathy Hanby-Sikora and advised by Jim Brown surveyed folk crafts around north Alabama. This Folkcenter South project then held craft demonstrations at Tannehill State Park featuring basket makers, potters, blacksmiths, net makers, and instrument makers.

In 1976 Henry Willett came to work for the Alabama State Council on the Arts and became the first state folklorist in Alabama. During his tenure, several National Endowment for the Arts–sponsored projects involving north Alabama material were undertaken, including the exhibit and catalog *The Traditional Pottery of Alabama* (1983) and the Jefferson County Quartet Reunion concert (1980), based on fieldwork by gospel scholar Doug Seroff. This project was the first of many honoring the Birmingham African American gospel tradition.

Brenda McCallum established the Archive of American Minority Cultures at the University of Alabama's Special Collections in 1979. The core of these audio recordings and related materials are from fieldwork she accomplished during her stay in Tuscaloosa and represent one of the largest collections of Alabama folklore materials in existence. In 1982 she produced the album *Birmingham Boys: Jubilee Gospel Quartets of Jefferson County, Alabama* with Henry Willett. This fieldwork also led her to develop plans for two radio series that explored the social fabric behind gospel music. The National Endowment for the Humanities–funded *Working Lives* (1985) is a thirteen-part radio documentary about Birmingham's industrial workers. Along with her husband Steve, McCallum then produced a six-part radio program entitled *In the Spirit* (1986), a profile of Alabama's black religious music funded by the National Endowment for the Arts. A planning report written just before her death in 1992 was the basis for *Spirit of Steel: Music of the Mines, Railroads and Mills of the Birmingham District* (1999), a documentary book and album published by Sloss Furnaces Museum of Birmingham.

In 1980 a group of folklore enthusiasts founded the Alabama Folklife Association. Since then, many projects have been produced by the group with federal and state funding. The first was a cassette publication of some of Byron Arnold's field recordings entitled *Cornbread Crumbled in Gravy*, with notes by Joy Baklanoff and John Bealle. Joyce Cauthen, an authority on traditional music, became director of the Alabama Folklife Festival (1989–93), a partnership between the folklife association and the arts council that invigorated fieldwork during those years. In 1995 the Alabama Folklife Association produced, under Cauthen's direction, the recording *John Alexander's Sterling Jubilee Singers of Bessemer, Alabama*, a profile of Jefferson County's oldest African American quartet. Later, Cauthen headed a research project on Primitive Baptist hymn singing and compiled the book and album *Benjamin Lloyd's Hymn Book: A Primitive Baptist Song Tradition* (1999). The film *Sweet Is the Day* (2001), produced by Jim Carnes and Erin Kellen with association support, documents the Sacred Harp tradition of the Wootten family of Sand Mountain. The association also publishes the annual journal *Tributaries*.

In the early 1980s, Robert J. Norrell directed an oral history project called "Birmingfind" at Birmingham Southern College. This project collected interviews among Birmingham's ethnic neighborhoods and published highlights in a series of booklets. In 1981 the Birmingham Museum of Art produced *Alabama Quilts*, based on research by Gail Andrews, Robert Cargo, and Janet Strain McDonald. This was the museum's first major folk art exhibition and raised the public's appreciation for this traditional art form. The *Made in Alabama* exhibition traveled from 1994 to 1996 and presented historic art from throughout Alabama. The catalog, published by the museum in 1995, has chapters on Alabama folk pottery, quilting, and weaving.

In 1985 Alabama State Council on the Arts director Al Head formed a special program to support folklore research and present Alabama traditional artists. The Alabama Folklife Program funds a wide range of projects including films, exhibitions, documentary recordings, festivals and an apprenticeship program. One of the first projects supported by a grant from the program was *Possum up a Gum Stump* (1988), Joyce Cauthen's recordings of Alabama fiddlers. Director Joey Brackner produced several north Alabama projects, including the exhibition and catalog *Pottery from the Mountains of Alabama* (1986) and the film *Unbroken Tradition: Jerry Brown's Pottery* (1989) with Appalshop, the mountain media center at Whitesburg, Kentucky. Maggie Holtzberg worked at the Alabama Folklife Program in 1988 and researched the gandy dancer (railroad track builder) work song tradition, especially among retired railroad workers around Birmingham. She organized and documented a reunion of these men in Calera and with Barry Dornfeld produced the film *Gandy Dancers* (1994), based upon her Alabama work.

In 1990 the Alabama Center for Traditional Culture was created as a department of the Alabama State Council on the Arts. The center has undertaken several projects presenting north Alabama material. The book and album *In the Spirit*, a sampling of Alabama's sacred music, was edited by center director Hank Willett. Center folklorist Anne Kimzey produced a radio series on aspects of Alabama folk culture and *Water Ways*, an exhibit on folkways associated with rivers. Aimee Schmidt produced the exhibition *Alabama Culture and Community*, a survey of the state's folk traditions.

See also: BALLADS (MUSIC); KORSON, GEORGE; SAND MOUNTAIN POTTERY (CRAFTS).

—Joey Brackner, *Alabama State Council on the Arts*

Byron Arnold, *Folksongs of Alabama* (1950); Joey Brackner, ed., *Spirit of Steel: Music of the Mines, Railroads and Mills of the Birmingham District* (1999); Stephen Martin, ed., *Alabama Folklife: Collected Essays* (1989).

North Carolina Public Folklore

In North Carolina, public folklore is a recent manifestation of a long-standing interest in documenting and presenting folklife. Written and pictorial records of traditional culture in the state began in the colonial period and span more than four hundred years. While traditions of the Appalachian region were not the first to be noticed, they have often attracted the most attention.

From their first arrival in what is now North Carolina, Europeans attempted to document cultural traditions. In the 1580s, John White made paintings of Indian dress and dance, sculpture and architecture, work, foodways, and worship. More than a century later, John Lawson left prose descriptions of beliefs and customs of Indians and white settlers and, unknowingly, included folktales he heard. In the nineteenth century, the humorist Harden E. Taliaferro preserved and burlesqued the talk and folklife of Surry County in *Fisher's River Scenes and Characters* (1859), and shape-note tunebook compiler William Hauser printed melodies he learned from black and white singers at Piedmont camp meetings in his books *The Hesperian Harp* (1848) and *The Olive Leaf* (1878). The first self-conscious field documentation, however, appeared in transcriptions of eight spirituals sung in the state during the Civil War and published in *Slave Songs of the United States* (1867), and the first serious fieldwork was ethnologist James Mooney's study with Cherokees in western North Carolina between 1887 and 1890. Mooney's subsequent publications, *The Sacred Formulas of the Cherokee* (1891) and *The Myths of the Cherokee* (1900), signal the beginnings of deliberate and intensive collection in the state on the part of governmental agencies. From that time, recognition of the social, historical, and artistic value of North Carolina's musical, narrative, and craft traditions, as well as its ethnic, religious, and occupational cultures, has steadily grown.

With establishment of the North Carolina Folklore Society in 1913, Frank C. Brown formally initiated an active program of collecting folklore within the state. For years, a small army of public school teachers, students, university faculty, and interested citizens amassed material that was eventually edited by a team of scholars and published as *The Frank C. Brown Collection of North Carolina Folklore* (1952–64). This massive seven-volume set is still notable as the largest state folklore collection ever published. Remarkable also is the work of English song collectors Cecil Sharp and Maud Karpeles, who visited singers in mountain communities and transcribed the tunes and texts of old songs and ballads while they sang. Sharp's *English Folk Songs from the Southern Appalachians* (1917; revised 1932) includes numerous songs collected in the North Carolina mountains during World War I.

As sound-recording equipment became available and reasonably portable, field collectors began using it to capture performances of traditional music and songs. Among the earliest of these collectors were Robert Winslow Gordon and John and Alan Lomax, who included North Carolina in their field trips to record authentic American folk song for the Library of Congress from the 1920s through the 1940s. Other collectors from within the state, including Brown, Jan Schinhan, Ralph S. Boggs, W. Amos Abrams, and Artus Moser, continued this work, but such collectors typically held the recordings they made in private collections. When universities and other institutions developed formal mechanisms for handling archival nonprint materials, many private collections gradually found their way to libraries and archives. Important Appalachian collections of sound recordings, artifacts, and photographs can be found at the Museum of the Cherokee Indian, the Museum of Early Southern Decorative Arts, the North Carolina Museum of History, the North Carolina State Archives, the North Carolina Arts Council, Mars Hill College, Appalachian State University, Western Carolina University, Duke University, and the University of North Carolina.

Three of these institutions have been key to the development of public folklore. The North Carolina Museum of History pioneered the collection and public display of artifacts, and it has for years had Appalachian materials scattered throughout its collections. Handmade items such as quilts, dulcimers, pottery, baskets, and carvings have formed a significant part of the museum's research collections along with photographs of craftspeople, objects, and vernacular architecture. In anticipation of opening the Folklife Gallery as a permanent part of its new facility, the museum created a position for a folklife curator in 1994 and increased its representation of folklife throughout the state. As the museum's first folklife curator, Sally Peterson supervised and conducted field research, helped develop major exhibits on topics such as health and healing, and organized programs that featured traditional arts and artists. The Museum of History has raised the visibility of folklife in the state and has helped validate the traditional focus of regional museums such as the Mountain Gateway Museum in Old Fort, which has included Appalachian folklife topics in exhibits, research, and programming for many years.

A second institution, the Curriculum in Folklore at the University of North Carolina in Chapel Hill, has been instrumental in establishing a place for folklore studies in higher education across the state, in training many of the folklorists now working in the mountain region, and in developing the Southern Folklife Collection, which has significant holdings of commercial and field recordings of Appalachian music. A master's level program, which offers a doctoral minor, was established in 1940 and was the nation's first graduate degree program in folklore. From the outset, it has been fed by literary and musical folklore interests and by social and political interests in improving conditions for people in the state. With many of its faculty and students engaged in field research, the curriculum developed strengths in folklife documentation and presentation that have attracted students interested in pursuing careers in public-sector folklore. Its graduates hold positions in colleges, universities, organizations, and state agencies across the Appalachian region, as well as throughout the state, the South, and the rest of the country. The writings of these students and of the faculty of the curriculum have helped establish folklore as a serious field of work for public folklorists.

The third institution, the Folklife Program of the North Carolina Arts Council, has been key to recent advances in public folklore. Just as the study, collection, and exhibition of folklore have become institutionalized, so has folklife programming. Popular events such as Bascom Lamar Lunsford's Mountain Dance and Folk Festival, begun in Asheville in 1928, and the early Dogwood Festival at the University of North Carolina featured performances by folk musicians and dancers. A team of dancers that appeared regularly at the Asheville festival brought national recognition to the state when it performed at the White House by invitation from First Lady Eleanor Roosevelt. The Folklife Program continues to encourage presenters to include authentic traditional artists in public programs, special events, and other performances. The arts council has raised the visibility of many traditional artists by listing them in directories that it circulates widely to presenting organizations within the state.

The Folklife Program of the North Carolina Arts Council is one of the few state folklore programs to originate as a state initiative, without salary support from the National Endowment for the Arts. Prompted by the success of the North Carolina bicentennial celebration in Durham, a folklife festival produced by George Holt, the North Carolina Department of Cultural Resources created a state-level position for a folklife coordinator in 1977. As its new director, Holt developed the Office of Folklife Programs in the Department of Cultural Resources and worked with a small staff to document traditional artists and produce folklife festivals and special events. A departmental reorganization in 1981 placed the Office of Folklife Programs in the North Carolina Arts Council, where it became the Folklife Program and continued its mission to document, preserve, interpret, and present the state's traditional arts and artists.

Acquisition of a grants-making capability in 1984 gave the Folklife Program a way to extend its work by supporting numerous people across the state who showed initiative in presenting performances and festivals and by producing publications, exhibits, documentary films, and sound recordings, a number of them with Appalachian subjects. Through a series of grants to summer interns, the program has also offered graduate students in folklore a wide variety of experiences in public folklife programs such as administering grants, staging awards ceremonies and festivals, editing publications, organizing conferences, and carrying out field research. Salary-assistance grants from the council have allowed organizations such as the John C. Campbell Folk School and the Hiddenite Center to create positions for folklorists. The North Carolina Folk Heritage Awards, perhaps the most visible and popular of the council's grants programs, have honored traditional artists—many of them outstanding musicians, ballad or gospel singers, storytellers, quilters, and instrument makers from the mountain region—in public ceremonies since 1989.

Support from the National Endowment for the Arts has also allowed the Folklife Program to plan and carry out ambitious projects that reach beyond state lines. One of these, Sustainable Folk Arts Programming, organized in collaboration with the Curriculum in Folklore at the University of North Carolina, offered a summer institute in which public folklorists and related professionals from across the nation met to explore major issues affecting their work. For the Folklife Program, that conference led to the creation of the Blue Ridge Music Trails and the Cherokee Heritage Trails in the late 1990s as part of the Blue Ridge Heritage Initiative in the southern Appalachian region of

North Carolina, Tennessee, Virginia, and Georgia. The trail projects have brought public folklorists in the four states together with a variety of state, federal, and local agencies, the Eastern Band of Cherokee Indians, nonprofit organizations, and interested individuals to plan for tourism that will celebrate and preserve important cultural traditions in the mountain region.

Other developments in the late 1990s offered even wider opportunities for folklorists when the Center for Documentary Studies at Duke University filled several staff positions, including that of director, with folklorists. The center serves the state and carries out documentary projects in the mountain region, but it also works at the national and international levels. Folklorists, whose work often focuses on the local and the particular, now have an opportunity to carry that perspective into larger contexts.

The pattern that has emerged over the long period of interest in folklore in North Carolina is one in which varied and unsystematic efforts to collect, preserve, interpret, and present folk traditions gradually become systematized and institutionalized. The sphere of this work continues to expand. This trend, especially notable in the mountain region, reflects the growth of folklore as a profession and greater public awareness and appreciation of cultural heritage and living traditions. Tensions have often developed between commercial, political, and public interests in folk culture, and sensitive resolution of such issues remains one of the greatest challenges for public folklorists.

See also: JOHN C. CAMPBELL FOLK SCHOOL (CRAFTS); SECTION OVERVIEW (TOURISM).

—Beverly B. Patterson, *North Carolina Folklife Institute*

Newman Ivey White et al., eds., *The Frank C. Brown Collection of North Carolina Folklore* (1952–64).

North Georgia Public Folklore

The section of the Appalachian Mountains that lies within the state of Georgia, mostly within the Great Smoky Mountains, is simply known as north Georgia. It is defined not only geographically but also by cultural traits shared with nearby areas of the upland South, particularly northern Alabama, east Tennessee, and the Carolinas. While the term *Appalachia* does not always bring Georgia immediately to the public mind, some of the best-known images of Appalachia have been drawn from north Georgia—including the publishing and cultural phenomenon Foxfire and the 1972 motion picture *Deliverance*.

The Foxfire Fund, based in Rabun County, started when high school teacher Eliot Wigginton had his students collect oral narratives from local elders. *Foxfire Magazine* has been produced uninterrupted since its founding in 1966. The collected stories of traditional ways of life led to a widely popular series of eleven *Foxfire* books, with seven additional books on specialized topics such as cooking, quilting, and Christmas traditions. Foxfire has preserved a group of historic log cabins as the Foxfire Museum and Center, which opened to the public in 1991 to share local history, a growing collection of artifacts, and the organization's educational mission with visitors.

Running counter to the image of north Georgia and Appalachia presented by Foxfire, writer James Dickey's novel *Deliverance* was released just four years after the founding of *Foxfire Magazine* and became an immediate best-seller. It served as the basis for a popular film by the same name in 1972. In the film, four respectable businessmen from Atlanta take a canoe trip on the wild Cahulawassee River, soon to be dammed. Deep in the woods and far from civilization, the suburbanites encounter two mountain men who prove to be sadists, rapists, and murderers and a child who is the obvious product of inbreeding. Against a backdrop of beautiful mountain scenery and the haunting tune "Dueling Banjos," the film shaped American impressions of the southern Appalachians for a generation after its release.

Popular images of the traditional culture of north Georgia notwithstanding, serious work in public folklore in Georgia is a relatively new phenomenon. In their *English Folk Songs from the Southern Appalachians* (1917; revised 1932), Olive Dame Campbell and Cecil Sharp included much of the state in their map of Appalachia but spent little time collecting within the borders of Georgia. In the 1920s, George Pullen Jackson examined the relationship between black and white religious singing in the South, with particular interest in northern Alabama and Georgia. In his *White Spirituals in the Southern Uplands* (1933), Jackson analyzed the origins of shape-note singing in the South and paved the way for future folklorists.

Public folklore in Georgia was born with the establishment of the Georgia Council for the Arts. In 1953 the state established a study commission to determine its appropriate role in supporting the arts. In 1965, just after the National Endowment for the Arts was established, the Georgia Commission on the Arts was created. Three years later, the commission began to fund programs. In 1972 the commission was replaced by the Georgia Advisory Council for the Arts, whose name was later changed to the Georgia Council for the Arts and Humanities. Finally, in 1986 the Georgia legislature changed the name to establish the Georgia Council for the Arts in its current form. Its mission, as currently stated, is to "encourage excellence in the arts, to support the arts' many forms of expression and to make the arts available to all Georgians by providing funding, programming and services."

The Georgia Folklife Program was created in 1987 with support from the National Endowment for the Arts, the Dekalb Council for the Arts, the Fulton County Council for the Arts, and the Governor's Office. In 1991 the folklife program found a permanent home in the Georgia Council for the Arts. The Georgia Folklife Program actively documents, supports, preserves, and educates the public about Georgia's traditional folk culture, defined as "the traditional expressive culture (music, craft, dance, verbal lore) maintained by groups of people who share a common family history, ethnic heritage, occupation, religion, or geographic region. Whether sung or told, hand-crafted or performed, a group's folklife signifies a tangible sense of belonging and identity."

In addition to the state-sponsored Georgia Folklife Program, a number of smaller public folklore organizations have arisen to collect and support folklife in north Georgia. The Georgia Humanities Council provides humanities outreach programs, grants, and services to schools and organizations. The Southern Arts Federation is a nonprofit regional arts organization whose Traditional Arts and Heritage Program works with state arts agencies to collect and support the folklife in Alabama, Georgia, Florida, Kentucky, Louisiana, Mississippi, North Carolina, South Carolina, and Tennessee.

North Georgia's folklife includes musical traditions such as fiddling, a capella gospel quartet singing, and Mexican American *norteños;* regional crafts such as coiled baskets and Piedmont utilitarian pottery; various forms of traditional dance such as flatfoot buck dancing and South Indian Kuchipudi; and food traditions such as dinners on the grounds, barbecues, and fish fries. North Georgia folklife also includes many healing practices, occupational traditions, and local architectural variations. Though people tend to identify north Georgia folklife with the state's older indigenous communities, folklife also includes the traditional culture of more recent groups. It is not uncommon for a group's folklife to remain virtually unknown beyond the local community in which it flourishes, largely because these traditional practices are found outside the usual media of art: in churches and other places of worship, at local auctions, and in workplaces.

See also: *DELIVERANCE* (MEDIA); FOXFIRE (EDUCATION).

—Cynthia Byrd Murtagh, *University of Pennsylvania*

Olive Dame Campbell and Cecil J. Sharp, *English Folk Songs from the Southern Appalachians* (1917; revised 1932); George Pullen Jackson, *White Spirituals in the Southern Uplands* (1933); Michael Ann Williams, *Great Smoky Mountains Folklife* (1995).

Occupational Folklore

Within the broader study of American regional cultures, a subfield of occupational folklore emerged from pioneering research in Appalachia by folklorists George Korson and Archie Green during the 1960s. Korson and Green both focused on verbal lore, particularly song traditions associated with Appalachian coal-mining communities. By the early 1970s, folklorists affiliated with the recently established Smithsonian Festival of American Folklife (later the Smithsonian Folklife Festival) attempted to represent to a broad-based audience the diversity of shared work experiences within specific American regional groups. Soon, folklorists across the United States began to explore the occupational folklife of modern-day working Americans.

Expanding upon the approaches of Korson and Green, folklorists in recent years have documented the occupational folklife of people across Appalachia primarily involved in work historically associated with the region—traditional trades such as hunting, foraging, farming, herding, blacksmithing, and moonshining, as well as such industrial occupations as railroading, timbering, coal mining, oil drilling, and milling. Folklorists have also explored the work-related culture of people living in Appalachia and working in mainstream jobs. Recent research shows that individuals and families in Appalachia continue to combine several work activities rather than relying upon a single specialized occupation. Many people in the region today are engaged in more than one type of work and, therefore, are bearers of multiple occupational traditions.

From the earliest days of European settlement in Appalachia to recent times, residents of the region have shared information about their work through a combination of orally communicated and physically demonstrated cultural expressions. The occupational traditions that evolved in Appalachia through the mid-nineteenth century blended old-world ideas about work with the knowledge of native peoples. For example, Appalachian architectural traditions combined German (and possibly Scandinavian) woodworking techniques with British design features, while Appalachian foodways incorporated numerous plants originally cultivated by Native Americans, including beans, corn, pumpkins, and squash.

Industrialization of Appalachia after the Civil War transformed the region's economy and ultimately changed the region's culture. The agent of that industrialization, the railroad, soon attained considerable symbolic significance in regional cultural expression, as people across Appalachia composed numerous folk and popular songs about trains, from the traditional disaster ballad "The Wreck of the Old 97" to such self-penned country music hits by the Delmore Brothers (of Elkmont, Alabama) as "Blue Railroad Train" and "Blow Yo' Whistle, Freight Train." Railroads created jobs that attracted people of various ethnicities to Appalachia and led to the dissemination of new cultural attitudes and expressions. For instance, African Americans migrating into the region brought their aesthetic sensibilities, which markedly influenced Appalachian verbal folklore (particularly the style and repertoire of music making and storytelling) as whites in the region borrowed tunes, songs, and stories from black culture. African Americans in Appalachia crafted enduring songs, such as the traditional blues ballad "John Henry," based on a legendary story about an African American laborer whose victory over a railroad company's steam-drill occurred either in West Virginia or northern Alabama.

Railroads rendered Appalachia more accessible to industries that sought to exploit the region's coal, minerals, or timber. People employed by industrial companies—Appalachian natives as well as newcomers—endured considerable hardships, and companies historically offered meager compensation for frequently life-endangering work. While few occupational traditions were created in the region's short-lived timber camps, coal towns in Appalachia fostered diverse work-related traditions, a result of the comparative stability of mining communities. Mill towns located both within and near Appalachia also maintained relatively stable populations, which likewise encouraged the development of a distinctive occupational culture. People living in these company towns drew upon traditional cultural expressions—particularly music and stories—to entertain themselves and to mobilize their communities in the effort to achieve positive social change. Coal miners and mill workers in Appalachia produced protest songs that criticized the injustices of the capitalist system as well as the companies' seeming disregard for human life and the natural environment. Well-known coal-mining protest songs from Appalachia have included Florence Reece's 1931 pro-union anthem "Which Side Are You On?" and such later songs as Billy Edd Wheeler's "Coal Tattoo" (1963). A popular protest song among Appalachian textile mill workers was "Weave Room Blues," composed by Dorsey Dixon in 1932.

Images of Appalachian culture, communicated through the occupational traditions of the region, have exerted a strong imaginative hold on people outside Appalachia. For example, songs about coal mining, farming, moonshining, and railroading, composed or reinterpreted by Appalachian and non-native musicians, continue to influence mainstream America's view of life in Appalachia.

See also: COAL-MINING AND PROTEST MUSIC (MUSIC); HILLBILLY (IMAGES AND ICONS); RAILROAD PROMOTION AND IN-MIGRATION (SETTLEMENT AND MIGRATION).

—Ted Olson, *East Tennessee State University*

Norm Cohen, *Long Steel Rail: The Railroad in American Folksong* (1981); Ronald D Eller, *Miners, Millhands, and Mountaineers: Industrialization of the Appalachian South, 1880–1930* (1982); Archie Green, *Only a Miner: Studies in Recorded Coal-Mining Songs* (1972); Ted Olson, *Blue Ridge Folklife* (1998).

Oral Narrative

The narrative folklore of the Appalachians, documented as early as the eighteenth century, became by the beginning of the twenty-first a major emblem of cultural self-identification and the subject of study by folklorists worldwide. Various Native American and European American storytelling traditions flourish in the region, but by far the most celebrated and stereotyped folk narratives are certain British American genres of the southern Appalachians: especially märchen (the German term for fairy tales, such as those of the Brothers Grimm) but also legends, jokes, tall tales, family sagas, and personal narratives. A comprehensive account of Appalachian oral narrative would be extensive in scope, but a survey of the genres and topics most often treated in folklore collections provides an introduction to mountain narratives.

Appalachia is famous for its märchen—long, multi-episodic narratives in which, characteristically, a single hero or heroine uses cunning and magical help to defeat a supernatural opponent (most often in Appalachia a giant or witch), winning wealth or a mate and coming of age in the process. Best known in English-speaking traditions are such tales as "Jack and the Beanstalk" and "Jack the Giant-Killer," both of which were extremely popular in both oral and printed versions in Britain in the mid-eighteenth century, the period of English, Scottish, and Scots-Irish migrations into the southern mountains.

The earliest surviving Appalachian account suggests that the first European American märchen enjoyed the same general popularity as their British sources. In his *Notes on the Settlement and Indian Wars* (1824), Joseph Doddridge describes the tales he heard as a boy around 1760 in what is now West Virginia as "dramatic narrations, chiefly concerning Jack and the Giant," which furnished young people with amusement during their leisure hours. Doddridge remembers that many of the tales were lengthy, embracing a range of incidents in which Jack, always the hero of the story, encounters many difficulties and performs great feats, including conquering the Giant.

Writing in the early nineteenth century, Doddridge expressed the belief that these tales had already been swept away by "civilization," which had "substituted in their place the novel and the romance." Yet it is now known that märchen were told throughout the nineteenth and twentieth centuries because folklorists heard many such tales when they first began asking for them in the 1920s and heard narrators identify them as part of local storytelling traditions stretching back to the early 1800s.

The family traditions of Appalachian storytellers and the internal evidence offered by the tales themselves indicate that many possess English sources. For example, the Harmon and Hicks families of western North Carolina and east Tennessee maintain that their tales came from England, and Easley Ratliff's "Jack the Giant-Killer," told to Leonard Roberts in Pike County, Kentucky, in 1954, has a plot and proper names featured in eighteenth-century English versions of the tale. Other Appalachian tales have strong affinities with Scottish and Irish märchen. For example, "Jack and the Bull" presents a unique hero who is both a giant-killer and a "male Cinderella": a young boy saves the life of a talking bull; the bull feeds and protects the boy as they wander through the world; the bull dies, leaving the boy with magic objects that help him kill giants and court a princess; the boy flees from a ball leaving behind a shoe, which the princess recovers and uses to identify the boy; and the two marry. In the United States, this tale has been collected almost exclusively in the southern Appalachians; elsewhere in the world, it is known almost solely in Ireland and Scotland.

Märchen are not particularly common in the Appalachians, but they have become a major symbol of Appalachian identity, largely because they have been collected from southern mountaineers far more frequently than from any other British American group in the United States. Of the major American märchen collections published in the twentieth century, all come either from the southern Appalachians or the Ozarks, with one exception: Emelyn Elizabeth Gardner's *Folklore from the Schoharie Hills, New York* (1937). Gardner's tales and others collected more recently (such as Jack tales told by the Lugg family of northern Pennsylvania) suggest that the northern Appalachian märchen-telling tradition has enjoyed greater popularity than folklorists once supposed.

Appalachian märchen became internationally famous through Richard Chase's book *The Jack Tales* (1943), a heavily edited collection based on the family repertoire of the Beech Mountain, North Carolina, branch of the Harmon-Hicks family, supplemented by tales collected by Chase and James Taylor Adams in Wise County, Virginia. *The Jack Tales* inspired teachers and folklorists to collect, publish, and retell tales throughout southern Appalachia. For example, Leonard Roberts, teaching in the Berea (Kentucky) Foundation High School shortly after World War II, read *The Jack Tales* to his students and discovered that their families had many similar tales to tell, stories that appear in his first collection, *South from Hel-fer-Sartin* (1955).

One reason why Jack tales and other märchen were collected so late and are still considered by some to be exceedingly rare is that historically they have belonged to intimate domestic performing contexts. Märchen tended to stay within the family and were shared during work sessions (such as hoeing rows, cleaning cotton, and shelling beans), evenings after work (on the front porch or front lawn, as the family enjoyed the evening breeze and waited for the house to cool), or at bedtime, as entertainment for children. Through most of the twentieth century the most public forum for telling märchen was the classroom, where teachers such as Marshall Ward of Boone, North Carolina, and Lige Gay of Hyden, Kentucky, shared stories with their students.

The measure of a märchen's popularity lay in the narrator's ability to adapt it to the tastes and values of the immediate audience. In the Appalachians, the armored warriors common in European folktales were transformed into poor farm boys. Kings, when they appeared, became gentlemen farmers, and giants lived in farmhouses and went to Wednesday-night prayer meetings, much as those who listened to the tales. Jack and other male heroes were social underdogs, poor boys who succeeded not through strength, but through their wits or inherent generosity. Female heroes generally resembled the Appalachian male heroes more than the heroines of Walt Disney's *Cinderella* or *Sleeping Beauty;* rather than sitting passively at home, girls wandered into the wilds, using their courage, brains, and virtue to overcome powerful adversaries.

In the late twentieth century, Appalachian märchen became widely known through electronic media and highly dramatic public performances, largely inspired by the same family that had told the Jack tales to Chase. In 1947 the Library of Congress issued recordings by Maud Gentry Long (whose mother, Jane Hicks Gentry, had told the first Jack tales collected by a folklorist, Isabel Gordon Carter, in 1925), and in 1964 Folkways records released Jack tales told by her distant relative Ray Hicks. In 1973 the first gathering of the National Storytelling Festival in Jonesborough, Tennessee, featured Hicks, who became a fixture of subsequent festivals and an inspiration to the amateur and professional storytellers who spread his reputation and tales. Acting troupes performed dramatized märchen in school pageants, and companies such as Appalshop, a media cooperative in Whitesburg, Kentucky, created video reenactments.

Jokes and tall tales are not only far more common in Appalachia than Jack tales but also possess a more thoroughly documented history. From the eighteenth century forward, most almanacs printed in the eastern United States featured dozens of short, largely humorous narratives, and early on these reflected and influenced an Appalachian taste for terse, often dry, narrative jokes.

Themes of Appalachian jokes, like those worldwide, are innumerable, but an early and often recorded subject is survival skill (or lack thereof). In the nineteenth and early twentieth centuries, "Irishman" jokes poked mild fun at one of the early immigrant groups to the region by presenting two numbskulls, Pat and Mike, who lacked rudimentary knowledge of farmwork. Many jokes draw upon stereotypes of mountain life to subvert them, as seemingly ignorant mountaineers get the better of outsiders. For example, a revenue agent offers a farm boy ten cents to tell him where a whiskey still is hidden in the nearby woods: "I'll give you a nickel now and a nickel when I come back." "Give me a dime," the boy answers. "You ain't coming back."

Many other jokes show a knack for social self-criticism. As illustrated by Loyal Jones in *The Preacher Joke Book* (1989), regional anecdotes often find humor in the long-windedness of preachers, the self-righteousness of some churchgoers, and the waywardness of other parishioners.

Tall tales, fictional narratives masquerading as accounts of true occurrences, were generally told by and to males, often in the first person, and sometimes were attached to well-known regional figures such as David Crockett and Daniel Boone or to a local hero, real or fictional, known only in the confines of the community. Unlike märchen, Appalachian tall tales enjoyed a healthy life in print tradition, dating back at least to the Crockett Almanacs of the 1830s.

Appalachian tall tales typically pit one man against the wilderness and celebrate both the dangers and the bounty of nature. One common tale, called "The Lucky Shot," has many variations and goes something like this version told to folklorist Dillon Bustin in West Virginia in 1992:

> I went down the road and down the creek and up the creek a piece, and I looked over the water and I saw an old fish a swimming around right at the top of the water. I thought I'd shoot it and then I hear something on the bank on the other side. A bear stood over there. And I kind of studied which one then to shoot. And then I heard something and I looked up and there was a limb running straight out over the creek and there was a whole gang of turkeys lit on that limb. And then I heard something behind me, and I looked back and there was a gang of quails under a stump where a tree had turned out. And I studied which one to shoot. And then finally I decided to point the gun at the fish and give him a sling. I did. And then the gun went off. I just give him a quick sling up, and I killed the fish. And the gun kicked so hard, it kicked my coat off, and it flew back over the quails, and I went and killed them. And [the gunshot] split the limb that lit the turkeys on it, and it caught their feet in the crack. They started to fly off and they broke the limb down, which killed them and killed the bear. I went back to the house and told Dad and we got the horse and wagon, and we went and hauled the game in.

Legends are narratives told as true, and their truth is sometimes accepted, sometimes debated by teller and audience alike. Some folklorists distinguish between belief and historical legend: the former dwells on supernatural beings and occurrences; the latter, on persons and events crucial to the local, regional, and national past. Some Appalachian communities make no such distinction, extending equal credence and historicity to both types of tales.

Among the most characteristic legends of the nineteenth and early twentieth centuries were witch tales, which generally featured accounts of sickness or poverty brought about through magic. In "Cooking a Witch's Shoulder," told by James Taylor Adams of Wise County, Virginia, and published in Thomas E. Barden's *Virginia Folk Legends*, a man's seemingly healthy sheep drop dead one by one. A neighbor "witch doctor" tells the man to skin one of the dead sheep, cook its shoulder in his oven, and to allow no one to borrow anything from the house while the shoulder is cooking. Several times an old neighbor woman rushes to the house in great pain and seeks to borrow something but is refused. On her last visit, she runs up screaming and rips off her clothes to reveal that her shoulder has been baked to the same "crisp golden brown as the mutton shoulder." In the later twentieth century, as most communities grew increasingly skeptical of witches, they continued to share such stories for entertainment and as history lessons illustrating the beliefs and lifestyles of their forebears.

Currently, ghosts, spirits, and extrasensory perception are much more commonly the subject of legends, and in many areas, as throughout the United States, belief in these phenomena is strong. The more dramatic ghost stories were sometimes shared by large groups in parlor and front-porch storytelling sessions; most tellings, however, were not set performance pieces but sprang up in everyday conversation. One of the most common themes remains the haunted house. In a widespread tale known internationally as "The Youth Who Went Forth to Learn What Fear Is," a boy accepts a dare to spend the night in such a house. He encounters many strange sights: skeletons descending down the chimney, coffins floating through the air. Finally he meets a ghost, who tells him that he was murdered in that house. There is a bag of gold hidden in the house; the ghost tells the boy to dig it up and give half to the ghost's survivors and half to himself. The boy's bravery is rewarded by wealth. Outside of Appalachia, this tale is often told as fiction, but Appalachian tellers tend to present it as a true local event.

Historical legend themes include the dangers of the wilds, encounters with Indians, Civil War stories, and exploits of great hunters. For example, stories may tell of how a hunter pursued by a panther threw pieces of meat behind him to delay and finally escape the animal, or how Daniel Boone tricked five Indians by having them reach their hands into the cleft of a log he was splitting and then removing the splitting wedges to trap their hands. Legend tellers often associate their stories with specific places, and many tales embed geography lessons, serving to explain, for example, how a given town or mountain got its name or the reasons behind certain social rivalries.

Family sagas and personal narratives, generally exchanged among family members and close friends, are probably the types of Appalachian tales most commonly told today. Through recounting the heroic and humorous acts of relatives, family raconteurs articulate their personal and their family's history, values, and sense of place. Typically woven into casual conversations, these tales have not been collected or publicized in proportion to their popularity, although there are several good collections. Laurel Shackelford and Bill Weinberg's *Our Appalachia* (1977) presents oral histories that embed family sagas and personal narratives, as do many of Eliot Wigginton's *Foxfire* books (1972–), which center on the folklife of north Georgia. Nancy J. Martin-Perdue and Charles L. Perdue Jr.'s *Talk About Trouble* (1996) contains family stories collected in the 1930s and 1940s by the Virginia Writers' Project; Patrick B. Mullen's *Listening to Old Voices* (1992) focuses on the life stories of the elderly. Both recount many Appalachian narratives, though neither focuses exclusively on Appalachia. Donald Davis's *Listening for the Crack of Dawn* (1990) and Sheila Kay Adams's *Come Go Home with Me* (1995) present literary adaptations of personal and family narratives by North Carolinians who grew up in post–World War II Appalachia.

Oral narratives of other Appalachian groups are rife, though less collected and studied. The Cherokee of the Great Smoky Mountain region are a notable exception: from James Mooney's *The Myths of the Cherokee* (1900) to tales collected nearly a century later in the Fading Voices Project from the Snowbird culture of North Carolina, folklorists have shown continued interest in Appalachia's Native American storytellers. The least documented oral traditions belong to African Americans and European Americans of non-British cultural background. Ruth Ann Musick's *The Telltale Lilac Bush* (1965), an anthology of West Virginia ghost legends, was one of the first books to draw upon the traditions of culturally diverse populations, including West Virginians of African American, German, Italian, Polish, and southern Slavic descent.

Until recently, most collectors of Appalachian oral narrative sought to uncover a "pure" oral tradition untouched by literacy. This fascination with and insistence upon orality was connected with the tendency to characterize Appalachian narrators as "our contemporary ancestors," their märchen as the ancient memories and property of a "folk" or "race," and their performances as little changed by the passage of centuries. Some writers continue this stereotype; for example, one study of storytelling published in 1999 labels the Appalachian Jack tales "the oldest, rarest, and fullest folktales to survive in North American oral tradition."

Although the plots of many southern Appalachian märchen possess demonstrably ancient precedents in medieval European manuscripts and printed chapbooks of the sixteenth through eighteenth centuries in Britain and Ireland, it is doubtful that many of them, once in Appalachia, persisted in an oral tradition utterly independent of writing. To be sure, at least before the 1940s, some family and community märchen traditions existed almost exclusively on an oral plane. Notably, the extended Harmon-Hicks family maintained a stable repertoire of oral Jack tales for a century before printed popularizations made it a major literary tradition as well. Others, however, such as the Farmer-Muncy family of eastern Kentucky, used written tales as a constant and valued source in the family repertoire at least from the 1920s.

The most common collections of Appalachian folktales also tended to stress those traits of the region perceived to be most old-fashioned. As collectors gathered the distant memories and traditions of the oldest storytellers, they created books and performances that emphasized the most archaic aspects of Appalachian culture and thus reinforced the impression that southern mountaineers were trapped in a time warp. More recent studies, such as Michael Ann Williams's chapter on "Verbal Lore" in her *Great Smoky Mountains Folklife* (1995) and the insider narrative art of Sheila Kay Adams and Donald Davis, offer a refreshing corrective to this trend and illustrate ways in which long-lived traditions and contemporary American cultural values intertwine in the tales told in Appalachia.

See also: JACK TALES, TRICKSTERS, AND MOUNTAIN FOLKLORE (IMAGES AND ICONS); STORYTELLING, HISTORY OF (PERFORMING ARTS); STORYTELLING IN THE TWENTIETH CENTURY, RENAISSANCE OF (PERFORMING ARTS).

—Carl Lindahl, *University of Houston*

William Bernard McCarthy, ed., *Jack in Two Worlds: Contemporary North American Tales and Their Tellers* (1994); Charles L. Perdue Jr., ed., *Outwitting the Devil: Jack Tales from Wise County, Virginia* (1987); Leonard Roberts, *Sang Branch Settlers: Folksongs and Tales of a Kentucky Mountain Family* (1974; reprint 1980).

Park Lore

In 1926 the United States government authorized the creation of three new national parks. Two, Shenandoah and Great Smoky Mountains, were in the Appalachians; the third, Mammoth Cave, was located in central Kentucky. The removal of local communities, the influx of a government bureaucracy, and the dramatic increase in tourism all combined to create "park lore."

Park lore includes the perceptions that various groups (tourists, local residents, park officials) who meet in and around the park have of each other. The occupational lore of park rangers frequently involves the misperceptions and hapless adventures of tourists, officially known as visitors. In the Smokies, the quintessential tourists are "Maud and Henry," whose antics are preserved by park rangers in both oral narratives and in notebooks. Maud and Henry are the folks who want to know if they will see giraffes on the Cades Cove loop road or ask if there is anything to see besides mountains in the park. More generically, there are "tourons," the especially moronic tourists that rangers and local people encounter.

Natural and cultural resources are the center of much park lore. Of the fauna found in the parks, bears play a particularly significant role in the lore of rangers, visitors, and local people alike. While in traditional Cherokee folklore bears were generally benevolent figures, in more recent times they have frequently taken the role of tricksters. Although overfed tourist bears are a genuine problem in the park and "bear jams" cause traffic congestion on park roads during the busy season, humorous stories of encounters with bears, particularly certain bears with quirky personalities, flourish among visitors and rangers alike.

Early superintendent reports are full of conflicts over fishing and hunting. Many local people did not look kindly on the government-mandated change in their relationship with the local environment, and use of natural resources became a source of conflict between local people and park officials. Some local residents maintained traditional use practices even though they had been rendered illegal within park boundaries. Surreptitious gathering of the flora, such as ramps and ginseng, still continues on parkland.

Conflict over cultural resources has been even more pronounced. Following the removal of local residents to create the parks, plans were made only to preserve the most sensitive reminders of the former communities, such as churches and cemeteries. In the Smokies, although not in Shenandoah, a more concerted effort was made to preserve some other culture resources, particularly the log architecture. The highly edited landscape now tells a story of a "unique" people caught forever in the nineteenth century. For those removed and their descendents, who still tell stories of government intrusion in their lives, the surviving cultural landscape has become the focus for family and community homecomings that assuage loss and assert personal connections to place. Disputes have arisen in the parks over access to former communities and cemeteries, as well as interpretation of these remnants of lost home and community.

See also: GREAT SMOKY MOUNTAINS NATIONAL PARK (GOVERNMENT); GREAT SMOKY MOUNTAINS NATIONAL PARK (TOURISM); SHENANDOAH NATIONAL PARK (TOURISM).

—Michael Ann Williams, *Western Kentucky University*

Charles L. Perdue Jr. and Nancy J. Martin-Perdue, "Appalachian Fables and Facts: A Case Study of the Shenandoah National Park Removals," *Appalachian Journal* (Autumn–Winter 1979–80); Michael Ann Williams, *Great Smoky Mountains Folklife* (1995).

Pennsylvania Public Folklore

In the Allegheny Mountains of Pennsylvania, arching from the southwestern corner of the state to the northeast, various vernacular monikers identifying subregions have found their way into common parlance: the northern tier, the Endless Mountains, the lumber region, the bituminous and anthracite coal regions, southwestern Pennsylvania, the Poconos, and God's country. In the west lies Pittsburgh, the historic urban capital of Appalachia.

The people who populate the various subregions have a keen understanding of the work that brought them to Pennsylvania and much of the public folklore research done in the area reflects this understanding. From the coal, slate, and lumber industries to the coke and steel companies, a relationship has been forged between work and between settlement patterns and ethnic identity.

Though Germans settled in the eastern counties and around St. Mary's in central Pennsylvania, only a few Appalachian counties are home to Pennsylvania German (popularly known as the Pennsylvania Dutch), Amish, or Mennonite communities. While much of the early academic folklore research focused on these populations, their primary settlement patterns favored the fertile rolling farmlands in the southeastern part of the state rather than Appalachia. In addition to Native American populations (various tribes of the Iroquois Confederacy as well as the Delaware, Susquehannock, Monongahela, and Lenni Lenape), Scots-Irish and English settled in the Appalachian region of Pennsylvania as early as 1790. By 1880 these populations were joined by Scandinavians eager to work the woods and the lumber mills. The Welsh followed, bringing their expertise to the early coal mines. By 1920, the development of coke and steel brought waves of workers from eastern Europe, including Hungarians, Poles, Austrians, Czechs, Slovaks, and Russians. Place names remain in the region as testimony to these early communities and their occupations: Ole Bull, French Asylum, Roulette, Carbondale, Ore Hill, Schuylkill Haven, Bitumen, Punxsutawney, Oil City, Sweden Valley, and Towanda, to name a few.

The Pennsylvania Folklore Society, now the Society for Pennsylvania Culture Studies, was organized in the early 1920s to "study and enjoy all forms of folklore and performance in both academic and non-academic atmosphere." Among its founders was Colonel Henry W. Shoemaker, a newspaperman and folklore collector with a love of the tall tale, local history, and fiction. Born in 1880, Shoemaker was a member of the Pennsylvania Historical Commission throughout most of the 1920s and served as the state archivist from 1933 to 1944. He held the office of state folklorist of Pennsylvania, the first such position in the country, between 1948 and 1952. Though his works are perceived by others to confuse folklore, fiction, and history, he is often credited with being the first to call attention to the traditional music and culture of Pennsylvania's mountain communities and highlight their connection to Appalachian communities to the south. He published several books on folk songs (*Mountain Minstrelsy of Pennsylvania, The Indian Steps and Other Pennsylvania Mountain Stories*, and *Susquehanna Legends: Collected in Central Pennsylvania)*, but most of his work found its way into his weekly newspaper articles and received broad distribution through newspapers that he owned. Perhaps his best-known collection is *South Mountain Sketches: Folk Tales and Legends Collected in the Mountains of Southern Pennsylvania* (1920).

Pennsylvania joined the folk festival movement when folklorists George Korson, Thomas Brendle, and William Troxell organized the first Pennsylvania State Folk Festival in Allentown in 1935. Though Allentown is not in the Appalachian region, Korson saw to it that the songs and culture of the nearby mountainous mining communities where he so avidly collected were as much a part of the festival as the Pennsylvania German culture studied by Brendle and Troxell. Thirty-two recorded discs containing more than one hundred songs, ballads, tunes, dances, and spoken performances from this First Annual Pennsylvania Folk Festival were deposited at the Archive of American Folk Song.

While the Pennsylvania State Folk Festival is no longer held, Pennsylvania is home to several other long-running folk festivals, including the Pennsylvania Dutch Folk Festival (now called the Kutztown Festival), begun by folklorist Don Yoder and others in 1950, and the Pittsburgh Folk Festival, first staged in 1956. With the creation of the Pennsylvania Dutch Folk Festival, Don Yoder also began publication of *Pennsylvania Folklife*, a magazine-style journal featuring articles about folklore, history, and culture in Pennsylvania. The early issues focused on Pennsylvania German culture, but the magazine has grown to include a much broader range of articles along with an indexed calendar of public programs and events at sites around the state.

Korson is perhaps one of the most prominent collectors of folklore in Pennsylvania. Working as a newspaper reporter for the *Pottsville Republican* before and after World War II, he came to know the people living and working in the mining communities up and down the Schuylkill River Valley area. He also became aware of how little mining lore and history were available in the local libraries. Outfitted with recording equipment on loan from the Archive of American Folk Song, he set out to collect the songs and stories of miners working the anthracite region of Pennsylvania's hills. His initial collection of mining songs and ballads appeared in the *United Mine Workers Journal* and was most likely the first folklore study to be published in an American trade union periodical. Collecting became his life's work as he canvassed the anthracite and bituminous coal regions of the Appalachian Mountains across twenty states. Korson produced three major publications: *Songs and Ballads of the Anthracite Miners* (1927), *Minstrels of the Mine Patch* (1938), and *Coal Dust on the Fiddle* (1943). He also edited *Pennsylvania Songs and Legends* (1949).

Coal Dust on the Fiddle was a pioneering work when it was first released in 1943, and it remains an exemplary account of occupational folklore. Korson not only collected the words and tunes of these songs, but he also wove into his text the folklore, history, and experiences of the miners in order to provide a more complete understanding of their lives and their music. Portions of his collection were published by the Library of Congress in 1947 as *Songs and Ballads of the Anthracite Miners*. Fifty years later, Rounder Records reissued Korson's tunes; one reviewer observed that the work contains "treasures for those who truly cherish folk music," including works by Irish ballad singer Daniel Walsh of Centralia and fiddler James Muldowney of Tamaqua.

A little further to the north and west, another folklorist was quietly collecting the fiddle tunes and dances of Pennsylvania's agricultural Appalachians. Samuel Bayard published *Hill Country Tunes* in 1944. Bayard is often considered a pioneer in the field of collecting and documenting instrumental folk music because his work includes substantial biographical data as well as stylistic observations about the fiddlers themselves. This approach prompted other folklorists to place greater emphasis on the fiddler as artist rather than the tune and its transmission.

Bayard continued to collect and analyze the traditional music of Pennsylvania's hill country until his death in 1997. His monumental work *Dance to the Fiddle, March to the Fife: Instrumental Folk Tunes in Pennsylvania* was published in 1982, culminating a lifetime of collecting, transcribing, and analyzing. The work includes 651 tunes collected between 1928 and 1963 and transcribed with detailed annotations, establishing Pennsylvania as a state vibrant with a fiddle tradition. It offers one of the first conscientious examinations of tune origins, development, and variation. Folklorists and old-time fiddle enthusiasts have continued to document fiddlers in central and western Pennsylvania. In the 1970s alone, more than seventy tapes containing interviews and music from fiddlers and fiddle contests in the region were deposited into the Archive of American Folk Song.

In the spring of 1956, the Pennsylvania Folklore Society published the first issue of *Keystone Folklore Quarterly* (later changed to *Keystone Folklore*). The journal contained articles, book and record reviews, and notes about Pennsylvania folklore or by folklorists working in Pennsylvania. It was published in conjunction with Lycoming College, Point Park College, the Pennsylvania Historical and Museum Commission, and West Chester University, moving with the editor between 1956 and 1989. The Pennsylvania Folklore Society (now the Society for Pennsylvania Culture Studies) continued to host an annual meeting into the 1990s but has been inactive since 1993.

Henry Glassie was the first to take a state-supported position as a folklorist. In 1966 he was hired as an associate historian by the Pennsylvania Historical and Museum Commission to undertake an ethnic culture survey at the behest of the Pennsylvania General Assembly. The purpose of the survey was not only to collect oral and written materials of various ethnic communities in Pennsylvania, but also to make these materials available through "organized collections, in print, festivals, and displays." A secondary goal was to encourage historical societies around the state to join in the collecting effort. To that end, in 1968 the Pennsylvania Historical and Museum Commission published *A Guide for Collectors of Oral Traditions and Folk Cultural Material in Pennsylvania*, written by Glassie and MacEdward Leach. The work of collecting oral and written materials on the contributions of ethnic groups continued at the commission under David Hufford until 1972, when the state-supported effort ended.

Throughout the 1970s, several ethnic studies programs and initiatives sprang up, most heavily in the southwestern part of the state, where many immigrants had settled to work the steel mills and coke ovens of the industrial era. Duquesne University, for instance, published several popular manuscripts on the folk arts and culture of Hungarians, Slovaks, Poles, Bulgarians, and Italians, to name a few. Bruce Weston at California University of Pennsylvania began editing *Southwestern Pennsylvania*, a magazine-style journal published by the Museum of Southwestern Pennsylvania featuring stories about the history, folklore, and experiences of the many ethnic and work communities in the region. John Bodnar directed the Historical Society of Western Pennsylvania to document the impact of the industry's ethnic history on Pennsylvania through exhibits and publications, and in 1981 the University of Pennsylvania released David Washburn's annotated bibliography of resource materials, *The Peoples of Pennsylvania*.

In this climate, the State Folklife Program was reestablished in 1982. With support from the University of Pennsylvania and Pennsylvania State University, Shalom Staub filled a position created at the Pennsylvania Heritage Affairs Commission. Under his direction, the commission hired contract fieldworkers and conducted a county-by-county ethnographic survey of folk arts in the state. The resulting photographs, taped interviews, field notes, and ephemera formed the foundation of the Pennsylvania Folklife Archives, a collection that has grown over the years and is still in use today.

Staub organized the South Central Pennsylvania Folklife Festival in 1983, featuring artists who are representative of the changing face of Appalachian communities in the central part of the state. From county-by-county fieldwork, Staub curated *Craft and Community*, a highly interactive exhibit that featured the breadth and depth of traditional arts in the state, including Hmong needleworkers, Amish carriage makers, hickory chair makers, hex sign painters, rural blacksmiths, and others actively practicing living cultural traditions. Subtitled *Traditional Arts in Contemporary Society*, the exhibit impressed upon visitors the very real and tangible presence of folk arts in the state. The exhibit opened in 1988 at the Balch Institute for Ethnic Studies in Philadelphia and traveled to several sites over a two-year period, augmented by public programs and a 140-page catalog featuring in-depth articles by many of the original fieldworkers. In 1987, during the development of the exhibit, Staub was hired as the executive director of the Pennsylvania Heritage Affairs Commission, and Amy Skillman joined the staff as the director of folklife programs.

In the late 1980s, the Pennsylvania Heritage Affairs Commission created a western folklife office with Doris Dyen at the helm. Housed at the Mon Valley Initiative and with three years of support from the National Endowment for the Arts, the program documented folk arts and occupational traditions in the greater Pittsburgh area. Dyen organized a series of events at several branches of the Carnegie Libraries that featured artistic and occupational traditions representative of each host site's community, and she developed an exhibit that traveled to each library. Dyen's work eventually became the basis of the Cultural Conservation program at the Rivers of Steel National Heritage Area, covering eight counties in southwestern Pennsylvania; it has become a national model for effectively incorporating folklore and folklife into heritage area planning and development.

The Pennsylvania State Apprenticeships in the Traditional Arts is a small but significant grants program that has continued successfully with state funding for more than twenty years. It has supported more than two hundred partnerships in nearly as many different art forms, with artistic traditions from the Appalachian region prominent among them. For the tenth anniversary of the program, a traveling exhibit that focused on the process of informal learning was targeted to youth. *Tricks of the Trade* included interactive stations and a treasure hunt that encouraged children to explore learning outside the classroom. In 1996 the exhibit, which features master-apprentice partnerships practicing the traditional arts found throughout Pennsylvania's Appalachian counties, became part of the Mid Atlantic Arts Foundation's *Appalachian Views* traveling exhibits program.

In 1989, in anticipation of the Columbus sesquicentennial, the commission embarked on a touring program that included old-time fiddle and bluegrass tunes, Hungarian gypsy dance music, polka and tamburitza music, Italian, Lithuanian, and Ukrainian songs, Scottish bagpiping, and songs from the lumber camps of northern Pennsylvania.

Being housed at the Pennsylvania Heritage Affairs Commission enables the folklife program to be flexible in developing its work. In particular, the program worked closely with a State Interagency Task Force to develop the cultural conservation component of a statewide heritage parks program. The first step was a three-year initiative beginning in 1988 with America's Industrial Heritage Project centered in Altoona. Working in partnership with local museums, colleges, and historical organizations, the commission facilitated several years of fieldwork and public programs that brought attention to the occupational and ethnic traditions of long-time residents. Funding from the National Park Service helped establish Folklife Documentation Centers within the nine-county service area. These include Seton Hill College (with a focus on gender studies), the Railroaders Memorial Museum in Altoona (with a focus on railroader's culture and history), the Somerset Historical Society, and the Johnstown Area Heritage Association. Long after the dissolution of the centers as formal entities, there exists a lasting awareness of and attention to the lives and experiences of workers whose stories make up the themes of the America's Industrial Heritage Project.

The success of the national project helped launch the Pennsylvania State Heritage Parks Project. Cultural conservation was identified as one of five goals of the program, and each potential heritage area was encouraged to include ethnographic fieldwork in its feasibility study and management action plan. As a result, the commission became the lead state agency to facilitate and review this portion of all studies, offering folklorists opportunities to conduct surveys and develop recommendations for cultural conservation strategies. Significant surveys were done throughout most of the Appalachian counties of the state, including the northern tier, the Scranton area, the Delaware and Lehigh Canal region, the oil region of northwestern Pennsylvania, and the Pittsburgh area, enhancing the work of each state heritage park as well as the Pennsylvania Folklife Archives.

See also: KORSON, GEORGE; NATIVE AMERICANS AND APPALACHIAN LITERATURE (LITERATURE); PITTSBURGH FOLK FESTIVAL (PERFORMING ARTS).

—Amy Skillman, *Institute for Cultural Partnerships, Harrisburg, Pennsylvania*

Simon J. Bronner, *Popularizing Pennsylvania: Henry W. Shoemaker and the Progressive Uses of Folklore and History* (1996); Henry W. Shoemaker, *Mountain Minstrelsy of Pennsylvania* (1931) and *Pennsylvania Mountain Stories* (1908).

Pittsburgh Folk Festival

See Pittsburgh Folk Festival (Performing Arts)

Plant Lore

See Medicinal Plant Use (Health)

Public Folklore in the Appalachians

Public presentation of folklore to audiences who are not exclusively academic has been an important aspect of folklore studies in the Appalachians since the early twentieth century. Public folklorists seek to enrich the lives of collectors, informants, and audiences through folklife festivals, recordings, radio programs, general-interest publications, craft shows, tourism, marketing, museum exhibitions, staged music performances, social advocacy, and workshops. The work of folklorists in the Appalachians has been particularly marked by an inclination toward public interests rather than strictly academic or theoretical concerns. Public folklore efforts have four primary functions or objectives: cultural preservation, presentation of folklore and folklife, commercial interests, and social advocacy.

In the first decades of the twentieth century, various individuals and institutions interested in preserving the culture of Appalachian peoples founded folklore societies, receiving federal funds for research and public folklore programs. Academically trained folklorists as well as lay enthusiasts scoured the peaks and valleys of the Appalachians to recover tales, ballads, and "quaint" folkways, which they believed were quickly vanishing in the face of modernity. Collections were deposited in archives of museums, universities, the Library of Congress, the Smithsonian Folkways Collection, documentary agencies, and historical societies to ensure their accessibility to future generations.

The preservation function of public folklore leads to the presentation function exemplified in teaching, publication of books, distribution of recordings, radio programs, performances at folk festivals, and exhibitions at museums and elsewhere. One of the main goals in presentation of folklore in the region is to expose a wider audience to the richness of Appalachian expressive culture for revitalization and perpetuation of those traditional practices.

Although folklore presentation seems to emerge from a desire to celebrate cultural diversity for its own sake, commercial interests often underlie such efforts and appear to belie folklorists' claims of disinterested research and presentation. Public folklorists working in the Appalachians have been involved in marketing and sale of local arts and crafts such as quilts and wood carvings and in promotion of local musicians and storytellers. Efforts to market folklore to new audiences can transform folk practices in form, content, and function. For example, traditional quilt designs often give way to designs more popular with the buying public.

Opponents of folklorists' involvement in the public sector (most notably folklorist Richard Dorson) have claimed that these interventions both disrupt the continuity of cultural processes and compromise the ideal of unbiased social research. However, some folklorists prefer social activism, taking a role in the lives of local residents and seeing community intervention as positive. Public folklore advocacy tends to engage contemporary issues facing the community being studied. For example, folklorists in some cases have interceded on behalf of Appalachian residents by presenting government officials with traditions of Appalachian land use and folkways to stop destructive activities of mining industries. This type of public folklore may more appropriately fall under the rubric of "applied folklore," characterized by application of folklore research to address social problems.

Public folklore thrives in the Appalachian Mountains because folklorists who research this region are often natives or residents of the region themselves or are outsiders drawn into the lives of their subjects. Public folklorists in the Appalachians generally have had a goal of developing the region's economy through appreciation, cultivation, and promotion of local cultural practices.

See also: FOLK MUSIC COLLECTIONS (MUSIC).

—Anika Wilson, *University of Pennsylvania*

Jane S. Becker, *Selling Tradition: Appalachia and the Construction of an American Folk, 1930–1940* (1998); Michael Owen Jones, ed., *Putting Folklore to Use* (1994); Nicholas R. Spitzer and Robert Baron, *Public Folklore* (1992).

Roberts, Leonard Ward

(1912–1983) Folklorist.

Leonard Ward Roberts, collector of Appalachian folktales, ballads, legends, and family traditions, was born in a log cabin on Toler Creek, Floyd County, Kentucky, the seventh in a family of eleven children. When he enlisted in the U.S. Army in 1930, he had completed one year of high school. His three-year military stint in Hawaii earned him the nickname "Sarge" on his return home. After finishing high school, he enrolled at Berea College, graduating in 1939. An aspiring novelist, he earned a master of arts from the University of Iowa, writing for his thesis a novel with autobiographical elements about an eastern Kentucky teacher. Shortly thereafter he met folklorists Stith Thompson and William Hugh Jansen, and under their influence he turned his attention to folklore.

Roberts's doctoral dissertation at the University of Kentucky was published in 1955 as *South from Hell-fer-Sartin: Kentucky Mountain Folk Tales;* it established him as the leading American folktale collector. His later publications included folktale collections, a volume of folk songs, and his magnum opus, *Sang Branch Settlers: Folksongs and Tales of a Kentucky Mountain Family* (1974), which included material collected in Harlan and Leslie Counties, Kentucky, from 1951 to 1955. He identified informants as members of the "Couch" family rather than using their real names. This volume was noteworthy at the time for providing not only texts but context as well. A book of legends was in the planning stages when Roberts was killed in a car wreck in 1983. This material, along with his other papers, is in the Southern Appalachian Archives at the Hutchins Library at Berea College in Berea, Kentucky.

See also: FOLK MUSIC COLLECTIONS (MUSIC); JACK TALES, TRICKSTERS, AND MOUNTAIN FOLKLORE (IMAGES AND ICONS); ORAL NARRATIVE.

—W. K. McNeil, *The Ozark Folk Center*

Schrock, Alta

(1911–2001) Educator and founder of folk institutions.

Born April 3, 1911, at Strawberry Hill Farm near Grantsville, Maryland, Alta Schrock lived most of her early life between there and Springs, Pennsylvania, in bordering Somerset County. Shrock was the daughter of devout Pennsylvania German Mennonites, and her Christian faith dominated her life. Educated in Pennsylvania at Grantsville's Yoder School and Salisbury High School, she earned an undergraduate degree in biology from Waynesburg College in 1937. After graduate studies at the University of Cincinnati, Kent State University, and Oberlin College, she received a doctorate in biology from the University of Pittsburgh in 1944, the first Mennonite woman in America to receive the advanced degree and stay in the church. Schrock taught at American University in Washington, D.C., Bluffton College and Goshen College in Indiana, and Frostburg State College in Maryland from 1960 to 1977.

The ideas that gave rise to her folklore accomplishments, she said, "began at age eight with stories of old farms being restored." She came by her fieldwork and marketing

Educator and entrepreneur Alta Schrock poses near a split-rail fence bordering Spruce Forest in Grantsville, Maryland, c. 1960. The founder of seventeen philanthropic organizations, Schrock is best known for establishing Penn Alps Restaurant and Crafts Shop, where local artisans market their work and visitors learn about the history and cultural traditions of the Allegheny highlands.

skills naturally. Her great-great-grandfather, Joel B. Miller, was a master craftsman and gave her an interest in handmade objects and life in the mountains. She considered it her mission in life to minister to the people of the Appalachian region, and in 1934 she began visiting mountain people in Garrett County, Maryland, and the Pennsylvania border regions to collect their stories, crafts, and songs. Her goal was to provide economic and spiritual means towards their self-sufficiency.

Schrock was inspired by her travels in Europe, where she observed "what crafts were able to do for the peasants." As she said, "I thought that if it could be done there, it could be done here." This lifetime avocation culminated in the founding of numerous regional institutions, including the Springs Historical Society, Springs Museum of Early Settlers, and Springs Folk Festival, all in Pennsylvania, and Penn Alps, Inc., and Spruce Forest Artisans Village, both in Maryland. She served as editor of the *Casselman Chronicle* (1961–76) and the *Journal of the Alleghenies* (1964–77), the publication of the Council of the Alleghenies.

Her dream of a mobile craft center that would visit remote communities to inventory existing craft activity and get people started on crafts they would "like to tackle" was never realized. Schrock died on November 7, 2001, after helping to serve the physical, mental, social and spiritual needs of people in one part of Appalachia throughout her life.

See also: CONTEMPORARY CRAFTS (CRAFTS); COUNTRY LIFE MOVEMENT (CRAFTS).

—Elaine Eff, *Maryland Historical Trust*

Sharp, Cecil

(1859–1924) Folklorist.

About 1900, Cecil Sharp (b. November 22, 1859), principal of the Hampstead Conservatoire of Music in England, developed a deep interest in British folk music. For the next decade and a half, he traveled the English countryside collecting traditional ballads and songs, many of which he transcribed for various published collections. During this period he also became an authority on British folk dance.

In 1915, while on a lecture tour in the United States, Sharp met Olive Dame Campbell, who informed him about balladry traditions still extant in Appalachia. Between 1916 and 1918, Sharp, with his assistant, Maud Karpeles, undertook three collecting trips in the Appalachian sections of North Carolina, Virginia, Kentucky, and Tennessee. There they recorded some five hundred traditional ballads and

Folklorists Cecil Sharp and Maud Karpeles visit a woman in Hindman, Kentucky, 1917. Between 1916 and 1918, Sharp and Karpeles undertook three collecting trips in the Appalachian sections of North Carolina, Virginia, Kentucky, and Tennessee, where they recorded approximately five hundred traditional ballads and songs and nearly three hundred singers of British ancestry.

songs (along with additional variants) from nearly three hundred singers of British ancestry, transcribing tunes and texts by hand. Their most prolific informant was Jane Hicks Gentry of Hot Springs, North Carolina, who shared seventy ballads and songs. Much of the material Sharp and Karpeles collected in Appalachia was published in *English Folk Songs from the Southern Appalachians* (1917; revised and expanded in 1932). Although it has been criticized for overlooking religious material (hymns and spirituals), instrumentals, and commercial songs that were an integral part of Appalachian singers' repertoires, their book, in the opinion of many folklorists, remains the most significant single collection of preindustrial Appalachian folklore.

Sharp died on June 23, 1924. Many years later, Karpeles, with A. H. Fox Strangways, wrote a biography of her mentor, *Cecil Sharp* (1955); Karpeles's revision of the book, retitled *Cecil Sharp: His Life and Work*, was published in 1967. *Songcatcher*, a movie released in 2000, is loosely based on Sharp and Karpeles's experiences in Appalachia.

See also: FOLK MUSIC COLLECTIONS (MUSIC); GENTRY, JANE HICKS, AND MAUD GENTRY LONG (MUSIC); KARPELES, MAUD.

—Ted Olson, *East Tennessee State University*

Signs

Just as telling stories and visiting neighbors are ingrained habits in Appalachian life, so is the practice of reading signs, a dynamic and expressive medium treated with varying degrees of seriousness. The symbolic language of signs comes from many sources, ranging from biblical passages and inexplicable events to omens, apparitions, dreams, and astrology. Signs lead people to attach special significance to objects, events, and patterns and to find in them messages such as insights into events past or warnings of things to come. These practices create a link between everyday life and presumed supernatural forces and between seemingly disparate realms of life. Believers in signs find omens in religion, in daily life, in existential moments such as birth and death, and in forms of attachment to places and people. The practice of planting crops with the guidance of signs has long been associated with the region. Signs were also used to plan activities as diverse as taking a hunting trip, harvesting crops, or repairing machinery. In ecstatic religious practices, "signs of the Spirit" are manifested in such occurrences as dramatic conversion experiences, trance states, or speaking in tongues. The experience of "getting a feeling" is considered a sign that something has just happened or is about to happen.

Signs can link the very concrete to the ephemeral—a felt sensation to an unfulfilled desire, an astrological pattern, a passage in the Bible, an imminent danger, or a life force passing. The nature of the links noted in signs is always open to argument. A link may be suggested by a mimetic resemblance (as when a woman's neighbors remark that the vegetables she grows in her garden are sweet because the woman herself has a sweet disposition) or by an accidental collision of events or a coincidence that seems significant (as in the saying that a bird flying into the house is a sign of impending death). Because it is thought that death often seems to "come in threes," one death can be taken as a sign of two more to come. Since graves are often dug under a pine tree, it may be said that to plant a pine tree in the yard is to invite the death of a family member.

Between certain signs, there is a logic of association and influence between things that somehow "work on" each other. This connection may also be a haunting resonance expressing absence, loss, and longing. A baby may be born with a sign, or birthmark, that resembles a food for which the pregnant mother had a craving. Signs of impending death can be interpreted from events that signal a breached boundary between nature and culture or between humans and animals: a picture falls off a wall for no apparent reason, a door opens by itself, there is a knocking on the walls of the house, a rooster crows in the middle of the night, a dog lies with his eyes looking out the door. Signs that relate to mining disasters have included dreams of fire or explosion, the apparition of a ghostly woman floating into the mouth of a mine, or the sight of a white dove perched on top of a tipple or flying into a mine.

Discussion of signs provides an opportunity for thinking about the deep impacts of events. Signs are a way of reading likenesses, frictions, antipathies, and impacts. Their logic, whether social, astrological, or mystical, opens the question of how they function as symbols in a conventional way and how they mimic or point to an association because of their structure or form. The idea of "planting by the signs," for example, is based on ancient astronomers' recognition of the Zodiac in which the twelve signs are divided into elements (fire, earth, air, and water) and body parts (head, neck, breast, bowels, loins, knees, feet, legs, thighs, kidneys, heart, and arms). Using a calendar or almanac that delineates days of the month by signs, a farmer picks the series of days with the most favorable signs for planting or harvesting his crops. For example, one should plant vegetables that grow downward (such as potatoes, beets, or carrots) when the stars are "in the feet" and "on the dark side of the moon" (when the moon is on the wane). Houses or cars should be painted in a dry sign. Bad habits should be quit on a new moon. Weeding should be done and trees girdled or harvested in the barren signs. Hogs should be slaughtered in the new moon so they will yield more lard. Similarly, there is a time for castrating hogs, catching fish, hunting, digging a well, and making sauerkraut.

Appalachia has a long history of inscribing place with the significance of home, history, and spirit. This tradition has grown more urgent in a region of economic boom and bust and sustained rural poverty, mass migrations, and cultural disruption. Signs can be used both as a reminder of tradition and as an expression or agent of social change. At different moments and in particular ways, signs can be used both to support and maintain a local way of life and as a means for registering the impacts of national and global forces on the region.

See also: FOLKLORE AND THE SUPERNATURAL; PREGNANCY AND CHILDBIRTH (FAMILY AND COMMUNITY).

—Kathleen Stewart, *University of Texas*

William Lynwood Montell, *Ghosts along the Cumberland: Deathlore in the Kentucky Foothills* (1975); Kathleen Stewart, *A Space on the Side of the Road: Cultural Poetics in an "Other" America* (1996); Eliot Wigginton, ed., *The Foxfire Book* (1972) and *Foxfire 2* (1973).

Southeastern Ohio Public Folklore

Appalachian Ohio officially includes twenty-nine counties, all located in the southern and eastern third of the state. Appalachian cultural traditions, however, are scattered throughout the state, particularly in urban centers with industries that have attracted migrants from the southern mountains. These migrants tended to maintain strong ties with the mountains, often returning there on weekends or as soon as a sizeable amount of money was earned. Frank Proffitt from Beech Mountain, North Carolina, from whom the ballad of "Tom Dula" was collected in 1940, for example, worked in a jeep factory in Toledo for two years in the 1940s before returning to his home in the mountains. Both temporary and permanent Appalachian residents left their mark on Ohio culture, frequently in the form of music jams, house parties, and festivals featuring bluegrass and country music.

Perhaps due to misperceptions surrounding Ohio's cultural identity as "middle America," those who study public folklore, along with the general American public, have paid scant attention to Appalachian Ohio, much less to these urban pockets of Appalachian culture. Systematic collecting of Appalachian traditions in Ohio has been on an individual basis, and it is only in the last two decades of the twentieth century that institutionalized efforts have been made to preserve and present Ohio's Appalachian traditions.

Alan and Elizabeth Lomax (the latter became well known as Bess Lomax Hawes) made two collecting trips to Ohio, one in November of 1937 and the second in March and April of 1938. During the first trip, they recorded twelve twelve-inch discs of the singing of Captain Pearl R. Nye in Akron. The Library of Congress recording *The Ballad Hunter: John A. Lomax: Parts V and VI* also includes excerpts from Nye, and he was recorded at the 1938 National Folk Festival in Washington, D.C., where he sang "The Old Skipper." Another collector, Ivan Walton, recorded him again in Akron in September 1938.

One of the most significant collectors of Ohio musical traditions was Anne Grimes, a musician, journalist, mother of five, and self-trained folklorist who lived most of her life in Granville, where her husband was a professor at Denison University. Focusing on ballads and the dulcimer, Grimes began recording traditional music, interviewing musicians, and collecting dulcimers in the early 1950s and continued into the 1990s. In 1992 she donated her extensive collection of recordings (a total of 140 in various formats) along with photographs, field notes, and ephemera to the Archive of Folk Culture at the Library of Congress. The Musical Instrument Division of the American History Museum of the Smithsonian Institution acquired her extensive collection of dulcimers. To celebrate this acquisition, the Smithsonian sponsored a lecture performance by Grimes at the museum.

Grimes's collecting activities were primarily in south-central Ohio, but she traveled throughout the state searching for music that she felt was unique to Ohio. One of her concerns was to demonstrate that Ohio had distinctive traditions that were not simply derivative of southern Appalachia but had a legitimate heritage of their own. A singer, pianist, and dulcimer player, she sought out ballads referencing Ohio events and characters and presented programs illustrating Ohio history and culture. She frequently performed on the dulcimer and argued for the importance of Ohio, particularly the Ohio River, in the development of the instrument. She located more than two hundred instruments representing various stages and offshoots of the dulcimer, demonstrating that it was probably disseminated by traders and travelers rather than passed down as a family tradition. She also found that a number of names were used for the instrument, including harmony box and dulcerine.

Grimes was also significant as a host to visiting students, musicians, and miscellaneous artists and scholars, including poet Carl Sandburg and folklorist Benjamin Botkin. Many of the people she welcomed as guests played significant roles in the history and profession of folklore as an academic discipline as well as in American culture at large. She was active in the Ohio Folklore Society and encouraged numerous students to become active, both as performers and folklorists. Most notable among these is Joe Hickerson, former head of the Archive of Folk Culture at the Library of Congress.

Fiddle and string-band traditions in southern Ohio became the focus of collecting in the early 1970s. An influential fiddler was Ward Jarvis, originally of Braxton County,

West Virginia, but later of Guysville, Ohio. Folklorist Carl Fleischhauer recorded him playing with Dan (Danlovich) Daggett and John Hutchison in 1973 as part of a fieldwork project sponsored by the American Folklife Center. Folklorist David A. Brose made recordings of Jarvis on banjo and fiddle in 1978 and 1979, and he gave the recordings, along with extensive logs and field notes to the Library of Congress. Folklore collectors Howard and Judy Sacks and Jeff Goering also recorded Jarvis and other southern Ohio fiddle players and produced a documentary recording of Ohio fiddle traditions. Jarvis's tunes entered the old-time revival scene through Appalachian Ohio–based bands such as the Red Mules (Jeff and Suzy Goering, Wally Goering, Lynn Frederick, and Beth Braden) and are still part of the old-time repertoire.

Howard and Judy Sacks have also studied African American vocal and instrumental traditions found in Appalachian Ohio. Since Ohio played an active role in the Underground Railroad, some of these traditions were brought from the South by escaping slaves. Freed blacks also brought some traditional music from the eastern states and in Ohio blended it with traditions brought by white Appalachians. In a fascinating study of Dan Emmett (1815–1904), a native of Mount Vernon, Ohio, and the originator of first minstrel show group, the Virginia Minstrels, the Sackses discovered that Emmet had had extensive interaction with African American neighbors, learning and adapting a number of their tunes, including the song "Dixie."

Students at Ohio State University, Ohio University, Kenyon College, Denison University, and others have collected Appalachian Ohio musical traditions. Fieldwork and research on the material, narrative, and customary traditions of the region have either been lacking or have not been given much public attention, but craft cooperatives and galleries are now attempting to remedy the situation.

Festivals and fiddle contests have been one of the primary venues for presenting Appalachian Ohio traditions. Cincinnati has held festivals since the late 1930s, including one specifically celebrating Appalachian heritage. Similarly, Dayton, which boasts a large number of migrants from the region, hosts a Mountain Days Festival. Fiddle contests provide a common venue for presenting music traditions, although many of them now encourage the western contest style of fiddling rather than local traditional styles. Contests in Nelsonville and Coshocton are probably the best known.

Preservation and promotion of traditional culture are also encouraged by agencies working for economic development in Appalachian Ohio, which is still the poorest region in the state. Coal mining and family farming have been the two primary industries for residents, and neither occupation lent itself to the accumulation of wealth. Cultural tourism, therefore, has become a way to create pride in heritage as well as job opportunities.

In 1994 the Ohio Arts Council established grant programs aimed specifically at Appalachian traditions, helping fund a number of organizations that promote the culture of the region. The Appalachian Arts Program serves artists, arts organizations, community leaders, and residents of Ohio's twenty-nine Appalachian counties, as well as urban Appalachians living in Columbus, Cincinnati, and Dayton. The Ohio River Border Initiative is a partnership with the West Virginia Commission on the Arts to dissolve political barriers and support communities along the Ohio River. The Foundation for Appalachian Ohio was established in 1998 to seek contributions for grants for charitable and civic purposes in designated Appalachian counties of Ohio. The foundation has funded arts and crafts cooperatives, cultural tourism projects, and conferences on economic development and Appalachian cultural traditions.

See also: AFRICAN AMERICAN INFLUENCES (MUSIC); DULCIMER, FRETTED (MUSIC); LOMAX, JOHN AND ALAN.

—Lucy M. Long, *Bowling Green State University*

Carl E. Feather, *Mountain People in a Flat Land: A Popular History of Appalachian Migration to Northeast Ohio, 1940–1965* (1998); Barbara V. Howe, "Paradise Found and Lost: Migration in the Ohio Valley," *Journal of American History* (December 1998); Howard L. and Judith Rose Sacks, *Way Up North in Dixie: A Black Family's Claim to the Confederate Anthem* (1993).

Southwest Virginia Public Folklore

By the early twentieth century, public folklore attention in Virginia was primarily focused on the ballad as exemplified in Francis James Child's *The English and Scottish Popular Ballads* (1882–98) and on material culture and handicrafts as influenced in America by the English Arts and Crafts movement. These separate strands, evident in the collecting activities of the Virginia Folklore Society and in Allen H. Eaton's later survey of handicrafts in the southern highlands, foreshadowed coming folk festivals, fiddling conventions, and crafts exhibits, as well as federally sponsored or funded programs for the collection, public presentation, or cultural conservation of folklore and folklife.

In 1913 C. Alphonso Smith, Edgar Allan Poe Professor of English at the University of Virginia, founded the Virginia Folklore Society and enlisted schoolteachers to collect Anglo-American ballads throughout the state. When British folk song collector Cecil Sharp came to the United States in 1915 on a lecture tour, he stayed briefly with Smith in Charlottesville.

Smith introduced Sharp to local musicians (some of whom appear in Sharp's *English Folk Songs from the Southern Appalachians*, 1917; revised 1932), including Jim Chisholm, listed variously as an Appalachian or mountain fiddler, who later played in the White House at Eleanor Roosevelt's request and at the 1938 National Folk Festival in Washington, D.C. The performances of Chisholm, singer Texas Gladden, and other Virginians at the folk festival were recorded for the Archive of Folk Song at the Library of Congress.

Arthur Kyle Davis Jr. of the University of Virginia English Department succeeded Smith as archivist and editor of the Virginia Folklore Society. Harvard University Press published the society's first volume under his editorship, entitled *Traditional Ballads of Virginia*, in 1929. Davis began a project in 1932 to record informants on aluminum discs. By 1935, Davis had added 180 aluminum disc recordings of sixty-six Virginia singers and musicians to the Virginia Folklore Society archive, making it a significant resource of early recorded folk song. In some cases, Davis recorded persons who were first collected in print twenty years before by Smith or Sharp.

Between 1934 and 1935, Davis sought funds from various agencies for collecting and recording projects. In addition to the American Council of Learned Societies, he solicited help from various New Deal programs. The more narrowly focused efforts of the Virginia Folklore Society overlapped very little with the broad range of folklore collected later by the Virginia Writers' Project, another New Deal program. When the Virginia Writers' Project closed in 1942, Davis arranged for its massive folklore collection to be deposited at the University of Virginia library with the hope of eventually establishing a single, unified archive of Virginia folklore.

In 1949, with the help of several graduate students, Davis published *Folk-Songs of Virginia: A Descriptive Index and Classification*. This was followed in 1960 by the publication of *More Traditional Ballads of Virginia*. Davis's long and dedicated association with the society ended with his death in 1972.

Allen H. Eaton's coverage of Virginia material culture in his *Handicrafts of the Southern Highlands* (1937) featured Rosemont—a local commercial effort to create markets for the area's surplus wool, training programs for trades, and make-work projects initiated by vocational schools or rural church missions. Eaton gave scant attention to traditional Virginia craftsmen, though he did mention Silas Nicholson and a dozen or so other unidentified basket makers of that surname in the vicinity of Old Rag Mountain in the Blue Ridge. The timing of Eaton's trips closely paralleled development between 1924 and 1936 of the Shenandoah National Park and removal of its inhabitants, including many Nicholsons; ironically, Eaton proposed teaching some of the people basketmaking to make a living outside the park.

A 1983 follow-up of Eaton's work in the Blue Ridge for the National Council for the Traditional Arts reconstructed six multigenerational lines of basket makers sharing a common descent from John Nicholson (who died in 1805). Some of these persons and their baskets are shown in the book *Appalachian White Oak Basketmaking: Handing Down the Basket* (1991).

Other onlookers went into the Shenandoah National Park area to record ballads and folk songs, congregational singing, and the speech of local residents in 1932. They included several dialect geographers, such as Mandel Sherman, coauthor of the book *Hollow Folk* (1933), which depicted the Blue Ridge communities and people in negative terms, and Miriam Sizer, a schoolteacher who later became the Virginia Writers' Project folklore supervisor. Photographer Arthur Rothstein documented material culture (including some Old Rag baskets), houses, and people of the national park area for the Resettlement Administration in 1935.

Between 1937 and 1942, the Virginia Writers' Project also interviewed former slaves and produced more than thirteen hundred life histories, many of which were from the Virginia highlands and included folklore in its natural context. The Virginia Art Project's participation in the federal Index of American Design produced a sizable body of watercolor plates documenting traditional quilts, pottery, furniture, and other material culture items, some of which resided in the Bascom C. Slemp Museum in Big Stone Gap.

As folklore fieldworkers in 1938, James Taylor Adams and Emory Hamilton of Wise County and Raymond Sloan of Franklin County were exceptions to the general rule in that they were both collectors and informants who saw their work as a chance to actively preserve their own culture. Out of about thirty Virginia Writers' Project folklore fieldworkers, Adams and Hamilton turned in almost half of the folklore and folk songs collected. Adams and various of his family members were the source for many of the stories published by Richard Chase in *The Jack Tales* (1943). When folklorist Herbert Halpert conducted a southern recording expedition for the Works Progress Administration Joint Committee on Folk Art and the Library of Congress in 1939, he also recorded songs and stories, as well as ballads and instrumental music, from a number of Adams's relatives and friends.

While the Virginia Folklore Society continued its almost exclusive interest in the ballad to the neglect of other forms of traditional music, a major shift occurred with the commercially important 1927 Bristol recording sessions of early country musicians, including the Carter Family of southwest Virginia. Other public folklore venues followed in the 1930s. The White Top Folk Festival, held at the southern end of the Virginia Blue Ridge, began in 1931, and the Galax Old Fiddlers' Convention, sponsored in 1935 by the local Moose Lodge No. 733, continues to the present.

A number of private collectors in the 1930s and 1940s made field recordings that were later deposited in the Archive of Folk Song at the Library of Congress. Among these collectors were Chase, various Lomax family members, and Sidney Robertson Cowell, all of whom recorded at the White Top and Galax festivals, some repeatedly. As a result, E. C. Ball, Dan Tate, Wade Ward and the Bogtrotters, Hobart Smith, Texas Gladden, John M. "Sailor Dad" Hunt, and other well-known traditional performers from Virginia are well represented in their collections. Later individual collectors concentrated mainly, though not exclusively, on traditional instrumental and string-band music from southwest Virginia and bordering areas of Tennessee and North Carolina. Also deposited in the Archive of Folk Song, the field recordings of collectors and folklorists Peter Hoover, Mike Seeger, Scott Odell, George Foss, Alan Jabbour, Blanton Owen, and Tom Carter overlap with the areas and musicians covered by earlier collectors; however, these new studies have more depth of research and analysis.

Cooperstown (New York) Folklore Program graduate J. Roderick Moore taught folklore at Mountain Empire College in Big Stone Gap for several years before moving to Ferrum College in Ferrum, Virginia, where he established the Blue Ridge Institute in the early 1970s. Under its sponsorship, a Blue Ridge Folklife Festival featuring regional foods, traditional crafts, music, and dance was organized in 1973. The festival has since expanded to include horse pulls, steam engine demonstrations, coon dog water races, and other events, drawing up to forty thousand people for the one-day event.

In the mid-1970s, Kip Lornell did field research for the Blue Ridge Institute to identify traditional musicians and craftsmen for the festival. Through public and private funding, an archive of manuscripts, photographs, recordings, and artifacts, a recording series, a farm museum, exhibition galleries, and an Elderhostel program have all been established under the institute's umbrella. In 1986 the Virginia General Assembly designated the Blue Ridge Institute as the State Center for Blue Ridge Folklore.

With the establishment of National Endowments for the Arts and Humanities and the American Folklife Center at the Library of Congress in the 1970s and 1980s along with other government and private funding bodies such as the National Park Service and the National Council for the Traditional Arts, it became more possible to support community or regional studies and large team-based folklore research projects. These developments, along with a growing number of academically trained folklorists interested in oral history and folklife, led to a growing number of collaborative and interdisciplinary studies in Virginia.

The Blue Ridge Parkway Folklife Project in 1978 was such a team-based folklife research effort undertaken by the American Folklife Center in cooperation with the National Park Service. The survey covered parts of seven counties on the border of North Carolina and Virginia, including Galax and Mabry Mill, close to the site of the present-day Blue Ridge Music Center. A group of folklorists and photographers produced written documentation, recordings on tape, audiocassettes, and video and photographic negatives and color transparencies; these documents form a core collection in the Appalachian Resource Center at the parkway's headquarters in Asheville, North Carolina. A book, *Blue Ridge Harvest*, and a record album, *Children of the Heav'nly King*, were also produced out of this body of material. A separate report for the National Park Service in 1979 surveyed instrument makers and other craftspeople in thirteen southwest Virginia counties regarding the impact of either the Blue Ridge Parkway or the developing Mount Rogers National Recreation Area upon their livelihoods. Virginia instrument makers Raymond V. Melton and Kyle Creed, Albert Hash, and later National Heritage Award winner Wayne Henderson were interviewed for this project.

The Patrick County Project, cosponsored in 1981 by the Blue Ridge Regional Library and Virginia Polytechnic Institute and State University and funded by a National Endowment for the Humanities grant, brought together a team of librarians, historians, and Virginia Tech folklorists Jean Haskell and Elizabeth Fine. The project's joint objectives were to gather oral histories and photographs from county residents for a series of public slide/tape presentations, public discussions, and a documentary film showing the history of continuity and change in the county's rural communities and to publish a bibliography entitled *The Appalachian Region of Virginia: A Guide to Library Materials*.

Lastly, a collaborative effort initiated by the Virginia Folklore Society in 1989 led to establishment of the Virginia Folklife Program in the Virginia Foundation for the Humanities and Public Policy with support from the Virginia Commission for the Arts and the National Endowment for the Arts Folk Arts Program. The Virginia Folklife Program has conducted seminars on folklore and oral history for the Southwest Virginia Folklore Society in Big Stone Gap, undertaken preservation of the Beth Van Over Collection of Appalachian Folksong in Wise County, and assisted the Monacan Indians in producing a video for the Monacan Ancestral Museum at Bear Mountain in the Blue Ridge.

A video documentary on old-time music around Galax began as a collaborative effort between the Virginia Folklife

Program, traditional musicians of the Carroll and Grayson County areas, and the Arts and Cultural Council of the Twin Counties (Carroll and Grayson). It is part of the interpretive program at the Blue Ridge Music Center, which opened on the Blue Ridge Parkway in 2000. The center is also an important venue for the Blue Ridge Music Trails, a cultural heritage tourism project. In 2003 the Virginia Folklife Program was a major participant in the Smithsonian Folklife Festival's salute to Appalachia, and activities included an apprenticeship program, production of albums and documentary films, an on-line guide to folklife resources in the state, a folk artist database, and public performances, lectures, and workshops.

See also: BALLADS (MUSIC); BLUE RIDGE MUSIC CENTER (CULTURAL INSTITUTIONS); SECTION OVERVIEW (TOURISM).

—Nancy J. Martin-Perdue, *University of Virginia*

Jane S. Becker, *Selling Tradition: Appalachia and the Construction of an American Folk, 1930–1940* (1998); Charles Camp, ed., *Time and Temperature: A Centennial Publication of the American Folklore Society* (1989) and ed., *Traditional Craftsmanship in America* (1983); Charles L. Perdue Jr., Thomas E. Barden, and Robert K. Phillips, *An Annotated Listing of Folklore: Collected by Workers of the Virginia Writers' Project, Works Projects Administration* (1979); Charles L. Perdue Jr., with Nancy J. Martin-Perdue, *The Archive of Folk Song Virginia Folklore Index* (1977); David E. Whisnant, "The White Top Festival, 1931–1939: An Introduction, Annotated Bibliography, and Guide to Resources," *Folklore and Folklife in Virginia* (1980–81).

Superstitions

See Folklore and the Supernatural

Trade and Barter

Trade and barter, in many forms, have been intrinsic to life and livelihood throughout Appalachia for at least two centuries, and probably longer. Indeed, this informal system of traditions and practices, falling outside the norm of the national economy, can be considered a "folk" economic system.

Traditional subsistence-based farms in the region relied on extended families and reciprocal farm labor. Contemporary Appalachian farms that hire labor and combine subsistence farming with cash crops still rely on unpaid family labor, and trade and barter relationships are perpetuated at places such as auctions and flea markets.

In coal camps of the past, survival would have been impossible without supplementing wages with a panoply of arrangements that involved pooling, sharing, and exchanging labor and goods. Even in communities of urban Appalachian migrants in northern cities, transformations of rural patterns of trade and barter manifest themselves.

Trade and barter have enabled people to create for themselves a sense of autonomy and control in the face of dominant local, national, and global economic forces. When local community practices of exchange break down, making many forms of trade and barter impossible, effects can be devastating, not only to individuals and families but to entire communities.

Trading and bartering operate at regional, community, household, and individual levels—and in both collaboration and conflict with mainstream capitalism. Because much trade and barter constitute an alternative and often hidden economy, rules and practices, as well as terminology surrounding these economic exchanges, are not always easy to discern. Often intricate combinations of monetary and nonmonetary exchanges are involved.

In rural Appalachia, farm families have traded labor, borrowed labor, and donated labor to kin and neighbors during harvest periods, whether for subsistence or cash crops. Harvesting burley tobacco, for example, requires arduous work in both picking and processing. Kin are expected by families and communities to help out, regardless of competing obligations. In this case, borrowed or donated labor is particularly valuable, for tobacco is a cash-producing crop and its value is influenced by getting it to market at the right time. Labor given by non-kin must be reciprocated, although not necessarily immediately. These are forms of barter and trade. Similarly, when groups of women get together to "put up" (can or freeze) fruits and vegetables such as tomatoes, beans, or corn, there is always an expectation that the labor involved will be returned either in goods or in services. Quilting is another form of reciprocal cooperative labor. No exact measures of time or effort are made for the help that will be given in return.

Child care is often traded and bartered in informal ways. In urban Appalachian communities, there is an expectation that adults will do what is necessary to ensure the maintenance and safety of the community. For example, if a child is locked out of the house and needs shelter and food after school, an adult in the neighborhood will offer to take in and feed the child. Spontaneous flow of such assistance constitutes a safety net in small-scale, face-to-face communities. Even the disciplining of children may work in a similar reciprocal fashion, especially when their safety is at stake.

Livelihood strategies in Appalachia have always included exchanges that supplement and parallel wage-earning jobs and function as replacements for these jobs when there are layoffs and uncertainties in mines and factories. Anthropologist Mary LaLone has written about Appalachian coal-mining families trading services, pooling incomes, and growing food (using reciprocal cooperative labor of neighbors and friends) for home consumption, trade, barter, and storage. People in coal camps also collected, processed, stored, and traded foods they gathered such as fruits (apples, pears, grapes), berries, and nuts. Various processing and storage techniques provided not only the opportunity to save food for use in winter, but also to lend flexibility to bartering and trading foods such as jams, jellies, and canned goods. Hogs, chickens, and cows consumed for eggs, meat, and other products were also sold and traded for goods ranging from clothing and other foods to services such as child care.

Swapping is the term used for the direct exchange of goods on the spot with no delay in the return. One Appalachian community member, Diane Reece, described swapping as follows: "You caught fish and you had too many and somebody had eggs, you'd swap. Or you needed milk or butter, you'd swap. Like if you had buttermilk and I had butter, or I had eggs or I had corn, you'd swap it out. And they traded guns, fishing reels and rods, and stuff like that all the time." People who live along the Ohio River in Cincinnati will do the same with fish, swapping them for other goods such as staples, or simply giving them away with the expectation of a return at a later time. As one man said, "I love to fish, but I can't stand fish." Fish can be bartered for many things, including other types of food, car repairs, and child or elder care.

Favors come in various forms. There may be a direct exchange of goods and services on the spot or there may be a delay in connection with a deal that has been struck. In flea markets, two vendors will give one another a better deal than either vendor will give to a customer. But if a customer is well known to a vendor, terms of exchange will become increasingly better. While a deal is struck for an exchange of goods in such settings, between individuals or families in communities these would be referred to as favors, as when folks cook a meal for someone or fix someone's car, knowing the favor will be returned in some form, someday.

"Being there" for someone involves even less return and permits longer delay. If someone's electricity has been turned off and a neighbor runs an extension cord to her house, there will be no expectation of a direct return. If someone's grandmother needs to go to the grocery store, anyone capable of driving her will be expected to make the trip and help her with the groceries. Natural disasters such as tornados and floods automatically mobilize community members to the aid of anyone in need. Cleaning mud out of basements, bringing water and food, and washing down houses are only some of the tasks with which people will help.

Natural resources such as ginseng have a long history in trade and barter in Appalachia. In the nineteenth and early twentieth centuries, ginseng was grown in the mountains and imported to New York's Chinatown. Mining families gathered bloodroot and ginseng from the mountains and took the items to a country store, where they were bartered for sugar, flour, baking soda, and the like. Physicians frequently accepted vegetables and other goods, including livestock, in exchange for health-care services. As country doctors left for the city, these arrangements began to wane.

In the twentieth century, the informal economy (outside the mainstream economy) of garage sales and flea markets has replaced many country stores as places for trade and barter. Exchanges in the informal economy generally involve money. The key difference between buying and selling in the conventional economy and trade and barter principally has to do with the nature of the institutions and principles expediting the exchanges.

In general, goods sold in flea markets are priced well below market rate. That is, the same pint of strawberries in a regular supermarket will probably sell for twice as much (or more) as it will in a flea market. At the end of the day, when a vendor does not want to take his strawberries home, he may trade them to a neighboring vendor for an electric frying pan or sell the berries for less than half of what they brought in the morning. Other items sold in flea markets include craft items, factory seconds, used furniture, tools, guns, work clothes, gloves and boots, and many other items. Since none of the sales are recorded, vendors have the freedom to sell at any price or not to sell at all. Prices are determined by numerous and changing variables: time of day, relation between the two parties, season of the year, and conditions of the local economy. Collecting sufficient goods to sell in flea markets often requires much time and labor on the part of family members. Auctions must be attended, goods transported, and children cared for, tasks that may themselves involve traded and bartered services.

The informal economy of helping out or being there works as long as a person or group does not overstep traditional limits. If a person in a community asks for favors such as rides, help with repairs, food, clothing, or child care without reciprocating for a period of several months, that person will be labeled a "taker." Members of the community will then stop helping the individual or will indicate that their own resources, including time, are limited. At the extreme, feuds can result if a person has taken something inappropriately, especially if the person has become involved with an outsider who is perceived to be exploiting local people.

See also: FARM FAMILIES (FAMILY AND COMMUNITY); FARMERS' MARKETS (AGRICULTURE); SUBSISTENCE FARMING (AGRICULTURE);

—Rhoda H. Halperin, *University of Cincinnati*

Rhoda H. Halperin, *The Livelihood of Kin: Making Ends Meet "The Kentucky Way"* (1990); Paul Salstrom, *Appalachia's Path to*

Dependency: Rethinking a Region's Economic History, 1730–1940 (1994); Altina L. Waller, *Feud: Hatfields, McCoys, and Social Change in Appalachia, 1860–1900* (1988).

Traditional Music and Dance

See Section Overview (Music)

Upstate South Carolina Public Folklore

The jagged blue skyline of upstate South Carolina is a magnificent surprise to travelers steeped in visions of Myrtle Beach's neon commercialism and Charleston's palm-lined historic streets. Rising abruptly from a lightly undulating Piedmont to heights of more than 3,500 feet, the front wave of the Blue Ridge marks the state's northwestern boundaries with Georgia and North Carolina, and shares elements of topography, history, and culture with the rest of the Appalachian region. This is vastly different from coastal South Carolina.

A sense of Appalachian identity has remained in the uplands, held deliberately and firmly against "foreign" (that is, flatland) influence yet enriched uniquely by cultures, particularly African American, on its fringes. The African banjo, for example, ranks with fiddle as a favored instrument, the moves of the ubiquitous buck dance owe as much to Africa as to Native America, and burgeoning numbers of shape-note choirs are interracial and widely interreligious.

Area institutions strive to save and foster heritage traditions. North Greenville College, a pioneer in Appalachian studies, is home to Upcountry Friends, a group involved in preservation of folkways, including the lore of the Dark Corner, a one-time moonshiners' mecca in northern Greenville and Spartanburg Counties. Another center of folk art and activity is the Pickens County Museum of Art and History through its satellite facility, Hagood Mill, which still grinds corn on an abbreviated schedule and hosts monthly performances of traditional music and programs in blacksmithing, moonshining, quilting, hearth cookery, spinning, dancing, wood carving, and other skills of mountain living. The mill's annual Upcountry Folklife Festival and Old Time Fiddling Convention draws thousands every year on the third Saturday in September.

In 1997 Alan Jabbour, director of the American Folklife Center at the Library of Congress, met with a diverse group at Clemson University and began planning the Piedmont Harmony Project, which has become a landmark in ongoing collection, study, preservation and performance of traditional music of the uplands. Dean Watson, the project leader, is one of the region's premier folk musicians and music scholars. Area fiddlers Nick Hallman and John Fowler, both also excellent storytellers, have been honored as traditional artists by the South Carolina Arts Commission. Members of the South Carolina Institute for Community Scholars and others in folklife work maintain contact through the state-sponsored South Carolina Traditional Arts Network.

Thunderously percussive feet of hundreds keep alive the rhythms (and rigors) of Appalachia at dances from Mountain Rest and Walhalla eastward to River Falls in the mountains north of Greenville. Such artists as painter and basket maker Gale McKinley of Anderson, the woodcarving Turner family of Pickens, potter Don Lewis of Cleveland, and kudzu and pine-needle basket specialist Nancy Basket of Walhalla are sought out not only for the quality of their work but also for their teaching.

Venues for the handmade products of Appalachia range from the country store beside the highway to the Smithsonian Institution in Washington, D.C., to the South Carolina Artisans' Center at Walterboro, on the southern coast. Interest in the history and culture of the Appalachian area of South Carolina continues to grow. In the building stage are the Greenville History Museum in downtown Greenville and a more rustic and modest Birchwood Center for Arts and Folklife at Table Rock Mountain near Pickens.

See also: CLOGGING IN COMMUNITY SETTINGS (PERFORMING ARTS); FESTIVALS, HUMOR AND STORYTELLING (HUMOR).

—Dot Jackson, *Pickens, South Carolina*

Michael Hembree and Dot Jackson, *Keowee* (2004); Robert Morgan, *Gap Creek* (1999); Ben Robertson, *Red Hills and Cotton: An Upcountry Memory* (1942).

Urban Appalachian Folklore

During what Appalachian historians call the Great Migration of 1940 to 1970, more than three million mountaineers left their homes to seek jobs. Although they sometimes moved first to the few factory jobs in Appalachia or to nearby southern cities such as Atlanta, Baltimore, and Washington, D.C., migrants usually followed major transportation arteries in chain migrations to midwestern industrial cities. Eastern Kentuckians primarily populated Cincinnati's seven Appalachian neighborhoods, West Virginians formed the largest migrant group in Columbus and Cleveland, and migrants from Kentucky, Tennessee, and West Virginia settled in greater metropolitan Detroit. Folklore of white Appalachian migrants includes traditions that grew out of the migration experience, mountain traditions adapted to urban contexts, and folklore newly created in city environments.

The migration experience generated jokes, nicknames, stories, and songs that reflect the life of a displaced people and their nostalgia for home. During the 1960s, Guy and Candie Carawan collected songs from Kentucky migrants, later published as *Voices from the Mountains* (1975). Titles such as "Blue Ridge Mountain Refugee" and "Ain't Goin' Home Soon" were sung to both newly composed and traditional tunes. An oft-told joke refers to the practice of returning for weekends, hunting, fishing, holidays, family reunions, funerals, or cemetery reunions on Memorial Day. A man died, went to heaven, and during an introductory tour from Saint Peter, he pointed out sections reserved for each denomination. As they came to a hillside with a fence around it, the new arrival asked who lived there. "Oh, these are our 'West Virginia people,'" said Saint Peter. "They still think they have to go home every weekend."

Appalachians' deep nostalgia for native county, town, or homeplace is expressed in countless ways. Memories of home are often preserved in symbolic displays of selected nostalgic items such as quilts, jars of stone-ground cornmeal, or a replica of the old log homeplace. At the now closed Ilene's Restaurant in Ecorse, Michigan, once patronized by displaced Appalachians, jars of dirt from each Appalachian state held places of honor.

In the city, Appalachian migrants experienced situations of culture contact and adjustment similar to those of foreign immigrants. Dubbed "the invisible minority" by sociologists and the media, Appalachian migrants have been labeled as hillbillies and ridgerunners when their folk speech, lifestyles, and other identifiable cultural differences set them apart. Perceptions of the region and its lore preceded migrants' arrival in urban areas during the Great Migration in the 1940s, having been shaped by pervasive hillbilly stereotypes disseminated by the mass media and popular press. Inevitably, ethnic jokes told about Appalachians continue to play on these stereotypical images.

Sizable Appalachian neighborhoods such as Uptown (Chicago), Lower Price Hill (Cincinnati), and "Hazeltucky" (Hazel Park, Michigan) have been called cultural islands or "urban hollers" because their people continue traditional community and family-centered lifestyles, folkways, regional dialects, and codes of neighborliness and hospitality that define them as Appalachian. Continuity of tradition usually is strongest in the initial migrant generation. Migrants have founded Pentecostal and Old Regular Baptist churches to sustain familiar worship practices, dinners on the grounds, and traditional music and preaching styles. Self-help organizations, social clubs, bars, and restaurants have provided contexts to maintain group ties and traditions, especially food and music. Until 1998, the Kentuckians of Michigan organized an annual Kentucky Picnic, with seating organized by counties of origin, allowing attendees to enjoy white corn bread made with meal from "down home," play horseshoes, and "shoot the breeze."

Old-time country music, dubbed "hillbilly music" during the early years of radio and commercial recordings, was a lifeline to the sounds of home for urban Appalachians. One of the earliest and most influential broadcasts of hillbilly music originated in Chicago, where the *National Barn Dance* began on WLS in 1924. By the late 1940s, WLW Cincinnati's *Midwestern Hayride* and *Boone County Jamboree* were second in size and importance only to the *Grand Ole Opry* in Nashville. WLW's television broadcast of *Midwestern Hayride* in the 1950s was one of the earliest programs of its kind in the new medium.

Bluegrass music, which grew out of the professionalization and urbanization of older forms of Appalachian music, was closely associated with urban Appalachians during its formative years and became an important identity symbol. Midwest-based record companies, including King and Vetco in Cincinnati and later Old Homestead in Brighton outside Detroit, catered to Appalachian migrant populations by disseminating recordings by local and nationally known bluegrass performers. Factory workers from Appalachia congregated in "hillbilly bars" that featured live and recorded music by local amateurs and by well-known bluegrass professionals who either toured the Midwest or were migrants themselves.

While migrants transplanted some rural traditions to the city, they adapted or eliminated others over time. Traditional cooks found it necessary to "put up" or preserve produce purchased at the grocery store rather than can vegetables grown in a kitchen garden. Traditional recipes intermingled with those borrowed from different ethnic groups encountered in the city. For instance, one Tennessee migrant to southeast Dearborn, Michigan, a city with a large Muslim population, eliminated ham and red-eye gravy and added Middle Eastern dishes to her traditional cooking. Similarly, traditional wood-carvers learned to fashion traditional balls and chains and toys from factory scrap wood, while metal craft workers adapted scrap to make knives and other items.

With ingredients for home medical remedies often unavailable in the city, urban Appalachians adapted folk treatments of earlier ethnic immigrants; practitioners who once picked dandelion root for arthritis now order it from catalogs or not at all. Over time, folk medical practices became mostly memories associated with older relatives left behind in Appalachia.

Generally, migrants did not bring traditional ballads, Jack tales, or mountain death lore associated with Appalachia to their urban lives. However, their new urban lifestyles generated a variety of urban folklore forms such as festivals celebrating Appalachian culture, music with titles such as "Uptown Chicago Kind of Blues," and personal narratives full of common urban folklore themes such as crime, innercity violence, danger, and racial tension.

See also: APPALACHIAN SOCIAL ISSUES OUTSIDE THE REGION (URBAN APPALACHIAN EXPERIENCE); SECTION OVERVIEW

(SETTLEMENT AND MIGRATION); SECTION OVERVIEW (URBAN APPALACHIAN EXPERIENCE).

—Janet Langlois, *Wayne State University*, and Laurie Kay Sommers, *Valdosta State University*

Ellen J. Stekert, "Focus for Conflict: Southern Mountain Medical Beliefs in Detroit," in *The Urban Experience and Folk Tradition*, ed. Américo Paredes and Stekert (1971); John R. Williams, "'Up Here, We Never See the Sun': Homeplace and Crime in Urban Appalachian Narratives," in *Usable Pasts: Traditions and Group Expressions in North America*, ed. Tad Tuleja (1997).

Vernacular Architecture

See Section Overview (Architecture)

Western Maryland Public Folklore

Even now considered remote by outsiders, the mountains of western Maryland were opened in the 1800s by construction of the Chesapeake and Ohio Canal, the National Road, and the Baltimore and Ohio Railroad. Those who made western Maryland home had begun arriving after 1765, however, coming from Germany and Switzerland, many migrating north from southern Maryland. From Pennsylvania, Amish settlers moved south to take advantage of the rich farmland. By 1850, Welsh, Scottish, and Irish workers came to build railroads and then to mine coal and cut timber. Higher elevations and resorts such as the stylish, railroad-owned Deer Park and church-centered Mountain Lake Park attracted summer communities of wealthy city folk. In modern times, Garrett County remains the most isolated and least urbanized area in Maryland; a majority of its forested land is owned by the state, and tourism its main economic hope for the future. Cumberland and Hagerstown became seats of county governments and were, until recently, the region's industrial and rail centers.

Though western Maryland's geographic isolation and ethnic and occupational enclaves allowed the area's entrenched traditions to flourish, folklore collectors overlooked the region. Cecil Sharp in 1917 went ballad hunting in neighboring West Virginia but, like most collectors of Appalachiana, bypassed the mountains of Maryland, commenting that, because of the disturbance of rural life by the coal industry, songs and ballads did not "lie so ready at hand as in the other states." Despite Sharp's pronouncement, Maurice Matteson, a Frostburg State Teachers College music professor in the 1940s and 1950s who collected folklore in Beech Mountain, North Carolina, and performed at the National Folk Festival in 1938, claimed to have collected folk songs in the western Maryland area. His Madrigal Singers went on national tours performing what he called "Appalachian songs."

Though residents of Georges Creek in Allegany County still sing traditional ballads, regional Maryland collections are virtually unknown to outsiders. Stories and songs collected in the Georges Creek Valley and around Frostburg in 1949–50 by Dorothy Howard and tapes of interviews and religious songs collected by Margaret and Gerald Parsons in 1977–78 are available at the Library of Congress's Archive of Folk Culture. There has long been a rich fiddling and string-band tradition in Garrett County, where the community of Friendsville has been the home of an annual Fiddle and Banjo Contest since 1966 and where state fiddle and banjo contests are staged every October as part of the Autumn Glory Festival, which was held for decades in the town of Accident. The event's renowned fiddling families include the heirs of acclaimed hunter and storyteller Meshach Browning and the Broadwater and Hare families, all of Garrett County.

Folklore enthusiasts, both natives and summer residents, began safeguarding local traditions, particularly in Garrett County, in the early twentieth century. Their work continues to find an audience in respected local journals such as the *Glades Star*, a publication of the Garrett County Historical Society since 1941. Annie Weston Whitney, a New Englander with a country home in western Maryland, was a member of the Council of the American Folk-Lore Society from 1904 to 1906. She was instrumental in the founding of the Maryland Folk-Lore Society and was charged with collecting superstitions and tales. In 1895 she and an Emmitsburg (Frederick County) member contributed the bulk of attributed entries in the first published collection of Maryland folklore. Encouraged by the society's offer in 1899 of prizes for the largest and most varied offerings, Whitney coedited *Folk-Lore from Maryland*, a publication of the American Folk-Lore Society, in 1925. Of the 2,844 entries, the only ones consistently identified by place are from western Maryland, Washington County, Emmitsburg, Allegany County, Cumberland, Hagerstown, Thurmont, and "Maryland Mountains."

District of Columbia socialite and author Madeleine Vinton Dahlgren, who summered atop South Mountain, compiled Washington County's only folklore collection. Her *South-Mountain Magic* (1882) details legends and beliefs collected from locals. Her work on local beliefs is also found in exhibits at the Boonesborough Museum of History, established in 1975 by Douglas Bast. The best-known moment in the folklore of the area is perhaps the 1908–9 frenzy brought on by reports of a dragon-like snallygaster (from the Pennsylvania Dutch *schnelle geist*, or "quick spirit"). For years thereafter, interest was fanned by editors at the *Hagerstown Mail* and Middletown's *Valley Register*, its competitor in adjacent Frederick County. Reported sightings continued into the 1970s despite the creature's alleged demise in a vat of moonshine. In 1972 a reborn Maryland Folklore Society (now defunct, its records donated to the Middle Atlantic

Folklife Association) named its short-lived newsletter the *Snallygaster*.

Photography has also played an important role in the preservation of western Maryland tradition and folklore. Between 1935 and 1943, U.S. Farm Security Administration photographers Arthur Rothstein, Theodor Jung, John Vachon, Edwin Rosskam, Esther Bubley, and Marion Post Wolcott did extensive work in rural Frederick, Washington, and Garrett Counties and the towns of Cumberland and Hagerstown. Their complete works are available at the Library of Congress. The Herman and Stacia Miller Photo Collection of two thousand images from Cumberland in the 1880s to mid 1900s is housed in the City Hall. A glass plate collection by disabled photographer Leo Beachy documenting life and work in Garrett County from 1905 to 1927 has also garnered considerable national attention since 1990; his work was named an endangered treasure by the Maryland Commission for Celebration 2000.

Natives of western Maryland have played the most important roles in preserving and perpetuating folklore of the area. Felix G. Robinson, a Lutheran minister, returned home to Oakland, Maryland, in 1949 from pulpits in New York and Arthurdale, West Virginia, and published eight volumes of *Tableland Trails* from 1953 to 1964 that focused on the history, folklore, and cultural interests of the Allegheny Mountains. Known for crafting ballads, often modeled on traditional songs, to celebrate special occasions, Robinson also played a major role in establishing the Friendsville Fiddle and Banjo Contest a year before his death.

Alta Schrock, a biologist and self-taught folklorist, was instrumental in identifying and saving the cultural heritage of the Maryland mountains, first within a fifty-mile radius of bordering Springs, Pennsylvania, and later from a base on the Casselman River at Grantsville, Maryland. Traveling on foot, on the back of a burro, and in a succession of trademark green automobiles, Schrock visited every corner of the state's western panhandle in search of excellence in stories, craft, and music. Beginning in 1934, Schrock traversed the Allegheny Mountains in search of weavers, potters, quilters, rug hookers, chair makers, wood-carvers, cooks, and makers of other living crafts. She helped place sewing machines and looms in some homes to boost the earning capacity of people she visited. She succeeded in making the State Board of Education establish weaving classes for mountain families. Dorothy Mills Howard taught folklore as part of her English course offerings at Frostburg State Teachers College, but her primary work with children's folklore locally resulted in publication of *Folk Rhymes and Jingles of Maryland Children* (1944). Much of her students' locally researched work may be found in reports and note card collections at the Maryland State Arts Council and the Folklore Archives of the University of Maryland's Hornbeck Library at College Park. Howard collaborated with Baltimore photographer Susie Fitzhugh on a series of exhibitions called *Soundings*, which documented living traditions in Amish and Mennonite communities. Fitzhugh's black-and-white images featured children's games and the work of split-oak basket maker James McCrobie of Garrett County, who was featured with rag-rug maker Irene Miller in statewide folklife festivals in the 1970s.

Folklorist Geraldine Niva Johnson, who began her career as a fieldworker for the Maryland State Arts Council's nascent Folk Arts Program, has documented western Maryland rug makers and brought wide recognition to women whose craft reaches an expanding and appreciative contemporary market. Johnson's work culminated in the 1985 publication *Weaving Rag Rugs: A Women's Craft in Western Maryland.*

The folklife of western Maryland's rich coal-mining history has been documented by the Maryland Historical Trust. Oral histories include the state preservation office's sponsored initiatives to document coal culture in Garrett County and railroad traditions in Hagerstown; a Coal Talk collection archived at Garrett County Community College; and ethnographic surveys in Allegany and Garrett Counties. Since 2000, grants from the trust, the arts council, and the National Endowment for the Arts have funded folklife field surveys in Frederick and Washington Counties under the auspices of Frederick Community College's Catoctin Regional Center. Canal Place in Cumberland, the first state-recognized heritage area, included a folklife survey as part of its management plan.

See also: MENNONITE AND AMISH COMMUNITIES (FAMILY AND COMMUNITY); RUG MAKING (CRAFTS); SCHROCK, ALTA.

—Elaine Eff, *Maryland Historical Trust*

Meshach Browning, *Forty-Four Years of the Life of Hunter* (1860); Madeleine Vinton Dahlgren, *South-Mountain Magic* (1882); Geraldine Niva Johnson, *Weaving Rag Rugs: A Woman's Craft in Western Maryland* (1985); Annie Weston Whitney and Caroline Canfield Bullock, *Folk-Lore from Maryland* (1925).

West Virginia Public Folklore

West Virginia broke away from Virginia and attained statehood in 1863 as a result of differences over Virginia's secession from the Union. The border between the states roughly delineates cultural differences, including folkways and social customs that underlie the original division. In an interesting bit of folk speech, older state residents still call people who are from east of the Blue Ridge "tuckahoes." At one point these tuckahoes (of English descent) referred to western Virginians (largely Scots-Irish) as "cohees." Tuckahoe (or Indian bread) is a marsh plant; the roots, a staple in the diet of Native Americans, became important in the early diet of James River colonists and synonymous with their culture. The word *cohee* referred to those west of the Blue Ridge whose apparent use of the Scots-Irish figure of speech *quoth he* eventually earned them the designation.

In West Virginia, interest in such folklore and folklife was first recognized by the West Virginia Folklore Society, formed in 1913. In the summer of 1915, C. Alphonso Smith, founder of the Virginia Folklore Society, stirred additional interest through several lectures he gave at West Virginia University, always concluding with a plea to organize a society to "collect and preserve whatever of this material might be recovered." Historically, West Virginia was seen as fertile ground for the collection of regional Appalachian folklore, with music at the forefront. Surprisingly, however, one of the Appalachian region's foremost early collectors of folk songs, Cecil Sharp, spent little time in the state, actually visiting only two counties. In the preface to his heralded work *English Folk Songs from the Southern Appalachians*, Maud Karpeles, his assistant, noted that the state "did not appear to be a promising field of research." Between Sharp's collecting period (1916–18) and the publication of the expanded version of his work in 1932, John Harrington Cox proved Sharp and Karpeles wrong. *Folk-Songs of the South*, which Cox edited and published in 1925 under the auspices of the West Virginia Folk Lore Society, is a monumental work that testifies to the depth of the state's ballad traditions. This work brought together the collecting efforts of twenty-two society correspondents from throughout West Virginia. Cox, a former student of ballad scholar George Lyman Kittredge at Harvard, assumed the position of president, archivist and general editor of the West Virginia Folk Lore Society. His 1939 publication *Traditional Ballads Mainly from West Virginia* built on his earlier work. At the same time Cox was in the field, the Federal Writers' Project in West Virginia played a part in the documentation of folk culture; the state was on the geographical fringe of a major southern initiative of cultural conservation by the New Deal–era project. Additional materials were collected in the state by the Resettlement and Farm Security Administrations in 1936–37 and are housed at the Library of Congress.

Cox's work paved the way for dozens of other music collection efforts throughout the twentieth century, and true to regional thinking of the early period, these efforts emphasized ballads (or "ballets," as the song's written words were called in folk parlance) with little relevance given to the tunes. Cox published 185 ballads and many variants but only twenty-six tunes to the ballads were noted. However, at about the time of Cox's publication, another West Virginia University professor working in the state, Louis Watson Chappell, was pioneering field recording as a collecting methodology.

Chappell's publication of *John Henry: A Folk-Lore Study* in 1933 earned him international fame. This field study of West Virginia's classic folk song offers a folkloric synopsis of the Industrial Revolution in Appalachia. Presented as a scholarly text, the documentation of the song and lore surrounding it are based on the voices of the people but include Chappell's thoughtful interpretation. But the most lasting impression that Chappell made to the study and understanding of folklore is through his collection of field recordings of folk songs and music made throughout West Virginia between 1937 and 1947. Acquired in the early 1970s by West Virginia University, this remarkable collection of 647 aluminum discs joined other significant field-recorded collections at the West Virginia and Regional History Collection, where a Sound Archive was formalized in 1972. Chappell's work joined other West Virginia collections by Cortez D. Reece (regional African American folk music, c. 1949–c. 1953), Kenneth L. Carvell (religious music in Monongalia County, 1957–61), and Thomas S. Brown (various folk music, mostly from central West Virginia beginning in 1970).

While music and song were the main thrust of collection and interpretive efforts throughout the first half of the twentieth century, other aspects of folklife slowly came into prominence. One early exception is the book *Marion County in the Making*. This 1917 work documents numerous aspects of rural West Virginia folklife and folklore through a project supported by James Otis Watson and written by the Fairmont High School class of 1916. Though this book devotes space to folk music, the subject is a minor aspect of the volume, which also includes documentation of manners and customs, homes and home life, remedies and superstitions, and legends as well as local oral history. The material was acquired and presented in the fashion made famous by the *Foxfire* series, but decades earlier than the Foxfire concept was introduced as an educational tool.

An early folk festival of sorts was held at the planned community of Arthurdale in 1936, through an economic-development project championed by Eleanor Roosevelt. In 1950 a folklife event was organized by Gilmer County native Patrick Ward Gainer at Glenville State College, with students asked to present artifacts, photos, or practitioners of folklore and folklife. This subsequently became the West Virginia State Folk Festival and had a lasting effect on traditional folk music and dance in central West Virginia. In the 1960s and 1970s, privately produced folk music festivals were organized at Pipestem, Ivydale, Huntersville, and elsewhere.

The Glenville event was the first folk festival that included aspects of folk culture other than music. Singers performed while working at a spinning wheel and presented other contextual situations based on somewhat romanticized images of folk culture. Ghost stories and tales were integrated into the presentations and local traditions, and events such as shape-note singings and spelling bees were staged.

Mainly a collector of folk songs, Gainer preferred to notate and publish the music and songs from his informants even though field recording technology was readily available. Gainer gained access to folk artists primarily through students in his English and folklore classes at West Virginia University and introduced many to the public stage. He published two volumes of folklore after retiring from West Virginia University: *Witches, Ghosts and Signs: Folklore of the Southern Appalachians* (1975) and *Folksongs from the West Virginia Hills* (1975). Before that, at the time of the West Virginia centennial in 1963, he assembled *The West Virginia Centennial Book of One Hundred Songs.* Marie Boette published *Singa Hipsy Doodle and Other Folk Songs of West Virginia* in 1971. Ruth Ann Musick added to the nonmusical genre of published lore with *The Telltale Lilac Bush* (1965) and *Green Hills of Magic* (1970). She was the first to collect and publish a considerable volume of non-Anglo-Celtic narrative folklore, concentrating for the most part on material of continental European origin brought to West Virginia by immigrant coal miners.

Serious state-supported efforts to identify and promote folklore began in the early 1960s, and the folk arts had a major place in official celebrations of the state's centennial in 1963. Governor W. W. Barron created the state Commerce Department in 1961 and appointed Hulett Smith the first commissioner. Smith assigned employees to explore the economic potential of handicrafts and to encourage artisans to produce and market their goods. By 1963 this effort had grown into a separate Arts and Crafts section within the Commerce Department. That same year, as part of the state's centennial observance, the department took the lead in organizing the first Mountain State Art and Craft Fair at Cedar Lakes. The following year, the Commerce Department included a strong selection of arts and crafts in the West Virginia pavilion at the New York World's Fair.

Smith succeeded Barron as governor in 1965 and continued to support folk arts by expanding the staff and scope of the crafts division. These and other efforts, combined with the national folklore revival, produced a lively folk arts scene in the state. The Art and Craft Fair, planned as a one-time centennial event, remains a major annual economic and artistic venue. By the end of the 1960s, at least four annual craft fairs were being held in the state, and several older events began to include some native folk music, a few shops were offering local handicrafts, and at least three albums of genuine West Virginia traditional folk music were publicly available. A decade later, fairs and festivals, recordings, and craft outlets, including the state-supported craft center at Tamarack, were commonplace, and awareness of West Virginia folk heritage had become firmly established.

During the 1960s and 1970s, West Virginia attracted a large number of young people interested in the state's folk culture. This introduced a new wave of folklife documentation, much of it conducted on a nonacademic, freelance basis. Foremost among this group was Pennsylvania native Gerald Milnes. Moving to Webster County in 1975, Milnes set about observing, learning, and preserving local traditions and lore, including music, architecture, foodways, burial practices, farming methods, storytelling, and many other aspects of rural mountain life. Through photography, audio recordings, film, and video, Milnes amassed a substantial body of documentation over a period of three decades.

After several years as a seasonal staff member, Milnes became full-time coordinator of Folklife Programs for the Augusta Heritage Center of Davis and Elkins College in Elkins. Much of his research and documentation is housed at Augusta, for which he has produced five films and more than twenty full-length audio recordings. Since 1989, Milnes has also coordinated and administered the West Virginia Folk Arts Apprenticeship Program. Milnes has authored two books: *Granny Will Your Dog Bite?* (1990) and *Play of a Fiddle: Traditional Music, Dance, and Folklore in West Virginia* (1999). He has also written numerous magazine articles on West Virginia folklife and frequently presents lectures and workshops on related topics.

The festival at Glenville, dating to 1950, is the state's oldest continual folklife festival. The summer Augusta Workshop at Davis and Elkins College, established in 1972, continues with a wide array of traditional arts and craft offerings as well as a festival and two seasonal traditional music programs. The Vandalia Gathering (established 1977) on state capitol grounds continues as a major traditional music event. The Footmad Festival and Allegheny Echoes are newer traditional music and dance venues providing hands-on learning opportunities. The state-sponsored annual Appalachian String Band Music Festival at Camp Washington Carver is a major regional music event and the Mountain State Arts and Crafts Show at Clifftop includes apprenticeship learning of traditional arts. An ongoing statewide project, the West Virginia Folk Art Apprenticeship Program, with initial support by the National Endowment for the Arts and subsequent support by the West Virginia Division of Culture and History, was designed by the Augusta Heritage Center in 1989. The Folklife Center (established 1999) at Fairmont State College provides an educational folklore study curriculum and training seminar for teachers. The Center for the Study of Ethnicity and Gender in Appalachia at Marshall University has supported folklife-related projects as well.

In the 1990s, the American Folklife Center undertook studies in the New River Gorge and the Coal River basin in southern West Virginia. Newly identified cultural preserves such as the Wheeling National Heritage Area and designated areas within the state park system such as the Cass Scenic Railroad support some folklife interpretation. The National Coal Heritage Area in southern West Virginia includes the Coal Heritage Trail. Other regional projects such as the Stanton Parkersburg Turnpike are establishing, documenting, and interpreting local and historic cultural information within the concept of heritage corridors.

Goldenseal, a quarterly folklife magazine established by the state in 1975, publishes nonscholarly articles covering a wide range of regional traditions and folklife practices. *Traditions,* Fairmont College's Folklife Center's annual periodical, contains articles and folk resources. The West Virginia University Press and Augusta Heritage Center produce and release traditional music recordings, and the Augusta Collection of Folk Culture at Davis and Elkins houses documentation of state and regional folklife and oral history. The state's major archives are the West Virginia State Archives in Charleston and the West Virginia and Regional History Collection at West Virginia University, an important repository of folklife documentation.

See also: FESTIVALS, HUMOR AND STORYTELLING (HUMOR); *GOLDENSEAL* (MEDIA); TAMARACK (CULTURAL INSTITUTIONS).

—John Lilly, *Goldenseal;* Gerald Milnes, *Davis and Elkins College;* and Danny Williams, *West Virginia University*

Louis W. Chappell, *John Henry: A Folk-Lore Study* (1933); Patrick W. Gainer, *Witches, Ghosts and Signs: Folklore of the Southern Appalachians* (1975); Ruth Ann Musick, *The Telltale Lilac Bush* (1965).

Food and Cooking

Section Editor: Mark F. Sohn

THE STORY OF FOODWAYS IN CONTEMPORARY APPALACHIA IS, AS WITH MUCH OF Appalachian culture, a saga of dislocation and change. During the last half of the twentieth century, the region evolved from agrarian self-sufficiency to a Wal-Mart, Winn-Dixie, and McDonald's culture. The image of a granny gathering ramps and creasy greens on the mountainside was no longer a suitable image of an Appalachian food provider; she had been replaced by the image of a man or woman in a business suit or work uniform dashing into a supermarket or fast-food restaurant to pick up a quick meal after a day on the job. Even though Appalachians have followed their fellow Americans out of the garden and into the grocery store, traditional Appalachian foods still loom large in memory and on holiday tables. Of all the markers of cultural identity, people cling to foodways most tenaciously (if tenuously) in the face of change. But cultural change is not a new phenomenon in the region, and dishes widely regarded as traditional Appalachian cooking actually represent an amalgamation of the foodways of many cultural groups who made their way into the region and left their mark on its cuisine.

The first Appalachian cooks were Native Americans who inhabited the region twelve thousand years ago and whose legacy to Appalachian cooking is quite transparent. From Native American farmers and cooks, Appalachia received corn, beans, and squash, three vegetables that remain at the heart of its cuisine. Supplementing this agricultural triad, which by A.D. 1200 had become the basis of horticulture throughout eastern North America, Native Americans hunted, fished, and gathered wild nuts, fruits, and greens, a practice that Euro-American settlers would follow. Since similar Native American foodways prevailed throughout the East, Appalachia's first white settlers probably were already familiar with these crops before they arrived in the mountains.

In post-European-settlement Appalachia, two general and somewhat overlapping subregional cuisines developed on top of this Native American foundation. In southern and central Appalachia, foodways show the influence of Scottish, English, Irish, African, and to some extent German traditions. Farther north, the ingredients and recipes of Germany and of eastern and southern Europe prevail. These culinary differences reflect immigration patterns. While southern and central Appalachia was settled largely by Scots-Irish, German, and English immigrants, northern (along with

Facing page: A ham being salt-cured, Copper, Virginia, 1956. Pork is a seasoning for cooking vegetables and dried beans, a medium for frying, and, in the form of lard, a shortening in bread making.

some parts of central) Appalachia manifests a large Pennsylvania German presence augmented by the late-nineteenth- and early-twentieth-century influx of Italians, Slovaks, Yugoslavs, Hungarians, and other southern and eastern Europeans to work in coal mines and urban industries. Whatever their country of origin, European immigrants in Appalachia adapted old-world recipes to new-world ingredients. Among British immigrants, for example, pork replaced mutton, corn replaced oats or wheat, and wild greens were substituted for the salad greens of northern England and Scotland.

In many ways, the food of the central and southern Appalachian heartland resembles classic southern cooking, although coastal and low-country ingredients such as seafood and rice are minimized. The linchpin is pork, which is used as a primary foodstuff, a seasoning for cooking vegetables and dried beans, and, in the form of lard, as a shortening for making bread and a medium for frying. Historically, the popularity of pork may have resulted from the adaptability of swine husbandry to frontier woodland conditions. Unlike dairy cows or chickens, pigs could simply be allowed to run free in the woods and gather their own food with little attention from their owners. Moreover, sows were efficient breeders, producing offspring in litters rather than single births. Frontier necessities and the exigencies of agriculture created taste preference, with pork dishes varying according to seasonal availability and economic conditions. Before modern refrigeration, fresh pork was available only at hog-killing time, typically late fall, when cool temperatures ensured that the meat would not spoil before it could be processed. Otherwise, diners were limited to hams, bacon, and sausages cured by salting or smoking, with country ham being the hands-down favorite. When hard times struck, fried fatback might become a family's only meat option.

Although pork may be central to traditional southern and central Appalachian cooking, it shares with other foods the status of regional icon. These iconic foods include soup beans, stack cake, ramps, green beans (and their dried incarnation, known as leather britches or shucky beans), apple butter, biscuits, and corn bread. Soup beans—not to be confused with bean soup, which mountain cooks also make—are pintos cooked with pork and served in their own broth, to be eaten with a spoon. Stack cake resembles the many-layered torte of German cooking; it is an assemblage of numerous layers of spicy cake or baked pastry alternated with a fresh or cooked apple or fruit filling.

The ramp, a wild member of the Allium family, is gathered in the early spring. Traditionally, cooks used ramps as a pungent seasoning. In the late twentieth century, as Appalachians turned toward commercial rather than local food sources, festivals celebrating the ramp became popular, and some mountaineers gathered ramps for sale. Commercialization widened their consumption, and overharvesting has become a threat to their survival in the wild.

Historically, southern and central Appalachian menus manifested distinct seasonality, another hallmark of the region's foodways. When fresh foods were available, they were consumed; otherwise, preserved foods dominated. A typical winter menu might have included soup beans, sliced onions, fried potatoes, turnip, collard, or beet greens, and buttermilk. Another favored winter menu featured fried pork chops or fried chicken, macaroni and cheese, mashed potatoes, gravy, baked beans, fried apples, and corn or corn pudding. A midsummer dinner might combine green beans, new potatoes, sliced tomatoes, fresh cucumbers, barbecued pork ribs, and cantaloupe, while a family may have dined on chicken and dumplings, skillet potatoes, green beans, and sweet potatoes, or meat loaf, gravy, mashed potatoes, shelled October beans ("shellies"), fried okra, and fried green tomatoes in the fall. Some sweets also had a season. For example, candy was associated with winter and fruit cobblers with summer. Whatever the time of year, dinners included either corn bread, biscuits, and, more recently, yeast rolls. During the summer, grated fresh corn might be stirred into the corn bread batter for "gritted" corn bread.

Traditional food and cooking in the Appalachian highlands have a strong association with self-sufficiency and hard times. Families in isolated areas were obliged to grow most of what they ate, buying only those products they could not raise, such as coffee and baking soda. Before the advent of food preservation technologies such as canning and freezing, mountaineers had to depend on root cellars or trenches for storing potatoes and cabbage, and the diet in winter could become seriously deficient in vegetables and fruits, leading in the worst cases to scurvy and other nutrient-deficiency diseases. Nineteenth-century travelers did not always speak kindly of Appalachian cooking even during the best of times. In *On Horseback: A Tour in Virginia, North Carolina, and Tennessee*, Charles Dudley Warner lamented the monotony of the mountain diet and declared, "[T]he traveler in this region must be content to feed on natural beauty." Even during lean periods, however, the mountain code of hospitality required that a family share its food with visitors to the house. Furthermore, some of the complaints might be attributable to regional tastes: southerners cook vegetables for what people outside the region consider an excessively long time, and frying, the favored cooking method in Appalachia (Sunday dinner might feature fried corn bread, fried pork chops, and fried chicken), goes through periodic cycles of disfavor nationally. Although the skillet and frying pan retain preeminence in the Appalachian kitchen, cardiovascular health has advanced with the retreat of pork lard as the frying medium.

A different cuisine emerged in northern Appalachia. Pennsylvania "Dutch," or German, cuisine, the cynosure of eastern Pennsylvania, is widely found throughout the state, and the iconic dishes associated with that tradition—shoofly pie, whoopee pie, potato filling—appear in Appalachian Pennsylvania as well. In addition, coal and industrial workers' culture has led to other subregional influences in Appalachia. Italian immigrants into Pennsylvania and West Virginia brought recipes for pasta, polenta, and rice and raised gardens containing herbs such as oregano and basil. In towns such as Clarksburg, West Virginia, bakeries still specialize in Italian breads and pastries. Slovak and Slovenian women's clubs in Virginia and Maryland prepare *gibanica* pastries and *potica* rolls for sale at community functions. Some auxiliaries in Pennsylvania sell Polish *pierogi*. Savory noodles, potato pancakes, and spicy sausages are also popular in these areas.

The regional cuisine of northern Appalachia is vividly illustrated in community-based cookbooks. For example, Johnstown, Pennsylvania, a coal-mining and historically a steel-producing city, has populations from Croatia, Germany, Greece, Hungary, India, Ireland, Italy, Mexico, Poland, Russia, Scotland, Serbia, Slovenia, and Ukraine. In 1989 the Johnstown Area Heritage Association identified about twenty local recipes for each ethnic group, which it published in a spiral-bound cookbook, *Ethnic Recipes of Johnstown*.

In addition to ethnic influences, climatic variation has also been responsible for differences between the foodways of northern and southern or central Appalachia. Cold winters made it possible for northerners to cut ice from ponds and lakes and use it in icehouses to preserve beef. Farther south, where ice accumulation was not appreciable, smokehouses were employed to preserve pork. Underground root cellars were commonly used for storing vegetables and canned goods in the North, while further south canned foods were placed in above-ground or semi-subterranean sheds, and cabbages were stored in trenches covered with straw. Climate also affected sweetening preferences. In northern Appalachia, maple syrup and maple sugar production were common; southern and central Appalachian farmers produced syrup from cane sorghum (although maple trees were sometimes tapped in the southern highlands as well).

The arrival of Hispanic immigrants and the rise of new ethnic communities in the late twentieth century brought with it yet another change in the availability of food products. Supermarkets in areas with large Hispanic populations began to offer an array of Mexican ingredients previously unfamiliar in Appalachia, including jicama, tomatillos, *masa harina*, and a wide variety of peppers. Mexican entrepreneurs and restaurateurs in Appalachia opened *tiendas* (stores) and *taquieras* (diners) that specialize in ethnic foods and merchandise. And Taco Bell and other fast-food outlets purveying Mexican specialties arrived to compete with McDonald's.

Across the twentieth century, waves of Appalachians migrated to find work in northern and midwestern urban areas. Just as Italian or Polish immigrants into Appalachia retained their fondness for ethnic foods, so Appalachian out-migrants to cities such as Cincinnati and Chicago expressed nostalgia for traditional mountain food. Urban Appalachians requested that people back home send care packages of special foods such as home-dried apples, and restaurants in urban Appalachian neighborhoods featured mountain dishes alongside standard dinner fare.

No traditional foodways are retained more zealously than those associated with special events such as holidays and weddings. Food is often a significant component of ritual, and rituals are inherently conservative. In northern Appalachia, Christmas Eve celebrations in Polish communities may feature *barszcz z uszkami* (borscht); Slovaks bake the customary *paska* bread for Easter. Sometimes food is at the center of a ritual. For example, in central and southern Appalachia, a traditional event in many churches is dinner on the grounds, an informal but elaborate meal shared in the churchyard, sometimes under a specially built picnic shelter, after church meetings, homecomings, and other special occasions.

Women are essentially in charge of dinner on the grounds, for which each cook contributes one or more dishes including fried chicken, chicken and dumplings, vegetables, potato salad, breads, and an enormous assortment of cakes and pies. At Old Regular Baptist Association meetings, women of several member churches assume responsibility for dinner on the grounds; the seriousness with which they take their job is reflected in the special aprons, which have their church's name embroidered on the bib, that they don for the occasion.

In general, food—both in ritual and in daily life—is one arena in which women, traditionally marginalized in Appalachia's androcentric culture, traditionally exerted control and gained status. Except during all-male forays such as hunting or fishing parties, women assumed responsibility for cooking. Frequently, they also worked the kitchen garden and, when families kept cows at home, were responsible for milking. Women could develop coveted reputations for the excellence of their cakes.

As food is often important in holiday or religious rituals, so too does ritual often surround the procurement and preparation of food. When people produced most food at home, certain large-scale food-related tasks such as hog killing, corn shucking, and making molasses or sorghum syrup were often accomplished communally. Tasks were assigned by gender, with men usually assuming such jobs as slaughtering the hogs or shucking the corn while women rendered lard and prepared a large meal to feed the workers. Communal canning tended to be an exclusively female activity.

Sometimes these work bees served as initiatory experiences for young people; for example, as boys matured, they might be tapped to kill or gut a hog.

Periodically, certain food crops have become commercially important to local Appalachian economies. The green bean, for example, so central to Appalachian cooking, became a valuable cash crop during the 1950s in extreme northeastern Tennessee and northwestern North Carolina. In the late twentieth century, southern Virginia and northern North Carolina developed an extensive cabbage industry. Dairying has been significant throughout many parts of the region.

In Appalachia, as elsewhere, much food today is preprocessed, and even with processed foods residents have certain preferences. Although the soft drink Mountain Dew is now a nationally popular beverage, it originated in southern Appalachia and originally displayed a stereotypical hillbilly on its label. MoonPies, produced in Chattanooga, Tennessee, have been a favorite packaged sweet. Southern Appalachians share the general southern fondness for canned Vienna sausages and potted meat. Local manufacturers of snack foods such as Moore's of Bristol, Virginia, and Snyder's of Hanover, Pennsylvania, have often garnered a large share of the regional market.

Appalachian cooking continues to change. The national fondness for restaurant dining has led to the recent development of Appalachian haute cuisine, in which chefs, many of whom are native to the region but trained elsewhere, incorporate into their complex recipes such traditional ingredients as ramps, fiddlehead ferns, lamb's-quarters, pawpaws, and elderberries. Local growers supply chefs with heirloom vegetables and fruits. At the opposite end of the spectrum, nostalgia for traditionally prepared foods has given rise to festivals celebrating dishes such as corn bread and apple butter. In addition, restaurants featuring traditional Appalachian food have become popular. Cracker Barrel, for instance, the interstate highway restaurant chain, offers an attempt at home cooking, and there are many locally owned restaurants that feature southern menus and family-style dining. One such eatery in the North Carolina foothills has adopted the name "Hillbilly Hideaway." Housed in a huge log building decorated with painted plywood cutouts of hillbilly caricatures, the Hideaway offers superb home-style cooking so popular that on weekends local and out-of-town diners arrive by the busload. An hour's wait for a table is not uncommon. Even in eateries otherwise devoid of an Appalachian theme, traditional foods sometimes crop up. In Johnson City, Tennessee, for example, a delicatessen—which is definitely not a traditional Appalachian-style restaurant—advertises in large lettering on its front window that it serves both subs, a non-Appalachian import, and soup beans, an Appalachian icon that is hardly typical deli fare.

Commercialized and blended into the national culture of mass production and consumption, Appalachia's distinctive foodways have become less conspicuous with passing time, but they remain at the core of mountain families' heritage, passed along in dog-eared cookbooks, time-tested recipes, and tips whispered at wakes and dinners on the grounds.

—Mark F. Sohn, *Pikeville College*

Linda Keller Brown and Kay Mussell, eds., *Ethnic and Regional Foodways in the United States* (1984); Joseph E. Dabney, *Smokehouse Ham, Spoon Bread, and Scuppernong Wine: The Folklore and Art of Southern Appalachian Cooking* (1998); Sidney Saylor Farr, *More Than Moonshine: Appalachian Recipes and Recollections* (1983); Theodore C. and Lin T. Humphrey, eds., *"We Gather Together": Food and Festival in American Life* (1988); John F. Mariani, *The Encyclopedia of American Food and Drink* (1999); John Parris, *Mountain Cooking* (1978); Mark F. Sohn, *Mountain Country Cooking: A Gathering of the Best Recipes from the Smokies to the Blue Ridge* (1996) and *Southern Country Cooking* (1992).

African American Foodways

African influence on the foods of Appalachia is manifest in okra, yams, black-eyed peas (or cowpeas), and watermelon. These foods were introduced by Africans arriving as servants with early settlers, by Africans who were slaves, and by slave traders in the early sixteenth century. Like the Huguenots, Germans, Scots-Irish, Italians, and other ethnic European groups who came and settled in Appalachia, African settlers also came to the region seeking independence and freedom from servitude. All of these groups brought with them their cultures and ways of life, including their foods. The Africans were not a homogenous group, but represented many different tribes, each with its own culture, language, and religion, from the west coast and western interior of Africa.

Since Africans had first been brought to the region by Spanish explorers in 1540, many blacks already resided in South Carolina when the English arrived. West African foods such as peanuts, yams, rice, and black-eyed peas came to the New World as trade commodities brought by the slave traders. Interestingly, the Spanish had earlier introduced peanuts to Africa's west coast, so many Africans who arrived as slaves in Appalachia were already familiar with the food. Other foods thought of as African in origin such as okra, plantains, and coconuts are actually Caribbean and American in origin. The black-eyed pea originated in North Africa and was introduced to America by African slaves, becoming a staple of the southern diet. One of the best-known southern dishes is "Hopping John," which is black-eyed peas cooked with fat pork and served with rice. Numerous stories of its origin have been handed down with a variety of recipes, but basic Hopping John includes another food that was a staple of the African and slave diet in America—rice. Rice brought by Africans became one of the main cash crops of South Carolina. This innocent introduction also contributed to slavery in the region, as Africans were brought en masse to work the rice fields.

In addition to food rations, the slave diet was generally augmented by foods discarded by the slave owners. Chitterlings (or chitlins), pigs' feet, oxtails, pigs' ears, and chicken feet became part of the slave diet and eventually part of the diet of central and southern Appalachia.

Because slaves had few cooking vessels, most foods were prepared in one big pot over an open fire. Gumbos, which can include shrimp, okra, rice and other ingredients, were cooked in such fashion.

Across America, African American staples are lumped together as "soul food." In rural Appalachia, hallmark soul foods such as catfish, collard greens, ham hocks, black-eyed peas, sweet potato pie, and many more dishes have become part of a regional cuisine.

See also: AFRICAN AMERICAN FAMILIES AND COMMUNITIES (FAMILY AND COMMUNITY).

—Leola A. Brown, *East Tennessee State University*, and Mary A. Waalkes, *Lee University*

Jessica B. Harris, *The Welcome Table: African American Heritage Cooking* (1996); William H. Turner and Edward J. Cabbell, eds., *Blacks in Appalachia* (1985).

Apple Butter

Apple butter is a mixture of peeled, cored apples, apple cider, spices, and sweetening slowly simmered and stirred to a thick consistency. Typical of other fruit butters such as peach and pear, apple butter contains a relatively small amount of sugar in proportion to fruit. Of middle European origin, apple butter recipes were probably brought to southern Appalachia by German settlers as early as the 1700s. North Carolina proved to be a fertile apple-growing region, as did Tennessee, Kentucky, West Virginia, and Georgia.

Different types of apples can be used to prepare apple butter. Sweet varieties such as the old-fashioned Cortland or the newer Yellow Delicious require little additional sweetener, while tarter varieties such as the McIntosh or Winesap need more. Sweetening agents have varied. Settlers in Pennsylvania used maple syrup; sorghum, molasses, and sugar are also used.

Making apple butter has traditionally been an important event at festive occasions throughout Appalachia. It is an all-day process, taking up to sixteen hours to properly cook down the apples as the aroma slowly permeates the surroundings. Specialized apple butter pots—iron, brass, or copper kettles suspended from a tripod over a slow but steady fire—are often used to make large quantities. In the past many families put an iron washpot to use, and today others use a dishpan on top of the stove, a crock-pot, or an oven-safe container in the oven.

Whatever the cooking vessel, the method is about the same. Apple cider (unfermented, or "soft," cider) is reduced to about one-half. Pared, quartered, and cored apples are added, and the reduced cider mixture is cooked and stirred. The amount of water loss is determined by spooning out a "glob" of apple butter onto a stainless steel surface and measuring it with a calibrated measuring stick. Constant stirring is necessary to keep the mixture from burning and sticking to the sides and bottom of the kettle. A long-handled (up to eight feet) perforated paddle is used for the task, keeping the mixture in constant motion and the stirrer far away from the steaming, bubbling mass. Oven and crock-pot variations reduce the need for stirring. Near the end of the cooking, spices such as ginger, cinnamon, or nutmeg are added. The finished product is then sealed into jars for storage or sale. Four or five bushels of apples yield approximately eight gallons of finished apple butter.

See also: APPLES (AGRICULTURE); COBBLERS; DRIED APPLE STACK CAKE.

—Ann Juttelstad, *International Association of Chef Professionals*

Joseph E. Dabney, *Smokehouse Ham, Spoon Bread, and Scuppernong Wine: The Folklore and Art of Southern Appalachian Cooking* (1998); Jeanne Lesem, *Preserving Today* (1992).

Bacon

See Pork

Berries

See Fruits and Berries

Big Game

Large species of wild game were an integral part of the early Appalachians' diet. Settlers of the 1700s and later years relied heavily on what was, at the time, an abundant natural resource. Even in years of good plant food harvests, some form of meat, often game, was served at most meals.

Native Americans of the southeastern United States had consumed black bear, elk, and buffalo for centuries before the Europeans arrived in Appalachia. Bear brains and livers were delicacies, as was the broiled tender meat of juvenile bears. Chunks of bear meat were also threaded onto thin rods with venison and poultry for roasting, and bear fat was valued for cooking.

Due to their large size, buffalo and elk were not popular game for Appalachian hunters, who found transporting and preserving such large quantities of meat (buffalo can weigh more than a ton) too difficult, particularly when other forms of game were so plentiful. However, if a buffalo was taken, the animal's rump, tongue, and hump were the choice parts; the rest of the carcass, minus its hide, was often left where the animal had fallen.

Smaller than buffalo or elk, white-tailed deer were easier to manage, and most of the animal could be eaten. In Appalachian kitchens, venison was served as roast, chops, or barbecued. Deer steaks were fried, often with onions. Less desirable parts of the animal were stewed or braised with vegetables or ground for sausages and, more recently, for chili.

Wild turkeys were another seemingly inexhaustible source of meat. These birds, which could reach forty pounds, were generally roasted; occasionally, the breast meat was fried. So common were they that farm-raised chickens were more expensive than turkeys in Kentucky markets of the early nineteenth century, and turkey breast was sometimes used as a bread substitute.

Feral hogs, sometimes called razorbacks in the Southeast, were a treasured food. When Europeans moved into Appalachia, their pigs were marked for later identification, and then turned loose in the forests to forage for themselves. Some of them went completely wild. Swift-running and dangerous, razorbacks offered meat that was so highly prized that it was reserved primarily for important social occasions.

Indiscriminate hunting and an increasing human presence eventually took their toll on Appalachia's big game. By the late 1800s, the populations of elk, buffalo, and black bear were seriously depleted, causing hunters to turn increasingly to deer and wild turkey. By the early twentieth century, the sole big-game animal to maintain its numbers after the encroachment of humans was the feral pig. The situation prompted one local forestry official in Georgia, Arthur Woody, to begin a replenishment program in his area. Later on, several Appalachian states developed elk restoration programs. Black bear and wild turkey populations also recovered. By the 1990s, the success of such restoration efforts had dramatically increased big-game populations in Appalachia. Thanks to state-controlled hunting, the food and cooking in this region once again include big game.

See also: HUNTING AND FISHING (SPORTS AND RECREATION); SMALL GAME.

—Rebecca Maksel, *Ashburn, Virginia,* and Stephanie D. Zonis, *Neshanic Station, New Jersey*

Linda Garland Page and Eliot Wigginton, eds., *The Foxfire Book of Appalachian Cookery* (1984); Waverley Root and Richard de Rochemont, *Eating in America: A History* (1976); Mark F. Sohn, *Mountain Country Cooking: A Gathering of the Best Recipes from the Smokies to the Blue Ridge* (1996).

Biscuits and Salt-Rising Bread

Biscuits (from the Latin words *bis,* meaning "twice," and *coctus,* meaning "to cook"), in various forms, are a staple in Appalachian kitchens and dining rooms, appearing at any meal, at festive occasions, or as leftovers. Prepared by mixing, they are buttered and served alone or with gravy, meat drippings, sorghum, jam, honey, molasses, or syrup. While biscuits may or may not be flaky, they are round, generally possess a melting quality, and should have lightness and a characteristic heft. In southern Appalachia, more substantial versions are called "cat-head" biscuits because of their enormous size.

Except for cream biscuits, which benefit from a little kneading, biscuits must be handled as little as possible during preparation. In this and other ways, they resemble piecrusts, for which the shortening and liquids used should be icy cold and the oven very hot during baking. It is the juxtaposition of temperatures that causes the shortening to explode between the layers of dough, giving good biscuits their airy and flaky texture.

Plain biscuits are often referred to as buttermilk biscuits, baking powder biscuits, or soda biscuits (short for baking soda biscuits). In Appalachia, biscuits, rather than sponge cake or pound cake, are classically used as the bottom building block for fruit shortcake desserts because their savory, buttery quality contrasts well with the sweet, juicy fruit.

The beaten biscuit was common in the mid-nineteenth century and throughout the Civil War. Comparable to the modern-day cracker—hard, flat, and crispy—this biscuit was valued for its storage longevity and not for its taste. Served plain or with very thin slices of aged country ham, these biscuits were so named because they were beaten with a rolling pin or mallet during preparation. Eliza Leslie, in her 1857 *Miss Leslie's New Cookery Book*, noted that children should not eat beaten biscuits at all and that grown-ups should choose "any other sort of bread" if given a choice.

With the introduction of chemical leaveners such as baking soda and baking powder in the mid-nineteenth century, biscuits and other types of breads grew in popularity, since cooks (particularly those living in rural areas) could prepare tasty breads, biscuits, muffins, and pancakes quickly and at little cost.

Salt-rising, or salt-risen, bread, also popular in Appalachia, is a white bread that develops its flavor from an unusual fermentation process. Believed to have first been prepared in the United States in the early to mid-1800s, the bread has achieved its greatest popularity in the central and southern Appalachian states of West Virginia, Virginia, and Kentucky. Historically, it was served with homemade apple butter or preserves. A common misconception about salt-rising bread is that the name is derived from the presence of salt in the recipe. In fact, salt is not a necessary ingredient for salt-rising bread and is not used at all in some recipes. Instead, the name comes from the original method of placing heated rock salt around the container of starter to maintain the temperature of the starter and keep it warm overnight.

An unusual characteristic of salt-rising bread is that it utilizes naturally occurring bacteria rather than commercial yeast as its rising agent. Pioneer women were often unable to purchase yeast for their bread baking, so they had to utilize an alternative means of fermentation. Because the bacteria necessary to ferment carbohydrates respond naturally to these foods, a starter recipe for salt-rising bread required either potatoes, cornmeal, or flour. Without these bacteria, the bread could not rise. Either warm milk or water was added to the starch to complete the starter.

Once the starter for salt-rising bread had successfully fermented, a distinct aroma similar to that of fermented cheese was detected. If the odor and a foamy and bubbly texture did not appear within sixteen hours, the starter was deemed a failure and discarded. Rising times for all stages varied greatly (as they still do) due to factors such as the weather, type of flour, and room temperature.

See also: CAKES AND COOKIES; CHICKEN AND DUMPLINGS; COBBLERS.

—Susan Brown, *Morgantown, West Virginia*, and Catherine S. Vodrey, *East Liverpool, Ohio*

Craig Claiborne, *The New York Times Food Encyclopedia* (1985); Prudence Hilburn, *A Treasury of Southern Baking* (1993); R. N. Kohman, *Baking Industry* (1953).

Boardinghouse Food

Before motels and restaurants were widespread in Appalachia, most towns had at least one boardinghouse, often identified by a woman's name, such as Mrs. Brown's or Mrs. Dale's. Few jobs were available for women in the late nineteenth and early twentieth centuries, so those who had large houses with extra bedrooms sometimes accepted regular boarders and prepared meals for local townspeople and tourists. The women packed lunches for the roomers who worked on the railroad or in industrial plants and served three meals daily in the dining room at specified times. Diners sat at long tables laden with seasonal foods that they passed around the table, family style.

A typical summer meal featured dishes such as fried green tomatoes and okra and squash, potatoes mashed with country butter and cream, green beans cooked with fatback, buttered peas and carrots, cooked cabbage or slaw, fried chicken and gravy, country ham in red-eye gravy, biscuits or homemade rolls, and corn bread. Dessert was fresh fruit or berry cobbler, rice or bread pudding, and a pie or cake.

During the winter months when gardens were dormant, the boardinghouse hostess served canned or dried fruits and vegetables. Other favorites included shuck beans, or beans dried and cooked in the hull, and shelled and dried beans called soup beans. These dishes were cooked slowly all day with seasoning meat and served over corn bread. Potatoes were served in some form at nearly every meal, sometimes mashed or fried in bacon drippings, sometimes mixed with chopped onion, or sometimes served as potato salad. The same meal might include macaroni and cheese, candied sweet potatoes, chicken and dumplings with dressing and gravy, or a pot roast surrounded by vegetables or fresh pork tenderloin once the weather was cold enough to kill hogs. Collards, kale, and turnip and mustard greens were harvested during cold weather, cooked with seasoning meat, and served with a drizzle of vinegar. Winter was also the time when jars of pickled beets and beans and corn that had been canned during the summer months were brought from the cellar and served. Homemade jellies, apple butter, and molasses were spooned onto hot biscuits. Desserts included fried pies made with dried apples or peaches, pound cake served with canned peaches, and cobblers filled with canned fruits and berries.

The group seated at the table, sharing news of the day in a family atmosphere, might include railroad workers, schoolteachers, laborers, bachelors, traveling salesmen, troupes of entertainers, and local merchants, all attracted by the quality meal. Ultimately, the hostesses' ability to consistently provide good meals determined the success of boardinghouses.

See also: COTTAGE INDUSTRIES (BUSINESS, INDUSTRY, AND TECHNOLOGY).

—Patty Smithdeal Fulton, *Johnson City, Tennessee*

John Egerton, *Southern Food: At Home, on the Road, in History* (1993); Patty Smithdeal Fulton, . . . *And Garnish with Memories: The Life, Times, and Recipes of a Great Cook and Raconteur* (1998).

Bread Pudding

See Cakes and Cookies

Buttermilk

When cream is churned, buttermilk is the liquid left in the churn after the butter has risen to the top. For many reasons, residents of Appalachia made their own butter. Buttermilk was therefore a dietary mainstay, whether used as an ingredient or consumed as a beverage.

Because of its acidity, buttermilk is less subject to spoilage than sweet milk, a great asset in the days before refrigeration. That same acidity allowed it to interact with baking soda, providing leavening for many baked goods. Moreover, buttermilk also imparted a slight tartness that was appealing to many.

In addition to countless biscuit recipes (both yeast-risen and leavened with baking soda) that called for it, buttermilk was traditionally popular in corn bread and cornmeal dishes such as cornmeal battercakes and hush puppies. It was also used in cake fillings, glazes, pie fillings, and sweet breads and was frequently an ingredient in cake batter, especially if the cake was devil's food or included jam or dried fruit.

As a beverage, buttermilk was served with meals. Sometimes, corn bread was crumbled into a glass of buttermilk, and this would be eaten as a supper. Local doctors were known to prescribe buttermilk for children who had fevers or could not tolerate sweet milk.

Because of its wide use, easy availability, and resistance to spoilage, buttermilk remained part of everyday Appalachian life well into the twentieth century and continues to have a place in traditional recipes.

See also: CORN; DAIRY FARMS (AGRICULTURE).

—Stephanie D. Zonis, *Neshanic Station, New Jersey*

Cabbage

Appalachians have grown, cooked, and preserved cabbage for more than two centuries, and in that time it has become a regional culinary staple. Brought to the mountains by European settlers, cabbage was cultivated by Jamestown colonists as early as 1625. In Appalachia, the popular cabbage varieties eventually included red and green head cabbage, broccoli, collards, and kale, as well as the less popular Brussels sprouts, cauliflower, and kohlrabi.

True head cabbages are dependable, easy-to-grow crops that can be harvested in the spring and fall in southern Appalachia and in the summer in the northern sections of the region. They grow best under uniformly cool, moist conditions in rich-soiled valleys and hollows. In addition to that grown in family gardens, cabbage is cultivated commercially in north Georgia, western North Carolina, east Tennessee, and Virginia. Cabbages are simple to store for winter; they may be buried in the ground or kept in root cellars or (for commercial producers) in warehouses.

Cabbage is served both raw and cooked. In New York and Pennsylvania, popular Dutch and German dishes include boiled cabbage with potatoes and red cabbage with apples. In the southern mountains a favorite cold-weather dish is cabbage (or turnip greens) boiled with pork to yield not only cooked cabbage and pork, but also pot likker, a broth that is eaten with crumbled corn bread. Coleslaw, usually raw grated cabbage, is perhaps the most popular use of cold raw cabbage. Other traditional dishes include fried head cabbage cooked with pork and potatoes or with tomato sauce. After the cook softens the leaves by blanching or braising, cabbage pie and stuffed cabbage—cabbage leaves or even whole cabbages filled with rice and ground beef—can be prepared.

Pickling chopped cabbage to make sauerkraut and chowchow allows for storage and later reheating. During the first half of the twentieth century, sauerkraut, or kraut as it was known, was made in large crocks, tubs, barrels, buckets, and bathtubs. It was stored in any convenient area, such as the back porch, cellar, or can house, a small cool building with shelves for storing canned foods. Kraut was served hot with sausages and frankfurters; cold kraut dishes included kraut salad, kraut slaw, and refrigerator slaw.

See also: RELISHES.

—Collen Engle, *Meridian Café, Prospect, Kentucky*

Cakes and Cookies

The immense variety of cakes and cookies found in modern Appalachian homes and at church socials and community festivals bears little resemblance to those made by early settlers in the region. The baking of delicate batters was not amenable to open-hearth cooking. Even after the introduction of wood- and coal-burning kitchen stoves, oven temperatures were difficult to regulate. Furthermore, in the days before refined sugar and leavenings such as baking powder were readily available, baked desserts were more like breads than modern-style cakes. In fact, old recipes handed down through several generations suggest their breadlike origins: nut bread, pumpkin bread, gingerbread, and shortbread (or shortenin' bread). Joseph E. Dabney, in his book *Smokehouse Ham, Spoon Bread, and Scuppernong Wine: The Folklore and Art of Southern Appalachian Cooking* (1998), describes an early Indian cake (also called bannock bread), a sweet bread made of cornmeal, sorghum syrup, shortening, salt, and hot water and baked in a pan on an open hearth. Sometimes stewed pumpkin was added for moisture and flavor.

Lacking both the amenities of modern kitchens and the choices of leavenings and flavorings, the pioneer housewife seeking to create sweet treats for the end of a meal layered rounds of baked pastry with fresh or stewed fruit to create "stack" cake. This enduring favorite could have as many as sixteen layers. One of the most popular versions of this cake, especially during the winter months, was made with stewed dried apples. In some parts of the region, bakers still refer to their layer cakes as "stacked" cakes. Similarly, the spring favorite, strawberry shortcake, had a very humble beginning as fresh strawberries layered with baked pastry or split leftover biscuits. Many longtime residents of the region still prefer this to the soft, spongy cake typical of restaurant offerings of the dessert.

Similar in origin, though not usually considered cake, are puddings made from leftover biscuits, eggs, and milk or cream and sometimes flavored with jam or dried fruit or with spirits such as rum or brandy. These bread puddings were often a specialty in boardinghouses and country inns. If flavored with spirits, they were known as whiskey pudding. Another old dessert known as Indian pudding was made from cornmeal, eggs, butter, milk, and sorghum. The ingredients were first boiled in a pot over the fire, then baked and served with cream or fruit sauce. Sometimes dried fruit or spirits were added to the batter. Other baked puddings were similar to very dense, moist cakes. The most common cake of this type is persimmon pudding, made from the fruit of the wild persimmon tree. Unlike the Japanese variety, wild persimmons are a highly astringent fruit when green, but when they ripen following a hard frost, the pulp is sweet and distinctively flavored. Persimmon-based desserts—pudding, cakes, and cookies—are prized by modern Appalachian families, as is persimmon bread, flavored with spices and dense with nuts and brandy-soaked raisins.

Many of these early cakes were close in form and texture to modern sweet breads or quick breads. Made of butter, eggs, flour, and sour milk or cream and sweetened with sorghum or honey, these sturdy cakes were often enriched with hickory nuts and black walnuts or dried or pureed fruits. Spices such as ginger often added flavor. In the southern Appalachians, sweet potatoes were often used in precursors of such contemporary favorites as banana nut bread and zucchini bread.

By the end of the nineteenth century, as refined sugar, more finely milled flour, and other pantry staples such as baking powder were more readily available, cakes became more delicate in texture, even though they were made from many of the same ingredients as before. The most common of the old-time recipes was the 1-2-3-4 cake, whose name reflected the measurement of the ingredients: one cup of butter, two cups of sugar, three cups of flour, and four eggs. These measures were adjusted, depending on availability. One documented variation, the two-egg cake, was made when eggs were scarce; sometimes, rendered pork fat (lard) was substituted for butter. Home bakers used this recipe as the basis for the many variations of the frosted layer cake. As with loaf cakes, nuts such as hickory nuts and black walnuts were added to the batter or sprinkled on top of the frosted cake. Cocoa was used to make rich chocolate cakes, the most popular of which was the dark, rich devil's food cake. Coconut layer cake, made with fresh coconut and boiled frosting, was especially popular at Christmas. Other holiday cakes had hearty fillings made of nuts, raisins, and coconut and flavored with rye whiskey or bourbon.

Another regional specialty (one more versatile than its name might suggest) is the pound cake. Originally a loaf cake, but later baked in a tube pan, the batter was a heavy mixture of one-pound measures of the main ingredients: butter, sugar, eggs, and flour. It was flavored with spices, as well as brandy, vanilla, or lemon juice. A holiday variation of the pound cake is the Christmas fruitcake. Families spent days cracking and shelling nuts, grating fresh coconut, and chopping dried fruits for this special cake, which required several hours of baking. The cooled cake was often wrapped in brandy- or bourbon-soaked cloths, assuring that it kept well during the cold winter months.

With the introduction of cake mixes in the 1940s, home baking became less time-consuming, but many Appalachian bakers shunned the boxed mixes and continued to make scratch cakes from favorite family recipes. Even after cakes were available at every grocery and specialty bakery, many in the region preferred to offer their families home-baked cakes.

Long before chocolate chips, Appalachian cooks were making small cakes, or cookies, for their families. Like cakes, cookies evolved with the availability of kitchen amenities and pantry staples. Immigrants brought their food traditions. Scottish shortbread and German ginger cookies, for example, were readily adapted in the region, as were nut and fruit drop cookies, which soon became standard fare in many lunchboxes. Generations of children have grown up enjoying homemade cookies with intriguing names: jumbles, snickerdoodles, gingersnaps, and hermits.

More time-consuming and labor-intensive, rolled cookies were nonetheless valued for their versatility, especially during the holidays, when they were cut into fanciful seasonal shapes and decorated with colored sugar or frosting. The icebox cookie was a time-saver for busy housewives, however. Made from rolls of dough, sliced into rounds, and baked, it eliminated the laborious cutting and re-rolling of the dough. Bar cookies such as brownies, baked in a shallow pan, cooled, and then cut into bars or squares, were even easier and just as tasty.

See also: DRIED APPLE STACK CAKE; SWEETENERS; SWEETS.

—Kenneth G. Gilbert, *Ohio Valley College;* June W. Hayes, *Hayes and Associates International, San Antonio, Texas;* Gabriele I. Kupitz, *Brigham Young University;* Rebeccah Kinnamon Neff, *Raleigh, North Carolina;* and Edelene Wood, *National Wild Foods Association*

Bill Neal, *Biscuits, Spoon Bread, and Sweet Potato Pie* (1990); Linda Garland Page and Eliot Wigginton, eds., *The Foxfire Book of Appalachian Cookery* (1992); Beth Tartan, *North Carolina and Old Salem Cookery* (1992).

Casseroles

Casserole is a term that describes both a utensil and a food cooked in that utensil. Although the name did not come into common use until the last half of the twentieth century, many early Appalachians used a traditional casserole cooking process to prepare many of their family meals. Typical early casserole utensils had shallow, sometimes bulging sides, easily grasped handles, and a slightly arched, tight-fitting lid. The Dutch oven, while not truly a casserole utensil in the modern sense, was frequently used to cook many one-dish-type meals in the homes of early settlers. Unlike modern casserole dishes, which are made of glass, coated alloy, or stainless steel, early casserole containers were made from clay, iron, or glass.

The traditional casserole cooking method is to cook raw food slowly in a casserole utensil with a tight-fitting lid. Generous amounts of butter, fat, or oil are used as well as a small amount of liquid, usually stock. As the food cooks, juice from the food condenses on the lid and supplies a measure of self-basting, although some hand-basting with the pan fats is often necessary. Cooking takes place at a low simmer, condensing the food juices into a delicious reduction.

In this fashion, early Appalachian settlers cooked wild game such as venison, rabbit, squirrel, birds, and wild turkey, as well as chicken, pork, mutton, and beef. Dried beans and other legumes were also combined with meats, and various vegetables could be added to make one-dish meals.

Contemporary cooks would find it difficult to recognize early settlers' casseroles. In recent times the term has come to mean a type of self-service dish—such as a bean, broccoli, or potato casserole—that is often served in American homes and on buffet tables at dinners on the grounds, family reunions, school banquets, and other gatherings. Consisting of a combination of precooked and quick-cooking foods, this type of casserole is a mixture of several foods, including pasta or rice, a protein source, and vegetables in a sauce. Many casseroles are oven-to-table dishes, meaning that the food is served in the dish in which it was baked. The modern-day casserole, while sometimes baked covered, is usually cooked uncovered in a moderate oven to avoid building up too much steam and breaking down the sauce in which it is served.

Casseroles often have a crumb topping that protects the food and absorbs fat. Popular Appalachian casseroles are made with ramps, hominy, and squash. Within Appalachian communities, cooks are known for their sweet potato, cheese grits, pork chop, onion, sausage, and oyster casseroles.

See also: CAST-IRON COOKWARE; FUNERAL FOODS; WOODSTOVE COOKING.

—Betty Greer, *University of Tennessee*

Better Homes and Gardens Heritage Cookbook (1975); Irma Rombauer, Marion Becker, and Ethan Becker, *Joy of Cooking* (1997).

Cast-Iron Cookware

Cookware made from cast iron, an alloy of iron and carbon, arrived in the Appalachian region with European settlement, and it remains highly valued for its durability and its ability to retain and evenly distribute heat. As the region was settled and industrialization proceeded, blast furnaces were built for smelting iron to make a product called pig iron; from this iron, manufacturers produced farm implements, stoves, decorative wrought-iron items, and cookware including cauldrons, Dutch ovens, chicken fryers, skillets, muffin pans, griddles, teapots, and cornstick bread pans.

Cookware such as the Dutch oven and cauldron was so valued that neighbors often borrowed from one another because not all families could afford to own the items. The Dutch oven was a three-legged pot that stood over the coals and had a flanged lid on which coals could be heaped. Late models had a swivel handle so the oven could be turned around for even cooking. Entire family meals could be cooked in this pot. According to legend, the item got its name from the Dutch peddlers who sold it door-to-door in colonial America. The cauldron, a large, three-legged, open kettle, was sometimes called a "rendering pot" because it was used in making lard. The cauldron was pressed into service on wash days for boiling clothes.

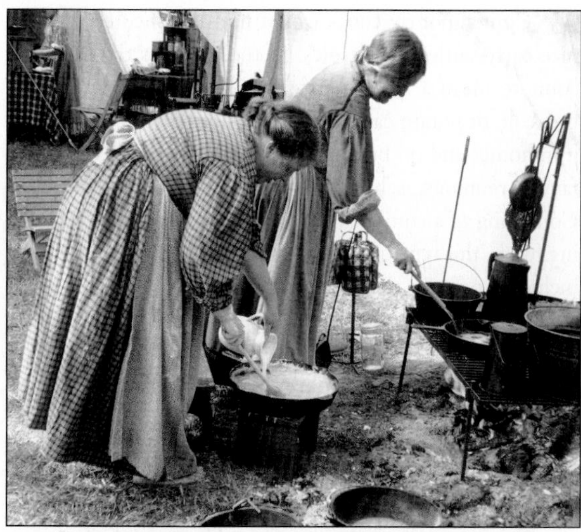

Civil War reenactors of the Georgia Southern Ladies Association demonstrate preparation of food using cast-iron cookware at Stone Mountain Park, Georgia, 2002. Cast-iron cookware is still highly prized by Appalachian cooks.

Other useful cast-iron items included spiders, saucepans, andirons, and lug poles. A long-handled skillet on legs, the spider was used over a small bed of coals pulled out from the main fire. Saucepans and griddles were also available with legs and long handles. Andirons not only held wood in the fireplace but also could be fitted to support an iron spit for roasting meat. Some fireplaces were equipped with a lug pole from which a notched rack, called a trammel, could be used to raise and lower pots. Interlocking pothooks were also used to adjust the height of the pot from the fire.

Cast-iron cookware continues to be popular with home-style cooks and is essential to traditional southern Appalachian cooking. Many cooks maintain a separate cast-iron skillet for baking corn bread and biscuits. If the skillets are properly seasoned, the bread will cook in them without sticking, and if they are used exclusively for baking, they can be washed without detergent.

In some families, pieces of cast-iron cookware passed down from parents, grandparents, and great-grandparents are priceless keepsakes. In retail stores, flea markets, and antique shops, customers continue to seek out cast-iron items. While old cast-iron pieces have increased in value, new items such as the holiday muffin pan, square skillet, and nine-inch grill pan have been recently developed to meet the changing food habits of Americans.

See also: CASSEROLES; OPEN-HEARTH COOKING; WOODSTOVE COOKING.

—Betty Greer, *University of Tennessee*

Molly Harrison, *The Kitchen in History* (1972); W. J. Keep, *Cast Iron: A Record of Original Research* (1902).

Cherokee Foods

See Native American Foodways

Chicken and Beef

Special breeds of chicken and methods of preparing them were brought to Appalachia by Scots-Irish, British, and German immigrants, and African slaves also introduced methods of cooking poultry. Roasted, boiled, fried, or baked into pies, chicken has been a common food for Sunday and holiday meals for guests, and for weddings, homecomings, and wakes.

Over the years, cooks have attempted to improve the flavor of chicken in various ways, soaking it in buttermilk or salting and seasoning it with paprika, parsley, hot pepper sauce, lemon juice, or even bourbon. In *The Virginia House-Wife*, first published in 1824, Mary Randolph advocated dredging cut-up chickens in flour, sprinkling them with salt, and frying them in boiling lard until golden brown. Gravy made from the pan drippings and parsley were proposed as garnishes. This technique, along with embellishments from the cook, was a common recipe for fried chicken. Others preferred coating chicken pieces with buttermilk batter to achieve a crispy crust during frying. The pan drippings were subsequently blended with flour and milk to make cream gravy, which was generously ladled over the chicken and a side dish of mashed potatoes. According to Mark F. Sohn, in his cookbook *Hearty Country Cooking: Savory Southern Favorites* (1998), it was an Appalachian tradition for the families of the newly deceased to be comforted with platters of fried chicken, while gravediggers were fed gravedigger's stew made of boiled chicken and homegrown vegetables.

Many early settlers to the region also brought cattle, which were primarily used for dairy production. When beef was used for food in rural Appalachia, it was dried, smoked, or preserved with salt. Beef did not become a popular part of Appalachian meals until after 1877, when Gustavus Swift and Philip Armour developed refrigerated railroad cars. Shipped from the Chicago slaughterhouses, beef began to replace lamb in such dishes as Kentucky burgoo and was added to squirrel and chicken in Brunswick stew, a coastal dish adopted into the eastern edges of Appalachia. Served with fresh produce, the mixtures were often cooked over open fires at fairs, church gatherings, and barbecues.

People in northern Appalachia often used German and Swiss techniques to dry beef, then soaked it in a vinegar-sugar-water solution before serving. In Tennessee, spiced round beef was usually available around Christmas and consisted of beef roast that had been threaded with pork fat, rolled in spices, and cured in brine.

When ground beef became more readily available, many casseroles were developed, including beef shepherd's pie and layered beef casseroles. As if to apologize for using beef, later cooks often called beef dishes by other animals' names. Pig in a blanket (northern Appalachia) is actually seasoned ground beef sealed in biscuit dough and baked, and beef birds are pounded steak rolled with a filling and braised in gravy. Sometimes beef with a bread stuffing was called mock duck or mock turkey.

See also: CATTLE (AGRICULTURE); CHICKEN AND DUMPLINGS; POULTRY (AGRICULTURE).

—Catherine D. Lucas, *Mere Catherine Cuisine, Boca Raton, Florida*

John T. Edge, *A Gracious Plenty: Recipes and Recollections from the American South* (1999); John Egerton, *Southern Food: At Home, on the Road, in History* (1993); Harold McGee, *On Food and Cooking* (1984); Mary Emma Showalter, *Mennonite Community Cookbook* (1950).

Chicken and Dumplings

Chicken and dumplings is one of the primary main dishes of the Appalachian kitchen, and most regional cookbooks contain recipes for it. Until the 1950s, rural families commonly killed, cleaned, and dressed their own chickens and cooked them on wood-burning stoves in cast-iron cookware.

For chicken and dumplings, the bird is stewed, cooled, deboned, and returned to the broth. While the chicken and broth simmer, the dumplings, colloquially known as dough balls, slipperies, or slickums, are prepared. Neither a biscuit nor a bread, dumplings are pieces of dough made with a base of flour or cornmeal mixed with varying amounts of milk, baking powder, and shortening. The most common dumplings eaten with chicken in this manner are drop, or slick, dumplings, dropped by the spoonful into the broth and cooked until they are light, tender, and biscuitlike. Some Appalachian cooks add butter and chopped giblets as well as boiled eggs to this mixture; others add one or more additional ingredients such as sherry, lemon peel, parsley, or pepper.

Besides the drop dumpling, which can also be cooked in soups, stews, or with vegetables such as tomatoes and beans, there are two other types of dumplings. The potato dumpling (or *Kartoffelkloesse*), originally prepared by Germans settling in Maryland, Pennsylvania, and New York, is served with beef, game, or cabbage. The slick, slickum, or flat sinker is a flour dumpling that becomes slippery to the touch during the cooking process. Unlike drop dumplings, the unleavened dough in the flat sinker is rolled thin on a floured surface and then cut into strips about two inches long before being added to a boiling broth.

Dumplings have also been prepared as desserts by putting leavened dough into pots of boiling rhubarb, blackberries, or other sweetened fruits of the season. Easy to prepare, the finished dish of stewed fruit and dumplings has long been served in the Appalachian region as an alternative to baked cobblers with a crust. Another version of a popular sweet dumpling is made by wrapping pastry dough around a cored or sliced apple with sugar and spices, tying the mixture together with cloth, and then boiling it in water. The recipe for this dumpling can be traced back through early recipe books such as Hannah Glasse's *The Art of Cookery Made Plain and Easy*, published in England in 1747 and widely used in Virginia and the other American colonies.

See also: CHICKEN AND BEEF; SWEETS.

—Sidney Saylor Farr, *Berea, Kentucky*, and Margaret C. Woolfolk, *Williamsburg, Virginia*

Joseph E. Dabney, *Smokehouse Ham, Spoon Bread, and Scuppernong Wine: The Folklore and Art of Southern Appalachian Cooking* (1998); Sidney Saylor Farr, *Table Talk: Appalachian Meals and Memories* (1995); Mark F. Sohn, *Mountain Country Cooking: A Gathering of the Best Recipes from the Smokies to the Blue Ridge* (1996).

Cobblers

The fruit cobbler may be the quintessential dessert of the Appalachians. Variations of this popular dish have long graced tables in mountain cabins, farmhouses, boardinghouses, and country mansions. Country inns in the region promote their prized peach cobblers. The name may derive from the "cobbling" together of commonly available ingredients or from the resemblance of the baked top to a cobblestone street. Possibly descended from the crackle or crisp, sweetened fruit baked with a crumbly topping, the cobbler is a cousin of the Betty (as in apple brown Betty, baked layers of spiced apples, bread crumbs, sugar, and butter). It is certainly in the same dessert family as New England grunts (desserts made by dropping biscuit dough on top of boiling berries) and buckles (coffee cakes baked with berries and a crumbly topping).

Cobbler recipes vary by the type of crust. They may require a soft batter of sugar, flour, eggs, butter, and milk; a simple pastry crust; or heartier biscuitlike dough. Some old recipes call for several layers of fruit and pastry. A lattice-top crust is traditional in some areas, and some cooks add a dusting of cinnamon or nutmeg. Whether it goes into the pan first or last, the fruit usually ends up on the bottom after baking although in some variants, the fruit is dispersed throughout the batter. Blackberries, blueberries, peaches, cherries, apples, and pears are most popular for cobblers, which are usually served warm with cream or ice cream.

See also: CAKES AND COOKIES; FRIED PIES; FRUITS AND BERRIES; PIES.

—Rebeccah Kinnamon Neff, *Raleigh, North Carolina*

Coffee

From the days of early Euro-American settlement in the mountains, Appalachians have enjoyed drinking coffee. Seventy-five to 150 years ago, coffee, along with salt, pepper, and sugar, was one of the few food items that mountain farmers purchased.

Prior to the advent of packaged coffee, fresh coffee beans were roasted in fireplaces, hearths, and stoves. In some areas families continued to roast coffee beans at home until the 1940s. Beans could be roasted in light pans, cast-iron skillets, or spiders, which are long-handled cast-iron pans with legs. Once the beans were brown, fully dry, and brittle, they were cooled and ground in a hand-turned mill or grinder.

In many homes coffee was made every morning, and because the process required time, the task was often shared. Like barnyard chores, coffee making often began before the sun came up. Some families used the hearth rather than a stove for making coffee, since the stove was occupied by biscuits, fried apples, pies, and eggs. Sometimes the coffee was boiled in a pan of water with a raw egg broken into the boiling mixture to help the grounds settle to the bottom.

During the Great Depression or other hard times, inventive cooks made coffee with wheat bran and cornmeal. They also made dandelion coffee and chicory coffee with the dried and ground roots of these plants. Other specialty blends have included coffee sweetened with honey, molasses, or sorghum; cinnamon coffee made by adding oil of cinnamon; chocolate coffee made with Mexican coffee chocolate; and southern comfort coffee enlivened with sour mash or bourbon whiskey. Black coffee ranges from a light, tealike drink to a deep black brew.

See also: SWEETENERS.

—Rebecca Maksel, *Ashburn, Virginia*

Joseph E. Dabney, *Smokehouse Ham, Spoon Bread, and Scuppernong Wine: The Folklore and Art of Southern Appalachian Cooking* (1998); Linda Garland Page and Eliot Wigginton, eds., *The Foxfire Book of Appalachian Cookery* (1984); Mark F. Sohn, *Mountain Country Cooking: A Gathering of the Best Recipes from the Smokies to the Blue Ridge* (1996).

Cookbooks

The first completely American cookbook appeared in 1796, when Amelia Simmons published a small and unprepossessing book entitled *American Cookery*. While there is no evidence that this work was used in Appalachia, it was important because Simmons focused on the food and cooking of the United States. Almost thirty years later, in 1824, Mary Randolph refined this focus on local foods with her classic book *The Virginia House-Wife*. Written especially for Virginia cooks, Randolph's book reflects both an English and a subtle French influence while introducing the importance of Native American and African traditions to the diet. Many dishes that have remained southern and Appalachian favorites, including sweet potato pudding, okra, black-eyed peas, catfish, Apoquinimic cakes (a form of beaten biscuit), boiled turnip tops, and pound cake, were carefully recorded in this popular book that went through nineteen printings before the Civil War.

For pioneers traveling down the Ohio River or across the Alleghenies and through the Cumberland Gap in the late 1700s and early 1800s, a diet of wild foods consisting of squirrel, venison, berries, and greens gradually expanded to include cultivated crops and domesticated animals. The fundamental knowledge of preparing such food often depended on observation and oral communication. In 1839, Lettice Bryan collected much of that wisdom in an inclusive volume entitled *The Kentucky Housewife*. Encyclopedic in scope, Bryan's book contained more than thirteen hundred recipes that embraced the best of wild and cultivated foods and included instructions for barbecued shoat (young hog), beans, biscuits, cakes, corn, bread pudding, and apple butter.

Following the Civil War, a uniquely American type of cookbook appeared when groups of women published the best of their recipe collections to benefit charitable causes such as hospitals, churches, temperance societies, and Confederate relief organizations. Reflecting the social and cultural fabric of their specific area, community cookbooks showed the meals that people were actually eating at home rather than the idealized recipes presented in many commercial cookbooks. Although varying tremendously in organization and size, these charity books frequently contained bits of local history and lore as well as advertisements for the town businesses and new appliances, gadgets, and food products of the time. The first charity cookbook published in Kentucky was *Housekeeping in the Bluegrass*, compiled by the women of the First Presbyterian Church in Paris in 1875. This treasure trove of true Kentucky recipes and household hints was so successful that it had at least nine printings with more than twenty thousand copies sold. These community cookbooks—including a 1911 Charleston, West Virginia, volume containing recipes for Dixie pie and hominy fritters and the 1907 *Knoxville Cook Book* with three pages devoted to the art of cooking pigeons—are valued as historical source material that preserve Appalachian recipes and foodways that otherwise might not have survived.

Two other important community-style cookbooks that reflect central and southern Appalachian cooking of the mid-twentieth century are *Smoky Mountain Magic* (1960) by the Junior League of Johnson City, Tennessee, and *What's Cooking in Kentucky* (1970) by Irene Hayes. Both books are still in print decades after initial publication and are widely comprehensive, having well over one thousand recipes each.

Two community cookbooks especially reflect the diversity of northern Appalachia. In 1950 the Community Folk Festival of New York's Triple Cities (Binghamton, Johnson City, and Endicott) published *The Folk Festival Cookbook*, a book of recipes representing the cooking of twenty-six different ethnic groups living in the Triple Cities. This pattern continued in Johnstown, Pennsylvania, with the publication in 1989 of *The Johnstown Area Heritage Association Cookbook*. It, too, is divided into chapters by ethnic group. Both books include chapters for German, Greek, Hungarian, Irish, Italian, Jewish, Mexican, Polish, Scottish, Slovak, and Ukrainian cuisines. Additional groups represented in the Triple Cities book are Armenian, Dutch, Finn, French, Korean, Lebanese, and Scandinavian.

In 1978 the Asheville Citizen-Times Publishing Company published John Parris's *Mountain Cooking*. This book is significant because it presents interview-based columns that Parris wrote for the *Asheville Citizen-Times* on topics such as ramps, taverns, honey, poke sallet, rye coffee, and molasses candy pullings. Each entry is anecdotal, and the book represents food topics important in the Asheville region. Sidney Saylor Farr's *More Than Moonshine: Appalachian Recipes and Recollections*, a 1983 book from the University of Pittsburgh Press, is also impressive. Here, Farr presents the traditions of her childhood and family from Stoney Fork in southeastern Kentucky.

In 1984 *The Foxfire Book of Appalachian Cookery* was published as one of a series of popular books documenting mountain customs and life. Wholly devoted to the foodways of southern Appalachia, this grassroots cookbook is interwoven with anecdotes, practical country wisdom, and more than four hundred authentic recipes that chronicle the honest pleasure of good eating. Eminently personal in the same way charity cookbooks are, this classic volume favors such regional recipes as poke salad, stack pie, and persimmon cake.

In recent years two Appalachian books have been recognized for excellence by the James Beard Foundation. In 1996 Mark F. Sohn's *Mountain Country Cooking: A Gathering of the Best Recipes from the Smokies to the Blue Ridge* received a Cookbook of the Year nomination in the category Foods of the Americas, and in 1999 Joseph E. Dabney's book *Smokehouse Ham, Spoon Bread, and Scuppernong Wine: The Folklore and Art of Southern Appalachian Cooking* was named the Cookbook of the Year. Sohn, a lover of food and a trained chef who started cooking at age eleven, presents some three hundred typically Appalachian recipes. He developed and tested the recipes to reflect their regionwide derivation and to make them workable in modern kitchens. Each recipe includes an updated version or healthy choice alternative. Dabney, who is a journalist, presents a sociocultural history. In the forward, John Egerton, author of *Southern Food: At Home, on the Road, in History*, calls Dabney's book a "patchwork" of people, places, stories, history, and recipes. With its long bibliography and extensive indexes, the book successfully records recent food history.

See also: FESTIVALS, FOOD; HAUTE CUISINE.

—Margaret Woolfolk, *Williamsburg, Virginia*

Joseph E. Dabney, *Smokehouse Ham, Spoon Bread, and Scuppernong Wine: The Folklore and Art of Southern Appalachian Cooking* (1998); Linda Garland Page and Eliot Wigginton, eds., *The Foxfire Book of Appalachian Cookery* (1984); Mark F. Sohn, *Mountain Country Cooking: A Gathering of the Best Recipes from the Smokies to the Blue Ridge* (1996).

Corn

Indigenous to the Americas, corn was both primary grain and vegetable for the Native American tribes who inhabited the Appalachian region centuries before the influx of European settlers in the eighteenth century. In Appalachian diet and culture, the importance of corn can hardly be overstated. This Indian grain was, for the early American settler from Europe, not only an acceptable substitute for those known abroad (wheat, barley, rye), but it was also more versatile and keenly adaptable to the rougher growing conditions encountered in the New World, particularly the Appalachian region.

These factors made corn the grain of choice in early settlements throughout the nation. But as land was cleared and agriculture evolved, the cultivation of other grains began in the New World, and wheat, in particular, became the primary ingredient for bread throughout most of the country by the nineteenth century. In the Appalachian Mountains, however, the high yield from corn plus its many uses and adaptable growing nature made it a cornerstone of the mountain diet.

Local cultures in Appalachia have often constructed menus around a grain, legume, and meat or dairy product that together provide a maximum of what dietician/food historian Frances Moore Lappé calls "usable protein." In the southern Appalachians, that combination appears as soup beans (pinto beans seasoned with a little meat) and corn bread. In the northern Appalachians, Native Americans and early settlers often prepared dried corn with dried beans and salt pork seasoning in a dish called succotash. A fresh version of succotash, made with green or butter beans and corn from the garden, is an important modern offering.

Corn has been used as a foodstuff in a variety of states. Fresh corn, traditionally called green corn, is consumed on the cob after light boiling in water. Native Americans of the region often built a fire in the cornfield itself, predating the modern culinary obsession with boiling corn as soon as it is picked. A more common, and arguably more flavorful, way of preparing fresh cob corn in the mountains is to roast it wrapped in shucks over the coals of a campfire, fireplace, or outdoor grill. So popular is this form of preparation that the term *roasting ear* (often elided and pronounced as one word: *rosineer*) is used throughout the middle and southern Appalachians to refer to any green corn for eating, even if the preparation method is to be boiling or frying.

Commonly called fried corn, perhaps the most popular method of preparation throughout Appalachia is actually fresh corn that is slow-simmered in a bit of pork fat. The dish is also sometimes made with butter, but bacon grease or lard is more common in the mountains. To make it, corn kernels are cut from the cob, and the cob itself is "milked" to extract juice. Then all is simmered in a heavy (generally cast-iron) skillet on top of the stove, with a bit of milk or water added, until it reaches a creamy, tender consistency. Although this dish is prepared throughout the United States, especially in the South, a specific version in which the whole skillet is then placed in a hot oven to crust on the bottom and top seems to be particular to the southern Appalachian region.

Corn was canned by itself and in combination with green beans throughout the region and also put up as a relish (commonly with peppers) called piccalilli. The influence of German settlers is seen in pickle corn, a canned product common from Pennsylvania all the way through southern Appalachia. *Sauerbohne* is a method of preserving green beans in sauerkraut-like brine that came to the mountains with settlers from the Palatinate Rhineland. Mountain cooks quickly added corn cut from the cob to their "pickle beans" and soon prepared corn alone in this salty brine as well. These "pickles" are not consumed as a relish but as a side dish, drained of brine and sautéed in bacon grease or lard before serving, often with corn bread.

In the Appalachians, dried corn was eaten out of hand as parched corn, used for popcorn, and treated with lye to be turned into hominy. Although whole hominy is rarely eaten elsewhere in the United States—the Southwest is an exception—it is still served in the southern mountains. And while the rest of the South favors grits—hominy ground to a cereal consistency, simmered in liquid, and served as a savory side dish at breakfast or other meals—most cooks in the mountains prefer quicker-cooking cornmeal mush, which is chilled into a loaf, sliced, and fried in bacon grease. This may be eaten as a side to breakfast, topped with something such as hash, or served with sorghum syrup poured over it as a light supper or breakfast.

The most significant use of corn in the Appalachians, however, is as meal for making bread. Indian bread, hoecake, johnnycake, ash-cake, dodgers, pone: there are a number of ways of turning ground corn into bread, and the vernacular of the region has many words to describe them, often varying from one area to another. Corn bread was the daily staff of life to such an extent that in the mountain South it was often referred to simply as "bread," with "light bread" signifying the common wheat loaves bought at the store. In addition to bread made from dried corn ground into meal, both Native Americans and early settlers of the region also made bread from a mixture of green corn kernels and milk, which was pounded and kneaded before baking. Gritted corn bread was made from corn allowed to dry, or partially dry, on the cob and cooked after the kernels were scraped across a heavy grater. Again, corn's versatility is demonstrated by this ability to make bread from the grain in a number of states.

Lula Conrad, following a recipe handed down from her mother and grandmother, makes a batch of gritted corn bread, Sugar Grove, Virginia, 1954.

Corn shuckings were an essential part of the Appalachian culture up until the mid-twentieth century. The community came together to shuck or strip the dried cobs of kernels that were then taken to the mill to be ground or ground at home by hand. Hog-slaughtering season brought crackling bread—corn bread containing cracklings, or the pieces of meat left in the pot after lard was rendered.

Biscuits were generally made for breakfast, but corn bread graced the table at most other meals and was sometimes baked more than once a day. The ease of preparation and short baking time were boons to busy mountain cooks. The portability of pones, dodgers, and cakes made them ideal, first for Native Americans on the trail, then for pioneers, and ultimately for miners and their children, who had to pack a meal in a tin lunch pail. Hot corn bread accompanied the other dishes at the main meal of the day, and a light supper was often made on corn bread alone, crumbled into a tall glass and covered with sweet milk or buttermilk. In some southern regions of the mountains, this dish is called "crumble-in."

White dent and white flint corn were most commonly grown and ground into meal in the region. People in the southern part of the mountains developed an affection for cornmeal's strong flavor and relative lack of sweetness. Although it is common farther north in Appalachia to add flour, more leavening, and sugar to the batter of corn bread, in the southern mountains these additions, particularly sweetening, are scorned.

See also: CORN (AGRICULTURE); GRISTMILLS; MOONSHINE.

—Ronni Lundy, *Asheville, North Carolina*

Joseph E. Dabney, *Smokehouse Ham, Spoon Bread, and Scuppernong Wine: The Folklore and Art of Southern Appalachian Cooking* (1998); Betty Fussell, *The Story of Corn: The Myths and History, the Culture and Agriculture, the Art and Science of America's Quintessential Crop* (1992); John Thorne, *Serious Pig: An American Cook in Search of His Roots* (1996).

Corn Bread and Hoecakes

See Corn

Country Ham

See Pork

Cushaw Squash

One of the oldest squash varieties eaten today is cushaw, a large, smooth, hard-skinned winter squash. It is Appalachia's dominant squash because of its size and because it has long been adaptable to the mountain climate.

Europeans who arrived in the early 1500s learned from native tribes how to cultivate and eat cushaw and other squash (which the explorers mistakenly called melons or pumpkins). Squashes are thought to be the first foods grown by indigenous Americans, even before beans and corn.

Green- and white-striped cushaws resemble yellow crookneck squash but weigh from ten to twenty-five pounds and reach twelve to thirty inches in length. All-white cushaws grow to twenty or thirty pounds and look like squat pumpkins. Indeed, some mountain people call them Indian pumpkins, but botanists are undecided about the relationship between the two.

The texture of the nutty-flavored flesh of the cushaw is a cross between the density of butternut squash and the looseness of spaghetti squash. Good for baking, cushaws readily absorb honey or sorghum, as well as butter. They are also used in soups, pies, and cakes. Planted as early as "Vine Day" (May 10, the traditional day of planting cucumbers and "kershaws" in some areas), cushaws ripen by September. In late fall, very large cushaws become fall decoration or food for a crowd—a twenty-pounder easily yields enough baked squash to feed sixty.

See also: NATIVE AMERICAN AGRICULTURE (AGRICULTURE); NATIVE AMERICAN FOODWAYS; PAWPAWS.

—Marilyn Canna, *Culinary Historians of Chicago*

Dinner on the Grounds

A common occasion throughout central and southern Appalachia, dinner on the grounds, particularly identified with more rural areas, is most often an event of late summer associated with church activities such as annual homecomings. Dinners are also spread in the same fashion at graveyard reunions and other community and family reunions. No matter what the event, dinner on the grounds is an opportunity for locals to provide hospitality for visiting friends and family.

Featuring large potluck dishes, such meals serve as showplaces for favorite recipes and inevitably feature iced tea, fried chicken, ham, casseroles, potato salad, corn bread, and homemade pies. Although these foods are no longer everyday fare, tradition dictates that they highlight dinners on the grounds.

At church homecomings dinner on the grounds customarily follows morning worship and precedes an afternoon of singing. While men may continue to be primarily responsible for the worship services in most traditional Appalachian churches, women have important roles in the culture and ritual of the community as they plan, prepare, and serve community meals. Women usually cook large portions of their favorite foods and leave the worship service early to set the food out on the tables. In some places, the tables are temporary, but permanent facilities are often created in anticipation of regular use. Since past members and other visitors are invited, attendance often exceeds seating space, forcing diners to sit on the ground or retreat to automobiles or church steps.

Dinner on the grounds at South Cleveland Church of God Tabernacle, Cleveland, Tennessee, c. 1910. At church homecomings, dinner on the grounds usually follows morning worship and precedes an afternoon of singing.

Although dinner on the grounds is a tradition in many denominations and independent groups in Appalachia, the practice probably originated with Presbyterians as they spread throughout the region. Likely going back to earlier Scottish roots, from at least the eighteenth century American Presbyterians developed the custom of holding joint communion services when an ordained minister was sent from the Synod of Philadelphia to serve communion to several congregations at once. In such settings, the church grounds become sacred space and the meal reflects John Calvin's emphasis on the covenanted community of the saints. In terms of theological importance, such meals are reminiscent of the sacrament of the Lord's Supper (communion) and New Testament–style love feasts; additionally, they point toward the future marriage supper of the Lamb. The meal becomes a sacred meal reflecting one's ongoing participation in the life of family, church, and community. With scattered family members returning for such special occasions, the meal represents an interweaving of both faith and family.

As churches are able to afford fellowship halls and gymnasiums, especially in the modern age of air conditioning, dinner on the grounds has been abandoned in many places. Recently, however, the practice has seen an upsurge as an integral part of the revival of Sacred Harp singings.

See also: FUNERAL FOODS; MEMORIAL SERVICES (RELIGION); WOMEN IN TRADITIONAL CHURCHES (RELIGION).

—David G. Roebuck, *Hal Bernard Dixon Jr. Pentecostal Research Center*

Dana Adkins Campbell, "Feeding Body and Soul," *Southern Living* (April 1996); Gwen Kennedy Neville, *Kinship and Pilgrimage: Rituals of Reunion in American Protestant Culture* (1987); Gwen Kennedy Neville and John H. Westerhoff III, *Learning through Liturgy* (1978).

Dried Apple Stack Cake

The dried apple stack cake is a distinctive southern Appalachian cake. Called by names such as apple stack cake, Confederate old-fashioned stack cake, and Kentucky pioneer washday cake, the apple stack cake is many layered, low in fat, and not sweet. It is made with layers of stiff cookielike dough flavored with ginger and sorghum and spread with a sweet, spiced apple filling. When served, the cake is tall, heavy, and moist.

The origin of the recipe is uncertain. According to one story, James Harrod, the pioneer who founded Harrodsburg, Kentucky, brought the stack cake directions with him when he traveled the Wilderness Road to Kentucky.

Following the original recipe is a long, tedious process requiring up to five hours. Dough for the cake is rolled or pressed out into very thin layers and baked in cast-iron skillets. Cooked, sweetened, and spiced dried apples are then spread between the layers. Some cooks, however, use regular cake layers and a filling of cooked fresh apples, applesauce, or apple butter. While stack cake made this easy way is tasty, it is hardly comparable to versions using apple butter and the flavorful dried apple filling.

Although sorghum was considered unsuitable for most traditional cakes and pies, it worked very well in the stack cake. Sometimes cooks varied the amount of sweetening by adding brown sugar to the sorghum.

The dried apple stack cake was a favorite pioneer wedding cake. Weddings were celebrated with "in-fares," where people gathered to party, dance, and eat potluck food. Because wedding cakes were expensive, neighbor cooks brought cake layers to donate to the bride's family, who cooked the dried apple filling. The bride's popularity was often gauged by the number of layers in her wedding cake. Sometimes there would be as many as twelve layers, but the average was seven or eight. Stack cakes were also served at family reunions, church suppers, Christmas dinners, and other large gatherings.

While modern Appalachian cooks purchase dried apples for the cake filling, their predecessors dried their own apples in the fall and winter months. After being cored and peeled, apples were quartered and cut into thin slices. Then they were dried by one of several methods. Sometimes they were spread on cloth or screens and placed on top of a shed or other flat area to dry in the sun; a fine wire screen put over them kept out insects. This method, however, was chancy because of high humidity, cloudy skies, and frequent rains. As a result, apples were also dried over gas stoves, near wood-burning stoves, in sunny windows, or in ovens at a low temperature. In addition, apple slices were strung with a needle and stout thread and hung in the air for drying. Whatever the method, the slices shriveled and turned brown as they dried. When completely dry, they were stored in cloth bags, glass canning jars, or the freezer.

When Appalachians migrated out of the region, they took recipes for dried apple stack cake with them. While modern versions are numerous, many mountain cooks still use traditional recipes.

See also: APPLE BUTTER; APPLES (AGRICULTURE); CAKES AND COOKIES.

—Sidney Saylor Farr, *Berea, Kentucky*

Joseph E. Dabney, *Smokehouse Ham, Spoon Bread, and Scuppernong Wine: The Folklore and Art of Southern Appalachian Cooking* (1998); John Egerton, *Southern Food: At Home, on the Road, in History* (1993); Ronni Lundy, *Shuck Beans, Stack Cakes, and Honest Fried Chicken: The Heart and Soul of Southern Country Kitchens* (1991).

Many-layered dried apple stack cake, 1999. This dessert is made from stiff dough layers spread with a sweet, spiced apple filling.

Eastern European–American Foodways

The cuisine of Appalachia often utilizes some of the fundamental ingredients found in eastern European dishes, namely potatoes, cabbage, wheat, pork, poultry, and dairy, and at times, wild mushrooms and freshwater fish. In sections of Appalachia heavily settled by immigrants from eastern Europe, recipes and cooking techniques have been adopted along with ingredients. Appalachians of eastern European origin have continually adapted their native foodways to the region, substituting newfound convenience foods in recipes if necessary.

The late 1880s saw the beginning of a wave of eastern European immigration to the United States, with the greatest numbers arriving between 1900 and 1915. The years of the Great Depression found families in Appalachia providing shelter and sustenance for many eastern European families recently moved into the region.

Slovaks, Slovenes, Yugoslavs, Serbs, Hungarians, and Croatians eventually found employment in the coal mines and steel mills of Pennsylvania and the Ohio River Valley. Others earned a living as farmers and farm laborers, while many took manual jobs in factories where knowledge of English was not required. Immigrants from Poland, Austria-Hungary, and the Ukraine also worked in the industrial and agricultural trades, settling in areas beyond western Pennsylvania, from eastern and southeastern Ohio to northern West Virginia. Communities were established in parts of Maryland, Virginia, and some southern Appalachian states.

The very nature of their labor made a hearty diet essential. Fats and starch—whether lard, butter, or vegetable shortening—were crucial sources of calories. Appalachian cooks often prepared noodles, dumplings, and breads from scratch for sopping up the skillet gravy from fried chicken, much like their eastern European counterparts did for soups and stews.

In contemporary Appalachian kitchens, traditional eastern European recipes frequently have American equivalents or adaptations. Stuffed cabbage leaves simmer in a tangy sweet-sour tomato sauce as Polish *golabki*, Czech *golumki*, Ukrainian *holubtsi*, or Americanized pigs in a blanket. Slovak-Slovenian *haluski* may be served with sautéed cabbage, while Polish *kluski* and Czech *nudle* are typically tossed with butter and farmer's cheese or poppy seeds—all these dishes are made with noodles. In Romania, cornmeal is used to prepare the staple *mamaliga*, a thick cornmeal mush or polenta that is topped with sour cream, grated cheese, meat, fish, or eggs; in Appalachia, it becomes fried cornmeal mush eaten with sorghum syrup.

Heads of cabbage are shredded into Ukrainian *kapusniak*, sauerkraut soup, or Appalachian stone jar kraut. Mashed potatoes are one of many fillings for Polish *pierogi* dough pockets, and leftovers become skillet-fried potato cakes or dumplings. In parts of Pennsylvania, Ohio, and New York, ground pork is seasoned and shaped into the Polish ring sausage *kielbasa*, while cured salt pork, fatback, or streak o' lean is used to season a pot of greens in many southern Appalachian states. Heavy cream is soured and used to thicken and enrich hearty Hungarian *guylás*, or goulash stew, whereas clabbered or sour milk is worked into fresh curds of homemade cheese in areas of rural Appalachia.

Traditional eastern European dishes highlight holidays, name days, and weddings and are often served alongside local Appalachian cuisine. In parts of Pennsylvania, Ohio, and New York, Poles often serve *barszcz z uszkami*, a meatless borscht with mushroom dumplings, at Christmas Eve dinner. The yeast-raised Ukrainian *kalach*, or *kolach*, is a bread that is braided into a wreath. Symbolizing the sun, the *kalach* is usually baked during the dark days of winter.

The Easter meal celebrates the arrival of spring with egg-rich baked goods. The Slovak *paska* bread is decorated with hard-boiled eggs or a bread-dough cross. Polish *babka* cake, laden with morsels of chocolate, cheese, or raisins, is popular in many of Appalachia's northern urban centers.

The influence of Jewish heritage is reflected in eastern European dishes such as *schav* borscht, or sorrel soup, and pickled or smoked fish. The ubiquitous bagel, derived from the Ukrainian *bublyk*, is a ring-shaped roll first boiled in water, then baked for a chewy crust.

Social and religious organizations play an important role in the demonstration and preservation of eastern European foodways. Slovak and Slovenian auxiliary groups in Virginia and Maryland prepare homemade cheese-filled *gibanica* pastries and nut- and raisin-filled *potica* yeast rolls for church bake sales and fairs. Communal organizations such as the Polish and Lithuanian clubs found in western Pennsylvania provide meeting places for drink and conversation.

See also: CABBAGE; HUNGARIANS (RACE, ETHNICITY, AND IDENTITY).

—Suzanne C. Weltman, *Foodways, Inc., Philadelphia, Pennsylvania*

Katherine S. and Thomas M. Kirlin, *Smithsonian Folklife Cookbook* (1991); Kay Shaw Nelson, *The Eastern European Cookbook* (1973); Stephan Thernstrom, ed., *Harvard Encyclopedia of American Ethnic Groups* (1980).

Fatback

See Pork

Festivals, Food

Appalachia's numerous food festivals highlighting both traditional and contemporary regional foodways have grown from simple swap meets to daylong and even weeklong events. While most of them occur in the fall, a number take place in the spring.

In mid-April, South Pittsburg, Tennessee, hosts the National Corn Bread Festival. Besides offering samples of corn bread and corn bread fritters, vendors try to outdo one another with creative corn bread recipes. Notable offerings have included corn bread baked with pinto beans, turnip greens, pork chops, or chicken, not to mention the ever-popular corn bread salad. As part of the celebration, Lodge Manufacturing Company, a local concern that has made cast-iron cookware since the nineteenth century, sponsors a cook-off.

To preserve the skills of tapping maple trees (also known as gathering "tree sugar" or "tree 'lasses"), Monterey, Virginia, hosts an early spring Highland Maple Festival. Maple sugar camps in the area introduce visitors to the entire syrup-making process, from tapping trees with plastic pipes to boiling kettles of sap into syrup and storing it in labeled bottles. Culinary highlights include a pancake breakfast with maple syrup, maple-flavored donuts, and funnel cakes. As is the case with many festivals, the Highland Maple Festival also sponsors car and craft shows and, occasionally, hog-calling and beard-growing contests.

Marathon, New York, hosts the Central New York Maple Festival each April which features, along with arts and crafts, talent shows, and a beauty pageant, a demonstration of the process of boiling down forty gallons of maple sap to make one gallon of syrup.

Also held in April, the Strawberry Festival in Cullman, Alabama, celebrates the berry amidst a car show, tractor pull, entertainment, and food and crafts vending, while Russellville, Alabama, and Water Valley, Mississippi, pay similar tribute in late summer to the watermelon.

The powerful flavor of ramps attracts festivalgoers who have the bravado to sample the dishes at the Ramp Cook-Off and Festival in Elkins, West Virginia. The two-day event begins with a grand ramp dinner. Festival attendees sample the products of the ramp cook-off and vote for the best ramp dish. Past efforts have included ramp burgers, ramp candy, and even ramp-flavored pies, cakes, and cookies.

One of the many fall food festivals is the South Carolina Apple Festival held in Westminster. This mid-September event features a Dutch oven cook-off for cast-iron kettles and in-ground cooking. In addition to apple butter, an apple-baking contest fills the air with tantalizing aromas of cinnamon and nutmeg. More apple butter demonstrations are held in Berkley Springs, West Virginia, in early October. On the town square, copper kettles and cast-iron vats hold gallons of slow-simmering apple butter redolent of cinnamon, allspice, and cloves. The finished product is for sale, as is freshly pressed apple cider.

Other apple-oriented festivals include those in Jackson County, Ohio; Hendersonville and North Wilkesboro, North Carolina; Moulton, Alabama; and Gilmer County, Georgia—a county that produces six hundred thousand bushels of apples each year.

September also sees the Barnesville Pumpkin Festival held in Belmont County, Ohio, complete with contests for size, carnival rides, games, crafts shows, and a Grand Pumpkin Parade in recognition of this important autumnal food source.

In McClure, Pennsylvania, pots simmer with bean soup at the McClure Bean Soup Celebration. Civil War Veterans of McClure first held the event to organize a Grand Army of the Republic post in 1883. After eight years the veterans invited the public, and the event grew. As the ranks of veterans thinned over the years, sons of the veterans and citizens of McClure took over the event. In modern times, bean soup is prepared as it was during the Civil War. Large cast-iron kettles hanging over wood-fired furnaces simmer thirty-five gallons of the beef and bean concoction. Festival literature claims the use of tons of beans, a ton of beef, and many, many crackers to serve more than seventy-five thousand attendees annually.

Every September citizens of London, Kentucky, dust off what festival promoters call the "world's largest stainless steel skillet" for the World Chicken Festival. This skillet, weighing seven hundred pounds and measuring ten feet, six inches wide by eight inches deep, can fry more than six hundred chicken quarters at a time. With the smell of chicken in the air, attendees are in the mood for the chicken-wing-eating contest or the rooster crowing, strutting, and clucking contest, in which musicians compete with chicken imitators for audience attention.

Various meats comprise the themes of several other festivals in Appalachia, including the Wild Turkey Festival in Vinton County, Ohio, and the Blue Ridge Barbecue Festival on the border of North and South Carolina. The Possum Town Pigfest in Columbus, Mississippi, is built around a heated competition between sixty-five teams of cooks vying for best pork barbeque.

Bardstown, Kentucky, the self-proclaimed Bourbon Capital of the World, hosts another mid-September event, the Kentucky Bourbon Festival. Here, from dawn to dusk, the spotlight is on bourbon. A bourbon breakfast includes sour mash pancakes, bourbon-marinated berries, and bourbon-enhanced honey butter, syrups, and preserves. Even bourbon-flavored coffee is served. An afternoon tea and fashion show feature foods cooked with bourbon. Jim Beam sponsors culinary arts school demonstrations and attendees sample the prepared dishes.

At the Moonshine Festival of Hocking County, Ohio, celebrants can dine on moonshine burgers, pies, and doggies at the five-day event that features a working moonshine still—for demonstration purposes only. The wine-producing Finger Lakes District of New York holds a wine festival in Watkins Glen each July complete with seminars, demonstrations, and live music in addition to arts, crafts, and wine-related merchandise.

October heralds the celebration of another agricultural product, buckwheat. Neither wheat nor grain, buckwheat is related to rhubarb, but its seed, or groat, is used like a grain and ground into buckwheat flour. Long a crop of the central and northern Appalachian Mountains, buckwheat grows well in poor soil on rocky, hilly land and is seldom bothered by insects. The citizens of Kingwood, West Virginia, prize its strong flavor and speckled appearance. They have celebrated the crop each fall since 1938 with festivals featuring a buckwheat pancake and sausage breakfast. During one record festival, community groups used more than two tons of buckwheat flour.

The small town of Corinth, Mississippi, is best known for its annual Slugburger Festival, featuring the slugburger, a depression-era soybean alternative to beef burgers.

Both Tennessee and West Virginia hold festivals to honor important sweeteners. The West Virginia Honey Festival in Parkersburg, West Virginia, seeks to educate the public in bee keeping, honey flavors, and the uses of honey. A baking contest, cooking demonstration, auction, and a beekeeper with a beard of live bees are presented. Mennonites from Muddy Pond, Tennessee, sponsor the Scott County Sorghum Festival in Oneida. At this September festival producers demonstrate the preparation of sweet sorghum using an old-fashioned, horse-powered mill. After sap is pressed from the sorghum, the juice is transferred to large evaporators. A sorghum bake-off features chili, cakes, pies, and meat dishes.

Centered on finding and preparing wild foods and herbs, the Annual Nature Wonder Wild Foods Weekend provides field trips, lecturers, and an evening banquet. This annual fall event is held in Cairo, West Virginia. This festival and others are featured in *Blue Ridge Country*, which publishes an almanac of coming events, and other regional magazines.

Although food-based festivals have existed in Appalachia for centuries—a major festival among the precontact

Cherokee, for example, celebrated the midsummer ripening of the corn—post–World War II Appalachia witnessed an unprecedented proliferation of small-town food festivals. During this era, life in the region changed dramatically as traditional foods were supplanted by national brands and as small-town Main Street culture gave way to suburban malls. Modern food festivals, characterized by nostalgia, suggest a desire to capture an idealized version of Appalachia's rural and small-town past. Thus, they function partly as a community's desire to preserve and invent memories. In addition, since festivals often draw large numbers of visitors, they also provide a way for communities to capitalize on Appalachia's increased tourism and recreational spending.

See also: FARMERS' MARKETS (AGRICULTURE); FESTIVALS, FOLK (FOLKLORE AND FOLKLIFE).

—Katherine G. Tufts, *Daisy, Maryland*

Fried Pies

Culinary cousin of the baked fruit turnover, fried pies were a winter favorite among old-time mountain residents when fresh fruit was not available. Still eaten, they are made from stewed, sweetened, and sometimes spiced dried fruit. Fried pies are served hot or cold and are usually eaten not with a fork but out of hand. Also called half-moon pies because of their half-circle shape, they are formed from circles of biscuit or pastry dough, the size of the circle determining the size of the finished pie. One side of the circle is spread with fruit; the other side is then folded over and the edges sealed. A recipe for "Fried Apple Jacks" in Beth Tartan's *North Carolina and Old Salem Cookery* (1992) specifies that the pastry be cut into saucer-sized rounds and filled with only a tablespoon of fruit. Early recipes called for frying the pies in lard, but modern cooks are more likely to use vegetable oil. While the pies can also be baked, frying gives a more authentic flavor. The hot pies can be sprinkled with granulated or powdered sugar.

Dried apples are the most common fried pie filling, but peaches, apricots, and prunes are also used. In *Smokehouse Ham, Spoon Bread, and Scuppernong Wine: The Folklore and Art of Southern Appalachian Cooking* (1998), Joseph E. Dabney notes that some Carolinians call fried peach pies "mule ears." He also cites a Tennessee version spiced with cinnamon, nutmeg, and ginger.

See also: CAKES AND COOKIES; COBBLERS; FRUITS AND BERRIES; PIES.

—Rebeccah Kinnamon Neff, *Raleigh, North Carolina*

Frog Legs

The abundance of frogs, amphibians found in freshwater ponds and rivers in the South, has made them a popular food delicacy in some restaurants. In Appalachia, frog legs, or frogs' legs, are also served at home when a family member is willing to harvest the frogs from a nearby pond or stream. The hunting is considered something of a sport and requires some skill since it is done at night with a long gigging fork. The gig is a metal, four-pronged fork that is mounted on the end of the cane pole. The basic motion used in gigging resembles a javelin throw, but the hunter uses less force and does not release the gig. This action requires a steady hand. Larger frogs are typically the targets, although smaller ones in large quantities can provide a meal. A bright light, similar to those worn by coal miners, is often attached to the gigger's hat. The light helps him or her to navigate through the weeds and serves to blind the frog, making it immobile while the hunter or his partner does the gigging. Once the frogs are caught, they are typically carried in a burlap bag attached to the hunter's belt.

The only edible parts of the frog are its legs. After being cleaned, frog legs are typically fried. Appalachian cooks frequently dip them in an egg, milk, and flour mixture and fry them in a heavy skillet, either in corn oil or lard. The legs have a flavor similar to chicken, although they have their own distinct taste and texture. The meat is not used in other dishes. Stories concerning the eating of frog legs often center on the hunting experience rather than the meal.

See also: HUNTING AND FISHING (SPORTS AND RECREATION); TURTLE.

—Janet S. Gilligan, *University of Kentucky*

Fruits and Berries

Wild fruits and berries have been an important food source for inhabitants of Appalachia from the animals that first roamed the wilderness to Native Americans to the English, Scots-Irish, and German immigrants who established permanent settlements in the region beginning in the early 1700s. Over time, the immigrants added a variety of old-world fruits to their homesteads. Fruits and berries that sustained the pioneers remain prominent among the foods of Appalachia.

Blackberries, most abundant of the wild berries, are prized for their versatility. Generations have enjoyed the tart-sweet berries fresh from the vine, in desserts, and in wine and jelly. Ground-hugging dewberry vines bear larger, redder berries that are more tart than blackberries but are used in much the same way. Dark blue huckleberries, sometimes called wild blueberries or whortlelberries, are a low-growing wild version of the cultivated highbush blueberry (which is larger and dusty blue). Although huckleberries are now rare, many varieties of blueberries thrive throughout Appalachia. Other wild berries of the region include strawberries; elderberries, most commonly used to make wine or jelly; currants; and ground cherries, little blueberry-sized yellow fruit from low-growing shrubs. Berry pickings, like other food-related events, were a popular form of socializing in the region well into the twentieth century.

The most exotic of the Appalachian wild fruits is the maypop (or "molly pop") fruit of the passionflower vine. A Cherokee favorite, the ripe lemon-colored maypop has a mellow taste suggestive of apricot and is sometimes called field, mountain, or wild apricot. Wild grapes, large blue-black muscadines and bronze scuppernongs, as well the smaller fox ("winter") and possum grapes, were common in the Appalachian wilderness and still grow in some areas. Highly prized for wine and jelly and sometimes used in pies and tarts, wild grapes were also preserved in sorghum or sugar syrup, a technique adapted from the Cherokees.

In addition to crab apples, pawpaws, and persimmons, other wild tree fruits in the region include the wild black cherry, the wild plum (also called August plum or goose plum), and the serviceberry, or Juneberry. Peaches, one of the region's most popular fruits, were probably brought to North American by sixteenth-century Spanish explorers. A favorite fresh fruit, peaches are used in a variety of desserts and enjoyed dried (especially as a sweet, chewy confection of sun-dried peach puree called peach leather), pickled, as jam, and as a spiced spread called peach butter. The fruit is also used to make a popular alcoholic drink, peach brandy.

Homesteaders introduced other fruits such as gooseberries and raspberries and many varieties of apples and cherries, as well as Kieffer and seckel pears and damson and greengage plums. These fruits were used in desserts and jams; in fruit-based syrups and conserves such as "pear honey"; and in a variety of alcoholic beverages, including an old favorite called "cherry bounce." In winter, preserved fruits such as damson plums and berries were used in pies and puddings, in which the fruit was combined with leftover bread or biscuits, eggs, and milk. When glass jars replaced pottery crocks in the early twentieth century, canning became the preferred method of preserving both wild and cultivated fruits. In the last half of the century, home freezers and plastic containers made freezing a convenient way of "putting up" food.

Appalachian fruit desserts range from simple to elegant. Pioneers ate fruit fresh, dried, poached, stewed and mixed, or topped with cream, a preparation the English called "fools." As ovens became more common, so did baked desserts such as crisps, cobblers, and pies. Boiled fruit dumplings were also popular. Sometimes cream or soft custard (dip) was poured over these pastry-based desserts. With the spread of railroads in the late nineteenth century, citrus fruits, bananas, and pineapples became available in Appalachia. A traditional dessert in many families is banana pudding: layers of sweet boiled custard, banana slices, and vanilla wafers topped with meringue. Other twentieth-century regional favorites include fruit whips and delights made with beaten egg whites, cream cheese, or gelatin.

See also: FRUITS (ECOLOGY); JAMS, JELLIES, AND PRESERVES; PAWPAWS.

—Noel Kinnamon, *Mars Hill College*, and Rebeccah Kinnamon Neff, *Raleigh, North Carolina*

Joseph E. Dabney, *Smokehouse Ham, Spoon Bread, and Scuppernong Wine: The Folklore and Art of Southern Appalachian Cooking* (1998); Sidney Saylor Farr, *More Than Moonshine: Appalachian Recipes and Recollections* (1983); Linda Garland Page and Elliott Wigginton, eds., *The Foxfire Book of Appalachian Cookery* (1984).

Funeral Foods

The practice of bringing foods to mourning family members of a recently deceased individual is a deeply engrained custom in the mountains. In the days following a death, neighbors, friends, and distant relatives often travel to the home of the deceased or another gathering place and typically contribute one or more dishes to the family.

When hospitals and funeral homes were less common, individuals often progressed through illnesses and into death in the home, and funerals were likely to take place in a nearby family cemetery. During a prolonged illness, neighbors and relatives often contributed food prior to the loved one's death. Since hospitals and convenience foods have become common, this practice has greatly decreased, but the custom of providing gathering foods is still widely practiced throughout Appalachia.

While funeral foods vary widely, common dishes are pies, rolls, cakes, and meats. These and other foods provided are simple to reheat or cook but filling and nourishing. For this reason, casseroles are popular items.

The importance of funeral foods is multifold. First, the donation of food takes the burden of preparing meals off the bereaved, who often houses and feeds extended family members who attend the funeral. The offered food also sustains a family or a widowed spouse through a difficult and emotional time. Moreover, the donation is an expression of grief and a gift for the family.

Other theories hold that the preparation and donation of funeral foods are symbolic of the ties between community members and that funeral foods act as a demonstration of the giver's relationship with and fondness for the deceased. The offering of food acts as a measure of the deceased's place within the community. For instance, those who only knew the deceased or his or her family in passing may offer one small dish such as a "funeral pie," a generic term encompassing many types of simple pies often given to bereaved families. Individuals who knew the deceased well are likely to offer more elaborate or homemade dishes—cakes, cooked hams, or chickens—or to bring more than one dish over several days. In this way, the amount of food brought in both before and after the funeral can serve as a gauge for the popularity of the deceased.

See also: CASSEROLES; DINNER ON THE GROUNDS; MEMORIAL SERVICES (RELIGION).

—Anna E. Bogle, *Tupelo Honey Café, Asheville, North Carolina*

Joseph E. Dabney, *Smokehouse Ham, Spoon Bread, and Scuppernong Wine: The Folklore and Art of Southern Appalachian Cooking* (1998); John Egerton, *Southern Food: At Home, on the Road, in History* (1993); Mark F. Sohn, *Mountain Country Cooking: A Gathering of the Best Recipes from the Smokies to the Blue Ridge* (1996).

Ginger

To early Appalachian families, ginger *(Zingiber officinale)* was one of the most highly prized and versatile spices after staples such as salt, pepper, and sugar. Drawing on a wide range of ethnic influences as well as local inspiration, cooks in this region have used ginger in a multitude of ways.

Ginger is used fresh, dried, candied, crushed, powdered, and sliced thin and is employed in dishes such as pickled vegetables, fruit preserves, biscuits, pies, cookies, cakes, and breads. It can be brewed as tea, used to flavor cider, ale, and wine, or to add strength to relishes, chutneys, and meat dishes. It also serves to mask the ripeness of wild game, and its tangy warmth makes it especially welcome in winter.

Although wild ginger (genus *Asarum*, of which there are at least two species native to Appalachia) is readily substituted for imported ginger, its flavor is not as strong, and it was used mainly when the commercial spice was not available. In the eighteenth and early nineteenth centuries, when imported goods were scarce and expensive, commercial ginger was reserved for special-occasion recipes such as dried apple stack cake and holiday gingerbread and cookies. Until recently, common use of ginger was more likely to involve the wild sort, usually gathered in late spring and early summer from shady wooded areas throughout the Appalachians.

Both types of ginger have traditionally been used medicinally, as well, for ailments such as nausea, cramps, digestive problems, and whooping cough. Native Americans in the region are known to have brewed a contraceptive tea from the wild plant.

See also: CAKES AND COOKIES; DRIED APPLE STACK CAKE.

—Troy Gowen, *East Tennessee State University*, and Gabriele I. Kupitz, *Brigham Young University*

Gravy

Gravies are commonplace within Appalachia, particularly in the southern and central portions of the region. The popularity of gravy as a side dish may be rooted in the need to stretch meals as far as possible and to provide a source of long-lasting energy, with calories from fat and often milk.

The majority of the common gravies are starch-bound, using either flour or cornmeal as a thickener. Most are also "white" as opposed to "brown" gravies, using milk instead of meat broth or stock as their liquid component. Gravy is frequently made in a cast-iron skillet after meat or vegetables have been fried. The most widely known Appalachian gravies, however, are sawmill gravy and red-eye gravy, and recipes for both can be found throughout the region.

Sawmill gravy may have acquired its name when a cook at a lumber camp ran out of flour and substituted cornmeal as the thickening agent for the morning gravy. Today, sawmill gravy is typically made from the pan drippings from fried sausage with flour or cornmeal as a thickener and milk as the liquid. Though sawmill gravy originally contained cornmeal, recipes calling for flour have become more common. Sawmill gravy is also called logging gravy, white gravy, sausage gravy, breakfast gravy, morning gravy, and cornmeal gravy, depending on the location. Whatever it is called, it is most often served with biscuits.

Red-eye gravy is made from the residual juices and fat from frying country ham and is one of the few Appalachian gravies that is neither starch-bound nor made with milk. It most commonly involves a mixture of ham drippings, strong black coffee, and water and is usually eaten with biscuits also.

The same general combination of meat drippings, flour or cornmeal, and milk used in sawmill gravy applies to most other Appalachian gravies. A cream or chicken gravy is made using some of the pan juices left from fried chicken. The same is true of rabbit, squirrel, pork chops and pork tenderloin, and fried potatoes. The name of each gravy correlates with the meat or vegetable that was cooked in the skillet prior to making the gravy. For example, gravy made in the same skillet used to fry potatoes is called potato gravy.

Chocolate gravy is common in parts of Appalachia, particularly eastern Kentucky. Made using sugar, flour, cocoa, and milk, chocolate gravy is thicker than other gravies and is served over biscuits either at breakfast or as a dessert.

Other less common but notable gravies include tomato gravy, containing onions and chopped tomatoes; egg gravy, made with the addition of an egg to the gravy mixture; Pepsi gravy, using cola instead of milk; and bologna gravy, made after frying bologna.

See also: CORN; LOGGERS' FOODS.

—Anna E. Bogle, *Tupelo Honey Café, Asheville, North Carolina*

Joseph E. Dabney, *Smokehouse Ham, Spoon Bread, and Scuppernong Wine: The Folklore and Art of Southern Appalachian Cooking* (1998); Linda Garland Page and Eliot Wigginton, eds., *The Foxfire Book of Appalachian Cookery* (1984); Mark F. Sohn, *Mountain Country Cooking: A Gathering of the Best Recipes from the Smokies to the Blue Ridge* (1996).

Green Beans

Long-stewed with fat pork or smokehouse ham and served fresh from the garden with corn bread, green beans are a staple of the Appalachian diet. The immature seedpods of a member of the legume family *(Phaseolus vulgaris)*, green beans have many varieties. As the name suggests, pods are usually green, though some varieties have yellow, purple, or mottled red and white pods.

Some green beans are called "string" beans, for the tough fiber running along the pods' sides; the process of removing this strip is called "stringing." Selective breeding, however, has mostly eliminated the string. Similarly, green beans are sometimes called "snap" beans since the ends are snapped off or the entire beans are snapped into segments for cooking. But the green beans favored by mountain people are so full, thick, and meaty that they have matured beyond the snap stage and more exactly are broken, not snapped. Shell, or shelly, beans (shucked fresh bean seeds) and dry beans come from still further stages of the bean's growth.

It is easiest to group beans by growing habits—bush, pole, or half-runner. Bush beans are short, bushy, and usually self-supporting. Pole beans, which grow upward to a height of ten feet or more, require external support. Often trained up trellises or cornstalks, they will also wind around sunflowers. Half-runners send out three-foot vining shoots, or runners.

Historically, frugal Appalachians rarely purchased bean seeds from catalogs or stores. People saved seeds gleaned from previous crops and traded them among neighbors. Seeds were also "imported," tucked into pockets and suitcases of immigrants. Of varieties grown, Kentucky wonder pole beans are cherished in the South. White half-runners (also known as mountaineer or state half-runners), blue lake, and slenderette are favored in West Virginia. Others include lazy wife (no strings); cornfield (grown up corn stalks); Romano (Italian origin; wide, flat pods); Logan giant; short-cut or cutshorts (short pods); greasy or greasyback (oily-looking seeds); goose; and cranberry, horticultural, or October beans, which mature late and are used most often as shellies.

Mountain green bean cookery has many variations, but robust beans, such as white half-runners, are often slow-simmered for hours with salt pork, country ham, streaky bacon, or ham hocks. Some cooks include a pod of dried hot pepper, some sugar; all add salt. Cooks speak of cooking green beans dry, or down to the grease, so that the pot likker evaporates, leaving the good, rich flavor and fat in the beans. Some people simmer white Irish potatoes atop beans, and some include okra. Beans are cooked three to four hours, pulled off the stove, allowed to rest, then reheated. Sometimes fresh shellies are simmered with young green beans. Often the mature beans have such well-developed seeds that their still-tender pods split apart when cooking, leaving the seeds visible. Home-canned beans are combined with seasoning meat and simmered at least twenty minutes.

In the past, mountaineers canned green beans by packing them into quart jars and processing jars in a kettle of boiling water. Sometimes the jars would seal, sometimes not. Because of its unreliability, this open-kettle method has been replaced by steam-pressure canning, which produces safe, wholesome green beans. Green beans can also be preserved by drying, salting, pickling, and freezing.

See also: GARDENING (FOLKLORE AND FOLKLIFE); SHUCK BEANS; SOUP BEANS.

—Miriam Rubin, *New Freeport, Pennsylvania*

Sidney Saylor Farr, *Table Talk: Appalachian Meals and Memories* (1995); John L. Marra, "Heirloom Seeds," *Huntington (W.Va.) Herald-Dispatch* (June 15, 1996); Linda Garland Page and Eliot Wigginton, eds., *The Foxfire Book of Appalachian Cookery* (1984).

Greens

The three most common wild greens found in Appalachia are lamb's-quarters *(Chenopodium album)*, pokeweed *(Phytolacca americana)*, and dandelion *(Taraxacum officinale)*. Other spring greens found in the region include chickweed, corn salad, dock, fiddleheads, purslane, ramps, shepherd's purse or St. James's wort, winter cress or creases, and mouse-ear.

Old-time Appalachian gatherers were known to give colloquial names to the wild greens they collected and consumed. In some families, special names for favorite wild greens have been passed down for generations. For example, some refer to the Virginia waterleaf *(Hydrophyllum virginianum)* as Shawnee salad, while others called the tall bellflower *(Campanula americana)* by the same name. Other Appalachians identified any plant used by the Shawnee tribe as Shawnee salad. Among European settlers, the granny apron was a common collecting bag for wild greens.

Wild greens mixtures differ according to the season and the preference of individual gatherers. Once gathered, many wild greens are tender enough to be used raw in salads; others, however, particularly older ones, are parboiled in one to three changes of water. They are then drained and sautéed in bacon grease, vinegar, water, and sugar. Hard-boiled eggs are chopped and sliced to add as garnish for both the raw salads and cooked greens.

Italian immigrants added wild greens such as purslane *(Portulaca oleracea)* to omelets. Germans and Scots-Irish ate poke (also known as pokeweed or poke sallet). Pokeweed shoots appear in early spring and are gathered for raw greens, cooked greens, and pickles when the plant is three to six inches tall. Poke can be parboiled, dipped in cornmeal, and fried; it is also boiled, chopped, and fried with eggs to make poke sallet. Poke is among the favorite pickled greens in Appalachia. Poke and other wild greens can be preserved in glass jars, dill crocks, and deep freezers.

Today, cultivated, or garden, greens are more widely consumed than wild greens. Throughout the Appalachians, gardeners plant a variety of greens, including mustard, turnip, collard, kale, and rape (broccoli rabe, a leafy green related to cabbage and turnips). In addition, spinach, beet, and watercress are grown in the spring in the southern mountains and later in the season farther north.

Spinach, beet greens, and watercress are eaten both raw and cooked, while mustard, turnip, collard, kale, and rape are usually cooked. The preparation of garden greens in Appalachia was heavily influenced both by slaves of African descent and Euro-American subsistence farmers. Collards, turnips, mustard, and kale are commonly either boiled, fried, or boiled and then fried. In gardens, different greens are often grown side by side, and cooks often combine different varieties, such as turnip and mustard or collards, kale, and rape. If greens are boiled and not fried, they are seasoned with country ham, smoked ham hocks, smoked hog jowls, salt pork, or fatback. The cooking water becomes a valued broth that is called pot likker. The likker is used to moisten corn bread or cook dumplings. Today, some chefs replace these pork parts with smoked turkey or even vegetable extracts. If garden greens are fried, they are boiled first, usually without pork flavoring, and then fried in bacon grease.

Over the last quarter of the twentieth century, greens such as Swiss chard, radicchio, Chinese bok choy, and *tatsoi*, or mustard spinach, were introduced to the region. While these new varieties have had some impact on Appalachian cooking, mustard, turnip, and collard remain the most popular greens.

See also: RAMPS; ROOT VEGETABLES; WILTED LETTUCE.

—Kenneth G. Gilbert, *Ohio Valley College;* Blanche Jackson Glimps, *Kentucky Christian College;* and Edelene Wood, *National Wild Foods Association*

Edelene Wood, *Taste of the Wild* (1991); Edelene Wood and Kenneth G. Gilbert, *Appalachian Wildfood Cookbook* (2000).

Gristmills

Originally, pioneer farmers in Appalachia ground grain by hand, using mortars or hand stones called querns. In the late 1700s, the waterwheel revolutionized the process, and millers from England imported the knowledge required to build gristmills. Soon, many small towns and communities throughout the Appalachians used gristmills in place of hand stones.

Although gristmills varied in size and efficiency, the waterwheel was the core of the operation. Some mills housed horizontal wheels inside, where they were called turbines or "tub" wheels. Other mills had vertical waterwheels on the outside. These vertical wheels could be either "overshot" or "undershot." The overshot wheel was turned when water spilling from the end of a flume above it filled a bucket or trough at the top of the wheel's rotation and then spilled into the buckets below, slowly rotating the wheel. In the undershot wheel, the lower part of the wheel rested in a trough of flowing water; the force of the water striking the wheel's evenly spaced baffles turned it.

There were two ways of conveying water to gristmills. One was for the owners to dam a stream with logs or rock, creating a millpond. From the pond, water rushed through a controlled sluice (a boxed-in channel) and passed over or under the wheel. The second method was to channel water from a nearby stream through pipes to the edge of the mill and then shoot it into the buckets in the waterwheel. In both instances, the turning wheel set in motion the cogs, shafts, and pulleys inside the mill and turned the heavy grinding stones.

Millstones usually came from local quarries, but a few buhrstones were imported from France. In a typical configuration, two stones about four feet in diameter were placed one on top of the other; the bottom stone was stationary. Half-inch grooves cut into the center of the stones enabled corn, fed from a hopper, to be ground between the stones and passed outward into a pulley-operated conveyor, which transported the meal to a box for sacking.

Millers established certain "mill days" for local residents to bring their grain. Farmers described the trip as taking a "turn" of corn to the mill on grinding day. The miller usually performed his services for a toll, typically a gallon of corn for two bushels of ground meal. In addition to being a necessity, the mill became a social meeting place.

Dangers of milling included fire and floods. Some mills burned to the ground, and others were washed away. During the Civil War, armies burned hundreds of mills to deprive communities of food. A few mills were rebuilt, but many were not, and the use of gristmills declined. In modern times, most of the rare waterwheel-powered gristmills still standing have become tourist attractions.

See also: CORN; HAGOOD MILL (ARCHITECTURE); MILLS (BUSINESS, INDUSTRY, AND TECHNOLOGY).

—Sidney Saylor Farr, *Berea, Kentucky*

Emory L. Hamilton, *Old Mills of Southwest Virginia* (1973); Donald Gregory Jeane, *The Culture History of Grist Milling in Northwest Georgia* (1974); Robert A. Powell, *Kentucky Covered Wooden Bridges and Water-Powered Mills* (1984).

Ham

See Pork

Haute Cuisine

The French phrase *haute cuisine* suggests food and cooking that is refined, expert, even lofty in its aspirations for taste and presentation. In stereotypical depictions of food in

Resort guests dine in the Windsor Dining Room at Skytop Lodge, Skytop, Pennsylvania, c. 2001. Appalachia boasts many exceptional restaurants and an emerging regional cuisine.

Appalachia, which evoke images of sausage, biscuits, gravy, and fried pies at best or variations of roadkill cooking (opossum, raccoon, and groundhog) at worst, the notion of haute cuisine has no place. In reality, however, Appalachia boasts fine chefs, exceptional restaurants, famous cooking schools, and an emerging gourmet regional cuisine.

The Appalachian region has produced numerous outstanding American chefs who learned cooking from their mothers and grandmothers in the mountains and then, with the help of cooking schools, large staffs, and dedicated clients, took that tradition to a higher level. Perhaps the most celebrated chef from Appalachia is Dean Fearing, executive chef of the posh Mansion on Turtle Creek in Dallas, Texas. Fearing has won such awards as the Culinary Institute of America's Chef of the Year, the James Beard Award, the Wine Spectator Grand Award, has authored cookbooks, and has cooked for queens and presidents. Reared in Ashland, Kentucky, Fearing credits his grandmother and great-grandmother in the mountains for his success as a chef.

Several other noted chefs learned to appreciate good cooking from their mothers and grandmothers in the region. After apprenticing with several renowned American chefs, Appalachian-born Jack McDavid opened two of his own restaurants in Philadelphia, Pennsylvania, to showcase a mountain-inspired cuisine based on his foremothers' cooking. His success led to a televised cooking program that brought him and his down-home style of clothing, speech, and food to national attention. Asheville, North Carolina–born chef Scott Howell opened Nana's, a popular restaurant in the Piedmont area of North Carolina named for his Tennessee grandmother and guided by her style and spirit of cooking.

Unlike these chefs, who made their mark outside the region, some native-born chefs practice their culinary art in Appalachia; still others are transplants to the mountains who have adapted their cooking to regional produce and regional tastes. One female chef returned to the mountains of her childhood in Ashe County, North Carolina, to establish an award-winning restaurant and inn. The chef of a highly acclaimed restaurant in Blowing Rock, North Carolina, brought his culinary skill to Appalachia from one of America's top restaurants in Miami, Florida, but quickly adapted dishes to take advantage of regional delicacies such as mountain trout and the produce of local farmers.

Tourist trade and an increasingly affluent and sophisticated population in Appalachia's urban areas have led to growth in the number of fine eating establishments throughout the region. Mountain resorts such as the Greenbrier in White Sulphur Springs, West Virginia, the Homestead in Hot Springs, Virginia, the Inn at Blackberry Farm in Walland, Tennessee, and Skytop Lodge in Skytop, Pennsylvania, have developed national reputations as purveyors of fine food. Rather than attempt to present haute cuisine in the French style, their chefs offer indigenous food that is as significant and refined as any other class of foods.

Accompanying the growth in outstanding restaurants has been an increasing number of culinary institutes and cooking schools throughout the region. Some type of cooking school is found in the Appalachian portion of nine of the thirteen Appalachian states, including professional culinary schools such as Pittsburgh's Pennsylvania Culinary Institute and its International Culinary Academy. These schools offer prestigious apprenticeships, continuing education, and, at the Greenbrier in West Virginia and other resorts, nonprofessional cooking classes for guests.

The development of an Appalachian haute cuisine has been grounded in regional ingredients that draw on traditions of Appalachian cooking. For example, one chef at a mountain resort uses ramps, a garlicky, onionlike wild lily found in the hills of Appalachia, in an elegant appetizer, while another chef pickles ramps to serve instead of *cornichons* (small sour pickles) with patés and as a substitute for onions in martinis. Another native-born chef makes a version of his grandmother's red-eye gravy for clients of one of the top restaurants in the country, and yet another introduces guests to chinquapins (the edible nut of a variety of beech tree). One Appalachian chef has designed dishes that echo foods more simply prepared in early mountain kitchens such as spicy venison sausage, trout (now paired with garlic shrimp and fried leeks), and fried chicken salad with buttermilk dressing. The Finger Lakes Culinary Bounty program in New York unites specialty agricultural producers with local culinary providers. A formal dinner on Capitol Hill in Washington for members of Congress, ambassadors, and other dignitaries in 2001 featured an Appalachian-inspired smoked quail in a black currant sauce and a dessert of individual apple stack cakes with crème fraîche. Often these elegant regional dishes are accompanied by regional wines that have developed hand-in-hand with the region's haute cuisine.

Entrepreneurs in the region have created fancy food products with an Appalachian flavor for sale in specialty shops and tourist meccas. In east Tennessee, one businesswoman, using her mountain grandmother's strawberry jelly recipe as the basis for her strawberry champagne butter with macadamia nuts, makes artisan jams and jellies for sale as corporate gifts and in gourmet shops. At West Virginia's state-operated regional craft center, Tamarack, shelves are filled with locally made, high-end food products. Turning regional foods into value-added products—that is, enhancing their value through restyling, packaging, and marketing—has been an important element in economic sustainability efforts in the region. The debate over whether an authentic Appalachian cuisine exists may continue, but the evidence demonstrates that there is an upsurge of interest in haute cuisine and chef training programs throughout the region that bodes well for the future of Appalachian-based fine food.

See also: COOKBOOKS; TAMARACK (CULTURAL INSTITUTIONS).

—Jean Haskell, *East Tennessee State University*

Jean Anderson, "Smoky Mountain Easter," *Food and Wine* (April 2001); Shaw Guides, *The Guide to Cooking Schools* (2002); Jean Haskell Speer, "Uppity Mountain Cooking," *Now and Then* (Spring 1998).

Hispanic Foodways

Hispanic culinary traditions first came to Appalachia when Mexican migrant coal miners arrived in the early twentieth century, and the influx dramatically increased starting in the 1960s with the arrival of Mexican migrant agricultural workers. But not until Hispanic communities were created in the 1980s did there emerge a substantial Mexican culinary influence in the region.

Traditional Appalachian cooking bears similarities to Hispanic cooking in both ingredients and cooking style, which helped to perpetuate traditional Hispanic foodways in the region. The preference for frying in lard was the same method used in Hispanic countries (introduced by the Spanish) to make crisp tortillas and refried beans. Gardening conditions favored corn, chilies, and tomatoes—the core of Mexican cuisine. Most Hispanic influence on Appalachian food and cooking in the early 1900s was from isolated Mexican families in the southern and central region. In the northern tier of Appalachia, non-Hispanics were believed to have introduced some Hispanic culinary influences. For example, the Empress food chain in Cincinnati, Ohio, which is owned by a Bulgarian family, began serving chili on spaghetti (later known as Cincinnati red or Cincinnati chili) in 1922.

Hispanic impact in some parts of Appalachia has been substantial, creating a demand for Mexican foods and ingredients. In all parts of the region, supermarkets feature fresh and processed Mexican food sections; many communities have locally owned Mexican restaurants and serve their own specialties such as tamales wrapped in corn shucks or peppers, fried banana peppers, and combinations of traditional Appalachian fare with ingredients from Hispanic tradition. The increased presence of Mexican food outlets in Appalachia was not entirely related to the expanding regional Hispanic community, though. The nationwide popularity of Mexican cuisine, Americanized to various extents by fast-food franchises, specialized restaurants, and food-packaging companies, also contributed to the acceptance of Mexican food by Appalachians.

In the North, the influence of Hispanic foodways became increasingly discernible as Latino migration spread west into Appalachia from New York, Philadelphia, and other metropolitan areas of the eastern seaboard. For example, in the late twentieth century, Mexicans had settled in the area of Johnstown, Pennsylvania, where they celebrate the Feast of Our Lady of Guadalupe each year with such traditional foods as enchiladas, refried beans, Spanish rice, chili, and mole. A Johnstown community cookbook published in 1989 includes recipes for enchiladas (using chili powder), chicken mole (without chocolate), tamales, guacamole (without jalapenos or cilantro), chili, tortillas, and arroz con pollo (using saffron). In Cincinnati, a Latino grocery sells candies dipped in chili power, tropical fruit baby foods, and Latin American canned goods. In Tennessee, immigrants from Cuba have introduced the Christmas pig roast. As communities of Hispanics have grown throughout Appalachia, so has the intermingling of Hispanic cuisines with older regional foodstuffs.

See also: HISPANICS (RACE, ETHNICITY, AND IDENTITY).

—Linda Murray Berzok, *International Association of Culinary Professionals*

John Egerton, *Southern Food: At Home, on the Road, in History* (1993); Sidney Saylor Farr, *Table Talk: Appalachian Meals and Memories* (1995); *Now and Then Special Issue: Food in Appalachia* (Spring 1998).

Italian Foodways

Although Italian food has been embraced in every corner of America, in Appalachia it is particularly important in southwestern Pennsylvania, West Virginia, and areas where large numbers of Italian immigrants were attracted by employment in coal mines.

Because traditional gender roles mandated that foodways were largely the domain of women, the types of foods prepared in immigrant households depended on the region of Italy from which the female members of the family hailed. Women from northern Italy, for instance, regularly prepared polenta (cornmeal mush) and risotto (rice cooked in broth) while southern Italian women relied on pasta with tomato sauce, or gravy, as a staple of the family diet. Whereas many recipes were brought directly to Appalachia from Italy, other foods common in Italian immigrant households actually evolved within the United States and are more accurately described as Italian American. Two of the most popular dishes were *pasta e fagioli* (pasta and beans) and *pasta alla carbonara* (pasta with eggs, pancetta, and black pepper), both known for their inexpensive and readily available ingredients and high nutritional value.

Reflecting the close relationship between food and spirituality in immigrant households, Italian women made food and cooking important parts of religious holiday observances. Southern Italians, for example, celebrated Christmas Eve with the Feast of the Seven Fishes, a lavish meal consisting of seven different types of seafood or one or two types of seafood prepared seven different ways. The difficulty of obtaining fish in remote regions of Appalachia sometimes forced Italian immigrants to replace this traditional dinner with other foods such as ravioli or lasagna, although the meal still remained meatless. In some rural areas, however, Italian immigrant storeowners arranged special shipments of seafood at Christmastime.

Food is equally important to lesser holidays. On Saint Joseph's Day, a Lenten holiday traditionally celebrated on March 19, immigrant women prepared a huge repast of traditional foods in honor of this particular Catholic saint. Many Italian families also celebrated Easter Sunday with a traditional meal consisting of roasted lamb or pork, meat pies, special pastas such as tortellini or ravioli, and Italian pastries and other baked goods.

While women were responsible for planning and preparing meals, Italian immigrant males played their own important role in development of Italian foodways. For example, most Italian men maintained small backyard gardens in which they raised tomatoes, lettuce, peppers, and a variety of cooking herbs such as oregano, basil, and parsley. Abundant with wild flora and fauna, the Appalachian region also provided the opportunity for immigrants to augment their diet through hunting and gathering. Many immigrant men regularly hunted small game such as rabbits, pheasants, and groundhogs while others scoured the forests in search of wild mushrooms, nuts, and berries. Another responsibility of husbands and fathers was the production of homemade wine. Each autumn, Italian men across Appalachia purchased California-grown grapes brought in by local Italian storeowners and made several barrels of wine for their extended families. Wine was so much a part of Italian tradition that even Italian children drank wine with their meals, albeit in a watered-down form.

Descendants of immigrants from Italy continue to observe many Italian culinary traditions, making foodways one of the few aspects of the old-world way of life that has survived the process of assimilation.

See also: CORN; GRAVY.

—Nicholas P. Ciotola, *Historical Society of Western Pennsylvania*

Edvige Giunta and Samuel J. Patti, eds., *A Tavola: Food, Tradition, and Community among Italian Americans* (1998); Frances M. Malpezzi and William M. Clements, *Italian American Folklore* (1992).

Jams, Jellies, and Preserves

John Egerton, author of *Southern Food: At Home, on the Road, in History*, notes that Native Americans used red sumac to make jelly and that a concoction resembling blackberry jam was prepared during the colonial era. In the succeeding centuries, mountain folk have satisfied their yearning for sweets with jams and jellies made with blackberries, elderberries, fox grapes, pears, damson plums, and apples. Across the twentieth century, biscuits with jam or jelly have been a staple of lunch boxes as well as kitchen tables.

Though the terms are often used interchangeably, jams, jellies, and preserves are different from one another. Preserves contain whole fruits, jams contain crushed or chopped fruit, and jellies are made from fruit juice. In addition, jams and preserves are cooked once; jellies, on the other hand, are cooked twice. After a first heating of the fruit and sugar, the hot juice is strained through cheesecloth. The clear juice is then cooked again to the jelling point.

Making any of these products—especially in the traditional manner without commercial pectin—takes patience, precise measurement, and practice. Cooks must learn about a fruit's pectin content in order to judge cooking time; undercooking results in a runny product, while overcooking renders jam, jelly, or preserves tough and grainy. Traditional Appalachian cooks learned which fruits have a high pectin content and which need the addition of either commercial pectin or natural pectin in the form of apple juice, apple peels, or unripe berries to aid in jelling.

See also: FRUITS AND BERRIES; SWEETENERS.

—Katie Hoffman Doman, *Tusculum College*

Loggers' Foods

In the logging camps that flourished in the mountains from about 1880 to 1920, food was a major preoccupation. Six days a week for ten hours a day, loggers engaged in the exhausting work of felling huge trees, peeling them, and transporting them to sawmills. Vast amounts of food were necessary to restore the calories that the loggers burned, but food also provided diversion and reward in an otherwise isolated, lonely, and arduous existence.

Logging as a business began in Appalachia about 1820. Before that it was an off-season pursuit of farmers. With the American Industrial Revolution, construction of cities and railroads drastically increased the demand for lumber, and Appalachia was the prime source.

After the Civil War, large commercial enterprises discovered the still expansive pine and hardwood forests. These companies bought or contracted large tracts of forested land, hired full-time logging crews, and by 1880 began systematically cutting vast areas.

A large percentage of Appalachian loggers were part-time farmers who commuted home to their wives and families whenever possible, but many were independent, single men who made the camps their homes. To itinerant lumberjacks who migrated from camp to camp, the quality of the meals was a factor in determining where to work.

In the early days, loggers took turns in the kitchen, but in commercial operations the cooking and dining facilities were separated from the sleeping quarters, and full-time, professional cooks were employed. The bull-cook, or boiler, as the main cook was known, was assisted by one or two so-called cookees and two or three waiters, referred to as flunkeys. Female cooks, known as she-cooks, she-boilers, or open-bottom cooks, were rare.

The cook held an exalted position in the camp, reflecting the significance of food in keeping workers satisfied. He earned more than any other worker with the exception of the foreman. Regarded almost as celebrities, cooks could be forgiven dirty habits and disagreeable personalities, providing their food was acceptable. Those who did not satisfy were quickly booted out at the insistence of the men.

The cook worked extremely hard and helped to regulate the activity of the camp. Rising at three or four o'clock in the morning, he typically served a huge breakfast to fifty or a hundred workers at half past five and was responsible for two enormous lunches, consumed at eleven o'clock and at three in the afternoon, and an equally expansive dinner, usually eaten at nine o'clock in the evening. He planned the daily menus, ordered supplies a week in advance, and baked all his own bread and pastries.

One grocery shopping list from 1907, when foremen and cooks earned about three dollars a day, shows a tally of almost $150 for a week's groceries to feed forty-five men. Among the items were 295 pounds of beef, two barrels of flour, and 112 pounds of cabbage.

With the exception of requests to pass the plates, meals were usually eaten in complete silence and generally lasted no more than half an hour, a phenomenon that testifies to the control that the cook exerted over the men. This practice probably was imposed by cooks to expedite eating, which allowed them to get out of the kitchen faster after a long day.

Loggers did not expect fancy meals, but they demanded food that was well prepared and properly seasoned. Most preferred plain Appalachian fare such as smoked ham, potatoes, and corn bread. Tales are told of a logger polishing off a dozen eggs at a sitting or piling an entire platter of steaks onto his own plate.

The cook's skill with pastry was often more important than his ability with the rest of the meal. The need for rib-sticking, high-energy foods put a premium on pastries, so biscuits, pies, and bread were highly esteemed.

In their colorful fashion, lumbermen coined nicknames for nearly everything, especially foods. In their jargon, biscuits became cat-heads. Coffee was called jerk-water or Arbuckles. Milk was cow or white line. Donuts were fried holes or doorknobs, and apple butter became Pennsylvania salve.

Food was not neglected even during the difficult and dangerous process of driving logs down mountain streams and rivers to the sawmills before the invention of log railroads. During the drives, which generally lasted from one to two weeks, the men lived in covered log rafts called arks that comprised both a bunkhouse and a separate cookshack and dining room.

Typically measuring seventy to a hundred feet long, the arks often accommodated as many as a hundred men. Foods commonly carried on these trips included corn bread, bacon, preserved vegetables, jellies, sorghum syrup, and corn liquor.

At the steam-powered sawmills where the logs were processed into lumber, the men may not have worked as strenuously as their lumberjack colleagues, but reportedly they ate as well. Sawmill gravy, supposedly invented when one Smoky Mountain sawmill cook ran out of flour and had to substitute cornmeal in the gravy, has been said to suggest a frugal existence. However, during the Appalachian lumber industry's peak years, loggers and sawmill hands generally were considered to be among the best-fed workers in the country.

See also: LUMBER INDUSTRY (BUSINESS, INDUSTRY, AND TECHNOLOGY); LUMBER SETTLEMENTS (SETTLEMENT AND MIGRATION); TIMBER AND LUMBER WORKERS (LABOR).

—Deanne L. Moskowitz, *Mount Washington, Massachusetts*

Chris Bolgiano, *The Appalachian Forest: A Search for Roots and Renewal* (1998); Roy B. Clarkson, *Tumult on the Mountains* (1964).

Miners' Foods

The arduous work of a coal miner requires hearty food in substantial quantities. Traditional coal miners' foods have reflected not only the everyday fare of Appalachia but also the diverse foods brought to the coalfields by immigrants from Europe and the Middle East and by African Americans from the South.

In the first half of the twentieth century, most coal-camp families tended their own vegetable gardens, producing tomatoes, corn, lettuce, onions, green beans, cucumbers, peppers, squash, cabbage, and potatoes. If their house lot had no space for a garden, they usually planted on a nearby hillside or cultivated an unused plot of land within reasonable walking distance. In addition, camp residents gathered potherbs, berries, mushrooms, and other edible wild plants. Many families also raised chickens and a hog each year. Flour, sugar, cornmeal, coffee, and other necessities that could not be grown had to be purchased from the company store. During strikes and other lean times, families subsisted on beans and potatoes or, in later years, on commodities such as cheese, peanut butter, and staples provided by the union or the federal government. Until electric and gas stoves became the norm, families used cast-iron cookware on wood or coal stoves. Single miners and those working some distance from home usually stayed in boardinghouses, where the woman of the house cooked and served meals from predawn to dusk and packed rows of lunch buckets before going to bed at night.

Coal miners' breakfasts have traditionally been large and hot: eggs; bacon, ham, or sausage; fried potatoes; biscuits and red-eye or sausage gravy; cooked apples; and strong coffee. The meal brought from home and eaten during a coal miner's work shift is usually called dinner, regardless of what time of day or night it is eaten. Appalachian miners usually carry more than enough food for one person in their dinner buckets. Those who pack miners' buckets follow a tradition of including an extra sandwich in case a roof fall or other catastrophe traps their loved ones underground. However, miners never hoard the excess food; they commonly share or trade their bounty, and if an accident occurs, the section foreman designates a crewmember to collect the food and water and place it in a central location for equal distribution.

Inside the mine, workers eat in what is called the dinner hole, an area supplied with benches located away from the production site. Purchased at the company store or a local hardware store, the miner's traditional metal dinner bucket is cylindrical and divided into three sections beneath the lid. The bottom compartment is designed to hold about two quarts of drinking water while a removable middle section contains most of the food and an upper pie tray holds desserts. The bucket is carried with a bailed handle. A necessity underground, fresh water sloshed freely in the cool lower section of the bucket and was sipped from the edge not only by the owner, but his friends. Today, commercially bottled water or plastic water bottles filled at home are more common. Although some miners carry bag

Metal dinner buckets once used by coal miners on display at the Exhibition Coal Mine Museum, Beckley, West Virginia, 2000. Some miners still carry the old-fashioned metal buckets.

lunches or a domed lunch box with a thermos in its hinged lid, present-day workers often carry small plastic insulated coolers. Old-timers and tradition-minded younger miners proudly continue to carry the old-fashioned metal bucket.

Until the mid-twentieth century, home-cooked foods typical of the region were the mainstays of the miner's dinner bucket: brown beans and corn bread, corn bread crumbled into a Mason jar of buttermilk, ham sandwiches on home-baked bread, cold fried chicken or pork chops, game meats such as rabbit, cat-head biscuits, fried apple pies, cakes, fruit cobblers, and coffee, milk, or buttermilk. Miners from immigrant families often packed ethnic foods or a raw onion with brown bread and strong coffee. Dinner underground frequently consisted of yesterday's leftovers.

In recent years, miners have viewed home-cooked leftovers as treats. As processed foods became common and miners' salaries rose, commercially prepared items replaced those traditionally made from scratch. A contemporary miner's lunch typically consists of at least two sandwiches on white bread (usually ham, salami, peanut butter and jelly, or bologna—humorously referred to as "coal miner's steak"), fresh fruit, packaged lunch cakes (the Little Debbie brand remains a favorite), a small bag of potato chips, and a can of soda or a thermos of coffee. Once wrapped in waxed paper, sandwiches are now carried in plastic sandwich bags. Some mines have even installed microwave ovens underground, introducing microwavable foods such as popcorn or frozen dinners.

Several foods and food traditions have originated in Appalachian mining communities. Among the better known are two popular desserts—a black walnut cake known as coal-camp cake and a three-layer jam cake known as John L. Lewis jam cake, supposedly because it was a favorite of the first president of the United Mine Workers of America.

By introducing novel tastes and traditions to the native Appalachians, newly arriving European immigrants greatly influenced coal miners' foods. Italian immigrant Giuseppe Agiro receives credit for inventing the pepperoni roll in 1927 as a convenient lunch treat for Fairmont, West Virginia, coal miners. Agiro's original pepperoni roll consisted of a six-inch tube of yeast dough wrapped around two pepperoni sticks. Since each pepperoni stick was individually encased in dough, the bread formed two tunnels around the pepperoni as it baked, allowing the spicy oil to soak into the bread. Seventy-five years later, the pepperoni roll remains a popular item at the Agiro family's Country Club Bakery.

In and around Wheeling, West Virginia, generations of coal miners have packed Lebanese meat pies called *spheha* in their dinner buckets. Purchased at a Lebanese bakery, the pies are baked triangular bread pockets folded over a seasoned beef filling. Miners placed the handheld pies on the hot motors of underground machinery to warm them before eating.

Coal miners who drank alcoholic beverages generally saved their consumption for the weekends. During prohibition, the moonshine business boomed. Many families made a malted "home brew" and elderberry or wild grape wine. After prohibition, many Appalachian counties remained dry, so coal-camp bars and liquor stores were rare. As a result, a few individuals with automobiles and the financial means bootlegged by driving to the nearest liquor store, buying pints of whiskey in quantity and illegally selling them from their homes or cars at a profit. Some boardinghouses illegally sold their renters beer from kegs delivered to the premises and often saved the empty kegs to make homemade sauerkraut.

See also: COAL SETTLEMENTS (SETTLEMENT AND MIGRATION); COAL TOWNS (FAMILY AND COMMUNITY).

—Annette Yurkovich Shumate, *Indiana, Pennsylvania*

Cheryl Ryan Harshman, "West Virginia Foodways: A Visit to the Lebanon Bakery," *Goldenseal Magazine* (Summer 1990); Jeanne Mozier, *Way Out in West Virginia* (1999); Mark F. Sohn, *Mountain Country Cooking: A Gathering of the Best Recipes from the Smokies to the Blue Ridge* (1996).

Moonshine

Immigrants to Appalachia from the British Isles and Northern Ireland brought distilling tools—copper pots and condensing coils—along with knowledge of still making and whiskey manufacture, introducing a craft and an eventually illegal enterprise that became a central element of the region's identity. The newcomers and their descendants—particularly the Scots-Irish from Northern Ireland—were delighted to find a new grain—Indian maize, or corn—and they quickly put it to use in their mash along with barley they had used in making Irish and Scotch whiskeys. They also found in the Appalachian interior abundant streams of limestone soft water, a primary whiskey-making component.

The corn-based whiskey soon had universal uses, becoming as valuable as Continental dollars. Spirits were used as barter to purchase the necessities of life on the frontier—salt, nails, and even farmland—and to pay property taxes. Corn whiskey became a popular social beverage and was used as the base for frontier medicines, often combined with herbs. George Washington, typical of many farmers across the South, built a still at Dogue Creek in Virginia and hired a Scottish distiller. His operation turned out generous quantities of rye whiskey and peach, persimmon, and apple brandy. In the interior, economics drove farmers to turn corn into whiskey. While frontier farmers could haul only

A small moonshine still, or "mountain coffee pot," near Sinking Creek, Virginia, 1959. This still can produce about twelve gallons of "straight corn" in a single night.

four bushels of grain to market on a mule or horse, they could transport the equivalent of twenty-four bushels of grain on a horse if distilled into what they called liquid corn.

With one exception, whiskey making in early America was free from taxation. That exception was an eleven-year period of federal regulation starting in 1791; resentment of this taxation precipitated the Whiskey Rebellion.

Although the word *moonshine* had been used in the 1600s to describe whiskey runners along the British coast who were evading English taxes, the terms *moonshiner* and *moonshine whiskey* were not in common use in America until the late 1860s, after the United States government imposed excise taxes on distilled spirits to pay Civil War expenses. Many farmers across the region, resentful of the taxes and wishing to sell their farm products freely, went underground and made whiskey illicitly, much of it by the light of the moon. Another term used in the late 1800s to describe Appalachian moonshiners was *blockaders*, a Civil War expression for persons running military blockades. Their product was called "blockade liquor."

While corn whiskey by United States government definition calls for the use of an 80 percent corn mash, moonshine had no standards, thus leaving to individual distillers the option to improvise recipes. Many used low-grade wheat shorts, for instance, along with sugar and sorghum syrup rather than the preferred corn, rye, or barley malt.

Moonshining expanded considerably during prohibition years. National prohibition lasted from 1920 to 1933, but southern states such as Georgia and Tennessee had enacted prohibition laws years earlier. Thus, for more than two and a half decades, moonshiners found a booming market for their illicit beverages. Much of the moonshine made in the Appalachians was transported to major cities across the region such as Chattanooga, Knoxville, Asheville, and Atlanta, as well as to metropolitan areas such as Chicago, Cleveland, and New York. While illicit whiskey making during this period flourished across Appalachia from Kentucky and West Virginia into north Alabama, three areas took turns as the nation's moonshine capital: Wilkes County, North Carolina; Dawson County, Georgia; and Cocke County, Tennessee. During the years following national prohibition, many southern states remained largely dry due to local-option liquor laws, and moonshining continued to boom.

Prohibition spawned drivers who developed racing skills while running moonshine whiskey in retooled cars on mountain roads at high speeds. Favorite early whiskey cars were the 1939 and 1940 Ford coupes. Many young drivers in Dawson County drove their whiskey to bootleg distribution outlets in Atlanta during the week and on Sundays raced their modified cars on the dirt Lakewood Speedway. These Sunday competitions marked the beginning of today's popular stock car racing operated by NASCAR, the National Association of Stock Car Automobile Racing.

After the mid-1950s, the number of mountain farmers making moonshine on simple copper pot–type stills had declined greatly. This decline was due to a changing economy and a slow reduction in the number of dry Appalachian counties. However, because of the high cost of commercially produced liquor, there remained a significant incentive for illegal liquor production, and a few maintained large operations that resembled modern businesses more than small-farm moonshining.

See also: CORN; SCOTS-IRISH (RACE, ETHNICITY, AND IDENTITY); WINE.

—Joseph E. Dabney, *Atlanta, Georgia*

Joseph E. Dabney, *Mountain Spirits: A Chronicle of Corn Whiskey from King James' Ulster Plantation to America's Appalachians and the Moonshine Life* (1974) and *More Mountain Spirits: The Continuing Chronicle* (1980); H. F. Wilkie, *Beverage Spirits in America* (1947).

Mushrooms

Mushrooms of all kinds thrive in the mixed forests of the Appalachians, and both wild and cultivated types are abundant today. Moving southward, the mushroom season gets

Bowl of morel mushrooms, 2001. In Appalachia, morels are also known as dry land fish, hickory chickens, markels, and bigfoot morels.

longer. One mushroom, the morel *(Morchella esculenta)*, is both widely distributed and especially prized.

Morels are conical, honeycomb mushrooms that grow on fat stems with the cap and stem constituting a continuous piece. In Appalachia, they are called dry land fish, hickory chickens, markels, and big-foot. For those who know them, morels are among the easiest and safest mushrooms to hunt. Morel hunters suggest that a person look for mushrooms while walking uphill, because they will be at eye level and easier to see. Those who are not experienced in mushroom identification may confuse morels with a look-alike—the *Helvella esculenta*, or beefsteak morel—and must be aware that some mushrooms are extremely poisonous.

Morels prefer rich soils mixed with ashes. They thrive in burned-over ground, old fencerows, tree-covered hills, and established orchards. Morels generally grow from an inch to six inches in height, and like other mushrooms, they spread by spores. Cutting the stalk with a sharp knife to gather the morels is the preferred method because it does not damage the roots and enhances the likelihood for morels to come back.

Dedicated morel hunters know when the time is right to gather these culinary prizes. In southern Appalachia, they mature in April after a warm rain and when blue violets are in bloom. As one moves north, the morel season begins later, especially at higher elevations.

Chefs from Paris to New York prepare morels in a variety of ways, but traditional Appalachian cooks tend to fry them in bacon grease either without a coating or dipped in a cornmeal batter.

Other mushrooms, including puffballs *(Calvatia gigantea)* and oak rabbits or lion's manes *(Hericium erinaceus)*, are also popular. More than 150 edible species are indigenous to Appalachia, but because several deadly species are common, most people are afraid to eat unidentified mushrooms. Mushroom clubs affiliated with the North American Mycological Association are active in a number of Appalachian states, and their members help others with wild mushroom identification.

Since 1980, some Appalachian states have initiated extensive cultivation of mushrooms. The most common cultivated mushroom is the shiitake (pronounced *shee-ta-key*). This firm, tasty, and easily stored mushroom is cultivated on dead hardwood logs by drilling holes in green logs, inserting starter mixture obtained from one of several laboratories in the region, and stacking inoculated logs in the woods where they originated. After about a year, the logs begin producing mushrooms, and they continue to produce as many as twelve crops for three to four years.

See also: GREENS.

—Sidney Saylor Farr, *Berea, Kentucky;* Paul Goland, *Franklin, West Virginia;* and Mark F. Sohn, *Pikeville College*

Sidney Saylor Farr, *More Than Moonshine: Appalachian Recipes and Recollections* (1983); David W. Fischer and Alan E. Bessette, *Edible Wild Mushrooms of North America: A Field-to-Kitchen Guide* (1992); Anna Lee Robe-Terry, *Bootstraps and Biscuits: Three Hundred Wonderful Wild Food Recipes from the Hills of West Virginia* (1997).

Native American Foodways

The Appalachian region was colonized at least twelve thousand years ago, if not earlier, as the glaciers that covered the northern portion of the region retreated. Temperatures remained several degrees colder than they are today, especially in the north, until about ten thousand years ago. The first human inhabitants hunted and gathered their foods and may have taken species of large animals that became extinct about 10,800 years ago, including mastodon and giant tortoise, although it is unclear how much they depended on these animals. More important to the diet in southern Appalachia, especially after the these species disappeared, were white-tailed deer, waterfowl, turkeys, squirrels, raccoons, and fish, among other animals. Nuts, berries, and probably greens were gathered. Hickories, black walnuts, acorns, grapes, hackberries, and persimmons were among the most important wild plant foods. North of central Virginia, where climatic conditions were much colder, people seem to have concentrated their efforts primarily on hunting caribou in addition to gathering wild plants. As the climate continued to ameliorate and caribou migrated north with the melting ice sheets, hunters in north Appalachia turned to deer and smaller animals as well.

Approximately eight thousand years ago, climatic conditions became markedly warmer and drier than they are today, a period referred to as the Hypsithermal Climatic Interval. Sea levels and river channels stabilized, making floodplains more attractive places to live than they had been previously. Along some rivers in southern Appalachia, such as the Tennessee and Green Rivers, extensive settlements were established between roughly seven thousand and three thousand years ago near river shoals, where shellfish could be easily harvested. These settlements included large artificial shell mounds, which probably served as markers of identity for the people who lived there.

As people began to live in settlements, especially near rivers, for greater portions of the year, their impact on their surrounding environment increased. Native peoples had likely managed the landscape since their arrival in Appalachia, particularly through the use of fire. This technique improves browse for deer, clears underbrush for easier travel and nut collection, and enhances the growth of some plant species. As settlements became larger and longer lasting, however, they created disturbed habitats that encouraged the growth of weedy plants. Through time, Native Americans cultivated some desirable weedy plants including squash, bottle gourd, goosefoot, sunflower, and sumpweed. Native Americans had been cultivating plants several thousand years prior to the arrival of the first European colonists to the New World. Domesticated specimens of squash date back nearly five thousand years, and bottle gourd about forty-three hundred. Sunflower and sumpweed were domesticated approximately four thousand years ago and goosefoot by thirty-five hundred years ago. Additional cultivated species include maygrass, knotweed, and little barley. These plants were probably grown in gardens near villages and were harvested for their seeds. In addition, the hard rinds of squash and bottle gourd were used as containers. These horticultural practices were initiated in present-day Tennessee, Kentucky, Ohio, and Illinois, later spreading west, south, and east. Garden plots were not cultivated in northern Appalachia at this time, however, due in part to the shorter growing season.

Among all groups in Appalachia, hunting and gathering of wild plants, especially hickory nuts and acorn, continued to be significant subsistence activities. In addition to game procured by hunting and fishing, Native Americans obtained meat through "garden hunting," taking advantage of the fact that animals such as rabbits and deer find plants grown in garden stands attractive food sources. By hunting these animals, Native Americans simultaneously protected their crops and procured meat.

Cultivation of native crops intensified over several thousand years as increasingly sedentary settlement patterns evolved. If they did not live near their fields year-round, native gardeners must have been present at least during the planting and harvesting seasons. This development of farming was to culminate after 1000 B.C. in more sedentary lifeways. It was into this well-established horticultural system that maize (corn) was introduced to the southeastern United States from Mexico, most likely via the Southwest, approximately seventeen hundred years ago. Maize did not become a common constituent of native fields until about a thousand years ago, however. At this time the practice of maize agriculture became widespread from northern Mississippi and Alabama through southern New York, especially with the introduction of hardy varieties that could tolerate the limited growing seasons of the Northeast. Other crops were beans, pumpkins, squash, and sunflowers. The common bean, also first domesticated in Mexico, quickly spread through eastern North America, around eight hundred years ago to the Southeast, reaching the Northeast about one hundred years later. With this last addition, the maize-bean-squash agricultural triad traditionally associated with eastern North American Indians was established. People supplemented these staples with native crops, nuts, wild fruits, and greens, as well as meat and fish.

Coincident with the adoption of maize agriculture was an increase in population, an increase in the size of settlements, and the formation of chiefdoms in the southern portions of Appalachia. While the mechanisms involved in the development of chiefdoms are numerous and complex, agriculture played an indirect role, as the surplus provided by maize harvests could be used to support an elite class. In northern Appalachia, however, where maize agriculture was not practiced as intensively as in the southern region, Native American groups maintained a more egalitarian social structure.

The adoption of maize agriculture also had an impact on the health of Native Americans. The starchy sugars in corn kernels stick to teeth, causing higher rates of cavities, periodontal disease, and tooth loss than do the nuts, seeds and greens that people had been eating previously. Rates of anemia also increased among populations practicing maize agriculture. This may be related to the low level of iron in maize or its property of binding with iron from other sources in the diet. Parasites, which spread quickly in close living conditions like villages, can also be associated with anemia by consuming iron or causing internal bleeding. Thus, although the production of maize supported larger populations in smaller areas, the general health of these populations declined.

The arrival of Europeans in the early sixteenth century had significant impact on Native American foodways. In their efforts to explore and colonize the New World, Europeans brought with them a variety of plants and animals. Native groups throughout the Appalachian region were quick to adopt old-world plants such as peaches, watermelons, and cowpeas. Watermelons and cowpeas were analogous to squash and beans in native subsistence systems and thus were easily incorporated into Native American diets. Despite the acceptance of these new plant foods by native groups, the traditional agricultural triad of maize-bean-squash continued to dominate native subsistence systems.

During the seventeenth century, Native Americans became heavily involved in the deerskin trade. To satisfy the demands of European traders, native hunters began to focus their efforts more heavily on deer in the Southeast and beaver in the Northeast, as well as other fur-bearing mammals such as bear and fox. This focus on fur-bearing mammals resulted in a shift away from the exploitation of aquatic habitats and a concentration on terrestrial species. White-tailed deer, wild turkey, and box turtle were important dietary mainstays, supplemented by smaller mammals and fish. Unlike old-world plants, European animal domesticates were not as readily adopted by Native American groups. While most plants introduced from the Old World were incorporated into southeastern native cuisines by the late sixteenth century, domesticated animals did not become common components of native diets until the late seventeenth century, somewhat later in the Northeast. Domestic cows and chickens became common to native foodways during this time, but pigs were rarely eaten until much later.

Gender is an important aspect of native identity to be considered in any treatment of foodways. Ethnohistoric documents from the Appalachian region indicate that native groups had a clear gendered division of labor. Although men provided meat through their hunting activities, most food-related tasks fell to women. Women farmed large communal tracts and small garden plots. They gathered foods, carried water, and guarded crops against predators. Women prepared and stored the food. They also produced the pottery that was used to cook and serve food.

Women prepared a variety of dishes from their inventory of grown, gathered, and hunted foods. Stews and breads compose the two most common recipes, both of which require a hominy base. Similar to grits, hominy (or corn gruel) required extensive processing. Hickory nut oil, or hickory milk, was also an important ingredient in soups and stews. Because hickory kernels are tightly encased in the interior shell, it was extremely time-consuming and labor-intensive to extract the nutmeats by hand. Instead, hickory nuts were generally pounded into pieces and boiled to extract the oil. This boiling process unlocked the nutmeats and oil, which were then skimmed off the top. Grain seeds (little barley, goosefoot, knotweed, amaranth) and oily seeds (sunflower and sumpweed) were generally toasted and then ground into flour before being added to breads and stews. Not surprisingly, fish and meat products also served as ingredients in these stews. In addition, they were dried and roasted fresh over open fires.

Access to food varied according to both gender and power. For example, Native American women planted, harvested, processed, and cooked maize. Their close involvement with this plant afforded them greater access to its consumption. As game hunters, native men had greater and more immediate access to fresh meat than to maize products. This differential access to plant and animal resources often culminated in gendered patterns of consumption. In the archaeological record, native women exhibit significantly higher incidences of dental cavities than men as a result of women's greater consumption of maize. In this case, differential access to food played a key role in dental health.

Access to food also tends to be more highly differentiated in ranked versus egalitarian societies. The chiefdoms that originated in southern Appalachia after A.D. 1000, characterized by a two-tiered hierarchy of noble and commoner classes, provide excellent examples of how power shapes access to food resources. Certain types of foods were produced and procured by commoners and then funneled to chiefs and their families in the form of tribute. Staple foods such as maize, dried fish, and venison were included in tribute payments and were sometimes accompanied by special ceremonial foods, the consumption of which was often restricted to elite members of society. Foods that were assigned ceremonial value varied from group to group but generally included species such as bear, passenger pigeons, raptors, carnivores, and yaupon holly leaves, the main ingredient in the ceremonial Black Drink. In addition to specific types of plant and animal foods, chiefs were also afforded access to certain parts of an animal. Often hunters would provide chiefs with the choicest cuts of animals such as deer and bear. In addition to gender, status clearly played an important role in determining the composition of an individual's diet in native Appalachian societies.

See also: NATIVE AMERICAN AGRICULTURE (AGRICULTURE); NATIVE AMERICANS (RACE, ETHNICITY, AND IDENTITY).

—Kandace R. Detwiler and Amber M. VanDerwarker, *University of North Carolina*

Judith A. Bense, *Archaeology of the Southeastern United States: Paleoindian to World War I* (1994); Brian M. Fagan, *Ancient North America: The Archaeology of a Continent* (2000).

Nuts

Black walnuts and pecans are the most common nuts in the contemporary Appalachian diet and in times past even served as currency and enhanced the value of land. Of the states included in Appalachia, Georgia is especially rich in pecan groves. Thought to have originated in the Mississippi River Valley, the pecan tree has a lengthy life span, with healthy specimens often living more than a century and some up to a thousand years. It takes at least ten years for a pecan tree to begin producing nuts, but a single tree subsequently can bring nearly a quarter ton of pecans in a single season. Pecans (whole or in pieces) have long been used extensively in the preparation of pies, cakes, and cookies and were often ground into a coarse flour or meal used to enrich breads, pie crusts, and meat and bean dishes. Pecan meal is also added to flour used for dredging fish or chicken before frying.

Black walnut trees can be found throughout Appalachia and as far south as Florida and Texas, their presence indicating fertile, loose soil with high limestone content. For this reason, early settlers in the region valued land where walnut trees grew. The Cherokees referred to the nuts as *se-di*, frequently frying them with corn.

Having a distinctive, sharp taste, the nuts continue to be used to flavor both savory and sweet dishes; they can also be pickled. In addition to their many uses in food, they can serve as a digestive lubricant. The process for shelling black walnuts is laborious. The sticky brown hull must first be removed before the nuts are dried and cracked. Early Appalachians used rocks, hammers, and clubs to open the nuts; later, the nuts were placed in bags and run over with a truck or tractor. After the shells are opened, the small nutmeats must be pried from the shell with a pick. Although the yield per bushel of nuts in the hull is low, a few black walnuts provide a considerable amount of flavor.

Hickory nuts (related to both walnuts and pecans), butternuts, and beechnuts are other popular nutmeats commonly used in Appalachian kitchens. Hickory nuts were originally used by the Algonquin Indians, who called the trees *powcohicora*—a name eventually shortened to pohickory then to hickory. Beechnuts, although sometimes used in cooking, are more commonly found in the barnyard—specifically for feeding pigs. They are generally regarded as foodstuffs only in times of calamity and famine.

The American chestnut, which was virtually wiped out by a fungus in the early 1900s, also played a major role in the early society and economy of Appalachia. Native Americans are believed to have cultivated the tree along with other nut trees; they mixed the nuts with corn to make bread and parched them to prepare a coffeelike beverage. Medicinally, the leaves of the tree were used to treat heart conditions, and the sprouts were made into a tea for treating cold sores and mixed with honey for a cough syrup. Because chestnuts contained tannic acid, which made them impervious to rot and insects, they were an extremely important food source for Appalachians, as well as a trade commodity. The nuts were frequently eaten plain, but more often they were roasted or boiled.

See also: CHESTNUT BLIGHT (ENVIRONMENT); FRUITS AND BERRIES; TREES, SHRUBS, AND NATIVE PLANTS (AGRICULTURE).

—Katie Hoffman Doman, *Tusculum College*, and Catherine S. Vodrey, *East Liverpool, Ohio*

Open-Hearth Cooking

For several centuries, open-hearth cooking (also known as fireplace cooking) was an essential means for food preparation. Cookstoves did not reach the mountains until the mid-1800s, and open-hearth cooking continued in certain rural or mountainous regions of Appalachia as late as the early to mid-twentieth century. Today, skilled interpreters at living history museums regularly practice it.

There were two types of cooking fireplaces built in Appalachia. The most common employed a lug pole, a horizontal bar installed about three feet above the hearth floor into the sidewalls of the chimney. The other type depended on an iron crane attached to a side of the fireplace wall. To protect the cook from being burned, the crane could be swung out over the hearth. The lug pole and crane were used similarly in the cooking process.

Other common cast-iron utensils included andirons or fire dogs to elevate the logs off the floor, bellows to give oxygen to the fire, a shovel to bring coals out onto the hearth, a stoker to stoke the fire, and tongs to pick up individual coals and arrange the logs.

Trammels and S-hooks attached to the lug pole or crane held and adjusted pots over the fire for boiling. Dutch ovens, placed on hot coals on the hearth with coals arranged on their lipped lids, were used for baking. To help bake their contents evenly, a trivet could be placed underneath the dish inside the oven. Pots usually had a bail or pothooks for hanging, and most had legs, which gave the cook the option of cooking directly over the fire or setting the pot over coals on the hearth. A kettle with water always hung in the fireplace for a constant source of hot water. Roasting was accomplished by using an iron spit that could be attached to the firedogs. For frying food, skillets were placed on top of the fire.

The kitchen hearth has always been an important part of a home. It was a primary source of heat and light as well as the main method of preparing food. Open-hearth cooking was dangerous, time-consuming, and labor-intensive for the cook, historically the woman of the household. However, those who have experienced the taste of food prepared on the open hearth will often insist that food tastes better when cooked over the fire.

See also: CAST-IRON COOKWARE; WOODSTOVE COOKING.

—Ginger Nicole Morelock, *Tyner, North Carolina*

Sally Eustice, *History from the Hearth: A Colonial Michilimackinac Cookbook* (1997); Doris E. Farrington, *Fireside Cooks and Black Kettle Recipes* (1976); Kay Moss and Kathryn Hoffman, *The Backcountry Housewife: A Study of Eighteenth-Century Foods* (1994).

Dishes of pawpaw pudding shown with ripe pawpaw fruit, 1996. Pawpaws are America's largest native edible fruit.

Pawpaws

Growing on trees in creek bottoms from Georgia to southern Ohio, the nutritious pawpaw *(Asimina triloba)* is America's largest native edible fruit. Twenty-seven varieties are grown in the United States and are available from about fifty commercial nurseries. Native to the Appalachian region, the pawpaw is a member of the tropical custard family, Annonaceae.

With large, tropical-like green leaves similar to those of southern magnolias, pawpaw trees bloom in the spring with a striking maroon flower that opens like a wild rose. The fruit is full-sized in the Appalachians between late August and mid-October. Pawpaws often fall from the tree while still green and need to ripen and sweeten off the tree. Once fully ripe, the fruit will keep up to a week refrigerated. Partially ripe, it can be kept for three weeks if refrigerated and then allowed to finish ripening at room temperature. The fruit also freezes beautifully, either whole or pulped. To make pulp, the fruit can be pushed through a ricer to remove the skin and seeds from the custardlike flesh.

The fruit has a powerful aroma and a unique, tropical flavor reminiscent of banana, mango, and pineapple. Shaped like giant peanuts, pawpaws feature a thin green skin similar to a mango. Like a banana's, the skin turns brown to black as it ripens. The fruit grows in clusters or singly; one stem can have fruit of varying sizes. When sliced open, the flesh contains many black seeds in a semi-random row down the center of the fruit. The seeds resemble oversized watermelon seeds. Although pawpaws thrive along creeks, they grow in open fields as well.

The fruit is nutritious with more vitamins, minerals, and amino acids than apples, peaches, or grapes. The plant's leaf, bark, and twig tissue also produces natural compounds (annonaceous acetogenins) that possess insecticidal and anticancer properties. Kentucky State University leads the country's pawpaw research at its Atwood Research Facility in Frankfort. In partnership with the Pawpaw Foundation (also located in Frankfort), Kentucky State University publishes information on variety trials, cultural recommendations, clonal propagation, germ plasm collection, molecular characterization of genetic diversity in existing cultivars, and native germ plasm as well as cooking with pawpaws. Atwood is also the site of the United States Department of Agriculture's National Clonal Germplasm Repository for pawpaws.

Pawpaws kept Lewis and Clark alive as they returned from their expedition to the Pacific in 1810. This was nearly three hundred years after Hernando de Soto and his army were saved from near starvation by eating pawpaws in the 1540s when they reached the Mississippi Valley. In the twenty-first century, the pawpaw remains an Appalachian specialty. The fruit is eaten raw and in breads, puddings, fruit sauces, and ice cream. In general, pawpaws are substituted for bananas in recipes. Pawpaws are featured on some of the most prestigious restaurant menus in America, including the pawpaw coulis at the Mobil Five Star Charlie Trotter's in Chicago and flamed pawpaws Foster at the Oakroom in Louisville, Kentucky's Seelbach Hilton.

See also: FRUITS (ECOLOGY); FRUITS AND BERRIES.

—Adam R. Seger, *Seelbach Hilton, Louisville, Kentucky*

Snake C. Jones and Desmond R. Layne, *Cooking with Pawpaws* (1997); Desmond R. Layne, "The Pawpaw [*Asimina triloba* (L.) Dunal]: A New Fruit Crop for Kentucky and the United States," *HortScience* (September 1996); R. N. Peterson, J. P. Cherry, and J. G. Simmons, "Composition of Pawpaw *(Asimina triloba)* Fruit," *Northern Nut Growers Association Annual Report* (1982).

Pies

Pies can be sweet and served as desserts or savory (made with fish, meat, vegetables, or poultry) and served as entire meals. Cooks in different locations in Appalachia traditionally prepared pies according to the fillings and type of cooking facilities available. Deep-dish meat, fish, or fruit and pot or spoon pies were cooked over an open fire, while shallow pies were made with fruit, custard, or nut fillings and baked in a wood-burning stove. A shallow pie might show the filling with an edge of crust indicating pastry on the bottom, or a top layer of pastry that was attached, or crimped, to the bottom pastry might cover a filling to make a double-crust pie. Some pies were topped with a sprinkling of sugar and nuts instead of pastry. The diversity of pie recipes reflects their makers' diversity of heritage, ingredients, creativity, and cooking skills.

Pies have always been served at barn raisings, baptisms, funerals, revivals, family reunions, harvest dances, and holiday parties. As families traveled throughout the Appalachian region, they shared recipes, many dating from the early nineteenth century. Cookbooks and recipe boxes today contain countless suggestions for crusts and inventive fillings cooks created based on whatever was available.

Shoofly pie, one of the best-known pies made in northern Appalachia, contains molasses and sugar (either brown or white) as sweeteners but varies slightly in sweetness or ingredients depending on whether it was created in Pennsylvania or Ohio. If prepared by someone in Alabama or Georgia, it may be called molasses pie. Chess, sugar cream, black bottom, and butterscotch or buttermilk pie are closely related to shoofly pie. Apple, plum, peach, nut, cherry, pumpkin, and sweet potato pies likewise vary somewhat in spices or sweetness according to the region. Cider, vinegar, Amish raisin, and Scots oatmeal pies are more prevalent in the upper half of the region; pawpaw, grape (or muscadine), and sweet potato pie are more common in southern Appalachia. Blueberry, blackberry, rhubarb, and strawberry pies are also popular from the far north to the south of the region.

Meringue toppings and lemon, coconut, and chocolate cream fillings emerged at the turn of the century; they became popular when electric mixers became widely available in the 1940s and cooks learned about recipes being made in metropolitan areas. Meat, fish, and game pies also have been important on Appalachian tables. Star-gazy pie and shepherd's pie, which originated in Cornwall, England, and fisherman's pie, which came with the Irish settlers, are examples of pies that have changed with available ingredients. Freshwater fish indigenous to the mountains and squirrel, rabbit, venison, vegetables, and chicken are used in place of lamb or seafood. Star-gazy pie is a deep-dish, double- or single-crust pie, while shepherd's- and fisherman's-style pies are made with or without a bottom crust and with a mashed potato topping. Other old-world influences include turnovers and pasties (British Isles) and empanadas (Spain, Portugal), small pies that can be carried in lunch pails and eaten without a fork.

See also: CAKES AND COOKIES; SWEETS.

—June W. Hayes, *Hayes and Associates International, San Antonio, Texas*

Anna Teresa Callen, *The Wonderful World of Pizzas, Quiches, and Savory Pies* (1981); William Harlan Hale, *The Horizon Cookbook and Illustrated History of Eating and Drinking through the Ages* (1968); *Time-Life Books Foods of the World, American Cooking: The Eastern Heartland* (1971).

Poke

See Greens

Pork

Pigs first appeared on the North American continent in about 1540, trailing along in an entourage of European explorers. From then until well after the Civil War some three centuries later, pork was a vital link in the continental food chain, as it had been on the Eurasian landmass since the Stone Age. It quickly became the domesticated meat of choice in the colonies, and it has remained the signature meat of the mountain and piedmont South to the present day. The ubiquitous chicken notwithstanding, pork in all its myriad and useful forms, from barbecue to bacon grease, is the nonpareil fleshy staple of the Appalachian kitchen and those farther south.

The food historian Waverley Root has documented the presence of pigs throughout most of Europe and Asia dating back thousands of years into antiquity. Pork, he declares, "is, and always has been . . . the most important butcher's meat in the world," in large part because of its no-waste utility and low maintenance. Pigs proved their value in early America. They could forage for food when necessary, they were extremely prolific, and they were almost totally edible from snout to tail. Even the few indigestible parts, such as hoof and hair, were useful in other ways. No animal food source could possibly have been better suited to the remote and rugged forests of Appalachia.

Pigs first came into the region with the expedition of Hernando de Soto (1539–43)—a total of thirteen boars and sows, led ashore by the Spaniard and his soldiers in Tampa Bay on the west coast of Florida. By the time the explorers had made it into and across the mountains of present-day Georgia, North Carolina, and Tennessee, uncounted dozens of piglets had been farrowed and left to propagate a new breed of farm animal for the South of the future. Thus, every American pig since then, wild boar and tame shoat alike, is descended, at least symbolically, from those Spanish-born, cloven-hoofed mammals.

The English families that began settling in Virginia in the early 1600s also brought pigs, and soon both domesticated and free-roaming droves of the beasts were abundant wherever there were people. More than two hundred years later, it was still commonplace to see pigs wandering in the streets of towns and cities—in New York no less than Richmond or Nashville. Officials who tried to end the practice sometimes encountered housewives willing to take up arms to protect their pork. Even Thomas Jefferson found it hard to impose policies affecting the freedom of pigs. When he was governor of Virginia in 1780, he incited such wrath in the butchers of Richmond for trying to control the price of market-bound hogs that they stirred up a noisy protest outside his house and festooned his picket fence with chitterlings.

Before the Civil War, the South was the center of the pork industry in America, but the Union army's need for meat caused production to double in the North while supplies were dwindling in Dixie. From that time forward, pigs on the hoof (and packinghouses to process them into pork cuts) have been far more abundant in Illinois or Iowa than in Georgia or North Carolina. Tennessee and Kentucky were primary exporters of salt-cured pork before the war, but not after. The Kentucky writer James Still recalled hard times when all his family had in the way of meat was salt pork (also known as white bacon or side meat), which was sometimes dredged in flour or cornmeal before frying. Thus upgraded, the dish became "Cincinnati chicken"—a humorous nod to its packinghouse place of origin.

To be sure, a sow and a few pigs remained essential on small and isolated family farms in the mountains of Appalachia—as the primary source of meat and lard, as a supplier of by-products such as soap and hairbrushes, and even as a valuable commodity for bartering. But when it came to making big money from hogs, Appalachians, by and large, would not be among those who profited most.

It was as clever utilizers of a seasonal hog or two, rather than as mass producers of pork, that these rural people developed their storied affinity for all things porcine. The pig as symbol and substance, as pet and provider, attained an exalted place among mountain dwellers, whites and blacks alike, whether they could afford to eat "high on the hog" (tenderloins, chops, hams) or only the "leavings" (intestines, jowls, feet).

In the lean and hungry decades that stretched from Appomattox to the end of World War II, people from Arkansas to Kentucky to Virginia and back across North Carolina, Tennessee, and the upper parts of Georgia and Alabama gradually refined and perfected the ancient techniques of smoking and curing hams and bacon, of rendering lard, of making sausage, and of slow-cooking ribs and shoulders over hickory coals—techniques that had been passed down from generation to generation for centuries.

It was in the mountain and piedmont landscapes of the South (and in lowland river cities such as Memphis, Louisville, and Little Rock) that the celebrated pork specialties of the region attained their highest state: country hams, dry-cured in salt, smoked, and then aged to perfection; expertly seasoned sausage, stuffed in cloth bags and dispensed fresh or smoked; and tangy, mouth-watering barbecue so tender that it could be pulled from the bone (hence the term *pulled pork*). Farther north, in West Virginia and the Appalachian regions of Pennsylvania and New York, the utilitarian pig yielded other popular specialties, from pork chops to scrapple (a blend of organ meat and other bits, chopped and shaped into a loaf to be sliced and fried). In 2000, more than a century after the center of American pork production had shifted to the Midwest, the most distinctively rich and flavorful renditions of cooked pig to be found anywhere still came from the upper South and the Appalachian highlands.

The overall excellence of these homegrown, home-processed, home-cooked pork foods came at a high price in time and effort. "Hog-killing day" could actually last several days, involving entire families and others who volunteered in return for fresh meat or for reciprocal help when their own day came around. This was cold-weather work, mostly outdoors, and it required strength, endurance, patience, and skill. A family might kill several hogs at once to produce their year's supply of meat for the smokehouse.

In pre–World War II times, before home-freezing was an option, there was a frenzied rush to get the job done—not only to trim the hams and slabs of bacon and put them into the salt bins for curing, but also to render the fat into lard and cracklings, to preserve some choice cuts in salt water or sealed jars or bury them in tubs of lard, to season and mix the sausage, and to make pickled souse (a blend of delicate meats from the hog's head). The highlight of this arduous time was the feast on fresh pork that began at noon of the first day and continued until the work was done. There was a festival air to this culinary orgy, an immediate gratification for hunger-inducing labor. The best cooks were in the kitchen, turning out the most cherished dishes at every meal—backbones and sauerkraut, brains and eggs, spareribs, liver, fresh sausage, all manner of chops and cutlets, and the most coveted of all: the aptly named tenderloin. Only the chosen few were favored with a slice.

Next to hog-killing day—as ritual and as eating experience—was the barbecue, a nightlong watch over slowly cooking shoulders and ribs, with perhaps a kettle of Brunswick stew or burgoo simmering on a separate fire nearby. These could be bonding times, when the greater truths and myths of barbecue and the meaning of life were as closely examined as the meat itself. On the rarest of occasions, they transcended the boundaries of race, class, age, gender, religion, politics, and place of origin, becoming communions of the spirit among all who partook. More often, though, the barbecue was simply a mundane chore of strong men, either black or white, who lightened the long hours of meat-tending with food, drink, and storytelling to help them make it through the night.

As dawn broke and the feasting time neared, there came the anticipated moment when the meat was declared ready, and the first charred, crusty, tender, smoke-anointed taste of pulled pork confirmed its superiority. An all-night barbecue was a singular event, not alone for the meat but for so much more besides: the preparation, the ceremony, the social and cultural interplay, the fellowship, the anticipation, the realization, the memory. For generations, this meaningful and memorable rite of passage was observed frequently—before weddings and anniversaries, births and funerals, church and lodge gatherings, political events, welcomes and farewells. Whenever, wherever, for whatever reason, people came together—and pork was their common bond.

In consequence of the rapid modernization of America since the end of World War II, most of the ritual and ceremonial aspects of pork preparation have faded into history. By century's end few farmers butchered their own hogs, or made and stuffed their own sausage in pokes (homemade cloth sacks), or made scrapple and souse, or rendered lard from fat, or cured and aged hams in a smokehouse, or barbecued ribs and shoulders for hours over a pit of hardwood coals. Commercially produced bacon, sausages, and hams became so readily available to the buying public that only nostalgia drove the dwindling few farmers, folklorists, chefs, food co-ops, and specialty food producers to keep the ancient practices alive. Old-fashioned pit barbecue became a lost art, replaced by faster and easier (though not tastier) cooking methods.

In time, when those who vividly recall the sights and smells and tastes associated with the noncommercial processing of pork have passed into history, these delicacies may be thought of only as supermarket items encased in Styrofoam and plastic wrap, emanating from some mechanical meatmaker rather than from the mortal but mystical and seemingly indestructible hog. One indication of that coming time is the disappearance of smokehouses. The few that remain are mostly on farms in Appalachia and the highland South.

See also: BIG GAME; HOGS (AGRICULTURE).

—John Egerton, *Nashville, Tennessee*

Harriette Simpson Arnow, *Seedtime on the Cumberland* (1960) and *Flowering of the Cumberland* (1963); Joseph E. Dabney, *Smokehouse Ham, Spoon Bread, and Scuppernong Wine: The Folklore and Art of Southern Appalachian Cooking* (1998); Linda Garland Page and Eliot Wigginton, eds., *The Foxfire Book of Appalachian Cookery* (1984); Mark F. Sohn, *Mountain Country Cooking: A Gathering of the Best Recipes from the Smokies to the Blue Ridge* (1996); Joe Gray Taylor, *Eating, Drinking, and Visiting in the South* (1982).

Potatoes

Potatoes came to North America by way of South America and Europe, reaching the Appalachians with Scots-Irish and English settlers. The vegetables are boiled, baked, fried, mashed, creamed, used in breads and pastries and for medicinal purposes; they are part of most Appalachian meals and dining occasions throughout the region. Irish potatoes, or white potatoes, belong to the deadly nightshade family, which includes tomatoes, tobacco, and eggplant. The stems and leaves of the potato plant are poisonous, but the swellings in the stems below the ground become tubers that grow into potatoes.

After plundering the Caribbean, Sir Francis Drake is said to have brought potatoes to Virginia from Colombia on his way to England in the late 1580s. He gave some of the tubers to Sir Walter Raleigh's agent, who sent them to Raleigh's Irish estate. (The English botanist, John Gerard, who mistakenly believed that potatoes originated in Virginia, named them *Batata virginiana* after most likely receiving specimens from Drake.) The official entry of potatoes into the North American colonies is believed to have been in the 1620s, when the governor of the Bahamas sent a ton of potatoes to the governor of Virginia. It was thought that they would make fodder for cattle and inexpensive slave food to be shipped to the Caribbean.

It was not until 1719, when Protestant Scots-Irish immigrants brought potatoes to Londonderry, New Hampshire, that common potatoes began to be known as Irish potatoes. The Scots-Irish grew successful potato crops and popularized them as food for the rest of the population. Scots-Irish and English settlers brought potatoes to Appalachia as they gradually settled the mountains. German settlers, who ate potatoes as early as the 1570s in their native land, brought their love of potatoes to the mountains as they migrated into southern New York, Pennsylvania, and on to the Carolinas, Tennessee, Ohio, and other southern Appalachian states.

Potatoes were popular because they grew in cool, damp, and rocky areas as well as in cleared fields. In times when fields were hand cleared, potatoes could produce almost double the amount of food in the same space as grains. Until the potato blight appeared in Ireland and Europe in the 1840s, molds and dry rot sporadically killed crops in some areas of Ireland. When the blight hit Ireland, it also reached the United States and destroyed nearly 40 percent of the crops. Many blight-resistant potatoes were developed as a result. Today, Kennebec, Cherokee, and Atlantic are just a few of the potatoes available in Appalachia.

See also: SCOTS-IRISH (RACE, ETHNICITY, AND IDENTITY); SWEET POTATOES.

—Catherine D. Lucas, *Mere Catherine Cuisine, Boca Raton, Florida*

Harold McGee, *On Food and Cooking* (1984); Maggie Oster, *The Potato Garden* (1993).

Potherbs

See Greens

Ramps

Also known as wild leeks, ramps *(Allium tricoccum)* are a perennial herb classified in the same family as onions, garlic, and lilies. For centuries, Native Americans, pioneers, and modern Appalachians have used the pungent bulb and leaves of the plant not only as a source of food but also for medicinal purposes. In recent years, upscale restaurants from New York to New Orleans have featured ramps on their spring menus.

Ramps grow wild throughout the Appalachians from New England south to the mountains in Georgia. Their flat, elliptical leaves typically attain a length of about ten inches and are among the first wild greens to appear in the late winter and early spring. In particularly rich woodlands, ramp patches sometimes cover acres. The display of greenery is fleeting, however. Before blooming in June and July, the foliage dies back only to be replaced by a fifteen-inch stem topped by a cluster of white bell-shaped flowers. Following the summer bloom, the stem also dies, leaving the small underground bulb to lie dormant until the following spring.

The digging of ramps during the late winter and early spring is an Appalachian tradition that predates the arrival of European settlers. In addition to eating the leaves and bulb of the plant, Native Americans used it as a spring tonic and to provide relief from cold symptoms.

When European settlers arrived during the late eighteenth century, they brought with them customs governing the use of leeks. Even the name *ramp* is a variation of the Old English word *ramson*, an alternate name for the European bear leek. The pioneers and their descendants used ramps as both a food and as an herbal remedy. Faith in its efficacy was expressed in an old European saying: *By eating ramps in May, all the year after physicians may play.* Superstitious individuals sometimes wore ramps around their necks in an effort to keep sickness at bay.

Although some people still tout the health benefits of ramps, the plant receives much more publicity as the focus of ramp festivals sponsored by sportsmen's clubs, civic groups, churches, and schools. In addition to the ramp dinner, the occasion frequently involves music, dancing, and other forms of entertainment.

Ramps are prepared for consumption in a variety of ways. Popular methods include panfrying, using them as salad greens, and adding them to soups and sandwiches. Considering that their flavor becomes increasingly more intense as spring progresses, some people preserve the more mild early plants for future use either by freezing or pickling. Several cookbooks have been devoted solely to the preparation and preservation of ramps.

Although ramps are rich in both nutrients and culture, anyone who eats more than just a few begins to smell like the odoriferous plant itself. For several days, the consumer exudes a pungent odor from his pores and breath, a condition that dissipates only with the passage of time.

See also: FESTIVALS, FOOD; GREENS; RELISHES.

—John Boback, *Alderson-Broaddus College*

Kevin Adams and Marty Casstevens, *Wildflowers of the Southern Appalachians* (1996); Earl Core, *Castanea* (1945).

Relishes

The practice of canning and preserving relishes and pickles, a necessity more than a century ago, is a creative and colorful way for cooks to display their talents while providing flavorful condiments for meals throughout the year.

Dozens of relishes still enjoy popularity in Appalachia. They constitute singular or various mixtures of vegetables, preserved in brine or in vinegar, sugar, and spices. Served with soup beans, shuck beans, fried chicken, pork—nearly any meal except breakfast—relishes trim any simple meal with a pleasant edge of tartness.

The region's prevalent relish is chowchow. Ingredients vary depending on the recipe, but chowchow usually includes a combination of cabbage, green tomatoes, onions, and green peppers. Various additions can include cauliflower, cucumbers, green beans, apples, or corn. The word *chowchow* has its origins from the Chinese *cha*, meaning "mixed." In times past, a straightened garden hoe attached to a short wooden handle was used to chop ingredients for relishes and kraut.

Corn relish—a mixture of corn and green and/or red bell peppers—is another variety ubiquitous in the region. Sometimes it is embellished with the addition of cabbage, tomatoes, or cucumbers. Other relishes include cucumber, pear, squash, or onion. Chutneys are relatives of relishes that generally marry a sweet fruit such as apples, pears, or peaches with savory flavorings such as onions or hot peppers in a spiced sweet vinegar mixture. Often paired with roasted meats and game, they enliven all manner of plain cooking. Other pickled condiments range from pickled beets—a sweet and sour mixture flavored with cinnamon and clove—to pickled beans, okra, green tomatoes, cucumbers, cabbage (kraut), corn, watermelon rind, and peaches.

See also: CORN; GREENS; JAMS, JELLIES, AND PRESERVES.

—Jackie Mills, *Jackson Heights, New York*

Root Vegetables

Because the temperate climate of Appalachia is ideal for root vegetables, beets, turnips, parsnips, and carrots have become favorites in the region's diet. Beets in particular are widely enjoyed because they thrive in the region's soils, take up little garden space, and have a long shelf life when pickled. Usually seed-planted along the spine of a small ridge, beets are harvested by being pulled up by their leaves. Once gathered, the vegetables are washed, cooked (to loosen the outer layer), and skinned. Due to the beet's distinctive flavor, pickling is the most common method of preparation, done in the traditional manner using pickling spices, vinegar, and sugar. The juice created in the processing is often used later to pickle eggs. Pickled beets can be stored for several years.

Turnips offer a somewhat greater degree of versatility, making them a food staple in the Deep South as well as throughout Appalachia. Easily grown and requiring little or no weeding or hoeing after sprouts appear, the turnip bulb can be eaten raw or cooked. Its characteristically sweet, sharp flavor is detectable in the plant's greens, which are also edible. Appalachian cooks sometimes use raw turnips as a crunchy additive to coleslaw and salads, and cooked turnips can be steamed or mashed like potatoes or combined with potatoes, cabbage, or chestnuts and then mashed. After a turnip is boiled, the resulting broth, or pot likker, can be eaten with corn bread.

Depending on the climate, both beets and turnips can be left in the ground through the winter months. In the warmer parts of Appalachia, growing a second fall crop of beets and turnips is common.

See also: POTATOES; SWEET POTATOES.

—Roger D. Mullins, *Pikeville College*

Joseph E. Dabney, *Smokehouse Ham, Spoon Bread, and Scuppernong Wine: The Folklore and Art of Southern Appalachian Cooking* (1998); John Parris, *Mountain Cooking* (1978); Mark F. Sohn, *Mountain Country Cooking: A Gathering of the Best Recipes from the Smokies to the Blue Ridge* (1996).

Salt Pork

See Pork

Sassafras

Historically known in Appalachia for its medicinal properties, sassafras is a genus of trees and shrubs of the laurel family (Lauraceae). The most noted of the sassafras species is the American sassafras *(Sassafras albidum)*. Usually a small tree (less than fifty feet tall) that prefers well-drained soils in areas such as abandoned fields and open, eroded slopes, it grows from southern Ontario south throughout the Appalachian region to central Florida and as far west as eastern Texas.

The sassafras tree is easily distinguishable by its leaf shape and aromatic leaves, bark, and roots. Sassafras may bear three types of leaves on the same tree: entire (not lobed), two-lobed (mitten shaped) and three-lobed. It is one of the most colorful fall trees found in Appalachia.

Dating from the Cretaceous period and long known to Native Americans, who used it in their tea brews and in other ways, sassafras was discovered by the Spanish in the early sixteenth century. Its name derived from the Spanish for "stone breaker" (in reference to kidney stones) and indicates one of the many medicinal qualities ascribed to the plant. The bark of the root and the oil distilled from it have long been popular for their alleged properties as stimulant, diuretic, blood thinner, and stomach relaxant. In colonial times, the root bark and oil were shipped back to Europe as cure-alls for various ailments. In Appalachia, the outer bark of the roots was routinely brewed for making tea or as a spring tonic. Mountain cooks also dried and powdered the early spring leaves of sassafras to use as a thickener for soups and stews. The oil has also been used to perfume soaps and rubbing lotions and to flavor candies and medicines.

Sassafras is best known, however, for its use in brewing teas and root beer. Root beer was originally a naturally effervescent beverage made by fermenting sugar and yeast with other variable flavoring ingredients often including sassafras root bark or its extract. However, with a 1960s Food and Drug Administration ban on extracts containing the active agent safrole, a putative carcinogen and the ingredient most closely associated with the root beer flavor, commercial beverage companies resorted to various combinations of other flavoring substances such as wintergreen, vanilla, and cinnamon. Some companies have reverted back to using safrole-free sassafras extracts, though, touting their products' traditional mountain origin.

See also: HEATHS (ECOLOGY); FOLK MEDICINE (FOLKLORE AND FOLKLIFE); TREES, SHRUBS, AND NATIVE PLANTS (AGRICULTURE).

—Jeffery J. Nordhaus, *Columbus Grove, Ohio*

Scottish, Irish, and English Immigrant Foodways

By far the largest number of settlers coming to Appalachia in the eighteenth century emigrated from Ireland, Scotland, and England, bringing with them cultural influences on all aspects of life, including food. They had to adapt their cooking to the resources of the new environment, but connections to foods and food preparation between Appalachia and Great Britain remain strong even today.

For most of the settlers who left the British Isles for Appalachian America, bread and vegetables, rather than meats, had been the staple diet. However, in most of the new region to which they came, corn became the dominant grain instead of the rye, barley, and oats to which they were accustomed. Settlers still cooked bread in flat cakes or softer, sweeter bannocks on the griddle (or girdle in Britain), but they were made of corn and sometimes sweetened with sorghum (the so-called Appalachian Indian cake or bannock bread). The familiar potato, turnip, and cabbage grew equally well in the mountains as in the Isles and the common methods of preparation—boiling or mashing and seasoning with salt and perhaps some potherbs or wild greens—remain common in both Britain and Appalachia today. These vegetables, which stored well, also added bulk to soups and stews to stretch meals for large families with few financial resources. Cabbage, kale, and wild greens such as ramps and sorrel, which were among the few greens to withstand the harsh winters of Scotland, Ireland, and northern England and the high elevation of much of Appalachia, consequently figure importantly in cooking on both sides of the Atlantic.

Abundant game and the introduction of pigs to the region at an early time gave settlers from the British Isles access to meats with which they were familiar but which were often reserved for only the more wealthy in their homelands. Venison, rabbit, and wild birds such as grouse were known to these settlers and quickly added to the diet, along with the abundant but less familiar squirrel, bear, and turkey. Roasting and stewing remained preferred cooking methods. Pork, long-favored in England as a meat staple, transferred well to the Appalachian mountains where pigs could fatten on wild nuts, berries, and roots, and the meat would last using the British tradition of salt preservation. Bacon, sausages, and hams, prized in Appalachian diets, reflect their British origins. While fish had been more abundant in the islands from which they came, these settlers did find the familiar trout and cooked it with a coating of cornmeal similar to the oatmeal breading in their countries of origin.

A voracious appetite for sweets is still a marker of life in Britain and Ireland, and the desire for sweet foods in the diet affected food traditions in Appalachia. The tradition of ending each meal with a "pudding" (dessert) in the Isles is reflected in the need for a "sweet bite" at the end of meals in the mountains. Cakes, sweet puddings, and desserts made with wild berries echo British and Irish roots. Gingerbread and dense cakes filled with raisins, sultanas, candied peel, and nuts and sometimes soaked in spirits (known by such names as black bun or Scotch bun and Dundee cake in Britain and fruitcake in Appalachia) became special treats, often for holidays. Marmalades, jams, and jellies, ever popular in British and Irish cooking, also became staples of Appalachian food preservation as another way to keep sweets on the table even after the fruit and berry season had faded. Honey, a sweetener brought with bees from Britain, not only appeared on morning biscuits but also aided farmers with crop propagation and provided wax for lighting cabins.

Washing down all this heavy food representative of colder climes were beverages brought to Appalachia by way of Ireland, Scotland, and England. Buttermilk, the tart milk residue left after making butter, had long been important in the diet of the Ulster-Scots and adapted well to mountain life, where making butter was a necessity, and lack of refrigeration made buttermilk's resistance to spoilage significant. Buttermilk became a favored drink and a powerful additive to other foods such as biscuits and corn bread.

The Scots-Irish proclivity for making spirits formed one of Appalachia's enduring icons—moonshine production. Scots had long made whiskey from barley and oats, and the Irish distilled poteen, or potheen, from potato skins. Settlers in Appalachia soon found that corn worked just as well and was a profitable enterprise. The traditional technology of distilling, well honed in the Isles, transferred elegantly to the mountains.

Many other food traditions in Appalachia emanate from Scotland, Ireland, and England (such as sweet and sour food accompaniments, which took the form of home canned relishes in Appalachia); suffice it to say that the region's most dominant settlement groups also heavily influenced the region's food and cooking.

See also: ENGLISH (RACE, ETHNICITY, AND IDENTITY); SCOTS-IRISH (RACE, ETHNICITY, AND IDENTITY).

—Jean Haskell, *East Tennessee State University*, and Susan M. Thomson, *University of Edinburgh*

Catherine Brown, *Scottish Cookery* (1999); Joseph E. Dabney, *Smokehouse Ham, Spoon Bread, and Scuppernong Wine: The Folklore and Art of Southern Appalachian Cooking* (1998); Richard Straw, "Food and Nutrition in Pre-Industrial Appalachia," *Appalachian Studies Conference Proceedings* (1992).

Shuck Beans

Shuck, or shucky, beans, also known as leather britches, are dried green beans. Unlike shelly beans, which are dried on the vine and then shelled, shuck beans include the entire dried pod and bean. Before the invention of preservation methods such as canning and freezing, drying was the only process for preserving beans. Among the favorite beans for drying were mountain white half-runners, striped cornfield beans, and Kentucky wonders.

Two drying methods were commonly used. For both, the bean was harvested when mature but while the pod was still edible. The first method involved stringing whole, unbroken pods, like stringing popcorn for Christmas tree garlands. Using a big darning needle, the processor carefully inserted strong thread between the two middle beans in a pod. When the string of whole beans was three or four feet long, the thread was knotted and the string of beans hung to dry, traditionally in such places as the porch, from roof rafters, or on a wall behind a wood burning kitchen stove. The beans slowly dried, turned straw colored, and shriveled. After drying, they were stored in cloth sacks or, more recently, in glass jars or freezers.

The second method was to snap the pods into bite-size pieces, then spread them on white cloths and place them in a sunny place to dry. Many women chose to break their beans before drying because it was nearly impossible to pull the threads out of beans dried by the stringing method.

A bean stringing was a popular social event in the first part of the twentieth century, providing a way for neighbors to socialize while doing important work. Word would go out to neighbors that a bean stringing was to take place, and neighbors and acquaintances would assemble, with someone usually bringing a guitar, fiddle, or banjo to provide music. Many hands made short work of bushels of green beans.

Even after the advent of canning and freezing, some mountain families, craving the intense flavor of shuck beans, continued to dry them for winter eating. Appalachian families who migrated elsewhere carried such fond memories of dried beans that it was not unusual for boxes of dried beans to be shipped to Chicago, Detroit, Indianapolis, or Cleveland to mountaineers homesick for old-time cooking.

The best method for cooking shuck beans is to soak them overnight in a kettle of cold water or to put them into boiling water, turn off the burner, and soak them for an hour and then rinse them and simmer with a piece of smoked slab bacon until the beans are fork tender.

Sometimes rituals have surrounded the cooking of shuck beans. In the Big Sandy region of southeastern Kentucky, for example, some families waited for the first snow to cook the first pot of shuck beans.

See also: GREEN BEANS; HEIRLOOM FRUITS AND VEGETABLES (AGRICULTURE); SOUP BEANS.

—Sidney Saylor Farr, *Berea, Kentucky*

L. Elisabeth Watts Beattie, ed., *Savory Memories* (1998); Sidney Saylor Farr, *More Than Moonshine: Appalachian Recipes and Recollections* (1983); Mark F. Sohn, *Mountain Country Cooking: A Gathering of the Best Recipes from the Smokies to the Blue Ridge* (1996).

Small Game

From the late seventeenth century through the early twentieth century, settlers lived off the plentiful wild game—including squirrel, raccoon, opossum, groundhog, and rabbit—that thrived in the woods of Appalachia. Even after hogs were raised and fattened, game remained a staple, providing fresh meat between hog-killing times and a change from salty preserved meats. For many mountaineers, hunting was a primary means of obtaining food and a way of controlling garden and field pests, not to mention a sport.

Hunting small game remains popular in Appalachia to the present day, and except for rabbit, these animals are still only found in the wild. Many related dishes, adapted to modern equipment and ingredients, continue to be prepared.

Historically, squirrel was considered one of the most flavorful wild meats in the region. After being skinned, a squirrel was usually soaked in salt water to draw out blood and to tame the "wild" flavor. Older specimens, sometimes tough and unpleasantly gamy, were stewed. They were first parboiled, then simmered in fresh water until tender. To make squirrel dumplings, a favorite dish, the soft, cooked meat was usually removed from the bones and the broth well seasoned with salt and pepper. Cooks prepared dumpling dough from flour, lard, and milk or water, rolled it thin, and cut strips or pinched off pieces to drop into simmering broth. Creamed squirrel, often spooned over biscuits, was another favorite.

Young, tender squirrels were rolled in seasoned flour or breadcrumbs, panfried in bacon grease or lard, and served with squirrel gravy, a flour-milk (or water) gravy prepared from pan drippings. Two squirrel dishes with Appalachian roots are Brunswick stew and Kentucky burgoo. As James Beard notes in *American Cookery,* no two recipes for these dishes are alike, though both are long-simmered stews that include squirrel, often with chicken or rabbit and plenty of vegetables.

While rabbit is commonly available in modern supermarkets, mountaineers of the past caught rabbits in the wild or raised them in cages. As with squirrels, a wild rabbit's age often dictated the cooking method. After skinning, it was generally soaked in water with salt or vinegar. Young, tender, mild-flavored rabbits were coated with seasoned flour and panfried, like squirrel (or chicken). Sometimes, water and/or vinegar and onions were added. The skillet was covered so the rabbit was cooked "smothered." Or rabbit gravy was prepared from pan drippings and browned rabbit pieces stewed in the gravy. Older, tougher rabbit meat was parboiled in salted water, dipped into egg batter, seasoned flour, or cornmeal, and then fried. Sometimes rabbit was simply boiled.

Raccoons, often a nuisance in the orchard or cornfield, yielded meat that was dark, rich, soft, and sweet. The strong-flavored fat was pared away. Settlers skinned raccoons carefully and sold or traded the valuable pelts. To reduce gaminess, raccoon was usually soaked in vinegar-water or milk, then parboiled in fresh water, often with vinegar, for tenderizing. Seasonings included salt, pepper, hot pepper pods, and spicebush twigs, snipped from the aromatic, native Appalachian bush *(Lindera benzoin)*. After parboiling, raccoon was sometimes rolled in seasoned flour or cornmeal and fried in lard, bacon fat, or bear grease; or it was baked with apples or sweet potatoes. Raccoon was also sometimes stuffed with a corn bread mixture and barbecued.

Another garden pest was the groundhog, also called woodchuck and, by mountain people, whistle pig (because the animal was thought to whistle through its teeth when chased). Its meat—fat, dark, and mild-flavored—was cooked much like raccoon.

After skinning, the groundhog was soaked in water with salt or vinegar then parboiled, sometimes with spicebush twigs to temper the flavor. The tender meat was often rolled in flour or cornmeal and panfried or baked with white potatoes or, more often, sweet potatoes. It was also enjoyed with ramps and corn bread. A practical use for dried groundhog hide was to knead it until pliable and cut it into thin strips for shoelaces.

The opossum is North America's only marsupial (an animal that carries its young in a pouch, like a kangaroo). Its light-colored meat is strong and gamy. After skinning or scalding it in water with wood-ash or lime then scraping off the hairs, the cook removed the opossum's musk glands and ample fat. Next it was soaked with salt water and/or vinegar and usually parboiled, sometimes with spicebush twigs. The meat was then coated and fried, stuffed and roasted, or baked with sweet potatoes. Appalachian mountaineers generally favored the latter method.

In his book *Southern Food: At Home, on the Road, in History,* John Egerton speaks about game feasts, or "critter suppers," still held throughout the South to celebrate the bounty of the hunt. Any game might be served, often baked or roasted. These feasts remain a tradition in many Appalachian states. In West Virginia, one of the most colorful festivals is the annual Road Kill Cook-Off held in Marlinton, West Virginia.

See also: BIG GAME; HUNTING AND FISHING (SPORTS AND RECREATION).

—Collen Engle, *Meridian Café, Louisville, Kentucky,* and Miriam Rubin, *New Freeport, Pennsylvania*

Joseph E. Dabney, *Smokehouse Ham, Spoon Bread, and Scuppernong Wine: The Folklore and Art of Southern Appalachian Cooking* (1998); Sidney Saylor Farr, *More Than Moonshine: Appalachian Recipes and Recollections* (1983); Linda Garland Page and Eliot Wigginton, eds., *The Foxfire Book of Appalachian Cookery* (1984).

Soup Beans

Soup beans and brown beans are made from the dry bean (*Phaselous vulgaris* L.), a pantry staple for Appalachians from upstate New York to northern Georgia. Whatever the name or method of preparation, this versatile bean is a readily available food source with a long shelf life. Early Appalachians probably did not know the nutritional value of dried beans, but they in fact provide an excellent source of protein and a high percentage of dietary fiber.

As with many other traditional foods, dried beans required a long preparation time. However, after the beans were on the stove, they did not need constant supervision, a plus for the Appalachian cook.

Preparation of dried beans varied with each area of the region. In the north, beans, salt water, and a soup bone became "brown beans." In the central and southern mountains, dried salt pork, sometimes called a sinker, was added to soup beans. During the 1920s and 1930s, many Appalachians adopted the practice of adding macaroni to stretch the dish for extra mouths and to thicken the soup. In addition, leftover beans were mashed, shaped, and fried into patties.

In every area of Appalachia, preparation began with washing, rinsing, and picking out grit and stones before soaking. Many cooks added a dash or two of soda during soaking process to reduce cooking time and act as a digestive aid.

The beans were often served with raw onion, fried potatoes, and corn bread. In early days, meat was not always available except in the fall when hogs were slaughtered. A fresh "mess" of pork, corn bread, and soup beans was often the reward to neighbors who came to help with chores such as hog killing, barn raising, and bringing in hay.

Early Appalachians grew their own beans, dried them, and stored them for winter. Later they were grown commercially in the Midwest, Southwest, and Mexico and sold in general stores. They were merchandised in one-hundred-pound cloth bags from which the grocer scooped, weighed, and sold them by the pound in brown paper "pokes." Today beans remain a favorite Appalachian food purchased in bulk by schools and other institutions and are available in family-size packages from one to twenty pounds in the dried bean section of most grocery stores.

See also: GREEN BEANS; SHUCK BEANS; SOUPS.

—Eloise Reynolds Delzer, *Paintsville, Kentucky*

Robert L. Myers, *Dry Edible Beans* (1999).

Soups

Soups are liquid foods, usually with a base of meat or vegetable stock or broth, often containing pieces of solid foods (meats, vegetables, beans, etc.). The flexible nature of soups, with their ability to use up leftovers and cook for long periods with little attention, ensured their place as a staple in the Appalachian diet.

Early settlers in the region learned some of their cooking from the Native Americans, who combined wild game or the occasional domestic animal with any seasonal or available vegetables in simmering salted water. Deer or rabbit might share the pot with raccoon, turkey, or an old chicken, and beef was always popular in soups. Meat scraps from previous meals or bones with bits of meat still attached also provided flavor and made for a richer broth.

Heartier meat soups were most often eaten during colder weather. In warmer months, vegetable soups predominated. A great number of vegetables were preserved for winter by canning, drying, or cold storage in the case of root vegetables or cabbage, but those eaten fresh frequently found their way into the soup kettle. Water and tomato juice were common bases for these vegetable soups. Carrots, celery, corn, onions, potatoes, okra, fresh beans and peas, and tomatoes were all recognized as vegetables well suited for summertime or harvest soups. There are occasional recipes for creamed vegetable soups, too. These contained only one or two types of vegetables, were sometimes thickened with flour, and had milk added.

Bean soups were a great favorite in Appalachia. Shelly beans (beans that required shelling, such as limas) were often used fresh, but peas and beans were dried for use in more substantial soups, too. In soups, beans could substitute for meat or stretch the amount of meat available, providing valuable protein and rendering the meal more filling.

Of course, the cook altered soups to suit personal and family tastes. They were comforting and hospitable without being fancy or formal; there are references to Appalachian families keeping a pot of soup simmering in the event that someone stopped by. In addition, because soups did not require constant attention while they cooked and could simmer for long periods of time without harm, the woman of the house was able to attend to other chores while the soups effectively made themselves. For women engaged in a constant round of domestic activities, this was a great boon.

Adaptability, ease of preparation, and frugality combined to make soups a common meal on Appalachian tables. Their usefulness in the diet has been handed down for generations as part of the American culinary tradition.

See also: SOUP BEANS.

—Stephanie D. Zonis, *Neshanic Station, New Jersey*

Joseph E. Dabney, *Smokehouse Ham, Spoon Bread, and Scuppernong Wine: The Folklore and Art of Southern Appalachian Cooking* (1998); Linda Garland Page and Eliot Wigginton, eds., *The Foxfire Book of Appalachian Cookery* (1984); Mark F. Sohn, *Mountain Country Cooking: A Gathering of the Best Recipes from the Smokies to the Blue Ridge* (1996).

Sweeteners

Of the many sweeteners used in the region's kitchens, sorghum and honey stand out because of their historic economic importance, numerous varieties, and multiple uses.

A member of the grass family and native to Africa, sorghum has been widely grown and used in Appalachia to produce a viscous syrup that is highly favored as a sweetener. While many varieties are grown around the world, the type that is best known in Appalachia is called sweet sorghum. With sweet, juicy stems, the plant is grown in Appalachia almost exclusively for the pressing and production of sorghum syrup, commonly called molasses.

In the early to mid-nineteenth century, various types of sorghum syrups were the leading sweeteners in America. Then as now, the amber to brown, delicious, and strong-flavored syrup was poured over pancakes or biscuits and used as a sweetener and flavoring in breads, cakes, pies, and candy. Sorghum remained the preferred sweetener in Appalachia and the South through the end of the nineteenth and well into the twentieth century. By the late 1800s total production of sorghum syrup in the United States reached an estimated 20 million gallons, and an encyclopedia listed Indiana, Ohio, Illinois, Kentucky, and Missouri as the leading producers of sorghum. While most people who enjoy sorghum do so because of tradition and the syrup's strong distinctive flavor, an added benefit to using sorghum in place of refined sugar products is its rich nutritional value as a source of iron, protein, and potassium.

The sorghum plant resembles corn and is grown in areas where corn is popular. Plants grow to a height of six to twelve feet with stalks that are between one and two inches thick. In the nineteenth and early twentieth centuries, most Appalachian farmers grew sorghum either for their own table use or as a cash crop. Most communities had at least one farmer who operated a sorghum mill and evaporating pans, which squeezed and cooked neighbors' cane into syrup. The process of rendering the stalks into syrup is relatively simple. Stalks of cane are gradually fed into rollers, which crush them and squeeze the juice into a tub or pan. Collected and taken to the evaporating pans, the juice is cooked down to thick syrup. For a century or more, sorghum making, like many other aspects of farm life in Appalachia, was a community activity that involved not only shared work but social gatherings as well.

Another popular Appalachian sweetener is honey. Like other Americans, Appalachians consume over a pound of honey per person annually. While Americans outside Appalachia prefer wild flower and sweet clover honey, Appalachians generally favor the thin, lightly colored, fragrant honeys from sourwood, tulip poplar, basswood, and honey locust trees.

Each of these native mountain trees produces a relatively light-colored honey with distinct qualities. Sourwood is pale amber and delicately sweet, lemony, and aromatic with a tangy aftertaste. Tulip poplar honey is somewhat darker and mild-flavored. Linn or basswood honey, the most prized honey in the central highlands, is produced from the flowering American basswood tree in the linden family. Like other preferred honey, this honey is light in color, runny in texture, and mild in flavor. It yields an immediate complex sweetness without any sharpness or aftertaste. Another mountain honey that is quite the opposite of linn is locust. Produced from the honey locust tree, this honey is several shades darker than sourwood (but still relatively light in color), thick, rich, full-bodied, and nutty-flavored with no sharp aftertaste.

Home-produced honey, robbed from hives and sometimes called beehive honey, or honey taken from wild bee gums or bee trees is spread with butter on biscuits, hot rolls, and corn bread. Sometimes these breads are served with honey in place of elaborate desserts. Mountain producers sell honey plain, with the comb, and as honey butter. For children they also produce honey straws—colored and flavored plastic tubes filled with honey. The waxy comb is used as a replacement for chewing gum or is served flattened on buttered biscuits and fried chicken.

During the twentieth century, as refined sugar products and sugar replacements became available, the use of honey and sorghum as everyday sweeteners declined. In contemporary Appalachia, the old favorites make up only a small fraction of sweeteners used, but traditions linger, and consequently, sorghum and honey continue to be produced and used throughout the region.

See also: JAMS, JELLIES, AND PRESERVES; MAPLE SYRUP (AGRICULTURE); SORGHUM (AGRICULTURE); SWEETS.

—Richard A. Straw, *Radford University,* and Jeanne Voltz, *Pittsboro, North Carolina*

Sidney Saylor Farr, *More Than Moonshine: Appalachian Recipes and Recollections* (1983); Mark F. Sohn, *Mountain Country Cooking: A Gathering of the Best Recipes from the Smokies to the Blue Ridge* (1996); Joseph S. Wall and William M. Ross, *Sorghum Production and Utilization* (1970).

Sweet Potatoes

Sweet potatoes *(Impomoea batatas)*, which flourish in the long summers of the southern Appalachians, are members of the morning glory family. How the sweet potato, a native of South America, came to the region is not precisely known. According to Joseph E. Dabney, the first European settlers in North Georgia named their community Tater Hill because of the Cherokees' practice of growing sweet potatoes in the area. Since the arrival of European settlers to the region in the second half of the eighteenth century, the vegetable has remained important in southern Appalachia because it is easily grown and highly productive.

Sweet potatoes are neither potatoes nor yams. The two dominant types of sweet potatoes are easily distinguished by color. The first type is pale with a thin, light yellow skin and pale yellow flesh; it is not sweet but has a dry, meaty, crumbly texture and is called a white sweet potato. The second and more dominant type is darker with thick orange skin and bright orange flesh. This latter type has a sweet, moist texture and is mistakenly called a yam. Yams are the tuber of a tropical plant *(Dioscorea batatas)* and are darker and redder than sweet potatoes.

Appalachian families have traditionally roasted, boiled, and baked sweet potatoes, but they also use them in casseroles, boil them with apples, grill, fry, or make them into soup, and even eat them raw. The vegetable is also used in making sweet potato cakes, cookies, fritters, pudding, bread, biscuits, pancakes, balls, and pies.

In the days of open-hearth cooking, Appalachians roasted sweet potatoes in the fireplace by covering them with hot ashes. They also cooked them underground, usually in the fall, by burying and building a fire over them. Eating roasted sweet potatoes was in some communities a Friday night social event. In some families, children took whole baked sweet potatoes to school and ate them for lunch.

The importance of sweet potatoes is due in part to their storage longevity. When placed in cool, dry areas, the vegetables can last an entire winter. According to *Table Talk: Appalachian Meals and Memories,* one method by which Appalachians stored sweet potatoes was to dig a hole in the ground, line it with straw, place the vegetables inside, and cover them with dirt. Planks were placed upright over the dirt to drain water away from the potatoes.

See also: POTATOES; ROOT VEGETABLES.

—Blanche Jackson Glimps, *Kentucky Christian College*

Joseph E. Dabney, *Smokehouse Ham, Spoon Bread, and Scuppernong Wine: The Folklore and Art of Southern Appalachian Cooking* (1998); Sidney Saylor Farr, *Table Talk: Appalachian Meals and Memories* (1995); Bill Neal, *Southern Cooking* (1985).

Sweets

No less than other Americans, Appalachians have a fondness for sweet foods. But in addition to baked desserts, candies, ice cream, and gelatin-based foods universally enjoyed, residents of the mountains have inherited their own regional sweets.

During the eighteenth and early nineteenth centuries in Appalachia, a sweet might be a piece of fresh or dried fruit or a leftover biscuit spread with honey or sorghum syrup. Fruit leather made of pureed dried fruit was also common. The prevalence of sweet sorghum led to the practice of making simple candies such as pulled taffy. To make this popular confection, sorghum syrup is boiled down until very thick, then spread in pans to cool slightly until it can be handled and pulled into long ropes. As the candy is pulled, it whitens and hardens. The long ropes are cut into smaller pieces and stored for later enjoyment. Taffy-pulling parties were common in the region into the last century.

A traditional sweet especially popular in winter was the popcorn ball, freshly popped corn coated with sorghum syrup and shaped by hand. Nut brittles, made by adding hickory nuts, pecans, or peanuts to boiled sorghum syrup, were also popular. The mixture was spread in flat baking pans and allowed to harden before being broken into smaller pieces. The advantage of all these sweets was that they kept well and long without refrigeration.

When refined sugar became available, the Appalachian fondness for sweets led to the creation of a number of other confections. Lacking precise instruments to measure temperature, housewives developed their own methods of judging when a sugar confection had been boiled to the appropriate level of doneness: "soft ball," "hard ball," "soft crack," or "hard crack" indicated what happened when a small amount of the mixture was dropped into cold water. Readily available ingredients were used to make variously flavored hard (rock) candies, fudge, and divinity, which one food writer has called "a first cousin to marshmallow and a second cousin to nougat."

Older residents still remember with fondness these homemade delicacies. Oral histories of the region describe a frozen winter treat: snow cream, or ice cream. Snow was collected in heavy pans and combined with milk or cream and sugar and flavorings to make a dish suggestive of the low-calorie twentieth-century dessert ice milk. In the absence of snow, families would nest a bucket of a mixture of milk, sugar, and flavorings in a bucket of ice cut from a stream and let it stand until frozen. With the introduction of hand-cranked ice cream freezers, making these frozen treats became the center of activity at summer ice cream socials that brought together families and entire communities.

Late in the nineteenth century, gelatin-based desserts such as fruit or wine jellies were sometimes served as an accompaniment to plain cake or cookies. As the Jell-O brand of commercial gelatin became a pantry staple, more elaborate congealed preparations with nuts, fruits, cream cheese, and sour cream were developed and continue in popularity.

See also: CAKES AND COOKIES; PIES; SWEETENERS.

—Brenda S. Bradds, *Hillsboro, Ohio,* and Rebeccah Kinnamon Neff, *Raleigh, North Carolina*

Linda Garland Page and Eliot Wigginton, eds., *The Foxfire Book of Appalachian Cookery* (1984); Mark F. Sohn, *Mountain Country Cooking: A Gathering of the Best Recipes from the Smokies to the Blue Ridge* (1996).

Swiss Foodways

When early German Swiss settlers came to the Appalachians in the mid-1800s, they adapted their native cookery to the abundant raw materials they found in the new land—wild greens, nuts, fruits, honey, and game. In America, they cultivated wheat, buckwheat, rye, grapes, apples, pears, cherries, walnuts, plums, potatoes, corn, and eventually, extensive vegetable gardens. The culture and foodways that emerged, part industrious Swiss, part American pioneer, are a special American amalgam.

From the Swiss side came the spicy sweet-and-sour flavors of sauerbraten and sauerkraut, rich quichelike onion pies, noodlelike dumplings, and spicy cookies. From the South came corn bread and ham, beans, cultivated turnip greens, and lard-crusted pies. However, it is not always clear which foodways the Appalachian Swiss brought from their native Switzerland and which they incorporated from America, for many were typical of both. Americans and Swiss made wines from blackberries, raspberries, elderberries, wild and cultivated grapes, wild cherries, and dandelion; both salted local fish to preserve it. In Appalachia, the Swiss foraged for wild greens such as mustard, poke, dandelion, nettle, sheep sorrel, and lamb's tongue. Many recipes would seem to be a fusion of cultures; such dishes include *turkenribel,* made of fried leftover corn bread served with sugar and rich cream, and sweet-sour coleslaw scented with caraway.

Home-raised pork, cheap and economical, was the linchpin of Appalachian-Swiss cooking. Slabs of panfried ham were a staple, and bacon fat was the cooking fat of choice. Along with the usual curing and smoking of hams, particularly Swiss treatments included the making of blood sausages, head cheese, and *krautliwurst,* in which sauerkraut was mixed into the stuffing, and an unusually delicious mincement made from a hog's head (which may be viewed as evidence of Swiss frugality and resourcefulness). Cows were used primarily for milk and milk products such as cottage cheese, sour cream, buttermilk, and butter. Many families made cheese similar to the *Appenzeller* of their native Switzerland.

The once-thriving Swiss communities that peppered the Appalachians declined sharply during the last half of the twentieth century due to complex economic changes and simple attrition. Third-generation Swiss who grew up on self-sufficient farms in the early part of the twentieth century are the last to speak the German Swiss dialect of their forebears. To a lesser degree, they kept alive the foodways of their youth—traditional recipes such as *rosti* (fried potato pancakes), *knopfli* (buckwheat dumplings with fried onions), *klossli* (potato dumplings stuffed with ham or sauerkraut), and an endless array of baked goods: *birnwecken* (pear bread), *berner biberli* (yeast-raised jelly donuts), and rosettes (a sugar sprinkled fried dough made by dipping a hot rosette-shaped iron into a batter).

Perhaps the most vibrant Appalachian Swiss community left in the early twenty-first century is Helvetia, a small town nestled in a lush valley near West Virginia's eastern panhandle. Settled by Swiss immigrants in 1869, Helvetia survived in large measure due to the efforts of Eleanor Fahrner Mailloux. She championed the preservation of its distinct culture and established the Helvetia Museum and a library with a rich archive of oral histories and other original material. In addition, she compiled *Oppis Guet's Vu Helvetia (Something Good from Helvetia),* a cookbook of traditional recipes and a repository of great insight into the area's unique foodways. Mailloux is also the proprietor of the Hutte, ("Little House"), a restaurant which features Helvetian Swiss cooking.

See also: GERMANS (RACE, ETHNICITY, AND IDENTITY); SWISS (RACE, ETHNICITY, AND IDENTITY).

—Sally Schneider, *Food and Wine Magazine, New York City, New York*

John Paul von Grueningen, ed., *The Swiss in the United States* (1940); Elizabeth A. Moize, "Turnaround Time in West Virginia," *National Geographic* (June 1976); David H. Sutton, *One's Own Hearth Is Like Gold: A History of Helvetia, West Virginia* (1990).

Turtle

Long considered a regional delicacy, snapping turtles are a source of succulent meat that connoisseurs swear is well worth the considerable obstacles involved in their capture. These aquatic turtles can be taken by using a hook baited with raw chicken or by grabbing them by the tail when they lurk near swampy areas or creeks. In either case, care must be taken in the capture because of the reptile's strength and stamina.

To slaughter a snapping turtle, enterprising Appalachians place the turtle on a log and entice it to bite into a twig. The twig is then used to pull the head out of the shell, making it possible to cut the head off with a sharp axe. Traditionally, the turtle is then plunged—shell and all—into a pot of boiling water. After a short boiling, the meat is separated from the shell and the skin and nails are removed from the legs. Supposedly, the meat can then be removed from the turtle and cooked. But as Georgian author Celestine Sibley writes in *A Place Called Sweet Apple*, preparing a turtle is as difficult as cleaning an armored truck.

Turtles range from saucer to dishpan size. To fry a mature turtle, most mountain recipes call for boiling the meat until tender, then coating it in seasoned flour or cornmeal batter and frying in grease until brown. Young turtle meat is fried without the initial boiling step. The meat is also stewed in milk and seasonings to make a dish similar to oyster stew or prepared in a casserole with rice.

See also: FROG LEGS; HUNTING AND FISHING (SPORTS AND RECREATION); SMALL GAME.

—Jackie Mills, *Jackson Heights, New York*

Wilted Lettuce

Although its origin is obscure, wilted lettuce, also called killed lettuce, has long been a popular and valued food in the region. Because a variety of greens thrive for months in Appalachia, the simple recipe can be used for much of the year.

Wilted lettuce is made by placing lettuce in a bowl and pouring hot bacon grease over the greens to cause them to wilt, or "kill" them; crumbled bacon and chopped green onions are sometimes added in. Oak leaf lettuce and black-seeded Simpson are the lettuce varieties commonly used in wilted lettuce dishes, although practically any type of greens or wild herbs can be substituted. As a stand-alone dish, wilted lettuce can be served in lieu of a salad before a meal. As a side dish, it is commonly served with pinto beans.

Wilted lettuce is not distinctly Appalachian or American; greens were cultivated and eaten in this manner in Europe for many years prior to the arrival of the colonists in the New World. The dish has also been found in some Native American diets.

See also: GREENS; RAMPS.

—Roger D. Mullins, *Pikeville College*

Wine

Wine production in Appalachia—as in other parts of the United States—was halted by prohibition (1920–33), although many areas in the region were dry (meaning that alcohol cannot be sold) long before and some remain dry today. Bans on production notwithstanding, Appalachia has both commercial and homegrown traditions of wine making, and the wines produced range from relatively sweet to dry flavors associated with France and California. At the close of the twentieth century, more than one hundred wineries operated in Appalachia, the largest concentration being in Pennsylvania and New York.

Wine making began in the Appalachians in the late eighteenth century, after Thomas Jefferson began importing grapevines from Europe to his Virginia estate, Monticello. His actions inspired others living in nearby Appalachian counties to follow similar pursuits. One of the more successful older wineries is Biltmore Estate Winery in Asheville, North Carolina, which continues to operate. The oldest winery in the Chautauqua region, the Johnson Estate Winery of Westfield, New York, opened for business in 1961. Because of the increasing popularity of wine in the 1980s and 1990s, Appalachian wine production increased, and many new areas started producing grapes. In the 1970s and 1980s, former strip-mining sites in Virginia and West Virginia were reclaimed as grape vineyards, helping to rejuvenate these communities. By the close of the twentieth century, a number of young wineries in Appalachia, such as the Chateau Morrisette, launched in 1982 in Floyd County, Virginia, had gained national recognition.

Appalachian wineries tend to produce more sweet grape wines, and many use native grapes, but some also use French hybrids, as both are well suited to Appalachian climates and soils. The native Catawba grape, for example, produces pink juice, which can be made into still wine and sparkling wine. Three other commonly grown white varieties are the Vidal Blanc and Seyval Blanc, which is used primarily for wines, and the Niagara, used for both wine production (especially dessert wines) and for grape juice. Other historical Appalachian grape wine recipes call for muscadine, scuppernong, possum, and purple, black, or pink fox grapes, all of which are indigenous. Concords, a grape varietal developed from indigenous stock, are the most common purple variety, and they are heavily planted for wine and grape juice in the Lake Erie viticultural region (a growing area recognized by the federal Bureau of Alchohol, Tobacco, Firearms, and Explosives). This region borders Lake Erie in Appalachian New York and Pennsylvania. Other important recognized viticultural regions include the Kanawha River Valley of Ohio and West Virginia, the Cumberland Valley of Pennsylvania and Maryland, and the Shenandoah Valley of West Virginia.

Appalachians were making non-grape wines at home long before grape wines became an important commercial crop. Blackberries, strawberries, elderberries, dewberries, gooseberries, and cherries were fermented into wine. Appalachian wineries continue this tradition, offering applejack, peach, and blueberry wines. Mead, or sourwood honey wine, is made in northeast Georgia. Certain vegetables, such as parsnips and rhubarb (also called wine-plant), are also used to make wine, and during the Great Depression even corncob wine was drunk when nothing else was available.

Homemade wines are still produced by traditionalists using the old recipes and equipment. Heavy stoneware crocks or butter churns are used for the initial stages of the process. Various fruits are cleaned and mashed and then yeast and sugar are sometimes added. Grapes require no added sugar or yeast, though winemakers sometimes add yeast to improve quality and sugar to increase sweetness.

See also: MOONSHINE.

—Katie Hoffman Doman, *Tusculum College*, and Mark F. Sohn, *Pikeville College*

Joseph E. Dabney, *More Mountain Spirits: The Continuing Chronicle* (1980) and *Smokehouse Ham, Spoon Bread, and Scuppernong Wine: The Folklore and Art of Southern Appalachian Cooking* (1998); Bill Thomas, *Northeast Georgia Cuisine: The Foods and Flavor of Northeast Georgia Revisited with a New Perspective* (1999).

Woodstove Cooking

Because of the variety of deciduous forests in the Appalachians, open-hearth cooking and woodstove cooking occupy an especially vital place in the region's culinary traditions. By 1760, woodstoves were being produced regularly in industrial nations around the world, but the bulky iron contraptions remained a luxury during early Appalachian settlement. With the opening of the frontier and the establishment of trade routes, settlers who wished to do so and were able financially could replace their family fireplaces with commercially produced iron stoves. By the mid-1800s, the number of Appalachian citizens cooking with woodstoves increased with the advance of the railroad into the region and establishment of mail-order supply houses.

Though not as easily controlled as the later coal, gas, or electric models, the wood cookstove was an improvement over the open hearth. The iron surface provided a surprisingly even heating surface, milder than that of most modern stoves. Since temperatures varied with the weather and the type of fuel, ovens commonly ran hot or cold; keeping a close watch on items being baked was a necessity. To this end, cast-iron pots and pans were desirable—the iron absorbed the heat and helped spread it more evenly on the surface of the food.

See also: CAST-IRON COOKWARE; OPEN-HEARTH COOKING.

—Roger D. Mullins, *Pikeville College*

Humor

Section Editor: Loyal Jones

In the summer of 1973, the unfolding Watergate scandal, which eventually forced the resignation of President Richard Nixon, produced one of its few heroes—an Appalachian mountain man whose warm humor brought insight and civility to a bitter national crisis. Nearing the end of his long political career, Senator Sam J. Ervin had long been known in his home state of North Carolina for an inexhaustible store of jokes and anecdotes that he used with devastating effect. But while presiding over nationally televised Watergate hearings that kept the country spellbound, Ervin became a national icon, vividly demonstrating the great value of humor in modern culture.

Sam J. Ervin, Johnson City, Tennessee, 1977. Appalachian humor helped ease the country through a national crisis when North Carolina Senator Sam Ervin, presiding over the Watergate hearings, shared an insightful story or witty observation from his heritage.

Reared in the Blue Ridge foothills around Morganton, Ervin began absorbing Appalachian stories during train rides with his father. Over the years, as he grew into a superb raconteur and humorist, he cultivated a deep appreciation of oral tradition and the power of well-timed jokes, homilies, and folktales. "An apt story," he once said, "is worth an hour of argument," and he could summon one, it seemed, at any moment. When United States Attorney General John Mitchell, one of the central figures in the Watergate affair, opined that he would like to do certain things over again, Ervin responded with a story. He told Mitchell:

> There was a girl down in North Carolina who had been dishonored by a rich man. The girl's father, rifle in hand, confronted the rich man. "You have dishonored my daughter," said the angry father. "But I am a rich man," said the accused and promised to pay for his indiscretion—$15,000 for a baby boy, $10,000 for a baby girl. "What if my daughter has a miscarriage?" demanded the father. "Will you give her another chance?"

Facing page: Uncle Juney, Little Clifford, and A'nt Idy Harper, Renfro Valley, Rockcastle County, Kentucky, c. 1939. The family trio played by Danny Duncan, Harry Mullins, and Margaret Lillie did much to establish the popularity of the *Renfro Valley Barn Dance* radio program and stage show during the late 1930s and early 1940s.

Through these rejoinders and observations, delivered as his eyebrows rose and fell like great white caterpillars crawling across his forehead, Ervin took gentle aim at figures mountain folk hold in great respect—preachers, teachers, doctors, and the elderly—not to mention less-esteemed lawyers, city folk, politicians, and sinners at large. Invariably, he looked homeward for his material. "We had a man down in my state that didn't agree with anybody about anything," he once said in a debate with an implacable colleague. "He found out that cabbage didn't agree with him, and after that he wouldn't eat anything but cabbage."

Ervin's nationwide popularity resulting from the hearings dramatically illustrated that the region's humor has universal qualities, even though it is drawn almost exclusively from rural experience. Stories told on courthouse benches and around grocery stores of Appalachia surface in altogether different cultures and even in different tongues. An old North Carolina joke about a stolen hog provides a compelling example of rural humor's durability and adaptability. The basic story is that the Johnson brothers steal a hog one night and put it between them on the seat of their flatbed truck:

> When the sheriff pulls them over, the boys quickly put a jacket and hat on the hog. The sheriff shines his light on the two boys and asks their names. They comply, after which the sheriff shines it on the hog, asking for his name. One of the boys hits the hog in the ribs with an elbow, causing it to oink.
>
> After the sheriff tells the brothers to drive on, he goes back to his cruiser and tells his deputy, "I've been sheriff here for twenty year, and I've seen some ugly people, but I'll be derned if that Oink Johnson ain't the ugliest S.O.B. that I ever saw."

This very same story was told by a group of Tibetans visiting Appalachia some years ago when they were asked for an example of their country's humor. Their version differed only in that the authority figures were Chinese soldiers rather than a country sheriff and his deputy. The story also appeared in the movie *Operation Petticoat*, except this time members of the U.S. Navy Shore Patrol were the authorities. The story has also been passed around by racists who portray the law officers mistaking the hog for a member of one minority group or another, depending upon where the joke surfaces.

Appalachian humor is usually more specific than the mountain version of the Johnson boys and the stolen hog. Generally, it reflects the region's culture, often making light of deeply held values, social icons, habits, and stereotypes. Ironically, hurtful stereotypical "Appalachian jokes" told by outsiders are gleefully used by natives and often employed to make a quite different point. The following story, for example, makes the rounds when mountain winters become a topic of conversation:

> In the terrible winter of 1959, a great snowstorm closed the back roads of southern Appalachia. The Red Cross workers sent in to help with the emergency set off in a four-wheel-drive vehicle to see if an isolated woman up on a mountain needed help. After spinning and slipping for most of the day, they arrived at her house and knocked on the door, announcing, "Howdy, ma'am, we're from the Red Cross." She responded, "I don't think I'm going to be able to he'p you any. We've had a right hard winter."

In homefolks' telling, the vignette is not about an old woman out of touch with the modern world, but about mountaineers' mythic and still treasured independence.

One particular strain of Appalachian humor concerns the relationship of the region's people, supposedly still isolated, to the rest of America, particularly urbanites and individuals in positions of authority. From stereotypical images and outside perceptions of mountain folk as uniformly backward and impoverished arose a form of wry self-deprecation used simultaneously to maintain self-respect and to turn hurtful barbs back upon authority figures and others presuming material, spiritual, or intellectual superiority. That jokes and anecdotes would take such a turn is not surprising, considering that previous generations of Appalachians witnessed a succession of land agents, revenuers, missionaries, and government officials whose occupations and missions presumed some higher status. Revenuers and law enforcement officials from afar tended to see Appalachians as devious and lawless or both. Missionaries often assumed mountain religion to be inferior and presumed to direct Appalachians onto a more enlightened path to salvation. Business entrepreneurs and government agents not infrequently assumed locals to be inherently incapable of developing their resources and economy. Sensitive to such perceptions, many Appalachians found solace in humor that employed nonsense and circular dialogue leading nowhere. The technique is revealed in apocryphal stories such as the following:

> A missionary rides by a mountain cabin and asks a woman standing in the doorway if there are any Presbyterians around there. She says she doesn't think so but that her husband hunts varmints and nails their hides to the barn wall, and that the visitor can go look if he wants. The missionary then says, "I see you're living in darkness," to which she replies yes but that she's already asked her husband John to cut a window in the cabin for some light. The missionary asks where John is, and she says he is out hunting. He says, "What! Out hunting on the Sabbath? Doesn't he know the day of judgement is coming?" She says, "Don't tell him. He'll get a quart of liquor and go tear that Judgement Day to flinders like he does ever' Election Day."

Rural people have long directed such joking not only at visitors from distant places, but townsfolk, even relatives and former neighbors, considered to be putting on airs or having forgotten their origins as well. A certain reverence for rural heritage and a sensitivity to negative images perpetuated by the media lead to instances where hillbilly stereotypes are purposely resurrected and exaggerated—sometimes for the sheer fun of it but often as a fund-raising gimmick. During the annual Hillbilly Days celebration in Pikeville, Kentucky, natives dress up and gleefully play the roles of toothless, barefoot louts, moonshiners, and corncob-pipe-sucking granny women. Country music comedians, made famous by such programs as the *WWVA Jamboree* and the *Renfro Valley Barn Dance*, have been and remain willing to play the foolish hillbilly role, doing perhaps more than movies and television to spread the image of rural Appalachians as variously lacking in the trappings of civilization. Because most country comedians are products of the very culture they lampoon and exaggerate, most Appalachians not only accept their stereotypical jokes but also find belly laughs in material that would be considered cruel if used by outsiders, particularly northerners or urbanites.

William Hugh Jansen, a University of Kentucky folklorist, wrote perceptively about the nature of in-group and out-group humor in an article, "The Esoteric-Exoteric Factor in Folklore" (*The Study of Folklore*, 1965). Esoteric humor is about us, he wrote, and comes out of our sense of belonging to a particular group and strengthens and defends that sense. Exoteric humor, on the other hand, is about groups different from our own and "may result from our fear of, mystification about, or resentment of the group to which one does not belong." The late Governor Bert Combs, a native of the Kentucky hill country, commented that one learns nothing from the second kick of a mule, and his logic is esoteric as Appalachian humor because rural-oriented folk readily see the sense in his statement. Asking the difference between a Kentucky hillbilly and an S.O.B.—the answer being the Ohio River—is an example of exoteric humor, although the distinction is muddled since part of Ohio above the river is also in Appalachia.

A form of humor that combines esoteric and exoteric elements is the country bumpkin/city slicker routine, much of which derives from early commercial entertainment such as minstrel, medicine, vaudeville, and other traveling shows. Minstrel shows date back to the mid-nineteenth century; medicine shows traveled from community to community more than a century ago. While vaudeville and variety shows mostly played larger towns that boasted theaters, minstrel, medicine, and traveling shows visited villages in many parts of Appalachia. Medicine shows usually stayed a week or two, providing entertainment in the form of music and comic skits and jokes while the proprietors peddled their cures for common complaints. Rural people in a mostly oral culture were adept at remembering jokes and other material that titillated them, and they shared this material with others for years to come. Numerous entertainers who came from Appalachia and succeeded as radio and recording artists told of building their humorous routines around the comedy they had heard in the old traveling shows.

A standard part of American entertainment of this sort was the "Toby" character, a red-haired country bumpkin who was part of the traveling tent show plays. Toby was transparently less intelligent than the ordinary folk in the audience, but he always triumphed over antagonists who were not only brighter but invariably devious. To rural people, such a character was a hero. In more modern times the comics' Li'l Abner or Jed Clampett in television's *Beverly Hillbillies* fits this role. Neither is overly smart, but both are good-hearted, and they nearly always come out better than those who try to outsmart them. Sidekick characters played by such actors as Smiley Burnett, Pat Buttram, and Gabby Hayes in the western movies of Roy Rogers and Gene Autry also fulfilled this role. Related characters are the "Grandpappy," or irascible, old-uncle types from country music shows, as well as the "Aunt," or old-maid characters, who were free to speak their minds on almost any subject in a comic way. Examples include Archie Campbell's Grandpappy on Knoxville, Tennessee's WNOX *Midday Merry-Go-Round;* Grandpa Jones and Minnie Pearl on the *Grand Ole Opry* and *Hee Haw;* and Old Joe Clark and A'nt Idy on the *Renfro Valley Barn Dance* in Kentucky.

The earliest humor of the Appalachian frontier included European folktales brought to the mountains in the memories of immigrants. Hunting tales similar to those related by the Baron Münchausen of Germany were popular, and they led to other native tall tales about the exploits of various hero types. Richard Chase (*The Jack Tales*, 1943, and *Grandfather Tales*, 1948) collected stories and wrote about the folk character Jack (as in "Jack and the Beanstalk"), a figure known throughout the Old World and whose exploits have been perpetuated for generations within Appalachian families such as the Hicks, Harmon, Ward, and Proffitt families of western North Carolina and the Kilgore, Shores, and Adams families of southwest Virginia. Leonard Roberts has collected and written about such tales from the "Couch" family of eastern Kentucky (in *Sang Branch Settlers*, 1974; reprint 1980, and *Up Cutshin and Down Greasy*, 1959; reprint 1988). James York Glimm collected a wide range of tales and funny stories from natives of the Pennsylvania mountains in *Flatlanders and Ridgerunners: Folktales from the Mountains of Northern Pennsylvania* (1983) and *Snakebite: Lives and Legends of Central Pennsylvania* (1991).

To understand the region's humor and its cultural importance, one must appreciate its religious history and the profound role that religion continues to play in contemporary life in Appalachia. Most of the earliest settlers were Calvinists—Baptists and Presbyterians—who generally had a pessimistic view of the human condition, believing that sin and the flesh are inextricably linked, that freedom from sin comes only with the end of earthly existence, and that salvation comes through the grace of God, not good works. Such beliefs instilled a profound humility. The Perfectionists, on the other hand—Methodist, Holiness, and Pentecostal believers—had hope of rising above sin and living a perfect or holy life. The drastically different views and the consequent tension between the two groups set up many opportunities for humor. Jokes about various denominations often revealed far more than the jokesters may have realized. "What's the difference between Baptists and Methodists?" is the question posed by one joke. Answer: "Oh, not much. They both sin, but the Methodists can't enjoy it."

Jokes about denominations, such as the story of the Johnson boys and the stolen hog, have a universal quality and a way of transcending geography as well as culture, but in Appalachia they are a staple of banter among friends:

> Two fellows meet at a Methodist convention. One asks the other if he is a Methodist. He responds, "No, I've been sick."

Or:

> A Baptist lady offers to keep six Methodists for their revival. When asked how many beds she has, she says two—but that Methodists are so narrow they can sleep three to a bed.

Methodists respond with such as the following:

> Two Baptist deacons are talking about how their preacher stole six hundred dollars of the church's money and ran off.
> "Did they catch him?" one asks.
> "Yeah, they got him," said the second.
> "Did they get the money back?"
> "No, he spent it all."
> "What do you think we ought to do with him?"
> "Why, I think we ought to make him preach it out, ever' cent of it!"

The great subject of predestination and limited atonement versus free will and universal atonement has inevitably received humorous treatment from succeeding generations of Appalachians, including the region's preeminent storyteller-philosophers such as Sam Ervin. Jokes on these core theological tenets are often intended to elicit amused reflection rather than guffaws. For example:

> A Methodist and Predestinarian Baptist work on the second floor of the courthouse. As they walk down the stairs one day, the Baptist stumbles and falls down the steps. The Methodist picks him up, brushes him off, and says, "I guess you're glad to have that behind you, aren't you?" The next day the Methodist trips and falls down the same stairs, and when he arises, he says to himself, "Now why did I choose to do that?"

Country people love to poke fun at the pretensions of town churches and their preachers. Typical in this vein is the story of a county-seat preacher who has worked all week on a great sermon, typing his final draft late on Saturday night. Sunday morning, as he hurriedly gets ready for church, he finds that his text has been chewed to ribbons by his dog. In the pulpit, he introduces an abbreviated message by saying, "I had a great sermon prepared for you but the dog chewed it up. So this morning I'll just have to rely on the inspiration of God. But I promise to do better next Sunday!" (An addendum to this story is that a visitor from another church, impressed by the short sermon, inquires of the preacher, "Does that dog of yours have pups, by any chance? I'd like to give one to my preacher.") Town preachers, on the other hand, speak in a jocular way about the untrained "called" preachers who rely on inspiration and revelation. At least three folk-type sermons were written by one William P. Brannan, a nineteenth-century itinerant newspaperman and typesetter who made fun of those preachers who in their sermons ventured beyond their knowledge of the scriptures. One is the "Peezeltree Sermon," supposedly preached by an old-time minister when he misunderstood the word *psaltery.* Another had the text of, "And they shall gnaw a file and flee into the mountains of Hepsidam, where the lion roareth and the whang-doodle mourneth for its first-born." These and other preposterous sermon parodies were part of the Appalachian oral tradition.

Even though there are many optimistic Christians in modern Appalachia, the heavy hand of John Calvin still rests on much of the population, and among the devout there remains a strong skepticism about the human condition. Thus humility is much prized and historically has been espoused by even politicians. One of the best-known stories in Kentucky concerns the legendary Fess Whitaker of Letcher County, who joined Theodore Roosevelt's regiment and served in Cuba during the Spanish-American War. Later, when running for jailer in Letcher County, he would relate this adventure, telling how he and Teddy had ridden stirrup-to-stirrup up San Juan Hill with their sabers flashing in the sun while the enemy fled before them. He always ended the story by quoting Colonel Roosevelt: "We've done a great thing here today, Fess, and one of us is going to be President." Fess had responded, "You go ahead, Teddy. All I want to be is jailer of Letcher County!"

Early settlers, whose lives were rough and close to nature, also loved bawdy and scatological jokes and stories, some brought from the old countries and refashioned to fit new experiences and some generating in their mysterious way from the forming culture. But church and custom have always frowned on the public telling of such stories in many communities, thereby relegating the risqué to separate gender groups such as gatherings of boys just discovering the allure of forbidden things. Still, off-color jokes constitute the most common of all folk humor in modern-day Appalachia, with most people hearing, if not telling, them. Even though many are told just because they are off-color, some are truly funny and tell us much about the vagaries of the human experience, especially concerning sex and a few other things that remain taboo in polite society.

In earlier times, there were gifted persons and sometimes entire families who were good at singing old ballads or telling traditional folktales. Today, although the old ballads and folktales have faded, there are still those persons who tell good jokes and humorous stories and have a ready supply of them. Some see great humor in everyday life and turn it into genuine insight. Some of these gifted people—such as Carl Hurley, who gives humorous motivational speeches; Betty Lou York, a comedienne on the *Renfro Valley Barn Dance;* and Sam Venable, humor writer for the *Knoxville News-Sentinel*—make a living with their comic stories and observations. Others, perhaps equally talented, remain humorists by avocation only, unknown beyond their community but appreciated as local resources.

Storytelling is treated elsewhere in this volume, and some of the storytellers as well as writers appear elsewhere. Within the following section, however, are entries on some of the better-known Appalachian humorists: Archie Campbell, Judge Ray Corns, Harry Caudill, Bonnie Collins, George Daugherty, Andy Holt, Carl Hurley, Paul and Bil Lepp, Doc McConnell, Roni Stoneman, and Betty Lou York. The reader will quickly note that there are only three women included here. This is not rank discrimination; there are simply not as many women trying to be funny as there are men, at least in this region. Rayna Green, who wrote the introduction to *Pissing in the Snow and Other Ozark Folktales* (1976), a stunning collection of bawdy humor by folklorist Vance Randolph, has noted that women do tell stories, including off-color and scatological ones. But they tend to do so within their gender group—partly because of modesty but also because so many of the jokes take withering aim at male vanity.

Also included here are entries that deal with both the psychology and sociology of Appalachian humor. Other articles explore the region's storytelling tradition, the role of off-color jokes, and the importance of humor in literature, politics, and daily life. The authors are scholars who have long enjoyed and shared Appalachians' affinity for jokes and stories that deflate the pompous, deliver delicious insight, and help always to keep circumstance in perspective. Among different ethnic groups working in various occupations across the subregions of Appalachia, humor is manifest in special and changing ways, some spontaneous, some contrived. The humor is both stinging and gentle. It is both traditional and trendy. Always it serves both the people who listen and the people who perform. And just as mountain culture continues to be expressed in music, food, Sunday sermons, needlework, and books, it also survives in laughter.

—Loyal Jones, *Berea, Kentucky*

James R. Aswell et al., *God Bless the Devil! Liars' Bench Tales* (1940; reprint 1985); Richard Chase, *Grandfather Tales* (1948) and *The Jack Tales* (1943); James York Glimm, *Flatlanders and Ridgerunners: Folktales from the Mountains of Northern Pennsylvania* (1983) and *Snakebite: Lives and Legends of Central Pennsylvania* (1991); Carl Hurley, *We Weren't Poor—We Just Didn't Have Any Money* (1995); Loyal Jones and Billy Edd Wheeler, eds., *Laughter in Appalachia: A Festival of Southern Mountain Humor* (1986) and *More Laughter in Appalachia: Southern Mountain Humor* (1995); Paul and Bil Lepp, *The Monster Stick and Other Appalachian Tall Tales* (1999); W. K. McNeil, *Ozark Mountain Humor: Jokes on Hunting, Religion, Marriage and Ozark Ways* (1989); Elliott Oring, *Jokes and Their Relations* (1992); Vance Randolph, *Pissing in the Snow and Other Ozark Folktales* (1976); Leonard Roberts, *Sang Branch Settlers: Folksongs and Tales of a Kentucky Mountain Family* (1974; reprint 1980) and *Up Cutshin and Down Greasy* (1959; reprint 1988); Herbert Strean, *Jokes: Their Purpose and Meaning* (1993); Richard Walser, ed. *Tar Heel Laughter* (1974).

Ball, Lucille

(1911–1989) Actress, comedienne, and television executive.

Born and reared in Appalachia on the southern shore of Lake Chautauqua in Jamestown, New York, Lucille Ball became one of the most recognized faces in the world during a fifty-three year career that included more than seventy films and hundreds of television appearances. Working closely with her husband, Desi Arnaz, Ball defined the art of television situation comedy during the 1950s, creating memorable, highly entertaining characters while pioneering techniques that have become the standard in television sitcom production today.

Ball was respected and admired for her superb comic timing, most notably in slapstick. Her best-known body of work is the television sitcom *I Love Lucy* (1951–57), in which she played Lucy Ricardo, a character loosely based on Ball who found herself in a series of outrageous predicaments, usually self-created. This character shared Ball's real hometown of Jamestown, and the comedienne often used the names of real people and places from her Appalachian childhood in the series. On several episodes, country singer Tennessee Ernie Ford appeared as Lucy's country bumpkin cousin from Bent Fork, Tennessee.

During her career, Ball was recognized as a brilliant innovator in the field of television production. In a time of live broadcast, Ball and Arnaz insisted on filming in a studio before a live audience for best capturing the comedienne's energetic performances. This method of production had the additional benefit of providing recordings that were used to rerun episodes at later dates, a lucrative practice for studios that is now a staple of television broadcasting. Desilu Studios, the company formed by Ball and Arnaz to produce *I Love Lucy*, became a huge financial success and produced other popular television series including *The Andy Griffith Show* and *Star Trek*.

See also: TELEVISION DEPICTIONS OF THE REGION (MEDIA).

—Troy Gowen, *East Tennessee State University*

Bawdy and Scatological Humor

The largest body of Appalachian humor is composed of bawdy and scatological jokes, the region's religious bent and social conservatism notwithstanding. Before the publication of Roger Abrahams's *Deep Down in the Jungle: Negro Narrative Folklore from the Streets of Philadelphia* (1964) and Vance Randolph's *Pissing in the Snow and Other Ozark Folktales* (1976), with its excellent introduction by Rayna Green, most publishers discouraged the printing of obscene stories. However, more permissiveness toward the end of the twentieth century allowed some inclusion of this type of material.

No gathering of Appalachian bawdy lore compares with Randolph's Ozark collection, although such raconteur-collectors as the late Josiah H. Combs and Cratis Williams did have repertoires of off-color Appalachian stories, and some of these have appeared in collections.

Off-color humor, exemplified by Chaucer's "The Miller's Tale" and Randolph's title story, has been collected widely over time. Jokes are the popular folklore told or heard by most people. They are more likely to be shared in separate gender groups, but they are increasingly heard in mixed circles. Although bawdy jokes have figured in several sexual harassment complaints, Howard Pollio, a scholar of such material, suggests a utilitarian function of off-color humor. If men "wanted to meet a young woman who is sitting at the bar, what did they do? . . . The technique was to begin by saying something cute or funny, and what they were looking for was some sort of laugh or reaction from the young woman . . . and if the woman laughs, the man moves a bit closer toward her. . . . He progressively gets more risqué, and he knows something is possible when she laughs as the risqué level of his humor goes up. It's a mating ritual among North Americans."

Sometimes obscene jokes are told more for their shock value than for their humor, just as four-letter words litter many otherwise unfunny movie scripts. However, some are truly funny and reveal much about human joys, hopes, and fears. Most jokes, as Sigmund Freud noted, are either aggressive or sexual. An aggressive joke is a way to get back at someone obliquely. A sexual joke is tied to instincts about romance, happiness, fulfillment, and procreation. Yet sex is fraught with the ludicrous, ridiculous, and absurd, inspiring jokes that reflect both hope of triumph and fear of failure. For example, there are many jokes about declining male potency:

> Two women were discussing religion. "Does your husband believe in life after death?" asked one.
>
> "Heck no," replied the other. "He doesn't even believe in life after supper."

> This old man got up early, went to the bathroom, shaved, came out, and said to his wife, "Boy, that makes me feel twenty years younger."
>
> His wife said, "Did you ever think of shaving at night?"

Bawdy and scatological jokes have undoubtedly brought laughter to more people than the efforts of all other humorists. The genre is roundly condemned in polite society; perhaps this condemnation accounts for its appeal.

See also: JOKES, EXOTERIC AND ESOTERIC; SOCIOLOGY OF APPALACHIAN HUMOR; STORYTELLING, HISTORY OF (PERFORMING ARTS).

—Loyal Jones, *Berea, Kentucky*

Gershon Legman, *The Rationale of the Dirty Joke* (1968); Elliott Oring, *Jokes and Their Relations* (1992); Herbert Strean, *Jokes: Their Purpose and Meaning* (1993).

Campbell, Archie

(1914–1987) Comedian and country singer.

Archie Campbell was a noted comedian and singer on the *Grand Ole Opry* and *Hee Haw,* a popular television show of the 1970s. Born in Bulls Gap, Tennessee, Campbell studied for two years at Mars Hill College in North Carolina. In 1936, after several lean years playing music, he landed a job as a singer and musician at Knoxville, Tennessee's WNOX radio station, where he was mentored by announcer Lowell Blanchard. He then tried his hand at comedy, playing a character called Grandpappy on the *Midday Merry-Go-Round.*

After stints at Bristol, Tennessee's WOPI and Chattanooga's WDOD and two years in the U.S. Navy during World War II, Campbell rejoined the *Midday Merry-Go-Round.* He then went to WROL-TV for a show called *Country Playhouse,* Knoxville's first country music television show.

In 1958 Campbell joined the *Grand Ole Opry* as a comedian on the *Prince Albert Show.* He bade farewell to his Grandpappy character, who had donned bib overalls and plaid shirts, and began doing comedy in regular street clothes. His best-known routines were "Rindercella" and "Pee Little Thrigs," spoonerism versions of folktales. In 1969 Campbell was named Comedian of the Year by the Country Music Association and was hired as a writer-comedian on the *Hee Haw* television show, which had a twenty-four-year run. The routines and characters that he developed were sometimes based on skits that he and Blanchard had written years earlier in Knoxville. He recorded several albums for the RCA and Electra labels, and *Archie Campbell: An Autobiography,* with Ben Byrd, was published by Memphis State University in 1981.

Campbell and his wife, Mary Elizabeth, had two sons: Steve, a teacher, and Phil, a comedian, who was also a regular on *Hee Haw.* In 1987 Campbell died of a heart attack in Knoxville.

See also: GRAND OLE OPRY (MEDIA); HEE HAW (MEDIA).

—Loyal Jones, *Berea, Kentucky*

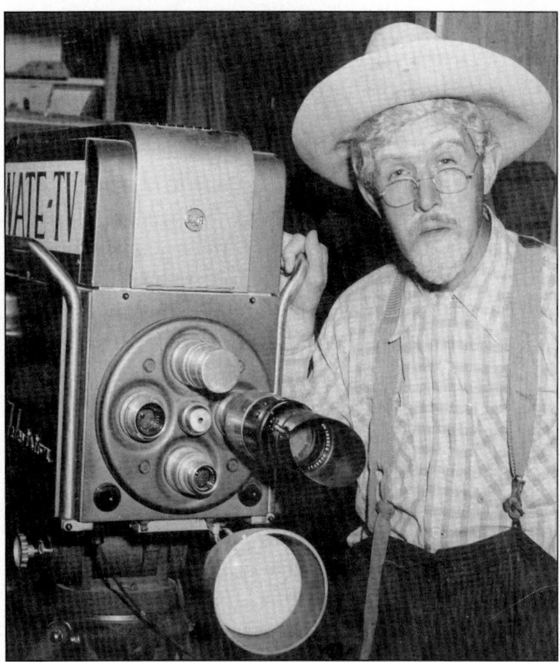

Archie Campbell, Knoxville, Tennessee, c. 1956. Campbell's "Grandpappy" was a popular character in both radio and television comedy.

Caudill, Harry

(1922–1990) Speaker and author.

Best known for *Night Comes to the Cumberlands,* his defining 1963 book addressing the environmental, social, and economic issues facing Appalachia, Harry Monroe Caudill is also recognized as a humorist and raconteur. As an attorney, he produced colorful and entertaining court arguments; as a writer, graphic and scathing prose on the social, political, and economic conditions of the region. His mastery of nineteenth-century rhetoric and lawyerly eloquence made him a spellbinding figure. On visits to Washington he drew open-mouthed officials, secretaries, and clerks out of their cubicles to hear his stories.

Caudill was born May 3, 1922, in Letcher County, Kentucky, and grew up heavily influenced by the oral traditions of the mountains. A wounded infantry veteran of the World War II Italian campaign, he married Anne Frye in 1946 and was graduated from the University of Kentucky law school in 1948. He then practiced law in Whitesburg and represented his district for three terms in the Kentucky legislature. After his twenty-eight-year law career, Caudill taught Appalachian history at the University of Kentucky between 1977 and 1985. He wrote a total of ten books and some 130 magazine and newspaper articles.

Some of his most popular stories, humorous or otherwise, are found in *The Mountain, the Miner, and the Lord* (1980) and *Slender Is the Thread: Tales from a Country Law Office* (1987). Caudill ranks with Sam J. Ervin of North Carolina and fellow Kentuckian A. B. "Happy" Chandler as a superb storyteller. He died in Letcher County on November 29, 1990, of a self-inflicted gunshot wound.

See also: POLITICAL HUMOR.

—Loyal Jones, *Berea, Kentucky*

Coal-Mining Humor

Although Appalachian coal miners are involved in a grim and dangerous occupation, they are prone to tell jokes and humorous stories, engage in pranks, and laugh at the foibles of their industrial work world. Because most miners in the region grew up in an oral culture, they tend to be superb storytellers, delighting in weaving irony, exaggeration, and wit into their otherwise intense lives. Although the broad categories of mining humor are similar to those found in other industrial occupations, many of the practical jokes, rookie pranks, initiation rites, tricks, mischief, gags, and witticisms are quite distinct.

One of the most common types of coal-mining humor is the initiation prank played on novice miners during their first days on the job. These pranks may include applying grease to the new miner's hair, ears, or face or sending him or her to fetch fictitious items such as a "sky hook" or a "side-goggling wobble bearing." Rookie surface miners have been sent for roof bolts, without thinking of the obvious—that there are no roof bolts in surface mines. Stories are told of a rookie who returned his cap light to the lamp house, declaring that he wouldn't need it because he was assigned to work the day shift. There are stories of new workers being told they are to be assigned duty as mine timbers.

Another category of mining humor involves gob rats. These are rodents that live in the mines, often feeding on scrap food discarded from miners' lunch buckets. Gob rat stories are often tall tales about the rats' ability to steal miners' food. A good example is an old miner's account of hiding behind a timber and watching a gob rat wrap his long tail around the lid of his round dinner pail as another rat pulled him around in a circle until the lid was unscrewed.

The narrow working space of the mine is also the subject of many jokes. One miner claimed that the seam where he worked was so low he had to carry his lunch in a fishing tackle box with sliding drawers. Another said the seam was so low that pancakes were the only food that could be taken into the mine and that they had to be dragged in with dynamite shot wire. Still another claimed the seam was so low that when he rolled toward the coal face with a shovel, he landed with his back to the seam. He would have to roll back out, flip over, and roll back again to see if he would land facing the coal.

Jokes frequently poke fun at the slow-wittedness of coworkers and the coal companies' lack of regard for them. The following joke illustrates both. A miner is ordered to drive his shuttle car faster when he approaches a particular area of suspect mine roof. "When you get to where that bad top is, speed up," says the foreman. "We don't want to get the company's shuttle car destroyed!"

For comedic relief, miners often engage in dark humor about real and present dangers such as roof falls. "Long John" Matyka, a Pennsylvania miner, once lugged a department store dummy to the mine and partially buried it in a coal pile. When another miner saw what appeared to a body sticking out of the coal, his screams could be heard throughout the mine.

Bathhouse pranks are imaginative and enduring. Because miners' faces are covered with coal dust by the end of each shift, they often use dishwashing liquid to wash their hair and face. When they are sufficiently lathered, coworkers might dump buckets of snow on them or throw a rubber snake into the shower room and yell, "SNAKE! RUN!"

Jokesters delight in "robbing" or "cutting" any lunch bucket they find unattended, and the owner of the sabotaged bucket will often go to great lengths to repay the mischief. Retaliation can be in the form of a hidden electrical wire attached to a bucket or laxative-laced food slipped into a lunch. One miner made a sandwich with dog food and left it for a potential thief.

Already colorful Appalachian language is enriched by contributions from the mining community. Miners have been heard to say, "He couldn't mine coal in a stockpile!" and "He could tear up a steel ball in a pile of rock dust!"

See also: COAL IMAGES (IMAGES AND ICONS); SOCIOLOGY OF APPALACHIAN HUMOR; SPECIALIZED LANGUAGE OF COAL MINING (LANGUAGE).

—James B. Goode, *Lexington Community College*

Collections of Appalachian Humor

As far as scholars know, the first collectors of Appalachian humor were travelers in the early nineteenth century. Their reports were usually not extensive, often consisting of accounts of an incident or two considered funny by the locals but decidedly not humorous by the traveler. An example is the Englishman Thomas Ashe, who in 1806 traveled via the Allegheny, Monongahela, Ohio, and Mississippi Rivers into what was then regarded as the Southwest. While passing through a Kentucky village, Ashe commented on a favorite backwoods entertainment—a fight, in this case between a Kentuckian and a Virginian. Ashe's report provided details about gouged eyes and chewed-off ears. Later that same day, after retiring from a frontier ball that had ended in a brawl, the English traveler returned to his tavern, where he listened to his landlord tell several anecdotes about the day's events that the landlord found greatly entertaining but which Ashe regarded with horror.

Newspapers and magazines also carried occasional items of traditional mountain humor. Beginning in the 1820s, a new type of newspaper arose that was not aimed primarily at the educated upper class. Instead of being filled with foreign news, these papers sought to provide entertainment as well as news for the local communities they served. Consequently, they included humor in various forms, ranging from conundrums to elaborate tales. In 1831 the *Spirit of the Times*, a weekly sporting paper that was for three decades the leading medium for humorous backcountry sketches, was established in New York. To be sure, this paper and similar ones included matters other than Appalachian or folk humor, but many of their contributors were from the southern mountains and more than a few borrowed heavily from folk tradition. For example, George Washington Harris, now best known as the creator of Sut Lovingood, contributed in 1840 a traditional tale titled "A Snake-Bit Irishman" about a man who thinks he has been bitten by a snake when he squats on his own spurs.

In the nineteenth century, several other publications appeared that relied to some extent on traditional Appalachian humor. Notable among these were a series of almanacs about Davy Crockett issued from 1835 to 1856. These booklets both borrowed from and influenced the tradition although their intent was simply to make money off Crockett's name. Three years after the last Crockett Almanac, the first major collection of Appalachian humor appeared in print. In 1857 Harden E. Taliaferro, a Baptist minister raised in Surry County, North Carolina, visited his home region after an absence of twenty years, and while there he decided to write out some of the narratives he had heard in the 1820s. The result was *Fisher's River (North Carolina) Scenes and Characters* (1859), a collection of character sketches followed by yarns from each storyteller. Included in this cache of humorous tales are classic Baron Münchausen tall-tale themes such as the steeple-tethered horse, the deer bearing a peach tree, and the split dog. Taliaferro related the stories in a not greatly successful attempt to capture the Surry County dialect. Even so, many of the sayings he put in the mouths of his characters ring true.

No collection of Appalachian humor comparable to Taliaferro's appeared in the remainder of the nineteenth century. American folklore collectors of the day were primarily interested in ballads and folktales and little inclined to deal with such topics as humor. This attitude continued well into the twentieth century, as evidenced by *The Frank C. Brown Collection of North Carolina Folklore*. This seven-volume opus includes different genres of folklore collected throughout the Tar Heel State but very little humor. Out of eighty-six pages devoted to folk narratives only six deal with humorous items, and most of these few texts come from outside Appalachia.

In the 1930s, a boost to Appalachian humor research and folklore collecting in general was provided by the Federal Writers' Project of the Works Progress Administration. As part of the effort to create jobs in music, drama, writing, and the arts, workers were encouraged to collect various genres of folklore as a means of getting at the "real" culture of the American people. Although books using the collected materials were published for many states, *God Bless the Devil! Liars' Bench Tales* (1940) was one of the few volumes devoted exclusively to humorous texts. This collection of twenty-five narratives recorded in Tennessee illustrates some of the problems folklorists have with much of the Works Progress Administration material. Documentation of sources is very casual, often informants are not even identified, and background details on their lives are missing. Because folklore was prized as a source of inspiration for creative fiction, texts were greatly "improved" and often presented with dialect reproduced somewhat amateurishly. Moreover, these tales are presented as though they were unique to Tennessee when, in fact, most are relatively widespread. On the positive side, this book and some other Works Progress Administration folklore volumes did present a body of traditional humorous tales to the general reading public. Furthermore, it was the first large, systematic Appalachian humor collection ever published.

Since the 1970s most Appalachian states have had official state folklorists, but these programs have not been particularly oriented towards humor research. As a result *God Bless the Devil!* is the only publication on Appalachian humor (and not all texts in the book come from Appalachia) resulting from a government-funded collecting project. In recent years, however, several raconteurs have published books of their own humorous material. Of these writers the most successful has been Donald Davis, a retired minister who has written several volumes, including *Listening for the Crack of Dawn* (1990). Davis often tells stories—sometimes funny, sometimes serious—based on childhood memories. Some, such as his essay on fourth-grade teacher Daisy Rose Boring, are more reminiscent than funny. Most of the humorous stories are unique to Davis rather than examples of folk humor.

Newspaper columnists such as Sam Venable of the *Knoxville News-Sentinel* and Bob Terrell of the *Asheville Citizen-Times* often include mountain humor in their columns and in books. Representative of such productions are Terrell's *Old Gold* (1981) and *Keep 'Em Laughing* (1985), which consist of tales he heard from friends and neighbors. Some of the stories have been rarely told. One of them is the story of an Ohio farmer who took future-President James Garfield to be an ordinary farmhand and refused Garfield's request to marry his daughter. Others, such as tales about Winston Churchill, are widely traveled.

Loyal Jones, then director of the Appalachian Center at Berea College, and Billy Edd Wheeler, a humorist and songwriter, were the first to compile volumes dealing with folk humor throughout Appalachia. Their *Laughter in Appalachia:*

A Festival of Southern Mountain Humor (1986), *Curing the Cross-Eyed Mule: Appalachian Mountain Humor* (1989), and *More Laughter in Appalachia: Southern Mountain Humor* (1995) are largely based on material contributed by participants in four Festivals of Appalachian Humor held at Berea College in 1983, 1987, 1990, and 1993. These three volumes are considerably superior to *God Bless the Devil!* in that informants are clearly identified and texts are generally given in their exact words. Unfortunately, the books lack comparative material (story type and motif, variants, etc.) since they are primarily intended for popular, not academic, audiences. As a result the impression is given that these tales, most of which are quite widely circulated, are unique to Appalachia.

Several printed works dealing with southern mountain humor have appeared over the last two centuries, but few have been the result of systematic collecting. Moreover, geographic coverage of Appalachia has been spotty, and most publications have been intended for popular audiences. Therefore comparative data are lacking, and from a scholarly standpoint Appalachian humor research is still in its infancy.

See also: CROCKETT, DAVID; HUMOR IN APPALACHIAN LITERATURE; NEWSPAPER HUMORISTS.

—W. K. McNeil, *The Ozark Folk Center*

James R. Aswell et al., *God Bless the Devil! Liars' Bench Tales* (1940; reprint 1985); Michael A. Lofaro, *The Tall Tales of Davy Crockett: The Second Nashville Series of Crockett Almanacs, 1839–1841* (1987); Norris W. Yates, *William T. Porter and the Spirit of the Times: A Study of the Big Bear School of Humor* (1957; reprint 1977).

Collins, Bonnie

(1915–) Storyteller, humorist, comedienne, and singer.

Prizewinning West Virginia storyteller and humorist Bonnie Collins was born Bonnie Mae Starkey on June 9, 1915, in Doddridge County and grew up in a large family from whom she learned to tell stories, read music, and play stringed instruments. She married Archie Carl Collins in 1942 and, after rearing her children, went to work as a cook in a Doddridge County school. When one of the children called her "the goodest cook," she wrote a poem by the same name that so impressed school administrators that they hired her to work with an early childhood program. Eventually, Collins developed a repertoire of stories and jokes that she was often asked to perform for groups of educators and civic groups. In 1963 she became a 4-H Club leader and began making appearances at folk festivals such as the Vandalia Gathering in Charleston, West Virginia, the Jackson's Mill Jubilee held near Weston, West Virginia, and the Festival of Appalachian Humor in Berea, Kentucky. When Collins's husband died, she quit performing for a time but eventually resumed her career at the urging of her daughter and friends.

Collins's stories and songs, drawn largely from her personal experiences and local lore, have brought her considerable recognition. She was named a Distinguished West Virginian by Governor John D. Rockefeller IV in 1980 and received the Vandalia Award—the highest folklore honor bestowed by the State of West Virginia—for her work with schoolchildren in 1990. She was also given the Good Samaritan Award at the Pinch (West Virginia) Reunion in 1995. Collins has judged the Vandalia Gathering's West Virginia Liars Contest every year since its inception in 1983. She has produced an audiocassette entitled *An Evening with Bonnie Collins* and coauthored a book with children's writer Marc Harshman entitled *Rocks in My Pocket.*

See also: FESTIVALS, HUMOR AND STORYTELLING; HUMOROUS STORYTELLING.

—Bil Lepp, *Charleston, West Virginia*

Corns, Judge Ray

(1934–) Lawyer, jurist, humorist, and ventriloquist.

Although his profession as lawyer, judge, and state official suggests a serious demeanor, Ray Corns is a noted stand-up comedian, ventriloquist, motivational speaker, and author of a syndicated humor column called "The Corn Crib."

Born near Cabin Creek in the hills of eastern Kentucky, Corns graduated from Berea College and Samford University law school. During his career, he served in many Kentucky offices, including commonwealth attorney, juvenile judge, chief legal counsel to the State Department of Education, and circuit judge in the capital city of Frankfort. He was also legal advisor to two governors, secretary of the Kentucky Justice Cabinet, and commissioner of the Kentucky State Police, as well as coauthor of a textbook on public school law. While serving as a circuit judge, Corns ruled that the state's system of financing public schools was unconstitutional because it did not provide equal financing across the state, bringing about landmark educational reform. The 1990 Kentucky Educational Reform Act added $800 million in new funds for education and made structural changes in the system.

While he was a circuit judge, Corns traveled on weekends to Chicago, Illinois, to study ventriloquism and honed this art as a regular comedian on the *Renfro Valley Barn Dance* in south-central Kentucky. He has also performed stand-up comedy across the country and given professional talks spiced with humor about lawyers, judges, and the legal profession.

See also: COUNTRY MUSIC COMEDY; *RENFRO VALLEY BARN DANCE* (MEDIA).

—Loyal Jones, *Berea, Kentucky*

Cast of the *Original WWVA Jamboree,* Wheeling, West Virginia, c. 1940s. Music and comedy intertwined in shows such as this long-running country music program.

Country Music Comedy

Comedy has always been a part of country music, and many Appalachian-born entertainers played the role of the comedian in the minstrel, vaudeville, and medicine shows that began in the nineteenth century and continued into the first part of the twentieth century. Such shows were opportunities for native musicians such as Tennessee's Roy Acuff, who began his career in a medicine show playing both blackface and white rustic characters known as rubes. Rod Brasfield and his brother Lawrence ("Uncle Cyp") from northern Mississippi were veterans of vaudeville when Rod joined the *Grand Ole Opry* and Lawrence became a fixture on the *Ozark Jubilee*, a country music show televised from Springfield, Missouri.

Road shows, popular staged radio shows of the mid-twentieth century such as WNOX's *Midday Merry-Go-Round* and the *WWVA Jamboree*, and radio barn dances required variety, and comedy became essential to their success. John Lair, beginning in 1928 at Chicago radio station WLS, later at radio stations in Cincinnati, and finally at the *Renfro Valley Barn Dance* in Kentucky, wrote comedy scripts that borrowed from minstrel, vaudeville, and medicine show routines as well as from traditional humor. These scripts were performed by entertainers such as Lulu Belle and Scotty (Wiseman) from North Carolina and the Coon Creek Girls, led by Kentuckian Lily May Ledford, over the *National Barn Dance* on WLS. Lair wrote for numerous comedians on his *Renfro Valley Barn Dance*. At Knoxville, Tennessee's WNOX radio, Lowell Blanchard also wrote voluminous comedy scripts at the *Midday Merry-Go-Round* for such entertainers as Archie Campbell ("Grandpappy") from Bull's Gap, Tennessee; Charles Elza ("Kentucky Slim") from Harlan County, Kentucky; and Kenneth Burns and Henry Haynes ("Homer and Jethro") from Knoxville. These and other entertainers took Blanchard's scripts with them when they left and used them at other venues, including the *Grand Ole Opry* and *Hee Haw*.

Although comedians had to use clean humor since they played to family audiences, there were innuendos in regard to sexual relations and knowing references to alimentary functions. The content of the humor, while seemingly light and frivolous, had political overtones as well. Adopting the city slicker/country bumpkin theme that had been a large part of American humor and theater in the nineteenth century, comedians found that their audiences loved jokes or routines that showed country people were as smart (or smarter) and as worthy as their urban contemporaries.

One function of country humor was to reinforce traditional rural values in the face of great social and economic change. The humor was pointed as it related to inequality in financial and political matters. Because of bewilderment caused by rapid industrialization, part of the humor gave country people assurance about their own abilities as they compared themselves to rubes encountering newfangled things that completely baffled them. Such humor helps people forget their own troubles for a time and reinforces their own sense of worth in relation to people who appear to think they are better than country people. It is a humor that reinforces the underdog.

Other Appalachian artists doing country comedy were Wade and J. E. Mainer, Red Rector, and Fred Smith from North Carolina; Pat Buttram and the Louvin Brothers from Alabama; Jim and Jesse McReynolds, Roni Stoneman, and Ron Thomason from Virginia; Josh Graves, Doyle Lawson, James "Sparky" Rucker, and Manuel "Old Joe" Clark from Tennessee; the Lilly Brothers, Melvin Goins, and Little Jimmie Dickens from West Virginia; and David "Stringbean" Akeman, Carl Hurley, and Betty Lou York from Kentucky.

Country comedy reached its peak with the television show *Hee Haw*, produced in Nashville for twenty-four years, beginning in 1969. The show was simple, rural, corny, and trite—characteristics that would seem to guarantee failure on modern television. However, rural audiences, as well as others, loved it. Comedy has largely faded from the country music business, but it is still sometimes heard at the *Grand Ole Opry*, at bluegrass festivals, and always at the *Renfro Valley Barn Dance*, as well as in newer venues such as the country music shows in Pigeon Forge, Tennessee, and the *Kentucky Opry* in Prestonsburg, Kentucky.

See also: *HEE HAW* (MEDIA); *RENFRO VALLEY BARN DANCE* (MEDIA); *WWVA JAMBOREE* (MEDIA).

—Loyal Jones, *Berea, Kentucky*

Douglas B. Green, *Country Roots: The Origins of Country Music* (1976); William Jensen Smyth, *Traditional Humor on Knoxville Country Radio Entertainment Shows* (1987); Pete Stamper, *It All Happened in Renfro Valley* (1999).

Crockett, David

(1786–1836) U.S. congressman and frontier humorist.

The life of the real David Crockett has become nearly inseparable from the mythic Davy Crockett created by fabrications and exaggerations by Crockett himself and wildly embellished in the twentieth century. Of his ability to tell a humorous story, however, there can be no doubt. The Appalachian-born frontiersman, congressman, and hero of the Alamo is the central figure in countless stories, novels, plays, and films and is also considered the first person to write in a style that was to become the Old Southwestern humor tradition.

During Crockett's life, the Southwest consisted of Tennessee, Alabama, Mississippi, and Arkansas. Elements of Old Southwestern humor include the use of dialect, crude physical humor, exaggerated claims of strength and cunning, and most importantly, a protagonist portrayed as folksy and naive who nonetheless triumphs over his adversaries—notably urban elitists. The character of Davy Crockett is a central figure in many of these tales, told both by Crockett and others. However, it is primarily the autobiography of David Crockett, written in collaboration with Thomas Chilton, that best illustrates the humor of the real Crockett.

A Narrative of the Life of David Crockett of the State of Tennessee, the autobiography published in 1834 primarily as a publicity tool of the Whig Party's opposition campaign against President Andrew Jackson, revealed an earthy wit that made Crockett enormously popular. Although the humorous side of Crockett was possibly contrived, it helped him win three terms in Congress despite his ineffectual performance there. In the generally accurate autobiography, Crockett employed slightly exaggerated, humorous anecdotes to present himself as a backwoods Everyman. "Fashion is a thing I care mighty little about, except when it happens to run just exactly according to my own notion," Crockett declared in prose style that is later emulated in works by writers such as Mark Twain.

This style served not only to entertain, but also to deflate the images of Crockett's political adversaries, notably Jackson and Martin Van Buren. In a twist on his autobiography, he wrote, or had his name put to, a scurrilous biography of Van Buren a year later. "What a pity I hadn't been [born] the seventh!" Crockett wrote in his autobiography. "For then I might have been, by common consent, called doctor, as a heap of people get to be great men. But, like many of them, I stood no chance to become great in any other way than by accident." This is an example of the slightly sarcastic humor with which he distinguishes himself as a man with no pretensions from the image of Jackson, who held an honorary doctorate from Harvard University.

This talent served Crockett in public speaking as well. At least once he memorized the speech of his opponent and recited it to the crowd before the other man had his turn. Another tactic was to take his turn last. After the crowd had been tired out by the other speakers, Crockett would tell one joke then offer to treat the crowd at the local tavern.

Once when he was asked to give an impromptu speech before a gathering of voters in west Tennessee, Crockett reported being "choaked up" with little to say, until he got himself started with the following story: "A man was beating on the head of an empty barrel near the road-side, when a traveler, who was passing along, asked him what he was doing that for? The fellow replied, that here was some cider in that barrel a few days before, and he was trying to see if there was any then, but if there was he couldn't get at it. I told them that there had been a little bit of a speech in me a while ago, but I believed I couldn't get it out."

Giving up on politics after Jackson's supporters helped to destroy his career, Crockett made his farewell by declaring that he "was done with politics for the present, and that they might all go to hell, and [he] would go to Texas." Crockett's sense of humor was instrumental to his popularity, and his nearly mythical fate cemented his folk-hero status. Crockett died as one of the last defenders of the Alamo during the Texas Revolution in March 1836.

See also: CROCKETT, DAVID (SETTLEMENT AND MIGRATION); CROCKETT ALMANACS (MEDIA); HUMOR IN APPALACHIAN LITERATURE; POLITICAL HUMOR.

—Troy Gowen, *East Tennessee State University*

David Crockett, *A Narrative of the Life of David Crockett of the State of Tennessee*, annotations by James A. Shackford and Stanley J. Folmsbee (1834); Michael A. Lofaro, ed., *Davy Crockett: The Man, the Legend, the Legacy, 1786–1986* (1985).

Daugherty, George

(1932–) Lawyer, actor, humorist, and musician.

While a practicing attorney, Mannington, West Virginia, native George A. Daugherty established himself as a noted humorist using material strongly reflecting his Appalachian roots. In addition to calling himself the "Earl of Elkview," Daugherty claims he is a psychoneuroimmunologist, which he defines as "a doctor of perpetual celebration." He further describes himself as "a minstrel who brings a message of love, peace, pride, heritage, and humor." Proud of his American, West Virginian, and Irish heritage, Daugherty has toured the United States, Ireland, England, and Germany, presenting more than three thousand shows that incorporate his patriotism, mountain humor, and original humorous songs. He also has performed community theater in Charleston, West Virginia, playing lead roles in productions of *Dylan*, *The Field*, and *Oliver!* He also produced and appeared in *A Touch of Ireland* with Irish actor James N. Healy.

Musician Buddy Griffin often accompanies Daugherty onstage when he tours, and occasionally other singers and musicians do as well. Daugherty sings and plays the guitar and banjo, but his crowd-pleaser is a rendition of "Danny Boy" performed on the handsaw. He has released two recordings, *The Relax Radio Show* and *The Irish Relax Radio Show*, both on the Braxton label.

Daugherty practices law in Elkview, West Virginia, with his law partner and wife, Suzanne. During the controversy over mountaintop removal in West Virginia coalfields, Daugherty became a popular performer at rallies and protests staged by environmental activists.

See also: HOLT, ANDY; IRISH (RACE, ETHNICITY, AND IDENTITY); MACON, UNCLE DAVE (MUSIC).

—Loyal Jones, *Berea, Kentucky*

Davis, Donald

See Davis, Donald (Performing Arts)

Festivals, Humor and Storytelling

Due partially to the isolation of its people for many decades, the Appalachian region has kept alive a strong oral tradition that continues to be a hallmark of its culture in the twenty-first century. Historically, the telling of stories, humorous and otherwise, was a form of entertainment, education, and cultural preservation. Storytelling, in times of joy and sorrow, was part of the workplace, family gatherings, and community events. In modern times, this anecdotal heritage has served many Appalachians well, often bringing them renown as politicians, preachers, writers, and entertainers.

In some locations in the region, the position of storyteller has been passed down through families. In Beech Mountain, North Carolina, for example, the most revered storytellers, even in the early twenty-first century, are descendants of Council Harmon, the great-grandson of

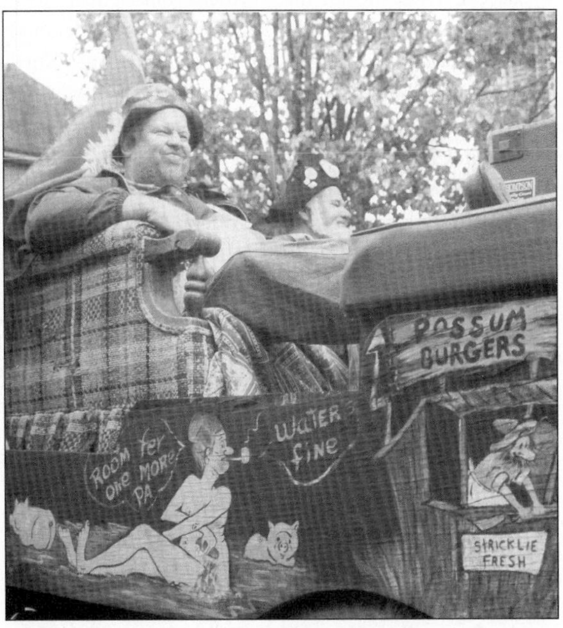

A customized "hillbilly vehicle" provides a lighthearted take on Appalachian images during the Hillbilly Days parade in Pikeville, Kentucky, 1999. The parade is a major component of this annual fund-raising festival for Shrine charities.

David Hicks (then Hix), who emigrated from England around 1760. They are noted for telling Jack tales ("Jack the Giant Killer") and humorous stories. Ray Hicks, approaching eighty at the turn of the century, continued to tell the same stories and live much as his ancestors had (without electricity or running water) on the side of Beech Mountain.

Numerous other humorists and storytellers such as Donald Davis, Doc McConnell, and Sheila Kay Adams (great-niece of famous ballad singer Dellie Norton) are both beneficiaries and contemporary conduits of Appalachia's strong oral tradition. Many of these tellers, along with newcomers (known as revivalist storytellers) who have adopted the tradition, continue to play a part in the burgeoning tourist industry in Appalachia. With the arrival of electricity, industrialization, and improvements in transportation to many parts of the region during the 1930s and 1940s, tourism became an increasingly important component of local economies. While storytelling continued to be important within families and communities, it also came to be viewed as an endearing and marketable aspect of Appalachian culture—a tourist attraction. The town of Jonesborough, Tennessee, staged the first National Storytelling Festival in 1973. Attracting national media coverage, the annual event drew soaring crowds, and by the mid-1980s it had become internationally known.

Towns throughout Appalachia have subsequently organized hundreds of similar events, with varying degrees of success. These include the Northern Appalachian Storytelling Festival of Mansfield, Pennsylvania (now defunct); the Beech Mountain Storytelling Festival in Boone, North Carolina; the Smoky Mountains Storytelling Festival in Pigeon Forge, Tennessee; the Cherokee Rose Storytelling Festival in Carrollton, Georgia; the Stone Soup Storytelling Festival in Woodruff, South Carolina; the Blue Ridge and Beyond Storytelling Festival in Mount Airy, North Carolina; and the Toe River Storytelling Festival in Spruce Pine, North Carolina. And there are countless other events—including music festivals and crafts fairs—that also feature stories as part of the entertainment such as the Townsend Heritage Festival and Old Timers Day in Tennessee and Merlefest (founded by folksinger Doc Watson), held in Wilkesboro, North Carolina.

Humorous stories are particularly prime tourist fare when offered as liars' contests, with the challenge being to "bring down the house" and overcome the competition with the funniest and most outrageous tale. These events generally draw big crowds, with the winners often becoming local as well as regional celebrities. Some of the most notable of these events include the Tall Tale Liars Contest held during the Autumn Glory Festival in Swanton, Maryland, and the National Storytelling Competition held in Hillsboro, Ohio. Started in 1983, the West Virginia Liars Contest, held in Charleston, West Virginia, is part of the Vandalia Gathering, one of the nation's largest folk festivals. During the competition, contestants vie for the positions of "Big Liar" (third place), "Bigger Liar" (second place), and "Biggest Liar" (first place), with the latter receiving the prestigious Goldenseal Shovel—a blue and gold barn shovel.

One of the best-documented events of this type was the Festival of Appalachian Humor, created in 1983 and subsequently held in 1987, 1990, and 1993. Sponsored by Berea College's Appalachian Center in Kentucky, it was the only event of its kind devoted exclusively to Appalachian humor. Besides featuring a storytelling competition, event planners also brought in noted humorists such as Doc McConnell, David Holt, Judge Ray Corns, Sam Venable, George Daugherty, Bonnie Collins, Paul Lepp, Carl Hurley, Roni Stoneman, Manuel "Old Joe" Clark, Joe Bly, Bill Foster, Anndrena Belcher, and Roy Blount Jr., to name a few. The stories from this event, recorded and placed in the Berea College Sound Archive, were later compiled by festival founders Billy Edd Wheeler and Loyal Jones and published in a collection of books—*Laughter in Appalachia: A Festival of Southern Mountain Humor* (1986), *Curing the Cross-Eyed Mule: Appalachian Mountain Humor* (1989), *Hometown Humor* (1991), and *More Laughter in Appalachia: Southern Mountain Humor* (1995).

Also worth a mention are the numerous successful humor-based festivals that play off stereotypical images that still exist about Appalachia. A prime example is Hillbilly Days, held in Pike County, Kentucky, which beckons as many as eighty thousand attendees each year to dress in hillbilly garb—while raising thousands for Shriners' charities. Likewise, the annual BubbaFest in Sugar Tit, South Carolina, has garnered national recognition since 1993 with its tongue-in-cheek Bubba-Q cook-off, Bubbalympics, and Bubba and Bubbette competition.

See also: INTERNATIONAL STORYTELLING CENTER (PERFORMING ARTS); NATIONAL STORYTELLING FESTIVAL (PERFORMING ARTS); STORYTELLING IN THE TWENTIETH CENTURY, RENAISSANCE OF (PERFORMING ARTS).

—Jill Oxendine, *East Tennessee State University*

William Bernard McCarthy, ed., *Jack in Two Worlds: Contemporary North American Tales and Their Tellers* (1994); National Storytelling Network, *National Storytelling Directory* (2002); "2000 Liars Contest," *Goldenseal Magazine* (Spring 2001).

Freeman, Barbara

See Freeman, Barbara (Performing Arts)

Hee Haw

See *Hee Haw* (Media)

Hicks, Ray

See Hicks, Ray (Performing Arts)

Hillbilly Jokes

Every nation has its own hillbillies, marginal rural people who are the butts of disdainful metropolitan humor, but the expression has a special resonance in central and southern Appalachia. According to the *Oxford English Dictionary*, the term *hillbilly* is an Americanism, first appearing in print in 1900, referring to "a person from a remote or mountainous area, *esp.* of the southeastern U.S.," with no indication given of its ultimate origins. *Billy* is an archaic word of Scottish and northern English provenance meaning "fellow, companion, comrade, mate," which first appeared in Scots literature in 1505 and was used by Robert Burns in several of his poems. Shortly after the American Civil War, southern mountaineers emerged in the national consciousness as a peculiar people with old-fashioned ways. But the estrangement of Appalachian mountaineers from the dominant traditions of the lowland South and the mainstream American culture may have been germinating long before then, as contemporary scholar Rodger Cunningham persuasively argues in his book *Apples on the Flood* (1987).

Poor people who migrate from rural peripheries to a metropolis looking for work are stereotyped in similar ways wherever their origin. Conceited city dwellers typically depict the inhabitants of the hinterlands as ignorant, backward, uncouth, and even animalistic. Much of the coarse humor directed at marginal people focuses upon their purported unfamiliarity with urban ways. Absurd misunderstanding is the most commonly found comic motif in American hillbilly jokes and their international counterparts. Backcountry humor counters allegations of rural stupidity and ignorance with the canny rustic—a trickster-hero who outwits thick-skulled townsfolk.

Jokes told about hillbillies in the United States become "Newfie" jokes in Canada. Physically isolated from the Canadian mainland on an enormous, remote island that is the northernmost extension of the Appalachian Mountain system running through eastern North America, Newfoundlanders are psychologically and culturally disassociated from mainland Canada by the island's long history as a separate British possession. Newfies became maritime hillbillies when they began migrating to the mainland looking for work they could not find at home. Hillbillies and Newfies share much in common, as shown by these two localized variants making fun of rural migrants wanting to go back home. First, an Appalachian example from folklorist Bill Lightfoot:

> A guy died and went to heaven. St. Peter was showing him around, and the guy thought it was wonderful. They went around the corner, and there was a bunch of people in chains, and the guy asked St. Peter why in the world these people were chained. St. Peter replied, "That's a bunch of hillbillies, and every Friday at 5 p.m., they want to head home for the weekend!"

This joke's Newfoundland counterpart appears in *We Rant and We Roar*, a self-published collection of jokes by Al Clouston:

> During the war boom in Newfoundland, American foremen were appalled that a man would leave a good job, just to be at home for four or five months. These foremen did not know that Newfoundlanders "went home in the fall." An Irishman, an American, and a Newfoundlander all arrived at the gate of heaven at the same time. St. Peter addressed the Irishman first and asked his nationality. He was told to take the next train north, and he would get to the community where all the Irishmen were congregated. The American was to take the next train south.
>
> When St. Peter came to the Newfoundlander, he said, "What are you?"
>
> "I'm a Newfoundlander," was the reply.
>
> And St. Peter said, "My son, you'd better stay right here by the gate because you'll want to go home in the fall."

Newfie and hillbilly jokes have numerous shared motifs centering around themes of intellectual, material, and moral deficit and feature absurd misunderstandings, fools, poverty, excessive indulgence in alcohol and sex, slovenliness, and the ultimate slurs, accusations of incest and bestiality. These same themes also appear in jokes about other marginal groups including Irishmen, Scottish Highlanders, natives of Aberdeen (renowned for excessive thriftiness and overfamiliarity with sheep), as well as French jokes about Belgians and Dutch jokes about the residents of the Frisian Islands. Jokes told about a marginal group may in turn be retold about an extremely peripheral segment of that very population. Jokes told about Scots in general are told about Aberdonians by other Scots; generic Irish numskull jokes become Kerry jokes in Ireland, while the jokes that other Americans tell about Appalachian people are often recast as West Virginia jokes. Here is one of the least nasty sheep jokes encountered in various local versions in the United States and its Aberdonian counterpart:

> Do you know they've discovered a new use for sheep in West Virginia/Arkansas/Carter County, Tennessee? Wool!
>
> Do you know they've discovered a new use for sheep in Aberdeen? Mutton!

The underlying message of these jokes is "Really, these people are no better than animals!" Rural people know better, and they tell their own jokes about the ignorance and stupidity of city people, particularly tourists in the countryside. The widely encountered theme of the lost tourist encountering the wisecracking rustic even has its own category as a character type among international folklorists.

Sometimes it is possible to score comic hits against more than one ridiculed group at a time, as in the following Scottish joke about the Irish tourist inspecting a hand-knit Fair Isles sweater in a gift shop:

> *Scottish shopkeeper:* "You know, it takes seven sheep to make one of these sweaters!"
> *Irish tourist:* "I didn't know they could knit!"

As Jerry Williamson notes in *Hillbillyland: What the Movies Did to the Mountains and What the Mountains Did to the Movies* (1995), all groups have their own hillbillies, even hillbillies, who make up jokes about even poorer and more isolated brierhoppers and ridgerunners. Thus the need to laugh at numskulls and to make light of dehumanizing images imposed by others explodes stereotypes in the very process of embracing them.

See also: HUMOROUS STORYTELLING; JOKES, EXOTERIC AND ESOTERIC; NORTHERN APPALACHIAN HUMOR.

—Richard Blaustein, *East Tennessee State University*

Ronald L. Baker, *Jokelore: Humorous Folktales from Indiana* (1986); Al Clouston, *We Rant and We Roar* (1988); J. W. Williamson, *Hillbillyland: What the Movies Did to the Mountains and What the Mountains Did to the Movies* (1995).

Holt, Andy

(1904–1987) Educator and humorist.

One of the great southern humorists and storytellers, Andrew David Holt, as president of the University of Tennessee (1959–70), oversaw the greatest expansion—in facilities, enrollment, faculty, and curriculum—in the history of the institution. Born December 4, 1904, in Milan, Tennessee, Holt received his bachelor's degree from Emory University in Atlanta and his master's and doctorate from Columbia University in New York. Before joining the University of Tennessee in 1950 as administrative assistant to the president, Holt had compiled an impressive list of professional accomplishments as an elementary and high school teacher, football coach, principal, college professor, executive secretary of the Tennessee Education Association (thirteen years), and president of the National Education Association (eight years).

One of his greatest skills was entertaining audiences. Whether speaking to a small-town civic club, addressing the student body, or wooing the Tennessee General Assembly—from which he regularly extracted millions of dollars for the university—Holt captivated listeners with his warm southern drawl and self-deprecating stories. His popularity was so universal that both the Republican and Democratic Parties urged him to run for governor in the early 1960s, an offer he declined—humorously, as usual—to remain in education.

For more than a decade after retirement, Holt stayed on the speaking circuit, displaying the talents that had served him so successfully throughout his educational career. In low-key, folksy performances, he always sang the praises of his native state and reminded audiences to display their "friendly faces." His stock-in-trade included a joke about the city slicker who stopped at a farm and asked for a drink of water:

> The farmer led his guest to the springhouse, removed a gourd dipper from its peg, ladled a cup of cool water, and offered it to the man. That's when the visitor noticed two dried streaks of tobacco juice running from the farmer's mouth. To avoid sipping from the same side of the dipper, he turned the gourd around and drank backward. "Well, I'll be John Brown!" the farmer exclaimed. "You're the first man I ever saw who drinks water the same way I do!"

Holt died August 7, 1987, after suffering a series of strokes in Knoxville. Andy Holt Avenue and the Andy Holt Administration Tower, both on the University of Tennessee's Knoxville campus, are named in his memory.

See also: PUBLIC COLLEGES AND UNIVERSITIES (EDUCATION).

—Sam Venable, *Knoxville News-Sentinel*

Humor in Appalachian Literature

Appalachia has a long-standing tradition of humorous writing. Although these texts sometimes draw on the oral tradition, they are distinct from that tradition and from published collections of amusing stories drawn directly from oral sources. At the center of this textual humor is the backwoods person; shifting attitudes toward this character delineate major changes that the genre has undergone in its evolution.

From the 1830s until the 1860s, sketches now known as Old Southwestern humor entertained readers with amusing depictions of life along the southern frontier. Deriving its name from the Old Southwestern Territory, the genre had a strong southern Appalachian component, and its vision of backwoods life influenced literary descriptions of the region well into the twentieth century.

Whether a confidence man or a mighty hunter, the genre's typical frontiersman narrator regales his audience with tales of his bodacious adventures. Despite a semiliteracy indicated by his use of substandard dialect, he is a master of verbal expression and boasting. In tension with this trickster is a secondary gentleman narrator, whose frame story contains (and thus tames) the frontiersman's verbal fandangos and moral dubiousness. Further distancing the frontiersman from polite readers is his ineptness when confronted by town life.

Old Southwestern humor's roots lie partially in the oral tradition. The tall tale, a staple of the genre, was also a popular form for American storytellers. Similarly, the backwoods narrator's brag talk was a characteristic verbal form on the nineteenth-century American frontier.

Despite the genre's attempt to replicate frontier speech and life, its literary antecedents are perhaps more significant than its roots in the oral tradition. Many of the tall tales collected on the frontier stem from print sources, particularly the adventures of the fictitious Baron Münchausen written by the German author R. E. Raspe. Additionally, Tidewater Virginian William Byrd II's eighteenth-century description of North Carolina backwoodsmen as lazy, pipe-smoking Lubberlanders prefigures later accounts of mountaineers as shiftless and morally lax.

New Yorker James Kirke Paulding's play *The Lion of the West* (1830) fixed the character of the humorous, verbally brilliant backwoods hunter on whom the niceties of polite society are lost. In writing *The Lion of the West*, Paulding drew on a trip he had made to Virginia and Kentucky and, even more importantly, on the verbal style and biography of David Crockett, one of Appalachia's native sons. Crockett was well known on the national level as a result of his political career and his ghostwritten autobiographies, both of which had made famous his colorful, metaphoric language as well as his "stretchers," such as his account of grinning down a bear. In the Crockett Almanacs, produced after Crockett died and featuring a fictional Davy Crockett narrator, these exploits assume epic proportions: Crockett can, for example, thaw the earth when it freezes on its axis and walk home with a slice of sunshine in his pocket.

With the 1830s publication of the Crockett Almanacs, Augustus Baldwin Longstreet's *Georgia Scenes*, and numerous humorous tales in William T. Porter's sporting magazine, the *Spirit of the Times*, Old Southwestern humor had arrived. Its Appalachian connection continued to be important. Joseph Glover Baldwin, whose *Flush Times of Alabama and Mississippi* (1853) was so popular that it was reprinted six times in six months, was born in the Shenandoah Valley, where he lived until migrating to the Old Southwest at the age of eighteen. Impresario and actor Solomon Smith set one of his finest humorous sketches, "A Tennessee Door-Keeper" (1868), in the Tennessee Valley town of Greeneville, where Smith, whose theater company traveled throughout the South and Midwest by riverboat, performed. Hardin Taliaferro wrote *Fisher's River (North Carolina) Scenes and Characters* (1859) after a visit to his boyhood home in the foothills of the Blue Ridge. Although William Gilmore Simms is best known for his historical romances set in the South Carolina low country, he did produce several humorous sketches set in the Balsam Mountains of southwestern North Carolina, where he had traveled and hunted.

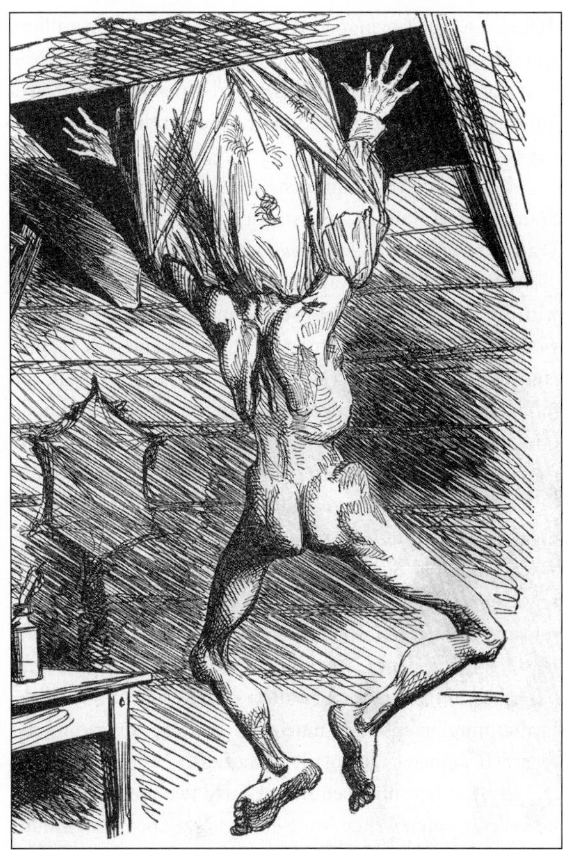

"Sut's New-Fangled Shirt," an illustration by Justin H. Howard from George Washington Harris's *Sut Lovingood: Yarns Spun by a "Nat'ral Born Durn'd Fool"* (1867). Sut Lovingood is a classic character in Old Southwestern humor, a genre depicting life along the southern frontier that influenced Appalachian humor well into the twentieth century.

By all agreement, the masterpiece of Old Southwestern humor is George Washington Harris's *Sut Lovingood: Yarns Spun by a "Nat'ral Born Durn'd Fool"* (1867). Born in Pennsylvania, Harris lived his adult life in the vicinity of Knoxville,

Tennessee. Sut Lovingood is a true backwoods rapscallion, and his exploits—which include putting lizards into the pants of a hypocritical preacher and wreaking havoc at a quilting party—suggest the importance of religion and gender to humor.

Post–Civil War humorists demonstrate a debt to Old Southwestern humor, as is evident in Charles Dudley Warner's *On Horseback: A Tour in Virginia, North Carolina, and Tennessee* (1888). Warner, who cowrote *The Gilded Age* with Mark Twain, tweaks bad mountain cooking, amateur women botanists vacationing at Roan Mountain's Cloudland Hotel, and the garrulousness of Big Tom Wilson, the mountaineer who discovered Professor Elisha Mitchell's body on Mount Mitchell and with whom a visit was de rigueur for literary tourists. Warner's text also maintains Old Southwestern humor's invidious distancing of gentleman narrator from local rube.

While Old Southwestern humor allows us to glimpse, however distortedly, the lives of men on the frontier, it remains silent about women's activities, tales, and jokes. The reason for this silence is twofold. Many of these sketches were published in male-oriented outlets such as sporting journals; furthermore, mainstream nineteenth-century American men regarded women as singularly humorless.

By the late nineteenth and early twentieth centuries, however, women writers were enlarging the scope of mountain humor in their local color writing about the region. Although not primarily a humorist, Mary Noailles Murfree penned occasionally amusing stories about mountain life such as "The 'Harnt' That Walks Chilhowee," which appeared in her 1884 text *In the Tennessee Mountains*. Educator and author Lucy Furman, who assisted Katherine Pettit at Hindman Settlement School in Kentucky, fictionalized the "fotched-on" women's experiences in texts such as *The Quare Women* (1923), which, although sometimes unsympathetic toward mountain customs, take a lively interest in Appalachian women's lives.

By the 1920s, humor in American literature was becoming pointed and urbane. Thomas Wolfe's satirical passages in *Look Homeward, Angel* (1929)—such as the portrayal of obsequious undertaker Horse Hines or the parodic synthesis of a description of "Altamont" (modeled on Asheville, North Carolina) with protagonist Eugene Gant's schoolboy obsession with literature—reflect this increasingly self-conscious literariness.

In much Appalachian literature, however, the tall tale and the comical exploits of mountaineers remained the stock in trade. But Appalachian textual humor began to register a shift in its attitude toward mountaineers. Instead of relentlessly portraying rural people as louts and bumpkins, many humorists adopted a nonelitist stance, aiming their satire at individual foibles, social injustice, or metaphysical complaints. Olive Tilford Dargan was a harbinger of this trend. Best known for her social realist protests against the exploitation of the working poor, Dargan made a foray into humor in *Highland Annals* (1925; reprinted as *From My Highest Hill*, 1941), a fictionalized autobiographical account of her relationships with her tenants and neighbors in southwestern North Carolina. Brilliant in capturing colorful mountain speech patterns, the text reserves its ridicule for snobs whose prejudices blind them to the essential humanity of mountain people. Dargan's narrator, Miss Dolly—whose voice structurally resembles that of the gentleman frame narrator in Old Southwestern humor—is redeemed by learning to respect her mountain neighbors, an awareness that the gentleman narrator of Old Southwestern humor never achieves.

As writers native to the region became the dominant voices in its literature, the trend toward nonelitist humor intensified. In Jesse Stuart's *Taps for Private Tussie* (1943), the Tussies may seem to be stereotypical degenerates; however, the real target of Stuart's right-wing satire is the New Deal, whose welfare programs Stuart believed promoted dependency. More recently, the biting wit of Lisa Alther's *Kinflicks* (1975) is directed against a variety of follies, from the conservatism of small-town Appalachia to the excesses of the counterculture. Michael Malone's *Foolscap* (1991), an academic satire, is set in a fictitious university in the North Carolina mountains, where professors in an English department wrangle over poststructuralist theory and other less lofty grievances.

In addition to nonelitism, contemporary literary humor is often inextricably, unexpectedly imbedded in pathos or bitterness. Jim Wayne Miller's "Brier," for example, is at once a humorous trickster and a deeply suffering refugee, sometimes literally displaced into the urban north, at other times psychologically displaced from his rapidly changing mountain environment or his own inner life. Similarly, Lee Smith's fiction often combines an essentially bleak philosophical vision with a sassy narrative voice and a cast of likeable characters who get themselves into amusing scrapes. In *Midquest* (1981), Fred Chappell, who infuses much of his dense, allusive poetry and fiction with humor, rapidly shifts from slapstick to somber.

Even though twentieth-century Appalachian authors failed to produce a clearly delineated genre of humorous writing, they nonetheless manifested a genuinely profound sense of humor, one that gestured toward traditional Appalachian characters and sensibilities at the same time that it struck out for new ground.

See also: COLLECTIONS OF APPALACHIAN HUMOR; CROCKETT ALMANACS (MEDIA); ORAL NARRATIVE (FOLKLORE AND FOLKLIFE).

—Theresa Lloyd, *East Tennessee State University*

Barbara Bennett, *Comic Visions, Female Voices: Contemporary Women Novelists and Southern Humor* (1998); Carolyn S. Brown, *The Tall Tale in American Folklore and Literature* (1987); M. Thomas Inge, ed., *Sut Lovingood's Nat'ral Born Yarnspinner: Essays on George Washington Harris* (1996).

Humorous Storytelling

Three types of humorous stories are prevalent in Appalachian culture: (1) traditional stories brought and kept alive orally by original Scots-Irish, Welsh, English, and German settlers; (2) stories with traditional themes and plotlines (including jokes), often retold with locally known characters and settings; and (3) original stories created by storytellers rooted in these traditions. Each type has humorous plot components and humorous descriptive components that can be easily identified.

Since a major thrust of Appalachian settlement was the Scots-Irish migration in which people left Scotland to preserve their own identity following the takeover of Scotland's parliament by the English government in the early eighteenth century, a major component of Appalachian storytelling consists of traditional stories brought to the region by these original settlers. Recounting these stories was one means the Scots-Irish had to preserve their identity—who they were, where they came from, and the values and points of view that were important to them.

Because the Appalachian Scots-Irish and Welsh carriers of these stories were political and cultural underdogs to the "wicked English," the plotline humor in the stories that were preserved often became a comedy of underdog prevalence over authority. Thus, the king is often stupid while the simple country dweller is clever. Authority is the subject of trickery, and the rural prevails over the cultured and educated. As time passes and the particular subjects of derision (the English kings, for example) are no longer immediately relevant, the same dynamic may be transferred to other figures of authority such as the sheriff, the preacher, or even elected political leaders. Other earlier settlers in the region, usually disenfranchised in their home countries, shared this political viewpoint.

In the old traditional tales the hero is often either Jack (who successfully seeks his fortune over and over again) or one of a variety of female main characters who each have a name related to a crisis dynamic in the story. The female main characters have usually lost their birth identity and have been reduced to near slavery (hence, names such as Cinder Girl, Cat Skins, Rush Cape, and Musty Maggie) but subsequently are restored to their appropriate positions (or better) in life.

As these stories unfold, a great deal of the humorous content is not related to plot turns, but rather to the way in which descriptiveness is carried out. Therefore, Jack, even at middle age, is still called "my baby" by his mama, and the king and his family are described as being so dumb that if they were birds they would fly north in the winter.

Heirs to these long traditional stories are the sorts of jokes, legends, and other short traditional themes that are no longer told about mythical characters (Jack, Musty Maggie, the king) but are retold in humorous form with local settings and with locally known characters. In such tellings, the worst tales are usually told on the best friends (often family and neighbors). If a person from outside the community or culture told the same stories on the same people, it would be considered insulting or unacceptable ethnic humor.

Thus, Uncle Frank and his neighbor Silas Jolly swapped such stories trying to outdo one another. Silas told about Uncle Frank throwing a dollar down the hole in the outhouse after he saw that he had accidentally dropped a dime down the same hole. The reason, Silas said, was because Uncle Frank said he didn't want to go down in that %#!@* for nothing but a dime! After that, Uncle Frank would tell about Silas fishing in a bucket of water. When told he wouldn't catch fish that way, Silas replied that he knew it would be hard but they needed the fish so badly he was going to give it a try. Such telling often had an almost competitive edge and easily provided porch or fireside entertainment for entire afternoons or evenings.

As in all culturally rich regions, Appalachia has produced a wealth of storytellers and writers of their own original humorous stories. Original Appalachian stories continue to humorously poke fun at neighbors and relatives, but kindly, and they continue to champion the final superiority of the rural and simple over the cosmopolitan and complex. Even in original Appalachian story and literature, the embodiments of humor are as often carried out through descriptive nuance as they are through the outworkings of plot and story line.

See also: JOKES, EXOTERIC AND ESOTERIC; ORAL NARRATIVE (FOLKLORE AND FOLKLIFE); STORYTELLING, HISTORY OF (PERFORMING ARTS).

—Donald Davis, *Ocracoke Island, North Carolina*

Richard Chase, *The Jack Tales* (1943); William Bernard McCarthy, ed., *Jack in Two Worlds: Contemporary North American Tales and Their Tellers* (1994).

Hurley, Carl

(1941–) Humorist, motivational speaker, and educator.

Carl Hurley grew up among a family of storytellers in a two-room cabin built by his father near East Bernstadt, Laurel County, Kentucky. He graduated from Eastern Kentucky University and, after earning a doctorate from the University of Missouri–Columbia, returned to teach for eight years in the Education Department of his alma mater. His ability to enliven speeches with humor from his native area made him a popular conference and after-dinner speaker, and soon he was traveling widely to entertain audiences.

In 1982, at the urging of his agent, Hurley became a full-time humorist and motivational speaker, billing himself as "America's Funniest Professor." Since then, he has traveled the country doing stand-up comedy, convention keynote addresses, seminars, and workshops. He has also appeared on Kentucky Educational Television, the Nashville Network, the Odyssey and Family channels, on Bill Gaither's gospel music videos, and at the *Renfro Valley Barn Dance* in Kentucky. In his work, Hurley often uses humorous traditional anecdotes from his rural background but also creates material from his own family and living situations, preaching the importance of laughter in times of miscommunication and change.

Hurley has recorded a number of humorous tapes, some of which are also on video, and has written one book, *We Weren't Poor—We Just Didn't Have Any Money*.

See also: COUNTRY MUSIC COMEDY; *RENFRO VALLEY BARN DANCE* (MEDIA).

—Loyal Jones, *Berea, Kentucky*

Jokes, Exoteric and Esoteric

Of all American groups subjected to regional ridicule, none has been more incessantly or harshly targeted than Appalachians, who are made the butt of harsh hillbilly jokes told by outsiders. Folklorists classify such jokes as exoteric, or out-group, meaning that they are told by one group about another, generally at the latter group's expense. At times, some Appalachians, especially entertainers, enjoy telling these derogatory jokes themselves. They also enjoy telling jokes about themselves that they rarely share with outsiders. These fall into the category of esoteric, or in-group, jokes.

Most hillbilly jokes are based upon persistent stereotypes of intellectual, material, and moral deficit and revolve around the hillbilly's putative stupidity, ignorance, foolishness, backwardness, poverty, slovenliness, laziness, and sensuality. Subjects include animalistic behavior such as overindulgence in food, drink, and sex and even dehumanizing slurs such as accusations of bestiality and incest. One frequently encountered joke of this type is the "Hillbilly Honeymoon":

> A hillbilly boy and girl get married. On their honeymoon night she reveals that she is a virgin. He gets angry and goes back home, where he explains to his pappy why he left her: "If she wasn't good enuf for her folks, she shore ain't good enuf for our'n!"

Numerous variants of this moldy chestnut can still be found on hillbilly and redneck humor Web sites on the Internet. The late Paul M. Fink, town historian of Jonesborough, Tennessee, recalled a salty variant of this joke in which the boy explains to his bemused father that he left his bride because she was not a virgin:

> *Pappy:* "How did you know?"
> *Son:* "Well, I figured that up-and-down came from nature, but that round-and-round had to be larnt!"

Appalachian people, like people everywhere, enjoy bawdy jokes, though outsiders rarely get to hear the genuine article. George Payne, born in the late 1880s and reared in a log cabin built by his father in the Paint Creek community in Greene County, Tennessee, remembered this naughty riddle from his Appalachian mountain boyhood:

> *Question:* The old man went to bed and he forgot it; the old woman went to bed and she forgot it. The old man woke up and remembered it and shoved it in nine inches. What is it?
> *Answer:* A door peg!

One not raised in a hand-hewn cabin with a whittled wooden latch, or door peg, would be unlikely to immediately get the point of this antiquated Appalachian esoteric joke.

Payne grew up on the very crest of the Appalachian range. As a child, he heard a joke about a little boy and little girl who lived so far back in the mountains that they had never seen a wheat flour biscuit; they did not even know what one looked like:

> One evening a traveler came by their cabin and asked their parents if he could spend the night with them. They wouldn't have to feed him, because he had already brought his own supper, including a pan of biscuits. The stranger ate his fill of supper and then went off to bed, leaving a few biscuits uneaten. The little boy and girl waited until the stranger began to snore, and then sneaked over to the glowing fireplace where he had left the remaining biscuits. The little boy picked up a biscuit and said to his sister, "Let's get a hot coal out of the fire and put it on this little terrapin's back and see if we can make him come out of his shell!"

This is a classic numskull joke hinging upon the motif of absurd misunderstanding. In fact, most so-called hillbilly jokes are actually localized variations on widespread international numskull motifs applied to almost any derided marginal group such as Poles, Belgians, Irish, Scottish Highlanders, or Newfoundlanders.

By contrast, esoteric jokes tend to emphasize what the in-group itself considers to be its most distinctive traits, especially its folk speech. This commonly told riddle is the definitive esoteric Appalachian joke:

> *Question:* Why were the Three Wise Men covered with soot and ashes?
> *Answer:* Because they come from afar!

Another frequently heard esoteric Appalachian joke makes light of the gap between vernacular folk speech and educated elite standards:

> A young man from the hills of West Virginia who received a scholarship to Harvard is trying to locate the admissions office. He stops a nattily attired upperclassman and asks, "Excuse me sir, could you please tell me where the admissions office is at?"
>
> "My dear boy, wherever did you learn to speak like that? Don't you know it's grammatically incorrect to end a sentence with a preposition?"
>
> "Sorry about that, sir!" replied the West Virginian. "Could you please tell me where the admissions office is at, asshole?"

Exoteric jokes about Appalachians generally portray them as numskulls. In their own esoteric jokes, however, Appalachian mountaineers are more often tricksters whose native wit enables them to get the best of outsiders, usually through clever retorts but sometimes through deliberate misunderstanding and feigned stupidity. Appalachian raconteurs particularly enjoy jokes about lost tourists, a perennial comic motif found in the famous "Arkansas Traveler" skit dating back to the 1840s and probably earlier. Most lost traveler jokes set in Appalachia are simply local variations on widely distributed international motifs, such as the one about the lost traveler who comes to a fork in a road and asks a mountain farmer conveniently standing nearby for directions:

> *Traveler:* "Does it matter which road I take to get to Chattanooga?"
> *Farmer:* "Not to me it don't!"

Sometimes life imitates art. Folklorist Bill Lightfoot has related a supposedly true encounter between a lost traveler and an elderly resident of western North Carolina: "The funniest one I've ever heard is about a guy sitting by the side of the road and a lost tourist drives up and asks rather rudely, 'How do you get to Boone?' The old man says, 'Well, sometimes I walk and sometimes my son-in-law takes me in his pick-up truck.'"

Appalachian jokes invalidate negative stereotypes through embracing them. In the end, the canny in-group trickster who makes a numskull of the "highfalutin' furriner" has the last laugh after all.

See also: SOCIOLOGY OF APPALACHIAN HUMOR; STORYTELLING, HISTORY OF (PERFORMING ARTS).

—Richard Blaustein, *East Tennessee State University*

Ronald L. Baker, *Jokelore: Humorous Folktales from Indiana* (1986); Christie Davies, *Ethnic Humor around the World: A Comparative Analysis* (1990); William E. Lightfoot, "Esoteric-Exoteric Dimensions of Appalachian Folk Humor," in *Curing the Cross-Eyed Mule: Appalachian Mountain Humor*, ed. Loyal Jones and Billy Edd Wheeler (1989).

Jones, Loyal

(1928–) Humorist, author, and educator.

Loyal Jones is a popular speaker, writer, and educator who helped advance the Appalachian studies movement of the 1970s and is recognized for his knowledge and use of Appalachian folk humor. Born in Marble, North Carolina, on January 5, 1928, Jones grew up among mountain people who loved to tell stories, and throughout his life he has collected humorous narratives and used them in his various careers.

As a young man Jones joined the U.S. Navy and later attended Berea College in Kentucky, where he completed a bachelor's degree in 1954. He also served for a time in the U.S. Army and went on to finish a master of education degree at the University of North Carolina in 1961. In the ensuing decade, Jones established himself as an advocate for Appalachian causes, serving as associate director and then executive director (1967–70) for the Council of the Southern Mountains, an agency established in 1913 that was prominent in the 1960s War on Poverty.

From 1970 until his retirement in 1993, Jones directed Berea College's Appalachian Center, where he taught Appalachian studies, organized workshops and festivals, administered student service programs, and established a sound archive of interviews, stories, and music. Due to his early work, which included editing a book entitled *Reshaping the Image of Appalachia* and writing numerous articles on the region, the educator helped facilitate the development of Appalachian studies as an academic field. While at Berea, he published biographies of musicians Bradley Kincaid and Bascom Lamar Lunsford, a collection of religious humor, and along with singer-songwriter Billy Edd Wheeler four collections of Appalachian humor: *Laughter in Appalachia: A Festival of Southern Mountain Humor* (1986), *Curing the Cross-Eyed Mule: Appalachian Mountain Humor* (1989), *Hometown Humor* (1991), and *More Laughter in Appalachia: Southern Mountain Humor* (1995). His books *Appalachian Values* (1994; with photographs by Warren Brunner) and

Don Knotts (left) with Hal Smith, *The Andy Griffith Show,* c. 1962. Morgantown, West Virginia, native Don Knotts is widely known for his Emmy-winning role as Deputy Barney Fife.

Faith and Meaning in the Southern Uplands (1999) deal with more serious regional topics but are still laced with humor.

See also: COLLECTIONS OF APPALACHIAN HUMOR; FESTIVALS, HUMOR AND STORYTELLING.

—Harry Robie, *Berea, Kentucky*

Knotts, Don

(1924–) Actor and comedian.

Best known for his television and movie roles, including Deputy Barney Fife on *The Andy Griffith Show* (1960–65) on CBS, Jesse Donald Knotts was born July 21, 1924, in Morgantown, West Virginia. The youngest of four sons of William Jesse and Elsie Knotts, a farm couple, Knotts graduated from Morgantown High School in 1942, already having developed a ventriloquist act with his dummy, Danny. He moved briefly to New York City but returned to Morgantown and enrolled at West Virginia University as a speech major after two unsuccessful appearances on *Major Bowes' Amateur Hour*. After his freshman year, Knotts joined the army and toured the Pacific islands during World War II as a comedian in "Stars and Gripes," a G.I. variety show. He returned to West Virginia University after the war, married Kathryn Metz in 1947, graduated the following year, and returned to New York.

Knotts resumed his show business career, performing at comedy clubs and radio shows and landing a role as Windy Wales on the *Bobby Benson* radio series. In 1955 he appeared in the Broadway hit *No Time for Sergeants*, his first collaboration with Andy Griffith and a role he reprised for the 1958 film of the same name. Knotts in the late 1950s became a regular on the *Tonight Show with Steve Allen*, doing his nervous man routine as part of the show's comedic ensemble. In 1960 he rejoined Griffith to play Deputy Barney Fife on the new situation comedy *The Andy Griffith Show*, winning five Emmys for Outstanding Performance by an Actor in a Supporting Role in a Series.

With a hit television series to his credit, Knotts starred in several motion pictures, including *The Incredible Mr. Limpet* (1964), *The Ghost and Mr. Chicken* (1965), *The Reluctant Astronaut* (1967), *The Shakiest Gun in the West* (1968), *The Love God* (1969), and *How to Frame a Figg* (1971). In 1969, he was divorced from his first wife, with whom he had a son, Thomas Allen, and a daughter, Karen Ann. After his contract with Universal Pictures expired, he had a short-lived variety show on NBC, performed in plays, made guest television appearances, and acted in several movies with Tim Conway for Disney. In 1974 he married Loralee Czuchna.

In 1979 Knotts landed the role of the eccentric landlord Ralph Furley on the popular television series *Three's Company*. He remained with the show until it was discontinued in 1984, a year after he was divorced from his second wife. In 1986 Knotts rejoined Griffith and Ron Howard for the television movie special *Return to Mayberry*. From 1988 to 1992 he had a recurring role on *Matlock*, Griffith's courtroom drama television series.

In the late 1990s, Knotts appeared in several plays and movies, including a role as the television repairman in the motion picture *Pleasantville*. He published his autobiography, *Barney Fife and Other Characters I Have Known*, in 1999. The following year, he made a special appearance at an antique show in Morgantown, where a street was renamed Don Knotts Boulevard in his honor. Knotts resides in Beverley Hills, California.

See also: *ANDY GRIFFITH SHOW, THE* (MEDIA); LINDSEY, GEORGE.

—Larry Sonis, *Arlington, Texas*

Neal Brower, *Mayberry 101: Behind the Scenes of a TV Classic* (1998); Louis B. Hobson, "Comedy Tied Up in Knotts," *Calgary Sun* (October 27, 1998); Don Knotts, with Robert Metz, *Barney Fife and Other Characters I Have Known* (1999).

Lepp, Paul and Bil

Storytellers.

Lepp, Paul (1961–1998) Humorist.

Lepp, Bil (1970–) Minister and humorist.

Paul and Bil Lepp are noted in Appalachia for telling humorous personal stories about life in West Virginia. Although not native to the region—Paul was born in Chicago and Bil in Bowling Green, Ohio—the brothers spent most of their later youth and early adult lives in West Virginia, first gaining public notice in the late 1980s, when they individually captured several first-place honors in the Vandalia Gathering's West Virginia Liars Contest in Charleston.

The Lepp brothers moved to Charleston in 1973, when their father became vice-president of Morris Harvey College (later the University of Charleston). After settling in the region, the brothers soon acquired the Appalachian propensity for lie-telling, enhancing a talent for storytelling learned from their grandfather, a German Mennonite from southern Russia. Having grown up hearing their grandfather's tales of fighting the Bolsheviks during the Russian Revolution, the brothers adopted his flair and story techniques and employed them in their own West Virginia lie-tales.

One of Paul Lepp's most popular stories is about hooking a marijuana-laden DC-6 while casting for catfish with his "Monster Stick," a theme that appears in many of Paul's fishing tales. Bil Lepp, on the other hand, is widely known for narratives about his dog, Buck, a cross between a German shepherd and a basset hound. The tales of both men generally originate from actual events that evolved into entertaining narratives.

Paul attended West Virginia University, served in the U.S. Army as a military policeman in Germany, and later joined the South Charleston Police Department. Paul performed at numerous festivals and on National Public Radio's *Whad'Ya Know?* with Michael Feldman. He died prematurely on January 13, 1998, after a long struggle with alcoholism.

Bil Lepp, who holds a theology degree from Duke University Divinity School, is a Methodist minister and serves on the staff of the West Virginia Department of Culture and History in Charleston. After Paul's death, Bil continued to tell the brothers' original stories at events across the region. In 1999 August House published their most notable stories in *The Monster Stick and Other Appalachian Tall Tales.*

See also: FESTIVALS, HUMOR AND STORYTELLING; STORYTELLING, HISTORY OF (PERFORMING ARTS).

—Loyal Jones, *Berea, Kentucky*

Li'l Abner

See *Li'l Abner* (Media)

Lindsey, George

(c. 1931–) Comedian and actor.

Following four years of small parts on the stage, in movies, and on television, George Lindsey was cast as a simple-minded gas station attendant on *The Andy Griffith Show* in 1964 and became forever known as Goober. After playing the role for more than seven years on Griffith's hit show and on the subsequent *Mayberry RFD*, Lindsey took Goober to the durable country comedy show *Hee Haw*. Continuing to appear regularly through the 1970s and 1980s, the actor became virtually indistinguishable from the character he had created. Like many sidemen in rural and Appalachian comedy, Goober became irresistibly lovable because his good nature and kind heart more than offset his mental handicap. His obvious vulnerability provided a setup to reveal Griffith as a kindly, self-effacing, even wise figure.

Born in Fairfield, Alabama, near Birmingham, Lindsey grew up poor in the north Alabama town of Jasper. He attended Florence State Teachers College, now the University of North Alabama, on a football scholarship. Interested in acting since his boyhood, he appeared in college stage productions, including the musical *Oklahoma!* After a tour in the air force and a short stretch as a high school teacher and coach, he studied acting in New York. His big break, the opportunity to create the Goober character, came after he auditioned for the part of Gomer Pyle and lost the role to Jim Nabors. Griffith reportedly told him to think of Goober as a person who would sit down to a meal and marvel, "This is great salt!"

Even as he pursued his acting career, Lindsey became an energetic fund-raiser for mentally handicapped children and for the Special Olympics. For his professional and charitable work, his alma mater bestowed an honorary doctorate of humane letters in 1992. In 1998 Lindsey helped establish the George Lindsey/University of North Alabama Film Festival, providing young filmmakers an opportunity to showcase their skills and make contacts in the entertainment industry.

See also: *ANDY GRIFFITH SHOW, THE* (MEDIA); *HEE HAW* (MEDIA); KNOTTS, DON.

—Rudy Abramson, *Reston, Virginia*

McConnell, Doc

(1928–) Storyteller and humorist.

A native of northeast Tennessee, Ernest "Doc" McConnell gained a national reputation as a storyteller in the late 1970s when he made appearances at the National Storytelling

Festival in Jonesborough, Tennessee. McConnell quickly became a favorite at the festival, which over several years launched a national revival of interest in the oral storytelling tradition. An early leader in the storytelling movement, McConnell helped found the National Association for the Preservation and Perpetuation of Storytelling and served on the organization's first board of directors. The National Association for the Preservation and Perpetuation of Storytelling is now known as two distinct organizations—the National Storytelling Network and the International Storytelling Center, both based in Jonesborough.

McConnell grew up in Hawkins County, Tennessee, where he often heard traditional stories shared by family members in his cabin home and from friends at the local general store. While working as a maintenance supervisor for the Hawkins County School System, he developed a repertoire of outlandish tall tales, fish stories, and anecdotes that examine Appalachians' tendency to exaggerate facts and misinterpret information. One of McConnell's staple tales, "The Snake-Bit Hoe Handle," is about a garden hoe that swells up so big after being bitten by a copperhead snake that there's enough wood to build a chicken coop. Earlier in his career, McConnell sometimes shared the stage with brother Cecil, better known as "Steamer," and daughter Hannah.

Into the twenty-first century, McConnell continued to perform and upon request will present his "Old-Time Medicine Show," which parodies nineteenth-century traveling barkers who went from town to town selling medicinal wares from a country wagon.

See also: INTERNATIONAL STORYTELLING CENTER (PERFORMING ARTS); STORYTELLING FESTIVAL (PERFORMING ARTS); STORYTELLING IN THE TWENTIETH CENTURY, RENAISSANCE OF (PERFORMING ARTS).

—Jimmy Neil Smith, *International Storytelling Center*

Newspaper Humorists

The thin ranks of Appalachian daily newspaper humorists reflect the national trend toward syndication and an increasingly limited market. Perhaps the most successful of the contemporary daily newspaper humorists in Appalachia is Tennessee's Sam Venable of the *Knoxville News-Sentinel*, whose popularity has led to four books of collected columns, an archived Web site, and a busy speaking schedule, in which he informs the audience "How to Tawlk and Rite Good."

Venable's assertion, shared by many, is that Appalachian humorists go out of their way to make themselves the butt of their own jokes and that the funniest stories are the ones the writer tells about himself. He considers this neither a cultural slight nor a reflection of low self-esteem but rather an affirmation that Appalachians are self-assured enough to tell jokes about themselves, just as family members love one another yet laugh at each other's goofs and flubs. Venable, born May 24, 1947, in Knoxville, has also written the non-humor study *Mountain Hands: A Portrait of Southern Appalachia* (2000).

Venable's predecessor on the *News-Sentinel* staff was Bert Vincent, who wrote a column called "Strolling" from 1933 until his death in 1969, covering topics ranging from the best biscuit recipe to "haints" to hilarious tales of mountain folks. Vincent's columns were collected into *The Best Stories of Bert Vincent: Sage of the Smokies* in 1968. Lesser known as a humorist was Don Whitehead (1908–1981), a hard-shelled journalist who went ashore with the troops on D-Day and won two Pulitzer Prizes for his reports on the Korean War before retiring to Knoxville in 1959 to write for the *News-Sentinel*. Whitehead's local columns were light and airy, in stark contrast to his somber war coverage, and his funniest pieces were about his mountain upbringing. Up the road in Kingsport is Sheila Moss, "The Tennessee Firefly," whose work appears in the *Kingsport Daily News*.

Across the Smokies in Asheville, North Carolina, two longtime columnists have sprinkled the pages of the *Asheville Citizen-Times* with mountain folklore and humor. The late, revered John Parris (1914–1999) wrote "Roaming the Mountains" for many decades. His columns were more about mountain people and mountain ways than about humor, but they reflected the gentle, wry, and dry humor of the self-sufficient people he chronicled. Parris's columns were collected into several books including *Roaming the Mountains* (1955), *My Mountains, My People* (1957), *Mountain Bred* (1967), *These Storied Mountains* (1972), and a cookbook titled, of course, *Mountain Cooking* (1978). After Parris, *Citizen-Times* columnist Bob Terrell, a former sportswriter and general columnist, became the house humorist. Among his many books are six filled with mountain humor.

In Kentucky, the late and much loved Joe Creason (1918–1974) of the *Louisville Courier-Journal* wrote frequently about Appalachian people and humor in his "Joe Creason's Kentucky" columns, as does current *Courier-Journal* columnist Byron Crawford, who also spent five years as host of Kentucky Educational Television's award-winning *Kentucky Life* series. *Lexington Herald-Leader* columnists Don Edwards and Dick Burdette, although primarily assigned to Bluegrass Kentucky, have written frequently about eastern Kentucky mountain humor. Jack Hicks of the *Kentucky Post* in Covington has also found the humor and folklore of Appalachian Kentucky prime material.

Beginning in the late 1980s, the *Richmond (Ky.) Daily Register* has been the primary outlet for Garry Barker's "Head of the Holler" humor column, also carried by a number of weekly papers. Born in 1943 as the third of nine children to a mountain family, Barker draws his humor from the people of the communities where he lives and works. His columns became part of a 1995 book, *Notes from a Native Son: Essays on the Appalachian Experience*, and continue to provide material for periodic National Public Radio commentaries. In Pikeville, Kentucky, satirist Larry Webster, who is also an attorney, writes a column of thorny political humor intended to offend Democratic Party leaders. Entitled "Red Dog," the column is published weekly in the *Appalachian News-Express* and monthly in the *Lexington Herald-Leader*. The newspaper humor of Russ Metz was so appreciated that columns by the Owingsville, Kentucky, writer continued to be reprinted by several weekly newspapers after his death.

Fiddler and longtime stage and radio comedian Clarence C. "Slim" Clere, born in Ashland, Kentucky, in 1914, wrote his "Mountain Echoes" column for the *Charleston (W.Va.) Gazette-Mail*. Clere, whose comedic name was "Nimrod," began his stage career in 1933 on WSAZ in Huntington, West Virginia, and did a solo act, playing the fiddle and performing stand-up comedy until his death in 2001. Clere explained his column thus: "I used to be a standup comedian, but now I'm getting so old I have to sit down, so I'm a sit down comedian." For years, legendary Jim Comstock filled columns of his *West Virginia Hillbilly* newspaper with folklore, life, and mountain humor and also found time to amuse readers with his books, *Best of Hillbilly* (1968) and *West Virginia Heritage Encyclopedia* (1974).

As more Appalachian newspapers are taken over by chain ownership, opportunities for regional humor columnists fade. Standardized and profit oriented, many papers under absentee owners reflect little local personality; humor columns are more likely to be the products of nationally syndicated writers such as Dave Barry. The most "southern" of all columnists, the late Lewis Grizzard, was the closest of the nationally recognized humorists to Appalachian humor, but more recognized Appalachian humorists such as Carl Hurley do not use the newspaper as an outlet.

See also: COLLECTIONS OF APPALACHIAN HUMOR; HUMOR IN APPALACHIAN LITERATURE.

—Garry Barker, *Morehead State University*

Northern Appalachian Humor

Even though their affinity for folklore and oral tradition is not as widely known, people of the northern Appalachians live in an oral society and rely upon word-of-mouth communication no less than their counterparts in the southern highlands. Television, newspapers, and the Internet notwithstanding, matters most vital to day-to-day existence are communicated person to person. In rural communities and small towns, Appalachians tend to "visit" with everyone they meet because it is the traditional means of finding out what is going on. The habit makes for a tight-knit, even gossipy, world. Jokes, anecdotes, folktales, and news are often imbued with cultural values and therefore serve a societal purpose beyond their obvious entertainment value and information content.

A good example of the way deep-rooted cultural value is maintained and spread through oral folklore can be seen in flatlander tales told by mountain people of Pennsylvania. A flatlander tale is a numskull story about an arrogant outsider who meets his comeuppance at the hands of a canny ridgerunner. Tales about outsiders and numskulls are thousands of years old, and most flatlander tales follow ancient tale types.

Anxiety is at the root of these tales. People living in isolated rural regions of the hill country can feel threatened by urban values, ultramodern culture, and slick outsiders. Aware that their world may be outdated, poor, and even laughable by comparison, they tell flatlander stories as defense mechanisms, anxiety relievers, and psychological equalizers. The ridgerunner always comes out on top, often hilariously.

In western Pennsylvania and elsewhere, flatlander tales developed over the last century as mobile and affluent city dwellers poured into the mountains to hunt, fish, vacation, and often to buy up inexpensive land. Competition between local people and outsiders for land deals, hunting spots, and even spouses took on a keen edge. This was especially true when major projects such as government dams or power plants threatened to bring massive and permanent change. Flatlander tales were one way of getting even, springing up almost overnight in barbershops and taverns with the flatlanders inevitably cast as rich and uppity but at the same time naive and inept. By contrast, the ridgerunner was quiet, modest, honest, and, above all, cunning and at home in the wilds. In these caricatures, the ridgerunner always comes out on top, while the cocksure flatlander is reduced to idiocy. Significantly, locals tell these tales to each other and not to outsiders. Besides serving as a defense mechanism, the stories help sustain cultural balance by taking something threatening and turning it into something harmless and silly.

The following Pennsylvania tale is an example of a flatlander story:

> My grandfather used to take dynamite and get trout for some of the restaurants. As this was illegal, authorities constantly tried to catch him. They never succeeded because Gramps knew all of the game wardens and their friends. Finally, a game warden was brought in from the flatlands, and he approached Gramps as though he was a restaurant owner. Gramps offered to help him out. They thought they had him this time for sure. As they went to the

> stream, Gramps pulled a quarter stick of dynamite from his pocket, rigged it up, and then asked the warden to hold it while he lit it, and then he just walked away with the warden hanging on to that lit dynamite. The only place he could throw it was into the stream right there. It went off and Gramps walked back. There was probably a hundred trout come floatin' up, and Gramps says, "There's your fish, you kilt them and you might as well net 'em out, Mr. Smarty-pants Warden."

This story about a ridgerunner mink farmer is another example:

> One of the first flatlanders brought his wife with him. . . . At the time of his arrival, there was an old mink farm around Tioga. His wife wanted to see the farm, so her husband talked to the owner, and he agreed to show them how they raise mink. As they were walking through the farm, Mrs. Flatlander interrupted the proprietor with a question: "How many times a year do you skin the mink?"
>
> The proprietor looked rather astounded and then calmly replied, "Just once, ma'am; anymore than that and they get meaner than hell."

In Pennsylvania, New York, and in parts of West Virginia, large established ethnic communities and recent immigrants have brought special richness and variety to evolving mountain humor. But ethnic humor often exploits stereotypes as mercilessly as mountain folk caricature flatlanders. Germans are considered to be hardworking, thus this story of one who observes, "Ja, you have to vork yourself to death—shust so dot ven dey come to your funeral, dey vill say, 'Ja, he vas a goot vorker.'" Wattie, an Irishman, takes a different view: "I have no reputation for being a very great worker—and be domned if I want such a reputation—because then I'd have to work like hell all the while to live up to it."

Being a social minority, the Amish were susceptible to stereotyping, and stories about them often relate to their honesty. For example, there is the tale about an Amish couple who drove two days in a wagon to buy a farm in Pennsylvania, bringing their money in a milk jug. However, when they counted out the money to the banker who was handling the sale, they were several dollars short. The man said, "Mom, we brought the wrong jug." The banker assured them that they could make up the difference later, but the couple would not hear of it, so they drove back home and returned a week later with the right jug.

As in ethnic humor the world over, the Irish in Appalachia find themselves ridiculed in jokes about excessive drinking. Likewise, jokes about Scots turn upon stinginess. A more modern joke has to do with several ethnic groups. A true heaven is a place where the French are the cooks, the Italians are the lovers, the British are the cops, and the Germans are the engineers. A pure hell would be where the Italians are the engineers, the British the cooks, the French the lovers, and the Germans the cops.

Of course, ethnic groups have intermarried for generations, and many of their differences have been smoothed away. However, one can hear quips and jokes that recall the views that people once held, or may still hold, about different ethnic groups. And one of the most persistent sources of humor is the perceived difference between the insiders and the outsiders—the flatlanders and the ridgerunners.

Adapted in part from *Flatlanders and Ridgerunners: Folktales from the Mountains of Northern Pennsylvania* by James York Glimm, copyright 1983, by permission of University of Pittsburgh Press.

See also: HUMOROUS STORYTELLING; JOKES, EXOTERIC AND ESOTERIC; SOCIOLOGY OF APPALACHIAN HUMOR.

—James York Glimm, *Mansfield College*, and Loyal Jones, *Berea, Kentucky*

John P. Ernenwein, *Germany Road and Beyond* (1973); James York Glimm, *Flatlanders and Ridgerunners: Folktales from the Mountains of Northern Pennsylvania* (1983) and *Snakebite: Lives and Legends of Central Pennsylvania* (1991).

Political Humor

Political humor is an important cultural form in nations around the world, but in the Appalachian South it has occupied—and retains—a status of extraordinary importance. Individual practitioners have become legendary in their own communities and states even though most of their remarks were never recorded. The structure of American politics and the relatively limited transportation and communication systems in Appalachia before 1900 encouraged this form of expression.

Competitive politics came to Appalachia in the 1820s with the rise of the Democratic Party and the organization of the opposition into the Whig Party. Political campaigns in this time period heavily relied upon oral presentations by the candidates. The usual format was for the candidates to follow the circuit court to each county seat for its session. These "court days" would bring most of the rural population into town, providing a large audience. Generally, the opposing candidates spoke in a debating style of alternating speeches with the entire program lasting five hours or more. These debates were expected to be a principal form of entertainment during the court session, and in this environment the most entertaining candidates enjoyed a significant advantage.

Some politicians used their mastery of traditional music to considerable effect. The most famous example of this feature of Appalachian campaigns was the 1886 Tennessee gubernatorial election. The two candidates, Democrat Bob Taylor and Republican Alf Taylor, were brothers from Greeneville. Each was an accomplished fiddler and each was a legendary humorist; together they set a new standard for campaign entertainment. Musical ability was still put on display by traveling candidates a century later. Among the more successful fiddling politicians in the region were Senator Robert C. Byrd of West Virginia and Senator Albert Gore Sr. of Tennessee.

For most politicians, however, humor was the chief component of their attempt to entertain. This was a welcome part of the political dialogue because the usual campaign speeches apparently were crude and personally offensive. In the 1830s, a western North Carolina congressman was killed in a duel by his opponent, who felt slandered by his remarks in a campaign. Zebulon Vance, a congressman, governor, and U.S. senator from western North Carolina, was challenged to two duels before his thirtieth birthday by political opponents—one of them his uncle.

Two east Tennessee politicians received the most notoriety for aggressive campaigning. William G. "Parson" Brownlow renamed his newspaper the *Knoxville Whig and Rebel Ventilator* during the Civil War. The title was an apt description of his rhetorical style. Brownlow's chief opponent for most of their careers was Andrew Johnson. In 1866, a year after becoming president, Johnson went on a national speaking tour that greatly weakened his political position because northern audiences were shocked by the crude and occasionally vulgar phrasing that he used.

As national communications networks improved and campaigning became an increasingly individual enterprise after 1900, the traditional aggressiveness of mountain electioneering declined. In the tense and bitter confrontations that often did take place in mountain politics, humor was an effective way to counterattack, as this story indicates:

> A local politician was speaking from the courthouse steps. A heckler interrupted by yelling, "Take a minute and tell us everything you know."
>
> "I'll tell all both of us know," the politician retorted. "And it won't take any longer."

Clement Dowd, a representative from North Carolina to the U.S. Congress from 1881 to 1885, reported the following incident from twenty-four-year-old Zebulon Vance's 1854 campaign for the legislature. Vance's political opponent objected to, among other points, Zeb's tender age. In response, Vance apologized for his youth and declared that he would have cheerfully been born at an earlier date if it had been in his power. He observed that his father and mother gave him no chance whatever about the matter and humbly begged everyone's pardon and said he would try to do better next time. The audience burst into laughter and applause at this retort.

Many political figures have also discovered that self-deprecating humor is particularly effective in winning public support. Popular eastern Kentucky political leader Bert Combs once recalled joining a bus tour that showed visitors around Frankfort and the state capitol during his term as governor:

> When he went down to board the bus, a group of patients from Eastern State Hospital, the mental hospital, got on also, and the governor sat down among them.
>
> The social worker decided to count his patients and so he started, "One, two, three, four, five, six . . . wait a minute, who are you?"
>
> Governor Combs said, "I am Bert T. Combs, Governor of Kentucky."
>
> The social worker said, "Seven, eight, nine. . . ."

And finally there are a large number of stories told by political figures and citizens alike that tend to hold politicians as a class up for ridicule. This genre includes the following account from eastern Kentucky:

> A politician was going up and down the roads campaigning when he saw a young girl milking a cow. He stopped to talk a while. Soon the girl's mother called from the house, "Who are you talking to?"
>
> "Just a politician," said the young woman.
>
> "You come here this minute," the old woman called back. "And bring the cow with you."

While modern campaigns have retained some of the meanness of previous generations, the widespread use of media advertising has overshadowed personal appearances by the candidates and reduced the opportunity for humor. Nevertheless, U.S. Senator Sam J. Ervin of Burke County, North Carolina, became something of a media star in the 1970s. Ervin's use of traditional mountain stories and wit defused a great deal of the tension during the televised Watergate hearings. Tennessee Senator Howard Baker, the ranking Republican on the committee, was a mountain humorist in his own right and joined Ervin in using regional tales and jokes to bring insight and laughter to an otherwise grim political drama.

See also: CROCKETT, DAVID; TENNESSEE'S WAR OF THE ROSES.

—Gordon B. McKinney, *Berea College*

Loyal Jones and Billy Edd Wheeler, eds., *Curing the Cross-Eyed Mule: Appalachian Mountain Humor* (1989), *Laughter in Appalachia: A Festival of Southern Mountain Humor* (1986), and *More Laughter in Appalachia: Southern Mountain Humor* (1995); Richard Walser, ed., *Tar Heel Laughter* (1974).

Regan-Blake, Connie

See Regan-Blake, Connie (Performing Arts)

Sociology of Appalachian Humor

What is defined as Appalachian humor grows out of the experience of living in Appalachia as differentiated from mainstream American life. Local group humor is produced and disseminated through face-to-face interaction in neighborhoods and not by humorists representing the national culture on television or in comedy clubs. While communications media have moved from being local to mass in the twentieth century, jokes about and for local people will never disappear, although they most certainly may change.

As with any cultural form, Appalachian jokes and other types of humor pass in and out of use depending on conditions. As elsewhere, the region's humor can be classified and analyzed as a form of communication with important social overtones and positive social functions. For instance, humor is a survival mechanism for any group, but this is especially so for Appalachians. When there is conflict, humor is sometimes used by one group to express aggression or hostility at the other's expense. The following story reflects the resentment mountain people can feel when educated folks condescend to them:

> A veterinary researcher comes to a mountain farm asking to inspect the bull he sees in the pasture. The owner warns that the bull is rather fractious. But the vet says, "I have credentials, a B.A., M.A., D.V.M., and Ph.D.," and enters the pasture.
>
> The bull charges, and the vet runs for the fence. Whereupon, the farmer yells, "Show him your credentials!"

As a means of fighting stereotypes, mountain people love humor that turns the tables on outsiders caught in an error resulting from prejudice or misperception. For example:

> Some visitors from Ohio decide to visit the "real" Appalachia and find themselves off the interstate in a county seat town that has one traffic light and a name they cannot agree how to pronounce. As they wait to be served at the only eating place in town, they ask a man at a nearby table, "Would you tell us real slowly how to pronounce the name of this place?"
>
> Using his best diction, the man responds, "Bur-ger King."

Humor is one way people bond with each other. A group laughing together shares this common sense of humor and becomes emotionally closer, even if the joke comes at the expense of others—such as this one from Appalachian Kentucky:

> *Question:* What's the difference between a Kentuckian and an S.O.B.?
> *Answer:* The Ohio River.

Another classic example of rural in-group bonding humor is the following bit of Appalachian wisdom:

> There is a lot to learn in life, but you don't learn anything from the second kick of a mule.

Because humor integrates people by providing relief from stress and strain, jokes are devices behind which groups hide and thus maintain dignity in difficult times. The following story, told by a mountain man, is a good example of this type of humor:

> During one winter, we had it rough and mainly ate turnips. I took to school fried turnips, mashed turnips, boiled turnips, until it got to be too much. One day I went to the cloakroom to get my lunch and decided to leave mine behind and take the heaviest bag for myself, no matter who brought it. When I looked inside, I found three walnuts and a claw hammer!

Humor also has the ability to control the behavior of members of the group when social criticism is masked in jokes. For example, when someone is the butt of a joke, the situation reminds everyone that they had better not commit this behavior. In Appalachia, a similar type of control is evident in humility jokes such as the following, about a visiting social worker:

> Back during the War on Poverty, this poverty worker, wearing a three-piece suit and driving a Buick Electra with tail fins, a lot of chrome, and electric windows, got lost over in eastern Kentucky. Seeing a local man standing along the road, he pulled over, put down the window on the man's side, and inquired about directions. He got them, thanked the man, put up the window, and started to proceed. The local man pecked on the window and, when the driver put it down again, asked, "What line of work are you in?" The visitor replied with some pride,

"I'm with the War on Poverty." The local man looked him and the car over and said, "It looks like you won!"

See also: HUMOROUS STORYTELLING; JOKES, EXOTERIC AND ESOTERIC.

—Tom Boyd, *Berea College*

Marvin R. Koller, *Humor and Society: Explorations in the Sociology of Humor* (1988); Hans Speier, "Wit and Politics: An Essay on Laughter and Power," *American Journal of Sociology* (March 1998).

Stoneman, Roni

(1938–) Country comedienne and musician.

Born in Washington, D.C., Veronica Loretta "Roni" Stoneman is the youngest daughter of country music pioneer Ernest V. Stoneman. She grew up in Carmody Hills, Maryland, within a large family of music-playing Appalachian migrants. As a member of the Stoneman Family, she played music and did comedy until early 1971, when she became a solo performer. As a musician, she reportedly was the first female bluegrass banjo picker to make a recording (for Folkways, c. 1956). In 1973 she joined the cast of *Hee Haw,* where she remained until 1991.

On *Hee Haw,* Stoneman won her greatest acclaim with her characterization of Ida Lee Nagger, a bedraggled housewife who engaged in a continual battle of the sexes with her shiftless husband LaVerne (played by Canadian comic Gordie Tapp). The character was drawn from the humorous side of Stoneman's own personal life—which has had its own share of tragedy and heartbreak—augmented by such earlier Hollywood female rural comics as Judy Canova and Marjorie Main ("Ma Kettle"). After the demise of *Hee Haw,* Stoneman continued to work as a solo comic and musician, often performing at the Nashville Palace.

See also: COUNTRY MUSIC COMEDY; *HEE HAW* (MEDIA); STONEMAN, ERNEST V./STONEMAN FAMILY (MUSIC).

—Ivan M. Tribe, *University of Rio Grande*

Tennessee's War of the Roses

In 1886 Bob and Alf Taylor, brothers from Carter County, Tennessee, opposed one another as candidates for governor. The campaign, known as Tennessee's War of the Roses, was marked by lively and often humorous debate and is recognized as one of the most colorful events in the history of American politics.

The sons of Nathaniel Green Taylor, a lawyer and Methodist preacher who served east Tennessee in Congress as a Whig (and later became a Union supporter), and Emmaline Haynes, whose brother was a Confederate senator, the two boys grew up in a home where sympathies were often divided. It is little surprise that the brothers adopted opposing political views as adults. Born in 1848, Alf was the older and became a Republican; Bob, born in 1850, became a Democrat. It was in 1878 that the political sibling rivalry really began. Shortly after being admitted to the bar, Alf tossed his hat into the ring as a candidate for Congress from east Tennessee. But the job went to his opponent. Alf's friends thought that he had gotten a raw deal. So Bob's Democratic allies—along with Alf's Republican supporters—launched a campaign to send Bob to Congress. Despite the fact that Tennessee was true-blue Republican, Bob was elected. It could not last, and Bob failed at the polls two years later. Despite defeat, neither brother gave up.

When the Republicans met in 1886 to nominate a candidate for governor, Alf was the hands-down favorite and was nominated on the first ballot. Two months later, the Democrats chose brother Bob as the Democratic standard-bearer. (In addition, the Prohibitionist Party tried to persuade their father to run on that ticket, but he respectfully declined.) And so the stage was set. Brother was vying against brother for Tennessee's governorship, an event rarely paralleled in American history. The pair tried to make the best of it. After getting their heads together, the two political factions developed a schedule of forty-one debates that took the two brothers from the Appalachians to the Mississippi River. At the first gathering in Madisonville, in east Tennessee, Bob declared: "I have a very high regard for the Republican candidate: he is a perfect gentleman because he is my brother. I have already told him to come with me and I would furnish him with crowds and introduce him to society. We are two roses from the same garden."

Despite the comment, the political battle became Tennessee's War of the Roses—an adaptation of the famous fifteenth-century struggle for the English throne. Bob's Democratic friends wore the white rose, while Alf's Republican supporters displayed the red rose. Seeing them together was as much a joy to the throngs who gathered to hear them as traveling together was to the two brothers themselves. They sought to entertain rather than confuse the crowds with issues. Both could get a tune from a fiddle, though Alf was the more accomplished musician. But Bob had the edge with his tales and sharp wit. The rivalry was sometimes harsh and biting, but the two always remained gentlemen and friends.

At the end of the race, Bob remarked, "I say to you now that after all those eventful struggles, I still love my brother as of old with an undying affection—but politically, my friends, I despise him."

A few days later, the Tennessee voters sent Bob to the state capital by a thirteen-thousand-vote majority. And Alf, after serving three terms in Congress, also realized his

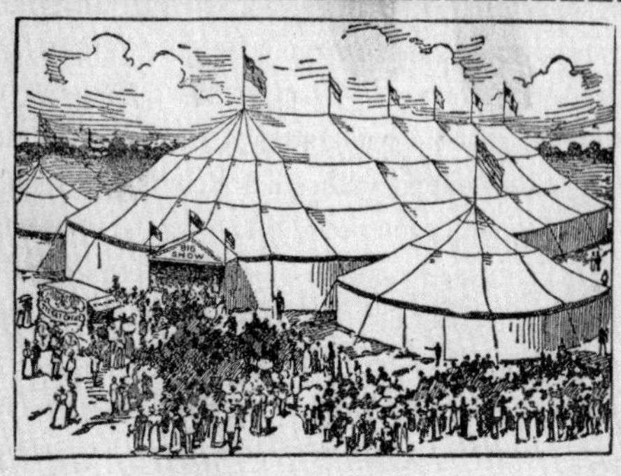

And We Don't Mean "Maybe"
Coming Soon!
Big Tent Theatre!
You'll Enjoy It!
TOM'S COMEDIANS
"So'll Your Old Man"
Singers : Dancers Entertainers
New Play and Vodvil Each and Every Night
LADIES FREE
WHEN ACCOMPANIED BY PAID ADULT TICKET
MONDAY NIGHT!

Handbill from an early-twentieth-century comedy troupe, c. 1920s. Tom's Comedians was one of several hundred comedy companies or tent repertoire troupes that performed melodrama and farce under canvas during the late 1800s and early 1900s. Primarily rural audiences were treated to different plays nightly, with brass bands and vaudeville-style performances between acts.

ambition to become governor in 1921—thirty-five years after the War of the Roses.

See also: POLITICAL HUMOR.

—Jimmy Neil Smith, *International Storytelling Center*

Traveling Shows

Traveling shows had a presence in Appalachia from its early settlement. By 1800, comedians, musicians, dancers, acrobats, fortune-tellers, and animal trainers were performing at court days and fairs and being employed to draw customers to taverns and inns.

By the 1830s, dramatic troupes such as the one mounted by actor-manager Solomon Smith were appearing in courthouses and hotels. Their audiences insisted on an evening's entertainment that generally included a tragedy, a farce, and between-acts dancing, singing, and comedy. Circuses that came to the region included the John Robinson Circus and Dan Rice's Great Show. Even before the minstrel boom of the 1840s, circuses were featuring blackface banjo players and comedians. Until clowning became primarily visually oriented in the mid-1800s, audiences were accustomed to clowns who sang and told jokes.

Blackface minstrel shows were regularly visiting even the smallest towns by the 1860s. Although their popularity had begun to fade by the turn of the century, groups such as the Silas Green Show and Van Arnam's Minstrels remained viable well into the 1900s. Adaptations, with and without blackface, of the genre's trademark comedic exchanges between end man and interlocutor became a key feature of vaudeville, commercial recordings, radio, and country music comedy.

Medicine shows began developing soon after the Civil War. The shows' glib-talking "doctor" worked with a cast of entertainers ranging from two or three to forty. Although admission was free, the shows had periodic timeouts for the doctor's lecture touting, for only a dollar a bottle, the wonders of such "great blood and nerve medicine" as Mokiton Tonic, Hamlin's Wizard Oil, or Wa-Hoo Bitters. The smaller shows often played towns too small to attract more elaborate productions. Performing from the back of a wagon or truck or on a simple outdoor stage, they typically featured rube and blackface comedy routines along with banjo and fiddle music and popular songs. The larger shows played in tents and featured full orchestras, vaudeville acts, and dramatic productions. Medicine shows proved especially good outlets for the comedic as well as musical talents of regional performers such as Roy Acuff, Clarence "Tom" Ashley, Snuffy Jenkins, Pappy Sherrill, Walkin' Mary McClain, and Greasy Medlin. The shows' comedian-emcee was often called "Jake." Usually in blackface and wearing oversized shoes and baggy pants with extra elastic suspenders, he was present throughout the show.

The rapid expansion of rail service after the Civil War made small towns even more attractive to traveling shows. To accommodate these groups, communities built theaters, which they often called "opera houses." Dramatic troupes stayed from three days to a week, each evening performing a different play drawn from a repertoire that included the likes of *The Two Orphans*, *East Lynne*, and *Katherine Mavourneen*. Other companies made one-night stands and specialized in performing widely popular works such as *Uncle Tom's Cabin* or *Ten Nights in a Bar Room*. All included comedy and music between acts. Vaudeville-type shows that most frequently made it to small towns were the musical tabloid companies, or "tab shows." These abbreviated versions of popular musicals provided live entertainment between silent film showings and continued to be popular briefly into the sound era.

Cinema's wide popularity and low presentation cost resulted in many performers' having to find work outside the opera houses. Showboats such as those of Billy Bryant and Charles Hunter became alternative venues for some. Bryant's was a small, family-owned showboat of the early twentieth century that ran the inland waterways of the Ohio River watershed from before World War I until 1942. These showboats brought a blend of melodrama and vaudeville into the lives of isolated people in rural communities. Most show people, however, chose tent performing, which allowed them to continue playing much the same territory. Additionally, the tent's mobility enabled performers to reach remote audiences that could not support indoor venues. Tent dramatic shows such as the Bud Hawkins Players, Boob Brasfield's Comedians, and the Princes Stock Company continued the pattern of melodrama, comedy, and between-acts entertainment. The rural-oriented comedy-dramas written by tent show performers yielded several well-liked and enduring stock characters. The most popular was the "silly kid," or "Toby," who first appeared about 1910 and continued thereafter as a tent show staple. Toby's persona varied to reflect the audience's particular ethnic or regional flavor, but his underlying essence was a laugh-provoking, rustic awkwardness coupled with a keen eye for seeing through the sham of conniving city slickers.

Some tent troupes, such as Billroy's Comedians and the Seabee Hayworth Show, were successful as vaudeville-only operations, emphasizing dancing girls, comedy, and music. Beginning in the early 1900s, the Chautauqua tent circuits provided a more refined option. The Redpath and other booking agencies provided small towns a week of low-cost education and culture in conjunction with local sponsors. Daytime children's activities included magic shows and chalk-talk artists. Evening programs offered lectures by noted orators and music ranging from opera singers to yodelers, harpists, and Hawaiian string bands. There were also dramatic readings and full-length plays such as *The Meanest Man in the World* and *Rebecca of Sunnybrook Farm*.

As the 1930s proceeded, economic hard times, radio and movie competition, and worn-out stage routines combined to inflict major box-office losses. This resulted in far fewer such shows on the road as better times arrived in the late 1930s and on into the 1940s. Helping to fill this void were the road shows mounted by popular radio barn dance programs such as the *Grand Ole Opry*, the *Renfro Valley Barn Dance*, and the *WWVA Jamboree*. Besides making major urban tours, these shows replaced the musical tabloids in small-town movie houses and rejuvenated the tent-show business throughout Appalachia. Kentucky's Renfro Valley organization and *Grand Ole Opry* performers such as Honey Wilds, Roy Acuff, and Bill Monroe consistently filled sixteen-hundred-seat tents during much of the 1940s with programs of music and comedy.

In the 1950s, television quickly replaced small-town-oriented traveling shows as the chief source of popular entertainment. As the twenty-first century began, only the circus preserved the overall flavor of traveling shows past. The comedic elements of these shows are to a great extent being continued on the stages of such country music entertainment centers as Branson, Missouri, and Dollywood in Tennessee. Traveling show genres in all their variety are good examples of the many disparate elements that have combined with British folk culture to yield the lore and song that define the Appalachian American experience.

See also: MINSTREL MUSIC/BLACKFACE MINSTRELSY (MUSIC); VENUES (MUSIC).

—Harry Rice, *Berea College*

Brooks McNamara, *Step Right Up* (1976); William L. Slout, *Theatre in a Tent* (1972); Solomon Smith, *Theatrical Management in the West and South* (1868).

Varney, Jim

(1949–2000) Actor and comedian.

Although not a native of Appalachia, Jim Varney launched his acting career in the region and went on to devise one of the most visible images of the hillbilly "good ole boy" in the twentieth century.

Varney was born June 15, 1949, in Lexington, Kentucky. At age sixteen, he played Puck in *A Midsummer Night's Dream* at Barter Theatre in Abingdon, Virginia. Small roles in television variety shows and sitcoms followed. Years as a stand-up comic and primarily unsuccessful auditions for off-Broadway roles ended when Varney returned to Kentucky during the New York actors' strike in 1979. In 1980 Nashville advertising agent John Cherry produced the first television ad featuring Varney's character Ernest P. Worrell. Over two thousand more advertisements followed.

The ads featuring Ernest followed a schema so strict it might be regarded as hillbilly haiku. Each ad was one continuous take, shot without interruption from the point of view of Vernon, Ernest's long-suffering, never-seen neighbor. "Hey Vern!" Varney would begin while leaning so far into the camera that the viewer's—and Vernon's—personal space was destroyed. Varney as Ernest pressed his well-intentioned but worse-than-useless assistance on Vern, found a way to profess a longing for the sponsor's product, did something memorably stupid, and usually exited the scene asking, "KnowwhutImean?" Because the ads aired in astonishing abundance in regional markets nationwide, viewers throughout America believed Varney was local.

Capitalizing on the popularity of his pitchman persona, Varney appeared in a number of tours de farce beginning with, "Hey Vern, It's My Family Album!" (1983), a network television special comprised of several skits in which Varney played most of the characters. Varney played the Ernest character in feature films including *Ernest Goes to Camp* (1987) and *Ernest Saves Christmas* (1988). In 1988 his short-lived children's program, *Hey Vern, It's Ernest!* aired on Saturday mornings. Although Varney's humor appeared to be pure slapstick, much of it actually relied on an appreciation of and familiarity with adult foibles. Ernest proved misplaced on kiddie television. Though Varney won the Emmy for Outstanding Performer in a Children's Series, the show was canceled after only thirteen episodes.

Jim Varney always expressed fondness for his alter ego, Ernest. Although he played in over thirty feature films and sought increasingly diverse roles, he never ventured far from the affable rube. So close was Varney's association with the hillbilly persona that he was selected to play Jed Clampett in the film version of *The Beverly Hillbillies* (1993). Varney's last live-action role was Uncle Hazel in *Daddy and Them* (released in 2002), and his final voice-over was wise-guy Cookie in *Atlantis: The Lost Empire* (2001), both released after his death from lung cancer on February 11, 2000.

See also: BEVERLY HILLBILLIES, THE (MEDIA); LINDSEY, GEORGE.

—David Cortner, *Lenoir, North Carolina*

Wheeler, Billy Edd

See Wheeler, Billy Edd (Music).

York, Betty Lou

(1938–) Comedienne.

Betty Lou (Davis) York, popular comedienne at the *Renfro Valley Barn Dance*, was born in Williamsburg, Kentucky, on February 20, 1938, although she grew up in Richmond, Indiana, where her family moved to find employment. York's first attempt at performing comedy was a skit for her TOPS weight-loss club. Her act, which included diet jokes, went over so well that she was soon sought after on the civic club circuit. After she performed at her husband's Lions Club variety show, she received considerable renown and numerous invitations to perform from businesses and organizations. Although many people encouraged York to go to Nashville to pursue a professional comedy career, she preferred to concentrate on raising her two young children and continued her regular employment.

Eventually, York was invited to perform at the *Renfro Valley Barn Dance* show that she and her family often attended on their visits to Kentucky. After two trial shows, she was invited to become a regular in 1991 and has performed there ever since. She believes that everybody needs humor in their lives and talks of the healthful effects of laughter. Her comedy reflects a woman's point of view—in her case the never-ending battle to lose weight—but she also recycles jokes, listens for bits and pieces of conversation that can be worked into her act, and makes up comedy that reveals the inconsistencies of human nature.

See also: COUNTRY MUSIC COMEDY; *RENFRO VALLEY BARN DANCE* (MEDIA).

—Loyal Jones, *Berea, Kentucky*

NOTICE
IF YOU ARE INJURED, NO MATTER HOW LITTLE, TELL
YOUR FOREMAN ABOUT IT RIGHT AWAY.
ZUR KENNTNISNAHME
BENACHRICHTIGEN SIE IHREN WERKFUHRER SOFORT
WENN IHNEN AUCH NUR DER GERINGFUGISTE UNFALL
ZUGESTOSSEN IST.
FIGYELMEZTETÉS
HA MEGSÉRULT, LEGYEN AZ BÁRMILYEN CSEKÉLY IS,
AZONNAL JELENTSE BE AZ ELOMUNKÁSÁNÁL.
AVVERTENZA
SE VI SIETE FATTO MALE, ANCHE SE LEGGERMENTE
DITELO SUBITO AL VOSTRO FOREMAN.
OBJAVA
AKO S MA I NAJMANJE OZLIJEDJEN KAŽI TO ODMAH
TVOMU NADSTOJNIKU (FORMANU).
POZOR
AKO SE POŠKODUJETE, ČE TUDI LE MALO, POVEJTE
TAKOJ SVOJEMU FORMANU.
BACZNOŚĆ
JEZELI ZOSTANIESZ POKALECZONYM, NIE ROBI
ROZNICY JAK TRYWIALNIE, DAJ ZNAC NATYCHMIAST
O M FORMANOW

Language

Section Editor: Michael Montgomery

Characterized by distinctive sounds, syntax, and originality, Appalachian speech has long served as an emblem of the region's natives—one that has inspired contradictory, fanciful, and sometimes far-fetched notions about the people and their culture. The linguistic dexterity of Appalachian speakers—storytellers, preachers, politicians, and common folk—and their seemingly archaic vocabulary and phrasing have fascinated outsiders for more than a century and a half. Appalachians have been romanticized as surviving speakers of Elizabethan English yet simultaneously ridiculed as backward users of a lower-class, substandard dialect reflecting the region's isolation and poverty. Whether fostering positive or negative stereotypes, the way Appalachians speak has frequently marked them as different, generating many attempts to explain still another aspect of the region's "otherness."

No single way of looking at the subject adequately explains the complex roles that the English language has played in the life and history of Appalachia and its people. Though mountain speech is often believed to be the most distinctively regional variety in America, Appalachia is not home to a single dialect. Research has shown that the ancestry of Appalachian speech is quite mixed and that in many ways it represents a microcosm of American English. Educator and social researcher John C. Campbell famously observed in 1921 that Appalachia was a land "about which, perhaps, more things are known that are not true than of any part of our country." This statement pertains particularly well to the English spoken there.

Europeans were relative latecomers to Appalachia, first engaging native speakers of Iroquoian languages about 1540, when the Spanish under Hernando de Soto encountered the Cherokee in the hill country and mountains of the present-day Carolinas. Within a century French traders had made contact with the Cherokee's Iroquoian-speaking cousins, including the Oneida and Seneca, in the foothills of New York. Neither Spanish nor French took hold, however, and it was not until the early eighteenth century, when Germans and English-speaking Scotch-Irish pressed into central Pennsylvania, that European languages took root in the region.

Dating from the late-seventeenth century, *Scotch-Irish* is the oldest name in the United States for emigrants from Ulster, the northernmost province of Ireland, and their descendants. Most of their earlier ancestors came from Lowland Scotland, where for centuries people were known as Scotch (but now usually as Scots). This

Facing page: Multilingual sign at a coal mine, Kempton, West Virginia, 1939. Although Appalachia was settled mostly by English speakers, this sign in English, German, Lithuanian, Italian, Hungarian, Czech, and Polish attests to the diversity of languages found in the region.

historical fact is preserved in *Scotch-Irish*, a name Americans have continued to employ. Also (but much less often) known as the Scots-Irish, most of the 150,000 or more Ulster emigrants who came in the American colonial period settled in the interior, where they and their culture and language became influential in much of Appalachia. Because *Scotch-Irish* has been the more common name for three centuries and remains so among descendants in Appalachia, it is used in this section in observance of the linguistic right a group has to name itself.

In the nineteenth century, small groups of Welsh, French, and other Europeans also came to Appalachia, but only English and German ever became community languages. The latter declined precipitously in the twentieth century, as did native languages. In modern Appalachia, English is known by all except for very recent migrants (such as Mexicans in north Georgia), though misconceptions, myths, and misinformed stereotypes about its speakers abound.

Indeed, the English language in Appalachia has long captivated journalists, travelers, and educators, and since the 1880s they have stressed one quality above all others—its conservatism. Writers have consistently been struck by the older usages retained in the mountains. An early and still frequent explanation for these archaic elements was that mountain speech was "Elizabethan" or "Shakespearean." Suggestions of such respectable roots have largely been discredited, though, and Appalachian speech is more often considered an inferior type of English and therefore an impediment to social mobility and educational progress. These conflicting views have simultaneously romanticized mountain speech (and by implication its users) as quaint while stigmatizing it as improper and ungrammatical. The public, scholars included, appears to have no difficulty holding contradictory ideas about the English language spoken in Appalachia.

Influenced by early backwoods humorists' use of dialogue, nineteenth- and early-twentieth-century writers such as humorist George Washington Harris and novelist Mary Noailles Murfree created generally negative images through their fictional portrayals of mountain speakers. Both employed contorted spellings to enhance their portrayals of illiterate, dialect-speaking characters. "Thar's nun ove 'em fas' enuf tu ketch me" is typical dialog from one of Harris's mountain characters. Many of these forms later made their way into the *Barney Google* comic strip after Snuffy Smith was introduced to it in 1934. Reinforcing this stereotypical image since that time have been countless books, movies, television programs, and tourist-shop caricatures conveying the popular but erroneous belief that such usages as *plumb* "completely," as in "He fell plumb to the bottom," and *right smart* "a good deal (of)," as in "They lost a right smart in that trade," among others, are found only in mountain speech. No matter how ludicrous, portrayals of mountain English in the media are often considered accurate outside Appalachia and consequently reinforce perceptions that mountain people are different and backward.

Writers have also pointed out the expressiveness and adaptability of mountain speech and the resourcefulness of its speakers, however. These positive qualities are appreciated in fresh metaphors such as *kick* "reject in courtship" and *can see to can't see* "dawn to dusk"; vivid similes (*meaner than a striped snake; as thick as fiddlers in hell*); abundant use of proverbs; descriptive place names such as Hell for Certain, Kentucky; novel conversions of one part of speech to another (the noun *manpower* as a verb meaning "move by brute effort," as in "We'll have to manpower that log up"); and in other ways.

Because the Appalachians cover a vast area from the Northeast to the Deep South, the region is too large to form a distinct or unified region in traditional culture or speech. Instead, linguists focus on the Midland dialect region, a smaller area stretching westward and southwestward from its cultural and linguistic seedbed in central Pennsylvania, where English was first planted in the region, to northern Alabama. This region is subdivided into the North Midland (northern West Virginia, northwestern Maryland, and most of Pennsylvania) and the South Midland (southern West Virginia, western Virginia, western North and South Carolina, eastern Kentucky, east Tennessee, north Georgia, and north Alabama).

Several factors worked against Appalachia's becoming a distinct, cohesive dialect area of its own. Settlement by different groups or different proportions of groups produced local variations within the region. Migration within the region has mixed the languages of the English, Scotch-Irish, Germans, and other settler groups in various ways, leveling differences in their speech and spawning innovations. Research by the American Linguistic Atlas Project, a systematic national survey of traditional vocabulary initiated in the 1930s, found only seventeen words and phrases by and large distinctive to the Midland region. Some of these are *bawl* "a calf's cry"; *blinds* "window shutters"; *hull* "to shell," as in "to hull beans or peas"; and *poke* "paper bag," as in "She bought a poke of peanuts." Six others are common to the North Midland (*jag* "armful of corn"; *run* "creek") and five (*jacket* "vest"; *fireboard* "mantel," as in "Lydia set her clock proudly on the fireboard") to the South Midland.

Another survey, conducted in the 1960s in connection with the *Dictionary of American Regional English*, found four strictly Appalachian terms: *spring house* "small building over a spring in which to keep foodstuffs cool," as in "Pickled beans and kraut were kept in the spring house"; *poke* "paper bag"; *whistle pig* "groundhog"; and *lay out* "to play truant from work or school." Since then, the dictionary has labeled 46 items "Appalachian" and 123 others "southern Appalachian" because they appear to be concentrated in those regions. Interestingly, the dictionary labels some items as "now Appalachian," including *gaum* "a mess," as in "He left everything in a gaum." This suggests that much of what is popularly thought to be Appalachian is simply disused, old-fashioned English outside the region.

This scarcity of evidence for geographically defined Appalachian English has led some scholars to consider whether such entities as "Appalachian English" and "Southern Appalachian English" exist or whether they are more strongly linked to cultural solidarity than geography and common usage. Mountain people's strong sense of place, cohesive communities, and attachments to traditional lifestyles and values, it is believed, make them less willing to change or accommodate to mainstream culture. This resistance to change is reflected in the tendency to retain speech habits, even a generation or more after a person has moved to a metropolitan area such as Chicago, Detroit, or Cincinnati. Like people who stayed back home, these migrants often consciously distinguish themselves from people outside their communities, as in pronouncing *Appalachia* with the third syllable as *latch* rather than *lay*, a development that has grown steadily since the 1960s and reflects regional consciousness and a reaction to the pronunciation of members of the media and government officials.

The existence of many archaisms in mountain speech has prompted more study of its origins than that of any other regional American English variety. Three sources of origin are commonly proposed: that these archaisms are traceable mainly to Elizabethan England, to eighteenth-century colonial America, or to Ulster (by way of the Scotch-Irish). It is easy to oversimplify this issue because no type of speech came to North America without mixing with others immediately after arrival, because retentions represent only part of the larger history of mountain speech, and because no type of American English, no matter how isolated, has remained static.

The Elizabethan, or Shakespearean, connection is the most popular but has the least historical and linguistic support. People from the British Isles who settled in Appalachia began arriving in North America more than a century after the Elizabethan period of the late sixteenth century. Furthermore, the source of most Appalachian vocabulary has been Britain in general (not just England) and to a lesser extent northern England (*galluses* "suspenders"; *palings* "fence posts"), western England (*counterpane* "bedspread," as in "We sleep under a counterpane"), and Scotland (*chancy* "doubtful," as in "Hit was a chancy sort of thing to do"; *sop* "gravy," as in "We ate light bread and sop").

The myth of Elizabethan English was formulated and promoted by people from areas outside the Appalachians who recognized some mountain usages (*afeared* "afraid," as in "He wasn't afeared of them in the least bit") as being also in the works of Shakespeare. Some came to know mountain people firsthand, and they attempted to counter negative stereotypes by highlighting their positive qualities. Although this Elizabethan connection has little scholarly basis, it and related ideas have flourished as cultural myths, possibly because the region retains immense value for countless Americans elsewhere who lack cultural roots. They view the language and culture—and especially the music—of Appalachia as valuable storehouses of tradition, less affected by mass society and more closely tied to the past. Historically, however, this romantic notion has not saved Appalachia from neglect, marginalization, and exploitation by the rest of the nation.

For both pronunciations and grammar patterns a better case can be made for colonial American than for English roots. For example, *blowed* and *knowed* as the past tense and past participle of *blow* and *know* do not occur in Shakespeare but were fairly common among eighteenth-century English immigrants to the American colonies. The use of these verb forms is still common in Appalachia, though they have long been considered nonstandard in the United States. Such colonial American forms in mountain speech are far more numerous than supposed Elizabethan ones.

Associated with both of these explanations is the alleged influence of geographic and cultural isolation on Appalachian speech. This is largely a myth, based on the false beliefs that Appalachia is culturally homogenous and that physical isolation caused life in the mountains to move slowly, even to become frozen in time. Archaic speechways, along with traditional ballads, Jack tales, folk dancing, and weaving, supposedly prove that Appalachian culture is static. Historians have pointed out that mountain communities are quite typical of rural America, however, and while these traditions might seem perfect examples of cultural preservations from centuries past, studies have found them to be living and dynamic. Mountain people still write ballads to recount modern tragedies, disasters, and star-crossed love, but these are timeless themes, not archaic ones.

The third commonly cited origin of Appalachian speech is that it derives mainly from people from Ulster, the Scotch-Irish. Most of the 150,000 or more emigrants who left Ulster in the eighteenth century settled in the American interior, becoming known as Scotch-Irish. Many of them moved into the hills and valleys of Appalachia, but only traces of modern-day Appalachian pronunciation are attributable to them. In vocabulary a few Scotch-Irish contributions to the region are *airish* "chilly," as in "It was an awful airish day"; *brickle* "brittle," as in "The dry leaves were brickle and crumbled easily"; *discomfit* "to inconvenience," as in "I wouldn't want to discomfit you"; and *ill* "bad-tempered," as in "That dog is ill as a hornet."

The Scotch-Irish contribution to regional grammar has been even more significant, as evidenced in the formation of words (by combining *'un* "one" with adjectives and pronouns, as in "young'un," "big'un," and "you'uns"); phrases (*need* followed by a verb past participle, as in "That boy needs taught a lesson"); compound helping verbs ("I wonder if you might could help me"); and clauses (*whenever* for "at the time that," as in "Whenever I was young, people didn't do such a thing"). The English of Appalachia resembles the language of Shakespeare's England not nearly so much as that of eighteenth-century Ulster.

Even so, only about 20 percent of Appalachian pronunciations, vocabulary, and grammatical patterns not shared by the rest of the nation can be traced to the British Isles. This percentage is higher than for most other varieties, but it indicates that the foremost component of American speech in general, and Appalachian speech in particular, is new vocabulary. Borrowings and inventions are continually needed as speakers face new challenges of environment and culture.

Most terms identified as Appalachian by the *Dictionary of American Regional English* and other sources were actually born in America (*bald* "treeless area on a mountaintop"; *flannel cake* "pancake"). Of the seventeen Midland items identified by the American Linguistic Atlas Project, most are unambiguously American in origin and represent responses to the New World (*lamp oil* "kerosene"; *sugar tree* "sugar maple"). Six at most (*piece* "snack"; *want in* "want to go/come in," as in "That dog doesn't know whether he wants in or out") may have come from Ulster (though much of the English of Ulster is shared with northern England and Scotland and is, historically speaking, derived from those regions).

Contributions to Appalachian speech from other languages have been insignificant. Other than many surnames in the region, few linguistic traces of German exist outside Pennsylvania, where the language shows in words such as *smearcase* "cottage cheese," from German *schmier* "spread" and *Käse* "cheese." Irish Gaelic/Scottish Gaelic inheritance is also scant and consists mainly of vocabulary. Terms such as *brogan* "heavy, homemade leather shoe," *bonny clabber* "curdled sour milk," and *muley* "hornless cow," as in "Let's get our muley cow from the field," already had been absorbed by the English-speaking Scotch-Irish before they left Ulster, and no evidence for a community of Gaelic speakers in Appalachia has been documented. Other European languages such as Spanish (*doney* "sweetheart") and French contributed even less to Appalachian speech. The lack of influence from Cherokee is both striking and puzzling. Because so much medicinal and other lore was borrowed by whites from the Cherokee in southern Appalachia, as well as the names of so many rivers, mountains, and other topographical features, there is no ready explanation for the absence of common vocabulary such as Cherokee names of plants.

Many features of grammar and pronunciation are also found elsewhere, especially in the Deep South, but occur with a higher frequency in Appalachian English, distinguishing it from other varieties. Some of these common grammatical patterns, such as *a-* as a prefix on verb present participles *(a-goin'; a-comin')* and possessive pronouns with the suffix *-n* (*hern; hisn; yourn*, as in "a book of yourn"), came from England. Emigrants from Ulster introduced others, such as personal pronouns *hit* "it" and *you'uns* "you (plural)" and *all* after pronouns to indicate inclusion: *who all* and *what all*, as in "Who all came and what all did they say?"

Verbs with the same form for the past tense and past participle as well as present tense *(come; eat; run)* and the addition of *-est* to form the superlative of adjectives ending in *-ing (workingest* "working the hardest or most," as in "the workingest fellow in town"; *singingest)* exhibit a general ancestry from the British Isles, while the reversal of word elements (*everwhat* "whatever"; *everwho* "whoever," as in "Everwho hears that will be surprised") and the use of prepositions in series

("There was several houses on up around on Mill Creek") are apparently American developments.

Many common patterns of pronunciation reflect the general English of colonial days. These include final *-a* pronounced as *-y* (*opry* "opera"; *extry* "extra," as in "The soup needs an extry pinch of salt") and heavy use of *r,* including addition of the sound to some words (*mater* "tomato"; *warsh* "wash").

Other pronunciations are more recent developments shared with the Deep South: prolonging and splitting of vowels into two syllables (*red* as *re-uhd* or *ray-uhd; rib* as *ri-uhb*, a pattern sometimes known as the "southern drawl"); shifting of accent to the first syllable of a word *(IN-surance; PO-lice)*; modification of "long *i*" to *ah* in certain contexts, so that *my right side* sounds like *mah raht sahd, wire* rhymes with either *car* or *war,* and *tile* rhymes with *tall;* and pronouncing the same vowel sound in word pairs such as *pen/pin* and *gem/Jim.*

Mountain speech has retained or created senses of words unfamiliar elsewhere in the United States that can result in miscommunication. In the Great Smoky Mountains someone might be heard to say, "A lot of mountain people are kind of backward, but I don't care to talk to nobody." By this is meant that while others are shy, the speaker does not mind (in fact, enjoys) talking to strangers. If someone says they are "hard to hear," they may mean, depending on the context, that they have difficulty hearing others, as well as that they are soft-spoken. Other common words having variant meanings in the mountains include *several* "quite a few," as in "We picked several blackberries this summer," *clever* "hospitable," as in "You'll find people very clever here in the mountains," and *ill* "bad-tempered."

Many social factors influence the use of Appalachian speech by individuals: formality of a given situation, respective ages and occupations, level of education, and so on. Less educated working-class speakers are more likely to use speech considered typically Appalachian, though some features of pronunciation are used at all social or educational levels (except in northern parts of Appalachia). Examples include modification of "long *i*" to *ah* in words like *time* and *my* and the pronunciation of words like *pen* and *gem* as *pin* and *Jim.* These are completely "standard" in Appalachia and in much of the South.

Vocabulary varies mainly by subregion within Appalachia or by the age or "ruralness" of the speaker. More modern, national terms have been rapidly displacing older, rural counterparts, especially among younger inhabitants. A recent study of students at a small western North Carolina college found a dramatic loss of regional vocabulary; for instance, *living room, gutters, mantel,* and *attic* had completely replaced *big house, eaves trough, fireboard,* and *loft.*

Because it brings speakers into contact with national norms, formal education enables speakers, especially younger ones, to shift between varieties of English according to a given situation. But it also produces self-consciousness or defensiveness about differences between their "home English" and "school English," pitting the values of family and place against the larger world and striving for the mobility to enter it. Because of the pressure to conform to local norms in much of rural Appalachia, an individual's level of education often does not strongly influence the way he or she speaks.

Too often one still finds the view that American dialects such as Appalachian speech are only modifications of Standard English "incorrectly learned" due to social backwardness or even mental deficiency. Educators and linguists have argued against these views for a long time, but the association of mountain English with impoverished, low-status speakers has resisted arguments of its respectable heritage. Unfortunately, some mountain people also have accepted this negative evaluation of their English.

No region, community, or person is uniform in speech, of course. Variation and change in languages are natural and universal. In Appalachia, language has been shaped by the region's history of frontier settlement, its geographic breadth, the diversity of peoples and cultures coming in contact there, and the constant adaptation by speakers to meet their needs. Like other types of American speech, language in Appalachia will continue to bend somewhat to the forces standardizing American culture. But in the end, it will persist because of the strong cultural cohesion and the sense of social and regional identity it provides to its speakers, even in the face of misunderstanding and pressure to conform.

—Michael Montgomery, *University of South Carolina*

Craig M. Carver, *American Regional Dialects: A Word Geography* (1987); Frederic G. Cassidy et al., eds., *Dictionary of American Regional English* (1985–); Hans Kurath, *A Word Geography of the Eastern United States* (1949); Michael Montgomery, "How Scotch-Irish is Your English?" *Journal of East Tennessee History* (1995) and "Myths: How a Hunger for Roots Shapes Our Notions about Appalachian English," *Now and Then* (Summer 2000); Michael Montgomery and Joseph S. Hall, *Dictionary of Smoky Mountain English* (2004); Anita Puckett, *Seldom Ask, Never Tell: Labor and Discourse in Appalachia* (2000); Walt Wolfram and Donna Christian, *Appalachian Speech* (1976).

African American Appalachian English

Appalachian English varies significantly between ethnic groups. Many scholars have studied African American English and Appalachian English, two of the most stigmatized English varieties in the United States, but there is almost no published information about the language of African Americans in Appalachia.

Linguists have begun to analyze recordings of younger and older African Americans in Appalachia, however, and they have identified several distinctive characteristics of African American English in the region. The language of African Americans is changing. Speakers born in the last decade of the nineteenth century had speech patterns different from those of their younger counterparts. Even so, there is a discernible variety of vernacular English of African Americans in Appalachia that includes traditionally European American Appalachian features.

One feature of both Appalachian and Lower Southern English speakers of both African and European ancestry is a two-part vowel becoming a single vowel in words such as *mine* (pronounced *mahn*), *mile (mahl)*, and *bide (bahd)*. In the past this practice diverged in words such as *like*, *light*, and *nice*, which European Americans pronounced *lahk*, *laht*, and *nahs*, but in which African Americans did not use *ah* before the consonants *k*, *t*, or *s*. More recently, however, some African American Appalachians have adopted the traditional Appalachian English pattern, albeit at lower rates than European Americans—an indication of the ancestry of their speech.

African American English in Appalachia has three types of features: one group found only in traditional African American English; a second group derived from Lower Southern dialect; and a third shared by African American and European American speakers of Appalachian English.

The first group, especially as used by older speakers, includes features such as the omission of word-final consonants, as in *tes' on Saturday* for *test on Saturday*, and the loss of *-n* at the end of words, as in *mã* for *man*. Both younger and older African Americans also use *be* in the traditional fashion of African American English to indicate an event happening on a repeated or regular basis, as in "Sometimes my ears be itching."

The second group includes features also not characteristic of European Americans in Appalachia but reflecting a background in the lower South. One such feature is making the final *r* sound more vowel-like (*four* becomes *fo-uh*). It is often in the small similarities between older and younger African Americans for the first two groups of features that a discernible Appalachian African American English can be recognized.

A third group, characteristic of both African American and European American Appalachian English, includes *was* with plural subjects, as in "We was there"; pronouncing *l* almost like a vowel *(oh* or *uh)* at the end of words such as *ball* and *boil;* and sounding the vowels of *pen* and *pin* alike.

African American English varies regionally within Appalachia. For example, West Virginia since its formation in 1863 has been divided into northern and southern cultures as a result of alliances during the Civil War, and the state tends to have a sharp dialect boundary dividing southern and northern dialect regions. This is reflected in African American speech; pronouncing the vowel in *mine* and *bide* as *mahn* and *bahd* is more frequent for African Americans in southern West Virginia. Cultural attitudes follow these dialect divisions: African Americans in southern West Virginia view themselves as both southern American and African American, while those in northern West Virginia identify themselves as African American only.

The patterns and features of African American Appalachian English provide evidence for the inherent richness and diversity of both African American English and Appalachian English. They permit Appalachian English to be defined more completely as a collection of varieties differing by subregion, generation, and ethnicity.

See also: AFRICAN AMERICAN TWENTIETH-CENTURY MIGRATION (SETTLEMENT AND MIGRATION); APPALACHIAN ENGLISH IN THE URBAN NORTH.

—Kirk Hazen, *West Virginia University*

Ralph W. Fasold et al., "Are Black and White Vernaculars Diverging?" *American Speech* (Spring 1987); Wolfgang Viereck, "The Rise of *Be* as an Aspect Marker in Black English Vernacular," *American Speech* (Winter 1988); Walt Wolfram and Dan Beckett, "The Role of the Individual and Group in Earlier African American English," *American Speech* (Spring 2000).

Appalachia

Just as the word *Appalachia* is generally pronounced *Ap-pa-LATCH-a* in the southern mountains, but more commonly *Ap-pa-LAY-cha* in the rest of the country, so too is there some dispute over the origin of the name given to the region.

Legend has it that Hernando de Soto or members of his 1539 expedition named the Appalachian Mountains. Surviving accounts of the de Soto expedition, however, offer no evidence that the conquistador or his companions intended to designate the eastern mountain chain for the Apalachee Indians, whom they encountered far to the south in what is now northern Florida. The first European contact with the Apalachee had been made by Alvar Nuñez Cabeza de Vaca's expedition in 1528 in the vicinity of Tampa Bay, Florida. One derivation of the name argues that in the Muscogee language *apala* means "great sea," and combined with the personal participle *chi*, *apalache* means "those by the sea."

Apparently early mapmakers, confused by vague stories of locations and distances, transposed the territory of the Apalachee farther north.

Diego Gutiérrez was the first mapmaker to record a variation of *Appalachian*. On his map of America, published in 1562, the region "Apalchen" appears to the north of a mountain range, far from Florida. Jacques le Moyne de Morgues, an artist who accompanied the French Huguenot expedition to Florida in 1564, never actually traveled north to the mountains, but he painted a scene of Indians collecting gold from streams running from the "Apalatcy Mountains" and also designated a village as "Apalatchi." Le Moyne's map was published in 1591 and, despite its errors, influenced many subsequent maps, including Gerardus Mercator's 1606 map, a standard for the next fifty years.

During the eighteenth century, the southern half of the eastern mountain chain was known as the Appalachians and the northern half the Alleghenies, with the overall designation alternating between the two. In a letter to the editor of the *Knickerbocker* in 1839, Washington Irving suggested that Appalachia or Alleghenia might be a more appropriate name for the United States, probably the first appearance in print of the term *Appalachia*. Geographer Arnold Henry Guyot established the scientific and popular usage for the entire mountain range with his article "On the Appalachian Mountain System" in 1861.

With the geographic nomenclature firmly established, Appalachia began to be defined as a cultural region and a social and economic problem area. Before the Civil War, there was little to distinguish the way of life in the Appalachians from life generally on the American frontier. Local color writers discovered the region in the mid-1870s, and educators and missionaries sought to define the southern Appalachians as a social problem area deserving the attention of church home mission boards and private philanthropic foundations. Berea College President William Goodell Frost made influential delineations of the region in 1894, as did John C. Campbell in *The Southern Highlander and His Homeland* in 1921. The federal government issued a comprehensive survey in 1935 *(Economic and Social Problems and Conditions of the Southern Appalachians)*, and the Ford Foundation supported an updated survey in 1962 *(The Southern Appalachian Region: A Survey)*. Since 1965, official designations have followed the Appalachian Regional Development Act and its subsequent amendments. Political considerations have extended the definition from physiographic highlands to lower-lying areas with similar socioeconomic profiles, as in northeastern Mississippi.

See also: APPALACHIAN REGIONAL COMMISSION (GOVERNMENT); DE SOTO, HERNANDO (SETTLEMENT AND MIGRATION); PLACE NAMES.

—David S. Walls, *Sonoma State University*

William P. Cumming, *The Southeast in Early Maps* (1958); David S. Walls, "On the Naming of Appalachia," in *An Appalachian Symposium*, ed. J. W. Williamson (1977).

Appalachian English and Ozark English

Although separated by several hundred miles, Appalachian English and Ozark English have long shared a close association in descriptions of language in the southern highlands. Writers have often assumed that the dialects of the two regions are similar because most of the original settlers of the Ozarks came from the southern Appalachians. Although precise origins are difficult to determine, nineteenth-century census records indicate that natives of Tennessee and Kentucky were especially numerous among early residents of the Ozarks, and recent linguistic analyses have indeed confirmed that Ozark English and Appalachian English are very closely related varieties.

Early treatments of Ozark English, similar to those of Appalachian English, focused on the supposed archaic quality of the region's dialects. As early as the 1890s, writers linked the regions in articles about the survival of Shakespearean or Elizabethan English.

The earliest systematic linguistic description of any part of the Ozark region appears in Rachel B. Faries's *A Word Geography of Missouri* (1967), which compares folk vocabulary collected in Missouri with that compiled in Hans Kurath's *Word Geography of the Eastern United States* (1949). The study is limited to vocabulary, and the Ozark portion is confined to southwestern Missouri, but Faries's work suggests that the Ozarks are an extension of Kurath's South Midland speech area, a dialect region strongly associated with Appalachian English. South Midland terms common in the Missouri Ozarks include *red-worm* "earthworm"; *brute* and *male brute* "bull"; *salat* "greens"; *johnny house* "privy"; *turn* "amount," as in "A turn of corn is the amount you would take to a mill"; *middlins* and *middlin meat* "salt pork (the side of bacon)"; *tow sack* "burlap bag"; and *fireboard* "mantel."

In his *American Regional Dialects: A Word Geography* (1987), Craig Carver suggests that a truly close relationship between Appalachian English and Ozark English folk vocabulary is limited to the Arkansas portion of the Ozarks. Some characteristic terms include *brickle* "brittle"; *bull tongue* "plow"; the preposition *fernent* "near to," "against," or "opposite"; *goober pea* "peanut"; *jarfly* "cicada"; and *redeye gravy*.

More comprehensive studies, the *Linguistic Atlas of the Gulf States* (1986–92) and *Variation and Change in Geographically Isolated Communities: Appalachian English and Ozark English* (1988), have disclosed overall similarities beyond vocabulary and indicate significant phonological and grammatical links between the two dialects. Ozark English seems to be closely related to dialects in the eastern half of Tennessee but not to the dialects of western Tennessee and eastern Arkansas.

Appalachian English and Ozark English share features that set these dialects apart from other varieties of American English. Characteristic pronunciations include *ghostes*, *th'owed*, and *potater*, as well as *oncet* "once," *idn't* "isn't," *hit* "it," and *far* "fire." Grammatical features include *a-* prefixing, as in "I'm a-goin' home"; completive *done*, as in "He's done been here"; double modal helping verbs, as in "might could"; *liketa*, as in "He liketa died"; positive *anymore*, as in "He works there anymore"; and present-tense agreement of plural noun subjects with *is* or verbs with the suffix *-s*, as in "people is," "people likes," "my two brothers lives," and "schools has." There are indications that some features may be declining more rapidly in Ozark English than in Appalachian English.

The dialects in southern Appalachia and in the Ozarks are closely related; however, this does not indicate that there is one Mountain dialect, with Ozark English a simple extension of Appalachian English. A more realistic view is that they are two relatively conservative descendants of a single dialect that was developing in the southern Appalachians during the late eighteenth and early nineteenth centuries and was carried by migrating settlers westward into the Ozarks, where it has developed independently since the nineteenth century.

See also: APPALACHIAN ENGLISH IN THE URBAN NORTH; ATTITUDES TOWARD APPALACHIAN ENGLISH.

—Michael Ellis, *Southwest Missouri State University*

Donna Christian, Walt Wolfram, and Nanjo Dube, *Variation and Change in Geographically Isolated Communities: Appalachian English and Ozark English* (1988); Lee Pederson et al., eds., *Linguistic Atlas of the Gulf States* (1986–92).

Appalachian English in Literature

Since the early nineteenth century, writers have portrayed spoken language in literature with Appalachian characters and settings. Many early literary dialects are of doubtful authenticity, and their overuse has helped create negative regional stereotypes. On the other hand, since evidence of earlier Appalachian English is limited, literary sources sometimes provide important clues to the development of dialects in the region. Insight into the linguistic or the social significance of Appalachian English in literature requires an understanding of literary dialects and their evolution over the last century and a half.

By the 1830s, American literary dialects had become fairly conventional. Writers employed an extensive common stock of words, phonetic spellings intended to represent words, spelling pronunciations, and grammatical forms to represent rustic speech without any specific regional identification. James Fenimore Cooper was perhaps the single most influential American writer to represent the speech of frontier characters, beginning with *The Pioneers* (1823), the first of his Leatherstocking novels. Cooper's novels, set mainly on the New York frontier, abound in spellings such as *larn*, *sarmon*, and *sarpent*, as well as *skear* "scare," *nater* "nature," *idee* "idea," *sitch* "such," *afeard* "afraid," and *wust* "worst." Nonstandard grammatical forms include verbs such as *know'd*, *catched*, *teached*, *seed* "saw," *fit* "fought," and *druv* "drove." Other grammatical forms include the pronoun *yourn*, the demonstrative *them*, as in "them fellers," and the prepositions *afore*, *again* "against," *atween*, and *betwixt*.

In the 1830s and 1840s, authors drew from this common literary dialect in works with settings from New England to Arkansas. Other examples from this common stock include phonetic spellings such as *swaller*, *tater*, and *yeller*; *hoss* "horse"; *bile*, *spile*, and *pizon* "boil," "spoil," and "poison"; verb forms such as *hearn* "heard," *rid* "rode," and *writ* "wrote"; *a-goin'* and other words formed with an *a-* prefix; the possessive pronouns *hisn*, *hern*, and *ourn*; and words such as *chimbly* "chimney," *yarb* "herb," and *catamount* and *painter* "panther." Most writers also employed a technique known as eye-dialect—spellings such as *wuz*, *sez*, *licker*, *minnit*, and *wimmin* that represent universal pronunciations and have no basis in phonological differences. Eye-dialect was often used for comic effect and served to emphasize the backwardness and illiteracy of characters.

The existence of a common stock of forms does not mean that all nineteenth-century authors employed exactly the same literary dialect, only that many writers borrowed rather than invented the features they used. Indeed, the primary purpose of a literary dialect was not to create an accurate record of regional speech but rather to define the social position, or perhaps the social divergence, of fictional characters. Contrasts between dialect speakers and non-dialect speakers delineated broad cultural differences: rural (or frontier) versus urban, uneducated versus educated, even irrational versus rational. By the mid-nineteenth century, dialect had become a convenient method for revealing social status through the use of dialogue.

Before the Civil War, examples of Appalachian English based on actual observation were rare and limited to scattered references in literature by northern travel writers such as Anne Newport Royall, James Kirke Paulding, and Frederick Law Olmsted. By the 1830s, however, a fictional version of Appalachian English began to appear. Paulding, for example, used literary dialect in *The Lion of the West* (1831), a comic drama partly inspired by the life of David Crockett.

There is little difference between the dialect of Paulding's literary frontiersman, Nimrod Wildfire, and that of Cooper's Leatherstocking.

Slightly more accurate is William A. Caruthers's *The Kentuckian in New York* (1834). Caruthers was a native Virginian and presumably had a more extensive knowledge than Paulding of the Appalachian region and its speech. He at least used one grammatical feature characteristic of present-day Appalachian English: present tense suffix *-s* on a verb with a plural noun subject, as in "But I'm told the yankees always sings a psalm before they go to battle" and "Our gals and boys stands up before the parson a few minutes."

The life of David Crockett also inspired the anonymous author or authors of various Crockett Almanacs, which began appearing soon after Crockett's death in 1836 at the Alamo and remained popular through the 1850s. These authors, many of whom were unfamiliar with the region, borrowed their literary dialect from earlier works, including those of Cooper and Paulding, as well as James Hall's *Letters from the West* (1828), which includes a character described as "half horse and half alligator," and *The Western Souvenir, a Christmas and New Year's Gift for 1829* (1828), which featured another frontiersman who could "whip his weight in wild cats." The literary dialect in the Crockett Almanacs is, however, generally undistinguished, with dozens of forms such as *enuff, laffing, speek, throte, tale* "tail," and *hare* "hair." Although the Crockett Almanacs may not represent an authentic version of Appalachian English, they were probably influential in setting the tone for much of what would follow.

Of more linguistic interest are the literary dialects used in works by native southerners from the 1830s through the 1860s, including the border romances of William Gilmore Simms and examples of the Old Southwestern humor genre by Augustus Baldwin Longstreet, Johnson J. Hooper, William Tappen Thompson, George Washington Harris, and Harden E. Taliaferro. Harris and Taliaferro are of particular interest since their works have specific Appalachian settings, making them among the earliest examples of Appalachian literature and certainly the earliest to contain extensive literary representations of Appalachian English. Taliaferro's *Fisher's River (North Carolina) Scenes and Characters* (1859) is set in western North Carolina, while Harris's *Sut Lovingood: Yarns Spun by a "Nat'ral Born Durn'd Fool"* (1867) is set in east Tennessee. Generally speaking, native southerners used at least some regionally distinctive features in their literary dialects, while northern authors portraying southern dialects did not. For example, most southern authors regularly employed present tense suffix *-s* on verbs with plural noun subjects (as in the examples above from Caruthers), a regionally distinctive feature absent from the work of northern authors.

Harris's Sut Lovingood stories are especially interesting from a linguistic standpoint since he used so many nonstandard features that were original rather than borrowed. Harris began contributing comic stories to William T. Porter's national weekly *Spirit of the Times* in the 1840s, and most of these stories later appeared in the 1867 *Sut Lovingood* volume. Judging Harris's authenticity presents challenges because his literary dialect is so dense and contains many features that are probably not authentic. Like the authors of the Crockett Almanacs, Harris made extensive use of eye-dialect, comic mispronunciations, and malapropisms (*dogratipe* "daguerreotype"; *Delicious Tremenjous* "delirium tremens"; *furnitur-takers* "fornicators"). A typical sentence, taken here from "Sut Lovingood's Daddy, Acting Horse," reveals a mixture of spelling-pronunciations and eye-dialect: "When we got the bridil fix'd ontu dad, don't yu bleve he sot in tu chompin hit jis like a rale hoss, an' tried tu bite me on the arm (he allers wer a mos' complikated durned ole fool, an' mam sed so when he warnt about)." In addition to the spelling-pronunciations *bleve, chompin, jis, rale, an', mos', ole,* and *hoss,* there are nearly as many examples of eye-dialect: *bridil, fix'd, ontu, yu, tu, complikated,* and *sed.*

Although Harris probably borrowed much of his literary dialect ("he . . . wer," "he warnt," "sot," and "allers" in the passage above), other usages, such as *hit* "it," are uncommon among his contemporaries. Some features used only by Harris, such as the plural forms *ghostez* and *postez,* are distinctive of Appalachian English. The most significant aspect of Harris's literary dialect is his use of folk vocabulary, since by comparison his contemporaries were fairly reticent about using distinctive regional expressions. Words such as *chinkipin, cowcumbers, dulcimore, furnint, gallinipper, gouber peas, lightning bugs, mud dauber, muley cow,* and *roasin ear* are among the dozens found in Harris's work. Indeed, his use of folk vocabulary was so extensive and often so obscure that one modern editor included a lengthy glossary at the end of his edition of *Sut Lovingood.*

The relative importance of Harris's work as a source of evidence about earlier Appalachian English is problematic. Following methods outlined by Sumner Ives in his 1950 article "A Theory of Literary Dialect," writers have sometimes attempted to authenticate the works of individual authors by comparing selected features from a literary source with evidence from modern linguistic studies. These investigations generally focus on pronunciation rather than vocabulary or grammar, and they usually fail to recognize the conventional nature of literary dialects. While some of Harris's vocabulary compares well with regional forms described in the *Dictionary of American Regional English* and the *Linguistic Atlas of the Gulf States,* others do not. Harris perhaps best represents the end of the first stage in the evolution of Appalachian English in literature: the comically exaggerated, first-person narrative intended primarily for a regional audience. His work is probably the last published fiction in the nineteenth century that provides a useful source of linguistic evidence.

In the same year that *Sut Lovingood* appeared, Sidney Lanier published *Tiger Lilies*, a novel set in the Smoky Mountains of Tennessee and reminiscent of the border romances of Simms. Although Lanier was a native southerner, his literary version of Appalachian English is fairly conventional and derives from the previous generation of southern writers. Lanier's work is, however, a good example of the tendency among nineteenth-century fiction writers to contrast the standard speech of educated outsiders with the dialect of Appalachian natives.

Local colorist Mary Noailles Murfree was probably the most influential author of the postbellum period to use a literary version of Appalachian English. Under the pseudonym "Charles Egbert Craddock," Murfree began publishing short stories with Appalachian settings in the 1870s, although her real success came with the publication of *In the Tennessee Mountains* (1884), soon followed by *The Prophet of the Great Smoky Mountains* (1885). Though she made heavy use of literary dialect, she, like Lanier, borrowed most of the features she used. She did not, however, reproduce the characteristic grammatical features that would have given her work authenticity. Instead, she relied upon frequent use of a fairly limited number of spelling-pronunciations and nonstandard grammatical forms.

Murfree was not the only late-nineteenth-century American writer to employ literary dialect, but a comparison of her work with that of her contemporaries reveals more extensive use of it. Murfree's work also shows a basic discontinuity between genre and style. In subject matter and tone, her work is akin to that of Simms and Lanier; her frequent use of dialect, however, has much more in common with the Crockett Almanacs and *Sut Lovingood*. Moreover, her novels were aimed at a general rather than regional audience, and since her fiction was romantic rather than humorous, she relied much less on eye-dialect and much more on spelling-pronunciation.

For a northern audience unfamiliar with the actual dialect, Murfree's technique may have contributed to a mistaken impression that her representation of speech was more realistic than it actually was. In any given passage of dialogue, Murfree used two or three times as many nonstandard features as writers who portrayed other regional dialects such as James Whitcomb Riley, Hamlin Garland, or Sarah Orne Jewett. Murfree used four to five times as many nonstandard features as Mark Twain did in *Huckleberry Finn*, published the same year as *In the Tennessee Mountains*.

A short passage from *In the Tennessee Mountains* illustrates the density of Murfree's technique: "Vander war a good blacksmith fur the mountings, but they sot him ter l'arnin' thar. They 'lowed, though, ez he war pearter'n the peartest. He got ter be powerful pop'lar with all the gyards an' authorities, an' sech." In this passage nearly half the words are nonstandard. Her only contemporaries to use literary dialect so heavily were those who portrayed African American speech, such as Thomas Nelson Page and Joel Chandler Harris. Murfree's literary dialect helped exaggerate the supposed cultural and linguistic divergence of her Appalachian characters.

John Fox Jr. adopted techniques used by Murfree in turn-of-the-century works such as *The Little Shepherd of Kingdom Come* (1903) and *The Trail of the Lonesome Pine* (1908). In his use of literary dialect, Fox was somewhat more restrained than Murfree, although the nonstandard features contained in his representation of Appalachian English were still excessive in comparison to American writers in general. The importance of Fox's literary dialect, however, goes beyond perpetuation of regional stereotypes through exaggeration. Fox was instrumental in establishing the notion that Appalachian English was a particularly archaic dialect as a consequence of extreme geographic isolation. For example, in his early novella *A Mountain Europa* (1892), Fox describes a moonshiner's daughter, Easter Hicks, as one "upon whose lips lingered words and forms of speech that Shakespeare heard and used." Fox also suggested an archaic Scotch-Irish influence in a 1901 *Scribner's* article in which he observed, "Scotch ballads are said to be sung with a Scotch accent."

The literary dialects used by Murfree and Fox are of little help in understanding earlier Appalachian English. Both borrowed extensively from earlier writers and are not particularly consistent with each other, but they are important because they influenced popular misconceptions about Appalachian English. Through their fiction, mountaineers and their language became inseparable.

Since the 1930s the techniques used by authors to represent Appalachian English have shifted away from the exaggeration characteristic of nineteenth-century authors. More recent writers who have used Appalachian settings have tended toward restraint in their literary dialects. A partial list of works published from the 1940s to the 1960s includes James Still's *River of Earth* (1940), Jesse Stuart's *Men of the Mountains* (1941), and Harriette Simpson Arnow's *The Dollmaker* (1954), all set in eastern Kentucky; James Agee's *A Death in the Family* (1957), Wilma Dykeman's *The Tall Woman* (1962), and Cormac McCarthy's *The Orchard Keeper* (1965), all set in east Tennessee; and John Ehle's *The Land Breakers* (1964), set in western North Carolina.

These authors all depicted dialect speakers but tended to suggest dialect through the occasional use of spelling-pronunciations or nonstandard grammatical features. This more subtle literary version of Appalachian English is apparent in a passage from Arnow's *The Dollmaker:* "Reuben warn't lyen. He's had a rifle since he was ten years old. They's bear and deer clost to our place back home. We're right nigh the edge of a gover'ment game preserve. One year the deer eat up my late corn."

The reaction against regional stereotypes, including the overuse of literary dialect, is characteristic of most recent Appalachian literature, and since the 1970s the trend seems to be toward a very minimal use of literary dialect. A selective list of works that generally reflect this trend includes Lee Smith's *Black Mountain Breakdown* (1980), set in southwestern Virginia; Denise Giardina's *The Unquiet Earth* (1992), set in West Virginia; Charles Frazier's *Cold Mountain* (1997), set in western North Carolina; and Sharyn McCrumb's *The Ballad of Frankie Silver* (1998), set along the Tennessee–North Carolina border.

It would be a mistake to overlook the stylistic diversity in the growing body of Appalachian literature, since writers continue to use a variety of techniques in portraying the regional speech of their characters. Ultimately, though, literary dialects are not the same as speech, and they are of very limited value as sources of linguistic evidence. Literary representations of Appalachian English are probably much more valuable in revealing how the work of nineteenth-century authors established common perceptions of the region and its speech.

See also: HUMOR IN APPALACHIAN LITERATURE (HUMOR); SECTION OVERVIEW (LITERATURE).

—Michael Ellis, *Southwest Missouri State University*

Paul Hull Bowdre Jr., "Eye Dialect as a Literary Device," in *A Various Language: Perspectives on American Dialects*, ed. Juanita V. Williamson and Virginia M. Burke (1971); Michael Ellis, "Literary Dialect as Linguistic Evidence: Subject-Verb Concord in Nineteenth-Century Southern Literature," *American Speech* (Summer 1994); Graham Shorrocks, "Non-Standard Dialect Literature and Popular Culture," in *Speech Past and Present: Studies in English Dialectology in Memory of Ossi Ihalainen*, ed. Juhani Klemola, Merja Kytö, and Matti Rissanen (1996).

Appalachian English in the Urban North

Mountain people from Tennessee, North Carolina, Virginia, West Virginia, and Kentucky began moving to northern cities such as Detroit and Chicago in large numbers in the 1920s and 1930s. Migration was a difficult choice because of the strong kinship ties and cultural cohesiveness of rural mountain communities, but remaining in the mountains often meant a life of unemployment or poverty. Economic survival and success came at the price of emotional pain, but many migrants and their descendants minimized this by maintaining a cultural, regional, and linguistic connection with the mountains decades after they left.

Appalachian English has common features wherever it is spoken, including in migrant communities in the northern United States. Initial unstressed syllables are often deleted, as in *taters* "potatoes" and *maters* "tomatoes." Another important pronunciation is that of "long *i*" in words such as *side*. In most of the country, the vowel usually consists of two sounds: *ah* as in *father* and *ee* as in *beet*. In Appalachian English, the second sound is absent, meaning that *pie* and *right* sound like *pah* and *raht*. Words like *tire* and *fire* are pronounced *tar* and *far*. Words ending in the unstressed "long *o*" sound are pronounced with *er*, as in *holler* "hollow" and *tobaccer* "tobacco." Words ending in an unstressed final sound are pronounced with *ee*, as in *extry* "extra" and *Georgy* "Georgia." The sound system of Appalachian English is unique and persists among migrant groups who have been in the North for decades.

The grammar of Appalachian English also differs from most other varieties of English. For example, Appalachian migrants in Detroit, as well as speakers remaining in the mountains, sometimes add an *uh* sound to the beginning of words ending in *-ing*, as in *a-talkin'* and *a-runnin'*. Both groups also make irregular verbs into regular ones, meaning that *knowed* and *throwed* or *th'owed* become the past tense and past participle of *know* and *throw*. Appalachian English speakers use some irregular verbs in only one or two forms as principal parts rather than three, as for *do (do, done, done* instead of *do, did, done)* and *give (give, give, give* instead of *give, gave, given)*. Appalachian English in the urban North and in the mountains employs double helping verbs, as in *I might could go* "I might be able to go" and *I might should go* "Maybe I should go," and two-word phrases that intensify an activity or a characteristic, as in *She's got a right smart temper* "She's got a very bad temper" and *The old Griggs house burnt plumb down* "The old Griggs place burned all the way to the ground." Another common feature is the use of multiple negatives, as in *I ain't seen nobody fix nothin' a-tall* "I haven't seen anyone fix anything at all" and *Ain't nobody can get on there* "No one can get a job there." Many Appalachian migrants in the North also maintain the pronoun *you'uns* "you (plural)."

In northern cities people continue to use such features of pronunciation and grammar to indicate their ties to the mountains, but their Appalachian speech makes them stand out in the North. Because many of its features are stigmatized outside the region, speakers of Appalachian English are frequently stereotyped in the North, where both whites and African Americans often refer to them as hillbillies.

See also: ATTITUDES TOWARD APPALACHIAN ENGLISH; CHICAGO, ILLINOIS (URBAN APPALACHIAN EXPERIENCE); UPPER OHIO VALLEY SPEECH.

—Bridget Anderson, *University of Georgia*

Harold F. Farwell Jr. and J. Karl Nicholas, eds., *Smoky Mountain Voices: A Lexicon of Southern Appalachian Speech Based on the*

Research of Horace Kephart (1993); Hans Kurath, *A Word Geography of the Eastern United States* (1949); Michael Montgomery and Joseph S. Hall, *Dictionary of Smoky Mountain English* (2004); Cratis D. Williams, *Southern Mountain Speech* (1992).

Attitudes toward Appalachian English

Appalachian English has long been a stigmatized language variety in American culture. Non-Appalachians often view Appalachian English as a quaint, antiquated type of English akin to Elizabethan English while maintaining that the variety is substandard and indicates a lack of proper education. For native Appalachians, however, attitudes toward their own language are considerably more complex.

Mainstream attitudes toward Appalachian English build on social stereotypes that have been ingrained into American society for more than a century and reinforced by modern mass media. Recent images include the 1960s television show *The Beverly Hillbillies* and the syndicated comic strip *Li'l Abner*, in which the characters are quite likeable and even possess a certain country wit, resourcefulness, and charm yet invariably display an ignorance of the wider world and a lack of formal education. These stereotype-reinforcing images create a link to Appalachian (especially southern Appalachian) culture directly through the dialect of the characters. Once the language has gained negative associations, the very sound of it can be exploited to convey further stereotypes of the culture. Thus, mainstream attitudes toward Appalachian English are deep-rooted social prejudices.

Even the pronunciation of the region's name is a distinguishing characteristic of Appalachian English, as this humorous poem dedicated to reminding non-natives how to produce it attests:

> "Snake," said Eve,
> "If you try to deceive,
> I'll throw this apple-atcha."

Just as an Appalachian dialect conjures up stereotypes and cultural prejudices about the speaker to outsiders, many native Appalachians decide from the pronunciation of the region's name whether or not the speaker is a community insider endowed with all of the defining and valued characteristics of Appalachian culture, including integrity and morality. Native attitudes toward Appalachian English are so indicative of group membership and positive community status within the region that Appalachian speakers often strive to maintain their dialect despite negative associations in mainstream culture, even when living outside the region. For example, a 1997 sociolinguistic study of Appalachian speakers transplanted to urban Ohio revealed that despite being surrounded by a more mainstream speech group with overt language prejudices, Appalachian speakers retained covert prestige language norms in line with non-relocated Appalachians.

Strong symbolic ties between language and group membership, however, can create complex issues with respect to native attitudes toward Appalachian English. Native Appalachians are not always comfortable with their language. While some speakers of Appalachian English, such as those in the Ohio study, actively retain their dialect, others attempt to conform their language to the mainstream. College students from Appalachia enrolled at non-Appalachian universities often renegotiate their identities in order to become socially acceptable. As their identities shift, so do their dialects, creating "identity ambivalence" for them and marking them as "elite outsiders" to their home community. Their shift in attitude away from Appalachian culture and its dialect puts them in line with the mainstream, despite the loss of community status.

See also: APPALACHIAN ENGLISH IN THE URBAN NORTH; LANGUAGE IDEOLOGY; SECTION OVERVIEW.

—Clare J. Dannenberg, *Virginia Polytechnic Institute and State University*

Rosina Lippi-Green, *English with an Accent: Language, Ideology, and Discrimination in the United States* (1997); Anita Puckett, *Seldom Ask, Never Tell: Labor and Discourse in Appalachia* (2000); Walt Wolfram and Donna Christian, *Appalachian Speech* (1976).

Cherokee

Cherokee is a member of the Southern branch of the Iroquois language family and is related to Mohawk, Seneca, and other Northern Iroquoian languages spoken in New York and Ontario. When Europeans began moving into the southern Appalachians in the eighteenth century, the Cherokee Nation occupied much of western North Carolina, eastern Tennessee, and northern Georgia and sometimes ranged as far north as Virginia and Kentucky. By the early 1800s a shift to Cherokee and English bilingualism had begun in these areas among the Cherokee, and since the early twentieth century a radical shift to English monolingualism has taken place.

By the beginning of the twenty-first century, fewer than 10 percent of North Carolina Cherokee, primarily middle-aged and older members, spoke the language, which is considered endangered. Major dialects are still found in areas of North Carolina reserved for the Cherokee by the federal government. There are about 1,000 speakers of the Kituwah, or Middle, dialect of the Qualla Cherokee of Swain and Jackson Counties, North Carolina, and close to 150 who speak the Overhill, or Western, dialect of the Snowbird Cherokee of Graham County. Descendants of those forcibly marched west during the tragic Trail of Tears in 1838–39, about 10,000 Cherokee speakers reside in Oklahoma.

Much of this decline of the language is attributable to prejudices of the dominant American culture. Into the 1950s

Psalm 23
in Cherokee

My shephed · is the · Lord · unwanting · I will be
green · pastures · to lie down · He makes for me
beside · still · water · He leadeth me
my soul · He restoreth · for His name sake
the paths · of · righteousness · He leadeth me
the valley · of the · shadow · of · death · I walk
evil · I will not fear

Cherokee translation of the Twenty-third Psalm. Although it can be written phonetically using the English alphabet, Cherokee, which is a member of the Iroquois language family, is often written using this syllabary created in 1821 by Sequoyah. Adopted that same year by the Cherokee Nation, the syllabary consists of six vowel sounds, the consonant *s*, and seventy-eight combinations of consonants and vowels.

Cherokee children could be beaten or punished severely if they spoke their ancestral language in federally run boarding schools, which had active policies designed to eradicate Cherokee language and culture. This treatment discouraged many Cherokee people from teaching the language to their own children for fear that they too would be punished and humiliated.

Written Cherokee uses a syllabary that is remarkable among written languages in that it was apparently developed by a single person, Sequoyah. Also known as George Gist, Sequoyah was born in 1760 west of Chilhowee Mountain in Tennessee. Though illiterate himself, Sequoyah was inspired to devise a system for writing Cherokee through his fascination with the "talking leaves" used by white traders communicating in English. Using both invented and borrowed characters, he experimented for twelve years and by 1821 had assigned symbols to the eighty-five sounds and sound combinations still used in Cherokee.

Within a year the Cherokee Nation adopted the syllabary as its official writing system. According to nineteenth-century ethnologist James Mooney, a Cherokee speaker could learn to read and write the language in a few months, and thousands quickly became literate. By 1828 a Cherokee press had been established; it published the *Cherokee Phoenix*, a newspaper using the syllabary, as well as translations of the Bible and other books in the language. Although a majority of Cherokee use the syllabary, Cherokee can also be written with English letters.

The syllabary consists of six vowel sounds, the consonant *s*, and seventy-eight combinations of consonants and vowels. Every syllable ends with a vowel sound. Vowel pronunciations are as follows: *a* as in *father*, *e* as in *day*, *o* as in *goat*, *i* as in *machine*, *u* as in *rule*, and a nasally produced *v* as the vowel sound in *tug*. Each vowel can have either strong or weak stress and either long or short duration. Long vowels take about twice as much time to pronounce as short vowels, as in the examples of the short vowel of *ama* "salt" and the long vowel of *aama* "water." There are also pitch differences in the pronunciation of vowels, with the last vowel of each word nasalized.

Cherokee has consonants similar to English *j*, *s*, *t d*, *k*, *g*, *m*, *n*, *l*, *y*, *w*, and *h*, but it differs from English in having no sounds resembling *p* and *b*. Cherokee has a glottal sound, which resembles a catch in the throat (as the middle sound in English *uh-oh*); a voiceless *l* (sounded like English *l* preceded by *h*); *tl* (like English *l* but with the tip of the tongue in position to make a *t* sound); *ts* (as in the end of the English word *eats*); *ch* (as in English *church*); *kw* (as in English *queen*); and *gw* (as in English *Gwen*).

Cherokee grammar is highly complex. Nouns are similar to those of English in that they represent a person, place, or thing, but Cherokee nouns are divided into two classes: animate and inanimate. In Cherokee, prefixes or suffixes added to nouns are equivalent to articles and adjectives in English. Although Cherokee pronouns do not specify *he*, *she* or *it*, nouns are gender specific, and there are content words for *mother*, *father*, *boy*, *girl*, *man*, *woman*, and similar equivalents in English.

Verbs are the most important part of every Cherokee sentence and are either active or stative. Active verbs refer to a definite action performed by someone, for example, *jiwoniha* "I am talking." Stative verbs refer to passive states or to actions performed by someone other than the speaker on a recipient individual or group. Each verb must have one or more prefixes followed by a root and at least one suffix. Additional prefixes and suffixes can alter the meanings further.

Verbs in Cherokee show great attention to details of the physical world and reflect a way of seeing and interpreting the world that is different from English. For example, the Cherokee way of expressing "to hand something to someone" depends on the nature of the object being handed: *gvnea* means "I hand you something nondescript" (probably solid); *gvdea*, "I hand you something long and inflexible"; *gvnvnea*, "I hand you something floppy or flexible" (such as a cloth); and *gvnevsi*, "I hand you something liquid."

The Cherokee are attempting to preserve and revitalize their rich and fascinating language, and it is recognized and taught in the schools within Cherokee communities. However, since many Cherokee still do not speak the language at home or on a regular basis, its future is by no means secure.

See also: IROQUOIAN LANGUAGES; SHAWNEE; SOUTHERN NATIVE AMERICANS (SETTLEMENT AND MIGRATION).

—Bridget Anderson, *University of Georgia*

Margaret Bender, *Signs of Cherokee Culture: Sequoyah's Syllabary in Eastern Cherokee Life* (2002); James Mooney, *History, Myths, and Sacred Formulas of the Cherokee* (1992); Sharlotte Neely, *Snowbird Cherokees: People of Persistence* (1991).

Colonial Survivals in Appalachian Speech

Contrary to the popular view that it is Shakespearean in character, Appalachian folk speech is much closer to the language of colonial America. It has preserved a record of colonial speech unequaled in any other American region, largely due to Appalachia's relative physical isolation during much of the nineteenth and twentieth centuries.

Differing agreement patterns between subject and verb (as in "We went to hunt for the horses which was lost"; "Snails is large and common"; and "Two files was demanded by the Indians"), which were once standard usage in the north of England and in the Scottish Lowlands, were also common in the writings of colonial America. Such constructions appeared in the speech of Appalachian natives well after their disappearance from mainstream American English.

In present-day Appalachia there are still survivals from colonial pronunciation. A final *r* in such mountain terms as *winder* "window" and *piller* "pillow" have their counterparts in colonial writings (*vaniller* "vanilla"; *holler* "hollow"; *musquetters* "mosquitoes"), as does the intrusive *r* so frequent in Appalachian speech (*corked* "caulked"; *orning* "awning"). The Appalachian tendency for *r* to modify the pronunciation of the preceding vowel (*tar* "tire"; *har* "hair"; *arish taters* "Irish potatoes") is similar to phonetic spellings found in colonial writings.

Other language peculiar to mountain speech appears in writings from the colonial period. *Tushes* "tusks," *hawlk* "hawk," and *harry-kin* "hurricane" are examples, as are *pizen* "poison" and *dost* "dose." Appalachian speech still has such expressions as *bubbies* "female breasts," and residents still hold a ladder to *study* "steady" it while another person climbs.

Colonial writings by literate but not highly educated people contain these and a host of other expressions still used in Appalachia that the remainder of the country thinks are quaint. Seemingly Elizabethan English can occasionally be found in the mountains (Shakespeare wrote *yers* for "ears," for example), but southern Appalachia has much more in common with the eighteenth-century language of the nation's founding fathers.

See also: APPALACHIAN ENGLISH IN LITERATURE; ATTITUDES TOWARD APPALACHIAN ENGLISH; LANGUAGE IDEOLOGY.

—Ted R. Ledford, *Lees-McRae College*

Nicholas Biddle, ed., *The Journals of the Expedition under the Command of Captains Lewis and Clark* (1814); Frederic G. Cassidy et al., eds., *Dictionary of American Regional English* (1985–); Harold F. Farwell Jr. and J. Karl Nicholas, eds., *Smoky Mountain Voices: A Lexicon of Southern Appalachian Speech Based on the Research of Horace Kephart* (1993); Michael Montgomery and Joseph S. Hall, *Dictionary of Smoky Mountain English* (2004).

German

Nearly three centuries ago, German dialects were habitually spoken in the Appalachian regions of Pennsylvania, Virginia, and North Carolina, and in the 1800s German dialects were commonly heard in Tennessee. While the emerging Standard German (written German) was the language of newspapers, almanacs, educational materials, and religious sermons, German immigrants used a type of spoken, colloquial German in their daily life regardless of religious affiliation. By contrast, the survival of the language in contemporary Appalachia is dependent on the survival of two conservative Anabaptist sects, the Old Order Amish and Old Order Mennonites.

William Penn's promise of religious tolerance in the colony of Pennsylvania first enticed German-speaking Protestant groups that did not enjoy the protection or toleration of political authorities in Europe. Mennonites, Amish, Dunkers, Schwenckfelders, and Moravians started new lives in Pennsylvania. From the first settlement at Germantown, northwest of Philadelphia, in 1683, these colonists settled the counties of southeastern Pennsylvania and ultimately extended into more western regions of Pennsylvania, such as Mifflin, Somerset, and Centre Counties. Lutheran and Reformed Germans, motivated by escape from wars and poverty, soon followed earlier seekers of religious freedom. Within a few decades, these so-called nonsectarian Germans would vastly outnumber all other German church communities. By 1776, persons speaking some form of German as their mother tongue made up one-third of the population of Pennsylvania, between 150,000 and 200,000 individuals.

German-speaking colonists originated primarily in the southwestern part of the German language area. The majority stemmed from the Palatinate, though there were significant numbers from Switzerland, Württemberg, Alsace, Westphalia, and Hesse. The lively interaction among speakers of varying background resulted in leveling their dialects towards a relatively homogenous, new dialect of German distinct from other German language varieties. The borrowing *(screen door; fence)* and adapting (*am tshumbe* for "jumping"; *shpell* for "spell") of American English lexical items contributed to this uniqueness. While Pennsylvania German is commonly referred to as Pennsylvania Dutch, this designation is misleading, having been produced by English speakers who misinterpreted the German dialectal form *Deitsch* "German."

By the end of the nineteenth century, 600,000 speakers of Pennsylvania German lived in the state, most of them nonsectarian German Americans. At this time, conservative Anabaptists, who were religious separatists, represented only a fraction of German speakers (for example, there were only 3,700 Old Order Amish in Pennsylvania in 1890). But at the close of the twentieth century, the Pennsylvania German language was nearly extinct among nonsectarian speakers, while the population of Anabaptist sects continued to increase. This group kept the German dialect alive by rigidly separating their world into two domains: inside the group, Pennsylvania German is the sole means of oral expression; outside the group, English serves as the medium of communication, and all forms of writing take place in English.

Even as Pennsylvania German approaches extinction among nonsectarians, the dialect continues to grow among Old Order Anabaptists, an estimated 26,000 of whom were speaking it regularly at the beginning of the twenty-first century.

A second large cluster of German dialect speakers was located in Virginia's Shenandoah Valley. The valley was settled almost exclusively by migration from southeastern Pennsylvania and Maryland. The Adam Miller family, formerly of Lancaster County, Pennsylvania, established the first permanent German settlement in 1726 near modern-day Elkton, Virginia. Many other families of various religious backgrounds followed. By the time of the American Revolution, German speakers from Pennsylvania inhabited large portions of Rockingham, Shenandoah, Frederick, Augusta, and Page Counties in northwestern Virginia, as well as Pendleton and Hardy Counties in present-day West Virginia. At that time, they comprised more than 5 percent of the total population of Virginia, with most German colonists having settled in the Shenandoah Valley. During the eighteenth century, the German language was used in both public and private domains, in newspapers, churches, and schools. Even a comprehensive collection of Virginia laws was translated into Standard German. By the mid-nineteenth century, however, English had replaced German in nearly all public functions. While the spoken language, a variant of the Pennsylvania German dialect, continued its vitality much longer, only a few very elderly individuals in Virginia belonging to Lutheran and Reformed churches were able to speak and understand it at the outset of the twenty-first century. Most lived in the Bergton-Criders area of Rockingham County or the Jerome-Orkney sections of Shenandoah County. A few others remained in the Propst Gap and Brushy Fork sections of Pendleton County, West Virginia.

In the 1940s, a small group of Pennsylvania German–speaking Old Order Amish settled in the Staunton–Stuart's Draft area of Virginia. But during the last forty years of the twentieth century, most of their young people left their conservative roots and lifestyle along with the German dialect.

Exact numbers of German speakers in the Shenandoah Valley are difficult to determine, but migration into the valley was numerically small, making these colonists highly susceptible to cultural and linguistic assimilation. As the language disappeared from Lutheran communities, however, a few Old Older Amish families who still learned Pennsylvania German as their first language moved into the mountain regions of Bland, Giles, Tazewell, and Washington Counties, assuring that German would continue to be spoken in southwestern Virginia.

In the mid-nineteenth century, Germans from the Shenandoah Valley and the North Carolina Piedmont established enclaves in Memphis, Nashville, Chattanooga, Knoxville, and elsewhere in Tennessee. Between 1848 and 1885, German was the main language spoken in Wartburg in Morgan County, for example. But marriages to English-only speakers and the replacement of German by English in church services signaled the demise of the German language. By 1970, only a few of the oldest residents in Wartburg and adjacent areas spoke any German dialect at all.

In North Carolina, there was no significant German presence until the Moravians arrived in 1753. By 1775, the state had an estimated 8,000 German-speaking settlers in its central and western reaches. Between 1789 and 1870, Salisbury, Lincolnton, Raleigh, and Salem had German printing offices at various times. Until the 1850s, spoken dialects of German—primarily variants of Alemannic and Rhine-Franconian—continued to be used, but the introduction of English into Moravian church services in the 1850s accelerated the decline of German dialects. By the late nineteenth century, the number of speakers in North Carolina was negligible.

See also: EARLY WHITE SETTLEMENT OF WESTERN PENNSYLVANIA (SETTLEMENT AND MIGRATION); GERMANS (RACE, ETHNICITY, AND IDENTITY); PENNSYLVANIA SPEECH.

—Silke Van Ness, *State University of New York at Albany*

Christopher Dolmetsch, *Deutsch als Muttersprache in den Vereinigten Staaten* (1985); C. Nelson Hostetter, *Anabaptist-Mennonites Nationwide USA* (1997); Silke Van Ness, *Changes in an Obsolescing Language: Pennsylvania German in West Virginia* (1990).

Hall, Joseph Sargent

(1906–1992) Scholar.

Joseph Sargent Hall was the first trained linguist to investigate Appalachian English in depth. From the 1930s to the 1970s he observed and recorded traditional speech in the Smoky Mountains of east Tennessee and western North Carolina. In his first area of study, phonetics, he produced the most detailed description of the pronunciation of any variety of American English, but as he came to know mountain people, his interests expanded rapidly. His collections were diverse, encompassing terminology of all kinds, hunting tales and other anecdotes, proverbs, folklore, instrumental and vocal music, and many other types of material.

When the federal government acquired the land that was to become the Great Smoky Mountains National Park, many older residents were allowed to remain on the property for the remainder of their lives. In 1937 Hall, who spent much of his academic career at Pasadena City College in California, was offered a summer job documenting the lives and lore of these mountain residents. Assisted by the Civilian Conservation Corps, he sought out and recorded mountain natives born as early as 1843 and documented the lives and speech of more than one hundred individuals in communities no longer on the map. Over half of his lifetime, he amassed a collection of material on mountain life unsurpassed in its richness, comprehensiveness, and detail.

Joseph Sargent Hall, 1974. A trained linguist who observed and recorded the culture and speech of Appalachian mountain people from the 1930s through the 1970s, Hall was one of the first scholars to discredit the notion that Appalachians spoke a variety of Elizabethan English. His extensive collection of materials, which includes anecdotes, proverbs, folklore, and instrumental and vocal music, many from people and communities long gone, is a rich resource for Appalachian scholars.

Prior to Hall's work, scholars were often interested only in confirming romantic notions about the archaic or supposed Elizabethan character of mountain English and had approached mountaineers en masse, generalizing about them and their speech. Hall approached his subjects without preconceptions and always identified the communities and the individuals from which his material came. Where he found local or generational differences in speech, he noted these. Not surprisingly, he discounted the view that mountain people spoke Elizabethan English, finding it much more varied and innovative than commonly thought. As the pioneer researcher of the speech and culture of the Great Smokies, Hall let people speak for themselves, setting the standard for scholarship in Appalachian English.

See also: ATTITUDES TOWARD APPALACHIAN ENGLISH; KEPHART, HORACE; WILLIAMS, CRATIS.

—Michael Montgomery, *University of South Carolina*

Joseph S. Hall, *The Phonetics of Great Smoky Mountain Speech* (1942); Michael Montgomery, "The Contributions of Joseph Sargent Hall to Appalachian Studies," *Journal of the Appalachian Studies Association* (1994); Michael Montgomery and Joseph S. Hall, *Dictionary of Smoky Mountain English* (2004).

Iroquoian Languages

A number of Northern Iroquoian languages were present in northern Appalachia during the 1700s. Best known are the languages of the Iroquois Five Nations of New York State located originally in the Mohawk Valley and consisting of the Mohawk, Oneida, Onondaga, Cayuga and Seneca tribes—all perched on the northernmost fringe of Appalachia. Whether these languages were spoken beyond the Mohawk Valley prior to European contact is unknown. In the 1720s, remnants of the Tuscarora, an Iroquoian tribe from eastern North Carolina, joined the Iroquois Confederacy.

Of these tribes, the Seneca were present from time to time in what is now Pennsylvania and West Virginia. At the beginning of the twenty-first century, a band calling themselves Mingoes and claiming Seneca descent still lived in West Virginia. The Susquehannocks, a Northern Iroquoian tribe separate from the original Five Nations, lived along the Susquehanna River in central Pennsylvania and thus would have the strongest claim to Appalachia, but they had disappeared by the mid-1700s as a result of European diseases such as smallpox and conflicts with other natives and American vigilante groups.

The Onondaga, Oneida, and one branch of the Seneca tribe have held on to portions of their ancestral lands in New York State while the Mohawk and Cayuga tribes are now divided between the United States and Canada. One branch of the Oneida tribe is now located in Wisconsin, and branches of the Seneca and Cayuga tribes are located in Oklahoma. Mohawk has the most contemporary speakers, as many as two thousand, but all tribes continue efforts to preserve interest in the language by publishing traditional narratives in bilingual editions.

The Wyandots, another Northern Iroquoian group that originated in Canada and had settled in Ohio by the late 1700s, moved into and out of Appalachia along with other displaced tribes. The grammatical structure of Wyandot is similar to the other Northern Iroquoian languages, which in turn are related to the Southern Iroquoian branch represented today only by Cherokee.

Wyandot, like the other Northern Iroquoian languages, is built around verb roots compounded in various ways. Prefixes specify location, direction, or repetition of an action, while suffixes indicate whether an action occurred a single time, has been completed, and the like. Additional prefixes identify the individual(s) involved in the action and, in the case of transitive verbs, both the subject and object.

Thus the root *-yo-* can mean "come" or "go" depending on the prefix. With *ta-* "toward" and *hi-* "the two," the form *ta-hi-yo-'* means "the two came here." With *ha-* "away" and *in-* "we two," the form *ha-in-yo-'* means "we two will go there." The final apostrophe represents a glottal stop (the sound that occurs in the English expression *uh-oh*) and signifies a one-time event as opposed to a recurring event or a completed event. The personal prefixes in these examples specify two people, a category distinct from both singular (one) and plural (three or more).

Personal prefixes denoting both subject and object can be illustrated by the forms *a-yom-ateduto-'* "I ask of you" and *a'-sk-ateduto-'* "tell me," in which the prefix *yom-* represents "I" as subject and "you" as object while *sk-* represents "you" as subject and "me" as object. The final apostrophe in both examples denotes a one-time event. The *a-* prefix indicates something desired while the *a'-* prefix suggests a demand.

The Wyandots were relocated to Kansas following the Indian Removal Act of 1830. One group, the Wyandot Nation of Kansas, remains in the Kansas City area, while the Wyandotte Nation of Oklahoma is based in northeastern Oklahoma. The language is known primarily from a compilation of forty narratives collected in 1911–12 by Canadian folklorist Marius Barbeau.

The last speaker of Wyandot died in Oklahoma around 1950. In recent years the tribe has used the Barbeau collection and other materials in a continuing effort to learn more about the language of its ancestors.

See also: CHEROKEE; NORTHERN NATIVE AMERICANS (SETTLEMENT AND MIGRATION); SHAWNEE.

—Bruce L. Pearson, *University of South Carolina*

Floyd G. Lounsbury, "Iroquoian Languages," in *Handbook of North American Indians, Vol. 15: Northeast*, ed. Bruce G. Trigger (1978).

Kephart, Horace

(1862–1931) Librarian, writer, and scholar.

Horace Kephart's contribution to the understanding of Appalachian speech consists of two published works and a considerable body of notes. His magnum opus, *Our Southern Highlanders*, published by Outing in 1913 and augmented by Macmillan in 1922, contains a chapter devoted to "The Mountain Dialect," and his article "A Word-List from the Mountains of North Carolina" appeared in *Dialect Notes* in 1917. Unpublished notes are housed in the Kephart Collection in the archives of the Hunter Library at Western

Horace Kephart, c. 1910. Kephart meticulously observed and recorded mountain life, particularly culture and speech, in southern Appalachia during the first three decades of the twentieth century. Although he was not a trained scholar, Kephart's copious notes, extensive reading, and determination to check and compare his observations set him apart from his contemporaries.

Carolina University in Cullowhee, North Carolina. A lexicon of Appalachian speech based on these materials and prepared by Harold Farwell and Karl Nicholas was published by the University Press of Kentucky as *Smoky Mountain Voices* in 1993.

Kephart lived and wrote in the Smoky Mountains of North Carolina during the first three decades of the twentieth century—a time when the distinctive dialect of the isolated mountaineers was still unsullied by mass communication or ease of travel. Trained as a librarian, Kephart compulsively recorded his daily observations of mountain life, first on note cards and then in notebooks. These notes were at first a restorative exercise for him, as he had come to the mountains in 1904 after suffering a nervous breakdown—very likely the result of his arduous duties as head librarian at the St. Louis Mercantile Library, the position he had held since 1890. Eventually his observations turned into a new occupation, for he never returned to library work, supporting himself instead by writing, chiefly articles for outdoor magazines dealing with camping, hunting, and woodlore.

Kephart lived first in Dillsboro and then in Hazel Creek, North Carolina, until 1907. He left these locales briefly to travel throughout the southern Appalachians, comparing the lives and folkways of the mountaineers he encountered with those he had become familiar with in the Smokies. Returning to North Carolina in 1910, he took up residence in Bryson City, where he remained until his death in an auto accident in 1931. The last years of his life were spent actively lobbying for the establishment of the Great Smoky Mountains National Park.

Kephart's painstaking scholarship—as evidenced by his copious notes, extensive reading, and determination to check and compare his observations firsthand—sets him apart from the local color writers of the time. To be sure, he read the local colorists, but his observations—particularly those dealing with mountain dialect—consistently exhibit a depth of analysis far beyond those of his contemporaries. His chapter in *Our Southern Highlanders* is the first serious treatment of Appalachian speech beyond a few desultory word lists. His fascination with relic forms (*betwixt* "between"; *fernent* "near to") helped to promote the erroneous notion that mountain speech was largely Elizabethan, but his equal attention to such matters as learned terms in mountain speech (*discern* "see"; *recollect* "remember") and linguistic innovations (*antigadlin* and *slantdicular* "out of plumb"; *hickey* "unknown object") clearly mark him as an uncommon and influential observer. Kephart's detailed and dispassionate observations relied on recorded fact, not fancy or impressions, making his contribution to the study of Appalachian English a lasting one.

See also: ATTITUDES TOWARD APPALACHIAN ENGLISH; HALL, JOSEPH SARGENT; LANGUAGE IDEOLOGY.

—Karl Nicholas, *Western Carolina University*

Harold F. Farwell Jr. and J. Karl Nicholas, eds., *Smoky Mountain Voices: A Lexicon of Southern Appalachian Speech Based on the Research of Horace Kephart* (1993); Horace Kephart, *Our Southern Highlanders* (1913; revised 1922).

Language and Gender

Scholars often view gender as a social category comparable to ethnicity and socioeconomic class rather than a biological description. In this context, traits of gender emerge from social interactions, with language playing a critical role. There has been little research in the area of language and gender relations in southern Appalachia, but existing studies suggest three areas in which language plays a significant role—requests, literacy, and verbal lore.

As elsewhere, men and women in Appalachia differ subtly but significantly in the way they make requests of others. The genders construct the grammar and rhetoric of requests according to the status of the persons making and receiving a request and the nature of the item or service requested. Requests are usually phrased as a want or need. *Want*-requests are more self-focused and political, frequently asserting authority, power, or privilege. *Need*-requests connote a social purpose in which compliance benefits a number of people. When someone says, "I want a truck," he or she is expressing a different intent and purpose than when he or she says, "I need a truck." Men tend to use *want*-requests more than women; young children use poorly formed *want*-requests extensively.

Requests in much of the region are indirect rather than direct. Residents of close-knit communities assume they know each other well enough to provide wants and needs without being asked. The use of order-requesting imperative forms (as in "Move your truck!") is highly restricted. They tend to occur when the right to make a *want*-request is clear or when a *need*-request is within the rights of the person demanding (for example, when a husband says to his wife, "Fix me my supper"). Otherwise, indirect verbal structures are used to make requests and may take the form of a narrative that parallels something the requestee can do or provide; a woman, for instance, may describe to another woman the way her mother cooked something in hopes the listener will cook the dish the same way. At other times a third party may make a need known to someone capable of meeting it. Direct requests using *ask*, *beg*, or other requesting verbs usually require the requestor to be in a close relationship with the requestee. The requestor then has the "right" to ask and is considered in her or his "place." Direct requests also occur when speakers have developed strong claims on each other and tend to take place among kin.

With few exceptions, research indicates that items or services women have the "right" to request fall into the following domains: the bearing, caring, and rearing of children; domestic spaces and activities; food preparation and related activities; healing and caring for the sick; literacy activities; and spiritual or moral matters involving church activities or the evaluation of people's behavior. Women answer and make most telephone calls. Men tend to have authority and control over matters related to money, machinery, politics, land transactions, and outdoor activities. Many patterns in request usage are changing as more women find jobs outside the home in which they work together with men.

In many southern Appalachian communities, gender also plays a role in literacy activity. Traditionally, men have tended to avoid reading and writing activities beyond those related to practical use, such as instructions. Women are more apt to read novels, write invitations or letters, send cards, or make extensive use of e-mail, among other reading and writing activities. Although the rise in information technology jobs has encouraged men to use computer keyboards, many still strongly resist writing extended prose. Women may be much more likely to do so.

These culturally influenced variations in literacy contribute to a gender-based division of labor (for example, men repair computers while women key in data). These patterns can negatively impact men's access to high-paying professional positions that require extensive reading or writing, but women also have limited access to jobs that require authority over others, especially men, despite their greater literacy. Many women will not take such a job, or do not keep it, if the position requires that they violate their "place" with respect to both men and women.

Studies suggest gender differences in verbal lore traditions as well. Women tend to learn singing and storytelling traditions from their mothers, grandmothers, or aunts; men acquire traditions from fathers, grandfathers, or uncles. Women often tell their tales only to their children or close family members and typically feature women resisting the patriarchal dominance that characterizes the region. Appalachian storytellers such as North Carolinians Angelyn DeBord and Bessie Eldreth and Kentuckian Octavia Sexton replace or usurp dominant male heroes or trickster figures with strong female leads. For example, one of Sexton's female characters uses male strategies to get back at her lazy husband, while Eldreth asserts women's self-worth by telling of women who perform kind and valuable services to others. In contrast, renowned storytellers Ray and Orville Hicks presented tales in which the central male character exercises straightforward guile, wit, or authority over others in ways that reinforce male dominance. Genderization of storytelling therefore suggests that many women use this form of oral literature to covertly contest or resist patriarchal norms.

See also: ATTITUDES TOWARD APPALACHIAN ENGLISH; LANGUAGE IDEOLOGY; WOMEN'S ROLES (FAMILY AND COMMUNITY).

—Anita Puckett, *Virginia Polytechnic Institute and State University*

Bill Ellis, "The Gentry-Long Tradition and Roots of Revivalism: Maud Gentry Long," in *Jack in Two Worlds: Contemporary North American Tales and Their Tellers*, ed. William Bernard McCarthy (1994); Elizabeth C. Fine, "'Lazy Jack': Coding and Contextualizing Resistance in Appalachian Women's Narratives," *National Women's Studies Association Journal Special Issue: Appalachia and the South: Place, Gender, Pedagogy* (Fall 1999); Anita Puckett, *Seldom Ask, Never Tell: Labor and Discourse in Appalachia* (2000).

Language Ideology

The term *language ideology* refers to implicit or explicit judgments or evaluations concerning speech. Most evaluations of Appalachian speech fall into three categories, or ideologies. First is prescriptivist, asserting that Appalachian speech deviates significantly from an American English standard. The second is romantic, arguing that Appalachian speech is a survival of Elizabethan English or some other antiquated form of speech. The last is relativistic, maintaining that Appalachian speech is equal to other forms of English in its linguistic functions.

Broad public acceptance of an ideology often leads to its being treated as true, regardless of linguistic evidence. A widely accepted language ideology can dictate political, economic, social, educational, and cultural policies and actions based upon language usages and practices, including Appalachian ones. This process leads to implicit rankings of superiority or inferiority by which schools, businesses, media, and governmental agencies judge individuals by their language usage.

With compulsory public education common by the late nineteenth century, most Appalachian children first encountered Standard Written American English. Teachers were trained to judge speech as correct or incorrect using class-based models of proper English grammar and usage. Their prescriptivist ideology assumed Standard English was immutable, correct, pure, inherently logical, and maintained by elevated written texts, as well as the intrinsic property of privileged and educated people. Language, captured in dictionaries defining acceptable American English words and in prescriptive grammars, possessed a moral component, distinguishing good speech from bad speech and good speakers from bad speakers. Good Americans, it was presumed, would speak the prescribed Standard American English. Like most Americans, however, speakers of Appalachian varieties exhibit numerous vocabulary and grammar usage variations labeled deviations by prescriptivists. Words such as *ain't*, *poke* "paper bag," *mater* "tomato"; verb constructions such as *might could*, *hit don't matter*, *I'm a-comin'*, and *I done fixed it;* and sound variations such as *kittle* "kettle" all became examples of these so-called deviations. As a result, Appalachian speech was devalued in public schools, newspapers, and popular media as corrupt, inferior, ungrammatical, pathological, and sometimes even an incoherent string of words rather than an actual language.

The first written expression of this ideology occurs in Will Wallace Harney's "A Strange Land and a Peculiar People," published in 1873. The ideology is often expressed in media through satiric or mocking depictions that associate nonstandard dialogue with undesirable character traits and negative stereotypes. Examples are readily found in comic strips *(Li'l Abner* and *Barney Google and Snuffy Smith)* and comic books; in fiction (Mary Noailles Murfree's *In the Tennessee Mountains*) and film *(Deliverance)*; in moralizing newspaper columns on "correct" workplace speech; and in the coinage of derisive labels such as *Hillbonics* in the wake of the 1997 Ebonics controversy sparked by the Oakland, California, school district's decision to treat African American Vernacular English as a variety significantly different from Standard American English and requiring special approaches to education for many African American students.

An evaluation of southern Appalachian speech as Elizabethan or Shakespearean arose in the late-nineteenth century as a counter to this prescriptivist stance. Writers of local color fiction, as well as regional educators and folklorists, published popular works and gave speeches advocating a romantic preindustrial view of Appalachia and Appalachian speech. Berea College President William Goodell Frost strongly presented this alternative ideology in his 1899 article "Our Contemporary Ancestors in the Southern Mountains."

Romantic ideology evaluated southern Appalachian speech as being a "survival" from the era of Shakespeare. The argument relied on a limited number of striking variations from Standard American English speech that are found in works using Chaucerian or Elizabethan English—word forms and meanings such as *pack* "carry"; plural constructions such as *nestes* "nests"; and past tenses such as *holp* "helped." Along with elements of folklore, such as log cabins, spinning wheels, and a cappella ballads, adherents used these language similarities to argue for Appalachians as racially and culturally pure Anglo-Saxon survivors from an earlier time. Schools and theatrical groups fostered this ideology in the region through readings or productions of Shakespearean plays.

The romantic ideology of Appalachian speech has been discredited for several reasons: its selective use of language forms as support, the diversity of origins for speech usages within the region, the overlap of many features with other dialects, and the historical fact that Appalachia was not settled exclusively by Anglo-Saxons. Most pronunciation and lexical variations noted as Elizabethan can be attributed to eighteenth-century southern England. Many other variations (especially grammatical ones) from Standard American English can be attributed to eighteenth-century northern England, Scotland, or Ulster.

In an attempt to undermine the ideology of prescriptivism, sociolinguists coined the term *Appalachian English* in the 1970s, identifying the nonstandard speech of Appalachian residents as a distinct variety of English. They argued for the integrity of local speech as a fully developed language system that fulfills the same functions as any other variety. In this view, it is neither superior nor inferior to Standard Written American English, merely different in certain lexical items and in a few features of grammar and punctuation that can be codified in rules like any language. Similar to the prescriptivist ideology, this relativistic ideology asserts a moralist stance. In this case, it is a democratic evaluation of speech that rejects presumptions of language superiority. Nonetheless, it, too, has its detractors. This ideology is politically idealistic in its goal of linguistic equality; it is authoritarian in that it is constructed by academics rather than by the speakers who use the variety; and it defines Appalachian English (or Englishes) by political borders decided upon by the Appalachian Regional Commission, rather than by communities of speakers.

No language ideology is without a political component, no matter how well-intentioned its proponents. Prescriptivist, romantic, and relativistic ideologies of Appalachian speech have had enormous political, economic, and social impact on how Appalachian residents are perceived by those outside the region and by themselves.

See also: ATTITUDES TOWARD APPALACHIAN ENGLISH; COLONIAL SURVIVALS IN APPALACHIAN SPEECH; KEPHART, HORACE.

—Anita Puckett, *Virginia Polytechnic Institute and State University*

Edward Finegan, *Attitudes toward English Usage: The History of a War of Words* (1980); Michael Montgomery, "In the Appalachians They Speak Like Shakespeare," in *Language Myths*, ed. Laurie Bauer (1998); Walt Wolfram and Donna Christian, *Appalachian Speech* (1976).

Logging Terminology

Logging has been a major industry throughout Appalachia since the mid-nineteenth century and, as in most specialized activities, has developed its own jargon. In spite of technological changes, much early logging terminology continues in use. Derogatory terms for loggers—such as *woodhicks* and *woodpeckers*—are no longer used, nor is *ridgerunner* applied to a farmer who logs part time. But old terms such as *cant hooks,* which refers to long poles topped with a hook for turning logs, are still used for loggers' tools. Some loggers' slang lingers in other contexts. *Ball-hootin',* a term that once referred to the dangerous practice of rolling cut timber downhill, has come to be used by teenagers to describe speeding around in cars on mountain roads: "He was ball-hootin' down 107."

As an industry, logging moved southward through Appalachia, with some of the biggest operations in the Great Smoky Mountains coming directly from Pennsylvania after timber supplies were exhausted there. Technical terms migrated along with the workers and as a result became fairly standard throughout the region. The Climax engine, a steam locomotive common on logging spurs in the South, was developed in Corry, Pennsylvania. A Maine blacksmith, Joe Peavey, improved on the cant hook by adding a spike on the end, and the "peavey" can still be used to "muscle" logs. Not surprisingly, many loggers from the southern Appalachians left for the Pacific Northwest after their timber was cut, taking their language with them. The slang term *boar's nest* for a lumber camp or almost any messy bachelor's residence is now more common in the West.

Regional differences have been probably less important than the passage of time in varying the language of logging. The three major epochs of lumbering are defined by the mode of transporting logs from forest to mill: streams and rivers in the nineteenth century; railroads in the early twentieth; and trucking in the late twentieth century into the twenty-first. The earliest phase was notable for the use of "splash dams" along upper streams; these were log dams that created temporary pools to which newly felled logs were "skidded," or dragged. When these dams were broken, the impounded logs would "splash" downstream to a holding pond near the mills. Where rivers could be used, the timber was "boomed," or bound, into "cribs" and floated downstream by "drivers." The use of steam engines brought steam-powered skidders: both "ground hogs" that dragged the timber on cables over the ground and later "overhead skidders" on a network of suspended cables that "flew" the timber over the forest to "scalers," who graded the timber in "loading areas" on spur railroads. "Hayburners," or horses, their "teamsters," and oxen driven by "bullwhackers" all became outmoded, as did "crosspoling" logs across trails to make them sturdy and "swamping," or cutting, new trails to "snake" logs out of the forest.

In both of the early phases, roughly until the 1930s, logging camps were the way stations between forest and mill. Linked only to distant mills by streams or narrow gauge rails, the isolated camps were home to about seventy-five loggers in a totally male society. The lore and language of these camps has not yet been fully recorded, but they were perhaps not as rough as circumstances might suggest. Swearing was forbidden in many southern Appalachian camps, and records indicate camp language was richly metaphoric. The boss, called a "bull," had to be tough, a "bull-roarer," or driver of men. During the workday, separate crews for each stage of the logging process fanned out in the forest, jokingly called "the sticks," where trees might be eight feet across. Most crews had a "push," or foreman. "Swampers" built roads maintained by "chickadees" and "grease monkeys," who kept them slick. Sawyers with their crosscut saws, called "misery whips" or "briars," formed crews with "buckers," who sawed timber in lengths. Bark crews had "spudders" and "rawhiders," who removed and stacked bark from felled trees.

In camp a "filer" kept all the saws sharpened while the "commissary clerk" ran the company store. He and the "time boss," who kept track of working hours, had to be able to add and subtract, apparently not universal skills. Men were paid in "scrip," or "doogaloo," and dropped "tokens," small company coins, into a pail before each meal. A "gut bell" announced the meals, which the cook, called a "gut robber," had prepared with the help of "cookees." Provisions were "bait," beans "firecrackers," and biscuits "cat heads." Adjoining the mess hall was a "lobby" where the men could socialize, ruled over by the "lobbyhog," usually a tough old lumberman who played both housekeeper and peacemaker.

This way of life and much of its special language has disappeared, but logging terms turn up in surprising places. As early as the 1940s, Riverview Amusement Park in Chicago boasted a flume water ride called, in good logger style, Shoot the Chute, the "chute" being an especially narrow rapids. Modern kayakers and whitewater rafters still speak of the "pitch," or height, of the river and identify as "rips" those sections of a stream not quite swift enough to be labeled rapids or narrow enough to be chutes.

See also: LUMBER INDUSTRY (BUSINESS, INDUSTRY, AND TECHNOLOGY); SPECIALIZED LANGUAGE OF COAL MINING; TIMBER AND LUMBER WORKERS (LABOR).

—Harold Farwell, *Western Carolina University*

Frederic G. Cassidy et al., eds., *Dictionary of American Regional English* (1985–); Harold F. Farwell Jr. and J. Karl Nicholas, eds., *Smoky Mountain Voices: A Lexicon of Southern Appalachian Speech Based on the Research of Horace Kephart* (1993).

Medical and Health Terminology

Effective communication between health-care providers and patients is often a critical dynamic of the healing process. Providers must be able to explain disease etiology and treatment, and patients must be able to articulate symptoms. In times past, the use of Appalachian English sometimes complicated health professionals' efforts to understand their patients' needs.

Health-care providers in contemporary Appalachia may still encounter antiquated medical terminology such as *phthisic* or *tizzy* "asthma," *grippe* "flu," *dyspepsia* "indigestion," *consumption* "tuberculosis," *piles* "hemorrhoids," *St. Vitus's Dance* "chorea," *flux* "diarrhea," and *dropsy* "heart disease." The term *smothering* refers to labored breathing, and an episode of labored breathing is a "drawing spell." *Swimmy headed* means "dizzy." One who is "peaked" (pronounced *pee-kid*) or "puny" feels ill; one who is "pert" feels energetic. The term *leader* refers to a ligament or tendon, particularly in the neck or ankle. The verb *creel* means "to sprain," as in "He stepped off the porch and creeled his ankle." Variant forms of *beal* refer to an infected sore ("My ear is bealed") or a boil ("I've got a bealin' on the back of my neck"). Other terms include *risin'* "a boil or carbuncle," *corruption* "pus produced by an infected lesion," and *kernel* "a swollen lymph node in an armpit, on the neck, or in the groin." The term *stove* can mean "to jam or stub a finger or toe" (as in "I stoved my finger when I caught the ball") or "to be bedridden by illness or exhaustion" (as in "She's been stoved up for a week now with the flu"). The term *pieded* is used to describe variegated skin color, as in "My legs are pieded and they hurt something awful." The term *fallen off,* or *falling off,* refers to loss of weight ("This past month I've fallen off a lot"). One who is slightly overweight is "fleshy," but "stout" if excessively fat (or strong and robust). Chafed areas of skin, especially in the groin, are described as a "galled" or "gallded." The expression *loss of courage* is used to describe impotency or diminished sexual drive in men.

In some situations, health-care providers and Appalachian patients may mistakenly think they are talking about the same thing. The term *bold hives,* for example, might be interpreted by a physician as urticaria, a skin disease caused by an allergic reaction to certain foods, drugs, and other agents. For some Appalachians, however, it refers to an infant-specific folk illness commonly known as "croup." Some Appalachian patients interpret a diagnosis of high blood pressure as "high blood," a folk illness caused by an abnormally high volume of blood in the body. Similarly, physician use of the term *blood thinner* to describe anticoagulant drugs is construed by some Appalachians to mean that they have "thick blood," a folk illness caused by abnormally viscous blood. The term *nerves* (as in "I've got a bad case of the nerves") is a label for a debilitating mental disorder.

The terms identified above, with the notable exceptions of *high blood, thick blood,* and *nerves,* are used almost exclusively by the older generation, making it likely that many of them will disappear with the passage of time.

See also: GRANNY MIDWIVES (HEALTH); MEDICINAL PLANT USE (HEALTH).

—Anthony Cavender, *East Tennessee State University*

Frederic G. Cassidy et al., eds., *Dictionary of American Regional English* (1985–); Anthony Cavender et al., eds., *A Folk Medical Lexicon of South Central Appalachia* (1990).

Melungeon

The word *Melungeon* (and its variant spellings) refers to individuals or families who are usually presumed to have mixed-race ancestries and whose ancestors generally settled in out-of-the-way areas of eastern and southeastern Tennessee, far southwest Virginia, northwestern North Carolina, and southeastern Kentucky. The dominant scholarly view is that their ancestries are combinations of Native American, African, and northern European, although a few scholars now include a southern European or Mediterranean component. Popular and folkloric accounts of Melungeon physical features often refer to combinations of white and non-white characteristics such as straight black hair and blue eyes. These presumed features often do not conform to members' actual physiques or to photographs of their ancestors and kin. Strong evidence exists that *Melungeon* has been used as an outsider's term and was highly derogatory from its beginning. Many descendants of Melungeons still living in areas where the term has been common refuse to use the word, at least as one referring to themselves.

The etymology of *Melungeon* is disputed, and more than fifty origins have been cited in published sources. Most of these lack any historical or linguistic support. Current historical research supports the commonly asserted French origin of *mélange* "mixture." A French origin is supported by the late-eighteenth-century presence of French Huguenots and other French speakers in the region where *Melungeon* emerged as a commonly used term. The first documented record of *Melungeon* is found in the minutes of the Stony Creek Primitive Baptist Church, Scott County, Virginia, in 1813. Various twentieth century accounts report that *Portegee* or *Portuguese* was used by members to designate themselves. These terms are not linked necessarily to modern-day citizens of Portugal, as they could also have been ethnic identifiers that simply circumvented stigmatized terms for African or African American ancestry. Also, many self-described Portegee did not define the word as meaning they had ancestors who came from Portugal or as having any meaning other than a term that referred to themselves.

Melungeon had largely fallen into disuse by the mid-twentieth century, in part because of diffusion of Melungeon community members into white populations through marriage and through other strategies that enabled them to be treated as white. The term occurred primarily in an occasional published literary or scholarly work or in restricted speaking contexts such as expressions or discussions of the genealogies of deceased residents. The outdoor drama *Walk toward the Sunset* of the 1960s rejuvenated the term *Melungeon,* however. The 1990s Melungeon identity movement and the Melungeon Heritage Association arising from it have given *Melungeon* an international recognition and are redefining it as a positive, respected word referring to mixed-heritage people who have suffered an oppressive and discriminatory past. Consequently, the current meaning of *Melungeon* is fluid, reflecting its changing usage by the different groups using it.

See also: MELUNGEONS (RACE, ETHNICITY, AND IDENTITY).

—Anita Puckett, *Virginia Polytechnic Institute and State University*

C. S. Everett, "Melungeon History and Myth," *Appalachian Journal* (Summer 1999).

Moonshining Terminology

The production and distribution of homemade corn whiskey (most often called simply "liquor" in the mountains) have a lively history in Appalachia, beginning with the earliest settlement of Europeans in the region. The Whiskey Rebellion of western Pennsylvania first brought Appalachian distilling to national attention in the early 1790s. More than two centuries later, revenuers, or "the revenue," continue to hunt for moonshiners, or "shiners," who manufacture the beverage illegally and for bootleggers and runners who market it, though the days of high-speed, midnight chases down "thunder road" and transactions at a "blind tiger," where a customer leaves or hands money to the proprietor but does not see him, are now in the past.

Within the extensive technical and descriptive terminology associated with distilling, the old-world roots of the process can be detected. These lie in Scotland and Ireland, where the beverage was usually made from barley and oats. Introduced by the Scotch-Irish from Ulster, Scottish terms still used in Appalachia include *flake stand* "a container with cold, flowing water in which a still's condenser is set," *low wine* "the low-proof liquor produced by the first distillation on a simple pot still," and *run* "a distillation cycle producing whiskey." From Ireland come terms formerly applied to poteen, such as *double* "to strengthen by distilling a second time" and *doublings* "whiskey produced by distilling it a second time" or "the second run of whiskey through a still."

Most terminology for the process as well as the equipment for distilling is not only American in origin, but also superregional in distribution, carried south and west into much of the country with people as they migrated. Within Appalachia one finds little variation in terms for technological components. Two notable exceptions are *coil, condenser,* or *worm* for the long, spiral-shaped, copper tube attached to the cap of a still and submerged in cold water and *thump keg, thump chest, thumper, thumping chest,* or *thump tank* for the second distillation unit sometimes added to a whiskey still.

Terms for the beverage itself are much more numerous. These emphasize its varying qualities, effect on the body, or appearance. They run the descriptive gamut from the derogatory *(busthead* and *rotgut)* to the sardonic (*scorpion juice, wobble water, panther sweat, headache medicine,* and *white mule*—the last because of its "kick") to the blissful *(glory juice* and *O be joyful)*. Some of these are local, others regional or national. *Splo* (a shortening of *explode*) is an east Tennessee term, *popskull* a southern Appalachian one. According to the *Dictionary of American Regional English,* other terms that are Appalachian in scope include *beer* "the fermented mash solution produced during the first stage of distilling," *groundhog still* "a still that is a metal cylinder with a wooded top and bottom placed in a hole dug into the side of a hill, usually on the bank of a creek," and *pot tails* "the mash left in the still after distillation." Though illegal distilling is increasingly mechanized, many traditional terms continue to be employed.

See also: MOONSHINE (FOOD AND COOKING); STOCK CAR RACING (SPORTS AND RECREATION).

—Michael Montgomery, *University of South Carolina*

Joseph E. Dabney, *Mountain Spirits: A Chronicle of Corn Whiskey from King James' Ulster Plantation to America's Appalachians and the Moonshine Life* (1974); David W. Maurer, "The Argot of the Moonshiner," *American Speech* (February 1949).

Pennsylvania Speech

Appalachia cuts a great swath across Pennsylvania, and central and western Pennsylvania speech is historically significant to the entire Appalachian region as the point of origin for many of the region's speech characteristics. Though settlers from Maryland and Virginia had established themselves in the Pittsburgh area by 1763, a wave of Scotch-Irish migration swelled westward from the ports of the Delaware Valley into Appalachia after 1785. These emigrants from Ulster left an indelible mark on language in Appalachian Pennsylvania and areas farther south and west in Appalachia in which they settled.

Appalachian Pennsylvania speech exhibits features of Ulster Scots, certain English dialects, and local eastern and central Pennsylvania dialects influenced by Pennsylvania German. These streams of language came together in the Pittsburgh region. Though part of the much larger Midland dialect region, Appalachian Pennsylvania speech has retained and developed words, sounds, and grammatical features distinct from the rest of Pennsylvania, as well as from Ohio, New York, and the rest of Appalachia.

The influence of Ulster Scots is most evident in Appalachian Pennsylvania's vocabulary. In the early twentieth century, western Pennsylvanians could poke fun at a *gillie* "an easily led person, fool" (from Scots *gillygawkie*) off *gallivanting* "wandering idly" (probably borrowed from New York and New England speech) for believing he had seen a *fetch* "a spirit that foretells early death" (a popular Irish term) or the *Deil* "Devil" himself alongside the road at midnight; or perhaps he fled from a *Jenny-in-the-wood* "will o' the wisp" (from Scots *Jenny* "generic young woman" and with closely parallel Scots forms such as *Jenny-bun-tail* and *Jenny-burnt-tail*). Other ancient Scots words once adopted by western Pennsylvanians, such as *usquebaugh* "whiskey" and *brickle* "brittle," have faded from use. No one speaks any longer of being *livergrown* "having enlargement or adhesion of the liver," and wounds rarely *beal* "fester, suppurate" (from *boil*) for western Pennsylvanians as often as they do for their southern Appalachian cousins.

But a farmer in Appalachian Pennsylvania still fills a "bucket" rather than a "pail" in order to *redd up* "clean" (in Scots usage from the sixteenth century) a *baachie* "filthy" (probably from Scots *bach* "cow dung") barn until the dirt is *all* "all gone" (borrowed from eastern and central Pennsylvania German neighbors). After work he or she may stop at a store for a *piece* "snack" and carry it home in a *poke* "paper bag" (both probably from Scots). Western Pennsylvanians still occasionally attend a *belling* "noisy celebration of nuptials," and they still put *carbon oil* "kerosene" (from a nineteenth-century trademark owned by a Pittsburgh oil company) in the lamps they carry to frighten the newlyweds. Comfortably wrapped in *haps* "quilts" (a Scotch-Irish term) on cool October mornings, they may still have *conniptions* "fits of anger" (borrowed from New York) at the noise *grannies* or *ground hackies* "chipmunks" make in the *spouting* "eaves" (of Ulster origin) outside their windows.

The speech of the Ulster Scots also contributed to the means by which Appalachian Pennsylvania speakers formed words. For instance, the diminutive suffix *-ie* so prevalent in Appalachian Pennsylvania vocabulary, as in *croppie* "girl with bobbed hair," *blackie* "small iron cooking pot," and *sprucie* "frizzled fowl," reflects a centuries-old formative habit of Lowland and Ulster Scots.

Pittsburghese, the name by which Pittsburghers know their own dialect, includes terms used by Appalachian Pennsylvanians generally, and some that are purely local. A Pittsburgher packs *jumbo* "bologna sausage" for lunch, then, like others in Appalachia generally, carries it to work in a poke, secured at the top by a *gum band* "rubber band." If her homeward road is *slippy* "slippery" and it is *going for* "approaching" seven o'clock, the rest of her family may *wait* "delay" dinner until she arrives.

Certain sounds are characteristic of Appalachian Pennsylvania speech. Pronunciations like *drooth* for *drought* and *food* to sound like *good* reflect Ulster-Scots influence. Western Pennsylvanians typically replace the suffix *-ing* with *-in' (sittin'* rather than *sitting)*, changing the final nasal sound—a tendency of English and Scots speech in the eighteenth century, when central and western Pennsylvania were first settled, and increasingly a tendency throughout American speech. They were the first to merge the vowel sounds of *cot* and *caught*, so that the two words are indistinguishable except in context, a tendency that did not spread into southern and western Appalachia, as one might expect, but through Ohio into the American Midlands. Appalachian Pennsylvanians also exhibit an aggressive *r*-fulness, so that words like *car* and *near* end in a recognizable *r*. This feature, surely planted in the region by Scotch-Irish settlers, distinguishes Appalachian Pennsylvania from New England, where *r* sometimes simply disappears (some Bostonians *pahk the cah* and Downeasters in Maine pronounce *near* in two syllables, as *nee-uh*), and from the South, including southern Appalachia, where *r* is voiced farther back in the mouth, almost as an afterthought.

Appalachian speech, including that in Pennsylvania, operates by rules markedly different from those that govern either Standard American English or contiguous dialects. Historically, speakers in the region have preferred various nonstandard forms for verbs in the past tense, as in "When I heared he eat all them pies at the fair, I run home as fast as I could, but when I told her, mama just sit there, shakin' her head." They have employed double modals, as in "I might could do it," another habit adopted from Ulster Scots. Concord between subject and verb has been flexible, allowing "The trees was all blown down" as well as the standard "The trees were all blown down." The auxiliary *done* can express verbal completeness, as in "She done put the baby to sleep."

Much of what characterizes Appalachian grammar has persisted from very old forms: *yourn* "yours," a form parallel to *mine*, was a feature of southern English dialects when Appalachian Pennsylvania was settled; *you'uns* and *yinz* "you (plural)" (parallel to southern American *y'all*) traveled to the area in the mouths of Scotch-Irish immigrants and persists in Pittsburghese to this day; and prefixed forms such as *a-huntin'* and *a-washin'* descend from Middle English (1100–1500) *on hunting* (as in "He went on hunting") and *on washing*. This last grammatical feature, like most of the others mentioned, is gradually becoming less frequent throughout all of Appalachia, and it has become especially rare in Pennsylvania—even though all such grammatical structures entered southern and western Appalachia from Pennsylvania.

The above examples by no means exhaust Appalachian Pennsylvania's contribution to American English. Southern Appalachia retains many features that were once used frequently in Pennsylvania but now have disappeared, for instance, *a*-prefixing and perfective *done*. Some forms that entered American speech through Appalachian Pennsylvania, including *supposeta* "supposed to" and *anymore* "nowadays," as in "Anymore people watch videos instead of going to the movies," have permeated other American English dialects. Still an independent dialect region, Appalachian Pennsylvania is perhaps most important historically as the port of entry for many regional and national features of American English.

See also: EARLY WHITE SETTLEMENT OF WESTERN PENNSYLVANIA (SETTLEMENT AND MIGRATION); GERMAN; UPPER OHIO VALLEY SPEECH.

—Michael Adams, *Albright College*

Frederic G. Cassidy et al., eds., *Dictionary of American Regional English* (1985–); Hans Kurath, *A Word Geography of the Eastern United States* (1949); Michael B. Montgomery, "Exploring the Roots of Appalachian English," *English World-Wide* (Winter 1989); Henry W. Shoemaker, *Thirteen Hundred Old Time Words* (1930).

Personal Names

As in much of the English-speaking world, names of persons in Appalachia consist of a first name (also called a Christian name), a surname, and often a middle name. First-name patterns resemble those in other regions of the United States. Names derive from the Bible (Joshua, Elizabeth), classical languages (Homer, Katherine), and other sources. Until well into the nineteenth century, as elsewhere in the United States and in the British Isles, first-born and sometimes second children were frequently named after grandparents, with subsequent children named after older relatives. This practice stressed family continuity, but it complicates the work of genealogists in reconstructing family trees because of the repetition of first names across generations. More recently, other practices have come into vogue, such as giving children (especially girls) faddish names or assigning all children of a generation names having the same initial letter.

Nicknames are useful in distinguishing people having the same legal name. For example, three men named John Sutton, who all lived in the same small, western North Carolina community, were known locally as Big John, Little John, and Lyin' John based on physical and personality characteristics. Nicknames are bestowed more commonly on men, and men are more often known by their middle names. Both children and adults are called by double names (Sara Jane, Joey Lee) in Appalachia more than in most other parts of the country as another means of distinguishing people with the same first and last names. Children are sometimes referred to by a parent's first name, as in "Pete's Liza is marryin' Ella's Jack."

Common European surnames date back only to the later Middle Ages, when European monarchs and their bureaucracies began documenting and taxing their subjects. Their origins fall into four principal groups: patronyms (based on the father's last name, as Adamson, MacAndrew, Williams), occupation (Carpenter, Weaver, Smith), location (Woods, Lancaster), or physical characteristics such as eye color (Brown) or body shape or size (Short). Since they are passed from one generation to another, surnames have been used to estimate the proportions of settlement groups in Appalachia. Historians posit that English, Germans, and Scotch-Irish were the three predominant European groups to settle the region, with subregional variations. For example, the English were more numerous in eastern Kentucky, the Germans in the northern Shenandoah Valley of Virginia, and the Scotch-Irish in southwestern Pennsylvania. Approximately half the surnames found in Appalachia historically are English in form, followed by German and Scottish (each about 10 percent), Irish, Welsh, and French.

Due to several factors, determining ethnicity from surnames is inexact, however. Many presumably English names, such as Robinson and Andrews, were found throughout England, Scotland, and Ireland. Others are indeterminate in origin. Finally, many surnames have been obscured intentionally or unintentionally. For example, while Myers and Shultz are self-evidently German, many others were anglicized through spelling (Snyder, from Schneider, meaning "tailor") or translation (Smith from Schmidt; Carpenter from Zimmerman). Even then, surnames indicate only one of a person's ancestors and thus reveal little for certain about his or her cultural background.

See also: PLACE NAMES; SPEECH PLAY.

—Michael Montgomery, *University of South Carolina*

John C. Campbell, *The Southern Highlander and His Homeland* (1921); William E. Mockler, "Surnames of Trans-Allegheny Virginia, 1750-1800," *Names: Journal of the American Name Society* (Fall 1956).

Place Names

Humans assign names to land features, whether natural or man-made, to give order, meaning, and familiarity to their environment. As elsewhere, place names in Appalachia may be literal (Big Stone Gap, Virginia; Bluefield, West Virginia), metaphorical (Hell for Certain, Kentucky), or even promotional (Saltville, Virginia; Jellico, Tennessee, the latter after the angelica root). Place names, especially those given by Europeans and their descendants, often commemorate prominent leaders (Boone County, West Virginia; Washington, Pennsylvania); founding families (Hillsville, Kentucky); English towns (Romney, West Virginia; Rugby, Tennessee); biblical sites (Berea, Kentucky); older American communities farther east (New Salem, West Virginia, after Salem, New Jersey, itself named after the city in Israel); or significant events (Fighting Creek, Tennessee).

Most Appalachian place names are comprised of a specific element (a personal name or a descriptive word) and a generic one (a common noun for a watercourse, mountain, town, or other feature on the landscape). Generic names sometimes vary by subregion. Community names ending in *-burg* or *-burgh* (Pittsburgh, Pennsylvania) are more common in northern Appalachia; those ending in *-ville* are more common in southern Appalachia (Asheville, North Carolina). Rivers are designated as such everywhere (though in southern Appalachia smaller ones are occasionally called "prongs" or "forks"), but streams are only sometimes "creeks." A stream is often called a "branch" in the southern half of Appalachia but a "run," as in Britain, in the northern half. Other generics found mainly in Appalachia include *bald* "a naturally bare or treeless area on a mountain or ridge summit"; *butt* "a steep slope that stands out at the end of a mountain or ridge"; *hollow* or *holler* "a small sheltered valley or open place between ridges"; *lead* "a long ridge extending from a main ridge of a peak"; and *cove* "an enclosed valley having a level floor, cultivatable land, and a single drainage outlet." *Diamond*, a generic name for a town square, is found in Pennsylvania but originated in Ireland.

Europeans also borrowed many Native American names, especially those for rivers and other watercourses (the Kanawha in West Virginia; the Allegheny in Pennsylvania). They applied others to their settlements (Chattanooga, Tennessee; Cullowhee, North Carolina) or political units (Otsego County, New York), or they combined them with generic names (Toccoa Falls, Georgia). The name for the entire region (Appalachia) possibly derives from a tribe much farther to the south. Four of the region's thirteen states have names transferred from native names of rivers (*Ohio* from Iroquoian, *Alabama* from Choctaw, *Tennessee* from Cherokee, and *Mississippi* from an unknown source, but clearly a native one). *Kentucky* is possibly from Shawnee, but its exact source has eluded scholars. Of the remaining states, six are named for British royalty (Georgia after George II, North and South Carolina after Charles I, Virginia and West Virginia after Elizabeth I, and Maryland after Henrietta Maria, wife of Charles I), one an English city (New York), and one an English landowner (Pennsylvania).

Many Native American names were adopted by the French or Spanish before entering English usage, and thus may no longer resemble closely the pronunciation of the original. *Tennessee*, for example, which first appeared in English as *Tinnase* in 1707, was recorded by the Spanish as early as 1567 as *Tanasqui* and derives from an ancient Cherokee town of the same name. Native names in northern Appalachia usually came from Iroquoian languages (Tioga County, New York) or from Delaware (Punxsutawney, Pennsylvania), those in southern Appalachia from Cherokee (Tellico, Tennessee; Etowah, Georgia). Other names were translated into English, so their native source is now disguised.

Place names derived from European languages other than English are not common in Appalachia. Those that occur usually represent or incorporate the name of an immigrant family such as Lesage, West Virginia (French), and Floyd County, Kentucky (Welsh). Some derive from place names in the Old World, like Wartburg, Tennessee (named after an area of Germany by German-Swiss settlers), Berea (from Greek), or Salem (from Hebrew). The origins of many place names (such as Kentucky) are unclear because they were used years before appearing on any map and will remain controversial. As a result, popular stories, or "folk etymologies," often arise to explain their unusual spelling or character. In recent decades the U.S. Board on Geographic Names, the U.S. Geological Survey, and other governmental agencies have attempted to standardize names, but many variants persist. For example, government maps of Haywood County, North Carolina, identify Cataloochee Valley, which is known locally as Cataloochee Cove. Wear Valley, Tennessee, is known alternately as Wear Cove, Wear's Cove, and Wear's Valley by locals. Despite efforts to document them, countless place names, perhaps the majority of them, are informal ones used locally for roads, hills, and other parts of the landscape.

See also: APPALACHIA; OLD IMMIGRANTS (RACE, ETHNICITY, AND IDENTITY); PERSONAL NAMES.

—Michael Montgomery, *University of South Carolina*

Hamill Kenny, *West Virginia Place Names: Their Origin and Meaning* (1945); William S. Powell, *North Carolina Gazetteer: A Dictionary of North Carolina Places* (1968); Robert M. Rennick, *Kentucky Place Names* (1984).

Shawnee

The Shawnee people, native to southern Ohio, eastern Kentucky, and western Pennsylvania, were the only indigenous representative of the Algonquian linguistic group in northern Appalachia at the time of European contact. They were pushed west of the Mississippi River by the 1795 Treaty of Greenville after Tecumseh was defeated in his effort to halt American expansion. Displaced along with the Shawnee were tribes such as the Delaware, who originally had lived in coastal areas of Pennsylvania and New Jersey before early Europeans pushed them into the mountains and valleys of northern Appalachia.

Shawnee and Delaware are related languages, both belonging to the Algonquian family centered around the Great Lakes and including Fox, Miami, Menominee, Potawatomi, Ojibwa, Cree, Blackfoot, Cheyenne, Arapaho, and numerous languages of New England.

As in other Algonquian languages, Shawnee sentences are built around a verb. The verb includes a root, which denotes the core meaning and which may be compounded to modify or elaborate the basic meaning. Prefixes and suffixes denote the subject and object of the verb, making separate pronouns unnecessary. A single verb often constitutes a complete sentence.

Interesting features of Shawnee grammatical structure can be illustrated by *-neew-*, the common verb root meaning "to see." (Hyphens before and after a form indicate that it cannot occur by itself.) *Nineewa*, meaning "I see him/her," consists of three elements: *ni-neew-aa*. The prefix denotes first person ("I") and the suffix (shortened to *-a* in final position) denotes verbal action normally flowing from the person marked in the prefix to the person marked in the suffix. In this case the absence of an overt suffix implies third person, which could be either "him" or "her" since gender is not specified in Shawnee.

The form for "he (or she) sees me" is *ninookwa*, which actually comes from an underlying form *ni-neew-ek-w-aa*. In Algonquian languages, first person, if present, always occurs as a prefix and third person as a suffix. The suffix *-ek* denotes a reversal of the action, which now flows from the third person suffix *-w* to the prefix, representing first person as object rather than subject. The suffix *-aa* again denotes verbal action and is shortened in final position as usual. The lip rounding associated with *w* causes the surrounding vowels to be pronounced as *o*.

The Shawnee people today live in three separate communities in central and eastern Oklahoma and southwestern Missouri. A fourth group claiming Shawnee ancestry still lives in Ohio. As many as two hundred members of the largest community near Oklahoma City continue to speak the language, and it is used by tribal elders on ceremonial occasions.

Although a number of scholars outside the tribe have studied the language over the years, the Shawnee community itself has not developed a written tradition and few tribal members under the age of fifty have grown up speaking the language. The future of the language is uncertain.

See also: CHEROKEE; IROQUOIAN LANGUAGES; SOUTHERN NATIVE AMERICANS (SETTLEMENT AND MIGRATION).

—Bruce L. Pearson, *University of South Carolina*

Bruce L. Pearson, "Shawnee as a Southeastern Language," *Southern Journal of Linguistics* (Fall 2000).

Spanish

Spanish speakers in the United States have typically been clustered in the Southwest or in large urban areas such as Los Angeles, New York, or Chicago. Appalachia is one of the new, atypical destinations for Spanish-speaking immigrants. With the exception of coal-mining areas such as southern West Virginia, which attracted African Americans, Italians, and others, industries in rural Appalachia have not needed to bring in many workers from outside the region in the past. However, since the 1990s, companies have increasingly relied upon workers migrating from south of the U.S. border, leading to the unprecedented use of a language other than English in Appalachia. This trend is most apparent in areas with strong economic growth, such as northern Georgia and western North Carolina. According to the census data, there were at least 464,441 Spanish-speakers in Appalachia in 2000, which equates to approximately 2 percent of the Appalachian population, although this figure is widely considered to be an undercount. The population of Spanish-speakers is not uniformly distributed, however, with a concentration of more than 7 percent in Appalachian Georgia.

Before the 1990s, Spanish speakers in mountain areas were mostly a transient population of young men who came temporarily to work. In the twenty-first century, growing numbers of Spanish-speaking immigrants began bringing their families and buying homes. They are drawn to Appalachia not only by jobs, but by the same factors that draw retirees to the mountains and keep longterm residents there: the sense of community and security found in small towns and the desire to escape from the urban problems of pollution, traffic, and noise. The trend toward more stable Hispanic communities in Appalachia has made it more likely that the Spanish language will become permanently established.

Immigrants from Spanish-language countries learn English as quickly as immigrants from other places and have done so in all eras, but they may be less likely to stop speaking Spanish. Many adult immigrants do not become fluent in English due to long hours of work and limited contact with English speakers. Their school-aged children, however, do learn and speak English regularly, while remaining bilingual. By the third generation, most of these families have become monolingual English speakers. Spanish speakers tend to retain their bilingualism longer than other immigrant populations due to a constant arrival of new monolingual Spanish speakers into communities.

Spanish speakers in Appalachia come from many different countries. The exact composition varies from community to community because of the way new immigrants are recruited, which is most often through an informal network of family and friends extending back to the country of origin. The largest group by far is from Mexico, followed by those from other Latin American countries. Many arrive in Appalachia after first living in other parts of the United States. Immigrants, who see themselves as Mexicans, Guatemalans, or other ancestry, often consider group labels such as *Hispanic* and *Latino* disagreeable.

As is common in areas of high immigration, new dialects of both Spanish and English have begun to emerge in Appalachia as newcomers become more integrated into the community and opportunities for interaction become more frequent.

See also: GERMAN; HISPANICS (RACE, ETHNICITY, AND IDENTITY); MIGRANT LABOR (AGRICULTURE).

—Ellen Johnson, *Berry College*

Arthur D. Murphy, Colleen Blanchard, and Jennifer A. Hill, eds., *Latino Workers in the Contemporary South* (2001); Barbara Ellen Smith, *The New Latino South: An Introduction* (2001).

Specialized Language of Coal Mining

The language of coal mining is extensive, often colorful, and, like the industry itself, evolving. An underground mine accesses coal seams from below the earth's surface, while a surface or strip mine exposes the seams from above. Underground mines are either designed for "room and pillar" or "longwall" extraction. In the former, miners work in pairs or small teams in highly restrictive individual rooms separated by pillars of coal left to support the mountain. The miners bore vertically into the coal seams, or "the face," manually with picks in the old "handloading" days or, in the contemporary era, with machines called "continuous miners" that use rotating drill bits to chew out the coal. When miners bore through the seams or when the seams become too thin for extraction, the workers back out of the various sections, "pulling pillars" as they go, that is, removing the blocks of coal left to support the mountain. In longwall mining a long length of coal seam, as much as five thousand feet at a time, is removed by a series of interlocked "longwall machines" with cutting blades that move back and forth in a horizontal motion, shearing the coal down from the face.

There are three basic types of underground mines: "shaft mines," "slope mines," and "drift mines." Workers in a shaft mine access the coal seams by riding an elevator, or "cage," down a vertical entryway that takes them deep underneath the earth. In a slope mine, workers walked (but now ride a "man-trip") down a sloping entryway that is not nearly as vertical as in a shaft mine but which still slopes downward. In a drift mine, the most common type in Appalachia, workers walked and now ride into an entryway that slopes gently upward, providing natural drainage.

There are several types of surface mines as well. In "pit mines," also called "area mines," workers use explosives and bulldozers to remove trees and other plant life as well as topsoil, or the "overburden," from a coal seam lying more or less level with the earth's surface. However, pit mining is rare in Appalachia because of the steep, mountainous topography of the Cumberland and Allegheny Plateaus, in which all of the region's coal lies. In "contour mining," also known as "bench mining" or "highwall mining," workers follow the contour or direction of a seam along a mountainside, cutting straight down to remove the overburden and expose the seam. This process creates a vertical highwall and then a level bench just below it on which machinery can maneuver. In an "auger mine," the exposed coal is extracted by drills or augers boring into the seam. In "mountaintop-removal mining," the tops of mountains are removed to expose the coal seams below, and the overburden is pushed into an adjacent hollow, creating a "valley fill." A "truck mine" is one in which the extracted coal is delivered from mine site to transportation link by coal trucks instead of being loaded directly onto a rail line at the work site.

The vernacular of the Appalachian miner has changed as the nature of the work itself has changed over the past century due to the introduction of new technology. Whatever the era, many terms make use of analogies to nature or to animals. A "horse's back" is the curved indentation left in a mine ceiling when a slab of rock or coal falls. "Bird's eye cannel" is a type of bituminous or "soft" coal (versus anthracite, also known as "hard" coal) that is imprinted with small concretions said to resemble a bird's eye. "Bug dust" is the coal dust lingering in the air in fine particles after a section of coal is "shot from the face." A "dog hole" is a small mine, generally unsafe and often nonunion (thus sometimes called a "scab mine"). "Possum piss" is the oil used underground to keep machine parts from rusting. Sometimes surface or strip miners apply the term to the hydraulic fluid poured into their bulldozers and front-end loaders.

In the old handloading days before the widespread use of machinery, the miner's workday involved the mastery of several skilled tasks and his lexicon was colorful. Upon entering his "working room" for the day, a miner "propped the roof," or "top," with "timbers" and then "laid track" right up to the face of the coal seam. After kneeling or lying on his side and "undercutting" the seam (which had to be further supported with short timbers, or "sprags"), the miner drilled blasting holes with a "breast auger," used a "tamping rod" to pack his black powder, inserted a "clay dummy" to ensure proper repercussion of the explosion, lit the fuse, and yelled, "Fire in the hole!" or perhaps "Shootin' coal!" to warn other miners of the impending blast. If the coal had been blasted from the face without undercutting, the mineral was "shot from the solid." After the dust had settled the miner loaded the coal into a "gon," hung his "weigh tag" on a nail, and then pushed the gon out into the entryway for delivery outside the mine site where the "checkweighman" credited it to the respective miner. The miner then cleaned his working room of waste rock, called "gob" or "bone" and eventually hauled outside and added to a massive "slag pile," and headed home for the day.

Every two weeks or month the miner collected his pay, often in the form of company money called "scrip" or "clacker" that had to be spent at the company store, or "pluck me store" as miners called it because of inflated prices. Often the miner collected nothing at payday because he had been advanced credit for groceries or mining supplies, so he essentially worked not for a wage but to pay off mounting debt. The next week he would do it all over again.

See also: ANTHRACITE MINERS, TWENTIETH-CENTURY (LABOR); LOGGING TERMINOLOGY; STRIP MINE WORKERS (LABOR).

—Stephen D. Mooney, *Virginia Polytechnic Institute and State University*

Douglas Crickmer and David Zegeer, eds., *Elements of Practical Coal Mining* (1981); Jack M. Jones, *Early Coal Mining in Pocahontas, Virginia* (1969; reprint 1983).

Speech Play

Appalachia is well known for the dexterity of its storytellers and its distinctive vocabulary. However, the region's speakers may be most noteworthy for their use of intermediate verbal forms—sayings, phrases, and short verses and rhymes that encapsulate experience, comment on daily life, and exhibit word play. These include proverbs and aphorisms, similes, riddles, tongue twisters, play verses (counting-out and other children's rhymes), figures of speech, and other types of concise verbal folklore. Most such forms are more or less invariable, making them easily memorized and handed down orally from generation to generation. Many are several hundred years old, but new ones are being created all the time.

Strictly speaking, proverbs are sentences that express general truths or popular beliefs based on shared experience and attitudes. Many proverbs used in parts of Appalachia are quite old and derive from classical or biblical sources or are traceable to medieval or Renaissance England. Used to instruct or impart an ethical perspective, they are most often expressed in present tense statements *(A stitch in time saves nine; A whistlin' woman and a crowin' hen always come to some bad end)* but not always: *Root, hog, or die* and *When you can't afford it, don't butter both sides of your bread* are imperatives. Frequently they make use of literary devices such as alliteration, meter (most often a four-beat line), rhyme, a balanced or parallel construction expressing an opposition, and ellipsis; *Waste not, want not* has all of these features. Personification and metaphor are seen in *The apple never falls far from the tree.* Proverbs are used to deal with a variety of recurrent social situations, including providing a short, pithy, moral comment on an event; emphasizing that a circumstance is familiar and has been successfully dealt with before; giving advice; summing up an argument; or reinforcing a point.

Proverbial exaggerations (usually in the pattern *so* + ADJECTIVE + *that*) express the extraordinary degree to which something is true or that something or someone possesses or embodies a quality, as does *It was so good you could taste the gal's feet in it that hoed the corn it was made out of,* a statement referring to moonshine.

Similes are also part of everyday discourse in Appalachia but lack the element of folk wisdom. They are proverbial phrases that take one of three general patterns (*as* + ADJECTIVE + *as* + NOUN; ADJECTIVE + *-er* + *than* + NOUN; or VERB + *like* + NOUN). Used most often to emphasize rather than compare, similes add color and expressiveness to speech by juxtaposing two things, qualities, or actions not usually associated with one another. Thus, *His wife was as ugly as a mud fence daubed with chinquapins* means that she was very ugly; *Joe is meaner than a striped snake* that he is very mean; and *She wanted to play as bad as a crippled pup* that she wanted to play very badly. *As thick as fiddlers in hell* means "plentiful." Likewise, *She went down that row like a hen a-peckin'* and *He just took off like a scalded dog* both mean that a person went very quickly.

Riddles are verbal puzzles used to tease, test, or entertain, as in sessions in which members of a group take turns trying to outwit one another or compete for telling the "best one." Often containing puns, they consist of a stated or implied question (usually prefaced by an invitation to "see if you can guess this one"), a short period to contemplate an answer, and then a guess at the answer, often with an explanation:

Question: What went to grandpa's house on Sunday, stayed a week, and came back on the same Sunday?
Answer: A man who rode a horse named Sunday.

As an aid to memorization, riddles may take the form of a short verse, most often several rhyming lines. Examples include the following:

Hit's as round as a ring,
and as deep as the spring,
and all the King's horses
couldn't pull it up.
Answer: A well.

As I went around my willy-go-whackum,
there I spied old Bow Backum,
and I went home after Tom Tackum,
to run Bow Backum,
out of my willy-go-whackum.
Answer: Going around the cornfield, I saw the old sow and went home to get the dog.

Children's verses also include rhymes for many types of play. A counting-out rhyme found in Appalachia is the following:

As I went up the crazy steeple;
there I met three crazy people;
one was black, one was blue;
one was the color of my old shoe;
what color is that?
(The child who is pointed at supplies the name of a color, and the counting out continues.)

The expressiveness of mountain speech and the resourcefulness of its speakers are also found in metaphorical language that is often mildly earthy but that captures human shortcomings. *To build the fence after planting the corn* means "to marry after a child is conceived," while *to drive one's ducks to a poor market* and *to fly over a field and settle on a cowpile* mean "to make a poor choice in marriage." Mountain phraseology can be striking visually (*can see to can't see* means "from dawn to dusk"; *bloom for the grave* means "to get gray hair, grow old"), aurally (*call the hogs* means "to snore loudly"), or psychologically (*charge it to the dust and let the rain settle it* means "to dismiss a loan considered small, unimportant, or impossible to collect").

See also: PERSONAL NAMES; PLACE NAMES.

—Michael Montgomery, *University of South Carolina*

Paul G. Brewster et al., eds., *The Frank C. Brown Collection of North Carolina Folklore, Vol.1: Games and Rhymes* (1952); Wolfgang Mieder et al., eds., *A Dictionary of American Proverbs* (1992); James Still, *Way Down Yonder on Troublesome Creek: Appalachian Riddles and Rusties* (1974).

Upper Ohio Valley Speech

The dialect of the Ohio River Valley has been studied for only sixty years, but observations about its distinctive features were made even in the earliest period of settlement. Travelers to the Ohio Valley, which extends from Pittsburgh to Cairo, Illinois, where the Ohio River joins the Mississippi, wrote about the words, pronunciations, and grammatical forms used in this area, contrasting them with New England, Virginia, and Philadelphia speech. In an 1878 issue of *Appletons' Journal,* Reverend N. C. Burt commented on the "Scotch-Irish" origins of the English of Pennsylvania, the Cumberland Valley of Virginia, and the trans-Allegheny region, noting the use of phrases such as *I want out, to wait on* (someone), *to take sick,* and *quarter till* (in telling time). Similarly, Burt observed that the "broad *a*" of New England gave way to a "narrower *a*" in words like *laugh, grass,* and *past,* and that the final *r* was pronounced in this middle region but dropped in both New England and the South. Referring to Ohio specifically, Burt traced three distinct regions, representing migration from New England in the northern area, Pennsylvania in the central area, and Virginia and Kentucky in the southern belt. These observations have been confirmed by recent studies, beginning with the American Linguistic Atlas Project in the 1930s and continuing with the *Dictionary of American Regional English* project in the 1960s and more focused studies since.

The Ohio Valley is part of what most linguists now call the South Midland dialect area; its dialect shares some features with both southern Appalachian speech and general Southern American English. The three largest cities in the valley—Pittsburgh, Cincinnati, and Louisville, Kentucky—differ largely because of the influx of people from different rural areas as well as from other regions of the country. Stable residence patterns in the areas surrounding these cities have, on the other hand, led to the retention of older forms of speech in a belt running north of the river through Ohio, Indiana, and Illinois (roughly south of the old Zane's Trace and the National Road) and throughout all of West Virginia and Kentucky south of the river. Crosscutting this South Midland region is the trans-Appalachian area of secondary settlement from western Pennsylvania and northern West Virginia to the upper Ohio Valley and from the Blue Ridge through the Cumberland Gap into southern Ohio.

Vocabulary items still common in the Ohio Valley include *gutter, mango, bucket, sack, lightning bug, crawdad, skil-*

let, blinds, spigot, snap beans, snake feeder, polecat, toboggan, redd up, and *Beggars' Night* (corresponding to the northern terms *eaves trough, green pepper, pail, bag, firefly, crayfish, frying pan, shades, faucet* or *tap, green beans, dragonfly, skunk, ski cap, clean up*, and *Trick-or-Treat*); some of these, however, now alternate frequently with northern or urban forms. The use of *mamaw* and *papaw* for grandparents is still common, even in young people's speech. Grammatical forms include the plural *you-all* (not *y'all*) and *you'ns* (in the Pittsburgh area, *y'uns* or *y'ins*), possessive *you-all's*, and reduced phrases *want off, want out, over top of*, and *upside*, as well as *needs washed* (as opposed to *needs to be washed* or *needs washing*). Vernacular past tense forms are common, as in "he come," "I done it," and "I done seen him." The subject relative pronoun may be absent, as in "He's the man stole my car"; and a personal dative pronoun is sometimes added, as in "I'm gonna get me a new car soon." Singular nouns of measurement are used with plural meaning: *ten mile, five bushel, six foot;* and an *a*-prefix before a progressive verb is still used by older and rural people: *He was a-dancin'; They come a-runnin'*.

Pronunciation features include the rhyming of *collar* (and sometimes *color*) with *caller, cot* with *caught*, and *Don* with *dawn*. Three other mergers of vowels advancing throughout Appalachia and now present in southern Ohio result in the rhyming of *steel* with *still, pool* with *pull*, and *sale* with *sell*. Also common is the tensing of vowels in *fish, push*, and *special (feesh, poosh, spacial)*; pronouncing *greasy* as *greazy;* inserting *r* in *wa(r)sh, l* in *draw(l)ing*, and *t* in *across(t)*; and using monophthongs in *I, buy, fire*, and *tired* (to rhyme with *ah, bah, far*, and *tarred*) and diphthongs in *dog* and *tall* (pronounced as *dawg* and *towel*). Stress on the first syllable, as in *IN-surance* and *UM-brella*, is common, and the reduction of two syllables to one also occurs, as in *sewer, Stewart*, and *Newark* (pronounced *sore, stort, nerk*).

While not all Ohio Valley residents use all of these vernacular forms, many use some of them, especially in rural and small-town areas. Older people tend to use them more than younger people, and men are more likely than women to use vernacular grammar in particular. While education and out-migration are promoting the adoption of non-local vocabulary and grammar, pronunciation is more resistant to change. Furthermore, these forms may spread as residents reassert their Appalachian identity and as General Southern American speech, the source of many Appalachian features, continues to influence Midland English. Out-migration from the valley has already carried regional forms throughout Ohio to Cincinnati, Dayton, Columbus, and Akron. The features described above should therefore be regarded not as relic forms in decline but rather as evidence that at least some traditional features of Appalachian English are still alive and well in the Ohio Valley.

See also: APPALACHIAN ENGLISH IN THE URBAN NORTH; CINCINNATI, OHIO (URBAN APPALACHIAN EXPERIENCE); PENNSYLVANIA SPEECH.

—Beverly Olson Flanigan, *Ohio University*

Robert F. Dakin, *The Dialect Vocabulary of the Ohio River Valley* (1966); Clyde T. Hankey, "Notes on West Penn–Ohio Phonology," in *Studies in Linguistics in Honor of Raven I. McDavid, Jr.*, ed. Lawrence M. Davis (1972); Walt Wolfram and Donna Christian, *Appalachian Speech* (1976).

Vulgarity and Profanity

While Appalachians are widely perceived as religiously inclined and conservative in personal habits, the region's speech, in given circumstances, manifests its own brand of vulgarity, profanity, invective, and innuendo. A good example of colorful, regionally distinct swearing was once provided by Cratis Williams, widely regarded as a founding father of Appalachian studies, quoting his grandfather's spontaneous reaction to a balky piece of farm machinery: "I wish, by God, that this son-of-a-bitching thang was in the fur fork of hell with its back broke." In polite company, Appalachians who become sufficiently provoked to use strong language are apt to utter innocuous euphemisms (sometimes called "by-words") such as *golly, dad burn it, gad*, or even *eye gollies* rather than unvarnished oaths in the style of Williams's grandfather. But in circumstances where off-color language can be employed without offense, rural Appalachian speech is often scatological, profane, and laced with sexual innuendo.

Though focused not on Appalachia but the Ozark Mountains, the best-known scholarly work on bawdy language in rural highlands is folklorist Vance Randolph's *Pissing in the Snow and Other Ozark Folktales.* This groundbreaking work raised eyebrows when the University of Illinois Press published it in 1976, but the sexual jokes contained in it collected over a period of many years are often hard to distinguish from those of the Appalachians. In the introduction to the volume, folklorist Rayna Green observes that the previous unavailability of realistic, common, and obscene material of the type collected by Randolph had contributed to a wide perception of a rural people as "quaint, archaic, courtly rustics removed from the realities of life in a contemporary world."

As elsewhere in rural America, the most common Appalachian invective uses various anatomical parts and scatological terms to express disapproval of character, to question veracity, or to ridicule. A person of dubious intelligence may be said to be unable "to grab his ass with both hands" or "too dumb to pour piss out of a boot." Notable terms of wide utility, though crude, can carry subtle nuances. *Horse-*

shit, *bullshit*, and *chickenshit* are not used interchangeably, for instance. While the first and second are often used as interjections, the second is also widely used to indicate loose talk or an untruth. *Chickenshit* often connotes a subject or individual beneath contempt though it, like other such terms, can be modified or embellished, as in "chickenshit sonofabitch." Many such words can serve equally well as nouns, verbs, adjectives, or interjections when used with expertise.

Just as off-color language is used to ridicule, dismiss, or express contempt, so is it employed in exaggeration and in expressions of humor, with sexual language having particular affinity for the latter. Again, nature provides the most common metaphors and similes. A summer downpour brings rain "like a cow pissing on a flat rock," for example. Sexual speech, being especially sensitive, is heavily metaphorical and also often drawn from behavior associated with various animals. A man known for sexual prowess is referred to as a "tomcat," a "stud hoss," or a "billy goat." By the same token, a woman thought to be available is "ready as a rabbit." Women who follow musicians to festivals have been called "weed monkeys."

In general, off-color language is taboo in mixed groups, especially when children are present. In segregated circumstances, though, both men and women use pungent language, which helps to account for children's learning such speech.

Notwithstanding the wider use of profanity and sexual innuendo by entertainers and unrestrained language on the Internet, many Appalachians, particularly in small towns and rural settings, continue to be appalled by any off-color speech, be it vulgar, profane, or even intemperate.

See also: APPALACHIAN ENGLISH AND OZARK ENGLISH; BAWDY AND SCATOLOGICAL HUMOR (HUMOR).

—Loyal Jones, *Berea, Kentucky*

Vance Randolph, *Pissing in the Snow and Other Ozark Folktales* (1976); Richard A. Spears, *Slang and Euphemism: A Dictionary of Oaths, Curses, Insults, Racial Slurs, Drug Talk, Homosexual Lingo, and Related Matters* (1981); Cratis D. Williams, *Southern Mountain Speech* (1992).

Williams, Cratis

(1911–1985) Scholar and folklorist.

Cratis Dearl Williams was the foremost native interpreter of the speech of Appalachia. In lectures, performances, and essays (especially a series of eleven articles in *Mountain Life and Work* in the 1960s), he brought an understanding of many aspects of the region's English untouched by other scholars before or since. These included such expressive and rhetorical devices as hyperbole, similes, metaphors, oaths, proverbs, and the pitch, rhythm, melody, and pace of speech. In his monumental doctoral dissertation, "The Southern Mountaineer in Fact and Fiction" (1961), he dealt extensively with how literary artists had portrayed mountain English over the previous century. In this and other writings he did more to present the individual speaker and to counter stereotypes about mountain speech than any other individual.

Not a professional linguist, Williams trained himself through self-study and observation and relied on intuition and memory for his originality and insight. A native of eastern Kentucky and a life-long educator, first in public schools and later on the university level, Williams traced his awareness of language to being humiliated for his rural speech by an English teacher upon entering Louisa County High School in 1925. He became acutely conscious of his own speech patterns and realized they were inseparable from the identity and character of native mountain people. In his long career teaching literature, speech, and drama at Appalachian State University, he took care not to embarrass his own students from the mountains. Fearing that teachers could "do damage" to their students' speech, he instead cultivated in them self-respect and appreciation for the expressiveness and history of their native language patterns.

Williams was keenly interested in the history of Appalachian speech. Calling traditional mountain English "the oldest living dialect" of English, Williams joined many other scholars in emphasizing its historical legitimacy. They often argued that mountain speech was Elizabethan or Shakespearean, but he was the first to claim a substantial Scotch-Irish component for it, believing that its historical character was determined by the predominance of that group in the eighteenth-century settlement of the region. His principal interest was not in identifying older usages (though he insisted that mountain speakers had "history on their side") nor in analyzing sounds, grammatical forms, and curious, often archaic vocabulary. Rather, Williams was intent on presenting the unique qualities of mountain speech and showing how the smaller elements of language were used in daily conversation as well as in storytelling and other forms of oral rhetoric. Mountain culture and values could be understood only when one saw that its language "expressed basic views of life, attitudes, ways of looking at things" and that it was a vivid, powerful medium for expressing the nuances and drama of mountain thought and everyday life. Professionally trained linguists who analyze speech using scientific concepts have objected to Williams's subjective description of mountain speakers as having "straight jaws" and traditional mountain vernacular as exhibiting "spare economy," "subtlety," "exactness," "strength," "respect for the individual," "pungency," and "melody." He illustrated these qualities with transcriptions and renditions of the region's speech and tales that were colorful, passionate, and memorable, if sometimes short on technical exactitude. His work brought Appalachian English to life more than that of any other scholar or writer.

See also: APPALACHIAN ENGLISH IN LITERATURE; HALL, JOSEPH SARGENT; WILLIAMS, CRATIS (LITERATURE).

—Michael Montgomery, *University of South Carolina*

Cratis D. Williams, "Appalachian Speech," *North Carolina Historical Review* (Spring 1978) and *Southern Mountain Speech* (1992).

Literature

Section Editors: Grace Toney Edwards and Theresa Lloyd

HISTORIAN HENRY D. SHAPIRO, AUTHOR OF THE SEMINAL *APPALACHIA ON OUR MIND: The Southern Mountains and Mountaineers in the American Consciousness, 1870–1920*, has noted that Appalachia is in many ways a textual construction more than two centuries in the making. It follows, then, that the various faces of the region are best revealed in the writings of authors, both native and non-native, whose texts are the primary materials for that process of regional invention. Directly and indirectly, these writings address such questions as what and where Appalachia is, who Appalachians are, and who legitimately speaks for them. Additionally, the region's literary output reveals the textual interplay among Appalachia's southern, central, and northern subregions.

It is far to the east of Appalachia, however, that one discovers the first depictions of what would become a primary Appalachian trope: the backwoodsman, best known today in his twentieth-century incarnation, the hillbilly. Although this early literature cannot be considered Appalachian per se, examination of it is crucial to an understanding of the subsequent literature of Appalachia. Early American texts are filled with anxious discussions of the supposedly barbarizing effect of the wilderness on white settlers. In 1729 William Byrd II, surveyor of the dividing line between Virginia and North Carolina and owner of a vast plantation in Tidewater Virginia, described eastern North Carolina frontiersmen as lazy lubberlanders who lived in hovels and foisted farmwork off on their wives. Hector St. John de Crèvecoeur, writing in 1782 from the New York frontier when it was east of Appalachia, concurred with Byrd, claiming that, once Euro-Americans on the frontier picked up a gun to go hunting, they said goodbye to the plow. As the less mountainous parts of the early American frontier were transformed from wilderness to pastoral or urban societies, the rugged, heavily forested Appalachians came to be seen as immune to the civilizing process. Furthermore, since the pre-romantic Western tradition had regarded mountains as the most dangerous type of wilderness, it was but one short step to associate the wild American frontiersman with the mountain dweller. Hence, the description of the Appalachian male devolved into one of three archetypes of the semi-civilized backwoodsman—the violent barbarian, the noble savage, or the comic rube. In *Letters from the South* (1817), New Yorker James Kirke Paulding, who like Byrd and Crèvecouer lived east of Appalachia, contrasts civilized eastern seaboard Tuckahoes with primitive mountain Cohees. The lead character in Paulding's *The*

Facing page: Engraving on woodblock from a drawing by Julian Walbridge Rix (1850–1903). This illustration accompanied the article "Through Cumberland Gap on Horseback" by James Lane Allen in *Harper's Monthly* (June 1886). Often received as more documentary than art, travel writing has influenced—and continues to influence—economic development and tourism as well as cultural perceptions of the region.

Illustration from an 1859 edition of James Fenimore Cooper's *The Last of the Mohicans,* first published in 1826. Cooper's Natty Bumppo was a prototype for the character of the frontiersman, antecedent of the mountaineer.

Lion of the West, Nimrod Wildfire, who is based in part on David Crockett, is a comic backwoods trickster who invades polite society.

In contrast to his fellow New Yorkers, James Fenimore Cooper, who spent much of his life in a small northern Appalachian town, presents an idealized portrait of the frontiersman in his character Natty Bumppo, hero of his five Leatherstocking novels, which were published between 1823 and 1841. Based in part on the legend of Daniel Boone, which in turn harked back to the idea of the noble savage, Natty is not only a skilled woodsman but also the moral exemplar of his society, indignant over the rapacity of the civilized world.

Another preoccupation of early Appalachian writings is the environment. Late-eighteenth- and early-nineteenth-century descriptions of the region's mountains reveal a shift from a perception of mountains as gloomy warts on the landscape—a point of view that lasted from the Greek and Roman classical period through eighteenth-century neoclassicism—to the romantic notion that mountains are among the most sublime of all natural features. Whereas Thomas Jefferson lauds its mountains for being laid out in regularly spaced ridges and valleys in *Notes on the State of Virginia* (1787), William Bartram, a naturalist who traveled through southern Appalachia on the cusp of the American Revolution, waxes eloquent on wild, scenic mountain views in his 1791 narrative of his expedition. In 1850 Susan Fenimore Cooper, daughter of James Fenimore Cooper, penned one of America's first significant environmental books, *Rural Hours,* celebrating a year's observations of nature in northern Appalachia.

As Native Americans fell under the critical eye of the explorers, they typically fared less well than did the idyllic "Garden of God" in which they lived. Though writers such as Lieutenant Henry Timberlake (1765) and Brothers Abraham Steiner and Frederick C. De Schweinitz (1799) attempted objectivity in their reports, Anne Newport Royall was openly negative and even cruel in her 1830 *Letters from Alabama on Various Subjects.* Bartram's admiration of the Cherokee was a notable exception.

Important Native American and African American voices spoke throughout the early and middle nineteenth century. The Cherokee, already in possession of a rich oral tradition that ethnographer James Mooney would later collect and publish in *The Sacred Formulas of the Cherokee* (1891) and *The Myths of the Cherokee* (1900), entered into print culture after Cherokee scholar Sequoyah invented a syllabary that enabled printing and literacy in the Cherokee language. In his "Address to the Whites" (1826), Elias Boudinot argued the Cherokee cause as he attempted to solicit funds for a printing press; later, he served as editor of the *Cherokee Phoenix,* a bilingual Cherokee-English newspaper. African Americans writing in the mid- to late nineteenth century focused on abolition and after emancipation on the lives of freedmen and women. Martin Delaney's *Blake; or, The Huts of America* (1859–61) is an antislavery novel. Part slave narrative, part classic American autobiography, *Up from Slavery* describes Booker T. Washington's upbringing as a slave child in the foothills of Virginia's Blue Ridge and his attempts to secure an education when, after the Civil War, he and his family moved to the saltworks region of West Virginia.

Appalachia in mid-nineteenth-century literature is distinguished from the larger southern or mid-Atlantic frontier faintly, if at all. During this time, most references to southern Appalachia appeared in the writings of the Old Southwestern humorists, whose "big lies" sprang from the oral tradition of the tall tale. The master of the genre was George Washington Harris, whose Sut Lovingood is an archetypal hillbilly trickster, akin to the medieval fool in his ability to mock the foibles of polite society. After the Civil War, southern and central Appalachia burst upon the American consciousness as a separate region, largely through publications in mass-market magazines such as *Harper's*, *Lippincott's*, *Appletons'*, and the *Atlantic Monthly*. Many of these texts were the observations of travelers, educators, and missionaries; others fit into the genre of local color fiction.

Local color depicted specific locales and customs with an emphasis on little-known, exotic spots where people were considered quaint and different. Writing in 1873, Will Wallace Harney dubbed Appalachia and its inhabitants "a strange land and peculiar people," a sentiment echoed by most other local color writers, who generally came from outside the region and took neither the time nor trouble to become acquainted with the subjects about which they wrote. Two exceptions to this superficiality were Rebecca Harding Davis, a resident of Wheeling, (West) Virginia, whose short stories such as "The Yares of the Black Mountains" (1875) are sympathetic portrayals of mountain culture, and Mary Noailles Murfree, a native of middle Tennessee who spent summers with her family in the Cumberland Mountains and, writing under the pseudonym "Charles Egbert Craddock," produced numerous sentimentalized short story collections and novels about Appalachia, including *In the Tennessee Mountains* (1884) and *The Prophet of the Great Smoky Mountains* (1885). Murfree's successor, John Fox Jr., son of a well-to-do family in the Bluegrass region of Kentucky, spent time in eastern Kentucky and Big Stone Gap, Virginia, at first pursuing family interests in mineral resources before embarking on a literary career depicting mountain people. In fiction such as the best-selling novels *The Little Shepherd of Kingdom Come* (1903) and *The Trail of the Lonesome Pine* (1908), Fox, like Murfree and less conscientious local colorists, depicts the mountains as primarily pastoral, isolated refuges where people make their living through subsistence farming, hunting, fishing, and moonshining. Although full industrialization, especially in the coalfields, contributed significantly to disruptions in established socioeconomic patterns and folkways, conflict in these novels is typically depicted as resulting from feuds.

Beginning in 1905, with the publication of Emma Bell Miles's remarkable *The Spirit of the Mountains*, came a series of book-length studies of Appalachia. Spawned by the earlier magazine pieces, many of these volumes amplified the idea of the southern mountaineer as contemporary ancestor. Although the classic among these texts is Horace Kephart's *Our Southern Highlanders* (1913; revised 1922), a study of the North Carolina mountaineers among whom Kephart lived in the Great Smokies, Miles, who spent her adolescence and adult life in southeastern Tennessee, is considered today to reflect more of the culture's regional essence than the work of the local colorists. Her book is therefore seen as a bridge from romantic local color to twentieth-century realism.

In the 1920s and 1930s, a general ferment of southern writing sprang up almost as a direct challenge to H. L. Mencken's 1919 assertion that the entire South was so devoid of aesthetic expression that it could be seen as a "Sahara of the Bozart." During this period, native Appalachian authors began to publish noteworthy serious fiction and poetry. Like American fiction of these decades in general, some of this writing exhibited the influence of modernism; other texts were social realist in orientation. In his poetic and experimental autobiographical novel *Look Homeward, Angel* (1929), high modernist Thomas Wolfe re-created his hometown of Asheville, North Carolina. Social realist Elizabeth Madox Roberts examined rural poverty. Jesse Stuart, who for many people is synonymous with Appalachian literature, began his long publishing career during this era with the poetry collection *Man with a Bull-Tongue Plow* (1934).

The profound damage that extractive industries wrought in Appalachia's culture and landscape led to a strong current of social protest in the region's literature, beginning with the 1861 publication of Rebecca Harding Davis's graphic *Life in the Iron-Mills*. The literature of social protest became particularly prominent with the development of the coal industry and the out-migration of Appalachians to the industrial cities of the non-mountain South, the Midwest, and the Northeast. Olive Tilford Dargan's *Call Home the Heart* (1932) deals with labor issues among mountaineers working in the textile industry; James Still's *River of Earth* (1940) poignantly describes the plight of a coal-mining family; and Harriette Simpson Arnow's *The Dollmaker* (1954) examines the impact of life in a Detroit industrial ghetto on a Kentucky mountain family. Perhaps the best-known outcry against the abuse of the Appalachian landscape and people is Harry Caudill's *Night Comes to the Cumberlands* (1963). Controversial for its harsh criticisms not only of industrialists but also mountaineers themselves, Caudill's book is a powerful jeremiad seeking to redeem a chosen people from imminent destruction. Denise Giardina continued the tradition of coalfield protest in her 1987 novel *Storming Heaven*.

Twentieth-century northern Appalachian literature echoes the social protest of central Appalachian authors and often focuses on miners and industrial workers. Probably the classic northern Appalachian text from this period is Thomas Bell's *Out of this Furnace* (1934), which describes the hardships of life in the western Pennsylvania steel industry.

Much post–World War II Appalachian literature has a pronounced historical bent. Many works of fiction by Wilma Dykeman, Mary Lee Settle, Lee Smith, and Robert Morgan look back to a pioneer or agrarian past. Having lived through the wholesale post–World War II transformation of Appalachia from farming, mining, and timbering to a modern industrial and service economy, poets such as Jim Wayne Miller and Jeff Daniel Marion lament the loss of an agrarian lifestyle and landscape.

Since the 1970s, so much good writing has emanated from southern and central Appalachia that the period is sometimes known as the Appalachian Renaissance. Contemporaneous with the rise of Appalachian studies as a discipline and sometimes motivated by the same desire to rectify negative attitudes toward the region, this literature presents Appalachia as a region of remarkable diversity. In addition to the agrarian historicizing of authors such as Smith, Morgan, and Miller, other Appalachian Renaissance authors, including Cormac McCarthy, Breece D'J Pancake, Lisa Alther, and Pinckney Benedict, are distinctly urban or presentist in orientation. Yet other of these authors, such as Jayne Anne Phillips and Dorothy Allison, manifest a postmodern tendency to ignore history altogether. Many authors, however, would agree with out-migrant poets such as Miller and Charles Wright that Appalachian origins should not be forgotten. Fred Chappell's narrative persona in the book-length poem *Midquest* (1981) is perhaps representative of the group: Ole Fred has moved out of the mountains to hobnob with intellectual and artistic luminaries yet frankly and fondly acknowledges his highland roots.

In contrast to the agrarian focus of much southern and central Appalachian literature, northern Appalachian writing since World War II has tended to be concerned with urban issues. Mary Roberts Rinehart set several of her early mysteries in her native Pittsburgh. John Edgar Wideman has described the urban African American experience in Pennsylvania, using subject matter that his nephew Albert French has also pursued.

Along with French and Wideman, Henry Louis Gates Jr. emerged as a significant late-twentieth-century chronicler of Appalachia's African American experience. Gates, a leading scholar of African American literature, was born and reared in Piedmont, West Virginia, in a segregated community nostalgically depicted in *Colored People: A Memoir* (1994). Despite Gates's affection for Piedmont, his text records indignities that African Americans in West Virginia suffered under Jim Crow and thus serves as a reminder that, despite the myth of a racially benign Appalachia, race relations in the region have mirrored those of the rest of the South. Kentucky poet Frank X Walker coined the term *Affrilachian* to describe African Americans in Appalachia, marginalized within a marginalized society.

One of the hallmarks of the Appalachian Renaissance is the appearance of important anthologies of the region's literature. The first of these was Robert J. Higgs and Ambrose N. Manning's *Voices from the Hills: Selected Readings of Southern Appalachia* (1975). In 1995 Higgs and Manning, along with Jim Wayne Miller, followed *Voices* with the two-volume *Appalachia Inside Out.* Joyce Dyer's *Bloodroot: Reflections on Place by Appalachian Women Writers* (1998) functions as a manifesto of regional pride.

This impulse to anthologize is part of the larger movement to construct southern Appalachian literature as a discreet entity, not merely the country cousin of southern literature. This movement began with Cratis Williams's magisterial 1,661-page dissertation, "The Southern Mountaineer in Fact and Fiction." Williams's ambitious project examines Appalachian literature from the early travel reports of the 1700s to Arnow's fiction of the 1950s. *Appalachian Journal*, published since 1972 at Appalachian State University, where Williams taught, has featured much literary criticism. Concerns of post-1960s Appalachian literary criticism have included the appropriate topics for Appalachian literature (Must it deal with rural settings? Must its characters belong to the non-elite classes?); the necessity of an author's having an insider's as opposed to an outsider's perspective (Must writing about Appalachian be done by natives?); mimetic accuracy (Does the desire for a positive portrayal of the region affect the presentation of images that might be considered stereotypical?); and postcolonial notions of cultural silencing and marginalization (How does Appalachia, a marginalized region within the larger marginalized South, manifest its "double alterity," or double otherness?). As all these definitional questions suggest, the invention of Appalachian literature is, like any cultural manifestation, a work perpetually in progress.

—Grace Toney Edwards, *Radford University*, and Theresa Lloyd, *East Tennessee State University*

Dwight B. Billings, Gurney Norman, and Katherine Ledford, eds., *Confronting Appalachian Stereotypes: Back Talk from an American Region* (1999); Elizabeth S. D. Engelhardt, *The Tangled Roots of Feminism, Environmentalism, and Appalachian Literature* (2003); Parks Lanier Jr., ed., *The Poetics of Appalachian Space* (1991); Danny L. Miller, *Wingless Flights: Appalachian Women in Fiction* (1996); Henry D. Shapiro, *Appalachian on Our Mind: The Southern Mountains and Mountaineers in the American Consciousness, 1870–1920* (1978); Cratis D. Williams, "The Southern Mountaineer in Fact and Fiction," Ph.D. dissertation, New York University (1961).

African American Literature

African American authors in Appalachia often manifest the same devotion to land and family that characterizes the work of their white counterparts, and the story of their literary output follows a trajectory similar to that of white Appalachian authors. However, the writing of black Appalachian authors also parallels that of African American authors living outside the region in addressing the major social, legal, and economic obstacles that blacks have faced throughout the history of the United States.

The earliest fully developed African American literary genre—one that some scholars call the first truly American literary tradition—was the slave narrative, written by escaped slaves and exposing the horrors of slave life. Although most Appalachian slave testimonies were collected from the oral tradition (particularly noteworthy were the Works Progress Administration's ex-slave interviews of the 1930s), some Appalachian slave accounts were printed prior to the Civil War. Most other black-authored Appalachian writings in the nineteenth century bore the imprint of the slave narrative or manifested a similar concern for the oppression of African Americans. Writer, editor, and physician Martin Delaney, born in 1812 to a slave father and free black mother in Charles Town, (West) Virginia, lived for much of his life in Appalachia's largest city, Pittsburgh, and was an ardent agitator for black rights and black cultural nationalism. In 1847 he founded and coedited the antislavery *North Star* newspaper with abolitionist leader Frederick Douglass; later, Delaney wrote *Blake; or, The Huts of America*, which portrayed life in slave society and was serialized in two African American newspapers between 1859 and 1861. Delaney's major work was *The Condition, Elevation, Emigration, and Destiny of the Colored People of the United States, Politically Considered* (1852), a scathing exposé of white racism and a separatist call for African Americans to rely on themselves, not whites, for advancement.

Possessing a conciliatory attitude toward whites that was the antithesis of Delaney's determined separatism, the noteworthy but controversial educator Booker T. Washington penned his autobiography, *Up from Slavery* (1901), within a few decades of the Emancipation Proclamation of 1863. Washington recounted his childhood as a slave in the foothills of Virginia's Blue Ridge Mountains and his subsequent freedom, education, and work at the Tuskegee Institute, the African American school that he founded in Alabama.

Unlike Delaney and Washington, the late-nineteenth-century poet Effie Waller Smith seldom overtly addressed the issue of race in her poetry, preferring to encode racial markers subtly. Born in 1879 in Pike County, Kentucky, of parents who were former slaves but had achieved middle-class status, the well-educated Smith published in prestigious magazines such as *Putnam's* and collected her poetry in three volumes. Smith's writings celebrate the natural beauty of the mountains, the cultural significance of artifacts and foodways, and the importance of women's independence. Smith eventually moved north to escape harsh southern segregation.

Despite the strong showing of Delaney, Washington, and Smith, black Appalachians generally remained unpublished throughout most of the late nineteenth and early twentieth centuries. During this era, however, African American characters did occasionally appear in white-authored texts about Appalachia. Generally their roles were minor ("real" mountaineers were portrayed as white), and they were rendered in broad, demeaning stereotypes that served chiefly to signify a southern location, as with the loyal black servant of a wounded Confederate veteran sequestered in the North Carolina mountains in Constance Fenimore Woolson's "The French Broad," published in *Harper's New Monthly Magazine* in 1875. As topics in rather than originators of the discourse surrounding them, black Appalachians during this era occupied a position analogous to that of white mountaineers, about whom a great deal of late-nineteenth- and early-twentieth-century local color literature was written but who wrote almost none of it themselves.

Although black Appalachians may have been largely absent from the written literary tradition of early Appalachia, their creativity flourished in the oral tradition, a pattern of literary output that, again, parallels that of white mountaineers, who also long enjoyed a rich oral culture. The legend of John Henry, for example, grew out of the experiences of an actual African American railroad worker in West Virginia; the tale quickly spread from that state to become a significant part of nineteenth-century African American lore throughout the South and later entered the Euro-American tradition as well. White folklorist William Lynwood Montell's *The Saga of Coe Ridge* (1970) draws heavily on the oral tradition to reconstruct the history of a post–Civil War African American settlement on Kentucky's Cumberland Plateau.

One would not want to carry the parallels between the black and white Appalachian literary traditions too far since, however marginalized white Appalachians may have been by the hegemonic culture surrounding them, African Americans in Appalachia have faced the additional burden of being oppressed by white mountaineers themselves. Consequently, Appalachian African American writers of the twentieth century, like their nineteenth-century forebears, tended to focus on racial injustice and the uniqueness of the African American experience in the region, topics not usually dealt with by many Appalachian-born white authors of the era. Like earlier, non-native local colorists, white Appalachian writers tended to portray the region as Euro-American.

Notable exceptions to the invisibility of black Appalachians in white-authored twentieth-century texts include, among others, Willa Cather's *Sapphira and the Slave Girl* (1940) and John Ehle's *Move Over, Mountain* (1957) and *The Journey of August King* (1971).

Since the mid-twentieth century, Appalachian African Americans have made strong showings in a variety of genres. Significant southern and central Appalachian fiction writers include William Demby and Virginia Hamilton. Set in West Virginia, Demby's novel *Beetlecreek* (1950) centers around the difficulty of interracial relations in a racist society. Hamilton's children's novel *M. C. Higgins, the Great* (1974) won the Newbery Medal and the National Book Award for its account of a young African American boy living in a strip-mined section of Appalachian Ohio.

Pittsburgh produced a number of noteworthy African American authors who were active in the late twentieth century. In fiction and nonfiction texts such as *Damballah* (1981), *Hiding Place* (1981), and *Sent for You Yesterday* (1983), John Edgar Wideman examines Homewood, an African American community in Pittsburgh. The writings of Wideman's nephew Albert French investigate racial injustice in the Deep South (*Billy*, 1993) and in Pittsburgh (*I Can't Wait on God*, 1998), a range that underscores the commonality of the African American experience both inside and outside Appalachia. The work of playwright August Wilson (*Ma Rainey's Black Bottom*, produced in 1984; *Fences*, 1987; *Joe Turner's Come and Gone*, 1988; and others) focuses on urban African American males seeking to balance relationships, personal ambitions, and the limitations placed on them by white society, providing a comprehensive history of African American experience in the twentieth century.

In the early 1990s, a group of African American authors known as the Affrilachians coalesced in Lexington, Kentucky. Hailing from throughout Appalachia, these authors, seeking to expand the notion that all Appalachians were white, tapped both their mountain and their African American roots. Poet Frank X Walker first began using the term *Affrilachian* to refer to his own experience and work; the Affrilachian group grew to include Nikky Finney, Kelly Ellis, Daundra Scisney-Givens, Bernard Clay, Crystal Wilkinson, and others.

Like many mountain whites, and like African Americans throughout the South, African Americans have often left Appalachia to seek work and a better life elsewhere. Consequently, many prominent twentieth-century African American authors with Appalachian roots are expatriates, and often their work does not reflect their regional origin. Into this group fall Alex Haley, Margaret Walker, Ishmael Reed, Julia Fields, Norman Jordan, and Sonia Sanchez. Although living as an expatriate for a number of years, poet Nikki Giovanni, reared in Knoxville, Tennessee, eventually returned to Appalachia to teach at Virginia Polytechnic Institute and State University.

The expatriate to give fullest tribute to his Appalachian origin is the well-known scholar Henry Louis Gates Jr., who was born and reared in West Virginia but has lived most of his adult life in the Northeast, where he chairs Harvard University's Afro-American Studies program. Gates's memoir *Colored People* (1994) is an affectionate portrait of his African American neighborhood in Piedmont, West Virginia, in the 1950s and 1960s. The text illustrates the complexity of the African American experience in Appalachia. Gates's friends and family love the mountains and small-town life, and they are tightly bound by ties of kinship, community, and religion. But just as significant in their lives as these iconic Appalachian attitudes and pursuits are their daily struggles with the racism and discrimination meted out by white Appalachia.

See also: AFFRILACHIANS (RACE, ETHNICITY, AND IDENTITY); WALKER, FRANK X.

—Theresa Lloyd, *East Tennessee State University*

Edward J. Cabbell and William H. Turner, eds., *Blacks in Appalachia* (1985); Wilma A. Dunaway, *The African-American Family in Slavery and Emancipation* (2003).

Agee, James

(1909–1955) Novelist and film critic.

James Rufus Agee was born in Knoxville, Tennessee, the son of Hugh James "Jay" and Laura Whitman Tyler Agee. After his father's death, which Agee immortalized in his novel *A Death in the Family*, he moved with his mother to Saint Andrew's School near Sewanee, Tennessee, where he lived and studied from age ten to fourteen. There he made a lifelong friend of Father James Harold Flye; Agee's letters to Father Flye were published in 1962. In 1925 Agee entered Phillips Exeter Academy in New Hampshire. In 1928 he went to Harvard, and in 1931 he was president of the *Harvard Advocate* when it presented a notoriously witty parody of *Time* magazine. This escapade did not prevent Agee from getting a job with *Fortune*, another magazine published by Time, Inc., after graduation.

While writing for *Fortune*, Agee won the 1934 Yale Younger Poets Award for *Permit Me Voyage*, which was later included in *The Collected Poems of James Agee* (1968). In 1936 *Fortune* sent Agee and photographer Walker Evans to Alabama to document the lives of sharecroppers during the Great Depression. The result was not a series of magazine articles but the acclaimed book *Let Us Now Praise Famous Men* (1941).

Agee began writing film reviews for *Time* in 1941. He also wrote film criticism for the *Nation* and feature articles for *Time* and *Life*. Agee's screenplays include *The African*

Queen (1951), directed by John Huston and starring Humphrey Bogart and Katharine Hepburn, and *The Night of the Hunter* (1955), directed by Charles Laughton and starring Robert Mitchum. Bogart won an Academy Award for his role in *The African Queen*, and Agee and Huston's script was nominated for an Oscar. For television, Agee wrote the script for an acclaimed five-part biography of young Abraham Lincoln for the *Omnibus* television series, and he took a small acting part in the drama as the town drunk. His articles about film were posthumously published in *Agee on Film: Reviews and Comments* (1958); this collection was followed by a collection of his screenplays, *Agee on Film: Five Film Scripts* (1960).

In 1950 Agee's health began seriously to deteriorate as he suffered disruptive angina attacks. Although during the decade before his death Agee dedicated much time to film and television work, he was also writing fiction. He published the novella *The Morning Watch* in 1951 as he was also completing *A Death in the Family*. The latter, published posthumously, received the Pulitzer Prize for Fiction in 1958.

In *A Death in the Family*, Agee casts his parents as Jay and Mary Follet and himself as young Rufus. The book sensitively portrays tensions between the mother's urban, Anglo-Catholic background and the father's humble, rural mountain origins. Young Rufus barely comprehends the antagonisms and arguments generated by his father's death in an automobile accident. He seeks to penetrate the mysteries of life and death, but his family, as the novel's prologue sings, "will not, oh, will not, not now, not ever tell me who I am." In one famous scene, the novel presents a visit to Rufus's great-great-grandmother in the Great Smoky Mountains; his father wants his son to know the family of which he is a part. Though Rufus has memories that might bind him to his rural mountain relatives, they are overwhelmed by his sense of alienation and conflict.

When *A Death in the Family* was published in 1957, the editors made a prologue of a lyrical segment, "Knoxville: Summer 1915." The piece was already famous from its earlier publication in *Partisan Review*. That initial publication had so impressed West Virginia–born opera singer Eleanor Steber that in 1947 she commissioned world-renowned composer Samuel Barber to set portions of the text to music as *Knoxville: Summer of 1915 for Soprano and Orchestra, Op. 24*. Steber recorded the work for the CBS Odyssey Legendary Performances series in 1962.

In 1960 Tad Mosel's theatrical version of *A Death in the Family*, entitled *All the Way Home*, also received a Pulitzer Prize. Philip Reisman Jr. in turn adapted the play for a 1963 film version of *All the Way Home*, a David Susskind production starring Jean Simmons and Robert Preston.

See also: AGEE FILMS (MEDIA); DOCUMENTARY FILMS (MEDIA).

—Parks Lanier Jr., *Radford University*

Laurence Bergreen, *James Agee: A Life* (1984); Ross Spears and Jude Cassidy, eds., *Agee: His Life Remembered* (1985).

Agrarianism

Although the term *agrarian* remains closely linked to the Twelve Southerners who published *I'll Take My Stand* in 1930 and to certain other individuals associated with the Vanderbilt University–based group, these writers (with the exception of Caroline Gordon) published little fiction that treats agrarian issues and themes at length. Mid-twentieth-century Appalachian writers, on the other hand, produced an important body of work that seriously considers agrarian themes.

The best agrarian literature involves a complex understanding of farming and an intimate knowledge of the joys and challenges of living close to the land in the subsistence pattern historically characteristic of Appalachia. Agrarian writing acknowledges the benefits—to the land and to the people—of careful stewardship and often depicts the ravages of shortsighted agricultural practices. Agrarian writers also recognize threats to the continued existence of a farm-based way of life posed by industrialization and urbanization, factors that have affected much of Appalachia, where extractive industries such as coal mining and timbering have damaged the land and disrupted traditional patterns of living and migration to urban centers has drawn people away from the region.

Many Appalachian writers have treated these tensions in their work. Kentuckians James Still (1906–2001) and Harriette Simpson Arnow (1908–1986) depict the forces threatening the continued existence of an agrarian way of life and at the same time demonstrate a complex understanding of the demands and benefits of careful, sustainable methods of farming. Although Still and Arnow articulate a preference for an agrarian way of life in the Appalachian Mountains, they express reservations about the feasibility of widespread survival of such a manner of living.

Still's 1940 novel *River of Earth* treats the tension between agrarianism and industrialization within the context of a marital conflict. The mother in the novel, Alpha Baldridge, longs to create a self-sustaining life on a farm with her family; her husband, Brack, prefers to follow the coal mines and work for wages. In the course of the novel, set in the mountains of eastern Kentucky in the 1930s, the family moves from farm to coal camp without ever establishing the permanent home Alpha desires. Still gives full credence to the complexity of the Baldridges' situation. He recognizes the desirability of Alpha's dream of a self-supporting life on the land but also acknowledges the social and economic forces encouraging Brack to seek work in the mines. The conflict remains unresolved at the novel's end, with only

Alpha's brother, Jolly Middleton, achieving a true agrarian self-sufficiency. Unlike his migratory relatives, Jolly carefully farms his own land, drawing both physical and spiritual sustenance from his vocation.

Arnow wrote four novels depicting the lives of rural Kentuckians. *Mountain Path* (1936), *Between the Flowers* (written in the late 1930s but not published until 1999), *Hunter's Horn* (1949), and *The Dollmaker* (1954) cover a particularly turbulent period in American history—roughly the mid-1920s to the mid-1940s. In the novels, Arnow depicts the escalating battle between the settled and self-reliant agrarian community and the outside capitalistic consumer world. This battle culminates in *The Dollmaker*, when the war and war-related industries force the native hill people away from their homes and their farms.

Arnow does not romanticize hill farming in her work, and she often depicts the life as particularly hard on women. However, her fiction also espouses a consistent, knowledgeable, and highly practical brand of agrarianism. Arnow's farmers work hard to restore land damaged by over-farming and other abuses, and they receive a genuine self-sufficiency and spiritual satisfaction in return for their labors. This mutually sustaining relationship between the land and those living from it stands at the heart of her agrarian vision.

Many other Appalachian writers have produced work that can be broadly termed agrarian. In the 1920s, Elizabeth Madox Roberts in *The Time of Man* (1926) and Edith Summers Kelley in *Weeds* (1923) presented detailed treatments of farm life, focusing on its impact on their female protagonists. Arnow and Still's contemporary, Jesse Stuart, wrote both agrarian fiction and poetry, as did Jim Wayne Miller a generation later. Wilma Dykeman's 1973 novel *Return the Innocent Earth* traces the personal and environmental consequences of the shift from family to industrial farming, and Lee Smith's *Fair and Tender Ladies* (1988) ends with the protagonist, Ivy Rowe, protecting her farm from Peabody Coal Company bulldozers.

This list remains partial, and if the definition of agrarian writing is expanded to include all literature dealing with the conflict between a settled, agriculturally based way of life and an ever encroaching industrial world, then the majority of Appalachian authors have worked within the tradition. However, Arnow and Still, contemporaries of the Nashville Agrarians, produced some of the most fully developed agrarian fiction of the region.

See also: ARNOW, HARRIETTE SIMPSON; SECTION OVERVIEW (AGRICULTURE); STILL, JAMES.

—Martha Billips, *Transylvania University*

Steven Mooney, "Agrarian Tragedy: Harriette Arnow's *The Dollmaker*," *Appalachian Journal* (Fall 1991); Gregory Morris, "The Agrarian Impulse in Contemporary American Fiction," *Michigan Quarterly* (Winter 1988); H. R. Stoneback, "Rivers of Earth and Troublesome Creeks: The Agrarianism of James Still," *Kentucky Review* (Autumn 1990).

Allison, Dorothy

(1949–) Novelist, poet, and essayist.

Dealing boldly with issues of gender, class, and sexual orientation, Appalachian-born and -reared Dorothy Allison identifies herself as a "Southern working-class writer." Though influenced by Toni Morrison and classic southern authors Flannery O'Connor, Carson McCullers, and Tennessee Williams, Allison has said that the central fact of her life—and a strong influence on her writing—is that she was born to an unmarried white woman from a desperately poor family in Greenville, South Carolina. Her writings go beyond being mere "victim" literature, however, despite drawing from childhood experiences of abuse and rape at the hands of her stepfather.

Allison's first book of poetry, *The Women Who Hate Me* (1983), explores betrayal, love, sexual desire, and bitterness. Her short story collection *Trash* won two 1988 Lambda Literary Awards for its exploration of themes related to class and sexuality. Four years later, Allison's semi-autobiographical novel *Bastard Out of Carolina* became a best-seller and finalist for the 1992 National Book Award. It was later adapted into a movie directed by Angelica Houston. Despite her autobiographical bent, her "memoir," *Two or Three Things I Know for Sure* (1995), which began as a performance piece, is not a direct telling of her life's story, since she has become convinced that it is impossible to know the truth about her family. Her second novel, *Cavedweller* (winner of 1998 Lambda Award for Lesbian Fiction), also explores autobiographical themes but transcends the anger of her earlier work to explore themes of forgiveness and redemption.

See also: GAY AND LESBIAN LIFE (FAMILY AND COMMUNITY); GAYS AND LESBIANS; WOMEN'S ROLES (FAMILY AND COMMUNITY).

—Marie F. Jones, *East Tennessee State University*

Ammons, A. R.

(1926–2001) Poet.

One of the most acclaimed contemporary American poets, Archie Randolph Ammons, reared in the lowland South, spent much of his adulthood living and writing in Appalachian New York. Born February 18, 1926, near Whiteville in coastal North Carolina, Ammons grew up there on his family's farm, which gave him consolation from deprivation and isolation during the Great Depression. From 1946 to 1949, he majored in biology at Wake Forest College.

Having first composed poetry on board a U.S. Navy destroyer during World War II, Ammons in 1951 enrolled in the University of California at Berkeley to study writing and literature. In 1952 he began a twelve-year residency in southern New Jersey, where, while working as a business executive, he composed the poems that appeared in his first three books. Although the first of these, *Ommateum* (1955), attracted little attention, Ammons's next two books, *Expressions of Sea Level* (1964) and *Corson's Inlet* (1965), established his reputation as a major poet. In 1964 Ammons accepted an instructorship at Cornell University. Virtually all his subsequent poetry was written while he lived in Ithaca, New York, and taught at Cornell, for years as the Goldwin Smith Professor of Poetry.

Ammons was encyclopedic in his range of interests. In many poems, including the acclaimed "Easter Morning," he explores his southern identity, while in other poems, such as "The Ridge Farm," he chronicles life in his adopted region. For his poetry Ammons received, among other accolades, the National Book Award (twice), the Bollingen Prize, a Guggenheim Fellowship, the National Book Critics Circle Award, and a MacArthur Fellowship. He died February 25, 2001.

See also: POST–WORLD WAR II POETS.

—Ted Olson, *East Tennessee State University*

Anderson, Sherwood

(1876–1941) Fiction writer and journalist.

Mentor to Ernest Hemingway and William Faulkner, who regarded him as the literary father of their generation of writers, Sherwood Anderson grew up in Ohio, made a name for himself in Chicago, and spent much of the final sixteen years of his life in southwestern Virginia's Grayson and Smyth Counties.

As a boy, Anderson attended school sporadically. When he became an adult, he established a company that sold mail-order paint. Although he was successful, an emotional breakdown at age thirty-six prompted him to forsake the business and move to Chicago, where he became a writer. The 1919 publication of *Winesburg, Ohio*, a collection of linked short stories using spare language to weave tales of defeated, stunted, and grotesque victims of small-town life, established Anderson as an important author.

By 1925 Anderson, fearing that he had lost his creative spark, rented a summer place in the highlands of Grayson County, Virginia, where he produced *Tar: A Midwest Childhood* (1926). He bought a piece of land in a nearby valley, and the next year he built a home of logs and fieldstone, naming it Ripshin after a creek that flowed through the property. In 1927 Anderson purchased two weekly newspapers in Marion, Virginia, the *Smyth County News* and the *Marion Democrat*. After years of writing about the dark side of small towns, he was optimistic about Marion and the surrounding countryside. He operated the papers as if Smyth County were the center of the universe, enthusiastically covering hog killings, corn plantings, and a hen's laying an egg on Main Street. His rustic alter ego, a columnist named "Buck Fever," commented on local people and politics.

Anderson enjoyed newspapering, but he was still restless. In 1929 his third marriage ended, and he turned the newspapers over to a son. He traveled widely after that, still using Virginia as a home base and occasionally writing for the weeklies. In 1933 he married Eleanor Copenhaver, a Marion native who worked across the South in support of organized labor. He joined her fight on behalf of textile workers demanding decent wages and conditions. His last novel, *Kit Brandon* (1936), tells the story of a Virginia moonshiner's daughter. Although it contains powerful scenes, it was a critical disappointment and evidence that his Appalachian years had ultimately failed to reverse his decline as a novelist.

Anderson's 1941 death was untimely. During a South American goodwill tour, he died of peritonitis in the Panama Canal Zone, apparently after swallowing a toothpick. Since 1976, the Sherwood Anderson Association, a volunteer group based in Marion, has worked to preserve his Virginia legacy, sponsoring an annual short story contest for children and adults.

See also: TEXTILE INDUSTRY (BUSINESS, INDUSTRY, AND TECHNOLOGY); TEXTILE WORKERS (LABOR).

—Michael Hudson, *Roanoke Times*

Sherwood Anderson, *Return to Winesburg* (1967) and *Sherwood Anderson's Memoirs* (1942); Ray Lewis White, ed., *The Achievement of Sherwood Anderson* (1966).

Armstrong, Anne W.

(1872–1958) Writer and businesswoman.

Anne Wetzell Armstrong's best-known novel, *This Day and Time* (1930), portrays the life, speech, and customs of mountain people in upper east Tennessee during the early twentieth century. Born September 20, 1872, in Grand Rapids, Michigan, Armstrong grew up in Knoxville, Tennessee. She attended Mount Holyoke College and the University of Chicago but apparently did not earn a degree.

Armstrong was personnel director at National City Company of New York City from 1918 to 1919, when she became assistant manager of industrial relations for Eastman Kodak Company, a position that she held until 1923. She began writing and lecturing on business and labor relations and became the first woman invited to speak before the Tuck School of Business at Dartmouth and the Harvard School of Business Administration.

In the late 1920s, Armstrong and her husband, Robert F. Armstrong, retired to their summer home on the Holston River across from the Big Creek section of Sullivan County, Tennessee. Big Creek and the mountain people of that area provided the setting and characters for *This Day and Time*. The story takes place shortly before construction of the Tennessee Valley Authority (TVA) dams and touches on their threat to the mountain people's way of life. Armstrong herself was forced to leave her home, Knobside, when TVA built South Holston Dam and the area was covered by a lake.

Armstrong's other novel, *The Seas of God* (1915), is set in Knoxville. She also left an unpublished autobiography, "Of Time and Knoxville," about her early life there. Her numerous nationally published articles include "The Southern Mountaineers" (*Yale Review*, March 1935) and "As I Saw Thomas Wolfe" (*Arizona Quarterly*, Spring 1946). Armstrong died March 17, 1958, in Abingdon, Virginia.

See also: APPALACHIAN ENGLISH IN LITERATURE (LANGUAGE); SECTION OVERVIEW (LABOR); TENNESSEE VALLEY AUTHORITY (GOVERNMENT).

—Linda Behrend, *University of Tennessee*

Arnow, Harriette Simpson

(1908–1986) Fiction and nonfiction writer.

Highly respected for her fictional portrayals of Appalachian hill people, Harriette Simpson Arnow set most of her fiction and nonfiction in and around the Cumberland Mountains of Kentucky, where she grew up. The second of six children of Elias Thomas Simpson and Mollie Jane Denney Simpson, she was born at home in Wayne County, Kentucky, and moved with her family from Bronston to Burnside in 1913. She attended public schools in Burnside and private schools while her father worked in the Kentucky oil fields, graduating from Burnside High School in 1924.

Two years later, soon after receiving a teaching certificate from Berea College, Arnow accepted a teaching position at the age of eighteen in a one-room school in Pulaski County, Kentucky. Her experiences there became the basis for her first novel, *Mountain Path*, about an inexperienced teacher named Louisa (Arnow's middle name) who teaches in a rural, subsistence-farming community and boards with the family of one of her pupils.

Arnow graduated from the University of Louisville in 1931 and worked as a teacher until she moved to Cincinnati in 1934. She held down odd jobs as a waitress, typist, and clerk to support herself as a writer. During the Great Depression, she had modest success as a short story writer, placing at least eight stories in such magazines as *Atlantic Monthly*, *Southern Review*, and *Esquire*. At this time, she also wrote her first two novels, *Mountain Path* and *Between the Flowers* (the latter published posthumously).

While employed by the Federal Writers' Project in Cincinnati, she met and married Harold B. Arnow, a former Chicago newspaper reporter who shared her dream of leaving the city and buying a farm, where they could be self-sufficient and write. They purchased 150 acres in Keno, Kentucky, and moved there in 1939. During the next five years, though the Arnows found little time for writing, they began a family. Their first child, a son, and their third, a daughter, died as infants and were buried in a family cemetery in Kentucky. Their second child, a daughter, was born in 1941. In 1945 the Arnows moved into wartime housing in Detroit, where their fourth child, a son, was born in 1946.

While living in wartime Detroit, Arnow began writing *Hunter's Horn* (1949), a novel she thought of as a sequel to *Mountain Path*. Her working title for *Hunter's Horn* had been "End of the Gravel" because the novel extends the story of "progress" and roads that change Kentucky mountain life. The novel presents strong-willed women who both gain and lose as their community changes. It is also about obsession—the dangers of single-minded pursuits that ultimately destroy people. Farmer and fox hunter Nunn Ballew chases the elusive red fox "King Devil" until he finally understands what the chase has cost him, his family, and his community. *Hunter's Horn* had an outstanding reception, with the *New York Times Book Review* calling it one of the year's ten best novels and *Saturday Review*'s national critics' poll voting it "Best Novel of the Year."

Arnow's third novel, *The Dollmaker* (1954), which Joyce Carol Oates has called "our most unpretentious masterpiece," received even greater acclaim as a national bestseller and runner-up for the National Book Award in 1955. The culmination of her trilogy on progress, the novel offers a particularly realistic and insightful portrayal of women who must adjust to social change, loss, and threats to their survival. In *The Dollmaker*, Gertie Nevels and her family move from the farming community of Little Smokey Creek, Kentucky, to Detroit during World War II. Although Arnow had thought of naming the novel "Highway" because it continues her story of the changes brought by roads to a Kentucky farming community, she chose *The Dollmaker* to focus attention on Gertie as a woman who finds a way to use her heritage to carve out a new life in the city.

Arnow wrote three other novels. *The Weedkiller's Daughter* (1970), her only book set entirely in Detroit, focuses on Susie Schnitzer, a teenaged environmentalist who rebels against pollution, her father, and McCarthyism. *The Kentucky Trace* (1974), set during the American Revolution, deals with a land surveyor with the androgynous name of Leslie who adopts a child and befriends a young Indian to create a makeshift family in the wilderness. The central characters of *Between the Flowers* (written in 1938, published in 1999) are Delphine Costello, an overprotected young Kentucky woman who has seen little of the world, and Marshall Gregory, an oil man who has done dangerous work and lived in South America. Each is attracted to what the other has, a pattern that replicates Arnow's frequent depiction of couples who work at cross purposes, failing to communicate and living with divided loyalties.

In addition to writing roughly twenty nonfiction essays and reviews, Arnow devoted years to producing two landmark studies of pioneer history, *Seedtime on the Cumberland* (1960) and *Flowering of the Cumberland* (1963). She described them as "companion" books rather than sequels, with the first describing the survival of the lone settler and the second presenting the community life of early pioneers. She also completed one autobiographical book, *Old Burnside* (1977), which describes her hometown and childhood.

See also: AGRARIANISM; APPALACHIAN ENGLISH IN LITERATURE (LANGUAGE); APPALACHIAN SOCIAL ISSUES OUTSIDE THE REGION (URBAN APPALACHIAN EXPERIENCE).

—Sandra L. Ballard, *Appalachian State University*

Harriette Simpson Arnow, *Old Burnside* (1977); Haeja K. Chung, ed., *Harriette Simpson Arnow: Critical Essays on Her Work* (1995).

Awiakta, Marilou

(1936–) Poet and nonfiction writer.

Of Cherokee and European heritage, Marilou Awiakta was born in 1936 in Knoxville, Tennessee, and grew up in Oak Ridge, a major center for nuclear research and one of the sites of the Manhattan Project, which produced the material for the first atomic bombs. These diverse influences would later become prominent in Awiakta's writings. As a child, Awiakta thrived "behind the fence" in Oak Ridge's regimented and science-dominated yet eclectic and culturally diverse community, which stimulated her thinking and nurtured her creative talents. She was educated at the University of Tennessee in Knoxville, where she met her husband, Paul Thompson, and earned a B.A. in French and English in 1958. She reared her three children and from 1964 to 1967 worked as a civilian liaison officer and French translator for the U.S. Air Force in France. She knew since childhood that she would write poetry after her mother asked, "What will you do for the people?"

In addition to numerous essays, Awiakta has written three books: *Abiding Appalachia: Where Mountain and Atom Meet* (1978), *Rising Fawn and the Fire Mystery: A Story of Heritage, Family, and Courage, 1833* (1983), and *Selu: Seeking the Corn-Mother's Wisdom* (1993). Her work deals with contemporary issues concerning the environment, gender relations, abortion, native cultures, and technology. She synthesizes scientific tradition with Cherokee philosophy, including the Cherokee belief that the universe is governed by harmony between nature and humans. In her depiction of Selu, the Cherokee corn goddess, Awiakta emphasizes a feminine source of mystical knowledge, as have Paula Gunn Allen and many other Native American women authors.

See also: CHEROKEE FAMILIES AND COMMUNITIES (FAMILY AND COMMUNITY); NATIVE AMERICANS AND APPALACHIAN LITERATURE; OAK RIDGE NATIONAL LABORATORY (BUSINESS, INDUSTRY, AND TECHNOLOGY).

—John C. Nemeth, *Oak Ridge Associated Universities*

Bartram, William

(1739–1823) Writer, artist, and naturalist.

Born in Kingsessing, Pennsylvania, William Bartram was the son of John Bartram, a Quaker farmer and internationally renowned botanist who established one of the first botanical gardens in English North America. William Bartram was an accomplished illustrator and naturalist, as well as a writer now known chiefly for his *Travels through North and South Carolina, Georgia, East and West Florida, the Cherokee Country, the Extensive Territories of the Muscogulges, or Creek Confederacy, and the Country of the Chactaws.* First published in 1791 in Philadelphia, the book is an account of an expedition that Bartram took from March 1773 to January 1777, during which he traveled widely, drew and collected botanical specimens, and wrote. Bartram's *Travels* holds an important place in American literary history, and the section that describes southern Appalachia has become standard source material for novelists and poets, as well as for botanists, anthropologists, and geographers interested in the region.

In May 1775, a month after the beginning of the Revolutionary War, Bartram followed a British trading path up the Savannah River into the valley of the Little Tennessee in the region of the Cherokee Middle Towns. He got as far into the southern mountains as the vicinity of present-day Andrews, in Cherokee County, North Carolina, before turning back. His accounts of the region appear in several chapters of the *Travels.* These chapters juxtapose scientific reports of flora and fauna, lyrical evocations of landscapes, and detailed descriptions of British traders and Cherokee inhabitants. Idyllic passages on the people of the town of Cowee are especially poignant because Cowee, along with other Middle Towns, was subsequently destroyed during the Revolutionary War.

Acknowledged as a valuable scientific document (the book records, for example, 215 birds native to the Southeast, the most complete list at the time), the *Travels* was nonetheless largely dismissed in America through the nineteenth century as too rhapsodic and too sympathetic with Indians. In Europe, however, it was reprinted in at least eight pirated editions within the first decade of its publication, and it influenced the European romantic vision of the American wilderness. Scholars have identified Bartram's influence in Samuel Taylor Coleridge's "Kubla Khan" and William Wordsworth's "Ruth," as well as in works by Dorothy Wordsworth, Charles Lamb, Percy Bysshe Shelley, Alfred, Lord Tennyson, and others. The French romanticist Chateaubriand also adapted entire passages from the *Travels.* American interest in Bartram's work was revived in the early twentieth century, and Bartram's *Travels* is now viewed as an example of the American transition from the Enlightenment to the age of romanticism. Modern readers also value Bartram for his celebratory writing about nature.

In 1976 a Bartram Trail Conference was established by the governors of eight southeastern states and charged with developing and maintaining a historic and recreational trail that roughly follows Bartram's route through the Southeast. Though it is unmarked and poorly maintained in places, some 220 miles of the trail run from Augusta, Georgia, into the mountains of western North Carolina.

See also: FLOODPLAIN FORESTS (ECOLOGY); NATURALIST ILLUSTRATORS (VISUAL ARTS).

—Kevin E. O'Donnell, *East Tennessee State University*

Francis Harper, ed., *The Travels of William Bartram: Naturalists' Edition* (1958); Thomas Slaughter, ed., *Bartram's Travels and Other Writings* (1996).

Benedict, Pinckney

(1964–) Fiction writer.

Pinckney Benedict has written two collections of short stories, *Town Smokes* (1987) and *The Wrecking Yard* (1992), and a novel, *Dogs of God* (1994). Born in West Virginia, he was educated at Princeton University (B.A., 1986) and the Iowa Writers' Workshop (M.F.A., 1988). He has taught at Princeton, Oberlin College, Hope College, and Hollins College and has published stories in the *Ontario Review, Granta, Gunzio,* and *The Oxford Book of American Short Stories.*

Because of their depiction of West Virginia mountain life as hopeless and violent, Benedict's first stories, collected in *Town Smokes,* often elicited comparisons to the fiction of Breece D'J Pancake, a young West Virginia writer who committed suicide in 1979. Benedict's subsequent works have demonstrated a wider variety of characters and subject matter. In *Dogs of God,* a Wagnerian superman druglord, Tannhauser, sets up a slave-labor marijuana plantation on the site of a former military installation that over the course of its history has also been a resort, a spa, a hippie commune, and a women's prison. Tannhauser blames his crop's failure on a buried space ship that is poisoning the ground, and the novel's denouement involves an apocalyptic shootout. Although the setting and a few of the characters are recognizably West Virginian, most seem to belong to a land closer to Hollywood. *Los Angeles Times* reviewer Chris Goodrich has called this surreal West Virginia of the imagination "Benedictland."

See also: POST–WORLD WAR II FICTION.

—Louis H. Palmer III, *Michigan State University*

Berry, Wendell

(1934–) Fiction writer, poet, essayist, and farmer.

After traveling over the world, Wendell Berry settled in his birthplace of Henry County, Kentucky, where he has lived most of his life with his wife and children. Berry's devotion to place has influenced people internationally to value themselves, their food, and their homeland. Though Berry is not from Appalachia, he has worked closely with Appalachian writers Harry Caudill, James Still, and Gurney Norman, and his text *The Unforeseen Wilderness* focuses on the Red River Gorge in the mountains of Kentucky. In addition, his work has inspired environmental activism throughout Appalachia.

Berry has published extensively in three genres. His fiction includes four novels and four collections of short stories. Among his twenty-five collections of poetry are *Collected Poems, 1957–1982* (1985) and *The Selected Poems of Wendell Berry* (1998). In nonfiction, Berry has produced more than twenty-three works, including *The Unsettling of America: Culture and Agriculture* (1977), a critique of agribusiness and American culture.

Berry contends that people must understand their dependence upon the natural world, and his agrarian ideology insists that a healthy democracy depends on active citizens and small farmers rather than large corporations. In his view, people need to act responsibly for the good of all, and health, not wealth, should be the principal value. Still, he laments how ignorance seems to abound in modern culture, even in regard to fundamentals such as the source of our food and its price in human labor, soil loss, and energy consumption. Berry has devoted much of his life to promoting healthy local economies.

Berry holds A.B. and M.A. degrees from the University of Kentucky, where he was a faculty member from 1964 to 1977 and 1987 to 1993. In more than fifty books, he has advanced his vision of a better world. For this steadfastness and gift of words, he has received many prizes, including a Guggenheim Fellowship and a Lannan Literary Award.

See also: GRASSROOTS ENVIRONMENTAL ACTION (ENVIRONMENT); SUSTAINABLE AGRICULTURE (AGRICULTURE).

—Jim Minick, *Radford University*

Black Mountain Poets and *Black Mountain Review*

The Black Mountain poets were a group of poets who in the 1950s were associated with Black Mountain College, an institution that flourished near Asheville, North Carolina, from 1933 until 1957 and was widely respected in avant-garde artistic circles.

Centering on Charles Olson, who was at the time an administrator of the college, and Robert Creeley, who edited the *Black Mountain Review*, the group included Denise Levertov, Robert Duncan, Ed Dorn, and others. Because the Black Mountain poets' work is so idiosyncratic, defining a rhetoric or aesthetic of Black Mountain poetry is difficult. Some commonalities among the poets are a sense of cultural resistance, explosive experimentation, and great formal concern with the line, the basic unit of their free verse. Many of the movement's poets point to their association with the college during these years as a distinct impetus to their work.

Black Mountain Review occupies a position of prominence in mid-century American literature. During the early 1950s, the journal was one of the few outlets publishing experimental poetry. Allen Ginsberg was among the authors who appeared on its pages, and he was listed as a contributing editor of its seventh volume.

Although the Black Mountain poets, like the college itself, had little interaction with local culture, the association of some of the century's most creative and experimental American authors with western North Carolina is suggestive of the diversity of people drawn to the mountain region and the variety of reasons for their coming.

See also: POST–WORLD WAR II POETS.

—Theresa Lloyd, *East Tennessee State University*

Buck, Pearl S.

(1892–1973) Fiction and nonfiction writer.

Born in Hillsboro, West Virginia, to Presbyterian missionary parents, Pearl Comfort Sydenstricker moved with her family to China when she was three months old. Her immersion in two cultures came full circle when she returned to the United States in 1910 to attend Randolph-Macon Woman's College in Lynchburg, Virginia. In 1917 she married John Lossing Buck, an agricultural economist, and moved back to China. Pearl Buck's best-known work, *The Good Earth*, set in a rural Chinese province, directly reflects her own experiences in Chinese culture.

Buck's works chiefly deal with Chinese culture, but her sense of storytelling, her portrayals of oppressed women, and her rural settings connect her to her Appalachian roots. Growing up, Buck heard stories about her mother's happy childhood in the foothills of the Appalachians, while Buck's Chinese governess, Wang, told her stories of fairies, dragons, and magic swords. Buck's father's distinctly patriarchal household, combined with her observations of the sexual caste system in place for Chinese women, strongly influenced her writings. Because Buck felt male writers were viewed more favorably than women, she published several works under the pseudonym "John Sedges."

The Good Earth won a Pulitzer Prize, even though the book generated considerable controversy, and Buck was the first woman to win the Nobel Prize in Literature. The Chinese press alternately adored and abhorred the work. The novel continues to be the flagship for Buck's enduring popularity. The West Virginia farmhouse in which she was born is now a public historical site.

See also: WOMEN AUTHORS.

—Mary Margaret Thompson, *Southwest Virginia Community College*

Byer, Kathryn Stripling

(1944–) Poet and essayist.

Known for her poems set in the mountains of North Carolina, Kathryn Stripling Byer was born and raised in Camilla, Georgia. In 1966 she graduated from Wesleyan College in Macon, Georgia, and in 1968 completed her M.F.A. at the University of North Carolina at Greensboro, where she studied with Allen Tate and Fred Chappell. In her first book of poetry, *The Girl in the Midst of the Harvest* (1986), Byer began her exploration of the lives of American women. The poems in this volume move between landscapes of the Georgia flatlands of Byer's childhood, the Black Hills of her ancestors, and the Appalachian Mountains of North Carolina.

In 1968 Byer accepted a position as an instructor of English at Western Carolina University in Cullowhee, North Carolina. She married James Byer in 1970, and in 1978 their daughter Corinna was born. Until she retired in 1998, Byer continued to teach at Western Carolina, where she also directed the visiting writers program and served as poet-in-residence.

In 1992 Byer's *Wildwood Flower* was published by Louisiana State University Press and received the Lamont Prize from the Academy of American Poets. Taking its title from the ballad popularized by A. P. Carter, *Wildwood Flower* tells the story of Alma, a woman who is abandoned by her husband and struggles to survive with her child in a remote cabin in the mountains of North Carolina. With her third volume, *Black Shawl* (1998), Byer continued to explore the complex culture and landscapes of early-twentieth-century North Carolina.

The subject of Byer's poetry is women's lives: love, pregnancy, the deaths of family members, solitude, and pleasures such as quilting and dancing. Byer often employs rhyme and traditional meter; some of her stanza forms are traditional and others experimental.

In addition to her full-length volumes, Byer has produced two chapbooks, *Alma* (1983) and *Eve* (1997). A poet, essayist, critic, and reviewer, she has been published in the anthologies *Sixty Years of American Poetry; Like a Summer Peach: Sunbright Poems and Old Southern Recipes; Dream Garden: The Poetic Vision of Fred Chappell;* and *Bloodroot: Reflections on Place by Appalachian Women Writers.*

See also: SENSE OF PLACE (IMAGES AND ICONS).

—Julie Kate Howard, *Caldwell Community College*

Carr, Jess

(1930–1990) Fiction and nonfiction writer.

Jess Carr was born on his grandparents' farm in White Gate, Giles County, Virginia. Much of his work derives from his early experiences there. He attended school in Chicago and served in the United States Marine Corps during the Korean War. When his father became ill, he was released from duty early to return home and run the family farm. Carr moved to Radford, Virginia, in the late 1950s and worked in publishing at the Commonwealth Press. Always an avid reader, he was convinced through his work at the press to try writing and eventually published twelve books.

Carr's first book, a collection of short stories entitled *A Creature Was Stirring and Other Stories,* was published in 1970. Carr is best known for *The Second Oldest Profession: An Informal History of Moonshining in America* (1972), a nonfiction account of the making of illegal whiskey during the period between the Civil War and the end of prohibition. Other nonfiction texts include *The Saint of the Wilderness* (1974), which details the life of the Reverend Robert Sheffey, a circuit-riding Methodist preacher, and *Murder on the Appalachian Trail* (1984), which deals with the 1981 murder of two hikers in Jefferson National Forest near Carr's childhood home. Carr also wrote *The Moonshiners* (1977), a novel about a young woman involved in making and trading illegal whiskey, and, under the pen name "Kathleen Carerra," *Nantahala Love Feast,* a romance novel.

See also: APPALACHIAN TRAIL (TOURISM); METHODIST CIRCUIT RIDERS (RELIGION).

—Phyllis A. Lyle, *Radford University*

Carson, Jo

See Carson, Jo (Performing Arts)

Carson, Rachel

(1907–1964) Writer and conservationist.

A native of rural western Pennsylvania, Rachel Louise Carson helped to inspire the modern environmental movement with her 1962 best-seller *Silent Spring,* which created national concern over the impact of synthetic pesticides on the environment and the human food chain. Focusing on the effects of the insecticide DDT and other chemicals labeled "elixirs of death," the book led to federal controls on pesticides and set the stage for environmental debates that persist decades after its publication and Carson's death.

Born in the rural community of Springdale near the Allegheny River about fifteen miles north of Pittsburgh, Carson acquired a passionate interest in nature from her mother. At Pennsylvania College for Women (now Chatham College), she set out to be a writer but changed her concentration to marine biology. She later received an M.A. degree in zoology from Johns Hopkins University. After working at the University of Maryland and the Woods Hole Marine Biological Laboratory in Massachusetts, Carson became a writer and biologist for the U.S. Bureau of Fisheries, eventually rising in 1952 to the position of top editor of publications for the U.S. Fish and Wildlife Service.

While in government service, Carson began to write books drawn from her expertise in marine biology. Her first, *Under the Sea-Wind,* appeared in 1941. It was followed by *The Sea Around Us* (1951) and *The Edge of the Sea* (1955). Her last book, *The Sense of Wonder* (1965), grew from a magazine article she had written in the 1950s and was published posthumously. Although Carson did not write about Appalachian subjects specifically, *Silent Spring* exerted a powerful impact in her native region, where stream pollution continues to be a major concern, as it did across the country and the world.

Carson died of breast cancer at her home in Silver Spring, Maryland, in 1964. In 1975 the Rachel Carson Homestead Association was created to preserve and restore the five-room farmhouse where Carson was born and reared and where her family lived until 1930.

See also: ENVIRONMENTAL WRITING; WOMEN AUTHORS.

—Rudy Abramson, *Reston, Virginia*

Linda Lear, *Rachel Carson: Witness for Nature* (1997).

Carter, Forrest

(1925–1979) Novelist and segregation activist.

Forrest Carter was born Asa Earl Carter in 1925 in Anniston, Alabama, and reared along Chocoloco Creek in the foothills of the Alabama Appalachians. Carter is best known for the controversies surrounding his book *The Education of Little Tree.*

Carter served in the U.S. Navy during World War II. After his discharge, he enrolled at the University of Colorado as a journalism student but soon took a position as a radio talk show host and dropped out of college. In 1953 he returned to Alabama to work in radio and began to build a reputation as an activist in the crusade against racial integration. Carter published a magazine called the *Southerner,* hosted radio talk shows, and ran unsuccessfully as a protest candidate for Birmingham city commissioner and for lieutenant governor and governor. As a speechwriter for Alabama Governor George Wallace, Carter was the author of Wallace's cry for "Segregation now, segregation tomorrow, segregation forever."

After agitation against integration died down, Carter moved to Florida in 1973 and began writing fiction. He took on the pen name "Forrest" in honor of Nathan Bedford Forrest, the Confederate general who founded the Ku Klux Klan. Carter published his first novel, *Gone to Texas*, in 1973. In 1976 the novel was made into the movie *The Outlaw Josey Wales*, starring Clint Eastwood. That same year, *The Education of Little Tree* was published. *The Vengeance Trail of Josey Wales* also appeared in 1976, and two years later *Cry Geronimo!* (later reprinted as *Watch for Me on the Mountain*) appeared. Carter died in Potosi, Texas, in June 1979.

In 1991, the controversy over *The Education of Little Tree*, which had been released in a new edition, erupted. Carter had claimed the book, which deals with a boy reared by his Cherokee grandparents in the mountains of Tennessee, was autobiographical; however, it was revealed that Carter had no authenticated Cherokee ancestors. As a result, the *New York Times* removed the book from its nonfiction best-seller list and placed it on the fiction list. Moreover, as details about Carter's segregationist background emerged, the book's celebration of racial tolerance seemed to some readers ironic.

Despite the controversies, Carter's books remained in print a generation after his death. In 1991 *The Education of Little Tree* won the first nationwide Abby Award as the book that booksellers most enjoy to recommend, and in 1997 the book was made into a movie of the same name. Carter's work appeals to readers who distrust government interference in personal life and espouse a deep respect for nature.

See also: CHEROKEE (RACE, ETHNICITY, AND IDENTITY); CHILDREN'S LITERATURE; NATIVE AMERICANS AND APPALACHIAN LITERATURE.

—George Brosi, *Berea, Kentucky*

Caudill, Harry

See Caudill, Harry (Humor)

Caudill, Rebecca

(1899–1985) Fiction writer.

Rebecca Caudill, who wrote fiction about Appalachian life for children and young adults, was born on a farm in Harlan County, Kentucky, in 1899. Within five years of her birth, her father moved the family to Tennessee in search of better educational opportunities. Education and a strong sense of community are two major themes in Caudill's writings.

Of her eighteen books for children, four are more aptly categorized as young adult novels. *Barrie and Daughter*, *The Far-Off Land*, *Susan Cornish*, and *Tree of Freedom* provide a rich picture of the strengths and challenges of Appalachian life in the early twentieth century. Each novel has a strong female protagonist, and each highlights four characteristics of the best in Appalachian culture: kindness displayed in hospitality and tolerance; freedom and independence; moral integrity; and belief in the importance of education.

All her works for children are loosely autobiographical. *Come Along!* describes the four seasons in Appalachia through haiku. Her nonfiction text *My Appalachia: A Reminiscence* (1966) offers a powerful exploration of the forces shaping both the negatives and positives of the region.

Caudill's legacy continues in the Rebecca Caudill Young Reader's Book Award, established in 1987 by several Illinois library and English associations to honor Caudill, who lived a major part of her life in that state in Urbana. Caudill's books continue to be read, and she remains among the major figures in Appalachian children's literature.

See also: CHILDREN'S LITERATURE; SECTION OVERVIEW (IMAGES AND ICONS).

—Mary Warner, *Western Carolina University*

Chappell, Fred

(1936–) Poet and fiction writer.

One of Appalachia's most notable poets and novelists, Fred Chappell was reared on a farm near Canton, North Carolina, home of the Champion Fibre Company, where he learned firsthand the contrast between agrarian and industrial life. A lifelong resident of North Carolina, he earned his B.A. and M.A. degrees at Duke University and has taught at the University of North Carolina at Greensboro since 1964.

Chappell published his first novel, *It Is Time, Lord* (1963), while still enrolled at Duke. Though that book's setting is outside the mountains, its protagonist, James Christopher, recalls his childhood in western North Carolina. Like *The Inkling* (1965) and *Dagon* (1968), *It Is Time, Lord* is an account of the conflict between will and appetite. While the later two novels are chiefly set in western North Carolina, neither makes the mountains crucial to the book's unfolding action. Much darker in outlook than Chappell's subsequent fiction, these novels of the 1960s contain little of the lively humor or detailed exploration of Appalachian life found in Chappell's later novels and poetry beginning with *The Gaudy Place* (1973), a comic novel set in a city based on Asheville.

Chappell's first book of poems, *The World between the Eyes*, appeared in 1971. But it was not until he published *River* (1975) that he discovered his richest, most evocative subject matter: the region of his birth. *River* was the first of four separate volumes of poems collected in 1981 under the title *Midquest*. Each of the volumes of *Midquest* is organized around one of the elements—water, fire, air, and earth—that ancient and medieval philosophers saw as fundamental to all life, and the book as a whole traces a spiritual quest based in part on Dante's *Divine Comedy*. The semi-autobiographical narrator, Ole Fred, interacts with his parents and grandparents, his wife, Susan, assorted literary friends, and other writers both living and dead. Appearing in several of the poems is the country storekeeper Virgil Campbell, who embodies the spirit of Appalachia itself. *Midquest* is Chappell's poetic masterpiece, a subtly structured celebration of both his mountain heritage and the Western literary tradition. The book's immense variety of poetic forms and genres confirms Chappell's virtuosity as a poet.

While composing *Midquest*, Chappell generated material that he could not incorporate into that book but that he did wish to publish. He thus came to envision a tetralogy of novels intended loosely to parallel the four volumes of *Midquest*. Although he renamed the novels' narrator, calling him Jess Kirkman rather than Ole Fred, Chappell claims that the family portrayed is the same. The title of the first of those novels, *I Am One of You Forever*, voices Jess's—and his creator's—intense love for Appalachia.

Each of the Kirkman novels—the others are *Brighten the Corner Where You Are* (1989), *Farewell, I'm Bound to Leave You* (1996), and *Look Back All the Green Valley* (1999)—is episodic in structure. Like *Midquest*, each displays a range of genres, from straightforward literary realism to rollicking tall tales to allegory and fantasy. Each book also portrays an array of engaging characters whose experiences are rich both in humor and in thematic implication. As a humorist, Chappell is strongly indebted to Old Southwestern humor and to Mark Twain, whose legacy he combines with native Appalachian storytelling traditions. Together, *Midquest* and the Kirkman tetralogy are considered by many critics to be the finest literary tribute to the people and culture of Appalachia published in the last quarter of the twentieth century.

During the years when Chappell was writing the Kirkman novels, he also continued to publish poetry regularly. These volumes are notable for their distinctive structures, their range of poetic forms, and their characteristic combination of lively humor and searching philosophical and moral vision. That humor is absent only from *Castle Tzingal* (1984), a collection of twenty-three poems spoken by nine different characters that reads more like a play than a conventional volume of poems. *Source* (1985) is a more loosely structured book of lyric poems, partially unified by its focus upon the varied origins of narrative. *First and Last Words* (1989) draws upon the seventeenth- and eighteenth-century practice of devising prologues and epilogues to other literary texts, though Chappell also includes musical compositions and paintings and even a film among the works examined. The opening and closing poems, with their biblical sources, highlight the moral and religious dimension of Chappell's work, also evident in *Midquest*. Chappell's use of other writers' and artists' compositions also testifies to his confidence in the past as a resource. That engagement with the literary tradition is equally apparent in *C* (1993), a collection of one hundred epigrams, a quarter of them translations, and in *Spring Garden: New and Selected Poems* (1995). Chappell's books of poetry have been exceptionally diverse—as *Family Gathering* (2000) and *Backsass: Poems of Fred Chappell* (2004) confirm—while demonstrating a consistently high level of achievement.

In addition to novels and poetry, Chappell has published two books of short stories—*Moments of Light* (1980) and *More Shapes Than One* (1991)—and two volumes of essays on poetry. His short stories range widely in subject and style, but among his finest accomplishments in this genre are his historical short fictions based on such figures as Benjamin Franklin, botanist Carl Linnaeus, astronomer William Herschel, and composers Franz Joseph Haydn and Jacques Offenbach.

Over the course of his career Chappell has won many awards, including the Bollingen Prize, the T. S. Eliot Award, the Aiken Taylor Award, the Sir Walter Raleigh Award, the University of North Carolina's O. Max Gardner Award for excellence in teaching, and the French Academy's Prize for the Best Foreign Book *(Dagon)*. In 1998 he began a five-year term as poet laureate of North Carolina.

See also: HUMOR IN APPALACHIAN LITERATURE (HUMOR); STORYTELLING, HISTORY OF (PERFORMING ARTS).

—John Lang, *Emory and Henry College*

Patrick Bizzaro, ed., *Dream Garden: The Poetic Vision of Fred Chappell* (1997) and ed., *More Lights Than One: On the Fiction of Fred Chappell* (2004); John Lang, *Understanding Fred Chappell* (2000).

Children's Literature

Like its adult counterpart, nineteenth-century Appalachian children's literature strongly reflects the enduring regional images largely created by journalists and popular authors writing in the local color tradition. Robert Montgomery Bird's *Nick of the Woods*, set on the Kentucky frontier after the Revolutionary War, was reputedly reprinted twenty times between 1837 and 1928. Its stereotypical views of Native Americans and frontier adventure made it one of the most successful books for juvenile boys. Another nineteenth-century juvenile title is Elisha Sterling King's *Wild Rose of Cherokee* (1895). Although its stilted dialogue and long descriptive sentences make this story of Cherokee history in northeast Tennessee inaccessible to young readers in the twenty-first century, its existence is proof that early writers did indeed produce children's literature about the region. That tradition, though largely ignored, now spans three centuries.

In the early 1900s, the number of books for juveniles began to increase. Joseph Alexander Altsheler's *Forest Runners* (1908) and Payne Erskine's *The Mountain Girl* (1912) are typical of the era. One of the most prolific writers was May Justus, who published more than fifty titles from the 1920s through the 1970s. Typical Justus works include *Children of the Great Smoky Mountains* (1923), *The House in No-End Hollow* (1938), *Lizzie* (1944), and *The Complete Peddler's Pack* (1957). The 1920s also saw the publication of Elizabeth Madox Roberts's *Under the Tree* (1922), a poetry collection whose title echoes the classic *Under the Window* by British poet and illustrator Kate Greenaway. For all its local color, Roberts's poetry is so accessible to modern readers that the University Press of Kentucky reissued it in 1985.

From the 1930s to the 1960s, the number of Appalachian children's books continued to grow, though with little variety in theme or character. Under the pseudonym "Maristan Chapman," the duo of John Stanton Chapman and Mary Isley Chapman produced dozens of juvenile books, including a highly popular series about a Tennessee mountain town called Glen Hazard. Begun in 1928 with *The Happy Mountain*, the series continued well into the 1940s. The work of another 1940s writer, Rebecca Caudill, spans four decades. *Happy Little Family* (1947) introduced Bonnie Fairchild, who appears in a series of books, and *Tree of Freedom* (1949) and *The Far-Off Land* (1964) are both set in the 1780s Kentucky wilderness. But her classics are *A Certain Small Shepherd* (1965) and *Did You Carry the Flag Today, Charley?* (1966). Among books by Ruth and Latrobe Carroll are *Beanie* (1953) and *Tough Enough and Sassy* (1958). Ellis Credle, beginning with *Down, Down the Mountain* (1934), produced books well into the 1950s, including *Big Doin's on Razorback Ridge* (1956) and *Tall Tales from the High Hills* (1957).

Two additional writers who made their appearance in the 1950s and 1960s, Jesse Stuart and Billy Curtis Clark, produced stories about Kentucky mountaineers for the middle grades. In addition to his adult novels, nonfiction, and poetry, Stuart wrote more than a dozen children's books, notably *The Beatinest Boy* (1953), *A Penny's Worth of Character* (1954), *Red Mule* (1955), *Andy Finds a Way* (1961), *A Ride with Huey the Engineer* (1966), and *Old Ben* (1970). Clark's first novel, *Song of the River* (1957), established him in the Stuart tradition, which he continued with *The Trail of the Hunter's Horn* (1957), *Useless Dog* (1961), and *Goodbye Kate* (1964). Clark and Stuart's fun-filled local color stories are adventuresome but at times also somber.

A contemporary of Stuart and Clark, William O. Steele from the 1950s to the 1970s wrote more than one hundred historical fiction titles with frontier themes and depictions of highly stereotypical attitudes toward Native Americans. Even though lacking originality, a few of these titles remain in print: *The Buffalo Knife* (1952), *Winter Danger* (1954), *Flaming Arrows* (1957), and *The Perilous Road* (1958). Steele's wife, Mary Q. Steele, writing under the pseudonym "Wilson Gage," produced excellent fiction for children, most notably *Big Blue Island* (1964). The Steeles are part of a distinctive literary family: Mary Q. Steele was the daughter of Christine Noble Govan, who wrote a series of mysteries set in the Chattanooga, Tennessee, area, coauthored with her daughter (Mary's sister) Emmy West.

Beginning in the 1930s, a plethora of juvenile biographies of Appalachian individuals appeared. *Stonewall* (1931) by Julia Adams, *Six Feet Six: The Heroic Story of Sam Houston* (1931) by Bessie and Marquis James, and *Davy Crockett* (1934) by Constance Rourke are typical. The lives of Daniel Boone, Andrew Johnson, Andrew Jackson, Rachel Jackson, Sequoyah, and Nancy Ward were also covered frequently and in predictable fashion. Not until the 1960s did biographers begin to explore the lives of other notable Appalachians such as Mother Jones, as in *Labor's Defiant Lady* (1969). Nor did children's literature show much change in themes, attitudes, characterization, setting, and style until the 1960s and 1970s, when the Great Society and the War on Poverty made their way into Appalachian children's fiction.

Vera and Bill Cleaver's classic *Where the Lilies Bloom* (1969) and its sequel, *Trial Valley* (1977), are among books that depict for the first time characters who are aware of the outsiders' perceptions of mountain people. Margaret Wise Shull's *The Children of Appalachia* (1969) is a fictionalized photo essay about government programs, isolation, deprivation, and strip mining. Beverly Courtney Crook's *Fair Annie of Old Mule Hollow* (1978) introduced the theme of strip mining and mountaineer activism to young adult Appalachian fiction. Lillie Chaffin and Conrad Stein's *A World of Books* (1970), Gail Hardin's *The Road from West Virginia* (1970), and Charles Geary's *What I'm About Is People* (1970) are nonfiction accounts of "hillbillies" who migrated to northern urban centers and struggled to fit into the majority culture.

It was also during this period that attention to folklore and the oral tradition grew. Perhaps inspired by the *Foxfire* books, rhymes and stories for a young audience emerged as a trend in the early 1970s. James Still's *The Wolfpen Rusties: Appalachian Riddles and Gee-Haw Whimmy-Diddles* (1975) and *Jack and the Wonder Beans* (1977) set the stage for the continued retelling of Jack tales in the 1980s and 1990s by such notable writers as Gayle Haley in *Jack and the Bean Tree* (1986) and *Mountain Jack Tales* (1992), William Hooks in *Snowbear Whittington: An Appalachian Beauty and the Beast* (1994) and *Three Little Pigs and the Fox* (1989), and Joanne Compton in *Ashpet: An Appalachian Tale* (1994).

Another trend begun in the 1960s and 1970s was the impetus toward Native American material. Forrest Carter's later controversial *The Education of Little Tree* (1976), Electa Clark's *Cherokee Chief: The Life of John Ross* (1970), and Peter Collier's *When Shall They Rest? The Cherokees' Long Struggle with America* (1973) were followed in the 1980s by fiction such as Robert J. Conley's *The Witch of Goingsnake* (1988), for which Wilma Mankiller wrote the foreword.

African Americans were largely ignored in the early decades of Appalachian children's fiction until Virginia Hamilton wrote the Newbery Award–winning *M. C. Higgins, the Great* (1974), *Arilla Sundown* (1976), and *The Magical Adventures of Pretty Pearl* (1983). Following Hamilton, more attention has been given to such classics as the poetry of Nikki Giovanni, to the extent that her poem "Knoxville, Tennessee" was illustrated in picture-book form in 1994. Michelle Greene's *Willie Pearl* (1990), about an African American family in a Kentucky coal-mining town, is unusual in its perspective on ethnic diversity in Appalachia.

Though every decade from the 1920s forward saw a proliferation of children's books about the region, the 1980s and 1990s can be viewed as a golden age. During those years, nearly 20 percent of the children's titles identified as Appalachian were published, and the authors most readily identified with the Appalachian children's market published their first books. Among those writers were Jo Carson, Connie Jordan Green, Gloria Houston, George Ella Lyon, and Cynthia Rylant. An important aspect of the work of these authors, and others in the 1990s, is that they investigate the past through a "re-vision" of the present, exploring new forms and new themes.

Carson's *Stories I Ain't Told Nobody Yet* (1989) is notable for its rich, fresh language. Green wrote one of the few children's books about the work on the atomic bomb in Appalachia in *The War at Home* (1989). Houston's historical fiction about western North Carolina, which includes *The Year of the Perfect Christmas Tree* (1988) and *My Great Aunt Arizona* (1992), illustrates the ethnic diversity of the region. Lyon experiments with subject and form in her picture books *A Regular Rolling Noah* (1986) and *Mama Is a Miner* (1994), as well as fiction for the middle grades such as *Borrowed Children* (1988) and *Here and Then* (1994). Both Lyon and Jeff Daniel Marion are among the new generation of children's writers who see the ready adaptability of poetry for the picture-book format, as in Marion's *Hello Crow* (1992). Rylant is best known for her picture books *When I Was Young in the Mountains* (1982) and *The Relatives Came* (1985), along with her Newbery Award–winning *Missing May* (1992). Rylant is one of the few contemporary Appalachian writers to produce poetry for children as well in volumes such as *Waiting to Waltz* (1984) and *Soda Jerk* (1990).

As Appalachian literature for children expanded, it included some weak and objectionable material, such as Thomas Noel Turner's *Hillbilly Night Afore Christmas* (1983) and Lois Gladys Leppard's religious *Mandie* series, which revived nineteenth-century didacticism at its worst. For the most part, however, the end of the twentieth century brought high-quality, nationally recognized writing such as Phyllis Reynolds Naylor's *Shiloh* trilogy, the first title of which won the Newbery Medal in 1992. Biographers began to move away from the expected and toward the unique and individual, as in Candice Ransom's 1993 biography of Rachel Carson.

The most promising trend in the twenty-first century is the willingness of writers to experiment with literary forms, as in George Ella Lyon's *Gina.Jamie.Father.Bear* (2002). In this novel, Lyon fuses an ancient folk-tale pattern with a contemporary family story, demonstrating to readers how they can view the past through a modern lens. While early

Illustration from George Ella Lyon's *Mama Is a Miner,* 1994. During the 1980s and 1990s, nearly 20 percent of Appalachian children's literature was published, making these two decades a golden age for the genre.

Appalachian children's literature may seem predictable and trite, the first writers established a literary tradition for twenty-first-century writers to expand.

See also: CAUDILL, REBECCA; CHILD LABOR AND THE COAL INDUSTRY (LABOR); LYON, GEORGE ELLA.

—Roberta Herrin, *East Tennessee State University*

George Brosi, *Appalachian Mountain Books* (1980–1995); *Book Links* (May 1991; May 1996; July 2000).

Christy

See *Christy* (Media)

Coal-Mining Literature

Creative writing about Appalachian coal mining first appeared in the late nineteenth century and has continued to the present. Early fictional efforts, even when praising the courage and durability of miners and their families, could be burdened by stereotypical and one-dimensional characters. Miners in groups were usually feared, unions frequently distrusted, and miners and their families often pitied.

Like many novels that would follow it, *A Mountain Europa* (1899) by John Fox Jr. employs its setting primarily as a backdrop for the pursuit of romance and local color. Middle-class characters continue to pursue one another in coal-mining areas in Marcellus E. Thornton's *My "Buddie" and I* (1899), although this novel, set in the southern Appalachians, is also filled with technical descriptions of various kinds of mining. During the first four decades of the twentieth century, labor disputes often joined romance as a dominant theme of mining novels. William W. Whalen's *The Lily of the Coalfields* (1910) is one of the first to look at women in a mining community, while his *Strike* (1927) stereotypes foreign workers. In *The West Virginian* (1926), H. E. Danford not only lobbies for the open shop but sensationalizes the much-publicized shootout between Sid Hatfield and Baldwin-Felts guards at Matewan, West Virginia.

The fictionalized exploration of coal mining came of age with the appearance of James Still's *River of Earth* (1940) and *On Troublesome Creek* (1941). These novels explore the impact of digging coal for a living on individuals, families, and communities in more sophisticated ways than anything published previously. Although Still disliked the artificial barriers coal mining created between human beings and nature, as well as mining's destruction of a traditional way of life by creating economic dependence on industrial labor, he neither stigmatized nor stereotyped his fictional characters. In *Vein of Riches* (1978) John Knowles describes hard times in the coal industry from management's perspective during the first two decades of the twentieth century. Endemic violence in Davis Grubb's portrayal of a 1930s strike in West Virginia, *The Barefoot Man* (1971), makes the entire region appear to be the nation's heart of darkness. Jesse Stuart, Jayne Ann Phillips, Richard Curry, and Breece D'J Pancake have all written short stories centering on coal mining but no full-length works.

The last two decades of the twentieth century saw significant writing about mining life. Cathryn Hankla's *A Blue Moon in Poorwater* (1988) provides a sensitive portrayal of a coal-mining father and his ten-year-old daughter that avoids categorizing miners as one-dimensional by-products of a difficult working environment. Lee Smith, like Still, writes more about mountain life than coal mining, but mining people and communities play significant roles in *Oral History* (1983) and *Fair and Tender Ladies* (1988). If ambivalent about the impact of coal mining on individuals and families, Smith avoids the use of conventional stereotypes or easy solutions, and her novels have a complexity not often found in other coal-mining fiction.

By far the two most important contemporary Appalachian writers to explore the coal-mining milieu are Mary Lee Settle and Denise Giardina. Settle's *The Scapegoat* (1980) explores a twenty-four-hour period shortly before the beginning of a strike in the vicinity of Paint Creek, West Virginia, in 1912. *The Killing Ground* (1982) is set in the 1970s in Charleston, West Virginia, while one of the four sections of *Choices* (1995) is located in the eastern Kentucky coal region in the 1930s. Although all three of these novels are too complex and multidimensional to be labeled coal-mining fiction, they raise penetrating questions about class, greed, memory, redemption, and resiliency.

Less complex but more directly focused on mining communities and personalities are Giardina's *Storming Heaven* (1987) and *The Unquiet Earth* (1992). Giardina's work explores the tumultuous events that dominated southern West Virginia from early-twentieth-century organizing efforts to the Buffalo Creek flood. Her characters are neither romanticized nor degraded but portrayed with the vast strengths and frailties of the human condition. Giardina's fiction is filled with a barely concealed anger against outside economic forces that have socially and environmentally scarred an entire region.

Miners also write about themselves. The *United Mine Workers' Journal* as well as other lesser-known publications are filled with miners' poetry and occasional short fiction. Jack Reese's *Grubbing the Bowels of the Earth* (1988) describes the life of an underground miner in Pennsylvania. Barbara Angle's *Rinker* (1979) offers a glimpse of a day in the life of a miner, and *Those That Mattered* (1994) is a profound examination of the world of a female miner.

See also: GIARDINA, DENISE; STILL, JAMES; FOX, JOHN, JR.

—David C. Duke, *Marshall University*

Stephane Elise Booth, "The American Coal Mining Novel: A Century of Development," *Illinois Historical Journal* (Summer 1988); David C. Duke, *Writers and Miners: Activism and Imagery in America* (2002); Evelyn Hovanec, "Readers' Guide to Coal Mining Fiction and Selected Prose Narratives," *Bulletin of Bibliography* (September 1986).

Cooper, James Fenimore

(1789–1851) Novelist and nonfiction writer.

Most famous for his series of five historical novels published collectively as *The Leatherstocking Tales*, James Fenimore Cooper was born into an affluent family in 1789. His father, a prominent politician and judge, founded Cooperstown, New York, which during James's childhood was still on the northern Appalachian frontier. Cooper attended Yale before being expelled in his third year, allegedly for excessive pranks. He then worked as a merchant seaman and was commissioned as a midshipman during a stint in the navy. He began writing at age thirty and eventually produced thirty-two novels as well as histories, biographies, and travel writing. The first major American novelist, he lived as an adult in Europe and Cooperstown.

The protagonist of the Leatherstocking novels is Natty Bumppo, whom Cooper introduces in *The Pioneers* (1823). Modeled in part on Daniel Boone, Natty is the noble savage in Euro-American guise, a virtuous, highly skilled, individualistic backwoodsman who prefers nature and the company of Native Americans to civilized life. *The Last of the Mohicans* (1826), the second novel to feature Natty, borrows elements of its plot from the captivity narrative, a popular genre recounting the capture of white Americans by Indians. In this novel Cooper foregrounds white America's contradictory tendencies both to anathematize and romanticize Native Americans. In *The Prairie* (1827), the old hero, having moved west in an unsuccessful attempt to escape the encroachment of civilization, meets his end. Cooper resurrected Natty in two subsequent novels, *The Pathfinder* (1840) and *The Deerslayer* (1841). In addition to the standard Cooper topics of adventure and war, these novels explore Natty's complicated relationships with women and suggest the essential loneliness of the lone American hero.

Cooper's depiction of the wise, independent-minded backwoodsman has influenced American literature and national mythology, particularly constructions of the Appalachian mountaineer and the western cowboy. The Leatherstocking novels are also noteworthy for their exploration of the political and socioeconomic divide between the gentleman farmer and the pioneering backwoodsman and the struggle between settlement and wilderness. Natty has been viewed as an early environmentalist, a person who understands the ethical value of preserving wilderness.

—Rebecca Tolley-Stokes, *East Tennessee State University*

Cooper, Susan Fenimore

(1813–1894) Writer, naturalist, and philanthropist.

Susan Fenimore Cooper, daughter of James Fenimore Cooper, was one of the first important nature writers in the United States. Although Cooper spent part of her youth in the New York City area and Europe, she lived most of her adult life in Cooperstown, New York, which had been founded by her grandfather.

Cooper is best known as the author of *Rural Hours* (1850), a book organized as a journal recording a year's observations of the Otsego County, New York, countryside. In addition to discussions of flora and fauna, the work includes descriptions of regional history, folklore, and Native American culture. *Rural Hours* was well received; Henry David Thoreau cited it with approval in *Walden*. Cooper wrote other texts about nature, including an essay in *The Home Book of the Picturesque; or, American Scenery, Art, and Literature* (1852), *The Rhyme and Reason of Country Life* (1854), and a series of essays published under the title "Otsego Leaves" in *Appletons' Journal* (1878). Cooper's nature writing suggests that although human intervention can improve the landscape aesthetically, modern engineering has the potential to damage nature radically. She also emphasized the importance of understanding the environment of a region before human alteration.

In addition to nature writing, Cooper composed fiction, poetry, history, and a memoir. She served as her father's copyist and after his death wrote important introductions to his novels. In 1890 she published the biography *William West Skiles: A Sketch of Missionary Life in Valle Crucis in Western North Carolina, 1842–1862* (1890), a story of the establishment of an Episcopalian mission in the southern Appalachian Mountains.

See also: EPISCOPAL CHURCH (RELIGION); NATURALIST ILLUSTRATORS (VISUAL ARTS).

—Clara Hasbrouck, *East Tennessee State University*

Dargan, Olive Tilford

(1869–1968) Fiction writer.

Olive Tilford Dargan, a native of Kentucky, chose western North Carolina as both her home and site of two of her best-known literary works—the novel *Call Home the Heart* (1932) and the story cycle *From My Highest Hill: Carolina Mountain Folks* (1941). Dargan began her professional life as a teacher, attended Radcliffe College, and then moved to New York City, where she published a series of plays. With proceeds from her work, she purchased land and settled in the Great Smoky Mountains.

Call Home the Heart, written under the pseudonym "Fielding Burke," is a response to the violent textile mill strike in Gastonia, North Carolina, in 1929. The book explores women's and workers' rights through the lives of southern mountain people. Republished by the Feminist Press in 1983, the novel traces the growing political consciousness of Ishma Waycaster, a mountain woman who migrates to a foothills textile town, where she becomes embroiled in labor struggles before returning to her beloved mountains.

Less overtly political, *From My Highest Hill*, first published in a more autobiographical vein as *Highland Annals* in 1925, emphasizes the daily lives of mountain women, exploring their work, social relationships, position in society, and personal desires within the context of "explaining" life in the mountains. Retaining her representation of mountain dialect, Dargan revised the collection of stories in 1941 and added photographs by Bayard Wootten, partly in response to the success of Muriel Earley Sheppard's *Cabins in the Laurel* (1935).

See also: APPALACHIAN ENGLISH IN LITERATURE (LANGUAGE); HUMOR IN APPALACHIAN LITERATURE (HUMOR).

—Katherine E. Ledford, *University of Kentucky*

Davenport, Doris Diosa

(1949–) Poet.

A performance poet, educator, and feminist thinker, Doris Diosa Davenport is best known for her poetry about the African American (also known as Affrilachian) communities in northeast Georgia in which she was reared. Her maternal ancestors (the Gibsons) have lived in this area since approximately 1830, and Davenport grew up in her maternal grandparents' house. She received a B.A. from Paine College, an M.A. from the State University of New York at Buffalo, and a Ph.D. from University of Southern California and has taught at colleges and universities across the United States. In 1992 Davenport returned to northeast Georgia and settled in the community of Sautee.

Davenport's work consists chiefly of four books of poetry: *it's like this* (1980), *eat thunder and drink rain* (1982), *voodoo chile/slight return* (1991), and *Soque Street Poems* (1995). She commemorates the four-room house in which she grew up—103 Soque Street—and the African American community of Cornelia (the "Hill") in many of her poems. Davenport's poetry highlights the verbal traditions of her community, the region's beauty, and the power in working-class people. She also has published numerous essays, including "All This, and Honeysuckles Too" in *Bloodroot: Reflections on Place by Appalachian Women Writers* (1998). Davenport has performed her poems at the Sautee-Nacoochee Arts and Community Center, Seven Stages Performing Arts Center in Atlanta, and numerous other sites.

See also: AFFRILACHIANS (RACE, ETHNICITY, AND IDENTITY); SECTION OVERVIEW (RACE, ETHNICITY, AND IDENTITY).

—Joyce Dyer, *Hiram College*

Davidson, Donald

(1893–1968) Poet, essayist, and educator.

Although he grew up just outside Appalachia and spent most of his adult life in Nashville, Donald Davidson played a significant role in the evolution of Appalachian literature during his long career as a teacher and writer. Born August 18, 1893, and reared in Giles County, Tennessee, Davidson attended local schools while studying classical literature and languages at home with his schoolmaster father, who also encouraged his son's interest in Tennessee folklore.

From older neighbors, Davidson learned many frontier and Civil War–era stories and songs. In several books, including the poetry volume *The Tall Men* (1927) and his acclaimed two-part Tennessee River study, *The Tennessee, Vol. 1: The Old River: Frontier to Secession* (1946) and *The Tennessee, Vol. 2: The New River: Civil War to TVA* (1948), Davidson explored his native state's cultural past. Aware of his own family's ancestral ties to Appalachia, he was fascinated by human efforts to live in mountainous environments. In other writings, such as his contribution to the Agrarian manifesto *I'll Take My Stand* (1930) and his essay collection *The Attack on Leviathan* (1938), Davidson sharply criticized the destruction of American regional identities during his era by such politically mandated pressures as cultural conformity and economic imperialism.

Davidson began his long affiliation with Vanderbilt University in 1909; after earning two degrees there, he taught in the English Department from 1920 to 1964. An active participant in two Vanderbilt literary groups (the Fugitives and the Agrarians), Davidson in his writings and lectures not only celebrated frontier and rural cultural values but also encouraged the emergence of distinctly regional literary works. As a Vanderbilt professor, Davidson mentored Appalachian writers, including Jesse Stuart and Mildred Haun, as well as such scholars of Appalachian culture such as George Pullen Jackson and Thomas G. Burton. Davidson died April 25, 1968.

See also: AGRARIANISM; HAUN, MILDRED; SECTION OVERVIEW (FOLKLORE AND FOLKLIFE).

—Ted Olson, *East Tennessee State University*

Deliverance

James Dickey's 1970 novel *Deliverance*, a harrowing account of a canoeing trip gone wrong, has been controversial in its depiction of mountaineers as savage, irrational brutes eager to prey upon unwitting lowland suburbanites. Yet in recounting the urban protagonists' fearful experiences, which include abduction, assault, and a literal manhunt, Dickey offers commentary on the arbitrariness of power, the strength of will, and the creative force of imagination coupled with logic.

The novel's protagonist, Ed Gentry, the owner of an Atlanta graphic arts studio, agrees to spend a weekend canoeing down an uncharted north Georgia mountain river with his survivalist friend, Lewis Medlock, and two fellow suburbanites, Bobby Trippe and Drew Billinger. While the men seek adventure and diversion from their everyday lives, they soon discover that both the natural world and the liberties that people (both themselves and the mountaineers they encounter) take when outside the mutual policing of society present major obstacles to survival. Separated from Lewis and Drew by river currents, Bobby and Ed are abducted by two mountaineer woodsmen; Ed narrowly escapes the sexual assault Bobby suffers at their hands only because Lewis kills one of the woodsmen at the last moment. This confrontation leads to the group's dangerous attempt to get downriver and to kill the remaining abductor. During this escape, Ed wrestles with conflicting ideas regarding law, justice, and ethics. His deliverance comes from his willingness to contend with the unforgiving terrain, the unguarded violence of some of its inhabitants, and his own heart of darkness.

See also: *DELIVERANCE* (MEDIA); POST–WORLD WAR II FICTION; SECTION OVERVIEW (IMAGES AND ICONS).

—Thomas Alan Holmes, *East Tennessee State University*

Dillard, Annie

(1945–) Fiction and nonfiction writer.

In her autobiographical *An American Childhood* (1987), Annie Dillard lyrically recalls growing up in affluence in 1950s Pittsburgh. Her deep engagement with the mountains of Appalachia began as an undergraduate in the late 1960s at Hollins College in Roanoke, Virginia, where she became closely involved with other future writers, including novelist Lee Smith, who became known as the "Hollins Group." She married and later divorced Hollins professor and novelist Richard H. W. Dillard, her mentor in writing.

After a bout of near-fatal pneumonia in 1971, Dillard, through journal writing, spiritual and environmental questing, and studying the transcendentalism of Henry David Thoreau and Ralph Waldo Emerson, produced the environmental classic *Pilgrim at Tinker Creek* (1974), winner of the 1975 Pulitzer Prize for Nonfiction. *Pilgrim* is a season-following sequence of lyrical essays linking inner and outer worlds, the sensuous and metaphysical, and describing the search for the spiritual source of nature's wonders and horrors. Rich with experience and observation of nature in the mountains, the book defined Dillard as an observer of the Appalachian environment rather than Appalachian culture. In subsequent years, she set her diverse works in many locales; her epic novel *The Living* (1992), for example, takes place in the Pacific Northwest. She also wrote the reportorial *Encounters with Chinese Writers* (1984) and the meditative *Holy the Firm* (1977) and *For the Time Being* (1999); the latter two texts recount her search for God in many religions and regions of the world.

See also: SECTION OVERVIEW (ENVIRONMENT); SMITH, LEE.

—Fred Waage, *East Tennessee State University*

Dykeman, Wilma

(1920–) Novelist, essayist, journalist, historian, and teacher.

Born and reared in Asheville, North Carolina, Wilma Dykeman has lived most of her life there and in Newport, Tennessee. One of the towering figures of Appalachian literature, Dykeman is notable for her fiction, historical writings, environmentalism, and concern for civil rights. Her Appalachian roots run back to the eighteenth century, when her mother's family settled in the mountains of western North Carolina. A graduate of Northwestern University, Dykeman married James R. Stokely Jr., whose family established the Stokely Canning Company. They have two sons.

Dykeman clearly expresses her commitment to Appalachian issues in her novels *The Tall Woman* (1962), *The Far Family* (1966), and *Return the Innocent Earth* (1973). Lydia McQueen, protagonist of *The Tall Woman*, refuses to be restricted to the domestic sphere and becomes active in community issues such as education. Dykeman's novels also reflect her love of place; *Return the Innocent Earth* touches on the environmental effects of industrial farming.

Appointed state historian in 1981 by Governor Lamar Alexander, Dykeman had previously heralded her interest in Tennessee history with the publication of *The French Broad* (1955), a nonfiction text that was part of the *Rivers of America* series. The book gracefully synthesizes history, sociology, environmentalism, and biography and includes such memorable accounts as the search for Professor Elisha Mitchell's body on Mount Mitchell. In 1976 she published *Tennessee: A Bicentennial History*. Dykeman's commitment to civil rights led her to cowrite two books with her husband—*Neither Black nor White* (1957), which is an account of *Brown v. Board of Education*, and *Seeds of Southern Change: The Life of Will Alexander* (1962). Biographies by Dykeman include *Too Many People, Too Little Love* (1974), devoted to Appalachian family-planning advocate Edna Rankin McKinnon, and *Prophet of Plenty: The First Ninety Years of W. D. Weatherford* (1966). Passionate about mountain culture as well as the landscape, Dykeman was an early advocate of Appalachian literature, and in 1962 she coauthored (with W. D. Weatherford) a pioneering essay on the subject published in *The Southern Appalachian Region: A Survey*.

Dykeman has received numerous awards and honors for her writings, including the Thomas Wolfe Memorial

Award and a Guggenheim Fellowship. A dynamic speaker, often taking on more than thirty public engagements per year throughout the United States, she has also taught on the faculty of the University of Tennessee in Knoxville. As of 2004, Dykeman had published eighteen book-length works.

See also: LITERARY SCHOLARSHIP; WOMEN AUTHORS.

—Theresa Lloyd, *East Tennessee State University*

Sandra L. Ballard and Patricia L. Hudson, eds., *Listen Here: Women Writing in Appalachia* (2003).

Earley, Tony

(1961–) Fiction writer and essayist.

Tony Earley has said that in his imagination all views have a mountain in them. Born in Texas but reared in Rutherfordton, North Carolina, Earley sets most of his writings in the mountains and Piedmont of his boyhood home.

The simplicity of Early's language belies the complexity of his ideas. The introspective characters in his short story collection *Here We Are in Paradise* (1994) search for meaning in their lives by sifting through memories of the past. The novel *Jim the Boy* (2000), inspired by E. B. White's *Charlotte's Web*, tells the story of a ten-year-old boy living at the foot of Lynn Mountain, North Carolina, with his widowed mother and three bachelor uncles during the Great Depression. Earley describes his North Carolina upbringing in the essay collection *Somehow Form a Family: Stories That Are Mostly True* (2001).

Earley's work has appeared in *New Stories from the South, Best American Short Stories, Esquire, Harper's*, the *New Yorker*, and the *Oxford American*. He won the PEN Syndicated Fiction Award in 1991. In 1996 the British literary journal *Granta* selected Earley as one of America's top twenty young fiction writers. The award heightened his critical acclaim, and he was featured as one of the *New Yorker*'s "Twenty Writers for the Twenty-First Century."

See also: POST–WORLD WAR II FICTION.

—Marianne Worthington, *Cumberland College*

Ehle, John

(1925–) Novelist.

John Ehle's literary reputation rests primarily upon his novels set in the mountains of western North Carolina, where his mother's family settled shortly after the American Revolution. Born and reared in Asheville, Ehle earned his B.A. and M.A. at the University of North Carolina. As a special assistant to Governor Terry Sanford in the early 1960s, he established the first Governor's School program in the United States and also founded the North Carolina School of the Arts.

Ehle's first two novels, *Move Over, Mountain* (1957) and *Kingstree Island* (1959), are set outside Appalachia, but with *Lion on the Hearth* (1961), set in Asheville during the 1920s and 1930s, Ehle began to explore the people, culture, and landscape of his native region. His next book, *The Land Breakers* (1964), focuses on the late-eighteenth-century pioneers who settled western North Carolina. Careful historical research likewise informs *The Road* (1967), which depicts the building of the railroad through the Swannanoa Gap in the late 1870s, *Time of Drums* (1970), a Civil War novel, and *The Journey of August King* (1971), a moving account of the title character's efforts to assist a fifteen-year-old fugitive slave girl. Though each of these books is meant to be read independently, together they create a broad portrait of the Wright, King, and Plover families over some two hundred years.

Except for *The Changing of the Guard* (1974), which is set in France and revolves around a Hollywood film project, Ehle's novels since *The Journey of August King* have continued to investigate, among other characters, descendants of these three families. *The Winter People* (1982), though set in the 1930s, evokes an earlier era of frontier living and clan loyalties, an ethos transcended by protagonist Collie Wright's act of self-sacrifice. Of his more recent novels, only *The Widow's Trial* (1989) is set in late-twentieth-century Appalachia.

Ehle's fiction is marked by lively storytelling, well-crafted dialogue, effectively structured dramatic scenes, engaging characters, and intelligent good humor. Ehle powerfully conveys the connection between landscape and character, affirming humanity's profound dependence on nature. His major subjects include conflict among family members, tension between individual conscience and community mores, and the ongoing quest for social justice. That quest not only shapes many of his novels but also pervades his books of nonfiction, especially *The Free Men* (1965), a portrait of the Civil Rights movement in Chapel Hill, and *Trail of Tears* (1988), a poignant history of the Cherokee people and their forced march to Oklahoma. Ethical and religious values play a central role in his work.

See also: APPALACHIAN ENGLISH IN LITERATURE (LANGUAGE).

—John Lang, *Emory and Henry College*

Environmental Writing

Literature set in the Appalachian region frequently invokes the natural environment and humankind's relationship to it. Through the development of ecocriticism in the 1980s, however, environmental literature has been more specifically defined as writing of any genre that gives at least equal standing to human culture and nonhuman nature. Much such writing also presents some degree of environmentalist advocacy and bases its presentation of the nonhuman environment on ecological principles.

But ecocriticism has also spurred re-envisioning of early Appalachian literature as "environmental," if not self-consciously so. Michael Branch and Daniel Phillipon's anthology of Appalachian Virginia nature writing, *The Height of Our Mountains* (1998), provides an excellent introduction to European American environmental writing from colonial times to the present; among some unfamiliar and some over-familiar names, important figures include John Bartram (1699–1777), Andre Michaux (1746–1802), William Gilmore Simms (1806–1870), and Bradford Torrey (1843–1912).

Kevin O'Donnell and Helen Hollingsworth's *Seekers of Scenery: Travel Writing from Southern Appalachia, 1840–1900* (2004) presents a broad array of Appalachian environmental writing and illustration, while Elizabeth Engelhardt's *The Tangled Roots of Feminism, Environmentalism, and Appalachian Literature* (2003) shows how Mary Noailles Murfree, Emma Bell Miles, and other turn-of-the century contemporaries used fiction and creative nonfiction to promote an ecofeminist agenda.

Horace Kephart's *Our Southern Highlanders* (1913; revised 1922) promoted Appalachian culture to a national audience and initiated a continuing debate over exploitation versus preservation of Appalachian nature and the harmony or disharmony between the "indwellers" and their physical environment. Appalachian environmental writing expanded in subsequent decades, both through the literature of labor and through new natural history writing, including Roderick Peattie's *The Great Smoky Mountains and the Blue Ridge* (1943), Wilma Dykeman's *The French Broad* (1955), and Harvey Broome's *Out under the Sky of the Great Smokies: A Personal Journal* (1975).

A crucial moment for Appalachian environmental writing came with the "discovery" of Appalachian poverty at the beginning of the 1960s. Books such as Michael Harrington's *The Other America* (1962) and Harry Caudill's *Night Comes to the Cumberlands* (1963) emphasized the disjunction between human deprivation or exploitation and Appalachia's natural beauty.

The 1970s brought a sometimes combative ecological consciousness to Appalachian writing. A signal work was Eliot Porter and Edward Abbey's *Appalachian Wilderness* (1973), which combined Porter's lyrically beautiful nature photographs and Abbey's acerbic environmentalist criticism. Kai T. Erickson's *Everything in Its Path* (1976) dramatized the Buffalo Creek flood as an Appalachian Love Canal, while Wendell Berry and Annie Dillard wrote powerful ecologically based prose and poetry. Other environment-centered Appalachian poets whose careers became significant in the 1970s are Jim Wayne Miller, Jeff Daniel Marion, and Robert Morgan.

As well as Berry, novelists of the last quarter-century such as Mary Lee Settle, Lee Smith, and Denise Giardina have given equal play to Appalachian nature and culture. The culminating (thus far) work of Appalachian environmental fiction is Barbara Kingsolver's *Prodigal Summer* (2002).

Innovative environmental nonfiction has become prominent since the later 1990s, centered perhaps by Donald E. Davis's *Where There Are Mountains: An Environmental History of Southern Appalachia* (2002). Travel writing such as that collected by O'Donnell and Hollingsworth has many recent practitioners, from superficial (Bill Bryson's *A Walk in the Woods*, 1998) to deep (Noah Adams's *Far Appalachia: Following the New River North*, 2002). Contemporary environmental nonfiction about Appalachia includes John Elder's *Reading the Mountains of Home* (1998) and Ian Marshall's *Story Line: Exploring the Literature of the Appalachian Trail* (1998).

A sign that Appalachian environmental literature will flourish in the future can be found in the University of Kentucky's Summer Environmental Writing Program, directed by Randall Roorda, whose student participants combine writing in all genres with ecological study in the field.

See also: SECTION OVERVIEW (ECOLOGY); SECTION OVERVIEW (ENVIRONMENT); TRAVEL WRITING.

—Fred Waage, *East Tennessee State University*

Michael Branch and Daniel Phillipon, *The Height of Our Mountains* (1998); Kevin O'Donnell and Helen Hollingsworth, eds., *Seekers of Scenery: Travel Writing from Southern Appalachia, 1840–1900* (2004).

Fox, John, Jr.

(1863–1919) Fiction writer.

John Fox Jr.'s novels and short stories about Appalachia belong to the genre of local color writing, which flourished from the late 1800s to the early 1900s. Born in 1863 to a prosperous family in the Bluegrass region of Kentucky, Fox was educated at Harvard University and then moved to Big Stone Gap, Virginia, at the time hailed as the "Pittsburgh of the South" because of the coal boom. There, he began to write local color fiction about mountain life. Although Fox's one-dimensional and romanticized view of mountain people and his use of dialect in mountain characters' speech are regarded by some readers as condescending, his writings deal with the effects of progress on the land and people, a continuing social and environmental issue in Appalachia.

The Trail of the Lonesome Pine (1908), perhaps Fox's most famous work, recounts the impact of the coal industry on Appalachia. The novel pits mountain culture against the culture of larger America (in this case, the Bluegrass of Kentucky) by introducing a love story between a mountain girl and a refined man from the flatlands who, like Fox, has come to the mountains to work. The novel also features feuding mountain families, an apparent attempt by Fox to emphasize what he saw as the lawlessness of mountain folk. Fox's other important novel, a somewhat more negative take on those living in the mountains, is *The Little Shepherd of Kingdom Come* (1903). Set during the Civil War and alternating between the mountains of Kentucky and the Bluegrass, the novel presents its young protagonist with the choice between a poor mountain girl and a flatland belle who both love him as he struggles with his divided heritage.

Fox remains influential in Appalachian literature. His novels, which helped shape the nation's perceptions of mountain culture, were among the first to sell a million copies in the United States, and several of them are still in print. A dramatized version of *The Trail of the Lonesome Pine*, which has been performed for several decades in Big Stone Gap, is the official outdoor drama of Virginia. The house that Fox built in Big Stone Gap now serves as a museum.

—Aaron Davis, *Big Stone Gap, Virginia*

Frazier, Charles

(1950–) Fiction and nonfiction writer.

Charles Frazier achieved national recognition when his first novel, *Cold Mountain*, reached the top of the *New York Times* best-seller list in 1997 and won the 1997 National Book Award for fiction. In creating the landscape for his novel, Frazier drew on his deeply rooted connection with the mountains of North Carolina.

Based on a family anecdote about a relative (given the name Inman in the book) who was wounded in the Civil War and walked from a hospital in Raleigh to his home in western North Carolina, *Cold Mountain* also draws freely from Homer's *Odyssey*. The novel explores the cultural and spiritual disruptions experienced by the civilian population, particularly in North Carolina, during the Civil War. To Inman, geography is symbolic; the lowlands represent the horror of war and the mountains respite and salvation. Meticulously recreating the language of the period, Frazier's novel provides a penetrating study of the folklore and music of the Appalachian region. *Cold Mountain* was made into a major Hollywood film released in 2003.

Frazier received a B.A. from the University of North Carolina, an M.A. from Appalachian State University, and worked on a Ph.D. at the University of South Carolina. During the summers of 1982 and 1983, he hiked through the mountains of Ecuador, Peru, and Bolivia and in 1985 published *Adventuring in the Andes: The Sierra Club Travel Guide to Ecuador, Peru, Bolivia, the Amazon Basin, and the Galapagos Islands*.

See also: APPALACHIAN ENGLISH IN LITERATURE (LANGUAGE); *COLD MOUNTAIN* (MEDIA).

—Donald Secreast, *Radford University*

French, Albert

(1943–) Novelist.

Albert French, an African American writer from Pittsburgh, is the author of three highly acclaimed but not widely known novels: *Billy* (1993), *Holly* (1995), and *I Can't Wait on God* (1998). He has also published a memoir of his experience of and trauma after serving in Vietnam entitled *Patches of Fire: A Story of War and Redemption* (1996).

Born in 1943, French grew up in Pittsburgh before going to Vietnam as a marine in 1965. Severely wounded in the war, he returned to Pittsburgh and worked as a photographer for the *Pittsburgh Post-Gazette* for thirteen years before starting his own magazine, the *Pittsburgh Preview* (1980–88). When the magazine failed, French struggled with depression and finally faced his traumatic experiences in Vietnam. He recovered through writing *Patches of Fire*. His cousin, noted author John Edgar Wideman, showed his agent some of French's work, and French's novel *Billy*, written in just six weeks, was published soon thereafter. *Billy*, the story of a ten-year old boy sentenced to death, received unusually strong reviews for a first novel.

Billy and *Holly*, both tales of southern racial injustice, are set outside of Appalachia, in 1930s Mississippi and 1940s coastal North Carolina, respectively. *I Can't Wait on God* takes on back-alley life in Pittsburgh's Homewood neighborhood of the 1950s. French's rhythmic, colloquial prose borrows more from the oral than the literary tradition of storytelling. His tight powerful scenes reveal the inner world of the characters through the tiny details of their outer world, creating emotional but unsentimental portraits of individuals and communities.

See also: AFRICAN AMERICAN FAMILIES AND COMMUNITIES (FAMILY AND COMMUNITY); RACISM (RACE, ETHNICITY, AND IDENTITY).

—Brandon Story, *King College*

Furman, Lucy

(1869–1958) Fiction writer.

One of the most comical of local color writers, Lucy Furman was born in Henderson, in northwestern Kentucky. She grew up in Evansville, Indiana, and worked there as a court reporter, an occupation that perhaps sharpened her ability to replicate local dialects and patterns of speech. Her first book, *Stories of a Sanctified Town* (1896), is a satirical treatment of religious practices in western Kentucky, but her other writing is centered in Hindman Settlement School in Knott County, where she was employed from 1907 to 1924. Her principal contribution to Appalachian literature is the series of five novels she published during her tenure there.

The Quare Women (1923), her best-known work, and its sequel, *The Glass Window* (1925), depend heavily on the turn-of-the-century diaries of Katherine Pettit and May Stone, the "fotched-on" women who came to the mountains from the Bluegrass to found Hindman Settlement School. *Mothering on Perilous* (1913) and *The Lonesome Road* (1927) are based on her own experiences as a housemother to the schoolboys. The comic episodes that dominate her fiction are based on fact.

Furman's stated intention in her writing was to provide publicity for the school. Her work has been justly criticized for being propagandistic and didactic, but it is also compassionate, witty, and well constructed.

See also: HUMOR IN APPALACHIAN LITERATURE (HUMOR).

—Nancy Carol Joyner, *Western Carolina University*

Gates, Henry Louis, Jr.

(1950–) Author, scholar, and cultural commentator. Henry Louis Gates Jr., born in 1950 in Keyser, West Virginia, is one of the leading intellectuals in the United States. He has been a key developer of African American studies as an academic discipline, with emphasis on recovering lost or neglected texts by African American women and discovering the African roots of African American cultural expression.

Gates began his undergraduate studies at Potomac State College in Keyser, completed them at Yale University in 1973, and became the first African American to receive a doctorate from Cambridge University in England. Gates's critical works include *Figures in Black: Words, Signs, and the "Racial" Self* (1987) and *The Signifying Monkey: A Theory of Afro-American Literary Criticism* (1988), a landmark work that won the American Book Award and helped to define the emerging discipline of African American studies. Gates is coauthor with Cornel West of *The Future of the Race* (1996) and has also written other books of cultural commentary, including *Loose Canons: Notes on the Culture Wars* (1992) and *Thirteen Ways of Looking at a Black Man* (1997). He is also author of *Wonders of the African World* (1999), a companion piece to his PBS series.

Gates's autobiography, *Colored People: A Memoir* (1994), recounts his upbringing in the mill town of Piedmont, West Virginia, and is especially important for documenting African American experiences in central Appalachia. Gates charts his development of personal and racial identity through school, reading, television, music, sports, and Methodist and Episcopal churches during the nation's march to desegregation. In the preface, which is addressed to his daughters, he emphasizes his desire to preserve a sense of community, family, and small-town life in a changing America. Although Gates was an active proponent of desegregation and makes it clear that racism and segregation had damaging effects on African Americans in West Virginia, he expresses nostalgia for the closeness and warmth of the segregated black society in which he grew up. *Colored People* was awarded the Lillian Smith Prize, as well as the W. D. Weatherford Award for significant work on Appalachia by Berea College and the Appalachian Studies Association.

Gates is the W. E. B. Du Bois Professor of the Humanities at Harvard University, where he chairs the Department of Afro-American Studies and directs the W. E. B. Du Bois Institute for Afro-American Research. He has also taught at Yale, Cornell, and Duke Universities and has served as general editor or coeditor for several key projects, including the *Oxford-Schomburg Library of Nineteenth-Century Black Women Writers* (1988, with a ten-volume supplement published in 1991) and the *Norton Anthology of African American Literature* (1996). Along with Kwame Appiah and Nobel Prize winner Wole Soyinka, Gates was coeditor of the groundbreaking book *Africana: The Encyclopedia of the African and African American Experience* (1999) and the accompanying CD-ROM *Encarta Africana* (2000), bringing to completion

Henry Louis Gates Jr., c. 2003. Born and reared in West Virginia, Gates is regarded as one of the leading intellectuals in the United States and has been instrumental in developing African American studies as an academic discipline.

Du Bois's dream of creating a comprehensive volume about African and African American history and culture. Gates has also edited a number of other volumes, including reprints of numerous primary texts by African American authors and collections of essays by prominent scholars, including *Black Literature and Literary Theory* (1987), *"Race," Writing, and Difference* (1986), and *Reading Black, Reading Feminist: A Critical Anthology* (1990). A cultural and political commentator, Gates writes for such publications as the *Village Voice*, *Harper's*, and the *New Yorker*, and he coedits *Transition*. He has been awarded a MacArthur Foundation grant and a National Humanities Medal.

See also: AFRICAN AMERICAN LITERATURE.

—Linda Tate, *Shepherd University*

Gays and Lesbians

Until the 1970s gays and lesbians were largely unacknowledged in Appalachia and Appalachian literature. Since then, however, homosexual characters have begun to come out of the literary closet.

Often a text depicting gay characters emphasizes their alienation. In *Black Mountain Breakdown* (1980), Lee Smith presents Jules Spangler, who is tormented by his sexual identity even though he has left the mountains for a metropolitan life. Likewise, in *Fair and Tender Ladies* (1988) Smith portrays a lesbian school teacher named Miss Torrington, who, in kissing her student Ivy Rowe, the novel's protagonist, drives the girl away, even though Ivy remembers the kiss passionately for the rest of her life. Yet another novel to explore gay isolation is Karen Salyer McElmurray's *Strange Birds in the Tree of Heaven* (1999), which describes Andrew Wallen as a lonely, desperate thirty-year-old man struggling to find his sexual identity in the face of his religiously conservative mother's condemnation of homosexuality as an abomination.

More positive accounts of gay life do exist, although even these often suggest the difficulty of being gay in Appalachia. In Denise Giardina's *The Unquiet Earth* (1992), friends and family of the gay couple Hassell Day and Junior Tackett treat the two men with love and respect, but the couple's "don't ask, don't tell" existence camouflages their relationship.

Abraham Verghese's *My Own Country* (1994), which focuses on the treatment of AIDS patients in a Johnson City, Tennessee, hospital, presents a nonfiction account of gays in Appalachia. Verghese indicates that the region is home to a diverse gay population, including a gay subculture that dates back at least to the 1950s in urban areas such as Johnson City and Knoxville, Tennessee; Huntington, Bluefield, and Charleston, West Virginia; and Asheville, North Carolina.

Appalachian lesbian authors include novelists Lisa Alther and Dorothy Allison. In Alther's *Kinflicks*, set in a fictionalized version of her native Kingsport, Tennessee, lesbianism is one of the many paths that the protagonist, Ginny, explores in her journey of self-discovery. Allison's *Bastard Out of Carolina*, which takes place in her hometown of Greenville, South Carolina, suggests that lesbianism can provide women with a compassionate, supportive antidote to heterosexual abuse.

See also: GAY AND LESBIAN LIFE (FAMILY AND COMMUNITY); VERGHESE, ABRAHAM (HEALTH).

—Danny Miller, *Northern Kentucky University*

Kate Black and Marc A. Rhorer, "Out in the Mountains: Exploring Lesbian and Gay Lives," in *Out in the South*, ed. Carlos L. Dews and Carolyn Leste Law (2001).

Giardina, Denise

(1951–) Fiction writer and activist.

Denise Giardina established herself as a powerful voice of the region with her award-winning historical novels set in the Appalachian coalfields, *Storming Heaven* (1987) and *The Unquiet Earth* (1992). A resident of Charleston, West Virginia, she teaches writing at West Virginia State University and plays an active role in regional politics, once appearing on the ballot as an environmentalist candidate for governor.

Her mother from eastern Kentucky and her father from Italy, Giardina was born in Bluefield, West Virginia, and grew up with a dual heritage. In the West Virginia coal camp where her father worked as a bookkeeper, Giardina witnessed the exploitation of miners and their families and discrimination against blacks and European immigrants who had come to work in the mines. She has published works set in England and Germany as well as Appalachia.

While majoring in history at West Virginia Wesleyan College, Giardina participated in a study-abroad program in England. Out of this experience came her first book, a historical novel about the young Henry V, *Good King Harry* (1984). An engaging character study, the book also reveals Giardina's deep concern with moral and ethical issues and her skill at creating a compelling fictional voice.

Although Giardina's first Appalachian book, *Storming Heaven*, is fictional, some of its characters and events have a basis in fact. In researching the novel, Giardina conducted numerous interviews with local people as well as reading exhaustively. This coalfields novel of social protest earned the writer immediate notice both inside and outside the region, winning the Appalachian Studies Association's W. D. Weatherford Award. It was, not surprisingly, attacked by mining and banking leaders.

Some of the characters from *Storming Heaven* also appear in *The Unquiet Earth*, Giardina's next novel. Again, Giardina's focus is the struggle of poor people against corporate leaders and political institutions that seek to exploit them. In this novel, however, she takes her characters beyond the coalfields to the skies over the South Pacific and the jungles of Central America.

Giardina's fourth book represents a change of setting, but its theme remains the struggle between the powerful and the powerless. *Saints and Villains* (1998) focuses on a single historical figure, Dietrich Bonhoeffer, the German theologian who died in prison after an unsuccessful attempt to assassinate Adolf Hitler. Giardina emphasizes the inner conflict of a good man confronted with absolute evil and the need for people to act according to their convictions. The book demonstrates Giardina's breadth of vision and the closeness of regional and universal concerns.

Giardina's *Fallam's Secret* (2003) is a fantasy-adventure novel, a departure from her usual themes. It features travel from present day West Virginia through a fault in the time-space continuum to seventeenth-century England, where the main character learns about her past, joins the resistance movement against Oliver Cromwell, and finds romance with a masked bandit. Although its tone is lighter than in previous works, *Fallam's Secret* contains themes of long-standing interest to Giardina.

Giardina began her work as a social and political activist while a graduate student at Virginia Theological Seminary. Her activities have included participation in the Appalachian Land Ownership Task Force (which eventually resulted in the book *Who Owns Appalachia?*) and work with the Sojourner Commune in Washington, D.C. She also played a key role in the work of the Kentuckians for the Commonwealth, which has sought to protect the eastern Kentucky landscape and people from abuses perpetrated by coal companies.

See also: APPALACHIAN ENGLISH IN LITERATURE (LANGUAGE); COAL-MINING LITERATURE; GAYS AND LESBIANS.

—Laurie K. Lindberg, *Ball State University*

George Brosi, *The Literature of the Appalachian South* (1992); *Iron Mountain Review: Denise Giardina Issue* (Spring 1999).

Giovanni, Nikki

(1943–) Poet and essayist.

Author Nikki Giovanni is a major voice for African Americans across the nation. Born Yolande Cornelia Giovanni Jr., in Knoxville, Tennessee, she was reared in Cincinnati, where her parents moved when she was still an infant. She returned to Knoxville while in high school to live with her maternal grandparents. After graduating with honors in history from Fisk University in 1967, she attended the University of Pennsylvania's School of Social Work and Columbia University. Her career as a poet and writer was launched during the late 1960s and early 1970s, when she made her home in New York City. In 1978 she moved with her young son to Cincinnati to care for her parents. Since 1987 she has been professor of English at Virginia Polytechnic Institute and State University in Blacksburg.

The author of more than twenty-five books of poetry and essays, Giovanni has seen her works widely anthologized. Some of her titles include *Black Feeling, Black Talk* (1968); *Black Judgement* (1970); *Spin a Soft Black Song* (1971); *A Dialogue: James Baldwin and Nikki Giovanni* (1973); *Ego Tripping and Other Poems for Young Readers* (1973); *Cotton Candy on a Rainy Day* (1978); *Those Who Ride the Night Winds* (1983); *Sacred Cows . . . and Other Edibles* (1988); *Selected Poems of Nikki Giovanni* (1996); *Love Poems* (1997); *Blues for All the Changes: New Poems* (1999); and *Quilting the Black-Eyed Pea: Poems and Not-Quite Poems* (2002). Giovanni's media performances include a PBS film, *Spirit to Spirit: The Poetry of Nikki Giovanni* (1987), and recordings such as *Truth Is on Its Way* (1971), *Like a Ripple on a Pond* (1973), *The Way I Feel* (1975), *Legacies* (1976), and *The Reason I Like Chocolate* (1976).

Giovanni is a popular teacher and reader of her own works, and her honors include the NAACP Image Award for Literature (1998) and the Langston Hughes Award for Distinguished Contributions to Arts and Letters (1996). She has been named Woman of the Year by *Ladies' Home Journal* and *Mademoiselle* and holds honorary doctorates from the University of Maryland, Fisk University, Indiana University, Albright College, and Smith College.

See also: AFRICAN AMERICAN LITERATURE; POST–WORLD WAR II POETS.

—April Asbury, *Pulaski, Virginia*

Godwin, Gail

(1937–) Fiction writer.

Born in Birmingham, Alabama, Gail Godwin moved with her mother to live with her maternal grandparents in Asheville, North Carolina, when she was two. She grew up in Asheville, which she later fictionalized as Mountain City. She received her bachelor's degree from the University of North Carolina and holds both master's and doctoral degrees from the University of Iowa. Although she has lived outside Appalachia for most of her adult life, the region figures prominently in Godwin's fiction as both setting and subject.

Godwin's representation of Appalachian women has focused on two types: the woman who stays in the region and struggles to define herself as an individual within the culture and the woman who leaves Appalachia but finds herself perpetually drawn back into the culture through family ties and the inescapable effects of memory and conditioning. In her third novel, *The Odd Woman* (1974), the types first emerged as a central concern; in *A Mother and Two Daughters* (1982) Godwin not only achieved extraordinary commercial success but also refined her earlier explorations of these female types in ways that make this novel essential reading for those interested in her view of urban Appalachian culture after World War II.

In both *A Mother and Two Daughters* and *A Southern Family* (1987), Godwin extended her exploration of Appalachian women beyond white women of the professional class to include portraits of African American women and those who come from less privileged, more isolated, rural backgrounds. In addition, she began a more focused examination of Appalachian males of both the World War II and baby boom generations.

In her companion novels *Father Melancholy's Daughter* (1991) and *Evensong* (1999), Godwin focused on another crucial aspect of the region's culture: religion. These novels examine a father and daughter, both Episcopal priests ministering to a minority denomination within the region and working to establish its place within a community that does not always understand their sense of faith. *Evensong*, in particular, explores the tensions and connections between the Episcopal faith and more dominant, conservative strains of southern Protestantism.

Aware of the ways in which provincialism has hurt Appalachians, Godwin has displayed an increasing respect for the lasting positive contributions of the region's traditional values to contemporary life, both within and outside the confines of Appalachia. Godwin, who lives in Woodstock, New York, is also author of two story collections and the recipient of numerous awards.

See also: POST–WORLD WAR II FICTION; WOMEN AUTHORS.

—Jane Hill, *State University of West Georgia*

Jane Hill, "Coming to Terms with the Appalachian 'Other' in the Novels of Gail Godwin," *Journal of Kentucky Studies* (September 1994) and *Gail Godwin* (1992); Lihong Xie, *The Evolving Self in the Novels of Gail Godwin* (1995).

Grey, Zane

(1872–1939) Fiction writer.

Born in Zanesville, Ohio, Pearl Zane Grey was an influential American novelist who wrote eighty-five books. Most concern the American West, but three are set in Appalachian Ohio. These Appalachian novels are uncomplicated stories with stilted dialogue, but they offer historical perspective on this part of northern Appalachia.

Grey, who dropped his first name as a young man, was an avid outdoorsman who fancied wide-open spaces and the romantic notion of heroes rescuing damsels in distress—elements that figure prominently in his writing. Among the first to settle eastern Ohio just after the Revolutionary War, the Zane family included entrepreneurs who owned turnpike rights in the state from present-day Zanesville to Aberdeen. Family stories about the challenges of pioneer life fired Grey's youthful imagination and helped form his adult views of frontier settlement.

Betty Zane (1903), *Spirit of the Border: A Story of Early Settlers in the Ohio Valley* (1906), and *The Last Trail* (1908) center on life-and-death struggles of pioneers in Appalachian Ohio while it was part of the Northwest Territory. In these novels, Grey portrays real-life people such as Simon Girty, who supported Native Americans against pioneer intruders, and Lewis Wetzel, a vengeful, if not psychopathic, killer of Native Americans; the novels also feature Moravian settlers and Grey's own ancestors. His work displays admiration for the hardiness of pioneers and is peppered with references to historical events.

In Grey's frontier world, women are loyal and courageous in dangerous situations but are subordinate to male characters, who run the gamut from a variety of military leaders to indomitable settlers resigned to hardship. Grey's dialogue follows the conventions of the time; lower-class characters speak in dialect signaled by misspellings and quaint words while main characters, usually Zane family members, use Standard English. Violence in Grey's fiction is sometimes gruesome (as in his account of a massacre of Moravian settlers or Girty's death in *Spirit of the Border*), but it is usually associated with issues of honor rather than hatred.

See also: EARLY WHITE SETTLEMENT OF SOUTHEASTERN OHIO (SETTLEMENT AND MIGRATION).

—Charles F. Moore, *East Tennessee State University*

Carlton Jackson, *Zane Grey* (1973).

Grubb, Davis

(1919–1980) Fiction writer.

Davis Alexander Grubb was born in the Ohio River town of Moundsville, West Virginia, on July 23, 1919. He was named for his mother's father, William Davis Alexander, a steamboat captain in the 1880s and a descendent of one of the oldest area families. Grubb's mother, Eleanor Louise Alexander, was an iconoclast who worked for the Department of Public Assistance and often came home with stories of needy families. His father was a conservative architect, Louis Delplain Grubb, who encouraged his first-born son to draw and write.

In 1938 the family moved to Clarksburg, West Virginia, where Grubb finished his senior year in high school. After dropping out of Carnegie Institute of Technology in Pittsburgh, where his color-blindness hampered his attempt to study art, he became a copywriter for radio, working in Florida and New York. In the early 1940s, he settled in Philadelphia, where he wrote advertising copy and pursued creative writing in his spare time. From the mid-1940s, his writing appeared frequently in a variety of magazines.

In the early 1950s, Grubb began writing novels. His first published work, *The Night of the Hunter* (1953), was both a critical and popular success. In 1955 United Artists released it as a movie starring Robert Mitchum and Shelly Winters, with the screenplay by James Agee. After a disappointing initial reception, it became one of the most acclaimed movies of the decade. Grubb's next two novels were also both set in West Virginia. *A Dream of Kings* (1955) is a Civil War story, and *The Watchman* (1961) is a murder mystery. The success of these first three books enabled Davis Grubb to leave advertising work and devote himself completely to writing. He moved to New York, near his brother, Louis, and entered a period of great creative accomplishment which resulted in the publication of seven more books, all but one set in West Virginia, culminating in 1971 with *The Barefoot Man*, a mine-war novel. These works included a collection of stories and six novels ranging from historical fiction to crime fiction and even a Christmas novel.

From 1973 until 1976 Grubb lived in Franklin, Louisiana, near his cousin Ruth Williamson. He then moved back to Clarksburg, remaining there—except for a year spent back in New York—for the rest his life. Often misperceived by Clarksburg townspeople as a drug-abusing homosexual, Grubb, in fact, sought medication primarily to treat the cancer he was battling. He died on July 24, 1980, at the age of sixty-one.

Grubb is considered one of the most successful and impressive Appalachian authors of the second half of the twentieth century. He was effective with a wide range of popular fiction, publishing ten novels and two collections of stories in his thirty-year writing career. At its best, Grubb's work combines the virtues of literary and popular fiction. His books deal with complex themes and are written in a poetic style, yet they are exciting and entertaining as well.

See also: COAL-MINING LITERATURE; MITCHUM, ROBERT (MEDIA).

—George Brosi, *Berea, Kentucky*

Hague, Richard

(1947–) Fiction and nonfiction writer and poet.

Richard Hague was born in Steubenville, Ohio, and lives in Cincinnati, where he has taught at Purcell Marian High School since the early 1970s. His poetry, fiction, and essays focus primarily on the Ohio River Valley, especially its mill towns. Hague's many collections of poetry include *Ripening* (1984), *Possible Debris* (1988), and *Mill and Smoke Marrow* (1991). *Milltown Natural: Essays and Stories from a Life* (1997) uses both fiction and nonfiction to examine childhood and adolescence in a place dominated by a river and towering smokestacks. In addition to his extensive publications, Hague as a teacher has had great success in developing young writers.

Hague has taught at the Appalachian Writers Workshop and has won numerous awards, including an Ohio Arts Council Fellowship in Poetry and a National Endowment for the Humanities Fellowship to Oxford University. He has served as editor of *Pine Mountain Sand and Gravel*, and his writing has appeared in many anthologies throughout the region and nation.

See also: POST–WORLD WAR II FICTION.

—Jim Minick, *Radford University*

Haun, Mildred

(1911–1966) Fiction writer and folklorist.

East Tennessean Mildred Eunice Haun is best known for the story collection *The Hawk's Done Gone*. Born in her paternal grandmother's home in Hamblen County, she was one of three children of Margaret Ellen Haun and James Enzor Haun. As the writer explained, her mother was a Haun from Cocke County who married a Hamblen County Haun. She grew up in the Hoot Owl District of Cocke County and attended public schools there.

Deciding that her community needed an educated midwife to deliver babies and care for women and children, Haun moved to Franklin, near Nashville, to live with an aunt and uncle and further her education. After graduating from Franklin High School in 1931, she was admitted to Vanderbilt University. Although she gradually abandoned her dream of medical school, she took an undergraduate advanced composition course with poet John Crowe Ransom, who encouraged her to write.

Haun continued to create stories about Cocke County while she taught high school in Franklin and then began graduate school. Under the direction of Donald Davidson and John Crowe Ransom, she completed "Cocke County Ballads and Songs," her 440-page M.A. thesis, still considered a valuable collection of east Tennessee folklore. She also studied writing, supported by a fellowship, at the University of Iowa. When she completed her collection of stories, *The Hawk's Done Gone*, it was accepted for publication by Bobbs-Merrill in 1940. The 1968 edition included ten previously unpublished stories.

Throughout her life, Haun supported her mother and herself with work as a writer and an editor. She was book review editor for the *Nashville Tennessean* (1942–43), editorial assistant to Allen Tate on the *Sewanee Review* (1944–46), and an information specialist in Memphis and Washington, D.C., writing and editing press releases, speeches, and technical information for the military and the Department of Agriculture (1950–66). She died in Washington and was buried beside her parents in the Dover Cumberland Presbyterian Church near Morristown, Tennessee.

Haun's stories show her keen ear for dialect and folk traditions as well as a willingness to explore the dark side of human nature. Her fiction captures natural images and local superstitions and explores such subjects as incest, racist attitudes toward Melungeons, gender inequities, infanticide, witchcraft, and miscegenation. *The Hawk's Done Gone* is narrated by Mary Dorthula White, a mountain "granny woman" who introduces herself in the prologue. The midwife casts her shadow across generations in the community and creates continuity and unity within the powerful collection.

See also: GRANNY MIDWIVES (HEALTH); SECTION OVERVIEW (FOLKLORE AND FOLKLIFE).

—Sandra L. Ballard, *Appalachian State University*

Robert Bain, Joseph M. Flora, and Louis D. Rubin Jr. eds. *Southern Writers: A Biographical Dictionary* (1980); Herschel Gower, ed., *The Hawk's Done Gone and Other Stories* (1968); *Mossy Creek Reader: Mildred Haun Issue* (Spring 1993).

Houston, Gloria

(1940–) Fiction writer.

Gloria Houston writes picture books and children's historical fiction set in Appalachia. Born in Marion, North Carolina, to James and Ruth Greene Myron, owners of the Sunny Brook General Store in Spruce Pine, Houston grew up observing the customers in her parents' store and listening to her father recount family stories and local history. She has used many of those stories in her fiction.

Houston is best known for her picture book *The Year of the Perfect Christmas Tree* (1988), illustrated by Barbara Cooney, which is set in a rural mountain town during World War I. This book, like most of Houston's work, celebrates Appalachian codes of honor, loyalty, and family. Three of Houston's books deal with the character Littlejim. Littlejim's desire to be seen as a man by his disapproving father underlies the plot of *Littlejim* (1990) and *Littlejim's Dreams* (1997). Written for older juvenile readers, these works of historical fiction center around Littlejim's love of learning; *Littlejim's Dreams* introduces the topics of mining and clear-cut logging. *Littlejim's Gift: An Appalachian Christmas Story* (1994), illustrated by Thomas B. Allen, is set during the World War II era. Rebecca Linkerfelt, a herbalist and wise-woman commonly purported to be a witch, makes appearances in *Mountain Valor* (1994) and *Heckum, Beckum Linkerfelt* (1995). Houston's novel *Bright Freedom's Song: A Story of the Underground Railroad* (1998) deals with a former indentured servant who, along with his southern Appalachian family, helps slaves escape to freedom.

See also: CHILDREN'S LITERATURE.

—Elizabeth Poe, *West Virginia University*

Kephart, Horace

See Kephart, Horace (Language)

Kingsolver, Barbara

(1955–) Fiction and nonfiction writer and poet.

Born in Maryland, Barbara Kingsolver grew up in Carlisle, Kentucky, where her parents—native Kentuckians—had established her father's medical practice. During 1963, the Kingsolvers and their three children moved to a village in the Republic of Congo to provide medical help and in 1967 moved to St. Lucia, a Caribbean island, for the same reason. The impact of these experiences shaped the young Barbara as much as did her pastoral life in eastern Kentucky.

After graduating from Nicholas County High School, Kingsolver attended De Pauw University on a music scholarship, graduating magna cum laude with a double major in music and biology. Several years in Europe were followed by graduate work in the University of Arizona's Department of Ecology and Evolutionary Biology, but she turned to scientific writing rather than complete the Ph.D. dissertation.

Kingsolver's fiction utilizes a blend of her scientific, artistic, and travel experiences. Her settings vary. The Kentucky protagonist of Kingsolver's first novel, *Bean Trees* (1988), which sold more than a million copies, escapes her homeland to live in the Southwest. Both *Animal Dreams* (1990) and *Pigs in Heaven* (1993) are set in Arizona. In *The Poisonwood Bible* (1998), a Baptist family from Georgia tries to live in Belgian Congo. But many of her stories are set in Kentucky or Virginia, as is *Prodigal Summer* (2000), generally considered to be her most directly Appalachian work.

Kingsolver's versatility as a writer is further proven by her journalism, published in *Holding the Line: Women in the Great Arizona Mine Strike of 1983* (1989) and *High Tide in Tucson: Essays from Now or Never* (1995). These works also speak of her love for her southern childhood, as does her poetry collection, *Another America: Otra America* (1992).

See also: POST–WORLD WAR II FICTION; WOMEN AUTHORS.

—Linda Wagner-Martin, *University of North Carolina*

Knowles, John

(1926–2001) Novelist.

Author of the acclaimed novel *A Separate Peace*, John Knowles was born in Fairmont, West Virginia. The son of a coal-mining executive, Knowles drew heavily on childhood experiences for the novel *A Vein of Riches* (1978), set in a small Appalachian coal-mining town in West Virginia.

At age fifteen, Knowles went to Phillips Exeter Academy in New Hampshire. Graduating in 1945, he served in the U.S. Army Air Corps, graduated from Yale, and worked as a journalist, writer, and editor before publishing *A Separate Peace* in 1959. By far the most read and admired of Knowles's eleven books, *A Separate Peace* is set in a New England preparatory school during World War II and explores relationships between adolescent boys, turning on one boy's fall from a tree—a crippling "accident" that may or may not have been purposefully caused by the victim's best friend. The novel received the William Faulkner Foundation Award and the Rosenthal Award from National Institute of Arts and Letters.

Knowles wrote for the balance of his life, traveling in the United States and abroad and teaching at the University of North Carolina, Princeton University, and Florida Atlantic University. He continued to pursue themes of corruption and greed among affluent Americans throughout his writing career. Knowles's other novels include *Indian Summer* (1966), *The Paragon* (1971), *Spreading Fires* (1974), and *Peace Breaks Out* (1981), a companion novel to *A Separate Peace*.

See also: COAL-MINING LITERATURE.

—Will Eudy and Julie Kate Howard, *Hickory Day School, Hickory, North Carolina*

Literary Periodicals

In the nineteenth and early twentieth centuries, "serious" authors (natives as well as non-natives) who wrote about Appalachian subjects generally saw their literary works published in periodicals produced outside the region. George Washington Harris, a writer of satirical fiction in the Old Southwestern humor mode associated with Appalachia, first conveyed the exploits of his now archetypal Appalachian character Sut Lovingood in an 1854 story published in the New York City–based magazine *Spirit of the Times*. Rebecca Harding Davis's acclaimed 1861 novella *Life in the Iron-Mills*—an early manifestation of literary realism set in the industrial city of Wheeling, (West) Virginia—first appeared in Boston's prestigious *Atlantic Monthly*. Also appearing in that periodical were stories written during the late 1870s and the 1880s by Mary Noailles Murfree (under the pseudonym "Charles Egbert Craddock"), the first important author of local color fiction set in Appalachia. In the 1890s, the *Century*, a magazine based in New York City, published the earliest Appalachian-based fiction (two novellas) of local colorist John Fox Jr., who soon became one of the nation's best-selling novelists.

During the first decades of the twentieth century, a new generation of nonfiction writers, such as Emma Bell Miles, and scholars, including John C. and Olive Dame Campbell, attempted to represent Appalachian culture in a more balanced, less stereotyped light than had nineteenth-century authors. Their work ultimately resulted in a literary renaissance within Appalachia. Yet into the 1960s the authors who embodied that renaissance—James Still, Jesse Stuart, and Don West, among others—sent much of their work outside the region for publication. Few periodicals primarily interested in promoting Appalachia's literature existed within the region during the first half of the twentieth century—the notable exception being *Mountain Life and Work* (initiated in 1925 at Berea College in Berea, Kentucky), which published literary works by authors from Appalachia alongside scholarly essays that explored the region from cultural or sociological perspectives. Two literary periodicals published within Appalachia—*Sewanee Review*, founded in 1892 at the University of the South in Sewanee, Tennessee, and *Virginia Quarterly Review*, established in 1925 at the University of Virginia in Charlottesville—were prominent nationally by the 1950s, but they were not specifically focused on Appalachian literature.

The Appalachian studies movement of the 1960s and 1970s inspired the establishment of numerous new periodicals dedicated to increasing understanding of Appalachia's people and culture. Several of these periodicals received sufficient community or institutional support to ensure their survival, and they offered opportunities for writers and scholars on Appalachian themes to reach readers within the region. While some of the leading periodicals among this group were multidisciplinary in order to explore Appalachian culture holistically, they generally granted considerable space to creative writing and to literary scholarship. *Appalachian Journal*, begun in 1972 at Appalachian State University in Boone, North Carolina, has consistently incorporated literary works into its blend of materials, including poems, short stories, literary criticism, interviews of leading regional authors, and book reviews. *Appalachian Heritage*, founded in 1973 at Alice Lloyd College, publishes creative writing by regional authors alongside regional literary scholarship and book reviews. *Now and Then: The Appalachian Magazine*, started in 1984 at East Tennessee State University in Johnson City, Tennessee, specializes in publishing thematic issues, with each one offering related creative pieces and book reviews. *Iron Mountain Review*, published since 1983 at Emory and Henry College in Emory, Virginia, is another thematic periodical, focusing each issue on the life and work of one contemporary Appalachian literary figure.

Several other periodicals have made significant contributions to Appalachian literature, including *Shenandoah: The Washington and Lee University Review* (based in Lexington, Virginia, and founded in 1950); the *Hollins Critic* (Roanoke, Virginia, 1963); *Wind* (Pikeville, Kentucky, 1971); *Cold Mountain Review* (Boone, North Carolina, 1972); *Asheville Poetry Review* (Asheville, North Carolina, 1994); and *New Millennium Writings* (Knoxville, Tennessee, 1996). The emergence of the Internet in recent years has rendered possible wider dissemination of literary materials across Appalachia, with the *Nantahala Review* (initiated in 2001) being among the earliest and best-known e-journals in the region.

See also: *APPALACHIAN JOURNAL* (MEDIA). LITERARY SCHOLARSHIP; PRINTING/PUBLISHING PRESSES (BUSINESS, INDUSTRY, AND TECHNOLOGY).

—Ted Olson, *East Tennessee State University*

Literary Scholarship

In *Voices from the Hills*, an influential 1975 anthology of writings about Appalachia, editors Robert J. Higgs and Ambrose N. Manning asserted that Appalachian literature must be approached differently from the literature of the American South in that the two regional literary traditions reflect the two regions' significantly different histories with regard to race and class. Several other scholars during the early years of the Appalachian studies movement in the 1960s and 1970s shared Higgs and Manning's belief that the literature of Appalachia is unique and worthy of formal study.

The first major scholarly study of Appalachian literature has also proven to be among the most influential: Cratis Williams's 1961 dissertation, "The Southern Mountaineer in Fact and Fiction" (abstracted during the mid-1970s in four issues of the periodical *Appalachian Journal*), which focuses on the representations of Appalachian people and culture in novels and narrative nonfiction works published through the 1950s. Williams ignored non-narrative literary genres such as certain types of nonfiction, poetry, and song lyrics.

In an essay written for the 1962 book *The Southern Appalachian Region: A Survey*, W. D. Weatherford and Wilma Dykeman discussed more genres of literature than had Williams in his dissertation. Nonetheless, the essay was strictly an overview of the region's literature, and some of the book's analyses of the various genres of Appalachian literature would today be considered romanticized or fallacious. Two of the most important anthologies of writings about Appalachia—the 1975 single-volume *Voices from the Hills* and its two-volume successor, the 1995 book *Appalachia Inside Out* (both edited by Higgs and Manning, with assistance from Jim Wayne Miller on the latter project)—combined regional "creative writing" with texts primarily of sociological interest. While not providing a sustained critical discussion of Appalachian literary history, these anthologies introduced a broad-based audience to a wide range of literature about Appalachia.

Incorporating responses to regional literary works from several scholars, the 1976 book *Appalachian Literature: Critical Essays*, a compilation edited by Ruel E. Foster, spurred critical debate regarding the relative merits of specific works and encouraged within the Appalachian studies movement further formal study of a growing canon of Appalachian literature. In an essay included in *Appalachian Journal*'s "A Guide to Appalachian Studies" issue (1977), Miller not only surveyed the region's literary legacy but also confronted a dilemma inherent in the interpretation of Appalachian literature. Should the main focus of Appalachian literary study, Miller asked, be on "the works themselves"? In other words, should creative writing from the region and/or by regional authors be analyzed primarily to discern its literary qualities? Or might Appalachian literature also be read for sociological reflection on the region's cultural life? While not denying the utility of certain literary works for providing information on the intricacies of Appalachian society, Miller cautioned that literary renderings of Appalachian culture are not precisely sociological representations.

Appalachian literary scholarship has evolved to keep pace with socioeconomic changes within the region, and scholars continue to assess the profusion of new works written about the region. In the 1960s and 1970s, for example, scholars constructing the Appalachian literary canon focused largely on the literature of the region's highland areas and the coalfields and devoted less attention to literature from valley and urban areas; scholars also tended to overlook the work of female writers. The new socioeconomic conditions and cultural attitudes that emerged within Appalachia beginning in the 1970s inevitably necessitated reconsideration of the region's literary canon and influenced the direction of the scholarship.

Avoiding the more general approach found in previous studies of Appalachian literature, scholarly works published in the 1980s and 1990s explored the region's literature from specific theoretical or philosophical positions. *Sense of Place in Appalachia* (edited by S. Mont Whitson), a publication resulting from a 1987 symposium at Morehead State University, featured essays by scholars from numerous disciplines in the humanities and the social sciences assessing the importance of understanding and preserving Appalachian cultural identity in the face of modernization and pluralization. *The Poetics of Appalachian Space*, a 1991 collection of critical essays, examined a cross-section of the region's literature from the perspective of Gaston Bachelard's theory of interior space, which, according to the book's editor, Parks Lanier Jr., may help scholars of Appalachian literature better understand how "regional writing . . . transcends its local habitation." Two other books focusing on major topics in Appalachian literary studies are Danny L. Miller's *Wingless Flights: Appalachian Women in Fiction* (1996) and the 1999 collection of essays *Confronting Appalachian Stereotypes: Back Talk from an American Region*, edited by Dwight B. Billings, Gurney Norman, and Katherine Ledford.

In recent years, some graduate students have conducted extensive research into Appalachian literature and have produced valuable written scholarship. Numerous doctoral dissertations have been revised and published in book form, generally by university presses. Important unpublished dissertations—in the spirit of Williams's doctoral work—have found readers through periodicals, interlibrary loans, and on-line database services. Examples of such dissertations include Stephen Mooney's analysis of representations of Appalachian coal-mining culture in American novels; Carol Boggess's scholarly interpretation of James Still's novel *River of Earth;* and Katherine Ledford's critique of nineteenth-century travel writing about Appalachia.

Collectively challenging academia's previous disapproval of formal study of Appalachian culture in academia, the aforementioned books, essays, and dissertations ultimately enabled Appalachian literature to gain wider acceptance as a distinctive American regional literary canon. With Appalachian literature receiving considerable attention nationally since the 1990s, it remains to be seen if future writings about Appalachia—regardless of their literary merit—will retain the regional distinctiveness of works already part of the Appalachian canon. Significantly, while Miller's 1977 essay did not forecast the remarkable diversification evident in Appalachian literature during subsequent decades, his 1990 essay "A People Waking Up: Appalachian Literature since 1960" not only anticipated the increasing national interest in Appalachian literature that became apparent during the 1990s and continued into the first decade of the twenty-first century, but it also provided insightful analysis of that growing popularity. Despite the implication of its title, Miller's 1990 essay was less a survey of the region's literature since 1960 than it was a philosophical discussion of literary regionalism and its contemporary manifestations. Exhibiting skepticism towards the current national embrace of "Appalachian" literature, Miller wrote: "What happened in the late 19th century [i.e., the local color movement] is happening again. . . . Much contemporary 'regional' writing is a packaging of 'otherness' and traditional culture for a mass audience outside the region." Miller's historically grounded, skeptical approach to studying the literature of Appalachia may well serve as an ideal model for future scholarly efforts to assess and interpret literary works from and/or about the region.

See also: LOCAL COLOR; MILLER, JIM WAYNE; SECTION OVERVIEW (IMAGES AND ICONS).

—Ted Olson, *East Tennessee State University*

Jim Wayne Miller, "Appalachian Literature," *Appalachian Journal* (Autumn 1977) and "A People Waking Up: Appalachian Literature since 1960," in *The Cratis Williams Symposium Proceedings: A Memorial and Examination of the State of Regional Studies in Appalachia,* ed. Barry M. Buxton et al. (1989); Cratis D. Williams, "The Southern Mountaineer in Fact and Fiction," *Appalachian Journal* (Autumn 1975–Summer 1976).

Local Color

Shortly after the Civil War there began in American fiction a movement known as local color. Paralleling a similar impulse in nonfiction, local color fiction continued to be in vogue for at least thirty years, and in some respects it continues to the present day. Local color provided a notable contrast to the fiction of Edgar Allan Poe, so remotely connected to any time and place—though he does provide an Appalachian setting for "A Tale of the Ragged Mountains" (1844)—or even to the fiction of New Englander Nathaniel Hawthorne, who urged in the preface to *The House of the Seven Gables* (1851) that it be read as a "Romance" having little to do with the real city of Salem, Massachusetts. Local color, by contrast, attempts to offer the reader a picture of a particular place—its scenery, its people, and its ways of doing, thinking, and talking.

Classic definitions of local color come from a time when the movement was well established. Hamlin Garland, in *Crumbling Idols* (1894), defines local color as a writer's reflection of the life that goes on around him. To Garland, local color fiction has a texture and background so distinctive that it could not have been written anywhere else or by anyone other than a native of the area. Mark Twain, in "What Paul Bourget Thinks of Us" (1895), declared that the "native novelist" was the only one qualified to write of the "ways and speech and life" of the people of his area. Twain's examples range from New England to Oregon but do not include Appalachia. His own depiction of the region in the opening chapter of *The Gilded Age* (1874) would hardly qualify as local color fiction by his definition, since he had never visited the "knobs of East Tennessee" that he describes so unfavorably.

In the years when the local color movement flourished, the principal regions dealt with were the West (Bret Harte), Midwest (Garland), New England (Harriet Beecher Stowe, Sarah Orne Jewett, Mary E. Wilkins Freeman), and the South. The last of these had several subsections: the plantation South of Virginia and Georgia (Thomas Nelson Page, Joel Chandler Harris), the French society of Louisiana (George Washington Cable, Grace King, Kate Chopin), and the southern Appalachians.

Foremost among the local color writers of Appalachia was Mary Noailles Murfree, whose *In the Tennessee Mountains* (1884) contains eight stories previously published in the *Atlantic Monthly*. The earliest of these, her first published story, "The Dancin' Party at Harrison's Cove" (1878), is set in the area around Beersheba Springs, Tennessee, where she and her family spent many summers. Murfree's first and probably best-known mountain novel is *The Prophet of the Great Smoky Mountains* (1885). In the years that followed she published numerous stories and novels—all under her masculine pseudonym "Charles Egbert Craddock"—in which she sought to depict the manners and speech of the people of the Cumberland and Great Smoky Mountains. Born and reared in Murfreesboro in middle Tennessee and educated in the North, she was far from being a Tennessee mountain woman like the ill-fated Cynthia Ware of "Drifting Down Lost Creek" (1884) or Celia Shaw of "The Star in the Valley" (1878). This is quite apparent in the distance between her narrator's overblown diction and the dialect of the characters of her stories. Nevertheless many readers undoubtedly took her depiction as a straightforward, accurate portrait of the people of the southern mountains, unaware of the degree of stereotyping and exaggeration to be found in it. The national image of Appalachia, especially in the nineteenth century, was highly influenced by the fiction of its local color writers.

Murfree was not the only local color writer inspired by southern Appalachia. Rebecca Harding Davis is usually identified as having written the first Appalachian local color story, "The Yares of the Black Mountains" (*Lippincott's*, July 1875), in which an outsider comes to the mountains near Asheville, North Carolina, some years after the Civil War and is taken in by a pro-Union family there. Another early writer was Constance Fenimore Woolson, whose "Crowder's Cove: A Story of the War" appeared in *Appletons'* (March 18, 1876). In 1881, Mississippi writer Katherine Sherwood McDowell, writing under the pen name "Sherwood Bonner," published four Appalachian stories in *Harper's Weekly*, beginning with "Jack and the Mountain Pink" (January 29, 1881), set in the Cumberland Mountains near Cookeville, Tennessee. Later in the century another female writer, Will Allen Dromgoole, published a number of local color stories, primarily in the Boston-based *Arena*, which were collected in *The Heart of Old Hickory and Other Stories of Tennessee* (1895) and *Cinch, and Other Stories* (1898). Yet another Tennessee woman, Sarah Barnwell Elliott, also wrote stories and novels set near the town of Sewanee in the mountains of Tennessee, including *The Durket Sperret* (1898). Elliott sought to avoid the excessive romanticizing and sentimentality that marked the work of other local colorists.

In time the local color vogue faded; indeed, the term became somewhat pejorative, suggesting fiction marked by concern for the picturesque and charming, by excessive use of dialect spelling, and by an undue emphasis on what the writer perceives as different or unique about the area. On the other hand, if defined broadly enough, the aims of local color are to be seen in the work of many Appalachian writers. Lee Smith, Denise Giardina, Sharyn McCrumb, and many others are concerned to portray accurately the scenery, people, and speech of the places where their novels are set. But unlike Murfree and local colorists of the past, they are far more intimately acquainted with the regions they write about and do not regard their characters as quaint, rustic, or especially different.

See also: HUMOR IN APPALACHIAN LITERATURE (HUMOR); LITERARY PERIODICALS; MURFREE, MARY NOAILLES.

—Allison R. Ensor, *University of Tennessee*

Henry D. Shapiro, *Appalachia on Our Mind: The Southern Mountains and Mountaineers in the American Consciousness, 1870–1920* (1978); Merrill Maguire Skaggs, *The Folk of Southern Fiction* (1972); Emily Toth, ed., *Regionalism and the Female Imagination* (1985).

Lyon, George Ella

(1949–) Fiction writer, poet, and playwright.

Born and reared in the mountains of Harlan County, Kentucky, George Ella Lyon uses her Appalachian heritage as inspiration for her writing. Her education includes a B.A. from Centre College of Kentucky (1971), an M.A. from the University of Arkansas (1972), and a Ph.D. from Indiana University in Bloomington (1978). Primarily known for her children's picture books, Lyon also writes novels for middle school readers as well as fiction and poetry for adults.

A prolific writer, Lyon began her career with the poetry chapbook *Mountain* (1983), which, like subsequent works, demonstrates her poet's eye for detail and metaphor. *A Wordful Child* (1996), an autobiographical account of her own love of language, indicates how family stories provide the background for some of her picture books. *Where I'm From: Where Poems Come From* (1999) provides interpretive details for many of her poems and serves as a workbook to help readers develop their own poetic voices.

Lyon collaborates with a variety of artists in her children's picture books and sometimes appears as a character in her own books, significantly in *Who Came Down That Road?* (1992) and *A Sign* (1998). This inclusion of herself and her family strengthens the connection between writer and readers, encouraging them to imagine their own lives. Lyon's novels for middle school readers usually feature a young girl facing some problem or situation that becomes a rite of passage into adulthood. These stories deal with families caught between their desire to protect their children from harsh realities (puberty, sex, parents' unemployment, alcoholism, war, or death) and the inevitability of these realities entering children's lives. Although most of Lyon's stories are realistic, *Here and Then* (1994) includes time travel from the present back to the Civil War.

Lyon also writes poetry and fiction for adults. Using simple language, *Choices: Stories for Adult New Readers* (1989) features very short stories about adult situations that involve making difficult decisions. *With a Hammer for My Heart* (1997) is a novel told from multiple points of view as it portrays several generations from two families who experience conflict, tragedy, and renewal.

Lyon has received many awards, and recognition of her work is growing. Her myriad interests are reflected in the wide range of her audiences, topics, and genres. Her primary focus, however, is Appalachian Kentucky—its people, landscape, and history.

See also: CHILDREN'S LITERATURE.

—Harriette C. Buchanan, *Appalachian State University*

Sally Holmes Holtze, ed., *Seventh Book of Junior Authors and Illustrators* (1996); *Iron Mountain Review: George Ella Lyon Issue* (Summer 1994).

Lytle, Andrew

(1902–1995) Novelist, essayist, and editor.

Generally considered a southern rather than an Appalachian writer, Andrew Nelson Lytle spent some of his formative years and many of his later years living on the margins of Appalachia in Tennessee and northern Alabama. His most famous novel, *The Velvet Horn* (1957), which explores the impact of modern civilization on traditional rural southern culture, is set in a rugged Appalachian landscape.

Born December 26, 1902, in Murfreesboro, Tennessee, Lytle attended nearby schools, including Sewanee Military Academy. He enrolled at Exeter College (Oxford University) briefly in 1921, but soon returned to Tennessee after a death in his family. Entering Vanderbilt University, Lytle studied under—and eventually joined the ranks of—that school's renowned literary circle, the Fugitives.

Graduating with a B.A. in 1925, Lytle operated his father's north Alabama farm for a year and then moved to New York City to write plays and to act. In 1929 he returned to Tennessee to write a biography of Confederate General Nathan Bedford Forrest. Simultaneously, he collaborated with members of a later literary group at Vanderbilt, the Agrarians, to produce *I'll Take My Stand* (1930), an essay collection defending rural southern culture in the face of impending modernization. In 1932 Lytle published his first fiction. Eventually producing four novels, he also wrote plays, essays, and reviews while teaching at several schools, most notably the University of the South in Sewanee and the University of Florida. The editor of the prestigious literary journal *Sewanee Review* from 1961 to 1973, Lytle received several literary honors during his long career, including three Guggenheim Fellowships, a *Kenyon Review* fellowship for fiction, and a National Institute of Arts and Letters fellowship.

In addition to teaching and writing, Lytle farmed in several locations. For the last several decades of his life he resided in Monteagle, Tennessee, at "the Log Cabin," a family house his father had purchased in 1907. Lytle died December 12, 1995.

See also: AGRARIANISM; LITERARY SCHOLARSHIP.

—Ted Olson, *East Tennessee State University*

Marion, Jeff Daniel

(1940–) Poet, editor, and educator.

Jeff Daniel Marion earnestly began writing poetry in 1968. These poems were grounded in the countryside and culture in and around his hometown of Rogersville, Tennessee. This longing for the familiar provides themes Marion visits repeatedly in his work—the importance of home, a human connection to the natural world, the rough beauty of rural speech, and the power of memory to rediscover ever-changing people and places.

Taught at a young age to be attentive to his surroundings by his maternal grandmother, who was blind from cataracts, and his father, who was a sharp-eyed ink specialist at Rogersville's Card and Label Company, Marion deftly applied that skill in his first poetry collection, *Out in the Country, Back Home* (1976). Here the speaker observes rural life, such as the ritual of an old woman, her sense of touch sharpened by blindness, preparing her daily bread. The poem "In a Southerly Direction" features what Loyal Jones, in *Laughter in Appalachia: A Festival of Southern Mountain Humor,* calls "personalism"—the tendency to think of landscapes in terms of the people who inhabit them.

Subsequent poetry collections include *Tight Lines* (1981), *Vigils: Selected Poems* (1990), *Lost and Found* (1994), *The Chinese Poet Awakens* (1999), *Letters Home* (2001), and *Ebbing and Flowing Springs: New and Selected Poems and Prose, 1976–2001* (2002), as well as the children's book *Hello, Crow* (1992). Marion's narrative voice becomes open and emotional when he describes the death of close friends and relatives and, with them, the passing of beloved rituals and places so much a part of his youth. "Ebbing and Flowing Spring" presents an elderly woman, Matilda, a repository of local lore whose spring still flows, suggesting that her lore will live on in the speaker's memory. "Tight Lines" also employs water metaphorically, making an analogy between fishing and writing poetry; in both, the "lure" is "what's beneath."

In addition to writing, Marion has been active as an editor and an educator. From 1975 to 1980, he published one of the first literary journals in the southern Appalachians, the *Small Farm,* which featured works by Robert Morgan, George Ella Lyon, Fred Chappell, and other authors from across the nation. In 1983 he founded Mill Springs Press, which produced chapbooks and broadsides from handset type. Marion was distinguished poet-in-residence, director of the Appalachian Center, and associate professor of English at Carson-Newman College in Jefferson City, Tennessee, where he edited the *Mossy Creek Reader*. He also taught in the Tennessee Governor's School for the Humanities; served as poet-in-the-schools in Tennessee, North Carolina, and Virginia; and lectured and conducted workshops on teaching and writing poetry throughout the Appalachian region. He has received numerous awards, including the first Tennessee Arts Commission's literary arts fellowship (1978).

See also: CHILDREN'S LITERATURE; POST–WORLD WAR II POETS.

—Linda Parsons Marion, *University of Tennessee*

Iron Mountain Review: Jeff Daniel Marion Issue (Spring 1995); Rita Sims Quillen, *Looking for Native Ground: Contemporary Appalachian Poetry* (1989); Lynne P. Shackelford, "Jeff Daniel Marion," in *Contemporary Poets, Dramatists, Essayists, and Novelists of the South*, ed. Robert Bain and Joseph M. Flora (1994).

McCarthy, Cormac

(1933–) Fiction writer.

Born in Rhode Island, Cormac McCarthy grew up in east Tennessee near Knoxville, where he attended the University of Tennessee during the 1950s. During this decade, he also spent four years in the U.S. Air Force. By the end of the twentieth century, he had authored eight novels.

McCarthy's first four novels form the "Southern" or "Appalachian group" and all deal with marginal, impoverished, or criminal members of the American underclass. Writing in an expressionistic prose style laced with archaisms, McCarthy uses social outsiders to expose the brutality by which the middle and upper classes in America maintain their power. In *The Orchard Keeper* (1965), an aging mountaineer and a bootlegger serve as father figures to a young boy; the older men are eventually incarcerated. *Outer Dark* (1968), set in nineteenth-century Appalachia, concerns a young mother's quest for a child abandoned by her brother, the child's father. The tone of the novel is fantastic and nightmarish. *Child of God* (1974) follows Lester Ballard, the disenfranchised son of a suicide who is described in the novel as "a child of God much like yourself perhaps" as he transforms into a subterranean, necrophiliac transvestite preying on the women of a Tennessee mountain town. *Suttree* (1979), the longest and most complex of McCarthy's Appalachian novels, follows a few years in the life of Cornelius Suttree, a former member of the upper class who chooses to live among the urban poor in Knoxville during the 1950s. The novel presents a richly detailed, often humorous, grotesque world peopled with colorful characters who are typically doomed and evoke readers' sympathies.

McCarthy's last four novels take place in the Southwest, where he has made his home in El Paso, Texas. Like the Appalachian novels, these books—*Blood Meridian, or the Evening Redness in the West* (1985), *All the Pretty Horses* (1992), *The Crossing* (1994), and *Cities of the Plain* (1998)—present vivid, often critical, reexaminations of the myths of the American West. McCarthy has also written one screenplay, *The Gardener's Son* (1996), and a play, *The Stonemason* (1994).

McCarthy has received grants from most major foundations offering support for writing, including the Guggenheim Foundation, the American Academy of Arts and Letters, the Rockefeller Foundation, and the MacArthur Foundation.

See also: APPALACHIAN ENGLISH IN LITERATURE (LANGUAGE); POST–WORLD WAR II FICTION.

—Louis H. Palmer III, *Michigan State University*

Edwin T. Arnold and Dianne C. Luce, eds., *Perspectives on Cormac McCarthy* (1999); Vereen Bell, *The Achievement of Cormac McCarthy* (1988); Dana Phillips, "History and the Ugly Facts of Cormac McCarthy's *Blood Meridian*," *American Literature* (June 1996).

McCrumb, Sharyn

(1948–) Fiction writer.

Best known for her "Ballad series" of novels set in the mountains of Tennessee and North Carolina, Sharyn Arwood McCrumb was born in Wilmington, North Carolina, to a mother who was a native of the flatland South and a father who was a descendent of circuit-riding preachers in the Great Smoky Mountains. McCrumb received a B.A. in communications and Spanish from the University of North Carolina and an M.A. in English from Virginia Polytechnic Institute and State University. She uses elements from these varied parts of her history to depict aspects of Appalachian life and culture realistically.

McCrumb began writing at an early age. She credits her family heritage of telling stories with fostering her talent for writing and storytelling, noting that she was particularly bolstered by her great-grandfathers' loquaciousness and her father's bedtime stories based on classics such as Homer's *Iliad* and *Odyssey*.

McCrumb is the author of eighteen novels and three collections of short stories. The Ballad novels, so called because their titles refer to song and ballad titles, include *If Ever I Return, Pretty Peggy-O* (1990), *The Hangman's Beautiful Daughter* (1992), *She Walks These Hills* (1994), *The Rosewood Casket* (1996), *The Ballad of Frankie Silver* (1998), and *The Song Catcher* (2002). Primarily these novels take place in the fictional town of Hamelin and county of Wake in northeastern Tennessee, although in *The Song Catcher* some events transpire in Scotland and Philadelphia.

McCrumb's skills as a writer have received regional, national, and international acclaim. Two of the Ballad novels were *New York Times* best-sellers, and all of the Ballad novels have been either *New York Times* or *Los Angeles Times* "notable books." Among other accolades, she has received the Appalachian Writers Association's Best Appalachian Novel and Outstanding Contribution to Appalachian Literature awards, and Shepherd College (West Virginia) honored her as 1999 Appalachian Writer of the Year. Because of the popularity of her work, McCrumb has been an influence on the way people both in the United States and abroad perceive Appalachia.

See also: APPALACHIAN ENGLISH IN LITERATURE (LANGUAGE); LOCAL COLOR; NATIVE AMERICANS AND APPALACHIAN LITERATURE.

—Kimberley M. Holloway, *East Tennessee State University*

Kimberley M. Kidd, *From a Race of Story Tellers: The Ballad Novels of Sharyn McCrumb* (2003).

McCullough, David

(1933–) Historian and author.

Historian David McCullough was born July 7, 1933, in Pittsburgh. Educated at Yale University, he worked from 1956 to 1970 as editor and writer for *Time* magazine, the U.S. Information Agency, and the American Heritage Publishing Company before embarking on a highly successful career writing histories and biographies.

McCullough's first book examined one of northern Appalachia's most infamous disasters, the devastating flood that occurred in Johnstown, Pennsylvania, in 1899. A sweeping, meticulously researched, and readable account that interweaves social history, economics, and politics, *The Johnstown Flood* (1970) set the pattern for his subsequent books.

McCullough's interests have ranged throughout American history and North America. *The Great Bridge: The Epic Story of the Building of the Brooklyn Bridge* (1972) tells the story of the construction of New York's Brooklyn Bridge. *The Path between the Seas: The Creation of the Panama Canal, 1870–1914* (1977), which won a National Book Award, is a similarly broad examination of another engineering feat.

With *Mornings on Horseback* (1981), which also won a National Book Award, McCullough turned to biography as he recounted the early life of Theodore Roosevelt. His next book, a Pulitzer Prize–winning biography of Harry Truman, appeared in 1992. In 2001 McCullough published his third biography, *John Adams*. Like the histories, these biographies cast a wide net, not only narrating the lives of their subjects but also fully contextualizing them by describing their times. McCullough's scholarly soundness and deft sense of narration and characterization have made him one of the most successful history writers of his time. His popularity was enhanced by his frequent television appearances, notably as host of *The American Experience* on PBS.

See also: JOHNSTOWN FLOOD (ENVIRONMENT); POST–WORLD WAR II FICTION.

—Theresa Lloyd, *East Tennessee State University*

McFee, Michael

(1954–) Poet, essayist, and editor.

Michael McFee was born in Asheville, North Carolina, and received his B.A. and M.A. from the University of North Carolina, where he teaches. His poems often explore the emotional and cultural influences of the Appalachian region. McFee has worked as an assistant poetry editor for *DoubleTake* magazine, reviewer for WUNC-FM, and editor of the poetry anthology *The Language They Speak Is Things to Eat: Poems by Fifteen Contemporary North Carolina Poets* and the fiction anthology *This Is Where We Live: Short Stories by Twenty-Five Contemporary North Carolina Writers*.

McFee has published six books of poems: *Plain Air* (1983), *Vanishing Acts* (1989), *Sad Girl Sitting on a Running Board* (1991), *To See* (1991), *Colander* (1996), and *Earthly* (2001). Sparsely elegant and illuminated by a gentle but penetrating wit, McFee's poems usually unfold as meditations on mundane objects or actions that ultimately demonstrate psychological or spiritual significance. McFee has won many awards for his poetry, including a National Endowment for the Arts fellowship and a Pushcart Prize.

As an essayist on popular culture, McFee addresses a variety of topics, from film, as in his "Guide to Directors" in *An Introduction to Film Criticism*, to academic analyses of television shows, which he satirizes in "*Via Ponderosa:* Notes Toward a Theology of *Bonanza*" in the *Journal of Popular Film and Television*.

See also: POST–WORLD WAR II POETS.

—Donald Secreast, *Radford University*

Melungeons

Melungeons have been marginalized in Appalachia by custom and sometimes by law for nearly two centuries. Designated "free persons of color" in more than one census, these dark-skinned, fine-featured people were denied education and suffrage. In fiction, the word *Melungeon* denotes mystery, unpredictability, isolation, prejudice, passion, volatility, superstition, and pride. It means moonshine "likker," attractive diminutive women, and handsome reckless men. *Melungeon* conjures images of life on lonely ridges, tongue-speaking preachers handling poisonous serpents, log cabins with arched windows, grave houses in family cemeteries, and genealogies that hint at exotic ethnic origins in the century between Christopher Columbus and the settling of Jamestown.

Although Appalachian fiction makes use of Melungeon characters, Jesse Stuart's *Daughter of the Legend* (1965) is the only work in which a Melungeon, Deutsia Huntoon, is a main character. Other Melungeon characters in novels and short stories usually serve as metaphors.

Melungeon characters appear in Mildred Haun's *The Hawk's Done Gone*, Lee Smith's *The Devil's Dream*, Wilma Dykeman's *The Tall Woman* and its sequel, *The Far Family*, Sharyn McCrumb's *She Walks These Hills*, Lisa Alther's *Kinflicks*, Adriana Trigiani's Big Stone Gap trilogy, Phyllis Reynolds Naylor's *Sang Spell*, Patrick Bone's *Melungeon Winter*, Sarah Shaber's *The Fugitive King*, and Silas House's *Parchment of Leaves*. There are Melungeon characters in short stories by John Fox Jr. and Chris Offutt, as well as the four Melungeon tales collected by the Works Progress Administration Tennessee Writers' Project. Kermit Hunter's outdoor drama about Melungeons, *Walk toward the Sunset*, played in Sneedville, Tennessee, in the 1970s.

See also: MELUNGEON (LANGUAGE); MELUNGEONS (RACE, ETHNICITY, AND IDENTITY).

—Katherine Vande Brake, *King College*

Miles, Emma Bell

(1879–1919) Fiction and nonfiction writer and poet.

Emma Bell Miles, a pioneer folklorist in Appalachia, was one of the first authentic cultural voices from within the region. Born to schoolteacher parents, B. F. and Martha Mirick Bell, Emma spent the first ten years of her life in Rabbit Hash, Kentucky, on the banks of the Ohio River. Her parents then moved south to "keep school" on Walden's Ridge in southeastern Tennessee, taking her into a mountain environment that she soon adopted as her own and came to love deeply.

As Miles grew into adulthood, she listened to and learned scores of songs, stories, and sayings from her mountain neighbors, and she observed the rituals and customs of a traditional agrarian lifestyle continued from earliest days of settlement in the mountains of Tennessee. These mental collections were to become the subject matter of her first and best-known book, *The Spirit of the Mountains*, published in 1905. Consisting of ten chapters with titles such as "Cabin Homes," "The Old-time Religion," and "Some Real American Music," Miles's ethnographic study details the life of people on "King's Creek." Her models can be traced to the Walden's Ridge area now known as Signal Mountain, Tennessee. Although *The Spirit of the Mountains* was published a mere six years after Francis James Child's definitive five-volume *The English and Scottish Popular Ballads* and twelve years before the 1917 appearance of Olive Dame Campbell and Cecil Sharp's *English Folk Songs from the Southern Appalachians*, Miles's book contained a variant of the Child ballad "The Wife of Usher's Well" that Miles had collected. The book also cited a tune called "Weevily Wheat," which she believed to be about Bonnie Prince Charlie. Although Miles never called herself a folklorist, she functioned in that capacity through the collection, transmission, and interpretation of the mountain people's lore and lifestyle.

Miles also wrote poems and short stories that were published in popular periodicals such as *Harper's*, *Lippincott's*, and *Putnam's* over a fifteen-year span. The short stories display a strong crusading theme on behalf of women's rights, marking Miles as an early feminist in an unlikely setting. Her personal writings in journals, however, indicate that she struggled with the public portrayal of the lot of women and her own private life on Walden's Ridge. In traditional manner, she married a mountain man, Frank Miles, descendant of one of the settling families, and gave birth to five children over the course of seven years. Much of her writing was motivated by the need to make money to support her family, as was the artwork she produced in the form of paintings, wall murals, and illustrations of her own poems and prose.

In 1919, just weeks before her untimely death from tuberculosis, Miles's *Our Southern Birds* was published. A posthumous collection of her poetry, *Strains from a Dulcimore*, appeared in 1930. She remains an authentic spokesperson for Appalachia even into the twenty-first century. Since its republication in 1975, *The Spirit of the Mountains* has never been out of print. Miles's works are popular choices in Appalachian studies courses and among a general audience.

See also: FOLK MUSIC COLLECTIONS (MUSIC); WOMEN AUTHORS.

—Grace Toney Edwards, *Radford University*

Grace Toney Edwards, "Emma Bell Miles: Appalachian Author, Artist, and Interpreter of Folk Culture," Ph.D. dissertation, University of Virginia (1981) and "Emma Bell Miles: Feminist Crusader in Appalachia," in *Appalachia Inside Out, Vol. 2: Culture and Custom*, ed. Robert J. Higgs, Ambrose N. Manning, and Jim Wayne Miller (1995); Kay Baker Gaston, *Emma Bell Miles* (1985).

Miller, Jim Wayne

(1936–1996) Poet, essayist, fiction writer, and teacher.

Jim Wayne Miller was one of the most influential writers, scholars, and teachers to explore and promote the literature and culture of Appalachia as distinct from those of the lowland South. He celebrated regional culture in his poetry, essays, and fiction and insisted that the history and values of Appalachian people be essential considerations in shaping the region's educational, political, and economic future.

A native of Leicester, Buncombe County, North Carolina, Miller completed studies in English and German at Berea College in 1958 and for the next two years taught both subjects in the Fort Knox Dependent Schools. In 1963

Jim Wayne Miller in his office at Western Kentucky University, c. 1990. A native of western North Carolina, Miller was one of the most influential writers, scholars, and teachers in promoting the literature and culture of Appalachia as distinct from those of the lowland South.

he joined the Department of Modern Languages at Western Kentucky University while completing a Ph.D. in German literature as a National Defense Education Act fellow at Vanderbilt University. Miller's thirty-year career as a teacher and translator of German literature paralleled and informed his emergence as both a poet of the Appalachian region and a commentator on stereotyped images of the southern mountaineer. His mastery of an adopted language and literature enhanced his appreciation for the beauty and complexity of his own language and lent a practical, international perspective to his passionate defense of the power of regional speech and literature. Until shortly before his death of lung cancer in 1996, Miller crisscrossed Appalachia, reading from his own and others' work, teaching, lecturing, and leading workshops on regional culture and writing.

Copperhead Cane (1964), *The More Things Change the More They Stay the Same* (1971), and *Dialogue with a Dead Man* (1974), along with numerous journal and anthology publications from 1965 to 1980, established Miller's reputation as a poet. During this period, as he was studying and writing about his region's history and culture as described by Horace Kephart, John C. Campbell, Harry Caudill, James Still, Jesse Stuart, Harriette Simpson Arnow, and Cratis Williams, Miller also translated German poetry.

When *The Mountains Have Come Closer* appeared in 1980, its central figure, a displaced mountaineer known only as "the Brier," was recognized by many as the ideal persona to express dismay at the decay and dismissal of traditional mountain culture. *Brier* was a disparaging term applied to Appalachian immigrants to the Midwest, where Miller's Brier also had moved. Alienated from both his people and himself as a result of this spatial change and the cultural change taking place in the mountains themselves, the Brier refers to himself in third person and inhabits spaces that reflect his isolation. Holding down a variety of occupations, including that of craftsman and impromptu sidewalk evangelist, the Brier recognizes the damage done to Appalachians by both negative and seemingly benign, romantic stereotypes of the region; he suggests that mountaineers pay for participation in mainstream American life by rejecting their traditional values or by acting out a degrading self-parody. His "Brier Sermon," the long conclusion to *The Mountains Have Come Closer*, criticizes the decay of traditional mountain culture, articulates the hope that mountain people can escape limitations of the "brier" image by learning to "think ocean to ocean" instead of "ridge to ridge," and establishes as his unofficial eleventh commandment the injunction to remember the past. In his second Brier volume, the optimistic *Brier, His Book* (1988), Miller continues to explore the relationship between past and present. Like one of Miller's favorite fictional characters, the rascally Sut Lovingood (created by George Washington Harris), the Brier is a product of his time and place; he is also a detached observer who perceives universal truths in local situations. The Brier as Appalachian archetype may be Miller's most enduring literary and social legacy.

Miller's other poetry collections include *Vein of Words* (1984), *Nostalgia for Seventy* (1986), and *The Wisdom of Folk Metaphor* (1988). Individual poems appeared in dozens of regional and national journals and anthologies. His nonfiction works are *Reading, Writing, Region: A Checklist and Purchase Guide for School and Community Libraries* (1984), *Sideswipes* (1986), *The Examined Life: Family, Community, and Work in American Literature* (1989), and *Round and Round with Kahlil Gibran* (1989). Works of fiction by Miller are the chapbook *His First, Best Country* (1987; adapted into a play and expanded to a novel in 1993) and the novel *Newfound* (1989). Miller contributed numerous short stories, articles, essays, and reviews to literary and professional journals, newspapers, and magazines.

Miller was intensely interested in the work of other Appalachian writers, both early and contemporary. He edited the anthology *I Have a Place* (1981), edited and introduced a reissue of Jesse Stuart's *Songs of a Mountain Plowman* (1986), and coedited reissues of Stuart's novels *A Penny's Worth of Character* (1988) and *The Beatinest Boy* (1989). Close friend and frequent traveling companion of poet and fiction writer James Still, Miller edited and wrote the introduction to Still's *The Wolfpen Poems* (1986). He was coeditor of Cratis Williams's *Southern Mountain Speech* (1992) and of the anthology *A Gathering at the Forks* (1993). Along with Robert J. Higgs and Ambrose N. Manning, he coedited *Appalachia Inside Out* (1995).

An early proponent of place-based education, Miller argued that readings and assignments should illuminate the environments in which students actually live rather than alienate them from their homes and communities. He received numerous awards for his teaching, writing, and advocacy of Appalachian literature and culture.

See also: CHILDREN'S LITERATURE; HUMOR IN APPALACHIAN LITERATURE (HUMOR); LITERARY SCHOLARSHIP.

—Ricky Cox, *Radford University*

Robert Morgan, "Clearing Newground," *Appalachian Heritage* (Fall 1997); Rita Sims Quillen, *Looking for Native Ground: Contemporary Appalachian Poetry* (1989).

Morgan, Robert

(1944–) Poet, fiction writer, essayist, and teacher.

Throughout his career, Robert Morgan has examined Appalachia's history, landscape, objects, people, work, and religion in poetry, fiction, and essays. Morgan was born near Hendersonville, North Carolina, on land settled by his great-great-grandfather. While studying science at North Carolina State University, he came under the influence of Guy Owen, who encouraged Morgan to switch to writing. Morgan transferred to the University of North Carolina, where he received his B.A.; he obtained an M.F.A. in 1968 at the University of North Carolina at Greensboro, where he studied under another Appalachian poet and fiction writer, Fred Chappell. In 1971 Morgan began teaching at Cornell University, where he was named Kappa Alpha Professor of English.

Morgan has produced ten volumes of poetry. His early poems are terse and concise, like mathematical proofs. Through microscopic attention to objects and startling juxtapositions, he attempts to evoke the specificity of those objects in an almost animistic fashion. *Zirconia Poems* (1969) and *Red Owl* (1972) reveal his controlled mastery of free verse. *Land Diving* (1976) and *Trunk and Thicket* (1978) constitute an exploration of narratives, longer poems, formal poetry, and his deeply Appalachian origins. *Groundwork* (1979), his most lyrical and most formal book, is devoted almost exclusively to Appalachian narratives, myths, superstitions, and Morgan family legends.

Morgan's next two books of poetry demonstrated that he was neither a regional chauvinist nor a nostalgic Appalachian. *At the Edge of the Orchard Country* (1987) and *Sigodlin* (1990) consider such subjects as plate tectonics, field theory, and shadow matter as well as American history, religion, and the Vietnam Memorial. These poems employ complex forms such as triolet, terza rima, chant royal, and pantoum.

In 1989 Morgan turned toward fiction with a volume of short stories, *Blue Valleys,* which was followed by the short stories in *The Mountains Won't Remember Us* (1992). These stories range from historical tales to contemporary scenes of trailer-park America. Set on the escarpment of the Blue Ridge bordering North and South Carolina, Morgan's first novel, *Hinterlands: A Mountain Tale in Three Parts* (1994), is a family saga tracing the Richards family from 1772 to 1845.

Morgan's next novel, *The Truest Pleasure* (1995), centers around the conflicts between Ginny, whose passion is for Pentecostal preaching and the ecstasy of speaking in tongues, and her husband, Tom, a practical man who believes in work, land, and money. The novel examines religious possession—its mysteries, gifts, and embarrassments; the struggles to endure childbirth, sickness, jealousy, and marital discord; and the restorative power of love. The early drafts of *The Truest Pleasure,* which were told from the male's point of view, were unsatisfactory to Morgan because he believed that this particular type of man would not have noticed the specific details of domestic life or talked readily about his feelings. To achieve the intimate, domestic observations Morgan knew from listening to women storytellers and watching his grandmother, mother, sister, and wife, he recast the novel so that it was told from Ginny's point of view. He had also used a female narrator in *The Mountains Won't Remember Us,* and he continued to employ this point of view in later texts such as *Gap Creek* (1999).

Like *The Truest Pleasure,* the novel *Gap Creek* explores the conflict between spouses of different temperaments, a tension Morgan traced back in his own family history. Named Book of the Year in 2000 by the Appalachian Writers Association, *Gap Creek* chronicles the pleasures and misfortunes of a young couple fighting to forge a life for themselves in the North Carolina mountains at the turn of the twentieth century. The story is told in the spare, uneducated voice of Julia Harmon, who recounts the terrible hardships and disappointments she has endured. Hers is the voice of a woman who does not speak easily and who feels inarticulate yet whose story is an emotionally complex, gripping account of the physical struggle of rural existence counteracted by the strength of the human spirit. Glowing reviews and Morgan's appearance on Oprah Winfrey's television show rocketed the novel onto the best-seller lists and touched off a contest for film rights.

Morgan's interest in the female narrative voice is also evident in *The Balm of Gilead Tree* (1999), a collection of new and previously published stories. Several are narrated by bright, feisty women who are survivors of the violence, sickness, and hardship in the North Carolina mountains shortly after the Civil War. In addition to this text, two other important collections of previously published material appeared in the 1990s. *Green River: New and Selected Poems* (1991) shows the evolution of Morgan's style from intensely sensory, imagistic poetry about common farm implements and actions to poems encompassing Appalachian and Cherokee history, family, narratives, and science. The interviews and essays in *Good Measures: Essays and Interviews on Poetry* (1993) explore, among other things, Morgan's family's North Carolina subsistence farm, which functions on the level of archetype throughout his writings. The title of Morgan's tenth volume of poetry—*Topsoil Road* (2000)—indicates his enduring interest in the land.

See also: POST–WORLD WAR II FICTION; POST–WORLD WAR II POETS.

—Newton Smith, *Western Carolina University*

William Harmon, "Robert Morgan's Pelagian Georgics: Twelve Essays," *Parnassus* (Fall–Winter 1981); John Lang, "Coming Out from under Calvinism: Religious Motifs in Robert Morgan's Poetry," *Shenandoah* (Fall 1992); P. H. Liotta, "Pieces of the Morganland: Recent Achievements in Robert Morgan's Poetry," *Southern Literary Journal* (Spring 1990).

Murfree, Mary Noailles

(1850–1922) Fiction writer.

Mary Noailles Murfree wrote novels and short stories about mountain people in the late 1800s and is credited with helping to shape a national perception of Appalachia that is still felt today. Born into wealth at Murfreesboro in middle Tennessee, Murfree grew up in a contradictory environment of privilege and disaster. A fever when she was four left her permanently lame; eleven years later Grantland, the family estate, was destroyed in the Civil War. She received an education typical of upper-class women of the time, including two years (1867–69) at Chegary Institute, a finishing school in Philadelphia. Upon her return to Nashville, her father, a lawyer with a predilection for the arts, encouraged her to write. After success with a few comic sketches in *Lippincott's*, she turned her attention to fiction. Writing under the pseudonym "Charles Egbert Craddock," she found through northern publications an audience eager to read about life in the southern highlands. In a prolific career that spanned nearly half a century, she produced some forty-five short stories and eighteen novels. These include juvenile works, such as *Down the Ravine* (1885) and *The Champion* (1902), and novels set in the plantation South, such as *Where the Battle Was Fought* (1884), but the majority of her work and her chief contribution to American letters are her fictional treatments of the mountain South. She is the preeminent practitioner of Appalachian local color.

Murfree was not a native of Appalachia, but she was far more than a tourist in her proximity to mountain people. Beginning at the age of five and continuing for fifteen years, she and her family spent each May through October in the Cumberland Mountains at their summer home in Beersheba Springs. Her first story using material from the mountains, "The Dancin' Party at Harrison's Cove," appeared in the *Atlantic Monthly* in 1878. It includes many elements of what have become Appalachian stereotypes: a feud, moonshine, puritanical social strictures, portraits of winsome mountain youth and their haggard elders, some humor, and purity in ancestry and attitudes. Often anthologized, it is one of eight short stories in her best-known volume, *In the Tennessee Mountains* (1884). That collection and the novel that followed, *The Prophet of the Great Smoky Mountains* (1885), were hailed by Cratis Williams as her most influential works.

During her lifetime Murfree was widely acclaimed, receiving extensive laudatory reviews in major publications and in 1922 an honorary degree from the University of the South. After her death her literary reputation faltered, and later scholars have objected to her florid style and authorial commentary about the mountain types she describes. Henry D. Shapiro argues in *Appalachia on Our Mind* that Murfree is the single most important writer in creating of the myth of Appalachia, bringing to the nation in the heyday of local color an image of a distinctly "other" region. Her writing continues to attract readers and controversy, with some seeing her work as a doorway and others a barrier to an understanding of Appalachia.

See also: APPALACHIAN ENGLISH IN LITERATURE (LANGUAGE); HUMOR IN APPALACHIAN LITERATURE (HUMOR); LOCAL COLOR.

—Nancy Carol Joyner, *Western Carolina University*

Native Americans and Appalachian Literature

The Appalachian region has historically been home and hunting ground for such tribal peoples as the Delaware,

Shawnee, Cherokee, Creek, and Choctaw. As a result, Native Americans have contributed to Appalachian literature as creators of oral and written texts and as historical and fictional subjects.

The Appalachian Mountains serve as a backdrop for ancient stories passed down through tribal oral traditions. One Cherokee creation myth, for example, describes a world of mud too wet to live on until the Great Buzzard flew over to dry it; wherever his wings struck the earth a valley appeared, and wherever his wings rose again a mountain stood. The mountainous terrain thus created became Cherokee country.

Early in the nineteenth century, Sequoyah's creation of a Cherokee syllabary led to the beginning of written work from a tribal people native to Appalachia. Soon after the syllabary was completed and type was created for its characters, the region saw the publication of the *Cherokee Phoenix* (1828–34), a bilingual newspaper in both the tribal language and English. This newspaper, edited by a Cherokee named Elias Boudinot, offered some of the period's most eloquent arguments for the tribal peoples to remain in their Appalachian homelands and not be driven west of the Mississippi River.

Recently, poet and essayist Marilou Awiakta, from Oak Ridge, Tennessee, has combined her Appalachian and Cherokee heritages to address contemporary regional challenges that are personal, tribal, and technological. Awiakta's central works are *Abiding Appalachia: Where Mountain and Atom Meet* (1978) and *Selu: Seeking the Corn-Mother's Wisdom* (1993).

As historical subjects, Native Americans appear in early memoirs set in the Appalachian region. In addition to their roles as guides and hunters in these narratives, the tribal peoples are also treated—alongside difficult terrain and wild animals—as a dangerous element of the mountains. Historical images of Native Americans appear in such works as Private John G. Burnette's nineteenth-century eyewitness account of their removal from Appalachia.

Some of the most applauded fiction from Appalachian authors contains images and influences of Native Americans as well. Thomas Wolfe created a Cherokee history for his baseball folk hero Nebraska Crane in *The Web and the Rock* (1939) and *You Can't Go Home Again* (1940). In the background of Sharyn McCrumb's *She Walks These Hills* (1994), the ghostly Shawnee captors of Katie Wyler lend a sense of danger to the mysticism of the mountains. Cherokee naturalism, folklore, and history contribute to the allure of Charles Frazier's *Cold Mountain* (1997), particularly enhancing the spiritual character of Inman, a Civil War deserter trying to get home to the mountains and his beloved Ada. Perhaps the best-known images of Native Americans in Appalachian fiction appear in Forrest Carter's controversial *The Education of Little Tree* (1976).

See also: CARTER, FORREST; CHEROKEE (LANGUAGE); CHEROKEE FAMILIES AND COMMUNITIES (FAMILY AND COMMUNITY).

—Michael Cody, *East Tennessee State University*

John Ehle, *Trail of Tears: The Rise and Fall of the Cherokee Nation* (1988); Laurence French and Jim Hornbuckle, eds., *The Cherokee Perspective* (1981); James Mooney, *History, Myths, and Sacred Formulas of the Cherokee* (1992); Theda Perdue, ed., *Cherokee Editor: The Writings of Elias Boudinot* (1996).

Naylor, Phyllis Reynolds

(1933–) Fiction writer.

Phyllis Reynolds Naylor, author of more than ninety books, mostly for children and young adults, has chosen the Appalachian Mountains of West Virginia as setting for several of her best-known works. Born in Anderson, Indiana, she published her first story for a church magazine at age sixteen, married at age eighteen, and graduated from Joliet Junior College before moving with her husband to Chicago. After five years of marriage, her husband developed an incurable mental illness; later, Naylor obtained a divorce and in 1960 married Rex V. Naylor, a native of West Virginia. In 1963 she earned a degree in clinical psychology from American University.

Naylor's writing reflects all the places she has lived; her connection to Appalachia comes through her husband and his family. Her 1992 Newbery Medal winner, *Shiloh*, was named for a West Virginia community where she found an abused dog that inspired the book and its sequels *Shiloh Season* and *Saving Shiloh*. Naylor's Appalachian novels also include *Wrestle the Mountain*, the story of a boy growing up in a West Virginia coal-mining community, and a popular series of six works focusing on the feuding antics of the Hatford boys and the Malloy girls *(The Boys Start the War, The Girls Get Even, Boys against Girls, The Girls' Revenge, A Traitor among the Boys,* and *A Spy among the Girls)*. A later Appalachian young adult novel, *Sang Spell*, is noteworthy for its depiction of Melungeons.

See also: COAL-MINING LITERATURE; WOMEN AUTHORS.

—Carolyn Mathews, *Radford University*

Norman, Gurney

(1937–) Fiction and nonfiction writer and editor.

Gurney Norman, born July 22, 1937, in Grundy, Virginia, is best known as the author of the novel *Divine Right's Trip*, for which he received a National Book Award in 1972, and the collection of short stories *Kinfolks: The Wilgus Stories* (1977).

From a coal-mining family that experienced the hard times of depression and war, Norman and his two siblings spent part of their childhood with grandparents in Hazard, Kentucky, and Pennington Gap, Virginia. In 1946 he and his brother enrolled at the Stuart Robinson School, a Presbyterian boarding school in Blackey, Kentucky, and he remained there until his graduation in 1955. Norman attributes his early interest in writing to the influence of Robinson teachers who first introduced him to the books of Jesse Stuart and James Still and encouraged his own writing. He edited the school paper, the *Stuart Robinson Highlights*, and wrote his first short stories at the school.

Norman attended the University of Kentucky, where he majored in journalism and English. In the late 1950s, four of his stories appeared in *Stylus*, the campus literary magazine. On the strength of these stories, he won a Stanford University Wallace Stegner Creative Writing Fellowship in 1960.

After serving in the U.S. Army from 1961 through 1963, Norman returned to Kentucky to work as a reporter for the weekly *Hazard Herald*. He covered such stories as the roving pickets, which were still active in 1964, the War on Poverty, and the beginnings of environmental activism against strip mining.

A return to California in 1967 brought work as an editor and writer for the *Whole Earth Catalog*. Out of that experience came Norman's first novel, *Divine Right's Trip*. Published in short chapters in the margins of the catalog, it became a national best-seller in 1971.

In 1979 Norman joined the faculty of the University of Kentucky, teaching creative writing. Since then, he has been a driving force for cultural activism in Appalachia, supporting young writers, filmmakers, actors, and teachers. He initiated and coedited an anthology of poetry, *Old Wounds, New Words* (1994), and the essay collection *Confronting Appalachian Stereotypes: Back Talk from an American Region* (1999). In 1999 Norman and his wife, Nyoka Hawkins, founded a small publishing house, Old Cove Press. The press's first book was *Affrilachia*, a collection of poems by Frank X Walker.

Norman has also been involved with television and film. He wrote and hosted three documentaries for Kentucky Educational Television: *Time on the River*, exploring the Kentucky River Valley; *From This Valley*, examining the literary and cultural heritage of the Big Sandy Valley; and *Wilderness Road*, retracing Daniel Boone's route into Kentucky. His play *Ancient Creek* was recorded by June Appal Records of Appalshop; later translated into Italian by Annalucia Accardo from the University of Rome, it was performed for video in a series of programs on *The South of the World*. Norman collaborated with director Andrew Garrison on the screenplay adaptation of three stories from *Kinfolks*: "Fat Monroe," "Night Ride," and "Maxine." The three resulting films were edited together into *The Wilgus Stories* (2000).

See also: COAL-MINING LITERATURE; POST–WORLD WAR II FICTION.

—Andrew Garrison, *University of Texas*

"Our Contemporary Ancestors in the Southern Mountains"

William Goodell Frost's *Atlantic Monthly* essay "Our Contemporary Ancestors in the Southern Mountains" (March 1899) was the definitive summary of views that Frost had been developing since becoming president of Berea College in 1892, and it was to have great influence on America's view of Appalachia for the next century. Frost's essay was the culmination of seven years of crafted appeals to his fellow wealthy northerners for financial support for Berea College; in that service, it deploys rhetorical strategies that appealed to establishment American values and assumptions of the time. The essay is thus not only a shaper of American attitudes but also an illuminating mirror of them.

Since its founding, Berea College had been a historically biracial and predominantly African American institution. White Appalachian students had long attended Berea with its administration's encouragement, but Frost greatly expanded this emphasis in a decade in which Jim Crow laws were proliferating in the South and endangering the future of biracial education. Frost claimed to be recruiting white students for the benefit of the black ones, but by the time mandatory segregation came to Kentucky in 1904, Berea's black enrollment had plummeted. Frost was trying to replace blacks with mountain whites in the affections of northern philanthropists and on campus.

Frost's essay pushes all the right buttons of his age, an era that stressed the civilizing mission of the Anglo-Saxon race, which white Americans felt was triumphant abroad but seemingly threatened at home by large-scale immigration of people from eastern Europe and the Mediterranean. The core of Frost's appeal is found in his use of "contemporary ancestors." Frost repeatedly asserts that although mountain people may seem peculiar, their apparent oddities are simply a result of being peculiarly American, peculiarly true to what his audience thought of as their own colonial and pioneer roots. Frost asserts that the mountaineer's "ancestry . . . is for the most part creditable" (meaning Anglo-Saxon). Furthermore, Appalachia's supposed isolation, he insists, has not, as many people said, led to degeneration but has caused mountain culture to remain static. Just as the mountaineer's homemade implement stands to the middle-class American's commercial product as "not a substitute, but an archetype," so it is for the cultural "anachronism[s]" of mountain life: they represent pure colonial virtues. Despite their pedigree and colonial values, Frost argues that mountain people are "consciously stranded" and that they must therefore be "enlightened and guided" by "saving aid" from Frost's audience—via Berea, for example. In short, as Appalachians now are, so white Anglo-Saxon Protestants once were; Appalachians can evolve with the help of their descendants.

Through this assistance, mountaineers can join the rest of white Protestant America and reinforce its ranks against the supposed barbarians without and within.

Recent critics have tended to feel that Frost's rhetoric in "Our Contemporary Ancestors" had destructive effects. These critics argue that the depiction of mountain people purely as objects of charity was disempowering and that the suggestion that they existed outside the flow of history implicitly dismissed the validity of their own perceptions and their attempts to help themselves, such as through labor actions. Furthermore, the idea of northern benefactors' facilitating Appalachians' natural destiny lent itself to a program of cultural assimilation, and the identification of mountain people with white Anglo-Saxon America in a racially charged context underscores the idea that mountaineers lived in a subculture of white racism.

See also: BEREA COLLEGE (EDUCATION); FROST, WILLIAM GOODELL AND ELEANOR MARSH (EDUCATION); SECTION OVERVIEW (IMAGES AND ICONS).

—Rodger Cunningham, *Alice Lloyd College*

William Goodell Frost, "Our Contemporary Ancestors in the Southern Mountains," *Atlantic Monthly* (March 1899); Elisabeth S. Peck and Emily Ann Smith, *Berea's First 125 Years: 1855–1980* (1982).

Our Southern Highlanders

First published in 1913, *Our Southern Highlanders* by outdoorsman Horace Kephart is one of the seminal works of Appalachian nonfiction and has been the foundation for numerous subsequent studies of Appalachia. Kephart's book paints a vivid picture of the mountains and their inhabitants, offering geographical, historical, cultural, socioeconomic, linguistic, and anthropological information. In the first few chapters, Kephart relates the history of the Appalachian Mountains, explaining their origin and identifying subchains, elevations, and notable peaks, as well as flora and fauna.

Kephart, a native of the Midwest, traveled to the Great Smoky Mountains in the early twentieth century and secluded himself for nearly ten years to study the mountaineer, then an often misunderstood and under-researched American. Kephart sought to characterize and demystify the Appalachian dweller, a person he portrays as a contemporary ancestor long isolated from modernism and preserving a vanishing way of self-sufficient life in the high hills and deep hollows. His mountaineers are lean, independent, and hardy, unfailingly loyal to family, prone to feuds with neighbors, and wary of change and outsiders. They cannot be simply stereotyped as ignorant and backward, however, for Kephart notes that in their character are an awe-inspiring stamina and wisdom not found in city dwellers or lowlanders. In describing the mountain way of life, Kephart provides enduring vignettes of Appalachia—a bear hunt, a moonshine still, a conversation between neighbors, a cabin hearth—but he ends his study with the image of a sleeper who must eventually wake, symbolizing the inevitable loss of this culture to the encroachment of development and industry.

See also: ENVIRONMENTAL WRITING; KEPHART, HORACE (LANGUAGE).

—Heather Rhea Gilreath, *East Tennessee State University*

Out of This Furnace

Out of This Furnace, a 1941 novel by Thomas Bell (1903–1961), addresses the social, political, and economic oppression of Slovak immigrants in Pennsylvania steel mills. The book is also a fictionalized family history of Bell, born Adalbert Thomas Belejcak to Slovak immigrants Mary and Micheal Belejcak.

Out of This Furnace follows three generations of Slovak steel mill workers around Bell's hometown of Braddock, Pennsylvania, from 1881 until 1937. Djuro Kracha, the protagonist, comes to America to work on the railroad, moves on to a steel mill, and eventually buys his own butcher shop before losing his money to a bad business deal and a thieving mistress. Kracha's daughter Mary weds hard-working, politically minded Mike Dobrejcak, but their happiness at home cannot transcend the harsh working conditions, poverty, and danger of millwork. Their son Dobie endures the Great Depression and fights for union representation for mill workers.

Out of This Furnace offers the tight Slovak family as an antidote to brutal mill-town life. Though the working conditions for men are more obviously horrific, the workload for women is no less impossible and claims as many young wives as the mill does young husbands. The destroyed landscapes of Braddock and Homestead show the mill consuming land as hungrily as lives. Each successive generation gains power to affect the decisions that determine working conditions, though, and the family evolves from Slovak immigrants to labor-minded mill workers to American union men in about fifty years.

See also: IRON AND STEEL MILL WORKERS (LABOR).

—Brandon Story, *King College*

Pancake, Breece D'J

(1952–1979) Fiction writer.

Breece Dexter Pancake's first and only collection of stories has been the subject of controversy but is generally regarded as among the best fiction to come out of Appalachia. Born on July 29, 1952, Pancake grew up in Milton, a small town in southern West Virginia. Though his home life was comfortably middle-class, he seems to have been most interested artistically in people living under harsh economic conditions.

After high school graduation, Pancake attended West Virginia Wesleyan College for a year and then enrolled at Marshall University in Huntington, West Virginia, where he completed an undergraduate degree in English in 1974. A year later, he began graduate courses at the University of Virginia; soon after, in 1977, his story "Trilobites" was accepted for publication by the *Atlantic Monthly*. Galley proofs for this story showed his middle initials set up with an apostrophe, as *D'J*. The young author, amused by the mistake, left them that way.

In April 1979, at the beginning of his literary career, Pancake killed himself outside his rented rooms near Charlottesville, Virginia. His suicide stunned not only his family and friends but also the editors who had come into contact with his work. Through their efforts, his short stories were published posthumously in 1983, and the collection was nominated for a Pulitzer Prize that year.

Pancake wrote about people struggling to hold onto something of value or to find something worth holding onto. Although his prose is spare, it is evocative, suggesting forces aligned against his characters. History—personal, social, even geological—is implicated in his characters' misfortunes and the matter-of-fact cruelty they endure and inflict on each other. Implicit in all of his stories, violence is made to seem ordinary. Set mostly in "Rock Camp" and its outskirts, where remnants of an agricultural economy mix with an industrial economy that is winding down, Pancake's stories dramatize the inner lives of characters in a particular place and time so poignantly they have been compared with James Joyce's famous early-twentieth-century short story collection, *Dubliners*.

Some critics have raised the question whether Pancake's reputation derives mostly from the romantic image that grew out of his suicide. As others have noted, however, Pancake's talent was recognized before his death. After he submitted "Trilobites," *Atlantic Monthly* editors solicited a whole collection, an editor from the *New Yorker* solicited a story, and Doubleday publishers asked him to submit a novel. Such attention to a beginning writer argues for the merit of his work. Certainly, many Appalachian writers express their artistic indebtedness to Pancake, and his readership continues to broaden. In the 1990s, collections of his stories were published in Great Britain and Portugal. One of his stories is in the anthology *Appalachia Inside Out*, and another is in *American Gothic Tales*, where it shares the company of writers ranging from Nathaniel Hawthorne to Ursula K. LeGuin.

See also: COAL-MINING LITERATURE; POST–WORLD WAR II FICTION.

—Edwina Pendarvis, *Marshall University*

Thomas E. Douglass, *A Room Forever: The Life, Work, and Letters of Breece D'J Pancake* (1998); Grace Toney Edwards, "Place and Space in Breece Pancake's 'A Room Forever,'" in *The Poetics of Appalachian Space*, ed. Parks Lanier Jr. (1991); Angela Freeman, "The Origins and Fortunes of Negativity: The West Virginia Worlds of Kromer, Pancake, and Benedict," *Appalachian Journal* (Spring 1998).

Phillips, Jayne Anne

(1952–) Fiction writer.

Born in Buckhannon, West Virginia, a small coal and college town, Jayne Anne Phillips is the author of two novels and two short story collections. While her work is not exclusively Appalachian in focus, Phillips frequently draws on her childhood experiences and environment.

Phillips began her career as a poet, a fact that may explain the startlingly lyrical quality of her work, but she soon found her niche in writing fiction. Her first collection of short stories, *Black Tickets*, appeared in 1979 to critical acclaim. The stories in *Black Tickets* provide a capsule of themes to which Phillips returned in later works: physical and emotional isolation, damaged people, sexual power, generational and familial conflict, loss of innocence, and the intersection between the political and the personal. Her first novel, *Machine Dreams* (1984), based loosely on her own childhood and adolescence, examines the complexity of small-town life in West Virginia of the 1960s and 1970s, as economic depression and international conflicts exacerbate already-strained family ties. In 1987 her second collection of short stories, *Fast Lanes*, explored the conflicting needs for security and escape. These conflicts are also the focus of her second novel, *Shelter* (1994). The story of four girls' loss of innocence at a summer camp in West Virginia in 1963, *Shelter* probes the nature of good and evil in a primal mountain setting.

Phillips feels she has patterned her own life around the escape-and-redemption motif that forms the thematic core of much of her work. In her view, escape means moving within the self for security; redemption requires circling back to grapple with reality. The commitment to preserving the emotionally real, however disturbing it may be, is paramount with Phillips, and the mountain settings she often utilizes provide appropriate backdrops.

An Appalachian expatriate, Phillips lives in Boston. She has received, among other awards, a Guggenheim Fellowship and two National Endowment for the Arts fellowships.

See also: COAL-MINING LITERATURE.

—Shannon Young Brooks, *National D-Day Memorial, Bedford, Virginia*

Joyce Dyer, ed., *Bloodroot: Reflections on Place by Appalachian Women Writers* (1998).

Post–World War II Fiction

Since World War II—and especially since the 1970s—the southern and central regions of Appalachia have spawned numerous fiction writers. Many of these authors—including Wilma Dykeman, Lee Smith, Robert Morgan, and Fred Chappell—have published widely and built national reputations. Others, while producing fewer texts, speak eloquently of Appalachian life, particularly the difficulty that people in the region face as they make the transition from an agrarian to an industrial society.

Reared in the mountains of eastern Kentucky, Chris Holbrook (1961–) writes of contemporary life in southern Appalachian communities where the past and present intermingle to form an eclectic mix of values and lifestyles. Holbrook's work mainly consists of short stories focusing on the daily struggles of strained marriages, mining operations that ruin the land, and people searching for lost lives and uncertain futures. *Hell and Ohio*, his first collection of short stories, was published in 1995; his stories have also appeared in the anthologies *Groundwater*, *A Gathering at the Forks*, and *Kentucky Voices*, as well as in a variety of small literary publications.

A resident of Berea, Kentucky, Gwyn Hyman Rubio (1949–) is best known for her first novel, *Icy Sparks*, published in 1998, which tells of a girl (Icy) growing up in eastern Kentucky coal-mining country. Diagnosed with Tourette's syndrome, Icy struggles with her "secret," coming to see herself as resembling the local pokeweed, a mixture of wholesome leaves (her beauty and goodness) and poisonous berries (her jerking and cursing). In a moving conclusion, Icy accepts her disorder as a gift.

Lisa Koger (1953–), born in Ohio and reared in West Virginia, is the author of *Farlanburg Stories* (1990), a collection of short stories set in fictional Farlanburg, West Virginia. The stories look at West Virginians facing unsettling but inevitable cultural change. In "Bypass," Koger lays out the options of a Farlanburg man: farming if he has the land, teaching if he does not, or driving a chemical company truck. Given these choices, many younger citizens move away, leaving behind parents who wonder what will happen to the family farm and its traditions once they are gone. For Koger's women, there is only one expectation: to marry and have children. Those who do not are suspect; those who do are often unduly constrained by family responsibilities. Koger writes of a world she knows, having grown up on land that has been in her mother's family for generations and having watched her father go north to work while the family remained on the homeplace.

Anna Egan Smucker, who was born in Steubenville, Ohio, in 1948 and moved to West Virginia in 1955, set her children's novel *No Star Nights* in Weirton, West Virginia. The book, which evocatively captures the gritty heyday and rapid decline of this Ohio River steel town, is seen through the eyes of a young girl remembering when round-the-clock factories cast their red glow into the night sky, obscuring the stars. The book conveys the glow and smoke of the mills, the rhythms of working-class life, and the hazy Appalachian landscape of the industrial upper Ohio Valley. Smucker has written one other children's book, *Outside the Window* (1994), and *A History of West Virginia* (1997), a book for new adult readers.

Lou Crabtree (1913–), best known for her short stories and poetry about rural Appalachia, began to publish after her seventieth birthday. She grew up in a remote corner of southwestern Virginia where even wagon traffic disappeared after the rerouting of the main road. Before retiring in 1975, Crabtree taught school for thirty-six years. Known as an excellent drama teacher, she inspired one young man to set up a stage in a barn to perform Shakespeare. Although she had written throughout her life, she never attempted to publish her work until she was "discovered" by novelist Lee Smith in a creative writing class at the Virginia Highlands Festival in Abingdon. Crabtree's first book, *Sweet Hollow*, a collection of short stories, was published in 1984. She went on to win the Edgar Allan Poe Award for Poetry and in 1985 received the Virginia Governor's Award for Outstanding Literature.

A native of the east Tennessee town of Elizabethton, Lou Kassem (1931–) has written a dozen novels for adolescents to dispel what she calls the myth of "Southern stupidity." She often sets her novels in the Blue Ridge Mountains of Virginia. *Listen for Rachel* is based on a legend about a Civil War–era healer; questions about women's roles during this period underlie the depiction of the protagonist, Rachel, as a spirited young woman who learns doctoring skills from a mountain granny woman and then treats wounded soldiers from both Confederate and Union armies. *The Treasures of Witch Hat Mountain* is a mystery about hidden treasure in a centuries-old house; *The Druid Curse* tells of an ancient Welsh curse and the young friends who plot to prevent its deadly outcome. Kassem's most popular book, *Middle School Blues*, uses Appalachian speech patterns to relate the chaos and confusion, mood swings and mortification of life in seventh grade.

Donald Secreast (1949–) was born, reared, and worked in the small industrial town of Lenoir, North Carolina. His short story collections *The Rat Becomes Light* (1990) and *White Trash, Red Velvet* (1993) depict the North Carolina foothills, where textile and furniture mills employ many Appalachians. *White Trash, Red Velvet* consists of twelve connected stories about the Holsclaw family of Hibriten, North Carolina, a fictional town based on Lenoir. The stories evoke respect and admiration for blue-collar values such as tolerance, discipline, and the building of community, qualities that emerge even though the mill work denigrates the basic humanity of the people.

Marcos McPeek Villatoro (1962–), whose father is from east Tennessee and whose mother is from El Salvador, explores what it means to be a Hispanic southerner. He had authored five books by 2001: *A Fire in the Earth* (a novel based in 1932 El Salvador); *Walking to La Milpa: Living in Guatemala with Armies, Demons, Abrazos and Death* (a memoir of his life in that country); *They Say That I Am Two* (a collection of poetry); *The Holy Spirit of My Uncle's Cojones* (a comic novel of discovery); and *Home Killings* (a crime novel set in Nashville).

Not all fiction writers born in the region have chosen to write about it. Expatriate novelists such as Tom Robbins, who was reared in Blowing Rock, North Carolina, and noted African American author Ishmael Reed, born in Chattanooga, Tennessee, record no traces of Appalachia in their writings. Similarly, a generation earlier, Gertrude Stein, a native of Pittsburgh, steadfastly turned her back on Appalachia after her family moved away during her adolescence. Overall, however, an Appalachian upbringing often leaves an indelible mark on a fiction writer.

See also: AFRICAN AMERICAN LITERATURE; CHILDREN'S LITERATURE; POST–WORLD WAR II POETS.

—Harriette C. Buchanan, *Appalachian State University;* Kathy A. Campbell, *East Tennessee State University;* Richard Hague, *Purcell Marian High School;* Jane Hill, *State University of West Georgia;* Jeanne Johnson, *Roanoke, Virginia;* Carolyn Mathews, Maria M. Melius, Jim Minick, and Ann H. Moser, *Radford University;* and Edward Whetstone Moser Jr., *Deep Springs College*

Post–World War II Poets

Nowhere is the recent flowering of Appalachian literature that has been dubbed the Appalachian Renaissance more clearly seen than in the outpouring of poetry from the region since World War II.

In southern Appalachia, Bettie Sellers (1926–), poet laureate of Georgia (1997–98), has published seven volumes of verse since beginning to write poetry after she moved to the mountains to teach at Young Harris College in 1965. Her works include *Westward from Bald Mountain* (1974), *Appalachian Carols* (1976), *Spring Onions and Cornbread* (1978), *Morning of the Red-Tailed Hawk* (1981), *Liza's Monday and Other Poems* (1986), *Satan's Playhouse* (1986), and *Wild Ginger* (1989). Concerns for place, family, and religion pervade the poems in each collection. She has also written *The Bitter Berry: The Life of Byron Herbert Reece* (1992), a study of the poet who lived and taught in Young Harris before his death in 1958.

The major African American feminist poet Sonia Sanchez (born Wilsonia Benita Driver in 1934) moved from her native Birmingham, Alabama, to New York at the age of nine and is typically not associated with Appalachian writing. However, poems such as "Dear Mama" reflect the language and experience of her early years in Birmingham. A pioneer in the field of black studies, Sanchez offered the first college seminar on the literature of African American women at the University of Pittsburgh in 1969 and was a professor of English and women's studies at Temple University until 1999. Dubbed "a lion in literature's forest" by Maya Angelou, Sanchez has won numerous awards for her poetry, including the 1985 American Book Award for *homegirls and handgrenades.*

Bill Brown's greatest contributions to Appalachian literature are his poetry and his teaching expertise. Born in Dyersburg, a small town in west Tennessee, in 1948, he spends annual vacations hiking, camping, studying, and writing in the Appalachian Mountains. Brown's poetry is richly vernacular and appears in four volumes: *Holding On by Letting Go* (1986), *What the Night Told Me* (1992), *The Art of Dying* (1996), and *The Gods of Little Pleasure* (2001). With Malcolm Glass, Brown coauthored *Important Words: A Book for Poets and Writers* (1991), a textbook on how to write poetry and teach writing.

R. T. Smith was born in the District of Columbia in 1947 and grew up in Charlotte, North Carolina, and the small textile town of Griffin, Georgia. He began writing as a graduate student at Appalachian State University, where he founded *Cold Mountain Review,* the school's literary magazine. His interest is rooted in southern and Irish literature, and he finds inspiration in those landscapes for his work. He also finds a deep connection between those places in their Celtic dreaminess, as W. J. Cash's *The Mind of the South* called it, invoking the Scots-Irish-settled South's long dependence on mythologies.

Heather Ross Miller (1939–) was born in Albemarle, North Carolina, near the Uwharrie Mountains. These mountains, along with the Ozarks and the Blue Ridge, have influenced her writing. A member of a southern literary family that includes authors Fred Ross, Eleanor Ross Taylor, Jean Ross Justice, and, by marriage, Peter Taylor and Donald Justice, Miller has published at least seven volumes of poetry, four novels, one volume of short stories, and a memoir of her experiences living and writing in state parks, where she spent many years with her late husband, Clyde Miller, who was a park ranger and forester.

Moving into the central portions of the region, one finds other well-regarded poets. David Huddle (1942–), a native of Ivanhoe in Wythe County, Virginia, uses experiences in his youth and young adulthood as the basis for much of his poetry and fiction. He has taught English at the University of Vermont since 1971 and as a faculty member of Bread Loaf School of English since 1985 and returns frequently to his Virginia environs to conduct workshops and writing seminars. Huddle has authored at least two novels and several collections of poetry, fiction, and nonfiction.

M. Ray Allen, a poet and Appalachian activist from Clifton Forge, Virginia, is a native of Martin, Kentucky, whose writing and teaching career led him to help Appalachian youth through literacy and the performing arts. A high school teacher since 1963, Allen is best known for his work as founding director of Appalfolks of America, a nonprofit corporation that promotes drug-free living through its writing and performance programs. Appalfolks owns and operates the historic Stonewall Theatre in Clifton Forge as a performance center for Appalachian youth. Allen's poems are widely published in literary arts magazines across the United States and in four book-length volumes.

The poetry of feminist author and Radford University professor Rita Sizemore Riddle, who was born in Fleming, Kentucky, in 1941 and reared in Dickenson County, Virginia, depicts a complex Appalachia defined by home, women crushed by violence, and the struggle to understand the nature of divine grace. These themes both ground her in the Appalachian region and connect her to the larger world. Her unflinching style demands careful attention and emotional response from readers.

Born in 1954 in Hiltons, Virginia, Rita Sims Quillen is the author of two volumes of poetry, both of which portray the contemporary rural Appalachian woman striving to retain connection to traditional mountain life while also exploring her own rich inner life, which sometimes encourages her to go in new directions. She has been a frequent workshop leader at the Hindman Settlement School Appalachian Writers Workshop in Hindman, Kentucky, and is also known for her contribution to Appalachian literary criticism. In 1985 she published an extensive bibliography of Appalachian poetry in *Appalachian Journal*, and in 1989 she served as associate editor for *A Southern Appalachian Reader*, published by the Appalachian Consortium Press. Her 1989 critical study, *Looking for Native Ground: Contemporary Appalachian Poetry*, examines the work of four Appalachian poets: Jeff Daniel Marion, Fred Chappell, Robert Morgan, and Jim Wayne Miller.

Jane Stuart (1942–) is best known for her lyrical and visionary record of rural Kentucky life. She lived in Gainesville, Florida, for many years after leaving her native Kentucky but returned to W-Hollow, where she now lives in the ten-room log house of her parents, noted author Jesse Stuart and Naomi Deane. Jane Stuart received a Ph.D. from Indiana University in 1971 and has studied in Italy, Greece, Kenya, and Uganda. She is the author of numerous books of poetry, three novels, a short story collection, and two children's books. Her themes and symbolism reflect her interest in the natural world of eastern Kentucky and her lifelong study of classical languages, cities, and other peoples. *Transparencies*, her book of remembrances about her father, was published in 1985.

Victor Depta was born in 1939 to a Czechoslovakian family residing in Accoville in the coalfields of Logan County, West Virginia. He has published at least eleven works, including seven volumes of poetry, two novels, and a collection of comedic plays, all set in his native Appalachia. Beginning with the publication of *The Creek* in 1973, Depta has attempted to explain the pull of place upon Appalachian people. In his plays, he uses humor to approach Appalachian stereotypes and then moves on to produce a serious consideration of the region.

Mark DeFoe's poetry is known for its attention to ordinary events in small-town life in contemporary Appalachia. Born in 1942 in Enid, Oklahoma, DeFoe moved to the Appalachian region in 1975 to teach at West Virginia Wesleyan College in Buckhannon. From 1977 to 1987, he edited the *Laurel Review*, which, under his editorship, earned a national reputation. His poetry often focuses on domestic life, infusing mundane events with a quiet sense of awe. "The Former Miner Returns from His First Days as a Service Worker," one of his best-known poems, identifies economic change as one of the forces that make ordinary life so tenuous in the small-town borderline between city and country. Much of DeFoe's poetry suggests what people living in Appalachia have in common with other contemporary Americans.

Muriel Miller Dressler (1919–2000) was a strong opponent of the image of Appalachia as an area of want and ignorance. Born in Witcher, West Virginia, the youngest of seven girls, Dressler credited her mother, Fannie Underwood Miller, as the strongest influence in her life. Coming from a long line of storytellers and musicians—her mother sang ballads as she worked—Dressler carried those traditions into her writing. Dressler was a performer as well as a writer. Dressed in period costumes, she recited her work and that of other regional writers for a wide variety of audiences. A line from her poem "Appalachia" was used in the title of *Wild Sweet Notes: Fifty Years of West Virginia Poetry, 1950–1999* (2000).

Poet laureate of West Virginia from 1979 until her death in 1993, Louise McNeill (b. 1911) grew up on a farm settled by her ancestors in 1769 near Marlinton in Pocahontas County. Beginning her education in the two-room school where her father taught, she eventually completed a Ph.D. at West Virginia University. In addition to eight books, the first of which was introduced by Stephen Vincent Benét, her work appeared in the *Atlantic Monthly*, *Harper's*, the *Saturday Evening Post*, *Poetry*, and *Good Housekeeping*. McNeill's poems, written primarily in traditional forms, record and celebrate the people and location of her heritage. Many critics, however, consider her masterpiece to be her autobiography, *The Milkweed Ladies*.

Llewellyn McKernan (1941–) is a transplant from Arkansas who now lives in rural West Virginia and teaches at Marshall University. In the 1970s she began writing poetry about Appalachia, a world she found reminiscent of her girlhood home. McKernan's work consists of poetry and children's books. She explores Appalachia as it existed before urban sprawl and technological upheaval, but she refuses to romanticize her subjects—rural rituals, extended families, evangelical religion, and seasonal shifts in landscape.

A widely published author of poetry, fiction, and nonfiction, Wisconsin-born Barbara A. Smith (1929–) has made West Virginia history and culture the heart of her work. Smith moved to Philippi, West Virginia, to become a professor of literature and writing at Alderson-Broaddus College. She founded the Barbour County Writers' Workshop and its publication, *Grab-a-Nickel*, which she edited for twenty years. She is a long-time member of the staff of the Appalachian Writers Conference at Hindman, Kentucky, conducts workshops throughout the region, and is well known to Appalachian writers as a mentor and perceptive critic. With Kirk Judd, she coedited *Wild Sweet Notes*.

Northern Appalachia also harbors many excellent poets. Larry Smith, born in 1943 and reared in the Appalachian Ohio steel town Mingo Junction, is author of at least twelve books of poetry, fiction, and literary biography and of documentary screenplays about James Wright and Kenneth Patchen. Director of Bottom Dog Press, a literary and educational organization, Smith has been instrumental in bringing the voices of northern Appalachian writers and working-class people to a regional and national readership. Much of his writing is set in industrial communities and deals with the plight of working people and the culture they struggle to maintain in and at the borders of northern Appalachia. His translation with Mei Hui Huang of Chinese poems entitled *Chinese Zen Poems: What Hold Has This Mountain?* (1998) reflects his ongoing relationship to the way of Zen.

Richard Hague was born in 1947 in Steubenville, Ohio, up the Ohio River from Cincinnati, where he has lived, written, and taught at Purcell Marian High School since 1969. His poetry, fiction, and essays explore the natural and human history of the Ohio River, focusing primarily on mill towns. In addition to his publications, Hague has won many teaching awards, which, along with publications and readings by his students, attest to his skill in developing young writers.

Pauletta Hansel (1959–) is an original member of the Soupbean Poets, a collective of activist Appalachian writers. Born and reared in eastern Kentucky, she has lived for many years in Ohio. Her poems are narrative and deal with her mobile childhood and the complexities of an urban Appalachian adulthood. Her 1998 one-woman performance piece *Sitting with Terry* uses poetry, journal entries, and monologues to chronicle a theater acquaintance's death from AIDS. Hansel also wrote *We Come Up from Kentucky* for Street Talk, a Cincinnati theater collective, and *Breathitt*, commissioned by the Breathitt County (Kentucky) Historical Society.

See also: BLACK MOUNTAIN POETS AND *BLACK MOUNTAIN REVIEW*; POST–WORLD WAR II FICTION.

—Jo Ann Asbury, Parks Lanier Jr., Jim Minick, and Ron Willoughby, *Radford University;* Joyce Dyer, *Hiram College;* Tom Frazier, *Cumberland College;* Richard Hague, *Purcell Marian High School;* Marie F. Jones, *East Tennessee State University;* Edwina Pendarvis, *Marshall University;* Madelyn Rosenberg, *Roanoke Times;* Barbara Smith, *Alderson-Broaddus College;* Peter Stillman, *Charlotteville, New York;* Linda Tate, *Shepherd University;* Robin O. Warren, *University of Georgia;* and Michael R. White, *Surry Community College*

Rash, Ron

(1953–) Poet, storyteller, and novelist.

Ron Rash was born in South Carolina and traces his ancestry to hardscrabble farms in Buncombe and Watauga Counties, North Carolina. His poetry is strongly narrative and features a variety of Appalachian speakers.

Rash's first volume of poetry, *The Night the New Jesus Fell to Earth* (1994), is a *Decameron*-like series of tales recounted by a group of narrators as they cope with a fire that has destroyed the only café in Cliffside, North Carolina. Tracey, the town's female carpenter, describes her sleazy ex-husband, who volunteered to be Jesus as a promotional stunt to sell used cars and ended up falling off the cross. Randy tells how his scheme to sell opossums to New York restaurants actually hit it big when environmentalists bought him out. Vincent remembers the family cars that his father bought—used Cadillac hearses.

The poems of *Eureka Mill* (1998), more poignant in tone than *The Night the New Jesus Fell to Earth*, tell the story of Rash's grandparents' move from the mountains to the textile mills of South Carolina. Rash weaves together their memories with the lives of others who long for the land they left, caught in a Piedmont textile town like machines filling with cotton dust and living on the promises of whiskey and revivals.

Among the Believers (2000) features poems narrated by people living in Watauga County. These narrators speak of enduring floods, sickness, child murders, bushwhackers, and massacres in bloody Madison County during the Civil War. The volume secured Rash's place in the Appalachian literary canon as a poet with a strong, alternately humorous and bleak voice and excellent narrative talent. Rash's first novel, *One Foot in Eden*, was published in 2002.

See also: POST–WORLD WAR II POETS.

—Newton Smith, *Western Carolina University*

Reece, Byron Herbert

(1917–1958) Fiction writer and poet.

Byron Herbert Reece, north Georgia poet, novelist, and farmer, drew on the Appalachian landscape, local ballads, and the King James Bible to write poems and novels rich in drama and natural images. Reece was born and reared at the foot of Blood Mountain in the Choestoe community of Union County. From 1935 to 1939, he attended Young Harris College intermittently before quitting to run the family farm.

The title poem of Reece's first volume of verse, *Ballad of the Bones and Other Poems* (1945), retells the Old Testament story of God's call to Ezekiel and takes its place beside other ballads relating biblical stories or tragic tales of jealousy, murder, and thwarted love. Sonnets and lyric poems evoking the land and nature's cycles fill the rest of the volume. Similar themes and forms predominate in *Bow Down in Jericho* (1950), *A Song of Joy* (1952), and *The Season of the Flesh* (1955).

Both of Reece's novels probe the darker side of human experience. Set on a small farm in the foothills of north Georgia, *Better a Dinner of Herbs* (1950) is a story of love and betrayal involving a country minister, his wife, and a farmworker. Moving from the hills to the flatlands, *The Hawk and the Sun* (1955) relates the lynching of a black man wrongly accused of raping a white woman.

Reece won two Guggenheim awards and lectured as writer-in-residence at the University of California at Los Angeles, Emory University, and Young Harris College. Suffering from tuberculosis, he took his own life in 1958.

See also: POST–WORLD WAR II FICTION; POST–WORLD WAR II POETS.

—Robin O. Warren, *University of Georgia*

Richter, Conrad

(1890–1968) Fiction writer.

Conrad Richter set many of his historical novels in northern Appalachia. Born in 1890 in Pine Mills, Pennsylvania, Richter was the son of a dedicated Lutheran minister who moved the family to several different parishes in the anthracite region.

Richter began his writing career working for newspapers in Johnstown and Pittsburgh. In 1913 he published his first short story, and he combined writing fiction with magazine editing until 1928, when he and his wife moved to New Mexico in search of a cure for her ill health. After the move, Richter began to write about this new region. In 1937 he published his first novel, *The Sea of Grass*, a saga of pioneer life set in the Southwest.

Although Richter eventually shifted his setting back to northern Appalachia, he continued to focus on pioneer life. In 1940 he published *The Trees*, the first novel in a trilogy that deals with frontier life on the Ohio-Pennsylvania border. The other two installments of the trilogy are *The Fields* (1946) and *The Town* (1950); the latter garnered Richter a Pulitzer Prize. In 1953 he published *The Light in the Forest*, a captivity narrative about a white boy reared by the Leni Lenapi and then forcibly repatriated into white society. A sequel, *A Country of Strangers*, appeared in 1966.

Richter set two autobiographical novels, *The Waters of Kronos* (1960), which won a National Book Award, and *A Simple, Honorable Man* (1962), in the coalfields of central Pennsylvania. Richter had hoped to write a third volume in this series, but he did not live to do so. On October 30, 1968, he died in Pine Grove, Pennsylvania, where he had lived for the last eighteen years of his life.

—Theresa Lloyd, *East Tennessee State University*

Rinehart, Mary Roberts

(1876–1958) Mystery writer.

Influential mystery writer Mary Roberts Rinehart was born into a family of modest means in 1876 in Pittsburgh. Trained as a nurse, she married a physician, Stanley Marshall Rinehart, and began writing after her husband's bankruptcy in 1903. In her heyday, Rinehart rivaled the English mystery writer Agatha Christie in popularity. Many of Rinehart's early works feature a Pittsburgh setting.

Rinehart's first two western Pennsylvania novels, *The Man in the Lower Ten* (1906) and *The Circular Staircase* (1908), are still highly regarded; they demonstrate her interest in combining mystery and adventure. Other of her mystery novels include *The Case of Jennie Brice* (1914), *The Red Lamp* (1925), *The Door* (1930), *The Yellow Room* (1945), and *The Swimming Pool* (1952). Rinehart also wrote for the stage; her play *Seven Days* (1909) became a Broadway hit, and in 1920 *The Circular Staircase* was dramatized as *The Bat*. A feminist who marched for woman's suffrage, Rinehart often depicted a female detective, the most famous of which is Tish. Many of the Tish stories were published first in the *Saturday Evening Post* and later collected in *The Best of Tish* (1955). Rinehart is credited with establishing the mystery cliché "the butler did it."

In 1932, after her husband's death, Rinehart moved away from the Pittsburgh area to Washington, D.C., and then to New York, where her sons had established the Farrar and Rinehart publishing company, which after 1930 handled most of her work. Rinehart died in 1958 in New York.

See also: WOMEN AUTHORS.

—Theresa Lloyd, *East Tennessee State University*

Roberts, Elizabeth Madox

(1881–1941) Fiction writer and poet.

Elizabeth Madox Roberts was a leading American novelist, poet, and short story writer during the 1920s and 1930s. Although she wintered in various parts of the country throughout her adult life, she returned each summer to her hometown of Springfield, Kentucky, on the western perimeter of the Appalachian region. This area provided the setting for all of her fiction.

Roberts was born in Perryville, Kentucky, on October 30, 1881. Both her parents were teachers, and her father was a veteran of the Confederate army. In 1884, when "Bess" was three, the family moved about fifteen miles west to Springfield, the seat of Washington County. There her father opened a store and later worked as a surveyor and engineer. From 1896 to 1900, Roberts lived with maternal relatives and attended high school in Covington. After entering the University of Kentucky, she became ill and was forced to withdraw before the end of her first term.

After returning home to recover her health, Roberts began giving school lessons in the front room of her family's home and later taught public school in both county seat and rural schools in Washington County. By 1915 her health had improved, and she re-enrolled at the University of Kentucky. In 1917, at the age of thirty-six, she entered the University of Chicago.

Roberts returned to Springfield in 1921 with a degree in English and began devoting herself in earnest to her writing. The following year she created an outstanding book of verse, *Under the Tree*. In 1926 she published *The Time of Man*, a novel that she never eclipsed in either critical repute or popular appeal. In compelling poetic language, the novel tells the story of Ellen Chesser, a farm wife who has become a memorable and beloved protagonist in southern fiction. Selected for the Book-of-the-Month Club, the novel was also published in England and translated into six languages.

After two more novels, Roberts published *The Great Meadow* in 1930. This historical novel concerning the migration of pioneers over the Wilderness Road to Kentucky is generally considered her second most important book. The inner journey of the book's protagonist, Dioy Hall, parallels the progress of her family's covered wagon. *The Great Meadow* was a commercial as well as a literary success.

In the following years, Roberts published two more novels and a collection of stories. In 1936 she was diagnosed with Hodgkin's disease. Despite this affliction, she published another novel, a book of poetry, and a collection of stories before her death on March 13, 1941, in Orlando, Florida, at the age of fifty-nine. In the era between the world wars, Roberts was a leading American female writer. She remains one of the most celebrated and popular Kentucky authors and an important Appalachian literary voice.

See also: WOMEN AUTHORS.

—George Brosi, *Berea, Kentucky*

Russell, Timothy

(1951–) Poet and millwright.

The poetry of Timothy Russell is set in industrial northern Appalachia, often in mill towns and along the Ohio River. In tone, it strikes a balance between fear of the environmental effects of heavy industry and celebration of the fleeting beauty and pathos of the ordinary. His work evokes Japanese poetry but replaces locust branches and plum blossoms with blue-orange flames above open-hearth furnaces, ailanthus trees struggling in mill yards, and the sudden beauty of a backyard oriole.

Russell was born in Steubenville, Ohio, and reared in Follansbee, West Virginia. He attended Follansbee High School, graduated from Weirton Madonna High School, and then served in the army. In 1973 he started college and began work at Weirton Steel Corporation. He graduated from West Liberty State College with a B.A. in 1977 and in 1979 received an M.A. in English from the University of Pittsburgh, where he was an early participant in the writing program. He retired from Weirton Steel in 1997.

Russell has found a wide audience for his poetry. After the appearance of a series of chapbooks in the 1980s and 1990s, his collection *Adversaria* was awarded the 1993 Terrence de Pres Prize by *TriQuarterly* and published by Northwestern University Press. He has been a writer-in-residence at Centrum, a nonprofit arts center in Port Townsend, Washington, and in 1999 won the fourth Shiki Internet Haiku Contest, for which he was awarded a trip to Matsuyama, Japan.

See also: POST–WORLD WAR II POETS; URBAN APPALACHIAN IDENTITY (URBAN APPALACHIAN EXPERIENCE).

—Richard Hague, *Purcell Marian High School*

Rylant, Cynthia

(1954–) Fiction writer and poet.

Cynthia Rylant, the author of more than sixty books for children and young adults, based her first book, *When I Was Young in the Mountains*, on her early years living with her grandparents in a house without electricity or running water. Because she writes about places and characters true to her own early experiences in the mountains of West Virginia, Rylant's works have a strong sense of place, depicting the dignity of mountain people and the joys of extended family.

Rylant's first book won the American Book Award in 1982 and was a Caldecott Honor Book, as was *The Relatives Come*, which celebrates a visit from the kinfolks. Rylant's adolescence in Beaver, West Virginia, inspired *A Blue-Eyed Daisy*, a novel for young adults set in a coal-mining town, and an autobiographical collection of free-verse poems, *Waiting to Waltz: A Childhood*. Particularly noteworthy, *Appalachia: The Voices of Sleeping Birds* renders in poetic descriptions of people, places, and animals the essence of the region. In her Newbery Medal–winning *Missing May*, she tells the stirring story of a foster child's acceptance of loss and death. Critics have called Rylant one of America's best writers of children's and young adult literature, praising the lyrical prose style and deft storytelling that makes young people's concerns vivid to her readers.

Rylant was born in Hopewell, Virginia. After her parents' divorce, she lived with her grandparents at Cool Ridge, West Virginia. Growing up in an area deprived of libraries, she read little as a child beyond comic books. Nonetheless, she went on to receive degrees from Morris Harvey College, Marshall University, and Kent State University. She lives and works in Oregon.

See also: CHILDREN'S LITERATURE.

—Carolyn Mathews, *Radford University*

Shelby, Anne

(1948–) Children's author, essayist, and poet.

Born in Berea, Kentucky, Anne Shelby draws on her Appalachian experience for much of her writing. All five of her books for children depict life in small towns and farms or reflect Appalachian roots. Her poetry, essays, and short fiction have appeared in *Appalachian Heritage* and *Appalachian Journal*, among other outlets.

Shelby's children's books dealing with rural life include *We Keep a Store* (1990) and *Homeplace* (1995). *We Keep a Store* depicts the daily activities of an African American family running a rural store. The youthful narrator describes the business of the store, such as ordering goods and waiting on customers, as well as the store's social function as a gathering place for community members. *Homeplace* traces the history of a family home from 1810 to the present, noting physical changes in the structure as well as changes in lifestyle of each generation. Shelby emphasizes both continuity and change in her characters' rural worlds, drawing connections of work and love between past and present life in the mountains.

Shelby's other children's books include *Potluck* (1991), *What to Do About Pollution* (1993), and *The Someday House* (1996), all of which (periodically) evoke Appalachia. She has served on the creative writing faculties of numerous writing programs in Kentucky. *We Keep a Store* received a Pick of the List citation by the American Booksellers Association, and *Homeplace* was a Junior Library Guild selection.

See also: CHILDREN'S LITERATURE; WOMEN AUTHORS.

—Shannon Young Brooks, *National D-Day Memorial, Bedford, Virginia*

Sinclair, Bennie Lee

(1939–2000) Poet and fiction and nonfiction writer.

Although Bennie Lee Sinclair, appointed poet laureate of South Carolina in 1986, was honored for her work as a novelist and essayist, it was her poetry, first published in *Foxfire Magazine* in 1968, that distinguished her powerful and eloquent Appalachian voice.

Born in Greenville, South Carolina, Sinclair received a B.A. degree in English and philosophy from Furman University. From 1976 onward, she and her husband, potter Don Lewis, lived at Wildernesse, their mountain wildlife sanctuary near Cleveland, in the Saluda Mountains of South Carolina.

Sinclair's four books of poetry are *Little Chicago Suite* (1971), *The Arrowhead Scholar* (1978), *Lord of Springs* (1990), and *The Endangered* (1992). *Lord of Springs* received the 1990 Appalachian Writers Association Book of the Year Award and a Pulitzer Prize nomination. *Appalachian Trilogy*, a chapbook of fiction, followed in 1991. In 1992 she published *The Lynching*, a novel based on the story of Willie Earl, the last man lynched in South Carolina.

Poetry, fiction, and essays by Sinclair appeared in numerous journals, including *Appalachian Heritage*, for which she also served as advisory editor. She received various awards and citations for her writing, among them acknowledgements of excellence in each of the three genres she attempted. She taught creative writing at Furman University, where she was Alumna Honorary Phi Beta Kappa, and at North Greenville College, where she was writer-in-residence. She edited *Taproots: A Study in Cultural Exploration* for the South Carolina Arts Commission and served across her home state in the Poet-in-the-Schools program and the Governor's School for the Arts. In 1999, for the inauguration of Governor Jim Hodges, she delivered "South Carolina 1999," a poem that celebrated the history and vigorous multiculturalism of her home state.

U.S. Poet Laureate Mark Strand praised Sinclair as a poet for whom content was essential, one who was able to write about issues without losing control. In "Appalachian Loaves and Fishes," anthologized in *Bloodroot: Reflections on Place by Appalachian Women Writers* (1998), Sinclair speaks eloquently of her own life and work in Appalachia.

See also: LITERARY SCHOLARSHIP; WOMEN AUTHORS.

—Parks Lanier Jr., *Radford University*

Slone, Verna Mae

(1914–) Fiction and nonfiction writer.

To her own surprise, Verna Mae Slone became a published author and spokesperson for Appalachia in her seventh decade. Born in a log house at the mouth of the Trace Fork in Caney Creek, Knott County, Kentucky, on October 9, 1914, Slone was the twelfth child of Sarah Jane and Isom Slone. Her mother lived only five weeks after her birth. Except for the time she attended Alice Lloyd School, where her father was a chair maker, Slone was reared by her sister Lorenda, or "Rennie." In 1936 Verna Mae married Willie Slone (not related), and they reared five sons in Bunyun Holler.

Proud of her heritage and happy with where she believed God had placed her to live, Slone wrote her first book—*What My Heart Wants to Tell*—for her grandchildren to help them understand and appreciate their legacy and to honor her father. Slone also hoped that by relating stories of her childhood she could dispel some of the myths and misunderstandings about mountain people. Doris Grumbach, reviewing *What My Heart Wants to Tell* for the *New York Times,* concluded that Slone had handsomely achieved these goals.

In May 1980, Slone began writing a weekly newspaper column, "Now and Then," for the *Troublesome Creek Times.* For a number of years she filled it with her natural wit, recollections of historical events, and narratives about the material culture of the region. Other books by Slone include *Common Folks* (1978), *Sarah Ellen* (1982), *How We Talked* (1982), and *Rennie's Way* (1994). She has been a regular participant in the Appalachian Writers Workshop at the Hindman Settlement School, has appeared in numerous radio and television interviews, and has published short stories in *Appalachian Heritage.*

Slone has long enjoyed quilting and making dolls. Fifteen of her quilts hang in the May Stone Building of the Hindman Settlement School. The two-hundred-year-old, one-and-a-half-story log house where her mother was born has been reconstructed on the grounds of the school. Slone's home is a short distance away in Pippa Passes, or Caney Creek, as many still refer to the area.

See also: QUILTS (CRAFTS); WOMEN AUTHORS.

—Diane W. Stuart, *Tampa, Florida*

Diane Watkins, "Verna Mae Slone," *Kentucky Living* (May 1990) and "A Visit with Verna Mae Slone," *Appalachian Heritage* (Winter 1989).

Smith, Lee

(1944–) Fiction writer and essayist.

A native of Grundy, Virginia, Lee Smith became recognized in the 1980s as one of the finest novelists to come from the Appalachian region and make it the setting of her fiction. Born in 1944, she is the daughter of a Tidewater Virginia schoolteacher who married a Grundy native when she arrived in the small town to teach. Smith's father owned the local dime store in Grundy, and as a result, Smith had ample opportunity to observe a range of people in her community and to listen to numerous stories. She began writing at a very early age, though most of her stories had little to do with her immediate surroundings. Not until she went to Hollins College and studied with Louis Rubin did she begin to develop a sense of her true potential as a writer. She belonged to an unusually talented Hollins class, and several of her classmates—including Annie Dillard—emerged as writers. Their years at the college are explored in Nancy Parrish's *Lee Smith, Annie Dillard, and the Hollins Group.*

Though Smith credits her reading of James Still's *River of Earth* (1940)—a novel which ends with a reference to Grundy—as awakening her understanding that her home community in southwest Virginia could serve as the focus for her writing, it was some time before she successfully put that discovery to work in her novels. Her first novel, *The Last Day the Dogbushes Bloomed* (1968), won a Book-of-the-Month Club fellowship, and she soon sold her second novel, *Something in the Wind* (1971), followed quickly by *Fancy Strut* (1973). By this time, however, the fact that her novels were not selling well discouraged her publisher and editor, and she was left to rebuild her writing career. Eventually, she persuaded another editor and publisher to take a chance with her fourth novel, *Black Mountain Breakdown* (1980), the first of her works to focus on Appalachia. Her fifth novel, *Oral History* (1983), established her reputation as one of the finest novelists ever to come from and write about southern Appalachia. The groundbreaking work was a featured selection in the Book-of-the-Month Club, giving Smith her first widespread fame.

Smith has published a number of other novels since that time, including *Family Linen* (1985), *Fair and Tender Ladies* (1988), *The Devil's Dream* (1992), *Saving Grace* (1995), *The Christmas Letters* (1996), and *The Last Girls* (2002), as well as three collections of short stories: *Cakewalk* (1981), *Me and My Baby View the Eclipse* (1990), and *News of the Spirit* (1997). In addition, Smith has written numerous essays and forewords to works by other writers. A collection of previously published interviews with Smith is available in *Conversations with Lee Smith* (2001).

Several of Smith's works have been adapted for the stage, and she has helped create a musical, *Good Ol' Girls,* which features the work of Smith and novelist and short story writer Jill McCorkle. Smith is a frequent workshop leader at the Appalachian Writers Workshop in Hindman, Kentucky, where she also volunteers in the adult literacy program.

Smith has been the recipient of the Lila Wallace–Reader's Digest Award, the Robert Penn Warren Prize for Fiction, a Lyndhurst Grant, the W. D. Weatherford Award for significant work in Appalachian literature, and the North Carolina Award for Fiction. She is a two-time winner of the O. Henry Award as well as of the Sir Walter Raleigh Award. In 1999 she received the Academy Award in Literature from the American Academy of Arts and Letters. She lives in Hillsborough, North Carolina, with her husband, journalist and essayist Hal Crowther.

See also: APPALACHIAN ENGLISH IN LITERATURE (LANGUAGE); COAL-MINING LITERATURE; HUMOR IN APPALACHIAN LITERATURE (HUMOR).

—Linda Tate, *Shepherd University*

Nancy C. Parrish, *Lee Smith, Annie Dillard, and the Hollins Group: A Genesis of Writers* (1999); Linda Tate, *A Southern Weave of Women: Fiction of the Contemporary South* (1994) and ed., *Conversations with Lee Smith* (2001).

Still, James

(1906–2001) Fiction writer, poet, and folklorist.

Although born and reared in Chambers County, Alabama, in the southernmost foothills of Appalachia, James Still is generally considered one of the finest writers to have lived and worked in Kentucky. Most of Still's writings—including his acclaimed novel *River of Earth* (1940), award-winning short stories, poetry, children's literature, and folklore collections—are set in the eastern Kentucky hills, where he lived from 1931 until his death on April 28, 2001.

Both sides of Still's family traced their ancestry to Appalachian Virginia. His father, J. Alex Still, a self-educated farmer and horse trader, married James's mother, Lonie Lindsey, in 1893; the union produced ten children. The sixth child overall and the first of five boys, James Still grew up in and near the town of Lafayette, Alabama. His parents' home contained four books, one of which (the *Cyclopedia of Universal Knowledge*) he claimed was his "introduction to a wider world." Listening as a youth to stories told by veterans of the Civil War, Still developed a romanticized view of the Confederacy. After witnessing a public hanging and a Ku Klux Klan cross burning during his adolescence, he denounced capital punishment and racism.

In 1924 Still left Alabama for Lincoln Memorial University in Harrogate, Tennessee, near the Cumberland Gap. He had made "a genealogical circle," he wrote later, as the school was close to the site of a paternal ancestor's former homestead. Among his classes at the college was a composition course taught by novelist Harry Harrison Kroll. After earning an A.B. degree in 1929, Still enrolled at Vanderbilt University. There, he studied under John Crowe Ransom and others in Vanderbilt's Fugitive/Agrarian literary circle. Taking an M.A. degree in literature from Vanderbilt in 1930, Still subsequently enrolled at the University of Illinois, where in 1931 he received a B.S. degree in library science.

Still's classmates at Lincoln Memorial and Vanderbilt included fellow writers Jesse Stuart and Don West; only the latter significantly influenced Still's career. In 1931 Still visited West, who was coordinating a summer Bible school in Knott County, Kentucky. Impressed by the locality's natural beauty and its people, Still accepted a librarian position at the nearby Hindman Settlement School. Serving the institution over the next several years, much of the time as a volunteer, he implemented a program in which he regularly walked books to nearby rural schoolhouses.

Upon arriving in Hindman, Still began to write prolifically, producing poems and short stories exploring the natural world and aspects of Appalachian regional folklife. Soon, his work was appearing in leading national periodicals, and in 1937 the Viking Press issued a volume of his poetry, *Hounds on the Mountain*. Two years later, wanting to devote more time to writing, Still moved eleven miles from Hindman into a remote log house. In 1941 Viking compiled a collection of his stories entitled *On Troublesome Creek*. During this period, Still's short fiction appeared several times in two prestigious anthologies: the *O. Henry Memorial Prize Stories* (in 1937, 1938, 1939, and 1941) and the *Best American Short Stories* (in 1946, 1950, and 1952).

Wedged between Still's poetry and short story collections was his novel *River of Earth*, published by Viking in 1940. Generally considered Still's masterpiece, *River of Earth* grew out of the author's summer stint as a social worker for the Federal Emergency Relief Administration, a New Deal program. Witnessing firsthand the plight of Kentucky coal miners during the Great Depression, Still decided to write a novel chronicling the changes wrought by industrialization on the traditional Appalachian way of life. Noted for its lyrical prose (a literary approximation of Appalachian folk speech), *River of Earth* was well received by literary critics, but nationally the novel soon fell into obscurity as scholars and readers championed John Steinbeck's *The Grapes of Wrath* as the most significant novel of the Great Depression. The 1978 republication of *River of Earth* by the University Press of Kentucky, however, secured for Still's novel an enduring place in Appalachian literature. Among his other books are a second novel (*Sporty Creek: A Novel about an Appalachian Boyhood*, 1977; revised 1999), two compilations of short stories (*Pattern of a Man*, 1976; *The Run for the Elbertas*, 1980), two poetry collections (*The Wolfpen Poems*, 1986; *From the Mountain, from the Valley: New and Collected Poems*, 2001), a study of Appalachian folklore (*The Wolfpen Notebooks: A Record of Appalachian Life*, 1991), and a number of works for children, including *Jack and the Wonder Beans* (1977), Still's retelling of "Jack and the Beanstalk."

Although he once claimed he was "more an autodidact than a classroom scholar," Still acknowledged several literary influences, including antebellum humorist Johnson Jones Hooper; novelists Thomas Hardy, Honoré de Balzac, and Alphonse Daudet; poets Geoffrey Chaucer, Percy Bysshe Shelley, John Keats, and Lord Byron; and playwright William Shakespeare. Otto Jespersen's *The Philosophy of Grammar*, Still said, enlivened his literary imagination, encouraging him to favor folk speech over more stilted formal language.

Drafted into the U.S. Army Air Corps in 1942, Still was stationed in Africa and the Middle East through the end of World War II. Upon his discharge, he returned to his Knott County log house to recover from psychic and physical wounds sustained during the war; in addition to ground warfare, he had survived a plane crash and bouts with dysentery and malaria. In 1952 Still resumed his affiliation with Hindman Settlement School, serving ten more years as the school's librarian. Thereafter, he accepted a teaching position in Morehead State University's English Department. In the 1970s, retired from academia, he spent several winters traveling in Mexico and Central America. During the 1980s and 1990s, residing in Knott County, he frequently accepted invitations to speak and read at regional schools.

Still's admirers feted him as "the dean of Appalachian literature." In the last decades of the twentieth century, authors as diverse as Wendell Berry, Fred Chappell, Wilma Dykeman, Jim Wayne Miller, Gurney Norman, and Lee Smith publicly declared their appreciation for Still and his work. For several years beginning in the 1990s, Hindman Settlement School hosted annual birthday parties in his honor that were attended by other authors, longtime readers of his work, his Knott County neighbors, and many of his relatives.

See also: APPALACHIAN ENGLISH IN LITERATURE (LANGUAGE); CHILDREN'S LITERATURE; COAL-MINING LITERATURE.

—Ted Olson, *East Tennessee State University*

Dean Cadle, "Man on Troublesome," *Yale Review* (Winter 1968); Laura Lee et al., "An Interview with James Still," *Foxfire Magazine* (Fall 1988); H. R. Stoneback, "Rivers of Earth and Troublesome Creeks: The Agrarianism of James Still," *Kentucky Review* (Autumn 1990).

Stillman, Peter

(1934–) Essayist, poet, editor, and teacher.

Peter R. Stillman is a chronicler of daily life in the northern Appalachian village of Charlotteville, New York, where he has lived off and on since moving there in 1970 to teach high school, and later, college English. A native of Norwalk, Connecticut, Stillman earned a B.A. from Central Connecticut University and an M.A. from the Breadloaf School of English at Middlebury College. Though pulled away from Charlotteville for months at a time by his career as a composition consultant, writer-in-residence, and editor and publisher of rhetoric texts, Stillman has maintained a spiritual and physical connection to the town in which he raised three children.

An exploration of a community and Stillman's place within it, *Planting by the Moon: On Life in a Mountain Hamlet* is a 1995 revision and expansion of a collection of poems and essays that first appeared as *Gilead: Notes on a Catskill Hamlet* in 1985. Gleaned from fifteen years of letters, notes, and journal entries, the poems and essays in *Planting by the Moon* deal with Stillman's discovery of a spiritual home in Schoharie County, New York. Stillman's experiences parallel those of thousands of post-1960s immigrants to rural Appalachia who sought a more firmly rooted, more slowly paced alternative to mainstream American life. His understanding of his adopted home is broadened by his immersion in the community, which he served as a teacher, a logger, and the president of the volunteer fire department.

Though somewhat less deferential than their southern counterparts, the Catskills mountaineers that Stillman describes in his essays and poems display many of the same cultural traits that have fascinated and frustrated the observers of the southern Appalachians. In Stillman's renderings of his community, people's choices and attitudes seem illogical, even comical, until considered and appreciated within the contexts of complex family histories and lengthy personal relationships. Interwoven with Stillman's observations of the natural and cultural environments of rural northern Appalachia is the narrative of his own gradual acceptance as a respected and respectful participant in the life and traditions of a mountain community.

A highly regarded speaker, writing consultant, and workshop leader, Stillman has been writer-in-residence at universities in and outside the Appalachian region. His other books include *Writing Your Way*, *Families Writing*, and *Introduction to Myth*.

See also: LITERARY SCHOLARSHIP; POST–WORLD WAR II POETS.

—Ricky Cox, *Radford University*

Stribling, T. S.

(1881–1965) Novelist.

A prolific writer of short stories and magazine articles as well as novels, T. S. Stribling was awarded the 1932 Pulitzer Prize for Fiction for *The Store*, the second volume of a trilogy set in Florence, Alabama, and spanning the years from the Civil War until the 1920s. Besides publishing fifteen novels and writing scores of magazine articles, he worked as a teacher, journalist, and lawyer in the course of his career.

Addressing racial violence and conflict and the dark corners of southern culture, Stribling's blunt realism departed from regional literary custom and romantic views of the South and broke ground for modern fiction about the region.

Thomas Sigismund Stribling was born in Clifton, a tiny community beside the Tennessee River in middle Tennessee, on March 4, 1881. At the age of twelve, he sold his first story for three dollars. After graduation from the Florence Normal School, now the University of North Alabama, he proceeded to law school at the University of Alabama and was admitted to the state bar after graduation in 1905. Practicing law only briefly, he soon took up the writing career he had planned since childhood. His first novel, *The Cruise of the Dry Dock*, was published in 1919.

Although Stribling's most important works are set in Appalachian north Alabama, his writing also reflects his extensive travels, which led to adventure and travel articles for numerous magazines. Two novels, *Birthright* (1922) and *Fombombo* (1923), first appeared as magazine serials. *Birthright* became a silent motion picture in 1924, and *Teeftallow* (1926) was dramatized in the 1928 Broadway production *Rope*, which closed after thirty-two performances.

The Forge, the first volume of Stribling's trilogy of the South, was published in 1931. A year later, *The Store* became a national best-seller and made Stribling famous. A review in the *New Yorker* likened him to Mark Twain in his ability to render small-town life. The trilogy, using the rise of Miltaides Vaden and his family from antebellum poverty to twentieth-century wealth and prominence, was completed with the appearance of *Unfinished Cathedral* in 1934. Stribling's last novel, *These Bars of Flesh*, appeared in 1938. His other novels are *East Is East* (1922), *Red Sand* (1924), *Bright Metal* (1928), *Clues of the Caribees* (1929), *Strange Moon* (1929), *Backwater* (1930), and *The Sound Wagon* (1935).

During the 1940s and 1950s, Stribling lived in Florida with his wife, Lou Ella Kloss Stribling, who had also grown up in Clifton and who had pursued a career as a music teacher. They returned to their hometown in 1959. In 1964 Stribling received an invitation to speak at the University of North Alabama and returned to the town where *The Store* had stirred such resentment that he had written an apology and explanation to the community. Thereafter, Stribling visited the community several times and returned there to live several months before his death on July 8, 1965. Stribling was buried in Clifton beneath a small marker reading "Through this dust, these hills once spoke."

Stribling left the manuscripts of several unpublished novels, a book of philosophy, and an autobiography. In 1982, seventeen years after his death, his autobiography, *Laughing Stock*, was published and nominated for the Pulitzer Prize. Stribling's papers are housed in the Tennessee State Library and Archives in Nashville, and in the Collier Library at the University of North Alabama.

See also: POST–WORLD WAR II FICTION.

—Rudy Abramson, *Reston, Virginia*

Edward J. Piacentino, *T. S. Stribling: Pioneer Realist in Modern Southern Literature* (1988); Thomas S. Stribling, *Laughing Stock: A Posthumous Autobiography* (1982).

Stuart, Jesse

(1906–1984) Educator and author.

The late poet laureate of Kentucky, Jesse Hilton Stuart is one of Appalachia's best-known and most anthologized authors, with many of his more than 2,000 poems, 460 short stories, and 60 books having been translated into numerous foreign languages. Yet his contributions are more than literary. He was a charismatic educator, a leader for the people of his mountain homeland, and a spokesman for values such as hard work, respect for the land, belief in education, devotion to country, and love of family. His life and works still attract hundreds of tourists to eastern Kentucky every year.

Stuart was born on August 8, 1906, in northeastern Kentucky's Greenup County, where his parents, Mitchell and Martha Hilton Stuart, were impoverished tenant farmers. From his father, Jesse learned to love and respect the land, an attitude that he maintained throughout his life and one that led him to donate more than seven hundred acres of his land in W-Hollow to the Kentucky Nature Preserves System in 1980.

Stuart's father could neither read nor write, and his mother had only completed the second grade, but they taught their two sons and three daughters to value education. Jesse graduated from Greenup High School in 1926 and from Lincoln Memorial University in Harrogate, Tennessee, in 1929. He also completed a year of graduate study at Vanderbilt University (1931–32), where he began his autobiographical *Beyond Dark Hills* (1938), a book that inspired readers to follow his example of overcoming great obstacles to obtain an education.

The bulk of Stuart's teaching career was spent in Greenup County. By the end of the 1930s, he had served as a teacher in the county's one-room schools, a high school principal, and the county school superintendent. These experiences served as the basis for his autobiographical book *The Thread That Runs So True* (1949), hailed by the president of the National Education Association as the finest book on education written in the previous fifty years. The book became a road map for educational reform in Kentucky. By the time it appeared, Stuart had left the classroom to devote his time to lecturing and writing. He returned to public edu-

Jesse Stuart with his dog Sir Birchfield at the W-Hollow Farm, near Greenup, Kentucky, 1954. Stuart was one of Appalachia's best-known and most anthologized authors, and interest in his life and works still attracts hundreds of tourists to eastern Kentucky every year.

cation as a high school principal in 1956–57, a story told in *Mr. Gallion's School* (1967). He later taught at the University of Nevada in Reno in the 1958 summer term and served on the faculty of the American University of Cairo in 1960–61.

While in high school and as an undergraduate in college, Stuart wrote stories and poems about Appalachia. At Vanderbilt, he received encouragement from Donald Davidson, one of his professors, to continue writing. Following the private publication of Stuart's poetry collection *Harvest of Youth* in 1930, *Man with a Bull-Tongue Plow* appeared in 1934. This volume of poetry was widely praised, with critic Mark Van Doren likening Stuart to the eighteenth-century Scottish poet Robert Burns. Stuart's ten volumes of verse also include *Album of Destiny* (1944) and *Kentucky Is My Land* (1952). He was designated poet laureate of Kentucky in 1954 and was made a fellow of the Academy of American Poets in 1961.

Stuart was a widely read fiction writer. His first novel, *Trees of Heaven,* appeared in 1940, followed by the short story collections *Head o' W-Hollow* (1936) and *Men of the Mountains* (1941). He published a dozen other short story collections during his lifetime. The novel *Taps for Private Tussie* (1943) was an award-winning satire of New Deal relief and its effect on Appalachia's self-reliance. *Taps* catapulted Stuart to popular success, but critical reaction was mixed. Some saw it as nothing more than a comical, almost stereotyped story of poor, lazy mountaineers on relief, while others explained that Stuart, a first-rate local colorist, wrote for a popular rather than a highbrow audience.

Stuart also wrote a number of children's books that are still read and highly regarded today. *The Beatinest Boy* (1953) and *A Penny's Worth of Character* (1954) are two of his eight junior novels for readers in third to seventh grade. *Hie to the Hunters,* a novel published in 1950, is a celebration of rural life that has been especially popular with readers in junior high and high school.

In 1954 Stuart suffered a major heart attack. During his convalescence, he wrote daily journals that formed the basis for *The Year of My Rebirth* (1956), a book recording his rediscovery of the joy of life. He later became an active spokesman for the American Heart Association.

For his work both as an educator and writer, Stuart received numerous honors. He was awarded the first of many honorary doctorates in 1944 by the University of Kentucky. The governor of Kentucky proclaimed October 15, 1955, "Jesse Stuart Day," and a bust of Stuart was unveiled on the Greenup County Courthouse lawn. In 1958 the author was featured on *This Is Your Life,* a popular television show. In 1972 the lodge at Greenbo Lake State Resort Park was named the Jesse Stuart Lodge. Stuart received Kentucky's Distinguished Service Medallion in 1981.

Stuart was disabled by a stroke in 1978, and in May 1982 he suffered another stroke that rendered him comatose until he died on February 17, 1984. He is buried in Plum Grove Cemetery in Greenup County close to W-Hollow, the Appalachian valley that was the setting for many of his works.

See also: APPALACHIAN ENGLISH IN LITERATURE (LANGUAGE); CHILDREN'S LITERATURE; HUMOR IN APPALACHIAN LITERATURE (HUMOR).

—James M. Gifford, *Jesse Stuart Foundation*

Ruel E. Foster, *Jesse Stuart* (1968); Jerry A. Herndon and George Brosi, *Jesse Stuart, the Man and His Books* (1988); J. R. Lemaster and Mary Washington Clarke, eds., *Jesse Stuart: Essays on His Work* (1977).

Sut Lovingood

A self-proclaimed "nat'ral born durn'd fool," Sut Lovingood is the fictional creation of George Washington Harris (1814–1869). Born in Allegheny City, Pennsylvania, Harris spent most of his adult life in the South, captaining a steamboat in Knoxville, Tennessee, and working as a railroad conductor and silversmith. In 1867 he published his only book, *Sut Lovingood: Yarns Spun by a "Nat'ral Born Durn'd Fool,"* an influential collection of short stories chronicling the hell-raising antics of an east Tennessee mountain man who creates chaos and confusion everyplace he goes. Harris brilliantly captured the oral tradition of mountain tale telling and committed it to paper in dialect.

Sut enjoys "cork-screw kill-devil whisky," flirting with young girls, and playing cruel pranks on figures of authority. In "Parson John Bullen's Lizards," he disrupts a camp meeting by releasing a bag of lizards, some of which find their way up the preacher's pants legs, and then peer out through his shirt collar. Placing circuit riders, sheriffs, educators, and Yankees in incongruous situations is Sut's way of reminding pretentious people that they are human, too.

Sut relates his stories to George, a neutral narrator, who sets Sut off into flourishes of exaggeration by asking a few leading questions. This frame-narrative technique, also employed by Mark Twain in "The Celebrated Jumping Frog of Calaveras County," was common in Old Southwestern humor, the genre to which the Sut Lovingood stories belong. Critics generally acknowledge that the Sut Lovingood yarns are masterpieces of nineteenth-century humor, surpassed only by Twain.

See also: APPALACHIAN ENGLISH IN LITERATURE (LANGUAGE); HUMOR IN APPALACHIAN LITERATURE (HUMOR); LITERARY PERIODICALS.

—Fred W. Sauceman, *East Tennessee State University*

Walter Blair, *Native American Humor* (1960).

Travel Writing

Travel writing about the Appalachian region mirrors development of the genre through the eighteenth, nineteenth, and twentieth centuries in literary complexity and intellectual depth. Often received as more documentary than art, travel writing has influenced—and continues to influence—economic development and tourism as well as cultural perceptions of the region.

Spanish military expeditions in the first half of the sixteenth century led to the first documented European activity in the region that would come to be known as the Appalachian Mountains. Members of the expedition led by Hernando de Soto wrote the first accounts. The best-known and most complete of these, a narrative by the writer known as the Gentleman of Elvas (a town in Portugal), provides a provocative glimpse of the region just after European contact. However, writers of the early Spanish narratives did not have good maps and did not use consistent place names. Their accounts are generally confusing and incomplete.

With the rise of British trade in the seventeenth century, Europeans began sending back more coherent accounts of the flora, fauna, geology, geography, and inhabitants of the region. The earliest description published for a European audience was John Lederer's 1672 text *The Discoveries of John Lederer*, in which the author relates his experience ascending Virginia's Allegheny Mountains. Expecting to see the Pacific Ocean beyond, Lederer was stunned by the sight of range upon range of mountains extending to the horizon. More than a century later, William Bartram described the region's natural diversity, beauty, and inhabitants in his classic account *Travels through North and South Carolina, Georgia, East and West Florida, the Cherokee Country, the Extensive Territories of the Muscogulges or Creek Confederacy, and the Country of the Chactaws* (1791). Bartram, a botanist and illustrator, devotes four chapters to the horticultural wonders of the southern mountains, employing a consciously artful rendering of the natural and cultural scenes he encounters. Isaac Weld's *Travels through the States of North America*, an account of a journey in 1795–97, also depicts the region in the waning years of the eighteenth century.

With greater access to the region in the early decades of the nineteenth century, the number of published travel accounts increased. People journeying west from the Atlantic seaboard crossed the mountains through a handful of developed access routes. Additionally, tourists increasingly chose the Appalachian Mountains as a destination, spawning development of accommodations and services. Texts from this period that devote significant attention to the region include Andre Michaux's *Travels to the West of the Alleghany Mountains* (1805); Thomas Ashe's *Travels in America, Performed in 1806* (1808); John Melish's *Travels through the United States of America* (1815); James Kirke Paulding's *Letters from the South* (1817); John Palmer's *Journal of Travels in the United States of North America and in Lower Canada* (1818); William Faux's "Memorable Days in America" (1823); Timothy Flint's *Recollections of the Last Ten Years* (1826); Henry Tudor's *Narrative of a Tour in North America* (1834); Charles Fenno Hoffman's *A Winter in the West by a New Yorker* (1835); Charles Joseph Latrobe's *The Rambler in North America* (1835); and George William Featherstonhaugh's *Excursion through the Slave States* (1844). As several of the titles indicate, tours of the region often occurred during larger explorations of the eastern United States. Europeans wrote several of the most extensive accounts (including a number in German) for the enlightenment of the European public.

Paulding's *Letters from the South* marks the emergence of a literary convention often used in American travel writing of the nineteenth century—a northerner touring the South reports back to his compatriots about cultural conditions in the region, often including a "report" on the southern mountains. Frederick Law Olmsted's letters from the South to a northern newspaper audience, collected in 1860 as *A Journey in the Back Country*, originated from this perspective. Charles Lanman's *Letters from the Alleghany Mountains* (1849), which appeared initially as a series of letters for the Washington, D.C.–based *National Intelligencer*, is also in this vein. While men wrote most published accounts during this period, a handful of significant texts were the work of women. Perhaps most famously, newspaper reporter Anne Newport Royall documented the region in *Sketches of History, Life, and Manners in the United States* (1826). Likewise, Anna Marie Wells recorded her impressions of the Asheville, North Carolina, area and her trip through Pigeon Gorge to Tennessee in "Sketches from Buncombe, N.C." (1838).

In the second half of the nineteenth century, America saw the rise of national-circulation periodicals, or "quality" magazines, including illustrated magazines such as *Harper's*, *Appletons'*, *Scribner's*, and *Lippincott's*, as well as the non-illustrated *Atlantic Monthly*. The rise of these periodicals went hand-in-hand with a golden age of illustrated American travel writing, much of which concerned the Appalachian region. Among the first significant American contributors to *Harper's Monthly* in the 1850s, for example, was David Hunter Strother, who illustrated his own works under the pen name "Porte Crayon." His popular, thinly fictionalized travel series about the southern mountains—including "Virginia Illustrated" (1854), "North Carolina Illustrated" (1857), and "A Winter in the South" (1857–58)—helped to increase the magazine's circulation from 75,000 to more than 200,000 during the 1850s. After the Civil War, publishers of the illustrated national magazines focused increasing attention on Appalachia. *Picturesque America* (two volumes, 1872 and 1874) grew out of an illustrated series of the same name published in *Appletons' Journal*. This nine-hundred-page folio, sold in parts by subscription, features lavish steel-plate and wood engravings. Subscribers included such influential northeasterners as Ralph Waldo Emerson, Henry Wadsworth Longfellow, Oliver Wendell Holmes, John Greenleaf Whittier, and Harriet Beecher Stowe. Out of thirty-four illustrated travel articles in the first volume, nine cover sites in central and southern Appalachia.

As Reconstruction drew to a close, the volume of American magazine travel writing about the southern mountains continued to increase. A sampling of significant Gilded Age writing in the genre includes Edward Pollard's "The Virginia Tourist" (*Lippincott's*, 1870); Edward King's "The Great South" (*Scribner's*, 1874); Rebecca Harding Davis's "By-Paths in the Mountains" (*Harper's*, 1880); and Charles Dudley Warner's "On Horseback" (*Atlantic Monthly*, 1885)—all of which were republished in book form. Also during the post-Reconstruction era, so-called local color fiction became popular. Much of the travel writing of the period is closely related to, sometimes indistinguishable from, local color fiction. Writers such as Constance Fenimore Woolson, Rebecca Harding Davis, and "Christian Reid" (Frances Fisher Tiernan) wrote fictionalized travelogues in the local color and genteel modes of the period. These articles brought national attention to the region. First serialized in *Appletons'* (1875–76), Reid's "The Land of the Sky" was particularly wide-read and is credited with boosting tourism to the mountains of western North Carolina.

Towards the end of the century, travel writing about the region often took the form of descriptive natural history. Such writing includes Bradford Torrey's series of articles in the *Atlantic Monthly* in the early 1890s, collected in *Spring Notes from Tennessee* (1896) and *A World of Green Hills: Observations of Nature and Human Nature in the Blue Ridge* (1898). John Muir, in *A Thousand-Mile Walk to the Gulf* (1916), gives a cursory account of the region. With an eye towards natural history, Emma Bell Miles also adopted conventions of travel writing. At the same time, Miles's writings both reflect and comment upon another tendency of the period. By about the 1890s, national evangelical and educational energies had turned towards the white inhabitants of Appalachia. With this trend, subsequently dubbed the "uplift movement," came a substantial body of nonfiction about the region written by missionaries, educators, and folklorists. Though this work is often more than simply travelogue, it emerged from the travel-writing tradition. It represents the region and its inhabitants as the objects of ethnographic curiosity, and it influenced travel to, as well as perceptions of, the region.

From the 1890s through the 1920s, for example, church and evangelical publications, including the *Christian Observer*, the *Home Mission Monthly*, and publications of the American Missionary Association, printed countless articles about Appalachia, many of which were travelogues. William Goodell Frost, president of Berea College in Kentucky for twenty-eight years (1892–1920), wrote about the region for evangelical publications, as well as for the *Atlantic Monthly*, in which he published his influential "Our Contemporary Ancestors in the Southern Mountains" (1899). James Watt Raine, head of the English Department at Berea for thirty-three years, published *The Land of the Saddle-Bags* (1924) and *Saddlebag Folk* (1942), both widely read "uplift" accounts that fit explicitly in the travel-writing tradition. During the same era, the *Journal of American Folklore* featured accounts of mountain whites and Cherokees alongside accounts of southern blacks and presented mountain whites as a regional ethnic group. Folklorists published full-length books, including *The Southern Highlander and His Homeland* (1921) by educator and folklorist John C. Campbell. This posthumous work appeared under the auspices of the Russell Sage Foundation, a philanthropic organization whose goals were ethnographic.

The next distinct body of travel writing about Appalachia arose with the increasing popularity of automobile tourism in the 1930s. Though the well-known state guides coordinated by the Federal Writers' Project tend to skirt the Appalachian region, a number of excellent full-length nonfiction works written explicitly for auto travelers appeared in the 1930s and 1940s. These books typically mix popular history, botany, and ethnology alongside automobile travel routes. Examples include Muriel Earley Sheppard's *Cabins in the Laurel* (1935) and Laura Thornborough's *The Great Smoky Mountains* (1937). Another is *The Great Smokies and the Blue Ridge* (1943), edited by Roderick Peattie, featuring chapters by Arthur Stupka, Donald Culross Peattie, and others. During World War II and the postwar decades, publishers continued to produce high-quality, book-length nonfiction, often illustrated with black-and-white photographs, for a travel readership. Significant books include *The Kentucky* by Thomas D. Clark (1942); Donald Davidson's *The Tennessee* (two volumes, 1946 and 1948); and Wilma Dykeman's *The French Broad* (1955), all three of which were from the Holt-Rinehart *Rivers of America* series. Michael Frome's *Strangers in High Places: The Story of the Great Smoky Mountains* (1966) covers the natural, social, and political history of the region and includes highway maps.

See also: APPALACHIA (LANGUAGE); ENVIRONMENTAL WRITING.

—Katherine E. Ledford, *Gardner-Webb University*, and Kevin E. O'Donnell, *East Tennessee State University*

Katherine E. Ledford, "The Primitive Circle: Inscribing Class in Southern Appalachian Travel Writing, 1816–1846," *Appalachian Journal* (Fall 2001–Winter 2002); Kevin O'Donnell and Helen Hollingsworth, eds., *Seekers of Scenery: American Travel Writing from Southern Appalachia, 1840–1900* (2004).

Trigiani, Adriana

(1964–) Novelist, playwright, and screenwriter.

Adriana Trigiani spent her formative years in the small mountain town of Big Stone Gap, Virginia, which serves as the setting for three of her novels: *Big Stone Gap* (2000), *Big Cherry Holler* (2001), and *Milk Glass Moon* (2002).

The protagonist of Trigiani's Big Stone Gap trilogy is Ave Maria Mulligan, a thirty-five-year-old self-described spinster who finds herself on an identity quest sparked by her realization of her minority status as an Italian, Roman Catholic, college-educated, female pharmacist in the Virginia mountains. Other colorful, multilayered characters include Fleeta Mullins, a chain-smoking cashier; Iva Lou Wade, the bookmobile librarian; and Jack MacChesney, a coal-mining bachelor who eventually becomes Ave Maria's husband.

In addition to fiction, Trigiani has written for the theater, film, and television. She majored in theater at Saint Mary's College at the University of Notre Dame in Indiana, where she was the first student to write and direct her own play, *Notes from the Nile*. In 1985 she wrote *Secrets of the Lava Lamp* for the Manhattan Theatre Club, followed in 1986 by the comedy screenplay *Three to Get Married.* Other television credits include *The Cosby Show*, *A Different World*, *Good Sports*, *Central Park West*, and *City Kids.* In 1996 she wrote an award-winning, feature-length documentary entitled *Queens of the Bigtime*, a tribute to her family. She also served as screenwriter and director for the movie version of *Big Stone Gap*. Trigiani lives in New York with her husband and daughter.

See also: POST–WORLD WAR II FICTION; WOMEN AUTHORS.

—Donia Stevens Eley, *Pulaski, Virginia*

Turnbull, Agnes Sligh

(1888–1982) Novelist.

A prolific and popular writer, the northern Appalachian author Agnes Sligh Turnbull was born on October 14, 1888, in New Alexandria, Pennsylvania, to parents of Scots-Irish descent. She attended Indiana Normal School (Indiana University of Pennsylvania) and taught high school English until she married James Lyall Turnbull in 1918. A year later, after his return from the war in France, the couple moved to Maplewood, New Jersey, where the author lived until her death on January 31, 1982.

After her marriage, Turnbull gave up teaching and began writing full time. Her first short story was published by *American Magazine* in 1920 and launched her long and successful career as a writer for adults and children. Her first novel, *The Rolling Years*, an imaginative account of her mother's family history, was published by Macmillan in 1936. Subsequent novels, often focusing on northern Appalachia, include *The Day Must Dawn* (1942), *The Bishop's Mantle* (1947), *The Golden Journey* (1955), *The Nightingale* (1960), *Whistle and I'll Come to You* (1970), and her last, *The Two Bishops* (1980). Turnbull also wrote four novels for juveniles—*Elijah, the Fish-Bite* (1940), *Jed, the Shepherd's Dog* (1957), *George* (1965), and *The White Lark* (1968)—and a memoir, *Dear Me* (1941). At a time when realism was making way for modernism and when authors were becoming more daring, often writing freely of psychology and sexuality, Turnbull offered stories of a simpler, more innocent life, where a kiss was detail enough. Her imagination was fueled by her love of history and heritage, and she commonly wrote of small-town and rural life, often in historical settings, where old-fashioned values of hard work, frugality, and loyalty to family prevailed. Though critics often dismissed her work as out-dated and sentimental, the public found the nostalgia of her tales appealing, and she remained widely read and admired throughout her career.

See also: CHILDREN'S LITERATURE.

—Heather Rhea Gilreath, *East Tennessee State University*

Walker, Frank X

(1961–) Poet, artist, and school administrator.

Frank X Walker created the word *Affrilachia* to join his rich heritage as an African American and an Appalachian. His first book of poetry, titled *Affrilachia,* explores these roots. Walker was born in Danville, Kentucky, received a B.A. from the University of Kentucky, and an M.F.A. from Spalding University. He has directed his home state's Governor's School for the Arts and in 2004 began teaching at Eastern Kentucky University.

Frank X Walker, c. 2000. A strong advocate of the arts and cultural heritage, Kentucky poet and educator Walker coined the term *Affrilachian* to describe the culture of African American Appalachians.

As a student at the University of Kentucky, Walker studied under and became friends with acclaimed Appalachian writer Gurney Norman. Fifteen years later, in 2000, Norman and his wife Nyoka Hawkins began a new press by publishing *Affrilachia* as their first book. In the collection, Walker urges his readers to claim their roots and their history, but he also urges them to act to solve the nation's problems. His poems value family, despite divorce; they hold onto history, despite its tragedies; and they challenge American politics and vision, encouraging differences. Walker's second book of poetry is *Buffalo Dance: The Journey of York,* in which he relates the story of the Lewis and Clark expedition from the perspective of Clark's slave, York.

In addition to writing, Frank X Walker is a strong arts advocate. He is a founding member of the Affrilachian poets, a group of African American poets from the region. In his work, Walker tries to ensure access to art and art education for all, regardless of race or income.

See also: AFRICAN AMERICAN LITERATURE; POST–WORLD WAR II POETS.

—Jim Minick, *Radford University*

Washington, Booker T.

(1856–1915) Author, orator, and educator.

One of the most famous autobiographies in American literature, *Up from Slavery* chronicles Booker Taliaferro Washington's personal transformation from a slave in Appalachia to an internationally recognized educator and social reformer. Upon its publication in 1901, the book became a best-seller, as both black and white readers were moved by its reinterpretation of the archetypically American Horatio Alger myth. In addition to presenting a narrative of Washington's "upward mobility," *Up from Slavery* offers an elaboration of his innovative educational ideas and a clarification of his views on race relations.

Highly didactic, plainspoken, and direct, *Up from Slavery* reflects the fact that its author was not only an accomplished orator but also a public figure with an overt political agenda. At the time of the book's publication, both northern and southern white Americans deemed Washington the unofficial spokesman for his race, a role he embraced.

Granted its larger intentions, Washington's autobiography includes some compelling recollections of his Appalachian childhood. According to biographer Louis R. Harlan, Washington was born in the spring of 1856 on a 207-acre Franklin County, Virginia, tobacco plantation. His mother, Jane, was a slave, so Washington's birth was not officially recorded. His father was a never-disclosed white man who lived in the vicinity. Emancipated after the Civil War, Jane and her children left Franklin County for West Virginia to join her husband, who was employed in the salt industry, near the town of Malden. There, Washington, not yet a teenager, worked stints as a salt packer, coal miner, and servant, attending school only intermittently. Nonetheless, he applied himself to his own course of study.

In 1872 Washington was admitted to Hampton Normal and Agricultural Institute, an experimental school in Tidewater Virginia offering a program of industrial education as a method for empowering postwar African Americans. Graduating with honors from Hampton in 1875, he returned to Malden to teach at an African American school; then, after studying theology in Washington, D.C., he accepted a teaching position at the Hampton Institute.

In 1881, at age twenty-five, Washington was hired to head a new school, Tuskegee Normal and Industrial Institute, in Tuskegee, Alabama. Loosely modeled on Hampton, the Tuskegee Institute flourished under Washington's leadership, eventually boasting approximately two hundred faculty and staff and more than one thousand students. The school featured a respected academic program in addition to industrial training.

By the end of the nineteenth century, Washington figured significantly in state and national politics. Governors and presidents consulted him for advice, newspapers nationwide quoted him, and prominent philanthropists made substantial donations to Tuskegee. Washington believed that African Americans of the post–Civil War period should pursue economic and moral empowerment before seeking social and political equality, an accommodationist position lauded by whites across the nation. This stance was strongly criticized by some individuals among the African American intelligentsia, however, most notably, W. E. B. Du Bois.

Washington, given his central if controversial position in American society, was arguably the most significant African American of his generation. Many historians still refer to the years between 1895 and 1915 as the "Era of Booker T. Washington."

See also: CIVIL RIGHTS MOVEMENT (RACE, ETHNICITY, AND IDENTITY); HISTORICALLY BLACK COLLEGES AND UNIVERSITIES (EDUCATION); CHRISTIANSBURG INSTITUTE (EDUCATION).

—Ted Olson, *East Tennessee State University*

Louis R. Harlan, *Booker T. Washington: The Making of a Black Leader, 1856–1901* (1972) and *Booker T. Washington: The Wizard of Tuskegee, 1901–1915* (1983).

West, Don

(1906–1992) Poet and labor activist.

Revered by many, reviled by some, Don West was a towering figure of regional pride who led labor organizers, defended those he considered oppressed, and wrote populist poetry for the masses. An ordained Congregational minister, he was burned out, shot at, subpoenaed by the House Un-American Activities Committee, chased down mountain highways, and jailed.

West was born in 1906 in Devil's Hollow in Gilmer County, Georgia, the son of a small mountain farmer and the grandson of Kim Mulkey, a Unionist and Radical Republican who strongly influenced West's worldview. As a high school student, West was invited to attend the Berry School in North Georgia but was expelled for protesting the showing of *The Birth of a Nation*, D. W. Griffith's controversial film about the founding of the Ku Klux Klan. As a student at Lincoln Memorial University, he was a popular athlete and student leader. Like his classmates in the class of 1929, Jesse Stuart and James Still, West went from Lincoln Memorial to graduate school at Vanderbilt, in his case to the Divinity School, which awarded him a travel grant to study Danish folk schools. Returning to Tennessee, he met Myles Horton, who had also traveled to Denmark, and together they founded the famous Highlander Folk School in 1932 in Monteagle, Tennessee. The following year West left Highlander to head up the defense committee for Angelo Herndon, a young African American communist who had been sentenced to twenty years in prison for leading a protest of unemployed people. Throughout the rest of the 1930s, West was a full-time social activist, receiving a jail sentence in Kentucky while working for the National Miners Union in Bell and Harlan Counties. All the while, he was publishing poems that appeared in the *Liberator*, *New Masses*, *Daily Worker*, *Christian Century*, and numerous other publications.

As the activism of the 1930s was swallowed up by preparation for World War II, West retreated to his family farm for a few years and then became superintendent of a nearby public school system. This job led to a teaching position at Oglethorpe University in Atlanta. In 1946 Charles Boni, the publisher who had brought out Ernest Hemingway's first story collection, chose West's fourth poetry book, *Clods of Southern Earth*, as the inaugural book for his new press. The book was a great success, with *Publishers Weekly* reporting eight thousand prepublication orders and the *Atlanta Constitution* calling West a "Walt Whitman in Overalls." Nevertheless, when West defended Rosalie Ingram, a poor African American woman sentenced to death for shooting a white man who attempted to rape her in front of her children, the same paper editorialized against him. He was fired from Oglethorpe, and his house was burned down. West then moved to Dalton, Georgia, where he worked for a church paper that was progressive in politics and conservative in theology. His efforts to unionize workers in the carpet industry resulted in severe "red-baiting" attacks against West, and he was literally run out of Dalton by gun thugs in a speeding car. Throughout the 1950s he taught school in Maryland.

In 1965 West established the Appalachian South Folklife Center at Pipestem, West Virginia. This center, inspired by Danish folk schools, combined local service projects with workshops and programs designed to encourage a positive Appalachian identity. At the same time, he quietly encouraged activists of the 1960s and raised money to support his efforts through poetry readings around the country. He also wrote a series of pamphlets for the Appalachian Movement Press celebrating the spirit of progressive politics in the Appalachian South. His eighth and last book of poetry was published in 1982, a decade before his death in 1992 and more than fifty years after the first, written while he was a student at Vanderbilt.

West was unexcelled as a regional writer of proletarian poetry. Although his political legacy may surpass his literary reputation, he remains one of Appalachia's most popular and original poets.

See also: FOLKLORE AND SOCIAL PROTEST (FOLKLORE AND FOLKLIFE); HORTON, MYLES (EDUCATION); LITERARY PERIODICALS.

—George Brosi, *Berea, Kentucky*

Wideman, John Edgar

(1941–) Fiction and nonfiction writer

Noted African American author John Edgar Wideman was born June 14, 1941, in Washington, D.C. Within a year of his birth, his family moved to Pittsburgh, where one of his female ancestors had settled after escaping from slavery in the mid-1800s. Initially the family lived in Homewood, a close-knit African American community, but relocated to the mostly white suburban community of Shadyside when Wideman was in high school so he could attend a top-ranked school. He became class president and captain of the basketball team, and he graduated first in his class in 1959. Continuing his academic excellence, he attended the University of Pennsylvania from 1959 until 1963 and earned a Rhodes scholarship to Oxford University in England. In the meantime, he also excelled on the basketball court.

Wideman published his first novel, *A Glance Away* (1967), one year after he left Oxford. The novel is set in Homewood, which continued to figure prominently in his other writings. His fourth, fifth, and sixth books—*Damballah* (1981, a collection of short stories) and *Hiding Place* and *Sent for You Yesterday* (1981 and 1983, novels)—are known as the "Homewood trilogy." The trilogy's interconnected narratives, which stretch from the nineteenth to the late twentieth century, focus on the descendants of a female slave who, like Wideman's grandmother, escaped to Pittsburgh. Wideman's first nonfiction book, *Brothers and Keepers* (1984), also looks toward Homewood, as do *Reuben* (1987) and *Two Cities* (1998), the latter set in both Pittsburgh and Philadelphia. Wideman's poetic writing style combines narratives of ordinary people's lives with myth and folklore, and critics have compared it to jazz, describing it as multivocal and improvisational.

In addition to writing, Wideman has had a distinguished career as an educator, teaching at the University of Pennsylvania, the University of Wyoming, and the University of Massachusetts. He has won the PEN/Faulkner Award for literature twice, and in 1993 he was awarded a MacArthur Fellowship.

See also: AFRICAN AMERICAN LITERATURE; POST–WORLD WAR II FICTION.

—Theresa Lloyd, *East Tennessee State University*

Williams, Cratis

(1911–1985) Scholar and folklorist.

Cratis Dearl Williams is widely considered the father of Appalachian studies. He is known for his eastern Kentucky roots, his Scots-Irish heritage, his breadth of knowledge of Appalachian folk speech and cultural traditions, and his great wit and humor. Born in his grandfather's log house on Caines Creek, in Lawrence County, Kentucky, he drew lifelong inspiration from his rural family and community culture. He initiated curricula and programs in Appalachian studies, became a professor of English and dean of the graduate school at Appalachian State University in Boone, North Carolina, and served as acting vice-chancellor for academic affairs and also acting chancellor before his retirement from that institution. A nationally recognized spokesperson for Appalachian culture, Williams documented and interpreted ballads, folktales, language, historical traditions, and religious customs.

The first child of Curtis and Mona Whitt Williams, Cratis Williams was educated in the one-room Hillside Elementary School on Caines Creek. Later, he boarded with relatives in the county seat of Louisa to attend high school, from which he graduated in 1928. His interest in ballads had been sparked at Louisa High School, and he began a lifelong study of historical and cultural traditions of the community into which he was born. He attended Cumberland College (1928–29), and then taught in one-room schools on Caines Creek (1929–33) while taking classes at Morehead State Normal School and Teachers College and the University of Kentucky, where he completed his B.A. degree in 1933.

After graduation, Williams moved to Blaine, Kentucky, to teach high school science and English (1933–38). In 1937 he married fellow teacher Sylvia Graham, and that same year he received the M.A. in English from the University of

Kentucky. In his thesis, Williams analyzed 471 ballads and songs from eastern Kentucky. Reproduced on microcard, his work was used extensively by folklore scholar Malcolm Laws in his revised edition of *Native American Balladry*. While serving as principal of Louisa High School (1938–41), Williams ran unsuccessfully for the board of education. Following his defeat, he and his wife Sylvia were unable to find work locally as teachers, and he had to leave the area and teaching for a time.

In 1942 Williams was hired as critic teacher at the Appalachian Demonstration High School, Appalachian State Teachers College. During their first year in Boone, his wife Sylvia succumbed to tuberculosis, a disease with which he had also been diagnosed. Recovering from the illness, he served the high school until 1949 as critic teacher, assistant principal, director of drama, and director of the first school counseling program established in North Carolina. In 1946 he was named assistant professor of English and speech at Appalachian State.

While continuing to teach, Williams pursued his Ph.D. at New York University and earned the degree in 1961 with a dissertation entitled "The Southern Mountaineer in Fact and Fiction" (abstracted in *Appalachian Journal*, 1975–76). Acclaimed by the *Journal of American Folklore* as "the most comprehensive and valuable current work on Southern Highland literature," his dissertation is unparalleled and remains the baseline work in the field of Appalachian literature.

In 1949 Williams married Elizabeth Lingerfelt, with whom he had two children, Sophie (b. 1953) and David Cratis (b. 1955). By the late 1940s Williams had developed curricula on traditional ballads and songs and worked with associates in a Saturday afternoon folk festival in Boone. In 1956 he initiated, with Professor Beulah Campbell, one of the first senior-level college curricula in Appalachian studies, a summer workshop called the Living Folk Arts of Southern Mountain People. It provided students an opportunity to participate in Saturday folk festivals, to conduct home visits to document local speech, songs, tales, folk remedies, and traditional crafts, and to study Appalachian literature, history, and sociology. In addition to his courses in ballads and songs and Appalachian literature in the English Department, he sparked development of new courses both among his colleagues throughout the region and through his students as they assumed teaching positions in secondary schools, colleges, and universities.

His abiding interest in mountain speech led to publication of a series of articles between 1961 and 1967 in *Mountain Life and Work*, reprinted in 1992 as *Southern Mountain Speech*. His devotion to the nuances and rich subtlety of mountain speech was matched by his meticulous knowledge of ballads and his artful capacity for telling tales learned in childhood. He treasured and taught ballads as literature and as a key to mountain aesthetics. He lectured widely and entertained diverse audiences with his perspective on Scots-Irish heritage as manifest in cultural values and speech.

Following his retirement in 1976 from a distinguished career as a teacher and administrator at Appalachian State University, he began to write about his life. His memoirs, most published posthumously, include *William H. Vaughan: A Better Man Than I Ever Wanted to Be* (1983); *I Become a Teacher* (1995); *The Cratis Williams Chronicles: I Come to Boone* (1999), which contains a biography, chronology, and bibliography of Williams's writings and videos; and *Tales from Sacred Wind: Coming of Age in Appalachia* (2003). Video treatments include *Cratis Williams: Living the Divided Life* (1999).

A retirement symposium held in Williams's honor sparked organization of the Appalachian Studies Association in 1977 in Berea, Kentucky. In 1993 the highest honor bestowed by the association, given annually to an outstanding regional scholar, was designated the Cratis Williams Award. The 1970s saw many of his interests bear fruit in formation of new curricula, outreach, and collaboration, including preparation of teachers and supervisors for instruction in rural Appalachia. He was a founding member of the Appalachian Consortium and the Appalachian Consortium Press, where he served on the editorial board. In 1972 *Appalachian Journal* was launched, with Jerry Williamson as editor and Williams as advising editor. He was the major catalyst behind creation of the Center for Appalachian Studies in 1978 and the M.A. degree in Appalachian studies in 1980 at Appalachian State.

His awards include the Founders Day Certificate for excellence, New York University (1962); North Carolina Historical Society's Achievement Award (1972); O. Max Gardner Award, University of North Carolina (1973); Honorary Citizen of Harlan County, Kentucky (1973); Brown-Hudson Award, North Carolina Folklore Society (1975); Laurel Leaves Award, Appalachian Consortium (1976); W. D. Weatherford Award, Berea College (1979); and honorary degrees in 1984 from Cumberland College, Morehead State University, College of Idaho, and in 1985 from Marshall University and Appalachian State University.

The Cratis Dearl Williams Papers are housed in the W. L. Eury Appalachian Collection in Belk Library at Appalachian State University.

See also: LITERARY SCHOLARSHIP; WILLIAMS, CRATIS (LANGUAGE).

—Patricia D. Beaver, *Appalachian State University*

Barry M. Buxton et al., ed., *The Cratis Williams Symposium Proceedings: A Memorial and Examination of the State of Regional Studies in Appalachia* (1989); Loyal Jones, "A Complete Mountaineer," *Appalachian Journal* (Spring 1986); David Cratis Williams and Patricia D. Beaver, eds., *The Cratis Williams Chronicles: I Come to Boone* (1999).

Willis, Meredith Sue

(1946–) Fiction and nonfiction writer.

Chronicler of the conflicts, questions, doubts, and commitments of the postwar generation of Appalachians, Meredith Sue Willis was born in Clarksburg in 1946 and reared in Shinnston, West Virginia. Willis's parents, the first in their families to go to college, trained as schoolteachers. Stalwart members of church and lodge, the Willises provided their daughter with a typical 1950s middle-class life in an Appalachian small town.

As a teenager, Willis began to challenge many of the assumptions in her life, and when she enrolled at Bucknell University, her questioning intensified. Leaving college after one year, she worked as a VISTA (Volunteers in Service to America) volunteer for a year in Norfolk, Virginia. She then moved to New York City, where she earned degrees from Barnard College and Columbia University. During this time, she joined the radical student movement Students for a Democratic Society and participated in the antiwar protests and student strikes at Columbia in the spring of 1968. Settling in New York City and then the New Jersey suburbs, Willis has continued to live out her early political commitments, teaching at New York University, conducting writing workshops for inner-city residents, and working in community literacy programs. She is also the author of numerous guides and other resources for writers.

Willis's novels *A Space Apart* and *Oradell at Sea* and the short story collections *In the Mountains of America* and *Quilt Pieces* explore the pressures that individualism, class, race, and gender exert on identities. These texts also deal with the ways that women resist the limits society and culture place on them. The centerpiece of Willis's literary landscape is her semi-autobiographical trilogy: *Higher Ground, Only Great Changes,* and *Trespassers*. Narrating Blair Ellen Morgan's coming of age, the trilogy begins with Morgan's childhood and adolescent struggles with the assumptions and values of her middle-class parents and her West Virginia hometown. Also contributing to the development of Morgan's identity are college, two years as a VISTA volunteer in Norfolk, her move to New York, antiwar demonstrations at Columbia, and a range of relationships and affairs.

Willis writes from an understanding of identity as a social process intimately involved with place, and in her trilogy and other fiction she struggles with the personal, political, cultural, and social meanings of Appalachian identity and place, as well as the promotion of social justice. Like her protagonist Morgan, who by the end of *Trespassers* realizes that, while claiming New York as her own place, she remains connected to the mountains of West Virginia, Willis suggests that in her own life the Appalachian landscape is still a compass for her.

See also: IDENTITY, CENTRAL AND SOUTHERN APPALACHIAN (RACE, ETHNICITY, AND IDENTITY); IDENTITY, NORTHERN APPALACHIAN (RACE, ETHNICITY, AND IDENTITY); WOMEN AUTHORS.

—Tal Stanley, *Emory and Henry College*

Thomas E. Douglass, "Interview with Meredith Sue Willis," *Appalachian Journal* (Spring 1993); *Iron Mountain Review: Meredith Sue Willis Issue* (Spring 1996); Meredith Sue Willis, *In the Mountains of America* (1994).

Wolfe, Thomas

(1900–1938) Fiction writer and dramatist.

Thomas Wolfe modeled his experimental modernist fiction on his own experiences, including his childhood in the urban mountain South. Wolfe was born in Asheville, North Carolina, to William Oliver Wolfe, a stone carver, and Julia Westall Wolfe, a boardinghouse proprietor. Wolfe's boyhood was divided between the Wolfe family home and his mother's boardinghouse.

In 1916 Wolfe entered the University of North Carolina at Chapel Hill. There, influenced by Professor Frederick H. Koch's idea of the "folk play," he penned dramas set in the mountains around Asheville, two of which were produced by Carolina Playmakers. After graduating in 1920, Wolfe began graduate studies at Harvard University, where he enrolled in George Pierce Baker's 47 Workshop. Wolfe's play *The Mountains*, set in western North Carolina, was produced by the workshop in 1921. In 1922 Wolfe completed his M.A. and moved to New York, where, aside from stays in Europe, he resided for the rest of his life. Initially he attempted a career as a playwright, supporting himself by teaching English at New York University's Washington Square campus. He began a long, tempestuous relationship with Aline Bernstein, a wealthy, married set designer, in 1925.

By 1927 Wolfe had turned from drama to fiction. His first novel, *Look Homeward, Angel* (1929), which drew on his Asheville and Chapel Hill years, recounted the boyhood of protagonist Eugene Gant. The novel met with great critical acclaim, although Wolfe's graphic depiction of Asheville outraged many of the city's citizens. Along with *The Hills Beyond* (1941), a collection of short stories with mountain settings, *Look Homeward, Angel* is the most Appalachian of Wolfe's fictional texts.

Of Time and the River (1933), Wolfe's second autobiographical novel, continued Gant's story through his Harvard and early New York days. In *The Story of a Novel* (1936), Wolfe described the composition of *Of Time and the River*. Some critics were disturbed to learn of the extensive role that Maxwell Perkins, Wolfe's editor at Scribner's, had played in structuring his first two novels. Indeed, Wolfe's writing tended toward the episodic, not the minutely crafted, and he relied on his editors to shape his texts. Just before his death in 1938 of miliary tuberculosis of the brain, Wolfe submitted a vast, amorphous manuscript to his new editor, Edward C. Aswell of Harper's. Aswell edited this manuscript, published in 1939 as *The Web and the Rock*, so heavily that some critics question whether it, along with Wolfe's last posthumously published novel, *You Can't Go Home Again* (1940), can be solely attributed to Wolfe.

In 2000 Arlyn and Matthew J. Bruccoli reopened the editing controversy by publishing Wolfe's original version of *Look Homeward, Angel.* This unedited version, which was issued under Wolfe's working title for the novel, *O Lost: A Story of the Buried Life*, is 22 percent longer than the edited version, from which Perkins removed passages and language that he found superfluous or offensive.

Wolfe's fiction generally retains the high critical regard with which it was first met. His rhapsodic, allusive, realistic, experimental prose helped to define American modernism. The city of Asheville has likewise come proudly to embrace its internationally famous son.

See also: HUMOR IN APPALACHIAN LITERATURE (HUMOR); NATIVE AMERICANS AND APPALACHIAN LITERATURE.

—Theresa Lloyd, *East Tennessee State University*

David Herbert Donald, *Look Homeward: A Life of Thomas Wolfe* (1987); C. H. Holman, *The Loneliness at the Core: Studies in Thomas Wolfe* (1975); Louis D. Rubin Jr., *Thomas Wolfe: The Weather of His Youth* (1955).

Wilma Dykeman, c. 1970s. A prolific author of fiction, nonfiction, histories, and literary criticism, Dykeman, who lived in the mountains of North Carolina and Tennessee, helped to define Appalachian literature as an entity.

Women Authors

During the two periods when Appalachian literature experienced its greatest flowering—the late nineteenth century and the mid- to late twentieth century—American women writers also gained greater acceptance in the national literary canon. This convergence was a felicitous development for Appalachian women writers, whose prominence in the region's literature is now well established.

Although women (including Susan Fenimore Cooper and Elizabeth Wright, two northern Appalachian authors now considered important early ecofeminists) actively published in the United States in the early and mid-1800s, it was not until the local color movement at the end of the century that the dons of American literature began to grant women authors the status of literary authors. Local color, which sought to depict lives of ordinary but supposedly quaint people in picturesque, rural areas that were fast disappearing due to urbanization, seemed eminently suited to a woman's pen, since it emphasized the domestic over the public sphere.

Appalachia was one of those rural areas mined by local colorists, and women were prominent among them, publishing in prestigious northeastern magazines such as the *Atlantic Monthly*, *Harper's*, *Scribner's*, and *Appletons'*. Local color influenced both fiction and nonfiction, and sometimes local color travelogues blurred the distinction between the two. Constance Fenimore Woolson's "The French Broad," for example, published in 1875 in *Harper's*, has a cast of fictionalized characters, but its descriptions of vegetation, geology, and the development potential of mountain land around Asheville, North Carolina, came straight from post–Civil War nonfiction travel accounts of the region.

Rebecca Harding Davis, best known today for the novella *Life in the Iron-Mills* (*Atlantic Monthly*, 1861), an exposé of the impoverished lives and inhumane working conditions of laborers in Wheeling, (West) Virginia, wrote several short stories set in the mountains of North Carolina. Although not as insistent and graphic as *Life in the Iron-Mills*, these stories also indicate Davis's concern for the poor and disenfranchised. Her story "The Yares of the Black Mountains" (*Lippincott's*, 1875) suggests the anxieties that beset successful women authors of her day, who, despite growing professional stature, still faced the charge of being unwomanly for entering a profession and supposedly neglecting their families. As if to distance herself from this charge, Davis portrays a woman journalist as an insensitive, superficial hack and hustles her off during the first half of the story, which focuses on a long-suffering mother who has brought her child to the mountains in hopes of curing his ill health.

The most successful of the Appalachian local colorists was Mary Noailles Murfree, who published under the pseudonym "Charles Egbert Craddock." Best known for the short story collection *In the Tennessee Mountains* (1884), Murfree based her fiction on her observations of mountain culture while vacationing in the Cumberland Mountains. Murfree's stories demonstrate strengths and weaknesses of a genre that, in searching for the picturesque, can sometimes reinforce patronizing ideas about the culture that it discovers, which is assumed to be inherently inferior to that of the reader. Perhaps cognizant of these problems, Murfree sometimes undercuts the supposed superiority of her non-mountain characters by revealing their obtuseness, which contrasts with the virtuousness of mountaineers whom the lowlanders have seen as bumpkins and ruffians.

Another problem with local color writing about Appalachia was that it did little to promote authorship by people from the region itself, even though it did bring prominence to a number of women authors. Although Davis was a native of Appalachia, most local colorists were not. Another exception was Emma Bell Miles, who moved to Tennessee's Cumberland Mountains as a child and considered the region her home. Miles's *The Spirit of the Mountains* (1905) is an insightful account of folklife, religion, and gender roles in southern Appalachia. Although not exactly a feminist text, Miles's book does emphasize the lives of women, including their secondary status in a strongly masculinist culture.

In the early twentieth century, the prominence of local color and other forms of realism gave way to modernist experimentation, and although Appalachian women authors were doing important work during this period, their significance has until recently been overlooked. Perhaps one reason for their marginalization is that rather than embracing modernism, Appalachian women writers tended to continue in a local color vein—as did Lucy Furman, who wrote *The Quare Women* (1923) and two other novels based on her experiences at Hindman Settlement School, and Muriel Earley Sheppard, who penned a nonfiction account of the Toe River Valley, *Cabins in the Laurel* (1935)—or to write social realism, which for much of the twentieth century was regarded as inferior to modernism. Ironically, one of modernism's most original and powerful writers, Gertrude Stein, was born in northern Appalachia but left the region as a child.

Appalachia boasts powerful social realist literature authored by women. In the novel *The Time of Man* (1926), Elizabeth Madox Roberts, a native of central Kentucky, tells of the grinding poverty that a sharecropper's daughter and her family endure. Other Appalachian proletarian novels by women of this era include Anne W. Armstrong's *This Day and Time* (1930), Olive Tilford Dargan's *Call Home the Heart* (1932), written under the pseudonym "Fielding Burke," and Grace Lumpkin's *To Make My Bread* (1932). These texts deal with mountain people forced by poverty out of an agrarian lifestyle to seek employment in factories. The powerful union organizer Mary Harris "Mother" Jones provided a nonfiction account of industrial poverty and the union movement of this period in her autobiography, which she published in 1925.

Despite the marginalization of women authors, strong female voices also emerged in the mid-twentieth century. In 1940 Mildred Haun, a native of Cocke County, Tennessee, published *The Hawk's Done Gone*, a searing account of women's oppression in a patriarchal culture. Kentuckian Harriette Simpson Arnow wrote her classic novel of Appalachian out-migration, *The Dollmaker* (1954), while living in Detroit. Janice Holt Giles, an Arkansas native who spent much of her adult life in eastern Kentucky, wrote historical fiction as well as other novels and two autobiographies set in Appalachia. Northern Appalachian women writers from this era included the popular western Pennsylvania–born novelists Mary Roberts Rinehart and Agnes Sligh Turnbull.

By the last third of the twentieth century, Appalachian literature was undergoing a period of strong outpouring that some have called the Appalachian Renaissance, a movement that self-consciously promoted authorship by natives of the region. The late twentieth century also saw the rise of feminist criticism in literary studies throughout the United States, one of the goals of which was the advancement of women authors. This confluence resulted in a remarkable, well-respected body of work by Appalachian women writers. Wilma Dykeman, who lived in the mountains of North Carolina and Tennessee, helped to define Appalachian literature as an entity. A prolific author most active from the 1950s through the 1980s, Dykeman published fiction, nonfiction, histories, and literary criticism. Another sign of women's movement into the forefront of literary authorship is the recognition of women authors as originators and members of all-female literary circles. One such circle was the "Hollins Group," composed of southwest Virginia novelist Lee Smith, Pittsburgh natives Annie Dillard (author of numerous texts including *Pilgrim at Tinker Creek*) and Lucinda MacKethan (a literary scholar now teaching at North Carolina State University), and literary scholar Anne Goodwyn Jones. These women met while attending the all-female Hollins College near Roanoke, Virginia, in the 1960s and have achieved nationally distinguished careers in literature.

Much Appalachian literature of the late twentieth and early twenty-first centuries has dealt with iconic regional issues such as agrarianism and has looked back to

Appalachia's past. In the poetry collections *Wildwood Flower* (1992) and *Black Shawl* (1998), Kathryn Stripling Byer (a south Georgia native transplanted to the North Carolina mountains) incorporates self-sufficient agriculture, folk medicine, quilting, and traditional families into her portrait of the mountains as a place apart from mainstream America. Mary Lee Settle's ambitious "Beulah quintet" of novels, seeking to recreate a vast sweep of Appalachian history, stretches from seventeenth-century England to modern urban West Virginia. Sharyn McCrumb, a North Carolina author noted for her "Ballad series" of mystery novels, often examines a similarly broad sweep of Appalachian history. Lee Smith's novel *Oral History* (1983) revolves around the desire to invent an Appalachian past.

In some parts of Appalachia, coal mining has long held sway, and the topic has figured prominently in texts by women authors from mining regions. Denise Giardina's *Storming Heaven* (1987) and *The Unquiet Earth* (1992) explore the rhythms of mining life—from underground disasters to strikes—in the lives of multiple narrators. Coal mining also informs Lee Smith novels such as *Fair and Tender Ladies* (1988).

Another topic of recurring interest to late-twentieth-century Appalachian women authors is the family and the woman's place in it. Rural matriarchs tower in novels such as Dykeman's *The Tall Woman* (1962). Other examinations of the family are more ambiguous. Jo Carson's haunting play *Daytrips* (1988) deals with a middle-aged woman who strives to hold on to her own identity as she accompanies her mother and grandmother on their mad journeys through Alzheimer's disease and senility. Gail Godwin, who sets many of her novels in a fictionalized version of Asheville, North Carolina, where she was reared, also looks at the complications of a woman's finding her own identity while immersed in family and culture. Insisting that readers acknowledge the dark sides of family life, Dorothy Allison's *Bastard Out of Carolina* (1992) is a searing account of child abuse set in Greenville, South Carolina. Allison suggests that one way out of dysfunctional family relationships is to form new types of families, including lesbian-centered ones.

As the cases of Godwin and Allison suggest, some Appalachian women authors have moved beyond agrarianism to explore life in small towns. Three regional expatriates whose fiction looks at the confinements of small-town life are Jayne Anne Phillips and Meredith Sue Willis, both natives of West Virginia, and Lisa Alther, who hails from northeast Tennessee. Willis's Blair Ellen Morgan, who appears in *Higher Ground* (1981), *Only Great Changes* (1985), and *Trespassers* (1997), rebels against her hometown values and ultimately moves out of the region. Alther's satirical novel *Kinflicks* (1975) follows its protagonist's quest for identity as she tries on various roles—from hometown cheerleader to student at a prim northeastern college to lesbian back-to-the-lander in Vermont—and finally returns to her Appalachian hometown as a mother confronting the death of her own mother.

Another new arena into which Appalachian women's literature entered in the late twentieth century was African American and Cherokee women's worlds. The prolific African American poet, feminist, and activist Nikki Giovanni has been a spokesperson for women of color both inside and outside of Appalachia. Nikky Finney, one of the founders of the Affrilachian group of poets, has published not only poetry but also a collection of short stories. Marilou Awiakta, born of Cherokee and European heritage and reared in the scientific community of Oak Ridge, Tennessee, has attempted to synthesize Cherokee spirituality and atomic theory in such books as *Selu: Seeking the Corn-Mother's Wisdom* (1993).

Contemporary Appalachian women authors often seek to reconcile memories of the region's agrarian past with the realities of late-twentieth-century life, which are transforming Appalachia in profound, sometimes exhilarating, sometimes painful ways. Barbara Kingsolver's ecofeminist novel *Prodigal Summer* (2000) contains four main characters—three female and one male—who epitomize the contemporary changing face of Appalachia: a Jewish-Muslim entomologist, a septuagenarian organic orchardist, a wildlife biologist who prefers coyotes to most people she knows, and a retired high school teacher trying to make sense of the changes that have come to his family and community. By the end of the novel, these characters have forged new family relationships, not always traditional but filled with love and mutual respect. The land and how to use it, the people and where they come from, and the family and how it will be composed are all issues that have concerned Appalachian women writers as they have wrestled with the questions of who will be allowed to author the Appalachian experience and what that experience will be.

See also: AGRARIANISM; COAL-MINING LITERATURE; LOCAL COLOR.

—Theresa Lloyd, *East Tennessee State University*

Sandra L. Ballard and Patricia L. Hudson, eds., *Listen Here: Women Writing in Appalachia* (2003); Joyce Dyer, ed., *Bloodroot: Reflections on Place by Appalachian Women Writers* (1998); Elizabeth S. D. Engelhardt, *The Tangled Roots of Feminism, Environmentalism, and Appalachian Literature* (2003).

Wright, Charles

(1935–) Poet.

Charles Wright is one of the most celebrated poets with roots in the Appalachian region. As his father worked as an engineer for the Tennessee Valley Authority, Wright was born in Pickwick Dam, Tennessee, and grew up in Hiwasee Dam, North Carolina, and Oak Ridge and Kingsport, Tennessee. Wright earned his B.A. at Davidson College, majoring in history, then became interested in poetry while serving as an U.S. Army intelligence officer in Italy. After being discharged from the military in 1961, he enrolled in the University of Iowa's Writers' Workshop, where he earned a master of fine arts degree.

Wright's first book, *The Grave of the Right Hand*, appeared in 1970. His subsequent poetic career can be divided into three major stages. The first culminated with the publication of *Country Music* in 1982, winning the National Book Award for Poetry. *Country Music* reprinted five prose poems from Wright's first book and selections from his three succeeding volumes: *Hard Freight* (1973), *Bloodlines* (1975), and *China Trace* (1977). Highly imagistic, tautly structured, and lyrical rather than narrative, these poems explore the experiences that shaped the poet's identity, including the landscapes of his childhood. These poems also present, especially in *China Trace*, the spiritual quest that marks Wright's often visionary poetry.

That quest plays a more prominent role in *The World of the Ten Thousand Things* (1990), which reprinted *The Southern Cross* (1981), *The Other Side of the River* (1984), and two volumes of journal poems, *Zone Journals* (1988) and *Xionia* (1990). In these poems from the 1980s Wright uses longer, more conversational lines, frequently employing what he calls a "downstep" line, a phrase or clause that begins at the point where the preceding line ends. The journal format of many of these poems also provides a greater looseness of structure, but Wright's careful choice of images and his mastery of the music of phrase and line attest to the discipline of his artistry in free verse.

During the 1990s Wright produced three additional books of poems—*Chickamauga* (1995), *Black Zodiac* (1997), which won the Pulitzer Prize, and *Appalachia* (1998)—that together comprise a third trilogy, *Negative Blue* (2000). All exhibit Wright's continuing preoccupation with what he considers his three principal themes: landscape, language, and the idea of God. These themes continue to be evident in his more recent books, *A Short History of the Shadow* (2002) and *Buffalo Yoga* (2004). Though Wright's influences are diverse—Dante, Emily Dickinson, Ezra Pound, Hart Crane, and the many painters, especially Paul Cézanne, to whom his poems pay homage—his interest in landscape and his spiritual concerns are deeply indebted to the region in which he was raised, as the title *Appalachia* indicates. His demanding, sometimes hermetic poems are richly rewarding.

In addition to the National Book Award and the Pulitzer Prize, Wright has received two Fulbright Fellowships, the PEN Translation Prize, and both the Lenore Marshall and the Ruth Lilly Poetry Prizes.

See also: POST–WORLD WAR II POETS.

—John Lang, *Emory and Henry College*

Tom Andrews, ed., *The Point Where All Things Meet: Essays on Charles Wright* (1995); Lee Upton, *The Muse of Abandonment: Origin, Identity, Mastery in Five American Poets* (1998).

Wright, Elizabeth C.

(c. 1832–?) Nature essayist and poet.

Although little is known about the life of Elizabeth C. Wright, her only published book, *Lichen Tufts, from the Alleghanies* (1860), opens with a narrative of a camping trip that Wright made with several companions along the Allegheny River in its northernmost reaches, where today it forms the northern and western borders of New York's Allegany State Park. Wright was born in Dutchess County and lived as an adult with her husband and two children in Dunkirk, New York. Sometime before 1870, she moved with her family to St. Louis. The year and place of her death have not been discovered.

Lichen Tufts is comprised of four prose essays and a collection of Wright's poetry. Collectively, the essays are among the first literary treatises on nature by American women writers. The first essay, "Into the Woods," is a jaunty satire against her friends who love poetry about nature more than nature itself. Wright argues that a deeper knowledge of nature by her contemporaries would "cure" most societal ills. She quotes Henry David Thoreau several times, praising his "deliberate philosophy," and aligns herself with the essentialist biologists who held that the human species marks the perfection of nature.

Wright's only other known publication, "Something about Fungi" (*Putnam's Monthly Magazine*, October 1869), attempts to popularize the study of mushrooms and other fungi. In it, she also reveals that she taught classes in botany and mycology.

See also: ENVIRONMENTAL WRITING; LOCAL COLOR; WOMEN AUTHORS.

—Daniel Patterson, *Central Michigan University*

Writing Workshops, Conferences, and Festivals

Appalachian writers often feel isolated, both geographically and figuratively. Therefore, writing workshops, conferences, and literary festivals provide important opportunities for them to gain needed information, to develop a sense of community, and to form supportive relationships with other writers who either live in the Appalachian region or write about it.

One of the best-known of these events in the region is the Appalachian Writers Workshop held each summer at Hindman Settlement School in Knott County, Kentucky.

Founded by native Appalachian poet and educator Albert Stewart, the gathering each year has a faculty whose names read like a "Who's Who" of Appalachian literature. Stewart, also founding editor of *Appalachian Heritage* magazine, began bringing in well-known Kentucky writers to hold summer writing workshops while teaching at Morehead State College (now University). He continued these workshops after he joined the faculty of Alice Lloyd College at Pippa Passes, Kentucky, and in 1978 he offered the first Appalachian Writers Workshop at Hindman.

Many conferences and workshops are functions of organized groups of writers. One such organization is the Southern Appalachian Writers Cooperative, formed in 1974 by a group of young writers who met while students or faculty at Antioch Appalachia, a branch of Antioch College (Yellow Springs, Ohio) in Beckley, West Virginia. In the early days, members of the group held an annual meeting at the Highlander Research and Education Center in New Market, Tennessee. Today, in addition to an annual conference, they maintain a Web site featuring Appalachian poetry, fiction, and essays and sponsor an on-line workshop for poets who wish to have their work critiqued.

The Appalachian Writers Association is open to writers who live outside the region as well as residents. Established in the summer of 1983, the association grew out of a series of programs at East Tennessee State University in Johnson City, Tennessee, in 1982–83. Annual conferences have been held at East Tennessee, Morehead State University (Morehead, Kentucky), Virginia Polytechnic Institute and State University (Blacksburg, Virginia), Western Carolina University (Cullowhee, North Carolina), Berea College (Berea, Kentucky), Cumberland College (Williamsburg, Kentucky), and Radford University (Radford, Virginia). Conferences include workshops, panels, readings, book sales and signings, a keynote address by a well-known Appalachian writer, and the presentation of awards to winners of an association-sponsored writing competition. Awards are given for short story, poetry, essay, playwriting, and for Appalachian Book of the Year. An Outstanding Contributions to Appalachian Literature award recognizes someone whose body of work has contributed significantly to the literature of the region. The association's records are housed in the Archives of Appalachia at East Tennessee State University.

Other writers' organizations similarly function through regular meetings. Blue Ridge Writers, a Virginia organization established in 1983, holds an annual conference. The North Carolina Writers' Network, founded in 1985, holds spring and fall conferences each year. The Tennessee Mountain Writers, an affiliate of the Tennessee Writers Alliance, has held an annual conference with workshops for both experienced and aspiring writers since 1989. West Virginia Writers, Inc., founded in 1977 and open to all writers living in West Virginia, sponsors workshops, writing competitions, and an annual state conference.

A number of groups sponsor writing contests and competitions in conjunction with their conferences and workshops, and some hold or sponsor retreats. The Selu Writers Retreat, cosponsored by the Appalachian Writers Association and the school's Department of English, is held each summer at Radford University. The Green River Writers (Louisville, Kentucky) hold an annual summer retreat with workshops and individual working time for writers. The Hambidge Center for Creative Arts and Sciences (Rabun Gap, Georgia) provides working residencies for creative artists, including writers, and was instrumental in the development of the Foxfire program.

Other writing events affiliated with institutions in the Appalachian region include the Chautauqua Writers' Workshop, held each summer since 1946 at the Chautauqua Institution (Chautauqua, New York). The annual Highland Summer Conference, established in 1978 and held at Radford University, promotes creative writing with an emphasis on regional culture. The University of Kentucky Council on Aging has sponsored an annual Writing Workshop for People Over 57 in Lexington since 1967. The Kentucky Women Writers Conference, also a University of Kentucky program, was first held in 1979.

Organizations sponsoring workshops, readings, and writing events include Appalfolks of America Association (Clifton Forge, Virginia), the Appalachian Center for Poets and Writers (Abingdon, Virginia), and the Writers' Workshop of Asheville, North Carolina. Poetry Alive!, an organization headquartered in Asheville, sends teams all over the United States to perform poetry for student audiences and to give in-service workshops on how to teach poetry and performance in the classroom. They also offer summer residencies for educators and sponsored an Asheville Poetry Festival from 1994 through 1997.

Writing-related festivals in the Appalachian region include the Emory and Henry Literary Festival, held annually since 1982 at Emory and Henry College (Emory, Virginia). Each year, this festival honors an outstanding Appalachian writer with two days of events including the presentation of papers on the writer's work, an interview conducted by a colleague in his or her field, and a formal reading by the author. Proceedings of the festival are published as an issue of the *Iron Mountain Review*.

Creative Writing Days, a literary event held each August during the Virginia Highlands Festival in Abingdon, begins with a day devoted to three or four well-known writers who give presentations and participate in readings, panel discussions, and a question and answer session. During the remainder of the week, individual authors lead workshops in their specific genres. A literary competition is also part of the event, and Creative Writing Day includes an awards ceremony for winners.

Other conferences, festivals, and workshops held in the region include the annual Sherwood Anderson Short Story Contest and Festival (Marion, Virginia); the Sewanee Writers Conference at the University of the South (Sewanee, Tennessee); the biennial Chattanooga (Tennessee) Conference on Southern Literature; a biennial Southern Women Writers Conference at Berry College (Rome, Georgia); and the Lost State Writers Conference (Greeneville, Tennessee). Major book festivals that feature Appalachian writers but are held on the outskirts of Appalachia include the Southern Festival of Books each fall in Nashville, Tennessee, and the Virginia Festival of the Book in Charlottesville each spring.

See also: CHAUTAUQUA INSTITUTION (TOURISM); HINDMAN SETTLEMENT SCHOOL (CRAFTS); SECTION OVERVIEW (EDUCATION).

—Linda Behrend, *University of Tennessee*

Bob Henry Baber, "The Southern Appalachian Writers' Cooperative," in *Interviewing Appalachia: The Appalachian Journal Interviews, 1978–1992,* ed. J. W. Williamson and Edwin T. Arnold (1994); George Ella Lyon, Jim Wayne Miller, and Gurney Norman, eds., *A Gathering at the Forks: Fifteen Years of the Hindman Settlement School Appalachian Writers Workshop* (1993); Eileen Malone, *The Complete Guide to Writers Groups, Conferences, and Workshops* (1996).

Music

Section Editor: Ted Olson

At the outset of the twenty-first century, few people—whether natives of Appalachia or "outsiders"—would question the assertion that music has been and remains the most widely known manifestation of Appalachian culture, both within and outside the region. Throughout most of the twentieth century, Appalachian music, having evolved in the eighteenth and nineteenth centuries as a regional musical blend combining various ethnic and popular musics, was Appalachia's most effective cultural ambassador and the region's chief cultural export, transported via the media—especially radio and recordings—and via concerts by touring Appalachian musicians. Despite the growing popularity of the region's music, many fans are unaware of its true diversity. Natives and non-natives alike tend to associate only two genres of popular music with Appalachia—bluegrass and country—while other more traditional and elite regional musics reach significantly smaller audiences. Several types of Appalachian traditional music, including ballad singing and string-band music, are still performed, informally within family and community circles and in such formal settings as concerts. Prominent contemporary performers include natives who learned Appalachian music from kin as well as non-natives whose initial exposure to Appalachian music generally came through radio and recordings. The enthusiasm of "revivalist" performers for particular genres of Appalachian music ensures that those genres will continue to be heard, studied, and enjoyed by people who otherwise might have little contact with, or knowledge of, the region that inspired them.

The oldest musical traditions in Appalachia are also the least known—in part because few recordings have been made of the music of the Cherokee and other indigenous groups and in part because the music of aboriginal peoples was integrally associated with secret rituals. The first European American musical traditions in Appalachia involved balladry and fiddling. Brought to the region by settlers from the British Isles, ballads were initially sung in Appalachia as they had been in the Old World: a cappella, in minor keys, with an unemotional presentation. Over time, Appalachian balladeers truncated the generally tragic narratives of the British ballads and incorporated instrumental accompaniment. As English folklorist Cecil Sharp and his assistant, Maud Karpeles, discovered during World War I–era collecting forays into Appalachia, the region still harbored a large repertoire of "Child ballads" of British origin. So called because they were categorized by nineteenth-century Harvard scholar Francis James

Facing page: Master craftsman Jethro Amburgey tunes his handmade fretted dulcimer, Hindman, Kentucky, c. 1955. Emerging in a few sections of Appalachia during the eighteenth century as an amalgam of European folk instruments, the fretted dulcimer was widely played during the folk music revivals of the latter half of the twentieth century.

Czechoslovak American Band, Pittsburgh, c. 1930. Eastern European musicians in northern Appalachia preserved the musical traditions of their native cultures while broadening the range and styles of Appalachian music.

Child, these traditional ballads were sung across Appalachia in multiple variants. Appalachian singers expanded the region's song repertoire by introducing new ballads composed entirely in the New World. These "native American" ballads, as folklorists have termed them, directly reflected social realities in Appalachia, and some of these ballads documented historic events. "Omie Wise," for instance, chronicles an actual early-nineteenth-century North Carolina murder. Many "traditional" ballads—both British and native American—were originally broadsides. Composed by individual songwriters commenting upon specific events, broadsides were written onto paper and sold locally. Some of them eventually entered oral tradition and public domain. By the late nineteenth century, Appalachian people also sang various composed ballads taken from commercial songbooks. Most of these later ballads—published to be performed in parlors for social occasions—were thematically sentimental rather than tragic. Ballads markedly declined within the region after World War I as a consequence of industrialization and out-migration as well as the emergence of radio, recordings, and other new forms of entertainment. Balladry, though, remained an influence on early commercial country music performers, and the popular "disaster song" repertoire (for example, "The Wreck of the Old 97") evolved from the ballad tradition. A separate type of traditional song, the lyric folk song, survived in Appalachia into the twentieth century. Unlike ballads, lyric folk songs accentuate emotion rather than narrative.

Other singing traditions historically found in the region have been associated with the church. Shape-note singing, which flourished across the southeastern U.S. during the nineteenth century, still lingers in Appalachia (especially in northern Alabama and Mississippi). Another older vocal tradition occasionally practiced in contemporary Appalachia is "lined-out" hymnody, wherein a minister presiding over a service speaks a line of a religious hymn, with that same line then sung in chorus by the congregation. These two traditions of sacred music, though different in terms of their musical structures, bear similar social functions in that both singing traditions are vehicles for the aesthetic expression of religious feelings. In the twentieth century, new forms of religious music prevailed in Appalachia. Mass-marketed songbooks containing notated tunes and texts of original sacred-themed songs were promoted throughout the region by quartet singing groups sponsored by commercial publishing companies. The earliest of these was the influential Ruebush-Kieffer Company, established in the Shenandoah Valley not long after the Civil War. Later, most such firms were located outside Appalachia.

Beginning in the 1920s, this music genre (known as southern gospel) reached even wider audiences in Appalachia through the new technologies of radio and commercial recordings. Popular white gospel quartets from the region have included the Speer Family (from Double Springs, Alabama), the Blackwood Brothers (from Choctaw County, Mississippi), and the Statler Brothers (from the Shenandoah Valley, Virginia). African Americans in Appalachia have created their own legacy of religious music, from spirituals and shape-note singing traditions to commercial quartet singing groups—including such nationally famous acts as the Dixie Hummingbirds (from Greenville, South Carolina)—and larger ensembles, such as the Five Blind Boys of Alabama (from Jefferson County) and the Birmingham Mass Choir.

As with many British ballads, some instrumental tunes from the British Isles continued to be played in Appalachia. Regional musicians performed such instrumental tunes when accompanying reels, waltzes, and other old-world dances; many of these tunes gradually acquired new titles and new tune variations. Throughout the nineteenth century, a dance would often be accompanied by a solo musician playing fiddle. Toward the end of that century, the combination of fiddle and banjo became common. By the twentieth century, instrumentalists performed together in larger ensembles, as recently introduced instruments, especially the guitar and the mandolin, were combined with those instruments already familiar in Appalachia. Called "string bands" for their emphasis on string instruments, such ensembles performed for dances and—after radio and commercial records allowed musical groups to build fan bases—concerts. String bands often boasted instrumentalists who displayed considerable virtuosity.

In the first decades of the twentieth century, developments in mass-media technologies across the United States (initially, widely distributed songbooks, and, later, radio and commercial recordings) accelerated the spread of Appalachian music to new audiences. Inevitably, the process of broadcasting a largely regional music to a mass, generalized audience changed the music's character. With the expanding market for print collections of traditional Appalachian ballads, songs, and instrumentals, occasioned by mainstream America's newfound interest in American folk music, arrangers often refashioned traditional texts and tunes. By the mid-twentieth century, native-born classical composers such as Lamar Stringfield were incorporating stylistic influences from the region's folk music into their compositions. Even German composer Kurt Weill at this time composed a piece featuring vocal arrangements of Appalachian folk songs.

Unavoidably, the versions of Appalachian material presented to broad-based, non-native audiences were different from the original sources. The Kingston Trio's hit song "Tom Dooley," for example, significantly modified the traditional North Carolina ballad "Tom Dula." Such mainstream versions of Appalachian folk music commonly became more popular than traditional versions and styles. Producers of commercial recordings as early as the 1920s encouraged traditional Appalachian musicians to alter their sound, whether subtly or overtly. Victor Talking Machine Company producer Ralph Peer, for instance, requested that most of the musicians he recorded at the 1927 and 1928 Bristol sessions avoid instrumental tunes and instead perform popular and folk songs. But even though he favored vocals, Peer discouraged the recording of traditional ballads, which he deemed as being too long for commercial 78 rpm recordings and too complex and thematically troubling for mainstream audiences.

The Bristol sessions and most other late-1920s and early-1930s field recording sessions in Appalachian and southern cities were motivated by commercial rather than documentary interest, and collectively they spawned the commercial country music industry. Although from the mid-1930s onward most country music recording sessions occurred outside Appalachia, a significant number of major country music singers (Roy Acuff), singer-songwriters (Don Gibson, Loretta Lynn, and Dolly Parton), and instrumentalists (Chet Atkins and Charlie McCoy) have been Appalachian natives whose regional styles were essential to the evolution of the genre. While bluegrass music originated outside the geographical boundaries of Appalachia (bluegrass's founding father, Bill Monroe, was from western Kentucky), the genre has received vital contributions since its inception from Appalachian musicians, including Earl Scruggs and Lester Flatt, who were early members of Monroe's band. Bluegrass was soon embraced by Appalachian audiences because it reflected the influence of the Appalachian string-band tradition and the inspiration of the harmony singing of Appalachian brother duos and gospel quartets. The high-pitched vocals employed in bluegrass singing—often described as "high lonesome"—invoke the angular vocal style within Appalachian balladry and shape-note singing. Many premier first- and second-generation bluegrass musicians, such as Flatt and Scruggs, the Stanley Brothers, Reno and Smiley, Jim and Jesse, the Osborne Brothers, Jimmy Martin, and Doc Watson, were native Appalachians—as are several of the most respected newer bluegrass acts, including Ricky Skaggs and members of such groups as the Lonesome River Band, Blue Highway, and Union Station.

Appalachian music was unmistakably influenced by African American culture, as white and black musicians within Appalachian communities long shared their knowledge of songs, tunes, and musical instruments. Several well-known songs from the region, such as the blues ballad "John Henry," and one instrument widely associated with the region (the banjo) were of African American origin. The blues had a considerable impact on both country and bluegrass music, a fact evident, for instance, in Jimmie Rodgers's "blue yodel" singing style and Merle Travis's and Bill Monroe's instrumental styles.

During the 1920s and 1930s, while the Carter Family and other white Appalachian musicians made influential "hillbilly" records, several black blues and jazz musicians from the region—especially Bessie Smith and W. C. Handy—were key figures in "race" music, attracting the attention of African American audiences nationally through concerts and recordings. Blues traditions thrived in Appalachia, particularly the foothills of Virginia and the Carolinas (which produced such musicians as the Reverend Gary Davis, Etta Baker, and John Jackson), urban and industrial centers within the region (Bessie Smith, Cow Cow Davenport, and Brownie McGhee), and the north Mississippi hills (Howlin' Wolf, Junior Kimbrough, and R. L. Burnside). Within Appalachia, jazz was heard primarily in cities with large African American populations. Pittsburgh produced such jazz stalwarts as Earl "Fatha" Hines, Erroll Garner, Ray Brown, Billy Eckstine, George Benson, and Stanley Turrentine, while Birmingham, Alabama, was home to Sun Ra and Chattanooga, Tennessee, to Bessie Smith and Jimmy Blanton.

By the late 1940s, African American popular music was generally referred to as rhythm and blues. Several important rhythm and blues performers originally from Appalachia found commercial success only after relocating to urban centers outside the region; these include Stick McGhee, Nina Simone, Bill Withers, and Lionel Richie. By the mid-1960s, soul music—a subgenre of rhythm and blues—was gaining attention nationally. Accentuating an emotionalism borrowed from gospel, soul boasted a number of singers from Appalachia, including Arthur Alexander, Percy Sledge, and Wilson Pickett. One of the most important recording centers for 1960s soul was in the Muscle Shoals area of northern Alabama. White musicians from the region provided instrumental accompaniment for soul artists who recorded in the Muscle Shoals studios. Since soul and bluegrass were the only commercial musics that offered steady economic sustenance to musicians in Appalachia, many soul and bluegrass performers remained in the region throughout their careers.

African American musicians from Appalachia have long been influenced by "white" music genres. Many regional black musicians often entertained white audiences and thus borrowed from the white repertoire and musical style. Conversely, many white musicians from Appalachia have acknowledged their indebtedness to black musicians they knew personally. Leslie Riddle and Arnold Shultz, for instance, have been acknowledged as influences by the Carter Family and Bill Monroe, respectively. However, the hybrid styles of such African American musicians failed to fit the early recording industry's idea of either "race" music or "hillbilly" music (the major identified markets in the South). The majority of African American string bands (for example, the Hillbillies, from Winston-Salem, North Carolina, which featured Willie Walker and Gary Davis) were never recorded.

Florence, Alabama, native Sam Phillips, founder of Sun Records in Memphis, publicly stated that his label's recording star Elvis Presley, a native of Tupelo, Mississippi, became a revolutionary cultural force in the mid-1950s precisely because his musical persona incorporated both white and black stylistic influences. Presley's trendsetting Sun singles were the first commercially successful recordings of rockabilly (a coinage derived from the conjoining of the term *rock*, which suggested that music's rhythmic drive, and *billy*, which referred to the term *hillbilly*). A major subgenre of rock 'n' roll, rockabilly was a high-energy hybrid music initially performed primarily by southern and Appalachian singers and instrumentalists. The country music establishment viewed rockabilly as a threat because of its appeal to younger Americans, including many Appalachians, who also embraced subsequent types of rock 'n' roll.

A racially colorblind music equally indebted to rhythm and blues and to country, rock 'n' roll (by then generally referred to as rock) was reflecting trend-conscious urban and suburban values by the 1960s. Accordingly, as a largely rural region, Appalachia was the site of few important recording or performance centers for rock music. Even so, significant musicians in various rock subgenres have hailed from the region, including such individual performers as Charlie Feathers (rockabilly), Dave Loggins (pop), Darrell Scott (Americana), and Trent Reznor (industrial rock), and such groups as the Chambers Brothers (psychedelic soul), the Marshall Tucker Band (southern rock), Goose Creek Symphony (country rock), Superdrag (alternative rock), and Drive-By Truckers (alternative country). Many of these musicians have explored regional themes and have exhibited overt Appalachian musical influences.

Due to its broad scope of influence both within and outside the region, Appalachian music has been a powerful perpetrator of regional stereotypes. Although originating outside Appalachia, nineteenth-century minstrel show performances featuring white musicians derisively exaggerating black culture adversely affected the social standing of African Americans in the region after emancipation. In the twentieth century, the barn dance—which achieved national popularity via radio and which sustained that popularity into the 1990s through such television programs as *Hee Haw*—provided steady work and significant exposure for many Appalachian musicians. But in order to represent rural culture, which held novelty appeal for mainstream audiences, producers directed Appalachian musicians to project a hillbilly identity. The stereotype inevitably left far-flung audiences with negative and inaccurate impressions of Appalachian people. These barn dances particularly misrepresented two aspects of the region's culture: Appalachian speech and Appalachian clothes. Musicians were encouraged to exaggerate their regional speech and to wear standardized hillbilly dress, including bib overalls and straw hats.

Likewise distorting general understanding of Appalachian regional culture during the twentieth century were attitudes toward Appalachian people of some of the musicians associated with the century's several folk revivals, whose representations of Appalachian culture, whether earnest or intentionally exploitive, were rendered untrustworthy by both positive and negative stereotyping. Positive stereotypes included the revivalists' romanticized portrayals of Appalachian musicians as mountain sages or noble savages; negative stereotyping involved the unfavorable characterization of Appalachian people as "rubes," "hicks," or "degenerates." Other revivalist musicians exhibited considerable dedication to understanding Appalachian culture and thus were more sensitive to regional issues. The first folk revival of Appalachian music began shortly before World War I, as the forces of modernization were threatening the continuity of traditional life in many Appalachian communities. At this time, various aficionados of Appalachian folk music—natives such as promoter and performer Bascom Lamar Lunsford as well as non-natives such as British folklorist Cecil Sharp—extensively collected traditional ballads and songs in the region. Through the work of such collectors, the extensive repertoires of many traditional Appalachian singers were permanently recorded, first on paper, then by the late 1920s via sound recording machines. A second surge in revivalist zeal occurred between 1930 and 1945, as several people—mostly non-natives, including performer and anthologist John Jacob Niles, ethnomusicologist Alan Lomax, and the husband-and-wife team of Frank and Anne Warner—collected and reinterpreted traditional Appalachian music.

A subsequent revival occurred after World War II through the 1970s, as young natives and non-natives alike embraced Appalachian traditions in reaction to the materialism and cultural modernism of mainstream America during postwar prosperity. Numerous revivalist musicians toured the U.S. and Europe performing faithful renditions of Appalachian folk music learned from old 78 rpm recordings. One prominent revivalist group, the New Lost City Ramblers, which featured non-native musicians Mike Seeger, John Cohen, and Tracy Schwartz, not only toured and recorded prolifically but also "discovered" several talented yet unheralded traditional Appalachian musicians (Roscoe Holcomb, Dock Boggs, and Kilby Snow), whose lives and music they documented through various recordings and films. Several other non-native revivalist musicians, such as Wayne Erbsen and David Holt, utilized various media in their effort to promote the music they loved. Others active in Appalachia, including Si Kahn and John McCutcheon, specialized in writing and performing folklike songs bearing strong social messages. Appalachian themes and imagery influenced many non-native musicians working within the popular urban country rock style during the late 1960s and early 1970s, while many musicians from the region infused their renditions of tradition-based music with rock instrumentation and attitudes.

Renewed interest in Appalachian music was evident by the mid-1990s, as a new generation was introduced to the region's musical heritage through reissued "classic" recordings of traditional Appalachian music on compact disc. While encouraging some younger musicians from Appalachia to learn and reinterpret their native region's musical legacy, renewed national attention toward Appalachian music ultimately had its biggest impact on non-Appalachian musicians and audiences. Although their personal affiliations with the region were either marginal or nonexistent, numerous leading contemporary musicians in the alternative country, Americana, and roots rock music movements were, by the mid-1990s, writing original songs that incorporated traditional Appalachian instruments and/or explored Appalachian themes. Some of these musicians went to considerable lengths to project an archetypically "Appalachian" public image. Non-native Gillian Welch, for instance, not only wrote and performed songs evoking the region stylistically and thematically but also adopted regional dress and even affected a regional accent. Ricky Skaggs, Dolly Parton, and Patty Loveless—prominent musicians from Appalachia who had achieved considerable success outside the region in commercial country music—returned to the more acoustic and traditional sounds they had known in their youth. By the early years of the twenty-first century, two soundtrack recordings featuring carefully produced, sympathetic interpretations of Appalachian music—from the movies *O Brother, Where Art Thou?* (2000) and *Songcatcher* (2000)—attracted a broad-based national audience; the former soundtrack sold several million copies. Media attention toward Appalachian music in recent years has had the effect of encouraging many young people within Appalachia to reinvestigate their region's musical traditions, even as they embrace mainstream popular musics.

—Ted Olson, *East Tennessee State University*

Thomas G. Burton, *Some Ballad Folks* (1978); Olive Dame Campbell and Cecil Sharp, *English Folk Songs from the Southern Appalachians* (1917; revised 1932); Cecelia Conway, *African Banjo Echoes in Appalachia: A Study of Folk Traditions* (1995); James R. Goff Jr., *Close Harmony: A History of Southern Gospel* (2002); Peter Guralnick, *Sweet Soul Music: Rhythm and Blues and the Southern Dream of Freedom* (1986); John Rice Irwin, *Musical Instruments of the Southern Appalachian Mountains* (1983); John Lilly, ed., *Mountains of Music: West Virginia Traditional Music from Goldenseal* (1999); Bill C. Malone, *Country Music, U.S.A.* (2002); Marty McGee, *Traditional Musicians of the Central Blue Ridge: Old Time, Early Country, Folk, and Bluegrass Label Recording Artists, with Discographies* (2000); Beverly Bush Patterson, *The Sound of the Dove: Singing in Appalachian Primitive Baptist Churches* (2001); Neil V. Rosenberg, *Bluegrass: A History* (1993); Jeff Todd Titon, *Old-Time Kentucky Fiddle Tunes* (2001); Anne Warner, ed., *Traditional American Folk Songs from the Anne and Frank Warner Collection* (1984); Peter Zimmerman, *Tennessee Music: Its People and Places* (1998).

Acuff, Roy

(1903–1992) Country singer, fiddler, bandleader, and music publisher.

Born September 15, 1903, in Union County, Tennessee, near the Great Smoky Mountains, Roy Acuff grew up listening to the traditional music of southern Appalachia. His father was an accomplished fiddler whose house was a popular meeting place where music was performed by family and neighbors.

Acuff's early aspiration to be a baseball player was thwarted by a sunstroke-related collapse. After a stint developing his performance skills and showmanship as a singer and fiddler with a medicine show, Acuff recruited a group of local musicians and landed a program on Knoxville's WROL radio station. In 1936 a talent scout for the American Record Corporation heard Acuff singing "The Great Speckled Bird" and signed him to a recording contract. In 1938 he joined the *Grand Ole Opry*. Changing his band's name from the Crazy Tennesseans to the Smoky Mountain Boys, Acuff became the *Opry*'s greatest star. In 1942 he teamed with songwriter Fred Rose to launch Acuff-Rose Publications, the first modern publishing company in Nashville to specialize in country music. Acuff also appeared in several B movies and even contemplated a political career. In 1948 both major political parties courted him as a possible Tennessee gubernatorial candidate, and he accepted the Republican nomination. Although he lost the general election, he received the highest vote that any Republican had received up to that time in Tennessee.

In 1962 Acuff became the first living performer elected to the Country Music Hall of Fame. Although he performed mostly ballads and songs from the regional repertoire and his singing style suggested the mountain church, his popularity extended beyond the Southeast. He received exposure to a new generation on the college circuit during the urban folk music revival of the 1960s and through his appearance on the Nitty Gritty Dirt Band's landmark collaborative album *Will the Circle Be Unbroken* in 1972. Despite his untrained tenor voice and limitations as a fiddler, Acuff attained stardom because of his showmanship and the great zeal and sincere emotion with which he performed. He died November 23, 1992.

See also: COUNTRY MUSIC; FOLK MUSIC REVIVALS; *GRAND OLE OPRY* (MEDIA).

—Charles F. Faber, *Lexington, Kentucky*

Elizabeth Schlappi, *Roy Acuff: The Smoky Mountain Boy* (1993).

African American Influences

African American musical tradition, characterized by riffs, polyrhythms, and call-and-response structure, has influenced all American music, including that of Appalachia. In contrast to the conservative continuity of European musical traditions (particularly old-world balladry) in the region, the African American aesthetic within Appalachia has accentuated improvisation, encouraging musical and verbal dexterity and variation.

Historically, African culture considered both sacred and secular music as fundamental to spiritual expression and everyday life. Two major African musical traditions arrived early in America: group singing and drumming came from tropical rainforests of West Africa, and the instrumental tradition of the griots (storytellers of Africa who reminded fellow villagers of their history and traditions) emerged from the savannah grasslands. Africans in America had to negotiate among themselves many African dialects and languages as well as learn English. Living in shanties, these various peoples began to exchange repertoires. Accustomed to the mouth bow and bowed harp in Africa, these newcomers adopted the fiddle and entertained both themselves and whites, playing their own melodies as well as European tunes. The bluesy fiddle style that black fiddlers created still persists in Appalachia.

When collectors, almost all of whom were white, first traveled through the southeastern United States (including parts of Appalachia) to document African American music, they concentrated on vocal music, which was less challenging to transcribe than instrumental music. Collectors were most interested in black spirituals but also documented some African American field hollers and work songs, the latter featuring call-and-response improvisation.

No music has been more influential in the region than the singing, dancing, and music surrounding the banjo, still often considered an Appalachian icon. By 1740, enslaved musicians from West Africa had brought to the New World some percussion instruments as well as a plucked lute with a hide-covered gourd sound chamber and several strings, including the short, thumb drone. Blacks were playing this *banjar* for white frontiersmen in Appalachia by 1800. Interaction between African American *banjar* players and white musicians resulted in the invention of the wooden-rim, five-string banjo, the genre of banjo songs, and blackface minstrelsy. Several twentieth-century banjo styles reflected African traditions, especially various clawhammer techniques.

African American music was transformed when, in the early years of the twentieth century, guitars became readily available and affordable via mail-order catalogs. Transferring stylistic elements from the banjo to this newly adopted instrument, black musicians performed the recently emerged genre known as the blues, initially as solo vocalists with their own guitar accompaniment and, in later years, in combination with other singers and instrumentalists.

White musicians in Appalachia had been influenced by black music long before the introduction of recorded sound technology; several major country music stars from

Appalachia, including Jimmie Rodgers, the Carter Family, and Hank Williams Sr., learned songs and stylistic technique from African American muscians. Other music genres associated with Appalachia—such as string-band music, bluegrass, and rock 'n' roll—also reflect the influence of black music.

See also: BANJO; BLUES; GOSPEL MUSIC, AFRICAN AMERICAN; JAZZ; RHYTHM AND BLUES.

—Cecelia Conway, *Appalachian State University*

Cecelia Conway, *African Banjo Echoes in Appalachia: A Study of Folk Traditions* (1995); Howard L. and Judith Rose Sacks, *Way Up North in Dixie: A Black Family's Claim to the Confederate Anthem* (1993); Newman Ivey White et al., eds., *The Frank C. Brown Collecion of North Carolina Folklore* (1952–1964).

Alabama

Country music group.

Having sold more than 60 million albums and accumulated approximately two hundred awards by the year 2000, the country group Alabama was a significant force in country music in the 1980s and 1990s, amassing forty-two number one hit singles and placing seven other songs in the top ten. First cousins Randy Yeuell Owen (lead vocals/songwriter/rhythm guitar; b. December 13, 1949) and Teddy Wayne Gentry (bass; b. January 22, 1952), distant cousin Jeffrey Alan Cook (multi-instrumentalist; b. August 27, 1949), and friend Mark Joel Herndon (drums; b. May 11, 1955) charted new terrain as the first self-accompanying band in Nashville's country music industry, which had previously been dominated by individual acts and vocal groups. Alabama's group persona paved the way for Nashville's acceptance of such later acts as Restless Heart, Exile, Sawyer Brown, and Shenandoah. Alabama became the first group to be named Artist of the Decade by the Academy of Country Music (1989) and was elected Group of the Century by the Recording Industry Artists Association in 2000.

Founded in 1969 as Wildcountry in Fort Payne, Alabama, the band moved to Myrtle Beach, South Carolina, in 1973 and began working the beach club scene performing cover tunes in southern rock and country pop styles while honing original songs. The long hours, low pay, and touring caused original drummer John Vartanian to leave the group in 1976. The band's rise to fame began after the remaining trio (Fort Payne natives Cook, Owen, and Gentry) signed with GRT Records in 1977, changed their name to Alabama, hired Mark Herndon, a drummer from Springfield, Massachusetts, and debuted on the country charts with "I Want to Be with You." After moving to the newly formed MDJ label, Alabama's first album, *I Wanna Come Over*, was released in 1979. The group's first significant hit, "My Home's in Alabama," entered the top twenty and led to an RCA contract in 1980. A string of hits soon followed, including "Tennessee River," their first number one hit, and "Mountain Music" and "The Closer You Get," which both won the Grammy for Best Country Vocal Performance by a Duo or Group, in 1982 and 1983, respectively.

Their collaborations feature recordings with fellow Alabaman Lionel Richie ("Deep River Woman") in 1986 and with 'N Sync ("God Must Have Spent a Little More Time on You") in 1999. The group received a star on the Hollywood Walk of Fame in 1998.

Alabama's audience includes people of all ages. Realizing the influence of their songs, Alabama consciously strove to project a positive image. During much of the 1980s and 1990s they hosted June Jam, raising more than three million dollars for regional charities in the Fort Payne area. Their lyrics avoid themes of licentiousness and drinking while celebrating the virtues of faithfulness, patriotism, honesty, and regional pride. The group disbanded in 2003.

See also: COUNTRY MUSIC; ROCK MUSIC.

—Dennis R. Davis, *Eastern Kentucky University*

Alternative Country/Americana Music Movements

Americana is an umbrella term used to categorize a variety of hybrid musical styles incorporating elements of genres considered native to America, including American folk, country, rock, blues, and jazz. *Alternative country*, a term often employed synonymously with *Americana*, refers more specifically to a contemporary subgenre of country music that finds influence and inspiration in earlier, traditional country music (including that from Appalachia), while rejecting the more polished crossover country music associated with Nashville since the 1960s.

Alternative country music (sometimes called alt.country) celebrates the rural-based, traditional sounds of the early years of recorded country music; the "hard-core" country music of the 1950s and early 1960s; and previous country and rock musicians who incorporated those earlier styles into such amalgams as country rock and progressive country music. The alternative country scene is also devoted to the ballad traditions of America's early settlers, as well as to blues, old-time music, bluegrass, and folk music (including labor and protest songs).

Within the context of its acknowledgment of earlier genres of rural music, the alternative country movement has embraced a number of Appalachian musicians. From its inception in 1995, *No Depression*, the magazine that most comprehensively chronicles the alternative country movement and the Americana sound, has published articles on numerous Appalachian musicians, including Dock Boggs, Sarah Ogan Gunning, Ralph Stanley and the Stanley Brothers, Merle Travis, the Louvin Brothers, Hazel Dickens, Jean

Ritchie, Roscoe Holcomb, Jimmy Martin, Doyle Lawson, Loretta Lynn, and Dolly Parton. To contemporary alternative country musicians, such Appalachian musicians, as well as particular musicians from other American regions, embody the cultural roots of country music.

While numerous musicians had offered alternatives to mainstream country and urban pop and rock styles since the late 1960s, the alternative country movement crystallized in the early 1990s around the fan base of the country-influenced rock group Uncle Tupelo. Many other musicians gained from the burgeoning interest in American roots music. Several natives of Appalachia who were formerly major commercial country music stars (including Ricky Skaggs, Dolly Parton, and Patty Loveless) by the turn of the century had embraced a more traditional sound and garnered renewed artistic and commercial success.

The alternative country movement's dramatically widened fan base was evident in the popularity of the 2000 soundtrack to the movie *O Brother, Where Art Thou?*, which over the next few years was one of the best-selling and most discussed albums in any genre. This soundtrack not only featured such Appalachian musicians as Norman Blake and Ralph Stanley, but also included a number of non-native musicians performing traditional and older commercial southern and Appalachian songs in arrangements strongly influenced stylistically by the Appalachian musical legacy. The soundtrack's success at the Grammy Awards—where it won in the Album of the Year and the Best Soundtrack Album categories for 2001—confirmed an unprecedented popular appreciation for Appalachian music.

See also: BLUEGRASS; COUNTRY MUSIC; ROCK MUSIC.

—Stephen D. Mooney, *Virginia Polytechnic Institute and State University*

Grant Alden and Peter Blackstock, eds., *No Depression: An Introduction to Alternative Country Music (Whatever That Is)* (1998); Peter Doggett, *Are You Ready for the Country: Elvis, Dylan, Parsons and the Roots of Country Rock* (2001); David Goodman, *Modern Twang: An Alternative Country Music Guide and Directory* (1999).

Ashley, Clarence "Tom"

(1895–1967) Banjo player and early country singer.

Born Clarence Earl McCurry on September 29, 1895, in Bristol, Tennessee, Clarence "Tom" Ashley grew up in Ashe County, North Carolina. At an early age, Ashley learned clawhammer banjo playing and traditional ballads from his Aunt Ary and his Aunt Daisy. Increasing his repertoire by learning songs from guests in his mother's boardinghouse, Ashley soon started singing on the street for money. He eventually married Hettie Osborne and settled outside Mountain City in Shouns, Tennessee. Earning a job in Doc Hower's medicine show, Ashley trained new recruit Roy Acuff. Ashley remained on the medicine show circuit intermittently until at least 1943. During these years, he and fiddler George Greyson played in the West Virginia coalfields and at circuses in Saltville, Virginia.

Ashley also worked with a popular string band, the Carolina Tarheels, which featured Ashley on guitar and lead vocal, Dock Walsh on banjo, and either Garley Foster or Gwen Foster on harmonica. From the 1940s to the 1960s, he sometimes performed as a comedian with Charlie Monroe and with the Stanley Brothers.

Much of Ashley's song repertoire, including "Red Rocking Chair" and "Walking Boss," reflected a strong African American influence, as did his banjo playing. His influential interpretations of "House Carpenter" and "The Coo-Coo Bird" in "sawmill" tuning were close in style to the versions played by his African American neighbor Dave Thompson.

In 1960 folklorist and musician Ralph Rinzler befriended Ashley. The album Rinzler soon recorded, *Old-Time Music at Clarence Ashley's* (which features guitarists Doc Watson and Clint Howard and fiddler Fred Price), was embraced by urban folk revivalists, and Ashley was invited to perform at the Newport Folk Festival and in Europe. Ashley continued to sing, play banjo, and win ribbons at music conventions in Appalachia, as well as to play on campuses and at other folk revival venues nationally, until his death on July 2, 1967.

See also: AFRICAN AMERICAN INFLUENCES; BANJO; CONTESTS AND CONVENTIONS.

—Cecelia Conway, *Appalachian State University*

Atkins, Chet

(1924–2001) Guitarist and record producer.

Born June 20, 1924, Chester Burton "Chet" Atkins grew up on a Luttrell, Tennessee, farm. His father was a music teacher and his older half-brother, Jim, was an accomplished pop and jazz guitar player. Atkins initially played the fiddle but soon turned to the guitar, influenced by Merle Travis, whose thumb-and-finger picking style Atkins heard on the radio. For many years Atkins traveled from one radio station to another, often encountering resistance to his eclectic repertoire, which incorporated country, folk, pop, and jazz stylings.

After signing a contract with RCA Records in 1947, he soon became one of Nashville's early "A-Team" session musicians, playing primarily the arch-top electric guitar. He subsequently recorded, as a solo artist or collaborator, more than a hundred predominantly instrumental albums in many styles, playing his thumb-and-three-finger style on both electric and acoustic guitars. He also appeared as a sideman on recordings by countless country and pop artists, including Hank Williams Sr., Elvis Presley, and the Everly

Brothers. Numerous awards attest to Atkins's stature as one of the preeminent guitar players of his era. In 1973 he became the youngest living musician to be inducted into the Country Music Hall of Fame.

Equally significant was Atkins's role as a record producer. From 1955 through the 1970s he directed most of RCA's Nashville studio work. Atkins produced artists as diverse as Eddy Arnold, Don Gibson, Dottie West, Bobby Bare, Jim Reeves, Waylon Jennings, and Perry Como. Named a vice-president of RCA in 1968, Atkins left the label in 1982 and continued to make predominantly instrumental recordings for Columbia, often in collaboration with celebrated guitarists from across musical genres and continents, including Mark Knopfler, George Benson, and Tommy Emmanuel.

Bringing sophisticated production techniques to the music industry in Nashville, Atkins was a central figure in the development during the late 1950s of the Nashville Sound, which featured string, horn, and choral backups instead of steel guitars and fiddles. His interest in technology and commercial acumen ensured the crossover success of these innovations. Atkins died of cancer June 30, 2001. He was inducted posthumously into the Rock and Roll Hall of Fame.

See also: COUNTRY MUSIC; GUITAR; JAZZ.

—Frederick E. Danker, *University of Massachusetts*

Rusty Russell, *Chet Atkins: The Life, Legend, and Legacy of a Musical Giant* (2003).

Autoharp

Many American singers in the late nineteenth and early twentieth centuries found the autoharp, a modification of the zither, to be an easy-to-use accompaniment instrument. Although utilized in various musical contexts, the instrument has most often been associated with folk music.

Philadelphia, Pennsylvania, resident Charles F. Zimmerman patented a modification of the zither, which he called the "autoharp," in 1882. Three years later, when he began manufacturing instruments bearing that appellation, he employed a design patented in 1883 in England by Germany's Karl August Gutter, possibly because it was easier to make and play than Zimmerman's own design. The autoharp's appearance has changed relatively little since 1885. The instrument consists of a wooden sound box, typically with thirty-six or thirty-seven strings and with three to twenty-one movable bars (called chord bars) suspended across the strings. When these bars are pressed down, the felts on the bars mute some strings while allowing others to ring. For each bar the ringing strings form a specific chord, which is sounded by strumming the strings with a flat-pick or with thumb- and fingerpicks; melodies may be played over a chord by picking individual strings.

Before the 1950s, most players held the autoharp on their laps or on a table and strummed or plucked the strings below the chord bars. During the second half of the twentieth century, Maybelle Carter of the Carter Family (based in Maces Spring, Virginia) popularized another autoharp style that was to become dominant. This method consisted of playing the strings above the chord bars while holding the instrument upright against the chest.

Although not an Appalachian instrument by origin, the autoharp owes much of its current popularity in revivalist folk music circles to Appalachian musicians who featured the instrument on early country music recordings. For example, multi-instrumentalist Ernest V. Stoneman (from Monarat, Virginia) made the first commercial recording to feature the autoharp. Kilby Snow (based near Galax, Virginia)—an influential autoharp player "discovered" in the 1960s by Mike Seeger—was one of the first three inductees into the Autoharp Hall of Fame, along with Maybelle and Sara Carter. These stylists inspired the autoharp playing of such Appalachia-based folk revivalists as multi-instrumentalists Seeger and John McCutcheon. Many major autoharp championships, workshops, and festivals are held in Appalachia, with one regional event—the Mountain Laurel Autoharp Gathering in Newport, Pennsylvania—devoted solely to the instrument.

See also: CARTER FAMILY; SEEGER, MIKE; STONEMAN, ERNEST V./STONEMAN FAMILY.

—W. K. McNeil, *The Ozark Folk Center*

Baker, Etta

(1913–) Blues guitarist.

Etta Reid Baker is a leading proponent of the fingerpicked guitar style known as the Piedmont blues. Born March 31, 1913, in the Appalachian foothills of Caldwell County, North Carolina, Baker came from a family of African American, Irish, and Native American lineage. As a child, she learned a diverse repertoire, primarily from her father, Boone Reid, as well as from other family members. Etta Reid soon became proficient on several instruments, including the banjo. Excelling on the guitar, she developed a precise playing style that featured complex thumb-and-finger picking patterns. Her arrangements of traditional, popular, and blues material have been consistently imaginative.

In 1936 she married Lee Baker, and they later moved to Morganton, North Carolina. For most of her adult life, Etta Baker worked in local textile mills. Although she discontinued playing music in public for many years, Baker eventually received increased attention for her musical talents and for being a repository of a disappearing musical tradition. Her 1956 recording of the traditional "One-Dime Blues," released on the LP anthology *Instrumental Music of the Southern Appalachians*, was widely admired and much imitated during the folk music revival of the 1950s and 1960s, though she personally avoided the limelight. After her husband's death in 1967, however, Baker increasingly devoted her time to touring and performing. In 1991 she recorded her first solo album, *One-Dime Blues*, for the Rounder label. That same year Baker received a National Heritage Fellowship from the National Endowment for the Arts.

See also: AFRICAN AMERICAN INFLUENCES; BLUES; GUITAR.

—John Lilly, *Goldenseal Magazine, West Virginia Division of Culture and History*

Baker, Kenny

(1926–) Bluegrass fiddler.

Kenneth "Kenny" Baker was born June 26, 1926, in Jenkins, Kentucky, into a family of fiddlers. Counting jazz among his early musical influences, he played guitar while in the military and worked as a coal miner before becoming a professional musician. Baker began his national country music performance and recording career in 1953 as a fiddler with Don Gibson's touring band.

In 1956 Baker joined Bill Monroe and his Blue Grass Boys, becoming one of Monroe's best fiddlers and helping to define the bluegrass style of fiddle playing. He recorded nearly two hundred sides with Monroe, including those on the critically acclaimed tribute album *Uncle Pen* (1972), which was dedicated to Pendleton Vandiver, Monroe's uncle and a fiddler who helped shape Monroe's bluegrass music style. Other Baker albums include *Kenny Baker Country* (1972), *Kenny Baker Plays Bill Monroe* (1976), and *Portrait of a Bluegrass Fiddler* (1968), with Monroe's mandolin featured on many cuts. Among Baker's signature fiddle tunes are "Jerusalem Ridge," "Windy City," and "Festival Waltz," the first composed by Monroe and the latter two by Baker. His fiddle playing is known for its distinctive tone and inventiveness.

Baker interspersed three stints with Monroe between the mid-1950s and the mid-1980s with work in eastern Kentucky coal mines. He has also partnered with dobro player Buck "Uncle Josh" Graves, formerly of Flatt and Scruggs and the Foggy Mountain Boys. The long collaboration between Baker and Graves, highlighted by frequent festival appearances and occasional recordings, continued into the 1990s in the instrumental bluegrass "supergroup" the Masters, also featuring Jesse McReynolds and Eddie Adcock.

See also: BLUEGRASS; FIDDLE; MONROE, BILL.

—Steve Hooks, *WMMT Whitesburg, Kentucky/WDVX Clinton, Tennessee*

Ballads

A ballad is a narrative song in which each stanza of text is sung to the same melody. Brought to the American colonies by the earliest British settlers, the ballad form has remained in oral tradition through the present day, particularly in rural parts of the southeastern United States. The two ballad repertoires most strongly identified with the Appalachian region—ballads of British origin (often referred to as Child ballads) and "native American" ballads—differ in their age, source, style, and means of dissemination.

The ballad form originated in Europe during the Middle Ages and was firmly established in the British Isles by the fifteenth century. By the early eighteenth century, the composition of new ballads in Great Britain had tapered off, but the British ballad tradition was transported to the New World by emigrants. Formal collection and study of the British ballad repertoire dates to the late nineteenth century, when Harvard scholar Francis James Child collected and categorized 305 ballads in a series of books, *The English and Scottish Popular Ballads* (1882–98).

Conveying courtly stories that explore such common themes as love, bravery, treachery, the supernatural, and legendary events, the Child ballads are told through a highly economical form generally marked by four-line stanzas, with a metrical scheme that usually alternates eight and six syllables per line. Rhymes are frequently employed in these ballads, with the rhyming of the final accented syllable of the second and fourth lines being the most usual scheme. Internal and external refrains (lines that are repeated in each stanza) sometimes appear in ballads, as do other forms of repetition, such as repeated lines of text or incremental and parallel structures used to emphasize elements of the plot or to create formal symmetry.

Child ballads generally utilize a single opening stanza to introduce the setting and the principal characters. The story then unfolds rapidly to a point of confrontation, followed by a resolution presented through third-person narrative or dialogue. The language of the ballad features hyperbolic imagery and is marked by the use of stock phrases that reappear in numerous ballads, including formulaic beginnings (for example, "All in the merry month of May"), floating motifs (phrases that appear in numerous ballads, such as "the rose and the briar"), and epithets ("lily white hand").

Two stanzas drawn from "The Wife of Usher's Well" (Child ballad #79), as sung by Kentucky musician Addie Graham, illustrate aspects of the balladic art:

> There was a lady and a lady gay,
> And children she had three.
> She sent them away to an orphan's home,
> To learn their grammary.
> They hadn't been gone but a very short time,
> Only three weeks to the day,
> Till death swiftly came running along,
> And stole my little babies away.

In Appalachia, Child ballads were traditionally performed by a solo singer without instrumental accompaniment, though in later years a fretted dulcimer, guitar, fiddle, or banjo was sometimes used to accompany the singing. Although the language of ballads is dramatic, the singing style in Appalachia tended to be objective and detached, allowing the story to tell itself without the influence of an emotional delivery. A stanza such as the following, from "The Brown Girl" (Child ballad #295) as sung by Virginia traditional singer Horton Barker, seems shocking in its violence, yet it would be sung without any particular dramatic emphasis:

> He took the brown girl by the hand,
> He led her through the hall,
> And with a sword he cut her head off,
> And kicked it against the wall.

During the late nineteenth and early twentieth centuries, Appalachia came to be viewed as a repository for a dying tradition, and collectors and folklorists traveled in the region searching for ballad singers and their repertoires. As a result, ballads that had been in circulation among Appalachian people through oral transmission were preserved in notation and published in various collections, including Cecil Sharp's *English Folk Songs from the Southern Appalachians* (1917; revised 1932) and Bertrand Bronson's *The Traditional Tunes of the Child Ballads* (1959–72).

While maintaining the essential narrative nature of the Child ballads, "native American" ballads are distinguished by their more recent vintage (eighteenth to nineteenth century), their American origins, their subjective musical style, and often by their initial dissemination by means of broadsides, sheets of paper peddled on the street that were printed with the song lyrics but without the melody (printed alongside the lyrics would be the name of popular tunes to which the lyrics might be sung). Unlike the Child ballads, which had been brought from the Old World and which usually relate to unascertainable events with details blurred by time, native American ballads are topical, since they tend to be based either on specific events (such as tragic accidents, battles, and sensational murders) or on adventurous occupations (those of the lumberjack, cowboy, or sailor, for example). Befitting their American heritage, the subject matter of native American ballads is more democratic, reflecting on the lives of ordinary people rather than of lords and ladies.

Since a native American ballad often recalls actual events, the narrative contains more expository detail, while the language is specific rather than formulaic. For instance, "Mollie and Tenbrooks" refers to a late-nineteenth-century horse race held in Kentucky, and "Floyd Collins" relates the true story of a cave explorer who was trapped in Sand Cave near Mammoth Cave, Kentucky, on January 30, 1925. The accuracy of the stories told within these two ballads can be verified by newspaper accounts. Several other ballads from Appalachia, such as "John Henry" and "Omie Wise," exist in two or more variants, suggesting more than one interpretation of historic events. Because of the close personal and temporal identification between the composer of a ballad and that ballad's subject matter, the lyrics of native American ballads tend to be more personal, sentimental, and subjective than those of Child ballads. Frequently, native American ballads employ first-person narration and conclude with a moral.

Widely sung native American ballads in Appalachia include "Tom Dooley" and "Hills of Roane County." A subgenre of the native American ballad, the blues ballad, includes a number of narrative songs credited to African American sources. "John Henry," "John Hardy," and "House of the Rising Sun" have nonetheless long been equally popular among whites, within and outside the region.

During the twentieth century, balladry was precariously maintained in some communities in the Appalachian highlands by such singers as Jane Hicks Gentry (from Hot Springs, North Carolina), Texas Gladden (Salem, Virginia), Frank Proffitt Sr. (Watauga County, North Carolina), and Nimrod Workman (Martin County, Kentucky). Several folk revival–era singers—including Jean Ritchie (from Viper, Kentucky), Sheila Kay Adams (a native of Madison County, North Carolina), and Bobby McMillon (based in Lenoir, North Carolina)—are most responsible for the survival of the Appalachian ballad as a living art form. Additionally, the ballad tradition of telling a story in song continues to be an essential ingredient of country and bluegrass music. Many popular traditional ballads, whether performed within folk-revivalist circles (for example, "Darling Cora") or in popular music circles all over the world ("House of the Rising Sun"), have reentered circulation or gained wider distribution following collection (and publication and/or recording) from Appalachian balladeers.

See also: FOLK MUSIC COLLECTIONS; NILES, JOHN JACOB; RITCHIE, JEAN; SHARP, CECIL (FOLKLORE AND FOLKLIFE).

—Ron Pen, *University of Kentucky*

Frank C. Brown, Thomas G. Burton, *Some Ballad Folks* (1978); Tristram Coffin, *The British Traditional Ballad in North America* (1977); G. Malcolm Laws Jr., *Native American Balladry* (1964); Newman Ivey White et al., eds.,*The Frank C. Brown Collection of North Caolina Folklore* (1952–64).

Banjo

A four- or five-string instrument with a head of hide or plastic stretched over a gourd sound box or a circular wooden rim, the banjo evolved in America from a related family of variously named instruments—*banjar, bandora, banza*—brought from Africa by slaves.

In the seventeenth century, West African nomadic musicians brought to the New World an instrument with a long pole neck attached to a gourd and strung with three or four strings of horsehair, hemp, or catgut. Enslaved musicians in the West Indies colonies were playing such an instrument in a "knocking" or "beating" style by the early eighteenth century. The later incorporation of tuning pegs and a flat fingerboard facilitated the sliding and bending of notes.

By the mid-eighteenth century, African American musical culture was well established to the east of the Appalachians. In Maryland and Virginia as early as 1740, musicians made and played pole-necked, or sometimes flat-necked, gourd *banjars* with a short thumb string, skin head, and, sometimes, tuning pegs. Blacks played *banjars* and sang improvised lyric songs into the nineteenth century.

Traditionally, *banjar* playing incorporated both rhythm and melody and interacted with percussion—especially the African talking drums. *Banjar*-drum ensembles dominated performances in the lowland South until drums and brass horns were outlawed in the English colonies after the 1739 Stono insurrection, in which slaves on a South Carolina plantation used the beating of drums to coordinate a rebellion against slave owners. Afterward, a solo *banjar* tradition began to flourish. Some black banjo songs still survive in Appalachia, including songs about animal tricksters (Dink Roberts's "Fox Chase" and Rufus Kasey's "Old Rattler"), which recall the plight and strategic subversions of enslaved people.

Written records document the presence of black banjo players on the Appalachian frontier—in Knoxville, Tennessee, by 1800 and in Wheeling, (West) Virginia, by 1806. In early-nineteenth-century Appalachia, African American banjo music began to influence white fiddle music and in turn to be influenced by it. By 1830, white (especially Scots-Irish) musicians had begun to play the gourd *banjar* in the African American style of playing known as thumping. Shared interest in the instrument among blacks and whites soon resulted in the invention of the five-string, wooden-rimmed, open-back banjo, which replaced the gourd-bodied instruments; this new modification retained the African short-drone thumb string.

Joel Walker Sweeney, a Virginian of Irish descent and an early minstrel performer (c. 1830s), is often credited with the addition of the fifth string to the banjo. Contrary to popular conception, this additional string was not the short drone string but likely a fourth melody string. Sweeney's role in the invention of this five-string model remains contested, but his role in popularizing the banjo is widely acknowledged. His influence was perpetuated further by minstrel performer Dan Emmett's group, the Virginia Minstrels, whose banjo player, Billy Whitlock, was tutored by Sweeney. The group traveled to Ireland and England, popularizing the banjo there.

Views differ as to whether blackface minstrelsy was the major source by which Appalachian white musicians learned the banjo. Into the twentieth century, blacks continued to play the banjo in such sections of Appalachia as the North Carolina foothills. With the rise of radio and the commercial recording industry in the 1920s, most Americans began associating the banjo with Appalachian white "hillbilly" musicians. Minstrelsy and subsequent developments in late-nineteenth-century popular music not only influenced the performance styles of early commercial country banjo players from Appalachia but also contributed up-picking banjo techniques to the repertoires of more traditional musicians from or active in the region, such as Charlie Poole (Randolph County, North Carolina) and Dock Boggs (West Norton, Virginia). Jesting and rube outfits—essential parts of the acts of such early commercial country banjo players as Uncle Dave Macon, Stringbean, Lily May Ledford, and Grandpa Jones—also had their roots in minstrelsy.

The other possible mode of transmission of banjo-playing techniques from black mentors to white Appalachian musicians has been inadequately documented. Some white traditional musicians who continued to play homemade, fretless, often gut-stringed instruments into the era of recorded music were likely beneficiaries of an oral tradition that whites had learned from direct contact with black banjo players. By the 1850s, an increase in steamboat travel on rivers had intensified cultural exchange across Appalachia, as blacks (leased out by slave owners) often worked side by side with Irish and German laborers. Blacks and whites entertained each other by performing on the banjo a variety of jigs and reels, breakdowns, and "jump up" songs. On some steamboats traveling in the region, African American cabin boys would play instrumental music on the banjo and would buckdance or cakewalk. Musical crosspollination in Appalachia continued when blacks and whites came into contact during the Civil War. Through the 1870s, black roustabouts and longshoremen interacted with whites in waterfront dancehalls (for example, in Cincinnati) and paired the fiddle and banjo; this particular combination of instruments would remain the most popular musical configuration in Appalachia into the twentieth century.

Some African American musicians (for example, Virginian Leonard Bowles) and numerous white musicians in Appalachia still play banjos in a down-stroking style known as strumming, thumping, or clawhammer; the style usually involves the right index finger, or index and middle fingers, striking down on the strings, with the right thumb mostly droning on the short fifth string through downstrokes. In the latter half of the twentieth century, black banjo players, including Hardy County, West Virginia, native Clarence Tross and Virginian Josh Thomas, along with such white players as Doc Watson (of Deep Gap, North Carolina), continued to use the older terms—*knocking* and *beating*—for this style.

By the early twentieth century, with the addition of the guitar, mandolin, upright acoustic bass, and sometimes other musical instruments, the banjo-and-fiddle configuration was widely expanded into the fuller sound of the string band. Undaunted by the popularity of string bands, many traditional Appalachian banjo players—including Roscoe Holcomb (from Daisy, Kentucky), Wade Ward (Saddle Creek, Virginia), Frank Proffitt Sr. (Reese, North Carolina), Hobart Smith (Saltville, Virginia), Clarence "Tom" Ashley (Mountain City, Tennessee), Kyle Creed (Surry County, North Carolina), and Fred Cockerham (Low Gap, North Carolina)—played primarily solo or with fiddle accompaniment. Some of these musicians were recorded in the 1920s and 1930s, both commercially and by folk music enthusiasts and collectors. Several banjoists from Appalachia—including B. F. Shelton (Corbin, Kentucky), Hayes Shepherd (Jenkins, Kentucky), and Dock Boggs—played with up-picking techniques and favored modal and blues tonalities not typical to the Anglo-American fiddle tune repertoire of the region.

By the 1940s, up-picking styles—for example, the three-finger styles of Rex Brooks and Smith Hammett, and their pupil Snuffy Jenkins (from Harris, North Carolina)—had evolved into the syncopated, bluegrass banjo picking characterized by the intricate three-finger rolls of Flint Hill, North Carolina, native Earl Scruggs, the banjo player for Bill Monroe's Blue Grass Boys; by the simpler yet hard-driving rolls of Ralph Stanley (from Dickenson County, Virginia); and by the complex single-string playing of Don Reno (of Spartanburg, South Carolina). Later banjoists, including Kentuckians Sonny Osborne and J. D. Crowe, from Hyden and Lexington, respectively, expanded the possibilities of Scruggs's original style, while Don Stover (from Ameagle, West Virginia) strongly influenced the complex melodic and chromatic playing of such younger non-native progressive bluegrass exponents as Bill Keith, Tony Trischka, and Bela Fleck. Bluegrass banjo styles also inspired Appalachian musicians to develop techniques on other instruments that attempted to emulate the cascading sound of the banjo rolls. Buck "Uncle Josh" Graves adapted the rolls to his resophonic guitar and Jesse McReynolds developed a mandolin cross-picking technique, while Doc Watson was a pioneer of cross-picking on the acoustic flat-picked guitar.

Although musicians from the region contributed to its evolution, the banjo was not considered an Appalachian musical instrument in the nineteenth and early twentieth centuries. Three factors that encouraged the association of the banjo with Appalachia were a decline in the popularity of earlier non-Appalachian musical styles that featured the banjo (such as minstrelsy, "classical" banjo styles, medicine shows, vaudeville, and Dixieland jazz); recording industry interest in—and urban folk revivalists' focus on—Appalachian music and culture; and major innovations in banjo-playing styles by such Appalachian musicians as Earl Scruggs and Don Reno, who helped to make the banjo particularly suited to impressive displays of instrumental virtuosity. By the 1960s, the banjo was the instrument most non-Appalachian people associated with the region's folk and country music. Not only did urban folk revivalists focus on the banjo (for example, Mike Seeger's first project as a producer was an album of banjo instrumentals, *American Banjo: Three-Finger and Scruggs Style*, which featured such Appalachian banjo players as Snuffy Jenkins), but the instrument was also commonly featured in American popular music to evoke Appalachian culture and imagery. The latter trend can be traced through the folk-pop group the Kingston Trio's 1958 hit version of the Appalachian murder ballad "Tom Dooley" to contemporary alternative country music. Many Hollywood movies and television shows—including *Deliverance*, *Where the Lilies Bloom*, and *The Beverly Hillbillies*—featured banjo instrumentals as theme music. The recent mainstream discovery of Appalachian bluegrass banjo pioneer Ralph Stanley's music (following the success of the soundtrack from the 2000 movie *O Brother, Where Art Thou?*) has strengthened the popular association of the banjo with Appalachia and Appalachian music.

See also: AFRICAN AMERICAN INFLUENCES; FIDDLE; MINSTREL MUSIC/BLACKFACE MINSTRELSY.

—Cecelia Conway, *Appalachian State University*

Cecelia Conway, *African Banjo Echoes in Appalachia: A Study of Folk Traditions* (1995); Phillip F. Gura and James F. Bollman, *America's Instrument: The Banjo in the Nineteenth Century* (1999); Karen Linn, *That Half-Barbaric Twang: The Banjo in American Popular Culture* (1991).

Bare, Bobby

(1935–) Country singer and songwriter.

One of the more influential musicians to fuse traditional sensibilities with contemporary American viewpoints in post-World War II country music, Robert Joseph "Bobby" Bare was born April 7, 1935, near the rural town of Ironton, Ohio, not far from that state's border with Kentucky and West Virginia. Enduring the death of his mother when he was five, he did farm and factory work in his teens to help support the family.

Besides his eye for talent (he recommended country musician Waylon Jennings to record executive Chet Atkins), Bare is known for his emotionally understated vocal delivery on literate songs (mostly written by others) that often have a strong storyline. One of his biggest hits, "Detroit City," chronicles the loneliness of rural southerners drawn to northern factory work in the 1950s and 1960s. Bare's other hits include "Marie Laveau," "Margie's at the Lincoln Park Inn," and "The Streets of Baltimore."

Bare placed hits on the country charts every decade from the 1950s through the 1990s. His *Lullabys, Legends and*

Lies (1973), featuring songs by songwriter Shel Silverstein, was one of Nashville's first concept albums. At the end of the 1990s, Bare was nominated for a Country Music Association award for producing *Old Dogs*, an album of Silverstein songs (performed by Bare, Jennings, Jerry Reed, and Mel Tillis) that ruefully and sometimes hilariously cataloged problems of aging.

See also: COUNTRY MUSIC.

—Jack Hurst, *Lancaster, Tennessee*

Bass

The string bass (also called the upright bass, double bass, or stand-up bass) and its recent relative, the electric bass guitar, provide the rhythmic and harmonic foundation for much Appalachian music. Originating in Europe in the sixteenth century, the string bass—an acoustic, wooden, four-stringed instrument, generally tuned E-A-D-G—is the largest member of the viol family. In colonial America, the string bass was often utilized in churches; usually bowed, the instrument would double the bass line played by the organ. Appalachian string-band music, already developing long before the Tennessee Valley Authority brought electricity to the region, employed the string bass to provide rhythmic pulse and harmonic underpinning. The string bass's timbre blended well with the other acoustic instruments used in Appalachian string bands—fiddles, banjos, mandolins, and guitars. Bassists usually plucked the strings, sometimes slapping them against the fretboard on upbeats for percussive effect. Before drum sets were introduced into the region, the string bass played the principal timekeeping role in Appalachian instrumental groups. Many later musicians playing country, rockabilly, western swing, and old-time string-band music have continued to rely on the string bass to provide a traditional sound.

When a string bass was unavailable, early string bands utilized either a washtub (or gutbucket) bass or sometimes a cello or an accordion to provide bass parts. The string bass was sometimes referred to as a doghouse bass or bull fiddle, due to its size and function. The Appalachian bluegrass or traditional country bassist typically played in a simple two-beat style; the player maintained the rhythmic pulse utilizing the root and the dominant note of each chord, sometimes slapping the strings as described above. The bassist would frequently connect chords with scalar "walking" patterns.

Many Appalachian bands in the 1920s and 1930s played for traveling tent shows; bassists in these shows often assumed a comic role, dressing in rube outfits and blackening their front teeth. The bass itself could be a prop, variously spun, hidden behind, or even ridden as if a horse. Exemplifying this tradition was comedian Cousin Wilbur (a.k.a. Willie Westbrooks), a bassist with Bill Monroe's Blue Grass Boys in the 1940s.

By the 1940s, such Appalachian string bassists as Howard Watts (a.k.a. Cedric Rainwater) were playing both traditional and commercial styles. Other Appalachian bassists active during this period include Hillous Butrum (from Lafayette, Tennessee), who played with Hank Williams Sr.'s Drifting Cowboys; Billy Linneman, the bassist with Merle Travis; and Sheffield, Alabama, bassist Dexter Johnson, who played with the Blue Seal Pals, mainstays on WSM Nashville's *Sunup Serenade* radio program. Country singer Carl Smith, a native of Maynardville, Tennessee, performed as a string bassist at WROL in Knoxville, while Florence, Alabama, native Buddy Killen, a leading Nashville record executive, began his career as a bassist on the *Grand Ole Opry* in 1951. In the 1960s, Henry Strzezlecki, of Birmingham, Alabama, became an active session bassist in Nashville studios, as did Knoxville's Roy "Junior" Huskey. In the late 1980s and early 1990s, the latter's son, Roy Huskey Jr., was a leading Nashville studio bassist whose playing incorporated a blend of bluegrass and rockabilly.

First- and second-generation bluegrass bassists from Appalachia—all of whom specialized in the string bass—include George Shuffler, from Valdese, North Carolina, who played with the Stanley Brothers in the 1950s and who introduced the "driving bass" (walking bass) style to bluegrass; John Palmer, born in Union, South Carolina; Jack Cooke (from Norton, Virginia), who played with Ralph Stanley and the Clinch Mountain Boys; Jake Tullock (of Etowah, Tennessee), who accompanied the Bailey Brothers and the Happy Valley Boys; Jason Moore (of Ruffin, North Carolina); and Ben Issacs (from La Follette, Tennessee). Mercer County, West Virginia–born singer and songwriter Hazel Dickens often played bass early in her career.

Contemporary bluegrass bassists with Appalachian connections include Missy Raines (from Short Gap, West Virginia), recipient of several International Bluegrass Music Association Bass Player of the Year awards; Mark Fain (from Rogersville, Tennessee), who worked with Ricky Skaggs and Kentucky Thunder; and Barry Bales, of Kingsport, Tennessee, who played bass with Alison Krauss's group Union Station. Oak Ridge, Tennessee, native Edgar Meyer, a classically trained bassist equally adept at jazz, country, and bluegrass, melded those styles on two collaborative albums, *Appalachian Waltz* (1996) and *Appalachian Journey* (2000), which also feature cellist Yo-Yo Ma and violinist Mark O'Connor.

Pittsburgh's jazz scene has fostered several nationally recognized string bassists. Eddie Safranski performed with Stan Kenton's band in the 1940s. Ray Brown, also a composer, recorded as a bassist with Charlie Parker, Dizzy Gillespie, Duke Ellington, and Quincy Jones. Paul Chambers (born in Pittsburgh but reared in Detroit) played bass with such jazz stalwarts as Wes Montgomery, Miles Davis, and John Coltrane. John Heard has been affiliated with jazz musicians Ahmad Jamal, Oscar Peterson, and Joe Williams. Birmingham, Alabama's jazz scene produced bassist Cleveland Eaton, who worked with the Ramsey Lewis Trio and the Count Basie Orchestra; Eaton also recorded a popular regional hit, "Bama Boogie-Woogie." Jimmy Blanton, from Chattanooga, Tennessee, was a virtuoso bassist whose melodic hornlike solos were featured on duo recordings with Duke Ellington.

The electric bass guitar appeared in the 1950s and soon became the standard bass instrument used in rock, rhythm and blues, and modern commercial country music. Best known as Nashville's premier harmonica player, Charlie McCoy, from Oak Hill, West Virginia, played electric bass on some important recording sessions—most famously on Bob Dylan's 1966 album *Blonde on Blonde*. While bluegrass is usually performed acoustically, several Appalachian players have preferred the electric bass, especially since the 1970s emergence of the progressive bluegrass style. George Shuffler played electric bass on a few Stanley Brothers' sessions in the 1950s. Other bluegrass bassists who have preferred the electric bass include Lawrenceville, Georgia, native Ray Deaton; Mount Airy, North Carolina, native Ronnie Bowman; Christiansburg, Virginia's Ronnie Simpkins; and Danbury, North Carolina's Lou Reid.

Many electric bassists have worked in the Muscle Shoals, Alabama–area studios, and several are from that area. Norbert Putnam, for example, was affiliated with the legendary FAME Recording Studios in the early 1960s before moving to Nashville, where he became an acclaimed session bassist, arranger, and producer. Guitarist/bassist Albert "Junior" Lowe of Florence, Alabama, worked as a session musician at FAME in the 1960s and 1970s. Tommy Cogbill created an influential electric bass style that is closely tied to Muscle Shoals, where he recorded with Aretha Franklin and Wilson Pickett. Cogbill and Memphis-born bassist Mike Leech, who also recorded at Muscle Shoals, participated in Elvis Presley's celebrated sessions at Memphis's American Studio in the late 1960s. David Hood of Sheffield, Alabama, another electric bassist who started at FAME, later gained international recognition for his contributions to hundreds of hit records as a member of the Muscle Shoals Rhythm Section. Bob Wray, a Wisconsin native, is another well-known session bassist in Muscle Shoals, where he played on such hits as Clarence Carter's "Patches." Three other non-Appalachian bassists—Jerry Jemmott, Lenny LeBlanc, and Gary Baker—have also recorded frequently in Muscle Shoals.

See also: BLUEGRASS; JAZZ; MUSCLE SHOALS.

—Peter B. Olson, *University of Memphis*

Leonard G. Feather, *The Encyclopedia of Jazz* (1984); Buddy Killen, with Tom Carter, *By the Seat of My Pants* (1993); Paul Kingsbury, ed., *The Encyclopedia of Country Music* (1998).

Battle, Kathleen

(1948–) Classical singer.

The youngest of seven children of a Portsmouth, Ohio, steelworker and his wife, Kathleen Battle (b. August 13, 1948) learned to sing, play the piano, and read music from members of her family. Battle graduated from the University of Cincinnati College Conservatory of Music. During this period, she studied music with professor Franklin Bens and taught music to inner-city children.

Battle made her professional debut as a soprano soloist in Brahms's *Requiem* at the 1972 Spoleto Festival in Charleston, South Carolina. In 1975 she made her opera debut with the Michigan Opera Theater. The following year, she appeared as Susanna in the New York City Opera's production of Mozart's *Le nozze di Figaro*. Her debut with the Metropolitan Opera came on December 22, 1977, in the role of the Shepherd in Wagner's *Tannhäuser*. In 1979 she made her first European appearance as Nerina in Haydn's *La fedeltà premiata*. She also sang the role of Zerlina in Mozart's *Don Giovanni*, Pamina in that composer's *Die Zauberflöte* (a performance hailed as one of the greatest Mozartean characterizations of Battle's generation), Sophie in Richard Strauss's *Der Rosenkavalier*, and Marie in Donizetti's *La fille du regiment*, among other roles.

In addition to being in demand internationally at premier opera houses, Battle has performed as a soloist with the world's leading orchestras, including the Vienna Philharmonic, New York Philharmonic, Boston Symphony Orchestra, Berlin Philharmonic, and Orchestre de Paris. She has appeared in concerts and on recordings alongside many acclaimed opera, classical, and jazz performers. Battle has received numerous awards from the music industry (including multiple Grammy Awards) as well as recognition from her hometown.

See also: OPERA; SYMPHONY ORCHESTRAS.

—Eric S. Strother, *University of Kentucky*

Blake, Norman

(1938–) Multi-instrumentalist, old-time singer, and songwriter.

Norman Blake, of Rising Fawn, Georgia, became a major practitioner of traditional music in the 1970s. Initially a much sought-after Nashville session musician, the multi-instrumentalist worked solely in acoustic formats for three decades, performing in solo, duo, and ensemble settings. Acknowledged as an influential flat-pick guitar stylist, Blake has demonstrated equal facility on the fiddle, mandolin, and dobro. The lyrics of several of his better-known original songs, most notably "Last Train from Poor Valley" and "Ginseng Sullivan," depict Appalachian themes and imagery.

Born March 10, 1938, in Chattanooga, Tennessee, Blake absorbed the traditional music played by family members in northwest Georgia; he also heard African American blues, white country music, and bluegrass. Blake dropped out of school at the age of sixteen to play music full-time. His first band, the Dixie Drifters, played on radio stations in Knoxville, Tennessee, and Rome, Georgia. He made several guest appearances on WSM's *Grand Ole Opry* before being drafted into the U.S. Army in 1961.

After completing his service in 1963, Blake returned to Chattanooga and taught guitar lessons. He also traveled frequently to Nashville to record on sessions by a number of artists, including Johnny Cash. Moving to Nashville in 1969, Blake was soon performing regularly on Cash's television show. He also appeared on Bob Dylan's *Nashville Skyline* album and played in Kris Kristofferson's band. Later, Blake joined John Hartford's influential band, Aereo-Plain, a group that helped launch the progressive bluegrass, or "newgrass," era.

In 1972 Blake began collaborating with his eventual wife, Nancy Short, a multi-instrumentalist who shared his passion for old-time music. The couple toured and recorded, performing original compositions and nineteenth- and early-twentieth-century folk, country, blues, and old-time music. Among her other contributions to the duo's sound, Nancy revived the use of the cello in old-time music (the instrument was not uncommon in old-time bands during the early twentieth century). Norman Blake's later albums have maintained the consistency and integrity of such acclaimed solo albums from the 1970s as *Back Home in Sulphur Springs, Old and New*, and *The Fields of November*. In the 1990s, he recorded and toured with Johnny and June Carter Cash and with Steve Earle.

See also: BLUEGRASS; GUITAR; OLD-TIME MUSIC.

—Karl Rohr, *Western Carolina University*

Bluegrass

Born of the traditions and experiences of the people of Appalachia and neighboring regions, bluegrass is an ensemble music placing equal emphasis on heartfelt vocals and instrumental virtuosity. The structure, delivery, and repertoire of bluegrass owe a debt to Anglo-, Scots- and Irish-influenced American folk music, to string bands that flourished in the nineteenth- and early-twentieth-century rural South, and to blues, ragtime, jazz, and gospel traditions.

Instruments conventionally associated with bluegrass are the mandolin, fiddle, five-string banjo, acoustic flat-top guitar, upright acoustic bass, and dobro (resonator guitar). The instruments alternate playing lead parts while the bass and the remaining instruments provide a rhythmic background. Traditionally, all instruments were acoustic, but efforts to attract urban rock audiences, especially from the 1960s through the early 1980s, often led to the incorporation of electric instruments, including the electric bass guitar, sometimes the pedal steel guitar, and occasionally drums and electric guitar. Instrumental virtuosity and improvisation are hallmarks of bluegrass music.

Bluegrass vocalization is characterized by a high-pitched and intense delivery, contributing to a sound often labeled "high lonesome." Voices generally combine to form two-, three-, and four-part harmonies. Vocal parts include the lead, which carries the melody; tenor, which is usually sung a third interval above the lead; baritone, which usually provides the fifth of the melody, usually below but sometimes above the lead (the latter is called a high baritone); and the lowest part, bass, which generally handles the root notes of each chord. In this way, bluegrass harmony singing is derived from the harmony duo and gospel traditions of Appalachia, while the tonal character is influenced by the modal vocalizations in traditional Appalachian balladry.

The bluegrass repertoire includes instrumental tunes; secular songs by known composers based on such themes as the vagaries of love, nostalgia, and comedic situations; folk songs; and gospel music. A typical bluegrass song consists of several verses sung by the lead singer, each of which is followed by a chorus in two-, three-, or four-part harmony. The verse-chorus pairings are interspersed with instrumental interludes, each one showcasing one or more of the lead instruments.

Bluegrass music evolved from the innovative musical efforts of mandolin player and native Kentuckian Bill Monroe, the acknowledged "Father of Bluegrass Music." Although he was born in western Kentucky, Monroe's cultural heritage was heavily influenced by the Appalachian region, and his musical influence was in turn felt throughout Appalachia. While Bill Monroe and his Blue Grass Boys debuted on the *Grand Ole Opry* in 1939, most scholars agree that the classic bluegrass sound emerged with the 1945 introduction of Earl Scruggs's three-finger banjo picking to the group. Key members in the various lineups of the Blue Grass Boys came from Appalachia, including Scruggs, Lester Flatt, Don Reno, Red Smiley, Mac Wiseman, Jimmy Martin, and Sonny Osborne. By the late 1940s, Monroe's group was inspiring other country string bands. However, *bluegrass* was not employed as a label for the genre until the mid-1950s. In the mid- to late 1950s, when many country musicians were either opting for the commercial Nashville Sound or incorporating elements of the new rock 'n' roll genre, the hard-core traditional country music audience embraced bluegrass and its acoustic string-band sound. In the 1960s, bluegrass enjoyed a spurt of popularity with urban youth audiences as folk revivalists were attracted to the genre's acoustic sound and its perceived traditional origination (bluegrass was described by folklorist and collector Alan Lomax as "folk music in overdrive").

The country music that originally influenced bluegrass had gained most of its popularity through live radio broadcasts, but the popularity of live radio was on the decline when bluegrass emerged and its performers had to find other ways to attract an audience. Bluegrass performers reached audiences via records, syndicated television shows (during the 1950s and 1960s), and stage shows (of which the bluegrass festival proved to be the most rewarding). In 1961, at Luray, Virginia, bluegrass musician and promoter Bill Clifton organized a one-day event that featured several major bluegrass acts on the same stage. The first multi-day bluegrass festival was held September 3–5, 1965, at Fincastle, Virginia, near Roanoke. Reminiscent of medicine shows, fiddlers' conventions, and folk festivals, the typical bluegrass festival is a two- to four-day weekend event, often featuring a dozen or more musical groups that perform in open-air venues for successive thirty- to sixty-minute segments from late morning until approximately midnight. Bands booked by festival promoters include both full-time professionals and amateurs who pursue music as a hobby. Performers set up tables from which they sell their latest recordings and other products, including T-shirts and photographs. Even while featured acts are performing onstage, spontaneous jam sessions—involving both professional and amateur musicians—continue in adjacent parking lots and camping areas. By 2000, some five hundred bluegrass festivals were being held annually in the United States, with smaller numbers staged in Canada, Japan, and a half-dozen European countries.

In the beginning, professional bluegrass musicians were mostly men. In addition to Bill Monroe and the Blue Grass Boys, Appalachia-based acts—such as the Osborne Brothers, Jim and Jesse and the Virginia Boys, and the Stanley Brothers—dominated the field. Women gradually infiltrated the ranks. Rose Maddox, a native of Boaz, Alabama, was the first woman to record a bluegrass album (in 1962); it featured Bill Monroe, Don Reno, and Red Smiley, among others. Starting in the mid-1960s, Hazel Dickens (of Mercer County, West Virginia) performed bluegrass in an influential duo with revivalist folk musician Alice Gerrard. The legacy of these pioneering women of bluegrass continues in the music of many contemporary bluegrass performers, including such women from Appalachia as Claire Lynch, Dale Ann Bradley, and Murphy Henry.

Five members of Zeke Morris and the Happy Mountaineers, pioneers of bluegrass music, posing by the microphone at radio station WJHL, Johnson City, Tennessee, 1945. The musicians are, front row, left to right: Red Smiley and Howard Thompson; and back row, left to right: Red Rector, Zeke Morris, and Fred Smith.

Bluegrass musicians—individuals and groups—with Appalachian connections who have made significant contributions to the genre include Red Allen, Kenny Baker, Norman Blake, Blue Highway, the Bluegrass Cardinals, Ginger Boatwright, Ray Deaton, Raymond Fairchild, Betty Fisher, Lester Flatt, Melvin and Ray Goins, Buck "Uncle Josh" Graves, Bill Harrell, the Lonesome River Band, Doyle Lawson, the Lilly Brothers, Lonesome Standard Time, Jimmy Martin, Del McCoury, Jim and Jesse McReynolds, Tim O'Brien, Bobby and Sonny Osborne, Don Reno, Carl and J. P. Sauceman, Ricky Skaggs, Red Smiley, Carter and Ralph Stanley, the Stoneman Family, Carl Story, Don Stover, Frank Wakefield, Doc Watson, and Mac Wiseman.

Despite the fact that the early evolution of the genre occurred beyond the region's boundaries, the music initially found its warmest and most enthusiastic reception among residents of Appalachia. Bluegrass soon spread far beyond its Appalachian stronghold, however. During the urban folk revival of the mid-1950s through the 1970s, many urban centers, including Boston, Washington, D.C., New York City, and Los Angeles, developed major bluegrass music venues; there, musicians with an equal affinity for rock and bluegrass brought bluegrass to new audiences. The Nitty Gritty Dirt Band's album *Will the Circle Be Unbroken* (1972), the group Old and In the Way's self-titled debut album (1974), and J. D. Crowe and the New South's eponymous 1975 album (featuring Appalachian Kentucky's Ricky Skaggs) were some of the major projects that hastened this crossover. After the late-1970s rise in popularity of slick, dance-oriented styles in mainstream music, bluegrass was sustained by such independent recording labels as Rounder, Flying Fish, Sugar Hill, and County Records. The International Bluegrass Music Association, a professional trade organization dedicated to promoting the music, was established in 1985, with its headquarters situated in Owensboro in western Kentucky.

The last decade of the twentieth century was particularly successful for bluegrass music as well as for its Appalachian practitioners. Such Appalachian-born country stars as Ricky Skaggs, Dolly Parton, and Patty Loveless returned to an acoustic sound that celebrated the connections between bluegrass and Appalachia. The new millennium provided the capstone to this trend with the unprecedented commercial success of the *O Brother, Where Art Thou?* soundtrack, which featured Ralph Stanley and other Appalachian and non-Appalachian performers seamlessly fusing earlier traditional Appalachian music with bluegrass-influenced styles.

See also: COUNTRY MUSIC; GOSPEL MUSIC, ANGLO-AMERICAN; MONROE, BILL; STRING-BAND MUSIC.

—Wayne W. Daniel, *Chamblee, Georgia*

Robert Cantwell, *Bluegrass Breakdown* (1984); Neil V. Rosenberg, *Bluegrass: A History* (1993).

Blues

Blues is a musical genre that developed among African Americans in the lowland South during the late nineteenth century. With the increasing migration of African Americans into Appalachia (particularly urban industrial centers) in the late nineteenth and early twentieth centuries, cross-pollination between African and European American cultures resulted in distinctive blues subgenres developing in different parts of the region. Piedmont blues, for instance, flourished in the Blue Ridge foothills of the Carolinas. Interactions between blacks and whites also led to the emergence across the South of blues–influenced country music styles such as hillbilly blues and hillbilly boogie. Appalachian musicians made vital contributions to several commercial blues subgenres (especially classic female blues), as well as to other southern-based musics bearing a strong blues influence, including rockabilly, bluegrass, rhythm and blues, soul, and southern rock.

Blues songs and tunes tend to share similar characteristics: a call-and-response form, the use of particular scales, and the establishing of musical tension through the juxtaposition of major and minor intervals. Eight-, twelve-, and sixteen-bar blues, as well as the less rigidly structured nine- and thirteen-bar blues, have their basis in pre–World War I rural blues songs. Florence, Alabama, native W. C. Handy, a pioneer composer of commercial blues songs, was largely responsible for the twelve-bar structure's becoming the dominant form of blues composition. Several classic female blues singers from Appalachia—including Ida Cox (of Toccoa, Georgia), Bessie Smith (a Chattanooga, Tennessee, native) and "Diamond Teeth" Mary McClain (from Logan County, West Virginia)—became popular on the vaudeville circuit, singing the blues to orchestral or jazz accompaniment.

Some of the most distinctive styles of fingerpicked acoustic guitar blues developed to the east of southern Appalachia in the Carolina Piedmont. In the early part of the twentieth century, increased employment opportunities in such cities as Greenville and Spartanburg, South Carolina, and Winston-Salem, North Carolina, attracted a large number of African Americans. Entertaining both black and white audiences, usually at separate venues, black musicians borrowed European American repertoire ("Spanish Fandango") and stylistic elements (especially an emphasis on melody and an alternating-thumb style of picking—that is, alternating between two of the lower strings for the playing of bass notes).

Piedmont blues musicians born within Appalachia include Willie Walker and the Reverend Gary Davis (both from Greenville, South Carolina), Brownie McGhee (from Knoxville, Tennessee), and Etta Baker (of Caldwell County, North Carolina). Most of these musicians greatly influenced the post–World War II urban folk revival. Other African American musicians from Appalachia likewise developed individual instrumental styles that incorporated major-scale melodies typical in the European American musical repertoire. Two regional musicians—singer-guitarist Leslie Riddle (from Kingsport, Tennessee, who assisted A. P. Carter and his family on their song-collecting trips) and the itinerant guitar player Arnold Shultz (who influenced the mandolin playing of Bill Monroe as well as the "Travis picking" guitar style)—featured alternating string thumb-style guitar picking that significantly differed from the riff-based Delta blues style, which usually featured bass notes picked on the same string. Mercer County, West Virginia, guitarist Nat Reese and La Follette, Tennessee, native Howard Armstrong, a string-band fiddler and mandolinist, are other important African American musicians who were grounded in blues traditions but who had eclectic repertoires that included other regional and popular musical styles.

Early white country musicians in Appalachia—Maybelle Carter, Jimmie Rodgers, Frank Hutchison, Cliff Carlisle, and the duo Darby and Tarlton—incorporated elements of the blues (song structures, scales, and vocal inflections) into their individual guitar styles. Country steel-guitar styles, from the 1920s forward, bore a strong blues influence, borrowed directly from bottleneck blues guitar playing and indirectly from Hawaiian steel-guitar styles that had already incorporated the blues. Later-emerging country music subgenres, such as bluegrass and hillbilly boogie, reflected the influence of the blues and foreshadowed rockabilly and rock 'n' roll. Country harmonica playing similarly incorporated the blues cross-harp style. The harmonica playing of pre–World War II *Grand Ole Opry* African American star DeFord Bailey (from Smith County, Tennessee) influenced not only the bluesy cross-harp style that defined the pre–rock 'n' roll hillbilly boogie music of the Delmore Brothers, but also the harmonica playing of such Nashville session musicians as Charlie McCoy (from Oak Hill, West Virginia).

Rock 'n' roll evolved from a similar melding. Florence, Alabama, native Sam Phillips, a record producer who operated out of Memphis, was responsible for some of the earliest rock 'n' roll recordings, which featured African American musicians from the Appalachian margins in northern Mississippi (including Jackie Brenston's 1951 performance of "Rocket 88" and Junior Parker's 1953 song "Mystery Train"). In the mid-1950s, Phillips achieved major crossover success when he recorded, for his Sun Records label, white musicians (such as Tupelo, Mississippi, native Elvis Presley) performing in a similar style known as rockabilly.

Other producers from the Muscle Shoals, Alabama, area envisioned a popular synthesis of the blues with white country music. By the late 1960s, Muscle Shoals had become a nationally renowned recording center for soul, a music that fused the blues, rhythm and blues, and African American gospel with country music, often joining black singers with white backup musicians. Later music subgenres such as southern rock, blues rock, and roots rock similarly drew from the wellspring of the blues. The Allman Brothers Band's Chuck Leavell (a Birmingham, Alabama, native) and Warren Haynes (from Asheville, North Carolina) as well as the Marshall Tucker Band (from Spartanburg, South Carolina) have been major Appalachian exponents of these subgenres.

Northeastern Mississippi and the adjoining counties along Appalachia's western margins have long been a fertile ground for the blues. Major blues musicians from the area include Chester Burnette (a.k.a. Howlin' Wolf), from West Point, Mississippi; Mississippi Fred McDowell (a resident of Como, Mississippi, in Panola County); and white rockabilly pioneer Charlie Feathers (from Holly Springs, Mississippi). Two other important African American blues stylists from the area—Junior Kimbrough (born in Hudsonville, Mississippi) and R. L. Burnside (a resident of Holly Springs)—attracted national followings during the 1990s, late in their careers. Northern Mississippi's "hill country blues" continue to influence the music of younger musicians from the area—such as the members of the group the North Mississippi Allstars—as well as the music of non-native musicians, including the alternative rock band Jon Spencer Blues Explosion, which recorded with Burnside.

See also: GOSPEL MUSIC, AFRICAN AMERICAN; JAZZ; RHYTHM AND BLUES.

—Steve Hooks, *WMMT Whitesburg, Kentucky/WDVX Clinton, Tennessee*

Bruce Bastin, *Crying for the Carolines* (1971); Robert Santelli, *The Big Book of Blues: A Biographical Encyclopedia* (2001); Charles K. Wolfe, liner notes, *White Country Blues: 1926–1938: A Lighter Shade of Blue* (1993).

Blue Sky Boys

Country music brother duo.

Bolick, Bill (1917–) Early country singer and mandolinist.

Bolick, Earl (1919–1998) Early country singer and guitarist.

Perhaps the best of the many brother duos that performed in country music during the 1930s and 1940s, the Blue Sky Boys featured Hickory, North Carolina, natives William A. "Bill" (b. October 28, 1917) and Earl A. Bolick (November 16, 1919–April 19, 1998). Beginning their career in 1935 on WWNC in Asheville with fiddler Homer Sherrill as "John, Frank, and George" of the JFG Coffee Company–sponsored Good Coffee Boys, the Bolicks soon parted from Sherrill and renamed themselves the Blue Sky Boys.

After a move to Atlanta's WGST in 1936, Bill and Earl appeared on numerous stations throughout the southeastern United States, including WPTF in Raleigh, North Carolina, and WFBC in Greenville, South Carolina. The brothers' precise close harmony singing and Bill's understated but lyrical mandolin playing—heard on radio, in personal appearances, and on records—won them a wide and dedicated following. Between 1936 and 1951, the Blue Sky Boys recorded more than 125 sides for RCA Victor. Several comeback appearances before college and festival audiences in the 1960s and 1970s and recording sessions for Starday (1963) and Capitol (1965) brought the Blue Sky Boys back to public attention.

Although they were lauded primarily as singers of broadsides and ballads of American origin ("Knoxville Girl," "Banks of the Ohio"), the Blue Sky Boys also recorded many nineteenth-century parlor songs ("Sweet Evalina"), twentieth-century popular songs ("Kentucky"), gospel songs ("Turn Your Radio On"), and contemporary country songs ("Sold Down the River"). The Blue Sky Boys' repertoire and style influenced many later brother duos, including the Louvin Brothers. Many of the Bolicks' recorded and radio performances have been reissued on compact disc.

See also: COUNTRY MUSIC; DUOS, BROTHER.

—David E. Whisnant, *Chapel Hill, North Carolina*

Boggs, Dock

(1898–1971) Early country banjo player and singer.

Born February 7, 1898, in West Norton, Virginia, Moran Lee "Dock" Boggs worked as a miner in the coalfields of southwestern Virginia and eastern Kentucky for most of his life. A member of a musical family, Boggs began to sing and play the banjo in his teens. In 1927 he recorded eight songs for the Brunswick label and enjoyed a modest semiprofessional career, but hard times during the early years of the Great Depression sent him back to the mines and forced him to abandon hope of sustaining a musical livelihood. Boggs was "rediscovered" and recorded again in the 1960s, whereupon he performed frequently before urban folk revival audiences.

A key figure in the transition from folk to commercial music making in Appalachia, Boggs learned songs from many sources. He adapted traditional a cappella ballads to banjo accompaniment, learned blues from records, and devised his own up-picking, three-finger banjo style from watching local African American musicians. His fingerpicking allowed him to sing and play the melody together in a sort of duet—a contrast to the more common frailing style of banjo playing.

Boggs's music embodies the mingling of black and white traditions. His repertoire included "Country Blues," a reworking of the lyric folk song "Darlin' Corey"; such British ballads as "Pretty Polly"; native American ballads, including "Omie Wise" and "Cole Younger"; blues ballads such as "John Henry"; and blues songs learned from records, including "Down South Blues" and "Sugar Baby." He died on his seventy-third birthday.

See also: AFRICAN AMERICAN INFLUENCES; BANJO; OLD-TIME MUSIC.

—Frederick E. Danker, *University of Massachusetts*

Bristol Sessions

The Bristol sessions were among the earliest and most successful attempts to make field recordings of rural musicians in Appalachia. The 1927 sessions took place over two weeks starting July 25 in Bristol, Tennessee, and were produced by Ralph Peer of the Victor Talking Machine Company. All told, seventy-six performances by nineteen different groups were recorded that summer in Bristol. These recordings showcased the full range of music popular in Appalachia during the early twentieth century, including old popular and vaudeville songs, traditional mountain ballads and songs, fiddle and banjo tunes, blues, and gospel songs.

Peer had invited some previously recorded musicians to these sessions, including Ernest V. Stoneman of southwest Virginia. When a newspaper reported that Stoneman was paid for his services, Bristol was inundated with musicians from Tennessee, Virginia, Kentucky, and West Virginia. Among those who auditioned and recorded for Peer in 1927 were two acts that emerged as among the most important in the history of country music—the Carter Family and Jimmie Rodgers. A. P. Carter, his wife, Sara, and his sister-in-law, Maybelle, were from nearby Maces Springs, Virginia. Rodgers, from Meridian, Mississippi, had moved to the Asheville, North Carolina, area after being diagnosed with tuberculosis; initially performing on WWNC radio, he joined forces temporarily with a group of Bristol-based musicians called the Tenneva Ramblers, though he recorded as a solo act at the sessions. Among other notable performers at the 1927 Bristol sessions were gospel singers Alfred G. Karnes and Ernest Phipps and traditional singer and banjo player B. F. Shelton, all from eastern Kentucky; West Virginia–born protest singer Blind Alfred Reed; and banjo-fiddle duo J. P. Nestor and Norman Edmonds, from Hillsville, Virginia. Witnessing the popularity of some commercial releases from the 1927 sessions, Peer returned to Bristol the next year for a second round of field recording sessions.

See also: CARTER FAMILY; FIELD RECORDING SESSIONS; RODGERS, JIMMIE; STONEMAN, ERNEST V./STONEMAN FAMILY.

—Charles F. Faber, *Lexington, Kentucky*

Charles K. Wolfe and Ted Olson, eds., *The Bristol Sessions: Writings About the Big Bang of Country Music* (2005).

Calhoun, Walker

(1919–) Cherokee singer and ceremonial leader.

Walker Calhoun is a major tradition bearer of the old Cherokee ways, especially ceremonial songs and dances. Born in 1919 into the Big Cove community in western North Carolina's Qualla Boundary, Calhoun is the nephew of Will West Long, who was the spiritual shaman and dance leader of Big Cove and a primary informant for ethnologist James Mooney, author of *History, Myths, and Sacred Formulas of the Cherokee.* From his uncle, Calhoun learned the songs and dances of his community. Despite being forbidden by a Bureau of Indian Affairs policy to speak Cherokee as a boy in school, Calhoun had a minimal knowledge of English when he entered the U.S. Army during World War II.

But English is not the medium for communicating traditional Cherokee songs, and some of the lyrics utilize nonsemantic sounds (known as vocables) rather than words. These songs, some dating back three millennia or more, depict a natural order of things informed by a spiritual relationship among all forms of life and celebrate all aspects of traditional Cherokee life (the harvest, hunting, and everyday life in general). After the brutal removal of the Cherokees along the Trail of Tears to Oklahoma in 1838–39, songs became a means of cultural resistance and survival for those few who had escaped into the security of their mountainous homeland in the Great Smokies. Calhoun recorded many of these traditional songs for an album entitled *Where the Ravens Roost*, produced and distributed by Western Carolina University's Mountain Heritage Center. As the current leader of sacred ceremonies in Big Cove, Calhoun is respected among his people as a leader who endeavors to preserve their valued cultural heritage.

See also: CHEROKEE (RACE, ETHNICITY, AND IDENTITY); CHEROKEE MUSIC; CHEROKEE RELIGIOUS TRADITIONS (RELIGION).

—H. Tyler Blethen, *Western Carolina University*

Carson, Fiddlin' John

(c. 1868–1949) Early country fiddler and singer.

Born March 23, c. 1868, in the north Georgia mountains, John William Carson as a boy learned to play fiddle on an instrument brought from Ireland by his ancestors. In 1879, at a political function in Copperhill, Tennessee, the young Carson was dubbed "Fiddlin' John Carson" by fiddler and governor of Tennessee, Bob Taylor. With fiddling as a sideline, Carson made his living in a variety of jobs, working as a farmer, railroad worker, jockey, and moonshiner. After moving to Atlanta in 1900 to work in a textile mill, he found increased opportunities to entertain as a fiddler. A 1913 strike caused Carson to turn to fiddling and singing on the streets.

A major figure at the Georgia Old-Time Fiddlers' Convention, held annually in Atlanta between 1913 and 1935, Carson received extensive coverage in the city's newspapers. He was a favorite among the competing fiddlers and a colorful character who attracted large audiences wherever he performed.

When Atlanta's first radio station, WSB, went on the air in 1922, Carson was among its first performers. The large number of letters, telegrams, and telephone calls from listeners who appreciated his repertoire of traditional fiddle tunes kept Carson on the station as a regular performer for the remainder of the decade.

Recording company executives discovered the profitability of Appalachian and southern "hillbilly" music after Carson's debut release became popular. Recorded June 14, 1923, by producer Ralph Peer for the OKeh label, it featured the song "The Little Old Log Cabin in the Lane" and the instrumental "The Old Hen Cackled and the Rooster's Going to Crow." Although Carson was a pioneer in the fledgling commercial country music industry, his sound was soon deemed too "primitive," and his subsequent recordings for the OKeh and Bluebird labels received less attention. He died December 11, 1949.

See also: CONTESTS AND CONVENTIONS; COUNTRY MUSIC; FIDDLE.

—Wayne W. Daniel, *Chamblee, Georgia*

Gene Wiggins, *Fiddlin' Georgia Crazy: Fiddlin' John Carson, His Real World, and the World of His Songs* (1987).

Carter Family

Early country family group.

Carter, Alvin Pleasant (A. P.) (1891–1960) Singer, songwriter, and folk song collector.

Carter, Sara Dougherty (1899–1979) Singer and autoharpist.

Carter, Maybelle Addington (1909–1978) Singer, guitarist, and autoharpist.

The Carter Family of Scott County, Virginia, ranks as the most significant pre–World War II country music recording act. Their legacy extended to later generations, and their impact upon traditional Appalachian music remained strong into the twenty-first century. A. P. Carter (b. December 15, 1891), his wife, Sara (b. July 21, 1899), and sister-in-law, Maybelle (b. May 10, 1909), sang a mixture of traditional ballads, Victorian popular songs, and old hymns with guitar and autoharp accompaniment. From their first recordings at the Victor Talking Machine Company's famous Bristol sessions in 1927, the Carter Family attracted a large audience. Although only part-time performers throughout much of their careers, the Carters introduced many now-standard songs into country music, including "Wildwood Flower," "I'm Thinking Tonight of My Blue Eyes," and "Foggy Mountain Top."

The marriage of A. P. and Sara Carter disintegrated in the early 1930s, and the couple soon divorced. However, the Carter Family's recording career continued without interruption. After 1934, they left Victor and made discs for the American Record Company, Decca, and Conqueror before recording their final sessions for Victor in 1941. By then, they had amassed a recorded legacy of approximately three hundred masters. During this period, they also performed over radio on Mexican border stations and on Charlotte, North Carolina's WBT.

Meanwhile, in 1939 Sara married A. P.'s cousin Coy Bayes and eventually relocated to California. A. P. and Sara's younger children, Janette (b. 1923) and Joe (1927–2005), inherited their musical talents, as did Maybelle's daughters, Helen (1927–1998), June (1929–2003), and Anita (1933–1999). After the final breakup of the Carter Family in 1943, Maybelle and her daughters worked as Mother Maybelle and the Carter Sisters on various radio stations across the South, eventually settling in Nashville and performing on WSM and the *Grand Ole Opry*. In addition to their family group, both Anita and June Carter had solo careers, with the latter also doing comedy. A. P., Sara, Janette, and Joe Carter also made some recordings for Acme. A. P. died November 7, 1960.

By the 1960s, the surviving Carters had begun to gain recognition for their pioneering roles in the industry. In 1970 the original Carter Family trio was elected to the Country Music Hall of Fame. Maybelle died October 23, 1978, while Sara passed away on January 8, 1979. In 1976 Janette and Joe Carter opened the Carter Family Fold near Hiltons, Virginia, on the site where A. P. had operated a country store in his last years. There, Janette continues to present traditional music shows on Saturdays. The deaths of Helen, Anita, and June (who married country singer Johnny Cash in 1968) left daughter Carlene Carter (from June's previous marriage to country singer Carl Smith) as the sole survivor of the Nashville branch of the musical dynasty.

See also: BRISTOL SESSIONS; COUNTRY MUSIC; FAMILY GROUPS.

—Ivan M. Tribe, *University of Rio Grande*

Mark Zwonitzer, with Charles Hirshberg, *Will You Miss Me When I'm Gone? The Carter Family and Their Legacy in American Music* (2002).

Celtic Influences

The traditions of the Celtic peoples together constitute the single most dynamic ethnic influence on Appalachian music. An estimated 70 percent of the early settlers on the Appalachian frontier emigrated from historically Celtic countries (Scotland, Ireland, and Wales). Many of these settlers intermarried with people from different ethnicities, thus exchanging cultural traditions and widely influencing Appalachian music.

Scottish and Irish settlers brought the baroque fiddle to Appalachia. The recently designed instrument had become widely popular in Celtic countries because it was easily carried and well suited for performing at dances. The fiddle was especially valued in Scotland when bagpipes were outlawed after the Scottish defeat at the battle of Culloden in 1746. American fiddle tunes with Scottish roots include "Hop Light Ladies" (a variant of the Scottish tune "Mrs. McLeod's Reel"), "Leather Britches" (derived from "Lord MacDonald's Reel"), and "Too Young to Marry" (which borrowed the melody from Robert Burns's song "My Love Is But a Lassie-O"). Many traditional Appalachian ballads, including "Wind and Rain," "Gypsy Laddie," "Jack Went A-Sailing," "Butcher Boy," and "Pretty Polly," stemmed from Scottish sources.

The Irish influence on Appalachian music became more prominent after people escaping the potato blight in Ireland immigrated to the United States in the 1840s. Soon many Appalachian musicians began playing variations of traditional Irish hornpipes, reels, and jigs. Reinterpretations of Irish tunes performed at minstrel shows in Appalachia included "Cotton-Eyed Joe" (based on the Irish tune "The Mountain Top") and "Buffalo Gals" ("Battle of the Boyne").

In the mid-nineteenth century, Celtic American music merged with African American music. Appalachian musicians of Celtic ancestry such as Joel Walker Sweeney, Dan Emmett, and the latter's banjo teacher, whose first name is not known but whose last name was Ferguson, were among the earliest white rural folk to learn banjo from African Americans. Emmett helped create the Virginia Minstrels, the first minstrel band that combined the fiddle and banjo.

A strong Scottish or Scots-Irish influence could still be heard in twentieth-century Appalachia in the traditional singing of Jean Ritchie (of Viper, Kentucky), for instance, and in the traditional fiddling of Tommy Jarrell (of Round Peak, North Carolina). Several prominent bluegrass musicians active in Appalachia have acknowledged their Scottish or Scots-Irish ancestry, including Jim and Jesse McReynolds, Howdy Forrester, Fiddlin' Cowan Powers, and Bill Monroe.

A number of folk-revivalist musicians born or based in the region have specialized in exploring the influences of Celtic music and culture on Appalachia. Waynesville, North Carolina–based singer Flora McDonald Gammon, for example, has been noted for her interpretations of Scotland's ballad and song heritage, while singer-songwriter and multi-instrumentalist Tim O'Brien has celebrated Irish-Appalachian cultural connections through a series of acclaimed recordings, including his 1999 album *The Crossing*.

See also: BALLADS; FIDDLE; FOLK MUSIC REVIVALS.

—Cecelia Conway, *Appalachian State University*

Celeste Ray, *Highland Heritage: Scottish Americans in the American South* (2001).

Cherokee Music

Cherokee music, like other Cherokee art forms, was and continues to be an integral part of special ceremonies as well as of daily life. In the past, Cherokee melodic instruments included panpipes, flutes, and whistles, while percussion instruments were either drums or rattles. Both men and women sang, often for the purpose of leading dancing. Over the past three centuries, Cherokee music not only adopted European American and African American traditions (fiddling, shape-note hymn singing, banjo playing, and string-band music), but influenced these traditions in return.

Archaeological sites have yielded various Cherokee melodic instruments, including panpipes estimated at one thousand years old. Flutes, made of river cane or the leg bones of deer, were played to accompany processions of chiefs, to greet visitors, and to encourage success in stickball games. Whistles, made from the leg bones of birds, were sometimes blown by warriors to produce their war call (often, a male wild turkey gobble).

Percussion instruments—drums and rattles—primarily accompanied dancing. Most commonly used by the Cherokee, as well as by neighboring tribes, was the water drum, which could be tuned and which was made from a section of hollowed log partially filled with water and covered by tightly drawn hide. Many rattles were made from gourds containing beans, corn kernels, or pebbles. These gourds were attached to wooden handles and decorated with feathers or rattlesnake rattles. Other rattles were made from turtle shells. Such rattles, after being attached to leather strips, were worn by women during dances. Tied just below the knee, the rattles created a rhythmic accompaniment to keep time with the drumming and singing as the women danced.

Walker Calhoun playing the rattle, Cherokee, North Carolina, c. 1990. Used by the Cherokee to provide rhythmic accompaniment for dancing, rattles were generally made from dried gourds filled with beans, corn kernels, or pebbles and were attached to wooden handles and decorated.

Cherokee men sang to lead dances (the Bear Dance, the Eagle Dance, the Quail Dance, and the Horse Dance) in various traditional ceremonies. Their songs, often pentatonic and major keyed, frequently were made up of short sections comprised of phrases sung four or seven times, the sacred numbers of the Cherokee. During dances, songs might begin and end with a shout or a whoop. Some dance songs followed a call-and-response pattern, with one person leading the song and dance and the rest of the group answering in short musical phrases.

Other traditional uses of song included the singing of prayer formulas. In the late nineteenth century, ethnologist James Mooney documented medicine formulas sung by shamans in healing rituals. Songs documented by Mooney were also associated with the going-to-water and sweat lodge ceremonies.

In the eighteenth century, new instruments were incorporated into Cherokee music. At the height of the deerskin trade, Scottish and English traders introduced fiddle playing to the Cherokee. By the early nineteenth century, tribe members were learning Christian hymns from Moravian, Presbyterian, and Baptist missionaries. Following the introduction of Sequoyah's syllabary in 1821, one of the first books printed in Cherokee language and orthography was a hymnbook. During the Trail of Tears in 1838–39, the Cherokee sang Christian hymns—"Amazing Grace" and "Guide Me, O Thou Great Jehovah"—in their native language while incarcerated in the stockades and while being marched westward. Cherokee people still sing these songs to acknowledge the experiences of their ancestors during the Trail of Tears.

Throughout the nineteenth and twentieth centuries, the Eastern Band of Cherokee Indians (the descendents of those who remained in the mountains of western North Carolina) kept alive traditions of instrumental fiddle music, of hymns in both the Cherokee and English languages, and of older, traditional Cherokee songs and dance music. In the early twentieth century, Cherokee fiddle playing (via such Cherokee fiddlers as Manco Sneed) influenced nearby white Appalachian fiddle traditions. Hymns in English and Cherokee, often from the shape-note tradition, are heard in the churches of the Cherokee, and those hymns are often performed by gospel quartets (a cappella or accompanied by guitar and bass). Walker Calhoun and others continue to preserve Cherokee songs and dances. Meanwhile, Cherokee carvers carry on the making of river-cane flutes and carved wooden flutes that are still played within the tribal community and in public performances.

Contemporary Cherokee musicians also play a variety of musics other than those of the Cherokee, including powwow-style singing and drumming (a tradition incorporating music from several Plains tribes), as well as old-time music, bluegrass, country, blues, and rock 'n' roll.

See also: CALHOUN, WALKER; CHEROKEE (RACE, ETHNICITY, AND IDENTITY); CHEROKEE RELIGIOUS TRADITIONS (RELIGION).

—Barbara R. Duncan, *Museum of the Cherokee Indian*

Charles M. Hudson, *The Southeastern Indians* (1976); James Mooney, *History, Myths, and Sacred Formulas of the Cherokee* (1992); Frank G. Speck and Leonard Broom, with Will West Long, *Cherokee Dance and Drama* (1951).

Civil War Music

With the Southern states' secession from the Union in 1860–61, excitement spread through the Appalachian region as young men reported for induction into the Union and Confederate armies amid a festive atmosphere. Impromptu dances and parties were common, and music could be heard at all hours. This was a time of great patriotism, confidence, and excitement, and the tunes written and played by new recruits reflected that enthusiasm.

When the call came for companies to leave their communities for the army camps, feelings of uncertainty, apprehension, and resolve increased. Many "leaving home" songs were composed during this period, including "The Southern Soldier," one of the more popular songs among Appalachian soldiers who fought for the Confederacy. "I'll place my knapsack on my back, / my rifle on my shoulder," it begins. "I'll march away to the firing line, / and kill that Yankee soldier."

Music was an important part of everyday life for soldiers in both armies, as many young men brought fiddles, banjos, concertinas, and whistles with them. As they became part of the larger armies, the men of Appalachia were exposed to unfamiliar music, including the martial music performed by drum and fife corps and military brass bands. Appalachian soldiers sometimes heard familiar tunes such as "Listen to the Mockingbird" played with different instrumentation. They were also exposed to the music of men from different ethnic backgrounds as well as to tunes popular in other regions and states. Similarly, Appalachian soldiers introduced comrades not familiar with the region to the musical traditions of Appalachia.

In the course of the war, music publishing houses were established in numerous cities in both the South and the North. Although few of these publishing companies were located in Appalachia, musicians and soldiers from the region learned new compositions such as "Dixie," "John Brown's Body," "The Bonnie Blue Flag," and several versions of "Wait for the Wagon."

The war began in earnest on July 21, 1861, at Manassas, Virginia, where Confederate soldiers routed the Union forces, inspiring happy tunes in Southern homes and in the camps. Songs celebrating the Southern victory and the Confederacy's seemingly bright prospects were written and sung with gusto; one of the most popular of these was "Flight of Doodles." At the same time, Appalachians loyal to the Union expressed their somber attitude with songs of patriotism and resolve such as "May God Save the Union."

The period from the battle of Manassas until the spring of 1862 was the "civil" time of the war. Many Southerners and Northerners alike still hoped for a peaceful resolution to the conflict. This mood was documented in several songs popular during this period (both outside and within Appalachia), including "The Compromise Song."

The battle of Shiloh on April 6–7, 1862, however, destroyed any prospect for an early end to the war. Many songs were written as the true cost of the war became clear. "Brother Green" is an Appalachian song describing the death of a Union soldier. Other songs popular in the region included "Somebody's Darling," "The Vacant Chair," "The Battle of Shiloh Hill," and "Virginia's Bloody Soil."

In Appalachia, as in other regions of the United States, the Civil War proved to be a major inspiration for musical composition. Appalachian Civil War soldiers are remembered for their courage, dedication, and perseverance, and the songs and instrumental tunes composed during the war have made an important contribution to the region's rich musical heritage.

See also: CIVIL WAR (GOVERNMENT); FOLK SONGS.

—Bobby Horton, *Birmingham, Alabama*

E. Lawrence Abel, *Singing the New Nation* (1999); Paul Glass and Louis Singer, *Singing Soldiers* (1968); Irwin Silber, ed., *Songs of the Civil War* (1960).

Classical Composers

In the late nineteenth century, classical music composers initiated a movement (based on late-eighteenth-century European antecedents) to create a distinctively American national music, often incorporating traditional melodies. In 1892 Bohemian composer Antonin Dvorak (1841–1904), who felt that any nation's most important musical legacy lay in its folk songs, came to the United States to head the National Conservatory of Music. Through such works as his *New World Symphony*, which utilized African American spirituals, Dvorak demonstrated to American composers how traditional songs might be used in classical compositions. Composers who immediately followed Dvorak tended to evoke Native American music, yet several composers reinterpreted traditional Appalachian music.

Most classical composers who worked with Appalachian folk materials made arrangements of traditional songs. Arthur Farwell (1872–1952) created a piano setting of "Sourwood Mountain" and Elie Siegmeister (1909–1991) arranged "The Deaf Woman's Courtship" for vocals, while Charles Seeger (1886–1979) and Ruth Crawford Seeger (1901–1953) arranged numerous traditional Appalachian ballads and songs for voice and simple instrumentation. More recently, Robert Beaser (b. 1954) composed the chamber work *Mountain Songs for Flute and Guitar* (1985), which was nominated for a Grammy Award.

Other composers borrowed regional folk melodies and expanded them into orchestral works. Raleigh, North Carolina, native Lamar Stringfield (1897–1959), for instance, wrote *From the Blue Ridge—Symphonic Sketches* and the suite *From the Southern Mountains;* John Powell (1882–1963) composed *From a Loved Past, A Set of Three,* and *In Old Virginia;* Harvey B. Gaul (1881–1945) is remembered for *String Quartet;* and the English composer Frederick Delius (1862–1934) was praised internationally for his orchestral piece *Appalachia* after its debut in 1902. A native of Texas, composer Annabel Morris Buchanan (1889–1983) spent her adulthood in southwestern Virginia, where she collected, promoted, and arranged Appalachian music.

Several more recent composers have based compositions on traditional melodies from the region. For example, John Duarte (b. 1919) composed *Appalachian Dreams* (1999), a five-movement suite based on nine songs collected in southern Appalachia. Oak Ridge, Tennessee, native Edgar Meyer (b. 1960), a bassist and composer, collaborated with fiddler and composer Mark O'Connor and cellist Yo-Yo Ma in producing *Appalachia Waltz* (1996) and *Appalachian Journey* (2000), two best-selling albums that blended those musicians' original compositions with their interpretations of traditional Appalachian instrumental tunes and such popular songs as Stephen Foster's "Hard Times Come Again No More."

Few American classical composers have been as fascinated with traditional music as Aaron Copland (1900–1990). Even in his only full-length opera, *The Tender Land* (1954), in which he does not quote any folk or popular material, Copland simulated folk music styles. In the "Hoedown" section of his 1942 ballet *Rodeo,* Copland based the melody on a Library of Congress field recording of the Appalachian fiddle tune "Bonaparte's Retreat," performed by eastern Kentucky fiddler W. H. Stepp. Copland's most celebrated use of folk music was in his score for Martha Graham's ballet *Appalachian Spring* (1944), for which he composed variations on the melody of the Shaker hymn "Simple Gifts" (also known as "The Gift to Be Simple"). Because of the great popularity of Copland's score for *Appalachian Spring,* "Simple Gifts" was frequently heard in schools, churches, and other venues during the urban folk revival of the 1950s and 1960s.

Composers of opera have generally been less attentive to Appalachian folk music. A notable exception is Carlisle Sessions Floyd (b. 1926), a South Carolina native whose third opera, *Susannah* (1955), while not actually utilizing any folk music, simulated traditional hymns and songs to provide atmosphere for the opera's retelling of a biblical story in an Appalachian setting. Also, renowned German composer Kurt Weill (1900–1950) produced *Down in the Valley,* a 1948 one-act opera written for school productions. Making extensive use of traditional melodies collected in Appalachia, Weill interpolated the title song and four other regional folk songs into his score. Although important as an example of Weill's involvement with folk and folk-influenced materials, the opera, because it was written for amateurs, has generally been overlooked.

Since the mid-1970s, there have been several overt efforts to conjoin bluegrass instrumentation and classical orchestration, including works from composers Phillip Rhodes, Peter Schickele (a.k.a. P. D. Q. Bach), and Newton Wayland written specifically for performance by the McLain Family Band with various orchestras across the nation. Other classical music composers from Appalachia include George Crumb (b. 1929), of Charleston, West Virginia; Ethelbert Nevin (1862–1901), born in Edgeworth, Pennsylvania; and Kenton Coe (b. 1930), of Johnson City, Tennessee.

See also: COE, KENTON; CRUMB, GEORGE; STRINGFIELD, LAMAR; SYMPHONY ORCHESTRAS.

—W. K. McNeil, *The Ozark Folk Center*

Jack Sullivan, *New World Symphonies: How American Culture Changed European Music* (1999).

Cline, Patsy

(1932–1963) Country singer.

Patsy Cline's renditions of country songs played a major role in breaking down the boundaries between country music and pop. Born Virginia Patterson Hensley in Winchester, Virginia, on September 8, 1932, Cline lived in the Appalachian region for much of her life. Cline's identification with her regional roots was evident in her sometimes vigorous altercations with her production team and others over her desire to make country recordings in a more traditional style despite the widespread feeling that her voice was better suited for crossover pop success.

Cline's talent, evident at an early age, was matched by her single-minded pursuit of a career in country music. In 1957 she won the competition on Arthur Godfrey's *Talent Scouts* television show with her performance of "Walkin' After Midnight." Godfrey signed Cline for future appearances on his show, and the song climbed both the country and pop charts when released as a single, making her the first female country singer to have a crossover hit. In 1960 she became a member of the *Grand Ole Opry.* These television and radio venues introduced Cline to a national audience.

Later hits in her eight-year career include "I Fall to Pieces," "Crazy," and "She's Got You."

Cline died on March 5, 1963, in an airplane crash while returning from a benefit with fellow country singers Hawkshaw Hawkins and Cowboy Copas. In 1973 Cline was the first female solo artist elected to the Country Music Hall of Fame. Her sensuous voice and gutsy persona have inspired many subsequent female country singers.

See also: COUNTRY MUSIC; *GRAND OLE OPRY* (MEDIA); HAWKINS, HAWKSHAW.

—Adrienne Hollifield, *Black Mountain, North Carolina*

Margaret Jones, *Patsy: The Life and Times of Patsy Cline (1999).*

Coal-Mining and Protest Music

In the decades following the Civil War, technological advances and industrial modernization accelerated throughout Appalachia as the New South creed became the dominant ideology of the region's political and economic elite. As the twentieth century approached, the subsistence agriculture lifestyle and economy of much of Appalachia gave way to a wage-labor economy based on industrial production, particularly in coal and textiles, but also in timber and chemicals. With the rise of this new industrial Appalachia during the Gilded Age came an increase in social and environmental abuse, and the region's working classes responded with protest music, creating a legacy that is arguably the best-known such repertoire in American labor history.

The difficult early days of the coal industry in Appalachia are well documented in protest-oriented songs. Common topics of songs composed during the early to mid-twentieth century include miners' work-related concerns, safety conditions, the per-ton payment system and the company checkweighman, the quality of life for both men and women, and the difficulty of adapting to such standard coal-camp features as the company store and the scrip and wage-deduction systems. Many songs of the era reflect the often troubled lives of their authors, including Frank Hutchison's "Miner's Blues" (1928), Jim Garland and Aunt Molly Jackson's "Hard Times in Coleman's Mines" (written c. 1910; variants recorded in 1924 and 1939), and Jackson's "Kentucky Miners' Wives' Ragged Hungry Blues" (written c. 1931–32 and recorded in 1939). Three of the most famous songs of the era—Merle Travis's "Dark as a Dungeon," "Sixteen Tons," and "Nine-Pound Hammer"—all had implications of protest.

Coal-mining protest songs have also chronicled workplace disasters that occurred in the region, especially the massive methane and coal dust explosions that sometimes took hundreds of lives. For example, C. L. Luallen's "The Fraterville Mine Explosion" documented the 1902 Tennessee disaster that left approximately 200 dead; James Sinnott's "The Monongah Disaster" (date unknown) and Hazel Dickens's "Mannington Mine Disaster" (1973) documented West Virginia explosions that killed 362 and 78 people, respectively. The 1972 Logan County, West Virginia, Buffalo Creek flood, which took approximately 123 lives, became the subject of several songs, including Doug and Ruth Yarrow's "Buffalo Creek" (1975).

The rise of the labor movement and the accompanying "coal mining wars" that exploded throughout Appalachia (especially from 1880 to 1940) are the subject of dozens of protest songs. Tennessee's Coal Creek War of the early 1890s, which stemmed from the opposition of native miners to the state's use of convict labor in privately owned mining operations, is the topic of a series of pre-twentieth-century song variants, including "Coal Creek Troubles," "Coal Creek War," and "Coal Creek Rebellion" (all authors unknown). Musicians who recorded songs about this uprising include Uncle Dave Macon, Pete Steele, and Dock Boggs. The West Virginia mine wars, from the 1912–13 Paint Creek–Cabin Creek strike to the 1920 Matewan Massacre and the 1921 Battle of Blair Mountain, are the topic of a number of well-known songs, including Ralph Chaplin's labor movement anthem "Solidarity Forever" (1915) and "In the State of McDowell" (c. 1920s) by the prolific West Virginia songwriter Orville Jenks. The "Bloody Harlan" depression years in eastern Kentucky and the mine wars that raged there throughout the 1930s are the subjects of several famous protest songs of the Appalachian coal-mining labor movement. Among these are "Come All You Coal Miners" (c. 1931–32; recorded in 1937) by Sarah Ogan Gunning; Jim Garland's "I Don't Want Your Millions, Mister" and "The Ballad of Harry Simms" (both c. 1930s); and Florence Reece's immortal "Which Side Are You On?" (c. 1931–32; recorded in 1937).

The historical coalfield developments of the post–World War II era are similarly documented in protest song and music. Mine mechanization, job loss, union and industry betrayal and abandonment, and the roving pickets movement, in which miners protested corrupt unions by organizing strikes throughout the Appalachian coalfields from 1958 to 1964, are the subjects, for example, of Jean Ritchie's "The L&N Don't Stop Here Anymore" (1963) and "The Blue Diamond Mines" (1964), Malvina Reynolds's "Clara Sullivan's Letter" (1965), and Hazel Dickens's "Clay County Miner" (1970). Automation, job loss, and out-migration are poetically treated in Billy Edd Wheeler's "Coal Tattoo" (1963). Dickens's "Black Lung" (1970) documents the black lung movement, a successful late-1960s grassroots effort by West Virginia coal miners to gain compensation for financial losses resulting from black lung disease; in "The Yablonski Murder" (1970), she recounts the 1970 killing of Joseph "Jock" Yablonski, a popular candidate for the presidency of the United Mine

Workers, and his wife and daughter by three assassins hired by then-incumbent union president W. A. "Tony Boyle." The female coal miner of the late twentieth century also found a strident and uncompromising voice in Dickens, especially in her feminist manifesto "Coal Mining Woman" (c. 1970s).

The even more environmentally disruptive practice of surface, or strip, mining—which began in the region as early as the World War II years but which dramatically increased during the period from 1950 to 1975 and which continued to be a source of controversy in Appalachia into the twenty-first century—is the subject of numerous protest songs. Among these are Ritchie's "Black Waters" (1967), Wheeler's "They Can't Put It Back" (1966), John Prine's "Paradise" (1971), Jim Wayne Miller's "The Ballad of Jink Ray" (1971), and Gurney Norman's "The Ballad of Dan Gibson" (1973). In 1999 Steve Earle's "The Mountain" became a theme song heard often at rallies against mountaintop-removal mining. Even as the coal industry declined in terms of overall employment, Appalachia's miners and coal-mining culture continued to exert a powerful hold on the consciousness of American musicians, both within and outside the region. Among the many songs about Appalachian coal-mining to appear in the past two decades or so are Dwight Yoakam's "Miner's Prayer" (1985), Earle's "Hillbilly Highway" (1986) and "Harlan Man" (1999), Gillian Welch and David Rawlings's "Miner's Refrain" (1998), and Karen Poston's "Lydia's Song" (2000).

Despite the pervasive influence of coal-related issues in Appalachian protest music, numerous songs from the region have addressed occupations or social issues apart from coal mining. Many songs were devoted to the struggles of poor farmers during the 1920s and 1930s. For example, "Down on Penny's Farm," by the Bentley Boys (recorded 1929), lamented the poverty and powerlessness of tenant farmers exploited by dishonest farm owners working in tandem with corrupt banking, judicial, and political institutions. Another song, "Got the Farm Land Blues," by the Carolina Tarheels (1932), articulated the impossibility of the poor farmer's making a living, given the dishonest policies of landowners, banks, and sheriffs.

Better known are the many Appalachian protest songs addressing textile industry working conditions and strikes, such as those at Gastonia and Marion, North Carolina, and Elizabethton, Tennessee. Other songs of the textile industry documented aspects of cultural life. "Factory Girl," said to be America's oldest industrial ballad, was modified by South Carolina textile worker Nancy Dixon in the 1930s; the song voiced the desire of a working-class factory girl to marry a management-class man to escape her predicament.

The Civil Rights movement of the 1950s and 1960s is the subject of several protest songs associated with Appalachia. Guy Carawan, while working at the Highlander Folk School, then located in Monteagle, Tennessee, in the late 1940s and the 1950s, reworked the old African American sacred songs "We Shall Overcome" and "Keep Your Eyes on the Prize" for striking textile and tobacco workers. Carawan's version of "We Shall Overcome" was adopted by Martin Luther King Jr. as the official theme song of the March on Washington, a central event in the 1960s phase of the Civil Rights movement. Carawan's achievement is indicative of the influential stature and unquestionable dignity of Appalachia's rich legacy of protest song.

See also: COAL MINING (ENVIRONMENT); SECTION OVERVIEW (LABOR).

—Stephen D. Mooney, *Virginia Polytechnic Institute and State University*

Guy and Candie Carawan, *Voices from the Mountains* (1975); Archie Green, *Only a Miner: Studies in Recorded Coal-Mining Songs* (1972); George Korson, *Coal Dust on the Fiddle: Songs and Stories of the Bituminous Industry* (1943).

Cockerham, Fred

(1905–1980) Traditional banjo player and fiddler.

Born November 3, 1905, reared near Low Gap, North Carolina, and later residing in Blues Creek, Fred Cockerham was an influential Appalachian instrumentalist best known as a fiddler. He married Eva Galyean, the daughter of Civil War veteran and fiddler Houston Galyean, who was the source for a local, Scottish-influenced fiddle tune called "The Drunken Hiccups." Cockerham learned the banjo style known as frailing (or framming) about 1912. Later he learned the double-noting clawhammer (drop-thumb) style from Charlie Lowe and Lowe's protégé Tommy Jarrell. Always playing a fretless banjo (at one point utilizing a banjo with a Formica fingerboard made by Kyle Creed), Cockerham performed with Jarrell on short-bow fiddle, achieving a high-pitched intensity and setting the standard for fiddle and banjo music in the Round Peak area of North Carolina. Often one of the musicians played on the high strings while the other played on the low strings; then they would switch.

Influenced by fiddler Arthur Smith in the 1930s, Cockerham adopted the fiddle as his primary professional instrument. Although this modern style was quite different from his earlier music, Cockerham continued to retune the fiddle in the old open-tuned way for tunes in the keys of A and D. His recordings document his modern fiddle style as well as his older approach to the banjo, a style echoing the bluesy bends and slides of that instrument's African American heritage. Cockerham died July 8, 1980, but his influence can be heard in the music of such younger instrumentalists as Gilmer Woodruff, Blanton Owen, and Mike Fishback.

See also: BANJO; FIDDLE; OLD-TIME MUSIC.

—Cecelia Conway, *Appalachian State University*

Coe, Kenton

(1930–) Classical composer.

Kenton Coe is a classical composer whose works have been significantly inspired by Appalachian melodies and themes. Coe's creations—operas, choral works, anthems, film scores, and orchestral compositions—reflect a strong sense of place (in terms of concept and function) and have been performed by major symphonies and other ensembles across the United States and in Europe.

The son of an U.S. Army Corps of Engineers officer and his wife, Coe was born November 12, 1930, in Johnson City, Tennessee. He began his formal musical training at age seven at the Cadek Conservatory in Chattanooga. After moving to Knoxville with his family, he took after-school folk dance classes directed by Ethel Capps, who later became a well-known music and dance instructor. During these sessions, Coe was first exposed to the traditional Appalachian music that would inspire him throughout his career.

The composer graduated with a degree in music history from Yale University in 1953, then spent three years in Europe at the Paris Conservatory and Fontainebleau School studying with Nadia Boulanger. Returning to the United States, Coe took a job as production manager at New York City–based Vox Records and, receiving a MacDowell Colony fellowship, began to work on his first major composition in collaboration with French playwright Julien Green. That work, an opera entitled *South*, was successfully premiered by the Opera of Marseilles in 1965. Staged by the Paris Opera in 1972, it remains the only opera by an American composer ever performed by that prestigious company.

Coe went on to produce numerous other works, including the opera *Rachel* (about the wife of President Andrew Jackson), for which fellow Tennessean and Emmy Award winner Anne Howard Bailey wrote the libretto. Coe has also composed film scores for James Agee Film Project documentaries, many of which explore topics related to Appalachia.

Coe returned to Johnson City in 1974. He received the prestigious Lyndhurst Prize in 1985 and the Tennessee Governor's Award in the Arts (individual artist category) in 1990.

See also: CLASSICAL COMPOSERS; OPERA; SYMPHONY ORCHESTRAS.

—Jill Oxendine, *Johnson City, Tennessee*

Contests and Conventions

Although often thought of as an isolated place populated with stubbornly self-sufficient people, Appalachia has in fact produced a human culture that has long valued harvest celebrations, barn raisings, camp meetings, political rallies, community singings, dances, and family-oriented play parties. The practice of mixing pleasure and work has led to a tradition of fiddlers' conventions and gatherings featuring both recreational and competitive singing and playing.

The first documented fiddlers' contest in America was held in Hanover County, Virginia, in 1736. Such contests soon became widespread and have been a popular part of Appalachian culture for more than two centuries. Among the best known of the regularly held fiddlers' contests in the region was the Georgia Old-Time Fiddlers' Convention staged annually in Atlanta from 1913 to 1935. Each year's first-place winner received a monetary award and was named Georgia state fiddle champion. In addition to the fiddling contest, these events featured noncompetitive entertainment by singers, dancers, comedians, string bands, yodelers, and virtuosos on banjo and guitar. The Georgia Old-Time Fiddlers' Convention provided a launching pad for the careers of such commercial country music pioneers as Fiddlin' John Carson, Gid Tanner, Clayton McMichen, and Riley Puckett.

The oldest Appalachian fiddlers' contest still being held at the beginning of the twenty-first century is the annual Old Fiddlers' Convention of Galax, Virginia. The first Galax convention—sponsored then, as now, by the local Moose Lodge as a fund-raiser—was held in 1935. In addition to awarding prizes to winners in the fiddling contest, the first convention also named winners in banjo, guitar, dulcimer, folk song, storytelling, band, and flatfoot dance competitions. Other categories added in subsequent years include clogging, square dance, novelty, bluegrass banjo, bluegrass band, mandolin, autoharp, dobro/resonator guitar, and bluegrass fiddle. The first convention, a one-evening affair held in the local high school auditorium, filled the house, with several hundred people being turned away. By the late 1990s, the Old Fiddlers' Convention, expanded to a weeklong event and moved to a local park, where it drew more than fifty thousand people a year.

With the increasing popularity of bluegrass in Appalachia and with the evolution of more accomplished styles on other instruments, contests ceased to focus on the fiddle. For example, the Georgia Official State Fiddlers' Convention, held each year in Hiawassee, features competitions in all individual bluegrass instruments as well as in other traditional country instruments and styles.

Historically, some Americans looked upon the fiddle as the "instrument of the Devil" and upon fiddlers as his pawns. For Appalachians who share this view, gospel singing provides an outlet for musical expression. Two different groups of gospel singers have employed local, state, and national conventions as a means of popularizing and preserving their musical styles: the four-shape-note singers, also called fa-sol-la or Sacred Harp singers, and seven-shape-note singers, sometimes referred to as do-re-mi singers. Sacred Harp singing conventions date back to 1845 and the formation of the Southern Musical Convention in Harris County, Georgia.

The oldest of the surviving Sacred Harp conventions is the Chattahoochee Convention, started in 1852, also in Georgia. In its early days, this convention attracted an annual attendance of as many as eight thousand people. Over the next century, Sacred Harp singing fell out of popularity. The last quarter of the twentieth century, however, showed an increase in enthusiasm for Sacred Harp singing compared to the immediate post–World War II years, and several local conventions dating back more than one hundred years, as well as a number of newly formed conventions, were meeting regularly. In 1998 statewide Sacred Harp conventions were held in Georgia, Alabama, Kentucky, and Mississippi. Still, the attendance at individual conventions barely reaches triple figures.

Singing conventions utilizing the more recent seven-shape-note method are more numerous and more heavily attended. While many local seven-shape-note conventions predate it, the oldest statewide convention is the Alabama State Convention, started in 1931. At the close of the twentieth century, Appalachian states holding a statewide convention included Alabama, Georgia, Mississippi, North Carolina, South Carolina, and Tennessee. The national convention of seven-shape-note singers was organized in 1937 as an outgrowth of the Alabama convention.

See also: FESTIVALS, MUSIC; FIDDLE; SHAPE-NOTE SINGING/SINGING SCHOOLS.

—Wayne W. Daniel, *Chamblee, Georgia*

Buell E. Cobb Jr., *The Sacred Harp: A Tradition and Its Music* (1978); Wayne W. Daniel, *Pickin' on Peachtree: A History of Country Music in Atlanta, Georgia* (1990); Herman K. Williams, *The First Forty Years of the Old Fiddlers Convention* (n.d.).

Cooper, Wilma Lee and Stoney

Country husband-wife duo.

Cooper, Wilma Lee (1921–) Country singer and musician.

Cooper, Stoney (1918–1977) Country musician.

Born Wilma Leigh Leary on February 7, 1921, in Valley Head, West Virginia, Wilma Lee Cooper began singing publicly at the age of five in her family's gospel music group. In 1938 the Leary Family Singers achieved national recognition when selected, through regional and state talent contests, to represent West Virginia at the National Folk Festival in Washington, D.C. As a result of this exposure, the family embarked on a career as radio performers, working on stations in Virginia and West Virginia.

In 1941 Wilma Lee married Dale Troy "Stoney" Cooper (b. October 16, 1918, in Harman, West Virginia). A fiddle player who had been hired to work in the Leary family group, Stoney Cooper brought to the act considerable experience as a performer on radio with other string bands. The newlyweds soon struck out on their own, performing on radio stations in the Southeast and Midwest. They joined the *Grand Ole Opry* in 1957. Wilma Lee, as a soloist and with Stoney, recorded extensively for such labels as Rich-R-Tone, Columbia, Decca, Rounder, and Leather. The Coopers' biggest hits were "Come Walk with Me," "There's a Big Wheel," and "Big Midnight Special." Following Stoney's death on March 22, 1977, Wilma Lee continued performing as a solo act, accompanying herself on guitar or backed by an acoustic band, keeping her musical style close to her Appalachian roots. During the latter years of her career, she received wide acceptance among bluegrass music enthusiasts and enjoyed steady work at bluegrass festivals.

See also: BLUEGRASS; DUOS, MALE-FEMALE; FAMILY GROUPS.

—Wayne W. Daniel, *Chamblee, Georgia*

Country Music

Although long associated with rural America, country music continues to thrive in an urbanized, postindustrial society. It was initially popular among working-class people but later attracted more affluent audiences. While the genre had a national following from its emergence in the 1920s, country music has been particularly popular in the South, especially in Appalachia. Early recordings now identified as country were marketed under such names as "songs from Dixie," "old-time tunes," "old familiar tunes," or "folk music." After Al Hopkins in 1925 referred to members of his band as "a bunch of hillbillies from North Carolina and Virginia," record producer Ralph Peer named the group "The Hill Billies," and the term *hillbilly* soon became the popular label for this type of music. The Country Music Association, feeling the term was derogatory, led an effort, successful by the 1950s, to replace it in the public consciousness with the coinage *country and western.* With a broadening of styles and themes, the word *western* was dropped, and the music became known simply as country music.

The origins of country music are diverse: British ballads, music of other European immigrants, native Appalachian ballads, spirituals, gospel music, minstrel and vaudeville songs, parlor songs, work songs, cowboy songs, the blues, and swing. Although most country music performers have been white, their songs and styles were heavily influenced by African Americans.

Commercial country music emerged with the development of radio and the growth of the recording industry in the 1920s. Although some country fiddle tunes had been recorded as early as 1922, most historians date the beginnings of the country music recording industry to the records of Fiddlin' John Carson (from Fannin County, Georgia) and Henry Whitter (of Grayson County, Virginia). On June 14, 1923, Carson recorded "The Little Old Log Cabin in the Lane" and "The Old Hen Cackled and the Rooster's Going to Crow" in Atlanta for the OKeh label. By that date, test recordings of Whitter had already been made. After the release of Carson's recording brought commercial success, Whitter was called back to New York for another session. His recording of "The Wreck on the Southern Old 97," backed by "Lonesome Road Blues," was released in January 1924. Other recording companies decided to tap into the emerging market for "hillbilly" recordings. The Victor label issued Texas singer Vernon Dalhart's cover of "The Wreck of the Old 97" coupled with "The Prisoner's Song," which became the biggest-selling country recording of the decade, with more than one million copies sold by the end of 1925.

Among the most successful of the other country music pioneers of the 1920s were several performers from Appalachia, including Ernest V. Stoneman; Charlie Poole and the North Carolina Ramblers; Gid Tanner, Riley Puckett, Clayton McMichen, and other members of the Skillet Lickers; Dock Walsh; and Doc Roberts. Appalachian natives Samantha Bumgarner and Eva Davis were the first successful female performers in country music. Most of these performers were from southwestern Virginia, western North Carolina, or northern Georgia. A seminal event in country music history occurred in 1927 in Bristol, on the Tennessee-Virginia line, when two of the genre's most famous acts, the Carter Family and Jimmie Rodgers, were discovered during the same field recording session (today known as the Bristol sessions).

Performers from Appalachia were prominent on the nation's leading country music radio programs, the *National Barn Dance* on WLS in Chicago and the *Grand Ole Opry* on WSM in Nashville. The top star of the early *National Barn Dance* was Kentuckian Bradley Kincaid. Other stars of the program, all Kentuckians brought to the station by promoter John Lair, were Lester McFarland and Robert Gardner (Mac and Bob), the Cumberland Ridge Runners, the Prairie Ramblers, and Bob Atcher. The first major star of the *Opry* was Uncle Dave Macon, who in 1938 was replaced as headliner by Roy Acuff; both of these performers were from Appalachian Tennessee. Harmonica player DeFord Bailey, born in Smith County, Tennessee, was the *Opry*'s first featured African American performer, and he inspired the incorporation of the blues cross-harp style into country harmonica playing. Red Foley, from Madison County, Kentucky, hosted the prime-time segment of the *Opry* on NBC radio from 1946 to 1954.

Family groups were common in Appalachian music, and during the early years of commercial country music, family groups from Appalachia—whether brother or husband-wife duos or larger ensembles—were very popular among country music fans. The Carter Family, the Stoneman Family, the Blue Sky Boys, the Delmore Brothers, Lulu Belle and Scotty, and the Louvin Brothers were some of the best known from Appalachia. The music of the close harmony duos and groups, popular throughout Appalachia and in neighboring regions, was influential in the evolution of bluegrass music. Bluegrass was viewed as a new genre of acoustic string-band music and was credited to western Kentucky mandolinist and bandleader Bill Monroe. Monroe's 1945 bluegrass group featured, in genre-defining roles, banjo player Earl Scruggs and guitarist Lester Flatt, both from Appalachia. Bluegrass continues to receive some of its greatest contributions and appreciation from Appalachian musicians and audiences.

Two factors greatly accelerated the spread of country music throughout the nation. One of these was World War II, when southerners—including many Appalachian men—joined the armed forces and introduced their music to their non-southern comrades, many of whom warmly embraced it. The other factor was the migration of Appalachian people, especially those from West Virginia, Kentucky, and Tennessee, into northern and western U.S. cities to work in factories and shops. Cities such as Cincinnati and Dayton, Ohio, and Detroit had whole sections largely populated by Appalachian migrants. Nor was the spread of country music limited by national boundaries. The music would eventually become popular in Australia, Japan, Germany, and Great Britain, among other countries.

Since World War II, Appalachia has contributed numerous important figures to country music. Hank Williams Sr. and Tammy Wynette came from the margins, while Loretta Lynn and Dolly Parton were from the heart of Appalachia. In their accomplished songwriting, the latter two often celebrated their Appalachian heritage. Some important behind-the-scenes figures in the country music recording industry, which was mostly based outside the region, were also from Appalachia. Florence, Alabama, native Sam Phillips played a vital role in fusing country music with the blues to generate rockabilly music in Memphis, while Chet Atkins (from Luttrell, Tennessee) and Billy Sherrill (from Phil Campbell, Alabama) were two of the most significant producers of the lush Nashville Sound, which brought new audiences to country music. Two of the major country music publishing companies were Acuff-Rose, cofounded by Maynardville, Tennessee, native Roy Acuff, and Tree, overseen by Buddy Killen of Florence, Alabama. Numerous Appalachian musicians, including Atkins, Zeke Turner, Hank Garland, Jimmy Day, Buddy Spicher, Vassar Clements, and Charlie McCoy, contributed their instrumental skills to Nashville's mainstream country recordings.

By the 1970s, various Appalachian and non-Appalachian musicians were infusing elements of country and other traditional southern musics into a rock format. While some country rock acts from Appalachia, such as the Earl Scruggs Revue and the Marshall Tucker Band, primarily aimed at a rock audience, other performers from the region—including Emmylou Harris, Ricky Skaggs, Exile, and Alabama—found more success in the early 1980s among country music fans as part of Nashville's neo-traditionalist movement; by the late 1980s, this movement was featuring other commercially successful musicians from Appalachia, including Keith Whitley, Dwight Yoakam, and Patty Loveless. In the 1990s, some Appalachian country music performers, such as Billy Ray Cyrus (from Flatwoods, Kentucky) and Kenny Chesney (of Luttrell, Tennessee), gained crossover success; others, including Parton, Skaggs, and Loveless, recorded in more tradition-influenced styles, garnering critical accolades while also enjoying significant commercial success.

During the 1920s, the country music recording industry focused on the southeastern United States. Not surprisingly, more than 90 percent of country performers born before 1905 hailed from the South, with many originating in Appalachia. As the popularity of the music spread across the United States, the percentage of country music notables emerging from other places gradually increased. For instance, major stars of commercial country music have been born in Canada (Hank Snow, Anne Murray, and Shania Twain) and Australia (Olivia Newton-John). Still, nearly two-thirds of country music recording artists born after World War II have come from the American South. According to one study, Kentucky, Tennessee, and West Virginia generate the nation's highest number of recording artists per capita. Six of the top nine U.S. counties producing country music recording artists are in Appalachia, with Kentucky's Madison, Johnson, and Clark Counties topping the list. Fourth and sixth rankings are held by Appalachian counties in Virginia—Carroll and Grayson—while Sevier County, Tennessee, ranks ninth.

Among the hundreds of country musicians with Appalachian connections, some of the most prominent are Red Allen, Pete "Bashful Brother Oswald" Kirby, Chris Bouchillon, Hylo Brown, Carl and Pearl Butler, Archie Campbell, Bill and Cliff Carlisle, Martha Carson, Earl Thomas Conley, Karl Davis, Uncle Eck Dunford, Barbara Fairchild, Donna Fargo, the Forester Sisters, Hank Garland, Crystal Gayle, Jack Greene, Rex Griffin, Kelly Harrell, Roy Harvey, Bert Layne, Rose Maddox and the Maddox Brothers, Asa Martin, Kathy Mattea, the McCarters, Ronnie Milsap, George Morgan, Jimmie Osborne, Brad Paisley, Hank Penny, Fiddlin' Cowan Powers, Jeanne Pruett, Blind Alfred Reed, Del Reeves, Mike Reid, Jeannie Seely, Jimmie Skinner, Carl Smith, Red Sovine, Uncle Bunt Stephens, Gary Stewart, Mel Street, Harty Taylor, Ernest Thompson, Uncle Jimmy Thompson, Aaron Tippin, Dottie West, Mark Wills, Marion Worth, and Steve Young. Scholarly interest in the history of country music was stimulated by the publication of the so-called "Hill-billy Issue" of the *Journal of American Folklore* (July–September 1965). Since then an increasing number of academic and popular publications have focused on country music, which has become one of the top-selling musical genres.

See also: ALTERNATIVE COUNTRY/AMERICANA MUSIC MOVEMENTS; BLUEGRASS; STRING-BAND MUSIC.

—Charles F. Faber, *Lexington, Kentucky*

Douglas B. Green, *Country Roots: The Origins of Country Music* (1976); Paul Kingsbury, ed., *The Encyclopedia of Country Music* (1998); Bill C. Malone, *Country Music, U.S.A.* (2002).

Cousin Emmy

(1903–1980) Early country banjo player and singer.

The first woman to win the National Old Fiddlers contest in Louisville in 1936, Cousin Emmy achieved national acclaim as a "banjo pickin' girl" from Kentucky. She was born Cynthia May Carver in 1903 in Barren County, Kentucky, near the Tennessee border. Carver began her radio career playing banjo in a string band with two of her cousins; later she taught a young Grandpa Jones how to play frailing-style banjo.

In 1941 Cousin Emmy caught the ears of millions of listeners when she was hired by radio station KMOX in St. Louis. Her visual presence was captured on celluloid when she appeared in two movies: *Swing in the Saddle* (1944) and *The Second Greatest Sex* (1955). In 1947 folklorist Alan Lomax arranged for Carver to sign with Decca Records and also included her music in his anthology of field recordings, *Kentucky Mountain Ballads*. On this collection she played banjo and sang "Pretty Little Miss Out in the Garden" and "I Wish I Was a Single Girl Again."

With the decline of live radio in the 1950s, Carver relocated to the West Coast. In 1961 she was "rediscovered" by the New Lost City Ramblers, whereupon she introduced younger musicians in the urban folk revival to traditional Appalachian material. In 1968 she participated on the collaborative album *The New Lost City Ramblers with Cousin Emmy* (Folkways). One of her compositions, the song "Ruby," was made famous by the Osborne Brothers.

Granted her comedic persona, Cousin Emmy was an accomplished musician who could play numerous instruments, as well as a savvy entrepreneur who held the copyright to all her recordings. She died April 11, 1980.

See also: BANJO; FOLK MUSIC REVIVALS.

—Susan A. Eacker, *Morehead State University*

Creed, Kyle

(1912–1982) Banjo player, fiddler, and instrument maker.

Born September 20, 1912, Andy Kyle Creed was one of the finest clawhammer banjo players and instrument makers in the Blue Ridge Mountains. Whether in solo or group situations, Creed played an accentuated banjo style that followed the melody note for note. He liked to play fiddle tunes on the banjo, and he later became an avid fiddler.

From Surry County, North Carolina, Creed grew up surrounded by traditional music. He married Callie Percy Hicks in 1932 and worked as a carpenter, made instruments, and ran a country store at Piper's Gap, near the Blue Ridge Parkway and not far from Galax, Virginia. Creed became well respected within Appalachia and nationally through performances and recordings. He was part of the Camp Creek Boys, a string band that included Fred Cockerham on banjo and fiddle, Paul Sutphin on guitar, Verlin Clifton on mandolin, Ronald Collins or Roscoe Russell on guitar, and Earnest East on fiddle. Members of the group won many individual and band prizes at the Union Grove and Galax fiddlers' conventions, and together they made two albums in the late 1960s.

Another album featured Creed and traditional fiddler and singer Tommy Jarrell as a duo. Creed's precise, focused banjo playing, ringing with harmonics, influenced Thomas Norman and revivalist musicians such as Tommy Thompson (of the Red Clay Ramblers string band) and Henry Sapoznik. Creed also performed at the Newport and Smithsonian Folk Festivals. He died November 26, 1982.

See also: BANJO; CONTESTS AND CONVENTIONS; JARRELL, TOMMY.

—Cecelia Conway, *Appalachian State University*

Crumb, George

(1929–) Classical composer.

Born October 24, 1929, in Charleston, West Virginia, composer George Henry Crumb acknowledged his indebtedness to traditional Appalachian music and to such folk instruments as the hammered dulcimer, banjo, musical saw, and jug. His early Appalachian environment likely contributed to the lyricism and overall accessibility of his work, to the structure of his compositions, to his interest in international folk music and traditional drama, and to his attention to physical movement (Crumb's work *Ancient Voices of Children*, for example, has been choreographed). Crumb's music has been described as a committed quest for philosophical and emotional balance.

After attending the University of Illinois and the University of Michigan, Crumb taught at the University of Colorado and the University of Pennsylvania. He cited composers Webern, Bartok, Dallapiccola, Messiaen, and Berio as major influences on his own work. In 1968 Crumb received a Pulitzer Prize in Music for his composition *Echoes of Time and the River*. Among his other compositions are *Songs, Drones, and Refrains of Death; Black Angels; Makrokosmos;* and *Quest*. Although Crumb is not usually identified with Appalachia, his work is a reminder of the diversity of musical expression associated with the Appalachian region.

See also: CLASSICAL COMPOSERS; OPERA; SYMPHONY ORCHESTRAS.

—Harry Gieg and Edwina Pendarvis, *Marshall University*

Dance Music

Music for square dancing and buckdancing has been an integral part of Appalachian culture from the early European settlement of the region to the present. Dance music in Appalachia reflects the musical traditions of the region's varied ethnic groups, whether Scots-Irish, English, German, African American, or Native American. Although the music has historically been dominated by men, women have also performed dance music.

The fiddle, introduced by European settlers, was the earliest—and remains the primary—Appalachian musical instrument for dance accompaniment. In the 1800s, dances were held in homes with friends, relatives, and neighbors. Occurring during holidays and family get-togethers or after work gatherings such as corn shuckings, barn raisings, or bean stringings, these "frolics" were common in African American and Native American as well as in white communities. The fiddle was often played solo, providing music for square dancing and buckdancing. Also known as flatfooting or hoedowning, buckdancing was the precursor of clogging. By the 1870s, the five-string banjo, of African American origin, had made its way into southern Appalachia and had been adopted by rural whites as an accompaniment to the fiddle. In the early 1900s, guitars and mandolins were added, though as late as 1917 English folklorist Cecil Sharp documented dances in eastern Kentucky at which music was played solely on fiddle or fiddle and banjo. By the 1930s, dances had moved to public venues, including grange halls, schools, fire halls, and community centers. Adapting to the larger crowds, the dance band grew bigger and louder with the addition of the string bass. The piano, accordion, and four-string banjo, though occasionally found in the South, were more common in northern Appalachia, where the piano was often the primary accompaniment instrument. By the end of World War II, musicians in some communities had begun to use electronic amplification and electric instruments when playing for dances.

While Appalachian dance music of the nineteenth century included a wide variety of reels, jigs, hornpipes, waltzes, schottisches, cotillions, marches, and polkas, few of these musical forms survived into the twentieth century. With the advent of the radio and recording industry, Appalachian music drew on other kinds of popular music, including ragtime, blues, jazz, bluegrass, country, and rock. Nevertheless, traditional fiddle tunes have remained at the heart of Appalachian dance music. Although tune repertoire varies from north to south, reels in 4/4 time (also called hoedowns or breakdowns), typically played at sprightly tempos of 130–50 beats per minute, are the predominant form of dance music in the region, along with some waltzes and two-steps. Some northern Appalachian fiddlers still play a few jigs and hornpipes as well. Among the more common dance tunes found throughout Appalachia are "Soldier's Joy," "Arkansas Traveler," "Leather Britches," "Turkey in the Straw," and "Sally Goodin."

See also: CLOGGING IN COMMUNITY SETTINGS (PERFORMING ARTS); SQUARE DANCING IN COMMUNITY SETTINGS (PERFORMING ARTS); STRING-BAND MUSIC.

—Phil Jamison, *Warren Wilson College*

Cecelia Conway, *African Banjo Echoes in Appalachia: A Study of Folk Traditions* (1995); Cecil Sharp and Maud Karpeles, *The Country Dance Book* (1918); Susan Eike Spalding and Jane Harris Woodside, eds., *Communities in Motion: Dance, Community, and Tradition in America's Southeast and Beyond* (1995).

Delmore Brothers

Early country brother duo.

Delmore, Alton (1908–1964) Singer, songwriter, guitarist, and fiddler.

Delmore, Rabon (1916–1952) Singer, songwriter, guitarist, and fiddler.

Natives of Elkmont, Alabama, Alton Delmore (b. December 25, 1908) and his younger brother, Rabon (b. December 3, 1916), were a popular and influential country music act in the 1930s and 1940s. The sound of the Delmore Brothers combined a close harmony vocal style and sparse instrumental accompaniment.

The Delmores grew up in the shape-note music tradition. After establishing themselves singing gospel in their native area, they signed with Columbia Records and later joined the *Grand Ole Opry;* from 1933 to 1938 they attracted a national following via the weekly *Opry* radio broadcast. During this period the Delmore Brothers had major hits including "Brown's Ferry Blues" and "Fifteen Miles from Birmingham." Their sound consisted of the brothers' intricate and delicate harmonies, backed by Alton's guitar and Rabon's tenor guitar, with each fiddling expertly when needed.

Among the qualities that set the Delmores apart from other brother harmony duos was a more overt African American influence, which especially manifested itself in various blues and boogie numbers. Blues influences appear prominently in the Delmore Brothers' mid-1940s recordings for the King label, on which they augmented their sound with various instruments, including the electric guitar. With Zeke Turner's lower string boogie guitar lines and Lonnie Glosson's or Wayne Raney's harmonica, the Delmores' music anticipated the sound of rock 'n' roll on songs such as "Hillbilly Boogie" and "Freight Train Boogie."

During the early 1940s, Alton and Rabon frequently performed with Grandpa Jones and Merle Travis in a quartet known as the Brown's Ferry Four, which specialized in gospel songs. Alton documented the early half of the Delmore Brothers' history in a fascinating autobiography entitled *Truth Is Stranger Than Publicity* (written 1958–63; published 1977). Rabon died on December 4, 1952; Alton passed away June 8, 1964.

The Delmores left a legacy of memorable songs, many of which became standards, including "Blues Stay Away from Me," "Gonna Lay Down My Old Guitar," and "Weary Lonesome Blues." Both brothers were posthumously elected to the Nashville Songwriters Hall of Fame in 1971 and to the Country Music Hall of Fame in 2001.

See also: AFRICAN AMERICAN INFLUENCES; DUOS, BROTHER; SHAPE-NOTE SINGING/SINGING SCHOOLS.

—Thomas L. Wilmeth, *Concordia University Wisconsin*

Dickens, Hazel

(1935–) Traditional country and bluegrass protest singer and songwriter.

Born on June 1, 1935, in Mercer County, West Virginia, the eighth of eleven children, Hazel Jane Dickens is a bluegrass pioneer. Known for her memorable songwriting and her "hard" singing style blending a cappella Primitive Baptist and bluegrass vocal styles, Dickens has been a role model for many female musicians since the 1960s.

Through her father, Dickens was exposed to old-time banjo playing and traditional Primitive Baptist singing. Growing up in West Virginia, she listened to the *Grand Ole Opry* and local radio programs. She took particular interest in Bill Monroe, the Stanley Brothers, and Molly O'Day, as well as in the duet singing style of such acts as the Louvin Brothers.

In 1954 Dickens joined her siblings in Baltimore, hoping to find work. She quickly became a part of the area's burgeoning music scene, singing with musicians Mike Seeger and Alice Gerrard, among others. Dickens and Gerrard began singing together publicly in the early 1960s and continued to perform as a duo for more than a decade. In 1973 Rounder Records released the landmark album *Hazel and Alice,* which represented the breakthrough of women into the previously male-dominated bluegrass music world and which inspired a number of women to make their own contributions to bluegrass, folk, and country music. In 1996 Smithsonian Folkways reissued the duo's early work as *Hazel Dickens and Alice Gerrard: Pioneering Women of Bluegrass.*

Dickens gained wide respect for her work as a songwriter, composing such songs as "West Virginia, My Home," "Working Girl Blues," "The Mannington Mine Disaster," and "Mama's Hand." The latter won Song of the Year in 1996 from the International Bluegrass Music Association. In 1999 country music star Dolly Parton recorded one of Dickens's songs, "A Few Old Memories." Dickens has also had a major impact as a solo performer.

Dickens's dedication to the cause of the working poor—particularly coal miners and members of labor unions, welfare rights organizations, and women's groups—is felt in the songs she has written and in her numerous benefit concerts. Especially notable are the songs she wrote and performed in the documentary film *Harlan County, USA* (1976), as well as her performance in the movie *Matewan* (1987).

The subject of an Appalshop documentary, *Hazel Dickens: It's Hard to Tell the Singer from the Song* (2000), Dickens was awarded an honorary Doctor of Humanities in 1998 by Shepherd College (Shepherdstown, West Virginia). In 1994 she received the Award of Merit from the International Bluegrass Music Association; the next year, she was inducted into the Society for the Preservation of Bluegrass Music in America's Preservation Hall of Greats, and in 2001 she was awarded the prestigious National Heritage Fellowship.

See also: BLUEGRASS; COAL-MINING AND PROTEST MUSIC; FOLK MUSIC REVIVALS.

—Linda Tate, *Shepherd University*

Neil V. Rosenberg, Alice Gerrard, and Hazel Dickens, liner notes, *Hazel Dickens and Alice Gerrard: Pioneering Women of Bluegrass* (1996); Charles K. Wolfe, liner notes, *Hazel and Alice* (1995).

Dickens, Little Jimmy

(1920–) Country singer.

James Cecil Dickens was born on December 19, 1920, in Bolt, a coal camp in West Virginia. The youngest in a family of thirteen children, he adopted the stage name "Little Jimmy" because of his small physical stature. With sentimental songs and brash humor, Dickens helped create popular images (while reinforcing stereotypes) of Appalachian life.

Dickens began his radio career by walking several miles daily to Beckley, West Virginia, to open a morning broadcast with an imitation of a rooster's crowing. His musical talent soon improved his prospects, and he moved from one radio station to another until, in 1948, he was signed by Columbia Records and soon afterward joined the *Grand Ole Opry*. He left the *Opry* in 1957 but rejoined in 1975.

Dickens is more often remembered for his humorous, up-tempo novelty songs than for his sentimental slow numbers. If his music is predictable, with similar bass lines and harmonics and the simplest of syncopated rhythms on many recordings, his lyrics are often imaginative. Some of his songs—"Take an Old, Cold Tater (and Wait)," "A-Sleeping at the Foot of the Bed," and "I'm Little but I'm Loud"—communicate a notion of Appalachian life as one of good-spirited adaptation to material hardship, but these recordings were overshadowed by his surprising 1965 crossover hit, the novelty song "May the Bird of Paradise Fly up Your Nose."

In 1983 the Country Music Association named Dickens to the Country Music Hall of Fame. He continued to be a favorite at the *Opry* through the 1990s.

See also: COUNTRY MUSIC; *GRAND OLE OPRY* (MEDIA).

—Harry Gieg and Edwina Pendarvis, *Marshall University*

Dobro/Resonator Guitar

Dobro is the brand name of a guitar-derived line of instruments owned by the Gibson Musical Instruments company, but the term is used generically for similarly styled resonator-equipped instruments from other builders. Appalachian musicians from the 1920s through the 1950s integrated Hawaiian and blues steel-guitar influences into a distinctively country style that not only informs modern-day electric pedal-steel playing but also plays an integral role in the primarily acoustic tradition-based dobro styles popular in Appalachia.

The resonator guitar was developed in California by Slovak immigrants John and Rudy Dopyera, who sought to mechanically amplify the acoustic flat-top steel-string guitar. In 1926 the Dopyera Brothers created the first resonator guitars featuring a metal body and three resonator cones. These were manufactured by the National String Instrument Corporation, from which the Dopyeras departed in 1929 to set up the Dobro Corporation. Most of the instruments produced by the latter company were wooden-bodied single-cone resonator guitars. Later, the generic nomenclature *dobro* was often employed in reference to all such wooden-bodied instruments. However, the Dobro Corporation also made steel-bodied instruments, and the Dopyeras used resonators on some of these as well.

With either twelve or fourteen frets on the neck beyond the body, resonator guitars come in square- and round-neck cross-section models, with the former suited exclusively for steel playing with a metallic slide. Generally, metal-bodied resonator instruments have been preferred in Hawaiian- or blues-influenced contexts, while wooden-bodied ones, with their mellower tone, have been favored in bluegrass and country music.

Cliff Carlisle, of Taylorsville, Kentucky, is generally regarded as the first resonator guitar player on country music recordings. He started out playing "lap-style" with a steel bar on a Martin flat-top guitar, then turned to a metal-bodied National guitar, before moving to a wooden-bodied Dobro. Carlisle backed up Jimmie Rodgers and also recorded prolifically on his own and with his brother Bill Carlisle, playing in a strongly blues-influenced style.

The early development of a distinctly country music style on the resonator guitar can be traced to the Hawaiian-style guitarist Dave Trask, who is credited with introducing the instrument to Appalachia in the mid-1930s after moving from San Francisco to Knoxville, Tennessee. Trask's student, Clell Summey, of Sevier County, Tennessee, recorded the original dobro parts on two Roy Acuff hits, "The Great Speckled Bird" and "Wabash Cannonball," in 1936, and in 1938 Summey became the first musician to play the instrument on the *Grand Ole Opry*. (He went on to pioneer the electric steel guitar on the *Opry* with Pee Wee King and to achieve greater fame as the comedic character Cousin Jody.) Summey's replacement in Acuff's group, Beecher Ray "Pete" Kirby (also of Sevier County and better known by his stage name, "Bashful Brother Oswald"), is more often credited with making the resonator guitar a part of the traditional acoustic country sound (he was playing a metal-bodied National guitar, not a Dobro, at the time of his recruitment in Acuff's unit).

Over the next two decades, the widespread popularity of the electric steel guitar in country music relegated the resonator guitar to more traditional, acoustic-based music. Several Appalachian dobro players—including Speedy Krise (playing with Molly O'Day), Ray "Duck" Adkins (with Carl Story and Johnnie and Jack), and Deacon Brumfield (with Alex Campbell and Ola Belle Reed)—made significant stylistic contributions during this period.

The next significant development on the instrument was in 1955, when the dobro was first featured on a bluegrass recording. Buck "Uncle Josh" Graves, playing with Lester Flatt and Earl Scruggs, gave the instrument a new fleshed-out sound by adapting three-finger banjo rolls learned from Scruggs to the resonator guitar. The dobro soon became an instrument strongly associated with bluegrass music.

The 1996 Grammy-winning album *The Great Dobro Sessions* brought Appalachian dobro pioneers Kirby and Graves together with significant subsequent stylists from across the United States. Influential Appalachian players who did not participate in the project, including multi-instrumentalist Norman Blake (from Chattanooga, Tennessee) and Ed Snodderly (of Johnson City, Tennessee), were acknowledged in the album's liner notes. Another dobro pioneer, Tom Swatzell (from Decatur, Alabama), was honored with his own line of signature series instruments (as were Kirby and Graves) by the Gibson Musical Instruments company.

Ever since the advent of the cosmopolitan Nashville Sound in the late 1950s, which displaced earlier, more acoustic traditional country styles, the dobro has been utilized by producers and instrumentalists to create a more down-home sound. Accordingly, many accomplished country session musicians added dobro to their studio arsenals. Innovations on the instrument have continued. Some dobro players, including Paul Franklin, have recorded on an eight-string resonator guitar, and others, such as Mike Auldridge and Jerry Douglas, have utilized the instrument in interpretations of jazz, bossa nova, and Indian classical music. Several players have tried to bring some of the possibilities of pedal steel guitar to the dobro by adding pitch-bending pedals to the instrument. Virtuosos of other instruments have sometimes tried to capture the sound of the dobro, often through playing customized resonator-equipped instruments; such innovations have included Jesse McReynolds's "mandolobro" and banjoist Allen Shelton's five-string "dobro."

See also: BLUEGRASS; COUNTRY MUSIC; STEEL GUITAR.

—Karl Rohr, *Western Carolina University*

Tom Gray, "Dobro: The Resonator Guitar That Refused to Die," *Bluegrass Unlimited* (January 1999); Tom Gray and John Paul Quarterman, *Dobro Guitars: A Pictorial History* (2002); Steve James, "National Anthem: A Musical History of the Resonator Guitar," *Acoustic Guitar* (January 1997).

Dulcimer, Fretted

The fretted dulcimer has long been associated with southern and central Appalachia to the extent that it has variously been referred to as the mountain, Appalachian, or Kentucky dulcimer. The instrument has also been called the plucked dulcimer to distinguish it from the hammered dulcimer, a trapezoidal instrument with a greater number of strings. Although they have separate histories, the two instruments sometimes appear together in folk music festivals and clubs and in popular publications.

Also known as the hog fiddle, music box, and harmony box, the fretted dulcimer is essentially a modified fretted zither approximately thirty-four inches in length and consisting of a narrow three- to six-stringed fretboard attached to a larger sound box. The history of the fretted dulcimer challenges common stereotypes of Appalachian culture since the instrument's development represents innovation rather than conservation.

The evolution of the instrument and its use can be divided into three periods. During the "transitional" period (from around 1700 to the mid-1800s), the instrument emerged in southwestern Pennsylvania and in the Shenandoah River Valley of western Virginia as an amalgam of various European folk instruments (primarily the German *Scheitholt* but also possibly the Swedish *hummel*, Norwegian *langeleik*, and French *epinnete des vosges*). Sound boxes of early versions of the instrument were long rectangles, and frets were placed only under selected strings, offering diatonic modes rather than chromatic scales. No historical records of repertoire or playing styles from this period have been discovered. The popular assumption has been that the fretted dulcimer was used for ballads, play-party songs, and religious hymnody from British tradition and that it required little musical skill. Recent research suggests the instrument was in fact used for a much broader repertoire. Additionally, since there were no instrument books, dulcimer players developed their own playing methods, frequently adapting techniques from other instruments. Drone strings, for example, were utilized to simulate bagpipes.

The fretted dulcimer's form became fixed in the "pre-revival" or "traditional" period (lasting from the mid-1800s to 1940). The standard narrow fretboard was attached to a larger sound box, with localized variants in design. The sound box was generally hourglass- or teardrop-shaped, but oval, diamond, and rectangular shapes were also used. During this period, two instrument makers marketed fretted dulcimers and were responsible for much of the instrument's dissemination within Appalachia. J. Edward Thomas, of Knott County, Kentucky, made dulcimers between 1871 and 1933, many of which he peddled from a mule cart. He also taught his design to a number of other craftsmen at the Hindman Settlement School in Kentucky. Another maker, C. P. Pritchard, of Huntington, West Virginia, manufactured "American dulcimers" and sold strings through mail order. Both makers built hourglass-shaped instruments with three strings. Also during this period, traveling salesmen occasionally carried fretted dulcimers throughout southern and central Appalachia, and instruments entered southeastern Ohio and possibly other areas via canals, trains, and individuals pursuing seasonal labor. The dulcimer repertoire at this time combined folk material with minstrel show tunes, popular sentimental songs, Civil War marching tunes, and, after 1900, gospel, blues, and commercial "hillbilly" music. The fretted dulcimer was also used in some string bands, where the instrument both carried melodies and provided harmony and rhythm (the latter through the slapping of the pick against the strings). During the pre-revival period, the dulcimer was played in scattered pockets, with no evidence of any regional dulcimer tradition existing at that time. Many Appalachian residents considered the instrument a novelty.

In the early decades of the twentieth century, settlement schools, the folk crafts movement, popular literature, scholars (I. G. Greer, Mellinger Henry), and folk music enthusiasts (Andrew Rowan Summers, John Jacob Niles) brought the fretted dulcimer to national attention. These movements encouraged a romanticized view of the instrument as emblematic of an imagined Appalachian culture. Such attention simultaneously encouraged the region's residents to preserve the dulcimer and discouraged them from developing the instrument further.

The third historical period, known as the "revival" or "contemporary" period (post-1940), began when Kentucky-born musician Jean Ritchie introduced the fretted dulcimer to urban folk revivalists. Ritchie published the first major instruction and repertoire book in 1963, and her usual playing style of strumming with a feather quill while noting the strings with a noter (a rounded wooden stick) became the standard approach. Revivalist musicians such as Richard Farina, Paul Clayton, Howie Mitchell, and Anne Grimes also exposed national audiences to the instrument (and to a wider variety of playing styles) in the 1950s and 1960s, as did later recordings and public appearances by traditional players such as the Proffitt, Presnell, and Hicks families of Watauga County, North Carolina, the Melton and Russell families of Galax, Virginia, and other members of the Ritchie family of Viper, Kentucky. Frets were extended under all the strings, and some makers have added frets to allow the playing of chromatic scales. Sophisticated techniques—including utilizing all the strings for melody, playing chords, and fingerpicking—have been developed by Appalachian fretted dulcimer players of both traditional and contemporary music, notably Frank Proffitt Jr. (Watauga County, North Carolina), Clifford Glenn (Sugar Grove, North Carolina), Lois Hornbostel (Bryson City, North Carolina), and Madeline MacNeil (Winchester, Virginia). Most modern dulcimer players emphasize the older British-derived repertoire, but many also play pieces and styles from other cultural traditions, particularly from jazz and Irish music. A few players, notably Don Pedi, of Marshall, North Carolina, use the dulcimer for performing traditional string-band music. The fretted dulcimer is played by both amateur and professional musicians, and numerous recordings, instruction books, and dulcimer clubs exist. A quarterly magazine, *Dulcimer Players News*, has celebrated the instrument since 1975.

See also: DULCIMER, HAMMERED; INSTRUMENT MAKERS AND INSTRUMENT MAKING; RITCHIE, JEAN.

—Lucy M. Long, *Bowling Green State University*

R. Gerald Alvey, *Dulcimer Maker: The Craft of Homer Ledford* (1984); Lucy M. Long, "The Negotiation of Tradition: Collectors, Community, and the Appalachian Dulcimer in Beech Mountain, North Carolina," Ph.D. dissertation, University of Pennsylvania (1995); Ralph Lee Smith, *Appalachian Dulcimer Traditions* (1997).

Dulcimer, Hammered

A multistringed instrument played with mallets, this instrument was traditionally known as the dulcimer, but in recent years, the descriptor *hammered* has been added to distinguish it from the unrelated fretted dulcimer. The hammered dulcimer is a shallow trapezoidal box with 40 to 120 strings arranged in groupings of two to six strings. The two bridges are made of wood but almost always have some sort of covering, such as wire, ivory, or brass.

Prototypes of the hammered dulcimer (known by such names as *santour*) were played in Asia for almost two millennia, and they reached Europe by the Middle Ages. The earliest reference to the instrument's existence in America dates from 1717, when Judge Samuel Sewall wrote of hearing one in Salem, Massachusetts. Hammered dulcimers were fairly common during the eighteenth and nineteenth centuries. Regional styles of construction and playing developed in the Great Lakes region of Michigan and western New York, in the Piedmont of North Carolina, and in West Virginia. Hammered dulcimers were used primarily to accompany dances, most dulcimer pieces being adapted from fiddle tunes. In the nineteenth century, several musicians published hammered dulcimer tunebooks that included transcriptions of dance tunes, minstrel songs, hymns, and popular songs. Some of the tunebooks even included transcriptions of European art music pieces in an effort to move the instrument into the parlor.

Hammered dulcimers faded from view in the early twentieth century. While the urban folk revival of the 1950s and 1960s sparked interest in the fretted dulcimer, the hammered dulcimer was rarely played. By the 1970s, however, several Appalachia-based musicians—including Sam Rizzetta, considered one of the leading makers of hammered dulcimers in the United States—had begun playing the latter. In 1975 Rizzetta, of Inwood, West Virginia, formed the acclaimed group Trapezoid, which introduced the hammered dulcimer to many music fans. Since 1979, Rizzetta has toured and recorded as a solo performer of the instrument; he has also taught lessons at the Augusta Heritage Center in Elkins, West Virginia.

One of the most influential hammered dulcimer performers since the 1970s is Wisconsin-born, Charlottesville, Virginia–based John McCutcheon. A multi-instrumentalist, McCutcheon began playing the hammered dulcimer in the mid-1970s. In 1977 he released the landmark album *The Wind That Shakes the Barley*, which showcased the instrument's versatility by featuring hammered dulcimer performances of tunes from Appalachian, British, and Irish musical traditions. Subsequent Appalachia-based performers on the hammered dulcimer include Evan Carawan (Knoxville, Tennessee), Jim Miller (Hampton, Tennessee), Madeline MacNeil (Winchester, Virginia), and John Mason (Shelby, North Carolina).

See also: DANCE MUSIC; DULCIMER, FRETTED; OLD-TIME MUSIC.

—Eric S. Strother, *University of Kentucky*

Nicholas Blanton, "The Origin of the Hammered Dulcimer Finally Not Explained," *Dulcimer Players News* (February–April 2001); Paul M. Gifford, *The Hammered Dulcimer: A History* (2001); Peter Pickow, *Hammered Dulcimer* (1979).

Duos, Brother

From the mid-1930s into the 1950s, harmony duos—often comprised of two brothers—constituted a major style in country music. Especially popular and influential in the Piedmont and Appalachian regions, such duos in the 1930s generally accompanied themselves on two guitars or on a guitar and a mandolin; by the 1940s, however, additional instruments were often added. Dozens of brother duos flourished via radio and recordings.

The first musicians to popularize the close harmony male-duo style were from Appalachia but were not brothers. Mac and Bob, the stage name of blind friends Lester McFarland, from Gray, Kentucky, and Robert Gardner, from Oliver Springs, Tennessee, won favor with Chicago radio audiences in the 1920s. Their recordings on the Brunswick and Vocalion labels featured traditional and popular ballads as well as hymns. In the early 1930s, two Rockcastle County, Kentucky, natives, Karl Davis and Hartford Taylor, known as Karl and Harty, also attained radio popularity in Chicago and modest recording success nationally (on the Paramount and the American Record Corporation labels). The first actual brothers to become major national figures as a duo were Alton and Rabon Delmore, from Elkmont, Alabama, who joined the *Grand Ole Opry* in 1933 and became widely known for their Bluebird recordings. The Delmore Brothers performed a variety of sacred songs, ballads, and blues-influenced numbers while popularizing such Alton Delmore–composed songs as "Brown's Ferry Blues" and "Gonna Lay Down My Old Guitar." The Delmores' career extended until Rabon's death in 1952; their later repertoire included more modern-sounding material such as "hillbilly boogie" songs.

In 1934 the American Record Corporation introduced the Asheville, North Carolina–based Callahan Brothers. Featuring higher-pitched vocals than the Delmore Brothers, Homer and Walter Callahan recorded several widely popular songs, including "She's My Curly Headed Baby." The Morris Brothers (Wiley and Zeke), from Old Fort, North Carolina, recorded such influential original songs as "Let Me Be Your Salty Dog."

The latter two duos were overshadowed—even within Appalachia—by the Monroe Brothers and the Blue Sky Boys. Bill and Charlie Monroe were western Kentuckians, but they reached their height of popularity through radio broadcasts from Charlotte and Raleigh, North Carolina, and Greenville and Spartanburg, South Carolina, and through recordings on the Bluebird label. Bill Monroe's fast mandolin playing and high tenor distinguished the Monroes' music. The pair broke up in 1938 to pursue separate careers. The Blue Sky Boys—Bill and Earl Bolick, from Hickory, North Carolina—had a mellower sound than the Monroe Brothers, though the Bolick brothers' instrumentation was less dynamic. Like the Delmores', the Blue Sky Boys' career on radio and Bluebird/RCA Victor Records extended into the early 1950s.

In the 1940s, the Bailes Brothers, from Charleston, West Virginia, were a favorite act on the *Grand Ole Opry* and the *Louisiana Hayride*, performing such original songs as "Dust on the Bible" and "I Want to Be Loved." There were four Bailes boys, Homer, John, Kyle, and Walter. Until 1947 the duo was composed of John and Walter; thereafter, Homer performed with John. The end of that decade brought the rise of perhaps the most popular brother duo of all, the Louvin Brothers. Ira and Charlie Louvin (born Loudermilk), from the Sand Mountain region of Alabama, recorded primarily for Capitol Records between 1947 and 1963, when they dissolved their partnership. As *Grand Ole Opry* regulars from 1955 until 1963, the Louvins represented a commercial peak in the brother-duo style.

A few non-brother harmony duos also had notable careers, including West Virginia's Bill Cox and Cliff Hobbs, North Carolina's Whitey and Hogan (Roy Grant and Arval Hogan), and, especially, Tennessee's Johnnie (Wright) and Jack (Anglin), who were brothers-in-law. Many characteristics of the brother-duo style survive in the music of such bluegrass musicians from Appalachia as the Stanley Brothers, the Lilly Brothers, the Goins Brothers, Jim and Jesse (McReynolds), and the Crowe Brothers. Although the brother-duo style has had much less influence in contemporary country music, many contemporary folk musicians have attempted to recreate the sound.

The Everly Brothers—rock 'n' roll pioneers from western Kentucky who worked on radio in Knoxville, Tennessee—displayed reverence for the brother-duo tradition throughout their careers. Their style of harmony singing—modeled on that tradition—proved influential to many subsequent rock and pop performers, including the Beatles.

Women have also adopted the duo style of performance. Most notable have been Hazel (Dickens) and Alice (Gerrard), as well as Ginny Hawker and Kay Justice. Mother and daughter Naomi and Wynonna Judd, who as the Judds became one of the most commercially successful duos in country music history, acknowledged the influence of Hazel and Alice on their own music.

See also: BLUEGRASS; COUNTRY MUSIC; DUOS, MALE-FEMALE.

—Ivan M. Tribe, *University of Rio Grande*

Alton Delmore, *Truth Is Stranger Than Publicity* (1977); Richard D. Smith, *Can't You Hear Me Callin': The Life of Bill Monroe, Father of Bluegrass* (2000); Charles K. Wolfe, *In Close Harmony: The Story of the Louvin Brothers* (1996).

Duos, Male-Female

Male-female vocal duos—often comprised of a husband and wife—were a popular singing configuration in country music beginning in the mid-1930s.

The first and most influential of the male-female duos was the team of Lulu Belle and Scotty Wiseman, who broadcast their music over radio programs on WLS Chicago. Natives of the North Carolina Blue Ridge, the two met and married in Chicago in 1934 and were based there throughout most of their professional careers (except for a brief stint in Cincinnati). Their recordings of such songs as "Remember Me" and "Have I Told You Lately That I Love You" became classics. In an altogether different vein, they performed songs such as "Madame, I've Come to Marry You" as comedy skits playing upon the theme of the battle of the sexes. Lulu Belle and Scotty also appeared in several motion pictures. Even after retiring to North Carolina in the late 1950s, they continued to record and to make sporadic appearances until Scotty's death in 1981.

Four other married couples also helped define the male-female duo style. Eastern Kentucky natives Lynn Davis and Molly O'Day (Lois LaVerne Williamson) married in 1941 and had a successful career as a duo on various radio stations (especially WNOX in Knoxville, Tennessee) and on Columbia Records before shifting to evangelistic endeavors in 1950. Wilma Lee and Stoney Cooper, from Randolph County, West Virginia, performed together from their marriage in 1941 until Stoney's death in 1977. Besides making numerous influential recordings for the Columbia and Hickory labels, the duo performed for a decade on radio station WWVA in Wheeling, West Virginia, and for twenty years on WSM and the *Grand Ole Opry* in Nashville. Kentuckians James and Martha Carson were a popular male-female, mandolin-guitar duo. Based at WSB Atlanta through most of the 1940s, the Carsons recorded sacred songs exclusively for the White Church and Capitol labels until their marriage ended in the early 1950s. Lee and Juanita Moore (from central Ohio and eastern Kentucky, respectively) were another harmonizing couple who became radio favorites—especially at West Virginia's WHIS Bluefield and WWVA Wheeling; the Moores recorded only sparingly and divorced in 1960.

Numerous other male-female harmony duos achieved varying degrees of success on smaller radio stations from the mid-1930s to the mid-1950s. West Virginia alone boasted such combinations as Radio Dot and Smoky (Swan), Ted and Wanda Henderson, Benny and Vallie Cain, Rex and Eleanor Parker, Cherokee Sue and Little John Graham, Doc and Chickie Williams, Charlie and Honey Miller, and the Davis Twins (a brother-sister duo). The male-female duo style has continued to thrive in commercial country music with record companies often matching two of their contracted artists for recordings and live performances. Examples of this include Porter Wagoner and Dolly Parton, George Jones and Melba Montgomery, Conway Twitty and Loretta Lynn, and George Jones and Tammy Wynette; in each of these instances, only the women had Appalachian backgrounds.

The male-female duo sound has endured in such contemporary folk groups as Tim and Mollie O'Brien, from

Wheeling, West Virginia; Mac and Jenny Traynham, of Willis, Virginia; and Carol Elizabeth Jones and James Leva, based near Lexington, Virginia. Musical duos from outside the region—such as Grandpa and Ramona Jones from western Kentucky and Indiana, respectively; Colorado's Ray and Ina Patterson; and Nashville-based Barry and Holly Tashian and Gillian Welch and David Rawlings—have displayed distinctly Appalachian influences in their stylings.

See also: COUNTRY MUSIC; DUOS, BROTHER; FAMILY GROUPS.

—Ivan M. Tribe, *University of Rio Grande*

Mary A. Bufwack and Robert K. Oermann, *Finding Her Voice: The Saga of Women in Country Music* (1993).

Fairchild, Raymond

(1939–) Banjo player.

Raymond Fairchild is known for a banjo picking style that became a standard in bluegrass music. Born March 14, 1939, near Burnsville, North Carolina, he has long lived near the Qualla Boundary, the tribal lands of the Eastern Band of Cherokee Indians in the Great Smoky Mountains. While not officially a member of the tribe, Fairchild is of Cherokee descent, and he greatly values the tribe's cultural heritage.

Fairchild identifies with the Appalachian landscape to such an extent that he often calls his style "mountain music" rather than bluegrass. Speed, clarity, and timing characterize his banjo technique, which, as demonstrated in his signature song "Whoa Mule," includes picking notes between the bridge and tailpiece and bending notes without the use of machine-made Scruggs pegs.

In the 1950s, the young Fairchild honed his craft by playing banjo for tips at the Hillbilly Campground in Maggie Valley, North Carolina. In 1975 he joined with the Crowe Brothers (Josh and Wayne) in forming a bluegrass band, the Maggie Valley Boys; the next year, Fairchild first performed on the *Grand Ole Opry.* Wayne Crowe eventually left the band and was replaced by Fairchild family members Shane, Quentin, and Zane. After 1988, Raymond Fairchild appeared regularly at the Maggie Valley Opry House, which he and his wife created to promote bluegrass music.

The Society for the Preservation of Bluegrass Music of America named Fairchild Banjo Picker of the Year from 1989 to 1991. In 1989 he was inducted into that organization's Hall of Greats. Country singer Tom T. Hall wrote a song entitled "The World According to Raymond," portraying Fairchild as "rough, tough, and free," an embodiment of the Appalachian spirit.

See also: BANJO; BLUEGRASS.

—Adrienne Hollifield, *Black Mountain, North Carolina*

Family Groups

Appalachian music has its basis in families and neighbors playing and singing together, as many of the region's people historically lived in relatively isolated small settlements. Appalachian people as diverse as African American banjoist Uncle Homer Walker, white singer, fiddler, and banjoist Lily May Ledford, and Cherokee singer Walker Calhoun all learned music from their older relatives. The custom of different generations of the same family playing and singing together has continued in Appalachia into the twenty-first century. Folk musician Jean Ritchie tells of her family singing together during work (such as while hoeing corn), while walking to school, and on summer evenings on the porch or winter nights by the fire. The Hammons and Carpenter families of West Virginia, the Hicks-Gentry family of western North Carolina, and the Ritchie and Sexton families of eastern Kentucky were all well known locally for their music. Later, these families achieved wider recognition as folklorists and recording company producers "discovered," recorded, and wrote about these traditional musicians and introduced them to folk festivals.

Historically, if Appalachian women wanted a career in music, they were much more likely to succeed if accompanied by family members. Rose Maddox (born in Boaz, Alabama), Wilma Lee Cooper (Valley Head, West Virginia), Sara (Flat Woods, Virginia) and Maybelle (Nickelsville, Virginia) Carter, and Myrtle "Lulu Belle" Wiseman (Boone, North Carolina) all made their biggest impact as part of family groups, though they were strong musicians in their own right.

Commercial country music has always included notable family groups, many of whom got their professional start by playing on live country music programs on local radio stations. In 1925, the first performers on WSM Nashville's new radio show, soon to be named the *Grand Ole Opry,* were Uncle Jimmy Thompson and his niece Eva Thompson Jones. Other family groups achieved considerable success through commercial records, including groups led by Ernest V. Stoneman and J. E. Mainer. The 1930s saw the emergence of a host of brother duos whose recordings continue to influence both professional and nonprofessional musicians. Most acclaimed were the Blue Sky Boys (Earl and Bill Bolick, from Hickory, North Carolina), the Delmore Brothers (Elkmont, Alabama), and the Monroe Brothers (Rosine, Kentucky). Subsequent Appalachian family groups clearly inspired by these early brother duos included the Louvin Brothers (Section, Alabama), the Lilly Brothers (Clear Creek, West Virginia), Jim and Jesse McReynolds (Carfax, Virginia), and the Stanley Brothers (Stratton, Virginia). More recent family groups on the country music scene have included the Forester Sisters, from Lookout Mountain, Georgia; the McCarters, from Sevierville, Tennessee; Tim and

Mollie O'Brien, from Wheeling, West Virginia; and the Judds, from Ashland, Kentucky. The McLain Family, from Berea, Kentucky, was for many years among the more popular touring groups in bluegrass music.

The most influential Appalachian family group was the Carter Family, from Maces Spring, Virginia. The group consisted of Alvin Pleasant (A. P.) Carter, his wife, Sara Dougherty Carter, and his sister-in-law, Maybelle Addington Carter, and specialized in traditional secular and gospel music as well as new compositions in those styles. All three sang, and "Mother" Maybelle is especially remembered for her exceptional instrumental talent on guitar and autoharp. Later, the Carter Sisters (Maybelle and her daughters, Helen, June, and Anita) continued the family musical tradition. Many later groups patterned themselves after the Carter Family, including the A. L. Phipps Family of Barbourville, Kentucky, who were active in the 1960s and 1970s.

Appalachian families excelled in other types of music as well. The Chambers Brothers, from Lee County, Mississippi, made a name for themselves in soul, funk, and rock in the 1960s. The Marshall Tucker Band—an eclectic southern country rock group from Spartanburg, South Carolina, popular in the 1970s and 1980s—was formed by brothers Toy and Tommy Caldwell and their childhood friends. Gospel groups in particular tend to be made up of family members, usually as quartets or trios. Innumerable local gospel groups comprised of various family members and friends thrive throughout Appalachia, performing at homes, churches, funerals, singing conventions, gospel concerts, and bluegrass festivals. The Speer Family (from Double Springs, Alabama), the Blackwood Brothers (Choctaw County, Mississippi), and the Lewis Family (Lincolnton, Georgia) are white Appalachian gospel groups with national reputations.

Family musical groups are so integral to traditional and commercial Appalachian music that some groups, such as the Harmony Brothers and the Brother Boys, adopt family names though group members are not actually related.

See also: DUOS, BROTHER; DUOS, MALE-FEMALE; GOSPEL MUSIC, ANGLO-AMERICAN.

—Deborah J. Thompson, *University of Kentucky*

Mary A. Bufwack and Robert K. Oermann, *Finding Her Voice: The Illustrated History of Women in Country Music* (1993); Bill C. Malone, *Country Music, U.S.A.* (2002); Gerald Milnes, *Play of a Fiddle: Traditional Music, Dance, and Folklore in West Virginia* (1999); Jean Ritchie, *Singing Family of the Cumberlands* (1955).

Festivals, Music

A festival is a means by which culture can be celebrated, preserved, and represented in a public forum before an audience. In the 1920s and 1930s, building on a heritage of traditional public gatherings (such as agricultural fairs, court days, camp meetings, gospel conventions, community workings, shape-note singings, and fiddle contests) dating back to the eighteenth century, festivals in Appalachia were organized to preserve and celebrate rural life at a time when urbanization, industrialism, and changing migration patterns threatened to transform traditional regional culture.

Influenced by the urban folk revival, festivals in Appalachia have promoted wider appreciation of regional traditions. Despite monolithic characterizations of Appalachia's musical heritage in the mainstream American media, the region has fostered a variety of musical genres and styles. Festivals in Appalachia highlight the true diversity of the region's music by showcasing jazz, blues, Celtic music, rock, Cherokee music, and world music, in addition to the types of folk music more commonly associated with the region. While some festivals, such as the W. C. Handy Music Festival in Florence, Alabama, emphasize regional legacies of specific musical genres, other festivals, such as the Pangaea World Music Festival in Jonesborough, Tennessee, reflect the cosmopolitan tastes in contemporary Appalachia.

Folk festivals across the region, whether they focus on music, crafts, occupations, and/or foodways, display traditional regional culture removed from its usual context; instead, Appalachian culture is repackaged as a generalized example of traditional life for an audience usually comprised of people from the region as well as of cultural outsiders. Festivals must attempt a balance between the need to entertain and the need to educate the public; as a result, organizers may consciously represent certain aspects of folk culture while excluding others.

Early festivals in Appalachia, such as the White Top Festival in Virginia, originating in 1931, and the American Folk Song Festival at Ashland, Kentucky (1932), concentrated on the region's British cultural heritage and excluded other influences. Such an emphasis at these early festivals shaped and altered the repertoire and presentation of traditional musicians. At the height of their popularity, the two festivals each drew as many as twenty thousand participants, including First Lady Eleanor Roosevelt.

Another festival originating during this era, the Mountain Dance and Folk Festival, organized by folklorist and performer Bascom Lamar Lunsford in 1928, projected a more "authentic" representation of Appalachian culture. Based in Asheville, North Carolina, this festival continues to nurture local talent and traditions (though it excluded African American performers for many years) while remaining open to emerging trends. Donald Davidson's novel *The Big Ballad Jamboree*, a fictional portrayal of the Mountain Dance and Folk Festival, depicts the conflicting forces of traditionalism and commercialism that together shaped the festival.

Soon, the concept of the regional festival was co-opted by Kentuckian Sarah Gertrude Knott in the establishment of a national, multicultural event. From its beginning in St. Louis in 1934, Knott's National Folk Festival was guided by idealistic precepts of diversity and democracy informed by scholarship and progressive political ideology. While the festival presented such aspects of traditional Anglo-American culture as fiddling, shape-note singing, and clogging, these folkways were juxtaposed against African American gospel choirs, blues artists, Native American dancers and musicians, Hispanic corrido singers, and Cajun bands, thus foregrounding the wide range of ethnic diversity in America. The National Folk Festival is still produced under the aegis of the National Council for Traditional Arts. The largest annual festival in the United States is the Smithsonian Folklife Festival, held each summer in Washington, D.C., on the National Mall. Under the auspices of the Smithsonian Institution's Center for Folklife and Cultural Heritage, this two-week festival, inaugurated in 1967, celebrates the full range of American ethnic and cultural diversity, with additional representation of various international cultures. The Smithsonian Folklife Festival showcased Appalachian music in 2003.

Whether celebrating music exclusively or including it as one aspect of a cultural milieu, many festivals in Appalachia explore previously underrepresented ethnicities. Festivals that celebrate regional African American cultural legacies include Jazz at the Hill House in Pittsburgh and Multi-Fest in Charleston, West Virginia. Birmingham, Alabama's City Stages festival and Wilkesboro, North Carolina's Merlefest, as well as many smaller festivals in the region, are notable for their eclectic lineups. A number of classical music communities within Appalachia offer festivals that sometimes feature workshops. Universities and institutions hosting educational programs in classical and jazz music often host summer festivals and workshops; these include the Brevard Music Festival at Brevard, North Carolina, and the Jazz Seminar at the University of Pittsburgh.

Music is an integral part of major regional festivals and gatherings that focus on other aspects of culture, such as the Grandfather Mountain Highland Games and Gathering of Scottish Clans, near Linville, North Carolina; the National Storytelling Festival, in Jonesborough, Tennessee; and the Vandalia Gathering, in Charleston, West Virginia. Concurrently, established annual musical events in the region—the Fiddler's Grove Ole-Time Fiddler's and Bluegrass Festival, at Union Grove, North Carolina; summer workshops at the Augusta Heritage Center, in Elkins, West Virginia; and the Swannanoa Gathering at Warren Wilson College, near Asheville—have expanded beyond their earlier focuses to encompass new varieties of musical and nonmusical activities (such as dancing and storytelling), in the process becoming more like festivals. Many cultural organizations in Appalachia sponsor festivals that highlight a single instrument, including the Mountain Laurel Autoharp Gathering, in Newport, Pennsylvania; the National Slide Guitar Festival and Competition, in Brevard, North Carolina; and the Upper Potomac Dulcimer Fest, in Shepherdstown, West Virginia.

Having been shaped by various past models, Appalachian festivals—from small local events such as the Dock Boggs Festival, near Wise, Virginia, to regional celebrations such as Appalshop's Seedtime on the Cumberland Festival, in Whitesburg, Kentucky, to newer festivals with a national following such as Wilkesboro, North Carolina's Merlefest, to the venerable Mountain Dance and Folk Festival—draw tradition bearers, folk interpreters, and audiences together into a meaningful exchange of regional cultural expression.

See also: CONTESTS AND CONVENTIONS; MUSIC ORGANIZATIONS; VENUES.

—Ron Pen, *University of Kentucky*

Loyal Jones, *Minstrel of the Appalachians: The Story of Bascom Lamar Lunsford* (1984); Neil V. Rosenberg, ed., *Transforming Tradition: Folk Music Revivals Examined* (1993); David E. Whisnant, *All That Is Native and Fine: The Politics of Culture in an American Region* (1983).

Fiddle

The fiddle was the chief musical instrument in Appalachia from the eighteenth century through World War I. During this period, the association of the fiddle with dancing—and other related activities—reinforced the feeling among some Appalachian people that the fiddle was connected to Satan and evil, resulting in its nickname, "the Devil's box." Nonetheless, the instrument only gained in popularity, with fiddlers in Appalachia and the lower South forging some of the earliest and most distinctive American musical repertoires and styles.

Ostensibly the same instrument as the violin, the fiddle in Appalachia featured such modifications as a flatter curve to the bridge; insertion of rattlesnake rattles—said to improve the sound—through the f-holes; and frequent use of nonstandard tunings, most commonly A-E-a-e. Old-time Appalachian fiddling techniques include holding the fiddle to the chest, as in European baroque practice; choking up on the bow or gripping it with the thumb under the frog; favoring rhythmic syncopation and vigorous bowing patterns; supplying cross-rhythms by means of a second person beating straw on the strings; achieving drones and double-stopped intervals via frequent playing on two (and sometimes three) strings simultaneously; and playing chiefly, if not exclusively, in first position and holding the fiddle with the left-hand palm resting against the fiddle-neck and the wrist backed up against the joint where the neck meets the body. Fiddlers who play old-time hornpipes as well as bluegrass and more modern music often maintain a more classical hold, utilize the keys of F and B-flat as well as the standard C, D, A, and G, and play higher up the neck.

Although bowed stringed instruments were used in medieval Europe to accompany dances, the modern violin dates from sixteenth-century Cremona, Italy; louder and more powerful than its ancestors, it quickly became a favorite of instrumental virtuosos and classical music composers. Gradually the violin came into use throughout Europe, until it was the predominant dance-accompanying instrument in the eighteenth century at courts and in the countryside throughout Europe and the American colonies. Popular among the upper classes (Thomas Jefferson was an amateur violinist) as well as a lower class of professional musicians, the instrument was also played by slaves and indentured servants.

The violin entered Appalachia with the earliest explorers and settlers. From frontier times into the twentieth century, communal activities such as house raisings and corn shuckings were followed by a frolic, or dance, with a local fiddler supplying the music. Local traditions developed as beginning fiddlers learned from family members and local master fiddlers. Some fiddlers composed tunes in the idiom they had inherited; these compositions seldom were written down, but many passed into oral tradition, and some spread to other areas. Youngsters who had constructed fiddles out of cornstalks turned their hands to crafting wooden violins later in life, and a number of these amateurs turned out commendable instruments.

In Appalachian towns, fiddlers often supplied public entertainment. These trading centers, with their constant streams of people, attracted traveling musicians who contributed new tunes to local repertoires. Some Civil War soldiers from Appalachia carried fiddles; their travels and interactions with soldiers from other regions resulted in an unprecedented musical sharing and cross-fertilization of local styles and repertoires. Returning veterans brought back marches, military music, dance tunes, and programmatic pieces that entered local traditions.

Old-time fiddling in nineteenth-century Appalachia exhibited regional characteristics. Northern Appalachia was heir to a tune tradition found from New England to the Ohio River. Among the entertainers who barnstormed on steamboats down the Ohio were French, Irish, British, and northern European musicians who helped create an elegant, melodically elaborate dance music comprised of jigs, reels, hornpipes, and schottisches. These fiddlers also encouraged a legacy of note-reading and tunebook compilation. Samuel Bayard's book *Dance to the Fiddle, March to the Fife* (1982) contains a northern Appalachian (chiefly Pennsylvanian) fiddle tune repertoire that Bayard collected and notated beginning in the 1920s.

In southern and central Appalachia, Scots-Irish settlers fashioned a different sort of melodic tradition. Favoring the mixolydian modal tunes of their ancestors, Scots-Irish fiddlers played dance breakdowns along with marches and programmatic pieces. Jigs and schottisches fell out of the repertoire, while the "limping" rhythm of old-world hornpipes became regularized reels. Songs and ballads often were accompanied on fiddle, with the fiddler usually alternating a few stanzas of singing with an instrumental interlude. The influence of the military music and marches of the Civil War remained longest in southern and central Appalachia; there, some of the most intense and archaic fiddle styles and tunes have endured.

In those areas of Appalachia with a significant African American population (such as the Cumberland Plateau), African melody types and instrument playing styles, the combination of five-string banjo and fiddle, and a legacy of tunes from African American fiddlers and banjo players all contributed to the development of a type of Appalachian dance music characterized by rhythmic syncopation and the repetition of short melodic phrases. Native American influence on old-time fiddling in Appalachia was likely considerable but has been harder to document; the "crooked," or nonstandard length, tune type may well be of such origin.

As transportation routes improved in the last decades of the nineteenth century, the five-string banjo became common in southern and central Appalachia. The African American presence in the region increased early in the twentieth century with the development of the mining industry, and the guitar as well as the banjo were incorporated into string bands, which usually included fiddle, banjo, guitar, and, later, mandolin. The guitar, strummed in a bass note and chordal style, gave the music an underlying harmonic foundation that contrasted with the lonesome cry or propulsive drive of the solo fiddle and the syncopated dance rhythms of the fiddle-banjo duo.

By the 1920s, Appalachians distinguished between nineteenth-century music and the more modern music of ragtime, jazz, and Tin Pan Alley. The older music—which included sentimental parlor songs and minstrel music as well as traditional songs, ballads, and fiddle tunes—was associated with fiddlers, fiddle contests, and square dances. While some string bands primarily performed the older music, many musicians, particularly younger ones, were absorbing modern influences through the new media—radio and 78 rpm records.

After World War II, with the gradual rise of the country music band sound (featuring electric guitar, pedal steel guitar, and drums), the fiddle's role in country music declined. The instrument remained prominent in bluegrass music, a virtuoso acoustic reinterpretation of old-time string-band music intended for listening rather than dancing. In the 1960s, fiddle-based old-time music entered a revival phase, as dedicated younger musicians—attracted to the sound, style, and repertoire of the older traditional musicians, but raised on the rhythms of jazz and rock 'n' roll, often outside Appalachia or the rural South—transformed old-time music into "festival music." This term refers to the fiddle tunes played in string-band jam sessions at various old-time music festivals in Appalachia. Outside the summer festival season, old-time fiddlers seek out other musicians with whom to jam informally; unlike bluegrass and country musicians, old-time fiddlers neither have, nor seek, commercial outlets. Among the many outstanding Appalachian old-time fiddlers, past and present, are Blind Ed Haley (from Logan County, West Virginia), Tommy Jarrell (Round Peak, North Carolina), Melvin Wine (Braxton County, West Virginia), Benton Flippen (Surry County, North Carolina), Clyde Davenport (Monticello, Kentucky), J. P. Fraley (Rush, Kentucky), Owen "Snake" Chapman (Canada, Kentucky), and Ralph Blizard (Blountville, Tennessee). Prominent bluegrass fiddlers from Appalachia include Kenny Baker (Jenkins, Kentucky), Curly Ray Cline (Gilbert, West Virginia), and Benny Martin (Sparta, Tennessee). Other Appalachian musicians, such as Clayton McMichen (Allatoona, Georgia), Fiddlin' John Carson (Fannin County, Georgia), Vassar Clements (Kinard, North Carolina), Buddy Spicher (Dubois, Pennsylvania), Norman Blake (Chattanooga, Tennessee), Ricky Skaggs (Cordell, Kentucky), Gordon Terry (Decatur, Alabama), and Tommy Jackson (Birmingham, Alabama), have played the fiddle on many commercial country recordings, while Clements, Spicher, and Blake have added fiddle accompaniment to some rock recordings.

See also: BLUEGRASS; DANCE MUSIC; OLD-TIME MUSIC; STRING-BAND MUSIC.

—Jeff Todd Titon, *Brown University*

Jeff Todd Titon, *Old-Time Kentucky Fiddle Tunes* (2001); Gene Wiggins, *Fiddlin' Georgia Crazy: Fiddlin' John Carson, His Real World and the World of His Songs* (1987); Charles K. Wolfe, *The Devil's Box: Masters of Southern Fiddling* (1997).

Field Recording Sessions

For more than seventy-five years, scholars working for the Library of Congress, individuals associated with regional universities, hobbyists, amateur enthusiasts, and commercial companies have all sought to document the rich Appalachian musical heritage on sound recordings. These recordings, numbering into the thousands, range from one-of-a-kind recordings preserved only in archives to recordings reproduced on mass-produced phonograph albums that have sold thousands of copies. While some important recordings of Appalachian performers have been made outside the region, the vast majority have been recorded within Appalachia on back porches and in front rooms, in churches and meeting halls, as well as in temporary studios set up in hotel rooms, rented buildings, and radio stations.

Although Thomas Edison invented the phonograph in 1877, phonograph recordings of Appalachian music were not made until the 1920s. In June 1923, Fiddlin' John Carson, from north Georgia, recorded two songs for the OKeh label, and the commercial success of this recording sparked interest among the makers of Victrola records in "old time" or "hill country" music. Record companies first sought to meet this demand by hiring New York City studio musicians such as singer Vernon Dalhart to imitate the old southern style, but it was soon apparent that many of their customers wanted the real thing. From 1924 to 1928, record companies coaxed a number of Appalachian musicians into traveling to studios in New York or Chicago to record. These musicians included such major figures as fiddler Uncle Am Stuart, banjoist and singer Samantha Bumgarner, singer Henry Whitter, singer and bandleader Ernest V. Stoneman, fiddler Dedrick Harris, guitarist Frank Hutchison, banjoist Dock Boggs, fiddler and singer G. B. Grayson, string bands the Hill Billies and Da Costa Woltz (with Ben Jarrell and Frank Jenkins), and the band led by Fiddlin' Cowan Powers. Such trips were expensive and time-consuming, and many older musicians simply refused to travel. Major record companies soon decided it was to their advantage to go to the musicians, and the era of commercial field recordings began.

By far the best known and most dramatic of these sessions took place in Bristol, Tennessee, in July and August of 1927. However, the first such session to take place within Appalachia was an expedition to Asheville, North Carolina, in late August 1925 sponsored by OKeh Records. Like the later Bristol sessions, the Asheville session was directed by Ralph Peer, a Kansas City–born, New York–based producer who had earlier supervised the first recordings of rural blues in 1920 and of Fiddlin' John Carson. Peer set up a "recording laboratory" in a small room on the roof of the George Vanderbilt Hotel and within two weeks had recorded some fifty-nine masters of local musicians, including Stoneman, Bascom Lamar Lunsford, Kelly Harrell, fiddler John D. Weaver, and other purveyors of what newspaper accounts called "folk lore songs of the mountain land." Although Peer himself told local reporters that "the superior quality of the air" around Asheville made for excellent recordings and that OKeh planned to record there again, this 1925 session would be the only commercial one held in the city. However, some six weeks later, folklorist Robert W. Gordon, later to become the first head of the Archive of Folk Song at the Library of Congress, came into the area with a cylinder recorder and recorded some of the same musicians for noncommercial archival purposes. Despite a vastly inferior sound than the OKeh commercial sides, the 202 cylinders that Gordon recorded featured a wider range of music, including unaccompanied ballads.

By the summer of 1927, Peer, then working for the Victor Talking Machine Company, had acquired new electric carbon microphones developed by Western Electric and had taken his recording crew to Atlanta, Memphis, and New Orleans. On July 22, he and his crew drove into Bristol, on

Can You Sing or Play Old-Time Music?

Musicians of Unusual Ability --- Small Dance Combinations--- Singers --- Novelty Players, Etc.

Are Invited

To call on Mr. Walker or Mr. Brown of the Columbia Phonograph Company at 334 East Main Street, Johnson City, on Saturday, October 13th, 1928—9 A. M. to 5. P. M.

This is an actual try-out for the purpose of making Columbia Records.

You may write in advance to E. B. Walker, Care of John Sevier Hotel, Johnson City, or call without appointment at address and on date mentioned above.

Advertisement for a Columbia Records field recording session, Johnson City, Tennessee, 1928. In the early days of the commercial recording industry, major companies set up temporary studios in strategically positioned towns and cities in southern Appalachia, seeking out and then recording previously undiscovered talent.

the Tennessee-Virginia border, for a two-week stay, renting the second and third floors of an empty building at 408 State Street (on the Tennessee side of that street). For the first week, Peer had scheduled specific musicians he wanted to record, including Stoneman. For the second week, he planned to hold open auditions and see who showed up. Sparked by colorful newspaper stories, musicians from as far as a hundred miles away came to audition, and Peer generated some seventy-six recordings. The results represented a cross-section of Appalachian music: vaudeville entertainers (the Johnson Brothers); gospel groups (Ernest Phipps and his Holiness Quartet); buskers and singers of topical ballads (Blind Alfred Reed); string bands (the Tenneva Ramblers and the West Virginia Coon Hunters); and family groups (the Shelor Family, Mr. and Mrs. J. W. Baker, and the Carter Family). Along with another unknown act, a young singer named Jimmie Rodgers, the Carter Family made the session legendary; within a year, both the Carter Family and Rodgers would have national reputations and see their records become some of the biggest sellers in the new country music industry. Peer did a follow-up session in Bristol in the fall of 1928, which produced an additional sixty-four recordings by some of the groups Peer had recorded in 1927 as well as by Clarence Greene, the gospel-singing Stamps Quartet, two African American musicians named Tarter and Gay, and banjoist Shortbuckle Roark.

Impressed by the sales success that Victor and OKeh had achieved with commercial releases of their field sessions, rival record companies wasted no time in initiating their own "old-time music" series and in sending their talent scouts into Appalachia. In late September 1927, shortly after Peer left Bristol, his former colleague Polk C. Brockman led an OKeh crew into Winston-Salem, North Carolina, for a session that drew such performers as the Aiken County (South Carolina) String Band, Wanda and Ruth Neal, Dudley Vance's Tennessee Breakdowners, Fiddlin' Cowan Powers and his Family, and Crockett Ward and his band (who recorded their well-known version of "Sugar Hill"). In February 1928, the Brunswick-Balke-Collender Company held a session in Ashland, Kentucky, in the back room of Carter's Phonograph and Music Shop on Sixteenth Street. There, artist and repertoire agent James O'Keefe supervised some thirty recordings of such musicians as Lunsford (including the first recording of the song "Mountain Dew"), Clark Kessinger, gospel singers Welling and McGhee, Roy Harvey, the Tennessee Ramblers, Caplinger's Cumberland Mountain Entertainers, and Jack Ready's Walker Mountain String Band. Most of these recordings were issued on the Brunswick label, and some of them sold well, but the company never returned to Ashland.

Victor's archrival, Columbia Records, apparently felt uneasy about following Ralph Peer into Bristol but did not hesitate to set up field recording sessions in nearby Johnson City, Tennessee, in October 1928 and October 1929. In charge of Columbia's program was Frank Walker, who had discovered the Skillet Lickers earlier in Atlanta and who would in later years become the recording supervisor for Hank Williams Sr. Locating his studio in an empty cream-separating station, Walker ran advertisements in the local newspapers asking, "Can You Sing or Play Old-Time Music?" Very few of the muscians who responded to these ads had been at the Peer sessions—a testimony to the depth of musical talent in the Tri-Cities area. In 1928 Walker recorded fifty-seven masters in Johnson City by, among others, the Grant Brothers, Jimmy McCarroll and his Roane County (Tennessee) Ramblers, Richard Greene, and Earl Shirkey and Roy Harper. The following year an additional sixty-five titles were recorded in Johnson City, including some of the best-known recordings of Appalachian music: Clarence "Tom" Ashley's banjo song "The Coo-Coo Bird," Byrd Moore's "Frankie Silvers," and the Bentley Boys' "Down on Penny's Farm." Virtually all of these titles were performed by white musicians, with the exception of "Buttermilk Blues," by black harmonica player Ellis Williams.

By 1929, field recording activity by commercial companies was starting to taper off—the depression would soon curtail such sessions altogether. In August 1929 and again in April 1930, the Brunswick-Balke-Collender Company brought equipment from its Chicago headquarters to Knoxville and set up temporary studios at radio station WNOX in the Saint James Hotel. Several "staff musicians," including fiddler Lowe Stokes and promoter Bill Brown, were hired to augment the local musicians on records. The company's arrival garnered a full page of stories in the local newspaper. Most of the performers in Knoxville came from the east Tennessee–southern Kentucky area and included the popular family band the Tennessee Ramblers, Ridgel's Fountain Citians, blues singers Leola Manning and Will Bennett, the Southern Moonlight Entertainers (comprised of the Rainey Family), and the harmony duo Lester McFarland and Robert Gardner (Mac and Bob). Two especially significant recordings were made by a local black string band headed by fiddler Howard Armstrong (called the Tennessee Trio) and by banjoist and songster Hays Shepherd (billed as the Appalachian Vagabond). The two Knoxville sessions yielded 157 sides, most of them released on the Vocalion label. In October 1929, OKeh staged a session in Richmond, Virginia, recording 92 sides; many of these were of non-Appalachian African American vocal groups, but some important mountain performers made recordings, including Bela Lam and his Green County Singers, fiddler Babe Spangler, and Fields Ward.

All told, commercial companies made slightly more than seven hundred high-quality sound recordings in Appalachia during the 1920s. This figure does not include those made outside the area by Appalachian musicians in Charlotte, Atlanta, New York City, Chicago, Memphis, and other sites. These recordings were not documents designed to preserve a region's music in an archive; they were commercial products that were widely distributed. Extant sales figures suggest that an average commercial release of these recordings sold approximately five thousand copies; more than a few sold in the twenty thousand range. Major hits by the Carter Family sold up to one hundred thousand copies. The 78s on which these recordings were released were playable mainly on Victrolas and were fragile and easily worn out. However, many of the 1920s-era recordings were reissued on LPs in the 1960s and 1970s and subsequently on compact discs; numerous of these recordings are currently available in various historical compact disc anthologies.

Commercial recording of traditional Appalachian musicians by no means ceased in the 1930s and 1940s, but it shifted to centers such as Charlotte and Atlanta. In the meantime, folklorists, inspired by the 1920s work of Robert W. Gordon, used early disc recording machines to document their own research in Appalachia. Of the recordings these folklorists made in the region, few were reproduced or made available on commercial releases, but most were housed in various public archives. In 1937 Alan and Elizabeth Lomax traveled through eastern Kentucky, where they recorded such musicians as banjoist Pete Steele and fiddler W. M. Stepp. The latter's recording of "Bonaparte's Retreat" became so well known it was later incorporated into a ballet by composer Aaron Copland. In 1939 folklorist Herbert Halpert recorded ballad singer Horton Barker, of Chilhowie, Virginia, for the Library of Congress. In 1941 and 1942, Alan Lomax recorded the woman he considered the state's finest singer, Texas Gladden, of Salem, Virginia, as well as her brother, instrumentalist Hobart Smith, of Saltville. In West Virginia, Professor Louis Watson Chappell began a private program of field recording that would last more than ten years. In Tennessee, another professor, William Kirkland, obtained a disc-cutting machine and documented the musical culture around Knoxville. Teams from the Library of Congress did extensive recordings of the Harmon Family in Cades Cove in Tennessee's Great Smoky Mountains. Mary Elizabeth Barnicle and her husband, Tilman Cadle, traveled through the Kentucky coalfields recording union and protest songs. After World War II, a new generation of folklorists entered Appalachia with tape recorders and video recorders. For example, in the 1960s, Thomas G. Burton and Ambrose N. Manning, working from their base at East Tennessee State University, chronicled the ballad singing tradition of the Beech Mountain area in nearby Watauga County, North Carolina.

The late 1940s also saw the rise of a number of independent record companies based in Appalachia. The most successful was Rich-R-Tone, owned and operated by Johnson City businessman Jim Stanton. Rich-R-Tone made the first recordings of several major performers, including the Stanley Brothers, Wilma Lee and Stoney Cooper, Buffalo Johnson, the Bailey Brothers, and the Church Brothers; a subsidiary label, Folk Star, released recordings by lesser-known performers. Acme Records, owned by Clifford Spurlock, of Columbia, Kentucky, flourished in the early 1950s and featured a series of new recordings by A. P. and Sara Carter. Meanwhile, the Blue Ridge and Cozy labels helped document early bluegrass. Through the 1950s, the Shadow label, based in Bristol, Tennessee, released recordings by local musicians on a series of 45 rpm singles.

See also: BRISTOL SESSIONS; COUNTRY MUSIC; RECORDING COMPANIES.

—Charles K. Wolfe, *Middle Tennessee State University*

Tony Russell and Charles K. Wolfe, "The Asheville Sessions," *Old Time Music* (Winter 1978–79); Ivan M. Tribe, *Mountaineer Jamboree: Country Music in West Virginia* (1984); Charles K. Wolfe, "Early Country Music in Knoxville," *Old Time Music* (Spring 1974). Charles K. Wolfe and Ted Olson, eds., *The Bristol Sessions: Writings About the Big Bang of Country Music* (2005).

Flatt and Scruggs

Bluegrass musicians.

Flatt, Lester (1914–1979) Bluegrass singer, guitarist, and bandleader.

Scruggs, Earl (1924–) Bluegrass banjo player, guitarist, and bandleader.

In 1948, after being part of the seminal version of Bill Monroe's Blue Grass Boys, lead singer and guitarist Lester Flatt (b. June 19, 1914, in Duncan's Chapel, Tennessee) and banjo player Earl Scruggs (b. January 6, 1924, in Flint Hill, North Carolina) started their own band, Flatt and Scruggs and the Foggy Mountain Boys, which soon became one of the most popular bluegrass groups of all time.

In 1953 Flatt and Scruggs gained Martha White Flour as a sponsor and shortly afterward joined the *Grand Ole Opry*. At various times the band included such musicians as singers Mac Wiseman and Jim Eanes, fiddler Curly Seckler, and dobro player Buck "Uncle Josh" Graves (who introduced the resonator guitar to bluegrass audiences). In the 1960s, Flatt and Scruggs appeared six times on *The Beverly Hillbillies* television series, and the group recorded the original soundtrack for the show, including the song "The Ballad of Jed Clampett," which became a number one country hit. Under the management of Scruggs's wife, Louise, Flatt and Scruggs enjoyed a successful career in the 1960s urban folk revival scene, and their repertoire slowly moved towards more contemporary material. They benefited from the success of the soundtrack for the movie *Bonnie and Clyde*, which featured "Foggy Mountain Breakdown," a recycled instrumental they had recorded nearly twenty years earlier. After parting in 1969, Scruggs launched a successful career with the Earl Scruggs Revue, a country rock group that included his sons, Gary, Randy, and Steve, while Flatt returned to his bluegrass roots, fronting the group the Nashville Grass, which at one time included future country star Marty Stuart. Flatt died on May 11, 1979. Flatt and Scruggs were voted into the Country Music Hall of Fame in 1985.

See also: BANJO; BLUEGRASS; MONROE, BILL.

—Christian Séguret, *Auxy, France*

Earl Scruggs, *Earl Scruggs and the Five-String Banjo* (1968).

Foley, Red

(1910–1968) Country singer.

Born in Blue Lick, Kentucky, on June 17, 1910, Clyde Julian "Red" Foley grew up in the nearby town of Berea. He was essentially a self-taught harmonica and guitar player, but for a brief time he took singing lessons. Winning a 1927 statewide talent contest helped him get a voice scholarship to Georgetown College in Kentucky, where he received formal training in singing. In 1930 a talent scout from radio station WLS Chicago heard Foley and recruited him for the *WLS Barn Dance*, renamed the *National Barn Dance* in 1933 when it was picked up by NBC.

During his more than three decades in country music, Foley achieved many important accomplishments. Helping to found the *Renfro Valley Barn Dance*, he became the first country musician to have a network radio show, *Avalon Time*, and he hosted the first successful network country music television show, *Ozark Jubilee, USA*. Additionally, Foley helped expand Nashville's nascent recording industry.

Foley's recording career lasted from 1933 to 1968, during which time he had sixty-five chart entries, nine of which reached the number one position. His rendition of Thomas A. Dorsey's "Peace in the Valley" was the first million-selling recording of a gospel song. Foley also scored with pop songs, bluesy numbers, boogies, and novelties. This diversity easily made him one of the most versatile of all country singers. His best remembered songs include "Old Shep" and "Chattanoogie Shoe Shine Boy," the latter a crossover hit topping both country and pop charts. Elected to the Country Music Hall of Fame in 1967, Foley died while touring on September 19, 1968.

See also: COUNTRY MUSIC; *NATIONAL BARN DANCE* (MEDIA); *RENFRO VALLEY BARN DANCE* (MEDIA).

—W. K. McNeil, *The Ozark Folk Center*

Folk Music Collections

At the dawn of the twentieth century, as industrialization was transforming rural Appalachian culture, collectors attempted to preserve regional folk music by transcribing songs in musical notation. Ranging from Lila Edmond's groundbreaking *Songs from the Mountains of North Carolina* (1893) to popular narratives such as Jean Thomas's *Ballad Makin' in the Mountains of Kentucky* (1939), these collections were a potent vehicle for shaping American myths and defining Appalachian identity.

Early attempts to describe Appalachian folklore by nonfiction writers, including Emma Bell Miles's *The Spirit of the Mountains* (1905), were based on representations of Appalachian life by novelists such as John Fox Jr. Miles noted the region's historical connections to British culture, but English folklorist Cecil Sharp's visits to Appalachia between 1916 and 1918 and the subsequent publication of his influential *English Folk Songs from the Southern Appalachians* (1917; revised 1932) inextricably linked the twin concepts of Appalachian identity and British heritage by collecting ballads and songs common to both old- and new-world repertoires.

In the summer of 1915, Sharp, founder of the English Folk Dance Society, met Olive Dame Campbell, who directed his nine-week collecting expedition throughout North Carolina, Kentucky, Virginia, and Tennessee the following year. Since Sharp and his assistant, Maud Karpeles, sought British cultural retentions in Appalachia, they selectively collected Child ballads and a few lyric songs of English derivation. However, Sharp and Karpeles failed to document a wealth of music performed in Appalachia simply because they did not consider dance music and work songs to be as significant as British ballads.

Subsequent collectors and transcribers were almost uniformly outsiders to Appalachia, with the notable exception of Josiah H. Combs, of Knott County, Kentucky. Similar in background to the northern social workers, missionaries, and educators who established a network of missions and settlement schools in Appalachia, these collectors and transcribers published their work in a preservation, performance, or recreational format. Preservation collections such as Combs's *Folk-Songs du Midi des Etats Unis* (1925), Dorothy Scarborough's *A Song Catcher in the Southern Mountains* (1937), and John Harrington Cox's *Traditional Ballads Mainly from West Virginia* (1939) presented melody-line transcriptions with text and scholarly commentary. Performance collections such as Mellinger Henry's *Beech Mountain Songs and Ballads* (1936), John Jacob Niles's *Seven Kentucky Mountain Songs* (1929), and Loraine Wyman and Howard Brockway's *Lonesome Tunes: Folk Songs of the Kentucky Mountains* (1916) presented tunes and texts arranged with piano accompaniment. Recreational collections such as Richard Chase's *Old Songs and Singing Games* (1938) and *Songs for All Time* (published by the Conference of Southern Mountain Workers, c. 1930s) reproduced songs in small inexpensive booklets suitable for group singing.

While they helped to preserve a sense of the melody and text of Appalachian folk tunes, songs, and ballads, these early-twentieth-century collections also helped shape an image of Appalachia defined by Anglo-Saxonism, racism, nativism, and isolationism. In contrast, later collectors attempted to document the evolution of traditional culture in more objective terms based on contemporary methodology. These collections, including Bertrand Bronson's *The Traditional Tunes of the Child Ballads* (1959), *The Frank C. Brown Collection of North Carolina Folklore* (1952–64), and Thomas G. Burton's *Some Ballad Folks* (1978), were more inclusive in their documentation of repertoire, more accurate in notation, more attentive to the bearers of folk tradition themselves, and more expansive in terms of melodic, harmonic, and textual analysis.

See also: BALLADS; FOLK MUSIC REVIVALS; FOLK SONGS.

—Ron Pen, *University of Kentucky*

W. K. McNeil, *Appalachian Images in Folk and Popular Culture* (1989); John Jacob Niles, *The Ballad Book of John Jacob Niles* (1960; reprint 2000); David E. Whisnant, *All That Is Native and Fine: The Politics of Culture in an American Region* (1983).

Folk Music Revivals

At the dawn of the twentieth century, amid industrial exploitation of the region's vast natural resources and abundant labor force, educators and social workers committed to uplifting the region's people extolled Appalachia's wealth of distinctive cultural traditions. In his often quoted 1899 *Atlantic Monthly* article "Our Contemporary Ancestors in the Southern Mountains," Berea College's third president, William Goodell Frost, affirmed the aesthetic value of traditional ballads and advocated the revival of spinning and loom weaving as profitable, wholesome pursuits for Appalachian youth. Under Frost's leadership, Kentucky's Berea College became the epicenter of the Appalachian folk arts and crafts movement.

Emulating Frost, teacher, poet, and folklorist Emma Bell Miles advocated handicrafts as an alternative to factory work for Appalachian people. An enthusiastic self-taught folklorist, Miles was also interested in ballads and play parties (singing games). Miles's evocative book *The Spirit of the Mountains* (1905) strongly influenced the founders of Pine Mountain Settlement School and Hindman Settlement School in southeastern Kentucky.

A cofounder of Pine Mountain Settlement School in 1913, Katherine Pettit was also an avid folklorist. In 1907 eminent Harvard scholar George Lyman Kittredge published ballads and play-party rhymes collected by Pettit in an article in the *Journal of American Folklore*. In 1916 English folklorist and musicologist Cecil Sharp and his assistant, Maud Karpeles, collected traditional ballads and songs from students at Pine Mountain and Hindman (in this era, collecting folk music entailed transcribing lyrics and notating tunes). Among these students was Edna Ritchie, older sister of renowned musician and writer Jean Ritchie, who became a leading exponent of authentic Appalachian music in the urban folk revival that flourished in the post–World War II era.

A lively revival of Appalachian folk music was already underway during Jean Ritchie's childhood, capturing the imagination of educated natives of the region such as Bascom Lamar Lunsford in western North Carolina and Jean Thomas in eastern Kentucky. In 1928 Lunsford established a major festival showcasing regional folk music and dance in Asheville, North Carolina. A scholar, collector, and performer who staunchly rejected hillbilly stereotypes, Lunsford recorded traditional songs for the Library of Congress and also made a few commercial recordings, including one of his classic song "Mountain Dew."

A native of Ashland, Kentucky, Jean Thomas in the 1920s moved to New York City, where she encountered future leaders of the urban folk revival. Returning to Kentucky, she began collecting local folk music and writing popular books about Appalachian musicians. She also established the American Folk Song Festival, which she directed from 1931 to 1972.

Academic folklorists of her day questioned Thomas's scholarship and were disturbed by the undercurrents of racism in her fanciful representations of Appalachian folk culture.

While some promoters of the revival of Appalachian folk music in the 1930s undeniably had reactionary political agendas, other influential scholars and promoters of Appalachian folk music at that time were politically liberal and progressive, while several were unabashedly radical. Teaching English at New York University from the early 1930s through the late 1940s, Mary Elizabeth Barnicle also served as a fieldworker for the Library of Congress Archives of Folk Song and espoused left-leaning political causes, including the Kentucky coal miners' strike organized by the communist National Miners Union. In the mid-1930s, she met and shortly thereafter married Tilman Cadle, a radical Kentucky miner closely associated with union organizers Aunt Molly Jackson, Jim Garland, and Sarah Ogan Gunning, whose powerful protest songs inspired the politically left-wing music group the Almanac Singers (which included future leaders of the urban folk revival such as Woody Guthrie, Leadbelly, and Pete Seeger). In 1947 Barnicle and Cadle moved from Greenwich Village in New York City to east Tennessee. Barnicle taught at the University of Tennessee in Knoxville for almost three years until she retired after having been accused of being a communist. Barnicle and Cadle continued to work with the Highlander Folk School, then located in Monteagle, Tennessee. Using topical songs based on folk music to raise consciousness of social injustices has been an integral feature of the Highlander program since its inception.

Awareness and appreciation of traditional Appalachian music greatly increased between the mid 1950s and early 1960s. The folk music boom created new audiences and markets for performers, instrument makers, and producers. The commercial success of the Weavers, a quartet featuring Pete Seeger on the five-string banjo, inspired the formation of a host of banjo-playing popular groups performing folk-inspired music, most notably the Kingston Trio, but also the Limeliters, the Chad Mitchell Trio, and the New Christy Minstrels. Issued in 1958, the Kingston Trio's first and biggest hit song was "Tom Dooley," adapted from the text of a traditional murder ballad that Frank Proffitt Sr., of Watauga County, North Carolina, had recorded in the field for folklorist Frank Warner in 1939. Folklorist Alan Lomax published the ballad in his 1947 book *Folk Song USA*, crediting Warner rather than Proffitt, and the Kingston Trio learned Warner's rearranged version of "Tom Dooley" from his 1950 Elektra recording. In 1962, after Warner intervened on behalf of Proffitt, the ballad singer finally received a small share of revenue from the hit version.

Proffitt was but one of many Appalachian musicians (known in revivalist circles as "source musicians") who were "discovered" (or "rediscovered") during the urban folk revival in the 1950s and early 1960s. Literally reviving the careers of such older musicians as Clarence "Tom" Ashley, Dock Boggs, and Clark Kessinger (who had recorded commercially during the 1920s), this revival also introduced new and highly appreciative audiences to younger Appalachian performers such as the Stanley Brothers and Doc Watson, who mixed traditional material with contemporary innovation.

The urban folk music boom appeared to have peaked by the mid-1960s, when many young urban musicians previously performing acoustic folk-style material began switching to electric formats and harder rock-oriented styles. However, interest in older and newer forms of Appalachian music was renewed in the late 1960s after the influence of the British Invasion and psychedelic rock began to diminish. Urban non-native folk rock and country rock musicians, such as the Nitty Gritty Dirt Band and the group Old and In the Way, brought a more comprehensive vision to acoustic Appalachian music. Such recording projects as the former band's influential 1972 album *Will the Circle Be Unbroken* featured traditional country music performers (such as Roy Acuff and Maybelle Carter) alongside bluegrass musicians (for example, Jimmy Martin and Earl Scruggs) and eclectic interpreters of Appalachian music (including Doc Watson and Norman Blake). A number of younger revivalist performers during this era maintained an even more traditional stance, interpreting Appalachian music on recordings, at concerts and festivals, and in publications. Some of these performers, such as David Holt, Mike Seeger, John McCutcheon, Alice Gerrard, Wayne Erbsen, and Betty Smith, were not originally from the region, while others—James "Sparky" Rucker, Hazel Dickens, Rich Kirby, and Sheila Kay Adams—were natives of Appalachia. During the 1960s and 1970s, a variety of performance venues, including festivals, conventions, and contests, attracted new and old devotees of traditional music. A resurgence of interest in country music dance halls and music barns also took place during this same period. A noteworthy example is the Carter Family Fold in Hiltons, Virginia, established in 1974 by Joe and Janette Carter to celebrate their family's musical heritage and to promote active interest in Appalachian music and dance traditions. Other notable individual promoters of Appalachian traditional music include John Rice Irwin, founder of the Museum of Appalachia in Norris, Tennessee, which stages the Tennessee Fall Homecoming, a major annual traditional music festival, and master old-time fiddler J. P. Fraley, who hosts an annual festival near his family home place of Denton, Kentucky.

Various organizations and institutions have also promoted interest in Appalachian music, including the John C. Campbell Folk School, in Brasstown, North Carolina; the Jubilee Arts Center, in Knoxville, Tennessee; the Birthplace of Country Music Alliance, in Bristol, Tennessee/Virginia;

the Blue Ridge Traditional Music Association, in Galax, Virginia; and the Appalshop Center, in Whitesburg, Kentucky. Regional schools, colleges, and universities have also played a substantial role in promoting appreciation of Appalachian music. Warren Wilson College, in Swannanoa, North Carolina, hosts highly acclaimed summer workshops in Appalachian music, as does Davis and Elkins College, in Elkins, West Virginia. East Tennessee State University, in Johnson City, Tennessee, offers a popular bluegrass and country music program, attracting students from across the United States and from various other countries.

Just as earlier urban folk revivals led to the dissemination of traditional Appalachian music (via limited-release recordings from specialized folk labels) and of hybrid forms of regional music (via more commercially successful recordings by major labels), the commercial success of tradition-influenced recordings both by Appalachia-born and non-native performers in the late 1980s led to the emergence of a far wider audience for various Appalachian musics. Dolly Parton, Ricky Skaggs, Patty Loveless, and Ralph Stanley, from within Appalachia, and Steve Earle and Gillian Welch, among non-Appalachian alternative country music performers, have achieved significant commercial success in recent years performing music overtly based on the region's musical traditions. While such musicians cannot rightfully claim to make authentic "folk music," they have surely contributed to increasing the receptivity of mainstream audiences toward more traditional Appalachian music.

After more than a century of rediscovery and revival, Appalachian music has achieved worldwide popularity while remaining firmly rooted within the region, a testament to the tenacity of generations of Appalachian people who have expressed themselves through their traditional music.

See also: FESTIVALS, MUSIC; MUSIC ORGANIZATIONS; OLD-TIME MUSIC; SECTION OVERVIEW (FOLKLORE AND FOLKLIFE).

—Richard Blaustein, *East Tennessee State University*

Neil V. Rosenberg, ed., *Transforming Tradition: Folk Music Revivals Examined* (1993); Jean Thomas, *Ballad Makin' in the Mountains of Kentucky* (1939); David E. Whisnant, *All That Is Native and Fine: The Politics of Culture in an American Region* (1983).

Folk Songs

The term *folk song* is used in two ways by folklorists: first, it is a generic phrase applied to all traditional songs; second, it is a term used to distinguish between narrative and nonnarrative songs in the repertoires of folksingers. *Ballad* is the term applied to traditional songs that tell a story, while *folk song* is used for those songs lacking a connected narrative (these are also referred to as "lyric songs"). Most folk song specialists have followed the assumption that in ballads action dominates over sentiment and that in folk songs sentiment is accentuated over action. In actual practice, though, classification is often arbitrary. For example, Celestin P. Cambiaire categorizes a version of "Wagoner's Lad" as a ballad, while the editors of *The Frank C. Brown Collection of North Carolina Folklore* list "Wagoner's Lad" as a folk song.

Because ballads feature narratives, they are relatively easy to identify and therefore have received considerable study. The first monumental classification system for various types of ballads was Francis James Child's *The English and Scottish Popular Ballads* (1882–98), an attempt to present "every valuable copy of every known ballad." To date, no work performs for folk songs the service that Child's magnum opus and later classification studies provide for ballads. Indeed, the few published works devoted exclusively to nonnarrative songs are collections rather than classification systems.

Because folk songs lack a narrative, they are often thought of as being without shape or meaning. Such a view is inaccurate. Folk songs are coherent and have distinctive characteristics, some of which they share with ballads. Folk song lyrics are organized around a central idea or ideas, and thus the stanzas in folk songs are arranged purposefully. In some instances, lyrics may be sung in any order as long as they contribute to the overarching sentiment of the folk song. In other folk songs, however, stanzas are arranged in a specific order so as to present certain definite ideas. Thus, most versions of "On Top of Old Smoky" begin with the idea of a slow courtship, then discuss the thief-like qualities of a "false-hearted lover," then state why such a love is worse than a thief. Folk songs are usually presented in the first person, meaning that a folk song projects the narrator's opinions.

Often a folk song provides little detail about the places referred to in the song. Also characteristic of folk songs are several types of repetition, a feature they share with ballads. Plain repetition (the simple repeating of phrases or stanzas) and the listing of family members (commonly used in religious folk songs) are the most popular types of repetition used in Appalachia. A folk song is generally advanced by means of a monologue addressed to an unnamed party—often a folk song addresses a lover or, less specifically, all lovers. In the case of some folk songs, especially humorous ones, it is difficult to determine exactly to whom the text is directed. Like ballads, folk songs often rely on formulas, but the latter are much more dependent on "floating" verses—verses that are found in numerous songs and that seemingly fit all equally well. Traditional singers use both formulas and floating verses as mnemonic devices. Because folk songs are more fluid than ballads and have been much less studied, it is more difficult to be absolutely certain about their age. Even so, most lyric folk songs from Appalachia are probably of relatively recent vintage, going back no more than a couple of centuries.

Of the many types of folk songs known in Appalachia, six categories dominate. The largest category includes songs about love and lovers, such as "On Top of Old Smoky." Ranking second in popularity are religious songs, including "Go Wash in That Beautiful Pool." Numerous songs, such as "Billy Shaftoe" and "Go Tell Aunt Rhody," have historically been intended primarily for children, though they are also sung and enjoyed by adults. Other songs, including "Skip to My Lou," "Cindy," and "Old Joe Clark," are generally performed at such social occasions as dances and, in years past, play parties. Although work songs, such as "Roll On, John," are found in Appalachia, folk song collectors have tended to overemphasize them. The sixth major category of Appalachian folk songs is comprised of comic songs, including "The Kicking Mule" and "Watermelon on the Vine."

See also: BALLADS; FOLK MUSIC REVIVALS.

—W. K. McNeil, *The Ozark Folk Center*

Ray B. Browne, *The Alabama Folk Lyric: A Study in Origins and Media of Dissemination* (1979); Leonard Roberts, *In the Pine: Selected Kentucky Folksongs* (1978); Art Rosenbaum, *Folk Visions and Voices: Traditional Music and Song in North Georgia* (1983).

Ford, Tennessee Ernie

(1919–1991) Country and gospel singer.

Born February 13, 1919, and reared in Bristol, Tennessee, Ernest Jennings Ford studied at the Cincinnati Conservatory of Music. After serving the the U.S. Army Air Corps during World War II, he settled in southern California, where he performed on various radio shows as a singer and as a hick comic character known as "Tennessee Ernie."

After signing with Capitol Records in 1948, Ford enjoyed a series of hits, with many of his records crossing over to the pop charts. Some of his biggest sellers, such as "Mule Train" and "The Cry of the Wild Goose," were written by New York City–based songwriters. He also recorded duets with pop singer Kay Starr. For these reasons, Ford was not accepted as a legitimate country singer by many people. Nonetheless, his signature song, "Sixteen Tons," written by Merle Travis, depicted life as experienced by Appalachian coal miners deeply in debt to the company store. Ford's recording of that song remained number one on the country chart for ten weeks and number one on the pop chart for eight weeks. From 1954 through the 1970s, Ford hosted his own television show and/or appeared regularly on other programs.

Ford recorded more than one hundred albums, the majority of which contained primarily sacred music; his 1956 album *Hymns* was among the best-selling albums of its era. In 1964 Ford won a Grammy Award for Best Gospel or Other Religious Recording. His induction into the Country Music Hall of Fame in 1990 marked his final acceptance by the country music establishment. Ford died October 17, 1991.

See also: COUNTRY MUSIC; GOSPEL MUSIC, ANGLO-AMERICAN.

—Charles F. Faber, *Lexington, Kentucky*

Foster, Stephen

(1826–1864) Popular songwriter.

Stephen Collins Foster was born July 4, 1826, in Lawrenceville, Pennsylvania. Few songwriters have had more impact on American popular music. Despite the fact that Foster spent little time in the South, he is identified with an antebellum world he himself knew only at second hand.

Foster spent most of his life in Pittsburgh. He is best known for minstrel songs and "American melodies." Foster wrote two types of minstrel songs: "Ethiopian" and "plantation." Songs of the latter type, despite their heavy dialect and what is now considered racist stereotyping, were Foster's effort to move away from the Ethiopian songs that first earned him fame when performed by the Christy Minstrels, a popular northeastern blackface group that performed faux African American spirituals across the United States. Foster's plantation songs include "Oh! Susanna," "Away Down Souf," "Old Uncle Ned," "Camptown Races," and "My Old Kentucky Home." Later songs of this type, such as "Nelly Was a Lady" and "Angelina Baker," reflect his attempt to portray African Americans more sympathetically.

Foster's "American melodies" tended to be parlor songs influenced by the folk tunes of Italian and Irish immigrants that Foster encountered in Pittsburgh. Such songs, including "Old Folks at Home," "Hard Times Come Again No More," and "Beautiful Dreamer," became popular parlor songs.

Foster's life has been subject to much mythologizing. Although often portrayed as a self-taught bumpkin, Foster had a middle-class education with formal training in music. He approached songwriting with the dedication of a professional, revising his works frequently. His songs were enormously popular, yet he died virtually penniless on January 13, 1864. Because of the lack of effective copyright protection for musical works in the nineteenth century, Foster's career failed to bring him financial rewards. He nevertheless succeeded in writing a much beloved and long-lasting collection of songs.

See also: CIVIL WAR MUSIC; MINSTREL MUSIC/BLACKFACE MINSTRELSY.

—Amy Cortner, *Caldwell Community College*

Ken Emerson, *Doo-Dah: Stephen Foster and the Rise of American Popular Culture* (1998).

Garner, Erroll

(1921–1977) Jazz pianist and composer.

Erroll Garner was born June 15, 1921, in Pittsburgh, where he played piano during the early years of his career. Although reared in northern Appalachia, Garner gained fame after moving to New York City in 1944. He remained associated with the Appalachian region thereafter primarily through touring, usually as the leader of his own trio.

Following a stint with Leroy Brown's orchestra in Pittsburgh from 1938 to 1941, Garner began working in New York, where in 1944–45 he played and recorded with the Slam Stewart Trio. Beginning in the early 1950s, Garner achieved wide recognition as a leader of his own trio. His popularity soon extended beyond the jazz scene to the general public, especially through such compositions as his signature tune, "Misty." He recorded widely for Columbia Records and continued to tour the United States and overseas until 1975. He died January 2, 1977.

A self-taught pianist, Garner is widely recognized as a virtuoso who possessed one of the most distinctive piano styles in jazz. His rhythmic conception was unmistakable (and virtually inimitable); he often stated the beat with left-hand block chords, over which he superimposed behind-the-beat right-hand figures. Another unique aspect of his technique was his highly ornamented approach to ballad playing. Garner was one of the few jazz instrumentalists to develop an individual style that held appeal both for avid jazz fans and for a wider audience.

See also: AFRICAN AMERICAN INFLUENCES; JAZZ.

—Raleigh Dailey, *University of Kentucky*

Gentry, Jane Hicks, and Maud Gentry Long

Gentry, Jane Hicks (1863–1925) Traditional singer and storyteller.

Long, Maud Gentry (1893–1984) Traditional singer and storyteller.

Jane Hicks Gentry played an important role in the perpetuation and collection of traditional southern Appalachian ballads, songs, and stories. She was born December 18, 1863, on Beech Mountain in Watauga County, North Carolina, the daughter of Ransom Merritt Hicks and Emily Harmon. Jane Hicks learned her repertoire directly from her grandfather Council Harmon, the renowned source of Jack tales (such as "Jack the Giant Killer"), and from other members of this extended family of singers and storytellers. In 1875 Ransom Hicks moved his family to Madison County, North Carolina, where Jane Hicks married Jasper Newton Gentry.

Jane Hicks Gentry's singing, storytelling, and engaging personality made her a favorite with local schoolchildren and also attracted the attention of a well-known writer and editor, Irving Bacheller, and of collectors of songs and stories. Bacheller wrote short stories and articles based on Gentry's life, most notably "The Happiest Person I Ever Knew," which was published in the nationally distributed *American Magazine* in 1924. In 1916 English folklorist Cecil Sharp collected seventy ballads and songs from Gentry, more than from any of his other Appalachian informants. Forty of Gentry's ballads were published in Sharp's *English Folk Songs from the Southern Appalachians*, and twenty-one were included in Bertrand Harris Bronson's *The Traditional Tunes of the Child Ballads*. Isabel Gordon Carter collected Jack tales, fairy tales, and riddles from Gentry in 1923; fifteen of these tales were published in the *Journal of American Folklore* in 1925, shortly after Gentry's death on May 29. In the town of Hot Springs, North Carolina, a historical marker in front of Gentry's last home, Sunnybank, recognizes the contributions of Jane Hicks Gentry and Cecil Sharp toward preserving Appalachian ballad traditions.

Maud Gentry Long, daughter of Jane Hicks Gentry and Jasper Newton Gentry, was born February 2, 1893, in Madison County, North Carolina. One of that couple's nine children, Long carried on her mother's oral traditions. As a teacher in public schools and at the Dorland Institute, a Presbyterian mission school in Hot Springs, Long was known for her repertoire of songs and stories. She was also one of the first women to be ordained an elder in the Presbyterian Church.

Long was an informant for such folklorists as Annabel Morris Buchanan, Richard Chase, Artus Moser, and Duncan Emrich. The latter collected eleven Jack tales and more than thirty songs from Long for the Library of Congress in 1947. Long died October 29, 1984. Today, Long's granddaughter Daron Douglas carries on the family ballad-singing tradition.

See also: BALLADS; HICKS FAMILY; SHARP, CECIL (FOLKLORE AND FOLKLIFE).

—Betty N. Smith, *Hot Springs, North Carolina*

Betty N. Smith, *Jane Hicks Gentry: A Singer among Singers* (1998).

Gibson, Don

(1928–2003) Country singer and songwriter.

Don Gibson was born in Shelby, North Carolina, on April 3, 1928. By the late 1940s, he was singing with a trio at a local radio station. His singing models were Red Foley, Eddy Arnold, and George Morgan—all had warm, smooth, crooning styles. After making a few unsuccessful early recordings, Gibson started to write songs. Despite major success as a country music hit maker, Gibson continued to consider himself a songwriter first and a singer second.

By the mid-1950s, Gibson was singing over radio station WNOX in Knoxville, Tennessee. He had written his first classic song, "Sweet Dreams," and he had secured a songwriting contract with the Acuff-Rose music publishing company in Nashville. In 1957 he composed, on the same day, the two songs that catapulted him to stardom as a singer:

"Oh Lonesome Me" and "I Can't Stop Loving You." Both were hits for Gibson on the country charts, and the latter song has been recorded more than seven hundred times, most successfully as a pop hit by Ray Charles in 1962. Gibson's songwriting led to his inclusion in the Nashville Songwriters Hall of Fame in 1973.

Gibson had a string of country hits through the 1970s on RCA and Hickory Records. He often worked with Chet Atkins at RCA, where they developed a stripped-down version of the lush Nashville Sound that dominated mainstream country music at the time. Gibson, though capable of a smooth crooning style, generally preferred a harder, more traditional vocal sound than that of such Nashville Sound singers as Jim Reeves and Eddy Arnold. Elected to the Country Music Hall of Fame in 2001, Gibson died November 17, 2003.

See also: ATKINS, CHET; COUNTRY MUSIC.

—Frederick E. Danker, *University of Massachusetts*

Goose Creek Symphony

Country rock group.

Deeply rooted in the music and lore of the Cumberland Plateau and consistently led by Charles Gearheart (a native of the community of Goose Creek, in Floyd County, Kentucky) and Paul Spradlin (born in Narvue, Ohio), the group known as Goose Creek Symphony contributed a distinctly Appalachian flavor to the country rock movement of the late 1960s and early 1970s. Disbanding in the late 1970s and re-forming a decade later, the group received recognition and acclaim in the 1990s from adherents of the alternative country and Americana movements.

Goose Creek Symphony was formed in Phoenix, Arizona, during the height of the counterculture movement, and its first five albums—recorded during its original 1968–75 incarnation—exuded a distinctly West Coast "hippie rock" sensibility. Yet from the beginning, Goose Creek's sound was also significantly influenced by Appalachian old-time music, often combining electric guitar and bass with such folk instruments as the fiddle, banjo, mandolin, and Jew's harp. Goose Creek Symphony was noted during its heyday for complex jazz-influenced improvisations, making it one of the earliest jam bands. In recorded and live performances of such songs as "Guitars Pickin', Fiddles Playin'," Goose Creek Symphony blended regional themes and old-time, country, rock, and jazz-influenced styles to create an immediately identifiable sound.

See also: ALTERNATIVE COUNTRY/AMERICANA MUSIC MOVEMENTS; COUNTRY MUSIC; ROCK MUSIC.

—Stephen D. Mooney, *Virginia Polytechnic Institute and State University*

Gosdin, Vern

(1934–) Country singer and songwriter.

Born August 5, 1934, in the small east-central Alabama town of Woodland, Vern Gosdin developed an early love for Anglo-American gospel music and for the harmonies of the Louvin Brothers from the northeastern Sand Mountain section of his home state. With his family, Gosdin sang gospel songs over the radio in Birmingham in the 1950s, and he later moved to California with his brother Rex and joined a moderately successful bluegrass band, the Golden State Boys (later renamed the Hillmen). Also during this period, the Gosdin Brothers sang as a duo and with country rock pioneer Gene Clark.

After dropping out of music for a while in 1972 to open a business in Atlanta, Vern Gosdin traveled to Nashville in 1976 to rekindle his music career. Afterward, he had numerous hit recordings on the country charts—three number one singles and several top ten hits. A cowriter of most of the songs he recorded, Gosdin excelled with songs of lost love and love gone wrong, many of which have an autobiographical cast. With his rich baritone voice and attention to emotional nuance, he is part of the "hard country" or honky-tonk tradition of country music.

His song "Chiseled in Stone," cowritten with Max D. Barnes, won the Country Music Association's Song of the Year award in 1989. Other Gosdin songs, including "That Just About Does It," "Is It Raining at Your House," and "Do You Believe Me Now," are slow ballads of heartbreak that he recorded with gospel-influenced harmony singing, creating a kind of white blues or country soul.

See also: BLUEGRASS; COUNTRY MUSIC; GOSPEL MUSIC, ANGLO-AMERICAN.

—Frederick E. Danker, *University of Massachusetts*

Gospel Music, African American

Modern African American gospel music was greatly inspired by the music of Thomas A. Dorsey of Villa Rica, Georgia. After moving to Chicago in 1916, Dorsey developed the modern gospel sound and wrote much of its seminal material. His songs, notably "Take My Hand, Precious Lord" and "Peace in the Valley," became standards in both black and white churches. Additionally, Dorsey founded the first publishing company for African American gospel music.

Some of the most influential pre-Dorsey gospel performers were from Appalachia, specifically African American groups in nineteenth-century American Missionary Association schools. One such group, the Tuskegee Institute Singers of Alabama, incorporated harmonic patterns borrowed from European musical tradition, anticipating and eventually influencing the African American quartet styles of the 1930s and 1940s. The community quartet tradition that developed in the early twentieth century stood apart from the university "jubilee" style because of its emphatic rhythms and close harmonies. Community quartets spread rapidly during World War I.

One Appalachian area that produced many important black gospel quartets is Jefferson County, Alabama, which includes the municipalities of Birmingham, Bessemer, and Fairfield. That area's style of gospel singing was influenced by R. C. Foster, who moved to Jefferson County in 1915. Musically trained by a Tuskegee Institute professor, Foster formed the Foster Singers, a group that, though never recorded, featured a style of harmony singing that was regionally influential. Group member Norman McQueen, of Bessemer, moved to Chicago and influenced the northern gospel scene. In 1931 he formed an association of more than twenty-five African American gospel quartets that would be the first such groups to perform on live radio. Other important quartet trainers in Jefferson County were Charlie Bridges and Son Dunham.

In 1926 Columbia Records, one of the first companies to make field recordings of black gospel music, traveled to Atlanta and recorded the Birmingham Jubilee Singers, disciples of the Foster Singers. The Birmingham Jubilee Singers' debut record sold almost five thousand copies, and the second sold thirteen thousand, establishing the singers as the first major recorded black gospel quartet. Other popular groups from Jefferson County included the Five Blind Boys of Alabama and the Famous Blue Jay Singers. The Five Blind Boys began singing at the Talladega Institute for the Deaf and Blind in the 1930s but did not record until 1948; the group gained attention through the commanding voice of Clarence Fountain.

Bessemer was the birthplace of Alex Bradford, who was attracted to the emotionalism of the sanctified church as well as to the smoothness of such quartet vocal groups as the Famous Blue Jay Singers and the Kings of Harmony. Bradford, an ordained minister of a sanctified church in Birmingham, had considered a career as a blues singer before moving to Chicago after World War II and devoting himself to gospel music. In 1954 he recorded "Too Close to Heaven," which sold more than a million copies and made him the "Singing Rage of the Gospel Age." Bradford was not only one of gospel music's most prolific songwriters but also one of its most flamboyant performers.

The upstate area of South Carolina spawned some significant quartets in the 1920s and 1930s. The Spartanburg Famous Four, featuring baritone Buster Porter, was the best-known local group, recording in Charlotte, North Carolina, for Decca Records in 1938–39; another upstate group, the Shelby Gospel Four, also made records for that label. In 1939 the Gospel Light Jubilee Singers recorded in Rock Hill, South Carolina, for Bluebird Records. Gospel Light tenor Robert Hardy soon joined the Heavenly Gospel Singers from Spartanburg.

The most influential South Carolina group was the Dixie Hummingbirds, of Greenville. Beginning as a jubilee quartet in 1928 under the leadership of James B. Davis, by 1938 the group included thirteen-year-old baritone Ira Tucker as well as Willie Bobo, a former member of the Heavenly Gospel Singers. The Hummingbirds recorded for the Decca label before moving to Philadelphia in 1942. Tucker's frenetic showmanship influenced a generation of soul musicians in the 1960s.

The Swan Silvertones, one of America's premier gospel groups, spent formative years in Appalachia. Alabama native Claude Jeter founded the Four Harmony Kings in 1938 in Coalwood, West Virginia, where he had moved to work in the mines. The group's name changed to the Swan Silvertones in 1942, when they joined a radio show (sponsored by the Swan Bakery) on Knoxville, Tennessee, station WBIR. Later recording for the King and Specialty labels, the Swan Silvertones achieved national acclaim through their smooth a cappella harmonies and Jeter's soaring falsetto.

Some African American gospel groups in Appalachia have remained affiliated with a single church, while other groups have represented many churches and communities. The United Fellowship Mass Choir, for instance, represents twelve churches of various denominations in the Knoxville area. This vocal group grew from a 1983 African Methodist Episcopal Zion conference performance by singers from different choirs. The instrumentation employed by the United Fellowship Mass Choir—featuring synthesizers and drum machines—shows how black gospel music in Appalachia has adapted to changing musical styles and tastes.

See also: AFRICAN AMERICAN INFLUENCES; AFRICAN AMERICAN RELIGIOUS TRADITIONS (RELIGION); GOSPEL MUSIC, ANGLO-AMERICAN.

—Karl Rohr, *Western Carolina University*

Horace Clarence Boyer, *How Sweet the Sound: The Golden Age of Gospel* (1995); Viv Broughton, *Black Gospel: An Illustrated History of the Gospel Sound* (1985); Michael W. Harris, *The Rise of Gospel Blues: The Music of Thomas Andrew Dorsey in the Urban Church* (1992); Tony Heilbut, *The Gospel Sound* (1971).

Gospel Music, Anglo-American

Gospel music in Appalachia has been part of a larger national movement toward the composition of original hymns. Along the eastern seaboard during colonial times, the Congregational churches in New England and the Presbyterian churches in the middle colonies insisted on singing only psalms as found in the Bible. No personal or subjective hymns were allowed during worship services. Both these denominations were Calvinist in orientation, and their restrictive use of psalms was consistent with their literal reading of the scripture. In those times, followers of John Calvin believed in salvation through predestination and the divine election of saints. Finding in the Book of Revelation a prophecy that of all the souls who had ever lived or would ever live only 144,000 were preselected by God to enjoy heaven, Calvinist ministers in early America held that all other souls were inevitably doomed to perdition.

The Great Awakening of the 1730s and 1740s initially attempted to revitalize Puritan and Presbyterian theology, but it ultimately attracted new parishioners who were seeking a less rigid outlook. Believing that in the new Garden of Eden on the American frontier it might be possible to overcome the curse of Original Sin, ordinary people began seeking salvation through the grace of God. The new theology promised that if a person sincerely repented and willingly embraced Christian values, God would grant eternal life. These "glad tidings" became the essence of the gospel movement and the primary message of gospel music. Other denominations that encouraged this way of thinking through the late eighteenth century included Methodists, Baptists, and the German Pietistic sects.

Important European sources for singers in America included John Cennick's *Sacred Hymns for the Children of God in the Days of Their Pilgrimage* (1741), Thomas Butts's *Harmonia Sacra* (1753), John Wesley's *Select Hymns for the Use of Christians* (1761), and John Newton and William Cowper's *Olney Hymns* (1779). Due to the influence of such hymnals, many songs composed and popularized in England later became strongly associated with Appalachia, including "Jesus, My All, to Heaven Is Gone" and "Amazing Grace."

During the same period that these and other hymn collections were being imported into the American colonies, homegrown composers were beginning to publish their own compilations. Parallel to the efforts of such New England singing masters as William Billings, Daniel Read, and Timothy Swan, who composed in standard, round-note notation, a number of publishers began to experiment with shape-note notation. In 1801 two singing-school teachers, William Smith and William Little, published *The Easy Instructor: A New Method of Teaching Harmony* in Philadelphia. Solmization in the past had recorded the full diatonic octave, as in *do, re, mi, fa, sol, la, ti, do*. Smith and Little's innovation—called the "fa-sol-la" method—divided the octave in two and relied on only four shapes—triangle, square, oval, and diamond—and four syllables: *fa, sol, la, fa, sol, la, mi, fa*. The intent of this change, aside from making typesetting less expensive, was to allow untrained singers to read music—and to recognize harmony vocal parts—more easily.

Although the fa-sol-la method was abandoned in the northeastern states within two generations, many northern-born singing masters and songsters soon migrated into Appalachia. John Wyeth, for example, was born in Cambridge, Massachusetts, but settled in Harrisburg, Pennsylvania, where he published the influential *Repository of Sacred Music, Part 2*, in 1813. Before long, southern-born composers were active in the fa-sol-la movement, including Ananias Davisson, a Virginian, who published *Kentucky Harmony* in 1816; James Carrell, also of Virginia, who prepared *Songs of Zion* (1821); and William Moore, of Tennessee, who was responsible for *Columbian Harmony* (1825). South Carolina's William Walker brought out *Southern Harmony* in 1835. Georgia's B. F. White and E. J. King published *The Sacred Harp* in 1844, and John McCurry, also of Georgia, compiled *The Social Harp* in 1855.

The flowering of the fa-sol-la method occurred in conjunction with the Great Western Revival, which was marked by open-air religious revivals known as camp meetings. Large-scale revivals represented the triumph of the doctrine of Salvation by Grace. Beginning in Logan County, Kentucky, in the summer of 1800, camp meetings soon spread throughout rural areas of the United States. Singers in these massive worship services relied on familiar folk melodies and call-and-response refrains. Their songbooks, therefore, did not include musical notation but solely provided lyrics. Examples of such books include Henry Alline's *Hymns and Spiritual Songs* (published in Connecticut in 1802); David Mintz's *Spiritual Song Book* (North Carolina, 1805); and John Totten's *A Collection of the Most Admired Hymns and Spiritual Songs* (New York, 1809). More complete treatments of camp-meeting spirituals soon began to appear in the fa-sol-la hymnals listed above.

Eventually, in some parts of Appalachia, such as northern Mississippi, the four-shape approach of the fa-sol-la method was replaced by new seven-shape formats based on the do-re-mi scale. Although also shape notes, the alternatives were more compatible with conventional round-note notation. The first compiler to advocate the shift was Jesse Aiken, who published *The Christian Minstrel* in Philadelphia in 1846.

Shape-note singing, which flourished across the southeastern United States during the nineteenth century, lingers in a few areas within Appalachia in the twenty-first century (especially in northern Alabama and Mississippi). Another tradition of sacred music still practiced in contemporary Appalachia is "lined-out" hymnody, wherein a minister presiding over a service speaks a line of a religious hymn, with that same line then sung by the congregation.

In the twentieth century, new forms of religious music prevailed in Appalachia. Mass-marketed songbooks containing notated tunes and texts of original sacred-themed songs were promoted throughout the region by

Avenell Abbott, in the center wearing a white dress, poses with her family and some friends in southern Appalachia, 1930s. Abbott, a child evangelist in the Church of God, traveled throughout Appalachia with her family, conducting evangelical meetings in tents and churches and employing music as a method for attracting potential converts.

quartet singing groups sponsored by commercial publishing companies. The earliest such firm was the influential Ruebush-Kieffer Company, established in the Shenandoah Valley in Virginia not long after the Civil War. Most later gospel music publishers were located outside Appalachia, the most notable being the company operated by James D. Vaughan in Lawrenceburg, Tennessee. Beginning in the 1920s, this music genre, known as southern gospel, reached even wider audiences in Appalachia via the new technologies of radio and commercial recording. Since then, popular Anglo-American gospel quartets from the region have included the Speer Family (from Double Springs, Alabama) and the Blackwood Brothers (from Choctaw County, Mississippi).

Recorded country music in the region, from its inception in the 1920s, featured a fair proportion of gospel and spiritual numbers. At the seminal Bristol field recording sessions in 1927, gospel singers Alfred G. Karnes and Ernest Phipps, from Corbin, Kentucky, were not the only ones to record spiritual numbers; Blind Alfred Reed (from Floyd, Virginia), Ernest V. Stoneman (Monarat, Virginia), and the Alcoa Quartet also recorded sacred songs. The Carter Family, who were among the most significant musicians to emerge from the Bristol sessions, prominently featured gospel songs such as "Will the Circle Be Unbroken" and "No Depression in Heaven" in their repertoire. Later country singers, and especially bluegrass musicians, from Appalachia have continued to perform gospel numbers. While many Appalachian bluegrass acts feature gospel songs in their concerts, some, such as Carl Story (from Lenoir, North Carolina) and Doyle Lawson (from Kingsport, Tennessee), built a reputation as bluegrass gospel acts. Appalachian country and bluegrass musicians have added to the repertoire of traditional gospel songs—"I'll Fly Away," "Rank Strangers," "Life Is Like a Mountain Railway," "Angel Band," "Unclouded Day," and "Cry Holy unto the Lord"—by composing popular new gospel-inspired songs, including "I'm Using My Bible for a Roadmap" (Reno and Smiley) and "White Dove" (the Stanley Brothers). Several recording acts from Appalachia, including the Louvin Brothers and Elvis Presley, while achieving their biggest success in secular music genres, also made beloved gospel recordings. Following the 1956 release of his album *Hymns,* Tennessee Ernie Ford's sacred recordings became better sellers than his secular releases.

The 1980s saw Kenova, West Virginia's Michael W. Smith emerge as one of the most successful contemporary Christian music artists. In 1999 an organization preserving the legacy of southern gospel, the Southern Gospel Music Association Hall of Fame and Museum, was established at the Dollywood theme park in Pigeon Forge, Tennessee. In 2000, Appalachian gospel music reached a national audience through the *O Brother, Where Art Thou?* movie soundtrack. Ralph Stanley's a cappella version of "Oh Death" received a Grammy Award, and the Stanley Brothers' "White Dove" was also featured on that album.

See also: GOSPEL MUSIC, AFRICAN AMERICAN; LOUVIN BROTHERS; SHAPE-NOTE SINGING/SINGING SCHOOLS.

—Dillon Bustin, *Emerson Umbrella Center for the Arts,* and Ted Olson, *East Tennessee State University*

James R. Goff Jr., *Close Harmony: A History of Southern Gospel* (2002); Gene E. Veith and Thomas L. Wilmeth, *Honky-Tonk Gospel: The Story of Sin and Salvation in Country Music* (2001).

Grand Ole Opry

See *Grand Ole Opry* (Media)

Grayson and Whitter

Early country duo.

Grayson, G. B. (1888–1930) Singer and fiddler.

Whitter, Henry (1892–1941) Guitarist.

G. B. Grayson and Henry Whitter were two of the most influential Appalachian musicians during the early days of recorded country music. They were popular among such depression-era performers as the Mainers and they influenced many bluegrass musicians of the 1940s and later, including the Stanley Brothers. Songs originally recorded by Grayson and Whitter were covered by the Kingston Trio, Bob Dylan, and other urban folk revivalists. Their finest recordings were made when a duo, with Grayson playing the fiddle and singing to Whitter's guitar accompaniment. Nonetheless, both had enjoyed successful careers before they met.

Whitter was born on April 6, 1892, in Grayson County, Virginia. After completing the sixth grade, he went to work in a textile mill. He taught himself to sing and play several musical instruments and aspired to a musical career. He saved enough money from his mill earnings to take a train to New York City to audition for the General Phonograph Corporation. His first record, "The Wreck on the Southern Old 97," issued on the OKeh label in January 1924, was among the most influential recordings in early country music. In July of the same year, Whitter formed the Virginia Breakdowners with a banjoist and a fiddler, a group that was the first Appalachian string band to record.

Grayson was born November 11, 1888, in Ashe County, North Carolina. Blind from childhood, he traveled throughout the area fiddling at dances. In 1927 he met Whitter. The two musicians immediately paired up, and within three years the duo had recorded approximately forty sides of traditional fiddle tunes, murder ballads, and Appalachian folk songs. Their best-known record featured the songs "Handsome Molly" and "Train 45." Grayson died August 16, 1930, fatally injured while riding on the running board of a car that collided with a logging truck. Whitter continued to record, but without commercial success. He died due to complications from diabetes on November 17, 1941.

See also: COUNTRY MUSIC; OLD-TIME MUSIC.

—Charles F. Faber, *Lexington, Kentucky*

Guitar

The guitar's origins are usually traced back to Spain, though some scholars have suggested Greek and Arabian influences. The instrument's enduring design features include a fingerboard on a neck and a peghead with tuning gears. Historically, most guitars have had a body shape inspired by the violin, a resonating chamber, six strings, and E-A-D-G-B-E tuning, though twentieth century innovations have rendered these features optional.

The most common acoustic guitar types played in Appalachia include steel-stringed flat-top and arch-top guitars and the smaller-bodied nylon- or gut-stringed classical and folk guitars. Electric guitars are mostly either hollow-bodied arch-top acoustic-electric instruments favored for their mellow tone or solid-bodied guitars of various descriptions. Solid-bodied instruments offer a range of tonal possibilities, employing "humbucking" or single-coil pickups, with the latter often preferred among country musicians for their twangy tone. Steel guitars usually utilize open-chord tunings and feature either electric pickups or employ metallic resonating devices for acoustic amplification. Electric steel guitars very often share few commonalities with other guitars except for a similar tonal range and a shared history.

Brought to the New World by the Spanish in the seventeenth century, the guitar made its appearance in Appalachia relatively late but quickly established itself in the traditional and popular music styles of the region. Several twentieth-century Appalachian musicians and innovators have contributed to the development of contemporary guitar stylings and also to the prominence of the instrument in American music.

Before the arrival of the guitar in Appalachia during the first decade of the twentieth century, traditional music within the region consisted of a cappella singing; singing accompanied by the fiddle and, later, the banjo; and instrumental performance on those two instruments. The guitar was first distributed across Appalachia as a mail-order item from Sears-Roebuck. By the dawn of recording activity within the region in the 1920s, the guitar had already become nearly as popular as the fiddle and the banjo. Among the first Appalachian musicians to play the guitar for recordings were Henry Whitter, of Grayson County, Virginia (in 1923); Rosa Lee "Moonshine Kate" Carson, who performed with her father, Fiddlin' John Carson, of Fannin County, Georgia (in 1925); and Frank Hutchison, of Raleigh County, West Virginia (in 1926). Hutchison performed in a style highly influenced by the blues. Other white Appalachian guitarists were influenced by African American musicians, including Jimmie Rodgers and the Carter Family's Maybelle Carter, both of whom recorded at the influential Bristol sessions of 1927. Meridian, Mississippi, native Rodgers, a former railroad brakeman, had learned to play guitar by observing black railroad workers. Combining elements of the blues with folk, popular, and jazz styles, Rodgers's accompaniment patterns and solo breaks solidified both the role of the guitar and the primacy of the guitar player in American popular music.

Maybelle Carter's widely imitated guitar style—featuring the melody played on the bass strings with a thumbpick, in alternation with higher-string strum patterns—helped bring

Women with guitars, Patrick County, Virginia, c. 1900. The composer Beethoven once referred to the guitar as a "miniature orchestra" for its versatility and wide tonal range. Appalachian musicians have used the guitar as a solo instrument to accompany folk and blues songs and in groups performing bluegrass, rock, and country music.

the instrument out of an essentially rhythm accompaniment function into a more prominent lead role. Carter was influenced by the African American guitarist Leslie Riddle, who assisted the Carters on their song-collecting trips. Also influenced by black players were Riley Puckett, Cliff Carlisle, and Jimmie Tarlton, white guitarists from the margins of Appalachia. Puckett's elaborate lower-string runs inspired several later guitarists, including Doc Watson, and Carlisle and Tarlton employed different slide-guitar styles, with the former having major impact on the evolution of steel-guitar playing in country music. Hawaiian steel-guitar styles likewise influenced the development of country steel-guitar and dobro (resonator guitar) playing; many early performers of those instruments were from Appalachia, including Clell "Cousin Jody" Summey and Pete "Bashful Brother Oswald" Kirby.

"Travis picking," the guitar-picking style that bears Rosewood, Kentucky, native Merle Travis's name, has been popular in both country and folk music circles from the 1950s to the present. Having studied with local guitar teacher Mose Rager, who was influenced by black guitarist Arnold Shultz (Rager had also tutored Ike Everly, the Everly Brothers' father), Travis played the melody on the higher strings and muted bass notes on the lower strings. Such noted musicians as Chet Atkins, Scotty Moore, Jerry Reed, Doc Watson, and Thom Bresh continued to refine the Travis picking style further. For instance, Atkins, of Luttrell, Tennessee, incorporated three right-hand fingers, and utilized that style—mostly on electric guitar—on a wide range of country, pop, rock, and jazz recordings.

Appalachian musicians were significant in the evolution of other electric guitar styles as well. Clell Summey was the first to feature the electric steel guitar on the *Grand Ole Opry*, while Arthur "Guitar Boogie" Smith, of Clinton, South Carolina, and the Delmore Brothers, of Elkmont, Alabama (featuring guitarist Zeke Turner, from Lynchburg, Virginia), made significant contributions to the development of rock 'n' roll with their 1940s "hillbilly boogie" tunes, which often incorporated electric guitar.

Flat-picking, a virtuosic style of acoustic flat-top guitar playing often associated with bluegrass, enjoys wide popularity internationally. Two of the guitarists who independently developed this style in the 1950s came from Appalachia. Don Reno, of Spartanburg, South Carolina—remembered more for his three-finger banjo picking style—was an early practitioner of flat-picking, as showcased on his tune "Country Boy Rock and Roll" (1959). Most influential, though, was Deep Gap, North Carolina, resident Doc Watson's playing on the 1961 recording *Old-Time Music at Clarence Ashley's*. Watson soon was identified as the major practitioner of the flat-picking style, and his influence broadened through many subsequent recordings for several labels. Watson's son, Merle Watson, and grandson, Richard Watson, have also contributed to the style, as have Norman Blake, of Chattanooga, Tennessee, and many other proficient bluegrass and country guitarists from Appalachia, including Tim Stafford, Jeff White, Chris Jones, Richard Bennett, and Steve Kaufman. A renowned teacher of the instrument, Kaufman organizes a popular annual guitar camp in Maryville, Tennessee.

Several Appalachian musicians have expanded the vocabulary of the blues guitar. The landmark 1956 recording *Instrumental Music of the Southern Appalachians* featured African American guitarist Etta Baker, from Caldwell County, North Carolina, playing blues and lyric folk songs of

African American origin as well as European American tunes. Other influential Piedmont blues guitarists from Appalachia have included the Reverend Gary Davis (reared in Greenville, South Carolina), Brownie McGhee (born in Knoxville, Tennessee), and Pink Anderson (born in Spartanburg, South Carolina). North Mississippi has produced several significant blues guitar stylists, including Junior Kimbrough and R. L. Burnside.

Several guitarists from Appalachia have been key contributors to the evolution of southern rock and country rock music, including the Marshall Tucker Band's Toy Caldwell, of Spartanburg, South Carolina, and the Allman Brothers Band's Warren Haynes, of Asheville, North Carolina. Guitarists Charlie Feathers, of Holly Springs, Mississippi, and Hasil Adkins, of Madison, West Virginia, earlier helped forge the rockabilly sound. The internationally acclaimed Muscle Shoals, Alabama–area music scene has produced a diversity of musical talent, including major session guitarists Jimmy Johnson, Eddie Hinton, and Wayne Perkins. One of jazz music's biggest crossover successes, guitarist George Benson was born within the Appalachian region in Pittsburgh. Several country and bluegrass guitarists from Appalachia have recorded jazz and swing material, including Hank Garland (of Cowpens, South Carolina), Chet Atkins, and Norman Blake.

Although Appalachian music is often characterized as being strongly rooted in tradition, the innovative use of the guitar by Appalachian musicians demonstrates that the region's music is in fact constantly evolving. European American balladry and fiddle music in Appalachia during the eighteenth and nineteenth centuries were largely monophonic. The introduction of the guitar, a polyphonic instrument, into the region encouraged Appalachian music to become even-metered and increased that music's emphasis on inflection and intonation. Although the aforementioned guitar styles have historically been dominant in the region, younger guitarists in Appalachia also perform guitar styles from outside the region, ensuring that these guitarists will continue to perform interesting hybrids of the traditional and the contemporary.

See also: DOBRO/RESONATOR GUITAR; INSTRUMENT MAKERS AND INSTRUMENT MAKING; STEEL GUITAR.

—Dennis R. Davis, *Eastern Kentucky University*

Richard Chapman, *The Complete Guitarist* (1993); Ralph Denyer, *The Guitar Handbook* (1992); Christian Séguret, *The World of Guitars* (1998).

Gunning, Sarah Ogan

(1910–1983) Traditional singer and songwriter.

The daughter of farmer, minister, and union activist Oliver Perry Garland and his wife, Sarah Elizabeth Lucas, Sarah Elizabeth Garland was born on June 28, 1910, at a coal camp near Elys Branch in Knox County, Kentucky. At age fifteen, Sarah married coal miner Andrew Ogan, with whom she had four children.

In 1935 folklorist Mary Elizabeth Barnicle accompanied Sarah's half-sister "Aunt Molly" Jackson to Kentucky, where Barnicle met Sarah. Not long afterward, Barnicle helped the Ogans relocate to New York City so that she and Andrew could receive treatment for tuberculosis. Times were little better on the Lower East Side, however, and Sarah lost both her husband and a child to the disease.

Bolstering her repertoire of traditional ballads, lyric songs, and hymns learned from her parents, Sarah began writing original songs while still in Kentucky. Her first, "Down on the Picket Line," based on the hymn "Down in the Valley to Pray," was inspired by a 1931 National Miners Union strike in Bell County, Kentucky. In response to the death of her husband and some of her children, she wrote "Girl of Constant Sorrow," which was based on Emry Arthur's "I'm a Man of Constant Sorrow." Additional songs such as "I Hate the Company Bosses" (originally titled "I Hate the Capitalist System"), "An Old Southern Town," and "Dreadful Memories" reflected the hardships she experienced in depression-era Kentucky.

In 1941 Sarah married Joe Gunning and eventually settled in Detroit. Folklorist Archie Green located her there in 1963. She sang in public for the first time in twenty years at the 1964 Newport Folk Festival and made subsequent appearances at such festivals as the Smithsonian Festival of American Folklife and the University of Chicago Folk Festival. Shortly thereafter, Sarah recorded the album *Girl of Constant Sorrow* for the Folk-Legacy label. She died in Knoxville, Tennessee, on November 14, 1983, and was buried in Hart, Michigan.

See also: COAL-MINING AND PROTEST MUSIC; FOLK SONGS; JACKSON, AUNT MOLLY.

—Ron Pen, *University of Kentucky*

Haley, Blind Ed

(1883–1951) Traditional fiddler.

Fiddler James Edward "Blind Ed" Haley exercised a major influence on other musicians in much of eastern Kentucky, West Virginia, and adjacent parts of Ohio. Born near Hart's Creek, Logan County, West Virginia, in 1883, Haley lost his eyesight at the age of three from a bout with measles, and he survived a difficult childhood. Using his musical skills to earn a living, he traveled to local fairs, court sessions, country dances, and other events where crowds might gather. In 1914 he married Martha Ella, a blind piano teacher, and thereafter was based in Ashland, Kentucky. He continued to travel and play his fiddle, with his wife accompanying him on mandolin. Despite their handicap, the Haleys reared a family of six children.

Haley is remembered not only for his musical skills, but also for his wide repertoire. Other fiddlers admired his talents and learned his tunes, style, and techniques. Those influenced by Haley include traditional fiddlers such as West Virginians Wilson Douglas and Clark Kessinger and Kentuckian J. P. Fraley, as well as professional country fiddlers such as Georgia Slim (Robert Rutland). Although Haley never made any commercial records, he made home recordings for his son Ralph in 1946 and 1947; these have been collected and released in two compact disc sets, *Forked Deer* and *Grey Eagle*, on the Rounder label. Haley also inspired the character "Blind Frailey" in poems by Jesse Stuart. Seldom playing in public after World War II, Haley died in his sleep from a heart attack on February 4, 1951.

See also: DANCE MUSIC; FIDDLE; OLD-TIME MUSIC.

—Ivan M. Tribe, *University of Rio Grande*

Hall, Tom T.

(1936–) Country singer, songwriter, and author.

Best known for writing and singing observant songs reflective of rural and small-town Appalachian life, Tom T. Hall (he gave himself the middle initial to make his name more distinctive) was born May 25, 1936, in a log cabin at Tick Ridge, near Olive Hill in eastern Kentucky. Forced to drop out of school at age fifteen to support his family after his mother died and his father, a brick plant worker and Baptist minister, became disabled, Hall furthered his education while serving several years in the U.S. Army. Later, he took classes at Roanoke College in Virginia, becoming an admirer of Mark Twain, Ernest Hemingway, and Sinclair Lewis.

Hall is best known for a series of songs composed in the late 1960s and early 1970s that combine realism, journalistic succinctness, and, often, dark or subtle humor. These include "Harper Valley P.T.A.," "Old Dogs, Children, and Watermelon Wine," "Homecoming," "The Year that Clayton Delaney Died," "A Week in a County Jail," "Me and Jesus," and many others. Hall's hundreds of songs earned him the sobriquet "The Storyteller." He has also written several books, including an autobiography, *The Storyteller's Nashville* (1979), two novels, a short-story collection, a book on songwriting, and a children's Christmas book.

Hall has won a Grammy, fifty songwriting awards from the Broadcast Music, Inc., licensing organization, and a Nashville Music Award.

See also: COUNTRY MUSIC; STORYTELLING IN THE TWENTIETH CENTURY, RENAISSANCE OF (PERFORMING ARTS).

—Jack Hurst, *Lancaster, Tennessee*

Hammons Family

Traditional musicians.

For two centuries, the Hammons family of Pocahontas County, West Virginia, has maintained a distinctive style of traditional Appalachian music. From its arrival on the American frontier in the 1770s until the 1920s, the Hammons family was migratory, living temporarily in various counties along the West Virginia border with Kentucky and Virginia and in upper east Tennessee.

Music was central to the Hammons family as early as the 1770s. A family musical tradition of fiddle and banjo playing as well as ballad singing and storytelling was carried on from generation to generation. For instance, Burl Hammons (1908–1993), great-great-grandson of the earliest known Hammons settler in Appalachia, was a traditional musician who learned fiddle and banjo from his father and from uncles on both sides of the family.

Unlike the string-band and ensemble traditions of nearby Kentucky and Virginia, the music the Hammons family played was part of a larger West Virginia tradition of solo performance, presumably due to the relative isolation that lingered within certain sections of West Virginia well into the twentieth century.

Best known of the family musicians was fiddler Edden Hammons (1887–1952), who is often cited as having been one of West Virginia's finest fiddlers. Fifty-four of Edden's tunes were recorded in 1947. The Library of Congress published a comprehensive oral and documentary history of the Hammons family in 1973.

See also: BANJO; FAMILY GROUPS; FIDDLE.

—Roy Andrade, *East Tennessee State University*

Handy, W. C.

(1873–1958) Early jazz composer and pianist.

Born on November 16, 1873, in Florence, Alabama, William Christopher Handy studied organ and music theory at an early age. By his early teens, he had learned to play the cornet, had sung with a local minstrel show, and had begun to hone his composing skills. Handy left home at the age of eighteen and went on to a variety of musical jobs, including leading his own band and teaching music at Alabama A&M College.

In 1908 Handy and Harry Pace founded a music publishing company in Memphis, and six years later Handy published his world-renowned composition "St. Louis Blues." Although not the first to publish a twelve-bar blues composition, Handy was one of the most prominent early composers in the genre. He also arranged numerous African American folk songs and spirituals. In September 1917, his small jazz ensemble recorded fifteen sides for Columbia, including several of Handy's own works. The next year the Pace-Handy company relocated to New York City to be closer to more African American composers. In 1920 Pace and Handy parted company, with the latter forming a new publishing company, Handy Brothers Incorporated, while Pace founded the first African American–owned phonograph record company, Black Swan. Handy Brothers continued to publish the musical works of African American composers, and Handy himself promoted musical events at venues as diverse as Carnegie Hall, the New York World's Fair, and San Francisco's Golden Gate Exposition.

Two years before a 1943 accident left him virtually blind, Handy published *Father of the Blues: An Autobiography*. From the late 1940s into the 1950s, his various musical activities continued, and his public reputation grew. Handy died March 28, 1958. In the early 1980s, the Blues Foundation, an organization dedicated to promoting that musical genre, initiated the W. C. Handy Awards, which honor significant contributions to blues music. The W. C. Handy Home and Museum in Florence celebrates the composer's life and musical legacy, and that city also hosts the annual W. C. Handy Music Festival.

See also: BLUES; JAZZ; MUSCLE SHOALS.

—Kip Lornell, *George Washington University*

Harmonica

Because of its affordability, portability, durability, and availability, the harmonica has been a popular instrument in Appalachia for more than 150 years. Its forerunner was probably a free-reeded instrument that evolved in Asia around 3000 B.C. In A.D. 1825, a free-reeded mouth organ with blow and draw notes was configured by a Bohemian instrument maker named Richter, whose scheme of tuning and design became the basis of the modern harmonica.

Surviving copies of an instruction manual that was published in New York indicate that the harmonica had reached North America by 1830. A handmade harmonica with the date 1837 carved on its comb is on display in the Ford Museum in Dearborn, Michigan.

The harmonica soon appeared in Appalachia. Extensive site excavations of a military outpost occupied in the 1840s along Whites Creek, near Chattanooga, Tennessee, revealed the brass remnants of a harmonica. Excavations of Civil War encampments in the east Tennessee counties of Claiborne, Greene, and Hamblen have uncovered numerous harmonica fragments.

By the 1920s, the harmonica was a prominent instrument in country and blues music. Harmonica players working in both these musical genres entertained mass audiences via recordings and radio. More than anyone else during this period, Smith County, Tennessee, native DeFord Bailey, an African American harmonica virtuoso, helped to popularize the instrument as a star of the *Grand Ole Opry*. Bailey specialized in showpieces that imitated steam trains and fox chases.

In the 1940s, harmonica player Saunders Terrell (better known as Sonny Terry), born just outside Appalachia in the Georgia Piedmont, teamed up with singer/guitarist Brownie McGhee, a Knoxville, Tennessee, native, to play Piedmont-style country blues and other folk songs. Terry and McGhee performed widely around Appalachia and across the nation, during which time Terry impressed audiences by playing the harmonica and vocalizing simultaneously. Terry and McGhee's influence can be heard in such current Piedmont-style guitar and harmonica duos as (John) Cephas and (Phil) Wiggins, who also incorporate Appalachian material into their repertoire.

Charlie McCoy, the most recorded session harmonica player in country music history, was born in Oak Hill, West Virginia, in 1941. From the 1960s into the new century, McCoy was one of the world's leading harmonica players. Participating in hundreds of recording sessions per year and touring worldwide as a solo act, he also worked on many television shows as a headline performer, music director, and sideman.

Many Appalachian musicians who specialize in other instruments also play harmonica. For example, renowned guitarist Doc Watson, of Deep Gap, North Carolina, occasionally plays harmonica, particularly when performing country blues songs. Folk revivalist David Holt, based in Asheville, North Carolina, often employs a rack-mounted harmonica worn around his neck while playing another instrument. Another folk-revivalist and multi-instrumentalist, Mike Seeger, based in Lexington, Virginia, also plays the harmonica.

Two popular styles of harmonica played in Appalachia are the older style, called straight or first position harmonica (usually used for playing melodies in the natural major scale, or the Ionian mode, in the specified key of the harmonica), and a bluesy style known as second position or cross-harp (which favors playing in the mixolydian mode and uses note-bending techniques to sound other notes in the blues scale). The latter style is the basis of all blues and most commercial country music harmonica playing.

See also: BLUES; COUNTRY MUSIC; OTHER INSTRUMENTS.

—Wailin Wood, *Nashville, Tennessee*

Kim Field, *Harmonica, Harps, and Heavy Breathers: The History of the Harmonica and Its Role in American Music* (1993); Peter Krampert, *The Encyclopedia of the Harmonica* (1998); David C. Morton, with Charles K. Wolfe, *DeFord Bailey: A Black Star in Early Country Music* (1991).

Harris, Emmylou

(1947–) Country singer.

Born April 2, 1947, in Birmingham, Alabama, and reared in Woodbridge, Virginia, Emmylou Harris is one of the few individuals to influence both the urban folk music revival and modern commercial country music. Throughout her career, Harris explored and expanded the boundaries of mainstream country music while maintaining an uncompromising dedication to bluegrass and other older country styles.

After working as a folk-pop performer in the late 1960s, Harris came to national attention in the early 1970s through her collaboration with Gram Parsons, a former member of two influential groups (the Byrds and the Flying Burrito Brothers) that blended country music and rock. After Parsons's 1973 death, Harris continued to perform this distinctive stylistic blend, often termed country rock.

Harris's ongoing interest in traditional music is evident in her choice of material and in the musicians she has hired for her band (including Ricky Skaggs). While showing particular interest in the repertoire of two Appalachian groups, the Carter Family and the Louvin Brothers, Harris has covered songs from nearly the entire spectrum of country music and American folk music, often employing rock music elements. Her melding of styles has had a strong influence in the alternative country and Americana music genres.

Harris's eclectic approach gained her considerable support from diverse audiences and musical communities. She has had eight gold albums, one platinum album, and more than twenty-five top ten songs. Her honors include seven Grammy Awards, the Country Music Association's Female Vocalist of the Year award for 1980, and membership on the board of the Country Music Foundation. Harris became a member of the *Grand Ole Opry* in 1992.

See also: CARTER FAMILY; COUNTRY MUSIC; LOUVIN BROTHERS.

—John N. Currie, *Jacksonville, North Carolina*

Jim Brown, *Emmylou Harris—Queen of Alternative Country: Red Dirt Girl* (2003).

Hawkins, Hawkshaw

(1921–1963) Country singer and guitarist.

Harold Franklin "Hawkshaw" Hawkins, an influential but somewhat overlooked country singer, is most often remembered as having been a victim of the March 5, 1963, plane crash that also killed Patsy Cline and Cowboy Copas. Hawkins was born December 22, 1921, and reared in Huntington, West Virginia. At age fifteen, he won his first radio competition as a country music performer. After serving in World War II, Hawkins joined the *Jamboree*, a popular program on the Wheeling, West Virginia, radio station WWVA.

Hawkins stayed on the *Jamboree* from 1946 to 1954, during which time he began recording for the King label. These early King sides, often cited as his best work, yielded several top ten chart hits between 1948 and 1952. In 1953 Hawkins switched from King to the RCA Victor label. His growing reputation earned him an invitation to join the *Grand Ole Opry* in 1955. While he remained a popular stage attraction during the 1950s, hit records eluded him, even after he left RCA and signed with Columbia. In the fall of 1962, Hawkins returned to King in hope of recapturing the success he had enjoyed with that label a decade before. His single "Lonesome 7-7203" was just entering the *Billboard* magazine country chart when he was killed. The song proved to be the biggest hit of his career, staying at number one for four weeks.

Hawkins brought elements of his West Virginia youth onto the stage. He included trained horses in his act and featured a spot where he demonstrated, à la Will Rogers, his skill with the Australian whip. Hawkins's work has been cited as a link between country music's honky-tonk legacy and the musical changes upon the horizon at the time of his death, including the advent of the smoother Nashville Sound.

See also: CLINE, PATSY; COUNTRY MUSIC; *WWVA JAMBOREE* (MEDIA).

—Thomas L. Wilmeth, *Concordia University Wisconsin*

Hicks Family

Traditional musicians.

Members of the Hicks family—all of whom lived in the Beech Mountain area of Watauga and Avery Counties, North Carolina—were significant proponents of traditional ballad singing, fretted dulcimer and banjo building and playing, and storytelling. The family traces its residency in that area to Samuel Hix, who in the mid-1700s emigrated from England to Valle Crucis, North Carolina, where he acquired several hundred acres of prime farmland.

Accounts of the family's participation in musical tradition go back to Samuel Hicks III (1848–1929), who was married to Rebecca, daughter of storyteller Council Harmon. Hicks may have made instruments, and he had four sons—Brownlow, Windsor, Ben, and Roby—who built and/or played dulcimers and banjos. During the 1930s and 1940s, Ben's son Nathan, an innovative musician who played commercial "hillbilly" music as well as traditional mountain music, hosted folk music collectors Frank and Anne Warner, Mellinger Henry, and Maurice Matteson. Nathan frequently played with folksinger and banjo and dulcimer player Frank Proffitt Sr. (of "Tom Dooley" fame), who was married to Nathan's sister Bessie. Nathan's son Ray, the recipient of a National Heritage Award in 1983, was famous for storytelling (particularly Jack tales). Ben's daughter Nettie, a dulcimer player, was married to dulcimer maker and wood-carver Edd Presnell and was frequently recorded by collectors in the

1950s and 1960s. Roby was an instrument maker and banjo player; he also sang ballads with his wife, Buna, a fiddler. Roby's son Stanley made and played dulcimers and banjos and was well known for his willingness to share his family's traditions. Honored with a National Heritage Award in 1983, Stanley frequently performed with Frank Proffitt Jr. and neighbors Leonard and Clifford Glenn, renowned for their banjo and dulcimer making and playing. Roby's daughters Hattie and Rosa were ballad singers, and his son Linzy was known for his church singing. Many of these individuals were recorded and documented by folklorists and folk music collectors.

See also: BALLADS; FAMILY GROUPS; HICKS, RAY (PERFORMING ARTS).

—Lucy M. Long, *Bowling Green State University*

Robert Isbell, *The Last Chivaree: The Hicks Family of Beech Mountain* (1996).

Hines, Earl "Fatha"

(1905–1983) Jazz pianist and bandleader.

Earl Kenneth "Fatha" Hines was born December 28, 1905, in Duquesne, Pennsylvania, and played piano professionally in northern Appalachia during his early career. Hines is best remembered as an innovative jazz pianist, but it was as the leader of a big band that he first achieved widespread recognition. He formed this band in Chicago and toured extensively across the United States, particularly in the Appalachian region and the Midwest.

Hines studied classical piano as a child and began performing professionally in the Pittsburgh area as a teenager. He moved to Chicago and worked as a pianist for several years; his most significant association in the 1920s was with Louis Armstrong, with whom Hines made several influential recordings, notably "West End Blues" and the trumpet-piano duet "Weather Bird." In 1928 Hines's band began a twelve-year engagement at the new Grand Terrace Ballroom in Chicago; the band continued to tour until 1948, when Hines quit. For the remainder of his career, Hines worked primarily with smaller groups and as a solo pianist. His career experienced a revival beginning in the 1960s, and he performed all over the world until shortly before his death on April 22, 1983.

Hines was a pivotal figure in jazz history, both as a pianist and as a bandleader. His big band featured future bebop giants Dizzy Gillespie and Charlie Parker. Hines's virtuoso piano style influenced countless jazz pianists; often called trumpet-piano style, it featured linear single-note lines, brilliant octave tremolos, and ingenious rhythmic displacements.

See also: AFRICAN AMERICAN INFLUENCES; GARNER, ERROLL; JAZZ.

—Raleigh Dailey, *University of Kentucky*

Stanley Dance, *The World of Earl Hines* (1983).

Holcomb, Roscoe

(1912–1981) Traditional singer, banjo player, and guitarist.

Born September 5, 1912, at Daisy in eastern Kentucky near Hazard, Roscoe Holcomb (Halcomb at birth) from an early age played guitar and banjo and sang Old Regular Baptist and Holiness church songs as well as African American blues. While employed in the mines and in construction, he found time to perform locally as a folk musician. In 1959, he was "discovered" by John Cohen of the urban folk-revivalist string band the New Lost City Ramblers; subsequently, Holcomb enjoyed a career on the folk festival circuit, made recordings for the Folkways label, and was featured in Cohen's film *The High Lonesome Sound.*

Holcomb's music was spare and intense. He sang in a piercing tenor at the top of his range. Sometimes playing clawhammer-style banjo but more frequently a two-finger style (with a thumbpick), he tended to play repeated patterns, or ostinati, behind his vocals so that he could sing in free meter. He sang old British and American ballads, but he favored sacred songs he learned in church, blues he heard on records, and the traditional lyric songs common in Appalachia. For blues he tended to use a lower and less strident vocal register. Songs associated with Holcomb include "Little Birdie" and "Trouble in Mind" (with banjo accompaniment); "House in New Orleans," "Little Bessie," and "Motherless Children" (with guitar); and "A Village Churchyard" (a cappella).

Holcomb's singing style exemplified the "high lonesome" sound, a coinage some have used to describe the vocal sound in eastern Kentucky but that others have employed when referring to the vocal style of bluegrass legend Bill Monroe from western Kentucky. Holcomb would sing a cappella in the same manner as he did when singing to the accompaniment of an instrument. His music incorporates some of the oldest traditions of religious and secular folk music from Appalachia.

See also: BANJO; BLUES; GOSPEL MUSIC, ANGLO-AMERICAN.

—Frederick E. Danker, *University of Massachusetts*

Homer and Jethro

Country music comedy duo.

Henry D. "Homer" Haynes (1920–1971) Guitarist and singer.

Kenneth C. "Jethro" Burns (1920–1989) Country and jazz mandolin player and singer.

Homer (b. July 27, 1920) and Jethro (b. March 10, 1920), natives of Knoxville and Conasauga, Tennessee, respectively, are among the best-known comedy acts in country music history. Originally known as "Junior" and "Dude," the duo began playing together as the String Dusters in 1932, performing and developing their talents as song parodists over WNOX in Knoxville. Their permanent nicknames were bestowed by a WNOX radio announcer who had forgotten their original names. In 1938 Homer and Jethro moved to the *Renfro Valley Barn Dance*.

Following military service during World War II, Homer and Jethro resumed their radio performance career and were signed by King Records in 1946, where they had their first hits. They moved to RCA Victor in 1949, remaining with that label until 1971. Their greatest successes came in the 1950s and 1960s, including their 1959 Grammy Award–winning song "The Battle of Kookamonga" (a parody of Jimmie Driftwood's "Battle of New Orleans"), their hit 1960 live album *Homer and Jethro at the Country Club*, and their popular commercials for Kellogg's Corn Flakes. Less well known were their RCA albums of string jazz, produced by Chet Atkins. Following Homer's death on August 7, 1971, Jethro began a second career appearing at folk and bluegrass festivals, often with singer-songwriter Steve Goodman. In the 1970s and 1980s, Burns served as a role model and inspiration for a new generation of bluegrass and jazz mandolinists. He died February 4, 1989.

Homer and Jethro's material, while often humorous in the country "corn" mode and aimed at a regional audience, was in fact innovative and musically sophisticated. The duo was inducted into the Country Music Hall of Fame in 2001.

See also: BLUEGRASS; COUNTRY MUSIC COMEDY (HUMOR); JAZZ; MANDOLIN.

—John N. Currie, *Jacksonville, North Carolina*

Hopkins, Doc

(1900–1988) Early country singer, banjo player, and guitarist.

Howard "Doc" Hopkins was a popular performer on midwestern radio in the 1930s and 1940s. His melodious voice and accomplished three-finger-and-thumb guitar style were showcased on some of the era's most popular country music broadcasts, including the WLS *National Barn Dance* and the WJJD *Suppertime Frolic*.

Rural traditions marked his life as well as his work. Hopkins's nickname, "Doc," reflected the belief that as the seventh son he had healing powers. Born January 26, 1900, in Harlan County, Kentucky, Hopkins began playing banjo during his boyhood on an instrument his father crafted for him from a cigar box, a cedar neck, and a possum skin. The Hopkins family moved to nearby Rockcastle County, where Doc's neighbors included his future radio colleagues John Lair, Karl Davis, and Harty Taylor. At the age of nine or ten, Hopkins met and sang for Dakota Jack Pearsley, a medicine show performer; after Hopkins's return from World War I, Pearsley gave him his first job as a musician.

In the 1920s, Doc played steel guitar in a U.S. military band and performed with Davis and Taylor in the Kentucky Krazy Kats. In 1930 Lair invited his schoolmates to Chicago, and Hopkins named the new band the Cumberland Ridge Runners. Hopkins also played solo, first recording in 1931 for Paramount and later for the American Record Corporation and Decca. The bulk of his recorded work, however, resided in numerous radio transcriptions for the music publisher M. M. Cole. During the urban folk revival of the 1960s, Doc began playing at college folk festivals and coffeehouses and was recorded for a performer-and-repertoire study by the John Edwards Memorial Foundation at UCLA. One of his last appearances occurred in 1982 at the National Folk Festival, where he was the event's oldest performer, still creatively combining the spoken words, music, picking styles, and sound effects of the medicine shows of his childhood.

See also: COUNTRY MUSIC; FOLK MUSIC REVIVALS; OLD-TIME MUSIC.

—Stephen Wade, *Hyattsville, Maryland*

Hutchison, Frank

(1897–1945) Early country singer and guitarist.

Among the many white musicians who made country music recordings in the 1920s, Frank Hutchison was probably the one most influenced by African American music. Born on March 20, 1897, in Raleigh County, West Virginia, he began his working life as a miner in Logan County. Following a leg injury, he devoted himself to music, becoming expert at playing guitar and harmonica. The repertoire acquired by Hutchison during his youth reflected the diverse musical influences found in the industrializing areas of Appalachia, including blues brought to the mountains from the Deep South by African American laborers.

Hutchison recorded for the OKeh label, making his first trip to New York City for a recording session in September 1926. He was among the earliest singers who recorded solo while accompanying themselves on the guitar, thus setting a precedent for the countless singer-guitarists to follow. Over the next three years, Hutchison made approximately thirty recordings in OKeh studios in New York, St. Louis, and Atlanta, including such songs as "Stackalee" and "Cannon Ball Blues."

Hutchison's releases were marketed in the "hillbilly" category, though several of his selections had been learned from black blues singers and ragtime guitarists. He was among the first white musicians to record black songs, and thus he helped inaugurate a subgenre that became known as hillbilly blues. The outset of the Great Depression curtailed Hutchison's recording career. He died on November 9, 1945.

See also: BLUES; COUNTRY MUSIC; STEEL GUITAR.

—Dillon Bustin, *Emerson Umbrella Center for the Arts*

Instrument Makers and Instrument Making

Appalachia has long been recognized for its diverse musical traditions, and over the past three centuries much of the region's music has been performed on handmade musical instruments. Not surprisingly, this musical environment has fueled a craft heritage of instrument making. Practically every type of instrument used in the playing of Appalachian folk music—including the fiddle, banjo, guitar, mandolin, fretted dulcimer, hammered dulcimer, mouth bow, ukulele, autoharp, bones, and piano—has at one time or another been built by an Appalachian instrument maker.

The earliest music makers in the region were Native Americans, but historical accounts shed little light on the instruments made by these various peoples. Documented instrument making within Appalachia begins with settlers from England, Scotland, Ireland, and Germany, whose traditions included both distinctive musical styles and selected types of instruments. As Appalachia's musical and instrument-making heritage evolved, regionality, industrialization, and popular culture influenced the preferences of local musicians and artisans for instrument forms and playing styles.

Researchers have faced a number of challenges in studying early Appalachian instrument-making traditions, especially in the documentation of instrument making prior to the 1900s. Since instrument making has been primarily a part-time craft in Appalachia, it has rarely been mentioned in historical documents and records. For example, the 1834 inventory of the estate of Jesse Henscher (Wythe County, Virginia) listed dulcimer-making tools (as well as gunsmithing and wheelwright tools), and John Scales Jr. (Floyd County, Virginia) in 1832 signed a dulcimer he made, but neither man was identified as an instrument maker in the manufactures census of the period. Many artisans did not sign their instruments, and often it is only through listening to family stories about particular instruments and through investigating regional instrument forms that researchers can deduce the instruments' origins.

Three instruments stand out in the Appalachian instrument-making tradition: the fretted dulcimer, the fiddle, and the banjo. Within the region, these instruments have been produced in the greatest numbers, across the broadest geographic range, and over the longest span of time. All three instruments predate the American industrialization of instrument making in the second half of the nineteenth century.

In the mind of the American public no instrument has been more strongly associated with Appalachia than the dulcimer. (The term *dulcimer* as used here refers only to the fretted dulcimer; the hammered dulcimer also has an Appalachian heritage but was made only in localized pockets, such as central West Virginia.) Along with the fiddle, the dulcimer was likely one of the first instruments made in the region. Early dulcimers are found most often in those areas of Appalachia where people of German ancestry settled.

The oldest dulcimer-family form is the *Scheitholt* (also referred to as the zither), a straight-sided instrument with frets mounted directly on the body of the instrument rather than atop a soundboard. Found in the Appalachian regions of Pennsylvania, Maryland, Ohio, West Virginia, Virginia, Tennessee, and Georgia, the *Scheitholt* was still being made by traditional artisans such as Lewis Radford in the Blue Ridge Mountains of Virginia as late as the 1950s.

The more popularly recognized form of the fretted dulcimer, sometimes called the Appalachian dulcimer in modern catalogs, also exhibited regionally specific differences in form. Early dulcimer makers in southwest Virginia, such as Steve Melton (most active in 1890 in Carroll and Lee Counties), favored a teardrop shape for the instrument. However, nineteenth- and twentieth-century craftsmen elsewhere in Appalachia adhered to an hourglass form. These include, in western North Carolina, Eli Presnell (most active c. 1880s, Beech Creek); in eastern Tennessee, James Holly (c. 1920s, Morristown); in eastern Kentucky, James Edward Thomas (c. 1870s, Knott County); in southern Ohio, John H. Lunsford (c. 1870s, Lawrence County); and in southern West Virginia, Lewis Hinkle (c. 1880s, Upshur County). Later dulcimer makers in Appalachia have usually followed the forms popular in their particular localities.

With few exceptions, Appalachian fiddle makers, such as Alabama's Gene Ivey (DeKalb County), have utilized the basic form established by European violin makers long before Appalachian settlement. Within that context, one of the most regionally influential of the Appalachian fiddle makers was Albert Hash (Grayson County, Virginia); before his death in 1983, Hash taught at least eight other makers of various instruments. His daughter, Audrey Hash Ham (Ashe County, North Carolina), is one of the few female instrument makers in Appalachia. An exception to the European violin form is the gourd fiddle, which features a fiddle-type neck attached to a body made from a gourd. Frank Couch (Hancock County, Tennessee) made gourd fiddles as early as 1840, and similar instruments have also been found in southwest Virginia. Such instruments were likely made elsewhere in Appalachia, but since musicians preferred the standard forms of instruments, surviving gourd fiddles are rare.

Banjo-making traditions in Appalachia probably developed later than regional dulcimer and fiddle traditions. Prior to the 1830s, the banjo was a homemade gourd instrument made and played by slaves primarily in eastern Virginia and Maryland. In the 1840s, during the popularity of the new minstrel genre of entertainment, white banjoists performing in blackface with frame (as opposed to gourd) banjos toured Appalachia, in many cases as part of circus troupes. White Appalachian musicians thereafter enthusiastically took up the banjo. Early-twentieth-century gourd banjos are mentioned in oral histories in North Carolina and Kentucky, but most artisans built instruments patterned closely after the factory-made banjos that became readily available through mail-order catalogs in the late nineteenth century. Again, folk instrument makers historically did not sign their work, and it is not until the first quarter of the twentieth century that prolific Appalachian banjo makers can be specifically identified.

One regional banjo variation is found in the construction of the so-called mountain banjo, which features a small animal-hide head drawn across a circular hoop with a broad wooden rim. Built primarily from the late 1800s to the 1950s, the mountain banjo was produced by instrument makers in southwest Virginia such as Bill Plummer of Smyth County, as well as by artisans of nearby counties in neighboring states, such as Stanley Hicks of Watauga County, North Carolina. Plummer is the only Appalachian African American banjo maker that researchers have specifically identified thus far. The more common version of the mountain banjo made in the Blue Ridge has a round body, yet makers in the valley system west of the Blue Ridge and into the Alleghenies also fashioned octagonal rims.

Despite local instrument-making traditions, most musical instruments used by Appalachian musicians have come from factory sources outside the region. By the end of the nineteenth century, musical instruments of many types could easily be ordered through the mail, and, in part because of catalog sales, "newer" instruments, such as the mandolin, the autoharp, and the guitar, became part of the Appalachian folk music environment. Still, the traditional instrument maker—almost always a male artisan working part-time at his craft—remained an important figure in Appalachian society, fulfilling local demand for the type of instrument he produced. The increased attention granted Appalachian folklife during the twentieth century led to the documentation of numerous regional instrument makers. Many modern-day Appalachian instrument makers are recognized as cultural resources. A few of the finest—such as Virginia guitar maker and champion guitarist Wayne Henderson (Grayson County), North Carolina dulcimer and banjo maker Leonard Glenn (Watauga County), and Kentucky dulcimer, banjo, guitar, ukulele, and mandolin maker Homer Ledford (Clark County)—have received special recognition from state or national arts councils.

See also: BANJO; DULCIMER, FRETTED; FIDDLE.

—Vaughan Webb, *Blue Ridge Institute*

John Rice Irwin, *Musical Instruments of the Southern Appalachian Mountains* (1983); L. Allen Smith, *A Catalogue of Pre-Revival Appalachian Dulcimers* (1983); Vaughan Webb, ed., *Blue Ridge Folk Instruments and Their Makers* (1993).

Jackson, Aunt Molly

(1880–1960) Traditional protest singer and songwriter.

During the 1930s, Mary Magdalene Garland "Aunt Molly" Jackson was a prominent activist in the struggle for the unionization of the Appalachian coalfields. Her performances at labor rallies featured original protest songs closely modeled on traditional mountain music.

The daughter of miner, preacher, and union activist Oliver Perry Garland and Deborah Robinson Garland, Jackson was born in Clay County, Kentucky, in September 1880. Her mother died of tuberculosis in 1886; eleven months later, her father married Elizabeth Lucas, with whom he had an additional eleven children, including union activists Sarah Ogan Gunning (1910–1983) and Jim Garland (1905–1978).

During the Great Depression, Aunt Molly Jackson presented speeches and performed songs such as "I Am a Union Woman," "Kentucky Miner's Wife," and "Dreadful Memories" on behalf of the National Miners Union. In 1931 she met with a delegation sent by the National Committee for the Defense of Political Prisoners and subsequently traveled to New York City, soon appearing before an audience of twenty-one thousand people.

After spending the next five years traveling on behalf of the labor movement, Jackson and her third husband, Gustavos Stamos, moved to New York City in 1936. She died on August 31, 1960, in Sacramento, California.

Jackson's political adaptation of folk songs coupled tradition and innovation, as revealed in her own definition of folk music: "This is what a folk song really is: the folks composes their own songs about their own lives and their home folks that live around them."

See also: COAL-MINING AND PROTEST MUSIC; GUNNING, SARAH OGAN.

—Ron Pen, *University of Kentucky*

Shelly Romalis, *Pistol Packin' Mama: Aunt Molly Jackson and the Politics of Folksong* (1999).

James, Sonny

(1929–) Country singer.

James Loden, who performed under the stage name Sonny James, was born May 1, 1929, into a show business family in Hackleburg, Alabama, and was given his first guitar, which was made by his father, at the age of three. The next year, the family won a folk music contest in Birmingham. By the time he was in his teens, James had performed on several regional country music shows.

During the Korean War, James informally entertained his fellow servicemen and Korean orphans by playing guitar and singing for them. After his discharge, he moved to Nashville and embarked upon a recording career. In 1956 his recording of the song "Young Love" reached the number one position on both the country and pop charts. For a time he was more at home with pop and rock 'n' roll, but he returned to country music with resounding success. From 1967 to 1972, he had a string of sixteen consecutive number one hits on the country charts. Known as the "Southern Gentleman" for his neat appearance and elegant manners, James was named Country Music's Male Artist of the Decade by *Record World* magazine for his 1960s work. He also appeared during these years in several low-budget movies, including *Second Fiddle to a Steel Guitar*, *Nashville Rebel*, *Las Vegas Hillbillies*, and *Hillbilly in a Haunted House*.

In 1983 James retired to his farm in Alabama. Although his records seldom reflected his Appalachian heritage, James's crossover appeal won many new fans for country music.

See also: COUNTRY MUSIC; ROCK MUSIC.

—Charles F. Faber, *Lexington, Kentucky*

Jarrell, Tommy

(1901–1985) Traditional fiddler, banjo player, and singer.

Born March 1, 1901, Thomas Jefferson "Tommy" Jarrell was a popular traditional fiddler and banjo player and a leading practitioner of the influential local instrumental styles from the Round Peak, North Carolina, area. Reared in Surry County, he was the oldest of the eleven children of fiddler Benjamin Franklin Jarrell and Susan Letisha Amburn. He completed six grades at the one-room Ivy Green schoolhouse, then worked on farms and at a sawmill, made liquor, and played music. Jarrell married Nina Barnett Lowe, the daughter of banjo player Charlie Barnett Lowe and Ardena Leftwich from nearby Lambsburg, Virginia. The couple moved to Mount Airy, North Carolina, and reared three children. For decades, Jarrell drove a road grader for the North Carolina State Highway Department, which left him little time to play music.

Learning banjo when he was seven years old from Bauga (pronounced "Boggy") Cockerham, Jarrell started playing on a homemade banjo with a pokeberry-stained neck and a calfskin hide. At thirteen, he learned fiddle from his father and his uncle, Charlie Jarrell, and was soon playing dances with them and with neighbors. Benjamin Jarrell recorded for Gennett Records in 1927, but Tommy acquired most of his repertoire and style before the influence of commercial recordings and radio, and thus he preserved the older instrumental styles and repertoires of the Blue Ridge. From Civil War veterans, Jarrell learned several unaccompanied fiddle pieces—including "Sail Away Ladies," "Flatwoods," "Devil in the Strawstack," and "The Drunken Hiccups"—that predated the local merging of the fiddle and banjo repertoires and styles. His intense fiddling style combined energetic short bow strokes with expressive double stops on open string drones.

A powerful and haunting vocalist, Jarrell also performed instrumental versions of ballads and Primitive Baptist hymns. His large repertoire of unusual fiddle and improvisational banjo songs included many pieces assembled from "floating" verses—some borrowed from African American singers—that other musicians performed only as tunes without texts. Playing music more frequently after his retirement, especially with Fred Cockerham and Kyle Creed, Jarrell inspired younger local musicians such as Earnest East, Benton Flippen, Verlin Clifton, and Paul Sutphin. Renowned for his friendliness, generosity, humor, and storytelling, Jarrell became a favorite in parking lot music-making sessions at nearby fiddlers' conventions. During these years, he performed in concerts and festivals as far away as Canada and received international visitors at family dances and music get-togethers. In 1982 the National Endowment for the Arts awarded him one of its first fifteen National Heritage Fellowships. He died January 28, 1985.

See also: BANJO; FIDDLE; FOLK MUSIC REVIVALS.

—Cecelia Conway, *Appalachian State University*

Les Blank, Cecelia Conway, Alice Gerrard, and Maureen Gosling, *Sprout Wings and Fly*, Flower Films (1983); Cecelia Conway, *African Banjo Echoes in Appalachia: A Study of Folk Traditions* (1995).

Jazz

Jazz is not often associated with Appalachia in the public mind, but the region boasts more than one city significant in the development of the genre. Moreover, other musics commonly identified with the region, especially country and bluegrass, have been invigorated by jazz influences, leading to hybrid styles bearing appellations such as newgrass, jazzgrass, new acoustic music, country jazz, and hillbilly jazz.

Despite its origin in New Orleans, jazz music is widely considered a northern urban phenomenon. Such Appalachian cities as Birmingham, Alabama, and Chattanooga and Knoxville, Tennessee, are often unrecognized as centers of jazz though Pittsburgh has long been known as a hotbed of the genre.

Many jazz legends were born or reared in the Pittsburgh area, including singers Billy Eckstine and Maxine Sullivan; composer Billy Strayhorn; pianists Earl "Fatha" Hines, Mary

Ahmad Jamal (born Frederick Russell Jones), performing at the Kay Boys' Club, Pittsburgh, c. 1945. A leading jazz pianist internationally, Jamal began his career in his native Pittsburgh at age eleven, playing at a variety of area venues.

Lou Williams, Erroll Garner, Ahmad Jamal, and Horace Parlan; drummers Art Blakey and Kenny Clarke; bassists Ray Brown, Paul Chambers, and John Heard; guitarist George Benson; trumpeters Roy Elridge and Tommy Turrentine; and saxophonists Stanley Turrentine and Bob Cooper. Though most of these musicians left the region to pursue their careers in larger cities, from the 1930s to the 1950s Pittsburgh's Hill District boasted a vibrant nightclub jazz scene. Such clubs as the Crawford Grill and the Hurricane Lounge not only served as springboards for the careers of local talent, but these venues also hosted touring jazz luminaries. The musical heyday of the Hill District ended in the mid-1950s after the federal government implemented urban redevelopment initiatives in the area. Since the 1970s, Pittsburgh has made significant efforts to reaffirm its place in the history and future of jazz. Such efforts have included the annual Jazz at the Hill House gathering, which celebrates Pittsburgh's role in the evolution of jazz by showcasing hometown heroes such as Benson and Stanley Turrentine alongside other regional talent. Since 1992, the University of Pittsburgh has offered its annual Jazz Seminar, one of the major jazz forums in Appalachia. Meanwhile, Pittsburgh public radio station WDUQ has received national recognition as a pioneer and leader in jazz radio programming.

Paul Winter, also from northern Appalachia (Altoona, Pennsylvania), played a pivotal role in the fusion of jazz with musics from around the world, helping to lay the foundation for new age and world-beat musical styles. His late-1960s and early-1970s groundbreaking instrumental ensemble, the Paul Winter Consort, also featured oboist Paul McCandless, of Indiana, Pennsylvania, who later cofounded the world fusion jazz group Oregon.

Birmingham is the birthplace of jazz innovator Sun Ra as well as of big band leaders Erskine Hawkins and Teddy Hill, among others. Chattanooga was the early home for such pioneering jazz talent as singers Bessie Smith and Valaida Snow, pianist Lovie Austin, and bassist Jimmy Blanton, who later played with Duke Ellington and Billy Strayhorn. Trumpeter Cat Anderson, a longtime member of Ellington's band, was born in Greenville, South Carolina.

Jazz is valued in many Appalachian cities as part of these communities' cultural and artistic heritages, and notable attempts have been made within the region to foster appreciation and furtherance of local jazz traditions. After big bands declined in popularity in the late 1940s, jazz was generally sustained within Appalachia by elite patronage in larger cities. An increasing desire to foster pride in jazz across the region has led individuals and organizations to promote jazz to younger generations. Trumpeter and veteran Sun Ra sideman Jothan Callins, of Birmingham, coordinated the Birmingham Youth Jazz Ensemble to provide middle and high school students with opportunities for performing jazz regionally, nationally, and internationally. Similarly, the Alabama Jazz Hall of Fame sponsors jazz appreciation programs in Birmingham-area elementary schools. Several universities in Appalachia display considerable interest in jazz, offering a range of scholastic and performance opportunities from jazz ensembles within classical music programs to specialized departments offering bachelor's (University of Alabama; Virginia Tech; and University of North Carolina at Asheville) and master's (University of Tennessee and West Virginia University) degrees in jazz .

Recent "live" radio shows from Appalachia—such as the Charleston, West Virginia–based, internationally broadcast show *Mountain Stage,* which features jazz-oriented musicians in its house band—have challenged public perceptions of Appalachian music by mixing jazz with more recognized regional musics.

Jazz has influenced both country and bluegrass music. Jazz percolated into commercial country music early, as evidenced by Louis Armstrong's playing on a Jimmie Rodgers recording. Improvisatory like jazz, western swing music, a subgenre of country music generally associated with Texas and the Midwest, has had notable Appalachian proponents such as Hank Penny (who was born and had initial success in Birmingham before moving to Nashville) and steel guitarist Billy Bowman of Johnson City, Tennessee (who played with Bob Wills in the 1950s). The group most responsible for the western swing revival in the early 1970s, Asleep at the Wheel, was formed in Paw Paw, West Virginia.

After the country music industry became predominantly based in Nashville in the late 1940s, many skilled studio musicians from Appalachian backgrounds integrated jazz with folk and country musical styles. For instance, beginning in 1952, Hank Garland (a native of Cowpens, South Carolina) recorded numerous jazz-influenced tracks, culminating in his acclaimed 1961 album *Jazz Winds from a New Direction*. Among other Appalachian instrumentalists, Jethro Burns (born in Conasauga, Tennessee) is often acknowledged as one of the fathers of jazz mandolin, while Chet Atkins (from Luttrell, Tennessee) recorded many jazz standards as a solo performer and with various other instrumentalists, including guitarist Les Paul.

Other Appalachian musicians, such as fiddlers Vassar Clements (of Kinard, South Carolina) and Buddy Spicher (of Dubois, Pennsylvania), have recorded as sidemen and leaders on swing and bluegrass recordings, as well as on various jazz- and rock-influenced musical blends sometimes labeled country jazz or hillbilly jazz. Eclectic mandolinist Butch Baldassari (of Scranton, Pennsylvania) has often performed jazz, as has classically trained bassist Edgar Meyer (from Oak Ridge, Tennessee).

These and many other practitioners of Appalachia-influenced musics continue to weave multiple strands, including jazz, into a seamless fiber of American music.

See also: AFRICAN AMERICAN INFLUENCES; BLUES; RHYTHM AND BLUES.

—Ajay Kalra, *East Tennessee State University*

Leonard Feather and Ira Gitler, eds., *The Biographical Encyclopedia of Jazz* (1999); Barry Kernfield, ed., *The New Grove Dictionary of Jazz* (1994); Bill Kirchner, ed., *The Oxford Companion to Jazz* (2000).

Jim and Jesse

Bluegrass brother duo.

McReynolds, Jim (1927–2002) Singer and guitarist.

McReynolds, Jesse (1929–) Singer and mandolinist.

Jim and Jesse McReynolds have received acclaim since the 1950s for their style of bluegrass. Rather than being generally mournful, bluesy, and lonesome like the music of Bill Monroe and the Stanley Brothers, the McReynolds' music is often joyful and positive.

Both brothers were born in Carfax, Virginia, Jim on February 13, 1927, and Jesse on July 9, 1929. Brought up in a musical family (their grandfather Charles McReynolds was a noted fiddler who participated in the historic Bristol sessions), the brothers started playing on radio in 1947 before embarking on their recording career in 1951. Their early style was inspired by the Louvin Brothers. Jim and Jesse recorded for Capitol in the 1950s; these recordings displayed Jesse's trademark mandolin cross-picking style (simulating banjo rolls with a flat-pick), which would inspire generations of mandolin and flat-picking guitar players. Jesse is also known for his split-string playing (fretting each of a pair of strings on different frets to play harmonies). In the 1960s, the brothers' association with the Epic label coincided with a more commercial orientation, leading to an album of Chuck Berry songs entitled *Berry Pickin' in the Country* and recordings with a definite country flavor such as the hit song "Diesel on My Tail." During this period the duo's recordings featured some electric instrumentation. In the early 1970s, the brothers returned to a more traditional bluegrass sound. Jim and Jesse and their band, the Virginia Boys, continued as one of the major groups in bluegrass, touring the festival circuit and frequently releasing albums for a variety of labels, including their own company, Old Dominion Records. The brothers received the national Heritage Fellowship in 1997. Jesse McReynolds has also been associated with the Masters, a bluegrass "supergroup" that includes fiddler Kenny Baker, banjo player and guitarist Eddie Adcock, and dobro player Buck "Uncle Josh" Graves. Jim McReynolds died December 31, 2002.

See also: BLUEGRASS; DUOS, BROTHER; MANDOLIN.

—Christian Séguret, *Auxy, France*

Jones, Grandpa

(1913–1998) Country banjo player and singer.

During a country music career that lasted almost seventy years, Louis Marshall "Grandpa" Jones was known as a comedian, as one of the leading advocates of traditional country music and old-time gospel singing, and for keeping the frailing style of five-string banjo playing alive during a period when it virtually disappeared from country music. Jones was born October 20, 1913, in Henderson County, Kentucky, to a mother who sang traditional ballads and a father who was a traditional fiddler. In 1929, at age sixteen, Jones started his professional career, performing on radio in Akron, Ohio, as "The Young Singer of Old Songs," specializing in the "blue yodels" of Jimmie Rodgers. While performing with Bradley Kincaid in Boston in 1935, Jones was dubbed "Grandpa." Although he was only twenty-two, his manner reminded Kincaid of an old man's.

In 1946 Jones began working on the *Grand Ole Opry*. With the exception of breaks from 1949 to 1952 and 1956 to 1959, he remained on the show until his death. Also in 1946, Jones married Ramona Riggins, a talented fiddler, singer, and mandolin player from Indiana whom he had met while working in Cincinnati. A year later, he learned to play frailing-style banjo from another Kentucky performer, Cousin Emmy (Cynthia May Carver), and soon performed the instrument on his hit recordings of "Old Rattler" and "Mountain Dew." A regular slot on the television show *Hee Haw* beginning in 1969 helped make Jones's persona one of the best known in country music. Jones was a member of the gospel groups Brown's Ferry Four and the Hee Haw Gospel Quartet, which made several commercially successful recordings. In 1978 he was elected to the Country Music Hall of Fame. After an *Opry* performance on January 3, 1998, Jones collapsed; he died on February 19.

See also: COUNTRY MUSIC; *GRAND OLE OPRY* (MEDIA); *HEE HAW* (MEDIA).

—W. K. McNeil, *The Ozark Folk Center*

Louis M. "Grandpa" Jones, with Charles K. Wolfe, *Everybody's Grandpa: Fifty Years behind the Mike* (1984).

Judds, The

Country mother-daughter duo.

Judd, Naomi (1946–) Singer and songwriter.

Judd, Wynonna (1964–) Singer and guitarist.

Naomi, born Diana Ellen Judd on January 11, 1946, and her daughter Wynonna, born Christina Claire Ciminella on May 30, 1964, have been one of the most successful duos in the history of country music. Both were born in Ashland, Kentucky, and loved the old-time music of the area. In 1968 they moved to California but returned to Kentucky in 1976. At the age of twelve, Wynonna got her first guitar and began to sing around the house with her mother. They soon moved again to California, where Naomi completed work for a nursing degree.

In 1979 the Judds moved to the Nashville area, where they secured a recording contract with the RCA label in 1983. In 1984, they won the first of their five Grammy Awards for Best Country Performance by a Duo or Group with Vocal. In the same year, they also won the first of their nine Country Music Association awards and the first of eight Academy of Country Music awards as Vocal Group of the Year. In 1991 Naomi shared the songwriter's Grammy for "Love Can Build a Bridge," named the Best Country Song of the Year.

In 1991 Naomi temporarily retired from show business because of hepatitis C, a liver disease. Wynonna embarked on a successful career as a solo artist; her first three singles all reached number one on the country charts. By 1999, Naomi had recovered her health, and the duo reunited for a televised concert, a subsequent tour, and new recordings.

See also: COUNTRY MUSIC; DUOS, BROTHER; FAMILY GROUPS.

—Charles F. Faber, *Lexington, Kentucky*

Kazee, Buell

(1900–1976) Traditional singer and banjo player.

Buell Hilton Kazee was a Kentucky Baptist preacher and also an extraordinary banjo player and singer of traditional ballads. Born August 29, 1900, in Burton Fork, Magoffin County, Kentucky, he grew up making music with neighbors and friends. After graduating from Kentucky's Georgetown College, he followed his call to preach, giving voice lessons on the side. One day in a music store, the store's manager, a scout for the Brunswick recording company, persuaded Kazee to travel to New York to record. There Kazee cut more than fifty sides, most of which were released commercially on the Brunswick, Supertone, Vocalion, and Decca labels.

Kazee was urged to play on radio stations and at state fairs to promote his records, but he returned to preaching, and while he occasionally gave concerts, he kept his ministry separate from his folk music. He served churches in Corbin, Morehead, and Lexington, Kentucky, and taught at the Lexington Baptist Bible College.

Kazee's early recordings, such as "Lady Gay," "Roll On, John," and "The Wagoner's Lad," were treasured by folk music enthusiasts and have been included in several important compilations of folk music recordings. When he retired from preaching, Kazee performed at folk festivals, including those at Newport, UCLA, Mariposa, the University of Illinois, and Berea College. In 1958 Folkways Records released *Buell Kazee Sings and Plays*, and in 1978 June Appal Records released *Buell Kazee*. He was also the author of several books: three religious texts, an instructional book on banjo playing, and an unpublished autobiography. Kazee, who died on August 31, 1976, was buried at Mash Fork, in his native Magoffin County. His son Philip Kazee continued to perform many of his father's songs.

See also: BALLADS; BANJO; FOLK MUSIC REVIVALS.

—Loyal Jones, *Berea, Kentucky*

Kessinger, Clark

(1896–1975) Traditional fiddler.

Clark Kessinger was an accomplished West Virginia fiddler who gained national prominence through his early recordings as half of the Kessinger Brothers duo and through his later contest successes and other public performances.

Born July 27, 1896, in rural Lincoln County, West Virginia, Clark Kessinger later moved to nearby Boone County. He eventually settled in the Charleston area, where he became legendary for his extensive repertoire, impressive technique, and lively stage presence. Even as a very young man, Kessinger dominated local fiddling contests and was highly sought after as a dance musician and radio performer.

In early 1928, Kessinger began a recording career with his nephew, guitarist Luches "Luke" Kessinger (1906–1944). As the Kessinger Brothers they cut more than seventy sides for the Brunswick label during the next two and a half years. Their best-selling record was a version of "Wednesday Night Waltz"; recordings of lively fiddle breakdowns such as "Turkey in the Straw" and "Hell among the Yearlings" were also popular. Their final Brunswick recording session took place on September 20, 1930.

After nearly three and a half decades of relative obscurity, Kessinger was rediscovered in 1964 by traditional music enthusiast and promoter Ken Davidson. During the 1960s folk music revival, Kessinger won numerous fiddling competitions, appeared on national radio and television programs, performed at many folk festivals, and recorded extensively. The first, and often considered the most significant, of these later recordings was the album *The Legend of Clark Kessinger,* released in 1964 on Ken Davidson's Folk Promotions label. In 1971 Kessinger suffered a stroke, which ended his performing career. He passed away on June 4, 1975.

See also: CONTESTS AND CONVENTIONS; FIDDLE; FOLK MUSIC REVIVALS.

—John Lilly, *Goldenseal Magazine, West Virginia Division of Culture and History*

Kimbrough, Junior

(1930–1998) Blues singer, guitarist, and songwriter.

Born July 28, 1930, David "Junior" Kimbrough—a singer-guitarist and juke joint operator from Holly Springs, Mississippi—became known late in life for his signature style of country blues. Until age sixty-two, Kimbrough was known only regionally, performing at his establishment near Holly Springs and at other north Mississippi clubs. In 1992 he gained fame through his appearance in the documentary film *Deep Blues* and through the release of his first album, *All Night Long,* produced by music critic Robert Palmer. Along with fellow blues musician R. L. Burnside, Kimbrough helped bring the Oxford, Mississippi–based blues label Fat Possum Records to national prominence.

Kimbrough recorded three other albums for Fat Possum: *Sad Days, Lonely Nights* (1993), *Most Things Haven't Worked Out* (1997), and the posthumously released *God Knows I Tried* (1998). Fat Possum also released *Meet Me in the City* in 1999, a collection of recorded live performances of Kimbrough as a solo artist and with his band, the Soul Blues Boys. In 1997 the Hightone label released *Do the Rump,* an album of Kimbrough recordings from 1982 and 1988 produced by ethnomusicologist David Evans.

Kimbrough's approach to blues mixed traditional folk forms such as field hollers with Memphis soul rhythms and rock sounds to create a style of music often referred to by reviewers as "hypnotic." Unlike more traditional acoustic country blues guitarists, Kimbrough primarily played electric guitar so that he could be heard over the loud crowds at his juke joint.

Kimbrough's influence on Appalachian music extended beyond the blues: rockabilly legend Charlie Feathers, before becoming an influential musician at Sun Records in Memphis, received guitar lessons from Kimbrough. The 1998 Feathers anthology *Get with It* features Kimbrough on some early demo tracks. Kimbrough died of a heart attack on January 17, 1998.

See also: AFRICAN AMERICAN INFLUENCES; BLUES; GUITAR.

—Randall M. Brown, *Knoxville, Tennessee*

Kincaid, Bradley

(1895–1989) Early country singer.

Born July 13, 1895, in Point Leavell, Kentucky, and educated at Berea Academy in Berea, Kentucky, and the YMCA College in Chicago, Bradley Kincaid grew up listening to regional traditional music. In 1926 he became an overnight star on WLS Chicago's *National Barn Dance* radio show. After his first performance of the British ballad "Barbara Allen" and various folk songs, Kincaid received thousands of fan letters. He continued to collect songs in the Appalachians and published thirteen songbooks during his career, selling many thousands of copies via radio and at personal appearances.

In 1929 Kincaid went to WLW in Cincinnati, then to KDKA in Pittsburgh. Over the next ten years, teaming at times with Grandpa Jones and "Harmonica" Joe Troyan, he played in the Northeast over WGY Schenectady, WEAF and the NBC Red Network in New York City, WBZ Boston, WTIC Hartford, and WHAM Rochester. In 1944 Kincaid joined WSM's *Grand Ole Opry* in Nashville, where he remained until 1950. After retiring from the *Opry* he bought radio station WWSO and operated a music store in Springfield, Ohio.

Kincaid recorded some 250 songs (with repetitions), of which about 220 were released on a wide range of national and international record labels (some under pseudonyms, including "Dan Hughey," "John Carpenter," and "Harley Stratton"). His best-known recordings are "Barbara Allen," "The Fatal Derby Day," "The Legend of the Robin's Red Breast," and "The Letter Edged in Black." Over four days in 1963, he recorded 162 songs, which were eventually released on six albums.

Kincaid was a bridge from folk music to commercial country. A wide variety of performers—including Scotty Wiseman, Doc Hopkins, Mac Wiseman, Eddy Arnold, Bill Monroe, and Grandpa and Ramona Jones—have acknowledged his influence.

See also: COUNTRY MUSIC; *GRAND OLE OPRY* (MEDIA); *NATIONAL BARN DANCE* (MEDIA).

—Loyal Jones, *Berea, Kentucky*

Loyal Jones, *Radio's "Kentucky Mountain Boy": Bradley Kincaid (1980).*

Lawson, Doyle, and Quicksilver

(1944–) Bluegrass and gospel singer, mandolinist, and bandleader.

A native of Sullivan County, Tennessee, Doyle Lawson established his reputation as a bluegrass vocalist and mandolinist during the 1960s and 1970s while working with major bluegrass groups headed by Jimmy Martin and J. D. Crowe, as well as with the Country Gentlemen. In 1979 Lawson formed his own group, Quicksilver, which distinguished itself as a preeminent bluegrass gospel group.

Born April 20, 1944, Lawson grew up listening to his parents singing in quartets whose repertoires consisted of gospel songs found in books sold by Stamps-Baxter, James D. Vaughan, and other publishers of shape-note music. Through records and radio, Lawson became acquainted with the African American gospel music tradition, whose influence came to permeate the gospel quartet stylings of Quicksilver. So great has been the gospel influence on Lawson's music that his stage performances and recorded output consist of equal parts sacred and secular material. Quicksilver's a cappella quartet singing (for which Lawson sings lead and tenor vocal parts) is especially popular with audiences.

As an instrumentalist, Lawson drew inspiration from such veteran bluegrass mandolin players as Bill Monroe, Red Rector, Bobby Osborne, and Frank Wakefield. Lawson's approach to bluegrass performance is characterized by precise harmony vocals and hard-driving instrumental delivery. Quicksilver has inspired and influenced a multitude of young bluegrass musicians, who particularly admire Lawson's mandolin playing.

Quicksilver has recorded extensively for several record companies specializing in bluegrass. The group's vibrancy and diverse repertoire have made Doyle Lawson and Quicksilver a top draw at both bluegrass festivals and gospel music venues.

See also: BLUEGRASS; GOSPEL MUSIC, ANGLO-AMERICAN; MANDOLIN.

—Wayne W. Daniel, *Chamblee, Georgia*

Ledford, Lily May

(1917–1985) Traditional and early country banjo and fiddle player and singer.

The seventh of fourteen children of Daw White and Stella May Tackett, Lily May Ledford was born March 17, 1917, beside the South Fork of the Red River in Powell County, Kentucky. Growing up on a sharecropping farm, Lily May learned banjo from her father and by age twelve was playing fiddle.

In 1937 Ledford was chosen by John Lair to perform on WLS Chicago's *National Barn Dance* radio program. Lair featured Ledford's singing and driving clawhammer banjo playing accompanied by the Coon Creek Girls. This group, one of the first all-female string bands, featured Lily May, her sister Charlotte "Rosie" Ledford on guitar, Evelyn "Daisy" Lange on bass, and Esther "Violet" Koehler on mandolin. In 1939 Daisy and Violet left the band and were replaced by another Ledford sister, Minnie "Black-Eyed Susie" Ledford. Popular recordings from this period included the songs "How Many Biscuits Can You Eat" and "Banjo Picking Girl."

After just one year in Chicago, the Coon Creek Girls followed Lair to Ohio to perform on his new program, the *Renfro Valley Barn Dance*. In October 1939, the show moved to its permanent location in Mount Vernon, Kentucky, and the group appeared there for the next eighteen years, finally disbanding in 1957.

Ledford was rediscovered during the folk music revival of the 1960s and was invited by folklorist Ralph Rinzler to appear at the 1968 Newport Folk Festival in Rhode Island. Subsequently, Ledford performed at various festivals and recorded the album *Banjo Picking Girl* (1983) on the Greenhays label. Presented the National Heritage Award in 1985, she died that same year on July 14.

Ledford's music continues to live through a new all-female band, the New Coon Creek Girls, and on a retrospective recording, *Gems: Lily May Ledford—Rare Concert and Studio Recordings, 1968–1983*, issued in 2000 on the June Appal label.

See also: FOLK MUSIC REVIVALS; *RENFRO VALLEY BARN DANCE* (MEDIA); STRING-BAND MUSIC.

—Ron Pen, *University of Kentucky*

Lilly Brothers and Don Stover

Bluegrass musicians.
Lilly, Mitchell Burt "B." (1921–)
Singer and guitarist.
Lilly, Charles Everett (1924–)
Singer and mandolinist.
Stover, Don (1928–1996)
Banjo player, singer, and songwriter.

From Clear Creek, West Virginia, in the coal fields near Beckley, Mitchell Burt "B." Lilly (b. December 15, 1921) and Charles Everett Lilly (b. July 1, 1924) learned old ballads and Appalachian folk songs from their family. The brothers were soon entranced by the Carter Family and especially such brother duos as the Monroe Brothers and the Blue Sky Boys. Beginning in 1940, the Lilly Brothers built their early radio careers in Beckley and Wheeling, West Virginia, and Knoxville, Tennessee, singing as a duo, with B. on guitar and Everett on mandolin.

In 1951 Everett joined Flatt and Scruggs, but fiddler Tex Logan soon persuaded the brothers and their banjo-playing neighbor, Don Stover (March 6, 1928–November 11, 1996), from Ameagle, West Virginia, to join him in Boston to play on the radio and in clubs. Stover had grown up using the clawhammer style, but after hearing Earl Scruggs in the mid-1940s, he decided to adopt the three-finger picking style that would define the new bluegrass music.

From 1952 to 1970, the Lilly Brothers and Stover played at Boston's Hillbilly Ranch to transplanted southerners as well as northerners, exposing the latter group not only to the energetic new bluegrass sound, but also to the brother-duo sound and a rich repertoire of older songs and ballads. Don Stover remains an influential musician in his own right, not only for his banjo playing but also for his singing and songwriting, best heard on his solo albums for the Rounder label.

See also: BANJO; BLUEGRASS; DUOS, BROTHER.

—Frederick E. Danker, *University of Massachusetts*

Louvin Brothers

Country and gospel brother duo.
Louvin, Ira (1924–1965) Singer, mandolinist, and songwriter.
Louvin, Charlie (1927–) Singer, guitarist, and songwriter.

Ira Loudermilk, born April 21, 1924, and his brother Charlie, born July 7, 1927, grew up in the town of Henegar, Alabama—close to the home community of the Delmore Brothers. Seeking a career in country music, the brothers left farming, adopted the name Louvin, and turned professional. Ira played mandolin and sang high tenor, while Charlie sang lead and played guitar.

Although the duo's early recordings consisted primarily of original religious songs, they were accomplished at performing various styles of music. At first, the Louvins seemed too mainstream country for the gospel circuit and too traditional for Nashville's country music industry, but legendary producer and songwriter Fred Rose obtained a recording contract with MGM Records for them and later placed the duo on the newly formed Capitol label. In early 1955, Ira and Charlie landed a spot on the *Grand Ole Opry*.

Considered to be among the finest brother harmony acts, the Louvins came onto the country music scene at a time when musical tastes were quickly and radically changing. Hence, the brothers never attained great commercial success. The duo parted company in 1963. Ira died in a car crash on June 20, 1965; Charlie continued to perform as a solo act.

Although most of their recordings fell out of print after the duo's breakup, the Louvin Brothers' affecting harmonies—with Ira's tenor singing a focal point—continued to influence performers in diverse genres, including popular duos such as the Everly Brothers, bluegrass acts such as Jim and Jesse, and, in the late 1960s and the early 1970s, country rock musicians such as Gram Parsons and Emmylou Harris. The duo was inducted into the Country Music Hall of Fame in 2001.

See also: COUNTRY MUSIC; DUOS, BROTHER; GOSPEL MUSIC, ANGLO-AMERICAN.

—Thomas L. Wilmeth, *Concordia University Wisconsin*

Thomas L. Wilmeth, *The Music of the Louvin Brothers: Heaven's Own Harmony* (1999); Charles K. Wolfe, *In Close Harmony: The Story of the Louvin Brothers* (1996).

Loveless, Patty

(1957–) Country singer.

A major country vocalist of the late 1980s and 1990s, Patty Loveless established herself as many music critics' favorite among mainstream women country singers. Born Patricia Ramey in Pikeville, Kentucky, on January 4, 1957, Loveless was a coal miner's daughter like her distant cousin Loretta Lynn. Her early break came when she replaced Lynn in the Wilburn Brothers' touring show in 1973. Loveless married the Wilburns' drummer, Terry Lovelace, in 1976 and spent the next decade singing in rock bands around his hometown of Kings Mountain, North Carolina. She embarked on her country career in 1985 when she moved to Nashville, a failed marriage and a bout with alcohol behind her.

Loveless was a torchbearer for country music's neo-traditionalist movement. After recording several hits for MCA, she signed with Sony/Epic in 1992. Emory Gordy Jr., whom she married in 1989, produced for Loveless a series of best-selling and critically acclaimed albums. She received the Country Music Association's Female Vocalist of the Year award for 1996, the Academy of Country Music's Female Vocalist of the Year awards for 1996 and 1997, and a 1998 Grammy Award for Best Country Collaboration with Vocals.

Loveless has repeatedly acknowledged her roots in Appalachian music. A contributor to two Ralph Stanley tribute projects—*Saturday Night and Sunday Morning* (1993) and *Clinch Mountain Country* (1998)—Loveless topped the *Bluegrass Unlimited* singles chart with "Pretty Polly," a duet with Stanley from the latter album. Loveless's album *Mountain Soul* (2001) was her effort to revisit the music of her rural Appalachian childhood. After joining the *Grand Old Opry* in 1988, Loveless collaborated vocally with such artists as George Jones, Dolly Parton, Vince Gill, Ricky Skaggs, John Prine, Emmylou Harris, and Mary Chapin-Carpenter.

See also: COUNTRY MUSIC; LYNN, LORETTA; STANLEY, RALPH.

—Ajay Kalra, *East Tennessee State University*

Lulu Belle and Scotty

Early country husband-wife duo.

Wiseman, Lulu Belle (1913–1999) Singer.

Wiseman, Scotty (1909–1981) Singer, banjo player, and songwriter.

Lulu Belle and Scotty Wiseman are best known for popularizing an image of Appalachia that emphasized hillbillies and mountaineers as good, family-oriented people. The duo purveyed that image via the Chicago radio show *National Barn Dance* on WLS from 1933 until their retirement in 1958. Hailing from western North Carolina, the two met as members of the *National Barn Dance* troupe and married in late 1934.

By that time, Lulu Belle (born Myrtle Eleanor Cooper in Boone, North Carolina, on December 24, 1913) was already a national star because of her music and comedic flair. Scotty (born Scott Greene Wiseman in Ingalls, North Carolina, on November 8, 1909) had been discovered by Bradley Kincaid. Specializing in the singing of traditional Appalachian ballads and of Scotty's original songs, the duo became the *National Barn Dance*'s most popular performers. Lulu Belle and Scotty spent most of their career at WLS, with a brief interlude at WLW Cincinnati in 1940–41. The duo also appeared in seven Hollywood films. Lulu Belle was the star of the duo, while Scotty wrote their most famous songs, including "Have I Told You Lately That I Love You" and "Remember Me (When the Candle Lights Are Gleaming)." He cowrote the classic song "Mountain Dew" with Bascom Lamar Lunsford. Family was a crucial theme in their act, and their daughter and son regularly performed with them.

Readers polled by a national radio magazine in 1936 named Lulu Belle "National Radio Queen." She served two terms in the North Carolina House of Representatives in the 1970s. Scotty was inducted into the Nashville Songwriters Association Hall of Fame in 1971. After Scotty's death on January 31, 1981, Lulu Belle married Ernest Stamey. She died February 8, 1999.

See also: KINCAID, BRADLEY; LUNSFORD, BASCOM LAMAR.

—Kristine M. McCusker, *Middle Tennessee State University*

Lunsford, Bascom Lamar

(1882–1973) Revivalist singer, banjo player, fiddler, folk music collector, and promoter.

Bascom Lamar Lunsford, the originator of the Mountain Dance and Folk Festival in Asheville, North Carolina, was also a performer, recording artist, and collector of folk music. Born on March 21, 1882, in Mars Hill, North Carolina, Lunsford began making music at an early age, adopting the five-string banjo as his primary instrument. He also played the fiddle. Lunsford collected old songs and tunes from friends and neighbors as he grew up. After attending Rutherford College in nearby Rutherford County, he taught in a one-room school, then became a fruit tree salesman and later an apiarist. These jobs enabled him to stay overnight with mountain people and learn their music and stories. Subsequently, Lunsford taught at Rutherford College, served as a supervisor at a private school, and worked as a newspaper editor. After studying law at Trinity College (later renamed Duke University), he was admitted to the bar in 1913. During World War I, Lunsford was a Justice Department agent, and he later practiced law in Asheville. He established the Mountain Dance and Folk Festival in 1928 and for many years assembled the talent for the festival.

In 1929 Lunsford and Lamar Stringfield published *Thirty and One Folk Songs from the Southern Mountains.* To complement the lore he had already committed to memory, Lunsford began a paper collection that later contained more than three thousand songs, tunes, square dance calls, and stories. This collection is housed in the archives of Mars Hill College. Lunsford recorded from memory more than three hundred songs, tunes, dance calls, and stories for Columbia University in 1935 and the Library of Congress in 1949. Commercially, he cut twenty-two sides for OKeh, Brunswick, Vocalion, and Columbia, and, later, he recorded four albums—one each for the Library of Congress, Folkways, Riverside, and Rounder. He also composed a number of songs, including the widely known "Mountain Dew" (co-written with Scotty Wiseman).

In 1934 Lunsford assisted Sarah Gertrude Knott in establishing the National Folk Festival, held that year in St. Louis, and he helped to organize other festivals, including the North Carolina State Fair and the Cherokee Indian

Fair. In 1939 he sang folk songs at the White House for the king and queen of England. Lunsford's work as a performer and promoter was influential in the urban folk revival of the 1950s and 1960s. He died on September 4, 1973. In 1996 Smithsonian Folkways released a commemorative compact disc, *Bascom Lamar Lunsford: Ballads, Banjo Tunes, and Sacred Songs of Western North Carolina*.

See also: FESTIVALS, MUSIC; FOLK MUSIC REVIVALS; STRINGFIELD, LAMAR.

—Loyal Jones, *Berea, Kentucky*

Loyal Jones, *Minstrel of the Appalachians: The Story of Bascom Lamar Lunsford* (1984).

Lynn, Loretta

(1935–) Country singer and songwriter.

Loretta Webb was born April 14, 1935, at Butcher Hollow (or "Butcher Holler") in Johnson County, Kentucky. Her father was a coal miner in nearby Van Lear. Growing up in a one-room cabin with seven siblings, Loretta married Oliver V. "Mooney" Lynn at age thirteen and soon moved to the state of Washington, where her husband could find better employment.

Loretta had sung around the house from an early age and was an avid fan of the *Grand Ole Opry*. In Washington, she continued to sing informally but was preoccupied with raising her several children. Eventually her husband bought her a guitar, and in the late 1950s he convinced her to sing in public. In 1960 Lynn cut her first record for the small Zero label and found success on the country music charts with her composition "I'm a Honky Tonk Girl." She and her husband traveled across the country promoting her single, and upon arriving in Nashville she achieved stardom almost immediately. Joining the *Grand Ole Opry*, she became the foremost successor to pioneering female honky-tonk stylist Kitty Wells. Lynn wrote some of her own songs and chose others from compositions that fit her strong feminist stance. She sang about her early hardships ("Coal Miner's Daughter") and about struggles over men and fidelity in "Don't Come Home a Drinkin' (With Lovin' on Your Mind)," "Your Squaw Is on the Warpath," "When the Tingle Becomes a Chill," and "After the Fire Is Gone," the latter song one of a series of popular duets with Conway Twitty. She broached topics of women's reproductive rights in "One's on the Way" and "The Pill."

Lynn's best-selling autobiography, *Coal Miner's Daughter*, published in 1976, became a hugely popular film starring Sissy Spacek as the singer in 1980. Lynn received the Country Music Association's first Female Vocalist of the Year award in 1967 and its first Female Entertainer of the Year award in 1972. A popular guest on network television talk and mainstream music shows through the mid-1980s, she continued to record country hits until she cut back her activities later in the decade. Lynn was elected to the Nashville Songwriters Hall of Fame in 1983 and to the Country Music Hall of Fame in 1988. Her sister, Crystal Gayle (Brenda Gayle Webb), has also enjoyed a significant career in country music, though in a more pop-influenced vein. In 2001 Lynn made a minor comeback with the album *Still Country*.

See also: *COAL MINER'S DAUGHTER* (MEDIA); COAL-MINING AND PROTEST MUSIC; COUNTRY MUSIC.

—Frederick E. Danker, *University of Massachusetts*

Loretta Lynn, with George Vecsey, *Coal Miner's Daughter* (1976); Loretta Lynn, with Patsy Bale Cox, *Still Woman Enough: A Memoir* (2002).

Macon, Uncle Dave

(1870–1952) Early country banjo player and singer.

David Harrison Macon was born October 7, 1870, in Warren County, Tennessee. When he was thirteen, his family moved to Nashville, where they ran a hotel that served as headquarters for many circus and vaudeville acts. Macon acquired his first banjo at the age of fourteen. After his father's death the family moved to rural Cannon County, Tennessee. There, Macon farmed and ran a mule-drawn transportation company.

Macon learned the traditional songs of the region as well as popular songs from vaudeville and medicine shows. At the age of fifty, he embarked on a musical career that lasted more than thirty years. He became the most popular performer on the early *Grand Ole Opry* and one of the first country music recording stars. Macon was a crucial link between the southern folk music and commercial country music. His repertoire included traditional ballads, vaudeville tunes, comic songs, gospel music, and topical songs ("The Bible's True," about the Scopes trial, and "All In, Down and Out Blues," about the depression). Many of his comic lyrics derived from black folk music. His first record to be released was "Chewing Gum," perhaps his most popular comedy song. Macon performed with other musicians, including Sid Harkreader and Sam and Kirk McGee, and his style influenced Stringbean and Grandpa Jones, among others. Macon's band recorded as the Fruit Jar Drinkers and as the Dixie Sacred Singers. He died March 22, 1952. In 1966 Macon was inducted into the Country Music Hall of Fame. Later generations continued to celebrate his music through such festivals as the Uncle Dave Macon Days Celebration in Murfreesboro, Tennessee.

See also: COUNTRY MUSIC; *GRAND OLE OPRY* (MEDIA); TRAVELING SHOWS (HUMOR).

—Charles F. Faber, *Lexington, Kentucky*

Mainer, J. E. and Wade

Early country musicians.

Mainer, Joseph Emmett "J. E." (1898–1971) Fiddler and singer.

Mainer, Wade (1907–) Banjo player and singer.

Joseph Emmett "J. E." Mainer was a traditional fiddler whose group Mainer's Mountaineers was one of the leading Appalachian string bands of the late 1930s. Born in Buncombe County, North Carolina, on July 20, 1898, Joseph Emmett Mainer and his younger brother Wade, born April 21, 1907, were both influenced musically by a fiddle-playing brother-in-law, Roscoe Banks. As a teenager, J. E. went to work in cotton mills; settling in the early 1920s in Concord, North Carolina, he formed Mainer's Mountaineers to play at local functions. J. E. was soon joined by Wade, whose two-finger style of banjo playing has been identified by music scholars as a stylistic link between the clawhammer and bluegrass banjo styles. This band's most influential recording was a rendition of Gussie Davis's 1880 lyric "Maple on the Hill," for which they supplied a new tune.

In 1936 Wade left to form his own band, the Sons of the Mountaineers. J. E. and Mainer's Mountaineers continued recording for various labels and working for a large number of radio stations. J. E. was most prolific as a recording artist after being rediscovered during the urban folk revival of the 1960s. Thereafter, he played festivals and concerts until his death on June 12, 1971.

In 1953 Wade left the music business and moved to Michigan to work for General Motors. For some years he and his wife, Julia, sang only in churches. After 1973, when he retired, Wade and Julia began performing at folk and bluegrass festivals, and they made several records. In 1987 Wade was awarded a National Heritage Fellowship for his life's work, and in 1992 he recorded his last album.

See also: BANJO; COUNTRY MUSIC; FIDDLE; STRING-BAND MUSIC.

—W. K. McNeil, *The Ozark Folk Center*

Mandolin

A fretted, eight-string instrument of European origin, the mandolin became available in Appalachia in the late nineteenth century through mail-order catalogs and thereafter was a mainstay of both traditional and popular musical styles within the region. By the time the country music recording industry arose in the 1920s, the mandolin was already used in many Appalachian string bands, including Ernest V. Stoneman's group. During the next decade, it became the primary lead instrument in the brother harmony duo style. Since then, mandolinists in the region have incorporated outside musical influences, yielding diverse mandolin-playing styles that draw on country, bluegrass, blues, jazz, and classical music.

The mandolin is tuned like a violin (GG-DD-AA-EE) but features a fretted fingerboard and four pairs of strings (each pair tuned in unison) that are usually picked with a plectrum. The instrument usually has a larger body than a violin. A member of the lute family, the mandolin originated in central Europe during the Middle Ages. In the early twentieth century, the instrument evolved in the New World from a round-backed ("taterbug") model to the flat-bodied, Florentine model designed by Lloyd Loar, renowned luthier for the Gibson Musical Instruments company.

The mandolin was commonly featured alongside the fiddle, the banjo, and the guitar in 1920s-era string bands. Early harmony duos, including Mac and Bob (who started performing professionally in 1922), and later brother harmony acts such as the Blue Sky Boys combined the mandolin with the guitar. In the harmony duos, mandolin leads usually consisted of variations on the melody played with a right-hand tremolo. The preeminent mandolinist during this era was Bill Monroe, whose technically dazzling playing (with the Monroe Brothers in the 1930s and with the Blue Grass Boys from 1939 onward) was extremely influential on his contemporaries and on subsequent generations of musicians in Appalachia and elsewhere. Monroe fused a European American fiddle-tune repertoire with the blues, forging a quick, flamboyant and improvised style of string-band music that was eventually labeled bluegrass.

Later mandolinists from Appalachia generally started by imitating Bill Monroe's style of bluegrass mandolin playing, but more accomplished musicians also added individual innovations to expand the possibilities of the instrument. Jesse McReynolds (of Carfax, Virginia) developed a cross-picking technique that simulated Earl Scruggs's three-finger banjo rolls and that has influenced countless mandolinists and flat-pick guitarists. McReynolds also perfected a split-string playing technique that allowed the playing of harmonies on an individual pair of strings by fretting each string on different frets. Frank Wakefield (from Emory Gap, Tennessee) was known for his hybrid pick-and-fingerpicking technique. Jethro Burns (a Conasauga, Tennessee, native) was regarded as a founding father of jazz mandolin. Other masters on the instrument from Appalachia include Bobby Osborne (Hyden, Kentucky), Red Rector (Marshall, North Carolina), Doyle Lawson (Kingsport, Tennessee), Ricky Skaggs (Cordell, Kentucky), Tim O'Brien (Wheeling, West Virginia), Butch Baldassari (Scranton, Pennsylvania), Shawn Lane (Fort Blackmore, Virginia), and Adam Steffey (Johnson City, Tennessee). Some mandolinists, especially Baldassari and O'Brien, have broadened the possibilities for the mandolin by utilizing the instrument for performing other American music genres and ethnic musics. Several mandolinists have also performed on related instruments of the lute family, including the mandola and the bouzouki.

See also: BLUEGRASS; HOMER AND JETHRO; JIM AND JESSE; MONROE, BILL.

—Steve Hooks, *WMMT Whitesburg, Kentucky/WDVX Clinton, Tennessee*

Marshall Tucker Band

Southern rock group.

The Marshall Tucker Band was formed in 1970 by six natives of Spartanburg, South Carolina. The group maintained its roster of original members—Toy Caldwell, Tommy Caldwell, George McCorkle, Paul T. Riddle, Jerry Eubanks, and Doug Gray—until 1980, when Tommy Caldwell was killed in a traffic accident. By 1984, three members had departed: Toy Caldwell (who died in 1993), McCorkle, and Riddle. Despite changes in personnel, the Marshall Tucker Band continued to be a vital presence in southern rock music into the twenty-first century.

Beginning with their 1973 self-titled debut album, the Marshall Tucker Band blended many genres of southern music into its distinct sound. In its earliest days, the group was particularly known for adding flute and saxophone to the standard guitar-driven southern country rock instrumentation.

Often compared to the Allman Brothers, the Marshall Tucker Band has a softer, more country-oriented sound featuring pedal steel guitar. The group over the years has worked with such artists as Charlie Daniels, Hank Williams Jr., and Garth Brooks. Several Marshall Tucker Band albums have gone gold and platinum; the group's 1976 instrumental "Long Hard Ride" received a Grammy nomination. A number of classic Marshall Tucker Band songs address Appalachian themes, including "Blue Ridge Mountain Sky" and "Hillbilly Band." With *Face Down in the Blues* (1998) and *Gospel* (1999), the Marshall Tucker Band continued to celebrate the group's original regional influences.

See also: COUNTRY MUSIC; ROCK MUSIC.

—Amy Cortner, *Caldwell Community College*

Martin, Jimmy

(1927–2005) Bluegrass singer, guitarist, and bandleader.

One of the most identifiable voices in bluegrass as well as a singular and strong-minded character, Jimmy Martin (b. August 10, 1927, in Sneedville, Tennessee) has long been an advocate of traditional bluegrass. Some of the best second-generation bluegrass artists, including Doyle Lawson, J. D. Crowe, and Bill Emerson, have passed through the ranks of Martin's band.

Making his debut in 1949 with Bill Monroe's Blue Grass Boys, Martin later worked with the Osborne Brothers before starting his own group, the Sunny Mountain Boys. With the help of some exceptionally talented sidemen (most notably Crowe on banjo and Paul Williams on mandolin and tenor vocals), Martin recorded a number of classic songs for the Decca label, including "Hit Parade of Love," "Ocean of Diamonds," "Hold Whatcha Got," "Widow Maker," and "Sunny Side of the Mountain." He participated on the Nitty Gritty Dirt Band's influential 1972 album *Will the Circle Be Unbroken;* many young listeners discovered his style of bluegrass through this milestone recording.

Throughout the 1990s, despite declining health, Martin was still appearing at a few select festivals. He was, along with Ralph Stanley, one of the few bluegrass pioneers to survive into the twenty-first century. In 1995 Martin was inducted into the International Bluegrass Music Association Hall of Honor. He died May 14, 2005.

See also: BLUEGRASS; MONROE, BILL; OSBORNE BROTHERS.

—Christian Séguret, *Auxy, France*

Tom Piazza, *True Adventures with the King of Bluegrass* (1999).

McGhee, Brownie

(1915–1996) Country blues singer and guitarist.

Walter Brown "Brownie" McGhee was born November 30, 1915, in Knoxville, Tennessee, and was reared in Kingsport. At the age of four, he contracted polio and was partially crippled. McGhee learned guitar from his father and could also play the organ and the piano by age eight. He plied his trade in church, traveling shows, roadhouses, and juke joints, playing a mixture of country blues and other folk songs. A 1937 operation sponsored by the March of Dimes restored most of McGhee's mobility.

In 1938 McGhee relocated to the North Carolina Piedmont, where he met Blind Boy Fuller, a famed blues singer and guitarist, and J. B. Long, a talent scout for OKeh Records. In Chicago, McGhee recorded his first song, "Me and My Dog," as the flip side to Fuller's "Bus Ride Blues." After Fuller's passing in 1941, McGhee wrote and recorded the song "The Death of Blind Boy Fuller" for OKeh. This single was credited to "Blind Boy Fuller No. 2."

Later in 1941, McGhee started a longterm collaboration with harmonica player Sonny Terry, Fuller's former sideman. Relocating to New York in 1942, the duo became a part of the city's burgeoning folk music scene, playing alongside Woody Guthrie, Pete Seeger, Leadbelly, and Josh White. The duo was equally popular with revivalist audiences in the 1950s and 1960s, recording numerous albums and performing at major folk music venues and festivals across much of the United States, Canada, and Europe. McGhee and Terry's association lasted approximately forty years, reaching a landmark in 1973 with *Sonny and Brownie*, an album featuring songs written by prominent songwriters such as Curtis Mayfield and Randy Newman and performed with popular musicians, including Arlo Guthrie, John Mayall, and John Hammond Jr., as sidemen. From the early 1980s until his death, McGhee continued as a solo performer while gaining a measure of success as an actor in such movies as *The Jerk* and *Angel Heart* and on television's *Matlock* series. He had previously worked in Broadway shows, including Tennessee Williams's *Cat on a Hot Tin Roof* and Langston Hughes's *Simply Heavenly*. McGhee died February 16, 1996.

See also: BLUES; FOLK MUSIC REVIVALS; GUITAR; HARMONICA.

—James "Sparky" Rucker, *Maryville, Tennessee*

Minstrel Music/Blackface Minstrelsy

Flourishing during the mid-nineteenth century, the minstrel show initially consisted of white male musicians performing broad caricatures of African Americans through wearing blackface (using burnt cork or a black substance known as mantan as makeup to give the performer the appearance of being an African American minstrel). Later nineteenth-century minstrel shows also included black performers and, sometimes, female performers. Traveling minstrel shows were common in Appalachia, and their influence on Appalachian music continues long after the genre itself faded from popularity.

Minstrelsy influenced Appalachian music in several ways. First, minstrel shows introduced the banjo to many Appalachians and also influenced the instrument's evolution. Second, the minstrel repertoire became popular in Appalachia; many minstrel songs and tunes continue to be played by contemporary old-time and bluegrass musicians within the region. Third, minstrel show performance styles were incorporated into country music and formed the basis of such country music barn dances as the *Grand Ole Opry*, *National Barn Dance*, *WWVA Jamboree*, and *Hee Haw*. The personae and performance styles of many early country music performers, including Uncle Dave Macon and Roy Acuff, owed much to minstrelsy, since those musicians started their performing careers in medicine shows, a form of entertainment strongly influenced by the minstrel show tradition.

Early minstrel performances featured short comedy skits and song-and-dance pieces and were usually featured as parts of circuses or of other traveling shows. Thomas Dartmouth "Daddy" Rice and Joel Walker Sweeney were two important performers from this early minstrel era. Appomattox, Virginia, native Sweeney has been widely credited with the invention of the five-string banjo. Although his modification of the originally African instrument was the addition of a melody string and not the short drone string, as long believed, Sweeney played a significant role in popularizing the banjo among white people. The first full minstrel show was staged by the Virginia Minstrels in February 1843 in New York City. Blackface minstrel shows during this phase featured dancing and songs with banjo, fiddle, tambourine, bones, and, occasionally, accordion accompaniment. The Virginia Minstrels' organizer, Daniel Decatur Emmett (born in Mount Vernon, Ohio, near the northwest margin of Appalachia), is credited with composing such minstrel songs as "Old Dan Tucker" and "I Wish I Was in Dixie's Land" (though recent scholarship has questioned Emmett's authorship of the latter song, better known as "Dixie," suggesting that an African American songwriter may have contributed to its composition). The Virginia Minstrels' banjo player, Billy Whitlock, who studied with Sweeney, helped popularize the banjo in the British Isles, where the group traveled.

A typical minstrel show by the 1850s was divided into three principal parts. In the first part the performers were seated in a semicircle. All the members of the "company" were similarly attired, with the exception of the comically clad "endmen," who played bones and tambourine and were respectively named Mr. Bones and Mr. Tambo, or Pat and Mike in the event that the Irish were the target of the humor. The endmen cracked jokes and hurled insults at the central performer—the "straight man," or the interlocutor—who performed in "whiteface" (without wearing the burnt cork makeup). The comic endmen were derived from the popular blackface characters Jim Crow (the unrefined plantation slave) and Zip Coon (the urban dandy), whose names derived from the titles of songs by Daddy Rice and George Washington Dixon (c. early 1820s), respectively, whose blackface acts were forerunners of the full-fledged minstrel show.

While early minstrel shows were often featured as part of circus or theater shows and focused on material mocking African American dialects and dances, by the 1850s songs from a more "genteel" tradition had entered the genre, and black elements were downplayed. The songs in the first part of a minstrel show were evenly distributed between up-tempo pieces, such as Stephen Foster's "Oh! Susanna," and sentimental ballads, such as "Lorena." A minstrel show's second part, the olio, was performed on the proscenium to allow for the changing of the set. The olio consisted of a varied mix of short skits and song-and-dance routines presented by a solo performer or in varying duo combinations, much like latter-day vaudeville acts or modern stand-up comedians. The third part—the afterpiece and a finale known as the walk-around—usually involved the entire cast, with members of the troupe participating in song, instrumental and choral music, and dance, in various combinations. The walk-around was generally accompanied by a musical composition such as Sam Lucas's "Hannah Boil Dat Cabbage Down."

Many minstrel songs and tunes entered oral traditions across Appalachia and continue to be performed. Tunes popular among contemporary old-time musicians that started as minstrel songs include "Old Joe Clark" and "Get Along Home, Cindy." Several songs from the American Civil War period—Henry Clay Work's "Grandfather Clock"; George Frederick Root's "Battle Cry of Freedom"; and James Bland's "Oh, Dem Golden Slippers" and "Carry Me Back to Old Virginny"—originated in minstrel shows and remain standards in the Appalachian song repertoire.

See also: BANJO; CIVIL WAR MUSIC; TRAVELING SHOWS (HUMOR).

—James "Sparky" Rucker, *Maryville, Tennessee*

Richard Jackson, ed., *Popular Songs of Nineteenth-Century America* (1976); David A. Jasen and Gene Jones, *Spreadin' Rhythm Around: Black Popular Songwriters, 1880–1930* (1998); Robert C. Toll, *Blacking Up: The Minstrel Show in Nineteenth-Century America* (1974).

Monroe, Bill

(1911–1996) Bluegrass mandolinist, singer, and composer.

Known as the "Father of Bluegrass Music," Bill Monroe is one of the few individuals credited with the creation of a new musical genre. Born on September 13, 1911, in the town of Rosine in western Kentucky, Monroe had a definite influence on the post–World War II revival of interest in the music of Appalachia due to his repertoire, which was drawn from the same sources as much of traditional Appalachian music.

Influenced by the fiddle tunes of his uncle Pendleton Vandiver, immortalized in Monroe's song "Uncle Pen," as well as the blues of itinerant African American guitarist Arnold Shultz, Monroe started playing professionally with his brother Charlie in the early 1930s as the Monroe Brothers. Bill Monroe's animated mandolin playing and high tenor voice contributed to this early brother duo's success. In the late 1930s, Monroe started his own band, the Blue Grass Boys, which in 1945 added Lester Flatt and Earl Scruggs; this lineup, completed by Chubby Wise on fiddle and Cedric Rainwater on bass, is considered by most historians as the first combination to play what came to be known as bluegrass. Many major figures in bluegrass were at one time Blue Grass Boys, including David "Stringbean" Akeman, Don Reno, Jimmy Martin, Sonny Osborne, Mac Wiseman, Del McCoury, and Peter Rowan.

In the mid-1950s, despite the fact that Elvis Presley covered Monroe's "Blue Moon of Kentucky," bluegrass suffered as rock 'n' roll exploded nationally. By the next decade, however, Monroe had not only emerged as a central figure in the urban folk revival, but he also was headlining bluegrass festivals. He died September 9, 1996. Monroe attained cult status within the bluegrass community and left hundreds of classic songs and instrumentals that will be played for generations to come.

See also: BLUEGRASS; DUOS, BROTHER; MANDOLIN.

—Christian Séguret, *Auxy, France*

Tom Ewing, ed., *The Bill Monroe Reader* (2000); Richard D. Smith, *Can't You Hear Me Callin': The Life of Bill Monroe, Father of Bluegrass* (2000).

Muscle Shoals

The small city of Muscle Shoals sits near the bank of the Tennessee River in northwestern Alabama, adjacent to three other cities: Florence, Sheffield, and Tuscumbia. The quad-city area, generally referred to as Muscle Shoals in music circles, emerged as an important regional recording center in the early 1960s, yielding a laid-back stylistic musical admixture of soul, country, rock, and rhythm and blues. Muscle Shoals's musical culture grew out of its vernacular traditional music—spirituals, ballads, and blues—fostered in the area by African American and Scots-Irish settlers.

At the beginning of the twentieth century, Florence-born William Christopher "W. C." Handy, a composer and publisher, ventured to Memphis and became renowned as the "Father of the Blues." Recording activity in the quad-city area dates from the 1940s, when Sheffield bassist Dexter Johnson opened his garage studio. Nevertheless, many of the area's early talent, including Florence natives Sam Phillips, founder of Memphis's Sun Records, and Buddy Killen, country musician, producer, and eventual owner of Nashville's Tree Publishing Company, were drawn to more prominent and lucrative commercial music centers.

In 1956 songwriter James Joiner and guitarist Kelton "Kelso" Herston formed the first Alabama-based recording company, Tune Records, in Florence. That label released Joiner's song "A Fallen Star" in 1957, sung by popular local singer Bobby Denton. Jud Phillips, brother of Sam Phillips, formed the short-lived Judd label in Florence, releasing Arthur Alexander's song "Sally Sue Brown" in 1958. Tom Stafford, also of Florence, started SPAR (Stafford Publishing and Recording) Music in 1959. Soon, Stafford, teaming with local musicians Billy Sherrill and Rick Hall, changed the organization's name to FAME (Florence Alabama Music Enterprises), recruiting aspiring local songwriters Dan Penn, Dewey Lyndon "Spooner" Oldham, and Donnie Fritts. In 1960 Sherrill, who later pioneered the "countrypolitan" sound in country music, moved to Nashville, and Hall then acquired FAME from Stafford.

In 1961 Hall moved FAME to a tobacco barn in Muscle Shoals and employed a house band comprised of pianist David

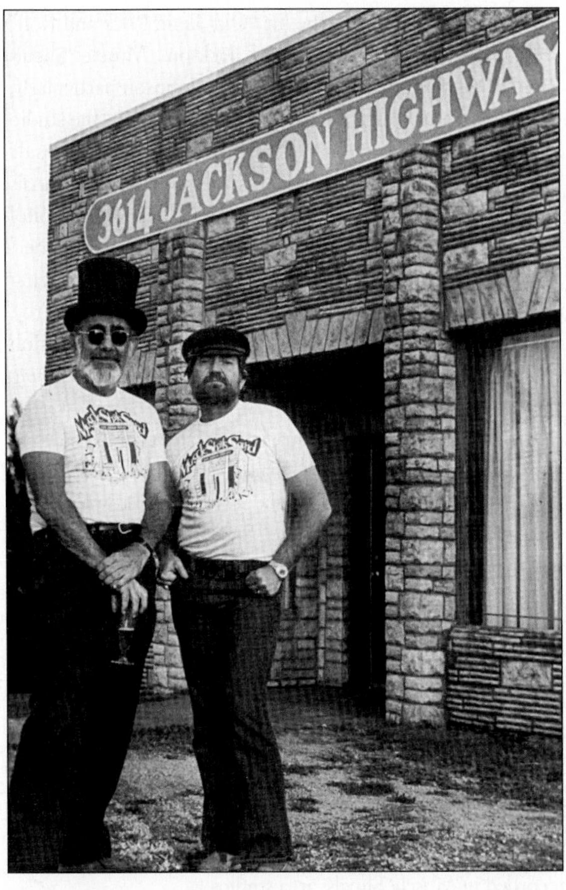

Jerry Wexler (left) and Willie Nelson at 3614 Jackson Highway, Sheffield, Alabama, 1974. Many of the most renowned musicians, songwriters, producers, and sound technicians in 1960s and 1970s popular music recorded at 3614 Jackson Highway, the first home of the Muscle Shoals Sound Studio.

Briggs, guitarist Terry Thompson, drummer Jerry Carrigan, and bassist Norbert Putnam. FAME's first regional hit was Alexander's influential "You Better Move On" in 1961. In 1962 Hall produced "Steal Away," written and sung by Jimmy Hughes of Leighton, Alabama, which reached number seventeen on the national pop charts in July 1964. FAME's success as a recording studio soon attracted to Muscle Shoals such singers as Tommy Roe, Ray Stevens, and the Tams, as well as Felton Jarvis, later an Elvis Presley producer.

In November 1964, Killen produced singer Joe Tex's top five pop hit "Hold What You've Got" at FAME. That song was released through Atlantic Records, initiating an alliance between Hall and that label's artist and repertoire representative Jerry Wexler. In 1964 Carrigan, Putnam, and Briggs left for Nashville, where they had successful studio careers. Hall hired a new studio band for FAME: guitarist Jimmy Johnson (nephew of Dexter Johnson), Spooner Oldham, drummer Roger Hawkins, and bassist Albert "Junior" Lowe. That band backed singer Joe Simon's Vee-Jay Records single "Let's Do It Over" in 1965, an early hit from the songwriting duo of Penn and Oldham. Concurrently, Quin Ivy, a local disc jockey, along with local guitarist Marlin Greene, opened Norala (later Quinvy) Recording Studio in Sheffield. In early 1966, Ivy produced Leighton, Alabama, singer Percy Sledge's recording of "When a Man Loves a Woman." Engineered by Jimmy Johnson and released through Atlantic Records, that song, backed by FAME's studio band, became a number one pop hit. Thereafter, Muscle Shoals was identified nationally as a center for racially integrated "soul" music, a genre of popular music combining elements of blues, country, gospel, and rhythm and blues.

In 1966 Atlantic's Wexler brought singer Wilson Pickett to FAME, where he recorded his chart-topping hit "Land of 1,000 Dances." Memphis-based guitarist Lincoln "Chips" Moman and bassist Tommy Cogbill augmented the FAME band for Pickett's hits "Mustang Sally" in 1966 and "Funky Broadway" in 1967. Wexler also produced Aretha Franklin's single "I Never Loved a Man (The Way I Love You)" backed with the Penn-Moman song "Do Right Woman, Do Right Man" at FAME; the former became a number one rhythm and blues hit in the spring of 1967. In January 1967, Otis Redding and Jimmy Johnson produced singer Arthur Conley's "Sweet Soul Music," a major hit that attempted to summarize the genre. Shortly afterward, Hall produced two more influential hits at FAME: Clarence Carter's "Slip Away" (released on Atlantic Records) and singer Etta James's Carter-penned "Tell Mama" (Chess Records).

Meanwhile, Ivy, Greene, and songwriter Eddie Hinton continued producing local soul artists such as Bill Brandon, Tony Borders, and Don Varner for Quinvy's Southcamp imprint. (David Johnson, Ivy's assistant engineer, eventually took over Quinvy Recording Studio, renaming it Broadway Sound.) In 1966 Pensacola, Florida, promoter "Papa" Don Schroeder brought singers James and Bobby Purify, along with Birmingham, Alabama, keyboardist Barry Beckett, to FAME, where the Purify brothers recorded the number six pop hit "I'm Your Puppet," written by Penn and Oldham.

In 1967 Beckett and local bassist David Hood joined FAME's band, replacing Oldham and Cogbill. FAME's new quartet (Beckett, Hawkins, Hood, and Jimmy Johnson) began freelancing for Atlantic Records, commuting to New York City and playing on recording sessions for Solomon Burke, King Curtis, Dusty Springfield, and Aretha Franklin. Often, additional guitarists appeared on Muscle Shoals sessions, including Hinton, Lowe, Duane Allman, Pete Carr, Will McFarlane, Wayne Perkins, Joe South, and Travis Wammack. Also in the late 1960s, trumpeter and arranger Harrison Calloway Jr. put together the Muscle Shoals Horns, a brass section featured on many recordings.

In 1969 the FAME rhythm section resigned from FAME to establish themselves as the Muscle Shoals Rhythm Section. They set up their own recording studio, Muscle Shoals Sound, at 3614 Jackson Highway in Sheffield. That year, singers Cher, Lulu, and Boz Scaggs recorded at the studio for Atlantic, while Jimmy Johnson engineered the Rolling Stones' "Brown Sugar" and "Wild Horses." The Muscle Shoals Rhythm Section's 1969 production of singer R. B. Greaves's number two pop hit "Take a Letter Maria" demonstrated the new studio's viability. By the early 1970s, Muscle Shoals had become an internationally respected recording center, with artists from diverse genres making records there. The studio hosted sessions for Jimmy Cliff, J. J. Cale, Don Covay, Art Garfunkel, Linda Ronstadt, Leon Russell, Tony Joe White, and Bobby Womack, as well as Memphis-based Stax label acts Luther Ingram, Mel and Tim, the Staple Singers, and Johnnie Taylor. Concurrently, FAME produced Clarence Carter's number four pop hit "Patches" (1970) as well as recordings for such nationally charting artists as Mac Davis, Paul Anka, and Lou Rawls. Hall's work at FAME earned him *Billboard* magazine's Producer of the Year award in 1971. The same year, Hall produced the Osmonds' number one hit "One Bad Apple," penned by FAME staff writer George Jackson.

As the Muscle Shoals scene diversified, a host of independent songwriters and producers emerged. Mickey Buckins wrote and produced the Osmonds' hit "Double Lovin'" at FAME in 1971. The following year, Muscle Shoals Sound publisher Terry Woodford and FAME keyboardist Clayton Ivey formed Wishbone Productions in Muscle Shoals, signing a contract with Detroit's Motown label to record the Commodores, Supremes, and Temptations. In 1976 Wishbone signed Red Bay, Alabama, songwriter and guitarist Mac McAnally. Other 1970s-era Muscle Shoals–area songwriters included Ava Aldridge, also a background vocalist for many Muscle Shoals recording sessions, and Walt Aldridge, a guitarist at FAME who later became an influential country songwriter and producer. Increased recording activity in Muscle Shoals during the 1970s prompted the emergence of competing studios, notably Music Mill and Widget.

In 1972–73 the Muscle Shoals Rhythm Section toured and recorded with British rock group Traffic. In 1973 Paul Simon's Muscle Shoals–recorded *There Goes Rhymin' Simon* received a Grammy nomination. White soul singer Bonnie Bramlett and southern rock artists Lynyrd Skynyrd (who immortalized the Muscle Shoals scene in the lyrics of "Sweet Home Alabama"), Blackfoot, Cowboy, and Wet Willie likewise recorded at Muscle Shoals Sound in the 1970s, as did country singer Willie Nelson, who in 1974 made his groundbreaking outlaw country album *Phases and Stages* there. Rod Stewart recorded his hits "Sailing" and "Tonight's the Night" at the studio in the mid-1970s. Bob Seger recorded often in Muscle Shoals, including the hit "Old Time Rock and Roll" (1978), also written by George Jackson. Muscle Shoals Rhythm Section members, Beckett and Johnson particularly, emerged as much sought-after producers. In 1978 the studio moved its facility to a vacant Naval Reserve building beside the Tennessee River in Sheffield. In 1979 Muscle Shoals Sound formed an independent label affiliated with Capitol Records, releasing recordings by Levon Helm and Delbert McClinton. In the late 1970s and early 1980s, the Amazing Rhythm Aces, Billy Burnette, Lou Ann Barton, Glenn Frey, and John Prine recorded at Muscle Shoals Sound, as did Bob Dylan, whose Grammy-winning album *Slow Train Coming* (1980) was recorded there.

In the 1980s, many country music stars recorded at Muscle Shoals, including Hank Williams Jr., the Oak Ridge Boys, Eddie Rabbitt, Sawyer Brown, and T. Graham Brown. Under Rick Hall's guidance, local band Shenandoah emerged as a major national country music act. In 1985 Jackson, Mississippi–based Malaco Records purchased Muscle Shoals Sound, reinvigorating interest in southern soul through issuing discs by such artists as Bobby "Blue" Bland, "Little" Milton Campbell, Tyrone Davis, Dorothy Moore, and Johnny Taylor—often utilizing the Muscle Shoals Rhythm Section. In 1992 Etta James recorded *The Right Time* at the studio; the next year Dan Penn made his acclaimed album *Do Right Man* there. More recently, rock and pop musicians including Melissa Etheridge, the Decoys, John Hiatt, and George Michael have recorded in Muscle Shoals–area studios.

Although many studios that sprang up in the area during the 1970s have closed, FAME and Muscle Shoals Sound remain active, and there has been a resurgence of activity. The renowned 3614 Jackson Highway studio, the former site of Muscle Shoals Sound, reopened in 2001 under new management; it was refurbished to resemble the original. In 1998 Mac McAnally's studio, one of several studios built in Muscle Shoals to serve its burgeoning publishing industry, yielded Jimmy Buffett's album *Beach House on the Moon*. Jimmy Johnson, who chairs the nearby Alabama Music Hall of Fame, operates a commercial recording studio in Sheffield. Mark and Rodney Hall, sons of producer Rick Hall, initiated Muscle Shoals Records, an offshoot of FAME Music Enterprises, with 2001 releases by Russell Smith and the Decoys. The popular W. C. Handy Music Festival, held each August in Florence, attests to continued interest in the vibrant musical legacy of Muscle Shoals.

See also: RECORDING COMPANIES; RHYTHM AND BLUES; ROCK MUSIC.

—Peter B. Olson, *University of Memphis*

Peter Guralnick, *Sweet Soul Music: Rhythm and Blues and the Southern Dream of Freedom* (1986); Jerry Wexler, with David Ritz, *Rhythm and the Blues: A Life in American Music* (1993); Richard Younger, *Get a Shot of Rhythm and Blues: The Arthur Alexander Story* (2000).

Music Organizations

Music has arguably been Appalachia's foremost cultural export, as the region's musical heritage has been celebrated by dedicated music organizations located throughout the United States and in many other countries. These organizations, many of which are outgrowths of twentieth-century folk revivals, have attempted to maintain the communal spirit that originally fostered the music. Technological innovations, including the Internet, have allowed these music communities to expand. Many clubs sponsor festivals and other live performances that preserve and perpetuate Appalachian musical traditions.

In the 1920s, the popularity of newer, commercially disseminated musical styles threatened to erode a rich legacy of traditional musical styles, including old-time fiddling. In response, enthusiasts of traditional music sponsored fiddlers' conventions, which spread through the South after World War I and became a popular form of entertainment. Sponsored by civic groups and local music clubs, these conventions not only raised money for charitable causes but also united communities in the process. The popularity of such conventions declined after World War II due to changing musical tastes and the migration of many rural Appalachian people to cities.

The urban folk revival of the late 1950s and the 1960s generated new interest in Appalachian music. Organizations dedicated to the region's music were founded where none had existed before, and fiddling contests grew more popular outside Appalachia. Bluegrass festivals, which began to flourish across the United States, brought together fans of a musical genre strongly influenced by traditional musics from Appalachia. By the early 1980s, bluegrass music organizations existed in at least twenty-seven states and three Canadian provinces.

Many organizations in Appalachia promote bluegrass alongside earlier traditional musical styles (usually referred to collectively as old-time music). The larger among these organizations publish newsletters, host festivals, create Internet chat sites, and sponsor workshops featuring well-known musicians. All types of music organizations in the region attempt to provide opportunities for members to play music. Indeed, jam sessions are the primary purpose of most smaller organizations. Appalachian music organizations vary in their mission and scope, from the Possum Town Bluegrass Network in Columbus, Mississippi, which provides listings of nearby bluegrass shows, to the eight-hundred-member Kentucky Friends of Bluegrass in Clay City, which sponsors several festivals each year.

Some music organizations in Appalachia focus on one instrument, such as the North Georgia Foothills Dulcimer Association, based in Flowery Branch. Another example is the Paul Pyle Dulcimer Association, based at the First Presbyterian Church in Tullahoma, Tennessee, which since 1990 has sponsored the town's annual Dulcimer Daze festival.

Other organizations in Appalachia commemorate local music heritages. The Birthplace of Country Music Alliance, based in Bristol, Tennessee/Virginia, seeks to promote the crucial role played by the city of Bristol and the surrounding area in the evolution of country music and bluegrass. Many urban areas within Appalachia host organizations dedicated to the preservation of the regional legacies of blues, jazz, and classical music. The Pittsburgh Jazz Society, Pittsburgh's Hill House Association, the Alabama Jazz Hall of Fame (Birmingham), and the Music Preservation Society (based in Florence, Alabama, and hosting the W. C. Handy Music Festival) celebrate regional contributions to jazz; the latter organization also focuses on blues and soul music.

The Pittsburgh Chamber Music Society, the Renaissance and Baroque Society of Pittsburgh, and the Piedmont Classic Guitar Society (Winston-Salem, North Carolina) are some organizations in Appalachia dedicated to various subgenres of classical music. The Piedmont Classic Guitar Society, reflecting a broader agenda not restricted by genre, features concerts that combine regional, national, and international guitar masters, ranging from renowned classical guitarists to local musicians such as eclectic flat-pick acoustic guitarist Doc Watson (from nearby Deep Gap, North Carolina).

In many Appalachian communities, college and university music departments are the primary organizations promoting specific genres of music.

See also: CONTESTS AND CONVENTIONS; FESTIVALS, MUSIC; FOLK MUSIC REVIVALS; VENUES.

—Karl Rohr, *Western Carolina University*

Joyce Cauthen, *With Fiddle and Well-Rosined Bow: Old Time Fiddling in Alabama* (1989); Neil V. Rosenberg, *Bluegrass: A History* (1993) and ed., *Transforming Tradition: Folk Music Revivals Examined* (1993).

Niles, John Jacob

(1892–1980) Singer, folk music collector, and composer.

John Jacob Niles was both a collector and arranger of traditional music and a composer who created well-known songs such as "Black Is the Color of My True Love's Hair," "I Wonder As I Wander," and "Go 'Way from My Window" by transforming fragments of traditional music into original compositions.

Born in Louisville, Kentucky, on April 28, 1892, Niles moved with his family in 1902 to rural Jefferson County, Kentucky, where he initiated his collecting work. By age fifteen, Niles had completed his first song, "Go 'Way from My Window," which was based on a single line of text collected from an African American worker on his father's farm.

In 1917 Niles enlisted in the aviation wing of the Army Signal Corps and served during World War I as a reconnaissance pilot. This afforded him the opportunity to collect songs from soldiers; these songs were later published as *Singing Soldiers* (1927) and *Songs My Mother Never Taught Me* (1929).

In 1925 Niles moved to New York City, where he began publishing collections of traditional music, including *Impressions of a Negro Camp Meeting* (1925) and *Seven Kentucky Mountain Songs* (1928). That same year, he met photographer Doris Ulmann, with whom he made four expeditions through the southern Appalachians to take photographs and collect music.

By 1933, Niles inaugurated his solo career, performing traditional and original repertoire self-accompanied on homemade instruments modeled after dulcimers. After briefly serving as music director at the John C. Campbell Folk School in Brasstown, North Carolina, Niles married journalist Rena Lipetz in 1936 and settled in rural Clark County, Kentucky. At the zenith of his popularity, Niles presented at least fifty concerts annually and recorded for RCA's Red Seal label, as well as for Folkways and Tradition.

Although he maintained an active concert career until shortly before his death, Niles increasingly focused his attention on composition, completing more than one hundred art songs and several extended works, including the oratorio *Lamentation* (1951) and *The Niles-Merton Songs* (1967–72). He died at his Clark County farm on March 1, 1980, and was buried at nearby Saint Hubert's Church.

Inevitably, Niles's twin vocations as collector and composer overlapped and created controversy. While many folklorists assumed that he plagiarized folk material, Niles heard his original, copyrighted songs plagiarized by performers who assumed the songs belonged in public domain because of their folklike characteristics.

See also: BALLADS; FOLK MUSIC COLLECTIONS; FOLK MUSIC REVIVALS.

—Ron Pen, *University of Kentucky*

John Jacob Niles, *The Ballad Book of John Jacob Niles* (1960; reprint 2000); Ronald Pen, "The Biography and Works of John Jacob Niles," Ph.D. dissertation, University of Kentucky (1987).

O'Brien, Tim

(1954–) Bluegrass, country, and traditional singer, songwriter, mandolinist, fiddler, and guitarist.

Known for his expressive singing, instrumental versatility, and sophisticated yet regionally rooted songwriting, Tim O'Brien has explored and synthesized several genres of American traditional music. Born in Wheeling, West Virginia, on March 16, 1954, O'Brien was first inspired to make music after hearing Jerry Lee Lewis, Merle Haggard, the Country Gentlemen, and others perform at his hometown's renowned music venue, the *WWVA Jamboree*.

O'Brien eventually became proficient on the mandolin, fiddle, guitar, and bouzouki. In 1978 he cofounded the influential bluegrass band Hot Rize, which played both traditional and progressive music. Touring extensively, the band revived a forgotten country music performance practice: Hot Rize would leave the stage, change outfits, and reemerge as a western group, Red Knuckles and the Trailblazers. This allowed O'Brien to expand his repertoire.

By the late 1980s, after country music star Kathy Mattea had hits with two of his songs, O'Brien pursued a solo career. He was recognized for a series of albums on the Sugar Hill label, including *Take Me Home* (1988), which featured duets with his sister Mollie, and *Red on Blonde* (1996), which showcased O'Brien's interpretations of Bob Dylan songs. O'Brien's songs have been recorded by Garth Brooks, the Dixie Chicks, the New Grass Revival, and Nickel Creek.

During the late 1990s, O'Brien worked on diverse projects, including recordings with singer-songwriter Darrell Scott. O'Brien also deepened his explorations of American roots music. He collaborated on an album of old-time Appalachian tunes entitled *Songs from the Mountain* (1999) as a complement to Charles Frazier's popular novel *Cold Mountain*. On two albums—*The Crossing* (1999) and *Two Journeys* (2001)—O'Brien explored his family's Irish ancestry and the cultural and musical connections between the Celtic world and Appalachia. In 2001 O'Brien became president of the International Bluegrass Music Association.

See also: BLUEGRASS; CELTIC INFLUENCES; MANDOLIN.

—Thomas Sneed, *Johnson City, Tennessee*

O'Day, Molly

(1923–1987) Country singer and banjo player.

Molly O'Day was called "the greatest female country singer ever" by Art Satherly, legendary producer for Columbia Records. Born Lois LaVerne Williamson on July 9, 1923, in McVeigh, Kentucky, near the West Virginia border, O'Day began her radio career in Charleston and Beckley, West Virginia, before moving to WHIS in Bluefield. Lynn Davis, the station's program director, was impressed by O'Day's voice and asked her to join his band when she was seventeen. Davis and O'Day married in 1941. They began their recording career as the Cumberland Mountain Folks, with Davis on guitar, O'Day's brother Skeets on fiddle, and O'Day on banjo and vocals. Between 1946 and 1951, the group recorded thirty-six sides for Columbia Records.

O'Day's hard-driving banjo frailing closely resembled that of Lily May Ledford, whom O'Day had heard on the radio. One of her most popular recordings, the ballad "Poor Ellen Smith," provides aural evidence not just of O'Day's vocal ability but also of her banjo prowess. Once, according to Davis, O'Day beat Earl Scruggs in a London, Kentucky, banjo contest.

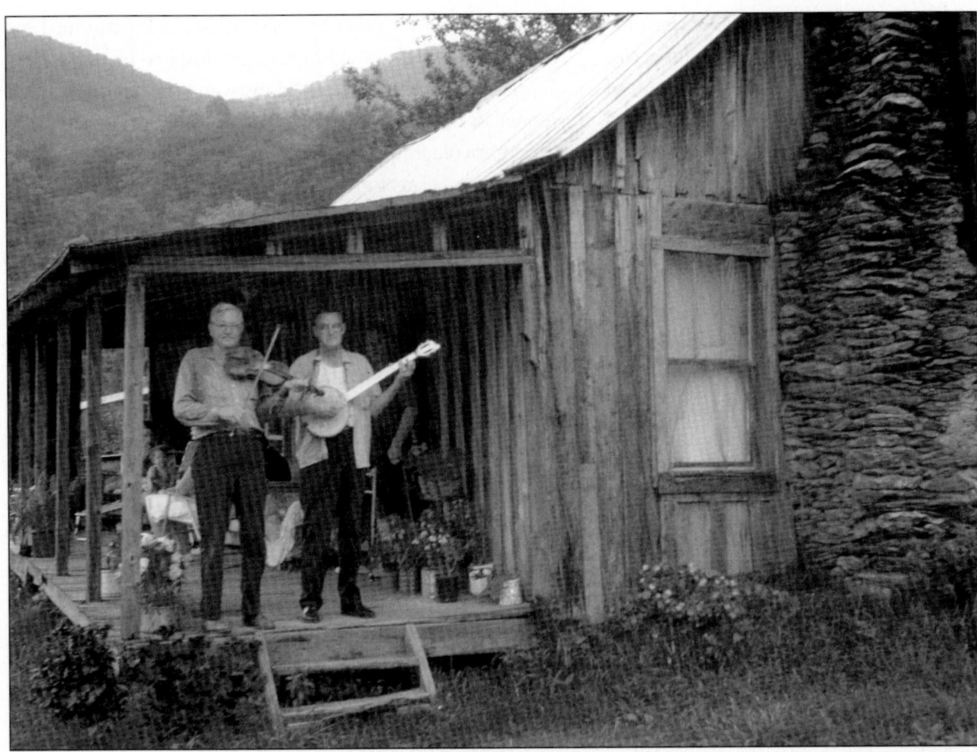

Tommy Jarrell (with fiddle) and Fred Cockerham (holding banjo), Low Gap, North Carolina, 1966. These two musicians, pictured at Cockerham's home, were two of the more revered old-time musicians from Appalachia.

O'Day suffered a nervous breakdown in 1949 and thereafter shunned secular songs and the music business. After a 1951 recording session, she never again performed publicly, unless it was in front of the congregation pastored by Davis, who had become a Church of God minister. O'Day died on December 5, 1987. In 1992 most of O'Day's recordings were reissued as a compact disc box set on Germany's Bear Family label.

See also: BANJO; COUNTRY MUSIC.

—Susan A. Eacker, *Morehead State University*

Old-Time Music

The term *old-time music* is a designation used by Appalachian musicians, singers, and enthusiasts in reference to the variety of traditional musical genres found in sections of Appalachia where regionally specific repertoires continue to be performed. Genres of old-time music include ballads and folk songs; instrumental music such as fiddle tunes and banjo tunes; traditional sacred songs and their instrumental versions; popular songs by known songwriters recorded in the late 1920s and 1930s and disseminated via 78 rpm records and the radio and eventually entering oral tradition; pre–World War II commercial country music by family groups such as the Carter Family and by brother duos such as the Monroe Brothers and the Blue Sky Boys; and blues.

Old-time music in Appalachia reflects many cultural influences. Traditional English, Scottish, and Scots-Irish ballads and lyric songs were eventually mixed with sacred songs such as spirituals and hymns as well as ballads, lyric songs, and, from African American tradition, the blues. Initially, traditional ballads and lyric songs were performed a cappella, yet by the mid-nineteenth century they were sometimes accompanied by the fiddle (of western European origin), the banjo (brought to the New World by African slaves), the guitar (of Spanish origin), the mandolin (an Italian instrument), the autoharp (of German origin), or the fretted dulcimer (probably of northern European origin). Other instruments utilized less frequently were nonetheless important to the vitality and diversity of old-time music. Inexpensive, easy to play, and portable, Jew's harps and harmonicas sometimes accompanied fiddlers and singers. While the hammered dulcimer was historically popular in some locales, such as western Pennsylvania, it has been a relative newcomer (since the 1960s and 1970s) to most parts of Appalachia. The plucked and the bowed psaltery, used regularly in medieval music, have occasionally surfaced in Appalachian old-time music, mainly to accompany ballads.

Musical accompaniment for the singing of ballads and lyric songs could come from a single instrument or from combinations such as duos, trios, quartets, and multi-instrument string bands. European settlers, after arriving in Appalachia, created new ballads and folk songs expressing themes relevant to their new environment; some of this material entered the regional music repertoire. Similarly, African Americans across the South composed their own ballads and folk songs, some of which, including "Frankie and Johnny," "John Henry," and "Stagolee," were adopted by Anglo-American musicians and singers in Appalachia.

African Americans in turn learned the fiddle from Anglo-Americans. African American fiddlers not only performed Anglo-American fiddle tunes (with their own syncopated approach), but also developed a distinctive African American tune repertoire. The African banjo was being played by Anglo-American musicians in Appalachia by the mid-nineteenth century. By the end of that century, the fiddle and banjo combination was widely utilized for both public and private gatherings. Neither instrument, when played as part of a duo, had a designated lead or accompaniment role. The guitar became easily available at the turn of the twentieth century as the result of mail-order companies and improved transportation in Appalachia. This revolutionized Appalachian music, as fiddle, guitar, and banjo took on specific roles—the fiddle playing the lead melody, the guitar providing rhythm and bass runs, and the banjo either carrying a melody or providing a rhythmic drive.

Sacred music, whether traditional or composed, has been a part of old-time music in Appalachia since at least the mid-nineteenth century. Sacred genres considered a part of old-time music include hymns, spirituals, gospel songs, and ballads and folk songs with religious themes. As with other genres of old-time music, sacred musical traditions evolved out of cultural exchange between blacks and whites.

During the twentieth century, several folk music revivals revitalized old-time music. A late-depression-era revival melded old-time music with often radical politics, as urban-born singers such as Pete Seeger interacted with rural-born performers such as Woody Guthrie and Aunt Molly Jackson, both of whom utilized traditional music from Appalachia as inspiration for their new compositions. During a late-1940s revival, folklorists and folk music enthusiasts, including Alan Lomax, Charles Seeger, and Pete Seeger, prompted the post–World War II old-time music boom by introducing audiences in the urban North to Appalachian old-time musicians through the release of commercial recordings and music-related publications and via radio and live performances.

In a revival that lasted from the late 1950s through the early 1970s, old-time musicians, many of whom were from Appalachia, performed alongside singer-songwriters and folk music interpreters at northern venues such as the Newport Folk Festival. During this period, urban-born musicians such as Mike Seeger and John Cohen of the revivalist ensemble the New Lost City Ramblers painstakingly studied and interpreted vocal and instrumental performance styles of Appalachian musicians. In the 1970s, other revivalist string bands performed and recorded Appalachian old-time music. Inspired by the work of a previous generation of folklorists and amateur collectors, thousands of fans of old-time music headed into Appalachia to learn from older Appalachian residents. Nationally, some of the younger musicians formed their own string bands, and several of these ensembles—the Highwoods Stringband, Fuzzy Mountain Stringband, and Hollow Rock Stringband—performed a primarily Appalachian old-time music repertoire.

Festivals featuring old-time music have existed since Bascom Lamar Lunsford started the Mountain Dance and Folk Festival in Asheville, North Carolina, in 1928. Other old-time music festivals were initiated and grew popular, including the National Folk Festival and the annually occurring festivals in Mount Airy, North Carolina; Union Grove, North Carolina; and Galax, Virginia.

The various revivals of traditional music led to the establishment of recording companies that issued new recordings (or reissued ones from earlier decades) of Appalachian old-time music. Some of these recording companies, such as County Records, were founded in Appalachia, while others, such as the Rounder, Folkways, and Folk-Legacy labels, were from outside of the region.

During the early years of the twenty-first century, Appalachian old-time music continues to flourish through the recent media of compact discs and videos. Digital computer communication technologies—including e-mail, Web sites, and chat rooms—permit wide dissemination of information about music, song lyrics, and performers to a new generation of old-time music fans.

See also: BALLADS; COUNTRY MUSIC; FOLK MUSIC REVIVALS.

—David A. Brose, *John C. Campbell Folk School*

John Cohen and Mike Seeger, eds., *The New Lost City Ramblers Songbook* (1964); Benjamin Filene, *Romancing the Folk: Public Memory and American Roots Music* (2000); Bill C. Malone, *Country Music, U.S.A.* (2002).

Opera

In Appalachia, opera is mostly limited to larger urban areas. Since cities do not usually figure in the popular conception of Appalachia as a largely rural region, opera has generally been excluded from assessments of the region's musical culture.

Although opera was not unknown in larger Appalachian cities of earlier times, most currently operating opera companies were established or resurrected after the 1930s. Many older opera houses do exist, but they are used for other purposes. The Elkins Opera House in Elkins, West Virginia, for instance, has been a clothing store since 1919, while a theater company currently occupies the Old Opera House in Charles Town, West Virginia.

Pittsburgh hosts the oldest continuously running opera company (established in 1939) within Appalachia, though Cincinnati's company, established in 1920, is the second oldest in the United States. Chattanooga, Tennessee, hosts the only combined professional symphony and opera company in the nation, as the Chattanooga Opera (founded in 1943) merged with the Chattanooga Symphony Orchestra in 1985. The acclaimed Tri-Cities Opera (established in 1949) of Binghamton, New York, collaborated with Binghamton University to offer the first Masters of Music program in the nation that offered specialization in opera. In Alabama, the Birmingham Civic Opera, founded in 1955, merged in 1986 with another opera company, the Southern Regional Opera, resulting in the formation of the Birmingham Opera Theater; in 1996 this company was rechristened Opera Birmingham. Opera came to Knoxville, Tennessee, in 1976 with the establishment of the Knoxville Civic Opera Company (shortened to Knoxville Opera Company in 1983). Other cities in the Appalachian region that feature opera companies are Winston-Salem, North Carolina (Piedmont Opera Theatre); Cooperstown, New York (Glimmerglass Opera); and Chautauqua, New York (Chautauqua Opera Company, which is affiliated with the Chautauqua Institution).

Opera luminaries from Appalachia have included Roland Hayes (1887–1976) of Curryville, Georgia, an African American tenor who performed internationally, and Grace Moore (1898–1947), who grew up in Jellico, Tennessee, and achieved fame as a star of New York City's Metropolitan Opera, Broadway, motion pictures, radio, and recordings. Eleanor Steber (1916–1990), a Wheeling, West Virginia–born soprano, and Kathleen Battle (b. 1948), a multiple Grammy Award–winning African American soprano from Portsmouth, Ohio, likewise worked with the Metropolitan Opera. Impresario Francis Robinson (1910–1980), from Mount Pleasant, Tennessee, served in different capacities with the company, working at various times as head of ticketing, supervisor of the Metropolitan Opera Touring Company, and host of the *Live from the Met* television show.

Most opera companies in Appalachia have placed considerable value on opera education and community outreach in an effort to generate wider public support and appreciation for an art form often thought of among uninitiated listeners as being foreign and boring. For younger students, interactive programs in classrooms (such as one offered by Knoxville Opera) provide a fun-filled introduction to the world of opera. Other companies, including the Tri-Cities Opera and Opera Birmingham, perform children's operas such as *Little Red Riding Hood* and *The Three Little Pigs* in schools. The Pittsburgh Opera, as part of its Student Matinee program, provides free tickets to full-length opera performances for economically underprivileged students. Also important to many opera companies are the development of new operatic talent through artist residencies and the integration of opera programming with school and university music departments. Other efforts aimed at expanding the popularity of the art form in Appalachia have included Pittsburgh Opera's introduction of simultaneous English translations of librettos projected above the stage.

Some composers have sought to chronicle the history of Appalachia through the medium of opera. Internationally acclaimed classical composer Kenton Coe, of Johnson City, Tennessee, has written operas with Appalachian themes including *Rachel* (about the relationship between President Andrew Jackson and his wife). Given its cultural and geographical distinctiveness, Appalachia has fueled the imaginations of numerous non-native composers attempting to create folk operas, a subgenre of American opera that falls between opera and musical theater. Some prominent works of this type include German composer Kurt Weill's *Down in the Valley* (1948), South Carolinian Carlisle Floyd's *Susannah* (1956), and Donald Davidson and Charles Faulkner Bryan's *Singin' Billy* (1952), which concerns William Walker, the author of the influential 1835 shape-note singing book *Southern Harmony*. These folk operas not only explore Appalachian themes but also incorporate into their scores stylistic elements borrowed from traditional Appalachian music.

See also: CLASSICAL COMPOSERS; SHAPE-NOTE SINGING/SINGING SCHOOLS; SYMPHONY ORCHESTRAS.

—Ajay Kalra, *East Tennessee State University*

Peter G. Davis, *The American Opera Singer: The Lives and Adventures of America's Great Singers in Opera and Concert, from 1825 to the Present* (1997); John Dizikes, *Opera in America: A Cultural History* (1993); Rowena Rutherford Farrar, *Grace Moore and Her Many Worlds* (1982).

Osborne Brothers

Bluegrass brother duo.

Osborne, Bobby (1931–) Mandolinist and singer.

Osborne, Sonny (1937–) Banjo player and singer.

The Osborne brothers were born near Hyden, Kentucky. Robert Van "Bobby" Osborne Jr. was born December 7, 1931, and Sonny Roland Osborne October 29, 1937. The family left Kentucky in 1941, and the boys were brought up in Dayton, Ohio. Their father was familiar with traditional mountain music, which he taught his sons. Both boys began performing professionally as teenagers. After appearing separately with other groups—Bobby played mandolin and guitar with the Lonesome Pine Fiddlers, the Stanley Brothers, and Jimmy Martin, while Sonny toured with Bill Monroe—the brothers began appearing as a team in 1953.

The Osborne Brothers' concert at Antioch College in 1960 sparked the spread of bluegrass music on college campuses. By broadening their repertoire and adding drums, electric bass, steel guitar, and piano, while retaining the mandolin and five-string banjo, they fused bluegrass with country music and enjoyed wider exposure than any other bluegrass group. They appeared on Wheeling, West Virginia's *WWVA Jamboree* for several years before joining the *Grand Ole Opry* in 1964. In 1971 the Osborne Brothers were named Vocal Group of the Year by the Country Music Association, the first bluegrass ensemble to be so honored. In 1973 they became the first bluegrass act to perform at the White House. They are best known for their recording of Felice and Boudeleaux Bryant's "Rocky Top" (1967), which became an official Tennessee state song.

Although at times the brothers' sound has been criticized for not being traditional, the Osbornes include many old-time songs in their repertoire. The Osborne Brothers especially deserve credit for attracting new audiences to bluegrass music.

See also: BLUEGRASS; DUOS, BROTHER; *GRAND* OLE OPRY (MEDIA).

—Charles F. Faber, *Lexington, Kentucky*

Other Instruments

While a number of musical instruments (including the fiddle, banjo, guitar, fretted dulcimer, mandolin, autoharp, bass, dobro, pedal steel guitar, and harmonica) are commonly associated with Appalachia, several other instruments—such as the mouth bow, psaltery, Jew's harp, and musical bones or spoons—have historically been important within the region.

The mouth bow, or musical bow, was one of the first musical instruments played in Appalachia. Closely resembling a hunting bow, the mouth bow includes a tuning peg utilized to change the pitch of the instrument's one string. A player plucks the string while using his mouth as a resonating chamber. Similar instruments have been historically found around the world (particularly in Africa). The mouth bow was common among Appalachian Native Americans, who shared their knowledge of the instrument with European settlers. The mouth bow is not often played in present-day Appalachia, having been displaced by more versatile stringed instruments.

Closely related to the zither and the harpsichord, the psaltery is a triangular- or trapezoidal-shaped instrument that is either plucked with fingers or bowed (with one or sometimes two bows); the instrument generally contains twenty-two to thirty-two strings. Mentioned in the Bible, the psaltery was once popular in some Appalachian localities because it was easy to learn, with strings tuned to a chord when played in the open position. While not widely played in modern-day Appalachia, the psaltery has experienced a revival, with several companies designing and building the instrument.

The Jew's harp (sometimes called juice harp or jaw harp) has been played in many cultures but is most closely associated with Europeans. In Appalachia, the instrument was traditionally played as both a solo and an ensemble instrument. The Jew's harp is played by using the mouth cavity as a sound chamber and by plucking a reed positioned inside the body of the instrument. Most Jew's harps found in Appalachia have been commercially manufactured out of metal.

Appalachian people have long utilized two expressly rhythmic instruments: bones and spoons. Both instruments consist of a pair of similarly sized objects that are held between different fingers of the same hand and are rapidly clanged together. Bones were originally made out of animal ribs, generally from a cow, while spoons were generally spoons or other household utensils. A skilled bones or spoons player could vary the pitch of the instrument by adjusting each of the two bones in the hand and knocking them together at different angles. Bones and spoons players in Appalachia often served as percussion players in musical ensembles featuring fiddles, banjos, and guitars. Household implements, such as pots and pans, have also been employed as percussion instruments.

Certain instruments not closely associated with Appalachia are nonetheless common, even mainstream, in the region. The piano, long popular among Appalachian people, has been played in some churches and in many homes. The popularity of rock 'n' roll in the 1950s and 1960s brought drum sets into the region as well as such instruments as the electric guitar, electric bass, and electric fiddle. The recent increase in popularity of two other instruments in Appalachia—the highland bagpipes and the Celtic harp—is an outgrowth of the ongoing revival of Celtic cultural traditions across the region and an acknowledgement of the important influence of Scottish and Irish cultures on Appalachia.

See also: AFRICAN AMERICAN INFLUENCES; CELTIC INFLUENCES; CHEROKEE MUSIC.

—Roy Andrade, *East Tennessee State University*

John Rice Irwin, *Musical Instruments of the Southern Appalachian Mountains* (1983).

Parton, Dolly

(1946–) Country singer and songwriter.

Born January 19, 1946, in a cabin just north of Gatlinburg in Sevier County, Tennessee, Dolly Parton grew up in the Great Smoky Mountains surrounded by musicians. Her mother sang old ballads and folk songs; her grandfather was a preacher, fiddler, and songwriter; her aunt was a gospel songwriter; and her uncle was an aspiring country musician. At age ten Parton began to appear on a Knoxville television variety show and debuted on the *Grand Ole Opry* three years later. Determined to attain country music stardom, she set off for Nashville after graduating from high school, and with her uncle Bill Owens's help she landed a songwriting contract.

Parton's initial success came as a songwriter. In 1967, after Porter Wagoner asked her to join his syndicated television show, her singing career took off. Soon she was writing prolifically and singing hit duets with Wagoner. In the early 1970s, Parton made the charts as a solo act with her cover of Jimmie Rodgers's song "Mule Skinner Blues" (which also exhibited the influence of Bill Monroe) and her own song "Joshua" (her first solo number one hit). Through 1974 she appeared on Wagoner's show and toured with him and his band, putting on performances as duet partner and as solo artist. Some of her songs were autobiographical, detailing her life and hard times in east Tennessee; many of these appeared on her 1973 album *My Tennessee Mountain Home*. Other songs, built upon folk song and ballad traditions, addressed heartbreak, abuse, and mental illness. Parton also wrote songs depicting the beauties of nature and celebrating mountain culture. Her signature song, "Coat of Many Colors," describes the simple dignity of confronting poverty. By the mid-1970s, hit songs such as "Jolene," "The Bargain Store," and "The Seeker" confirmed Parton's status as the leading female songwriter in country music.

In 1974 Parton ended her collaboration with Wagoner. Also that year, her first recording of what would become her most successful song, "I Will Always Love You," topped the country charts (a 1992 version of the song sung by Whitney Houston rose to the top of the pop charts). Parton went to Hollywood to appear in movies and find management that could help her cross over to pop audiences. The strategy worked for several years: she acted in five films and even had a short-lived television show. As a guest on television specials and talk shows, Parton became a national celebrity with her easy conversational manner and striking appearance.

By the mid-1990s, Parton's Hollywood star had waned. With a younger generation of country singers dominating the charts, Parton cut back her music making and focused on entrepreneurial projects, including the Dollywood theme park in Pigeon Forge, Tennessee. She eventually returned to her musical roots with the Grammy Award–winning albums *The Grass Is Blue* (1999) and *Little Sparrow* (2001). Elected to the Country Music Hall of Fame in 1999, Parton remains one of country music's most recognized performers.

See also: COUNTRY MUSIC; DOLLYWOOD (TOURISM).

—Frederick E. Danker, *University of Massachusetts*

Alanna Nash, *Dolly: The Early Years* (1978); Dolly Parton, *Dolly: My Life and Other Unfinished Business* (1994).

Phillips, Sam

(1923–2003) Record producer and music promoter.

Best known for his discovery of Elvis Presley, record producer Samuel Cornelius "Sam" Phillips during the 1950s helped pioneer the rockabilly style (a blend of white country music with black rhythm and blues). Born January 5, 1923, in Florence, Alabama, Phillips became a disc jockey at age fifteen for radio station WLAY in Muscle Shoals, Alabama, then worked as a broadcaster in Decatur, Alabama, and at WLAC Nashville. In 1945 he took a job as a broadcast engineer for WREC Memphis; in 1950 Phillips started the Memphis Recording Service, building a studio at 706 Union Avenue. That same year, he formed the "It's A Phillips" label and worked as a freelance producer for Modern and Chess.

Establishing Sun Records in 1952, Phillips recorded many important blues artists at his Union Avenue studio, including B. B. King, Howlin' Wolf, "Little" Walter Horton, James Cotton, and "Little" Milton Campbell. Phillips's Sun productions included, in 1951, "Rocket 88," a seminal early rock 'n' roll record by Jackie Brenston, and, in 1952–53, a string of rhythm and blues recordings by Junior Parker, Rufus Thomas, and the Prisonaires. Elvis Presley began his career at Sun, recording five singles and several other tracks before Phillips sold Presley's contract to RCA in 1955. That year, Phillips started WHER, a Memphis radio station featuring an all-female talent roster. Subsequently at Sun he produced a catalog of definitive rockabilly recordings by such musicians as Carl Perkins, Jerry Lee Lewis, Johnny Cash, Charlie Rich, and Roy Orbison, before selling the label in 1969. In later years, Phillips headed the Big River Broadcasting Corporation in Florence, Alabama, operating three stations serving the Shoals-area community. He died July 30, 2003.

See also: PRESLEY, ELVIS; RHYTHM AND BLUES; ROCK MUSIC.

—Peter B. Olson, *University of Memphis*

Colin Escott, with Martin Hawkins, *Good Rockin' Tonight: Sun Records and the Birth of Rock 'n' Roll* (1992).

Phipps, Ernest, and Alfred G. Karnes

Phipps, Ernest (1900–1963)
Gospel singer and bandleader.
Karnes, Alfred G. (1891–1958)
Gospel singer and guitarist.

Ernest Phipps and Alfred G. Karnes were both preachers from the Corbin, Kentucky, area. Their recordings from the famed Bristol, Tennessee, recording sessions of 1927 and 1928 were among the earliest recorded examples of Anglo-American gospel music.

Phipps (b. May 4, 1900) and members of his Free Holiness Pentecostal Church congregation recorded six songs at each of the two Bristol sessions. At the 1927 sessions, Phipps's group, labeled the Holiness Quartet, featured two singers and a standard string band. At the 1928 sessions, Phipps fronted a larger group, known as Ernest Phipps and his Holiness Singers, consisting of four singers with piano, fiddle, banjo, guitar, and mandolin accompaniment. The resulting twelve commercial recordings, with their evangelical lyrics, repetitions, strong rhythms, improvised harmonies, hand clapping, and guitar backup, provide a rare record of the fervent, intense Holiness style of gospel singing heard in many Appalachian churches in the early twentieth century.

Phipps's recordings, including "Do, Lord, Remember Me," "Old Ship of Zion," and "Don't Grieve after Me," were among the first 78s issued from the Bristol sessions. Phipps's "If the Light Is Gone Out of Your Soul," backed with "Bright Tomorrow," sold almost twelve thousand copies and stayed in print into the 1930s. He died April 17, 1963.

Karnes, born February 2, 1891, in Bedford, Virginia, served as a Baptist preacher at several rural churches near Corbin. Although he often performed in churches with his children, for the Bristol sessions he sang solo, accompanying himself on a Gibson harp guitar. Karnes may also have played that instrument on some of Phipps's recordings.

Of the thirteen sides Karnes recorded at the Bristol sessions—six in 1927 and seven in 1928—only four were released during his lifetime. His Bristol recordings included "To the Work," "I Am Bound for the Promised Land," "When They Ring the Golden Bells," and an original song about missionary work, "Called to the Foreign Field." Karnes never recorded again, but he continued to perform music and preach until his death on May 18, 1958.

See also: BRISTOL SESSIONS; GOSPEL MUSIC, ANGLO-AMERICAN; GUITAR.

—William Bernard McCarthy, *Pennsylvania State University*

Polka

The polka, a couples' dance in 2/4 time, was in vogue in much of Europe during the second half of the nineteenth century. European immigrants who settled in Appalachia, particularly in Pennsylvania, retained the polka dance and the music associated with it as part of their cultural legacy. Germans, Poles, and Czechs were the most active ethnic groups to perpetuate the polka in Appalachia, but Italians, Ukrainians, Hungarians, Slovenians, Slovaks, and Croatians also maintained polka traditions. The nineteenth-century polka craze spread from Europe to Mexico, and numerous Mexican musicians eventually interacted with musical German, Polish, and Czech immigrants in Texas, creating the polka style of the Texas-Mexican *conjuntos.* During the twentieth century, Mexican Americans migrated to Pennsylvania, bringing with them the *conjunto* style of polka music and dancing, adding to the variants of polka music in the region.

Polka musicians in Appalachia play a number of distinctive styles. The most influential styles are named after ethnic groups—Czech (or "Bohemian"), German (or "Dutchman"), Polish, Slovenian, and Mexican. Each of these styles is maintained by a core constituency of dancers and players from the namesake ethnic group; however, people from a variety of ethnic backgrounds participate in every polka scene in the region.

Both the Czech and German polka styles use brass and reed instruments in interaction with an accordion or concertina, with the tuba frequently providing the bass notes. German polka bands have tended to strive for a smoother, more blended brass and reed sound, while Czech bands favor an incisive brassy or reedy tone from the wind instruments.

In Appalachia, Polish- and Slovenian-style polka bands have been most common in urban centers such as Pittsburgh and in mining and mill towns where Slavic, Italian, and Ukrainian immigrants have settled. Historically, Polish bands in the region were influenced by such semiprofessional East Coast Polish orchestras as the one led by Frank Wojnarowski. For the last thirty years, however, Chicago-based Polish musicians such as Li'l Wally Jagiello and Eddie Blazonczyk have been much more influential. From these Chicago musicians, Appalachia-based Polish polka bands have learned to combine the Chemnitzer concertina with brass and reeds, playing these instruments together in a raucous and polyphonic style over syncopated drumming. In modern Polish bands, the accordion is often used only as a rhythm instrument.

Slovenian bands generally emphasize the accordion (either a diatonic button-box or a "piano" accordion) accompanied by the tenor banjo. In the Slovenian style, a second accordion often plays fills between the melody lines. Many such bands also employ a saxophone to alternate with accordion on lead parts. The most influential musician in shaping the contemporary Slovenian style was Cleveland, Ohio–based Frankie Yankovic, who was born in Davis, West Virginia. Slovenian and Polish bands avoid the tuba, utilizing instead an acoustic upright string bass, an electric bass guitar, or, more recently, a MIDI bass synthesizer operated by the accordion player.

Numerous polka bands were active in the Appalachian section of Pennsylvania at the beginning of the new millennium, including the ATM Band (based in Greensburg), John Stanky and the Coal Miners (Nanticoke), the Karl Lukitsch Band (Pittsburgh), and the Polka Jets (Forest City).

See also: GERMANS (RACE, ETHNICITY, AND IDENTITY); HISPANICS (RACE, ETHNICITY, AND IDENTITY); POLES (RACE, ETHNICITY, AND IDENTITY).

—Rick March, *Wisconsin Arts Board*

Poole, Charlie

(1892–1931) Early country singer, banjo player, and bandleader.

In a recording career that spanned only six years (1925–31), Charles Cleveland "Charlie" Poole (b. March 22, 1892, in Randolph County, North Carolina) created a distinctive and influential style of string-band music.

Poole was attracted to the banjo while very young. Partly through a relative's influence and partly through a youthful accident that left him with several broken fingers, Poole developed a style of three-finger playing which resembled the sophisticated styles of such "classical" banjo players as Vess Ossman and Fred Van Eps. Poole's banjo style was the centerpiece of the "chamber music" style of his band, the North Carolina Ramblers, which included fiddlers Posey Rorrer and Lonnie Austin and guitarists Norman Woodlieff and Roy Harvey. Poole was particular about the quality of the musicians he hired, all of whom were chosen to reinforce his musical vision. While it might be inaccurate to characterize the Ramblers as the link between old-time music and bluegrass, in many ways their playing influenced later musicians. The complexity and sophistication of interplay between the instruments on the Poole-Austin-Harvey recordings, for example, reveal the effect that popular music was having on the old-time style, resulting in a blending that would eventually influence bluegrass.

During his six-year recording career, Poole cut more than seventy songs for the Columbia, Brunswick, and Paramount labels. Poole's best-known recordings are "Don't Let Your Deal Go Down Blues" and "White House Blues." Poole led a flamboyant lifestyle that made him a household name as his band traveled the country entertaining audiences with their music and antics. He died on May 21, 1931, after years of hard living. Poole's musical legacy has persisted over several generations of old-time musicians.

See also: BANJO; OLD-TIME MUSIC; STRING-BAND MUSIC.

—John N. Currie, *Jacksonville, North Carolina*

Presley, Elvis

(1935–1977) Singer.

Born January 8, 1935, in Tupelo, Mississippi, Elvis Presley spent his first thirteen years in that small city in the Appalachian foothills. His family moved to Memphis in 1948, whereupon Presley developed his talents as a singer, blending different types of racial and regional music. To the north and east were the country, bluegrass, and Anglo-American gospel music of Tennessee and Kentucky, to the south and west were the blues styles of Mississippi and Arkansas, and further southwest was the western swing of Texas and Oklahoma. These styles could be heard on commercial recordings and radio broadcasts in Memphis during the early 1950s, and Presley absorbed them all. Such blending was obvious from Presley's first release for Sam Phillips's Sun Records in 1954, recorded when he was nineteen. One side of this release featured his version of Bill Monroe's bluegrass standard "Blue Moon of Kentucky," while the other side contained a cover of "That's All Right," originally written and recorded by Mississippi bluesman Arthur Crudup. In his recordings for Sun Records, Presley and his accompanists created a new stylistic fusion—combining elements of gospel, country, blues, rhythm and blues, pop, and rock 'n' roll—that revolutionized the music industry, first regionally, then nationally.

Despite the singer's cultural orientation toward the lowland South, Appalachian music fans were crucial in Presley's emergence on the national scene. At that time it was extremely difficult for unknown singers from the South to break through to national audiences and to attract the attention of national record labels. Sun Records was a regional label, with distribution reaching no more than six hundred miles from Memphis. Significantly, however, the label's range of distribution encompassed east Tennessee. The area between Knoxville and the Tri-Cities of Kingsport, Bristol, and Johnson City was part of the territory for Brad McCuen, a field agent for RCA Records. The response to Presley's first Sun release in that specific area was so favorable that McCuen sent a copy of the record to corporate executives in New York City, advising them that something unexpected was happening with musical taste in America. Within a year, RCA had purchased the rights to Presley's contract from Sun, and he was on his way to fame and fortune.

Even after his death on August 16, 1977, Presley remained the most influential individual figure in American popular music, regionally, nationally, and internationally. He was inducted into the Rock and Roll Hall of Fame in 1986 and the Country Music Hall of Fame in 1998.

See also: GOSPEL MUSIC, ANGLO-AMERICAN; RHYTHM AND BLUES; ROCK MUSIC.

—Dillon Bustin, *Emerson Umbrella Center for the Arts*

Peter Guralnick, *Last Train to Memphis: The Rise of Elvis Presley* (1994).

Proffitt, Frank, Sr.

(1913–1965) Traditional singer and banjo player.

Born June 1, 1913, in Laurel Bloomery, Tennessee, Frank Proffitt Sr. moved with his family when a child to the Beaver Dam area of Watauga County, North Carolina. He left school after the sixth grade to work on the family farm. Best known as the source of the song "Tom Dooley," Proffitt was a talented traditional singer and fretless banjo player.

In 1938 singer and folklorist Frank Warner and his wife, Anne, met Proffitt during a song-collecting trip. The first number Proffitt performed for them, "Tom Dooley," was the first he remembered hearing his father, Noah, play on the banjo, as well as the first song he himself learned to play. The song's lyrics told the story of Tom Dula (pronounced "Duley") from Wilkes County, North Carolina, who had murdered Laura Foster in 1866. Proffitt's grandmother, Adeline Pardue, who knew both Dula and Foster, passed the song down through the family. Frank Warner performed the song in programs and taught it to folklorist Alan Lomax, who included it in his 1947 book, *Folksong U.S.A.* In 1958 the Kingston Trio recorded "Tom Dooley" for Capitol Records. That group's version eventually sold several million copies and is credited with expanding public interest in American folk music. Controversy soon arose over the song's copyright. In 1962 an out-of-court settlement divided royalties among Warner, Lomax, and Proffitt—long after the song's popularity had peaked. Nevertheless, the success of "Tom Dooley" drew attention to Proffitt's music. Before his death on November 24, 1965, he performed at folk festivals around the country and recorded three albums of traditional songs and ballads. His son Frank Proffitt Jr. continues to perform much of that repertoire.

See also: BALLADS; BANJO; FOLK MUSIC REVIVALS.

—Geoff Eacker, *Miami University*

Recording Companies

In the early days of the record industry, commercial recording companies sent engineers into Appalachia to locate and record string bands and so-called hillbilly singers in the field. Some Appalachian performers were recorded in Appalachia—at the Victor label's famous field recording sessions in Bristol, Tennessee, for instance—yet many musicians traveled from the region to record in temporary studios in such cities as Atlanta and Charlotte.

After a slowdown during the Great Depression, the American record industry was again flourishing by the 1940s. New companies—most located outside of Appalachia—recorded many Appalachian performers. One such label was King Records in Cincinnati. Although not within Appalachia, the city was home to countless Appalachian migrants. Concentrating heavily on country, blues, and bluegrass music, King owner Sydney Nathan signed and recorded dozens of Appalachian performers, including the Delmore Brothers, the Stanley Brothers, Cowboy Copas, and Hawkshaw Hawkins. In the 1940s and 1950s, Appalachia's stores were stocked with 78, 45, and 33-⅓ rpm discs from King and many other national labels.

Perhaps because the region was comparatively poor and largely rural, few major recording companies emerged in Appalachia during the twentieth century. Two Pittsburgh labels, Calico and World Artists, released national hits that contained no hint of the country twang associated with the popular conception of Appalachia; like their counterparts in New York and Los Angeles, the two companies concentrated on pop music. Calico's biggest hit, still heard widely nearly half a century later, was the Skyliners' "Since I Don't Have You" (1959). World Artists Records achieved its high point in 1964 with the English duo Chad and Jeremy, whose hits included "Yesterday's Gone," "A Summer Song," and "Willow Weep for Me."

In 1962, unable to convince another label to release a song recorded by black singer-songwriter Jimmy Hughes, white musician and entrepreneur Rick Hall, owner of FAME Recording Studios, launched FAME Records in Muscle Shoals, Alabama. Hughes's song, "Steal Away," charted on both the rhythm and blues and pop charts, and Hall continued to release recordings on his label, mostly soul songs by black artists such as Candi Staton. FAME's stellar cast of musicians and singers and its national distribution established the label as Appalachia's most recognizable. In 1979 a nearby studio, Muscle Shoals Sound, started its own label, Muscle Shoals Sound Records, distributed by Capitol Records; the label's biggest success was the top ten hit "Givin' It Up for Your Love" by Delbert McClinton (1980). Although Appalachia's indigenous national recording companies were few, they were significant, serving crucial roles in the development of their communities' record industries and providing much-needed work for musicians in local studios.

In the second half of the twentieth century, Appalachian folk, old-time, and bluegrass recording musicians generally followed a career path exemplified by Doc Watson. Like many Appalachian performers, Watson recorded for a wide variety of recording companies, ranging from major national labels to smaller independent labels, from those with few Appalachian performers (such as Vanguard Records) to those that specialize in promoting Appalachian performers (such as Sugar Hill Records).

Many national companies have released recordings by Appalachian roots musicians. Rounder Records of Cambridge, Massachusetts, has reissued historically significant folk, old-time, and country recordings as well as new releases by many prominent bluegrass groups with some strong connection to Appalachia (including Alison Krauss and Union Station, IIIrd Tyme Out, and the Dry Branch Fire Squad). Rounder has strengthened its catalog by purchasing the Flying Fish label (of Chicago), thus ensuring the continued availability of important releases by such Appalachian musicians as the father-son duo Doc and Merle Watson and country bluesmen John Cephas and Phil Wiggins.

Another national company, the Washington, D.C.–based Smithsonian Folkways label (formerly Folkways Records, founded by Moses Asch in 1948), likewise maintains a strong commitment to Appalachian music. The Smithsonian Folkways catalog features Harry Smith's influential *Anthology of American Folk Music*, which ignited the urban folk revival of the 1950s and 1960s, as well as releases by such stalwarts of traditional Appalachian music as Dock Boggs, Roscoe Holcomb, Bascom Lamar Lunsford, and Clarence "Tom" Ashley. Smithsonian Folkways releases contain extensive liner notes that often provide musicological and ethnographic information, transcribed interviews with performers, and lyrics.

Responding to the increasing interest in bluegrass music nationally since the 1950s, several independent labels located in or near Appalachia release bluegrass material exclusively, often from musicians with strong Appalachian ties. The largest of such labels is Rebel Records, based in Charlottesville, Virginia, which has issued recordings by such first- and second-generation bluegrass musicians as the Stanley Brothers and Ralph Stanley and the Clinch Mountain Boys, as well as early works by later bluegrass groups, including Blue Highway and the Lonesome River Band. As recording technology has become more accessible and affordable, smaller independent Appalachian labels, including Hay Holler Records (Blacksburg, Virginia) and Doobie Shea (Boones Mill, Virginia), have released some of the most respected recordings in contemporary bluegrass.

Other independent companies in or near the region have maintained a more broad-based catalog, releasing recordings of Appalachian folk and old-time music as well as bluegrass. Sugar Hill Records of Durham, North Carolina, has sustained the careers of many contemporary Appalachian musicians (Doc Watson, Doyle Lawson and Quicksilver, and Tim O'Brien, for example), while Copper Creek Records of Roanoke, Virginia, releases recordings by current Appalachian performers as well as reissues of older material by artists including the Blue Sky Boys, Reno and Smiley, and the Louvin Brothers.

Several companies are exclusively committed to releasing recordings of historic performances. One such Appalachia-based label is County, located in Floyd, Virginia, which has issued recordings of many pioneers of country and string-band music, including Gid Tanner and His Skillet Lickers, Grayson and Whitter, and Charlie Poole (most remastered from original copies of 78 rpm records). Similarly, the Yazoo label, owned by Shanachie Records of New York City, produces recordings that contain collections of old blues and country 78s. Bear Family Records of Germany releases box sets showcasing the entire recording careers or significant portions of the careers of many historically important artists, including Appalachian figures such as the Carter Family, Flatt and Scruggs, Jimmy Martin, and Jim and Jesse.

In recent years some of the finest performers of traditional Appalachian music have recorded for little-known independent labels such as June Appal (Whitesburg, Kentucky), Old Homestead (Brighton, Michigan), Marimac Records (Crown Point, Indiana), and Yodel-Ay-Hee Records (Asheville, North Carolina).

See also: BRISTOL SESSIONS; FIELD RECORDING SESSIONS; MUSCLE SHOALS.

—Randy McNutt, *Hamilton, Ohio,* and Thomas Sneed, *Johnson City, Tennessee*

Rick Kennedy and Randy McNutt, *Little Labels—Big Sound: Small Record Companies and the Rise of American Music* (1999); Jerry Wexler, with David Ritz, *Rhythm and the Blues: A Life in American Music* (1993).

Reed, Ola Belle

(1916–2002) Early country singer, banjo player, and songwriter.

Born August 17, 1916, in Lansing, Ashe County, North Carolina, Ola Belle (Campbell) Reed was a traditional clawhammer banjo player and singer and a prolific songwriter. Her father, Arthur Harrison Campbell, a schoolteacher and storekeeper, played fiddle, banjo, piano, and organ; her mother, Ella Mae Osborne (from Grayson County, Virginia), sang ballads; and her uncle, Bob Ingraham, led singing schools. After losing both their farm and family store during the depression, the family followed other local families to the Maryland-Pennsylvania-Delaware border area, where there were farms for rent and jobs in factories.

Music was a source of strength and continuity within the community of displaced musicians. Ola Belle got her first job as a musician in the late 1930s with the North Carolina Ridge Runners; the band, made up of transplanted mountaineers, was constantly in demand at dances, carnivals, music parks, and on local radio. Their repertoire and style mingled the traditional and popular repertoire, instrumentation, and performing styles of the North Carolina and Virginia mountains with those of the region to which they had relocated.

In 1949 Ola Belle married Ralph "Bud" Reed, who was from a local musical family. For many years thereafter, the couple promoted traditional and commercial country music at two country music parks: first at Rainbow Park in Lancaster, Pennsylvania, in 1950 and then at the New River Ranch near Rising Sun, Maryland, which throughout the 1950s drew outstanding bluegrass, gospel, and country performers, as well as prominent revivalist musicians such as Mike Seeger and Ralph Rinzler. Throughout these years, Reed also performed on the radio with her brother Alex Campbell and other well-known performers (Bill Monroe, the Louvin Brothers, Reno and Smiley) on *Campbell's Corner*, first on WASA (Havre de Grace, Maryland) and later on WCOJ (Coatesville, Pennsylvania). In 1960 the Reeds began a lengthy stint as regular performers at Sunset Park in West Grove, Pennsylvania.

The 1960s folk revival brought Ola Belle and Bud a new audience. With son David they played to enthusiastic new audiences at the National Folk Festival, the Festival of American Folklife (the Smithsonian Folklife Festival), state folklife festivals, and the Kennedy Center.

Ola Belle Reed's repertoire included ballads, traditional fiddle and banjo tunes, commercial country and popular songs, and her own compositions, including "High on a Mountain," "Go Home, Little Girl," "Springtime of Life," "I've Endured," and "My Epitaph." Her music reflected social dislocation, loss, and change but also continuity, vitality, and irrepressible creativity. Not performing after a stroke in 1987, Ola Belle died August 16, 2002.

See also: BANJO; COUNTRY MUSIC; FOLK MUSIC REVIVALS.

—David E. Whisnant, *Chapel Hill, North Carolina*

Reno and Smiley

Bluegrass duo.

Reno, Don (1927–1984) Banjo player, singer, guitarist, and composer.

Smiley, Arthur "Red" (1925–1972) Singer, guitarist, and songwriter.

Donald Wesley Reno and Arthur Lee "Red" Smiley rank with Bill Monroe, the Stanley Brothers, and Flatt and Scruggs as significant contributors to the development of bluegrass music. Reno was born in February 21, 1927, in Spartanburg, South Carolina, while Smiley, born May 17, 1925, hailed from Marshall, North Carolina. Reno's distinctive three-finger banjo style, harmony vocals, original songs, and occasional flat-pick guitar playing coupled with Smiley's vocal lead gave the duo a distinct sound that made them popular figures on daily morning television at WDBJ in Roanoke, Virginia, from 1957 until 1964. Between 1952 and 1964, they recorded more than two hundred numbers for the King and Dot labels.

The two musicians were both World War II veterans who had accumulated varied radio-based musical experience prior to meeting in 1949, when they worked together in Tommy Magness's band. Reno and Smiley along with their group, the Tennessee Cutups, became a studio recording band in 1952, but they did not tour as a unit until they began their television program, *Top of the Morning*.

Reno and Smiley's numerous original songs included "I'm Using My Bible for a Roadmap," "Trail of Sorrow," and "I Know You're Married but I Love You Still." With Arthur "Guitar Boogie" Smith, Reno composed the instrumental "Feuding Banjos," which, retitled "Dueling Banjos" for use in the movie *Deliverance* (1972), became a major pop hit for Eric Weissberg and Marshall Brickman. In the late 1950s Reno composed the flat-pick guitar instrumental classic "Country Boy Rock 'n' Roll."

After ending their partnership, Smiley continued with the WDBJ television program until 1969. Reno played with Bill Harrell from 1966 to 1976, also reuniting with Smiley for a few concerts in 1970 and 1971. Beginning in the late 1970s, Reno performed with his three sons (who continue to work as the Reno Brothers). Smiley passed away on January 2, 1972, while Reno died on October 16, 1984.

See also: BANJO; BLUEGRASS; GUITAR.

—Ivan M. Tribe, *University of Rio Grande*

Rhythm and Blues

A dance-oriented African American music, rhythm and blues emerged in the mid-1940s as a major genre within American popular music. Rhythm and blues developed concurrently with and in response to the urbanization of rural southern blacks who sought prosperity in northern industrial cities during and following the Great Depression. Advancements in recording technology ensured that black music (of such diverse genres as blues, gospel, and jazz) would reach an enlarged audience base, particularly via the jukebox. This amalgam of music styles was initially cast by record marketers as the "Harlem Hit Parade" or "race music," but immediately following World War II, as segregation was increasingly questioned, a more enlightened term was needed. In 1949 influential record producer Jerry Wexler, then a writer for *Billboard* magazine, suggested *rhythm and blues*.

Rhythm and blues stuck as a description for the sophisticated urban dance music—a fast-paced jive hokum blues—that was being performed in the late 1940s by such singer/bandleaders as Wynonie Harris and Louis Jordan. Those who composed songs for this emerging genre often spoofed their rural roots. In 1946 Vicksburg, Mississippi–born songwriter and bassist Willie Dixon, a member of the Chicago-based Big Three Trio, had a southern regional jukebox hit with the song "Signifying Monkey." This pattern—northern-made blues-oriented music interpreting black southern experience—became increasingly present in American entertainment in the decade after World War II.

The musical roots of rhythm and blues can be traced to the early twentieth century. As rural blacks moved from northern Alabama and Mississippi to find work in Memphis, they brought an ear for the blues, and some people sought to make a living through music. During World War I, Memphis-based musician Gus Cannon (from Red Banks, Mississippi) formed the Jug Stompers, a group that pioneered the self-contained multi-instrumental combo format that would become, in terms of instrumental roles, a standard in rhythm and blues. W. C. Handy, a Florence, Alabama, native, organized several popular bands in Memphis before relocating to New York City in 1920.

During the early twentieth century, recently urbanized rural transplants formed Pentecostal and sanctified churches in such cities as Birmingham and Memphis. Unlike many dissenting white churches in Appalachia, most black churches encouraged instrumental music. Black preachers in and near the region fostered a "growling" singing style that was both florid and declamatory. In the late 1920s, African American vaudeville-blues singers such as Chattanooga, Tennessee–born Bessie Smith developed a large fan base through live performances and recordings. At the same time, Birmingham-based pianist Clarence "Pine Top" Smith popularized the riff-based boogie-woogie style that was influential in the evolution of the popular jump blues style of the 1940s. While jazz in the post-depression years became increasingly sophisticated and urbane, jump blues retained an accessible rhythmic and riff-oriented appeal that became the staple of such Midwest-based singers as Jimmy Rushing and Big Joe Turner.

The black gospel quartet singing style featured close harmonies, gliding tones, blue notes, and a deep and independent bass voice. This vocal style—combined with a heavy dance-oriented backbeat on the drums, a strong riff-structured boogie-woogie bass part, and a preference for up-tempo jump swing or slow triple rhythms—became the foundation of the rhythm and blues genre. By the mid-1940s, the electric guitar was being incorporated into blues combos (notably in Muddy Waters's recordings for the Chess label in Chicago), cutting lead riffs in alternation with (or in place of) the harmonica and saxophone.

By the late 1940s, rhythm and blues had surpassed blues in popularity among African American listeners due to the former genre's optimistic, contemporary attitude and its utility for dancing. Rhythm and blues songs, such as Knoxville, Tennessee, native Granville "Stick" McGhee's "Drinkin' Wine, Spo-Dee-O-Dee," addressed themes common in black adult urban life. Many Chicago-based blues musicians from the South—including Sam Lay from Birmingham (Muddy Waters's drummer)—played on early rhythm and blues records, a trend that continued into the 1950s, when pianist Johnnie Johnson (a Fairmont, West Virginia, native) graced Chuck Berry's recordings.

By the 1950s, rhythm and blues had become the most popular black music through the mass media. Independent record labels—such as Florence, Alabama, native Sam Phillips's Memphis-based Sun Records—fed product to Memphis-based black-format radio station WDIA. Soon, clear-channel radio broadcasts of rhythm and blues music were emanating from stations such as WLAC in Nashville, reaching listeners throughout the southern Appalachians. A national musical style popular in urban parts of northern Appalachia at this time was doo-wop, a smooth four-part vocal harmony-based style drawing from African American gospel and rhythm and blues and using nonsensical phrases in the harmony parts. Pittsburgh-based groups recorded some of the classic doo-wop hits of that era, including "Come Go with Me" (the Del-Vikings), "Blue Moon" (the Marcels), and "Since I Don't Have You" (the Skyliners). While the majority of rhythm and blues artists in the 1950s, both black and white, had southern or Appalachian roots, by the 1960s the style had migrated to such northern cities as Cincinnati and Pittsburgh. Detroit's Motown Records, despite its Top 40 leanings, was a major rhythm and blues label, while Washington, D.C., New York, and Los Angeles hosted active rhythm and blues scenes.

By the late 1950s, the popularity of novelty material within the rhythm and blues genre was surpassed by increased interest in material suggesting the emotional depth of gospel music (likely a response to the increasing frivolity of rock 'n' roll and its appeal to white teenagers); soul music, as that type of rhythm and blues came to be called, was gaining a national audience. Initially based in Atlanta, Memphis, and New Orleans, and, inside Appalachia, in Birmingham and Muscle Shoals, Alabama, soul music was noted for its gut-wrenching honesty. Southern soul's impact continued to grow through the late 1960s, with Stax Records in Memphis and FAME Studio in Muscle Shoals attracting international recognition. The soul movement drew participation from both blacks and whites, ensuring the presence of elements from blues, country, and gospel music.

In the 1970s, funk and disco, with their urban sophistication and contemporary concerns, superseded soul's southern ethos among national audiences. Muscle Shoals kept up with the shift in rhythm and blues styles, producing recordings for James Brown, Luther Ingram, Millie Jackson, Candi Staton, and Johnny Taylor, among others. Meanwhile, jazz players George Benson and Stanley Turrentine (both from Pittsburgh) made commercially successful crossovers into rhythm and blues and pop music territory.

Other Appalachian rhythm and blues musicians include such female singers as Dinah Washington (from Tuscaloosa, Alabama) and Syreeta Wright (from Pittsburgh), as well as such male singers as Howlin' Wolf (born Chester Burnett in West Point, Mississippi), Wilson Pickett (a Prattville, Alabama, native), Rufus Thomas (from Cayce, Mississippi), Arthur Alexander (of Florence, Alabama), Percy Sledge and Jimmy Hughes (both of Leighton, Alabama), Lionel Richie (from Tuskegee, Alabama), and Bill Withers (from Slab Fork, West Virginia). Birmingham was the birthplace of Paul Williams and Eddie Kendricks of the Temptations and Eddie Levert of the O'Jays, two major 1960s and 1970s rhythm and blues groups, as well as of soul singer and producer Frederick Knight.

Rhythm and blues recording in Appalachia has witnessed a high degree of interracial collaboration. Many of the key studio musicians associated with the Muscle Shoals–area studios have been white Alabama natives, including guitarist Jimmy Johnson, drummer Roger Hawkins, bassist David Hood (all from Sheffield), and keyboardist Barry Beckett (from Birmingham)—all four were members of the Muscle Shoals Rhythm Section—as well as singer-songwriter-producer Dan Penn (from Vernon) and songwriter-keyboardist-singers Donnie Fritts (from Florence) and Spooner Oldham (of Center Star). Several white rhythm and blues singers are Appalachian, including Billy Price, Donnie Iris, and Johnny Daye, all of Pittsburgh, and Eddie Hinton, a Tuscaloosa native; the latter was also a sought-after session guitarist and a respected songwriter and producer in the Muscle Shoals soul music scene. Johnny Sandlin, a Decatur, Alabama, producer and multi-instrumentalist, has also made significant contributions to the legacy of rhythm and blues, working with Johnny Jenkins, Bonnie Bramlett, Jimmy Hall, and Gregg Allman.

See also: BLUES; JAZZ; MUSCLE SHOALS.

—Peter B. Olson, *University of Memphis*

Stanley Booth, *Rythm Oil: A Journey through the Music of the American South* (1991); Peter Guralnick, *Sweet Soul Music: Rhythm and Blues and the Southern Dream of Freedom* (1986); Gerri Hirshey, *Nowhere to Run: The Story of Soul Music* (1984).

Ritchie, Jean

(1922–) Traditional singer, fretted dulcimer player, and songwriter.

Jean Ruth Ritchie, the youngest child of Balis and Abigail Hall Ritchie, was born on December 8, 1922, in Viper, Perry County, Kentucky. Although her thirteen siblings were educated at Pine Mountain and Hindman Settlement Schools, Jean attended Viper High School and graduated from the University of Kentucky in 1946 with a degree in social work. Moving to New York City in 1947, she took a position at the Henry Street Settlement; there she met photographer George Pickow, whom she married in 1950.

Ritchie's mellifluous voice, her vast repertoire of mountain folk songs and ballads, and her striking fretted dulcimer accompaniment soon caught the attention of folklorist and song collector Alan Lomax, who recorded her for the Library of Congress's Archive of Folk Song and presented her in a 1948 concert at Columbia University. In 1950 Ritchie inaugurated her commercial recording career with Elektra Records; her debut album was the first-ever release by that label. In 1952 she was awarded a Fulbright Fellowship to seek the roots of her family's music through travel in England, Scotland, and Ireland. She also published *The Swapping Song Book*, a transcribed collection of her family's song repertoire with photography by her husband.

Ritchie was one of the leading figures of the folk revival of the 1950s and 1960s. Her ability to recreate the musical context of home and family in a concert situation made her a popular performer at concerts and festivals. She was closely identified with the Newport Folk Festival, having been appointed to its original board in 1963.

Ritchie's fretted dulcimer accompaniment, featuring subtle countermelodies, was largely responsible for the widespread national popularity of that instrument. Although known principally as a traditional singer of ballads, lyric folk songs, play-party songs, and Old Regular Baptist hymnody, she also extended the tradition by writing original songs, many of which were composed under the pseudonym "'Than Hall." Her songs "Black Waters," "The L&N Don't Stop Here Anymore," and "Blue Diamond Mines" projected an articulate contemporary Appalachian voice that focused attention on the problems associated with the coal industry and the abuses of strip mining.

In her five-decade career, Ritchie recorded more than forty albums and published ten books, including the 1955 autobiographical work *Singing Family of the Cumberlands*. Dividing her time between homes in New York and Kentucky, she continues to perform. Her 1995 album *Mountain Born*, released on her own Greenhays label, features her sons, Peter and Jonathan.

See also: BALLADS; DULCIMER, FRETTED; FOLK MUSIC REVIVALS.

—Ron Pen, *University of Kentucky*

Karen Carter-Schwendler, "Traditional Background, Contemporary Context: The Music and Activities of Jean Ritchie to 1977," Ph.D. dissertation, University of Kentucky (1995).

Rock Music

Rock music, an international cultural phenomenon involving numerous subgenres of music, can trace some of its roots to the geographic and cultural environs of Appalachia's southern margins, where black and white musical traditions flourished. As early as the late 1920s, Meridian, Mississippi, native Jimmie Rodgers's "hillbilly" recordings revealed the absorption of the blues into white commercial music genres. By the late 1940s, young white audiences in parts of Appalachia were listening to rhythm and blues broadcasts via such radio stations as WLAC Nashville and WDIA Memphis. Simultaneously, migrating white Appalachians and southern blacks converged on cities such as Memphis, Cincinnati, Philadelphia, and Chicago, propelling an unprecedented cultural exchange.

By the early 1950s, rhythm and blues musicians were absorbing country and western influences (in large part by listening to *Grand Ole Opry* radio broadcasts), which resulted in the emergence of a subgenre known as country soul music. White country musicians adopted blues influences, producing rockabilly, a style composed of blues riffs, electric guitar solos, strident vocals, and, often, predominant drumbeats—all components of black musical expression. In the mid-1950s, two white performers, one from near each end of Appalachia, emerged on the national stage with Appalachian roots and also a passion for black music. Bill Haley, a Chester, Pennsylvania, singer whose eastern Kentucky ancestry initially led him to perform country and western music, was introduced to rhythm and blues music as a disc jockey. Haley's 1954 international hit "Rock around the Clock" became an anthem for youthful rebellion after the song's appearance in the 1955 film *Blackboard Jungle*. That same year, Elvis Presley, a native of Tupelo, Mississippi, began his extraordinary career with Sun Records in Memphis. That label also launched the career of rockabilly guitarist Charlie Feathers, of Holly Springs, Mississippi.

Sun Records, started by Florence, Alabama, native Sam Phillips in 1952, was the most significant record company near the southern fringes of Appalachia during the early rock 'n' roll era. Most of the regional recording studios utilized the studio-band formula and often employed Appalachian musicians. For instance, Sam Phillips hired Muscle Shoals, Alabama–area musicians Quinton Claunch and Bill Cantrell to record with Carl Perkins beginning in 1954. A number of these musicians went on to have significant behind-the-scenes recording careers. Fiddler Cantrell and guitarist Claunch left Sun to establish the influential Hi Records in 1960; Claunch later started the Goldwax label. Fiddler Jim Stewart and guitarist and songwriter Chips Moman, both from the southernmost section of Appalachia, started Memphis's Stax Records and American Studio, respectively.

The first studios dedicated to the new hybrid music actually located in Appalachia were in Muscle Shoals. Recording for the Tune and Judd labels took place there in the late 1950s, but Rick Hall's FAME Studio and Muscle Shoals Sound Studio made that part of the region a national recording center in the 1960s and 1970s.

Cultural exchange in Appalachia flowed in various directions. Soul was an African American subgenre that resulted from the fusion of rhythm and blues with gospel and country music. Muscle Shoals–area black soul singers Arthur Alexander and Percy Sledge not only recorded with white backup musicians but also freely acknowledged their country influences. A Pittsburgh-based group, the Del-Vikings—one of the first racially integrated groups in rock—had a major hit in 1957 with "Come Go with Me." Another integrated group, the Chambers Brothers, of Lee County, Mississippi, rose to prominence at the height of rock's psychedelic movement, transfiguring African American gospel and folk music into their 1967 protest hit "Time Has Come Today." Country singer Sonny James (James Loden) of Hackleburg, Alabama, whose song "Young Love" was a crossover hit in 1956, continued to enjoy mainstream success by subsequently recording covers of rock, pop, and rhythm and blues standards.

The experimentalism and return-to-roots zeitgeist of the 1960s resulted in the emergence of various revivalist rock styles in the Northeast and on the West Coast. In the South, these styles and other traditional musical influences were fused into two regional rock subgenres, southern rock and country rock. Southern rock can be traced to the formation in Decatur, Alabama, in 1967 of the group Hour Glass, featuring Duane and Gregg Allman, Pete Carr, Paul Hornsby, and Johnny Sandlin (the latter two were later producers for the premier southern rock label, Capricorn Records). The Allman Brothers Band, an offshoot of Hour Glass, became the most influential southern rock group. While not comprised of Appalachian musicians, the Allman Brothers in a mid-1970s lineup featured the keyboard talents of Birmingham, Alabama–resident Chuck Leavell, who went on to later success with his jazz-influenced rock group Sea Level. Spartanburg, South Carolina's Marshall Tucker Band crafted another variant of the southern rock sound by skillfully mixing country, rock, and jazz influences. Guitarist Warren Haynes, an Asheville, North Carolina, native, contributed to a popular resurgence of southern rock in the late 1980s with a reformed Allman Brothers Band and later with the group Gov't Mule.

The coinage *country rock* identifies rock amalgamations that are overtly country-influenced. The country rock phenomenon started with non-southern urban musicians recording with country instrumentation in the 1960s. Appalachian musicians—including harmonica player Charlie McCoy (from Oak Hill, West Virginia), keyboardist David Briggs (Killen, Alabama), fiddlers Buddy Spicher (Dubois, Pennsylvania) and Vassar Clements (Kinard, North Carolina), multi-instrumentalist Norman Blake (Chattanooga, Tennessee), and pianist Hargus "Pig" Robbins (Spring City, Tennessee)—were often called upon as session musicians to provide "authentic" traditional sound to such recordings. Recognizing country rock's popularity, Appalachian artists by the early 1970s were attempting the fusion on their own. McCoy, Briggs, and Spicher appeared in Nashville "supergroups" Area Code 615 and Barefoot Jerry. Earl Scruggs (Flint Hill, North Carolina) and his sons, Randy, Gary, and Steve, toured widely as the Earl Scruggs Revue. Craig Fuller (Portsmouth, Ohio) formed the groups Pure Prairie League and American Flyer. Singer-songwriter Russell Smith (Lafayette, Tennessee) fronted the Amazing Rhythm Aces, a group that added blues and soul to the country rock sound. Singer-songwriter Eric Andersen, a Pittsburgh native, incorporated country elements into his folk rock style, achieving artistic success with the 1972 album *Blue River*.

With the urban folk revival's interest in agrarian themes, Appalachian images and influences appeared regularly in pop and rock recordings by both Appalachian and non-Appalachian artists. In the 1950s, several such songs topped the charts, including Bill Hayes's "The Ballad of Davy Crockett," Bristol, Tennessee, native Tennessee Ernie Ford's "Sixteen Tons," and the Kingston Trio's reworking of the nineteenth-century Appalachian murder ballad "Tom Dooley." Pop hits from the 1960s by Appalachian singers included Marietta, Georgia, singer Billy Joe Royal's cover of Joe South's "Down in the Boondocks" and Chickasaw County, Mississippi, singer-songwriter Bobbie Gentry's "Ode to Billy Joe."

In recent years, many Appalachian rock musicians have incorporated traditional elements into their individual styles. In the 1980s, for example, several former rock bands from the region, including Alabama (based in Fort Payne, Alabama) and Exile (formed in Richmond, Kentucky), found commercial success after pursuing a more country sound. Non-native Appalachian musicians have recast Appalachian themes for a broader audience. Steve Earle, for instance, has written songs such as "Hillbilly Highway" and "Copperhead Road" and recorded an album-length bluegrass collaboration with the Del McCoury Band.

Appalachia has not only spawned distinctively regional rock sounds but has also produced more mainstream rock music. The northern Appalachian city of Pittsburgh has long yielded nationally popular music acts—including the Del-Vikings, the Marcels, the Skyliners, the Jaggerz (led by Donnie Iris), Tommy Hunt (of the Flamingos), Shanice Wilson, Syreeta Wright, George Benson, and pop-metal band Poison's frontman, Brett Michaels—that seem little influenced by older regional traditions. Young musicians from Appalachia feel the increasing draw of nontraditional musics, evidenced, for example, in the industrial rock sounds of Trent Reznor (Nine Inch Nails), a native of Mercer, Pennsylvania. Countless audiences across the region likewise display cosmopolitan tastes.

Other musicians from Appalachia who have distinguished themselves in some rock subgenre include Alabamans Odetta, Emmylou Harris, and Bill Justis (all from Birmingham), Eddie Hinton (reared in Tuscaloosa), Pierce Pettis (Fort Payne), the Gosdin Brothers (Vern and Rex, from Woodland), and Patterson Hood and Mike Cooley of the alternative country group Drive-By Truckers (Muscle Shoals); Steve Young, brought up in Appalachian sections of Georgia and Alabama; Travis Wammack, from Walnut, Mississippi; Marshall Chapman, from Spartanburg, South Carolina; Asheville, North Carolina–based David Wilcox; Dave Loggins, of Mountain City, Tennessee; Hasil Adkins, of Madison, West Virginia; Gary Stewart, born in Letcher County, Kentucky; Perry Como and Bobby Vinton, from Canonsburg, Pennsylvania; Jules Shear, Chuck Pyle, and Amy Rigby, of Pittsburgh; and Natalie Merchant, of Jamestown, New York.

See also: ALTERNATIVE COUNTRY/AMERICANA MUSIC MOVEMENTS; MUSCLE SHOALS; PHILLIPS, SAM; RHYTHM AND BLUES.

—Peter B. Olson, *University of Memphis*

Colin Escott, with Martin Hawkins, *Good Rockin' Tonight: Sun Records and the Birth of Rock 'n' Roll* (1992); Charlie Gillett, *The Sound of the City: The Rise of Rock and Roll* (1996); Peter Guralnick, *Feel Like Going Home: Portraits in Blues and Rock 'n' Roll* (1994).

Rodgers, Jimmie

(1897–1933) Early country singer, guitarist, and songwriter.

Singer, guitarist, and songwriter James Charles "Jimmie" Rodgers was an enormously successful and influential figure during the early years of the country music recording industry. Born September 8, 1897, in Meridian, Mississippi, Rodgers began his career as a railroad laborer. In 1924 he was diagnosed with tuberculosis, and in 1927 he moved to Asheville, North Carolina, where the elevation and mountain air were thought to be beneficial. He performed over local radio station WWNC and elsewhere in western North Carolina before achieving his career breakthrough at a pivotal recording session for the Victor Talking Machine Company in Bristol, Tennessee, on August 4, 1927.

Appearing regularly throughout the southern Appalachians over the next several years, Rodgers attained near legendary status regionally, nationally, and internationally through his recording successes and popular personal appearances. Known as the "Singing Brakeman" and "America's Blue Yodeler," he was later called the "Father of Country Music" due to his immense influence on the genre. In 1961 Jimmie Rodgers was the first individual inducted into the Country Music Hall of Fame.

Rodgers's approximately 110 recordings include blues, jazz, sentimental Tin Pan Alley songs, and novelty numbers. He frequently sang about trains, cowboys, home, and hard times, and his trademark yodeling is instantly recognizable and has been widely imitated. For years, aspiring country singers across Appalachia not only covered Rodgers's songs but also emulated his unorthodox guitar style and tried their best to duplicate his unique singing.

"Blue Yodel (T For Texas)" was Rodgers's first successful recording, followed by such classics as "Waiting for a Train," "In the Jailhouse Now," and "Miss the Mississippi and You." These and many other songs popularized by Rodgers are still frequently performed across the Appalachian region. Rodgers died May 26, 1933, from tuberculosis.

See also: BLUES; BRISTOL SESSIONS; COUNTRY MUSIC.

—John Lilly, *Goldenseal Magazine, West Virginia Division of Culture and History*

Nolan Porterfield, *Jimmie Rodgers: The Life and Times of America's Blue Yodeler* (1979).

Seeger, Mike

(1933–) Revivalist singer, multi-instrumentalist, folk music collector, and educator.

Arguably the single most influential figure in the late-twentieth-century traditional music revival, Mike Seeger (b. August 15, 1933, in New York City and reared in Washington, D.C.) is the son of composers and musicologists Charles and Ruth Seeger, who introduced their children (including sister Peggy Seeger and half-brother Pete Seeger) to American folk music at a very early age.

In 1956 Mike Seeger produced his first important documentary recording, *American Banjo: Three-Finger and Scruggs Style*, sometimes cited as the first bluegrass album. The following year, he cofounded the New Lost City Ramblers, a revivalist string band that had a profound effect on the course of the urban folk revival. The Ramblers were his primary performance vehicle for the next twenty-one years; thereafter Seeger continued to perform on his own and with other musicians. Additionally, Seeger produced countless field recordings, documenting virtually the entire range of traditional Appalachian and southern music. He played a crucial role in introducing younger audiences to such older traditional musicians as Dock Boggs, Kilby Snow, and Elizabeth Cotten. Seeger has served on the board of directors for the Newport and the National Folk Festivals, has been a recipient of a Guggenheim Fellowship (1984) and the Rex Foundation's Ralph J. Gleason Award (1984), and is a four-time Grammy Award nominee. Seeger's work as a collector, researcher, promoter, and performer of Appalachian musical traditions has helped ensure their continuation into the twenty-first century.

See also: FOLK MUSIC REVIVALS; OLD-TIME MUSIC; STRING-BAND MUSIC.

—John N. Currie, *Jacksonville, North Carolina*

Sexton Family

Traditional musicians.

Sexton, Morgan (1911–1992) Banjo player.

Sexton, Lee (1928–) Banjo player and fiddler.

Sexton, Phillip (1953–2000) Banjo player and fiddler.

For several generations, members of the Sexton family played traditional Appalachian music in Line Fork, Kentucky. As a child, Morgan Sexton (b. January 28, 1911) began to play a banjo made of "an old molasses bucket and tanned groundhog hide," learning from his father, Shaderick, and his sister, Hettie. After retiring from the coal mines at age sixty-five, Morgan began playing publicly at such festivals as Seedtime on the Cumberland and the Augusta Heritage Festival. His two recordings, *Rock Dust* and *Shady Grove* (both on the June Appal label), display an unusual two-finger picking technique, frequent use of nonstandard tunings, and repertoire of older songs and tunes. Morgan received the National Heritage Award in 1991. He died on January 30, 1992.

Morgan's nephew Lee (b. March 23, 1928) played the banjo clawhammer style as a child, but at age twenty-three, his right hand was crushed in a coal-mining accident, and he was forced to develop an original variation of the drop-thumb style. Also becoming an accomplished fiddler, Lee performed on radio and at square dances with the Jolly Mountain Boys in the 1940s. After retiring from his job in the mines, Lee pursued music full-time. In 1960 he was documented on the album anthology *Mountain Music of Kentucky* (Smithsonian Folkways), and in 1987 he recorded an album, *Whoa Mule* (June Appal), with noted fiddler Marion Sumner. Lee received the Kentucky Governor's Arts Award in 1999.

Lee's son Phillip (b. August 26, 1953) absorbed and then personalized his father's style and mountain fiddle tune repertoire. Phillip made two traditional recordings, *The Banjo Still Rings* and *Fifth Generation* (both on June Appal), before devoting himself to gospel music and making several recordings for the Master's Harmony label. Phillip died in an automobile accident on September 9, 2000.

See also: BANJO; FIDDLE; OLD-TIME MUSIC.

—Ron Pen, *University of Kentucky*

Shape-Note Singing/Singing Schools

Shape notes were invented to improve the quality of church singing. The system's originators, by making patently clear the intervals between notes without requiring singers to learn all the key signatures, intended their innovation to teach people how to sight-read sacred music without instrumental accompaniment. Although originally used as a teaching aid, shape notes proved so popular that they spawned an evangelical subculture that continues to frame the lives of many Appalachians.

Shape notes were invented in the late eighteenth century. Instead of standard round notes, each of the scale's seven notes was turned into one of four shapes: a triangle-, square-, oval-, or diamond-shaped note, depending upon its position in the scale. Each of these shaped notes went by a name (fa, sol, la, mi); when learning a new piece, singers started by singing these names instead of the words. As the system gained popularity, publishers and composers began experimenting with different shapes and names until settling upon a uniform seven-shape scale shortly after the

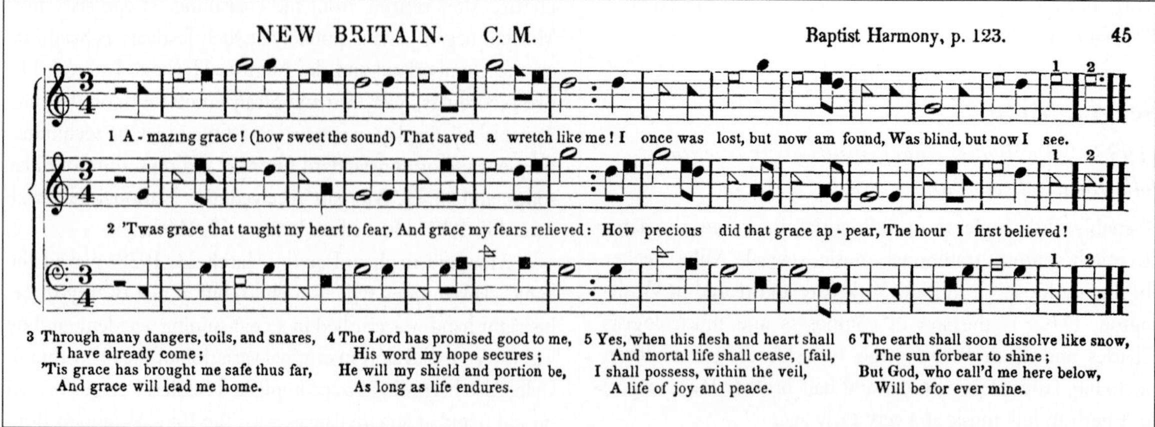

An example of shape-note hymnody from *The Sacred Harp*, 1859. Invented in the early nineteenth century as a method for teaching simplified sight-reading of sacred music, shape notes identify tones on the scale via triangle-, square-, oval-, and diamond-shaped notes.

Civil War. To this day, a divide remains between those who favor the four-shape method (often called "fa-sol-la" or "Sacred Harp") and those who use the seven-shape method (often called "do-re-mi" or "new book").

Throughout the antebellum South, shape-note singing enjoyed widespread popularity. Dozens of books, including *Kentucky Harmony, Harmonia Sacra, Southern Harmony, New Harp of Columbia*, and *The Sacred Harp*, competed for the public's attention by catering to broadly held evangelical beliefs and by courting singers from all Protestant denominations. The 1835 *Southern Harmony*, for example, like dozens of its competitors, declared itself "well adapted to Christian churches of every denomination" as well as to "singing schools and private societies." The lyrical repertoire upon which these tunebooks relied borrowed heavily from the works of the English hymnists Isaac Watts and Charles and John Wesley, as well as from poems by lesser-known American hymnists. The melodies to which these lyrics were set (by such earlier New England composers as William Billings) reflected a commingling of fiddle tunes, psalms, ballads, camp-meeting tunes, and anthems. From these materials, teachers crafted books that they sold as they traveled from community to community teaching three-week-long "singing schools" in which they explained the rudiments of music. These teachers' efforts were often rewarded by the establishment of regular "singings" that took place at a set day or weekend every year, bringing the community together to sing, eat, and visit. By the early twentieth century, many of these annual singings had become highly organized conventions, complete with constitutions, bylaws, and printed minutes of their proceedings. Some of these conventions attracted thousands of singers.

The antebellum books sold remarkably well. *Southern Harmony* reputedly sold six hundred thousand copies between 1835 and 1866. Yet such sales paled in comparison to the popularity of shape-note books published after the Civil War. Technological innovations increased the speed of printing presses, and the number of shape-note books increased exponentially. The new books differed from their antebellum predecessors in important ways. Not only did the new books favor the recently developed seven-shape system over the older four-shape method, but they also reflected a changing musical and religious sensibility. Inspired by the gospel hymnody flooding the northeastern urban revivals of preachers such as Dwight Moody, the new books spoke more of golden streets and Christ's mercy than they did of earthly vanity and death's proximity. Equally importantly, the new tunes moved away from the rough-hewn compositions of an earlier era and incorporated rolling bass sections, flexible rhythms, and close vocal harmonies. These later books, issued by such publishing houses as Ruebush-Kieffer, Stamps-Baxter, and James D. Vaughan, came out at a furious pace to keep up with the demand. Ironically, the number of people actually singing shape-note music soon declined. Publishers sent out quartets to help sell new books, and the more polished sound of these quartets caught the ear of the listening public, who gradually began to prefer hearing professional singers.

It has been difficult to trace the involvement of African Americans in the fa-sol-la shape-note tradition. The available evidence suggests that before the Civil War black singers, both slave and free, participated avidly in shape-note singings (particularly during interracial camp meetings), often having a marked impact on the style of music the antebellum books contained. After the Civil War, many African Americans created their own independent singing conventions, and, like many whites, began switching from the older tunebooks to the popular "new book" style. Black interest in the fa-sol-la style did not completely die out, however. The most dynamic manifestation of this interest came with the 1934 publication of *The Colored Sacred Harp*. After the compositions of its author, Judge Jackson, were rejected for inclusion in a revision of *The Sacred Harp*, Jackson published this companion book, made up almost entirely of tunes by black composers. This book's adherents, however, have tended to live outside Appalachia in such areas as southeastern Alabama and northwestern Florida. Many African Americans in Appalachia have traditionally used a version of the old *Sacred Harp* called the "Cooper book" (named after its white Alabama editor, W. M. Cooper). Some Appalachian blacks have enthusiastically embraced the "new book" style and have established singing conventions to support this interest.

Despite lingering divisions between seven- and four-shape adherents and white and black singers, shape-note music and its attendant traditions have for two centuries retained a strong hold on the religious and musical sensibilities of many Appalachian people. Some denominational hymnals still publish shape-note editions; far more common are nondenominational tunebooks printed especially for singers. Publishing houses still put out new books arranged in shape notes to satisfy the demands among shape-note singers for new tunes, and older antebellum tunebooks, especially *The Sacred Harp*, have experienced a remarkable resurgence in popularity. All-day "singings" continue to attract large and enthusiastic crowds, especially during the summer, when conventions are held in numerous Appalachian communities. Shape-note singing provides participants with an important artistic, social, and religious framework within which to understand their relationship to one another and to God.

See also: GOSPEL MUSIC, AFRICAN AMERICAN; GOSPEL MUSIC, ANGLO-AMERICAN; SECTION OVERVIEW (RELIGION).

—Gavin James Campbell, *University of North Carolina*

Buell E. Cobb Jr., *The Sacred Harp: A Tradition and Its Music* (1978); George Pullen Jackson, *White Spirituals in the Southern Uplands* (1933).

Skaggs, Ricky

(1954–) Country and bluegrass singer, mandolinist, and fiddler.

During his musical odyssey, Ricky Skaggs has influenced mainstream Nashville country music, hard-core bluegrass, and even the national pop consciousness. He was born July 18, 1954, in Cordell, Kentucky, the son of a construction worker. As a child, Skaggs learned songs from his mother while being tutored on stringed instruments by his father. His progress, particularly on the mandolin and the fiddle, was so rapid that he performed on a concert stage with bluegrass patriarch Bill Monroe at the age of five and on the syndicated television show of two other bluegrass pioneers, Lester Flatt and Earl Scruggs, at seven.

Skaggs's professional career began at fifteen, when he was hired as a regular member of the band of another bluegrass groundbreaker, Ralph Stanley. Moving steadily in more progressive directions—first into the Washington, D.C.–based Country Gentlemen, then back to Kentucky to join J. D. Crowe and the New South—Skaggs also teamed briefly with boyhood friend and fellow Stanley band member Keith Whitley. In 1977 Emmylou Harris enlisted Skaggs in her country rock group, the Hot Band, where he influenced her interest in vintage country music and bluegrass.

Skaggs has enjoyed national prominence of his own since the early 1980s. Nashville's nearly simultaneous discovery of him and Texas cowboy George Strait returned the focus of mainstream country music to the music's roots after a period of musical adulteration in the crossover-preoccupied 1970s. Strongly Appalachia flavored, Skaggs's singles—including such refashioned bluegrass standards as "Crying My Heart Out over You" and "Uncle Pen" as well as traditional-styled newer songs such as "Heartbroke" and "Country Boy"—played pivotal roles in the rise of Nashville's neo-traditionalist country movement in the 1980s. A multiple Grammy Award winner, Skaggs garnered the Country Music Association's pinnacle honor, Entertainer of the Year, in 1985.

As his mainstream popularity waned in the 1990s, Skaggs reverted to bluegrass. Claiming to have been inspired by the death of Monroe and returning to the mandolin from the electric guitar he had played during his mainstream heyday, Skaggs founded the bluegrass group Kentucky Thunder, with whom he released several best-selling bluegrass albums.

Skaggs's influence stems not only from his instrumental and vocal abilities but also from his exacting production standards. In addition to painstakingly crafting his own albums, he has produced records by such other important acts as Dolly Parton, the Whites (featuring Skaggs's wife, Sharon White, and her sister and father, Cheryl and Buck White), and Blue Highway.

See also: BLUEGRASS; COUNTRY MUSIC; MANDOLIN.

—Jack Hurst, *Lancaster, Tennessee*

Skillet Lickers

Early country string band.

Tanner, Gid (1885–1960) Singer, fiddler, and bandleader.

Puckett, Riley (1894–1946) Guitarist and singer.

McMichen, Clayton (1900–1970) Fiddler and songwriter.

The Skillet Lickers were a popular string band from north Georgia whose recordings, made during the late 1920s and early 1930s, influenced old-time musicians for generations. Formed around local fiddler and comedian James

Gideon "Gid" Tanner (June 6, 1885–May 13, 1960), the Skillet Lickers were the creation of Columbia recording executive Frank Walker, who sought to capitalize on the burgeoning popularity of rural southern music throughout the region at that time.

Tanner and his accompanist of several years, blind guitarist and singer Riley Puckett (May 7, 1894–July 13, 1946), were joined by virtuoso fiddler Clayton McMichen (January 26, 1900–January 4, 1970) and banjoist Fate Norris (dates unknown) for the first Skillet Lickers recording session, held in April 1926 in Atlanta. Over the next several years, the group, with varying personnel and under different names, recorded hundreds of infectious fiddle breakdowns, raucous comedy skits, and upbeat songs. Many other individuals were also part of the loose-knit group through the years, including fiddlers Lowe Stokes and Bert Layne, guitarist Slim Bryant, mandolin player Ted Hawkins, and other talented north Georgia musicians.

The Skillet Lickers' best-selling release was a lively 1934 recording of the instrumental "Down Yonder," which reportedly sold more than a million copies. Group members were rediscovered during the folk music revival of the 1950s and 1960s, leading to a resurgence of interest in the Skillet Lickers' music. Many string bands of the past twenty-five years have derived their style, repertoire, and personas from the group's early recordings. Puckett's guitar style, with distinctive syncopated bass runs, was highly influential. McMichen, the most technically accomplished musician in the band, went on to studio work with such artists as Jimmie Rodgers (who recorded McMichen's "Peach Pickin' Time in Georgia"). Gid Tanner's grandson Phil Tanner and other family members and friends have kept the style and much of the repertoire of the original group alive, appearing around north Georgia as the Skillet Lickers.

See also: FOLK MUSIC REVIVALS; OLD-TIME MUSIC; STRING-BAND MUSIC.

—John Lilly, *Goldenseal Magazine, West Virginia Division of Culture and History*

Smith, Bessie

(1894–1937) Blues and jazz singer.

Born April 15, 1894, in Chattanooga, Tennessee, Bessie Smith was among the best known and most accomplished of the vaudeville blues singers. Her parents, William (a laborer and Baptist preacher) and Laura, died before Smith's tenth birthday, by which time she had taken to singing on the street. Her professional career began around 1912 with a job as chorus girl with the Moses Stokes Show at the Ivory Theater in Chattanooga. Smith soon took to the road, singing with a series of vaudeville shows that toured small cities and towns throughout the South to bring vaudeville to various audiences. By the late 1910s, Smith had become popular enough to warrant a featured billing, and she began working in larger cities such as Baltimore and Philadelphia in the segregated theaters that proliferated during the period.

In 1923, just as Smith began to gain status as a headlining artist, she launched her recording career with the Columbia Record Company; thereafter, she emerged as one of the brightest and best-selling "race" artists. Between 1923 and 1933, Smith recorded with some of the best jazz and blues artists of the day, including Charlie Green (trombone), Louis Armstrong (trumpet), and Fletcher Henderson (piano). Memorable and influential performances by Smith include "Back Water Blues," "Soft Pedal Blues," and "Gulf Coast Blues."

Left without a recording contract when she was dropped by Columbia in 1931, Smith continued to perform at numerous theaters from coast to coast as a headliner and sometimes as part of a larger musical and comedy revue. In mid-September 1937, while on the road with the Broadway Rastus Revue, a vaudeville show touring the Deep South, Smith was involved in an automobile accident near Clarksdale, Mississippi. She died from her injuries on September 26, 1937. Smith was inducted into the Rock and Roll Hall of Fame in 1989 as an "early influence." She also had a significant impact on jazz, particularly on later generations of female jazz vocalists.

See also: BLUES; JAZZ.

—Kip Lornell, *George Washington University*

Jackie Kay, *Bessie Smith* (1997).

Smith, Hobart

(1897–1965) Traditional singer, banjo player, fiddler, guitarist, and pianist.

Born May 10, 1897, Hobart Smith, the son of King and Louvine Smith from Saltville, Smyth County, Virginia, was a skilled banjo, fiddle, guitar, and piano player, as well as a seventh-generation ballad singer. In the 1930s, Smith and his sister, the influential traditional singer Texas Gladden (1895–1967), performed at many festivals (including the White Top Festival) and at the White House. During the 1940s, the siblings made recordings for folklorist and collector Alan Lomax and the Library of Congress as well as for Folkways Records.

Smith first learned music from his mother and father, who were both banjo players. By age seven, he had picked up the traditional "rapping" style on the banjo from his father; soon after, he learned from neighbor John Greer to "double-note" by dropping his thumb—a technique he displayed especially on "The Cuckoo Bird" and "Banging Breakdown." At the age of fourteen, Smith bought a guitar, having been moved by the music of black men working on nearby railroads. Smith also took up the fiddle, an instrument played by both of his grandfathers before he was born; Smith's fiddle style was influenced by the playing of once enslaved Jim Spencer, a black musician who performed old tunes at dances in white homes. Smith learned a large repertoire of fiddle and banjo tunes at these dances.

Making a living as a farmer, wagoner, and butcher, Smith played music all his life. He formed a band with Clarence "Tom" Ashley and became a leading musician in the urban folk revival of the early 1960s. Smith died January 11, 1965.

See also: AFRICAN AMERICAN INFLUENCES; ASHLEY, CLARENCE "TOM"; BANJO.

—Cecelia Conway, *Appalachian State University*

Stanley, Ralph

(1927–) Bluegrass singer, banjo player, and bandleader.

Following the death of Carter Stanley in December 1966, Ralph Stanley continued playing the kind of music exemplified by the Stanley Brothers and their band, the Clinch Mountain Boys. Stanley's new band, as before named the Clinch Mountain Boys, included former members of the Lonesome Pine Fiddlers, Curly Ray Cline and Melvin Goins, and a young guitarist from Ohio's Appalachian migrant community, Larry Sparks, together with longtime Clinch Mountain Boy George Shuffler. By February 1967, Stanley and his band began recording for both the King and Jalyn labels. With the rising popularity of bluegrass festivals, this Stanley aggregation achieved greater commercial success than the original Stanley Brothers had attained.

Ralph Stanley's Clinch Mountain Boys re-created much of the musical sound identified with the Stanley Brothers, featuring heavy emphasis on fiddle, lead guitar, and Stanley's own banjo, together with "high lonesome" solo and harmony vocals. Although Goins, Shuffler, and Sparks had left by 1970, Cline stayed with the band until retiring in 1994. Other musicians who have played with the Clinch Mountain Boys include bassist Jack Cooke and such lead singers as Roy Lee Centers, Keith Whitley, Ricky Skaggs, Charlie Sizemore, Ernie Thacker, and Ralph Stanley II. The elder Ralph Stanley and his band have recorded prolifically, mostly for the Charlottesville, Virginia–based Rebel label, ultimately surpassing the total number of studio recordings made by the Stanley Brothers.

As the twentieth century came to a close, Ralph Stanley easily ranked as the leading active figure in bluegrass music. Two albums recorded in the 1990s, *Saturday Night, Sunday Morning* and *Clinch Mountain Country*, paid tribute to Stanley's influence on younger musicians. Among other awards, Stanley received a National Heritage Fellowship and an honorary doctorate from Lincoln Memorial University and was been inducted into the International Bluegrass Music Association Hall of Honor. In January 2000, he and his band became official members of the *Grand Ole Opry*. Two years later Stanley won a Grammy Award for his a cappella performance of the traditional song "O Death," featured on the *O Brother, Where Art Thou?* movie soundtrack.

See also: BANJO; BLUEGRASS; STANLEY BROTHERS.

—Ivan M. Tribe, *University of Rio Grande*

John Wright, *Traveling the High Way Home: Ralph Stanley and the World of Traditional Bluegrass Music* (1993).

Stanley Brothers

Stanley, Carter (1925–1966) Bluegrass singer, guitarist, and songwriter.
Stanley, Ralph (1927–) Bluegrass singer, banjo player, and songwriter.

The Stanley Brothers were the most traditional sounding of the first generation of performers in bluegrass. Natives of Smith Ridge in mountainous Dickenson County, Virginia, where Carter was born on August 27, 1925, and Ralph on February 25, 1927, the Stanleys formed the Clinch Mountain Boys band in 1946 following their World War II military service. The group featured Ralph on banjo, Carter on guitar, Leslie Keith on fiddle, and Pee Wee Lambert on mandolin and forged a trio harmony sound with Carter singing lead, Ralph singing tenor, and Lambert singing an even higher third part. Carter also contributed many original songs (a number of which became classic songs in bluegrass and country music repertoires). The Stanley Brothers' music was, in essence, a merging of the older traditional mountain string-band styles with the sound of Bill Monroe's Blue Grass Boys. Initially, the Stanleys' musical base was WCYB radio in Bristol, Tennessee/Virginia, and they periodically returned there, though they also worked out of other locales, most notably the *Suwanee River Jamboree* on radio station WNER in Live Oak, Florida.

The Stanley Brothers were the most recorded of the early bluegrass acts, with nearly four hundred masters to their credit. Their first offerings appeared on the Rich-R-Tone label in 1947, but the group soon moved on to Columbia (1948–52), Mercury (1953–58), Starday (1958–61), and King (1958–65). In between contracts they recorded sessions for smaller firms, including Blue Ridge, Wango, Rimrock, and Cabin Creek. In 1966 Carter and Ralph returned to western Virginia, where Carter's health deteriorated rapidly. However, they continued making appearances until a few weeks before Carter's death on December 1, 1966. Shortly afterward, Ralph revitalized the Clinch Mountain Boys and continued performing and recording.

See also: BLUEGRASS; DUOS, BROTHER; STANLEY, RALPH.

—Ivan M. Tribe, *University of Rio Grande*

Statler Brothers

Country music group.

One of the longest-lived and most successful vocal quartets in country music, the Statler Brothers hailed from the Shenandoah Valley of Virginia. Harold Reid was born near Staunton in Augusta County on August 21, 1939; Don Reid in Staunton on June 5, 1945; Phil Balsley in Staunton on August 8, 1939; Lew DeWitt in Roanoke on March 8, 1938; and Jimmy Fortune in nearby Nelson County, southeast of Staunton, on March 11, 1955. In 1961 Harold Reid formed a quartet called the Kingsmen with Don Reid, Balsley, and DeWitt; the friends sang some pop and country music but concentrated on gospel music in the style of white country gospel quartets such as the Statesmen and the Blackwood Brothers. In 1963 Johnny Cash heard the Kingsmen when he was touring near Staunton and shortly thereafter invited the group to join his road show. Renaming themselves the Statler Brothers (after a popular brand of tissue) upon learning of another group called the Kingsmen, the quartet stayed with Cash from 1964 to 1972. With his help the Statlers landed a recording contract with Columbia Records and in 1965 scored a crossover hit with the song "Flowers on the Wall." After only moderate success with Columbia, the quartet signed with Mercury Records in 1970 and had many hits on the country music charts.

The success of the Statlers during the 1970s and 1980s was attributable to strong original songwriting (notably by the Reids and by Fortune) that projected themes of nostalgia, small-town values, and the everyday tensions and conflicts of ordinary people. The quartet's work captured three Grammy Awards and nine selections as Vocal Group of the Year by the Country Music Association. Their best-known songs include "Bed of Roses," "The Class of '57," "Do You Remember These?" and "Whatever Happened to Randolph Scott?"

Suffering from a gastrointestinal disorder, DeWitt left the Statler Brothers in 1981 (he died on August 15, 1990) and was replaced by Jimmy Fortune. In 1991 the quartet started a weekly variety television show on the Nashville Network that soon became the network's highest rated show, running until 1999. The Statlers returned to touring, keeping quartet singing alive in contemporary country music until the end of 2002, when they discontinued their act.

See also: COUNTRY MUSIC; GOSPEL MUSIC, ANGLO-AMERICAN.

—Frederick E. Danker, *University of Massachusetts*

Steele, Pete

(1891–1985) Traditional banjo player.

Of all the early banjo players recorded for the Library of Congress's folk music archive, none commanded as many techniques or employed as many tunings as Simon "Pete" Steele. A dazzling array of frailing, two-finger, and up-picking styles defines his extensive repertoire of instrumentals, folk songs, and ballads. Born in Woodbine, Kentucky, on March 5, 1891, Steele gave few public performances outside his home community in Hamilton, Ohio, yet he had considerable influence on musicians of the urban folk revival during the 1950s and 1960s.

Steele began playing the banjo when he was six or seven on a fretless instrument made for him by his fiddle-playing father. While much of Steele's instruction came from his father, other local musicians also passed along tunes. One of these, "Coal Creek March," a parlor-based banjo instrumental with a series of ascending and descending arpeggios, commemorated mining troubles that occurred in the early 1890s in Coal Creek, Tennessee.

In 1938 Steele recorded "Coal Creek March" for the Library of Congress. With the tune's publication in 1942, Steele's playing came to be known to a wider audience, and by the mid-1950s, Pete Seeger had made the "March" an integral part of his concerts, urging his listeners to learn directly from the music's authentic sources. This led to Steele's 1958 solo album on the Folkways label, *Banjo Tunes and Songs*. In later years, those who traveled to his home were rewarded with his performance of "Coal Creek March," which had become a signature piece among the many he had mastered. Steele died November 21, 1985.

See also: BANJO; COAL-MINING AND PROTEST MUSIC; FIELD RECORDING SESSIONS.

—Stephen Wade, *Hyattsville, Maryland*

Steel Guitar

Steel-guitar playing includes all guitar performance styles where a steel bar is used to intonate a note in place of fretting with fingers. However, the term *steel guitar* is often associated exclusively with the pedal steel guitar most often heard in country music. Appalachian musicians contributed significantly to the development of a country music vocabulary on the instrument, channeling influences from Hawaiian and blues steel-guitar styles.

Probably originating in Hawaii and crossing to the mainland around 1915, steel-guitar playing entered Appalachian music via both Hawaiian music and the blues. Early examples of steel-guitar playing in commercial "hillbilly" music were heard in the blues-influenced recordings of such white Appalachians as Frank Hutchison (born in Raleigh County, West Virginia) and Cliff Carlisle (based in Knoxville, Tennessee).

Initial attempts at mechanically amplifying the steel guitar led to the development of resonator-equipped instruments by the Dopyera brothers and of Kona guitars with hollow necks by instrument makers including Weissenborn. Electric steel guitars were commercially introduced in 1931 with Rickenbacker's "Frying Pan" model. However, many pioneering steel guitarists started with electric pickups mounted on regular acoustic flat-top steel-string guitars. During the 1930s and 1940s, the non-pedal steel guitar was featured prominently in the major country music styles of the era—from western swing to "silver screen" cowboy music to honky-tonk. Western swing bandleader Hank Penny, of Birmingham, Alabama, featured major steel-guitar players in his bands. Also in this era, Appalachian musicians such as Clell "Cousin Jody" Summey (from Sevier County, Tennessee) pioneered the electric steel guitar at venues where it had formerly been unacceptable, including the *Grand Ole Opry*. Since the mid-1950s, the pedal steel guitar has been one of the instruments most strongly associated with country music. Often employed to add a country flavor to other popular music genres, the instrument can be heard on many country rock and some pop recordings.

A highly complex and demanding instrument that features knee levers and foot pedals to alter pitch and volume while playing and often two or more necks (each usually featuring ten strings tuned to different open chords, the E9 and the C6 tunings being the most common), the pedal steel requires a high level of dexterity. Indeed, pedal-steel duties at major recording centers are usually dominated by a small number of accomplished session players. For instance, Jimmy Day (of Tuscaloosa, Alabama) accompanied many major country artists during the 1950s and 1960s. Other notable pedal-steel players from Appalachia have included Billy Bowman (of Johnson City, Tennessee), a member of Bob Wills's western swing band in the 1950s, and Buddy Charlton (of New Market, Virginia), who played in Ernest Tubb's band.

Appalachian musicians have contributed to the development and popularization of steel-guitar playing through their imagination, innovation, and experimentation. Such contributions include Hacker Valley, West Virginia, native Eddie Alkire's crafting of a ten-string lap steel around 1939, which was intended to expand the harmonic possibilities of the instrument before pedals were widely used for that purpose. Additionally, many acoustic-oriented musicians from Appalachia—including the Osborne Brothers, Earl Scruggs, Jean Ritchie, Phyllis Boyens, and Vassar Clements—have at times incorporated the pedal steel into their recordings. Not limited to country-related music, the steel guitar has been featured on recordings of rock, new age, blues, gospel, world, and even classical music.

See also: COUNTRY MUSIC; DOBRO/RESONATOR GUITAR; GUITAR.

—Ajay Kalra, *East Tennessee State University*

Rich Kienzle, "Steel Guitar: The Western Swing Era," *Guitar Player* (December 1979); Tom Mulhern, "The Pedal Steel Guitar: What It Is, How It Works," *Guitar Player* (September 1979); Lorene Ruymar, comp., *The Hawaiian Steel Guitar and Its Great Hawaiian Musicians* (1996).

Stoneman, Ernest V. / Stoneman Family

(1893–1968) Early country singer, guitarist, autoharpist, and bandleader.

Ernest Van Stoneman, born May 25, 1893, in Carroll County, Virginia, ranks among the most significant recording artists in the early years of country music. He sang a variety of old folk and popular ballads and songs as well as sacred numbers, accompanying himself on either guitar or autoharp and harmonica. Sometimes he worked with a larger string band that included fiddle and banjo. Between 1924 and 1934, Stoneman cut some two hundred recordings for such companies as OKeh, Victor, Edison, and Gennett. His best-known song was "The Titanic." Other favorites included "The Poor Tramp Has to Live," "Two Little Orphans," and "Hallelujah Side." He was already an accomplished veteran of recording studios when he participated in the 1927 and 1928 Bristol sessions.

After the Great Depression curtailed his recording career, Stoneman moved his large family to the Washington, D.C., area, where they endured several years of dire poverty. However, he stayed as musically active on the local scene as conditions would permit. "Pop," as he became known, eventually rebuilt his career with the help of his thirteen surviving children, the most notable being Patsy (b. 1925), Scott (1932–1973), Donna (b. 1934), Jimmy (1937–2002), Veronica (b. 1938), and Van (1940–1995). As a concert act, the Stoneman Family demonstrated a charismatic brand of showmanship. The family's second career peaked in 1967, when they won the Country Music Association's Vocal Group of the Year award. Their popularity declined during the 1970s as some family members left to pursue individual careers, but the Stoneman Family group remained musically active into the early 1990s. Many of Stoneman's original recordings have been reissued on vinyl albums and compact discs.

See also: AUTOHARP; BRISTOL SESSIONS; FAMILY GROUPS.

—Ivan M. Tribe, *University of Rio Grande*

Ivan M. Tribe, *The Stonemans: An Appalachian Family and the Music That Shaped Their Lives* (1993).

String-Band Music

From the mid-nineteenth century to the present, musicians in Appalachia have played music together utilizing various combinations of stringed instruments. At one time, Lester Flatt noted, "It used to be that a band was just a fiddle and banjo," but as Appalachian society was increasingly affected by outside influences from 1900 to the 1930s, the makeup of string bands, like many others aspects of Appalachian culture, adapted to fit the times.

Early settlers in Appalachia brought fiddles with them. By the mid-nineteenth century, the banjo, an instrument of

African origin, had joined the fiddle to produce a new sound. By 1900, the guitar—which became more popular in Appalachia as a result of availability through mail-order catalogs—was added to the mix primarily as a rhythm instrument. By the mid-1920s, when the first commercial recordings of string bands were made, other instruments, notably the mandolin and autoharp, had also been added by some groups to further enliven the ensemble sound.

Until the 1920s, string-band performances were mostly limited to families, homes, and small dances, with occasional competitions held away from home by local civic or social organizations. The musicians at these competitions were rarely paid in money for their services. The early string bands' repertoires were comprised mostly of dance tunes, southern folk songs, and nineteenth-century popular songs. As their instrumentation changed in the 1920s, string bands began to perform songs from the mainstream popular repertoire.

In the early years of the commercial recording industry, numerous string bands were recorded with many different combinations of instruments and sounds. During this experimental "golden age" of recording, which lasted through the early 1930s, two important tendencies in string-band styles emerged. Some bands displayed great control and complexity, and they strove for an almost polished, parlor sound. The best example of this type of string band was Charlie Poole and the North Carolina Ramblers. Poole's band was much admired and much imitated because of its sophisticated and disciplined playing. One group that emulated Poole's sound was Ernest V. Stoneman's Blue Ridge Cornshuckers. In stark contrast to Poole stood the unrestrained style of Gid Tanner and His Skillet Lickers. This band generated a notably spontaneous sound that resulted from a strong fiddle lead, intense singing, and rhythmically loose backup on banjo and guitar. The approach of the Skillet Lickers influenced many early string bands, including the Georgia Crackers and Earl Johnson's Clodhoppers.

String-band music remained a mainstay of country music into the early 1940s, as evidenced by the popularity of such groups as Mainer's Mountaineers and Roy Acuff and the Smoky Mountain Boys. Since the 1950s, the string-band tradition's strongest influence has been on bluegrass. String-band music enjoyed renewed interest within the broad boundaries of the urban folk revival movement of the 1950s and 1960s, as groups such as the New Lost City Ramblers performed faithful interpretations of the string-band repertoire. Far from the country music mainstream, string-band music remains a vibrant subculture, with many practitioners in Appalachia. For example, in the Galax, Virginia, and Mount Airy, North Carolina, locales, rural string-band music is commonplace and popular at local dances, contests, festivals, community gatherings, and informal private functions.

See also: BLUEGRASS; FOLK MUSIC REVIVALS ; OLD-TIME MUSIC.

—Richard A. Straw, *Radford University*

Bill C. Malone, *Country Music, U.S.A.* (2002) and *Southern Music—American Music* (1979); Neil V. Rosenberg, *Bluegrass: A History* (1993); Gene Wiggins, *Fiddlin' Georgia Crazy: Fiddlin' John Carson, His Real World and the World of His Songs* (1987).

Stringbean

(1916–1973) Early country banjo player and comedian.

David "Stringbean" Akeman parleyed his slender physique, old-time banjo songs, and droll humor into a lengthy entertainment career. "String," as he was known to friends, appeared on radio's *Grand Ole Opry* in various roles for thirty-one years, and for the last four years of his life he was an ensemble member on television's *Hee Haw*.

Born on June 17, 1916, in Annville, Kentucky, Akeman worked on Civilian Conservation Corps projects in the mid-1930s. About 1938, after winning a talent contest sponsored by radio musician Asa Martin on WLAP Lexington, Akeman joined Martin's musical group, and the veteran entertainer nicknamed him "String Beans" (soon shortened). Stringbean, who played clawhammer banjo, eventually teamed up with Grandpa Jones and became a protégé of Uncle Dave Macon.

In 1942 Akeman arrived in Nashville to perform on radio station WSM as the first banjo player in Bill Monroe's Blue Grass Boys. In 1945 Akeman went solo but often traveled with veteran entertainer Lew Childre. Although recording albums for Starday, Nuggett, and Cullman in the 1960s, along with singles for the Cullman label, Akeman was too unpolished for the contemporary country market and not "folk" enough for the urban revivalist audiences (his signature song, "Barnyard Banjo Pickin'," a traditional number previously recorded by Martin as "Hot Corn, Cold Corn," did not chart). Ironically, "String" had found a whole new audience via *Hee Haw* when he and his wife were murdered on November 10, 1973, at their modest country home near Nashville during a robbery attempt.

See also: BANJO; COUNTRY MUSIC COMEDY (HUMOR); *GRAND OLE OPRY* (MEDIA).

—Ivan M. Tribe, *University of Rio Grande*

Stringfield, Lamar

(1897–1959) Classical composer, flautist, and symphony conductor.

Born October 10, 1897, in Raleigh, North Carolina, into a musical family, Lamar Edwin Stringfield attended Mars Hill and Wake Forest Colleges. He served in the 105th Engineers regimental band in France during World War I under Joseph DeNardo, a music teacher from Asheville. After discharge, he remained in Paris to study composition with Nadia Boulanger. When he returned to the United States, Stringfield entered New York's Institute of Musical Art (now the Juilliard School), studying flute, conducting, composition, and music theory. He graduated in 1924 with an artist's diploma in flute performance.

A prolific composer of solo as well as large orchestral compositions, Stringfield based much of his music on folk tunes, especially those from Appalachia. He received a Joseph Pulitzer Scholarship Prize for his symphonic suite *From the Southern Mountains* (1928). With Bascom Lamar Lunsford, Stringfield published a book of arrangements of Appalachian folk songs (1929). Interested in Appalachian, African American, and Native American music, he organized the Institute of Folk Music at the University of North Carolina in Chapel Hill in 1930. Stringfield collaborated with playwright Paul Green on the music for at least five dramas, including *The Lost Colony*, typically using Elizabethan English and American folk tunes.

Founder and conductor of two orchestras, the Asheville Symphony (founded in 1927) and the North Carolina Symphony (1932), Stringfield also conducted the Charlotte and Knoxville Symphonies in the 1940s. Considered one of the finest flautists in the United States, Stringfield was a flute builder, as well as a composer for the instrument. He died January 21, 1959, in Asheville.

See also: CLASSICAL COMPOSERS; LUNSFORD, BASCOM LAMAR; SYMPHONY ORCHESTRAS.

—Paul C. Hager, *Berea College*, and E. Wayne Pressley, *Mars Hill College*

Sun Ra

(1914–1993) Jazz keyboardist, bandleader, and composer.

Born Herman Poole Blount in Birmingham, Alabama, on May 22, 1914, Sun Ra led an innovative jazz big band that toured Appalachia as well as much of the country over a period of forty years. Although this band, usually called the Arkestra, was most influential through its work in Chicago and New York, Sun Ra remained associated with Appalachia throughout his career. He relocated near northern Appalachia in the 1970s and continued to give concerts across the region into the early 1990s.

Sun Ra worked as a freelance pianist in the 1930s, touring in Tennessee, Kentucky, Virginia, and the Carolinas. Following a brief tenure as a pianist and copyist with jazz bandleader Fletcher Henderson in the late 1940s, Sun Ra became active in the Chicago jazz scene, making his mark as a distinctive composer and arranger. After several years in New York City, he and the Arkestra relocated to Philadelphia in 1970. The band became well known internationally, recording frequently and touring Europe, Asia, and Africa.

Sun Ra maintained his group for forty years despite encountering racism and enduring financial hardships. He saw himself as a mystic; his interests went beyond music into the fields of mythology, numerology, and African American history. Often stating that he was from the planet Saturn, Sun Ra led his "space orchestra" in concerts that included elaborate costumes, light shows, slide presentations, and dance. A pioneer in free jazz and electronic music, he anticipated later developments in aleatoric music (music that incorporates elements of chance in its structure), microtonality, and minimalism. Sun Ra died May 30, 1993.

See also: AFRICAN AMERICAN INFLUENCES; JAZZ.

—Raleigh Dailey, *University of Kentucky*

John F. Szwed, *Space Is the Place: The Lives and Times of Sun Ra* (1998).

Symphony Orchestras

Symphony orchestras maintain a vital cultural presence in the Appalachian region. With annual operating budgets ranging from more than ten million dollars (Pittsburgh Symphony Orchestra) to less than thirty-five thousand dollars (the Allegheny Civic Symphony in Meadville, Pennsylvania), Appalachia's orchestras can be divided roughly into the following categories: professional orchestras, volunteer/community orchestras, orchestras affiliated with educational institutions, and summer music festival orchestras. The following list, while far from exhaustive, identifies representative Appalachian orchestras from each category.

Professional orchestras in Appalachia include the Pittsburgh Symphony, West Virginia Symphony (Charleston), Alabama Symphony (Birmingham), Maryland Symphony (Hagerstown), Binghamton Philharmonic (New York), Winston-Salem Piedmont Triad Symphony (North Carolina), Wheeling Symphony (West Virginia), Asheville Symphony (North Carolina), Knoxville Symphony (Tennessee), Kingsport Symphony (Tennessee), and Greenville Symphony (South Carolina). These professional orchestras generally operate on comparatively large budgets that enable them to procure world-renowned guest soloists. While professional orchestras tend to be located in larger metropolitan areas, the Wheeling Symphony, with a budget of more than one million dollars, serves a home city of approximately thirty thousand people.

Appalachian volunteer/community orchestras include the Nittany Valley Symphony (Pennsylvania) and the Anderson Symphony (South Carolina). This type of orchestra is usually found in smaller communities; however, in larger cities with a professional orchestra in residence, a volunteer/

Pittsburgh Symphony Orchestra, Heinz Hall, 1997. Orchestras in Appalachia range from community and college ensembles, largely composed of amateur musicians, to internationally recognized professional orchestras such as the Pittssburgh Symphony.

community orchestra can provide playing opportunities for nonprofessional musicians. Quite frequently, community orchestras are affiliated with educational institutions, especially colleges and universities.

Orchestras affiliated with educational institutions in Appalachia serve as training grounds for musicians, offering technical instruction and performance opportunities. Occasionally these orchestras incorporate musicians from the community, as is true of Virginia Polytechnic Institute and State University's New River Symphony. The Appalachian region boasts a large number of college and university orchestras, among them the Marshall University Symphony (Huntington, West Virginia), Anderson College Symphony (Anderson, South Carolina), Westminster Orchestra (New Wilmington, Pennsylvania), Penn State Philharmonic (University Park, Pennsylvania), Marywood College Community Orchestra (Scranton, Pennsylvania), Wake Forest University Symphony (Winston-Salem, North Carolina), Millbrook Orchestra (Shepherdstown, West Virginia), Eastern Kentucky University Symphony (Richmond), and Carnegie Mellon Symphony (Pittsburgh). A variant of this type of orchestra can be found at the North Carolina School of the Arts in Winston-Salem; this institution's orchestra attempts to prepare students at the high school level for professional careers in music performance.

Another type of educational orchestra in Appalachia is the summer music festival orchestra. For sixty years, Brevard Music Center (Brevard, North Carolina) has taught talented teenaged and young adult students through a rigorous seven-week summer program in which students play alongside faculty in the Brevard Festival Orchestra. The Sewanee Summer Music Center (Sewanee, Tennessee), which offers a five-week summer training program for advanced music students aged twelve to adult, emphasizes performance experience; selected students play alongside the faculty and staff in the Sewanee Festival Orchestra. In New York, the Chautauqua Institution, founded in 1874, features the Chautauqua Festival Orchestra.

A number of Appalachia's symphony orchestras employ educational outreach programs to introduce and promote the symphonic repertoire as well as to encourage the study of music. Mainly targeting schoolchildren, many symphonies travel to present concerts in localities otherwise unrepresented by orchestras. Some orchestras, such as Symphony of the Mountains in Kingsport, Tennessee, mail videos and compact discs to schools across their states, sponsor youth orchestras, and offer scholarships. The Chattanooga Symphony and Opera Association (Tennessee) presents curriculum-related multi-arts performances for students, using small ensembles from the orchestra as well as other performing artists. The Lexington Philharmonic (Kentucky), though based outside of Appalachia, travels to Kentucky's Appalachian region to perform in such towns as Pineville, Paintsville, Hazard, Prestonsburg, and Pikeville. Other orchestras, including the West Virginia Symphony, perform throughout their respective states. Whether playing in their own concert halls or traveling to play for those who would not otherwise hear them, Appalachia's symphony orchestras add to the broad spectrum of musical experiences that enrich the region's culture.

See also: CLASSICAL COMPOSERS; OPERA.

—Nancy Jane Earnest, *East Tennessee State University*

Travis, Merle

(1917–1983) Country guitarist, singer, and songwriter.

Although remembered primarily as the chief proponent of what came to be known as the "Travis picking" style of guitar playing, Merle Robert Travis was also an accomplished singer, songwriter, and cartoonist. Born in Rosewood, Kentucky, on November 29, 1917, he learned his thumb-style guitar-playing technique from coal miners in the region, the two most influential being Mose Rager and Ike Everly (father of the Everly Brothers, Don and Phil). This style enabled the simultaneous playing of a tune's melody and rhythmic, harmonic, and bass accompaniment. Travis was largely responsible for this guitar-playing method's becoming a significant part of the commercial country sound of the 1940s and 1950s. He was also an important influence on several Appalachian guitarists, most notably Doc Watson (who named his son Merle in honor of Travis) and Chet Atkins.

In addition to his instrumental talents, Travis was influential as a singer and songwriter. His repertoire consisted of folk songs such as "John Henry" and "I Am a Pilgrim," traditional-sounding original songs such as "Dark as a Dungeon" (which has been published in at least one folk song collection), and honky-tonk songs such as "No Vacancy" and "Divorce Me C.O.D." Many of his own folk-based songs dealt with the lives of Kentucky coal miners during the 1930s. The most commercially successful of these was "Sixteen Tons," a number one hit on both the pop and country charts for Tennessee Ernie Ford in 1955.

For several years after World War II, Travis was a fixture on the West Coast country music scene. Later, he moved to Nashville and eventually settled in Tahlequah, Oklahoma, where he died October 20, 1983.

See also: COAL-MINING AND PROTEST MUSIC; COUNTRY MUSIC; GUITAR.

—W. K. McNeil, *The Ozark Folk Center*

Venues

The first musical venues in Appalachia were the gathering places most often associated with close-knit, isolated rural communities: churches, Saturday night square dances in homes and barns, and county fairs. While churches remain popular centers for musical activity, the other sites for music making are less common than such contemporary musical venues as informal music jams in homes and stores, open mike nights at restaurants and clubs, and festivals.

Traditional venue settings have also been integrated into some modern tourist attractions. At theme parks such as Dollywood, in Pigeon Forge, Tennessee, traditional Appalachian and commercial country music are incorporated into multidimensional acts featuring costumes, comedy, dancing, and animals to create a circuslike atmosphere designed to appeal to visiting tourists more interested in entertainment than in authentic Appalachian culture. On the other hand, various cultural institutions in the region are committed to showcasing traditional Appalachian music in more representative settings. At the Museum of Appalachia in Norris, Tennessee, for example, gospel groups often perform in the sanctuary of a one-room, restored mountain church. However, both types of venues emphasize a connection to Appalachia.

One trend in venues has involved the restoration of movie theaters built during the 1920s and 1930s, highlighting their original, ornate furnishings. These theaters, rescued from disuse and dilapidation, are attractive musical performance halls, drawing suburban audiences to urban centers. Examples of such auditoriums—all restored in the 1980s and 1990s—are the Paramount Center, in Bristol, Tennessee; the Palace Theatre, in Maryville, Tennessee; the Tennessee Theatre, in Knoxville; and the Alabama Theatre for the Performing Arts, in Birmingham. Promoting such older musics as the blues and bluegrass as well as more contemporary musical genres, these venues seat from several hundred to more than a thousand people.

Another musical venue from Appalachia's past, the barn, is currently being revived in the region. Performance halls fashioned out of or in the style of barns, popular from the 1930s to the 1950s, are found in several locations in Appalachia, including the Carter Family Fold in Hiltons, Virginia (home of the Carter Family), and Everett's Music Barn in Suwanee, Georgia. Both of these establishments schedule festivals featuring both national performers and local talent on the bill. Another Appalachian venue is the community center—usually a former schoolhouse operated by a nonprofit organization that offers a place for regularly scheduled jam sessions and stage performances. Community centers in the region include the Bradbury Community Club in Roane County, Tennessee; Anderson House in Blountville, Tennessee; and the Stecoah Valley Center in Graham County, North Carolina.

The heritage trail—a system of marked roadways with accompanying literature for self-guided tours—is a relatively new type of venue in Appalachia, a concept that acknowledges both the benefits of tourism and the need to preserve regional cultural heritage. The Blue Ridge

Heritage Trail Project—a joint effort of state and federal arts-supporting agencies—is being established to link the Blue Ridge Parkway to marked roadways, enabling visitors to experience cultural traditions (including local music scenes) in the Blue Ridge. Meanwhile, North Carolina and Tennessee are working together to develop heritage trails that will showcase Cherokee culture, especially the tribe's traditional music. The heritage trail concept is also being developed enthusiastically in other places. The Cradle of Country Music Tour, which started as a self-guided walking tour in Knoxville, Tennessee, will eventually be linked to a heritage trail connecting Knoxville and Bristol, Tennessee/Virginia. When completed, these combined heritage trails will mark music-related attractions in and between the two cities. The heritage trail concept is also represented in eastern Kentucky along U.S. Highway 23. Known as the Country Music Highway, this heritage trail recognizes musicians from eastern Kentucky who have gone on to Nashville and country music stardom. Along the Country Music Highway in Prestonburg is the Mountain Arts Center, a new one-thousand-seat auditorium that features national and regional performers.

Other musical genres and styles in the region, often incorporating traditional elements in their musical admixtures, are showcased at concert halls, opera houses, stadiums, campus grounds, campgrounds and festival sites, coffeehouses, nightclubs, university auditoriums, libraries, and bookshops.

See also: CULTURAL HERITAGE TOURISM (TOURISM); FESTIVALS, MUSIC; MUSIC ORGANIZATIONS.

—Steve Hooks, *WMMT Whitesburg, Kentucky/WDVX Clinton, Tennessee*

Wallin Family

Traditional singers.

Residing in Madison County, North Carolina, members of the Wallin Family have for decades been some of the finest traditional singers in Appalachia; Doug Wallin (1919–2000), one of the ten children of Lee and Berzilla Wallin, is the most widely known. In 1990 Doug received a Heritage Fellowship from the National Endowment for the Arts; he was lauded for being "the finest living singer of unaccompanied British ballads in southern Appalachia." The performance of such songs is a family tradition. Doug's great uncle Mitchell and great aunt May Sands contributed twenty-six ballads to Cecil Sharp's collection between 1916 and 1918. Several family members, including Doug's mother, Berzilla, cousin Dillard Chandler, and aunt Dellie Norton, appeared in the 1963 documentary film *The End of an Old Song*. These singers—along with Doug's father, Lee, and uncles Cas Wallin and Lloyd Chandler—were featured on four albums issued between 1963 and 1978. Doug appeared briefly in the aforementioned film and was also heard on the albums *The End of an Old Song* and *Crazy About a Song*. His brother Jack Wallin (b. 1932) was not in these productions but did appear with Doug on a Smithsonian Folkways compact disc, *Family Songs and Stories from the North Carolina Mountains*.

Whereas Jack Wallin always accompanied himself when singing, Doug frequently sang a cappella. When Doug did accompany himself, it was with the fiddle, using similar embellishments and ornamentations to those he employed in his singing. The broad range of Wallin brothers songs included old ballads ("The House Carpenter"), nineteenth-century popular songs ("After the Ball"), religious songs, old-time fiddle tunes, and modern country songs. Doug and Jack also sang some of the comic songs that were their father's favorites.

In 1989 Doug received the North Carolina Folk Heritage Award. During the last decade of his life, he and Jack performed at a wide variety of venues.

See also: BALLADS; FIDDLE; SHARP, CECIL (FOLKLORE AND FOLKLIFE).

—W. K. McNeil, *The Ozark Folk Center*

Ward, Fields and Wade

Ward, Fields (1911–1987) Guitarist and early country singer.

Ward, Wade (1892–1971) Banjo player.

Fields Mac Ward and his uncle Benjamin Wade Ward were talented musicians who performed traditional Appalachian music from the early years of commercial recording through the urban folk revival of the 1960s. Born in Saddle Creek, near Independence, Virginia, on October 15, 1892, Wade was one of the nine children of Enoch and Rosamond Carico Ward. Enoch and his son David Crockett Ward played fiddle, while another son, Joe Ward, played the banjo, and Rosamond sang ballads and songs. Wade started playing the banjo at age eleven and the fiddle at sixteen. He later helped form the Buck Mountain Band, which eventually included Fields as a member. Besides learning music from his parents, Fields—born January 23, 1911, on Buck Mountain, Virginia—was also heavily influenced by the recordings of Riley Puckett, from which he learned guitar technique.

Crockett Ward's son and Wade's nephew, Fields Ward made his first commercial recordings in the mid-1920s for the OKeh label and recorded later for Gennett. In the late 1930s and early 1940s, he made recordings for the Library of Congress with a string band called the Bogtrotters, which featured Wade on banjo; several performances from those sessions were issued commercially. In 1940 the Bogtrotters performed for a national audience on the CBS radio program *American School of the Air*.

Shortly after World War II, the Bogtrotters broke up. Both Fields and Wade temporarily quit performing on a regular basis; the former moved to Maryland, where he worked as a house painter, while the latter continued to farm. Rediscovered by folk music revivalists in the 1960s, both musicians appeared at festivals and on several albums as respected practitioners of Virginia's old-time music. Wade died May 29, 1971, while Fields passed away October 26, 1987.

See also: BANJO; FOLK MUSIC REVIVALS; STRING-BAND MUSIC.

—W. K. McNeil, *The Ozark Folk Center*

Watson, Doc

(1923–) Guitarist, singer, banjo player, and harmonica player.

Reared in the western North Carolina community of Deep Gap, Arthel "Doc" Watson is an internationally treasured interpreter of Appalachian music as well as an acclaimed innovative guitarist. Born March 2, 1923, and blind from infancy, Watson is the product of a musical family. His mother sang traditional ballads while she worked around the house, his father played the banjo, and other family members and friends regularly joined in music making at the Watson home. At age six, Watson took an interest in music, starting with the harmonica, on which he played familiar church songs. When he was nine years old, his father made him a fretless banjo, and by age thirteen Watson ("Doc" was a nickname he acquired as an adult) had begun playing the guitar.

Watson's guitar playing was initially influenced by thumb-and-finger-style guitarists such as Merle Travis, Riley Puckett, and Maybelle Carter. He first played music publicly in the early 1950s, when he joined a local popular music group and started experimenting with playing fiddle lines on the electric guitar. In the late 1950s, musician friends Clint Howard and Fred Price introduced Watson to well-known banjo player and singer Clarence "Tom" Ashley. In 1960 folklorists Ralph Rinzler and Eugene Earle came to western North Carolina to record Ashley and in the process met and heard Watson, who was providing guitar accompaniment. The resulting album, *Old-Time Music at Clarence Ashley's*, spread Watson's reputation outside the region. The following year, Watson and Ashley performed in New York together, and by 1963 Watson's solo career had been launched, sparked by the enthusiastic response to his performance at the Newport Folk Festival that year. Two years later, Watson's only son, Merle, also a talented guitar player, joined him, and the duo delighted audiences across the country and abroad for two decades. In 1972 Doc Watson expanded his following after appearing as a guest musician on the Nitty Gritty Dirt Band's best-selling *Will the Circle Be Unbroken* album. Merle Watson was killed in a farming accident in 1985. Doc Watson continued to record and perform both as a solo act backed by one or more accompanists and in collaboration with other notable musicians.

In addition to gaining worldwide popularity and acclaim as one of the most accomplished and influential acoustic flat-pick guitarists, Watson has been the recipient of numerous awards, including five Grammy Awards, an honorary doctorate degree from the University of North Carolina, and the National Medal of the Arts.

See also: BLUEGRASS; GUITAR; OLD-TIME MUSIC.

—Roy Andrade, *East Tennessee State University*

Wheeler, Billy Edd

(1932–) Country songwriter and singer.

Billy Edd Wheeler, born December 9, 1932, in Boone County, West Virginia, won wide acclaim as a songwriter, musician, poet, playwright, and humorist. His recording of "Ode to the Little Brown Shack Out Back," which he also wrote, was a number three country hit in 1964.

Wheeler's songs have been recorded by approximately ninety artists, including the Kingston Trio; Peter, Paul, and Mary; June Carter and Johnny Cash; Elvis Presley; Nancy Sinatra and Lee Hazelwood; Judy Collins; and Kenny Rogers. The best known of Wheeler's songs are "The Reverend Mr. Black," "The Coming of the Roads," "Jackson," and "Coward of the County" (written with Roger Bowling). Wheeler has composed several Appalachia-related songs, including "Coal Tattoo" and "They Can't Put It Back." He has won twelve American Society of Composers, Authors, and Publishers awards and *Billboard* magazine's Pacesetter Award for Music and Drama, and he has been nominated for the Nashville Songwriter Association International Hall of Fame.

Educated at Warren Wilson College, Berea College, and Yale Drama School, Wheeler has written twenty plays, including several long-running outdoor dramas: *Hatfields and McCoys*, staged in Beckley, West Virginia; *Young Abe Lincoln*, in Lincoln City, Indiana; and *Johnny Appleseed*, in Mansfield, Ohio. He is author or coauthor of five books of Appalachian humor. Wheeler has also published two volumes of poetry, and he has made records for the Monitor, United Artists, Kapp, Capitol, and RCA labels.

Wheeler lives in Swannanoa, North Carolina. When not writing, he depicts Appalachian life in paintings, drawings, and sculpture.

See also: COLLECTIONS OF APPALACHIAN HUMOR (HUMOR); COUNTRY MUSIC; OUTDOOR DRAMA (PERFORMING ARTS).

—Loyal Jones, *Berea, Kentucky*

Whitley, Keith

(1955–1989) Country singer.

Keith Whitley, despite his untimely death, was a major influence on 1980s neo-traditionalist movement in mainstream country music. Born on July 1, 1955, in Sandy Hook, Kentucky, Jessie Keith Whitley made his first mark in country music at the age of eight with a guest appearance on the *Buddy Starcher Show* at WCHS-TV in Charleston, West Virginia. By 1969, Whitley and Ricky Skaggs, both teenagers, formed a bluegrass duo performing Stanley Brothers material. This led to both boys' obtaining jobs as sidemen in Ralph Stanley's Clinch Mountain Boys during the summers of 1970, 1971, and 1972. From 1972 to 1974, Whitley played with the bluegrass group New Tradition before rejoining the Clinch Mountain Boys in May 1974 as guitarist and lead vocalist. In 1978 he moved on to the progressive bluegrass group J. D. Crowe and the New South.

When Ricky Skaggs became a star of mainstream country music, Whitley followed him to Nashville and signed a contract with RCA Victor. After a slow start and only modest chart success in 1984 and 1985, his career accelerated rapidly when his singles—"Ten Feet Away," "Homecoming '63," and "Hard Livin'"—reached the *Billboard* country top ten in 1986. That same year Whitley married *Grand Ole Opry* star Lorrie Morgan. In the summer of 1988, his single "Don't Close Your Eyes" became the first of five consecutive number one hits. Unfortunately, the last two of these hits reached their peak only after Whitley's death from alcohol abuse on May 9, 1989, at age thirty-three. "I'm No Stranger to the Rain" won the 1989 Single of the Year award from the Country Music Association, and the same organization voted the posthumously released duet (with Morgan) "Till a Tear Becomes a Rose" Vocal Event of the Year in 1990.

See also: COUNTRY MUSIC; SKAGGS, RICKY; STANLEY, RALPH.

—Ivan M. Tribe, *University of Rio Grande*

Williams, Hank, Sr.

(1923–1953) Country singer and songwriter.

More often identified with south Alabama, where he grew up, Hiram "Hank" Williams is also associated with Appalachia, where he died. His influence on post–World War II country music probably exceeds that of any other figure.

Williams was born on September 17, 1923, in Butler County, Alabama. His father, a World War I veteran, worked as an engineer for small logging company railroads, while his mother, Lillie, operated boardinghouses. After numerous relocations and a divorce, Lillie, Hank, and sister Irene settled in Montgomery in 1937. Hank displayed interest in country music from childhood, singing at local entertainments and sporadically on local WFSA radio. His major musical influences during these years included the music of Roy Acuff and the blues.

During World War II, Hank alternated between performing music and laboring in the Mobile, Alabama, shipyards. He also met several music figures who recognized his knack for songwriting. In 1946 Fred Rose of Acuff-Rose Publications, searching for appropriate song material for Molly O'Day, not only bought some Williams songs, but also landed him contracts with Sterling Records and, later, with MGM. In 1947 Williams had a major hit with "Move It On Over" and began performing on the *Louisiana Hayride* radio show on KWKH Shreveport. Early in 1949, he experienced even bigger success with "Lovesick Blues," one of the few songs he recorded that he did not compose.

In June 1949, Williams moved on to the *Grand Ole Opry* and recorded a string of hits including "Long Gone Lonesome Blues," "I'm So Lonesome I Could Cry," and the Cajun-flavored "Jambalaya." Meanwhile, his personal life deteriorated as a result of increasing alcohol abuse. Many of his songs have been attributed to inspiration resulting from his stormy relationship with his wife, Audrey.

In 1952 *Opry* officials dismissed Williams from the show, and he returned to the *Louisiana Hayride*. He died at the end of that year—perhaps in Knoxville, though he was pronounced dead in Oak Hill, West Virginia, January 1, 1953—en route to an appearance in Canton, Ohio. Two of his biggest hits, "Your Cheatin' Heart" and "Kaw-Liga," were released after his death. Williams's son, Hank Williams Jr., also a major country music star, has spent much of his career reinterpreting his father's legend and repertoire. Daughter Jett Williams and grandson Hank Williams III, both singer-songwriters, have also recorded Hank Williams songs and are among countless musicians who continue to mine his legend.

See also: BLUES; COUNTRY MUSIC; *GRAND OLE OPRY* (MEDIA).

—Ivan M. Tribe, *University of Rio Grande*

Colin Escott, *Hank Williams: The Biography* (1994).

Wiseman, Mac

(1925–) Bluegrass and country singer and music promoter.

While generally considered a bluegrass singer, Mac Wiseman regularly and unapologetically crossed the boundaries between bluegrass, country, and pop music. In his career, he worked as a disc jockey, record company artist and repertoire director, and concert promoter. Born Malcolm B. Wiseman on May 23, 1925, in Crimora, Virginia, Wiseman was influenced by traditional, popular, and classical music. He attended the nearby Dayton (Virginia) Conservatory of Music; specific influences ranged from turn-of-the-century popular music to the early country music of the Carter Family, Vernon Dalhart, and Bradley Kincaid. In 1946 Wiseman joined Molly O'Day's band as a bass player before moving to Flatt and Scruggs's Foggy Mountain Boys as a guitarist and singer in 1948 and Bill Monroe's Blue Grass Boys in 1949. Leading his own group, the Country Boys, Wiseman achieved a popularity equal to that of Monroe and Flatt and Scruggs during the period of 1951 to 1957, when he recorded numerous bluegrass hits that demonstrated his mastery of both traditional and contemporary material, including "Love Letters in the Sand," "I Wonder How the Old Folks Are at Home," and "Little White Church."

Wiseman has been identified with three of the most influential radio programs in the bluegrass and country music genres, serving as a cast member in Bristol, Tennessee/Virginia, on the WCYB *Farm and Fun Time* show in 1947, joining Bill Monroe's band on WSM Nashville's *Grand Ole Opry* from 1949 to 1951, and serving as program director (and often featured performer) of WWVA's *Wheeling Jamboree* for the latter half of the 1960s. Wiseman's recording career continued successfully into the 1970s, as he began to use country-pop backing on country hits such as "(If I Had) Johnny's Cash and Charlie's Pride." Thereafter, he continued to tour the bluegrass festival circuit and to record.

See also: BLUEGRASS; MONROE, BILL; *WWVA JAMBOREE* (MEDIA).

—Robert Russell, *East Tennessee State University*

Workman, Nimrod, and Phyllis Boyens

Workman, Nimrod (1895–1994) Traditional and protest singer.

Boyens, Phyllis (1947–) Traditional, protest, and country singer.

Nimrod Workman and his daughter Phyllis Boyens, both Martin County, Kentucky, natives, are important figures in Appalachian music because of their topical songs on coal mining and unions. Workman was born November 5, 1895, into a family with English, Scottish, and Cherokee ancestry. He went to work in the coal mines at age fourteen for minimal wages. Impressed by Mother Jones and the United Mine Workers of America when they came to organize the miners in his county, Workman became a staunch union loyalist and activist. Developing black lung disease during forty-two years in the coal mines, he was active in the campaign to gain compensation for miners suffering from that debilitating and often fatal malady.

Workman mostly sang a cappella. His repertoire combined traditional Appalachian ballads and topical self-composed songs dealing with coal mining, religion, and current events ("The Watergate Boogie"). He recorded three albums, one of which, *Passing thru the Garden* (1974), featured Phyllis Boyens, the next-to-youngest of the eleven children that Nimrod and Molly Workman raised to adulthood.

Workman's other albums are *Mother Jones' Will* (1976) and *Lay Down My Pick and Shovel* (c. early 1970s). He is also featured on the album *Come All You Coal Miners* (1973) and is the subject of an Appalshop film, *To Fit My Own Category* (1975). Some of his songs and advice can be found in the book *Voices from the Mountains*, compiled by folklorists and musicians Guy and Candie Carawan. Workman died November 26, 1994.

Phyllis Boyens sings traditional ballads, gospel, and topical coal-mining songs, as well as country, blues, and rock. She performed often at folk revival venues in the 1960s with her sister and later formed a quartet. In 1983 Boyens recorded a solo album entitled *I Really Care* and later contributed material to the 1997 recording anthology *Coal Mining Women.* Both Workman and Boyens were featured in the movie *Coal Miner's Daughter* (1980); Boyens, who had previously appeared in the Academy Award–winning documentary *Harlan County, USA* (1976), played Loretta Lynn's mother.

See also: BALLADS; COAL-MINING AND PROTEST MUSIC.

—Sean McCollough, *University of Tennessee*

Wynette, Tammy

(1942–1998) Country singer.

Virginia Wynette Pugh, better known as Tammy Wynette, was born May 5, 1942, on a farm in Itawamba County, Mississippi. As a child she learned to play several musical instruments that had been owned by her father, a local musician who died when Wynette was eight months old. She took music lessons with the hope of a career in music.

Married for the first of five times at the age of seventeen, Wynette worked as a beautician and a receptionist. In order to supplement her income, she began singing in clubs and on radio stations. In 1966 she moved to Nashville and secured a record contract. The next year she recorded the first of twenty number one hits, a duet with David Houston entitled "My Elusive Dreams." Three other hits were chart-topping duets with one-time husband George Jones. Wynette received Grammies in 1967 and 1969 for Best Country Vocal Performance, Female. From 1968 through 1970, she was named Female Vocalist of the Year by the Country Music Association. In 1969 she was also voted the Female Vocalist of the Year by the Academy of Country Music.

Her biggest hit, "Stand By Your Man" (1968), was cowritten with Billy Sherrill, a producer for Columbia Records who was largely responsible for Wynette's image as the "Queen of Country Music." Many of her other songs likewise stressed women's faithfulness to their men and forgiveness for their transgressions. Although her glory days were behind her by the end of the 1970s, Wynette had a resurgence in popularity in the 1990s through the success, in collaboration with the British duo KLF, of the single and video "Justified and Ancient" (1992), a pop chart-topper in the United Kingdom. In 1993 she recorded an album with Dolly Parton and Loretta Lynn entitled *Honky Tonk Angels.* Wynette died on April 6, 1998.

See also: COUNTRY MUSIC; LYNN, LORETTA; PARTON, DOLLY.

—Charles F. Faber, *Lexington, Kentucky*

Tammy Wynette, with Joan Dew, *Stand By Your Man* (1979).

Yoakam, Dwight

(1956–) Country singer and songwriter.

Dwight Yoakam, born October 23, 1956, in Pikeville, Kentucky, was viewed as one of the most promising of country music's "new traditionalists" when he came to national attention in 1986. Yoakam's music is heavily influenced by the Bakersfield sound of such artists as Buck Owens, yet he did not forget the Kentucky coal-mining area where he was born. In interviews, he frequently mentions his grandfather, who worked in the mines, and to whom he dedicated his self-composed song "Miner's Prayer." Although based in Los Angeles, Yoakam possesses wide knowledge of his native region's history and lore. His song "South of Cincinnati" reflects his love of Appalachia, just as "I Sang Dixie" is a lament not only for a lost friend, but also for the American South.

Playing a style of hard-edged honky-tonk music that had disappeared from mainstream country, Yoakam booked himself into Los Angeles punk rock bars during the early 1980s just to have a place to perform. That audience thought him a parody act, but Yoakam soon connected with fans of traditional country music with his first album, *Guitars, Cadillacs, Etc., Etc.* (1986). His version of the Johnny Horton hit "Honky Tonk Man" brought critical accolades and extensive radio play.

Although Yoakam focused his attention on acting after the release of his 1993 album *This Time*, appearing in such movies as *Sling Blade* (1996), he continues to record strong albums in his unmistakable style, and his music is highly esteemed among newer fans of the honky-tonk style of country music.

See also: COUNTRY MUSIC.

—Thomas L. Wilmeth, *Concordia University Wisconsin*

Performing Arts

Section Editor: Robert H. Leonard

THE GENERATIONS OF EUROPEANS WHO MIGRATED TO THE APPALACHIANS WHEN the mountains represented America's western frontier brought their cultures with them in songs and stories, musical instruments, and dances. As early as 1817, Appalachians were building permanent theaters in their towns. By the twentieth century, every sort of professional performance was being presented in the region, in both grand old opera houses and new civic centers. Alongside this growth of professional performance, each new generation has strengthened folk traditions so that they have become even richer and more deeply embedded in the region's cultural life.

The performing arts are social in nature. Whether presented in professional venues or in casual locations by everyday people, storytelling, dancing, and theater provide the excitement of public interaction and the stimulation of people imagining together. They are bonding rituals that preserve and strengthen both personal identity and sense of community. For some people, certain performances are ceremonial, welcoming the change of seasons or honoring the forces of the universe. For others, they are sheer fun. To Americans living on the frontier, the many rituals of gathering together—to tell stories, to dance, to be amazed by artists from distant places—were as central to shaping a new life as were the excitement of political self-determination and newly acquired freedoms from old-world structures.

As deeply rooted as these cultural rituals were, they were still influenced by the new realities of frontier life. The frontier was a place for extraordinary cultural creativity and change fed by the interaction of native peoples with immigrants, the intermingling of widely differing European and African cultures, languages, and traditions, and the peculiar invigoration of entering a land with the express purpose of transforming it.

Stories and storytelling techniques were shared, borrowed, and otherwise disseminated among different cultures and traditions—German to Welsh and English, Cherokee to Scots-Irish. Likewise, dances and dance designs were so fluid that the history of a single dance may include ancient African traditions, old-world Irish forms, and popular American steps.

One particularly striking cultural interchange that originated on the frontier was the treaty council. These councils were carefully orchestrated meetings between native peoples and immigrating Europeans intended to reach formal agreements (or

Facing page: Ray Hicks performs in a circus tent at the long-running National Storytelling Festival, Jonesborough, Tennessee, 1987. The oral narrative tradition, commonly associated with Appalachia and its people, is one of many types of performance observed on stages or "among the folk" in the region.

treaties). Beginning in the colonial period and continuing throughout the nineteenth century, many treaty councils were conducted in the Appalachian frontier at places such as Fort Bedford, in what is now southwest Pennsylvania, and Sycamore Shoals in northeast Tennessee. These highly ritualistic meetings between native and migratory peoples reached across vast cultural distances. They were extraordinary cultural phenomena as much as they were diplomatic summits. The meetings progressed according to careful scripts that took days, even weeks, to enact. Food, dress, social gesture, and language all became performance in the context of international diplomacy. Dance, song, and story were exchanged, as well as official rhetoric. The treaty language itself evolved over time with roots in both native oral traditions and European written traditions.

While the actual agreements were written down for safekeeping in offices of first colonial and then federal authority, they also had a surprising continued life as public performance. It was common practice for the treaties, together with the cultural practices of the several parties engaged in the treaty councils, to be reproduced as publicly performed events in Boston, Philadelphia, and other cities and towns in this country and in Europe, far away from the original treaty council sites.

These historical treaty councils were thereby transformed into popular performances that signified moments of cultural interaction in a way that is perhaps unique. They offer the curious student a fruitful area in which to investigate the intersection of social history with the performing arts. Appalachian history contains myriad such naturally occurring interchanges. This history records how such cultural interactions have shaped and influenced Appalachian peoples' traditions over generations, even as they have remained connected to their roots.

Though encounters of differing cultures created new expressions on the frontier, each of the separate cultures maintained its own traditions, which endure to the present day, thanks to imagination and the artistic impulse to explore and invent. The interchange of dance forms between the circle dances of African slaves and the courtly dance steps of their masters is testament to the resilience of both, confirming that cultural integrity and interchange conspire to perpetuate vitality in the performing arts.

The following section includes three specific categories of the performing arts: dance, storytelling, and theater. All have histories and current expressions in the Appalachian region that are at times widely separate and distinct, while at other times almost entirely blurred. For purposes of clarity and accessibility, they are presented here as distinct.

Storytelling and dance have histories in Appalachia that are predominantly folk in nature. Storytelling originated as an intimate activity within families and close-knit congregations of neighbors who perpetuated old, even ancient, stories from across the seas and down through generations. These stories reveal the deep cultural roots of those telling them, preserving the extraordinary and celebrating the ordinary. Tall tales, lies, and elaborate accounts of commonly shared events are important elements in a folk tradition of unusual vitality. In the mid-twentieth century, a renaissance of public appreciation for storytelling, initiated in Jonesborough, Tennessee, added professional storytelling to the cultural mix.

Dance has a similar history, though professionals have played a larger role. For centuries, community gatherings in the region have been filled with traditional dance forms, handed down from generation to generation. These include native ceremonial dances, English-derived reels, African circle dances, clogging, and a variety of traditional forms. Early frontier accounts tell of itinerant dance masters and even dancing schools set up in larger communities where the locals could learn the complex steps of old court dances and of popular contemporary dances being invented elsewhere for the pleasure of the general public. In addition, throughout the region's history, specific dance traditions have from time to time been presented by accomplished touring professional dancers. These and other professional expressions create a fruitful dynamic with folk traditions, enriching both forms despite the fact that one is intended primarily for an audience to experience and the other as an experience intended strictly for those dancing.

Elephants from the John Robinson Circus parade down Main Street in Johnson City, Tennessee, c. 1900. Traveling circuses brought entertainment to cities and small towns across Appalachia throughout the nineteenth and well into the twentieth century.

Theater presents a somewhat different case. First, not all cultures have practiced this particular art. The traditions of native peoples include a wide range of theatrical expressions, but the written stage play as it is experienced in Appalachia is predominately European in origin. Unlike dance, which in its folk expression can be satisfyingly complete with only the dancers themselves, the theater requires an audience. In this, it is like storytelling. Unlike storytelling, however, theater generally calls for a multitude of performers and other art makers who must come to some consensus through rehearsal.

Throughout the region, from the time of the earliest pioneers, local groups of amateur actors performed plays for the enjoyment of family and neighbors. Thespian Societies (named after Thespis, the first known actor in ancient Greek dramas) were organized in communities of the eighteenth- and early-nineteenth-century Appalachian frontier. Sam Houston, the politician and military officer from Maryville, Tennessee, who earned national fame as president, then governor of Texas, performed as an actor with professional companies in Tennessee. In the early twentieth century, the "little theater" movement gave birth to what is now called community theater and reinvigorated the local impulse for nonprofessionals to produce plays in the mountain towns of the region.

Professional actors have been a part of Appalachian history from the earliest days as well. Indeed, itinerant entertainers appeared in frontier communities virtually from the beginning of the westward white migration. Fire-eaters, tumblers, tight- and slack-rope walkers, magicians, jugglers, and clowns traveled from town to town, performing in inns, taverns, and people's homes. There were presentations of wax figures manipulated by wires and ribbons that simulated famous people and events. Lecturers and inspirational speakers dispensed knowledge, hope, and bunkum. Magic shows crisscrossed the region aboard wagons. Medicine shows drew crowds to street corners and opera houses, where entertainers whetted appetites for potions and elixirs.

In some communities, the most popular entertainment event was the circus, which, with a history dating back to the English colonies, took to the roads and eventually the rails of Appalachia. At first, the circus was generally confined to feats of horsemanship, but the shows grew to gigantic proportions. One prominent nineteenth-century circus manager, Gil Robinson, was born in a Buchanan, Virginia, hotel during a regular tour of his father's circus. From his birth, Robinson traveled to the towns and byways of Appalachia in the circus he and his brothers eventually inherited. Robinson shares his stories of the traveling circus in his book, *Old Wagon Show Days* (1928).

In addition to the theater produced by and for Appalachian audiences, the region itself has often been the subject of plays and theatrical events for audiences around the nation. Citizens on the Atlantic seaboard enjoyed pantomimes and theatricals about the far frontier. The backwoodsman was both a hero and a comedic character in early American drama. Throughout the past two centuries, plays representing the characters and cultures of Appalachia have reached the world's finest stages. They have also played their part in stereotyping and stigmatizing the people and traditions of the region.

History shows that people in Appalachia have always savored good performances. Early actors' diaries remark that audiences would gather as if by magic, arriving on horseback or on foot at the notice of something unusual. If movies and television have since claimed a portion of the Appalachian's regular cultural life, the old traditions still retain their special values, and a fine performance can gather a crowd in most any Appalachian community.

—Robert H. Leonard, *Virginia Polytechnic Institute and State University*

Marston Balch, Robert E. Gard, and Pauline B. Temkin, *Theater in America: Appraisal and Challenge* (1968); Joseph Bruchac, *Our Stories Remember: American Indian History, Culture, and Values through Storytelling* (2003); Charlotte Heth, ed., *Native American Dance: Ceremonies and Social Traditions* (1992); Barnard Hewitt, *Theater U.S.A., 1668 to 1957* (1959); Richard Kraus, Sarah Hilsendager, and Brenda Dixon, *History of Dance in Art and Education* (2000); Brooks McNamara, *Step Right Up* (1976); Constance Rourke, *The Roots of American Culture* (1942); Ruth Sawyer, *The Way of the Storyteller* (1942; reprint 1977); William L. Slout, *Theatre in a Tent* (1972); Joseph D. Sobol, *The Storytellers' Journey: An American Revival* (1999); Susan Eike Spalding and Jane Harris Woodside, eds., *Communities in Motion: Dance, Community, and Tradition in America's Southeast and Beyond* (1995); Marshall and Jean Stearns, *Jazz Dance: The Story of American Vernacular Dance* (1968).

Alabama Ballet

The Alabama Ballet of Birmingham, under the artistic direction of Alabama native Wes Chapman since 1996, performs a classical repertoire rooted in the European tradition and shaped by artistic ties with recognized greats of that tradition. The company was begun in 1981 by renowned dancers Dame Sonia Arova and Thor Sutowski and within twenty years had grown to support more than thirty professional dancers and apprentices. The company performs five main-stage productions annually in Birmingham and tours throughout the United States, attracting more than forty thousand patrons each year.

Chapman, who performed with the company early in his career (1983–84), is recognized for his expertise as a dancer and for extensive international connections gained from a ten-year tenure with the American Ballet Theater under the direction of Mikhail Baryshnikov. Chapman's leadership has energized the company with his commitment to regional artists as well as accomplished dancers from abroad. He has developed a challenging and popular repertoire that includes the horror ballet *Dracula*, created by Chapman and ballet master Roger Van Fleteren, who came to the Alabama Ballet from the London City Ballet in 1996.

The Alabama Ballet grew out of three community dance organizations: the Birmingham Civic Ballet, the University of Alabama at Birmingham Ballet, and Ballet Alabama. Coupled with its artistic excellence, the company's strength lies in its commitment to local audiences, the engagement of regional dancers and choreographers, and an ability to reach and hold a larger national audience.

See also: DANCE.

—Judith DeWitt, *Chattanooga, Tennessee*

Alternate ROOTS

Alternate ROOTS was founded in 1976 by a small group of southern Appalachian theater companies who convened at the Highlander Research and Education Center in New Market, Tennessee, at the invitation of writer Jo Carson. Created as a not-for-profit service organization, ROOTS (Regional Organization of Theaters/Artists South) supports theaters performing original pieces rooted in local and regional story and history. As the organization became more established, however, it attracted other artistic disciplines, including dance, music, storytelling, and the visual arts, and reached well beyond its twelve-state southeastern region, serving as a national leader and a model for organizing community arts.

The initial conveners (which included the Carpetbag Theatre, the Play Group, the Road Company, and Roadside Theater, among others) began to meet annually to share work, discuss common problems, and devise mutual solutions. By 1981 ROOTS had established an office in Atlanta, hired staff, and developed a diverse membership base that included theater, dance, music, and mime companies, as well as educators and individual artists such as choreographers, playwrights, directors, and critics. As the only regional artist-driven organization in the South, ROOTS has played a prominent role in the national and regional dialogue about arts policy and practice, working with state and regional arts agencies, the National Endowment for the Arts, and many regional and national foundations concerned with arts policy and funding.

More than the legally required convening of its board, Alternate ROOTS's annual meeting is a retreat for artists interested in critical feedback on their work, in teaching and learning new skills, and in sharing resources and information. ROOTS also produces occasional performance festivals that connect the new work being created in the South with various audiences and sponsors, often featuring a component that focuses on social change, critical writing, or community engagement.

Other ROOTS programs include subsidies to support the touring of professional companies across the South, publications (including a public newsletter and an anthology of southern plays), small grants to encourage communities and artists to create and sustain longterm relationships, and a training program for community arts practice. ROOTS also promotes an active network of artists and community partners that have contributed to independent initiatives such as the Community Arts Network, founded at Virginia Polytechnic Institute and State University in Blacksburg.

ROOTS supports the creation and presentation of original performing art rooted in a particular community of place, tradition, or spirit. As a coalition of cultural workers, the organization is committed to social and economic justice and the protection of the natural world, addressing these concerns through its programs and services.

In addition to networking, resource sharing, and alliance building, ROOTS members are also attracted by the organization's active engagement with issues of oppression (especially as defined by race, gender, and class), consistent leadership by women and people of color, and policies and practices grounded in participatory democracy. The organization's commitment to the principles of conflict resolution, power sharing, and consensus building are reflected in many members' art-making processes.

See also: THEATER, GRASSROOTS/COMMUNITY-BASED; THEATER, HISTORY OF; THEATER, PROFESSIONAL RESIDENT.

—Kathie deNobriga, *Atlanta, Georgia*

Tom Boeker, "Rooting for Alternatives," *Southern Exposure* (Fall–Winter 1986); Kathie deNobriga, "An Introduction to Alternate ROOTS," *High Performance* (Winter 1993); Kathie deNobriga and Valetta Anderson, eds., *Alternate ROOTS: Plays from the Southern Theater* (1994).

Appalachian State University Theater Program

Appalachian State University supports a college theater program that influences and is influenced by its immediate cultural surroundings. Located in Boone, North Carolina, the university was still known as Appalachian State Teachers College when a young professor of physics organized an extracurricular drama club in 1929. From its modest beginning, the program has grown to shape the development of theater in the region.

The university added theater coursework in 1944. In 1963 speech and theater courses were moved from English into the Department of Speech, and a theater major was offered beginning in 1972. It was integrated into the Department of Theatre and Dance in 1989. The program currently offers the bachelor of arts and bachelor of science degrees, the latter designed to prepare graduates for a K–12 teaching career. Typically, eighty-five to ninety students are enrolled as theater majors.

Appalachian State University has had considerable influence on theater developments in the region, despite its relatively isolated location. As summer tourism grew, an outdoor historical drama, *Horn in the West*, was begun in 1952 with regular participation by Appalachian State students, faculty, and alumni. Appalachian State theater program personnel have also supported both the Blue Ridge Community Theater and the Blowing Rock Stage Company, a professional theater in neighboring Blowing Rock. University graduates often teach in area high school theater programs. Appalachian State also provides theater for young audiences by touring their productions and theater workshops to regional schools through an outreach program.

In turn, the theater program has benefited from its Appalachian location. Nationally recognized playwright Romulus Linney, who spent a part of his childhood in the Boone area, has elected to premiere three of his plays at Appalachian State. Local audiences have embraced other Linney plays produced at the school, as well as works with North Carolina mountain settings such as *Dark of the Moon* and *Look Homeward, Angel*.

See also: CARNEGIE MELLON UNIVERSITY THEATER PROGRAM; CONVERSE COLLEGE THEATER PROGRAM; THEATER, COLLEGE AND UNIVERSITY.

—Philip G. Hill, *Furman University*

Asheville Contemporary Dance Theatre

The Asheville Contemporary Dance Theatre, under the leadership of founding artistic director Susan Collard, began in 1979 as western North Carolina's first resident modern dance company. Collard works with her dancer husband, Giles, blending his performance and design skills with her choreography in multidisciplinary collaborations. Having emerged from Collard's New Studio of Dance, the company produces theatrical extravaganzas, large-scale historical works, and intimate dramatic portraits.

The Collard team claims hard work and good humor as core values. They maintain an artistic emphasis on craft and technical excellence. Their artistic vision derives choreographic inspirations from the movement of natural elements, animals, people, and machines. The structure of their works echoes the complex layers and textures of narrative storytelling.

Laurel Legends, developed in collaboration with African American and Cherokee storytellers, is a time-traveling depiction of local history that includes dances at Methodist camp meetings and a battle between white settlers and Cherokees. It remains in the company's repertoire for school audiences through Asheville's Center for Diversity. *Zelda* is an intimate re-creation of Zelda Fitzgerald's recuperation in a psychiatric hospital and last days in Asheville.

In its international collaborative exchanges, the company immerses artists from other countries in the history, culture, and natural beauty of Appalachia, as well as in the company's own artistic processes. The company has been honored by the support of the French government through residency exchanges with artists of that nation. In addition to France, the company has traveled to Turkey, Guatemala, and Mexico, and the Cuban Ministry of Culture invited them to perform *Zelda* at a festival in Havana.

The Asheville Contemporary Dance Theatre has inspired and assisted the emergence of several other dance companies in Asheville, the most prominent of which is Wall Street Danceworks, the first western North Carolina company to pay dancers for touring. Traveling throughout the Southeast, Wall Street Danceworks offers a diverse repertoire of original choreography by both company artists and nationally recognized choreographers such as Weaverville, North Carolina, native Mark Dendy.

See also: DANCE.

—Judith DeWitt, *Chattanooga, Tennessee*

Bailey Mountain Cloggers

The Bailey Mountain Cloggers Folk Dance Company was organized in 1974 by students at Mars Hill College in North Carolina and has since established a national and international reputation for American clog dance excellence. The company has won national championships in a variety of dance styles and has performed throughout the United States and in Canada, Mexico, England, Scotland, Austria, and Ireland. Mars Hill is one of the few colleges to offer scholarships for members of a clogging team.

The college clog team took its name from the Bailey Mountain Square Dance Team, a championship group that performed at the Mountain Dance and Folk Festival in Asheville, North Carolina, beginning in the 1930s. The founder and promoter of the festival, Bascom Lamar Lunsford, named that older team after a mountain adjacent to the college campus.

The Bailey Mountain Cloggers were initially influenced by the Green Grass Cloggers, a team that originated in 1971 at East Carolina University in Greenville, North Carolina, and used precision steps and high kicks. During the 1980s, Bailey Mountain began competition clogging and expanded its repertoire to include traditional Appalachian clog dance routines such as Big Circle Smooth, Southern Appalachian Traditional Freestyle, Country Hoedown, and Kentucky Running Set. They also added contemporary precision, show, and percussive dance routines. Besides competing, the Bailey Mountain group showcases traditional and contemporary dance routines in an annual spring concert. They serve as ambassadors of goodwill for the college and for the folk dance traditions of the southern mountains.

Bailey Mountain has performed at the Kennedy Center (1996), at the Austrian Alps Performing Arts Festival (1997), four times at the Ulster-American Folk Park's Appalachian Festival, and on Broadway (2000). The group is featured in the dance video *Mountain Legacy* (1998) and appeared in "Making a Difference," a live television program aired in 2000 by the British Broadcasting Corporation from Belfast, Ireland. The latter honored those making significant contributions to cultural understanding and was viewed by more than five million people across Europe.

See also: CLOGGING IN COMMUNITY SETTINGS; GREEN GRASS CLOGGERS; LUNSFORD, BASCOM LAMAR (MUSIC).

—Richard Dillingham, *Southern Appalachian Center, Mars Hill College*

Barter Theatre

Barter Theatre of Abingdon, Virginia, founded by native son Robert Porterfield in 1933, is one of the earliest forerunners of the regional theater movement. It owes its place in American theater to its admission policy: "35 cents or the equivalent in produce." Porterfield offered the idea of a barter-based theater to his hometown chamber of commerce when his professional career in New York dried up during the Great Depression. The company took up residence in the Stonewall Jackson College for Women and performed in the old Abingdon Opera House.

The Abingdon Opera House was constructed in 1831 as a church, but in 1835 it was converted to a temperance hall and then, in 1890, to a town hall. In 1953 Porterfield brought furnishings from the defunct Empire Theater in New York to renovate the space. In 1961 the company added a second stage for children's theater and more artistically adventurous works. In 1996–97, both theaters underwent major renovation.

The Barter Theatre was immediately successful in its community and in making a reputation in New York, where Porterfield recruited actors and directors. Hume Cronyn, Gregory Peck, and Patricia Neal are alumni from the first decade. Theater cartoonist Al Hirschfield produced a *New York Times* cartoon of patrons lined up with hams, chickens, and vegetables to feed the actors. The Barter received a Tony award in 1948 for its place as an early pioneer of the regional theater movement.

Porterfield died in 1971 and was succeeded by Rex Partington, who served until 1992. Rick Rose led the company into the twenty-first century. Though the bartering practice does not continue, the name remains for a theater that performs year-round and reaches students, tourists, and community residents.

See also: THEATER, HISTORY OF; THEATER, PROFESSIONAL RESIDENT.

—Barbara Carlisle, *Virginia Polytechnic Institute and State University*

Belcher, Anndrena

(1951–) Storyteller.

Anndrena Belcher is a noted performing storyteller whose work focuses heavily on Appalachian heritage and culture. Often dressed in granny shoes and vintage clothing, Belcher presents original monologues that integrate her personal experience of growing up in the heart of the Kentucky coalfields with poetry and narratives that juxtapose contemporary views and the nostalgia of mountain life. One reporter described her as "a Minnie Pearl with track shoes."

Belcher describes her most recent work, entitled "Ridin' Route 23," as an oral history performance in which she relates her own rural-to-urban migration experience of the 1950s. Another monologue, "Emma: Wings Again Wide and Free," recounts the life of Appalachian artist and poet Emma Bell Miles.

Born in Pike County, Kentucky, on February 5, 1951, Belcher moved with her family while she was still a young girl to the Appalachian Uptown neighborhood of Chicago, where she recalled being stigmatized for her mountain ways. Her life as an Appalachian in Chicago forced her to evaluate her identity based on the culture and traditions passed down by her mother and grandmother. In 1976 Belcher returned to Pike County to live.

Belcher attended Northern Illinois University, receiving a degree in English, and went on to complete a master of arts degree in social sciences with a focus on Appalachian studies and rural in-migration. Her consciousness of her Appalachian identity prompted her to express herself creatively, usually using the format of storytelling in combination with poetry, song, dance, art, and her mother's and grandmother's personal artifacts.

Also recognized as a producer, writer, and actress, Belcher has appeared in nine films or productions and currently works primarily in postsecondary education and the arts, frequently accepting speaking invitations from colleges, conferences, and conventions. The founder and director of a multimedia performance company called For Old Times' Sake, Belcher has been featured at the National Storytelling Festival in Jonesborough, Tennessee, and was a touring artist for the Virginia Commission for the Arts during the 1990s.

See also: STORYTELLING, HISTORY OF; STORYTELLING IN THE TWENTIETH CENTURY, RENAISSANCE OF.

—Adam Sanders, *East Tennessee State University*

Berea College Country Dance Program

Berea College, located in Berea, Kentucky, has widely influenced folk dance teaching since the 1930s and continues to be an international center for English dance. Oscar Gunkler, a physical education teacher at the college, introduced folk dancing in the 1920s. In the early 1930s, Frank H. Smith, a recreation leader with experience in folk schools, joined the recreation extension program founded at Berea in conjunction with the Conference of Southern Mountain Workers. One part of the program involved sending traveling instructors into Appalachian schools and communities to teach dancing as a form of cooperative recreation and to promote aspects of Anglo-Saxon heritage. Children learned English country dances, morris and sword dances, wooden-shoe clog dances, and Danish folk dances. In the 1950s, versions of Appalachian square dancing were added to the repertoire and, in the 1970s, Appalachian clogging.

In 1935 Smith established the Spring Mountain Folk Festival to bring regional students together to demonstrate dances they had learned. Three years later, he established Christmas Country Dance School to train schoolteachers how to become dance leaders. At about the same time, the Berea College Country Dancers were established as a traveling demonstration team. In the 1960s, the group performed at the White House and toured Central America as the only student group sponsored by the U.S. State Department.

The influence of the Berea College Country Dance program has been extensive, with hundreds of dance leaders and teachers receiving dance education through the Berea College Country Dancers, Christmas Country Dance School, and related programs.

See also: CLOGGING IN COMMUNITY SETTINGS; DANCE; SQUARE DANCING IN COMMUNITY SETTINGS.

—Susan Eike Spalding, *Berea College*

Bloomsburg Theatre Ensemble

The Bloomsburg Theatre Ensemble of Bloomsburg, Pennsylvania, one of five contemporary theater ensembles that have originated in Appalachia, is a leader in the national ensemble theater movement, having established its own distinct style of classic, contemporary, and original drama in a nonurban setting. One of seven charter members in the nationwide Network of Ensemble Theaters, Bloomsburg is

The Bloomsburg Theatre Ensemble performs *Letters to the Editor,* an original work based on a century of letters to the newspaper in Bloomsburg, Pennsylvania, 1996. The ensemble is recognized nationally for its success in integrating theater into the life of its northeastern Pennsylvania community.

a community-based, nonprofit professional theater serving rural north-central Pennsylvania.

The ensemble was inspired by Alvina Krause, a legendary acting teacher from Northwestern University, who taught that theater could, with courage and conviction, be a part of the healthy institutional infrastructure of the ordinary American town. Krause's last class of student actors founded the ensemble in 1978 when they followed their mentor to her retirement home in Pennsylvania. Currently, the group's theater space is an old movie house in downtown Bloomsburg refurbished by ensemble members and renamed the Alvina Krause Theatre.

Following Krause's ideal, members of the group have committed not only to a life of working together as artists but also to making theater a vital part of its local community. When Bloomsburg's newspaper asked local residents to name its most essential community assets, the ensemble was at the top of the list. Its nationally acclaimed original production of *Letters to the Editor* exemplifies this commitment, gleaning excerpts from a century's worth of letters to the local newspaper as the text for telling rich stories of Bloomsburg's life.

Having worked together as an artistic group for some twenty-five years, ensemble members have become noted for their commitment to self-management and governance. They offer workshops on collective decision making that are popular in corporate management programs.

As it has grown, the Bloomsburg Theatre Ensemble has broadened its artistic goals and horizons. Prominent guest artists with diverse aesthetic and cultural roots have refreshed the ensemble's own artistic visions while offering a wide variety of theatrical experiences to their community. In 1991 the ensemble toured five African nations. At home, they maintain a full year-round schedule of performances and theater workshops in local public schools. During the summers, the theater hosts professionally led training in various performance styles for theater students and professionals from across the United States. The Bloomsburg Theatre Ensemble has become nationally prominent as a model for other ensemble-based theaters, inspiring the integration of theater into the fabric of community life.

See also: THEATER, GRASSROOTS/COMMUNITY-BASED; THEATER, HISTORY OF; THEATER, PROFESSIONAL RESIDENT.

—Andrew Belser, *Juniata College*

Buck Dancing

See Clogging in Community Settings

Carnegie Mellon University Theater Program

Carnegie Mellon University in Pittsburgh was founded in 1900 by Andrew Carnegie as a technical school for the sons and daughters of Pittsburgh steelworkers. It became the first college program in the United States to offer a bachelor of arts degree in theater, and its School of Drama has become one of the largest professional training programs in the nation.

Theater started at Carnegie Mellon in 1914, when the School of Applied Arts invited Thomas Wood Stevens to develop a "technical school of stage craft" offering a liberal bachelor of arts degree. The program, which graduated its first students in 1917, included all phases of theater and required students to study and work in all of them.

Today, the School of Drama trains career-oriented students in film, electronic media, and arts administration, as well as in theater. The undergraduate program enrolls about two hundred majors in six career tracks leading to a bachelor of fine arts degree. The graduate program enrolls about forty students in eight master of fine arts tracks. Despite the influence of these career tracks, all undergraduates are still required to gain experience in all phases of the dramatic arts. A large resident faculty is augmented by extensive use of part-time adjunct faculty from the professional world. The university opened a new theater facility in 1999.

See also: APPALACHIAN STATE UNIVERSITY THEATER PROGRAM; CONVERSE COLLEGE THEATER PROGRAM; THEATER, COLLEGE AND UNIVERSITY.

—Philip G. Hill, *Furman University*

Carpetbag Theatre, Inc.

Created as part of a national movement toward community-based professional theater, the Carpetbag Theatre, Inc., is one of the oldest continually operating African American theaters in the Southeast. Founded in 1969 in Knoxville, Tennessee, by Knoxville College resident artist and playwright W. F. Lucas, Carpetbag is one of a handful of African American ensemble theaters currently producing in the United States. The theater takes its name from the popular nineteenth-century travel tote that was favored for being sturdy, affordable, and easy to carry—all qualities attributed to Carpetbag Theatre.

Under the artistic leadership of Linda Parris-Bailey since 1974, Carpetbag tours its productions across the United States and abroad, featuring original plays by Parris-Bailey and others (including international playwrights of color) as well as company-developed work. Carpetbag plays are heavily infused with music, generally a cappella, featuring tight harmonies influenced by spirituals, blues, folk, and, more recently, hip hop.

Signature pieces include *Cric? Crak!* (a play for young audiences based on folktales from the African Diaspora), *Red Summer* (a history play about the Knoxville race riots of 1919), *Dark Cowgirls and Prairie Queens* (about the historic

The Carpetbag Theatre, Inc., performs *Red Summer,* Knoxville, Tennessee, c. 1993. The Carpetbag Theatre is one of the oldest continually producing African American theaters in the southeastern United States. *Red Summer,* about the Knoxville race riots of 1919, is characteristic of the theater's attention to issues affecting the elderly, youth, and people of color.

role of African American women and westward expansion), *Ce Nitram Sacul* (a contemporary "praise poem" to black women mentors), *Nuthin' Nice* (about environmental racism), and *SWOPERA* (influenced by spoken-word performance, about the living legacy of poetry in the Harlem Renaissance and Black Power movement). Consistent with their mission "to give artistic voice to the underserved," Carpetbag has been deeply engaged in issues relating to the elderly, youth, and people of color. They have focused recent activities on adult literacy, youth development, women in transition, and the intersection of arts and activism. The company is supported through touring fees and grants to underwrite educational workshops and outreach activities. Since May 1999, Carpetbag has been the professional theater in residence at historically black Knoxville College.

See also: ALTERNATE ROOTS; THEATER, GRASSROOTS/COMMUNITY-BASED; THEATER, PROFESSIONAL RESIDENT.

—Kathie deNobriga, *Atlanta, Georgia*

Carson, Jo

(1946–) Playwright, performer, poet, and author.

Born in Johnson City, Tennessee, Jo Carson has been creating award-winning theater works since the 1980s. As a playwright, she is best known for *Daytrips*, a drama about duty, madness, and Alzheimer's disease set in east Tennessee. Her distinctive east Tennessee voice has also been heard in her commentary for National Public Radio and on stage in performance pieces drawn from her own life and from stories told to her by the people of central Appalachia and the Southeast. She has performed her monologues and dialogues across the United States under the titles *Liars, Thieves, and Other Sinners on the Bench* and *Stories I Ain't Told Nobody Yet*, the latter also the name of Carson's book of story-poems, which was created from actual conversations and published in 1989.

The playwright's interest in the theater can be traced to her college days at East Tennessee State University, where she completed degrees in speech and theater in 1973. During this period, Carson also worked for a time for Broadside Television, an independent station that produced educational videos, and began (in 1972) a twenty-year stint as an actress and dramatist with the Road Company, a touring stage company based in the Johnson City area for which she wrote two plays: *HorsePower: An Electric Fable* (1978) and *Little Chicago* (1981). In the 1980s and 1990s, Carson produced several books and award-wining plays. Among her many awards are the Kesselring Award for the Best New American Play of 1989 from the National Arts Club for *Daytrips;* the Roger L. Stevens Award from the Fund for New American Plays for *Preacher with a Horse to Ride* (1993), which is about Theodore Dreiser and 1930s coal-mining conflicts; a National Endowment for the Arts playwright's fellowship for *The Bear Facts* (1993), about Davy Crockett; and an AT&T Onstage: New Plays for the '90s Award for *Whispering to Horses* (1997). In 2000 Carson was recipient of a Theatre Communications Group/National Endowment for the Arts residency award to work with 7 Stages in Atlanta, a collaboration that resulted in *If God Came Down*—a play about alternative healing and the archetype of the wounded healer.

Carson's work reflects a deep sense of place. Her knack for discovering the true story of a place has led her to work with more than twenty communities, developing theater pieces based on their own oral histories, including *Swamp Gravy* for Colquitt, Georgia, and *Cross Tides*, for Newport News, Virginia. She has also produced three picture books: *Pulling My Leg* (1990), *You Hold Me and I'll Hold You* (1992), and *The Great Shaking* (1994). *The Last of the "Waltz across Texas" and Other Stories* (1993) is a collection of short fiction. Carson's writings about her home territory are frequently taught in Appalachian studies courses in the United States and abroad.

See also: ALTERNATE ROOTS; ROAD COMPANY, THE; THEATER, GRASSROOTS/COMMUNITY-BASED.

—Linda Frye Burnham, *Saxapahaw, North Carolina*, and Marianne Worthington, *Cumberland College*

Chautauqua

See Chautauqua Institution (Tourism)

Cherokee Traditional Dance

Cherokee traditional dance refers to the oldest dance forms performed in southern Appalachian Cherokee communities. The persistence of this centuries-old dance tradition on and around western North Carolina's Qualla Boundary reservation attests to the pivotal place dance has long held in Cherokee culture.

Originally, all-night ceremonial dances, now called stomp dances, were a central part of Cherokee religious rituals observed in conjunction with hunting, war, and with six seasonal festivals tied to the growing season. During the eighteenth century, smallpox epidemics and decades of Cherokee involvement in European conflicts over control of the North American colonies had taken their toll. Cherokee society was in disarray. While a powerful minority of Cherokee favored conforming to United States policy promoting acculturation as they attempted to recover and rebuild, a majority did their best to hold on to traditional culture.

Beginning in the early nineteenth century, there were several attempts to revive and preserve older dance forms. From about 1811 until 1830, the Cherokee brought back ancient dances as part of an effort to reinvigorate their indigenous religious practices and culture. In the late nineteenth and early twentieth centuries, the arrival of the lumber industry and railroads into the North Carolina mountains sparked a period of cultural upheaval among the Eastern Band, descendents of those who remained in the East following the 1838–39 removal of most Cherokees to Oklahoma. Eastern Band traditionalists such as the medicine man Swimmer and, later, Will West Long worked to keep traditional dance alive.

During the first half of the twentieth century, Long established the Qualla Boundary community of Big Cove as a center for these revival efforts. He taught the old dances, organized all-night social dances, brought back the Festival of Green Corn ceremonial dances in connection with the harvest, and performed at the newly established Great Smoky Mountains National Park. In addition, Long collaborated with several investigators, including the late-nineteenth-century pioneering ethnologist James Mooney and anthropologists Frank G. Speck and Leonard Broom in the 1930s.

Along with Richard Crowe and Lloyd Sequoyah, Long's nephew Walker Calhoun has been an important figure in the late-twentieth-century movement to reclaim Cherokee heritage by preserving the old dance forms. Catalysts for this movement included a resurgence of Native American pride in the 1960s and a desire to counter the fabricated Indian culture often marketed to tourists visiting the Qualla Boundary. Cherokee traditionalists taught the older dance forms in schools, while various troupes danced for community events and for visitors. Performed to rhythmic chants accompanied by percussive instruments such as gourd or turtle-shell rattles and drums, the dances today are either animal dances such as the Bear, the Eagle, or the Beaver Dance or non-mimetic dances such as the Friendship or Peace Pipe Dance. Often dances such as the Friendship Dance incorporate figures—the winding of dancers into a tight spiral, for example—that have a striking resemblance to square dance figures. Such similarities hint at considerable cross-fertilization between Cherokee and European American dance traditions, a rich ground for future investigation.

What began as an effort to reclaim an authentically Cherokee dance tradition has evolved into an attempt, led initially by Calhoun, to reconnect the dance with the ancient Keetowah religion. Members of Oklahoma's Cherokee Nation have aided North Carolina's Eastern Band in this endeavor. Currently there are ceremonial fires burning on the Boundary, where Cherokee traditional dance is once again performed within the context of religious ritual.

See also: CHEROKEE (RACE, ETHNICITY, AND IDENTITY); CHEROKEE RELIGIOUS TRADITIONS (RELIGION); NATIVE AMERICAN THEATRICAL TRADITIONS.

—Jane Harris Woodside, *East Tennessee State University*

Susan Eike Spalding and Jane Harris Woodside, eds., *Communities in Motion: Dance, Community, and Tradition in America's Southeast and Beyond* (1995); Frank G. Speck and Leonard Broom, with Will West Long, *Cherokee Dance and Drama* (1951).

Clarence Brown Theatre

The Clarence Brown Theatre, founded at University of Tennessee's Knoxville campus in 1974, is one of a limited number of professional regional theaters in Appalachia. It is unusual in that it is affiliated directly with the professional training program at the University of Tennessee. The theater is named for Massachusetts-born alumnus, patron, and film director Clarence Brown (1890–1987), who is noted for his direction of *National Velvet*, *Ah, Wilderness!*, and *The Yearling*. The company opened with a production of *The Headhunters*. The original artistic director, Sir Anthony Quayle, led that production in collaboration with the Kennedy Center for the Performing Arts in Washington, D.C.

Currently headed by producing artistic director Blake Robinson and associate general manager Thomas A. Cervone, the company offers theater ranging from the classic to the avant-garde, featuring internationally known guest artists and originating world-class productions. These include Zoe Caldwell's *Medea*, which went on to New York and won a Tony Award; Liviu Ciulei's *A Midsummer Night's Dream;* Peter Muller's *Shadow of the Vampire;* and George Tabori's *The Brecht File*.

One of the few professional theaters affiliated with a university program, the Clarence Brown allows master of fine arts candidates and undergraduates opportunities to work with professional actors while earning union membership in the Actors' Equity Association. The company maintains its professional status with memberships in both the League of Resident Theaters, the national association of professional theater companies, and Theatre Communications Group, the national service organization for not-for-profit theaters. The company annually stages seven productions in two performance venues: the Clarence Brown Theatre and the Ula Love Doughty Carousel Theatre—the oldest arena stage south of the Mason-Dixon Line.

See also: THEATER, PROFESSIONAL RESIDENT.

—Melody A. Zobel, *Blacksburg, Virginia*

Clogging in Community Settings

Strongly identified with the Appalachian region, clogging, also known as flatfooting, buck dancing, or hoedowning, is a dance of rhythmic footwork that usually minimizes other movements of the body. Cloggers may use percussive or light footwork, alternately involving the toes, the heels, or the whole foot. The footwork is generally kept close to the floor but often involves kicks, hops, jumps, or chugs. The steps may emit sounds or be silent. In clogging, the knees bend and stretch with each beat, and the emphasis is downward on the beat.

Clogging and its related forms are social dances within some European American, Native American, and African American communities, especially in the central Appalachian region. These footwork dances are believed to blend Native American dance styles with those from Africa and the British Isles.

Social and theatrical forms of clogging have existed in the United States since at least the early 1800s, mutually influencing each other. Historically, men clogged or buck danced informally, sometimes showing off and trying to outdo each other, after community work events such as corn shuckings or at family or neighborhood gatherings. Clogging was also a customary feature of minstrel and medicine shows.

Contemporary precision clogging grew out of social clogging in the mid-twentieth century. Promoted by national organizations, precision clogging involves dancers performing memorized sequences of synchronized steps to recorded music, sometimes played at increased speed. It rarely includes the individuality and improvisation of social clogging.

Community-based social clogging, regular recreation for many individuals and families, is learned through traditional processes of imitation while absorbing elements from popular dances of the day. Individual improvisation within a local community aesthetic is valued. Social clogging may be a solo, couple, or group activity and involve live old-time string-band, bluegrass, and country music. No special costumes are worn for social clogging, although some dancers wear taps on their shoes. Clogging may be found at old-time dances on Friday or Saturday nights in such places as school cafeterias, Lions Clubs, and fire department halls. It is often part of a larger social event that may involve other dances such as old-time square dancing, two-stepping, waltzing, and cake walks. Sometimes these dance events are fund-raisers for local causes.

Each community or area has developed its own characteristic style of clogging. For example, in the Blue Ridge Mountains of southwest Virginia, dancers call their dancing flatfooting, and keep their feet close to the ground, saying they "pat a tune to the music." Two hours to the west in Dante, Virginia, dancers use a stomping swivel step reputed to come from the Charleston and dance in couples in a form reminiscent of the jitterbug. In northeastern Tennessee, cloggers incorporate precision-style steps into their personal improvisations. Many of these dancers associate the individual style of social clogging with local Appalachian aesthetics or beliefs. In a coal strike in the 1980s, local residents clogged on the picket line as a symbol of pride in local culture.

See also: BAILEY MOUNTAIN CLOGGERS; GREEN GRASS CLOGGERS; LUNSFORD, BASCOM LAMAR (MUSIC).

—Susan Eike Spalding, *Berea College*

Frank Hall, "Improvisation and Fixed Composition in Clogging," *Journal for the Anthropological Study of Human Movement* (Winter 1984–85); Susan Eike Spalding and Jane Harris Woodside, eds., *Communities in Motion: Dance, Community, and Tradition in America's Southeast and Beyond* (1995).

Cocke, Dudley

(1946–) Theater artist, stage director, writer, teacher, and media producer.

Dudley Cocke, a practitioner and leader in grassroots theater, is the director of Roadside Theater and a board member of Appalshop, both in Whitesburg, Kentucky. Born in Norfolk, Virginia, of a southern lineage from the 1600s, he has family roots in the mountain regions of Virginia, as well as the Tidewater. Access to oral traditions of history and tale telling—first, as a child at the knees of accomplished family storytellers and later as a teenager on front porches and next to stoves in country stores—shaped his approach to performance. Cocke earned an undergraduate degree in English from Washington and Lee University in 1968 and did graduate work at Harvard University.

Cocke directs original Roadside Theater productions. Among his many directing credits are *New Ground Revival*, a bluegrass musical with the Mullins Family Singers, and the 2002 Winter Olympics production of *Why the Cowboy Sings*. His publications include essays in *Voices from the Battlefront: Achieving Cultural Equity* (1993), *From the Ground Up: Grassroots Theater in Historical and Contemporary Perspective* (1993), and *Journeys Home: Revealing a Zuni-Appalachia Collaboration* (2002). *Red Fox/Second Hangin'*, which he coauthored, is one of the selections in *Alternate ROOTS: Plays from the Southern Theater* (1994). He has taught at Arizona State University, the College of William and Mary, Cornell University, and the International Baltic Dance Festival. At Appalshop, in addition to the extensive tours of Roadside productions, he produces television specials, radio dramas, music recordings, and film festivals.

Cofounder of Alternate ROOTS (Regional Organization of Theaters/Artists South) and cocreator of the American Festival Project and the Global Network for Cultural Rights, Cocke is a tireless ambassador and preserver of the rich Appalachian performance tradition. His philosophy is expressed in his oft-quoted observation: "To deny a people their cultural expression is to deny them their existence." Cocke received the 2002 Heinz Award in the arts and humanities category, which is given annually to honor the late U.S. Senator John Heinz.

In his commitment to art that documents, empowers, and gives voice to those who are excluded by the narrow purview of institutional art, Cocke is known for his collaborations with unlikely partners—for example, a storytelling exchange with the Arizona State Police in 1997–99. The artist bases his theater on narrative traditions and the function of storytelling as a trustworthy tool for community dialogue. He cites the Civil Rights movement of the 1950s and 1960s as a major influence in his life choices, especially the murder on June 12, 1963, of the Mississippi activist and organizer Medgar Evers.

See also: ALTERNATE ROOTS; THEATER, GRASSROOTS/COMMUNITY-BASED; THEATER, PROFESSIONAL RESIDENT.

—Melody A. Zobel, *Blacksburg, Virginia*

Community Theater

Nonprofessional community theater groups have existed in the Appalachian region for more than a hundred years. Most were formed to present dramatic works significant to their local communities while others developed to present conventional Broadway fare. They are as diverse as the regions that have spawned them and reflect the energy and enthusiasm as well as the interests and talents of the individual actors, directors, and designers who participate in their productions.

Scholars consider the community theater movement in the United States during the first half of the twentieth century to be one of the more significant developments in theater history. Hundreds of "little theaters" were formed between 1900 and 1950 all over the country. Some of the most successful evolved in rural areas, including in Appalachia.

The increase in theatrical activity at the beginning of the twentieth century coincided with three other important developments: the independent theater movement, the "new stagecraft," and naturalistic drama. Many American theaters tried to emulate the success of the Moscow Art Theater in Russia, the Théâtre Libre in France, and Otto Brahm's Freie Bühne in Germany. In doing so, the new little theaters in the United States claimed an independence from the commercialism of the early-twentieth-century mainstream theater, which typically produced and toured huge spectacles in the melodramatic format. Little theaters used realistic, three-dimensional scenery in relatively small playhouses and presented the newly emerging realistic and naturalistic dramas being written, first in Europe, and eventually in this country by playwrights such as Eugene O'Neill. Although many tried to emulate Broadway theater, most were organized with the goal of creating quality arts experiences that would serve their own communities by utilizing native talent.

Theatre Magazine, a national monthly launched in 1900, began including a section on "the amateur stage" in the early 1920s that profiled successful community and university theaters across the country. The publishers realized that there were theater audiences and readers beyond the New York theater world who were active and committed theater participants.

The Appalachian region shared in the growth of amateur theatrical activity in the early 1900s. Professor Alexander M. Drummond, director of theater at Cornell University in Ithaca, New York, from 1912 to 1947, was one of the pioneers in the little theater movement and started a small, "country" theater at the New York State Fair in 1919. Drummond fostered the creation of new plays that reflected life in rural America and were written and produced by local people according to the highest standards of drama and theater. Many of his students went on to become directors and teachers in community and university theaters, some in the Appalachian region.

Among the oldest community theaters in the country are several in Appalachia. These include the Johnson City Community Theatre in Johnson City, Tennessee (formed in 1912); the Erie Playhouse in Erie, Pennsylvania (formed in 1916 and originally called the Erie Civic Theatre); the Kanawha Players in Charleston, West Virginia (1922); and Clemson Little Theatre in Clemson, South Carolina (1931). All four are still operating.

Two Appalachian theaters, the Barter Theatre in Abingdon, Virginia (formed in 1933), and Flat Rock Playhouse in Flat Rock, North Carolina (1952), were among the first "community/professional" theaters in the country. These playhouses used professional actors from New York as well as amateur actors from their own communities to present theater of high caliber. Both theaters are recognized as pioneers in the regional theater movement in the United States and continue to make significant cultural and economic contributions to their respective communities.

The community theater movement in Appalachia experienced another growth spurt in the 1940s. Successful theaters formed during this period included Oak Ridge Community Playhouse in Oak Ridge, Tennessee (1943); Huntsville Little Theatre (now Theatre Huntsville) in Huntsville, Alabama (1947); Altoona Community Theater in Altoona, Pennsylvania (1948); Charleston Light Opera Guild in Charleston, West Virginia (1949); Portsmouth Little Theater in Portsmouth, Ohio (1949); and Asheville Community Theatre in Asheville, North Carolina (1946).

Boasting some of the finest community theaters in the nation, the Appalachian region has experienced enormous artistic growth in its community-supported performing arts groups since the 1970s. Some of the more ambitious and noteworthy Appalachian community theaters include: Theatre Huntsville and Theatre Tuscaloosa in Alabama; Holly Theatre Company (Dahlonega) and Rome Little Theatre in Georgia; Middlesborough Little Theatre (Middlesboro) in Kentucky; Starkville Community Theatre in Mississippi; Olean Community Theater, Ti-Ahwaga Community Players (Owego), and Orange Tree Theater Company (Ithaca) in New York; Asheville Community Theatre, Blowing Rock Playmakers, and Brevard Little Theatre in North Carolina; Chillicothe Civic Theatre and Zanesville Community Theatre in Ohio; Area Community Theater (Carbondale), Apple Hill Playhouse (Delmont), and Bradford Little Theater in Pennsylvania; Spartanburg Little Theatre and Phillis Wheatley Repertory Theatre for Youth (Greenville) in South Carolina; Theatre Bristol in Tennessee; and the Actors Guild of Parkersburg and Towngate Theatre (Wheeling) in West Virginia.

In recent years, Appalachian community theaters have represented the southeast region at the American Association of Community Theatre's national festivals. Oak Ridge Community Playhouse won the 1995 festival competition with its production of *Falsettoland* by William Finn and James Lapine, marking the first time an Appalachian theater had placed first in this prestigious theater competition. Charleston Stage Company from West Virginia took the first-runner-up award in the 1999 festival (held in Memphis) for its production of *The Complete Works of William Shakespeare, Abridged* by Adam Long, Daniel Singer, and Jess Winfield. Both Oak Ridge Community Playhouse and Charleston Stage Company have been invited to represent the United States at various international theater festivals throughout the world.

See also: THEATER, GRASSROOTS/COMMUNITY-BASED; THEATER, HISTORY OF; THEATER, PROFESSIONAL RESIDENT.

—David Wohl, *West Virginia State College*

Gertrude S. Burley and Robert E. Gard, *Community Theater: Idea and Achievement* (1959); Robert E. Gard, *Grassroots Theater: A Search for Regional Arts in America* (1999); Barnard Hewitt, *Theatre U.S.A., 1668 to 1957* (1959).

Converse College Theater Program

Converse College, a small private liberal arts college for women located in Spartanburg, South Carolina, offers a typical example of a college theater program with a generic focus and a history dating back more than one hundred years. The earliest recorded faculty-directed theater activity at the college was in 1897, when a member of the Department of Expression took the lead in the presentation of extracurricular plays. These plays, often including an annual Shakespeare production, were frequently presented in a still extant outdoor theater that was then a popular campus feature. At the time, Converse was primarily a finishing school for young women, and thus the plays were as much exercises in elocution and deportment as they were works of theatrical art. Nevertheless, they won high praise in the local press and enjoyed strong support from the college administration.

In 1927 Converse employed a faculty member to create a bachelor of arts degree with a major in theater within the Department of English. Until 1936 only women performed in onstage roles, but since then men from outside the all-female student body have regularly appeared. At the start of the twenty-first century, the theater faculty reported that the program's location in Appalachia had no particular influence upon its work, either positive or negative.

See also: APPALACHIAN STATE UNIVERSITY THEATER PROGRAM; CARNEGIE MELLON UNIVERSITY THEATER PROGRAM; THEATER, COLLEGE AND UNIVERSITY.

—Philip G. Hill, *Furman University*

Cumberland County Playhouse

The Cumberland County Playhouse in Crossville, Tennessee, is a nonprofit professional company serving the state's largest audience for Tennessee-produced theater. Founded in 1965 by local citizens led by Broadway and Hollywood veterans Paul and Mary Crabtree, the organization operates a four-theater facility, which it built and owns. The facility includes rehearsal studios, classrooms, a storage warehouse, and a large annex on Crossville's Main Street. The Cumberland County Playhouse takes single shows to rural counties and has performed extended runs at Nashville's Ryman Auditorium, Knoxville's Bijou Theatre Center, and Chattanooga's Tivoli Theatre.

Under the leadership of Jim Crabtree, the founders' son, since 1981 (when Crabtree became tandem producing director with his mother), the company annually hosts 145,000 patrons for nearly 500 performances and 1,600 arts classes in dancing, acting, and other performance skills. The young Crabtree began his theater career at the playhouse in 1965, working for his father in technical production and as an actor. Now the operation's $2.3-million budget includes 80 percent earned revenue with an average ticket price under fifteen dollars. Combining its professional acting company with local volunteers, the playhouse produces both Broadway and Appalachian works, including Paul Crabtree's *Tennessee, USA!*—the company's founding musical comedy, a celebration of the state's heritage. Performed frequently in the playhouse's early years, *Tennessee, USA!* was revived most recently in 1995.

Jim Crabtree and Nashville and Hollywood composer/songwriters Dennis Davenport, George S. Clinton, and Bobby Taylor have created new works for the playhouse's Living History Series. These works include *A Homestead Album: A Musical Story of the Cumberland Homesteads; Spirit of the Mountains; Second Sons: A Story of Rugby, Tennessee; Old Hickory; Tennessee Strings; Good Neighbors;* and *Cumberland Mountain, USA.*

See also: THEATER, PROFESSIONAL RESIDENT.

—Melody A. Zobel, *Blacksburg, Virginia*

Dance

Never as isolated as it has often been portrayed, the Appalachian region has been the site of constant interaction among dance forms and dancers. From national and international forms, Appalachian people have created their own distinctive dance preferences grounded in the region's cultures and values.

People dance to fulfill a variety of artistic, social, and ceremonial purposes. Ceremonial or sacred dancing is less common than other forms in the Appalachian region. Nevertheless, for Native Americans and in certain African American and European American churches in the region, dance continues as an important component of spirituality. Though in Appalachia, as across the nation, professional dance artists do not often achieve great financial success, evidence of the importance of professional dance in the region lies in the fact that even small Appalachian communities support professional dance activities. Professional dancers performing Irish, Scottish, English, African, European, and Native American dances, modern and experimental dance, movement theater, and ballet have all found their places in Appalachia. Social or recreational dances, meant solely for the enjoyment of the participants, include such varieties as square dancing, waltzing, swing dancing, and clogging.

Through dance, communities often express beliefs or demonstrate cultural pride. For example, the traditional Cherokee Bear and Quail (also known as Partridge) Dances recognize the bond between hunter and prey and are still performed to recognize humankind's place in the environment. African American fraternity steppers express principles of fraternity life such as unity and identity with their totally synchronized movement and confident personal presentation. Dance may link a group with its history, as does the Swiss dancing in Helvetia, West Virginia. Perhaps the most obvious way that dancing builds community in Appalachia is through social interaction. Square dancing and a related form called contra dancing are generally social rather than performance activities. The same is true of ballroom and swing dancing. Social dance draws people together and builds intercultural or social bonds important to community cohesiveness.

Among the upper classes of the region during early white settlement, dancing was a skill cultivated to help one maintain social and political position. Itinerant dancing masters traveled the Wilderness Trail to find clients among the new arrivals on the western slopes of the mountains. In Lexington, Kentucky, John Davenport offered dancing classes in 1788 at Captain Thomas Young's home, and a Professor Harvey opened a dancing school at Wood's Tavern around 1790 in Reading, Pennsylvania. Besides teaching the minuet, the cotillion, country dances, hornpipe steps, jigs, and reels, such masters taught discipline, manners, and deportment to genteel boys and girls. Enslaved black dancing masters were often hired out by their owners for this purpose.

Dancing was also crucial to common folk, though they usually learned from participation rather than classes. Bees, frolics, and workings, at which several households came together to complete tasks such as husking corn or shucking beans, were typically followed by a meal and dancing.

From the onset of white migration and the forced transplantation of Africans into the lands of the indigenous peoples of the region, all three groups borrowed from each other. Europeans brought figure dances (based on the shapes or movement patterns formed by the dancers) that blended with African and Native American circle dances, and all three groups participated in footwork dances, taking on each other's rhythms, dynamics, and use of space. So-called traditional dancing may incorporate elements of the Charleston, jitterbug, flatfooting, and patting juba. People in the mountains have always borrowed across cultural boundaries, appreciated itinerant performers, patronized dance teachers, traveled and lived in other places, and taken movements from popular dance such as ballet and waltz into their repertoire. Some forms, such as clogging, square dancing, and the Cherokee Bear Dance, evolved within the region.

During the nineteenth century, a wide assortment of dance forms and styles were introduced to the region by various means: through religious practice, the stage, community social dancing, and the interchange of new peoples. African Americans exerted a profound effect on dance, both in the mountains and elsewhere. At plantation dances, the fiddler was often of African descent, and it is likely that the rhythms of his music reflected his heritage. These fiddlers originated the practice of "calling" the figures of a dance, giving the dancers directions in rhyme. One might chant, "Swing Mr. Adam and swing Miss Eve, / Swing old Adam before you leave." By the 1840s, dance calling was common practice. Numerous accounts between 1770 and 1853 in such places as Knoxville, Tennessee, Lynchburg, Virginia, and Wheeling, (West) Virginia, describe whites dancing to black music, as well as blacks and whites observing and experimenting with each other's dances.

The national religious revival that began in Kentucky in the late 1790s had a particularly strong impact on the development of vernacular dance in the southern mountains. People of all classes and ethnic groups attended weeklong camp meetings. The large numbers of blacks in attendance introduced circular dance and processionals, and blacks and whites danced together in "shouting rituals." This blending of styles and rhythms is believed to have contributed significantly to contemporary Appalachian footwork dancing known as clogging, flatfooting, or buck dancing.

As increasing numbers of people migrated into and through the mountains, stage dancers traveled the region offering entertainment. Some followed the innovations of John Durang, the first stage dancer born on American soil. In 1785 he performed a dance combining ballet steps with dance steps taken from English, Irish, and American step dancing. Minstrel shows also used vernacular dance as entertainment but incorporated caricatures of African Americans into their performances. These shows toured the mountains as well as the rest of the country by wagon, riverboat, and rail from 1830 well into the early 1900s, both reflecting the social dancing of the mountains and influencing its evolution.

Foreign performers also toured the region. The Ravel family came from France in 1832 and regularly toured into the 1860s, following river routes. They presented a fast-paced program of acrobatics, *tableaux vivants* (academic poses based on Greek statues), contortionism, French vaudeville, pantomime, and comedy. Rope dances, their signature pieces, were performed on long thick ropes suspended above the ground.

After the introduction of French ballet in New York in 1827, European ballet dancers often performed between acts of theatrical productions in towns of all sizes. Their repertoire tended toward selections from *Giselle*, *La Sylphide*, or other major romantic ballets popular in Europe. Typical dance tours stopped in Pittsburgh, Cincinnati, and smaller towns along the way. In 1846–47 the Appalachian region and adjoining states were thrilled by the performance of Mary Ann Lee, the first American-born ballerina, recently returned from study in France.

Throughout the nineteenth century, social dancing continued to evolve from the variety of sources that commingled in the region. Square dancing and footwork dancing (clogging, buck dancing, flatfooting, and hoedowning) were documented in the region by 1840, and variations among communities could be found in figures, footwork style, and general structure of the dance. Some communities in the late nineteenth century are known to have enjoyed "play parties," or singing games in which the words dictated the movement of the participants. Many of these games, such as "Goin' to Boston" or "Old Bald Eagle" from eastern Kentucky, were documented by folk musicians Jean and Edna Ritchie in the early twentieth century. Some of the play party games, such as "Weavilly Wheat" or "Johnny Brown," have been traced to European or African roots. These dances have structural and movement similarities to country dances or square dances, which use circles or lines of dancers.

New social dances arriving from Europe included popular couple dances such as the waltz (1820s) and polka (1840s). Upon seeing the polka for the first time, Mary Cosby Shelby, daughter of Kentucky's governor, expressed distaste at the intimacy and abandon demonstrated by the whirling couples, but dancing masters continued to be in demand, teaching these new diversions and the accompanying social skills. In 1852 Kentucky dancing master Henry Meyen wrote the first American dance manual using footprints to indicate the pattern traveled by the feet. Swiss immigrants settled in Helvetia, (West) Virginia. Croatians, Hungarians, Bulgarians, Slavs, Germans, and Italians settled in communities from southwest Virginia to western Pennsylvania. All contributed their dance traditions to the mix.

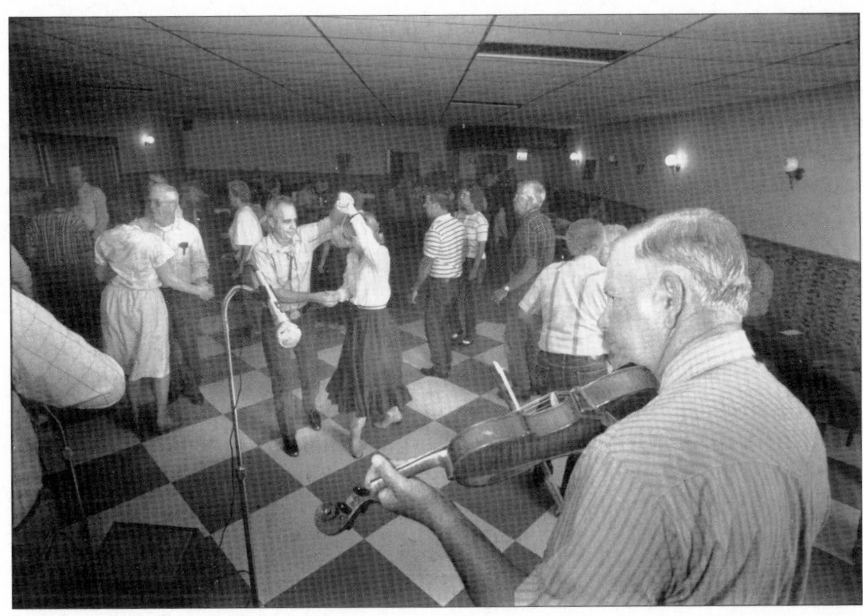

Old-time square dancing at the Lions Club, Chilhowie, Virginia, c. 1980s. Square dancing has been a popular social activity in Appalachia since the middle of the nineteenth century, with individual communities developing distinctive styles and traditions.

In the early twentieth century, Appalachian square dance came to the attention of people outside the region through the writings of British folk music collector Cecil Sharp. In 1917 Sharp described the dancing he dubbed the Kentucky Running Set and proposed that it had existed unchanged since pre-Elizabethan days. His description undermines this claim, however, with references to rhythmic characteristics more African than British. Oral historians working for the Works Progress Administration documented Appalachian square dancing and clogging through extensive interviews in the mid- to late 1930s. Square dancing and clogging continued in homes and at workings until the 1950s, when they moved to public dance halls, school cafeterias, and other community buildings such as fire halls. Often, evenings included other kinds of dances, such as country and western line dancing, waltzes, two-step, polka, and novelty dances. Residents of the region have enjoyed many other kinds of social dancing as well, including disco, hip hop, contra, and ballroom dancing. Cherokee people square danced regularly in their homes and communities, but in the early part of the twentieth century Will West Long, a medicine man of the Eastern Band of Cherokee Indians, led a revival of traditional Cherokee dance, seeing its value in maintaining the Cherokee belief system.

In the early 1900s, large numbers of central European immigrants settled the mountains to work in the timber, coal, and steel industries, contributing their dance traditions to local styles. Hungarians in the coal town of Dante, Virginia, held an annual "Grape Arbor" celebration each fall during the 1930s.

As thousands of African American southerners migrated to the coalfields, they brought the Charleston and the lindy hop with them. From the 1920s to the 1960s, popular music greats such as Cab Calloway, Duke Ellington, and the Ink Spots brought swing music and rhythm and blues and such popular dances as the lindy, hucklebuck, jitterbug, foxtrot, and twist to towns as small as Abingdon, Virginia, and as large as Pittsburgh.

In the Appalachian region as elsewhere, dance education during the first part of the twentieth century focused primarily on folk dance and aesthetic dance. Folk dance was taught for a variety of reasons. Settlement and folk schools such as the John C. Campbell Folk School in Brasstown, North Carolina, used English country dancing, Danish folk dancing, and morris dancing as a means of acquainting children with the customs of other nations and easing the assimilation of recent immigrants into American culture. Colleges supported folk dance with performance groups and teacher preparation programs. In 1937 Duquesne University assumed support of the Tamburitzans, a student group performing dances reflecting Slavic heritage in the Pittsburgh area. Around the same time, the Berea College Country Dancers started performing English country dances and morris dances. Along with folk dance classes, colleges also initiated modern dance classes for women, based upon the techniques of Isadora Duncan and Ruth St. Denis and upon the visionary dance education work at Columbia University Teachers' College in New York City. One of the first colleges in the nation to offer classes in modern dance was the University of Tennessee at Knoxville in 1936.

By mid-century, dance performance was established within the region. Clogging and square dancing had emerged as performance dance by 1928 with Bascom Lamar Lunsford's Mountain Dance and Folk Festival in Asheville, North Carolina. Western North Carolina became a center of flashy, more audience-oriented dancing. Clogging and square dancing moved Appalachian dance to national attention a decade later when they were presented as regular features of the *Grand Ole Opry.* James Kesterson, a dancer from Henderson County, North Carolina, is credited with developing a new exhibition style of clogging in the 1950s. In this precision clogging, everyone on a team performs the same steps in unison.

The pioneers of modern dance found a home in the region during the 1930s, partly with the help of the Works Progress Administration's Federal Arts Project. One of the great artistic forces of modern dance, Ruth St. Denis brought her company to Asheville in the 1930s, performing her only speaking part, in the title role of Salome, on the stage of the summer theater held in the Asheville Women's Club. Ted Shawn, dance innovator and founder of the internationally known dance retreat Jacob's Pillow in Lee, Massachusetts, taught and performed at Black Mountain College near Asheville. Asheville natives Fred Hearn and Foster Fitzsimmons danced with Shawn's Men's Company and later with the Denishawn Company, performing throughout the United States and abroad. Modern dance great Martha Graham performed in Asheville with her company several times. Black Mountain College was also the site of early artistic collaborations among the innovative dancer/choreographer Merce Cunningham, experimental composer John Cage, and painter Robert Rauschenberg during the 1950s. The influence of these pioneers continues, as regional dance schools and companies contribute to the development of the dance profession. In the first half of the twentieth century, Asheville was also an important touring destination for the Ballet Russe de Monte Carlo and the Littlefield Ballet, featuring such internationally known stars as Alexandra Danilova and Leonide Massine. Pittsburgh, besides contributing much to American social dance through its immigrants from many European countries, was the home of Gene Kelly, who revolutionized dance in musical theater.

Dance performance opportunities have proliferated since 1960, spurred in part by the availability of arts funding in the late twentieth century. Modern dance and ballet companies have formed all over the region. Appalachia is home to two ballet companies with international reputations, the Pittsburgh Ballet Theatre and the Alabama Ballet. Along with these two major companies, civic ballet companies from northern Mississippi to southwestern New York usually employ at least some professional dancers, produce a version of Marius Petipa's ballet *The Nutcracker* at Christmas, and hold a student recital each spring. Jazz is almost always an important second dance form in these companies, as it is across the nation. Regional modern dance, postmodern experimental dance, and movement theater groups have achieved international recognition.

Several southern Appalachian dance artists have drawn audiences and national attention to the region. The Asheville Contemporary Dance Theatre and Donna Rizzo's Tennessee Dance Theater toured nationally and won awards during the 1970s and 1980s. At the Contemporary Performing Arts of Chattanooga, Tennessee, artistic director Ann Law's visionary method of creating and presenting dance in collaboration with actors, musicians, visual artists, and writers has expanded an understanding and appreciation for experimental dance in Tennessee and northern Alabama.

In northern Appalachia, many companies create experimental work and preserve historical choreography. The internationally recognized Bill T. Jones/Arnie Zane Dance Company was launched in Binghamton, New York, in the 1980s, and Therese Anne Joseph established a second home in the same area for her Manhattan-based modern dance company, Isadora's Dance Legacy, one of the very few to preserve the works of the modern dance innovator.

Hand in hand with performance opportunities, dance education has grown in the last half of the twentieth century. Colleges offer majors and/or minors in dance in all thirteen Appalachian states. Examples include Denison University in Granville, Ohio, and James Madison University in Harrisonburg, Virginia. A dance studio exists in almost every town. Schools throughout the region host performances and workshops by artists from state-level arts in education programs. Kentucky and North Carolina are national leaders for dance education in public schools.

In many parts of the region, East Indian, Middle Eastern, African, and Irish performance groups preserve their heritage through dance. For example, the Pittsburgh Folk Festival has presented dancers from the many ethnic and cultural groups that reside in the area since 1956. The John Henry Festival, established in 1969 by Ed Cabbell in Morgantown, West Virginia, presents African American dance and music traditions. Many communities are home to precision clogging teams, and universities boast African American fraternity stepping teams. In Cherokee, North Carolina, Walker Calhoun, following the footsteps of his uncle Will West Long, led a revival of traditional Cherokee dance in the 1980s, and his Raven Rock Dancers, along with other groups from the reservation, perform at festivals and other public events to share Cherokee culture and values. Appalachian dance continues to evolve as Hispanics, Hmong, and people of other nationalities make the region their home. Annual Cinco de Mayo and Dieciséis de Septiembre celebrations, traditional to Mexico and featuring salsa, merengue, and other Latin dancing, are held in Appalachian towns of many sizes.

The story of dance in the Appalachian region involves complex multidimensional interplay between social dance and dance performance, between traditional and popular cultures, and among people of many classes and ethnic groupings, effectively demonstrating the diversity and fluidity of Appalachian culture.

See also: SECTION OVERVIEW; STORYTELLING, HISTORY OF; THEATER, HISTORY OF.

—Judith DeWitt, *Chattanooga, Tennessee*, and Susan Eike Spalding, *Berea College*

Cecelia Conway, *African Banjo Echoes in Appalachia: A Study of Folk Traditions* (1995); Loyal Jones, *Minstrel of the Appalachians: The Story of Bascom Lamar Lunsford* (1984); Patrick E. Napier, *Kentucky Mountain Square Dancing* (1960; reprint 1983); Susan Eike Spalding and Jane Harris Woodside, eds., *Communities in Motion: Dance, Community, and Tradition in America's Southeast and Beyond* (1995).

Dance Alloy

With a name that suggests the amalgamation of metals at the heart of economic life in its home of Pittsburgh, Dance Alloy is known nationally and internationally for merging modern dance with other sometimes ancient dance forms to create new artistic and cultural experiences. Often structured around intercultural collaborations, these experiences involve an exchange of residencies hosted by Dance Alloy and its partner companies. One notable example is the company's 1998 *Roots/Crossroutes* project, a residency exchange between the company's five American dancers with Caribbean artists at the University of the Virgin Islands in St. Thomas. Under the leadership of artistic director Mark Taylor, the project addressed the multifaceted impact of immigration on the island. Oral histories were gathered from people whose lives were altered by the process of immigration, and the structure of the dance was derived from those accounts. The project included dance, storytelling, and music composed by Leroy Calliste (also known as Black Stalin), a leading Calypso musician and outspoken activist for Caribbean unity.

In 2001 a new dance, entitled *Dust*, was added to the company's repertoire through collaboration between Dance Alloy and Madras-based choreographer Anita Ratnam, director of Arangham Trust in India. *Dust* was inspired by the writings and story of Alexandra David-Neel, who, after disguising herself as a beggar, became the first European woman to enter the forbidden city of Lhasa, Tibet, where she studied tantric rituals in Tibetan Buddhism.

Since 1984, under the artistic direction of Elsa Limbach (1984–89), Mark Taylor (1990–2003), and Beth Corning (2003–), Dance Alloy has conducted performance seasons at major venues in Pittsburgh. The company tours in its immediate rural surrounding region as well as across the country and maintains a dance school at the Carnegie Museum, providing education services to schools throughout the area.

See also: DANCE.

—Judith DeWitt, *Chattanooga, Tennessee*

Dance in Education

Since the early part of the twentieth century, the Appalachian region has fostered many kinds of dance through education in colleges, schools, and dance studios. Colleges have stimulated the growth of contemporary concert dance and the preservation of traditional dance. The University of Tennessee in Knoxville was among the first to offer a major in dance, and Binghamton University in New York has attracted noted professionals to its faculty and produced cutting-edge choreographers and performers. Randolph Macon Women's College in Ashland, Virginia, had a long and fruitful connection with the highly influential Martha Graham Dance Company, bringing in company members to teach and sending students to the company to train. In Pittsburgh, the Duquesne University Tamburitzans perpetuate the history and heritage of southern and southeastern Europe, and the Berea College Country Dancers from Kentucky and the Bailey Mountain Cloggers from Mars Hill College in North Carolina preserve dance traditions of Appalachia. All three groups tour internationally and their members continue dancing and teaching dance after graduation, further disseminating their traditions.

With the recruitment of dance educator Dorothy Evelyn Koch in 1936, the University of Tennessee became one of the first colleges in the South to develop courses in modern dance, a form that emerged during the first three decades of the twentieth century. Emotionally expressive and built upon fundamental movements of the body such as walking, running, and leaping, the unusual form gained its growing following as a result of innovations by Isadora Duncan, Ruth St. Denis, Ted Shawn, Martha Graham, and others. During the late 1930s and 1940s, Koch worked intensively to promote modern dance both on campus and in the Knoxville community, offering lecture demonstrations and performances. One performance was a collaboration with a local African American high school choir. In 1941 the Modern Dance Club presented a piece entitled *A Saga of East Tennessee*, portraying such events as the forced removal of the Cherokee to Oklahoma, pioneer settlements, the advent of industrial enterprise, and African American life. Frequent concerts involved as many as one hundred students, drew favorable reviews from the press, and began building an enthusiastic audience for modern dance in the region.

The dance program at Binghamton University is the training center for dancers of significant contemporary influence on the national dance scene, including Bill T. Jones and

Arnie Zane, who have brought to dance the idea of the community story and the personal journey. The work of Jones and Zane is recognized widely for helping shape postmodern dance with its inclusion of theater, spoken text, technology, masks, stories drawn from the personal lives of the dancers, and contemporary political and social issues. Their work also continues to influence and inspire dancers in and around the Binghamton program, including Lois Welk, artistic director of the American Dance Asylum, who chooses to develop dance in her home region of Corning, New York.

Institutions of higher learning also promote and preserve traditional dance in Appalachia through festivals and summer learning opportunities. Davis and Elkins College in Elkins, West Virginia, has made a particular contribution to the promotion of traditional arts with its Augusta Heritage Center. Every week throughout the summer, adults come from all over the United States to learn crafts, music, and dance from many traditions. Throughout the region, institutions of higher learning organize Appalachian festivals that include dance and music. In a similar vein, Hindman Settlement School in Kentucky has for many years offered a Family Folk Week, teaching traditional Appalachian music, dance, storytelling, and crafts.

Private dance schools and studios have contributed to the promotion of dance, teaching forms from ballet to African dance, from clogging to hula, and from improvisation to Irish step dancing. Dedicated dance teachers have built dance programs in both urban and rural communities. Constance Hardinge founded the Bristol Ballet School in the 1950s in Bristol, Tennessee/Virginia. Concert dance was unknown in the area when she arrived, and she built the program with innovative approaches, including ballroom dance lessons and cotillions. The company that grew out of the school flourished independently for many years and now is part of Virginia Intermont College. The Tennessee Children's Dance Ensemble of Knoxville is the vision of former University of Tennessee dance professor Dorothy Floyd, who believed in nurturing the abilities of children. This unusual group tours internationally with technically strong contemporary dance. Graduates from the Pittsburgh Youth Ballet regularly receive scholarships and apprenticeships with major national ballet companies. At Heartwood in the Hills, located in Calhoun County, West Virginia, children attend classes in a wooded rural setting to study dance technique and improvisation, theater, mask making, and visual arts, learning much about themselves and about community in the process.

Some states in the Appalachian region have been leaders in the movement to incorporate dance into the curricula of elementary and secondary schools. In 1954 Peggy Evans-Thomas founded Terpsichord, now part of the Chattanooga Girls' Preparatory School fine arts program. This program was recently selected by the National Endowment for the Arts as one of the most outstanding high school arts programs in the country. The North Carolina School of the Arts in Winston-Salem, founded in 1963, was one of the earliest performing arts high schools. North Carolina was also among the first states to certify teachers in dance. The Kentucky Education Reform Act of 1990 mandated that the state establish requirements for all children in dance content areas. Professional performing artists contribute to dance education in the schools, often with the support of state arts education programs. Schools in the Pittsburgh area can choose workshops by groups as diverse as the African Dance and Drum Ensemble and the Coal Country Cloggers.

Dance education in the Appalachian region encompasses all ages and many styles of dance. Professional dancers, college dance programs, private studios, and elementary and secondary schools all contribute to dance learning. Students who are educated in dance become better participants and audiences, thus nurturing dance of all kinds.

See also: DANCE; SECOND HAND; TENNESSEE CHILDREN'S DANCE ENSEMBLE.

—Jeanne Palmer-Fornola, *State University of New York at Buffalo,* and Susan Eike Spalding, *Berea College*

Judy Dash, "Steppin' Lively," *National Geographic Traveler* (May–June 1997); Marian Horosko, "North Carolina School of the Arts," *Dance Magazine* (September 1997).

Dancin' Demons

The Dancin' Demons were an old-style tap dance duo based in Pittsburgh that toured Pennsylvania and neighboring states. During their careers, Henry Belcher and Nazeeh Hameed were highly regarded for their efforts to preserve and promote the traditions of African American footwork dance. They were given a Folk Arts Fellowship Award in 1997 by the Pennsylvania Council on the Arts and a state Folk Arts Apprenticeship Award in 1999.

Belcher was born in Pendleton, South Carolina, in 1915. Hameed (formerly known as Irvin Taylor), his Dancin' Demons partner, was born in Pittsburgh in 1921. Both began dancing at an early age (Belcher at thirteen and Hameed at seven) in the vernacular dance community of the late 1920s and 1930s on the street corners and stages of the Hill District, a predominantly African American neighborhood of Pittsburgh. Though they did not dance together until much later, tap dancing took each of them to stages in Chicago, Detroit, New York, and many other cities.

Belcher formed a group with James Hambrick and Henry Kelly called first the Three Hot Shots and then the Three Magandis, which eventually performed at the Apollo Theater in New York in 1940. Hameed's first group was called the Nitwits. He also performed with the Candy Kids, the Fish Brothers, and the Esquires. His career culminated at the Apollo in 1952, when he danced with Eddie Jefferson

The Dancin' Demons performing at a community concert, Allegheny County, Pennsylvania, 1995. Tap dancers from childhood, Henry Belcher and Nazeeh Hameed became a team in 1981, performing old-style routines that drew on African American footwork dance.

in the Jefferson and Taylor act. Not long after their respective Apollo appearances, both Henry and Nazeeh stopped dancing.

In 1981 the renowned tap dancer and actor Gregory Hines performed in Pittsburgh and wanted some old-style tap dancers to perform with him. Belcher and Hameed responded, created a routine, and called themselves the Dancin' Demons. They continued to perform as a team until Hameed's death from bladder cancer at age eighty-one in June 2002. The duo performed with the state's Artists in Education program and conducted tap dance residencies in schools and communities throughout the region. They were also listed in the program for Pennsylvania Performing Arts on Tour.

See also: DANCE.

—Andrew Frazier, *Pittsburgh, Pennsylvania*

Davis, Donald

(1944–) Storyteller.

Donald Davis is a noted Appalachian storyteller who grew up in the North Carolina mountains hearing stories told by his Grandmother Walker and Uncle Frank. With a childhood immersed in Jack tales, mountain lore, and Welsh and Scottish folktales, Davis later integrated stories into his work as a minister and became skillful at manufacturing seemingly true narratives about his own neighbors and kin. His "personal narrative" tales have distinguished him on the festival circuit and helped popularize a performance genre often emulated by other tellers. He is recognized as a leader in the storytelling renaissance of the late twentieth century.

After completing a bachelor's degree from Davidson College, Davis earned a master of divinity degree from Duke University in 1969 and began a twenty-year career as a minister for the Western North Carolina Conference of the United Methodist Church. Gradually his love of the oral tradition moved him from the pulpit to the stage, where he now performs as a professional storyteller approximately three hundred days each year.

Davis is a frequent performer at the National Storytelling Festival in Jonesborough, Tennessee, and served as board member for the festival's sponsoring organization, the National Association for the Preservation and Perpetuation of Storytelling, for six years and as chairperson from 1986 to 1989. A prolific author, he has produced more than forty audiotapes of his stories and eleven books, including *Listening for the Crack of Dawn*, *Barking at a Fox-Fur Coat*, and *Southern Jack Tales*.

Now living in Ocracoke Island with his wife, Merle, Davis is also a popular workshop leader and has been guest host for the National Public Radio program *Good Evening*. Davis maintains that storytelling is at the center of his life. "We're all full of stories," he says. "Stories aren't just what we make up. Our stories are part of who we are."

See also: STORYTELLING, HISTORY OF; STORYTELLING IN THE TWENTIETH CENTURY, RENAISSANCE OF.

—Flora Joy, *East Tennessee State University*

deNobriga, Kathie

(1950–) Theater artist and consultant.

Kathie deNobriga is a freelance consultant and facilitator for not-for-profit arts organizations, Appalachian states' arts agencies, and the Mary Reynolds Babcock Foundation. Her career is rooted in the production of community-based art, and she has strong artistic and family ties to the Tri-Cities area of Tennessee.

Born in Atlanta in 1950, deNobriga was reared in Kingsport, Tennessee. She earned bachelor's and master's degrees in speech communications and theater arts at Wake Forest University in Winston-Salem, North Carolina. From 1974 to 1976 she served as a visiting artist for the North Carolina Arts Council in Johnston County. She was an ensemble member of the Road Company in Johnson City, Tennessee, from 1976 to 1979. There she created roles in productions about southern Appalachian mountain history, tradition, and issues. For nine years (1979–88), she managed Footlight Players/Temple Theatre, the community performing arts center in Sanford, North Carolina. As producing artistic director, she directed both the community and the youth theater. She also was instrumental in the leadership of a successful campaign to renovate the historic Temple Theatre. In Sanford, she provided leadership for hundreds of community members, serving as an officer for the local arts council and initiating a nationally recognized Girl Scouts youth theater project. In 1986 deNobriga was named Sanford Rotary Woman of the Year.

From 1988 to 1997 deNobriga undertook an influential leadership position as executive director of Alternate ROOTS (Regional Organization of Theaters/Artists South), a multidisciplinary artist-driven service organization nurturing and supporting original performance rooted in local and regional stories, history, and contemporary issues. In this capacity, she became widely respected regionally and nationally for her advocacy of community-based art and artists. She has gained a national reputation for an innovative approach based in collective decision making and collaborative processes of production for not-for-profit management structures. She is coeditor of an anthology of seven plays under the title *Alternate ROOTS: Plays from the Southern Theater* (1994). Recipient of a 1999 Rockefeller Foundation Fellow/Next Generation Leadership Award, deNobriga serves as a site evaluator for both the National Endowment for the Arts and the Association of Performing Arts Presenters.

See also: ALTERNATE ROOTS; THEATER, GRASSROOTS/COMMUNITY-BASED; THEATER, PROFESSIONAL RESIDENT.

—Melody A. Zobel, *Blacksburg, Virginia*

EcoTheater

Based in Lewisburg, West Virginia, EcoTheater (from the Greek for "home viewing place") is a nonprofit theater group founded in 1975 to bring street theater to rural communities in Appalachia. The premise behind street theater is that dramatic play is a natural form of expression and a powerful vehicle for communities to share the stories relevant to them. EcoTheater is the brainchild of founder Maryat Lee, an accomplished actor, writer, director, and musician who honed her street theater skills in New York City during the 1950s. Convinced that the truth of a story can only be told by the people who live it, Lee conceived a play performed by actors from the streets of East Harlem entitled *Dope!* for their own neighborhood. The results were critically acclaimed, with street theater companies springing up throughout the city, and Lee went on to form the Soul and Latin Theater from a group of untrained black and Puerto Rican young people, ages sixteen to twenty.

A native of Covington, Kentucky, Lee left New York for rural West Virginia in 1970. Adapting street theater to a rural environment, she formed EcoTheater with fifteen low-income youths from the Governor's Summer Youth Program in 1975. Their first production was *John Henry: A Drama with Music,* which played on a converted hay wagon. Success prompted the addition of adults to the program, resulting in locally developed productions such as *Ole Miz Dacey, Four Men and a Monster,* and *The Hinton Play,* all performed at Pipestem State Park in southeastern West Virginia.

Participants in EcoTheater are primarily nonprofessionals who collect oral histories, organize, write, and stage public performances for their local communities. Personal connections to the stories and the people presenting them energize audiences in a way traditional theater rarely does. The productions often inspire community pride in all involved—crew, cast, and audience alike.

EcoTheater's successes have spawned companies throughout Appalachia and beyond. Among the companies the organization oversees are those in White Sulphur Springs, West Virginia; Hazel Green, Kentucky; Hickory, North Carolina; Abingdon, Virginia; Quincy, Illinois; and Bonham and Dallas, Texas. These companies are advised by playwrights and directors trained at a series of workshops, and the companies emphasize dramatic performances drawn from oral histories of local families and communities in accordance with Lee's vision. Lee died in 1989, but a board of directors carries on her work, keeping EcoTheater and genuine community theater alive and well in the heart of Appalachia.

See also: THEATER, GRASSROOTS/COMMUNITY-BASED.

—Troy Gowen, *East Tennessee State University,* and Emily A. Green, *Nashville, Tennessee*

Erie Playhouse

Erie Playhouse in Erie, Pennsylvania, began its life as the Peoples Theatre in 1882, rivaling the Johnson City Community Theatre (which originated in Johnson City, Tennessee, in 1885) as the oldest community theater in Appalachia. The Peoples Theatre presented shows at the H. V. Claus Block Building on State Street. Productions were sporadic during the next thirty years, but the group was officially incorporated as the Erie Civic Theatre Association in 1916 (four years after the Johnson City group incorporated). Henry B. Vincent served as director of the theater company at that time, leading the community group from 1898 until 1941.

Productions were staged at various sites in downtown Erie during the early twentieth century, including the Reed Hotel and the Keystone Brass Foundry. A permanent playhouse was built in 1929 on West Seventh Street. The theater was sold in 1965, and the group occupied the Wesleyville Penn Movie House for several years until fire safety regulations forced its closing in 1975. The troupe became known as "the brave little theater without a home" and performed in various local venues until 1983, when the Strand Theater was purchased. Managing directors since World War II have included Newell Tarrant and David Matthews, who began his tenure in 1974.

The Erie Playhouse has an annual budget of more than a million dollars and in 1993 completed a capital campaign that raised an additional one million dollars for theater renovations. The group performs about twelve shows annually, mostly musicals. Contemporary productions have included *Funny Girl*, *Steel Magnolias*, *Nunsense*, *High Society*, and *The Importance of Being Earnest*. In 2000 Erie Playhouse celebrated its one-thousandth production, *The Sound of Music*.

See also: COMMUNITY THEATER; JOHNSON CITY COMMUNITY THEATRE; THEATER, HISTORY OF.

—David Wohl, *West Virginia State College*

Flat Rock Playhouse

Founded in Flat Rock, North Carolina, in 1952 by actor/director/producer Robroy Farquhar, the Flat Rock Playhouse is a regional theater that presents about eleven productions annually—Broadway musicals, comedies, drama, theater for young people, and a holiday production. The western North Carolina town was a final artistic stop for Farquhar, who had managed the Vagabond Players, a touring theater in the Northeast, since 1937. He began relocating to the Hendersonville–Flat Rock area in 1941, and Flat Rock Playhouse grew from a tent to become one of the top ten summer theaters in the nation, performing for 3.7 million patrons in more than 445 productions in its first fifty years. Notable productions have included *The Rainmaker*, *The Odd Couple*, *Pump Boys and Dinettes*, and musicals *1776*, *The Music Man*, and *Singin' in the Rain*. Acknowledging its artistic achievement and economic impact, the North Carolina General Assembly designated the Flat Rock Playhouse the State Theater of North Carolina in 1961.

Flat Rock's seasonal company of actors has included such nationally recognized names as Lee Marvin, Kim Hunter, Pat Hingle, and Burt Reynolds. Working under one of the country's largest resident contract agreements with the Actors' Equity Association, the union of actors and stage managers, Flat Rock employs union performers from May to December. The founder's son, Robin Farquhar, assumed leadership of the organization in 1981. The year-round administrative and artistic staff is largely comprised of former apprentices and interns. In addition to its regular production schedule, Flat Rock hosts a Theater for Young People that includes studio classes and performances. An extensive intern-training program continues the founder's dream under the name Vagabond School of Drama.

In 1958 poet Carl Sandburg, who had relocated to the Flat Rock community, gave a benefit performance for the playhouse. Thus began a long relationship between the playhouse and the life and work of one of America's most respected poets. Sandburg was known sometimes to bring his guitar to the theater and play for the crowd from his *American Songbag* before performances. In the early 1960s, the playhouse initiated a tour of Norman Corwin's *The World of Carl Sandburg* in North Carolina's secondary schools. A shorter version of the play has become a regular offering at the Carl Sandburg National Historic Site in Flat Rock along with *Rootabaga Stories* and *Sandburg's Lincoln*.

See also: FLAT ROCK–HENDERSONVILLE AREA, NORTH CAROLINA (TOURISM); THEATER, HISTORY OF; THEATER, PROFESSIONAL RESIDENT.

—Melody A. Zobel, *Blacksburg, Virginia*

Folkmoot USA

Folkmoot USA, held annually in and around Waynesville, North Carolina, is one of the largest international folk dance festivals in the United States. *Folkmoot* comes from an old English word meaning "gathering of the people." Named since 1987 by the Southeast Tourism Society as one of the top twenty attractions in the Southeast, the event brings together as many as 190 groups from more than ninety-five different countries for two weeks every July. With hundreds of musicians and dancers performing in several locations nightly, the main objective of Folkmoot is to share cultural aspects of music and dance by providing educational opportunities and promoting international understanding and goodwill.

Unique in its reliance on foreign dance groups, the festival was started by local surgeon Clinton Border, who envisioned Haywood County as the site of an international dance festival of the sort to which he had accompanied Appalachian folk dancers in England and other countries. The first festival was held in 1984 and duplicated classic European festivals held during summer months in England, Denmark, France, Germany, Spain, and Italy.

Besides daily and nightly performances, Folkmoot events include a Parade of Nations opening ceremony, a candlelight closing ceremony, and children's activities. On the second Saturday of the festival, Waynesville's Main Street is transformed into a European festival scene with mini-performances of music and dance and international food and craft sales.

See also: DANCE.

—Myrna Schild, *Southern Illinois University at Edwardsville*

Freeman, Barbara

(1944–) Storyteller.

As the Folktellers, Barbara Freeman and her cousin Connie Regan-Blake were two of the earliest traveling professionals in the storytelling renaissance of the 1970s. The Folktellers left secure jobs as librarians at the Chattanooga Public Library in Tennessee to take their storytelling to audiences across the United States and Canada.

The cousins developed a style of tandem storytelling while working as children's librarians. Appearances at the first National Storytelling Festival in Jonesborough, Tennessee, in 1973 encouraged Freeman and Regan-Blake to take up storytelling as full-time traveling performers. Beginning in 1975, the duo traveled and often lived in the back of their pickup truck and camper, appearing at schools, college campuses, and folk music festivals.

The Folktellers received many honors over the years, especially for their two-act play, *Mountain Sweet Talk*. The play wove a series of traditional and personal stories into one tale of mountain life about two cousins' great-aunt Jenny and other family members. Its popularity made it the longest-running play at the Blue Ridge Parkway's Folk Art Center in Asheville, North Carolina. A second play, *Christmas at the Homeplace*, was a holiday favorite and incorporated regional ballad singing into a tale of a simple Appalachian Christmas. The duo also produced numerous award-winning recordings and videos, including *White Horses and Whippoorwills* (audiocassette, 1981) and *Pennies, Pets and Peanut Butter* (video, 1994).

Generally performing solo since 1994, Freeman has developed projects in educational curricula related to storytelling. She has developed new stories of the faith of Christian saints and martyrs and brings humorous twists to traditional Appalachian tall tales and Jack tales.

An important contributor to the revival of storytelling since the 1970s, Freeman has devoted significant energy to promoting the National Storytelling Festival. She was a charter member of the National Association for the Preservation and Perpetuation of Storytelling, also serving as a board member for a number of years. Through performance and workshops, Freeman continues to convert people to an appreciation for storytelling.

See also: REGAN-BLAKE, CONNIE; STORYTELLING, HISTORY OF; STORYTELLING IN THE TWENTIETH CENTURY, RENAISSANCE OF.

—Carol Roberts, *Tennessee State Library and Archives*

Green, Paul

(1894–1981) Playwright.

Appalachia was a significant source of material for Paul Eliot Green, an influential playwright whose body of work included several outdoor dramas written for Appalachian presentations. Three of Green's outdoor dramas have been produced seasonally for many years in Appalachia: *Wilderness Road* in Berea, Kentucky; *The Stephen Foster Story* in Bardstown, Kentucky; and *Trumpet in the Land* in New Philadelphia, Ohio.

Born March 17, 1894, in Harnett County, North Carolina, Green grew up on a rural cotton farm where he knew hard physical labor but developed a love of reading, playing the violin, and baseball. At twenty-two he entered the University of North Carolina in Chapel Hill, where his writing skills were so sufficiently developed that he was assigned to teach freshman English.

Following service with the British Engineers in World War I, he resumed his studies, including graduate work in philosophy at Cornell University in Ithaca, New York, before returning in 1923 to the University of North Carolina to teach philosophy and English. He remained on the faculty at Chapel Hill until 1944, when he retired to follow his already busy writing career. Though he wrote principally for theater and film, the full range of his work includes essays, books of folklore, and several novels. With much of his writing Green espoused a popular literature that arose out of the folklore, history, and day-to-day life of a specific place or immediate region. He shared this orientation with several other recognized leaders in the American theater, including Alexander M. Drummond at Cornell University and Robert Gard at the University of Wisconsin.

In 1937 Green was asked to write a play commemorating Sir Walter Raleigh's colony on Roanoke Island. *The Lost Colony* was performed in Manteo, North Carolina, and proved to be a distinct contribution to the American theater as he developed what he named "symphonic drama," a form of epic theater that involves all of the performing arts to present the story of a particular event or person. The oldest and longest-running of America's outdoor dramas, *The Lost Colony* established the pattern for many outdoor historical dramas in subsequent years. Green introduced his student, Kermit Hunter, to the outdoor drama form by arranging for Hunter to dramatize the story of the Cherokee removal from their ancestral home. Hunter, a native of McDowell County, West Virginia, wrote the Cherokee, North Carolina, outdoor drama *Unto These Hills* under Green's tutelage. Hunter went on to become one of the country's most prolific playwrights in the twentieth century, producing more than forty outdoor dramas.

Green's work was widely recognized. Through his writings and his personal commitment to a form of theater that voiced the local story, he was a profound influence on the social values of Appalachia and the country. There were times when he stood almost alone as a white southern man of letters preaching equality of the races, the richness of southern tradition, and the perfectibility of every human being. His 1927 play *In Abraham's Bosom* was awarded the Pulitzer Prize. He received two Guggenheim Fellowships, the National Theater Conference Award, and nine honorary degrees.

Green died on May 4, 1981, and was posthumously inducted into the Theater Hall of Fame in New York and the North Carolina Literary Hall of Fame in 1996. Throughout his life, Green battled against the death penalty. He also traveled the world on behalf of the U.S. National Commission for the United Nations Educational, Scientific, and Cultural Organization, lecturing on drama and human rights.

See also: HUNTER, KERMIT; OUTDOOR DRAMA; *TRUMPET IN THE LAND*.

—David W. Weiss, *Charlottesville, Virginia*

Laurence G. Avery, ed., *A Southern Life: Letters of Paul Green, 1916–1981* (1994).

Green Grass Cloggers

The Green Grass Cloggers clogging team was formed in 1971 by students at East Carolina University in Greenville, North Carolina. From 1977 until 1987, part of the group, which relocated in Asheville, toured full-time nationally and internationally as a professional dance company. Inspired by traditional mountain-style clogging teams, but more influenced by older flatfoot and buck dancers at fiddlers' conventions, the Green Grass Cloggers developed an original, eclectic style that was a radical departure from traditional North Carolina team clogging of the time.

In contrast to the "big-set" mountain square dance figures of traditional freestyle clogging teams, the Green Grass Cloggers used choreography based on four-couple western square dance figures in short energetic routines consciously designed for audience appeal. While the group's footwork was synchronized, as in precision clogging, their free-spirited performances included head-high kicks and other unconventional steps. Dressed in old-time calico dresses, blue jeans, and black shoes, they provided sharp contrast to the clean-cut polyester outfits and white tap shoes worn by other groups.

By 1974, the group had an established reputation for audience appeal and was invited to perform at major folk festivals throughout the United States and Canada. By the end of the 1970s, clogging groups inspired by the Green Grass Cloggers had formed in many places across the country far from the Appalachians. Overseas, the Green Grass Cloggers' style was adopted by groups in Japan and in England, where by the 1990s it had become the predominant style of "Appalachian" clogging. The Green Grass Cloggers still perform occasionally. In 2003 they were part of the Appalachian program at the Smithsonian Folklife Festival in Washington, D.C.

See also: CLOGGING IN COMMUNITY SETTINGS; DANCE; SQUARE DANCING IN COMMUNITY SETTINGS.

—Phil Jamison, *Warren Wilson College*

Hangar Theatre

Named after the airport hangar in which it was housed, the Hangar Theatre was founded in 1975 in rural Tompkins County, New York, by Robert Moss, a respected director of new plays. Despite being in northern Appalachia and offering more serious theater as opposed to typical "summer stock" fare, the Hangar Theatre has managed to break geographic barriers and initiate innovative programs to become a highly successful regional professional theater. The theater relies on a strong audience base in Ithaca and the surrounding Finger Lakes region.

Through Robert Moss, the Hangar developed an in-depth artistic relationship with New York's Playwrights Horizons, an off-Broadway theater Moss had founded a few years earlier as a means of nurturing the work of young as well as established contemporary playwrights. Moss conceived the Hangar Theatre as a place where professional actors, directors, designers, and playwrights attracted to Playwrights Horizons could work on new plays in summer residencies. The Hangar's production seasons also include classic and established contemporary scripts.

The Lab Company, an intensive summer training program mentored by the theater's artists in residence, produces plays written by young guest playwrights. The Hangar encourages a learning environment in which no social distinctions are made between professional artists, Lab Company artists, and the educational staff. The theater's focus on education continues during the school year with the Artists-in-the-Schools Program, in which professional theater artists spend daily and weekly residencies in the largely rural school districts throughout Tompkins, Seneca, and Tioga Counties.

See also: THEATER, PROFESSIONAL RESIDENT.

—Andrew Belser, *Juniata College*

Hatfields and McCoys

See *Honey in the Rock* and *Hatfields and McCoys*

Hicks, Ray

(1922–2003) Storyteller.

Ray Hicks was internationally recognized by historians and cultural authorities as the patriarch of traditional Appalachian storytelling. He was best known for his stories about Jack, a rambunctious mountain boy who infamously planted a bean tree. Hicks learned these Jack tales from his grandfather Ben Hicks, whose own storytelling abilities were documented by folklore collector Richard Chase. For most of his life, Hicks seldom ventured from the wood-frame house built by his father located more than four thousand feet up Beech Mountain, near Banner Elk, North Carolina, where he was born, reared, and educated through the seventh grade.

Although Hicks never pursued storytelling as a profession—he supported his wife and five children by farming and working a few months each year as a carpenter, mechanic, or sawmill operator—he received some of the industry's highest honors, including the National Storytelling Association's first Lifetime Achievement Award in 1995. Since he rarely performed in public, much of Hick's acclaim stemmed from his popular appearances at the National Storytelling Festival held annually in Jonesborough, Tennessee. He was the only performer to have been featured at every festival since its conception in 1973, missing only one due to illness.

Hicks's performances attracted the attention of such publications as the *New Yorker* and *National Geographic*. He

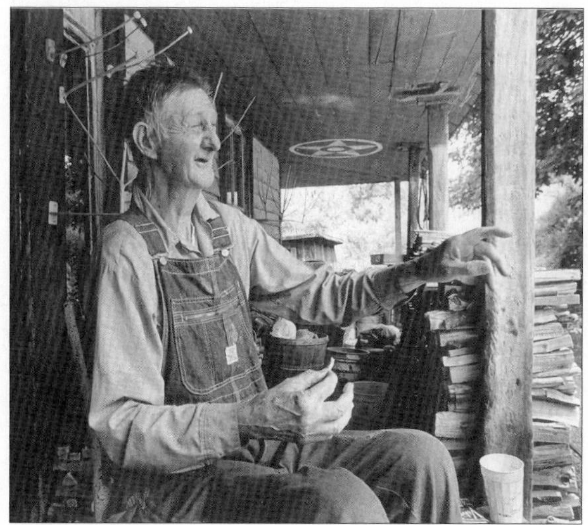

Ray Hicks on the porch of his ancestral home, Beech Mountain, North Carolina, 2000. Internationally recognized by historians and cultural authorities as the patriarch of traditional Appalachian storytelling, Hicks, who died in 2003, was best known for his Jack tales, passed down to him by his grandfather Ben Hicks.

was also featured on the Public Broadcasting Service series *The Story of English*. In 1983 Hicks was awarded a National Endowment of the Arts National Heritage Fellowship. He died April 20, 2003, at the age of eighty in a nursing home in Boone, North Carolina.

See also: FESTIVALS, HUMOR AND STORYTELLING (HUMOR); NATIONAL STORYTELLING FESTIVAL; STORYTELLING IN THE TWENTIETH CENTURY, RENAISSANCE OF.

—Kara Carden, *Hermitage, Tennessee*

Holt, David

(1946–) Musician, singer, storyteller, and radio and television host.

A storyteller and performer of traditional music, David Holt of Fairview, North Carolina, is internationally known as a television and radio host and for efforts to preserve the music and folklore of the southern Appalachian Mountains.

Holt was one of the first performers to appear on the main stage at the National Storytelling Festival in Jonesborough, Tennessee, establishing himself as a pioneer of the 1970s storytelling revival in the United States. He has also spent more than thirty years traveling the rural byways of the Appalachian region, collecting mountain tunes and narratives that are now housed at the Library of Congress in Washington, D.C.

Born in Gatesville, Texas, Holt grew up in Garland, Texas, in a family of informal storytellers whose musical talents were limited to playing bones and spoons (the clicking together of bones, pieces of wood, or spoons to sound out musical rhythms). As a teenager, he was drawn to traditional music and at age twenty-two sought out Carl Sprague, one of the first recorded singing cowboys. Sprague shared stories with Holt and taught him to play harmonica. After graduating from the University of California at Santa Barbara in 1968 with a degree in biology and art, Holt moved to western North Carolina, where he began seeking out other traditional musicians and storytellers. Eventually, he amassed a small library of on-site recordings. Holt's preservation efforts also led him to found the Appalachian Music Program at Warren Wilson College in Swannanoa, North Carolina, in 1975. The program is one of the few in the country in which students collect and study traditional music, storytelling, and dance.

In 1981 Holt launched a full-time career as an entertainer, which, due to his frequent appearances on national radio and television in the mid- and late 1980s, gave impetus to America's storytelling movement and to the emerging popularity of traditional and bluegrass music.

While Holt's first recordings featured stories from the southern Appalachians *(The Hairyman and Other Wild Tales* and *Tailybone and Other Strange Stories)*, his subsequent works have focused more on contemporary storytelling *(Spiders in the Hairdo: Modern Urban Legends* and *Stellaluna)* and traditional folk music (*Grandfather's Greatest Hits*, which he recorded with Chet Atkins, Doc Watson, and Duane Eddy). Holt, who plays ten acoustic instruments, has served as host of several television and radio series, including the Nashville Network's *Fire on the Mountain*, *Celebration Express*, and *American Music Shop* and the Public Broadcasting Service's *Folkways* program. He has performed frequently on such prime-time television shows as *Hee Haw*, *Nashville Now*, and the *Grand Ole Opry* and was a musician in the hit movie *O Brother, Where Art Thou?* in 2000.

Holt has made numerous recordings for his High Windy label and has garnered multiple Grammy nominations, winning for *Stellaluna* in 1996 and *Legacy* (with Doc Watson) in 2002.

See also: INTERNATIONAL STORYTELLING CENTER; STORYTELLING IN THE TWENTIETH CENTURY, RENAISSANCE OF.

—Jill Oxendine, *Johnson City, Tennessee*

Honey in the Rock and *Hatfields and McCoys*

Theatre West Virginia, located in Beckley, annually presents two historical outdoor musical dramas. *Honey in the Rock*, written by West Virginia native Kermit Hunter with music by Jack Kilpatrick and Ewel Cornett, opened in 1961. Set during the Civil War, the play celebrates the founding of West Virginia. While most of the action relates to the establishment of the new state, Hunter also includes elements of history before the white man's arrival. The title refers to the discovery of natural gas by the Native Americans who lived in the area.

Ewel Cornett collaborated with songwriter and playwright Billy Edd Wheeler to create the musical drama *Hatfields and McCoys*, with Wheeler producing the script and lyrics and Cornett writing the music. This play, which opened in 1970, brings to life the feud between these two mountain families. Both families arrived in Appalachia in the 1820s, the Hatfields settling in what is now West Virginia and the McCoys in Kentucky. While the reasons for the feud are in dispute, the two sides remained bitter enemies for forty years, their conflict becoming the best known of all mountain feuds.

When this play proved to be popular with the Appalachian audience as well as visitors to the area, it was added to the repertoire and continues to be presented each summer. The dramas are presented in Cliffside Theatre in Grandview Park on the New River Gorge National River.

See also: HUNTER, KERMIT; OUTDOOR DRAMA; WHEELER, BILLY EDD (MUSIC).

—David W. Weiss, *Charlottesville, Virginia*

Hunter, Kermit

(1910–2001) Playwright and educator.

Born in McDowell County, West Virginia, on October 3, 1910, Kermit Hunter wrote more than forty outdoor dramas, becoming one of the most produced playwrights in the United States. Much of his work concerns the people and events of Appalachia. Though principally a dramatist and educator, he was also an accomplished musician.

Hunter graduated from Ohio State University in 1931 and went on to hold a variety of jobs throughout the 1930s, including working for two newspapers, as business manager for a professional baseball team, and as an organist and choir director for a Methodist church. In 1940 he joined the army and served for five years, rising to the rank of lieutenant colonel. Following World War II, Hunter worked for two years as business manager for the North Carolina Symphony Society and in 1947 enrolled at the University of North Carolina in Chapel Hill to pursue graduate work in drama and theater. Hunter's first outdoor drama, *Unto These Hills*, which he was commissioned to write for the Cherokee Historical Association, was completed in 1949 and served as his master's thesis.

Unto These Hills premiered in 1950 at the Mountainside Theatre in Cherokee, North Carolina, and continues to run seasonally. The play enacts events leading to the removal of the Cherokee people to Oklahoma on the infamous Trail of Tears. *Unto These Hills* was followed by Hunter's *Horn in the West* in Boone, North Carolina, which centers on Daniel Boone and others involved in settling the Appalachian region. In 1961 the playwright's *Honey in the Rock* was produced in Beckley, West Virginia, celebrating the founding of that state during the Civil War.

These plays are still performed, but others have come and gone over the years. One of the more intriguing of Hunter's outdoor dramas was *Walk toward the Sunset*, performed in Sneedville, Tennessee. *Walk toward the Sunset* depicted the Melungeons of east Tennessee, especially those in Hancock County, who were families thought to be of mixed racial heritage who moved to the mountains of east Tennessee and far southwestern Virginia to live apart from the racial prejudices of the valleys and towns. The origin of this group remains a mystery, but Hunter attempted to bring its story to light. The remote site of the production limited the audience, however, and the play survived for only a few short seasons.

Hunter remained at the University of North Carolina as an English professor while working on a doctorate, which he completed in 1955. He then took a position as professor of drama at Hollins College in Virginia. In 1964 the playwright left Hollins to become the first dean of the Meadows School of Arts at Southern Methodist University in Dallas, Texas. In 1993 Hunter was given the Mark R. Sumner Award for Distinguished Service by the Institute of Outdoor Drama. He continued to write for the theater until his death in 2001.

See also: *HONEY IN THE ROCK* AND *HATFIELDS AND MCCOYS*; OUTDOOR DRAMA; *UNTO THESE HILLS*.

—David W. Weiss, *Charlottesville, Virginia*

Institute of Outdoor Drama

Founded in 1963 under the leadership of playwright Paul Green, the Institute of Outdoor Drama is a state-supported public service agency located at the University of North Carolina at Chapel Hill. It is the only advisory and research organization in the United States dedicated to the advancement of the outdoor drama movement. In 2003 the 118 groups affiliated with the institute performed for a combined annual audience of 2.5 million with an estimated economic impact of $500 million. Twenty-seven of these groups were in Appalachia in 2003, presenting twenty-one history plays, two religious dramas, and four Shakespeare festivals.

Serving principally as a resource for groups planning or producing outdoor dramas, the institute also works with government agencies that have an interest in existing and potential productions. Offering assistance of all kinds to any organization involved with producing theater outdoors, the institute is governed by an administrative board composed of distinguished faculty from the College of Arts and Sciences of the University of North Carolina. In addition, the organization has an advisory board of American theater professionals, some of whom reside in Appalachia and serve as consultants and assist in research and planning.

The institute offers professional advisory services in every phase of planning and production. It may call on professionals in playwriting, management, theater architecture, directing, and design, who then assist in such areas as planning, script evaluation, board retreats, fund-raising, marketing, promotion, and facility design and renovation. Representatives of the institute often conduct reviews of the overall operation of productions. The director of the institute and his staff visit twenty to thirty of the companies each summer to maintain contact and offer assistance.

An annual conference for directors and managers nurtures artistic and managerial excellence as well as continued expansion of outdoor drama in the United States. Representatives of existing dramas join planning groups to share ideas and experiences and to discuss new approaches to the task of presenting outdoor dramas. Each year a different outdoor drama hosts the annual conference; Appalachian hosts have included *Unto These Hills* in Cherokee, North Carolina, and *Honey in the Rock* and *Hatfields and McCoys* in Beckley, West Virginia.

Many outdoor dramas depend upon the institute for assistance in filling staff positions, and the institute maintains a list of available personnel for that purpose. Each spring auditions are held in Chapel Hill for actors wishing to be employed in the productions planned for the following summer. Typically more than 150 actors, singers, and dancers audition for twenty or more outdoor dramas across the United States.

See also: OUTDOOR DRAMA.

—David W. Weiss, *Charlottesville, Virginia*

International Storytelling Center

The International Storytelling Center is a nonprofit organization based in Jonesborough, Tennessee, that encourages the preservation and telling of stories to promote positive change in society. Due to its long association with Jonesborough, located in southern Appalachia, many of the organization's participants and programs have been strongly influenced by the region's oral narrative tradition.

Founded in 1975, the center, originally named the National Association for the Preservation and Perpetuation of Storytelling (NAPPS), grew out of the National Storytelling Festival, which is recognized as the first festival in America devoted exclusively to the oral narrative tradition. While Appalachian tellers largely dominated early performances, the event and its sponsoring organization had moved beyond their Appalachian roots by the early 1980s, attracting diverse performers and a national audience. Historically, the festival and NAPPS are credited with starting a national renaissance of storytelling that continues into the twenty-first century.

In the mid-1990s, NAPPS was renamed the National Storytelling Association. The group then underwent a major restructuring that resulted in two separate sister organizations: the National Storytelling Network, created to address the needs of members, and the International Storytelling Center, for furthering the application of stories in the workplace and world community. Both entities jointly own the National Storytelling Festival, although the event is produced solely by the center.

The International Storytelling Center, which was constructed from 1999 to 2002, consists of administrative offices in Jonesborough's Chester Inn (the oldest inn in Tennessee) and a performance hall for programs and activities surrounded by a three-acre community park.

See also: NATIONAL STORYTELLING FESTIVAL; STORYTELLING, HISTORY OF; STORYTELLING IN THE TWENTIETH CENTURY, RENAISSANCE OF.

—Jill Oxendine, *Johnson City, Tennessee*

Johnson City Community Theatre

Johnson City Community Theatre in Tennessee has the distinction of being the oldest amateur theater in the Appalachian region. Although officially formed at the start of the twentieth century under the name Johnson City Dramatic Club, the group began performing short plays at Jobe's Opera House in Johnson City as early as 1885. The players originally charged five cents for admission and in 1900 performed a benefit to raise money to buy uniforms for the city's fire department. Between 1904 and 1910, a loosely knit company of actors performed at the Mountain Home veterans' facility. The first verified production was of *American Girl*, staged on June 13, 1912.

In 1924 the group renamed itself the Johnson City Little Theatre Guild and committed to the performance of at least one production annually. The group changed its name again in 1946 (becoming the Johnson City Little Theatre Players) and finally settled on its current identity in 1968. The company has utilized several performance spaces during its long history, including a downtown turn-of-the-century opera house, a local country club, and a junior high school. In 1958 the theater found a permanent home in a building at the corner of East Maple and Afton Streets in downtown Johnson City.

The theater group currently performs at least five shows annually, including contemporary plays such as *Driving Miss Daisy*, *Moon over Buffalo*, and *Grease*. The theater's mission has changed little since 1912. The company strives to present quality live theater to the Johnson City Community and to provide an opportunity for local actors and actresses to showcase their talents.

See also: COMMUNITY THEATER; ERIE PLAYHOUSE; THEATER, HISTORY OF.

—David Wohl, *West Virginia State College*

Kanawha Players

In the summer of 1922, a small group of drama enthusiasts formed the Kanawha Players in Charleston, West Virginia, with the assistance of Rose Fortier, a local elocution teacher. The theater became a classic example of the independent "little theater" movement in Appalachia, typically producing realistic drama with local talent. After the company's first season of plays at a local high school, Fortier departed. The group sought help from George Pierce Baker, a professor at Harvard University widely recognized as the originating source and guide of the early-twentieth-century movement for a new, locally generated American theater. Shortly thereafter, one of Baker's students, Perceval Reniers, went to West Virginia from Harvard to direct the group's second season of plays.

Over the next several years, the group performed in a variety of locations, including churches, schools, and even on a riverboat docked in the Kanawha River. In 1941 the company was designated "the official state theater of West Virginia" by Governor Mansfield Neely. The Kanawha Players built their own theater workshop for set construction and rehearsals in 1951. Since the 1960s, they have performed at the Charleston Civic Center Little Theatre.

The Kanawha Players mount four major productions each season and produce touring and dinner theater shows as well. Some of their productions have included *Ten Little Indians*, *Sylvia*, *One Flew over the Cuckoo's Nest*, *Big River*, *Inherit the Wind*, and *Driving Miss Daisy*.

See also: COMMUNITY THEATER; THEATER, HISTORY OF.

—David Wohl, *West Virginia State College*

Linney, Romulus

(1930–) Playwright.

Romulus Linney is best known for his lyrical social-issue plays that reflect his deep concern about questions of morality. Linney's plays fall into three categories: historical plays such as *Ambrosio;* personal journey plays such as *April Snow;* and Appalachian plays. His plays about Appalachia include: *Can Can; The Captivity of Pixie Shedman; F. M.; Gint; Gold and Silver Waltz; Goodbye, Howard; Heathen Valley; Holy Ghosts; Yancey; Mountain Memory; Sand Mountain; Tennessee; True Crimes; Unchanging Love;* and *A Woman without a Name.* While many of these are generated directly out of stories and people of the region, his play *Gint,* an adaptation of Henrik Ibsen's *Peer Gynt,* reveals much about Linney's artistic vision. He senses that the Appalachian culture and folklore, like Ibsen's Norwegian social landscape, is at its core stark and unvarnished. He recreates Ibsen's folk-based legend of a poor boy who becomes a rich man, "who loses himself trying to find himself, and who is closer to us than we think." Deep religious and spiritual overtones are mixed with humor and excitement.

Though he was born in Philadelphia, Pennsylvania, Linney's connection to Appalachia goes back to his childhood years spent with his father's family in Boone, North Carolina, and Madison, Tennessee. Linney's student years during the 1950s yielded him a bachelor's degree from Oberlin College and a master of fine arts degree from the Yale School of Drama.

Linney has published more than forty plays, three novels, and numerous short stories, essays, and poems. He has taught at the Universities of North Carolina and Pennsylvania, as well as at Columbia University. He currently teaches at the Actors Studio Drama School, New School University, and the Sewanee Writers' Conference.

Linney's numerous achievements include playwriting fellowships and grants from the National Endowment for the Arts, the New York Arts Council, the Guggenheim and Rockefeller Foundations, and the Pew Charitable Trust/Theatre Communications Group. He holds Obie Awards for Continued Excellence in Playwriting and for Best Play *(Tennessee).* Yet the response to his Appalachian plays has been mixed, as some critics note a lack of depth in regional understanding.

Linney holds honorary doctorates from Oberlin College and from Appalachian State and Wake Forest Universities. He is a member of the Council of the Dramatists Guild, Ensemble Studio Theater, Fellowship of Southern Writers, National Theater Conference, College of Fellows of the American Theater, American Academy of Arts and Sciences, and Yaddo.

See also: PLAYS AND PLAYWRIGHTS.

—Melody A. Zobel, *Blacksburg, Virginia*

Lunsford, Bascom Lamar

See Lunsford, Bascom Lamar (Music)

McConnell, Doc

See McConnell, Doc (Humor)

McMillon, Bobby

(1951–) Traditional singer and storyteller.

Robert Lynn "Bobby" McMillon of Lenoir, North Carolina, was honored in 2000 with a North Carolina Folk Heritage Award from the state arts council, which recognized him as one of the most knowledgeable Appalachian singers and storytellers of his generation. As a child, he absorbed the Primitive Baptist hymnody and ballads of his father's family and the "booger" and "haint" tales and legends of his mother's family. By his teen years he had begun tape-recording family members and friends and compiling a manuscript of four hundred traditional songs, all of which he sings. He was also storing uncounted tales, riddles, and sayings in his memory.

After high school, he took jobs in furniture factories but became widely known as a performer. From 1978 until 1988 he worked in the North Carolina Arts Council's Visiting Artists program. Through the years, he has appeared at many national events, including the Smithsonian Festival of American Folklife and the World's Fair in Knoxville, Tennessee, and at hundreds of local venues. In 1995 the North Carolina Folklore Society honored his contributions with its Brown-Hudson Award.

McMillon has recorded two audiocassettes, *Carolina Sampler* and *A Deeper Feeling*. Filmmaker Tom Davenport's video *The Ballad of Frankie Silver* features McMillon's performances and includes an epilogue about the performer and his singing partner Marina Trivette. An exploration of the performer's interpretation of the Silver murder (McMillon is a descendent of Charlie Silver, who was murdered by his wife, Frankie, in 1831) is also included in the book *A Tree Accurst* by Daniel Patterson. McMillon's deep roots in the region make him an eloquent interpreter of Appalachian lore.

See also: STORYTELLING IN THE TWENTIETH CENTURY, RENAISSANCE OF.

—Daniel W. Patterson, *University of North Carolina*

Minstrelsy, Jim Crow, and Medicine Shows

The tradition of the American minstrel show (blackface performers singing, dancing, and making jokes out of stereotypes of African slaves on southern plantations and freed African Americans in northern cities) has many roots in early American theater history. It began with the performances of Thomas Dartmouth Rice, a white actor/singer who worked the Appalachian Ohio River Valley from Pittsburgh to Cincinnati and Louisville during the late 1820s and 1830s. Rice based the character, song, and dance of old "Jim Crow" on a man he watched one day working on the docks. He turned the imagery of the enslaved laborer, with a hobbling gait due to a malformed leg, into a characterization that was happy, funny, and untroubled. Rice's Jim Crow song and dance routines entertained the entire nation through minstrel shows that toured both cities and farm towns from Rice's day well into the twentieth century. There were local companies of minstrels and national ones. In the decade leading up to the Civil War, minstrelsy became a performance craze, attracting crowds and amassing fortunes for the managers. It continued in an even stronger vein after the war, following the rail lines and circuits of the legitimate theater. The form borrowed from vaudeville and burlesque to create a set format of song, patter, dance, and rough comedy. Rice's Jim Crow gave his name to an official national policy of paternalistic oppression of African American people while creating a popular entertainment form that graced (or disgraced) American stages for more than a century.

There were many other nineteenth-century examples of what is now recognized as cultural and racial insensitivity on the American stage. Medicine shows often presented Native Americans performing fabricated approximations of ceremonial life, including dancing and singing and even concocted "scalping" ceremonies. A pervasive racist climate made these humiliating demonstrations viable entertainment.

In 1836 the chiefs of the southeastern tribes, including Chief John Ross of the Cherokee, traveled to the nation's capital to present their case against their removal from their Appalachian home. As it happened, the National Theater in the city was presenting a revival of the play *Pocahontas* that included wholly invented "native" dances and entirely erroneous depictions of "savage" culture. Production promoters went so far as to suggest in newspaper advertisements that the delegation of the chiefs would participate in these performances under the name of "John Ross and his merrie men . . . doing real War dances." The painful irony was intensified by Ross's published denial of any participation or approval, stating, "We have too high a regard for ourselves—too deep an interest in the welfare of our people, to be merry-making under our misfortunes."

See also: THEATER, HISTORY OF.

—Robert H. Leonard, *Virginia Polytechnic Institute and State University*

Rosemarie K. Bank, *Theatre Culture in America, 1825–1860* (1997); Benjamin McArthur, *Actors and American Culture, 1880–1920* (1984); Brooks McNamara, *Step Right Up* (1976); Carl Wittke, *Tambo and Bones: A History of the American Minstrel Stage* (1930; reprint 1968).

Mountain Dance and Folk Festival

See Festivals, Music (Music); Lunsford, Bascom Lamar (Music)

National Association for the Preservation and Perpetuation of Storytelling

See International Storytelling Center

National Storytelling Festival

The National Storytelling Festival takes place every October in Jonesborough, Tennessee, headquarters of the sponsoring

International Storytelling Center. Designed as a celebration of the oral tradition, the weekend-long event features professional and amateur storytellers who perform for as many as ten thousand attendees from all over the world.

The festival has been hailed in major media, including *USA Today* and *Smithsonian* magazine, as the genesis of a storytelling revival in America. Since its inception, similar events have been established nationwide, including the Northern Appalachian Storytelling Festival in Mansfield, Pennsylvania; the National Storytelling Competition in Hillsboro, Ohio; and the West Virginia Storytelling Festival at Jackson's Mill. In addition, an entire storytelling industry has emerged, spawning books, magazines, tapes, Web sites, and organizations dedicated to the subject.

The festival is also credited with helping to revitalize Jonesborough after the town experienced economic decline in the 1960s and the early 1970s. The impact continues: a multimillion-dollar International Storytelling Center opened on Main Street in 2001. The center operates as an affiliate of the Smithsonian Institution, offering cultural and educational programming. A comprehensive storytelling library is also a component of the center.

Jimmy Neil Smith, president of the International Storytelling Center since 1998, organized the first National Storytelling Festival in 1973 after hearing Mississippi humorist Jerry Clower tell a story on the radio. Clower, who died in 1998, performed at both the first and twentieth festivals, entertaining crowds with his famous coon-hunting tales.

See also: INTERNATIONAL STORYTELLING CENTER; NATIONAL STORYTELLING NETWORK; STORYTELLING IN THE TWENTIETH CENTURY, RENAISSANCE OF.

—Kara Carden, *Hermitage, Tennessee*

National Storytelling Network

Based in Jonesborough, Tennessee, the National Storytelling Network is a not-for-profit membership organization formed when the National Storytelling Association underwent major restructuring in 1998. The organization has several thousand members across the United States and works to improve the quality of storytelling at many levels—in public venues, in classrooms and libraries, and wherever storytelling can be used to improve quality of life.

The network is the membership branch of what was once known as the National Association for the Preservation and Perpetuation of Storytelling (NAPPS), an organization founded in 1975 by the early planners of the National Storytelling Festival, an annual event started in 1973. The NAPPS board of directors renamed it the National Storytelling Association in 1995.

In its early years, NAPPS advanced the cause of storytelling through publications such as *Yarnspinner* and *Storytelling Magazine;* the creation of a publishing house, the National Storytelling Press; and by establishing an archive of storytelling resources. In the late 1990s, when the National Storytelling Association conceived the building of a $10-million storytelling center, its board voted to restructure the organization into two entities: the National Storytelling Network for addressing the needs of its membership and the International Storytelling Center for building stronger programming and an international outreach. The National Storytelling Network has continued to publish *Storytelling Magazine* and sponsors a National Storytelling Conference each year at different locations. The organization also provides support and networking for storytellers who work in specific areas such as festival production, youth storytelling, and health care.

An early board of directors for the National Association for the Preservation and Perpetuation of Storytelling (NAPPS) convenes in Jonesborough, Tennessee, c. 1977. NAPPS was the predecessor of the National Storytelling Network and laid the groundwork for a historic revival in the oral tradition during the final decades of the twentieth century. Front row, left to right: Connie Regan-Blake, Jimmy Neil Smith, Barbara Freeman, and Harriet Allen. Back row: Kathryn Windham, David Holt, and Doc McConnell.

See also: INTERNATIONAL STORYTELLING CENTER; NATIONAL STORYTELLING FESTIVAL; STORYTELLING IN THE TWENTIETH CENTURY, RENAISSANCE OF.

—Jill Oxendine, *Johnson City, Tennessee*

Native American Dance Traditions of Western New York

The Haudenosaunee, called the Iroquois by French colonists, are a confederation of nations that once resided on land that includes the Appalachian areas of southwestern New York, western Pennsylvania, and eastern Ohio. *Haudenosaunee* means "People of the Longhouse," referring to the long bark structures that were their traditional homes.

The Haudenosaunee still practice their ceremonies in longhouse structures. They share two kinds of dance, social and ceremonial.

The term for social dance, *o-wen-tsia-ke on-wa-te-re-watohn-te*, means "the dances for the celebration of things that happen on the earth that are not of spiritual significance." The social dance helps to develop leadership skills, cooperation, and responsibility. It also provides an opportunity for socializing and making new friends and for strengthening the bonds within each clan. Children are introduced to dancing from infancy. Their parents carry them and pass them to other extended family members as they dance.

The social dance opens with an address recognizing people's relationship to all of life and to the entire universe. Every part of nature is included: the earth, the grasses, the medicinal bushes, the waters, and the living things that need water. A person called the "House Keeper" or "Pusher" organizes the dances. The music is provided by singers who occupy a special bench and musicians who play a small water drum and cow horn rattles. Formerly, all singers were men, but women singers have emerged in recent decades.

There are approximately nineteen social dances of different lengths and tempos. The Stomp Dance is usually the first. It is a slow-paced shuffle dance, about fifteen minutes long, with call-and-response singing. The second dance is usually the Women's Dance. One such dance has a song with verses telling about specific events. Other dances are named after animals as a way of honoring their contributions to society. Among these are the Fish Dance, the Robin Dance, and the Snake Dance. Other dances relate to growing things, such as the Corn Dance, the Shaking Bottle or Pine Tree Dance, and the Shaking the Bush Dance. The dances have different structures: a man and a woman, two men and two women, women only, or men and women in separate lines or circles. Some dances have been borrowed from other Indian nations. Examples are the Alligator Dance, the Delaware Skin Dance, and the Rabbit Dance.

Ceremonial dance is an important part of ceremonies among those who belong to the traditional Code of Handsome Lake religion, named after the eighteenth-century Iroquois prophet. Turtle rattles and elm-bark and gourd rattles are only used in ceremonial dances. The Great Feather Dance is often part of ceremonies in the longhouse. In the Women's Shuffle Dance, a young woman carries a basket holding the "three sisters," corn, beans, and squash. She leads the other women in a procession as the Givers of Life. These dances, along with prayer and song, express gratitude for the gifts from the Creator and reflect the Haudenosaunee belief in the balance between life and death, positive and negative energy.

See also: DANCE; IROQUOIS (RACE, ETHNICITY, AND IDENTITY); NATIVE AMERICANS (RACE, ETHNICITY, AND IDENTITY).

—Ron LaFrance and Linley Logan, *Seneca Nation*

Native American Theatrical Traditions

For the native peoples of the Appalachians, everyday life was heightened by the drama of worship and ritual. These practices were directly connected with the cycles of the lives of human, animal, plant, and other beings of physical or spiritual realms. Farming, done by women, was the mainstay of these communities, and important rituals marked the time for planting and harvesting. Men groomed the outer regions of fields by burning off meadows. There was a time for fishing and hunting, gathering other provisions, and engaging with enemies. All of these activities involved times set apart for prayer and communion with greater forces.

Features of these dramas included carefully chosen settings, constructed set pieces, masks, and other artwork using fiber, wood, cane, or copper. Songs were integral to many of these events, accompanied by gourd (now sometimes coconut) rattles and water drums, as were dances, both circular and meandering. Emblems were added to enhance costumes.

Settings varied with intent. Those involving the entire community, such as the farming rituals, took place around a central fire burning in an open plaza. These still culminate in the Green Corn Ceremony that lasts all night in the engulfing dark. Intensely competitive games that unleashed extreme emotions were played out at the edge of town. Warfare rites once occurred at the edge of the forest, with later purification held in a sweathouse. At the very end of most ceremonies, in the past and now, everyone involved "went to water," washing or submerging in the nearest river to begin life anew.

Each ritual or ceremony had its own time. The plant series began in the spring with first growth, often strawberries, then progressed through the planting and hoeing of the field crops. Men and women played a game to advance this growth with their energies. In team games, such as the form of football played by the Shawnee and Yuchi or the two-stick lacrosse played in the northern part of the region, dramatic suspense was created by team medicine men, who attempted to benefit their own side by mystically weakening the other.

As fall harvest approached, masks appeared. Among the Iroquois, those representing farming beings (spirits) were woven of cornhusks, while Cherokees used gourds, particularly for the lewd hilarity of the Booger Dance. After the harvest, when emphasis shifted to male activities such as hunting and warfare, ritual visitors wore carved wooden masks.

The Iroquois had a variety of healing societies associated with these "false faces," which have a dozen forms.

Traditions regarding the making of carved wooden masks among southern native peoples are harder to document because these practices lapsed under pressure on the tribes from missionaries to convert to Christianity. Throughout the region, human faces were also carved on standing posts set at the borders of villages and near temples, which were often raised on earthen mounds. A profusion of masks occurs within female-based (matrilineal) kinship systems, in which the father is believed only to contribute his child's "face."

Male-only dramas involved fasting, praying, and dancing to prepare for killing either four- or two-legged animals. The most serious ballgames, often with injuries and fatalities, engaged teams of men. Players dressed in bits of animals, birds, and bats to enhance their own abilities, though they wore little else.

Most of the natives of the Appalachians, such as the Onondaga, Susquehanna, and Cherokee, spoke languages and practiced rituals of the Iroquoian stock. To the east and west were speakers of Algonquian, such as the Delaware and Shawnee. To the south towards the Gulf of Mexico, people spoke languages and practiced traditions of the Muskogee, Choctaw, Creek, Yuchi, and Apalachee, a strong nation living in Florida whose name became applied to the Appalachian region. Among all these groups (except the Yuchi), kinship was traced through mothers rather than fathers, emphasizing their farming economy. Except for some Cherokee still in their original home, these native traditions continue today far away in Ontario and Oklahoma.

See also: NATIVE AMERICAN DANCE TRADITIONS OF WESTERN NEW YORK; THEATER, HISTORY OF.

—Jay Miller, *Portland, Oregon*

Robert J. Conley, *The Peace Chief: A Novel of the Real People* (1998); Charles M. Hudson, *The Southeastern Indians* (1976); Frank G. Speck, *The Tutelo Spirit Adoption Ceremony: Reclothing the Living in the Name of the Dead* (1942).

North Carolina Black Repertory Company

Located in Winston-Salem, North Carolina, the North Carolina Black Repertory Company was founded in 1979 by Larry Leon Hamlin. The first professional black theater company in North Carolina, its stated mission is to promote and increase accessibility to black theater on a national level, especially in traditionally underserved communities. The company produces three to four African American–authored productions per season—new works and classics—and tours both nationally and internationally. The acting company, including professionals from all over the country, is involved in the community through outreach programs such as Arts-in-Education.

In 1989 Hamlin and his company, with the support of poet Maya Angelou, founded the National Black Theatre Festival with the goals of uniting black theater companies across the United States and preserving the tradition of African American theater. The festival is now a biennial event and includes black theaters from all over the country as well as numerous international black theater artists and scholars. On its tenth anniversary in 1999, the festival brought more than fifty thousand people to Winston-Salem to see more than ninety performances during a six-day period.

In addition to the productions, the festival offers workshops, seminars, readings of new works, international colloquia, and forums addressing the relationship between the arts and community development. The event attracts a large number of black celebrities, both in the audience and as speakers. The Youth/Celebrity Project gives young people at the festival the opportunity to interact with and learn from major names in the field. The festival has continued to grow, adding a Midnight Poetry Jam and a film festival to its offerings.

See also: THEATER, HISTORY OF; THEATER, PROFESSIONAL RESIDENT.

—Susanna Rinehart, *Virginia Polytechnic Institute and State University*

North Carolina School of the Arts

Located in Winston-Salem, the North Carolina School of the Arts is a world-renowned residential professional arts training institution. Although its reputation draws students from all parts of United States as well as from abroad, the school retains its emphasis on serving the regional community, the impetus for its formation in 1962.

Established in 1963 by the North Carolina General Assembly, the North Carolina School of the Arts welcomed its initial students in September 1965, becoming the first state-supported residential professional arts training institution for middle and high school students alongside undergraduate and graduate college students in the nation. In 1972 the school was incorporated into the University of North Carolina system.

Comprised of five professional schools—dance, design and production (including a visual arts program), drama, filmmaking, and music—the North Carolina School of the Arts emphasizes professional training geared toward performance and production. It has integrated general studies to encourage holistic development of its students. Staging more than four hundred public performances and screenings annually, across the nation and abroad, the school continues to serve its city and region as a local center for the arts. The institute's own performance and exhibition venues host a majority of these events. Despite the school's national reputation, a regional emphasis is evident in its enrollment, with North Carolina students comprising 50 percent of the student population. Programs such as the Community

Music School bring training opportunities to all ages within the regional community.

An impressive alumni list includes members of the New York Philharmonic, the Metropolitan Opera, American Ballet Theatre, and the Academy of Motion Picture Arts and Sciences, as well as Tony and Emmy Award winners.

See also: THEATER, COLLEGE AND UNIVERSITY.

—Ajay Kalra, *East Tennessee State University*

Outdoor Drama

Although the performance of drama outdoors goes back to ancient times, the modern outdoor drama movement in America began in 1937 with the production of Paul Green's *The Lost Colony* in Manteo, North Carolina. The success of *The Lost Colony* encouraged many communities around the country to establish outdoor dramas, especially after World War II, to stimulate tourism while telling the story of a significant event or individual related to a locale. The movement quickly took root in Appalachia. Nearly half of America's outdoor historical dramas are performed in the Appalachian region. It is probably no coincidence that the two prime movers of the movement, Green and his student Kermit Hunter, had strong connections to Appalachia. Hunter was born and reared in the West Virginia coalfields, and though Green was a lowland North Carolinian, he found himself connected artistically to many Appalachian stories. Green developed a pattern of dramatic writing that he called "symphonic drama." It raised presentations past simple pageantry and spectacle into a form involving all of the performing arts to tell a story with specific characters involved in a dramatic action.

The second major outdoor symphonic drama, Hunter's *Unto These Hills*, opened in Cherokee, North Carolina, in 1950. It continues to be presented in a 2,800-seat amphitheater on the Qualla Boundary reservation, relating events leading to the removal of sixteen thousand Cherokees to Oklahoma and the death of four thousand on what came to be known as the Trail of Tears.

The Lost Colony and *Unto These Hills* established a style of presentation for outdoor historical dramas that continues to the present time. Drama, music, and dance blend to offer an evening of entertainment coupled with a vivid lesson in history. Spectacle that is difficult, even impossible, to offer convincingly in an indoor theater—battles with cannons and cavalry, burning forts, large masses of people—gives these dramas a special appeal. A particular strength of these productions is a sense of pilgrimage created by seeing events reenacted that would have occurred on or near the very ground of the amphitheater. This connection can produce a powerful emotional impact on viewers.

Over the years, approximately fifty outdoor dramas have been presented in Appalachia; twenty-one continue to be performed each summer. Several other productions are in various stages of development throughout Appalachia, including a possible revival of Green's *Wilderness Road*.

Many of the plays in Appalachia have honored heroic individuals such as Tecumseh, Daniel Boone, and Abraham Lincoln. Two plays focus on the harrowing capture and return of abducted pioneer women. *The Legend of Jenny Wiley*, in Prestonsburg, Kentucky, tells of Wiley's capture by Cherokees and her eventual escape. *The Long Way Home*, in Radford, Virginia, relates the story of Mary Draper Ingles, who was taken by the Shawnee and eventually fled from them, covering 850 miles in forty-two days. Virtually any significant event or individual can come to life through these dramas.

The scale of production of the dramas in Appalachia ranges from that of *Unto These Hills* and *Tecumseh!*, playing to more than one hundred thousand patrons annually, to *The Trail of the Lonesome Pine* in Big Stone Gap, Virginia, playing to fewer than four thousand in a season. Size of audience or production has little to do with the enthusiasm with which all of these plays are offered. Most of the stories focus on events and characters from the frontier days in Appalachia with which audience members are already familiar only as words on a page. The drama brings those words, people, and events to life.

Outdoor historical dramas have been popular through the years, but in the twenty-first century they face growing competition from attractions that did not exist in their heyday of 1950s and 1960s. Nevertheless, community leaders throughout Appalachia and elsewhere see an outdoor drama as a significant addition to the cultural fabric of the area and as a positive device for economic development.

Historical dramas are no longer the only outdoor theater in America. Of the 118 outdoor venues listed by the Institute of Outdoor Drama in 2003, forty-three were historical dramas, eleven were religious plays, and sixty-four were Shakespeare festivals. At least one religious drama and four Shakespeare festivals could be found that year in Appalachia, but new productions and festivals were also being developed in these categories.

See also: HUNTER, KERMIT; INSTITUTE OF OUTDOOR DRAMA; THEATER, GRASSROOTS/COMMUNITY-BASED.

—David W. Weiss, *Charlottesville, Virginia*

Jill Charles, "Getting a Jump on the StrawHat Circuit: Non-Equity Combined Auditions for Summer Stock," *Back Stage* (January 9, 1987); Randy Mink, "America's Great Outdoor Dramas," *Travel America* (May–June 2003).

Pittsburgh Ballet Theatre

Pittsburgh Ballet Theatre maintains an internationally recognized repertoire that includes the giants of classical ballet and the work of some of the most significant modern dance artists of the twentieth century, three of whom—Martha Graham, Paul Taylor, and Glen Tetley—had roots in the Pittsburgh area. From the company's inception in 1969, cofounders Loti Falk and Nicholas Petrov struck a balance between artistic achievement and organizational stability. The succeeding artistic director, ballerina Patricia Wilde (1982–97), continued their strong leadership, building a classical repertoire and a precise ballet technique while raising financial support for more than thirty world premiers as well as for the renovation and expansion of the company's facility.

In the twenty-first century, under the artistic direction of Terrence Orr, the Pittsburgh Ballet Theatre has honored the city's modern dance pioneers by celebrating the works of founders Taylor and Tetley in the *Pittsburgh Choreographers* project during the 2000–2001 season. The company is also one of a select few ballet companies to have been given permission to perform Graham's 1948 work *Diversion of Angels*.

The current leadership of the company has been successful in attracting national and local sponsorship of local arts activities. The company has formed a partnership with the Manchester Craftsmen's Guild, a multidiscipline, minority-directed center for arts and learning in Pittsburgh, to commission three distinguished American contemporary choreographers to create *Indigo in Motion*, a suite of original ballets focusing on Pittsburgh's jazz heritage. This remarkable accomplishment, in a time of the dwindling cultural dollar, reflects the depth and diversity of the artistic work as well as the vision of the organizational leadership.

See also: DANCE.

—Judith DeWitt, *Chattanooga, Tennessee*

Pittsburgh Folk Festival

The Pittsburgh Folk Festival was founded in 1956 to preserve and perpetuate national customs and traditions of cultural groups in southwest Pennsylvania. Originally a two-day festival, the event is now a three-day event involving twenty-five nationality groups, five thousand participants, and one hundred thousand audience members. Children's Day attracts as many as five thousand children from public and private schools. This was the first festival to celebrate explicitly the multicultural heritage of the Appalachian region.

Over the years, the concept of the festival has expanded. Besides representing such local national groups as Bulgarians, Ukrainians, Lebanese, Croatians, Germans, Chinese, Israelis, and Slovenians, the festival also celebrates African and Hispanic cultural heritages. The event aims to promote the American ideal expressed in the motto *E Pluribus Unum*, unity out of diversity. Every year, each nationality group prepares dance and music programs, foods, exhibits of crafts and traditional objects, and original or authentic costumes. After performances by six groups, each evening concludes with a finale of American dance, such as early American dances or Appalachian clogging, and the singing of Woody Guthrie's "This Land Is Your Land." The festival leadership envisions the festival as an example of world unity.

The festival began as the vision of Reverend John Schlicht of the Congregation of the Holy Ghost Fathers at Duquesne University; Duquesne's folk music and dance troupe, the Tamburitzans, provided administrative support. In 1962 sponsorship moved to Robert Morris College. In 1992 all the groups decided to form a private nonprofit corporation and became the owners of the festival.

The yearlong preparation for the festival has helped groups sustain their ethnic identity through involvement in research, rehearsals, crafts, food preparation, and costume making. Besides educating the community, the festival has contributed to the vitality of many ethnic groups in this area of the Appalachian region.

See also: DANCE; TAMBURITZANS, THE.

—Susan Eike Spalding, *Berea College*

Pittsburgh Public Theater

The Pittsburgh Public Theater is one of four professional theaters in the Appalachian region affiliated with the League of Resident Theaters, a national organization of regional theater management. By funding and audience size, Pittsburgh Public is the largest of the four League of Resident members in the Appalachian region. The theater serves more than one hundred thousand people annually, usually in a thirty-week, 230-performance season, and is supported by grants from the National Endowment for the Arts and by corporate and local private benefactors.

The Pittsburgh Public Theater was founded in 1974—a time when some of the city's grand old theaters were being demolished, lessening Pittsburgh's appeal as a touring stop for New York productions on their way to or from Broadway. With the hope of joining the burgeoning regional professional theater movement begun in the early 1960s in Minneapolis, Minnesota, and Washington, D.C., local theater supporters Joan Apt and Margaret Rieck conceived the Pittsburgh Public Theater as a way to fill the cultural vacuum created by the city's demolition program. The Pittsburgh Public Theater is artistically focused on providing the city with quality professional productions that have become respected on other stages around the nation. This is distinct from many professional theaters in the Appalachian region that derive artistic vision from the stories or culture of their immediate locale. In an effort to be a prominent player nationally, Pittsburgh Public has worked with such renowned artists as Andrew Lloyd Weber and native son August Wilson to create pieces with aspirations for commercial success in New York.

The Pittsburgh Public Theater is an established piece of Pittsburgh's cultural landscape, operating the 650-seat O'Reilly Theater, which opened in 1999 in the heart of the city's growing downtown cultural district.

See also: THEATER, PROFESSIONAL RESIDENT.

—Andrew Belser, *Juniata College*

Play Group

The Play Group, a professional theater ensemble based at Laurel Theater in Knoxville, Tennessee, emerged in the late 1970s as a leader in the performing arts culture of the southern Appalachian region, and its influence extended throughout the Southeast. Started in 1974 by a group of ten students at the University of Tennessee, the company was noted for creating diverse and innovative theater that examined topics ranging from local folklore to regional environmental issues such as the movement to protect the snail darter, a small fish at the center of a major struggle over the Endangered Species Act. The company was a strong and unifying community presence for Knoxville's Fort Sanders neighborhood, a historic area populated with working-class families, artists, and students. It became one of the leaders and founding members of Alternate ROOTS (Regional Organization of Theaters/Artists South), an arts organizing force working with artists and their partners in communities throughout the Southeast.

The Play Group divided its creative focus between developing alternative theater forms for new adult audiences and creating children's material. The ensemble created plays related to Appalachian topics such as music and stories from coal-mining communities, traditionally treasured tales such as *Snow White* and *Alice in Wonderland*, and plays by contemporary authors. One of the Play Group's most notable productions was *200 RPMs*, written by poet/musician and labor organizer Si Kahn in collaboration with the ensemble. The company added a women's acting ensemble in the late 1970s, which concentrated on health and social issues.

The Play Group ensemble performed widely in elementary schools across the South and at major festivals, including the Spoleto Festival in Charleston, South Carolina, and at the 1982 World's Fair in Knoxville. The group disbanded in the late 1980s. The ensemble's home, Laurel Theater, remains a popular venue that continues the inclusive community spirit of the Play Group, a spirit that still permeates the work of Alternate ROOTS and the community-based arts movement throughout the Southeast.

See also: ALTERNATE ROOTS; THEATER, GRASSROOTS/COMMUNITY-BASED; THEATER, PROFESSIONAL RESIDENT.

—Mac Pirkle, *Earnhardt & Co. Productions, Nashville, Tennessee*

Plays and Playwrights

Many theater histories of the Adirondack, Allegheny, Cumberland, and Blue Ridge Mountains read like cautionary tales of places that featured wild beasts, rough terrain, and even rougher people. These uncivil and intemperate characteristics were quick to take on a dramatic life of their own in popular plays in the influential East Coast theater market. As early as 1794, a grand historic pantomime was presented in Philadelphia entitled *The Western Expedition, or The Whiskey-Boys' Liberty Pole*. This theatrical event depicted the farmers' rebellion of western Pennsylvania and Virginia over federal taxation of whiskey, which was put down by a federal force under then-Colonel Alexander Hamilton. Hamilton was portrayed as the hero, while the frontiersmen fighting for the same independence that had fueled the creation of the young nation only eighteen years earlier were characterized as an unruly rabble.

The earliest dramatic renderings of Appalachia relied on local color conventions and an easily identified plot structure such as melodrama. Tempered by romanticism's ideal of the earthy "noble savage," early-nineteenth-century mountaineers became stock characters on popular stages and tended to fall into two camps: rugged, idolized frontiersmen such as Davy Crockett and humorous rustics from Kentucky who craftily make their way in the big city. Crockett's memoirs from the 1830s spawned several stage incarnations that satirized President Andrew Jackson and ultimately peaked in popularity with Frank Murdoch's 1873 production of *Davy Crockett, or Be Sure You're Right, Then Go Ahead.* Also cloaked in buckskin and coonskin cap, the popular character of Nimrod Wildfire in James Kirke Paulding's *The Lion of the West* (1831) was the country cousin who comically upstaged his effete and pompous city brethren to win the girl's hand.

By the late nineteenth century, a new dramatic form called realism began to take the stage from the worn-out formulaic playwriting and generalized local color conventions of mid-century melodramas. Appalachian-born William Clyde Fitch was an early proponent of the realist movement that led the American theater into the twentieth century. Born and reared in Elmira, Chemung County, New York, in 1865, Fitch was considered the best American dramatist of his day. He wrote a total of sixty plays before he died at the age of forty-four. He believed his works were dramas of ideas. His last play, *The City*, tells of the struggles of the members of a rural upstate family as they move into New York City for fame and fortune, only to be set back by drug addiction, corruption, and family secrets. Building his plays on adroit but nonetheless contrived situations and interesting but less than realistic characters, the playwright excelled in what might be called realistically crafted melodrama, and it won him great success in his short but prolific life. Another turn-of-the-century Broadway playwright, Charles T. Dazey, wrote *In Old Kentucky* (1893). This play, essentially a romance, shed much of the frontier mystique, reinforcing both fiction and nonfiction's use of moonshine and feuding as natural extensions of Appalachian character.

By the 1920s, the new realism on the popular stage began to focus on mountain violence and isolation when portraying Appalachian subjects. Spurred by regional and folk drama movements such as Frederick Koch's Carolina Playmakers, mountain dramas exhorted the righteousness of the feud, damned government "revenuers," and generally apologized for a people who, as Rufe Cagle in Lula Vollmer's immensely popular *Sun-up* (1923) stated, "need larnin'." A native of western North Carolina, Vollmer packaged mountain brutishness with core family values as well as gender disparities in other works, including *The Shame Woman* (1923), *The Dunce Boy* (1925), and *Trigger* (1927). Fellow North Carolinian and Columbia University professor Hatcher Hughes took broader, more melodramatic swipes and cashed in on religious fundamentalism with his Pulitzer Prize–winning *Hell-Bent fer Heaven* (1924) and *Ruint* (1925). Also contributing to the backward image of southern Appalachia was Percy MacKaye, an academic, poet, and proponent of the nascent Blue Ridge Parkway, whose travels through the Cumberlands and Blue Ridge were witnessed on Broadway with *This Fine Pretty World* (1924), a latter-day melodrama laden with regional speech and mannerisms.

If the nineteenth century is considered as a time of romanticized individualism and the twentieth as one of isolation and violence in mountain dramas, an exception would be the 1930s, a decade rife with labor issues. Appalachia gave voice to national concerns during depression-era America in *Power* (1935), a "living newspaper" touring production of the Federal Theatre Project that promoted the Tennessee Valley Authority and the benefits of electricity distribution. Coal miners echoed the country's employment woes and unionization attempts in Albert Maltz's *Black Pit* (1934). Grace Lumpkin's *To Make My Bread*, a novel contending with Appalachian displacement to low-country mills, was adapted for the Broadway stage by Albert Bein in *Let Freedom Ring* (1935). "Steeltown" was the dramatized locale for western Pennsylvania's steel industry in the highly controversial and satirical musical drama *The Cradle Will Rock*, presented by Orson Welles and his famed Mercury Theatre in 1937.

The Broadway musical began its ascendancy as an American art form during the years between the world wars, but noticeably absent from any list of early Broadway hits were musicals about the Appalachian region. This distinction ended in 1956 with the national and international success of *Li'l Abner*, a musical based on Al Capp's comic strip set in the hillbilly world of Dogpatch. The staged characters of Daisy Mae, Marryin' Sam, Earthquake McGoon, and Moonbeam McSwine caricatured Appalachia as a place of primitive urges and ambiguous religious fundamentalism, a slapstick reality that would soon become even more popular through television situation comedies.

Far from the Broadway productions of New York, curious new comedies called Toby shows became a favorite theatrical form popular in Appalachia from the early 1900s well into the 1950s. Featuring the rural character and antics of Toby, a red-haired, freckle-faced farm boy, these formula pieces were created by rural theater artists performing for local audiences. Usually performed in the summer under a tent, they were often also called tent shows. Toby was usually confronted with characters who seemed at first to be smarter than the young country fellow. In the end, Toby's common sense and "natural" wit always surmounted his challenges, and he inevitably came out a winner. Scores of Toby show companies traveled Appalachia during summers of the early twentieth century, especially in Ohio, Pennsylvania, and New York, but into central and southern Appalachia as well.

Restlessness, questioning, and character depth typified the changing nature of the national popular theater after World War II. Embodying many of these qualities, Howard Richardson and William Berney's *Dark of the Moon* (1945) had its lead character search for a new soul in this adaptation of an old-time ballad set in the Great Smoky Mountains. With even greater character depth and motivation, Romulus Linney's work began attracting off-Broadway and regional theater attention by the late 1960s. A native of Philadelphia, Pennsylvania, Linney spent part of his childhood in Boone, North Carolina, where he was exposed to white working-class values and religiosity, as witnessed in *Holy Ghosts* (1989). With an eye on history, Linney has also dramatized nineteenth-century southern Appalachia in *Tennessee* (1980), *Heathen Valley* (1988), and *True Crimes* (1996).

Beginning in the 1960s, cultural diversity, or multiculturalism, came to the fore in theaters around the world. Appalachia continued to be uniformly portrayed as a culture indebted to the past, however, and traditional mountain ways were often outdone by modern contrivances, as in Susan Cooper and Hume Cronyn's 1982 Broadway hit *Foxfire*.

Though several of his plays are set in Pittsburgh, the works of two-time Pulitzer Prize–winning playwright August Wilson primarily chronicle African American experiences in twentieth-century America and are not necessarily a comment on Appalachian diversity. But as the playwright contends and its critics decry, Robert Schenkkan's *The Kentucky Cycle*, which won the Pulitzer Prize in 1992, does belong to the multicultural landscape, giving African Americans, American Indians, and women kinder representations and greater stage time. Many scholars and activists see *The Kentucky Cycle* as an epic continuation of stereotypes where violence and poverty repeatedly place Appalachians on the fringe of contemporary society. Newspaper articles, academic journals, and, most notably, the collected essays in

Confronting Appalachian Stereotypes: Back Talk from an American Region (1999) have made regional attempts at redressing Schenkkan's doomed rendering of eastern Kentucky history.

Like other information and entertainment sources that influence public opinion, the mainstream theater has a long history of stereotyping Appalachians in limited and pejorative terms. It is a history that continues to this day, though several professional companies in the region, such as Roadside Theater in Whitesburg, Kentucky, and the Carpetbag Theatre in Knoxville, Tennessee, have made inroads at representing Appalachia with a truer, more native voice. One need look no further than the *New York Times* and other international publications as they shower praise upon *Bat Boy: The Musical* (2001), a musical fantasy that features a half-bat/half-boy found in a cave and shunned by a town's insensitive residents. Not surprisingly, the setting is West Virginia.

See also: THEATER, GRASSROOTS/COMMUNITY-BASED; THEATER, HISTORY OF; THEATER, PROFESSIONAL RESIDENT.

—James Manning, *Western Carolina University*

Dwight B. Billings, Gurney Norman, and Katherine Ledford, eds., *Confronting Appalachian Stereotypes: Back Talk from an American Region* (1999); Laurence Hutton, *Curiosities of the American Stage* (1891); Jordan Y. Miller and Winifred L. Frazer, *American Drama between the Wars: A Critical History* (1991); Arthur Hobson Quinn, *A History of the American Drama from the Beginning to the Civil War* (1943).

Regan-Blake, Connie

(1947–) Storyteller.

Connie Regan-Blake, who originally performed with her cousin Barbara Freeman in the Folktellers, was one of the first in American storytelling's modern-day renaissance to turn her art into a full-time career and take it on the road. Performing in tandem, Regan-Blake and Freeman took their storytelling programs to audiences across North America, gaining a wide popularity and inspiring many others to begin storytelling careers.

Born January 20, 1947, in Mobile, Alabama, Regan-Blake was inspired as a child by her father's Irish folktales. A graduate in political science and mathematics, she had just returned from traveling in Europe in 1971 when she successfully applied for a storyteller's position in the Chattanooga Public Library where Barbara Freeman was working. While working with reading programs for children at the library, Regan-Blake was concerned with making books more interesting for her young audiences and from 1972 to 1975 coordinated a reading outreach program. Developing a style of tandem delivery during their work, Regan-Blake and Freeman decided to forsake their day jobs to become professional traveling storytellers; appearances at the National Storytelling Festival in Jonesborough, Tennessee, in 1973 and 1974 encouraged them to make the move.

The Folktellers traveled across the country taking the art of Appalachian storytelling to schools and colleges, also introducing storytelling to folk music festivals. For more than twenty years, the Folktellers shared their careers and styles of storytelling through educational workshops and videotapes. They also succeeded in blending a series of traditional stories into two plays, *Mountain Sweet Talk* and *Christmas at the Homeplace.* Both were popular in Asheville, North Carolina, Regan-Blake's hometown.

Since 1994, Regan-Blake has worked largely as a solo performer and continues to explore ways of expanding the storytelling art, including collaborating with the chamber music group the Kadinsky Trio. The storyteller was a member of the founding board of directors of the National Association for the Preservation and Perpetuation of Storytelling and served as the organization's artistic director for nearly ten years. Regan-Blake also directed Asheville's Tell It in the Mountains storytelling festival for seven years and has produced numerous award-winning recordings and videos.

See also: FREEMAN, BARBARA; STORYTELLING IN THE TWENTIETH CENTURY, RENAISSANCE OF.

—Carol Roberts, *Tennessee State Library and Archives*

Road Company, The

The Road Company, a professional theater ensemble founded by Robert H. Leonard and based in Johnson City, Tennessee, created two dozen original plays during its twenty-six year existence. These plays explored history, heritage, and current events in the communities of upper east Tennessee and central Appalachia. The company was formed in 1972 as part of the People's Bicentennial Commission, a national populist response to the two-hundredth anniversary of the American Revolution. Incorporated in Tennessee in 1975, the Road Company was rooted in the tradition of political protest theater associated with civil rights and antiwar agitation. The ensemble used improvisational games and other collaborative techniques to create much of their original work; other plays were scripted, notably by Johnson City native Jo Carson.

The Road Company supported itself by touring widely, performing in churches, community halls, university theaters, public parks, and town squares. From 1990 to 1998, the company operated at Beeson Hall in cooperation with the Johnson City Parks and Recreation Department, presenting professional performances, offering youth arts programs, and sponsoring creative community projects. Motivated by a desire to reach new audiences, the company developed partnerships with the National Endowment for the Arts and the Tennessee Arts Commission, as well as local school systems and businesses.

Signature pieces include *We Refuse to Speculate!* (a play recounting the history of the "lost" State of Franklin), *Echoes and Postcards* (an oral history play celebrating music as the fabric of community), *Mountain Whispers* (based on a traditional Appalachian ballad), *Blind Desire* (a future fantasy about single women in the workplace), and *HorsePower: An Electric Fable* (a play about energy in its many forms, written after the oil crisis of the 1970s).

A sudden loss of national touring subsidies following program and policy changes at the National Endowment for the Arts destabilized the Road Company, as well as many other grassroots arts organizations across the country. In 1998 the company officially suspended operations.

In 1976 the Road Company was one of a handful of theater companies to found Alternate ROOTS (Regional Organization of Theaters/Artists South), a service organization for artists creating original, community-based work in the Southeast. A nonprofit organization based in Atlanta, Alternate ROOTS is an extensive network of cultural workers, community organizers, and others interested in using art in the service of progressive social change.

See also: ALTERNATE ROOTS; CARSON, JO; THEATER, GRASSROOTS/COMMUNITY-BASED; THEATER, PROFESSIONAL RESIDENT.

—Kathie deNobriga, *Atlanta, Georgia*

Roadside Theater

Roadside Theater, a professional theater ensemble based in Whitesburg, Kentucky, was founded in 1975. Roadside Theater is part of Appalshop, a nonprofit arts and education organization created as a result of the federal War on Poverty in the late 1960s. Under the leadership of Dudley Cocke since 1976, the theater has created a nationally recognized repertoire of original works, expressive of the culture and interests of the group's central Appalachian home.

Roadside's members, many native to the region, have called on their shared heritage of song and story to create a distinct theatrical form. They combine archetypal images from traditional Jack tales, Appalachian oral histories, original stories, traditional ballads, hymns, and original tunes for the fiddle, guitar, and banjo. As of 2000, Roadside has created more than twenty original plays and toured more than forty states, produced plays for radio and television, and published several texts and recordings. Roadside had also appeared off-Broadway in New York and has represented the United States at international theater festivals from Sweden to the Czech Republic.

The ensemble's repertoire includes several signature pieces. *Junebug/Jack* (a collaboration with Junebug Productions of New Orleans) explores issues of race, class, and place. *South of the Mountain* dramatizes the changes faced by two generations of a family as hillside farming yields to coal mining. *Red Fox/Second Hangin'* recounts the establishment of coal-mining operations by northern speculators in the nineteenth century. *Corn Mountain/Pine Mountain* is based on Roadside's fifteen-year collaboration with the Idiwanan An Chawe theater of Zuni, New Mexico. *New Ground Revival* is a collaboration with the Mullins Family Singers of Dickenson County, Virginia, who have passed along a tradition of family harmony singing for one hundred years. A new touring musical, *Promise of a Love Song*, is a collaboration with Teatro Pregones, a Puerto Rican ensemble from the South Bronx, New York, and Junebug Productions.

Roadside Theater performances are always presented with accompanying residency activities such as "story circles," which give local audiences an opportunity to share their own stories and songs. Roadside assists community groups in creating their own local productions. Roadside Theater is a founding member of Alternate ROOTS (Regional Organization of Theaters/Artists South), a service organization for artists creating original, community-based work in the Southeast.

See also: COCKE, DUDLEY; THEATER, GRASSROOTS/COMMUNITY-BASED; THEATER, PROFESSIONAL RESIDENT.

—Kathie deNobriga, *Atlanta, Georgia*

Roadside Theater production of *Leaving Egypt*, Whitesburg, Kentucky, 1987. A component of Appalshop, a nonprofit arts and education organization developed as a result of the War on Poverty, Roadside Theater performs a repertoire of original works and conducts theater residencies in communities across the United States. Its distinct theatrical form is rooted in the traditions of Appalachian story and song.

Rucker, James "Sparky"

(1946–) Musician, storyteller, and educator.

James "Sparky" Rucker, who resides in Maryville, Tennessee, is a popular storyteller and musician who gained recognition during the 1970s and 1980s, when storytelling experienced a revival as an entertainment medium. A talented blues and gospel singer and guitarist, Rucker assembled his storytelling repertoire from material from Appalachia and the black oral tradition, including tales about animal and human tricksters such as Br'er Rabbit and High John, the Conqueror.

Born in Knoxville, Rucker grew up singing in church and school choirs, playing in rock 'n' roll bands, and listening to stories from family members. With the rise of the Civil Rights movement in the 1960s, Rucker, who had attended segregated schools as a youth, began singing freedom songs and speaking at rallies and sit-ins. Strongly influenced by performers Guy Carawan and Pete Seeger, Rucker developed a musical storytelling style influenced by two of his uncles, preachers with dynamic oral delivery, and Bessie Jones, a noted storyteller from Sea Island, Georgia.

Rucker graduated from the University of Tennessee and taught art in Chattanooga, but he was soon on the road as a performer at festivals and in schools. He has appeared throughout the United States and Canada, as well as in Europe. In recent years, he has performed at major storytelling events, including the National Storytelling Festival at Jonesborough, Tennessee, and the Smithsonian Folklife Festival in Washington, D.C.

An interest in the Civil War led him to develop a program featuring stories and songs on the subject and an album, *The Blue and Gray in Black and White*. Other recordings include *Cold and Lonesome on a Train; Heroes and Hard Times;* and *Patchwork Tales*.

See also: BLUES (MUSIC); STORYTELLING IN THE TWENTIETH CENTURY, RENAISSANCE OF.

—Loyal Jones, *Berea, Kentucky*

Second Hand

Second Hand, a contemporary dance company based in Binghamton, New York, was founded in 1987 by dancers Andy Horowitz, Paul Gordon, and Greg O'Brien and performed for fifteen years throughout the United States and the world. Named for its use of materials found in dumpsters, alleys, and thrift shops, the ensemble often expressed opposition to environmental abuses in the programs as well as admiration for their northern Appalachian surroundings. Dissolving in 2002, the company was known for its athleticism and ingenuity.

The ensemble's three male dancers used their bodies and an odd assortment of props and costumes—popcorn poppers, vegetables, and flashlights, for example—to create a blend of dance, humor, and muscle. Now on faculty as artists-in-residence at Binghamton University, the men met during their studies there and founded the ensemble. Highly collaborative, the group created dance pieces using improvisational pattern-breaking games that required a high level of trust and total group awareness. Their intertwining bodies melded to form "sculpture in motion," which they augmented with comedy, audience participation, and food to create innovative theatrical presentations.

Second Hand extended its cutting-edge choreography beyond Appalachia through worldwide television programs

Second Hand, a contemporary dance ensemble based in Binghamton, New York, performing at Centre Pompidou in Paris, 1991. Physical comedy, audience participation, and improvisation combined with acrobatic "sculpture in motion" characterized the ensemble's innovative choreography.

and in live performances throughout the United States, Canada, Europe, Russian, Israel, Chile, and Japan.

See also: DANCE; DANCE IN EDUCATION.

—Paul Gordon, *Binghamton University*

Shona Sharif African Drum and Dance Ensemble

Organized in 1982, the Shona Sharif African Drum and Dance Ensemble of Pittsburgh performs music, dance, costuming, storytelling, and art from the traditions of Africa, the Americas, and the Caribbean. The ensemble tours throughout the Appalachian region, sponsored by the Department of Africana Studies at the University of Pittsburgh.

The ensemble was conceived as a performing arts group by Willie Anku, then professor of music at the University of Ghana and a doctoral student in ethnomusicology at the University of Pittsburgh. Anku and his wife, dancer Akosua Anku, created the ensemble to teach and perform traditional Ghanaian dancing and drumming throughout the Pittsburgh area. They eventually partnered with American choreographer Shona Sharif and her fellow dancers, Angela Ingram and Ron Hutson. When the Ankus returned to Ghana in 1987, Sharif became artistic director of the ensemble, adding two drummers, George Jones and Suliman Rucker. Under Sharif's direction until her death in 1999 and now under the direction of her son Oronde Sharif, the ensemble performs the dances and rhythms of Senegal, Ghana, and Guinea.

The group also performs Shona Sharif's choreography, which combines elements of traditional African dance, ballet, African rituals, and American jazz rhythms and is frequently patterned after the work of dancer and anthropologist Katherine Dunham. Some of Sharif's best-known works are *Swing Low, Sweet in the Mornin'*, and *African Fables*. Her most enduring work is her choreographed interpretation of Langston Hughes's poem "Black Nativity," which has become a Christmas tradition in Pittsburgh, telling the story of Christ's birth through song and dance.

See also: DANCE.

—Judith DeWitt, *Chattanooga, Tennessee*

Silent Partners Movement Theater

Established in 1986 in Asheville, North Carolina, by artistic director Hilarie Burke Porter, Silent Partners Movement Theater creates original pieces that emphasize the importance of social change. Silent Partners is a contemporary expression of Asheville's historic support of innovative dance. The company's performances combine storytelling, dance, mime, large puppet masks, and physical comedy with inventive costuming, props, and sound. A hallmark of the group's performances is its ability to create intimacy with the audience while presenting universal metaphors and addressing themes of sharing, nonviolence, tolerance, and self-esteem through artistic commentaries on contemporary life. Residencies encourage discussion for all ages on human interactions and values.

Fables, one of the group's best-known works, uses adaptations of contemporary animal stories to present thematic material to young children. Other pieces that have a social theme are *Haiku Suites* and *Montage*. Residencies emphasize both physical training and creative processes, rigorously following the teaching of each technical skill with an improvisation, placing the skill into a theatrical context. In weeklong workshops, participants learn cooperation and critical thinking, applying the skills they have gained to the creation of a final performance project. A longer-term collaborative residency, called Sliding Through the Comfort Zone, is designed for teenagers. This residency works in partnership with communities and educational institutions to explore cultural differences and stereotyping.

The close relationship of Silent Partners with Alternate ROOTS (Regional Organization of Theaters/Artists South), a network of performing artists and arts organizations with a mission to emphasize the functions artists play in building communities, is reflected in its work. Silent Partners has performed in theaters, festivals, and institutions throughout the United States, South America, and Northern Ireland. Nevertheless, the company's primary focus is on working at home, using their art to enhance and improve the quality of life.

See also: ALTERNATE ROOTS; DANCE.

—Judith DeWitt, *Chattanooga, Tennessee*, and Hilarie Burke Porter, *Asheville, North Carolina*

Smith, Jimmy Neil

(1947–) Arts organizer and founder of storytelling institutions.

Born April 13, 1947, on a farm in Jonesborough, Tennessee, Jimmy Neil Smith created the nation's first festival devoted to storytelling in 1973 and founded the National Association for the Preservation and Perpetuation of Storytelling. Smith guided both the festival and the association, later called the National Storytelling Association, through their early years, establishing his hometown as a mecca for storytellers in the late twentieth century.

Smith received a bachelor of science degree in English, history, and journalism at East Tennessee State University in Johnson City. While attending high school, he was a feature writer for the *Jonesborough Herald and Tribune*, and as a college student, he worked as a reporter for the *Johnson City Press*. In the early 1970s, he taught English and journalism at a local public high school. Always interested in local politics, he suggested to Jonesborough's town leaders that hosting an event featuring traditional storytelling might spur tourism and boost the local economy. The first festival was held in 1973 and featured Appalachian storyteller Ray Hicks and country humorist Jerry Clower.

Almost immediately, people across the nation responded with an interest in the preservation of stories and the networking of tellers. In 1975 Smith and storytellers Doc McConnell, Connie Regan-Blake, Barbara Freeman, Lee Pennington, and Kathryn Windham, along with writer Ardi St. Clair, established the National Association for the Preservation and Perpetuation of Storytelling and served as its first board of directors. Smith was board chairman for several years; in 1984 he became the organization's director. During the 1970s and 1980s, Smith served three two-year terms as Jonesborough's mayor and ran several local businesses.

By the mid-1990s, interest in storytelling had grown to international proportions, giving rise to an extensive network of professional storytellers, educators, librarians, ministers, health-care workers, and others who used stories in their lives and work. In 1998, when the National Storytelling Association split into two entities, the National Storytelling Network and the International Storytelling Center, Smith became president of the latter.

See also: INTERNATIONAL STORYTELLING CENTER; NATIONAL STORYTELLING FESTIVAL; STORYTELLING IN THE TWENTIETH CENTURY, RENAISSANCE OF.

—Phyllis Crain, *Jonesborough, Tennessee*

Square Dancing in Community Settings

Square dancing has been popular among Native, African, and European American communities of central Appalachia since at least the 1850s. It has continuously evolved, taking in characteristics from popular dances. British folk music and dance collector Cecil Sharp first documented square dancing in 1917 at Pine Mountain Settlement School. He mistakenly believed it to be an ancient form of dance predating English country dancing, misnaming it the Kentucky Running Set because the dancers said they were "running a set."

The most common form is known as old-time square dancing. Danced in a circle for any number of couples, the "square" is formed when two couples dance together. Square dance sets of four couples are found in some areas of Appalachia, such as in West Virginia and Pennsylvania. Live string-band music is the usual accompaniment, and a caller directs the dancers.

In the early 1900s, square dances were often "visiting couple" dances, in which the first couple would dance a figure with each of the couples in the circle. Then the second couple would do the same figure with each couple, then the third couple had a turn, and so on. One dance might take two hours. Today, in many communities, the entire circle divides into sets of two couples to execute the same figures at the same time, so that the dance lasts only twenty minutes or so.

In old-time square dancing, newcomers learn by doing, and each community continues to evolve its own traditions of figures and names for the figures. A figure called "Swinging on the Garden Gate" in Virginia may be "Ocean Wave" in Kentucky. "Dive for the Oyster" is danced differently in the two states. Each community also evolves its own style. For example, some communities use a smooth walking step for square dancing, some use a running step, and some clog, doing rhythmic footwork throughout the dance.

Old-time square dancing differs from western square dancing, which was developed from elements of southern, northeastern, and western square dance traditions. It has been formalized through a national organization and is taught in a series of classes of increasing difficulty rather than being a community-based dance form.

Historically, square dancing was an important community social event. In the early twentieth century, neighbors walked as far as five miles to dance in someone's home. Sometimes square dancing was associated with workings such as corn shuckings, and sometimes it was simply social. By the middle of the twentieth century, it had moved to public venues such as lodge halls. It lost favor as a regular recreation with the rise of partner dances such as the jitterbug, but it continues or has been revived in some areas of Appalachia, including the Blue Ridge of Virginia and North Carolina and the Great Valley of Virginia and Tennessee. In many places, square dancing is the centerpiece of regular community fund-raising events.

See also: BEREA COLLEGE COUNTRY DANCE PROGRAM; CLOGGING IN COMMUNITY SETTINGS; LUNSFORD, BASCOM LAMAR (MUSIC).

—Susan Eike Spalding, *Berea College*

Burt Feintuch, "Dancing to the Music: Domestic Square Dances and Community in Southcentral Kentucky (1880–1940)," *Journal of the Folklore Institute* (January–April 1981); LeeEllen Friedland, "Traditional Folk Dance in Kentucky," *Country Dance and Song* (1979); Susan Eike Spalding and Jane Harris Woodside, eds., *Communities in Motion: Dance, Community, and Tradition in America's Southeast and Beyond* (1995).

Stepping

Stepping is a complex performance involving synchronized percussive movement, such as stomping and clapping, as well as singing, speaking, chanting, and drama. Step shows have become popular community entertainment and fund-raising events in the Appalachian region and occur at both predominantly white as well as historically black colleges and universities and at many high schools.

Stepping, also called blocking and marching, developed in the early twentieth century among African American fraternities and sororities in order to express group identity and unity. It is practiced by youth and community groups in African American churches and public schools, as well as in the Greek-letter organizations of African Americans, Latinos, and Asian Americans.

The most apparent African and African American aesthetic influences on stepping include percussive dominance, multiple meters, a call-response format, and moving low to the ground. Stepping has elements from a number of earlier dance and movement traditions, including drill team marches and slave dances such as ring shouts and patting juba.

Stepping may also have elements of Irish step dancing. The leading black minstrel dancer of the nineteenth century, William Henry Lane, billed as "Master Juba," lived in the Five Points district of lower Manhattan in the 1840s with other free blacks and poor Irish immigrants. Lane competed with Irish jig dancers in dance clubs in Five Points and amazed audiences in London, England, with his virtuoso performances of a new style of jig dancing that blended Irish and African American dancing styles. Lane had a profound influence on American vernacular dance. By the mid-nineteenth century, the phrase *jig dancing* came to be applied to African American dance in general.

Stepping draws on a variety of communication patterns, such as call-response, rapping, the dozens, signifying, marking, spirituals, handclap games, and military chants. Stepping also incorporates advertising jingles, television theme songs, popular music, break dancing, and gymnastic moves.

See also: CLOGGING IN COMMUNITY SETTINGS; DANCE.

—Elizabeth C. Fine, *Virginia Polytechnic Institute and State University*

Elizabeth C. Fine, *Soulstepping: African American Step Shows* (2003); Jacqui Malone, *Steppin' on the Blues: The Visible Rhythms of African American Dance* (1996); Marshall and Jean Stearns, *Jazz Dance: The Story of American Vernacular Dance* (1968).

Storytelling, History of

The earliest European settlers carried their stories and storytelling traditions with them as they swept onto the Appalachian frontier. The Germans brought stories called märchen, which fueled the children's fairy-tale traditions, and the character Baron Münchausen, who foreshadowed the American tall tale. The Scots-Irish contributed folktales, stories of the border wars, and morality stories called exempla by folklorists. More importantly, these immigrants brought the impulse to create out of the immediate experience and to record local events in narrative form as ballads or legends. The Welsh added exotic stories of sin eaters, old gods, and a magical past. The Scots brought their history, folktales, and tradition of second sight. Settlers from the north of England offered saints, kings, queens, and nursery rhymes. French Huguenots carried a hint of medieval songs and poetry, called minstrelsy, and animal fables. The Cornish miners, last among the first wave of European settlers, added tales of sin, sex, and the supernatural. Often forgotten beneath the narratives of the immigrating Europeans lie the myths, sacred formulas, and legends of the native peoples, especially the Cherokee, Creek, Choctaw, Shawnee, Delaware, Wyandot, and Iroquois.

While the ancient history of Europe can show that the seven different European roots of early white Appalachian immigrants shared a common Celtic heritage originating in the cultural hearth of the high Swiss mountain valleys, it is only reasonable to assume that the actual settlers were not aware of this. Separated by language, dialect, religion, economics, and habit, they would have seen their differences and not their similarities. It is an accident of American history that these seven ethnic European groups and the native peoples (primarily Cherokee, who intermarried with the European mix in large numbers) ever found each other. These eight groups met, mingled and coalesced on the frontier to become the Appalachian people; their stories, so different in eighteenth-century America, would blend together into the tradition of Appalachian storytelling.

As people migrated from New York and Pennsylvania to Kentucky, Tennessee, and Alabama, they moved together in family groups and congregations, cleaving to their own kind, preserving their ethnic differences, and taking some measure of identity from their specific European origins. Even today, along the old migration routes ethnic legacies are written on the landscape.

Stories mirror populations, and separation led to identifiable ethnic variations among storytelling traditions. Yet even during that first century in the backcountry, from about 1725 to 1825, there was a subtle blending, a growing acceptance of neighboring traditions, and an appreciation of the other. However, significant melding of storytelling traditions awaited two important developments in the 1820s: the rise of the tall tale as the preeminent trend in American storytelling and the Georgia land lottery system, which broke traditional migration patterns on the Appalachian frontier.

There are few written records of the narrative tradition. Julius Caesar's legions found Jack tales already being told in Cornwall. Early histories of Scotland portrayed storytelling as a vital tradition on long winter nights. Popular authors such as Sir Thomas Malory in the fifteenth century and Sir Walter Scott in the early nineteenth century imbued storytellers with almost mythic qualities. However, it is in letters, diaries, and scattered local records that individual stories may be traced. For example, the first written record foreshadowing the story known as "Mutzmag" was in the 1100s in Scotland. By the 1400s, it was known there as "Molly Whuppie."

Since there were even fewer written sources for stories on the Appalachian frontier, it was difficult to know which ethnic groups added what and when. Certainly "Molly Whuppie" was told in early Virginia. F. B. Kegley's *Virginia Frontier: The Beginning of the Southwest* (1938) attributed it to the Scots-Irish in the 1750s. By 1800 that story reached southwest Virginia, where it was called "Mutzmag." Mona Williams, mother of Appalachian scholar Cratis Williams, handed down her text of the story, which she could trace back in her family to 1805. However, the story's Scottish antecedents puzzled her; she thought the story was German, as the spelling of the heroine's name and certain internal clues suggest. By 1805 "Mutzmag," a feminist tale about a resourceful young girl, showed distinct signs of ethnic blending.

By the 1820s, the tall tale was the dominant oral narrative in America. It expressed the values of Jacksonian democracy, celebrated the mores of the frontier, and gave voice to the rude, raucous humor of the backcountry. Appalachia contributed to this most egalitarian of narratives. David Crockett rode his self-spun exploits into the U.S. Congress, and George Washington Harris made the rambunctious Sut Lovingood the most famous frontiersman in America.

Children born in Appalachia in the early twentieth century were surrounded by the sounds of many cultures. Their ears distinguished Welsh appositives—a figure of speech setting a second word next to the first as description, as in "Owens, shoemaker, pitched the first ball"—from the very different German nickname system based on adjectives, adverbs, and physical attributes—"Blue Billy" or "Slough-eyed Sue." In those days, one could hear Cherokee place names and English riddles. There were differences between Scots-Irish and Cornish legends, as well as those of Scotland or Wales. Cherokee myths lay hidden behind the settlers' tall tales for the discerning ear to hear.

In those days, men told tall tales, women told legends, and both told folktales and myths. Education was oral. Story set the parameters of the world so that ever after people there and then would think in story form. From the time of waking in the morning until sleep at night, someone was talking or singing or playing at riddles or games throughout the workaday life.

In some four-generation Appalachian households at the onset of the twenty-first century, family stories were wedded to the land in the Indian way. Great-grandfathers were known to hold up newborns to the mountains within hours of birth. In their earliest years, children were taught the names of the mountains and learned their stories. An old man would raise his walking cane, point to a mountain, and it was the youngster's job to name the mountain to which he pointed, in English and in Cherokee, and recite stories about it.

In such ways, children learned from their elders both to collect and to create, coming to know the relationship of product with process. It is not uncommon for such children to have thousands of stories in their own repertoire by the time they reach their sixth decade. This kind of oral education is life defining. In some it fosters what can be described as a lifelong obsession with the Appalachian region, the mountains, the people, this special place, this storied land.

See also: SECTION OVERVIEW; STORYTELLING IN THE TWENTIETH CENTURY, RENAISSANCE OF.

—Charlotte T. Ross, *Boone, North Carolina*

Joseph Bruchac, *Our Stories Remember: American Indian History, Culture, and Values through Storytelling* (2003); Ruth Sawyer, *The Way of the Storyteller* (1942; reprint 1977).

Storytelling in the Twentieth Century, Renaissance of

In 1973 Jimmy Neil Smith, a local entrepreneur in Jonesborough, Tennessee, initiated a storytelling festival in his hometown, naming it the National Storytelling Festival. Within its first decade, the event became the ceremonial center of a national revival devoted to the oral storytelling tradition.

The renaissance of storytelling in the latter part of the twentieth century was a folk revival movement in a long line of such movements, and it borrowed images, styles, and stances from many of its predecessors. An important, though largely forgotten, storytelling movement at the beginning of the twentieth century produced several influential texts and led teachers to inspire later generations of revivalists. Later storytellers took their craft to festival and coffeehouse circuits pioneered by the political folk song movements of the 1930s and 1940s and the popular folk music boom of the 1950s and 1960s. Key figures such as Ray Hicks, Richard Chase, Pete Seeger, and others enjoyed long careers that bridged the various eras. Modern-day storytellers also draw from earlier movements a heritage of political and social engagement while adding a new emphasis on psychological and spiritual transformation drawn from popular movements of the 1970s and 1980s. But a significant thread connecting the folk music and storytelling movements of the twentieth century is the use of Appalachian themes and images as key source material.

The first storytelling revival movement of the twentieth century was heralded by the founding of the National Story Tellers' League in Knoxville, Tennessee, southward along the same western Appalachian ridge as Jonesborough. This was in 1903, at a summer gathering of schoolteachers at the University of Tennessee. It was a period of great interest in things Appalachian by local color writers, Presbyterian missionaries, settlement school educators, and serious students of the region such as Horace Kephart and John C. Campbell. The tone of the early storytelling movement itself was strongly missionary. It was heavily inflected with the pre–World War I bourgeois faith in the progress of the European "higher races"; yet it proselytized for the cultural and educational value of arts drawn from the supposed "child races"—Africans, Native Americans, and the European peasantry. As such, the first wave of storytelling revivalism concerned itself with bringing "classics" of orally derived literature—stories from Homer, Anglo-Saxon epics, Norse sagas, and nineteenth-century folktale collectors and creators such as the Brothers Grimm, Hans Christian Andersen, and Joel Chandler Harris—to the children of Appalachia and the immigrant inner cities.

Only after that wave of revivalism began to wane after the First World War and the passage of restrictive immigration laws in the mid-1920s did it begin to penetrate the milieu of restless cultural activists that Appalachia might have some powerful oral literature of its own. Around the time of Cecil Sharp's first published collection of British ballads from the southern Appalachians, the *Journal of American Folklore* printed its first Appalachian Jack tale texts, collected by Isabel Gordon Carter from Jane Gentry, one of Sharp's most valuable informants. The realization that the supposedly savage backwoods of Appalachia contained flourishing oral traditions that could be validated by Oxford and Harvard scholars began to deepen the mystique of the region as a neo-Elizabethan cultural preserve.

Drawn by the romance of these discoveries, Richard Chase visited Pine Mountain Settlement School in the 1920s to learn ballads and folk dances. During the Great Depression he worked as a folklore collector for the Federal Writers' Project in Virginia and also as a lecturer for a North Carolina Works Progress Administration agency called the Institute of Folk Music. During his travels around the region he met storytellers such as Marshall Ward and his father, Monroe Ward, of Beech Mountain, North Carolina, and realized that the mountaineers' repertoires of oral folktales had cultural and historic significance that matched that of their old-world ballads. Chase's *The Jack Tales*, published in 1943, along with his later books, *Grandfather Tales* and *American Folk Tales and Songs*, promoted the region and also its wonder-tale hero, Jack, as representative of an authentic, deep-rooted Americana lost or obscured virtually everywhere else. This mythic identification of Appalachia with authentic Americana has persisted and bloomed afresh in the most recent storytelling revival.

At the beginning of the 1970s the nation was emerging from a period of intense iconoclastic ferment. The social movements of the previous decade were fraught with radical antagonisms, highlighting divisions among generations, races, religions, genders, and particularly between official culture and a host of crusading countercultures. As the Vietnam War gradually wound to an end, the flames of the inner cities died, and young radicals began to grow up, popular culture took a more inward turn. Children of the 1960s began seeking avenues of increased awareness, communication, and expression. In a hothouse climate of alternative religion, meditation retreats, encounter groups, and psychological self-help, storytelling groups began to emerge, both for the direct pleasure they gave their devotees and for the artistic camouflage they provided for people to continue the struggles of the previous decade in gentler, less confrontational forms.

This struggle is exemplified by Roadside Theater, a storytelling theater based in Whitesburg, Kentucky. Founded in the early 1970s by a group of young artist-activists from the Appalachian coalfields, Roadside strives to give contemporary theatrical form to the traditional stories and music of its area. At the same time it sets those traditional arts into dialogue with contemporary political issues such as economic exploitation, cultural stereotyping, and regional self-determination. Roadside's artistic enterprises grew out of a media collective, Appalshop, whose work with film, television, radio, and recording has had an important impact both locally and regionally, as well as influencing the national debate over the relationship of arts and communities. Along with allied groups such as Johnson City's Road Company and Knoxville's Carpetbag Theatre, Roadside exemplifies the intersection of the storytelling movement with grassroots political, economic, and artistic activism in Appalachia.

When Smith was looking for performers for the first National Storytelling Festival in 1973, he went to a Nashville talent agent and to East Tennessee State University folklore professor Thomas G. Burton for leads. The agent gave him Jerry Clower, in addition to a number of ephemeral acts who never made another ripple in the storytelling scene. Burton gave him Ray Hicks. Hicks came from the same Beech Mountain family from whom Chase had collected most of his Jack tales and other traditional stories. Nearly seven feet tall, beanpole thin, and at once mischievous and otherworldly in aspect, Hicks, who died in 2003, exuded a deep identification and infectious joy in his hero Jack. Others from that Beech Mountain clan have appeared at the National Storytelling Festival over the years, including Stanley Hicks, Woodrow Roland, and Marshall Ward. But only Ray Hicks's performances became an annual autumn ritual in Jonesborough. The figure he cut as a mountain man whose speech and folkways were a revelation to modern audiences elevated him to the status of an icon of the festival and of the storytelling revival enterprise as a whole.

Another southern Appalachian native who has had an important formative influence on the national storytelling movement is Donald Davis. Reared in Waynesville, North Carolina, in the years just after the Second World War, Davis imbibed tall tales, fool tales, and local character yarns from his father's side of the family and Jack tales and other Euro-American wonder tales from his mother's. Educated at Davidson College and Duke Seminary, he gained a cosmopolitan perspective on his family traditions. But he moved

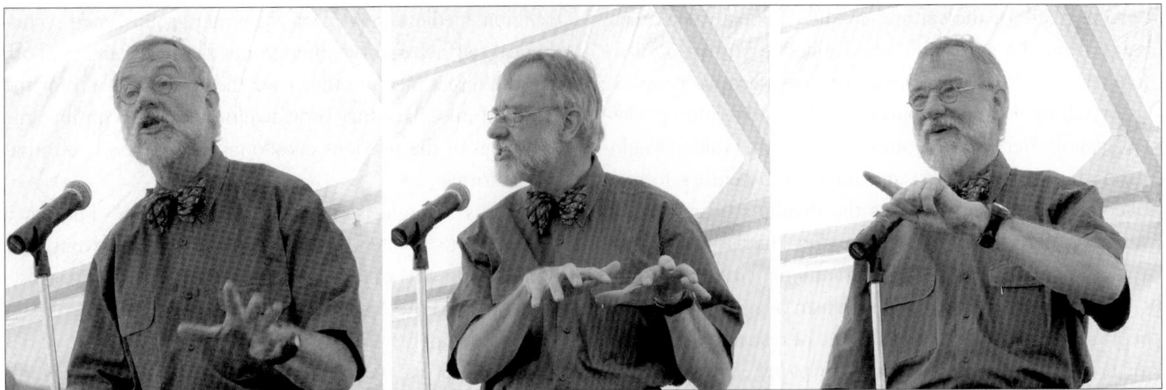

Donald Davis at the Stone Soup Storytelling Festival, Woodruff, South Carolina, 2003. A retired Methodist minister, Davis is noted for popularizing the "personal narrative" story. He played a significant role in perpetuating the storytelling art in the late twentieth century.

far beyond this traditional legacy to develop a remarkable and seemingly inexhaustible series of autobiographical tales of growing up in Haywood County. In them, he blended his masterful oral traditional technique with a literary and psychological sense of creative form. Along with Garrison Keillor, Spalding Gray, and others, Davis has helped to make the crafted personal story a centerpiece of the contemporary revival scene.

The town of Asheville, North Carolina, has long been a cultural gateway, a crossroads to which outsiders could come to draw on mountain air and traditions and from which Appalachian folk arts have long been collected for export. Asheville fulfilled this function for the storytelling revival as well. First cousins Connie Regan-Blake and Barbara Freeman, originally from Alabama and Tennessee, respectively, based themselves in Asheville when they decided to go on the road as the first full-time traveling tandem storytelling duo in the mid-1970s. For twenty years they served as influential missionaries of the storytelling movement, attracting talented neophytes and experienced crossover performers from theater and folk music to the expanding storytelling scene. David Holt, originally from Texas, moved to Asheville in the late 1960s to learn traditional mountain music but soon became absorbed in the storytelling world as well. Several more accomplished performers from around the mountains and beyond have relocated in Asheville, making it a regional storytelling center and cosmopolitan counterpart to Jonesborough.

Meanwhile, the National Storytelling Festival continues to be the most visible and prestigious forum for storytelling performance in the United States. It draws on the rural, antiquarian mystique of its Appalachian site for important elements of its allure, even as the movement itself has grown increasingly pluralistic and professional. The festival and the national storytelling organizations that have grown out of it have also become important engines for the economic redevelopment of downtown Jonesborough, which was placed on the National Register of Historic Places in 1969. Since then storytelling has been embraced as a local import-export cottage industry, a perfect accompaniment to the idealized image of preindustrial America that the downtown strives to present. Storytellers from around the country have eagerly embraced the town as an emblem of the transfigured communal past that the revival movement would have had to invent, had it not been offered up whole in east Tennessee.

See also: HICKS, RAY; INTERNATIONAL STORYTELLING CENTER; NATIONAL STORYTELLING FESTIVAL; SMITH, JIMMY NEIL.

—Joseph Sobol, *East Tennessee State University*

Richard Chase, *The Jack Tales* (1943); William Bernard McCarthy, ed., *Jack in Two Worlds: Contemporary North American Tales and Their Tellers* (1994); Joseph D. Sobol, *The Storytellers' Journey: An American Revival* (1999).

Swiss Dance in Helvetia, West Virginia

Settled by Swiss immigrants in the mid-1800s, Helvetia, West Virginia, has retained a distinctive Swiss culture, which includes traditional dancing and music. The immigrants brought with them their concertinas, accordions, cellos, and violins, and nearly every home contained both an upright piano and a parlor organ. As neighbors gathered to play music and sing Swiss songs, tables and benches were removed from kitchens to facilitate spontaneous dancing.

The earliest dances were polkas, schottisches, mazurkas, and waltzes, but Appalachian culture began to influence Helvetia with square dancing. Local people recall that the best places for dancing were on large beech floors in farmhouses. Timber cutters from the camps were notorious for coming and "cutting a shine." It has been said that somebody would throw matches under a dancer's boots and holler "Make it spark!" and the fire would fly. The village built the Star Band Hall in 1910 and the larger Helvetia Community Hall in 1939 to accommodate its residents' passion for dancing.

The Helvetia Polka, the community's most treasured dance, is a simple open-couple schottische. It can be danced to any schottische tune but is most frequently danced to a three-part tune recognized by old West Virginia fiddlers as "The Rochester Schottische."

In the 1930s folk dance collector Jane Farwell discovered Helvetia's rich folk dance tradition and helped the village organize the Helvetia Folk Dancers, who since have faithfully learned, preserved, and performed the dances and music of their ancestral home.

See also: DANCE; POLKA (MUSIC); SWISS (RACE, ETHNICITY, AND IDENTITY).

—Bruce Betler, *Helvetia, West Virginia*

Tamburitzans, The

The Tamburitzans are an internationally famous folk music and dance troupe at Duquesne University in Pittsburgh. Performing traditional music and dance of eastern and southeastern Europe, including material from Armenia, Azerbaijan, Bulgaria, Croatia, Georgia, Greece, Hungary, Lithuania, Macedonia, Poland, Romania, Serbia, Slovenia, Ukraine, and other areas, the group is known for having pioneered the use of folk music and dance in theatrical art. Vigorous dancing, challenging steps, meticulously researched and colorful costumes, and traditional vocals and instruments all contribute to the Tamburitzan experience.

Named for the tambura, a lutelike eastern European instrument, the group was founded in the early 1930s. After short residencies at Saint Thomas College of St. Paul, Minnesota, and Saint Edward's College, Austin, Texas, the Tamburitzans relocated in 1937 to Pittsburgh, a city with a strong Slavic community.

At the start of the twenty-first century, the troupe consisted of nearly forty young men and women who performed eighty shows a year while studying full-time. Students applying for Duquesne and the Tamburitzans simultaneously participate in a rigorous audition process. Those selected attend the university on a partial fellowship and study in their chosen field. Each July, a three-week summer camp provides the opportunity for the Tamburitzans to train for the annual show with internationally known choreographers and instructors. The result is a production that is intense, vibrant, and memorable.

See also: DANCE; DANCE IN EDUCATION.

—Dena Thomas, *University of New Mexico*

Tecumseh!

Written by Allen W. Eckert with music composed by Carl T. Fischer, *Tecumseh!* is an outdoor drama based on the life of the Shawnee chief. Performed near the site of a Shawnee village, the play premiered in the Sugarloaf Amphitheater outside Chillicothe, Ohio, in 1973 and is still performed there annually.

Unlike many outdoor dramas, *Tecumseh!* does not follow Paul Green's "symphonic drama" model, which usually blends dramatic action with music and dance. It includes no singing and only a war dance and a brief wedding dance. These standard elements are replaced with skillfully choreographed battle scenes that are remarkable in their intense realism.

The play begins with the young Tecumseh discovering the white man's threat in the form of settlers sweeping down from the Appalachians intent on western expansion. As Tecumseh matures, so does his strength as a leader. He develops a plan to organize all the tribes he can reach in his frequent travels, preaching that by unifying as one group, rather than struggling as individual tribes, the Indians will prevail.

The story takes on classical overtones as Tecumseh tragically puts too much faith in his ambitious younger brother, who betrays him, thereby bringing about the famous battle of Tippecanoe, where the Shawnees are mercilessly defeated. Tecumseh finally sides with the British in a desperate effort to drive out the Americans, but this only results in his death at the battle of the Thames. The play ends as Tecumseh's corpse is carried off to be buried "where no white man will ever know."

See also: OUTDOOR DRAMA.

—David W. Weiss, *Charlottesville, Virginia*

Tennessee Children's Dance Ensemble

Founded in Knoxville in 1981 by Dorothy Floyd, the Tennessee Children's Dance Ensemble was the first professional children's dance company in the United States. Under the leadership of artistic director Irena Linn since the founder's death in 2002, the twenty-four artists in the ensemble range in age from eight to seventeen years. It is the only children's company accepted into Dance/USA, a juried organization of professional dance companies. The ensemble has performed at the Kennedy Center for the Performing Arts in Washington, D.C., and has toured Japan, Norway, England, Scotland, Taiwan, Singapore, Indonesia, and Canada. It has been proclaimed an official ambassador of goodwill for the State of Tennessee.

The company was founded on the principle that children are capable of achieving artistic and personal excellence. Founding director Floyd and artistic director Linn have choreographed more than fifty dances that form the core of the repertoire. In addition, thirty dances have been commissioned by guest artists, including such internationally known figures as Eleo Pomare and Ze'eva Cohen. The ensemble's dances focus on issues of importance to the dancers themselves, such as the quest for freedom and sharing in times of hardship.

The company performs for schools and for local, state, and national audiences, sometimes appearing as many as four times a day. Membership in the company is open, without regard to cultural or ethnic background or economic status. Commitment to excellence as a dancer is required, as is commitment to the concept of honor on which the ensemble is founded. The goal of the company is "to change the way people think about what young people can achieve in the arts and to add a new dimension to how people think about Tennessee and her cultural resources."

See also: DANCE; DANCE IN EDUCATION.

—Susan Eike Spalding, *Berea College*

Theater, College and University

The study of theater at the college level in the United States was pioneered in the Appalachian region. In 1914 Carnegie Mellon University in Pittsburgh created the country's first bachelor of arts degree program in theater. Today, most of the 222 colleges and universities in the region offer theater in some form, in many cases as an undergraduate major, sometimes as coursework within other majors, and sometimes simply as an extracurricular activity. Several larger universities provide professional training with a master of fine arts degree in theater as a terminal degree. Scholarly training is also sometimes available through a master of arts degree in dramatic studies. Only a few Appalachian institutions grant doctorates in dramatic studies.

Nearly all the colleges and universities in the Appalachian region began their theater programs in liberal arts departments, but many of the larger ones have followed the post–World War II national trend of creating professional training programs in theater alongside or in place of the liberal arts program. Although its initial undergraduate degree program clearly had a liberal arts approach, Carnegie Mellon has led the way in preparing students for a career in the theater. Likewise, theater programs at Pennsylvania State University, the University of Tennessee, Virginia Polytechnic and State University, and West Virginia University all offer professional training as well as liberal arts programs. Some smaller colleges, although solely awarding a bachelor of arts degree, often include some training of theater artists for the profession through a liberal arts approach.

Nationally, coursework in theater was well established by 1940, but Carnegie Mellon remained at that time one of only a few colleges in Appalachia to list curricula leading to a degree. Still, drama courses were a part of college curricula as early as 1885 in departments of English and elocution and similar academic units.

The University of Tennessee reports the earliest date (1840) for any faculty-directed play production on a college or university campus in the region. Most other schools date such activity to the 1920s. This followed a national trend initiated by George Pierce Baker as early as 1903 with the introduction of a playwriting course at Radcliffe and Harvard Universities. One of Baker's students, Thomas Wood Stephens, pioneered the degree program at Carnegie Mellon. Baker and Stephens insisted that every theater student, whatever his or her special interest, must study and practice all phases of the field and that theater is best learned through practical experience in stage production.

Despite the fact that the Appalachian region contains distinctive cultures and local histories, most college and university theater programs perceive themselves as relatively isolated and consider it a challenge to present quality theater to audiences that would not otherwise be served. However, because some colleges perceive such audiences to be conservative or unsophisticated, they feel restricted in their selection of scripts. At the same time, several college programs contend that indigenous artists often make meaningful contributions to their particular theater program and that presenting plays of local or regional significance enhances their programs.

See also: APPALACHIAN STATE UNIVERSITY THEATER PROGRAM; CARNEGIE MELLON UNIVERSITY THEATER PROGRAM; CONVERSE COLLEGE THEATER PROGRAM.

—Robert H. Leonard, *Virginia Polytechnic Institute and State University*

Shannon Jackson, "Professing Performance," *Drama Review* (Spring 2001); Thomas W. Loughlin, "University Theatre Departments Are Showing the Dark Side of Success," *Chronicle of Higher Education* (April 11, 1997).

Theater, Grassroots / Community-Based

Community-based theater, also known as grassroots theater, is generally considered to be theater "*of*, *by*, and *for* the people." It is characterized by original plays, written by people (often working-class) rooted within a community and dealing with subjects drawn from local history, stories, and concerns. Appalachia is home to several prominent national leaders in this field, including Jo Carson, Dudley Cocke, Kathie deNobriga, Robert H. Leonard, Linda Parris-Bailey, and Jerry Stropnicky, as well as several community-based theater ensembles that have been recognized nationally for their pioneering accomplishments in advancing the field. These include the Bloomsburg Theatre Ensemble, Carpetbag Theatre, EcoTheater, the Play Group, the Road Company, and Roadside Theater.

A core premise of community-based theater is that cultural expression and creativity reside within a community. Other characteristics are a strong commitment to collaboration and an active relationship between the audience and the artist. While traditional theater usually treats the audience as passive spectators, community-based theater seeks to engage the audience actively in a number of possible ways—as performers, as the source of song or story, or as citizens motivated to action. Community-based artists tend to reject the romantic ideal of the artist as separate and elevated from society, instead considering themselves integral to community life. Community-based theater often seeks to inform as well as to entertain.

Community-based theater differs from community theater (sometimes called "little theater" or civic theater), also a widespread activity in Appalachia. While community-based theater focuses on original work, community theater usually focuses on Broadway musicals, classic world dramas in the realistic or naturalistic style, or light comedies. However, the distinction is not always clearly drawn, as community theaters also occasionally produce original plays set in their communities, often depicting the celebration of a local historical event.

Community-based theaters are customarily nonprofit organizations. They usually pay their artists, often creating a resident professional ensemble. Beginning in 1975, Roadside Theater developed a core of local artists in the Whitesburg, Kentucky, area; conversely, a group of professionally trained artists took up residence in Pennsylvania in 1978 to start the Bloomsburg Theatre Ensemble. While touring is often an economic necessity for such companies, community-based theaters generally reject the tradition of whistle-stops and one-night stands used by early American theater and opera troupes who traveled by river or rail to remote outposts. Instead, community-based theaters prefer to spend several days, weeks, or even months in a host community, offering workshops and activities in addition to performances. Theaters such as Roadside may also engage the community in the making of their own performances during these extended residencies.

The contemporary practice of community-based theater in Appalachia blossomed in the 1970s due to a combination of factors. Politically engaged artists who were active in the Civil Rights and women's liberation movements created theater pieces about contemporary social problems (often in historical context) or explored racial, ethnic, sexual, or cultural identities. The confrontational street theater of the 1960s, with its antiwar protests, evolved into a more inclusive approach following the end of the Vietnam War. Theater "*of*, *by*, and *for* the people" now included "*with* the people."

The celebration of the American bicentennial in 1976 also contributed to the emergence of many contemporary community-based theaters. This period was roughly concurrent with the availability of funds from the Comprehensive Employment and Training Act, a federal employment program. According to research reported by Arlene Goldbard, the act allocated more than $200 million to the arts in 1979. Although arts organizations in Appalachia accessed only a small portion of its funds, the program's impact was significant. For example, the Road Company depended heavily on funds provided by the initiative in its earliest years.

An early advocate of locally produced and controlled theater, Kentucky-born Maryat Lee moved to West Virginia after twenty years of making street theater in New York City. She founded EcoTheater in 1975 on the central premise that "theater is a natural, simple, and universal ability in everyone, and the telling of your own story has powerful and life-changing impact." For EcoTheater, as for many community-based theaters, the value of making the play is equal to the finished product or performance. Artistic virtuosity is often secondary in importance to the community participants' experience, both collectively and individually. Although Lee died in 1989, several EcoTheater chapters remain active in Kentucky and North Carolina.

Historical precedents for community-based theater include the life work of Professor Frederick Koch, who was deeply influenced by Irish dramatists Lady Gregory, John Synge, and William Butler Yeats. Koch taught at the University of North Carolina in Chapel Hill beginning in 1918, introducing his students to the idea of the "folk drama." Koch's advocacy for homegrown theater across the South was amplified by his students, who wrote scores of plays, and by regional tours of the Carolina Playmakers, the producing arm of Koch's Department of Dramatic Art.

Pulitzer Prize–winning playwright Paul Green, a North Carolina native, studied with Koch and also briefly with Alexander M. Drummond of Cornell University. Drummond was one of several men who were interested in dramas written by and relevant to the lives of ordinary citizens; others include Robert Gard and his Wisconsin Idea Theater, Baker Brownell at the University of Montana, and E. C. Mabie at the State University of Iowa in Iowa City, now the University of Iowa. Such theaters flourished for a time before, during, and especially after World War II, before radio and television reduced the sense of rural isolation, and before the agrarian economy and culture were superceded by the industrial sector.

Green is best known for his outdoor dramas (or "symphonic dramas," as he called them), which later became a profitable tourist industry for many small towns in Appalachia. Don Baker's *Stonewall Country* at the Theater at Lime Kiln in Lexington, Virginia, and Kermit Hunter's *Unto These Hills* in Cherokee, North Carolina, are two of many such plays. Green's first outdoor drama, *The Lost Colony*, was written in 1937 with assistance from the Federal Theatre Project (1935–39), a component of the Works Progress Administration, part of President Franklin D. Roosevelt's New Deal. Because Appalachia had relatively few professional artists whose chronic unemployment could be officially relieved, the Federal Theatre Project itself had little direct impact on the region. However, the Federal Writers' Project, which collected oral histories and folktales, may have helped to revitalize an interest in storytelling, a common aesthetic component of many community-based theaters.

The Federal Theatre Project was dismantled in 1939 as the country prepared for war, but some remnants of prewar cultural activities survived, notably in rural areas, as at the Highlander Folk School, now Highlander Research and Education Center, in Tennessee. Highlander hosted the first meeting of Alternate ROOTS (Regional Organization of Theaters/Artists South), for instance, which continues to be an organizing force among community-based artists in the South working in all disciplines, particularly theater.

See also: ALTERNATE ROOTS; THEATER, HISTORY OF; THEATER, PROFESSIONAL RESIDENT.

—Kathie deNobriga, *Atlanta, Georgia*

Don Adams and Arlene Goldbard, *Crossroads: Reflections on the Politics of Culture* (1990); James Flannery, "Southern Theater and the Paradox of Progress," *Southern Exposure* (Fall–Winter 1986); Robert E. Gard, *Grassroots Theater: A Search for Regional Arts in America* (1999).

Theater, History of

From its earliest days, theater in the Appalachian region has employed many forms of expression. Native people told stories and celebrated life with theatrical rituals that included masks, dance, and character impersonation. White migration into the region brought European traditions of theater based on human conflict (whether serious or comedic) enacted through characters in dialogue. The Spanish, French, and English each brought their own form of European theater to their colonies established on the Atlantic and Gulf Coasts, but political, economic, and military events determined that primarily English-speaking people would settle the Appalachian region after the American Revolution.

On April 10, 1790, the first known performance of a play west of the Alleghenies was given by students at the Transylvania Seminary in Lexington, Kentucky. The production included a tragedy and a farcical comedy, both unnamed in existing records. A week later, Pittsburgh announced productions of *Cato,* a popular tragedy from England, and *All the World's a Stage,* an equally popular English farce. Theatrical histories suggest that plays produced and enjoyed in the Appalachians throughout the nineteenth century were contemporary popular hits in London and New York, especially melodramas and comedies. In addition to formal plays, Appalachian theater history is marked by a broad variety of other types of performance.

As the flow of migration accelerated, taverns, inns, and other public houses in developing communities attracted a wide variety of itinerant performers. Jugglers, pantomimes, reciters of verse and dramatic literature, slack-rope and tight-rope dancers—virtually anyone with a performance skill sought their fortunes in the tide of pioneers. One such traveling actor, a Mr. Rannie, is reported to have performed in a Lexington tavern during April 1805, having traveled from Canada and performing in exchange for food and shelter throughout his journey. Similar wayfaring artists undoubtedly performed in taverns and public houses through the valleys of western Pennsylvania, Maryland, and Virginia, as well as along the National Road.

Records show that in 1808 Luke Usher, a successful umbrella maker in Lexington, and his actor son, Noble Luke Usher, built and opened the first permanent theater in Kentucky. It was probably the first west of the Alleghenies. Located on the second story, the theater shared the brick building with one of the Ushers' other businesses, a brewery, on the first floor. In 1815 the Ushers contracted for their theater to be managed by Samuel Drake Sr., the actor/manager of an upstate New York traveling company of actors built around the Drake family members. Drake and company traveled by wagon and barge to Kentucky, performing for river towns and farm villages along the way. Noah M. Ludlow, an actor in the company, recorded richly detailed accounts of the proceedings of this first professional theater in Kentucky in his book, *Dramatic Life As I Found It.* Ludlow went on to become one of the most successful actor/managers of the Old West. In 1819 he was the first to bring professionally produced theatricals into Alabama, before it became a state, performing in Florence, Tuscumbia, and Huntsville, the state's first capital.

In these same years, Solomon Smith left his home village of Solon, in the Appalachian county of Cortland, New York, in search of a career in the theater. He took the same route as the Drakes but traveled alone, rowing and floating a skiff five hundred miles on the Allegheny River from Olean Point, New York, to Pittsburgh, where he found makeshift theater enterprises in taverns and hastily built halls that were little better than sheds. Smith, not yet seventeen when he set out, learned the acting trade over the next few years through short engagements in Ohio River towns. His work led eventually to professional membership in the Drake family company in Kentucky. Like Ludlow, Sol Smith was destined to become one of the region's most illustrious actor/managers. Not to be outdone by his contemporary, Smith published his memoirs in a book called *Theatrical Management in the West and South.*

In his memoir, Smith recalled his wagon journey across eastern Kentucky, as well as performances in Richmond, London, and Barbourville, where the shows were presented in taverns. Smith's troupe labored across the Cumberland Gap to perform Shakespeare's *As You Like It* in a small Tazewell, Tennessee, hotel. Traveling on, the company played in Greeneville, Tennessee, in a carpenter's shop. They intended to play only one night, but, since a religious revival was going on, they stayed on for three, awaiting an audience. In the end, the religious people of Greeneville finished their devotions and some 160 to 180 souls attended the play, giving the performances much shouting and stomping of approval. However, the local man whom Smith asked to "cover the door" took up only seven tickets. When pressed on the point, the man avowed that, indeed, only seven people had come through the door. The rest, he asserted, entered the building through the windows. From Greenville, Smith and company traveled on to Buncombe County, North Carolina, and onward into the South Carolina uplands, tracing one of the earliest touring circuits in the southern mountains and bringing their art to satisfied if tightfisted audiences.

In 1831 another acting family came down the Ohio River, as the Drakes had sixteen years earlier. The William Chapman family did things much differently, however. In Pittsburgh, they fitted out a barge to permit plays to be staged onboard. They performed all along the banks of the Ohio in Steubenville, Ohio, Wellsburg and Wheeling, (West) Virginia, and other Appalachian river towns, big and small. Thus, the Chapman Family Floating Theater inaugurated a fabled era of the showboat in American theatrical history.

After several years of floating downriver to New Orleans, selling the barge and traveling back to Pittsburgh by stagecoach for the next year's downstream float, the family eventually took advantage of the advent of the steam-driven riverboat and began performing in both directions. The showboat became an institution and an economic engine along the rivers for several decades, until the railroads made theatrical travel into the interior towns and villages easier and more profitable. Reminders of the romance and excitement of Chapman's theater barge are preserved in tourist attractions along the Ohio's Appalachian riverbanks, as well as far downstream.

Off the river, some frontier theatrical managers, such as Drake, traveled overland by wagon in the early nineteenth century and supported their company of actors through a circuit of theaters within a close region. Others built their business by traveling more broadly. Ludlow and Smith moved from one likely venue to another, staying as long as they attracted audiences. These stays, lasting for a few days, weeks, or even months, were called "seasons." While ticket buyers were the first consideration, weather, health, and other circumstances helped determine the itinerary of frontier theatrical ventures.

In the early days, locals would transform any likely room into a theater for the night or even build a temporary hall, to be taken down as soon as the company moved on. From the 1830s on, however, Appalachian towns supported permanent theaters; Pittsburgh's first permanent theater was built in 1833. As the rail network expanded in the 1880s and 1890s, theater construction rapidly increased. In larger cities, some theaters were virtual palaces, and even small Appalachian towns often had their own opera house—usually a simple hall with a raised stage framed by a proscenium arch, the standard theatrical format of the nineteenth century. By 1912, at least 273 theatrical houses were operating in Appalachia, 162 in the northern four states and 111 from West Virginia southward. By 1921, there were at least 324 theaters in the region, with the increase slightly more in the southern states.

Some of these old houses are still in use as producing theaters. The Directory of Historic American Theaters identified 38 that still existed in Appalachia in 1987, and the list was incomplete. Among them, the Bijou Theatre in Knoxville, Tennessee, has been producing theater almost continuously since it was built in 1817. Though Pittsburgh's first permanent theater was torn down in 1870, that city has preserved at least 5 of the dozen or more grand theaters in its history. Even some small towns still support these old houses. Among them are Stuart's Opera House (1879) in Nelsonville, Ohio, and the Stonewall (formerly Masonic) Theatre (1905) in Clifton Forge, Virginia.

Larger houses such as the Bijou in Knoxville, the Burlew Opera House in Charleston, West Virginia, and the Alvin in Pittsburgh presented major productions from New York or overseas. These productions became increasingly elaborate, requiring regular updates in the theater technology. The New York hit production of *Ben Hur* (1899), which traveled the nation for several years, included a fully staged chariot race, which required the use of a huge treadmill built flush with the stage floor, allowing the horses to run at a full gallop while they remained more or less secure on the stage. Such major productions followed the rail lines from city to city for weeklong stays, with one-night stands in smaller urban centers along the way.

Companies operating in a wide variety of formats from regional or local bases served towns not on the rail lines. Unconstrained by technical demands, these small touring professional companies, some based in New York City but many others in towns throughout the region, brought a wide menu of theatrical fare to even the smallest of towns. Local so-called stock companies, much like Drake's early efforts, built shows for established circuits, performing the same show at each venue for a week at a time. Repertory companies carried with them several shows at a time, again touring in established circuits with weeklong "seasons" but offering a new title or performance bill each night of the week. Toward the end of the nineteenth century, circle stock companies were instituted by innovative management. These companies set up a home base, where performers lived and rehearsed. Traveling outward from this base, the company performed a show one night in each of five or six surrounding towns, returning back home after each performance. The circle stock company produced a new show each week in a grueling schedule throughout the fall, winter, and spring. With the advent of the automobile in the twentieth century, the number of circle stock companies exploded, with entertainers using cars with trailers as well as the bus and truck combination to get from site to site. In the summer months, for audience comfort, similar circuit and circle operations performed shows under tents. Whatever the management design, traveling shows brought current dramas, comedies, and, most of all, melodramas to rural and urban communities throughout Appalachia during the nineteenth and early twentieth centuries. Shakespeare and the high comedy of the English classics filled out the usual bill of fare.

In addition to this so-called legitimate theater, there were numerous other forms of theater for Victorian Appalachians to enjoy. Until the movies overwhelmed the form in the mid-twentieth century, vaudeville was a consistently popular form of entertainment. These variety shows featured music, comedy, dance, special feats of expertise (or specialty acts), and dramatic skits. In Appalachia, they traveled to the same opera houses that presented legitimate theater. New York vaudeville companies traveled the nation, while local vaudeville teams worked only in their immediate region. One well-known local act was the Lua Amusement Company, operating out of Rome, Georgia, in the 1930s.

Burlesque, originating in the tradition of parody and mockery of serious theater, was another favorite form in the region throughout the nineteenth century. Although "leg shows" featuring dancing women in dresses shorter than fashion proscribed were added to burlesque fare late in the century, it was only after the advent of movies that burlesque found itself reduced to "girlie" shows, gaining an unsavory reputation before it passed away altogether.

As the twentieth century progressed, the dominance of technically spectacular traveling shows from New York and Chicago began to isolate and marginalize the small-town opera house. Vaudeville and burlesque tours became the sole fare for most. Finally, the movie industry took over, refurbishing many of the small houses for the silver screen. Some venues survived in other roles, but many were demolished. Thus ended the era of local and regional companies bringing local talent to local audiences. It was only when Robert Porterfield created the Barter Theatre (1933) in his hometown of Abingdon, Virginia, that twentieth-century Appalachian audiences could again enjoy locally produced professional theater.

However, in a popular aesthetic revolt at the outset of the twentieth century, audiences throughout the nation, rural as well as urban, demanded more depth and value than the syndicates and producers of New York were providing. The "little theater" movement took matters into local hands, producing the best of the new realistic plays with well-disciplined but unpaid local talent. The trend swept Appalachia as it did other regions. In fact, Alexander M. Drummond, a teacher of theater at Cornell University in Ithaca, New York, during the first half of the twentieth century, was one of its foremost proponents in Appalachia, promoting the idea that the stories of local people, written and produced by local people, were the single greatest treasure of American theater. The Erie Playhouse in Erie, Pennsylvania, was another of the leaders in this important national movement. As the century progressed, the outdoor drama movement adopted these ideas, fostering original plays that depicted local history performed on-site for local audiences. Many Appalachian communities responded to the movement by creating productions of plays about local history and characters. Several of these efforts quickly went beyond local audiences to become national tourist attractions.

In the tradition of locally produced theater expressing the perspectives and cultures of local peoples, late-twentieth-century Appalachia became the home of several national leaders in professional ensemble theater, starting in the 1970s. These ensemble companies, which include the Carpetbag Theatre and the Play Group in Knoxville, Bloomsburg Theatre Ensemble in Bloomsburg, Pennsylvania, the Road Company in Johnson City, Tennessee, and Roadside Theater in Whitesburg, Kentucky, link contemporary social concerns with local stories and culture, establishing standards of excellence based on the resonance of truth in the hearts and minds of local audiences. Several of these Appalachian ensembles, finding their artistic maturity at the beginning of the twenty-first century, give voice to the shared interests, concerns, joys, and community struggles of friends and neighbors. These efforts in Appalachia have resulted in nationally recognized leaders in community-based theater who are honored for their successes at securing the art form in the very roots of home.

See also: PLAYS AND PLAYWRIGHTS; THEATER, GRASSROOTS/COMMUNITY-BASED; THEATER, PROFESSIONAL RESIDENT.

—Robert H. Leonard, *Virginia Polytechnic Institute and State University*

Dudley Cocke, Harry Newman, and Janet Salmons-Rue, eds., *From the Ground Up: Grassroots Theater in Historical and Contemporary Perspective* (1993); Robert E. Gard, *Grassroots Theater: A Search for Regional Arts in America* (1999); Glenn Hughes, *A History of the American Theatre: 1700–1950* (1951); Joseph Wesley Zeigler, *Regional Theatre: The Revolutionary Stage* (1973).

Theater, Professional Resident

The Appalachian region is home to numerous professional theaters, some of which reflect the region while others are indistinguishable from theaters found anywhere in the United States. Some professional theaters in the Appalachian region identify local history and culture as crucial elements of their work. Others concentrate on professional local productions of classics and other works.

Two particular expressions of professional theater in the Appalachian region are especially notable: first, ensembles that create original plays out of the history, culture, and interests of their home, such as Roadside Theater in Whitesburg, Kentucky, whose original work is built from traditional tales and local stories of eastern Kentucky and southwest Virginia; and second, outdoor dramas that chronicle the history of a particular area, such as *Unto These Hills* in Cherokee, North

Carolina, dramatizing the removal of the Cherokee people from the southern Appalachian Mountains to Oklahoma.

Besides these two particular forms of theater, the region is home to a number of distinctive independent efforts. Perhaps the best known is the Barter Theatre in Abingdon, Virginia. Founded in 1933, the Barter is the oldest resident professional theater in the South and a national pioneer in the mid-twentieth-century movement of resident professional theater away from New York. Other theaters in the region produce new plays and present more experimental forms. These include the Contemporary American Theater Festival in Shepherdstown, West Virginia, a theater organization dedicated solely to giving new and emerging contemporary American playwrights professional productions, and City Theatre in Pittsburgh, known for taking risks both in choice of scripts and in its production values.

With a few exceptions, audiences in Appalachia and across the United States depended on touring groups, mostly from New York City, for local access to professional theater well into the 1950s. But before the decade ended, economic factors resulted in the fading of these far-ranging tours of Broadway shows from the national scene. In place of the disappearing road shows, resident professional theater companies began to emerge in every region of the country. Appalachia has its share of these resident, or "regional," theaters. The regional theater movement, an imprecise description of the professional theaters that began to spring up in many larger cities across the country during the mid-twentieth century, made its way to Appalachia in the early 1970s with the founding of the Pittsburgh Public Theater. The Pittsburgh Public Theater continues to thrive with generous financial support and a large new theater building (O'Reilly Theater) in downtown Pittsburgh. The Clarence Brown Theatre, affiliated with the University of Tennessee in Knoxville, is another example of an established regional theater to emerge in Appalachia during the 1970s.

In the late twentieth century, emergent theater ensembles in the Appalachian region were at the forefront of a national arts movement that recognized the artist's place as a member of the community and as a part of the community's cultural infrastructure. This movement, sometimes referred to as community-based or grassroots theater, departs from the more conventional notion of the artist as an outsider, a separated and uninvolved observer of life. In community-based theater, ensembles of actors and theater artists devote their careers to working in a specific place. Ensemble-based theaters depart from the conventional model of theater organization in which a producer casts actors and designers from far and wide, show by show (or sometimes season by season). An ensemble of theater artists works together over the years and looks to its members and its relationship with its audiences to develop a style of performance that is specific to the group.

Five nationally known ensemble-based theaters have originated in the Appalachian region over the past thirty years: the Bloomsburg Theatre Ensemble in Bloomsburg, Pennsylvania; Carpetbag Theatre and the Play Group in Knoxville, Tennessee; the Road Company in Johnson City, Tennessee; and Roadside Theater in Whitesburg, Kentucky. While the production aesthetic and mission of each of these theaters vary, one common denominator among them is their commitment to their own communities. In addition to creating original plays, artists in each of these ensembles have risen to leadership positions of regional and national prominence.

See also: ALTERNATE ROOTS; THEATER, GRASSROOTS/COMMUNITY-BASED; THEATER, HISTORY OF.

—Andrew Belser, *Juniata College*

Oscar G. Brockett and Robert R. Findlay, *Century of Innovation: A History of European and American Theatre and Drama since 1870* (1973); Felicia Hardison Londré and Daniel J. Watermeier, *The History of North American Theater* (1998); Julius Novick, *Beyond Broadway* (1968).

Theatre Bristol

Theatre Bristol, in Bristol, Tennessee, was founded in 1965 by Cathy DeCaterina as the Bristol Children's Theatre. DeCaterina's original idea of focusing on theater for youth has been the guiding vision that has made Theatre Bristol an exceptional community theater in the Appalachian region. With community and family support, DeCaterina began offering acting and music lessons in a studio in her basement. As involvement and participation grew, the company incorporated in 1970 and formed a board of directors. In 1980 it produced its first adult season and changed its name to Theatre Bristol.

Theatre Bristol's activities fall into three primary fields: arts education and youth programming; community outreach; and producing main-stage seasons of quality adult and family musicals and dramas. The group operates the Catherine F. DeCaterina School of the Arts, which offers a series of classes and workshops for all ages. Theatre Bristol participates in several partnerships with schools in Virginia and Tennessee and involves K–12 students in many of its activities. It regularly develops study guides for area schools and is actively committed to promoting theater education.

The theater's main-stage season consists of three musicals and one drama. While some of the group's performances take place in the ARTspace, a multipurpose, black box space, the majority are produced at the Paramount Center for the Arts, a restored 756-seat movie theater. Productions have included *Cabaret*, *Scrooge*, *Annie Get Your Gun*, *Das Barbecue*, and *The Miracle Worker*.

See also: COMMUNITY THEATER; THEATER, HISTORY OF.

—David Wohl, *West Virginia State College*

Torrence, Jackie

(1944–2004) Storyteller.

Recognized nationally as "the Story Lady," Jackie Torrence became a prominent figure in the mid-1970s in the emergence of storytelling as a professional performance art. Born in Chicago on February 12, 1944, but reared at Second Creek near Salisbury, North Carolina, Torrence appeared at major festivals and venues throughout the United States and the world. Known for her stage presence and animated style, she began drawing media attention early on, which helped fuel a national revival in storytelling in the late twentieth century. Her African American parables utilizing characters such as Br'er Rabbit and Uncle Remus represent an important legacy of oral histories and dialects from pre-emancipation America.

Encouragement from her teachers and corrective surgery for impacted teeth allowed Torrence to overcome a speech impediment while in school; writing and reading stories in class also helped the young girl overcome her diffidence. Later exposure to public speaking and performance for Torrence came in the form of reading scripture at high school assembly programs, through participation in the drama club while in college, and relating Bible stories in churches as she traveled across the South with her minister husband. Torrence's marriage had disintegrated and she was struggling to raise a child when, during her work as an uncertified reference librarian in High Point, North Carolina, she was asked to substitute for the absentee storyteller. Torrence was an immediate success and soon her services were sought for birthday parties and community functions.

Exposure to the burgeoning professional storytelling community at the 1977 National Storytelling Festival encouraged Torrence to take her act on the road. By this time, Torrence was able to support herself through storytelling and enjoyed success unknown in the field. Traveling across the United States and to Canada, Mexico, and England, Torrence appeared in major national media outlets, including the *Wall Street Journal* and *Late Night with David Letterman.*

Jackie Torrence also extended her talents to the print medium. She researched and wrote the story of Delta blues musician Robert Johnson. Her 1992 play *Bluestory*, which relates the story of the evolution of blues music, was turned into performance with the help of Piedmont blues musicians John Cephas and Phil Wiggins. Torrence produced numerous commercial recordings and authored a book, *Jackie Tales: The Magic of Creating Stories and the Art of Telling Them.*

Torrence became mostly homebound due to illness during the late 1990s and gave only occasional performances until her death in 2004.

See also: STORYTELLING IN THE TWENTIETH CENTURY, RENAISSANCE OF.

—Carol Roberts, *Tennessee State Library and Archives*

Jimmy Neil Smith, ed., *Homespun: Tales from America's Favorite Storytellers* (1988); Jackie Torrence, *Jackie Tales: The Magic of Creating Stories and the Art of Telling Them* (1998).

Trumpet in the Land

Paul Green's outdoor drama *Trumpet in the Land* tells of David Zeisberger, a Moravian missionary who lived among a band of Delaware Indians and established Ohio's first white settlement in 1772. Opening in 1970 near New Philadelphia, Ohio, the play follows Green's "symphonic drama" format, in which dramatic action, music, and dance blend to offer an evening of entertainment coupled with a vivid lesson in history. Spectacle that is difficult, even impossible, to offer convincingly in an indoor theater—battles with cannons and cavalry, burning forts, large masses of people—gives this outdoor drama a special appeal. The music for *Trumpet in the Land*, composed by Frank Lewin, employs a variety of instruments, rather than the more common electric organ, to accompany the singing and dances. Otherwise this symphonic drama (the tenth written by this playwright) is similar in many respects to its predecessors.

The subject particularly appealed to Green because the Moravian congregation had the singular objective of establishing a community where the races could live together in peace. As the story evolves, however, the community is caught up in the fury of the Revolutionary War. The peaceful relationship is destroyed as both warring factions are angered by the refusal of the Indians to take sides. The consequences of this decision create the dramatic conflict. Designated as Ohio's official state play, *Trumpet in the Land* is performed in the eleven-hundred-seat Schoenbrunn Amphitheater, especially built for the production.

In recent years *The White Savage*, by Joseph Bonamico and Mark Durbin, has been performed with *Trumpet in the Land.* The play tells of Simon Girty, a legendary and heroic frontiersman who allied with the Native Americans and the British during the American Revolution.

See also: GREEN, PAUL; OUTDOOR DRAMA.

—David W. Weiss, *Charlottesville, Virginia*

Unto These Hills

Unto These Hills is an outdoor drama that relates the tragedy and triumph of the Cherokee people in their long struggle against oppression. Produced by the Cherokee Historical Association, the play opened in 1950 on tribal land in Cherokee, North Carolina. The association asked Paul Green to write and produce a play in the style of "symphonic drama" he established with his previous success, *The Lost Colony*, in eastern North Carolina. Green was unable to free the time and passed the opportunity to Kermit Hunter, his student. An amphitheater was built for the production. With twenty-eight hundred seats, it remains one of the largest facilities built for an outdoor drama. It is located adjacent to a replica of a Cherokee village that offers an insight into how the Cherokee lived in former times.

Still performed, the play begins with the initial encounter of the Cherokee with Hernando de Soto as he journeys through Appalachia in search of gold. From that first meeting with Europeans, the story moves forward to the nineteenth century when, with the support of President Andrew Jackson, the United States government forced the Cherokee to sign a treaty compelling them to give up their land and move to Oklahoma on the infamous forced march known as the Trail of Tears.

More than one hundred performers and technicians make up the production company of the drama. Half of these are local Cherokee. Although the play was long considered to be a truthful representation of the history, more recent perspectives question the treatment of some issues and events. Some modern critics argue that the sacrifice of the lead character, Tsali, for the people to remain in their traditional mountain homeland is inaccurate, as many Cherokee actually had the legal right to stay. In this, some critics say, the play is inconsistent with historical fact. Others take exception to the hiring of non-native people as actors portraying native characters. There is also tension around the original intentions of the Cherokee Historical Association, a primarily white organization. Critics accuse the association of initiating the idea of the play as a tourist attraction and, consequently, of creating a kind of white colonialism over native history and its retelling. Nevertheless, the play remains a popular and emotionally effective depiction of the plight of these displaced people.

See also: HUNTER, KERMIT; NATIVE AMERICAN THEATRICAL TRADITIONS; OUTDOOR DRAMA.

—David W. Weiss, *Charlottesville, Virginia*

Wheeler, Billy Edd

See Wheeler, Billy Edd (Music)

Wilson, August

(1945–2005) Playwright.

One of the most prolific and successful African American playwrights of this century, August Wilson was born in the Hill District of Pittsburgh, one of six children. His father, a white German baker, abandoned the family early on, leaving his mother to raise the children alone in a small apartment. Wilson dropped out of school at age fifteen after experiencing racial harassment when his family moved to Haglewood, a predominantly white community. He educated himself, reading everything he could in the tiny "Negro" section of the public library, as well as numerous white poets and fiction writers. Ralph Ellison, Langston Hughes, Richard Wright, and Amiri Baraka were major early influences.

Wilson is best known for his ambitious commitment to a ten-play cycle about the African American experience: one for every decade of the twentieth century. He has completed nine, to critical and popular acclaim: *Ma Rainey's Black Bottom* (1984), *Fences* (1985), *Joe Turner's Come and Gone* (1986), *The Piano Lesson* (1989), *Two Trains Running* (1992), and *Seven Guitars* (1996). In 1996 he revised and produced *Jitney* (originally written in 1982), and *King Hedley II* premiered in 1998. His most recent is *Gem of the Ocean*, completed in 2003. He has won multiple New York Drama Critics' Circle, Tony, and Pulitzer Awards. Most of his plays take place in his hometown of Pittsburgh or in Chicago.

Cofounder of Pittsburgh's Black Horizons Theatre in 1968 and close colleague of Lloyd Richards (at the Eugene O'Neill Theater Center and Yale Repertory Theater), Wilson is a strong advocate for funding black theaters and a vocal critic of colorblind casting as a denial of black culture and identity. His writing is noted for its complex and intimately drawn characters and vivid evocation of African American culture and language. He speaks of his plays as celebrations, illuminating specific cultures and histories that have not always been valued in American society.

See also: PITTSBURGH PUBLIC THEATER; THEATER, HISTORY OF; THEATER, PROFESSIONAL RESIDENT.

—Susanna Rinehart, *Virginia Polytechnic Institute and State University*

Zanesville Community Theatre, Inc.

Though a latecomer to the community theater movement in Appalachia, Zanesville Community Theatre, Inc., located in the historic McIntire Terrace district of Zanesville, Ohio, continues the tradition of independent theater production and is unusual for producing original pieces by new or unpublished playwrights. Zanesville, with a population of approximately twenty-six thousand, is one of the larger communities in the rural southeastern Ohio region. Many of the original founders of the theater in 1963 were professional people, among them a judge, a college professor, and an engineer.

The oldest continuously operating theater in the area, Zanesville Community Theatre owns an early-twentieth-century building that originally served as a synagogue and later a church for Christian congregations prior to becoming the company's permanent home. The company produces five to seven theatrical pieces annually and, due to a heavy emphasis on education, generally includes at least one classic such as a Shakespeare play. The theater is known for nurturing young actors and has inspired many to make careers in the theater.

See also: COMMUNITY THEATER; THEATER, HISTORY OF.

—Amy and Carleton Underwood, *Zanesville, Ohio*

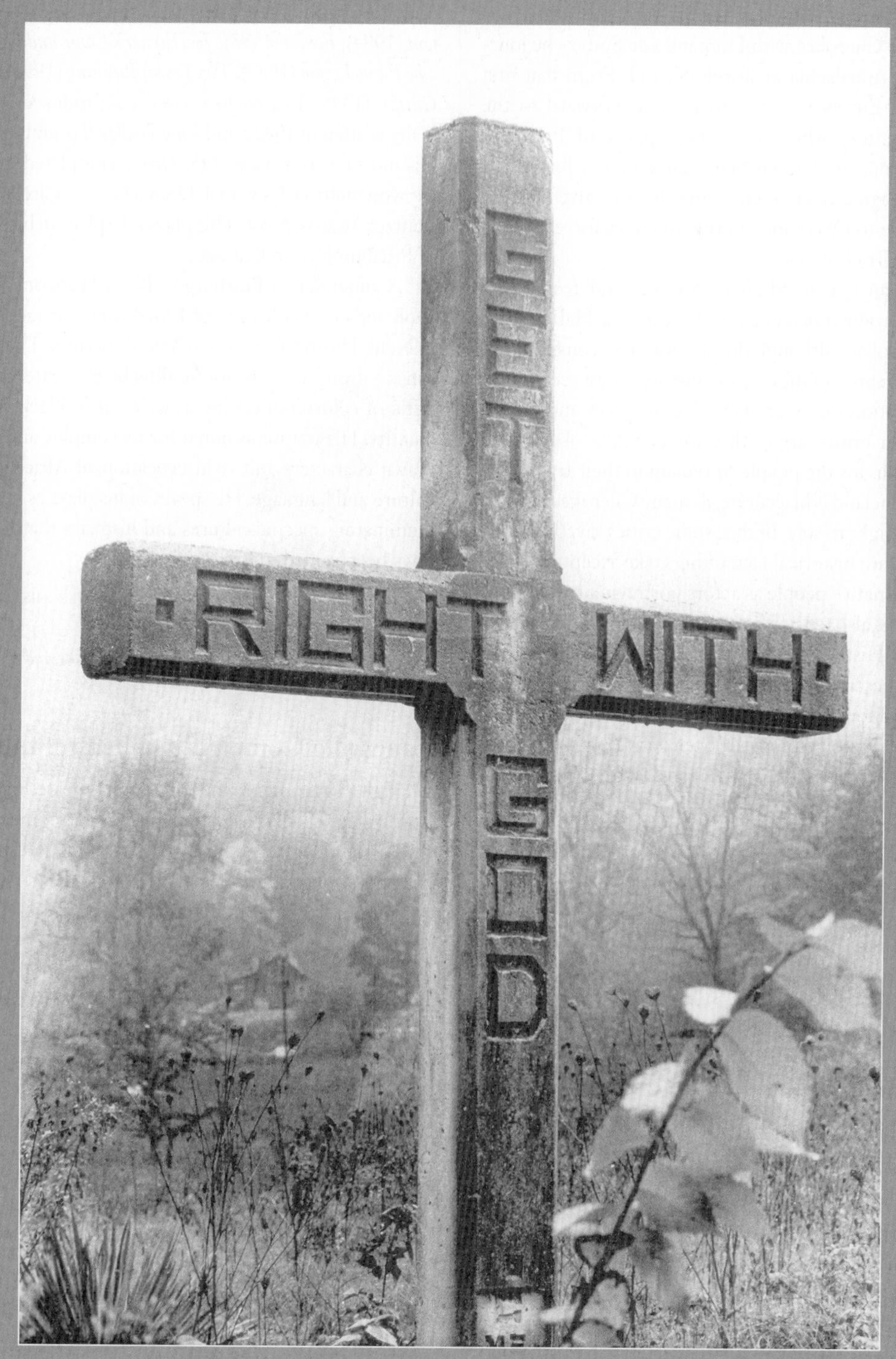
GET
RIGHT WITH
GOD

Religion

Section Editor: Howard Dorgan

FROM THE EARLIEST DAYS OF APPALACHIAN SETTLEMENT TO THE CONTINUING urbanization and industrialization of the twenty-first century, religion has been one of the most powerful and definitive forces in the region's culture. Because of three widely held assumptions, it emerges early in any serious discussion of Appalachian life and experience. The first assumption is that many eighteenth- and nineteenth-century religious practices have been preserved in the mountains relatively intact; the second, that the population of the region is far more religious than the rest of the nation; and the third, that these spiritual beliefs and worship exercises have been largely a response to the bleak sides of the area's economic and social conditions, the old Marxist postulate that religion is the opiate of the common man.

This first assumption has truth in it, especially as it relates to those congregations collectively referred to as Old-Time Baptists. Groups such as Regular Baptists, Old Regular Baptists, United Baptists, Separate Baptists, and old-school Primitive Baptists doggedly preserve traditional practices that include foot washing, lined singing, and living water baptisms. They continue to sing extemporized sermons and hold to many Pauline gender codes such as disallowing female participation in church governance. They frequently maintain gender separation, particularly during foot washing, and prohibit divorce and double marriage (remarriage after a divorce while the original spouse still lives). Within the Holiness-Pentecostal movement there also are worship practices that have been carried over from late-eighteenth- and early-nineteenth-century frontier camp meetings: revival exercises such as running in the Spirit, perishing in the Spirit, rolling in the Spirit, dancing in the Spirit, and shouting in the Spirit. Nevertheless, the reader is cautioned against stereotypes that cast all forms of Appalachian religious expression into a two-hundred-year-old mold. Modern ways may not have overwhelmed Appalachia, but their presence is still vividly felt.

Given current statistical data, the second assumption, that religion has a greater presence in Appalachia than elsewhere, is difficult to prove or disprove, since the federal census has for many decades collected no information concerning respondents' religious affiliation. The gathering of such information has been left to private agencies, such as the Glenmary Research Center in Atlanta, which canvass the nation's religious affiliations every few years. Participation in this study is voluntary, however, and the collection methods favor more established mainline denominations that are zealous in compiling and reporting membership records. In contrast,

Facing page: Henry Mayes devoted more than sixty years to erecting signs and monuments throughout the region such as this cross, which stands in Scott County, Virginia.

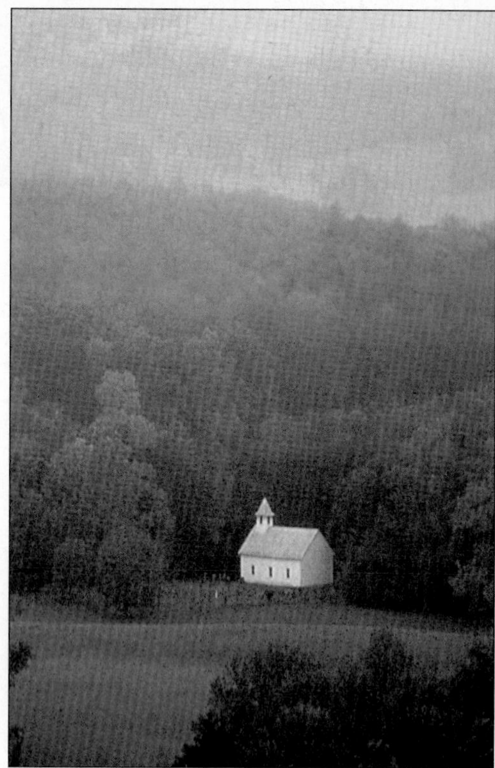

Methodist church in Cades Cove, Tennessee, 1992. Religion has long been a defining force in the Appalachian cultural landscape.

small independent congregations in such factions as the Holiness-Pentecostal movement often do not maintain formal membership roles and are reluctant to divulge them even when they do. One result of this dilemma was that both the 1980 and 1990 Glenmary census reported a number of county populations in central Appalachia as being as much as 70 percent unchurched, this in spite of the fact that the back roads of those counties are crowded with the small nonaligned churches mentioned above.

The third assumption, that of a perpetual cause-and-effect linkage between Appalachia's economic health and the region's religious traditions, has troubled a number of scholars, notably Loyal Jones, Deborah Vansau McCauley, and Melanie Sovine, all recognized authorities on Appalachian religion. Jones's position is that Appalachian religion has too often been perceived as a crutch that does nothing more than help people endure crippled lives. Somewhat as a corollary to Jones's view, Sovine and McCauley have argued that Appalachian religion has been studied primarily as a consequence of poverty rather than an end unto itself. All three have declared the need for more respectful treatment of mountain faith and practice.

To be sure, an understanding of Appalachia's religious traditions is critical to fathoming the region's overall culture. Therefore, Jones, McCauley, and others have reasoned that objective study of these spiritual traditions should coincide with any examination of the area's social, economic, and political profiles. Jones in particular has urged students of Appalachian culture to understand how spiritual practices influence the broader value systems of the southern mountains. In addition, these scholars have expressed the view that both the "religion as consequence" and the "religion as crutch" interpretations have negative connotations that emphasize old-time and emotionally expressive modes of worship and assume that such displays indicate a backward and troubled regional thinking.

Outside images of contemporary Appalachia tend to ignore the rich religious diversity of the region, creating an impression of the area's religious culture as monolithic. Indeed, Appalachian religion is often seen as a conglomeration of lined-singing Old Regular Baptists, tongue-speaking Pentecostals, double-predestination Primitive Baptists, and serpent-handling Holiness. Although all four of these traditions continue to have strong presences in the region, it is erroneous to conclude that the culture's religious base is dominated by these groups.

Nevertheless—at least in central Appalachia—six common characteristics can be identified as having substantial relevance to the region's religious base:

- a strong sense of spiritual independence that pervades the behavior of both individual worshipers and their churches;
- a distrust of religious hierarchies, especially when governing structures are outside the region;
- a lean toward congregational polity, with the individual church often having the final say on all matters of faith and practice;
- a God-called and God-trained clergy that operates under the premise that he whom God elects, God equips;
- a demand for a personal experience of redemption, constantly reinforced by worship that is explosively emotional and joyous, thus giving evidence of that redemption; and
- a modified Calvinism that accepts God as the controlling force in life.

Each of these characteristics can be traced to the experiences of the Great Awakening (1726–56) immediately preceding heavy settlement of the Appalachian frontier, to the common problems faced on that new frontier, and to other events played out in the introduction of Anglo-European religious traditions.

Near the close of America's colonial period, a thirty-year revival (the Great Awakening) swept through the colonies, generating an outpouring of religious emotionality that frequently disturbed the mind and challenged the authority of the more established and sedate churches and denominations. Early settlers of the trans-Allegheny wilderness found this field-preaching, independent, antihierarchical, and cross-denominational movement well suited to circumstances on the frontier. In addition, this earlier extended revival experience functioned well as a partial model for the camp-meeting practices of the Great Western Revival, also known as the Second Great Awakening (1787–1805), which began the nineteenth century and established much of the region's religious tone for the next one hundred years and beyond.

Since two of the most common problems on the frontier were general isolation and the absence of many community services, controls, and regulations ordinarily provided by civilization, the preacher and the church congregation frequently filled the void, governing local behavior and occasionally going far beyond purely spiritual matters. Even when there was no church, the assistance provided by traveling preachers extended to secular needs. In addition to his Bible and a hymnal, the early Methodist circuit rider, for example, usually carried a copy of John Wesley's *Primitive Physic*, a book on herbal medicines.

During the eighteenth and nineteenth centuries the Appalachian terrain and the general isolation of the region led to four major patterns in the introduction of Anglo-European religion to the region. The first of these centered on the activities of lone preachers wandering the mountains to bring ministerial services to individual homes or to small settlements. During these visits, common law marriages were validated, earlier deaths and burials were memorialized, baptisms were carried out, traditional prayer and preaching services were conducted, and occasionally churches were established. In addition, numerous secular needs were met, not the least of which was the bringing of news from the outside world.

By necessity the spiritual services became quite ecumenical, given the intermingled denominational backgrounds of the early settlers—Anglican, Baptist, Congregational, Methodist, Presbyterian, and the like. Within this mixed environment, many of the early religious communities were not as strongly sectarian as they later became.

Furthermore, these fluid and malleable religious circumstances proved advantageous in the formation of early mountain denominational associations, since the small numbers of certain denominations encouraged alliances with other groups. One result was that the Separate Baptists and the Regular Baptists, rather serious opponents at the close of the Great Awakening, seemed to have little trouble in coming together in 1786 to form the Holston Association, the second Baptist association organized west of the Alleghenies. Similar motivations were operative during the great camp meetings that forged the Great Western Revival.

A second pattern involved preachers migrating to the region with at least partly established flocks, typically reaching the mountains through a succession of moves. After the Separate Baptists emerged out of the Great Awakening, for instance, they moved from Connecticut under the leadership of Shubal Stearns, made their way to North Carolina, and then tracked across the Blue Ridge into east Tennessee and beyond, where they still can be found.

A third pattern was more prevalent among Brethren, Mennonite, Mormon, Moravian, and Quaker communities and often involved the migration of entire settlements, or at least significant portions thereof. One of the best examples of such a transplantation was the 1753 move of part of a Bethlehem, Pennsylvania, Moravian community to a Carolina wilderness later known as Wachovia, now part of the city of Winston-Salem, North Carolina.

The fourth pattern emerged as a later development, encouraged by early-nineteenth-century home-mission passions and promoted initially by such individuals as William Carey, Luther Rice, and most notably, John M. Peck. Driven by the assumption that the religious traditions that had been developing on the Appalachian frontier were primitive and even heretical, mainline churches in the eastern part of the nation organized missionary societies to educate the Appalachian mountaineer and validate his religious doctrines and practices. Inevitably the missionaries came into conflict with the independence of local churches, their tendency towards congregational polity, and their reliance upon a purely God-called and God-trained ministry. As a result, there may have been even stronger adherence to the traditions the missionaries hoped to change, especially that of distrusting religious hierarchies from outside the region.

Indeed, the missionary movement produced decidedly mixed results. Schools and settlement centers established by missionaries were often deeply appreciated by frontier inhabitants, but attacks upon existing mountain religious traditions were profoundly offensive. Furthermore, the entire idea of "spread the Gospel" efforts being imposed upon the region was anathema to strongly Calvinistic religious elements, believing as they did that God had elected his church before the beginning of time. In this view all forms of evangelism were futile usurpations of God's role.

By the 1820s missionary/anti-missionary disputes so consumed the region that sub-denominational splits, especially among the Baptists, rapidly increased, with all topics relating to evangelism or church outreach (Sabbath schools, revivals, tract societies, religious education, social gospel efforts, and the like) constituting dangerous grounds for discussion. Thus the missionary movement inadvertently became one of the factors contributing to Appalachian religious diversity.

Nevertheless, the missionary movement did work advantageously for some denominations, particularly for the Episcopalians. Though wide establishment of the Episcopal Church in the mountains was more difficult than it was for the Baptists, Methodists, and Presbyterians, its hierarchical structure allowed congregations to raise money, find teachers and administrators, and establish the schools and social services that mountain communities often needed. And although much of the mission movement later came under attack for having waged war on mountain culture, the efforts in education, medicine, and vocational training led by individuals such as Reverend William West Skiles at the Valle Crucis, North Carolina, Episcopal Mission have received considerable praise.

Many obstacles to the broader missionary movement in Appalachia were insurmountable, however. Circumstances encouraged—indeed, almost demanded—a regionally homegrown ministry that was of the God-called and God-trained variety. Even the mainline faiths, as they found their ways into the mountains, frequently were forced to depend heavily on lay ministers, who occasionally veered from established canons of faith and practice, thus engendering new schisms.

In the following section, readers will see diversity in almost every denominational entry. The Baptists are the best example of the marked proliferation in subtypes. Because of the presence within the region of the wide array of Old-Time Baptist groups, it becomes relatively easy to identify more than forty divisions of the Baptist family in Appalachia. All of the Baptist branches usually called "mainline" are represented: the Southern Baptists (the largest of this group), the American Baptists (originally the Northern Baptists, the second half of the 1845 split), the General Association of Regular Baptists (a conservative offshoot from the Northern Baptists and the product of a 1932 split that arose out of the Fundamentalist/Modernist controversy), and the National Baptists (actually three primarily African American organizations that traditionally are grouped together, although separate in structure).

Another cluster of Baptists can be formed around several sub-denominations that are not thought of as mainline. Collectively they are quite numerous and share somewhat similar general-atonement doctrines. These include Free Will Baptists, General Baptists, Missionary Baptists, and Old Missionary Baptists. Moreover, the

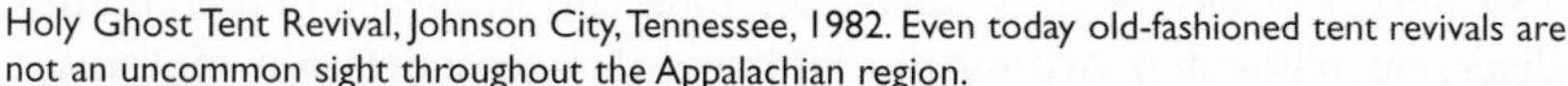
Holy Ghost Tent Revival, Johnson City, Tennessee, 1982. Even today old-fashioned tent revivals are not an uncommon sight throughout the Appalachian region.

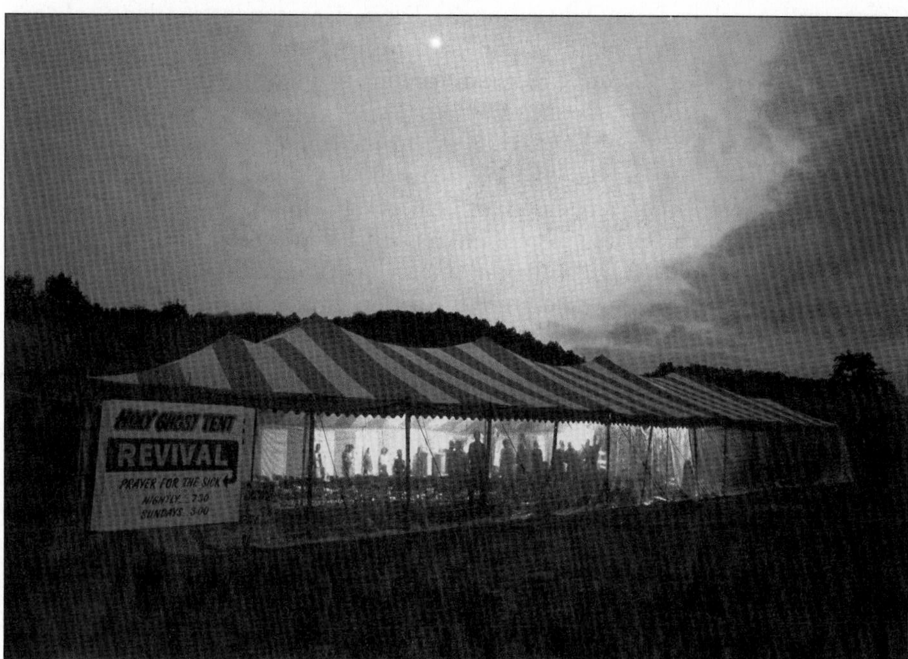

units in these groups can be partitioned to create a number of other titles, particularly from the Free Will Baptists and the Missionary Baptists.

The Baptist cluster that has become known in Appalachia as the Old-Time Baptists or Old Baptists has been the most prolific through its numerous splits. It is nearly impossible to count separate divisions of the denomination with any degree of accuracy, much less to cover them individually. In one way or another, all members of this group can trace their lineage back to the Regular Baptists, the Separate Baptists, or both. Separates and Regulars are themselves counted among the Old Baptists and are the products of their own division that occurred during the Great Awakening. Today relatively pure strains of these two early Baptist sub-denominations can be found in Appalachia.

Three of the most widely recognized of this Old Baptist cluster are the Old Regulars, the Uniteds, and the Primitives. The first two are largely limited to central Appalachia and to a number of midwestern states where emigrations have taken these fellowships. The Primitives, however, are found throughout the region, and are themselves a highly fractured group.

In fact, Primitive Baptists serve well to illustrate how each of these Old Baptist sub-denominations can themselves be partitioned to produce additional factions. There are scores of Primitive Baptist associations scattered across the Appalachian region that have no correspondence with more than one or two other associations. This means they do not recognize the legitimacy of any other Primitive Baptist groups. These highly traditional believers have squabbled over all issues relative to predestination, precise interpretations of election doctrine, and having or not having Sabbath schools. They have disagreed over the acceptability of cross-gender foot washing, over the nature of hymnody in their services, and over a host of other issues relating to both theology and worship practices.

Appalachian religious diversity, however, does not stop with the Baptists. Their tendency to splinter is rivaled by the Pentecostals, especially as a result of their numerous and divergent fellowships within the Holiness-Pentecostal fusion movement. Controversies include Jesus Only versus the Trinitarians; tongue speaking only versus tongue speaking with interpretation; serpent handling and fire handling versus the absence thereof; full acceptance versus banning of women preachers; and a multitude of other doctrine or practice variations.

The more establishment Pentecostal groups, reflecting the diversity within the movement, include Assemblies of God; Church of God (Cleveland, Tennessee); Church of God of Prophecy; Church of God of the Mountain Assembly; International Church of Foursquare Gospel; International Pentecostal Church of Christ; Open Bible Standard Church; Pentecostal Church of God; and Pentecostal Holiness Church. Several of these groups also have experienced their own schisms.

No further list of subunits is provided here, but when examining the entries on denominational families, some readers may be surprised to find several splinter groups discussed under such mainline clusters as the Methodists, Presbyterians, and Lutherans. While no claim is made that all of these breakaway units are indigenous to Appalachia, the distribution of a wide range of faiths does make the region's religious map exceptionally rich and colorful. In addition, readers should take note of the large number of these divisions that are, or were, unique to Appalachia.

To manage this distribution of diverse faiths, this section employs a denominational-family approach, for which the editor is indebted to Clifford A. Grammich Jr., who uses this cataloging system in his *Appalachian Atlas: Maps of the Churches and People of the Appalachian Region.* However, because of the large number of Baptist groups needing to be addressed, Grammich's organizational scheme has been modified to include the three major partitions already discussed. In addition, because of space, not all of the various denominations and sub-denominations mentioned by Grammich have been included.

This section is not devoted entirely to denominational families. In fact, some of the more important entries have little to do with denominationalism. Still, these entries say something significant about the essence and distinctiveness of Appalachian religion. It should be noted, however, that the search for the essence of Appalachian religion becomes nearly impossible given that the region extends from northeastern Mississippi to southern New York State.

Thus, a number of entries focus on what might be called Old Appalachia, the central part of the region given the most attention by regional scholars. For example, Charles H. Lippy's entry "Popular Religion" is relevant here. As Lippy explains, studies of popular religion attempt to reach beyond denominationalism in a quest for a region's true religious nature. In the process, shared principles, values, and basic morality pronouncements are examined to uncover the essence of a culture's spiritual character. If this thesis is valid, such studies may hold the most hope for genuine understandings of a culture's spiritual makeup.

Many of the same observations can be made about an area of study that has captured the interest of Loyal Jones. Although Jones's studies frequently examine a scriptural base for each value, he has still focused on the cultural principles that cut

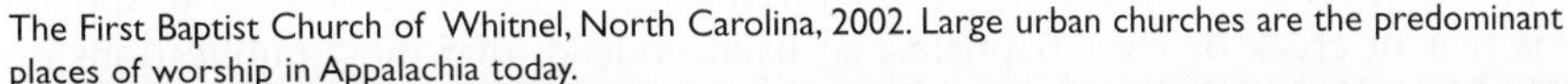

The First Baptist Church of Whitnel, North Carolina, 2002. Large urban churches are the predominant places of worship in Appalachia today.

across the broad range of at least Old Appalachia. Therefore, there is considerable similarity between his approach and Lippy's popular-religion focus. Both attempt to understand a culture's spiritual fare without becoming bogged down by sectarianism.

A third major entry in the section, McCauley's essay on the Holiness-Pentecostal fusion, is important to discovering the core or essence of religion in central Appalachia. Originally two separate and very different campaigns in American religious history, Pentecostalism and the Holiness movement have managed to find a comfortable but informal union in much of southern and central Appalachia. Pentecostalism focuses on powers gained from Holy Spirit possession, especially glossolalia (speaking in tongues), while the Holiness movement features a Wesleyan doctrine upholding a second blessing sanctification that can emerge after an extended practice of purity in thought and behavior. Despite their differences, the relationship between these two movements can be considered one of the core elements of this part of the region.

Another way of looking for *essence of* elements in the region's religious base is to focus on practices that appear on the verge of extinction elsewhere but seem to remain essential to many of the religious factions of Old Appalachia.

Lined singing is certainly rare outside the region, but in central Appalachia there are many Old Baptist factions that refuse to relinquish the tradition, proclaiming that note book singing (the use of either a shape-note or regular-note hymnal) will never satisfy. Furthermore, even when these groups do not practice lining, they still refuse to allow musical instruments within their services, except for some Regular Baptist and United Baptist weeknight sings and prayer services.

Another practice that has become strongly fixed to the religion of Old Appalachia is that of creek or river baptisms, so fixed, indeed, that most publications on Appalachian religion feature a photograph of at least one such event. In addition, a highly popular piece of religious art displayed in traditional Appalachian churches is one of the many renderings of Christ being baptized in the Jordan River. The image is perhaps second in popularity only to pictures of the Last Supper.

Often referred to in southern and central Appalachia as either living water baptisms or natural water baptisms, these creek immersions so capture the essence of old-time religion that accounts abound of non-immersion denominations occasionally feeling compelled to practice the custom when a new convert demands it. McCauley, in *Appalachian Mountain Religion: A History*, reports a story offered by a Methodist minister of one of his newly won souls rejecting sprinkling in favor of immersion.

Foot washing is another religious practice that has become strongly identified with Old Appalachia, so much so that preservation of the practice is a defining symbol for the "old" part of this entire culture. Moreover, an attitude of ready and eager participation in this rite appears essential for individuals who seek to be totally involved in any of the denominations or sub-denominations that preserve the practice.

Nevertheless, the ritual provokes a multitude of sensitive issues. There is debate over crossing of gender lines in the service, even whether a husband and wife may wash each other's feet. There is the question of whether two members of a fellowship may repeatedly wash each other's feet to the exclusion of the feet of other church members. There is an issue of closed communion, whether the service should be open only to members of the individual church or association. And even more delicate, there is a modern day question of whether a female participant can involve herself in the rite while wearing stockings or pantyhose. Some of the most traditional of the Old Regular Baptists view the latter as a clear deviation from the procedural requirements suggested by the Gospel of John.

Two final practices that should be included among those *essence of* factors relate to preaching expectations. The first is the insistence that the preacher extemporaneously deliver all sermons, thus precluding any formal preparation. Second is the assumption that truly blessed preaching is recognizable through its speed, passion, and rhythmical delivery. The general rationale is that human-prepared sermons can only be human discourse, while extemporaneous preaching at least gives God the opportunity to control the message. Then these expectations about delivery styles imply that one way of recognizing blessed preaching is through its transcendent mode of address, a rising to chant or song. These expectations are found not only within the various Old Baptist sub-denominations (including in this case many Free Will and Missionary Baptist factions), but also very broadly among the Pentecostal and Holiness-Pentecostal persuasions.

Future studies of religious traditions may discover ties that run throughout the Appalachian Mountains. Until then, diversity may be viewed as the most distinctive characteristic of the region's religion.

—Howard Dorgan, *Appalachian State University, Emeritus*

Dickson D. Bruce Jr., *And They All Sang Hallelujah: Plain-Folk Camp-Meeting Religion, 1800–1845* (1974); Paul K. Conkin, *American Originals: Homemade Varieties of Christianity* (1997); Loyal Jones, *Faith and Meaning in the Southern Uplands* (1999); Bill J. Leonard, *Christianity in Appalachia: Profiles in Regional Pluralism* (1999); Deborah V. McCauley, *Appalachian Mountain Religion: A History* (1995).

Adventist Denominational Family

Adventism refers to belief in the Second Coming, or Second Advent, of Christ in recorded history. Among Adventist groups Christ's return is thought to be imminent or already underway, and many adherents espouse particular practices, doctrinal statements, and behavioral guidelines in the conviction that following them will prepare the faithful for, if not speed the arrival of, the Second Advent.

Most Adventist bodies in Appalachia have roots in the early 1840s Millerite movement associated with William Miller (1782–1849). Aided by publicist Joshua Himes, Miller became a popular lecturer, primarily in the region just beyond the northern reaches of Appalachia. Miller set a precise date for the Second Advent, October 22, 1843, revising it to October 22, 1844, when nothing transpired. That the Advent never occurred is sometimes referred to as the Great Disappointment. Those caught up in the Millerite movement later provided Seventh-Day Adventist founder Ellen White with her first followers.

A more moderate Adventism emerged from the Restorationist movement that for a time in the nineteenth century had its major center in Bethany, West Virginia, where Alexander Campbell and the Disciples of Christ had established a home base. Over time, the millennialist doctrine of the Campbellites became muted, although some smaller offshoots of the Campbellite movement, such as the Christadelphians, still have clusters of adherents within Appalachia who sustain a lively belief in the imminent return of Christ.

Among groups in Appalachia with direct links to Millerite Adventist expectation, two are very small. The Advent Christian Church, with headquarters in Charlotte, North Carolina, was one of the first coherent clusters to emerge following the Great Disappointment; it has fewer than 350 congregations nationwide. The Primitive Advent Christian Church, with fewer than a dozen congregations, broke off from the Charleston, West Virginia, Advent Christian Church following a debate over foot washing and the rebaptism of backsliders who returned to the church. The Primitive Advent Church, now centered near South Charleston, West Virginia, supports both practices; the parent body does not.

A third group, the Church of God General Conference (Abrahamic Faith) has more tenuous connections to the Millerite movement but some ties to the Advent Christian Church. It began among independent Adventist congregations in the area stretching from Lancaster, Pennsylvania, to central Indiana. Solidly Adventist but non-Trinitarian in theology, this group insists that only those found worthy at the Last Judgment will receive immortality. The Christadelphians also espouse many distinctive ideas of the Church of God General Conference. Their founder, John Thomas, worked briefly with Alexander Campbell, absorbing his brand of millennialism. Thomas is commonly associated with Richmond, Virginia, where his followers first adopted rudimentary organization. Thomas also lived for a time in Waterloo, Iowa, where in 1888 a Church of God General Conference gathering adopted articles of faith similar to Christadelphian beliefs.

The largest denomination issuing from the Millerite movement, the Seventh-Day Adventist Church, is also the largest Adventist group in Appalachia. What set this group apart from others emerging from the Great Disappointment was founder White's conviction that much of ancient Hebrew law remains binding. Her followers thus worship on the Sabbath (Saturday, or the seventh day) and keep to the dietary codes set out in Leviticus. White also had a profound interest in health and health care. The early sanitariums in Battle Creek, Michigan, and the dietary interests of Adventist J. H. Kellogg (later of cereal fame) reflected these concerns. This interest in health issues remains central to Seventh-Day Adventists today.

Especially striking is the expansion of Seventh-Day Adventists deep into central and southern Appalachia. Most Adventist churches owe their genesis to traveling preachers or persons who went on lecture tours, usually speaking in cities where lectures were popular forms of entertainment. In some cases, Adventism took hold because families holding such beliefs relocated and attracted others to their way of thinking. Then, too, salesmen of religious books, also known as colporteurs, traveled across the nation, including into Appalachia, selling Adventist literature. All these were vital to bringing the Seventh-Day Adventist message to the heart of Appalachia. But the significant Seventh-Day Adventist presence in central and southern Appalachia also owes much to evangelists who used the typical southern tent revival and camp meeting to promote Adventist views.

The earliest documented Seventh-Day Adventist presence still continuing in the South dates to 1876 in the area around Quitman, Georgia, where Adventist tent meetings were held through the 1880s. In 1876, too, a congregation formed in Sparta, Tennessee, on the Cumberland Plateau. Colporteurs were at work through the 1880s, sparking enough interest that the publishing arm of the denomination established a branch in Atlanta in 1889 that remained a separate agency for nearly a century. Four years earlier, a thriving congregation had emerged in Graysville, Tennessee, about thirty miles north of Chattanooga. That congregation became a symbolic center of Adventist activity in Appalachia, especially after a training school was established in 1892. The school is the direct antecedent of Southern Adventist University, located now in Collegedale, Tennessee. Camp meetings continued to spur Adventist growth in Tennessee; one such 1900 meeting in Harriman resulted in a congregation that soon boasted more than four hundred members.

Elbert B. Lane preached the Adventist gospel around the Nashville area as early as 1871, holding meetings in the Edgefield Junction railroad station. African Americans who came to these meetings, though sitting in a separate area of the station, organized a congregation in the 1880s. African American congregations remain administratively segregated in the South Central Conference, which includes churches in Kentucky, Alabama, Tennessee, Mississippi, and parts of Florida.

Early in the twentieth century, the Adventists' commitment to health care led to the establishment of the Madison Rural Sanitarium near Nashville (now the Tennessee Christian Medical Center). As Adventists became more numerous, they also became more visible in the public eye. The practice of keeping a Saturday Sabbath but endorsing Sunday work made them especially suspect, and Adventist annals record occasional arrests during the first few decades of the twentieth century for violating local Sunday ordinances.

Evangelistic meetings were responsible for planting a Seventh-Day Adventist presence in Kentucky in the 1870s, where early success came in Hardin County, south of Louisville. Rapid growth led to the formation of the Kentucky-Tennessee Conference in 1876. Evangelist G. K. Owen crossed the border from Kentucky to bring the Adventist message to the Springville, Tennessee, area in 1881.

Distribution of Adventist publications provided the main impetus for establishing Adventist congregations in West Virginia by the late 1870s. Soon after, Isaac Sanborn, a Seventh-Day Adventist evangelist from Virginia, came to the Charleston area; the first congregation established in the state, in Jerry's Run, near Charleston, dates to 1881. Camp meetings around Parkersburg later that decade extended Adventist influence across the state as attendance sometimes exceeded one hundred persons. At the same time, Adventist gatherings around Asheville, Brevard, Mount Pisgah, and elsewhere in the French Broad River Valley assured that Adventism would become a permanent part of the religious culture of North Carolina's Appalachian region.

By the close of the twentieth century, Seventh-Day Adventists had marked out a distinguished history in the heart of Appalachia. There were enough white congregations to have three separate conferences (Georgia-Cumberland, Kentucky-Tennessee, and Mountain View) with nearly thirty-five thousand members in the late 1990s in central and southern Appalachia. The African American South Central Conference took in almost twenty-four thousand more. This nationally largest of Adventist bodies has carved a solid place for itself in the Appalachian religious landscape.

Jehovah's Witnesses represent yet a different strand of Adventist thinking. They owe their birth to a Bible study group started by Charles Taze Russell in Pittsburgh in 1872. Russell, fascinated with the idea of Christ's impending return, posited a heavenly Second Advent in 1914. It then became imperative to preach the imminent return of Christ to Earth, which some believe will come before the generation living in 1914 has died. According to Jehovah's Witness doctrine, when Christ finally establishes God's reign on Earth, only 144,000 will attain heavenly existence; most Witnesses will spend eternity in an earthly paradise.

After Russell died in 1916, Judge Joseph F. Rutherford became the unquestioned leader of the Jehovah's Witnesses. Blessed with keen organizational ability, Rutherford restructured the movement into the Watch Tower Bible and Tract Society, still the formal designation for the movement. Headquarters remain in Brooklyn, New York, where Russell moved them in 1909.

Witnesses tend to be concentrated in urban areas, even in Appalachia. They owe their growth to an aggressive program of door-to-door evangelism, achieving much success among African Americans. Because they believe Christ's rule has already begun for believers, Witnesses (known internally as publishers) have little use for any human government. Their refusal to bear arms, salute the flag, or otherwise participate in any political activity has brought general suspicion, occasional persecution, and numerous court cases involving members. Nonetheless, Jehovah's Witnesses continue to flourish wherever they have set up a Kingdom Hall.

Whether rooted in the millennialist speculation of William Miller, the Restorationist convictions of reconstituting the New Testament church with its apocalyptic expectation, or the unique Bible teaching of Charles Taze Russell and later Witnesses, Adventism remains a multifaceted and enduring component of Appalachian religious life.

See also: CAMPBELL, ALEXANDER; CHRISTIAN DENOMINATIONAL FAMILY.

—Charles H. Lippy, *University of Tennessee at Chattanooga*

Dennis Pettibone, *A Century of Challenge: The Story of Southern College, 1892–1992* (1992); *Seventh-Day Adventist Encyclopedia* (2nd edition, 1996); Arthur W. Spalding, *The Hills o' Ca'liny* (1921).

African American Religious Traditions

Although they first came into the mountains as slaves, freemen, or maroons (former slaves who had escaped bondage), little is known about the religious life of African Americans who lived in eighteenth- and early-nineteenth-century Appalachia.

Typically, white Appalachians did not own slaves, and those who did owned few. Even in the larger valleys, the

Mrs. Fred Brim leading choir, Ararat Church, Patrick County, Virginia, 1978. Originating in African American churches, gospel music has become a significant aspect of worship throughout Appalachia.

slave population in southern Appalachia never approached that of the lower South. In most cases, slaves worked alongside members of their owners' families and worshiped, often in segregated seating, at their owners' churches. Most were either Methodist or Baptist although some were Presbyterian, Episcopalian, Lutheran, or other denominations. Documents from this period indicate that a few black pastors preached to both blacks and whites and that, in rare churches in which black members became the majority, separate services for slaves were sometimes initiated.

After the Civil War, blacks created their own churches, where they could freely practice their own versions of Christianity, which often combined elements of African religion with those drawn from evangelical Christianity. These separate churches were established either with the assistance of white congregations or associations (the New Covenant Baptist Association of northwestern North Carolina and adjacent Virginia was sponsored by the white Mountain Union Baptist Association founded by pro-Union Baptists), by white denominations (Colored Methodist Episcopal), or solely through the efforts of local blacks who wanted to control their own spiritual and religious lives. In the years immediately following the Civil War, published popular accounts described lengthy candle- and torch-lit services in remote mountain locations that incorporated dancing, singing of melancholy dirge-like hymns, and shouting that could be heard for miles.

Although most Appalachian African Americans have historically been Baptist, many chose the Methodist faith, of which the African Methodist Episcopal and African Methodist Episcopal Zion Churches are representative. While most Baptist churches were created through spontaneous organization by local preachers and laity (the African Zion Baptist Church of Malden, West Virginia, is said to have spawned 386 additional Baptist churches in that state), the Methodist churches were founded through the active planning and missionary efforts of those denominations.

The African Methodist Episcopal and African Methodist Episcopal Zion denominations were founded in the North prior to the Civil War. The Colored Methodist Episcopal Church—later the Christian Methodist Episcopal Church—separated from the white Methodist Episcopal Church South. Others remained in the Methodist Episcopal Church North, an organization active in missionary work and in establishing new churches among urban African Americans. Some, but never many, Appalachian blacks have been Presbyterian, Congregationalist, Episcopalian (Reverend James Kennedy, an African American, was appointed Archdeacon of the Diocese of Western North Carolina in 1920), Roman Catholic, and Cumberland Presbyterian.

Denominations such as the Christian Church in east Tennessee and southeastern Kentucky were particularly active in Appalachia, attracting many black converts and establishing numerous black churches. One black Christian preacher, Samuel Allen Russell, established three churches in Tennessee and one each in North Carolina and Kentucky and claimed to have baptized more than thirteen hundred converts. Also notable in Appalachia is the Krimmer Mennonite Brethren mission, of which the North Carolina District is the denomination's sole African American district.

There is also a history of more interracial religious activity in several areas of Appalachia as compared to the lowland South. This appears to be especially true in the coalfields of central Appalachia, where blacks and whites have historically worked and worshiped together. Conversely, Charles Horace Hamilton, who cowrote *The Role of the Church in Rural Community Life in Virginia*, discovered attendance at white-only churches in Virginia rose proportionately to the percentage of blacks in the local population.

By the beginning of the twentieth century, Holiness and Pentecostal churches were becoming increasingly popular with African Americans. In Appalachia, some of these denominations began as interracial fellowships, as was the case with the Fire Baptized Holiness Church founded in Anderson, South Carolina, in 1898. Due to the spread of Jim Crow legislation, the black members withdrew and founded the Colored Fire Baptist Holiness Church in 1908, with headquarters in Greer, South Carolina. Today, black charismatic churches in Appalachia remain a minority. More commonly found in urban areas, they are usually racially homogenous and often affiliated with major black charismatic organizations such as the Church of God in Christ.

Americans in the early decades of the twentieth century experienced the rise and rapid spread of African American gospel music. The gospel blues soon replaced the older black spirituals and lined-hymn singing as well as the assimilated denominational music of the dominant majority culture. Isolated instances of the older traditions persist, but gospel music holds sway in most of Appalachia's black churches regardless of affiliation. From the influential hotbeds of quartet singing in Birmingham, Alabama, and Spartanburg, South Carolina, to the solo recording careers of artists such as the Reverend Gary Davis, Blind Gussie Nesbit, and Sister O. M. Terrell, to West Virginia's Black Sacred Music Festival founded by singer/pianist Ethel Caffie-Austin, African Americans of Appalachia have significantly contributed to gospel music.

African American Christians in Appalachia have incorporated much African music, oratory, worldview, and religious rituals into their faith, leading some to observe that black Christians did not so much convert to God as converted God to themselves. Black Appalachian religion also reflects American democratic independence in the tendency of its practitioners to subdivide their churches and associations over small differences in belief or ritual. Blacks in Appalachian Virginia, for example, are reported as having more churches, fewer members per church, and more preachers than elsewhere in the state. Studying African Americans in a small West Virginia community, one black anthropologist even wondered if there were not a Methodist hell and heaven separate from the Baptist hell and heaven.

The black church in Appalachia serves the spiritual needs of African Americans and continues to be a primary social institution for the maintenance of community. It also serves as school, social club, mutual support and protection agency, and, especially in urban areas, as the hub of civil rights activity.

See also: GOSPEL MUSIC, AFRICAN AMERICAN (MUSIC); KENNEDY, JAMES; MENNONITES.

—Fred J. Hay, *Appalachian State University*

Wilson Fallin Jr., *The African American Church in Birmingham, Alabama, 1815–1963: A Shelter in the Storm* (1997); Loyal Jones, "Interracial Harmony in Three Eastern Kentucky Churches and Communities," *Appalachian Quarterly* (March 1997); Katherine Siemens Richert, *Go Tell It on the Mountain: The Story of the North Carolina–Tennessee Mennonite Mission* (1984).

Anointment

See Baptism of the Holy Spirit

Appalachian Ministries Educational Resource Center

Appalachian Ministries Educational Resource Center is a nonprofit organization based in Berea, Kentucky. Founded in 1985 by Mary Lee Daugherty, the center promotes cross-cultural and field-based education for theology students, faculties, and other Christian leaders. Through funding, resources, and consultation, the center enables the training of persons for church leadership in Appalachia and in similar rural and urban settings. Integrating practical experience with theology, courses expose participants to Appalachian rural culture, economic and social issues, and religious traditions.

Within the United States, this is the largest consortium-sponsored effort in the history of theology education. Students in the center's courses have represented fifty-two denominations and include Protestants, Catholics, and Eastern Orthodox Christians. The consortium members come from colleges, universities, and theology schools in the United States and Canada. Denominational judicatories or other church organizations overseeing the development of congregational leaders are also eligible to be consortium members. The broadly based ecumenical membership includes conservative and traditional mainline denominations.

Prior to 2000, the center conducted educational programs for seminarians and other religious leaders interested in ministry in Appalachia and other rural areas. Focus on forms of in-the-field and in-contact education led by knowledgeable guides and interpreters helped participants experience regional culture, economics, ecology, and religious traditions.

Thereafter, the center redirected its resources to fund and support courses organized and run by consortium member schools. Seminars focus on issues such as small church pastoring, religious and social contexts of Appalachia, economic systems of rural America, community development, and living in healthy balance with the land. Appalachian Ministries Educational Resource Center provides funding for the seminars, assists in identifying course leaders (mentors), and also provides technical assistance and library resources. The library, which is available to center-funded classes, contains around two thousand volumes focusing on issues that coincide with the center's mission.

See also: COALITION FOR APPALACHIAN MINISTRY.

—Lisa Rosenbarker, *Appalachian Ministries Educational Resource Center*

Asbury, Francis

(1745–1816) Methodist bishop and circuit rider.

Francis Asbury is best known as the founder of American Methodism. As the first Appalachian circuit rider, or itinerant preacher, Asbury traveled on horseback, gathering congregations in boardinghouses, schools, cabins, orchards, mills, taverns, and even at public hangings, preaching throughout the eastern United States and across the Appalachian Mountains. Asbury, born in Birmingham, England, volunteered to go to Pennsylvania in 1771 as an evangelist for the founder of Methodism, John Wesley.

Although he never renounced his British citizenship, Asbury remained in the United States after the Revolutionary War to lead the establishment of the Methodist movement in the American frontier. He preached from three hundred to five hundred sermons each year. During his career, he covered a total of 270,000 miles, perhaps the greatest mileage ever compiled by a horseman, and crossed the Appalachian Mountains sixty times. Incapacitated by rheumatism, asthma, and pleurisy, he was unable to stand to preach for the last seven years of his ministry, though he continued to ride.

In 1784 Asbury was ordained a superintendent, or bishop, of the Methodist Episcopal Church. When Asbury arrived in the colonies, he found about a dozen Methodist preachers. By the time he died in 1816, more than four thousand Methodist ministers had been ordained in America, and the number of practicing Methodists had increased from 1,200 to 214,000.

See also: METHODIST CIRCUIT RIDERS; METHODISTS.

—Heather Ann Ackley Bean, *Azusa Pacific University*

Associations, Baptist

American Baptists inherited the designation *associations* from their British General and Particular Baptist forebears who during the 1640s and 1650s gathered their individual churches into alliances that promoted the common good of all members. Consisting of delegates from local churches who elected officers and established deliberative processes, these association bodies instituted bylaws, articles of faith, and rules of decorum that unified the individual churches into each respective doctrinal camp while preserving considerable local church autonomy.

Philadelphia Association, a Particular Baptist body founded in 1707, was not the first such organization established in the colonies, but it became the most influential, notably for those Baptists who found their way onto the trans-Allegheny frontier. Subscribing to the Philadelphia Confession of Faith (1742), these Baptists spawned a number of Particular or semi-Particular divisions that now constitute the Old-Time Baptists of southern and central Appalachia.

Elkhorn (1785) and Holston (1786) became the first Baptist associations established west of the Alleghenies, the former holding to Particular election doctrine and the latter combining fellowships from both Particular and General election traditions, even though at its formation Holston adopted the Philadelphia Confession. Following their late-nineteenth-century beginnings, each of these early Appalachian Baptist alliances either split several times, "armed off" (amicably separated) associations, or influenced the foundation of other groups. These now constitute the line of Appalachian Old-Time Baptists called Regulars, Old Regulars, Uniteds, and several varieties of Primitives, plus a number of the region's more Arminian Baptist clusters.

Scheduled over a weekend in late summer or early fall, Baptist Association Times are intense three-day gatherings for worship, business, and fellowship. Typically, the Friday morning sitting of delegates opens with singing, followed by prayer and one or more sermons. Statements of peace and love, or letters, are then received from member churches, accompanied by annual reports on membership statistics. Church letters also list delegates and alternates, who, after being seated, elect officers for the ensuing year. The remainder of Friday morning is devoted to such standard business as appointing committees, receiving reports, seating messengers from corresponding associations, and approving any new member churches. Following the midday dinner on the grounds, committees meet while the remaining delegates and visitors enjoy additional singing and preaching. Further business is conducted on Saturday, and Sunday is devoted to worship and celebration of the association's unity.

One of the first reports heard Saturday morning is that of the Committee on Arrangements, which may place on the agenda issues that engender controversy: queries concerning faith and practice or concerning relationships with other associations or member churches. Associations may go for years in total harmony, then face an issue that splits the organization into two or more divisions. The history of Appalachian Old-Time Baptists is marked by separations of this kind that have permanently changed the course of doctrinal developments.

See also: BAPTISTS, THE OLD-TIME GROUPS.

—Howard Dorgan, *Appalachian State University, Emeritus*

F. W. Sacks, *The Philadelphia Baptist Tradition of Church and Church Authority, 1707–1814* (1989); W. B. Shurden, *Associationalism among Baptists in America, 1707–1814* (1980); William Warren Sweet, *Religion on the American Frontier: The Baptists* (1964).

Backsliding

The term *backsliding* is used not only in Appalachia but throughout the South, and to a large extent wherever in the United States there are Christian churches following an Arminian (free will) atonement doctrine. In direct contrast to Calvinism (the doctrines of John Calvin), Arminianism (the doctrines of Jacobus Arminian) argues that individuals, of their own free will, choose salvation through acceptance of the Christian faith and its concomitant behavioral codes. As a direct corollary to that free-will choosing, backsliding is when the Christian elects to stop believing and falls away into sin and faithlessness.

The concept of backsliding is viewed very differently by Calvinistic believers who see salvation/regeneration/ redemption as the consequence of God's having elected the individual to a state of grace. Cycles of salvation, then falling away, followed by a return to the faith and perhaps more backsliding constitute evidence of that person's not having been elected in the first instance. Calvinists usually insert into their articles of faith a statement to the effect that the truly redeemed can never fall away.

See also: ELECTION; MISSIONARY/ANTI-MISSIONARY SPLIT.

—Howard Dorgan, *Appalachian State University, Emeritus*

Balch, Hezekiah

(1741–1810) Presbyterian minister and educator.

Hezekiah Balch, a prominent pioneer Presbyterian minister in east Tennessee, was the founder and president of Greeneville College, which united with Tusculum Academy after the Civil War and ultimately became Tusculum College. Although inoperative with no college courses offered until 1805, Greeneville was called by some the first college west of the Appalachians, that distinction later passing on to Tusculum.

Born in Maryland, graduated from Princeton, Balch taught school before being licensed by the New Castle Presbytery in 1768. After ministering in South Carolina, Maryland, and Virginia, he moved in 1782 to what is now Tennessee. He spent much of the next few years involved in creating a separate trans-Appalachian presbytery and in engaging in various theological disputes. He also spoke against slavery and in 1807 emancipated his own slaves.

Soon after arriving in Tennessee, Balch began to raise money for and to seek the chartering of Greeneville College. He accomplished this goal in 1794, apparently before Blount College, the forerunner of the University of Tennessee, was established. Charles Coffin, Balch's longtime aide, succeeded him as president at Greeneville and served until his own death in 1827. After that, the college continued in a weakened state until forced by financial considerations to unite with Tusculum Academy. It was not until the twentieth century that the institution formally became known as Tusculum College.

See also: DOAK, SAMUEL; PRESBYTERIAN DENOMINATIONAL FAMILY.

—Ira Read, *Appalachian State University*

Baptism of the Holy Spirit

Also known as *anointment*, the phrase *baptism of the Holy Spirit* refers to the experience of being endowed with special powers as a consequence of Holy Ghost possession. Associated with several Appalachian religion families, but most pointedly with Pentecostal denominations, this belief is that during intense spiritual moments the worshiper may become anointed by the third Trinitarian entity, the Holy Spirit. Thus the worshiper is able to feel, understand, or act as the ordinary human condition would not permit. Such people have been known to shout ecstatically; fall into trances or faint (perishing in the Spirit); practice glossolalia (speaking in tongues); prophesy; heal or be healed; and experience any of the revival exercises. Among these exercises are running in the Spirit, jerking in the Spirit, and dancing in the Spirit.

Pentecostals draw this doctrine from the Acts 2 account depicting the anointment of Christ's twelve disciples. They hold that baptism of the Holy Spirit occurs as a blessing distinct from both salvation and sanctification. To believers, proof of its having occurred is the ability to speak in tongues, which is the special empowerment given to Christian witnesses in the last days before the Second Advent of Christ. Charismatic groups operating in other Protestant and Roman Catholic traditions have also embraced baptism of the Holy Spirit.

See also: HOLINESS-PENTECOSTAL FUSION; PENTECOSTALS; REVIVAL EXERCISES.

—Diane Price, *Appalachian State University*

Baptist Denominational Family, the Mainline Groups

As a movement originating in Protestant Separatism, Baptists came into existence in the early 1600s and arrived in North America not long after. By the 1700s, they had found Appalachia to be fertile soil for the faith. Today, Baptists number more than 30 million, with a sizeable representation in the northern and southern regions of Appalachia. Indeed, many Baptist divisions in Appalachia are unaffiliated with any nationally based denomination. However, four national branches of the denomination do have a presence in Appalachia: the American Baptist Churches, the General Association of Regular Baptist Churches, the National Baptists, and the Southern Baptist Convention.

Although ethnically, regionally, and theologically diverse, these four Baptist divisions have a shared belief in personal autonomy concerning doctrinal decisions; in local church autonomy; in reliance on the Bible rather than creeds; and in religious liberty. This commitment to local church autonomy places congregational concerns above organizational ones.

Excluding the formation of those early trans-Allegheny Baptist associations such as Elkhorn (1785) and Holston (1786), the beginning of denominational life in Appalachia and elsewhere in America centered on the emergence of national agencies supportive of home and foreign missions. America's first national Baptist organization was the General Missionary Convention of the Baptist Denomination in the United States for Foreign Missions. Formed on May 18, 1814, in Philadelphia, this society, popularly known as the Triennial Convention, solicited membership from congregations, other entities, and individuals, primarily to pool funds in support of missionaries. Soon, Baptists formed other organizations for benevolent endeavors, and collectively these alliances became the basis of a de facto denomination. Because of the Calvinistic and anti-missionary leanings of many Appalachian Baptists, there was some regional resistance to affiliation with these new national and urban-based structures. However, other congregations joined in the development of Baptist denominationalism with enthusiasm.

The Southern Baptist Convention was formed in 1845 after two separate instances in which the Triennial Convention and the closely related American Baptist Home Mission Society excluded slaveholders from participation. During a meeting in Augusta, Georgia, leading Baptists in the South withdrew from these organizations and formed the convention. Unlike divisions in the Presbyterian and Methodist denominations, this split did not involve a centralized denomination; Baptists did not have such at the time. Instead, this was a break from the two mission societies. Nevertheless, the Augusta gathering, in addition to withdrawal from these agencies, resulted in the creation of a centralized denomination.

Formed with a special interest in both home and foreign missions, the Southern Baptist Convention quickly established a presence outside the eleven states of the Confederacy and in the twentieth century embraced an agenda of national expansion. Today, approximately forty-one thousand churches and more than 15 million members make it the largest Protestant denomination in the nation. Southern Baptist churches can be found in all fifty states, and the denomination has a significant presence in all of Appalachia.

Since 1979, Southern Baptists have faced conflicts centered on internal politics and biblical interpretation. Their leadership strictly supports biblical inerrancy, which, among other consequences, has resulted in the exclusion of women as pastors. Large numbers of progressive Southern Baptists who do not share such beliefs or who do not believe they should be binding on local congregations have shifted their involvement with the Southern Baptist Convention to the Cooperative Baptist Fellowship, which also has a strong presence in Appalachia, although exact statistics are difficult to determine.

Withdrawal of Southern Baptists from the aforementioned mission societies contributed significantly to a regionalism in America's Baptist identity; the two societies remained in existence, but with their financial support now coming largely from the North. Then, while southerners were in the process of forming a centralized denomination, Baptists outside the South retained the society approach to denominational life: they did not immediately join a central denomination but instead sent their money to several different Christian-outreach agencies. In 1905, however, the more centralized Northern Baptist Convention was organized, renamed in 1950 the American Baptist Convention and then, in 1972, the American Baptist Churches in the USA.

Although smaller than the Southern Baptist Convention, the theologically diverse American Baptist Churches in the USA has a strong national presence, with more than five thousand churches and approximately 1.5 million members. This membership includes a major presence in northern Appalachia, but it also encompasses West Virginia as the majority Baptist community.

Early in the twentieth century, Northern Baptists faced theological conflicts similar to those faced by Southern Baptists in the 1980s. In the end, the factions opposed to fundamentalism prevailed. As a result, in 1932 a pro-fundamentalist caucus within the Northern Baptist Convention, the Baptist Bible Union, formed a new denomination, the General Association of Regular Baptists, claiming to hold the historic "regular" doctrinal positions of Baptists, as opposed to the "irregular" positions of the Northern Baptists. While the first organizational meeting was in Chicago and did not include Appalachian representatives, the General Association of Regular Baptists today has a presence in Appalachia, although rather small.

When in the 1700s large numbers of enslaved African Americans became Christians, they tended to choose the loose structures and spirited worship of frontier Baptists. However, only in the late 1800s did African American Baptists form national denominations. Today, most African American Baptists are referred to as National Baptists, a term that identifies three different denominations: the National Baptist Convention of the United States of America, Inc.; the National Baptist Convention of America; and the Progressive National Baptist Convention. The oldest of these, the National Baptist Convention of the United States of America, Inc., formed in 1895 when a foreign mission society, a home mission society, and an educational society merged. Today, this denomination has more than seven million members and thirty thousand churches. A 1915 division over the ownership of the denomination's publishing agency resulted in the formation of a second denomination. Unofficially known as the National Baptist Convention, Unincorporated, the denomination has close to three million members and eleven thousand churches.

In the 1950s, the National Baptist Convention of the United States of America, Inc., faced another period of strife over the power concentrated in the office of the convention president and the question of limiting the president's time in office. Connected to this debate were differences in the proper role ministers should play in the growing Civil Rights movement. After a heated 1960 convention, several prominent National Baptists, including Martin Luther King Jr., gave their support to the creation of the Progressive National Baptist Convention. This denomination has worked to establish shared leadership in its structure, with clear limits on the powers of denominational leaders. While this denomination has only one million members—considerably smaller than its parent body—it operates in the mainstream of American life and has had many nationally prominent ministers besides King, including Jesse Jackson.

See also: ASSOCIATIONS, BAPTIST; BAPTISTS, THE GENERAL-ATONEMENT, NON-MAINLINE UNITS; BAPTISTS, THE OLD-TIME GROUPS.

—Merrill M. Hawkins Jr., *Carson-Newman College*

William H. Brackney, *The Baptists* (1988); Leon McBeth, *The Baptist Heritage* (1987); Robert Torbet, *A History of the Baptists* (1950).

Baptists, the General-Atonement, Non-Mainline Units

Baptist denominations such as Free Will, General, and Missionary Baptists do not fit well under either the mainline or the Old-Time Baptist headings. *Mainline* traditionally references the larger sub-denominations of this faith, and *Old-Time* labels those smaller Baptist sects that have strong historical connections to either the Regular Baptists or the Separate Baptists and have preserved high degrees of eighteenth- and nineteenth-century traditionalism. Although several reasons exist to call some of the mountain Missionary Baptists "Old-Time," that sub-denomination as a whole groups more easily with Free Will and General Baptists, primarily because of doctrinal connections. Also, General Six-Principle Baptists are certainly Old-Time in terms of origins, but they do not meet that second criteria of being derived from either Regular or Separate Baptists. In fact, they actually predate both. Consequently, a grouping has been established simply on the grounds that Free Will, General, and Missionary Baptists share a theology grounded in Arminian general-atonement doctrine but are not mainline.

General Baptists

In England, the General Baptists originated in Gainsborough, Lincolnshire County, during the first decade of the seventeenth century, initially under the leadership of John Smyth. *General* was adopted to signify the movement's acceptance of an Arminian general-atonement doctrine that contrasted with the Calvinistic doctrine avowed by Particular Baptists. Generals are credited with establishing in 1612 the first Baptist church in England. Particulars did not organize there until 1633.

British General Baptists, however, had little direct influence on the institution of American General Baptists, who emerged from splits occurring in colonial churches that earlier had become Particular fellowships: Providence (split 1652), Newport (split 1665), and Swansea (split c. 1680). Also, these early colonial-era General Baptists emerged as Six-Principle Baptists, since their doctrines required six things—repentance, faith, baptism, a practice of laying hands on new converts, a belief in the resurrection of the dead, and an affirmation of eternal life for the redeemed. The laying-on-of-hands rite strongly distinguished the Generals from the Particulars, the latter being uncomfortable with these procedures because of what they seemed to symbolize concerning human involvement in the salvation process. The belief was that the hands ceremony allowed the convert to receive the Holy Spirit. During the colonial period, Particulars often were called Five-Principle Baptists, given their rejection of this one practice.

The only General Baptists in Appalachia today are the General Six-Principle Baptists of Susquehanna County, Pennsylvania, part of a minuscule remnant of the original colonial Six-Principle Baptists. Like their forebears, the Pennsylvania cluster, only twenty-five members (1990 statistics), still holds to the six doctrinal positions. The only other General Baptists close to Appalachia are the churches of the General Association of General Baptists, midwestern fellowships who have several churches in western Tennessee and western Kentucky. These congregations are not Six-Principle Baptists.

Although General Baptists have almost disappeared from Appalachia, they are significant in the influence they have had on the Free Will movement and indirectly on the Missionary movement.

Free Will Baptists

Free Will Baptists trace their American origins to two widely separated beginnings. The first (in North Carolina, 1727) evolved from the leadership of Paul Palmer, a General Baptist; the second arose (in New Hampshire, 1780) from the efforts of Benjamin Randall. This latter preacher had been a Great Awakening convert who initially joined the Particular Baptists (1776) but came to his own general-atonement position by rejecting the Calvinistic leanings of preachers such as George Whitefield.

The Palmer and Randall movements did not merge until 1935 in Nashville, Tennessee, remnants of both movements formed the National Association of Free Will Baptists. Nevertheless, it was the Palmer movement that became more strongly influential in Appalachia and the lower South, with adherents sometimes being called General Baptists and at other times labeled Free Will Baptists. Histories of both the Free Will churches and the General churches include Palmer in their stories. Meanwhile, much of Randall's movement ultimately fused after 1845 with the Northern Baptists, later American Baptists.

Currently, Free Will Baptists are strongly represented in Appalachia, although it is impossible to attach a precise number to their presence. This counting problem is due to the region's large distribution of wholly independent Free Will fellowships, many of which have adopted some Pentecostal practices (speaking in tongues, healing, perishing in the Spirit, running in the Spirit, and the like). There is a formal organization named the Pentecostal Free Will Baptist Church, but these fellowships are found in eastern North Carolina. The Appalachian independent Free Will fellowships are Free Will first and Pentecostal second, usually not having the latter term in their official names.

Two formal Free Will Baptist associations do operate in Appalachia, the larger of which is the National Association of Free Will Baptists, headquartered in Antioch, Tennessee, with churches in 122 of the 410 Appalachian counties in 2002. Clifford A. Grammich Jr., who conducted a 1990 enumeration of Appalachian region Associated Baptists, reports 94,271 National Association of Free Will Baptists memberships within Appalachia. One especially strong affiliate is the West Virginia State Association of Free Will Baptists, with more than 180 fellowships. A second group, the John-Thomas Association of Freewill Baptists (*freewill* as one word), has strong representation in southwest Virginia and eastern Kentucky, with additional churches in Ohio and Indiana. A final Free Will association is the United American Free Will Baptist Conference, an African American organization operating primarily in Florida and which apparently has no churches in Appalachia.

Missionary Baptists

Missionary Baptists in Appalachia are also difficult to canvass, again because of the large number of independent fellowships affiliated with no larger association or convention. Highly traditional in their worship practices, these small independent fellowships usually select their pastors from among non-seminary-trained preachers, reject the use of artificial baptisteries in favor of creek baptisms, practice foot washing as an extension of their annual communion services, occasionally reject instrumental music, and sometimes employ hymnals that use shaped notes. In addition, their preachers frequently deliver completely extemporized sermons that follow the song/chant pulpit style so notable among Appalachian Old-Time Baptists.

Missionary Baptists became prominent in Appalachia as early as the 1820s as a consequence of the missionary/anti-missionary split. Supporting the Arminian position on atonement and the concomitant evangelistic practices, these fellowships parted from the strongly Calvinistic Baptists who called themselves Old Line, Old School, or Primitive.

Some Appalachian Baptists do belong to Missionary associations; perhaps the largest is the Baptist Missionary Association of America, which has churches in at least seventeen counties and a total regional membership of approximately ten thousand. There also are smaller Missionary associations in the region, such as the Enon Missionary Baptist Association and the Old Missionary Baptist Association. The latter maintains traditional practices that make them similar to the Old Regular Baptists and the United Baptists, the main difference being that the Old Missionaries are Arminian in theology. Grammich places 5,432 Old Missionary Baptists in the Appalachian regions of Tennessee, Kentucky, and West Virginia.

See also: BAPTISTS, THE OLD-TIME GROUPS; ELECTION; MISSIONARY/ANTI-MISSIONARY SPLIT.

—Howard Dorgan, *Appalachian State University, Emeritus*

W. F. Davidson, *The Free Will Baptists in America, 1727–1984* (1985); Clifford A. Grammich Jr., *Appalachian Atlas: Maps of the Churches and People of the Appalachian Region* (1994); B. R. White, *The English Baptists of the Seventeenth Century* (1983).

Baptists, the Old-Time Groups

The Appalachian region, particularly its central portions, has a rich diversity of small Old-Time Baptist churches and associations. Although not always counted in religious affiliation canvasses, these churches and their associations are among the leading religious bodies in several central Appalachian counties. Much recent scholarship has examined the origins of these groups, their current theologies, their size in the region and elsewhere, and their prospects for the future.

United Baptists, Old Regular Baptists, and Primitive Baptists are prime examples of Old-Time Baptists. Such groups are direct descendants of the first Baptists to cross the Appalachian Mountains in the late eighteenth century, and they still maintain many eighteenth- and nineteenth-century traditions. Among these are lined a cappella singing, rhythmically chanted impromptu preaching, congregational shouting, tactile worship behavior, foot washing, natural water baptism, traditional gender codes, restrictions on divorce and remarriage, and roughly similar liturgical formats. Additional characteristics include the belief in the King James Bible, an emphasis on the ancient origins of their faith, a nonprofessional clergy without formal religious education, opposition to missions, rural origins and membership, and stable growth at home with some losses through migration. Their theological beliefs lie between predestination and free will, generally holding that the plan of salvation is preordained but individual outcomes are not. The *Old-Time* label is not just for scholarly convenience. Some of these Baptists refer to themselves as "old-time" or "old-fashioned," principally to contrast themselves with Southern Baptists and with other "modern" Baptists who generally are more aggressive in evangelization.

These characteristics are not exclusive to Old-Time Baptists, and not all such churches and associations share them. These characteristics, however, do reflect the core doctrine and practice of these churches, particularly those fellowships whose only organization outside the local congregation typically is an association of neighboring churches of like faith and order. Among some representative bodies comprising the Old-Time associations of central Appalachia are United, Old Regular, Primitive, Central, and Enterprise Baptists.

Histories and Theologies

Many characteristics of these Baptists can be traced to Separate Baptists and Regular Baptists who settled the region in the late eighteenth and early nineteenth centuries. From a 1755 settlement in what is now Randolph County, North Carolina, Separate Baptists expanded into southwestern Virginia, across the Blue Ridge into east Tennessee, and along the Cumberland River in Tennessee and Kentucky. By the mid-1780s, the South Kentucky Association of Separate Baptists was formed. Separate Baptists originally held Calvinistic beliefs, but their evangelistic zeal and suspicion of written creeds led them to emphasize free will and general atonement. From practices of Separate Baptists, Appalachian Baptist associations have developed traditions of emotional services led by lay clergy who have had no formal theological training.

From their first congregations near Baltimore and in Pennsylvania, Regular Baptists moved into the Shenandoah Valley in the mid-eighteenth century, then into southwestern Virginia, North Carolina, east Tennessee, and eastern Kentucky. Elkhorn Association, the first Regular Baptist association west of the Alleghenies, was founded in 1785. Regular Baptists relied on the Philadelphia Confession for their Calvinism, and from these Regular Baptist traditions, Appalachian Baptist associations developed strains of Calvinism in a theology today that for most is between predestination and free will.

Drawing on Separate and Regular roots, Appalachian Baptists developed their own particular histories and theologies. Among the first instances of this practice was the formation of the United Baptist tradition, which has its origins in a movement for unity among Separates and Regulars along the southern Appalachian frontier in the late eighteenth century. These churches sought a greater sense of Baptist community, but without encroachments by outside authority. Separates in the movement agreed to de-emphasize their free will doctrines, while the more Calvinistic Regulars agreed to allow special customs such as foot washing.

Among the first United Baptist associations was Burning Spring of eastern Kentucky, still extant today. The journey of this association from its United Baptist origins to its current Primitive Baptist theology indicates how many of these associations have developed their own indigenous theologies.

The oft retold history of New Salem Association, which began by "arming off," or separating amicably, from Burning Spring Association in 1825, provides details of how the indigenous theologies of these associations can develop. New Salem, like Burning Spring, began as United Baptist, but by 1870 was styling itself as a more traditional Regular or Old Regular association. Throughout most of the last half of the nineteenth century, New Salem held a doctrine of limited rather than general atonement during a time when it also developed, as did Primitive Baptists, opposition to institutions such as missionary societies, Sunday schools, and Masonic lodges. In 1891 New Salem stopped short on its apparent path toward absolute predestination, resolving it could not endorse a doctrine that could hold God to be the author of sin. Since then Old Regular doctrine has occupied a place between predestination and free will, holding that humans do not control, by will or work, their own salvation. Rather, the call and salvation come from God, while still requiring certain behavioral responses from the recipient of the call.

The story of the Eastern District Primitive Baptist Association and the Central Baptist Association illustrates further themes of indigenous theological development. Eastern District separated from the Mulberry Gap Association of United Baptists in east Tennessee in a dispute over support of foreign missions. Eastern District initially became an orthodox Primitive Baptist association, but in 1956 several churches left to start the Central Baptist Association. Taking their name from strictures in the Book of Joshua to vary neither to the right nor to the left in following the laws of scripture, Central Baptists seek to do works of charity and evangelization that Primitive Baptists do not undertake. Eastern District, while retaining an article of faith supporting election according to the foreknowledge of God, later modified its own theology to the point that its beliefs and practices are now closer to those of the Southern Baptist Convention than to those of other Primitive Baptists.

These histories are illustrative rather than definitive for these groups as a whole. There are elements of faith and practice common to all Old-Time Baptists—most notably a literal, though still varying, interpretation of the King James Bible, an approach that allows flexibility and does not lead to unwavering legalistic formulas. Unlike many evangelical fundamentalists, they do not feel a need to resolve biblical ambiguity or to employ theological semantics to find scriptural answers to all problems of daily life. Rather than emphasizing an unchanging Bible, these Baptists are more likely to engage in their own indigenous theological development, recognizing new lessons from their faith as time and circumstances change. The ambiguity of such faiths, when coupled with emphasis on local church autonomy, can lead to these varying interpretations, each held with equal fervor. A traditional joke about Baptists generally holds particularly well for these associations: two brethren engaging in doctrinal discourse are likely to end up with four theologies.

Present and Future

The "old-time" image of these churches may lead observers to question whether these associations will soon pass from the Appalachian scene. Although there are few reliable statistics to document long-term trends and prospects, the indicators that do exist show these faiths are likely to persist in the Appalachian region for quite some time, particularly in the rural parts of central Appalachia.

United Baptists are the largest of these groups, comprising 77,396 adherents in 476 churches of 120 counties nationwide in 1990—nearly three in five members of Old-Time Baptist churches in Kentucky belong to United Baptist congregations. The largest concentration was counted in a group of fifteen contiguous counties in northeastern Tennessee and southeastern and south-central Kentucky, the second-largest concentration in a group of twelve counties near the border between Kentucky and West Virginia. About half of all United Baptists are in these two areas, but United Baptist churches have also been established as far apart as Arizona, Idaho, Florida, and Wisconsin.

In the same year, Old Regular Baptists numbered 19,257 adherents in 326 churches of 94 counties in states spread as far apart as Arizona, Florida, Maryland, and Washington. Three-quarters of Old Regular Baptists lived in a small band of eleven contiguous counties in Kentucky, Virginia, and West Virginia. Central Appalachian emigres have established Old Regular Baptist churches in areas of Indiana, Michigan, and Ohio.

Of approximately 49,000 Primitive Baptist adherents enumerated in the 1990 church membership study, about one-third were in Appalachia, most prevalently in eastern Kentucky, southwestern Virginia, and northeastern Tennessee. Primitives are generally recognized as being split into different groups. The most numerous are single-predestinationists, who believe in the predestination of the elect but reject the idea that God has predestined all things.

As noted, the doctrine of the Eastern Primitive Baptist Association has evolved to the point that this group, while comprising about one in seven enumerated Primitives nationwide and more than a third of those in Appalachia, barely remains inside the single-predestinationist tradition. Eastern District Primitives are most concentrated in southwestern Virginia and northeastern Tennessee. The Central Baptists who separated from them are centered in the nearby Tri-Cities area of east Tennessee and are unique among Old-Time Baptist groups for their comparatively urban concentration.

Again, as in the histories noted above, these statistics are illustrative rather than definitive. With a complete enumeration of these churches and their adherents unavailable and perhaps impossible to compile, only illustrative data can be offered. Nevertheless, the available statistics do indicate some characteristics that probably apply to these particular groups as a whole.

Old-Time Baptists are rural or have clearly rural origins. The overwhelming majority of them are in nonmetropolitan counties. Even in rural counties their churches tend to be located in the countryside, away from the county seat. Some of these churches are now in urban areas, either because rural migrants to urban areas started new congregations or, less frequently, because urban areas have encroached upon these rural churches.

With very few statistics available for comparisons across time, growth patterns are difficult to discern. The limited indicators show that these groups have had stable and proportional growth within their areas. Many of these areas have experienced declines or fluctuations in population or have not otherwise kept up with national population growth. Because of these trends and because of the loss of migrating members to areas without communing churches, it is likely that these groups have not kept up with national population growth.

There is no evidence indicating any drastic loss of membership over the years. What one sees instead are churches that have maintained their presence in home areas. These churches have been a unique part of the Appalachian religious scene for many years, as well as one of the most important religious influences in some core parts of the region. While this degree of importance is not always recognized, their presence and influence is likely to persist for many years to come.

See also: ASSOCIATIONS, BAPTIST; FOOT WASHING; LINED SINGING; LIVING WATER BAPTISM.

—Clifford Grammich, *Downers Grove, Illinois*

Howard Dorgan, *The Old Regular Baptists of Central Appalachia: Brothers and Sisters in Hope* (1989) and "Old-Time Baptists of Central Appalachia," in *Christianity in Appalachia: Profiles in Regional Pluralism*, ed. Bill J. Leonard (1999); Clifford A. Grammich Jr., *Local Baptists, Local Politics* (1999); Deborah V. McCauley, *Appalachian Mountain Religion: A History* (1995); John H. Spencer, *A History of Kentucky Baptists* (1886).

Barking

See Revival Exercises

Brasher, John Lakin

(1868–1971) Holiness evangelist and Methodist Episcopal minister.

In 1900 in Birmingham, Alabama, John Lakin Brasher's heritage of upland South, plain-folk revivalism, coupled with the Wesleyan doctrine of sanctification as a second work of grace, led him to identify with the Holiness movement. He thereafter traveled more than seven hundred thousand miles to preach in hundreds of camp meetings and revivals. Nevertheless, he remained a minister in the Methodist Church throughout his life.

Born in Greasy Cove, near Attalla, Alabama, Brasher grew up in an abolitionist, Unionist, Republican family. His father, Reverend John Jackson Brasher, voted against secession at the Alabama Secession Convention and chartered in Alabama the reorganized (northern) Methodist Episcopal Church. After serving ten years as pastor of Methodist Episcopal churches in northern Alabama and Tennessee, Brasher graduated as valedictorian from U. S. Grant University School of Theology, Chattanooga, in 1899.

Acclaimed by many as the premier Holiness preacher from the South, Brasher drew upon a repertoire of traditional Appalachian tales to augment the eloquent, formulaic themes he employed in preaching. He served as president of both John H. Snead Seminary, a Methodist Episcopal secondary school in Boaz, Alabama, and Central Holiness University (later John Fletcher College) in Oskaloosa, Iowa. His diverse Holiness itinerancy took him to primitive "brush-arbor" meetings and to such middle-class resort towns as Ocean Grove, New Jersey, where he shared the preaching with William Jennings Bryan. Brasher preached with vigor through his 102nd year and claimed to have expounded the Wesleyan doctrine of sanctification longer and later in life than any other person.

See also: CHURCHES OF GOD–HOLINESS; GREAT WESTERN REVIVAL AND CAMP-MEETING MOVEMENT; HOLINESS-PENTECOSTAL FUSION.

—J. Lawrence Brasher, *Birmingham-Southern College*

Brethren

The Brethren have deep roots in Appalachia. Indeed, many members of this historic peace church migrated to the mountains of Pennsylvania, Maryland, Virginia, North Carolina, and South Carolina soon after the Brethren initially settled near Germantown, Pennsylvania, in the 1720s. From these first Appalachian settlements, the Brethren then spread westward in the early 1800s to what became West Virginia, Tennessee, and Kentucky. Today, roughly 45,000 of the nation's 145,000 Brethren nurture their spiritual lives in the Appalachian region.

The Brethren originated from an Anabaptist and Pietistic faith community that ultimately splintered into several separate denominations. Today, only two of those church bodies are active in Appalachia: the Church of the Brethren, considered the original German Baptist Brethren fellowship, and the Old German Baptist Brethren who moved their separate way in the 1880s.

Anabaptists were radical sixteenth-century Reformationists who believed only in adult baptism and who refused to bear arms, use force of any kind, or serve in government positions. German Pietism dates to the seventeenth and eighteenth centuries, springing from a German Lutheran movement to restore, among other objectives, the devotional and personal piety goals of the Christian faith. Touched by both of these influences, the Brethren originated in Schwarzenau, Germany, in 1708 during the religious persecutions of the Thirty Years War. Alexander Mack founded an initial community of only eight believers; because of the continual persecution waged against them, however, these Brethren immigrated in 1729 to Pennsylvania, where Mack joined his coworker, Peter Becker, who had fled to the colony a decade earlier. The original Germantown congregation of Brethren had been founded on Christmas Day 1723.

In Pennsylvania, Brethren were able to worship more freely, an essential condition for them since their faith compelled them to create communities based on the membership's interpretation of New Testament Christianity. Prominent among their beliefs was a commitment to nonviolence rooted in the principle that all people are God's people. They also cultivated their version of a simple lifestyle modeled on their interpretation of the Sermon on the Mount beatitudes.

In terms of sacraments, the Brethren developed a unique form of baptism that earned them the derisive title *Dunkards*. They believed that the New Testament called them to baptize through immersion three times forward in the name of the Father, Son, and Holy Spirit. In addition, as in Jesus' recorded baptismal experience, they believed that baptism should involve an adult decision. Finally, the Brethren developed a unique communion service: a foot washing, followed by the communion meal, and then the bread and cup.

Brethren governance structures evolved over the years. Their first Annual Meeting, also called Big Meeting, was instituted in 1742. At these yearly gatherings, Brethren developed a practice of presenting queries to be considered by the whole body. These questions dealt with such issues as the church's peace witness, slavery, the simple life, church governance, and a whole host of spiritual concerns. The first Annual Meeting of the Brethren in an Appalachian setting was staged in 1794 in Virginia's Shenandoah Valley. Then the Blackwater Brethren of Franklin County, Virginia, hosted an Annual Meeting in 1797. At this later gathering, the Brethren drafted a historic document detailing their opposition to slavery.

In the early years of the church, the location of the Annual Meeting represented Church of the Brethren strongholds such as Huntingdon, Pennsylvania, or Roanoke, Virginia. The Old German Baptist Brethren have chosen smaller rural communities for their sites, convening their Big Meetings in Virginia locations such as Hollins Station, Burnt Chimney, and Boones Mill, where huge tents were pitched on Brethren farms.

In recent times, both the Church of the Brethren and the Old German Baptist Brethren have resorted to districts in an attempt to address their spiritual and geographical growth. This has enabled Brethren to voice their faith stances within local forums first. If district queries are consensually accepted, they are then presented to the voting delegation, consisting of district representatives, at the Annual Meeting.

Church of the Brethren ministers are both men and women and are called from their local congregations, paid for their services, and often educated at Bethany Theological Seminary. Within the Old Order Brethren, elders are men only, and though local bodies also call them to serve, there is no paid ministry or formal preparation.

Though few in number, the Brethren have made many contributions to the Appalachian region and beyond. Within Appalachia, for example, the Brethren have established two liberal arts colleges. In 1876 Andrew B. Brumbaugh, a physician, founded the first in Huntingdon, Pennsylvania, along with his two publisher cousins, Henry and John Brumbaugh. Today known as Juniata College, this small, independent school enrolls thirteen hundred students on a one-hundred-acre campus. The second institution, Bridgewater College, founded in 1882, became the first coeducational liberal arts school in Virginia. This college enrolls about a thousand students.

One of Bridgewater's most noted graduates, Michael Robert Zigler of Broadway, Virginia, helped develop several pan-Protestant relief organizations such as the Heifer Project International (founded by a Brethren, Dan West) and the Christian Rural Overseas Program. As the Brethren's delegate to the World Council of Churches in 1950, Zigler also helped to establish the Brethren Service Committee that enabled Brethren to go into many war-ravaged countries in order to distribute millions of dollars worth of clothing, food, and medicines. Many Appalachian Brethren youth have participated in Brethren Volunteer Service, the model program for America's Peace Corps, to help with projects as varied as overcoming racial intolerance to relief work in the Third World.

Young and old have been nurtured in Appalachia by Brethren institutions. The denomination's youth enjoy camps such as Camp Galilee in West Virginia, Camp Bethel in Fincastle, Virginia, and Camp Harmony in western Pennsylvania. Brethren retirement homes, such as Friendship Manor in Salem, Virginia, can also be found in Appalachia.

Many Brethren farms, handed down for generations, still exist in Appalachia. Brethren farming communities have been prominent in state soil and water conservation initiatives and have experimented with numerous alternative conservation farming practices.

See also: KLINE, JOHN; LOWE, WILLIAM; MOOMAW, B. F.

—Beatrice Naff Bailey, *Clemson University*

Donald F. Durnbaugh, *Fruit of the Vine* (1997) and ed., *The Brethren Encyclopedia* (1983).

Call to Preach

See Preachers and Preaching: Old-Time Baptist Exhorters

Campbell, Alexander

(1788–1866) Religious reformer and educational leader.

Alexander Campbell and his father, Thomas Campbell, along with the leader of the Cane Ridge revival, Barton W. Stone, were influential in the Presbyterian theological shifts that established the Christian denominational family, which consists of the Christian Church (Disciples of Christ), the Christian Churches, and the Churches of Christ, all present in Appalachia.

Born in the north of Ireland, Alexander immigrated to western Pennsylvania with his mother and siblings in 1809, where he reunited with his father, who had made the trip two years earlier. Originally members of the Old Light, Anti-Burgher Seceder branch of the Church of Scotland, both father and son became distressed by Presbyterian divisions and created a unity organization named the Christian Association of Washington, Pennsylvania. Later, this organization became the Brush Run Church, affiliating with the Redstone Baptist Association in 1815. However, within fifteen years Alexander Campbell had parted ways with the Baptists over issues such as the legitimacy of creeds and the purpose of baptism. Campbell had begun to refer to his followers simply as "disciples of Christ," emphasizing the reunification of all Christians in local churches that mirrored the primitive Gospel fellowships.

Following his marriage in 1811 to Margaret Brown, Alexander Campbell moved to Brooke County, Virginia (now West Virginia), where he became owner of the Brown family farm. There he lived until his death in 1866, not only running the farm, but also operating a printing business and the local post office, which he named Bethany. Between

1820 and the mid-1850s he and his reform views became widely known through his debates with Presbyterians John Walker, William Maccalla, and Nathan Rice and with agnostic Robert Owen and Roman Catholic Bishop John Purcell. He disseminated his views in two periodicals, *The Christian Baptist* (1823–30) and the *Millennial Harbinger* (1830–70), as well as in books such as *The Christian System* (1839) and *Christian Baptism* (1851).

Campbell represented western populist sentiments in the 1829 Virginia Constitutional Convention. Opposing the Tidewater gentry, he advocated universal suffrage for white males as well as universal education of youth. In 1840 Campbell obtained a charter from Virginia for the establishment of Bethany College, now in West Virginia.

After a meeting in Lexington, Kentucky, in 1832, many congregations in Stone's Christian movement united with Campbell. In 1860 the total national membership of the Stone-Campbell movement was approximately 200,000, with most of its 2,100 congregations located in Appalachia. Congregations of the Christian Church (Disciples of Christ), Christian Churches, and Churches of Christ could be found in 384 of the 410 counties included in the Appalachian Regional Commission's map of Appalachia in 2002.

See also: CHRISTIAN DENOMINATIONAL FAMILY; STONE, BARTON W.

—Douglas A. Foster, *Abilene Christian University*

Perry Epler Gresham, *The Sage of Bethany: A Pioneer in Broadcloth* (1960); Robert Richardson, *Memoirs of Alexander Campbell: Embracing a View of the Origin, Progress and Principles of the Religious Reformation Which He Advocated* (1868–70); James Seale, ed., *Lectures in Honor of the Alexander Campbell Bicentennial, 1788–1988* (1988).

Camp Meetings

See Great Western Revival and Camp-Meeting Movement

Cane Ridge Revival

See Great Western Revival and Camp-Meeting Movement

Carried Out (Blessed, Quickened, Revelated)

See Preachers and Preaching: Old-Time Baptist Exhorters

Cartwright, Peter

(1785–1872) Methodist circuit rider.

Peter Cartwright, central to the growth of Appalachian Methodism, was one of the most colorful preachers America ever produced. Born in Amherst County, Virginia, he moved with his family to Logan County, Kentucky, where Methodist circuit preachers often visited the family's frontier cabin. At sixteen Cartwright experienced a camp-meeting conversion and joined the Methodist Episcopal Church. In 1802 he was licensed as an exhorter by Jesse Walker and began riding a circuit of his own, preaching wherever people would open their homes.

In 1806 Bishop Francis Asbury ordained him as a deacon, and in 1808 he became an elder. Then in 1812 he was appointed a presiding elder (now district superintendent), a position he held for fifty years, longer than any other minister in the Methodist Church. During fifty-three years of preaching throughout Kentucky, Tennessee, Ohio, Indiana, and Illinois, Cartwright received ten thousand members into the Methodist faith, baptized twelve thousand, conducted more than five hundred funerals, and preached more than fifteen thousand sermons.

To avoid raising his children in a slave-owning state, Cartwright moved from Kentucky to Illinois in 1824, remaining there the rest of his life, helping in 1824 to found the Illinois Annual Conference. He was elected to sixteen General Conferences and served for sixteen years as a member of the Illinois state legislature. In 1846 Abraham Lincoln defeated him in a bid for a congressional seat. Cartwright also helped found McKendree and MacMurray Colleges and Illinois Wesleyan University.

See also: ASBURY, FRANCIS; METHODIST CIRCUIT RIDERS; METHODISTS.

—Heather Ann Ackley Bean, *Azusa Pacific University*

Catholicism

The Catholic Church is the second largest of the Christian groups found in Appalachia. That statistic, however, may be misleading. The Appalachian Regional Commission defined Appalachia in 2002 as including 410 counties covering all or part of thirteen states stretching from the lower tier of counties in New York to the northeastern corner of Mississippi. In this region, Catholicism has more than 2.5 million church adherents, the majority of whom can be found in New York and Pennsylvania. The remaining are concentrated in the counties of West Virginia's two panhandles, one near Wheeling to the west and the other in the counties along the Maryland state line near Harpers Ferry and Berkeley Springs. A significant concentration of Catholics can also be found in the suburban counties north of Atlanta with lesser numbers located in the larger cities of Appalachia such as Chattanooga and Knoxville, Tennessee. In the late 1990s approximately 230,000 Catholics lived in central Appalachia.

Europeans began settling Appalachia in the second half of the eighteenth century. Catholics probably made up a small proportion of these settlers. However, since the U.S. Census was not begun until 1790, there is little evidence beyond a study of surnames found in the region to support this conjecture. It is known that a wide spectrum of European immigrants settled in northern Appalachia—Germans, Belgians, French, Swiss, and Anglophones from various regions—while in central and southern Appalachia a proportionately larger number of Anglophones (Irish, Scots, Welsh, and English) made their homes. As time passed, northern Appalachia experienced an even stronger influx of Catholics, particularly in the second half of the nineteenth century. By the mid-twentieth century the majority of the people who lived in northern Appalachia were Catholic.

Catholicism historically has been a small statistical minority in central and southern Appalachia. However, the first Catholic bishop to reside in the South, John England of Charleston, South Carolina, observed in 1829 that more than three million people who were once Catholic lived in his diocese, which embraced the Carolinas and Georgia. While his figures were probably inflated, one can surmise that Catholics made a notable presence in the southern mountains.

The earliest Appalachian Catholic parishes were found in the north. The first important pioneer of Catholicism in the region was Prince Gallitzin, known as Father Augustine Smith. A member of the Russian nobility, Gallitzin began a mission at Latrobe, Pennsylvania, in 1789. From there he worked in the areas around Pittsburgh and even ventured into the hills of Maryland and Virginia (now West Virginia). There is evidence that Catholics lived in the southern mountains in 1800 in what is now Nicholas County, West Virginia. It was here that a prominent family named Duffy owned an estate and ardently sought the services of a priest. This particular migration of the faith probably occurred by way of the Shenandoah Valley.

In 1815 Catholic churches existed in what today is White Sulphur Springs, West Virginia; the first parish in Wheeling, now Saint Joseph Cathedral, was founded in 1821–22. While parish churches were not established until later, by 1790 priests were regularly visiting and ministering to the needs of local Catholics in Harpers Ferry and Gallipolis–Point Pleasant (Ohio–West Virginia). In this early period of settlement, people were trekking into the mountains from both the east and west. For Catholicism, these excursions originated from heavily Catholic settlements in Maryland; Somerset, Ohio; and Bardstown, Kentucky. In addition, Carolina migrants made their way into Fentress and Sumner Counties in Tennessee during the period from 1741 to 1791. John Sevier, living near Knoxville in 1799, petitioned the Bishop of Baltimore for a priest to serve the needs of a hundred Catholics in this area. The unavailability of priests was a difficulty for mountain Catholics and probably played a role in the denomination's minimal presence in Appalachia.

The first diocese to serve the southern mountains was established in 1850 at Wheeling, (West) Virginia. Significant strides were made as resident bishops began serious efforts to serve the scattered Catholics west of the mountains. However, when a bishop finally moved to the area, there were already at least four parishes: Wheeling, Weston, Wytheville, and one at Harpers Ferry. Parishes without resident pastors could be found at Howesville, Summersville, and Parkersburg.

The first Catholic schools established in the mountains were Visitation Girls Academies at Wheeling in 1846 (a high school followed in 1865) and at Parkersburg in 1864. A third Visitation school was established at Abingdon, Virginia, in 1867. Elementary schools were organized in widely separated areas of the Virginia mountains: Clarksburg, 1866; Grafton, 1859; Proctor, 1854; and Wellsburg, 1857—all of these located in present-day West Virginia. Catholic nuns from Pittsburgh, along with the Visitation sisters and later the Sisters of Saint Joseph from Wheeling, played a major role in these educational efforts.

As the nineteenth century drew to a close, the region became increasingly less isolated. Mining began to flourish in the southern Appalachians, and coal workers were recruited from among recent immigrants from throughout Europe. Soon the region became home to peoples from eastern Europe and the Mediterranean, many of whom were Catholics. Religious order priests began to serve Catholics in the area, with a fair share of these being Benedictines from Alabama (Saint Bernard Abbey) and Latrobe (Saint Vincent Archabbey). Later, Redemptorists and their offshoot, Paulists, frequently roamed the mountains offering revivals to Catholic congregations.

These recruits to the coal-mining region of Appalachia faced great difficulties. Unlike immigrant Catholics to the north, southern Appalachian Catholics seemed unable to establish a strong homogeneous parish community uniquely their own within which to worship while transitioning into their new cultural setting. Although the coal companies often provided church buildings and priests, these parishes were often viewed by mine owners as homogeneously Catholic, rather than mixtures of Hungarians, Poles, Czechs, and so on. With little opportunity to indulge in their own specific cultural traditions, mountain Catholics frequently moved on to more hospitable neighborhoods in the Northeast or simply assimilated as best they could. Their numbers were never sufficient to establish the stronghold ethnic parishes and identities that shaped Catholicism in the urban North.

In 2005 central and southern Appalachia was served by Catholic dioceses in Wheeling-Charleston; Knoxville; Lexington, Kentucky; Steubenville, Ohio; Charlotte, North Carolina; Richmond, Virginia; and Atlanta. The first four primarily served the mountains with approximately 230,000 Catholics registered (1994 statistical estimates). This represented a Catholic population of approximately 7 percent in

West Virginia; in the dioceses of Lexington, 3 percent; Knoxville, 2 percent; and Steubenville, 10 percent. The other three dioceses registered about 455,000 Catholics, but the majority of these resided in the Atlanta, Norfolk, and Charlotte areas, outside of Appalachia. Fewer than 8,000 lived in the Appalachian sections of these dioceses.

While few in numbers, Catholics have made considerable contributions to the region and continue to do so. For more than 150 years, education in small Appalachian towns has been enriched by the presence of Catholic sisters and their schools. Catholicism has also marked a consistent presence of an alternative religious practice. It may represent the most ethnically and socially diverse church tradition to exist in the Appalachian region.

See also: GLENMARY HOME MISSIONERS; GLENMARY SISTERS.

—Lou McNeil, *Georgian Court College*

James H. Bailey, *A History of the Diocese of Richmond* (1959); Christopher J. Kauffman, *Mission to Rural America* (1991); Michael McNally, "The Parish in the Southeast," in *The American Catholic Parish*, ed. Jay Dolan (1987); Lou F. McNeil, "Catholic Mission and Evangelization," in *Christianity in Appalachia: Profiles in Regional Pluralism*, ed. Bill J. Leonard (1999).

Cherokee Religious Traditions

In southern Appalachia, Cherokee religious traditions developed as part of a larger belief system that encompassed religion, psychology, politics, environmental science, and health. Although most Cherokee have been Christians for two centuries, many of their older traditions still survive and are practiced along with their new faith.

Cherokee religion has always focused on a monotheistic belief in the Creator. This deity was all-powerful and omniscient, the one God of the universe. Believed to be present in humans, animals, plants, minerals, and everything else in the world, the Creator was affirmed to be the ambience that connected everyone and everything. Identified in Cherokee language as neither male nor female, this spiritual entity was judged to be the same god worshiped by all religions.

However, most early European observers were misled by the Cherokee integration of religious beliefs and the natural world and reported the native faith to be polytheistic. For example, Cherokee prayers at sunrise were interpreted as supplications to a sun god, when in fact they were to the Creator, offered at sunrise simply because this was the beginning of the day. Likewise, Kanati and Selu were described as gods when in fact they were the Cherokees' first man and first woman.

In addition to being monotheistic, Cherokee religion was integrated with the physical world and daily life; the physical world was seen as a gateway to the Creator rather than as a barrier to that spirit. Unlike much of traditional Christian thought, there was no nature/spirit dichotomy in Cherokee theology.

Cherokee religious traditions built on one unifying principle, *duyuktv*, a concept that has been variously translated as "balance," "the right way," and "truth." The consensus of the Cherokee elders and scholars who collaborated on exhibit text for the Museum of the Cherokee Indian, Cherokee, North Carolina, further explained being in balance as assuming responsibility for one's actions, focusing on the good of the whole (family, tribe, and land), taking only what is truly needed, and existing in harmony with nature. Additionally, Cherokee thought recognized three aspects of human life: physical, mental, and spiritual. Therefore, being in balance also meant recognizing these aspects of oneself, listening to them, and responding to their needs. In addition, balance suggested being in harmony with one's neighbors—treating them in a way one wanted to be treated. This worldview was based on the premise that people are part of the one great life made by the Creator. Rather than being separate from nature, people were viewed as part of nature. Nevertheless, humans were seen as having a unique responsibility in being caretakers of the earth.

Several religious practices helped the Cherokee maintain balance: "going to water," using the sweat lodge, employing prayer formulas, dancing, and celebrating the annual Green Corn Ceremony. Historically, going to water was performed at sunrise by all Cherokee people, facing east across running water. Prayers were said and people entered the water, emerging purified and ready for another day.

The sweat lodge ceremony took place in an *asi*, a low log building covered with earth. The ceremony could be accompanied by drums and dancing, or it could be a lone act of spiritual renewal. Its purpose was the purification of the body, mind, and spirit. At one time, every household had an *asi* among its dwellings, while the medicine person of the village had a larger *asi* that he or she used. A combined religious and secular facility, the *asi* was both a place for religious ceremonies and also a structure for winter warmth.

Other ceremonies were also observed. Originally, prayer formulas were employed only by people who possessed special knowledge of their forms and powers, but after the creation of a Cherokee written language, some medicine people recorded these prayers, which subsequently became used before hunting, before a ball game, to cure diseases, and to effect healing. Cherokee traditional dances were considered sacred, educational, and social. Many dances were themselves a form of prayer. Smoking the pipe was a ceremony that specifically offered prayers to the Creator. Finally, the annual Green Corn Ceremony—still performed—was staged in the fall of the year and combined purification ceremonies, dances, marriages, fasting, feasting, and thanksgiving for the harvest.

In addition to these traditions, religion permeated every aspect of life. For example, balance was maintained in hunting and gathering and in interpersonal relations. Only the fourth plant (or one in four) was harvested, and some were carefully cut above their roots so they would regenerate. Fish and game were taken only as they were needed. Individuals were expected to take responsibility for their actions, and personal freedom was balanced with respect for elders, children, and the rights of all. Differences were valued, and competition in game was balanced with cooperation as a whole.

Cherokee religious traditions have changed over time. From about A.D. 900 to 1550 the Cherokee, along with other southeastern tribes, participated in what is known as Mississippian culture, identified by its agriculture, art forms, technology, and common ceremonies and religious activities. Scholars hypothesize that a surplus of corn and beans enabled some individuals to function solely as a priestly class. Indeed, a Cherokee myth relates the rise to power of such a class, the Ani-Kutani, who abused their authority only to be killed by the people, after which hereditary priesthood was abolished. This myth may recount the end of the Mississippian period.

In 1800 missionaries began living among the Cherokee. Moravians were the first, followed by Presbyterians and Baptists. By 1828 the Cherokee were printing Bibles and hymnbooks translated into the Cherokee language. Baptist missionary Samuel Worcester was jailed for remaining on tribal lands in defiance of a repressive Georgia law, and his case was pursued all the way to the U.S. Supreme Court, resulting in the decision affirming the sovereignty of Native American nations (*Worcester v. Georgia*, 1832). Some missionaries accompanied the Cherokee on the Trail of Tears, along with the Cherokees' own Cherokee Christian ministers.

Today, most members of the Eastern Band of Cherokee Indians (a federally recognized tribe of 12,500 people living on the Qualla Boundary in western North Carolina) are Christian. Their churches include Baptist, Methodist, Catholic, Pentecostal, and Church of Jesus Christ of Latter-Day Saints. Many hymns are still sung in English and in Cherokee. While some ministers preach against Cherokee religious traditions, many church members combine traditional beliefs and the Christian message with little sense of contradiction.

See also: CHEROKEE MUSIC (MUSIC).

—Barbara R. Duncan, *Museum of the Cherokee Indian*

Marilou Awiakta, *Selu: Seeking the Corn-Mother's Wisdom* (1993); Michael Tlanusta Garrett, *Walking on the Wind: Cherokee Teachings for Healing through Harmony and Balance* (1998); James Mooney, *History, Myths, and Sacred Formulas of the Cherokee* (1992).

Christian Denominational Family

In the late 1700s several groups that shared a desire to reform Christianity by restoring its primitive beliefs and practices arose on the Appalachian frontier. Most used the label *Christian* to emphasize their nonexclusive character. These groups included the Christian movement led by Baptists Elias Smith and Abner Jones; the Christian Church of Methodist James O'Kelly in Virginia and North Carolina; the Kentucky Christians under Presbyterian Barton W. Stone; and the Disciples movement led by Thomas and Alexander Campbell in western Pennsylvania and western Virginia.

The Smith-Jones Christian Churches were located primarily in Vermont and New Hampshire but were connected with the Appalachian O'Kelly and Stone churches. O'Kelly's movement emerged from a controversy over authority in the recently constituted (1784) Methodist Episcopal Church. Francis Asbury had organized American Methodism along Episcopalian lines with bishops having final decision-making authority in church matters. Many Americans, however, favored a more democratic structure. O'Kelly led the opposition to Asbury, introducing a resolution at the 1792 General Conference that would have given ministers the right to appeal their appointment.

When O'Kelly's resolution was defeated, he withdrew from the Methodist Episcopal Church, taking with him around ten thousand members. The following year O'Kelly and his followers organized themselves as Republican Methodists at Manakintown, Virginia. However, in August of 1794 at Old Lebanon in Surry County, Virginia, they rejected all names but *Christian* and made allegiance to the Bible the only test of fellowship. By 1810 the movement had churches from Pennsylvania to Georgia.

The Barton-Stone movement originated in central Kentucky near Paris, in Bourbon County. Stone was a Presbyterian minister who migrated to Kentucky via North Carolina and Tennessee in 1796. Influenced by America's liberty rhetoric, Stone rejected the fatalism of the Westminster Confession and divisions perpetuated by denominational structures. He hosted the famous Cane Ridge sacramental meeting at his church in August 1801. Opposition to such meetings by the Synod of Kentucky led to his withdrawal in 1803, when he and other Presbyterian ministers formed the Springfield Presbytery. In June 1804, however, they ended the organization's life by publishing the *Last Will and Testament of the Springfield Presbytery.* The signers urged readers to take the Bible alone as the only sure guide to heaven. Despite the early desertions of other original leaders, by the late 1820s Stone's movement had spread across Appalachia and beyond.

The other major movement was led by Thomas and Alexander Campbell. Emigrants from the North of Ireland

and members of the Associate Synod, a dissident branch of the Church of Scotland, the Campbells, too, were deeply affected by what they saw as a possibility in America of bringing the church back to a pure and united state. Their main goal was to restore the beliefs and practices of the early church as spelled out in the Bible. They understood the New Testament to function as a constitution for the church as the Old Testament had functioned as a constitution for the Israelites.

The Campbell movement drew heavily from Baptist ranks after Alexander Campbell's adoption of adult immersion in 1812. Eventually expelled from Baptist associations, the churches of the Campbell movement most often used the generic term *disciples* because of Campbell's uncertainty about the doctrinal orthodoxy of some of the groups that used the label *Christian*. The spheres of influence of the Stone and Campbell movements began to intersect in the 1820s. After a meeting in Lexington, Kentucky, in late December 1831, many congregations of the two movements united.

Stone's churches had identified themselves loosely with the O'Kelly and Smith-Jones Christians early in the century; however, many in these groups objected to Stone's union with the Campbell movement, accusing Campbell of holding a cold and rational religion. The Stone churches that refused to enter the union remained in communion with the other two Christian movements, in what is often referred to as the Christian Connexion. This body eventually merged with the old Congregational Church in 1931 to form the Congregational Christian Church. This latter group in turn merged with the Evangelical and Reformed Church in 1957 to form the United Church of Christ, which has a presence in Appalachia through the existence of congregations connected to the O'Kelly and Stone bodies.

By the 1830s churches of the Stone-Campbell movement had spread throughout Appalachia from New York to Mississippi. Then, by 1860, the Stone-Campbell movement had become one of the most significant religious bodies in the United States with a total national membership of approximately two hundred thousand and with most of its twenty-one hundred congregations located in Appalachia.

In more recent times, however, the movement has suffered two divisions. By the early 1900s congregations that rejected the use of instrumental music in worship and the legitimacy of extra-congregational organizations such as missionary societies were identified separately as Churches of Christ. The second division crystallized when congregations that refused to accept the 1968 restructuring that produced the Christian Church (Disciples of Christ) withdrew to form the nondenominational Fellowship of Christian Churches and Churches of Christ, often known as Independent Christian Churches. In both cases the divisions were more complex than were the surface issues and took decades to run their course. The three Stone-Campbell groups were represented in 384 of the 410 counties of Appalachia in 2002.

See also: CAMPBELL, ALEXANDER; STONE, BARTON W.

—Douglas A. Foster, *Abilene Christian University*

Charles Harnbrick-Stowe, ed., *The Living Theological Heritage of the United Church of Christ: Colonial and National Beginnings* (1997); Richard Hughes, *Reviving the Ancient Faith: The Story of Churches of Christ in America* (1996); James B. North, *Union in Truth: An Interpretive History of the Restoration Movement* (1994).

Churches of God–Holiness

Within the Appalachian region, the Church of God (Holiness) denominational family is represented most heavily by congregations affiliated with Church of God (Anderson, Indiana), the oldest Holiness denomination in the United States and a movement not to be confused with the Church of God (Cleveland, Tennessee), a Pentecostal contingent. In addition to the tenets of Wesleyan Holiness movement, members of Church of God (Anderson, Indiana) acknowledge roots deeply grounded in the Protestant Reformation, the Anabaptist free-church tradition, the Puritan-Pietist movements, and Arminian (general-atonement) theology.

According to statistics compiled by Clifford A. Grammich Jr. in 1990, the Church of God (Holiness) family—which includes not only Church of God (Anderson, Indiana) but also Church of God–Seventh Day of Denver, Colorado, and the Churches of God, General Conference—had approximately 282,000 adherents across the nation, with 48,734 of those followers found within 188 counties of Appalachia. The heaviest Appalachian concentrations of these churches are in Pennsylvania, Kentucky, and Ohio, in that ascending order. Representative central Appalachian fellowships of the Church of God (Anderson, Indiana) can be found in Johnson City, Tennessee, as well as Blacksburg, Christiansburg, and Radford, Virginia.

Although not a member of the Church of God (Holiness) denominational family, the Church of the Nazarene also should be mentioned because of this faith's strong affiliation with Wesleyan Holiness theology. The largest of the nation's formal Holiness denominations, the Church of the Nazarene is well represented throughout Appalachia, with 122 fellowships in West Virginia alone, 35 of which are in Kanawha County.

The Church of God (Anderson, Indiana), founded by Daniel S. Warner in 1881, was the first Holiness body to call itself by that name. However, confusion quickly developed when, between 1880 and 1923, numerous small, independent churches having no affiliation with the Church of God (Anderson, Indiana) or the Pentecostal-rooted Church of God (Cleveland, Tennessee) also took that title.

Warner's church body resulted from a split from the northeastern and midwestern Winebrenner Church of God (also known as the Churches of God in North America). Warner and his associates set out to reestablish Holiness theology within all of their churches and to restore unity to the movement. Foremost in their reformation efforts was the forsaking of all denominational hierarchies and formal creeds.

Warner, son of a tavern-keeper turned farmer, was reared in Ohio. A frail man afflicted with tuberculosis from an early age, he had a talent for ministry and began preaching before he ever joined a denomination. Upon discovering the narrow, sectarian Winebrennerian communion in 1878, Warner thought he had found his idea of the apostolic church. However, he was bitterly disappointed when the elders brought charges that he was practicing outside their authority. His subsequent affiliation with a different eldership within the movement lasted only a short time. He soon adopted what became a lifelong spiritual principle: a belief in the visible and invisible church as a congregation of Christians from which no believer was excluded by any human-instituted creeds, rules, or corporate forms of organization. Warner and his followers saw all Christians as members of the Church of God; therefore, even though its adherents could organize to carry out the work of the movement, the Church of God itself could not be organized.

Warner spent most of his spare time in research and writing, and he was also an editor. In that role, he became involved with a newly consolidated paper, the *Gospel Trumpet*, a publication that allowed him to spread Holiness teachings. However, his insights were not always greeted positively. While on a campaign through the South, he and his workers were mobbed and beaten by rival Holiness groups because of stands he had taken against tobacco and in favor of justice for southern blacks.

The Church of God went through several early schisms. Some resulted from the movement's struggles over the meanings of and belief in sanctification, an early Methodist principle that lay at the heart of John Wesley's concept of the second blessing. Other splits occurred over issues, such as the wearing of neckties, that to outsiders may have seemed trivial. Around 1945 the movement was shaken by the attacks of a minority of the group's ministers who believed that the Church of God positions on both social and theological issues had become far too liberal.

The Church of God still has no formal membership, considering all true Christians among its flock. Followers rely heavily on the church's emphasis on conversion, holiness, and attentiveness to the Bible. Congregational in church polity, the Church of God (Anderson, Indiana) has state and regional assemblies that govern its pastors. Each church is locally autonomous, selecting its own Church of God–ordained minister, who may serve as long as is agreeable to both parties.

The movement has welcomed women as ministers since its inception, when fully one-third of its pastors were female. Adherents accept salvation through belief in Christ and also in the second work of sanctification, when all inbred sin is cleansed away. Services usually are informal with expository preaching. Among its practices are energetic singing and the ordinance of foot washing.

National program boards coordinate ministries and resource materials, which include an annual Bible conference in Montreat, North Carolina, and a monthly newsletter, *People to People*. In keeping with its mission, the Church of God (Holiness) also emphasizes "bearing witness" and "making disciples of all nations." Its adherents have congregations in 85 foreign countries, with its heaviest concentration in Kenya. The Church of God (Holiness) also carries out international broadcast ministries comprised of a weekly radio program heard in 165 countries in eight languages.

See also: HOLINESS-PENTECOSTAL FUSION; METHODISTS; PENTECOSTALS.

—Diane Price, *Appalachian State University*

Charles Ewing Brown, *When the Trumpet Sounded: A History of the Church of God Reformation Movement* (1951); Clifford A. Grammich Jr., *Appalachian Atlas: Maps of the Churches and People of the Appalachian Region* (1994); Vinson Synan, *The Holiness-Pentecostal Movement in the United States* (1971).

Churching

Churching, or *exclusion*, is a term employed by many highly traditional southern and central Appalachian church congregations to signify the act of expelling an individual from membership. The term is particularly popular among Old-Time Baptists for whom many behavioral or doctrinal breaches warrant removal from church membership and sometimes from social fellowship. Traditionally not as harsh as shunning, the Amish version of this action, churching still may institute emotional divisions within families, church fellowships, and even the much larger associations. Banishments from fellowship that result from charges of doctrinal irregularities may become especially divisive, frequently generating permanent splits in churches and associations. Thus, individual membership exclusions have occasionally resulted in the ultimate creation of an entirely new subdenomination.

Churching still is practiced among the more traditional Appalachian religious congregations. In 1998 the Union Association of Old Regular Baptists reported fifty-six exclusions among its seventy-four churches. In each of these instances someone in the respective fellowship had to bring formal charges against the errant member, charges that then were deliberated at one of the church's monthly business meetings. The resulting shame experienced by the family of an expelled member may be excruciating.

See also: ASSOCIATIONS, BAPTIST; BAPTISTS, THE OLD-TIME GROUPS.

—Howard Dorgan, *Appalachian State University, Emeritus*

Coalition for Appalachian Ministry

The Coalition for Appalachian Ministry is the largest Presbyterian-Reformed mission agency in Appalachia. Supported by five denominations—Christian Reformed Church, Cumberland Presbyterian Church, Cumberland Presbyterian Church in America, Presbyterian Church (USA), and Reformed Church in America—the coalition's mission is "to make a positive impact wherever the Reformed Tradition and Appalachian culture come together."

In 1964 Presbyterian minister and author Jack Weller convened the Presbyterian Appalachian Council to discuss and coordinate the efforts of judicatories throughout the region. Presbyterian interest in Appalachia swelled with the nationwide War on Poverty, but a restructuring of the two largest Presbyterian denominations in the early 1970s provided the council with little opportunity to voice its concerns.

In 1974 representatives from the Presbyterian Appalachian Council and the restructured synods met to form the Coalition for Appalachian Ministry, a new body given a budget and staff. Six needs were affirmed as the ministry's special responsibility: (1) to devise strategies for the church in Appalachia; (2) to give visibility of the region to the judicatories and to the church at large; (3) to highlight the needs of the small church; (4) to help recruit, train, and support the Appalachian pastor; (5) to offer united strength, through ecumenical channels, to Appalachian missions; and (6) to address pressing social and economic issues facing the region.

Work immediately began on the implementation of these responsibilities. An orientation seminar for new church workers in the region was held, and promotion of the Appalachian Regional School for Church Leaders at West Virginia University was intensified. Attention was given to the "Discovering the Bible with Children" church school curriculum, designed particularly out of the experience with small churches in Appalachia. A newsletter was published.

In 1985 the "Mission Strategy in Appalachia for the Reformed and Presbyterian Churches" was adopted, providing renewed impetus to the coalition's work. The statement began with an interesting confession: "While we have offered much to the region, particularly in the field of education, we have failed to listen for the Word of God in the voice of the people. We have not moved with the people, perceiving their gifts and learning from their spiritual journey." Thereafter, the coalition made understanding the Appalachian experience central to its work.

The Coalition for Appalachian Ministry is located outside Townsend, Tennessee. Its work includes Cabin Crafts, which retails items made by low-income Appalachian families; the Volunteer Recruitment Program, which matches volunteers from churches and universities with community-based sites throughout the region; and the Center for the Study of Religion in Appalachia, which houses publishing and educational work. The coalition's Center for the Study of Religion in Appalachia also encourages and facilitates research and dialogue pertinent to church and community in Appalachia.

See also: PRESBYTERIAN DENOMINATIONAL FAMILY; WELLER, JACK.

—Paul Rader, *Presbyterian Church (USA)*

Commission on Religion in Appalachia

The Commission on Religion in Appalachia was created in 1965 to initiate, support, and coordinate secular and church-based antipoverty projects at the grassroots level throughout Appalachia. It was formed in response to three major impulses of the 1960s: the federal War on Poverty, a broader social movement for economic justice, and criticism from sociocultural commentators who faulted the traditional approaches to underlying issues in the region—approaches that ignored local customs and folkways.

The Commission on Religion in Appalachia includes nineteen denominations, three councils of churches, five other ecumenical organizations, and eight at-large community representatives, all recruited from northern, central, and southern Appalachia. Annual meetings alternate between locations in the northern and the southern sections and focus on the religious and moral implications inherent in economic, social, and cultural conditions. Three themes evident throughout the commission's existence have been the recognition of structural causes for problems in Appalachia, the acceptance of churches' roles in fostering economic change, and close cooperation with indigenous groups.

In the 1960 Democratic primary election, presidential candidate John F. Kennedy first pledged to attack poverty in West Virginia, drawing national attention to economic conditions in Appalachia. In 1964 President Lyndon Johnson's administration declared the War on Poverty, and one year later the commission met for the first time, in Morgantown, West Virginia, to discuss effective ways to organize cooperation among indigenous churches and groups in implementing social programs in Appalachia. In 1980 the Social, Economic, and Political Issues task force issued a more explicit call for economic justice in the region, igniting discussions concerning the need for a more rigorous, biblically based understanding of the churches' roles. The

Social, Economic, and Political Issues task force held hearings at the community level, engaging the Commission on Religion in Appalachia in local dialogues that resulted in extensive grassroots exposure for the commission's role in Appalachia.

As the commission grew, tensions developed between its administrative organization at the national level and its indigenous task forces at community level. Ironically, the unresolved tensions provided a source of energy that enabled the commission's survival through the 1970s and 1980s, when other ecumenical associations were declining. The commission debated whether it should coordinate programs in cooperation with area religious communities, provide financial and technical support for Appalachian ministries, or serve as an advocate in legislative, union, and natural crises. Many consider these apparent differences within the organization to be the key to its adaptability and survival.

The commission accomplishes its purposes through four strategies: consultations with entities working within communities; research, study, and education to expand knowledge of local conditions; coordination of staff and programs; and engagement in both secular and church-based projects. Since the 1960s the Commission on Religion in Appalachia has addressed issues of social and economic justice in Appalachia through cooperation of the indigenous people in church and nonchurch groups within constituent communities.

See also: COALITION FOR APPALACHIAN MINISTRY; WAR ON POVERTY (GOVERNMENT).

—Schuyler Kaufman, *Appalachian State University*

Congregational Denominational Family

While Appalachia was being settled, geography, isolation, and a general spirit of independence favored the development of local church autonomy, or congregationalism. In this nondenominational sense, a church that adopted a congregational polity secured its own pastor and ran its own affairs. While laity and clergy of various churches occasionally met to discuss matters of common concern, usually only the local fellowship made church decisions. During Appalachia's early settlement, distances from other denominationally affiliated churches and seats of hierarchy tended to deter other approaches to church governmental structure, at least temporarily. Furthermore, during the eighteenth century, the congregationalist tradition of freedom and self-government bolstered the independent spirit of American revolutionaries.

Still the Congregational denomination itself, present in the colonies long before the American Revolution, was somewhat slow in its Appalachian implantation. By the 1800s Congregational churches had joined with the Presbyterians in a Plan of Union for joint missionary endeavors on the western frontiers of Appalachia and beyond. However, Congregationalists later pulled out of this arrangement when, after fifty years, a large number of Presbyterian, not Congregational, churches had been built in these states.

In the early twentieth century many individual Congregational churches formed the National Council of Congregational Churches, which later merged with several groups, including the Congregational Christian Church, to form the United Church of Christ, which existed from 1931 to 1957. However, between 1950 and 1957 some Congregational Christian Churches sued the United Church of Christ's General Council to preserve their Congregational identity, asserting that while individuals, churches, and agencies are endowed with temporal power, none wields authority over another except through the biblical authority of God in Jesus Christ. About two hundred Congregational Christian Churches remained independent. Most of these joined either the National Association of Congregational Christian Churches or the Conservative Congregational Christian Conference, both of which had never joined the United Church of Christ and are represented in Appalachia.

Churches within the Congregational denominational family are free churches that, under the leadership of Christ, are bound to others by the Congregational Way of love rather than law. This Congregational Way promotes maximum religious, philosophical, and moral freedom for the rule of God in each church, so that each can follow Christ, led not by a creed but by the Spirit. This freedom requires both unity and liberty, balancing theological diversity with biblical respect. No church is required to teach and practice a viewpoint against the conviction of that particular assembly. Seventy-seven Congregational family churches with nearly thirteen thousand adherents exist in twenty-eight Appalachian counties, accounting for about 7.5 percent of the national Congregational membership.

Evangelical Congregational Church

Although the original Congregationalists were strict Calvinists, the Evangelical Congregational Church is Wesleyan. While it is the largest Congregational body in Appalachia, this group of churches is only the third-largest Congregationalist cluster in the nation. With thirty-nine churches in ten Appalachian counties, the Evangelical Congregationalists comprise about 23 percent of the denomination's national membership. In the 1890s theological controversies, leadership problems, and social friction divided the Evangelical Association of North America (now part of the United Methodist Church). One result was the United Evangelical Church, which today partially continues as the Evangelical Congregational Church.

National Association of Congregational Christian Churches

The second-largest Congregational denomination in Appalachia is the National Association of Congregational Christian Churches, the nation's largest Congregational body. Twenty-eight churches in seventeen Appalachian counties have about thirty-three hundred adherents in Appalachia and seventy thousand nationwide. Formed when two hundred Congregational Christian Churches refused to join a 1955 merger with the United Church of Christ, this voluntary association of free churches is designed to have no power, so that local churches may enjoy the benefits of national fellowship without compromising their freedom, maintaining full control of their own affairs.

Conservative Congregational Christian Conference

The nation's second-largest Congregational body, the Conservative Congregational Christian Conference, is the smallest Congregational denomination in Appalachia. This denomination explicitly identifies with the Christian churches that in 1931 merged with the National Council of Congregational Churches. The Christians were a group of churches almost identical to those of the Congregationalists, but laying more importance on the use of the name *Christian* to identify followers of Christ. Located in six Appalachian counties, the ten churches of the Conservative Congregational Christian Conference represent about eighteen hundred of this group's thirty-six thousand adherents nationwide. Though founded in 1948, this denomination identifies historically with the Separating Congregationalists of England (more commonly known as Puritans). The Conservative Congregational Christian Conference practices strict Reformed theology, holds conservative evangelical Christian doctrines, and is explicitly fundamentalist. Each church is responsible to the conference financially and doctrinally.

See also: METHODISTS.

—Heather Ann Ackley Bean, *Azusa Pacific University*

Martin B. Bradley et al., eds., *Churches and Church Membership in the United States, 1990* (1992); Clifford A. Grammich Jr., *Appalachian Atlas: Maps of the Churches and People of the Appalachian Region* (1994); Leon O. Hynson, "Congregational! Evangelical! Wesleyan: The Evangelical Congregational Church, 1922–1950," *Methodist History* (July 1998).

Correspondence

See Associations, Baptist

Dancing in the Spirit

See Revival Exercises

Doak, Samuel

(1749–1830) Presbyterian minister and educator.

Samuel Doak was perhaps the earliest Presbyterian minister in the Appalachian region but is best known as the founder and first president of Washington Academy (1783) and as one of the founders of Tusculum College (1794). Born in Augusta County, Virginia, Doak graduated from the College of New Jersey (Princeton) and taught briefly at one of the Presbyterian "log colleges" in Pennsylvania and, also briefly, at Hampden-Sydney College in Virginia.

After being licensed to preach, Doak moved with his new wife, Esther H. Montgomery, to Limestone, Tennessee, becoming the first minister to settle permanently in the state. There he became a friend of John Sevier and attained a certain prominence, although he continued to farm to make a living. In 1783 he established Martin Academy, which in 1795 was renamed Washington College, in honor of George Washington. This institution remained primarily an academy after failing to secure the significant land grant that went to Blount College in Knoxville (ultimately the University of Tennessee).

In 1818 Doak turned over Washington College to his eldest son, John Whitefield Doak, and then joined another son, Samuel W. Doak, who had founded Tusculum Academy. Samuel Doak spent his final years teaching at Tusculum, which ultimately merged with Greeneville College to become Tusculum College. Established in 1794, Tusculum claims to be the oldest college west of the Appalachians. Doak's sons also had distinguished careers as ministers and educators in eastern Tennessee.

See also: PRESBYTERIAN DENOMINATIONAL FAMILY.

—Ira Read, *Appalachian State University*

Double Marriage

Among numerous highly traditional southern and central Appalachian Baptist sub-denominations, the term *double marriage* refers to a person's being divorced and remarried while the original spouse still lives—an offense that can result in exclusion from church membership.

Especially prevalent among Appalachian Old-Time Baptists, the double-married edict is grounded in prohibitions against divorce found in Mark 10:11 and 1 Cor. 7:10–11. Occasionally an exception is made for a wronged party whose original spouse violated the marriage vow by an adulterous relationship. However, a less egregious breach in a marriage contract usually does not permit the second marriage prior to death of the original spouse. The latter is particularly true for an elder or a deacon.

Throughout much of the 1990s the Union Association of Old Regular Baptists debated a development in one of its out-migrant Michigan churches. There a well-loved, but divorced, male was permitted in the pulpit. His status as a liberated brother (called but not yet ordained) allowed this man to preach, argued his Michigan church, without violating the association's edict against divorced elders. Not persuaded, the association finally demanded a divesting of the individual's preaching rights, much to the grief of the Michigan fellowship.

See also: BAPTISTS, THE OLD-TIME GROUPS; MARRIAGE CUSTOMS (FAMILY AND COMMUNITY).

—Howard Dorgan, *Appalachian State University, Emeritus*

Double Predestination

Among the more Calvinistic Baptist denominations of southern and central Appalachia, the terms *single predestination* and *double predestination* are employed to signify two sharply variant doctrinal positions relative to the absolute determinism of life's circumstances. Single-predestination theology claims that God has preselected, since before the beginning of time, the precise body of individuals who ultimately will become the beneficiaries of Christ's atonement for Adamic sin. Double predestination takes a more inclusive deterministic position by asserting that in addition to election God has predetermined all of the circumstances of mankind's temporal and extra-temporal existence.

The doctrinal split that has occurred between these two predestination positions appears more prevalent among Primitive Baptists than among other denominational units of the Appalachian region. One example of such a theological division can be found in the beliefs of the Mates Creek Primitive Baptist Association (with churches in eastern Kentucky and West Virginia) and the Original Mates Creek Primitive Baptist Association (with churches in eastern Kentucky and southwestern Virginia). The latter group adheres to the single-predestination doctrine and the former supports the double-predestination tenet.

See also: ASSOCIATIONS, BAPTIST; ELECTION.

—Howard Dorgan, *Appalachian State University, Emeritus*

Dow, Lorenzo

(1777–1834) Camp-meeting evangelist.

Lorenzo Dow was important in the establishment of the outdoor camp meetings of the early nineteenth century, and throughout his career he continued to support their development. The emotional excesses of these early encampments suited Dow's style as a preacher and worship leader. Camp meetings remain as an institution of Appalachian religious life.

Dow is best known for his eccentric appearance, flamboyant preaching, and emotional exploitation of his audiences. Though a native of New England, Dow preached extensively in the Deep South and Appalachia. It is believed he preached the first Protestant service in Alabama.

Dow rejected the Calvinism of his youth after he heard Methodist itinerants extol unconditional saving grace. Though he never received the official endorsement of the Methodist Conference, he evangelized under its banner and sent converts to its churches. He was not above huckstering or manipulating an audience, using elaborate tricks or feigning death in an effort to win converts. However, despite his eccentricities, he enjoyed a loyal following and the fame he craved. He even acquired wealth through the sale of his writings and a medicine he patented.

This colorful exhorter took his sensational preaching style into all parts of the United States and Great Britain. During the first decade of the nineteenth century, Dow crusaded in Alabama, North and South Carolina, Tennessee, and Virginia. En route to New England, he closed the decade in 1810 with a campaign in both Georgia and North Carolina. Dow died in Georgetown, Maryland, in 1834.

See also: GREAT WESTERN REVIVAL AND CAMP-MEETING MOVEMENT.

—James S. Baugess, *Ohio State University*

Election

Finding its validation in such scriptural passages as John 15:16, Rom. 8:29, and Eph. 1:4–5, staunch election theology proclaims that a limited body of humankind, known by God before the foundation of time, will constitute his church in the temporal world and subsequently become the beneficiaries of Christ's atonement for Adamic sin. A key element in this doctrine is the argument that God alone chooses—not man. Therefore, God elects his church, rather than depending upon it being won to him through free-will responses to human-instituted evangelism. Proponents of a strict election doctrine look with suspicion on Sabbath schools, revivals, foreign and home missionary programs, radio or television ministries, and all other forms of evangelistic outreach.

Election doctrine may also heavily influence preaching style, content, and audience. For the general-atonement Pentecostals, Methodists, Free Will Baptists, Missionary Baptists, and similar groups, the primary purpose of any sermon may be the "winning of souls for Christ." However, the limited-atonement Primitive Baptists would probably argue not only that the Word of God must be reserved for the elect but also that it should be delivered without undue emotion, in fear that for the non-elect it might produce a sense of a call (to worship) when none actually exists. As for who numbers among the elect, most Old-Time Baptists refer to themselves as "Brothers and Sisters in hope," reflecting the belief that no one but God knows for certain.

See also: DOUBLE PREDESTINATION.

—Howard Dorgan, *Appalachian State University, Emeritus*

Elkhorn Association

See Associations, Baptist

Episcopal Church

The presence of the Episcopal Church in Appalachia predates the formation of the nation. As inheritors of the Anglican tradition in the United States, committed laity and clergy brought *The Book of Common Prayer* with them as they settled the foothills of the Blue Ridge and the southern highlands. Itinerant Episcopal clergy moved the Anglican tradition into the backcountry of South Carolina, the Shenandoah Valley of Virginia, and eastern Kentucky decades before the American Revolution.

These early efforts were sparse, inconstant, and dependent upon the initiative of individuals committed to the harsh work on the frontier. There was no formal mission plan of the Anglican/Episcopal Church for the Appalachian region until the early 1800s. Neither was there overwhelming grassroots support for this expression of the Christian faith. Furthermore, these obstacles were magnified in Appalachia due to the geographic ruggedness, the isolation from communities of support, and the political and cultural climate of the early mountaineers. Specific problems included the Episcopal association with the Church of England and the related distrust with anything related to the Realm; the fact that no bishops were present before the Revolution and few until the early 1800s; the additional reality that there were few to no clergy in the foothills and mountains prior to the Revolution; and, finally, the especially crippling circumstance that after the Revolution the Episcopal Church had no money.

The lack of organization and the burden of church structure did not hamper the personal initiative of the first Episcopal missionaries who crossed the Blue Ridge. Noteworthy in those early years was the Reverend James Moore of Kentucky, who conducted services and brought organization to the Episcopal Society of the Kentucky territory as early as 1775. Likewise, the Reverend Robert Johnstone Miller injected a unique ecumenical flavor into early missionary work throughout southern Appalachia. This same fervor inspired a faithful few to stretch beyond denominational anxieties in the early 1800s. The Reverend James Otey worked in Tennessee and Alabama while Otey and the Reverend Stephen Elliott together led the work in Georgia. These efforts were paralleled by the visionary ministries in Pennsylvania, western New York, and Ohio of the Reverend Jackson Kemper (later the church's first missionary bishop) and the Reverend Philander Chase.

Education was always a common denominator of Episcopal work all along the Appalachians. Throughout the nineteenth century, the typical mission strategy began with the establishment of schools, which also served as places for worship. The church also worked with Native Americans and African Americans. One of the earliest missionary outposts in the Appalachians was established in 1842 by the Reverend Levi S. Ives, second bishop of North Carolina. Called Valle Crucis, it was founded on a monastic model of prayer, study, and work. Under the leadership of the Reverend William West Skiles, the ministry in Valle Crucis included academic, spiritual, and vocational training.

Unlike other denominations, the Episcopal Church did not formally split over the issue of slavery and the Civil War. Even though mission expansion in the mountains was hampered by the postwar poverty that gripped so many, these unbroken ties within the church were essential for the institution's continuing work. Funds and material from Episcopalians "up north" and "down east" helped fuel mission efforts as the organizational structure of the church began to catch up with other denominations.

As the tumultuous century came to a close, the country and the church were grasped by a concern for social welfare. Most states did not provide formal education, poverty assistance, or organized health care. These basic needs were even more neglected in the mountains. To these pressing human needs, the Episcopal Church brought compassion, establishing its presence among mountain inhabitants. The great social gospel movement found life and expression in Appalachia during the years from 1890 to 1940, and this era saw the will to serve and the organization of the church work as one, with enormous quantities of energy, people, and money focused on the mountains. Episcopalians established schools, orphanages, hospitals, and vocational training centers. Groups ranging from the Sewing Society of Saint John's in Knoxville to the dauntless health-care workers Mary Hughson and Maria Allen in the North Carolina foothills did this work. Other tireless workers were Archdeacons B. W. Spurr in West Virginia, Fredrick Neve in Virginia, and the Reverend LeRoy Baker in Pennsylvania. Among the many leaders in African American ministries were the Reverend James Kennedy and the Reverend Henry McDuffy, both archdeacons.

These social gospel efforts continued throughout the Great Depression and the 1940s; however, due to population shifts and changing needs in the mountains, work often was reorganized or integrated into government-backed programs. Episcopalians were at the heart of ecumenical efforts to integrate resources and speak with a common voice on a variety of issues from economics to justice. The Appalachian People's Service Organization and the Commission on Religion in Appalachia were products of such joint efforts. Most dioceses now weave aspects of these ministries into the work of their particular region. Changing populations, regional development, the Hispanic presence, and growth of resort communities have inspired the Episcopal Church to adapt once again. In West Virginia, lay vicars, vocational deacons, and cluster ministries now do the work of ministry.

In 1983 Episcopal membership in the Appalachian region showed a decline of more than 7 percent. Though it remained one of the ten largest Christian expressions there, Episcopal membership continued to fall, losing a total of 10 percent by 1992. However, during the mid-1990s these patterns changed. Twelve of the seventeen dioceses in Appalachia showed growth, with ten of these growing faster than the total population.

See also: KENNEDY, JAMES; MILLER, ROBERT JOHNSTONE; SKILES, WILLIAM WEST.

—Scott A. Oxford, *Episcopal Diocese of Western North Carolina*

Susan Fenimore Cooper, ed., *William West Skiles: A Sketch of Missionary Life at Valle Crucis in Western North Carolina* (1890); Clifford A. Grammich Jr., *Appalachian Atlas: Maps of the Churches and People of the Appalachian Region* (1994); Francis Keller Swinford and Rebecca Smith Lee, *The Great Elm: Heritage of the Episcopal Diocese of Lexington* (1959).

Falling Exercises

See Revival Exercises

Fire Handling

The handling of fire, specifically the exposing of hands, feet, arms, and necks to the flames of alcohol- and kerosene-filled lamps, propane torches, and hot coal, is most often associated with the serpent-handling Holiness services of Georgia, Alabama, Tennessee, Virginia, Kentucky, and West Virginia. Fire handling is one of many signs that are followed by the serpent-handling believers and is based on literal interpretations of the biblical scriptures of Isa. 43:2, Heb. 11:33–34, 1 Peter 1:7, and Daniel 3:20–27. The handling of fire by Christians in North America is a relatively recent development when compared to the fire-handling practices that have existed for centuries among some Egyptian and Indian religious sects.

The origin of fire handling among sign followers is unclear. However, the development of serpent handling in the South and, more specifically, in Appalachia has been traced to the first decade of the twentieth century. Whether this form of fire handling began with George Hensley, the east Tennessee evangelist who initiated the handling of serpents in the early twentieth century, remains uncertain. It is clear, however, that some of the important elements necessary for the perpetuation of the practice had already been established throughout the South: a fervent fundamentalist religious community coupled with a literal approach to biblical interpretation.

Individuals may be moved to handle fire by either the strength of their faith or through spiritual anointment. This anointing, sometimes referenced as baptism of the Holy Spirit, is what such believers proclaim to be a possession by the Holy Ghost (or Holy Spirit): a coming down upon, an entering, a filling, and a taking control of a spiritually worthy individual. Anointment is viewed as a blessed state that allows individuals to do what they ordinarily could not do. They may speak in tongues, prophesy, heal the sick, handle serpents, drink deadly liquids, or handle fire. No two experiences are the same. Some receive the blessing to exhibit one sign but not another, such as the handling of serpents but not fire, or speaking in tongues but not healing. One believer's spiritual experience may last only a few seconds, while another's may extend over a much longer period.

The anointing can occur at any time during a church service. It may be initiated by the Spirit in a number of ways, including through the singing of a favorite gospel song, the listening to or preaching of a moving sermon, the laying on of hands on the sick, or the administering of a foot washing. Whatever activity precipitates the anointing and practice of the sign, the believers always attribute their experiences to an unshakable faith in the Holy Spirit.

Research conducted in 1992 seemed to show that the attendant physiological and psychological behaviors of those who handled fire during a church service in Baxter, Kentucky, fell outside of normal tolerances. Believers claimed that due to the power of the anointing, individuals were able to expose their hands, arms, and necks to the flame of a kerosene lamp with temperatures exceeding 675 degrees Fahrenheit for periods of nearly two minutes, in no instance being harmed or experiencing pain. Scientists, however, do not agree with this explanation for the handling of fire without harm, a practice common in many traditions around the world and one that can be readily explained in scientific terms.

Research conducted during 1993 on a single male serpent and fire handler established that the euphoria and altered pain perceptions associated with spiritual anointment can be attributed to specific types of neurochemical agents produced by the pituitary and adrenal systems (epinephrine, norepinephrine, dopamine, cortisol, and beta-endorphin). The net effect of these responses and other emotional and physical stimuli could have been so strong that the message (perception of discomfort) failed to be transmitted to higher brain centers and thus blocked natural reflexes. The results of this chemical analysis support electroencephalographic observations in earlier studies that show the anointing experience to be a state of high physical and psychological arousal. However, the significant increases of all these naturally produced chemicals within this particular test subject did not adequately explain his apparent ability to handle fire without tissue damage.

See also: BAPTISM OF THE HOLY SPIRIT; HENSLEY, GEORGE; SERPENT HANDLING.

—Scott Schwartz, *Smithsonian Institution*

Thomas G. Burton, *Serpent-Handling Believers* (1993); David Kimbrough, *Taking Up Serpents* (1995); Scott W. Schwartz, *Faith, Serpents, and Fire* (1999).

Flower Service

An annual tradition in Missionary Baptist Churches in the southeast corner of Watauga County, North Carolina, the Flower Service functions as the congregations' rededication to love and unity. Staged in early September, the rite features a general exchange of flowers, with each member of the fellowship swapping a blossom with every other church member. At these moments, each reciprocating pair of individuals will seek forgiveness for any breach in love and fellowship that might have occurred between the two. Based loosely on the admonition provided in Matt. 5:23–24 concerning being "reconciled to thy brother" prior to making an offer to God, the ceremony involves the placing of flowers before the altar, followed by a preaching service that emphasizes the theme "Get right with thy neighbor." Only then are members told to retrieve their flowers for the exchange.

The powerful symbolism of these reciprocal transactions occasionally precipitates scenes of emotional purgation and reconciliation as conflicts and misunderstandings are resolved. Indeed, an individual's avoidance of a Flower Service in order to escape responsibility for such healing encounters will generate congregational concern and may warrant a correcting admonition from the church's minister.

See also: BAPTISTS, THE GENERAL ATONEMENT, NON-MAINLINE UNITS.

—Howard Dorgan, *Appalachian State University, Emeritus*

Foot Washing

A wide range of Christian denominations practice the communal rite of washing feet. However, in southern and central Appalachia, the convention is most frequently associated with the highly traditional Baptist sects of the region. Following the model recounted in John 13:3–15, where Christ concludes his last Passover feast by washing the feet of his disciples, Appalachian Baptists such as the Primitives, Regulars, Old Regulars, Separates, and Uniteds typically end their annual communion services with a round of highly emotional ablution ceremonies in which foot washing is done. This ritual is considered a faith ordinance, similar to the ceremonies of baptism and communion.

Generally closed to all but members of the respective fellowship and corresponding fellowships, foot-washing services may last only a few minutes with individual members pairing with other members for a round of reciprocating washes. However, sometimes the services may continue for an hour or more and entail frequent re-pairings, until every member washes the feet of every other member of the same gender. Although some congregations allow the crossing of gender lines for this ritual, such is not the norm. Indeed, decorum may require that the meeting space be temporarily partitioned, with sections of church pews facing different directions, to ensure gender privacy.

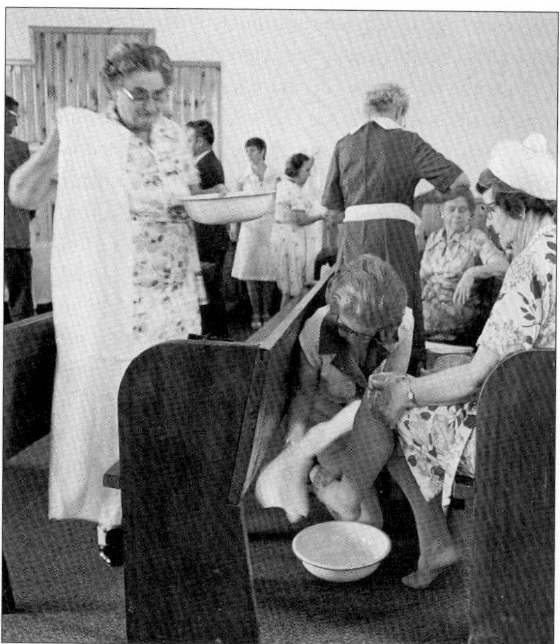

The women of Cross Roads Primitive Baptist Church, Baywood, Virginia, washing one another's feet during communion service while the men participate across the aisle, 1978. Gender segregation is common in the ritual of foot washing.

See also: BAPTISTS, THE OLD-TIME GROUPS.

—Howard Dorgan, *Appalachian State University, Emeritus*

Glenmary Home Missioners

Founded in 1939 by Father William Howard Bishop, Glenmary Home Missioners of America worked to establish the Catholic Church in small towns and rural areas of Appalachia and the South. Never larger than 109 fully professed brothers and priests, the society focused its primary work in Catholic parishes, but later its mission broadened through research, ecumenism, and social justice ministry. As a mission group through the 1940s to the 1960s, Glenmary initiated creative techniques that reflected indigenous religious expressions such as tent meetings and street preaching. The group's innovative spirit also inspired the writing of mountain music for the Mass and the institution of numerous ecumenical endeavors both locally and regionally.

By the late 1960s Glenmary had established a research arm that now publishes a U.S. church membership study every ten years. Analysis of the religious data gathered in Appalachia has revealed, among other findings, that mountain religions do not easily fit the categories of national denominational groups.

By the mid-1970s Glenmarians had become a catalyst for two pastoral letters from the Appalachian bishops: "This Land Is Home to Me" (1975) identified Appalachia as a special region where absentee ownership of the resources oppressed the people, and "At Home in the Web of Life" (1995) called for sustainable development in light of the global economy. Both documents validated the voice of ordinary people and changed the church's view of ministry in Appalachia.

See also: CATHOLICISM; GLENMARY SISTERS.

—John S. Rausch, *Glenmary Home Missioners*

Glenmary Sisters

Founded in 1941, the Glenmary Sisters have served southern and central Appalachia since 1944. While their religious work has been with members of their own Catholic faith, the Sisters' social service assistance and advocacy have covered the entire region, particularly in regard to the underprivileged.

Between 1944 and 1976 the Sisters lived among people of southeastern Ohio, from Otway/Pond Creek to Portsmouth, initiating programs that involved religious instruction, helping the poor, home nursing, and other works of charity. In the late 1940s similar services were extended to counties of far-western Virginia (Lee, Wise, Dickenson, Scott, and Russell Counties). In 1947 the Glenmary Sisters established a mission at Big Stone Gap, Virginia, which continued until 1967, at which time forty-four of the sisters broke from the order to form the Federation of Communities in Service. This latter group then assumed responsibility for the Big Stone Gap service efforts.

The Glenmary Sisters established a presence in western North Carolina in 1957 and by 1961 were operating a clinic in Haysville, North Carolina; the clinic was made a public facility in 1976. By the early 1970s, the Sisters had moved into six counties in Kentucky, starting with the establishment of the Christian Social Service Center of Morehead. A similar facility was begun in 1987 in Owingsville, and another is planned for Frenchburg. Other Kentucky Glenmary missions exist in Guthrie, Livermore, and Smithland. Their central office and motherhouse are located in Owensboro, Kentucky.

See also: CATHOLICISM; GLENMARY HOME MISSIONERS.

—Sister Christine Beckett, *GHMS, The Glenmary Sisters*

Glossolalia

Also known as speaking in tongues, glossolalia is ecstatic religious speech in which vocal patterns are not familiar or recognizable as a human language. It is important to any discussion of Appalachian religion because it is widely practiced among Pentecostal Holiness fellowships of the region and because it also is exercised within some Appalachian Pentecostal-influenced Independent and Free Will Baptist fellowships. It is believed the presence of glossolalia in Appalachia can be traced to the formative Appalachian religious practices, notably the enraptured religious expression of the Cane Ridge revival of 1801, and perhaps to the even earlier influences of Scottish sacramental revivalism. Acts 2:1–13 and Mark 16:17 commonly are cited as biblical justification for the exercise. However, glossolalia should be distinguished from xenolalia, the miraculous use of a known human language not learned by traditional methods.

Glossolalia's robust existence in Appalachia may have been one source of the international rise of speaking in tongues from the Azusa Street (Los Angeles) Pentecostal revivals of 1906 and onward. C. H. Mason brought the Azusa movement to Tennessee, and G. B. Cashwell similarly introduced it to North Carolina, where the new impetus for glossolalia likely met and invigorated older practices. Holiness churches were most affected by the Azusa movement, and eventually several major Holiness bodies, each with roots or presence in Appalachia, came into the Pentecostal camp: the Church of God (Cleveland, Tennessee), the Pentecostal Holiness Church, the Fire Baptized Holiness Church, and the Church of God in Christ.

Speaking in tongues, however, is a practice with a lengthy history in religious expression. The Montanists in second-century Italy, the Albigenses in twelfth-century France, and the Waldensians in thirteenth-century Italy exhibited the practice. John Wesley noted the custom among the seventeenth-century Camisards in France, and the Shakers spoke in tongues in England and America beginning in the late seventeenth century. In addition, Pietism and ecstatic practices during the Great Awakening brought forth the phenomenon.

Glossolalia has had a favorable environment in the more independent fellowships and revival practices of Appalachia, both Pentecostal and Baptist; and it has become one of the many signs of the Fire Baptized Way, the ecstatic expression of being anointed by the Holy Spirit. Nevertheless, it is by no means an exclusively Appalachian phenomenon. First radio and then other media became instrumental in spreading the practice. Today glossolalia, with its Appalachian roots and branches, is a key identifying mark of a worldwide Pentecostal movement that has kept Christianity growing in the Southern Hemisphere and invigorated many traditional Christians and their institutions.

See also: BAPTISM OF THE HOLY SPIRIT; PENTECOSTALS; REVIVAL EXERCISES.

—Gilson A. C. Waldkoenig, *Lutheran Theological Seminary at Gettysburg*

Deborah V. McCauley, *Appalachian Mountain Religion: A History* (1995); Watson E. Mills, *Glossolalia: A Bibliography* (1985); Vinson Synan, *The Holiness-Pentecostal Movement in the United States* (1971).

Great Western Revival and Camp-Meeting Movement

The Great Western Revival was in fact a series of revivals that swept the South between 1787 and 1805. It constituted a watershed in the history of southern religion and formed much of the character of Appalachian religion that exists today. Focusing on the individual whom God would judge, the revivals sought to bring persons to a felt, dateable conversion that opened a path toward perfection pursued via a strict moral code. Elements of Appalachian religion fostered by the Great Revival (often called the Second Great Awakening) include individualism, emotionalism, perfectionism, anti-institutionalism, scriptural literalism, lay empowerment, tendencies toward schism, folk hymnody, and (earlier) antislavery sentiment.

In the wake of the American Revolution, southern religion suffered a depression that has been linked in part to wide-scale migration and economic and political disruption in the emerging nation. The faithful, however, perceived this religious drought as a temporary punishment from God and confidently expected imminent divine renewal of the Church. In 1787 a revival broke out at Hampden-Sydney College in Virginia that presaged sporadic spiritual outpourings that culminated in astonishingly large revivals in southwest Kentucky from 1798 to 1805.

The primary catalyst for the Kentucky revivals was James McGready, a Presbyterian minister from North Carolina who arrived in Logan County in 1796. McGready's powerful, emotional preaching, performed in the context of traditional Presbyterian sacramental meetings, ignited his congregations to intense fervor and attracted crowds of visitors. These revivals climaxed in the famous Cane Ridge camp meeting of August 1801 near Paris, Kentucky, which lasted several days and drew perhaps twenty thousand people, both blacks and whites. Although Cane Ridge was initiated by Presbyterians, Methodist and Baptist preachers joined in exhorting the crowds simultaneously from numerous improvised pulpits on the makeshift campground. A tumult of preaching, singing, and shouting was augmented by physical "exercises" (later widely publicized) of the emotionally charged participants, which included falling, jerking, rolling, barking, and laughing.

These mass meetings, for which people planned and provisioned to spend several days at the place of preaching (usually near a water source with a grove of trees), served as models for camp meetings that followed in Kentucky and rapidly spread throughout the South. Scheduled for a time that would not interfere with the farming cycle (between "laying-by and fodder-pulling time"), camp meetings evolved into highly regularized, seasonal rituals of spiritual renewal and reunion for rural southern folk.

The intense phase of the Great Revival had concluded by 1806, but one of its immediate results was a rapid growth in church membership. Methodist rolls in the South doubled between 1800 and 1806. Also, residents and visitors alike universally remarked on a reformation of morals after revivals. Presbyterians and, to a lesser degree, Baptists eventually withdrew support from the free-spirited camp meetings, leaving them primarily to the Methodists. But the long-term legacy of the revival was the evangelical pietism that came to characterize the Protestant South, especially the people of Appalachia, as well as a religion centered on the individual, promoted through revivalism, marked by intense emotionalism, and which transcended doctrinal and denominational differences.

The first phase of camp-meeting fervor abated by the 1840s, but after the Civil War, Holiness groups within the Methodist Church again adopted camp meetings as a vehicle to revive a neglected emphasis on perfection and to recapture the tenor of the earlier revivalism. Holiness camp meetings that convened in and around the Appalachians in the closing decades of the nineteenth century reinvigorated the ideals of the Great Revival: emotionalism, perfectionism, physical manifestations of the Holy Spirit, biblical literalism, rejection of learned preaching for Spirit-led utterance, and empowerment of the laity—especially of women. When, in the 1890s, the Methodist Church officially distanced itself from its Holiness constituency, many Holiness folk formed new Holiness churches, some of which became Pentecostal in the early twentieth century. Holiness and Pentecostal sects, true progeny of the Great Revival, have proliferated in Appalachia.

See also: GLOSSOLALIA; MCGREADY, JAMES; REVIVAL EXERCISES.

—J. Lawrence Brasher, *Birmingham-Southern College*

John B. Boles, *The Great Revival, 1787–1805* (1972); Dickson D. Bruce Jr., *And They All Sang Hallelujah: Plain-Folk Camp-Meeting Religion, 1800–1845* (1974); Leigh Eric Schmidt, *Holy Fairs: Scottish Communions and American Revivals in the Early Modern Period* (1989).

Hensley, George

(1881–1955) Serpent-handling evangelist.

George Went Hensley reputedly initiated the practice of handling serpents as a Christian ritual in modern times. According to report and tradition, he first took up a serpent near Ooltewah, Tennessee, in response to reading about signs of believers in Mark 16:17–18 sometime between 1908 and 1910, or perhaps as late as 1913. Originally a member of the Baptist faith, he was converted in 1908 by the preaching of the son of the general overseer of the Church of God (Cleveland, Tennessee).

Two years later Hensley himself started preaching. The first contemporary report of his handling serpents is that of a 1914 revival in Cleveland. He along with other preachers evangelized, "confirming the word with signs following" (Mark 16:20). These signs included the taking up of serpents. Hensley, however, resigned his ministry in the Church of God (c. 1922), the year he separated from his first wife and family. (He also separated from the next two of his later three wives and families.)

After a short abandonment of his religion, or apostasy, he resumed preaching and during the last thirty-odd years of his life continued his ministry in Ohio, Kentucky, southwest Virginia, Tennessee, Georgia, and Florida. In 1945 he helped found the Dolly Pond Church of God with Signs Following, which became in 1947 the focus of a test case for the newly passed Tennessee code restricting the handling of serpents. While holding a revival in Calhoun County, Florida, he was bitten by a rattlesnake and died.

See also: GLOSSOLALIA; REVIVAL EXERCISES; SERPENT HANDLING.

—Thomas Burton, *East Tennessee State University*

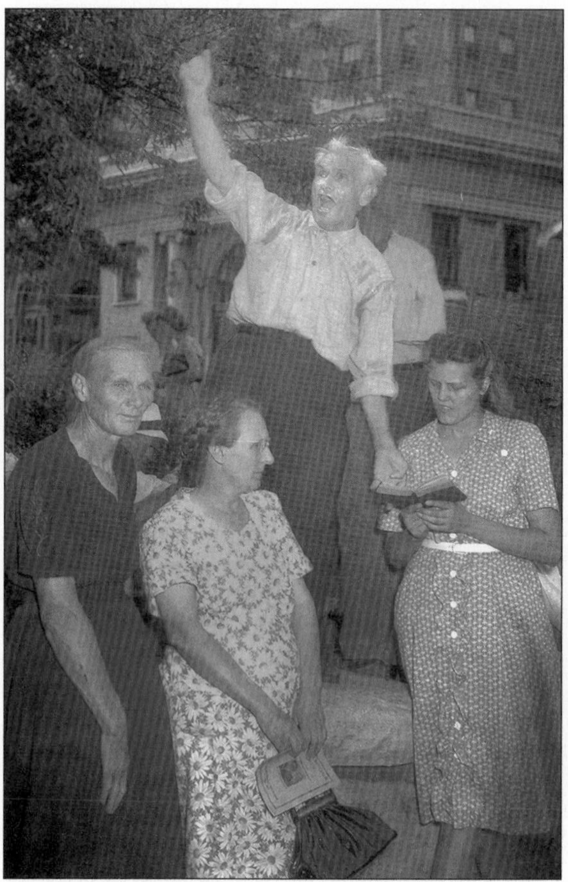

George Hensley preaching in front of the Hamilton County, Tennessee, Courthouse, 1947. An influential preacher and cofounder of the Dolly Pond Church of God with Signs Following in Birchwood, Tennessee, Hensley is credited with inspiring the practice of serpent handling in modern times.

Holiness-Pentecostal Fusion

Scattered throughout Appalachia, especially in the southern and central parts of the region, are small, independent, one-room churches called Holiness, Holiness Pentecostal, or Pentecostal Holiness. These congregations practice acts of ecstatic religious expression associated with Pentecostalism's Spirit baptism (possession by the Holy Spirit) while also upholding some version of the Wesleyan Holiness doctrine. So numerous are the examples of this Appalachian phenomenon that they suggest an informal fusion of two religious movements that have separate origins and discrete doctrines.

By the early twentieth century, the Holiness and Pentecostal movements—which had been in foment throughout much of the nineteenth century—settled into two distinct institutional trends. One trend, the Holiness movement, emphasized the Wesleyan Methodists' theology of perfectionism and sanctification—that state of purity in heart, mind, and deed that also was called the "second blessing." The other trend, the Pentecostal movement, also incorporated the idea of second blessing or sanctification, understood, however, as the baptism of the Holy Spirit, a state that enabled the practicing of such gifts as glossolalia (speaking in tongues).

On a national level, this basic theological difference gave rise to two separate institutional structures, or denominations. The oldest Holiness denomination today is the Church of God (Anderson, Indiana), and the largest is the Church of the Nazarene. The oldest Pentecostal denomination is the Church of God (Cleveland, Tennessee), and the largest is the Assemblies of God. Like other Protestant denominations in the United States, these formal Holiness or Pentecostal denominations have adopted fixed organizational structures that have solidified each as distinct administrative and theological entities. In addition, they have established missions at home and overseas and have practiced self-documentation, maintaining close counts of membership, number of churches, church attendance, money collected, and so on.

With the emergence of these denominations, the late-nineteenth-century tendency toward unification between the Holiness and the emerging Pentecostal movements waned, except in terms of theological and institutional antecedents. Historically, however, both the Holiness and Pentecostal movements were characterized as the religion of the poor and dispossessed, a label that middle-class followers would dismiss in the late twentieth and early twenty-first centuries.

Nevertheless, in southern and central Appalachia independent and largely nondenominational congregations still gather in freestanding, one-room buildings or storefront structures and claim for themselves the name *Holiness*, *Pentecostal*, or combinations of both titles. The people who worship in these facilities tend not to be the growing economic elite claimed by the larger Holiness and Pentecostal denominations. No centralized organization, no membership rolls, not much money, often no clear-cut doctrine or polity, but a lot of prayer, praise, singing, and expressive or even ecstatic worship traditions—such are the dominant characteristics found in many of these independent churches. Wholly independent congregations that remain generally uncounted in such canvasses as the Glenmary Research Center's *Churches and Church Membership in the United States, 1990*, these small fellowships hold little formal relationship with each other except as the individual units of a collective genre. In Appalachia these independent, nondenominational churches number not in the hundreds but in the thousands, especially in eastern Kentucky, southwest Virginia, southern West Virginia, east Tennessee, western North Carolina, and the foothills of South Carolina, Georgia, Alabama, and Mississippi.

Appalachia's independent Holiness or Holiness Pentecostal churches make up one of the region's largest church traditions, perhaps the largest. It is impossible to get a hard count of the number of such churches and how many people worship in them because of the absence of written documentation. Regardless of the literacy of the people who worship in these churches, Appalachia's independent Holiness churches are a product almost entirely of oral tradition. These churches rarely keep membership rolls and are usually started by an individual who feels called by God to preach and pray with his or her family, friends, and neighbors.

Although these congregations, which defy institutional categories and lack the trappings of denominationalism, may be seen as the remnants of a religion of the poor, there are other factors by which they can be understood. Many scholars of institutional church history assume that these independent churches are a by-product of organized denominations of the Holiness and Pentecostal movements that came early into Appalachia. They also assume that the so-called poor folks' churches reflect what is commonly identified as Appalachia's individualistic, divisive, sectarian approach to religion. However, other scholars of American religious history believe that Appalachia's independent churches' calling themselves Holiness, yet also practicing traditions identified with the Pentecostal movement, preceded the development of Holiness and Pentecostal denominations throughout the United States. The latter is a viable alternative to the assumptions that Holiness and Pentecostal movements were brought into Appalachia primarily by denominational developments. In addition, this second theory projects an environment in which the discussed fusion could more easily have occurred, vacant as that environment would have been of any deterring denominational controls.

Although mountain people who worship in Appalachia's independent Holiness churches may call themselves Pentecostal because they practice speaking in tongues, these same people also call themselves Holiness, a tradition that regionally reaches back to plain-folk camp-meeting religion which took root and flourished with the explosion of the Great Western Revival (or Second Great Awakening) on the Appalachian frontier at the beginning of the nineteenth century. Today, mountain Holiness services are held one or more nights a week for at least three hours, a practice that continues, in miniature, the tradition of plain-folk camp-meeting night services. In addition, by 1850, shouting, leaping, clapping, running, jerking, and being "slain in the Spirit" (falling to the ground) were worship behaviors that characterized much of the camp-meeting movement and later solidified as the Holiness-Pentecostal touched-by-the-Holy-Spirit style.

Geography and belief may have worked together to bring about the Holiness-Pentecostal fusion in Appalachia. During the nineteenth century, many mountain churches tended largely toward local autonomy. Distances were too great and populations too sparse for extensive national, regional, or even subregional control over a majority of mountain churches, regardless of their denominational traditions. By the end of the nineteenth century, when the term *Holiness* had come to the fore in the emerging Holiness-Pentecostal movements, the independence of mountain worshipers enabled them to be sensitive to the similarities shared by the two movements. However, the commonalities most important to the mountaineers were not in doctrine or polity, but in their intense religiosity and style of worship.

Certain Holiness and Pentecostal theological traditions that developed outside of Appalachia have taken root in the region. The most prominent is the divide between the Pentecostal Oneness or Jesus Only tradition (Unitarian) in contrast to the Pentecostal churches upholding Trinitarian theology. Church names often reflect this controversy: Shade's Creek Jesus Church (for Jesus Only) is down the road from Shade's Creek Holiness Trinity, and both were named by local, individual founders. However, if contemporary Appalachian

Holiness people are asked to define their beliefs, they will generally not mention any written articles of faith or a Nicene Creed, and talk about perfectionism, sanctification, or tongues speaking may be sparse. Instead, the adherents mention the power of their worship practices, a power that resembles the communal conversion experience of early-nineteenth-century plain-folk religion.

See also: BAPTISM OF THE HOLY SPIRIT; GREAT WESTERN REVIVAL AND CAMP-MEETING MOVEMENT; PENTECOSTALS.

—Deborah Vansau McCauley, *East Orange, New Jersey*

Troy D. Abell, *Better Felt Than Said: The Holiness-Pentecostal Experience in Southern Appalachia* (1982); Dickson D. Bruce Jr., *And They All Sang Hallelujah: Plain-Folk Camp-Meeting Religion, 1800–1845* (1974); Eleanor Dickinson and Barbara Benziger, *Revival!* (1974); Bill J. Leonard, ed., *Christianity in Appalachia: Profiles in Regional Pluralism* (1999); Deborah V. McCauley, *Appalachian Mountain Religion: A History* (1995); James Rutenbeck, *Raise the Dead*, First Run/Icarus Films (1998).

Holston Association

See Associations, Baptist

Holy Kiss

The holy kiss is a Christian greeting and salutation consisting of a brief touching of the lips. Extended as a gesture of love and fellowship to "one another" (Rom. 16:16; 2 Cor. 13:12) and "to all the Brethren" (1 Cor. 16:20; 1 Thess. 5:26), the practice dates from the New Testament era (Acts. 20:37). In the early church a kiss of charity was also used at baptism and during communion. By the fourth century, however, these actions had disappeared as common greetings within the Christian community and became limited to liturgical practices.

Sixteenth-century Anabaptists, seeking to imitate practices of the early church, reinstituted a kiss of greeting among members as a sign of brotherhood and at rituals such as foot washing or baptism. Today the kiss is practiced more among plain-dress Anabaptist groups who maintain a high degree of separation from society. These include the Old Order Amish, Beachy Amish, and Old Order and Conservative Mennonites, all of whom have congregations in Appalachia.

The Brethren (Dunkards, Church of the Brethren, and related groups), with roots in both Anabaptism and seventeenth-century Pietism, have observed the kiss as a greeting at worship services, the love feast, and on social occasions. By the mid-twentieth century, however, these practices had been largely discarded, except by the nonconforming Old German Baptist Brethren, who also have a presence in the Appalachian region.

See also: BRETHREN; LOVE FEAST; MENNONITES.

—David B. Eller, *Elizabethtown College*

Jerks

See Revival Exercises

Judaism

Jews were a small minority among the early colonial American settlers, and they moved west with their neighbors as the frontier settlements moved into the Appalachian region. However, throughout most of the eighteenth century Jews comprised less than 1 percent of the American population, and the little existing evidence suggests that for most of the eighteenth and nineteenth centuries they were an even smaller proportion of the Appalachian populace. Substantial Jewish communities were established in Savannah, Georgia; Charleston, South Carolina; Richmond, Virginia; and Philadelphia, Pennsylvania; but the movement of Jews into Appalachia was slow.

While most American Jews came from Orthodox communities in Europe, the majority found that the lack of kosher butchers, Hebrew schools, and rabbinic leadership forced them to desert or greatly modify the faith of their ancestors. Sephardic (Mediterranean) Jewish communities in the Caribbean provided most of the liturgical materials for southern Jewish communities, and consequently, Sephardic rituals dominated the large Jewish communities on the periphery of Appalachia until the mid-eighteenth century.

Most early Jewish settlers were single—younger sons or widowers—or displaced migrants such as Abraham Mordecai. After first settling in Philadelphia, Mordecai fought in the Carolinas during the Revolution and stayed to search for land and wealth by operating a number of mills and trading posts in southern Appalachia. Believing some Native Americans descended from the lost tribes of Israel, he married several Indian women and trained one wife to provide him with an Orthodox burial.

During the 1830s and 1840s, several major persecutions and failed revolutions brought a new wave of German, Austrian, and eastern European Jews to America, and many new communities began to coalesce as rabbis, kosher butchers, and cantors trained in Europe followed their countrymen to the land of opportunity. During the middle decades of the nineteenth century, two major Jewish figures, Rabbi Isaac Meyer Wise and Rabbi Isaac Leeser, greatly encouraged the growth of Reform and Conservative Jewish congregations. Centered in Philadelphia, Leeser made five major tours of the South from the Ohio Valley to Atlanta, organizing congregations, performing weddings, training butchers, and promoting the Jewish Sunday school movement. Through the pages of Leeser's *Occident*, Appalachian Jews could hire clergy, appeal for donations, read sermons, acquire spouses, and debate the contentious issues of American Judaism. Settling in Cincinnati in 1854, Rabbi Wise

The Tree of Life Synagogue, Clarksburg, West Virginia, 1994. While a few Jewish settlers were among the earliest to come to the region, waves of European immigration during the nineteenth century established the faith in larger communities throughout Appalachia.

established the first Jewish seminary in America, published his German-English *Israelite*, organized the Union of American Hebrew Congregations, and saw to it that his *Union Prayer Book* and his vision of Reform Judaism came to dominate Appalachia through the First World War.

The Asheville, North Carolina, congregation, Beth Ha Tephila (House of Prayer), was formed in 1891, operating under the Reform tradition. Twenty-seven businessmen and professionals organized for the purposes of building a sanctuary, conducting Jewish services, establishing a cemetery, creating a Sunday school, and providing charity. Their first spiritual leader, Reverent A. Jacoby from Charleston, West Virginia, provided High Holiday Service (Rosh Hashanah and Yom Kippur observances). In 1902 the congregation acquired its first building, and in 1908 it officially affiliated with the Union of American Hebrew Congregations. Eight years later, Asheville hosted the annual meeting of the rabbinate of the union.

The beginning of the twentieth century saw many Jewish merchants establish businesses throughout Appalachia, thus attaining a degree of social prominence in the region. However, immigration acts of the early 1920s, followed by the economic downturns in the 1930s, greatly diminished Jewish life in Appalachia, although Jewish migration to northern and western Appalachia increased toward the close of the thirties. In turn, New Deal programs such as the Tennessee Valley Authority brought Jewish professionals to the region, as did the expansions of state colleges and universities during the 1930s, 1940s, and 1950s, with European Jewish scholars finding the region an appealing refuge from Nazi persecution. The post–World War II decades brought a further expansion of Jewish congregations in the northern part of Appalachia as the so-called Borsht Belt developed in the mountains of New York and Pennsylvania. Many small Jewish communities sprang up to serve the resorts and campgrounds that hosted a generation fleeing the summer heat of the greater New York and Philadelphia areas.

While the rise in heating costs during the 1970s oil embargo and the growth of retirement and medical facilities brought a massive migration of older Jewish residents to southern states such as Florida and Arizona, it produced a parallel but different migration within Appalachia: a movement of Jews from the northern part of the region to retirement communities farther south. Of the dozens of small communities in the Adirondacks that began in the post–World War II decades, only two—the century-and-a-quarter-old congregation at Lake Placid and the one at Tupper Lake—remain open, with neither employing a rabbi.

In West Virginia, Rabbi Cooper and the Sisterhood of B'nai Jacob Synagogue tracked the demographic changes in Charleston's Jewish population. Between 1958 and 1980, Jewish residents dropped from 1,623 to 1,076, and—as the study predicted—continued to drop through the 1990s. As is true in Kentucky and Tennessee, the remaining West Virginia Jews are more frequently marrying outside their religion, are becoming significantly older, and are finding their support services declining. In a somewhat comparable situation, the only North Carolina Jewish retirement facility—the Blumenthal Retirement Home—was sold because most of its residents were non-Jewish.

On a positive side, the growth of spirituality in America, the religious networking facilitated by the Internet, and the increased flexibilities provided by Social Security and better pensions mean that many baby boomers are returning to their original hometowns. Also, numerous Jewish retirees have summer homes in the mountains and, like the Rosen family of Boone, North Carolina, have become benefactors of community cultural and artistic projects, thus continuing to play a vital role in Appalachia.

See also: JEWS (RACE, ETHNICITY, AND IDENTITY).

—Sheldon Hanft, *Appalachian State University*

Kennedy, James

(1865–1956) African American Episcopal archdeacon.

James Kennedy served western North Carolina's African American Episcopalians for more than fifty years. Eventually the Episcopal Diocese of Western North Carolina appointed him archdeacon, with jurisdiction of Asheville's African American community.

Born a slave in Columbia, South Carolina, James Kennedy joined that city's Saint Mary's Episcopal Church in 1883, beginning his life of religious service. He became Sunday school superintendent and later was licensed as a Protestant Episcopal minister serving Columbia's African American associate mission.

In 1887 Kennedy accepted a teaching position at the African American school in Franklin, North Carolina. There, he worked with Reverend John Deal to build Saint Cyprian's Chapel for Franklin's black population. After being ordained as deacon, Kennedy became Saint Cyprian's minister-in-charge in 1890. His wife, the former Florence Kyer, directed women's auxiliary activities and taught school.

Kennedy's skills and devotion brought notice from the Episcopal leadership, and in 1911 he accepted the position of deacon in charge at Saint Matthias, the Episcopal African American church in Asheville. Subsequently he was formally ordained to the priesthood, becoming Saint Matthias's first rector. In 1920 he was promoted to archdeacon of the Episcopal Diocese of Western North Carolina. Later, he was placed in charge of St. Stephen's Church (black) of Lincolnton, but also assisted at the predominately white Saint Agnes Church of Franklin. Eventually he became the longest-standing minister in his diocese. Although he retired in the early 1950s, he remained active in the Episcopal Church until his death.

See also: AFRICAN AMERICAN RELIGIOUS TRADITIONS; EPISCOPAL CHURCH.

—Kathryn Staley, *Appalachian State University*

Kline, John

(1797–1864) Brethren church leader.

Before and during the Civil War, John Kline served the Appalachian Brethren movement as an outspoken pacifist, as an antislavery advocate, as a pamphleteer in defense of the creed's nontraditional form of baptism (immersal forward three times), as a church leader, and ultimately as a symbol of martyrdom for the movement.

Kline moved with his family to mountainous Rockingham County, Virginia, when he was about fourteen. His great-grandfather had been a prominent Pennsylvania Brethren. Kline's own Brethren ministry took several forms. First, he gave land to establish the Linville Church of the Brethren, and his own records show that he traveled one hundred thousand miles as a minister, providing not only religious but also some medical services.

As a Brethren leader, Kline served as moderator of the Annual Meetings during the politically charged years of the Civil War, vigorously opposing both slavery and military service. Kline wrote many letters to his friend Governor John Letcher of Virginia, explaining the Brethren peace position. His efforts, in part, enabled Brethren to secure exemption from military service by paying a fee of five hundred dollars.

On June 15, 1864, shortly after returning from that year's Brethren Annual Conference, he was ambushed near his home and killed, apparently because of his strongly defended Brethren beliefs. Today, children's books about the faith portray Kline as a Brethren martyr, a courageous prophet who considered his view of patriotism to be an outgrowth of love for the whole human family.

See also: BRETHREN.

—Beatrice Naff Bailey, *Clemson University*

Lined Singing

Characteristic of Old Baptist denominations, particularly in the coal-mining regions of central Appalachia, lined singing is the oldest continuously practiced style of English- language hymn singing in the United States. In Appalachian practice, the song leader sings the very first line of text, and the congregation joins in when they recognize the song. After that the song proceeds line by line: the leader alone briefly chants a line, and then the group repeats the words to a tune that is much longer and more elaborate than the leader's chant or lining tune. Music scholars call this procedure "lining out" or "lining." The term *lining* is not generally used by Old Baptists, who call what the leader does "giving out" the song.

Antiphony, or call-and-response performance of ritual language, traces its ancient lineage from Africa, Greece, and the Middle East. A group responding to what a leader says, chants, or sings most likely entered Christian worship from Jewish practice. According to musicologist Nicholas Temperley, lined singing in Appalachia derives from the music of the sixteenth-century English parish church. In 1644 the Westminster Assembly of Divines appointed by

Cromwell's Parliament recommended the practice of lining out, and it was adopted in Massachusetts a few years later. By the end of the century it had become the common way of singing among Anglicans and in other Protestant denominations (except Lutherans) throughout Britain and her colonies. It survives also in Scottish Gaelic on the Isle of Lewis. As settlers moved during the eighteenth and nineteenth centuries into the frontier South, they carried this way (now called the "old way") of singing with them.

Old Baptists in the central region of Appalachia opposed modern ways in singing, just as they withstood other forms of modernization in belief and practice. They resisted a nineteenth-century music literacy movement in which some of the melodies they used and continue to use were written out, boxed into regular musical meters, and harmonized in shape notation in songbooks such as *The Sacred Harp*. Camp-meeting folk hymns, spiritual songs, gospel songs, harmonization, note-reading (whether round notes or shaped notes), and the use of musical instruments such as organs in church all represented departures from the tried and true texts of their favorite eighteenth-century devotional hymn writers such as Isaac Watts and from the practice of lining out.

Gradually, however, the old way of singing retreated to the point where, in Appalachia today, lined hymnody is practiced in its most conservative manner only in Old Regular Baptist churches, those of the Thornton Union Association excepted. It is also practiced among a minority of Primitive Baptists (particularly in African American congregations), United Baptists, and a few churches of smaller denominations. These groups do not sing lined hymnody exclusively, however; a visitor to any of these churches might also hear more modern compositions, particularly gospel songs, sometimes lined out and sometimes not.

Lined singing among Old Baptists in Appalachia shares many features with Christian hymnody generally. The singing takes place in church, at memorial meetings, at baptisms, and in homes. The entire congregation of men, women, and children is invited to sing. The purpose is to praise God. Like almost all Christian hymns, Old Baptist lined-out hymnody consists of rhymed, metrical verse in a series of stanzas to which a repeating tune is set. The metrical verse patterns include common meter—alternating lines of 8 and 6 syllables (8, 6, 8, 6)—long meter (8, 8, 8, 8), short meter (6, 6, 8, 6), and others.

This lined singing also has distinctive characteristics. Among Old Regular Baptists, songbooks are kept at the pulpit and passed around to the song leaders. The books contain no musical notation. Among Old Regular favorites are *The Sweet Songster* (1854) and E. D. Thomas's *Hymns and Spiritual Songs* (1877), both containing hymn texts written chiefly by eighteenth- and nineteenth-century devotional poets. The singing is very slow and has no regularly recurring accent that invites foot tapping. No musical instruments are permitted. The melodies derive from the British-American folk music tune stock, not from classical music or from popular songs; thus, the melodies and singing style show an affinity with the British and American ballad tradition in Appalachia.

Tunes are passed along informally from one generation to the next. Singers learn by following and imitating others, not by reading notes. Characteristically, the group sings not in harmony but in heterophonic unison. That is, each singer elaborates a basic melodic line in his or her own way, singing one, two, or a few "in between" tones while the group moves from one principal melodic tone to the next. These melismatic melodic elaborations can also be heard in bluegrass (particularly gospel music) and to a recognizable extent in modern country music; they are among the defining features of the central Appalachian singing style. In a small minority of churches harmony singing by ear is condoned.

The rhythmic framework is governed not by metronome time but by breath-time. Outsiders are mistaken if they think the intent is singing with unified precision and the result falls short; rather, this singing is in step but deliberately just a little out of phase. Old Baptists say that this musical freedom has a "drawing power": it encourages both a unique melody and a quickening of spiritual feelings. As Elder I. D. Back puts it, "We believe in being tuned up with the grace of God and his Holy Spirit; and when that begins, it makes a melody, makes a joyful noise."

See also: AFRICAN AMERICAN RELIGIOUS TRADITIONS; BAPTISTS, THE OLD-TIME GROUPS.

—Jeff Todd Titon, *Brown University*

Primitive Baptist Hymns of the Blue Ridge, 2 LP recordings (1982); *Songs of the Old Regular Baptists: Lined-Out Hymnody from Southeastern Kentucky*, CD recording (1997); Jeff Todd Titon, "'The Real Thing': Tourism, Authenticity, and Pilgrimage among the Old Regular Baptists at the 1997 Smithsonian Folklife Festival," *The Worlds of Music* (1992).

Living Water Baptism

In much of southern and central Appalachia, *living water baptism* is a phrase employed to denote baptisms by immersion in natural bodies of water such as streams, rivers, ponds, or lakes, rather than in non-natural indoor or outdoor baptisteries. Treated as an absolute requirement in many Appalachian traditional denominations, living water baptism generally will be demanded for all converts other than perhaps those of advanced age or those who for any physical reasons are confined to home, hospital, or nursing-care environments.

This insistence upon a natural water site makes the close proximity of a baptismal spot—ideally within walking distance of the meetinghouse—highly important to a

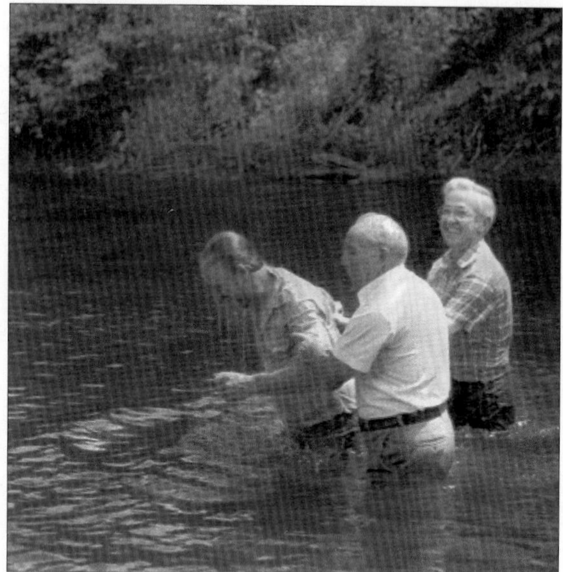

Baptism in the North Fork of the New River, Warrensville, North Carolina, 1991. Many Appalachian churches stand near rivers and lakes because of the need for natural, or "living water," baptismal sites.

fellowship. Thus multitudinous mountain churches rest beside and bear the names of their respective baptismal sites: Grassy Creek, Stoney Fork, Bent Branch, Beaver Dam, Mouth of Laurel. Unfortunately, some congregations in the coalfield regions of Appalachia have had their original baptismal streams declared unfit for such use because of various contaminants now present in the water. Such is currently the case for Bull Creek Old Regular Baptist Church near Grundy, Virginia.

—Howard Dorgan, *Appalachian State University, Emeritus*

Love Feast

Simple, shared, communal dining based on the New Testament–era *agape* (love) meals (Jude 12, Acts 2:46), love feasts were almost certainly connected with early Christian development of the Eucharist but were also distinct from it. However, by the end of the third century such meals had gradually disappeared.

Love feasts were reintroduced in Western Christianity by seventeenth-century German Pietist Brethren (Dunkards, Church of the Brethren, and related groups), who have observed the custom since their origins in 1708. Moravians followed in 1727 and passed the custom to John Wesley in the late 1730s; it became a feature of early Methodism. These traditions had no sacramental meaning, focusing instead on love and fellowship.

Brethren use the term *love feast* for a special worship service (or series of services) patterned after a literal reading of John 13. Traditionally held twice a year, it includes self-examination and individual confession, foot washing, passing the holy kiss, a shared meal, and communion. The menu varies but usually includes bread, water, and a beef (or lamb) broth.

Among Moravians a love feast may be observed on several special occasions, but the best known are at Christmas Eve and the Friday before Easter. The service consists of an opening prayer, hymn singing, and a meal of sweetened rolls and coffee or tea. For early Methodists the service often preceded communion and included a collection for the poor, but the practice underwent a gradual decline and became limited to conference gatherings. Wesleyan Holiness movements, particularly the Free Methodist Church, retained the service well into the twentieth century.

See also: HOLY KISS; METHODISTS; MORAVIANS.

—David B. Eller. *Elizabethtown College*

Lowe, William

(1756–1835) Brethren preacher of universal salvation.

Although William Lowe's religious career was not exclusive to the Appalachian region, the legacy of his work is important there because of his involvement in the planting of Universalist theology on the trans-Allegheny frontier. Lowe is credited with organizing Consolation Church, the first Universalist church west of the Allegheny Mountains.

A native of Virginia, Lowe lived as a young man in Orange County, North Carolina, where he married Margret Fair. He joined the Church of the Brethren in South Carolina, probably under the influence of David Martin. He may also have been placed in the ministry under Martin's tutelage. By the late 1780s he was living in Sumner County, in middle Tennessee. Then, in the mid-1790s, he relocated to Drakes Creek in Warren County (later Simpson County), Kentucky, where he spent the remainder of his life. Here he became part of a Brethren congregation led by John Hendricks and Gasper Roland Jr. from North Carolina, both preachers of universal salvation.

An itinerant preacher, Lowe helped organize Consolation Church at a location near Hopkinsville in Christian County, Kentucky, in 1819. Although there is no record that this congregation observed traditional Brethren ordinances (triune immersion or love feast), it did profess the universal salvation doctrine. After Lowe's death, the congregation gradually allied itself with the Universalist denomination and became the mother church of other Universalist congregations in southwest Kentucky.

See also: BRETHREN; LOVE FEAST; PRIMITIVE BAPTIST UNIVERSALISTS.

—David B. Eller, *Elizabethtown College*

Lutherans

Lutherans were among the earliest European settlers of Appalachia and have constituted a large and consistent religious presence in the region until modern times. Drawing on both indigenous roots and denominational connections beyond the region, religiously motivated Lutherans continue to contribute to the quality of life in Appalachia.

Appalachian Lutherans are primarily of German descent. Migrating from eastern Pennsylvania and adjacent areas in the 1720s, they began settling in the Shenandoah Valley, extending themselves into east Tennessee and western North Carolina by the 1780s. From their many Virginia settlements, Lutherans and their missionary pastors worked their way over the mountains into the territory of present-day West Virginia and southern Ohio. From Tennessee and North Carolina, they immigrated in lesser numbers into the reaches of southern Appalachia, supplemented by German settlers moving westward from South Carolina ports. Other Pennsylvania Lutherans followed the path that became the national pike through western Maryland, joining the Scots-Irish in populating western Pennsylvania, northern West Virginia, and southern Ohio. Still more German Lutherans journeyed north along the Susquehanna River and its branches, thus becoming well represented in northern Appalachia. They shared many of their first church buildings there with the German Reformed, the other major German Protestant family.

People of the land, Lutheran immigrants in Appalachia remained largely rural, usually leaving settling of towns to others. While more often choosing bottomland for their farms, Lutherans also numbered among the upland peoples. Some scholars estimate that Germans made up about a fifth of the Appalachian population during white settlement, second in number only to the Scots-Irish.

As industrialization swept the region, Lutheran numbers grew. While some urban members of the faith belonged to the business and professional classes, the vast majority of Lutherans either joined the forces of labor or continued their ancestral vocation of farming. Those of Slovak and Swedish descent, in particular, came to northern Appalachia to work the mines, mills, and land.

By the 1990s there were more than 450,000 Lutherans in Appalachia, about 5.4 percent of the total Lutheran population in the United States and 2.2 percent of the population of Appalachia. Judging by these figures, the 1,326 Lutheran congregations in Appalachia in 1990 had not held their portion of the German-descended population, nor had they made much evangelistic progress. Deindustrialization in Appalachia hit Lutheran churches hard. Many rural and old-industrial-town congregations shrank, and some closed. Despite a historic presence in Appalachia, the distinctive theological and cultural traits of Lutheranism stood in stark and unpopular contrast to the revivalism and independence of most Appalachian religious groups.

The Lutheran religious message emphasizes the forgiveness of God as a free gift established by Jesus Christ, and Lutherans uphold the scriptures and creeds of the Catholic Church. The group took its name from sixteenth-century German monk Martin Luther, who broke from the medieval Roman Catholic Church and touched off the widespread Protestant Reformation. Lutherans in northern Europe and North America preserved Catholic traditions to various degrees, thus setting themselves apart from many other Protestant groups. Confessional theology, ordained ministry, sacraments, and churchly order differentiated Lutherans from a majority of Appalachian Christians. However, Appalachian Lutherans developed from styles of the faith that were more Protestant than Catholic and often assimilated the traits of neighboring Protestant movements. Consequently, many Appalachian Lutherans are distinct from Lutherans elsewhere but still are more conforming to churchly order than most Appalachian Protestants.

An example of the strong twentieth-century connection between Lutheranism and its Appalachian context was the mission work of Kenneth Killinger in Smyth, Washington, and Grayson Counties in southwestern Virginia. A gristmill owner turned preacher who later received official certification and wide denominational support for his ministry, Killinger founded several remote mountain congregations, health clinics, and schools during the first half of the twentieth century. A native Appalachian, Killinger is representative of how indigenous Appalachian Lutheranism connected with other Lutherans and resources outside the region; he also provides an example of a mainline Protestant social service that did not originate from paternalistic impulses outside Appalachia. Lutherans—among the most energetic in religious social service through the nineteenth and twentieth centuries—established schools and community service organizations throughout the region.

Ninety percent of Appalachian Lutheran congregations belong to the Evangelical Lutheran Church in America, the largest denomination of Lutherans in North America, while most of the remaining 10 percent belong to the Lutheran Church–Missouri Synod. Both groups were members of the Commission on Religion in Appalachia upon its founding in 1965–66, with the evangelicals represented at the time by its two predecessor denominations before their merger. One of those predecessors formed the Appalachian Regional Intersynodical Coordinating Committee in 1967, and that work continued with the 1990 institution of the Evangelical Lutheran Coalition for Mission in Appalachia.

In 1967 Lutheran clergyman and rural sociologist B. B. Maurer founded the Appalachian Regional School for Church Leaders within the extension service of West Virginia

University. One of only four such programs in the nation, the school brought the educational resources of the state university to the under-serviced population of pastors and enhanced the community development role of local churches. Lutherans led the school until it closed in 1988. When the Appalachian Ministries Educational Resource Center was founded in 1987, Lutherans J. R. Hale and, later, John A. Rodgers were involved. These men directed the Town and Country Church Institute (founded 1981) at the Lutheran Theological Seminary at Gettysburg, Pennsylvania, which maintained a commitment to research and training for Appalachian ministry.

See also: CATHOLICISM; GERMANS (RACE, ETHNICITY, AND IDENTITY).

—Gilson A. C. Waldkoenig, *Lutheran Theological Seminary at Gettysburg*

H. George Anderson, *Lutheranism in the Southeastern States* (1969); C. W. Cassell et al., *History of the Lutheran Church in Virginia and East Tennessee* (1930); William. E. Eisenberg, *The Lutheran Church in Virginia* (1967); Sherree R. Tannen, *Kenneth Killinger: Mountain Missionary* (1995).

Mayes, Henry

(1898–1986) Evangelist.

Henry Harrison Mayes dedicated more than sixty years of his life to erecting road signs that declare "Prepare to Meet God," "Jesus Is Coming Soon," and similar religious messages. His evangelical declarations still are found along roadsides in forty-four states.

Born in Goins, Tennessee, Mayes became a coal miner at age thirteen; however, after a serious mining accident (c. 1920), he promised God that were he to recover he would dedicate his life to this version of Christian evangelism. His first efforts involved painted messages on railway cars and rocks. Then, in the early 1940s, he began erecting the fourteen-hundred-pound concrete crosses and hearts for which he became best known. Nine feet high, these monuments declared "Get Right with God" on one side and "Jesus Is Coming Soon" on the other. Aluminum, wood, and corrugated metal also were among materials he used in his evangelism. In addition, Mayes made one-of-a-kind signs: a "Give God Your Heart" painted on a discarded boiler, an 80-foot metal sign stretched across a gorge near Tazewell, Tennessee, and a 150-foot illuminated cross overlooking Middlesboro, Kentucky.

The house Mayes built in Middlesboro also embodied a religious statement. Constructed in the shape of a cross, it displayed "Jesus Saves" on the roof for the benefit of passengers in low-flying airplanes. He also sent his messages out in fifty-six thousand whiskey bottles. Transcribed in a number of languages, an effort for which he received help from the University of Tennessee, these floating messages were tossed into rivers or oceans. One such bottle was returned from the Philippines sixteen years after being set adrift.

Much of Mayes's work is on permanent display at the Museum of Appalachia in Norris, Tennessee.

—Ronnie Seals, *Monroe, Michigan*

Catherine Mayes, *A Coal Miner's Simple Message* (1999).

McGready, James

(1763?–1817) Camp revivalist preacher.

James McGready is generally credited with introducing the frontier camp meeting and as being one of the principal forces behind the Great Western Revival (or Second Great Awakening) of 1787–1805, a wave of emotionally intense revivals in Kentucky and Tennessee that greatly influenced the distinctive nature of Appalachian religion. When his vehement, emotional sermons full of denunciations of sin and vivid descriptions of hell as brimstone and a lake of fire offended upper-class families in his Stony Creek, North Carolina, congregation, he relocated to Logan County, Kentucky.

Unlike other Presbyterian revivalist preachers in Kentucky at the time, McGready held to the Westminster Confession and its doctrines of total depravity, irresistible grace, and election. Scholarship in the 1980s and 1990s linked New Light theology, and thus McGready, to beliefs prevalent in southwest Scotland in the late sixteenth century. His beliefs about conversion and eschatology, or the last days of mankind, were traditionalist, reflecting those of eighteenth-century revivalists such as Jonathan Edwards and George Whitefield.

Following a particularly large revival at Red River in June 1800, McGready introduced the frontier camp meeting, which featured wagons, campsites, food and drink, an outdoor preaching stand, long benches, and four days of continuous preaching and worship. Kentucky's great revival period climaxed with the August 1801 Cane Ridge camp meeting, a six-day event attended by an estimated twenty thousand. In 1810 McGready and other suspended revivalists founded the Cumberland Presbytery, which became the foundation for the Cumberland Presbyterian Church.

See also: GREAT WESTERN REVIVAL AND CAMP-MEETING MOVEMENT; STONE, BARTON W.

—Glenn Ellen Starr Stilling, *Appalachian State University*

Memorial Services

Three types of annual memorials for the deceased are found among the practices of central Appalachia's more traditional churches, particularly Old-Time Baptist fellowships: home, graveside, and within-the-church memorials. The first of these is primarily a family affair. Kin gather at a patriarch's home for a one-, two-, or three-day celebration of all departed members of the lineage, especially those of the more recent three or four generations. A combination of both reunion and memorial conventions, these events frequently involve a ceremonial calling out of the names of the deceased, and may even include the reading of obituaries published in church association minutes, at least for individuals who died that year.

Graveside memorials are similar to what are more popularly known as "decoration days," events that entail an annual cleaning and redecorating of respective cemeteries. However, the more traditional graveside memorials involve a full preaching service (including several exhorters) and the calling out of names. Within-the-church memorials have the potential of becoming the most emotional of these commemorative events. Some fellowships accompany the traditional calling out of names with brief oral history narratives concerning selected deceased church members that remind the congregation of behaviors that made these individuals so cherished. Living family members prize these accounts and may respond with cries, shouts, or other expressions of jubilation.

See also: ASSOCIATIONS, BAPTIST; BAPTISTS, THE OLD-TIME GROUPS.

—Howard Dorgan, *Appalachian State University, Emeritus*

Mennonites

The Mennonite family includes various groups that trace their heritage to the radical wing of the Protestant Reformation. Sometimes classified as Anabaptists, these believers emphasized adult or "believer's" baptism and a discipleship generally defined in terms of nonconformity to the world, nonresistance, and abstention from holding governmental office. The Mennonite family consists of two major branches. The southern branch traces its heritage to Switzerland, southern Germany, and the Alsace region; the northern to the Netherlands, northern Germany (Prussia), and especially Russia. With few exceptions, Mennonite congregations in the Appalachian region derived from the southern branch.

Old Order Amish

Old Order Amish originated during the late seventeenth century from a split led by Swiss Mennonite elder Jacob Ammonn. Historically, the Amish have defined nonconformity to the world in absolute terms, including strict observance of church discipline, a plain-dress code, and a ban on the use of tractors, cars, and telephones. Worship services are held in members' homes, and adherents reject not only church buildings but also most formal church organizations. Education beyond eighth grade is carried on outside the schools, integrating life and learning in an agricultural and religious community. *Old Order Amish* is strictly a North American term, distinguishing those traditionalists who have resisted innovations promoted by more progressive groups. Within Appalachia, approximately half of the Old Order Amish congregations are in Pennsylvania. The others are in Ohio, New York, and Kentucky.

Beachy Amish

Composed of some one hundred or more congregations in more than twenty states and six countries, of which fourteen Appalachian congregations were listed in 1997, Beachy Amish separated from the Old Order during the first half of the twentieth century. In 1927, prior to the official split, this group began its separate worship, led by a southwestern Pennsylvania bishop, Moses M. Beachy, who was reluctant to enforce the strict ban in church discipline. Then, with the introduction among Beachy followers of automobiles, electricity, telephones, and church meetinghouses, Amish tensions led to the formal institution of the Beachy Amish Church. This faith has supported missions and, through the Amish Mennonite Aid Society, sponsored relief work in both post–World War II Europe and Latin America. Except for a heavier presence in Ohio and Pennsylvania, there are few Beachy congregations in the Appalachian region.

Conservative Mennonite Conference

Another group that traces its heritage to the Amish community is the Conservative Mennonite Conference (known prior to 1957 as the Conservative Amish Mennonite Conference). It maintains fraternal ties with the Mennonite Conference (mentioned later), but remains independent. Appalachian congregations are located in Kentucky, Maryland, Ohio, and Pennsylvania.

Wayne and E. Mae Wenger and children, Breathitt County, Kentucky, 1955. Mennonite and Amish families incorporate nonconformity to worldliness into their daily lives, most notably through simplicity of dress and bans on the use of some technology.

Church of God in Christ Mennonites

Formerly identified as Holdeman Mennonites, the Church of God in Christ Mennonites originally were named after John Holdeman from Wayne County, Ohio, who (influenced by Methodist revivalism) broke with his Mennonite church in 1859. Holdeman attracted few followers until Russian Mennonite immigrants began to join in the 1870s. The group has attempted to maintain strict church discipline and the principle of nonconformity, defined in part as regulation of dress and facial hair styles, with men growing beards and women wearing black head coverings. Along with revivals, they have historically emphasized the validity of dreams, visions, and revelations and are active in relief efforts, missions, and tract distribution. Seven Church of God in Christ Mennonite congregations are found in the Appalachian region: three in Mississippi, two in Pennsylvania, and one each in Tennessee and Georgia.

Mennonite Conference/ General Conference Mennonite Church

The oldest and largest faction of Appalachian Mennonites is composed of the churches of the Mennonite Conference, who are in the process of merging with the General Conference Mennonite Church. Therefore, these two are treated collectively. Originating primarily from the original settlements of Mennonites in Pennsylvania who were part of the seventeenth- and eighteenth-century Swiss/southern German movement of Mennonite and Amish immigrants, the Mennonite Conference has been characterized by a diversity in faith and practice. This has led to groups breaking off formal ties while often maintaining fraternal relations with the conference. There are five or more congregations within each of the Appalachian regions of New York, Ohio, North Carolina, and Mississippi. In addition, there are more than fifty fellowships in Pennsylvania.

The General Conference Mennonite Church, organized in 1860 at West Point, Iowa, was composed of both southern German and Alsatian Mennonites who migrated after 1815. In the 1870s a number of Russian Mennonite immigrants joined the conference, making it truly a merger of both the northern and southern branches of the family. Within Appalachia there are probably fewer than five General Conference congregations, all located in Ohio and Pennsylvania. Both conferences have exercised leadership in the broad Mennonite community in promoting colleges and missions, in enunciating the meaning and significance of the Anabaptist vision, and in directing the work of the Mennonite Central Committee, an inter-Mennonite relief and service agency.

In addition, there are a number of Mennonite conferences that, while retaining fraternal relations, do not participate in the Mennonite Conference General Assembly. A majority of these have been founded since 1970, often in response to what some believe are overt modernizing tendencies in the Mennonite Conference.

Eastern Pennsylvania Mennonite Church

The Eastern Pennsylvania Mennonite Church was founded in 1968 when several congregations left the Lancaster Conference, one of the conferences in the Mennonite Conference. At issue was a debate over maintaining biblical practices, including questions concerning whether men should enter professions, women cut their hair, couples divorce or remarry, children attend public schools, and even whether members should purchase commercial, health, and life insurance. More than thirty of the fifty-eight congregations listed in 1997 were located in Pennsylvania, of which approximately six were in the Appalachian region.

Evangelical Mennonite Church (United States)

The Wadsworth Avenue Evangelical Church at Meadville, Pennsylvania, is part of the Evangelical Mennonite Church (United States). Previously known as the Defenseless Mennonite Church, it was founded in Ohio in 1864. Originally marked by its conservative dress and doctrine, the Evangelical Mennonite Church (United States) has dropped many of the external markings of Mennonite traditionalism.

Brethren in Christ Mennonites

The Brethren in Christ denomination, founded in Pennsylvania around 1780, grew out of a revival movement in Lancaster County. Known originally as the River Brethren, this group registered with the U.S. government as a peace church during the Civil War and changed its name to Brethren in Christ. One of the first Brethren in Christ churches in Appalachia was founded near Bedford, Pennsylvania, around 1830. The group stressed revivals, a simple lifestyle, and church discipline. Unique to the group was its emphasis not only on a crisis conversion experience but also an acceptance of the Wesleyan concept of holiness. It emphasizes both missions and a call for social justice. While there are several churches in Ohio, Kentucky, middle and east Tennessee, Virginia, and West Virginia, nearly 75 percent of Brethren in Christ churches in the Appalachian region are located in Pennsylvania.

Mennonite Brethren Church

The Mennonite Brethren Church, third largest of the Mennonite conferences, originated in Russia in 1860. It combines both an Anabaptist heritage and evangelical emphasis. Except for one church on the border of the Appalachian region in New York, the only Appalachian Mennonite Brethren churches are located in the Boone, North Carolina, area. The churches in the Boone area are distinctive in two respects: (l) they came into the Mennonite Brethren Conference due to a 1960 merger of the Krimmer Mennonite Brethren (originating in the Crimea in 1869) with the Mennonite Brethren; (2) the group of five congregations in the Boone, Lenoir, and Newland, North Carolina, area hold membership in the African American Mennonite Association. The association, a successor to the Black Caucus in the Mennonite Church, includes Mennonite congregations whose membership is 80 to 100 percent African American. Among its goals are the fostering and recruitment of African American males for leadership positions in the church as well as a full recognition of the African American heritage within the Mennonite churches. Begun as a mission outreach by the Krimmer Mennonite Brethren, the Boone area Mennonite Brethren churches have moved towards greater independence under the leadership of Rondo Horton, an African American who began preaching in 1933 and served as moderator of the North Carolina Conference from 1955 until his death in 1986.

Bruderhof (Society of Brothers)

The six Bruderhofs (individual communal associations) in Pennsylvania and New York belong to a group known as the Society of Brethren. Unlike their counterparts in the western states, these six have not joined the Hutterian Brethren. The Brethren practice a way of life marked by communal landownership and clearly enunciated lines of authority and responsibilities based on the members' understanding of God's order as it affects property, child-rearing, education, and interpersonal relationships.

See also: AFRICAN AMERICAN RELIGIOUS TRADITIONS; GERMANS (RACE, ETHNICITY, AND IDENTITY); SWISS (RACE, ETHNICITY, AND IDENTITY).

—Harvey Neufeldt, *Tennessee Technological University*

Cornelius J. Dyck, *An Introduction to Mennonite History* (1993); *General Conference Brethren in Christ Church: Official Annual Directory* (1999); James E. Horsch, *Mennonite Yearbook and Directory* (1997); *Mennonite Encyclopedia* (1955–90); Conrad Ostwalt, "The Junaluska Community of Boone," Center for Mennonite Studies (1991); C. Henry Smith, *Smith's Story of the Mennonites* (1981).

Methodist Circuit Riders

Methodism began at Oxford University in England in 1729 simply as a Lincoln College holiness movement that showed no initial intention of becoming a new Protestant denomination. However, a half-century later the new faith had reached much of the settled region of Appalachia and was building a base for what eventually would become the second- or third-largest denomination in the region. This rapid American expansion of Wesleyanism was due in part to the efforts of Bishop Francis Asbury and the hundreds of horseback-riding Methodist preachers whom he enlisted to travel the rugged mountain circuits linking individual cabins and small settlements. Only much later did these circuits become networks of actual churches.

The type of evangelism practiced by Methodist circuit riders meshed well with both the emerging religious temperament and the sparsely settled environments of Appalachia.

Circuit riders were welcome guests to the isolated families and communities of Appalachia.

Methodism's free-grace theology was comforting to settlers who faced harsh survival concerns that made more elaborate dogmas seem less applicable. The lone circuit rider did not threaten that sense of religious independence that had early begun to develop in the mountains. In addition, the circuit rider often provided services other than purely spiritual ones: news from afar; perhaps an application of some remedy from John Wesley's *Primitive Physic* (1747), a volume on herbal medicines; the sanctification of a common law marriage; the memorialization of a death; or the passing along of some domestic skill or agricultural knowledge enjoyed elsewhere.

In England, Wesley had himself been an untiring itinerant preacher, traveling by horseback as much as five thousand miles a year. In America, Asbury gave the traveling Methodist preacher a more structured purpose by formally organizing networks of cabins and settlements (and eventually formal churches) into "circuits" that a preacher would service at regular intervals.

In 1783 the Holston Circuit in east Tennessee and southwest Virginia became one of the earliest of such networks. It tied together settlements on the Watauga, Nolichucky, and Holston Rivers, covering geographic locales that now lie in Carter, Greene, Hawkins, Johnson, Sullivan, and Washington Counties, Tennessee, and in Lee, Russell, Scott, Smyth, and Washington Counties, Virginia. To reach the Holston Circuit region, Asbury crossed the Appalachians near the present community of Elk Park, North Carolina. He is reported to have transited the Appalachian range sixty times during his American preaching career.

By 1784, especially in North Carolina, a number of Methodist circuit riders had become known as Republican Methodists, identified as such because they opposed slavery and even went so far as to bar slaveholders from communion. This contribution to the social consciousness of the region, tied to the secular roles also played by the visiting preachers, suggests that Methodist circuit riders of the late eighteenth and early nineteenth centuries should be measured by regional influence other than just the building of a denomination.

See also: ASBURY, FRANCIS; CARTWRIGHT, PETER; METHODISTS.

—Howard Dorgan, *Appalachian State University, Emeritus*

Methodists

This movement began with Oxford University students whose methodical and enthusiastic religious asceticism earned them the nickname *Methodists.* Around 1760 Irish Methodist Robert Strawbridge immigrated to America, settling on Sam's Creek in Appalachian Maryland to preach. The log meetinghouse he built was the first American Methodist church building. In 1769 Robert Williams became the first Methodist itinerant preacher in the New World, spreading Methodism southward through Appalachia, from New York to Virginia and North Carolina. Methodist groups still maintain Bible-based emphases on free will, individual personal responsibility before God, spiritual revival, and missions.

Methodists comprise the third-largest denominational family in the Appalachian region and the United States. Of the nearly 12.6 million Methodists nationwide, about 15 percent were in Appalachia, with Methodist family churches in 396 of the 406 Appalachian counties in 2000. Overall, Methodists comprise 9.2 percent of the region's population, distributed among seven Methodist denominations.

African Methodist Episcopal Zion Church

In 1796 African American parishioners of the John Street Methodist Episcopal Church in New York City, disconcerted by their exclusion from church management, organized a separate congregation with the approval of Anglo-American Bishop Francis Asbury of the Methodist Episcopal Church. The group continued to meet in the John Street church until 1800, when they erected their own building, Zion. In 1820 the group withdrew from the Methodist Episcopal Church. The following year, congregations from New York, Connecticut, New Jersey, and Pennsylvania held an annual conference and elected James Varick (1750?–1828), their original leader, as their first bishop. The name *African Methodist Episcopal Zion Church* was adopted in 1848, and though the denomination spread rapidly throughout the North, mostly after the Civil War, the greatest growth was in the Southeast, including southern Appalachia. Between 1866 and 1868 membership quadrupled. Church doctrine and polity are Methodist. Its chief policymaking body is the quadrennial General Conference. A bishop presides over each of the twelve episcopal areas. The church supports Livingstone College in North Carolina, missions in the United States, Africa, the West Indies, and South America, and publications including *Star of Zion*, *Quarterly Review*, and *Missionary Seer.*

The African Methodist Episcopal Zion Church is the second-largest Methodist church in the region and nation. Of the nation's 1.42 million AME Zion members, 9.5 percent are in Appalachia. The denomination has 277 churches in ninety-one Appalachian counties, concentrated in the southern areas of the region, especially around Birmingham, Alabama. The denomination has been growing slightly faster than the population in forty-eight Appalachian counties.

Allegheny Wesleyan Methodist Connection

Though John Wesley and American Methodist leaders vigorously denounced human slavery, its economic advantages seduced many of the Methodist Episcopal Church's ministers and members. When a group of ministers in the New England

Conference began to preach abolition, the bishops sought to silence them to avoid schism, causing many churches and ministers to withdraw from the denomination. On May 13, 1841, a new annual conference formed the Wesleyan Methodist Church, free from episcopacy and slavery. Its first convention was held in 1843 to organize a "Connection" of local churches in annual conferences. It avoided bishops, providing equal ministerial and lay representation in all governing bodies. The church advocated moral and social reform, especially prohibitions on slaveholding and intoxicating liquors. When the Civil War ended, some members returned to larger Methodist denominations. The rest were split to become the Allegheny Wesleyan Methodist Connection, based in Appalachia, and the evangelism-focused Wesleyan Church. Members must be "regenerated" adults (made new by the Holy Spirit) seeking or having attained sanctification (perfection in holiness).

Of its 2,500 national adherents, the Allegheny Wesleyan Methodist Connection has 1,858 in the region—74 percent of the denomination's membership. The denomination has eighty-one churches in thirty-six Appalachian counties.

Evangelical Methodist Church

Founded in 1946 after breaking from the larger Methodist Church, the Evangelical Methodist Church preaches the biblical imperatives of early Methodism. The denomination endorses congregational church government, affording greater freedom for local churches to set their own budgets, call their own pastors, and operate their own programs. Based in Indianapolis, Indiana the denomination exists as a resource for its local churches. It upholds standards of professional conduct for pastors and conference officials and endorses a committed belief in the Bible-based tenets of early Methodism. Members of the denomination denounce what they view as other Methodists' liberalism, charismatic worship, and emphasis on social action.

More than twenty-five hundred members of the Evangelical Methodist Church—about one-fourth of the denomination's national enrollment of eleven thousand—are in Appalachian counties. The church has twenty-two churches in twenty Appalachian counties. About a third of its members are in Georgia.

Free Methodist Church of North America

In Pekin, New York, in 1860, the Free Methodist Church was founded by ministers and laypeople expelled from the Methodist Episcopal church in the Genesee New York Conference because of their dissatisfaction over other Methodists' departure from Wesleyan teaching. Free Methodists emphasized basic biblical freedoms, promoting equal rights (especially for women) and holiness. Headquartered at Indianapolis, the denomination adheres to the doctrines and practices of early Methodism. Its polity is similar to the Methodist Church. The chief policy-making body is a general conference. Like the Evangelical and Wesleyan Methodist Churches, the Free Methodist Church emphasizes the doctrine of Christian perfection, known also as "perfect love," sanctification, or holiness. Unlike other Methodist Holiness churches, however, the group also emphasizes education and social concern. The denomination supports several institutions of higher education, a seminary, a worldwide radio ministry, and an international missionary program.

The Free Methodist Church is the nation's fourth-largest Methodist denomination, third largest in Appalachia. Of nearly eighty-three thousand national members, nearly twelve thousand members, 14.2 percent, are in Appalachia. The denomination has 197 churches in eighty counties. About 80 percent of its congregations and 86 percent of its members are in northern Appalachia—New York, Pennsylvania, and Ohio. Free Methodists are most prevalent in Ohio's Monroe County, comprising 4.1 percent of the population.

Primitive Methodist Church

In 1807 British Wesleyan leaders dismissed two Methodist preachers who led an outdoor revival without permission, refusing church membership to their converts. After waiting two years for acceptance into the established church, the converts formed the Society of Primitive Methodists, aspiring to return to the roots of the Methodist movement. In 1829 Primitive Methodist missionaries began ministries among English and Welsh immigrants living in American industrial and mining areas, especially Appalachia. On September 16, 1840, the American Primitive Methodist Church was established. The denomination's beliefs include biblical inerrancy, spiritual regeneration and sanctification, premillennialism (a doctrine emphasizing the imminent coming of Christ and the destruction of the world), and the importance of Christian service.

The majority of the members of the Primitive Methodist denomination are Appalachian. Of eight thousand national members, 61 percent are in thirty-nine churches in nine Appalachian counties.

United Methodist Church

Formed in 1968 by merger of the Methodist church and the primarily Appalachian Evangelical United Brethren church, the United Methodist Church supports more than 125 secondary schools, colleges, and universities; fourteen seminaries; two publishing houses; and missions in the United States and fifty-one other countries. The denomination is an episcopal democracy. Local congregations form districts governed by superintendents and supervised by bishop-led annual conferences. A bishop's "area" may include more than one conference. Conferences meet every four years for a legislating General Conference, composed of lay and clerical delegates. Doctrines, laws, and liturgies are contained in a book of discipline and are revised following each General Conference. A judicial council hears appeals when disagreements or needs for clarification arise. Though United Methodists endorse the Apostles' Creed, they are the most liberal of the Methodist groups.

The United Methodist Church is the third largest of all denominations in Appalachia and the United States. It had churches in 396 of 406 Appalachian counties in 2000. Of the United Methodists' 11.1 million national adherents, nearly 1.75 million (15.7 percent) are Appalachian. United Methodists comprise 90 percent of national and regional Methodist family members. Regionally, they are most prevalent on the eastern edge of Appalachia, from Scranton, Pennsylvania, to Tennessee's Tri-Cities.

Wesleyan Church

After the Civil War ended slavery, many members of the abolitionist Wesleyan Methodist Connection felt there was no need for the Connection to continue, and they returned to larger Methodist bodies. At the 1867 Wesleyan Methodist General Conference, those remaining affirmed the continuing need for their denominational protest against the effects of slavery, alcohol, and secret societies. At its first General Conference in 1843, the Connection officially adopted the doctrine of sanctification, becoming the first Methodist denomination to do so. In 1867 its first national camp meeting was held, leading to the formation of the National Holiness Association. Personal holiness, rather than social and political reform, became the Connection's major focus. In 1883 the General Conference adopted a resolution requiring the preaching of entire sanctification (perfect holiness), and by 1893 new articles of religion on regeneration and entire sanctification had been adopted by the General Conference, the annual conferences, and local churches. By 1891 denominational evangelism led to the gradual development of a more formal church organization, the Wesleyan Methodist Connection (or Church) of America, led by a general missionary superintendent. In 1947 it became the Wesleyan Methodist Church of America, supervised by a general conference president and board of administration. Headquartered in Marion, Indiana, the church has been led jointly by three general superintendents since 1959 and supports the Hephzibah Faith Missionary Society, the Missionary Bands of the World, the Alliance of the Reformed Baptist Church of Canada, and many other missions around the world.

The Wesleyan Church is the third-largest denomination in the Methodist denominational family nationally. Of nearly 261,000 Wesleyans in the nation, 37,440 (14.3 percent) are Appalachian. Fifty-five percent of regional members are in the northern Appalachian region of New York, Ohio, and Pennsylvania, with 304 Wesleyan churches in 127 Appalachian counties.

See also: AFRICAN AMERICAN RELIGIOUS TRADITIONS; ASBURY, FRANCIS; CARTWRIGHT, PETER.

—Heather Ann Ackley Bean, *Azusa Pacific University*

The Discipline of the Primitive Methodist Church (1995); *The Discipline of the Wesleyan Church* (1996); *Evangelical Methodist Church Book of Discipline* (1998); *Free Methodist New Life Discipleship Series* (1989); Clifford A. Grammich Jr., *Appalachian Atlas: Maps of the Churches and People of the Appalachian Region* (1994); Sandy Dwayne Martin, *For God and Race: The Religious and Political Leadership of African Methodist Episcopal Bishop James Walker Hood* (1999); *The United Methodist Book of Discipline* (1996).

Miller, Jacob

(1735?–1815) German Baptist Brethren leader and emancipationist.

Active in the Blue Ridge and Roanoke Valley areas of Appalachia, Jacob Miller established himself as a leader of German Baptist Brethren and as an advocate for the freeing of Brethren-owned slaves. Born in Franklin County, Pennsylvania, Miller was ordained in the Antietam Brethren Church in 1762. Sometime before 1775, he moved to Franklin County, Virginia, where he established the second permanent Virginia Brethren settlement. He then baptized an English pacifist, William Smith, who helped found Brethren churches for both German- and English-speaking settlers in Franklin and Floyd Counties, Virginia.

Miller developed such a reputation that the Brethren held their 1797 Annual Meeting in Franklin County. At that gathering these German Pietists passed a resolution which forbade Brethren to own slaves. The ruling first stipulated that no brother or sister should purchase slaves and further judged that if such an ownership already existed, then the respective slaves should be emancipated as soon as—by their own labors—they had repaid their purchase prices. The determination that such a repayment had been achieved was to be made by the nearest Brethren church. The ruling continued by prescribing that the freed slave should be provided a "good suit of wearing apparel," just as acceptable as those clothes that might be allotted a white servant. Under Miller's leadership, Appalachian German Brethren thus participated in this significant declaration of human rights.

See also: BRETHREN; MOOMAW, B. F.

—Beatrice Naff Bailey, *Clemson University*

Miller, Robert Johnstone

(1758–1834) Episcopal missionary.

Perhaps no other person affected the early years of the Episcopal witness in Appalachia as did Robert Johnstone Miller. It is equally true that no leader in this tradition has been so overlooked. Miller was one of the first Episcopal frontier missionaries in southern Appalachia, and he was an anomaly regarding ecumenical relations.

Born July 11, 1758, in Baldovie, Scotland, Miller came to America in 1774. He served in the Continental Army before moving to Lincoln County, North Carolina, in 1786, where he functioned as a catechist to a small group of Episcopalians. However, as there was no organized Episcopal diocese in North Carolina at the time, Miller soon aligned himself with the Lutheran Church. Subsequently, he was ordained by that faith in 1794, but with a unique stipulation: he would remain Episcopalian, and once that denomination organized in the region, he would seek ordination with them.

In 1811 Miller was appointed traveling missionary for the North Carolina Lutheran Synod. During his first year, he covered three thousand miles in Tennessee, southwestern Virginia, and the western reaches of North and South Carolina, establishing numerous congregations. Finally, on 28 April 1821, Miller was ordained an Episcopal deacon in the morning and an Episcopal priest on the same afternoon. For the next thirteen years he ministered in Burke County, North Carolina, providing a training ground for Episcopal missionaries who then ventured deeper into Appalachia.

Miller's ministry was contrary to fears of interfaith cooperation and doctrinal fusion. His founding of the "Fraternal Union" between Lutherans and Episcopalians anticipated the ecumenical atmosphere two centuries later.

See also: EPISCOPAL CHURCH.

—Scott A. Oxford, *Episcopal Diocese of Western North Carolina*

Missionary/Anti-Missionary Split

During the 1820s a controversy erupted among central and southern Appalachian Baptist churches over biblical authority for intercongregational organizations, particularly the appropriateness and biblical validity of missionary programs. Off and on through the remainder of the nineteenth century, this dispute divided fellowships who adhered to John Calvin's belief in particular atonement (that Christ's atonement includes only those elected individuals whom God chose before time began), on the one side, from the congregations who believed in general atonement (that Christ died for all humanity's sins and God's grace extends equally to all humanity), on the other. Frontier Calvinists pronounced that if God had already elected his church, then missionary work was only man's futile effort to usurp God's role.

However, evangelism had not always been dismissed by Calvinists. During the Great Awakening (1726–56), particular-election orators such as George Whitefield and Jonathan Edwards played dramatic roles in instituting a thirty-year revival. Although some parish-based churches resisted the emotionalism of this renewal, Methodist, Presbyterian, and Baptist denominations used the movement to increase their numbers and solidify their doctrines. By traveling from one church to another with the message of spiritual rebirth, itinerant preachers created networks of doctrinal unity within the denominations.

Not being bound to their geographic locations by a parish system, these Baptist, Methodist, and Presbyterians then spread westward with the early Appalachian settlers. The rugged life in frontier communities demanded self-reliance, which in turn facilitated a gospel of individual salvation and local church autonomy—basic tenets especially of the Baptists. Thus, during the late 1700s and early 1800s, Baptists grew both in numbers and strength, due in part to the strong surge of camp-meeting revivalism that accompanied much of the early-nineteenth-century Appalachian frontier experience. Known as the Great Western Revival or the Second Great Awakening (and occurring between 1787 and 1805), this beginning of the later and longer lasting camp-meeting movement generated a form of intensely emotional worship that meshed well with the largely unstructured, voluntary, and nonhierarchical forms of religious polity and expression that frontier Baptist congregations were enjoying. Indeed, the evangelism that sprang from camp-meeting revivalism proved far more satisfactory to most Appalachian Baptists than did the more hierarchically driven, northern-based, mission-work evangelism that came to the mountains approximately two decades later.

The beginnings of this home-missionary movement came near the close of the eighteenth century when Timothy Dwight, a grandson of Edwards, began preaching to his Yale classmates, reawakening a spiritual consciousness in university circles. At about the same time, such evangelists as William Carey, Luther Rice, and John M. Peck called for a new commitment to spreading the Gospel. Beginning in the early 1800s, church-based organizations of all sorts initiated various forms of evangelism and revivalism. The Baptist Board of Foreign Missions became a leading force in directing home missions toward the scattered church associations of the Appalachians. Tract societies, Bible distribution groups, and more missionary boards formed to support these efforts.

However, just as missionary societies started spreading their message westward—raising money for their work, recruiting additional missionaries, and ministering to what were perceived as the "unchurched" communities of the frontier—individual Appalachian churches began to question the societies' motives and biblical authority. Particular-election Baptist congregations, who somewhat earlier may have embraced the revivalism of the more spontaneous Great Western Revival, seemed threatened by the externally driven missionary movement. In 1818 the Wabash Association received a query from one of its constituent churches concerning the biblical legitimacy of the Baptist Board of Foreign Missions and subsequently declared this institution's operations as scripturally out of Gospel order.

By the early 1820s, a series of anti-mission movements led by, among others, Alexander Campbell, John Taylor, and Daniel Parker declared that organizations outside the individual churches were "unbiblical," and that human efforts to save the heathen violated Calvin's doctrine of predestination. Consequently, the whole idea of reaching out to save souls, at home or abroad, seemed not only redundant but also blasphemous. The anti-mission churches thus split from congregations that leaned more toward Jacobus Arminius's doctrine of salvation through faith. Nevertheless, many of the Arminian-leaning Baptists also felt insulted by the suggestion that their religious practices and doctrines were found wanting and in need of missionary endeavors.

When splits erupted over the missionary versus anti-missionary question, churches struggled concurrently over titles. In the beginning, many Baptist fellowships were simply identified as missionary Baptists, the lowercased *m* suggesting no more that an affiliation with the pro-mission side of this controversy. Later, however, that lowercased *m* gradually grew to an uppercased *M*, indicating the development of a new Baptist sub-denomination.

In a similar way, many anti-missionary Baptist churches, searching for the proper title to apply to themselves, found validation in the designator *primitive*, a term that actually predated the missionary versus anti-missionary controversy in the sense that it had been applied to those churches that adhered most closely to the mandates of the Pauline church. Thus began yet another Baptist sub-denomination, the Primitive Baptists.

Today, Baptist sub-denominations can be thought of as occupying positions on a spectrum, with those teaching strict predestination at one end and those holding with the Arminian doctrine of salvation through faith available to all at the opposite end. Primitive Baptist churches generally practice no outreach ministries at all. Old Regular Baptists also preach election by grace and hold neither Sunday school nor revivals, while Regular Baptists hold Sunday school and revivals but field no missionaries outside their own churches. Near the center of the spectrum, Union Baptist churches (formed in the late 1860s of Union sympathizers) support no missionary outreach but are not anti-missionary. Toward the Arminian end of the spectrum, Free Will Baptists preach salvation for any human who asks for it, although they rarely send out missionaries, and Missionary Baptist churches proselytize actively but remain small and generally independent.

See also: CAMPBELL, ALEXANDER; PARKER, DANIEL; TAYLOR, JOHN.

—Schuyler Kaufman, *Appalachian State University*

Henry Holcombe, "A Sermon, Containing a Brief Illustration and Defence of the Doctrines Commonly Called Calvinistic" (1793); William Warren Sweet, *The Baptists, 1783–1830: A Collection of Source Material* (1931) and *Religion in the Development of American Culture, 1765–1840* (1963).

Moomaw, B. F.

(1814–1900) Brethren antislavery and pacifism activist.

Benjamin Franklin Moomaw was born in Botetourt County, Virginia. He and his wife, Mary Ann Crouse, became Brethren shortly after their marriage in 1840. Within twenty years, he was called to the Brethren ministry, and long before 1861 he opposed slavery. In 1843 a prospective Brethren member freed his slaves so he could join the fellowship. Since freed slaves had to leave Virginia after one year, Moomaw escorted one of them, Samuel Weir, to Ohio. Weir later joined the Brethren church, secured an education, and eventually became a minister. In support of his antislavery sentiments, Moomaw donated his inheritance from his slave-owning father to the African Colonization Society.

During the Civil War, Moomaw's antislavery and pacifist positions were well known. His efforts helped secure exemptions from Confederate service for Brethren men who could provide a five-hundred-dollar substitution fee. However, in July 1861, when eight hundred Confederate troops came to the Roanoke vicinity to train, community leaders jokingly suggested that the soldiers use Moomaw's farm. Ironically, Moomaw was contacted, and he agreed to assist the young fighting men. He subsequently won the friendship of the officers and men without compromising his positions. He even preached at the camp, and when an epidemic of measles swept among the men, the Moomaw family nursed many of the soldiers back to health.

Moomaw's son, John Crouse Moomaw, was largely responsible for bringing the Norfolk and Western Railroad to Roanoke and for southern relief work following the Civil War.

See also: BRETHREN; MILLER, JACOB.

—Beatrice Naff Bailey, *Clemson University*

Moravians

The Moravian presence is important in Appalachian history primarily for the eighteenth-century settlement of the areas in and around Winston-Salem, North Carolina, and Tuscarawas County, Ohio.

The Moravian Church in America traces its origins to the reform work of Jan Hus in fourteenth- and fifteenth-century Bohemia; to the followers of Hus who were known as the Unitas Fratrum; and to the Renewed Unitas Fratrum that arose in the 1720s among the Hussite refugees who took shelter on the Saxon estate of Nicholas Ludwig Count von Zinzendorf. A charismatic figure, Zinzendorf became the leader of the Moravians and advanced their worldwide missionary efforts, including their 1740 establishment of Bethlehem, Pennsylvania, from whence a party of settlers embarked in 1753 to found Wachovia in the western Carolina wilderness. Wachovia later became Salem, and eventually Winston-Salem, North Carolina.

The German-speaking Moravians were among the first people of European descent to populate the area of Winston-Salem. In an organized, communal pattern they built the economy and society. Initially, they lived in separatist villages, following certain faith-oriented codes of behavior and ceding control of property leases to the church. Their communal lifestyle was economically potent on the frontier, providing stability and growth in enterprise for the entire area. By 1759 non-Moravians were permitted into their thriving communities, and in 1856 this interchange with the outside world progressed to the point that church control over property leases ceased altogether. Although pacifistic, with exemption from military service until 1831, the Moravians nevertheless participated in local and early state politics. In addition, some African American slaves became Moravians, and Salem's African American St. Philip's Church is today one of the oldest black congregations in North America.

Farms, mills, crafts, and taverns were the base of the early Moravian economy in western North Carolina. By the 1760s the Moravians of Wachovia were operating fully in world trade, making use of their international network of faith members in the West Indies, Europe, and North America. They also benefited from continued migration of Germans along the eastern side of the Appalachians from Pennsylvania southward. Well into the nineteenth century there was a distinctive Moravian presence in western North Carolina, with Wachovia seen as a refuge for godly living. However, by the eve of the Civil War much of the distinctiveness of the Moravian community had disappeared: the church had become a voluntary organization like other American denominations; intermarriage and residence among non-Moravians was accepted; Salem was a busy market town and part of non-Moravian Winston; and the German language was seldom heard. Today there are nearly forty Moravian congregations in western North Carolina.

There are also three congregations in southern Virginia that stem from the first official home mission effort of the Moravian Church in America in the 1830s. During that time, governing officials of the church in Germany did not approve of new missions. American Moravians proceeded on their own, founding Mount Bethel at Cana, Virginia, in the early 1850s. Later the nearby congregations of Willow Hill and Crooked Oak developed as missions aimed specifically at migrant farm workers.

The Moravian religious witness centers on the joy that believers receive from the love of God expressed through Jesus Christ. Recognized widely for their beautiful hymns and expert attention to music, Moravians were among the earliest proponents of ecumenism among the Protestants of North America and strongly influenced a number of other churches through their practices of piety and service.

In 1745, near Tuscarawas Creek in eastern Ohio, the Moravians positioned David Zeisberger as a missionary to the Delaware Indians. He worked in the Delaware language and published German-Delaware and English-Delaware works. A pacifist throughout the Revolutionary War period, Zeisberger followed the Indian refugees to new settlements after massacres by both British and American troops. Zeisberger founded Schonbrunn in 1772 and Gnadenhuften in 1777. Today six Moravian congregations exist in the same general area. One other Appalachian presence for Moravians was a mission among the Cherokee at New Spring Place in northern Georgia, in operation from 1801 until the removal of the Cherokee to Oklahoma in 1838–39.

See also: GERMANS (RACE, ETHNICITY, AND IDENTITY); *TRUMPET IN THE LAND* (PERFORMING ARTS); WINSTON-SALEM, NORTH CAROLINA (URBAN APPALACHIAN EXPERIENCE).

—Gilson A. C. Waldkoenig, *Lutheran Theological Seminary at Gettysburg*

Earl P. Olmstead, *Blackcoats among the Delaware: David Zeisberger on the Ohio Frontier* (1991); Jon J. Sensbach, *A Separate Canaan: The Making of an Afro-Moravian World in North Carolina, 1763–1840* (1998); Daniel B. Thorp, *The Moravian Community in Colonial North Carolina* (1989).

Mormons

Northern Appalachia, particularly parts of New York and Pennsylvania, was important to the beginnings of the Church of Jesus Christ of Latter-Day Saints. Indeed, it was at the Susquehanna County, Pennsylvania, farm of his father-in-law that Joseph Smith allegedly translated the Book of Mormon from a set of tablets he claimed to have found on a hill near Palmyra, New York. Shortly after the completion of this task, the Mormon Church was organized, with some initial membership efforts expended in these northern Appalachian locales. By 1838 the movement's missionaries were seeking converts in southern and central Appalachia, especially in Tennessee, North Carolina, and Virginia.

As these conversion efforts progressed, mountain people became aware of the movement's conflicts with non-Mormons in the communities where the faith first established its Zion—Kirkland, Ohio; Independence, Missouri; and later Nauvoo, Illinois. Nevertheless, there were features of Mormon missionary work that softened Appalachian opposition to the persuasion. First, the church rejected judgments of mountain people as being lazy, backward, and unintelligent. Also, the Mormon family-centered life, self-sufficient agrarian culture, and independence resonated well with Appalachians. Finally, in contrast to many other efforts at converting the mountain people, Mormon missionaries showed respect for the basic values and traditions that set the region apart from most of mainstream America.

Following the establishment of its capital at Nauvoo (1840), the church experienced the flowering of the "gathering" doctrine. Since Mormons saw America as the Promised Land and Christ's seat of government, converts were encouraged to travel to the location of the main body of the church. Following the 1844 assassination of Joseph Smith, most missionaries left their fields to gather in Illinois. However, in the absence of Smith's strong leadership, the church developed a split that eventually produced the Missouri and Utah branches of the faith. Led by Brigham Young, the main body of the church relocated to Utah, and large numbers of the Appalachian converts joined that migration.

Until the 1860s, there was little information about the Mormons who stayed behind in the southern mountains. After the Civil War, missionaries with family connections in Appalachia returned to the region, but they encountered considerable anti-Mormon prejudice in the vicinity. Yet the Mormons persevered, and their first postbellum mission near the Appalachian region opened at Shady Grove, Tennessee, in 1875.

After church officials renounced polygamy (1890), Appalachian prejudice against Mormons slowly abraded, allowing the church to reach out not only to southern mountaineers but also to the Cherokee. Indeed, Mormon doctrine has held that Native Americans are descended from the Lamanites, who were, according to the Book of Mormon, a lost tribe of Israelites promised a restored gospel by God. In more recent years American blacks have also received the attention of the faith.

Mormon populations are organized, from smallest to largest, into branches, wards, and stakes. By the early 1990s, branches considerably outnumbered wards in the Asheville Stake, suggesting that the faith was still spreading out in western North Carolina. A similar growth pattern developed in southwest Virginia, from Bristol north through Roanoke and Charlottesville. Such expansion in southern and central Appalachia has been one factor motivating the 1999 establishment of a Mormon temple in Raleigh, North Carolina.

See also: CHEROKEE RELIGIOUS TRADITIONS; PROTESTANT MISSIONARY COMMUNITIES.

—Schuyler Kaufman, *Appalachian State University*

Parker, Daniel

(1781–1844) Baptist anti-missions leader.

Daniel Parker, who served as a pastor in Dickson County, Tennessee, from 1806 to 1817, exerted influence upon frontier Baptists through his strong opposition to missions and through his "Two Seeds in the Spirit" doctrine. Parker began to articulate his dislike of missions around 1815, when he was moderator of Tennessee's Concord Association. Himself uneducated, Parker resented the fact that missionaries were required to be educated, and he believed that only God could prepare preachers. He also held that missions were not provided for in the Bible.

Parker's "Two Seeds in the Spirit" doctrine has been called the most extreme of anti-mission theologies. Based on Gen. 3:15–16 and Matt. 13:29–30 and 36–43, it holds that Eve contained both good seed and bad seed. Individuals in subsequent generations were therefore either good or evil depending on the seed from which they originated. The non-elect could not be redeemed and would return to hell, so missionary efforts with them were useless. Similarly, the elect needed no missionary attention because God would save them at the time of His own choosing.

Parker also disliked religious tracts, newspapers, and books, which he saw as efforts to replace the Bible. He condemned theological seminaries and benevolent societies as just additional efforts by man to replace the will of God. He preached his beliefs in Tennessee, Kentucky, North Carolina, Illinois, Indiana, and Texas. Between 1820 and 1840 numerous Appalachian congregations coalesced over his doctrine.

See also: BAPTISTS, THE OLD-TIME GROUPS; MISSIONARY/ANTI-MISSIONARY SPLIT; TAYLOR, JOHN.

—Glenn Ellen Starr Stilling, *Appalachian State University*

Pentecostals

The Pentecostal faith is one of the dominant influences on Appalachian religious culture, with up to 420,000 formally counted adherents in the late twentieth century. This number does not include memberships of many independent Pentecostal fellowships scattered throughout southern and central

Appalachia, memberships that cannot be totaled since they do not report to administrative bodies higher than themselves. Consequently, their tallies do not appear in such canvasses as Glenmary Research Center's *Churches and Church Membership in the United States, 1990.*

A Restorationist Christian movement, Pentecostalism has flourished in Appalachia since the turn of the twentieth century and has been traced to Charles Fox Parham's Bethel Bible School in Topeka, Kansas. A former Methodist preacher influenced by the Holiness movement, Parham (1873–1929) taught that glossolalia (speaking in tongues) was evidence that one had received the baptism of the Holy Spirit recorded in the Bible in Acts 2. For Parham, Spirit baptism would empower the church for the "last days harvest," and tongues was to be a gift for evangelizing the world. Although earlier episodes of tongues speech had been reported, the modern Pentecostal movement became clearly established when Parham's student, Agnes N. Ozman (1870–1937), practiced glossolalia on January 1, 1901. Then, in 1906, divine healing became integral to Pentecostalism when Parham's African American disciple William J. Seymour established the Azusa Street Mission in Los Angeles. From Azusa Street, Pentecostalism spread around the world, spawning new churches and changing numerous existing ones.

Pentecostals believe Jesus is savior, sanctifier, healer, baptizer with the Holy Spirit, and coming king. Some groups reject the Trinity in favor of a "oneness" or "Jesus Only" theology, and a few encourage serpent handling. Today Pentecostals view glossolalia as a supernatural heavenly language rather than as a supernaturally learned human language.

Pentecostalism exists in Appalachia in both denominational and independent churches, as well as in a variety of theological expressions. In his *Appalachian Atlas,* Clifford A. Grammich Jr. reported that in 1990 Pentecostal churches were present in 385 of Appalachia's (at the time) 399 counties, primarily in central and southern Appalachia. As previously suggested, however, his total for the faith underrepresents Pentecostalism because it cannot include all of the independent Pentecostal congregations worshiping in homes, storefront facilities, and other makeshift quarters. In addition, groups not represented in Grammich's count include the Jesus Only United Pentecostal Church and such African American denominations as the Church of God in Christ.

The Church of God (Cleveland, Tennessee)—not to be confused with the non-Pentecostal Church of God (Anderson, Indiana)—is the largest of the nine denominations in Appalachia, with 189,360 adherents in 1,410 churches. The roots of this Appalachian-born denomination go back to 1886, when Missionary Baptist preachers Richard Spurling (1810–1891) and his son R. G. Spurling (1857–1935) established the Christian Union in Monroe County, Tennessee. The Spurlings chafed at the exclusivity of Baptist Landmarkism and called for union around faith in Christ and the priority of the New Testament.

A revival at nearby Camp Creek, North Carolina, introduced the doctrine of sanctification as a second work of grace that moved the believer far beyond initial regeneration and into or at least towards a more perfected spiritual existence. Under the leadership of Baptist William F. Bryant (1863–1949), these Holiness believers met in homes and the Shearer Schoolhouse for Sunday school and prayer meetings. About 130 reportedly experienced speaking in tongues, and there were numerous alleged healings. Coming under the influence of Benjamin Hardin Irwin's (1854–?) Fire Baptized Holiness Association, they adopted the more radical elements of the Holiness movement. But radicalism and the resulting persecution decimated the group. In 1902 sixteen people organized the Holiness Church at Camp Creek under the leadership of R. G. Spurling.

When Indiana-born A. J. Tomlinson (1865–1943) joined in 1903, his vision transformed the movement. The center of activities moved to Cleveland, Tennessee, home of an important north-south railroad, which allowed for expansion of missionary efforts. Although continuing many practices of Appalachian Baptists such as believer's baptism, shouting, and foot washing, Tomlinson developed an Episcopal form of church polity. By the end of the twentieth century, the Church of God (Cleveland, Tennessee) was highly organized, with overseers, standing boards, and departmental leadership of specialized ministries. Their official voice is the *Church of God Evangel,* and in 1948 the denomination adopted a Declaration of Faith as its doctrinal statement.

The Church of God of Prophecy, also with headquarters in Cleveland, Tennessee, came out of the Church of God (Cleveland, Tennessee) in 1923. Tomlinson's increasing authoritarianism clashed with growing diversity within the church, and the elders' council removed him. Undaunted, Tomlinson continued to hold annual assemblies, published the *White Wing Messenger,* and began anew to establish the Church of God. Disputed claims about the name *Church of God* resulted in legal action, which ultimately demanded that Tomlinson's group use *Tomlinson's Church of God.* Finally, in 1952, the courts ruled that Tomlinson's followers could use the name *Church of God of Prophecy.* This was acceptable, as they had always considered themselves the Church of God cited in biblical prophecy.

Upon Tomlinson's death in 1943, his son Milton became general overseer. Milton served until 1990 when the church chose Billy D. Murray for the position. This selection of someone outside the Tomlinson family signaled moderation of exclusivity and isolationism. When Murray resigned in

2000, the Church of God of Prophecy reported 520,000 members worldwide. There were 23,612 Appalachian adherents in 503 churches, according to 1990 figures.

In addition to the 1923 division, a series of schisms have developed in the Church of God/Church of God of Prophecy movement. In 1919 J. L. Scott led a faction called the Original Church of God and established headquarters in Chattanooga. Opposition to the leadership of Milton Tomlinson then resulted in two further divisions. In 1943 A. J. Tomlinson's eldest son, Homer, established The Church of God. Although first established in New York, offices for many years were in Huntsville, Alabama. In 1957 Grady R. Kent bolted the Church of God of Prophecy to form the Church of God of All Nations, more popularly known as The Church of God, Jerusalem Acres, relating to its particular location in Cleveland, Tennessee. Kent practiced New Testament Judaism—emphasizing Saturday worship and the celebration of Jewish feast days. Finally, in 1993, a group calling for a return to early practices of a Holiness theocracy left the Church of God of Prophecy and established another The Church of God, which is often distinguished by the parenthetical appellation *Zion Hill*, a reference to their headquarters church in Cleveland.

The Church of God, Mountain Assembly, has parallel but distinct origins and development from the Church of God. With offices in Jellico, Tennessee, the denomination began in the early 1900s when ministers in the South Union Association of the United Baptist Church sought and experienced sanctification as a second work of grace. After the South Union Association excluded ministers for teaching that one could sin following regeneration, several congregations met in 1906 at Jellico Creek in Whitley County, Kentucky, to discuss forming a new association. They held their first assembly in 1907. Calling themselves the Church of God, this group added *Mountain Assembly* to their name for distinction in 1911. A. J. Silcox served as the first moderator. Since 1919 a Board of Twelve Elders has served between annual assemblies as the primary governing body. Although there are churches in other states, the denomination is strongest along the I-75 corridor from Florida to Michigan. Appalachian members number approximately 3,020 in forty-five churches.

The International Pentecostal Holiness Church is a movement that developed out of a merger of three Pentecostal groups. Benjamin Hardin Irwin established the Fire Baptized Holiness Association in Anderson, South Carolina, in 1898. A Baptist turned Wesleyan Methodist minister, Irwin had experienced sanctification and then a third blessing called "the fire," a baptism of the Holy Spirit for which the most immediate sign was to be speaking in tongues. By 1902 the offices of the movement were located in Royston, Georgia, where the publishing ministry of the International Pentecostal Holiness Church remains.

Meanwhile, Methodist minister Ambrose Blackman Crumpler was sanctified and organized the North Carolina Holiness Association in 1897. Under Crumpler's leadership, the first Pentecostal Holiness church was organized in Goldsboro, North Carolina, in 1898. After being disciplined by the Methodist church for his Holiness activities, Crumpler organized the Pentecostal Holiness Church of North Carolina in 1900.

Also under fire for his sanctification doctrine, Presbyterian minister Nickles John Holmes in 1898 founded an independent congregation and Bible college in Greenville, South Carolina. Other ministers soon joined him in forming the Brewerton Presbyterian Church, which later became Tabernacle Pentecostal Church.

All three of these Holiness denominations became Pentecostal under the ministry of Gaston Barnabas Cashwell. As minister in Crumpler's Pentecostal Holiness Church of North Carolina, Cashwell traveled in 1906 to Seymour's Azusa Street revival in Los Angeles. After receiving the baptism of the Holy Spirit with the accompanying tongues, Cashwell began a Pentecostal revival in Dunn, North Carolina; that event swept these three groups into the Pentecostal movement.

Mergers in 1911 and 1915 brought all three denominations under the International Pentecostal Holiness Church. Their polity reflects Methodist roots with a quadrennial meeting of the General Conference and ministerial credentialing in annual regional conferences. In 1998 the organization reported 2.6 million members and 7,330 churches worldwide. Grammich's 1990 count showed Appalachia with 21,438 members in 218 churches.

International Pentecostal Church of Christ was formed in a 1976 merger of two Pentecostal organizations, the first of which was International Pentecostal Assemblies, a group that had grown out of independent Pentecostal groups influenced by G. B. Cashwell in the Atlanta, Georgia, area. The second body was the Pentecostal Church of Christ begun in Advance, Kentucky, at a meeting called by Methodist elder John Stroup. With offices in London, Ohio, this group, which practices foot washing and is pacifistic, has approximately 1,750 Appalachian adherents in thirty-seven churches.

Outside the Holiness camp, the Assemblies of God is the largest Pentecostal denomination in Appalachia, with 135,690 followers in 861 churches. Assemblies organized in Hot Springs, Arkansas, in 1914, bringing together Pentecostal ministers from diverse backgrounds. Initial offices were in Findlay, Ohio, but by 1918 they had been moved to Springfield, Missouri. The group is a fellowship of ministers with congregational polity.

Although early Assembly ministers emphasized a holy lifestyle, most were not part of the Holiness movement and did not teach sanctification as a second work of grace. Instead, they adopted the "finished work of Calvary" doctrine of William H. Durham, who held that the Christian was both pardoned and cleansed at conversion. Rather than seek a second work of grace for sanctification, one should live an "overcoming" lifestyle, resisting all sinful temptation. Assemblies congregants do not practice foot washing.

Doctrinal division occurred early in the organization when some rejected the Trinity in favor of a oneness form of Pentecostalism. However, in 1916 the Assemblies disavowed this "New Issue" and adopted a Statement of Fundamental Truths. Out of the subsequent division came several Jesus Only denominations and independent congregations, who often identify themselves as "Apostolic."

Pentecostals have tended to be anti-creedal, and not all who were affiliated with the Assemblies of God approved of the Assemblies' adoption of the Statement of Fundamental Truths. Pentecostal Church of God was formed when John C. Sinclair gathered together ministers who shared Assemblies beliefs but rejected the adoption of a doctrinal statement. Organized in 1919 as the Pentecostal Assemblies of the U.S.A., they adopted the name *Pentecostal Church of God* in 1922. In 1950 they located their offices in Joplin, Missouri. For 1990, Grammich reported 3,565 Pentecostal Church of God Appalachians in fifty-two churches.

The International Church of the Foursquare Gospel also has Assemblies of God roots. Aimee Semple McPherson (1890–1944) joined the Assemblies of God under the ministry of future husband Robert Semple. Following Robert's death, she married Harold McPherson and began her evangelistic career. Although most Pentecostal denominations either ordain or license women, Sister—as she preferred to be called—found the Assemblies of God stifling. In 1923 she established Angeles Temple in Los Angeles and incorporated the denomination in 1927. The term *foursquare* comes from an interpretation of Ezek. 1:4–10, from which McPherson takes the four cherubim to typify Jesus as Savior, Baptizer with the Holy Spirit, Healer, and Coming King. The International Church of the Foursquare Gospel in Appalachia numbers approximately 4,860 in forty-four churches.

The Open Bible Standard Churches have only a small presence in Appalachia (twenty-seven churches). With roots in Eugene, Oregon's Apostolic Faith (Trinitarian) and in the International Church of the Foursquare Gospel, both the Bible Standard Mission and the Open Bible Evangelistic Association formed in reaction to certain polices of their parent denominations. These two then merged in 1935, with doctrine and practices similar to those of the Assemblies of God. Their official publication is *Message of the Open Bible*.

See also: HOLINESS-PENTECOSTAL FUSION; SPURLING, R. G.; TOMLINSON, A. J.

—David G. Roebuck, *Hal Bernard Dixon Jr. Pentecostal Research Center*

Stanley M. Burgess, Gary B. McGee, and Patrick H. Alexander, *Dictionary of Pentecostal and Charismatic Movements* (1988); Clifford A. Grammich Jr., *Appalachian Atlas: Maps of the Churches and People of the Appalachian Region* (1994).

Perishing in the Spirit

See Revival Exercises

Popular Religion

Although religion is commonly defined in terms of organizations and institutions—from traditions and denominations to churches and temples—such an approach obscures a dimension of religion not limited to or bound by such structural arrangements. Anthropologists highlight this more elusive side of religion when they speak of "folk religion." Historians talk about "popular religion," or expressions of religion emerging from the experiences of ordinary women and men rather than from organized groups (though at times new religions or denominations do develop from these expressions). Others refer to "lived religion," because this noninstitutional side of religion concerns itself with beliefs and practices that deal essentially with how people actually go about the business of living their lives day after day. Some of these beliefs and practices may stem from organized religious institutions. But the particular mix is often highly idiosyncratic and thus difficult to analyze precisely. This popular religiosity or lived religion flourishes alongside the institutions of religion throughout the world.

At the same time, however, some recurring ideas inform the personal religiosity of many people, particularly if common influences shape their lives as individuals and as a collectivity. The experience of living in central Appalachia, for example, provides a common base for looking at some features of popular Christian religiosity. These may not be unique to central Appalachia; indeed, they may shape much personal religiosity throughout the entire region. But central Appalachia presents an opportunity to illuminate this subtle dynamic of religious life. The following characteristics of central Appalachian Christian religiosity are not exhaustive; they are, instead, representative of the phenomenon.

One idea running through many expressions of popular Christian religiosity in central Appalachia, especially deep in the mountains, is a conviction that supernatural forces or powers are constantly at work in the world. This makes ordinary life a realm of power, often experienced as an arena of conflict between good and evil. Even more, what gives rise to this sense of power are experiences, either those of the individual or those witnessed by the individual, that draw him or her into the presence of divine power. Simply put, if divine power undergirds all of life, then there is a confidence that countervailing power can be conquered.

On the simplest level, this sense of the world as a realm of power manifests itself in the knowledge of what natural plants and herbs offer in terms of healing for human afflictions. Those who have this knowledge, generally among the elderly of mountain communities, are regarded with tremendous respect, for their knowledge is a key to one form of supernatural power that can have positive consequences for those on whose behalf it is used. Some analysts point to this aspect of popular religiosity as an example of folk religion; today many recognize its affinity with holistic medicine and other alternative approaches to treating disease.

In central Appalachia perhaps the most overt examples of experiencing the reality of supernatural power come from Holiness-Pentecostal circles. In numerous religious communities, speaking in tongues is part of religious life. When one speaks in tongues, one has the sense of being taken over by a superior, supernatural power that for the moment controls one's life. One does not speak in tongues at will, but only when seized by the Spirit. Nor does an individual need to have a personal experience of speaking in tongues in order to appreciate the reality of the power at work. Witnessing others speak in tongues reinforces the reality of the experience and the power behind it.

The same may be said for those who believe they are commanded by scripture to take up serpents. In many communities where serpent handling is practiced, those who handle will not do so every time they gather for worship. Often the most experienced handlers will not do so unless they feel the power of the Spirit present in the service and within their own bodies. They recognize that the serpents themselves represent a power, literally a power of life and death, and that to handle when not infused with divine power is to invite the opposing powers of death to take over should they be bitten. Others believe that they handle as a sign of their faith and may not always need assurance of a special divine presence.

Outside the Holiness-Pentecostal orbit, supernatural power may manifest itself in less dramatic, but equally compelling ways. For example, among Primitive Baptists and Old Regular Baptists, phenomena like glossolalia and serpent handling are eschewed, for here the Calvinist notion of predestination shapes much thinking. The very idea that God elects some for salvation calls attention to a supernatural power that holds one's eternal destiny in its control. In such circles the experience of conversion, when one confronts the reality of divine power in the confidence that one has been chosen by God for salvation, becomes a reminder of the reality of this power. Not every individual who espouses predestination has to have a direct personal experience to accept the reality of the power that lies behind it. Seeing others in the throes of conversion or hearing testimonies to the work of God provides ample reinforcement that such supernatural power is at work.

Even more basic is personal prayer. For countless folk in central Appalachia, prayer is fundamentally a means of accessing the realm of power, of leaving this world behind and granting control to God. Prayer provides an entree into the realm of the supernatural, where one can tap into the omnipotence of the Almighty on behalf of not only oneself, but also one's family and others in the community. Hence, one prays for rain when drought threatens crops; one prays for healing when illness comes; one prays for guidance if one loses a job. This function of prayer is by no means limited to expressions of popular religiosity in the mountains, but it is of extraordinary import in giving ordinary folk a way to endow their lives with meaning.

The reality of evil, however, is often as vital as the reality of a beneficent supernatural power. For many, daily life is not easy. There are temptations constantly luring believers into immoral behavior. Sickness and death strike with a ferocity that too often escapes human control. For the generations who struggled to tease sustenance from the rocky soil, nature itself could be fickle, if not sometimes malevolent. Floods could destroy hopes for a good yield one year, while drought could follow the next. In other words, supernatural forces are at work that can undermine all human effort. The reality of these unseen demonic powers in daily existence makes it all the more imperative that the faithful be able to access the realm of divine power.

When one can affirm that the supernatural powers of the world are aiding the journey through life, the perils of the present pale. Here the second dominant feature of mountain popular Christian religiosity comes into focus. It is a sense that life as we know it is lived on two levels. Daily life, what philosophers dub empirical reality, is one level. Far superior is the realm of God, the heavenly realm that awaits us in eternity. Yet every manifestation of divine power here and now is a window into this realm.

Where can this aspect of popular religiosity be seen? One place is in the hymns and songs that are common in many mountain congregations. Countless allusions to a future in heaven when all the travails of this life will finally make sense are a major feature of popular religious songs in central Appalachia. It is there, too, in the emphasis on individual moral behavior. For example, taboos against the use of alcohol, wearing makeup, or participating in certain amusements and leisure activities do not merely produce a style of life that seems anachronistic to outsiders; they are the stuff of life in heaven. The present is marked by temptation and evil; the future will be free of such burdens. Likewise all hardships, from illness to hard work to unemployment, are ephemeral and fleeting when viewed from the perspective of eternity.

The devaluing of the present comes through even among those who look to an idealized past as setting the norm for the present. Among those who have their religiosity informed by the Old Regular Baptist style, for example, there is a conviction not only that the formal beliefs and practices of associated congregations reflect precisely the patterns of New Testament Christianity without change or transformation over time, but also that the values underpinning daily life are those of the first Christians. At the same time, the way of life, both personal and corporate, that follows is what will prevail in the heavenly sphere in the future. So the future and the idealized past are mirror images of each other that encase the present.

Popular religiosity knows no boundaries or denominational labels. It knows little of fine theological distinctions or divisions of social class. But it knows that supernatural power pervades all of life and carries with it the promise of life in a heavenly realm of power for eternity.

See also: GLOSSOLALIA; PENTECOSTALS; SERPENT HANDLING.

—Charles H. Lippy, *University of Tennessee at Chattanooga*

Troy D. Abell, *Better Felt Than Said: The Holiness-Pentecostal Experience in Southern Appalachia* (1982); Charles H. Lippy, "Popular Religiosity in Central Appalachia," in *Christianity in Appalachia: Profiles in Regional Pluralism*, ed. Bill J. Leonard (1999); Deborah V. McCauley, *Appalachian Mountain Religion: A History* (1995).

Preachers and Preaching: Old-Time Baptist Exhorters

One of Appalachia's best-known icons is the mountain preacher, especially the Old-Time Baptist exhorter, chanting out his sermons in a highly rhythmic and partially sung delivery style that writers occasionally identify as the prototypic Appalachian sermonic sound. It is not typical, of course, because even central Appalachia is so religiously diverse that there is no archetype for that region's pulpit artistry. Still, the symbol is such a strong one that this preacher and his preaching warrant examination.

After professing his call to preach, the aspiring Old-Time Baptist preacher is granted permission by his local congregation to try out this call by occupying the stand (the pulpit) of that church and those of corresponding fellowships and/or associations. Depending on the specific subdenomination, this permission to preach may be identified as licensed, liberated, or "libertized," and will last as long as the local church needs for confirmation of the call, but rarely more than a year. There are instances when the process never culminates in ordination.

During his licensed stage the beginning preacher will seek to master those requisite gifts needed for his pulpit career, including but not limited to improvisational speaking, his version of the traditional chanted style, a soaring emotional modality, and the congregation/preacher interactive format so much demanded by these fellowships.

Nothing is quite so basic to Old-Time Baptists as the belief that prepared sermons represent men speaking, while improvisational preaching gives God the chance to inspire what are variously called "blessed," "quickened," "carried out," or "revelated" modes of delivery. It is recognized, however, that there is no guarantee that God is present in all unprepared sermonic expressions.

One possible sign of this God-inspired "blessed" state is the preacher's eventual rise to his version of the traditional chant/song delivery mode. At this time the preaching ascends to an enhanced chant composed of rhythmically delivered short lines of poetic expression, the cadence of which then rises and falls with the passions of the moment. Frequently, this style also includes an end-of-each-line "huuh" or "haah," produced when the speaker regulates his breathing by explosive exhalation immediately after deeply and silently inhaling.

The simplest of these styles include only these rapidly delivered rhythmic expressions, with each short line closed by the explosive exhaling of air. More complicated patterns involve lines that rise sharply in inflection and sail off into lyrical variations, occasionally transforming into crescendos of undulating wails, shouts, outcries, or exaltations that hold for seconds before cascading through a series of equally melodic inflection falls.

These chant/song patterns do not develop immediately at the beginning of sermons. Indeed, they may emerge only after long "waiting for the Lord to speak" moments marked by hesitancy and stumbling uncertainties. Some sermons may never reach a blessed state, leaving the respective preacher to conclude that God did not choose to use him that day.

To be quickened or carried out is also to experience soaring passion for one's message: those scolding, urging, or rejoicing words that these believers expect from God, pronouncements delivered with all the ardor, animation, or affection believed worthy of God's dispatches. Emotion is not itself the message, but it may validate that message if its sentiments are otherwise acceptable. The preacher who perpetually falls flat in this area of this delivery may ultimately be judged as having received a false call.

Old-Time Baptists require personal involvement in their worship services, and that involvement must include something other than just the perfunctory singing of hymns. Women cry, shout, or "praise," and men move about the church embracing or shaking the hands of fellow male celebrants, frequently themselves crying. Furthermore, both genders often engage in these activities while a sermon is actually being preached, especially during those moments when the preacher is revelated. That may include moving to the stand to hug the exhorter of the moment.

The libertized speaker must learn to work with this interactive system, even developing techniques that orchestrate its dynamism; for not only are regular church members expressing themselves at will, but also his fellow preachers supply their own verbal and nonverbal responses from their semicircle behind the stand, all while he is attempting to speak extemporaneously. If he finds these behaviors distracting rather than motivating, he will have trouble adjusting to the traditional milieu of Old-Time Baptist services. If his growth in preaching skills suggests a genuine call, the young preacher will be ordained by his home church in a service that starts with oral examinations on doctrine, practice, and personal dedication, followed by the formal ordination conferred by a laying on of hands.

Now the elder is ready for his unsalaried service of travel, preaching, and church and association leadership, perhaps as an assistant-moderator or moderator. If his association is large and "corresponds" with several similar organizations, the total number of churches to which this elder can be summoned to preach for special-service events can reach two hundred or more, scattered across several states. For the average elder, the circle of his preaching obligations will extend to only six or eight congregations that lie near his home church. However, since that home fellowship convenes only one Saturday and Sunday each month, he will be expected to make himself available to other churches the remaining weekends. This procedure is especially necessitated by the fact that Old-Time Baptists hear three or more preachers each service.

Old-Time Baptist elders are not called to one church as that fellowship's pastor, but they may be called by the church as its moderator, even though the respective elder is not a member of that congregation. The same is true for an assistant-moderator. These two individuals, in combination with a clerk, who functions as both secretary and records-keeper for the church, then lead that fellowship, officiating over monthly business meetings and worship services, moderating during the addition or dismissal of members, arranging for the ordination of other elders or deacons, and supplying the leadership for all matters concerning the church's affiliation with an association. So loyal are these congregations to their moderators that an elder occasionally spends most of his preaching lifetime moderating one church.

See also: ASSOCIATIONS, BAPTIST; BAPTISTS, THE OLD-TIME GROUPS.

—Howard Dorgan, *Appalachian State University, Emeritus*

Howard Dorgan, *Giving Glory to God in Appalachia* (1987); Bruce Rosenberg, *The Art of the American Folk Preacher* (1970).

Presbyterian Denominational Family

With the arrival of the Scots-Irish and other Reformed Christians in the eighteenth century, Presbyterianism began to influence the Appalachian religious landscape. Since that time the Presbyterian family in the region has fragmented and reformed, addressing such issues as diversity in denominational affiliation, views on polity, theological tendencies, and worship practices. Presbyterian diversity in Appalachia is evidenced by the Associate Reformed Presbyterian, Cumberland Presbyterian, Second Cumberland Presbyterian, Evangelical Presbyterian, Presbyterian Church of America, and Presbyterian Church (USA) sub-denominations. Perhaps the Presbyterian group with the greatest regional identification with Appalachia is the Cumberland Presbyterian Church.

Presbyterianism finds it roots in the Reformed branch of the Protestant Reformation movements and includes traditions with a Presbyterian polity and a Calvinistic theology. The French reformer John Calvin attempted to establish a theocracy in Geneva, Switzerland, during the sixteenth-century reform movements and made his theological system, based on the unchallenged sovereignty of God, the cornerstone of the religious-social experiment. Calvin's theology was based on the notion that humankind is totally depraved and sinful. As a result, human beings cannot save themselves and are completely dependent on the grace of a sovereign God. God elects certain individuals to salvation, but this election is limited in number and is completely unconditioned by the actions or status of individuals. This theological system provided the framework for Reformed churches that spread from Switzerland through France and Holland to England and Scotland.

Those in the Reformed tradition who followed Jacobus Arminius modified Calvin's theological system. The Arminian position tends to question the principle of unconditional election and allows an element of human free will into the divine election process. This modification set up a theological controversy that would at times impact the Reformed traditions and eventually lead to denominational splits. The Reformed theology was coupled with a Presbyterian form of church governance wherein local congregations elect representatives who oversee churches through a series of ecclesiastical organizations and councils. This form of representative church government challenged the hierarchical arrangements of the Roman Catholic Church as well as the episcopacy of the Anglican Church.

John Knox, a contemporary and disciple of Calvin, led the conversion of many in Scotland to Presbyterianism. The Scots Presbyterians played a significant role in the British Parliament's Westminster Assembly from 1643 to 1648. This assembly produced the Westminster Confession of Faith, which became the doctrinal rule of faith for Presbyterianism. This confession is based on Calvin's theology, and with the Presbyterian dominance of the assembly came considerable governmental control, so much so that by the late seventeenth century the Church of Scotland was organized in Presbyterian form. During that period, political and religious upheaval continued in Britain and eventually led to the migration of many Presbyterians from Scotland to Northern Ireland. Although there were Presbyterian congregations in the colonies earlier, these Ulster Scots were a major factor in introducing Presbyterianism to North America during the middle portion of the eighteenth century when they emigrated from Ireland to the American colonies.

Though owing much to this Scots-Irish migration into Appalachia, Presbyterianism in America and in Appalachia was also greatly shaped by revivalism. Just as the eighteenth-century Great Awakening generated Presbyterian controversies and divisions, nineteenth-century revivalism combined with other concerns to foster a new set of shifts in the Presbyterian denominational family. The Cumberland Presbyterian movement that originated in Kentucky and Tennessee during the first decade of the nineteenth century nicely illustrates this dynamic quality of Presbyterianism. Because this movement grew out of the Great Western Revival (also known as the Second Great Awakening), the Cumberland Presbyterian Church is the division of this faith most clearly associated with Appalachia, although the church has its strength in the South and Midwest in general.

Perhaps James McGready is as responsible as anyone for setting the stage for the beginnings of the Cumberland Presbyterian Church. This Presbyterian revivalist had ignited reawakening fires in Kentucky by 1800, and the rapid spread of revival sparked a need for churches and preachers. As a result of the impassioned meetings in Kentucky and Tennessee in 1800, new churches were organized with revivalist tendencies and preferences.

Many of the Cumberland County, Kentucky, churches ordained preachers who did not have the usual ministerial training. The Kentucky Synod of the Presbyterian Church, USA, refused to recognize the legitimacy of these preachers or of the Cumberland Presbytery. By 1810 in Dickson County, Tennessee, Cumberland fellowships reorganized as a body independent of the Presbyterian Church, USA, with ministers Finis Ewing, Samuel McAdow, and Samuel King leading the movement. The formation of this new Cumberland Presbytery intensified the controversies generated by the revivals, especially relative to the Arminian theological positions being taken by the revivalist elements of the Presbyterian family. However, disputes also erupted concerning polity issues, authority matters, and other theological questions arising from interpretations of the Westminster Confession of Faith.

The Cumberland Synod was officially instituted in 1813 and followed with the recognition of a confession of faith intended to revise the Westminster Confession. This confession was intended to strike a mediating position between the extremes of Calvinism and Arminianism. Main differences between the two confessions of faith involve eternal reprobation (which the Cumberland Confession denies) and atonement (which the Cumberland group regarded in universal terms). Thus, the Cumberland Confession challenged the more fatalistic aspects of the Westminster Confession and allowed the entrance of Arminian elements into the group.

Though much contemporary scholarship on Appalachia has tended to focus on the Calvinistic and fatalistic tendencies of the region's religions, the Cumberland Presbyterians propound an Appalachian doctrine that challenges the fatalism inherent in Calvinistic theology. This challenge, of course, is due to the revivalistic beginnings of the Cumberland movement. Revival preachers were dependent on human free will and choice as an integral part of election theology and thus championed the cardinal tenets of the Cumberland Confession.

By 1829 a Cumberland Presbyterian General Assembly had been organized, and by 1874 in Tennessee, a General Assembly of the Cumberland Presbyterian Church, Colored (later changed to the Second Cumberland Presbyterian Church in the United States), had been instituted. This Second Cumberland Presbyterian Church follows the Confession of Faith of the Cumberland Presbyterian Church.

The Cumberland tradition grew rapidly during the nineteenth century and revised its confession in 1883 to further remove the language of Calvinism. Then in 1906 the Cumberland Presbyterian Church reunited with the Presbyterian Church in the USA following a revision of the Westminster Confession that was agreeable to a majority of the Cumberland group. However, a minority of Cumberland Churches did not accept the merger, partly for doctrinal reasons. The Cumberland Presbyterian Church continued through this dissension.

Of the other Presbyterian bodies represented in Appalachia, the Presbyterian Church (USA), the Presbyterian Church in America, and the Associate Reformed Presbyterian Church should be mentioned. The Presbyterian Church (USA) was formed in 1983 by the reunion of the Presbyterian Church in the United States (Southern Presbyterian

Church) and the United Presbyterian Church in the United States of America (Northern). On the other hand, the Presbyterian Church in America, organized in 1973, is a conservative group of dissent from the Presbyterian Church in the United States (Southern). This church reaffirmed its Reformed theology and a fundamentalist view of scripture. Finally, the Associate Reformed Presbyterian Church (General Synod) constitutes a small Presbyterian group located in the South that is interesting to the region because of its strong connection to Scottish Seceder and Covenanter groups (collections of Presbyterian groups that promoted spirituality or rebelled against the established church).

While Presbyterianism may not come to mind when one thinks of Appalachian religious traditions, this denominational family marks, for several reasons, an important element of the religious and theological landscape. Because of a strong commitment to Reformed theology, some forms of Presbyterianism stand in stark contrast to Holiness traditions and all of the more Arminian groups, thus adding theological diversity to the region. In addition, the theological tenets on God's sovereignty, election, and grace provide an interesting element in a region that displays a Calvinistic influence outside of Presbyterianism. The Scottish history of the movement and the connection to Scots-Irish migration provide an important cultural element to the movement, and the existence of the Cumberland Presbyterian Church gives insight to a crucial period of religious development in the history of Appalachia.

See also: MCGREADY, JAMES; SCOTS (RACE, ETHNICITY, AND IDENTITY); SCOTS-IRISH (RACE, ETHNICITY, AND IDENTITY).

—Conrad Ostwalt, *Appalachian State University*

Ben M. Barrus, Milton L. Baugh, and Thomas H. Campbell, *A People Called Cumberland Presbyterians* (1972); Yeuell H. Davis and Marcia Clark Myers, "The Presbyterians in Central Appalachia," in *Christianity in Appalachia: Profiles in Regional Pluralism*, ed. Bill J. Leonard (1999); William Warren Sweet, *The Presbyterians: A Collection of Source Materials* (1964); Ernest Trice Thompson, *Presbyterians in the South* (1963–73); Leonard J. Trinterud, *The Forming of an American Tradition: A Re-examination of Colonial Presbyterianism* (1970).

Primitive Baptist Universalists

Primitive Baptist Universalists are arguably the most distinctive of Appalachia's Old-Time Baptist sub-denominations. Mislabeled by opponents as the "No-Hellers," Primitive Baptist Universalists proclaim a theology that promises an afterlife in heaven for all humankind, regardless of any and all temporal behavioral or doctrinal transgressions. Indeed, this faith is characterized by Calvinistic determinism at both ends of its theology. Just as the doctrine proclaims the curse of Adamic sin to be universally unavoidable, it also pronounces the redemptive consequence of Christ's atonement as equally universal and equally unavoidable. "For as in Adam all die, even so in Christ shall all be made alive" (1 Cor. 15:22) has become the unofficial scriptural motto of the movement.

The No-Heller title is misleading, for Primitive Baptist Universalists do believe in hell; however, they simply claim that condition to be solely a factor of the temporal world, a tormented state of mind and soul engendered by the individual's separation from God. This view of hell as an earthly entity also makes Satan equally terrestrial and humanity centered, the natural (Adamic) side of man at war with spiritual man. Still, by doctrine, all of the consequences of Adam's fall are erased at the believers' resurrection. Thus sin, punishment, death, and humankind's separation from God are terminated by a redemption that restores all of Adam's descendants to a new Eden of spiritual perfection and union with God (heaven).

Universalism reached Appalachia during the first quarter of the nineteenth century, influencing a wide range of denominational thought; however, it was either the Restorationist theology of Elhanan Winchester or the ultra-Universalism of Hosea Ballou, both from Baptist beginnings, that most influenced a limited number of trans-Allegheny Baptist associations. Restorationist Universalism promised only a limited-duration afterlife hell, a purgatory-like place where sinners would stay until retribution had been made for temporal-world wrongdoings. Ultimately all of humankind would be restored to union with God. Ultra-Universalism, on the other hand, proclaimed a heaven for all, beginning immediately after Resurrection, all sins having been punished in the earthly life. In nineteenth- and early-twentieth-century Appalachian Baptist association minutes, Restorationist influence was referenced as "short hell heresy," while ultra-Universalism was labeled "No-Hell heresy." It was toward the final decade of the 1800s that the latter of these doctrines began to affect churches in the Washington District Primitive Baptist Association, located in east Tennessee and southwestern Virginia. In 1924 Washington District formally split and formed what would become known as Heller and No-Heller sides.

Today a relatively small number of Primitive Baptist Universalist fellowships are found in east Tennessee, eastern Kentucky, southwestern Virginia, and southern West Virginia, with a scattering of out-migrant churches in Ohio and Pennsylvania. These fellowships are clustered in four associations: Regular Primitive Baptist Washington Association, Three Forks of Powell's River Regular Primitive Baptist Association, and two Elkhorn Primitive Baptist Associations (not in correspondence with each other).

See also: BAPTISTS, THE OLD-TIME GROUPS; SHORT HELL DOCTRINE.

—Howard Dorgan, *Appalachian State University, Emeritus*

Howard Dorgan, *In the Hands of a Happy God: The "No-Hellers" of Central Appalachia* (1997).

Protestant Missionary Communities

During the Civil War, Protestant missionaries from the North set their sights on improving life for southern blacks. After the war (c. 1870), evangelical churches began seeking new home missionary projects at about the same time that Appalachia began to be perceived as its own, identifiable frontier region—a region of poverty and need with natural resources and an increasing population. These churches saw growth potential and sent out missionaries, even as industrialization added to the Appalachian expansion.

The histories of the missions and mission communities that soon formed are similar to one another: northerners from mainline churches, full of altruistic spirit and a desire to increase the size of their denominations, went to live among the "unchurched" in the mountains, Bibles and textbooks in hand. Often these missionaries were women educated in New England. They traveled to Appalachia to open Sunday schools and teach ABCs to mountain children and home economics to parents. They served as brokers for Appalachian crafts. They built schools and community centers and lived among those they hoped to help.

Of course, missionaries had been in Appalachia since the very beginning of the nineteenth century, but they had not always been met with open arms. Appalachians had their own small churches and frequently took offense at the assumption that they needed religious instruction. In addition, there was that strong strain of Calvinism present in the mountains, with its distrust for any form of evangelization, including Sunday schools, revivals, and tract societies. Indeed, by the 1870s the region had already experienced fifty years of the missionary/anti-missionary split.

However, there were families who wanted the schools, health clinics, and vocational training that missionary communities eventually offered. Some of the more established Appalachian families donated land for the missions and helped with construction, as was the case with the Presbyterian-affiliated Sunset Gap mission in Cosby, Tennessee. This mission, begun in 1924, started with a school, but now sponsors everything from clothing and home repair to Little League sports. Other missionary settlement centers were established to help in agriculture and other vocational activities.

Although county governments eventually took over some mission schools, just as private hospitals occasionally replaced mission health care, churches have continued to see need in Appalachia. Indeed, missions remain, and some have grown into small communities unto themselves. There is no town hall at Red Bird Mission in Beverly, Kentucky, but it is nearly its own town now, with eighty-two buildings, 130 staff members, and a full life of outreach. Episcopal Grace House on the Mountain in Sandy Ridge, Virginia, was a large community when it was established near the turn of the twentieth century. Now outreach continues with only one staff member, who organizes work groups of volunteers for home repair and the like.

Protestant missionaries who came to Appalachia as trained carpenters, health-care specialists, or administrators often stayed for decades, raising families and retiring in the region. Today, however, the missionary may be a member of a temporary work group run by such organizations as Episcopal Grace House on the Mountain or the Shack Neighborhood House, a mission that offers recreation, daycare, and home repair in the coal community of Scott's Run, West Virginia. Although missions still maintain denominational ties, volunteers of today often are ecumenical and serve few if any sectarian purposes.

See also: MISSIONARY/ANTI-MISSIONARY SPLIT; SETTLEMENT, MISSION, AND SPONSORED SCHOOLS (EDUCATION).

—Madelyn Rosenberg, *Roanoke Times*

Quakers

During the second half of the eighteenth century, members of the Society of Friends, commonly called Quakers, migrated to northern and southern Appalachia from the regions east of the mountains. They founded Quaker meetings in western Pennsylvania, Virginia, Tennessee, North and South Carolina, and Georgia. The Society of Friends established several Appalachian communities that flourished into the first half of the nineteenth century, when many of that region's Quakers then moved on to midwestern states such as Ohio, Indiana, and Iowa.

Quaker origins stem from the religious radicalism of the 1640s that resulted from the English Civil War. George Fox founded the Society of Friends in 1652, drawing members particularly from the northwestern part of England and other regions of the British Borderlands. Later many of those Borderland peoples settled in Appalachia.

During the seventeenth century, English Quakers were severely persecuted for their beliefs, many of which collided with early modern tenets of hierarchy and patriarchy. For example, Quakers recognized both men and women as having the gift of ministry, refused to tip their hats to their "betters," addressed all ranks of society with the second person "thee" or "thou," rejected all sacramental observance, refused to swear oaths, and emphasized the continuing revelation of truth by the Holy Spirit. Eventually persecution and a faulty economy led many Quakers to leave England. In 1682 William Penn established the colony of Pennsylvania as a refuge for religious dissenters; that cultural openness attracted Quakers, as well as many other religious sects. Other American colonies, such as Virginia and North Carolina, also saw pockets of Quakers settled within their borders.

In the first half of the eighteenth century, Quaker families found particular success in the Delaware Valley, developing rich farmlands and exporting crops to the West Indies. Relatively inexpensive land allowed Quaker parents to accumulate property and give their children enough to establish their own farms. However, not all Quaker families prospered, especially second- and third-generation American Friends and those who immigrated later. By the 1750s, land in southeastern Pennsylvania had become too expensive for many families to set up children on their own farms. In addition, conflicts with the French and Native Americans wreaked havoc on the economy. Thus, some Quakers felt the only way to preserve their families and stay a part of the Society of Friends was to seek places where land was plentiful and inexpensive. Many moved south or west.

Those Quakers who left Pennsylvania and New Jersey moved to Virginia and the Carolinas, forming communities in the Piedmont region and inching their way toward Appalachia. In the South, they encountered other members of the Society who had lived in Virginia and the Carolinas since the beginning of the eighteenth century. The first Quakers to settle in Appalachia did so as early as the 1730s; however, after the Revolutionary War and the opening of land in the Appalachians and beyond, Quakers pushed west in greater numbers, settling in the Appalachians and forming several thriving Quaker communities.

From the end of the seventeenth century, the Society of Friends organized itself into congregations called "meetings." Local meetings met two or three times a week for worship. Monthly, quarterly, and yearly meetings, made up of representatives from the local congregations, were later established to oversee the activities of broader regions. During the eighteenth century the largest of the yearly assemblies was the Philadelphia Yearly Meeting, attracting Quakers from Pennsylvania, New Jersey, and Maryland. Later, other yearly gatherings were established in New York, New England, North Carolina, and Ohio, the last of which, in 1813, was the first yearly meeting west of the Appalachians.

Local gatherings usually were one- to two-hour silent services, sometimes interrupted with Friends speaking spiritual messages if moved by the Holy Spirit to do so. In addition, monthly local meetings would be held to handle Quaker business such as consenting to marriages, forming committees to investigate infractions of the Society's Discipline (a book containing rules of behavior relative to all matters of the Society), meting out punishment, and appointing representatives to attend the larger quarterly and yearly meetings.

Friends who established themselves in Appalachia resembled Quakers from other parts of the eastern United States in their practices. For example, they kept their silent worship and continued to uphold the Society's Discipline and the Quaker Peace Testimony. Nevertheless, Appalachian Friends encountered some distinctly regional difficulties, including inadequate transportation routes, ongoing military campaigns against Native Americans, and long travel distances to other Quaker meetings. Those westerly Quakers also saw their meetings composed of Friends from all over Europe and the eastern states, leading in some cases to disagreement over traditions. During much of the eighteenth century, the Appalachian meetings were often mentioned as a concern to the larger Society of Friends because of their inaccessibility and the fear that Quakers in the West might not be upholding the Society's Discipline. In reality, frontier Friends maintained as strong a faith as any of the movement's eastern factions.

Quakers established monthly meetings throughout Appalachia. In Virginia, Quakers instituted the earliest meetings in Bedford, Campbell, Loudon, and Fredrick Counties. In South Carolina, Quakers moved toward the interior from Charleston, organizing the Bush River Monthly Meeting in Newberry County in 1770 and the Cane Creek Monthly Meeting in Union County in 1799. Some Quakers migrated as far south as Georgia and settled Wrightsborough just over the South Carolina border. By 1784, Friends had found their ways to Tennessee.

Although the larger Quaker community voiced concern about Friends moving onto land that might not have been officially purchased from the earlier Native American owners, Quakers continued their westward movements, settling three meetings in Tennessee: New Hope, Greene County, 1795; Lost Creek, Jefferson County, 1797; and Newberry, Blount County, 1808. In northern Appalachia, Quakers located in the Allegheny Mountains and settled two communities in western Pennsylvania. By the 1780s, Friends had instituted communities on both sides of the Monongahela River.

Families composed the greatest number of Quaker settlers in Appalachia; however, a number of single women, particularly widows, also moved west, finding assistance and support from their community of Friends. Also emerging among Appalachian Quakers were the Public Friends, or men and women who had been recognized by their own monthly meeting as having the gift of truth and who subsequently traveled to other communities giving advice. Often when a Public Friend visited a meeting, non-Quakers also attended, both for the message and the social interaction. Other denominations' ministers, especially Baptists and Methodists, often visited Quaker communities, although few Friends converted to these faiths.

During the first decades of the nineteenth century, Quakers throughout Appalachia (as well as the rest of the South) began migrating across the Appalachian Mountains. Quakers moved to Ohio, Indiana, Iowa, and Kansas, where new meetings were established. In fact, one area in Wayne County, Indiana, had so many east Tennesseans among the settlers that the community was called the "Tennessee Settlement." Reasons for migration included ongoing concerns about slavery and a desire for more inexpensive and fertile land. By the Civil War, meetings in the mountains of Georgia,

Tennessee, South Carolina, Virginia, and North Carolina had either been "laid down," that is, they no longer existed or only had a few families who continued to meet for worship. While records are sketchy about how Quakers in Appalachia responded to the Civil War, most Friends remained true to their peace testimony despite pressure from both the Union and Confederate armies. In Winchester, Virginia, Friends held meetings in members' homes when their meetinghouse was occupied on different occasions by both armies, who used it as a barracks and hospital.

In the mid-nineteenth century, education became a priority, especially in the southern Appalachians. Friends from the North and the newly established meetings in the Midwest sent funds to establish schools for training teachers. In Blount County, Tennessee, Friends established two schools, the Friendsville Institute for boys and the Newberry Female School for girls. Both Quakers and non-Quakers attended the schools, which the state eventually took over in the 1880s.

While the number of Quakers had drastically declined by the twentieth century, members of the Society of Friends still held a place in Appalachia. During the 1920s and 1930s, members of the American Friends Service Committee (which formed in 1917 in response to World War I) assisted unemployed coal miners and their families in a food-assistance program. The committee worked in Appalachia throughout the Great Depression and was instrumental in retraining coal miners for craft manufacturing. Friends also assisted in the establishment of the Mountain Craftsmen Cooperative Association in Morgantown, West Virginia.

Today, Quaker meetings are again visible in many Appalachian communities. However, most of the meetings consist of members who were not born into the Society but have joined as "convinced" Friends. The meetings often draw members from the growing number of non-native Appalachians who now reside throughout the region.

See also: TOMLINSON, A. J.

—Neva Jean Specht, *Appalachian State University*

Errol T. Elliott, *Quakers on the American Frontier* (1969); Thomas D. Hamm, *The Transformation of American Quakerism* (1988); Barry Levy, *Quakers and the American Family* (1988).

Religious Conference Centers and Retreats

Influenced by the success of the Chautauqua Assembly, first held in 1874 on the shore of Lake Chautauqua, New York, various denominations established religious retreat centers in Appalachia in the late 1800s and early 1900s. Most of the retreat founders chose western North Carolina sites.

Chautauqua Assembly, itself in Appalachia, was founded by John Heyl Vincent, an editor of Methodist Sunday school publications who envisioned it as a vehicle for advanced training for Sunday school instructors. Early on, Chautauqua attracted participants from other Protestant denominations and added programs to address nonreligious topics. By 1900 there were nearly four hundred summer institutes that called themselves "chautauquas"—though not affiliated with the New York assembly—in small towns throughout the United States. The original assembly, renamed Chautauqua Institution, still focuses on both religious and intellectual renewal and on the arts. Its nine-week season draws around 142,000 people.

Montreat, founded in 1897 by John C. Collins, a Congregationalist minister from Connecticut, was intended as an interdenominational retreat center where New England churchgoers could combine meetings and Bible study with rest and relaxation. Located in a forty-five-hundred-acre cove two miles from Black Mountain, North Carolina, the center was sold to the Presbyterian Church of the United States in 1897. Montreat added privately owned cottages for family gatherings, a summer camp for girls, a normal school (now Montreat College), and more. Its programming has expanded from Bible conferences to include a forum for ministers, a young people's conference, a music conference, and—since 1911—a women's conference.

Lake Junaluska Assembly, a Methodist facility west of Asheville, North Carolina, opened in 1913 with four thousand people in attendance. Originally called the Southern Assembly Grounds, it was proposed by James Atkins, who had visited John Heyl Vincent at Chautauqua. Its original focus was on training Sunday school teachers and missionary workers. The headquarters for the American section of the World Methodist Council is on the property, as well as the Commission on Archives and History/The Heritage Center.

Hall in the Grove at Lake Chautauqua, New York, c. 1880. The Chautauqua Assembly, one of the first religious retreats in Appalachia, influenced the establishment of hundreds of imitation "chautauquas" throughout the United States.

The Western North Carolina Conference of the United Methodist Church meets annually at Lake Junaluska.

In 1907 Baptists opened Ridgecrest on a thousand acres near Black Mountain. Bernard Washington Spilman, the Sunday school secretary of the North Carolina Baptist State Convention, had been holding Sunday school chautauquas patterned on the New York model for some time, but when a session held at Red Springs attracted more than two thousand people, he began to envision something larger. A boys' camp was added in 1930 and a girls' camp in 1935. Attendance was strong during World War II, and facilities were expanded and modernized in the 1950s. The facility is now named Ridgecrest Conference Center and is operated by LifeWay Christian Resources, a Southern Baptist Convention agency.

A more recently developed western North Carolina center is the Billy Graham Training Center at the Cove. Consisting of Cove Camp, as well as year-round conference and retreat facilities that can be used by other church groups, it offers fifty-five of its own biblically based seminars for lay Christians each year. The fifteen-hundred-acre site in Potter's Cove is eight miles from Montreat. The center opened in 1987 and was dedicated in 1993. Its buildings include a stone chapel with an eighty-seven-foot steeple, a seventy-five-hundred-square-foot conference center, two lodges, cabins for guest lecturers, and a summer camp.

Other retreat centers in western North Carolina include the YMCA Blue Ridge Assembly, founded in 1906 at Black Mountain; Cragmont Assembly, established 1945 in Black Mountain for the state's Free Will Baptists; an Episcopal center in Black Mountain called In the Oaks; an African Methodist Episcopal Zion center in Black Mountain, established before 1927 and later renamed Camp Dorothy Walls; the Blowing Rock Assembly Grounds, established in the 1950s by the Southern Conference of the United Church of Christ; the Valle Crucis Conference Center, established in the 1970s by the Episcopal Church; Christmount, founded in Black Mountain in 1947 by the Christian Church (Disciples of Christ); and Kanuga, an Episcopal facility in Hendersonville established around 1909.

A nondenominational center located outside the main clustering in western North Carolina is the Kirkridge Retreat Center in Bangor, Pennsylvania. John Oliver Nelson, a Presbyterian minister and professor of Christian vocation at Yale Divinity School purchased Kirkridge in 1942. Its programs reach out to both clergy and laypeople and have always been designed to combine faith with social justice and attention to the needs of people from diverse backgrounds. The center's vast array of program offerings include a Peacemaker Training Institute; an interfaith series on teaching children tolerance; workshops for the gay, lesbian, bisexual, and transgender communities; and individual programs on nuclear disarmament and consumerism.

Retreat centers specializing in meditation are found throughout Appalachia. Examples include the Southern Dharma Retreat Center in Hot Springs, North Carolina; Heavenly Mountain and the Maharishi Spiritual Center of America, both devoted to Transcendental Meditation, in Blowing Rock, North Carolina; Bhavana Society, a forest meditation center in High View, West Virginia; Himalayan Institute in Honesdale Pennsylvania; Satchidananda Ashram (or Yogaville) in Buckingham, Virginia; the Center for Spiritual Awareness in Lakemont, Georgia; and the Center for New Beginnings in Dahlonega, Georgia.

The rapid growth of religious retreat centers between 1897 and the 1920s demonstrated the need for a level of education and enrichment between degree-granting seminaries and church camping programs. Most of Appalachia's centers have since moved from summer to year-round operations and have opened their facilities to other denominations and to nonchurch groups. Many of them have dropped the denominational part of their name and added *conference* and/or *retreat center*. Whether founded in 1897 (Montreat) or 1987 (the Billy Graham Training Center), all were placed in the Appalachian Mountains because of the draw of their remote beauty and the certainty that the location would facilitate spiritual renewal.

See also: CHAUTAUQUA VILLAGE, NEW YORK (ARCHITECTURE); MONTEAGLE ASSEMBLY (ARCHITECTURE).

—Glenn Ellen Starr Stilling, *Appalachian State University*

Elmer T. Clark, *Junaluska Jubilee* (1963); William Bean Kennedy, "Montreat: An Educational Center of the Presbyterian Church," *American Presbyterians* (Summer 1996); James H. McBath, "The Emergence of Chautauqua as a Religious and Educational Institution," *Methodist History* (October 1981).

Revival Exercises

The phrase *revival exercises* denotes a collection of preternatural physical behaviors motivated by spiritual enthusiasm, behaviors that supposedly transcend conscious awareness and produce an altered state not controlled by the practitioner. These behaviors include perishing in the Spirit, running in the Spirit, rolling in the Spirit, twirling in the Spirit, and others. These practices had their American origins both during the Great Awakening (1726–56) and the Great Western Revival (1787–1805), the latter also known as the Second Great Awakening. In Appalachia and elsewhere, these behaviors can be observed within contemporary Pentecostal traditions, within various nondenominational charismatic movements, and within some Appalachian Free Will Baptist worship.

Appalachia's revival-exercise traditions originated in Tennessee and Kentucky camp meetings, most notably in the Cane Ridge revival (Bourbon County, Kentucky, August 1801). Like many of the western-frontier sacramental meetings immediately before and after the start of the nineteenth century, the Cane Ridge experience exploded with such emotionalism that Presbyterian ministers working with the event became concerned about an absence of controls at the scene. Indeed, some of these ministers accused fellow Presbyterians, such as Reverend Richard McNemar, of acting "like Methodists" when they themselves fell under the meeting's emotional power.

Observers, both at Cane Ridge and at subsequent turn-of-the-century camp meetings, reported scene after scene of distraught worshipers falling helplessly to the ground, some remaining for extended periods of time either unconscious or moaning over the condition of their souls. Some rolled about on the ground as in pain. Others tried to rise, but fell again as if having lost control of their bodies. Some attempted to run from the scene and yet seemed incapable of moving from the spot. Repentant individuals occasionally howled in despair, while others made repetitive explosive sounds described as "barks." Being observed by 1804 were "the jerks," a behavior marked by the distraught person's being overtaken by convulsive movements similar to those associated with epileptic seizures.

First-person descriptions of these revival meetings suggest that the central cause for these physical disturbances was sinners' great fear of the afterlife punishments they heard described by some preachers. Intensifying these fears was the heavy Calvinism of many exhorters; a doctrine of absolute determinism made the torments of a literal hell seem inescapable. While the Cane Ridge versions of these exercises appeared to have been motivated by fear and remorse, however, comparable contemporary practices are more often associated with ecstasy.

"Falling" was the most prominent of the exercises exhibited at Cane Ridge. In fact, accounts suggest that it was this one physical behavior from which other revival exercises had their beginnings, at least during the Great Western Revival. By 1803 and 1804 other variations of this unusual behavioral family began to be reported, including the jerks, dancing, barking, running, and rolling, some of which were preceded by a fall. Reverend John Lyle's diary accounts of the 1801 Cane Ridge meeting tell of individuals who collapsed to the ground early in the day and were still there at nightfall. Individuals who remained conscious after falling occasionally were described as rolling about and also as attempting to rise and run, only to fall again.

To suggest motivation for these falling behaviors, observers sometimes mentioned the great feeling of destitution being experienced by the prostrate mourners, convinced as these fallen were that they were headed for the awful hell occasionally described by preachers. Today's falling exercises, usually practiced by believers who proclaim an Arminian doctrine of atonement, are prone to be more hopeful, even joyful.

At Pentecostal revival meetings in Appalachia, individuals still fall to the ground during heights of religious enthusiasm, sometimes simply as an emotional swoon and other times as a result of having twirled themselves into dizziness. Far more frequently, however, the individual falls as a result of having hands laid upon her or him by a preacher. This second phenomenon is referenced as being slain by the Spirit or as perishing in the Spirit, and once on the ground the fallen individual may lie there for five minutes to an hour, seemingly unconscious.

Two versions of running exercises appear in Great Western Revival accounts. The first depicts some sinner as having started to run away from her or his fallen state but being caught in a frantic and futile running in place, while the second apparently suggests a running for joy, usually in a circle. A witness has described this second version being practiced in the Thornton Freewill Baptist Church in Letcher County, Kentucky (1989). The individual involved said that he never remembered the beginning of his runs, only their ending.

Contemporary Appalachian versions of dancing, or "twirling exercises," often look like buck dancing if practiced by a male or arms-on-high twirling if practiced by a woman. Frequently performed by Holiness-Pentecostal groups, the behavior looks more joyous than emotionally disturbed, and the action occasionally will result in an eventual fall. *The Holy Ghost People*, a documentary filmed in West Virginia in the late 1960s, includes examples of this behavior, in one case accomplished by a male and in the other case by a woman. The documentary also captured three examples of the jerks, one of them especially interesting because it involved a small boy who appeared to be learning how to perform the exercise.

In 1991, at a Pentecostal tent meeting in Iaeger, West Virginia, a researcher witnessed several examples of dancing, falling, rolling, jerking, and even one version of what might have been called barking, in the sense that the woman involved released a series of explosive vocal sounds totally unrelated to any recognizable verbalizations but instead identifiable more as very guttural whoops or coughs.

See also: GLOSSOLALIA; GREAT WESTERN REVIVAL AND CAMP-MEETING MOVEMENT.

—Howard Dorgan, *Appalachian State University, Emeritus*

John B. Boles, *The Great Revival, 1787–1805* (1972); Paul K. Conkin, *Cane Ridge: America's Pentecost* (1990); Ellen Eslinger, *Citizens of Zion: The Social Origins of Camp Meeting Revivalism* (1999).

Running in the Spirit

See Revival Exercises

Scopes Trial

State of Tennessee v. John Thomas Scopes, also known as the Scopes Evolution Trial or the Scopes Monkey Trial, is considered one of the most significant religion-related events to transpire in Appalachia. This case marked the nation's first challenge to the anti-evolution laws emerging across the nation, and the resulting publicity subjected a small section of southern Appalachia to an intense national and international scrutiny, perhaps unfairly so.

The trial took place in Dayton, Tennessee, in July of 1925, yet the principal players in the drama were almost all outsiders. John Scopes, the defendant, and George Rappelyea, who brought against him the charge of teaching evolution in school, were both newcomers to Dayton. Visiting legal counsel on both sides, as well as scientists and Christian fundamentalists, arrived from all over to battle over the teaching of evolution while the entire town lay under the scrutiny of the national press. In the end, the entire region was pushed into the national spotlight as a symbol of theology versus science.

Tennessee's anti-evolution statute originated in the foothills of Appalachia, from the mind of State Representative John Washington Butler. Butler, a fourth-generation Macon County farmer, grew concerned about the teaching of evolution after hearing that a member of his church had gone to college and returned believing in evolution and not in God. In response to this perceived threat to his faith, Butler introduced a bill outlawing the teaching of evolution in Tennessee public schools.

The Butler Bill encountered virtually no opposition. Legislators could not oppose it for fear of appearing irreligious. Academics dared not protest because legislators were debating the largest appropriation ever given the University of Tennessee. Some hoped Governor Austin Peay would veto the bill, but he desired a U.S. Senate seat and would not risk being labeled an atheist. Thus, only supporters were heard, and the Butler Bill entered Tennessee law.

Upon learning of the legislation, the American Civil Liberties Union (ACLU) took steps to challenge it, placing a notice in Tennessee newspapers offering support in challenges to the Butler law. This notice caught the attention of a number of people in Dayton, including Rappelyea.

Dayton, a mining town in Rhea County between Knoxville and Chattanooga, had seen better times. With mines flagging, the county seat relied on the surrounding farms for its livelihood. Rappelyea, a New Yorker who had come to Dayton as a mine engineer, read the ACLU's notice and suggested challenging the anti-evolution law to bring the town to national attention. Rappelyea asked Scopes, the high school's substitute science teacher, to agree to stand trial for having taught evolution. Scopes was from western Kentucky and was working in Dayton as a football coach and substitute teacher to earn money for graduate school. He disapproved of the Butler law and agreed to stand trial.

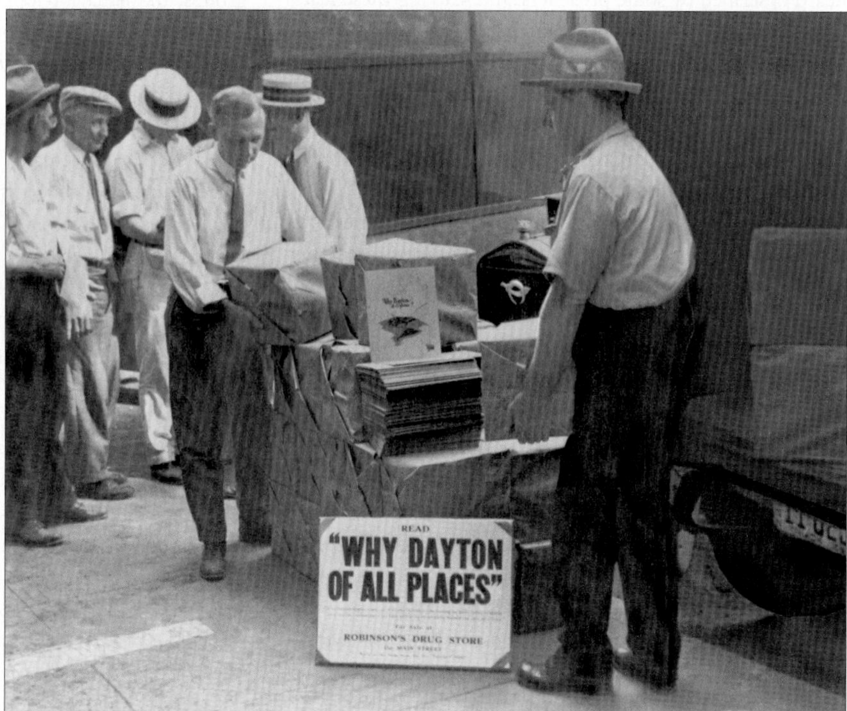

Local businessman and school board president Fred Robinson (left center, bare-headed) selling copies of a booklet promoting his town during the Scopes trial, Dayton, Tennessee, 1925.

Rappelyea and an assortment of local businessmen pushed to have the trial held as soon as possible. There was urgency, as other towns also had challenges to the Butler law planned. A special session of the county court had to be called to prevent the trial's being delayed.

Although local lawyers technically led the prosecution and defense, the visiting attorneys proved far more conspicuous. The ACLU brought the nationally known and controversial Clarence Darrow to assist in the defense. Darrow had grown up in northern Ohio and brought with him a reputation for representing unpopular defendants whom he saw as victims of the law. *Tennessee v. Scopes* proved to be one of his highest-profile cases. With Darrow came scientists from across the nation. Experts in geology, biology, anthropology, and linguistics volunteered their services to assist the defense.

The defense attempted to dismiss the charges on state and national constitutional issues and on the law's ambiguity, but the judge disallowed all of these arguments. Next, the defense wanted to allow an explanation of evolution to the jury to show evolution did not conflict with the Bible. The judge would not allow the jury to hear this, only permitting the explanation to be inserted in the record, where the press did not miss a word. If the defense could not strike down the Butler law, Darrow hoped to educate the public with testimony.

The prosecution received the assistance of William Jennings Bryan, the former presidential candidate and religious figure originally from Illinois. Bryan used this opportunity to speak about religion, advertise his books and real estate, and test the waters for forming a new political party. Religious activists flocked behind his banner of fundamentalist Christianity.

Through the massive national and international publicity, the Scopes trial fulfilled the backers' hopes of putting Dayton on the map. The case became the first major trial broadcast live over radio, while the judge even set aside time for reporters to take pictures. The national press came to cover both the trial and those gathered to attend the spectacle, and when news proved sparse, some invented reports of local color that included blurred lines between native religion and that of fundamentalist visitors.

Buildings in Dayton received fresh paint. Local people opened their homes to boarders, while both area and visiting entrepreneurs started booths selling hot dogs, lemonade, or books on religion. Overnight, what had been a quiet town developed a carnival atmosphere. Local inhabitants found themselves caught between science, religion, and salesmanship while under the eyes of the nation.

In the end, the defense asked for a summary judgment of guilty and hoped for an appeal. None was granted, and the Butler law would stand until repealed in 1967. While the Scopes trial did put Dayton on the map, it did so in a questionable light.

—Richard C. Evey Jr., *Appalachian State University*

Ray Ginger, *Six Days or Forever?* (1958); Mary Lee Settle, *The Scopes Trial* (1972); Jerry D. Tompkins, *D-Days at Dayton: Reflections on the Scopes Trial* (1965).

Second Great Awakening

See Great Western Revival and Camp-Meeting Movement

Serpent Handling

Serpent handling as a modern Christian religious ritual emerged among southern Appalachian fundamentalists, principally Holiness-Pentecostal groups, within the first twelve years of the twentieth century. Instrumental in the initiation and proliferation of this ritual were George Hensley in Tennessee and Kentucky and Jim Miller in northern Alabama and southern Georgia. Appalachian serpent-handling preachers, many of whom in the initial years were associated with the Church of God (Cleveland, Tennessee), have evangelized their belief throughout the South and beyond, as well as transporting it to northern industrial cities.

Participants designate this practice as one of the five signs listed in Mark 16:17–18 that Jesus said would follow those who believe. Sign followers, often perceived as tempting God, instead see themselves as pursuing biblical precedent and "confirming the word" by taking up serpents, casting out devils, speaking in tongues, drinking deadly poisons, and healing the sick. Serpent handlers closely associate these practices with those manifestations of the Spirit (which they describe as the "nine spiritual gifts") in 1 Cor. 12:8–10 and with the handling of fire referenced in Heb. 11:34. Although some believers handle serpents solely by faith in the authority of biblical text to protect them, most prefer to wait on direction given through anointment of the Holy Ghost.

In most aspects, members and services of serpent-handling congregations vary little from those of Pentecostal groups in which serpents are not handled. Thus, a description of serpent handlers resembles that of other Holiness people with the addition of the belief in all the signs. They are sincere fundamentalist believers, principally white males and females from low to moderate social, economic, and educational levels. Modest in dress and appearance, they also restrict the consumption and use of all substances, such as alcohol, considered harmful to the body (which is viewed as the temple of the soul) and are restrained in activities deemed worldly. Although stable emotionally and psychologically, they are given to great expression in informal, emotionally charged, participatory worship services. Their religious and church commitments are reinforced through various means, including kinship, frequent attendance at

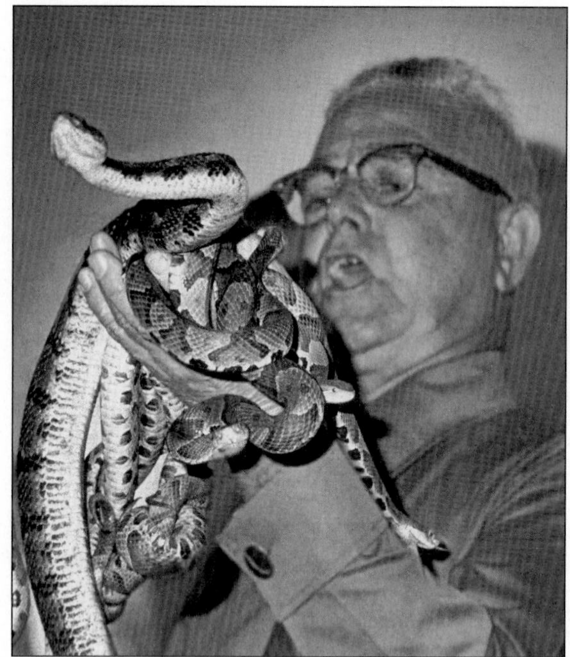

A member of the congregation at Holiness Church of God in Jesus' Name, Cocke County, Tennessee, 1971. The ability to safely handle poisonous serpents is viewed as one of the signs of a true believer.

services, and testimonials of personal experiences affirming, both physically and spiritually, God's apparent direct power. Their interpretation of the Bible, principally the King James Version, is independent.

In general, snake handlers are influenced greatly in preaching, ritual, gesture, and public worship by tradition, which has been established by oral and demonstrative means. This profile varies with individuals and is changing, as is that of many other conservative religious groups, with the increased liberalization and secularization of contemporary American culture.

Religious doctrine based on belief in the direct intervention of divine power is well established in Christian faith; however, the practice of following the signs by small, autonomous churches is frequently considered by the general public as bizarre and incomprehensible. A more objective view toward serpent handling is one that incorporates an historical perspective of southern rural culture in general and religious faith in specific, including the influences of Wesleyanism, Calvinism, and the revival movements of the nineteenth and twentieth centuries.

The influence of traditional beliefs and codes of conduct are especially significant. Characteristically, communities where serpent handling is active believe strongly in the literal truth of the Bible and in the presence of the supernatural, not only stemming from their belief in scripture but also from what is passed down in oral tradition. They believe in and identify with heroes of the Old Testament, and they believe in codes of heroic behavior—proving oneself and disdaining death. These traditions are among those central to the understanding of serpent handling and why it sprang up in the southern Appalachians.

Congregations that believe in serpent handling may be divided into two groups, sometimes distinguished as Jesus' Name and Trinity, a division based partially on their interpretation of biblical nomenclature. Ordinarily, only a small percentage of congregational members handle serpents. The count of practitioners (fewer than a thousand) is largely guesswork because of, among other factors, their autonomous structure, isolation, and fluidity in church attendance. There is also a considerable ebb and flow in the number of both individuals and congregations that practice the taking up of serpents.

Serpent handlers are sometimes bitten and sometimes die from the bites. Their multiple interpretations of these events, which include attitude of the victim, absence of anointment, sinfulness, evidence of lethality to unbelievers, and being called to heaven, all fall within the compass of Providence. The danger to life that the practice imposes and perhaps the threat to mainstream religious belief have effected prohibitive legislation in a limited number of states, although in certain instances these laws have been removed. Cases against serpent handlers have been appealed to state supreme courts on constitutional rights to religious freedom. These appeals have been denied, citing that although the right to believe is absolute, the right to practice is conditional. Serpent handlers, however, persist in obeying what they deem God's law.

Scholarly analyses of serpent handling are varied. Some observers argue that the practice is a manifestation of sexual repression; others see it as an expression of a psychological need for religion and ritual, or to expand on that view, an archetypal experience common to humanity and expressed in correlative rituals throughout the world. It has also been described as a meaningful religious experience eliciting phenomenological research, or as an individual and collective response to socioeconomic forces within a distinctive subculture. Some of the approaches are essentially reductionist theories more nearly relative to the overall question of religion than to serpent handling as a Christian ritual.

In their worst light, serpent handlers may be viewed as extremists who are naive, illiberal, simplistic, and foolhardy. In their best light, they may be seen as Holy Ghost believers experiencing a profound emotional religious confrontation with death, both tangible and symbolic, and as Christian mystics who by taking up deadly serpents achieve an epiphany—an intuitive perception of the reality of themselves, the world in which they live, religion, and God.

See also: FIRE HANDLING; HENSLEY, GEORGE; PENTECOSTALS.

—Thomas Burton, *East Tennessee State University*

Thomas G. Burton, *Serpent-Handling Believers* (1993); Steven M. Kane, "Snake Handlers of Southern Appalachia," Ph.D. dissertation, Princeton University (1979); Paul Williamson, Howard R. Pollio, and Ralph W. Hood Jr., "A Phenomenological Analysis of the Anointing among Religious Serpent Handlers," *International Journal for the Psychology of Religion* (October 2000).

Sheffey, Robert

(1820–1902) Itinerant preacher.

Even though Robert Sayers Sheffey, a Methodist, was one of central Appalachia's most beloved itinerant preachers, his style was extremely unconventional, and he was never licensed by his denomination. Functioning as an independent exhorter, Sheffey traveled by horseback through much of central Appalachia. Although not recognized for his oratory, he had a reputation for gaining remarkably successful results in his prayer requests to God. Apparently, this special gift was greatly appreciated during the heyday (1870–90) of the Wabash camp meetings in Giles County, Virginia, where his unrestrained prayer style became legendary.

Born in Ivanhoe, Virginia, Sheffey was orphaned and sent to Abingdon, Virginia, to live with an uncle. Shunning family wealth and educational traditions (though he briefly attended Emory and Henry College), he gained an early reputation for revivalistic zeal. While still a young man, he began his itinerant ministry, preaching whenever asked, assisting with altar calls, conducting hearth-side devotions in mountain cabins, and waging a fervent campaign against moonshiners. Surrounding this latter effort, a colorful set of folk accounts circulated concerning results of his prayers, which called for the supernatural destruction of mountain distilleries. According to reports, an oak tree fell on one still, and another burned under mysterious circumstances, while many were leveled and replaced with more acceptable structures, including churches.

Sheffey died close to Wabash, only a few years after the Wabash campground facilities burned down. In 1979 the annual Robert Sheffey Memorial Campmeeting was established on a site next to the Wesley Chapel Cemetery in Trigg, Virginia, where the preacher was buried.

See also: GREAT WESTERN REVIVAL AND CAMP-MEETING MOVEMENT; METHODIST CIRCUIT RIDERS.

—J. Brent Carrick, *Mount Airy, North Carolina*

Short Hell Doctrine

Also identified as hell redemption doctrine and restoration doctrine, this version of Universalist theology occasionally was found among the beliefs of nineteenth century and later central Appalachian Old-Time Baptists. The theology probably originated from the preaching of Elhanan Winchester (1751–1797), who in the late eighteenth century established in Philadelphia a small movement known as the Universal Baptists. It defined a purgatorial type of hell—a place where sinners spent only such time as was necessary to the expiation of their respective earthly transgressions, later joining the "purer at heart" in an eventually universal and eternal heaven.

This "short hell heresy" received a number of references in nineteenth-century Old-Time Baptist association minutes. Identified as an especially egregious theological error that should be avoided at all costs, it could result in an expulsion of errant preachers or a splitting away from the infected elements of the named churches. In particular, the South Kentucky Association of Separate Baptists allegedly suffered from the infiltration of this doctrine. The theology also occasionally received mention in annual minutes of Primitive Baptist, Regular Baptist, and United Baptist associations.

See also: PRIMITIVE BAPTIST UNIVERSALISTS.

—Howard Dorgan, *Appalachian State University, Emeritus*

Skiles, William West

(1807–1862) Episcopal missionary.

William West Skiles was the epitome of the Episcopal missionary spirit in nineteenth-century Appalachia. He arrived in Valle Crucis, North Carolina, in 1844. Episcopal Bishop Levis S. Ives had envisioned a missionary outpost among the mountain people and recruited the agronomist Skiles to assist in the mission's development. Ordained at the Valle Crucis seminary in 1847, the following year Skiles became the first Anglican since the English Reformation to take monastic vows in the newly created Order of the Holy Cross.

Until his death on December 8, 1862, Skiles was a faithful pastor to the mountain people of what was then an isolated region of Appalachia. He provided services as physician, farmer, schoolteacher, carpenter, veterinarian, and friend. The integrity of his character was recognized throughout North Carolina. He kept the Valle Crucis Mission alive after the conversion of Bishop Ives to the Roman Catholic Church in 1852. Although some church leaders suspected he had Catholic leanings, Skiles continued his ministrations with the Episcopal Church until his death.

Even today Skiles is regarded as a local saint. The greatest testimony to his legacy is the congregation of Holy Cross Church that continues in the same missionary spirit as a century and a half earlier.

See also: EPISCOPAL CHURCH.

—Scott A. Oxford, *Episcopal Diocese of Western North Carolina*

South Kentucky Association

See Associations, Baptist

Speaking in Tongues

See Glossolalia

Spurling, R. G.

(1857–1935) Cofounder of the Church of God (Cleveland, Tennessee).

Richard Green "R. G." Spurling, with the assistance of his father, Richard Spurling, formed a church in the late nineteenth century that represented the beginning of the Church of God (Cleveland, Tennessee). Born in Kentucky and reared in Tennessee, Spurling was converted in the religious tradition of his father, a Missionary Baptist minister. He came of age under the influence of the Landmark Baptist movement in east Tennessee and, following his marriage, became licensed to preach through a North Carolina Missionary Baptist church.

The beginnings of the Church of God can be traced back to the early 1880s, when Spurling began to resist certain tenets of Landmarkism in his Missionary Baptist church, which resulted in his being excluded from the church and revocation of his license. Subsequently, he took shelter among the Methodists but did not formally unite with them. He soon concluded that the apostolic church had fallen and needed restoration, and, on August 19, 1886, after he had preached a challenging sermon, his wife, his seventy-five-year-old father, and six others responded by forming an independent church they called Christian Union.

Due to factors surrounding the start of the Church of God, Spurling has sometimes been confused in the church's developing historiography with his father, Richard. However, the records clearly show that the younger Spurling was the primary inspiration and thinker behind the church's founding and early development, although the elder Spurling is considered a cofounder.

Spurling's extreme individualism and loose form of organization prevented him from finding any lasting success until 1902, when he established a small western North Carolina congregation. This fellowship attracted A. J. Tomlinson, a former Quaker, who thereafter provided charismatic leadership for the movement and centralized its government. In 1907 the general assembly of the churches adopted the name *Church of God*. After the organization divided in the early 1920s, Spurling remained detached from both branches until 1931, when he reconciled with Tomlinson and his followers in the Church of God of Prophecy.

See also: PENTECOSTALS; TOMLINSON, A. J.

—Wade H. Phillips, *Church of God of Prophecy*

Stearns, Shubal

(1706–1771) Baptist preacher.

Shubal Stearns is considered the founder of the Separate Baptist denomination prominent in certain areas of Appalachia. He began his career in Tolland, Connecticut. Influenced by the Great Awakening, he left the Congregationalists and eventually founded a Separate Baptist Church in that community, serving as its pastor until 1754.

In 1755 Sterns moved his family to the Sandy Creek area of Guilford County (now Randolph County), North Carolina. He established Sandy Creek Baptist Church with sixteen members. Under Stearns, the Separates allowed eldresses and deaconesses as well as elders and deacons. They also believed in seven Christian rites rather than the customary two: love feast; laying on of hands after baptism; foot washing; anointing the sick with oil; the right hand of fellowship; the kiss of charity; and the "devoting" of children, a dry christening in which the infant's name is bestowed but with no baptismal sprinkling. Stearns made preaching trips through North Carolina, establishing new Separate Baptist congregations. In 1760 he organized the Sandy Creek Baptist Association, comprised of seven Separate churches in North Carolina and Virginia, the first such organization in the South and the third oldest in the United States. When Stearns died in 1771, Sandy Creek Baptist Church had grown to 606 members and had promulgated forty-two churches and 125 ministers.

Stearns believed converts should have undergone an emotional conversion experience. A highly effective evangelical preacher with a strong but musical voice and expressive, piercing eyes, he had the ability to move converts to tears, screaming, and shouting. The Regular Baptists were averse to Stearns and Separate Baptists because they allowed women to pray in public, used uneducated men as preachers, and conducted noisy, disorderly meetings.

See also: BAPTISTS, THE OLD-TIME GROUPS.

—Glenn Ellen Starr Stilling, *Appalachian State University*

Stone, Barton W.

(1772–1844) Religious reformer.

Barton W. Stone was the leader of a populist Christian movement that significantly affected a number of religious denominations in Appalachia. Born near Port Tobacco, Maryland, Stone moved to Pittsylvania County, Virginia, in 1779, then to Guilford Courthouse, North Carolina, in 1790, where he began legal studies at David Caldwell's academy. Though baptized Anglican, he experienced a conversion while in

North Carolina after hearing the preaching of Presbyterian ministers James McGready and William Hodge.

Licensed by the Orange Presbytery in 1796, Stone preached in North Carolina and Tennessee before being called to the Cane Ridge and Concord congregations near Paris, Kentucky. In 1798 Stone was ordained by the Transylvania Presbytery despite his expressed misgivings about Calvinist doctrine. After witnessing McGready's revival in Logan County, Kentucky, in the spring of 1801, Stone organized a similar meeting in August around the annual sacrament service at Cane Ridge. The gathering was highly charged and drew thousands from across denominational lines. Facing censure by the Synod of Kentucky, Stone and four other ministers then formed the Springfield Presbytery in 1803 but declared it dissolved a year later with the publication of the *Last Will and Testament of the Springfield Presbytery*. The ministers labeled their independent congregations as Christian Churches or Churches of Christ. The movement numbered between fifteen and twenty thousand by 1823.

Stone published a religious journal called the *Christian Messenger* from 1826 until his death in 1844. In the 1830s many of Stone's churches united with congregations of the Alexander Campbell movement. In the twenty-first century, Stone's ideological influence can still be evidenced in the Christian Church (Disciples of Christ), Churches of Christ, and Christian Churches, as well as in part of the United Church of Christ.

See also: CHRISTIAN DENOMINATIONAL FAMILY; GREAT WESTERN REVIVAL AND CAMP-MEETING MOVEMENT; MCGREADY, JAMES.

—Douglas A. Foster, *Abilene Christian College*

Taylor, John

(1752–1835) Baptist anti-missions leader.

John Taylor's most significant contribution to Appalachia was his leadership in the anti-missionary movement. Born in Fauquier County, Virginia, Taylor was "awakened" at age seventeen by the preaching of John Marshall, a Separate Baptist. Once ordained, he spent ten years as an itinerant evangelist in backwoods Virginia before moving to Kentucky and eventually becoming an advocate for the Calvinistic anti-missions campaign.

Taylor's migration to Kentucky followed his marriage and a 1783 substantial inheritance. This move was similar to that of many young families who, attracted by the chance for free land, were traveling west in groups. Once in Kentucky, Taylor organized churches in Woodford, Boone, and Trimble Counties. He also became actively involved in Kentucky Baptist associations, and he established Baptist congregations in western North Carolina, West Virginia, and Tennessee.

In 1820 he made a major contribution to the anti-mission literature with *Thoughts on Missions*, in which he made the argument that the Baptist Church should not undertake missionary work. At age seventy he also wrote *A History of Ten Baptist Churches* (1823), which is considered a highly useful record of early frontier Baptist life. Some of the activities Taylor describes are the movement of his family's belongings sixty miles by boat down the Ohio River; the clearing of timber, planting crops, putting up fences, and constructing buildings; conversions, including his own and that of his teenaged sister; baptisms; laying on of hands; the calling of pastors; and the expulsion of church members.

See also: BAPTIST, THE OLD-TIME GROUPS; MISSIONARY/ANTI-MISSIONARY SPLIT; PARKER, DANIEL.

—Glenn Ellen Starr Stilling, *Appalachian State University*

Tomlinson, A. J.

(1865–1943) Pentecostal pioneer and first general overseer of the Church of God (Cleveland, Tennessee).

Born and educated in a Quaker community in Indiana, Ambrose Jessup "A. J." Tomlinson came under Holiness influence in about 1892 and professed to have experienced "entire sanctification." Thereafter, he became dissatisfied with his Quaker tradition and began to search for a church affiliation that could satisfy his growing passion to restore apostolic Christianity. In 1899 he came to Appalachia as a missionary under the auspices of the American Bible Society. There he met R. G. Spurling, who, beginning in 1886, had organized several small congregations based on a Restorationist view of the church. Tomlinson became deeply impressed by Spurling's doctrine and in 1903 united with his movement.

Tomlinson's leadership ability was readily recognized, and he was ordained by Spurling and William F. Bryant. In 1904 he moved to Cleveland, Tennessee, basing the church's government and activities there. Convinced of the validity of speaking in tongues as the evidence of Spirit baptism, he thereafter led the Church of God into the Pentecostal movement.

In the early 1920s the leadership became divided on several issues, particularly on Tomlinson's exalted position as general overseer. After being impeached by a majority of the ruling elders in 1923, Tomlinson disputed the validity of the proceedings and, with his followers, formed the Church of God of Prophecy. He continued to lead this body until his death.

See also: GLOSSOLALIA; PENTECOSTALS.

—Wade H. Phillips, *Church of God of Prophecy*

Union Baptists

Within Appalachia, Union Baptists are found in three northwest counties of North Carolina (Ashe, Watauga, and Wilkes) and in a limited area of southwest Virginia. Theologically they are Regular Baptists, but they derive their name from having sided with Unionist positions during the Civil War. Union Baptists expound an atonement theology that lies roughly midway between the staunch Calvinism of their Primitive cousins and the Arminianism of their Free Will and Missionary kin. In terms of worship practice, they preserve the same conventional ways of their Regular Baptist forebears: foot washing, impromptu rhythmical preaching, limited lined singing, living water baptism, multi-sermon services, and a host of similar traditions.

By 1858, the Senter Association (now Primitive Baptist) was already experiencing discord between its pro-slavery and antislavery churches; however, the association did not formally split until 1867 when Silas Creek Church (Ashe County) led other Senter pro-Union fellowships into what would become the Mountain Union Association, the first Union Baptists of the region. Later, two additional Union Baptist clusters were instituted: the Friendship (Union Baptist) Association and the Primitive (Union Baptist) Association. This region of North Carolina now has an Old-Time Baptist presence fairly evenly distributed among Primitive, Regular, and Union Baptists, with one association of Separate Baptists also present.

See also: BAPTISTS, THE OLD-TIME GROUPS; LINED SINGING.

—Howard Dorgan, *Appalachian State University, Emeritus*

Unitarian Universalists

The Unitarian Universalist Association of Congregations came into being when the Universalist Church of America and the American Unitarian Association merged in 1961. Both denominations resulted from the eighteenth-century American Enlightenment and were in opposition to an Edwardian Calvinism that still pervades much of the Appalachian religion. Coeval with the new nation, both Unitarianism and Universalism developed liberal, humanistic, and scholarly approaches to scriptural Christianity but from differing social bases. In addition, how each denomination spread through Appalachia differed significantly.

Universalists preached a gospel of universal salvation. During the first decade of the nineteenth century, Universalist churches, primarily composed of rural and small town yeoman farmers and artisans, appeared in northern Appalachia (New York and Pennsylvania). Itinerant preachers, tracts, and word of mouth spread the movement rapidly through the backcountry. However, Universalists lacked a strong national organization to support their numerous and scattered congregations. Conscious efforts to found Appalachian churches (as in Harriman, Tennessee) or missions (Inman's Chapel, North Carolina) suffered from a scarcity of personnel and lack of funds. At the start of the twentieth century, the Universalist Church in the southern Appalachians barely existed, but the influence of its message did influence the ideologies of some religious groups, notably the Primitive Baptist Universalists.

The American Unitarian Association (1825) migrated slowly beyond the urban Northeast. Its members came predominantly from the well-educated upper middle class. The group's message was similar to the Universalists and emphasized the unity of God, basic human goodness and free will, and the necessity of reasonable scholarship in interpreting scripture. They began as Christians, then moved towards Transcendentalism, and by the late nineteenth century included a humanistic wing.

Until the second half of the twentieth century, the Unitarian influence in Appalachia was due primarily to coincidence. However, after World War II, Unitarianism moved more directly to the southern mountains. Fellowships were established that were intentionally small, humanistic, and possessed of an anticlerical bias. They formed in college towns, at research centers, and in retirement communities: in Blacksburg and Harrisonburg, Virginia; in Oak Ridge and Kingsport, Tennessee; and in Asheville and Hendersonville, North Carolina. Initially most fellowships remained small since they had a tendency to be made up of outsiders, to be intellectual, and to have limited interactions with the local culture. While some fellowships retain these practices and remain isolated, other congregations have reflected the larger movement and have evolved into more inclusive communities.

At the turn of the twenty-first century, Unitarian Universalism was enjoying a healthy growth rate both regionally and nationally. As intentionally inclusive, non-creedal religious communities, Unitarian Universalist churches in Appalachia seek to provide a welcoming, safe place for open-minded seekers, for all types of minorities, and for interfaith dialogue. As modern congregations move toward greater engagement with traditional Appalachian society and culture, they learn from the significant overlap of values. Thus, the future of Unitarian Universalism in Appalachia rests on the discovery of a mutually beneficial path for the denomination and the regional culture.

See also: PRIMITIVE BAPTIST UNIVERSALISTS.

—Barry Thomas Whittemore, *Holston Valley Unitarian Universalist Church*

Values and Religion in Central Appalachia

Religion both reflects and shapes the values by which people live, and the case in Appalachia is no different. Because the religious practices and beliefs of central Appalachians are easily the most documented and studied in all of Appalachia, they are useful in examining how apparent cultural traits and values have been influenced in the region by the religious heritage of its people. Similar relationships between values and religious beliefs can be found throughout the region, and even the world.

Central Appalachian values, to a large extent, are based not only on the scriptures that suggest life's meaning to mountain people, but also on the religious experience of their forebears. Old-Time Baptists and others have depended heavily on the Apostle Paul's letters for their theological grounding and thus for their values. Writers such as Emma Bell Miles, Horace Kephart, John C. Campbell, Thomas R. Ford, Jack Weller, Jim Wayne Miller, and Howard Dorgan have identified several of these values, which include independence, humility, familism, personalism, egalitarianism, and hospitality.

The independent nature of central Appalachian mountain people has the least scriptural authority but is nonetheless pervasive. The mountaineer has been described as possessing extreme personal independence in terms of actions. However, he is also independent in terms of his spiritual life, and this attitude dates back to the Reformation, when many Christians eschewed priests and hierarchies and asserted the freedom to interpret the scriptures on their own. Few groups are more intellectually independent of earthly authority than Primitive and Old Regular Baptists, whose spiritual and intellectual resistance to hierarchical authority is shared by many relative newcomers in the Holiness-Pentecostal faith.

Humility is perhaps the most prominent value in Appalachian life, so much so that it has become part of the manners system. Central Appalachians think it unseemly to brag on themselves or even to agree with someone who compliments them generously. They defer to others and say disparaging things about themselves in regard to ability and reserve their praise for others. Dorgan has written that in one church group an individual can rise to a leadership position only by disclaiming any qualities that would assure effectiveness in the role. Dorgan points out that this stance is rooted in a belief that humankind can never be confident that behavior will be acceptable to God, only that there is hope.

A church minister with his family, Hamilton County, Tennessee, 1947. Appalachian family roles are often defined by religious beliefs.

There is ample scriptural authority for this value. The Old Testament has many references to humility before the Almighty God, as in "The fear of the Lord is the instruction of wisdom; and before honour is humility" (Prov. 15:33). But the New Testament adds another requirement, that of humility before one another, as in "Yea, all of you be subject to one another, and be clothed in humility: for God resisteth the proud, and giveth grace to the humble" (1 Peter 5:5). There are numerous verses in the New Testament that exalt humility and warn that pride is of the world and the devil.

The family is important in central Appalachian life, and, in general, the Pauline model is accepted, with father at the head and wife and children obedient to him. In actuality, however, studies have shown that while the father is conservative and resistant to change, women are usually better educated and often take more progressive leadership in regard to such matters as education, health care, and innovations that improve the quality of living. The model children are obedient to both parents but may in later life almost deify their mothers. Reverence for mothers is so prevalent in sermons that the moderator of a Baptist association confided that he had to remind the preaching brothers that the church is founded on Jesus Christ and not on mother. Some mountain women reject this Paulinian family system. However, some who go on to higher education and liberation values often speak fondly of their childhood churches even as they at the same time join more liberal churches as a way of accommodating their changing values.

Extreme personalism among mountaineers has often been noted. Most rural people do relate more personally than abstractly. Central Appalachian Christians often talk of Jesus as a "personal Savior," and they are fond of such scripture as Acts 10:34–35: "God is not respecter of persons: But in every nation he that feareth him, and worketh righteousness, is acceptable with God." God, as no respecter of persons, does not look on outward appearances and attributes but on the heart.

The same scriptures that support humility and personalism also engender egalitarianism, and the manners system based on these beliefs has had a leveling effect on the people. For example, James 2:1–10 instructs us to have as much respect for the poor as we do for the rich.

The regard for hospitality grew as much out of the needs of the frontier, when life often depended on the hospitality of strangers, as it did from a scriptural requirement. Yet Paul mentions hospitality four times in his list of Christian attributes (Rom. 12:13; 1 Tim. 3:2; Titus 1:8; and 1 Peter 4:9).

Central Appalachian people have relied as much as any other group on the Bible for meaning and for ordering the values in their lives; but the knowledge of the experiences of their ancestors, coming down through their churches' articles of faith, rules of decorum, and other church documents, as well as their own personal experiences, have also had a substantial influence.

See also: PENTECOSTALS; POPULAR RELIGION; WOMEN IN TRADITIONAL CHURCHES.

—Loyal Jones, *Berea, Kentucky*

Howard Dorgan, *The Old Regular Baptists of Central Appalachia: Brothers and Sisters in Hope* (1989); Loyal Jones, *Faith and Meaning in the Southern Uplands* (1999); Deborah V. McCauley, *Appalachian Mountain Religion: A History* (1995).

Weller, Jack

(1923–2000) Presbyterian minister.

Author of a controversial examination of Appalachian character, *Yesterday's People*, Jack Weller was a Presbyterian minister who received both praise and condemnation from the region he served. Born in Rochester, New York, and graduated from the University of Rochester, Weller enrolled in Union Theological Seminary, from which he graduated in 1948. His interest in Appalachia began with a seminary internship in West Virginia. Later, during his first pastorate, in Lima, New York, he met and married Jeanette Merritt, a nurse who was planning to work with Frontier Nursing Service in Hyden, Kentucky. In 1952 the couple moved to Clear Fork, West Virginia.

Puzzled by the inability of the Presbyterian Church to produce significant results in Appalachia, Weller used a 1962 sabbatical at Colgate Rochester Divinity School to reflect upon the matter. The resultant manuscript, *Yesterday's People*, was published by the University Press of Kentucky in 1965, almost immediately becoming a target of critics who believed its author had demeaned Appalachian people. Yet Weller did not flee the region, moving to Hazard, Kentucky, the year his book was published. As minister-at-large for the Presbyterian Churches of Eastern Kentucky, he became an advocate for Appalachia and a vocal critic of strip mining. He founded the Coalition for Appalachian Ministry and was active in the Commission on Religion in Appalachia. In 1989 Weller was awarded an Honorary Doctor of Divinity by Pikeville College in tribute to his contributions to the people of the region.

See also: COALITION FOR APPALACHIAN MINISTRY; COMMISSION ON RELIGION IN APPALACHIA; PRESBYTERIAN DENOMINATIONAL FAMILY.

—Paul Rader, *Presbyterian Church (USA)*

Women in Traditional Churches

In most of Appalachia's traditional Old-Time Baptist and Pentecostal churches, women's roles traditionally are circumscribed, a practice that mirrors the region's generally conservative stance on gender issues. Like Christians historically, Appalachian church leaders cite biblical precedents for restrictions against women—particularly the account of Eve's guilt in the Fall (Gen. 3), Paul's denunciation of women's speaking in church, cutting their hair, and adorning themselves (1 Cor. 11 and 1 Tim. 2), and his insistence that women submit themselves to their husbands (Eph. 5). The degree of female subordination varies from quite pronounced among the Old-Time Baptists to fairly insignificant among many Pentecostals; a few of the region's independent denominations allow women full participation in church government and the ministry. Despite these restrictions, however, women have found ways to attain power, status, and personal fulfillment in a religious context.

Exclusivity in gender roles was characteristic of the first denominations in Appalachia, a practice that mirrored early-nineteenth-century Christianity throughout America. Camp meetings—the first major venue for group religious expression on the Appalachian frontier—reinforced sexual as well as social and racial distinctions. Throughout most of the service, white male leaders initiated all verbal expression. During the conversion ritual, however, audience members assumed an active role. Women, like children and blacks, were permitted to function as exhorters, singers, or reciters of prayers.

Most Old-Time Baptist denominations such as the Primitives and Old Regulars maintain male leadership and a separation of the sexes, even though the specific rules binding women have changed over the years. Older church buildings had two front doors, which provided separate entrances for men and women, although this practice, along with separate seating, has waned. More tenacious, however, is the Old-Time Baptist prohibition against women's speaking in church. Obliged to remain silent during policy debates and forbidden from initiating hymn singing, women are also not allowed to preach or (with some exceptions) to hold positions in church government.

Despite the injunction to remain silent in church, Old-Time Baptist women discuss theology in informal settings. Often, though, they preface their remarks with qualifying phrases such as "I'm not sure about this idea." If an Old-Time Baptist woman desires to influence church policy, however, she must attempt to persuade her husband to uphold her point of view, a practice that affords but marginal control and that provides no recourse for the unmarried woman.

Strict rules govern female appearance. In some associations, women are not permitted to cut their hair or wear makeup, trousers, or short-sleeved shirts. Old Regulars explain these dicta as necessary so that women will not be temptations to men and will refrain from dwelling on the physical world to the neglect of the spiritual.

Such prohibitions are fraught with controversy, and disagreement over them has divided Old-Time Baptist associations. Furthermore, the rules are enforced with varying degrees of strictness. For example, some associations of Old Regulars officially forbid women to wear pants but have female members who nonetheless wear trousers under certain circumstances. Similarly, Old Regular women in some associations are told that they can wear makeup in the home for their husbands but not in public. In short, although the rules may fluctuate, the premise underlying them—that men, not women, should lead in the church and home—remains constant.

Since Old-Time Baptists also lack the missionary societies and choirs that provide opportunities for women's participation in some denominations, female roles can seem almost nonexistent. In actuality, however, Old-Time Baptist women do have significant institutionalized functions. For example, women are expected to participate in hymn singing, and they sometimes compose songs, although in church their compositions will be introduced and performed by a male singer. During sermons, certain women unofficially work with a preacher to inspire the congregation by energetically shouting, clapping, raising their arms, or walking about the church. At foot washings, decorum leads women to wash only one another's feet.

Above all, Old-Time Baptist women carve out significant roles in the preparation of food. Most Sundays during warm weather, a congregation will linger after the service for dinner on the grounds; women provide the food. When no dinner on the grounds is scheduled, women will often extend an invitation at large for fellow worshipers to join them at home for dinner. During association meetings, women from selected churches are responsible for feeding the entire gathering, a highly honored responsibility. In some churches, women bake unleavened bread and occasionally make wine for communion.

In the Pentecostal tradition, one finds a much wider array of roles for women than among the Old-Time Baptists. In particular, the Pauline prohibition against women's speaking in the church is sometimes interpreted in such a way as to offer women a public voice. For example, at its early-twentieth-century inception, the Church of God (Cleveland, Tennessee), citing Joel 2:28 ("Your daughters shall prophesy"), allowed women to serve as ministers. By 1913, however, the church's General Assembly had ruled against women's ordination; later rulings forbade women's performing marriages and serving on the Body of Elders. As a result, the number of women ministers in the church fell from 30 percent in 1913 to 3 percent in 1987. Similarly, in the Church of the Nazarene, 20 percent of all ministers were women in 1908 but only 6 percent in 1973. In this respect, the Holiness and Pentecostal churches illustrate Max Weber's theory that in the first stages of a religion aimed at the disenfranchised, women may be allowed extensive roles, but that as these religions become more institutionalized and the ministry professionalized, women lose ground.

Holiness leader John Larkin Brasher similarly held to traditional ideas about female submissiveness and piety, arguing that women's roles were chiefly domestic. However, Brasher also believed that "indwelling spirit" was nongendered; consequently, he allowed women to serve as missionaries, testifiers, and preachers. Examples of women preachers with large and loyal followings can be found throughout the Holiness-Pentecostal denominations, as Deborah Vansau McCauley *(Appalachian Mountain Religion)* and Howard Dorgan *(The Airwaves of Zion)* note. However, women preachers in these denominations do not always have equal institutional power with men, and the churches' general attitude toward women mirrors that of Brasher: women should find fulfillment in the home as wives and mothers.

Women Pentecostals do routinely function as song leaders, and in this capacity they are responsible for setting a service in motion. Female musicians compile extensive songbooks and perform solo, with other women, or in mixed groups. Furthermore, women usually are permitted to testify and to serve as Sunday school teachers and perform charitable work if these functions are present in a church.

Since in their secular lives Appalachian women hold a variety of positions from homemakers to elected officials and educated professionals, it may seem puzzling that some of them are willing to join churches that openly subordinate them to men. In addition to theological considerations, probably the greatest incentive to women's continuing participation in these denominations is the close sororal bonding that occurs among female members. These close relationships palliate the prohibitions against female agency. Furthermore, women in many mainstream denominations serve in similarly restricted and subordinate roles.

See also: FOOT WASHING; HOLINESS-PENTECOSTAL FUSION.

—Theresa Lloyd, *East Tennessee State University*

Mickey Crews, *The Church of God: A Social History* (1990); Howard Dorgan, *The Old Regular Baptists of Central Appalachia: Brothers and Sisters in Hope* (1989); Deborah V. McCauley, *Appalachian Mountain Religion: A History* (1995).

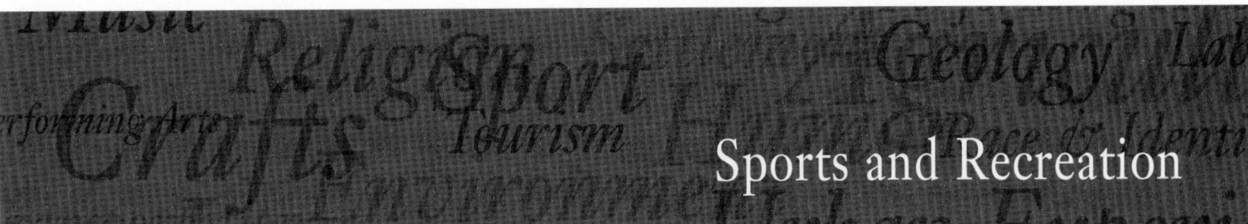

Sports and Recreation

Section Editors: C. Robert Barnett and Michele Schiavone

EXTRAORDINARY TOPOGRAPHY, VARIED CLIMATE, RICH NATURAL RESOURCES, AND racial, ethnic, and occupational diversity have made sports and recreation activities treasured elements of Appalachian life, attracting tourists from across the nation to far-flung corners of the region. In ways sometimes subtle and often conspicuous, the Appalachian Mountains define both competitive sports and leisure pursuits.

Covering the ridges and slopes, forests and the streams that drain them have made hunting and fishing an immutable part of the cultural fabric generations after fish and game were procured of necessity. The rural and rugged terrain that historically attracted independent-minded settlers still lures modern lovers of the outdoors who value self-sufficiency, physical ability, and individual challenge. These qualities, so prized in both competitive and leisure activities, are also manifest in traditional Appalachian occupations such as farming, lumbering, coal mining, and steelmaking. In both work and play, physical performance is to countless Appalachians a prerequisite to both social and financial success.

In spite of the rigors of daily life on the mountain frontier, sports and games were important in Appalachia from the 1700s through the mid-1800s. The earliest and longest continuously played sport is Cherokee stickball. Similar to lacrosse, it was a ritual event often used to settle disputes peacefully between tribes, but it was also dangerous: a favored strategy was to injure the best player on the opposing team. The Cherokees of the Qualla Boundary section of the Great Smoky Mountains still compete in a tamer version of the game.

Among European settlers the ability to hunt and shoot was crucial to survival, and successful hunters became local legends whose feats were often embellished and exaggerated. In 1796 a hunting party near Irving's Lick, Kentucky, bragged that they had killed 7,941 squirrels in only one day of hunting.

Appalachian frontiersmen participated in a variety of contests to demonstrate their skill. The most prevalent were turkey or beef shoots, in which contestants shot at a paper target on a tree. The prizes were usually a side of beef, a turkey, or perhaps a barrel of whiskey. "Shooting the cup" was popular in the Appalachian section of the Carolinas. In this sport, one man would shoot a cup from the head of his partner at thirty paces for the prize of a quart of whiskey.

Facing page: Legendary Appalachian frontiersman Davy Crockett is depicted in a no-holds-barred fight with a "Puke" (a Missourian) in this illustration from one of the many "almanacs" to capitalize on Crockett's name. Rough-and-tumble fighting reflected the fierceness and even cruelty of life on the frontier.

In some events, the only reward was victory over an opponent. Rough-and-tumble fights permitted the use of any means except weapons to force an opponent to quit. Kicking, biting, eye gouging, and groin kicking were standard techniques, and fighters often sharpened and hardened their long fingernails so they could gouge an opponent's eyes from their sockets. Sport historian Elliott Gorn asserts that this sport was most popular in the central and southern Appalachians because it fulfilled a manly need to face constant danger and unpredictable violence with unflinching toughness and immediate action.

In the late 1800s, Appalachian recreational pursuits began to change from folk activities to organized sports. Golf and baseball, both popular into modern times, were two of the first organized sports played in Appalachia. The first recognized golf club in the United States was established in 1884 on a golf course built at Oakhurst, the estate of Russell Montague near White Sulphur Springs, West Virginia. The course at the nearby Greenbrier Resort was constructed in 1913. There, Sam Snead was later the golf professional and a leading player on the Professional Golfers' Association tour during the 1940s and 1950s. Other outstanding professional golfers from Appalachia include Arnold Palmer and Tammie Green. Hilly terrain makes courses throughout the region especially challenging. Three courses—the Oakmont Country Club in Oakmont, Pennsylvania, the Wade Hampton Golf Club in Cashiers, North Carolina, and the Honors Course in Chattanooga, Tennessee—have been ranked among the forty best courses in America by *Golf Magazine*.

As in the rest of the country, Appalachia's love for baseball was especially fervent during the first half of the twentieth century. Ranging from the major league and Negro League teams in Pittsburgh to the minor league teams in small cities, towns, and coal camps, the game absorbed communities during long summer days.

Pittsburgh fielded its first major league team in 1882, participated in the first World Series in 1903, and has since won five World Championships. During the segregated era of the 1930s and 1940s, Pittsburgh was the center of African American baseball. The Homestead Grays and Pittsburgh Crawfords, with stars such as pitcher Satchel Paige and home run king Josh Gibson, not only played a Negro League schedule but also barnstormed through much of the Appalachians, taking on white as well as African American teams. Another legendary figure who played in the Negro Leagues of Appalachia was Willie Mays, who signed with the Birmingham Black Barons at the age of seventeen. Born in Fairfield, Alabama, Mays went on to become one of the great sports figures in America in a long career with the New York and San Francisco Giants and the New York Mets.

Appalachian teams have participated in minor league baseball from the early days of the modern minor leagues. Chattanooga, Tennessee, has the longest continuous history of minor league baseball in the region, having first fielded a team in 1902. Minor league baseball reached its peak of popularity in 1949, when more than forty towns in Appalachia had teams. Four leagues—the Appalachian, the Blue Ridge, the Mountain State, and the Western Carolina—were comprised entirely of towns in Appalachia. After a short decline in popularity, the first years of the twenty-first century have seen a resurgence in minor league baseball, with twenty-six Appalachian teams playing in five leagues.

Amateur baseball was an important presence in most small towns and coal camps from about 1920 through the 1950s. Companies sponsored teams to boost employee morale and provide entertainment in the small coal camps of West Virginia and Pennsylvania, the steel towns along the Ohio River, and the textile towns of North and South Carolina. In the late 1940s, nearly every town and village had at least one company or town team that played in a league of nearby rival towns. Television, growing interest in other sports, and development of youth baseball in the 1950s signaled the beginning of a rapid decline in the minor leagues and adult amateur baseball.

Football has enjoyed extraordinary popularity in Appalachia since the late 1800s as well. The sport's demands for rugged physical performance, teamwork, and the defense of one's own territory while invading the opponent's seem to mesh with deeply rooted Appalachian values.

The first professional football team in America was formed in 1892, when the Pittsburgh Athletic Club paid Pudge Heffelfinger, a former All-American center at Yale, five hundred dollars to help beat its archrival club, the Allegheny Athletic Association. Thereafter, professional football spread through the industrial towns of eastern Ohio and western Pennsylvania and down the Ohio River Valley. Two of the most successful professional teams of the 1920s were Ohio's Ironton Tanks and Portsmouth Spartans. The Spartans joined the National Football League (NFL) in 1929 but moved to Detroit and became the Lions in 1934. The disbanding of the Tanks following the 1930 season and the Spartans' move were a result of the Great Depression. Ironically, the Pittsburgh Steelers joined the NFL during the worst of the depression in 1933 and remain Appalachia's only NFL team.

The popularity of college football in the region has been enhanced by the success of college teams and athletes on the national level. National champions and All-American players are a source of pride and an affirmation of the region's ability to achieve on a national stage. The strongest of the early Appalachian teams was the University of Pittsburgh, undefeated from 1915 through 1917 against a schedule of major eastern powers.

The first Appalachian college to play in the Rose Bowl was Washington and Jefferson College, a private school of only three hundred students in Washington, Pennsylvania. Following an undefeated season in 1921, the Washington and Jefferson Presidents were selected to represent the East in the Rose Bowl against the mighty University of California, setting up a "David and Goliath" contest that captured the imagination of the country. Ending in a 0-0 tie and a stunning moral victory for the Presidents, the game remains one of the classic upsets in college football history.

College football developed more slowly in the southern Appalachians, but by the mid-1920s teams in that area were competing for national championships. The University of Alabama was the first to become established as a power when it was voted national champion following the undefeated seasons of 1925 and 1926 under head coach Wallace Wade. The Crimson Tide was again undefeated and won Rose Bowl games in 1930 and 1934. The University of Tennessee won its first national championship in 1938 with an undefeated season. Success continued for the Volunteers as the 1939, 1940, 1950, and 1951 teams also went undefeated in the regular season. The 1951 team was voted national champions.

The early success of Appalachian teams continued with national championship teams at Alabama (1961, 1964, 1965, 1973, 1978, 1979, and 1992), Tennessee (1998), Pitt (1976), Clemson (1981), and Penn State (1982 and 1986). Some of the legendary

Varsity squad of the Science Hill High School, Johnson City, Tennessee, 1921. Since the early twentieth century, high school football has often served as a focus for community identity and morale, especially in smaller towns and cities throughout Appalachia.

professional football players from Appalachia include Bobby Dodd, Sam Huff, Joe Montana, Dan Marino, Tony Dorsett, and Joe Namath.

The teams closest to the hearts of Appalachians, however, were the local high school squads whose games transcended simple athletic competition. By the 1930s and 1940s, the high school had become the center for culture and entertainment in virtually every mountain town and village. Successful teams promoted community identity and morale, often to the advantage of the mine or mill owners, at taxpayer expense. Football became especially popular in larger high schools in western Pennsylvania, eastern Ohio, and northern West Virginia. Participation helped Americanize the sons of southern and eastern European immigrants.

Some writers on mountain life have expressed concern that the popularity enjoyed by high school athletics detracted from the education of Appalachian children. In his polemic *Night Comes to the Cumberlands*, Harry Caudill asserted that the glitter of sports distracted students from academic work. In *Yesterday's People*, West Virginia minister Jack Weller contended that many mountain children went to school only to play sports.

In small mountain schools and rural communities of southern West Virginia, Kentucky, and Tennessee, basketball has historically reigned supreme. There, high schools not large enough to support winning football teams could successfully compete with big schools on the basketball court. Two small high school teams that became legendary were those from Carr Creek, Kentucky, and Waterloo, Ohio. In 1928

Carr Creek High School, which had only eight male students and no gym, reached the Kentucky State Basketball Finals. Although Carr Creek lost in quadruple overtime to Ashland, a "big city" of 14,000, both teams went on to play in the National High School Basketball Championship in Chicago. Carr Creek lost in the quarterfinals, but Ashland won the national high school championship. Likewise, the Waterloo High School Wonders from a small village of 150 in eastern Ohio swept undefeated through the state's small school tournament in 1934. The journey to Columbus was a huge adventure for the boys from Appalachia. In 1935 word of the Wonders' speed and dazzling play preceded them, and they drew big crowds playing against larger high schools. At the end of the 1935 season, the Wonders had a two-year record of 97-3 and two state championships. Waterloo, Carr Creek, and other schools like them fanned interest in basketball in hundreds of small Appalachian towns.

In the second half of the twentieth century, rapid social and economic changes—interstate highways, television, racial integration, and the women's movement—drastically altered sports and recreational activities in the region. The decline in population, racial integration, improved roads, and education reform led to extensive school consolidation. Larger high schools were able to offer additional sports.

Prior to the *Brown v. Board of Education* Supreme Court decision in 1954, ten of the thirteen Appalachian states had segregated schools and, consequently, segregated school sports (New York, Ohio, and Pennsylvania were already integrated). In West Virginia, the twenty-four African American high schools established what is believed to be the first African American high school state tournament in 1925. The number of schools grew to almost fifty, and regional and state tournaments were held annually until 1957. In 1958 the remaining African American high schools began to play in the "white" state tournament until 1966–67, when all of the schools in West Virginia were finally integrated. Similarly, the first integrated state high school basketball tournament in Tennessee was not held until 1966.

The integration of some college teams took even longer. Among the pioneers who broke the color barrier in basketball were Hal Greer, who integrated Marshall College as a student and basketball player in the fall of 1954 before going on to a Hall of Fame career in the National Basketball Association (NBA), and Earl Lloyd, who played at West Virginia State College and was the first African American player in the NBA's initial season in 1950. Football and basketball teams in the Southeastern Athletic Conference did not fully integrate until the 1970s. In the 1950s and 1960s, the Appalachian region produced a number of outstanding basketball players, including Greer, Lloyd, Jerry West, Frank Selvy, and Clarence "Bevo" Francis.

The development of women's sports in Appalachia closely followed national trends. In the 1920s, both Kentucky and Tennessee had girls' state high school basketball tournaments. But both were disbanded along with most other sports programs for girls and women because of the belief held by physical education teachers that intense competitive sports were harmful to women. Counter to that trend, some high schools in Tennessee continued girls' sports teams, and in 1958 the girls' state tournament resumed. The strongest influence on the emergence of girls' and women's sports programs was passage of the 1972 Educational Amendments Act, Title IX of which mandates equal school sports programs for women. By the late 1970s every state in Appalachia began establishing state championship events for girls.

Because Appalachia has few large cities, professional sports have changed little in the past fifty years. Pittsburgh remains the only major league city and has added the National Hockey League Penguins to baseball's Pirates and the NFL's Steelers. Minor league baseball remains popular, and the Appalachian region has also experienced a growing interest in minor league hockey and NASCAR.

College and high school sports still predominate, but participants have become more diverse and the types of teams more varied. College football remains the most popular spectator sport in the region and the most successful, continually producing contenders for the national championship. Because of school consolidation and Title IX, schools and colleges in Appalachia have parallel athletic programs for women and a greater variety of sports teams. Gymnast Mary Lou Retton and basketball players Tamika Catchings and Chamique Holdsclaw are among the nationally known female sports stars from the region.

Contemporary recreation in Appalachia is diverse. The region's combination of forests, lakes, streams, parks, and trails has made Appalachia the leading area for outdoor recreation in the eastern United States.

Hunting remains the primary recreational use of Appalachian forests, thanks to the lush habitat created by reforestation programs begun in the 1930s. Among the region's most popular hunting areas are the Monongahela National Forest in West Virginia, the Cherokee National Forest in Tennessee, the Daniel Boone National Forest in Kentucky, and the Jocassee Gorges area along the North and South Carolina border.

The white-tailed deer is the most popular and plentiful big game species, followed by black bear and wild turkey. Wild boar hunts take place in the southern mountains, particularly in the Nantahala National Forest in western North Carolina. Rabbits and squirrels are hunted in every part of the region; pheasants, grouse, and quail are shot in the uplands; and ducks and geese are taken on lowland lakes and streams. Each state regulates its own hunting seasons.

Fishing in Appalachia can be divided into two types: mountain stream fly-fishing and spin-fishing on ponds, lakes, or rivers. Appalachia has the best fly-fishing streams in the eastern United States, with upland streams teeming with native brook trout or stocked brown and rainbow trout. Lakes, rivers, and ponds have numerous species of fish, including lake trout, large- and smallmouth bass, bluegill, and catfish. Trophy fish such as sauger, muskies, and walleye are also found in some areas.

Excellent fishing spots can be found in the Monongahela National Forest in West Virginia, along the Kentucky and Tennessee Rivers, and around Deep Creek Lake in western Maryland. The Tennessee Valley Authority and the U.S. Army Corps of Engineers have built a number of large lakes, creating their own angler's paradise.

Appalachia boasts some of the best areas in the United States for the increasingly popular outdoor sports of whitewater rafting, mountain biking, and rock climbing. The Tallulah and Chattooga Rivers in Georgia, the Ocoee River in Tennessee (the site of the 1996 Olympic whitewater events), and the Gauley and New Rivers in West Virginia are the most popular whitewater rivers in the eastern United States.

Numerous areas are available for mountain biking, rock climbing, hiking, and camping. Most national forests, such as the Finger Lakes National Forest in New York, have trails where biking is permitted. Rock-climbing sites in Appalachia are extremely varied. Three examples are the Shawangunks, less than a hundred miles from New York City, Bucks Pocket in northern Alabama, and the multiface, granite

Seneca Rocks in West Virginia. Hiking remains popular in the Appalachian region. The Appalachian Trail, which stretches more than 2,150 miles from Katahdin, Maine, to Springer Mountain, Georgia, is the most famous of the thousands of trails that cross the region.

—C. Robert Barnett, *Marshall University*

Anthony J. Badger, *The New Deal: The Depression Years, 1933–1940* (1989); C. Robert Barnett, "The Finals," *Goldenseal Magazine* (Summer 1983); Harry M. Caudill, *Night Comes to the Cumberlands: A Biography of a Depressed Area* (1963); Foster Rhea Dulles, *A History of Recreation: America Learns to Play* (1965); Ronald D Eller, *Miners, Millhands, and Mountaineers: Industrialization of the Appalachian South, 1880–1930* (1982); Danny Fulks, "Hardwood Heroes," *Timeline* (February–March 1988); Elliott J. Gorn, "Gouge and Bite, Pull Hair and Scratch: The Social Significance of Fighting in the Southern Backcountry," in *Sport in America: From Wicked Amusement to National Obsession*, ed. David K. Wiggins (1995); Robert J. Higgs, Ambrose N. Manning, and Jim Wayne Miller, eds., *Appalachia Inside Out, Vol. 1: Conflict and Change* (1995); Lloyd Johnson and Miles Wolff, eds., *The Encyclopedia of Minor League Baseball* (1993); Ted Olson, "Cherokee Stickball: A Changing Tradition," *Journal of the Appalachian Studies Association* (1993); *Now and Then Special Issue: Sports in Appalachia* (Fall 1992); Jack Weller, *Yesterday's People: Life in Contemporary Appalachia* (1965).

Aethlon

Aethlon: The Journal of Sport Literature, published at East Tennessee State University, is a scholarly journal devoted to sport. Intrigued by the use of sport-related themes and characters in the work of noted writers and poets, a coalition of university faculty and friends led by Lyle Olsen at San Diego State University created the Sport Literature Association in 1983. The primary purpose of the association is to sponsor and direct *Aethlon*, which celebrates the marriage of serious, interpretive literature with the world of play, games, and sport. Published twice a year, the journal offers a varied menu of fiction, poetry, scholarly essays, and critical reviews, as well as commentary on drama and cinema.

In the fall of 1984, the journal (issued under the name *Arete* until 1987) was taken over by East Tennessee State University, with Don Johnson as general editor. Since that time the university has become a center for the study of sport literature, taking advantage of work already being done in the field by faculty member Jack Higgs, one of the leading scholars of the subgenre.

—Don Johnson, *East Tennessee State University*

Anderson, Paul

(1932–1994) Weightlifter.

Paul Edward Anderson gained widespread recognition in the 1950s as the world's strongest man and maintained that reputation throughout his lifetime. Although he spent most of his adulthood in Vidalia, Georgia, Anderson was born in Toccoa, in the foothills of the southern Appalachians, and did most of his early training in Elizabethton, Tennessee, under the guidance of legendary deadlifter Bob Peoples.

Nicknamed the "Dixie Derrick," Anderson was best known for his leg strength, but in the 1952 Tennessee State Meet he established his competitive credentials by breaking all heavyweight records and then performing a 660-pound squat. In 1955 he set a world record with a clean and jerk of 436 pounds at the national championships in Cleveland and later gained international acclaim by pressing 402 pounds at a meet in Moscow. The Russians called him *chudo pirody*, a wonder of nature, and at the height of the Cold War era this mountain man became a symbol of American strength. Anderson won the world heavyweight championship at Munich in 1955 and an Olympic gold medal at Melbourne in 1956. He returned to his hill-country home as a conquering folk hero. Anderson then became a professional strongman and, after committing his life to Christ, performed five hundred exhibitions annually to fund his Christian youth home in Vidalia.

Although Anderson's 1,200-pound squat and 6,270-pound backlift (previously listed in *The Guinness Book of World Records*) cannot be verified, weightlifting pundits believe he could have done them. In 1974 he was inducted into the Georgia Sports Hall of Fame, and at the USA Power and Strength Symposium in Orlando, Florida, in 1992, Anderson was named "Strongest Man of the Century."

As a result of a bout with Bright's disease in childhood, Anderson suffered from kidney ailments in later life. Although he received a kidney transplant in 1983, he eventually succumbed in 1994 to complications from a long series of illnesses.

—John D. Fair, *Georgia College and State University*

Baseball

Known as America's national pastime, baseball is manifestly Appalachia's sport as well. Such legendary players as Ty Cobb, Willie Mays, "Shoeless" Joe Jackson, Bill Mazeroski, Lew Burdette, and Stan Musial all were born and reared in Appalachia. Fans drive for miles to root for teams in nearby cities such as Atlanta, Cincinnati, Cleveland, and Baltimore, and the many minor league teams of the region have tremendous support from local communities.

Pittsburgh, however, is the only Appalachian city to host a major league baseball franchise. In the late 1800s, Pittsburgh had teams in the American Association and the Players League, both of which were considered major leagues. Pittsburgh joined the National League in 1887, and the team was named the Pirates in 1889. The current Pirate organization dates from 1900.

The team's playing facilities, all in central Pittsburgh, have included the Recreation Park, Exposition Ground, Forbes Field, Three Rivers Stadium, and PNC Park. Pittsburgh has won nine National League Championships and five World Series. The Pirates participated in the first modern World Series in 1903, losing five games to three to the American League's Boston Pilgrims.

Pirates in the National Baseball Hall of Fame are shortstops Joseph "Arky" Vaughn and eight-time National League batting champion Honus Wagner; third baseman Harold "Pie" Traynor; outfielders Max Carey, Hazen "Kiki" Cuyler, Paul and Lloyd Waner, Hank Greenberg, Willie Stargell, Roberto Clemente, and seven-time National League home run leader Ralph Kiner; second baseman Bill Mazeroski; and managers Fred Clarke and Bill McKechnie.

Minor league baseball has had an extensive presence in Appalachia. The Southern League, begun in 1885, is the most notable of the pre-twentieth-century operations and has survived into the twenty-first century after several interrupted periods. Appalachian cities in the league include Knoxville and Chattanooga, Tennessee, and Birmingham

Baseball team composed of coal miners in Welch, West Virginia, 1946. From its rise in the early 1920s through the end of World War II, coalfield baseball was a catalyst of social activity for miners, owners, and families, as towns and companies united in support of favorite teams.

and Huntsville, Alabama. The highest-ranked minor leagues, the American Association and the International, have fielded teams in Charleston, West Virginia, Scranton/Wilkes-Barre, Pennsylvania, and Binghamton, New York.

Most identified with the region, however, is the Appalachian League. Founded in 1911, it functioned intermittently until 1937 and since then has operated continuously to the present. This league is primarily comprised of cities in eastern Tennessee, southwestern Virginia, southeastern Kentucky, and southern West Virginia. Longtime members include Johnson City, Kingsport, and Elizabethton, Tennessee; Bristol, Virginia; and Bluefield, West Virginia. On May 13, 1952, Ron Necciai of Bristol struck out all twenty-seven batters of the Welch (West Virginia) Miners in a nine-inning Appalachian League game, a feat unsurpassed in organized baseball. The Bristol staff pitched five no-hitters that same season. Richard "Hobie" Brummett is the most noted manager in the league's history, having won six pennants (five at Elizabethton and one at Kingsport) in the late 1930s and early 1940s. Major league players who began their careers in the "Appy" include Cal Ripken (Bluefield), Tony Oliva (Wytheville), Kirby Puckett (Elizabethton), and Dale Murphy (Kingsport).

Other minor leagues featuring Appalachian communities functioning at the turn of the new millennium included the Eastern, the New York–Pennsylvania, and the South Atlantic Leagues. Others that once included Appalachian communities but had ceased operations were the Alabama State, Alabama-Tennessee, Bi-State (North Carolina and Virginia), Blue Grass (Kentucky), Blue Ridge (Pennsylvania, Maryland, and Virginia), Carolina, Middle Atlantic, Mountain State (West Virginia), Mountain States (Kentucky, West Virginia, Ohio, Tennessee, and Virginia), New York State, North Carolina State, Ohio State, Ohio-Pennsylvania, Pennsylvania–West Virginia, Piedmont, the South Carolina, the Virginia, Virginia Valley, Virginia–North Carolina, the West Virginia, and Western Carolina Leagues.

In the era of segregated black professional baseball, several teams played in the Appalachian region. Prior to the formation of the Negro National League in 1920, the Pittsburgh Keystones, Pittsburgh Giants, and Homestead Grays played in western Pennsylvania while also maintaining independent and barnstorming schedules.

Pittsburgh was the stronghold of two rival Negro League teams. The Pittsburgh Crawfords, named for the Crawford Grille on Crawford Avenue, was owned by W. A. "Gus" Greenlee. Formed initially by black steelworkers in 1910, the Crawfords were an amateur team until 1930. Greenlee built Greenlee Field for his club's games in Pittsburgh. He was a backer of the reorganization of black baseball with the new Negro National League of 1933. The second club, the Homestead Grays, was a member of the league from 1934 through 1950. The club played many games at Forbes Field and was directed by Cumberland

"Cum" Posey. The Grays won nine championships and five Negro World Series titles. These teams were powers of the 1930s; their rosters included Oscar Charleston, William "Judy" Johnson, Satchel Paige, Josh Gibson, and James "Cool Papa" Bell. All have been elected to the National Baseball Hall of Fame. Other Appalachian teams included Birmingham's Black Barons and the Chattanooga Black Lookouts, who played in the Southern Negro League, the Negro Southern League, and the Negro National League in the 1920s. The Asheville Blues and the Knoxville Grays played in the Negro Southern League in 1945.

Company-backed coalfield baseball teams in Appalachia developed in the early twentieth century, reaching their peak of popularity in the 1920s and 1930s. The teams were a catalyst of social activity for miners, owners, and families, as towns and companies united in support of favorite teams. Communities had well-maintained fields and good equipment. The teams were financed in part through paycheck contributions beginning at fifty cents; companies such as the Rochester and Pittsburgh Coal Company in western Pennsylvania and the Glen White and the Pocahontas operations in West Virginia also partially subsidized teams. League games were well attended, as were special contests against barnstorming black teams, since few other outlets for entertainment existed. Many men gained or improved their jobs in the coal companies as a result of their baseball abilities. Even during the Great Depression, when the workweek was shortened for the typical miner, ball-playing miners continued to be paid for a full week's work.

The decline of baseball in the coalfields began with unionization of the mines in the late 1930s, ending special privileges for players. Changes in mining practices reduced the number of miners. During World War II, leagues and teams began disbanding, and as the postwar era brought competing forms of entertainment to the region, coalfield baseball as a major focus in Appalachia slowly died.

See also: MUSIAL, STAN; SPORTS HALLS OF FAME; WALKER, MOSES "FLEET."

—John Schleppi, *University of Dayton*

Dick Clark and Larry Lester, eds., *The Negro Leagues Book* (1994); Lloyd Johnson and Miles Wolff, eds., *The Encyclopedia of Minor League Baseball* (1993); David Nemec, *The Great Encyclopedia of Nineteenth-Century Major League Baseball* (1997).

Basketball, College

College basketball has never achieved the prominence that college football programs have enjoyed in Appalachia. This may be attributed in part to the demographic character of the region (mostly rural, dotted with small towns) and the premium that football places upon ruggedness, strength, and teamwork, traits often associated with the people of Appalachia. Nor has college basketball experienced the popularity of basketball in high schools, where personal associations and generations of family ties create intense community interest and loyalty. Yet over the years, Appalachian colleges have produced some outstanding basketball teams and players, and college teams outside of Appalachia, such as the legendary program at the University of Kentucky in Lexington, have benefited from generations of talented Appalachian players.

During the 1940s, the University of Pittsburgh, West Virginia University, Marshall College, and West Virginia State College basketball teams were highly successful on the national level. In 1941 Pitt advanced to the Final Four of the NCAA Division I Championships and finished third. West Virginia, seeded last among eight teams, won the National Invitational Tournament in 1942 by defeating Western Kentucky State College. West Virginia was led by Rudy Baric, named Most Valuable Player of the tournament, and All-American Scotty Hamilton. Marshall won the National Association of Intercollegiate Basketball Championship in 1947 by defeating Mankato (Minnesota) 73-59. That season Marshall had the most NCAA victories with a 32-5 record.

Led by teammates Earl Lloyd and Bob Wilson, West Virginia State went undefeated in the 1947–48 season with a 33-0 record and was considered the "National Negro Champion" by winning the Central Intercollegiate Athletic Association Championship. Lloyd became the first African American to play in the National Basketball Association (NBA) and later became the league's first African American coach. Wilson followed Lloyd to play in the pros. In the late 1940s, West Virginia State traveled to California and became one of the first all-black teams to play against white teams during the era of segregation.

During the 1950s and 1960s, only one team from the Appalachian region made it to the NCAA basketball finals. West Virginia University advanced to the 1959 Division I championship game against the University of California, who had upset the University of Cincinnati. Much of the nation was dismayed by Cincinnati's loss to California because fans had anticipated the matchup between Jerry West of West Virginia and Oscar Robertson of Cincinnati. In the final, West Virginia lost on a last second tip-in, giving California a dramatic 71-70 upset victory. In addition to West Virginia, Penn State (1954) and Wake Forest (1962) advanced as far as the Final Four during this period. Both finished third.

Noteworthy individuals from the Appalachian region during this era include West, Hal Greer of Marshall College, Frank Selvy of Furman University, and Clarence "Bevo" Francis and Coach Newt Oliver of Rio Grande College in Rio Grande, Ohio.

University of Tennessee Lady Volunteers playing at home in Knoxville, 2002. The popularity of high school basketball in the region has produced many outstanding players for college teams in and around Appalachia, including Tennessee's Lady Vols, who won national championships six times from 1987 to 1998.

West was selected as an All-American twice during his college career. After graduation, he was drafted by the Minneapolis Lakers, who moved to Los Angeles before the season began. The second overall pick in the NBA draft in 1960, West went on to a stellar career as an NBA player, coach, and administrator. In 1996 he was named one of the fifty greatest players in NBA history.

In 1955 Hal Greer became the first African American to play for a major college team in West Virginia when he accepted a basketball scholarship at Marshall College. At Marshall, Greer was selected to the All-American Team in 1958. He began his professional career with the Syracuse Nationals (later the Philadelphia 76ers). A ten-time NBA All-Star, Greer was awarded a spot on the NBA's Fiftieth Anniversary All-Time Team.

Frank Selvy went to Furman University in Greenville, South Carolina, where he set a single-game NCAA Division I record of 100 points against Newberry College on February 13, 1954. During his career, Selvy set twenty-four major college records and scored 50 or more points eight times. After graduation, he played seven seasons in the NBA.

Clarence "Bevo" Francis was recruited to play for tiny Rio Grande College in southeast Ohio by his former high school coach, Newt Oliver. At the turn of the twenty-first century, Francis's 113 points against Hillsdale College on February 2, 1954, still stood as the single-game scoring record. After two seasons at Rio Grande, including a 39-0 campaign in 1952–53, Francis followed Coach Oliver again to become a player on the world-famous Harlem Globetrotters tour, playing under Oliver on the Boston Whirlwinds, the traveling team that provided the Globetrotters' opposition. Abe Saperstein, originator and owner of the Globetrotters, later described Oliver as "the greatest college basketball promoter who ever lived."

Two other excellent players from the modern era of college basketball in Appalachia include Tim Duncan and Keith Jennings. Duncan, of Wake Forest University, received the James A. Naismith Award, the John R. Wooden Award, the U.S. Basketball Writers Association Award, and the National Association of Basketball Coaches Award in 1997. Jennings, of East Tennessee State University, received the Frances Pomeroy Naismith Award (for players shorter than six feet tall) in 1991.

The most successful college basketball team in Appalachia has been the University of Tennessee Lady Volunteers. Coached by Pat Summitt, who took leadership of the program in 1974 at age twenty-two, the Lady Vols had made an unprecedented fifteen NCAA Final Four appearances and won six NCAA national championships (1987, 1989, 1991, 1996, 1997, and 1998) as of 2004. Summitt, who also coached the United States women's team to a gold medal at the 1984 Olympic Games, was enshrined in the Women's Basketball Hall of Fame in Knoxville, Tennessee, in 1999 and the Naismith Memorial Basketball Hall of Fame in Springfield, Massachusetts, in 2000. The only other women's team from the Appalachian region to appear in the Final Four during the twentieth century was the University of Alabama, a semifinalist in 1994. Lady Vol Chamique Holdsclaw received the Naismith Trophy in 1998 and 1999, the Broderick Award in 1997 and 1998, and the Women's Basketball Coaches Association Award in 1998 and 1999. The Women's Basketball Hall of Fame is located in Knoxville in part because of the phenomenal success of the University of Tennessee Lady Volunteers basketball team.

See also: BASKETBALL, HIGH SCHOOL; HENDERSON, CAM; WEST, JERRY.

—John R. Kiger, *Marshall University*

Peter C. Bjarkman, *The Biographical History of Basketball* (1998); Morgan G. Brenner, *College Basketball's National Championships* (1999); Bill Gutman, *The History of NCAA Basketball* (1993).

Basketball, High School

High school basketball rose to prominence in the 1910s and 1920s, when most high schools began to field teams and state championship tournaments were established. Interest increased in rural and small-town teams during the period from the late 1920s through the 1950s; occasionally a small school with five good players could bring recognition and fame to a community. Events in West Virginia, Kentucky, and Ohio epitomize the role of the sport in the region.

West Virginia was racially segregated, and most of its African American high schools, concentrated in the southern coalfields and northern steel towns, were extremely small. At West Virginia State College in March 1924, eleven of the twenty-four African American high schools in West Virginia played in what the *Pittsburgh Courier* called the first African American state high school basketball championship in the nation. Lincoln High School of Wheeling, the former state capital in the northern part of the state, defeated Kimball, a small town in the southern coalfields, in the final game to win the championship.

The tournament was held annually until 1957. Many of the early championship teams came from southern coalfields, but by the 1940s the locus of power had shifted, and Clarksburg's Kelly Miller High School, in the north-central part of the state, rose to dominance under legendary coach Mark Cardwell, who later coached at West Virginia State College. By the 1950s schools in the larger cities, such as Charleston Garnett and Huntington Douglass, dominated the tournament.

After the 1954 *Brown v. Board of Education* Supreme Court decision mandating the integration of public schools, the number of African American high schools quickly declined. The last African American tournament was played in 1957, and thereafter the remaining African American schools began to play in the formerly all-white state tournament. Williamson Liberty, the last African American high school in West Virginia, closed in 1967, a year after finishing as runner-up in the integrated state basketball tournament.

In March 1928, the Kentucky State High School Basketball Tournament matched Ashland against Carr Creek in the championship game before a record crowd of four thousand. The crowd was not there to see Ashland, a powerful undefeated team (28-0) from a city of fourteen thousand, but Carr Creek, a school so small that it had only eight boys in the entire high school, all of whom were on the basketball team. Carr Creek was located in eastern Kentucky's Knott County, more than twenty miles from a railroad line, and the team practiced outdoors because the school had no gymnasium.

The game lived up to the dreams of the underdog's fans. Tied 9-9 at the end of the fourth quarter and still deadlocked after three overtime periods, it finally ended with a 13-11 Ashland win. Both Ashland and Carr Creek were invited to play in the National High School Basketball Championship Tournament sponsored by the University of Chicago. Carr Creek won three games but was eliminated in the quarterfinals. Ashland reached the final and defeated Canton, Illinois, 15-10 for the national championship. That season was a landmark in Kentucky high school basketball history. Carr Creek showed that a small school could compete successfully, and Ashland demonstrated that Kentucky basketball was as good as any in the country.

Kentucky had no monopoly on heroics by tiny schools, however. In 1932 Waterloo High School, which had only twenty-five boys, rolled undefeated through the small schools in Appalachian southeastern Ohio. The Wonders took a 31-0 record to Columbus to the Class B (small school) state championship tournament, where some of the team rode an elevator for the first time. After three more wins, the Wonders, representing a depression-ridden community of 150, were the 1932–33 state champions.

All the team members returned the following season, and Coach Magellan Hairston scheduled up to five games a week with big city schools throughout Ohio in addition to local league games. The Wonders attracted packed houses everywhere they played and adopted tricks like those of the famed Harlem Globetrotters to use on the other teams when they got ahead. The Wonders ended their run in Columbus in 1934 with a second state championship and a two-year record of 97-3.

Stewart Wiseman, who played for Rio Grande College, was the only Wonder to go to college. The other players turned professional and barnstormed the country, playing teams such as the Globetrotters, the New York Rens, and the New York Celtics. Though World War II brought an end to the playing careers of the Wonders, their legend lives on.

See also: BASKETBALL, COLLEGE; CIVIL RIGHTS MOVEMENT (RACE, ETHNICITY, AND IDENTITY).

—C. Robert Barnett and Danny Fulks, *Marshall University*

C. Robert Barnett, "The Finals," *Goldenseal Magazine* (Summer 1983); Danny Fulks, "Hardwood Heroes," *Timeline* (February–March 1988); Thomas Kunkle, "The Wonder Years," *Sports Illustrated* (February 6, 1995).

Bear Hunting

Hunting black bears for sport in Appalachia is a combination of time-honored traditions and modern techniques. It typically involves a group of hunters using hounds to pursue a bear until it is brought to bay. Knowledge of mountain terrain and the habitat and behavior of bears is crucial to success.

The black bear *(Ursus americanus)* found in the eastern United States is a large omnivore that reaches 54 to 72 inches in length, 24 to 36 inches in height at shoulder, and generally weighs 125 to 400 pounds at full maturity. An adult male bear can cover 20 miles in his territory daily and range up to 150 miles.

Although the time when bear hunts provided sustenance is long past, hunters still take great care in the distribution of meat. A lasting tradition is for one hunter to select cuts of meat for an individual portion while another hunter, out of sight of the first, calls out the name of the hunter to whom the selected portion goes.

State fish and game and wildlife resources departments supervise bear hunting, determining the hunting season and setting regulations such as lands accessible for hunting and the weapons and ammunition allowed. All states in the Appalachian region require hunters to be licensed and to wear fluorescent orange clothing while afield.

A prompt report of a kill is mandated, often with location, sex, and field weight of the bear. Many states request a premolar tooth be extracted to help determine the animal's age. Wildlife officials carefully monitor the status of the bear population to assist in future regulations and game management.

Dogs that make up a pack tend toward hound and hound-mixed breeds, with offspring bred specifically for the purpose of bear hunting. Good hunting dogs often cost thousands of dollars. Among recognized bear-hunting breeds are Black and Tans, Plotts, Blue Ticks, and Treeing Walkers.

Dogs are also bred and trained for specific tasks in the hunt. Hounds with good scent ability are called "strike dogs." They must be able to detect and follow a scent trail and initiate the pursuit of a bear. A good strike dog is sometimes expected to find and follow an old scent track, or "cold trail." Dogs used to bring a bear to bay are called "catch dogs." These are aggressive, agile dogs that physically challenge a bear, fighting it and keeping it from escaping until hunters arrive. Breeds other than hounds, such as Airedale terriers, are sometimes used as catch dogs.

All of the dogs must have stamina and be fearless. The number of dogs varies throughout the hunt, with one or two strike dogs used initially and other dogs added once the pursuit, or "bear chase," begins. Up to a dozen dogs ultimately may join the chase. Listening to the sound of the chase is a key aspect of the hunt. From the tone and frequency of individual dogs' bawling barks, hunters identify the hounds in closest pursuit and discern the direction the bear is headed and how near the pack is to it.

Bear hunters use rifles almost exclusively, usually variations of the .30 caliber. Carbines, lever actions, and semiautomatics that are light and maneuverable without sacrificing accuracy and power are preferred. Bow hunting and the use of pistols and black-powder weapons are rare in bear hunts in Appalachia.

Modern technology assists the hunter in many ways. Citizens band radios and cellular phones enable hunters to communicate over mountainous terrain, making it possible for them to establish a base for the hunt, alert others to a pursuit, contact veterinarians when dogs are injured, let family members know of their whereabouts, or report a kill. Tracking collars and handheld telemetry devices are used to locate dogs both during and after a hunt.

Four-wheel-drive pickup trucks are specially outfitted with dog carriers and a platform for strike dogs to ride on in order to detect airborne scents. Vehicles must be able to navigate a variety of terrain including highways, rural unimproved roads, logging roads, and forest paths.

Many bear hunters belong to hunt clubs, which provide more than simple camaraderie. Members' hounds form a hunting pack, and club fees cover veterinary costs. Clubs also host dinners featuring bear meat as social functions for hunters' families.

See also: CROCKETT ALMANACS (MEDIA); HUNTING AND FISHING; SHOOTING SPORTS.

—Geoffrey Cantrell, *Asheville, North Carolina*

Richard Farner, *Black Bear Hunting in the Southeastern Appalachian Mountains* (2002); Jim Gasque, *Hunting and Fishing in the Great Smokies* (1948); Donald W. Linzey, *Mammals of Great Smoky Mountains National Park* (1995).

Bee, Clair

(1896–1983) Basketball coach and author.

Clair Francis Bee, the son of James Edward Bee and Grace Louise Skinner, was born March 2, 1896, in or near Grafton, West Virginia. He was one of the greatest college basketball coaches of the 1930s and 1940s and a prolific author of both fictional sports books for young adults and technical basketball books. Bee spent his early years in Kansas. Following his mother's death, he returned with his father to Grafton. His father remarried and had four children, but Bee never fit into this second family. He roamed the hillsides above Grafton, played basketball, and participated in other sports at every opportunity. Bee was graduated from Grafton High School in 1920 and Waynesburg College in Pennsylvania in 1925.

As a young coach at Rider College in New Jersey, Bee compiled a three-year record of 55-7. He went on to national prominence at Long Island University, where he coached from 1931 to 1951. There, his teams won the National Invitation Tournament twice (1939, 1941) and had two undefeated seasons (1936, 1939) and a 43-game winning streak. His winning percentage at Long Island University was .818, and his career winning percentage was .826. Bee left the university in 1951 after three of his players were implicated in a scheme to fix games and the institution discontinued intercollegiate athletics. He coached for the National Basketball Association's Baltimore Bullets until 1953, before becoming the athletic director at New York Military Academy, where he ended his career in 1967.

Bee began his writing career in high school when a "hero story" he wrote was published in the school yearbook. Grosset and Dunlap published his first book of sports fiction, *Touchdown Pass,* in 1948. Bee published twenty-two more volumes in the Chip Hilton Sports Series, following Chip and his friends through their high school and college sports careers. Bee reached back into his childhood in Grafton for the setting of these books, always centering his stories on moral values. His sports heroes exemplified small-town Appalachian values of loyalty to their coaches and teammates, respect for family and elders, courage in adversity, and inner strength. In addition to this series, Bee wrote twenty technical books on the fundamentals of basketball, including *The Science of Coaching.*

Through his technical books and as a member of the NCAA rules and tournament committees Bee had an important influence on college basketball. Coaches at all levels of the game attended his coaching clinics and camps. The recipient of numerous awards, Bee was inducted into the Basketball Hall of Fame and the West Virginia Sportswriter's Hall of Fame. He died in Cleveland, Ohio, in May 1983 and is buried in Sullivan County, New York.

See also: HENDERSON, CAM; WEST, JERRY.

—Rogers McAvoy, *West Virginia University*

Neil D. Isaacs, *All the Moves: A History of College Basketball* (1984); Ronald L. Mendell, *Who's Who in Basketball* (1973).

Bryant, Paul "Bear"

(1913–1983) Football coach.

Born on a farm in Morro Bottom, Arkansas, Paul William "Bear" Bryant is best known as the football coach of the University of Alabama Crimson Tide. While growing up, he tried his hand at a number of endeavors to help earn money for his family, including wrestling a bear on stage in Fordyce, Arkansas, thus earning his legendary nickname. Bryant entered the University of Alabama on a football scholarship in 1933 and helped his team win the Southeastern Conference championship in 1933 and 1934.

After serving in the navy during World War II, Bryant began his long coaching career as the head coach at the University of Maryland in 1945. In 1946 he moved to the University of Kentucky, where he spent seven years. This was followed by a four-year stint at Texas A&M. Returning to his alma mater as head coach in 1958 because, as he said, "Mama called," Bryant remained with the Crimson Tide until he retired in 1982.

As a coach, Bryant set numerous records. Rather than innovating, he was at his best reforming and developing the ideas of others and adapting game plans to fit the skills and talents of his teams.

Bryant was named National Coach of the Year on three different occasions (1961, 1971, and 1973) and Southeastern Conference Coach of the Year eight times and is a member of the College Football Hall of Fame. His career record of 323-85-17 made him history's most successful college football coach at the time of his retirement, having broken the record of Amos Alonzo Stagg. The Crimson Tide won six national championships under Bryant (1961, 1964, 1965, 1973, 1978, and 1979). In 1997 Bryant was one of those honored in a new series of postage stamps entitled "Legendary Coaches."

Bryant retired after the 1982 season and suffered a fatal heart attack in January 1983. His passing was marked by the football world as a major event. As a tribute to the coach, the University of Alabama opened the Paul W. Bryant Museum in 1988. Documenting the history of Alabama football, the museum houses a wide array of exhibits and recognizes every player for the Crimson Tide. A series of standing exhibits is highlighted by *Echoes of Heroes* and *The Path to Glory,* as well as a Waterford Crystal reproduction of the Bear's signature houndstooth hat.

See also: FOOTBALL, COLLEGE.

—Leslie Heaphy, *Kent State University, Stark Campus*

Paul W. Bryant, with John Underwood, *Bear: The Hard Life and Good Times of Alabama's Coach Bryant* (1975); Mickey Herskowitz, *The Legend of Bear Bryant* (1987); James A. Peterson, *Bear Bryant: Countdown to Glory* (1983).

Burdette, Lew

(1926–) Baseball player.

Selva Lewis Burdette Jr., the son of a chemical plant worker in Nitro, West Virginia, was an outstanding major league baseball pitcher, spending most of his career with the Milwaukee Braves. Burdette, at six feet, two inches, and 190 pounds, was known as a control pitcher and won between 17 and 21 games each year from 1957 through 1961, leading the National League in a number of categories. At his best he won 20 games in 1958 and 21 games in 1959, and he won 203 games overall, losing only 144.

Though a star high school football and basketball player, Burdette did not play baseball at Nitro High School because the school had no team. He learned to pitch in 1944 with the American Viscose Rayon Company team, which played in the chemical and coal leagues around Charleston, West Virginia. Burdette signed his first professional contract with the New York Yankees in 1946 but became a regular only in 1952 with the Boston Braves.

In 1957 Burdette had a 17-9 record and won three games in the World Series to lead the Braves to victory over the Yankees. After being named the World Series Most Valuable Player, he returned to Nitro for Lew Burdette Day. In 1967 Burdette ended his playing career with the California Angels, having played eighteen major league seasons.

See also: BASEBALL.

—C. Robert Barnett, *Marshall University*

Camping

Native American tribes, ranging from the Iroquois Confederacy in the north to the Creek in the south, preceded the frontier settlers as early campers in the Appalachian region. Early settlers' camping grounds were located along Indian trails and near strategic locations such as the Cumberland Gap, where the Warriors Path south from the Potomac River provided access to Kentucky and Ohio. Daniel Boone, famous for opening up what later became known as the Wilderness Road, and other long hunters were representative of campers who preceded settlers on the frontier.

Modern recreational camping is primarily done on publicly owned lands—in county, state, and national parks and forests. Camping is enjoyed in many forms, from spending the night in or beside a vehicle parked at a carefully maintained recreational vehicle campground such as West Virginia's Pipestem Resort State Park to backpacking and sleeping on the ground in wilderness areas such as the Sipsey Wilderness of Alabama's Bankhead National Forest.

Car camping is the term used for overnight outings in the woods, whether in a tent pitched near a minivan, a sleeping bag in the camper of a pickup, or a forty-five-foot recreational vehicle with the amenities of home. Most car camping is done at organized campgrounds with designated sites and facilities that range from primitive outhouses to heated bathrooms with showers. Fees are usually charged at such sites, most of which are located in scenic areas that also may offer hiking, fishing, swimming, or boating. The Civilian Conservation Corps, a national work program initiated by President Franklin D. Roosevelt, constructed many national forest campgrounds in the 1930s. Rock Creek Campground in the Cherokee National Forest of Tennessee features a swimming pool lined with local stone that attempts to capture the look of a mountain stream. Private campgrounds usually do not provide recreational opportunities equal to those of public campgrounds but do feature other facilities such as camp stores.

Backcountry campers strike out with nothing but a pack on their backs or in a loaded canoe. These campers must take everything they might need with them since they do not have the option of driving back into town for supplies. Though the means of transportation differ, both kinds of backcountry campers look for the same thing: a flat spot with water nearby. Mountain backcountry campsites are generally located in the occasional level area along clear streams or high in gaps along ridges where water is accessible.

The spine of backpackers' paths in the Appalachians is the Appalachian Trail, where three-sided wood or stone shelters are available within a day's hike of one another. Backpackers are known to hike in all seasons, even in winter, taking a respite from the cold in trail shelters such as Thomas Knob in Virginia's Mount Rogers National Recreation Area. Canoe campers obviously have water nearby, but they need a site far enough off the water to avoid flooding. Both Georgia and South Carolina lay claim to the Chattooga, a national river with some of the most scenic camping in the nation. Other Appalachian canoe camping locales include West Virginia's New River Gorge and North Carolina's Fontana Lake, which borders the Great Smoky Mountains.

See also: HIKING; SECTION OVERVIEW (TOURISM); SUMMER CAMPS.

—Johnny Molloy, *Knoxville, Tennessee*

Johnny Molloy, *The Best in Tent Camping* (1999); *Woodall's 2000 Mid-Atlantic Camping Guide* (2000); *Woodall's 2000 South Camping Guide* (2000).

Cardwell, Mark

(1901–1964) Football and basketball player and coach.

Mark Hanna Cardwell, an exceptional football player and coach in the segregated schools of West Virginia, led West Virginia State College to the National Negro College Championship in 1922. The son of Nathaniel and Cornelia Cardwell, he was the youngest child in a family of three boys and two girls. The Cardwells worked a farm near Columbus, Ohio.

An outstanding athlete at Columbus East High School, Cardwell was best known as a running back on the football team. Ironically, he had to leave Ohio, which had integrated schools, to attend segregated West Virginia State to get his chance to play college sports.

Nicknamed "the Fox," he was elected team captain in 1922, and West Virginia State went undefeated on its way to the national championship. Cardwell was named to the Negro All-American team as a halfback the next two seasons. He graduated in 1925 with a degree in physical education.

Connections at West Virginia State landed Cardwell a position at segregated Kelly Miller High School in Clarksburg, West Virginia, where he proved to be as good a coach as he had been an athlete. Between 1925 and 1945, Cardwell led Kelly Miller to six state football and five state basketball championships in the segregated West Virginia Athletic Union.

Under his leadership, Kelly Miller became so formidable that fellow coaches, despairing of losing to his teams, signed a petition demanding that the West Virginia State coaching position be given to Cardwell when it became vacant. Cardwell was no less successful in the college ranks. His West Virginia State football teams won the Central Intercollegiate Athletic Association Championships in 1948 and 1951. His basketball teams were even better. In 1947–48 the Yellow Jackets went undefeated, winning thirty-two games, and were conference and tournament champions as well as being voted the national Negro champions. The 1948–49 team defended their championships, winning twenty-six straight conference games. Those teams were among the best in the nation but had little opportunity to play white colleges. Two of the players from those teams, Earl Lloyd (one of three African Americans to integrate the National Basketball Association in the league's first season) and Bob Wilson, went on to NBA careers.

When West Virginia State was integrated into the formerly all-white West Virginia Intercollegiate Athletic Conference, Cardwell's success continued. His basketball team won the 1961 and 1963 conference championships and a spot in the National Association of Intercollegiate Athletics National Tournament.

Cardwell is representative of the hundreds of African American coaches who toiled in the obscurity of small high schools and colleges of a segregated Appalachia in the period from 1920 to 1960. Such men kept alive the idea of character and fair play in a society that often seemed devoid of both. Through his leadership and foresight he helped prepare a generation of African Americans who would become pioneers in the integration of American sports and ultimately American society. Cardwell died from a heart attack while he was attending the 1964 state high school basketball tournament.

See also: FOOTBALL, COLLEGE.

—C. Robert Barnett, *Marshall University*, and Rod Bradley, *Charleston, West Virginia*

Caving

With its extensive karst topography and tens of thousands of known caves, the southern Appalachian region is home to some of the best caving in the world according to enthusiasts, who generally prefer the term *caving* to *spelunking*. The caves of Appalachia were mostly created by water eating through the soluble rock of the region, and they offer a variety of challenges for the adventurous. Some caves provide an easy ramble through caverns large enough to sail a ship through, while others require crawls through tight squeezes or rope descents as deep as six hundred feet.

People in the Appalachian region have been caving for thousands of years. Torch fragments and strands of cords up to three thousand years old have been found in several caves in the region. There is also evidence of sustained mining activities in some caves in the region as early as 500 B.C. Native Americans apparently harvested epsomites and other minerals from cave walls, though there is some speculation that this activity was partly a religious ceremony or a rite of passage. Torch fragments have been found miles into some caves, an indication of how far these first spelunkers explored the dark, underground passages. Indians of the Mississippian period (A.D. 900–1550) seem to have given up the deep caving of their ancestors, concentrating their activities near cave entrances. The next periods of intense usage came in modern times, first during the War of 1812 and then during the Civil War, as caves were mined for saltpeter, a source of nitrate used in the manufacture of gunpowder.

After the Civil War, the exploration and use of caves dropped off for nearly a century until the 1950s and 1960s, when levels of caving increased dramatically. More leisure time for many Americans coupled with improvements in technology may account for this renewed interest. Among important developments were reliable light sources adapted for cave exploration from miners' carbide lamps. Unfortunately, this period also saw a massive rise in vandalism, including the destruction of historic saltpeter works, plundering of prehistoric remains, and damage to delicate natural formations in the caves.

Many caves are located on private property, and landowners became concerned about their potential liability for accidents as they saw increasing numbers of people heading into them. Accordingly, some cave entrances were closed by dynamite or bulldozers in an effort to decrease the perceived liability of the owners. To protect landowners and lessen cave destruction, many states passed laws that removed landowners' liability for any injuries suffered in a cave (as long as no fee was charged for entrance). Protection for caves was provided when most of the states in the region passed conservation laws that set fines for cave vandalism and molestation of cave-dwelling animals.

Basic equipment of modern cavers includes a good visorless helmet with a lamp bracket and a chinstrap, a pack worn on either the shoulder or back, and a reliable source of light. The modern light of choice is a headlamp with a lead-acid battery that straps to the waist, commonly a Wheat light, which is also approved for use in mines. A fresh, fully charged battery will last up to eight hours. Backup lights usually include a carbide lamp with enough carbide to last for many more hours and a Mini-Maglite or two with spare batteries. Even candles are often included for illumination at lunch breaks. Light is so important that cavers usually carry enough spare parts to fix lighting equipment. In wet caves, prudent explorers wear wetsuits while rappelling down through underground waterfalls or navigating the cold underground streams that stay around sixty degrees Fahrenheit year-round.

Vertical cavers require ropes and special skills to descend into the pit caves and "rope walk" back up. Several types of ascending devices and setups can be used. The large numbers of cavers who visit a six-hundred-foot-deep pit near Chattanooga, Tennessee, indicate the increasing popularity of vertical caving in the region. Most cavers, however, stick to the horizontal portions of the caves into which they can walk, squeeze, or free climb.

Cavers often organize into local groups to share techniques, teach beginners the basics of safe caving, and advocate cave preservation, among other activities. The National Speleological Society is the preeminent caving organization in the United States, with approximately fifty local chapters, or grottoes, located in Appalachia.

See also: ROCK CLIMBING; SECTION OVERVIEW (GEOLOGY).

—Stuart Carroll, *Fall Creek Falls State Park, Tennessee*

Thomas Calhoun Barr, *Caves of Tennessee* (1961); David R. McClurg, *Adventure of Caving* (1998); Tom Rea, *Caving Basics* (1992).

Cherokee Stickball

The Cherokee have played stickball in southern Appalachia for centuries. While it was formerly a ritualistic contest played to settle conflicts between townships or differences between the Cherokee and some neighboring tribe, the game has been played primarily as an exhibition event for nearly a century.

Around 1900 Cherokee stickball was banned by the United States government, which cited the game's roughness and spectators' rowdiness and excessive wagering on the outcome. At the first annual Cherokee Indian Fair in 1914, a revised exhibition version of stickball was introduced, and this tamer version of the game was featured at subsequent Cherokee-sponsored events, including the Cherokee Fall Festival. Thereafter, as the economy of the Qualla Boundary (the Cherokee's self-purchased "reservation" in the Great Smoky Mountains) became economically dependent on tourism, stickball increasingly functioned as a money-making exhibition sport. Since stickball in this form needed to appeal to white people's standards of propriety, the game's elaborate ritualism (involving numerous pregame and post-game ceremonial procedures) was not performed for tourists. Soon, younger Cherokee were mainly familiar with exhibition stickball; toward the end of the twentieth century, few Cherokee practiced, or remembered much about, the original version of the game.

In present-day Cherokee stickball, as in the older version, the team on offense must transport a ball one inch in diameter (traditionally made of deer skin and stuffed with deer hair) through the opposing team's goal (marked by two poles placed apart at the opposite end of the field from the offensive team's own goal poles). Players on the offensive

A stickball game on the Qualla Boundary in western North Carolina, 1932. Now primarily an exhibition event, Cherokee stickball was once a hazardous sport played to settle disputes.

team must carry this ball by means of two sticks (traditionally made of hickory with a webbing of bear sinew) and may pass the ball to teammates, who must catch or pick up the ball with their sticks. As in American football, members of the offensive team try to block opponents so that their own ball carrier can run unimpeded across the opposing team's goal line to score. After each point is scored, the players of both teams return to the center of the field, and an umpire starts a new round of play by tossing the ball up between two tall players, one from each team. The first team to score twelve points wins the game.

Prior to the twentieth century, a medicine man led ritualistic conjuring before the start of a game and served as umpire once play began. Ballplayers' wives and girlfriends, to show support for their men, would wager various material items. Each team was permitted one or two drivers, who could identify the ball's location to teammates but who were not allowed to score points. Stickball was never called off because of inclement weather, and there was no time limit. If darkness rendered continuation impossible, a game would be resumed the next morning. Whereas the number of participants is generally set at twenty (ten players per team) in the modern game, the older version permitted wide variation. One obvious rule change in Cherokee stickball has been that the high level of physical aggression formerly associated with the game is no longer tolerated. In another development, women, who were banned from playing stickball around 1870, were once again allowed to play beginning in 2000.

See also: CHEROKEE (RACE, ETHNICITY, AND IDENTITY); CHEROKEE TOURISM (TOURISM); QUALLA ARTS AND CRAFTS MUTUAL (CRAFTS).

—Ted Olson, *East Tennessee State University*

Charles Lanman, "Indian Ball 1848 Version," *The State* (1955); James Mooney, "The Cherokee Ball Play," *American Anthropologist* (April 1890); Ted Olson, *Blue Ridge Folklife* (1998).

Cobb, Ty

See Baseball

Cockfighting

Although not limited to Appalachia, cockfighting persists as a lucrative profession, hobby, spectator sport, and gambling opportunity in some hollows and out-of-the-way places in the region.

Cockfighting traces its origins to ancient Babylonia and aficionados take pride in calling it "the oldest sport in the world." The earliest recorded cockfight dates from 517 B.C. in China, and it is likely that fighting birds came to the New World on Columbus's second voyage in 1493 and moved into the Appalachians with the first European settlers.

It is estimated that more than half of all cockfighters in the United States reside in the Southeast, where the sport is particularly popular among Cajuns, Mississippi River Delta blacks, Mexican Americans, and rural whites. Trainers, handlers, and spectators are attracted to the bloody fights for a variety of reasons. Camaraderie—particularly male bonding—and gambling are the primary drawing cards. To accusations of cruelty, fans respond that it is cruel not to allow the birds to fight, as it is their nature to battle for territory.

The federal Animal Welfare Act Amendments of 1976 prohibit interstate commerce of animals intended for blood sports, and forty-seven states expressly prohibited cockfighting by 2002—a felony offense in twenty of them. Many of these prohibitions date from the 1800s, and fines can reach more than two thousand dollars. Still, in many areas, particularly in the rural parts of the South and in the hills of Appalachia, cockers, as the handlers are called, appear unafraid of the law or confrontation with members of area humane societies and animal rights groups.

Fighting cocks achieve victory by killing their opponent. This rule has less to do with the nature of the breed in the pit than it does with the nature of the humans in the stands, and fights can be "fixed" when conditions exist for wounded birds to be removed during the fight. In the gruesome matches, birds, which compete for expansive territory in the wild, are forced to compete for a dirt square approximately two feet wide. Cocks instinctively aim for their opponent's most vulnerable areas, attacking the head, the eye, and the beak. When a combatant is injured, the handler signals for a time-out, sucks the blood from the cock's beak, aerates his feathers, and props him up to reenter the fray. If neither cock kills his opponent in the allotted time, both birds are removed to an external drag pit to finish the task.

Cockfighting is an expensive enterprise. In 2001 a single fighting cock sold for approximately one hundred dollars, and a dozen eggs could fetch up to twenty-five dollars. Gaffs, the razor sharp metal spurs that are attached to the birds' legs, sold for about seventy dollars. Individual metal teepees to which the birds are tied to keep them separated when not in battle required additional expenditure. The entry fee for each bird in a match was typically about two hundred dollars. On the other hand, cockfighting with all its accouterments has been estimated to produce more than $10 million in profits nationally each year.

Attendance at cockfights is often a family affair. Men, women, teenagers, and small children are allowed as long as each pays the ten-dollar-or-so admission fee. Bettors communicate verbally or with hand signals across the pit, and reneging on a bet is a serious violation of etiquette.

In spite of legal sanctions and public disapproval, the prospect of easy money, the ritual sacrifice, and the excitement of life-and-death struggle enable the sport to continue and even to flourish.

See also: RECREATION (IMAGES AND ICONS).

—Joyce Duncan, *East Tennessee State University*

Alan Dundes, ed., *The Cockfight: A Casebook* (1994); Charles R. Gunter, "Cockfighting in East Tennessee and Western North Carolina," *Tennessee Folklore Society Bulletin* (December 1978).

Disc Golf

At the turn of the twenty-first century, disc golf was a rapidly growing form of recreation around the world, especially in the United States and particularly in Appalachia. In the 1990s, the number of permanent courses increased from 250 worldwide to more than 900. At least 133 of the courses are located in Appalachian states, where the hilly, forested terrain presents a special challenge.

Disc golf, sometimes called Frisbee golf, is played according to the rules and etiquette of traditional golf with slight modifications. Players throw plastic discs of varying weights and diameters from tee to target with the object of traversing the course in the fewest possible strokes. A majority of courses are on public land, and play is free. A few courses are on private property, where the owners seek nominal payment to assist with upkeep.

The Professional Disc Golf Association, with a membership of nearly six thousand in 2002, sanctions tournaments in the United States. Members register in a variety of divisions based upon skill level and age. According to a 1998 association survey, approximately four million people had played disc golf since its invention in the early 1970s, and it is estimated that fifty thousand to seventy-five thousand play the game each year. Fifty-two percent of association members were reported to be between the ages of thirty-one and forty, with 55 percent having at least one college degree.

Disc golf is played at different levels in different areas of Appalachia. Virginia and the Carolinas are hotbeds for the sport while the number of players in West Virginia and southern Ohio is relatively small. One notable aspect of disc golf is its accessibility and attraction to people of all ages and socioeconomic classes, who often play at the same time.

See also: HANG GLIDING; MOUNTAIN BIKING.

—Donald C. Kleppe, *Huntington, West Virginia*

Ditka, Mike

See Football, College

Dorsett, Tony

See Football, College

Football, College

American football was born amid the wealth and social privilege of Ivy League campuses during the 1870s and 1880s, and the less affluent colleges and universities of the Appalachian region did not adopt the sport until the late 1880s and early 1890s. Though this late start and budgetary constraints made it difficult for Appalachian teams to achieve national prominence, they began to do so by the 1910s. Several football programs in the region have perennially ranked among the best in the nation, and numerous others have enjoyed significant levels of success. As of the end of the 2000 season, three Appalachian teams stood among the nation's top ten programs in total victories. Pennsylvania State University was fifth with 739, the University of Alabama sixth with 737, and the University of Tennessee eighth with 707. This success is based on strong grassroots participation. Geographer John Rooney's study of the geographic origins of major college football players during the 1960s found that of the twenty counties that produced the largest number of scholarship football players per capita, eight were in Appalachia. Six of the eight lie in the coal-mining and industrial regions of western Pennsylvania, eastern Ohio, and northern West Virginia.

The University of Pittsburgh, winner of eight national championships, has historically drawn most of its players from that area. Pitt became regionally competitive after 1900 and achieved national prominence between 1915 and 1923 under Coach Glenn "Pop" Warner. One of football's coaching legends, Warner compiled a record of 60-12-4 at Pitt, which included national championships in 1915, 1916, and 1918. John "Jock" Sutherland, a native of Scotland who immigrated to the United States at age sixteen, succeeded Warner in 1924 and served as head coach until 1938. His 111-20-12 record included national championships in 1929, 1931, 1934, and 1937. In 1976 the Panthers won another national championship with a team coached by Johnny Majors and featuring running back Tony Dorsett. A Pittsburgh native, Dorsett won the 1976 Heisman Trophy and shattered the NCAA career rushing record, gaining 6,526 yards between 1973 and 1976. Other outstanding Panther players from the Pittsburgh area were Mike Ditka, an All-American tight end and defensive lineman from 1958 to 1960, and 1981 All-American quarterback Dan Marino. Ditka especially personified the tenacity, intensity, and blue-collar work ethic that have always formed the core of the Panthers' image.

Pennsylvania State University began playing football in 1887, but its early teams were loosely organized and underfunded. The Nittany Lions (Penn State is located in the Nittany Valley of central Pennsylvania, where mountain lions once roamed) rose to national prominence after World War I under Coach Hugo Bezdek, who stabilized the program's finances. The team played in the 1923 Rose Bowl, losing to Southern California. From 1950 through 1965, Rip Engle served as head coach, compiling a 104-48-4 record. Joe Paterno succeeded him in 1966, and he led Penn State to sustained success while maintaining high academic standards. Between 1967 and 1970, the Nittany Lions compiled a thirty-one-game unbeaten streak. Their undefeated and untied 1973 team was led by running back John Capelletti, who became the first player at an Appalachian school to win the Heisman Trophy. Penn State won its first national championship in 1982, capping an 11-0 regular season with a Sugar Bowl victory over the University of Georgia. It won a second national title in 1986 with a 12-0 season that included an upset victory over the University of Miami in the Fiesta Bowl. Entering the 2003 season, Paterno had a 336-99-3 career record, making him the all-time leader in career victories by a major college coach.

Washington and Jefferson University, in Washington, Pennsylvania, southwest of Pittsburgh, had a generally strong program between 1900 and 1930. Its high point came under head coach Greasy Neale in 1921, when the Presidents compiled a 10-0 regular season and fought the University of California to a scoreless tie in the 1923 Rose Bowl. Washington and Jefferson is the smallest school ever to have played in the prestigious game.

Cornell University, in Ithaca, New York, is located at the northern edge of Appalachia. It became nationally competitive during the 1910s and claimed national championships in 1915 and 1922. Cornell de-emphasized football and joined the Ivy League in 1956. Nevertheless, in 1971 Ed Marinaro was the runner-up for the Heisman Trophy and set the NCAA career rushing record of 4,715 yards that was later broken by Dorsett.

The faculty and students of Marshall University demonstrated the kind of resilience so admired by Appalachians after suffering the worst disaster in college football history in 1970. On November 9, a plane carrying seventy-five football players, coaches, athletic staff, and fans crashed near the Huntington, West Virginia, airport, killing everyone on board. Marshall fought back from the tragedy to win NCAA Division I-AA national championships in 1992 and 1996. The school began competing at the Division I-A level in 1997.

Southern Appalachia has produced several strong football programs. Clemson University in South Carolina overcame decades of budgetary constraints, winning a national championship in 1981 under head coach Danny Ford. The University of Tennessee began playing football in 1891 but remained a second-rank power in the South until the 1926 arrival of Robert Neyland as head coach. A career army officer who ultimately rose to the rank of brigadier general, Neyland led the Volunteers until 1952, except for stretches on active duty in 1935 and again from 1942 to 1945. His conservative style of play emphasized defense and the kicking game. He compiled a 173-31-12 record, won eight Southern and Southeastern Conference championships, and captured national championships in 1938 and 1951. In 1998 Tennessee captured another national championship under Phillip Fulmer, head coach since 1993.

Of all the schools in southern Appalachia, the University of Alabama claims the richest football tradition. The program was undistinguished prior to the 1920s, but head coach Wallace Wade guided the Crimson Tide to national championships in 1925, 1926, and 1930, capping each of those seasons with a Rose Bowl appearance. Wade's successor, Frank Thomas, led Alabama to another national title in 1934 and to Rose Bowl appearances in 1935, 1938, and 1946. Paul "Bear" Bryant, who played under Thomas from 1933 through 1935, took the Alabama program to even greater heights during his tenure as head coach from 1958 through 1982. Under Bryant, Alabama won national championships in 1961, 1964, 1965, 1978, and 1979. Bryant compiled a 232-46-9 record at Alabama and broke Amos Alonzo Stagg's record for career victories by a major college coach before retiring in 1982 with 323 victories. Under Gene Stallings, Alabama won another national championship in 1992.

Joe Namath, a native of Beaver Falls, Pennsylvania, starred at quarterback for Bryant at Alabama from 1962 through 1964. While culture and background separated this young man from a Pennsylvania mill town from his predominantly southern teammates, they shared the toughness and perseverance that have historically characterized players for scores of college football programs in Appalachia.

See also: BRYANT, PAUL "BEAR"; SECTION OVERVIEW.

—Andy Doyle, *Winthrop University*

Mike Bynum, Larry Eldridge, and Sam Sciullo, *Greatest Moments in Pitt Football History* (1994); Francis J. Fitzgerald, *Greatest Moments in Tennessee Vols Football History* (1998); John Watterson, *College Football: History, Spectacle, Controversy* (2000).

Francis, Clarence "Bevo"

(1932–) Basketball player.

A star basketball player for Rio Grande College (Gallia County, Ohio) from 1952 to 1954, Clarence "Bevo" Francis attracted national attention by scoring 444 field goals and 1,225 points, averaging an unheard-of 46.5 points per game in the 1953–54 season.

Francis grew up on a farm near Hammondsville in the hills of Columbiana County, Ohio. He was the seventh child of an Appalachian farm family in which hoeing corn, slopping hogs, shoveling manure, and hunting wild game were common activities. He and his family moved to Wellsville, a small town on the Ohio River, when he was sixteen. Three years later, playing basketball with the Wellsville Tigers under Coach Newt Oliver, Francis scored 776 points in the 1951–52 season by combining a soft shooting touch and unusual agility for someone standing six feet, nine inches tall. Six times that season he outscored the entire opposing team. That one outstanding season put him on the recruiting list of sixty-three colleges and universities. In 1952 President Charles Davis of Rio Grande College hired Oliver as the head basketball coach, and Francis, who was awarded an athletic scholarship, followed.

Oliver organized his college team in the fall of 1952 with Francis as the star of a high-scoring offense. In January 1953, Francis scored 116 points against Ashland Junior College in Kentucky, 55 of which came in the last quarter. Major news organizations sent reporters and film crews to Rio Grande, and at the end of the season Francis and Oliver were feted by major sports figures in New York City for Rio Grande's undefeated season and Francis's prolific scoring. That summer, however, the National Association of Basketball Coaches voted to remove from the record books the games Rio Grande had won and the points that Francis had scored against two-year colleges, as the NCAA only recognizes games played against four-year schools.

The following season, with little support from the college's conservative administration, Rio Grande and Francis became a road show. Games were booked with Villanova, Providence, North Carolina State, Butler, Southeast Louisiana, and other schools across the nation. At Madison Square Garden the team lost to Adelphi, ending its thirty-nine-game winning streak, but it did beat Wake Forest, Creighton, Arizona State, and Miami of Florida. When Rio Grande played Hillsdale College of Michigan, Francis scored 113 points, a record that still stood early in the twenty-first century.

In the spring of 1954, in a whirl of controversy over Francis's academic records and Oliver's conflicts with school administrators, both left to join the Harlem Globetrotters tour. After two years of hectic schedules and big money, tired of the road and homesick, Francis returned home to Columbiana County, where he worked as a laborer and played with industrial teams until he was thirty. Long after his retirement, he returned to Rio Grande each year for the Bevo Francis Classic basketball tournament.

See also: BASKETBALL, COLLEGE; SELVY, FRANK.

—Danny Fulks, *Marshall University*

Larry Donald, "A Dream Gone Bad," *Basketball Times* (December 31, 1987); Danny Fulks, "Bevo's Odyssey," *Timeline* (February–March 1992); William Nack, "Who the Heck is Bevo Francis?" *Sports Illustrated Classic* (Fall 1992); Newt Oliver, *Basketball and the Rio Grande Legend* (1995).

Gatski, Frank "Gunner"

(1922–) Football player.

Frank "Gunner" Gatski, inducted into the National Football League Hall of Fame in 1985, never missed a game or practice in his many years of high school, college, and professional football.

A native of Farmington, West Virginia, Gatski played center and linebacker under Coach Cam Henderson at Marshall College from 1940 to 1942, when he left school to join the military. After World War II, he transferred to Auburn University and played for the Tigers.

From 1946 to 1956, Gatski starred at center for the Cleveland Browns, anchoring the Browns' powerful offensive line during the years it dominated the All-American Football Conference and, later, the National Football League (NFL). Known as a strong, consistent, exceptional pass blocker, he was singled out by the Browns' legendary coach Paul Brown as professional football's greatest center ever. He was chosen as a member of the All-NFL Team four times and played in the 1957 Pro Bowl.

In 1957 Gatski played his final season of professional football for the Detroit Lions, who beat the Browns that year to take the NFL championship. In his twelve years of professional ball, he played in eleven championship games, with his teams winning eight times. Following his professional football career, he retired to West Virginia to coach football at the state Boys Industrial School.

See also: GREER, HAL; HENDERSON, CAM.

—James E. Casto, *Huntington, West Virginia*

Gibson, Josh

(1911–1947) Baseball player.

Josh Gibson, renowned for his catching and powerful hitting, spent most of his life and career in Appalachia, playing baseball in the Negro Leagues for seventeen years. Sometimes called the "Black Babe Ruth" and considered one of the game's greatest all-time players, Gibson was elected into the National Baseball Hall of Fame in 1972. He was the second Negro Leaguer elected, after Satchel Paige.

Joshua Gibson was born in 1911 in Buena Vista, Georgia, to Mark and Nancy Woodlock Gibson. In the mid-1920s, his family moved to the Pleasant Valley section of Pittsburgh, and his father, a former sharecropper, got a job at the Carnegie-Illinois Steel Company. The Gibsons were typical of African American families that migrated north in the early twentieth century. Gibson attended the Allegheny Pre-Vocational School and Conroy Pre-Vocational School in Pittsburgh. At age fifteen, he joined his father, working after school in the steel mills. He later worked as an apprentice electrician at Westinghouse Airbrake.

Gibson spent most of his professional baseball career in Pittsburgh. At age sixteen, he began playing for the Pittsburgh Crawfords, then a semiprofessional team. From 1930 through 1946 he played mostly in the Negro National League for either the Homestead Grays (1930–31, 1937–39, and 1942–46) or the Crawfords (1932–36) with short stints in the Dominican Republic (1937) and for Veracruz of the Mexican League (1940–41). Gibson also played winter baseball in Latin America and Puerto Rico.

The six-foot-one-inch, 210-pound catcher had his best seasons in 1938 and 1939, when he posted batting averages of .433 and .440 and led the Grays to Negro National League championships. Gibson is best known for the home runs he hit in major league parks, most notably Pittsburgh's Forbes Field and New York's Yankee Stadium. Although Negro League statistics were informally kept, he is credited with 962 home runs in his career.

Gibson had many personal problems during his final years in baseball. After his wife, Helen Mason, died in childbirth in 1930, he left his twin children, Josh Jr. and Helen, with their maternal grandparents. Heavy drinking and drug use began to affect his performance on the field. Accounts of his ill health vary, but in 1943 severe headaches led doctors to diagnose a brain tumor. He declined an operation and continued to play baseball. The integration of major league baseball, first announced in 1945 with the signing of Jackie Robinson to the Brooklyn Dodgers' farm team in Montreal, came too late for Gibson. He suffered a stroke and died in 1947 at the age of thirty-five.

See also: BASEBALL; CIVIL RIGHTS MOVEMENT (RACE, ETHNICITY, AND IDENTITY); WALKER, MOSES "FLEET."

—Michele Schiavone, *Marshall University*

Mark Ribowsky, *The Power and the Darkness: The Life of Josh Gibson in the Shadows of the Game* (1996); John Schulian, "Laughing on the Outside," *Sports Illustrated* (June 26, 2000).

Gliding

See Soaring

Green, Tammie

(1959–) Professional golfer.

Tammie Green, a native and resident of Somerset, Ohio, joined the Ladies Professional Golf Association (LPGA) Tour in 1987 and made an immediate impact. She was named the LPGA Rookie of the Year after winning $68,346 and finishing ranked thirty-ninth on the tour. Green's first tournament victory came in 1989 when she captured the du Maurier Classic, one of the tour's four major tournaments. She narrowly missed winning another major that year, the Nabisco Dinah Shore, with a second-place finish. *Golf Digest* named her the LPGA's Most Improved Player in 1989.

Green, who learned to play golf on the hilly courses of the eastern Appalachian foothills, is a graduate of Marshall University, where she lettered in both golf and basketball. She won four collegiate golf events, including three as a senior. In October 1999, Green was inducted into Marshall's Athletic Hall of Fame.

In 1997 Green competed in twenty-five events, won two tournaments (Sprint Titleholders Championship and Giant Eagle LPGA Classic), and finished the year ranked fifth on the tour in prize money with $595,077. In 1998 she won her seventh career tournament (LPGA Corning Classic), crossed the $3-million mark in career earnings, and shot a career-low stroke average of 71.24.

Green also helped lead the United States to Solheim Cup victories in both 1994 and 1998, and she was a member of the LPGA Executive Committee from 1992 to 1994.

See also: PALMER, ARNOLD; SNEAD, SAM.

—Clark Haptonstall, *Rice University*

Greer, Hal

(1936–) Basketball player.

When he retired in 1973, Harold Everett "Hal" Greer, a member of the Naismith Memorial Basketball Hall of Fame in Springfield, Massachusetts, had appeared in more games (1,122) than any other player in National Basketball Association (NBA) history. His 21,586 career points ranked among the all-time top ten, as did his totals for minutes played, field goals attempted, and field goals made. His efforts earned him a place on the NBA's Fiftieth Anniversary All-Time Team in 1996.

Greer grew up in Huntington, West Virginia, where he starred for the all-black Douglass High School. He broke the color barrier for black college athletes in West Virginia in 1955, when he was awarded a basketball scholarship at Marshall University. At Marshall, he averaged 19.4 points per game in his three varsity seasons and was an all-conference selection in 1957 and 1958 and an All-America pick in 1958.

Selected by the Syracuse Nationals in the second round of the 1958 NBA draft, Greer remained with the same franchise throughout his career, moving with the Nationals when they became the Philadelphia 76ers in 1963. In his first season, Greer already showed the skills that would make him a star: a deadly jump shot, quick penetration to the basket, and tenacious defense. He played even better his second season, and by his third he had moved into a starting role. He was an All-Star for ten straight seasons and a seven-time member of the All-NBA Second Team. He was also the second-leading scorer on Philadelphia's vaunted championship team of 1966–67 behind Wilt Chamberlain.

Both Marshall and the 76ers retired Greer's jersey. The Huntington City Council honored him by renaming Sixteenth Street, which runs past the Marshall campus, Hal Greer Boulevard. Greer was named as one of the NBA Fifty Greatest Players of All-Time at the 2001 All-Star Game.

See also: GATSKI, FRANK "GUNNER"; HENDERSON, CAM.

—James E. Casto, *Huntington, West Virginia*

Peter C. Bjarkman, *The Encyclopedia of Pro Basketball Team Histories* (1994).

Hamilton, Steve

(1943–1997) Baseball and basketball player and coach and athletic administrator.

Appalachian-born Steve Absher Hamilton achieved national fame as an athlete and made a great regional contribution as a coach and athletic administrator. Hamilton was born on November 30, 1934, in Columbia, Kentucky. In 1958, after lettering for four years in basketball, baseball, and track, he received a B.A. from Morehead State University in eastern Kentucky. A six-foot-seven-inch center/forward, he was an All-American basketball player and was the second draft choice of the Minneapolis Lakers, for whom he played for two years.

Hamilton also played professional baseball. After winning fifty-two games in the minors, he arrived in the American League with the Cleveland Indians in 1961. In a twelve-year major league career, he played for five teams: the Indians, the Washington Senators, and the New York Yankees in the American League and the San Francisco Giants and Chicago Cubs in the National League. He pitched in 421 major league games, winning forty and losing thirty-one. He also was credited with forty-two saves, eleven of them with the 1968 Yankees. Highly respected by players and management, Hamilton was an early leader of the major league players' union.

Hamilton retired in 1973 and served as pitching coach with the Detroit Tigers. He later managed the Johnson City team in the Appalachian League. In 1975 he became head baseball coach at his alma mater and later athletic director. Hamilton died December 2, 1997, of colon cancer.

Hamilton held the rare distinction of having played in the NCAA basketball tournament, the National Basketball Association Championship, and the World Series.

See also: BASEBALL; BASKETBALL, COLLEGE.

—James M. Gifford, *Jesse Stuart Foundation*

Hang Gliding

Ideally suited to much of the Appalachians, hang gliding—flying an unpowered, ultralight air vehicle that can be launched on foot—made its appearance in the region in the 1970s. Early flights were short glides often made with home-built aircraft from the top of hills and mountains. Notable long-distance glides include Chris Starbuck's flight from Mount Washington, New Hampshire, in 1973 and John Harris's flight from Grandfather Mountain, North Carolina, in 1974.

Evolving equipment and techniques later allowed long, soaring flights above mountain ridges. In 1984 World Hang Gliding Championships silver-medalist Stu Smith flew 112 miles from Grandfather Mountain to Lynchburg, Virginia, for the longest flight along the Appalachian system, while in 1997 Pete Lehmann flew 182 miles from near Pittsburgh to Maryland to cross the entire range for the first time.

The popularity of hang gliding in the Appalachians is a consequence of both the region's topography and meteorology. Until the advent of tow launching techniques, hang gliders were entirely reliant upon the availability of hills and mountains from which to begin their flights. As a result, hang gliding in the eastern United States was concentrated in areas of sharp topographic relief.

The structure of the Appalachians creates ridge lift and waves, two of the atmospheric phenomena that make soaring flight possible. The ridges' alignment in a northeast to southwest direction presents a barrier to the prevailing winds of the eastern United States. The resulting rising air masses generated on the upwind side of the ridges permit hang gliders to fly for extended periods and great distances.

The presence of parallel ridges also enables the formation of amplified waves of ridge lift that grow in size as the air flows over successive ridges. Such waves enable flights to go as high as twelve thousand feet above sea level. Complementing these topographically induced forms are the common thermal updrafts generated by localized solar heating of the ground.

In 1999 there were between two thousand and three thousand hang glider pilots in the Appalachian region. Hang gliding within Appalachia is largely organized by local clubs that acquire and regulate sites on public and private land.

See also: RIDGE AND VALLEY PROVINCE (GEOLOGY); SOARING.

—Pete Lehmann, *U.S. Hang Gliding Association*

Dennis Pagen, *Performance Flying: Hang Gliding Techniques for Intermediate and Advanced Pilots* (1993); Jim and Maggie Palmieri, *Sky Adventures: Stories of Our Heritage* (1998).

Hang glider launching from the top of Tuscarora Mountain, overlooking McConnellsburg, Pennsylvania, 2002. This popular launch site, jointly owned by the Capital Hang Gliding and Paragliding Association and the Maryland Hang Gliding Association, is less than one hundred yards from the Appalachian Trail.

Henderson, Cam

(1890–1956) Basketball and football coach.

Eli Camden "Cam" Henderson is best known as an innovator in basketball and football. In basketball, he is widely credited with pioneering the zone defense as well as the modern fast break.

Born in 1890, Henderson grew up just outside of Salem, West Virginia. After college he became principal of Bristol High School in Clarksville, where he initiated the school's athletic program. During a basketball game against the YMCA team from Grafton, West Virginia, a leaky roof made the gym floor slippery, and Henderson instructed his players to guard an area of the floor instead of a man. It was the creation of the zone defense.

Henderson's first college coaching position was at Muskingum College in Ohio. He later coached for twelve years at Davis and Elkins College until 1935, when he left for Marshall College, again coaching both football and basketball. In his second year, his football team won the Buckeye Conference.

The high point of his basketball coaching career came in 1947, when Marshall won the National Association for Intercollegiate Basketball National Tournament in Kansas City, Missouri. Henderson resigned as Marshall's football coach following the 1949 season, but during his tenure, he coached ten players who later played professionally, including Frank "Gunner" Gatski, who was inducted into the National Football League Hall of Fame in 1985.

In Henderson's final season (1954–55) as basketball coach, he recruited Harold "Hal" Greer for Marshall. Greer, a National Basketball Association Hall of Famer, was the first African American to play integrated college sports in the state.

Henderson remains Marshall's all-time winningest coach in basketball (362-160) and held that record in football (68-46-5) until Bob Pruett surpassed him in 2001.

See also: BASKETBALL, COLLEGE; GATSKI, FRANK "GUNNER"; GREER, HAL.

—Clark Haptonstall, *Rice University*

Sam Clagg, *The Cam Henderson Story: His Life and Times* (1981); Fred R. Toothman, *Wild Wonderful Winner: Great Football Coaches of West Virginia* (1991).

Highland Games

The large number of people of Scots and Scots-Irish ancestry in the region perhaps accounts for the popularity of the Highland games held throughout Appalachia. Scots music, dance, and athletic competitions form the core of the festivals that some historians believe were originally part of the Celtic Highland clans' martial training. Clan chiefs often held competitions testing strength, endurance, and accuracy to keep the clan's physical edge. Although pride in family and community still motivates participants and supporters alike, the games in Appalachia are purely social festivals celebrating all things Celtic.

The Highland Society of New York is reported to have held a Sportive Meeting in 1836, marking one of the first American productions of competition believed to have originated with clans in the Scottish Highlands. Societies in other cities such as Boston and Philadelphia held games before and after the Civil War. In the ensuing years, as Scots entered Pennsylvania, Virginia, and the Carolinas, many such gatherings developed in Appalachia.

At the center of these festivals are the Scottish heavy athletic events, which emphasize strength and endurance over speed and agility. For turning, or tossing the caber, a wooden pole of a size between nineteen and twenty feet long and weighing 100 to 130 pounds is held upright at the narrow end of its tapered length. Balancing the pole vertically against his shoulder, the contestant takes a short run, stops, and flips the pole so that the small end carries over the large end, now on the ground. The objective is to make the pole land pointing to the twelve o'clock position, with six o'clock at the thrower's back. The event is judged for accuracy, not distance.

In the fifty-six-pound weight toss for height, the weight, with a handle, must be tossed with one hand (in any manner desired) over a horizontal bar, usually with the competitor's back to the bar. The height of the bar is adjusted, and the competition proceeds, just as the bar is raised in high jump or pole vault events. Both the twenty-eight- and fifty-six-pound weight throw for distance require a spherical metal weight with an attached ring and chain totaling eighteen inches in length. A short run-up is allowed, but the weight must be thrown with one hand. A rotating body motion is usually used to gain momentum. For the twenty-two-pound hammer throw, a round metal plate or sphere is attached to a flexible cane handle approximately forty-two inches long and tossed for distance. Also thrown for distance is the clachneart, a roughly spherical stone weighing between sixteen and twenty-two pounds.

An event that clearly reflects the agrarian nature of the games' originators is the sheaf toss, in which a twenty-pound burlap sack of straw is heaved with a pitchfork over a bar that is adjusted for height until a winner emerges. Other events include Highland wrestling, the object of which is to take the opponent to the ground, and a mile race run in kilts.

These physical contests are only part of the festivals, which include pipe and drum bands, traditional music concerts, sheep dog competitions, tartan parades, and Highland dancing, as well as offerings of Celtic foods, goods, and crafts. Large annual games are held in various areas of Appalachia, including Gatlinburg, Tennessee; Grandfather Mountain and Catawba Valley, North Carolina; Leesburg and Dumfries, Virginia; Wheeling, West Virginia; Hunter Mountain, New York; and Elizabethtown, Pennsylvania. Throughout the twentieth century the games expanded beyond Appalachia as far as California and Canada.

See also: GRANDFATHER MOUNTAIN (TOURISM); SCOTS (RACE, ETHNICITY, AND IDENTITY).

—John Schleppi, *University of Dayton*

Emily Ann Donaldson, *The Scottish Highland Games in America* (1986). E. F. Holcombe, ed., *Official Athletic Rules: North American Scottish Games Association* (1985).

Hiking

In the rugged, diverse Appalachian highlands lie some of America's premier recreational hiking trails. Within a day's drive of more than half the total U.S. population, the abundant wildlife and varied terrain of the region attract hikers of all ages from around the world to the ancient Appalachian Mountains and their hardwood forests. The mountain system runs more than 2,000 miles, is 250 miles wide in some places, and offers short, easy footpaths as well as long, arduous climbs through forests, past spectacular waterfalls, and along rocky ridges and open balds.

Many, if not most, of the region's recreational trails follow the extensive network of paths created by Native Americans living in Appalachia and enlarged by Europeans, who found them convenient avenues for trade and settlement. One such is the Natchez Trace National Scenic Trail, which parallels an ancient Native American pathway that carried early pioneers westward into Mississippi.

The trail systems of Appalachia have been preserved in large part by the 1911 Weeks Act, which gave the federal government authority to acquire land for national forests, parks, and wildlife areas. These areas now provide the majority of hiking paths available in Appalachia—more than thirty-five hundred miles of trails cross federal lands alone.

Recreational trails are a major attraction for the 9 million annual visitors to the Great Smoky Mountains National Park. With only one major road through the half million acres of protected forest in the park, visitors must access remote areas along more than eight hundred miles of footpaths and hiking trails that wind through its mountains. Likewise, 1.4 million visitors each year hike the five hundred miles of trails and footpaths of the Shenandoah National Park in Virginia.

Trails in Appalachia offer varying degrees of visitor accommodation. Trail systems near urban areas usually provide the broadest access and the most amenities, while wilderness trails restrict the use of motorized vehicles and have no physical developments or artificial conveniences. North Carolina, West Virginia, Georgia, Tennessee, and Alabama all contain official federal wilderness areas. The Cranberry

A hiker encounters campers in the Great Smoky Mountains near the border of North Carolina and Tennessee, 1914. Appalachia has long been a popular destination for hiking and camping enthusiasts.

Wilderness Area is one of five small federal wilderness areas in West Virginia that provide rugged backcountry hiking opportunities. Relatively short wilderness hiking trails can be found in North Carolina's Linville Gorge Wilderness Area, while more lengthy trails are available in the nearly thirty-seven thousand acres in the Cohutta Wilderness Area of northern Georgia and southern Tennessee.

Best known of all trails in the region is the federally protected Appalachian Trail, stretching more than twenty-one hundred miles between Maine and Georgia. First proposed in 1921 and officially completed in 1937, the famous trail passes through portions of fourteen states. Millions of hikers enjoy parts of the trail locally, and each year thousands of thru-hikers make the attempt to complete the entire route, walking steadily from early spring until fall.

The newest of Appalachia's major trail attractions is the Hatfield-McCoy Recreation Trail, a multiple-use trail in southern West Virginia. When completed, this trail will extend into western Virginia and eastern Kentucky and will total two thousand miles. In 1999 the White House Millennium Council and the U.S. Department of Transportation designated the Hatfield-McCoy Recreation Trail as one of only sixteen National Millennium Trails.

Although hiking and walking are the most common trail uses, other popular activities are horseback riding, mountain biking, and off-highway vehicle trekking. The Ohiopyle State Park in southwestern Pennsylvania has forty-one miles of day-hiking trails and nine miles of equestrian trails.

The increasing popularity of hiking in the region has created overcrowding problems in some high-traffic areas. Near the end of the twentieth century, for example, volunteer organizations began erecting outhouses along the Appalachian Trail to accommodate the growing number of travelers. Other volunteer organizations work year-round to maintain and protect the hiking trails of the region from excessive and irresponsible use. In the future, a continued balancing of public access and environmental protection will be necessary to sustain hiking as an important regional sport and leisure activity.

See also: CAMPING; MOUNTAIN BIKING.

—Raymond L. Busbee, *Marshall University,* and Ryan S. Otto, *East Tennessee State University*

Barry Buxton and Malinda Crutchfield, *The Great Forest: An Appalachian Story* (1985); Thomas Connelly, *Discovering the Appalachians* (1968); Clyde Smith, Wilma Dykeman, and Dykeman Stokely, *Appalachian Mountains* (1980).

Hill, Harlon

(1932–) Football player.

Harlon Hill, born in Florence, Alabama, to Frank and Bessie Simpson Hill, made his mark in the football world with a nine-year National Football League (NFL) career that ended in 1962. Growing up poor in a rural community, Hill chose to stay close to home for college after graduating from Lauderdale County High School. At Florence State Teachers College (now the University of North Alabama) from 1950 to 1953 he earned small college All-American honors, but he was an unknown when the Chicago Bears drafted him in the fifteenth round.

The unlikely choice from an obscure teachers' college paid huge dividends, for Hill led the Bears in yards and touchdowns and was named the NFL's Rookie of the Year. In his second season, Hill went to the Pro Bowl for a second time and won the Jim Thorpe Trophy (equivalent to the Most Valuable Player award). Though he finished his career in 1962, playing seven games each for the Pittsburgh Steelers and Detroit Lions, Hill established a number of records for the Bears, including that for the most one-hundred-yard receiving games in a season with seven.

Hill was inducted into the Helms Athletic Foundation Hall of Fame in 1958, the Alabama Sports Hall of Fame in 1976, and the University of North Alabama Hall of Fame in 1990. The Harlon Hill Trophy, named in his honor and awarded to the best player in the NCAA's Division II each year, is one of the most prestigious awards in college sports.

After his football career ended, Hill became principal of Brooks High School in Killen, Alabama.

See also: FOOTBALL, COLLEGE.

—Leslie Heaphy, *Kent State University, Stark Campus*

Huff, Sam

(1934–) Football player.

As a college player, Robert "Sam" Huff earned numerous college football accolades, including being named second-team All Southern Conference (1954) and co-captain of the 1955 West Virginia University football team. He was selected to play in the Senior Bowl (1955), the North-South Game (1955), and the college football All-Star Game (1956). As a pro, Huff spent twelve stellar years in the National Football League (NFL), playing first for the New York Giants (1956–63) and then for the Washington Redskins (1964–69), where he also served two seasons (1969–70) as a player and assistant coach to the legendary Vince Lombardi. During his professional football career, Huff played in six Pro Bowl games. In 1959 he was named Most Valuable Defensive Player in the NFL and won the Most Valuable Player Award in the 1961 Pro Bowl Game.

Huff was born in Morgantown, West Virginia. His father was a coal miner, and Huff's early childhood experiences were tied to the coal industry in West Virginia. In 1952 Huff enrolled at West Virginia University and played football and baseball for the Mountaineers. During his four-year varsity football career, Huff played offense and defense at guard and tackle positions. He gained national recognition as one of the game's most ferocious hitters during college and built on that reputation throughout his pro career. In 1960 CBS produced a documentary titled *The Violent World of Sam Huff.*

Huff was elected to the West Virginia State Hall of Fame (1976) and the National Football Foundation's College Hall of Fame (1980), and in 1982 he was inducted into the Pro Football Hall of Fame. At West Virginia University he is a member of the School of Physical Education Hall of Fame (1988), Academy of Distinguished Alumni (1990), and Sports Hall of Fame (1991). In addition to his athletic exploits, Huff made contributions to football literature with his book *Defensive Football* (1963) and his autobiography, *Tough Stuff* (1988), written with Leonard Shapiro of the *Washington Post.*

After retiring from professional football, Huff became a successful businessman and worked as an analyst on radio broadcasts of Redskins games.

See also: FOOTBALL, COLLEGE.

—Dana D. Brooks, *West Virginia University*

Tony Constantine, *A Record of West Virginia University Football: The First One Hundred Years* (1991) and *Mountaineer Football, 1891–1969* (1969); Kent Kessler, *Hail West Virginians!* (1959).

Hunting and Fishing

From the time the first humans ventured into the Appalachians approximately twelve to fifteen thousand years ago, hunting and fishing were essential human activities in the uplands. Even though these activities—hunting, in particular—are controversial in some quarters of modern American society, they remain popular with thousands of people in the Appalachian region.

At first, hunting and fishing were necessary for survival, but they evolved into recreational activities as humans learned to control their environment through advances in agriculture and technology. In the last half of the twentieth century, these activities spawned multimillion-dollar industries including sales, service, and manufacture of increasingly sophisticated equipment. Sales of fishing rods, reels, lures, boats, rifles, shotguns, ammunition, and camping gear through local outfitters and catalogs are significant to the region's economy. In 1996 hunting-related retail sales in Pennsylvania totaled more than $757 million; in Georgia the total for the same year was almost $889 million. Additionally, the sale of hunting and fishing licenses along with outdoor equipment produces taxes and revenue that state wildlife agencies can use for habitat conservation and other natural resource improvements.

Hunting and fishing in the Appalachian region also serve as resource-management tools for controlling the size of game populations. In the past, virtual extinction of natural predators such as mountain lions and wolves by hunters allowed populations of deer and other species to increase, in some places beyond the ability of the range to sustain them.

A fisherman on the South Fork of the Holston River in southwest Virginia, 2002. Appalachian rivers and streams provide some of the best fly-fishing in the eastern United States.

Managed hunting, based upon data resulting from environmental surveys and biological science, has been used to offset the absence of natural predators on some game species.

The ready availability of game species to hunt and fish in the region has allowed people to exploit these resources heavily over time, and this exploitation has produced numerous negative effects. Of particular importance in the past was overhunting (the taking of game without any limits). Before the first quarter of the twentieth century, there were few, if any, hunting regulations or game wardens in many areas of the Appalachians. Overhunting, along with habitat loss and habitat fragmentation due to human intrusion in the region, caused some big game species, such as black bear and mountain lion, to decline significantly in their historic range.

The popularity of hunting has consequences beyond impacts on wildlife populations. The use of firearms in remote mountain country under sometimes extreme weather conditions is inherently risky. Numerous firearms injuries and deaths of hunters occur annually across the nation during hunting seasons. Because it involves the killing of animals, the sport is subject to opposition by both individuals and organizations.

But the exceptional game and fish resources provide irresistible appeal for enthusiasts in Appalachia. With mountains more than six thousand feet rising above marshy wetlands and bogs in valleys and coves, the area offers fishing opportunities as varied as deepwater panfishing on large basin lakes (Summersville Lake in West Virginia) and fly-casting for native brook trout in mountain streams (Hazel Creek on the North Carolina side of Great Smoky Mountains National Park). Hunting opportunities range from upland wild turkey and grouse habitat in the Catoosa Wildlife Management Area in Tennessee to lowland deer habitat in the Shenandoah Valley in Virginia. There are thousands of places to hunt and fish in Appalachia. All the Appalachian states have wildlife resource officers or game wardens who enforce state fish and wildlife laws, and each state publishes hunting and fishing regulation booklets that are available to the public.

Hunting with firearms in the Appalachian area has a long history, and modern hunters use a variety of rifles, shotguns, and handguns. Certain hunters prefer to use black-powder weapons such as antique or reproduction muzzle-loading muskets and rifles. These black-powder weapons do not use jacketed bullets loaded from the breech or a magazine; rather, they use gunpowder and projectiles loaded from the muzzle and ignited by either flintlock or percussion caps. Hunters who use these weapons seek the challenge of stalking wild animals in the fashion of the early southeastern long hunters and Allegheny frontiersmen. Most states in the Appalachian region have muzzle-loading hunting seasons in addition to modern rifle and shotgun seasons.

In addition to hunting with firearms, some persons in the Appalachian region hunt game animals with bows and arrows. Although some hunters still use the traditional bow, most modern archers wield compound bows that bear little similarity to the handmade longbows of the past. Specific archery seasons are set by each state's game and fish agency.

The Appalachians' extraordinary fishing opportunities arise not only from mountain creeks and natural lakes but also from reservoirs built by various land-management agencies. Live-bait fishing draws visitors from across the country to U.S. Army Corps of Engineers and Tennessee Valley Authority (TVA) lakes such as Norris and Tellico in Tennessee and Dale Hollow and Lake Cumberland in Kentucky. For fly-fishermen there are clear mountain streams in national parks and forests such as the Shenandoah National Park in Virginia and Monongahela National Forest in West Virginia.

In addition to the TVA and Corps of Engineers lakes in the central and southern Appalachians, excellent fishing can be had in the northern mountains. The Adirondack Mountains of New York offer a plethora of sporting opportunities for fishermen. Speckled with alpine lakes and streams, the northern mountains provide both easy access for those who enjoy roadside fishing and challenging backcountry hikes for those who prefer a wilderness environment.

See also: BEAR HUNTING; SHOOTING SPORTS.

—Arthur McDade, *National Park Service*

American Sportfishing Association, *The Economic Importance of Sport Fishing* (1996); International Association of Fish and Wildlife Agencies, *The Economic Importance of Hunting* (1996); U.S. Fish and Wildlife Service, *1996 National Survey of Fishing, Hunting, and Wildlife-Associated Recreation* (1996).

Jackson, "Shoeless" Joe

(1887–1951) Baseball player.

Born on July 16, 1887, in Appalachian Pickens County, South Carolina, Joseph Jefferson Jackson grew up in neighboring Greenville, where he began his professional baseball career. He is best known as one of the eight Chicago White Sox players banned from organized baseball for life as a result of the sport's notorious "Black Sox" scandal. Although Jackson was acquitted in court, his standing as one of the greatest baseball players of all time is eclipsed by the allegations that he conspired with gamblers to intentionally lose the 1919 World Series.

A six-foot-one-inch left-handed batter, Jackson began his professional career in 1908 with the Carolina Association and won an offer from the Philadelphia Athletics later that year. An illiterate who had earned the nickname "Shoeless" by playing barefoot in a minor league game because of sore feet, Jackson was often mocked by his teammates.

Over the next five years, Jackson matured as a professional. He was traded to the Cleveland Naps (later renamed the Indians) in 1910 and achieved one of the highest lifetime batting averages in history (.356). During this period, Jackson learned to interact more confidently with teammates and fans, possibly through the help of his well-educated wife, Kathryn Wynn Jackson.

In August 1915, Jackson was traded to the Chicago White Sox and helped lead the team to American League pennants in 1917 and 1919. The White Sox were, however, a fractious and unhappy club. Charles Comiskey was well known as a tightfisted owner who underpaid most of his players. Moreover, the team was split into two factions: the players with formal education tended to disassociate from their less well-educated and typically underpaid teammates. Jackson naturally gravitated toward the latter, whose members became associated with gamblers seeking to engineer a Chicago loss of the World Series to Cincinnati.

Although declared ineligible to play major league baseball for the rest of his life by the commissioner of baseball, Judge Kenesaw Mountain Landis, Jackson continued to play for various unsanctioned teams. He later operated a dry-cleaning business and a liquor store in Greenville, South Carolina. Jackson died on December 5, 1951, leaving his wife, Katie, but no children.

See also: BASEBALL.

—Richard A. Swanson, *University of North Carolina at Greensboro*

Eliot Asinof, *Eight Men Out* (1963); Harvey Frommer, *Shoeless Joe and Ragtime Baseball* (1992); Donald Gropman, *Say It Ain't So, Joe!* (1979).

Jett, James

(1970–) Olympic sprinter and football player.

Born in Charles Town, West Virginia, James Jett represented the United States at the 1992 Olympic Games in Barcelona, Spain, winning a gold medal as a member of the four-man one-hundred-meter relay team. In addition to this Olympic feat, Jett achieved athletic success at the high school, intercollegiate, and professional levels.

At Jefferson High School, in West Virginia's eastern panhandle, he was a three-sport star in basketball, football, and track. Twice a West Virginia state high school champion in the one-hundred- and two-hundred-meter dashes, Jett also received the 1989 Kennedy Award, which is given to an outstanding high school football player in West Virginia.

Jett enrolled at West Virginia University, where he was a four-year letterman in both football and track. Because of his speed, he was a considerable asset for the Mountaineers, both in returning kicks and as a wide receiver. Jett experienced even more success on the track team, where he became a seven-time All-American and set five school records. In 1992 he was named West Virginia Track and Field Athlete of the Year.

The National Football League's Oakland Raiders drafted Jett in 1993. He won the league's fastest man competition in 1996, and in 1997 he caught forty-six passes for 802 yards and led the American Football Conference with twelve touchdown receptions.

See also: FOOTBALL, COLLEGE.

—R. Michael Burr, *Santa Barbara, California*

Johnson, Junior

(1931–) Stock car driver and team owner.

Named the greatest driver of all time by *Sports Illustrated* in 1998, western North Carolina native Robert Glenn "Junior" Johnson epitomized the legendary figure of a daring moonshine runner turned professional stock car racer. Johnson accumulated fifty NASCAR Winston Cup Series wins from 1953 to his retirement in 1966 and still placed eighth on the all-time win list in 2000. As an owner, Johnson also found success, his teams winning 119 races and six series championships with drivers such as Bobby Allison, Cale Yarborough, Darrell Waltrip, Geoff Bodine, and Bill Elliott.

Johnson's father, Robert, is alleged to have been the leading moonshiner in Wilkes County, North Carolina, and his son, known as Junior, the most celebrated runner in the area. Junior Johnson's audacious flair, quick reflexes, and highly developed driving skills acquired on the dusty mountain roads of North Carolina outrunning federal agents served him well on the local dirt racetracks. Johnson was eventually caught and served just under a year in jail, and his reputation as a legendary moonshine runner brought him as much fame as his skill brought him success when he began racing professionally in 1953. The novelist Tom Wolfe labeled Johnson the "last American hero" in an essay for *Esquire* magazine, and a movie by that name was loosely based on Johnson's life.

After the 1995 NASCAR season, Johnson left racing to work his North Carolina farm. He is a member of several racing halls of fame, including the International Motorsports Hall of Fame and Bristol Motor Speedway's Heroes of Bristol Hall of Fame, and is the subject of the biography *Junior Johnson: Brave in Life* by Tom Higgins and Steve Waid.

See also: MOONSHINING TERMINOLOGY (LANGUAGE); SPORTS HALLS OF FAME; STOCK CAR RACING.

—Troy Gowen, *East Tennessee State University*

Justice, Charlie "Choo Choo"

(1924–2003) Football player.

Charles "Choo Choo" Justice is best known for his outstanding college football career (1946–50), in which he led the University of North Carolina to three major bowl games and a third-place national ranking in 1948. He was named to the All-American team in 1948 and 1949.

Justice was born on May 18, 1924, and reared in Asheville, North Carolina. He became a local legend during his football career at Lee Edward High School in Asheville, where in his senior year his team outscored the opposition 400-6 and finished a second undefeated season. Graduating in 1943, he joined the U.S. Navy and starred on military teams over the next three years. There he acquired the nickname "Choo Choo"—it was said he ran like a train. Following the 1945 season, he was a highly sought-after recruit by colleges throughout the nation. Enrolling at the University of North Carolina in the fall of 1946, the 176-pound tailback led the Tar Heels to the greatest period of football success in the school's history. He continues to be revered throughout the state as perhaps the greatest player produced in the Appalachian region of North Carolina.

Following his college career, Justice played the second half of the 1950 season for the Washington Redskins of the National Football League. After serving as an assistant coach at North Carolina for the 1951 season, he again joined the Redskins for a three-year period (1952–54), leading the team in rushing. Following his football career, Justice became a businessman in North Carolina.

See also: FOOTBALL, COLLEGE.

—Richard A. Swanson, *University of North Carolina at Greensboro*

Majors, Johnny

See Football, College

Marino, Dan

See Football, College

Mays, Willie

See Baseball

Mazeroski, Bill

(1936–) Baseball player and coach.

Bill Mazeroski, an outstanding defensive second baseman for the Pittsburgh Pirates from 1956 to 1972, was born in Wheeling, West Virginia, in 1936. The son of a coal miner, Mazeroski grew up in a wooden house with no electricity or running water. As a child, he would fill a bucket with stones and spend hours by himself hitting the stones with broken broom handles. After graduating from Warren Consolidated High School in Tiltonsville, Ohio, Mazeroski played shortstop for the minor league team in Williamsport, Pennsylvania. In 1955 he joined the Hollywood Stars of the Pacific

Coast League, and the following year, at age nineteen, he was promoted to the Pirates.

Mazeroski is considered by many to be the best second baseman of all time. Known primarily for his fast and graceful double plays, he won the Gold Glove eight times and led the National League in double plays for a record eight seasons (1960–67). Although not usually known for his hitting, Mazeroski became a legend in 1960 when he hit a dramatic home run in the ninth inning of the seventh game of the World Series to beat the New York Yankees. Pittsburgh erupted into joyful chaos that day, and Mazeroski and his home run became enshrined in the city's lore.

After his playing days, Mazeroski became a coach for the Pirates (1973) and the Seattle Mariners (1979–80). Mazeroski was inducted into the Pennsylvania Sports Hall of Fame in 1985 and the National Baseball Hall of Fame in 2001.

See also: BASEBALL; SPORTS HALLS OF FAME.

—Michele Schiavone, *Marshall University*

Mountain Biking

One of the newest outdoor recreation activities in the Appalachians, mountain biking dates from the mid-1970s, when several California cross-country bicycle racers combined the durability of fat-tired, one-speed American bicycles with the lightness and gear shifting capabilities of racing bikes. The result was a durable hybrid capable of handling rugged backcountry trails. What began as a few bikers experimenting with new designs in their garages became a multimillion-dollar industry, with mountain bike use growing in popularity all over North America.

In Appalachia, many public parks and forests allow mountain biking, and paths and logging roads provide extensive access and challenges. There are restrictions on the use of mountain bikes on most public lands, however. The Great Smoky Mountains and Shenandoah National Parks limit bike use to paved or gravel roads. The New River Gorge in West Virginia and the Big South Fork Recreation Area in Tennessee and Kentucky allow mountain bikes only on designated trails.

The widely varied topography of Appalachia provides many opportunities for mountain biking, and the sport has thus joined other activities such as kayaking, canoeing, and hang gliding in regional popularity.

See also: CAMPING; HIKING; ROCK CLIMBING.

—Arthur McDade, *National Park Service*

Musial, Stan

(1920–) Baseball player.

Born November 21, 1920, to a Polish immigrant zinc miner and a Czech mother in the western Pennsylvania mill town of Donora, Stanley Frank Musial went on to have one of the most distinguished careers in baseball history. When he retired in 1963 after twenty-two years with the St. Louis Cardinals, Musial was at or near the top of almost every batting category, holding twenty-nine National League records, seventeen major league records, and nine All-Star records.

While Musial's father wished him to get a college education to escape working in the mines or steel mills, his mother encouraged his sports ambitions. He began his career as a left-handed pitcher in the Cardinal organization, but a shoulder injury sustained in 1940 ended his hopes on the mound. He quickly attracted attention with his hitting, however, swinging from a peculiar crouched posture. In 1942 Musial's skill with the bat led St. Louis to a World Series triumph over the New York Yankees. Until his retirement in September 1963, he played for the Cardinals every year except one for twenty-two seasons (missing only the 1945 season for navy duty at Pearl Harbor), leading the team to three World Championships. Among the many records "Stan the Man" set in an exceptionally consistent batting career are sixteen consecutive .300 seasons (second best in history); 6,134 total bases (second-highest all-time total); and 1,951 runs batted in (fourth highest). Winner of seven National League batting titles (third highest in history) and three Most Valuable Player awards, Musial was commemorated with a bronze statue at Busch Stadium in St. Louis in 1968. He was inducted into the National Baseball Hall of Fame the following year.

After his retirement, the "Donora Greyhound" was named the director of the National Council on Physical Fitness in 1964 and general manager of the Cardinals in 1967 although he stepped down after one season and continued as vice-president. Musial was also awarded the Polish government's highest sports award, the Merited Champions Medal, becoming the first foreigner so honored.

See also: BASEBALL; SPORTS HALLS OF FAME.

—Ajay Kalra, *East Tennessee State University*

Namath, Joe

See Football, College

Neale, Greasy

(1891–1973) Football coach.

Alfred Earle "Greasy" Neale was a highly successful football coach during the first half of the twentieth century. His contributions to both college and professional football earned him honors in both camps.

When Neale, the son of a produce operator, was a boy in Parkersburg, West Virginia, he called a playmate "Dirty." The boy responded by calling him "Greasy." The nickname stuck; many fans never knew Neale's real name. Although an indifferent student, Neale excelled in baseball, football, and basketball at Parkersburg High School and then at West Virginia Wesleyan College. In baseball, he went on to spend eight seasons in the major leagues (1916–23) as a fast, fine-fielding outfielder. Though his career batting average was a mediocre .259, he hit .357 for Cincinnati in the 1919 World Series, the infamous series in which eight Chicago players conspired to throw games.

The same year he reached baseball's major leagues, Neale became head football coach at West Virginia Wesleyan. He also secretly moonlighted with the professional Canton Bulldogs, led by Jim Thorpe. In 1918, when most professional teams did not play because of World War I, Neale coached and played fullback for the undefeated Dayton Triangles.

Neale coached Washington and Jefferson College to a Rose Bowl appearance in 1922. Pitted against the University of California, considered the country's top team, the Presidents fought to an amazing 0-0 tie. He went on to coach at the University of Virginia (1923–28) and West Virginia University (1931–33). From 1934 to 1940, he was assistant coach at Yale, then a football power.

In 1941 Alexis Thompson, a wealthy sportsman and Yale graduate, purchased the downtrodden Philadelphia Eagles, a National Football League (NFL) team that had never had a winning season. Thompson chose Neale to lead the team out of the doldrums. Neale slowly crafted a winner, turning former tailback Tommy Thompson into one of the NFL's top quarterbacks and drafting running back Steve Van Buren, who went on to set league rushing records. His "Eagle Defense" was copied by most NFL teams and became the standard type of defense used by college and professional teams.

The Eagles won the Eastern Division in 1947 but lost the NFL Championship game to the Chicago Cardinals, 28-21. Overcoming both opponents and weather, Philadelphia triumphed in title games in 1948, defeating the Cardinals 7-0 in the midst of a blizzard in Philadelphia, and again in 1949, defeating the Rams 14-0 during a heavy rainstorm in Los Angeles.

After the Eagles were sold in 1950, Neale fought with the new owners over what he considered interference with his coaching. At the end of the 6-6 season he was fired. Subsequently, his coaching greatness was recognized by his election to the National Football Foundation (College) Hall of Fame in 1967 and Pro Football Hall of Fame in 1969. He died in Lake Worth, Florida, in 1973.

See also: CARDWELL, MARK; FOOTBALL, COLLEGE; GATSKI, FRANK "GUNNER."

—Bob Carroll, *Pro Football Researchers Association*

Bob Carroll et al., eds., *Total Football II: The Official Encyclopedia of the National Football League* (1999); Harold Claassen, ed., *Ronald Encyclopedia of Football* (1961); David L. Porter, ed., *Biographical Dictionary of American Sports: Football* (1987).

Newsome, Ozzie

(1956–) Football player and general manager.

In December 2002, Appalachian-born and -reared Ozzie Newsome Jr. was named general manager of the Baltimore Ravens, making him the highest-ranking African American executive with a National Football League club. Newsome was born in the northern Alabama city of Muscle Shoals on March 16, 1956, and graduated from Colbert County High School in neighboring Leighton. Recruited in 1974 by legendary football coach Paul "Bear" Bryant to play for the Crimson Tide at the University of Alabama, the tight end was named All-American his senior year and was drafted in the first round by the NFL's Cleveland Browns in 1978.

Nicknamed "Wizard of Oz," Newsome had notable accomplishments on and off the field in his thirteen-season, 198-consecutive-game career with the Browns. Newsome was the first rookie in twenty-five years to be named the Browns' Offensive Player of the Year (1978). He earned All-Pro honors in 1979 and 1984 and was inducted into the College Football Hall of Fame in 1994 and the NFL Hall of Fame in 1999. Newsome received the NFL Players Association Byron "Whizzer" White Award for community service in 1990 and the Ed Block Courage Award for continuing to play in spite of injuries.

In 1991 Newsome moved from the playing field to the front office and coaching staff, and when the Browns left Cleveland in 1996 to become the Baltimore Ravens, he was appointed the director of player personnel. Recognized as the architect of the Raven team that won the Super Bowl in 2001, Newsome was subsequently named the NFL's Executive of the Year by the *Dallas Morning News*. He served as the Ravens' senior vice-president of football operations from the fall of 2001 until December 2002, when he became the Ravens' general manager.

See also: BRYANT, PAUL "BEAR"; FOOTBALL, COLLEGE.

—Sändra Henson, *East Tennessee State University*

Neyland, Robert R.

(1892–1962) Football coach.

Robert Reese "Bob" Neyland Jr. was the head football coach at the University of Tennessee for twenty-one seasons (1926–34, 1936–40, 1946–52), compiling a record of 173 wins, 31 losses, and 12 ties. It was under Neyland that the Volunteers gained national prominence. Neyland's 1931 team, led by such players as Herman Hickman, Gene McEver, and Beattie Feathers, all from southern Appalachia, defeated New York University in a charity game at Yankee Stadium. This milestone event brought national attention to the University of Tennessee football program and to east Tennessee.

Neyland was born in Greenville, Texas, in 1892 and received an appointment to the United States Military Academy while attending Texas A&M in 1912. He graduated with a degree in engineering in 1916 but excelled in sports as well, participating in baseball and boxing. Neyland had tours of duty in Washington, D.C., France, and Texas. After receiving a bachelor of science degree in civil engineering from the Massachusetts Institute of Technology in 1921, he returned to West Point as an education and recreation officer and as a personal adjutant to General Douglas MacArthur, the superintendent of the academy.

After five years in those roles, he accepted a position with the University of Tennessee in 1925 as senior Reserve Officers Training Corps instructor and assistant football coach. The following year, he became head coach. Neyland is known for drawing on his military education and experience in developing his coaching style.

Neyland's leadership on the sidelines produced numerous All-America players and a consensus national championship team in 1951. Neyland left coaching after the 1952 season but remained the athletic director at Tennessee until his death in 1962. The university has honored him by way of the stadium and thoroughfare that bear his name and through the Robert R. Neyland Scholarship program, which makes awards to outstanding non-athletes.

Neyland's coaching career was interrupted twice by military service. He served in Panama in 1935 and was called back into service during World War II. Between 1941 and 1946 he held commands at four posts, retiring with the rank of brigadier general.

See also: FOOTBALL, COLLEGE.

—Andy Kozar, *University of Tennessee*

Paige, Satchel

See Baseball

Palmer, Arnold

(1929–) Professional golfer.

Born in 1929 in Youngstown, Pennsylvania, in the foothills of the Allegheny Mountains, Arnold Palmer became one of history's greatest professional golfers and a prime mover in popularizing the game. The son of a golf professional and course superintendent, Palmer grew up near the sixth hole of the Latrobe Country Club. After dominating the western Pennsylvania amateur ranks, Palmer moved on to Wake Forest University in Winston-Salem, North Carolina. Distraught over the death of one of his closest college friends, Palmer left Wake Forest before his senior year and joined the United States Coast Guard. After a three-year stint with the Coast Guard, he returned to Wake Forest to finish his education.

After winning the 1954 U.S. Amateur Championship, Palmer joined the Professional Golfers' Association (PGA) and won the first of his sixty-one tournaments, the 1955 Canadian Open. The bulk of his wins came between 1958 and 1967, when he won forty-four tournaments, including four Masters Tournaments, two British Open Championships, and one U.S. Open Championship.

Because of his impact on the golf world during this time, Palmer is given much of the credit for the growth of professional golf's mass appeal during the late twentieth century. With his trademark habit of hitching up his pants and taking risky, aggressive shots, Palmer gained the nickname "the King," and his huge following became known as "Arnie's Army." As his popularity grew, so did the tournament purses. In 1962 he became the first player on the PGA tour to win one hundred thousand dollars in tournament purses. He also became the first player to eclipse the million-dollar mark in career earnings. Palmer was a four-time leading money winner on the tour (1958, 1960, 1962, and 1963), and in 1980 the Senior PGA Tour trophy, awarded annually to the tour's leading money winner, was named after him. In 1960 and 1962 he was named PGA Player of the Year.

Palmer participated in seven international Ryder Cup events, six times as a player and once as captain of the U.S. team. In 1994 he was named captain of the United States team in the inaugural Presidents Cup tournament. He was inducted into both the World Golf Hall of Fame and the PGA Hall of Fame.

After retirement Palmer continued to participate on the Senior PGA events, served as honorary national chairman of the March of Dimes Birth Defects Foundation, and played an active role in the work of the Arnold Palmer Hospital for Children and Women. He remained in the public eye through numerous television commercials.

See also: GREEN, TAMMIE; SNEAD, SAM.

—George M. Reger, *Huntington, West Virginia*

Larry Guest, *Arnie: Inside the Legend* (1993); George Peper, *Golf in America: The First One Hundred Years* (1988).

Paterno, Joe

(1926–) Football coach.

The coach of Pennsylvania State University's Nittany Lions football team, Joseph Vincent Paterno is affectionately known as JoePa to the residents of State College and the team's fans throughout the state. He coached five undefeated, untied teams, won two national championships (1982 and 1986), and was selected the nation's best coach in a 2000 survey of NCAA Division I-A coaches. Paterno's teams ranked in the top ten twenty times, and in 2001 he surpassed the University of Alabama's Paul "Bear" Bryant's record of 323 career wins.

Paterno enjoyed remarkable longevity at the school surrounded by the Nittany highlands once roamed by mountain lions. Assistant to Rip Engle for sixteen years, he became head coach in 1966. While the nation's Division I-A programs saw 709 head coaching changes over the next thirty-five years, Paterno remained a constant at Penn State. More than 250 of his players went on to the National Football League, 25 of them drafted in the first round.

Born in Brooklyn, Paterno played quarterback at Brown University and after graduation became an assistant coach at Penn State. His reputation derives not only from his outstanding coaching record but also from his loyalty to Penn State and his dedication to academic and lifestyle issues. Paterno's football program boasted a 70 percent graduation rate for the freshman class of 1994—at a time when the national average was only 49 percent. All five of Paterno's children graduated from Penn State, and in 1998 the family gave the university $3.5 million, which has been used to fund faculty positions, scholarships, libraries, and several building projects.

See also: BRYANT, PAUL "BEAR"; FOOTBALL, COLLEGE; NEYLAND, ROBERT R.

—Troy Gowen, *East Tennessee State University*

Retton, Mary Lou

(1968–) Olympic gymnast.

Born in the coal-mining town of Fairmont, West Virginia, Mary Lou Retton was an athlete of many firsts: the first American woman to win an individual gold medal in Olympic gymnastics; the first gymnast and youngest inductee to the Olympic Hall of Fame (1985); and the first woman featured on a box of Wheaties.

Four years old when she began training in West Virginia, Retton moved to Houston, Texas, at thirteen to work with Bela Karolyi, trainer of more than five hundred gymnasts. She captured five medals in the 1984 Olympics in Los Angeles, the most medals won by any competitor—a feat accomplished in her first international competition and only six weeks after major surgery on her knee.

Going into the vault exercise, Retton trailed the leader by 1.5 points. She needed 9.95 points to tie for the gold medal. Using the full-twisting layout double Tsukahara, a move attempted by few men and virtually no women, Retton scored a perfect 10. Earlier that year, as an alternate on the team, she had scored 39.50 points of a possible 40, winning the gold medal for individual all-around performance at the McDonald's American Cup at Madison Square Garden.

The four-foot-eight-inch, ninety-eight-pound Retton was named 1984 co-Sportsman of the Year by *Sports Illustrated.* Olympic success brought many commercial endorsements, including the Wheaties box cover. After retirement from competition she wrote a book about her life and became a successful motivational speaker, actress, and national chairperson for Children's Miracle Network. She retained close ties with her Appalachian hometown, where a street was named for her, and she has remained a popular figure in the sports world. According to an Associated Press national survey, she was the Most Popular Athlete in America in 1993. Retton was inducted into the International Gymnastics Hall of Fame in 1997.

—Barbara Smith, *Alderson-Broaddus College*

Rock Climbing

In the late twentieth century, rock climbing emerged as a popular activity across the Appalachians thanks to distinctive terrain presenting a wide variety of challenges. Although there are no high, rugged, alpine-type mountains in the region and no mesas such as those found in the arid West, there are numerous ideal formations, including Seneca Rocks in West Virginia and the Red River Gorge in Kentucky.

In the northern Appalachians, the Shawangunks, or the "Gunks," located less than a hundred miles from New York City, have routes of varied difficulty. The Tuscarora (Clinton) sandstone formation of Seneca Rocks also offers a range of climbing challenges, and its location makes it accessible to large numbers of climbers from the Baltimore-Washington-Richmond urban complex.

Numerous sites exist along the New River, including several in the New River Gorge in West Virginia. The "Endless Wall" has several miles of climbing face in a variety of patterns. Also in West Virginia, Pinnacle Rock, close to the border between southern West Virginia and Virginia, is a wall-like eroded remnant of Medina sandstone that is ideal for novice climbers.

Western North Carolina boasts many popular climbing sites with colorful names such as Looking Glass Rock and Devil's Courthouse, offering climbing routes from moderate to very difficult. Other sites may be found in the Breaks of the Sandy area, around Natural Bridge, Kentucky, and in a series of cliffs near Natural Tunnel State Park in western Virginia. In the southern Appalachians, rock-climbing areas

Climbers on Seneca Rocks in the Monongahela National Forest, Pendleton County, West Virginia, c. 1990. Distinct and unusual formations within easy reach of major metropolitan areas, including the Seneca Rocks and the Shawangunks of New York, have made the Appalachians a popular climbing destination.

are found near Chattanooga, Tennessee, including parts of Lookout Mountain. Bucks Pocket in northern Alabama is also a popular site.

See also: CAVING; HIKING; MOUNTAIN BIKING.

—R. T. Hill, *Concord College*

Stefani Ellen Jackenthal, *The Complete Idiot's Guide to Rock Climbing* (1999); Turlough Johnson, *Rock Climbing Basics* (1995); Don Mellor and Ron Hilderbrand, *Rock Climbing: A Trailside Guide* (1997).

Rooney, Art

(1901–1988) Football executive.

Arthur Joseph Rooney Sr. was an athlete and sports executive best known as the founder and longtime owner of the Pittsburgh Steelers. Born in Coultersville in the coal-mining and agricultural section of western Pennsylvania, Rooney was the oldest of nine children of a Welsh father, Daniel, and an Irish mother, Kathleen. When he was one year old, the family moved to the working-class north side of Pittsburgh, where they ran a hotel and saloon. Rooney lived the rest of his life in that same section of the city.

As a child Rooney played near the eventual site of Three Rivers Stadium, the home of the Pittsburgh Steelers from 1970 until 2000. From 1917 through 1927 he attended Duquesne Preparatory School, Duquesne University, Georgetown University, and Indiana State Normal School. He earned no college degree and played professional and semiprofessional football and baseball while participating in college sports.

Rooney founded the Pittsburgh Steelers during the depths of the Great Depression in 1933, quickly taking advantage of the state legislature's repeal of a law that had prohibited professional sports contests on Sunday. Through the 1960s the team was neither a very lucrative investment nor an athletic success. However, it was a reflection of Pittsburgh and the region in that many of the players were second-generation Americans who were hard drinking and played a tough, physical brand of football. Even though the team won infrequently, Rooney was fiercely loyal to both coaches and players, valuing personal relationships over winning. Pittsburghers admired Rooney's tenacity and loved the Steelers while suffering the team's mediocrity.

In the late 1960s Rooney turned the operation of the team over to his sons, Daniel and Arthur Jr., who hired Chuck Noll, a former Baltimore Colts assistant, as the Steelers' head coach in 1969. Noll created a dynasty, winning Super Bowl Championships in 1974, 1975, 1978, and 1979.

Rooney's willingness to compromise and support innovations in the National Football League, often to the detriment of his Steelers, led to the phenomenal rise in popularity of professional football. Even during the Steelers' years of futility, Rooney was a beloved figure, for he epitomized the ethnic, hard-drinking, hardworking city and region where loyalty and forthrightness were more important than material success.

See also: PITTSBURGH, PENNSYLVANIA (URBAN APPALACHIAN EXPERIENCE).

—C. Robert Barnett, *Marshall University*

Roy Blount Jr., *About Three Bricks Shy of a Load: A Highly Irregular Lowdown on the Year the Pittsburgh Steelers Were Super but Missed the Bowl* (1974); Joe Tucker, *Steelers' Victory after Forty* (1973).

Selvy, Frank

(1932–) Basketball player.

Frank Delano Selvy, the son of an eastern Kentucky coal miner, earned a place in college basketball history by scoring one hundred points for Furman University in a game against Newberry College on February 13, 1954. During the twentieth century, only one player in NCAA Division I came within twenty points of Selvy's record.

Selvy scored his hundredth point with a shot from mid-court with two seconds remaining on the clock. In the stands to witness the feat were his mother, who had never seen him play in a college game, and several hundred supporters who had traveled by bus caravan from his hometown of Corbin, Kentucky, to the game at Greenville, South Carolina. By coincidence, the contest was the first college basketball game ever televised in South Carolina.

Selvy missed an opportunity to play for the University of Kentucky because he had already committed to Furman by the time legendary Kentucky coach Adolph Rupp first saw him play as a high school senior.

When his collegiate career ended, Selvy held twenty-four college records and had scored fifty or more points eight times. After graduation, he played professionally for seven seasons in the National Basketball Association.

See also: BASKETBALL, COLLEGE; FRANCIS, CLARENCE "BEVO."

—John R. Kiger, *Marshall University*

Shooting Sports

Target shooting has a long tradition in Appalachia, and it is not unusual to find three or four generations of a family participating in a Sunday afternoon shoot. The term *Kentucky windage*, a method of correcting for wind and gravity by aiming a weapon to one side of the target instead of by adjusting the sights, honors the skill of early marksmen in the region. Among sharpshooters of the U.S. armed forces, Appalachians outnumber recruits from any other region in the nation.

Shooting sports can be traced back to the bows and arrows, knives, and tomahawks of Native Americans and to European settlers with their muskets and black-powder rifles. Celebrated historical marksmen include Daniel Boone, David Crockett, and Mike Fink, a champion at "shooting the tin cup," an event in which the target is placed atop a man's head. According to the National Rifle Association, more than four million Americans participate in shooting sports of one kind or another.

Modern shooting sports, marked by regulation and organization, feature a wide variety of equipment including rifles, shotguns, pistols, muzzleloaders, air guns, bows and arrows, knives, and tomahawks. Various organizations and Web sites support each of these and promote safe practice of the sport, ethical behavior, personal responsibility, and development of technical proficiency. The largest such organization, the National Rifle Association, annually sponsors approximately eleven thousand competitions and fifty national championships for men, women, and youth. The association also publishes extensive educational materials and sponsors youth camps, coaches' schools, and training clinics. Gun classes for all ages and both genders are often held in schoolrooms or community centers. However, much of the recruitment and training of shooters takes place on-site at shooting events and competitions, with children becoming interested at early ages.

In Appalachia, most hunters are also target shooters, but generally the most competitive target shooters are not hunters. Skeet and trap shooters use shotguns and rifles to shoot at clay or plastic "birds" launched mechanically from "houses." Archers may shoot arrows at stationary paper or fabric bull's-eye targets, but in field competition, mechanized animal targets appear unpredictably from behind trees or shrubs. Silhouette shooting employs pistols or rifles, the targets being collapsible metal shapes set before a backstop. Pin shooting involves rifles, with discarded bowling pins serving as targets. In knife and hawk throwing, the equipment is usually handmade, but manufacturers of throwing knives catalog hundreds of varied items. Targets vary from official, meaning that they are manufactured and relatively costly, to improvised items such as playing cards tacked on logs.

Muzzleloaders, or black-powder rifles, are generally handmade by experts, the design modeled on the weapons of early settlers. Targets are paper bull's-eyes. The goals of muzzleloader organizations such as West Virginia's Barbour County 36ers include the preservation of history as much as the sport of shooting. As safety is a primary concern in these groups, range officers, or target men, and shell men are appointed to oversee shoots. Their responsibility is to ensure that all targets, guns, and ammunition meet approved standards and that shooting does not endanger shooters or spectators.

The activities of most shooting sports are publicized only among regular participants, but turkey shoots are an exception. One of the oldest of the shooting sports, the turkey shoot takes its name from the original target and reward. Held year-round, often near holidays, turkey shoots often serve as fund-raisers for volunteer fire departments or community centers. Modern shoots use targets made of paper bottle caps or other easily acquired objects, and the rewards may be money, barrels of whiskey, or turkeys, hams, or cuts of beef purchased at the local supermarket.

Champions in target sports are numerous in Appalachia. Hiram Bradley of Hindman, Kentucky, at one time held seven world records in trap shooting. Kitty Frazier of Cross Lanes, West Virginia, was the national women's archery champion in 1982 and a seven-time member of the U.S. Archery Team, which won the gold medal in the 1991 Pan American Games. Ed Etzel of Morgantown, West Virginia, three-time All-American and 1984 Olympic gold-medalist in riflery, served for years as coach of the West Virginia University team, winners of eighteen NCAA national championships between 1980 and 1999. Carol Waddell of Philippi, West Virginia, is a six-time state women's champion skeet shooter and a Class D world champion.

See also: BEAR HUNTING; HUNTING AND FISHING.

—Barbara Smith, *Alderson-Broaddus College*

Foster Rhea Dulles, *A History of Recreation: America Learns to Play* (1965); Wayne C. McKinney, *Archery* (1975); David E. Petzel, ed., *The Experts' Book of the Shooting Sports* (1972).

Snead, Sam

(1912–2002) Professional golfer.

In 1933 Samuel Jackson Snead decided to play golf professionally and in 1937 won five major tournaments, finishing second in the United States Open. The following year he won seven tournaments, including the first of eight Greensboro Open tournaments. A life-long resident of Hot Springs, Virginia, near the West Virginia border, Snead was blessed with a natural swing and won a record eighty-one Professional Golfers' Association (PGA) tournaments, earning the nickname "Slammin' Sammy" with his powerful drives from the tee. His victories included three Masters Tournaments, three PGA Championships, and one British Open Championship. Noticeably absent from his impressive list of victories is the U.S. Open, where he finished second on four occasions. His failure to win the tournament was the greatest disappointment of his career.

In 1936 Snead was named the golf professional at the Greenbrier Resort in White Sulphur Springs, West Virginia. There, he often played to the Appalachian stereotype with his southern drawl, signature straw golf hat, and the rumor that he buried his money in vegetable cans in his back yard. As club pro at the famed resort, he golfed with princes, presidents, and captains of industry. At the same time he was a Greenbrier attraction, he continued to play in tournaments around the nation on the fledgling PGA tour.

With Ben Hogan and Byron Nelson, Snead dominated the early days of the tour, winning the Vardon Trophy for low scoring average four times. He was also the leading money winner on tour in 1938, 1949, and 1950. During his golfing career Snead was named to nine United States Ryder Cup teams between 1937 and 1959. Additionally, he captained the U.S. Ryder Cup team three times, in 1953, 1959, and 1969. He was also the oldest person to win on the tour, taking the 1965 Greater Greensboro Open when he was fifty-two.

Snead is a member of the World Golf Hall of Fame, the PGA Hall of Fame, the Helms Athletic Hall of Fame, the Virginia Hall of Fame, and the West Virginia Sportswriters Hall of Fame. In 1993 Snead was welcomed back by the Greenbrier when the resort owners named him the golf pro emeritus.

See also: GREEN, TAMMIE; PALMER, ARNOLD.

—George M. Reger, *Huntington, West Virginia*

George Peper, *Golf in America: The First One Hundred Years* (1988); Sam Snead, with Fran Pirozzolo, *The Game I Love: Wisdom, Insight, and Instruction from Golf's Greatest Player* (1997).

Soaring

The sport of soaring, or sustained flight in a glider or sailplane, got an auspicious start in Appalachia with a number of flights setting national distance records. Among them were flights of 15.75 miles in 1929, 122 miles in 1933, and 240 miles in 1940, all made wholly or partially in Pennsylvania and Virginia.

In 1968 Karl Striedieck of Port Matilda, in west-central Pennsylvania, set a 476.6-mile world record for out-and-return distance along Appalachian ridges. Striedieck also made the world's first 1,000-mile soaring flight, traveling from Lock Haven, Pennsylvania, to near Knoxville, Tennessee, and back in 1977. Such long fights require sailplanes of advanced technology able to fly more than one hundred miles per hour at a low rate of sink, keeping as close as fifty feet above the ridgeline, where the vertical air motion is strongest.

Soaring is possible anywhere that open, level terrain permits launching and landing sailplanes or gliders. (The terms are used interchangeably, although *sailplane* connotes higher performance.) Ridge lift (air deflected upward by windward-facing ridges) and thermal lift (rising columns of air heated by the sun) are the normal means used to stay aloft. Other sources of lift are atmospheric waves that form under certain meteorological conditions and can extend to the upper stratosphere. In the Appalachians, these waves form in the lee of mountains and are common near Mount Mitchell, North Carolina, and near Petersburg, West Virginia. In both these areas, glider flights have climbed to altitudes of more than twenty thousand feet.

Most soaring is done within clubs that provide necessary equipment and gliding instruction. Clubs are active throughout the region, but would-be pilots of gliders or sailplanes can begin the sport by taking instruction and renting equipment from commercial businesses.

Tom Knauff and Doris Grove opened a notable commercial soaring facility called Ridge Soaring Gliderport in 1975 near Julian, Pennsylvania, and Bald Eagle Ridge. Ridge flight training is their specialty. Hundreds of pilots flying from the facility have completed flights in the 300- to 1,000-mile range to earn internationally recognized proficiency awards. Knauff and Grove each hold several national and world soaring records and have significantly contributed to ridge soaring in Appalachia.

Predictions of 600-mile ridge flights, made as early as 1933, were fulfilled in the 1970s. By the turn of the century, experts foresaw soaring flight from mid-Pennsylvania to Florida. In April 1997 Karl Striedieck soared from Port Matilda, Pennsylvania, to Selma, Alabama, setting a national distance-to-goal record of 800.82 miles, about 40 miles past his goal of Marion, Alabama.

See also: HANG GLIDING; RIDGE AND VALLEY PROVINCE (GEOLOGY).

—Robert H. Ball, *National Soaring Museum*

Thomas Knauff, *Ridge Soaring the Bald Eagle Ridge* (1995); Paul A. Schweizer, *Wings like Eagles* (1988).

Sports Halls of Fame

Located throughout Appalachia are facilities devoted to recognizing significant contributors to various sports popular in the region. These halls of fame honor outstanding athletes, coaches, and innovators and also function as museums and archives housing artifacts and memorabilia of various sports. Most hold annual induction ceremonies eagerly anticipated by fans and athletes alike. In essence, sports halls of fame are celebrations of sport rather than place and draw visitors from around the country.

One of the first of such halls, and perhaps the best known, is the National Baseball Hall of Fame and Museum located in Cooperstown, New York. As one of the nation's largest and most popular halls of fame, the facility boasts an annual attendance of close to four hundred thousand. According to popular legend, Cooperstown is the location where, in 1839, Abner Doubleday invented and played in the first baseball game. The center officially opened in 1939, on the presumed one-hundredth anniversary of that game.

The genesis of the National Baseball Hall of Fame was the construction of a baseball stadium, Doubleday Field. The discovery of baseball artifacts near the stadium and the desire to call attention to Cooperstown's role in the development of the national game led Stephen C. Clark, a local philanthropist, to open a one-room exhibit featuring early baseballs, bats, uniforms, photographs, and other memorabilia. The display prompted Alexander Cleland, a business associate of Clark, to suggest the establishment of a national baseball museum.

In 1935 baseball aficionados in Cooperstown and major league baseball officials began planning for a baseball centennial celebration. At these deliberations, National League President Ford Frick proposed that a hall of fame also be included in plans for the baseball museum. The centennial celebration planning committee enlisted the cooperation of the Baseball Writers Association of America to select the honorees. The Hall of Fame also established the Committee on Baseball Veterans to select players from the nineteenth century, before the official establishment of major league baseball in 1903, and from the Negro Leagues.

By 2001, the Hall of Fame had 253 members, including 188 former major league players, 23 executives, 18 Negro Leaguers, 16 managers, and 8 umpires. The museum honors inductees with plaques, photographs, artifacts, and other memorabilia. The history of the game can be traced through more than a thousand photographs and artifacts. Also at the hall is the National Baseball Library, the world's largest repository of baseball reference materials.

While the facility at Cooperstown celebrates professional baseball, the Little League Hall of Excellence recognizes the significance of youth baseball, not only to the sport, but to society in general. The hall is located in one of the galleries at the Peter J. McGovern Little League Baseball Museum in Williamsport, Pennsylvania, where Carl Stotz and George and Bert Bebble established Little League Baseball in 1939. Situated in north-central Appalachia, the Little League Hall of Excellence was established in 1988 to recognize former Little League players who have demonstrated a commitment to excellence in their adult professional lives, exemplifying the values of sportsmanship and teamwork learned as youngsters in Little League. The Little League Museum Advisory Board elects inductees to the Hall of Excellence, and the induction ceremonies are held each year before the Little League World Series championship game, also held in Williamsport.

The Hall of Excellence features illuminated panels of the honorees as well as photographs, memorabilia, equipment, and trophies. Former and current baseball players honored at the Little League Hall of Excellence include Dale Murphy, Jim Palmer, Cal Ripken Jr., Nolan Ryan, Mike Schmidt, and Tom Seaver. Among the other notables inducted into the hall are actor Tom Selleck, astronaut Story Musgrave, golfer Hale Irwin, syndicated columnist and political analyst George Will, United States Senator and New York Knick Bill Bradley, and Vice President Dan Quayle.

Devoted to the history of Little League Baseball, the museum not only focuses on rules and regulations and championship games, but also highlights issues facing young athletes, from proper nutrition to the abuse of performance-enhancing drugs.

Perhaps the most Appalachian of the sports halls of fame is the International Motorsports Hall of Fame (IMHOF). A nonprofit organization dedicated to the preservation of the history of motorsports, the center opened in 1983 as a cooperative venture between Alabama Governor George Wallace and NASCAR (National Association for Stock Car Auto Racing) founder Bill France Sr. It was built and is operated by the state on land donated by the France family adjacent to the Talladega Superspeedway and hosts more than one hundred thousand visitors a year.

The IMHOF recognizes individuals who have made a lasting contribution to all forms of motorized racing. At the heart of the facility is a museum containing more than a hundred vehicles and a large collection of racing memorabilia, with special emphasis on stock car racing. The cars, motorcycles, and boats on exhibit are vehicles associated with major achievements of champion drivers. The IMHOF also contains the McCaig-Wellborn International Motorsports Research Library.

The Women's Basketball Hall of Fame opened in June 1999 in Knoxville, Tennessee, a site chosen both for the phenomenal success of the women's basketball team at the University of Tennessee and because of the efforts of Gloria Ray of the Knoxville Sports Corporation. Attractions at the thirty-two-thousand-square-foot facility feature a number of historical exhibits, including a film that traces the 107 years of the women's game. A Winners' Wall features the best teams of years past, and an old-time locker room is displayed. Computer-driven exhibits present players, coaches, and others giving personal accounts of basketball in earlier times; a modern locker room where successful contemporary coaches give halftime talks; videos of great players sharing their experiences; and taped talks by coaches during timeouts in actual games. The Hall of Honor features plaques and information on the inaugural class of twenty-five inductees into the hall.

Other notable halls of fame located in Appalachia include the National Soccer Hall of Fame in Oneonta, New York; the Pennsylvania State Football Hall of Fame in State College, Pennsylvania; and the State of Alabama Sports Hall of Fame in Birmingham.

See also: BASEBALL; BASKETBALL, COLLEGE; STOCK CAR RACING.

—Adam R. Hornbuckle, *Alexandria, Virginia;* M. Joan Paul, *University of Tennessee;* and Suzanne Wise, *Appalachian State University*

Stock Car Racing

Stock car racing, which began as competition among automobiles with "stock" parts available from dealers, was born in the 1930s in southern Appalachia and from these humble origins rose to become one of America's foremost spectator sports. The sport has its roots in prohibition and the Great Depression, when hard-pressed subsistence farmers turned to the lucrative distilling of untaxed, and thus illegal, spirits. Frustrated in their efforts to find and destroy stills in the mountains, government agents turned their attention to the supply lines and the moonshiners who hauled loads of alcohol along dark, twisting roads to Knoxville, Tennessee, Atlanta, and other urban distribution points. Moonshine runners customized family sedans and developed astonishing driving skills. Inevitably the skills led to competition, and soon moonshiners were matching their cars against each other on dusty dirt tracks in cow pastures and at local fairgrounds.

William Henry Getty "Big Bill" France Sr., a gas station owner and sometime race driver and promoter, saw promise in the growing number of drivers pursuing a sport without standardized rules and often losing winners' purses to shady promoters. France convened a group of about thirty-five men influential in the sport on December 14, 1947, in Daytona Beach, Florida. Three days later NASCAR (National Association for Stock Car Auto Racing) was formed with France as president.

The first NASCAR-sanctioned race was held at Daytona Beach on February 15, 1948. All fifty-two races that year were in the Modified division, which allowed extensive customization of older cars. France thought that NASCAR would draw more fans if the cars on the track looked like the cars driven by the spectators, so he formed the Strictly Stock division. The first Strictly Stock race was held at the Charlotte Speedway on June 19, 1949, in the Grand National (later Winston Cup) division of NASCAR. Modified racing is still popular, especially at local tracks, but it is the modern high-profile version of Strictly Stock racing that epitomizes the sport. Shortly after the Charlotte race, the first superspeedway was constructed at Darlington, South Carolina, and the inaugural race on Labor Day 1950 drew more than thirty thousand fans.

Automobile manufacturers soon recognized promotional opportunities, for cars that won races instantly gained value, creating the "win on Sunday, sell on Monday" phenomenon. To increase their sales on dealer lots, major manufacturers became active participants in stock car racing. Their infusion of money and technical support in the 1960s revolutionized the sport. Cars became stock in name only, as

The Bristol Night Race at Bristol Motor Speedway, Bristol, Tennessee, 2002. This event draws more than 160,000 visitors annually to the Tri-Cities area along the Tennessee-Virginia border.

modifications made them faster and safer. Factory support became essential to compete successfully.

In the early years, media coverage of stock car racing was mostly local, with regional radio broadcasts and occasional television tidbits on ABC's *Wide World of Sports*. A breakthrough into national consciousness came in 1979, when an East Coast snowstorm found millions of people at home on the afternoon of the first live, flag-to-flag broadcast of a NASCAR event. Viewers saw a hair-raising Daytona 500 that ended with a fight in the infield between drivers Cale Yarborough and Bobby and Donnie Allison. Stock car racing gained the beginning of a national following. By the turn of the century, every race of NASCAR's top three divisions (Winston Cup, Busch Grand National, and Craftsman Truck Series) was nationally televised.

France operated a benevolent dictatorship at NASCAR, using savvy marketing, skillful manipulation of the sport's image, and rules creating parity among competitors to create a stupendously successful enterprise. The France family retained control after management of NASCAR passed to Bill France Jr. and other family members. While other organizations and venues for stock car racing appeared, NASCAR continued to dominate the sport. Its success made stock car racing second only to the National Football League in televised sports ratings.

Stock car racing has traditionally been strongest in the rural communities and mill towns of the Appalachian foothills, home to many drivers and race team owners, including Junior Johnson, Todd Bodine, David Pearson, Bill Elliott, and Glen and Leonard Wood. Farmers, small business owners, and factory workers of the region are fiercely independent and relish individual competition, making heroes of drivers such as Richard Petty and Dale Earnhardt, quintessential "good ol' boys" with little formal schooling who became very successful. In many rural areas, racing was for years the only easily accessible professional sport.

The sport's economic impact has grown apace with its public popularity. Marketing studies have found that stock car racing fans are intensely brand loyal. When Procter and Gamble introduced a forty-two-ounce box of Tide featuring Darrell Waltrip's car, the company sold 7.5 million boxes rather than the expected 1.5 million. Coca-Cola has made multimillion-dollar investments in sponsorship of single races. The sport's fan base has changed dramatically from the male blue-collar beer drinkers of the early days. About 40 percent of modern race fans are women, and more than half are white-collar professionals. Sponsors, keenly sensitive to the demographics, adorn cars with the logos of breakfast cereals and Internet-based companies, as well as breweries and auto parts stores.

As corporate pressure for wider exposure increased, the sport left its Appalachian roots in favor of major national markets. Races at North Wilkesboro, North Carolina, an original NASCAR track, were moved to Texas and New Hampshire. New venues in Kansas City, Chicago, and Cincinnati increasingly threatened smaller Appalachian circuits such as Martinsville, Virginia, and Pocono, Pennsylvania. Latter-day drivers come from Maine, Michigan, and California, as well as Tennessee, Virginia, and the Carolinas. The stock car may be, as legendary driver Junior Johnson once observed, simply a refined 1940s moonshine car, but the sport's Appalachian personality has been changed by Madison Avenue, millionaire drivers, and worldwide exposure.

See also: JOHNSON, JUNIOR; MOONSHINING TERMINOLOGY (LANGUAGE); SPORTS HALLS OF FAME.

—Suzanne Wise, *Appalachian State University*

Greg Fielden, *Forty Years of Stock Car Racing* (1992) and *Forty Plus Four, 1990–1993* (1994); Mark D. Howell, *From Moonshine to Madison Avenue: A Cultural History of the NASCAR Winston Cup Series* (1997); Sylvia Wilkinson, *Dirt Tracks to Glory: The Early Days of Stock Car Racing as Told by the Participants* (1983).

Summer Camps

Summer camping for schoolchildren began in the middle 1800s to provide a residential outdoor experience for children from eastern cities. Into the twentieth century, the summer camp movement represented an attempt to teach rugged individualism to urban youth by replicating the American frontier experience. By 1920, more than 106 summer camps were in existence, most located in New England. Since then, the summer camp movement has spread across the United States, with more than 8,500 day and residential camps in operation. In Appalachia, hundreds of summer camps give children, adults, and families the opportunity to experience the region's natural beauty.

Traditionally, residential camps for children offered swimming, hiking, archery, and arts and crafts. Today, campers are just as likely to participate in challenge and rope courses, climbing and rappelling, and wilderness trips. Some adventure camps even include activities such as hang gliding and scuba diving. Many camps have moved into specialized areas of academics and the arts. Students can choose from camps that emphasize general academics, computer science, languages, or math and the sciences. Students of the arts can attend camps for dance, music, and art instruction.

One of the oldest girls' camps in the region, Camp Alleghany in Lewisburg, West Virginia, offers traditional outdoor activities plus dance, drama, and nature and environmental studies. Established in 1922, the camp also teaches girls how to be good citizens and good sports. A notable example of a specialized camp in the Appalachian region is the U.S. Space Camp, located in Huntsville, Alabama. This coed residential academic program has been teaching young people about engineering and science since 1982.

Camps for children who are physically or mentally challenged can be found throughout the Appalachian region. Some concentrate on individuals with one particular problem, such as diabetes; others, upon those with a variety of challenges. Camp ARC of Beaver County in Emlenton, Pennsylvania, provides both day and residential camps for children and adults with mental retardation and offers crafts, outdoor living, swimming, horseback riding, and other activities.

Residential programs also strive to meet the needs of children and teenagers with behavioral and emotional problems. These programs work to develop campers' teamwork and leadership skills while providing structured environments and learning experiences. Since 1977, for instance, Ashe County 4-H Wilderness Experience, located in Jefferson, North Carolina, has taken young people on wilderness camping trips in order to help them develop self-esteem and a sense of personal and social responsibility.

Well-known organizations such as the Girl Scouts, Boy Scouts, Woodmen of the World, and the YMCA also sponsor traditional camps for both members and nonmembers throughout the region. YMCA Camp Horseshoe in St. George, West Virginia, has fostered youths' team leadership skills since 1940, seeking to help young people reach their full potential through working together and enjoying a wide range of activities.

Religious organizations also support camps. Buffalo Mountain Camp in Jonesborough, Tennessee, for example, is affiliated with the United Methodist Church and includes traditional activities along with religious instruction.

The trend toward adult learning and inclusion is evident in the proliferation of specialized camps. Adults may choose from archaeology, arts and crafts workshops, campus vacations, working schools, and volunteer research vacations in every Appalachian state. One adult camp emphasizing Appalachian culture is the John C. Campbell Folk School located in Brasstown, North Carolina. Founded in 1925, the school teaches basketry, beadwork, blacksmithing, quilting, rug making, and weaving. Participants enjoy family-style dinners featuring regional Appalachian fare in sessions that are offered year-round. Adults interested in Appalachian culture can also attend a variety of workshops at centers such as the Penland School of Crafts in Penland, North Carolina, and the Appalachian Center for Crafts in Smithville, Tennessee.

See also: CAMPING; JOHN C. CAMPBELL FOLK SCHOOL (CRAFTS).

—Jill Case, *Dublin, Ohio*

Edwin DeMerritte, "The Emergence of the Camping Movement," *Camping Magazine* (November 1999); *Fodor's Great American Learning Vacations* (1997); *Peterson's Summer Opportunities for Kids and Teenagers* (1999).

Summitt, Pat

(1953–) Basketball coach.

From the time she was named head coach of the women's basketball team at the University of Tennessee in 1974, Pat Head Summitt has accomplished feats that place her among the greatest college coaches of any sport. In a twenty-eight-year span through 2002, Summitt amassed a win-loss record of 788-158, including six NCAA national championships (with three consecutive titles in 1996, 1997, and 1998), and showed no sign of slowing down. Summitt has won two Olympic medals for the United States—silver in 1976 as a player and the nation's first women's basketball gold medal in 1984 as the team's coach. In 2000 she was named the Naismith College Basketball Women's Coach of the Twentieth Century.

Though originally from Henrietta, in central Tennessee, Summitt is a significant presence in Knoxville, where she was named the 1998 Woman of the Year, not only for her success in basketball, but also for her dedication to the community. Summitt has been active in Big Brothers/Big Sisters, served as spokesperson for the Juvenile Diabetes Foundation, the United Way, and the Komen Race for the Cure, and as chairperson for the Tennessee branches of the Easter Seal Society and American Heart Association. Her work has been recognized and honored by groups as diverse as the Boy Scouts of America, the Lupus Foundation, and *Working Mothers* magazine.

See also: BASKETBALL, COLLEGE; SPORTS HALLS OF FAME.

—Troy Gowen, *East Tennessee State University*

Wagner, Honus

(1874–1955) Baseball player.

Johannes Peter "Honus" Wagner, considered one of the best baseball players of all time, rose to greatness while playing shortstop for the Pittsburgh Pirates. Nearly half a century after his death, he still ranked third in triples, seventh in doubles, seventh in total hits, and eighth in stolen bases and at-bats in lifetime offensive statistics. Defensively, he was a legend, with a strong arm and excellent range.

A son of Russian immigrants, Wagner left school at the age of twelve and began working with his father in the coal mines of western Pennsylvania, earning seventy cents per ton of coal shoveled. He estimated that he brought home $3.50 per week. In his spare time, Wagner played baseball with his brother and other boys from the town.

Wagner signed his first professional baseball contract in 1895 with Steubenville, Ohio, of the Inter-State League. His first major league season, 1897, was with the National League's Louisville Colonels, where he spent three years. He then joined the Pittsburgh Pirates, playing for them from 1900 until 1917.

Wagner was a great all-around player, able to play infield or outfield. However, shortstop seemed to be his natural position, and it has been argued by many that he was the greatest shortstop ever to play the position. While renowned for his fielding ability, Wagner was also impressive as a batter, leading the National League in hitting eight times from 1900 to 1911. His .329 batting average is the highest of any shortstop, and he is still listed in eight of the top twenty individual batting categories in many baseball encyclopedias.

An ungainly two-hundred-pounder with broad shoulders, long arms, and bowed legs, Wagner was not a graceful athlete. Besides "Honus" and "Hans," he was also known as the "Flying Dutchman" because of his surprising speed.

After his playing career ended in 1917, Wagner briefly managed the Pirates, and for the next sixteen years he held a variety of jobs, including coaching baseball at Carnegie Institute of Technology (now Carnegie Mellon University). While he seemed to enjoy the peace and quiet of the hills of western Pennsylvania, his love for the game and financial hardships led him to accept a job in 1933 as a coach with the Pirates, a position he held until 1951.

Wagner was known as a man of integrity and was well liked. In 1936 he was one of the five charter members elected to the National Baseball Hall of Fame in Cooperstown, New York. He has often been mentioned as a bridge connecting the early and modern games of baseball.

See also: BASEBALL; PITTSBURGH, PENNSYLVANIA (URBAN APPALACHIAN EXPERIENCE).

—Clyde Partin, *Emory University*

Dennis and Jeanne Burke DeValeria, *Honus Wagner: A Biography* (1996); Arthur D. Hittner, *Honus Wagner: The Life of Baseball's Flying Dutchman* (1996).

Wagon Trains

Since the 1950s, teamsters and riders throughout the upper South have participated in recreational wagon trains. Essentially weekend or weeklong trail rides, wagon trains typically travel from six to twelve miles daily. A few rides move camp nightly; most, however, return to a base camp, where drivers and riders relax in comfortable recreational vehicles, swap stories, and party. Although participants occasionally don period costumes for parades, they generally make little attempt to achieve historical authenticity. Teamsters pull their covered wagons with either mules or horses; riders favor horses, although some use saddle mules.

Wagon training emerged in the 1950s among rural southerners interested in preserving the use of draft horses and mules after the mechanization of agriculture; another significant influence was media imagery of cowboys and covered wagons. Appalachian wagon training began in 1958 with a weeklong drive from Tellico Plains, Tennessee, to Murphy, North Carolina. Operating as the Western North Carolina Wagon Train, this annual ride labels itself the oldest continuously held wagon train in the United States. Strongholds of Appalachian wagon training include North Carolina's northern foothills and southwestern counties; northern Georgia; upper east Tennessee; and the Blue Ridge counties of southern and central Virginia.

The activity is not without controversy, as the alcohol consumption and rowdiness of some participants sometimes alienate onlookers. Enthusiasts, however, extol the sport's family orientation and its role in preserving traditional knowledge of wagons and draft animals.

See also: FLORENCE WAGON WORKS (BUSINESS, INDUSTRY, AND TECHNOLOGY); HORSES AND MULES (AGRICULTURE).

—Theresa Lloyd, *East Tennessee State University*

Walker, Moses "Fleet"

(1857–1924) Baseball player.

More than sixty years before Jackie Robinson broke the color barrier and ushered in the modern era of integrated major league baseball in America, Moses Fleetwood "Fleet" Walker played as the sport's first African American. For forty-two games during the 1880s, Walker was a catcher for the Toledo Blue Stockings, but he was forced from the major leagues by the color line in 1889.

A lifelong resident of eastern Ohio, Walker was an inventor, civil rights activist, editor, author, and entrepreneur. Born in Mount Pleasant to one of the first black physicians in Ohio, Walker grew up in Steubenville on the Ohio River, which separated Appalachian blacks into free and enslaved. The city was a place of contrast, with scores of saloons, gambling establishments, and houses of prostitution coexisting alongside its many denominationally diverse churches. These apparent contradictions of his hometown were reflected in Walker himself, a mulatto who for his entire life was torn between black and white, vice and virtue, hope and despair.

He attended Oberlin College and the law school at the University of Michigan though he earned degrees from neither, abandoning his studies in 1883 to play baseball for Toledo's entry in the Northwestern League. When the team was accepted into the more competitive American Association the following season, Walker and his brother Weldy (who played six games near season's end) became the first black major leaguers. Fleet subsequently played on high-level white teams for Cleveland, Waterbury, Newark, and Syracuse.

Difficult situations dotted his baseball career: Cap Anson and his Chicago White Stockings played against him once but refused on two later occasions; racial taunts and threats marred his appearances in the South; in 1888 he was arrested after an incident in which he threatened contentious Toronto fans with a revolver.

After his exit from baseball Walker stabbed a man to death in 1891 during an alcohol-fueled argument in Syracuse. Acquitted on grounds of self-defense, Walker returned to Steubenville with his first wife, Arabella, and their three children. Working as a postal clerk for a rail line, he was convicted in 1898 of theft from the mails and sentenced to a year in prison. In 1902 he edited the *Equator*, a civil rights newspaper, and, with his brother, proposed a Liberian emigration venture. In 1904 Walker and second wife, Ednah, began a fifteen-year period as managers of the local opera house in nearby Cadiz.

In 1908 Walker published *Our Home Colony*, a forty-eight-page tract on Negro history that advocated the return of all American blacks to Africa. Like his inventions of an artillery cartridge and, later, a device to improve film reel loading, the plan brought him neither success nor fame. Walker moved to Cleveland in 1922, where he died of pneumonia within two years.

See also: BASEBALL; GIBSON, JOSH; RACISM (RACE, ETHNICITY, AND IDENTITY).

—David W. Zang, *Towson University*

David W. Zang, *Fleet Walker's Divided Heart: The Life of Baseball's First Black Major Leaguer* (1995) and "Fleeting Evidence: A Case Study of Handwriting and History," *Journal of Sport History* (Spring 1997).

Warner, Glenn "Pop"

See Football, College

West, Jerry

(1938–) Basketball player, coach, and executive.

A native of Cheylan, West Virginia, Jerry Alan West is an icon of both his home state and professional basketball. He was elected to the Basketball Hall of Fame in 1979 and later selected as one of the fifty best players in the history of the National Basketball Association (NBA). For years his silhouette has served as the NBA logo. After a long career with the Los Angeles Lakers, West was named president of basketball operations for the Memphis Grizzlies in 2002, extending his professional basketball career to more than forty years.

Son of an electrician for a coal mine, West learned to shoot baskets by using a hoop nailed to a neighbor's shed. He led his East Bank High School team to the state championship in 1956 and became the first West Virginia high school player to score more than nine hundred points in a season. He was twice named All-American at West Virginia University. In 1959, his junior year, the Mountaineers lost the NCAA championship to the University of California, but West was named Most Outstanding Player. While in college, he scored an average 24.8 points per game and set seventeen school records. West co-captained the 1960 United States Olympic team that defeated the Soviet Union for the gold medal.

The second player chosen in the 1961 NBA draft, West played for fourteen seasons with the Los Angeles Lakers, leading the team to one NBA championship and winning a place on the All-NBA team ten times. In 1962 West established the NBA single-game scoring record for guards—63 points—and in 1969 he was named Most Valuable Player in the NBA finals. He participated in more than a thousand Lakers games, scoring 25,192 points in regular season play and 4,457 in the play-offs. He was named to the All-Star squad in each of his fourteen years as a professional player and set new records for career postseason scoring and for highest average in a play-off series (46.3 points per game).

West served as head coach for the Lakers from 1975 to 1978, as a scout from 1979 to 1982, and as general manager from 1982 to 1984. He then became executive vice-president. During the eighties the Lakers won NBA championships four times—1982, 1985, 1987, and 1988. The NBA named him Executive of the Year in 1995. Throughout his career in professional sports, West has maintained close ties to his home state, and he remains one of its most revered citizens.

See also: BASKETBALL, COLLEGE; BEE, CLAIR; GREER, HAL.

—Barbara Smith, *Alderson-Broaddus College*

Paul J. Deegan, *Jerry West* (1974); Jerry West, with Bill Libby, *Mr. Clutch: The Jerry West Story* (1969).

Whitewater Sports

The rivers of Appalachia range from steep creeks that tumble precipitously through the rhododendron forests of north Georgia to the broad family-friendly rivers of the Catskills in New York. With an average of more than sixty inches of rain per year, close proximity to urban centers of the East Coast and Ohio Valley, and—at least in the South—fairly mild winter temperatures, the region is a virtual playground for recreational boaters.

River running, beginning with the first descents in canoes early in the twentieth century, has become a major attraction. In the southern mountains, summer camps such as Camp Mondamin and Camp Merrie-Woode in North Carolina and Camp Tate in Georgia were instrumental in training early generations of eastern whitewater enthusiasts. In 1972 the movie *Deliverance*, filmed on the Tallulah and Chattooga Rivers in north Georgia, captured the beauty of the mountains and the exhilaration of whitewater canoeing. Though it presented negative stereotypes of southern mountaineers as violent degenerates, the film created an interest in southern rivers. Predictably, the new popularity of whitewater sport had unfortunate consequences. The Chattooga is challenging and dangerous even for advanced paddlers, and the number of fatalities on the river skyrocketed following the release of the film. Sixteen boaters, almost all of them ill equipped and inexperienced, died on the river between 1972 and 1975.

By the end of the century, more than a million paddlers took to Appalachian rivers each year in rafts, kayaks, or canoes. The vast majority of them were passengers in commercial rafts. Among the most popular rafting rivers are the Ocoee in east Tennessee (220,000 rafters annually), the Nantahala in North Carolina (220,000 rafters), the Youghiogheny in Pennsylvania (110,000 rafters), and the New (160,000 rafters) and Gauley (65,000 rafters) in West Virginia.

Commercial rafting in the Appalachians began in the 1970s and grew into a major industry in some mountain counties. For example, the Nantahala Outdoor Center, with six hundred summer employees and a permanent staff of about one hundred, was the largest private employer in Swain County, North Carolina, by the end of the twentieth century. Founded in 1972 as a small rafting venture, the company eventually took in $15 million a year, operating outposts on six rivers plus a retail store, a mail-order business, an outdoor instruction school, an international adventure travel operation, and three restaurants.

This template has been repeated in other areas of the mountains. Nearly a quarter of a million people each year run the rapids of the Ocoee River, the site of the whitewater events in the 1996 Olympic Games. According to the Tennessee Valley Authority, each Ocoee rafter spends an average of $150 in the region, which translates into direct spending of nearly $40 million a year in east Tennessee. Southern West Virginia has also reaped the benefits of whitewater tourism. Visitors to the New and Gauley Rivers spend about $50 million in the region each year. In Fayette County, river-related services now employ more workers than coal mines, historically the area's biggest industry.

As elsewhere, the waterways of Appalachia are a limited resource. On summer weekends popular rivers can resemble amusement parks jammed with convoys of rafts and legions of jostling kayakers. Locals have sometimes resented the influx of outsiders. In North Carolina, landowners restricted access to the Green River, and the

Rafters negotiate Fayette Station Rapid on the New River Gorge National River, Fayette County, West Virginia, c. 1994. Whitewater sporting has become a major industry in Appalachia since the 1970s. Fayette County now has more workers in this industry than in the traditional occupation of coal mining.

Cherokee Tribal Council has banned kayaking on Raven's Fork, a reservation stream in the Smoky Mountains. Many rivers popular with paddlers have been dammed for electrical generation and flood control. Although water releases are scheduled by power companies to meet the needs for electricity, a few companies have accommodated the need of the paddling community by arranging regular water releases for recreational purposes.

See also: DELIVERANCE (MEDIA); NANTAHALA NATIONAL FOREST (TOURISM); TALLULAH GORGE (TOURISM).

—Harold Herzog, *Western Carolina University*

John Connely et al., *Appalachian Whitewater: The Northern States* (3rd edition, 1999); Bob Sehlinger, ed., *Appalachian Whitewater: The Southern States* (1998); Monty Smith, *Southeastern Whitewater* (1995).

Visual Arts

Section Editor: M. Anna Fariello

AMONG THE OLDEST OF HUMAN ACTIVITIES, VISUAL AND MATERIAL ARTS PREDATE writing by thousands of years, forming an unbroken human tradition that continues into contemporary life. From earliest times, human beings have explored the limits of the unknown and expressed their understanding of the world through visual form. A work of art can be expressive or introspective; it can communicate and celebrate ideas; it can push the boundaries of understanding into uncharted space.

The factors that distinguish the arts in Appalachia from those in the rest of the country are similar to those that distinguish the region in other disciplines. A sense of place or connection to the land is expressed in visual renderings. A tradition of storytelling is evident in the region's wealth of narrative pictures. An independent spirit keeps artists at work in remote areas and contributes to an expansion of their repertoire beyond fashionable trends. The arts try to make sense of the world and our place in it. Native artistic traditions mesh with the ceremonial and spiritual; fundamentalist Christian faith yields eclectic and visionary forms. Paintings, drawings, sculpture, crafts, photographs, and new media serve a documentary purpose, recording national events or family or community history. In Appalachia, many of the region's most appreciated material forms have grown from folklife traditions.

Contemporary ideas concerning the arts originated in the European Renaissance, a period in which the arts flourished as a result of increased trade and wealth. Today's art world—which includes educators, critics, historians, curators, patrons, dealers, and artists—continues to focus on individuality, artistic personality, and talent, as well as the status and economic value of aesthetic forms. The practical need for artistic patronage, as well as the artist's need to engage a critically aware audience, has contributed to a concentration of artistic activity in populated regions. Throughout American history, cultural activity that departed from this urban model has been at a disadvantage. In Appalachia, artistic production and appreciation present challenges to makers and scholars alike.

The earliest Appalachian artists were native peoples, primarily the Cherokee, who lived in the southern Appalachians a thousand years before the arrival of Europeans. While other tribes bordered the region, native Appalachian culture was primarily transmitted through Cherokee artists, from mother to daughter and from

Facing page: Edgar Tolson, *The Garden of Eden,* 1969. Poplar, pine, water birch, cedar, and paint. Although the visual arts in Appalachia encompass a variety of forms and styles, its folk art perhaps best embodies the characteristic qualities of the region. Edgar Tolson was one of the first self-taught artists to gain national attention during the 1970s as a booming art market and the United States bicentennial interested larger audiences in folk art.

father to son. Both representational and abstract images were derived from traditional beliefs and conveyed a sense of spiritual and communal identity. Although objects produced by native peoples were regularly used in day-to-day life, they still possessed a spiritual aura. To outsiders, pots and baskets are merely functional, but to traditional Cherokee the use of such containers adds a spiritual dimension to daily living. After European contact, Cherokee artworks increasingly became objects of trade rather than forms of ceremonial significance. With the development of the Great Smoky Mountains National Park at the periphery of native lands, the market for Cherokee art grew apace with the rise of tourism. Contemporary Native American artists frequently mix elements from native and contemporary cultures, creating work that addresses the social and political dimension of a multicultural region. For example, a Cherokee artist, aware that turquoise is not a traditional regional material, may use it anyway for its value as a "Pan-Indian" symbol.

Until the advent of photography, skills of observation and rendering were crucial to the documentation of the New World. Using these skills, European artists recorded the North American landscape on exploratory expeditions in the sixteenth and seventeenth centuries. Although many of the earliest renderings made in America and in Appalachia appeared as amateur sketches in travel journals, professional artists were increasingly employed as part of exploratory teams traveling into new territories. As communities were settled, artists found employment as cartographers as well. The identities of many of these early artists remain unknown, but their work survives. The few known naturalist illustrators—Mark Catesby and William Bartram in the eighteenth century and T. Addison Richards and Edward Beyer in the nineteenth—form the basis for contemporary scholarship of this period. Artists depicted Appalachian flora and fauna, as well as the magnificent landscape. Thomas Jefferson's praise of sites in Virginia drew attention to places such as Natural Bridge and Harpers Ferry; both became popular subjects for artists. Farther south, painter William C. A. Frerichs explored the Great Smoky Mountains. His uninhabited landscapes contributed to an image of the Appalachians as an untamed and unending territory. Along the Hudson River and in the western regions of the northern Appalachians, America's first recognized school of painting, the Hudson River school, glorified the American landscape. Its depictions of vanishing and awe-inspiring views were seen as evidence of the Divine in nature and set the standard for landscape painting in America.

Demographics are an important factor in the development of art forms that depend upon the public for direct support. Portrait artists settled in towns and cities with sufficient populations to provide a patron base. In rural areas, itinerant artists traveled from town to town making portraits and hand-lettered family records for those who could afford them. Decorated documents and portraits have preserved significant information about eighteenth-century events, including births, marriages, and anniversaries. Schoolgirls attending early-nineteenth-century academies contributed to this legacy of antebellum decorative handwork in the form of stitched and painted surfaces. Although not unique to Appalachia, such art forms are historically and regionally important since few other aesthetic forms then existed in the region. With the nineteenth-century invention of photography, the tradition of itinerant portraitists extended to "picture men," photographers who traveled from town to town making family portraits and documenting Appalachian life. Itinerant portraits, memorial portraits, decorative paintings, silhouettes, stitched samplers, and miniatures were common in the region, but many of their makers remain anonymous.

The first generation of truly professional illustrators emerged just prior to the Civil War, fulfilling a need for illustration that grew with the expanded availability of

William C. A. Frerichs, *The Falls of Tamahaka,* Cherokee County, North Carolina, c. 1865. Oil on canvas. Frerichs painted the wild, uninhabited landscapes of the North Carolina mountains in the mid-nineteenth century, portraying a rugged, unspoiled region of striking physical beauty.

printed material. As *Harper's Monthly* emerged as America's first national magazine, it employed graphic artists to illustrate articles, especially travelogues. Regional artists such as David Hunter Strother found a national voice producing stories for *Harper's*. During the Civil War, artists from outside the region and outside the country—Englishman Frank Vizetelly, for example—were sent to Appalachia to cover battles. Throughout the conflict eyewitness accounts and artists' renderings were dispatched from battlefields to publishers by horse, ship, and train. Eyewitness sketches from battles in faraway places such as Martinsburg, West Virginia, and Lookout Mountain, Tennessee, reached national audiences.

The invention of photography produced an immediate impact on the role of art in society, eclipsing the documentary status of painting and drawing so evident during the Civil War. Technological developments in photography and improvements in mass-print technology allowed faster printing and wider distribution of books and magazines. In 1870 *Appletons' Journal* began its "Picturesque America" series, depicting remote Appalachian sites such as the Cumberland Gap for a national audience. By the early twentieth century, a proliferation of literature about Appalachia covered the spectrum of stereotypes. Artists and their works were no different. Thomas Hart Benton portrayed mountain people as lounging about on ramshackle porches, while Clare Leighton romanticized them as hard-working earthy laborers. Their depictions were reproduced in books, elaborating on stereotypical images of Appalachian people and places that were widely circulated. A need for graphic images contributed to the development of national printmaking firms that reproduced thousands of images via chromolithography, creating an abundance of inexpensive images for public consumption. Individual artists—Rockwell Kent and Grandma Moses, for example—took advantage of reproduction technologies to disseminate images of Appalachia well beyond the region. Art, adapted to reproduction and popular consumption, continues today with the work of well-known artists such as P. Buckley Moss and Bob Timberlake, who mass-produce prints from original paintings.

Photography, as a new field, was not limited to historically embedded practices, but it developed in rural areas of the country and allowed for women and minorities to enter the field more easily. Many American photographers who portrayed the distinctiveness of the American landscape and its people worked in the Appalachian region. In the early twentieth century, photographer Doris Ulmann used glass plates, a technique more common in the previous century, to produce images of Appalachian people. Working for the Resettlement and Farm Security Administrations during the 1930s, Dorothea Lange and Walker Evans photographed sharecropper families, creating such compelling pictures that Appalachia has found it difficult to escape from their portrayal of its people as impoverished and downtrodden, even though many of their photographs were made outside the region. During the 1950s and 1960s, Appalachian photographers teamed up with writers to create community portraits of a changing region, from War on Poverty images published in journalistic accounts to community-based projects such as *Voices from the Mountains*. Contemporary photographers, through venues ranging from sidewalk art fairs to museum exhibitions, continue to interpret the region for a national audience.

The technological support to produce large-scale sculpture in bronze or marble was not available to artists in any part of America prior to the twentieth century. American artists who aspired to make sculpture generally relocated to Europe to work. At the close of the Civil War and after World War I, the nation commemorated fallen loved ones by building commemorative monuments. Public monuments were commissioned to mark important battlefield sites—such as Antietam in Maryland—or for specific groups—such as Confederate, Union, and unknown soldiers. Citizens' groups that sacrificed and contributed to the war effort on either side—mostly women and African Americans—were commemorated as well. Individual memorials are found throughout the region's cemeteries, contributing to a rich iconography of graveside imagery that ranges from native burial mounds to the tomb-top angels carved by author Thomas Wolfe's father around Asheville, North Carolina.

The commissioning of public artworks was given a boost during the 1930s and 1940s when the federal government hired artists to create murals for U.S. post offices. Approximately 250 such murals grace post offices in Appalachia. While many communities approved of the murals installed in their town centers, others resented the sanitized images of rural life as caricatures of reality. In the 1980s and 1990s, a variety of public art programs made it possible for the general community to enjoy sculpture in federal and corporate buildings, in airports, and along interstate highways. Because of a low incidence of vandalism in the mountains, public sculpture programs were established at several sites across the region. Appalachian colleges, for example, instituted outdoor sculpture programs during the 1980s at the University of Tennessee in Knoxville, Appalachian State University in Boone, North Carolina, and Radford University in Radford, Virginia. Larger Appalachian cities such as Chattanooga, Cincinnati, and Pittsburgh revitalized their urban centers, placing public works on permanent view as part of the Appalachian cityscape.

Perhaps the most recognized three-dimensional art form to come out of Appalachia is handcraft. Traditional forms—especially quilts, baskets, and musical instruments—continue to be made, while some contemporary craftsmen have extended the forms into innovative directions, stretching traditional motifs through color, scale, and narrative. In Appalachia, as in other parts of the country, artists are increasingly making works that defy traditional categorization. Hybrid or crossover forms are

Doris Ulmann, *Portrait of Evelyn Bishop,* Sevier County, Tennessee, c. 1933. Photograph. Ulmann left a privileged urban life in New York to travel through the southern Appalachian highlands. Using glass plate technology characteristic of an earlier era, she created impressionistic portraits, such as this photograph of the director of the Pi Beta Phi Settlement School.

grounded in contemporary artistic theory but built using traditional methods or traditional materials. Usually three-dimensional and of smaller scale, these hybrid forms can often be found in communities near regional craft schools.

At the turn of the twentieth century, alternative ways of exploring the subconscious and the microscopic influenced the way artists interpreted the world. Artists attempted to portray layered realities of understanding, abandoning realistic observation for non-objectivity, fantasy, and meditative introspection. Catherine Wiley, an American impressionist from Knoxville, painted figures in natural settings where light played a significant role. Will Henry Stevens spent summers in the Blue Ridge Mountains, painting abstracted elements from nature. Elliot Daingerfield made religiously inspired paintings from his studio in Blowing Rock, North Carolina. Black Mountain College, established just east of Asheville in 1933, was an important center for artistic modernism until it closed in 1956. Although experimental and short-lived, Black Mountain was an influential school that functioned as a retreat for artists to come together to focus on enhancing creativity. Thinkers and artists such as Walter Gropius, Clement Greenberg, and Josef Albers established their reputations as national, if not international, figures while living and working in the Black Mountains of western North Carolina. Although Black Mountain College strengthened the position of America as a serious participant in the international arts community, it had little effect on the Appalachian culture where it was located.

The term *expatriate* is usually applied to artists such as Mary Cassatt, who, born in Pittsburgh, left the United States to work in Europe. But it also describes artists who were born and reared in rural Appalachia but were lured to larger cultural centers in their own country. As they assimilated into mainstream modernism, the regional flavor of their work disappeared. Many African American and women artists left the region to participate in a growing national aesthetic dialogue that questioned their traditionally prescribed roles and allowed them more leeway in personal expression. Beauford Delaney, for example, left his home in Knoxville to become part of the Harlem Renaissance. As the century progressed, artists increasingly obliterated regional content from their work in favor of a universal voice. Shedding their hometowns, many suppressed regional identities as well. Noted artists such as Andy Warhol (from Pittsburgh) and Cy Twombly (from Lexington, Virginia) are included in mainstream art history texts, but they are rarely identified as Appalachian artists.

Ironically, one of the most commercially successful art forms to come from the Appalachian region is folk art, work that emanates, for the most part, from a private, authentic, and aesthetic impulse well removed from commercial intent. Popular with collectors, folk art is sold through antique dealers and art galleries and is written about by folklorists, cultural anthropologists, and art historians. Because the "folk" do not tend to fit neatly within academic categories, definitions can be controversial. Depending on who is asked, folk artists are labeled as naive, outsiders, visionary, self-taught, rural, nonacademic, primitive, and/or popular. Aside from the plurality of names by which they are known, folk artists are recognized by certain similar visual characteristics and approaches. Their work employs ordinary materials, such as house paint applied to plywood or tin. Some claim to create in response to a divine calling, citing a higher power that compelled them to begin making art. Their inner visions are realized using materials at hand, resulting in eclectic artworks that often include literal visual descriptions of scriptural passages. Religious, popular, and personal motifs are mixed freely.

In the early twentieth century, a national interest in folk art was prompted in part by a desire to establish an American cultural identity, resulting in a number of important folk art exhibitions. Since that time, folk artists have been routinely included in museum collections and exhibitions. Tennessee artist Bessie Harvey made sculptures from tree roots and found objects, transforming them into fantastic creatures. Harold Green, another Tennesseean, began his work with a chainsaw, rough-cutting timbers before applying layers of colorful spots. Kentucky artist Edgar Tolson carved biblical scenes in wood, depicting figures with detailed expressions. Though he turned to creating art late in life, Georgia artist Howard Finster, whose paintings reflect his strong religious beliefs, may be America's best-known folk artist, having appeared in national magazines and on television. Like Finster, some contemporary folk artists have stepped beyond anonymity, and their works sell in a network of galleries nationwide. Others have arranged their accumulated works into colorful outdoor roadside museums. Regardless of public reception, their tenacious fidelity to private vision places them distinctly outside the art-historical Euro-American continuum.

Even into the twentieth century, students who aspired to be artists had to leave the region for an education. As universities evolved to provide artistic training, artists within newly opened art departments influenced students and subsequent generations of regional artists. Their influence extended well beyond their campuses into the communities or states in which they taught. Aaron Douglas, an artist whose work received recognition as part of the Harlem Renaissance, came to Nashville, Tennessee, in the 1930s to paint a series of murals focused on the African American experience. He remained at Fisk University as head of the Art Department. Similarly, Lamar Dodd, a Georgia native, returned from New York's Art Students League to establish the Art Department at the University of Georgia. While Douglas and Dodd worked at the outer edges of Appalachia, their work filtered into the region through their influential professional activities and through their students. This first generation of Appalachian artists and professors had to travel to New York, Chicago, or Paris for an art education, but their repatriation to universities at the region's edge allowed Appalachian students to study closer to home.

On a map of the United States, the South as a whole—along with the diagonal swath of the Appalachian region cutting across it—marks an area of the country much maligned and misunderstood. Historically, criticism of the region's cultural output has been published under the guise of mainstream academic objectivity. Authors have claimed that the region has no true culture at all. In 1926 an essay in the *Saturday*

Review titled "The Artist as Southerner" attempted to analyze the conflict facing serious regional artists. Should an artist embrace a regional identity and subject matter and be exposed to accusations of provincialism? Or should one pursue innovation and a more universal voice, thereby abandoning one's aesthetic roots? This dilemma, articulated during the 1920s, still faces artists today.

At the start of the twenty-first century, except for a prevalence of visionary art forms and an emphasis on handcraft, the visual arts in Appalachia are not much different from those in other parts of the country. Professional artists in Appalachia receive similar training and read the same professional periodicals as artists in the rest of the country. Likewise, they maintain studios, exhibit their work, enter competitions, approach galleries, meet collectors, give lectures, present demonstrations, read books, earn degrees, teach students, attend conferences, and discuss art. What changed dramatically during the last century was not how art was made but the way it was taught and studied. Scholars began to examine the underlying assumptions and judgments about quality and exclusivity. New scholarship explored folk art, popular culture, and crafts, as well as works by women, ethnic minorities, and outlying regions such as Appalachia. But a persistent lack of regional documentation has created a particular set of challenges for those scholars documenting and analyzing the visual arts for the *Encyclopedia of Appalachia*. While many sections in this volume have drawn from a broad body of published scholarship, the writers on visual arts have depended upon disparate materials to create a cohesive picture of the region's visual expression.

—M. Anna Fariello, *Virginia Polytechnic Institute and State University*

Bruce W. Chambers, *Art and Artists of the South: The Robert P. Coggins Collection* (1984); David C. Driskell, *Two Centuries of Black American Art* (1976); Barbara Duncan, *The Cherokee Artist Directory* (2001); M. Anna Fariello and Paula Owen, *Objects and Meaning* (2003); Ramona and Millard Lampell, *O, Appalachia: Artists of the Southern Mountains* (1989); W. K. McNeil, ed., *Appalachian Images in Folk and Popular Culture* (1989); Barbara Shissler Nosanow, *More Than Land or Sky: Art from Appalachia* (1981); Jessie Poesch, *The Art of the Old South: Painting, Sculpture, Architecture, and the Products of Craftsmen, 1560–1860* (1983); Virginia Museum of Fine Arts, *Painting in the South: 1564–1980* (1983); Charles Reagan Wilson and William Ferris, eds., *Encyclopedia of Southern Culture* (1989).

African American Artists

Among challenges faced by African American artists during the nineteenth and twentieth centuries were the struggles for equality and a sense of individuality. In the southern Appalachians, African American artists also had to contend with state-sanctioned segregation that severely limited choices in regard to education and exhibition opportunities. Despite such restrictions, African American artists in the region made significant contributions to the visual arts, producing diverse works ranging from the classically inspired to the folk or primitive. While some addressed issues related to racial identity, others took a more mainstream view.

There is little documentation related to the works of African Americans before the Civil War, although a few such artists stand out. One of these exceptional artists was Robert S. Duncanson (1821–1872), who modeled his work after the acclaimed Hudson River school. Painting landscapes in the Ohio River Valley, Duncanson established himself as one of the first African American artists to attain international recognition. His most famous work can be found in the Taft Museum of Art in Cincinnati, where he was commissioned to paint a suite of eight large murals while the museum was still a private residence. Another nineteenth-century African American artist was Henry Ossawa Tanner (1859–1937). Born in Pittsburgh, Tanner attended the prestigious Pennsylvania Academy of Fine Arts and studied with renowned teacher and painter Thomas Eakins. Tanner's 1893 painting *The Banjo Lesson* has been hailed as an icon of African American life in the nineteenth century. Tanner spent most of his career in Europe, where the French government purchased his *Resurrection of Lazarus* for the Louvre in 1897.

In the early twentieth century, African American artists continued to relocate in order to pursue careers in places that held more potential for success. Born in Knoxville, Tennessee, Beauford Delaney (1901–1979) began his formal training in Boston, where he studied at the Massachusetts Normal Art School, the South Boston School of Art, and the Copley Society. In 1929 Delaney moved to Harlem, where he befriended such notable African American leaders as James Baldwin during the Harlem Renaissance. While in Harlem, Delaney painted such works as *Abstraction* (1938) and *Portrait of a Man* (1943). In 1953 he moved to Paris, where he painted *Portrait of Darthea Speyer* (1966) and *Portrait of Jean Genet* (1970) and was described as the "Dean of African American Artists Living in Europe."

Joseph Delaney (1904–1991) was also born in Knoxville but, unlike his older brother Beauford, maintained ties to the region. In 1930 Joseph Delaney moved to New York and attended the Art Students League, where, while studying with Thomas Hart Benton, he began painting scenes depicting the everyday lives of American people and landscapes. As the Great Depression worsened, he completed art projects with the Works Progress Administration and the Index of American Design. During the 1940s, Delaney painted such works as *Penn Station in War Time* (1943) and *Waldorf Cafeteria* (1945). After Beauford's death, Joseph traveled to Paris and brought back many of his brother's paintings. In 1985 he moved back to Knoxville, where he worked as an artist-in-residence at the University of Tennessee.

In 1925 the first art department at a historically black college was established in Washington, D.C., at Howard University. Fisk University (Nashville, Tennessee) followed suit in the 1930s after Aaron Douglas (1898–1979), already an established artist, settled there. Douglas had been part of the Harlem Renaissance, during which artists of all races drew from African American culture to develop a repertoire of aesthetic forms as a comment on the American experience. Douglas followed the pattern of many African American artists who moved from rural regions of the country to northern or European cities, where there was more opportunity for them to show their work. This situation was somewhat ameliorated in the 1930s with the establishment of the Atlanta Annual, a competitive exhibition that included the work of black southern artists.

At the opposite end of the aesthetic spectrum from professionally trained artists are those known as outsider, naive, or folk artists. Without formal training, these artists often gain notoriety and enjoy successful careers once they are discovered. A notable example is Bill Traylor (c. 1856–1947), who was born into slavery in Benton, Alabama, and did not begin his artistic endeavors until the age of eighty-three. After leaving Benton in 1939, Traylor traveled to the state capital of Montgomery, where, virtually homeless, he began drawing animal figures on scraps of cardboard while sitting on street corners. He was discovered by Charles Shannon, a local artist, and supplied with materials. In 1940 the New South, an artist-run organization in Montgomery, sponsored Traylor's first exhibit. Some of his works include *Figures and Construction* (1941–42) and *Arched Drinker* (1939–40).

Bessie Harvey (1929–1994), a north Georgia native, was a self-taught artist whose unusual sculptural pieces captured the imagination of a national audience during the 1980s. Made from found wood and enhanced with paint, wood putty, shells, hair, cloth, and other items, her works have been collected by major museums such as the National Museum of American Art (now the Smithsonian American Art Museum) in Washington, D.C., and the Whitney Museum of American Art in New York City.

Another notable black folk artist is Lonnie Holley (1950–), who began his artistic career carving tombstones. Born in Birmingham, Alabama, Holley carved his first tombstones for his sister's children, who died in a house fire. After overcoming this personal tragedy, Holley continued to make

Bessie Harvey, *Washwoman,* c. 1981. Painted wood and attachments. African American artists in Appalachia range from self-taught visionaries such as Harvey to the formally trained and classically inspired.

art, working mostly with sandstone augmented with found materials. His images emphasize the spiritual world and his ancestral heritage. Holley was one of a few African American artists to be included in the Smithsonian Institution's landmark project *More Than Land or Sky,* an exhibition that attempted to capture the scope of contemporary art in the Appalachians.

See also: AFFRILACHIANS (RACE, ETHNICITY, AND IDENTITY); EXPATRIATE ARTISTS; SECTION OVERVIEW (RACE, ETHNICITY, AND IDENTITY).

—M. Anna Fariello and Sonny Smith, *Virginia Polytechnic Institute and State University*

Romare Bearden and Harry Henderson, *A History of African-American Artists from 1792 to the Present* (1993); David Adams Leeming, *Amazing Grace: A Life of Beauford Delaney* (1998); Steven Otfinoski, *African Americans in the Visual Arts* (2003).

American Scene Painting

American Scene painting, a major movement in American art in the 1930s and early 1940s, emphasized commonplace rural and urban subjects rendered in realistic styles. Commonly known as regionalism, within art-historical scholarship it is associated with the three major midwestern American Scene painters: Thomas Hart Benton, Grant Wood, and John Steuart Curry. As the movement swept America, many artists made sketching trips into Appalachian areas.

The history of American Scene painting in Appalachia actually begins earlier, in the 1920s, with oils and travel sketches by Benton, a Missourian and perhaps the best-known American artist of the period between the world wars. In the 1930s and 1940s, he traveled again in the region from Pennsylvania to Georgia, drawing steel mills, sawmills, and country musicians, among other subjects. Benton used his sketches as starting points for canvases and murals, including the mural project *America Today* (1930) for the New School for Social Research in New York. He anticipated other artists, including Howard Cook of Massachusetts and Chicago native Aaron Bohrod, who also executed works developed from sketching trips in the region.

Overshadowing artists' reliance on European modernism, the American Scene aesthetic reflected the national inclination during the Great Depression to focus on American life. Richard Coe and Roderick McKenzie of Alabama executed paintings of steel mills in Birmingham. Lamar Dodd, after moving back to his native Georgia, ventured into painting scenes of the coal and copper industries in Tennessee. The art colony of Woodstock, located in the Catskill Mountains of New York, became a center of the American Scene movement. There and in nearby communities, Alexander Brook, Arnold Blanch, Andrée Ruellan, John Taylor, and others painted quiet, realistic landscapes and townscapes laden with atmospheric effects of nature.

The most far-ranging, visible aspects of American Scene painting in Appalachia are the post office murals sponsored by the federal government's Section of Fine Arts (1934–43) and scattered in the region in small cities and towns. Subjects include views of workers, especially in industry or farming, scenes of the countryside or town, and events of local historical significance. Artists chosen to create murals were frequently well-known painters trained at leading American art schools.

See also: BENTON, THOMAS HART; DODD, LAMAR; REGIONALISM.

—Patricia Phagan, *Vassar College*

Matthew Baigell, *The American Scene: American Painting of the 1930s* (1974); Marlene Park and Gerald E. Markowitz, *Democratic Vistas: Post Offices and Public Art in the New Deal* (1984); Patricia Phagan, ed., *The American Scene and the South: Paintings and Works on Paper, 1930–1946* (1996).

Appalachian Expositions

The Appalachian Expositions were part of a number of extensive regional fairs that took place in America in the late nineteenth and early twentieth centuries. Between 1881 and

1915, regional expositions were held in Atlanta (1881, 1895), New Orleans (1885), and Norfolk (1907) and Richmond (1915), Virginia. In Knoxville, Tennessee, the city's Commercial Club funded two influential expositions in 1910 and 1911 with displays reflecting the theme "The Pride of the Appalachians." These expositions provided an opportunity to show that the South had recovered from the devastation of the Civil War and was committed to national loyalty and the abatement of racial tension. Emphasis was placed on presenting the South and southern Appalachia as sophisticated regions.

The Knoxville fair opened in 1910 in Chilhowee Park with six main buildings and several smaller structures containing business, industrial, agricultural, and cultural displays. During the 1910 and 1911 expositions, the art section was relegated to the Administration Building, which limited the size of exhibitions. Knoxville painter Lloyd Branson chaired the 1910 exhibition with the assistance of James Henry Moser, an artist from Washington, D.C., who organized an exhibition of painting from that city. Knoxville photographer Joseph Knaffl organized the photography exhibition, and members of the Nicholson Art League, a local arts appreciation organization, served as the art committee. Artists from south of the Ohio River were solicited to participate.

As with the Nashville Centennial Exposition of 1897, the Appalachian Expositions were the first opportunity for many Knoxville residents to see work by artists of both regional and national distinction. In 1910 a gold medal was given to William Gilbert Gaul for his painting *Skirmish Line;* to Lloyd Branson went the Nicholson Art League award for the best original oil; and impressionist painter Catherine Wiley won the Dr. H. J. Cook medal for "most meritorious collection from the Appalachian territory."

The following year, Branson took advantage of the Nicholson Art League's membership in the American Federation of Art. A national organization that provided loan exhibitions to member groups at reduced rates, the American Federation of Art supplied the bulk of the artwork for the 1911 exhibition. Unlike the art exhibition of the previous year, which had emphasized realist painting, the Appalachian Exposition of 1911 was dominated by the more contemporary work of the nationally recognized American impressionists, including Childe Hassam, Mary Cassatt, and Robert Reid. Works were again solicited from south of the Ohio for the "Appalachian Territory" section. Nashville-based Ella S. Hergesheimer won the award for the best group of paintings by a southern artist.

In 1913 the National Conservation Exposition was held in Knoxville, and again the American Federation of Art provided a contemporary art exhibition for the fair, this time incorporating the work of urban realists. Catherine Wiley chaired the art exhibit, which had its own building. In 1914 the exposition was little more than a Labor Day picnic and in 1915 the first East Tennessee Fair took place, beginning a tradition that continues to this day. The next major exposition to take place in Knoxville was the World's Fair of 1982.

See also: ART ASSOCIATIONS AND CLUBS; KNOXVILLE, TENNESSEE (TOURISM); PUBLIC ART PROGRAMS.

—Celia S. Walker, *Cheekwood Museum of Art*

Art Associations and Clubs

Membership associations and clubs founded to support an appreciation of the arts flourished in America at the turn of the twentieth century. Association members met regularly to discuss art and exhibit their work. Some redirected their focus to the community and devoted their organizations to the development of citywide art education. Eventually, many were subsumed by privately or state-funded institutions such as university art programs and museums.

Most larger cities in and outside of Appalachia were able to support art associations and clubs. Many were initiated after the Civil War, as communities set to the important work of Reconstruction. The Nashville Art Association (1883) and the Knoxville Art Circle (c. 1885) were two of the earliest Tennessee-based groups. Others were founded later but were long lasting, including the Associated Artists of Pittsburgh, which began in 1910 and continued its existence until 1985. Many art associations were all-volunteer groups; some left few records of their activities.

The art collections of many such associations and clubs became the core of their cities' art museums. For example, the Mississippi Museum of Art in Jackson developed out of the Mississippi Art Association (founded in 1911); the Montgomery Museum of Fine Arts began as the Alabama Society of Fine Arts (founded in 1930); and Atlanta's High Museum of Art formed from the Atlanta Art Association (founded in 1905).

In Knoxville the Nicholson Art League grew out of the Sketch Club (1881), an organization of art students led by painter Lloyd Branson, who traveled to nearby locales to paint outdoors in the Barbizon style. The group became the Knoxville Art Circle in the mid-1880s, later changing its name to the Nicholson Art League in memory of Major Calvin Hunter Nicholson, a financial patron and former club president. The league was instrumental in organizing regional art exhibitions as part of the Appalachian Expositions held in Knoxville in 1910 and 1911. When the Great Depression wiped out the league's treasury in the early 1930s, its art collection became the property of Hans Dulin. The collected works later formed the basis of the Dulin Gallery of Art, founded in 1961, the predecessor of the Knoxville Museum of Art.

See also: APPALACHIAN EXPOSITIONS; SOUTHEASTERN COLLEGE ART CONFERENCE; SOUTHERN STATES ART LEAGUE.

—Celia S. Walker, *Cheekwood Museum of Art*

Art Museums

See Art Museums (Cultural Institutions)

Benton, Thomas Hart

(1889–1975) Painter and printmaker.

Thomas Hart Benton made many drawings of Appalachia in the 1920s and 1930s. Born into a political family in Neosho, Missouri, in 1889, Benton studied at the Art Institute of Chicago in 1906–7 and the Académie Julian in Paris from 1908 to 1911. He taught at the Art Students League in New York from 1926 to 1934 and afterwards at the Kansas City Art Institute from 1935 to 1941.

In the 1930s and 1940s, the farm scenes of American life painted by Benton and fellow midwesterners John Steuart Curry and Grant Wood attracted great popular attention and exerted a strong influence on American artists. Their midwestern regionalism became a major part of the American Scene movement. Less well known is Benton's relationship to Appalachia through family ties to the mountainous regions of Tennessee and the Carolinas and through his art.

Beginning with his first sketching trip to Appalachia in 1928, Benton documented industrial and rural scenes and captured pastimes that were slowly disappearing. Steel mills, mines and miners, paper mills, lumber operations, Holiness services, and country musicians were among his subjects. Many works from this and subsequent trips became the basis for well-known prints and paintings (such as *Cradling Wheat*) and murals. Benton traveled in the Appalachian areas of Pennsylvania, West Virginia, Virginia, Kentucky, Tennessee, Georgia, and North Carolina. His impressions and several drawings can be found in his autobiography, *An Artist in America*, first published in 1937, in a chapter entitled "The Mountains."

See also: AMERICAN SCENE PAINTING; REGIONALISM.

—Patricia Phagan, *Vassar College*

Beyer, Edward

(1820–1865) Painter.

German artist Edward Beyer created the sketches and paintings of Virginia published as lithographed copies in the influential *Album of Virginia*, issued in 1857 and 1858. Trained in Dusseldorf, Beyer worked in Dresden before leaving Germany during the revolutions of 1848–49. He settled first in Philadelphia but moved to Cincinnati in 1853. In 1854 Beyer began to sketch the Virginia landscape to prepare for the publication of a portfolio of prints. In 1857 the first copies were shipped from Germany, where the lithographs were made, to Richmond, Virginia.

The portfolio contains a title page and forty plates. The title page includes vignettes of Monticello, Mount Vernon, a farm, a train emerging from a tunnel, and the Roman goddess Virtus holding an American flag. The views pictured on the portfolio plates focus on three aspects of Virginia: natural landscapes, vacation resorts, and feats of engineering. Beyer portrayed the natural landscape romantically; views of Natural Bridge, Weyers Cave, and mountain vistas in western Virginia are typical examples. Beyer also depicted the many resorts that developed around natural hot springs in the Blue Ridge Mountains. These images feature handsome hotels and cottages, coaches, and people riding horses and strolling on foot. Beyer also drew several engineering feats, including the James River and Kanawha Canal and the railroad bridge near Farmville.

In 1858 Beyer traveled to Germany, never again returning to America. He settled in Meissen and exhibited a cyclorama based on his American views. Beyer's *Album* remains an important source for visual information about the antebellum Virginia landscape and is regarded as one of the finest series of landscapes of nineteenth-century America.

See also: ITINERANT PAINTERS; NATURALIST ILLUSTRATORS; SCENIC ILLUSTRATION.

—Georgia B. Barnhill, *American Antiquarian Society*

Black Mountain College

See Black Mountain College (Education)

Catesby, Mark

(c. 1680–1749) Naturalist and illustrator.

Born in England, Mark Catesby contributed some of the most influential observations on the natural history of North America, including Appalachia, in the eighteenth century. His interest in horticulture stemmed from visits to his uncle Nicholas Jekyll's botanical garden and was nurtured by relationships with renowned naturalist John Ray and apothecary Samuel Dale.

During a period of scientific and cultural exchange between England and the American colonies, Catesby visited Virginia and the Carolinas (present-day North and South Carolina and Georgia) to gather information on native plants and animals. Between the years 1712 and 1726, he interacted with influential colonial Americans who were also interested in the promotion of natural history. Catesby conducted field research, collected seeds and specimens, and sketched and drew a variety of native plants, birds, fish, insects, snakes, and other forms of American animal life. Upon

Mark Catesby, *The Mock-Bird,* c. 1730. Hand-colored etching. Catesby's meticulous illustrations of flora and fauna provide some of the most useful documentation of Appalachia's natural history available from the eighteenth century.

his return to England, he sought financial backing to publish his observations and drawings. After finding the cost of hiring a professional engraver prohibitive, Catesby taught himself to etch and produced nearly 220 illustrations.

Catesby was the first artist to document North American plant and animal life in their natural habitat. The culmination of his efforts resulted in the two-volume *Natural History of Carolina, Florida, and the Bahama Islands.* First published between 1731 and 1743, it remains a seminal work of natural history.

See also: NATURALIST ILLUSTRATORS.

—Laura Pass Barry, *Colonial Williamsburg Foundation*

Civil War Illustrators

Appalachia saw its share of fighting throughout the Civil War, and artists were there to document for publication and posterity the drama and horror of the nation's most devastating conflict. They witnessed small skirmishes and major battles across the mountains of Virginia, West Virginia, Maryland, Tennessee, Kentucky, Georgia, and North Carolina. They produced eyewitness sketches portraying the battles of Philippi, Rich Mountain, South Mountain, Antietam, Cumberland Gap, Resaca, Winchester, and Cedar Creek, among many others. These sketches add immeasurably to the understanding of military life during the Civil War, giving character to the soldiers and citizens of Appalachia and the land where they lived, fought, and died.

Compelling and distinctive, Civil War drawings were the only means by which the public could have ready access to images of the war. From encampments and battlefields, drawings were dispatched by horse, ship, and train to the publisher's office, where teams of engravers copied them into woodblocks for printing in weekly newspapers. Usually it took three to four weeks for the drawn image to appear in print. Photographers and printmaking firms, such as Currier and Ives, also made thousands of images for public consumption, but at the time the technology did not exist to reproduce either photographs or lithographs as newspaper illustrations. Shutter speeds were too slow to capture movement, while lithographs took more time and money to produce than wood engravings. Therefore, newspaper editors depended on a network of salaried, freelance, and amateur artists in the field to sketch the war and define its progress for their readers.

Among the "special artists" who drew the war for the nation's illustrated newspapers were nationally celebrated artists and illustrators Winslow Homer, Thomas Nast, Alfred Waud, Edwin Forbes, and Theodore Davis. While Homer and Nast ventured only intermittently to the front, Waud and Davis were among the few intrepid sketch artists who relentlessly followed Union armies through four years of warfare on foot and in the saddle. Due to chronic paper shortages and a severely limited publishing industry during the war, Confederate sketch artists were rare; the most prominent and prolific among them was the Englishman Frank Vizetelly.

Eyewitness sketches of the Civil War produced for the American pictorial press remain an invaluable reference tool for students of American history. Although some drawings were derived from photographs or accounts given to the artist after the fact, the majority were accurate, eyewitness records of historic figures and events. These on-site sketches provide a comprehensive visual record of military life from the entrance of Union recruits into Washington, D.C., in the spring of 1861 to the surrender of Confederate General Robert E. Lee at Appomattox Courthouse four years later.

See also: CIVIL WAR (GOVERNMENT); GLASS PLATE PHOTOGRAPHY; STROTHER, DAVID HUNTER.

—Harry Katz, *Library of Congress*

Robert T. Cochran Jr., "Witness to a War: Century-Old Woodcuts and Words Preserve a British Correspondent's Experiences in the U.S. Civil War," *National Geographic* (April 1961); Allen L. Tischler, *Alfred R. Waud in the Shenandoah Valley* (1997).

Contemporary Crafts

See Contemporary Crafts (Crafts)

Contemporary Native American Art

Contemporary Native American art in the Appalachian region is often associated with the Qualla Boundary in North Carolina, home to a population of approximately nine thousand Cherokee. Members of other Native American nations found in Appalachia include the Chickasaw, Choctaw, Creek, Catawba, Lumbee, Seminole, and Shawnee. Native Americans from other regions, such as the Southwest or Canada, have also settled in Appalachia due to relocation programs of the 1940s and 1950s as well as employment opportunities in the region. This has contributed to at least as many, if not more, native people living off of the reservation than on it. Native associations such as the Native American Alliance and the American Indian Movement are represented throughout the region, working to preserve cultural heritage, maintain native ties, and explore social, political, and cultural issues.

During the late nineteenth century, many Native Americans assimilated western European ideas about art and crafts into a variety of artistic forms and aesthetic expressions. Contemporary Native American art explores a multitude of social, cultural, and political issues that may or may not use native symbols, challenging the public to consider what it means to be a Native American artist. At one time, galleries refused to accept contemporary work that explored issues of Indian identity, assuming that the public would not accept anything other than recognizably traditional forms.

Contemporary Native American artists have multiple choices regarding styles, forms, materials, signs, and symbols. Some re-create inherited forms and patterns such as baskets, pottery, beadwork, blankets, quilts, wood and stone carvings, rattles, paintings, sculptures, and jewelry. Cherokee river-cane basket weaver Rowena Bradley is one of many such artists whose goal is to maintain tradition. For other artists, traditional designs, colors, and materials serve merely as guidelines to produce hybrid forms. Contemporary artist Joel Queen is noted for award-winning handcrafted clay pottery with angular structures that blends traditional and modern influences. Scholars claim that native art no longer adheres to aboriginal significance but serves economic, therapeutic, cultural, or identity functions.

Intertribal exchanges of materials and symbols are referred to as Pan-Indian. Cherokee artists such as the Teesatuskie brothers are known for their silver and turquoise Pan-Indian jewelry, even though turquoise is not indigenous to the Appalachian region but to the Southwest. Cooperatives such as the Qualla Arts and Crafts Mutual and outlets such as the Medicine Man Shop on the Qualla Boundary encourage the development and distribution of Native American arts and crafts.

See also: NATIVE AMERICAN ART, PRECONTACT; NATIVE AMERICAN ARTS AND CRAFTS (CRAFTS).

—Christine Ballengee-Morris, *Ohio State University*

Barbara Duncan, *The Cherokee Artist Directory* (2001); Laurence French and Jim Hornbuckle, eds., *The Cherokee Perspective* (1981).

Contemporary Painting

Though the region is widely known for its crafts, contemporary Appalachian painting remains all but unnoticed on a national level. Many who come to the region to teach in universities and colleges struggle for recognition outside of the network of university galleries across the country. A number of artists born in Appalachia have left home in search of professional training, artistic community, and career opportunity; others, in search of solitude, cheap studio space, and proximity to the natural world, have settled in pockets of the region.

After the end of national and regional National Endowment for the Arts fellowships in the mid-1990s, it became more difficult to take the pulse of regional contemporary art. Few identifiably Appalachian artists were exhibited by galleries or museums in art centers such as Pittsburgh, Cincinnati, Lexington, Louisville, Knoxville, Asheville, and Charlotte. Published catalogs on regional artists became relatively rare. The Southeastern Center for Contemporary Art (SECCA) in Winston-Salem, North Carolina, once focused on contemporary art in an eleven-state region, now covers the national art scene. While such long-running juried shows as the Mint Museum's *Biennial* and the *Dulin* (now Knoxville Museum of Art) *National Works on Paper Competition* have fallen by the wayside, others continue to serve as entry points for local talent. Some of these annual or biennial competitions include *Appalachian Corridors* at West Virginia's Sunrise Museum (now Avampato Discovery Center), *Positive/Negative* at East Tennessee State University, and the *Red Clay Survey* at the Huntsville Museum of Art. In such exhibitions, artists who choose to employ identifiable Appalachian subject matter—capturing the mountains and valleys, the people, or customary activities such as day-to-day labor, family or religious life, or storytelling and superstition—communicate their allegiance to place. But many works created in Appalachia purposely eschew a regional connection. Furthermore, large numbers of artists, following the national trend, have moved beyond pure painting to embrace digital technology, mixed-media installations, and video art.

The 1981 exhibition *More Than Land or Sky: Art from Appalachia* included sixty-nine artists from thirteen states. Approximately half of them were painters. Many of the older artists—such as George Cress (Tennessee), Angelo Ippolito (New York), Lester Pross (Kentucky), and William Kortlander (Ohio)—rendered the landscape in the stylized gestures of modernism. A number of the next generation, born in the 1930s and 1940s, whether transplanted or homegrown, gravitated towards realism and storytelling.

Painters working in the region today seem to divide along similar lines. Larry Chappelear (Maryland), William

Dunlap (Virginia), and Herb Jackson (North Carolina) capture the tangible power of the Appalachian landscape with a distanced elegance and varying degrees of abstraction. North Carolinians Maud Gatewood, Bob Timberlake, and Noyes Capehart Long offer visual diaries of fast-fading settings and people of the North Carolina mountains. Ed Kellogg and Jim Ann Howard, masterful observers working in the southeast corner of Tennessee, present exactingly realistic views of forest streams and rocky outcroppings at the southern end of the Appalachian system. Many artists who move into the region to teach at colleges and universities become energized by their surroundings and tune into cultural undercurrents. Figurative expressionists such as Art Rosenbaum, of Athens, Georgia, create backwoods narrative scenes; Virginia Derryberry, in Asheville, North Carolina, deals with human response to the elements of nature in nearly biblical terms.

During the 1980s and 1990s, the late folk preacher-artist Howard Finster's Paradise Gardens Park near Pennville, Georgia, became a regular mecca for arriving artists, opening their eyes to "outsider art" and influencing many to experiment with the folk idiom. Many folk painters in the region have been discovered and appreciated by trained artists who value their untouched imaginative and creative instincts.

As expatriate artists and writers have always known, distance often provides creative perspective. Two notable Appalachian-born artists, Michael Paxton (West Virginia) and Belinda Di Leo (Virginia), who moved away to earn advanced art school degrees, have produced strong bodies of work echoing their Appalachian heritage. Paxton's exhibition *From Enoch to Strange Creek* consisted of drawings and ghostly montages that traced generations of family history on gold-stained canvases. The exhibit previewed at the Chicago Cultural Center in 2000 before coming to West Virginia University in 2002. Di Leo's 1994 master of fine arts thesis exhibition for the University of California at San Diego, a series of somberly expressive canvases paired with family anecdotes and commentary on topics ranging from maiden aunts to belief in the afterlife, was posted on the Internet and spawned an international response.

See also: CONTEMPORARY SCULPTURE; EXPATRIATE ARTISTS; *MORE THAN LAND OR SKY.*

—Susan W. Knowles, *Nashville, Tennessee*

Barbara Shissler Nosanow, *More than Land or Sky: Art From Appalachia* (1981).

Contemporary Photography

Contemporary photographers have focused on documenting struggles and triumphs in the Appalachian Mountains as well as presenting the natural beauty of the region to the world. The number and variety of photographs have increased with the availability of better cameras and film, easier access from improved roads, and higher income levels of residents. Just as Walker Evans created a lasting picture of Great Depression–era Alabama while on assignment in the 1930s, many later photographs of the Appalachian region were produced by journalists covering the War on Poverty in the 1960s. These photographers generally sought out the poorest residents and focused on the negative aspects of the region, contributing to stereotypes still prevalent today. A number of photographers have captured the region and its people with dignity and understanding, however.

Joe Clark (1904–1989) was an Appalachian native who became a newspaper photographer in Detroit. Clark, who referred to himself as the "Hillbilly Snap Shooter," or "HBSS," returned home to Cumberland Gap, Tennessee, where he photographed his family and friends. His work was published in a 1965 book, *Back Home*, and in *Tennessee Hill Folk* in 1972. Clark's photographs were also published in prominent magazines, including *Life*, *Look*, and *Time*, making his work as an Appalachian photographer known worldwide. Non-native photographers have also captured images of Appalachian people with compassion. New York City schoolteacher Builder Levy spent several summer vacations with coal miners in West Virginia, Kentucky, and Pennsylvania, making photographs later published in *Images of Appalachian Coalfields* (1989). *Voices from the Mountains* (1975) combined song lyrics collected by Guy and Candie Carawan with photographs showing the changing world of the Appalachian people. It introduced the photography of Levy, along with that of Gordon Baer, Kris Mendenhall, Earl Palmer, Mike Clark, and Bill Strode to a large audience.

A number of photographers have continued the tradition of centering their work on issues of social justice. The ongoing work of Earl Dotter, photographer for the United Mine Workers of America's *UMWA Journal* from 1972 to 1977, documents the lives of workers in hazardous occupations. Rob Amberg works for nonprofit organizations such as the Farmer's Legal Action Group and has documented the effects of the construction of Interstate 26 through Madison County, North Carolina. Newspaper photographer Kenneth Murray has used a journalistic approach to capture images of farmers, miners, snake handlers, and other regional icons. His black-and-white photographs were published in two books by the Appalachian Consortium Press: *Down to Earth: People of Appalachia* (1974) and *A Portrait of Appalachia* (1985).

William Bake, a Michigan native living in North Carolina, specializes in color nature and scenic photography using a large-format camera. Bake is one of a number of photographers who have worked with writers to produce books with a regional focus, collaborating with James Dickey on *Wayfarer: A Voice from the Southern Mountains* (1988). Others include Shelby Adams, whose book *Appalachian Portraits* (1993) contains an essay by Lee Smith, and Warren Brunner, who worked with writer Loyal Jones on the book *Appalachian Values* (1992).

A contemporary photographer from the Appalachians, Sally Mann, is perhaps best known outside the region. Born in Lexington, Virginia, Mann achieved national prominence exhibiting a series of black-and-white images of her three children. Mann's work, which includes *At Twelve: Portraits of Young Women* (1988) and *Immediate Family* (1992), has been called controversial because her images of children contain references to violence and sexuality. Her later work focuses on the landscape, captured in large format prints.

Contemporary Appalachian photography can be found in several regional magazines, including *Blue Ridge Country*, *Now and Then*, and *Appalachian Heritage*. National magazines such as *Country* and *National Geographic* occasionally feature photographs of the region. Appalachian photographers continue to record daily life, social change, and natural beauty in the mountains for future generations.

See also: DIGITAL ARTS; FARM SECURITY ADMINISTRATION PHOTOGRAPHY; GLASS PLATE PHOTOGRAPHY.

—Randy Ball, *Rogersville, Tennessee*

Guy and Candie Carawan, eds., *Voices from the Mountains* (1975); Joe Clark, *Back Home* (1965); Builder Levy, *Images of Appalachian Coalfields* (1989).

Contemporary Sculpture

The Appalachian region is home to some of the nation's preeminent venues for the support of contemporary sculpture. Universities such as Alfred University in Alfred, New York, known for its exemplary training in the ceramic arts, Carnegie Mellon University, which encourages sculptors to break ground with new technologies in the arts, and the University of Georgia, which has facilities to support training in all major sculpture media, are representative of the range of sculptural opportunities encompassed in the region.

Great diversity, both conceptually and technically, distinguishes sculpture made by artists from the region. Some artists, such as the late self-taught Tennessee sculptor Bessie Harvey, are considered folk artists. Inspired by her faith, Harvey found materials such as sticks and tree roots on roadsides and made figures based on her experience as a domestic worker and mother of eleven children. Horace Farlowe, known for his outdoor installations, selects marble from the quarries of northwestern Georgia and uses traditional carving techniques to create massive abstract sculptures.

As elsewhere, Appalachian artists have increasingly made works that defy categorization. While traditional forms continue to be made, contemporary artists have extended both the historic and traditional to innovative directions, stretching motifs with variations on color, scale, and narrative. Such hybrid or crossover forms are grounded in contemporary artistic theory but built using traditional methods or traditional materials. Usually three-dimensional and of smaller scale, sculptural craft is found in communities that have evolved around regional craft schools such as the Penland School of Craft in North Carolina and the Appalachian Center for Crafts in Tennessee.

Contemporary southern Appalachian sculptors are supported by a number of regional organizations and institutions. The Tri-State Sculptors Guild hosts annual conferences and exhibitions, while a number of universities have organized outdoor sculpture programs and competitions. Appalachian State University in Boone, North Carolina, hosts the annual Rosen Outdoor Sculpture Exhibition, which draws entrants from throughout the region and the country. Each year ten new pieces are selected to grace the campus grounds. Throughout the 1980s, the University of Tennessee sponsored an annual sculpture purchase, placing contemporary sculpture throughout its Knoxville campus.

Contemporary sculpture by internationally recognized artists is represented in venues throughout the region; these include numerous sites in Pittsburgh, including the largest Louise Bourgeois sculpture in the United States, a large bronze fountain in a city park. The Birmingham Museum of Art in Alabama houses a sculpture collection that includes work by well-known sculptors such as Rodin, Beverly Pepper, Jacques Lipchitz, and Elyn Zimmerman. The Hunter Museum of American Art Sculpture Garden in Chattanooga, Tennessee, displays the sculpture of George Segal, John Henry, Alexander Calder, and Kenneth Snelson, among others.

See also: ART POTTERY (CRAFTS); FOLK ART; PUBLIC ART PROGRAMS; VISIONARY ENVIRONMENTS.

—Catherine Murray, *East Tennessee State University*

Daingerfield, Elliott

(1859–1932) Painter.

Best known for his mystical, poetic works, Elliott Daingerfield focused on the spiritual and symbolic value of painting. Prior to beginning a painting, he would reportedly pray to God "to produce pictures which would inspire the highest good." Daingerfield felt his artistic spirit was derived from the South, the subject of his truly symbolic works. He was influenced by Albert Pinkham Ryder's expressive brush strokes and George Inness's interest in religion. Daingerfield not only studied with these artists but also wrote about their art.

Also a printer, illustrator, teacher, writer, and lecturer, Daingerfield was born in Harpers Ferry, (West) Virginia, and reared in Fayetteville, North Carolina. At age twenty-one, he moved to New York City but began spending time in Blowing Rock, North Carolina, in 1866. Many of Daingerfield's paintings are allegorical. One of his major works is a series of mystical paintings set in the Grand Canyon that resulted from a commission by the Sante Fe Railway Company to paint images of the American Southwest. He also executed religious paintings, including a number of Madonnas, as well as a series of murals in the chapel of the Church of Saint Mary the Virgin in New York City. Daingerfield was elected to the Society of American Artists in 1903 and the National Academy of Design in 1906.

In 1884 Daingerfield married Roberta French, the daughter of a judge in Wilmington, North Carolina, and moved to Blowing Rock two years later to recuperate from an attack of diphtheria. In 1891 Roberta died during childbirth. Daingerfield remarried in 1895. In 1900 he completed Winwood, his second home in Blowing Rock. Daingerfield and his family moved to Carmel, California, in 1913. In 1916 he built his third summer home, Westglow, in Blowing Rock, and two years later he presented an altar picture to his church there. He died in 1932 of a heart attack.

See also: LANDSCAPE PAINTING; VISIONARY PAINTING.

—Frank E. Thomson, *Asheville Art Museum*

Decorative Painting

Decorative painting, which includes painted furniture, architectural features, and hand-lettered family records, is often overlooked as an art form. Although not unique to Appalachia, decorative painting could be found there at a time when few other visual art forms existed in the region, and examples are still found in homes of well-to-do families. In the absence of any institutional decorative painting centers, painters passed their skills from individual to individual. Because their work was not signed, the exact identity of many painters is unknown. Traveling artists, working on commission from home to home, created much of the region's early artwork. In the case of illustrated family records, decorative painting was most often the work of a schoolmaster or local minister.

Eighteenth- and nineteenth-century illustrated family records were created as documentation as well as a showcase for the maker's skill. Decorative documents provided information about such domestic events as births, marriages, and deaths. Meant primarily for the family, these records nevertheless were full of creativity and often occupied an important place in the home. They were lettered and painted by hand, sometimes with glitter paint, and penned with swirling lines and feathery designs.

Some family record forms, such as the fraktur, directly reflected European heritage. A fraktur combines calligraphic notations of important events with decorative watercolor painting utilizing German and Swiss traditional motifs, commonly the iron cross, tulips, hearts, and birds. Though fraktur artists' names are not known, in some instances it is clear that the same artist decorated several pieces. For example, many fraktur works from Wythe County, Virginia, are believed to be the work of the painter known as "the wild turkey artist." The fraktur is commonly found in Appalachian regions with populations of German heritage, especially in western Pennsylvania and the Shenandoah Valley of Virginia.

The valentine—a forerunner of the modern store-bought card—is another calligraphic form incorporating decorative painting that was often drawn and scripted by untrained suitors. Usually, a handwritten romantic message was framed by elaborate decorative motifs illustrated with colored inks and cutout patterns. An 1857 valentine by artist Lewis Miller is in the collection of the Montgomery Museum in Christiansburg, Virginia.

The form of decorative painting used to adorn family records and other paper-based calligraphic work extended to other surfaces, especially wood. Woodwork and furniture were often enhanced with painted symbols and motifs. Coloring a complete piece of furniture with single or multiple colors of paint was one such common practice. This technique allowed a piece of furniture to stand out from its surroundings or emphasized architectural details such as cornices and moldings. Other techniques, including paint graining (including marbleizing and smoke graining), were employed to make an inexpensive wood such as poplar or pine pass for mahogany or walnut. Sometimes furniture painting took on more intricate and elaborate forms. Decorative symbols and motifs—painted freehand, with a template and compass, or with stencils—embellished chests, boxes, and other pieces of furniture throughout the South in the early nineteenth century. A number of intriguing examples have been discovered in Appalachia, including an 1830s paint-decorated mantel from Washington County, Virginia.

See also: FOLK ART; ITINERANT PAINTERS; SCHOOLGIRL ART.

—Betsy White, *William King Regional Arts Center*

Cynthia Elyce Rubin, ed., *Southern Folk Art* (1985); Cynthia V. A. Schaffner and Susan Klein, *American Painted Furniture: 1790–1880* (1997).

Digital Arts

Appalachia is no longer a back road on the information superhighway. Advances in powerful computing technology and broadband access to the Internet, along with cutting-edge projects and programs, have helped make Appalachia's digital artists internationally competitive.

Much of the impetus in this field comes from the region's colleges and universities. Several schools have digital media programs, ranging in focus from simple image manipulation and desktop publishing to architectural 3-D tours and the creation of entirely new forms of art. Carnegie Mellon University in Pittsburgh maintains two programs, the Entertainment Technology Center and the Human Computer Interaction Center, that specialize in connecting artists and technologists. East Tennessee State University in Johnson City was one of the first colleges in the region to offer a four-year degree program in digital media. Because of these two institutions and others like them, Appalachian artists have gained recognition in the creation of multimedia works seen around the world.

K–12 schools in Appalachia also teach through computers. Some schools use videoconferencing (two-way video transmitted over the Internet) to link their schools to outside experiences that children cannot access otherwise, such as zoos, art museums, technical experts, and classes from other states and countries. Other programs, such as the Appalachian Media Institute, a project of Appalshop, teach students to record their experiences and culture using cameras and audio recording equipment. Through such activities, digital arts have had a profound impact on education in Appalachia.

Part of the impact of efforts such as these has been to provide new outlets for the creative arts that have long been a hallmark of Appalachian culture. Traditional as well as contemporary artists and craftsmen use digital media to share techniques and resources with others located throughout the world. This same connectivity also helps to increase the market for the products these artists create.

Digital photography, while an end in itself for some artists, also helps to market the products of craftsmen who work in purely physical media. Digital photography no longer requires equipment that is priced out of the reach of most artists, as digital still cameras have steadily increased in quality and decreased in price. Many photographers now supplement their film work with digital cameras. While the latter require some skill, they do not require expensive darkroom equipment and extensive knowledge of traditional photography. A powerful personal computer with the appropriate software, a high-resolution printer, and good training manuals allow artists to produce images that can be captured easily, manipulated artistically, reproduced indefinitely, and marketed globally.

Digital video has allowed many Appalachian filmmakers to expand the scope of both their work and their audience. Digital movie cameras have followed digital still cameras in the trend towards higher quality and lower price. Combined with the increased processing power of personal computers, this has allowed people to produce films of higher technical sophistication by eliminating time-consuming and expensive film processing and postproduction editing. Digital video has made films about or by Appalachians both more accessible and more professional in appearance. An increasing number of filmmakers whose works are distributed by Appalshop and Bullfrog Films use digital video cameras and editing techniques. These include director Teresa Konechne's *This Black Soil: A Story of Resistance and Rebirth* and Tom Hansell's *Coal Bucket Outlaw*.

Digital audio has also benefited from the increase in processing power and reduction in price of the equipment. While the seminal fieldwork of Joseph Sargent Hall, who in the 1930s recorded the life stories of hundreds of individuals in the Great Smoky Mountains, was done with equipment that filled the back of a pickup truck, the equipment used by contemporary researchers to capture stories and songs has shrunk in size to recorders that fit in a shirt pocket.

See also: CONTEMPORARY PHOTOGRAPHY; ON-LINE MEDIA (MEDIA).

—Todd O. Doman, *East Tennessee State University*, and Greg Wallace, *Bluff City, Tennessee*

Dodd, Lamar

(1909–1996) Painter and educator.

Working and teaching at the southern edge of the Appalachian region, Lamar Dodd provided opportunities for generations of art students to study closer to home than was previously possible and influenced those Appalachian artists who sought mainstream acceptance. Born in 1909 and reared in LaGrange, Georgia, Dodd studied briefly at the Georgia Institute of Technology before leaving the South in 1928 to pursue professional art training at the Art Students League in New York. In 1937 he moved to Athens, Georgia, to teach at the University of Georgia, where he became head of the new Department of Art, a position he held for thirty-five years. While at the University of Georgia, Dodd went on sketching expeditions into the mountains of Georgia and Tennessee. One of his most famous works is a view of the blasted hillside of Copperhill, Tennessee, an area so ravaged by copper mining that nothing green appears in his image of what was once a lush Appalachian vista.

Early in his painting career, Dodd, along with Anne Goldthwaite of Alabama, was hailed by *Life* magazine as a leader in the "arts renaissance" in the South. His paintings and drawings from the 1930s and 1940s betray the synthesis of the Ashcan school's reliance on a dark, somber palette with the American Scene's lighter subjects and themes. Influenced by abstract expressionism, Dodd's mature style became looser, brighter, and more expressive during this period.

Throughout his career, Dodd oversaw the consolidation and growth of the Department of Art at the University of Georgia and, in that capacity, served as president of the College Art Association for two terms in the early 1950s. In the 1960s, he served as an official artist for the National Aeronautics and Space Administration and recorded the earliest flights of the nation's astronauts. Arts advocate, administrator, educator, and artist, Dodd died in 1996, the year he was honored by the transformation of his beloved department into the Lamar Dodd School of Art at the University of Georgia.

See also: AMERICAN SCENE PAINTING.

—William Underwood Eiland, *Georgia Museum of Art*

Evans, Walker

(1903–1975) Photographer.

Walker Evans's photographic style was direct, almost confrontational, especially in the pictures of the dispossessed and poverty-stricken sharecroppers of rural Appalachia. His work with writer James Agee reveals a narrative urge behind his photographs, but Evans preferred stories without incident and without pretense, the bare facts of an unflinching vision.

Born in St. Louis at the beginning of the twentieth century, Evans spent his youth in Chicago, New York City, and Toledo, Ohio. Although he was not Appalachian, Evans's photographs came to define the region for much of the American public. In 1935 he began working for the Resettlement Administration, later the Farm Security Administration, and made photographs in the South over the next four years as part of the survey of rural America undertaken by the agency. On leave from the Resettlement Administration in the summer of 1936, he joined Agee in a text-photo project for *Fortune* magazine on sharecroppers in the Appalachian South. The two lived for two months in Hale County, Alabama (Agee with a family of sharecroppers and Evans at a local hotel), but the editors at *Fortune* rejected the article for publication. The project was eventually expanded and published as *Let Us Now Praise Famous Men* in 1941. The highly influential book focused on a group of families whose poverty and ties to the soil became synonymous with life for white tenant farmers in southern Appalachia.

See also: AGEE, JAMES (LITERATURE); FARM SECURITY ADMINISTRATION PHOTOGRAPHY; FEDERAL ARTS PROJECT.

—William Underwood Eiland, *Georgia Museum of Art*

Expatriate Artists

Appalachian expatriate artists are those born and/or reared in Appalachian states but who left their birthplaces in order to pursue artistic endeavors. Financial considerations are one of the primary reasons artists have left the region; however, sexism and racial prejudice have also played key roles. From the early nineteenth to the mid-twentieth century, many artists left to study in various European countries, while others opted to stay in the United States and pursue art careers outside Appalachia. Although diverse in their artistic works, many of these expatriates shared a common bond: most did not return, and the art of those who did reflected where they had gone to rather than where they had come from originally.

Many African American and women artists left the region for areas that generally allowed them more freedom of personal expression. Beauford Delaney (1901–1979) left his home in Knoxville, Tennessee, to study painting in Massachusetts and eventually moved to France, where he died in 1979. Delaney is regarded as one of America's leading abstract painters and was friends in Paris with other American expatriates, including writers Henry Miller and James Baldwin, whom he painted in 1965.

As the century progressed, artists increasingly obliterated associations to the region from their work in favor of a universal voice. Shedding their hometowns, many shed regional identities as well. Cy Twombly, born in Lexington, Virginia, in 1928, is often included in mainstream art history texts, but he is rarely identified as an Appalachian artist. Twombly is best known for expressionist and surrealist paintings and drawings, though he also creates abstract sculptures. After studying art in Boston and New York, Twombly returned to Appalachia in 1951 to study at Black Mountain College, near Asheville, North Carolina. Although he lives part-time in Lexington, Twombly has a reputation as an international artist, and spends considerable time in France, Germany, and Italy.

During the nineteenth and twentieth centuries, Pittsburgh was birthplace of three well-known artists who are not usually associated with Appalachia: Mary Cassatt, Henry Ossawa Tanner, and Andy Warhol. Mary Cassatt (1844–1926) left the United States in 1865 and traveled to Europe to study art. Given that men largely dominated the arts during the nineteenth century, Cassatt's family was surprised by her career decision. From 1865 to 1874, Cassatt studied in Paris, Rome, Parma, and Seville, finally making Paris her home in 1874. It was during this period that the French painter Edgar Degas noticed Cassatt's works and invited her to join the impressionists. She became the only American whose works, including *Woman in a Loge* (1878–79) and *Driving* (1881), appeared in the impressionist exhibitions of 1879, 1880, 1881, and 1886. Although greatly influenced by the impressionists, Cassatt continued to paint modern depictions of mothers and children. After 1886, she became involved in the *peintres-graveurs* (painters-printmakers) movement and went on to produce such work as *The Letter* (1890–91).

Pittsburgh was also the birthplace of Henry Ossawa Tanner (1859–1937), who began his art studies in 1879 at the Pennsylvania Academy of Fine Arts. In 1891 Tanner left America for Paris and began his studies at the Académie Julian. Early in his career, Tanner's racial identity influenced his artistic style, through which he created sympathetic portrayals of African Americans in works such as *The Banjo Les-*

son (1893). After a brief trip to Philadelphia in 1893, Tanner returned to Paris, abandoned his early African American art influences, and began painting biblical scenes such as *Daniel in the Lions' Den* (1895), for which he would later become famous. Although Tanner spent the majority of his life in France, he kept close ties to the United States and contributed greatly to African Americans' struggle for racial equality. In 1923 the French government named him a chevalier of the Legion of Honor.

Arguably the most prominent of the Pittsburgh artists, Andy Warhol (1928–1987) defined the movement known as pop art during the 1960s. Warhol began his formal art studies at the Carnegie Institute of Technology. In 1949 he moved to Manhattan and began a career doing illustration work for magazines and store windows. His first exhibition in an art gallery took place in 1962, when the Ferus Gallery in Los Angeles showed his *32 Campbell's Soup Cans* (1961–62). By using techniques previously associated with commercial art production, Warhol opened a new avenue of expression for artists worldwide.

See also: ANDY WARHOL MUSEUM (CULTURAL INSTITUTIONS); PITTSBURGH, PENNSYLVANIA (URBAN APPALACHIAN EXPERIENCE).

—Sonny Smith, *Virginia Polytechnic Institute and State University*

Romare Bearden and Harry Henderson, *A History of African-American Artists from 1792 to the Present* (1993); Victor Bockris, *Warhol: The Biography* (1997); Debra N. Mancoff, *Mary Cassatt: Reflections of Women's Lives* (1998).

Farm Security Administration Photography

Franklin D. Roosevelt was elected to the presidency in 1932 on the promise of "a new deal for the American people." Intended to promote economic recovery and social reform, numerous programs and federal bureaucratic agencies were set up under the New Deal to lift the nation from the Great Depression. Many of these relied on photography to document both the need for federal aid and its positive impact on communities. Appalachia, as a particularly underprivileged rural region, became the subject of many photographic assignments by federal agencies.

The photography projects undertaken by the Resettlement Administration, later renamed the Farm Security Administration, have come to exemplify New Deal documentary photography and have become part of the iconography of the Great Depression. New Deal projects were funded through other federal departments as well. The United States Department of Agriculture, the Tennessee Valley Authority, and such New Deal agencies as the Treasury Department Section of Painting and Sculpture (renamed the Section of Fine Arts in 1938), the Work Progress Administration, the Bureau of Agricultural Economics, the Rural Electrification Administration, and the Civilian Conservation Corps all employed photographers to document the region.

The Resettlement Administration began in 1935 to coordinate rural relief activities and land-use administration. In 1937 the agency was subsumed under the Department of Agriculture and renamed the Farm Security Administration. The agency's photographic project, officially titled Historical Section–Photographic, was part of the Information Division responsible for all publicity pertaining to the Resettlement and Farm Security Administrations.

Project director Roy Stryker ensured wide distribution of the photographs by creating an extensive network involving journalists, editors, and publishers. He employed professional photographers, including Walker Evans, Marion Post Walcott, Ben Shahn, Arthur Rothstein, John Vachon, Jack Delano, and Dorothea Lange, all of whom shot assignments in the Appalachian region. The Farm Security Administration set a high artistic standard that landed its photographs on the pages of *Time*, *Life*, *Fortune*, *Today*, and *Look*. The parent agency's Information Division also utilized the images for its own publicity exhibits and publications.

Mining and miner's strikes from the coal mines of West Virginia to the copper mines in Ducktown, Tennessee, were favorite Appalachian subjects for Shahn and Walcott; Evans's images of sharecroppers in Hale County, Alabama, on the southern edge of Appalachia, were some of the most widely circulated. These Farm Security Administration photographs captured a wide variety of subjects against rural backdrops including homes, front porches, farms, town halls, courthouses, general stores, and railway stations.

While good will for the parent agency was a major justification for the photographic projects, the photographs' captions, their selective use in exhibits, and their distribution to national media often reflected a bias toward certain kinds of images. Still, the scope of these photographs attests to the broad latitude Stryker accorded the photographers in subject choice and composition, resulting in a wider spectrum of images than strictly required for government propaganda.

See also: EVANS, WALKER; FEDERAL ARTS PROJECT; MURALS, NEW DEAL.

—Ajay Kalra, *East Tennessee State University*

James Agee and Walker Evans, *Let Us Now Praise Famous Men* (1941); Andrea Fisher, *Let Us Now Praise Famous Women: Women Photographers for the U.S. Government, 1935 to 1944* (1987); F. Jack Hurley, *Portrait of a Decade: Roy Stryker and the Development of Documentary Photography in the Thirties* (1972).

Federal Arts Project

Established in 1935 under the Works Progress Administration, the Federal Arts Project was the first U.S. Government project substantially to subsidize the visual arts. Under the leadership of Holger Cahill, the massive program employed more than six thousand artists across the nation for a period of eight years. Federal Arts Project artists and bureaucrats promoted art education, established community art centers and galleries, and produced an enormous amount of original artwork. Employing painters, sculptors, muralists, craftsmen, and folk artists, the project popularized American folk art and celebrated the nation's frontier heritage.

The project worked in conjunction with other agencies—the Federal Music Project, Federal Writers' Project, and the Federal Theatre Project—to promote a distinctly American culture. Affiliated artists designed jacket covers for vinyl records, book covers, and posters and produced public art in post offices and other federal buildings; all of these works attempted to instill national pride in the midst of the Great Depression. Perhaps the most memorable products of this collaboration were Aaron Copland's musical tribute *Appalachian Spring* and the images used to promote it. Copland used the traditional Shaker hymn "Simple Gifts" as his leitmotif, while Federal Arts Project artists designed posters advertising the composition as well as its record jacket.

In Appalachia, traditional crafts such as split-oak baskets and patchwork quilts were rediscovered and elevated from the realm of the necessary to *objets d'art*. Responding in part to an increased interest in traditional and historic aesthetic forms from 1935 until 1942, the Federal Arts Project hired younger artists to catalog folk art specimens from European settlement through 1900 for the Index of American Design in order to document regional material culture. Additionally, the federal government employed folk artists in Appalachia, paying them a wage of $23.50 per week to teach at community centers and workshops. The program played a crucial role in promoting Appalachian folk art, showcasing the work in public exhibits in the region and throughout the country.

The Works Progress Administration constructed a number of public buildings in Appalachia, including federal courthouses, post offices, and national park structures. Professional artists received commissions to decorate these structures, many of which still exist. Murals, bas-reliefs, sculptures, prints, decorative metal work, and friezes were incorporated into the design of the buildings. Artists and craftsmen used graphic representations of local themes, motifs, and historic events to reflect regional distinctions. Typical examples of public art created by Federal Arts Project artists include works such as *Daniel Boone's Arrival in Kentucky* and *The Dark and Bloody Ground* (Kentucky); *Barn Raising* (New York); *Gathering Tobacco* (North Carolina); *Great Smokies and Tennessee Farms* and *The Partnership of Man and Nature* (Tennessee); and *The Miners* and *Old Time Camp Meeting* (West Virginia).

American Scene painting, which was a reaction against the modern European style, brought many artists to Appalachia. Producing mimetic and stylized representations of everyday life in the area, they celebrated the ideals of community, hard work, historical continuity, and democracy. Employed by the Federal Arts Project, artists specifically created works meant to appeal to working-class Americans. American Scene artists depicted men and women working, playing, and worshiping together. Appalachian images included scenes of coal mining, logging, gristmills, textile mills, steel mills, and farming. Some artists created a visual bridge between the past and present, as in Glenn M. Shaw's *Romance of Steel, Old* and *Romance of Steel, Modern* in Ohio. They incorporated historic-mythic figures such as Daniel Boone to embody the ideals of the region.

Federal Arts Project artists reverentially depicted New Deal programs in their public art. Many works of art, such as the play *Power* and the dozens of murals and posters celebrating the work of Tennessee Valley Authority, praised the work of the Roosevelt administration by depicting the federal government as a friend to the downtrodden.

Though the Federal Arts Project was short-lived, it produced an enormous body of work, much of which has never been displayed. While the project enhanced the careers of celebrated artists such as Diego Rivera, Thomas Hart Benton, and Jackson Pollock, it also legitimized the preservation of traditional crafts and regional material culture. The program enhanced the general public's awareness of art while promoting a positive image of America and regional identity. Though the Federal Arts Project began as an economic stimulus program, ultimately it fostered the notion that America could develop a national culture and that that culture should be celebrated.

See also: AMERICAN SCENE PAINTING; FARM SECURITY ADMINISTRATION PHOTOGRAPHY; FEDERAL FUNDING (CULTURAL INSTITUTIONS); MURALS, NEW DEAL.

—Michael E. Birdwell, *Tennessee Technological University*

Belisario R. Contreras, *Tradition and Innovation in New Deal Art* (1983); Francis V. O'Connor, *Federal Art Patronage, 1933–1943* (1966) and ed., *The New Deal Art Projects: An Anthology of Memoirs* (1972).

Finster, Howard

(1916–2001) Folk artist.

The Reverend Howard Finster was one of America's most widely recognized folk artists. His visionary works reflect strong biblical values and themes formed from his forty years as a Baptist preacher in Alabama and Georgia. Born in Valley Head, near Fort Payne in northeast Alabama, Finster pastored his first church in 1941. In 1961 he moved to Pennville, a small community outside of Summerville, in the mountains of northwest Georgia.

In 1970 Finster reported having a vision directing him to build Paradise Gardens Park around his home. The park features found objects that Finster embedded into mosaics, welded into sculptures, and painted with Bible verses. The Paradise Gardens Park and Museum, spanning more than two acres, has become the principal tourist attraction of Chattooga County.

Finster began his career as an artist in 1976, when he reported another vision inspired by a face he saw in the white paint he got on his thumb while painting a bicycle. The face told him to "paint sacred art." Many of Finster's works depict numerous copies of these visionary faces, which he called "resting souls." Finster is known for his "talking art," which preaches to the viewer through the biblically inspired words that decorate his works. The First Annual Howard Finster Fest began in Paradise Gardens in 1999 and is held in late May every year.

Finster's art has been shown at major galleries around the world. In 1984 his work was represented in the Venice Biennial. He appeared on *Good Morning America* and with Johnny Carson on *The Tonight Show* and was featured in numerous newspapers and magazines.

See also: FOLK ART; RELIGIOUS IMAGERY; VISIONARY ENVIRONMENTS; VISIONARY PAINTING.

—Elizabeth C. Fine, *Virginia Polytechnic Institute and State University*

J. F. Turner, *Howard Finster, Man of Visions: The Life and Work of a Self-Taught Artist* (1989).

Folk Art

The term *folk art* can refer to two fundamentally different forms of artistic creation. In its most traditional sense, folk art has been associated with the art of people who live in relatively remote places, such as the mountains of Appalachia, or those who live within a dominant society but maintain their own artistic, ethnic, social, religious, and racial identities, such as the Moravians who settled in North Carolina in the eighteenth century. Such artists pass technique and form from generation to generation within their group. In the twentieth century, however, the term *folk artist* has come to identify a different type of artist. These folk artists are prolific producers and have been embraced by American art institutions despite the fact that they possess little knowledge of the mainstream traditions of western European art. While such artists demonstrate little stylistic influence from academic traditions, they create similar material forms, including painting, sculpture, architectural decoration, and utilitarian objects. They are also known as self-taught, outsider, naive, or visionary artists.

Based on craft and Euro-American heritage, the preeminent traditional folk art practiced in Appalachia includes the making of baskets, furniture, carvings, pottery, textiles, and quilts. Although the making of handcrafted objects was a customary pioneer activity, by the mid-nineteenth century mass production had reduced the need for their creation. Yet folk art forms survived in parts of Appalachia and began to be noticed in the late nineteenth century. Kentucky's Berea College established a work-study program known as Fireside Industries, which taught students to make handmade objects that were offered for sale, thus promoting a revival of craft traditions. Other important institutions that encouraged this revival were the John C. Campbell Folk School in North Carolina (1925), the Hindman (1902) and Pine Mountain (1913) Settlement Schools in Kentucky, and the Pi Beta Phi Settlement School (1912) (now Arrowmont School of Arts and Crafts) in Tennessee.

Out of the settlement, folk, and missionary school movements, folk carving emerged as a dominant expressive form. Growing out of the pastime of whittling, this type of carving was redirected toward making saleable items. Under the direction of Murrial "Murray" Galt Martin (1902–), members of the community surrounding the John C. Campbell Folk School formed a group known as the Brasstown Carvers, among whom are represented several generations of the Brown and Hall families. The Brasstown Carvers are known for small animal figures and an occasional human form carved in a variety of woods supplied by the folk school. At the Pleasant Hill Academy in Tennessee, Margaret Campbell (c. 1896–1996) introduced carving to a mission school on the edge of the Sequatchie Valley. Polly Page (1913–) is known for her carvings of "Uncle Pink" and "Aunt Jenny," legendary ancestors who settled Pleasant Hill. Another Tennessean, Roy Pace of Greenbrier, makes human figures engaged in activities common to rural life.

While many carvers remain anonymous, the twentieth century has produced a plethora of gifted and celebrated self-taught folk artists. Best known among these is Edgar Tolson (1904–1984) of Kentucky. His celebrated *Fall of Man* series depicts eight biblical scenes, from Genesis to Revelation. Steeped in the Christian values that characterize much of Appalachia, Tolson's carvings relate directly to the paradoxical nature of southern fundamentalist religious doctrine. The spartan wooden figures, usually unpainted in a reductive and rigid style, stare without expression beyond the viewer. To balance such economy of means, a decorative and erotic tendency can be seen in his sculptures of animals and in his graphic portrayals of Adam and Eve in various sexual positions.

Shields Landon "S. L." Jones (1901–1997) of Hinton, West Virginia, was another wood-carver of distinction. Jones, familiar with whittling since boyhood, did not turn his attention full-time to the craft of wood carving until 1969. Using yellow poplar, black walnut, and maple highlights, Jones created animals and figures in a blocky, dynamic style.

An accomplished fiddler, he often depicted musicians and musical groups. Most notable, however, are his sculptures of life-sized heads. While the male heads seem to be self-portraits, the artist maintained that they are "everyman." Minnie (1934–) and Garland (1928–1997) Adkins began carving in Appalachian Kentucky in the early 1980s at their farm. Both created magical, sleek animal sculptures of unmatched elegance. Minnie's signature carving is the long-nosed majestic red fox. Garland's hallmark is the long-necked horse, often painted black.

Pottery making flourishes in Kentucky, North Carolina, and Georgia, where families such as the Meaders, from Mossy Creek, Georgia, have been making pottery since 1892. Lanier Meaders (1917–1998), Burlon Craig (1914–2002), a North Carolina potter, and Jerry Brown (1945–), an Alabama potter, have received National Folk Heritage Fellowships in recognition of the importance of their work to American culture. Self-taught folk artists sometimes take traditional materials and processes and create nontraditional forms. Georgia Blizzard (1919–2002), from Glade Spring, Virginia, made ceramic vessels that superficially appear as dark effigy figures unearthed from a pre-Columbian archeological site. Blizzard fashioned rounded women in traditional squatting poses from clay found near her home and gave them contemporary names such as *Annie from the Mountain* (1991).

Tennessee's William Edmondson (1874–1951) is celebrated for his limestone sculpture and was the first African American to have a solo exhibit at the Museum of Modern Art (1937). His work shows little similarity to folk art traditions, yet Edmondson is called a folk artist because he was self-taught. Many other self-taught artists, such as painter and sculptor Thorton Dial Sr. (1928–), from Bessemer, Alabama, demonstrate little connection to mainstream fine art. Howard Finster (1916–2001), for instance, constructed the visionary Paradise Gardens Park and Museum in northwest Georgia, and Bessie Harvey (1929–1994) made fantastic figures from tree branches and roots she found on roadsides near her home in Alcoa, Tennessee.

Folk art thrives in Appalachia in many forms. Unique sculptures continue to be made and appreciated for their ingenuity, beauty, and humor. More traditional forms thrive as well in the form of musical instruments, walking canes, whirligigs, and toys. Appalachian quilts, characterized by the use of vibrant colors and contrasting prints, are worked in a wide variety of materials. White oak is still used to make the classic Appalachian basket—simple, elegant, and functional in design.

See also: JOHN C. CAMPBELL FOLK SCHOOL (CRAFTS); SETTLEMENT, MISSION, AND SPONSORED SCHOOLS (EDUCATION); VISIONARY PAINTING.

—Annie Carlano, *Museum of International Folk Art,* and Carol Crown, *University of Memphis*

Lynda Roscoe Hartigan, *Made With Passion: The Hemphill Folk Art Collection in the National Museum of American Art* (1990); Chuck and Jan Rosenak, *Museum of American Folk Art Encyclopedia of Twentieth-Century American Folk Art and Artists* (1990).

Frerichs, William C. A.

(1829–1905) Painter.

William Charles Anthony Frerichs was one of the first painters to venture into the rugged wilderness of western North Carolina. Born in Ghent, then part of the Netherlands, Frerichs began his art studies at a young age at the Academy in The Hague. He later studied medicine at the University of Leyden and art at the Brussels Academy, completing his art studies with the Grand Tour of Europe.

Frerichs arrived in America in 1850. He lived for several years in Greenwich Village in New York City, where he came to know many of the artists associated with the Hudson River school. In 1854 Frerichs accepted an offer to teach art at Greensboro Female College (now Greensboro College). Relocating to North Carolina to assume his duties, he spent close to ten years teaching in Greensboro and traveling to western North Carolina on painting expeditions. Many of Frerichs's paintings were destroyed in a fire at the college in 1863.

During his ten years in North Carolina, Frerichs painted *Hiwassee Falls* in Cherokee County, North Carolina, and the French Broad River's *Falls of Tamahaka.* Both of these large oil paintings reveal a wild and active landscape, unspoiled and unpopulated. His similarly sized *Storm over the Blue Ridge* depicts an expansive landscape infused with mystery. Such an emotional approach links Frerichs to the nineteenth-century American landscape tradition in which painters attempted to capture the beauty of nature as industrial exploitation plundered natural resources.

During the Civil War, Frerichs was appointed to special duty with the Confederate Corps of Engineers to inspect iron mines and other works in the mountains. But the economic hardship of the Civil War and the loss of his artwork in the fire took their toll. In 1865 Frerichs returned to New York City and later moved to Staten Island, where he died in 1905.

Forty years after leaving North Carolina, in an interview with the *Newark News,* Frerichs vividly recalled his travels in the mountains of North Carolina and their rugged beauty. In the mid-nineteenth century, western North Carolina was still a frontier, travel was difficult, and Frerichs had his art materials and sketches stolen on more than one occasion.

See also: LANDSCAPE PAINTING; SCENIC ILLUSTRATION.

—Frank E. Thomson, *Asheville Art Museum*

Peter Hastings Falk, ed., *Who Was Who in American Art: 1564–1975* (1999); Estill Curtis Pennington, "Southern Landscape Painting, 1865–1925," *American Art Review* (November–December 1999).

From Africa to Appalachia

From Africa to Appalachia is a series of events organized by the From Africa to Appalachia Foundation and the Rose Center and Council for the Arts in Morristown, Tennessee, to celebrate Black History Month. Initiated in February 1989, the series was designed to increase awareness of and pride in the cultural heritage of the African American communities of upper east Tennessee. To convey the blending of African and Appalachian cultures, the celebration's logo is a map of the African continent overlaid with that of Tennessee.

A community-based organization, the From Africa to Appalachia Foundation was cofounded by grant writer Jovita Wells and Sammie Nicely, a visual artist from Russellville in east Tennessee, who works in various media including sculpture, drawing, and clay. In his pit-fired ceramic masks, Nicely fuses African and southern Appalachian art traditions to create visual images based in ritual and everyday life.

From Africa to Appalachia events are held at the Rose Center and Council for the Arts in Morristown, a community cultural center and museum serving the people of Hamblen County and the surrounding Lakeway area. The center, housed in an 1892 former school building, began operation in 1975. The annual celebration includes a monthlong visual arts exhibit; an evening performance by musical groups or storytellers; an opening reception with gospel music, guest speaker, historic recitation, and presentation of a community service award; an artist residency and other programs in the Hamblen County schools; and a closing reception featuring displays of artwork and crafts, secular and gospel music, and traditional foods prepared by community members.

See also: AFFRILACHIANS (RACE, ETHNICITY, AND IDENTITY); AFRICAN AMERICAN ARTISTS; SECTION OVERVIEW (RACE, ETHNICITY, AND IDENTITY).

—Bill Kornrich, *Appalachian Spring Cooperative*

Glass Plate Photography

Most early photographs of the Appalachian region were made using glass, or "wet," plate photography techniques. While a few larger cities had photographic studios, traveling photographers created glass plate photographs as they moved from community to community in Appalachia making and selling images. Few traveling photographers are remembered by name, as photography was regarded as a vocation more than an art. Many glass plate images were lost when the fragile glass negatives were broken, ruined by the elements, or cleaned and reused.

Beginning in 1851, photographers produced negative images on glass coated with a mixture of collodion and light-sensitive salts by bathing the plate in silver nitrate. Once sensitized, the plate had to be exposed before the resulting silver iodide solution dried. After exposure in the camera, the plate was developed and fixed, producing a negative image that allowed photographers to make several copies. The process initially demanded a nearby darkroom, but soon photographers ventured into more remote parts of the Appalachian Mountains by carrying the required equipment in packs or in wagons. The collodion process was the primary method of visual documentation until the early 1900s.

After the glass plate photographic process was replaced by the development of lighter-weight film, some photographers continued to use the cumbersome glass plates into the twentieth century. Their reasons varied. Some were more familiar with the traditional process, while others thought the results richer than the quicker, cheaper, newer processes. Doris Ulmann was one photographer who worked in the region using glass plates long after the new methods were available. At her death in 1934, she left thousands of glass plate images.

See also: PICTURE MEN; ULMANN, DORIS.

—Randy Ball, *Rogersville, Tennessee*

Aaron Sussman, *The Amateur Photographer's Handbook* (1973).

Graphic Arts

In the late eighteenth and early nineteenth centuries, when landscape scenery became popular in the United States, European and American artists made picturesque engravings, aquatints, and lithographs of Appalachian landscapes and towns. In their views of mountainous regions, they represented the American wilderness in compositions that relied on European traditions. Many of these prints recall the dramatic landscapes of contemporary English watercolorists.

The graphic arts include various printmaking processes such as engraving, etching, woodcutting, and lithography. Printed from a carved plank of wood, an incised metal plate, or a crayon-drawn lithographic stone, prints are generally made in multiples from an original work of art. They first appeared in Europe around the middle of the fourteenth century when paper became widely available; their major uses then were for playing cards and devotional images. In time, they became a means for circulating information.

In the nineteenth century, Americans purchased prints, especially inexpensively produced lithographs, with growing enthusiasm. In the 1820s, early Hudson River school painters in New York such as Thomas Cole designed lithographs featuring the Catskill Mountains. By mid-century, lithographs of Appalachia generally became more naturalistic,

Claire Leighton, *Untitled (Chopping Wood),* 1941. Wood engraving. Printmaking processes such as engraving, etching, woodcutting, and lithography provided a way for images of Appalachia to reach wide audiences. This example is an illustration from Leighton's book *Southern Harvest.*

with softer tones and expansive vistas. At this time, the successful company of Currier and Ives made lithographs of popular Appalachian views, including the Catskills, Natural Bridge in Virginia, the Susquehanna River in Pennsylvania, Lookout Mountain in Tennessee, and Tallulah Falls in Georgia. Throughout the century, newspapers featured the region in wood engravings.

In the early twentieth century, the presence of numerous artist-printmakers living in the art colony of Woodstock transformed the Catskill region of New York into a center of American printmaking. Peggy Bacon, Yasuo Kuniyoshi, and Konrad Cramer were among the better-known artists who made prints there. Artists also contributed vital woodcuts and linoleum cuts to local journals such as the *Plowshare* and *Hue and Cry*.

The early twentieth century also saw a proliferation of literature about the southern Appalachians, and although photography became the most frequently used medium for illustrations, the prints of graphic artists such as Thomas Hart Benton and Clare Leighton were reproduced as book illustrations. Continuing the tradition of their nineteenth-century counterparts by sketching the Appalachian region during the 1920s, 1930s, and 1940s, Benton produced lithographs and Leighton wood engravings that offer contrasting impressions of the region.

The artists toured some of the same Appalachian areas, and it is clear from their writings that both were acquainted with prevailing ideas used to categorize mountain people, including their "otherness." Benton published his impressions in a chapter titled "The Mountains" in *An Artist in America* (1937). In her book *Southern Harvest* (1942), Leighton likewise included a chapter entitled "The Mountains." In addition, Leighton's wood engravings for the multivolume *Frank C. Brown Collection of North Carolina Folklore* (1952–64) brought the customs and daily living of the mountain people to the public eye.

Benton's and Leighton's visual and literary impressions of mountain people were markedly diverse. Benton toured the Appalachian region beginning in 1928 to gather ideas for a pictorial history of industrial America and observed the effects that coal mining and textile mills were having on the native people. In "The Mountains," he wrote about the vices that accompanied industry, the natives' displacement, and their penchant for ecstatic religion. A few sympathetic character studies of individuals illustrate the text, but the remaining lithographs show families resting on the porches of derelict shacks or loitering at industrial sites. Lithographs and drawings not used in *An Artist in America* show that Benton observed the agricultural landscape in the mountains, yet the publication focused on the lawless, sensationalistic aspects of Appalachian people.

Leighton, by contrast, embraced mountain people and romanticized their agrarian way of life. An Englishwoman who helped revive the art of wood engraving, she viewed the relationship between man and manual labor, whether in craft or farming, as a sacred bond. *Southern Harvest* conveys the simple agrarian existence of Appalachian people that bound them with laborers of the soil worldwide. Leighton depicted them as "contemporary ancestors," a people whose values remained uncorrupted by modern civilization. Her visual and verbal images are intertwined to confirm her passion and empathy for the toilers of the earth. In the wood engraving known as *Chopping Wood,* Leighton's distinctive graphic style, which consists of flowing, rhythmic lines and strong contrasts of light and dark, depicts the woodchopper as one with the earth, as rooted to the soil as are the trees.

Howard Cook and his wife, Barbara Latham, were among other artists in the 1930s and 1940s who were interested in the distinctiveness of the region and who enthusiastically portrayed Appalachian culture. Traveling in 1934 and 1935 on Cook's Guggenheim Fellowship, they visited North Carolina, Kentucky, and Alabama, making prints documenting craft activities of mountain people and scenes in Birmingham's steel mills. Benton, Leighton, and Cook's insightful portrayals of the people of the southern Appalachian region were not to be matched during the second half of the twentieth century. However, centers for printmaking in Appalachia continue to thrive, especially at the Penland School of Crafts in Penland, North Carolina.

See also: AMERICAN SCENE PAINTING; BENTON, THOMAS HART; SCENIC ILLUSTRATION.

—Caroline M. Hickman, *Washington, D.C.*, and Patricia Phagan, *Vassar College*

Gloria-Gilda Deak, *Picturing America, 1497–1899* (1988); Caroline M. Hickman, "Graphic Images and Agrarian Traditions: Bayard Wootten, Clare Leighton, and Southern Appalachia," in *Graphic Arts and the South: Proceedings of the 1990 North American Print Conference*, ed. Judy Larson and Cynthia Payne (1993); Patricia Phagan, ed., *The American Scene and the South: Paintings and Works on Paper, 1930–1946* (1996).

Graveyard Art

Appalachian cemetery sculpture and graveyard traditions are shaped by many influences, among them location and resources, ethnicity, societal status, religion, technology, and artistic taste. The region's graveyards range from small family burial plots to large, professionally managed urban cemeteries, and grave monuments run the gamut from humble fieldstone and wooden markers to imposing mausoleums and marble statuary. In these respects Appalachian graveyards are not atypical, yet the region harbors many distinctive traditions.

The first traditions belonged to Native American groups. Burial mounds dotted the ancient landscape and were the subject of much later speculation, including by Thomas Jefferson. Some groups erected pitch-roofed burial sheds that have been proposed as a source for the gravehouses later erected by Appalachian whites and blacks as well as natives. Within a few decades of European settlement talented folk carvers emerged. The Scots-Irish Bigham family stonecutters settled on the Carolina frontier in the 1760s and adorned their soapstone memorials with exquisitely carved animals, coats of arms, and patriotic symbols.

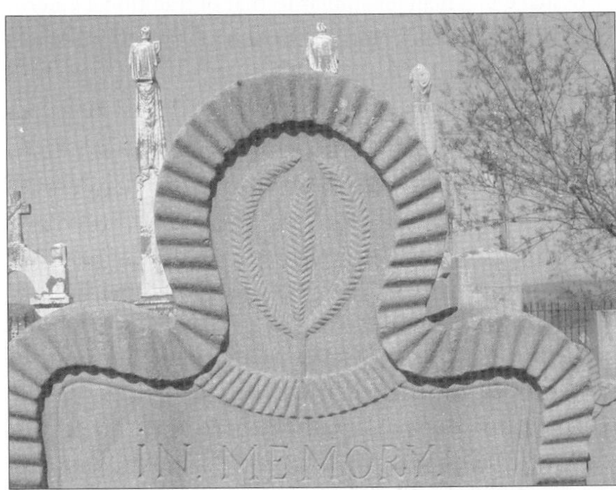

Gravestone, probably carved by Laurence Krone, McGavock Family Cemetery, Wythe County, Virginia, 2001. Local materials and personalized symbols characterize many gravestones in Appalachia, with distinctive traditions evident in many locales.

Vigorous Germanic traditions developed in the late eighteenth and early nineteenth centuries. Introduced principally through southeastern Pennsylvania, Germanic hearts, stars, and flowers spread westward into Ohio and southwestward into the Virginia and Carolina backcountry. Laurence Krone, B. F. Spyker, and a host of anonymous carvers used Germanic pagan symbols in western Virginia and eastern West Virginia. A British folk form popular in the region was the coffin stone; a 1774 example survives in western Virginia, and coffin-shaped slabs capped box tombs in Tennessee and Alabama. In the late nineteenth and early twentieth centuries, stoneworkers from Italy and eastern Europe introduced new forms to the region's coalfield graveyards.

Homegrown traditions arose in remote locales. Tennessee's Highland Rim counties feature comb graves formed by sandstone slabs leaned against each other in a gabled configuration, often with wraithlike effigy markers at the ends. North Georgia has box tombs constructed of long stones squared and corner-notched like logs. Local industries provided alternative materials. Cast-iron grave markers abound near furnaces, and potters from Virginia to Alabama made ceramic markers, some in mimicry of stone memorials, others turned on the wheel and decorated like flower pots.

Elites in towns and cities supported professional marble cutters such as Asheville's W. O. Wolfe, who stocked the angel statuary that inspired his novelist son, Thomas. Railroad and industrial development pulled the region into the mainstream by the mid-twentieth century, and standardized memorials supplanted most vernacular traditions. However, the region's folk spirit lives on in occupational markers (for example, a guitar on a musician's tombstone), grave goods, meticulously maintained scraped (bare-earth) graveyards, and decoration days, the summertime ritual of graveyard sprucing up and socializing.

See also: FOLK ART; ICONOGRAPHY; MONUMENTS.

—J. Daniel Pezzoni, *Lexington, Virginia*

Gregory Jeane, "Rural Southern Gravestones: Sacred Artifacts in the Upland South Folk Cemetery," *Markers IV: The Journal of the Association for Gravestone Studies* (1987); M. Ruth Little, *Sticks and Stones: Three Centuries of North Carolina Gravemarkers* (1998); *Southern Quarterly Special Issue: The Southern Cemetery* (Winter 1993).

Harvey, Bessie

(1929–1994) Folk artist.

A folk artist with no formal training, Bessie White Harvey created uncounted thousands of highly prized sculptural pieces at her east Tennessee home from the mid-1970s until her death in 1994. Inspired by a deep Christian faith, Harvey often depicted biblical characters and themes. Her early works (until about 1983) were "spirit pieces," so called for

Harvey's claim that she merely brought out the natural spirit of the piece of wood. These simple yet expressive representations of people and animals were enormously popular with art collectors, some of whom exploited the naive artist by acquiring large numbers for little or no payment. In the mid-1980s, Harvey began a series of more intentional sculptures entitled *Africa in America*, making a significant shift from finding the spirit of a piece to commenting on specific elements of African American history. These latter pieces are valued not only for their aesthetic qualities but for the artist's candid perspective on race and gender relations in the rural South.

One of thirteen children, Harvey was born Bessie Ruth White in Dallas, Georgia. Her father died in the mid-1930s, and her formal education ended in the fourth grade. At age fourteen she married Charles Harvey, by whom she eventually had three children. Separating from her husband, Harvey moved to Knoxville, Tennessee, in the early 1950s. The couple divorced, Harvey relocated to nearby Alcoa, and by 1964 she was the mother of eleven children. Her status as an uneducated, poor, African American woman living in Appalachia contributed to a difficult life for Harvey. The beginning of her artistic career is traced to the traumatic death of her mother in 1974.

In her artwork, Harvey frequently expressed the tragedies of her life, including experiencing poverty and racism, the death of both her parents, and having a daughter murdered and two sons sent to prison. Her technique was almost exclusively additive, constructing sculptural pieces by applying found objects such as small bits of wood, plastic, and glass, shells, beads, fabric, feathers, hair, and glitter to tree limbs and roots. Light sanding, shallow holes for eyes, and a flat base for mounting were the extent of sculpting she allowed. *Medicine Man* (c. 1979), *Thunder* (1979), and *Adam and Eve* (1981) are among notable early Harvey sculptures. From the *Africa in America* series, *Black Church* (1984), *The Hanging Tree* (1984), and *Master Please* (c. 1985) are examples of Harvey's frank appraisals of African American experiences with slavery and segregation in the United States.

Harvey received much recognition for her work during her lifetime. Journalist Morley Safer interviewed her in 1993 for the CBS television program *60 Minutes*. The Whitney Museum of American Art, the Smithsonian American Art Museum, the Tennessee State Museum, and the Knoxville Museum of Art, among others, have collected her pieces. Despite her personal hardships and exploitation at times by collectors and dealers, Harvey maintained a sense of optimism in her artwork.

See also: AFRICAN AMERICAN ARTISTS; FOLK ART; RELIGIOUS IMAGERY.

—James A. Hoobler, *Tennessee State Museum*

Iconography

In Appalachian visual and material arts, iconography (the use of traditional or familiar images and symbols) is commonly found and most apparent on pre-twentieth-century artifacts. For instance, the tree of life, a prominent motif in origin-of-death symbolism, as in the biblical Garden of Eden story, can be found on Appalachian gravestones of Lutheran and German Reformed congregations in Wythe, Botetourt, Bland, and Tazewell Counties in southwestern Virginia. Although diverse in form, the motif is often stylized, symmetric, and characterized by drooping lower branches, signifying death and decay, and arching, triple-branched, flowering upper leaves to show that life goes on. A heart, symbolizing love and affection, is often shown as the source of the fruit of the tree of life. Besides the tree of life and Germanic heart motif, graveside memorials in Appalachia also include coats of arms, patriotic symbols, and carved animals, especially the lamb. Central to the core of Christian teaching, the lamb alternately symbolizes the purity of a sacrificial Jesus and his human flock seeking spiritual leadership from the Good Shepherd.

Although snake symbolism is global, it has specific meanings in the Appalachians. In some fundamentalist congregations, the image is associated with the practice of snake handling. The rattlesnake featured on "Don't tread on me" Revolutionary War banners represented fearlessness. In Cherokee culture, the rattlesnake can be found on traditional masks used in preparation for war. Cherokee stickball players were known to eat rattlesnake flesh before a game in order to intimidate their opponents. In Cherokee mythology, Uktena, a large horned snake, wore a diamond-shaped blazing crest on its forehead. The rattlesnake is linked with life, death, terror, and anger. Some African American–made objects use the rattlesnake in a manner similar to that of traditional Cherokee practice, and snake forms are common on African American walking sticks.

Color symbolizes the spirits of the cardinal directions in Cherokee art and concepts such as power, peace, death, and defeat. Red and black are the traditional and principal colors used in Cherokee basketry. Red is the sacred color of the east and symbolizes power, war, strength, success, triumph, and the spirit of protection; black indicates the west and death. The four directions form a spiral of life with a sacred fire at the center of a universal circle. The spiral of life moves clockwise from southeast, each direction corresponding to a stage of life. Corresponding colors for the south are white for purity and green for plants, both also associated with health. The colors of the north are white, blue, or purple.

Appalachian coverlets and quilts held symbolic meanings for their creators and owners. Though not every motif was a symbol, a rich iconography appears in such artifacts. The tree of life and heart appear repeatedly. Pineapples, whether appliquéd or stitched, were a sign of hospitality. The Princess Feather pattern, often described as a modification of the feathered insignia of the Prince of Wales, also resembles a mountain wildflower in West Virginia quilting. Classical symbols such as the laurel crown (a symbol of victory and poetry) and the lyre (a symbol of lyric poetry) are also found. Quilts were made for hope chests, as wedding presents, to memorialize the dead, to commemorate friendships, and as family mementos.

Coverlet weaving had a renaissance during the late nineteenth and early twentieth centuries with an interest in material arts on behalf of settlement schools, industrial institutes, and other forms of what was termed "mountain work." The iconography of coverlet patterns demonstrates a wide variation, with names describing events such as Bonaparte's Retreat, natural phenomena such as Pine Bloom, or even square dance patterns such as Lady's Fancy.

Pattern names varied from region to region and in different time periods, leading to shifting meanings, and while the relative scarcity of examples of pre-twentieth-century Appalachian art bearing identifiable symbols makes iconographic study challenging, the examples that do survive point to an interesting and rich history of symbolism in Appalachian visual and material forms.

See also: FOLK ART; GRAVEYARD ART; RELIGIOUS IMAGERY.

—Betty J. Crouther, *University of Mississippi*

J. T. and Michael Garrett, *Medicine of the Cherokee: The Way of Right Relationship* (1996); Fawn Valentine, *West Virginia Quilts and Quiltmakers: Echoes from the Hills* (2000); Klaus Wust, *Folk Art in Stone: Southwest Virginia* (1970).

Impressionism

Impressionism in American painting has not been associated with Appalachia as often as it has with other distinctive geographic regions such as New England and California. Yet between the late 1880s and the mid-1930s, a significant number of painters, both natives and outsiders, created a body of important impressionist paintings unique to the region. The Appalachian Expositions of 1910 and 1911 and the related National Conservation Exposition in 1913, all of which were held in Knoxville, Tennessee, accorded impressionism a special status in exhibitions.

In northern Appalachia, impressionists Christian Walter, John Flender, and Joseph Woodwell centered their work on pastoral subjects, as had the earlier painters of the Scalp Level area east of Pittsburgh in southwestern Pennsylvania. The Pittsburgh cityscapes of Arthur Watson Sparks and Aaron Henry Gorson, the latter reminiscent of Whistler, reveal a markedly different view of northern Appalachia. The landscape and portrait painter Joseph Hugo worked in Pittsburgh before moving to Charleston, West Virginia. Charleston was also home to the portrait and figure painter Ashton Wilson, who was part of the White Sulphur Springs artist colony.

Impressionist painting in the southern Appalachians occurred mostly in western North Carolina and east Tennessee. Knoxville's Appalachian Expositions linked impressionism, the most progressive art movement to be accepted by American artists before World War I, with a progressive political agenda focused on conservation of the region's forests and other natural resources. At the 1910 Knoxville exposition, Catherine Wiley, the most important figurative impressionist of the southern highlands, was awarded a gold medal for her "meritorious" group of paintings. On the same occasion Chattanooga's William P. Silva was awarded a silver medal for a group of seventy impressionist landscapes in which paintings of Tennessee mountain subjects were surrounded by canvases depicting Venice, Florence, and the French countryside.

Augmenting the regional artists' works in 1911 and 1913 were two remarkable exhibitions organized by the American Federation of Art featuring paintings by some of the most notable American impressionists of the era, including Childe Hassam, Robert Reid, Ernest Lawson, Mary Cassatt, Cecilia Beaux, Robert Vonnoh, J. Alden Weir, Joseph De Camp, and Irving Wiles. The silver and bronze medals at the Conservation Exposition went to Karl Beuhr and Richard Miller, who were associated with the American artist colony at Giverny, the village that was home to greatest of the French impressionists, Claude Monet. The 1913 Conservation Exposition included a fine arts exhibition that was chaired by Wiley and housed in its own building on a hilltop overlooking the fair. The impressionist presence effectively reinforced the high moral and educational tone of the exposition's other exhibits, described as "lessons that will make history in the progress of civilization."

In the years following the National Conservation Exposition, when Congress debated and finally passed the National Park Service Act, impressionist artists helped draw public attention to the southern Appalachians. The New England impressionist Chauncey Ryder (Silva's teacher) had exhibited in the 1910 exposition and in the 1920s created a series of paintings in the Great Smoky Mountains. During the 1920s, public sentiment in favor of a national park in the Great Smoky Mountains began to build. About this time two immigrant impressionists with ties to Chicago came to paint in the Appalachians. Rudolf Ingerle created appealing, colorful canvases that strongly aided in the preservation of the Smoky Mountains, while Lawrence Mazzanovich celebrated the beauties of the Tryon, North Carolina, area. Although more avant-garde modernist styles eclipsed impressionism after the First World War, it retained a strong and increasingly romantic connection to the conservation movement.

See also: APPALACHIAN EXPOSITIONS; LANDSCAPE PAINTING; WILEY, CATHERINE.

—Jay Williams, *University of South Carolina*

Paul A. Chew, *Southwestern Pennsylvania Painters, 1800–1945: Collection of Westmoreland Museum of Art* (1989); William H. Gerdts, *Art Across America: Two Centuries of Regional Painting, 1710–1920* (1990); Estill Curtis Pennington, ed., *Southern Impressionist: The Art of Catherine Wiley* (1990).

Itinerant Painters

Sometimes known as limners, itinerant painters were traveling artists active in America from the late 1760s until the end of the nineteenth century. While these folk artists were more numerous in the northeastern states, many journeyed extensively through Pennsylvania and into Virginia, Kentucky, and Tennessee. Itinerant painters left a rich, if often anonymous, record of emerging middle-class values through the portraits they painted.

The term *limner* was generally applied to any painter of pictures, whether the painter worked out of an established city studio or traveled to the countryside homes of patrons. The media of limners included oils, pastels, pen and ink, and watercolors. Aspiring artists were largely self-taught, beginning their careers as house and sign painters or carriage decorators. Most eventually progressed to portraiture, practicing on friends or family members. When confident that a sufficient level of skill had been reached, a painter would set out on the road to ply his new trade. Facing bad roads and harsh weather on foot or horseback, itinerant artists carried their supplies with them. The roving limner would visit prosperous-looking homes, persuading householders to have portraits made for the family. Food and lodging for the artist were usually part of his fee, and his nomadic experiences and encounters with other patrons often made him an entertaining and sought-after guest. Some of these itinerants eventually were in such demand that they were able to open permanent studios.

Itinerant painters made it possible for Americans of lesser means to purchase likenesses of their loved ones, as had long been the custom of wealthier families. These paintings were more than mere wall decorations; they served as sentimental keepsakes as well as serious documentation of family history. The portraits usually included various objects reflecting the occupation or interests of the sitters: children were often depicted holding pets or toys, women with flowers or books, and men with symbols of their profession, such as account ledgers or apothecary jars. The quality of the surviving folk portraits varies greatly in the relative skill with which they were executed, as the line between academically trained and self-taught folk painters was indistinct, especially in the eighteenth century.

Among the artists who traveled in the Appalachian regions and whose identities are known was Jacob Frymire, a Pennsylvania painter who is known to have plied his trade in Virginia in 1805 and in Kentucky in 1806. Lewis Miller, another nineteenth-century itinerant painter from Pennsylvania, made more than two thousand sketches on trips between western Pennsylvania and southwestern Virginia to visit family. It was not customary for itinerant artists to sign their work, so many remain anonymous. Although most of the artists were men, some women were known to have had successful careers as itinerant artists.

The introduction of the daguerreotype in 1839 heralded the age of photography and the decline of itinerant painters, but their resourcefulness and improvisational techniques had a lasting effect on the Appalachian region, where an especially rich culture of self-taught artistic expression survives.

See also: NATURALIST ILLUSTRATORS; PICTURE MEN; PORTRAITURE.

—Debra Blundell, *University of Memphis*

Robert Bishop, *Folk Painters of America* (1979); Beatrix T. Rumford, ed., *American Folk Portraits* (1981); Clara Endicott Sears, *Some American Primitives* (1941).

Landscape Painting

The Appalachian landscape, with its once seemingly endless virgin forests, began attracting artists to the region from the beginning of the nineteenth century. At a time when forests were vanishing from the eastern United States, artists romantically sought out pristine locales where nature appeared to remain in its original state. Paintings of natural vistas had become significant in seventeenth-century Europe. In America, the Hudson River school (1825–75), the first school of American painting, established the significance of the landscape as subject during the second quarter of the nineteenth century.

Whereas Native Americans viewed all of nature, including humans, as interdependent, European colonists in America saw nature first as a wilderness of natural resources to be exploited. Only later did aesthetic tastes embrace a view of nature as beautiful or picturesque. Hudson River school artists canvassed the Allegheny, Catskill, Adirondack, White, and Green Mountains, as well as the Hudson River Valley of New York, for picturesque views. The first central and southern Appalachian sites to attract landscape interest were natural phenomena such as Natural Bridge in Rockbridge County, Virginia, medicinal and resort springs such as the White Sulphur Springs of Greenbrier, (West) Virginia, and historical and topographical sites such as Harpers Ferry, (West) Virginia. These sites attracted such artists as Edward

Beyer of Germany and English-born Sir William Fox during the mid-nineteenth century.

Among the Hudson River school, Philadelphia's Thomas Doughty, cofounder of the school with Thomas Cole, sketched at Harpers Ferry during the 1820s; Cole sketched along the Monongahela River in Pennsylvania before moving to New York in 1825. Second-generation Hudson River school artist Worthington Whittredge, born in Ohio, painted early views of Hawk's Nest and Crow's Nest, (West) Virginia, during the 1840s. William Sonntag, born in Allegheny County, Pennsylvania, concentrated on views of western Virginia. The African American landscapist Robert S. Duncanson sketched along the Ohio River from Cincinnati to Pennsylvania (1850–52) and the French Broad River in western North Carolina. Whittredge, Sonntag, and Duncanson, also considered founders of the Ohio River Valley regional landscape group, were based in Cincinnati. Frederic Edwin Church, a leader of the Hudson River school's second generation, painted Natural Bridge in 1852; it was painted by David Johnson in 1860. Other Hudson River school artists working in Appalachia included George Hetzel, James Hope, Charles W. Knapp, Russell Smith, and William Sheridan Young. The Richmond, Virginia, artist William Ludwell Sheppard produced picturesque and sublime views of Natural Tunnel, the New River, Rainbow Arch, and Goshen Pass in western Virginia during the early 1870s for *Picturesque America*, a publication on American scenery.

Doughty and his Hudson River school generation, influenced by European classical landscapes, often produced views of water and distant mountains framed by trees. Self-taught, Doughty emphasized detail and tonal gradation in his landscapes. Cole preferred allegorical, poetic views in which nature provided a background for didactic, moralizing themes. Second-generation Hudson River school masters, though inspired and influenced by their elders, preferred intimate scenes of nature instead of panoramic views, and their images tended to be softer and less defined. Whittredge's light-filled canvases combine naturalist detail with sweeping views and poetic sentiment. Sonntag was noted for his tight, linear detail, while Duncanson produced natural scenery that included poetic elements. The latter's *Landscape with Rainbow*, for instance, depicts an Eden-like environment with a rainbow illuminating a secluded cabin.

As the Hudson River school of landscape painting declined in the 1870s, it was replaced by Barbizon-inspired pastoral views (part of the French realist movement), broadly painted in a limited palette. During the early twentieth century, further decline in interest in painted landscapes was due to the influence of new modernist styles originating in Europe. But in the 1930s, Richmond-based Nora Houston traveled as far as West Virginia seeking restorative views, and by mid-century Spanish émigré Pierre Daura and Virginian Marion Junkin were painting views of Rockbridge County, Virginia.

The Appalachian landscape that inspired and educated artists of America's first school of painting, the Hudson River school, early in the nineteenth century continued to inspire artists of the late twentieth century, in part due to artists' pastoral longing for and anxiety about the loss of America's wild places. Recent landscape artists include those painting in Appalachia since the 1970s: David R. Craft of Elbert County, Georgia; George Ayers Cress of Calhoun County, Alabama; William Dunlap of Webster County, Mississippi; Lowell Hayes of Johnson County, Tennessee; Athens, Ohio, residents John W. and William Kortlander; Jerry L. Noe of Harlan County, Kentucky; and longtime Kentucky resident Lester F. Pross.

See also: BEYER, EDWARD; FRERICHS, WILLIAM C. A.; SCENIC ILLUSTRATION.

—Betty J. Crouther, *University of Mississippi*

John Driscoll, *All That Is Glorious around Us: Paintings from the Hudson River School* (1997); James C. Kelly and William M. S. Rasmussen, *The Virginia Landscape: A Cultural History* (2000); Barbara Shissler Nosanow, *More Than Land or Sky: Art from Appalachia* (1981).

Link, O. Winston

(1914–2001) Photographer.

Ogle Winston Link's documentary photographs of steam trains in the 1950s not only celebrate the power and beauty of train technology but also magically capture a particular time and place in rural Appalachia. Popular for some time among train buffs and museum curators, Link's photographs garnered wider appreciation through the publication of two books, *Steam, Steel and Stars: America's Last Steam Railroad* (1987) and *The Last Steam Railroad in America* (1995). In his pictures, Appalachia is an idyllic place where machines, humans, and nature exist in harmony. Alongside the quaint station in Green Cove, Virginia, for example, a horse pulling a wagon of logs pauses to let a train pass. In *Hawksbill Creek Swimming Hole, Luray, Virginia* (1956), swimmers play in a creek as a train passes high overhead on a scenic bridge.

Link was born in Brooklyn, New York, in 1914 and graduated from the Polytechnic Institute of Brooklyn in 1937. During World War II, as a project engineer and photographer in military research, Link experimented with night photography. In 1946 he started his own freelance photography business, specializing in industrial subjects. Between commercial projects, Link made railroad scouting forays and plotted his photographs with military precision. For his famous series on the Norfolk and Western Railway, Link covered the entire twenty-three-hundred-mile line through Virginia, West Virginia, and North Carolina. He photographed mainly at night in black and white using complex lighting equipment, including a specially designed synchronized series of strobe lights. Railroad officials permitted Link access to any location but offered no compensation. He created more than two thousand negatives during the five-year project, which ended shortly before Norfolk and Western retired its last steam engine in 1960. His photographs comprise an important archive of both steam trains before the conversion to diesel and the small railroad towns in the Shenandoah Valley and Appalachia.

Link spared no effort once he decided to go for a particular shot. He spent four days stringing a 150-foot rope bridge over the Maury River at Gooseneck Dam to transport lights for a nighttime image of cascading water and distant train. For a photograph outside Luray, Virginia, in 1956, Link strung more than one-third mile of wire to set off thirty-six flashbulbs for one picture. With multiple flashbulbs, he got only one shot before the train was gone. The difficulty of his technique and his determined perseverance heighten the beauty and arresting spontaneity of his work. Link received unwelcome publicity late in life during a widely publicized divorce trial and the later conviction of his ex-wife for stealing fourteen hundred of his prints.

See also: CONTEMPORARY PHOTOGRAPHY; NORFOLK AND WESTERN RAILWAY (TRANSPORTATION); RAILROADS (TRANSPORTATION).

—Russell T. Clement, *Northwestern University*

Modernism

See Daingerfield, Elliott; Dodd, Lamar; Wiley, Catherine

Monuments

Public artworks created to commemorate individuals, citizens' groups, or events, monuments are often commissioned to recognize bravery during times of war, social upheaval, or tragedy. A variety of monuments commemorating various aspects of Appalachia's history dot the region's landscape. The first monument erected in honor of George Washington stands in the mountains of western Maryland. Dedicated in 1827 by the citizens of Boonesboro, the thirty-four-foot stone tower stands beside the Appalachian Trail in Washington Monument State Park. Civil War memorials are among the most common in Appalachia, since many battles were fought in the region. Western Maryland has many such monuments that honor both Union and Confederate soldiers. Antietam National Battlefield in Sharpsburg has ninety-four monuments, erected primarily by veterans between 1890 and 1900. Monuments at the battlefield take various forms, from engraved commemorative stones, with or without additional engraved plaques or sculpture work, to statues on pedestals to pillars adorned by such battle-related motifs as the eagle and elaborate architectural pieces (such as the domed octagonal Maryland State Monument).

An elaborate and unusual Civil War memorial is located in Gathland State Park, near Burkittsville, Maryland. Erected in 1896 by Civil War correspondent George Alfred Townsend (the park derives its name from his pen name, "Gath"), the War Correspondents Memorial Arch is an asymmetrical architectural work standing fifty feet tall and forty feet wide. Three nine-foot-high limestone Roman arches top a sixteen-foot-high Moorish arch built of Hummelstown purple stone. A square crenellated tower flanks the arches on one side. Niches in different places shelter the carvings of two horses' heads and terra cotta statuettes of Mercury, Electricity, and Poetry. Inscribed tablets embedded in the east facade name 157 journalists and artists who reported from the Civil War battlefields. In 2003 a plaque containing the names of four journalists killed in Iraq was added.

Another significant Civil War monument is a statue of a recumbent Confederate General Robert E. Lee housed in the Lee Chapel at Washington and Lee University in Lexington, Virginia. The chapel was built at Lee's request during his tenure as president of the college from 1865 until his death in 1870. The marble statue was created by Richmond, Virginia, sculptor Edward V. Valentine between 1870 and 1874, although it was Lee's wife who chose the recumbent pose because it represented the general asleep, not in the sleep of death. At one time called the "Shrine of the South," the monument continues to be a tourist attraction. The remains of Lee's horse, Traveller, are interred in a plot outside the chapel.

Women have also been recognized as serving their Appalachian communities, especially during times of historic conflict, such as the Revolutionary War. In 1778 Mary Ludwig Hays ("Molly Pitcher") kept her husband's cannon firing against the British after he collapsed during the battle of Monmouth, near Freehold, New Jersey. A statue was erected in Hays's honor in 1876 adjacent to her grave in Carlisle, Pennsylvania. In Martin's Ferry, Ohio, stands a statue of Elizabeth "Betty" Zane holding a keg of gunpowder commemorating her bravery in battle against British and Native American forces at Fort Henry, Ohio, in 1782. A more recent memorial to honor past, present, and future women war veterans was erected by the Combined Veterans Council of Berks County, Pennsylvania, in City Park Veterans' Grove in Reading, Pennsylvania. Like the Hays and Zane memorials, this monument features a metal statue on a stone pedestal.

Monuments honoring minorities, although not as common as other memorials, also exist in Appalachia. For example, a monument to the United States Colored Troops was erected in Cumberland, Maryland, at Sumner Cemetery

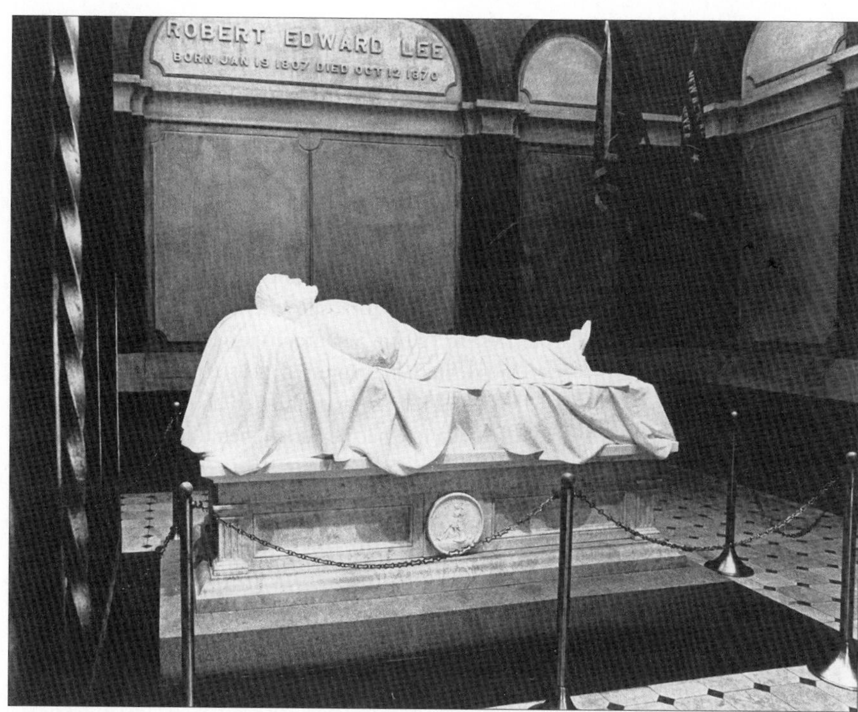

Edward V. Valentine, Lee Monument, Lee Chapel, Washington and Lee University, 1870–74. Marble. Monuments commemorating Civil War history are common in Appalachia, including this statue of Confederate General Robert E. Lee in what was once known as the "Shrine of the South."

in 1991. Other monuments have commemorated Cherokee leaders. A monument built at the turn of the twentieth century by James Abraham Walker honored a Cherokee native, Nanye-hi (Nancy Ward). The statue was made of gray granite, stood about five feet high, and depicted Ward holding a lamb to represent peace. It also had a plaque with the inscription *Nancy Ward, Watauga, 1776*, referring to the first known occasion when she helped pioneers. Walker intended the statue to be placed at Ward's grave, but financial difficulties caused him to sell it to his brother, who used it for his daughter's gravestone in Arnwine Cemetery near Liberty Hill in Grainger County, Tennessee. The statue was stolen in 1981 and has not been seen since. The Chattanooga chapter of the Daughters of the American Revolution also honored the memory of Nanye-hi, erecting a stone pyramid in 1923 and installing a fence to protect her actual gravesite near Benton, Tennessee. A state marker and ramp has been added and the monument is an official state historical site.

Sentiments following World War II generated a number of monuments throughout the country, with a few striking examples located in the Appalachian region. The War Memorial Monument and Chapel at Virginia Polytechnic Institute and State University is a hallmark of its Blacksburg campus. Eight massive pylons depict allegorical figures sculpted in bas-relief; they are positioned over an underground chapel with a sculptural frieze by Donald DeLue. Initiated in 1945 to pay homage to students and alumni who fought and died during World War II, the monument was not completed until 1960. The National D-Day Memorial is located in Bedford, a rural Virginia town that lost a disproportionate amount of men on that watershed day. Dedicated in 2001, the site features a plaza and sculpture and an English garden designed to resemble a World War II insignia rendered in horticultural plantings.

Artist Maya Lin designed the Civil Rights Monument in Montgomery, Alabama. Dedicated in 1989, the monument consists of two separate pieces of engraved black granite, each of which also features a fountain. The first is an inverted cone with a flat tabletop into which are inscribed the names of civil rights workers. A large wall serves as a backdrop for the smaller fountain. The words of Martin Luther King Jr., etched on the monument's wall, can be read through a sheet of water that pours over them: ". . . until justice rolls down like waters and righteousness like a mighty stream."

Not all memorials are dedicated to civil leaders or wartime events. Performing artists have also been recognized through commemorative monuments or statues. Appalachia's famous musical sons W. C. Handy, "Father of the Blues," and Elvis Presley, the "King of Rock and Roll," have memorial statues dedicated to them in their hometowns of Florence, Alabama, and Tupelo, Mississippi, respectively.

See also: CIVIL WAR (GOVERNMENT); GRAVEYARD ART; PUBLIC ART PROGRAMS.

—Pamela Simpson, *Washington and Lee University*, and Ima J. Stephens, *Auburn University*

Doug Gelbert, *Civil War Sites, Memorials, Museums and Library Collections: A State-by-State Guidebook to Places Open to the Public*

(1997); James W. Loewen, *Lies across America: What Our Historic Sites Get Wrong* (2000); David J. Meltzer, ed., *Ancient Monuments of the Mississippi Valley* (1998).

More Than Land or Sky

More Than Land or Sky: Art from Appalachia, an exhibition organized by the National Museum of American Art (now the Smithsonian American Art Museum), opened in Washington, D.C., in 1981, before touring the Appalachian region. The exhibition attempted to present a comprehensive and unprecedented survey of Appalachian contemporary fine arts.

During exhibition planning the show's curator traveled from the southern counties of New York to the northern counties of Mississippi and Alabama, examining hundreds of works for possible inclusion in the exhibition. Not limited to works by native Appalachians, the exhibition also included pieces by non-native artists living and working in the region. Selected works spanned styles from representational to non-objective, including those of both professionals and "outsider" artists with little or no formal training. Artistic quality was paramount, but a significant relationship to Appalachia was also mandatory.

The completed exhibition included 105 works by sixty-nine artists. Artists were invited to make a statement for a catalog that formed the basis for extensive programs promoting the project; concerts, poetry readings, workshops, and symposia provided a rich cultural context for understanding the art in the exhibition. For example, the symposium "Ties that Bind" examined the work of women artists of the region.

The exhibition attempted to understand the spirit of place and its influence on art. Many of the represented Appalachian artists mentioned the influence of novelist William Faulkner, the Mississippi-born Nobel laureate, long noted for evoking a sense of place. Many of the selections showed a strong influence of earlier art forms on contemporary works. While all artists draw on a vast reservoir of images, Appalachian artists frequently intermixed theirs with ideas drawn from traditional crafts and folklore. For purposes of exhibition, the works were divided into three major categories: "Images of the Land," "Images of People," and "Images Incorporating Myth and Folklore," with some works incorporating all of these themes. Landscapes inspired by Appalachia's exceptional natural beauty formed a major section of the works on display. Many works utilized storytelling in a visual form. Others expressed anxiety regarding changes wrought by modernization and the erosion of cultural traditions.

See also: APPALACHIAN EXPOSITIONS; CONTEMPORARY PAINTING; CONTEMPORARY SCULPTURE.

—Barbara Shissler Nosanow, *Keswick, Virginia*

Barbara Shissler Nosanow, *More Than Land or Sky: Art from Appalachia* (1981).

Moses, Grandma

(1860–1961) Painter.

Anna Mary Robertson Moses, better known as Grandma Moses, became famous in the 1950s for folk paintings depicting rural American life. Although Moses lived most of her life in upstate New York, she and her family spent the years from 1887 to 1905 in Staunton, Virginia.

Moses initially expressed her creativity through embroidery work but began painting in her late seventies when arthritis made fine needlework difficult. Her brushwork was sold at local fairs and area businesses. A collector purchased one of her paintings and brought it to the attention of Otto Kallir, owner of the Gallerie St. Etienne in New York City. Kallir sold her work and marketed the image of "Grandma" Moses, a farmwife who painted scenes of rural America unspoiled by technology. Riding on a wave of post–Great Depression and post–World War II interest in naive art and its depiction of less troubled times, Moses became a major celebrity and appeared on the covers of *Time* and *Life* magazines. When she died on December 13, 1961, at the age of 101, Moses left behind more than fifteen hundred paintings, tiles, and book illustrations. Her paintings have been reproduced on a variety of commercial products, including prints, fabric, porcelain plates, tiles, and greeting cards.

Moses painted Virginia landscapes and genre scenes from memory in the 1940s and 1950s, decades after her stay in the Appalachian region. She painted numerous landscapes of the Shenandoah Valley, as well as mills in the area. *Gypsy Hill Park* (c. 1940) depicts the Moses home in Staunton. Moses eschewed the conventions of linear perspective and spatial relations, instead favoring changes in scale to depict her subjects with maximum detail and indicate their relative importance to the rural scene.

See also: FOLK ART; POPULAR ART; WOMEN ARTISTS.

—Carissa A. Amash, *Bennington Museum*

Murals, New Deal

Between 1934 and 1942, the federal government conducted the largest public art project in United States history. More than eleven hundred "decorations" were placed in new federal buildings, most of them murals in small town post offices. Of these, roughly a quarter were located in the Appalachian region. Contrary to popular opinion—and sometimes contrary to signs in the post offices themselves—the murals were not funded by the Great Depression–era Works Progress Administration but by the Treasury Section of Fine Arts (known as the Section of Painting and Sculpture, or "the Section," until the name was changed in 1938). The purpose of the murals was less for economic relief than to bring quality art into the purview of all citizens.

People in Appalachia, especially southern Appalachia, responded vigorously to the art in their federal buildings. As a result, the National Archives has a rich collection of correspondence among artists, post offices, and citizens of towns where murals were placed. Some local citizens were exceedingly grateful that their government had provided a major work of art at a time when they could ill afford to commission artwork themselves. Others reacted defensively, suspecting that the government had joined the general population in underestimating the value of their own contributions to national culture. Artists had a difficult time because they had to contend both with Section form restrictions and community content suspicion. The Section accepted the mountain cabin scene painted by muralist Frank Long for Morehead, Kentucky, only after Long made the daughter less svelte and the matriarch less overweight. In Appalachia, Virginia, residents familiar with coal mines, coal dust, and hard labor did not recognize the sanitized scenes of idyllic trees and mountains depicted in the mural placed in their town. Nonetheless, the program was an overall success—so much so that most of the murals are still in place, even as some buildings have taken on other functions. Technically, the murals belong to a combination of federal agencies, and theoretically, all remaining murals will be preserved in the community or in the Smithsonian American Art Museum.

See also: AMERICAN SCENE PAINTING; FEDERAL ARTS PROJECT; PUBLIC ART PROGRAMS; REGIONALISM.

—Sue Bridwell Beckham, *University of Wisconsin–Stout*

Native American Art, Precontact

The Native American art history of Appalachia is rich in form and function. Through time, artists used materials from the animal, plant, and mineral kingdom to create an array of utilitarian and sacred objects. The earliest Paleo-Indians spent a majority of their time securing food and shelter for survival. They used animal skins for clothing and crafted simple tools from stone. The warmer climate of the Archaic period (8500–1200 B.C.) enabled increasing populations of hunter-gatherers to live in seasonal villages. Local and imported stone was sculpted into beads, pipes, and ritual tablets with stylized designs. Fabric and baskets were woven of plant fibers, and clay was shaped into bowls and small figurines.

Huge shell middens and mounds, created near rivers in Tennessee, Kentucky, and Georgia, contain a remarkable array of ceremonial items, including tubular pipes, tortoise-shell rattles, and flutes, as well as large quantities of personal adornment. Copper was shaped into beads, pendants, bracelets, and headdresses. Long-distance exchange and social ranking of the late Archaic created new demands for art, bringing marine shell from the Atlantic and Gulf Coasts, copper from the Great Lakes, and fine-grained slate and jasper from more distant regions.

Early Woodland societies included the Adena (800–100 B.C.), centered in Ohio, and the Hopewell (200 B.C.–A.D. 500), stretching from Mississippi to Minnesota and from Missouri to West Virginia. Woodland culture developed increasingly complex burials, more elaborate grave goods, and extensive earthworks and burial mounds, some in geometric, human, or animal shapes. Ceramists shaped clay containers with symbolic designs, particularly bird motifs; other artists used mica, copper, shell, animal teeth, and freshwater pearls to create artworks. Such objects circulated in the Hopewell exchange network, which linked native people across sections of the east through cultural beliefs and art forms.

Some of the most exceptional art of precontact North America was created in the Mississippian period (A.D. 900–1550). Settled populations in the ceremonial centers of Moundville, Alabama, and Etowah, Georgia, were characterized by massive, flat-topped earthen mounds. Powerful male and female chief-priests exerted their influence over the use, circulation, and cycle of art production. Sculpture, vessels, war implements, objects of adornment such as feather cloaks and painted leather garments, and other finely crafted objects were associated with the elite and were frequently buried with them in mortuary mounds. Human figures, supernatural beings, and symbols of the cosmos, status, and war formed the iconography of the Southeastern Ceremonial Complex.

Many types of art were shared throughout the Appalachian region. Smoking pipes, sculptures, carved wooden and clay bowls with rim effigies, and various types of clothing and adornment were similar in form and function. In the early sixteenth century, beads of purple and white shell (wampum) were traded prolifically and became especially favored in northern Appalachia. Fur trade and imported goods, particularly glass beads, metal objects, and trade cloth brought by European explorers and traders, changed forever the form and function of regional art. Colorful beaded garments, bags, and sashes with designs unique to each tribe were among the newly created types of art that emerged.

See also: CONTEMPORARY NATIVE AMERICAN ART; FRANK H. MCCLUNG MUSEUM (CULTURAL INSTITUTIONS); ICONOGRAPHY.

—Susan C. Power, *Marshall University*

Richard Balthazar, *Remember Native America! The Earthworks of Ancient America* (1992); David S. Brose et al., *Ancient Art of the American Woodland Indians* (1985); Charles M. Hudson, *The Southeastern Indians* (1976).

Naturalist Illustrators

The first European artists to record the North American landscape were those who accompanied exploratory expeditions in the sixteenth and seventeenth centuries. Before the advent of photography, skills of observation and rendering were valued as necessary to the documentation of the New World. Although many of the earliest renderings made in America and in Appalachia appear as amateur sketches in travel journals, professional artists were often part of exploratory teams traveling into new territories. As communities were settled, artists were employed as cartographers as well. The identities of many early artists remain unknown although their work survives. Nevertheless, though fewer in number, the works of known artists form the basis for contemporary scholarship of this period.

In 1585 English artist John White accompanied an expedition to the Roanoke colony in eastern Virginia, where he made images considered to be among the earliest renderings of life in the New World. White documented Native American life, albeit filtered through the distorted lens of European imperialism. His subsequently published work formed the basis for a European vision of the American colonies. The first systematic visual record of the New World came more than century later when Mark Catesby came to Virginia in the early 1700s. Born in England, Catesby was more field botanist than artist, but the publication of his many renderings in *The Natural History of Carolina, Florida, and the Bahama Islands* (1731–34) has given him a firm footing in American art history. Catesby followed the James River upstream into the Appalachians and traveled south to the Carolinas, where he recorded the flora and fauna of the mountains. His work, notably sketches of birds and small animals in their native habitat, is admired not only for its faithful imitation of nature but also for its botanical content. John James Audubon's *The Birds of America* (1827) was published almost a century later. Although produced in a limited edition of just a few hundred portfolios, Audubon eclipsed Catesby as America's premier wildlife illustrator. Both naturalists traveled the countryside, venturing into the remote wilderness beyond relatively populated areas.

Although works by Catesby and Audubon are admired for their aesthetic qualities today, prior to the nineteenth century their renderings of the natural world were considered documentary evidence rather than art. Others would continue the tradition of making a visual record of the natural environment. T. Addison Richards and Edward Beyer each made important contributions to the antebellum landscape tradition. Both artists were born in 1820, Richards in England and Beyer in Germany. Around 1838, Richards settled in Penfield, Georgia, where his father was a school principal. With his brother William, Richards published a volume entitled *Georgia Illustrated in a Series of Views Embracing Natural Scenery and Public Edifices* (1842), which celebrated the beauty of the north Georgia mountains. "The upper part of the State abounds with romantic and picturesque views," he reported. "Mountains and vallies, glens and waterfalls, caverns and cliffs, with pastoral landscapes . . . Nature has lavished her beauties." Beyer may be the first professionally trained artist to have traveled through Appalachia. In the mid-nineteenth century, Beyer immigrated to America, working first in Cincinnati and, later, in Virginia. He is best known for the impressive volume entitled *Album of Virginia*, issued in 1857. James Cameron recorded the dramatic terrain of the lower Tennessee Valley while working in Chattanooga; later, Flavius Fisher, living in Lynchburg, Virginia, recorded the more open landscape of the Dismal Swamp.

In nineteenth-century America, there was a growing interest in establishing a distinct national identity, and the unique landscape features of the American continent gained recognition as important to this idea. In northern Appalachia, a group of artists working along the Hudson River in New York painted the American landscape exclusively. Their depictions of awe-inspiring epic landscapes were seen as evidence of the Divine in nature and set a standard for landscape painting in America. In western Virginia, Natural Bridge was one site frequently painted because of its unique features. William C. A. Frerichs shared in the spirit of those nineteenth-century landscape painters who fashioned the image of America as an untamed and unending territory. Frerichs came to the region to teach at the Greensboro Female College and settled in western North Carolina. He braved the wilderness of the Great Smoky Mountains at a time when they were inaccessible, rugged, and sparsely populated and may have been the first painter to venture into this remote territory to capture the drama and magnificent beauty of the landscape. Left ill and penniless after the Civil War, Frerichs left North Carolina and lived the rest of his life outside the region.

Because of the popularity of naturalist and landscape painting, good examples can be found in virtually every museum in the region.

See also: BEYER, EDWARD; CATESBY, MARK; RICHARDS, T. ADDISON.

—M. Anna Fariello, *Virginia Polytechnic Institute and State University*

O, Appalachia

The traveling exhibition *O, Appalachia* began as a quest to set aside stereotypes of Appalachia, to present the reality of the region, and to share the work of self-taught mountain artists with the public. Ramona Lampell, a West Virginia native, began collecting indigenous works and championing the creators as artists. With her husband, screenwriter and novelist Millard Lampell, she cowrote *O, Appalachia: Artists of the Southern Mountains* (1989), a coffee-table resource on folk artists of the Appalachian region that celebrates artistic creation unfettered by the rules of form and genre. In the introduction to the book, Millard Lampell writes, "Starting out, painting and sculpture are just something [the artists] try because they feel a need to make a statement that words cannot express."

After the publication of *O, Appalachia: Artists of the Southern Mountains*, curators Eason Eige and Ramona Lampell designed an exhibition with the same name. This show opened at the Huntington Museum of Art in Huntington, West Virginia, in 1989, beginning a three-year tour to fourteen other institutions. The exhibition included 141 pieces by twenty-five self-trained artists, many of whom did not consider themselves artists or their work "art." The exhibition presented their work to a broad range of museum audiences for the first time. The works conveyed impressions of natural beauty, individual fortitude, and community strength to a public unfamiliar with such positive perceptions of the region. Thus, *O, Appalachia* contributed to an increased awareness of the traditional and visionary skills of Appalachian artists.

See also: FOLK ART; *MORE THAN LAND OR SKY.*

—Kimberly Pulice, *Roanoke, Virginia*

Palmer, Earl

(1905–1996) Photographer.

Calling himself a mountain man and mountain photographer, Earl Palmer made photographs of Appalachia for more than fifty years. Born in 1905 in Straight Creek Hollow in Kentucky, Palmer spent his youth farming and mining but became a storekeeper for his life's vocation and a photographer for his passionate avocation.

Although Palmer took pictures as early as the 1930s, he shot the bulk of his work from the late 1940s to the 1970s, when he moved from Kentucky to Cambria in southwest Virginia to run a general store. Most of his freelance photography consisted of nostalgic images of Appalachia that used pictorialism, incorporating such techniques as posing, props, and retouching. Palmer's photographs are prized for their composition and documentation of traditional mountain processes such as apple butter making and moonshining. He also created portraits of famous Appalachians such as writer Jesse Stuart as well as local folks.

Palmer published his work in newspapers, popular photographic magazines such as *Look* and *Life*, and automobile travel magazines produced by various gasoline distributors, such as Standard Oil's *Scenic South*. Also the subject of a 1990 book entitled *The Appalachian Photographs of Earl Palmer* (1990), his photographs chronicled the region's rich folklife, including crafts, foodways, vernacular architecture, work lore, and religion. His pictorial legacy can be found in private collections and archives at such institutions as Berea College in Berea Kentucky; Ferrum College in Ferrum, Virginia; and Virginia Polytechnic Institute and State University in Blacksburg.

See also: CONTEMPORARY PHOTOGRAPHY; PICTURE MEN.

—Jean Haskell, *East Tennessee State University*

Picture Men

Picture men is a term that has been applied to rural, southern Appalachian, part-time, and usually self-trained portrait photographers. The term was popularized by Ann Hawthorne and Bruce Morton, whose 1993 book *The Picture Man* described and presented the work of Paul Buchanan of Hawk, North Carolina. In addition to Buchanan, who worked from the 1920s through the early 1950s as a sawmiller, miner, and farmer as well as a photographer in the four-county area around his home, other known picture men included W. R. Trivett of North Carolina and T. R. Phelps in Virginia. Hawthorne, in her preface to *The Picture Man*, contrasts Buchanan with the more famous pictorialist Doris Ulmann: "Ulmann was a photographer and artist; Paul Buchanan was the Picture Man."

The pictorial photographs of Doris Ulmann and Bayard Wootten, included in such books as *Handicrafts of the Southern Highlands* (1937) and *Backwoods America* (1934), defined the visual environment of early-twentieth-century Appalachia. Ulmann and Wootten's interest in depicting mountain people as living survivors of the pioneer age attracted book publishers and national audiences. Their work appealed to those who agreed with William Goodell Frost, president of Berea College, who popularized the image of Appalachians as "our contemporary ancestors." Ulmann and Wootten frequently depicted craft workers, the poverty-stricken, and the elderly and are reported to have asked those sitting for portraits to pose in their grandparents' homespun clothes rather than their own store-bought clothing. To create romantic images, Ulmann and Wootten manipulated their pictures through depth of focus, tint, background, and detail to produce the look they desired and were not obligated to produce a finished product for the sitter's approval.

The so-called picture men had a different relationship with their subjects, who were also their clients, patrons, and audience. As commercial photographers, picture men had to produce satisfactory photographs for their sitters in order to earn a living. The work of these photographers, when done well, more accurately showed how sitters perceived themselves. Picture men allowed the sitters to arrange themselves, to choose the way they dressed, and to show themselves to the advantage that they considered best. In contrast to Ulmann and Wootten, whose portraits connected their subjects to the past, the picture men's sitters often emphasized their connections to modernity and urbanity through clothing or by appearing with automobiles. They showed their piety by holding Bibles, their education through the display of pens and pencils in their pockets, and their concern for efficiency through the watches pinned or chained to their clothes.

In contrast, the work of the more romantic pictorial photographers reveals less about Appalachia and more about the way the nation perceived the region and the people who lived there. Their patrons were book publishers and an educated public who bought books. The work of the picture men is an insider's view of the region and a more accurate visual document than the work of so-called documentary photographers. For much of the twentieth century, scholarly studies that focused on documentary photographers omitted picture men or treated them as an anonymous marginal group. More recently, they are gaining increased recognition as important photographers in their own right.

See also: EVANS, WALKER; ULMANN, DORIS; WOOTTEN, BAYARD.

—Charles Alan Watkins, *Appalachian State University*

Ralph Lentz, *W. R. Trivett, Appalachian Pictureman: Photographs of a Bygone Time* (2000); David Moltke-Hansen, "Seeing the Highlands, 1900–1939: Southwestern Virginia through the Lens of T. R. Phelps," *Southern Cultures* (Fall 1994); William Stott, *Documentary Expression and Thirties America* (1973).

Popular Art

Unlike art taught in universities, exhibited in museums, and collected by elite patrons, popular art is created for mass audiences. It tends to be aesthetically conservative and usually appeals to people whose tastes and interests make them art consumers rather than art connoisseurs. It is specifically neither folk art, naive art, nor reproduction art, although all of these impulses may be present in its total character. Appalachian popular art draws on sentimental family scenes and pastoral landscapes and wildlife. Often sold in reproduction, where multiple prints are made from an original painting or drawing, popular art is disqualified from the "legitimate" art market. Critics have referred to it as mere "illustration" or as "commercial art" and generally exclude it from aesthetic analysis.

The roots of popular art extend back to the nineteenth-century development of the process of chromolithography, which mechanically reproduced images in great numbers. A complicated technical process, chromolithography required a separate stone for each color, sometimes using up to twenty different stones in a single print. Appearing in the mid-nineteenth century, chromolithographs became common to millions of American homes due to their availability and low cost. As an art form it has been called a "democratic art."

In the mid-twentieth century, Anna Mary Robertson Moses (1860–1961), known as Grandma Moses, practically defined the modern popular art movement. Beginning late in life as an untrained or naive painter, Moses transformed a folksy style into a conscious artistic expression. She painted western Virginia landscapes based on her memories of time spent in Staunton from 1887 to 1905. Her combination of romantic rural scenes and distinctive primitivism caught the attention of the public. The personality cult of Grandma Moses became a marketable commodity with high-priced original paintings and widely available reproduction prints.

Rockwell Kent (1882–1971), a world traveler who visited the Appalachian area from his upstate New York home, is credited with bringing art into advertising. His 1956 oil on canvas entitled *Child under Tree, Virginia* depicts a large tree in an open field; its expansive branches shelter a family group and the majestic Blue Ridge Mountains fill the background. This Nelson County, Virginia, scene became a visual prototype for a whole class of nostalgic landscapes. Combining themes of nature and nurture, Kent successfully merged commercialism with idealism, creating a paradigm for aspiring popular artists.

Contemporary artist Bob Timberlake (1933–) makes paintings that evoke traditional themes and utilize Appalachian motifs, including quilts, log cabins, and split-rail fences. The originals are made in his studio in the Piedmont region of North Carolina and sold there and in a second gallery in Blowing Rock. Prints made from his original paintings are advertised widely in regional magazines.

P. Buckley Moss (1933–) is one of the most commercially successful popular artists to work in the Appalachian region. Moss was born and reared in New York City, where she obtained a classical art education at the prestigious Cooper Union. Her fame came with her 1964 move to Waynesboro, Virginia, where she began her career by showing at festivals and art fairs. Once she "discovered" the Amish people of the Valley of Virginia, a subject appropriate to her style and sense of spirituality, she became known as the "plain" artist of the "plain people." Moss depicts her subjects as stylized individuals and steadfast traditionalists both at work and play. In time, with luck, planning, and considerable sales ingenuity, her distinctively linear, elegantly simple, and patently moralistic paintings and original prints were enthusiastically received by a public hungry for art they could understand and admire. Spurred on by popular acceptance, Moss produced edition after edition of hand-signed and numbered offset prints. Charles Kuralt dubbed her "The People's Artist," and her loyal public continues to agree.

Popular artists, in general, have maintained that they are not necessarily concerned with either aesthetic criticism or the academic content of their work. On the contrary, they attract large numbers of consumer-collectors who are interested in art as a purchase to be enjoyed, rather than art to be understood as a challenging statement. Limited edition prints (numbered reproduction prints) are signed and personalized on request by even the best-known popular artists. Such personal attention adds to the close and loyal relationship between creator and consumer. Much popular art, in its original and reproduced form, is inclined to be generic. Similar works appear at local festivals and exhibitions as amateur artists strive for public recognition and monetary validation. Though few of these artists achieve the success they desire, their efforts add vibrancy to many local art scenes.

See also: FOLK ART; GRAPHIC ARTS; MOSES, GRANDMA.

—Peter M. Rippe, *Roseland, Virginia*

Becky Johnston, ed., *P. Buckley Moss: Painting the Joy of the Soul* (1997); Joshua C. Taylor, *The Fine Arts in America* (1979).

Portraiture

Prior to the advent of photography, painted portraiture functioned as a visual document, perhaps the only one a family possessed. Because portrait artists viewed their works as important records, they often sought to achieve accuracy rather than idealistic depictions. For this reason, early American portraits often appear unflattering to modern eyes. Although family portraits were made, artists were often hired to render posthumous portraits of loved ones, frequently at the bedside of the recently deceased. In an age when infant mortality ran high, such portraits were often of young children.

In Appalachia, a number of successful artists made portraiture a focus of their careers. In 1858–59, James A. Whiteside, one of the founders of Chattanooga, Tennessee, commissioned a family portrait by James Cameron, a Scottish itinerant painter. Legions of itinerant artists traveled to less populous areas, while painters who kept studios in larger towns advertised in local newspapers for well-to-do clients. Susan F. Quarles and her second husband, Jacob Cannon Nicholson, also an artist, announced in 1839 that they had rented a house in Amherst Court House, Virginia, and were prepared to paint miniatures and portraits. Nicola Marschall, an itinerant German painter, became famous in the South, where he worked in Alabama and designed Confederate uniforms. Many nineteenth-century American artists were trained in Europe. Kentucky's Frank Duveneck traveled to Munich in 1870 to study art, rapidly executing portraits and figure studies. In 1888 Duveneck returned to America, becoming an influential teacher at Cincinnati's Art Academy.

Twentieth-century painter Eugene H. Thomason, born in South Carolina but reared in Charlotte, North Carolina, studied at the Art Students League, worked in New York in the 1920s, and became a close colleague of George Luks and his circle. Returning to Nebo, North Carolina, in the 1930s, he was called "the Ashcan Artist of Appalachia" for his unembellished paintings of mountain people and landscapes. Betty McArthur (1865–1944) headed the Art Department at the Mississippi College for Women in Columbus for most of her career. Her portraits are part of a collection in the Old Capitol Museum in Jackson, Mississippi.

Self-taught portrait artists often worked from what they knew rather than what they saw. Kentucky's Milford Miller combined a career in high-tech concrete products with carving portraits of eastern Kentucky folk artists. Larry Hamm, born in Carter County, Kentucky, in 1937, moved to Morehead in 1963 and, while managing a gas station, became a self-taught wood-carver. He practiced the art form until his death in 1996. His sense of humor can be seen in subjects as diverse as Presidents Dwight D. Eisenhower, Franklin D. Roosevelt, and Bill Clinton, Kentucky Fried Chicken founder Colonel Harland Sanders, and singer Elvis Presley.

See also: ITINERANT PAINTERS; PICTURE MEN.

—Sharon Mullins, *Elkview, West Virginia*

Patti Carr Black, *Art in Mississippi, 1720–1980* (1998); John A. Cuthbert, *Early Art and Artists in West Virginia: An Introduction and Biographical Directory* (2000); A. Everette James Jr., A. Everette James III, and Edwin E. Ritts Jr., *Eugene Healan Thomason: The Ashcan Artist of Appalachia* (1987).

Public Art Programs

In comparison to larger metropolitan areas, contemporary public art in Appalachia was slow in coming. Once it arrived, though, programming and services to the community assumed interesting and varied courses. Public art is displayed both indoors and outdoors, in front of government offices and in public parks, and in a range of styles and media, from paintings and tile work to outdoor sculpture. Celebrating the lives of famous people and memorializing war veterans, public statuary and monuments can be found throughout Appalachia.

There were several models for public art in the late twentieth century. As early as the late 1960s, state and local arts councils, museums, and contemporary art centers began placing selected works within cities throughout Appalachia. Funding for these projects was generated through state organizations, cultural institutions, and the private sector. These projects were usually commissioned through juried competitions, some focusing on regional artists and others open to artists throughout the United States. Federal agencies such as the Tennessee Valley Authority, large corporations such as Coca Cola, and private foundations such as the Doris Duke Charitable Foundation have had a significant impact.

Another approach that states have employed to fund public art is the percent-for-the-arts model. State art councils with this structure are able to execute public art using a percentage of the total building costs for state construction

James G. Buonaccorsi, *Armor Pierce,* 1987. Steel and bronze. Public art is displayed throughout Appalachia in parks, outside government offices, and on college campuses. *Armor Pierce* is one of more than two hundred sculptures installed at the University of Tennessee in Knoxville.

projects. Many universities and public spaces throughout Appalachia have benefited from this program. The State of Tennessee, for instance, created public art projects at its entry rest areas during the 1980s using percent-for-the-arts funds.

Perhaps the model of most service to Appalachia has been the academic one. Knoxville, Tennessee, hosted the 1982 World's Fair, which prompted the University of Tennessee's Jack Reese and Dennis Peacock to establish a campus sculpture tour. Pieces of art from various artists were loaned to the tour, which placed the art on the university campus to greet fair visitors. The original exhibition was modest in scale and budget, yet from the initial success of the 1982 exhibition, the university continued the program for an additional fifteen years and installed more than two hundred sculptures, including Jim Buonaccorsi's *Armor Pierce*. During this period, the university maintained a close relationship with Walters State Community College of Morristown and Cleveland State Community College of Cleveland, Tennessee, by loaning art to these rural institutions.

Numerous other academic institutions throughout Appalachia have established public art programs. Notable among them are Appalachian State University in Boone, North Carolina; the University of North Carolina at Asheville; Western Carolina University in Cullowhee, North Carolina; Chattanooga State Technical Community College in Tennessee; the University of Alabama in Tuscaloosa; and Radford University in Radford, Virginia. Many of the programs flourished in the late 1980s and early 1990s, but budget cuts have since curtailed their activity. Still, with the region's ample outdoor spaces and low incidence of vandalism, for a period, public art programs thrived in Appalachia, and the legacy of late-twentieth-century public art programs is still evident on Appalachian college campuses.

See also: CONTEMPORARY SCULPTURE; MONUMENTS; MURALS, NEW DEAL.

—LeeAnn Mitchell, *Artist-Blacksmith's Association of North America*

Regionalism

Kentucky writer Wendell Berry, poet-advocate of the return to rural ways and community life, has defined regionalism as "local life aware of itself." A work of art can be the tangible proof of such awareness. A truly regional art might portray the local landscape and its inhabitants, reflect shared local beliefs or stories, or be fashioned from local materials. While one can still hear distinctive regional speech and taste regional culinary specialties in isolated portions of the country, the spread of mass-market advertising, franchise restaurants, and retail outlets, in combination with a mobile population, poses a threat to regional culture.

As the twentieth century progressed, discussions about regionalism grew in reaction to the rapidity of change that marked the times. The Fugitives, a group of modernist thinkers based in Nashville, Tennessee, complained that large-scale corporate interests would soon erode the civility of daily life in the South, reducing art to a nonessential by severing it from its everyday roots. Donald Davidson's seminal essay "A Mirror for Artists" in the Fugitive and Agrarian anthology *I'll Take My Stand* (1930) posited that southern culture—once rich in folk arts, music, and crafts—was shrinking into isolated pockets. Without strong community traditions, a close contact with nature, and spiritual or religious impulses, Davidson wrote, the authentic artistic endeavor would fail, to be replaced by surrogate mass-market commodities masquerading as authentic. Advocacy for an aesthetic regionalist approach remained viable between the wars and approached a national consensus with the work of midwestern regionalist painters Thomas Hart Benton, John Steuart Curry, and Grant Wood, who were able, for a while, to influence the direction of American mainstream painting. Thereafter, regionalist issues lost influence as America consolidated its art activity in New York City after World War II.

Later in the twentieth century, there were several attempts to catalog art making in the Appalachian region, defined by the federal government as parts of thirteen states spanning the spine of a mountain system running from New York State to northern Mississippi—an almost impossible task. The 1981 exhibition *More Than Land or Sky: Art from Appalachia*, organized by the National Museum of American Art (now the Smithsonian American Art Museum), included an admirably disparate selection of artists from many walks of life who were, in the words of the museum's director, Harry Lowe, "united by content." In statements collected for the catalog, many exhibiting artists cited the influence of the rugged mountain landscape and its resilient people, referred to the power of community in sustaining their efforts to live humanely, and acknowledged the spiritual impact of closeness to nature. To the show's three broad subject categories: land, people, and myth and folklore, one might suggest adding material inventiveness, the sort of make-do ingenuity born of want, thereby acknowledging the impoverished nature of much of the Appalachian region.

To greater or lesser degrees, regional characteristics can be found in the works of the self-taught artists and craft artists whose works exist in the Appalachian region in plentiful supply, and in works by trained artists, both inside and outside of major art centers. When artists come together in more rural community settings, distinctions such as economic class, education level, and distinctions between art and craft fall away. Instances of artistic bridge building, particularly between academic artists and self-taught or "outsider" artists in the southern Appalachian region, attest to the shared vitality that results from coming face to face with the creative endeavors of one's neighbors. In an example described by sociologist Julia Ardery in *The Temptation* (1998), University of Kentucky sculpture professor Michael Hall and his students were drawn to the creative persona of self-taught Kentucky artist Edgar Tolson, whose wood carvings they found at rural Appalachian craft cooperatives organized by VISTA volunteers in the 1970s. Hall's own career as an advocate for what would soon become known as "outsider art" was propelled by his introduction of Tolson's work to the fine art world.

More than seventy years after *I'll Take My Stand*, the once monolithic New York art world is slowly becoming decentralized. Following the example of Wendell Berry, many writers have returned to their home ground or have settled in other fertile pockets of nature. By the same token, many visual artists are also electing to work in small-town and rural settings.

A growing number of twenty-first-century artists are able to survive financially outside of the gravitational pull of New York City by carrying their wares to satellite markets closer to home, such as Atlanta, Pittsburgh, Louisville, and Asheville. The effect is cyclical. As regional hubs create a self-sustaining infrastructure of nonprofit art institutions and sales galleries, the local audience for art grows and artists find patronage nearer at hand.

See also: AMERICAN SCENE PAINTING; BERRY, WENDELL (LITERATURE); *MORE THAN LAND OR SKY*.

—Susan W. Knowles, *Nashville, Tennessee*

Jim Wayne Miller, "A Cosmopolitan Regionalism," *Border States: Journal of the Kentucky-Tennessee American Studies Association* (1991); Rick Stewart, "Toward a New South: The Regionalist Approach," in *Painting in the South: 1564–1980* (1983).

Religious Imagery

Evangelical Protestantism is a dominant force in religious life in Appalachia, and the religious work of the region's self-taught artists is primarily Christian in subject matter. Evangelical Christians regard the Bible as the authoritative voice of God, and many interpret scripture literally. Consequently, the Bible plays an integral role in the work of self-taught artists, who often cite scripture in their art to validate and emphasize an image's meaning. Imagery ranges from scenes directly inspired by the Bible and events relating to everyday church life to teaching charts and banners and visions said to be inspired by God. Lettering is also employed to enhance the literal interpretation and decorative nature of an artwork.

Bible stories, events, and prophecies often assume concrete reality, even though the style of untrained artists often simplifies natural objects, abstracts the human form, and uses color in a non-naturalistic fashion. Heaven is pictured with turreted mansions, broad streets, and formal gardens, reminiscent of upper-class residential districts of earthly cities. Hell is occupied by naked (and sometimes racially differentiated and gender-specific) human bodies tormented by droves of cackling demons. Angels usher Adam and Eve out of Eden and attend Christ's Second Coming. Common biblical subjects include Adam and Eve, Noah's ark, Jonah and the whale, Christ as the Good Shepherd, the life of Christ, scenes from the Books of Daniel and Revelation, and the New Jerusalem. The variety of animals pictured in such images suggests a profound love of nature and a belief in the world's fundamental goodness. By contrast, the many depictions of the fall of Adam and Eve point to the central belief in Appalachian religious thought of humanity's estrangement from God. The numerous portrayals of Christ crucified emphasize the pivotal role of Jesus in humankind's salvation and the immensity of God's love.

Among scenes of church life, baptism scenes, referring to the Christian ritual that marks the birth of a person into a life of faith and love, are common. The whole gamut of religious experience has been documented by regional artists: scenes of worship include preaching, prayer, singing, speaking in tongues, foot washing, and snake handling, as well as related social events such as church picnics, people honoring the graves of the dead, weddings, wakes, and funerals.

Much religious work by self-taught artists is evangelical and didactic in purpose and intended to reach a large public. Howard Finster, southern Appalachia's most famous untrained artist, considered himself to be a preacher first and an artist second. The influence of a tradition using charts and banners to teach prophecy since the mid-nineteenth century can be seen in the work of South Carolina artist William Thomas Thompson. Many untrained artists, such as Myrtice West from northern Alabama, are known as visionary artists, claiming to be inspired by God. Many of these artists also seek to proselytize with art.

See also: FOLK ART; ICONOGRAPHY; VISIONARY ENVIRONMENTS; VISIONARY PAINTING.

—Carol Crown, *University of Memphis*

Chuck and Jan Rosenak, *Museum of American Folk Art Encyclopedia of Twentieth-Century American Folk Art and Artists* (1990).

Richards, T. Addison

(1820–1900) Illustrator and author.

Thomas Addison Richards illustrated and wrote several works in the 1840s and 1850s describing the mountain regions of Georgia and the Susquehanna River area in Pennsylvania, encouraging tourists to visit and artists to depict them. Born in England, the son of a Baptist minister, he came with his parents to the United States in 1831. In 1838 they settled in Penfield, Georgia. In 1844 he moved to New York City, where he had a long career as an artist, teacher, and staff member of the National Academy of Design. He is best known as the author-editor of *Appletons' Illustrated Hand-Book of American Travel* (1857), the first major illustrated guidebook to the United States and Canada. He introduced many mid-nineteenth-century Americans to the natural wonders of Appalachia and other areas during an expansive phase of American history.

Richards wrote and illustrated articles for several magazines throughout his career. In 1842 he produced thirteen illustrations for *Georgia Illustrated in a Series of Views Embracing Natural Scenery and Public Edifices*, a volume edited by William Carey Richards, his brother. Rock Mountain (now Stone Mountain), Tallulah Falls, and the Falls of Toccoa are among the natural wonders illustrated as worthy of attracting vacationers "in search of the picturesque." His essay "The Landscape of the South," published in *Harper's New Monthly Magazine* in May 1853, described the southern continuity of the Allegheny chain as more varied than its northern counterpart. Scenes depicted in steel engravings based on his original drawings include Coweta Creek in the Blue Ridge Mountains, the French Broad River, and the Valley of Nacoochee, Georgia. Even as he extolled the virtues of these places, Richards recorded that there were few inns and that the food often was "indigestible pork." He surmised, "With the increase of travel, these little material discomforts will be, of course, abated." His article "The Susquehanna," published in *Harper's* in October 1853, included a short history of the valley and two illustrations of a coal mine, as well as picturesque scenery near Nanticoke. His writing, optimistic and romantic, focused on descriptions of places, not on the life of the people.

As an artist, Richards was part of the first generation of American landscape painters, broadly defined as the Hudson River school. Though romantic in concept, his drawings have topographic accuracy. A number of his Appalachian works are in the Georgia Museum of Art in Athens, the Morris Museum in Augusta, Georgia, and in private collections. From the late 1840s, he exhibited regularly at the American Art Union and later the National Academy of Design.

See also: LANDSCAPE PAINTING; NATURALIST ILLUSTRATORS; SCENIC ILLUSTRATION.

—Jessie J. Poesch, *Tulane University*

Scenic Illustration

In the nineteenth century, Americans became familiar with the scenic features of the Appalachian region primarily through illustrations in books and periodicals. Such images and their texts implied that the region's mountains and river valleys were on a par with the Northeast's better-known ones and thus promoted travel and further settlement.

The Appalachian region was little known to outsiders until the mid-nineteenth century, except for such easily accessible features as the Delaware Water Gap and the natural wonders of Natural Bridge and Harpers Ferry, praised by

John A. Hows, *Juniata River, Near Huntingdon,* c. 1870, from the *Aldine,* February 1874. Wood engraving by C. Maurand. Americans outside the region were first introduced to Appalachian scenery and natural resources during the mid- to late nineteenth century through illustrations in books and periodicals such as *Harper's Monthly, Appletons' Journal, Scribner's Monthly,* and the *Aldine.*

Thomas Jefferson in his book *Notes on Virginia.* The English viewbook *American Scenery* (1837–39) included only these few Appalachian locales. American publications, however, soon showed the region's more remote steep-banked rivers and mountains. In keeping with the contemporary interest in geology and picturesque landscapes—with much variety and contrast—these images most often depicted peaks, waterfalls, rock formations, caves, and gorges. Sites associated with history or literature, such as the Cumberland Gap, were also featured. By mid-century, general works such as *The Home Book of the Picturesque* (1852) included Appalachian views, while specialized publications highlighted specific areas. For example, *Georgia Illustrated in a Series of Views Embracing Natural Scenery and Public Edifices* (1842), edited by William Carey Richards and illustrated by T. Addison Richards, *Mountain Scenery: The Scenery of the Mountains of Western North Carolina and Northwestern South Carolina* (1859) by Henry Colton, and *Album of Virginia* (1858) by Edward Beyer featured areas becoming ever more accessible by railroad.

Less expensive than these viewbooks were periodicals launched in the 1850s such as *Harper's Monthly.* Their wood engravings occasionally featured Appalachian scenery, notably in *Harper's* articles on Virginia (1853 and 1854) and North Carolina (1857) written and illustrated by "Porte Crayon" (David Hunter Strother). After the Civil War, new periodicals such as *Appletons' Journal, Scribner's Monthly,* and the *Aldine* gave attention to the scenery and natural resources of Appalachia. In 1870 *Appletons'* began its "Picturesque America" series, promoting national reconciliation, landscape appreciation, and tourism to lesser-known and relatively accessible areas such as West Virginia. The series was expanded and published as a book from 1872 to 1874. *Picturesque America* included numerous wood engravings of many sections of Appalachia: the French Broad River, Natural Bridge, Cumberland Gap, Lookout Mountain, Weyers and Mammoth Caves, and the Virginia and West Virginia mountains; and, farther north, the Delaware Water Gap, the picturesque coal region Mauch Chunk, Cayuga Lake (New York), and the Juniata, Ohio, Susquehanna, and Upper Delaware Rivers. Another important magazine series, written by Edward King and illustrated by James Wells Champney, appeared in *Scribner's* in 1873 and 1874. Later published as *The Great South* (1875), the series contained numerous views of southern Appalachia and promoted the economic potential of the region.

Artists frequently added drama to their pictures by exaggerating a mountain's steepness or waterfall's height; yet the images were widely accepted as accurate, a claim often supported by including an artist drawing the scene in the picture itself. The cumulative impression created of Appalachian scenery was overwhelmingly positive and enhanced by figures of admiring tourists, while the inclusion of local residents engaged in traditional pursuits added to the "picturesque" interest. This tradition of scenic views persists in magazine features, tourist brochures, and coffee-table books.

See also: BEYER, EDWARD; RICHARDS, T. ADDISON; STROTHER, DAVID HUNTER.

—Sue Rainey, *Imprint: Journal of the American Historical Print Collectors Society*

Sue Rainey, *Creating Picturesque America: Monument to the Natural and Cultural Landscape* (1994); T. Addison Richards, *The Romance of American Landscape* (1854).

Schoolgirl Art

From the colonial period until the time of the Civil War (c. 1770–1860), the creation of ornamental needlework and decorative painting was an essential part of a girl's education. Curricula of schools in the region during that time period list sewing, knitting, tambour embroidery, and satin stitch along with music, dancing, painting, and drawing among the subjects taught. Such skills were acquired by well-to-do students at female academies or at home under the instruction of a private teacher. Although schools for girls were more common in the eastern and northern sections of the country, elaborate needlework and paintings made by girls in the Appalachians have been found. Clearly made by nonprofessionals, sometimes under the direction of another, such amateur artwork has attracted collectors drawn to its innocence and sentimentality. To the contemporary scholar, schoolgirl art provides a window into understanding the expectations and limitations placed on young women, many of whom invested their work with thoughtful creativity, time, and care. These works constitute a distinct body of nonprofessional art of the period.

Examples of schoolgirl art offer an important perspective on history because stitched samplers traditionally included family names, national symbols, scenes of local importance, scripture, and poetry, as well as birth and death dates in the design. These works provide information in establishing geographic and social history. Particular borders and motifs in needlework and paintings were associated with certain schools, indicating that designs were often not original but were made from stencils or patterns. Some designs could indicate which school a girl attended or the identity of the teacher.

Perhaps the best-known school of this era in or around Appalachia was the Moravian-operated boarding school for girls in Salem, North Carolina. Established in 1772, it is now Salem Academy and College, the oldest Protestant institution for female education in continuous operation in America. The educational program for young women included academic subjects along with needlework, drawing, embroidery on silk and satin, painting on velvet, ebony work, and the making of decorative objects such as mirror cases, pincushions, and pocketbooks. Another school in southern Appalachia was Greenville (South Carolina) Female Academy, which opened in 1823. The school offered instruction in drawing, embroidery, beadwork, fancywork, and tufted flowers. The Charles Town ([West] Virginia) Academy admitted women in 1836; at that time the Female Department offered English, music, drawing, and painting, which were considered proper and genteel accomplishments to round out a useful domestic life.

Examples of wool-embroidered samplers stitched in the early 1800s have been found in Virginia, Kentucky, Pennsylvania, and North Carolina. These are prized examples of schoolgirl art of the early 1800s since embroidering with wool thread was not common. One such sampler was done by Mary Ann Asbery (1818) from Tazewell County, Virginia, and another by Mary Warren (1847) in Asheville, North Carolina. A needlework picture of wind-tossed trees and center mausoleum was stitched by Sarah Childress in 1818 while she was a student at the Salem Girls' Boarding School. From a prominent family in Murfreesboro, Tennessee, she married James K. Polk, who became the eleventh president of the United States, in 1824.

The Industrial Revolution was instrumental in liberalizing the view of women's education, creating opportunities for an expanded academic curriculum in which ornamental needlework, painting, and other decorative arts ceased to be a priority.

See also: DECORATIVE PAINTING; WOMEN ARTISTS.

—Clara Hasbrouck, *East Tennessee State University*

Mary Jaene Edmonds, *Samplers and Samplemakers: An American Schoolgirl Art, 1700–1850* (1991); Olive Blair Graffam, *Youth Is the Time for Progress: The Importance of American Schoolgirl Art, 1780–1860* (1998); Kathryn Babb Vossler, "Women and Education in West Virginia, 1810–1909," *West Virginia History* (July 1975).

Southeastern College Art Conference

The Southeastern College Art Conference, known by the acronym *SECAC,* covers a twelve-state area; nine of these are part of southern Appalachia. As a nonprofit organization, SECAC seeks to promote artistic excellence and scholarship in higher education by facilitating cooperation among teachers and administrators in universities, colleges, junior colleges, professional art schools, and museums. With more than five hundred individual members and one hundred institutional members, SECAC is the largest and most active art conference in Appalachia.

Founded in 1942 at a meeting held at Sweet Briar College in Sweet Briar, Virginia, the organization took its current name in 1948. SECAC sponsors an annual conference, which is organized by a host institution, and publishes the *SECAC Review* annually, featuring scholarly articles, reviews, and abstracts of papers presented at the conference, as well as a membership newsletter. Each year, the organization sponsors a fellowship to an accomplished visual artist and presents awards for published scholarship.

An affiliate of the College Art Association, SECAC collaborates with its national parent organization and its many discipline-specific affiliates—including Foundations in Art: Theory and Education; the Visual Resources Association; the Southern Graphics Council; and the Southeastern Society of Architectural Historians—and other regional art organizations, such as the Mid-America College Art Association. By bringing scholars and art professionals together in an atmosphere of collegiality, the Southeastern College Art Conference provides opportunities for contact and stimulation to enrich the world of art in Appalachia and nearby areas.

See also: ART ASSOCIATIONS AND CLUBS; SOUTHERN STATES ART LEAGUE.

—Martha B. Caldwell, *James Madison University*

Southern States Art League

Organized in 1921 under the leadership of the Carolina Art Association and continuing for almost three decades, the Southern States Art League was an integral part of the cultural life of Great Depression–era Appalachia and brought about the only contact with the visual arts in some remote areas of the region. It bridged late-nineteenth-century associations that promoted an appreciation of the arts and the Southeastern College Art Conference, a contemporary regionwide organization made up of scholars and professional artists.

Initially called the All Southern Art Association, the league was created to promote and encourage the visual arts in culturally deprived areas of the South. Much of the activity of the Southern States Art League took place in the Deep South, but since it was the only professional and regional visual arts organization of the period, its influence was felt in Appalachia as well. Eight of its member states were later named as part of the Appalachian region as defined by the Appalachian Regional Commission: Mississippi, Alabama, Georgia, North and South Carolina, Tennessee, Kentucky, and Virginia.

At its meeting in Memphis, Tennessee, in 1922, the league elected officers and made plans for its future, eventually including a move of its administrative offices to New Orleans, where its president, Ellsworth Woodward, served as dean of the Newcomb College School of Art. The league championed regionalist art and preached a gospel of greater exposure for regional artists in all venues, even unorthodox spaces in communities from the lowlands through Appalachia to the Texas plains. The league was committed to uniting southern artists and their supporters and to encouraging a regional art that would accurately depict the region's peoples, history, landscape, and industry. The story of the Southern States Art League forms a significant chapter in the history of the American Scene movement of the 1930s and early 1940s that emphasized commonplace rural and urban subjects in realistic styles.

To meet its goals, the league held annual conventions, maintained a membership that at its height included some six hundred individuals in 1933, and sponsored two annual circuit exhibitions of members' works that traveled to rural towns as well as to large cities. These exhibitions allowed artists to sell their works, with the league charging a small commission. Unbothered by criticism that the league fostered parochialism, Woodward said without apology, "No Yankee artist, however skillful, can paint the South."

After Woodward died, the Southern States Art League ceased being an effective group. Its last convention held in 1947, the organization dissolved in 1950. However, the league left a legacy of accomplishment in bringing together artists and patrons, in proselytizing the cause of the southern artist, and in establishing a tradition of circuit exhibitions that traveled to Appalachian cities such as Birmingham, Alabama, Knoxville, Tennessee, and Asheville, North Carolina, and into more remote, poorer areas of the South. Perhaps most significantly, the league publicized and defined a southern presence in the mainstream of twentieth-century American art.

See also: AMERICAN SCENE PAINTING; ART ASSOCIATIONS AND CLUBS; SOUTHEASTERN COLLEGE ART CONFERENCE.

—William Underwood Eiland, *Georgia Museum of Art*

Stevens, Will Henry

(1881–1949) Painter and educator.

Will Henry Stevens is widely considered the most important modernist to have worked in the South. Born in Vevay, Indiana, Stevens read the literary works of Ralph Waldo Emerson and Henry David Thoreau with his grandmother as a young man and took long walks in the countryside; both activities shaped his philosophy and inspired an appreciation for nature. He attended local schools and one year at a preparatory school before entering the Cincinnati Art Academy in Ohio.

In 1907, at age twenty-six, Stevens went to New York City, where he spent time with artists such as Albert Pinkham Ryder, Van Dearing Perrine, and Jonas Lie and studied at the Art Students League. By 1912, he and his wife had developed a pattern of dividing their time between his hometown of Vevay and Louisville, Kentucky, where he taught art classes, painted, and regularly exhibited his work under the auspices of the Louisville Art Association. The family also began spending summer months in the mountains of western North Carolina, where Stevens hiked and painted. His 1920 one-man show at the Closson Galleries in Cincinnati included several mountain titles and his work *Morning on Sapphire Lake.*

Around this time, Stevens executed the theater design for a New Orleans production by playwright Hilliard Booth, and it is not clear whether this commission or other factors eventually led the family to visit the Gulf Coast. However, while there, Stevens met Ellsworth Woodward, head of the Newcomb College School of Art (now part of Tulane

University), who offered him a teaching position. Stevens accepted and in 1921 moved to New Orleans, where he taught at Newcomb until his retirement in 1948. He died the following year after moving back to Indiana.

Through the years, art critics have described Stevens' work as poetic, lyrical, and subjective and consistently praise his use of color. He worked simultaneously in two styles—one abstract and the other more traditional. Most art historians consider his non-objective and abstract work dating from the early 1930s to be his most important. Although he included components of abstraction in his earlier representational works, it was not until 1936 that scholars documented his non-objective abstracts. While Stevens's love of nature and the natural world is evident in his work both from Louisiana and the mountains, his summer sojourns in the Appalachian highlands were obviously significant. With paintings in major museums such as the Smithsonian American Art Museum and the Museum of Fine Arts in Boston, Stevens has begun to receive more serious study.

See also: LANDSCAPE PAINTING; REGIONALISM.

—Andrew Glasgow, *The Furniture Society*

Laurence Binyon, *The Flight of the Dragon: An Essay on the Theory and Practice of Art in China and Japan* (1911; reprint 1972); Jessie Poesch, "Will Henry Stevens—Modern Mystic: Beginnings to 1921," *Southern Quarterly* (Fall 1986).

Strother, David Hunter

(1816–1888) Illustrator and author.

David Hunter Strother wrote and illustrated articles for *Harper's New Monthly Magazine* under the pen name "Porte Crayon." Born in Martinsburg, (West) Virginia, Strother briefly attended college in western Pennsylvania and studied art in New York City. Following additional study in Europe, he found employment as an illustrator during the mid-1840s.

In 1853 Strother was commissioned by *Harper's* to write and illustrate a fictionalized article about a sporting expedition into the Allegheny Mountains of (West) Virginia. The essay proved to be so popular that Strother received a standing commission from the magazine. He proceeded to write more than two dozen additional illustrated travelogues before the outbreak of the Civil War. These included the five-part "Virginia Illustrated," which was reprinted in book form in 1857, and "A Winter in the South" (1857–58), which is set largely in southwestern Virginia and northeastern Tennessee. Strother's works feature characters such as the self-sufficient mountaineers and rifle-bearing frontiersmen that would become iconic in late-nineteenth-century local color writing. His travelogues made him one of the best-known and highest-paid artistic and literary figures of his day.

When the Civil War erupted, Strother remained neutral until political pressures and threats persuaded him to join the Union army. Between 1866 and 1868, *Harper's Monthly* published eleven installments of Strother's "Personal Recollections of the War," also written as "Porte Crayon." Accurate, detailed, and critical of both factions, the series contains an objectivity often lacking in the Civil War reminiscences of other writers.

Strother's most significant postwar effort was the ten-part *Harper's* series "The Mountains," which introduced America to the rural character and folkways of West Virginia. A staunch supporter of the fledgling state, Strother was one of the first writers to fully articulate the dilemma of encouraging the state's development while preserving its rustic beauty.

From 1879 to 1885, Strother served as United States consul general to Mexico; he died of pneumonia in Charles Town, West Virginia, in 1888.

See also: CIVIL WAR ILLUSTRATORS; SCENIC ILLUSTRATION.

—John A. Cuthbert, *West Virginia University*

Symbolism

See Daingerfield, Elliott

Tolson, Edgar

(1904–1984) Folk artist.

Edgar Tolson of Wolfe County, Kentucky, achieved notoriety for his wood carvings of starkly delicate single figures, animals, and scenes from the Old Testament. He was one of the first twentieth-century self-taught artists to gain national attention during the 1970s, as a booming art market and the United States bicentennial interested larger audiences in folk art.

Tolson worked as a farmer and carpenter until age fifty-three, when he suffered a stroke. As recreation and physical therapy, he turned to wood carving, whittling canes and human figures he called "dolls" out of local poplar. He sold some early pieces through the Grassroots Craftsmen of the Appalachian Mountains, a crafts cooperative begun by the Appalachian Volunteers, a service group established by the Council of the Southern Mountains during the War on Poverty. Through the cooperative display at the 1967 fair of the Kentucky Guild of Artists and Craftsmen in Berea, Tolson's works drew the admiration of Miriam Tuska, an art collector from Lexington. Tuska encouraged him to produce more carvings, and her husband, sculptor John Tuska, then a faculty member at the University of Kentucky, asked Tolson to carve an image of Adam and Eve beneath the Tree of Knowledge, a piece that, with many subsequent renderings, became Tolson's signature.

Sculptor Michael Hall befriended Tolson in 1968 and avidly promoted the carver's work. Through Hall's efforts,

Tolson's *Expulsion* was accepted into the Whitney Museum of American Art's 1973 exhibition *Contemporary American Art*, and Herbert W. Hemphill Jr., whose collection came to define the field of twentieth-century folk art, included Tolson's works in a trailblazing series of shows. The wood-carver also participated in three Smithsonian Folklife Festivals in Washington, D.C., produced by the Smithsonian Center for Folklife and Cultural Heritage and cosponsored by the National Park Service. Tolson's carvings appear in many public collections, including the Smithsonian American Art Museum and the Milwaukee Art Museum.

See also: FOLK ART; RELIGIOUS IMAGERY; WOOD CARVING (CRAFTS).

—Julia Ardery, *Austin, Texas*

Ulmann, Doris

(1882–1934) Photographer.

Doris Ulmann's first published portraits, of physicians and surgeons on the university faculties of Columbia (1919) and Johns Hopkins (1922), reflect her social standing. Having studied photography at the Clarence White School of Photography and at Columbia University, Ulmann was a founding member of the Pictorial Photographers of America. Included in the group's first exhibition was her photograph *The Blacksmith* (1916), an early indication that Ulmann's portrait lens would not remain long focused on the privileged. On the contrary, during the last two years of her life, Ulmann completed a comprehensive collection of Appalachian portraits that have come to dominate much of the scholarship on her work.

In the mid-1920s, Ulmann began making portraits of anonymous individuals, mostly people of the laboring classes, and increasingly sought out what she called "vanishing types." Beginning in the Northeast, she traveled south into the Shenandoah Valley of Virginia and the mountains of Kentucky, making her first images of Appalachia, which were subsequently published in 1928. Through her association with novelist Julia Peterkin, she traveled to South Carolina to coproduce *Roll, Jordan, Roll* (1933), which pictured the activities and religious ceremonies of rural southern blacks.

Ulmann spent the last two years of her life traveling by car more widely throughout the Appalachian highlands, photographing craftsmen and those who worked to promote a regional revival of handwork. Ulmann continued to use cumbersome glass plates long after lighter-weight photographic equipment came into use. Her method rendered "snapshot" photographs impossible; Ulmann's subjects had to pose motionlessly through relatively lengthy film exposures. She also continued her habit of carefully staging her photographs, as she had when making a portrait series of writers who posed in her Manhattan apartment with any number of props she kept on hand.

Ulmann's work is often linked with well-known Great Depression–era photographers who documented rural American life on behalf of the Farm Security Administration. But her work preceded that of Dorothea Lange and Walker Evans, and her portraits remained impressionistic. Ulmann collaborated with Allen H. Eaton during his craft survey in the Appalachian highlands, and after her death, fifty-eight of her images were published in Eaton's text *Handicrafts of the Southern Highlands* (1937).

See also: FARM SECURITY ADMINISTRATION PHOTOGRAPHY; PICTURE MEN; WOMEN ARTISTS.

—M. Anna Fariello, *Virginia Polytechnic Institute and State University*

Allen H. Eaton, *Handicrafts of the Southern Highlands* (1937); Philip Walker Jacobs, *The Life and Photography of Doris Ulmann* (2001).

Visionary Environments

Although visionary environments have been documented all over the world, they have especially flourished in the southern United States, including the southern Appalachian region, beginning in the last half of the twentieth century. Though the term *visionary* implies that such works convey a particular spiritual message, artists who create visionary environments are not necessarily inspired by a religion. These untrained artists, sometimes referred to as self-taught or folk artists, embellish the surroundings of their yards and homes as a lifelong pursuit. By transforming a physical space with images, objects, and text, such artists communicate messages about life, death, and devotion.

The proliferation of visionary environments is perhaps related to the South's narrative tradition, as well as the strong fundamentalist character of Christianity in the region. Both of these factors played a role in the most famous of Appalachian visionary environments, Howard Finster's Paradise Gardens Park, located in the wooded mountains outside of Pennville, Georgia. As both Baptist preacher and untrained artist, Finster (1916–2001) created a visual sermon consisting of pathways, buildings, hand-painted signs with references to biblical texts, and cement monuments embedded with shells, colorful glass, and stones.

Outside Prattville, Alabama, another preacher and artist transformed his yard into a haunting environment with thousands of wooden crosses interspersed with hand-painted signs that warn the viewer of impending death. William Carlton Rice (1930–) began preaching by driving around his rural community in a truck carrying a large wooden cross in the truck bed. After receiving a vision, he started his Cross Garden. As with many artists who create such environments, his work began simply, as Rice tacked three crosses to his back door. Today the site includes hundreds of crosses made of telephone poles, two-by-fours, and found wood, along with messages such as "It's hot, hot, hot in hell! And there ain't no ice water" painted on abandoned household appliances and handmade signs. The Cross Garden occupies more than an acre of hillside along both sides of a county road.

The Ave Maria Grotto at Saint Bernard Abbey in Cullman, Alabama, also developed over many years of dedicated work. In 1932 lay brother Joseph Zoetl (1878–1961) began making scale models of famous European cathedrals after his workday in the abbey's power plant. His hobby soon grew into an obsessive and dedicated service to God. Zoetl created more than 125 replicas of Holy Land sites, as well as Roman and American landmarks, many embellished with shells, cold cream jars, reflectors, and curious rock formations. Constructed within the hillside location are several grottos, though the main site is the large glittering, stalactite-encrusted Ave Maria Grotto.

African American Lonnie Holley (1950–) began making art after the tragic death of his sister's children in a house fire. At first constructing tombstones, Holley created what he referred to as "one square acre of art" near Birmingham, Alabama, until the Birmingham International Airport expanded into his property. Eventually, he received a settlement that allowed him to move his art twenty-five miles away to Harpersville. Holley's carvings, which include both human and animal forms, are made from industrial sandstone incorporated with found objects and emphasize the spirit world and his ancestral heritage. His work was included in the 1981 *More Than Land or Sky: Art from Appalachia* exhibition.

"Cedar Creek" Charlie Fields (1883–1966) of Lebanon, Virginia, painted the interior and exterior of his house, as well as its furnishings, with red, white, and blue polka dots. The Polka Dot House was ransacked after his death, though photographs and a few remaining pieces of the house may be viewed at the Museum of Appalachia in Norris, Tennessee.

See also: FINSTER, HOWARD; FOLK ART; VISIONARY PAINTING.

—Dixie Webb, *Austin Peay State University*

John Beardsley, *Gardens of Revelation: Environments of Visionary Artists* (1995); Lisa Stone and Jim Zanzi, *Sacred Spaces and Other Places: A Guide to Grottos and Sculptural Environments in the Upper Midwest* (1993); J. F. Turner, *Howard Finster, Man of Visions: The Life and Work of a Self-Taught Artist* (1989).

Visionary Painting

Terms for self-taught art such as *visionary art, folk art, naive art, intuitive art,* and *outsider art* are often used interchangeably. However, most academics and museum professionals in the United States and Canada define visionary art as a subcategory of self-taught art in which there are deep religious or spiritual overtones. Curiously, many visionary painters come to this art form late in life. Never having thought about the visual arts, they profess to receive a calling from God to create art. Many of the best-known twentieth-century artists working in this genre come from southern Protestant fundamentalist churches, including many in Appalachia. Visionary art in Appalachia takes the form of painting as well as sculptural environments.

Bill Traylor (1854–1947) began painting in 1939 in Montgomery, Alabama, at the age of eighty-five. He often used cardboard from discarded shirt boxes as a painting surface, and is known for his animated and abstract style. A freed slave, Traylor created paintings and drawings that are invaluable for the glimpses they provide of the artist's life, including depictions of riverboats, blacksmiths, and domestic scenes.

Throughout her life in North Carolina, Minnie Evans (1892–1987) experienced powerful recurring dreams that permeated her waking hours. When she began her "subconscious doodling" in 1935, she had no recollection of the origin of her imagery or skill. Much scholarship has focused on the parallels between Evans's work and African art, implying an unconscious, collective ethnic iconography. Evans produced a colorful and diverse body of work, the primary subjects of which are faces, insects, flora, and fauna.

Howard Finster (1916–2001) of Pennville, Georgia, was the first visionary painter to receive national attention; his remarkable "preacher-painter-shaman" output was prodigious. A predilection for words is apparent in his paintings, which incorporate biblical sayings and colorful images of a variety of saints, politicians, and figures from popular culture.

Cardboard, masonite, tin, plywood or other vernacular materials are often the "canvas" for visionary paintings, which juxtapose subject matter from everyday life with religion and dreams.

See also: FOLK ART; ICONOGRAPHY; RELIGIOUS IMAGERY.

—Annie Carlano, *Museum of International Folk Art*

Paul and William Arnett, eds., *Souls Grown Deep: African American Vernacular Art of the South* (2000); Elsa Weiner Longhauser, Harald Szeemann, and Lee Kogan, *Self-Taught Artists of the Twentieth Century: An American Anthology* (1998).

Wiley, Catherine

(1879–1958) Painter and educator.

Anna Catherine Wiley is considered the most important painter and art educator to have worked in eastern Tennessee between 1905 and 1925. Born in Lake City (Coal Creek), Tennessee in 1879, Wiley was the daughter of Mary Catherine McAdoo and Edwin Floyd Wiley, a coal-mine operator. She attended public schools in Knoxville and pursued higher education at the University of Tennessee. After graduating in 1903, she went on to New York's Art Students League for two years of further study.

Catherine Wiley, *The Letter,* c. 1907. Oil on canvas. Influenced by European impressionism of the late nineteenth century, Wiley's work is characterized by its brushwork, attention to light, and subject matter—human figures shown individually or in small groups.

Having begun her artistic career as an illustrator while in New York, she encountered impressionism, a style of painting developed in Europe during the late nineteenth century and characterized by painterly brushwork and an interest in the effects of light on color and form. Throughout her career, Wiley concentrated on portraying human figures, singly and in small groups, in both indoor and outdoor settings. Although sometimes considered a "genteel" impressionist, Wiley revealed her understanding of regional culture in unsentimental works such as *Morning Milking Time* (c. 1920) and *Indian Woman at Wolf Creek* (1915). Wiley's later figurative paintings, such as *By the Arbor* (1923), which depict refined women in conventional garden settings, are enlivened by aggressively broken brushwork and patterned color.

When Wiley returned to Knoxville in 1905, she taught art classes through the School of Home Economics at the University of Tennessee. She was awarded first prize for impressionist paintings shown at the Appalachian Exposition of 1910. Three years later, Wiley directed the fine arts section of the 1913 National Conservation Exposition. After being denied several applications for admission to the National Academy of Design, she suffered an emotional collapse in 1925 and never painted again.

See also: APPALACHIAN EXPOSITIONS; IMPRESSIONISM; WOMEN ARTISTS.

—Jay Williams, *University of South Carolina*

Women Artists

Women artists in Appalachia have faced all the same obstacles as women artists in other parts of America, with the additional challenges posed by isolation and provincialism. Historically, women have had to contend with limited access to education, restrictions imposed by social customs, a lack of financial resources, and the burden of multiple family responsibilities. While certain limitations encountered by women artists have changed over time, others remain persistent and reappear at various junctures.

The de facto prohibition of higher education for women in the eighteenth and nineteenth centuries meant that professional artistic training was difficult to acquire. Most women artists learned from family members who were artists or apprenticed to sympathetic family associates. Women learned and practiced portraiture and landscape painting, although much of it remains unidentified. Expressive forms that were open to women were those associated with domestic skills, such as needlework.

The lives of two female impressionist artists who were born in Appalachia illustrate the choices that women faced at the turn of the twentieth century. Mary Cassatt (1844–1926), often heralded as the greatest woman artist of the nineteenth century, was born into a wealthy family in the northern Appalachian center of Pittsburgh. Cassatt's upbringing allowed her to enroll in the Pennsylvania Academy of Fine Arts when she was just seventeen years old. In spite of such opportunity, Cassatt did not remain in the region, preferring instead the life of an expatriate among cultured literati in Europe. Cassatt's paintings of women and children in impressionistic environments leave little to associate her with the region.

After the turn of the century, institutions such as the Art Students League in New York City opened their doors to women. Catherine Wiley (1879–1958) completed her studies there and returned to her hometown to paint and teach at the University of Tennessee in Knoxville. Wiley's career as a professional artist was supported, in part, by the academic position she held and the support of an active community of artists in east Tennessee. But this was not enough to prevent her from suffering a mental breakdown. After repeatedly being denied application to the National Academy of Design, Wiley abandoned painting altogether. There is no documented evidence to support the claim that Wiley's rejection was based on gender, but the National Academy of Design was a male-dominated institution, as were most during much of the twentieth century.

Issues of propriety—what was and what was not the proper female sphere—also restricted women artists, especially those who attempted to step outside prescribed boundaries. Living on the edge of northern Appalachia, sculptor Belle Kinney (1890–1959) designed a monument to honor Confederate women. Her design was to be replicated with copies placed in southern capital cities. The ambitious commission dissolved over time; some have suggested that Kinney's female figures were too robust to win approval from commission judges. Much later, during the heyday of percent-for-the-arts commissions, regional women faced similar situations when ambitious designs were rejected due to a lack of faith in the artist's ability to complete them rather than the work's artistic merit. But options have improved for contemporary women, especially in fields previously dominated by their male peers. In Appalachia, women study and teach decorative blacksmithing and metal sculpture at such schools as Penland School of Crafts in Mitchell County, North Carolina. Likewise, women filmmakers at Appalshop in Whitesburg, Kentucky, have focused their careers on making documentaries about women in Appalachia such as *Coal-mining Women* (1982) and *Fast Food Women* (1991).

As a new field, photography was not as bound to historically embedded practices as were painting and sculpture. It was not restricted to urban areas of the country and allowed women and minorities to more easily enter the field. Attempting to portray the distinctiveness of the American landscape and its people, many photographers traveled and photographed the Appalachian region. But in publishing and widely disseminating their work, they sometimes inadvertently contributed to regional stereotypes. Doris Ulmann traveled into the mountains of Kentucky, Virginia, and North Carolina in a chauffeur-driven car with an array of cumbersome photographic equipment. Women artists such as Ulmann were able to pursue professional careers because family wealth supported their artistic freedom and financed their travel.

Few women have the resources of a Cassatt or an Ulmann; most have had to balance their artistic careers with demanding obligations of family and finances. Bessie Harvey (1929–1994), an African American who lived much of her life in Alcoa, Tennessee, was the mother of eleven children. Harvey made sculptures from found objects and bits of nature, and her work has been collected by the Whitney Museum of American Art and the Smithsonian American Art Museum. Poverty and adversity affect many women artists, especially those in the Appalachian region. One exhibition catalog described Georgia Blizzard as living "in the hardscrabble mountains of southwest Virginia on next to nothing." While her expressive ceramic vessels captured the attention of the region's museums, periodic purchases were never enough to lift her above bare subsistence.

The most significant movement to affect women's art in the twentieth century was the feminist art movement that swept the country beginning in the 1970s. Noting their lack of representation in museums, textbooks, and faculty positions, women artists, independently and collectively, began to challenge the assumptions upon which artistic judgments were made. Rather than assimilating into male-defined aesthetic arenas, women created ideologies and organizations in which to function more freely. Through lectures and exhibitions, women artists sought to define and position themselves as a greater presence in the American mainstream. For the most part undocumented, the feminist art movement was expressed in pockets throughout the Appalachian region. In middle Tennessee, the Red Hot Wimmen's Exchange sponsored exhibitions and symposia at various sites, exploring women's collective identity. In the mid-1980s, an informal association of six women artists formed Web 6. Centered in Blacksburg, Virginia, they created a showcase for political performance and exhibitions in a small community where few such expressive productions existed.

A strategy adopted by professional women was to establish parallel professional organizations, claiming they could more effectively address issues of parity in groups specifically focused on women's art and women's issues. The regional Southeastern Women's Caucus for Art (SEWCA) emerged out of the Southeastern College Art Conference to ensure that the annual conference adequately represented the ideas and scholarship of its female membership. For more than a decade, SEWCA sponsored panels of scholars, female and male, who presented new research on feminist theory, female historical figures, living women artists, and feminist art forms. In the late 1980s, SEWCA disbanded, having declared its goal achieved; women's issues had been well integrated into the programs of its parent organization. In Roanoke, Virginia, the regional journal *Artemis* followed a somewhat similar trajectory. Premiering in 1977, *Artemis* was launched by a group of women as a journal for and about women's art. It eventually abandoned its gender focus to develop into a regional voice that provided a forum for artists and writers of the Blue Ridge region via the production of an annual journal and exhibition.

Some activities and organizations that began during the 1970s and 1980s heyday of feminist art have maintained their strong feminist voice. The *Woman's Art Journal* was founded in Knoxville to encourage scholarship on women's art and women's issues. Maintaining its original focus, the *Woman's Art Journal* has become an important source of feminist writing and scholarship that continues to inform the American mainstream. In the twenty-first century, women artists continue to produce artwork in spite of entrenched sexism or

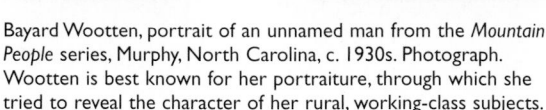

Bayard Wootten, portrait of an unnamed man from the *Mountain People* series, Murphy, North Carolina, c. 1930s. Photograph. Wootten is best known for her portraiture, through which she tried to reveal the character of her rural, working-class subjects.

obstacles in their paths. But women in Appalachia are less bound by gender restrictions than by the perceived limitations of regionalism. As women have gained a voice in the national aesthetic dialogue, that voice remains loudest in urban centers well outside the Appalachian region.

See also: EXPATRIATE ARTISTS; SCHOOLGIRL ART; SOUTHEASTERN COLLEGE ART CONFERENCE.

—M. Anna Fariello, *Virginia Polytechnic Institute and State University*

Nancy G. Heller, *Women Artists: An Illustrated History* (1987); Charlotte Streifer Rubinstein, *American Women Artists* (1982); *Southern Quarterly Special Issue: Art and Feminism* (Winter 1979).

Wootten, Bayard

(1875–1959) Photographer.

Mary Bayard Morgan Wootten, a photographer of southern Appalachia and the South and an advocate of equal rights for women, was born in New Bern, North Carolina, on December 17, 1875. She attended the State Normal and Industrial School in Greensboro, North Carolina, and taught art in Arkansas and Georgia in the 1890s before returning to her home state.

Wootten's career in photography began in New Bern about 1904, and her training in art contributed to her pictorial photographic style. Pictorialism, with its emphasis on artistic content even at the expense of technical quality, dominated photography during the first decade of the twentieth century. Although gifted as a landscape and architectural photographer, Wootten is best known for portraiture. Her subjects included working-class men, women, and children—both black and white—living in rural agrarian areas. She sought to reveal character and in doing so crafted images that are at times nostalgic and evocative.

Wootten's earliest Appalachian photographs date from the 1920s in western North Carolina, but she also worked in Tennessee, South Carolina, and Alabama. Her career peaked in the 1930s, when she was in demand as an exhibitor, illustrator, and lecturer. Wootten was also active in advancing the photographic medium, especially for women. She was a member of the Women's Federation of the Photographers' Association of America, serving as the group's secretary-treasurer. Her photographs were published in *Backwoods America* (1934), *Cabins in the Laurel* (1935), *Charleston: Azaleas and Old Bricks* (1937), *Old Homes and Gardens of North Carolina* (1939), and *From My Highest Hill: Carolina Mountain Folks* (1941). Wootten died in New Bern on April 6, 1959. Her photographic archives are in the North Carolina Collection at the University of North Carolina Library at Chapel Hill.

See also: PICTURE MEN; ULMANN, DORIS; WOMEN ARTISTS.

—Jerry W. Cotten, *University of North Carolina*

Works Progress Administration

See Farm Security Administration Photography

INSTITUTIONS

FRICK & LINDSAY Co

Cultural Institutions

Section Editor: Beverly B. Patterson

FOR MORE THAN A CENTURY, APPALACHIA HAS WITNESSED SOME OF THE MOST fervent and enthusiastic attempts to improve cultural, social, and economic conditions seen in any American region. Especially influential in the southern mountains have been institutions such as settlement and folk schools, which focused on reviving mountain crafts. Festivals have featured local music and dance, and organizations have promoted pride and well-being. Three general trends have emerged in institutions that grew out of such efforts. The first, and one that has long been dominant in the region, is the effort to bring education, the arts, and culture into a region thought by many to be both culturally and economically impoverished. This strategy, according to Marian Godfrey, director of the culture program at the Pew Charitable Trusts, guided major foundation support of the arts throughout the United States during the 1960s and 1970s. It is based on the belief that all Americans should have access to professional and high-quality arts and artists and the conclusion that such access has been inadequate outside the largest cities. In contrast, a second trend has been to increase support for the appreciation and preservation of the region's own culture—especially for its rich traditions of music, dance, crafts, and storytelling. Most recently this has taken the form of heritage tourism projects and cultural and historic preservation programs that feature the distinctive cultural resources of Appalachian communities. A third trend accommodates a variety of cultural interests through energetic institutional involvement in education, arts, and culture in ways recognizing both regional and national resources. Whatever the motives, these various efforts have resulted in the establishment of a wide array of institutions honoring and strengthening cultural life in Appalachia.

With a mission to perpetuate arts and culture in the region, institutions such as art museums, public libraries, arts councils, theaters, concert societies, and colleges have taken root in Appalachian communities, as in the rest of the nation. A closer look at their origins, however, sometimes reveals a special Appalachian story in attempts to promote cultural and social awareness among mountain residents. One widespread concern around the turn of the twentieth century, for example, was providing library services. In the late nineteenth and early twentieth centuries, Andrew Carnegie funded nearly two thousand public libraries in the United States, a number of them in the Appalachian region. That legacy lives on in communities such as

Facing page: One of the four Carnegie Museums of Pittsburgh, the Andy Warhol Museum features the Pittsburgh-born artist's 1986 *Self-Portrait* in its entranceway.

Packhorse librarians in Hindman, Kentucky, 1938. Riding horses and mules into remote areas of Appalachia to deliver books was an opportunity for female heads of households to earn an income while promoting social and cultural awareness. Begun in 1935, the Pack Horse Library Project ended in 1943.

Murphy, North Carolina, where the old Carnegie library building still stands, though it was remodeled as a county historical museum when the library moved to new and larger quarters. The need for library services for remote rural areas stimulated creative thinking across the region. In 1905 the first horse-drawn wagon took a collection of books to readers in Washington County, Maryland. A generation later, a New Deal initiative created jobs for female heads of households, paying them to serve as packhorse librarians in remote regions of eastern Kentucky. Women who took these jobs rode horses or mules fifty to eighty miles a week along footpaths and through creek beds to deliver reading materials to homes and schools in mountain hollows.

For many years, institutional programs designed to recognize and legitimate the region's cultural resources have provided a counterpoint to the trend of importing culture into Appalachia. Such programs have included preservation of the region's own historical artifacts and documents in museums and archives, as well as presentation of its most distinctive traditions at festivals, special exhibits, and other venues. A number of institutions in the region, some organized in reaction to the image of Appalachia as a region bereft of culture, see recognition of local culture as their foremost mission. Local heritage centers, historical societies, folk schools, archives, and historical museums document, interpret, celebrate, and advocate the value of regional history and culture. Grassroots events have also become durable institutions in Appalachian communities. These range from the popular Old Fiddler's Convention in Galax, Virginia, and the National Storytelling Festival in Jonesborough, Tennessee, to little-publicized community gatherings such as homecomings, cemetery decoration days, and informal musical jam sessions.

In many cases, individual institutions serve multiple interests. The John C. Campbell Folk School, which celebrated its eightieth anniversary in 2005, highlights local artists and regional culture while introducing arts and crafts from elsewhere. The school houses an archive and supports research and documentation of traditional cultures in the region. Similarly, the Penland School of Crafts, established in the 1920s with a mission to serve the local population, has changed with the times. In its early days, the school supplied looms and materials to local women and marketed their handwoven goods as the Penland Weavers. Eventually the Penland School adapted its program to a new audience and became a national center for crafts that attracts fourteen thousand visitors each year, houses a resident artist program, and operates a gallery that sells the work of resident artists, instructors, and others.

The conflicting impulses that influenced the development of these and other Appalachian cultural institutions have long attracted the interest of regional scholars. In one of the best-known critical assessments, *All That Is Native and Fine: The Politics of Culture in an American Region,* David E. Whisnant explores such impulses as part of a larger study of the dynamics and implications of cultural change. Using case studies, Whisnant contends that the interventions of various cultural missionaries such as ballad collectors, handicraft revivalists, and folk festival promoters in the early 1900s produced mixed results. Cultural problems arise, for example, when products offered to the public as authentic mountain crafts and music are not rooted in Appalachian traditions, even though created in the region.

Critics such as Whisnant further argue that cultural institutions, in their efforts to improve conditions in the region, have contributed to the very stereotypes that continue to plague it. Like the institutions themselves, stereotypes draw on the region's legacy of poverty and uneven development. When the Appalachian Regional Commission was established in 1965, one in three Appalachians lived in poverty, a rate 50 percent higher than the national average. By 1990 development had cut the poverty rate in half and significantly reduced the difference between the regional and national poverty rates. Improved economic conditions have had remarkably little impact on negative stereotypes, however, especially in film and television. Mass-media characterizations of Appalachian people as backward, lazy, ignorant, and prone to violence continue to sustain the image of the region as both economically and culturally impoverished.

On the other hand, positive stereotypes have promulgated a romanticized view of Appalachian culture. Numerous writers, photographers, ethnographers, folklorists, and others from the early 1900s to the present have made Appalachia one of the best-documented cultural areas in the United States, and that rich cultural legacy has been a boon to the advertising and the tourism industries. Marketing specialists have long recognized and used the power of images such as banjos and fiddles, log cabins and mountain farmsteads, and homespun coverlets and patchwork quilts to attract travelers to the region and to sell its products. In the late 1990s, HandMade in America's marketing campaign for its Craft Heritage Trails created an inviting poster that featured photographs of a mountain vista, a potter at work, a mountain dulcimer, and other beautiful handmade objects along with a text that described the "fiercely independent people of the North Carolina high country" as resourceful, creative, and hospitable raconteurs. None of these images individually, or even the positive and negative stereotypes combined, can approximate the actual cultural complexity of the region, however. Characterizing even a part of this diverse region as a homogeneous culture reinforces the stereotypes that play into various political agendas for reform or exploitation.

Many issues besides stereotypes affect the nature of cultural institutions in Appalachia. Although the Appalachian region is largely rural, it is also home to metropolitan areas, where a number of major cultural institutions are well established in the American mainstream. The Carnegie Museum of Art, founded in Pittsburgh in 1895, as well as the city's world-renowned symphony orchestra, for example, enjoy prestige far beyond the Appalachian region. In the southern tier of upstate New York, the Chautauqua Institution has offered summer programs in literature and the fine arts for more than one hundred years, and the Glimmerglass Opera, established in 1975 at Cooperstown, has become one of the nation's premier summer opera venues. By the close of the twentieth century, most observers considered hopelessly out of date any statement such as one in a 1964 report by the President's Appalachian Regional Commission convened by John F. Kennedy in 1963. It described Appalachia as "a region apart, geographically and statistically," and concluded that the focus of an Appalachian program should be "the introduction of Appalachia and its people into fully active membership in the American society."

In a region as large and diverse as Appalachia, questions of regional identity and authenticity become blurred. Many people who have lived in communities in the Appalachian region all their lives, especially Native Americans, residents of urban centers, and people living at the northern and southern extremes of the region, do not think of themselves as Appalachian. While the Andy Warhol Museum in Pittsburgh and the Birmingham Civil Rights Institute in Alabama may not represent themselves as Appalachian cultural institutions, they originated in the region and have important ties to it. An understanding of these ties provides a larger framework for understanding an institution and its legacy. That an institution such as the Appalachian Cultural Museum, which opened in 1989, would mount permanent exhibits focused on entrepreneurs and feature patent models and race cars as well as displaying dough trays, plow points, and other farm tools as objects of art opens viewers to a more comprehensive cultural view of the Appalachian region.

A sampling of other Appalachian cultural institutions further illustrates the region's cultural diversity. The Museum of the Cherokee Indian in western North Carolina, the Sequoyah Birthplace Museum in east Tennessee, the Seneca-Iroquois National Museum in the Allegany Mountains of New York, and the Choctaw Museum of the Southern Indian in Mississippi represent Native Americans, who generally think of themselves as tribal members rather than as Appalachians. Nevertheless, they have extraordinary ties to the region. The Cherokees, for example, who once controlled much of the area that is now the southern Appalachians, believe their people have always lived in present-day western North Carolina. Stories of their origin describe the first man and woman, Kanati and Selu, who were born in the area now called the Shining Rock Wilderness near the Blue Ridge Parkway. In addition, the Kituhwa Mound site, which Cherokees identify as the site of the first Cherokee town, is located on the Qualla Boundary near Cherokee, North Carolina, present home of the Eastern Band of Cherokee Indians.

Occupational cultures that have constituted a significant part of Appalachian heritage—farming, coal mining, logging, glassmaking, iron and steel manufacturing, and railroading, in particular—also add to the cultural diversity of the region. In an approach typical of American outdoor museums, the Farmers' Museum in Cooperstown, New York, re-creates a moment in time. Visitors are invited to stroll through a village and working farm where crafts demonstrators and others interpret daily life in the year 1845 in Appalachia's northernmost section. A more unusual outdoor presentation, that of the Frontier Culture Museum (formerly the Museum of American Frontier Culture) near Staunton, Virginia, showcases the diversity embedded in Appalachian agriculture by featuring farmsteads not only from Virginia, but also from the Ulster region of Ireland, the West Midlands of England, and the Rhine Valley of Germany. By demonstrating architectural styles, farm practices, and cultural traditions that intersected in the region, the museum helps visitors understand the complexity behind Appalachian farming practices.

A number of cultural institutions focus on industrial activities not always associated with Appalachia in the popular mind but of great importance to one part or another of the region. The Rivers of Steel National and State Heritage Area, designated by Congress in 1996, received funding that allowed development of projects in a seven-county area around Pittsburgh to draw attention to the region's heritage of steel and iron production. Besides preserving industrial artifacts, these projects have solicited the views and perspectives of steelworker families and perpetuated their experience. The Rivers of Steel Archives, public tours, special programs, and a regional folklife center are part of this development along with redevelopment plans for the Carrie Furnace Site that include establishing a new national park. In Alabama, culture and tourism specialists have worked with government agencies and others to transform abandoned ironworks into tourist destinations that tell the story of heavy industry in the Birmingham area. In West Virginia, where mining long dominated the economy, veteran miners lead tours of underground passages at the Exhibition Coal Mine of Beckley, showing visitors an authentic coal seam and helping them trace the evolution of mining in the region.

A desire to recognize Appalachia as a complex region also prompted the development of fourteen centers and institutes that specialize in Appalachian studies. These programs grew out of defensive impulses as well as new opportunities that emerged in the last half of the twentieth century. During that time, scholars and activists articulated the need to identify the region as geographically and culturally distinct. This, they believed, would facilitate efforts to preserve its authentic culture and produce well-documented descriptions of the region so that outsider stereotypes of mountaineers and hillbillies would not define Appalachia by default. New resources became available when Congress established the Appalachian Regional Commission in 1965. This funding, together with the support for new perspectives on the region that occurred in the wake of the Civil Rights movement and with the organization of the Appalachian Studies Association in 1977, made possible the development of these centers and institutes and their affiliations with colleges and universities in the region.

A few institutions—such as Highlander Research and Education Center in New Market, Tennessee (formerly the Highlander Folk School in Monteagle, Tennessee), and Appalshop, a major producer and distributor of documentary films in Whitesburg, Kentucky—carry out their cultural missions with explicit political activism. Highlander Center, for example, has a rich and controversial history, including inquiries into its alleged subversive activities by the Special Investigating Committee of the Tennessee General Assembly and the FBI. In the 1988 documentary film *We Shall Overcome*, Pete Seeger, Myles Horton, and others discuss Highlander's training of activists, its use of music to unite people, and its role in helping "We Shall Overcome" become an anthem of the Civil Rights movement. The current version of the song, like Highlander itself, reflects many years of interactions between blacks and whites.

These and other cultural institutions described in the following pages and throughout the *Encyclopedia of Appalachia* are a representative sampling of many others that currently exist in the region. Beginning in the 1960s, especially with the establishment of the National Endowments for the Arts and Humanities and the Appalachian Regional Commission, interest in the arts, cultural heritage, and historic preservation combined with new opportunities for funding from federal, state, and local agencies and from private foundations to fuel an explosion of educational nonprofit institutions. With their help, Appalachian cultural institutions, formal and informal, have achieved critical mass in both numbers and sophistication.

Emerging trends in cultural policy research suggest directions that energetic development may take Appalachian cultural institutions in the future. Despite the increase in their numbers over the past forty years, cultural institutions operate for the most part as decentralized and private-sector enterprises. No regional or national policymaking organization yet exists to help guide the creation of a strong institutional infrastructure. Nevertheless, interest in cultural policy research continues to increase at national and international levels. Researchers are interested in gaining a better understanding of how arts and cultural organizations and activities contribute to the health of American communities. They are interested in positioning the arts and culture alongside other policy areas such as economic development, housing, education, and employment. The potential exists for the creation of an infrastructure in which these institutions can work together across state lines to identify and preserve the distinctive cultural resources of Appalachia.

—Beverly B. Patterson, *North Carolina Folklife Institute*

Andrew M. Isserman, "Appalachia Then and Now: An Update of 'The Realities of Deprivation' Report to the President in 1964," *Journal of Appalachian Studies* (Spring 1997); Ruth Ann Stewart and Catherine C. Galley, "Appendix: The Research and Information Infrastructure for Cultural Policy: A Consideration of Models for the United States," in *Informing Cultural Policy* by J. Mark Schuster (2002); David E. Whisnant, *All That Is Native and Fine: The Politics of Culture in an American Region* (1983).

African American Heritage Family Tree Museum

The African American Heritage Family Tree Museum in Ansted, West Virginia, was created to collect, exhibit, and preserve the African American history and culture of West Virginia. Established in 1991, the museum occupies an original company house constructed by the Gauley Mountain Coal Company in 1900 and purchased by an African American couple, George and Artie Murray, in 1946. The recruitment of black laborers in the early 1890s significantly increased the African American population of Ansted, and a community began to develop.

Through artifacts such as tools, household items, toys, apparel, photographs, and documents, the museum exhibits African American history and culture in Ansted and southern West Virginia. The museum also displays historical items from Camp George Washington Carver, the nation's first 4-H camp for blacks, as well as artifacts associated with prominent African Americans in West Virginia's history. These individuals include Booker T. Washington, who lived and taught school in Malden; Minnie Buckingham Harper of McDowell County, who was the first female African American state legislator in the United States; and Carter G. Woodson, historian and founder of Negro History Week (the precursor to Black History Month), who worked and went to school for many years in West Virginia.

Open during the summer months, the museum welcomes youth groups and tourists, as well as expatriate West Virginians who have returned for family, school, church, and community reunions.

See also: WASHINGTON, BOOKER T. (LITERATURE).

—Brucella Jordan, *Marshall University*

Andy Warhol Museum

The Andy Warhol Museum in Pittsburgh houses the world's most comprehensive collection of pop artist Andy Warhol's work and memorabilia. Warhol, who was born in Pittsburgh, was one of the most influential American artists of the second half of the twentieth century.

Andrew Warhola (1928–1987), who later changed his name to Andy Warhol, was the son of Julia and Andrej Warhola, Carpatho-Rusyn immigrants from Mikova, in the Medzilaborce region of Czechoslovakia, now in the Slovak Republic. They settled in the Oakland section of Pittsburgh, where Andrej was a construction worker. Warhol's mother encouraged him to develop his artistic talent. Starting in the fourth grade, Warhol attended Saturday morning art classes conducted by Joseph C. Fitzpatrick for four years and at age seventeen he enrolled at the Carnegie Institute of Technology (now Carnegie Mellon University). The training Warhol received in Pittsburgh gave him the self-confidence and determination to become a professional artist, and upon graduation in 1949 he moved to New York City, where he became one of the country's leading commercial artists.

The Andy Warhol Museum is one of the four Carnegie Museums of Pittsburgh and is a collaborative project of the Carnegie Institute, the Andy Warhol Foundation for the Visual Arts, and the Dia Center for the Arts in New York City. Its holdings include films and videos, paintings and drawings, sculptural works, and archives. Each year the Warhol also presents special exhibitions of work by Warhol and other artists. Friday evening programs include bands, lectures, and other performances. The Weekend Factory on Saturday and Sunday afternoons offers hands-on experiences for the entire family.

See also: ART MUSEUMS; CARNEGIE MUSEUM OF ART; PITTSBURGH, PENNSYLVANIA (URBAN APPALACHIAN EXPERIENCE).

—Colleen Russell Criste, *Andy Warhol Museum*

Appalachian Center for Community Service

Located in Emory, Virginia, Emory and Henry College's Appalachian Center for Community Service and its academic department, Public Policy and Community Service, have engaged in place-based education, integrating service with learning, since 1996. This approach to education, which emphasizes a holistic understanding of place, requires attention to three critical educational and political practices: reflection, social justice, and collaborative partnerships, through which the center seeks to equip students with the civic, moral, and intellectual tools to care for and serve the places they might settle. For example, students who work directly with schools and communities in Washington County, Virginia, experience firsthand the gulf that often exists between the intent of public policy and its actual effects on people's lives.

The Public Policy and Community Service program emphasizes the interdisciplinary nature of the study of public policymaking and community service. This includes consideration of social, cultural, political, economic, and religious influences on the long development of a place. The center coordinates all of the service components for the academic major in Public Policy and Community Service and other service learning courses offered throughout the college's curriculum that integrate structured work in the community with classroom instruction and practices of critical reflection.

The center oversees three scholarship programs that require students to perform community service in exchange for their financial assistance: the Bonner Scholars Program, the Appalachian Center Associates Program, and an AmeriCorps program. Moreover, the center coordinates the Emory and Henry Student Tutoring Program, placing more than fifty college students in public schools as math and reading tutors. The center's staff has responsibility for campuswide service projects and events, as well as ongoing partnerships with agencies and organizations throughout southwest Virginia.

See also: APPALACHIAN CENTERS AND INSTITUTES; METHODISTS (RELIGION).

—Tal Stanley, *Appalachian Center for Community Service*

Appalachian Centers and Institutes

Fourteen public or nonprofit Appalachian centers and institutes are located across the Appalachian region. Components or affiliates of universities and colleges, these centers engage in a wide variety of projects, from scholarly research to community development.

The development of Appalachian centers parallels the evolution of Appalachian studies generally. For many years, institutions outside the region led studies of Appalachia, and their perspective was often that of the missionary, social reformer, or outside investor. This trend continued into the 1960s and early 1970s with such books as Michael Harrington's *The Other America* (1962). Harry Caudill, a native of eastern Kentucky, was one of the first nationally prominent authors to articulate a colonial model of Appalachian development although his book *Night Comes to the Cumberlands* (1963) was criticized by some as perpetuating an approach that emphasized Appalachians as victims without considering the history of resistance and struggle that has characterized the coalfields.

An impetus to consider Appalachia from within came when Congress established the Appalachian Regional Commission in 1965 to support economic and social development in the region. Concurrently, support for a new perspective on the region came from the Civil Rights movement. Appalachian migrants to urban centers such as Chicago, Detroit, Cleveland, and Cincinnati found themselves in ghettos next door to other minorities who were protesting and redefining their identities. The Urban Appalachian Council in Cincinnati was incorporated in 1974 to improve the lives of Appalachians in the Cincinnati area. The People's Appalachian Research Collective was organized by urban Appalachians who had gone to college in these cities and other urban areas with large numbers of Appalachian migrants. The collective's journal, *People's Appalachia*, begun in 1971, was one of the first to publish serious critical research of the region from the perspective of those who were themselves Appalachian.

In addition to these efforts, which were keyed to political activism and encouraged by parallel development of programs in black, women's, and Latin American studies, faculty on Appalachian campuses began to develop curricula related to the region. In response to the need for an umbrella organization, the Appalachian Studies Association was formed in 1977 by a group of scholars, teachers, and regional activists who believed that shared community was important to those writing, researching, and teaching about Appalachia. The Appalachian Studies Association's mission was to encourage study, advance scholarship, disseminate information, and enhance communication between Appalachian peoples and their communities, governmental organizations, and educational institutions. The association, in turn, legitimized the demand for on-campus Appalachian centers, as did a concurrent trend toward the publication of Appalachian scholarship by university presses in Illinois, Kentucky, Tennessee, North Carolina, and Georgia.

Thirty-five years after the Appalachian Regional Commission's creation, Appalachian centers and institutes were active on fourteen area campuses in the region: Appalachian State University (Center for Appalachian Studies); Berea College (Appalachian Center); East Tennessee State University (Center for Appalachian Studies and Services); Emory and Henry College (Appalachian Center for Community Service); Marshall University (Center for the Study of Ethnicity and Gender in Appalachia); Morehead State University (Institute for Regional Analysis and Public Policy); Ohio University (Institute for Local Government Administration and Rural Development); Radford University (Appalachian Regional Studies Center); Southeast Community College at Cumberland, Kentucky (Appalachian Center); University of Kentucky (Appalachian Center); University of Tennessee (Center for Community Partnerships); Virginia Polytechnic Institute and State University (Appalachian Studies Program); West Virginia University (Regional Research Institute); and Western Carolina University (Mountain Heritage Center).

These centers participate in a large number of activities, including educational reform, electronic-based course development for rural Appalachia, poverty studies, health education awareness, forest development, music and dance education, literacy training, volunteer development, preservation of Appalachian archives, entrepreneurial training and development, infrastructure evaluation for economic development, publication of the *Atlas of Appalachia*, folk art, herbal medicine, museum maintenance, wildlife preservation, crafts, regional welfare reform, community networking projects, home construction, cultural tourism, and ethnic and gender studies.

In the summer of 1999, the Appalachian Regional Commission formally brought together the directors of these fourteen centers. The outgrowth of an initiative developed by Ronald D Eller of the University of Kentucky Appalachian Center, this and subsequent meetings sought to develop and maintain a network of exchange and cooperation among the centers.

Collaboration has proved difficult, though, since each center faces its own institutional problems, has its own particular focus, and responds to the needs of its own subregion. As a means of pooling resources and carrying out projects over wider areas, however, cooperation remains an important objective.

See also: APPALACHIAN REGIONAL COMMISSION (GOVERNMENT).

—Lynda Ann Ewen, *Marshall University*

Appalachian Community Development Association

The Appalachian Community Development Association is a not-for-profit cultural and educational organization located in Cincinnati. Approximately one-third of the population of metropolitan Cincinnati, which includes parts of southwestern Ohio, northern Kentucky, and southeastern Indiana, is of Appalachian heritage.

The organization has its roots in the Appalachian Festival begun by the Junior League of Cincinnati in 1970 to provide an annual showcase for Appalachian artists. In 1974 the Appalachian Community Development Association was incorporated to take over the program. The purpose of the new organization expanded beyond the festival as it sought to provide a wide range of support for Cincinnati's Appalachian community, sponsoring many educational and cultural events that encouraged urban Appalachians and non-Appalachians to appreciate the cultural heritage of the region.

The Appalachian Festival, which soon expanded to fill Cincinnati's Convention Center, finally found its home as an annual outdoor festival at Coney Island, a popular picnic park in Cincinnati, on Mother's Day weekend. The festival includes more than a hundred handicraft exhibitors, fifteen special demonstrators, sixty living history interpreters, numerous Appalachian food vendors, three continuous music stages, storytelling programs, and workshops. A festival-supported Youth Activities Day features hands-on activities and draws as many as forty-five hundred students from the tri-state area.

In addition to the annual festival, the association sponsors concerts and other cultural events, including exhibits of art and photography and readings by rural and urban Appalachian writers. It also cosponsors events with organizations such as the Urban Appalachian Council, Greater Cincinnati Junior League, and Appalshop, all of which share the association's mission.

Through an annual grants program, the Appalachian Community Development Association disburses proceeds from the festival to organizations working for the Appalachian community in the metropolitan Cincinnati area. Funds totaling more than $150,000 have been distributed to more than forty organizations for a wide range of educational, cultural, and social programs.

See also: CINCINNATI, OHIO (URBAN APPALACHIAN EXPERIENCE); OHIO ARTS COUNCIL; URBAN APPALACHIAN ENCLAVES (URBAN APPALACHIAN EXPERIENCE).

—Donald W. Drewry, *Appalachian Community Development Association*

Appalachian Cultural Museum

Appalachian State University's Appalachian Cultural Museum in Boone, North Carolina, opened in 1989 with a commitment to fostering an understanding of Appalachian regional culture. The primary purpose of the museum's ten-thousand-square-foot permanent exhibit, *Time and Change: Centuries of Living in the Blue Ridge Mountains*, is to dismantle Appalachian stereotypes. Created by the New York design firm Purpura and Kisner from research developed by a team of scholars led by Cratis Williams, *Time and Change* represents one of the first, if not the very first, efforts by an Appalachian museum to move beyond a primarily folkloric format for interpreting mountain history and culture. Instead, *Time and Change* focuses on middle-class entrepreneurs across time. The exhibit includes information about people who owned mountains, general store operators who held patents for inventions, mica miners, commercial musicians, stock car racers, composers of symphonies, and African American ex-slaves.

In addition to the froes, fiddles, looms, and coverlets that have long comprised the conventional material culture canon of Appalachia, the exhibit exposes patrons to lesser-known Appalachian objects. Thus, patent models, Winston Cup race cars, Munchkin houses from the Land of Oz theme park, ski slope snowblowers, and self-portraits painted by local people are on display next to dough trays and iron plow points presented as works of sculpture. Though the innovative exhibit sparked some controversy, the Western North Carolina Historical Association gave the museum its 1990 Achievement Award.

Since the museum's opening, two thousand square feet of gallery space have been added to house temporary exhibits, and a native wildflower garden has been developed on the grounds. The museum staff continues to seek ways of providing a continuing reinterpretation of its service region and to serve as a teaching laboratory for the university's Public History graduate program.

See also: APPALACHIAN SPECIAL COLLECTIONS; APPALACHIAN STATE UNIVERSITY THEATER PROGRAM (PERFORMING ARTS).

—Charles Alan Watkins, *Appalachian State University*

Appalachian Regional Studies Center

The Appalachian Regional Studies Center of Radford University, located in Radford, Virginia, was founded in 1994. Growing out of the academic Appalachian Studies program in place since 1981, the center serves as an umbrella organization for numerous functions. The overall mission is to advance knowledge about the region by promoting appreciation of Appalachia's rich culture.

Within the Appalachian Regional Studies Center, four dominant strands of action have emerged. First is the Appalachian studies curriculum, which includes an undergraduate interdisciplinary minor, courses for various majors, and graduate courses supporting master's degrees in English, education, social work, health-related fields, and the arts.

The second major endeavor is programming. The Appalachian Events Committee, a collaboration of students, faculty, and staff, plans and implements three to five major activities annually, all of which are open to campus and larger communities. These include the fall Appalachian Folk Arts Festival during Family Weekend, Appalachian Awareness Day each February, and a major spring bluegrass concert.

The center's third objective is the compilation of research and resource materials. Since the inception of Appalachian studies at Radford, student fieldwork and other research efforts have produced more than 950 original projects in folklore, literature, history, anthropology, sociology, health care, education, music, and the arts. Complete with written reports, analyses, and transcriptions of interviews and supplementary materials such as audiotapes, videotapes, photographs, slides, maps, and artifacts, these research findings have been cataloged, indexed, and archived for use by center patrons. Other resources include books, periodicals, vertical files, and videotapes, including approximately 140 interviews and performances by Appalachian authors taking part in the Highland Summer Conference at Radford University since 1978.

Outreach, in the form of community work, is also a major objective of the Appalachian Regional Studies Center. For example, the ongoing Appalachian Arts and Studies in the Schools program has developed a partnership with public schools in southwest Virginia to encourage Appalachian youth to attend college. Another major initiative is the Selu Living History Museum. Located in Radford's Selu Conservancy, the museum is an interpretation of farm life in the 1930s.

See also: APPALACHIAN REGIONAL COMMISSION (GOVERNMENT); WRITING WORKSHOPS, CONFERENCES, AND FESTIVALS (LITERATURE).

—Grace Toney Edwards, *Radford University*

Appalachian Special Collections

The establishment of special library collections and archives devoted to the Appalachian region is a recent phenomenon. Librarian and journalist Horace Kephart complained in 1905 that he could not find so much as a magazine article written within his generation that described the Appalachian land and its people, and in 1921 Alfred Perrin stated that all the fiction and nonfiction books ever written about the southern mountains could be gathered on one desk. By 1966, however, noted Appalachian bibliographer Robert F. Munn could write in *Mountain Life and Work* that "the sheer tonnage of writing on the Southern Appalachians alone is staggering."

In his surveys of research materials on the region, Munn found that most of this material was housed in state-oriented collections and in the Southern collections of Duke University in Durham, North Carolina, and the University of North Carolina at Chapel Hill. At that time, only two strong Appalachian regional collections existed, those at Berea College in Berea, Kentucky, and West Virginia University in Morgantown. Noting the presence of good state history collections, two extensive bibliographies (E. E. Edwards's 1935 *References on the Mountaineers of the Southern Appalachians* and Munn's 1961 *The Southern Appalachians: A Bibliography and Guide to Studies*), and growing interest in the region, Munn predicted in 1966 that comprehensive collections on the Appalachian region would be forthcoming shortly.

Seven years later, Richard B. Drake, historian and editor of the important but short-lived journal *Appalachian Notes*, identified twenty-five "major" collections and twenty-nine other "significant" ones. Drake attributed this virtual renaissance in Appalachian regional bibliography and librarianship to an increased recognition and acceptance of Appalachian studies and to a broader interpretation of what constitutes Appalachia. Drake also included local collections that did not cover the region as a whole. Fourteen of his major collections were located within the broadly defined Appalachian region and eleven of them—including such international research collections as the Library of Congress and Harvard University's Houghton Library—were located outside the region. Four out of the five most important regionwide repositories in the year 2000 were included in Drake's 1973 list of major collections: West Virginia University's West Virginia and Regional History Collection; Berea College's Weatherford-Hammond Collection; the University of Kentucky's Special Collections (which now includes its Appalachian Collection); and Appalachian State University's W. L. Eury Appalachian Collection. The fifth primary Appalachian collection, the Archives of Appalachia, was founded at East Tennessee State University in 1978.

In late 1982, the Appalachian Consortium's Heritage and Folklife Committee initiated a program to study the needs of regional archives and manuscript repositories. In June 1984, a regional collections committee sent a questionnaire to 947 institutions, including colleges and universities, historical societies, public libraries, selected businesses and religious organizations, museums, and relevant libraries operated by federal, state, and local governments; 352 responded to the survey.

The results of the survey prompted developments that included several publications. *Archives in Appalachia: A Directory* (1985) described 181 repositories in seven states (Georgia, Kentucky, North Carolina, South Carolina, Tennessee, Virginia, and West Virginia) that held historical records pertaining to the region. The Appalachian Consortium established a permanent regional collections committee, and its publication, *The Curator: The Newsletter of Appalachian Regional Collections* (published irregularly since 1986), has served as a forum for regional collections to communicate their needs and mutual concerns and to share information about the organization and preservation of documentation in Appalachia.

Public (28.5 percent) and academic (24.7 percent) libraries comprised the two largest groups of respondents to the consortium's 1984 survey. "Other" was the third most frequent category; museums comprised the fourth. Business and religious organizations accounted for less than 2 percent of all responding repositories. Typically, archival holdings were small, with 51 percent of the 141 repositories reporting fewer than 50 linear feet of records. Fifteen repositories (10.6 percent) with holdings greater than 1,000 feet together with eleven (7.8 percent) with between 301 and 999 linear feet constituted less than 20 percent of repositories surveyed but contained at least 69 percent of all manuscript sources relating to the region.

Types of researchers using the region's archives are varied. Genealogists are reported to be the largest group by far. Students from colleges, universities, and secondary and elementary schools also make up a substantial number of patrons. Academic researchers have been less frequently reported as primary patrons. Only 20 percent of repositories ranked them as either their first or second most common type of user. Historian Valentina Maiewskij-Hay of Appalachian State University, however, observed that the line separating academic researchers and students from genealogists has become blurred. Historical scholarship on the region such as Altina Waller's *Feud: Hatfields, McCoys, and Social Change in Appalachia, 1860–1900* (1988) and British historian Martin Crawford's work on Ashe County, North Carolina, for example, has increasingly relied on genealogical research materials and methods.

Two major regional bibliographies have appeared since Munn's 1961 publication: *Bibliography of Southern Appalachia* (1976) and *Appalachian Bibliography* (2nd edition, 1980), the latter updated tri-annually by *Appalachian Outlook*. Special topic bibliographies have also been published. Notable among these are Sidney Farr's *Appalachian Women* (1981) and Edward Cabbell's *Like a Weaving: References and Resources on Black Appalachians* (1984). A number of special topic or special format bibliographies have been published in *Appalachian Journal*, and the *Journal of Appalachian Studies* publishes an annual "Appalachian Studies Bibliography."

Appalachia is a region characterized by decentralization and diversity. Appalachian documentation can be similarly characterized: significant research materials are scattered throughout the region, and no comprehensible bibliographic roadmap exists for them. If one intends to do primary research on the Cherokee Indians, a trip to Western Carolina University is a necessity. Research on coal-mining accidents requires a stop at the National Mine Health and Safety Academy in West Virginia. For material on President Andrew Johnson, researchers should visit archives at Tusculum College in Tennessee, and so forth throughout the region. That diversity of subject matter, decentralization of collections, and lack of adequate bibliography have had a profound impact on Appalachian scholarship is manifest in the nearly total absence of reference books and synthetic scholarly overviews of the region.

See also: ART MUSEUMS; CHURCH ARCHIVES.

—Fred J. Hay, *Appalachian State University*

Richard B. Drake, ed., *Appalachian Notes* (1973–74); Ellen Garrison, ed., *Archives in Appalachia: A Directory* (1985); Robert F. Munn, "Research Materials on the Appalachian Region," *Mountain Life and Work* (Summer 1966).

Appalshop

See Appalshop (Media)

Archives of Appalachia

Part of the Center for Appalachian Studies and Services at East Tennessee State University in Johnson City, the Archives of Appalachia collects and preserves historical materials that promote academic and public understanding of the southern Appalachian region. The archives hold hundreds of collections, including personal papers of families and individuals and institutional records of businesses and organizations in the region. The facility's large photographic collection contains nearly a quarter of a million images, and its oral history and folklore collection consists of thousands of sound and moving image recordings.

Originating from an earlier folklore collection started by university professors Thomas G. Burton and Ambrose N.

Manning, the Archives of Appalachia was officially created in 1978 as part of the inauguration of the university's president, Arthur De Rosier. When the Center for Appalachian Studies and Services was created in 1984, the archives' services and staff were expanded and functioned as part of the Center for Appalachian Studies and Services and the East Tennessee State University Sherrod Library. In January 1998, the Archives of Appalachia was fully integrated into the Center for Appalachian Studies and Services.

The facility's collections are encompassed in three units: Appalachian Archives, a multimedia collection of materials that documents the political, economic, social, and cultural history of the southern Appalachians; the University Archives, which documents the history of East Tennessee State University since its founding in 1911 as East Tennessee State Normal School; and Special Collections, focusing on local, Tennessee, and regional culture and history as well as Scottish and Irish studies.

The Archives of Appalachia offers audio and videotape loans covering specific Appalachian topics such as social and economic development, music, crafts, folklore, railroads, and local history. Other services include subject bibliographies, public presentations, information on conservation of materials, and research assistance. The collections are accessible to researchers and the general public.

See also: APPALACHIAN SPECIAL COLLECTIONS; B. CARROLL REECE MEMORIAL MUSEUM.

—Malcolm E. Blowers, *University of North Carolina at Asheville*

Archives of Industrial Society

Established in 1963, the Archives of Industrial Society collects and preserves records concerning the development of urban industrial society with an emphasis on Pittsburgh and western Pennsylvania. The repository holds 626 collections of papers, records, microforms, photographs, and oral histories. It is a part of the Archives Service Center of the University of Pittsburgh's University Library System. Other elements of the Archives Service Center include the United Electrical, Radio, and Machine Workers of America Archives and Labor Collections, the University Archives and Records Management, and the Dick Thornburgh Collection (including the papers of the former Pennsylvania governor and U.S. attorney general).

The archives hold two collections of special value for the study of Appalachian history. The collection of Henry Shaw (7 linear feet, 1965–72), a political and social activist who organized the Student Action Against Poverty at West Virginia University and participated in coal-mining, antiwar, and labor-related organizations, contains correspondence related to social issues in Appalachia, essays by Shaw, statistical studies, and publications from the period. The collection of U.S. Representative Elmer J. Holland (132 linear feet, 1956–68) contains subject files related to Appalachia, especially the 1967 amending of the Appalachian Regional Development Act (adopted in 1965).

Other archive collections with Appalachian information include those of labor unions and organizations such as the United Electrical, Radio, and Machine Workers of America and the Tri-State Conference on Manufacturing. Miscellaneous information about the region also appears in the records of the University Archives, which include economic and social studies, reports, and papers.

Materials are accessible through unpublished inventories, catalogs, and indexes. Collections are included in the National Union Catalog of Manuscript Collections, Online Computer Library Center, and Pittcat, the University of Pittsburgh's on-line catalog, which is available via the Internet.

See also: APPALACHIAN SPECIAL COLLECTIONS; PITTSBURGH, PENNSYLVANIA (URBAN APPALACHIAN EXPERIENCE).

—Dennis East, *University of Pittsburgh*

Art Museums

From 1895 through the early twenty-first century, approximately thirty-five art museums were established in the Appalachian region. Their development roughly follows that of similar organizations throughout the Western world and, more specifically, such development since the nineteenth century in the United States. While European museums were usually established to house the great collections of the nobility and remained for quite some time semiexclusive, their American counterparts generally were based on ideals of democracy, designed to appeal to the general public, and were often funded and gifted through private donations. Scholar and essayist Stephen Weil has defined the essential functions of museums as preservation, research, and communication. Appalachian art museums embrace these common goals while displaying diversity in the focus of their programs.

Emerging metropolitan centers housed the first art museums in the United States in the late nineteenth century. Of the art museums in Appalachia, one was founded before the twentieth century, and several art associations of the time later became museums as well. The remaining art museums in the Appalachian region were established after 1948.

The first was the Carnegie Museum of Art, established in 1895 in the manufacturing and transportation center of Pittsburgh. While most art museums established around the turn of the century focused on the Old Masters, Andrew Carnegie envisioned a museum consisting of "old masters of tomorrow." His goal was to introduce the people of Pittsburgh to paintings by contemporary American and European artists. The museum organizes the longest-running survey of international contemporary art in North America. Housed in an 1896 American Renaissance–style building with major additions made in 1907, 1974, and 1994, the museum's collection is distinguished by American art from the mid-nineteenth century to the present, French impressionist and post-impressionist paintings, and late twentieth-century works. Also included are American and European decorative arts from the late seventeenth century to the present.

Many of the early art museums in the United States were outgrowths of associations first formed to promote learning and to introduce outside culture to remote communities. In 1898 a group of artists formed the Art Club of Erie, Pennsylvania, to organize exhibitions, present papers, and raise funds to collect artwork for the public library in which they met. The club purchased a building in 1956 and hired a professional director in 1968. The next year, they began a year-round schedule of exhibitions and educational programs and became known as the Erie Art Center. In 1983 the organization's name changed again, to the Erie Art Museum. Still connected to its roots, the museum is now a member-supported, community-based organization. It promotes art making by providing studios, classes, artist services, and artworks to schools. The museum features a diverse collection of four thousand objects and presents exhibitions and lectures.

Similarly, in Alabama the Birmingham Museum of Art traces its inception back to the organization of the Birmingham Art Club in 1908. Affiliated with the City of Birmingham in 1950, the museum opened in five rooms of the City Hall in 1951 and is now the largest municipal museum in the Southeast. With a mandate to be comprehensive in its outlook, the museum began collecting in 1956 and houses more than 21,000 thousand objects from ancient to modern times in an 180,000-square-foot facility.

The Asheville Art Museum was founded in 1948 in western North Carolina more than five decades after the Carnegie Museum of Art. The scale, context, history, collection, and mission of the Asheville Art Museum provide a useful model from which to explore the range of art museums founded in the Appalachian region in the ensuing fifty years.

Asheville holds a remarkable place in Appalachia and the national arts movement. Since the mid-nineteenth century, this hub of the western North Carolina region has been known as a center for arts in America and is one of the top arts destinations in the country. The Asheville area is home to the Southern Highland Craft Guild and the Penland School of Crafts and is the birthplace of the modern studio glass movement. From 1933 to 1957 it was the site of Black Mountain College, an extraordinary educational institution that trained many renowned American modern artists.

Artists founded the Asheville Art Museum as a place to show their own work and the work of others, to call attention to the arts in the community, and to prompt discussion. The museum, the third oldest in North Carolina, serves the Asheville urban area and is the only visual arts facility of its kind in the twenty-three mostly rural counties of western North Carolina.

The Asheville Art Museum collects, preserves, and interprets twentieth- and twenty-first-century American art. Its collection, including nearly 2,000 objects in all media, explores major aesthetic trends with works by George Innes, Romare Bearden, George Luks, Robert Rauschenberg, Josef and Anni Albers, Bessie Harvey, Alex Katz, native sons Kenneth Noland and Donald Sultan, and others. One focus of the museum is historical and contemporary art specifically related to the region, including traditional and studio craft objects. These works are integrated into the larger American story of creativity. The museum's collection has been built primarily through gifts from generous community members. The Asheville Art Museum presents ten to twelve exhibitions annually in its complex of historic and contemporary structures in the heart of downtown. Exhibitions are at the center of an active schedule of in-house and outreach educational programs that include teacher training, curriculum development, adult and school tours, and workshops, films, and lectures developed to educate, entertain, and inspire urban and rural residents and visitors of all ages.

Like the Asheville Art Museum, many other Appalachian museums follow the model of a strong educational component, focus on American art, and emphasis on regional works. Substantial benefactor gifts—sometimes supporting both the buildings and the collections they house—supplement a number of Appalachian museums.

The Greenville County Museum of Art serves as an arts and cultural center for upstate South Carolina. It offers outreach programs and a Museum School of Art and attempts to preserve the culture of its geographic setting through specific collections. In the early 1980s the museum began collecting works depicting southern history or culture by both native southerners and by non-southerners working in the South. At the time, no other museum's collection focused specifically on the South. The museum's Stephen Scott Young collection features the artist's watercolors, temperas, and drawings depicting Greenville landmarks. The Greenville Museum houses works ranging from the nineteenth-century portraiture of Thomas Sully to a contemporary collection that features such revered American artists as Josef Albers, Jasper Johns, Andy Warhol, Romare Bearden, and Jacob Lawrence. The Andrew Wyeth collection includes 24 watercolors from the contemporary American master.

West Virginia's Huntington Museum of Art—which houses a substantial collection of Appalachian folk art in addition to its non-regional works—was founded almost solely on private local donations, beginning with a substantial gift from philanthropist Herbert Fitzpatrick. Fitzpatrick not only donated a collection of American and European paintings and prints, Georgian silver, and Islamic prayer rugs, but also the land on which the museum was built. Other donations include the historical Herman P. Dean Firearms Collection, the Daywood Collection (featuring paintings, drawings, prints, sculptures, and glass), and the C. Fred Edwards Conservatory, a unique outdoor nature exhibition featuring two and a half miles of hiking trails.

Chattanooga's Hunter Museum of American Art, which opened its doors in 1952, features holdings that range from colonial to contemporary, with artists from Thomas Cole to Robert Rauschenberg represented. The museum is housed in two buildings: the 1904 Classic Revival–style Faxon-Hunter mansion, which holds the bulk of its nineteenth-century collection, and a contemporary structure built in 1975, which houses the museum's twentieth-century collection. The Benwood Foundation, a private charitable trust, donated the mansion to the Chattanooga Art Association as the site for the city's first art museum.

In Winston-Salem, North Carolina, in 1964, the family of R. J. Reynolds Tobacco Company founder Richard Joshua Reynolds donated the mansion that Reynolds and his wife, Katherine Smith Reynolds, built in 1917 along with twenty acres to house a nonprofit organization dedicated to education and the arts. The Reynolda House, Museum of American Art, opened its doors in 1967. The American art collection includes more than 130 paintings, prints, and sculptures. In a comfortable domestic setting, the home's original furnishings are displayed along with a separate gallery for family furnishings, tableware, linens, toys, and clothing. The museum's acclaimed collection features eighteenth-, nineteenth-, and twentieth-century works by such notables as John Singleton Copley, Mary Cassatt, Thomas Eakins, Andrew Wyeth, and Jacob Lawrence.

The educational focus that marks many Appalachian museums is at the core of the Southeastern Center for Contemporary Art, also in Winston-Salem. A non-collecting museum, the center is dedicated to interpreting the diversity of American contemporary art and fostering relationships between art and society at large. Its exhibitions of American contemporary art encompass music, drama, dance, film, lectures, conferences, and symposiums. The center places a particular emphasis on its innovative educational outreach programs and sponsors a project called "Artist and the Community," a series of residencies in which participating artists focus their creative energies on crucial community issues. Opened in 1956 in response to local artists' need for exhibition space, it had expanded its range to include work by artists from all eleven southeastern states by 1972, when industrialist James G. Hanes willed his thirty-two-acre estate to the center.

The Art Museum of Western Virginia, located in Roanoke, also places a distinct emphasis on American art and houses an impressive collection of works depicting the Blue Ridge Mountains. Founded in 1951, the museum boasts a permanent collection that includes paintings by Asher B. Durand, T. Worthington Whittredge, and Winslow Homer. The museum also holds a substantial collection of American nineteenth- and twentieth-century sculpture, prints, photographs, and decorative arts—the latter featuring outstanding examples of folk art, furniture, and ceramics from western Virginia. A later addition to the museum is a growing collection of African art, with a special focus on West Africa. Through its ArtVan program, the Art Museum of Western Virginia takes art to rural audiences, including schools and senior centers, throughout the region.

Corning, New York's Rockwell Museum of Western Art was founded in 1976 as the Rockwell Museum, the venue for business owners Bob and Hertha Rockwell's vast collection of art and artifacts of the American West, along with Carder Steuben glass, firearms, and antique toys. When the collection became too large for continued display in their family store, the couple donated the collection to a new museum, founded with the financial support of Corning Glass Works. In 2000 the museum was extensively renovated. It houses an expansive permanent collection of both contemporary and traditional works that explore the American West, including paintings by Frederic S. Remington and Charles M. Russell.

The majority of Appalachian museums feature works by a variety of artists, but the Kate Freeman Clark Art Gallery, located in Holly Springs, Mississippi, features the largest collection of paintings by a single artist in the world—a total of 1,050 works. Freeman, the great-niece of Confederate Major General Edward Cary Walthall, refused to sell her paintings during her lifetime but left them in her will, along with the old General Walthall home, to create the Kate Freeman Clark Art Gallery. Clark, who studied as a teenager at the New York School of Art, lived and painted in New York until returning to Holly Springs late in her life.

Impressive art collections in Appalachia are also housed in university-affiliated museums. Greenville, South Carolina's Bob Jones University boasts one of the largest collections of religious art by Old Masters in the country. More than 400 works by such luminaries as Rembrandt, Rubens, Van Dyke, Tintoretto, Veronese, Sebastiano del Piombo, Ribera, and Murillo are part of the museum's permanent collection. Other notable university-run museums in Appalachia include Pennsylvania State University's Palmer Museum of Art, which features a collection of 4,000 works spanning thirty-five centuries and running the gamut from Baroque paintings to Asian and African ceramics. Ohio University's Kennedy Museum of Art is nationally acclaimed for its commitment to multiculturalism, with a particular emphasis on Native American art. The University of Alabama's Sarah Moody Gallery of Art, in operation since 1967, began with a small collection of works by contemporary artists and has grown to feature 450 pieces of some of the strongest American art created between the early 1950s and the early 1970s, including works by Karen Appel, Alice Neel, Lee Krasner, Alexander Calder, Fairfield Porter, Alfred Leslie, and Ansel Adams.

See also: BLACK MOUNTAIN COLLEGE (EDUCATION); SECTION OVERVIEW (VISUAL ARTS).

—Pamela Myers and Marsha Barber, *Asheville Art Museum*

William T. Alderson, ed., *Mermaids, Mummies, and Mastodons: The Emergence of the American Museum* (1992); Sherman E. Lee, ed., *On Understanding Art Museums* (1975); Stephen E. Weil, *Rethinking the Museum and Other Meditations* (1990).

Arts Center of Cannon County

The town of Woodbury, home of the Arts Center of Cannon County in middle Tennessee, is a small rural county seat with a long-standing tradition of white oak basket and chair making. Cannon County baskets and chairs have gained the attention of collectors and museums worldwide. Examples of this work can be found in places as diverse as the Tennessee State Museum, the Smithsonian Institution in Washington, D.C., and the Museum of Folk Culture in Hunan Province, China. In 1992 the community won the Tennessee Governor's Award in the Arts for supporting the construction of a permanent multifunctional arts center to bolster the local crafts industry and house a flourishing community theater.

Annual attendance grew from two thousand in 1991 to more than thirty-seven thousand in 2000. By 2003 the center was serving more than one hundred craft artists, four hundred performing artists, and more than nineteen thousand students annually in its recently expanded facility. The center has increased its programming to include community oral history projects, traditional craft and music exhibition and instruction, programs by regional and national touring artists, open studio tours of Cannon County artists and crafts producers, community theater, and educational programs.

The annual White Oak Crafts Fair, established in 1991, has become a showcase for the burgeoning local crafts community. With more than fifty booths, the juried fair includes both local artists and a sampling of craftsmen from around the region. In an area that has long been known as the cradle of Tennessee craftsmen, traditional white oak basket and chair makers, joined by modern potters, sculptors, and woodworkers, have created a vibrant crafts community. Because of the center's success and the community's rich craft heritage, Woodbury is featured in John Villani's book *The One Hundred Best Small Art Towns in America.*

See also: BASKETS, OAK (CRAFTS); CULTURAL HERITAGE TOURISM (TOURISM); SECTION OVERVIEW (CRAFTS).

—Patricia Atkinson Wells, *Murfreesboro, Tennessee*

Arts Councils and Agencies

See Federal Funding

Augusta Heritage Center

The Augusta Heritage Center, an integral part of Davis and Elkins College, is a hub for activities that relate to traditional folklife and folk arts. Located in the small town of Elkins, West Virginia, in the Allegheny Mountains, it attracts more than two thousand people annually for intensive weeklong programs, with thousands more attending public concerts, dances, and festivals. The center serves as a clearinghouse for information on traditional folk arts and music. It maintains a Web site with links to numerous individual artisans and musicians and produces an annual free catalog describing its classes and activities.

Since 1972, Augusta's workshops have brought together master artists, musicians, dancers, craftspeople, and enthusiasts of all ages. Ranging from novices to professional artists, participants come from nearly every state and from several countries. Topics covered in the workshops include vocal traditions, old-time music, blues, swing, guitars, dulcimers, crafts, and dance forms. Workshops have also explored Irish, Cajun and Creole, and French Canadian culture.

Augusta's mission includes documenting, promoting, and nurturing folk traditions. The year-round West Virginia Folk Art Apprenticeship program helps to preserve West Virginia's traditions through the funding of one-on-one apprenticeships. Ongoing research and documentation have resulted in the production of more than forty compact discs, audiocassettes, and video documentaries of West Virginia's traditions and culture. These and other documentary materials can be found in the Augusta Collection of Folk Culture in the Davis and Elkins Booth Library, which offers scholars access to a large collection of field recordings, oral histories, and concert tapes.

See also: SECTION OVERVIEW (CRAFTS); WEST VIRGINIA PUBLIC FOLKLORE (FOLKLORE AND FOLKLIFE).

—Margo Blevin, *Augusta Heritage Center*

B. Carroll Reece Memorial Museum

The B. Carroll Reece Memorial Museum is a component of East Tennessee State University's Center for Appalachian Studies and Services in Johnson City and is accredited by the American Association of Museums. Named for U.S.

Ninety-two-year-old fiddler Melvin Wine and two participants in Augusta Heritage Center's Youth Scholarship Program perform at the center's annual Fiddlers' Reunion, 2001. Part of Davis and Elkins College in Elkins, West Virginia, the center serves to document, promote, and nurture folk traditions of the region.

Congressman Brazilla Carroll Reece of Tennessee's First District, the museum began as a repository created by a campus history project in the late 1920s, and the collection grew when it became part of the university's library. In 1965 the collection was transferred to its present location, and it was further enlarged when the Art Department's permanent collection became the core of the Reece Museum's fine arts collection. The Reece was dedicated on October 10, 1965.

The Reece presents exhibits designed to enhance the intellectual and cultural climate of the area it serves. Exhibits explore social, political, and historical themes through a variety of media and are complemented with programming such as gallery talks, public lectures, panel discussions, and artist receptions. Additional programming includes children's art classes, musical programs, and workshops and lectures on a variety of subjects.

The museum's historical collection preserves the story of the settlement of Johnson City, Washington County, and the surrounding region. Significant east Tennessee pieces include an anvil used by early settler William Bean, a family buggy from Tennessee Governors Bob and Alf Taylor, and a Washington handpress from Rogersville. The art collection consists of more than a thousand pieces and includes works by Picasso, Whistler, and Renoir. The Reece collects works in various media by contemporary artists and crafts from the Appalachian region.

See also: APPALACHIAN CULTURAL MUSEUM; ART MUSEUMS; CENTER FOR APPALACHIAN STUDIES AND SERVICES.

—Cynthia L. Lucas, *Tusculum College*

Berea College Appalachian Center

At the request of a faculty committee, President Willis D. Weatherford Jr. established the Berea College Appalachian Center in July 1970. Loyal Jones, former executive director of the Council of the Southern Mountains, was hired as the director of the center.

Jones quickly established the center as a research and service facility. In 1971 it began its sponsorship of the Weatherford Award for the best publication about the region. Jones contracted with Thomas Parrish for publication of the center newsletter in 1972, and Parrish continued in that role as of 2005. Starting in the summer of 1973, Jones instituted a summer seminar on Appalachian history and literature. This innovative program featured Richard B. Drake and Wilma Dykeman as instructors and educated an entire generation of public school and collegiate teachers in regional studies. The next year Jones introduced the Celebration of Traditional Music, which featured nationally known performers as well as unknown but talented musicians.

The center has published important regional books since 1980. In 1983 Jones and Billy Edd Wheeler initiated a series of four Humor Festivals that concluded in 1993. Between 1990 and 1993, archivist Steve Green made a wide variety of field recordings of traditional music that became available to the public through tapes published by the center. Jones retired in 1993 and was succeeded by Helen Lewis, who held the position until Gordon B. McKinney became director in 1995. The center has continued to house the programs mentioned above as well as *Appalachian Heritage* magazine, the Appalachian Gallery, and the Brushy Fork Institute.

See also: FESTIVALS, HUMOR AND STORYTELLING (HUMOR); JONES, LOYAL (HUMOR); UNIVERSITY OF KENTUCKY APPALACHIAN CENTER.

—Gordon B. McKinney, *Berea College*

Birmingham Civil Rights Institute

Birmingham, Alabama, the largest city in southern Appalachia, witnessed many crucial events in the Civil Rights movement of the 1950s and 1960s. The Birmingham Civil Rights Institute, one of America's most impressive museums documenting the era, stands across the street from the Sixteenth Street Baptist Church, the site of the September 15, 1963, dynamite blast that killed four young African American girls and energized the Civil Rights movement against segregation in the South.

Established in 1992 with funds from public, individual, and corporate sources, the institute houses interactive multimedia displays and exhibits. One display recreates the cell where Martin Luther King Jr. wrote his "Letter from a Birmingham Jail." In this letter the eventual Nobel Peace Prize winner passionately explained why he felt compelled to push on with the struggle against segregation despite the risk of civic unrest and violence. In another display, 1960s television sets broadcast archival news reports showing demonstrators being attacked by police with dogs, water hoses, and billy clubs. Other exhibits depict life in the South for African Americans during the age of racial segregation.

The institute is more than a museum of history. It includes an Archives and Education Division where employees and volunteers collect oral histories of the Civil Rights movement, provide research opportunities, and develop curriculum materials for schools. Serving as a site for seminars and workshops and offering public programs on civil and human rights issues, it is also the focal point of Birmingham's Civil Rights District, which includes the Sixteenth Street Baptist Church, Kelly Ingram Park, the Fourth Avenue Business District, and the Alabama Jazz Hall of Fame. A tour of the institute and the Civil Rights District reminds visitors how the courage of participants in the Civil Rights movement changed America and the world.

See also: BIRMINGHAM, ALABAMA (URBAN APPALACHIAN EXPERIENCE); CIVIL RIGHTS MOVEMENT (RACE, ETHNICITY, AND IDENTITY).

—David Campbell, *Northeast Alabama Community College*

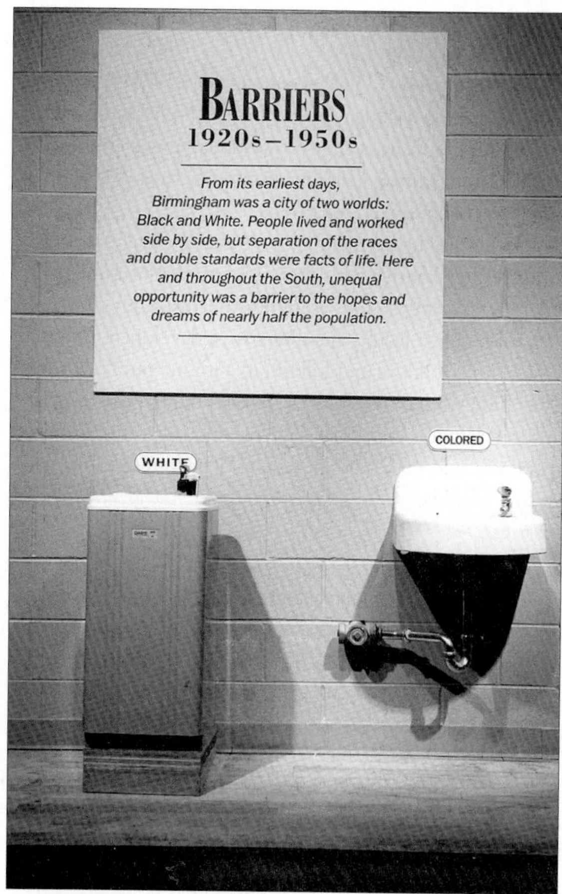

An exhibit of segregated drinking fountains is one of the many ways Alabama's Birmingham Civil Rights Institute documents the injustices that gave rise to the American Civil Rights movement. Many of the movement's pivotal events occurred in Birmingham.

Blue Ridge Institute and Museum

Established in the early 1970s by Ferrum College in southwestern Virginia, the Blue Ridge Institute and Museum was designated Virginia's State Center for Blue Ridge Folklore in 1986. The institute sponsors folk arts exhibits, the Blue Ridge Heritage Archives, Grammy-winning recordings of traditional music, outreach and heritage education programs, an 1800 Blue Ridge farmstead, and a folklife festival attended annually by more than fifteen thousand people.

The institute's purpose is to document, interpret, and present the native arts and culture of the Blue Ridge region, emphasizing western Virginia. The staff prepares exhibits for the institute's galleries, other Virginia museums, and the Internet. Exhibits feature historical and contemporary artifacts from domestic, artistic, agricultural, recreational, and social spheres.

The Blue Ridge Heritage Archives preserves documents, images, and recordings significant to Virginia's folk culture. Holdings include Galax Old Fiddler's Convention recordings, the Elmer Smith Collection of Shenandoah Valley folklore, the Lornell Collection of Virginia African

American folk music, and the Earl Palmer Collection of Appalachian photographs.

The annual Folklife Festival, begun in 1973, is the institute's best-known endeavor and has been covered in many travel guides. Visitors enjoy traditional foods, musicians, artisans, and animal-handling events such as draft horse, mule, and coon dog competitions.

In addition, the institute promotes heritage-arts education by consulting with schools, arts organizations, and community groups. For example, the institute's staff and Ferrum College faculty members have developed materials for teaching folklore and folklife in Virginia public schools. The Blue Ridge Institute also documents the region's cultural changes, such as the late-twentieth-century influx of Hispanics, and makes use of technological innovations with on-line exhibits such as *Deathly Lyrics: Songs of Virginia Tragedies*.

See also: FESTIVALS, FOLK (FOLKLORE AND FOLKLIFE); SOUTHWEST VIRGINIA PUBLIC FOLKLORE (FOLKLORE AND FOLKLIFE).

—Lana A. Whited, *Ferrum College*

Blue Ridge Music Center

The Blue Ridge Music Center, located on the Blue Ridge Parkway just north of the Virginia–North Carolina state line, is a natural area and interpretive site honoring traditional music and musicians of the southern Appalachians. In cooperation with the National Park Service, the National Council for the Traditional Arts, a private nonprofit corporation, operates the center. An outdoor amphitheater serves as a venue for performances of traditional music of the region from spring through October.

At the proposed interpretive center, tourists will hear and learn about the many different types of Blue Ridge music and their place in American cultural history and meet people and performers associated with traditional music in the area. Center programs and activities will include films, museum-quality exhibits, a listening library, lectures, and discussions. A selection of books and sound and video recordings will be sold in the gift shop.

Plans for the Blue Ridge Music Center began in discussions between the Blue Ridge Parkway and the National Council for Traditional Arts in 1985. In 1993 the city of Galax, Virginia, long known for its link to traditional and old-time music, donated 1,045 acres of land to the Blue Ridge Parkway for the purpose of building a music center devoted to the preservation and interpretation of regional music. Traditional performing genres of the Blue Ridge include bluegrass and old-time string-band music, blues, shape-note singing, and Cherokee fiddling, as well as flatfoot dancing, clogging, and square dancing. Instrument makers have also played a significant role in the continuance of the Blue Ridge musical tradition. As part of its work, the center directs visitors to places and events in the area where they can see and hear examples of music, dance, and instrument making.

See also: BLUE RIDGE PARKWAY (TOURISM); CULTURAL HERITAGE TOURISM (TOURISM); SECTION OVERVIEW (MUSIC).

—Patricia Atkinson Wells, *Murfreesboro, Tennessee*

Bookmobiles

The bookmobile is one of the most effective means through which library extension and reading have been promoted in geographically remote regions of Appalachia. Traveling collections of books emanating from a central agency to remote users, an early-nineteenth-century British innovation, were introduced in the United States by New York State Librarian Melvil Dewey in 1895. By 1897 Ohio also had adopted traveling collections, while in Tennessee and Kentucky the State Federation of Women's Clubs began sending books by rail and by horseback to remote mountain regions. In 1905 librarian Mary Titcomb of Hagerstown, Maryland, designed the first horse-drawn wagon to deliver books directly to isolated users in Washington County.

Southern Appalachia developed library service more slowly than the northern part of the region due to low population density, racially segregated services, parochialism, and resistance to taxation. A 1932 American Library Association survey reported that 77 percent of the population of the southern Appalachian region was without library service of any kind. Custom-fitted book trucks in Knox and Hamilton Counties in Tennessee and in Jefferson County, Alabama, accompanied demonstration grants of countywide library extension services by the Julius Rosenwald Fund in 1929. Not until 1934, however, when Knoxville librarian Mary Utopia Rothrock proposed collaborative federal-local partnerships within multicounty regions under the auspices of the Tennessee Valley Authority, were minimal extension services politically feasible.

The modern, professionally staffed bookmobile remained a rarity throughout Appalachia until the federal government focused attention on educational inequality through the Library Services Act (1956) and the Library Services and Construction Act (1964). Whereas in 1937 only sixty book trucks operated throughout the United States, their number had risen to more than two thousand by the time government funding leveled off in the 1970s.

See also: PUBLIC LIBRARIES.

—James V. Carmichael Jr., *University of North Carolina at Greensboro*

Campus Martius Museum

The Campus Martius Museum is the Ohio Historical Society's interpretive center for the history of settlement and migration in Ohio from 1780 to 1970. Museum exhibits explain how three important waves of migration helped make Ohio an economically and culturally diverse state. The museum is located in Marietta, in the Appalachian southeastern corner of the state at the confluence of the Muskingum and Ohio Rivers.

Under the leadership of General Rufus Putnam, the Ohio Company of Associates arrived to establish a town in the Ohio wilderness in 1788. The company was composed primarily of New England Revolutionary War officers and soldiers. General Putnam's home was a part of the fort called Campus Martius, built to protect the civilian inhabitants from Native American attack. Following the signing of the Treaty of Greenville with Native Americans in 1795, the fort was dismantled, but General Putnam continued to live in his fort house, the sole surviving remnant of the compound. The State of Ohio purchased the house in 1917 as a state memorial and erected the museum building adjacent to it in 1928. The state added a wing over the house in 1933 to protect it and in 1957 added another wing. In 1953 the original Ohio Company Land Office building was moved onto the museum grounds. Museum visitors can tour both buildings.

The museum's main floor, which contains a land model depicting the area in 1792, focuses on late-eighteenth-century white pioneer migration to Marietta. Exhibits on the main floor feature prehistoric and historic Native American cultures, early French traders, pioneer settlement life, the Northwest Ordinance (1787), area fauna, and surveying. In addition, a changing exhibit gallery offers temporary exhibits on subjects such as high school art, quilts, powder horns, and World War II artifacts.

Ground-floor exhibits look at two other Ohio migrations: the massive movement from farms to cities between 1850 and 1910 and the influx of Appalachians from Kentucky and West Virginia into Ohio's urban industrial centers between 1910 and 1970. These exhibits, which include audio and video, highlight the conflict many people felt as they left familiar rural surroundings and moved to the new urban environment for economic security and supposedly better lives.

See also: EARLY WHITE SETTLEMENT OF SOUTHEASTERN OHIO (SETTLEMENT AND MIGRATION); OHIO ARTS COUNCIL.

—John B. Briley, *Campus Martius Museum*

Carnegie Museum of Art

Founded by Andrew Carnegie in 1895, the Carnegie Museum of Art is one of the four Carnegie Museums of Pittsburgh, which also include the Andy Warhol Museum, the Carnegie Museum of Natural History, and the Carnegie Science Center. Carnegie envisioned a museum collection consisting of the "old masters of tomorrow" and initiated a series of exhibitions of contemporary art that included works by Winslow Homer, James McNeill Whistler, and Camille Pissarro. Most art museums of this period featured Old Masters; Carnegie is thus considered the founder of the first museum of modern art in the United States.

Works of American art from the late nineteenth century, French impressionist and post-impressionist paintings, and European and American decorative arts from the late seventeenth century to the present are among the featured collections. In addition, the museum exhibits Asian (notably Japanese prints) and African art.

In 1993 the Heinz Architectural Center, which includes the Hall of Architecture and the Hall of Sculpture, opened as part of the museum. The center houses an exhibition of architectural drawings and models, the largest collection of plaster casts of architectural masterpieces in America, and a replica of the interior of the Parthenon.

The collection of contemporary art includes film and video works. The museum hosts an active program of presentations in the galleries and in its two-hundred-seat theater.

See also: CARNEGIE, ANDREW (BUSINESS, INDUSTRY, AND TECHNOLOGY); CARNEGIE MELLON UNIVERSITY THEATER PROGRAM (PERFORMING ARTS); PITTSBURGH, PENNSYLVANIA (URBAN APPALACHIAN EXPERIENCE).

—Clara Hasbrouck, *East Tennessee State University*

Catskill Center for Conservation and Development

Dedicated to preserving the environmental and economic well-being of the Catskill Mountain region, the Catskill Center for Conservation and Development in Arkville, New York, serves an area encompassing six counties and more than six thousand square miles of mountains, forests, rivers, and farmland. Often referred to as the "First American Wilderness," the Catskill Mountains include six major river systems and nearly three dozen mountain peaks more than thirty-five hundred feet in elevation. Founded in 1969, the center works with local communities and organizations to improve the quality of life in the Catskills. It has nearly four thousand members.

Through its Natural Resources and Land Conservation program, the center collaborates with other organizations to identify land suitable for conservation. It facilitates purchase and conveyance of these parcels to the state for incorporation into the Catskill Forest Preserve or works directly with landowners to customize conservation easements. The center also advises the state on its land-acquisition policy in the Catskills and works with other environmental organizations on regional issues of common concern.

The center's Community Outreach and Planning program focuses on projects that encourage appropriate economic development. The staff provides communities with information and direct technical assistance on land use, planning, community revitalization, smart growth, and sustainable economic development. The center hosts training workshops and conferences for local officials, offers grant-writing services for community-based projects, and provides technical assistance for Main Street revitalization efforts.

An education initiative entitled *The Catskills: A Sense of Place* fosters appreciation of the Catskills as a place of environmental grandeur and historic significance. An accompanying curriculum guide for nineteen school districts in the region incorporates the New York State Board of Regents Learning Standards. A related Streamwatch program teaches students to assess the viability and ecological health of area streams through hands-on instruction by Catskill Center educators.

Arts and cultural programs focus on the rich creative history of the Catskills. The center's Platte Clove Artists in Residency program provides a rustic retreat for artists in the area where the first distinctive American art movement, the Hudson River school, began. The Erpf Gallery offers juried exhibitions of the work of area artists and craftspeople throughout the year, and a lecture series features topics of regional interest during the summer months.

See also: ART MUSEUMS; FOREST MANAGEMENT AND CONSERVATION (ENVIRONMENT).

—Helen Budrock, *Catskill Center for Conservation and Development*

Center for American Music

The Center for American Music is a research center, library, and museum at the Stephen Foster Memorial at the University of Pittsburgh. Established within the University Library System in 1996, the center includes the Foster Hall Collection, founded in 1937 as the earliest research facility devoted to American music at an institution of higher education. The Foster Hall Collection contains more than thirty thousand publications, manuscripts, artworks, and other materials documenting the life, music, and influence of America's first professional songwriter, Stephen Foster (1826–1864), who composed most of his works in and around Pittsburgh. Papers include those of his father, William Barclay Foster (1779–1855), a mayor of Allegheny City.

Other collections include printer's plates from the Charles H. Pace Old Ship of Zion Gospel Music Company in Pittsburgh from the 1940s to 1960s; the collected works of the Edgeworth, Pennsylvania, pianist and composer Ethelbert Nevin (1862–1901); the works of composer Adolph Foerster (1854–1927), who was active with the early Pittsburgh Symphony in the 1890s; the songs of Pittsburgh architect and satirical songwriter Robert Schmertz (1898–1975); and the manuscripts of jazz guitarist Joe Negri (b. 1926), a regular performer on *Mister Rogers' Neighborhood* on Pittsburgh's WQED-TV. Together, the collections document musical composition from the Pittsburgh region distributed nationally mostly through popular media from the 1840s to the present.

Chief among the center's educational projects is the *Voices across Time* curriculum. This package for secondary schools provides songs within their context in U.S. history. Appalachia is strongly reflected in the content, which includes songs that originated and were known and sung in the region.

See also: FOSTER, STEPHEN (MUSIC); PITTSBURGH, PENNSYLVANIA (URBAN APPALACHIAN EXPERIENCE); PUBLIC COLLEGES AND UNIVERSITIES (EDUCATION).

—Deane L. Root, *Center for American Music*

Center for Appalachian Studies

The Center for Appalachian Studies in Boone, North Carolina, was established at Appalachian State University in 1978 to coordinate and promote curriculum offerings, public programs, and research activities concerning the Appalachian region. Built on the work of generations of Appalachian scholars, including folklorists and literary scholars Amos Abrams and Cratis Williams, the center was established at the initiative of Chancellor Herbert Wey, who served from 1969 to 1979. Its directors have included Patricia D. Beaver, Carl Ross, David Sutton, and John Alexander Williams.

The center offers the nation's only master of arts degree in Appalachian studies, and it coordinates coursework that leads to an undergraduate minor and a major concentration (through Interdisciplinary Studies) in Appalachian studies. The center encourages research and collaborative projects with local scholars, community groups, and other organizations concerned with the region's past, present, and future. Collaborations have focused on projects such as the coordination of the Appalachian Land Ownership Study, microfilm preservation of regional newspaper back issues and historical documents, supervision of multiple oral history projects, production of a syndicated radio program, organization of a regional cultural festival, formation of the Matewan Development Center, research on ethnic Appalachia, and sustainable development initiatives.

The center is staffed by a director and secretary and has additional support from graduate assistants and student employees. Members of the Appalachian Studies faculty—drawn from fourteen academic departments on campus—serve in an advisory capacity to the center and provide instruction both within their home departments and in specially designated Appalachian Studies courses. *Appalachian Journal*, published quarterly, is administratively located within the center. Together, the Center for Appalachian Studies, *Appalachian Journal*, the Appalachian Cultural Museum, and the W. L. Eury Appalachian Collection comprise the four primary Appalachian Studies administrative units within the university.

See also: APPALACHIAN CULTURAL MUSEUM; CENTER FOR APPALACHIAN STUDIES AND SERVICES; W. L. EURY APPALACHIAN COLLECTION.

—Patricia D. Beaver, *Appalachian State University*

Center for Appalachian Studies and Services

The Center for Appalachian Studies and Services, established in 1984, is one of fourteen research hubs created by the State of Tennessee around different subject areas in the mid-1980s. Located in Johnson City on the East Tennessee State University campus, the center's purpose is to preserve Appalachian heritage and to foster an accurate vision of the region through research, teaching, publishing, and various special projects.

The facility consists of three main divisions: the Regional Resources Institute, the B. Carroll Reece Memorial Museum, and the Archives of Appalachia. The Reece Museum, formally dedicated in October 1965, is an art and history museum with six galleries. Three of the galleries house permanent exhibits on regional history, and three host exhibits of regional arts and crafts. The Archives of Appalachia is a multimedia collection of manuscripts, photographic images, sound recordings, moving image recordings, books, and collectibles that focuses on the culture and history of the Appalachian region.

Now and Then magazine, a center publication, tells the story of Appalachia through articles, personal essays, fiction, poetry, and photography. Widely known for its Bluegrass, Old Time, and Country Music program, the only one of its kind in the nation, the center also sponsors an Appalachian, Scottish, and Irish Studies program, which develops connections between Appalachia and the region's major cultural progenitors, Scotland and Ireland, through formal study, cultural events, and field experiences.

See also: ARCHIVES OF APPALACHIA; B. CARROLL REECE MEMORIAL MUSEUM.

—Lee Phillips, *East Tennessee State University*

Center for the Study of Ethnicity and Gender in Appalachia

The Center for the Study of Ethnicity and Gender in Appalachia was established at Marshall University in Huntington, West Virginia, in the fall of 1996 with support from the Rockefeller Foundation for the Humanities. As its name suggests, the center's primary purpose is to encourage scholarship focused on gender and ethnicity in the Appalachian region and thereby counter stereotypical images. The center brings together resources and scholars from several units of the university, notably the John Deaver Drinko Academy, the Carter G. Woodson Bibliographic Center, the Oral History of Appalachia Program, and Morrow Library Special Collections.

Research supported by the center explores the realities of Appalachia as a region of diverse populations whose histories are often obscured in official historical records. The original Rockefeller grant supported research projects on topics such as Cherokee heritage, a gendered history of the banjo, social relations in a glass factory, Italian coal miners in West Virginia, African American women in West Virginia, sexual minorities in the Appalachian region, and the lives of textile mill workers. A major conference highlighted that work and brought together more than thirty scholars for presentations. The Rockefeller Foundation extended the center's funding for additional research and an on-line database with a specific focus on ethnicity and gender in Appalachia.

In addition to supporting the research of selected scholars, the center has established categories of affiliation for scholars whose research is congruent with the goals of the center but who obtain their own funding. In this way, it provides collegial support for students and scholars engaged in research on topics traditionally ignored by many Appalachian scholars, and it has organized programs to highlight this research. Center-affiliated work has been presented at Appalachian Studies Association meetings and at other conferences.

See also: BIRMINGHAM CIVIL RIGHTS INSTITUTE; SECTION OVERVIEW (RACE, ETHNICITY, AND IDENTITY).

—Lynda Ann Ewen, *Marshall University*

Choctaw Museum of the Southern Indian

The Choctaw Museum of the Southern Indian presents and interprets the history, culture, and traditions of the Mississippi Band of Choctaw Indians, a federally recognized tribe whose lands include parts of Winston and Kemper Counties, Mississippi, at the southern end of the Appalachian region. The Choctaw Museum is located near the tribal headquarters in the Pearl River Community, just west of Philadelphia, Mississippi. In its thirteen-hundred-square-foot exhibit space, permanent displays address the tribe's social and governmental structure before and after removal and examine the Choctaws' highly successful economic-development programs. Swamp-cane basketry, Choctaw social dance, and stickball, a game still played by tribal members, are the focus of other exhibits. Photographs and text document more than fifty years of the Choctaw Indian Fair and decades of community life. The museum frequently sponsors demonstrations by traditional artisans and cooks, as well as sessions with chanters and storytellers. A sales shop features baskets, stickball sticks, beadwork, and traditional clothing made by Choctaw craftspeople.

See also: CHOCTAW (RACE, ETHNICITY, AND IDENTITY); MUSEUM OF THE CHEROKEE INDIAN; SENECA-IROQUOIS NATIONAL MUSEUM.

—Deborah Boykin, *Tribal Archives of the Mississippi Band of Choctaw Indians*

Church Archives

The Appalachian region's religious diversity, obvious in its ubiquitous church buildings, is just as deeply revealed in a host of church archives and collections. Mainstream denominations such as the Baptists, Methodists, and Presbyterians have established major archives in or near the region. These formal collections exist alongside smaller and less formal sectarian church archives, including archives where records are privately kept, often for generations. In many scattered sources, these collections document church membership, baptisms, confirmations, marriages, deaths, ordinations, and church activities and include minutes of church business meetings, committee reports and recommendations, and financial records.

Although Baptists, Methodists, and Presbyterians have been the most prominent denominations in Appalachia, distinctive branches exist within them. Among the largest branches of Baptists in the region are those churches affiliated with the Southern Baptist Convention. While the majority of the convention's records are housed in the Southern Baptist Convention Library and Archives in Nashville, Tennessee, others are located at the six major Southern Baptist seminaries; the Women's Missionary Union of the Southern Baptist Convention in Birmingham, Alabama; the International Mission Board of the SBC in Richmond, Virginia; and special collections located in Baptist and Baptist-affiliated colleges such as Samford University in Birmingham, Mercer University in Macon, Georgia, and Wake Forest University in Winston-Salem, North Carolina.

Other Baptist branches established churches in the Appalachians long before the Southern Baptists gained prominence. Congregations of Independent Baptists, Old Regular Baptists, Primitive Baptists, and others not affiliated with a parent organization remain scattered through much of the southern Appalachians. Researchers will find the historical records of these churches carefully preserved and maintained by church members and often housed in private residences.

The International Headquarters of the World Methodist Council and Museum at Lake Junaluska, North Carolina, holds one of the largest collections of letters, journals, and manuscripts from John Wesley and the founding fathers of the Methodist Church, including Wesley's original fifty-volume set of the *Christian Library*, edited 1749–52. The museum also includes materials related to Francis Asbury, the first bishop of American Methodism, who traveled and preached extensively in the Appalachians. The nearby Heritage Center at the Lake Junaluska Assembly, which also houses archives and a museum, holds material related to Methodism in the southeastern United States in addition to the historical records of the Lake Junaluska Assembly. Methodist church records are also found at affiliated colleges and seminary repositories such as Asbury Theological Seminary in Wilmore, Kentucky, Duke University's Divinity School Library in Durham, North Carolina, and Vanderbilt University's Divinity Library in Nashville.

Several branches of Presbyterians thrive in the Appalachians. These include the Cumberland Presbyterians, with denominational headquarters in Memphis, Tennessee, and the Presbyterian Church (USA). The latter's archives are headquartered in Philadelphia, Pennsylvania, with a regional branch at the Presbyterian Historical Society in Montreat, North Carolina. Collections at Montreat include photographic documentation of Presbyterian home mission work in the southern Appalachians from the 1890s to the 1930s, records of individual congregations and ministers in the region, and copies of the *Home Mission Monthly*, a periodical published from the 1870s to 1924, in addition to other mission publications.

A few other denominations that are well represented in the Appalachians also maintain archives in or near the region. These include the Pentecostals and the Disciples of Christ. The main resource for Pentecostal studies, including the charismatic and Holiness movements, is the Hal Bernard Dixon Jr. Pentecostal Research Center in the William G. Squires Library at Lee University in Cleveland, Tennessee. Other Pentecostal materials, including documents pertaining to the Assemblies of God, can be found at the Flower Pentecostal Heritage Center in Springfield, Missouri. Information about the Disciples of Christ is archived at the church's historical society in Nashville.

Although major faiths such as Catholicism, Judaism, and the Church of Jesus Christ of Latter-Day Saints are present in the Appalachian region, their numbers are relatively small, and they generally house their archival information outside the region.

See also: APPALACHIAN SPECIAL COLLECTIONS; RELIGIOUS CONFERENCE CENTERS AND RETREATS (RELIGION).

—Susan Jennings, *Appalachian State University*

Commission on Religion in Appalachia, *Atlas of the Church in Appalachia* (1983); Ellen Garrison, ed., *Archives in Appalachia: A Directory* (1985); Bill J. Leonard, ed., *Christianity in Appalachia: Profiles in Regional Pluralism* (1999).

Coal Mining Heritage Association

The Coal Mining Heritage Association of Montgomery County in Virginia's New River Valley was formed in 1994 by former coal miners, their wives, and their descendants. The association is a community-based cultural institution that continues to preserve Appalachian coal heritage through efforts to educate the public on the richness of that heritage. Additionally, the association honors and memorializes miners and their families who labored in dangerous and difficult circumstances to give their families and descendants improved standards of living.

By 1993, appreciative New River descendants of hard-coal miners had begun collecting artifacts, oral histories, and photographs related to local coal mining. That year, *Roanoke Times* reporter Robert Freis wrote two newspaper articles recounting the valley's coal-mining heritage that helped inspire local mining families to initiate observances, create miner memorials, and organize the Coal Mining Heritage Association.

In February 1994, a Coal Miners Memorial Committee, formed at Blacksburg, met with Montgomery County officials, who designated April 18 as the date of an annual Coal Miners Day. Twelve miners in McCoy, Virginia, lost their lives in the Great Valley Mine explosion on that date in 1946.

Researchers documented local mine fatalities of the twentieth century for a Coal Miners' Monument and, using firsthand reports of miners, cemetery markers, and family Bibles, certified forty-three men and a twelve-year-old boy for inclusion. Within sixty days, local citizens had contributed more than twenty-two thousand dollars for the monument, completed in 1994. Annual Coal Miners Days have been held since that first year and are marked by artifact displays, cultural demonstrations, entertainment, and contests. Deceased miners are honored at memorial services.

A joint project between the association, Radford University's Anthropology program, the state's heritage preservation office, and the Montgomery County Planning Office, which owns the property, resulted in a Coal Mining Heritage Park, dedicated on the site of the historic Merrimac Coal Mine in 2000. This mine supplied coal to the Confederate ironclad ship *Virginia* (formerly the USS *Merrimack*), which famously battled the Union ironclad *Monitor* on March 9, 1862. The Huckleberry Trail, part of the state's rails-to-trails system popular with local hikers and bikers, bisects the Heritage Park.

See also: COAL HERITAGE TOURISM (TOURISM); COAL MINING (ENVIRONMENT).

—Jimmie L. Price, *Coal Mining Heritage Association*

Coon Dog Cemetery

Begun in 1937, the Coon Dog Cemetery, located twelve miles south of Cherokee, Alabama, in Colbert County, is a manifestation of the area's love of coon hunting. The first animal interred there was a dog named Troop. Key Underwood, Troop's master, also owned the land, and he allowed others to be buried there after word about the cemetery spread among coon hunters. Only coon dogs are eligible for burial in the cemetery where, as of 2001, nearly two hundred of the hunting dogs lay.

The cemetery is located in a secluded rural area but is formal and well maintained. Many of the graves are marked

The grave of Queen, one of hundreds of dogs buried at the Coon Dog Cemetery near Cherokee, Alabama. Hunting raccoons with dogs has a long history in Appalachia, and hunters often develop a deep respect for their dogs, as reflected in the memorials erected at this cemetery.

with elaborately carved headstones. A board of directors, along with the Tennessee Valley Coon Hunters Association, maintains the grounds and hosts an informal Labor Day picnic in honor of departed hunting dogs. The cemetery was featured in the 2003 film *Sweet Home Alabama*.

Throughout the year, men (and sometimes women) of all occupations hunt ring-tailed raccoons with trained dogs. The sport is primarily an exercise for the dogs, and hunters sometimes do not even take a gun. They claim most of the fun is watching or hearing the dogs work. A network of dog breeders keeps the local population supplied with able dogs. Some local hunters and dogs compete in regional and national competitions. Champion dogs sell for thousands of dollars and are highly prized, and after a lifetime of companionship many are honored with a place in the Coon Dog Cemetery.

See also: HUNTING AND FISHING (SPORTS AND RECREATION); HUNTING AND FISHING LORE (FOLKLORE AND FOLKLIFE).

—Joey Brackner, *Alabama State Council on the Arts*

Cultural Initiatives

See Cultural Heritage Tourism (Tourism)

East Tennessee Historical Society

The East Tennessee Historical Society is dedicated to the preservation and interpretation of the history of east Tennessee, the area of the state that borders Virginia and eastern Kentucky to the north, North Carolina to the east, Georgia to the south, and the eastern edge of the Cumberland Plateau to the west. The entire section lies within the Appalachian region. Headquartered at the East Tennessee History Center in Knoxville, the society is located in a building constructed in 1874 as the U.S. Custom House, which also houses the Calvin M. McClung Historical Collection of the Knox County Public Library, the Knox County Archives, and the Tennessee Society of the Sons of the American Revolution. The society maintains a museum, publishes the tri-annual *Tennessee Ancestors* and the annual *Journal of East Tennessee History* (formerly the East Tennessee Historical Society's *Publications*), supports genealogy research, and offers public programs. Its print and archival materials are held at the McClung Historical Collection.

An antecedent of the present East Tennessee Historical Society was the East Tennessee Historical and Antiquarian Society, founded by J. G. M. Ramsey in 1834. Ramsey served as leader, librarian, and curator of this early organization, amassing a large collection of books, manuscripts, and artifacts at his house, Mecklenburg. All were lost during the Civil War in 1863 when Union forces burned Ramsey's home. In 1883 a group of Confederate veterans reorganized the antiquarian society as an auxiliary of the Southern Historical Society; under these auspices, the East Tennessee organization was active into the early 1890s. Finally, through the efforts primarily of University of Tennessee faculty and Knox County librarians, the East Tennessee Historical Society was established in 1925.

During the society's first decades, the McClung Historical Collection supplied office space and staff support, and the society sponsored lectures, published occasional monographs, and established a journal. A new direction was taken in the early 1980s, when the society moved to the Old Custom House and hired a professional director. Since then, it has developed an affiliate chapter program (with more than forty members in 2000), published local histories of east Tennessee communities, opened a museum on the history of the region, and established the highly successful "First Families of Tennessee" membership program.

The East Tennessee Historical Society Museum opened in 1993 with a permanent exhibit, *The East Tennesseans*, which covers two hundred years of history in the region. The museum receives approximately fifteen thousand visitors each year. "First Families of Tennessee," launched in 1993 as a Tennessee bicentennial project, has become a permanent program of the society, recognizing direct descendants of persons living in Tennessee prior to June 1796. The program had registered nearly thirteen thousand descendants by 2000 and published *First Families of Tennessee: A Register of Early Settlers and Their Present-Day Descendants*, with a foreword by historian Wilma Dykeman, in 2001.

See also: APPALACHIAN SPECIAL COLLECTIONS; HISTORICAL SOCIETIES; TENNESSEE OVERHILL HERITAGE ASSOCIATION.

—Ann Toplovich, *Tennessee Historical Society*

Ethnic Cultural Institutions in Southwestern Pennsylvania

Until the Civil War, southwestern Pennsylvania's population was mostly British and northern European. But by 1900, immigrants from many countries, rural whites from the southern and central Appalachians, and African Americans from the South were pouring into southwestern Pennsylvania to work in steel mills and steel-related industries such as coal and coke production, iron foundries, and river and rail transportation. The Pittsburgh region was transformed into an area of great ethnic diversity.

These foreign and domestic immigrants often banded together with those of similar background for social and economic support and sometimes for survival. Companies encouraged this inward-focused socialization, seeing the formation and maintenance of ethnic enclaves as a way to control the workforce. Turned away by most banks of the day, immigrants started their own financial cooperatives—

benefit and burial societies at first, such as the Bulgarian-Macedonian Beneficial Association, and, later, credit unions such as the First Slovak Building and Loan Society—to help one another through crises. They built their own churches by hand, using styles, symbols, and decorations remembered from home. Associated with the ethnic parishes were chapters of church-based social organizations such as the Ukrainian Orthodox National Women's League of America. Immigrants also founded fraternal clubs and orders such as the Croatian Fraternal Union, the Serb National Federation, and the Italian Sons and Daughters of America, whose national headquarters are still in the Pittsburgh area. Fraternal orders customarily built neighborhood lodges or halls where workers and their families could speak their native language or dialect, enjoy traditional music, dances, and sports, and teach children the traditions of their ancestors.

Before the 1940s, these ethnic organizations were usually located in the same mill communities or company-owned mining towns, or "mine patches," in which their members lived and worked. After World War II, however, ethnic communities began to disperse as second-generation workers, more financially secure and socially assimilated than their parents, bought cars and moved their families to new homes in the quieter, cleaner suburbs, away from the noise and grime of the plants. Postwar workers had company-paid pension plans, banks were more willing to lend immigrants and their children money for major purchases, and language barriers were crumbling. Marriage out of the ethnic group also became more common. Although the new suburbanites still returned to the old neighborhoods for weddings, worship, holidays, special occasions, and funerals, their daily lives no longer revolved around the old institutions. Those who maintained a strong ethnic identity did so by choice.

With succeeding generations' drift away from traditions, customs fell into disuse and folk arts declined. By the 1980s, most of the older ethnic clubs had become drinking establishments for diminishing numbers of aged cronies. With steadily dwindling congregations, neighborhood ethnic churches closed their doors, and parishes consolidated. New churches built in the suburbs downplayed ethnic connections, focusing instead on attracting young people from a wide geographic area without regard to ethnicity or tradition. However, the steep decline and subsequent restructuring of the steel industry in the 1980s once again changed the course of ethnic consciousness in the Pittsburgh region. Within a decade, as most of the mills closed, plants were demolished, and thousands lost their jobs, people in the region began to look to cultural identity as a way to maintain psychological balance amid precipitous change.

In the final two decades of the twentieth century—echoing the burst of organization building a hundred years earlier—many ethnic groups established new organizations or refashioned old ones with the aim of continuing ethnic traditions. Some even started new financial organizations such as the Kuumba Trust (catering to African Americans) to seek and coordinate funding for their group's activities. Most of the organizations, however, became oriented toward sponsoring social events and cultural programs. For example, the Bulgarian-Macedonian Beneficial Association became the Bulgarian-Macedonian National Educational and Cultural Center. The Slovene National Benefit Society, while maintaining some of its older halls, established a separate little village for larger events.

These redesigned older clubs, along with new ethnic cultural organizations such as the Irish Centre of Pittsburgh and the Antiochian Center (Syrian Orthodox) in Ligonier, tend to be regionally oriented, not neighborhood based. They often include museum-style exhibits featuring the history of the ethnic group in the region. Sometimes, they hold old-country language and arts classes and sponsor children's performance groups to learn ethnic songs and dances. To draw members together, organizations may have monthly or annual special events highlighting their ethnic group's foodways, arts, or religious customs (for example, lamb or corn roasts, saint's day parades, food fairs, button-box accordion or fiddle contests, polka dances, reunions, choir anniversaries, and holiday sales of old-country crafts). Ethnic groups who arrived more recently to the Pittsburgh area have bypassed the older neighborhood-hall concept altogether, going straight to the regional model. The Sri Venkateswara Temple in Monroeville, for example, provides a regional cultural center for Hindus from southern India, wherever they live in southwestern Pennsylvania.

Along with regionalism, another frequent characteristic of the newly established organizations is a pan-ethnic approach. The Latin American Cultural Union was founded to serve the many technical and professional immigrants to the Pittsburgh region who are from any Spanish-speaking country in the Western Hemisphere. Multicultural organizations that showcase or archive diverse ethnic traditions, such as the Pittsburgh Folk Festival, the University of Pittsburgh's Nationality Rooms Program, the Pittsburgh History Center's Ethnic Committees, and the Rivers of Steel Regional Folklife Center, have also grown in importance.

Acknowledging the reality of ethnically mixed families and the need for financial solvency, membership in these new ethnic cultural centers is often no longer limited to those whose ancestors came from the old country but can include friends and supporters of any ethnic background. Audiences for programs are also drawn from the wider public. In the new century, the challenge is no longer physical survival of the ethnic community, as it was when these groups first arrived in southwestern Pennsylvania, but the cultural survival of ethnic identity. The new ethnic cultural centers seek to give their members a way to resist cultural and social homogenization while educating the public about the area's diverse cultural heritage.

See also: IDENTITY, NORTHERN APPALACHIAN (RACE, ETHNICITY, AND IDENTITY); IRON AND STEEL INDUSTRY (BUSINESS, INDUSTRY, AND TECHNOLOGY); PITTSBURGH, PENNSYLVANIA (URBAN APPALACHIAN EXPERIENCE).

—Doris J. Dyen, *Rivers of Steel National Heritage Area*

Federal Funding

Federal monies support a wide variety of Appalachian arts and humanities programs with direct grants and with funds channeled through numerous state agencies. These federally funded programs include exhibitions, concerts, festivals, tours, theatrical productions, arts instruction in schools, folk arts apprenticeships, lectures, teacher institutes, and film series, to name a few. Federal support for historical societies, arts organizations, educational institutions, museums, and performing arts groups allow the study, preservation, and growth of diverse aspects of Appalachian culture.

The Museum of the Cherokee Indian in Cherokee, North Carolina, the AppLit program at Ferrum College of Ferrum, Virginia, educational and jazz programming at Manchester Craftsmen's Guild in Pittsburgh, the statewide apprenticeship program in folk arts administered by the Augusta Heritage Center of Davis and Elkins College in Elkins, West Virginia, and many other organizations devoted to the preservation and promotion of Appalachian culture have benefited in countless ways from federal support in the arts and humanities.

Such support is rooted in the idealism of early America. Thomas Jefferson, son of upland Virginia and vocal advocate of the arts and humanities, proposed as early as 1805 that revenue from taxes in times of peace be used to advance the arts, education, and public works in the nation. More than 160 years passed before sustained federal support for the arts and humanities was forthcoming, however. During that time the federal government was only sporadically involved in arts and humanities projects, notably in the creation of the Library of Congress (1800), the commissioning of the murals for the Capitol Rotunda (1817), and the chartering of the Smithsonian Institution (1846). With the Great Depression of the 1930s, the government's role expanded dramatically. New activities funded by the New Deal included initiatives such as the Federal Arts Projects, the Federal Theatre Project, and the Farm Security Administration documentation efforts, all of which left behind a vast cultural legacy.

Out of this activity a joint committee on the subject of folk arts was formed from the Works Project Administration. Collaborating with the Library of Congress in 1939, the committee sent folklorist Herbert Halpert on a three-and-a-half-month recording journey through Virginia, North Carolina, Tennessee, Alabama, Georgia, and neighboring states. In addition to producing valuable recordings of Appalachian and southern musicians, this expedition laid the groundwork for future folklore fieldwork and oral history documentation of local and regional culture in the various federal writing and arts projects.

In the final months of President John F. Kennedy's administration, Congress initiated serious discussion of a national foundation and council on the arts. Responding to the hearings on the subject, Kentucky folksinger and cultural activist Jean Ritchie wrote to the Senate's Special Subcommittee on the Arts on behalf of the Newport Folk Foundation urging the passage of legislation to establish a national arts foundation. In her letter she cited the need for supporting the cultural resources of the nation, noting her embarrassment at attending an international folk festival in Spain at her own expense as the sole U.S. participant, marching behind an American flag carried by a Frenchman.

Following two more years of debate, on September 29, 1965, President Lyndon Johnson signed into law the National Foundation on the Arts and Humanities Act establishing the National Endowment for the Arts and the National Endowment for the Humanities. These agencies, each advised by a national council and headed by a chair appointed by the president, are charged with providing support with appropriated public monies for programs in their respective cultural domains.

A significant institutional spin-off of this federal legislation was the parallel development of an infrastructure of state-based arts and humanities councils. Although eighteen state arts councils, including those in New York, Georgia, and North Carolina, existed before the National Endowment for the Arts was created, the enabling legislation required the existence of a state arts agency for the receipt of federal funds. This led to the almost immediate establishment and support, through state appropriation, of state arts councils. By 1974, every state had created some form of arts agency.

State humanities councils were not put into place until the mid-1970s, and they were created as independent not-for-profit organizations; consequently, they have not benefited in nearly the same way as arts councils from state-appropriated support. State humanities councils typically serve as both a source of funds and as fund-raisers. This is in addition to initiating and managing their own programming.

As well as funding state arts and humanities agencies, federal endowments give direct grants to organizations and projects within the region. These funds are allocated through an application process that involves peer-panel review of proposals. Individual historical societies, arts organizations, educational institutions, museums, and performing arts groups within the Appalachian region are able to carry out projects with this support.

In the case of the National Endowment for the Humanities, grants have supported work on the presidential papers of James Madison at the University of Virginia in Charlottesville and preservation of the newspapers of several states in Appalachia, including North Carolina, Virginia, and Tennessee. Regionwide projects funded by the National Endowment for the Humanities have included funds to support faculty at private colleges of central Appalachia through the Appalachian College Association of Berea, Kentucky; support for Appalachian State University of Boone, North Carolina, to endow an Appalachian Studies program; and a grant to East Tennessee State University in Johnson City for the *Encyclopedia of Appalachia*.

The National Endowment for the Arts has funded numerous projects with regional impact, including a broad array of activities sponsored by Appalshop, a multidisciplinary arts, education, and cultural center in Whitesburg, Kentucky. Appalshop projects have included film and video programs documenting Appalachian culture, training courses in media, and touring theatrical productions and workshops by its professional company, Roadside Theater. The National Endowment for the Arts also has underwritten, through the Mid Atlantic Arts Foundation, a touring exhibits program called *Appalachian Views*, which features the folk arts and cultures of people living in the Appalachian region.

Both national endowments also support awards recognizing individuals who have made significant contributions to the arts and humanities. Through the National Humanities Medal, known until 1997 as the Charles Frankel Prize in the Humanities, the National Endowment for the Humanities has honored Appalachian-born individuals such as playwright August Wilson, historian David McCullough, and literary and cultural scholar Henry Louis Gates Jr. The National Medal of Arts has been given to bluegrass and early country music pioneers Bill Monroe, Earl Scruggs, and Doc Watson. These musicians, along with Ralph Stanley of Coeburn, Virginia, have also received the National Heritage Fellowship from the National Endowment for the Arts in recognition of ongoing contributions to the folk and traditional arts. Other Appalachian recipients have included fiddler Tommy Jarrell from Mount Airy, North Carolina; storyteller Ray Hicks from Banner Elk, North Carolina; potter Lanier Meaders from Cleveland, Georgia; cooper Alex Stewart from Sneedville, Tennessee; weaver Dorothy Thompson from Davis, West Virginia; luthier and guitarist Wayne Henderson from Mouth of Wilson, Virginia; old-time fiddler Ralph Blizard of Blountville, Tennessee; and Jean Ritchie, folk musician and songwriter from Viper, Kentucky.

This multifaceted approach to the support of the arts and humanities has served to realize in a small way Thomas Jefferson's vision of a nation free and able to engage in the pursuit of knowledge and happiness. Nearly two centuries after Jefferson's plea for governmental engagement in the arts and humanities, federal funds have helped support research for the publication of the Pulitzer Prize–winning biographical series *Jefferson and His Time* by Dumas Malone, a historical exhibition at his home, Monticello, and the conservation of his writings.

See also: AUGUSTA HERITAGE CENTER; NORTH CAROLINA ARTS COUNCIL; OHIO ARTS COUNCIL.

—Barry Bergey, *National Endowment for the Arts*

National Endowment for the Arts, *Creative America: A Report to the President by the President's Committee on the Arts and the Humanities* (1997) and *A Legacy of Leadership: Investing in America's Living Cultural Heritage since 1965* (2000); National Endowment for the Humanities, *Rediscovering America: Thirty-Five Years of the National Endowment for the Humanities* (2001).

Folk Art Center

See Southern Highland Craft Guild Collection

Folklore Societies

Following the founding of the American Folklore Society in 1888, a dozen folklore societies were formed in as many years to discover, collect, publish, and preserve the area's folklore. Few of these early branches survived very long into the twentieth century or produced substantial Appalachia-related folklore materials.

In the next generation, however, folklore societies were founded in states located wholly or in part in the Appalachian region: Kentucky (1912); North Carolina and Virginia (1913); South Carolina (1914); and West Virginia (1915). These state societies were all organized in academic settings, and many held meetings with state teachers' organizations, upon whom they depended heavily for membership and support, extending their collective reach throughout the state or region. Teachers and other professionals or interested laypersons were actively recruited to collect folklore with the focus primarily on traditional folk songs and ballads. In the *Journal of American Folklore*, folklorist Wayland Hand described the efforts in this period as perhaps illustrating the highest order of early corporate folklore scholarship.

Following a relatively dormant period between World War I and the late 1920s, state folklore societies were established in Mississippi and Pennsylvania (1927), Tennessee (1934), New York (1944), and Ohio (1950). Several of these societies were affiliated with state historical associations, and inevitably these ties broadened the scope of possible activities and subject matter to include folklife and material culture.

The most recently formed folklore societies—in Maryland (1972), Georgia (1976), and Alabama (1980)—developed in the aftermath of the Civil Rights movement and the War on Poverty, which focused concern on the South generally but also drew specific attention to, and renewed interest in, Appalachian history and culture.

Through time, state folklore societies have undergone various periods of expansion or contraction and, in some cases, significant reorganization by members having different motivations or new missions. Others, including the Pennsylvania Folklore Society, simply disbanded in response to economic factors, changing interests, or significant loss of membership. Examination of the structure of the earlier state folklore societies reveals some broad historical patterns, including the impact and influence of various universities and pervasive social networks connecting both individuals and organizations.

The founding officers of the early organizations were, by and large, professors affiliated with English or language departments at state or private universities, and their interests, experience, and training shaped their respective folklore societies' purposes and programs. For instance, the influence of Harvard University professors Francis James Child and George Lyman Kittredge on later scholars can be seen in the number of societies collecting English and Scottish popular ballads. Harvard University Press also published some early state societies' collections, including John Harrington Cox's *Folk-Songs of the South* (1925), Reed Smith's *South Carolina Ballads* (1928), and Arthur Kyle Davis Jr.'s *Traditional Ballads of Virginia* (1929).

The Kentucky Folk-Lore Society was organized on December 3, 1912, at a meeting of the Kentucky College Association in Lexington. Professor Hubert G. Shearin of Transylvania University was its first president. In 1911 Shearin, with his student Josiah H. Combs (a native of Hazard, Kentucky, and a Hindman Settlement School alumnus) listed as collector, published *A Syllabus of Kentucky Folk-Songs* and "Some Superstitions in the Cumberland Mountains" in the *Journal of American Folklore*.

Another Kentucky Folk-Lore Society founder and president, Eber C. Perrow (Harvard, 1908), published a series on songs and rhymes from the upland South in the *Journal of American Folklore* between 1912 and 1915. Before becoming head of the English Department at the University of Louisville in 1911, Perrow served briefly as an instructor of English at the University of Mississippi, where he influenced student Arthur Palmer Hudson. In turn, Hudson played an important role in the Mississippi Folk-Lore Society and later the North Carolina Folk-Lore Society.

Gordon Wilson served more than three decades as head of the English Department at Western Kentucky University in Bowling Green and spent a number of those years as Kentucky Folk-Lore Society treasurer and editor. For a decade or more dating from about 1935, Wilson wrote a column for the society called "Tidbits of Kentucky Folklore," which appeared weekly in more than eighty newspapers throughout the state. Wilson was an invited speaker at the third meeting of the Hoosier Folklore Society in 1940, and Kentucky native Stith Thompson, who founded the Indiana University folklore program, likewise visited and spoke at several Kentucky Folk-Lore Society meetings.

By 1954, Kentucky Folk-Lore Society officers included folklorists Herbert Halpert of Murray State College, president; William Hugh Jansen of University of Louisville, vice-president; and D. K. Wilgus of Western Kentucky University, secretary-treasurer. The Kentucky Folk-Lore Society meeting, held in conjunction with the Daniel Boone Festival in Barboursville in October 1956, featured an address on "Kentucky's Living Folk Traditions" by Halpert and a program of songs by Wilgus. Both Halpert and Jansen were graduates of Indiana University and former presidents of the Hoosier Folklore Society.

An Ohio native, Wilgus studied under Francis Lee Utley (Harvard, 1934) and completed his undergraduate and graduate degrees in English at Ohio State University. Wilgus's M.A. thesis was the first academic work to focus on commercially recorded country music (now popularly referred to as roots music), and his dissertation later became the basis for the authoritative *Anglo-American Folksong Scholarship Since 1898* (1959). He began collaborating with Hubert Shearin's former student, Josiah Combs, shortly before Combs died suddenly in 1960. In 1967 Wilgus published the first English translation of Combs's dissertation, *Folk-Songs du Midi des États-Unis* (*Folk-Songs of the Southern United States*), completed at the Sorbonne in Paris in 1925, and he later deposited Combs's ballad collection along with his own collection of Kentucky folklore at Berea College.

The Kentucky Folk-Lore Society irregularly published a *Bulletin of the Kentucky Folk-Lore Society* until January 1938 and a quarterly, the *Kentucky Folklore and Poetry Magazine*, between 1926 and 1931. In 1955 the society began publication of a journal, the *Kentucky Folklore Record.* Under the direction of W. Lynwood Montell (Indiana University, 1964), a Center for Intercultural and Folk Studies was established at Western Kentucky University in 1970; it became an M.A.-granting department headed by him in 1979. Three of Montell's early publications—*The Saga of Coe Ridge: A Study in Oral History* (1970), *Ghosts Along the Cumberland: Deathlore in the Kentucky Foothills* (1975), and *Kentucky Folk Architecture* (with Michael Morse, 1976)—reflect the widening range of folklore scholarship. Both Montell and his successor as center director, Camilla Collins (Indiana University, 1978), served as president of the Kentucky Folk-Lore Society. Under the latter's direction, the curriculum in folklore expanded further to include subject areas such as occupational and feminist folklore. With Collins's guidance and support from the American Folklore Society in 1988, the former Southeastern Folklore Society's journal, *Southern Folklore Quarterly*, was transferred to Kentucky, where it merged with the *Kentucky Folklore Record* and was renamed *Southern Folklore*. Presently, the Kentucky Folk-Lore Society is inactive, and *Southern Folklore* is no longer published.

The major associations between the Kentucky Folk-Lore Society and other state folklore societies east of the Mississippi River tended to follow geographic lines north and south. Thus, in terms of hosting joint meetings or giving presentations at other societies' gatherings, there were significant ties between the Kentucky Folk-Lore Society and societies in Indiana, Ohio, and Tennessee.

The *Tennessee Folklore Society Bulletin* remains the oldest regional folklore journal continuously published from its beginning to the present. Despite changes in the circumstances of state folklore societies over time, the numerous publications produced by successions of scholars and editors in connection with these organizations constitute a substantial body of Appalachian folklore scholarship.

The organizational structures of state folklore societies in the late twentieth century (and the restructuring of some of the earlier ones) reflect new social realities and trends that include the institutionalization of folklore as a distinct academic field and as public-sector work; the growth of the nonprofit organization, dependent in whole or in part on grants-in-aid from state or federal sources for programming; and the incorporation of members or representatives of folklore societies into state agencies as cultural program officers. These officers, in many cases, work in collaboration with the societies, which, in turn, receive some institutional support or serve as quasi-official partners in the state's programs and objectives. The state folklore societies that remain in New York, Ohio, Virginia, North Carolina, Tennessee, and Alabama fit into one or more of these categories. While the evidence is not yet in, it is possible in the near term that the institutionalized state cultural programs will take over the purposes for which early state folklore societies were initially established and supplant them entirely.

See also: FOLK MUSIC COLLECTIONS (MUSIC); SECTION OVERVIEW (FOLKLORE AND FOLKLIFE).

—Nancy J. Martin-Perdue, *University of Virginia*

Jan Harold Brunvand, ed., *American Folklore: An Encyclopedia* (1996); Thomas A. Green, ed., *Folklore: An Encyclopedia of Beliefs, Customs, Tales, Music, and Art* (1997); Wayland D. Hand, "North American Folklore Societies," *Journal of American Folklore* (July–September 1943) and "North American Folklore Societies: A Supplement," *Journal of American Folklore* (October–December 1946).

Folkways Center of the Georgia Mountains

The Folkways Center of the Georgia Mountains is located in Dahlonega, Georgia. Housed in the Mountain Music Hall (formerly the Dahlonega Baptist Church), this nonprofit corporation is devoted to the preservation and cultivation of the history and folkways of the peoples of the north Georgia mountain region. The center encourages residents of the area to participate in the perpetuation of traditional Appalachian performing and visual arts.

Building on a tradition of festival gatherings in Dahlonega dating back nearly a century, the center began producing programming in collaboration with a number of local and regional partner organizations in 2000, when it was chartered as a nonprofit organization. Annual events include the Bear on the Square Mountain Festival, in honor of a bear cub that once wandered into Dahlonega, and the Dahlonega Bluegrass and Folkways Festival. In addition to festival events, the center coordinates community square dances and a number of art and craft classes. The live, two-hour *Dahlonega Mountain Music and Medicine Show* is broadcast on the first Saturday of each month on WKHC-FM. This program features traditional music and storytelling, commercial jingles, and regional folklore. On the fourth Saturday of each month, the center hosts the Folkways Mountain Music Revue, which includes live performances of Appalachian bluegrass, country, gospel, and other acoustic roots music.

The center includes a visitor center and art gallery that sells regional contemporary and traditional arts such as pottery, weaving, and painting. It also holds one of the region's finest collections of visionary arts, including works by Howard Finster, Mary Proctor, and Billy Roper.

See also: BLUEGRASS (MUSIC); FINSTER, HOWARD (VISUAL ARTS); RADIO BROADCASTING (MEDIA).

—Teresa Hollingsworth, *Southern Arts Federation*

Foundations and Funding Agencies

See Federal Funding

Foxfire Museum and Center

The Foxfire Museum and Foxfire Center, located in Mountain City, Georgia, are part of a larger nonprofit organization, the Foxfire Fund, Inc. Open year-round, the museum and center focus on the artifacts and culture of southern Appalachia. The Foxfire organization began in 1966 when Rabun County students interviewed their relatives and neighbors and the resulting publications became national best-sellers. Over the years, Foxfire grew from a local project to a national education reform effort. Though it

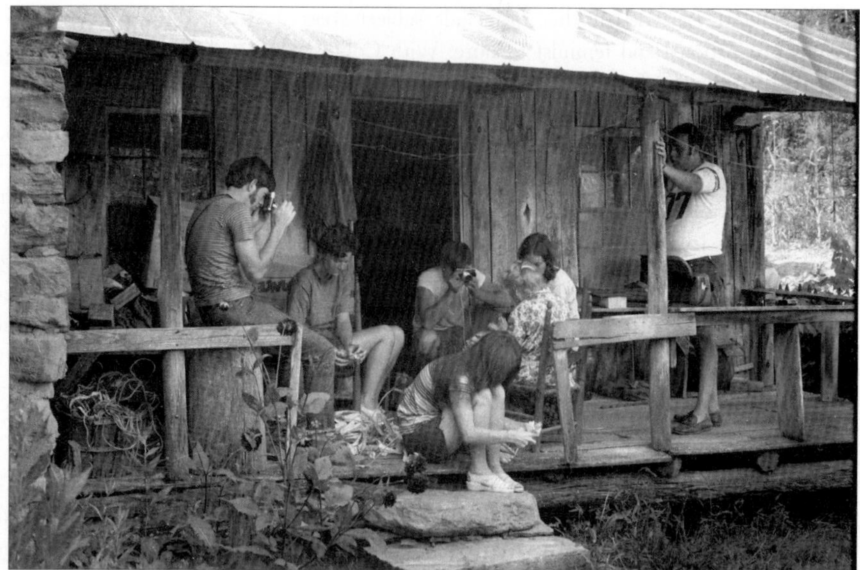
Foxfire students interviewing Aunt Arie Carpenter at her home in northern Georgia, 1972. The Foxfire Museum and Center provide public access to the work of hundreds of high school students who have documented the local history and culture of the southern Appalachians.

continues to work nationally on a limited basis, Foxfire focuses on Georgia and the surrounding region through a learner-centered approach to education that is academically sound and promotes continuous interaction between students and their communities.

The Foxfire Museum, which opened in 1991, provides public access to historical collections based on the work of hundreds of high school students who have undertaken projects to document their own local history and culture. The museum is housed in a log cabin constructed by students. Inside the museum are exhibits of artifacts, a one-room log cabin, gristmill, and gift shop. Collections include toys, wagons, farm equipment, and tools used in blacksmithing, woodworking, hunting, trapping, shoemaking, and logging. Artifacts collected from Aunt Arie Carpenter, one of Foxfire's best-known characters, are included in the exhibits.

The Foxfire Center, located near Black Rock State Park about a mile from the museum, includes a major collection of more than twenty log buildings. Its historic cabins, dating to the early 1800s, were moved from locations throughout the southern Appalachians and reconstructed by Foxfire students. Replicas of traditional vernacular design are also included. A chapel, blacksmith shop, mule barn, wagon shed, gristmill, one-room cabin, dogtrot cabin, and other cabins occupy several wooded acres.

See also: APPALACHIAN SPECIAL COLLECTIONS; FOXFIRE (EDUCATION).

—Barbara Duncan, *Museum of the Cherokee Indian*

Frank H. McClung Museum

Built with money bequeathed by Judge John Green as a memorial to his father-in-law, the Frank H. McClung Museum, which opened in 1963, is located on the campus of the University of Tennessee in Knoxville. The museum's collections and exhibitions include objects related to archaeology, anthropology, decorative arts, and natural history. They focus especially on Tennessee's culture, history, art, and geology.

Archaeological artifacts and data form the McClung Museum's largest research collection and are the basis for its premier permanent exhibition, *Archaeology and the Native Peoples of Tennessee*. The exhibit showcases the story of Tennessee's native peoples from Paleo-Indian times, more than twelve thousand years ago, to the present, with emphasis in the historic section on east Tennessee sites and inhabitants. Interwoven in the story is the process of archaeological discovery and investigation. Artifacts on display include some of the finest examples of prehistoric Native American art in the United States.

Other principal exhibitions are *Geology and Fossil History of Tennessee*, containing dinosaur bones found in Tennessee and a rare 300-million-year-old amphibian trackway from east Tennessee; *The Decorative Experience*, featuring fine decorative arts objects from around the world; and *Ancient Egypt: The Eternal Voice*. The museum also features a continuing program of temporary exhibitions as well as several smaller exhibits on selected topics.

In addition to the extensive archaeological collections, two other holdings comprise the museum's research collections. The archaeobotanical collection (ancient plant remains) documents the development and use of domesticated plants in the region. The freshwater mussel collection, numbering more than thirty-two thousand specimens, aids in regional riverine environment studies.

See also: APPALACHIAN CULTURAL MUSEUM; B. CARROLL REECE MEMORIAL MUSEUM.

—Deborah Woodiel, *University of Tennessee*

Frick Art and Historical Center

The Frick Art and Historical Center, located in the Point Breeze section of Pittsburgh, is the site of Clayton, former home of industrialist Henry Clay Frick, as well as several museums housing his antique car and art collections. Born in Westmoreland County, Pennsylvania, Frick made his fortune in the steel and coke industries that dominated the Pittsburgh area during the late nineteenth and early twentieth centuries.

Restored in the late 1980s, Clayton remarkably exemplifies the manner in which wealthy Victorians lived. As Frick's first family home, Clayton contains most of his early art collection as well as more than 90 percent of the family's original furnishings, including the bed in which Frick recovered after he was wounded during the Homestead Steel Strike riots in 1892.

The Frick Art and Historical Center is also home to the Frick Art Museum, the Car and Carriage Museum, a greenhouse, a visitor center and museum shop, and a café. Built by Frick's daughter Helen Clay Frick in 1970, the Frick Art Museum contains a collection of paintings, sculpture, and decorative arts dating from the twelfth to the eighteenth century. Opened to the public in 1997, the Car and Carriage Museum houses more than thirty-five antique cars and carriages, most of which were built in the Pittsburgh area.

See also: ART MUSEUMS; FRICK, HENRY CLAY (BUSINESS, INDUSTRY, AND TECHNOLOGY); PITTSBURGH, PENNSYLVANIA (URBAN APPALACHIAN EXPERIENCE).

—Jessica Bacon, *Frick Art and Historical Center*

Frontier Culture Museum

The Frontier Culture Museum (formerly known as the Museum of American Frontier Culture) is an outdoor museum near Staunton, Virginia. Opened in 1988 and located beside the route of southwestward migration in the eighteenth century, the museum presents four farmsteads through which visitors can explore English, Irish, and German influences on America's first western frontier. It is the American counterpart of the Ulster-American Folk Park in Northern Ireland.

In 1976, at a time of intense unrest in Northern Ireland, the Ulster-American Folk Park opened in County Tyrone. Planned by Eric Montgomery, secretary of the Scotch-Irish Trust of Ulster, the museum aimed to provide employment while unifying the people in an appreciation of Ulster's contribution to American history. Montgomery's museum, which continues to expand and develop, has two sections. In one, old buildings from Ulster have been dismantled and painstakingly rebuilt. In the other, log buildings of the American frontier have been faithfully replicated. Visitors move from the Old World to the New World, imaginatively experiencing the process of migration and settlement.

At the time of the American bicentennial, Montgomery dreamed of a version of the Ulster-American Folk Park for the United States. The idea was not the one usual in European countries such as Sweden and Holland, where old buildings are reconstructed to display regional diversity. Nor was it the American idea, realized at places that evoke a past moment of history, such as Colonial Williamsburg, Virginia, and Old Sturbridge Village, Massachusetts. Rather, four complete farmsteads from different areas and eras were brought together in the Shenandoah Valley of Virginia to enable the visitor to make comparisons among them to see how the culture of Appalachia, and thus of the American frontier, was at once a derivation from European sources and a new American amalgam.

One set of farm buildings, including a log saddlebag house and a finely crafted log double-crib barn, was brought from Botetourt County in the southern Shenandoah Valley. A second farmstead of low, stone, thatched buildings came from Northern Ireland. The third, from southern England, features a magnificent framed barn. The fourth, taken from the Rhine Valley in Germany, contains buildings similar to those Pennsylvania structures that proved influential on the vernacular architecture of the upland South.

See also: IRISH (RACE, ETHNICITY, AND IDENTITY); OUTDOOR MUSEUMS; SHENANDOAH NATIONAL PARK (TOURISM).

—Henry Glassie, *Indiana University*

Henry Glassie, *A Museum of American Frontier Culture: A Proposal* (1978); Eric Montgomery, *The Ulster-American Folk Park: How It All Began* (1991).

Glass Museums

Although few remain in Appalachia, hundreds of glass factories once flourished in the region. Glass museums tell their story. The museums are largely clustered in Ohio, Pennsylvania, West Virginia, and New York, where glass manufacturing was especially prevalent.

Abundant fuel (timber, coal, and natural gas) coupled with river and rail transportation, skilled labor, and ready availability of ingredients made these states the leading locations for the production of plate glass, windows, glass containers, and tableware. Individual entrepreneurs—including many who held patents on various machines, created innovative glass colors, or were skilled in design—dominated the industry throughout the nineteenth century. During the 1880s, the growing strength of labor unions stimulated these manufacturers to form trusts. Together, the National Glass Company and the United States Glass Company conglomerates controlled more than 80 percent of the tableware output for the nation at the outset of the twentieth century.

By 1910 the trusts foundered, and successful glass plants became closely held stock companies that relied on distinctive products for market share or on mechanization for economies of scale. After World War I most manufacturers embraced automation, but tableware producers used both hand processes and semiautomatic machines. The Great Depression claimed numerous plants in the 1930s, and the impact of imports affected the tableware industry in the 1950s. By 1990 much glass manufacturing was concentrated in the South and Southwest although tableware production remains centered in the Ohio Valley.

Eager collectors have organized clubs to promote the study of bottles and tableware made in Appalachia. Some groups, along with historical societies, maintain modest, well-focused museums to display local products. Examples of these can be found in Cambridge and Newark, Ohio; Indiana, Pennsylvania; and Moundsville, West Virginia.

Many well-established museums outside the region, such as the Chrysler Museum of Art in Norfolk, Virginia, and the Toledo Museum of Art in Ohio, have extensive American glass collections that include Appalachian pieces. Museums within the region offer much more information on Appalachian pieces for both the casual observer and the scholarly researcher, however. The Corning Museum of Glass in Corning, New York, boasts the world's foremost collection of glass objects, ranging from ancient to contemporary. Bottles and tableware produced by many Appalachian manufacturers are accessible in its study galleries. The museum's Rakow Library holds books and periodicals devoted to glass history and technology as well as trade journals and thousands of original catalogs.

The Carriage House Glass Museum and the Oglebay Institute's Glass Museum in Wheeling, West Virginia, display glassware made in the Wheeling area from 1830 to 1940. The extensive collection of decorative and utilitarian tableware associated with designer and manufacturer Harry Northwood (1860–1919) at the Carriage House is particularly noteworthy. The Fenton Museum in Williamstown, West Virginia, houses more than fifteen hundred pieces made by the Fenton Art Glass Company between 1905 and the present as well as late-nineteenth- and early-twentieth-century tableware from the Ohio Valley. The Senator John Heinz Pittsburgh Regional History Center in Pittsburgh and the West Virginia Museum of American Glass in Weston have wide-ranging collections of handmade and machine-produced bottles and tableware attributed to factories from their respective areas.

See also: GLASS INDUSTRY (BUSINESS, INDUSTRY, AND TECHNOLOGY); GLASSWORKERS (LABOR); WEST VIRGINIA GLASSWARE (CRAFTS).

—James Measell, *Fenton Art Glass Company*

Ann Madarasz, *Glass: Shattering Notions* (1998); Gerald I. Reilly, ed., *Wheeling Glass, 1829–1939* (1994).

Halls of Fame

Halls of fame are specialized museums or exhibits that recognize achievement in a particular field. In addition to being tourist attractions, they are often important elements of their communities. By 2000, more than 274 halls of fame existed in the United States, and they formed one of the fastest-growing segments of the museum world, with more than 70 opening since 1970. Approximately 20 halls of fame are located in the Appalachian regions of Alabama, Georgia, New York, Pennsylvania, South Carolina, and Tennessee.

Most halls of fame honor outstanding individuals, but the displays take different forms depending on each hall's origin, selection process, content, operation, site, size, and attendance. Many are freestanding museums, while others are galleries in museums or permanent exhibits at sports arenas, civic centers, association headquarters, or other sites. Some halls of fame are not site-specific and consist simply of luncheon or dinner award ceremonies.

Sports are the focus of the majority of halls of fame in the United States and the Appalachian region. The Alabama Sports Hall of Fame in Birmingham focuses on numerous sports, but other Appalachian region museums are devoted to one particular sport. These include the Little League Baseball Hall of Excellence in Williamsport, Pennsylvania; the Pennsylvania State Football Hall of Fame in State College; the International Motorsports Hall of Fame in Talladega, Alabama; and the popular Paul W. Bryant Museum at the University of Alabama in Tuscaloosa, which pays homage to legendary football coach "Bear" Bryant and players from the University of Alabama football program.

Among the non-sports halls of fame, the most popular regionally as well as nationally are those that feature aviation and music. The Alabama Aviation Hall of Fame and the Alabama Jazz Hall of Fame Museum, both in Birmingham, and the Alabama Music Hall of Fame in Tuscumbia attract thousands of visitors. Taking a more inclusive approach, the Appalachian Hall of Fame at the Museum of Appalachia in Norris, Tennessee, honors Appalachian individuals who have excelled in diverse fields; some of these people are relatively unknown while others have national reputations.

Hall of fame museums date from the National Baseball Hall of Fame in Cooperstown, New York, which opened in 1939. However, the precedent for these institutions was set much earlier with statuary halls such as the National

Statuary Hall in the U.S. Capitol in Washington, D.C. (1864), and the Hall of Fame for Great Americans in the Bronx (1900). Growth of the movement accelerated in the 1950s and 1960s, but the largest increase occurred from the 1970s to the 1990s, when approximately two-thirds of all American halls of fame were established.

See also: MUSEUM OF APPALACHIA; SPORTS HALLS OF FAME (SPORTS AND RECREATION).

—Valerie J. Wheat, *Smithsonian Institution Libraries*

Victor J. Danilov, *Hall of Fame Museums: A Reference Guide* (1997); Paul Dickson and Robert Skole, *The Volvo Guide to Halls of Fame* (1995); Paul Soderberg and Helen Washington, eds., *The Big Book of Halls of Fame in the United States and Canada* (1977).

Hiddenite Center

The Hiddenite Center is a folk and cultural arts center for exhibition and education. Chartered in May of 1981, the center is located in the small community of Hiddenite, North Carolina, at the foot of the Blue Ridge Mountains in Alexander County.

Since it began, the center has worked to preserve and perpetuate local history and culture and to foster self-expression in the arts and crafts. Because of its rural setting, the center serves a region of six counties: Alexander, Burke, Caldwell, Catawba, Iredell, and Wilkes. These counties are affiliated with Appalachian State University through the Sharpe Chair of Fine and Applied Arts, which brings arts programming from the university to a rural audience.

The Lucas House, restored mansion of James Paul Lucas, a successful diamond merchant who settled in Hiddenite, is the focal point of the center. The mansion serves as a history museum and an art gallery, and it houses the staff. Exhibits change on a monthly basis and include folk arts, such as handmade musical instruments, quilts, and pottery; fine arts, such as the National Watercolor Traveling Exhibit; and programs devoted to the history and ethnicity of the region, such as the art and crafts of local Hmong residents.

The Hiddenite Center's Educational Complex contains a performance area, classrooms, craft areas, exhibits, meeting space, and storage. Activities that take place in the complex include an annual festival of local arts and crafts, a Heritage Fair for fourth-grade students that features hands-on demonstrations of crafts found throughout the southern Appalachian region, and an Ethnic Fair for sixth-grade students, where students meet local residents from many different cultures.

See also: ART MUSEUMS; SECTION OVERVIEW (RACE, ETHNICITY, AND IDENTITY).

—Lucy H. Allen and Dwaine C. Coley, *Hiddenite Center*

Highlander Folk School

See Highlander Research and Education Center (Education)

Historical Societies

The Appalachian region was long viewed as a distant backcountry by the settlers of the British colonies, and to a significant extent the region was viewed in a similar fashion by the first state historical societies, which began to form in the early 1800s.

With the exception of West Virginia, which lies entirely within Appalachia, the region tends to straddle the western edges of the original states or the eastern portion of the first states formed from the colonies' old frontiers. Settlement patterns and population growth favored the nonmountainous regions of these states, leading to the establishment of state capitals outside Appalachia. (Tennessee is an exception, as its capital was in Knoxville through 1812.) When state historical societies formed, they too were located in more populated sections, usually in the state capital. It was not until the late 1800s that regional and local historical societies began to form within the Appalachian region.

Since the early nineteenth century was an era when most historians were genteel amateurs with discipline and high purpose, the first historical societies were usually a combination of a learned society and a private gentlemen's club. The first such society in a state now part of Appalachia was the New-York Historical Society, formed in 1804 in New York City. Eventually that society would build one of the largest private library collections in the country, but its early focus was on the city, at the expense of the rest of the state.

By 1860, the Historical Society of Pennsylvania (1824), Virginia Historical Society (1831), Kentucky Historical Society (1836), Georgia Historical Society (1839), Maryland Historical Society (1844), Tennessee Historical Society (1849), South Carolina Historical Society (1856), and Mississippi Historical Society (1858) had been chartered. Through most of this period, the learned-society model continued. The core of the societies' work was based on guardianship of an honored past, and most of the societies were restarted several times before their current iterations. The Tennessee Historical Society is one such example. It was initially formed as the Tennessee Antiquarian Society in 1819 to collect the history of the founding of the state, especially of the earliest settled area in Appalachian east Tennessee. After publishing this history, the group disbanded, reformed as the Society for the Diffusion of Knowledge in 1835, and then organized as the Tennessee Historical Society four years later.

Early state and regional societies shared the ideal of guarding the young republic's history from oblivion. They also desired to preserve historical documents and to bolster their state's history in comparison to that of rival states. Many of the societies' founders were young, and they tended to focus on exploration and pioneers. In states east of the mountains, much of the societies' early collecting took place in the area of first exploration and settlement—the Appalachian region—although the collections were taken to the state capital.

The idea of historical society as learned society soon yielded to the concept of the society as library, and many historical societies constituted the first libraries of any significance in their area. Avidly collecting artifacts, manuscripts, and oral histories, they also began publishing papers based upon their work. Many state journals, such as the *Register of the Kentucky State Historical Society* (1903), have their origins in the period from 1890 to 1910.

New societies formed in Appalachia, which had begun to feel neglected by societies based outside the region. Among them were the East Tennessee Historical and Antiquarian Society (1834); Livingston County, New York, Historical Society (1877); Historical Society of Western Pennsylvania (1879); Filson Historical Society (Kentucky, 1884); Ohio Historical Society (1885); and New York State Historical Association (1899). The U.S. centenary in 1876 and the approaching century's end also spurred new interest in local and regional history.

In the late 1800s, the progressive model for historical societies developed, following the example of the State Historical Society of Wisconsin. The ideal historical society was seen not only as a library but also as an educational institution and public agency, an organization that would stress academic enrichment for students and programs for the general public in addition to scholarly research. In some states, the formerly private state historical societies merged with state agencies, as did the Ohio Historical Society. In others, such as North Carolina and West Virginia, state agencies eventually assumed major leadership for state history. However, in reaction, some societies moved back toward the purely academic role of the learned society. For example, a Virginia Historical Society official stated that he would rather see one university professor spend fifteen days in the library than have a single junior high pupil there for fifteen minutes.

In the first half of the twentieth century, the model of historical society as museum became prevalent. A leader in the movement was the New York State Historical Association, which in 1938 had moved to Cooperstown, where it began to develop a museum community. Reflecting the growing national interest in folklife and American studies, these museums often featured living history demonstrations and visitor participation. The era saw a sudden appearance of new Appalachian county and regional historical societies such as the Tennessee Valley Historical Society in Sheffield, Alabama (1923), the Upper (South) Carolina Historical Society (1928), and the Delaware County, New York, Historical Association (1945).

By the 1950s, issues emerged that still affect historical societies in the region. Academic historians began to de-emphasize regional, local, and celebratory history, and many academics concluded that local historical societies were irrelevant except for collecting documents. As the museum model for societies increased through the 1960s and 1970s, scholars saw the organizations' attempts to appeal to a broad audience as a threat to resources for academic research and publication. From the 1980s into the early twenty-first century, issues of cultural diversity also embroiled many historical societies. Groups that had originally formed to extol the virtues of their white pioneer ancestors struggled with how to broaden their exhibits and programs to include African American, Native American, women's, and industrial history. However, one benefit of the historical and interpretive movements of the last fifty years has been a new emphasis on the history of Appalachia and its peoples, as historians' interests shifted from mansions to mill towns, from plantations to hardscrabble farms, and from Indian fighting to Native American lifeways.

Few of the historical societies still in existence were formed before 1900, and estimates place 75 percent or more as founded since 1960. The centennial of the start of the Civil War in 1961, the U.S. bicentennial celebration in 1976, and various anniversaries of county formation and statehood in the Appalachian region greatly encouraged the organization of local historical societies, mainly on the county level. A large proportion of the new groups focused primarily on genealogy. Examples from this period include the Greenbrier Historical Society in Lewisburg, West Virginia (1963); Tennessee Valley Genealogical Society in Huntsville, Alabama (1966); Red River Historical Society in Clay City, Kentucky (1966); Cherokee County, North Carolina, Historical Museum (1977); Allegheny County, North Carolina, Historical-Genealogical Society (1978); Union County, Tennessee, Historical Society (1980); Henderson County, North Carolina, Genealogical and Historical Society (1983); Allegheny Regional Family History Society in Elkins, West Virginia (1992); Wise County, Virginia, Historical Society (1993); and the Alcorn County Genealogical Society (1993) and Prentiss County Genealogical and Historical Society (1998) in northeast Mississippi.

Regardless of whether the organization was founded in the early 1800s or in the 1990s, the mission statements of virtually all regional and local historical societies stress the importance of collecting materials related to local history—documents, manuscripts, artifacts, and genealogies. Local historical societies also mark historic sites, sponsor programs or lectures, and publish newsletters, articles, journals, and books. Many operate museums, often in historic buildings acquired by the organizations, while some maintain research libraries or a history room in a local library. A few societies undertake the direct preservation of local landmarks. Societies that focus on family history often undertake cemetery surveys, transcribe local records, and maintain Web sites featuring primary documents. A small percentage of local and regional historical societies also present programs and other activities for schoolchildren, both in the classroom and at their museums. In short, the great majority of these organizations strive to promote an interest in history among the societies' members and the general public, and in Appalachia the societies typically stress their desire to protect the cultural heritage of the mountains.

Examples of these activities are seen in the Tennessee Valley Genealogical Society, which publishes the quarterly *Valley Leaves* and places its holdings in the Heritage Room of the Huntsville Public Library, and the Historical Society of Frederick County, Maryland, which maintains a museum and library in the c. 1820 Miller House. The Delaware County Historical Association (New York) maintains historic buildings, including a historic farmstead, gun shop, blacksmith shop, cemetery, church, and a Catskill Turnpike tollgate house. The Wise County Historical Society (Virginia) publishes the *Appalachian Quarterly*, covering the genealogy and history of the southern Appalachians of Kentucky, North Carolina, Tennessee, Virginia, and West Virginia, and hosts the Southern Appalachian Ancestral Registry, a database of family charts, and the National Melungeon Registry.

New historical societies are still being created within Appalachia, each striving to preserve local history. Many challenges confront them. Segregation—although voluntary—occurs when predominately African American or Native American historical organizations form separately from European American societies. New Hispanic and Asian residents of Appalachia are rarely included at all. Competition for artifacts and manuscripts has intensified as organizations within the region attempt to add prized items to their collections. The academic community still complains that local historical societies do not value their guidance, and vice versa. Overall, however, historical societies have preserved much of what is known about Appalachia.

See also: FOLKLORE SOCIETIES; SECTION OVERVIEW (SETTLEMENT AND MIGRATION).

—Ann Toplovich, *Tennessee Historical Society*

John Alexander Williams, "Introduction: American Historical Societies," in *A Culture at Risk: Who Cares for America's Heritage?* by Charles Phillips and Patricia Hogan (1984).

Historic Sites

See Section Overview (Tourism)

Institute for Regional Analysis and Public Policy

In 1998 the Kentucky General Assembly established "Programs of Distinction" at public universities. These programs are nationally recognized centers of academic excellence. The Institute for Regional Analysis and Public Policy became a Kentucky Program of Distinction at Morehead State University in 1999.

The institute's goal is to integrate university and regional resources in ways that will benefit the region. Academic programs, research initiatives, and service activities connect Morehead State faculty and students with local citizens, educators, civic leaders, and policymakers in the hopes that together these groups will promote sustainable economic development. The institute's Division of Academic Programs enables undergraduate students majoring in government, geography, sociology, social work, and environmental science to take extra courses and receive a B.A. or B.S. degree with emphasis in regional analysis. Graduate students in biology and sociology have similar options. Major and graduate degrees in regional analysis are planned for the future. In addition to the institute's degree programs, its Division of Applied Research, Service, and Policy works on understanding and solving problems in the Appalachian region.

See also: KENTUCKY EDUCATION REFORM ACT OF 1990 (EDUCATION).

—Michael W. Hail, *Morehead State University*

Johnstown Area Heritage Association

Highly responsive to its community, the Johnstown Area Heritage Association of Johnstown, Pennsylvania, has become a vehicle for community change in addition to conducting traditional museum programs. The organization promotes the interpretation and management of the area's cultural resources and serves as a clearinghouse for revitalization efforts tied to cultural tourism. It has worked to preserve and interpret such significant aspects of the Johnstown community as historic buildings and occupational and ethnic traditions. Since 1990, the association has presented the Johnstown Folkfest, a celebration of the multicultural traditions of southwestern Pennsylvania and the United States.

Incorporated in 1971 as the Johnstown Flood Museum Association, its original theme was the 1889 Johnstown Flood, a catastrophe that claimed more than twenty-two hundred lives when a dam failed during heavy rains. A four-million-dollar capital investment in 1989 included restoration of its building and installation of a permanent exhibition and film. Reorganized in 1991 as the Johnstown Area Heritage Association, the organization began working

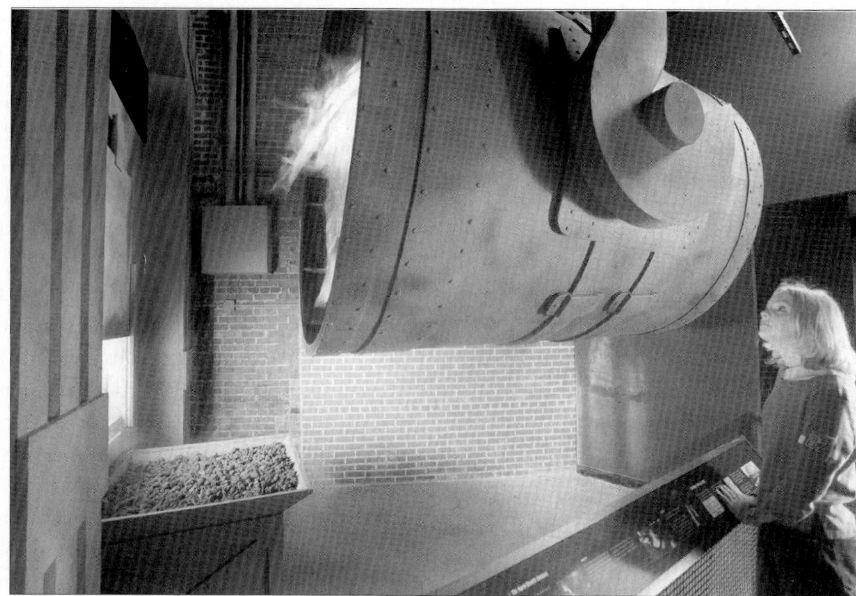

A replica of an open-hearth steel furnace is one of the many exhibits at the Frank and Sylvia Pasquerilla Heritage Discovery Center in Johnstown, Pennsylvania.

to expand beyond the story of the flood and to develop new programs and facilities to interpret Johnstown's social and industrial history.

The association operates several facilities. The Johnstown Flood Museum, housed in a historic Carnegie library building, encompasses exhibits and art that graphically depict the flood story. The Wagner-Ritter House, an 1860 immigrant steelworker's residence, is operated as a house museum. The visitor center at the house documents the restoration process and uses a portion of the archaeological collection from the site to present the Wagner-Ritter family's experience. A sixty-thousand-square-foot 1907 brewery building has been developed as the Frank and Sylvia Pasquerilla Heritage Discovery Center. This facility functions as a city museum and houses the permanent exhibit *America: Through Immigrant Eyes*, which interprets the way of life created by immigrants in industrial Johnstown.

A partner in a collaborative effort to preserve and develop the Cambria Iron and Steel National Historic Landmark, the association will manage and interpret the 1862 Cambria Blacksmith Shop. Its longterm goal is to develop the Johnstown Discovery Network, linking heritage museums and historic districts by an interpretive pedestrian greenway and an auto tour route.

In working to improve Johnstown's visibility as a tourist destination, the association has emphasized the story of the workingmen and -women of Johnstown—their struggles and their achievements.

See also: IRON AND STEEL INDUSTRY (BUSINESS, INDUSTRY, AND TECHNOLOGY); JOHNSTOWN FLOOD (ENVIRONMENT).

—Troy Gowen, *East Tennessee State University*

Mining Museums

Mining has played a significant role in defining and shaping Appalachian culture and economics. Lead was mined as early as 1756 in Wythe County, Virginia, but with the exception of a few isolated pockets, such as the massive copper and iron deposits at Ducktown, Tennessee, and Birmingham, Alabama, metals are relatively scarce in the region. The mining heritage of Appalachia is predominantly one of coal mining, and museums dedicated to the industry throughout the region reflect its cultural and economic significance.

Despite reduced mining employment since the mid-twentieth century, coal remains a major source of revenue for much of Appalachia. A few scattered coal mines operated in the region as early as the late 1700s, and by the 1820s small mining operations existed throughout the mountains. With the proliferation of railroads and mechanized mining techniques in the 1870s, coal mining became the dominant force in the Appalachian economy. Museums help communities interpret the industry and the way of life it created.

West Virginia is home to a number of coal-mining museums. The Exhibition Coal Mine of Beckley offers a sit-down tour that is unique among mine museums, as visitors board mine cars and tour 1,500 feet of winding underground passages following an actual coal seam. The tours, which are led by veteran miners, trace the evolution of mining from its earliest days to modern mechanized operations.

West Virginia's other coal-mining museums offer more conventional presentations. The Comer Museum, located on the ground floor of the Mineral Resources Building at the Evansdale campus of West Virginia University, seeks to preserve the social, cultural, and technological history of the coal, oil, and natural gas industries. It features artifacts such as miners' lamps, protective gear, mining equipment, photographs, railroad maps, and canary cages. The Eastern Regional Coal Archives of Bluefield, housed within the Craft Memorial Library in Bluefield, West Virginia, features exhibits of artifacts, miners' diaries, photographs, mining equipment, films, research materials, and other coal-mining memorabilia.

The Harry W. Meador Jr. Coal Museum, owned by the Westmoreland Coal Company, is located in Big Stone Gap, Virginia. The exhibits focus on coal and the impact mining has had on the community. Southwest Virginia is also home to the Pocahontas Exhibition Coal Mine, a national historic landmark near Bramwell that is open seasonally from April until the end of October. It features 875 feet of a coal seam that was reserved by the Pocahontas Operators Association for hand-loading, an early method of coal mining.

One of the most comprehensive coal-mining museums is located in Benham, Kentucky, a town that was designed and built as a coal town by International Harvester in 1911. The Kentucky Coal Mining Museum first opened in 1994 and displays early mining tools, the floor plans of an underground coal mine, and a photography collection. Loretta Lynn, a country music singer known as the "coal miner's daughter," donated many items from her personal collection. The museum also includes an electric locomotive modeled after the machines used to haul miners in the 1940s. A two-ton block of coal, specially carved for the museum, is prominently displayed in front of the facility.

A few museums in Appalachia focus on mining materials other than coal. The Gem and Mineral Museum in Franklin, North Carolina, for example, is maintained by volunteers, preserving the history of an area where there has been a large concentration of gem mines, some of which are open to the public.

North Carolina is home to several other gem and mineral museums, including the Museum of North Carolina Minerals, which reopened in 2002 after extensive renovation. The museum contains exhibits related to the Spruce Pine Mining District and is open year-round. The Colburn Gem and Mineral Museum, also open year-round, is located in Asheville and houses some forty-five hundred mineral specimens and more than one thousand cut gemstones.

In Lumpkin County, Georgia, the Dahlonega Courthouse Gold Museum offers a view of the mining history in the area that saw the United States' first gold rush between 1829 and 1847. Gold coins minted at the Dahlonega Branch Mint, gold nuggets, and other items of interest are on display along with a short film documenting the lifestyles of prospectors and mining families. Built in 1836 with local stone and mortar containing trace amounts of gold, the courthouse is the oldest public building in northeast Georgia and is designated a state historic site.

See also: COAL HERITAGE TOURISM (TOURISM); COAL MINING (ENVIRONMENT); COAL SETTLEMENTS (SETTLEMENT AND MIGRATION).

—Kim O'Connor, *University of Chicago*

Mounds

See Moundbuilders (Settlement and Migration)

Moundville Archaeological Park

Moundville Archaeological Park is the best-preserved Mississippian mound center in North America. Located in west-central Alabama at the southern end of the Appalachians, Moundville was once the largest, most powerful political and religious seat in the eastern United States. Nobles ruled thousands of people, directing construction of earthen mounds while fostering a thriving economy based on corn agriculture.

Around A.D. 800, Native Americans began growing vast amounts of corn and settling in large villages in what is now the southeastern United States. A rich, complex culture arose. Archaeologists call these people Mississippians. By about 1200, Moundville was an impressive city fortified on three sides with a mud-plastered, wooden wall studded with guard towers. A high bluff overlooking the Black Warrior River formed Moundville's northernmost boundary. Approximately one thousand people lived in Moundville at the community's peak, another ten thousand or so living within a sixty-mile radius along the Black Warrior River. Between 1200 and 1350, the Moundville people erected about thirty flat-topped pyramidal mounds in a roughly rectangular pattern around a central plaza. The site's largest mound is fifty-eight feet high and contains roughly 111,700 cubic yards of dirt.

Moundville Archaeological Park features a museum, a reconstructed Native American village, nature trails, picnic areas, a fully equipped campground, and a riverside conference center. The annual Moundville Native American Festival in October celebrates the culture and heritage of southeastern Native Americans and hosts approximately twenty thousand visitors. Other programs include guided tours, craft classes, Heritage Days (a springtime arts fair), and the Moundville Knap-in, a stone-tool-making meet.

See also: ARCHAEOLOGICAL SITES (SETTLEMENT AND MIGRATION); MOUNDBUILDERS (SETTLEMENT AND MIGRATION).

—Betsy Gilbert, *Moundville Archaeological Park*

Mountain Heritage Center

From its beginning in 1889, Western Carolina University in Cullowhee, North Carolina, has collected regional manuscripts and artifacts to celebrate its Appalachian history. In 1975, stimulated by a nationwide interest in heritage in general and a rediscovery of Appalachia in particular, Appalachian-born Chancellor H. F. Robinson announced plans for the creation of a formal museum and research center dedicated to Appalachian studies. The Mountain Heritage Center moved into its permanent home on the ground floor of the new H. F. Robinson Administration Building in 1979.

The center studies, documents, and interprets the culture and history of southern Appalachia and provides museum services to western North Carolina. To that end, it collects artifacts, builds exhibitions, documents and presents traditional craft demonstrations and musical performances, produces books and musical recordings, and enhances the curricula of elementary, secondary, and university classrooms. Its collection of more than ten thousand regional artifacts is especially rich in agricultural implements, logging and woodworking tools, textiles, and transportation equipment.

The center is committed to public history, especially to interpreting current academic studies of Appalachia for the public. Its programs highlight traditional music and textiles and the history of Appalachia. The Smithsonian Institution and the American Folklife Center of the Library of Congress have adopted some of that programming. Major research exhibits have examined regional handicrafts, mountain trout, and Scots-Irish immigrants and culture. Mountain Heritage Day, an annual presentation of traditional mountain culture, is a fall festival that attracts tens of thousands of visitors.

See also: APPALACHIAN CENTERS AND INSTITUTES; APPALACHIAN CULTURAL MUSEUM; NORTH CAROLINA ARTS COUNCIL.

—H. Tyler Blethen, *Western Carolina University*

Museum of Appalachia

The Museum of Appalachia, located in Norris, Tennessee, sixteen miles north of Knoxville, is the creation of John Rice Irwin, a descendant of early setters in the area. Irwin began his work in the 1960s with a single log cabin and eventually developed a living history farm and village of more than sixty-five acres, thirty-five historic structures, and a quarter of a million items. The museum is an outgrowth of Irwin's interest in the people of Appalachia and in collecting and displaying objects related to Appalachian heritage and culture with their respective histories.

Among the buildings are a cabin occupied by Mark Twain's parents in Tennessee just before their move to Missouri and the primitive one-room cabin built shortly after 1800 by a settler named Wes Arnwine and occupied by generations of Arnwines until 1936. The Arnwine cabin is listed on the National Register of Historic Places. Other structures include corncribs, smokehouses, barns, blacksmith shops, a one-room school, a church, and privies. The People's Building, which is constructed from early handmade bricks, features an exhibit on Henry Mayes, a Kentucky coal miner who received national attention when he waged a one-man religious crusade on the roadsides of America with homemade signs proclaiming "Jesus Saves," "Get Right with God," and other messages.

The Appalachian Hall of Fame, a three-story brick building, is dedicated to both famous and not-so-famous Appalachian artists and craftspeople. Exhibits include an extensive collection of Cherokee and other Native American artifacts from the mountain region, hundreds of handmade and unusual musical instruments, and handmade baskets. Also on display are items belonging to historically prominent Appalachians such as World War I hero Alvin York, Nobel Peace Prize winner Cordell Hull, and the first president of the Republic of Texas, Sam Houston.

Special events at the museum draw tens of thousands of visitors every year. The annual Tennessee Fall Homecoming is held the second full weekend in October and features old-time musicians and mountain craftspeople from the region. Other events include the July Fourth Celebration and Anvil Shoot and, in December, the celebration of Christmas in Old Appalachia.

See also: MAYES, HENRY (RELIGION); OUTDOOR MUSEUMS.

—Misty Yeager, *Museum of Appalachia*

Museum of Early Southern Decorative Arts Collection

The Museum of Early Southern Decorative Arts is located on the campus of Old Salem, a Moravian living history town in Winston-Salem, North Carolina. Its mission is to exhibit and research the decorative arts of the early South. The museum focuses its collection on three regions and argues that the Chesapeake, the low country, and the backcountry showed sharp cultural contrasts by the second quarter of the eighteenth century. The backcountry, which includes Winston-Salem, encompasses Appalachian areas.

The twenty-four period rooms and seven galleries of the museum contain furniture, paintings, textiles, ceramics, silver, and other objects made and used through 1820 in Maryland, Virginia, North and South Carolina, Georgia, Kentucky, and Tennessee. The museum's backcountry collection shows distinct characteristics attributed to the blending of ethnic styles that infuse that region's decorative arts. Germans, Quakers, Scots, Irish, and Scots-Irish all settled in the backcountry and brought with them different skills and designs that appear in the furniture and other objects they created. The Gallery at Old Salem, which shares an

The Basket Exhibit in the Appalachian Hall of Fame at the Museum of Appalachia in Norris, Tennessee, 1995. Housing more than a quarter of a million artifacts of folk, mountain, and rural Appalachian life, the Museum of Appalachia consists of a sixty-five-acre frontier village and farm comprised of dozens of fully furnished pioneer cabins relocated from around the region.

entrance with the museum, occasionally presents exhibitions with objects from one or the other's permanent collections.

In addition to maintaining and exhibiting its collections, the museum supports ongoing efforts to locate and record examples of southern material culture and conducts research in public and private records of every county of the early South. One outgrowth of this research is a database containing biographical information on nearly sixty thousand artisans and artists working in more than one hundred different trades. Object files and databases are open to the public.

See also: ART MUSEUMS; MORAVIANS (RELIGION); WINSTON-SALEM, NORTH CAROLINA (URBAN APPALACHIAN EXPERIENCE).

—Neva Jean Specht, *Appalachian State University*

Museum of the Cherokee Indian

The Museum of the Cherokee Indian was founded in 1948 to preserve and perpetuate Cherokee history, culture, and stories. Originally based on the collections of Samuel Beck and housed in a log cabin in downtown Cherokee, North Carolina, the museum has become one of the most visited and successful tribal museums in the United States. Now a nonprofit organization, it represents the Eastern Band of Cherokee Indians, a federally recognized tribe living on the Qualla Boundary in the mountains of western North Carolina.

Initially, the museum was part of the Cherokee Historical Association, organized to promote tourism in Cherokee through an outdoor drama entitled *Unto These Hills* and a living history museum, the Oconaluftee Indian Village. It became a separate nonprofit organization in 1971 and moved into a new building in 1976. Renovations in 1998 included the addition of an exhibit that combines artifacts, graphics, text, and computer-generated images to tell the story of the Cherokee people from eleven thousand years ago to the present day.

The museum pursues its mission in a variety of ways, including exhibits, publications, archives, and innovative programs. Its award-winning exhibit on Cherokee life, open year-round, attracts more than 125,000 American and international visitors annually. The museum gift shop sells handmade Cherokee crafts, books, sound recordings, and prints. Extensive archives, which are available to researchers, contain books, manuscript materials, photographs, and a microfilm collection of material on the Cherokee in foreign archives. Since 1976 the museum has published the *Journal of Cherokee Studies*, the first peer-reviewed scholarly journal dedicated to a single tribe; it occasionally publishes books on the Cherokee as well. Education programs include annual festivals, courses for teachers, and experiential programs for visiting groups. The museum's outreach staff provides programs for schools within a one-hundred-mile radius. Temporary exhibitions feature Cherokee artists and craftspeople. The museum has partnered with the North Carolina Arts Council and other organizations to create Cherokee Heritage Trails, a cultural and heritage tourism project for which it serves as the main interpretive center. It is also an official interpretive site for the Trail of Tears National Historic Trail developed by the National Park Service.

See also: CHEROKEE (RACE, ETHNICITY, AND IDENTITY); CHOCTAW MUSEUM OF THE SOUTHERN INDIAN; SENECA-IROQUOIS NATIONAL MUSEUM.

—Barbara Duncan, *Museum of the Cherokee Indian*

National Mine Health and Safety Academy Technical Information Center and Library

The National Mine Health and Safety Academy at Beaver, West Virginia, is a federal academy, just as are the United States FBI and military academies. Under the authorization of the Federal Mine Health and Safety Act of 1977, it is responsible for training mine safety and health inspectors, mining personnel, and others designated by the secretaries of labor and the interior.

The academy's Technical Information Center and Library covers health and safety, mining engineering, interpersonal communications, mine management, mining history, and other subjects. Special collections include Bureau of Mines publications, including Open File Reports dating from 1910 to the present; Kentucky and West Virginia topographical maps; and a wide selection of geological and mining maps and charts from the United States and foreign countries. Archival materials include photographs, mining equipment, and other artifacts. The collection also holds accident investigation files from all districts for the past twenty years.

The reference services of the academy's Technical Information Center are not limited to the boundaries of the United States and its territories. Several cooperative programs enable mining representatives and inspectors from other nations to take part in the academy's mine health and safety training programs. International requests are received regularly at the center from mining representatives and officials in Russia, Ukraine, Poland, China, Peru, Thailand, South Africa, and other nations.

See also: ANTHRACITE COAL INDUSTRY (BUSINESS, INDUSTRY, AND TECHNOLOGY); COAL MINING (ENVIRONMENT); MINER PHYSICAL REHABILITATION PROGRAM (HEALTH).

—Melody Bragg, *National Mine Health and Safety Academy*

National Youth Science Camp

The National Youth Science Camp, initiated as a youth activity during West Virginia's Centennial Celebration in 1963, is located near the National Radio Astronomy Observatory at Green Bank in Pocahontas County, West Virginia. It honors high school seniors who are outstanding science students. Participants come from throughout the United States, and the program is highly selective: each state may send only two students, who must be invited by their state governors. Criteria for selection include academic achievement, demonstrated leadership qualities, and an expressed intention to enter a scientific field of study.

Activities at the camp are varied. A lecture series features nationally recognized scholars who discuss their research. The topics range from the pure and applied sciences to the social sciences and the arts and represent most disciplines found in a liberal arts college. The camp's Appalachian setting in the Monongahela National Forest provides opportunities for exploring the natural and cultural landscape. A visit to the nearby Cass Scenic Railroad, for example, gives students the opportunity to learn about lumbering activity in the region during the early twentieth century. Students combine recreation with the study of regional flora and fauna as they engage in rock climbing, caving, snorkeling in mountain pools, and hiking.

A project of the National Youth Science Foundation, the National Youth Science Camp receives major support from the State of West Virginia. Funding covers all the students' expenses except personal items. In conjunction with the camp, students are honored in Washington, D.C., at a luncheon hosted by West Virginia's senior senator; many other senators join the group for lunch or come by to congratulate the youthful leaders from their states. Students describe the monthlong camp as a highly stimulating experience.

See also: HUNTSVILLE, ALABAMA (URBAN APPALACHIAN EXPERIENCE); SUMMER CAMPS (SPORTS AND RECREATION); U.S. SPACE AND ROCKET CENTER.

—Roderick W. Wilson, *West Virginia University Institute of Technology*

North Carolina Arts Council

The North Carolina Arts Council was established to enrich the cultural life of the state by nurturing and supporting creative excellence and by providing opportunities for all North Carolinians to experience the arts. The state has long been recognized for rich traditions in crafts, literature, historical drama, and music, and nowhere are these traditions more evident than in the Appalachian region of the state.

Governor Terry Sanford created the North Carolina Arts Council by executive order in 1964, and it became a statutory state agency in 1967. A division of the North Carolina Department of Cultural Resources, it is governed by a twenty-four-member board of directors appointed by the governor. The council provides more than thirteen hundred grants annually and also offers technical assistance and other services to nonprofit organizations and artists statewide. In a typical year, the council awards more than three hundred grants totaling more than \$1.5 million in the state's twenty-nine Appalachian counties. Funds are provided by the North Carolina General Assembly and the National Endowment for the Arts.

The council's approach to stimulating arts development has always been populist in nature. From its inception, the council has supported municipal and volunteer arts groups' organizing, staffing, and investing in arts facilities. Of the more than 2,000 arts organizations and 100 local arts councils operating in the state, approximately 650 of those organizations and 28 arts councils are in the Appalachian region.

Several Appalachian arts councils incorporate the region's rich cultural heritage into their programming. The Surry Arts Council uses traditional music from the area in many programs, including sponsorship of weekly live radio broadcasts. Surry, Ashe, Haywood, Wilkes, and Caldwell Counties collaborate with the council and the University of North Carolina at Chapel Hill on a Curriculum, Music, and Community project that draws on the state's traditional music and musicians for the North Carolina Standard Course of Study.

Blue Ridge music and Cherokee heritage are the subjects of the Blue Ridge Heritage Initiative, a cultural tourism project developed by the council with partners in North Carolina, Tennessee, Virginia, and Georgia. This initiative serves communities that want to highlight their own cultural heritage as an economic development strategy. Guidebooks and Web sites lead travelers to culturally important sites and artists in the region.

To recognize the talents and lifetime contributions of the state's folk artists, the council initiated the Folk Heritage Awards in 1989. Half of the artists who have been honored over the life of the program have come from the Appalachian region, confirming the extraordinary heritage found in the western third of the state. Several of these artists have also received the prestigious National Heritage Fellowship from the National Endowment for the Arts.

In the mid 1990s, the council, like many arts agencies across the nation, faced political efforts to eliminate government funding for the arts. The failure of such efforts resulted in renewed support for the council's work. The council's role in developing tourism based on traditional and contemporary Appalachian culture is but one of many examples of the value of public funding for the arts.

See also: ART MUSEUMS; OHIO ARTS COUNCIL; PUBLIC ART PROGRAMS (VISUAL ARTS).

—Miriam Sauls, *Raleigh, North Carolina*

North Carolina Arts Council Quadrennial Report, 1995–99 (2001).

Northern Tier Cultural Alliance

The Northern Tier Cultural Alliance, located at Mansfield, Pennsylvania's Mansfield University, supports folk arts and artists, heritage initiatives, and educational and cultural projects throughout eight northern Pennsylvania counties. The alliance is a volunteer organization composed of representatives of historical societies, libraries, schools, museums, and education councils, as well as individuals committed to heritage preservation.

The alliance developed from a 1992 Heritage Commission grant that resulted in a cultural plan, reports and video footage of tradition bearers, and ultimately the Center for Arts and Folklife at Mansfield University in 1996. Two books and three videos also grew from the original work. Ongoing projects of the alliance include an annual exhibit featuring the region's artisans, a mentorship for secondary students in heritage documentation, and sponsorship of national folk artist appearances.

Local-heritage curriculum courses, taught collaboratively by university and community experts, create interdisciplinary resource guides for K–12 teachers on topics such as the Underground Railroad, the tanning industry, the Civilian Conservation Corps, coal mining, and lumbering. Stories collected by students in these classes become part of the repertoire of alliance-affiliated storytellers who, along with other artists, make forty to fifty personal appearances in schools and other public venues each year.

First funded by the Center for Rural Pennsylvania, the Northern Tier Cultural Alliance receives support from the Pennsylvania Council on the Arts, National Endowment for the Arts, Pennsylvania Humanities Council, Pennsylvania Historical and Museum Commission, and local corporate and charitable foundations. The alliance participates in cultural planning and interpretation with two heritage parks and local museums. Pennsylvania's Institute for Cultural Partnerships recognizes it as one of three regional folk art centers in the state.

See also: APPALACHIAN CENTERS AND INSTITUTES; HISTORICAL SOCIETIES.

—Bonelyn L. Kyofski, *Mansfield University*

Ohio Arts Council

Since 1994, the Ohio Arts Council has worked extensively to celebrate the rich cultural and artistic traditions of Appalachian Ohio, which is home to approximately 1.4 million people and includes twenty-nine of Ohio's eighty-eight counties. The council's mission is to build the state economically, educationally, and culturally through the arts, to preserve the past, to enhance the present, and to enrich the future for all Ohioans. Established in 1965 and governed by a fifteen-member board with four nonvoting legislative members, the council accepts the premise that the arts arise from public, individual, and organizational efforts. With funds from the state legislature and the National Endowment for the Arts, the council provided nearly eight hundred grants in 2002 and offers assistance in research and professional development to arts organizations and artists statewide.

Guided by director and founder Patty Mitchell (right), artists with and without developmental disabilities collaborate at Passion Works Studio, Athens, Ohio, 2003. The Ohio Arts Council's Appalachian Arts Program gives financial support to Passion Works and to other artists and arts organizations of all kinds throughout the state's Appalachian counties.

The council supports two main programs in the Appalachian region. One is the Appalachian Arts program, which serves artists, arts organizations, community leaders, and residents of Ohio's Appalachian counties, as well as urban Appalachians living in Columbus, Cincinnati, and Dayton. The other, the Ohio River Border Initiative, is a partnership between the Ohio Arts Council and the West Virginia Commission on the Arts that gives the two state arts agencies a creative way to dissolve political barriers and support communities on both sides of the Ohio River. In addition, the council has published the *Directory of Appalachian Artists and Craftspeople*.

Through grant funds, the council supports a variety of community mural projects in Ohio, including the murals on the floodwall in Portsmouth. This twenty-two-hundred-foot stretch of murals attracts tourists to the community and instills pride in its history. The council also supports festivals in the region such as the Louis Mountain Old Thyme Herb Fair in Adams County by providing funding for artists to demonstrate their talents. In Morgan County, the non-profit agency Morgan Options uses council funds to provide after-school arts experiences for children living in government-subsidized housing. The Foothills School of American Crafts in Nelsonville is helping to promote the work of local artists and craftspeople by offering tours of artists' studios in the region.

See also: NORTH CAROLINA ARTS COUNCIL; PUBLIC ART PROGRAMS (VISUAL ARTS); SOUTHERN OHIO MUSEUM.

—Jami Goldstein, *Ohio Arts Council*

Outdoor Dramas

See Outdoor Drama (Performing Arts)

Outdoor Museums

The outdoor, or open-air, museum concept, embodied most notably by Colonial Williamsburg in Virginia, has taken root in Appalachia with sites such as the Farmers' Museum in Cooperstown, New York, and Old Salem in Winston-Salem, North Carolina. According to museum historian Edward P. Alexander, the first genuine outdoor museum was Skansen, founded in 1891 by Artur Hazelius in Stockholm, Sweden, when he was offered buildings and other objects too large to display indoors. Hazelius provided a template for future outdoor museums worldwide by moving buildings to museum sites, providing them with garden settings and interior furnishings, and staffing them with costumed craftspeople, musicians, and other interpreters to recreate an authentic environment.

The earliest examples in Appalachia, though not technically museums, were probably the region's various craft schools. Penland School of Crafts (formerly Penland School of Handicrafts) and John C. Campbell Folk School, both located in North Carolina, constructed log buildings—considered appropriate to the mountain theme—on rural campuses and practiced traditional crafts. Penland began attracting students from outside the region in the late 1920s to study weaving, and Campbell initiated craft teaching at about the same time. Such schools have become tourist attractions as much for their buildings as for their craft production, though Penland has since become oriented toward contemporary crafts.

The creation of the Blue Ridge Parkway, starting in 1934, was another important step in the development of Appalachian outdoor museums. The parkway is a 469-mile outdoor nature museum that connects the Shenandoah and

Great Smoky Mountains National Parks. Along the parkway are a number of open-air sites, including the Humpback Rocks farm exhibit, the Johnson Farm at the Peaks of Otter, a string of log cabins at various mileposts, and an assemblage of structures at the Mabry Mill site. Along the parkway near Blowing Rock, North Carolina, is Flat Top Manor, "Denim King" Moses H. Cone's elaborate Colonial Revival retreat, which was donated to the National Park Service following World War II.

As with the history of open-air museums generally in the United States, the post–World War II period saw rapid growth in Appalachia. In the early 1950s, the Cherokee Historical Association developed Oconaluftee Indian Village in Cherokee, North Carolina. Oconaluftee offers re-creations of an eighteenth-century Cherokee council house and homes typical of the 1750s along with costumed Native American interpreters and demonstrators. In 1969 John Rice Irwin began assembling the log buildings, furnishings, and other historical materials that have become the Museum of Appalachia in Norris, Tennessee. These buildings, including a school, an 1840 chapel, a gristmill, a number of barns, and several cabins, range in period from the eighteenth to the early twentieth century. Similar assemblages of log structures, though less extensive in acreage and collections, can be found throughout the region. Among the best are Hickory Ridge Homestead in Boone, North Carolina; the Cades Cove sites near Gatlinburg, Tennessee; the Mountain Farm Museum near Cherokee that, like Cades Cove, is part of the Great Smoky Mountains National Park; and the Mountain HomePlace in Paintsville, Kentucky.

While projects such as the Museum of Appalachia are organized to suggest communities, other museums focus more specifically on agriculture. In 1979 Ferrum College, located in Ferrum, Virginia, opened the Blue Ridge Farm Museum, a part of the Blue Ridge Institute and Museum. The log main house and attendant buildings depict German American farm life in the year 1800. Nearly a decade later, the Frontier Culture Museum (formerly known as the Museum of American Frontier Culture) began operation near Staunton, Virginia. This museum advances the idea that the major ethnic groups settling the southern colonial backcountry—Germans, Scots-Irish, and English—blended to produce a distinct American culture. The museum identified and imported three seventeenth- and eighteenth-century farmhouses from Northern Ireland, Germany, and England and erected them on the museum's 220-acre site along with a farmstead from Botetourt County, Virginia, to illustrate the diverse farming patterns that immigrants brought to colonial America. As is the case with almost all open-air museums in Appalachia, the Blue Ridge Farm Museum and the Frontier Culture Museum offer a rich variety of programs and demonstrations. Both museums make an effort to provide farm animals consistent with the periods being interpreted.

Biltmore House, constructed by George W. Vanderbilt in Asheville, North Carolina, presents grounds of such size and elaboration as to warrant defining this historic house as an outdoor museum. Operated as a commercial enterprise, Biltmore is the nation's largest private home, and the elaborate gardens and landscaped grounds are as important to many visitors as the main house. Near the entrance to the estate is the community of buildings called Biltmore Village, originally constructed to house and serve the needs of the workers brought to Asheville to erect and finish Biltmore House. Today, retail tenants occupy most of the structures within the village. Nonetheless, Biltmore Village is an outdoor architectural museum of the first rank even though it, like Biltmore House itself, is in private hands.

Biltmore House, Oconaluftee Indian Village, and Historic Rugby, the facility in Rugby, Tennessee, that preserves part of the town created by English reformer and author Thomas Hughes, are unique places dedicated to specific subjects. The vast majority of the region's outdoor museums, however, have attempted to interpret Appalachian history more generally as a story involving subsistence agriculture, isolation, self-sufficiency, and log-cabin architecture. While understandable, this perspective has become increasingly unhelpful for a variety of reasons.

Most of the region's influential interpreters have been outsiders, and their interpretations have painted the region as a preindustrial folk society. Much of this attitude derives from the original outdoor museum of Artur Hazelius. In establishing Skansen, Hazelius was attempting to preserve what he believed the Industrial Revolution was destroying: a distinctive and pastoral way of life. For this reason, the outdoor museum as a type has always been part history and part nostalgic romance.

At about the same time that Hazelius was creating Skansen, America was experiencing the Colonial Revival movement, also a reaction to the perceived evils of the Industrial Revolution. The waves of immigrants that accompanied that revolution were thought by some to threaten the American way of life, and Colonial Revivalists viewed Appalachia as a region where the pure Anglo-Saxon character of America's first immigrants had survived more or less intact and could be studied. Revivalists believed Appalachia to have endured a useful isolation that enabled the inhabitants to continue into the modern era as a peasant society. A nineteenth-century president of Berea College in Kentucky, William Goodell Frost, echoed this sentiment by describing mountain people as "our contemporary ancestors."

As the region's craft schools began teaching skills such as weaving to outsiders, they reinforced the idea that these crafts were generally ongoing activities in the mountains that had never been interrupted. This is as misleading as would be a claim that musket making had never died out within the city limits of Colonial Williamsburg. These early interpretations of Appalachia as a folk culture were intended to fit the needs and goals of those seeking to use Appalachia for their own purposes. A number of the region's open-air museums have based their programs on these earlier Colonial Revivalist visions of Appalachia as an antique society.

The romantic focus of open-air museums on craft production and subsistence agriculture has elevated the log cabin to a primacy as the region's enduring and pervasive symbol of Appalachian architecture. Focusing on a narrow slice of Appalachian life, many of the region's outdoor museums do not represent general architectural change in the region very effectively. A large number of outdoor museums, especially farm museums, are accumulations of log buildings. These necessarily reflect that part of Appalachia that did not change very much until the 1930s or so. By their omission of the history that did involve change, however, and by their suggestion that Appalachia has a homogeneous history, these museums reinforce in the minds of their visitors the idea of the region as a peasant society. Interestingly, examples of Victorian house styles, found in areas near most of these museums, reveal the region as a market for prefabricated window sashes, mantles and moldings, stick framing, and weatherboarding.

Appalachia's outdoor museums increasingly are attempting to correct these misconceptions. Nowhere is this more evident than in the interpretation programs of the various sites along the Blue Ridge Parkway, which has historically been the organization in Appalachia most aggressively offering the romantic folkloric view of the region. Few people driving down the parkway realize that the frame dwelling of Mabry Mill owner Ed Mabry has been replaced with a log cabin in order to meet visitors' romantic notions of the living conditions of mountain people. Now, however, the parkway is attempting to balance historic accuracy with its previous romantic visions of isolation, and visitors can learn about the relationships the original inhabitants had with the outside world—that turnpikes ran nearby and that the whistles of railroad trains could be heard. They are shown items that might have been purchased from a store or sent away for by mail order rather than only rustic handmade items.

Appalachia's outdoor museums must incorporate contemporary research into their public programs and either expand their interpretational reach or market the material they present to a particular group if they wish to compete in an increasingly competitive cultural marketplace. Outdoor museums provide some of the most vivid and effective formats for communicating regional history, but those that cannot change are likely to face increasing marginalization as the story they tell becomes a smaller and smaller aspect of the region's past.

See also: CULTURAL HERITAGE TOURISM (TOURISM).

—Charles Alan Watkins, *Appalachian State University*

Pennsylvania Lumber Museum

When Europeans began settling Pennsylvania in the seventeenth century, 90 percent of the land was forested, mostly by white pine and eastern hemlock. As lumber demands increased over the next century, lumbering became a well-established industry in Appalachian Pennsylvania, resulting in the state's becoming the nation's top lumber producer by 1850. The rise of large-scale timber industry in the second half of the century spawned lumber camps, towns, and sawmills, most temporary, throughout north-central Pennsylvania. By 1920 all the timber had been cut. The lumbermen moved on, and a way of life disappeared.

The Pennsylvania Lumber Museum, located in the heart of the regenerated Susquehannock State Forest, is dedicated to preserving the heritage of this bygone era. More than three thousand artifacts are on display, from everyday implements and logging tools to a seventy-ton steam locomotive. The recreated lumber camp on the museum grounds features a sawmill and loading shed, as well as typical camp buildings such as a blacksmith shop, horse barn, bunkhouse, and mess hall.

General admission includes a film on the heyday of logging and a walking tour through the camp. The museum, which publishes a quarterly newsletter, offers group tours, educational workshops, and classes. Each July the museum hosts the annual Bark Peelers' Convention, a two-day celebration modeled on the Fourth of July gatherings of lumbermen a century ago. Though closed during the winter except by special arrangement, the museum is open daily the rest of the year.

See also: LOGGING TERMINOLOGY (LANGUAGE); LUMBER INDUSTRY (BUSINESS, INDUSTRY, AND TECHNOLOGY); LUMBER SETTLEMENTS (SETTLEMENT AND MIGRATION).

—Troy Gowen, *East Tennessee State University*

Public Gardens

Gardens open to visitors throughout Appalachia generally fall into three categories: formal gardens that are part of historic sites and/or homes; gardens developed for knowledge and appreciation of plants and the environment; and those established to preserve native plants of a particular area.

Perhaps the most visited gardens are those on Biltmore Estate in Asheville, North Carolina, designed by Frederick Law Olmsted in the 1890s. Richmond Hill, also in Asheville, features period-style gardens surrounding a Victorian mansion. The Pittsburgh Civic Garden Center is on the Andrew Mellon estate. Although the mansion no longer exists, the original carriage house and stable enhance the attractive grounds that include rock, herb, and ground-cover gardens. In Ashland, Kentucky, the public can visit remnants from six hundred acres of formal gardens and orchards on an estate where Henry Clay lived during the 1800s.

Many of the botanical gardens are associated with universities and offer educational programs along with large varieties of plants from around the world. Others, not based at universities, include the Birmingham, Alabama, Botanical Gardens, which cover sixty-seven acres and include a Japanese garden; the Huntsville–Madison County, Alabama, Botanical Garden, with more than sixty educational workshops and programs for visitors; and the Phipps Conservatory and Botanical Gardens in Schenley Park, Pittsburgh, featuring a Victorian glasshouse and exhibition galleries with collections from all over the world.

Natural settings for native plants are the focus of the gardens of Roan Mountain, Tennessee, which have a large natural rhododendron display and an extensive collection of native plants. Other native plants are featured as part of the Oconaluftee Village Botanical Gardens and Nature Trail in Cherokee, North Carolina, and the Medicine Trail at the Junaluska Museum in Robbinsville, North Carolina. Wildflowers, rhododendron, and azaleas are featured at Craggy Gardens on the Blue Ridge Parkway north of Asheville, as is a bog garden at the Daniel Boone Native Gardens in Boone, North Carolina, in addition to collections of native trees, shrubs, wildflowers, and ferns. Four hundred species of native plants thrive at Rock City Gardens in Lookout Mountain, Georgia. At Callaway Gardens and Resort in the Appalachian foothills in Pine Mountain, Georgia, visitors can enjoy sixteen native species of azaleas, a seven-acre field of more than four hundred varieties of fruits, vegetables and herbs, and a butterfly center with more than one thousand butterflies from fifty species.

Visitors will find terraced gardens with more than one hundred ornate fountains at Prabhupada's Palace of Gold in Moundsville, West Virginia. In Cullman, Alabama, the Ave Maria Grotto at Saint Bernard Abbey contains 125 miniature replicas of sacred sites found around the world sculptured from cement, stone, and shells. At Greek-themed Jasmine Hill Gardens in Montgomery, Alabama, visitors can see replicas of nearly forty noteworthy artworks, lily pools, and colorful plantings of azaleas, camellias, jasmine, and cherry trees.

See also: OUTDOOR MUSEUMS; SECTION OVERVIEW (TOURISM).

—Clara Hasbrouck, *East Tennessee State University*

Mary Zuazua Jenkins, *National Geographic Guide to America's Public Gardens* (1998); Lois G. Rosenfeld, *The Garden Tourist, Northeast* (2001) and *The Garden Tourist, Southeast* (2001).

Public Libraries

Public libraries are an integral part of contemporary Appalachia, playing a significant role in the cultural, social, and educational life of the region's communities. Offering traditional library services such as recreational reading materials and children's story times as well as providing Internet access, Appalachian libraries meet the information needs of those in even the most remote areas.

Illiteracy rates historically have been high in this region. Margaret Morley noted in her 1913 book *The Carolina Mountains* the disturbingly high number of illiterate mountain people. At the time, it was estimated that only one-third of school-age children attended school in the southern Appalachian region. Early library advocates in Appalachia perceived public libraries as a means to address this problem, and the library's connection with literacy efforts continues. Appalachian libraries commonly have significant literacy collections, as well as providing space for tutors and their students, and it is not unusual for a community's literacy activities to be coordinated by the local public library.

Individuals and institutions have long recognized the importance of reading and have sought to incorporate the library into Appalachian life. A few citizen-organized circulating libraries existed in late-eighteenth-century Appalachia. In the nineteenth and early twentieth centuries, local schools and private church-affiliated institutions provided reading opportunities in the mountain areas. Social groups such as the Women's Christian Temperance Union established book-lending services in rural areas. Private educational institutions such as Berea College and Hindman Settlement School in Kentucky and the Berry School in Georgia offered library services to those nearby. As people throughout Appalachia began to realize the importance of reading, increasing numbers of citizens' groups organized to create circulating libraries. These citizens' library movements were found in several Appalachian states.

Schools, missions, and community centers promoted the citizens' movements, which in some cases had a positive impact on their state governments. In North Carolina, for example, a citizens' group that formed in 1927 convinced state legislators to appropriate funds for new libraries several years later. State library associations began organizing after the American Library Association's creation in 1876 and continued the work begun by the citizens' groups. The philanthropy of Andrew Carnegie also contributed to growth in library services throughout the Appalachian region in the first part of the twentieth century, with most new Carnegie library construction occurring in the northern Appalachian regions of Pennsylvania, Ohio, and New York. In spite of these encouraging developments, only 23 percent of the people in southern Appalachia in 1930 had library services of any kind.

Not surprisingly, the Great Depression slowed library growth, but it also had some unexpected positive effects. Many unemployed people with time on their hands availed themselves of library offerings. Library materials and programs grew in popularity, and library use increased. Another benefit of the depression was the creation of the Works Progress Administration (WPA), which provided funds for materials, staff, buildings, and expansion of services to new locations, as well as a bookmobile services. In the southern Appalachian area of North Carolina, the WPA service began in 1938 with one bookmobile. When this service ended in 1942, eighty-five of the one hundred counties in North Carolina had taken advantage of the program, and more than thirty counties operated their own bookmobiles.

Federal support continued to be an important source of funds for Appalachian libraries as the nation recovered from the depression. In 1933 Congress created the Tennessee Valley Authority (TVA), primarily to provide flood control and electricity to the Tennessee River basin. However, this massive project also included monies for library service to this largely poor, rural area, and the regional library networks—such as the Nantahala Regional Library in western North Carolina—created during this period still are functioning. The WPA provided a bookmobile and twenty-two hundred books for the new regional library, which was funded mainly by TVA. The Federal Library Services Act passed by Congress in 1956 created a system in which federal funds, administered through state libraries, provided materials, personnel, and equipment to rural America. The scope of the act was broadened in 1964 to include non-rural areas and construction projects and its name was changed to the Library Services and Construction Act. This act continues to be a major source of funds for Appalachian libraries.

State-of-the-art computer equipment, on-line databases, and automated circulation systems are common in Appalachian libraries. The demographics of Appalachia have changed over the past century, and the region's libraries now serve a much more ethnically diverse population. The library's role as provider of Internet and other technological services has grown, aided greatly by the donation by the Bill and Melinda Gates Foundation of thousands of computers to public libraries in low-income areas. Library staff have added instruction in the use of these new and powerful resources to their traditional duties. In spite of these changes, Appalachian libraries still reflect the distinct culture of their mountain regions and often assume responsibility for the preservation of their community's history, traditions, and handicrafts.

See also: BOOKMOBILES; CARNEGIE, ANDREW (BUSINESS, INDUSTRY, AND TECHNOLOGY); TENNESSEE VALLEY AUTHORITY (GOVERNMENT).

—Mary M. Sizemore, *Appalachian Regional Library*

George S. Bobinski, *Carnegie Libraries: Their History and Impact on American Public Library Development* (1969); William Eury, *The Citizen's Movement in North Carolina* (1951); Mayrelee Newman, *Library/Media Services in Appalachia: An Overview* (1972).

Railroad Museums

Few modern innovations have equaled the impact of easily accessible transportation on the Appalachian region. Railroads hauled out natural resources and brought in workers for the mines, mills, and logging companies. Many of the workers who laid the rails were eastern and southern European immigrants and blacks seeking employment in post–Civil War America. A number of organizations and institutions are dedicated to preserving and displaying the relics of this increasingly vanishing mode of transportation throughout Appalachia.

In 1997 the Leatherstocking Railway Historical Society and the Leatherstocking Chapter of the National Railway Historic Society purchased the Cooperstown and Charlotte Valley Railway, which first began service in 1869. Leatherstocking began service in 1999 with the goal of providing visitors an opportunity to experience railway travel through a sixteen-mile round trip in southwestern New York between Cooperstown Passenger Station and the Milford Depot and Museum on diesel-powered trains. The Engine House, Milford Park Railway, and Oaksville Depot are located near the museum. Scheduled to open in 2008, a museum in Cooperstown Junction planned to house railroad archives, artifacts, and an outdoor display of antique engines and railroad cars.

Scranton, Pennsylvania, has two transportation museums. Steamtown National Historic Site, part of the National Park Service, was created in 1986 to preserve and interpret the role of steam railroading in the history of the United States. The visitor center provides park orientation. Exhibits in the History Museum focus on the people who worked on the railroad and the economics of railroading. In the c. 1937 roundhouse, visitors can watch demonstrations of routine maintenance, inspection, and light repairs on locomotives. The Technology Museum features exhibits on the mechanical side of railroading, from laying track to signaling and safety devices. Educational programs include living history and other interpretive programs, outreach programs, brief interpretive train rides, and excursions on steam-powered passenger trains.

Created by the Lackawanna Heritage Valley Authority, the Electric City Trolley Museum is also located on the Steamtown National Historic Site. Known as the Electric City, Scranton was the first city in the United States to have a streetcar system operated entirely by electricity. The museum houses a display of vintage trolleys, features interactive exhibits for adults and children, and offers excursions.

Allegheny Portage Railroad National Historic Site, on 1,249 acres in Gallitzin, Pennsylvania, preserves a portion of the first railroad constructed over the Allegheny Mountains. This rail line stretched nearly four hundred miles from Philadelphia to Pittsburgh, linking sections of canal by rail, and used stationary steam engines to tow cars up and down mountain slopes. Operating between 1834 and 1854, the railroad played an important role in opening the Midwest to trade and settlement. Engine House #6 Exhibit Shelter houses the remains of the original building at the head of Inclined Plane 6, a full-scale model of a stationary steam engine, and interactive exhibits on railroad technology. The site also contains a nineteenth-century house, originally operated as a tavern and rest stop for travelers by its builder, Samuel Lemon, which has been restored to its 1840s appearance. The Summit Level Visitor Center contains additional artifacts, exhibits, and models related to the history of the railroad.

Altoona Railroaders Memorial Museum in Pennsylvania focuses on the life of railroad workers and the communities in which they lived. The Pennsylvania Railroad built Altoona in 1849 as a maintenance facility for its locomotives. Within a few years an army of workers at the Altoona Works was building and repairing railroad cars and locomotives. The purpose of the museum is to honor the significant contribution of these workers and preserve the cultural heritage of Altoona for the education, enjoyment, and enrichment of present and future generations.

Cass Scenic Railroad, located in Pocahontas County, West Virginia, is a museum of lumber railroading. In the early years of the twentieth century, when logging was a major industry in West Virginia, Shay locomotives, engineered for flexibility on rough mountain rails, climbed steep grades to haul heavy loads of timber to the mill in Cass. West Virginia Pulp and Paper owned the rail system from 1901 until the Western Maryland merged with the company in 1927 and renovated the lines to haul coal. The Mower Lumber Company acquired the Cass operation in 1942, using it in the company's second-growth timber cutting operation on Cheat Mountain and Back Allegheny Mountain. In early 1961 Cass Scenic Railroad became a part of the West Virginia State Park System and received twenty-three thousand visitors that first year. The museum in Cass contains artifacts of logging and lumber railroading. At the depot visitors board old logging cars refurbished and made into passenger cars. Carefully restored Shay locomotives pull the passenger cars up the steep grade to Whittaker Station, where the Mountain State Railroad and Logging Association has recreated a 1940s logging camp. A longer trip takes visitors to Bald Knob, the second-highest point in West Virginia.

Etowah, Tennessee, is the home of the Louisville and Nashville Depot and Railroad Museum. The Victorian depot, listed on the National Register of Historic Places, houses railroading artifacts and memorabilia from life in a railroad town. In 2002 the Tennessee Overhill Heritage Association, which is housed in the depot, became the owner of the CSX, a forty-three-mile rail line. Commonly known as the old-line railroad, the CSX was built in 1890 and runs through the Hiwassee River Gorge between Etowah and Copperhill in southeastern Tennessee. One of its best-known features is the Bald Mountain Loop, an 8,000-foot section of the track that rises 426 feet as it curves around the dome-shaped top of Bald Mountain. Scenic excursions have become part of a new plan for this rail line that only a few years earlier transported sulfuric acid.

The Tennessee Valley Railroad Museum was formed in 1961 when a group of railroad enthusiasts became concerned about the disappearance of steam locomotives and passenger trains in the United States. Members sought donations of equipment and a permanent site for its collection. Nearly twenty years of work went into the reconstruction of the railroad right-of-way, the turntable and shop, and the c. 1910 depot at East Chattanooga, Tennessee. The 1890s Grand Junction Depot at Cromwell Road was opened in August of 1984. Visitors to the museum can experience travel on a steam or diesel passenger train, visit the backshop where work is done on equipment, or view artifacts and tour train cars and locomotives.

Chase, Alabama, is the home of the North Alabama Railroad Museum. The waiting room, freight room, and agent's office of the restored Chase Depot are used to exhibit railroad photographs and artifacts. The Chase Depot is one of the smallest existing union depots (depots serving more than one railroad) in the country. One line ran between Memphis and Chattanooga. The other railroad ran between Dechard, Tennessee, and Gadsden, Alabama, although passengers had to take a ferry across the Tennessee River in order to complete their journey to Gadsden by rail. In Gadsden, passengers could transfer to a mainline railroad for other destinations. Historic freight cars, passenger cars, and locomotives are displayed on the museum grounds. Train excursions are scheduled several times a year on the museum's own Mercury and Chase Railroad, which uses a vintage diesel locomotive to pull a sixty-seat air-conditioned passenger car, a baggage car converted into an observation car, and a dining car that once was an army hospital car. The museum also offers educational programming through its school excursion program.

See also: CULTURAL HERITAGE TOURISM (TOURISM); MINING MUSEUMS; SECTION OVERVIEW (TRANSPORTATION).

—Mary Grace Meador, *East Tennessee State University*

Rivers of Steel Archives

Located in southwestern Pennsylvania, Rivers of Steel National and State Heritage Area was developed with a mandate from the U.S. Congress and the Commonwealth of Pennsylvania. Renowned for more than a century as the "Steel Capital of the World," the area includes Pittsburgh and seven counties: Allegheny, Armstrong, Beaver, Fayette, Greene, Washington, and Westmoreland. The Steel Industry Heritage Corporation, a regional nonprofit organization, coordinates Rivers of Steel. It works with communities throughout the region to identify, conserve, promote, and interpret the cultural, historical, natural, recreational, and economic resources associated with steel and steel-related industries.

The collections of the Rivers of Steel Archives are rich. They include ethnographic surveys that document the industrial communities in the heritage area, slides and photographs taken at town meetings and other events, videotapes, oral history interviews with area residents, blueprints and plans of industrial sites, company records, and personal papers. One set of photographs documents Soviet Premier Nikita Khrushchev's 1959 tour of the Mesta Machine Company plant in West Homestead. Another collection features the fifty-year history of the Homestead Steel Works Male Chorus, which gave its first public performance in 1935 at the Homestead Carnegie Library for the one-hundredth anniversary of the birth of Andrew Carnegie. Many artifacts, including tools, clothing, equipment, buttons, and identification badges, are also part of the archives.

See also: APPALACHIAN SPECIAL COLLECTIONS; CULTURAL HERITAGE TOURISM (TOURISM); IRON AND STEEL INDUSTRY (BUSINESS, INDUSTRY, AND TECHNOLOGY).

—Ronald A. Baraff, *Steel Industry Heritage Corporation*

Roberson Museum and Science Center

Roberson Museum and Science Center, located in Binghamton, New York, is a regional museum of art, folklife, and history and a center for science education serving the upper Susquehanna Valley region of New York and Pennsylvania. Roberson's mission is to preserve and communicate aspects of the region's cultural heritage and diversity, to present issues on topics such as the environment, economics, and the arts from an interdisciplinary perspective, and to use its collections, historic buildings, planetarium, and other resources for programs that are accessible and relevant to its diverse audiences.

Roberson Museum initiated its folklife program in 1982 to identify, document, and present the varied folk traditions of New York's southern tier. The program focuses on community and family-based traditions that develop a common ethic through several generations. Though its primary focus is on living traditions, the program also emphasizes historical antecedents.

The folklife curator has carried out extensive fieldwork and research in African American gospel singing, eastern European embroideries, and Catskill storytelling. This research formed the basis for exhibitions, programs, and publications such as *Three Catskill Storytellers* and *Harvesting Heritage*. Additional projects have focused on memory paintings, puppets, and Hmong needlework. *Catskill Memories: The Artistry of John McLean* explored Catskill life in the early 1900s through thirteen watercolor drawings by a dairy farmer in Andes, New York. McLean's memory drawings documented logging, maple sugaring, gardening, and other traditional work activities in the region. The *Puppetworks* exhibition and program series explored the artistry of a local resident, German-born puppet maker and marionettist Bernd Ogrodnik, placing his work in the larger context of traditional puppetry throughout the world.

During the 1990s Roberson received several important folk art collections: baskets made by local Polish, Estonian, and Ukrainian immigrants; carved canes and paintings by a Lithuanian immigrant; memory paintings of life in the Catskills in the early twentieth century; embroideries representing several regions of eastern Europe; iconography by a Russian refugee; blacksmithing tools; and an extensive quilt collection. These collections are usually accompanied by photographic, sound-recorded tape, and videotape documentation. Through exhibitions, programs, an archive, publications, and collections, the museum encourages the public to preserve the region's heritage.

See also: BINGHAMTON, NEW YORK (URBAN APPALACHIAN EXPERIENCE); CATSKILL CENTER FOR CONSERVATION AND DEVELOPMENT; NEW YORK SOUTHERN TIER PUBLIC FOLKLORE (FOLKLORE AND FOLKLIFE).

—Catherine Schwoeffermann, *Roberson Museum and Science Center*

Science and Technology Centers

The Appalachian region is home to an increasing number of science, technology, and discovery centers. The growth of these institutions in the region reflects an international trend.

In the museum world, science and technology centers are relatively new institutions, and their format reveals a major shift in museum ideology that puts visitors rather than objects or collections at the forefront of the experience. Their predecessors, the collections-based natural history museums and technology museums of the early 1900s, limited their missions to collection, conservation, and research on objects in their possession. Contemporary science centers have broader educational missions that emphasize interactive, hands-on learning. These centers focus on visitors' experiences with artifacts, specimens, and exhibits. Visitors are encouraged to touch, explore, question, and investigate scientific or natural phenomena in the exhibits. In most science centers, guides or docents help visitors interpret the exhibits.

Science and technology centers employ a variety of educational techniques. Traditional public lectures, museum classes, and school programs form the base of most programs. Centers often house a planetarium and offer multimedia astronomy programs under a dome. In the planetarium, starfields are either projected with the traditional optical starball or are computer generated. Larger science centers, including the Carnegie Science Center in Pittsburgh and the McWane Center in Birmingham, Alabama, have incorporated large-format films such as IMAX movies into their programs. The large-screen projection system and the seventy-millimeter film format provide a multisensory viewing experience. These movies take visitors inside the human body, into outer space, under the sea to swim with the dolphins, and into the depths of the Egyptian pyramids.

Innovative and nontraditional programs such as overnight camp-ins are popular in centers throughout the country. These informal learning experiences have opened the exhibit halls to thousands of students and their families. Girl Scouts and Cub Scouts are among the many community groups that have spent the night in science centers. Science centers also involve teens in a variety of roles. Working as teaching assistants, program presenters, and administrative assistants, teens contribute thousands of volunteer hours. Some science centers include theatrical performances in which actors present scientific facts, historical vignettes, and related issues. For example, SciWorks in Winston-Salem, North Carolina, stages a dramatization of the life of Madame C. J. Walker, an early-twentieth-century African American entrepreneur and developer of hair-care products. The presentation emphasizes Walker's creativity and her desire to succeed despite many challenges.

Science centers in Appalachia vary in size and generally reflect their individual communities in design, exhibits, and appearance. In the northern Appalachian region, the Carnegie Science Center in Pittsburgh houses a planetarium and an IMAX theater and offers a variety of exhibits and programs. Nearby is the Pittsburgh Children's Museum. In Charleston, West Virginia, an expansion of Sunrise Museum provided a focal point in a downtown redevelopment effort. Also in West Virginia are the Science Center of West Virginia, located in Bluefield, the Children's Discovery Center in Parkersburg, and the Youth Museum of Southern West Virginia in Beckley.

In North Carolina, the Health Adventure in Asheville emphasizes health science. SciWorks, in Winston-Salem, is a multidisciplinary institution that houses a planetarium and also offers exhibits in physics, health, and natural science. The Highlands Nature Center is a small center near the Georgia border that interprets the flora and fauna of the Blue Ridge Mountains. A larger facility in Asheville, the Western North Carolina Nature Center, covers more broadly the natural and environmental sciences. The Appalachian region of Tennessee is home to several centers: the Hands On! Regional Museum in Johnson City, the Creative Discovery Museum in Chattanooga, the East Tennessee Discovery Center in Knoxville, and the Children's Museum of Oak Ridge. The northwestern regions of South Carolina are served by the Imagine Nation Children's Museum and the Roper Mountain Science Center in Greenville. The McWane Center in Birmingham is part of a downtown redevelopment project.

According to the Association of Science Technology Centers, science centers in the United States had hosted more than 127 million visitors by 2001. These centers and museums benefit their communities in several ways. They support the formal educational system through exhibits, school programs, and teacher workshops, and they provide informal science education and recreation for families. As focal points for community service, science centers are becoming part of the cultural fabric of local areas, and as tourist destinations they are having an impact on the economic and cultural development of communities.

See also: MARSHALL SPACE FLIGHT CENTER (BUSINESS, INDUSTRY, AND TECHNOLOGY); ROBERSON MUSEUM AND SCIENCE CENTER; U.S. SPACE AND ROCKET CENTER.

—Beverly Sanford, *Winston-Salem, North Carolina*

Walter Witschey, "Many Roles to Play: The Science Center as Community Powerhouse," *ASTC Dimensions* (January–February 2001).

Senator John Heinz Pittsburgh Regional History Center

The Senator John Heinz Pittsburgh Regional History Center is a museum and research facility devoted to interpreting the history of western Pennsylvania. Owned and operated by the Historical Society of Western Pennsylvania, established in 1879, the center, which exhibits the society's collections, opened in 1996 in a newly renovated 160,000-square-foot building, the former headquarters of the Chautauqua Lake Ice Company.

The museum's permanent exhibit focuses on domestic life and industries in the region since the mid-eighteenth century. *Points in Time: Building a Life in Western Pennsylvania, 1750–Today* uses furniture, costumes, and other artifacts and interactive videos to interpret the domestic lives of past generations in the region. A history of the H. J. Heinz Corporation is featured in *Heinz 57*, an interactive exhibit in which visitors can pack pickles and create advertisements.

Another continuing exhibit, *Glass: Shattering Notions*, interprets Pittsburgh's reign as America's Glass City and features antique glassware, industrial and scientific glass, and interactive displays that trace the history of the region's glass industry since 1797.

Archival collections at the center hold more than five hundred thousand photographs related to western Pennsylvania, including photographs of Pittsburgh from the late 1800s. Family records and documents from industries in the region make up another substantial part of the archive. The library and archives are open to the public.

See also: GLASS MUSEUMS; HISTORICAL SOCIETIES; PITTSBURGH, PENNSYLVANIA (URBAN APPALACHIAN EXPERIENCE).

—Megan Tressler, *Senator John Heinz Pittsburgh Regional History Center*

Seneca-Iroquois National Museum

Located on the Allegany Reservation of the Seneca Nation of Indians, the Seneca-Iroquois National Museum is about sixty miles south of Buffalo, New York. Nestled in the Allegany Mountains and adjacent to the Allegheny River, the museum is dedicated to the honorable presentation and preservation of the prehistory, history, and contemporary culture of the Seneca (Onondaga) and other member nations of the Iroquois (Haudenosaunee) Confederacy, the indigenous peoples of New York State and much of the northeastern United States.

The museum represents groups that include the Allegany and two other reservations of the Seneca Nation of Indians in the Appalachian region of southwestern New York State: the Cattaraugus Reservation in Cattaraugus County and the Tonawanda Band of Senecas, whose reservation is near Akron. Differences in government distinguish the Seneca Nation from the Tonawanda Band. The Seneca Nation has an elective form of government founded in 1848, while the Tonawanda Band of Senecas has retained the old chieftain system. The two groups together have a tribal enrollment of about eight thousand. Enrollment is an official census based on matrilineal descent. Both groups of Senecas are federally recognized tribes. Four of the five other Iroquois Nations represented (Mohawk, Onondaga, Oneida, and Tuscarora) have reservations throughout New York State; the fifth, the Cayuga, were still fighting to regain their lost lands in the early years of the twenty-first century.

The Seneca-Iroquois National Museum opened to the public in 1977 with a 6,400-square-foot building that includes six gallery spaces and a central seating area for videos and lectures. The museum contains many old or prehistoric items and also supports and showcases contemporary Iroquois artists. Exhibits include a partially rebuilt prehistoric Iroquois-style longhouse, a clan animal display, a reconstructed log cabin, and displays of traditional and contemporary Iroquois and Seneca arts, both functional and aesthetic. Items of a sacred nature are prohibited from public display, as ancient traditional ceremonies are still practiced and the items are for ceremonial usage only. The Kinzua Room is devoted to the forced relocation of the Alle-

A demonstrator at the Seneca-Iroquois National Museum makes cornhusk dolls as part of the museum's Living Artist Series, Salamanca, New York, 1981. Dedicated to the preservation of Seneca and Iroquois culture, the museum features demonstrations and lectures, prehistoric and historic artifacts, and traditional and contemporary art.

gany Senecas in the mid-1960s by the completion of the Kinzua Dam. Built to stop annual flooding in Pittsburgh, where the Ohio, Monongahela, and Allegheny Rivers meet, the dam resulted in the inundation of some 10,469 acres of fertile bottomland and in the displacement of almost all Allegany Reservation Senecas. A hands-on children's exhibit area is the museum's newest addition. Special exhibits are scheduled intermittently, and demonstrations and lectures by native artists occur throughout July and August. The museum is entirely staffed by Seneca community members. Funding is very limited for special exhibits and functions and comes primarily from the Seneca Nation, small grants, public donations, and admission fees.

See also: CHOCTAW MUSEUM OF THE SOUTHERN INDIAN; MUSEUM OF THE CHEROKEE INDIAN; SENECA (RACE, ETHNICITY, AND IDENTITY).

—Midge Dean Stock, *Seneca-Iroquois National Museum*

Sequoyah Birthplace Museum

The Sequoyah Birthplace Museum is a tribute to Sequoyah, inventor of the Cherokee syllabary. Located on the shores of Tellico Lake in Vonore, Tennessee, and owned by the Eastern Band of Cherokee Indians, it is the only tribally owned enterprise in the state.

According to tradition, Sequoyah's father, a white trader, abandoned the family when Sequoyah, born about 1776, was an infant, leaving the child to be reared by his Cherokee mother. Sequoyah began work on a Cherokee writing system after he saw how effectively white men used the written word. He first tried to create symbols for entire sentences and then for words but finally settled on developing a symbol for each sound in the Cherokee language. He worked twelve years to complete the syllabary, a system of eighty-five symbols that represent six vowels, one consonant, and seventy-eight consonant-vowel combinations. No other person in recorded history has been solely responsible for developing a complete writing system. Soon after the syllabary was introduced in 1821, almost the entire Cherokee Nation became literate. Most modern Cherokees speak and write in English, but the Cherokee language and syllabary are still in use.

The museum, located near Sequoyah's birthplace, was built following a controversy surrounding the construction of the Tellico Dam and Reservoir. During the 1960s and 1970s, environmentalists protested the completion of Tellico Dam as they drew national attention to their fight to protect the endangered snail darter, a three-inch fish thought at that time to live only in the Little Tennessee River. The Eastern Band protested the flooding of former Overhill Cherokee towns and sacred burial grounds. In an effort to resolve the controversy, the Tennessee Valley Authority donated the land and funds for the Eastern Band to establish a museum, which opened in 1986. Some information and artifacts from archaeological digs conducted prior to closing Tellico Dam's floodgates in 1979 became part of the museum's exhibits.

Approximately one hundred yards west of the museum is the Cherokee Memorial, the final resting place for eighteenth-century Cherokee people whose remains were recovered during excavation for the dam. During the eighteenth century, Cherokee towns of the Tennessee Valley had been centers of tribal political and cultural activity. Two towns where excavations were conducted—Chota, the Cherokee capital, and Tanasi (from which *Tennessee* is derived)—were located within twelve miles of the current museum.

The museum provides ongoing educational programming and sponsors an annual fall festival that features Native American art, crafts, and entertainment. The museum's long-range goals include expanding exhibits on Sequoyah, the Overhill Cherokee, and the Trail of Tears.

See also: CHEROKEE (LANGUAGE); CHEROKEE (RACE, ETHNICITY, AND IDENTITY); TRAIL OF TEARS (SETTLEMENT AND MIGRATION).

—Mia Anderson Rhodarmer, *Vonore, Tennessee*

Southern Highland Craft Guild Collection

The Southern Highland Craft Guild's permanent collection, library, and archives are housed at the Blue Ridge Parkway's Folk Art Center in Asheville, North Carolina. By preserving objects and historical documents and educating the public and craftspeople who use its archives and library, the collection helps the guild, chartered in 1930, carry out its mission of conserving and promoting southern mountain crafts.

The collection began with a donation in 1938 of early Appalachian crafts and implements from Frances Goodrich, a founding member of the guild. It now includes more than twenty-four hundred artworks and artifacts that date from the late nineteenth century to the present and contains extensive holdings in textiles, wood carvings, pottery, furniture, and baskets. With very few exceptions, objects in the collection are the work of current or past guild members or craftspeople working in southern and central Appalachia. A small number of objects are from important American craftspeople from outside the region.

The guild archive, which has significant holdings from the 1890s to the present, includes photographs, personal papers of early guild members, and organizational papers for all guild activities. In 2000 the guild hired an archivist to assist with this important group of materials on the Appalachian craft revival movement.

The guild's Robert W. Gray Library Collection serves the general public, researchers, and guild members. Its most extensive holdings focus on fiber arts, but all craft media are represented. The collection includes a rare book section, an extensive holding of exhibition catalogs, regional craft newsletters, and numerous craft periodicals.

See also: APPALACHIAN SPECIAL COLLECTIONS; GOODRICH, FRANCES (CRAFTS); SOUTHERN HIGHLAND CRAFT GUILD (CRAFTS).

—Andrew Glasgow, *The Furniture Society*

Southern Ohio Museum

The Southern Ohio Museum, located in downtown Portsmouth, is southern Ohio's premier visual arts institution. It is housed in a stately neoclassical building that was, until 1977, the largest bank in the community. Renovations in the late 1970s and again in the late 1990s created more than five thousand square feet of gallery space. The museum also contains a reading room and library, a one-hundred-seat theater, a large classroom, and a gift shop.

Programming at the museum features a dozen temporary exhibitions each year; these range from regional folk art and local history to contemporary craft and nationally recognized artists. Exhibits have included quilts by Nancy Crow, watercolors by Charles Burchfield, collages by Romare Bearden, paintings by Emma Amos, and photographs by William Wegman. A wide array of satellite programming—gallery tours, lectures, workshops, classes, theater, and musical events—orbits around the exhibitions.

The museum's collections emphasize the artistic and historic heritage of the community. The centerpiece of the permanent display is a collection of forty-five paintings by native son Clarence Holbrook Carter, a nationally known regionalist artist whose work focuses on twentieth-century Appalachian life. The Carl Ackerman Collection of Historic Photographs spans 150 years of local history. These photographs are available on disk for public research at the museum's library computer station. Thematic groups of photographs dealing with topics such as Portsmouth's Ohio River floods, river transportation, and historic architecture are frequently exhibited. Another permanent collection will deal with the Native Americans who inhabited prehistoric southeastern Ohio and created earthworks such as Serpent Mound, seventy miles east of Portsmouth.

See also: ART MUSEUMS; OHIO ARTS COUNCIL.

—Sara R. Johnson, *Southern Ohio Museum*

Space Camp and Museum

See U.S. Space and Rocket Center

Special Collections, Western Carolina University

The Special Collections unit of Western Carolina University's Hunter Library houses a regional collection of personal manuscripts, business and organizational records, photographs, books and other printed materials, and maps. Although the school endeavored to organize a regional museum and historical collection as early as the 1920s, not until 1970 did the library, with university support, establish Special Collections.

Holdings emphasize the cultural and natural history of southern Appalachia, Cherokee Indian history, and literary works of regional authors. Most collections pertain to western North Carolina, north Georgia, and east Tennessee and document the range of human activity, including agriculture, industry, tourism, cultural pursuits, literature, politics, and economic development. Inclusive dates for the overall manuscript holdings are primarily 1800 to the present, except for the Cherokee Documents materials that cover the period from 1680 to 1800. Special Collections also serves as the archives of Western Carolina University.

Collections of importance to Appalachian history include the papers of Horace Kephart (1862–1931), an author, woodsman, and observer of Appalachia's cultural and environmental heritage who left extensive journals and writings. The Cherokee Documents in Foreign Archives collection consists of eight hundred reels of microfilm containing records and other primary documents from Great Britain, France, Spain, Canada, and Mexico dealing with the Cherokee. *A Guide to Cherokee Documents in Foreign Archives* is the finding aid for the collection. Literary papers include the works of journalist John Parris (1914–1999), who wrote on Appalachian foodways and other aspects of mountain life.

See also: APPALACHIAN SPECIAL COLLECTIONS; KEPHART, HORACE (LANGUAGE).

—George Frizzell, *Western Carolina University*

Tamarack

Located in Beckley, West Virginia, and operated by the West Virginia Parkways Authority, Tamarack displays an array of West Virginia–made craft items, food products, recordings, and publications that are offered for sale to the public. The unusual structure, prominently located on a small hill overlooking a travel plaza off the West Virginia Turnpike, features a number of architectural innovations, including several bright red triangular spires on the building's exterior and a circular interior floor plan. Incorporated into its fifty-nine thousand square feet of floor space are craft studios, a restaurant, a theater, and an art gallery. Constructed at a cost of $16 million, the building was completed in 1996.

The idea of selling West Virginia–made products along the state's highways was initiated in 1991 by Governor Gaston Caperton to capitalize on the growing tourism and crafts industries. At first products were distributed and sold through highway rest stops and travel plazas across the state, but the decision was soon made to centralize these activities, leading to the establishment of Tamarack. In its first four years of operation, Tamarack recorded two million visitors and $20 million in sales. While some within the state have questioned the center's longterm viability and the appropriateness of its apparent upscale appeal, Tamarack continues to be a popular stop for turnpike travelers and has a considerable economic impact both locally and throughout the state.

See also: CULTURAL HERITAGE TOURISM (TOURISM); WEST VIRGINIA TURNPIKE (TRANSPORTATION).

—John Lilly, *West Virginia Division of Culture and History*

Tennessee Overhill Heritage Association

The Tennessee Overhill Heritage Association is an innovative nonprofit organization devoted to cultural and tourism development in three counties of rural southeastern Tennessee. It was formed in 1990 as a pilot project among Monroe, McMinn, and Polk Counties under the Heritage Tourism Initiative, a local assistance effort of the National Trust for Historic Preservation. It has gained national recognition as a model program for its creative approaches to sustainable tourism and its resourceful pursuit of support from federal, state, and regional partners.

The association is headquartered in a restored Louisville and Nashville Railroad depot in Etowah, where its founder and director, Linda Caldwell, first became active in arts and preservation work. Its mission is to showcase the area in ways that are agreeable to area residents. Interpretive and promotional efforts have keyed on the theme "From Furs to Factories," which eschews Appalachian stereotypes to portray a realistic regional identity molded by railroads, mill towns, mines, and industrial deforestation. In its Cultural Legacy Project, the association strengthened area resources through the work of a folklorist who identified and helped create opportunities for local artists and delivered technical assistance to cultural groups and events.

In an area previously known for traditional recreational attractions, the Overhill Heritage Association has expanded the base and vision for tourism through diverse activities—commissioning documentary photography, developing cultural programs for the 1996 Olympic whitewater competition on the Ocoee River, hosting historic railroad excursions, and recognizing local African American history through programming at a restored theater. Creative marketing projects include an agricultural trail brochure and a regional products guide.

The organization takes its name—specifically the term *Overhill*—from the area's precontact Cherokee settlements, and its work has addressed this legacy. In 1997 the association became a partner in the Cherokee Heritage Trails project of the Blue Ridge Heritage Initiative, working with the Eastern Band of Cherokee Indians and other partners to reinterpret the story of the tribe's original homelands. In 1999 it successfully nominated a section of the Unicoi Turnpike, an ancient route across the mountains, as a National Millennium Flagship Trail.

While some cultural advocates oppose tourism as a destructive influence, the Tennessee Overhill Heritage Association seeks to tap its potential for strengthening communities by focusing on local resources and control and by trying to broaden economic impact. In its successful pursuit of this approach, the association has attracted more than a half-million dollars in outside grant support. The organization looks ahead to expanded Web site capabilities and other decentralized strategies for managing tourism in ways that benefit the quality of life in rural Appalachia.

See also: CHEROKEE (RACE, ETHNICITY, AND IDENTITY); NATIONAL TRUST HERITAGE TOURISM INITIATIVE (TOURISM); RAILROAD MUSEUMS.

—Robert Cogswell, *Tennessee Arts Commission*

University of Kentucky Appalachian Center

Established in 1977, the University of Kentucky Appalachian Center was one of the first multipurpose centers devoted entirely to Appalachian issues to be located in a large public university. Its mission includes research, instruction, and service. The Rockefeller Foundation funded planning for the center, and a grant from the National Endowment for the Humanities supported the development of courses in Appalachian studies. The Andrew W. Mellon Foundation and Pew Charitable Trust supported the Appalachian College Program, which brought faculty from the private colleges of southern Appalachia to the University of Kentucky for advanced study in the humanities, social sciences, and natural sciences.

Appalachian Center research topics have included the coal industry, landownership, poverty, economic development, education, transportation, and public policy evaluation, including taxation and welfare reform. In the 1990s a Kellogg Foundation–funded leadership training program in cooperation with Berea College's Brushy Fork Institute sought to facilitate grassroots discussion of public policy issues by identifying and supporting emergent, nontraditional community leaders and efforts. The Appalachian Center also helped form the Kentucky Appalachian Advisory Council (a citizens' organization) and the Appalachian Kentucky Commission (an officially appointed government advisory group) to advise the governor of Kentucky on policy issues relevant to the commonwealth's Appalachian counties. Beginning in the late 1990s, the Appalachian Center gave attention to new forms of participatory research, especially community-based efforts to respond to environmental issues and economic globalization.

See also: BEREA COLLEGE (EDUCATION); FEDERAL FUNDING.

—Dwight B. Billings, *University of Kentucky*

Upland South Carolina Institutions

Though Appalachian South Carolina was once known as "the dark corner," it has grown into one of the more culturally and economically significant regions of the state and the region. From the six counties in the northwest corner (Oconee, Pickens, Spartanburg, Cherokee, Greenville, and Anderson), Appalachian cultural traditions have spread across the rest of the state due largely to migration from the mountains to urban centers and mill towns during the early part of the twentieth century. Consequently, both state and local cultural institutions offer a diversity of materials and information on Appalachian traditions.

State institutions such as the South Carolina Archives and History Center, the libraries of the University of South Carolina, the University of South Carolina's McKissick Museum, the state's Arts Commission and Humanities Council, and the South Carolina State Museum devote a portion of their respective programs and holdings to the histories and cultural characteristics of the Appalachian counties. Other statewide organizations, including the South Carolina Traditional Arts Network, the South Carolina Bluegrass and Traditional Music Association, and the Eastern Cherokee, Southern Iroquois, and United Tribes of South Carolina, offer their members access to scholars, tradition bearers, cultural programmers, and artists whose work includes the Appalachian region.

Each of the Appalachian counties has at least one regional art, history, or cultural center. For example, the Spartanburg Regional History Museum highlights Spartanburg County's history and culture, offering a collection of antique dolls from the area and exhibits on historic battlefields in the region, and the Pickens County Museum features artwork from upstate South Carolina as well as exhibits highlighting Pickens County history. The focus of cultural institutions in these areas is varied and diverse, ranging from Kings Mountain National Military Park and Cowpens National Battlefield in Cherokee County—both of which feature visitor centers illuminating the region's role in the American Revolution—to Greenville's Nippon Center, which celebrates the Japanese immigrant culture as one of the more recent groups to settle in Greenville County. Both Spartanburg's Museum of Art and Bob Jones University in Greenville offer collections of fine art; the former features works by local artists along with examples of folk and decorative arts, while the latter includes one of the most significant collections of Old Master religious art in the United States, including works by Rembrandt, Rubens, and Van Dyke. The Hagood Mill of Pickens County preserves the milling traditions of early farm life in the region; the mill is also the site for the annual Upcountry Folklife Festival and Old Time Fiddlin' Convention, which celebrates the region's traditional music, foodways, and folk arts.

Various plantations and historic homes in the Appalachian counties attempt to preserve the Old South. Anderson County has the Woodburn and Ashtabula Plantation House Museums, which document early-nineteenth-century life, while Spartanburg's Jamie Seay House preserves eighteenth-century farm life. Cherokee County is home to the Possum Trot School, a nineteenth-century one-room schoolhouse.

Popular culture is celebrated in sites such as Shoeless Joe Jackson Memorial Park in Greenville and the Anderson Jockey Lot, perhaps one of the best places to fully experience the diversity of culture in the region. The Jockey Lot is one the South's largest flea markets and attracts patrons and vendors of a stunning array of products from across the state and beyond. The influence of the New South economy in the region is evident at Duke Power's World of Energy in Oconee County and at Greenville's Zentrum Museum, which celebrates the automobiles of one the area's newest and largest employers, BMW.

The Appalachian counties of South Carolina are also home to a number of local cultural organizations. One of the most active is the Piedmont Harmony Project. The membership of this organization includes representatives from the major arts, educational, and cultural institutions in the state as well as local musicians, church choirs, and music enthusiasts. Its mission is to document, preserve, and promote past and current folk music traditions of South Carolina's Appalachian counties, including bluegrass, shape-note singing, spirituals, and blues.

The rise of cotton mills during the late nineteenth and early twentieth centuries transformed this farm country into a region boasting several prosperous cities whose promise of steady pay drew workers from the fields and from the mountains. The region continued to thrive in the late twentieth century as German and Japanese companies, drawn by a ready labor pool with a general distrust of unions, opened manufacturing plants in the area. Economic developments have attracted various groups to these counties, giving this region of Appalachia a rich diversity of cultures, evident in the variety of cultural institutions in the area. The older Appalachian heritage survives, however, in organizations such as the Pickens County Museum, the Upcountry Folklife Festival, and the Piedmont Harmony Project.

See also: ART MUSEUMS; AUTOMOTIVE INDUSTRY (BUSINESS, INDUSTRY, AND TECHNOLOGY); MILL SETTLEMENTS (SETTLEMENT AND MIGRATION).

—Stephen Criswell, *Benedict College*

U.S. Space and Rocket Center

The National Aeronautics and Space Administration (NASA) and the State of Alabama established the U.S. Space and Rocket Center in Huntsville in 1968 to acknowledge the contributions of Redstone Arsenal, the Marshall Space Flight Center, and Alabama to America's space program. The center highlights the contributions of Marshall, which brought an influx of scientists and hundreds of other technology specialists from around the world to Huntsville, changing the character of the area and giving the small city a cosmopolitan flavor.

Noted rocket designer Wernher von Braun arrived in Huntsville in 1950 along with a team of scientists and engineers brought to the United States from Germany at the end of World War II. There they developed ballistic missiles for the army and, subsequently, launch vehicles for NASA spaceflights. Huntsville-developed rockets put the first U.S. satellite in orbit and sent men to the moon. Marshall engineers played a prominent role in development of the space shuttle and design of living modules for the International Space Station. Von Braun instigated the first permanent exhibition of rocket technology in 1968 during the Apollo program, and the Space and Rocket Center opened two years later. On exhibition at the center are the Apollo 16 command module, one of the space shuttle *Columbia*'s main engines from its inaugural flight, and hundreds of other artifacts.

The center is a major tourist attraction and home to the U.S. Space Camp, often described as the world's largest youth science activity program. Thousands of young people have participated in the camp. It is designed to encourage participants to pursue careers in science, technology, and aerospace industries.

See also: AEROSPACE INDUSTRY (BUSINESS, INDUSTRY, AND TECHNOLOGY); MARSHALL SPACE FLIGHT CENTER (BUSINESS, INDUSTRY, AND TECHNOLOGY); NATIONAL YOUTH SCIENCE CAMP.

—Joey Brackner, *Alabama State Council on the Arts*

Weatherford-Hammond Mountain Collection and Southern Appalachian Archives

Housed in Berea College's Hutchins Library in Berea, Kentucky, the Weatherford-Hammond Mountain Collection and Southern Appalachian Archives is a pioneering repository of published and unpublished materials on the southern Appalachian region. Berea's librarians began systematically to collect books on Appalachia in 1914, and nine years later Berea College President William J. Hutchins expressed

Rocket Park at the U.S. Space and Rocket Center in Huntsville, Alabama, c. 1995. In addition to the U.S. Space Camp, the center features one of the world's largest collections of space artifacts, including many rockets currently or previously used by NASA.

an interest in building a research-level collection on the southern mountains. In 1964 the collection was given a new footing when it was endowed by W. D. Weatherford, a trustee of the college, and William A. Hammond, an Ohio businessman. At the end of the twentieth century, the Weatherford-Hammond Mountain Collection numbered more than eighteen thousand volumes, with hundreds of new titles added annually.

Complementing the book collection, the Southern Appalachian Archives consists of manuscripts, newspaper clippings, photographs, and sound recordings documenting key aspects of the region's social and cultural development. Among its most significant holdings are the papers of the Council of the Southern Mountains (1912–70); records of the Appalachian Volunteers (1963–70), Appalachian Regional Survey (1962), and E. O. Robinson Mountain Fund (1922–78); and thousands of documents and photographs copied from the collections of Appalachian settlement schools. The region's musical and oral heritage is particularly well represented, with printed sources of ballads and hymns and approximately seven thousand sound and video recordings of traditional music, oral histories, folklore, and sermons.

Together with the papers relating to the founding and development of Berea College, the Weatherford-Hammond Mountain Collection and Southern Appalachian Archives constitute one of the premier research collections for the study of Appalachia.

See also: APPALACHIAN SPECIAL COLLECTIONS; BEREA COLLEGE (EDUCATION).

—Steve Gowler, *Berea College*

West Virginia and Regional History Collection, West Virginia University Libraries

The West Virginia and Regional History Collection of the West Virginia University Libraries in Morgantown is the primary historical information repository in West Virginia. The collection's roots date back to 1930, when the university library allocated space and facilities to organize and preserve the university's first important manuscripts acquisition, the papers of U.S. Senator Waitman T. Willey (1811–1900), a founding father of West Virginia. The papers of several other key early political and industrial leaders, including Francis H. Pierpont, provisional governor of Virginia from 1861 to 1863 (elected governor in 1863), and capitalist titans Henry Gassaway Davis and Johnson N. Camden, soon followed.

The West Virginia University Board of Governors formally authorized the library's growing Division of Documents, as the collection was initially known, in 1933. The collection was designated as a depository for public records by an act of the state legislature the following year. This status enabled it to become a center for preserving the court records of many of West Virginia's oldest counties during the Works Progress Administration period. From the 1950s to the 1970s, the collection's scope gradually expanded to include printed matter, audiovisual materials, and other historical information resources regardless of format.

The West Virginia and Regional History Collection preserves documents in many fields and formats. Its library of West Virginia books, periodicals, and newspapers is unmatched, as are its holdings of early West Virginia photographs, maps, broadsides, and sound recordings. The collection's archives and manuscripts division holds papers of West Virginia's political leaders from the first governor, Arthur I. Boreman, to later politicians such as Governor Arch Moore and Senator Robert C. Byrd; it also contains outstanding archival resources on virtually all aspects of the state's economic, cultural, and social history.

See also: APPALACHIAN SPECIAL COLLECTIONS; ARCHIVES OF APPALACHIA.

—John A. Cuthbert, *West Virginia and Regional History Collection*

Wildacres

Wildacres is a conference center located in the Blue Ridge Mountains near the town of Little Switzerland in McDowell County, North Carolina. Since 1946, when I. D. Blumenthal dedicated it to the betterment of human relations, Wildacres has offered its facilities to nonprofit groups that conduct educational or cultural programs compatible with the center's mission. Accommodations include two lodges, a dining hall building, a library and auditorium, a mineral and lapidary workshop, and a pottery studio.

Before Blumenthal bought the property in 1936, it had been owned and partially developed by Thomas Dixon, author of the pro–Ku Klux Klan novel *The Clansman,* which served as the basis for D. W. Griffith's controversial film *The Birth of a Nation.* Dixon envisioned Wildacres as a refuge for creative thinkers and a resort with a hotel, tennis courts, stables, golf courses, and swimming pools. In 1929, however, Dixon lost his money in the stock market crash. Blumenthal, a deeply religious man, saw divine guidance at work when he was able to purchase the property at auction for only $6,500.

In its early years, the facility's primary users were church and interfaith groups such as the North Carolina B'nai B'rith Institute (which was founded at Wildacres), civic organizations such as Civitan youth groups, and the Ringling School of Art and Design. Since then, Wildacres has attracted a wide range of groups and has expanded its buildings and services. From mid-April through October, the center hosts more than fifty nonprofit organizations such as the Hickory

Humanities Forum, Blue Ridge Center for Lifelong Learning, North Carolina Storytelling Guild, Wildacres Writers Workshop, North Carolina State Park Superintendents, and Southern Appalachian Highlands Conservancy.

In 1995 the Wildacres Leadership Initiative was established to help create leaders committed to promoting improved human relations and expanded opportunities for all North Carolinians.

See also: BLACK MOUNTAIN COLLEGE (EDUCATION); LITTLE SWITZERLAND, NORTH CAROLINA (TOURISM); NORTH CAROLINA ARTS COUNCIL.

—Beverly B. Patterson, *North Carolina Folklife Institute*

William King Regional Arts Center

William King Regional Arts Center is a private, nonprofit visual arts organization located in Abingdon, Virginia, and serving southwestern Virginia and northeastern Tennessee. A museum partner of the Virginia Museum of Fine Arts, Richmond, the center is governed by a volunteer trustee board and managed by professional staff. Its primary programming site is the 1913 William King High School building and the surrounding twenty acres.

The annual program includes exhibitions, art education, working studios for artists, and a museum gift store. Installed in three high-security galleries, exhibitions change every three to six months and feature a balance of original historic and contemporary art from the world and the region. An outdoor sculpture exhibit is located on the grounds. Educational programs include tours, classes, workshops, lectures, and demonstrations for adults and children. Youth programs feature classes for public and school audiences, including a full-day program at the center for third-graders called Art Express and a program for second-graders called Van Gogh Outreach.

The Cultural Heritage Project conducted a field survey of regional material culture of southwestern Virginia and northeastern Tennessee, documenting and photographing more than two thousand objects created prior to 1940. Research data for the project, held in a permanent archive at the center, is used to create exhibitions and programs and to develop a permanent collection of regional decorative arts. The collection is displayed at the Fields-Penn 1860 House Museum, a satellite site located approximately one mile away in Abingdon's historic district. The William King Regional Arts Center is open to the public year-round.

See also: CULTURAL HERITAGE TOURISM (TOURISM); SECTION OVERVIEW (VISUAL ARTS).

—Betsy White, *Abingdon, Virginia*

W. L. Eury Appalachian Collection

In 1968 the Appalachian Room was established as a special collection in Appalachian State University's Belk Library. It was renamed the W. L. Eury Appalachian Collection in 1971 to honor the former Appalachian State University librarian and early supporter of the collection. With the goal of becoming a comprehensive collection of Appalachia-related materials, the Eury Appalachian Collection has grown into one of the premier regional repositories.

As of 2002, the collection included more than 26,000 books, 2,300 sound recordings, and 850 videocassettes, housed approximately 1,000 linear feet of manuscript collections (with an extensive newspaper clippings file), and received more than 100 regional periodicals. Additionally, the collection owns more than 5,000 regional maps, including topographical maps for each quadrant in each Appalachian Regional Commission–defined county. Also available are more than 9,000 rolls of microfilm and 5,300 microfiche, which include census records, many western North Carolina newspapers and county court records, more than 900 Appalachia-related dissertations, Highlander Folk School's FBI file, Freedmen's Bureau records, and the International Genealogical Index.

The Appalachian Collection's subject strength includes Appalachian minorities, tourism, folklore, ethnography, genealogy, and western North Carolina. The manuscript collection stresses folk songs and Watauga County, North Carolina, subjects. Key manuscript collections include the papers of James T. Broyhill (U.S. congressman, 1963–86), Cratis Williams (a pioneer of Appalachian studies and dean of the graduate school), and W. Amos Abrams (folklorist and longtime instructor at Appalachian State), as well as ballad collector I. G. Greer's Folksong Collection. The collection Web site contains additional historical information, including bibliographies and pathfinders on various topics.

See also: APPALACHIAN CULTURAL MUSEUM; APPALACHIAN SPECIAL COLLECTIONS; SPECIAL COLLECTIONS, WESTERN CAROLINA UNIVERSITY.

—Kathryn L. Staley, *Appalachian State University*

ARTIN LUTHER KING AT COMMUNIST
TRAINING SCHOOL
KING
OZIER

Education

Section Editors: Alan J. DeYoung, Michele Glover, and Mary Jean Ronan Herzog

THE SCOPE OF EDUCATION IN APPALACHIA IS AS BROAD AS THE REGION ITSELF. From New York and Pennsylvania through the central states of the region to Alabama and Mississippi, schooling is shaped by statewide policies, initiatives, and mandates, as well as by place-bound types of education. Both formally and informally, from birth through adulthood and old age, the process of education takes many shapes. Subscription schools, church schools, public schools, colleges, and community centers are just a few of the many educational institutions in Appalachia.

Historians and philosophers have argued about the aims and purposes of education for generations. Depending on the era, such important social theorists as Jean-Jacques Rousseau and Maria Montessori, John Dewey and Elwood Cubberly, and Alfred North Whitehead and Robert Hutchins have all debated the prominence of local versus national and/or applied versus theoretical means and ends of schooling. Primarily, education has served three broad purposes: socialization of the student into society; personal growth and development; and improvement of society. All three objectives have been at play in schooling in the Appalachian region.

The aims and missions of community schools have changed continuously over the twentieth century, and contests over what is to be taught in Appalachian schools and who is to teach are well documented in regional history. To be understood, schools and education in Appalachia should be regarded as part of the American experience, not as something outside of the norm, as critics often claimed early in the last century. Entries in the following section cover a variety of topics that are illustrative, rather than exhaustive, of the places, people, traditions, and issues related to mountain schooling.

The history of public schooling in America has unfolded in the context of major cultural and social themes, influenced by religion, place, practicality, race, economics, and government. The ways Americans have understood and addressed these themes have shaped perceptions of education and the course of school policy. National changes have been dramatic in each of these areas over the last century, as have the influences that shape schooling aims and outcomes. Stories of schooling in Appalachia are at various times depressing, uplifting, heartwarming, and contradictory. Generally, they are variations of stories that have played out elsewhere in America and indeed in the world.

Facing page: A billboard, posted to suggest Martin Luther King Jr.'s association with communist causes, denounces the civil rights leader's appearance at the twenty-fifth anniversary celebration of the Highlander Folk School, Monteagle, Tennessee, 1957. During the 1950s, the school trained civil rights workers and taught African Americans to read and write well enough to pass literacy tests required to vote.

Morality and religion have been key factors in the evolution of American and Appalachian education and continue to be problematic. The first laws on education in the colonies were passed in New England and required that children be educated about the Bible in order that the "Old Deluder" Satan not get their souls. Many Appalachian schools from their inception were likewise organized around the teaching of Christian morality; most schools were in fact affiliated or formally attached to some congregational church. Their primary function was to teach reading, and what was to be read was most often the Bible. As secular twentieth-century trends took hold, schools often became battlegrounds for conflicts over moral instruction. Evolution, the posting of the Ten Commandments in schools, school prayer, and book banning have been frequent sources of controversy. School censorship issues have given special flavor to this theme and struggle in Appalachia.

Place and community have been historic and definitive concerns in Appalachian schools. Seeking independence and workable land, early mountaineers intentionally distanced themselves from neighbors, but by the late nineteenth century both regional demographics and notions of schooling had begun to change. Continued in-migration and growing families created larger communities; extractive industries led to new settlements and company towns. States began to support local education efforts, in part because more affluent families wanted formal schooling. One- and two-room schools controlled by local trustees mushroomed. Larger communities created and supported elementary and high schools as symbols of progress in the mountains. Besides serving as places for educational instruction, schools became sites for church services, political rallies, dramatic performances, band concerts, and ball games. Often the town's largest employer, schools were the focus of community political wrangling, and teaching jobs often became political plums.

The imperatives of place and community changed twentieth-century education. Year after year, school consolidation was a source of strident controversy in Appalachia and across the country as schools moved away from small communities and neighborhoods to more central locations. Improved highways and movement away from rural hollows and toward towns undercut most of the demographic reasons for retaining and celebrating formerly remote and isolated community schools. Movies, radio, and television replaced many of the social and cultural functions of the local schoolhouse. Yet the struggle over whose community the schoolhouse serves is a classic one for both urban and rural America. By the late twentieth century, the mission of the school was increasingly seen as a way to enable children to escape from their communities to pursue place-independent careers. Struggles over definitions of place, community, and nation are well represented in the history of Appalachian education.

Practicality has been a critical theme in educational policy and politics in Appalachia. Questions regarding "what schooling is good for" are culturally linked in the United States to the way schools relate to the economy. When America was predominantly rural, the schoolhouse was often thought of as a distraction from the world of work. Until the late nineteenth century, advanced schooling was understood in many Appalachian communities to lead to a move away from rural areas to the city, where a university degree might mean access to emerging middle-class occupations. Since many rural Americans remained hopeful that their children would find work locally and remain near home, the promise that high school graduation would enable their children to leave for the university and then the wider world was sometimes viewed suspiciously. Schools, some believed, taught children to "get above their raisin'" by challenging the farming, mining, or working-class roots of their fore-

A boy attending school in Harlan County, Kentucky, 1946. Before the 1960s and the War on Poverty, the state of education and the economy in Appalachia received little national attention. Many Appalachians either migrated out of the region or left school before graduation to work on farms, in coal mines, or in the oil and gas industry.

bears. Therefore, some communities were skeptical of education beyond the eighth grade, even into the middle of the twentieth century. In coal-mining communities in particular, practical work and vocational studies were viewed as positive because they could teach skills necessary to provide for a family close to home. Preparing for middle-class, administrative, or professional occupations (with the exception of teaching at the local school) was less popular in many remote mountain communities. This was also the case in the rest of the country until the early 1960s. Local parental support of public education beyond basic reading and writing and patriotism was often missing in mountain communities (other than in the homes of the few elites) until vocational programs funded by the federal and state governments emerged in the 1930s and 1940s.

Before the 1960s and the War on Poverty, the state of education and the economy in Appalachia received little national attention. Many Appalachians left school before graduation to work on farms, in the mines, or in the oil and gas industry or to migrate to the factories of Michigan and Maryland or to the Northwest to work in the timber industry. Mountain schools often got "bad press" by default as Appalachian children went with their families to the cities, where their culture and dialect were stereotyped by city residents. Back home, what was learned in school was often seen as secondary to having a good work ethic, good values, and a strong back.

Nevertheless, members of many extended middle-class families have highly valued education, taken professional jobs, and served as community leaders. In communities throughout the region solid schools were developed by local people who desired education and progress for their children. The story of education in Jackson County, North Carolina, provides an illustration. In the 1880s, residents of the town of Cullowhee organized a high school for mountain children that evolved first into a normal and industrial school, then a teaching college, and finally Western Carolina University. Though there were many mountaineers who did not pursue much formal education, there were also many who graduated from high school, received some higher education, and became teachers, lawyers, and doctors. Jackson County was a microcosm of educational life in the early twentieth century. Out in the hollows and coves, there remained one-room schools, while larger communities and towns had graded schools. From the 1950s, however, both rural schools and town schools were steadily closed and/or consolidated. The situation put children in buses for long, daily rides to schools out of their communities. Old school buildings were either taken over by other county agencies or abandoned. In the remote area of Little Canada, for example, the school was abandoned when it was consolidated in the 1960s, but in 2002 the community began working to reclaim and refurbish it as a community center.

Jackson County had a population of about thirty-three thousand in 2003 and was divided into northern and southern sections. The northern section had superhighways and the county seat of Sylva, while the southern section was only accessible by winding, two-lane roads. There was one high school of roughly one thousand students located in the more populated northern section, along with four K–8 schools. The southern section had one K–12, or union, school with about three hundred students—one of very few left in the entire Appalachian region—and it was located in the most inaccessible section of the area.

When observers from outside came to Appalachia early in the twentieth century, they often found mountain children deficient in skills or lacking opportunities generally available to children educated in the Northeast or Midwest. A number of settlement or mission schools and/or colleges were established for what were perceived to be these disadvantaged youth. Adult education and increasing awareness of the links between schooling and economic advancement were the focus of other programs and institutions. The Highlander Folk School in Tennessee and "moonlight schools" in Kentucky are excellent examples of institutions that combined social concerns and basic education.

Higher education in the Appalachian region includes a rich variety of institutions from the past and present that have had a significant impact: normal and teachers' colleges; work-study schools such as Berea and Warren Wilson Colleges; land-grant universities; private colleges; historically black colleges; and community colleges. Throughout the region, colleges and universities often evolved from normal and teachers' colleges. The State University of New York at Cortland, for example, was founded in 1868 as the Cortland Normal School, and over the next century became a teachers' college and eventually a regional college. The Normal School in Indiana, Pennsylvania, was founded in 1875, became a teachers' college in 1927, a state college in 1960, and a state university in 1965. Land-grant colleges have also played an important role in the region, and many that began as products of the Land Grant College Act of 1862 continue to the present as institutions important to the region. Examples include Cornell University in New York, Mississippi State University, and Pennsylvania State University.

The Appalachian region also has an important place in the history of African American education in America. Though it is not widely recognized, the famous Tuskegee University, founded by West Virginia–educated Booker T. Washington, lies within southern Appalachia in Macon County, Alabama. Native Americans have also always been an important presence in the region, long before it became known as Appalachia. Although there are many tribes throughout the region, schooling for Native Americans in Appalachia can be illustrated by the experiences of the Cherokee. At the beginning of the nineteenth century, Cherokees had a great desire for education and literacy for their children, as can be seen in documents such as their newspaper, the *Cherokee Phoenix*. As time passed, however, various attempts were made under the guise of education to persuade Cherokee children to reject their own heritage and culture and fully assimilate into the white man's world.

Women who received advanced education during the early twentieth century were primarily educated for teaching and nursing, and both local women and philanthropists and missionaries from outside the region ("fotched-on" women) served as leaders and educators. Women were also influential in founding and working with settlement, mission, and normal schools and colleges in the late nineteenth and early twentieth centuries.

Many educational issues faced throughout America take on additional difficulties in much of Appalachia. For example, geographic isolation is a fundamental theme in many stories of mountain schools, although some Appalachian scholars object to this generalization since many communities were accessible by rail and radio.

Another primary issue, well rehearsed in vernacular stories about Appalachian education, is the corruption of the educational process in some schools and school districts by political maneuvering. Nepotism and cronyism, for example, were frequent targets of state legislatures involved in several famous major statewide school reform efforts—in West Virginia in the 1980s (the "Recht decision"), for instance, and in Kentucky in the 1990s (the Kentucky Education Reform Act).

Schools in Appalachia have been forced to implement state and national policies, particularly accountability policies, in the late twentieth and early twenty-first centuries, regardless of the fit of those policies with individual locales. Several states with Appalachian counties have been involved in lawsuits over funding formulas. In the Kentucky case and in Pennsylvania, many reforms seem to have been sensitive to local needs, enabling Appalachian school districts to be agents of social change and gain increased autonomy as well as accountability.

With national policies closely connected to federal funds, schools must fall in line to collect, and this sometimes presents problems. Rural areas of the Appalachian region, for instance, faced difficulties fulfilling the requirements of the federal No Child Left Behind Act of 2001, which allowed students to transfer out of failing schools into schools of their choice. Such districts often have no other option but local public schools, and transferring means traveling long distances to other counties.

Consolidation and busing present continuing problems for Appalachian schools as well. The unwritten national policies guiding educational development throughout the twentieth century that "bigger is better" and "one size fits all" have not abated, and communities continue to resist losing their schools. More and more, however, scholars and policymakers are engaged in objective analyses of these policies, and they have been making strong cases for smaller, community-based schools. At the beginning of the twenty-first century, the importance of community schools seems to have come full circle throughout the Appalachian region.

—Alan J. DeYoung, *University of Kentucky*, and Mary Jean Ronan Herzog, *Western Carolina University*

Robert Bickel, "Post–High School Opportunities and High School Completion Rates in an Appalachian State," *Youth and Society* (September 1989); Alan J. DeYoung, *The Life and Death of a Rural American High School: Farewell, Little Kanawha* (1995) and *Struggling with their Histories: Economic Decline and Educational Improvement in Four Rural Southeastern School Districts* (1991); John R. Finger, *Cherokee Americans: The Eastern Band of Cherokees in the Twentieth Century* (1991); Diana L. Haleman and Alan J. DeYoung, "A Reflective Essay Concerning Something Better: Experiences of Appalachian Rural Trust Schools," *Journal of Research in Rural Education* (Spring 2000); Ellis Hartford, *The Little White Schoolhouse* (1977); Mary Hoffschwelle, *Rebuilding the Rural Southern Community: Reformers, Schools, and Homes in Tennessee, 1900–1930* (1998); David C. Hsiung, *Two Worlds in the Tennessee Mountains: Exploring the Origins of Appalachian Stereotypes* (1997); Henry Perkinson, *The Imperfect Panacea: American Faith in Education, 1865–1990* (1991); Alan Peshkin, *Growing Up American: Schooling and the Survival of Community* (1978); David E. Whisnant, *Modernizing the Mountaineer: People, Power, and Planning in Appalachia* (1980); Max R. Williams, ed., *The History of Jackson County* (1987); Curtis W. Wood and H. Tyler Blethen, *A Mountain Heritage: The Illustrated History of Western Carolina University* (1989).

African American Education

The education of Appalachian blacks has drawn little scholarly attention. Since the subject must be disentangled from studies of education in Appalachia or of blacks in the United States, current conclusions are largely inferential.

Before the Civil War, slavery was legal in Appalachia save for Ohio after 1803, New York after 1827, and Pennsylvania from the 1840s. The vast majority of slaves remained illiterate. Those who achieved literacy did so via self-study or tutoring by masters' families or fellow literate slaves. In Appalachia, schools that served both blacks and whites were rare. Ohio abolished segregated schools in 1887, while New York (until 1900) and Pennsylvania (1881) authorized but did not require separate schools for blacks. In northern Appalachia, schools for blacks (operated mostly by abolitionists) could be found, for example, in Binghamton, Elmira, and Bath, New York, around Pittsburgh, and in southern Ohio. From the 1830s to the 1850s, however, states from Virginia to Mississippi, except Kentucky and Tennessee, expressly forbade educating slaves. These laws were widely evaded, notably by many Baptist, Methodist, and Presbyterian churches in Appalachia. A few slaves learned secretly, while some masters wanted selected literate slaves for economic reasons or believed they should be taught to read the Bible. Still, among slave and freed blacks combined, illiteracy before the war stood at about 90 percent nationwide.

With emancipation, a thirst for education gripped southern blacks. Makeshift "schools" proliferated. The Freedmen's Bureau and the American Missionary Association (affiliated with Northern Congregationalists) soon moved in, eventually founding more than 4,000 schools. Blacks thronged to the hastily built, woefully equipped facilities. Teachers, mostly northern white females, were in desperately short supply. Inevitably, most schools were built where large numbers of blacks lived, especially in the "Black Belt" lowlands. How much Appalachian blacks benefited is uncertain—probably modestly. Because they steadily drifted from farms into towns and cities, their chances of finding schools vastly increased. This pattern of movement and concentration has continued to the present, to the benefit of blacks' educational opportunities.

By the mid-1870s, the southern states mandated public school systems, but education was pitifully funded by a populace that doubted the value of schooling beyond the rudiments and resented paying taxes, especially to educate blacks. Schools became legally segregated after a decade of a de facto racial separation, which had met with approval from many blacks who wanted "their" schools and distrusted whites' intentions. Berea College (Kentucky), which educated blacks and whites together from 1866 until passage of the segregationist Day Law in 1904, was an exception. With Jim Crow legislation rampant from the 1880s, black schools were starved of teachers, facilities, and prescribed attendance days. (Mississippi in 1929 spent 5.3 times as much per capita on white students as on blacks; in 1940, 9.9 times as much. Other states did little better.) Appalachian blacks in particular suffered further neglect when, in the 1890s, missionaries—frustrated by Jim Crow laws and the magnitude of the problem of educating blacks—turned to working among poor whites.

The black educational system survived because of blacks' generous contributions, financial and moral; outreach by Methodist, Baptist, and Presbyterian churches; support from northern philanthropists; and because, under the inspiration of Booker T. Washington and the Hampton (Virginia) and Tuskegee (Alabama) Institutes, black schools began to emphasize "industrial" (vocational) education. The rise of vocational training attracted northern philanthropists and allayed southerners' fears that blacks might not remain a caste of laborers if they were "classically" educated.

Supportive charitable foundations included the Peabody Fund (1867), the John Fox Slater Fund (1882), John D. Rockefeller's General Education Board (1904), the Anna T. Jeanes Fund (1907), the Phelps-Stokes Fund (1909), and the Julius Rosenwald Fund (1917). The Slater Fund, for example, established County Training Schools ("high schools") for blacks in 384 southern counties; the Jeanes Fund provided skilled supervisory teachers in rural areas; and the Rosenwald Fund built 5,357 schools in 883 counties. There is no research available to indicate how many of these County Training Schools or Rosenwald schoolhouses were built in Appalachia.

The second Morrill Act (1890) provided new money for land-grant universities, which helped found black institutions emphasizing industrial training (the "A&M" or agricultural and mechanical schools). The more than 100 black private colleges (or "institutes") founded by 1900 nevertheless retained a leading role in higher education. Well into the twentieth century, however, they offered mostly high school and even elementary preparatory courses rather than standard college fare, in addition to vocational courses. Still, the dispute between Washington's concept and the classical curriculum advocated by scholar and civil rights leader W. E. B. Du Bois persisted. By the 1920s the classical curriculum was ascendant in the private colleges. The strong emphasis on teacher training in black higher education—and for decades in secondary education—encouraged this classical trend.

Today there are a number of historically black colleges and universities in Appalachia. They include: Mary Holmes College and Rust College in Mississippi; Tuskegee University, Alabama A&M University, Talladega College, Stillman College, Miles College, Oakwood College, J. F. Drake State Technical College, and Lawson State Community College in Alabama; Knoxville College in Tennessee; Winston-Salem

State University in North Carolina; and Bluefield State College in West Virginia. More black colleges and universities are found on the fringes of Appalachia.

Historically, black teachers in southern schools have varied significantly in quality, with the best ordinarily found in urban settings. On the more positive side, blacks equaled or surpassed their white counterparts in credentialed training and probably in dedication to their mission. Nevertheless, black teachers typically received 25 to 35 percent less pay than whites (50 to 60 percent in Alabama and Mississippi) and were deliberately kept in inferior status by the white establishment. By 1958, for example, 82 percent of black schools still had not sought accreditation.

Poverty and distance were the silent enemies of southern black education. One leading authority, Henry Bullock, asserts that by 1933 virtually any black child could get at least two years of public high school without walking too far. Yet in 1934, only 18 percent of age-eligible black children attended high school, as compared to 54 percent of whites. In Alabama steel towns, companies that wanted a low-wage job pool provided elementary schools generously but no high schools. In Tennessee in 1950, 20 of the state's 95 counties had enough blacks to justify a high school, but none did; in Georgia 105 of 155 counties in 1941–42 offered no transportation for black students. If such figures were cited for Appalachia alone, they would doubtless be worse, since small numbers of black students were generally scattered across sparsely populated areas.

In a landmark unanimous decision on May 19, 1954, the United States Supreme Court in *Brown v. Board of Education of Topeka, Kansas*, declared racial segregation in public education unconstitutional and ordered it ended "with all deliberate speed." Virtually all higher education desegregated by 1960. But desegregation of primary and secondary education provoked bitter resistance in all the southern Appalachian states—except Kentucky and West Virginia, where integration was achieved by the mid-1960s with minimal legal resistance. The Civil Rights Act (1964) and the Elementary and Secondary Education Act (1965) finally furnished the federal government sufficient powers to force compliance in resisting states, although litigation about details of desegregation continues to the present. For example, the use of busing to overcome residential segregation occupied courts from 1970 *(Swann v. Charlotte-Mecklenburg Board of Education)* through the 1990s.

In Appalachia, violence flared in 1956 and 1960 in Clinton and Chattanooga, Tennessee, and exploded in Birmingham, Alabama, in the 1960s. Elsewhere the region was spared, mostly because of the absence of large cities, where busing between suburbs and the inner city, for example, became a heated issue in some cases. Minorities in rural and small communities are the most integrated in American schools—and Appalachia is arguably the prime example.

The state of education of blacks in Appalachia until late in the twentieth century is strikingly illustrated by statistics showing in 1985 that adult Appalachian blacks were twice as likely as the general populace to have five or fewer years of schooling. If urban areas are excluded, half of blacks over age twenty-five had fewer than five years of schooling—greater than the national black norm. At the same time, however, the enrollment of both blacks and whites nationwide was—finally—equal to their proportions in the total population. This statistic argued convincingly that access to primary and secondary education after desegregation was equal—a fundamental change since *Brown*, and strikingly so in Appalachia. (The case with higher education is more complicated, though legal racial exclusion of blacks has been abolished.)

Desegregation has not of itself solved the problems of educating blacks in Appalachia. Black teachers, administrators, and coaches have declined in number. Many if not most black schools were closed following integration (frequently with historical records destroyed or relegated to obscure locations), and non-tenured teachers were released; tenured teachers were retained but often assigned non-classroom or remedial-group positions. Black teachers, principals, and superintendents meanwhile lost prominence as leaders in black communities and as role models for students. Desegregation also aroused suspicion among blacks that white teachers might not understand or care about their children.

A 1998 survey of some Appalachian black students underscored these consequences and fears. Students indicated that they wanted more black teachers; more parental encouragement of achievement, help with homework, and provision of money and clothing; and to be held to higher expectations by teachers, especially whites, regarding their academic potential. The lack of these things contributes to discipline problems, low test scores, and dropouts. Such results, however, are not confined to Appalachian blacks but occur among all races in the Appalachian region and elsewhere.

See also: AFRICAN AMERICAN FAMILIES AND COMMUNITIES (FAMILY AND COMMUNITY); AFRICAN AMERICAN TWENTIETH-CENTURY MIGRATION (SETTLEMENT AND MIGRATION).

—David S. Newhall, *Centre College*

James D. Anderson, *The Education of Blacks in the South, 1860–1935* (1988); Henry Bullock, *A History of Negro Education in the South* (1970); William H. Turner and Edward J. Cabbell, eds., *Blacks in Appalachia* (1985).

Alvin C. York Institute

Located on the Cumberland Plateau in Jamestown, Tennessee, Alvin C. York Institute was founded by World War I hero Alvin Cullum York to bring educational advantages to local youth. Originally named the York Industrial Institute and later the York Agricultural and Industrial Institute, the school began as a nonprofit organization in 1920 and received fifty thousand dollars from the Tennessee legislature in 1925 toward construction of a building. The school officially opened in 1929, although classes were conducted as early as 1925 in what had been the local poorhouse for Fentress County.

York raised the initial funds to construct the facilities and operate the secondary school, which existed as a private institution until 1937, when he became too ill to travel and raise funds. The Tennessee legislature subsequently took over the facility, placing it under the governance of the state board of education. York Institute continues to operate with funds appropriated by the state.

In 1986 the school was given the mission of studying programs specifically geared to rural education. In this role, it has pioneered several educational programs, sharing the findings with school systems throughout the region. In 1986 York Institute was named the Tennessee Center for Rural Education and in 1989 was designated a National School of Excellence (one of 218 schools selected in the nation) by the U.S. Department of Education. In 1992 *Redbook* magazine named it one of America's best schools.

See also: HISTORICAL HEROES (IMAGES AND ICONS); *SERGEANT YORK* (MEDIA).

—Doug Young, *Jamestown, Tennessee*

Appalachian College Association

Formally established in 1990, the Appalachian College Association is a nonprofit organization of thirty-four private liberal arts teaching institutions located across five states in the central Appalachian region. Collectively, the schools serve an annual enrollment of approximately thirty-five thousand students and employ more than three thousand faculty members in Kentucky, North Carolina, Tennessee, Virginia, and West Virginia. The association encourages members to foster Appalachian history and culture; to share ideas, information, programs, and resources; and to support the economic development of the region by acting as a resource for agencies formulating regional and national policies. Appalachian College Association member schools are distinctive because they combine highly individualized academic programs with low student-to-faculty ratios and an emphasis on instilling strong traditional values in students. Because of the locations of the colleges throughout central Appalachia, they attract and serve many who might not otherwise have an opportunity to pursue higher education. More than 85 percent of students receive some form of financial assistance, and 30 percent are the first in their families to attend and graduate from college.

Member colleges are Alice Lloyd College, Berea College, Brevard College, Campbellsville University, Cumberland College, Kentucky Christian College, Lindsey Wilson College, Pikeville College, and Union College in Kentucky; Lees-McRae College, Mars Hill College, Montreat College, and Warren Wilson College in North Carolina; Bryan College, Carson-Newman College, King College, Lee University, Lincoln Memorial University, Maryville College, Milligan College, Tennessee Wesleyan College, Tusculum College, and the University of the South in Tennessee; Bluefield College, Emory and Henry College, Ferrum College, and Virginia Intermont College in Virginia; and Alderson-Broaddus College, Bethany College, Davis and Elkins College, Ohio Valley College, the University of Charleston, West Virginia Wesleyan College, and Wheeling Jesuit University in West Virginia.

Begun in 1980 as a grant-funded project at the University of Kentucky under John B. Stephenson, then director of the Appalachian Center, the program grew from a summer fellowship program for humanities faculty (named to honor author James Still) to a program providing yearlong fellowships for faculty in all arts and sciences fields. Stephenson, who later became president of Berea College, had envisioned periodically placing faculty from small campuses at large universities when he was a faculty member at a small college in the mountains of North Carolina. He knew firsthand the benefits of teaching in the intimate setting of a private liberal arts college, but he also knew the benefits of having access to resources at the libraries and laboratories of major universities.

In the mid-1980s, funding became available to expand the program to enable faculty to receive fellowships to attend any of six major universities in the five-state region: the University of Tennessee, the University of Virginia, the University of North Carolina, West Virginia University, Virginia Polytechnic Institute and State University, and the University of Kentucky. The graduate deans or their associate deans from these major institutions formed a panel to review applications for the awards.

In the late 1980s, John Chandler, then director of the Association of American Colleges and Universities, conducted an evaluation of the program at the University of Kentucky and concluded that there were ways the colleges could collaborate to reduce costs as well as improve efficiency. As a result of that evaluation, the presidents of the participating private colleges met with University of Kentucky officials and decided that the time had come to become independent. In the fall of 1990, those presidents met at Bluefield College to establish the Appalachian College Association.

The new association was incorporated in 1991 as an independent association with tax-exempt classification and governed by a board of directors composed of presidents of the member colleges. Warren Wilson College contributed office space, and Alfred Canon, who had just retired as president of Warren Wilson, was hired as a half-time director. The faculty-development program continued to operate at the University of Kentucky, and the new association began to focus on other needs of the colleges.

In 1993 the board hired its first full-time director and moved the headquarters to Berea, Kentucky. At that point, the program at the University of Kentucky began the formal procedures for closing. Funds remaining at the university from the program were moved to the graduate school for student graduate fellowships from the member colleges. Since that time, funding has grown to more than $10 million, with an annual budget of roughly $2 million. In 1999 an advisory council of prominent regional leaders was established to give additional guidance to the association.

Appalachian College Association programs continue to focus heavily on faculty. The fellowship program continues to make awards for faculty to complete degrees, conduct research independently or with students, make presentations at professional meetings, or learn new technologies relevant to their teaching. Fellowships and grants honoring Stephenson, author-historian Wilma Dykeman, and traditional folksinger and songwriter Jean Ritchie are awarded in amounts of $500 to $30,000. These awards are made possible by an endowment funded by the National Endowment for the Humanities and organizations such as the Andrew W. Mellon, Kenan, Hearst, and McCune Foundations, as well as by numerous individuals and corporations. Fellowship recipients are selected by a review committee consisting of twelve members: six graduate deans or their associate deans from the affiliated research universities in the region and six academic administrators from the Appalachian College Association member colleges.

Recent initiatives have focused on utilizing technology to enhance teaching and learning and to enable intercollegiate collaboration among faculty in these often geographically isolated institutions. Two grants from the Andrew W. Mellon Foundation totaling $5.4 million have supported this effort. The first, called "Teaching and Technology: Capturing the Promises; Avoiding the Problems," was begun in January 1996 and had five major goals: to reduce the isolation of the faculty at Appalachian College Association schools by increasing their ability to use technological informational resources; to provide new ways to access information for instructional purposes, providing a "quantum leap" in improved learning for students; to enable faculty to develop skills necessary for utilizing technology in their classes to bring new approaches to their teaching; to encourage the formation of teams composed of faculty teaching in arts and sciences divisions, where members can provide both expertise and encouragement for one another in the area of technology; and to facilitate planning for future improvements in campus technology that will avoid obsolescence and increase sustainability. Workshops, training, faculty-development projects, and infrastructure building resulted in markedly increased e-mail, listserv, and database usage; information retrieval from Internet sites; familiarity with applications software; and resource allocation to technology hardware and personnel. A technology summit was the final showcase activity of the first grant. About 15 percent of the total faculty of Appalachian College Association institutions attended the conference, representing thirty-two of the thirty-four colleges. The program included seventy-six presentations by eighty-seven Appalachian College Association faculty members working individually or in teams and often showcasing the integration of technology in their classroom teaching.

A second technology summit, called "Teaching and Technology: Stage II," was begun in 1999 and was one of the first activities of the second Mellon grant. This three-year grant built on the training, consultation, workshops, and collaborative projects of the first summit by furthering the development of institutional infrastructures, sustaining training initiatives, identifying cost-effective uses of technology for quality learning, and providing for the development of new and demonstrably superior modes of technology-assisted pedagogy through collaborative faculty-development projects. These collaborative grants involve faculty members from at least three different Appalachian College Association colleges or at least three different disciplines in a single college in the joint development of a new or enhanced course or program of study that infuses information technology in ways that demonstrate the potential for improved student learning and involve expanded pedagogical approaches.

A further focus of the second grant was the development of a Virtual Teaching and Learning with Technology Center (Virtual Center), an on-line resource being developed by Appalachian College Association faculty and information technologists. Its mission is to encourage and support efforts to improve teaching and learning by fostering collaboration and sharing resources among Appalachian College Association institutions. The primary goal is to facilitate faculty development through technical collaboration and instructional design.

Most of the colleges have histories dating to the 1800s, with such commonalties that provide a basis for collaboration as a strong Christian commitment, size, governance, complementary degree and academic programs, and a shared belief that faculty development strengthens the institutions broadly, as well as individually. The colleges offer a liberal arts education with emphasis on a strong work ethic, combining education, leadership development, and service to prepare students for responsible citizenship and lifelong learning.

See also: APPALACHIAN CENTERS AND INSTITUTES (CULTURAL INSTITUTIONS); PRIVATE COLLEGES AND UNIVERSITIES.

—Alice W. Brown, *Appalachian College Association*

Appalachian School of Law

The Appalachian School of Law was organized in 1994 by a group of lawyers, judges, and community leaders in southwest Virginia and the Tri-Cities area of upper east Tennessee. In late 1993, Norton, Virginia, attorney Joe Wolfe began discussing his idea for a law school in the area with colleagues who shared his concern that many talented young people had either to give up their dreams of a career in law or leave the area, often permanently. The founders of this independent, not-for-profit institution, located in Grundy, Virginia, hoped to reverse the trend. The steering committee, organized in the fall of 1994 with Wolfe as chair and Lucius Ellsworth as executive secretary, had more than eighty members from five states.

With a commitment to prepare lawyers for the twenty-first century and a curriculum that emphasizes dispute resolution, ethics, professional responsibility, and community leadership, the Appalachian School of Law opened its doors to the charter class of seventy-one students in September 1997. The school's community service program is a fundamental part of the curriculum, and all students must complete twenty-five hours of service work each semester. Embraced by the local community from the beginning, the school steadily grew and by 2005 had a faculty of twenty led by Dean W. Jeremy Davis.

On January 16, 2002, tragedy struck the school. Peter Odighizuwa, expelled for failing grades, killed Dean Anthony Sutin, Professor Thomas Blackwell, and student Angela Dales with a .380 semiautomatic pistol. Three other students were wounded as he continued on a rampage through the building. Upon hearing the shots, students Mikael Gross and Tracy Bridges retrieved guns from their cars and, assisted by Ted Besen, subdued Odighizuwa. The Appalachian School of Law, the community of Grundy, and the nation were horrified by the murders. Odighizuwa went on trial in September 2003. He pled guilty in April 2004 in order to avoid the death penalty and was sentenced to six consecutive life terms plus twenty-eight years on firearms, capital murder, and attempted capital murder charges. The three students wounded in the shootings sued the school, claiming it was negligent in protecting students and faculty from Odighizuwa, who was known to be prone to outbursts.

The law school, which received provisional accreditation from the American Bar Association in February 2001, enrolled 350 full-time students in August 2005, 70 percent of them from Kentucky, North Carolina, Tennessee, Virginia, and West Virginia.

See also: PUBLIC COLLEGES AND UNIVERSITIES; SECTION OVERVIEW.

—Sändra Henson, *East Tennessee State University*

Benham School

Benham, Kentucky, "The Little Town That International Harvester Built," was typical of corporate coal towns built

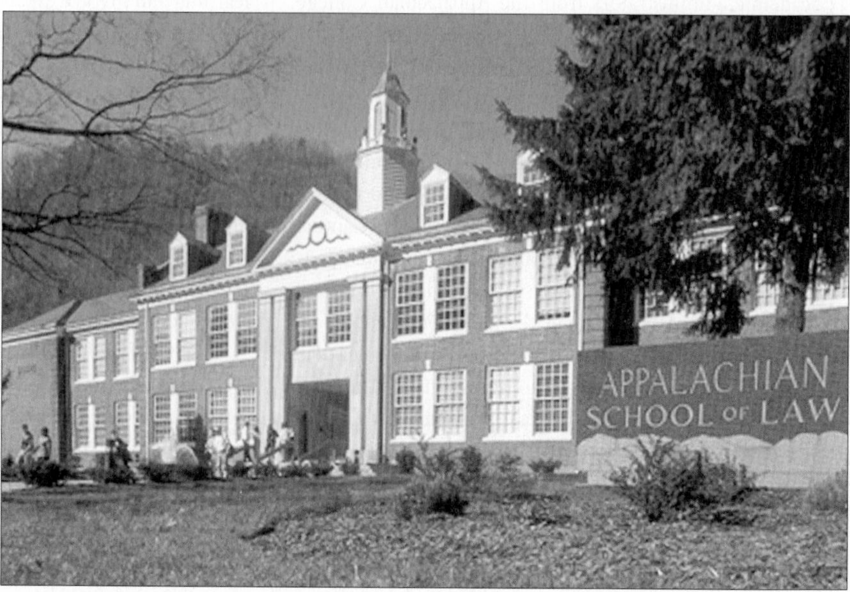

The Appalachian School of Law campus in Grundy, Virginia, 2002. Organized in 1994 by a group of lawyers, judges, and community leaders in central Appalachia, the school was established as an educational avenue for talented Appalachian youth. Seventy percent of students enrolled in August 2005 came from the five states of Kentucky, North Carolina, Tennessee, Virginia, and West Virginia.

from just prior to 1900 to the early 1960s. The Cyrus McCormick family, originally from Steeles Tavern, Virginia, invented the grain reaper and founded International Harvester Company in Chicago. This company became the largest farm implement manufacturer in the world, producing an array of farm equipment, trucks, and earthmoving machinery. Because the McCormicks wished to control every step of the manufacturing process, they established a coal-mining operation at Benham in the far southeastern tip of Kentucky in Harlan County near the Virginia border to provide a steady supply of coal for their Wisconsin Steel mills.

In order to maintain a steady and disciplined workforce in the mountains, International Harvester built a social infrastructure that included a private school system financed by the company and subsidized by public tax dollars. In 1910 a small wood-frame building was built and staffed with eight faculty members. Later, in 1928, a modern brick building modeled after Jeffersonian architecture was erected near the center of town. Another was built nearby to house African American students. Staffed by professional teachers and administrators, the schools offered a comprehensive curriculum including mathematics, physics, and chemistry. John A. Dotson, who held a doctorate from Peabody College, served as superintendent of Benham schools from 1922 to 1944.

Benham was one of the top academic secondary schools in Kentucky, particularly from the 1930s through the 1950s. The last high school class graduated in 1961, and ninth through twelfth grades were then consolidated with the county public school system. The original building continued to be used as an elementary and junior high school until 1992, when it was closed permanently as an education facility.

In the 1990s, a group of alumni purchased, restored, and opened the building as a full-service inn. The Benham School House Inn is currently owned by the Southeast Education Foundation, a nonprofit organization created in 1981 to support Southeast Community College. In 1998 the foundation accepted management responsibility on behalf of the Harlan County Fiscal Court for Benham School House Inn, which operates as a training facility for students enrolled in a two-year Hospitality Management program offered at Southeast Community College.

See also: COAL COMPANY SCHOOLS.

—James B. Goode, *Lexington Community College*

Berea College

Berea College, founded in 1855 by abolitionist John G. Fee and others, began as a district school located in southern Madison County, Kentucky. Built by Fee and some neighbors on ten acres of land donated by emancipationist Cassius Marcellus Clay, the college was the only institution of higher education for Kentucky blacks during the antebellum period and the only biracial institution in any slaveholding state. However, Berea closed in 1859 when its cofounders were forced out of state by slavery sympathizers. Classes did not resume until 1866, after the Civil War had ended. The college thereafter committed itself to interracial education, drawing students from two immediate constituencies: African Americans freed by the Civil War and "loyal" white mountaineers. In Berea's early years, at least half of the students were African American, and the college maintained its diversity until forced to segregate in 1904 with the passage of the Kentucky Day Law, which forbade interracial education in the state.

Berea College came to national attention during the presidency of William Goodell Frost, who was originally from New York. Arriving in Berea in 1892, Frost quickly emphasized work among mountain people, and the college's publicity literature promoted Berea's "discovery" of the people of the southern Appalachian Mountains, whom he called "our contemporary ancestors." While expanding the college's educational program, Frost also built up the school's endowment, engaging the philanthropic support of such luminaries as Andrew Carnegie and Woodrow Wilson. The labor program, based in part on the revival of Appalachian handicrafts, provided students with employment in order to help them meet the costs of education. In 1911 the college's charter declared the study of Appalachia Berea's primary area of concentration.

At the start of the twenty-first century, Berea's educational efforts in Appalachia continue, with 80 percent of all enrolled students coming from the region. Reintegrated in 1950, Berea renewed its commitment to interracial education. The labor program, including handicraft industries, complements a strong liberal arts curriculum, making Berea one of Appalachia's leading colleges.

See also: FIRESIDE INDUSTRIES (CRAFTS); FROST, WILLIAM GOODELL AND ELEANOR MARSH; KENTUCKY DAY LAW AND THE BEREA COLLEGE CASE (GOVERNMENT).

—Shannon H. Wilson, *Berea College*

Blab Schools

Blab schools—so called because students studied lessons by repeating, or "blabbing," them aloud in unison or individually—were common throughout America in pioneer times and continued longer in Appalachia than in other parts of the country. The supporting pedagogical belief was that children learned better by doing lessons aloud. Because schools were usually confined to one room, the teacher had several age groups studying different subjects at the same time. While the teacher was involved with one group, the other children were directed to recite their lessons aloud, thus assuring the teacher that they were studying.

One report about a Marshall County, West Virginia, school explained that children read, spelled, and ciphered "out loud" in part because there was a shortage of paper, pencils, and slates. In 1890 one teacher in an Appalachian church mission school told about children "studying at the top of their voices," noting that the students in his more progressive school, except for the younger ones, had previously been in blab schools.

Abraham Lincoln attended a blab school in Kentucky, and it made such an impression on him that he later reportedly irritated his law partner by reading his newspaper aloud, claiming that he remembered the content better if he used "two senses." In *Theirs Be the Power: The Moguls of Eastern Kentucky*, Harry Caudill wrote that John C. C. Mayo, Kentucky's homegrown coal baron, learned his letters in a blab school "presided over by a teacher that had never seen a college." Blab schools dwindled over time, disappearing from Appalachia by the early twentieth century.

See also: CAUDILL, HARRY (HUMOR); ONE-ROOM SCHOOLS.

—Loyal Jones, *Berea, Kentucky*

Black Mountain College

Black Mountain College was a small, progressive, experimental liberal arts institution founded in 1933 near Black Mountain, North Carolina. Owned and operated by its faculty, it was committed to democratic governance and to the idea that the arts are central to the experience of learning. Black Mountain set no course requirements and gave no grades until grading became necessary to facilitate its students' admission into graduate school. All members of the college community participated in its operation and upkeep through agricultural work, construction projects, kitchen chores, and other duties. The result was a close-knit community committed to experiencing life with intensity and passion.

Among the early faculty members were Bauhaus artists Josef and Anni Albers, who had fled Germany and brought with them an emphasis on abstract art. The designer-craftsman ideal was emphasized in workshops in woodworking, weaving, and other crafts. The first American presentations of "performance theater" in the mid-1930s emerged from classes at Black Mountain. In addition to working on the property, each student developed an individual program of study in consultation with an advisor.

Beginning in 1944, the college hosted summer institutes characterized by groundbreaking work in the arts. Composer John Cage and Merce Cunningham of the Martha Graham Dance Company experimented with music and choreography independent of feeling or narrative and developed compositional strategies using chance and indeterminacy. Buckminster Fuller, noted architect and designer, experimented with alternative materials for dome construction. The published work of the "Black Mountain poets," a group that came to include such noted writers as Charles Olson, Denise Levertov, and Robert Creeley, helped to establish the legendary status of the college.

After 1949, Black Mountain College became primarily a community of artists working in an atmosphere of experimentation. Although the institution closed in 1956, the powerful influence of Black Mountain College continues to reverberate. Having attracted and cultivated maverick spirits, many of the school's faculty and graduates went on to become well-known and influential individuals in the arts in the latter half of the twentieth century. The Black Mountain College Museum and Arts Center was established in 1993 to commemorate and publicize Black Mountain College's legacy of educational and artistic innovation.

See also: SECTION OVERVIEW (PERFORMING ARTS).

—Alice Sebrell and Susan Eike Spalding, *Berea College*

Campbell, Alexander

See Campbell, Alexander (Religion)

Campbell, John C. and Olive Dame

Campbell, John C. (1867–1919) Educator and social researcher.

Campbell, Olive Dame (1882–1954) Educator and ballad collector.

John Charles Campbell was born in Indiana and studied education and theology. He is best known as a minister, educator, and social researcher who led the way for a greater understanding of the culture and geography of Appalachia. Olive Dame Campbell, his wife, was born in Massachusetts and is known for founding the John C. Campbell Folk School in North Carolina, as well as for her collection of Appalachian folk music.

During the early 1900s, when the southern mountains attracted a number of educational, social, and religious missionary workers, John Campbell followed his calling to help the people of Appalachia. Along with Olive, he traveled from 1908 to 1909 in a covered wagon collecting information about the social conditions of mountain residents from Georgia to West Virginia. His findings led to the establishment of the Council of the Southern Mountains, a venture funded by the Russell Sage Foundation, and the creation of the first map identifying Appalachia as a distinct region in the United States. While John met with farmers and recorded the history, geography, and culture of Appalachia, Olive spent her time gathering the creative handiwork of these people.

She learned techniques and designs of their arts and crafts, and she collected hymns, ballads, and folk songs. Along with Cecil Sharp, a leading English musicologist, Olive published *English Folk Songs from the Southern Appalachians* in 1917.

Two years after John's death in 1919, his research on the history, geography, and culture of Appalachia was published in *The Southern Highlander and His Homeland.* The book prepared the way for further studies on the people of Appalachia. Meanwhile, Philander P. Claxton, executive secretary of the Conference for Southern Education, recommended that Olive consider starting a school similar in format to the northern European *folkehøjskole* (folk high school). During the early 1920s, she traveled throughout Scandinavia with Marguerite Butler studying education. Denmark had established the folk high school as a means to educate local people while at the same time preserving their ways of life. After considering several locations, she presented her plan to Fred Scroggs, a business leader in Brasstown, Cherokee County, North Carolina, and Scroggs donated about seventy-five acres for school property. The local community responded with overwhelming enthusiasm, and with support from the Carnegie Corporation, the John C. Campbell Folk School was incorporated in 1925 and opened in December 1927.

The John C. Campbell Folk School quickly became a center for learning about wood carving, basketry, weaving, pottery, music, dance, art, and related handiwork of southern Appalachia. The Campbells had always believed that education was the key to improving the quality of life among southern Appalachians, and they were concerned that too many mountain folk were leaving their family farms to work in textile mills. The folk school provided an alternative form of education to preserve Appalachian culture and to keep young people in the region. Following up the early successes of the school, Olive published *The Danish Folk School: Its Influence in the Life of Denmark and the North* in 1928 and was instrumental in the founding of the Southern Highland Handicraft Guild.

See also: JOHN C. CAMPBELL FOLK SCHOOL (CRAFTS); SHARP, CECIL (FOLKLORE AND FOLKLIFE).

—Eric G. Lovik, *Pennsylvania State University*

Richard B. Drake, *A History of Appalachia* (2001); John Alexander Williams, *Appalachia: A History* (2002).

Cherokee Education

Living today in Swain, Cherokee, Graham, and Jackson Counties in North Carolina, the Eastern Band of Cherokee Indians is comprised of the descendants of those tribe members who remained in Appalachia after the U.S. Army forced the Cherokee to relocate to present-day Oklahoma in 1838–39. The area, often referred to as the Qualla Boundary, consists of some 56,500 acres held in federal trust for the Cherokee. Prior to the influence of European settlers, traditional education for Cherokee children was a family and tribal responsibility. Children were taught in many ways, including through storytelling and experiences. Like most Native American people, however, the Cherokee were subjected to governmental and missionary acculturation programs that attempted to make them like neighboring white people. These civilization programs were most conspicuous in educational programming.

"Civilizing" the Cherokee was thought to be a method of saving them from their culture by making them more like white Anglo-Saxon Protestants. At that time, the dominant culture defined civilized people as Christians who knew how to read and write in English. Missionaries and their educational programming were the government's primary agents of change. Their actions, coupled with international, national, southern, state, regional, and internal events, completely transformed the world of the Eastern Band Cherokee.

During the late 1700s and early 1800s, missionaries established mission posts and opened schools for the Cherokee in western North Carolina. These schools placed strong emphasis on rigid cultural controls and saw educating youth as the primary vehicle for resocialization. While the Cherokee were primarily interested in having their children learn to read and write in English, some of the missionaries wanted only to convert the Cherokee to Christianity. Consequently, the Cherokee in 1880 threatened to evict the Quakers unless their educational demands were met.

The Indian Peace Commission, established by Congress in 1867 to investigate the conditions of Native Americans, issued a report the following year that indicated a lack of success with some civilization programs due to the diversity of languages. The solution, the commissioners concluded, was to teach in English, thus eliminating native languages. This led to a decision by the Bureau of Indian Affairs to require that only English be spoken in the schools, an edict strictly enforced by the late 1880s.

The General Appropriations Act of 1870, passed not long after the report of the Indian Peace Commission, provided funds for Indian education and was regarded as a milestone. Specifically, it mandated fewer subsidies for missionaries operating Indian schools and fostered the development of off-reservation boarding schools. The main objective of these schools was to remove children from family and tribal influences and to instill values and perspectives of white Americans. Parents were often coerced into sending their young children to boarding schools on the grounds that they would become better equipped to survive in the white man's world.

Quakers from Indiana opened the first boarding school on the Qualla Boundary in 1881 and operated it under a ten-year contract with the Cherokee. In 1892 the school was taken over by the Bureau of Indian Affairs, which ran it in a military manner, with students being required to wear uniforms and report for roll call at various times throughout the day. The facility had its own bakery, kitchen, dairy, and garden, and students actively competed for assignment to the most desirable jobs. Students provided most of their own food products and performed much of the maintenance of their school facilities. Classes consisted primarily of basics in mathematics, reading, and English usage. Students caught speaking Cherokee would have their mouths washed with soap and in some instances were beaten. Boys took courses in agriculture while girls were taught home economics. Not all students attending the school were live-in students. Those who lived nearby often came to the school during the day, went home each evening, and wore their own clothing rather than uniforms provided by the school.

When community-based schools became firmly established in the 1930s, attendance at boarding schools began to decline, which led to their closing in the 1950s. The modern-day school system of the Eastern Band Cherokee is locally governed. There are three schools in the system, all located on the Qualla Boundary: Cherokee Elementary School, Cherokee Middle School, and Cherokee High School. The new $7.5-million high school was designed to encourage Cherokee youth to remain in school. The schools' mission includes reiterating an awareness of cultural identity through instruction in Cherokee language, arts and crafts, games, and history.

See also: CHEROKEE (RACE, ETHNICITY, AND IDENTITY); QUAKERS (RELIGION).

—Elizabeth Rodgers Coulter, *Western Carolina University*

Laurence French and Jim Hornbuckle, eds., *The Cherokee Perspective* (1981); Joan Greene, "Civilize the Indian: Government Policies, Quakers and Cherokee Education," *Journal of Cherokee Studies* (Fall 1985); Theda Perdue, *The Cherokee* (1989).

Christiansburg Institute

Christiansburg Institute in Montgomery County, Virginia, was established in 1866 to provide an education for recently freed slaves and operated until 1966, ending a one-hundred-year history as a distinctive Appalachian institution. State records reveal that Christiansburg Institute was recognized for its academic excellence, receiving state and regional accreditation long before local white schools.

Charles Schaeffer, a Union captain assigned to the Freedmen's Bureau, established the school in a small frame building in Cambria, just outside the town of Christiansburg.

Booker T. Washington speaks to a crowd at Christiansburg Institute in Montgomery County, Virginia, 1909. Washington served as school supervisor at Christiansburg from 1896 until his death in 1915. Established in 1866 to educate recently freed slaves, the institute was one of only four high schools in Virginia that served African Americans in the early twentieth century.

With the impending dissolution of the Freedmen's Bureau, the Friends Freedmen's Association of Philadelphia, a philanthropic arm of the Society of Friends (Quakers), began to support the school. In the 1870s, the school expanded into a new two-story wooden schoolhouse, and in 1885 a large brick structure was built for classrooms on what became known as Zion's Hill. In 1896 noted educator Booker T. Washington became the institute's school supervisor, a position he held until his death in 1915. Washington, founder of the Tuskegee Institute, brought his philosophy of practical education and a vocational element to the existing curriculum. In 1896, in order to provide room for added trades and a growing school population, a nearby farm was purchased. Christiansburg Institute moved to an 85-acre tract of land two miles away, where a former plantation house served as the main classroom building and renovated slave cabins as male dormitories.

In 1904 Christiansburg Institute was one of only four high schools for African Americans in Virginia. Under the leadership of Charles Lives Marshall and Edgar Allen Long, two of the institute's most distinguished African American principals, the campus grew to include 185 acres by the early 1920s and boasted three Georgian brick halls that housed dormitories, classrooms, a library, and a hospital. Near these were two faculty cottages, a dairy, a barn, and a shop building, all surrounded by fields, gardens, and an orchard.

By 1924 the institute was accredited by the Virginia State Board of Education and in 1932 by the Southern Association of Colleges and Secondary Schools. During the 1930s and 1940s, the Friends Freedmen's Association convinced public school board officials to take responsibility for educating African American citizens. In 1934 the association donated the elementary department of the institute to Montgomery County. It also leased the farm campus as a public regional high school, eventually donating it in 1947 to the school boards of Montgomery and Pulaski Counties and the city of Radford.

The passage of the 1964 Civil Rights Act, which called for integration of the nation's schools, brought an end to Christiansburg Institute, as the public school boards involved voted to abandon the school rather than integrate it. As a result, the campus was eventually sold, neglected, and largely demolished. In 1976 an alumni organization was formed to recapture the school's history, and in 1996 Christiansburg Institute, Inc., was founded to restore and reopen the historic Edgar A. Long Building as an archive, museum, and learning center focused on African American education after emancipation.

See also: AFRICAN AMERICAN FAMILIES AND COMMUNITIES (FAMILY AND COMMUNITY); CIVIL RIGHTS MOVEMENT (RACE, ETHNICITY, AND IDENTITY).

—M. Anna Fariello, *Virginia Polytechnic Institute and State University*

Coal Company Schools

At the beginning of the twentieth century, privately and corporately owned coal camps began to move into the coal-rich regions of Appalachia in large numbers. Because most of these areas lacked an appropriate infrastructure to support laborers and their families, coal companies often constructed entire cities in the middle of a wilderness. In 1917, for example, the U.S. Coal and Coke Company, a subsidiary of U.S. Steel, built the community of Lynch, Kentucky, then the world's largest coal camp. The town's public buildings were constructed of cut sandstone and included a company commissary, post office, theater, hotel, hospital, churches, and schools. Providing an education for the children of coal laborers was important because doing so helped facilitate having a stable workforce. However, because most mine laborers in the late nineteenth and early twentieth centuries were single males, the construction and maintenance of schools did not come to the mining districts until after 1910, when coal companies found it desirable to seek a more permanent, family-based labor force.

Coal companies generally built schools on land they owned and provided supplies and teachers, which were financed by an "education fee" deducted each month from miners' wages. The design of schools often resembled that of churches in the towns. Because segregation was common until the 1960s, two small buildings were usually constructed —one for educating white children and another for blacks. The school for white children generally consisted of a two-story, four-room structure; the black school was usually a two-room, one-story structure.

Although these schools were privately owned and received their primary financial support from family or corporate entities, they were also subsidized from county school system tax revenues. Teachers and administrators often met or, in many cases, exceeded the state standards for school personnel. One teacher who worked in the mining camps of eastern Kentucky during the 1920s recalled that she received compensation of twenty-five dollars more per month than did the county teachers. Although the quality of education in such schools varied widely, some were exceptional. For example, Benham School, located in Benham, Kentucky, became one of the top academic secondary schools in the state, particularly from the 1930s through the 1950s. Other coal company schools had ultramodern athletic facilities with elaborate gymnasiums and football stadiums and offered foreign languages, industrial arts, home economics, forensics, and other specialized courses.

The more prominent companies that operated coal-camp schools included Bethlehem Mines Corporation; Blue Diamond Coal Company; Consolidation Coal Company; Elkhom Coal Company; Fordson Coal Company; Inland Steel Company; International Harvester Company; Island Creek Coal Company; Koppers Coal Company; Monongahela River Consolidated Coal and Coke Company; Pocahontas Fuel Company; Tennessee Iron and Railway Company; United States Coal and Coke Company; Virginia Iron, Coal and Coke Company; West Virginia Coal and Coke Corporation; United States Steel Corporation; and Youghiogheny and Ohio Coal Company.

As coal companies began to divest themselves of non-mining interests beginning in the late 1950s, many company schools were merged with public school systems.

See also: BENHAM SCHOOL; COAL SETTLEMENTS (SETTLEMENT AND MIGRATION); COAL TOWNS (FAMILY AND COMMUNITY).

—James B. Goode, *Lexington Community College*

Ronald D Eller, *Miners, Millhands, and Mountaineers: Industrialization of the Appalachian South, 1880–1930* (1982); Crandall A. Shifflett, *Coal Towns: Life, Work, and Culture in Company Towns of Southern Appalachia, 1880–1960* (1991); W. P. Tams Jr., *The Smokeless Coal Fields of West Virginia: A Brief History* (1963; reprint 2001).

Cordia School

Cordia School is a public-private educational organization jointly operated by the Knott County Board of Education and Lotts Creek Community School, Inc., a private, nonprofit corporation, tracing its roots back to 1933, when the school was founded by Alice Slone. The school is the center of and serves Lotts Creek, a once isolated community in Knott County, Kentucky, some ten miles north of Hazard. Because poor roads made daily travel an obstacle for many students, Cordia continued to operate as a residential school into the 1970s.

Originally, the school was one of many settlement schools in southeastern Kentucky that were public-private collaborations; however, today it is the only such school still operational. Other settlement schools were absorbed into consolidated systems by the early 1970s or assumed new roles in their respective communities. In 1998 Cordia moved into a modern classroom complex built by Lotts Creek Community School, Inc., and funded entirely by contributions of private donors. Nearly three hundred students were enrolled as of 2003.

Augmenting Cordia's conventional preschool and K–12 educational offerings, the Lotts Creek Community School Corporation provides financial assistance to all Cordia graduates who continue their studies in college or vocational school. As many as 75 percent of Cordia's graduates go on to college, and many of them go on to professional schools, becoming physicians, lawyers, pharmacists, nurses, engineers, police officers, and educators. Several of the school's former students have returned to teach at Cordia.

See also: SCHOOL CONSOLIDATION; SETTLEMENT, MISSION, AND SPONSORED SCHOOLS.

—Alice S. Whitaker, *Lotts Creek Community School, Inc.*

Council on Appalachian Women

In October 1976, approximately two hundred women representing seven Appalachian states gathered at Appalachian State University at Boone, North Carolina, to discuss issues and needs of women and girls in the region. Enthusiasm generated by the meeting, held under the auspices of the National Advisory Council on Women's Educational Programs, led to further consultation with thirty-five women at Mars Hill College in December 1976 and creation of the Council on Appalachian Women in February 1977. The nonprofit organization was dedicated to the advancement of Appalachian women in the areas of education, services, and research.

In 1979 the Appalachian Regional Commission awarded the council a $54,630 grant, marking the first federal support of women's efforts to improve their situation throughout the Appalachian region. Each Appalachian governor appointed a state representative to the council.

Among the council's activities were two series of forums funded by the North Carolina Humanities Committee: "Images of Appalachian Women" (1978–79) and "The Essence of the Appalachian Woman" (1979–80). At least one forum was held in each of North Carolina's twenty-nine Appalachian counties and consisted of presentations, individual or panel respondents, and general discussion. The abstracts of some of these presentations were published as *The Appalachian Woman: Images and Essence*, edited by Pauline Cheek (1980).

The primary goal of the council was "to set up a communication network for women in the region." The council published a newsletter with information about employment, legislation, conferences, training and educational workshops, and other issues of relevance to women in Appalachia. In 1978 the council purchased *MAW: A Magazine of Appalachian Women* from its editor-publisher Miriam Ralston but published only two issues. In order to remain solvent, the council's board of directors agreed to give the magazine to the Women's Counseling Center of West Virginia in February 1981.

The Council on Appalachian Women remained in operation until May 1981, when the office closed due to lack of funding. The council was served by three executive directors: Jeanne Hoffman, from May 1978 until June 1979; Constance Mahoney, from January until June 1980; and Ethelene Brasington, selected in January 1981 to serve as executive director for the duration of the contract with the Appalachian Regional Commission.

During its tenure, the council spawned a number of local activities for women participants and contributed to the establishment of the national nonprofit group Rural American Women. As an umbrella organization that included rural women, academics, businesswomen, and political and social activists, the council struggled to find a political and social agenda to satisfy its disparate constituencies and disbanded due to inadequate funding. The papers of the Council on Appalachian Women are located in the Archives of Appalachia at East Tennessee State University.

See also: APPALACHIAN REGIONAL COMMISSION (GOVERNMENT).

—Patricia D. Beaver, *Appalachian State University*

Pauline Cheek, ed., *The Appalachian Woman: Images and Essence* (1980); Council on Appalachian Women, *MAW: A Magazine of Appalachian Women* (Fall and Winter 1979).

Fotched-on Women

Fotched is the obsolete past tense of the verb *to fetch* (Old English *feccan*), which meant "to go in quest of and convey or conduct back." Hence was created the descriptive *fotched-on*, the colloquial root meaning of which is "brought from a distance." The term appears fairly frequently in print after 1910, its tone ranging from mildly to strongly pejorative, although not necessarily so.

The term was used (principally in eastern Kentucky, it appears) among local people to refer to women who came from outside the region (mainly Bluegrass Kentucky and New England) beginning in the 1890s to found and work in educational, cultural, medical, recreational, and religious programs and institutions. Their work was frequently intertwined with and supported by state and national church, women's, and philanthropic organizations. In often repeated accounts, they sometimes came at the behest of a venerable old man of the mountains: the shaggy, anonymous patriarch who as early as 1891 implored Susan Chester, founder of the Log Cabin Settlement (Asheville, North Carolina), to find help for his ailing granddaughter; Uncle Sol Everidge (Hindman Settlement School, Hindman, Kentucky, 1901); Uncle William Creech (Pine Mountain Settlement School, Kentucky, 1913); and Uncle Luce Scroggs (John C. Campbell Folk School, Brasstown, North Carolina, 1925).

So diverse were these women in background, personality, perspective, mission, and method that few generalizations about them withstand scrutiny. In many fictional treatments by local color and other writers (for example, in Lucy Furman's *Mothering on Perilous* [1913] and *The Quare Women* [1923]), fotched-on women are depicted as virtuous and high-principled Christians and altruistic servants of mountain people—bringers of the blessings of modernity. Among actual women who exemplified these ideals were Mary Breckinridge (Frontier Nursing Service), Olive Dame Campbell (John C. Campbell Folk School), Frances Goodrich (Allanstand Cottage Industries), Alice Lloyd (Caney Creek School, now Alice Lloyd College), Katherine Pettit (Hindman and Pine Mountain Settlement Schools), and May Stone (Hindman Settlement School).

In other works, local mountain people are not infrequently depicted as resenting and distrusting fotched-on women. In John Fox Jr.'s *The Heart of the Hills* (1913), a fotched-on woman who "had given up her beloved Bluegrass land, . . . left home and kindred, and . . . settled, two days' journey from a railroad, in the hills" to help mountaineers is characterized by local people as a distrusted "furriner." Some recent commentators have argued that some of the women served as unwitting legitimizing agents of an advancing industrial capitalism that entailed high social and cultural costs for mountain environments, communities, and people.

A broader meaning of *fotched-on* as "artificial, inferior, culturally incongruent" is evident in Charles Neville Buck's *Call of the Cumberlands* (1913), which refers to the superiority of moonshine liquor to the "fotched-on substitute" and to the "fotched-on" clothing and thoughts of a local mountain boy just returned from attending law school "down below." Related usages occur in two Ann Cobb poems from the 1920s. "Kivers" refers to natural, authentic "home-dyed colors" that "kindly meller [mellow] down," unlike the synthetic, manufactured "fotched-on ones from town." In "Up Carr Creek," the term stands broadly for the alien and suspect "ways of the world" as opposed to familiar and trusted local ones: "Biled shirts and neckties, / Powder-pots and veils, / Pizen fotched-on liquor, / Doctor-pills, and ails."

The term continues to have some currency. Pejorative uses survive, as do neutral and descriptive ones, as in one scholar's suggestion that it might be applied to members of the widely and justifiably admired Glenmary Sisters who came to do outreach work in the region beginning in the early 1940s. Phil Primack, a former reporter for the *Mountain Eagle* newspaper in Letcher County, Kentucky, recently described himself as "a Yankee newcomer, fotched-on, as it were," when he arrived in the county in the late 1960s. *Harlan Daily Enterprise* writer Charlotte Nolan recalls that when a new local hospital opened in the 1950s, "someone compiled a little dictionary of words and expressions often used by the local gentry which confused the hospital's 'fotched-on' doctors . . . and other personnel." Such a usage implies that they were merely innocent and not conversant with local culture.

See also: FRONTIER NURSING SERVICE (HEALTH); OUTSIDERS AND SUMMER PEOPLE (IMAGES AND ICONS); SETTLEMENT, MISSION, AND SPONSORED SCHOOLS.

—David E. Whisnant, *Chapel Hill, North Carolina*

Charlotte Nolan, "Mountain Expressions Confusing to Outsiders," *Harlan Daily Enterprise* (August 20, 2003); David E. Whisnant, *All That Is Native and Fine: The Politics of Culture in an American Region* (1983) and "Second-Level Appalachian History: Another Look at Some Fotched-On Women," *Appalachian Journal* (Winter–Spring 1982).

Foxfire

In 1966, students in Eliot Wigginton's high school language arts classes at Rabun Gap–Nacoochee School in northeast Georgia started a publication about Appalachian folklore called *Foxfire Magazine*, named after the colloquial designation for a fungus commonly found in the region's forests. Eventually, the term *Foxfire* came to refer to a series of best-selling books about Appalachian folkways, then later to a general approach to teaching imitated across the nation.

Wigginton's idea of a student publication about regional folkways began when his classes started transcribing interviews they had conducted with local residents and turning them into narratives for the magazine. When the people in Rabun County liked the magazine's contents, Wigginton realized he had "stumbled onto something that made sense" pedagogically. As the students worked to produce quality narratives for a real audience, their reading and composition skills improved dramatically. The experiences also led the classes to appreciate the skills and resilience of their own culture, causing them to shed hillbilly stereotypes.

Foxfire attained national prominence beginning in 1972 with Doubleday's publication of *The Foxfire Book*, an anthology of the best narratives from the magazine. Released just as Americans yearned for connections to the past to offset the depersonalization of modern life, the book quickly became a best-seller and a how-to manual for back-to-earth pioneers. As of 2003, Doubleday had published eleven volumes of the *Foxfire* books, with a twelfth volume soon to be released. E. P. Dutton has also published five single-topic volumes, including *The Foxfire Book of Toys and Games* and *A Foxfire Christmas*.

Classroom teachers, hungry for innovative and effective instructional strategies, approached Wigginton to learn how to "do Foxfire" in their own classrooms. In 1972 a $196,000 grant from the Ford Foundation funded a collaboration between Foxfire and the Institutional Development and Economic Affairs Service to provide systematic training to twelve culturally distinct areas, including Native American reservations, remote towns in Alaska, rural areas in South Carolina, and African American neighborhoods in major cities. This initiative stimulated a deepening of the theoretical underpinnings of Foxfire, beginning a particularly fruitful engagement with John Dewey's concepts of education.

At its peak in this "cultural journalism" phase, Foxfire tracked more than 130 similar high school programs around the country, plus seventeen in nations abroad. As a means of keeping the various programs connected, the staff created a newsletter called *Hands On*.

Wigginton and students created a nonprofit organization, the Foxfire Fund, Inc., and used it to guide distribution of the royalties from the Foxfire books. In 1971 and 1973, Wigginton and the fund purchased 110 acres on the side of Black Rock Mountain in Rabun County. Over the next several years, Foxfire students and local craftsmen moved to "the Land," twenty-four old log structures donated by people interested in the preservation of Appalachian culture. With a continuous flow of donated tools and artifacts, the ensemble of buildings took on the form of a mid-nineteenth-century Appalachian village.

In 1976 Wigginton moved the program to Rabun County High School, and the following year a newly constructed comprehensive secondary school was opened, with some teachers using Wigginton's approach to teaching. There the Foxfire program expanded to six classroom teachers at its peak in 1990, launching the separate series of single-focus books published by Dutton.

In 1977 Hume Cronyn and Susan Cooper approached Wigginton with the concept of a play inspired by Aunt Arie, one of the books' most distinctive interlocutors. After refinements by students, *Foxfire* opened in New York in 1982. In 1987 Cronin and Jessica Tandy reprised their roles for a television version of the play. The Foxfire Museum and Center in Mountain City, Georgia, opened in 1991.

As Foxfire's primary entry in the national debate over how to improve schooling, Wigginton wrote *Sometimes a Shining Moment* (1985), combining his narrative of how Foxfire happened with an exposition of its pedagogical possibilities. Immediately afterward, in 1986, the Bingham Trust for Charity awarded $1.5 million to Foxfire to initiate a major teacher outreach program. The outreach program grew to twenty-two networks in sixteen states at its peak and included teachers from all grade levels and all subject fields.

Foxfire exerted considerable influence on the instructional practices of individual teachers interested in implementing authentic learning to replace rote, textbook-driven teaching. The program anticipated many of the more recent progressive strands of pedagogic revisionism, including experiential education, active learning, democratic classrooms, constructivism, authentic assessment, and place-centered schooling. Participants in the program developed a set of "core practices," pulling together the accumulated wisdom of Foxfire practitioners into ten general concepts toward which teachers could align their instructional practices. These practices included doing class work that related to students' interests and concerns and that incorporated their community's values. Wigginton's work and that of the thousands of Foxfire-inspired teachers clearly indicate that students acquire the fundamentals best when they apply them to an enterprise in which they are invested.

See also: WIGGINTON, ELIOT.

—Hilton Smith, *Piedmont College*

Linda Garland Page and Eliot Wigginton, *Aunt Arie: A Foxfire Portrait* (1983); John L. Puckett, *Foxfire Reconsidered: A Twenty-Year Experiment in Progressive Education* (1989); Eliot Wigginton, *Sometimes a Shining Moment: The Foxfire Experience* (1985).

Frost, William Goodell and Eleanor Marsh

Frost, William Goodell (1854–1938) College president and education reformer.

Frost, Eleanor Marsh (1863–1950) Educator.

William Goodell Frost, president of Berea College in Kentucky from 1892 to 1920, regarded himself as the discoverer of the southern Appalachian people and their culture. He is noted for coining the phrase "our contemporary ancestors," which first appeared in an article Frost wrote for the March 1899 edition of the *Atlantic Monthly*. Entitled "Our Contemporary Ancestors in the Southern Mountains," the piece significantly influenced the way larger America viewed Appalachian people for several decades into the twentieth century.

The eldest son of the Reverend Lewis P. and Maria Goodell Frost and the grandson of abolitionist William Goodell, Frost grew up in Leroy, New York. Educated at Oberlin College, he taught Greek for several years before moving to Berea. Frost was known as a scholar, reformer, orator, evangelist, politician, and enthusiast, and he was a charismatic leader.

Early in his presidency, Frost explored the mountain areas to learn about the region and its people. This exploration inspired his focused commitment to mountaineer education and "uplift." Frost's second wife, Eleanor Marsh Frost (1863–1950), whom he met while at Oberlin College, was a powerful helpmate to him and established herself as a sympathetic and enthusiastic advocate for Berea College and its students. Following the birth of the couple's two children, Eleanor assumed an increasing role in speaking on behalf of the college to raise money. Noted for helping to shape the college's domestic science curriculum, the educator frequently made trips to the mountains and advocated that the school's offerings more actively reflect the realities of life in the mountains.

William Frost was particularly interested in mountain handicrafts, regarding them as symbolic of mountaineer independence. He purchased several homespun coverlets during his visits into the mountains and displayed them during his fund-raising trips. Finding that donors wanted to buy the weavings, Frost encouraged the making of linens, rugs, and coverlets for sale, and homespun items became a way by which students could offset their school expenses. In 1896 the first Homespun Fair was held during the college's commencement week. Prizes were given for the best work, and exhibitors were allowed to sell their wares, which, in addition to various weavings, included kettle dyes, baskets, knitting, leatherwork, and handmade furniture.

Berea College's Fireside Industries (known internationally as the Berea College Student Crafts Program) was a significant catalyst in the revival of handicrafts in southern Appalachia. While the crafts program was driven by the market and the need to provide work for students, Frost and others at Berea believed it was essential to preserve mountain arts from obscurity, if not from extinction. Thus the coverlet, the basket, and the axe handle became important symbols in the efforts to bring financial and educational support to Appalachian people.

In 1895 Frost launched the *Berea Quarterly*, the earliest periodical devoted to southern mountain life and culture. By 1911, Berea College's constitution had been amended to make the college's special field the study of Appalachia. Frost's efforts brought national attention to the region and to the college, expanding its academic, vocational, and extension programs and increasing enrollment from 350 to 2,400 students and the school's endowment from $100,000 to more than $2 million. Plagued by illness for much of his career, Frost retired in 1920. His memoir, *For the Mountains*, was published shortly before his death in 1938.

See also: BEREA COLLEGE; FIRESIDE INDUSTRIES (CRAFTS); "OUR CONTEMPORARY ANCESTORS IN THE SOUTHERN MOUNTAINS" (LITERATURE).

—Deborah L. Blackwell, *Texas A&M International University;* Sidney Saylor Farr, *Berea College;* and Shannon H. Wilson, *Berea College*

William Goodell Frost, "Our Contemporary Ancestors in the Southern Mountains," *Atlantic Monthly* (March 1899); Elisabeth S. Peck and Emily Ann Smith, *Berea's First 125 Years: 1855–1980* (1982).

Hambidge Center for Creative Arts and Sciences

See Hambidge Center for Creative Arts and Sciences (Crafts)

Highlander Research and Education Center

Located twenty-five miles east of Knoxville, Tennessee, the Highlander Research and Education Center is a residential adult education center dedicated to democratic instruction and social change. Founded in 1932 during the Great Depression, the center has thrived for seventy years in Tennessee in three locations. The educational philosophy has always been that mountain people are best suited to solve problems they face in their own communities. Highlander has sought to help these people gain information and to meet others working on similar issues.

First known as Highlander Folk School and located on the Cumberland Plateau in Monteagle, the center was founded by Myles Horton, who had grown up in rural Tennessee and studied at Union Theological Seminary and the University of Chicago. Horton's ideas for an adult education center crystallized when he spent a year visiting Danish folk schools, observing community people gathering to discuss problems and using music, history, and stories to strengthen their knowledge and confidence. He concluded that a similar approach might work in the southern mountains.

In its earliest years Highlander developed both a community program for farmers and unemployed coal and timber workers and their families and an extension program for industrial and rural workers. As the depression deepened social unrest in the 1930s, the staff at Highlander encouraged students to view their efforts as part of a growing labor movement. The school became known as a regional center for workers' education. Horton's wife, Zilphia Johnson Horton, and others infused the program with music and theater.

Racism and Jim Crow laws hindered the work of the school throughout the 1930s and 1940s. In the early 1950s, the staff decided to confront issues of segregation more directly. Septima Clark, fired from her job as a schoolteacher in South Carolina for belonging to the National Association for the Advancement of Colored People, became Highlander's director of education. From communities across the South, workshops brought together leaders and activists who were challenging racist laws and restrictions against voting. Rosa Parks visited Highlander shortly before she refused to give up her seat on a Montgomery bus, triggering the historic boycott that heralded the Civil Rights movement in the South. In April 1960, Highlander hosted the first regionwide gathering of students involved in sit-ins. Myles Horton challenged the students to consider the longterm implications of their campaign, including dropping out of school or spending periods in jail. Staff member Guy Carawan taught them the song "We Shall Overcome" and other tunes that had been important at Highlander throughout the labor period.

Highlander's staff, along with a community leader named Esau Jenkins, created the Citizenship School Program, which gave people the literacy skills needed to pass a voter registration test and the encouragement to organize politically to use the vote strategically. The program began in the South Carolina Sea Islands but eventually spread throughout the South.

Challenging the entrenched southern power structure and holding integrated residential workshops, the school became increasingly controversial and its ideas were resisted as "a cancer spreading over the South." In the late 1950s, several southern governors and white leaders conspired to close the "Communist training school" by bringing charges against it, and in 1961 the Monteagle enclave was closed by the State of Tennessee. The school's state charter was revoked, and its land and buildings were confiscated and sold at public auction. However, the staff secured a new charter and moved the school to Knoxville, where the Highlander Folk School became the Highlander Research and Education Center.

In the mid-1960s, the staff at Highlander shifted the center's focus to the social and economic problems in Appalachia, believing that blacks in the Deep South needed allies working for democracy and equality. Highlander's renewed commitment to the region dovetailed with the federal War on Poverty. The Highlander program evolved to include three approaches. First, workshops were convened at the center on specific issues such as strip mining, industrial health and safety, landownership, tax reform, school reform, and welfare rights. Second, it initiated a strong program of research and advocacy examining the major institutions in the region and their relation to ordinary citizens. Third, it continued its commitment to developing local leaders.

Specific programs were created to address specific needs. Staff member Helen Lewis guided a program to strengthen community control of regional health clinics organized by the United Mine Workers of America. She also pioneered efforts to pressure regional colleges to develop Appalachian studies courses. Highlander joined with the Appalachian Alliance in a major collaborative land study. Activists and community groups researched land ownership in eighty counties in six states, confirming that much of the land and mineral resources were in corporate and absentee hands. Over the next decade, community groups used data collected in the study to challenge unfair taxation, inadequate education and health systems, and environmental abuse. The Southern Appalachian Leadership Training program worked to strengthen local grassroots leadership, and cultural workshops encouraged regional artists, musicians, dance callers, and poets to link their work with community organizations. John Gaventa and Juliet Merrifield, coordinators for Highlander's resource center, expanded the research work into a participatory research program, which trained grassroots groups to access official records.

Highlander conferences on common problems such as environmental destruction gradually added an international dimension by increasing understanding that local communities in the South were deeply affected by global developments and decisions. Specifically, the center sought to use economic education to help local groups function in the global economy. Music continued to underpin both workshops and fieldwork, and poetry, humor, and dance enabled groups divided by race and geography to begin to build trust as they worked on difficult problems. Facing the prospect of an urban renewal project that would either raze the headquarters or leave no room for expansion, the faculty moved in 1972 to a 104-acre farm near the town of New Market, twenty-five miles east of Knoxville.

In the early 1970s, Horton retired as director, though he continued to live at the school and contribute ideas until his death in 1990. While administrative leadership has since passed to others, Highlander adheres to the founder's belief that local challenges must be linked to broader movements for justice in order to achieve social change. Noted for its historic role in providing education on behalf of human rights in the region, the center was nominated for a Nobel Peace Prize in 1982 and in 1990 was called "one of the South's most influential institutions of social change" by *Time* magazine.

See also: CIVIL RIGHTS MOVEMENT (RACE, ETHNICITY, AND IDENTITY); COMMUNITY ACTION GROUPS (FAMILY AND COMMUNITY); HORTON, MYLES.

—Candie Carawan, *Highlander Research and Education Center*

John M. Glen, *Highlander: No Ordinary School, 1932–1962* (1996); Myles Horton, with Judith and Herbert Kohl, *The Long Haul: An*

Autobiography (1990); Lucy Massie Phenix and Veronica Selver, *You Got to Move*, First Run/Icarus Films (1985).

Hindman Settlement School

See Hindman Settlement School (Crafts)

Historically Black Colleges and Universities

Historically black colleges and universities are accredited institutions of higher education that were established prior to 1964 and have as their principal mission the education of African Americans. Often referred to as HBCUs, the schools are generally affiliated with an umbrella organization known as the HBCU Network. Cheyney State University in Pennsylvania (1837) is often cited as the first such school.

Much of the financial support for black colleges and universities came from the black community with funds raised at bazaars, fairs, plays, lectures, church suppers, and church parades. Abolitionist and religious groups such as Quakers and Presbyterians made significant contributions as well. In 1846 the American Missionary Association was incorporated for the purpose of establishing black schools and colleges. After the Civil War, the new Freedmen's Bureau joined in bringing relief to freed slaves, poor whites, and refugees, working in conjunction with northern missionary societies that made substantial financial contributions to black education.

Historically black colleges and universities were largely established in the South after the end of the Civil War. Several of the oldest are located in the Appalachian region. These include Knoxville College (1875) in Tennessee; West Virginia State University (1891) in Institute; and Tuskegee University (1881) in Tuskegee, Alabama.

These schools have faced a variety of economic and social challenges, including achieving and maintaining economic viability and realizing a social and educational equality within the larger society. Shortly after Reconstruction, the South embraced Jim Crow laws and de facto segregation, denying blacks the right to equal education. In an attempt to remedy this injustice, the U.S. Supreme Court, in *Brown v. Board of Education* (1954), ruled that public schools be integrated. Ten years later, the Civil Rights Act of 1964 went further in guaranteeing blacks the right to equal education. These were hard-fought victories followed by years of difficult and often violent struggle before the laws were implemented and blacks had equal access to public education.

In the 1960s and 1970s, historically black institutions experienced a bitter debate over their continued relevance in an integrated society. Black Power advocates opposed the idea of complete integration and assimilation into white society. Although some African American leaders and educators questioned the need for historically black colleges and universities, at the turn of the twenty-first century they continued to be considered significant within the African American community. An article in a 2002 issue of *Education* magazine noted that they served "as the primary depository of the history and culture of peoples of African American descent in the United States" and played "a critical role in 'filling the gap' in U.S. higher education and in moving closer to its pluralistic ideal." Now racially integrated, these colleges and universities have succeeded in providing African American students with a supportive academic environment.

See also: PRIVATE COLLEGES AND UNIVERSITIES; PUBLIC COLLEGES AND UNIVERSITIES.

—Bernadette Ronan, *Tacoma, Washington*

W. E. B. Du Bois, *The Education of Black People: Ten Critiques, 1906–1960*, ed. Herbert Aptheker (1973); Tilden J. LeMille, "The HBCU: Yesterday, Today and Tomorrow," *Education* (Fall 2002); Julian B. Roebuck and Komanduri S. Murty, *Historically Black Colleges and Universities: Their Place in American Higher Education* (1993).

Horton, Myles

(1905–1990) Educational leader and innovator.

Born in Savannah, Tennessee, Myles Horton was one of the cofounders of the Highlander Folk School (later the Highlander Research and Education Center). He played a crucial role in the empowerment of the people in Appalachia, as well as helping to educate many people from economically or racially oppressed groups from around the country and world.

Horton grew up in poverty in east Tennessee but learned from the example of his mother, Elsie Falls Horton, who never neglected to share what she had with those who had even less. His father, Perry Horton, by joining unions and cooperatives, illustrated to Myles the importance of collective struggle. His parents brought him up in the religious milieu of the Cumberland Presbyterian Church, planting the religious seed that continued to influence him throughout his career.

Horton enrolled in Cumberland University in Lebanon, Tennessee, in 1924, where he began reading prodigiously and became involved in the struggle for racial equality and economic justice in the local chapter of the Young Men's Christian Association (YMCA). After college, he worked as a staff member for the YMCA, even organizing an integrated banquet, unheard of in that area. Working later for the Cumberland Presbyterian Church, Horton organized a community meeting in Ozone, Tennessee, where he realized that people were able to talk about their own problems and that they had the power and desire to fight injustice on their own behalf.

Myles Horton (right) with noted Brazilian educator Paulo Freire and workshop participants at the Highlander Research and Education Center in New Market, Tennessee, 1989. The center evolved from Highlander Folk School, which Horton founded in 1932 in Monteagle, Tennessee, to address pressing social, environmental, and economic issues facing Appalachians.

Horton's interests continued to include popular education. After college, he traveled to a number of cooperatives and even visited an expired utopian community. In 1929 he entered Union Theological Seminary in New York, where one of his professors and friends was noted theologian Reinhold Niebuhr. There he read socialist philosophy and became a member of the Socialist Party, continuing his action by participating in strikes and demonstrations. Marxist philosophy convinced him of the importance of collective over individual action. John Dewey's educational model also strongly influenced Horton, teaching him that empowered people are able to help themselves.

After Union, Horton spent some time at the University of Chicago, where he met Jane Addams and became interested in the Hull House. His later travels to Denmark on a tour to study folk schools gave him even greater clarity, demonstrating to him the necessity of an educational model that is culturally understandable to the participants. Many of the Danish programs included cultural elements such as dance, song, and stories. Gathering together all of his experiences, Horton became convinced that education must be communal and democratic and must emanate from the people. Change coming from an outside entity cannot possibly take into account the cultural needs of any group. Education should be a process of creating a forum where people solve their own problems.

The Highlander Folk School opened in 1932 with Horton as the first education director. He and the rest of the staff encouraged respect for local culture by setting aside one night a week for dance, song, and forums. The school initiated residence terms, an intensive method to train community activists better to deal with the problems of their communities. Informal weekend workshops also served to draw out problems, and community members began discussing them on a grassroots level rather than through a top-down hierarchy.

As well as influencing such strikes as those in McColl, South Carolina, and Lumberton, North Carolina, Highlander contributed to many smaller actions. After the anti-industrial movement of the 1930s and 1940s, Highlander recognized the importance of the incipient Civil Rights movement and trained people such as Martin Luther King Jr. and Rosa Parks in modes of resistance. The center helped to establish citizenship schools to train blacks to read so that they could pass literacy tests required to vote. Horton recognized the importance of mass movements and helped to inspire them by working with more isolated community organizations. When no mass movement had momentum, Highlander planted the seeds for later action. After the Civil Rights movement, Horton turned his eyes to international as well as Appalachian issues, visiting with Brazilian educator Paulo Freire and traveling to Nicaragua.

Through his highly democratic educational philosophy, Horton empowered many by encouraging collective learning based on social equality and freedom of speech. He retired from Highlander in 1970.

See also: CIVIL RIGHTS MOVEMENT (RACE, ETHNICITY, AND IDENTITY); COMMUNITY ACTION GROUPS (FAMILY AND COMMUNITY); HIGHLANDER RESEARCH AND EDUCATION CENTER.

—Adam Sanders, *East Tennessee State University*

Stephen L. Fisher, ed., *Fighting Back in Appalachia: Traditions of Resistance and Change* (1993); John M. Glen, *Highlander: No Ordi-*

nary School, 1932–1962 (1996); Myles Horton, with Judith and Herbert Kohl, *The Long Haul: An Autobiography* (1990).

Jesse Stuart Foundation

The Jesse Stuart Foundation is a regional press and bookseller that helped to introduce Appalachian life and culture to a national readership. Founded in 1979 in Louisville, Kentucky, by Harold E. Richardson, a professor at the University of Louisville, the foundation is devoted to preserving the legacy of Kentucky author Jesse Stuart (1906–1984) as well as other Kentucky and Appalachian writers. Since launching a publishing operation in 1986, the organization, which controls rights to all of Stuart's published and unpublished literary works, has produced more than one hundred printings and editions of texts by Stuart and other writers.

The nonprofit foundation's main purpose is to publish works that supplement the educational system at all levels. The foundation also promotes Stuart's legacy by producing videotapes and by bringing dramas, readings, and other presentations to school and civic groups. During the 1980s, the foundation assisted with the management and preservation of W-Hollow, the Stuart family's homestead in Greenup County. Shortly thereafter, the acreage became the Jesse Stuart Nature Preserve under the ownership and management of the Kentucky Nature Preserves Commission, an agency of the Commonwealth of Kentucky.

Although primarily known for his work as a poet, novelist, and conservationist, Stuart was also a passionate educator. "First, last, always," he once said, "I am a teacher." Stuart considered education a form of conservation, a way of preserving the nation's most precious resources and cultural viability. This commitment to education made Stuart a national folk hero during his lifetime, and his work has continued to inspire generations of teachers.

Stuart's books portray teachers as liberators and nurturers and himself as teacher-hero, rescuing the hill children and their families from degeneration, backwardness, and poverty. *Beyond Dark Hills* chronicles his own education and earliest teaching experiences, beginning at age seventeen. *The Thread That Runs So True*, winner of the National Education Association's book of the year in 1949, recounts his years as a teacher and superintendent in Greenup County. His more than sixty published works include *Man with a Bull-Tongue Plow* (poems), *Men of the Mountains* (stories), *God's Oddling* (biography), *Hie to the Hunters* (novel), and *Kentucky Is My Land* (poetry). Stuart also wrote eight children's books that have enjoyed national sales for more than fifty years.

See also: STUART, JESSE (LITERATURE).

—James M. Gifford, *Jesse Stuart Foundation*, and Newton Smith, *Western Carolina University*

John C. Campbell Folk School

See John C. Campbell Folk School (Crafts)

Kentucky Education Reform Act of 1990

In 1985 the Council for Better Education filed a civil action suit charging that Kentucky's systems for funding and operating schools were unconstitutional. This group represented a number of districts, school boards, and students, most of whom were poor, rural, and Appalachian. Led by Bert Combs, a former governor and federal judge, the plaintiffs achieved a relatively swift and remarkable response from the highest levels—the Kentucky Supreme Court declared the entire state system of education unconstitutional. The governor, general assembly, and Task Force on Education Reform's coordinated response was the 1990 Kentucky Education Reform Act, known as KERA.

The Kentucky Education Reform Act established a far-reaching infrastructure. Core elements included curriculum, governance, and finance reforms. In the decade after its inception, the Support Education Excellence in Kentucky Fund narrowed the per-pupil spending gap among districts, a critical issue for districts poor in property tax. Both academic and noncognitive (e.g., daily attendance rate) results, as measured through the Kentucky Instructional Results Information System and later the Commonwealth Accountability Testing System, showed significant gains, although race and gender differences persisted. More parents began to meet with teachers and principals to discuss school policies. In an effort to have more diverse representation in school decision making, the legislation also established school councils—consisting of the school principal, three teachers, and two parents (teachers and parents being elected representatives)—to make decisions on curriculum, instruction, materials, discipline, extracurricular programs, and the school budget. The councils would also hire principals if the position was vacant and consult with principals about the hiring of faculty.

Several provisions of the Kentucky Education Reform Act held particular relevance for Appalachian Kentucky. Extended school services offered students personalized tutoring in academic areas. Family Resource Centers (elementary) and Youth Service Centers (upper grades) created an on-site safety net for students and their families who might be in need of medical help, social services, employment or internships, or (teen) parenting programs. Many offered child care linked to dropout-prevention and health-education programs. The act's provisions for multi-age primary programs affirmed the legacy of one-room schools, where students learned on a flexible schedule with peers of varying ages and abilities. Professional development, continued training for school-based councils, and new curriculum initiatives received support through the regional service centers and the expanding Kentucky Education Technology System. Such elements of reform proved particularly important for remote districts in mountain areas where travel times and geography tended to impede effective communication and sharing of best practices. While the legislation established financial rewards for high-performing districts, officials were given additional authority to intervene in districts declared to be in crisis.

The result of the Kentucky Education Reform Act has been an increase in both accountability to the state and increased autonomy to respond to local concerns and priorities. Appalachian districts particularly struggle to retain students to graduation, achieve high standardized test scores among all students, and provide an advanced curriculum through technology and sharing resources while preserving the benefits that accompany reasonably sized community-based schools. Appalachian districts have been agents of social change in initiating the lawsuit, ratcheting up the stakes of educational achievement, and leading the way in modeling best practices in many provisions.

See also: COMBS, BERT (GOVERNMENT); SCHOOL EQUITY FUNDING (GOVERNMENT).

—Maureen Porter, *University of Pittsburgh*

"Education Reform Act of 1990," in *The Kentucky Encyclopedia*, ed. John E. Kleber (1992); Kentucky Department of Education, *Results Matter: A Decade of Difference in Kentucky's Public Schools 1990–2000* (2000).

Land-Grant Colleges

On July 2, 1862, President Abraham Lincoln signed into law the Morrill Act, which established the land-grant university system. The legislation, introduced by Representative Justin Smith Morrill of Vermont, granted each state and territory thirty thousand acres of public land for each senator and representative based on the 1860 census or at the time the state was admitted to the Union. Proceeds from the sale of these lands were to be invested in a perpetual endowment fund that would provide support for colleges of agriculture and mechanical arts in each of the states. Land-grant colleges within Appalachia or providing extensive service to the region are Alabama A&M University, Auburn University, and Tuskegee University in Alabama; Fort Valley State College and the University of Georgia in Georgia; Kentucky State University; Alcorn State University and Mississippi State University in Mississippi; Cornell University in New York; North Carolina A&T State University and North Carolina State University; Ohio State University; Pennsylvania State University; Clemson University and South Carolina State University in South Carolina; Tennessee State University and the University of Tennessee; Virginia Polytechnic Institute and State University and Virginia State University; and West Virginia State University and West Virginia University.

Interior shot of the A. D. White Library at Cornell University, Ithaca, New York, 1970. The federal land-grant institution of New York, Cornell was founded after President Abraham Lincoln signed the Morrill Act on July 2, 1862, creating the land-grant university system for assisting rural communities through education, research, and outreach services.

The original mission of the colleges and universities receiving benefits from this legislation was to provide members of the working classes with a liberal, practical education that included agriculture, military tactics, and the mechanical arts as well as classical studies. Since that time, nearly fifty subsequent legislative actions have extended the mission and support of these land-grant institutions. The Hatch Act of 1887 incorporated research into the land-grant mission by providing for the establishment of agricultural research stations at each college or university. The Smith-Lever Act of 1914 established extension work as the third element of the land-grant mission by creating the support and organization to reach out to serve the state in such areas as sustainable agriculture, food safety, and energy conservation. The land-grant system therefore encompasses three tasks within its mission: academic instruction in the classroom, informal education and information dissemination through outreach extension programs, and basic and applied research. Such practical instruction and outreach have been especially beneficial to lagging regions such as Appalachia.

Prior to the land-grant system, higher education in the United States focused on the classics and prepared students in areas of religion, law, and medicine. Colleges mainly served the urban male leisure class, government workers, and professionals. But society and the economy were primarily agricultural, with more than 80 percent of the population living in rural areas. Residents of rural areas such as Appalachia had few opportunities for formal instruction; illiteracy was widespread, and farming was inefficient. The land-grant system was established to deal with issues facing rural communities through education, research, and outreach services. With each state having at least one land-grant university, endeavors of the individual institutions naturally focused on issues facing their respective communities and region. Nowhere is this more evident than with the land-grant universities located in the states linked to the Appalachian region. These institutions regularly house organizations that specifically enhance the literacy, employment, political awareness, and cultural preservation of the region.

For example, the Appalachian Center at the University of Kentucky was established in 1977 to carry out the land-grant mission of research, instruction, and service for the region. Like similar organizations, the Appalachian Center brings people and resources from various areas of expertise to create and disseminate knowledge. Of specific importance to the Appalachian Center is the intersection of academia, citizen action, and public policy formulation. To achieve this, the center publishes current research findings and organizes annual meetings on issues such as children's poverty, health, and education. Similar work can be found at other land-grant institutions serving the region. At West Virginia University, the Regional Research Institute strives to advance understanding of social, economic, and political differences across regions with a particular focus on Appalachia. Many other universities serving the region increase understanding and awareness of Appalachia by providing academic programs that specialize on the complex cultural, historical, environmental, and economic issues of this distinctive region.

While providing education and service to rural communities was an original intent of the land-grant system, improving the productivity of farming was also a key concern. Policymakers understood that increased efficiency on farms was vital to the continued development of the United States. In the mid-1800s, farm production was at subsistence levels, with one farm typically producing enough food for five people. Half of all people lived on farms, and approximately 60 percent worked on farms. The land-grant system eventually increased productivity and allowed people to work off the farm, thus moving the country beyond an agricultural-based economy. Nearly 150 years later, one farm, on average, produced enough food for 140 people. Over the last half of the twentieth century, the productivity of farm labor increased sevenfold. By the early twenty-first century, 1 percent of the population lived on farms and only 2 percent worked on farms, allowing 75 percent of the population to live in urban and suburban areas. This evolution proceeded under a variety of influences, but the land-grant system was an important catalyst, as Representative Morrill envisioned.

See also: AGRICULTURAL EDUCATION (AGRICULTURE); APPALACHIAN CENTERS AND INSTITUTES (CULTURAL INSTITUTIONS).

—Todd L. Cherry, *Appalachian State University*

National Association of State Universities and Land-Grant Colleges, *The Land-Grant Tradition* (1995); U.S. National Research Council, *Colleges of Agriculture at the Land Grant Universities: A Profile* (1995).

Moonlight Schools

Started in 1911 in Rowan County, Kentucky, by Cora Wilson Stewart (1875–1958), moonlight schools were intended, in the words of their founder, to "emancipate from illiteracy all those enslaved in its bondage." Because potential students for the school worked during the day and bad roads and episodes of violence made it dangerous to travel at night, Stewart opted to teach only on the brightest evenings—hence "moonlight" schools.

Stewart, who was from Montgomery County, conceived the idea for moonlight schools while serving as the first woman superintendent of schools for Rowan County. Frequent requests to read and write for illiterate citizens made Stewart want to teach people to read and write for themselves. She responded by calling together county teachers and requesting that they volunteer to teach adults in the evenings.

Generally consisting of two-hour sessions four evenings per week over a total of eight weeks, the program offered condensed courses in history, civics, English, health and sanitation, geography, home economics, agriculture, horticulture, and good roads. Reading lessons presented in the form of a weekly school newspaper encouraged community pride and inspired intercommunity competition. Schoolhouses became gathering places for the many clubs (such as those devoted to agriculture and home economics) that grew out of courses of study.

In 1914, in response to Stewart's lobbying, Governor James McCreary established the Kentucky Illiteracy Commission. No funding was provided to the moonlight schools at first, but with the support of several women's groups, Stewart eventually raised funds to publish a book, *The Country Life Reader*, and provided a copy to every moonlight school student.

In 1918 Stewart introduced a bill in the Kentucky General Assembly to provide the Kentucky Illiteracy Commission with twenty-five thousand dollars per year over a three-year period, most of which went toward educating the thirty thousand Kentucky men who had registered by mark rather than signature for service in World War I. Stewart created *The Soldier's First Book*, a patriotic primer, and the federal government distributed it to training camps throughout the country. After the armistice was signed, *The Soldier's First Book* was replaced by *The Country Life Reader*, which was sent overseas to prepare soldiers for returning home to a life of peace and productivity.

But when the literacy campaign was at its height, critics began to question the moonlight schools and Stewart herself. Some teachers expressed dissatisfaction at being asked to volunteer by Stewart, who was superintendent of schools. Others resented the fact that the Kentucky Illiteracy Commission used its funds to hire illiteracy agents, who organized the work in individual counties, instead of compensating teachers. Additionally, the development of professionalism in state teaching standards placed further demands on teachers, leaving little time to volunteer for moonlight classes. Women's club members served as volunteers.

Moreover, several superintendents began to question whether anyone actually learned to read or write through the program, since no documentation was kept. Some contended many students learned little more than how to write their own names. Despite the controversy, the classes reflected the energy and enthusiasm of their founder. Stewart crusaded against illiteracy, and many states joined the campaign, continuing the mission of moonlight schools long after the schools themselves had disappeared.

See also: SECTION OVERVIEW; SETTLEMENT, MISSION, AND SPONSORED SCHOOLS.

—Kate Northcott, *University of Kentucky*

Yvonne Honeycutt Baldwin, "Cora Wilson Stewart and the Illiteracy Crusade: 'Moonlight Schools' and Progressive Era Reform," Ph.D. dissertation, University of Kentucky (1996); Florence Estes, "Cora Wilson Stewart and the Moonlight Schools of Kentucky, 1911–1920: A Case Study in the Rhetorical Uses of Literacy," Ed.D. dissertation, University of Kentucky (1988); Cora Wilson Stewart, *Moonlight Schools: For the Emancipation of Adult Illiterates* (1922).

New Opportunity School for Women

The New Opportunity School for Women, founded in 1987, provides an intense, though brief, educational experience for low-income central Appalachian women seeking job and social skills to take them beyond traditional roles of housework and mothering. Each year, the school in downtown Berea, Kentucky, accepts two groups of about fifteen students for three weeks of classes ranging from Appalachian literature to résumé writing and job interviewing. Besides providing a sharply focused educational experience, the curriculum is designed to elevate self-esteem and engender confidence. A writing workshop and practical work experience, for example, serve dual purposes of developing skills and cultivating a sense of self-worth. Each student receives a comprehensive health examination, clothing assistance, grooming tips, and both formal and informal personal counseling. Applicants are required to have a high school diploma or certificate of equivalency, but motivation and personal need are major factors in selecting students for the expense-paid course. Typical students are women who married very young and have never worked outside the home. Some have been widowed; others may be divorced or subjected to spousal abuse. Most graduates proceed to jobs, and many go on to college or vocational training. The program's success has led to a biennial "satellite" session held in other communities near the eastern Kentucky mountains.

Between 1987 and 2003, the New Opportunity School graduated 385 women from sixty-seven different counties in ten states, more than 95 percent from Kentucky. Of these, 100 went on to take college courses. Twenty received bachelor or associate degrees, one had earned a master's degree, and two others continued graduate studies.

Upon entering the program, 60 percent of the women were either single or divorced, and 6 percent were widows. Thirty-four percent were married. Eighty-five percent of them came from homes with incomes below the poverty level. Their ages ranged from their late twenties well into middle age, and many were grandmothers.

Although the school ended its informal affiliation with Berea College in the late 1990s, it remains a part of the college community and tradition. Indeed, it sprang from Berea's long-standing commitment to the Appalachian region. Jane Stephenson, the school's founder, was the wife of John B. Stephenson, an Appalachian scholar who became president of the college in 1984. A native of Banner Elk, North Carolina, Jane Stephenson got the inspiration for the New Opportunity School from Gurney Norman, an Appalachian writer and professor of English at the University of Kentucky, who called her about the plight of a particular unskilled eastern Kentucky woman facing financial crisis. Stephenson quickly found both a name and a precedent for the project. Early in the twentieth century, Berea College, taking its cue from Danish folk schools, had operated an "Opportunity School," which invited citizens to come to the campus in January and informally take any courses that interested them.

With her husband's help, Stephenson raised the project's initial funding for the New Opportunity School from the California-based Educational Foundation of America. Grants from other charitable foundations subsequently provided funds to operate the school, maintain its staff, and cover students' expenses and tuition. In April 2003, Stephenson appeared on the popular television program *Oprah*, hosted by Oprah Winfrey. In addition to national recognition, the New Opportunity School for Women received a $100,000 award

Wolfe Pen School near Pineville, West Virginia, 1960. Partly as a result of President Lyndon Johnson's Great Society, many one-room schools were consolidated into larger facilities in the 1960s and 1970s. Later, multiple-age groupings and peer teaching, hallmarks of successful one-room schools, came to be championed in some urban school systems. Wolfe Pen was one of the last one-room schools in West Virginia to close.

from Winfrey's Angel Network. Stephenson served as the school's president through its first decade, and thereafter, in emeritus status, she continued to be its principal fund-raiser as well as a director.

See also: BEREA COLLEGE.

—Rudy Abramson, *Reston, Virginia*

Rudy Abramson, "Just Remember My Name," *Appalachian Heritage* (Summer 1994); Jane B. Stephenson, *Courageous Paths: Stories of Nine Appalachian Women* (1995).

One-Room Schools

The typical rural school on the western frontier of Appalachia was the one-room, ungraded primary school. Normally, state governments in the region only partially subsidized formal education until the late nineteenth century. Before that, a community or an extended family could petition the state government to send some portion of the education budget to a district where local people were providing some or most of the facilities and funds necessary for education. Subsistence and small-scale farming communities required only part-time schooling, and the number of children within walking distance of a school was often quite small. The teaching of reading and writing and some "ciphering" was deemed important, but it was done primarily when children were not needed by their parents to assist with farming, hunting, caring for younger children, or doing domestic chores. Instructional activities were not considered age dependent. Children would attend school when they were permitted by their parents to do so. One-room schools were often administered by a local untrained "trustee," and the teacher was frequently a young woman or man from a local family with little instructional training, save for the education they may have received themselves in a one-room school or a town high school. Pupils were required to memorize and recite their lessons.

By 1900, two new types of schools had replaced the one-room schoolhouse in the mountains. In towns, there were often enough students available to justify new schools with multiple classrooms. "Progressive" instructional theories of the day suggested that the developmental and mental abilities of children should be taken into account when planning and teaching. Age differences were the easiest to measure, and "graded" schools became popular for both pedagogical and administrative reasons. The argument was also made that twentieth-century learning outcomes demanded more than simple reading and writing. The memorization and recitation exercises of the one-room school were castigated as being out of date and harmful to children. The other emerging types of schools were junior and senior high schools. These institutions were clearly differentiated by age and subject matter, which also undermined the logic of retaining one- and two-room schools in the countryside. By the middle of the twentieth century, the rural one-room school was often considered an embarrassing remnant of the past in those few places where they remained. Partly as a result of President Lyndon Johnson's Great Society, school reforms were made. Many one-room schools were closed and consolidated into larger schools. Communities lost one of their main pillars. Much later, however, multiple-age groupings and peer teaching, the forte of successful one-room school teaching, came to be championed in some urban school systems.

See also: BLAB SCHOOLS.

—Alan J. DeYoung, *University of Kentucky*

Pettit, Katherine

(1868–1936) Settlement school founder and teacher.

Katherine Pettit's lifelong interest in the living conditions of the eastern Kentucky mountains led her to establish two settlement schools in the region: Hindman Settlement School in 1902 and Pine Mountain Settlement School in 1913. Devoted particularly to the hands-on work of teaching children, Pettit was an influential leader of progressive reform efforts in Appalachia.

A member of a prominent Kentucky family, Pettit began her life's work after attending Sayre Female Institute in Lexington for two years. As early as 1895, she and others conducted walking tours of the mountains, handing out flower seeds and books from traveling libraries sponsored by the Kentucky Federation of Women's Clubs. Under this organization's auspices, Pettit recruited volunteers and organized three summer tent settlements between 1899 and 1901. The following year she and May Stone arrived in Hindman to begin their school there, offering an ambitious program that included general education, industrial education, Sunday schools, and health outreach services. In 1913 Pettit fulfilled a promise to the people of Pine Mountain to bring a settlement school to them as well, this time with the assistance of Ethel DeLong Zande. At Pine Mountain, she promoted agricultural ventures so avidly that she became known as "the blossom woman." Although outspoken and courageous, she disdained publicity for herself, even as she received numerous awards and accolades for her work. Pettit retired in 1930 from Pine Mountain and continued to promote conservation projects until her death in 1936.

See also: FOTCHED-ON WOMEN; HINDMAN SETTLEMENT SCHOOL (CRAFTS); PINE MOUNTAIN SETTLEMENT SCHOOL (CRAFTS).

—Deborah L. Blackwell, *Texas A&M International University*

Private Colleges and Universities

At the start of the twenty-first century, approximately 149 private institutions of higher education, including some of the nation's oldest and most prestigious colleges and universities, were operating in the Appalachian region. As elsewhere in the United States, the development of higher education in Appalachia followed the region's gradual settlement and population growth. The earliest institutions were founded in valleys along the eastern borders of the region. Typically, these early colleges were intended to serve particular religious denominations or ethnic groups. Approximately half of existing private institutions were founded before 1900. Throughout much of the late eighteenth and early nineteenth centuries, an advanced education included European classical literature and usually Protestant religious teachings. The ranks of college students were overwhelmingly male, and the curriculum focused preparation of students for careers in the ministry, law, and medicine. Catholic institutions were established in Appalachia between the mid-nineteenth and mid-twentieth centuries with the influx of large numbers of the faith. Following the Civil War, an increasing need for training in scientific and technical fields led, beginning in the late nineteenth and throughout the twentieth century, to the establishment of private universities with broadened curricula that included sciences and engineering. Black colleges and universities were another product of the post–Civil War era. Bible colleges strongly imbued with Protestant evangelism were established throughout the twentieth century. The century was also marked by the replacement of single-sex education by coeducation.

Eighty-six of the private Appalachian institutions at the turn of the twenty-first century were four-year colleges, and twenty-seven were universities. Also included in the region were fifteen Bible colleges, located for the most part in the southern and central subregions of Appalachia, eleven two-year private colleges, one independent law school, and nine theological seminaries, including one affiliated with the Orthodox Christian Church and a Jewish Rabbinical school. More than 50 percent of all postsecondary students who attended private institutions in Appalachia were enrolled in four-year colleges. About 40 percent were enrolled in universities and 5 percent in two-year colleges. Although Bible colleges make up 10 percent of the private institutions, they generally enroll only about 1 percent of the region's private college students. Nearly three-quarters of the private institutions continued religious affiliations, among them nineteen Protestant and seventeen Catholic schools. Three institutions were all male, and nine were exclusively for women. Forty-four of the 149 private institutions offered master's degrees, and thirteen had doctoral programs.

Four private Appalachian institutions trace their origins to schools that were established before 1800—Washington and Lee University in Virginia, Salem College in North Carolina, Washington and Jefferson College in Pennsylvania, and Tusculum College in Tennessee. The oldest of these, Washington and Lee, was founded as a classical academy by Scots-Irish settlers in 1749. The school came to be known as Washington Academy after George Washington donated twenty thousand dollars' worth of James River Canal stock to save the school from financial ruin. The name was changed to Washington and Lee in 1871 to commemorate Robert E. Lee's tenure as university president following the Civil War. A historically all-male institution, Washington and Lee began admitting women undergraduates in 1985. Salem College is the oldest college for women in the United States. In 1772 the Moravians, an early Protestant sect from central Europe, established a school for girls at their settlement of Salem, North Carolina. In the 1700s, the Single Sisters, as unmarried women of the Moravian community were called, were expected to be educated and economically self-sufficient, a rare circumstance for women of the time.

Berea College (Kentucky), Alice Lloyd College (Kentucky), and Warren Wilson College (North Carolina) are all known for their comprehensive work-study programs. Students lacking financial resources may enroll tuition-free, and all students are expected to work at various campus facilities. Berea College is also notable for its association with the antislavery movement before the Civil War. Founded in 1855 by John G. Fee, a fervent abolitionist, Berea College saw its mission evolve after the Civil War from an emphasis on educating African Americans to one of liberal arts education for the children of Appalachian mountaineers.

The first Catholic institutions in Appalachia were Saint Vincent College and Saint Francis College, founded in 1846 and 1847, respectively, in Pennsylvania. Fourteen Catholic institutions are located in Pennsylvania, including Duquesne and Gannon Universities. The remaining three Catholic schools are located in New York, Ohio, and West Virginia. Protestant evangelical institutions, generally called Bible colleges, have had a modest educational impact in the region. The most successful of this type of institution is Bob Jones University, which opened in Greenville, South Carolina, in 1947. The inspiration for the university and its namesake was an evangelist, the son of an Alabama sharecropper, who became alarmed by the paucity of Christian teaching in American higher education. Biblical inerrancy is a cornerstone of the Bob Jones University Creed.

Private Appalachian institutions are generally small, with an average enrollment of 1,200. However, one of the largest private institutions in the region is Cornell University, which has a full-time enrollment of more than 13,500 students. Cornell may be the region's most distinguished educational institution. Founded in 1865 at Ithaca, New York, it is a private comprehensive university, a member of the Ivy League, and the federal land-grant institution for New York. It is a partner with the State University of New York system, and three of its seven undergraduate colleges are operated with assistance from the state. Cornell awarded the nation's first university degree in veterinary medicine and the first doctorates in electrical engineering and industrial engineering. It endowed the nation's first chairs in American literature, musicology, and American history. Cornell University Press was the first university publishing enterprise in the United States and remains one of the nation's premier scholarly presses. Cornell was also the first American university to teach modern Far Eastern languages. Twenty-seven Nobel laureates have been affiliated with Cornell as faculty members or students.

The United States has forty-eight historically black private colleges and universities; eight of these are located in Appalachia. Although Talledega College, founded in 1867, is older, Tuskegee University is the largest historically black private college in Alabama and the best known, owing to its illustrious founder, Booker T. Washington. An emancipated slave, Washington became the most influential spokesperson for African Americans in the United States during the late 1800s and early 1900s. He founded Tuskegee Normal and Industrial Institute in 1881; it later became Tuskegee University. Washington's philosophy of education stressed that African Americans would benefit most from vocational education focused on teaching and the industrial arts.

See also: BEREA COLLEGE; HISTORICALLY BLACK COLLEGES AND UNIVERSITIES; PUBLIC COLLEGES AND UNIVERSITIES.

—Edward B. Reeves, *Morehead State University*

E. Grady Bogue and Jeffery Aper, *Exploring the Heritage of American Higher Education: The Evolution of Philosophy and Policy* (2000); MacMillan Reference USA, *The College Blue Book* (2001); Frederick Rudolph, *The American College and University: A History* (1962).

Public Colleges and Universities

At the beginning of the twenty-first century, 126 public institutions of higher education were located in the 410-county Appalachian region. However, this count underestimates the prevalence of public higher education in the region, as there are also 29 branch campuses affiliated with state institutions. In addition, the State of New York supports 8 colleges located on the campuses of various private institutions. For example, the College of Veterinary Medicine, the nation's oldest veterinary school, established in 1894, is affiliated with Cornell University, an ostensibly private institution. A comprehensive listing totals 163 distinct public-supported campus entities in the region.

The Cathedral of Learning, the second-tallest education building in the world, on the University of Pittsburgh campus, 2002. The University of Pittsburgh, founded in 1787, is the oldest public educational institution in the region. The rise of public higher education in Appalachia began after the Civil War and continued into the twentieth century, spurred by state and federal legislation that improved access to all citizens.

The earliest public institutions in Appalachia were the University of Pittsburgh (1787) and the University of Tennessee (1794) in Knoxville. Despite these early dates of the first public institutions, private colleges and universities generally led to the establishment of higher education in the region. Half of the region's still-existing private institutions were established before 1900, while only 30 percent of the current public institutions were established by that point. The founding of private institutions for higher education surged throughout the nineteenth century, largely due to religious sectarianism. The rise of public higher education began after the Civil War and continued unabated in the twentieth century, spurred by the efforts of state and federal governments to improve educational access to all citizens.

Modern-day public institutions in Appalachia are larger than their private counterparts, enrolling an average of 3,600 students, compared with 1,200 in private institutions. Of all students enrolled in Appalachian institutions, nearly 80 percent are in public universities and colleges. There are several reasons for the lopsided enrollment in public institutions. First, public institutions generally have higher acceptance rates than private institutions and much lower tuition. Toward the end of the 1990s, the average annual tuition for a private institution in Appalachia was approximately $9,000, while a public institution cost less than one-third of that amount. State governments in every Appalachian state have used public funds to subsidize low-cost, accessible higher education by creating a system of two-year community colleges. The region has 84 two-year colleges, enrolling approximately one-third of all public higher education students. Tuition costs at the community colleges are typically very low, and the acceptance rate averages around 95 percent.

In addition to the two-year colleges, Appalachia has 24 four-year colleges, 48 universities, 2 colleges of technology affiliated with the State University of New York system, and a School of the Arts in North Carolina. Today, all state-supported campuses in the region are coeducational. Nationwide, of the 47 public colleges and universities that are historically black institutions, 5 are in Appalachia—Alabama A&M University and Lawson State Community College in Alabama; Winston-Salem State University in North Carolina; and Bluefield State College and West Virginia State University in West Virginia.

The structure of public higher education in Appalachia has been strongly influenced by the federal system of land-grant institutions as well as by the hierarchical system within state higher education that includes a flagship university, regional universities, and community colleges. Initiated with the passage of the first Morrill Act in 1862, land-grant institutions were mandated to bring higher education of a practical nature to ordinary citizens, especially farmers, engineers, and skilled industrial laborers. The land-grant mandate stood in contrast to the orientation of most academic institutions of the time, which were finishing schools for the gentry emphasizing subjects such as philosophy, theology, law, medicine, and classical literature. The original Morrill Act provided for the establishment of colleges of agriculture in all U.S. states and territories. When the second Morrill Act was passed in 1890, it provided annual federal appropriations to land-grant institutions. It also stipulated that no appropriations would go to states that denied admission to these colleges because of race—unless they set up separate but equal facilities. Southern states responded by creating separate land-grant colleges for African American students.

Eight of the public institutions, or campus entities, in Appalachia are products of the Land Grant College Act of 1862 and subsequent, related legislation—Alabama A&M University, Clemson University, Mississippi State University, Pennsylvania State University, State University of New York College of Agriculture and Life Sciences at Cornell University, the University of Tennessee, Virginia Polytechnic Institute and State University, and West Virginia University.

Penn State, one of the earliest land-grant institutions, enjoys national prominence in academics and research and in sports. It traces its origins back to 1855, when the Commonwealth of Pennsylvania chartered the Farmer's High School in Centre County. The school was proposed by the state's agricultural society with the goal of promoting the application of scientific principles to farming. Its first president, Evan Pugh, was a proponent of land-grant legislation, and when the Morrill Act was passed in 1862, Pugh immediately set out to have Farmer's High named a land-grant college. In 1863 the institution's name was changed to the Agricultural College of Pennsylvania and some years later to Pennsylvania State College. During the 1880s, engineering studies were added, and the liberal arts curriculum was strengthened with the creation of a course in American literature, the nation's first. The Agricultural Experiment Station was founded after passage of the 1887 Hatch Act mandating congressional funding of college research activities.

During the Great Depression of the 1930s, the Penn State College system of branch campuses was created to serve students who could not afford to leave home to get an education. Penn State also pioneered classes at county agricultural extension offices throughout the state, allowing farmers to take courses via correspondence. In 1953 the college became Pennsylvania State University.

During the 1930s the need to lower costs and enhance accessibility to higher education was recognized by legislatures in Appalachian states and became a driving force during the post–World War II era. The passage of the G.I. Bill (Servicemen's Readjustment Act of 1944) and subsequent federal educational benefit measures expanded the educational opportunities of veterans. In the 1960s, Penn State responded to the first wave of the baby boom generation with greatly expanded enrollments. Subsequently, accommodations were made for minorities who previously had found a college education beyond their means and, more recently, for adults beyond the traditional college age who usually attended college part-time while working. Doctoral programs expanded to meet the need for increased numbers of faculty.

New programs of continuing education were developed in the 1960s and 1970s to serve the lifelong educational interests of both personal and professional development. During these same decades some private colleges were transformed into public institutions. In Alabama, Athens College, a private liberal arts college affiliated with the Methodist Church, became Athens State College, catering to nontraditional students. Similarly, the University of Chattanooga evolved from a Methodist-affiliated private liberal arts college into the University of Tennessee at Chattanooga, a campus in the state university system. Similar private-to-public transformations occurred in other areas of Appalachia.

Regional public institutions, such as Morehead State University in Rowan County, Kentucky, became prominent in higher education in Appalachia during the twentieth century. Founded as a normal school in 1887, Morehead was first operated by the Kentucky Christian Missionary Society. It struggled financially until 1923, when the state assumed control. In 1926 the name of the school was changed to Morehead State Normal School and Teachers College, and its new mission was training "white elementary school teachers" for the eastern Kentucky region. During the Second World War, the campus served as a training site for U.S. Navy personnel. In the 1950s and 1960s, enrollment increased tenfold, new academic programs proliferated, and the physical plant expanded. The Kentucky legislature granted the college university status in 1966.

During the 1960s, while Morehead State University was developing as a regional public university, five community colleges were established in eastern Kentucky. The Kentucky legislature charged the community colleges with a three-part mission: to offer career-oriented programs that prepare students for immediate employment upon graduation; to provide an inexpensive means for students to satisfy the first two years of a baccalaureate degree by attending colleges near their homes; and to offer general and adult educational opportunities to the local population.

Financial aid to students, enlargement of existing educational facilities, expansion of curricula, and unprecedented construction of new campuses were major policy objectives in the last half of the twentieth century. This change in American higher education has had an impact on all the Appalachian states. The modern three-tiered hierarchy of major research universities, regional universities, and community colleges is a product of this historical trend. Emergence of this complex, multitiered system of higher education has brought many benefits and many problems due to competition and lack of coordination among campuses. Each Appalachian state has answered these challenges by creating an overarching system of governance, such as Kentucky's Council on Postsecondary Education. The council is responsible for setting statewide higher educational policy, allocating resources to the various campuses, ensuring adequate curricular offerings, and ascertaining that curricula of all state-supported colleges and universities are compatible.

See also: PRIVATE COLLEGES AND UNIVERSITIES.

—Edward B. Reeves, *Morehead State University*

E. Grady Bogue and Jeffery Aper, *Exploring the Heritage of American Higher Education: The Evolution of Philosophy and Policy* (2000); Donald E. Heller, ed., *The States and Public Higher Education: Affordability, Access, and Accountability* (2001); Frederick Rudolph, *The American College and University: A History* (1962).

School Censorship

The Appalachian region, particularly the central and southern portions, is often referred to as part of the "Bible Belt," an area defined by the *Oxford English Dictionary* as "those parts of the United States reputed to be fanatically puritanical or fundamentalist." Appalachia is much more diverse than this stereotype implies, however, and People for the American Way, an organization that has documented school censorship episodes since the 1980s, found that they occurred rather equally across all regions of the country. A few noteworthy cases may have contributed to the belief that school censorship occurs more often in the region, but these episodes reflect conflicts over values and beliefs across the nation.

The most famous case culminated in the Scopes trial of 1925 in Dayton, Tennessee, which tested an anti-evolution law that had been passed by the state legislature earlier that year. It became a sensational media event that drew national attention to the issue and the locale. The guilty verdict against John Scopes, a young high school science teacher, was reversed a year later on a technicality. The theory of evolution has continued to be controversial until the present day, with religious fundamentalists contending that "creation theory" should have equal time with evolution in science classrooms.

Another important case with its roots in the Appalachian region was the precedent-setting *West Virginia Board of Education v. Barnette* in 1943. The U.S. Supreme Court found a state law requiring students to say the Pledge of Allegiance while saluting the flag of the United States unconstitutional. The penalty for not adhering to the rule was expulsion from school. The case was brought against the state by Jehovah's Witnesses who claimed it was against their religion to worship graven images. The *Barnette* case was used as the case law when the Ninth Circuit Court of Appeals in San Francisco ruled against reciting the pledge in schools in 2002.

In 1974 the region again gained notoriety when families in Kanawha County, West Virginia, objected to school textbooks on religious grounds. This case centered on language arts textbooks, though it began as a protest against sex education. The school board voted to adopt the textbooks, but the adoption was delayed when Alice Moore, a school board member who had been elected on a fundamentalist platform, demanded that they be studied further. Her objection sparked a controversy that became violent and included picketing, fire bombings, and shootings.

In the 1980s, a case dubbed "Scopes II" made national headlines in the mountains of Hawkins County, Tennessee. "Secular humanism" became an issue for fundamentalists, who claimed it was a religion inherent in school textbooks. Several fundamentalist Christian families objected to the use of the reading series adopted for the elementary schools. They protested the "humanistic, anti-Christian bias" of the books, claiming that the books offended their religious beliefs. Around the same time, Federal Judge Brevard Hand ruled that some forty-four textbooks approved by the state board of education should be removed from the schools throughout Alabama. Throughout the 1990s and into the twenty-first century, conflicts over values occurred periodically in the schools on issues ranging from the posting of the Ten Commandments to reading Harry Potter books to gay student rights.

Each case exemplified conflicts over the aims and purposes of schooling between groups holding differing values. Although such conflicts are not unique to the Appalachian region, when they occur in such locations, they are often portrayed as products of the region.

See also: SCOPES TRIAL (RELIGION).

—Mary Jean Ronan Herzog, *Western Carolina University*

Edward B. Jenkinson, *The Schoolbook Protest Movement: Forty Questions and Answers* (1986); Eli M. Oboler, ed., *Censorship and Education* (1981); Franklin Parker, *The Battle of the Books: Kanawha County* (1975).

School Consolidation

Appalachia had tens of thousands of schools in the early twentieth century, including thousands of small community schools and high schools. States had the legal responsibility to provide for schooling, but typically the operational and funding schemes to run them devolved to local counties and self-taxing school districts within the counties. West Virginia had more than three hundred fiscally independent school districts before the Great Depression began in 1929; Kentucky had more than one thousand. Between 1910 and 1960, about 90 percent of rural schools in the United States were either closed or consolidated. In Appalachia, the decline of rural schools was precipitous before 1960, and it continued even into the 1970s and 1980s. Even after the turn of the twenty-first century, West Virginia continued to pursue an aggressive school consolidation policy.

Among the more obvious reasons for consolidation have been out-migration from the region, improved roads and highways that enabled parents in more remote communities to send their children to larger schools, and the need to improve economic efficiency. The operation of numerous small schools in a district, each with its own library, cafeteria, playground, and administrative staff, seemed unnecessarily expensive when these functions could all be shared in a larger facility. County seat schools usually had more resources, and parents consequently wanted their children to attend those with better facilities and better teachers. Smaller one- and two-room schools run by local trustees and staffed by itinerant teachers or relatives of a local family began to lose their attractiveness as schools (especially high schools) began to appear as avenues to better jobs. Economic and demographic factors and demands by parents thus did much to undermine the attractiveness of small community schools.

At the same time, the ideology of professionalism and national security and economic issues created a climate hostile to small schools in America from the middle of the twentieth century. Even earlier, professional educators had called for graded schools with specialized teachers, and in their view the modern school demanded a separate teacher for every grade, as well as a professional administrator to supervise instruction and scheduling. "Unsupervised" teachers in multiple-grade classes in small schools were portrayed as limited and backward. Town schools in Appalachia were able to resist consolidation into the 1950s as long as they were prosperous, but smaller schools were increasingly vulnerable. Towns with graded schools large enough to sustain athletic and cultural programs attracted and generated community support.

By 1960, new ideological and political pressures combined with economic trends to diminish the viability of rural schools. Accepted pedagogical wisdom held that schools needed to be bigger and better and should offer a more sophisticated college-oriented curriculum.

Soon afterwards, the War on Poverty targeted education for reform. Schools were to teach academic skills that would help children leave home and find higher-paying work. The needs of local communities became less important. This belief was fortified by increased state funding to schools in an effort to equalize educational opportunities.

With state dollars came accountability and a demand for higher achievement-test scores, which resulted in educators' paying less attention to community needs.

The case of West Virginia provides a good illustration of the recent logic of school consolidation. The "Recht decision," a state supreme court ruling in 1982, found that students in Lincoln County were receiving an education inferior to those in metropolitan areas. The court mandated that all children receive an equal education, and the state education department used this ruling to close many small schools, arguing that such schools were too costly because more teachers were required for small numbers of students. In the modern perspective, it is assumed that all students should be in graded classes. Equal education is interpreted to mean that resources and class sizes must be similar across the state. At the same time, West Virginia schools, like all others in the region, are expected to provide a diverse high school curriculum that allows for different student choices. In addition, many high schools are required to have college-level math and science courses even if all students do not desire them. These factors (among others) push schools to grow larger and larger.

An additional factor contributing to consolidation has been the cost of maintenance and repair. Since money for school repair and replacement comes from state budgets, local communities must show why smaller schools should remain open, when students can be bused to another site.

Rather than a community undertaking, education by the end of the twentieth century had become a state (and national) responsibility. Instead of schools serving as sites for both community participation and celebration, they were redefined almost exclusively as instructional centers. Although professionals now agree that smaller schools can be better schools, it is unlikely that Appalachia will return to having community schools.

See also: WAR ON POVERTY (GOVERNMENT).

—Alan J. DeYoung, *University of Kentucky*

Alan J. DeYoung, *The Life and Death of a Rural American High School: Farewell, Little Kanawha* (1995); Alan J. DeYoung and Craig B. Howley, "The Political Economy of Rural School Consolidation," *Peabody Journal of Education* (Winter 1990); Alan Peshkin, *The Imperfect Union: School Consolidation and Community Conflict* (1982).

School Dropouts

In 1980 the national census showed that 25.3 percent of the adults in Appalachia aged eighteen to twenty-four did not have a high school diploma or equivalent. By the 1990 census, this dropout figure had decreased slightly (23.3 percent), but the level reported in the 2000 census was almost identical (23.9 percent). Thus, one in four eighteen-to-twenty-four-year-olds in Appalachia is likely to have dropped out of school, a situation that has remained largely unchanged over the past two decades. For policymakers who seek insight into the dropout processes of high school students in Appalachia, these statistics indicate a serious problem.

In 2000, 80.4 percent of the U.S. population over the age of twenty-five had finished high school, whereas only 75.1 percent of the similar group in the Appalachian region had finished. For college completion, the figures were 24.4 percent for the United States and 17.7 percent for the region. Not surprisingly, a similar discrepancy existed for per capita income, which was \$21,587 for the entire country and \$18,229 for Appalachia. Furthermore, 17.4 percent of Appalachian children under the age of eighteen were classified as living in poverty.

In a region where the economy is historically dominated by low-skill, low-wage jobs that require little education, a situation is perpetuated in which education seems to be unimportant in attaining and keeping employment. In homes lower on the economic and educational scales, less emphasis is placed on schooling and academic performance, and this attitude is generally passed from one generation to the next. Lack of support for academics in the home, coupled with other handicaps such as individual learning disabilities, almost guarantees that difficulties will arise in the classroom. As time passes, problems that may have been minimal or sporadic become a common part of the student's academic experience. Eventually, the child views schooling in a negative light and withdraws intellectually and emotionally. Confidence, success, and school become concepts with little relevance.

In some situations, such a negative perspective can be counterbalanced by social networks within the school environment. If learning is important within the general context of these networks, a student may develop a social identity in which academic performance has a prominent place. In contrast, if close friends view learning as unimportant or not an integral part of their lives, then the student may perceive the school environment as having little value.

The student is bound to the school by academic, social, and legal ties. If there is no social network centered around school or school activities, no strong academic bond to motivate the child to some goal in which education is important, and no home environment that emphasizes the importance of education, then the child is more likely to drop out as soon as is legally possible.

See also: SECTION OVERVIEW.

—Robert B. Pittman, *Western Carolina University*

J. D. Finn, "Withdrawing from School," *Review of Educational Research* (Summer 1989); R. Rumberger, "Dropping Out of Middle School: A Multilevel Analysis of Students and Schools,"

American Educational Research Journal (Fall 1995); Vincent Tinto, "Dropout from Higher Education: A Theoretical Synthesis of Recent Research," *Review of Educational Research* (Spring 1975).

Settlement House Movement

The settlement house movement originated in Great Britain in the late 1800s, and the first settlement houses in the United States were established in the late 1880s. In 1889, when an increasing number of women college graduates were seeking professionally challenging and socially useful work, the first two women's settlement houses opened, including Hull House in Chicago. Bent upon bringing literacy and scientific knowledge to uplift and modernize mountain folks, as well as to protect them from the vices of industrialization, college-educated women from the Kentucky Bluegrass region and the Northeast came to work in the Appalachian Mountains, especially in eastern Kentucky. Numerous religious schools were established in Kentucky, including Red Bird Mission School (Bell County), Kingdom Come School (Letcher County), and Booneville Settlement School (Owsley County), as well as a few independent schools such as Carr Creek Community Center and Caney Creek School (both in Knott County, Kentucky) and Pi Beta Phi Settlement School (in Sevier County, Tennessee).

Elsewhere in the southern Appalachians, seven settlements opened before 1900, including the Log Cabin Settlement in Asheville, North Carolina. The American settlement movement expanded rapidly in response to industrialization, immigration, and class polarization. By 1916, there were more than five hundred houses staffed primarily by white, middle-class, college-educated women. Although settlement houses varied widely in their activities, a unifying requirement of settlement work was residence in poor neighborhoods, which undermined the customary insularity of professional workers and brought them into more meaningful professional and social contact with the poor. Under the banner of neighborliness, settlement workers implemented a range of reform and educational activities informed by a broad range of cultural and class politics. Activities included ethnic cultural programs centered on folk arts and handicrafts, citizenship classes, labor organizing, Americanization classes, and events to foster the adoption of middle-class, Anglo-American values and behaviors. Other programs included social surveys and exposés of neighborhood and working conditions; lobbying efforts on behalf of reform legislation; sponsorship of recreational activities that cultivated "wholesome" alternatives to dance halls, saloons, and movie theatres; and establishment of clubs and social and medical services to strengthen community life within poor, working-class, and immigrant neighborhoods.

Two prototypical nonsectarian settlement schools in eastern Kentucky were the Hindman Settlement School, established by May Stone and Katherine Pettit in 1902, and Pine Mountain Settlement School, founded by Pettit and Ethel DeLong Zande in 1913. Armed with faith in the redemptive power of education and middle-class notions of mothering, domesticity, and family as prescriptions for transforming mountain life, these women reformers offered an array of programs including manual and domestic training, home visitation, mothers' clubs, preventive medical work, and arts and crafts distribution through fireside industries. Efforts to preserve selected folk traditions included ballad singing and creation of community social centers. As primarily single, childless women whose own lives disrupted traditional gender expectations, settlement women of both Pine Mountain and Hindman nonetheless were largely committed to programs that maintained the gender status quo. Because their emphasis was on the special needs of neighborhoods and communities they served, the local context shaped the activities of individual settlement houses. Hindman offered public school education from kindergarten through high school while Pine Mountain, which was not part of the public education system at first, preferred a less prescribed curriculum. Both Hindman (in 1911) and, later, Pine Mountain helped to pioneer the treatment of trachoma, an eye disease that often resulted in blindness, by sponsoring specialized medical clinics that eventually led to government-supported regional hospitals. The women of Pine Mountain also worked to raise money to build a road to Harlan, Kentucky. Over the years, both settlement schools introduced program changes, including environmental education, vocational guidance, and teacher institutes.

Scholars continue to debate the legacy of settlement work. Some have portrayed the reformers as romantic benevolent heroines, while others have viewed them as villains imposing their own cultural and class agendas. Recent research suggests that both impulses were present and that relations between settlement workers and local mountain people involved negotiation, search for consensus, and rejection.

See also: HINDMAN SETTLEMENT SCHOOL (CRAFTS); PINE MOUNTAIN SETTLEMENT SCHOOL (CRAFTS); SETTLEMENT, MISSION, AND SPONSORED SCHOOLS.

—Karen W. Tice, *University of Kentucky*

Ruth Hutchinson Crocker, *Social Work and Social Order: The Settlement Movement in Two Industrial Cities, 1889–1930* (1992); Karen W. Tice, "Social-Work and Mother-Work: The Interplay of Maternalism and Cultural Politics in the Educational Narratives of Kentucky Settlement Workers, 1910–1930," *Journal of Appalachian Studies* (Fall 1998); David E. Whisnant, *All That Is Native and Fine: The Politics of Culture in an American Region* (1983).

Settlement, Mission, and Sponsored Schools

In the late nineteenth and early twentieth centuries, more than two hundred private schools sprang up in remote rural areas of Appalachia where there was either no public education or only basic instruction for a few months of the year. Protestant religious denominations sponsored most of these schools, though other organizations and even individuals founded some of them.

The earliest sponsored schools in Appalachia began as mission work by a spiritual leader who saw the need for education. In 1855 the Reverend John G. Fee came to Kentucky and began work that would result in establishing Berea College on a ridge in southern Madison County. From the beginning Berea offered education to all who sought instruction—all races and both genders. The Reverend William Thurston opened the Classical and Agricultural School for boys at Valle Crucis, North Carolina, in 1845 with contributions from Episcopalians. Although this venture did not last long, the Episcopal diocese revived the idea for a mission and school at Valle Crucis toward the end of the century.

Many other church-sponsored schools originated in the late 1800s. The Reverend Luke Dorland and his wife moved to Hot Springs, North Carolina, in 1886. They soon abandoned their planned retirement and started the Dorland Institute under the sponsorship of the Presbyterian Church (USA). Martha Berry organized Sunday schools near her home in the north Georgia hills that later grew into day schools. In 1902 she combined several of her educational outposts into a boarding school for boys, with girls' facilities added in 1909 to form the Berry Schools.

In the first quarter of the twentieth century, many privately run schools sprang up in the mountains and were called variously institutes, academies, seminaries, halls, and colleges (although the word *college* did not necessarily denote higher education); settlement, industrial, agricultural, farm, training, and mission schools also proliferated. Most of the schools offered elementary instruction, with others including high school classes and even some college. The sponsored schools did not compete with publicly funded education but provided services not available locally. Blue Ridge Industrial School near Dyke, Virginia, for instance, offered courses in agriculture, homemaking, and hand skills such as carpentry and weaving.

While these private schools accepted students within walking distance, many provided boarding arrangements. Mary Ann Lipscomb perceived the need for education near her summer home and interested the Georgia Federation of Women's Clubs in sponsoring the Tallulah Falls Industrial School in Habersham County, Georgia. The school first opened in 1909 for area students, expanded rapidly, and by 1912 accepted boarding students.

Sometimes church support for the schools came through a mission effort; at other times it was administered by a regional governing board or through the strong denominational affiliation of a school founder. Although the schools charged tuition, most students attended under work-study programs or with scholarships provided by patrons or the sponsoring organization. A few of the independent schools formed public-private partnerships with local educational authorities. The teachers at Rabun Gap–Nacoochee School just outside Dillard, Georgia, received payment from county funds to run the local high school, while tuition and philanthropic contributions supported boarding students and enrichment programs.

Many of these sponsored schools based their work on the principles of the settlement house movement of large cities, which provided services to immigrant populations. Copying the English model for working among London's

The Knott County Opportunity Center, one of eight buildings located on campus at Hindman Settlement School, Hindman, Kentucky, 2003. The first rural social settlement school in the country, Hindman still serves central Appalachia through various programs, including year-round classes for students with dyslexia.

unfortunates, the reform workers lived among the poor as beacons of a better lifestyle, influencing by example. They believed in the power of progressive education, organized collective action, recreation, modern hygiene, and preventive medicine—all cloaked in activist liberal Christianity. The settlement schools of Appalachia retained these ideals, seeking to be responsive to conditions found in remote rural areas. Although operating under the banner of a school, settlement workers organized community activities, provided basic heath care, and promoted sustainable lifestyles.

Beginning first with summer camps in eastern Kentucky that taught basic literacy and homemaking skills, May Stone and Katherine Pettit established the Hindman Settlement School at Hindman in 1902. They organized clinics with visiting doctors and helped eradicate blindness caused by trachoma. Nurses on staff tended to health concerns of students and educated mothers about infant care. Hindman, like many of the schools, began by providing education to children in the surrounding area but soon offered boarding facilities. In 1912 Pi Beta Phi, the first women's college fraternity, opened their settlement school in Gatlinburg, Tennessee. Within a year, the school had a full-time nurse on staff and encouraged the development of crafts to increase the income of local families. The Appalachian Industrial School at Penland, North Carolina, followed the settlement model even though it was controlled by the Episcopal Diocese of Western North Carolina. The instruction followed a progressive education model, the school sponsored plays involving the community, and in 1923 its Department of Fireside Industries began teaching weaving and selling pieces made by area women.

Though men began the early missions, educated women dominated the creation, managing, and staffing of the schools in the twentieth century. The southern mountains attracted many young women who planned to spend a year or two in meaningful work before assuming the traditional roles of wife and mother. While some of these women returned home, others spent the rest of their lives teaching and organizing in the mountains.

The sponsored schools of the southern Appalachians received support from a women's network of arts organizations, church groups, and community social service associations. While a few schools received direct contributions, the broader women's network provided a forum for fund-raising and the sale of handicrafts produced under school direction. Crossnore School of Crossnore, North Carolina, received aid from the Daughters of the American Revolution and regularly sold weaving made by students and community women at the organization's conventions. Most of the women donors could not be counted on for large sums, but they gave consistently in response to benevolent appeals.

While researching the southern mountains as regional director for the philanthropic social service Russell Sage Foundation, John C. Campbell identified many sponsored schools that knew very little of one another. He brought them together for a conference in 1913, where they realized the similarity of their guiding principles. With the formation of the Conference of Southern Mountain Workers, representatives from schools, missions, and community centers met yearly to share ideas, study common problems, and reinforce their objectives.

Sponsored schools professed a goal of training leaders for the mountains and encouraged advanced learning at other regional institutions. The Caney Creek Community Center in Kentucky, which eventually became Alice Lloyd College, helped students continue their education at the University of Kentucky.

These Appalachian sponsored schools educated thousands and declined only with the spread of universally available public education. As roads improved, students could be bused to regional educational facilities. Many of the schools, with their large physical plants, rededicated themselves to another but often aligned purpose. Pine Mountain Settlement School in Kentucky became a center for environmental education, for instance, and schools such as Mars Hill and Lees-McRae in North Carolina now serve as institutions of higher education.

See also: CAMPBELL, JOHN C. AND OLIVE DAME; HINDMAN SETTLEMENT SCHOOL (CRAFTS); SETTLEMENT HOUSE MOVEMENT.

—Philis Alvic, *Lexington, Kentucky*

Philis Alvic, *Weavers of the Southern Highlands* (2003); John C. Campbell, *The Southern Highlander and His Homeland* (1921); Henry D. Shapiro, *Appalachia on Our Mind: The Southern Mountains and Mountaineers in the American Consciousness, 1870–1920* (1978).

Settlement Schools, Catholic

Since the nineteenth century, Roman Catholics have operated numerous boarding and day schools throughout Appalachia. Catholic "academies," which offered scholarships to the needy and served as nuclei of charitable activities in their respective areas, were generally founded and staffed by religious orders of nuns, priests, and brothers, as opposed to Protestant "settlement schools," which were usually established by laypeople.

The first lay-operated rural Catholic settlement school in Appalachia, Saint Theresa School in Lee County, Kentucky, opened in 1929. Part of a larger project called the Contrary Creek Catholic Community Center, its founder was a Catholic laywoman, Helen E. Keating. Born in Pennsylvania, Keating first came to Kentucky to serve as a teacher and principal for Alice G. Lloyd, founder of one of Appalachia's most celebrated settlement schools, Caney Creek at

Pippa Passes, Kentucky (now Alice Lloyd College). Due to prejudice against Catholics, Lloyd asked Keating not to reveal her religion to others. Seeking to continue her mountain work and still openly practice Catholicism, Keating wrote to Bishop Francis W. Howard of Covington, Kentucky. Howard, who had studied sociology at the graduate school of Columbia University and was one of the founders and first executive secretary of the National Catholic Education Association, welcomed Keating's offer to work among the poor of Appalachia. His diocese included thirty-eight Appalachian counties in Kentucky. With Howard's financial support, Keating established the Contrary Creek Catholic Community Center. Philanthropists from New York and other urban areas contributed financially to the center through monetary donations, as well as through purchases of mountain handicrafts. The center included an elementary school, dormitories, a farm employing students and local citizens, four second-hand clothing stores, programming for all ages, home visitations, and some medical care. A victim of the Great Depression, the opening of more public schools, and Keating's declining health, the school closed in 1936. Three years later, Keating moved to Montana to be near her twin sister. Nevertheless, other activities remained alive at the center into the 1940s, including summer "vacation schools."

Myrtle V. Kesheimer founded the second Catholic settlement school in Appalachia, the Saint Cecilia School of Music and Art in Hazard, Perry County, Kentucky. A friend of Keating, Kesheimer was also supported financially by Bishop Howard and by donors from urban centers. Originally, Howard and Kesheimer were intent on establishing an elementary school but altered their plans in order to avoid needless competition with "Class A-ranked" Hazard schools, as well as nearby settlement schools at Caney Creek, Hindman, and Irishman Creek. The Hazard Catholic community included a second-hand clothing store, a lending library, boarding for mountain students attending the Hazard city schools, catechism and music classes, home visitations, and other charitable work. In 1936 Kesheimer opened Saint Cecilia School of Music and Art, which continued until 1944, when she moved to Lexington. By that time, the heyday of settlement schools had passed, and nuns adopted much of the Appalachian work of Catholic laywomen. Foremost among these was Gertrude Kimmich of the Diocese of Covington, the first member of the Glenmary Sisters (Home Missioners of America), established in 1941 to work among the rural poor of the United States.

See also: SETTLEMENT, MISSION, AND SPONSORED SCHOOLS.

—Paul A. Tenkotte, *Thomas More College*

Paul A. Tenkotte, David E. Schroeder, and Thomas S. Ward, "To Be Catholic and American in Northern, Central, and Appalachian Kentucky: The Diocese of Covington, 1853–2003," unpublished paper, Archives of the Diocese of Covington (2004).

Stewart, Cora Wilson

See Moonlight Schools

Stone, May

(1867–1946) Settlement school founder and teacher.

Given the nickname of "the ladyest" by mountain residents because of her genteel manners and deeply religious nature, May Stone devoted her life to educating Appalachians in both the general school curriculum and in industrial pursuits while also conducting health outreach programs and fireside industries craft work. A native of the Kentucky Bluegrass, the Wellesley College–educated Stone moved to the mountains with Katherine Pettit in 1902 to establish Hindman Settlement School. She remained the school's codirector for the rest of her life.

Born in Owingsville, Kentucky, and reared in Mount Sterling and Louisville, Stone was the daughter of the chief counsel for the Louisville and Nashville Railroad. She became involved with the Kentucky Federation of Women's

May Stone with her students at Hindman Settlement School, Knott County, Kentucky, 1912. Stone, along with fellow educator Katherine Pettit, founded Hindman in 1902 at the invitation of Solomon Everidge, a mountain patriarch who wanted his grandchildren to be educated.

Clubs in the 1890s after attending college for three years, rising to the position of the organization's secretary by 1899. She later traced her first interest in the mountains to the reports of club members who accompanied traveling libraries in the region. Stone was one of the first volunteers to pledge her assistance to Pettit in creating the first of three summer tent settlements in the mountains, where she taught sewing and Sunday school lessons. Stone played a key role in the founding of Hindman under the auspices of the Women's Christian Temperance Union. Although Stone did not graduate from Wellesley, she found the connection to be invaluable for securing volunteers from this and other colleges. She assumed an increasingly visible role after Pettit left to found Pine Mountain Settlement School in 1913. Stone retired as principal of Hindman Settlement School in 1936 but remained on its board of directors until her death in 1946.

See also: FOTCHED-ON WOMEN; HINDMAN SETTLEMENT SCHOOL (CRAFTS); PETTIT, KATHERINE.

—Deborah L. Blackwell, *Texas A&M International University*

Stuart, Jesse

See Stuart, Jesse (Literature)

Teacher Corps

The Teacher Corps was a federally funded program of the Higher Education Act of 1965. Noted economist John Kenneth Galbraith originated the idea, President Lyndon Johnson named the program, and Senators Gaylord Nelson of Wisconsin and Edward Kennedy of Massachusetts drafted the legislation. Authorized $100 million by Congress, the Teacher Corps was designed to strengthen educational opportunities for children who lived in low-income areas, to attract and prepare persons for teaching in these areas through coordinated work-study experiences, and to encourage colleges and universities, schools, and state departments of education to work together to broaden and improve teacher-education programs. East Tennessee State University in Johnson City was selected to pilot the program in 1966. Initially, students were to be assigned to a selected school in Carter County, Tennessee. In 1967 students were placed in Washington County, and in 1968 the program expanded to Bristol, Virginia.

Through the Teacher Corps project at East Tennessee State University, approximately 175 interns were initiated into teaching between 1966 and 1973. Teachers serving as team leaders from the local schools could also earn a graduate degree, and approximately twenty did so. Outside agencies evaluating the projects determined them to be viable and to have reduced the pupil-teacher ratio to as low as eight to one in some schools. Many of the former interns now teach in the local schools, while others have moved on to schools throughout the country.

From the late 1960s to the mid-1970s, the Teacher Corps ran internship programs at numerous colleges and universities throughout the United States, with several programs in the Appalachian region. These institutions included Western Carolina University and Marshall University in West Virginia, which were opened to increase educational efforts of various Appalachian Regional Commission programs. All of these programs followed similar methods in attempting to improve the educational opportunity of students in underprivileged and underfunded school systems while preparing new teacher candidates to enter the educational profession.

The program ran its course and ended as scheduled in the mid-1970s, except for a small presence in Mississippi and California, where it continues to serve low-income populations.

See also: SECTION OVERVIEW.

—George A. Finchum, *East Tennessee State University* and *Milligan College*, and G. Allen Finchum II, *Oklahoma State University*

Teacher Education

Until the turn of the twentieth century, teaching was considered a part-time, temporary job throughout much of rural Appalachia. It was long thought that teaching required no special training, and as late as the 1920s many Appalachian elementary teachers lacked even a high school education. Teacher institutes, summer normal schools, and state normal schools appeared in the Appalachian states somewhat later than in other parts of the country, and they were often poorly funded.

In the nineteenth century, young men with only elementary schooling themselves were often chosen as teachers based on their ability to keep the older boys under control. Others secured teaching positions through nepotism or political patronage. In isolated one-room schools, they taught as they had been taught—by hearing recitations memorized from a variety of handed-down readers. Sometimes teachers were required to pass written examinations for a license to teach, but the questions were often capricious, unrelated to teaching ability, administered haphazardly, and subject to corruption.

Following the Civil War, teacher institutes (some lasting only a week) became widespread. Though popular in the antebellum Northeast, the only location in which they were found in Appalachia prior to 1867 was in western North Carolina. With a gift of two million dollars from investment banker George Peabody, former governors of northern and southern states gathered in 1867 to establish the Peabody Education Fund, which essentially led to the creation of a public education system for the American South. Thereafter, the Peabody Fund organized teacher institutes throughout the region. By the 1870s and 1880s, teachers were often required to attend county and district teacher institutes. Separate institutes were held for African American teachers, often using the same white faculty. These itinerant institutions were well suited to the mountainous terrain, where transportation was difficult, and they helped break down isolation by providing a place to share teaching methods and craft wisdom. The curriculum consisted primarily of talks by the county superintendent, textbook salesmen, and visiting public school advocates.

In Appalachia, state summer normal schools, including separate (but more poorly financed) institutions for African Americans, were established in the 1870s and 1880s. University and out-of-state normal school faculty taught the summer normal schools, and they were a step above county and district institutes in professional training. The summer sessions lasted from four to ten weeks, but the academic requirements were low. Examinations were usually optional. In Tennessee, for example, a student who scored 65 percent received a one-year teacher's certificate, and attendance for three summers was rewarded with a lifetime certificate. Students were attracted with promises of amusements and diversion. In a region of limited outside entertainment, the institutes and summer normal schools were often attended by more laypersons than teachers, and speakers took the opportunity to evangelize the gospel of better schools.

A desire for professionally trained teachers led to the establishment of state normal schools in the northern and western states beginning in the late 1830s; by 1875 there were around seventy in the United States, and approximately one hundred more were established by 1900. In Appalachia, West Virginia created a state normal school system in 1867, but there were concerted efforts in the 1870s to abolish it. North Carolina followed in 1891, when the legislature created the North Carolina Normal and Industrial School for Women. During intensive better-public-school campaigns throughout the South, Kentucky established two state normal schools in 1906, and Tennessee opened four during 1911–12, one for whites in each of the three grand divisions of the state and one for African Americans in Nashville. African American state normal schools often used federal land-grant funds provided by the second Morrill Act of 1890, but they were even more poorly supported than the underfunded white institutions.

Normal schools were not scholarly institutions. The two-year curriculum often consisted of secondary-level coursework with a smattering of courses in pedagogy. Rather than academic studies, state authorities required black normal schools to adopt an industrial, agricultural, and domestic science curriculum.

Conflict over modernization and economic development accompanied campaigns to establish normal schools. Progressive business leaders and educators were chief supporters of state normal schools, and there was much competition among towns to be the site for a normal school campus. Traditionalists feared that normal school proposals were a way of importing outside ideas and wresting school control from parents and the local community. Local patriarchs, who controlled the schools, feared that normal school education would make young women teachers more difficult to control. Parents were also concerned that normal schools would damage their daughters' femininity and morals.

Public normal schools in the Appalachian states competed with proprietary teacher education schools. In Kentucky, for instance, thirty-four private schools received state charters and engaged in teacher training before 1905. North Carolina had dozens of small, private, often church-supported normal schools at the beginning of the twentieth century. In Tennessee, the private Holbrook Normal School of Knoxville trained more teachers than the University of Tennessee in the late 1890s. Knoxville also had a Masonic normal school during the same period.

State universities and state normal schools throughout Appalachia were rivals and frequently came into conflict. Universities, whose administrations and faculties feared that the normal schools would take resources, expand their roles, and become serious competitors, often opposed the establishment of state normal schools. In the minds of university officials, the proper role of the normal schools was limited to training elementary teachers (mainly women), while the universities were to educate high school teachers and school administrators (mainly men).

Coming at the end of the national normal school movement, normal schools in Appalachia enjoyed only brief prominence. Following national trends, most were designated degree-granting teachers' colleges in the 1920s; within another generation, they became general-purpose state colleges.

See also: PRIVATE COLLEGES AND UNIVERSITIES; PUBLIC COLLEGES AND UNIVERSITIES; SECTION OVERVIEW.

—Clinton B. Allison, *University of Tennessee*

Clinton B. Allison, *Teachers for the South: Pedagogy and Educationists in the University of Tennessee, 1844–1995* (1998); Charles H. Ambler, *A History of Education in West Virginia, from Early Colonial Times to 1949* (1951); James L. Leloudis, *Schooling the New South: Pedagogy, Self, and Society in North Carolina, 1880–1920* (1996).

Two-Year Colleges

More than 260 two-year colleges are located in states of the Appalachian region. Two-year schools—comprehensive community colleges, junior colleges, and technical schools—make up a distinctive and diverse section of public higher education separate from four-year colleges and universities. Technical colleges prepare students for careers upon graduation. Junior colleges provide the first two years of four-year transfer programs. Comprehensive community colleges deliver both of these curricula, as well as community-oriented programs. Each state system of two-year colleges has its own structure, history, and mission, but all provide opportunities for low-cost higher education close to students' homes.

Specific programs offered by two-year colleges underscore their ability to serve their populations. Until 2003, for example, Haywood Community College in Clyde, North Carolina, located within a heavily timbered area, offered the nation's only accredited sawyer program in a two-year college. The college also takes into account the large tourist industry associated with the nearby Great Smoky Mountains National Park and the Blue Ridge Parkway, incorporating an entrepreneur component into all of its accredited programs. The combination allows students to gain classroom competencies and simultaneously to develop entrepreneurial skills.

In New York, Onondaga Community College responds to the community's cultural diversity by offering a degree in community professions that integrates community mental health and social services and ethnic studies with other traditional human service programs. Ashland Community College in Ashland, Kentucky, reflects the broad spectrum of community college programs by extending learning across many ages and requirements. The college maintains a Kinder College/Learning Academy to acquaint area young people with higher education and also serves as host to one of the nation's premier teaching/learning conferences to encourage professional development for community college personnel.

Further emphasizing the diversity of the region's two-year colleges, West Virginia University Institute of Technology in Montgomery operates a community and technical college as one of its three colleges. This type of structure allows students to complete an associate degree and a baccalaureate in engineering technology on the same campus.

Various groups and consortia have been developed to enhance access to education as a means of promoting economic vitality in the region. The organization Community Colleges of Appalachia focuses on education in the most economically distressed counties. One of its principal goals is to provide two-year colleges for students who have no family history of attending institutions of higher education. The Rural Community College Initiative has several Appalachian two-year colleges as members and also works to bring economic development to rural areas by addressing community problems and working to bring about institutional change by strengthening partnerships between college and community.

See also: HAYWOOD COMMUNITY COLLEGE PROFESSIONAL CRAFT PROGRAM (CRAFTS).

—Kevin Pennington, *Western Carolina University*

G. A. Baker III, ed., *A Handbook on the Community College in America: Its History, Mission, and Management* (1994); A. M. Cohen and F. B. Brawer, *The American Community College* (3rd edition, 1996); Allen A. Witt et al., *America's Community Colleges: The First Century* (1994).

Warren Wilson College

Warren Wilson College emerged from the home missionary movement that swept across the southern Appalachians in the late nineteenth century. After the Presbyterian Church (USA) opened schools for young women in Asheville and Hot Springs, North Carolina, in the mid-1880s, students from those schools asked mission officials to establish a similar school for boys. In 1894 the Presbyterian Board of Home Missions opened Asheville Farm School on a large tract of Swannanoa Valley bottomland. These schools attracted students from throughout the southern Appalachian region. Their "three-sided" emphasis on academics, manual labor, and Christian service won acclaim and left a distinctive legacy.

By the mid-1920s, dramatic changes posed challenges for the Presbyterian schools. As the Appalachian region came into closer contact with broader American society, changes in mainline Protestantism undermined missionary enthusiasm and funding, and pressing needs elsewhere led Presbyterian officials to consider terminating their western North Carolina work. Asheville Farm School, in particular, was struggling when Henry S. Randolph was named superintendent in 1927. A native Appalachian, Randolph applied the ideals of John Dewey's "progressive education" to the needs of his home region. In the midst of the Great Depression, he attracted a creative faculty, and together they formally integrated academic, work, and service emphases in a program that achieved national acclaim. In 1942 Presbyterian officials, citing improved public schools in the region, consolidated the church's western North Carolina work at the former Asheville Farm School campus and opened the new coeducational Warren Wilson Junior College.

Even more dramatic developments soon challenged the school. By the early 1950s, many students expressed preference for a four-year program rather than the vocationally oriented two-year program. New public schools and improved transportation and communications systems quickly made a purely Appalachian mission school obsolete. In a bold move, school officials in the early 1950s convinced supporters that they could best serve young people from the mountain region by exposing them to the ever-shrinking broader world. Warren Wilson opened its doors to students from around the globe and across the United States and in 1952 became one of the first southern colleges to enroll African Americans. Presbyterian officials in 1962 endorsed a four-year college plan that gradually turned the school over to its own trustees with the stipulation that it serve deserving young people and retain its distinctive work program, service emphasis, and commitment to the region.

Since graduation of its first baccalaureate class in 1969, Warren Wilson has refined its distinctive "triad." Believing that a balanced education is best, the school requires students to participate in mandatory work and service programs, which consist of more than a hundred work crews that provide assistance on campus, in the local community, or in distant locations. Each student is expected to perform fifteen hours of work weekly and to complete at least one hundred hours of service before graduation. Noted nationally for its programs, the school has been ranked by *Mother Jones* magazine as one of the top activist campuses in the country for the past twenty years and was included in the 2004 edition of *The Unofficial, Unbiased Guide to the 328 Most Interesting Colleges*, the only school in western North Carolina so recognized.

See also: PRIVATE COLLEGES AND UNIVERSITIES; SETTLEMENT, MISSION, AND SPONSORED SCHOOLS.

—Mark T. Banker, *Knoxville, Tennessee*

Reuben A. Holden and Mark T. Banker, *Warren Wilson College: A Centennial Portrait* (1994).

Wigginton, Eliot

(1942–) Educator and nonfiction writer.

Eliot Wigginton was founder of the Foxfire program, a teaching approach he devised while instructing language arts at Rabun Gap–Nacoochee School in northeast Georgia in the late 1960s. Eventually, the term *Foxfire* came to refer to both a series of best-selling books about Appalachian folkways that Wigginton's students compiled and to an educational approach eventually adopted by many K–12 classroom teachers around the United States.

Born in 1942 in Wheeling, West Virginia, Wigginton completed a bachelor's degree in English and earned a master's in teaching from Cornell University, as well as a graduate degree in English from Johns Hopkins University. Often called "Wig" by students and associates, Wigginton became a charismatic teacher and an effective advocate for a student-centered approach to classroom instruction. His *Sometimes a Shining Moment* was a major entry into the educational reform movements of the 1980s and 1990s. He served as the president of the Foxfire Fund, Inc., the tax-exempt organization he founded to manage the royalties from the series of *Foxfire* books generated by his students.

In the classroom, Wigginton combined an unrelenting attention to the quality of academic performance with an intense sensitivity to the backgrounds of his students as the beginning point of instruction. Though he possessed a strong classroom presence, he skillfully transferred the responsibility for their learning to the students. Except for short sabbaticals, Wigginton continued as a full-time high school language arts teacher throughout his career.

Awards include John D. Rockefeller III Youth Award, Kurt Hahn Award of the Association for Experiential Education, and a MacArthur Foundation Fellowship, as well as several honorary doctorates. In 1992 Wigginton pled guilty to a single charge of sexually molesting a minor, was sentenced to a year in jail, and resigned from the Foxfire Fund.

See also: FOXFIRE.

—Hilton Smith, *Piedmont College*

Eliot Wigginton, *Sometimes a Shining Moment: The Foxfire Experience* (1985); Eliot Wigginton, ed., *Foxfire: Twenty-Five Years* (1991) and *Refuse to Stand Silently By: An Oral History of Grass Roots Social Activism in America, 1921–1964* (1991); Eliot Wigginton et al., *The Foxfire Book* and *Foxfire 2* through *Foxfire 10* (1972–93).

Women as Educational Leaders

Women have been central to Appalachian education, both formal and informal, for as long as people have occupied the mountains of the eastern United States. Native Americans in the region at the time of European contact lived in matrilineal societies in which guardianship of children—including instruction in many domestic and community responsibilities—fell to women. The earliest white settlers established patterns of education derived from European models. Literate whites in more densely settled areas often taught children the fundamentals of reading and writing in community subscription schools organized, paid for, and administered by parents. Most of these schools' teachers were men, as were most Anglo-American teachers in the colonial and early national eras. Women held important responsibilities in organizing schools and choosing teachers.

But community schools, which had short calendars adapted to the needs of the farming and gathering seasons, were not the primary educational settings for Appalachian children—even for most of the children of literate parents—until after the Civil War. White Appalachians and their neighbors of color shared an emphasis on informal, oral learning in the eighteenth and nineteenth centuries. Recent scholarship suggests that Native American women may have resisted or sought to adapt to their own purposes changes brought by whites. Thus women appear to have played a primary role in preserving and passing on native cultural traditions during and after the colonial period. Children of black Appalachians, denied opportunities for most formal schooling before the Civil War, learned at home from mothers. Occupying primarily an oral culture, Appalachia's African American communities passed on their sustaining social mores and subsistence-related knowledge through verbal instruction and stories. White women also played important roles as bearers of oral tradition and home educators, especially for girls and for boys too young to work at men's tasks. Appalachian Christians received oral instruction in a number of forms; churches in which women testified or taught offered yet another opportunity for children to learn from women. Informal education's importance placed women at the center of most Appalachian children's early learning experiences.

In the years after the Civil War, Appalachian education (formal and informal) underwent fundamental transformations in which women again played central roles. Increased attention to the material and human resources of the Appalachians brought not only entrepreneurs from extractive industries, but also missionaries determined to help mountain residents negotiate the social, political, and economic changes created by the new wave of industrialization. Generally interested in some combination of changing and preserving Appalachian culture to reflect what was perceived as the best of both old and new, missionaries (many affiliated with Protestant churches in the Northeast or lowland South and many operating out of the semi-secularized ethos of the emerging social work profession) relied upon women to "uplift" Appalachia. Middle-class women constituted the largest number of mission workers who traveled into the southern Appalachians, and these women did most of their uplift work in schools. Women frequently held positions of leadership in missions and schools established after the Civil War, sometimes even founding their own.

Reflecting the union of progressive thought and political action, the great wave of mission-sponsored education coincided with a push for increased efficiency and reforms in many public services that often led to a greater role for the state in education. The mission boom also coincided with a return of Democratic politicians to local and state power in southern Appalachia. For these leaders, education for all white children proved a corollary to the systematic disfranchisement of the black community. Regardless of their motivation, early-twentieth-century educational reformers tended to ignore or denigrate the types of learning that took place in Appalachia's small community schools. They also tended to look down upon some of the subsistence practices and folk beliefs passed between Appalachian parents and children as "superstitions." Thus in many ways the educational reformers attempted a revolution in rural Appalachian ways of knowing, one that profoundly changed education in the region even as it was imperfectly realized.

Women were central to the projects of all the educational boosters working in Appalachia in the early twentieth century. Reformers often targeted women as the most promising constituency for uplift since academic training was but a part of this educational project. Instruction in work habits, morals, manners, and tastes also figured heavily into their goals, and women, as future mothers shaping the perceptions and ideas of their children, appealed as a primary outlet for school reformers' zeal. This was true not only of efforts at educating white Appalachian children, but also of schools for children of color. Whether Native American girls in private or state boarding schools or African American girls in segregated common schools, young women often became the special targets of educational uplift efforts.

Women proved key to educators for another reason: they were increasingly regarded as the future teachers who would put reforms into classroom practice. By the 1920s, in step with national trends, most Appalachian teachers in public as well as private schools were women. Women embraced teaching as a profession, valuing the chance for independent living, a socially important role deemed appropriately "maternal," and an increased level of personal academic training. Women's importance as future teachers assured that women in Appalachia enjoyed early access to education beyond high school. In the early twentieth century, when colleges mushroomed in the mountains, collegiate women carved niches in women-only or coeducational private missions colleges.

The Appalachian teaching force (like the teaching force elsewhere) has remained overwhelmingly female throughout the twentieth century. In their teaching role, women have proved central to several educational trends of profound importance to the region: the increase of state control over schools; desegregation; and the end of native boarding schools. Women have also helped engineer the steady consolidation of public schools, which has altered the definition of community life in many Appalachian areas. Moreover, women have continued to play an important role as preservers of elements of oral traditions in their capacities as primary child-care providers.

See also: FOTCHED-ON WOMEN; SETTLEMENT, MISSION, AND SPONSORED SCHOOLS.

—Sandra Hayslette, *Warren Wilson College*

James L. Leloudis, *Schooling the New South: Pedagogy, Self, and Society in North Carolina, 1880–1920* (1996); Theda Perdue, *Cherokee Women: Gender and Culture Change, 1700–1835* (1998); Karen W. Tice, "School-Work and Mother-Work: The Interplay of Maternalism and Cultural Politics in the Educational Narratives of Kentucky Settlement Workers, 1910–1930," *Journal of Appalachian Studies* (Fall 1998).

Zande, Ethel DeLong

(1878–1928) Settlement school founder and teacher.

Born and reared in Montclair, New Jersey, Ethel DeLong arrived in eastern Kentucky in 1901 to teach at the high school at Hindman Settlement School. In 1913 she helped

Katherine Pettit found the Pine Mountain Settlement School in Pine Mountain, Kentucky, where she met and married, in 1918, Luigi Zande, a worker on the school's farm. She remained at Pine Mountain until her death from cancer in 1928, exemplifying the many idealistic young women who had come to the mountains for a summer of reform work and stayed for a lifetime of service.

Zande graduated from Smith College in 1901, after balancing her studies with the care of her invalid family. Following several years of teaching English in Massachusetts and Indiana, she went to the mountains at the invitation of a former colleague. She began publicizing and fund-raising for Hindman even before she accepted a position at the school, and the skills she developed in that work proved invaluable when she and Pettit left to begin the Pine Mountain School. As codirector, Zande made speeches on the school's behalf and ran the main office. When Pine Mountain contracted with the state to build a road, she took a leading role in trying to safeguard the school's investment in the project. She also represented the school in a variety of forums, from talks before women's clubs to the court system after the murder of a school worker.

See also: HINDMAN SETTLEMENT SCHOOL (CRAFTS); PETTIT, KATHERINE; SETTLEMENT, MISSION, AND SPONSORED SCHOOLS.

—Deborah L. Blackwell, *Texas A&M International University*

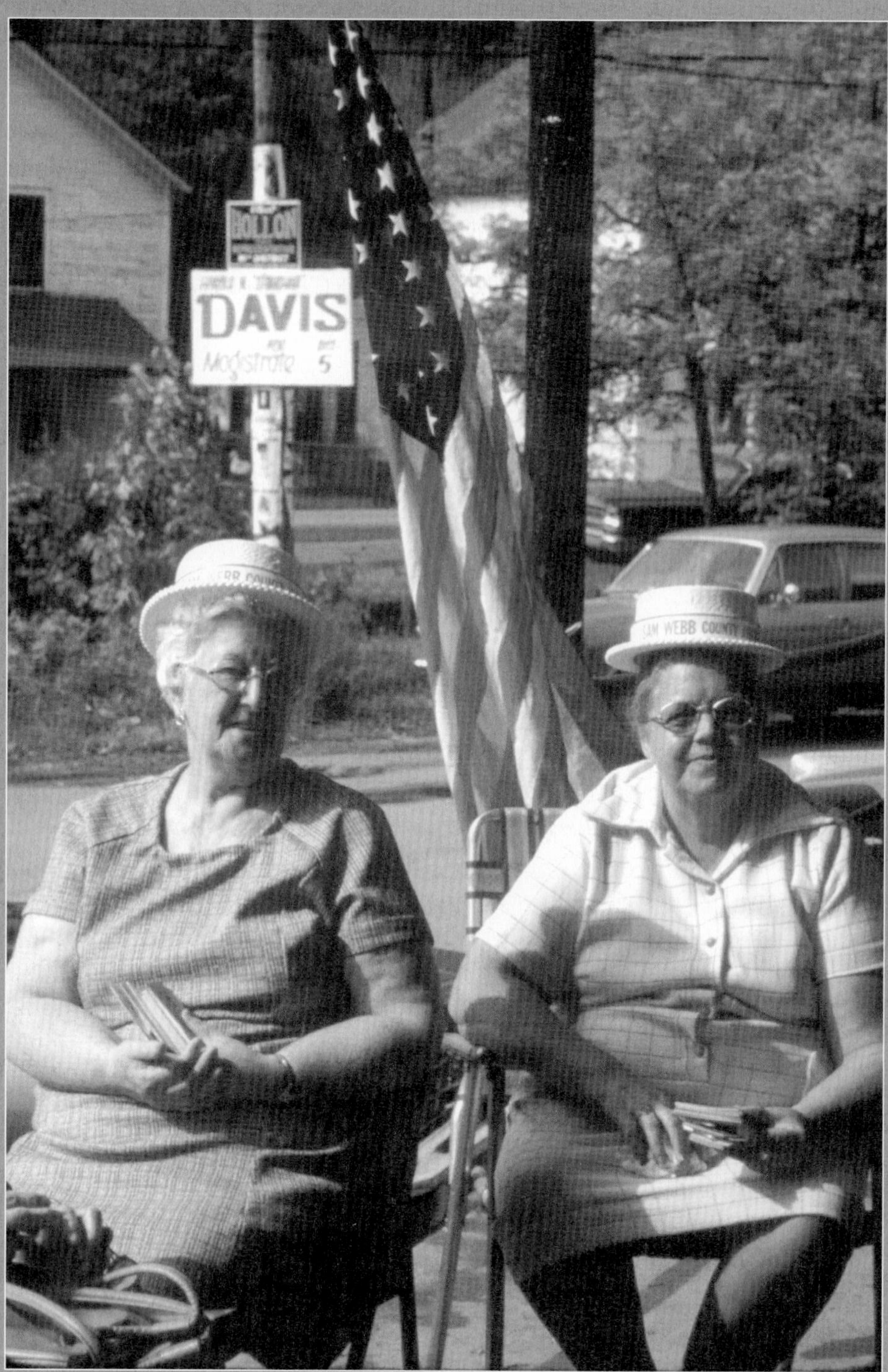
DAVIS
Magistrate
5
SAM WEBB COUNTY

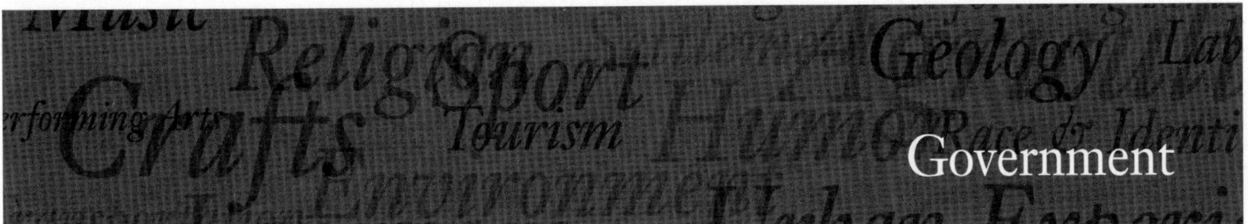

Government

Section Editor: Gordon B. McKinney

The role of government in Appalachia has expanded steadily since the eighteenth century, but developments in politics, law, and the military have followed no set pattern and have often been deeply influenced by forces from outside the region. At the same time, it is fair to say that both state and local governments have been dominated by local elites who followed policies that ensured their continued dominance and that voters have exhibited certain enduring characteristics, including strong partisan loyalty and racial prejudice. Entries in the following section examine longterm influences and significant individual events of both historical and contemporary interest.

To the earliest European settlers, Appalachia seemed a place without government. Native Americans who inhabited the region had no written laws and appeared to have no formal legal system or governing structure. Europeans did recognize that the Indians had a significant military presence, however. The result was a series of aggressive military expeditions into western North Carolina, western Virginia, and western Pennsylvania during the French and Indian War of 1754–63. The most significant of these incursions was that of British General Edward Braddock, who failed to capture Fort Duquesne, on the site of present-day Pittsburgh. Many Indian groups rejected the Treaty of Paris that ended the fighting. In an effort to secure peace and to limit the cost of running its now vast empire, the British government established the Proclamation Line of 1763, issuing an edict forbidding European colonists from settling in or crossing the Appalachian region. This policy angered settlers and became one of the irritants that would fuel later hostilities. When the American Revolution began, Native Americans, not surprisingly, sided with the British. Expeditions from Virginia, North Carolina, and Tennessee broke the military power of the Cherokee in 1776 and opened up part of the southern mountains. Three years later, colonists in this part of the Appalachians faced a British-Tory invasion. Local militias fiercely responded to the threat, and the Overmountain Men from Tennessee, North Carolina, and Virginia defeated the British at the battle of Kings Mountain, South Carolina.

With American independence secured in 1783, European American settlers streamed into and through Appalachia. The Great Valley of Appalachia continued to be a major migration route for people in western Pennsylvania looking for fertile

Facing page: Election day in eastern Kentucky, 1977.

soil to the south. In an effort to secure peace with the Indians who remained in many parts of Appalachia and beyond, the United States government signed a series of treaties that set specific boundaries, including the Treaty of Hopewell with the Cherokees in 1785. Two years later, the national government passed the Northwest Ordinance, opening the Midwest, including the mountain counties of southeastern Ohio, to settlement. Thereafter, the European population grew rapidly, and people in the mountains began to demand local political control. In 1792 Kentucky was separated from Virginia and entered the Union as the fifteenth state. Activists led by John Sevier unilaterally created the State of Franklin, but North Carolina refused to give up sovereignty. Intense negotiations followed, and in 1796 the new state of Tennessee was created with Sevier as governor. Like British authorities before them, American politicians found the mountain region difficult to govern. In 1794 President George Washington sent an army into western Pennsylvania to secure payment of the recently imposed internal revenue tax. A similar confrontation in western North Carolina was averted only by the failure of the national government to send troops. The Whiskey Rebellion, as the Pennsylvania episode is known, did not result in open violence, but the national government found it expedient to repeal the tax.

As the American population expanded, conflict with the remaining Indians continued. During the War of 1812, midwestern tribes under the leadership of Tecumseh, including some in western Pennsylvania and southeastern Ohio, allied with the British. When a peace treaty removed the British influence from the region, the Indians were forced westward in 1814. The Creek Indians in Georgia and Alabama were routed at the battle of Horseshoe Bend by a combined American and Cherokee force led by Andrew Jackson. After 1815 only the Cherokees in western North Carolina, eastern Tennessee, northern Georgia, and northern Alabama remained as a major Native American presence in Appalachia. A small group of Cherokees assimilated, creating a written language, holding slaves, and in 1827 establishing a written constitution. The discovery of gold in western North Carolina and—particularly—in northern Georgia led to a civilian invasion of Cherokee lands. Harassment of the Cherokees' supporters escalated to serious proportions and led to the United States Supreme Court case *Worcester v. Georgia*, in which the Court found for the Cherokees. Jackson, now president, refused to enforce the *Worcester* decision and continued to pressure the Cherokees to leave their lands. In 1835 a minority group of Cherokees signed the Treaty of New Echota, which was approved by the United States Senate. In 1838–39 the Cherokees were forced to migrate to present-day Oklahoma on the "Trail of Tears." Large numbers of Cherokees perished during this disgraceful episode.

European American settlers who replaced the Indians interacted with their own local governments but had little contact with either state or federal governments. Throughout the mountain region, county governments were set up as the population increased. Nearly always, local elites dominated these governments. In states south of the Ohio River, officeholders and other political leaders usually owned slaves. In the years after 1800, many of them were aligned with the Democratic-Republican Party of Thomas Jefferson and James Madison. Local courts were established to handle most of the legal disputes, and school systems were formed in every county. The elites generally favored a market economy and often sought help at the state and national levels for their efforts. An early federal construction project—the Chesapeake and Ohio Canal—connected western Maryland with the Potomac River near the city of Washington, but this was one of the very few examples of this type of positive government action in Appalachia.

The frustrations of the elites who wanted more positive government played a major role in the creation of political parties in Appalachia in the 1820s and 1830s. In the mountain counties of New York, Pennsylvania, and Ohio, local leaders resisted the influence of politicians associated with business groups and generally joined the Democratic Party. In the South, the majority of mountain politicians and voters aligned themselves against the downstate plantation elite and favored the Whig Party. In all parts of the region, the chief complaint of mountain politicians was discrimination against their own sections.

In many areas, the failure of the state governments to support improvements in transportation was particularly resented. In *State of Pennsylvania v. Wheeling and Belmont Bridge Company* in 1852, the U.S. Supreme Court ruled that no company could claim a state-sponsored transportation monopoly, setting a landmark precedent in defining the legal rights of all Americans within the transportation system. On the issue of slavery there was no difference between the two parties in southern Appalachia: politicians of both parties and at all levels staunchly supported it. Yet where whites were concerned, the political system appeared to be open enough that individuals from humble backgrounds such as Andrew Johnson of east Tennessee and Joseph E. Brown of northern Georgia could win elections and become part of the ruling class.

As the tensions between the North and South escalated after the war with Mexico, Appalachia's citizens and political leaders found themselves caught in the middle. While nearly all southern Appalachian politicians supported slavery, many of them rejected both the extremism of the Deep South and the radical abolitionist advocacy of separation from the Union. As the political system disintegrated in the 1850s, partisan lines remained intact in Appalachia. After the demise of the Whig Party, its adherents briefly joined the Know-Nothings in the middle of the decade. When this party disappeared, the former Whigs and antislavery Democrats formed the Republican Party in western New York, western Pennsylvania, and southeastern Ohio. Below the Ohio River, the former Whigs created a series of opposition parties and won occasional elections in the mountains.

John Brown's raid on Harpers Ferry, Virginia, in 1859 brought the crisis of the Union home to Appalachia and made the region an important part of the political crisis surrounding the election of 1860. As the national political system split, so did politics in Appalachia. In the mountain counties of New York, Ohio, and Pennsylvania, Republican candidate Abraham Lincoln confronted Stephen Douglas, who had gained the regular Democratic Party nomination. In the southern mountains, John Bell of Tennessee ran as the candidate of the Constitutional Union Party and John C. Breckinridge of Kentucky as the choice of the southern Democrats. After Lincoln's election and the secession of South Carolina, many mountain political leaders urgently sought a peaceful solution to the crisis. They were among the individuals who had attended conventions in early 1861 and tried to find a compromise between the sections. They often ran for election to state conventions as opponents of secession. These Unionists, as they were sometimes characterized, won majorities in the mountain counties of Alabama, Georgia, northwestern Virginia, North Carolina, and Tennessee. But when war came, the majority of political leaders and voters in western North Carolina, northern Georgia, and northern Alabama supported the Confederacy.

The Civil War had an enormous impact on all parts of Appalachia. In the 1860–61 crisis that followed Lincoln's election, mountain people generally sought to avoid conflict. After secession, the majority accepted the new Confederate government with varying degrees of reluctance. A minority—particularly in east Tennessee and northwest Virginia—militantly resisted the new nation. In the latter location, pro-Union leadership created a new state that entered the United States as West Virginia in June 1863. During the war, the mountain regions south of the Ohio River experienced persistent internal warfare. Thousands of civilians were killed by neighbors and kin—the best known such episode being the Shelton Laurel Massacre in Madison County, North Carolina.

Many other Appalachians suffered greatly when large armies fought in their midst. There were two main arenas for this level of activity. The first was the fertile Shenandoah Valley of Virginia. From 1861 through the summer of 1864, Confederate forces consistently defeated Union armies in this region. The best known of the commanders was Thomas "Stonewall" Jackson, a native of the area that became West Virginia. In the fall of 1864, a Union army eventually gained control of the region and destroyed most of the farms in the valley. The second area of major military activity was in southeastern Tennessee and northwestern Georgia. In the summer of 1863, Union armies advanced into east Tennessee, occupied Chattanooga and Knoxville, and then marched into northwestern Georgia. At the battle of Chickamauga, the Confederate army defeated Union forces and besieged them in Chattanooga. A successful Union assault on Missionary Ridge in November 1863 compelled the Confederates to retreat. In the spring of 1864, a large Union force under the command of William T. Sherman maneuvered and fought its way to the city limits of Atlanta. In both of these instances and in smaller military actions, the civilians in the region suffered great material losses.

The aftermath of the Civil War was a trying period in all parts of Appalachia. Northern states industrialized rapidly, and in the steel mills and coal mines of western Pennsylvania widespread labor unrest followed. Among the most significant crises were the railroad strike of 1877, the activities of the Molly Maguires in the 1860s and 1870s, and the Homestead strike of 1894. Similar tensions arose in the iron and coal districts around Chattanooga and Birmingham, Alabama. In eastern Kentucky, southwestern Virginia, east Tennessee, and West Virginia, corporations based in New York, Pittsburgh, and elsewhere secured vast coal deposits and tracts of timber. In all of these instances, local, state, and federal agencies and officials either worked closely with the outsider industrialists or were directly controlled by them. Among the leading examples of these industrial politicians were U.S. Senators Henry Gassaway Davis and Stephen B. Elkins of West Virginia.

Efforts to reach an adjustment of race relations after the Civil War were usually acrimonious, notwithstanding the fact that Andrew Johnson, the incumbent president of the United States, was from east Tennessee. Johnson's efforts to find a conservative policy acceptable to whites in the southern states were rejected by the Republican leadership in Congress. Congressional Republicans adopted forward-looking civil rights legislation in the Thirteenth, Fourteenth, and Fifteenth Amendments to the Constitution, and conservative southern whites reacted with violent opposition. The most conspicuous instrument of their opposition was the Ku Klux Klan, formed in Tennessee in 1866. The original Klan was strongest in upper South Carolina and bordering counties of North Carolina and northern counties in Georgia, Alabama, and Mississippi. Although forced to disband by the army, Klan members conducted campaigns of intimidation and lynching against black males for supposed violations of community mores. Among the largest outbreaks of violence in Appalachia was the Roanoke riot of 1893, in which police opened fire on a lynching party, leaving eight whites dead.

The excesses of the Klan encouraged white political leaders to seek less sensational ways of imposing racial control. Two policies were quickly developed to implement this strategy—segregation and disfranchisement. Under the direction of state and local governments, southern segregation required rigid separation of blacks and whites. This policy prevailed in public accommodations, transportation, education, the workplace, and elsewhere. For example, in 1908 the U.S. Supreme Court upheld Kentucky's Day Law, which required segregation in higher education in the state.

Disfranchisement was a political strategy regularly written into law. Starting with Mississippi in 1890 and ending with Georgia in 1908, former Confederate states passed laws mandating literacy tests, poll taxes, and other means to effectively prevent voting by African Americans (and poor whites) in many parts of southern Appalachia. These policies ensured elite control of state and local politics and enabled the Democratic Party to maintain control at the state level and in many counties in the southern mountains. Partially in reaction to such undemocratic tactics and abuses, most voters in northern Appalachia supported the Republican Party.

As parts of the region industrialized, business leaders seized firm control of their parties. Textile and coal companies built company towns to house their workers, creating a captive labor force and enabling the owners and management to dominate political as well as economic life of the region. While business leaders controlled both parties, they tended to be more numerous in the Republican ranks. One by-product of business leadership of party organizations was the dominant influence of money in political campaigns and in spreading corruption in mountain elections.

This elite control of the political and economic system provoked two sharply different reactions—progressivism and conservatism. Progressives were found in both major parties and were an important faction in the mountain counties. In general terms, the progressives were middle-class urban dwellers who sought to bring order to their communities. Among the reforms they supported were prohibition, woman suffrage, electoral reform, regulation of abusive business practices, and especially improvement of education. Perhaps the most important piece of progressive legislation at the national level was the Weeks Act of 1911, which encouraged the growth of national forests in Appalachia. When the Republican Party split in 1912, most mountain Republicans—north and south—voted for Theodore Roosevelt and the Progressive Party rather than the regular Republican candidate.

Conservatives were usually residents of more rural areas. Often distrustful of business and skeptical about urban ways, they sought to return the region to a less complicated past. They also endorsed prohibition, but their crusades took them away from the middle-class mainstream of American politics. Many thousands of men and women with conservative allegiances joined the revived Ku Klux Klan, which enjoyed growing strength in the North as well as the South. In the mid-1920s, the Klan was as strongly anti-Catholic as anti-black. During the 1928 presidential election, conservative Democrats revolted against the candidacy of Al Smith of New York, a Roman Catholic. Ironically, Smith had gained the party's nomination by demonstrating that he could compete in the South by winning the West Virginia primary. At the same time, conservatives dramatized the chasm between progressives and conservatives by trying to eliminate the teaching of evolution in public schools. The famous Scopes trial put the issue on display in Dayton, Tennessee, in 1925 and captivated the nation.

The Great Depression brought enormous expansion of the federal government throughout Appalachia. Many of President Franklin D. Roosevelt's New Deal programs were national in scope and not particularly directed at the region. Among the most important of these was the Civilian Conservation Corps, which employed out-of-work young men in forests throughout the region to restore exploited and neglected land and water resources. Other programs sought to help additional segments of the population. The Work Projects Administration, for example, employed all kinds of workers on local construction and cultural initiatives. Many public and educational buildings were constructed, and artists were commissioned to decorate these structures. Other artists were employed by the Resettlement Administration's Music Program. For the elderly and disabled in Appalachia, the Social Security Act was the beginning of federal support that has extended to the present day. For industrial laborers, the most important innovation was the Wagner Act—formally the National Labor Relations Act—providing labor unions the legal machinery needed to gain a foothold in the coal industry in particular.

Other New Deal actions had a greater impact on Appalachia than the remainder of the country. The Tennessee Valley Authority (TVA) was created to control flooding on the Tennessee River and to improve the lives of the people who lived in the vast Tennessee Valley. Constructing large hydroelectric dams and working in conjunction with the Rural Electrification Administration, TVA provided tens of thousands of mountain families with electricity for the first time. The creation of new national parks and forests brought an even greater federal presence to the region. Among these were the Shenandoah National Park, the Blue Ridge Parkway, and the Great Smoky Mountains National Park. These federal initiatives came at a fearful price for some Appalachian residents, who were uprooted by the national parks and forests and by lakes created by TVA dams. Many of those displaced were willing to move, but others decried the loss of community and objected to being expelled from lands their families had owned for generations. Despite the largely positive reaction to the New Deal in the mountain regions, partisan loyalties remained largely intact into the twenty-first century. Although President Roosevelt carried many traditionally Republican counties in Pennsylvania and Ohio and converted coal miners in West Virginia and Kentucky, Republicans had regained much of their strength in northern and central Appalachia by 1940.

The Great Depression was ended by huge government expenditures in preparation for World War II. As in the previous decade, the wartime impact of the federal government was immense. Selective Service was instituted in 1940, and Appalachians flocked to military service after the bombing of Pearl Harbor on December 7, 1941. The patriotism of mountain men was exemplified in Breathitt County, Kentucky, where enlistments made a draft unnecessary throughout the war. Military camps and reservations were placed in a number of mountain locations. The most significant of these facilities was the remote complex at Oak Ridge, Tennessee, where enriched uranium was produced for early atomic weapons. The pressure of patriotism led to the celebrated Supreme Court decision in the case of *West Virginia Board of Education v. Barnette* (1943). In this controversy the Court held that the state could not force children who were Jehovah's Witnesses to pledge allegiance to the flag of the United States—a violation of their religious beliefs. Following the war, the passage of the G.I. Bill extended educational opportunities to a greatly expanded number of Appalachian residents. This also led to the rapid expansion of public college systems throughout the region.

The next major impact upon life in Appalachia by the government came in the 1960s. Among the most significant landmarks were the Civil Rights Act of 1964 and the Voting Rights Act of 1965. Prompted by reports of economic distress in the region and protests across the Deep South, the administrations of Presidents John F.

President Franklin D. Roosevelt speaking at the dedication of the Great Smoky Mountains National Park, 1940. Controversy over land acquisition, funding, and development delayed dedication of the park until fourteen years after passage of legislation authorizing its creation. The Smokies welcome more visitors annually than any other national park.

Kennedy and Lyndon Johnson launched a number of new initiatives that Johnson labeled the "War on Poverty." Among these programs were Medicare and Medicaid, Head Start, and Volunteers in Service to America. The first of these was designed to ensure that the elderly and poor across the nation had access to health care. While the impact may have been greater in Appalachia than elsewhere, the program was not aimed directly at the region. The Appalachian Regional Commission, passed through the efforts of Governor Bert Combs of Kentucky and others, was significantly different in that respect. Created by Congress in 1965 to provide the infrastructure necessary to revive Appalachia's economy, its primary contribution has been to greatly improve the highway transportation system of the entire region. At the same time, local elites have used these funds to help secure their dominant position.

Despite the efforts of the federal, state, and local governments, the economic distress in many parts of the region remained a persistent problem, and growing dissatisfaction was directed toward these governments. Many citizens in all parts of Appalachia viewed their local governments as inept or corrupt. Their perceptions of their state governments were often hardly more sanguine. In all of the states except West Virginia, people in the mountain counties felt that their interests were being sacrificed for the benefit of more urban centers. There was also a significant dissatisfaction with the federal government. For many whites in southern Appalachia, the federal civil rights laws and court decisions of the 1960s brought unwelcome changes in race relations. Starting with the 1972 presidential election, this dissatisfaction led to a massive migration of voters out of the Democratic Party into the Republican Party. This created a new highly competitive political environment in areas of previous dominance by Democrats.

Increasingly, Appalachians took sharp issue with specific policies. In the 1960s and 1970s, relatively small numbers of college students in Appalachia protested against the Vietnam War, and the vast majority of mountain youth accepted the government's policy and once again participated in the fighting in large numbers. But throughout the entire mountain region, citizens objected to the *Roe v. Wade* decision on abortion. Their concerns led many previously uninvolved citizens to become activists in regional politics. Ironically, this increasing dissatisfaction came at a time when Appalachian political figures had unprecedented access to power. During the administration of President Jimmy Carter, West Virginian Cyrus Vance was secretary of state, and eastern Kentucky native Juanita Kreps was secretary of commerce. In the Senate, the Democratic leader was Robert C. Byrd of West Virginia, and the Republican leader was Howard Baker of Tennessee. Powerful House of Representative members included Roy Taylor of western North Carolina, Daniel Flood of western Pennsylvania, and Carl D. Perkins of eastern Kentucky. Despite the prominence of regional political figures, increasing numbers of regional citizens came to view the government with indifference or hostility. As the twentieth century came to a close, fewer Appalachians were voting or participating in political activities. These perceptions were part of a broad national trend that indicated a lack of faith in democratic politics in both the region and the nation.

—Gordon B. McKinney, *Berea College*

Michael Bradshaw, *The Appalachian Regional Commission: Twenty-Five Years of Government Policy* (1992); Erwin C. Hargrove, *Prisoners of Myth: The Leadership of the Tennessee Valley Authority, 1933–1990* (1994); Gordon B. McKinney, *Southern Mountain Republicans, 1865–1900: Politics and the Appalachian Community* (1978); Wilbur R. Miller, *Revenuers and Moonshiners: Enforcing Federal Liquor Law in the Mountain South, 1865–1900* (1991); Jerry Bruce Thomas, *An Appalachian New Deal: West Virginia in the Great Depression* (1998); David E. Whisnant, *Modernizing the Mountaineer: People, Power, and Planning in Appalachia* (1980).

American Revolution

Although few important battles occurred anywhere near the Appalachians, the American Revolution profoundly affected the region, and almost every time the fighting did approach the mountains, it was disastrous for the British.

In 1777 American and British forces met at Saratoga in New York, where the British offensive to cut off New England was defeated by massed local militias from the Hudson Highlands. The battle of Saratoga was a major turning point in the war, as a French alliance with the Americans soon followed. Britain's next major military offensive was in the South in 1780, and it ended in defeat at the hands of backwoodsmen at Kings Mountain in South Carolina, as did a battle at nearby Cowpens a few months later.

European colonists living in the Appalachians during the Revolution were generally sympathetic to the patriot cause, for they wished to continue the region's aggressive land speculation and open settlement. There were also important British loyalists in the region, but Appalachia largely avoided the local bitterness that led down-country Carolina into a virtual civil war.

Probably the most significant effect of the American Revolution in the region was the defeat of Indian tribes allied with the British, namely, the Six Nations of the Iroquois, who dominated northern Appalachia, and the Cherokee, the principal Indian power in the southern mountains. In two brutal campaigns, one in 1776 and the other in 1780, the Cherokee were defeated and their major towns decimated. To the north, the Iroquois were effectively destroyed by a massive campaign led by the New York militia in 1779 under the command of the Generals George Clinton and John Sullivan. Neither Indian nation was able effectively to resist intruding settlers following these devastating defeats.

Native American opposition to settlement was more successful in Kentucky and Ohio, where a Shawnee-Mingo force won what was the last battle of the American Revolution at Licking River in northern Kentucky, against a Kentucky militia led by Daniel Boone.

See also: CHEROKEE (RACE, ETHNICITY, AND IDENTITY); IROQUOIS (RACE, ETHNICITY, AND IDENTITY); SHAWNEE (RACE, ETHNICITY, AND IDENTITY).

—Richard B. Drake, *Berea College*

John R. Alden, *The American Revolution, 1775–1783* (1954); John Mack Faragher, *Daniel Boone: The Life and the Legend of an American Pioneer* (1992); Francis Jennings, *The Invasion of America: Indians, Colonialism, and the Cant of Conquest* (1975).

Appalachian Development Highway System

See Appalachian Development Highway System (Transportation)

Appalachian Regional Commission

Created in 1965 by the Appalachian Regional Development Act, the Appalachian Regional Commission is a joint state-federal agency established to coordinate regionwide planning and the allocation of federal funds for highways, water facilities, and other public infrastructure for economic development. Since 1965 the commission has channeled more than $16 billion of federal money into the thirteen-state region designated as Appalachia.

In the late 1950s and early 1960s, mountain counties and communities from Pennsylvania to Alabama were plagued by low per capita income, high unemployment, and weak economies dominated by the coal, timber, and textile industries. Roads, schools, public-health services, and public institutions in general lagged far behind standards in the nation at large. These problems were the result of a sharp decline in jobs in the region after mining and other dominant industries displaced people with improved machinery, national and international demand for Appalachian coal declined, and a massive number of workers migrated out of the region to seek jobs elsewhere. A spate of devastating floods added to the region's misery.

As early as 1951, staff at the Council of the Southern Mountains had called for regional collaboration and the establishment of a multistate agency to address the growing social and economic problems. The council believed that partnerships between the Appalachian states and the federal government held the key to coordinated development and more efficient use of public resources to promote growth. Late in the decade a group of businessmen and educators in eastern Kentucky led by John D. Whisman of the Kentucky Jaycees drafted Program 60, a plan for area recovery that included a call for Appalachian governors to work together to address their mutual concerns and raise the plight of Appalachia on the national agenda. When eastern Kentucky attorney Bert Combs was elected governor of his home state in 1959, he adopted the plan as a goal for his administration. In the spring of 1960, Combs and Governor Millard Tawes of Maryland formed the Conference of Appalachian Governors, which called upon congressional and presidential candidates that year to endorse a special program of development for Appalachia and to establish a federal commission to coordinate its implementation. After John F. Kennedy defeated Richard Nixon in the November election, the nine participating governors hoped that the young president would follow through on their initiative.

While campaigning for the Democratic Party nomination in West Virginia, Kennedy encountered living conditions that he found appalling in a prosperous nation, and he promised to help the people of the Mountain State if elected. As president, he sponsored the Area Redevelopment

Act, which provided limited funding for distressed communities across the country, but this legislation proved inadequate to the needs of Appalachia. Under increased pressure from the Appalachian governors and growing media awareness of poverty in the mountains, Kennedy finally established the President's Appalachian Regional Commission in 1963. Chaired by Franklin D. Roosevelt Jr., the President's Appalachian Regional Commission prepared the political framework for a separate Appalachian development program by working with academics, local officials, and state government leaders. Following Kennedy's assassination, the Appalachian governors gained President Lyndon Johnson's support for the Appalachian initiative. Shortly after declaring a national assault on poverty, Johnson submitted the Appalachian Regional Development Act to Congress, and although the legislation died in the House of Representatives in 1964, it eventually passed in March 1965.

The act established the Appalachian Regional Commission as a unique government program that not only designated special funds for the "underdeveloped" region but also created a joint policymaking and funding partnership between state and federal governments. Composed of a federal cochair appointed by the president and the governors of the original nine states of the President's Commission plus those of Mississippi, New York, Ohio, and South Carolina—added to ensure political support for the act's passage—this arrangement gives governors a direct voice in allocation of federal funds in their states. Each year governors submit a list of requested projects to the commission; allocation decisions require a majority vote of the governors plus the vote of the federal cochair. The commission determines the formula by which the annual appropriation from Congress is distributed among the states and approves each state's developmental plan. Much of the work of the commission is done by appointed state alternates and program officers in close consultation with their governors. Initially, multicounty local development districts were created in each state to facilitate area planning and the administration of funded projects. Over time, each state has developed its own system for receiving and prioritizing proposals, and in some states the planning and public participation functions of local development districts have diminished.

Programs for which the Appalachian Regional Commission provides funding have varied from decade to decade, governor to governor, and federal administration to federal administration. More than 80 percent of total funding has been allocated to the construction of the thirty-two-hundred-mile Appalachian Development Highway System, but funds have also been utilized for the construction of health and vocational education facilities, public housing, and sewage-treatment plants; timber development and mining area restoration; water resource planning, research, and technical assistance; land stabilization; and conservation control. Though not often acknowledged by ordinary citizens, the Appalachian Regional Commission has played a major role in building much of the modern physical infrastructure that helped to transform Appalachia in the late twentieth century. Commission resources have helped to create jobs, improve transportation, expand health services, and increase access to education for millions of Appalachians, substantially narrowing the gap in economic disparity between the region as a whole and the rest of the nation.

The program has not been without controversy, however, and critics have challenged the commission's policies and investment strategies throughout its history. During the 1960s and 1970s the commission drew close scrutiny from critics in government, academia, and the social activist community within Appalachia. Conservative opponents in Congress felt that the commission granted unfair advantage to one area of the country over other deserving regions; scholars and activists in Appalachia argued that the commission, based in Washington, D.C., had little understanding of the region's real needs and failed to be truly responsive to grassroots concerns. Appalachian writer Harry Caudill believed that it had simply turned over the distribution of millions of dollars of federal aid in the mountains to the local political bosses and business interests who had created the problems in the first place. Other critics decried the lack of any real regionwide strategy for comprehensive development, questioned the emphasis upon highways and infrastructure development at the expense of human and social development programs, and noted the failure of the commission to address structural problems involving land ownership, taxation, and political corruption.

Presidential support remained high throughout the 1970s, but the commission suffered major budget reductions and struggled to survive in the 1980s. President Ronald Reagan earmarked the commission for extinction, but bipartisan support from regional governors and powerful congressmen restored appropriations, albeit at a much reduced level. Consequently, the commission adopted a "finish up" policy that included a set-aside of special funds for the most persistently distressed counties. Years of funding infrastructure projects in the larger towns and county seats of the region at the expense of rural districts had produced disproportionate wealth. Investment in "growth centers," initially mandated by legislation and sustained by state and local politics, helped many counties on the periphery of the region to approach national standards of per capita income and employment, but a core of counties at the heart of Appalachia (primarily in eastern Kentucky and southern West Virginia) remained severely distressed. By 2004, 82 of the commission's 410 counties were still eligible for distressed county funding.

Although non-highway allocations never returned to their pre-1980 levels, appropriations stabilized in the 1990s, and the commission was reinvigorated under the leadership of Jesse White, appointed by President Bill Clinton. In addition to expanding the Distressed Counties Program, White launched several special initiatives to promote entrepreneurship, encourage the development of small businesses, enhance investment capital, and strengthen telecommunications technology in the region. In 1996 the commission issued a new strategic plan that emphasized workforce development, physical infrastructure, job creation, health care, and civic leadership. The latter goal represented growing recognition within the commission of the importance of social capital to community growth.

By the beginning of the twenty-first century, the Appalachian Regional Commission had contributed significantly to the modernization of Appalachian life and culture. Highways, industrial parks, water lines, health clinics, and other facilities improved the quality of life in many communities across the region, reducing the socioeconomic disparity between the nation and Appalachia as a whole. Despite these changes, however, other mountain communities continued to lag behind the rest of the country much as they had forty years before. The persistence of distress in the heart of Appalachia motivated Congress in 2000 to reauthorize the commission for another five years. Launched as an experiment in regional planning and government cooperation, the Appalachian Regional Commission has survived criticism, budget reductions, and presidential neglect to remain an enduring symbol of regional identity and politics.

See also: APPALACHIAN CENTERS AND INSTITUTES (CULTURAL INSTITUTIONS); APPALACHIAN DEVELOPMENT HIGHWAY SYSTEM (TRANSPORTATION); COMBS, BERT.

—Ron Eller, *University of Kentucky*, and Glen Edward Taul, *Georgetown College*

Appalachian Regional Commission, *Setting a Regional Agenda* (1996); Michael Bradshaw, *The Appalachian Regional Commission: Twenty-Five Years of Government Policy* (1992); David E. Whisnant, *Modernizing the Mountaineer: People, Power, and Planning in Appalachia* (1980).

Asheville Armory

The Asheville Armory was started by Robert W. Pulliam, Ephraim Clayton, and George Whitson of Asheville, North Carolina, in 1861. By November 1862, the firm employed 107 workers and had produced two hundred rifles for the Confederate army.

Inexplicably, this activity took place without the knowledge of Confederate authorities. When Josiah Gorgas, chief of Confederate ordnance, discovered the factory, he ordered an inspection. The devastating report concluded that the guns made there were useless and the labor performed was worse than thrown away. As a result of the investigation, Captain Benjamin Sloan was appointed to take direct control of the armory. Sloan found, to his dismay, that he could do little to improve the situation. The materials needed to manufacture the rifles had to be transported over a totally inadequate transportation system. In addition, the quality of local iron was judged to be miserable by another Confederate official. Equally significant was the fact that many local workers would not adjust to the discipline required in the specialized manufacturing procedures created by Sloan.

Federal incursions into western North Carolina in the fall of 1863 seemed to be aimed at disrupting the armory's operation. Confederate authorities decided to transfer the equipment in the armory to Columbia, South Carolina, and the armory building itself was destroyed by the Union army in the spring of 1865. This attempt to create a modern manufacturing concern in the mountains—a complete failure—was an early indication that complex industrial development would be dependent upon outside expertise and resources.

See also: ASHEVILLE, NORTH CAROLINA (TOURISM); CIVIL WAR.

—Gordon B. McKinney, *Berea College*

Baker, Howard, Jr.

(1925–) U.S. senator and ambassador.

Howard Henry Baker Jr. was born in Huntsville, Tennessee, on November 15, 1925, to Howard Henry Baker Sr., a future U.S. congressman, and his wife, Dora Ladd Baker. After graduating from a military preparatory school in Chattanooga in 1941, Baker enlisted in the U.S. Navy and through an officer training program studied electrical engineering at the University of the South and at Tulane University. During summers and school breaks, he was assigned naval duties. After leaving the navy, Baker earned a law degree from the University of Tennessee.

In 1951 Baker married Joy Dirksen, daughter of Everett Dirksen, U.S. senator from Illinois. Forty-five years later, following the 1993 death of his first wife, he wed Senator Nancy Landon Kassebaum of Kansas, daughter of Kansas Governor Alf Landon, the Republican Party's unsuccessful candidate against President Franklin D. Roosevelt in 1936.

As the Republican nominee for the U.S. Senate in 1964, Baker lost to U.S. Representative Ross Bass in a race to fill the unexpired term of Estes Kefauver, who had died in office. Two years later, he defeated former Governor Frank Clement to become the first Republican popularly elected to the Senate from Tennessee. He was reelected in 1972 and 1978 and retired from the Senate after his third term. In 1980 he made a bid for the Republican nomination for president eventually won by Ronald Reagan, but he was never in serious contention.

In 1973 and 1974, Baker served as vice-chairman of the U.S. Senate Select Committee on Presidential Campaign Activities in its investigation of the Watergate scandal, which culminated in the resignation of President Richard Nixon. During the committee's nationally televised hearings, Baker crystallized the investigation by repeatedly asking, "What did the President know, and when did he know it?"

Baker served as Senate minority leader from 1977 to 1981, Senate majority leader from 1981 to 1985, and White House chief of staff for President Reagan in 1987–88. In 2001 he became the U.S. ambassador to Japan.

Baker's practice of law included a partnership in the firm Baker, Donelson, Bearman, and Caldwell. An avid photographer, he published pictorial works on Washington, D.C., and the Big South Fork of the Cumberland River.

See also: KEFAUVER, ESTES; REPUBLICAN PARTY.

—Ed Speer, *Elizabethton, Tennessee*

J. Lee Annis Jr., *Howard Baker: Conciliator in an Age of Crisis* (1995); Bruce A. Ragsdale and Kathryn A. Jacobs, eds., *Biographical Directory of the United States Congress, 1774–1989* (1989).

Battle of Buffington Island

The battle near Buffington Island in Meigs County, Ohio, on July 19, 1863, marked the climax of Confederate General John Hunt Morgan's colorful but ill-conceived raid into Indiana and Ohio during the Civil War. In early July, Morgan led more than twenty-five hundred troops across the Ohio River into Indiana, taking the war to Northern civilians. Outdistancing Union pursuers under General Edward Hobson, his men destroyed or captured millions of dollars worth of property as they crossed southern Indiana and Ohio.

Morgan's exhausted men intended to re-cross the Ohio at the ford near Buffington Island into West Virginia. Waiting at the ford, however, was a detachment of militia. The ensuing delay allowed Hobson's forces, joined by several gunboats and cavalry brought up the Ohio on transports, to converge on the spot. The battle, in which more than fifty Confederates and five or six Federals died, showed Morgan that escape across the river was impossible. Leaving about half his command, artillery, and wagon train for a subordinate to surrender, he fled north with the remainder, who also surrendered a week later near Lisbon, Ohio.

Although the raid had little lasting military significance, it loomed large in local lore. Accessible only by poor roads, the site of the battle was visited primarily by local residents. In 1993 the Civil War Sites Advisory Commission recommended the spot for state protection, but six years later, three state agencies brushed aside local protests and signed an agreement with Shelly Materials to permit gravel dredging on all but forty acres of the largely unspoiled site.

See also: CIVIL WAR; CIVIL WAR TOURISM (TOURISM); MONUMENTS (VISUAL ARTS).

—Phyllis F. Field, *Ohio University*

Battle of Chattanooga

Stung by its defeat at Chickamauga in northwest Georgia at the hands of General Braxton Bragg on September 19–20, 1863, the Union army under General William S. Rosecrans retreated across the Tennessee line to Chattanooga. Bragg then cautiously marched his army north to Missionary Ridge and Lookout Mountain, and despite the pleas from his generals to attack immediately, laid siege to the town below. Keenly aware of Chattanooga's importance as a railhead, President Abraham Lincoln ordered significant Union reinforcements to the town. He then relieved Rosecrans of command and appointed Major General Ulysses S. Grant as commander of all Union forces west of the Appalachians. Grant arrived in Chattanooga near the end of October and four days later opened a supply route known as the "Cracker Line" to relieve the siege. In the meantime, he developed a simple, but effective, plan for breaking the Confederate grip on Chattanooga. On November 23, he ordered Major General George Thomas's Army of the Cumberland to take Orchard Knob, a foothill in front of the center of the Confederate stronghold on Missionary Ridge.

The next day, Major General Joseph Hooker boldly captured Lookout Mountain on the Confederate left under cover of heavy fog in an action to be forever known as the "Battle above the Clouds." Then, on November 25, Major General William T. Sherman's Army of the Tennessee assaulted the right of Bragg's line but ran into stubborn resistance from General Patrick Cleburne's Rebels at Tunnel Hill. On the Confederate left Hooker's assaults bogged down as well. By 3:30 p.m., Grant, realizing that the attacks were not going well, ordered Thomas to move his army to the first line of Rebel defense on Missionary Ridge to apply pressure on Bragg's center. The first line fell quickly, but the Federals were exposed to a withering fire from above. Refusing to remain exposed, Thomas's soldiers charged up the steep face of Missionary Ridge without orders and smashed through the Confederate defenses.

Bragg tried to rally his men, but they fled in panic as the Yankees continued to pour over the crest of the ridge. The siege of Chattanooga was lifted. Grant had won another stunning victory and was soon named general-in-chief of all Union forces. Bragg was relieved of command, and within a few months Chattanooga became the initial base of operations for Sherman's invasion of Georgia and the eventual capture of Atlanta.

See also: BATTLE OF CHICKAMAUGA; CIVIL WAR.

—Charles F. Bryan Jr., *Virginia Historical Society*

Battle of Chickamauga

The battle of Chickamauga was the largest battle to take place in the Appalachian Mountains during the American Civil War. One of the greatest tactical victories and strategic defeats in the history of the Confederacy, this engagement was waged in northwest Georgia along the banks of Chickamauga Creek on September 18–20, 1863.

After several weeks of maneuvering, the opposing forces stumbled into each other in the deep woods just west of Chickamauga creek on the morning of September 19, and fierce but inconclusive fighting followed. Confederate General Braxton Bragg renewed the attack the next morning, hoping to turn the Union left flank and get his forces between General William S. Rosecrans and the Union base in nearby Chattanooga, Tennessee. Poor communications and faulty staff work caused the Confederates to launch piecemeal assaults, which were repulsed by stiff Union resistance.

Meanwhile, General James Longstreet's corps successfully struck the Union center at the precise moment that a Federal division was ordered to another sector, creating a massive gap in the Union defenses. Longstreet exploited the opening, precipitating a panic and nearly cutting the Army of the Cumberland in two. Only a dogged rear-guard action by General George Thomas saved the Union forces from destruction. Casualties were horrendous. Confederate losses amounted to 18,454, while Union losses were 16,170, including nearly 5,000 captured.

Rosecrans's defeated army fled the battlefield, but Bragg's dilatory pursuit allowed the Union forces to withdraw safely into Chattanooga. Ulysses S. Grant replaced Rosecrans as commander, and a large number of additional troops were added to the Union forces, who drove the Confederates back into Georgia in November 1863.

See also: BATTLE OF CHATTANOOGA; CIVIL WAR.

—W. Todd Groce, *Georgia Historical Society*

Battle of Knoxville

With Union and Confederate forces locked in a stalemate at Chattanooga, Tennessee, President Jefferson Davis approved a plan in early November 1863 to detach twenty thousand Rebel troops under Lieutenant General James Longstreet to march up the Tennessee Valley and crush the Union army under Major General Ambrose Burnside at Knoxville. The move caused thousands of east Tennessee Unionists who had returned to their native region to flee into Kentucky, fearful of reprisals the Confederates might inflict if they regained the region. Under orders from Ulysses S. Grant, who commanded Federal forces at Chattanooga, Burnside cautiously moved troops south of Knoxville to delay the Confederates. But outnumbered almost two to one, the Federals stubbornly pulled back into the defenses of Knoxville on November 17. The Confederates invested the town and immediately began siege operations. Within days, the Federals ran short on supplies, but loyal citizens from the surrounding area floated large quantities of foodstuffs down the French Broad and Holston Rivers to the Tennessee River through Knoxville at night despite Confederate efforts to stop them. On November 29, Longstreet launched a powerful assault on Fort Sanders, one of the strongest points in the Knoxville defenses. Struggling across icy ground, tangled with telegraph wire, and facing a withering fire from musketry and canister, the Rebels were forced to retreat with heavy losses after only twenty minutes. Five days later, after receiving word that Braxton Bragg's Confederate army had been routed at Chattanooga and that a thirty-thousand-man army under William T. Sherman was marching north to relieve Burnside, Longstreet lifted the siege of Knoxville. Rather than face the combined Union armies, the Rebel general retreated to upper east Tennessee, where he set up winter quarters. The Confederate failure in front of Knoxville, combined with the loss of Chattanooga, secured Unionist east Tennessee for the Federals for the rest of the war.

See also: BATTLE OF CHATTANOOGA; BATTLE OF CHICKAMAUGA; CIVIL WAR.

—Charles F. Bryan Jr., *Virginia Historical Society*

Blue Ridge Parkway

See Blue Ridge Parkway (Tourism); Blue Ridge Parkway (Architecture)

Broad Form Deed

Broad form deeds were legal instruments that formalized the sale of mineral deposits and gave purchasers of coal deposits rights superseding those of the surface property owners. Businessmen living in the mountains, particularly Kentucky's John C. C. Mayo and Walter S. Harkins, designed the deeds in the late nineteenth century as a way of encouraging major American capitalists to invest in the region. These documents conveyed only ownership of the coal, oil, gas, and other minerals lying below the ground and not the land's surface. By separating mineral ownership from surface ownership, mineral speculators gained control of the region's resources at minimal cost and made widespread, intensive coal mining both possible and profitable.

Broad form deeds, as opposed to the much less detailed short form deeds, spelled out over several typed pages a wide variety of rights conveyed to the buyer. These included the absolute right to enter the surface still retained by the seller, to build tram roads and railroads, to divert and pollute watercourses, and to do anything else "necessary and convenient" to profitably remove the minerals lying underground. The "necessary and convenient" clause of the deeds guaranteed that the rights of mineral owners would take legal precedence over the rights of the surface owners, who were generally small farmers. The deeds specified that farmers could use the surface however they saw fit, but only insofar as they did not infringe on the rights of mineral owners. Based on the language of the broad form deeds, mining companies later insisted that the use of new technologies such as strip mining and longwall mining required no additional compensation for surface owners, even when they led to the destruction of farms and timber.

With the rapid spread of surface mining, court action in most states, starting in the 1950s, limited this application of the broad form deed. In Kentucky, however, the courts consistently upheld the mining companies' position. In 1988 public pressure finally led to the adoption of a constitutional amendment requiring companies to negotiate new deeds with surface owners before strip mining the property. The movement generating public concern and support for the amendment was spearheaded by an environmental group, Kentuckians for the Commonwealth.

While stories abound of speculators intimidating or defrauding mountain farmers, most such transactions were voluntary. Farmers sold mineral rights on their property because of personal circumstances arising from the weak preindustrial economy. That economy combined small-scale, household farming with commodity production in cattle and timber. The combination of household and market production generated only limited success, and most farmers lived under a heavy burden of debt. Already familiar with a wide range of legal instruments, farmers saw mineral rights as yet another commodity that could be sold to pay off debts and secure ownership of farmland, finally achieving the mythical independence so important to yeoman societies. Farmers did not foresee the fundamental alterations in society that coal mining would bring. While their decision to sell made rational sense at the time, it ushered in an age of corporate domination and poverty that defines the coalfields to the present day.

See also: BITUMINOUS COAL INDUSTRY (BUSINESS, INDUSTRY, AND TECHNOLOGY); COAL MINING (ENVIRONMENT).

—Robert S. Weise, *Eastern Kentucky University*

Joe Szakos, "Practical Lessons in Community Organizing in Appalachia: What We've Learned at Kentuckians for the Commonwealth," in *Fighting Back in Appalachia: Traditions of Resistance and Change*, ed. Stephen L. Fisher (1993); Robert S. Weise, *Grasping at Independence: Debt, Male Authority, and Mineral Rights in Appalachian Kentucky, 1850–1915* (2001).

Brown, Joseph E.

(1821–1894) Governor, U.S. senator, and entrepreneur.

Born April 15, 1821, in Dickens District, South Carolina, to Mackey and Sally Rice Brown, Joseph Emerson Brown grew up in northern Georgia. In spite of his relatively modest origins, he attended Yale Law School and became a prominent attorney and real estate speculator. In the 1850s he served as a Democratic state senator and judge for Georgia's Blue Ridge District. Although he represented an area with few large plantations, he strongly defended slavery.

In 1857 Black Belt Democrats selected Brown as a compromise candidate for the governor's seat, and he defeated the American Party candidate, Benjamin H. Hill. As governor, Brown modeled himself on Andrew Jackson and attacked the state's banking system as a symbol of privilege. At the same time, however, he invested in railroads and supported state aid for internal improvements.

Securing the support of non-slaveholders in the state's Appalachian foothills in the north, Brown helped lead Georgia into secession from the Union. But once the Civil War began, he criticized the policies of Confederate President Jefferson Davis, denouncing military conscription, Davis's suspension of habeas corpus, and impressment of property by the Confederacy. Nevertheless, Brown remained loyal to the Confederacy, delivering men and supplies to Richmond.

In 1865 Brown urged cooperation with President Andrew Johnson's plans for Reconstruction, but when the growing power of Radical Republicans in Washington became apparent, he backed the Republican administration of Governor Rufus B. Bullock in 1868. By the mid-1870s, the chameleonlike politician had abandoned the Republicans.

During the post-Reconstruction period, Brown practiced law and invested in coal, railroads, and real estate. Returning to the Democratic fold, he became a prominent advocate of segregation. In 1880 he was appointed to a U.S. Senate seat, which he retained until his retirement in 1891. Brown died November 30, 1894, in Atlanta.

See also: CIVIL WAR; RECONSTRUCTION.

—Wallace Hettle, *University of Northern Iowa*

Burr, Aaron

(1756–1836) Revolutionary soldier and politician.

Aaron Burr, Revolutionary soldier, politician, and adventurer, was born February 6, 1756, at Newark, New Jersey, son of Aaron Burr Sr. and Esther Edwards, daughter of Jonathan Edwards, the famous colonial preacher and theologian. His father, also a theologian, was the second president of the College of New Jersey (Princeton). Orphaned at an early age, Burr graduated from Princeton and began preparing for a law career.

In the first winter of the Revolutionary War, Burr marched with General Richard Montgomery and General Benedict Arnold on their ill-fated campaign into Canada. Returning to New York, he served briefly on the staff of General George Washington though the two developed a dislike for each other. His antipathy to Washington and his admiration for General Charles Lee may have determined his future Republican attachment.

He returned to the study of law and was admitted to the bar in New York in 1782. He then promptly married a widow, Theodosia Prevost. His only child, also named Theodosia, was the joy of his life but was lost at sea in 1812. Burr entered politics as attorney general under Governor George Clinton in 1789 and was subsequently elected to the U.S. Senate in 1791. Due to his efforts in electing a Republican majority to the state legislature in 1800, Burr was nominated as a candidate for the vice-presidency. He and Thomas Jefferson each received seventy-three electoral votes, and the Congress declared a tie, with the decision to be made by the Federalist-controlled House of Representatives. Though Jefferson eventually was chosen president, he never forgave Burr, whose disclaimers of competition were deemed inadequate.

U.S. Senator Robert C. Byrd, Democrat from West Virginia, 1988. One of the most powerful advocates for Appalachia ever to serve in Congress, Byrd rose to the Senate's highest leadership positions through tireless work and encyclopedic knowledge of the history of that body and the U.S. Constitution.

In 1804, near the end of his term, Burr killed his New York rival, Alexander Hamilton, in a duel. With no future in American politics, he devised a grand strategy to establish a personal empire in the Southwest on lands that he intended to capture from the Spanish. In 1805–6 he traveled throughout the western region soliciting support from disaffected politicians, including John Adair and Andrew Jackson. Among those whom he enlisted in his scheme was Harman Blennerhassett, an eccentric Irish aristocrat who had built a beautiful mansion on Blennerhassett Island, one mile below Parkersburg, (West) Virginia, in the Ohio River. In 1807 both Burr and Blennerhassett were arrested and brought to Richmond for trial on charges of treason. Chief Justice John Marshall, in whose circuit the case was heard, directed a verdict of "not proven," since the prosecutors had been unable to present more than one witness to any overt act of treason, as required by the Constitution. Blennerhassett was then released without trial, though much of his fortune had been squandered on the Burr intrigue.

Burr traveled in Europe for a time, then returned to practice law in New York. He died September 14, 1836, on Staten Island.

See also: AMERICAN REVOLUTION; DEMOCRATIC-REPUBLICAN PARTY.

—Philip Sturm, *Ohio Valley College*

Byrd, Robert C.

(1917–) U.S. senator.

Robert Carlyle Byrd, a durable and powerful U.S. senator from West Virginia, used his seniority to strengthen the infrastructure of the Appalachian region and to channel federal funds into his home state. Recognized as the Senate's foremost expert on rules and procedures, Byrd served in its two most influential posts—as majority leader and as chairman of the Committee on Appropriations. He has written a history of the Senate and compiled a statistical profile of it as well.

A recognized scholar of the U.S. Senate and the U.S. Constitution, Byrd completed his law degree at American University while serving in the U.S. House of Representatives. He was elected to the Senate in 1958 and quickly took advantage of the reforms proposed by Senate Majority Leader Lyndon Johnson. A freshman member of the Appropriations Committee, Byrd was also appointed to the Washington D.C. Oversight Committee. He came into direct conflict with the Civil Rights movement just then beginning and, despite much pressure from the West Virginia labor lobby, voted against the 1964 Civil Rights Act. Byrd's segregationist past died hard, but he repudiated his earlier association with the Ku Klux Klan as an "indiscretion of youth." Later, he supported civil rights legislation as being in the interest of all minority groups, making no distinction among them.

A tireless worker and voracious reader, Byrd rarely appeared on the Washington social circuit. While serving as majority leader, he traveled around the world, meeting with heads of state and participating in efforts that led to a normalization of relations with Eastern Bloc nations.

Byrd effectively shifted federal aid for his region away from handout programs that encouraged economic dependency to projects that contributed infrastructure improvements as well as longterm employment. Speaking to a West Virginia audience in the late 1990s, he acknowledged his nickname as Washington's "King of Pork," but he also laughingly advised the crowd, "[T]hey don't know how much I love it." His most lasting contribution to the Appalachian region may indeed be his success in channeling support and funding to government agencies and enterprises that relocated there.

Byrd was a protégé of Georgia Senator Richard Russell and proved an apt student, learning how to exploit parliamentary procedures and Senate rules to great advantage and becoming an unchallenged master of those maneuvers. His knowledge of U.S. Senate history—and that of the ancient Roman senate—enabled him successfully to take risky positions and defend unpopular ideas. Known for his devotion to Congress and particularly to the Senate, he zealously guarded their prerogatives. Byrd never feared to break with majority positions. He voted against equal opportunity employment in the House, for example, citing the doctrine of separation of powers.

Byrd declined a Nixon administration nomination to the U.S. Supreme Court, believing he would be more effective as a powerful senator than as a justice. His nomination would also have presented the Senate with a difficult choice between loyalty to a colleague and insistence upon a standard of legal experience since Byrd had never actually practiced law.

Born Cornelius Calvin Sale Jr. on November 20, 1917, in Wilkesboro, North Carolina, to Ada and Cornelius Sale, Byrd was left motherless by the 1918 influenza epidemic. He was reared by an aunt and uncle, Vlurma Sale and Titus Dalton Byrd, of Crab Orchard, West Virginia, who renamed him. Despite a bleak childhood of grinding poverty, he was the valedictorian of his 1934 high school class at the age of sixteen. He learned the butcher's trade and married his high school sweetheart, Erma Ora James, daughter of a coal miner, in 1937. On the eve of World War II, Byrd went to work as a welder in the Florida and Maryland shipyards. He has also worked at a gas station and a coal company store. Against the recommendation of the local Democratic executive committee, Byrd entered politics in Raleigh County in 1947. He used his skill as a traditional Appalachian fiddler to draw campaign crowds, a strategy that gave him victory in the crowded primary race, and he successfully unseated a long-entrenched local politician. As his political stock soared, Republican observer and Benedum Oil executive Samuel T. Mallinson quipped that "Byrd fiddled and Rome burned." Byrd's fiddling subsequently provided much fodder for good-natured banter between the political parties in West Virginia.

He pursued a college education part-time while opening a grocery store and serving in the West Virginia State Senate, a seat he won in 1950. He entered the U.S. House of Representatives in 1952. Byrd was first elected to the U.S. Senate in 1958. As the new century began, Byrd was in his eighth term, a West Virginia icon who had avoided splits between home state factions and cultivated diverse constituencies. Supporting both the state's extractive industries and the labor lobby, he has also helped broaden West Virginia's economic base with payrolls from federal installations and government contractors.

See also: DEMOCRATIC PARTY.

—Barbara Rasmussen, *Fairmont State College*

Frank Ahrens, "The Unyielding Robert Byrd," *Washington Post* (February 11, 1999); Robert C. Byrd, *The Senate of the Roman Republic: Addresses on the History of Roman Constitutionalism* (2001).

Cherokee Constitution of 1827

The Constitution of 1827 illustrated how acculturated Cherokees had become to the white man's world. Encouraged by the 1791 Treaty of Holston's civilization clause, the Cherokees recorded their laws, established a written language, centralized their government, and established a supreme court. The fact that five different religious denominations established schools among them in the early nineteenth century indicates that the Cherokees were becoming widely Christianized. Some Cherokees considered these changes to be for the better while others envisioned them as the only way to prevent the further loss of land.

The Cherokee Constitution, drawn up primarily by mixed bloods, was modeled closely after the United States Constitution. It created three branches of government and defined their powers. The National Committee and the National Council made up a bicameral legislature. Executive power was entrusted to a principal chief, assistant chief, treasurer, and national marshal. Most personal liberties were borrowed from the U.S. Constitution, but all land remained "the common property of the Nation." Imitating their white neighbors, the Cherokees extended voting rights to males who were at least eighteen and limited the right to hold office to males at least twenty-five. Neither women nor offspring resulting from intermarriage with blacks could vote. Ministers were also excluded from office.

The Constitution of 1827 culminated the Cherokees' movement to nationalize and centralize their government. But because the document defined boundaries and claimed supreme control within them, it was denounced as illegal by white Georgians and others. In a real sense, rather than solidifying Cherokee autonomy, the constitution acted as a catalyst for Cherokee removal.

See also: CHEROKEE REMOVAL; TRAIL OF TEARS (SETTLEMENT AND MIGRATION); TREATY OF HOPEWELL.

—William L. Anderson, *Western Carolina University*

Cherokee Removal

Cherokee removal was part of a federal initiative to open land in the Southeast—including Appalachia—to European American settlement. By the 1830s, Cherokee resistance to this policy brought federal troops to the mountain South and set the stage for the infamous coerced march of sixteen thousand Native Americans to the Indian Territory in the West.

Removal of the Cherokee was the culmination of a broader federal policy going back to Thomas Jefferson, who believed that the expanding white population required tribes living in the East to cede their lands and move to the recently acquired region west of the Mississippi River. Despite the absence of a congressionally mandated program, Presidents James Madison, James Monroe, and John Quincy Adams also encouraged Indian removal; like Jefferson, they insisted that it be voluntary.

By 1820 several thousand Cherokee had accepted periodic federal inducements and moved to present-day Arkansas, but the majority remained on tribally owned lands in Alabama, Georgia, North Carolina, and Tennessee. All of these state governments favored complete Cherokee removal, but Georgia was particularly insistent, pointing out that the state's 1802 concession of its western lands to the United States had required the federal government to clear the state of all Indian claims. Officials increasingly employed states' rights arguments to the effect that the Cherokee, despite federal treaties to the contrary, were mere tenants-at-will and could be removed at any time. Georgia began a systematic campaign to deny all Cherokee treaty rights.

Andrew Jackson's 1828 election as president brought matters to a head. A longtime supporter of removal, Jackson believed that Indian treaties had never been more than expedients. In his first annual address to Congress, he emphasized that Indian removal was necessary both for white America and for the preservation of Indians. After a vigorous debate in the spring of 1830, Congress made removal official U.S. policy. In exchange for their homelands, eastern Indians would receive land from the unorganized public domain in the West, and the United States would provide assistance in moving and compensation for their improvements in the East. Any Indians remaining in the East would come under the laws of the states in which they resided.

Though the new legislation renounced the use of force in negotiating treaties of removal, Jackson was willing to employ almost any measure short of actual violence. Federal officials withheld Indian annuities, emphasized the dire consequences of Indians' remaining in their homelands, and resorted to the bribery of compliant Indian leaders. Other major southeastern tribes signed removal treaties, but the Cherokee continued to resist. They had organized politically as the Cherokee Nation in 1827, and a generation of selective acculturation had made them adept in coping with the demands of white society. In 1832 they even won a U.S. Supreme Court victory *(Worcester v. Georgia)*, which upheld the validity of federal treaties recognizing Cherokee rights. But the political pressure intensified, and in December 1835 U.S. commissioners negotiated a removal treaty with a small number of Cherokee whose authority was unrecognized by the Cherokee Nation. The Treaty of New Echota stipulated that the tribe would give up its lands in the Southeast and move to a new home in the West; the United States would pay the Cherokee five million dollars and assist them in making the move. The Indians promised to relocate within two years of the treaty's ratification.

John Ross, the principal chief of the Cherokee Nation, denounced the Treaty of New Echota, but the U.S. Senate ratified it by the bare two-thirds vote required on May 23, 1836. By the spring of 1838, Ross and the vast majority of the tribe still refused to leave. The United States then forced tribal members into concentration camps and coerced the Cherokee into a long trek across the upper South and lower Great Plains during the winter of 1838 and 1839. The total number of Cherokee moving west as a result of the Treaty of New Echota was probably sixteen to seventeen thousand; about fifteen hundred remained in isolated areas of the southern mountains. Federal actions and Cherokee suffering along the route subsequently known as the Trail of Tears made this the most notorious example of American Indian removal. Historians have generally believed that about four thousand Cherokee died on the journey west, although some modern scholars assert the toll was much higher.

See also: CHEROKEE (RACE, ETHNICITY, AND IDENTITY); CHEROKEE CONSTITUTION OF 1827; TREATY OF HOPEWELL.

—John R. Finger, *University of Tennessee*

William L. Anderson, ed., *Cherokee Removal: Before and After* (1991); Theda Perdue and Michael D. Green, eds., *The Cherokee Removal: A Brief History with Documents* (1995); Ronald N. Satz, *American Indian Policy in the Jacksonian Era* (1975).

Cherokees during the American Revolution

The Proclamation Line of 1763 forbade whites from settling in Indian territory, but thousands of European Americans moved onto Cherokee land nevertheless. When the American Revolution broke out, the Cherokees naturally sided with the British.

In June 1776, the Cherokees launched an attack on illegal settlements as well as legal ones in North Carolina, South Carolina, and Georgia. General Charles Lee, commander of the southern Continental forces, urged punitive expeditions by the states most involved. In late July, Major Samuel Jack led two hundred men against the Cherokee in upper Georgia. Colonel Andrew Williamson attacked the South Carolina Lower Towns and marched northward to join General Griffith Rutherford in striking many of the Middle and Valley Cherokee Towns in North Carolina. Colonel William Christian attacked the Overhill Towns in Tennessee. Perhaps the only pitched battle was at Black Hole, where six hundred to one thousand Middle and Overhill Cherokees engaged Williamson's forces. The Americans destroyed about fifty towns throughout the Cherokee Nation, plus nearly one hundred thousand bushels of corn and potatoes. Williamson and Rutherford razed thirty-seven Middle and Valley Towns, with the remainder being leveled by Jack in the Lower Towns and by Christian in the Overhill Towns. Several peace treaties followed, marking the first forced land cessions and costing the Cherokees almost ten thousand square miles of territory. Even though the Chickamauga Cherokees continued to fight under Dragging Canoe through 1792, most Cherokees remained at peace.

The impact of the war was tremendous. In addition to lost land, the fighting caused a schism between the old chiefs and young warriors that continued into the nineteenth century. Other southern tribes were frightened by the devastation inflicted on the Cherokees, preventing any major cooperative resistance against the Americans.

See also: CHEROKEE (RACE, ETHNICITY, AND IDENTITY); PROCLAMATION OF 1763 (SETTLEMENT AND MIGRATION); TREATY OF HOPEWELL.

—William L. Anderson, *Western Carolina University*

Civilian Conservation Corps

The work of the Civilian Conservation Corps (CCC) in Appalachia was dramatic and lasting. Created in 1933 by President Franklin D. Roosevelt as part of the New Deal strategy of using public works to ease unemployment, the CCC was charged primarily with helping to preserve natural resources. Its achievements established it as an American icon. By 1942, when the program was discontinued, some 4,500 CCC camps had been built across the United States. Military in their structure and daily discipline, the camps employed about 3 million young men, who were paid thirty dollars a month. All were required to send twenty-five dollars back home to wives and dependents. Nicknamed "Roosevelt's Tree Army," the CCC planted some 2.5 billion seedlings, strung 89,000 miles of telephone line, restocked the nation's streams, rivers, and lakes with 972 million fish, built 125,000 miles of road, opened 13,100 miles of trails, began 800 state parks, and renovated nearly 4,000 historic buildings. Tasks varied from teaching illiterate citizens to read and write to controlling mosquitoes in woodlands. The rigors of the work led to another nickname, especially meaningful to the young men who wore the uniform: "Colossal College of Calluses."

The 469-mile Blue Ridge Parkway, a scenic motorway linking the recently opened Shenandoah National Park in Virginia and the Great Smoky Mountains National Park in Tennessee and North Carolina, evolved from a CCC project which brought work to unemployed engineers and architects as well as laborers. In the Smokies, CCC "boys" cleared trails and campgrounds and erected buildings and bridges from stone, enhancing the beauty of what would become the nation's most visited national park, now covering more than 520,000 acres. The park's Laurel Falls Trail was built by CCC labor in 1935.

In Georgia and Tennessee, CCC members conducted restoration and repair work at the Chickamauga and Chattanooga National Military Park, the site of several significant Civil War engagements. They also constructed fire towers, shelters, and lodging along the 2,174-mile Appalachian Trail running between Maine and northern Georgia. The majority of Appalachia's state parks are also products of CCC manpower. In 1933 thirteen states had no state park system, and about half of those, mainly in the South, were without a single park property within their borders. By 1939 ten of the states previously without parklands had the beginnings of park systems.

In Cumberland County, Tennessee, a dam and arch bridge started in 1935 still stands as the largest masonry project ever built by the CCC. World War I hero Alvin C. York was superintendent of the project until 1940, when he left to help with the filming of the motion picture *Sergeant York*.

The U.S. Forest Service directed the work of 188 CCC camps in the Tennessee Valley, where Tennessee Valley Authority technicians guided efforts in erosion control, reforestation, and forest protection. In the CCC's southern region, workers acted as firefighters and helped protect 47 million acres of land from forest fires in 1933. Through CCC labor, 75 million acres were protected by 1942.

In Appalachia, the number of men working for the CCC averaged about 75,000 per state, and expenditures of federal funds averaged about $70 million per state. In North

Carolina, workers sent home $16.4 million to their dependents. In Kentucky, the corps planted 26.5 million trees, and in West Virginia it stocked 4.4 million fish. In Virginia, CCC fire-suppression efforts reduced the average size of fires from 84.5 acres in 1929–33 to 24.1 in 1937–41. "It is impossible to calculate the favorable impact on public recognition of the need for fire protection and control, reforestation, and better management of the timberlands," said George W. Dean, state forester for Virginia from 1944 to 1973.

General George C. Marshall credited the training young men received in the CCC as a major factor for the Allied victory in World War II. A monument in Nashville's Bicentennial Park reads: "Few men have the satisfaction of knowing they have made a contribution in their lifetime that will last through the ages and touch the lives of thousands. Men of the CCC know that feeling well."

See also: NEW DEAL COMMUNITIES (FAMILY AND COMMUNITY); SECTION OVERVIEW (ARCHITECTURE); TENNESSEE VALLEY AUTHORITY.

—Fred W. Sauceman, *East Tennessee State University*

Perry H. Merrill, *Roosevelt's Forest Army: A History of the Civilian Conservation Corps: 1933–1942* (1981).

Civil War

The years between 1860 and 1865 were a time of extraordinary personal and social disruption and discord in the southern mountains. Nearly every aspect of life underwent enormous change as the war tore communities and families asunder, bringing about financial collapse and political turmoil as well as the end of slavery. Despite all of the apparent revolutionary changes in the region during these years, however, there were also strong threads of continuity.

During the secession crisis that followed the election of Abraham Lincoln to the presidency in 1860, the majority of mountaineers opposed the move to create a separate Southern nation. This sentiment was strongest in east Tennessee, northwestern Virginia, western Maryland, and southeastern Kentucky. In western North Carolina, northern Georgia, northern Alabama, and the Shenandoah Valley of Virginia, voters usually opposed immediate secession as well.

Despite the opposition to secession, the people of the region found themselves almost instantly at war. A Federal army promptly entered the northwestern counties of Virginia and in a series of small battles in June 1861 cleared the mountainous area of Confederate troops. Thereafter, a convention met and began the process of creating a separate state in northwestern Virginia. After the state convention approved an amendment that mandated gradual emancipation of the slaves, the Lincoln administration recognized the new state of West Virginia on June 20, 1863.

Mountain Unionists were active in other locations early in the war. In western Maryland, pro-Union candidates swept to victory in elections that ensured that their state would remain in the Union. In Greeneville, Tennessee, a convention sought a separation of east Tennessee from the remainder of the state. The state government in Nashville rejected the request, but east Tennessee militancy continued to burn, and in November 1861 Unionists joined a campaign to sabotage the region's railway bridges.

Confederate military initiatives in the spring of 1862 brought large armies to the mountain regions for the first time. The most spectacular of these was the campaign of Thomas "Stonewall" Jackson in the Shenandoah Valley of Virginia. Jackson, a native of the area that became West Virginia, won decisive victories at Winchester and Front Royal. In August, the small Confederate army of Kirby Smith was part of a broad movement of Rebel troops into Kentucky. Smith won a decisive victory at Richmond, but he was forced to retreat after the wider Confederate offensive failed.

Robert E. Lee led his veteran Army of Northern Virginia into the foothills of western Maryland in September 1862. At Antietam Creek, near Sharpsburg, the two main armies fought to tactical draw on September 17, the bloodiest day in American history. In danger of destruction, Lee's army escaped across the Potomac River and withdrew into Virginia. Five days after this battle, President Lincoln issued the Emancipation Proclamation, transforming the conflict into a crusade against slavery.

In September 1863, a Union army under the command of Ambrose Burnside marched unopposed into Knoxville, Tennessee, and a larger Federal army led by William S. Rosecrans forced Braxton Bragg's Confederate army out of Chattanooga and into northern Georgia. Reinforced by regiments from Lee's army, Bragg counterattacked and badly defeated the Union forces, driving them back into Chattanooga. In late November, however, a heroic charge up Missionary Ridge in Chattanooga by Federal forces routed Bragg's army and sent it back into northern Georgia. The following May, William T. Sherman started his army forward against the Confederate lines. Skillfully maneuvering his forces around the Confederates, Sherman reached the outskirts of Atlanta, taking the city in September 1864.

The final major campaign of the war in Appalachia took place in the Shenandoah Valley, where Union leadership placed a large army under the command of Philip Sheridan. With massive resources at his command, Sheridan attacked Jubal Early's army at Winchester, Virginia, in September 1864 and won a major victory, which he followed by winning another significant battle at Fisher's Hill. In October, Early counterattacked, but his army was nearly wiped out. Sheridan led his men to a sweeping victory that destroyed the Confederate forces. These campaigns by both large and small armies produced heavy civilian damage throughout the war, as both sides seized supplies from local populations and wantonly destroyed buildings and crops.

Large sections of the highlands far from large battles also suffered deprivation and hardship as the war trickled down to the community level. Throughout the region there were neighborhoods, families, and individuals who supported one side's government and army and neighbors who despised them. Moreover, events of the war created substantial numbers of mountaineers who simply became disillusioned by the demands made by conscription, the disruption of communities, and the injuries and deaths suffered by family members. The result was a growing level of violence and despair in the mountain areas by 1864.

Many Appalachians had recognized the potential for this type of difficulty even before the fighting began but nonetheless flocked to defend the government they supported. In western Maryland, northwestern Virginia (West Virginia), eastern Kentucky, and east Tennessee, large numbers enlisted in the Federal army. In southwestern Virginia, western North Carolina, northern Georgia, and northern Alabama, substantial numbers of men joined the new Confederate army.

Although most of the recruits were enthusiastic, much planning went into decisions to enlist. Generally, unmarried men from households with other male laborers were most likely to join the army. Collaborative decisions were made to ensure that neighborhoods and families retained sufficient male labor to survive as viable economic units. In keeping with this type of planning, neighborhoods tried to arrange that skilled craftsmen were among those who stayed behind.

This balancing of national and local needs continued through the winter of 1861–62. In the spring of 1862, the Confederate government faced a severe manpower crisis and resorted to the first conscription in American history. Recognizing that the South needed to keep its economy functioning, this act provided a number of occupational exemptions. The most notorious of these provisions was the exemption of one potential soldier for each twenty slaves owned by a family. This policy angered many yeoman and tenant farmers in the mountains who argued that the conflict had become "a rich man's war, and a poor man's fight."

The war also disrupted traditional trade routes in the mountain counties, causing significant shortages of necessities. The commodity most prized was salt. The center of production in Appalachia was Saltville, Virginia, where deposits were located near railroad lines, making distribution to many county seats and larger towns relatively easy. People who lived in rural areas and remote communities were in greatest peril from shortages of salt. Desperate farm families often resorted to boiling planks from their smokehouse floors to recover salt accumulated from cured meat. In Madison County, North Carolina, the infamous Shelton Laurel Massacre began as a dispute over the distribution of this critical commodity.

Mountain families faced another relentless foe in inflation. This was particularly true in areas where Confederate currency circulated. For goods that had to be purchased, prices increased rapidly, placing necessities beyond the reach of many families. State governments sought to alleviate some of the suffering in highland counties by providing money and necessities to the needy, but distribution was often unfair and drove some to desperate measures. For example, in Yancey County, North Carolina, about fifty women broke into a Confederate warehouse in April 1864 and carried off sixty bushels of government-owned wheat.

For others the only option was flight, a course that often led to disastrous results. In northern Georgia and western North Carolina, some escaping families were intercepted and massacred by Confederate sympathizers. In Johnson County, Tennessee, pro-Union farmers drove away Confederate-sympathizing neighbors and occupied their farms. In West Virginia and eastern Kentucky, Confederate sympathizers organized themselves into local defense groups.

Despite the disruption and hardship, slaves, the population most justified in fleeing, rarely did so. As far as can be determined, the institution of slavery underwent relatively little change during the war years. In Maryland, voters approved a new constitution in September 1864, ending slavery in that state, and West Virginia amended its proposed constitution to provide for gradual emancipation of slaves. Elsewhere, the two governments provided continuing support for the institution. Confederate state and local governments continued to enforce slave codes in southwestern Virginia, western North Carolina, northern Georgia, northern Alabama, northern Mississippi, and east Tennessee as long as they maintained control.

The most frightening manifestation of this fraying of mountain society was the rise of guerrilla warfare throughout the mountains. In western Maryland, (West) Virginia, eastern Kentucky, and, after 1863, east Tennessee, irregular troops often claimed affiliation with the Confederacy. In southwestern Virginia, western North Carolina, northern Georgia, and northern Alabama, partisans often claimed to be associated with the Federal war effort. Many other groups claimed no affiliation at all. Some of those involved in this activity were trying to protect their communities and families. But there were others whose violent tendencies were unleashed by the barbarism inherent in war.

By the spring of 1865, Appalachian society appeared to be on the verge of disintegration. The collapse of the Confederacy had left substantial portions of the mountains with little political structure. Raids by both organized armies and guerrilla bands disrupted the society and economy even further. Only in the decades that followed would the war years assume the romantic image that later generations associated with the nation's greatest tragedy.

See also: CIVIL WAR GUERRILLAS; CIVIL WAR TOURISM (TOURISM); RECONSTRUCTION.

—Gordon B. McKinney, *Berea College*

Noel C. Fisher, *War at Every Door: Partisan Politics and Guerrilla Violence in East Tennessee, 1860–1869* (1997); John C. Inscoe and Gordon B. McKinney, *The Heart of Confederate Appalachia: Western North Carolina in the Civil War* (2000); Kenneth W. Noe and Shannon H. Wilson, eds., *The Civil War in Appalachia: Collected Essays* (1997); Phillip Shaw Paludan, *Victims: A True Story of the Civil War* (1981).

Civil War Guerrillas

Guerrilla warfare was well suited to Appalachia's terrain and political environment, and it was historically familiar to inhabitants whose forebears had fought against Indians and the British. During the Civil War, guerrillas, or "bushwhackers," drew strength from the divided loyalties of mountaineers in a conflict that literally set neighbor against neighbor. Guerrilla operatives further capitalized upon resentment of plundering armies and the presence of deserters, draft dodgers, and refugees hiding in remote areas. The Federal army's rapid conquest of western Virginia, Union saboteurs' burning of railroad bridges affecting 270 miles of track between Bristol, Virginia, and Chattanooga, Tennessee, in November 1861, and the Confederacy's adoption of conscription in April 1862 ignited guerrilla warfare in earnest.

Areas most affected by guerrillas—authorized, unauthorized, Union, and Confederate—included southern West Virginia, western North Carolina, northwestern Georgia, northern Alabama, and particularly east Tennessee, where the devastation rivaled that suffered by Missouri and Kansas. Initially, both Union and Confederate authorities thought the war could be waged while largely sparing civilian lives and property, but by 1862 that hope had evaporated, principally a victim of guerrilla attacks on armies foraging amidst hostile populations. In April 1862, the Confederacy authorized the formation of the Partisan Rangers, while Union commanders sanctioned equivalent units or looked the other way when they were formed. Both sides soon concluded that guerrilla efforts were uncontrollable distractions, however. At General Robert E. Lee's request the Partisan Ranger Act was nullified in February 1864, with exception made for Colonel John S. Mosby's and Captain John "Hanse" McNeill's units, which were operating effectively in northern Virginia. Guerrilla bands nevertheless continued and even escalated their depredations until well after Appomattox. A number of individuals spawned usually romanticized stories and achieved varying degrees of fame.

Among Unionists (real or reputed) were Captain Goldman Bryson, Colonel George W. Kirk, Reverend William B. Carter, and David "Tinker Dave" Beatty in Tennessee; Keith and Melinda Blalock in North Carolina; the Destroying Angels and William "Black Fox" Looney in Alabama; John P. Buggs and his Snake Hunters in West Virginia; and Horatio Hennison in Georgia. Confederate guerrillas included Champion "Champ" Ferguson, Major Harvey Bingham, and Colonel John M. Hughs in Tennessee; Perry Conley and his Moccasin Rangers, Nancy Hart, and Colonel John D. Imboden in West Virginia; Jack Colquitt and John P. Gatewood in Georgia; and the Buggers, Reverend Miles E. "Bushwhacker" Johnson, Captain Frank B. Gurley, and Captain Joseph M. Hembrick in Alabama. Guerrilla bands under less notorious leaders plagued Appalachian Maryland, Virginia, Kentucky, South Carolina, and Mississippi. Pennsylvania and New York were spared. After the war, surviving guerrillas were allowed to surrender without punishment—save for Champ Ferguson, a killer consumed by vengeance and bloodlust who was captured, tried, and, on October 20, 1866, hanged.

Strategically, guerrilla fighters accomplished little. Unionists did not hasten victory; of Confederates only Mosby's Rangers had a perceptible impact in delaying defeat. Guerrilla operations were generally directed against other guerrillas and their supporters, and defense against them was usually left to militiamen or home guards. For the most part, their activities failed to divert mainline troops to defend against them or protect their favorite targets, supplies and communications facilities. Guerrillas did have an influence, though: armies, often in retaliation, increasingly adopted their harsh measures against civilians. This trend led to the use of "hard war" methods by Ulysses S. Grant and William T. Sherman in 1864–65.

Economically and socially the guerrilla war in southern Appalachia wreaked havoc. The economy, probably slipping in the 1850s, declined precipitously during the war years. Starvation threatened thousands of homes. Light manufacturing and especially agriculture suffered blows felt for decades. The guerrillas' looting, burning, torturing, and killing significantly desensitized mountain people to violence. Hatreds wracked families and communities and led to feuding. Law and order crumbled over large areas and remained shaky for years while vigilantism flourished and native suspicion of outsiders intensified. On the positive side, some communities pulled together in the face of unconventional threats. Gender roles blurred, and women assumed more independence, finding themselves defending their families and property and taking opportunities to provide intelligence and aid to fugitives and refugees.

See also: CIVIL WAR.

—David S. Newhall, *Centre College*

Albert E. Castel, "The Guerrilla War, 1861–1865," *Civil War Times Illustrated* (October 1974); Noel C. Fisher, *War at Every*

Door: Partisan Politics and Guerrilla Violence in East Tennessee, 1860–1869 (1997); Sean Michael O'Brien, *Mountain Partisans: Guerrilla Warfare in the Southern Appalachians, 1861–1865* (1999).

Clingman, Thomas Lanier

(1812–1897) U.S. senator and congressman.

Born in Huntsville, North Carolina, Thomas Lanier Clingman was the dominant political figure in western North Carolina during the two decades before the Civil War. In 1836 he moved to Asheville to advance his legal career and promote his political fortunes. Four years later, he was elected as a Whig to the state senate and became a vocal advocate of state-financed transportation improvements. He was elected to the U.S. House of Representatives in 1843 and, except for one term, served continuously until his appointment to the U.S. Senate in 1858.

Through his numerous public letters and newspaper articles, Clingman was among the first to call attention to the beauty and natural resources of the southern Appalachians. A tireless explorer, he gave his name to Clingman's Dome in the Great Smoky Mountains and engaged in a debate with Elisha Mitchell, maintaining that the crest in the Black Mountains of North Carolina, then called Black Dome, was the highest peak in the Appalachian chain.

During the 1850s Clingman achieved notoriety as a strident proponent of states' rights, and he eventually defected to the Democrats. Like Clingman himself, the majority of mountain voters were not slaveholders. But they resented northern interference with slavery and accepted his argument that a strong stand on southern rights was compatible with support for the Union. Clingman's endorsement of disunion in February 1861 placed him at odds with his constituents and impaired his efforts to make a political comeback after the Civil War.

See also: DEMOCRATIC PARTY; MOUNT MITCHELL (TOURISM); WHIG PARTY.

—Thomas E. Jeffrey, *Rutgers University*

Combs, Bert

(1911–1991) Governor and lawyer.

Bert T. Combs, one of Kentucky's most successful governors, is most noted for helping to establish the Appalachian Regional Commission. Born into a family of modest circumstances near Manchester in southeastern Kentucky, Combs attended local schools and worked for ten years to gain his higher education, earning a law degree in 1937 from the University of Kentucky.

When Combs became governor in 1960, the Appalachian area of Kentucky was experiencing chronic problems: a weak economy, substandard education, inadequate roads and public services, meager per capita income, and high unemployment. Soon after his inauguration, Combs adopted the policy goals of Program 60, a strategic ten-year plan prepared by the Eastern Kentucky Regional Planning Commission to diversify eastern Kentucky's economy, upgrade its physical infrastructure, and improve its educational and public services. Since Program 60's comprehensive approach to development required resources greater than Kentucky could provide, Combs and John D. Whisman, Program 60's principal author, pursued a strategy of tapping the resources of the federal government. Combs led a confederation of eleven states (although New York chose not to become a member and South Carolina later withdrew) known as the Conference of Appalachian Governors in pushing the creation of a federal-state development agency, which eventually became the Appalachian Regional Commission.

After his governorship ended in 1964, Combs continued his professional career as a federal judge and as a senior partner in Kentucky's largest law firm. As a result of his successful legal representation of Kentucky's poorest school districts in the state's courts in 1988–89, the Kentucky Supreme Court ordered the legislature to reorganize the state's entire school system, which it did through the Kentucky Education Reform Act of 1990.

Although Combs reached his eightieth year, his life was cut short on December 4, 1991, when he drowned during a flood that washed his automobile into the Red River near Rosslyn, Kentucky.

See also: APPALACHIAN DEVELOPMENT HIGHWAY SYSTEM (TRANSPORTATION); APPALACHIAN REGIONAL COMMISSION.

—Glen Edward Taul, *Georgetown College*

Cooper, John Sherman

(1901–1991) U.S. senator and diplomat.

John Sherman Cooper, a native of Appalachian Kentucky, is considered one of the more influential U.S. senators of the twentieth century. Born in Somerset in Pulaski County to a family that had produced six county and two circuit judges, Cooper graduated from Yale University in 1923 and then studied law at Harvard.

Following a single term in the Kentucky legislature, Cooper was elected at age twenty-eight to the post of Pulaski County judge. His eight-year service (1930–38) during the Great Depression deeply affected the young jurist, who often reached into his own pockets to help the destitute. In 1942 the forty-one-year-old Cooper enlisted as a private but eventually rose to captain in General George S. Patton's Third Army.

A Republican running in a predominantly Democratic state, the popular Cooper won short terms in the U.S. Senate twice (1946–49, 1952–55) but initially failed to capture a full term. Presidents of both parties recognized his talents, however, and tapped him for diplomatic posts. Under President Harry Truman, he assisted Secretary of State Dean Acheson in the negotiations leading to the formation of the North Atlantic Treaty Organization. In 1955 President Dwight D. Eisenhower named him to the sensitive post of ambassador to India and Nepal.

The beneficiary of the Eisenhower landslide the following year, Cooper returned to the Senate, where he served for sixteen years. Never an orator, the soft-spoken Kentuckian is best remembered for his early support of civil rights legislation, Medicare, and Medicaid, as well as his efforts to end the Vietnam War. He was a champion of the Tennessee Valley Authority and rural electrification and water projects throughout the Appalachian region. In 1965 he cosponsored the Appalachian Regional Development Act.

Declining to seek reelection in 1972, Cooper joined the prestigious Washington law firm of Covington and Burling. At the request of President Gerald Ford, he agreed in 1974 to become the first United States ambassador to East Germany (German Democratic Republic), serving until 1976. Afterwards he and his wife, Lorraine, made their home in Washington, D.C., where he died in 1991. He is buried at Arlington National Cemetery.

See also: DEMOCRATIC PARTY; REPUBLICAN PARTY.

—Thomas H. Appleton Jr., *Eastern Kentucky University*

County Government

It was quite natural for colonists to bring to America the institutions that were familiar to them, and county government throughout the South was modeled after that of the English shire. As the population spread inland, the Virginia House of Burgesses created the first eight counties in the colony beginning in 1634. These included Accawmacke, Charles City, Charles River, Elizabeth City, Henrico, James City, Warwick River, and Warrosquyoake Counties (though some of these were later extinguished). The boundaries for counties were drawn so that colonists did not need to travel more than a single day to attend county court sessions.

The officials of early Virginia counties were the same as those in the English shire: sheriff, county lieutenant, coroner, clerk, and justice. All but the clerk were appointed by the governor of the commonwealth. The senior justice was typically appointed as first sheriff of a new county. Justices initially exercised great power in county government. They recommended the sheriff, chose the clerk, sat as a jury in many cases, appointed militia officers, and commanded deference throughout the county. Their appointment by the chief executive gave the governor a great deal of control over local matters and politics. Gubernatorial appointment, a grievance of westerners, was continued in Virginia until the state constitution was revised in 1850. Thereafter, county officials were elected by popular vote.

Trans-Allegheny counties were exceptionally large. When Monongalia County was created in 1776, it encompassed the entire northern half of what is now West Virginia. Botetourt and Fincastle Counties stretched from the Blue Ridge to the Ohio River. The entire future state of Kentucky was included in Kentucky County, created in 1776.

County government was the basis of the settlement system not only in Virginia but throughout the South. Typically, colonists of a new area petitioned the state legislature to create a new county when their numbers were large enough to demand a courthouse closer to their settlements. Since all judicial business, recording of deeds, and even voting were conducted at the county seat, it was difficult if not impossible for many persons to make a long journey to the courthouse over treacherous roads. One group of petitioners complained of the "Distance from the Center of our Settlements to the courthouse of Seventy-four Miles the way Mountainous and many dangers [and] no comfortable accommodations."

See also: REGULATORS AND THE BATTLE OF ALAMANCE.

—Philip Sturm, *Ohio Valley College*

Davis, Henry Gassaway

(1823–1916) Industrialist and U.S. senator.

Henry Gassaway Davis was one of the Big Four, a group of powerful figures who played a dominant role in the development of West Virginia. His career illustrates the great influence of external forces and individuals upon the state's—and the region's—politics and economy.

Davis was born November 16, 1823, in Baltimore, Maryland, to Caleb Davis, a merchant and construction contractor, and Louisa Warfield Brown, a teacher. From 1842 to 1858, he worked for the Baltimore and Ohio Railroad as a brakeman, conductor, station agent, and superintendent. In 1853 he married Katharine Anne Bantz, by whom he would have eight children. The following year, he and his brothers opened a profitable store in Piedmont, (West) Virginia. During the Civil War, Davis, a strong Unionist, supplied goods to railroads and the government. After the war he engaged in farming, banking, timber, and coal businesses, and by 1871 he was one of the richest men in West Virginia.

Though he resided in Baltimore and at a Maryland retreat at Deer Park, where he and son-in-law Stephen B. Elkins entertained prominent politicians and businessmen, Davis was elected to the West Virginia House of Delegates in 1865, the state senate in 1868 and 1870, and the United States Senate in 1871 and 1877. He and ally Johnson N.

Camden rebuilt the Democratic Party after its recent decline by using modern methods of organization and communication (especially newspapers) together with money and private and government patronage. Neither man was an effective speaker, relying instead on astute maneuvering and negotiation. Being prudent businessmen who disliked paying more than was necessary to win, they spent money—but not nearly as much as legend claimed. Their biggest impediment was the party's incurable factionalism.

Fearing defeat, Davis retired from the Senate in 1883. Through the latter 1880s, Elkins led the rejuvenation of the state's Republican Party and was himself elected to the Senate in 1895. Davis, meanwhile, became disgusted with the Democrats' feuding and their support of tariff reform under Representative William L. Wilson, an erstwhile protégé. To help protect the tariff on bituminous coal, he even sabotaged the Democrats and helped Republicans attain office. When the Democrats suffered a schism after 1896 over candidate William Jennings Bryan and free silver, Davis suppressed his dislike for Bryan and reemerged as the leader of the mainline party in West Virginia.

But Republicans seemed set to dominate state politics for years to come, and after 1900 Davis focused on national party politics, working to oust the Bryanites. In 1904, at age eighty-one, he was named Alton B. Parker's running mate against Theodore Roosevelt. He campaigned very little nationally and suffered the humiliation of witnessing the Democrats' worst defeat in West Virginia since 1864. He then retired from politics.

In 1904 Davis and Elkins gave land for a college named for them in Elkins (formerly Leadsville). Davis, honored by a statue in Charleston while still living, died in Washington in his ninety-third year in 1916, outliving Elkins by five years.

Davis played a leading role in developing central and northern West Virginia enterprises, usually working with Elkins despite their political differences. In particular, they built railroads, notably the West Virginia Central and Pittsburgh and the Coal and Coke Railroads, connecting central West Virginia with the trunk lines of the Baltimore and Ohio and the Chesapeake and Ohio. Their principal business headquarters, however, were in New York—thus helping to make West Virginia's a kind of colonial economy, controlled from the outside.

See also: CAMDEN, JOHNSON N. (BUSINESS, INDUSTRY, AND TECHNOLOGY); ELKINS, STEPHEN B.; SCOTT, NATHAN B. (BUSINESS, INDUSTRY, AND TECHNOLOGY).

—David S. Newhall, *Centre College*

Charles M. Pepper, *The Life and Times of Henry Gassaway Davis, 1823–1916* (1920); John Alexander Williams, *West Virginia and the Captains of Industry* (1976).

Davis, John W.

(1873–1955) U.S. congressman, ambassador, and lawyer.

A native of Clarksburg, West Virginia, John William Davis was the Democratic Party's 1924 nominee for president of the United States. Although he was one of the outstanding lawyers of his time, he is best remembered for winning his party's nomination on the 103rd convention ballot and for losing the presidential race to incumbent Calvin Coolidge by a popular vote margin of two to one.

Born on April 13, 1873, Davis was the son of James and Anna Kennedy Davis. His father was a prominent attorney and former member of Congress. After graduation from law school at Washington and Lee University at Lexington, Virginia, Davis practiced law with his father, representing a number of coal, timber, and railroad companies. He was elected to Congress in 1910 and again in 1912, and in 1913 he was appointed solicitor general of the United States. During five years representing the federal government before the Supreme Court, Davis won 48 of the 67 cases that he personally argued. Among them was his successful defense of the government's authority to regulate interstate pipelines. Several members of the Court—Justices Oliver Wendell Holmes, William Howard Taft, Learned Hand, and Hugo Black—referred to Davis as one of the most persuasive attorneys they had ever known.

In September 1918, President Woodrow Wilson nominated Davis to be U.S. ambassador to Great Britain, a post he held for two and a half years before returning to the United States to practice law on Wall Street.

Davis became the Democrats' presidential nominee after the party's nominating convention deadlocked over William G. McAdoo of California and New York Governor Alfred E. Smith. The standoff lasted for two weeks (starting June 24, 1924) before Davis emerged as the victorious compromise candidate. His race for the presidency was marked by his efforts to unite the fractious party and his reluctance to call unequivocally for United States membership in the League of Nations. The campaign was complicated by the independent candidacy of Senator Robert La Follette of Wisconsin. In the end, President Coolidge received about 16 million votes to 8 million for Davis and nearly 5 million for La Follette.

After returning to his law practice, Davis was often at odds with the leadership of his party. Although he supported Franklin D. Roosevelt in 1932, he joined other disaffected Democrats in organizing the American Liberty League to oppose New Deal programs. Later, he supported the Cold War foreign policies of Harry Truman's administration but opposed Truman's Fair Deal domestic programs.

Increasingly a marginal political figure after his presidential campaign loss, Davis remained one of the country's blue-chip lawyers. His greatest victory came in 1952 when he successfully challenged President Truman's takeover of the nation's steel industry. Davis represented atomic scientist J. Robert Oppenheimer when Oppenheimer sought to reclaim his top-secret security clearance, which had been withdrawn by Atomic Energy Commission. During the landmark Supreme Court school desegregation case *Brown v. Board of Education*, Davis represented the State of South Carolina, unsuccessfully advocating separate but equal schools for blacks and whites.

By the end of his career, Davis had argued 140 cases before the Supreme Court, more than any other twentieth-century lawyer at the time of his death. Although his political views seemed to be sometimes contradictory, Davis was unwavering in his belief that human rights and property rights are inseparable. "History furnishes no instance," he once said, "where the right of man to acquire and hold property has been taken away without the complete destruction of liberty in all its forms."

Davis died in Charleston, South Carolina, on March 24, 1955.

See also: DEMOCRATIC PARTY.

—Rudy Abramson, *Reston, Virginia*

William H. Harbaugh, *Lawyer's Lawyer: The Life of John W. Davis* (1973).

Democratic Party

The Democratic Party claims Thomas Jefferson as its founder, but its full-fledged appearance in Appalachia dates from the Jacksonian period. Andrew Jackson and his enemies, by forming rival coalitions divided by disagreements on fiscal and monetary issues, internal improvements, and the relative balance between states' rights and federal authority, created what historians now call the Second American Party System. The Civil War led to a party realignment during the 1860s, but a new version of the system whereby Democrats competed with Republicans rather than Whigs emerged after Reconstruction and has evolved by stages into its present-day form.

Democratic advocacy of expanded political rights for white males became a party hallmark with special significance for Appalachia. Even where restrictions on white male suffrage and office holding remained in force, as in Virginia before 1851, the competition between Democrats and their Whig rivals served to increase voter turnout and widen participation in politics. Participation intensified between 1872 and 1900, when political parties developed more or less continuously functioning organizational machinery and fought frequent military-style campaigns meant to increase turnout among voters who tended to cast straight tickets. After 1901 presidential factions emerged to compete with congressional and state leaders for control of party machinery. These Democrats drew strength from presidential access to mass media and from the expansion of federal government functions and personnel during the Great Depression and two world wars. Presidential Democrats were more liberal than their state or congressional counterparts, and the civil service requirements of federally financed or mandated programs eroded the patronage available to state and local leaders. Finally, the rise of television campaigning tended to place party machinery in the hands of professional political consultants or interest group organizers with expertise in fund-raising or campaigns.

Party politics in Appalachia, whether considered as the vast region served by the Appalachian Regional Commission or as a smaller mountain and valley core in the six states of Georgia, Kentucky, North Carolina, Tennessee, and the two Virginias, has been shaped by each of these transitions, yet certain elements of continuity persist. First, two-party competition has been a relatively consistent feature of regional politics, even though lopsided local majorities have been frequently evident. During the formative period of the party system, this competition was extremely close, with the Democratic share of presidential voting in the Appalachian core growing from 44 percent in 1840 to 57.5 percent in 1856. In the three intervening elections, the region's voters were almost evenly split, with Democratic strength in Virginia and Georgia balanced by Whiggish loyalties in Kentucky, North Carolina, and Tennessee.

The same degree of competition characterized the post-Reconstruction period. Although Democrats won a majority of the core region's presidential votes in 1876, the rise of a competitive Republican Party in the mountain sections of each state led the Democratic share of the vote to fluctuate between 46 and 50 percent between 1880 and 1892, then to fall below 45 percent in 1896 and remain there until Franklin D. Roosevelt won a 55 percent majority in 1932. The Democrats remained the dominant party in Appalachia in the era of Roosevelt and his successor, Harry Truman. They returned to minority status in 1952 and have retained it, with the notable exception of the 1964 race, when the party benefited from a national Democratic landslide.

Until the 1970s, national political parties functioned as federations of state parties. Thus, there is no multistate Appalachian entity within the formal Democratic Party, and mountain Democrats have never developed the informal identity that attaches to mountain Republicans. At the state level it became difficult to generalize about the Democrats' role in Appalachian political history. Regardless of the degree of interparty competition, mountain Democrats were always a minority within statewide organizations, and their level of strength reflected differences among the states in the issues, personalities, and interest groups that shaped politics. Jackson, for example, had powerful and prominent enemies in Henry Clay and Hugh White, and these rivals laid the foundations for enduring opposition to Democrats in Kentucky and east Tennessee, respectively.

The slavery debate in Virginia led eastern Democrats to emphasize their loyalty to the institution to the exclusion of most other issues. Westerners such as the two Governors John Floyd, father and son, and the last antebellum governor, John Letcher, moderated or repudiated earlier critical positions on slavery in order to win statewide support. Western Virginia voters, reflecting the same ambivalence, voted Democratic but by consistently narrow margins. Antebellum north Georgia remained the most solidly Democratic section of Appalachia—reflecting, no doubt, Jackson's role in Cherokee removal—with majorities of 65 percent or better in all but one presidential election between 1840 and 1860. Joseph E. Brown, the state's Civil War governor, won as a dark-horse candidate in 1857, by which time the Democrats were thoroughly committed to states' rights. Democrats gained strength in Kentucky during this period while retaining their minority status in western North Carolina and east Tennessee, even in 1860.

Differences in Democratic strength among the states remained fairly consistent after the Civil War. Virginia and Georgia mountain counties usually produced large majorities for Democratic presidential candidates, but they invariably failed to carry east Tennessee. West Virginia and western North Carolina counties remained the Appalachian core's swing districts along with eastern Kentucky. Generally, the Democratic share of the Appalachian presidential vote tended to increase whenever the level of voter participation fell. However, this region is more complicated when examined on a state-by-state level. The 92 percent of voters who turned out in West Virginia in 1888 and Kentucky in 1900 took part in the closest elections in the history of their respective states. Republican east Tennessee approached these participation levels until the state adopted Jim Crow restrictions designed to curb black voting, which also had the effect of screening out many working-class whites. By 1920, east Tennessee voter turnout was between 33 and 45 percent, in the same range as that of Appalachian Virginia and Georgia until the impact of the Civil Rights movement began to be felt during the 1960s.

The intense two-party competition that characterized Appalachian politics during the century that followed Reconstruction served to distinguish the mountain region from the rest of the South, but it limited the statewide influence of Democratic leaders from the mountain counties. An interesting exception to this rule was Tennessee's Bob Taylor, but his success owed much to the notoriety of his first gubernatorial campaign in 1886, when the Republicans nominated his brother Alf as his opponent. The campaign the fiddling and storytelling Taylors waged was extremely entertaining, and Bob eventually earned three gubernatorial terms and one in the U.S. Senate. Georgia's Joseph E. Brown emerged from Reconstruction as one member of a Democratic oligarchy known as the "Bourbon Triumvirate" and served as a U.S. senator. Another Civil War governor, Zebulon Vance of North Carolina, formerly a Whig, became a prominent Democrat after the war. Elected governor in 1876, he also served in the U.S. Senate from March 4, 1879, until his death on April 14, 1894. While Vance retained many ties to his native mountains, he resided in Charlotte during this phase of his career. The highland counties along the Virginia border furnished West Virginia with a roster of undistinguished Democratic governors between 1876 and 1940. U.S. Senators Harry Flood Byrd of Virginia and Sam Ervin of North Carolina were generally thought of as southern because of their conservatism, particularly on civil rights, even though they were born, reared, and spent their lives in Appalachia.

More typical Appalachian Democrats who achieved national reputations started as congressmen. These included William L. Wilson, John W. Davis, and Harley Staggers of West Virginia, Fred M. Vinson and Carl D. Perkins of Kentucky, and Cordell Hull of Tennessee. The fact that mountain Democrats had to scramble for votes in their home districts while the Democratic nomination was "tantamount to election" in lowland counties limited their opportunities for statewide offices in Virginia, Georgia, and North Carolina. Mountain Democrats generally supported liberal federal programs of interest to the region such as the Tennessee Valley Authority, social welfare transfer payments, and the Appalachian Regional Commission. Because of their inability to establish longterm tenure in the House of Representatives, they rarely became committee chairman. Thus, they were unable to bring home patronage prizes such as defense installations that were scattered across northern Alabama and the non-mountain sections of Georgia, Virginia, and the Carolinas.

Since 1972 the degree of two-party competition historically found in Appalachia has become characteristic of southern states generally. The Republican Party gained adherents among rural segregationists and migrants to cities such as Atlanta and Dallas and achieved statewide parity with or superiority to Democrats. Because of their previous greater flexibility on racial matters and generally weaker economic growth in their sections, Democrats in Kentucky and West Virginia retained their base of support. In all of these states, however, Democrats are subject to other leavening factors, including a decline in party loyalty and voter participation. The recent success of mountain Democrats such as Senators Robert C. Byrd of West Virginia and Zell Miller of Georgia has less to do with their regional origins than to the push that media campaigns and weak party identification give to talented and powerful individuals.

See also: DEMOCRATIC-REPUBLICAN PARTY; REPUBLICAN PARTY; WHIG PARTY.

—John Alexander Williams, *Appalachian State University*

V. O. Key Jr., *Southern Politics in State and Nation* (1949; reprint 1984); William G. Shade, *Democratizing the Old Dominion: Virginia and the Second Party System, 1824–1861* (1996); John Alexander Williams, *West Virginia and the Captains of Industry* (1976).

Democratic-Republican Party

The Democratic-Republican Party was a political coalition created by Thomas Jefferson and James Madison in the 1790s to oppose policies promoted by Alexander Hamilton. Between 1800 and 1824, this party dominated the national government and Appalachian local governments as well.

The Democratic-Republicans thought of themselves as champions of the small white farmer and opposed strong central government. The impact of this policy perspective on Appalachia was first evident during the Whiskey Rebellion of 1794, when President George Washington sent troops into western Pennsylvania and threatened to send others to the North Carolina backcountry to collect the unpopular liquor tax. The Democratic-Republicans opposed this action and won the allegiance of the majority of the voters in mountain regions. Despite their assertion that they represented the common people, however, the party leadership was drawn from the economic and social elite.

The Appalachian population also appreciated the party's willingness to use the power of the government to acquire new land for settlement. Jefferson's purchase of the Louisiana Territory in 1803 was very popular. Similarly, highlanders welcomed the willingness of the Democratic-Republicans to seize land from American Indian tribes that bordered on white settlements. This was especially true during the War of 1812, when the Indian leader Tecumseh sought to unite midwestern and southern Indians.

The party became so dominant that it began to split into factions after 1820. The factionalism at the national level led to a confused presidential election in 1824 and to the development of the Democratic and Whig Parties in the late 1820s and 1830s. Within Appalachia, loyalties to party leaders and local economic interests ensured that Democratic-Republicans would split into competing organizations by 1828. Although the party existed for little more than three decades, it played a crucial role in establishing the political culture of Appalachia.

See also: DEMOCRATIC PARTY; REPUBLICAN PARTY; WHIG PARTY.

—Gordon B. McKinney, *Berea College*

Elkins, Stephen B.

(1841–1911) Industrialist and U.S. senator.

Stephen Benton Elkins was—with Johnson N. Camden, Henry Gassaway Davis, and Nathan B. Scott—one of the so-called Big Four, who shaped West Virginia in the state's formative years, when its economy came largely under the control of corporations run from New York, Philadelphia, and Baltimore. Elkins's career illustrates the rise to power of out-of-state interests and non-native persons in West Virginia's (and much of Appalachia's) economy and politics.

The eldest of the six children of Philip Duncan Elkins and Sarah Pickett Withers, Elkins was born September 26, 1841, in Perry County, on the fringe of Appalachian Ohio. In 1844 the family moved to Westport (Kansas City), Missouri, where Philip became a slave dealer. Stephen was graduated from the University of Missouri in 1860, taught school for a year, and then served in the Civil War as a Union cavalry captain in the Missouri militia, narrowly escaping death after being captured by William Quantrill's guerrillas. Frustrated by confinement to Missouri's wretched border war, he resigned July 3, 1863, went to the New Mexico Territory, studied law and Spanish, and set up practice in Mesilla. In short order he began to litigate, acquire immense Old Spanish land grants, and involve himself in banking.

He moved to Santa Fe, married Sarah Jacobs in 1866, and was appointed attorney general (1867–73). After Sarah died in 1872, he served as New Mexico's delegate to Congress (1873–77). He decided to remain in Washington as a lobbyist, having married Hallie Davis, daughter of Henry Gassaway Davis, senator (1871–83) from West Virginia, in 1875. In 1878 he moved to New York to manage his expanding business interests, which greatly profited from his connections with Davis, a coal, lumber, and railroad magnate. He also continued to speculate in New Mexico land and western mines. Davis and Elkins owned large coal-bearing tracts in the upper Potomac and upper Cheat River basins, and they helped found the giant Consolidation Coal and Coke Company (1893). They also built railroads connecting central West Virginia with the trunk lines of the Baltimore and Ohio and the Chesapeake and Ohio.

Meanwhile, Elkins remained active in national politics. While New Mexico's delegate, he became an intimate friend of James G. Blaine and a member of the Republican National Executive Committee. In 1884 he managed Blaine's unsuccessful presidential campaign against Grover Cleveland. In 1888 he worked in Benjamin Harrison's victorious campaign for the presidency and later served as Harrison's secretary of war. He was especially active in improving weapons, particularly a new infantry rifle. From the early 1880s he aspired to serve in the Senate, where he could most influence national policies on business. West Virginia appeared to offer his best possibility. Although he continued to reside principally in New York, he built Halliehurst, a mansion in Leadsville, West Virginia (now Elkins and the home of Davis and Elkins College), in 1889. Years of astute maneuvering in West Virginia politics brought him to the leadership of the state's Republicans—while his father-in-law remained at or near the top of the Democratic Party—and election to the U.S. Senate in January 1895. He died of stomach cancer on January 4, 1911, while still in office.

In the Senate Elkins stoutly defended business interests, notably supporting protective tariffs. But he was a "conservative realist," receptive to reforms in the relations between government and large corporations. He also advocated higher pay and benefits for workers. The Elkins Act (1903) attacked the rebate system used by railroads to manipulate rates. In 1906 he helped strengthen the Hepburn Act, designed to curb railroad management abuses, and in 1910 he sponsored the Mann-Elkins Act augmenting the powers of the Interstate Commerce Commission.

Elkins preferred subtle political maneuvering to outright confrontation and seldom made a misstep. His wealth helped, but he disliked spending an inordinate amount of money on campaigns. He was a consummate opportunist, using his political success in New Mexico and Washington and his marriage to Hallie Davis to reap a golden harvest in business. Around 1900, he and the others of the Big Four comprised four of West Virginia's five millionaires.

See also: REPUBLICAN PARTY.

—David S. Newhall, *Centre College*

Oscar Doane Lambert, *Stephen Benton Elkins* (1955); John Alexander Williams, *West Virginia and the Captains of Industry* (1976).

Ewing, Thomas

(1789–1871) U.S. senator and cabinet officer.

One of southeastern Ohio's most prominent politicians, Thomas Ewing served in the cabinets of two presidents and advised a third. Born near Charleston, (West) Virginia, of a farm family, Ewing moved to Athens County, Ohio, in 1798. He worked at a Kanawha Valley saltworks to earn money to attend Ohio University, graduating in 1815. After studying law under the prominent lawyer and politician Philemon Beecher in Lancaster, Ohio, he was admitted to the bar in 1816.

A man known for his intellect, determination, and leadership, Ewing invested heavily in real estate and local industry in addition to practicing law. Advocating canal building, education, and protection of domestic industry, he was elected to the U.S. Senate in 1830, and there his forceful, logical argumentation made him one of the chief Whig opponents of President Andrew Jackson. President William Henry Harrison rewarded him for his partisanship with the post of secretary of the treasury in 1841. Ewing wrote two bills attempting to reestablish a national bank, but both were vetoed by Harrison's successor, John Tyler. President Zachary Taylor made Ewing secretary of the interior in 1849, but he resigned in 1851 to fill a vacant Senate seat. A nationalist who deplored the sectionalizing effects of slavery, he disappointed antislavery Whigs, who stymied his further political career. During Reconstruction, he reemerged as one of President Andrew Johnson's chief advisors, writing messages accompanying Johnson's veto of several congressional Reconstruction measures.

Ewing's conservative nationalism influenced a generation of politicians, including his son-in-law, William T. Sherman, and Abraham Lincoln. For Ewing, education and economic development pointed the way to national fulfillment.

See also: JOHNSON, ANDREW; WHIG PARTY.

—Phyllis F. Field, *Ohio University*

Federalist Party

Part of the First Political Party System in Appalachia, the Federalists were generally viewed as supporters of urban and commercial interests. Subsequently, they had few supporters in the mountain counties.

The Federalist Party dominated the early government of the United States. Its leaders had been responsible for the writing and adoption of the Constitution, and the voters gave this alliance of politicians the opportunity to operate the new government. The nation's first two presidents, George Washington and John Adams, were Federalists.

During Washington's administrations, Alexander Hamilton became essentially a prime minister, and Hamilton's policies on funding, the national debt, support of local manufacturers, and formation of a national bank all supported the emergence of an aggressive commercial class. During Washington's second administration, agricultural interests increasingly opposed Hamilton's policies, and Thomas Jefferson and James Madison became leaders of the opposition Democratic-Republican Party.

Except for Indian issues, policies of the new government seemed quite remote to people of the Appalachians until the Federalists passed a steep tax on the making of whiskey. Opposition to this new tax centered in Appalachian Pennsylvania, and several counties around Pittsburgh rose in rebellion. Hamilton, with Washington's support, leaped at the opportunity to demonstrate the power of the new government and raised a force of approximately thirteen thousand, as large as the one the Continental Army had marshaled at Yorktown. Though the rebellion evaporated, the political effect was to turn Appalachian backwoodsmen into avid Democratic-Republicans. They strongly supported Jefferson's successful bid for the presidency in the election of 1800, and his victory ended Federalist hegemony.

See also: DEMOCRATIC PARTY; DEMOCRATIC-REPUBLICAN PARTY; REPUBLICAN PARTY.

—Richard B. Drake, *Berea College*

Felton, Rebecca Latimer

(1835–1930) U.S. senator and political activist.

Rebecca Latimer Felton was the nation's first female senator and an influential political activist and writer. She was born on June 10, 1835, near Decatur, Georgia.

The child of a prosperous family, Felton was able to secure a fine education. She was graduated first in her class at Madison Female College in 1852, and the next year she married William H. Felton, a physician and Methodist minister. The couple moved to Bartow County, Georgia, where she resided for the remainder of her life and bore five children, only one of whom survived into adulthood. The family suffered greatly during the Civil War, as both Confederate and Union armies passed through their neighborhood in the spring of 1864.

The Feltons entered politics in 1874, when William ran for Congress as an Independent Democrat in opposition to the dominant Democratic Party. Rebecca acted as publicist and campaign manager for her husband. The team proved quite successful, and William won three terms in Congress and election to the state legislature from 1884 to 1890. The two of them attacked the convict-lease system and supported prohibition as part of a general reform platform.

After William left politics, Rebecca continued to be active on her own. She became a crusader for woman suffrage, prohibition, and a separate penitentiary for women convicts. Starting in 1899, she wrote a column for the *Atlanta Journal* on topics of interest to women until 1927. She also wrote two books, *My Memoirs of Georgia Politics* (1911) and *Country Life in Georgia in the Days of My Youth* (1919). William's death in 1909 did not end Rebecca's political activities. She was a delegate to the 1912 Progressive Party national convention in 1912 and campaigned for the party's candidate, Theodore Roosevelt, in Georgia.

During her later years, Felton became an avid supporter of Georgia Senator Tom Watson, openly backing his attacks on Jews, Catholics, and African Americans. She even went so far as to endorse selective lynchings as a means of social control. After Watson's death in 1922, Felton was appointed to take his place. She served only one day in office in November 1922, but that service made her the first woman to serve in the U.S. Senate and the oldest person—at age eighty-seven—to enter the body. During the years before her death in 1930, she worked actively to promote compulsory school attendance and the right of women to attend the University of Georgia.

See also: LYNCHING; PROHIBITION; SUFFRAGE.

—Kim O'Connor, *University of Chicago*

Feminism

During the last decade of the nineteenth century, women in the larger towns and cities of Appalachia began to form

Prominent political women celebrate the arrival of Rebecca Latimer Felton in Washington, D.C., 1922. A longtime activist in Georgia politics, Felton was the first woman to become a member of the U.S. Senate, serving for a single day.

equal suffrage clubs. In 1894 suffrage supporters in western North Carolina gathered at the Buncombe County Courthouse in Asheville and soon formed the North Carolina Equal Suffrage Association. One year later, in West Virginia, activists from nine equal suffrage clubs met in Grafton and formed a state association. These equal suffrage clubs and associations were in many cases small and short-lived, and their quick decline paralleled that of the national movement during the last years of the nineteenth century.

During the 1910s, however, suffragists throughout Appalachia reinvigorated their campaign for the vote. Those who became the most active leaders and supporters of the movement tended to be relatively well educated, urban, and in many cases professional, working as schoolteachers and librarians. Working-class women also participated in the campaign. In Appalachian Virginia, for example, garment workers joined the Equal Suffrage League, and some suffrage leaders likened the disfranchised status of women to that of the working class in general.

Suffrage proponents tended to find a more favorable reception in the northern Appalachian states of Ohio, Pennsylvania, and New York. Further south, suffrage activism often pitted urban proponents of a "New South" against the advocates and beneficiaries of the plantation regime. The latter included not only traditional planter elites but also textile manufacturers and railroad entrepreneurs, whose economic interests and social backgrounds were usually tied to those of the planter class. These opponents viewed suffrage as a threat in part because of women's leadership in major progressive causes such as municipal reform, abolition of child labor, and public welfare provision. Joining them was the liquor lobby, which opposed woman suffrage because of the highly visible and successful advocacy of the Women's Christian Temperance Union for prohibition.

Infusing the most vicious arguments over suffrage in the southern mountains were fearful predictions about the presumed relationship between woman suffrage and white supremacy. White supporters and opponents both used racist arguments in favor of their position. Supporters argued that white female voters would ensure that black males would not again become politically significant. Opponents said that black females would greatly increase black political strength. Complicating the politics of suffrage even further, particularly in the South, were states' rights feminists who believed in the right to vote (at least for some women) but sought to sabotage the strategy of a federal amendment to the Constitution.

In 1920 the mountains of southern Appalachia became a crucial battleground, as Kentucky and West Virginia (along with the states of northern Appalachia) ratified the Nineteenth Amendment, while all of the states in the Deep South defeated it. Tennessee made woman suffrage a reality when a twenty-four-year-old legislator from east Tennessee, Harry T. Burn, switched sides in an evenly divided House (after receiving a note from his pro-suffrage mother) and voted in favor of ratification. Thereafter, women's activism in Appalachia took new forms. The National American Woman Suffrage Association renamed itself the League of Women Voters and drew former suffragists into continued activism over a diverse reform agenda, only a portion of which focused on gender-specific goals such as protective legislation for women workers. Black women, regardless of whether they were allowed to vote, continued their traditional efforts to improve the social conditions of their segregated communities and to contest degrading images of black womanhood. In 1927 Minnie Buckingham-Harper became the first African American woman to serve as a state legislator when the West Virginia governor appointed her to fill the term of her deceased husband. A form of labor feminism also arose during the late 1920s and the Great Depression, when women workers in industries such as textiles challenged convention and their male bosses by organizing unions and going on strike.

The "second wave" women's movement that emerged in the 1970s led to a more singularly feminist, or at least women-focused, activism in Appalachia. Chapters of the National Organization for Women and the National Abortion Rights Action League formed in many urban areas of the region. Activists developed women's health centers, domestic violence shelters, and other institutions run by and for women. In addition, rural women formed their own organizations separate from national groups. Examples include the Mountain Women's Exchange of Jellico, Tennessee, and the regionwide Appalachian Women's Alliance.

Working-class women in Appalachia also created feminist advocacy organizations that focused on employment discrimination and other issues related to economic survival. As more women found it necessary to enter the labor force in the 1970s, they were still consigned to working in low-wage jobs, but even opportunities to work as waitresses, secretaries, and sales clerks were relatively limited in rural Appalachia. Many of the region's dominant industries—coal in central Appalachia, steel in the north, heavy manufacturing in certain areas such as the Kanawha Valley in West Virginia, and construction throughout—barred women from employment altogether. Working-class women therefore organized to gain access to these relatively high-wage but male-dominated industries.

The first and probably best known of these working-class feminist organizations was the Coal Employment Project, founded in 1977 by Betty Jean Hall. Using affirmative action levers that required contractors with the federal government to hire women and minorities, the organization initially targeted companies that supplied coal to the Tennessee Valley Authority. Other groups soon developed similar strategies. Women and Employment of Charleston, West Virginia, a statewide organization founded by Chris Weiss, focused in part on gaining women access to jobs in construction. The Southeast Women's Employment Coalition, founded in 1979 by Leslie Lilly and leaders of the Coal Employment Project, Women and Employment, and similar groups, pursued a regional strategy to open up federally financed road construction jobs to women. In northern Appalachia, women sought jobs in heavy industries such as steel and automobile manufacturing, as well as in building trades.

Opposing their efforts were employers who resisted this feminist infringement on their hiring authority, as well as labor unions, male workers, and in some cases other women. Craft unions, which traditionally controlled apprenticeship training and members' assignments to worksites, opposed women's demands because of their feared loss of authority over hiring and entry into the trades. In industrial unions such as the United Mine Workers of America, opposition was significant but less entrenched, and allegiance to the union by women coal miners—who were often the daughters or other relatives of United Mine Workers members—was resolute.

Deindustrialization and the loss of employment in precisely the basic industries that these working-class women's organizations targeted, combined with declining federal support for affirmative action, gradually undercut feminists' nontraditional employment strategies during the 1980s. Plant closings and the abrogation of collective bargaining agreements increasingly spurred joint, class-based efforts among women and men. Women in some of these contexts developed their own organizations and tactics, however. During the Pittston Coal Company strike, for example, women organized to form the Daughters of Mother Jones, occupying the company's headquarters in southwest Virginia and providing significant strike support on picket lines, in rallies, and elsewhere.

In addition, community economic development—the effort to define and generate sustainable jobs (and other social necessities) in the face of severe economic dislocation—became a new locus of activism for many working-class women. Organizations such as the Dungannon (Virginia) Development Commission, Ivanhoe (Virginia) Civic League, and Big Creek (West Virginia) People in Action—although neither exclusively women's organizations nor explicitly feminist—were led by women, who were also among their most active participants. Taking a public role in defining and fighting for their communities' future, often through a maternal ethos that emphasized the well-being of children, became a path to empowerment for many female participants and leaders.

Feminist activism in Appalachia has challenged popular images of women's rights as an exclusively middle-class and urban cause, expanding the social base and content of feminism to include the concerns of working-class and rural women. Moreover, Appalachian women's distinctive activism—even when their cause has been labor, racial justice, or their working-class community—raises important but largely unanswered questions about the multiple meanings of feminism and the interactions of gender, race, and class in the region.

See also: SUFFRAGE; WOMEN AND EMPLOYMENT (LABOR).

—Barbara Ellen Smith, *University of Memphis*

John Gaventa, Barbara Ellen Smith, and Alex Willingham, eds., *Communities in Economic Crisis: Appalachia and the South* (1990); Elna C. Green, *Southern Strategies: Southern Women and the Woman Suffrage Question* (1997); Barbara J. Howe, "West Virginia Women's Organizations, 1880s–1930, or 'Unsexed Termagants . . . Help the World Along,'" *West Virginia History* (1990).

Fence Laws

In England, owners of farm animals were required to fence them in. If an animal damaged someone else's property, the owner of the animal was liable in court. In comparatively thinly settled colonial America, however, animals were allowed to run free, and farmers had to build fences around their crops or gardens. If an animal damaged property without a fence around it, the owner of the animal was not guilty of a tort. As settlement patterns became more dense, however, movements to adopt laws requiring owners to fence their livestock spread. Proponents maintained that they would conserve increasingly scarce land and timber and produce better supervised and healthier farm animals.

In contrast, opponents of fence laws claimed that forests and farmland were still plentiful and that requiring animals to be fenced in would hurt the landless or land-poor. Both sides were correct at different times and in different places.

In the postbellum South, the more intensively farmed lowland areas and those near cities began to adopt fence laws by referendum or by special legislation. Only late in the nineteenth century did struggles over this question come to rapidly developing Appalachia, and the fights were often bitter. Even within counties that generally benefited from fence laws, there was opposition since many voters, especially livestock raisers, suffered in the short run.

Although some historians have treated these battles as cultural or class conflicts, others have convincingly shown that they chiefly turned on material self-interest, which did not divide people neatly into economic classes.

See also: CATTLE (AGRICULTURE); FENCE LAWS (AGRICULTURE); HOGS (AGRICULTURE).

—J. Morgan Kousser, *California Institute of Technology*

Feuds

The term *feud* in the United States usually has been associated with a dozen or so conflicts that occurred in southern Appalachia, especially in eastern Kentucky, between 1880 and 1900. These include the French-Eversole, Baker-White, and Martin-Tolliver feuds, as well as the most famous of all—the Hatfield-McCoy feud in southern West Virginia and northeastern Kentucky. Although the term *feuding* has also been applied to a series of cattle wars and outlaw gangs in Texas, Montana, and Wyoming at about the same time, the feuds of southern Appalachia endured as American cultural icons. Yet the conflicts that came to be so labeled in the United States were very different from feuds in other regions of the world—both historically and in modern-day tribal societies. Despite Americans' image of feuding as a primitive and usually chaotic product of poor education and the absence of strong governmental institutions, scholars of premodern Europe and present-day tribal societies in Africa and Latin America have shown that feuds are based on widely recognized and accepted rules of behavior. Such conflicts, however violent, function to preserve order within or between communities.

In United States history, there is no clear understanding or definition of the term *feud* (or *vendetta*) as in other societies. Indeed, the term was not generally used until the early nineteenth century, and when it appeared in the press, it usually referred to the practice of southern dueling—an affair of honor between two aristocratic gentlemen. Rarely did such conflicts become ongoing family vendettas. The rigid set of rules and expectations associated with duels made these conflicts more like the European model, but they were not typical of the famous feuds of the post–Civil War era. In fact, in the antebellum era, there are few examples of feuds, although the term began to be popularized with the proliferation of newspapers and popular literature. Among early feuds that were conducted more like duels, the most famous was the Hill-Evans conflict in Kentucky during the 1850s, in which two wealthy families disputed over the treatment of a slave woman. In literature, Mark Twain popularized feuds with his story of the Grangerford-Shepherdson feud, which he incorporated into both *Huckleberry Finn* and *Life on the Mississippi*. Twain's feud was based on incidents in the Darnell-Watson feud he had witnessed in the 1850s while working on a riverboat on the Mississippi River. Neither the Hill-Evans nor the Darnell-Watson conflict conformed to the stereotype that later emerged in the press: neither occurred in the mountain South; neither involved poor, uneducated people; and neither was termed a feud by the participants themselves. Both did resemble the European model of aristocratic feuds (in Scotland and Corsica, for example) more than did the more famous feuds of the late-nineteenth-century United States.

Examination of the context and course of events in the approximately one dozen social conflicts that came to define feuds in America reveals some surprising patterns that have more to do with economic and social conflict than the inherited family hatreds of ignorant mountain folks. The earliest occurred in the mid-1870s in the eastern Kentucky mountains. In Breathitt County the Strong-Little feud and in Carter County the Underwood-Holbrook war emerged as clearly related to the Civil War and its racial politics. In both cases, one side had been organized as Union guerrillas during the war and afterwards supported votes for the few black men who lived in those counties. Although both sides engaged in violence, they were also in each case determined to assume the high ground by using the electoral and judicial system to control local government. In Breathitt County this resulted in the fatal shooting of a local judge and a battle at the courthouse door. The press response to this violence was to assume that this political and racial violence was deplorable but no more so than in other parts of Kentucky or, indeed, the South. The term *feud* was used (only by the press, not the participants) rather loosely and interchangeably with terms such as *vigilantism*, *lynching*, *war*, and *riot*. Feuds had not yet been stereotyped as a specific kind of interfamily violence unique to the mountain South.

But in the mid-1880s there erupted a series of conflicts in the southern mountains that redefined Appalachian feuding for American culture. All were located in Kentucky or on its borders: the Martin-Tolliver feud took place in Rowan County; the French-Eversole in Perry County; the Howard-Turner in Harlan County; the Hatfield-McCoy in Pike County, Kentucky, and Logan County, West Virginia; the Baker-White in Clay County; and the Hargis-Cockrell (or Cockrill) in Breathitt County. By 1884, when most of these feuds began, Democrats had regained power at the national level with the election of Grover Cleveland, and mountain Democrats had reason to hope they could regain political ground from Republicans. The political aspect of these conflicts is confirmed by the fact that election-day battles were a common denominator in all the feuds. Fueling those political battles, however, was an economic revolution bringing industrialization to the South. The nation's economic depression of the 1870s had been particularly severe in the South, which was already in serious economic decline after the Civil War. The rich yet undeveloped coalfields of Kentucky and West Virginia were proving highly attractive to New York capitalists as well as state political leaders in Kentucky and West Virginia. It was in this context that local politics became important far beyond the local community. Issues such as taxation, local financial support of railroad building, and the purchase of mineral rights by outside speculators all became crucial to the future of these mountain communities, and all the famous feuds involved conflict over how this development should proceed.

The Martin-Tolliver war of Rowan County is notable because it marked a turning point in the way regional and national press interpreted mountain violence. It began with clearly political violence, an 1884 election-day gunfight between partisans of candidates for a local office. At first, the press attributed the violence to politics, but within a year most Americans were being told by the *New York Times* that it was actually a case of irrational family hatreds in a primitive, ignorant culture. Ignoring the fact that the feudists were leading politicians and that there were already a railroad and considerable industry in Rowan County, the regional and national press concluded that the mountain South desperately needed the "civilizing forces of railroads and other economic development."

Although the Martin-Tolliver feud lasted several years and generated considerable national newspaper coverage, it never gained the long-lasting folkloric reputation of the Hatfield-McCoy feud, fought out between inhabitants of Pike County, Kentucky, and Logan County, West Virginia. This notorious feud began with a dispute over some land, which had quickly gone from being virtually worthless (too steep for farming) to extremely valuable when coal was discovered beneath it, and revived the political conflict of the Civil War, in which a few McCoy relatives had sympathized with the Union and the Hatfields had fought for the Confederacy. Economic alliances, however, were much more important than family loyalties, as there were Hatfields on the McCoy side and McCoys on the Hatfield side. The McCoys were poorer than the Hatfields, who were moderately well-to-do if not wealthy. This economic conflict led to a series of confrontations between 1878 and 1890 involving accusations of pig stealing, a fatal election-day shooting, and a Romeo-and-Juliet romance between Johnse, a son of the leading Hatfield, "Devil" Anse, and Roseanna, the daughter of Randolph McCoy. These more colorful events obscured the economic undercurrent in which the poorer McCoys joined with wealthy outside developers and state officials to bring legal action against the Hatfields. However, the real agenda was to force Devil Anse Hatfield to sell his newly valuable timber and coal lands along the Tug Fork of the Big Sandy River—an agenda that succeeded.

This pattern was repeated in the other so-called feuds. In the French-Eversole conflict, for example, Benjamin French was rapidly buying up mineral and timber rights to land in Perry County and was opposed by Joseph Eversole, a local merchant. Eversole was killed, and a series of gun battles in mountain hollows followed. In the press, both sides were described as "desperadoes" or "bandits" who were representative of the entire population of the mountains. In such descriptions, distinctions were lost between those who sought to keep economic development within local control and outsiders who saw local people as obstacles to their plans. The pattern that emerged was that the wealthier side in these feuds, usually Republicans and relative newcomers to the region, hired the poorest young men in these mountain communities to conduct violent warfare in the streets, courthouses, and hollows while the locals, usually Democrats of middling economic standing, responded with violence in kind. In any case, the usual objective was control of the political system and economic resources, rather than personal revenge.

The labeling of these conflicts as feuds between backward mountaineers served to obscure the economic struggle over development that one historian has termed the "incorporation" of America. As this process accelerated in the post–Civil War era, it inspired violence in a variety of places from the Appalachian South to the frontier West. Modern-day historians have begun to see that cultural myths featuring feuds, cattle wars, gunfights, and outlaw gangs were part of a pattern of political and economic development—not just stories about aberrant personal behavior on a lawless frontier.

See also: FEUDS AND VIOLENCE (MEDIA); VIOLENCE AND VENGEANCE (IMAGES AND ICONS).

—Altina L. Waller, *University of Connecticut*

Dwight B. Billings, Gurney Norman, and Katherine Ledford, eds., *Confronting Appalachian Stereotypes: Back Talk from an American Region* (1999); John Ed Pearce, *Days of Darkness: The Feuds of Eastern Kentucky* (1994); Altina L. Waller, *Feud: Hatfields, McCoys, and Social Change in Appalachia, 1860–1900* (1988).

Fighting Ninth District

The counties in southwestern Virginia comprising the Ninth District form the only geographical region in the United States known by its congressional district number. Created by the Virginia redistricting act of 1872, the "Fighting Ninth" has included fifteen to nineteen counties east and northeast of Cumberland Gap in Lee County. Construction of the Virginia-Tennessee Railroad during the 1850s linked the area's economy to eastern Virginia and led to an increase in the use of slave labor, distinguishing it from the counties to the north that became West Virginia in 1863. Arrival of the Norfolk and Western Railway and other improvements in transportation opened up the district's coalfields at the turn of the twentieth century and transformed the economy again. Livestock raising and extractive industries have long been major components of the district's economic base, and by the late twentieth century the area was also widely known for its lively folk music and folklore traditions.

Unionism was strong in the region during the Civil War, and the Republican Party established a firm foundation there afterward. During the 1870s and 1880s the district elected three Readjusters to Congress, more than any other district in Virginia. Democrats and Republicans fought a succession of close elections during the 1880s and 1890s. Republican Congressman C. Bascom Slemp (1907–23) became one of the most influential Republicans in the South by virtue of his base of power in the Fighting Ninth, which earned its name from the heated battles fought there at every election for decades, long after Republicans ceased to be a serious threat to Democrats elsewhere in Virginia.

The Democrats repeatedly failed in efforts to recapture the district from the Republicans, but in 1922 Harry Flood Byrd and Russell County political operative Everett Randolph Combs united behind the candidacy of George Campbell Peery, whose victory helped put Byrd in control of the state Democratic Party apparatus and make him governor from 1926 to 1930 and senator from 1933 to 1965.

Maintaining its contrarian tradition, the Fighting Ninth sometimes voted Democratic when the rest of the state voted Republican and vice versa. It elected John W. Flannagan (1931–49), Virginia's only consistent New Dealer in Congress. Republicans from the Fighting Ninth were often virtually the only ones in the Virginia General Assembly, and Abner Linwood Holton, originally from the Ninth District, was the first Republican elected governor of Virginia in modern times (1970–74). In 2004, Democrat Rick Boucher had held the Ninth District congressional seat for eleven terms.

See also: DEMOCRATIC PARTY; REPUBLICAN PARTY.

—Brent Tarter, *Library of Virginia*

Joseph A. Fry and Brent Tarter, "The Redemption of the Fighting Ninth: The 1922 Congressional Election in the Ninth District of Virginia and the Origins of the Byrd Organization," *South Atlantic Quarterly* (Summer 1978); Kenneth W. Noe, *Southwest Virginia's Railroad: Modernization and the Sectional Crisis* (1994); William C. Pendleton, *Political History of Appalachian Virginia, 1776–1927* (1927).

Fort Loudoun

Fort Loudoun, on the south bank of the Little Tennessee River in present-day east Tennessee, was from 1756 to 1760 the first British outpost west of the Appalachians. Its purpose was to safeguard from the French the control of trade with the Cherokee, who exchanged deerskins for salt, clothing, weapons, powder, and shot. The outpost was erected and commanded in succession by brothers Raymond and Paul Demere, both captains of British regulars.

Fort Loudoun was doomed almost from its inception. The nearest British garrison was Fort Prince George in upper South Carolina. Even worse, Paul Demere after August 1757 experienced endless difficulties in obtaining food, supplies, and trading goods, which led to numerous disputes with Governor William Henry Lyttelton of South Carolina and also served to alienate the Indians when they did not receive desired commodities.

On August 25, 1759, Oconastota, the Great Warrior of the Cherokees, broke off relations with Fort Loudoun. Thereafter the garrison was effectively besieged. Its fate was sealed in June 1760, when a British expedition of about thirteen hundred men under Colonel Archibald Montgomery turned back after meeting strong resistance in the Cherokee Middle Towns in western North Carolina.

Under agreement with the Cherokees, Demere's garrison of more than a hundred men, who had run out of food, departed for South Carolina on August 9, 1760. The next day, a few miles away, they were ambushed. Demere and many of his men were massacred. Only the expulsion of the French from North America a few years later accomplished what Raymond and Paul Demere and the Fort Loudoun garrison had been unable to achieve.

See also: CHEROKEE (RACE, ETHNICITY, AND IDENTITY).

—Richard G. Stone, *Western Kentucky University*

French and Indian War

The French and Indian War (1754–63) was the last of four wars fought between the French and the British over North America. The scope of the war differed vastly from the previous conflicts. Instead of small-scale engagements, it involved large armies, local militias, and shifting alliances between both the French and the British and various Indian tribes. It also expanded to include conflicts in Europe and India—the Seven Years' War and the Third Carnatic War.

In North America, the conflict took place in three main theaters of operation: northern New York and Canada; the upper Ohio River Valley (what is now southwestern New York, western Pennsylvania, eastern Ohio, and West Virginia); and the western Carolinas, including what is now east Tennessee. The first of these, while vitally important to the war, is not discussed here since it is outside Appalachia.

In the 1740s both the British and the French claimed the upper Ohio River Valley. The latter had trade relations and alliances with many of the Indian tribes of the region and depended heavily on the fur trade. The influx of traders from Pennsylvania and the affiliation of settlers with land companies chartered by Virginia (such as the Ohio Land Company) concerned the French greatly. Moreover, the British cut into French trade and allied themselves with the Iroquois Confederacy, whose tribes were enemies to the Indian allies of the French.

The war began in 1754, when Virginia Governor Robert Dinwiddie, a major shareholder in the Ohio Land Company, sent an expedition to build a fort at the Forks of the

Ohio, the site of present-day Pittsburgh. The French also sent an expedition, which drove the British out, and proceeded to build Fort Duquesne on the site. A party of Virginia militia under the command of George Washington, which had been sent to support the British expedition, attempted to retake the site and failed. Washington fell back to a hastily built strong point he called Fort Necessity, but it was easily taken by the more numerous and experienced French on July 4, 1754.

Dinwiddie then convinced the British government to send two regiments of the British army under General Edward Braddock to attempt to take Fort Duquesne. On July 9, 1755, the French and their Indian allies ambushed Braddock's force of two regiments, augmented by colonial militias and a few Indian allies. The British were defeated, and Braddock died of injuries sustained in the battle.

The French maintained their ascendancy until 1758. British difficulties were due to several factors, among them the lack of financial and political support for the war in the highest levels of government and military commanders' difficulties in dealing with the colonial leadership and citizenry. The British also had trouble dealing with the Indians, many of whom supported the French because of either actual or perceived British injustices. During this period, British settlers and traders in the trans-Appalachian areas were subject to attacks by both the French and their Indian allies. As a result, many settlers and traders who survived the attacks moved back east to safer, more settled areas.

When William Pitt became secretary of state for the Southern Department in 1757, the British forces in America began to receive the financial and political support they required. Pitt sent thousands of new troops with new generals to North America. He also made concessions to the colonists, and these concessions made the colonial governments and militias more eager to cooperate with the British army.

In 1758 a large force under General John Forbes comprised of several regiments of the British regular army, militia units from various colonies, and a group of Catawba and Cherokee Indians marched on Fort Duquesne. The French commander, realizing that the fort was seriously undermanned and that the local Indians would not come to his support, conceded defeat. He evacuated the fort and blew it up on November 24, 1758. The British forces promptly took control of the area and began the construction of Fort Pitt. This effectively marked the end of the war in the upper Ohio Valley.

Thereafter, the focus of the war in Appalachia moved south, as the Cherokee War erupted in the western Carolinas. In 1756 the Cherokees had agreed to construction of a British fort in their territory to protect them from the French and the Spanish. Fort Loudoun, in what is now southeastern Tennessee, was completed the following year, along with a supporting outpost, Fort Prince George. Later, however, the fort became a focal point for the troubles that emerged between the British and the Cherokees.

After the destruction of Fort Duquesne in 1758, British settlers and militia, perhaps unnerved by the heavily armed Cherokees, treated warriors returning to their homes from the battle savagely. At least thirty were killed by whites, who suspected them of theft. In addition, when the survivors arrived home, they discovered that white hunters had taken advantage of their absence to poach game in Cherokee territory. Negotiations between the Cherokees, represented by Attakullakulla (Little Carpenter), and Governor William Henry Lyttleton of South Carolina failed. The British sent a force under Colonel Archibald Montgomery to the Lower Towns of the Cherokee, where they killed or captured more than one hundred warriors and burned five villages. They proceeded toward the Middle Towns but lost so many men and supplies to the Cherokees that they were forced to retreat. Fort Loudoun, under siege by the Cherokees, was forced to surrender, and many of the soldiers were killed as they attempted to reach Fort Prince George.

In 1761 a much larger British force under Colonel James Grant entered the Cherokee lands in North Carolina. Over a period of several months, they destroyed hundreds of acres of Cherokee crops, burned all fifteen of the Middle Towns, and killed many Cherokee. In August the Cherokee sued for peace, ending the French and Indian War in Appalachia. The conflict continued in Canada until 1760 and elsewhere in the world until 1763, when the Treaty of Paris was signed. The French had lost their chance to control North America. The destruction of French influence was also the beginning of the end for the Iroquois Confederacy, since they had relied on the French to balance the power of the British. During the war, British leaders had also begun to negotiate alliances directly with individual tribes rather than rely on the Iroquois Confederacy to act as middlemen. After the war, the British government issued the Proclamation of 1763, forbidding settlement beyond the Appalachian Mountains, creating, in theory, a huge Indian reservation. Trans-Appalachian settlement by Europeans was thereby delayed, but only for a few years.

See also: CHEROKEE (RACE, ETHNICITY, AND IDENTITY); FORT LOUDON; FORT NECESSITY NATIONAL BATTLEFIELD (TOURISM); IROQUOIS (RACE, ETHNICITY, AND IDENTITY).

—Katherine A. Libby, *East Tennessee State University*

Fred Anderson, *Crucible of War: The Seven Years' War and the Fate of Empire in British North America, 1754–1766* (2000); Richard B. Drake, *A History of Appalachia* (2001); Gregory H. Nobles, *American Frontiers: Cultural Encounters and Continental Conquest* (1997).

Gender and Reform in the Progressive Era

In response to socioeconomic changes brought by industrialization, immigration, and increasing numbers of women in colleges and the wage-labor force, progressive reform activities by women soared in the early decades of the twentieth century. In Appalachia, women reformers came together for trachoma prevention, child labor surveys, community studies, literacy campaigns, school improvement leagues, social settlements, public-health nursing, community clubs, cottage industries, craft guilds, and preservation of folk traditions. Besides establishing their own women-centered institutions in the mountains, women reformers worked under the auspices of groups such as the Russell Sage Foundation, Young Men's Christian Association, and General Federation of Women's Clubs.

Middle-class women used their education and class standing to legitimize their authority as agents of social and cultural reform. These reformers professed a faith in the redemptive powers of education and science as well as the value of adopting middle-class standards for mothering, domesticity, hygiene, health, and leisure to heal a variety of social and economic ills. Following no linear pathway into public life and differentiated by class, region, and racial differences, they created myriad institutions and reform networks, including missionary efforts, settlement schools, colleges, and health programs throughout Appalachia. Many of these continued into the twenty-first century.

Social reformers differed in their explanations of poverty and dysfunction, their methods, and their relationships to those targeted for uplift and protection. "Maternalism," the nineteenth-century ideology of women's special fitness for mothering, nurturance, and rearing children, allowed many middle-class women to exercise class- and gender-based authority in ways that avoided disrupting the gender status quo while justifying their presence in the public arena as civic housekeepers. Ironically, middle-class women used notions of women's special morality to increase their own freedom of movement outside of the home while advocating strict domesticity for poor women.

New career fields for females and the expansion of state-supported social programs allowed women to advocate for the perceived needs of others while engaging in struggles for professional recognition. Claims to expertise legitimized by scientific ideologies and based on similarity, not difference, to men coexisted with earlier notions of women's special moral authority. Many of the college-educated single women who ventured into Appalachia from the Northeast and the Bluegrass, the closest region with an educated female elite, came as teachers, missionaries, health workers, and cultural workers in search of professional fulfillment. Although embracing middle-class motherhood and marriage as the prescription for transforming mountain life, they modeled a very different set of gender positions in their own careers, sometimes providing a counterpoint to local middle-class clubwomen engaged in similar reform efforts.

See also: FEMINISM; SUFFRAGE; WOMEN AND EMPLOYMENT (LABOR).

—Karen W. Tice, *University of Kentucky*

Sandra Lee Barney, *Authorized to Heal: Gender, Class, and the Transformation of Medicine in Appalachia, 1880–1930* (2000); Jane S. Becker, *Selling Tradition: Appalachia and the Construction of an American Folk, 1930–1940* (1998); Molly Ladd-Taylor, *Mother-Work: Women, Child Welfare, and the State, 1890–1930* (1994).

G.I. Bill

On June 22, 1944, President Franklin D. Roosevelt signed into law the Servicemen's Readjustment Act of 1944. Even before passage, the term *G.I. Bill of Rights* had replaced the formal title, and afterward popular usage shortened it to simply the *G.I. Bill.* The purpose of the G.I. Bill was to help veterans readjust to civilian life and to avoid the unemployment and other problems the nation had experienced following demobilization after World War I. Of the G.I. Bill's six titles, the first and sixth covered administration. Title Three concerned home, business, and farm mortgages. Employment came under Title Four; unemployment came under Title Five. Title Two dealt with education and training at all levels and of all types. More veterans in Appalachia used their G.I. Bill to finish high school and gain job skills than to attend college. Of West Virginia veterans, for example, 14.8 percent studied below the college level, 10.6 percent took on-the-job training, and 9.5 percent went to colleges.

From 1944 through 1956, the G.I. Bill cost approximately $18.9 billion, of which $14.5 billion went to education and training. Seventy-four percent of almost 16 million World War II veterans utilized one or more titles. Veterans who studied or trained earned higher salaries and paid more taxes than veterans who did not, and these higher tax revenues repaid the cost of the G.I. Bill. Of the G.I. Bill veterans, 22.7 percent attended schools below the college level; 14.3 percent studied at institutions of higher learning; 9.1 percent underwent on-the-job training; and 4.5 percent pursued on-the-farm training.

—Keith W. Olson, *University of Maryland*

Gore, Albert, Jr.

(1948–) U.S. vice-president and senator.

Vice-president of the United States from 1993 to 2001, Albert Arnold Gore Jr. was the Democratic Party nominee for president in 2000, losing to George W. Bush by a 271-266 vote of the Electoral College, even though he won the national popular vote by about 544,000.

Gore was born in Washington, D.C., while his father, later a three-term senator from Tennessee, was serving as a member of the U.S. House of Representatives. He grew up in the nation's capital and on a farm near Carthage, Tennessee, which was also the home of Cordell Hull, the U.S. secretary of state during World War II. After graduation from Harvard in 1969 and army service as a reporter for *Stars and Stripes* in Vietnam, Gore joined the *Nashville Tennessean*, where he was an investigative reporter and editorial writer for five years. In 1976 he was elected to the U.S. House of Representatives from Tennessee's Fourth Congressional District, then including several counties of the Appalachian region. In both the House and the U.S. Senate, where he served from 1985 to 1993, Gore was an aggressive spokesman for environmental concerns such as the global climate change and technological innovations such as the Internet. His 1992 book, *Earth in the Balance: Ecology and the Human Spirit*, became a national best-seller.

Although Gore rose to prominence through his involvement with national issues, he was involved in state and regional politics from childhood. His father was a country fiddler who used his skills to attract crowds to his early political rallies. The elder Gore, coauthor of the National Highway Act of 1956, was a leader in the creation of the Interstate Highway System. He became a stalwart among southern moderates in the Senate and was an early opponent of the war in Vietnam.

Al Gore Jr. began his political career holding the same House seat his father had occupied for fourteen years before entering the Senate, launching his first campaign from the steps of the Smith County Courthouse, where he returned to begin his races for the Senate and the vice-presidency.

Gore's quest for the White House in 2000 ended in Florida, where the final tally showed him losing the state by a mere 537 votes of nearly 6 million cast, giving Bush the state's 25 electoral votes. The U.S. Supreme Court sealed the outcome by refusing the Democrats' appeal for a selective manual recount of disputed ballots. Opting not to seek his party's nomination in 2004, Gore returned to Tennessee. He lectured on university campuses and undertook private business ventures.

—Rudy Abramson, *Reston, Virginia*

Great Smoky Mountains National Park

The establishment of the Great Smoky Mountains National Park marked one of the earliest major endeavors of the federal government in the southern Appalachian region. By most measures, the park has proved to be a huge positive asset for the region. It attracts more annual visits than any other national park and generates more than $600 million in consumer spending in the surrounding area. Inevitably, it has also generated significant controversy over the years.

Although individuals and groups had been promoting the establishment of national parks in the southern Appalachian region since the late 1890s, more than two decades passed before interests of the National Park Service, regional boosters, and politicians converged sufficiently to make a major park a real possibility. The National Park Service wished to establish parks closer to the concentration of population in the East and gain the support of southern politicians; regional boosters and politicians saw a park as a source of urgently needed revenue, a stimulus for better roads in the area, and an opening for additional federal projects and federal money for their constituents. Indeed, by 1923 communities and cities all across the region had begun petitioning the government, demanding consideration for their favored sites. In 1924 the National Park Service responded by appointing the Southern Appalachian National Park Committee to investigate potential sites.

Acting on the committee's recommendations, Congress passed a bill on May 22, 1926, calling for the establishment of national parks in the Great Smoky Mountains and the Blue Ridge Mountains of Virginia (Shenandoah National Park). The measure required that the respective states purchase the necessary land, however, and turn it over to the government to be managed by the National Park Service. Despite the enthusiasm of local residents, this proved a daunting task in a particularly impoverished region of the country. The states were able to raise the necessary funds ($10 million for the Smokies) primarily through the largesse of John D. Rockefeller Jr., who donated $5 million for the Smokies and $1 million for Shenandoah in 1928.

In convincing the nature-loving Rockefeller to make this historic donation, park boosters touted the rich biological diversity of the Smokies rather than the usual economic arguments. Indeed, it was the presence of the largest stands of remaining old-growth forests east of the Rockies, the 125 species of native trees, the 125 species of shrubs, the 1,500 vascular plants, the 60 ferns and fern allies, the 280 mosses and 250 species of lichens, the 200 species of birds, 40 reptiles, 40 amphibians, 80 species of fish, 50 mammals, and uncounted species of insects and other arthropods—not the millions of tourists that a park would attract—that swayed Rockefeller.

Celebrations by park boosters were premature, for special park commissions in both Tennessee and North Carolina still had to complete the purchase of the needed land, often from unwilling owners. Five major timber companies owned the bulk of the land designated by the National Park Service as suitable for inclusion in a national park in the Smokies. In order to acquire this land, the state park commissions were forced to spend hundreds of thousands of dollars in condemnation proceedings that often dragged on for years.

The most controversial aspect of land acquisition in the Smokies involved the purchase of an estimated twelve hundred farms and the removal of more than four thousand residents scattered throughout the mountains and hollows. For many mountain residents, their first close contact with a federal agency came in the form of an eviction notice. The dismantling or burning of most of the buildings in the park, with the exception of a few cabins and churches, further antagonized many residents of the Smokies. As Durwood Dunn observed in his book on the Smokies community of Cades Cove: "It was as though, having destroyed the community of Cades Cove by eminent domain, the community's corpse was to be mutilated beyond recognition."

The election of Franklin D. Roosevelt and the coming of the New Deal in the 1930s marked a major change in federal policy toward the Great Smoky Mountains National Park and national parks in the East. By the early 1930s, due to the expense of litigation and the inability to collect on pledges, the Tennessee and North Carolina park commissions had exhausted their funds. Using his executive powers, Roosevelt, along with Interior Secretary Harold L. Ickes, circumvented the 1926 park bill that prevented the federal government from purchasing land for the park, arguing that the $1,550,000 designated for the purchase of land was actually intended to enhance and enlarge employment opportunities in the Civilian Conservation Corps. Between 1933 and 1942 the corps established twenty-three camps, employing thousands of young men. Enrollees provided fire protection and built hiking trails, picnic areas, campgrounds, and roads.

The New Deal years also saw the beginning of development in the park and a major departure from previous policy. The early days of the National Park Service had seen a great emphasis on providing tourist facilities such as extensive road systems and grand lodges. Park boosters proposed many such "improvements" for the Smokies, including a skyline drive and a dam on Abrams Creek to create a lake in Cades Cove. Under Ickes's leadership and the effective lobbying of the newly formed Wilderness Society, such intrusive development was averted within the park. "I do not happen to favor the scarring of a wonderful mountainside just so we can say we have a skyline drive," Ickes said when he vetoed the proposed highway. "It sounds poetical, but it may be an atrocity."

On September 2, 1940, more than fourteen years after the passage of the original park act, President Roosevelt dedicated the Great Smoky Mountains National Park. Since then, the majority of residents of western North Carolina and east Tennessee have viewed the federal presence in the Great Smoky Mountains as beneficial. But for a significant minority of area residents, the park has been more curse than blessing. This has been especially true of mountain counties (particularly Swain and Haywood in North Carolina and Cocke in Tennessee) that lost significant amounts of land from their tax base and have been bypassed by much of the tourist traffic.

Despite the heavy-handedness of some government actions—particularly in the removal of families and communities—and challenges of budget shortfalls, invasive species, and air pollution in recent years, the park has largely fulfilled the dreams of its creators, harboring extraordinary biodiversity while attracting millions of visitors and generating hundreds of millions of dollars in tourist revenue for the surrounding region.

See also: ECOTOURISM (TOURISM); GREAT SMOKY MOUNTAINS NATIONAL PARK (TOURISM).

—Daniel S. Pierce, *University of North Carolina at Asheville*

Margaret L. Brown, *The Wild East: A Biography of the Great Smoky Mountains* (2000); Durwood Dunn, *Cades Cove: The Life and Death of a Southern Appalachian Community, 1818–1937* (1988); Daniel S. Pierce, *The Great Smokies: From Natural Habitat to National Park* (2000).

Greenback Party

The Greenback Party was an active political body between 1874 and 1884. Most party members were farmers in the South and the West who were experiencing severe financial distress. Their primary platform was the promotion of currency expansion.

The party held its first national convention in 1876 and enjoyed its greatest success during the 1878 congressional elections, when it elected fourteen representatives to the House of Representatives. This latter success was due in part to an alliance with labor organizations. Although the party broadened its platform to include tax reform and woman suffrage, its popularity declined, and the organization disappeared soon after the 1884 election.

In Appalachia, the Greenback Party was primarily a vehicle for white farmers to protest the conservative economic policies and elite leadership of the dominant Democratic Party. The new party won substantial support in western North Carolina in 1878 when the Republicans failed to nominate candidates for many offices and their supporters voted for the Greenback Party instead. In West Virginia, the Greenbackers worked closely with Republicans and even received funding from the Republican National Committee in 1880. They won 10 percent or more of the vote in many counties that year and helped to elect a Republican congressman two years later.

The Greenback Party had its greatest impact in northern Alabama, where William M. Lowe of Madison County won election to Congress as the Greenback candidate in 1878 and 1880. His support came from both Republicans and Democrats in one of the few successful biracial coalitions in the South after Reconstruction. Democratic state legislators amended Alabama's elections laws and used fraudulent practices to end this threat to their hegemony. Many embittered Greenbackers joined the Populist Party in the 1890s.

See also: DEMOCRATIC PARTY; REPUBLICAN PARTY.

—Kim O'Connor, *University of Chicago*

Head Start Program

The national Head Start program, an enduring initiative of the 1960s War on Poverty, operates in all areas of Appalachia, providing developmental services to preschool children, pregnant women, and social services for their low-income families. These programs are funded through grants from the federal government, which are awarded to local public or private nonprofit agencies. They are designed to meet the early educational, social, and health needs of children in specific communities based on each community's ethnic and cultural characteristics. The agency was begun in 1965 in the U.S. Office of Economic Opportunity and is now administered by the Administration for Children and Families.

The American Indian Head Start program, initiated for the Eastern Band of Cherokee Indians in Cherokee, North Carolina, and the Seneca Nation of Indians in Irving, New York, offers a wide range of services to families living on these Appalachian reservations. Twenty-three other states also participate in this program, which encourages the integration of language and culture into the curriculum.

Communities in Alabama, North Carolina, Pennsylvania, South Carolina, and Tennessee have received federal grants to serve migrant families living in Appalachia while performing seasonal farm labor. The Migrant Head Start program specifically meets the needs of migrant farmworker families. This program provides care for infants and toddlers as well as preschool-age children while parents are working in the fields.

See also: SCHOOL EQUITY FUNDING; WAR ON POVERTY.

—Clara Hasbrouck, *East Tennessee State University*

Heroes of America

One of the most militant expressions of Unionism in Civil War Appalachia, the Heroes of America actually emerged in the central Piedmont of North Carolina soon after the beginning of the conflict. A secret society with trappings derived from Freemasonry, the order's goal was to undermine the Confederate war effort and bring about a Union victory. Members, sometimes called "Red Strings" for their badge of identification, passed information to Union authorities, conducted sabotage, promoted desertion within the Confederate army, and helped escapees from Confederate prisons reach Union lines. Headquartered in Raleigh, the organization attracted perhaps ten thousand members in the central part of the state. Heroes of America spread into the mountains of western North Carolina and western Virginia late in 1862. By 1864 reports of its activities had alarmed Confederate authorities enough that they attempted to investigate and stamp out the order. Those attempts proved generally unsuccessful.

While the organization was a factor in the mountains, Confederate officials probably overestimated its size and importance there. Most Appalachian Unionists shied away from organized resistance, acting instead through family or neighborhood groups. Heroes of America did provide a foundation for the postwar Republican Party in many sections of the southern mountains, however. A similar but larger group, the Peace Society, operated simultaneously in northern Alabama, northern Georgia, and east Tennessee.

See also: CIVIL WAR.

—Kenneth W. Noe, *Auburn University*

Jackson, John George

(1777–1825) U.S. congressman, judge, and land developer.

The life of John George Jackson, an early-nineteenth-century politician and developer, indicates the importance of the connection between politics and economic development in early Appalachian history. Jackson was born September 22, 1777, in Buckhannon, (West) Virginia, to Elizabeth von Brake and George Jackson, a leading landowner in Harrison County who served three terms in the U.S. House of Representatives during the 1790s. John George added to his father's landholdings, became an attorney, purchased slaves, manufactured iron, processed salt, invested in private and chartered banks, and became a leading figure in the Monongahela Navigation Company, which planned to open northwestern Virginia to river commerce.

Jackson improved his economic and political position through marriages to women related to important national figures. His marriage to Mary Coles Payne, the sister of Dolley Madison, made him a correspondent and guest of President James Madison. When Mary died, he married Mary Sophia Meigs, the daughter of Return J. Meigs, who served as postmaster general in the Madison and Monroe administrations.

Wealth, position, and connections all aided Jackson's political career. He served in the Virginia House of Delegates between 1798 and 1801 and again in 1811–12. While in Richmond he broke with his eastern Virginia associates when he backed western demands for extended suffrage and constitutional reforms, internal improvements, and higher legislative salaries. Jackson served six terms in the U.S. House of Representatives, from 1803 to 1810 and 1813 to 1817, supporting the Jefferson and Madison administrations against the Federalists and Republican dissidents. Always interested in economic development, he backed national internal improvements, high tariffs, and the second Bank of the United States. He ended his career as the first U.S. district judge for western Virginia. Jackson died March 28, 1825, one of the wealthiest and most important men in Appalachian Virginia.

—Van Beck Hall, *University of Pittsburgh*

John Brown's Raid

John Brown (1800–1859), a radical white abolitionist, led his historic 1859 raid on Harpers Ferry, Virginia, hoping to exploit the supposed sympathy of Appalachian whites and to provoke a black uprising against slavery. The operation failed and resulted in Brown's execution, but it helped set the stage for the Civil War.

Located at the strategic confluence of the Shenandoah and Potomac Rivers, Harpers Ferry was the site of a major federal arsenal and armory, from which Brown planned to seize stores of weapons. In choosing to attack Harpers Ferry, Brown surely had in mind a strategy to arm potential supporters in a war against slavery. Historians have tended to speculate that he expected to secure support among white non-slaveholders as well as slaves and free blacks in the area. He may have also viewed the topography of the mountains to the south and west as a potential haven from which to launch attacks on slavery in the plantation regions of the South.

Brown and his small biracial band of abolitionists crossed the Potomac from Maryland into Virginia and entered the town on the night of October 16, 1859. They were trapped there, and Brown was captured and later hanged. His trial and execution led to his virtual sanctification in much of mainstream public opinion in the North. Abraham Lincoln's election to the presidency the next year was widely seen in the South as confirmation that many in the North agreed with Brown's objectives, if not his methods.

At the beginning of the twenty-first century, Harpers Ferry (now in West Virginia) is a tourist attraction, preserving artifacts of its rich industrial past as well as relics and reminders of John Brown's raid.

See also: HARPERS FERRY, WEST VIRGINIA (TOURISM); SLAVERY AND ABOLITION.

—Peter Wallenstein, *Virginia Polytechnic Institute and State University*

Johnson, Andrew

(1808–1875) U.S. president.

Andrew Johnson was the only Appalachian political figure to become president of the United States, taking office following the assassination of Abraham Lincoln in 1865. He is best known for his impeachment by the House of Representatives and his narrow acquittal after a trial by the Senate.

Johnson was the leading Democrat in antebellum east Tennessee and was elected to local, state, and national offices. He spent his formative years in Raleigh, North Carolina, where he was born. The death of his father, when he was only three years old, compounded the already severe economic circumstances his family faced. Johnson's mother apprenticed him to a tailor in Raleigh when he was ten. There he learned a trade that he would follow for much of his life.

The difficulties of Johnson's early life compelled the adventuresome teenager to seek a better situation elsewhere. In the fall of 1826, he arrived in Greeneville, Tennessee, and made the town his permanent home. Part of the attraction there was sixteen-year-old Eliza McCardle, whom he married in May 1827. Eventually they became the parents of two daughters and three sons.

The world of the young Johnson was a small Appalachian town where he was in daily contact with merchants, farmers, fellow artisans, and occasionally with physicians and lawyers. He was not associated or familiar with wealthy

President Andrew Johnson, c. 1860s. The only Appalachian to serve as president of the United States, Johnson was catapulted into the presidency after Abraham Lincoln's assassination. He served a tumultuous term and was eventually impeached and narrowly acquitted by the U.S. Congress.

planters or with plantation slavery. Indeed, he displayed an early antipathy toward persons of wealth or influence, and he adhered to this attitude in political life. The irony of this hostility, perhaps lost on Johnson, was that he himself subsequently acquired domestic slaves, prospered at his tailor's business, and became something of an entrepreneur as he invested in property and banks.

Still, he perceived himself a champion of the common man and parlayed this stance into a highly successful political career, winning election as mayor, alderman, and state legislator. In 1843 and continuing for ten years thereafter, Johnson served in the U.S. House of Representatives. During that tenure he first promoted the Homestead Bill, which provided that any man or woman twenty-one years of age or head of a family could have 160 acres of land by living on it for five years, a cause he would return to in his U.S. Senate days in the late 1850s. Between his House and Senate terms, he served an uneventful four years as Tennessee's governor.

In the Senate, Johnson not only championed the Homestead Bill but, more importantly, argued against Southern secession. He ardently believed that wealthy planters were promoting secession against the interests of the common man. In 1861 Johnson returned to Tennessee to campaign against the secession referendum that year. Although he rallied support in east Tennessee, the state voted to leave the Union. Shortly thereafter, under fear for his personal safety, he left Tennessee.

Because of the acclaim Johnson received for his pro-Union stance, President Lincoln selected him to become the military governor of Tennessee in early 1862, a post he held for three difficult years. During that time he exhibited particular hostility to Confederates who were prosperous and influential and became an advocate for the emancipation of slaves.

In an unusual strategy, Lincoln placed Johnson on the ticket as his vice-presidential running mate in the 1864 election. Johnson returned to Washington for the March 1865 inauguration. Just six weeks later, Lincoln's assassination thrust Johnson into the presidency, where he was confronted with the momentous challenge of reuniting the country.

Johnson's four years in that office were filled with controversy. One conflict revolved around his largely unsuccessful restoration of ex-Rebel citizens and states as provided by his Amnesty Proclamation, which exempted certain powerful and affluent ex-Confederates from its otherwise almost blanket pardon. In addition, the president established provisional governors in seven of the former Confederate states.

Rejection of Republican-backed civil rights legislation earned Johnson the special enmity of the congressional leadership, to say nothing of blacks. His objections were rooted in two things: his racist views and his notion that preferential treatment should not be given by the federal government to anyone, black or white. In 1868 the House voted to impeach Johnson, and the Senate convened to hear the case against him. The Senate acquitted Johnson of the impeachment charges but on one of the eleven articles came within one vote of the two-thirds majority necessary for conviction. His leadership was even more ineffective thereafter.

Johnson returned to Tennessee in March 1869 and devoted the next six years to political vindication. He almost succeeded in the fall of that year but lost a narrow vote for election to the U.S. Senate. His quest to return to political office was rejected a second time in 1872, when he lost a bid for election as congressman-at-large, but on a third try, he was elected to the Senate again in 1875. This victory returned him to the chamber where he had undergone his greatest travail and embarrassment.

A few months later, on July 31, 1875, while visiting his daughter in Carter County, he suffered a stroke and died. Wrapped in an American flag with his hand clasping a copy of the U.S. Constitution, Johnson was buried in Greeneville, Tennessee.

See also: CIVIL WAR; RECONSTRUCTION; REPUBLICAN PARTY.

—Paul H. Bergeron, *University of Tennessee*

Albert E. Castel, *The Presidency of Andrew Johnson* (1979); LeRoy P. Graf, Ralph W. Haskins, and Paul H. Bergeron, eds., *The Papers of Andrew Johnson* (1967–); Hans L. Trefousse, *Andrew Johnson: A Biography* (1989).

Johnson, Frank M., Jr.

(1918–1999) Federal judge.

The author of legal opinions that profoundly influenced the civil rights struggle in the South, Judge Frank Minis Johnson Jr. was once described by a legal scholar as "the John Marshall of the federal District courts." U.S. Supreme Court Associate Justice William J. Brennan wrote after retirement, "I cannot imagine the state of our civil liberties without him."

Johnson was born October 30, 1918, in Haleyville, Alabama, a tiny community in the Appalachian foothills of Winston County. His father was a postmaster, probate judge, and legislator and his mother, Alabama Sivilla Long Johnson, a teacher. Frank Jr. was the eldest of seven children. In a traditionally Democratic state, Winston County was strongly pro-Union in the Civil War and remained a bastion of "mountain Republicans" into the twenty-first century. Johnson, a self-styled hillbilly and lover of bluegrass music, fishing, and strong tobacco, attributed to Winston County "a very, very decisive effect" on his formation: "People in that part of the country have a fiercely independent attitude and personality. . . . They came to the hills without anything. They had only what they were willing to work for. I expect that plus a strong sense of fair play and respect for the individual . . . served me in great stead as a lawyer and as a judge."

After attending public schools and spending one year at Gulf Coast Military Academy in Gulfport, Mississippi, and another at Massey Business College in Birmingham, nineteen-year-old Johnson married Ruth Jenkins and decided to become a lawyer. He attended the University of Alabama and received a law degree in 1943. Having joined the U.S. Army, he served in France as an infantry officer, was wounded twice, and received the Bronze Star. In July 1946, he began practice in Jasper. He led Alabama Veterans for Eisenhower in 1952 and in 1953 was named United States attorney for the Northern District of Alabama (Birmingham). Outstanding performance as prosecutor plus excellent Washington connections brought him appointment as judge for the Central District (Montgomery) in October 1955. At thirty-seven, he was the youngest federal judge in the country. President Nixon was reported to have favored him to succeed Hugo Black on the Supreme Court, but Alabama's Republican congressmen objected. In 1977 Johnson was President Jimmy Carter's choice to head the Federal Bureau of Investigation, but surgery and a long recovery forced Johnson to withdraw himself from consideration. In April 1979, however, Carter nominated him to the U.S. Fifth Circuit Court of Appeals, and he was commissioned on June 21, 1979. Shortly thereafter, the circuit was split, with Johnson joining the new Eleventh Circuit (Alabama, Georgia, Florida). He assumed senior status, effectively retiring on October 30, 1991, and died in Montgomery on July 23, 1999.

Johnson readily ascribed his prominence to chance. In less than a month after his appointment as district judge, Rosa Parks refused to give her seat to a white woman on a Montgomery bus, igniting the famed bus boycott led by Martin Luther King Jr. During the struggle over segregated buses, Montgomery and Alabama became centers of the civil rights struggle in the South, with the eye of the legal storm often in Judge Johnson's hushed courtroom. (He was a stickler for courtroom decorum. As an observer put it, you could feel the rangy, rawboned, hawk-nosed, mountain man judge "looking at you like he's aiming down a rifle barrel.") As district judge, he issued a long list of verdicts, orders, and injunctions that determined the direction and tone of the civil rights revolution of the 1950s through the 1980s.

Johnson's decisions put the law on the side of the protesters in the bus boycott in 1955–56, integrated southern bus terminals in 1961, and cleared the way for the massive Selma-to-Montgomery march in 1965. He ordered desegregation of public accommodations and spaces, upheld the voting rights of black Americans, and mandated legislative redistricting. With Judge Richard Rives, he produced the nation's first court-designed legislative reapportionment plan when Alabama's legislature refused to redraw boundaries so as to enfranchise blacks. Other landmark decisions broadened constitutional protections for prisoners, aliens, and the mentally ill; directed hiring of blacks by the state government, notably the Alabama State Police; ended exclusion of women and blacks from Alabama juries; confirmed the rights of female soldiers' spouses; and provided for public payment for lawyers representing indigent defendants. Among Johnson's opinions overturned on appeal was a ruling voiding the death penalty. Outside his normal duties, Johnson conducted lengthy investigations concerning the appeal of serial killer Ted Bundy and the bribery case leading to the impeachment of Federal Judge Alcee Hastings. Such was his authority that President Johnson once quipped, "You know, I wouldn't have to be President if my name was Frank Johnson instead of Lyndon Johnson."

Johnson considered his decisions rendered in *Browder v. Gayle* (1956) and *United States v. Alabama* (1961) to be the most important of his career. In *Browder*, he and Judge Rives, the majority of a three-judge panel, held that the school desegregation ordered by the Supreme Court in *Brown v. Board of Education* (1954) overturned the 1896 high court ruling *(Plessy v. Ferguson)* that sanctioned "separate but equal" schools. Originating in the Montgomery bus boycott, *Browder* led to desegregation of public spaces, thus putting the axe to the root of the Jim Crow system. In *United States v. Alabama*, Johnson ordered registration of black voters—they had been systematically excluded—using the same standard applied to the least qualified whites. Congress later used this "freezing principle" in the Voting Rights Act of 1965.

While Johnson admired Martin Luther King's courage, he took "a dim view" of the civil rights leader's use of street protests. He also thought that well-intentioned northerners who traveled to the South to stage protests used "poor judgment." Though he upheld the right to demonstrate, Johnson believed that civil rights issues appropriately belonged in the courts. A civil rights lawyer described him as "a reserved Southerner suspicious of litigation with an explicit policy orientation." The judge himself denied he took positions in order to effect social change. "I approach the things strictly from a legal standpoint," he said, "and I have no interest in the social change as a judge."

Johnson's decisions, especially in the desegregation of public schools, subjected him to continual threats and vituperation, notably by segregationist Governor George Wallace, a law school classmate. The home of the jurist's mother was bombed in the mistaken belief that he lived there, and for nearly fifteen years he had to be protected day and night by federal marshals. Yet even his foes admired his unflinching courage and admitted he gave all who came before him a Winston County–inspired "fair day in court." Fellow federal judges praised his creativity in finding ways to make the law work in difficult circumstances, and in 1984 they conferred on him their highest honor, the Edward J. Devitt Distinguished Service for Justice Award. He also received the nation's highest civilian award, the Presidential Medal of Freedom, and the State of Alabama, the target of many of his historic rulings, inducted him into its Hall of Fame. "I have never thought of myself as a trailblazer or one who sets landmarks," Johnson observed in retirement. "I merely follow the law. I applied the facts to the law and made a decision."

See also: CIVIL RIGHTS MOVEMENT (RACE, ETHNICITY, AND IDENTITY); KENTUCKY DAY LAW AND THE BEREA COLLEGE CASE; RACISM (RACE, ETHNICITY, AND IDENTITY).

—David S. Newhall, *Centre College*

Jack Bass, *Taming the Storm: The Life and Times of Judge Frank M. Johnson, Jr., and the South's Fight over Civil Rights* (1993); Frank Sikora, *The Judge: The Life and Opinions of Alabama's Frank M. Johnson, Jr.* (1992).

Kefauver, Estes

(1903–1963) U.S. senator and congressman.

Carey Estes Kefauver was a lawyer and Democratic politician with a passion for consumer rights and antitrust law. Born July 26, 1903, to Phredonia Estes and Robert Cooke Kefauver in a small farming community in Madisonville, Tennessee, Kefauver went on to serve as a U.S. representative, win a senatorial election that significantly altered the political scene in Tennessee, and make two unsuccessful bids for his party's presidential nomination.

After attending the University of Tennessee in Knoxville as an undergraduate, Kefauver went to law school at Yale, where he graduated with honors in 1927. Afterward, he worked at Cooke, Swaney, and Cooke, a Chattanooga law firm. There, he dealt with a number of clients who had been mistreated by their employers, and the experience caused him to develop an interest in corporate law. A scholarly paper he published in the *Tennessee Law Review* led to his hiring by the firm of Sizer, Chambliss, and Sizer in 1927. Three years later, he became a junior partner. Kefauver married Nancy Patterson Pigott, a native of Scotland, in 1935.

Kefauver's involvement with government increased significantly in the ensuing years. He became deeply interested in the Tennessee Valley Authority, a New Deal program designed to develop hydroelectric power and navigation on the Tennessee River. In 1938 he ran for the state senate but was defeated.

A year later, he successfully ran for the U.S. House of Representatives on a platform supporting the Tennessee Valley Authority, federal aid to education, congressional reform, and other New Deal programs. He remained in the House until 1949, when he embarked on a campaign for the U.S. Senate. He won the 1948 election, causing a significant shift in Tennessee politics, long dominated by Edward H. "Boss" Crump's Memphis machine. After Crump compared him to a nocturnal raccoon working with subversive liberal elements, Kefauver responded by putting on a coonskin cap during a speech in Memphis and saying, "I may be a pet coon, but I'm not Boss Crump's pet coon." The coonskin cap became Kefauver's trademark during this campaign.

Kefauver gained national recognition as chairman of the U.S. Senate Crime Investigating Committee in 1950 and 1951, presiding over televised organized crime hearings that attracted a huge audience. Encouraged by his new popularity, he sought the Democratic nomination for president in 1952 and defeated President Harry Truman in the New Hampshire primary. Despite this early success, however, Kefauver lost the Democratic presidential nomination to Illinois Governor Adlai Stevenson. He sought the nomination again in 1956 and again lost to Stevenson but became Stevenson's vice-presidential running mate in a losing campaign against President Dwight D. Eisenhower and Vice-President Richard Nixon.

Kefauver remained in the Senate until the end of his life. In the late 1950s, he chaired the Antitrust and Monopoly Subcommitte, and in his final years he fought for fair drug pricing practices. Incensed by pharmaceutical companies' huge markups, he led a political battle that resulted in the Kefauver-Harris Drug Control Act (1962). Kefauver supported America's role in the United Nations, the North Atlantic Treaty Organization, and the Atlantic Union, which was a proposed federal union of the western democracies. He also cosponsored the Twenty-fourth Amendment, which abolished the poll tax for federal elections. Kefauver was on the Senate floor arguing an antimonopoly position when he suffered a heart attack on August 10, 1963; the senator died two days later and was buried at his family's farm in Madisonville.

See also: DEMOCRATIC PARTY; TENNESSEE VALLEY AUTHORITY.

—Kim O'Connor, *University of Chicago*

Charles L. Fontenay, *Estes Kefauver: A Biography* (1980); Joseph Bruce Gorman, *Kefauver: A Political Biography* (1971); Harvey Swados, *Standing Up for the People: The Life and Work of Estes Kefauver* (1972).

Kentucky Day Law and the Berea College Case

Named for its author, Representative Carl Day of Breathitt County, the Kentucky Day Law segregated public and private schools throughout the state. Day's bill was aimed at Berea College, which had promoted interracial education as one of its principal objectives since its founding. The measure made it unlawful for any school to engage in the coeducation of black and white students. Passed overwhelmingly by the Kentucky legislature, it took effect in July 1904. On

October 8, 1904, a Madison County grand jury indicted the college for violating the Day Law, beginning a series of court cases that lasted until 1908.

The college argued that the law violated the school's constitutional right to due process by abridging the law of contract and the freedom to engage in a lawful calling. But the Kentucky Court of Appeals found the law to be a reasonable protection of the public welfare, claiming that "the purity of racial blood" was "deeper and more important than the matter of choice." The U.S. Supreme Court also upheld the law, asserting that the state, in incorporating Berea College, reserved the right to "alter or repeal" the school's charter. The Court further ruled that the law did not "destroy the power of the college to furnish education to all persons" but simply required that the races either be educated at separate times or in different locations at least twenty-five miles apart.

Berea College reintegrated in 1950, admitting "qualified Negro students" from within the southern Appalachian region, and the Day Law was invalidated in June 1954 by the U.S. Supreme Court.

See also: BEREA COLLEGE (EDUCATION); EUGENICS PROGRAMS (FAMILY AND COMMUNITY); RACISM (RACE, ETHNICITY, AND IDENTITY).

—Shannon H. Wilson, *Berea College*

Knoxville Race Riot of 1919

See Race Riots

Ku Klux Klan

A terrorist organization with mutations that have survived into the twenty-first century, the Ku Klux Klan targeted African Americans in Appalachia during Reconstruction and Roman Catholics during the organization's revival in the 1920s.

The Klan was formed in Pulaski, Tennessee, in 1866 and first led by former Confederate General Nathan Bedford Forrest. It began as a social club for young men but was quickly transformed into a collection of night-riding terrorists associated with the postwar Democratic Party. The vast majority of Klan members were located in Piedmont counties—the less flamboyant Knights of the White Camelia were dominant in the Deep South—but there were some active klaverns in the mountain counties as well. These groups attacked Republican leaders, prevented African Americans from voting, and destroyed the offices of Republican newspapers. The most active Appalachian Klan group was in Rutherford County, North Carolina, where newspaperman Randolph Shotwell directed the activities of several hundred followers. The passage of federal Ku Klux Klan Acts of 1870 and 1871 led to the formal dissolution of the group in Appalachia, but many former Klansmen continued to participate in terrorist activities without the imprimatur of a formal organization.

While the Klan had disbanded by 1872, a resurgence of racism in the United States brought the organization back to life. The person most responsible for this revival of interest was North Carolina novelist Thomas Dixon, who published a savage attack on African Americans in a 1905 book entitled *The Clansman.* In 1915 D. W. Griffith made the book into an enormously successful and influential movie, *The Birth of a Nation.*

Apparently inspired by the movie, William J. Simmons, an Alabama physician, revived the Klan in November 1915 at Stone Mountain, Georgia. Simmons, who served as imperial wizard until 1922, and his associates were primarily interested in selling memberships and insurance rather than influencing politics. While it continued to target African Americans, the rejuvenated Klan sought to intimidate and limit the influence of immigrants in the United States—particularly Roman Catholics and Jews. By 1924 there were an estimated 2 to 4 million Klan members throughout the country, and the organization had become politically powerful in some areas. Although there were relatively few immigrants in Appalachia, the second Klan grew rapidly in the region after 1920. The largest concentrations were found in the urban areas, with estimates of 14,000 members in the Birmingham, Alabama, area; 3,000 in Knoxville and 2,500 in Chattanooga, Tennessee; and 2,000 in Charleston, West Virginia. An examination of membership rolls in Knoxville indicates that most members were blue-collar employees of large industrial companies and had left school after the seventh grade. Charges of financial corruption at the national and state levels were proven in 1925, and membership quickly declined.

The Klan has never entirely disappeared in Appalachia. Small groups of Klan members make periodic appearances—particularly when local controversies offer an opportunity for widespread publicity. Strong federal law enforcement efforts and internal divisions have limited Klan groups to the fringes of Appalachian society.

See also: LYNCHING; RACE RIOTS; RACISM (RACE, ETHNICITY, AND IDENTITY).

—Bill Archer, *Bluefield Daily Telegraph*

Lynching

Like much of the rural United States in the nineteenth and early twentieth centuries, Appalachia experienced collective violence, lethal and nonlethal, that complemented and sometimes replaced legal agencies. The region's intense localism sometimes precipitated lynchings, as communities retaliated against gangs of outlaws and against those who informed on moonshiners. Appalachians used a range of informal means, including mob killings, to punish those who transgressed communal values associated with gender and sexual roles as well as to punish serious crimes such as murder. The racial phobias of Appalachian whites also provoked lynchings of blacks in mountain districts, particularly in growing urban centers. Yet lynching in Appalachia never became the harrowing and systematic means for implementing racial control that it was in the Deep South.

In the nineteenth century, violence committed by organized mountain groups such as outlaw gangs sometimes spiraled into lynchings. In Breathitt County, Kentucky, for example, lynchers in 1877 killed an alleged member of the Strong gang as well as an African American man allegedly allied with the gang. Perhaps even more skeptical of centralized governmental authority than most rural Americans, Appalachians responded to the incursion of federal revenue agents in the 1890s with a form of organized collective violence known as whitecapping, the removal of blacks from an area for economic reasons. In north Georgia, moonshiners lynched several people accused of informing federal agents of the location of illegal stills.

Economic and social changes associated with the industrialization and urbanization of Appalachia in the late nineteenth and early twentieth centuries produced a spate of racially motivated lynchings. Half of the thirty-eight lynchings of African Americans that occurred in Georgia's upper Piedmont involved allegations of rape. On the outskirts of Atlanta and Rome, whites resorted to collective violence to assert racial supremacy, reflecting the tensions of urbanization as the races mixed in unfamiliar ways in public spaces. In southwest Virginia, twenty-eight lynchings occurred, with twenty-four black victims. This violence was concentrated in the 1890s in growing towns in Virginia—such as Wytheville, Bluefield, Richlands, Clifton Forge, and Roanoke—that served as market centers for the surrounding countryside. For example, a mob of eighty whites lynched five black railroad workers accused of robbing and beating two white storeowners in Richlands in February 1893. Whites then ordered African Americans out of Tazewell and Buchanan Counties. Sites of rural industrialization—where whites and blacks, many of them recent migrants, worked in coal mines and lumber mills—were less frequently locales for collective violence.

Lynching declined and then ended in Appalachia in the early decades of the twentieth century as the practice encountered community division, national antilynching campaigns, and state antilynching laws (enacted, for instance, in Kentucky in 1897 and 1920).

See also: RACE RIOTS; RACISM (RACE, ETHNICITY, AND IDENTITY).

—Michael J. Pfeifer, *Evergreen State College*

W. Fitzhugh Brundage, *Lynching in the New South: Georgia and Virginia, 1880–1930* (1993); George C. Wright, *Racial Violence in Kentucky, 1865–1940: Lynchings, Mob Rule, and "Legal Lynchings"* (1990).

Maxwell, Edith

(1914–1979) Celebrity defendant.

Scores of northern journalists flocked to Appalachia in 1935 and 1936 to cover the trials of schoolteacher Edith Maxwell, who was twice convicted by all-male juries of murdering her father in Wise County, Virginia. The case drew national attention—including commentary from James Thurber, Ernie Pyle, and Walter Winchell—because it touched on broad social themes of women's equality, domestic violence, and progress in the face of tradition. Sensational coverage by the Hearst newspapers and other media was favorable to Maxwell, yet it created a negative perception of the region and evoked comparisons to the State of Tennessee's prosecution of John Scopes for teaching evolution in 1925. Relying on stereotypes gleaned from turn-of-the-century romantic novels, Hearst writers saw college-educated Maxwell as an innocent victim of Appalachian culture, which they characterized as being patriarchal, against education, and hostile to progress. A Warner Brothers movie released in 1937 called *Mountain Justice* amplified those themes.

The incident that led to Maxwell's celebrity occurred shortly after midnight on July 21, 1935, when the attractive twenty-one-year-old teacher returned to her parents' house in the village of Pound after a date. She and her father, Trigg, a fifty-two-year-old coal miner, allegedly argued and engaged in a physical fight. Trigg died that same night of apparent head injuries. Police arrested both Maxwell and her mother, Ann. After initially claiming that the death was accidental, Maxwell admitted that a struggle had taken place. She testified that Trigg had tried to whip her while in a drunken rage and that she had defended herself with a high-heeled shoe. The prosecution accused her of deliberately bludgeoning him with a heavier instrument because he objected to her independent lifestyle.

Maxwell's 1935 murder conviction carried a twenty-five-year sentence. Two Washington, D.C., newspapers hired a prominent lawyer to appeal. The Virginia chapter of the National Woman's Party also recruited attorneys who unsuccessfully challenged the constitutionality of Virginia's law prohibiting women from jury service. Maxwell was retried in 1936 and again convicted, this time receiving twenty years. Charges against her mother were dropped. The former schoolteacher remained in state prison from

1937 until 1941, when she was pardoned by Governor James Price, partly through the intervention of Eleanor Roosevelt. Maxwell then left Virginia and lived a private life until her death in 1979.

See also: MOUNTAIN JUSTICE (media).

—Sharon Hatfield, *Athens, Ohio*

Miller, Izetta Jewell Brown

(1883–1978) Politician, activist, and actress.

Actress, journalist, and political activist Izetta Jewell Brown Miller is best known for being the first southern woman to run for the U.S. Senate, campaigning in 1922 and 1924. Also a West Virginia delegate to the Democratic National Convention in 1924, she became the first woman to second the nomination of a presidential nominee, John W. Davis of West Virginia. In 1930 she made another bid for Congress in New York's Thirteenth District at the insistence of Governor and Mrs. Franklin D. Roosevelt. U.S. Senator Jennings Randolph of West Virginia touted Miller as a realistic possibility as a Democratic presidential candidate.

Born November 24, 1883, Miller was also a renowned actress. Newspapers in Washington, D.C., reported she was the favorite actress of Presidents William Howard Taft and Woodrow Wilson. In 1928 she appeared in a leading role in the first televised play, *Queen's Messenger*, which was transmitted to experimental screens. Her other activities included participating in the women's rights leadership, agriculture and animal husbandry studies at West Virginia University, and the establishment of a commercial dairy in Preston County, West Virginia. She was later an accomplished reporter and radio commentator in California.

Miller was the widow of West Virginia Congressman William Gay "Junior" Brown, who died shortly after the birth of their only daughter. In 1927 she married Hugh G. Miller of George Washington University.

See also: DEMOCRATIC PARTY.

—Sharon Wills Brescoach, *Marshall University*

National Road

See National Road (Settlement and Migration)

Northwest Ordinance

The Northwest Ordinance of 1787 created the territorial system of the United States. Its provisions established the procedures by which conquered or acquired regions could become equal members of the North American Union. Because the ordinance only applied to the region north of the Ohio River, its impact on Appalachia was limited. However, its provisions, most notably its prohibition of slavery, ensured that the landscape and institutions of the southeastern counties of Ohio would develop differently from those south of the river.

An act of the Congress under the Articles of Confederation, the ordinance originated in the need to organize the land north of the Ohio River ceded by Virginia in 1783. Congressmen saw the vast expanse running from the Ohio River to the Great Lakes and west to the Mississippi River as a potential bonanza for the financially strapped government of the United States, even though it was inhabited by tens of thousands of Indians and Frenchmen. By establishing U.S. authority north of the Ohio River, Congress could sell millions of acres of land and not only retire the huge debt run up in winning the War for Independence but also support other projects designed to develop the North American interior.

The Northwest Ordinance provided for three stages of government. Initially, an appointed governor and three judges would supervise the territory; then, when there were five thousand free adult male residents, a legislature consisting of one appointed and one elected house would work with the appointed governor. A territory could apply for admission to the Union once it had sixty thousand free people and its residents had developed a constitution in accord with basic republican principles. Congress was the final arbiter of the statehood process; it and it alone had the power to decide whether or not to admit applicants. Following these procedures, Ohio, Indiana, Illinois, Michigan, and Wisconsin became states in the nineteenth century, and their experience became the model for the expansion of the United States as a whole.

The Northwest Ordinance also functioned as a charter document for the region north and west of the Ohio River, establishing the principles of freedom of religion, trial by jury, common law, and sanctity of private property and contracts. "Religion, Morality and knowledge being necessary to good government and the happiness of mankind," declared Article Three, "schools and the means of education shall forever be encouraged." The same paragraph called for the "utmost good faith" in dealing with the Indians, that is, securing "their consent" before taking land and waging only "just and lawful wars authorized by Congress" against them. Most famously, Article Six prohibited the practice of slavery and indentured servitude. Congress undermined some of the impact of the ordinance by making huge land sales to eastern speculators in the late 1780s. Meanwhile, territorial officials frequently ignored the presence of slaves, and Indians were hardly treated with "good faith," as a series of wars and treaties led to their eventual removal.

Still, the Northwest Ordinance was critical in dividing trans-Appalachian North America by differentiating the Old Northwest (or Midwest) from the region south of the Ohio River. While upland southerners flooded across the Ohio

River in the 1800s, the absence of both legal slavery and significant numbers of African Americans gave the states carved out of the Northwest Territory a distinctive self-image. Almost from the start, the ordinance's prohibition on slavery led many people to imagine the Ohio River as a significant boundary between two different worlds and to describe the Old Northwest as a land of freedom and honest labor, even though many people in southeastern Ohio were demographically and culturally similar to people south of the river. In other words, the ordinance created the perception of a sharper boundary between Virginia and Ohio than existed between other states.

Otherwise, the Northwest Ordinance's impact on Appalachia was minimal. Little of the region was federal territory; indeed, most of it lies within the borders of some of the original thirteen states or states created from them. These include Kentucky and West Virginia, which were never federal territories but parts of Virginia. Tennessee was originally a section of North Carolina but became the Southwest Territory in 1790. With a resolution having been drafted in 1784, Congress passed the Northwest Ordinance in 1787, shorn of the antislavery provision, to guide Tennessee's progress from territory to statehood, which occurred in 1796. The same version applied when Congress created the Mississippi Territory in 1798 to organize the region that would become the present-day states of Alabama and Mississippi. South of the Ohio River, aside from outlining procedures for achieving statehood, the ordinance was not as decisive in the development of the region as it was north of the river.

See also: AMERICAN REVOLUTION; WEST VIRGINIA STATEHOOD.

—Andrew Cayton, *Miami University*

Andrew R. L. Cayton, *The Frontier Republic: Ideology and Politics in the Ohio Country, 1780–1825* (1986); Peter S. Onuf, *Statehood and Union: A History of the Northwest Ordinance* (1987)

Overmountain Men

The Overmountain Men, a band of local militias from the mountains of Virginia, North Carolina, and the Tennessee section of North Carolina, defeated a British force at Kings Mountain, South Carolina, on October 7, 1780, effectively ending the Revolutionary War in Appalachia.

After the British seized control of Charleston, South Carolina, in 1780, they sought to gain control of North Carolina as well. They defeated regular American forces decisively at the battle of Camden, but this did not stop American irregulars from harassing them. In an effort to end this guerrilla activity, British General Charles Cornwallis ordered Major Patrick Ferguson to assemble a force to clear out the troublesome Americans.

Ferguson organized a force of an estimated one thousand men—many of whom were American Tories—and established a base in Rutherford County, North Carolina. After some initial success, Ferguson sent a message to guerrilla leaders threatening destruction of property and death to partisan leaders. In response, the aroused patriots agreed to meet at the Sycamore Shoals of the Watauga River. Led by Isaac Shelby, John Sevier, William Campbell, Charles McDowell, and others, they set out across the mountains to confront Ferguson's force. Learning of the patriot advance, Ferguson retreated to Kings Mountain, just across the state line in South Carolina. The mountain militia attacked Ferguson's forces, decisively defeating them and killing Ferguson. The British made no further efforts to gain control of the Appalachian region.

Two hundred years later, grassroots efforts by descendants and friends have resulted in an annual reenactment march of the campaign route to commemorate the exploits of the Overmountain Men. The original route is followed as much as possible, and campsites are built in the same areas as the original ones. To further recognize the backwoods militiamen, an Overmountain Victory National Historic Trail was incorporated into the official trail system maintained by the National Park Service.

See also: AMERICAN REVOLUTION.

—Borden Mace, *Pittsboro, North Carolina*

Perkins, Carl D.

(1912–1984) U.S. congressman.

Carl Dewey Perkins was a powerful congressman who represented eastern Kentucky in the U.S. House of Representatives from 1948 until his death in August 1984. After 1960 Perkins, a Democrat, played a leading role in the passage of the most comprehensive array of social legislation since the New Deal and was an unrelenting advocate for federal aid to education.

Perkins was born on a farm near Hindman in Knott County on October 12, 1912, the son of Dora Calhoun and James Elbert Perkins. His parents were prominent members of the local community—his mother a schoolteacher and his father a lawyer, county attorney, and school superintendent. Perkins attended the Hindman Settlement School, Caney Junior College, Lees Junior College, and the Jefferson School of Law in Louisville. In 1938 he married Verna Johnson of Knott County; they had one son, Carl Christopher, who succeeded his father in Congress.

Perkins served as Knott County attorney, state representative, and commonwealth attorney, and in the U.S. Army in central Europe during World War II. After his election to Congress in 1948, he focused his energy on the House Education and Labor Committee and became chair of that committee in 1967. He was author of the Vocational Education Act of 1963 and floor manager of the Elementary and Secondary Education Act of 1965, which made federal aid available to the schools for the first time. Perkins also helped to shape such programs as those controlling federal aid to libraries, Head Start, and student loans. He was also an early advocate of the Appalachian Regional Commission.

See also: APPALACHIAN REGIONAL COMMISSION; DEMOCRATIC PARTY.

—William R. Weinberg, *Hindman, Kentucky*

Pritt, Charlotte

(1949–) Politician.

Born in Charleston, West Virginia, on January 2, 1949, Charlotte Jean Pritt was the first female to run for governor in her home state. In 1992 Pritt came within a few percentage points of winning in the Democratic primary against Gaston Caperton, a strong Democratic incumbent. In the general election, she ran a controversial write-in campaign against Caperton. Four years later, she won the primary in a field of eleven candidates with 48 percent of the vote and was voted one of "America's Twenty Most Fascinating Women in American Politics" by *George* magazine. Although national pundits predicted Pritt would win, she met with a surprising upset by the Republican candidate, former governor and coal executive Cecil Underwood.

Pritt's campaign highlighted her Appalachian heritage as the daughter of a coal miner from Buzzard Rock, West Virginia. Pritt graduated from Marshall University in 1973, earned a master's degree in 1976, and taught English in West Virginia before entering politics. She was elected to the West Virginia House of Delegates in 1984 and 1986 and to the state senate in 1988. Although Pritt fought for education and health care, she is probably best known for her support of labor unions and environmental reform. Her campaign to prevent out-of-state dumping of toxic waste won her the Mother Jones Award from the West Virginia Environmental Council.

See also: WOMEN AND EMPLOYMENT (LABOR).

—Sharon Wills Brescoach, *Marshall University*

Prohibition

The Eighteenth Amendment to the U.S. Constitution, which prohibited the manufacture, sale, or transportation of alcoholic beverages in the nation and its territories, became effective January 17, 1920, and was repealed by the Twenty-first Amendment in 1933. Appalachian states had experimented with alcohol prohibition before that time, however, and many continue to have local prohibitions in the twenty-first century. New York had a statewide prohibition on the sale and manufacture of alcohol from 1845 to 1847, and New York and Pennsylvania adopted laws in 1884 and 1885, respectively, that required the teaching of anti-alcohol topics in public schools. Six Appalachian states were already under statewide prohibition before the national law took effect in 1920: Georgia (1907), Tennessee (1909), Virginia (1916), West Virginia (1914), South Carolina (1915), and Kentucky (1919).

Temperance movements that advocated restrictions on drinking had support in most of Appalachia prior to 1920. A long tradition of Protestant Christianity moved some Appalachians to regard the abuse (or even use) of alcohol as sinful, and many viewed it as socially destructive. During the Civil War, states such as North Carolina and Virginia enacted temporary prohibitions in order to conserve grain for the war. In the late nineteenth century, many Appalachian states already had local statutes that prohibited drinking near churches or similar locales that effectively restricted alcohol from larger areas. Tennessee enacted a "four-mile" law in 1877 that barred drinking establishments from the vicinity of chartered schools. Carrie Nation, who was arguably the most recognizable prohibition activist, was born in Garrard County, Kentucky, in 1846, and the two leading temperance organizations of the day, the Women's Christian Temperance Union and the Anti-Saloon League, both had their roots in Ohio.

Appalachians were not wholehearted in their support of national prohibition, however. The region had a history of open hostility to government-imposed restrictions on personal liberties—Appalachian Pennsylvania was the location of the Whiskey Rebellion of 1794, in which George Washington was obliged to call in the military to enforce taxation on distilled spirits. Many descendants of Scots, Irish, German, and other immigrant groups in Appalachia took generational pride in brewing beer and distilling whiskey and found these occupations to be convenient sources of agricultural income. Moonshining was both more dangerous and more lucrative after prohibition. However, in an effort to meet demand, quality generally declined to the point where bootleg liquor was frequently toxic. While moonshiners thrived, legal distilleries and breweries suffered from prohibition. Many that had operated for generations in Kentucky, Tennessee, Pennsylvania, and Ohio were forced out of business or acquired by opportunistic entrepreneurs who smuggled the warehoused stock to bootleggers and "medicinal" suppliers.

When the repeal of national prohibition in 1933 returned control of liquor to state and local governments, many Appalachian states continued statewide prohibition. Georgia was dry until 1935 and Tennessee until 1939, while Mississippi, the first state to ratify the Eighteenth Amendment and the last to ratify the Twenty-first, kept statewide prohibition on the books until 1966. Though South

Carolina never ratified the Twenty-first Amendment, today alcohol is sold legally in all counties. In Mississippi, North Carolina, Ohio, Pennsylvania, Virginia, and West Virginia, alcoholic beverages can only be purchased legally from state-operated stores. Counties throughout Appalachia still vote to remain "dry" or go "wet" in local elections, and often these contests are very close, causing great friction within communities, as the original issue of national prohibition did in its time.

See also: MOONSHINE (FOOD AND COOKING); MOONSHINING TERMINOLOGY (LANGUAGE); SUFFRAGE.

—Troy Gowen, *East Tennessee State University*

Paul E. Isaac, *Prohibition and Politics: Turbulent Decades in Tennessee, 1885–1920* (1965); Gordon B. McKinney, *Southern Mountain Republicans, 1865–1900: Politics and the Appalachian Community* (1978); Daniel J. Whitener, *Prohibition in North Carolina, 1715–1945* (1945).

Project Torchlight

Project Torchlight was a federal pilot project developed at Berea College in 1966 to help disadvantaged youth in nearby Appalachian counties. One of the first examples of educational innovation in that era, the project served as a model for similar outreach programs across the country in the 1960s and 1970s.

Initiated by Berea College faculty and staff members, Project Torchlight was developed to replace college programs eliminated in the early 1960s. The purpose was to reach financially challenged young people who had few opportunities for achieving academic or professional success. Students, faculty, and staff recruited 200 high school students from Clark, Estill, Madison, and Powell Counties in Kentucky for an eight-week summer program in 1966. The curriculum emphasized the arts and focused on doing and reflecting as a means of building self-knowledge and confidence. The following summer, 125 students from the same counties took part in the program. Due to lack of continued funding from the Office of Economic Opportunity, Project Torchlight was discontinued after 1967, with its educational principles adopted by Upward Bound, another federal program of the 1960s that targeted low-income high schoolers.

A follow-up study conducted thirty years after Project Torchlight found that most participants had achieved significant success, having entered professional careers in teaching, health care, civil service, business, science and technology, and the military. Four died in the Vietnam War. Most viewed their Project Torchlight experiences as a significant turning point in their lives, when negative expectations were shed and potentials discovered.

See also: BEREA COLLEGE (EDUCATION); SECTION OVERVIEW (EDUCATION).

—Bill Best, *Berea College*

Race Riots

Although they have not been as bloody as those of the Deep South and some urban centers, Appalachia has been the setting for a number of racial conflicts. Most occurred in the late nineteenth and early twentieth centuries and fit into national patterns reflecting white efforts to keep African Americans in a subordinate, segregated status. In the mid- and late twentieth century, very few incidents of race rioting occurred in Appalachia, where interracial violence typically has taken the form of communal purges, labor conflicts, or battles growing out of attempted lynchings.

Race riots of the late nineteenth and early twentieth centuries generally derived from two often interrelated sources: partisan political conflict and economic competition. Because the relatively low percentage of black voters mitigated white paranoia regarding black political influence, politically based race riots did not occur in Appalachia. Most riots were spawned by economic tensions instead, but even when they pitted blacks and whites against each other, such incidents were not necessarily race riots. For example, a battle between striking black miners and a group of Hungarian strikebreakers in 1887 in the Pocahontas field of western Virginia might be more accurately termed a labor riot, in spite of its racial overtones. Less ambiguous was a conflict in Winding Gulf Colliery, West Virginia, in 1916. There, an altercation between an African American and a white led to the jailing of two blacks. A black mob proceeded to attack the jail, killing the sheriff and freeing the prisoners.

Most race riots featured white mobs, however. Attempted lynchings precipitated the region's two major urban riots, which occurred in Roanoke, Virginia, in 1893 and Knoxville, Tennessee, in 1919. In both cases, economic downturns heightened racial tensions. Roanoke, which had grown from a crossroads hamlet to an industrial city of twenty-five thousand residents in the span of twelve years, exploded when a young black man named Thomas Smith was accused of beating and robbing a white woman. Mayor Henry S. Trout called out the local militia to prevent a mob from lynching Smith. Barricading themselves within the prison, militiamen opened fire on the mob, killing eight whites instantly and injuring many others. Enraged, the mob looted the city and then turned their attentions to the mayor, who barely escaped. Smith was eventually lynched.

Knoxville's 1919 riot began under similar circumstances but featured an attack upon the city's black community. As in so many other American cities during the "Red Summer," Knoxville, which had enjoyed a reputation for relatively peaceful race relations, experienced a rising tide of racial bitterness, culminating with a black sheriff's deputy's being charged with murdering a white woman. After failing to seize the prisoner, a white mob looted the city's stores and targeted the black section of town. There, they met the resistance of well-armed residents, who stationed snipers in the upper floors of buildings. A major street battle ensued. National Guardsmen restored order, but they did so mainly by siding with the white mob and disarming as many blacks as they could.

In some instances, African Americans were expelled from communities or even whole counties. White mobs in the northern Georgia counties of Forsyth and Dawson emptied their areas of blacks in 1912, and in 1919 whites forced all black newcomers out of the town of Corbin, Kentucky. Similar expulsions occurred in Ravenna and Cary, Kentucky, around the same time. Many other areas of the region may have enforced racial homogeneity in similar ways.

In the second half of the twentieth century, racial conflict, though no stranger to the region, was less common. Efforts to desegregate Clinton High School in Anderson County, Tennessee, in 1956 led to rioting similar to that which occurred in Little Rock, Arkansas, the following year. Whites, spurred by a northerner named John Kasper, attacked cars driven by African Americans and threatened the courthouse before being quelled by tear gas. The sins of Forsyth County, Georgia, were revisited upon its residents in 1987, when civil rights leader Hosea Williams led a protest march to the county, which was becoming a bedroom community of Atlanta, to shed light on its lily-white demographics. Marchers were repelled by crowds of rock-throwing whites, many, but not all of them, outsiders. The violence in Forsyth indicated a persistent shadow of racism and pointed up the region's similarity with the rest of the country in race relations.

See also: CIVIL RIGHTS MOVEMENT (RACE, ETHNICITY, AND IDENTITY); LYNCHING; RACISM (RACE, ETHNICITY, AND IDENTITY).

—Bland Whitley, *University of Florida*

Ann Field Alexander, "'Like an Evil Wind': The Roanoke Riot of 1893 and the Lynching of Thomas Smith," *Virginia Magazine of History and Biography* (April 1992); W. Fitzhugh Brundage, *Lynching in the New South: Virginia and Georgia, 1880–1930* (1993); Paul A. Gilje, *Rioting in America* (1996); Ronald L. Lewis, *Black Coal Miners in America: Race, Class, and Community Conflict, 1780–1980* (1987).

Reconstruction

Reconstruction was the name given to the process of reintegrating the states of the Confederacy into the Union after the Civil War. It is also the period extending from the conclusion of the Civil War in 1865 to the final withdrawal of federal troops from southern states in 1877. The Appalachian sections of several states played crucial roles in this process, and Andrew Johnson, an east Tennessee political figure, was president of the United States during the early part of Reconstruction.

The political situation at the end of the Civil War was wholly unsettled. The assassination of President Abraham Lincoln and the collapse of state governments in the South left a political void and pervasive uncertainty, particularly in areas where loyalty had been sharply divided during the conflict. Andrew Johnson—a former Democratic congressman and senator and military governor of Tennessee during the war—assumed the presidency April 15, 1865, and attempted to continue Lincoln's lenient policies toward the defeated region. Johnson pardoned the vast majority of southerners for their participation in the rebellion and appointed provisional governors, naming persons who had demonstrated support for the Union during the war. Former Confederate states were required to abolish slavery, nullify ordinances of secession, and repudiate public debts incurred to support the war. Then the states were allowed to hold elections and choose governors, members of Congress, and representatives to state legislatures. The president also required the legislatures to approve the Thirteenth Amendment to the U.S. Constitution that abolished slavery. Legislatures also elected U.S. senators. Generally, these elections returned the antebellum elite to power and once again left the Appalachian sections of Alabama, Georgia, Virginia, and North Carolina politically weak. Tennessee, where a coalition of Unionists elected William G. "Parson" Brownlow of Knoxville as governor, was an exception.

Throughout 1866 the Republican Congress worked to overturn President Johnson's program of Reconstruction. One reason was that the new southern state governments greatly restricted the rights of the former slaves. In reaction, Congress proposed the Fourteenth Amendment, which would grant the freedmen citizenship and limit the political participation of certain groups of former Confederates. Johnson challenged the Republicans in the congressional elections of 1866, and the Republicans won a sweeping victory. Now dominant in Congress, the Republicans took control of Reconstruction policies and overturned Johnson's plan. The Reconstruction Act of March 2, 1867, placed ten southern states under military control; Tennessee was exempted because Unionists were in power. The act required states to draft new state constitutions enfranchising freedmen, to hold new elections, and to ratify the Fourteenth Amendment. The Republicans controlled the constitutional conventions that created the new governments, and Appalachian political leaders were prominent among them. Many of the policies that had limited state economic and social programs in Appalachian counties were reversed in new state constitutions that included democratic and liberal provisions such as universal male suffrage, improved public education, and state laws preventing the loss of land for indebtedness. The yeoman farmers of Appalachia especially welcomed these last two reforms.

During this period of disruption and change, the modern political system developed in southern Appalachia. The Republican Party remained strong in northern Georgia, east Tennessee, southeastern Kentucky, northern West Virginia, and western Maryland, areas that had maintained loyalty to the Union during the Civil War. The upland areas of Virginia and Alabama tended to favor the Democratic Party, as did the pro-Confederate counties of southeastern West Virginia. In 1868 and 1869, Republicans dominated the state governments in this part of the South. At the local level, however, Democrats were either competitive or dominant in the mountains. Increasingly, Democrats relied on racist appeals and the activities of organizations such as the Ku Klux Klan to persuade mountain voters to support their candidates. While divisions among white voters continued, Democrats won enough votes to gain control of state governments and most local governments in the southern mountains as well.

The aftermath of Reconstruction was detrimental to the interests of the Appalachian South. White Republican voters in the mountain counties in each state were the only substantial numbers of white Republicans in the South. As the home of the political "enemy," southern Appalachia was neglected by lowland politicians. Public works projects, public education, transportation improvements, and the distribution of public funds all favored non-Appalachian portions of states. Some scholars argue that a significant cause of Appalachian poverty in the years after 1870 was the neglect of the region by the dominant Democratic Party and lowland political leaders of both parties. The political parties also were the vehicles through which outside business interests came to control the process of industrialization in the mountains in the decades after Reconstruction.

Although Reconstruction was a trying experience for the entire Appalachian region, there were some positive outcomes. Among changes for the better were the abolition of slavery and the provision for basic civil and social rights of African Americans. In addition, the principle of public education for all children was established—even if the policy was poorly implemented until the twentieth century. In general, the Reconstruction period was a time of political experimentation in which the non-elite sought to shape government institutions to address the needs of ordinary people. This effort ultimately failed, but it left a legacy to be redeemed much later.

See also: CIVIL WAR; JOHNSON, ANDREW; REPUBLICAN PARTY.

—John L. Bell, *Western Carolina University*

Richard O. Curry, ed., *Radicalism, Racism, and Party Realignment: The Border States during Reconstruction* (1969); Gordon B. McKinney, *Southern Mountain Republicans, 1865–1900: Politics and the Appalachian Community* (1978); Kenneth W. Noe and Shannon H. Wilson, eds., *The Civil War in Appalachia: Collected Essays* (1997).

Regulators and the Battle of Alamance

The Regulation was a political movement in the backcountry of North and South Carolina arising about 1768 and ending with the Regulators' defeat at the battle of Alamance, North Carolina, on May 16, 1771.

Based in Orange County, North Carolina, the Regulators protested the abuses of local officials, which included extortionate court fees, corrupt attachment of property, and the inability of freemen to get fair value for seized property. The Regulators desired to "regulate" county officers and to stop the abuses of power by refusing to pay taxes until officials published legal fees and accounted for public expenditures. They based their action on the British constitutional principle specifying that no grants of money could be collected by the crown until it designated how the money would be spent.

Governor William Tryon encouraged the Regulators to obtain legal redress of grievances, which they attempted to do. However, lawyers and judges frustrated their civil suits by changing the venue of cases to eastern counties and by packing juries. The Regulators elected assemblymen, but as a minority in the colony, they were unable to secure reform legislation.

Despairing of legal reforms, the Regulators became unruly and violent. Leaders such as Herman Husband and James Hunter could not control them. The worst violence occurred in September 1770, when Regulators prevented court from meeting in Hillsboro, North Carolina. They forced the judge from the bench, assaulted lawyers, including the hated Edmund Fanning, whose house was torn down, and terrorized the town.

Unable to abide riot and opposition to royal officials, Governor Tryon called out the militia to restore order. His thirteen hundred militia attacked and routed two thousand Regulators at Alamance Creek, thus ending the movement. Tryon hanged seven leaders but pardoned more than six thousand men. By 1772 over fifteen hundred former Regulators had moved westward, many into Appalachia.

See also: COUNTY GOVERNMENT.

—John L. Bell, *Western Carolina University*

Republican Party

When the Republican Party first appeared in Appalachia, it was limited to the northern part of the region. Formed in the wake of the collapse of the Whig Party, it was not a fully structured national or local party when it nominated its first presidential ticket in 1856, yet it carried nearly half of the Appalachian counties of Maryland, New York, Ohio, and Pennsylvania. Because it was viewed as advocating the restriction of slavery, the Republican Party did not exist as an organization in central and southern Appalachia. By 1860 Republicans were strong enough to take advantage of the split among Democrats to carry most of the counties in northern Appalachia. In Virginia, a Democratic Party stronghold, approximately one thousand citizens around Wheeling voted Republican and sustained the *Wheeling Intelligencer* as a party newspaper.

The secession crisis and the Civil War solidly identified the Republicans as the party of the Union, and the association with unity gave the party appeal in mountain areas of slave states in the region. A probable majority of people in western Maryland, northwestern Virginia, eastern Kentucky, and east Tennessee supported the Union during the war. The most significant result of this Appalachian Unionism was the creation of the state of West Virginia. Even in the Deep South, some mountain areas, including Winston County, Alabama, Fannin County, Georgia, and Wilkes and Mitchell Counties, North Carolina, refused to support the Southern rebellion. During the period that followed the war, Republicans in central and southern Appalachia were part of a coalition that included the former Unionists and recently emancipated slaves. For most whites, the enfranchisement of African Americans was a radical step. Some former Unionists, such as William G. "Parson" Brownlow of east Tennessee, endorsed the liberal policies of the national party, but the racist pressure of terrorist organizations such as the Ku Klux Klan reduced the Republican vote across central and southern Appalachia. Even so, the party remained active and viable in West Virginia, east Tennessee, eastern Kentucky, and western North Carolina.

After 1876 the Republican Party in Appalachia consolidated its organization at the local level. Generally, its structure adapted a military model. Party members received patronage appointments as rewards for their partisan work, and as a result, Republicans gained voter support. This was particularly true in central Appalachia, where dissatisfied Democrats sought a new political home. The most important of these revolts created the Readjuster Party in Virginia, led by Senator William Mahone. The Readjusters joined the Republican Party in 1884 and established the Republicans as a presence in southwestern Virginia for the first time. In several southern states, Democratic hegemony was threatened by the Populist Party during the 1890s. North Carolina Populists and Republicans won control of the state government and elected mountain Republican Jeter C. Pritchard to the U.S. Senate. Populists and Republicans were also especially active in northern Alabama.

The success of the Populists was only one manifestation of voters' reaction to the "Democratic" depression of the 1890s. The other major development was the election of Republicans as local and state officials, congressmen, and U.S. senators in northern and central Appalachia. These new Republican leaders were often connected to the industrial elite then seizing control of the Appalachian economy. One example of this new breed of Republican leader was Stephen B. Elkins of West Virginia. Elkins used his financial resources to oust locally oriented party leaders and replace patronage with financial rewards as the basis of party cohesion. In central and southern Appalachia, Democratic leaders felt threatened by Republican success. Starting in Mississippi in 1890 and ending in Georgia in 1908, Democrats passed laws that severely restricted the voting rights of two Appalachian Republican constituencies—African Americans and poor whites. As a result, statewide parties became moribund even though the Republicans in the mountain counties remained successful. An excellent example of the continued viability of mountain Republicans was Congressman C. Bascom Slemp, who represented the "Fighting Ninth" District of southwestern Virginia between 1907 and 1923.

The growth of business influence in politics led to a countermovement called progressivism. Although progressives were relatively weak in Appalachia in the absence of a large middle class, they did achieve some significant victories. Under the leadership of Governor Ben W. Hooper, east Tennessee Republicans combined with the rural Democratic faction to bring statewide prohibition to Tennessee in 1909. Appalachian Republicans voted overwhelmingly for Theodore Roosevelt and the Progressive Party rather than regular party nominee William Howard Taft in the 1912 presidential election. Mountain Republican legislators in West Virginia and Tennessee provided the decisive votes that propelled the Nineteenth Amendment to national victory in 1920. One result of this latter commitment was a heavy turnout of Republican women voters in east Tennessee later that year and the unexpected election of mountain Republican Alf Taylor as governor.

The association of the Republican Party with economic growth in the 1920s led to larger Republican majorities in central and northern Appalachian counties. The expanding power of large business corporations in company towns was a prominent factor in the Republican domination. Calvin Coolidge's decisive victory over the Progressive Party candidate in the Appalachian counties in the 1924 presidential election confirmed the power of the business leadership of the Republican Party. The 1928 presidential candidacy of Democrat Al Smith, an Irish Catholic from New York, distressed many conservative Democrats and led to sweeping Republican victories in northern and central Appalachia. These triumphs included a totally unexpected win in the western North Carolina congressional race of that year.

This pattern of success was undercut by the "Hoover," or "Republican," depression of the 1930s. Two important segments of the Republican coalition left the party during these years. Violent confrontations between textile workers and coal miners and industrialists drove many labor voters from Republican ranks, particularly in central Appalachia. Moreover, African Americans began to perceive that the Democratic New Deal offered programs that benefited them, and black Republicans shifted party allegiances throughout the 1930s. The switch to the Democrats reached its high point in the landslide victory of President Franklin D. Roosevelt in 1936. Roosevelt carried a small majority of northern Appalachian counties—the first Democrat to do so since 1856. The Republicans were also decisively defeated in central and southern Appalachia although they won a majority of counties in east Tennessee. Despite these losses, Appalachian Republicans fared better than the party did elsewhere, except in northern New England. President Herbert Hoover won only 300 of 3,200 counties in the country in 1936, and 101 of those Republican counties were located in Appalachia.

The party regained its dominant position in northern and parts of central Appalachia after World War II. In 1948 the developing civil rights issue split the Democrats and alienated southern supporters—including many in southern Appalachia. The overwhelming personal popularity of Dwight D. Eisenhower was a huge asset for the Republicans. In the 1960 election, the candidacy of Irish Catholic John F. Kennedy polarized the electorate, and the Republicans won decisively in northern and central Appalachia. The 1964 presidential election defined and changed mountain Republicanism. Republican candidate Barry Goldwater was perceived to be hostile to the moderate consensus of national politics. The result was a party disaster in northern Appalachia, where Goldwater won only four of ninety-eight counties. Republicans in central Appalachia also suffered significant losses, only winning a majority of votes in east Tennessee. In southern Appalachia, however, the previously moribund party suddenly came to life. Large numbers of white voters voted Republican for the first time to protest the alliance between national Democrats and the Civil Rights movement.

The last three decades of the twentieth century saw continuing Republican success in all three parts of Appalachia. The independent presidential candidacy of George Wallace in 1968 provided a bridge for many racially conservative Democrats in southern Appalachia to move over to the Republican Party. Four years later, the liberal Democratic candidacy of Senator George McGovern led to an overwhelming Republican victory in all parts of Appalachia for the first time in history. The Republican successes took place at all levels as the party won county, congressional district, and state contests, and some Appalachian Republicans, notably Howard Baker of east Tennessee, majority leader of the U.S. Senate, became nationally prominent. Despite these successes, the presidential election of 1996 indicated that some mountain Republicans were dissatisfied. A significant minority of the party supported the third-party candidacy of Ross Perot, and this allowed the Democrats to carry more counties than any election since 1964. Nevertheless, the history of the Republican Party in Appalachia has been one of considerable success and longterm voter loyalty.

See also: DEMOCRATIC PARTY; DEMOCRATIC-REPUBLICAN PARTY; WHIG PARTY.

—Gordon B. McKinney, *Berea College*

Paul E. Isaac, *Tennessee Republicans in the Era of William McKinley, Theodore Roosevelt, and William Howard Taft: Factions, Leaders, and Patronage* (1998); V. O. Key Jr., *Southern Politics in State and Nation* (1949; reprint 1984); Gordon B. McKinney, *Southern Mountain Republicans, 1865–1900: Politics and the Appalachian Community* (1978); Samuel L. Webb, *Two-Party Politics in the One-Party South: Alabama's Hill Country, 1874–1920* (1997).

Revenue Officers

Although moonshiners of Appalachian folklore regularly outwit "revenuers," mountain whiskey makers have found federal agents their principal nemesis from the creation of the Bureau of Internal Revenue in 1862 into the twentieth-first century.

By the time the bureau's agents began their raids on stills, taxes on liquor production had already been an issue for decades. The federal government first imposed a tax on liquor production in 1791. Farmers of mountainous western Pennsylvania resisted payment, and President George Washington dispatched troops to end riots in the Whiskey Rebellion of 1794. Though the rebellion was suppressed, the excise tax was repealed in 1802 and only temporarily revived during the War of 1812. From 1813 until 1817, retailers' and distillers' licenses bore a federal tax, but beginning in 1818 the industry enjoyed a tax-free era that lasted until 1862. By the outbreak of the Civil War, mountain farmers had been freely making and selling corn whiskey and fruit brandy for more than forty years.

During the war, whiskey makers in the Union were again taxed, and in the Confederacy they were prohibited from using grain for any purpose except animal feed. In 1862 the U.S. Congress established the Bureau of Internal Revenue to collect a new excise tax on liquor and tobacco. The tax became permanent, and by 1876 the bureau was operating an elaborate enforcement machinery. States were divided into districts headed by collectors who appointed deputies to take in taxes in local areas. With numerous subordinates, the collectors became leaders of their own political patronage organizations.

Revenue officers policed both large and small distillers. Even though enforcement was sporadic, the bureau hunted moonshiners in places as diverse as Brooklyn alleys and Appalachian hollows. Revenuers exposed a conspiracy between major distillers and public officials that led to the notorious Whiskey Ring tax evasion and bribery scandal of 1872. The Whiskey Ring reached into the highest levels of government and operated from 1864 to 1875 before it was dismantled. Dishonest government officials and distillers were convicted and sent to prison.

Systematic enforcement began when Green B. Raum became U.S. commissioner of Internal Revenue in 1876. Raum directed some operations in Appalachia as military expeditions, with soldiers serving in revenue raids until 1878, and sometimes organized revenuers from several states to sweep through moonshiner strongholds along the borders. Although revenuers occasionally captured moonshiners in these raids, usually they depended on informers, whose testimony was the basis for federal warrants. Revenue deputies could not make arrests without warrants, so they were normally accompanied by deputy U.S. marshals, who could arrest people on the spot. Moonshiners resisted with all means available, hiding stills, deploying clever warning systems, and even shooting raiders and assassinating informers. Nevertheless, when Raum resigned in 1883, he declared the government victorious.

Raum's successors continued the war against moonshiners. During the depression of the 1890s, when people found moonshine whiskey a better source of income than farming, revenuers again waged an uphill battle. The South's gradual adoption of prohibition forced federal officers to work much harder. When prohibition became national on midnight of January 16, 1920, moonshining thrived and became more commercialized. Stock car racing traces its heritage to the era's nighttime chases along narrow mountain roads. With repeal of prohibition, revenuers still had to collect the tax and prevent evasion. The mid-1960s witnessed Operation Dry-Up, a massive campaign against moonshiners. Although the conflict between revenuers (now the Bureau of Alcohol, Tobacco, Firearms, and Explosives, a division of the Department of Justice) and moonshiners has not abated, they sometimes meet to reminisce over the old days.

See also: MOONSHINE (FOOD AND COOKING); PROHIBITION; STOCK CAR RACING (SPORTS AND RECREATION).

—Wilbur R. Miller, *State University of New York at Stony Brook*

Jess Carr, *The Second Oldest Profession: An Informal History of Moonshining in America* (1972); Wilbur R. Miller, *Revenuers and Moonshiners: Enforcing Federal Liquor Law in the Mountain South, 1865–1900* (1991).

Roanoke Race Riot of 1893

See Race Riots

School Equity Funding

The funding of public schools in rural Appalachia has been inequitable historically because the majority of financing for both elementary and secondary schools comes from local property taxes, as it does elsewhere in the United States. The problem is that not all property is of equal value; consequently, schools do not all receive comparable funding. The major determinant of a property's value is its perceived economic worth. Generally, properties located in urban areas in proximity to industrial and service sectors are deemed to be far more valuable and provide more tax revenue than those located in rural and agricultural areas. For example, the limited industrial base of southern Ohio results in lower economic value for property, whereas in northeastern Ohio, a major concentration of industrial and service concerns produces greater economic value, and therefore higher tax revenues, for land.

Schools with limited property tax revenue are faced with issues that have a direct impact on the quality of education. Rural Appalachian school districts have had chronic problems attracting and retaining quality teachers and administrators. They have limited funds to build new schools, improve existing facilities, and acquire such educational technology as computers. These funding issues produce a marked difference between the education of students in rural Appalachia and their contemporaries in urban and suburban areas. Often the quality of education varies among rural, suburban, and urban areas.

One of the most notable examples of such disparities existed prior to 1990 in Kentucky, where gross inequities in education had been present for decades among the state's 180 school districts, clearly violating Section 183 of the Kentucky Constitution. In 1988 the situation changed dramatically when the boards of education in 66 Kentucky school districts incorporated as the Council for Better Education and, along with twenty-two public school students, filed suit against the Kentucky General Assembly in the Franklin County Circuit Court. Judge Ray Corns ruled that the general assembly was required by the constitution to provide equal support to conduct an efficient educational effort in all Kentucky schools. This case was later appealed to the state supreme court in *Council for Better Education, Inc. v. Wilkinson* and *Rose v. Council for Better Education, Inc.* In a sweeping decision, the Kentucky Supreme Court ruled in June 1989 that the existing system of public education in the state was unconstitutional.

The Kentucky General Assembly subsequently organized a task force, which led to the passing of House Bill 940, the Kentucky Education Reform Act of 1990, considered the most sweeping education initiative ever taken by a state.

While education inequities are less frequently seen in urban areas, funding crises also occur in these locations, as well as in suburban schools, some of which face financial difficulties due to low property values. Various efforts have been made to alleviate this funding disparity. In Ohio, the state supreme court decreed that the state's manner of funding public education is unconstitutional because it does not provide thorough and efficient education for each child.

See also: HEAD START PROGRAM; SECTION OVERVIEW (EDUCATION).

—James J. Sheehan, *Cleveland State University*

"Education Reform Act of 1990," in *The Kentucky Encyclopedia*, ed. John E. Kleber (1992).

Shelton Laurel Massacre

One of the worst atrocities of the Civil War occurred in the mountains of North Carolina on January 18, 1863, at a place called Shelton Laurel in Madison County. The incident, now known as the Shelton Laurel Massacre, involved the brutal murder of thirteen captured Union sympathizers at the hands of Confederate soldiers, an event that not only fueled the war but also remains a part of the historical legacy of Appalachia.

Shelton Laurel was home to Unionists, refugees, bushwhackers, and deserters of the Confederacy's Sixty-fourth North Carolina Regiment. When a band of Union raiders from the mountain area attacked nearby Marshall, primarily to obtain salt (a commodity often withheld from Union sympathizers by the Confederacy), they broke into several stores, taking what they wanted, and invaded the home of Confederate Colonel Lawrence Allen. At the time, Allen's wife was home caring for their three children, two of whom were ill with scarlet fever. The raiders were said to have stolen blankets from the sick children's beds.

When Colonel Allen and Lieutenant Colonel James A. Keith, both of the North Carolina Sixty-fourth, heard about the raid, they moved quickly to retaliate, acting under the authority of General Henry Heth, Confederate commander of east Tennessee at Knoxville. Keith reached the vicinity first and arrested fifteen old men and young boys, only five of whom, by some accounts, were believed to have been among the actual raiders in Marshall. The prisoners were told they would be marched to Knoxville the next day for a trial. Two in the group managed to escape during the night, and the march began the next morning with the remaining thirteen. As the group approached Laurel Creek, however, the prisoners were stopped and shot dead in groups of five, five, and three. Victims included Elison King; Joe Woods; Will Shelton, age twenty; Halen Moore, age twenty-five or thirty; Wade Moore, age twenty or twenty-five; Old Jim Shelton, age fifty-six; James Shelton Jr., age seventeen; James Metcalf, age forty; Stob Rod Shelton; David Shelton (brother of Stob Rod); Jasper Chandler, age fifteen or sixteen; David Shelton, age thirteen; and another, unnamed.

When North Carolina Governor Zebulon Vance heard the "rumors and reports of a brutal mass murder of prisoners" at Shelton Laurel, he requested an official investigation. Keith was allowed to resign, but only on the grounds of incompetence. In self-defense, he maintained that General Heth gave him verbal orders not to take any prisoners, although Heth "vigorously denied" the accusation. While the controversy raged over what happened at Shelton Laurel, militia units were chasing "marauders" elsewhere in Madison and Yancey Counties.

See also: CIVIL WAR.

—Georgia M. Greer, *East Tennessee State University*

Slavery and Abolition

Slavery infiltrated nearly every part of the southern Appalachians, though it did so more sporadically and much more sparsely than in most of the South. Without the large-scale, cash-crop agricultural system that made the institution essential to the plantation South, slaves in Appalachia were employed in a variety of ways by those who owned them and by others who hired them out. With the exception of several mining and manufacturing enterprises, slave labor was never dominant in the antebellum economy of Appalachia. As such, the presence of slaves evoked mixed responses from southern highlanders, especially as the institution became the source of increased sectional tensions in the 1840s and 1850s.

Central to the mythology of preindustrial Appalachia has been the assumption that when the sectional crisis emerged and the Civil War erupted from it, southern highlanders were solidly Unionist in their political sentiments. A corollary to this assumption is the belief that they opposed slavery. Only in recent years have historians begun to explore the realities behind those myths, and they are emerging with a far different and more complex view of what Appalachians thought of slavery and how the practice shaped regional politics during the late antebellum period.

Much of the myth of strong antislavery sentiment on the part of white mountain residents stems from another myth—that the mountains were settled by poor whites squeezed off of lowland farms or jobs by the dominance of large plantations and with slave labor. Resentful that opportunities were denied them elsewhere, highlanders in this scenario were assumed to have become champions of liberty and individualism, despising the privilege and class differences that drove them into the hills. Such was not the case. While slaveholders in the mountain South were relatively few, they were men of means who served their regional interests—economically and politically—well enough to earn the loyalty of the vast majority of non-slaveholding constituents, clients, and customers. While political leaders in some parts of the region—particularly east Tennessee and what would become West Virginia—played on the resentments and suspicions of their constituents toward those lowland areas so dominated by powerful and privileged "slaveocracies," such oppositions stemmed more from class- and region-based insecurities more than from any belief in the immorality of slavery or sympathy for slaves. Racism was as pervasive among white Appalachians as among other white southerners. The fact that many of the region's most influential politicians and journalists, whether secessionist or Unionist, were also slaveholders kept any real abolitionist sentiments out of the political debate during the sectional crisis.

Yet there were pockets of antislavery activity in the region, and they planted the seeds for later assumptions of widespread abolitionism throughout the mountain South. Indeed, the idea that organized abolitionism began in Appalachia rests on early efforts by Benjamin Lundy in Wheeling, (West) Virginia, and then in northeastern Tennessee just after the turn of the nineteenth century. In Tennessee, Lundy joined with Elihu Embree and other "New Light" Presbyterians and Quakers from Pennsylvania and Ohio to establish the nation's first manumission societies and produce the earliest antislavery newspapers. By 1827, according to one claim, east Tennessee had one-fifth of the abolitionist societies in the United States and nearly a fifth of the national membership. But most organized efforts were phased out or had moved elsewhere by the early 1830s. Maryville College, in the southeastern part of the state, remained the only substantial base of antislavery activity for the rest of the antebellum period. In Kentucky, abolitionist John G. Fee established Berea College in the early 1850s. Though just beyond the foothills of the Appalachians and less explicitly abolitionist in purpose than Maryville, Berea College stood as a model of interracial education throughout most of the rest of the century, the product of Fee's quest for "a practical recognition of the brotherhood of man."

The Appalachian region also took on the aura of a refuge for escaped slaves. It is often assumed to have been a vital part of the Underground Railroad out of the South though such claims are suspect, and none of the major works on the Underground Railroad include any reference to highland routes or stations. Militant abolitionist John Brown long saw the highlands as central to his scheme for liberating southern slaves, both as an escape route and sanctuary and as a base of operations from which to orchestrate uprisings against lowland plantations. His raid on Harpers Ferry in 1859, a site squarely within the Allegheny Mountains of Maryland and western Virginia, rested on a plan that included moving with those slaves he would free into mountain bastions from which they would operate a large-scale war of liberation. While nothing came of this ill-conceived venture, its romanticization in northern abolitionist circles added to the idea of Appalachia as a bastion of liberty and Unionism.

Such ideas remained impressionistic and far removed from the reality that, for most highlanders, any dislike of slavery did not stem from sympathy for those enslaved. Rather, fear of emancipation and its impact on their region outweighed any distaste for a system that relegated them to a lower class than they might otherwise have enjoyed. In western North Carolina and southwest Virginia, political leaders were quick to play on fears of federal interference with slavery to win majorities for secession in 1861. Governor Joseph E. Brown effectively mobilized his fellow north Georgians to support secession by warning them of the numerous blacks who would swarm into their peaceful valleys and hills wreaking havoc once freed from the constraints that slavery provided. Even Unionist leaders in the mountains, many of them slaveholders themselves, insisted that they were not abolitionists. Many were quick to state that if the North ever sought to end slavery, they would side with the Confederacy. It was by instilling a fear of the slaveocracy, so dominant in middle and west Tennessee, that men like Andrew Johnson, Thomas A. R. Nelson, and William G. "Parson" Brownlow, slaveholders all, convinced two-thirds of east Tennesseans to stick with the Union.

In short, while resentment of the planter class in the lowland South was intense and widespread among Appalachians, a fear of the impact of slavery's demise was often a stronger influence on their political alignments during the sectional crisis. The difference in how parts of southern Appalachia reacted to secession and the Civil War probably stemmed less from divergent feelings toward slavery and slaves than it did from the various circumstances of interstate sectionalism and the agenda of the political leadership in the mountain sections of the several states involved.

See also: CIVIL WAR; SLAVE LABOR (LABOR); SLAVERY (RACE, ETHNICITY, AND IDENTITY).

—John C. Inscoe, *University of Georgia*

Richard B. Drake, "Slavery and Antislavery in Appalachia," *Appalachian Heritage* (Winter 1986); Durwood Dunn, *An Abolitionist in the Appalachian South: Ezekiel Birdseye on Slavery, Capitalism, and Separate Statehood in East Tennessee, 1841–1846* (1997); John C. Inscoe, "Race and Racism in Nineteenth-Century Southern Appalachia: Myths, Realities, and Ambiguities," in *Appalachia in the Making: The Mountain South in the Nineteenth Century*, ed. Mary Beth Pudup, Dwight B. Billings, and Altina L. Waller (1995) and ed., *Appalachians and Race: The Mountain South from Slavery to Segregation* (2000).

State of Franklin

Called the "dangerous example" by some of its opponents and viewed as such by some of America's Founding Fathers, the movement to create a fourteenth American state called Franklin was an illuminating and influential episode in United States political history. It proved important to other politically restive areas of the early American republic, including western Virginia, Kentucky, Vermont, and Maine. Franklin, as model and anti-model, provided an example of the way states would not be created in the newly minted country.

The origins of the Franklin movement lay deep in the early settlement of the western country of North Carolina and southwest Virginia. Feeling isolated and often ignored by their distant seats of government, the early settlers in what later became Tennessee formed a political organization to provide local government known as the Watauga Association in 1772. Isolation bred community; neglect bred self-reliance; an independent spirit bred resolve. All these factors, gestating on the frontier from the early 1770s, gave birth in the mid-1780s to an attempt by citizens of the North Carolina trans-Appalachian counties of Washington, Sullivan, and Greene to secede and create a new state.

Residents declared their purpose at a Jonesborough (Tennessee) convention in August 1784. A provisional convention held there in December reaffirmed this action and adopted as a temporary measure the existing North Carolina Constitution (with slight revision) under which to govern until a new constitution was approved. Such a proposed constitution, believed to have been largely composed by Virginians Arthur Campbell and the Reverends William Graham and Samuel Houston (relative and namesake of Sam Houston of later Texas fame), was presented at the constitutional convention held at Greeneville (Tennessee) in November 1785.

Called one of the most democratic constitutions ever composed by Americans, the so-called Frankland constitution provided for universal male suffrage without property qualifications, proportional representation, a unicameral legislature, popular election of all government officials (including militia officers), limited terms of office, and a state university. Influenced heavily by Protestant, especially Presbyterian, clergy, it also had a strong ethical and moral tone. Elected officials were required to believe in God and the Bible and could not hold office if they gambled or were profane, lewd, drunken, or of immoral character.

From scant surviving evidence, it is not clear why the proposed Frankland constitution was not approved by the convention. Possibilities include resentment that the document was largely the creation of men not resident in the formative state, as well as resistance to the clerical tone of certain parts of it. Perhaps most influential may have been the delegates' desire to adopt something with which they were already comfortable—the existing North Carolina Constitution and Declaration of Rights of 1776. The name Frankland (meaning "land of free men") proposed by Campbell was dropped in favor of naming the state Franklin in honor of statesman Benjamin Franklin. Though defeated at home, the Frankland document, published in Philadelphia at the time America's leaders were discussing the need for such a document for the new nation, had some influence upon certain elements of the United States Constitution framed soon afterward.

With John Sevier's election as Franklin's governor in 1785, two sets of officials and two state governments were operating in the same place. The existence of two governments created a virtual state of civil war for the ensuing three years. While trying to fend off opposition at home, Franklin's leaders sought recognition from the national government and support from the empire of Spain (in what came to be called part of the "Spanish conspiracy"). It is unclear whether the leaders of Franklin were serious about a union with Spain or merely using it as a ploy to win congressional approval for statehood. At Philadelphia, the statehood effort received close scrutiny from George Washington, James Madison, Alexander Hamilton, and Benjamin Franklin himself. For the Virginians especially, it was a watchful time. Led by Arthur Campbell, there was a movement to include southwest Virginia in a "Greater Franklin," an effort strongly opposed by Patrick Henry, the state's governor, and other prominent Virginians. Still, Franklin came very close to winning its case. It failed by only one vote in Congress from becoming the country's fourteenth state.

This defeat, the number of anti-Franklinites led by John Tipton opposing the effort, and a clever pardon offer made by the North Carolina government eventually doomed the Franklin movement. It was only left for Sevier's ultimately unsuccessful siege of Tipton's farm in the so-called battle of the State of Franklin, fought in a snowstorm at the end of February 1788, to leave Franklin stillborn. Sevier's term as governor ended March 1, 1788, a day after the skirmish, in which two men were killed and six wounded. He did not seek reelection, and no one could be found who was willing to take his place. Thus, the pioneering attempt at state making ended less than five years after it began.

The repercussions of this attempt had a permanent impact on subsequent American political history and the system for creating new states. The "dangerous example" showed the Founding Fathers that a specific method for state making needed to be included in the United States Constitution, drafted the same year Franklin failed. Otherwise, confusion, conflict, and even bloodshed would not be avoided in the future. The Civil War awaited that generation who forgot the lessons Franklin taught.

Following Franklin's collapse, North Carolina in 1789 ceded the land that became Tennessee to the United States government, which in turn created the Territory South of the River Ohio in 1790 to administer it. This prepared the way for a peaceful transition to statehood for Tennessee in 1796. John Sevier, Franklin's only governor, became Tennessee's first.

See also: EARLY WHITE SETTLEMENT OF EAST TENNESSEE (SETTLEMENT AND MIGRATION); SEVIER, JOHN (SETTLEMENT AND MIGRATION).

—Ned L. Irwin, *East Tennessee State University*

James William Hagy, "Democracy Defeated: The Frankland Constitution of 1785," *Tennessee Historical Quarterly* (Fall 1981); Ned L. Irwin, "The Lost Papers of the 'Lost State of Franklin,'" *Journal of East Tennessee History* (1997); Samuel Cole Williams, *History of the Lost State of Franklin* (1924; revised 1933).

Suffrage

Woman suffrage became the law of the land in the United States in 1920. By ratifying the Nineteenth Amendment to the U.S. Constitution, six of the thirteen states in the Appalachian region—New York, Pennsylvania, Ohio, Kentucky, West Virginia, and Tennessee—contributed to this victory. Tennessee achieved celebrity status as the thirty-sixth state to ratify, the last needed to assure women the right to vote. Four of these states had already passed woman suffrage in some form before 1920. Kentucky granted woman suffrage in school elections as early as 1838, New York granted full suffrage to women in 1917, and in 1919 both Ohio and Tennessee granted suffrage to women for presidential elections. Maryland, Virginia, North Carolina, South Carolina, Georgia, Alabama, and Mississippi remained opposed to woman suffrage.

The fight for woman suffrage, which lasted from the mid-nineteenth century to 1920, was organized into individual state movements tied together at the national level after 1913 by the National American Woman Suffrage Association. Many early leaders developed organizing and public speaking skills through the abolition movement, but the later growth of the suffrage movement is attributed to the influences of industrialization and urbanization. These developments, which occurred most rapidly in the northern and midwestern areas of the nation, contributed to the growth of a class of women with sufficient leisure time to organize and question women's roles in society. Additionally, many of the negative social effects of industrialization fostered a reformist culture among this class of women that brought familiarity with government and public action for change.

State studies of woman suffrage rarely focus on activities in Appalachia, making it difficult to trace any distinctly Appalachian participation in these movements. But the regional pattern of support for suffrage evident in West Virginia, the suffrage movement of which has been studied in some detail, mirrors the division on the issue evident in the area's ratification votes.

In West Virginia, the suffrage movement came earliest and remained strongest in the most urban commercial, transportation, mining, and manufacturing centers of the northern and western parts of the state. By the 1890s, suffragists began to form local clubs, hosting traveling pro-suffrage speakers sponsored by national organizations. Groups continued to expand in the next two decades but remained consistently strong only in the northern and western areas of the state. That regional concentration of support was painfully reflected in a 1916 state referendum, which failed nearly three to one. Only five counties, all of which were industrial and commercial centers in the northern and western region bordering Ohio, Pennsylvania, and Kentucky, voted in favor of or split nearly evenly on woman suffrage.

The strongest votes against suffrage, between 80 and 90 percent, occurred in the most isolated, rural south-central counties and in the counties along the southern and eastern borders, where ties to the former Confederacy were strong. The eastern counties resisted suffrage based on traditional conservative attitudes, and anti-suffrage speakers there frequently associated woman suffrage with the dangerously radical movements of feminism and socialism. Commentary also alluded to the effect of woman suffrage on enfranchisement for blacks, though this was a much less publicly debated position.

In the most rural areas, poor transportation and a general lack of economic development also kept residents isolated from the speakers and organizing that fostered activity in other parts of the state. Many of those opposed to woman suffrage emphasized traditional religious views of woman's proper role in society and the family, and their language also reflected suspicion of the urban, reformist associations of many of the pro-suffrage leaders.

As noted, the West Virginia pattern appeared on a larger scale throughout Appalachia: northern and western states in the Appalachian region—New York, Pennsylvania, Ohio, West Virginia, Kentucky, and Tennessee—supported woman suffrage, while the eastern and southern states—Maryland, Virginia, North Carolina, South Carolina, Georgia, Alabama, and Mississippi—opposed it. This parallel suggests that voters in the Appalachian areas of these states shared the majority views on woman suffrage reflected in ratification votes. Confirmation of this suggestion, however, must be left to future research, as the history of woman suffrage for most of Appalachia has yet to be written.

See also: FELTON, REBECCA LATIMER; GENDER AND REFORM IN THE PROGRESSIVE ERA; WOMEN AS EDUCATIONAL LEADERS (EDUCATION).

—Anne B. W. Effland, *U.S. Department of Agriculture*

Anne Wallace Effland, "'Exciting Battle and Dramatic Finish': West Virginia's Ratification of the Nineteenth Amendment,"

The Tennessee Valley Authority's Norris Dam, Norris, Tennessee, c. 1937. By producing hydroelectric power and controlling seasonal flooding of the Tennessee River, the Norris Dam and others like it in the TVA system had a broad impact on life throughout the entire Tennessee Valley region.

West Virginia History (1989); Eleanor Flexner, *Century of Struggle: The Woman's Rights Movement in the United States* (1975).

Tennessee Valley Authority

For much of Appalachia, the Tennessee Valley Authority (TVA) was the most important of all the New Deal agencies created in response to the Great Depression, and it has been widely regarded as one of the landmark accomplishments of Franklin D. Roosevelt's presidency. Though TVA was also envisioned as a prototype for regional development elsewhere, it was primarily created to end the flooding of the Tennessee River, provide electricity, conserve the region's resources, and to improve the quality of life of citizens in the impoverished, predominantly rural Tennessee Valley. But as the agency evolved and energy-intensive industry was attracted to the region, TVA concentrated increasingly on power production. Over time, the resulting strategies and technologies contributed to air and water pollution, the destruction of the landscape in central Appalachia, and the eventual disillusionment of longtime supporters. Once a beacon of progressive and successful regional development and creative federalism, TVA is now generally viewed by political, scholarly, and environmental critics, consumer activists, and customers as a mix of successes and failures.

Roosevelt's legislation establishing the agency was sent to Congress on April 10, 1933, and the act was signed into law on May 18, precipitating an avalanche of reform bills. The effort to harness America's fifth-largest river had already been a subject of federal interest and debate for decades. As early as 1824, Secretary of War John C. Calhoun had proposed that the national government improve navigation on the river. The need for rapid expansion of nitrate production for weapons during World War I finally led the government to begin construction of the Muscle Shoals Dam in northern Alabama in 1916. After the war, industrialist Henry Ford sought to purchase the dam and associated facilities, but political and public opposition prevented the deal. Led by Republican Senator George Norris of Nebraska, Congress twice passed legislation authorizing expansion of the Muscle Shoals facilities and construction of additional flood-control dams. The bills, passed in 1928 and 1931, were vetoed by Presidents Calvin Coolidge and Herbert Hoover, respectively.

The Tennessee Valley Authority Act of 1933 called for the federal government to finance, plan, and carry out broad revitalization of the Tennessee Valley region by constructing a series of dams employing the Tennessee's potential for generating electricity while preventing chronic flooding and opening it to commercial navigation. The legislation included 42,000 square miles of the river's watershed in parts of seven states—Alabama, Georgia, Kentucky, Mississippi, North Carolina, Tennessee, and Virginia. Approximately two million people lived in the area in 1933. After years of piecemeal flood-control projects on tributary streams, the United States invested $300 million in TVA projects, building eight dams along the river's 652-mile course from Knoxville, Tennessee, to its confluence with the Ohio River at Paducah, Kentucky. By 1945 the number of dams on the Tennessee and its major tributaries had been doubled, with thousands of people put to work in the process.

Taming the river had immediate and far-reaching consequences for the region's economy and living conditions. Before TVA, 97 percent of the valley's residents lived without electricity; by 1955, 90 percent of the area's households had electrical service. Electrification and the arrival of wartime industry had set the stage for continued industrial growth. Moreover, nutrition and health had been vastly improved across the region. The scourge of malaria, for example, had been virtually eradicated. The river itself had been transformed into the efficient commercial waterway that visionaries had foreseen for generations. With economic development and conservation, the early TVA also sought to provide the visual aesthetic of well-managed land. The new discipline of landscape architecture brought cohesive form to TVA projects and impressed Americans with its attention to appearance.

But the agency's potential to accomplish broader cultural goals envisioned by Roosevelt and Norris was stifled by conflicting views and infighting among its leadership, beginning in its earliest years. Arthur E. Morgan, the first chair of the governing board of directors, was a former president of Antioch College in Tennessee and a visionary engineer with extensive experience in river management. While he sought to make TVA "a picture of the world as it might be," the other two members of the board favored more concrete, less utopian objectives. Together, Harcourt A. Morgan, an agriculturist and former president of the University of Tennessee, and David E. Lilienthal, a veteran of the Wisconsin Public Service Commission, were able to prevail over the chairman. Lilienthal secured an agreement to give each board member control over a major TVA initiative. Accordingly, Arthur Morgan assumed control over the construction program, Harcourt Morgan over agriculture and forestry, and Lilienthal over power production. Arthur Morgan continued to promote a cultural agenda including better education, improved labor relations, town planning, model communities, and expanded health care. Harcourt Morgan and Lilienthal emphasized economic initiatives—agricultural assistance and improvements to individual living standards—that generated strong grassroots support. To end the increasingly contentious relations between the three board members, Roosevelt dismissed Arthur Morgan in March 1938, making Harcourt Morgan chairman, and filling the vacancy with James P. Pope, a former U.S. senator from Idaho. Following Morgan's departure, Lilienthal emerged as the most powerful influence on TVA's course until the mid-1940s. Manifested in various ways, the philosophical issues that divided the original board remained with the TVA for the rest of the century.

Despite the advances that came with control of the river, many people in the valley paid a personal price for the agency's accomplishments. Directly affected were farm families forced to relocate from land inundated by the lakes created from the damming of the river. Some of the most fertile farmland in the valley was lost to flooding, and the displaced owners usually could find no comparable soil in their area. Discouraged by the agricultural depression of the 1930s, many farmers willingly sold their holdings at minimal prices due to the national economic collapse. In some cases, families intent on holding onto their land were forced off of generational homesteads. In other cases, such as the highly praised model town constructed as a refuge for displaced people in Norris, Tennessee, TVA officials were forced to expend great effort to relieve the social and cultural upheaval they caused. In the Norris example, however, those without the capital to purchase homesites in the community were not helped by such efforts.

To the disappointment of African Americans living in the Tennessee River Valley, TVA made few efforts to challenge racism in the region. Since it was dependent upon congressional support—particularly from powerful senators and House committee chairmen from the South—the agency was under constant pressure to maintain racial segregation. Its leadership acquiesced, as did leaders of other federal agencies in the South and elsewhere. Although TVA employed African Americans in proportion to their presence in the valley's population, most were assigned to menial jobs. In May 1942, only one of nineteen hundred TVA carpenters was black while virtually all of the custodians were. Blacks were segregated in company towns in inferior locations with inadequate schools. But in some instances, TVA leadership refused to countenance open discrimination. Despite violent protests by whites, for instance, the construction community near Fontana Dam in North Carolina was forced to accept black workers.

The advent of World War II dramatically changed the agency, as power production became its overwhelming priority. At Oak Ridge, Tennessee, a secret government complex for enriching uranium for the atomic bomb became TVA's most important customer. Soon after the war came new high-priority missile and aerospace installations at Huntsville, Alabama, Tullahoma, Tennessee, and elsewhere. Already recognizing that hydroelectric power sources would be inadequate for industrial development in the future, TVA turned to coal-fired "steam plants," and by the mid-1950s such plants were generating more electricity than the mighty dams on the river. In 1959 Congress gave new impetus to power production, passing the Bond Revenue Act granting TVA authority to sell bonds (and take on debt) for expansion of its facilities. Until then, the agency had relied upon congressional appropriations and its own revenues for such funds. With the new law, its power programs proceeded with far less oversight from Washington.

To fuel the increasing demands of their fossil-fueled boilers, TVA directors made huge purchases of mineral rights in Appalachia. By 1975 the agency owned 375 million tons of coal reserves in southeastern Kentucky and eastern Tennessee. In time, most of its coal came from these reserves, where surface mining rapidly replaced old-fashioned underground coal digging. Beginning in western Kentucky and advancing into the Appalachians, strip miners under contract to TVA extracted coal at a fraction of the cost of underground mining, enabling the government utility to maintain historically low electric rates. In addition to mining its own reserves, TVA began to buy large amounts of coal from private companies, negotiating supply agreements extending for as long as thirty years in order to ensure price stability. In an attempt to remain competitive, the private companies promptly resorted to surface mining as well, replacing legions of miners with increasingly efficient diesel-powered machines. By 1970 fully 80 percent of TVA's electricity was being generated by coal-fired boilers.

Anticipating sustained growth in the demand for electricity, officials in 1965 made a fateful commitment to nuclear power, mistakenly believing that the atom offered the agency its most profitable and dependable longterm option. Planning documents forecast that nuclear plants would generate most of TVA's power as early as 1985. Using its authority to take on massive bonded indebtedness, the agency began to build nuclear plants—Browns Ferry and Bellefonte in Alabama and Sequoyah, Watts Bar, and Hartsville in Tennessee. Tightened safety regulations, environmental opposition, and increasing technological sophistication dramatically increased costs in the construction of these plants. Overruns forced abandonment of four other nuclear plants that were still in the planning stage, causing a loss of more than a billion dollars. In addition, the partially constructed Bellefonte and Hartsville plants were cancelled. The policy disaster caused the cost of TVA power to rise sharply, angering consumers and bringing a deluge of criticism from local, state, and federal political officials.

Afterward, critics of the agency's environmental record became more vocal on a variety of issues, and criticism intensified as the twentieth century drew to a close. The organization created with conservation as one of its touchstones found itself targeted not only by environmental activists but also by the federal Environmental Protection Agency, which cited it for high-temperature water releases at its nuclear facilities and for excessive sulfur dioxide releases from coal-burning plants. TVA reached agreements on both issues only after contentious public debates and growing public pressure from regional and national environmental groups.

In late 2002, despite easing of Environmental Protection Agency emission rules for older power plants, TVA announced a $1.5-billion contract award to construct and install smokestack scrubbers in several of its coal-fired power plants in Tennessee, Alabama, and Kentucky to control pollution. All of the scrubbers, which remove the contaminate sulfur dioxide from the plants' emissions, were expected to be operating by 2011. TVA's eleven coal-fired power plants released six hundred thousand tons of sulfur dioxide in 2001, but the new equipment was designed to reduce that amount by two hundred thousand tons per year.

Public controversy arose in 2003 when the TVA-owned Watts Bar Nuclear Plant, located fifty miles southwest of Knoxville, became the nation's new source of tritium, a hydrogen isotope that enhances the explosive force of thermonuclear weapons. Despite objections from environmental groups and concerned citizens, the government struck a deal with TVA to produce about 1.5 to 3 kilograms of tritium annually for the next four decades, making Watts Bar the only commercial nuclear station in the country to produce both electricity for homes and isotopes for weapons.

Water projects were no longer sacrosanct. During the mid- and late 1970s, controversy over the construction of the Tellico Dam near Knoxville reached the U.S. Supreme Court. After discovery of an endangered species, the snail darter, in the stream to be impounded by the dam, the high court ruled that the project could not be completed. This prompted legislative intervention by Tennessee Senator Howard Baker and U.S. Representative John Duncan of Knoxville, creating an exception allowing TVA to complete the dam and reservoir.

After nearly seventy years of existence, TVA's evolution had taken it far from its New Deal roots, leaving it in many ways very similar to the private utilities that once bitterly opposed its creation.

See also: CIVILIAN CONSERVATION CORPS; MUSCLE SHOALS POWER (BUSINESS, INDUSTRY, AND TECHNOLOGY); NEW DEAL COMMUNITIES (FAMILY AND COMMUNITY).

—Brian Black, *Pennsylvania State University at Altoona*

Brian Black, "Organic Planning: Ecology and Design in the Landscape of TVA," in *Environmentalism in Landscape Architecture*, ed. Michael Conan (2000); Erwin C. Hargrove, *Prisoners of Myth: The Leadership of the Tennessee Valley Authority, 1933–1990* (1994); David E. Whisnant, *Modernizing the Mountaineer: People, Power, and Planning in Appalachia* (1980).

Thomas's Legion

Thomas's Legion of Indians and Highlanders, also known as the North Carolina Sixty-ninth Regiment, served in the Confederate Army from April 9, 1862, until the end of the Civil War. William Holland Thomas, a civilian businessman, Democratic member of the state senate from 1848 to 1861, member of the North Carolina secession convention, and full-blooded white chief of the Eastern Band of Cherokee Indians in North Carolina from 1839 to 1867, organized the regiment primarily to protect his Cherokee friends and to function as a home guard in eastern Tennessee and western North Carolina.

When the Civil War began, Thomas raised a company of two hundred Cherokees to protect their section of the state, calling them the Junaluska Zouaves. He accepted numerous more volunteers until September 1862, when General John P. McCowan named him colonel. Thomas was commander over more than two thousand officers and men distributed among eleven companies of infantry (two of these companies were Cherokee), eight companies of cavalry, and one light battery of artillery. Primarily responsible for guarding railroad bridges and mountain passes, the regiment saw action in Tennessee at Baptist Gap, September 13–15, 1862, and Sevierville, November 1863, and at Deep Creek, North Carolina, February 1864. Governor Zebulon Vance and General Alfred E. Jackson had Thomas court-martialed three times for taking in Cherokee deserters, but Confederate President Jefferson Davis pardoned him. Command passed from Thomas to James R. Love II on September 1, 1863. Thomas's Legion disbanded in early May of 1865, after the Confederate surrender in April.

See also: CHEROKEE (RACE, ETHNICITY, AND IDENTITY); CIVIL WAR; VANCE, ZEBULON.

—E. Stanly Godbold Jr., *Mississippi State University*

Vernon H. Crow, *Storm in the Mountains: Thomas's Confederate Legion of Indians and Mountaineers* (1982); John R. Finger, *The Eastern Band of Cherokees, 1819–1900* (1984); E. Stanly Godbold Jr. and Mattie U. Russell, *Confederate Colonel and Cherokee Chief: The Life of William Holland Thomas* (1990).

Tom Dula Murder Trial

On May 25, 1866, Laura Foster of Wilkes County, North Carolina, one of several girlfriends of Thomas Dula, was murdered near her home. Foster's body was not located for three months, but Dula came under immediate suspicion following her disappearance. Four weeks after Foster disappeared, he fled to a neighboring county in Tennessee. Authorities arrested him there and returned him to Wilkesboro.

Dula's lead attorney was former Governor Zebulon Vance, who persuaded the court to transfer the trial to Statesville. The most damaging pieces of evidence against Dula were his statements that he would kill the person who gave him syphilis and that Foster had infected him. In addition, he was seen in the area near her grave with a digging tool on the day of the murder. The state also claimed that Dula was involved in a conspiracy with another girlfriend—Ann Melton—to commit the murder. The jury found him guilty, but the verdict was overturned by the state supreme court. A second trial resulted in the same verdict, and Dula was hanged in Statesville on May 1, 1868. On the evening before his death, Dula wrote a note exonerating Melton of the murder.

According to tradition, Dula composed a lament on his way to his execution. This song was preserved by the Proffitt family and recorded by the Library of Congress. The song was adapted by the Kingston Trio in the late 1950s, and "Tom Dooley" became one of the signature ballads in the national folk music revival of the 1950s and 1960s.

See also: BALLADS (MUSIC); PROFFITT, FRANK, SR. (MUSIC).

—Gordon B. McKinney, *Berea College*

Treaty of Hopewell

The Treaty of Hopewell marked the first treaty between the Cherokee Indians and the new republic of the United States. Signed November 28, 1785, in the northwest corner of South Carolina on the family plantation home of General Andrew Pickens, a militia commander and later a member of the South Carolina General Assembly, the agreement brought peace between most Cherokees and white Americans, although the Chickamauga Cherokees continued to fight until 1794. Significantly, the tribe did not cede more land, though it recognized that which had been lost earlier. In exchange for this recognition, the Cherokees were to receive one thousand dollars annually, the first of many annuities promised them.

The Cherokees made several crucial concessions. They agreed that the United States would have sole control over trade and authority for "managing all their affairs." For many whites, this phrase suggested that the Cherokees had given up their sovereignty. The treaty also stipulated that the Cherokees were not to make agreements with foreign nations or individual states. Furthermore, the Cherokees were placed under the protection of the federal government, which would send an agent to live among them.

Even during the treaty negotiations, North Carolina and Georgia protested against the Cherokees' being allowed to keep land already assigned in bounty claims to Americans who had fought in the Continental Army. In most cases the United States government was unable to evict whites already settled on land acknowledged by the treaty as belonging to the Cherokees. The government's failure to live up to treaty commitments and the desire for more land necessitated the Treaty of Holston six years later.

See also: CHEROKEE (RACE, ETHNICITY, AND IDENTITY); CHEROKEE CONSTITUTION OF 1827; TRAIL OF TEARS (SETTLEMENT AND MIGRATION).

—William L. Anderson, *Western Carolina University*

Vance, Zebulon

(1830–1894) Governor and U.S. senator.

Zebulon Baird Vance was born on May 13, 1830, into an elite family in Buncombe County, North Carolina. He was elected to the state legislature as a Whig in 1854, and in 1858 he was elected to the U.S. House of Representatives in a special election and easily reelected in 1859. Vance possessed an effective campaign style that featured crude good humor.

In 1861 Vance actively opposed secession, but he became an enthusiastic supporter of the Confederacy after the shelling of Fort Sumter. He was elected colonel of the Twenty-sixth North Carolina Regiment and came under enemy fire at the battles of New Bern and Malvern Hill. In 1862 Vance was overwhelmingly elected governor of North Carolina. He requested that state and Confederate troops be stationed in North Carolina's mountain counties to deal with the growing disaffection and violence taking place in that section. Vance was reelected by a wide margin against a peace candidate in 1864.

Vance was arrested in May 1865 and remained in jail in Washington until July of that year. He was pardoned in 1867 and quickly plunged back into politics. In 1870 he was elected to the U.S. Senate, but the Radical Republicans refused to let him take his seat. Vance was elected governor of North Carolina in 1876 in a famous campaign against Republican candidate Thomas Settle. During his term in office, Vance put many of the state's resources into the construction of the Western North Carolina Railroad into the mountain counties. In 1879 he was again elected to the Senate, where he served until his death on April 14, 1894.

Zebulon Vance, c. 1880. Appalachian-born governor of North Carolina during the Civil War and later a U.S. senator, Vance initially opposed secession but following the attack on Fort Sumter became an enthusiastic supporter of the Confederacy.

See also: CIVIL WAR; SHELTON LAUREL MASSACRE; TOM DULA MURDER TRIAL.

—Gordon B. McKinney, *Berea College*

Vinson, Fred M.

(1890–1953) Chief justice of the U.S. Supreme Court.

Born in the mountain town of Louisa, Kentucky, Fredrick Moore Vinson rose from part-time city attorney in his birthplace to hold numerous federal positions before ending his career and his life as the thirteenth chief justice of the United States. During World War II and its aftermath, the White House called upon Vinson for important assignments so often that he acquired the nickname "Available Vinson." In 1943 he resigned a lifetime appointment as an associate justice of the federal Court of Appeals for the District of Columbia to serve in a succession of leadership posts in wartime agencies, including those of director of the Office of Economic Stabilization and director of the Office of War Mobilization. In 1945 President Harry Truman named him to his cabinet as secretary of the treasury, and the following year he succeeded Chief Justice Harlan Stone on the United States Supreme Court.

An outstanding athlete in both high school and college, Vinson considered playing professional baseball, but upon graduation from Centre College at Danville, Kentucky, he proceeded to Centre's law school. While practicing law back in Louisa, he was appointed to fill a vacant seat in the U.S. House of Representatives. The following year, 1924, he won a special election and remained a member of the state's congressional delegation until 1938, except for the 1929–31 term following his defeat in the 1928 Republican landslide led by Herbert Hoover. Membership on the House Ways and Means Committee enabled Vinson to have an important voice in legislation important to his state's coal, tobacco, and liquor industries and to play a role in the passage of the Social Security Act in 1935.

In nominating Vinson as chief justice, Truman hoped that the Kentuckian's leadership could unify a Supreme Court troubled by personal differences among several associate justices. It was generally conceded that Vinson failed to do that, and his harshest critics considered him a failure as chief justice. Vinson's most notable opinions were those upholding the federal government's right to bar a strike in coal mines (then under federal control), affirming the rights of racial minorities, and dissenting from the majority's decision invalidating President Truman's 1952 "seizure" of strike-threatened steel mills. The historic school desegregation decision, *Brown v. Board of Education*, remained for the Supreme Court to decide under Vinson's successor, Earl Warren.

Vinson died of a heart attack at his residence in Washington on September 8, 1953. After funeral services at Washington National Cathedral and in Louisa, he was buried in the town cemetery, across the square from the small house where he was born while his father was serving as jailer of Lawrence County.

—Rudy Abramson, *Reston, Virginia*

Vinton, Samuel F.

(1792–1862) U.S. congressman.

Samuel F. Vinton represented southeastern Ohio for eleven terms in the United States House of Representatives before the Civil War, advocating Senator Henry Clay's American System of protective tariffs, internal improvements, and banks as a way to develop the region. Born in South Hadley, Massachusetts, of a farming family, he attended Williams College and read law in the office of Stephen Titus Hosmer. Following admission to the bar, he moved to Gallipolis, Ohio, in 1816 to establish his practice.

Better trained than most western lawyers, Vinton successfully argued cases in other states and before the U.S. Supreme Court. He invested his earnings in regional enterprises such as mines, banks, real estate, and railroads, and in 1822 he was elected to Congress, serving from 1823 to 1837 and, following a brief retirement, from 1843 to 1851. He was a follower of President John Quincy Adams and Senator Clay and, after its formation in 1834, the Whig Party. He proposed letting states sell their school lands to establish trust funds to benefit public education, forming a cabinet-level Department of the Interior, and raising the tariff to pay Mexican War expenses.

Disliked by antislavery Whigs because he preferred sectional and party harmony to the championing of abolition, he was crushingly defeated when he ran for governor of Ohio in 1851. He is remembered principally for his devotion to Whig economic principles as a way to improve his community.

See also: WHIG PARTY.

—Phyllis F. Field, *Ohio University*

War on Poverty

Although the federal government's "War on Poverty" was conceived as the centerpiece of President Lyndon Johnson's national social agenda, the initiative was significantly inspired by stark and intensely publicized economic conditions in central Appalachia in the 1960s. Three months after declaring "unconditional war on poverty" in his 1964 State of the Union address, Johnson traveled to Martin County, Kentucky, and launched his public campaign for the program. His appearance in eastern Kentucky provided the defining and enduring image of the entire effort. Serving as the president's backdrop was the front porch of Tom Fletcher, a chronically unemployed coal miner and sawmill worker with eight children.

The Johnson poverty program had roots in John F. Kennedy's 1960 campaign, as West Virginia provided the crucial victory in his quest for the Democratic presidential nomination. Thereafter, dire economic circumstances in the coalfields led to massive national publicity about poverty in the region, particularly in eastern Kentucky. One of the first initiatives in what eventually came to be generally understood as the War on Poverty was the Area Redevelopment Act, signed by Kennedy in May 1961, providing loans, technical assistance, and funds for public facilities in depressed areas, Appalachia prominently among them.

Responding to Johnson's vow to eliminate poverty, Congress adopted the Economic Opportunity Act (Public Law 88-452) in August 1964, creating the Office of Economic Opportunity and mandating it to coordinate government-wide antipoverty efforts. Initiatives included vocational training, work-study programs for disadvantaged college students, adult literacy efforts, and the organization of foster grandparents to work with neglected and handicapped children. More conspicuous were Volunteers in Service to America (VISTA), viewed as a "domestic" Peace Corps; Head Start, a program for preschoolers; and the Community Action Program, designed for maximum citizen participation and viewed as the heart of the crusade.

But in Appalachia and elsewhere, the War on Poverty came under attack by critics who found it wasteful, politically motivated welfare. Forced to make compromises from the beginning, the Johnson administration had to drop plans for expensive programs designed to generate immediate employment.

Political controversy, budget demands of the Vietnam War, and flaws still debated undermined the Office of Economic Opportunity, and ten years after its creation it was dead. A significant number of its programs, including Head Start, continued into the twenty-first century, however, even though the United States turned sharply away from the liberal social activism that inspired the War on Poverty. In Appalachia, some of the most important antipoverty efforts were carried on outside of the galaxy of Office of Economic Opportunity programs. Among them were the far-reaching efforts of the Appalachian Regional Commission, created by the Appalachian Regional Development Act, and programs of the Elementary and Secondary Education Act, both adopted in 1965.

From the beginning, architects of the War on Poverty considered educational improvement to be one of its bedrock objectives. In addition to Head Start, a number of other education programs created by the Economic Opportunity Act continued to function in Appalachia four decades later—among them Adult Basic Education, the Job Corps, and Community Action. The Appalachian Regional Commission's continuing education activities included construction and equipping of about seven hundred vocational schools, support of teacher education through an Appalachian Education Satellite Program, and the delivery of coursework to students. Although school consolidation was not one of the objectives of the War on Poverty, the initiative nevertheless led to larger schools and school districts.

In retrospect, many scholars, including some of its creators, concluded that the decade-long War on Poverty had been a failure. Although some activists in the Johnson administration believed that the elimination of poverty was possible, others believed the program had misunderstood and distorted the real nature and causes of poverty. For example, Saul Alinsky, a famous community organizer, dismissed it as nothing more than "political pornography." In any case, poverty remains a problem in American society, and it continues to be manifest in Appalachia.

See also: APPALACHIAN REGIONAL COMMISSION; WEST VIRGINIA 1960 DEMOCRATIC PRESIDENTIAL PRIMARY.

—Craig B. Howley, *Ohio University and Appalachia Educational Laboratory*

Daniel Patrick Moynihan, *Maximum Feasible Misunderstanding: Community Action in the War on Poverty* (1969); Lana Muraskin, *Education in Appalachia: Accomplishments and Prospects in a National Context* (1991); David E. Whisnant, *Modernizing the Mountaineer: People, Power, and Planning in Appalachia* (1980).

Weeks Act

The Weeks Act of 1911 provided the first legal justification for the purchase of land by the federal government for forest reserves east of the Mississippi River. The act grew out of concerns in the southern Appalachian region and in New England during the Progressive Era over destructive logging practices in the eastern forests and the resultant deforestation, wildfires, and flooding.

The earliest organized movement to lobby and encourage the United States Congress to establish forest reserves in the East began with the organization of the Appalachian National Park Association in Asheville, North Carolina, in 1899. This group later joined forces with the Appalachian Mountain Club and the American Forestry Association to lobby Congress to purchase forest reserves.

A number of congressmen opposed the act on states' rights and constitutional grounds, arguing that the U.S. Constitution did not allow Congress to purchase land for the purpose of protecting forests. Indeed, House Speaker Joseph Cannon asserted that Congress would spend "not one cent for scenery."

Supporters of the act, including Gifford Pinchot, director of the U.S. Forest Service, argued that purchase of forest reserves would prevent flooding and protect the navigability of rivers, a power designated to Congress under the Commerce Clause. Congress finally passed the Appalachian–White Mountains Forest Reservation Bill in 1911, largely due to the efforts of Representative John W. Weeks of Massachusetts. The so-called Weeks Act authorized the federal government to purchase lands to be "permanently reserved, held and administered as national forest lands" for protection, development, and use of their natural resources. Weeks is known as the "Father of the Eastern National Forest System."

The first land purchased under the Weeks Act was a tract on Curtis Creek in McDowell County, North Carolina. Almost all lands currently under the management of the U.S. Forest Service in the Appalachian Mountains were purchased under the authorization of the Weeks Act and by the amendment to it, the Clarke-McNary Act of 1924.

See also: CHEROKEE NATIONAL FOREST (TOURISM); FOREST MANAGEMENT AND CONSERVATION (ENVIRONMENT); MONONGAHELA NATIONAL FOREST (TOURISM); NANTAHALA NATIONAL FOREST (TOURISM).

—Daniel S. Pierce, *University of North Carolina at Asheville*

West Virginia Board of Education v. Barnette

West Virginia Board of Education v. Barnette (1943) was a landmark United States Supreme Court decision that significantly affected America's classrooms and limited the ability of all institutions to enforce citizen compliance in certain areas. Following the Supreme Court's decision in *Minersville School District v. Gobitis* (1940) upholding the right of local school districts to compel children to salute the American flag, the West Virginia State Board of Education ordered daily flag exercises in all public, private, and parochial schools. The board treated refusal to participate in the compulsory flag salute as insubordination punishable by expulsion. When a number of Jehovah's Witness schoolchildren resisted the flag decree, citing the biblical proscription against worshipping graven images, they were expelled and threatened with confinement in reformatories. Their parents, including Walter Barnette, won an injunction from the federal district court in Charleston, prompting a board appeal based on *Gobitis*. The board, however, faced a Supreme Court whose philosophical ground had shifted.

Presidential candidate John F. Kennedy speaks to a crowd in the Welch Municipal Parking Building during the 1960 Democratic primary campaign, Welch, West Virginia, 1960. When Kennedy, a Roman Catholic, won the primary in this overwhelmingly Protestant, Bible Belt Appalachian state, it was a turning point in his quest for the presidency.

Justices Hugo Black, William O. Douglas, and Frank Murphy, who had sided with the majority in *Gobitis* on the basis of deference to local officials' prerogative, had since elevated the First Amendment to primacy in the constitutional hierarchy. In *Jones v. Opelika* (1942) they rejected compulsory flag salutes, joining lone *Gobitis* dissenter, Harlan Stone, in a five-four minority. By the time *Barnette* was decided, Justices Robert Jackson and Wiley Rutledge had joined the *Opelika* dissenters and the West Virginia flag decree was overturned, six to three. Jackson wrote the opinion, declaring that no state could prescribe orthodoxy or force citizen compliance in matters of politics, nationalism, religion, or "other matters of opinion."

See also: SCOPES TRIAL (RELIGION).

—John C. Hennen, *Morehead State University*

West Virginia 1960 Democratic Presidential Primary

The 1960 democratic presidential primary in West Virginia, sometimes called "the primary that made a president," pitted Senator Hubert H. Humphrey of Minnesota against Senator John F. Kennedy of Massachusetts. Kennedy's victory helped to consolidate his position with party liberals and to counteract the notion that southerners would not vote for a Roman Catholic.

Well funded as well as possessing great personal wealth, Kennedy enjoyed several advantages over the financially strapped Humphrey. Kennedy's brain trust, led by Lawrence O'Brien, mobilized thousands of volunteers and recruited Franklin D. Roosevelt Jr. to link the young senator with the powerful legacy of the New Deal in the minds of West Virginia's working-class voters. Throughout the state, O'Brien cultivated Democratic courthouse regulars and party power brokers. Kennedy himself campaigned tirelessly, promising to battle poverty and unemployment with new jobs in a state that had lost more than 60 percent of its coal-mining employment since 1947.

The primary took on national significance because respected political observers concluded that a victory by the Roman Catholic Kennedy in a Protestant, Bible Belt state would confirm his electability in the country at large. Kennedy's internal polls suggested that his religion was largely irrelevant to West Virginia voters, but his campaign managers skillfully manipulated the issue, implying that a vote against Kennedy was a vote for religious intolerance. The tactic infuriated Humphrey supporters and campaign strategists, who had sought to avoid the religious issue altogether.

Humphrey's organization was no match for Kennedy's personal appeal and the sophistication of his primary machine. Kennedy won 60 percent of the vote on the May 10, 1960, primary day, claiming that West Virginia voters had "buried the religious issue once and for all." Humphrey withdrew from the race that night, and Kennedy went on to the nomination and the presidency.

See also: CATHOLICISM (RELIGION); SECTION OVERVIEW (RELIGION).

—John C. Hennen, *Morehead State University*

West Virginia Statehood

The creation of West Virginia was brought about by the Civil War. Statehood was preceded by decades of sectional conflict between leaders of eastern and western Virginia, but sectionalism was a staple of politics in many Appalachian states. While other states saw occasional calls for "dismemberment," that is, division into two or more states, only Virginia actually split. East Tennessee, western North Carolina, and north Georgia remained geographical descriptions; West Virginia became a state.

The process of West Virginia's formation was shaped by both the war's political and military contexts. Politically, the election of Abraham Lincoln, followed by the secession of seven Deep South states to form a southern Confederacy, precipitated a crisis in Virginia. A special convention sitting in Richmond to consider the issue seemed at first to favor keeping Virginia in the Union. However, when Confederates attacked Fort Sumter on April 12 and President Lincoln called on the states for volunteers to suppress the rebellion, the Richmond convention approved secession by a vote of eighty-eight to fifty-five—with delegates from counties later included in West Virginia casting twenty-eight of the negative votes. In theory, secession would not take effect until voters had ratified it in the regular spring election on May 23, but authorities began acting as though the matter were settled. State officials called county militias into state service in early May and directed them to gather at key railroad junctions such as Grafton. Many local officials, even in western Virginia, went along with these actions, despite the fact that Virginia had not officially joined the Confederacy. The exception was in the Wheeling area, where local government continued to function and young men left the state militia to form companies of Union volunteers.

Unionist leaders rallied in Clarksburg on April 22 and summoned their own convention to meet in Wheeling on May 13. Initially, they concentrated on defeating the secession ordinance at the polls, but when this failed they debated other options. Meanwhile, Federal troops crossed the Ohio River and joined with Unionist Virginia volunteers to push Confederate forces back from Grafton and eventually—at the battle of Rich Mountain on July 11—from the entire northwest corner of the state. A parallel invasion in the Kanawha Valley followed shortly. The swift Union conquest gave pro-Union politicians a safe place to deliberate, in contrast to east Tennessee, where, despite a large Unionist majority, activists were by this time going underground or fleeing northward for their lives.

The Second Wheeling Convention met in June 1861 to consider western Virginia's options. Some leaders wanted to proceed directly to the formation of a new state; others thought it unwise to take such a step during wartime. A third group, led by Waitman T. Willey of Morgantown, effected a compromise whereby the Unionist remnant of Virginia's government was reconstituted as a "loyal" or "restored" state government, complete with governor, legislature, and representation in Congress. Key members of the Lincoln administration indicated their approval of this strategy but sent ambiguous signals about the notion of a new state. Nevertheless, a majority led by Willey decided to follow the complicated procedures that the U.S. Constitution requires for the formation of a new state out of the territory of another. While the Restored Virginia government under Governor Francis H. Pierpoint worked to raise troops and to restore local governments whose officials had "gone South," the Second Wheeling Convention approved a "dismemberment ordinance" in August that provided for a new state called Kanawha. This new state consisted of thirty-nine counties extending from the Kanawha Valley north and east to Randolph, Tucker, and Preston Counties. In November, a third convention assembled in Wheeling to write a constitution for the new state. This convention changed the name to West Virginia and added five more counties to the state in December and another four in April 1862, even though some of the additions were still under Confederate control. In May the Restored Virginia legislature gave dismemberment its approval, as did the U.S. Congress after the Constitutional Convention took steps to abolish slavery within the borders of the state.

President Lincoln's cabinet divided evenly on the issue of West Virginia statehood. Attorney General Edward Bates led opposition to the "revolutionary" statehood process while Treasury Secretary Salmon P. Chase defended the process as both constitutional and politically wise. Lincoln decided in favor of statehood. Countering the argument that relatively few voters had participated in the referenda that punctuated various steps of the statehood process, Lincoln pointed out that it was customary everywhere "to give no legal consideration whatever to those who do not choose to vote," for whatever reason. Following the ratification of West Virginia's antislavery amendment, in April Lincoln proclaimed West Virginia ready to take its place in the Union, which it did on June 20, 1863. Two additional counties (Berkeley and Jefferson) were transferred to the new state later that year.

The new state was constructed from blocks of counties, preserving the established borders with Kentucky, Ohio, Pennsylvania, and Maryland and creating a new border with Virginia based on existing county lines. Thus, while sectional differences and mountain barriers were often cited to justify dismemberment, the new border, in fact, cut diagonally across geographical features in many places and followed the dividing ridge between eastern and western rivers for only seventy-five miles out of four hundred. This was the only permanent boundary change to result from the Civil War.

See also: CIVIL WAR; WHEELING, WEST VIRGINIA (URBAN APPALACHIAN EXPERIENCE).

—John Alexander Williams, *Appalachian State University*

Daniel W. Crofts, *Reluctant Confederates: Upper South Unionists in the Secession Crisis* (1989); Richard O. Curry, *A House Divided: A Study of Statehood Politics and the Copperhead Movement in West Virginia* (1964).

Wheeling Bridge Case

This case, first heard by the U.S. Supreme Court in 1852, decided a major American nineteenth-century transportation issue—whether bridges for land-based traffic could block steamboats on rivers. An important concern for settlers heading west, river and railroad interests, and especially merchants at Wheeling, (West) Virginia, and Pittsburgh, the dominance of one transportation technology over another also affected states that had financed internal improvements (Pennsylvania and its Main Line Canal System) and states that had granted corporate charters to investors to build transportation improvements (Virginia and the Wheeling and Belmont Bridge Company).

In 1849 the Wheeling and Belmont Bridge Company opened a suspension span over the Ohio River at Wheeling that connected the eastern and western portions of the National Road. Built on a slope from the bluff on the Wheeling side of the river to the low-lying Wheeling Island in mid-river, the bridge's clearance over the channel was 92 feet. Steamboat owners at Pittsburgh declared that the bridge blocked their boats on high stages of water and convinced the State of Pennsylvania to sue the bridge company.

Because the dispute involved a state suing a "citizen" (the bridge company) of another state, the case was initially heard in the U.S. Supreme Court. Justice John McLean's majority opinion in *State of Pennsylvania v. Wheeling and Belmont Bridge Company* (1852) found that the bridge was a public nuisance that obstructed the river and ordered that it be removed or raised to 111 feet. Six months later Congress designated the bridge a post road, lawful at its 92-foot height. In 1854 the bridge blew down in a windstorm and was rebuilt at its original elevation. Pennsylvania brought suit again (*State of Pennsylvania v. Wheeling and Belmont Bridge Company*, 1856), and Justice Samuel Nelson, writing for the Supreme Court, held that because of the federal statute, the bridge did not constitute an obstruction to navigation on the river. Throughout the remainder of the nineteenth century and well into the twentieth century, the dimensions of the Wheeling Bridge determined the clearances of bridges across navigable rivers of the United States.

See also: NATIONAL ROAD (SETTLEMENT AND MIGRATION); WHEELING SUSPENSION BRIDGE (TRANSPORTATION).

—Elizabeth Brand Monroe, *Indiana University at Indianapolis*

Whig Party

The American Whig Party originated in the early 1830s to oppose the policies and actions of President Andrew Jackson. For years, it was the predominant party in many mountain counties of both North and South, where its members supported commercial development and improved transportation.

Assuming the name *Whig* to signify concern about the accretion of executive power by "King Andrew I," the party was initially an amalgam of anti-Jackson factions: nationalists who favored economic activism by the federal government, constitutional conservatives dismayed by Jackson's treatment of South Carolina nullifiers, and Antimasons alarmed by the influx of foreigners and the perceived power of the Roman Catholic Church. At one time the political haven of John C. Calhoun and others committed to states' rights, the Whig Party by the 1840s came to embrace the nationalism of Henry Clay and Daniel Webster.

For nearly twenty years (1832–52), during what political historians have designated the Second American Party System, Whigs contested with Jacksonian Democrats on a competitive basis. Between 1836 and 1852, the Democrats elected three presidents and the Whigs two. Control of state governments and Congress fluctuated as well. In general, Whigs favored activist governments, modernization, and economic development. Drawing inspiration from Clay's American System, they sought to promote national banking institutions, government-sponsored internal improvements, and protective tariffs. The Whig constituency included groups associated with the burgeoning market economy: merchants, manufacturers, shipping magnates, bankers, lawyers, and large agriculturalists. The Democratic Party usually drew its voters from the laboring classes, shopkeepers, and small farmers, especially those working marginal land. There were exceptions in each party, depending on factors such as local circumstances, influential newspapers, popular local leaders, and family political affiliations.

Appalachian politics mirrored the national two-party system, but there were notable contradictions to generalizations about party constituencies and voting patterns. The mountainous rural and small-town environments of eastern Kentucky, western North Carolina, east Tennessee, and southwestern and northwestern Virginia would seem to have been likely Democratic bastions. In fact, only in Virginia did the mountain electorate vote for Democratic candidates consistently. Western North Carolina and east Tennessee were solidly Whig. Only in eastern Kentucky were the two parties consistently competitive.

The Whig hegemony in east Tennessee and western North Carolina resulted from similar circumstances. Commercial interests in Asheville, Knoxville, and Chattanooga lobbied for state-supported railroads to open their regions to a broader market, but ambitious western North Carolinians and east Tennesseans were frustrated by underrepresentation in their respective state legislatures. Other similarities between the mountain Whigs in the two states were the dynamic leadership of Thomas Lanier Clingman of North Carolina and William G. "Parson" Brownlow of Tennessee.

The great political contests of the 1830s concerned banks and fiscal policy, while in the 1840s the Mexican War and the acquisition of western territories were the touchstone of party loyalty. In general, mountain Whigs supported the national party position in favoring banks and opposing "Mr. Polk's war." In the 1850s, when the slavery controversy destroyed the Whig Party, political realignment in the mountains followed patterns discernible elsewhere. Some mountain Whigs became Democrats, some joined the American, or Know-Nothing, Party, and some persisted in calling themselves Whigs. In the crisis of 1860–61, former mountain Whigs generally opposed secession and were staunchly Unionist. The Confederate capture of Fort Sumter and Abraham Lincoln's subsequent call for troops forced mountaineers to choose sides as no political issue had done previously. Some fought for the Union, some for the Confederacy, and some avoided service in either army. In the political realignment after 1865, former Union Whigs became the backbone of the Republican Party in the Appalachian states.

See also: CLINGMAN, THOMAS LANIER; DEMOCRATIC PARTY.

—Max R. Williams, *Western Carolina University*

Michael F. Holt, *The Rise and Fall of the American Whig Party* (1999); Daniel Walker Howe, *The Political Culture of the American Whigs* (1979); Charles G. Sellers Jr., "Who Were the Southern Whigs?" *American Historical Review* (January 1954).

Wilson, William L.

(1843–1900) U.S. congressman, postmaster general, and educator.

William Lyne Wilson, who introduced free rural mail delivery in the United States, was born May 3, 1843, on a farm near Smithfield, Jefferson County, (West) Virginia, to Benjamin Wilson, a teacher and farmer, and Mary Anne Whiting Lyne. A brilliant student, he graduated from Columbian College (later George Washington University) in 1860. During the Civil War, he saw heavy action as a private in the Confederate cavalry. Returning, he taught Latin at Columbian (1865–71) while studying law at night. He began practice in 1871 at Charles Town and became active in Democratic politics. Named president of West Virginia University in June 1882, three months later he accepted a nomination to run for Congress and won. He remained there until defeated in 1894. He then served (1895–97) as postmaster general under President Grover Cleveland, to whom he was a confidential advisor. After leaving the Cleveland administration, he became president of Washington and Lee University at Lexington, Virginia. He died there of tuberculosis on October 17, 1900.

Wilson won fame in Congress and the nation as a polished, informed orator. He was considered for Speaker of the House in 1891 and as a presidential prospect in 1896, had tariffs emerged as the dominant campaign issue. His political philosophy combined Jeffersonian individualism and suspicion of a large central government with Adam Smith's economics and Herbert Spencer's social Darwinism. He nevertheless voted, with reservations, for the Interstate Commerce Act of 1887, the Sherman Antitrust Act of 1890, and federal subsidies for education, all of which increased federal power. His introduction of rural free delivery during his service as postmaster general was publicly popular, but it left him uncomfortable because of its huge expense.

In Congress, Wilson was most identified with tariff reform, a burning issue dividing the political parties. He thought tariffs favored trusts, hurt consumers, agriculture, shipping, and trade, and unnecessarily taxed an overtaxed populace. He did not advocate totally free trade, however, partly because of interests supporting coal, lumber, and struggling industries in West Virginia. Working furiously, he got tariff-reduction legislation through the House, but the Senate shredded it with more than 630 amendments. Although the final bill still lowered many duties and contained a 2 percent tax on yearly gains over four thousand dollars from invested wealth (later declared unconstitutional), the Wilson-Gorman Tariff Act of 1894 was left unsigned and thus effectively vetoed by Cleveland, bitterly disappointing Wilson.

Wilson's defeat in the 1894 election resulted from the depression following the Panic of 1893, the tariff controversy, and the growth of populist and free-silver forces in his constituency. He joined the secessionist gold-standard National Democratic Party opposed to Bryan in 1896 but supported Bryan in 1900 against McKinley's expansionism following the Spanish-American War. Wilson was also a renowned advocate of North-South reconciliation and of elevating the South by forming an educated leadership.

See also: DEMOCRATIC PARTY.

—David S. Newhall, *Centre College*

Festus P. Summers, *William L. Wilson and Tariff Reform* (1953) and ed., *A Borderland Confederate* (1962) and *The Cabinet Diary of William L. Wilson, 1896–1897* (1957).

BLACK LUNG KILLS
BLACK LUNG KILLS
BLACK LUNG LAW NOW
BLACK LUNG KILLS
BLACK LUNG KILLS
BLACK LUNG LAW NOW

Health

Section Editors: Gary L. Burkett, Richard P. Mulcahy, and Pamela M. Zahorik

For decades health care has been one of the most challenging issues in American social policy, and into the twenty-first century it stands as an increasingly daunting national problem with huge political and economic implications. Historically, delivery of health-care services in rural settings has been problematic for both public and private institutions, and so it remains: portions of Appalachia continue to exemplify the gap between underserved communities and urban areas where health-care institutions form the core of thriving economies. The United States Congress has debated national health insurance many times, but advocates of a comprehensive government-mandated approach to health-care financing have never been able to surmount implacable opposition from organized medicine, the insurance industry, and citizens concerned about quality of care. The inability to bring efficiency and equity to health-care delivery and financing has had profound impacts across the nation, particularly in rural areas and especially in Appalachia. Ironically, the impasse persists in a country that spends twice as much on health care than any other developed nation and leads the world in medical research, science, technology, and specialized care. Statistics for the last one hundred years show steadily increasing life expectancy and declining maternal and infant mortality. In the course of the twentieth century, infant mortality fell from an average of 162 deaths for every 1,000 live births to around 10 in the United States, and around the world human life expectancy increased more than it had in all previous recorded history.

In important respects, Appalachia has followed these general trends. But while such figures are impressive, they are misleading. Because health statistics are generally averages, they hide disparities regarding general health, access to services, facilities, and quality of treatment. They create an illusion of national uniformity relative to health and health-care delivery. The reality is much different, and the idea that America has a single uniform medical system is fallacious. Instead, the country has two or more systems that work simultaneously but with different levels of effectiveness in rural and urban settings. Nowhere are the contrasts greater than those within Appalachia: the region has nationally known medical complexes in Birmingham, Alabama, and Pittsburgh, but it also has scores of counties without medical services that have been taken for granted for decades in much of America.

Facing page: Members and friends of the United Mine Workers of America rally at the U.S. Capitol in Washington, D.C., for federal black lung legislation, 1975. Because coal dust does not contain sharp-edged particles that cut lung tissue (as with silicosis), many physicians failed to see it as a health hazard. This attitude was changed by the combined efforts of diverse groups, including individual chapters of the Black Lung Association and UMWA Welfare and Retirement Fund.

The disparity between rural and urban health care has existed since colonial times. While residents of early New York and Philadelphia enjoyed access to trained physicians, people in remote areas relied upon folk medicine, home remedies, or medical compendiums such as John Wesley's *Primitive Physic* and William Buchan's *Domestic Medicine.* These books offered information on illness and how it could be treated. Given the state of medical knowledge at that time, however, there was actually no great difference in the efficacy of treatment or in outcomes.

This changed dramatically with the rise of modern medical science. Although breakthroughs such as the discovery of chloroform and confirmation of the germ theory came earlier, modern medicine did not emerge until after the Civil War. Between 1870 and 1900, reforms in medical education and expanding scientific knowledge ushered in a new era in which illness was effectively treated. But as these events unfolded, it was obvious that cities would benefit far more than rural areas such as backcountry Appalachia. What took root was a two-tiered system, with cities having an abundance of physicians and an extensive treatment infrastructure and rural areas suffering a chronic lack of service.

Although uneven distribution of resources was a problem across the nation, the effects were acute in Appalachia, especially in the mountainous central portion of the region. There, physical isolation and the exigencies of a coal- and timber-based economy weighed upon every aspect of life, family health and medical services included. Health care, particularly in the coalfields, was controlled by corporate policies and company management. In company-owned towns, physicians were company employees who were paid through a monthly wage deduction, or check-off, from miners' salaries. These medical plans provided office care only and limited coverage of severe conditions. Until the early 1950s, these company doctors provided the only treatment available to many of the region's rural inhabitants.

Another reason for the wide disparities in American health care was—and is—that the for-profit system forces medical practitioners to abide by the imperatives that govern all small business operators. Although group practice was introduced in the United States in the 1890s, most American physicians continued to be solo practitioners, accepting fees for services rendered. It has been long known that this fee-for-service system, avidly promoted by the American Medical Association as a means of assuring quality treatment and avoiding the "socialization" of medicine, is the most expensive way of purchasing medical care. The fee-for-service system has led to continuing concentration of both physicians and hospitals in urban areas. In a cycle that has proved to be unbreakable, doctors locate their practices in cities to have access to modern hospitals, and new hospitals are built in cities to have access to a wide range of physicians.

As health-care institutions gravitated to urban communities, the medical profession for years continued to promote the image of the wise and all-knowing country doctor. While some country doctors in Appalachia and the rest of rural America were professionally able, many were incompetent. This was demonstrated by a 1910 study conducted for the American Medical Association that exposed the situation and revealed why so many physicians were ill prepared to practice. Officially titled *Medical Education in the United States and Canada: A Report to the Carnegie Foundation for the Advancement of Teaching* but also known as *Bulletin Number Four* and the "Flexner Report," for its author, Professor Abraham Flexner, it resulted in the closing of medical schools still offering two-year degrees. By the early 1920s, all such institutions had been shut down, though their final graduates were allowed to practice. It was a particularly important development for rural communities, as they had often been served by the two-year doctors. Unable to compete with graduates of colleges and universities requiring four years of undergraduate study and four years of medical school, many two-year graduates opened offices in rural areas. Indeed, in some areas of Appalachia, it was not unusual for an individual to practice medicine without the benefit of any formal medical education. Usually such persons had informally acquired a certain amount of knowledge and had been awarded an M.D. by their state's legislature. According to a study of rural medicine published in 1948, rural physicians sometimes evidenced not only incompetence, but such other problems as alcohol and drug abuse. Some of these personal difficulties were attributed to the professional and social isolation and other frustrations resulting from rural practice.

Because Appalachian coal mining was a rural industry, a large proportion of company doctors came from the ranks of the inadequately prepared, and company practices effectively served as dumping grounds. Knowledge of the situation generated deep dissatisfaction among many coal miners and caused Walter Polakor of the United Mine Workers of America to observe in 1938 that the company-doctor system was the "bastard" of American medicine. Such anger was directed not only at inept treatment, but also at coverage limitations that were included in most check-off plans. Many companies disallowed treatment for a host of needs, ranging from obstetrical services to treatment for venereal diseases. Under the circumstances, most coal miners viewed company doctors as nothing more than agents of their employers, hired on the strength of their loyalty rather than medical ability.

With regard to hospital facilities, the situation was no better. But like the medical profession, hospitals also went through profound changes in the latter half of the nineteenth century. Improvements in medical knowledge transformed hospitals from warehouses for the incurable to centers of effective treatment featuring a variety of new technologies. With technology came increasing costs, and larger hospitals, including those operating on a nonprofit basis, located in urban areas, where they had a better chance of remaining solvent. The result was that rural Appalachian hospitals were usually considerably smaller than their urban counterparts and operated on a proprietary, or for-profit, basis.

A regional hospital in a large city typically had an inpatient capacity of 350 beds, while a community hospital in a small city would possibly have a 100-bed capacity. Hospitals in rural Appalachia, on the other hand, were generally no larger than 25 beds. Many of these institutions, when surveyed in 1947, were found to be deficient in several categories including staff, housekeeping, records, and lab services. Because most of these institutions operated on a proprietary basis, cutting corners was essential for profitability.

As these facts came to light, the United States was in a sustained period (1938–52) of heightened political interest in national health insurance. The leading reform proposal, the Murray-Wagner-Dingell bill, which called for a single-payer national health plan, died in Congress by 1952, but the debate helped illuminate rural health needs. In Appalachia, those needs were critical, and in 1946 they helped to bring about creation of the United Mine Workers of America Welfare and Retirement Fund. At the United Mine Workers' request, the U.S. Department of the Interior had conducted an extensive health survey, known as the "Boone Report," concerning the nation's coal-mining regions, including Appalachia, and the findings were stark. The region lagged behind the rest of the nation in several significant categories, including doctor-patient ratio and infant mortality. While the national doctor-patient ratio averaged one physician for every 748 people, Appalachian states, including Tennessee, Kentucky, Virginia and Mississippi, had only one physician for

1,138 to 1,758 people. This disparity loomed even larger when rural areas were compared to cities with populations of 50,000 or more.

The pattern regarding infant mortality was similar. By 1942, the national average had fallen to 40.4 deaths per 1,000 live births. Of the Appalachian states, only New York and Ohio (in 1942) could boast of rates lower than the national average. For the region's other states, the average stood significantly higher, at roughly 49.25. Virginia, West Virginia, and Alabama reported even higher rates of 55, 53, and 50.4.

Adult mortality was the only bright spot. The two principle causes of death in the United States in 1948 were heart disease and cancer, and death rates for both categories were higher in cities of 100,000 persons or more than they were for rural communities of 2,500 persons or fewer. While the death rate for both categories was 354.8 and 145.9 per 100,000 in large cities, rural death rates were 240 and 95.5. Although the higher rate of heart disease was attributed to urban stress, the cancer differential could not be explained. At least one commentator cautioned that statistics concerning rural areas needed to be viewed with skepticism because of possible misdiagnoses and non-diagnoses at inadequate medical facilities.

Possessing firm evidence of massive deficiencies, reformers and government agencies began to include provisions specifically addressing rural needs in national health insurance proposals. These included such initiatives as grants to encourage health professionals to locate in medically underserved areas. Some were enacted as individual pieces of legislation, making incremental improvements even as national health insurance remained out of political reach. The Hill-Burton Hospital Survey and Construction Act, for example, provided federal funding for modern hospitals in rural communities. Passed in 1946, the legislation was supporting construction of 1,827 hospital projects by 1952. But while Hill-Burton was crucial to scores of communities, its effectiveness was limited because it only provided matching funds. To receive federal assistance in building a hospital, a community was required to raise half of the estimated construction costs. This requirement placed Hill-Burton assistance beyond the reach of many of Appalachia's smaller towns.

Hill-Burton was the last major federal effort in health care until the middle 1960s. In central Appalachia, health-care leadership was significantly assumed by the United Mine Workers' Welfare and Retirement Fund. Moving beyond paying bills, the fund undertook several initiatives to improve health-care delivery. By far the most dramatic was creation of the Miners Memorial Hospitals. Formally opened in 1956, this chain of ten institutions was sold to the Board of National Missions of the United Presbyterian Church (USA) in 1963 and eventually renamed Appalachian Regional Healthcare. In addition to the hospitals, the fund and groups working with it opened primary-care and specialty clinics throughout the region in the 1950s and 1960s and through them extended important health-care services beyond those of the hospitals.

In 1965 the American health-care system was dramatically changed with the creation of Medicare and Medicaid to assure medical care for the elderly and for Americans in poverty. Moreover, the government began using grants and scholarships to increase the numbers of physicians working in medically underserved areas. From the surge of federal involvement came sustained improvements in Appalachian health care. By 1988, the region's overall infant mortality rate matched the national rate of 10.4 deaths per 1,000 live births. Even more heartening was the disclosure that the region's northern section had a rate lower than the national average.

Equally significant systematic improvements have continued. For instance, a study prepared for the Appalachian Regional Commission showed that the region's

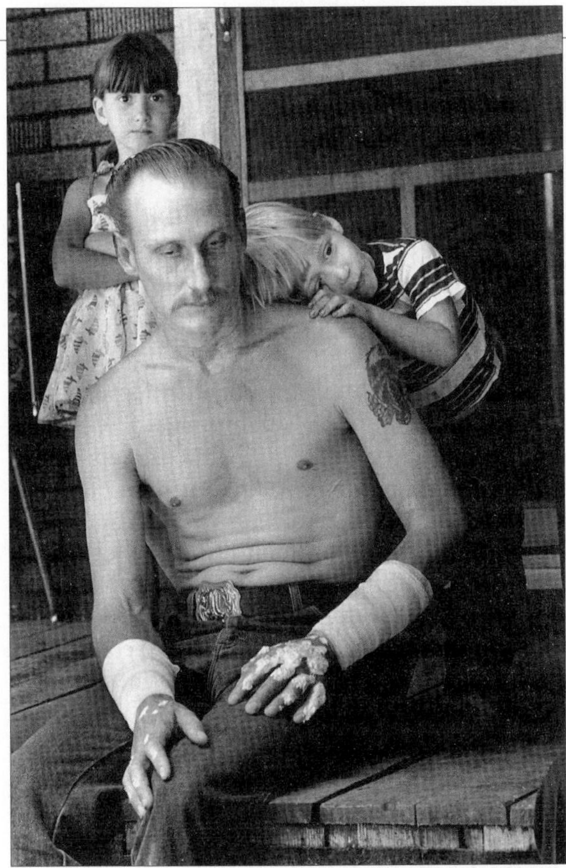

Coal miner Emory Howard recuperates from a methane gas explosion that occurred at a Pittston Coal Company mine in McClure, Virginia, 1983. Seven coal miners died in the blast. Despite technological change, mining was named the most dangerous industry in 2001 by the National Safety Council.

supply of physicians increased between 1990 and 1999, as distressed counties attracted more urgently needed primary-care physicians.

But the good news continues to be tempered by persistent problems. Since 1969, the federal government has acknowledged the coal miners' scourge of black lung disease. With funds authorized that year under the Coal Mine Health and Safety Act, the Health Research and Services Administration makes grants to sixteen public and private agencies that provide screening, treatment, rehabilitation, and counseling services at forty-three clinics serving miners afflicted with respiratory ailments.

The continuing affinity for tobacco in rural areas no doubt adds to the region's respiratory disease burden. In the late twentieth century, Kentucky stood number one in the nation in lung cancer mortality rates among white males. The region also has the highest cervical cancer mortality rate of any part of the country, and its oral health has been described by a specialist at the University of Pittsburgh School of Dental Medicine as the worst in the United States.

But more revealing than statewide statistics or general comparisons of Appalachia and other parts of the nation are glaring disparities between the region's urban communities and its "distressed" counties. More than twenty years after the Appalachian Regional Commission established a special program for counties with unemployment rates 150 percent above the national average, 111 counties remain in the "distressed" category. Inevitably, these counties, concentrated in Kentucky, West Virginia, Ohio, Mississippi, Alabama, and Tennessee, have the most acute health needs.

Nearly two-thirds of these counties lack a hospital that offers obstetrical services. More than three-fourths of them lack facilities for the treatment of mental illness. Nearly 90 percent are without programs to address drug and alcohol abuse issues. Also, the region's smaller hospitals, regardless of their location, appear to be having greater financial difficulty than larger institutions.

While distressed counties became more successful in attracting primary-care physicians during the 1990s, their doctor-patient ratio is far less favorable than in the rest of Appalachia. The region's more urbanized and economically competitive counties, on average, have about one primary-care doctor for every 1,099 persons and one specialist for every 588. The comparable supply of doctors in the distressed counties is one primary-care physician for every 2,128 persons and one specialist for every 2,857 individuals. The shortage of dentists is similar, and distressed counties have had even less success attracting dental practitioners than they have had recruiting other doctors.

Finally, there is the issue of adult mortality. Over the years heart disease has remained the nation's primary killer, followed by all forms of cancer. Taken at the aggregate level, research indicates that death rates, when adjusted for age, race, and gender, are almost uniformly higher for Appalachian residents than for the rest of the nation. There is also a generally higher-than-average rate of mortality among the distressed counties.

Superimposed upon the special problems of Appalachia, and particularly those of the distressed counties, are the pervasive national issues of the cost and availability of health insurance. With millions of Americans having no health insurance, hospitals and other providers cover their care by increasing charges to insured patients. The effect is to drive insurance rates inexorably higher, putting coverage out of reach for more and more families, and increasing the numbers of employers who provide no coverage for their workers. After the failure of the Clinton administration's effort to create a comprehensive national health-care insurance program in the 1990s, the federal government once again turned to incremental approaches to health-care legislation while public officials, the news media, and insurance experts pointed to continuing evidence of a mounting health-care crisis. In 2003 Congress approved the largest change in Medicare since its inception, adding a complex provision to partially cover prescription drug costs. Looming over the entire health-care delivery system was the aging of the post–World War II "baby boom," which will cause the nation's health-care needs to rise dramatically in the first several decades of the twenty-first century.

In the summer of 2003, reporting by the *Charleston Gazette* in West Virginia indicated the gravity of the health insurance dilemma in Appalachia. In 2001, the newspaper reported, one of every four working-age West Virginians was without health insurance, even though 60 percent of the uninsured were employed. By 2008, it predicted, the rolls of the uninsured would grow by as many as 60,000, and the cost of a family's coverage would approach eighteen thousand dollars a year.

—Richard P. Mulcahy, *University of Pittsburgh at Titusville*

Richard A. Couto, Nancy K. Simpson, and Gale Harris, eds., *Sowing the Seeds in the Mountains: Community-Based Coalitions for Cancer Prevention and Control* (1994); James M. Fallows, "A Triumph of Misinformation," *Atlantic Monthly* (January 1995); Joel Halverson, *An Analysis of Disparities in Health Status and Accessibility to Health Care in the Appalachian Region* (2003); C. Horace Hamilton, "Health and Health Services," in *The Southern Appalachian Region: A Survey*, ed. Thomas R. Ford (1962); Interdepartmental Committee to Coordinate Health and Welfare Activities, Josephine Roche, Chairman, *Proceedings: National Health Conference, July 18, 19, 20, 1938* (1938); Frederick W. Mott and Milton I. Roemer, *Rural Health and Medical Care* (1948); Richard P. Mulcahy, "A New Deal for Coal Miners: The UMWA Welfare and Retirement Fund and the Reorganization of Health Care in Appalachia," *Journal of Appalachian Studies* (Spring 1996) and *A Social Contract for the Coal Fields: The Rise and Fall of the United Mine Workers of America Welfare and Retirement Fund* (2001); The President's Commission on the Health Needs of the Nation, *Building America's Health* (1952); Project Hope, *An Analysis of the Financial Conditions of Health Care Institutions in the Appalachian Region and Their Economic Impacts* (2002); Paul Starr, *The Social Transformation of American Medicine* (1982); U.S. Department of the Interior, *A Medical Survey of the Bituminous Coal Industry: Report of the Coal Mines Administrator* (1947); White House Domestic Policy Council, *Health Security: The President's Report to the American People* (1993).

Allied Health and Public-Health Education

As of 2002, approximately 520 accredited programs of study in allied health professions were being offered at 241 public and private universities, community colleges, technical schools, and medical centers across the Appalachian region. Among the institutions offering accredited programs, only 8 belonged to the Association of Schools of Allied Health Professions. These are the School of Health Related Professions, University of Alabama at Birmingham; College of Health Sciences, Eastern Kentucky University (Richmond); College of Applied Sciences, Western Carolina University (Cullowhee); School of Health Sciences and Human Performance, Ithaca College (Ithaca, New York); College of Health and Human Services, Ohio University (Athens); Rangos School of Health Sciences, Duquesne University (Pittsburgh); College of Public and Allied Health, East Tennessee State University (Johnson City); and Waldron College of Health and Human Services, Radford University (Radford, Virginia).

Allied health education programs prepare students for a wide range of careers in the medical and health fields and encompass fields of study not included in nursing, medicine, or public health. Graduates become athletic trainers; medical assistants; laboratory technicians and technologists; radiation and ultrasound technicians, technologists, and therapists; dental assistants, technicians, and hygienists; physician's assistants; occupational therapists and assistants; physical therapists and assistants; and audiologists and speech-language therapists. Programs for these professions span the education spectrum from basic certification to graduate degrees.

The scope of programs offered by these institutions illustrates the variability of allied health education in the region and the nation at large. While Radford University concentrates on communication disorders, for example, East Tennessee State University, Duquesne University, Eastern Kentucky University, and the University of Alabama at Birmingham all offer a range of programs at the associate's, baccalaureate, and master's degree levels. However, these schools are not the only providers of allied health education in the Appalachian region. Community colleges awarding degrees in a wide variety of programs at the associate level include Wallace State Community College in Hanceville, Alabama; Greenville Technical College in Georgia; and Chattanooga State Technical Community College in Tennessee. The University of Pittsburgh and West Virginia University in Morgantown, along with their associated hospitals, offer a variety of programs as well, emphasizing baccalaureate and graduate education. The most broadly available programs are for radiographers (available at 73 institutions), medical assistants (57), medical laboratory technicians (40), and physical therapy assistants (33), with programs in each state. Programs that require graduate study are less likely to be available in each state. Allegheny County, Pennsylvania, the largest metropolitan area in the Appalachian region, is home to 58 programs in 20 different institutions.

Reflecting a lack of positions, education for public-health professions is limited in Appalachia to a handful of universities. Both of the accredited schools of public health in the region are in metropolitan areas. These are the University of Pittsburgh School of Public Health and the School of Public Health at the University of Alabama at Birmingham. Both offer a full range of professional and research-oriented graduate degrees at the master's and doctoral levels. Students at the University of Alabama at Birmingham can prepare for careers in epidemiology, international health, maternal and child health, health-care organization and policy analysis, biostatistics, and health behavior. Courses of study at the University of Pittsburgh include health promotion and education, health administration, health-policy analysis, a range of specializations in epidemiology, environmental and occupational health, biostatistics, and infectious diseases and microbiology. The school also offers a multidisciplinary master's degree for individuals with previous doctoral preparation in related health fields. These schools, among only 28 schools of public health in America, serve a national constituency. Neither specifically focuses on Appalachia, although the University of Pittsburgh does include service to the region as part of its mission. At present there are no schools of public health in West Virginia, Virginia, Tennessee, or Mississippi. The well-known schools of public health in North Carolina, South Carolina, and New York are not in the Appalachian region, nor are newer schools of public health recently established in Kentucky and Ohio.

In addition to the schools of public health in Birmingham and Pittsburgh, East Stroudsburg State University, East Tennessee State University, West Virginia University, and the University of Tennessee at Knoxville offer accredited programs leading to the master's of public health degree. The scope of professional preparation is limited in these programs. The University of Tennessee and East Stroudsburg offer concentrations in community health education, and East Tennessee State and the University of Tennessee offer concentrations in community health and administration. The University of Tennessee also has a concentration in gerontology. West Virginia University awards a generalist public-health degree. In their mission statements both East Tennessee State and West Virginia University explicitly target improvement of the health of the Appalachian region through faculty and student community service projects. The need for entry-level public-health educators and sanitarians at the baccalaureate level is met through a variety of channels, and specific training is not always required, depending on state requirements.

See also: SECTION OVERVIEW.

—Evelyn A. Knight, *Ermine, Kentucky*

R. David Lankes and Hugh W. Bonner, “Building an Education Infrastructure for Allied Health,” *Journal of Allied Health* (Spring 2003).

Appalachia Cancer Network

In 2000 the Center to Reduce Cancer Health Disparities, an organ of the National Cancer Institute, announced a \$60-million Special Population Network for Cancer Awareness Research and Training program for addressing higher morbidity and mortality from cancer within certain special populations in the United States. The Appalachia Cancer Network, a component of this initiative, grew out of an earlier program, the Appalachian Leadership Initiative on Cancer, which was funded by the National Cancer Institute from 1992 through 2000. Both the Appalachian Leadership Initiative on Cancer and the current Appalachia Cancer Network program recognize the importance of using community-focused efforts and partnerships to build intervention strategies for accomplishing cancer-control objectives.

The principal investigator institute, the Markey Cancer Center at the University of Kentucky, collaborates with West Virginia University and Pennsylvania State University in guiding a \$6.7-million grant toward research, education, and outreach to address cancer-control challenges in rural, medically underserved populations in Appalachian counties in Kentucky, West Virginia, Tennessee, Virginia, Ohio, Pennsylvania, Maryland, and New York.

The National Cancer Institute observed that certain sections of the American population suffered higher incidence, morbidity, and mortality from some forms of cancer and that this increased burden of cancer among special at-risk populations was related to socioeconomic and behavioral factors. “Special populations” identified as more prone to such discrepantly high cancer burden were largely Hispanic, African American, Native American, or rural and were medically underserved. With 266 of its 410 counties categorized as rural and a majority of them federally designated as health professional shortage areas, Appalachia constitutes a region with significant barriers to effective cancer prevention and control.

Recognizing a high incidence of cancer in the region, the National Cancer Institute in March 1992 issued a request for proposals for cooperative agreements to help establish a strong cancer-control outreach program, the Appalachian Leadership Initiative on Cancer. Through four grantee research universities (Pennsylvania State University, West Virginia University, the University of Kentucky, and North Carolina State University) in four geographical regions (northern, north-central, central, and southern Appalachia) covering the Appalachian counties of eleven states, the initiative aimed at achieving behavioral changes in both individuals and local health-care systems to reduce the regional burden of disease from cancer. The program focused on cancer of the breast and the uterine cervix, and its aim was to enhance local capacity and competence in cancer control through development of regional cancer-control partnerships and community coalitions. Development of regional partnerships involved coalition organizers, including investigators at twelve research universities, and county-based staffs of such national organizations as the American Cancer Society and the Cooperative Extension Service. A leadership-development phase was followed by community-participation strategies, including recruitment of local residents, civic leaders, students, teachers, cancer survivors, health professionals, and members of organizations such as the Grange, American Association for Retired Persons, Head Start, libraries, churches, and local health departments, hospitals, and health centers.

Sixty-three county coalitions totaling 1,662 members were developed during the implementation phase of the initiative. With the help of thousands of community participants, these coalitions organized cancer screenings, health fairs, media activities, grant proposal writing and presentation, and other efforts to increase cancer awareness.

The Appalachia Cancer Network program took over where the Appalachian Leadership Initiative on Cancer left off, building upon and expanding the latter’s community-based infrastructure. The focus was expanded to include colorectal and lung cancers. Other main objectives of the five-year, three-phase Appalachia Cancer Network program included increasing community awareness of clinical trials, as well as recruitment and retention in such trials, and increasing recruitment of Appalachian and minority students and scientists to cancer research and control.

See also: CANCER; REPRODUCTIVE CANCERS AND WOMEN’S HEALTH.

—Ajay Kalra, *East Tennessee State University*

Richard A. Couto, Nancy K. Simpson, and Gale Harris, eds., *Sowing Seeds in the Mountains: Community-Based Coalitions for Cancer Prevention and Control* (1994); National Institutes of Health, *NIH Guide: Appalachian Leadership Initiative on Cancer* (1992).

Appalachian Leadership Initiative on Cancer

See Appalachia Cancer Network

Appalachian Health Providers

Appalachian Health Providers was an informally structured, multidisciplinary network of community-based health-care providers in parts of the Appalachian region in the late 1970s and early 1980s. The organization was established in 1978 with the assistance of Richard A. Couto from the Center for Health Services at Vanderbilt University. The network served as a support group where members could share common experiences, problems, and solutions; as a discussion group for informal continuing education on clinical and social aspects of the region; and as a means of communication for promoting quality health care in Appalachia.

By 1982 Appalachian Health Providers had more than 150 members representing more than sixty communities from Kentucky, North Carolina, Tennessee, Virginia, and West Virginia. Meetings were held regularly at sites throughout the central Appalachian region until 1986. Much of the success of this relatively short-lived organization was due to its multidisciplinary membership and its focus on problems specific to the region such as coal workers' lung disease, malnutrition, and environmental health concerns.

See also: COMMUNITY-INITIATED HEALTH EFFORTS.

—Raymond H. Feierabend, *East Tennessee State University*

Appalachian Preceptorship Program

The Appalachian Preceptorship Program, established by the Department of Family Medicine at East Tennessee State University in 1985, provides opportunities for medical students to work in southern Appalachian communities, research alternative health and illness beliefs and practices, and become familiar with rural health-care delivery. The program addresses health needs in southern Appalachia by drawing medical students from around the nation to gain experience in rural practice. The mission of this program is to integrate culturally sensitive practices and care into rural medicine with special emphasis on the Appalachian context.

This summer program consists of a weeklong series of educational sessions held on the university campus and placement of students with physicians in rural communities. Sessions are organized around core concepts including cultural appreciation through an awareness of the history, economic development, religious beliefs, and health practices of the region; development of skills to explore the beliefs and practices of students and patients; and the nature of rural medical practice with workshops on medical communications, developing health projects, and the quality of life for rural health providers. Recreational activities that showcase the region's natural beauty and culture are incorporated into the program. The three weeks that students spend with a physician in a rural community provide modeling of patient care and community relationships.

During its first seventeen years, more than two hundred students from ninety-four medical schools participated in the program. Several individuals who took part continued their medical training at East Tennessee State University, established practices in the area, and became community physicians.

See also: EAST TENNESSEE STATE UNIVERSITY JAMES H. QUILLEN COLLEGE OF MEDICINE.

— Forrest Lang and Pamela M. Zahorik, *East Tennessee State University*

Appalachian Student Health Coalition

Formed in 1968 at Vanderbilt University, the Appalachian Student Health Coalition compiled a remarkable history of innovation in community health, community development, and university-community collaboration. In its twenty-five-year lifespan, the coalition assisted scores of community organizing efforts in the central Appalachian region.

During the first summer of work, students and faculty participated in a health fair in Clairfield, Tennessee, conducted by volunteers from a local Presbyterian church. This summer experience shaped the model employed by the coalition, in which student organizers assisted local leaders in planning and staging the health fair. Teams of nursing and medical students visited for a week and conducted health histories, medical exams, and referrals. Other team members included law students, who provided rights and benefits counseling and helped enroll people in programs for which they were eligible. After the fair, student organizers helped community residents secure resources and organize clinic services.

This formula brought about more than twenty clinic startups in Kentucky, east Tennessee, and southwestern Virginia, provided training for at least a thousand student participants from around the country, many of whom went into public service of different forms, and gave impetus to several other community organizations, including the environmental group Save Our Cumberland Mountains.

At Vanderbilt, the Center for Health Services learned from the coalition's work and adapted it to the fields of environmental and occupational health. It assisted in development of student health coalitions in other states, supported policy needs for the emerging set of community clinics, and backed new community initiatives in health care.

See also: COMMUNITY-INITIATED HEALTH EFFORTS.

—Richard A. Couto, *University of Richmond*

Area Health Education Centers

Area Health Education Centers evolved in the late 1960s and early 1970s in the wake of escalating national and state concern about the supply, distribution, retention, and quality of the health-care workforce. States throughout Appalachia and the rest of the country had long experienced shortages of physicians and other health-care providers, and a number of initiatives were developed to expand the training of primary-care practitioners and improve their distribution into underserved communities.

In 1970 the Carnegie Commission on Higher Education issued a report entitled *Higher Education and the Nation's Health.* One of its recommendations was for the creation of 126 Area Health Education Centers throughout the nation. The commission reasoned that the development of education and training centers for health-related professions at community hospitals would result in regional workforce-development programs, decrease the isolation of underserved communities, and improve the capacity of such communities to recruit and retain needed practitioners.

In 1971 Congress passed the Health Manpower Act, authorizing programs designed to improve the distribution, efficiency, effectiveness, and quality of the health workforce. In 1972 the Department of Health, Education, and Welfare funded the first eleven Area Health Education Centers, including those in North Carolina, West Virginia, and South Carolina.

The program has continued to grow at the national level, with forty-one states, including every state in the Appalachian region, operating such programs. Federal funds for Area Health Education Centers, within the Bureau of Health Professions of the Health Resources and Services Administration, are targeted primarily at starting new centers. Once programs rotate off core funding, usually after nine years, they are sustained through a combination of state and local funding, including a modest amount of federal funding available through a matching grant program.

The mission of the Area Health Education Centers program is to meet the nation's health and health-workforce needs by providing educational programs in partnership with academic institutions, community health-care agencies, and other organizations committed to improving citizens' health. Educational programs and services are targeted toward improving the distribution and retention of health-care providers with a special emphasis on primary care and prevention; increasing the diversity of the health-care workforce; enhancing the quality of care and improving health-care outcomes; and addressing the health-care needs of underserved communities and populations.

Area Health Education Centers throughout Appalachia have demonstrated significant success in addressing health-care access problems of underserved regions and populations. For example, the affiliated family-practice residency programs in the mountains of North Carolina, South Carolina, and Kentucky have graduated more than five hundred family physicians since 1978, and more than half of the family practitioners graduating from these programs have remained in mountain communities. Centers from Pennsylvania to Alabama and from Ohio to Maryland coordinate the community placements of thousands of health-science students each year in order to give them exposure to real-world health care, as well as to increase their awareness of opportunities for future practice sites. In North Carolina, 30 percent of the pharmacy students who train in the mountain region stay on to practice in a community there.

Besides offering thousands of hours of continuing education each year to health practitioners, the centers throughout the region provide health-related programs to elementary and secondary students, reaching more than twenty-five thousand young people each year. In addition, the centers in Kentucky, South Carolina, and West Virginia operate Health Education Training Centers as companion programs. These training centers focus on meeting the needs of historically underserved and indigent populations with a special focus on health promotion and disease prevention.

The Area Health Education Centers program is an integral part of training programs designed to meet the special needs of Appalachia. By connecting the resources of the academic health centers in their respective states to the needs of rural and other underserved communities, the program offers a network of educational services that have significantly improved access to quality health care for the citizens of the region.

See also: SECTION OVERVIEW.

—Thomas J. Bacon, *University of North Carolina at Chapel Hill School of Medicine*

Carnegie Commission on Higher Education, *Higher Education and the Nation's Health: Policies for Medical and Dental Education* (1970); Eugene S. Mayer, "Academic Support for Rural Practice: The Role of Area Health Education Centers in the School of Medicine," *Academic Medicine* (December Supplement, 1990); S. R. Wilson, V. K. Fowkes, and P. Campaeu, *Evaluation of the Impact of the National Area Health Education Center Program* (1989).

Black Lung Associations

Coal miners and miners' wives and widows began organizing the fight over black lung disease in West Virginia in 1968. Specifically, the purpose of the first Black Lung Association was to secure passage of a law that would recognize black lung as a compensable occupational disease under the West Virginia workers' compensation statute. Pressured by a three-week strike that shut down coal production throughout the state, the West Virginia legislature passed a weak version of the bill that coal miners had backed. The new law recognized coal workers' pneumoconiosis as a work-related lung disease; subsequently, a small number of coal miners in West Virginia began receiving workers' compensation for disability caused by this disease.

Following passage of the Federal Coal Mine Health and Safety Act of 1969, Black Lung Associations once again emerged to advocate for miners. This law established a federal compensation program financed with general tax revenues from the U.S. treasury for coal miners disabled by black lung and for the widows of miners who had died from the disease. A narrow interpretation of what constituted black lung and restrictive disability standards once again meant that relatively small numbers of coal miners and miners' widows received compensation. The Black Lung Associations, having organized on a county-by-county basis, challenged the eligibility criteria for compensation by assisting individual claimants who sought federal benefits and by lobbying in Washington, D.C., for reform of the program.

During the early to mid-1970s, Black Lung Associations sprang up throughout the central Appalachian coalfields. A few even developed in cities outside the region to which coal miners and their families had migrated. Although the original Black Lung Association in West Virginia was composed largely of male coal miners, their wives, widows, and daughters participated in and sometimes emerged as leaders of the new county-based chapters and statewide associations. The associations also tended to be racially diverse in both membership and leadership. The president of the original Black Lung Association in West Virginia was Charles Brooks, an African American coal miner.

By the late 1970s, Black Lung Association chapters were on the decline in most areas, though a few stalwart individuals continued to be active years later. The associations were in part victims of their own success in liberalizing eligibility standards for compensation, which undercut their base of aggrieved claimants. When union reformer and black lung activist Arnold Miller won the presidency of the United Mine Workers of America in 1972, the associations also became entangled in complex and divisive union politics.

Black Lung Associations served as an inspiration and model for workers in other industries who faced dusty working conditions and disabling occupational lung diseases. Organizations such as the Brown Lung Association, representing textile workers, adopted many features of the Black Lung Associations, perhaps most importantly their inclusive, community-based approach to workplace health problems.

See also: BLACK LUNG DISEASE AND THE BLACK LUNG MOVEMENT; MINERS FOR DEMOCRACY (LABOR).

—Barbara Ellen Smith, *University of Memphis*

Brit Hume, *Death and the Mines: Rebellion and Murder in the UMW* (1971); Barbara Ellen Smith, *Digging Our Own Graves: Coal Miners and the Struggle over Black Lung Disease* (1987).

Black Lung Disease and the Black Lung Movement

Black lung is a disabling, potentially fatal respiratory disease resulting from prolonged exposure to coal dust. The condition became the subject of intense political, medical, and legal controversy in 1968, when coal miners in West Virginia organized to demand recognition of and compensation for black lung.

Nonmedical sources suggest that coal miners all over the world have suffered from work-related lung disease since the beginning of large-scale underground mining. However, medical recognition of black lung was erratic and delayed in the United States. Although Great Britain began compensating coal miners disabled by black lung in 1943, by the late 1960s miners in most areas of the United States still received no such compensation. Physicians tended to label miners' complaints of respiratory problems "compensationitis" or "fear of the mines." They attributed medical evidence of respiratory impairment in coal miners to cigarette smoking and other nonoccupational factors.

Experts consider it likely that the incidence of black lung among Appalachian coal miners increased with the introduction of continuous-mining technology after World War II. The machines' rotating drill bits clawed into the underground coal seam, releasing clouds of dust. Increased productivity that came with such machinery led to widespread layoffs and out-migration. Miners who kept their jobs during this period of technological transformation found their union, the United Mine Workers of America, largely unresponsive to complaints of health and safety hazards and other workplace problems. High unemployment diminished miners' bargaining leverage with their employers, the coal operators, as well. By the late 1960s, the generation of coal miners who had worked together in these mechanizing mines began to retire en masse. Many suffered from black lung but typically received no workers' compensation for any related disability. Those disabled before working a sufficient number of years in the mines were denied a pension; some were ineligible for Social Security benefits as well.

In 1968 older miners in southern West Virginia began to organize to demand workers' compensation coverage of black lung disease. Word of the campaign circulated rapidly through networks of local unions, but the hierarchy of the United Mine Workers of America opposed this rank-and-file initiative as "dual unionism." Despite well-founded fears of reprisal from the union, activists such as Woodrow Mullins, Lyman Calhoun, and Earl Stafford persisted. Local support for the miners came from a physician in Charleston, I. E. Buff, and participants in an assortment of volunteer service programs such as Volunteers in Service to America

(VISTA) and the Appalachian Volunteers and other participants in the War on Poverty.

The Farmington, West Virginia, mine explosion in November 1968 galvanized the black lung movement and drew national attention to coal-mine health and safety. Buff, who had been joined by physicians Donald Rasmussen and Hawey Wells Jr., traveled throughout southern West Virginia, speaking at black lung rallies and lending medical legitimacy to the miners' cause. By February 1969, the West Virginia legislature had failed to pass any black lung legislation. Miners struck for three weeks, shutting off coal production throughout the state, until the legislature passed a bill recognizing black lung under the West Virginia workers' compensation statute.

Miners' activism inserted black lung disease and control of respirable dust into the national debate over coal-mine health and safety. The Federal Coal Mine Health and Safety Act of 1969 included a strict, unprecedented respirable-dust standard designed to prevent black lung; it also authorized payment of benefits from the federal treasury to miners disabled by black lung and to the widows of miners who died from the disease. This new federal benefits program spurred a continuation of black lung activism in the central Appalachian coalfields. When the Social Security Administration began awarding black lung benefits in the fall of 1970, its determinations of eligibility seemed completely arbitrary. Miners who appeared desperately disabled by lung disease were denied benefits while others, who seemed by comparison relatively healthy, received compensation. During this second phase in the black lung movement, miners and miners' wives and widows aggressively contested the eligibility criteria for federal black lung compensation.

At stake in this controversy were competing medical views of what constitutes black lung. After 1968, dominant medical opinion in the United States shifted from outright denial of occupational lung disease among coal miners to a narrow construction of the respiratory conditions that could be considered related to work and disabling. According to this perspective, *black lung* was an unscientific lay term for coal workers' pneumoconiosis, a disease that involved progressive destruction of lung tissue by dust inhalation over a prolonged period of time. The disease was by definition only diagnosed through X-ray evidence and was disabling only in advanced ("complicated") stages. An estimated 3 percent of miners suffered from this advanced stage and deserved compensation. Minority medical opinion, studied and argued most persistently by Rasmussen, held that black lung involved a pulmonary vascular process that impaired the ability of the small vessels in the lungs to exchange oxygen with the bloodstream. This process was not visible on X-rays and could be disabling in miners with little evidence of pneumoconiosis. Indeed, miners could contract bronchitis, emphysema, and possibly other, unrecognized diseases in the workplace. *Black lung* in this sense referred to diverse work-related respiratory problems.

Utilizing medical arguments for this broader definition of black lung, miners and their wives and widows challenged the Social Security Administration's processing of black lung claims. Through local Black Lung Association chapters, activists provided lay advocacy for individual claimants seeking federal benefits and organized to amend the program through new legislation. Their efforts resulted in the Black Lung Benefits Act of 1972 and a set of interim eligibility standards, which temporarily liberalized the claims process. Black Lung Association chapters flourished in the wake of the new law as the lay advocates became increasingly successful in winning benefits, and attendance swelled.

However, by the mid-1970s, complex political developments began to diminish the movement's vitality. Many black lung leaders simultaneously participated in the movement for union reform through the Miners for Democracy. When Miners for Democracy candidate and black lung activist Arnold Miller was elected union president in 1972, key chapter leaders who were United Mine Workers of America members became entangled in union politics. Women who had emerged as leaders and activists in many black lung chapters were not union members and had no access to the new administration. Meanwhile, federal black lung benefits became increasingly hard to secure. New permanent standards greatly restricted eligibility, and coal industry liability for new claims meant that lay advocates now had to fight corporate lawyers to win benefits. By the late 1970s, the black lung movement was no longer a political force in the coalfields.

See also: BLACK LUNG ASSOCIATIONS; BUFF, I. E.; RASMUSSEN, DONALD.

—Barbara Ellen Smith, *University of Memphis*

Alan Derickson, *Black Lung: Anatomy of a Public Health Disaster* (1998); Barbara Ellen Smith, "Black Lung: The Social Production of Disease," in *The Sociology of Health and Illness: Critical Perspectives*, ed. Peter Conrad (5th edition, 1997) and *Digging Our Own Graves: Coal Miners and the Struggle over Black Lung Disease* (1987).

Breckinridge, Mary

(1881–1965) Nurse-midwife and health reformer.

Born February 17, 1881, Mary Carson Breckinridge was the granddaughter of presidential candidate John C. Breckinridge and daughter of Katherine Carson and Clifton R. Breckinridge, an Arkansas congressman and diplomat. Although she came from an aristocratic background, she eventually dedicated her life to helping Appalachian women survive childbirth.

Breckinridge's first marriage ended in two years with her husband's death; her second ended in divorce in 1920. Her two children both died young, and this circumstance, coupled with her devotion to the ideal of service, led in 1925 to her founding of the Kentucky Committee for Mothers and Babies—renamed the Frontier Nursing Service three years later. Established on the idea of using professionally trained nurse-midwives, the organization provided health care to isolated mountain areas where none existed. A persuasive speaker and successful fund-raiser, Breckinridge was sometimes criticized for excessively emphasizing negative aspects of the region in order to raise money, but the organization she successfully created also accomplished much for the people it served from its headquarters at Wendover, Kentucky. Eventually, the Frontier Nursing Service also included a hospital and one of the first schools of midwifery in the nation. She recounted these successes in her autobiography, *Wide Neighborhoods: A Story of the Frontier Nursing Service* (1952).

A strong and forceful leader as well as a registered nurse, Breckenridge presided over an entirely female professional group, whose use of horses in the mountains caused the caregivers to be pictured, almost romantically, as "angels on horseback." By 1965, the year of Breckinridge's death, the Frontier Nursing Service had performed nearly fifteen thousand deliveries with an obstetrics-related death rate of 11.0 per 10,000 deliveries, versus the national average of 36.3. Although it has undergone significant changes since Breckinridge's death, the organization still continues as a testament to her vision of helping others.

See also: COMMUNITY-INITIATED HEALTH EFFORTS; FRONTIER NURSING SERVICE.

—James C. Klotter, *Georgetown College*

Buff, I. E.

(1908–1974) Physician.

A crusader for the recognition and prevention of black lung disease, Isidore E. Buff practiced medicine in Charleston, West Virginia, for more than forty years. The son of a Jewish tailor, he was born in Utica, New York, but soon moved with his family to Charleston. Buff was graduated from the University of Louisville School of Medicine in 1931. Following a residency at the former Chesapeake and Ohio Hospital in Huntington, West Virginia, he established a medical practice in Charleston, where he worked until his death in 1974.

Buff emerged as a public figure in 1965, when he lambasted the Kanawha Valley chemical industry for air pollution. His subsequent appointment to the Air Pollution Control Commission enhanced his visibility when he took up the black lung cause in 1968. In meetings and rallies throughout southern West Virginia, Buff railed against the coal industry for its indifference to workplace health and safety problems and exhorted miners to strike if necessary to secure compensation for disability due to black lung.

Soon after the Farmington, West Virginia, mine explosion on November 20, 1968, Buff joined two other doctors, Donald Rasmussen and Hawey Wells Jr., in forming the Physicians Committee for Miners' Health and Safety. Together they traveled the state, agitating for black lung compensation and prevention and lending their professional medical credibility to miners' self-identified problems with occupational lung disease. An impassioned speaker, Buff often provided the inspirational climax to these black lung rallies.

See also: BLACK LUNG ASSOCIATIONS; BLACK LUNG DISEASE AND THE BLACK LUNG MOVEMENT; RASMUSSEN, DONALD.

—Barbara Ellen Smith, *University of Memphis*

Cancer

Cancer is the second most common cause of death for people living in Appalachia. According to an analysis of age-adjusted mortality data from the National Center for Health Statistics for 1994–98, the five-year age-adjusted cancer death rate for people living in Appalachia was 173 per 100,000 population compared to 167 per 100,000 in the nation at large. In particular, males living in Appalachia die from cancer more often than males in the U.S. population. The cancer death rate for men living in Appalachia was 221 per 100,000 compared to a national rate of 207 per 100,000 for men. Women die from cancer less often than men. The cancer death rate for women living in Appalachia was 140 per 100,000 compared to 139 per 100,000 for women living in the United States.

The health status of people in the Appalachian region has been a focus of concern for many years, with cancer particularly significant. Cancer is not one disease but a collection of different diseases characterized by abnormal cell growth that can spread throughout a person's body and result in death. Each type of cancer has different causes and requires different treatments. Thus, the burden of cancer in a population can best be understood by examining how often people get and die from specific types of cancer. Cancer-incidence data (the rate with which people get specific types of cancer) are not uniformly collected across Appalachia. Therefore, discussions of the burden of cancer in Appalachia are limited to mortality data (the rate with which people die from specific types of cancer).

Lung cancer appears to be of greatest concern for people in the region. The five-year age-adjusted lung cancer mortality rate for 1994–98 for people living in Appalachia was 54 per 100,000 population. The lung cancer mortality rate for people living in the United States was 49 per 100,000. Men living in Appalachia die from lung cancer much more often than men in the United States population (80 per 100,000 compared to 68 per 100,000). On the other hand, women living in Appalachia die from lung cancer at about the same rate as women in the general U.S. population (34 per 100,000).

The death rates for breast and colorectal cancer in Appalachia appear to be similar to those for the United States. There are, however, significant variations in the death rates for specific types of cancer within regions of Appalachia. The male lung cancer mortality rates, for example, are highest in the Appalachian counties of Kentucky, Mississippi, and Tennessee (108, 95, and 93 per 100,000, respectively). Cancer of the uterine cervix occurs much less often than lung cancer. However, the cervical cancer death rate among women in Appalachia varies from 3.8 per 100,000 in Kentucky to 2.1 in North Carolina. Both lung and cervical cancer death rates have been linked with factors such as poverty and low literacy, which may present barriers to prevention, early diagnosis, and treatment. Though the causal links are not well understood, the traditional coal-mining areas of central Appalachia have historically exhibited both the highest rates of poverty and the highest rates of specific cancers as well as other diseases. Programs directed to the region, including the Appalachian Leadership Initiative on Cancer and the Appalachia Cancer Network sponsored by the National Cancer Institute, have stimulated community cancer-control activities in Appalachia as a way of addressing prevention, early diagnosis, and treatment of cancer.

See also: APPALACHIA CANCER NETWORK; REPRODUCTIVE CANCERS AND WOMEN'S HEALTH; TOBACCO AND HEALTH.

—Thomas C. Tucker, *University of Kentucky*

American Cancer Society, *Cancer Facts and Figures* (2002); Gilbert H. Friedell, Thomas C. Tucker, and Frances E. Ross, "The Impact of Poverty and Education on Lung and Cervical Cancer in Appalachian Kentucky," *Journal of Registry Management* (November 1999); National Center for Health Statistics, *Cancer Mortality Rates for Appalachia* (1994–98).

Community Health Centers

For more than thirty years, community health centers—subsidized by federal grants under the U.S. Public Health Service Act—have provided a vital system of health care in the Appalachian region. These health centers are located in medically underserved areas that have high levels of poverty and few health-care providers. About 66 percent of those served by the centers fall below the poverty line. They are most frequently women of childbearing age, children, and low-income families. Community and public housing health centers, as well as those for migrants and the homeless, serve more than 12 million citizens annually at more than 3,300 delivery sites in all fifty states, the District of Columbia, Puerto Rico, Guam, and the Virgin Islands, providing care for one of every five low-income children and one of every twelve rural residents. For many Appalachian communities, the centers are the main source of comprehensive primary health-care services.

Designed to complement the newly enacted Medicaid program, the Community Health Center program originated in the Johnson administration's War on Poverty in the mid-1960s. Politically bold for its time, the health-center model offered medical services traditionally limited to private physician practices and empowered community boards to make important organizational decisions. By the early 1970s, when it was phased out, more than 100 neighborhood health centers had been established under the Economic Opportunity Act. The Public Health Service began funding the health centers in 1969. Under the Nixon administration, the health-center program was moved to the Department of Health, Education, and Welfare, and its name was changed to the Community Health Center program. At the same time, the National Health Service Corps program was established to help provide physicians and nurses for the centers. Throughout the 1970s, the program continued to expand, growing to 937 centers nationwide by the end of the decade. Under the Carter administration's rural-health initiative, many new health centers were established, and it was during this period that the Appalachian Regional Commission helped initiate many health centers in the area. In 1978 alone, the commission started 41 clinics for provision of primary medical and dental care. During the Reagan administration in the early 1980s, the Community Health Center program was severely diminished, and some 250 centers lost federal funding. In the late 1980s, however, the program was revived and began to grow once again.

Publicly subsidized nonprofit organizations governed by community-based boards of directors, community health centers are funded through federal grants, Medicaid, Medicare, and commercial insurance and serve large numbers of uninsured patients. The federal grants help subsidize operating costs, allowing the center to serve all patients regardless of ability to pay through the use of a sliding fee scale. These grants also help cover the costs of offering comprehensive primary care and various other services, including environmental health risk reduction (such as solid-waste disposal, sewage treatment, and ensuring a safe water supply), food banks, health education, housing assistance, translation services, and transportation.

The Federally Qualified Health Center provision created by Congress in 1989 allows reimbursement of up to 100 percent of the operational cost for the qualifying health centers through Medicaid and Medicare programs. Increased reimbursement for community health centers has allowed them to serve more uninsured patients, expand their services, and increase their geographical coverage.

See also: APPALACHIAN REGIONAL COMMISSION (GOVERNMENT); NATIONAL HEALTH SERVICE CORPS; WAR ON POVERTY (GOVERNMENT).

—Kathy Wood-Dobbins, *Tennessee Primary Care Association*

Stuart Altman, Uwe Reinhardt, and Alexandra Shields, *The Future of the U.S. Health Care System: Who Will Care for the Poor and Uninsured?* (1998); Milton I. Roemer, *Ambulatory Health Services in America: Past, Present, and Future* (1981).

Community-Initiated Health Efforts

A long series of community-based health-care initiatives developed in the Appalachian coalfields after World War II later became models for community health for the nation. These programs embraced the World Health Organization's broader inclusion of the patient's psychological and social well-being and increased personal control in defining health issues. They involved both community-based professional innovations, such as the hospitals built by the United Mine Workers of America, and community-led initiatives, such as the community health centers created as part of the War on Poverty.

Some of the early community-based professional innovations of the twentieth century included the Frontier Nursing Service developed by Mary Breckinridge, which sent trained nurse-midwives with medical equipment into isolated mountain areas on horseback. Breckinridge eventually set up outpost nursing centers, founded a hospital, and created the Frontier Graduate School of Midwifery. The work of settlement schools and clubwomen also helped improve standards of health care and introduced prevention measures such as child inoculation and courses in basic hygiene.

After World War II, the United Mine Workers of America, a leader of health-care innovation in coal-mining regions, stimulated health reforms with its assistance in the preparation of *A Medical Survey of the Bituminous Coal Industry*, widely known as the "Boone Report," which was conducted and published by the U.S. Department of the Interior. The study found that the region's company-based health-care system had created a series of medical monopolies of proprietary hospitals whose staffs were closed to younger physicians. Armed with evidence of the need for improved health care, the United Mine Workers negotiated a contract that contributed a royalty per ton of coal produced to pay for a comprehensive range of health services through the union's Welfare and Retirement Fund. A short-lived part of the fund provided disabled miners with high-quality rehabilitation services. The fund built ten state-of-the-art hospitals in the region and brought in new health-care professionals to staff them. The demand for rehabilitation services outstripped the financial resources of the United Mine Workers' medical funds, though, and the fund stepped back from its commitment to the hospitals just ten years after it had started them. By the mid-1960s, the National Board of Missions of the United Presbyterian Church (USA) bought them and continued their operation as the Appalachian Regional Hospitals and later as Appalachian Regional Healthcare.

Union members and their dependents protested cutbacks in the Welfare and Retirement Fund's health benefits and its inattention to the prevention of coal workers' pneumoconiosis (black lung) and rehabilitation for those miners whose breathing had been damaged by inhaled coal dust. A similar movement developed among textile mill workers who were at risk for byssinosis, or brown lung. The black and brown lung associations balanced community and professional contributions and demonstrated the power of grassroots health movements by bringing about changes in workplace regulations and compensation policies, but they were vulnerable to changes in state and federal regulations.

Another part of the fund's initiative, however, continued and changed health care regionally and nationally. Comprehensive primary health-care clinics in Bellaire, Ohio, Fairmont, West Virginia, and Russelton, Pennsylvania, established a new standard of care by combining group practice, preventive services, and appropriate referrals. Just as importantly, the boards of directors of these clinics brought residents into the clinics' decision-making process along with the salaried health professionals. Thus, the fund's clinics pioneered in blending, very often in a stormy way, professional innovations with community-led health initiatives.

By the late 1960s, a field of community health emerged from these and other precedents. New federal initiatives, such as the Office of Health Affairs, began the development of community health centers that mandated consumer board members. Beginning in 1970, the Appalachian Student Health Coalition and the Center for Health Services at Vanderbilt University, with support from the Appalachian Regional Commission, stimulated the development of more modest primary health-care centers, often staffed primarily by nurse practitioners. The now reformed United Mine Workers of America also supported the development of four community health centers in West Virginia. The Robert Wood Johnson Foundation supported the development of one of the community health centers in New River, West Virginia, and another clinic in Hindman, Kentucky.

Craig Robinson, the founding director of the New River clinic, had participated in the black lung movement and the United Mine Workers' clinic-development program. He outlined four principles of community health:

responding to client needs; bringing as many services as possible under one roof; incorporating a range of health and social services; and using nonprofessionals and nonmedical personnel in providing services. Experience led Robinson to two more goals: meeting all the principles of community health efficiently and getting paid for them. Eventually, these last two objectives necessitated formation of statewide associations of community health centers to defend their practices—such as the employment of nurse practitioners—and their funding bases.

From disparate origins, other community health centers evolved to community-based health initiatives. The Center for Health Services and the Highlander Research and Education Center in New Market, Tennessee, for instance, responded to the emergence of community leadership around environmental risks with programs of training and support for community leaders. Workers took up issues of occupational health and safety by forming associations such as the Tennessee Committee on Occupational Safety and Health and continued efforts directed at black and brown lung control and rehabilitation with more physician support. The Maternal and Infant Health Outreach Worker program at the Center for Health Services uniquely combines the four principles of community health. Local women, trained as outreach workers, provide support for pregnant women at risk for pregnancy-related complications, advocate for women and children in the local system of health care and other social services, and organize programs of child development for mothers with young children. The model has been emulated in family resource centers and in public-health programs in several states. Women first trained as outreach workers have become administrators of school health programs and social services agencies. Partly in recognition of the needs, resources, and traditions of community organizing, the National Cancer Institute developed the Appalachian Leadership Initiative on Cancer, a prevention and screening program that followed two other institute innovations aimed at building coalitions among African Americans and Hispanics.

The region boasts national models of community health services. In addition, the large number of community groups protesting environmental degradation continue a long and distinguished history of community-initiated health efforts.

See also: APPALACHIAN HEALTH PROVIDERS; BLACK LUNG DISEASE AND THE BLACK LUNG MOVEMENT; MATERNAL INFANT HEALTH OUTREACH WORKER PROGRAM.

—Richard A. Couto, *University of Richmond*

Sandra Lee Barney, *Authorized to Heal: Gender, Class, and the Transformation of Medicine in Appalachia, 1880–1930* (2000); Barbara Berney, "The Rise and Fall of the UMW Fund," *Southern Exposure* (Summer 1978); Robert E. Botsch, *Organizing the Breathless* (1993); Mary Breckinridge, *Wide Neighborhoods: A Story of the Frontier Nursing Service* (1952).

Dentistry

As is the case across America, dentistry in Appalachia has been relegated to a secondary position, both in social policy and in the health insurance marketplace. This is evidenced in various reports published by the federal government over the course of the twentieth century. The Medicaid program, despite its stated intention of providing the poor with access to health services, does not effectively reimburse dentists, meaning that many people in desperate need of treatment go without. Although the reason for Medicaid's failure in this area is not entirely clear, it is reasonable to assume that the program was designed primarily to reimburse physicians and hospitals without much consideration for the rest of the health-delivery system.

The rise of modern dentistry followed a path similar to that of medicine. Although some medical schools offered rudimentary training in dental work, most dental practitioners in early America were untrained. Licensure was not required in every state, and states that did require certification generally lacked any machinery to enforce it. There was a prejudice against formal licensure, especially during the Jacksonian era (roughly between 1820 and 1840), because it appeared to many politicians that trained providers were attempting to set themselves apart as an aristocracy by limiting who could practice. At this time, anyone who was interested in doing so could work as a dentist. Although techniques to achieve basic tooth restoration through fillings had been practiced since the seventeenth century, most early-nineteenth-century dental work consisted of extraction and the fashioning of dentures. While materials varied, the actual teeth used in the best of these appliances were carved from ivory.

In 1840, however, things began to change with the establishment of the Baltimore College of Dental Surgery by the Maryland legislature. Similar institutions were created in Pennsylvania, Ohio, and New York over the course of the next ten years. Even more important was the introduction of ether as a general anesthetic. It was first used for dental purposes by William T. G. Morton in Boston in September of 1846. A year later, a group of British researchers led by Sir James Simpson successfully demonstrated the effectiveness of chloroform, an even stronger anesthetic. These events by themselves were major breakthroughs, since they made painless surgery possible. Around the same time, Louis Pasteur confirmed the germ theory, showing that bacteria caused disease. It was demonstrated shortly thereafter that tooth decay was a bacterial process. Following medicine's example, trained dentists formed the American Dental Association in 1859. The association sought to do for dentistry what the American Medical Association, which had been founded in 1846, was doing for medicine: promote scientific advancement, regularize professional education, establish licensure across the nation, and drive untrained charlatans out of business. Modern dentistry emerged in the United States around 1900.

Essentially, the same problems that plague health-care delivery in contemporary America apply to dental care, only more so. These problems include lack of insurance, disparities in wealth and household income, and uneven availability of providers. Like their colleagues in medicine, dentists have tended to work in fee-for-service solo practices concentrated in cities. The net result of these problems has been the creation, as in medicine, of a double-tiered service delivery system. Affluent urban and suburban residents have access to high-quality care, while rural inhabitants and less affluent people are left behind.

This reality has had a negative impact upon rural areas across the nation, but it has hit Appalachia especially hard. The reasons for this situation are due to lifestyle patterns and structural inequity. In terms of lifestyle, three major factors come into play: poor diet, lack of fluoridation for water supplies, and the extensive use of smokeless tobacco. Each of these is a contributory factor to tooth decay and gum disease.

Health risks associated with a poor diet, particularly one with a high level of saturated fat, which can lead to cardiovascular disease, are generally well known. Poor diet also affects oral health, especially in failing to provide the nutrients necessary to maintain healthy teeth. Although fluoridation of water supplies has been shown to be an effective preventative measure, many small Appalachian communities do not have the economic resources to provide it. Consumption of smokeless tobacco products is endemic in the region and in some instances considered a male rite of passage into adulthood. Although the health risks associated with smoking have received a great deal of attention, the risks presented by smokeless tobacco have not been as widely publicized. In addition to promoting tooth decay, all smokeless tobacco products are carcinogenic and a major cause of oral cancer.

Some of these lifestyle problems could be easily addressed, particularly use of smokeless tobacco, through public service messages and informational campaigns. Far more difficult, however, are the problems associated with structural inequity. Although the question of access to general medical care has received a great deal of attention from social-policy advocates and the insurance industry over the past one hundred years, dental concerns have either gone unaddressed or have been relegated to a secondary position. The result has been the creation of a disparity of service and access between affluent and poor people, as well as between urban and rural areas, that is greater and more extensive than what currently exists with medical care.

This situation is best illustrated by the following statistic: for every eighteen-year-old person currently without health insurance, there are two more who lack dental coverage. Although dental plans such as United Concordia are available, many employers with an eye towards keeping payroll costs to a minimum simply do not offer them. In addition, the Medicaid program, which was designed primarily to cover physician and hospital costs, does not adequately reimburse dental providers.

The federal government could go a long way toward improving matters with very little effort. Better coverage could be provided through the Medicaid program simply by developing a reimbursement formula specific for dental treatment. The government could also look at expanding any service-based scholarship or loan-forgiveness programs it may have for dental education in order to encourage more dentists to locate their practices in underserved rural areas. As it is, Appalachia already has the basic infrastructure in place for such initiatives in terms of educational facilities and service models. Four major dental schools are either located in, or in close proximity to, the region: the University of Pittsburgh School of Dental Medicine; University of Alabama School of Dentistry; West Virginia University School of Dentistry; and University of Kentucky College of Dentistry.

The University of Pittsburgh School of Dental Medicine, founded in 1896, is the oldest of these four institutions. It is organized into four divisions: oral biology, surgical dental sciences, restorative dental sciences, and pediatric and developmental dental sciences. Its primary service area covers western Pennsylvania, and student dentists treat some sixty-five thousand patients annually. In addition, it maintains the Cleft Palate–Craniofacial Center, which provides treatment for children with craniofacial abnormalities. The center annually treats more than fifteen hundred patients from all over the world.

The University of Alabama School of Dentistry, established in 1945 by the Alabama legislature, is a unit of the university's medical center in Birmingham. The school offers not only degree programs but also postdoctoral study in biomaterials, caries research, endodontics and pulp biology, pediatric dentistry, oral and maxillofacial surgery, and other areas. The school's students participate in several programs that serve low-income patients. An example is the Student/Resident Experiences and Rotations in Community Health program. Coordinated through the Alabama Department of Public Health, the program allows for supervised dental students to provide dental care to the young, elderly, and disabled at community health centers. Other programs that attempt to provide care for Alabama's low-income rural counties include Guard Care and All Kids.

West Virginia University School of Dentistry is of more recent origin, having opened its doors in 1957. The school's curriculum covers all of the major subject areas such as orthodontics and oral and maxillofacial surgery. Moreover, it offers undergraduate and graduate degrees in dental hygiene, a graduate program in endodontics, and an advanced program in general dentistry. Dental students may participate in the West Virginia Rural Health Education Partnerships program, which gives students hands-on experience in rural communities and carries a service commitment of at least six weeks.

University of Kentucky College of Dentistry was established in Lexington in 1962. Although not located in Appalachia, it draws a number of its students from the region and sponsors educational and service programs operating in several of the region's counties. Most notable are the school's dental outreach efforts that provide oral health screenings, prevention, and treatment for indigent and underserved children. The Seal Kentucky program offers on-site dental screening and preventative sealant applications at eastern Kentucky elementary schools in twenty-nine counties through a mobile dental unit. Through this program and similar efforts, the college has made a commitment towards improving dental health through prevention. At the turn of the twenty-first century, the college was developing a Center of Rural Health Research, which, in conjunction with the Kentucky School of Public Health, will further goals of providing community-based health services research, education, and opportunities and improving access to dental care for all Kentuckians.

See also: PROFESSIONALIZATION OF MEDICINE; SECTION OVERVIEW.

—Theobald Minani and Pamela M. Zahorik, *East Tennessee State University*, and Richard P. Mulcahy, *University of Pittsburgh at Titusville*

Appalachian Regional Commission, *An Analysis of Disparities in Health Status and Accessibility to Health Care in the Appalachian Region* (2003); C. Horace Hamilton, "Health and Health Services," in *The Southern Appalachian Region: A Survey*, ed. Thomas R. Ford (1962); Jeffrey Stensland et al., *An Analysis of the Financial Conditions of Health Care Institutions in the Appalachian Region and Their Economic Impacts* (2002).

East Tennessee State University James H. Quillen College of Medicine

East Tennessee State University's James H. Quillen College of Medicine, located in Johnson City, was established in 1974 by the state legislature to alleviate a critical shortage of primary-care physicians in the Appalachian area of east Tennessee. The college admitted its first class in 1978 and was named in honor of former Tennessee Congressman James H. Quillen, who was instrumental in the school's development. The school has historically emphasized health needs for the rural elderly, specifically through its Center of Excellence for Geriatrics and Gerontology and Center for Nutrition Research. In the 2004 "Best Graduate Schools" issue of *U.S. News and World Report* magazine, the college ranked third in the nation for excellence in rural medicine education, sixteenth in family medicine, and seventeenth in primary care.

The James H. Quillen College of Medicine is affiliated with many of the hospitals located in the Tri-Cities area of Johnson City, Bristol, and Kingsport and in surrounding rural communities. The medical school has a strong working relationship with the Veterans Affairs medical center at Mountain Home, which houses the majority of its clinical and administrative departments, as well as the medical library.

Dedicated to excellence in the field of primary care, the Quillen College of Medicine offers numerous programs designed to attract students who are interested in practicing in rural areas. The premier program of this nature is the Rural Primary Care Track, a program resulting from a grant from the W. K. Kellogg Foundation under their Community Partnership for Health Professions Education program. The program serves the communities of Hawkins and Johnson Counties and gives students opportunities to work in clinical settings from the onset of their medical education. Another program designed to attract students to the Appalachian region is the Appalachian Preceptorship Program. Students interested in family medicine are placed in predetermined sites throughout the region to expose them to the health-care needs of underserved areas.

See also: APPALACHIAN PRECEPTORSHIP PROGRAM.

—J. Scott Wilson and Pamela M. Zahorik, *East Tennessee State University*

Families and Health

While its members having been born in the Appalachian region is a conventional way of identifying a family as Appalachian, persons with parents and grandparents born and reared in the region may have a deeper identification that influences their health. Families with stronger ancestral lineages to the mountain regions tend to have health patterns considerably different from families who have newly arrived. Family health patterns may also differ depending upon influences of higher education, the media, work environments, and whether or not family members have resided in places outside the region.

Many Appalachians view health as the mere absence of illness and the ability to be physically active. Others attach importance to family relationships, the ability to cope with everyday problems, and a sense of spiritual wholeness and therefore view health as a means to an end and not a goal in itself. Popular views of Appalachia continue to perpetuate misconceptions concerning the state of health awareness and health care in the region. Many people in Appalachia tend to be more focused on the present and postpone seeking health care until symptoms become severe. Others turn to alternative healing systems including herbalism, faith healing, and home remedies. However, no evidence exists that Appalachians are more likely to postpone seeking professional care or to become attached to alternative remedies than people elsewhere. In many cases, Appalachians tend to associate their health with inherited traits.

Many Appalachians view family health as a balance in the physical, emotional, psychological, spiritual, and social well-being of multiple family members, while others are primarily concerned with their ability to respond to the needs of individual members as they arise. However, families with an ill, disabled, or dying member may still view themselves as a healthy family. Family health is often seen as the ability of family members to cooperate, protect, and promote individual health. While families are unique in their characteristics and health practices, common culture influences some behaviors. For instance, when a member is gravely ill, the family often needs to discuss future actions with extended family members before finalizing decisions.

In Appalachian families, caregiving roles related to illness and health care generally belong to women, and mothers are usually the primary decision makers. While male dominance is conspicuous in some areas of Appalachian culture, men are likely to view health matters as the provenance of women. Appalachian mothers most often teach children about health, see that family members take medicines, arrange for medical appointments and treatments, and make decisions about daily health-care needs. Mothers often seek advice from other female family members prior to seeking professional medical care.

Appalachian families' concerns about health-care costs and delivery are similar to those of others nationwide. Many rural regions lack physicians and other health services. Some families have limited access to public transportation and private vehicles. Access to affordable health-care services and availability of fewer medical treatment options are issues for many families with limited incomes or no health insurance. Rural health systems in some Appalachian regions are largely supported by Medicare and Medicaid and are not always able to provide services comparable to urban areas, potentially increasing families' health risks.

See also: FARM FAMILIES (FAMILY AND COMMUNITY); PREGNANCY AND CHILDBIRTH (FAMILY AND COMMUNITY); SECTION OVERVIEW.

—Sharon A. Denham, *Ohio University*

Gary Burkett, "Status of Health in Appalachia," in *Sowing Seeds in the Mountains: Community-Based Coalitions for Cancer Prevention and Control*, ed. Richard A. Couto, Nancy K. Simpson, and Gale Harris (1994); Anthony P. Cavender and Scott H. Beck, "Generational Change, Folk Medicine, and Medical Self-Care in a Rural Appalachian Community," *Human Organization* (Summer 1995); S. A. Denham, "The Definition and Practice of Family Health," *Journal of Family Nursing* (May 1999).

Frontier Nursing Service

Mary Breckinridge had seen her own two children die young; she had been trained as a nurse; she had worked in devastated France after World War I; she came from a family with a tradition of service; and she saw a need. All those parts of her life converged in 1925 when she founded the Kentucky Committee for Mothers and Babies, renamed the Frontier Nursing Service three years later. For the next four decades, she and the organization were one.

Breckinridge saw that isolated areas of Appalachia (specifically areas in Kentucky) had little access to health care. Her solution focused on working with local people to build community involvement and bringing in trained nurse-midwives—initially from England and Scotland, since few Americans had the requisite training. Traveling on horseback in sky-blue uniforms, the nurses carried their medical equipment in saddlebags and provided prenatal and maternal care to all who requested it.

When raising funds outside the region, Breckinridge displayed a strong speaking ability and pointed to statistics indicating that maternal mortality and morbidity rates with her nurse-midwives in attendance fell one-third below national rates, and below those of any other patient population. Utilizing such figures as well as shocking pictures of disease and powerful silent movies, she demonstrated the need in Appalachia and raised six million dollars to keep the pioneering organization going. The organization's accomplishments came despite opposition from many in the medical profession who did not yet support the concept of the professional nurse-midwife.

At the same time, Breckinridge set up outpost nursing centers closer to the people being served; founded a hospital in Leslie County, Kentucky, in the middle of the organization's service area; and created the Frontier Graduate School of Midwifery in 1939, one of the first in the nation to train Americans in the field. Over time, jeeps replaced horses as the method of transportation, increasing efficiency but detracting from the mystique and aura of "angels on horseback."

Breckinridge recounted many of the successes of the Frontier Nursing Service in her 1952 autobiography, *Wide Neighborhoods*, and in articles published across the nation,

Mountain residents in eastern Kentucky at a clinic operated by the Frontier Nursing Service, 1940s. Nurses and midwives rode horses and mules across the mountains to make home visits. The woman in the center, framed by the door, is Mary Breckinridge, founder of the Frontier Nursing Service.

Nola Blair (seated), of the Frontier Nursing Service, talks to a child she delivered on Munch Creek near Hyden, Kentucky, 1941. In the early days of the Frontier Nursing Service, nurses served a seven-hundred-square-mile area, riding horses and mules and later driving jeeps.

demonstrating how her Appalachian experiment had become a model overseas as well. After she died in 1965, the organization faced increasing challenges as the changing health-care climate moved in directions Breckinridge had not envisioned. Later directors Helen E. Browne, W. B. Rogers Beasley, and Deanna Severance found that delivering care at a reasonable cost to a medically underserved group had become more and more difficult. Despite increasing costs, the organization tried to survive while still remaining independent of federal funding. But survival meant significant change. Initial Medicaid regulations required the same charges for all patients regardless of need. Patients were reimbursed only if they saw a doctor, not a nurse-midwife, and deliveries outside a hospital were excluded from coverage. These changes ensured that more women would give birth at hospitals than at home, even though the national mood seemed to be shifting in favor of less clinical settings for deliveries such as "birthing centers."

By the beginning of the twenty-first century, the organization had attended to more than twenty-five thousand maternity cases, chiefly concentrating on operating its small rural hospital, where most births now took place, and on running the Frontier School of Midwifery and Family Nursing, along with community-based educational programs. Though significantly changed, the organization continued serving the region in eloquent testimony to the vision of its founder.

See also: BRECKINRIDGE, MARY; COMMUNITY-INITIATED HEALTH EFFORTS.

—James C. Klotter, *Georgetown College*

Carol Crowe-Carraco, "Mary Breckinridge and the Frontier Nursing Service," *Register of the Kentucky Historical Society* (July 1978); Nancy Dammann, *A Social History of the Frontier Nursing Service* (1982); James C. Klotter, *The Breckinridges of Kentucky, 1760–1981* (1986).

Granny Midwives

Granny midwives were the primary providers of birthing care for women and their families in Appalachia until the middle decades of the twentieth century. Midwives were members of the local community who learned about delivering infants by apprenticing with experienced midwives. Also called granny women or neighbor ladies, they were the usual attendants at home births in the region until they were gradually displaced by formally trained physicians and by women from organizations such as the Frontier Nursing Service of eastern Kentucky. These predecessors of contemporary midwives were educated in the European model of midwifery. They eventually moved into clinics and under the aegis of a physician. Although granny midwives are not common today in Appalachian communities, lay midwives, sometimes called direct-entry midwives, still practice in Amish and Mennonite communities and have some popularity among those who seek an alternative to the contemporary medical establishment.

Prior to the late twentieth century, rural mountain people had little access to physicians. Not only did older women often take on the job of bringing babies into the world, but they also tended to sick family members, taught health as they knew it, and comforted the dying and their families. Most pregnant women could call on an aunt or mother who was a midwife and who often felt a calling from God to practice.

Many families greatly respected these women, preferring them to physicians. If a family had a horse and buggy, it would be sent to pick up the granny, but often families were too poor to provide transportation and the midwife had to walk to the cabin. (Occasionally, midwives, even in modern times, may travel at night over poor roads to houses that lack running water, electricity, and telephone—albeit with a flashlight and not a lantern to light the way.) Early midwives were paid little, if anything, for attending to the laboring woman, often staying a week to help the mother and the family. If there was no money, payment was sometimes in the form of food. Most grannies did not ask for payment, leaving that decision to the family's discretion.

Granny midwives varied greatly in experience and expertise. Concern for improving care of pregnant women, increasing numbers of nurse-midwives, and legislative actions requiring certification of midwives led to classes taught by representatives of health departments in the early decades of the twentieth century and to the development of maternity centers in some regions. Such centers in the Appalachian region were first founded in Kentucky. The Frontier Graduate School of Midwifery began in 1939 and has been in operation ever since. The Community-Based Nurse-Midwifery Education Program trains prospective nurse-midwives who cannot leave their communities to obtain education. The program began in 1989 and is part of the Frontier School of Midwifery and Family Nursing. Another such maternity center was established in 1943 in the extreme northeastern corner of Georgia in Rabun County. Many midwives availed themselves of the opportunity to learn more by attending classes or receiving training in one of the maternity centers. As delivery-associated infections such as puerperal sepsis, commonly known as childbed fever, continued to be a significant cause of perinatal mortality even into the 1940s, an important emphasis in classes at the maternity centers was on noninterference. Educators taught midwives, for example, to wear gloves when conducting internal exams since bare hands increased the risk of infection.

Bonnie Fillers, a midwife who practiced in northeast Tennessee, described her early midwifery experiences as rather primitive, including such improvisations as using her own string to tie cords and substituting cloth sterilized in an oven for diapers. In some instances, there was just enough water to wash her hands and none to wash the baby. Though Fillers believed in providing services to all women in labor, some midwives, because of their religious beliefs, refused to assist unmarried women. In 2001 midwife Lucinda Flodin refused to attend to women who smoked because she believed smoking increases the need for medical intervention.

Grannies have long used herbs for healing and soothing. Wildcrafting, or the art of selecting leaves, flowers, stems, or roots of plants at the correct time for making herbal preparations, is a part of Appalachian culture. The use of herbs continues to be part of granny midwifery. For instance, raspberry leaf tea, believed to have specific effects on the uterus and to be high in vitamins and minerals, is recommended for pregnant women and laboring mothers. Nettle tea is also recommended by midwives for its vitamin K and calcium content, which helps contain bleeding. The use of herbal preparations has been questioned as nonscientific, but research continues in an effort to determine the efficacy of many herbs. Legislation to control herbs as drugs rather than food substances has been proposed and may affect lay midwives' practice.

Many states have outlawed lay midwifery, allowing only physicians or certified nurse-midwives to conduct a delivery. The tension between lay midwives and certified nurse-midwives is apparent in the professional literature of both groups. The lay midwife is defined as a woman who has apprenticed with an experienced midwife, who may have also attended additional workshops and classes, and who focuses on assisting a woman and her family in home births. Detractors, however, have described lay midwives as self-taught, having "unpredictable" levels of education, experience, and expertise, and practicing by the granny midwife dictum of "Have one, see one, do one."

Lay midwives as well as certified nurse-midwives have experienced pressure from legislative bodies seeking to limit or control midwifery. In addition, powerful lobbies such as the American Medical Association have attempted to influence legislatures to outlaw the practice. Ironically, in Tennessee lay midwives are specifically exempted from the Medical Practice Act. Certified nurse-midwives, on the other hand, are highly regulated. An attempt by two certified nurse-midwives in 1980 to join an obstetrician in a professional partnership to establish a family-centered maternity practice led to a protracted legal battle and an adverse effect on the nurse-midwifery movement in Tennessee. The certified nurse-midwives were denied privileges at three hospitals, and the obstetrician was notified by his malpractice insurance carrier that his policy was being cancelled because he was assuming too much risk. The certified nurse-midwives then sued the insurance company, which controlled more than 80 percent of Tennessee's malpractice insurance market and was owned and operated by physicians. It was not until 1993 that the suit against the company, the physicians, and the hospitals was settled out of court. In contrast, nurse-midwifery service in other states, such as Kentucky, has been recognized as a valuable part of the health-care delivery system.

Midwives' history in the Appalachian region is documented at the University of Kentucky Oral History Program's Frontier Nursing Service Collection, which contains information on the influence and experiences of grannies and nurse-midwives as recollected by people in Kentucky and the Ohio Valley region. Many poor women in the South, especially mountain women, used midwives and were perceived as backward compared to middle-class urban women who gave birth in hospitals. Hospital delivery and perinatal care has since become increasingly available and popular in the region, though a wish to control their birthing experiences has led some women to choose home births.

Today there are few granny midwives—the last generation having passed away, become very aged, or discontinued practice because of restrictive legislation. Yet midwifery continues to be a significant force in the Appalachian region. Research studies by the American Nurses Association and the U.S. Congress carried out by the Office of Technology Assessment concluded that patient outcomes in certified nurse-midwife-assisted deliveries compared favorably with those conducted by physicians. Midwives of today stress that labor is a natural, not a medical, process and bemoan what they view as an excessive resort of invasive procedures in the medical practice. In the past, having a midwife attend a woman giving birth was a necessity; today, it is an option considered by some Appalachian women.

See also: FRONTIER NURSING SERVICE; GRANNIES, MIDWIVES, AND HEALERS (IMAGES AND ICONS).

—Carol Ann Mitchell, *Veterans Affairs Medical Center, Mountain Home, Tennessee*

Pat Arnow, "Lucinda Flodin," *Now and Then* (Spring 1989); Lucinda Flodin, "Childbirth: Back to the Future," *Now and Then* (Spring 1989); Eliot Wigginton, ed., *Foxfire 2* (1973).

Hall, Eula

(1927–) Community health-care organizer.

Eula Hall represents a central Appalachian tradition of dynamic women leaders that includes Mother Jones, the noted labor activist, and "Widow" Combs, who heroically resisted the strip mining of her land in 1965. Best known as the founder and coordinator of the Mud Creek Clinic in Floyd County, Kentucky, Hall has been prominent in almost every grassroots movement for miners, black lung victims, victims of domestic violence, and poor people in eastern Kentucky since 1960.

Born in Pike County, Kentucky, Hall came to Floyd County at twelve years of age and with only three years of schooling to work as a domestic. Married at seventeen, she escaped a violent and abusive husband and raised five children in abject poverty with the help of neighbors and friends—a debt that she has spent a lifetime paying back to the residents of Mud Creek.

The War on Poverty of the 1960s inspired Hall's sense of community leadership. During this period, she worked with the Appalachian Volunteers, a service and advocacy group that used college students and others to establish lasting programs and organizations such as the Eastern Kentucky Welfare Rights Organization. As an advocate for poor people and workers, Hall demanded accountability from those with responsibility for school lunches, clean water supply, strip-mine regulation, black lung benefits, and medical care for the poor. For three decades she worked as coordinator and social worker at the Mud Creek Clinic. She summarized her continued active involvement simply: "I tried to make happen everything that didn't happen when I was a child."

Awards span Hall's distinguished career, from a presidential citation from the American Public Health Association in 1975 to the Kentucky Commission on Women award in 1999. Both *People* and *Family Circle* magazines have listed her among the most notable Americans. One of her most cherished appreciations is a client's poem entitled "Kentucky's First Lady," which reads, in part: "She found a clinic, / where you can get help you can afford, / there's no doubt, / it's blessed by the Lord."

See also: BLACK LUNG DISEASE AND THE BLACK LUNG MOVEMENT; MUD CREEK CLINIC; WAR ON POVERTY (GOVERNMENT).

—Richard A. Couto and Elizabeth Greene, *University of Richmond*

Richard A. Couto, *Poverty, Politics, and Health Care* (1975); Lynda McDaniel, "Eula Hall: A Driving Force for Change," *Appalachia Magazine* (May 1999); Dorothy Hall Peddle, "To Do What's Right," *Southern Exposure* (March–April 1983).

Hill-Burton Hospital Construction Act

Named for its two cosponsors, U.S. Senators Joseph Lister Hill of Alabama and Harold Burton of Ohio, the Hill-Burton Hospital Construction Act was designed to bring urban hospitals to medically underserved rural areas. Passed in 1946, Hill-Burton was a remnant of a national health insurance plan first offered in 1938 by Assistant Secretary of the

Treasury Josephine Roche. The original proposal featured several initiatives for meeting a variety of rural health needs in addition to construction of modern hospitals. According to available statistics, rural areas were medically underserved both in terms of physicians and adequate hospital facilities.

These problems were especially acute in south-central Appalachia's mining communities. In many cases, physicians working in these communities were either underqualified or incompetent, and hospital conditions were generally poor. According to a medical survey published in 1947, most hospitals in south-central Appalachia, usually accommodating fewer than fifty beds, were deficient in every measured category, from obstetrical facilities and staffing to records and housekeeping. In addition, since they were for-profit, they offered minimal care for inflated charges. The Hill-Burton Act addressed this problem by making federal monies available for the construction of community hospitals.

Federal support was provided through matching funds, and interested communities raised start-up capital themselves. Once a specific threshold was reached, Hill-Burton funds were awarded on a dollar-per-dollar basis, covering half of all costs.

Responses were mixed. For example, the State of Alabama created a coordinated plan for the use of Hill-Burton funding. The plan was authored, in part, by physician John Newdorp, who eventually worked for the United Mine Workers of America Welfare and Retirement Fund. Using a hierarchical approach, the plan created an integrated network of community hospitals linked to a central medical research center. Each institution would work together in terms of keeping up with the latest medical innovations while offering increasingly sophisticated care as a patient moved up the hospital network's ladder.

It is not clear whether any other Appalachian states developed such plans. While Hill-Burton could be utilized by the region's small to mid-level cities, mining communities were left out since they were unable to raise the required initial revenue. Thus, while the legislation had an impact in the region, that impact was blunted.

This made private-sector organizations devoted to hospital improvement very important to the region. Most notable of these was the United Mine Workers of America Welfare and Retirement Fund, which created a chain of ten modern hospitals in south-central Appalachia in 1956. Originally named the Miners Memorial Hospital Association, the chain was sold to the Board of National Missions of the United Presbyterian Church (USA) in 1963. Renamed Appalachian Regional Health Care, the hospital chain continues to be a major asset to the region.

See also: COMMUNITY-INITIATED HEALTH EFFORTS; MINERS MEMORIAL HOSPITAL ASSOCIATION; UNITED MINE WORKERS OF AMERICA HEALTH AND RETIREMENT FUNDS.

—Richard P. Mulcahy, *University of Pittsburgh at Titusville*

Daniel M. Fox, *Health Policies, Health Politics: The British and American Experience, 1911–1965* (1986); C. Horace Hamilton, "Health and Health Services," in *The Southern Appalachian Region: A Survey*, ed. Thomas R. Ford (1962); Richard P. Mulcahy, "Health Care in the Coal Fields: The Miners Memorial Hospital Association," *Historian* (Summer 1993).

HIV/AIDS

Since the first U.S. cases of acquired immune deficiency syndrome (AIDS) were reported in 1981, the disease has rapidly spread from urban centers to smaller cities and rural areas. The human immunodeficiency virus (HIV) that causes AIDS is most commonly acquired through sexual contact with an infected partner or the sharing of needles contaminated with infected blood. Although Appalachian people engage in the same risky behaviors as Americans elsewhere, little research has been conducted on the number and characteristics of Appalachians living with HIV.

The first published accounts of HIV/AIDS in Appalachia appeared in 1989. Health professionals from regional medical centers in West Virginia and east Tennessee described their HIV-positive patients as being primarily white, male, and homosexual. Most of these patients had left the state for employment, education, or lifestyle reasons and returned home after being diagnosed with advanced symptoms of HIV.

Between 1981 and December 2000, an estimated 19,222 adults and adolescents from the Appalachian region were diagnosed with AIDS. Fifty-four percent lived in southern Appalachia, 42 percent lived in northern Appalachia, and 4 percent lived in central Appalachia. The regional AIDS incidence rate in 2000 was 6 cases per 100,000 population, as compared to a U.S. rate of 14.3 per 100,000.

Like many other parts of the country, Appalachia experienced a second wave of the HIV/AIDS epidemic among women, minorities, and people infected through injection drug use or heterosexual contact. One of every 7 Appalachian adults and adolescents diagnosed with AIDS between 1981 and December 2000 was a woman. Although African Americans comprise only 8 percent of the Appalachian population, they accounted for 35 percent of the AIDS cases diagnosed during this twenty-year period.

Sixty-three percent of the Appalachian men diagnosed with AIDS through December 2000 acquired HIV through male-to-male sexual contact. However, the percentage of men contracting HIV through injection drug use ranged from 14 percent in southern Appalachia to 25 percent in northern Appalachia. While most AIDS-diagnosed women residing in central and southern Appalachia reported heterosexual contact as the mode of exposure, 43 percent of the women residing in northern Appalachia said they acquired HIV through injection drug use.

Ten of the thirteen Appalachian states are located in the South. In 2001 this region accounted for 40 percent of the people estimated to be living with AIDS and 46 percent of the estimated number of new AIDS cases. Since 1993, the South has led the nation in the percentage of adolescent and young adult AIDS patients who reside in small cities and rural areas. Statewide incidence rates for syphilis and gonorrhea—sexually transmitted diseases that increase the risk of contracting HIV by three to five times—are highest in the South.

Cervical cancer rates provide an additional indicator of risk for HIV. Because the human papillomaviruses that cause cervical cancer are spread through sexual contact, women who become sexually active at a young age and/or who have multiple sexual partners are more likely to develop this disease. Between 1994 and 1998, Appalachian counties had an average annual age-adjusted cervical cancer mortality rate only slightly higher than the overall U.S. cervical cancer mortality rate (2.8 as opposed to 2.7 per 100,000). However, cervical cancer mortality rates in rural Appalachian counties and in the Appalachian regions of three states (Kentucky, Ohio, and West Virginia) were significantly higher than the national mortality rate.

Poverty, unemployment, and low rates of high school completion in many Appalachian counties suggest that this region may be particularly vulnerable to the spread of HIV. These environmental conditions encourage high-risk behaviors such as the exchange of sex for money or drugs and reduce access to HIV-prevention services. Additional research on risk behaviors, migratory patterns, and HIV prevalence will be needed better to project regional HIV/AIDS trends.

See also: GAY AND LESBIAN LIFE (FAMILY AND COMMUNITY); REPRODUCTIVE CANCERS AND WOMEN'S HEALTH; VERGHESE, ABRAHAM.

—Martha M. McKinney, *Community Health Solutions, Inc.*

Amy Lansky and Shari Steinberg, "Epidemiology of AIDS in Appalachia," *Health Education Monograph on HIV/AIDS Education and Prevention in Rural Communities*, ed. Mohammad Torabi (2003); Abraham Verghese, *My Own Country: A Doctor's Story of a Town and Its People in the Age of AIDS* (1994).

Hutchins, Louise

(1911–1996) Physician.

Louise Frances Gilman Hutchins was a doctor of medicine best known for her work with the Mountain Maternal Health League, an Appalachian family-planning organization. She was born in China on February 2, 1911, to American missionaries and spent the first fifteen years of her life there. She returned to America to attend Wellesley College and, inspired by the example of service set by her parents and grandparents, continued her education at Yale University Medical School, receiving a diploma in 1936.

Soon after beginning medical school, she became engaged to Francis Hutchins. Her professors debated whether to allow her to complete her training, saying that a married woman would never practice medicine. She defied their predictions, working first in China, where she completed an internship in pediatrics at Hunan Hospital in Changsha. She then moved to Berea, Kentucky, with her husband in 1939, when he became president of Berea College. Between 1939 and 1967, Hutchins was the town's only pediatrician.

In the early 1940s, she became involved in the fledgling Mountain Maternal Health League. Through her work with this family-planning organization, she helped thousands of women in the Kentucky mountains obtain contraceptives. She resigned as director of the league in 1967, the same year her husband retired from Berea College. They spent the next three years in Hong Kong, where she remained active in family planning. Hutchins continued to speak on birth control in the United States and Asia until her death in 1996.

See also: BEREA COLLEGE (EDUCATION); MOUNTAIN MATERNAL HEALTH LEAGUE.

—Melanie Beals Goan, *University of Kentucky*

Indian Health Service

The Indian Health Service is an agency of the United States government responsible for delivery of health services to federally recognized American Indians and Alaskan Natives. The agency was established by the U.S. Constitution and resulted from various Supreme Court decisions, treaties, legislation, and executive orders dating back over more than one hundred years of Native American and U.S. governmental relations. The Snyder Act of 1921 provided the authority for funding of health services to American Indians. Today, the Indian Health Service operates a health-care delivery system serving approximately 1.6 million of the estimated 2.6 million American Indians and Alaskan Natives in the United States.

Most Indian Health Service funds are appropriated for American Indians who live on or near reservations, although Congress has also authorized programs that provide some access for American Indians and Alaskan Natives who live in urban areas. The agency's general mission is to improve the physical, mental, social, and spiritual health of these groups in partnership with the more than 560 federally recognized tribes in the United States. In the Appalachians, the largest tribes are the Eastern Band of Cherokee Indians located in North Carolina and the Seneca in New York. The main office of the Indian Health Service for the eastern tribes is located in Nashville, Tennessee.

In Appalachia, the Indian Health Service operates and provides outpatient and inpatient health services through a thirty-two-bed hospital located in Cherokee, North Carolina, one of thirty-six federally operated Indian Health Service hospitals in the United States. Many Native American tribes in the Appalachians are served by urban or other tribally operated health facilities funded through the Indian Health Service.

Historically, American Indians and Alaskan Natives have had a disproportionate number of health problems compared to other Americans. Although the last quarter of the twentieth century saw improvements due to increased availability of health care, many disparities remain. Educational and socioeconomic inequality strongly affects the health status of American Indians living in Appalachia. The five leading causes of death among American Indians and Alaskan Natives are cardiovascular disease, cancer, accidents, diabetes, and chronic liver disease.

The passage of the Indian Self-Determination and Education Assistance Act in 1975 and the Indian Health Care Improvement Act in 1976 gave tribes the option of assuming the administration and operation of health services and programs or remaining within the Indian Health Service's direct health system. This option of tribal self-governance has significantly affected the health and well-being of Native Americans, resulting in increased accessibility to health services, improved care, increased efficiency in the health system, and development of preventive programs that recognize traditional Native American healing practices.

See also: CHEROKEE (RACE, ETHNICITY, AND IDENTITY); CHEROKEE FAMILIES AND COMMUNITIES (FAMILY AND COMMUNITY); SENECA (RACE, ETHNICITY, AND IDENTITY).

—J. T. Garrett, *Beaufort, North Carolina*

Kenny, Sister Bernadette

(1938–) Family nurse practitioner.

Sister Bernadette Kenny, or "Sister Bernie," as she is known to patients and colleagues, is a family nurse practitioner who has provided health care to the residents of Dickenson and Buchanan Counties in southwest Virginia since 1984. Born in Massachusetts, Kenny received training as a nurse and midwife in Ireland in the early 1960s and completed an undergraduate degree in nursing from Boston College in 1971. She later obtained certification as a family nurse practitioner from the Medical College of Virginia in 1983.

With the support of Saint Mary's Hospital in Norton, Virginia, and the Catholic Medical Missionaries of Mary, Sister Bernie founded Saint Mary's Health Wagon in 1983, a service that she continued into the twenty-first century. The Health Wagon is a modified recreational vehicle that serves as a mobile medical office. From this office, Kenny has cared for numerous individuals who would otherwise not have access to medical care. Along with a staff of three, she has established annual health fairs serving numerous southwest Virginia communities. These fairs involve local health departments and other community agencies, as well as area medical students, resident physicians, and other health-care providers.

In addition to providing direct health-care services to meet the needs of southwest Virginia, she has provided leadership and inspiration for numerous local organizing efforts aimed at improving the health and welfare of the people of southwest Virginia. In 1990 she addressed the Southern Conference of Governors on access to perinatal care, and in 1994 she led a delegation to the United Nations Year of the Family, where she delivered an address on measures needed to support families. In 1998 she received the annual Lumen Christi Award, a national Catholic charities award for community outreach.

See also: COMMUNITY-INITIATED HEALTH EFFORTS.

—Raymond H. Feierabend, *East Tennessee State University*

Marshall University Joan C. Edwards School of Medicine

Established under the Veterans Administration Medical Assistance and Health Training Act passed by Congress in 1972, the Marshall University School of Medicine is a state-supported, community-based medical school founded in Huntington, West Virginia, in 1977. A shortage of primary-care physicians in the state led the board of regents to specify a sixteen-county region in central and southern West Virginia as the initial focus for the school. Renamed the Joan C. Edwards School of Medicine in May 2000, the institution strives to meet the health needs of all rural areas in the state.

Historically, Marshall University has specialized in rural health problems, recruited students from rural West Virginia, and regularly placed graduates in clinical practice in rural areas. Clinical and basic research has also focused on health issues related to rural populations. As of 2003, the Joan C. Edwards School of Medicine ranked fifth in the nation for the percentage of graduates entering primary-care fields.

The Edwards School of Medicine is affiliated with the Cabell Huntington Hospital, Saint Mary's Hospital, and the Huntington Veterans Affairs Medical Center, all of which serve as clinical training grounds for students. In addition, all students spend at least three months of their undergraduate medical education at rural sites statewide through the West Virginia Rural Health Education Partnerships. Students and residents also participate in a mobile pediatric clinic operated by Marshall and Valley Health Systems, delivering medical care to children in six rural counties.

Marshall operates the first of two rural family practice residency programs in the state. It has the nation's first Wilderness Medicine track in a family practice residency program, as well as a highly regarded International Health program.

The school has taken a leadership role in using technology to overcome geographical barriers, creating specialized services including RuralNet, an Internet information resource designed to meet the needs of rural providers and health-professions students on rotation in rural communities. Marshall also is home to the Robert C. Byrd Center for Rural Health, a resource supporting rural health-care providers and infrastructure.

See also: OFFICE OF RURAL HEALTH AT WEST VIRGINIA UNIVERSITY; WEST VIRGINIA UNIVERSITY SCHOOL OF MEDICINE.

—J. Scott Wilson and Pamela M. Zahorik, *East Tennessee State University*

Maternal Infant Health Outreach Worker Program

Since its beginning in 1982, the Maternal Infant Health Outreach Worker (MIHOW) Program has worked with communities and low-income families to improve maternal and infant health and early child development for more than ten thousand families across the Mid-South, including central and southern Appalachia. Based in the Center for Health Services at Vanderbilt University in Nashville, Tennessee, the project was initiated in 1982 in four Appalachian communities: Campbell County, Tennessee; Whitley County, Kentucky; and Fayette County and McDowell County, West Virginia. Operating out of locally run clinics and nonprofit agencies, the program now has more than twenty Appalachian sites. Incorporating the traditional Appalachian value of self-sufficiency, the MIHOW effort is based on the premise that women who live in hard-to-reach communities have specific knowledge and skills, along with energy and integrity, that enable them to be effective in improving maternal and child health in their own communities.

The program has grown steadily, becoming a partnership between Vanderbilt and twenty-five local grassroots agencies in Appalachia, as well as in sites in the Mississippi Delta and across the Mid-South. Vanderbilt provides assistance in fund-raising, planning, training, and evaluation. The local clinics and agencies recruit local mothers to become outreach workers. Working together, the local partner and Vanderbilt provide training for these women to become paid MIHOW paraprofessionals who assist pregnant women and families with young children. This training, combined with their existing empathy and judgment about the needs and strengths of local families, enables them to develop the relationships necessary to assist families dealing with extreme poverty and geographic and social isolation. Home visits are structured to improve the self-esteem of low-income women; workers identify strengths in the mother's situation and provide positive reinforcement. Efforts to reach out to fathers have been emphasized as well.

The key to the program's success has been its use of local parents as home visitors in conjunction with an effective partnership in which the local community has a strong and meaningful role. Several evaluations have shown, for example, that participants are more likely to know how to access affordable medical care and to obtain assistance with alcoholism, drug abuse, and depression. Participating mothers consume more vitamins and iron and less tobacco and caffeine during pregnancy. They receive more medical visits and are more likely to breast-feed. Children in participating families score higher on inventories indicative of later school success. The program is also beneficial for the outreach workers, many of whom are dropouts who have returned to high school or earned a high school equivalency diploma. A few have gone on to college. Several have felt empowered enough to leave abusive relationships.

Originally funded by a Ford Foundation grant, the MIHOW Program has received national and international attention, including awards by the Annie E. Casey Foundation, the Points of Light Foundation, and Lamaze Outreach. It was the first American program to win the prestigious Oscar van Leer Award, which is presented to one community organization worldwide by the Netherlands-based Bernard van Leer Foundation every two years.

See also: COMMUNITY-INITIATED HEALTH EFFORTS.

—Barbara Clinton, *Vanderbilt University*

Medicinal Plant Use

Medicinal plants have been used in the Appalachians since prehistoric times, but historical accounts document the practice of Native American medicinal plant use to the early eighteenth century. One of the earliest plants gathered in the Appalachian forest was American ginseng, a valuable commodity on the world market since the mid-1700s. The Cherokees were extremely familiar with the plant since they, like the Chinese who readily purchased the root, believed it to have important medicinal qualities. Ginseng was used by the Cherokees for a variety of ailments, including headaches, "weakness of the womb," nervous infections, and as a general health tonic.

The influence of Cherokees on medicinal plant use by settlers in the mountains is without question. Not only did they educate newcomers on the medicinal properties of native plants, but they also facilitated the mountaineers' participation in the trade and sale of these plants to markets outside the region. Root and plant digging in the mountains has provided an important source of income since at least the early nineteenth century. The Civil War increased the cultivation and digging of many native plants. One of the first "crude-drug" firms, as they were then called, in North

Carolina was established in Lincolnton during the height of the conflict.

After the war, the crude-drug industry became concentrated in the southern and central Appalachians, particularly in Tennessee, North Carolina, Virginia, West Virginia, and Kentucky. By the end of the nineteenth century, the enterprise was fast becoming an important source of supplemental income for individuals otherwise living on subsistence agriculture. By the turn of the century, the collection of plants for medicinal uses became important enough for the United States Department of Agriculture to create the Bureau of Plant Industries in 1901. The bureau produced numerous publications describing American leaves, herbs, roots, barks, and weeds used in medicine. These publications were designed to be guides and reference books for farmers, drug collectors, druggists, students, and others interested in the collection of medicinal flora.

Although medicinal plants were collected in the wild, many were also cultivated as agricultural crops. In fact, a Bureau of Plant Industries publication, *American Medicinal Plants of Commercial Importance*, gave specific instructions in the growing and preparation of plant material for the crude-drug market. The economic importance of collecting medicinal plants for commercial profit is strongly emphasized in the bulletin, and some plants were commonly sold in quantities ranging from a few pounds to many tons. To ensure potency and quality, many of the larger firms claimed adherence to provisions found in the Pure Food and Drug Act of 1906, one of the very first American laws designed to regulate the marketing and distribution of medicinal herbs.

By the end of the first decade of the twentieth century, numerous drug buyers had come to the region, where they opened processing facilities and collection points for growers and gatherers. One such collection point was operated by S. B. Penick and Company through offices in Asheville and Boone, North Carolina. Penick contracted with enterprising small farmers and local businessmen to collect medicinal plants ranging from bloodroot to wild sarsaparilla.

By the late 1920s, Penick was a major supplier of crude drugs to the world market, which had become largely dependent upon the Appalachian region. In a company price list and manual published in 1929, Penick claimed that in Appalachia 85 percent of all American drugs were gathered and prepared for the market and that Asheville was the heart of the collecting area. One of Penick's close competitors was the Wilcox Drug Company, established in Boone in 1900 by General Grant Wilcox. According to company records, the Wilcox firm purchased roots, herbs, and barks from across the Appalachian region, with most sales carried out through New York brokers.

The extensive collecting activities of such firms and individuals may well have contributed to the decline of many medicinal plants in the mountains, several of which are presently listed as federally endangered or threatened species. In the 1960s, Edward Price, who published an important article on the geography of botanical drugs in the Appalachians, claimed that these collection centers greatly encouraged the depletion of forest ecosystems. In one year alone, one firm in the region collected some thirteen thousand pounds of ginseng. By the late 1960s, most of the major crude-drug houses established in the mountains earlier in the century had moved to other regions of the United States.

Despite the decline of Appalachia as the regional cornerstone of the American plant-medicine industry, the mountains remain an important source for numerous commercial botanicals. Goldenseal and ginseng from the mountains continue to contribute a considerable portion of the world market for these two plant species. Numerous other species are still widely collected in the Appalachians, including black cohosh, mayapple, boneset, seneca snakeroot, Indian pinkroot, and witch hazel. Wilcox Natural Products, a private corporation now owned by a Swiss pharmaceutical firm, Zuellig Group North America, is the region's largest botanical supplier, buying more than fifty plant varieties from local collectors and processing them at their regional headquarters in Boone.

Historically, the crude-drug and multinational pharmaceutical companies and their collection practices bear a share of the blame for the decline in some species of mountain plants. Today, however, the choice between collecting and not collecting is not the only issue. In the late twentieth and early twenty-first centuries, more habitat and thus more native plants in the Appalachians were lost to suburban and industrial development than in the past two centuries. The biological heritage of the region and its value to the health of future generations make the problem of habitat loss one of increasing urgency.

See also: FOLK MEDICINE (FOLKLORE AND FOLKLIFE).

—Donald E. Davis, *Dalton State College*

Donald E. Davis, "Medicinal and Cultural Uses of Plants in the Southern Appalachians: Past, Present, and Future," *Ethnopharmacologia* (September 1999); Edward T. Price, "Root Digging in the Appalachians: The Geography of Botanical Drugs," *Geographical Review* (January 1960).

Mental Health

The history of mental health in Appalachia has been marked by the misguided blaming of mental illness on alleged characteristics of Appalachian culture and confusing the effects of economic distress and poverty with the causes. There has also been an undersupply of mental health professionals. The term *mental health* refers to the psychological, emotional, social, and biological well-being of people in their personal and work relationships. *Mental illness*, by contrast, refers to problems in realism and clarity of thinking, disturbances in mood or emotion, or behavior problems that result in social impairment. Examples of mental illness include schizophrenia, depression, anxiety, post-traumatic stress disorder, and personality disorders. Substance abuse and dependence are also included among mental health problems. The standardized reference of mental illnesses is *The Diagnostic and Statistical Manual of Mental Disorders* of the American Psychiatric Association. Mental health problems are diagnosed and treated by a variety of mental health professionals, including psychologists, psychiatrists, clinical social workers, marriage and family counselors, and chemical dependency counselors.

Individual mental disorders have different causes, and most have been found to have genetic as well as environmental components. Genetic factors alone do not cause disorder, but they can create a susceptibility that is triggered or worsened by life events. Poverty or affluence, the availability of employment opportunities, and other social conditions contribute to the way mental health problems are experienced throughout Appalachia, as elsewhere.

Like all communities, Appalachia struggles with problems presented by mental illness. However, there was a tendency in the past to view Appalachian people as especially predisposed to mental disorder due to alleged genetic factors and the social conditions imposed by perceived regional isolation, fatalism, ignorance, and violent temperament. Many early efforts to understand and treat mental illness in the region during the 1960s and 1970s led to erroneous and stigmatizing accounts by professionals about Appalachian culture and its identification with mental illness. Improved psychiatric classification, sophisticated epidemiological tools, and more rigorous Appalachian research and scholarship by indigenous and outside workers have changed this view. For example, the belief that Appalachians have greater genetic predisposition to mental illness has been disproved.

While there is a lack of reliable data, the prevalence of mental illness in rural America appears to differ little from urban settings. Likewise, the extent of substance abuse appears to be remarkably similar in rural and urban areas although specific drugs of choice may vary. While overall rates in Appalachia may not differ from national levels, the region's legacy of political and economic exploitation, poor access to transportation, unimproved schools, and poor housing have all contributed to the way mental illness is experienced. The loss of local or personal control over essential resources, a long-standing problem in Appalachia, may aggravate mental disorders and substance abuse problems.

A scarcity of mental health professionals has long characterized the more rural and economically depressed communities of the region. The dearth of such care contributes to the increased severity and chronicity of most mental illnesses. The Appalachian family medical practitioner often fills this resource gap and may carry a heavy caseload of mental health patients.

Economic distress and its relationship to mental and physical health problems may help explain heavy prescription painkiller and tranquilizer use in many Appalachian communities. Mining, farming, logging, and factory work bring high rates of injury and chronic illnesses that affect mental health, and unemployment has been shown to be an important contributor to mental illness. Not surprisingly, many clinicians in Appalachia report high levels of chronic pain and mood disorders among their clients.

To meet the needs of Appalachians with mental illness and substance abuse problems, traditional treatment services are combined in many communities with services that help with housing, other health-care services, and employment or training. Innovative and culturally sensitive outreach and community-based services are needed to supplement hospital- and clinic-based services for persons who would not otherwise be served. Enhancement of mental health in the more economically depressed parts of the region depends on measures that will improve economic conditions, enhance the overall quality of life, and increase the degree of control individuals have over their lives.

See also: SECTION OVERVIEW.

—James Clark, Robert Walker, and Carl Leukefeld, *University of Kentucky*

Robert Coles, *Children of Crisis, Vol. 2: Migrants, Sharecroppers, Mountaineers* (1967); Gerald N. Grob, *The Mad among Us: A History of the Care of America's Mentally Ill* (1994); Susan Emily Keefe, ed., *Appalachian Mental Health* (1988); U.S. Department of Health and Human Services, National Institutes of Health, and National Institute on Drug Abuse, *Rural Substance Abuse: State of Knowledge and Issues* (1997).

Miner Physical Rehabilitation Program

The Miner Physical Rehabilitation Program was established by the United Mine Workers of America (UMWA) Welfare and Retirement Fund (now the UMWA Health and Retirement Funds) in 1947 and marked the beginning of the fund's work as a health insurer. The rehabilitation program was initiated by Royd R. Sayers, the fund's original chief medical officer, and brought to fruition by his successor, Warren F. Draper.

Sayers discovered that company towns and mining communities were filled with miners disabled by work-related injuries suffering from longterm neglect. Viewing the situation as an appropriate area for the fund, he resolved to seek out such people and get them medical attention. Using all available records and word of mouth, the fund went into the field to find clients. In addition, the fund secured the services of Howard Rusk, a pioneer in rehabilitative medicine, as a consultant.

In many cases, disabled miners were found in Appalachia's most isolated sections. Most had been injured years earlier and suffered a variety of problems including muscular atrophy, infections, and bedsores. Because such areas were often without adequate roads, ailing workers were sometimes taken down from the mountains by stretcher teams. Eventually, they were placed aboard trains with Pullman cars designed for hospital care and sent to various "special centers" for rehabilitation.

When the program started, the fund made arrangements with nine rehabilitation hospitals, including the Kabat-Kaiser Institute in Vallejo, California; the Kessler Institute of Physical Rehabilitation in West Orange, New Jersey; and the Woodrow Wilson Rehabilitation Center in Fisherville, Virginia. In addition to treatment, the fund secured training for miners so they could become self-supporting.

The results were impressive. By 1953, 1,200 injured miners had been treated, with 224 having become self-supporting. After 1953 the volume of rehabilitation cases fell because the backlog had been diminished. Nevertheless, the program continued into the 1970s, ending only when the fund's medical program itself was terminated in 1977.

See also: MINERS MEMORIAL HOSPITAL ASSOCIATION; UNITED MINE WORKERS OF AMERICA (LABOR); UNITED MINE WORKERS OF AMERICA HEALTH AND RETIREMENT FUNDS.

—Richard P. Mulcahy, *University of Pittsburgh at Titusville*

Joseph E. Finley, *The Corrupt Kingdom: The Rise and Fall of the United Mine Workers* (1972); Maier B. Fox, *United We Stand: The United Mine Workers of America, 1890–1990* (1990); Richard P. Mulcahy, "'They Shall Walk Again!': The Physical Rehabilitation Program of the UMWA Welfare and Retirement Fund," *Journal of the Appalachian Studies Association* (1994).

Miners' Clinics

Organized by a coalition of the United Mine Workers of America (UMWA) Welfare and Retirement Fund, local unions, and civic organizations such as the Federation of Women's Clubs, miners' clinics were group-practice facilities created to replace company doctors in the coal industry. Health reformers, led by activist Josephine Roche, had promoted group practice as superior to solo practice during the New Deal's drive for national health insurance. Although their efforts failed, many of the individuals involved in that drive eventually worked for union-sponsored health insurance programs such as the UMWA Welfare and Retirement Fund (now the UMWA Health and Retirement Funds). Roche, a former assistant secretary of the treasury, joined the fund's staff in 1947 and was appointed its director shortly thereafter.

Roche managed the fund as a privatized version of the national health insurance program that she and her colleagues wanted to create. True to their beliefs, Roche and other members of the fund's staff, including physicians Lorin E. Kerr, John Newdorp, and John Winebrenner, paid for miner health care and sought to improve its quality. Promotion of group practice was one part of this. Group-practice facilities provided miners with more sophisticated care than was ordinarily available in traditional solo-practice settings. They also made minor surgery possible in the clinics, thereby avoiding excessive hospitalization and lowering costs.

Essentially, the fund cooperated with other organizations interested in improving the standard of medical care in their communities. This was done with at least three facilities organized during the middle 1950s: the Bellaire Clinic in Bellaire, Ohio; the Pruden Valley Clinic in Pruden Valley, Tennessee; and the Russelton Health Center in McKeesport, Pennsylvania. Under this arrangement, local groups organized the clinic while the fund recruited physicians, offered managerial expertise, and ensured a guaranteed income through a retainer agreement.

Rural areas that were previously underserved gained access to quality medical care. Company doctors, who had often been individuals of dubious professional competence, rapidly faded from the scene. Moreover, due to the success of these first institutions, many similar clinics sprang up throughout the region between the late 1950s and 1970. What had once been a widening gap between rural and urban health care for Appalachia in terms of access and quality was significantly narrowed.

See also: MINERS MEMORIAL HOSPITAL ASSOCIATION; ROCHE, JOSEPHINE; UNITED MINE WORKERS OF AMERICA HEALTH AND RETIREMENT FUNDS.

—Richard P. Mulcahy, *University of Pittsburgh at Titusville*

William A. Massie, *Medical Services for Rural Areas* (1957); Richard P. Mulcahy, "Replacing the Company Doctor: Pruden Valley, Tennessee, and the Development of the Miners' Clinics," *Tennessee Medicine: The Journal of the Tennessee Medical Association* (March 1999); U.S. Department of the Interior, *A Medical Survey of the Bituminous Coal Industry: Report of the Coal Mines Administrator* (1947).

Miners Memorial Hospital Association

Established through the auspices of the United Mine Workers of America Health and Retirement Fund, the Miners Memorial Hospital Association built ten hospitals in the mid-1950s, introducing significantly improved health care for coal miners and their families in south-central Appalachia. Dedicated officially at Beckley, West Virginia, on June 2, 1956, by United Mine Workers of America President John L. Lewis, the hospitals were located in Beckley and Man, West Virginia; Wise, Virginia; and in Harlan, McDowell, Hazard, Whitesburg, Pikeville, Middlesboro, and South Williamson, Kentucky. Construction of these hospitals brought modern facilities along with well-trained medical and ancillary personnel into the heart of the region's bituminous coalfields.

The hospital system was considered a success by miners and their families and has served as a model for similar health-care organizations. Its novel administration ideas, including new kinds of nursing services, supply plans, and efficiency efforts, were integrated into the hospitals' designs to impress and recruit staff. All ten facilities, including the hospital plus apartment complexes for nurses and other staff, were built at a cost of approximately $33 million. Other features included training schools for professional nurses and nurse anesthetists, a school for medical technology, additional training programs for various health-care specialists, and in several places the creation of sewage and water treatment facilities. Frederick W. Mott was the first chief administrator of the Miners Memorial Hospital Association; he was succeeded by John Newdorp.

Although the facilities were much needed, some physicians already working in West Virginia and Appalachian Kentucky and Virginia objected to the construction, feeling an intrusion on their territory. Many disliked the idea of salaried Miners Memorial Hospital Association colleagues competing with the traditional fee-for-service structure. Objections to the association were especially acute in Kentucky, where a strong antiunion bias prevailed politically and where the Kentucky State Medical Association fought the hospitals and their physicians. Kentucky county medical societies, controlled by the Kentucky State Medical Association, refused membership to physicians in the Miners Memorial Hospital Association, effectively excluding them from membership in the American Medical Association and potentially damaging their careers.

Almost from the beginning, the hospitals operated at a loss. Mechanization of the coal industry brought lower employment, and reduced coal production lowered royalties to the United Mine Workers of America Welfare and Retirement Fund, which relied upon such monies to finance the hospitals. Other problems contributed to the woes of the Miners Memorial Hospital Association system. Recessions hurt receipts, coal sales fell, beds were underutilized by beneficiaries, and a large indigent population drained away resources. In 1963 the hospitals were sold to the United Presbyterian Church (USA). The hospitals continued to operate under the name Appalachian Regional Hospitals, a nonprofit corporation, until 1986, when the company was renamed Appalachian Regional Healthcare.

See also: LEWIS, JOHN L. (LABOR); UNITED MINE WORKERS OF AMERICA HEALTH AND RETIREMENT FUNDS.

—Rick Smoot, *University of Kentucky Lexington Community College*

Joseph E. Finley, *The Corrupt Kingdom: The Rise and Fall of the United Mine Workers* (1972); Richard P. Mulcahy, *A Social Contract for the Coal Fields: The Rise and Fall of the United Mine Workers of America Welfare and Retirement Fund* (2001).

Hazard Memorial Hospital in Hazard, Kentucky, 1956. Built by the UMWA Welfare and Retirement Fund through its subsidiary, the Miners Memorial Hospital Association, Hazard Memorial was one of a coordinated chain of ten institutions established in Kentucky, Virginia, and West Virginia to provide health care for coal miners and their families.

Mountain Maternal Health League

Founded in 1936 by concerned women affiliated with Berea College, the Mountain Maternal Health League was one of the first organizations to bring contraceptives and family-planning information to eastern Kentucky. Despite significant difficulties with funding, access, and acceptance, the league and its dedicated women workers distributed birth control to thousands of women trapped in a "baby a year" cycle.

Inspired by the federal government's decision to allow contraceptive distribution through the mail and word of similar efforts in West Virginia, the Berea group came together as the Mountain Maternal Health League when Philadelphia physician Clarence Gamble proposed to conduct research on effective birth control for rural women. Gamble agreed to pay for a full-time nurse, a car, and spermicidal jelly if the league would keep careful records for his study. Over the next two years, hundreds of families received in-home visits and contraceptive information and supplies.

The withdrawal of Gamble and his funding at the close of his study in 1938 left the organization scrambling for donations. It received an important boost in 1939 with the arrival in Berea of Louise Hutchins, a Yale-educated physician who had served her residency in China and was the wife of Berea College President Francis Hutchins. Hutchins was appalled to find that although she could give out family-planning information as a private physician, the State of Kentucky made no provision for such assistance through its public-health service. The state health commissioner promised to look the other way, however, and Hutchins and the league managed to distribute contraceptives to thousands of eastern Kentucky women. Although still on shaky ground financially, Mountain Maternal established a clinic at Berea Hospital in 1944 and became affiliated with Planned Parenthood in 1945. Throughout the years, both clinic and outreach programs primarily employed women doctors such as Hutchins and Mary Pauline Fox as well as certified nurse-midwives who provided prenatal and obstetrical care in addition to their family-planning work.

Surviving documents relate emotional tales of the opposition faced by the league. Hutchins recalled one woman whose seventy-one-year-old minister husband had beaten her for having had an intrauterine device inserted. Another woman, the mother of twelve, faced a husband who objected to the use of contraceptive foam, even though she had been told by her doctor that another pregnancy would threaten her life.

Although restrictions on birth control eased in the 1960s, Mountain Maternal continued to provide for the needs of the medically underserved mountain region in Kentucky. More than sixty-five years after its founding, the league still serves eastern Kentucky as the Berea Planned Parenthood clinic, offering basic reproductive heath care, including birth control, and educational counseling.

See also: BEREA COLLEGE (EDUCATION); HUTCHINS, LOUISE.

—Deborah L. Blackwell, *Texas A&M International University*

Louise G. Hutchins, "Three Decades of Family Planning in Appalachia," *Hartwick Review* (Spring 1967); Jim Warren, "Birth Control Pioneers," *Lexington Herald-Leader* (April 9, 1989).

Mountain Surveillance, Counseling, and Outreach Project

The Mountain Surveillance, Counseling, and Outreach Project (Mountain SC-Out Project), developed by the University of Kentucky in 1991, was a collaborative two-year health-promotion effort that addressed barriers to cancer screening for women in Appalachian Kentucky.

Beginning in 1986, several focus groups of community women in eastern Kentucky revealed a range of barriers to seeking and obtaining optimal cancer screening, diagnosis, and treatment, as well as the women's hope to address these problems. Discussions about increasing screening rates were held in 1991 by Markey Cancer Center staff members with health department personnel and representatives of Appalachian Communities for Children and Whitley County Communities for Children, two autonomous, community-based organizations in eastern Kentucky focused on family health and welfare issues. These discussions led to the planning and implementation of the Mountain SC-Out Project in the Kentucky counties of Clay, Jackson, and Whitley.

The project was designed as a community-based, low-cost intervention aimed at improving low-income women's participation in available screening and early-detection regimens for cervical and breast cancer offered by local health departments. Five women from the community organizations were selected and received a brief period of training on breast and cervical cancer, screening methods, and health department procedures. The Mountain SC-Outs were paid an hourly rate for their part-time work with funds from a small private foundation.

Their work as community health advisors consisted of identifying women in their communities who were eligible for the program, providing meaningful, relevant, and understandable information to their peers in a variety of settings, and facilitating their entry into local health department screening programs. An evaluation of the Mountain SC-Outs clearly showed that the project was extremely effective during its two-year intervention in increasing screening for women forty-five years of age or older. All of the local health departments involved extended the projects with their own funds.

See also: APPALACHIA CANCER NETWORK; REPRODUCTIVE CANCERS AND WOMEN'S HEALTH.

—Angel Rubio, *University of Kentucky*

Mud Creek Clinic

The Mud Creek Clinic, located in Grethel, Kentucky, was founded in 1972. After three decades, it continues to serve as a national example of community health service.

In the 1960s, Office of Economic Opportunity staff members sought the political support of powerful eastern Kentucky Democratic Congressman Carl D. Perkins by locating a War on Poverty program in his district. Floyd County medical providers accepted the federal program of health care only after limiting it to screening clients and then transporting them to local doctors. The program also covered the cost of health care when patients had no other means of payment. The Eastern Kentucky Welfare Rights Organization protested these processes and secured one of only two closures of a War on Poverty program.

The Eastern Kentucky Welfare Rights Organization, under the direction of Eula Hall, then moved to begin its own health-service clinic. Clinic services soon outgrew their first humble home, and Hall moved from her own home so the clinic could have a larger facility. In 1977 the clinic merged with Big Sandy Health Care, the successor of the Office of Economic Opportunity health program. This merger brought federal dollars and more stability to its operation. In June of 1982, an arsonist burned the clinic to the ground. Operations resumed the next day, as staff attended to twenty patients beneath a tree adjacent to the smoldering embers. After the clinic moved to a local school for the summer months and then to trailers, a grant from the Appalachian

Regional Commission and matching funds from the community made construction of a new facility possible. More than twenty years later, the 5,200-square-foot clinic continued to serve more than seven thousand patients annually with a staff of more than twenty people. The adjacent Mud Creek Help Center, a 1,800-square-foot building, contains dental facilities, a food pantry, and a donated-clothing closet.

See also: COMMUNITY-INITIATED HEALTH EFFORTS; HALL, EULA; WAR ON POVERTY (GOVERNMENT).

—Richard A. Couto and Elizabeth Greene, *University of Richmond*

National Health Service Corps

The National Health Service Corps, created under the Emergency Health Personnel Act of 1970, is a federal program created to address shortages of health-care professionals in areas of high need. Formally stated, its mission is "to increase access to primary care services and reduce health disparities for people in health professions shortage areas by assisting communities through site development and by the preparation, recruitment, and retention of community-responsive, culturally competent primary care clinicians." Since its inception, more than twenty-two thousand health professionals—physicians, dentists, physician assistants, nurse practitioners, certified nurse-midwives, and others—have participated nationally in the program. From New York's Chautauqua County on the shores of Lake Erie to the banks of the Tombigbee River in Itawamba County, Mississippi, the National Health Service Corps has assisted communities throughout Appalachia in recruitment and retention of health-care professionals with the goal of developing self-sufficient health-care delivery systems.

The National Health Service Corps initially utilized a scholarship program to help recruit health-care professionals for communities in need, and a loan repayment program was added in the late 1980s. At the start of the twenty-first century, scholarships were provided for students in the health sciences who agreed to practice in communities of greatest need after graduation with one year of service required for each year of scholarship support. The loan repayment program provides a maximum of twenty-five thousand dollars of repayment of qualifying educational loans for each year of service in a designated federal health-professions shortage area.

The National Health Service Corps is now part of the Bureau of Health Professions in the Health Resources and Services Administration. In addition to recruiting health-care professionals, the program emphasizes working with communities to assist them in building sustainable health-care systems and with students and health-care professionals to help them acquire skills for practice in underserved communities. The National Health Service Corps focuses on primary care using an interdisciplinary team approach, which includes attention to oral, mental, and behavioral health.

In Appalachia, a longterm benefit of the National Health Service Corps is that clinicians have often decided to remain in the region after they leave the program. Some have become faculty members at institutions such as East Tennessee State University, Marshall University, and the University of Kentucky, where they are training the next generation of primary-care clinicians who will serve the region.

See also: SECTION OVERVIEW.

—Donald Weaver, *National Health Service Corps*

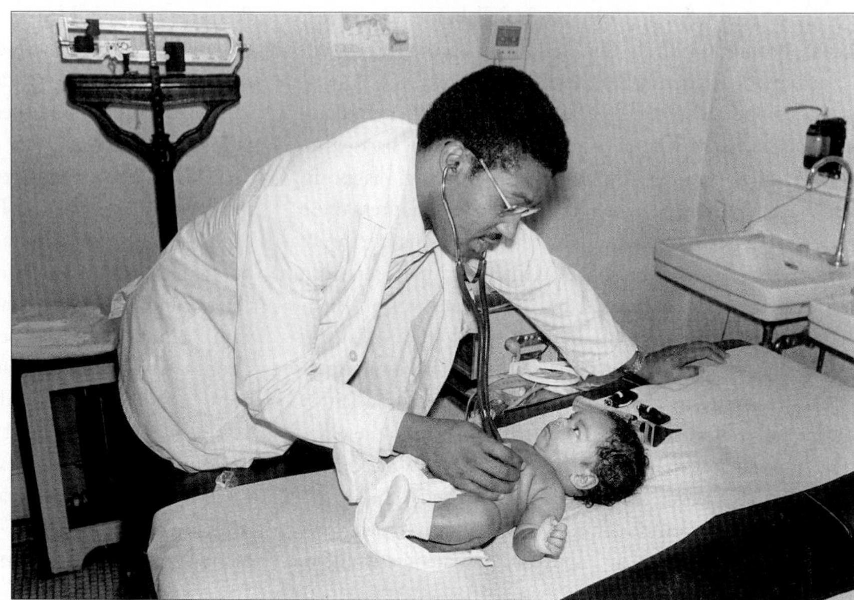

A physician examines a baby at the Tug River Health Clinic (now Tug River Health Association), Gary, West Virginia, 1978. The doctor was recruited through the National Health Service Corps, a federal program created under the Emergency Health Personnel Act of 1970 to address shortages of health professionals.

Neville, Linda

(1873–1961) Health reformer.

Born April 23, 1873, to a prominent Lexington, Kentucky family, Linda Neville became a leader in the movement to eliminate blindness in Appalachia in the early twentieth century. Neville earned a degree from Bryn Mawr College in 1895. Like many women of her generation who chose not to marry, she searched for meaningful work. She became interested in combating blindness after her father, a professor, suffered from eye troubles. A trip to eastern Kentucky in 1908 further sparked Neville's interest in blindness. She was appalled to see men and women infected with trachoma—a highly contagious, but easily preventable infection—desperately shielding their eyes from the sun. It is estimated that some thirty-three thousand residents in the remote areas of eastern Kentucky were affected by the disease.

Conscious of her position as a woman and a nonphysician, Neville carefully avoided actions that would cause her medical friends to think she was meddling in affairs outside her sphere. Nevertheless, she became the driving force behind the movement to eradicate trachoma. She helped organize the Kentucky Society for the Prevention of Blindness in 1910, lobbied the federal government for funds, and inspired the major political parties to wage war on the disease. By 1920, trachoma was rare in Appalachia, due largely to Neville's efforts, and was considered eradicated by 1952, when the last permanent clinic, at Richmond, Virginia, was closed. Neville's work, however, was not complete. Until her death in 1961, she remained committed to eliminating other forms of blindness and to serving the people of Kentucky as a member of the State Board of Charities and Corrections and as a trustee of the Frontier Nursing Service.

See also: BRECKINRIDGE, MARY; FRONTIER NURSING SERVICE.

—Melanie Beals Goan, *University of Kentucky*

Nursing

The first schools of nursing were founded by American reformers in the early 1870s as part of existing hospitals, predominately in the northeastern United States. These early schools were influenced by the innovations of English nurse Florence Nightingale and the work of lay nurses during the Civil War. In the late nineteenth and early twentieth centuries, schools of nursing generally provided care in hospitals. In rural areas, hospitals were often small, containing perhaps fifteen to fifty beds. Until the mid-twentieth century, most graduates of hospital nursing schools worked as private-duty or public-health nurses. Only a few graduates worked in hospitals as administrators or instructors.

Ironically, Appalachia's problem of being medically underserved provided opportunities for nurses to move beyond traditional confines. For example, public-health nurses were used by various women's clubs in the region to teach classes on healthy living. Diseases such as typhoid fever and tuberculosis were a constant problem in the region due primarily to overcrowding and poor sanitary conditions in coal camps and mines.

In 1925 Mary Breckinridge developed a model that relied on an expanded role of nurses when she established the Frontier Nursing Service in a poor, rural, sparsely populated area of southeastern Kentucky. Frontier nurses had public-health and midwifery training in addition to generalized nursing education before providing health care to families in assigned geographic areas. Despite documented successes in improving maternal and infant health, this model failed to spread to other areas. It did, however, demonstrate the value of an expanded role for nurses. Nurse practitioners remain essential for improving access to health care throughout Appalachia.

In terms of formal training, nurses were for many years educated primarily through schools of nursing associated with established hospitals. Although individual programs varied, the regimen followed by one nursing school in a West Virginia hospital around 1915 consisted of two years of formal classroom instruction accompanied by practicum work in the hospital's wards. Most schools of nursing were associated with hospitals as late as the mid-1950s. In fact, Frederick W. Mott, the physician who oversaw the establishment of the Miners Memorial Hospital Association, insisted that the hospital chain include nursing schools. However, nursing programs were already beginning to shift away from hospitals toward a college-based setting.

At the end of the twentieth century, registered nurses made up the largest group of health-care providers in the region, although workforce trends revealed a shortage of baccalaureate- and graduate-level trained nurses. Nurses currently enter the profession by obtaining a nursing diploma or an associate, bachelor, master, or doctor of science degree in nursing. At the close of the twentieth century, ninety associate-degree nursing programs were available in the region, as were fifty-six baccalaureate nursing programs and at least twenty-one diploma programs. Most nurses currently serving the region were educated at community colleges or universities.

Graduate education of nurses is increasing in Appalachia through programs that prepare advanced practice nurses such as nurse practitioners and clinical nurse specialists. Graduate programs for preparing advanced practice nurses exist in Appalachian counties in New York, Tennessee, Pennsylvania, South Carolina, North Carolina, Virginia, West Virginia, Mississippi, Alabama, and Georgia. The University of Pittsburgh opened the first doctoral nursing program in the region in 1954. Other doctoral nursing programs are at universities in Alabama, New York, Tennessee, and West Virginia.

Significant trends in nursing education include modification of curricula from a focus on acute hospital inpatient care to encompass a broader consideration of the community. While registered nurses continue to be a major employee group in hospitals, more nursing opportunities are expected to come in community-based agencies. Nurses will manage care along a continuum of health settings, work as members of interdisciplinary teams, and be required to integrate knowledge of communities with clinical care. Educators will assist nursing students to think critically, develop communication and problem-solving skills, and become better educated in population-focused care, behavioral health, health promotion, leadership, management, and interdisciplinary collaboration. Nurse educators will strive to prepare graduates to provide culturally competent nursing care to clients of diverse backgrounds and to build a basic nursing workforce that reflects the cultural diversity of society.

See also: BRECKINRIDGE, MARY; FRONTIER NURSING SERVICE.

—Sonda Oppewal, *University of North Carolina*

Sandra Lee Barney, *Authorized to Heal: Gender, Class, and the Transformation of Medicine in Appalachia, 1880–1930* (2000); Claude A. Frazier, with F. K. Brown, *Miners and Medicine: West Virginia Memories* (1992); Richard P. Mulcahy, "Health Care in the Coal Fields: The Miners Memorial Hospital Association," *Historian* (Summer 1993); Marilyn H. Oermann, *Professional Nursing Practice* (1997).

Office of Rural Health at West Virginia University

The Office of Rural Health at West Virginia University assists rural health providers across the state and provides administrative and management support for the West Virginia Rural Health Education Partnerships, a state-funded community-campus partnership that strives to increase the number of primary-care professionals in rural areas and to improve the health of all West Virginians.

The director of the Office of Rural Health serves as executive director for the West Virginia Rural Health Education Partnerships and as associate vice-president for rural health at the Robert C. Byrd Health Sciences Center, which is part of West Virginia University in Morgantown. The professional and support staff of the Office of Rural Health provide administrative support, information, and training to rural leaders in health information management, recruitment, and retention. The office also provides placement services for medical residents and mid-level providers and linkages to community opportunities. It manages financial support programs for students pursuing health-related professional degrees who are also interested in rural health care. The office works in collaboration with the Office of Rural Health Policy in the Office of Community and Rural Health Services, West Virginia Bureau for Public Health, on many projects that serve rural providers in the state.

The Office of Rural Health oversees funds allocated to the vice-chancellor for health sciences to support the West Virginia Rural Health Education Partnerships and is responsible for direct disbursement of $2.8 million annually in state funds to the more than three hundred rural training sites in the program. Established under the Rural Health Initiative Act of 1991 and its subsequent revisions in 1995 and 2000, the West Virginia Rural Health Education Partnerships program is now one of the largest community-academic collaborations in the country. Charged with implementing the program, the Higher Education Policy Commission of West Virginia received a grant in 1991 under the W. K. Kellogg Foundation Community Partnerships and Health Professions Education Initiatives that helped the state develop the program's principles and foundation. Student participants are required to spend 80 percent of their time in clinical services and 20 percent in community service, community-based research, and interdisciplinary case management.

Funded by the National Health Service Corps and managed under a contract from the West Virginia Bureau for Public Health, the Office of Rural Health also manages the Student/Resident Experiences and Rotations in Community Health program, which provides stipends to students and residents desiring to pursue their interests in primary care and rural health. Roughly fifty stipends averaging fifteen hundred to two thousand dollars are granted each year to students enrolled in programs in dentistry, dental hygiene, medicine, physician assistant training, nurse practitioner training, nurse-midwifery, and clinical psychology. Students must complete a community service-learning project at a rural training site in the West Virginia Rural Health Education Partnerships program to receive these stipends.

See also: WEST VIRGINIA UNIVERSITY SCHOOL OF MEDICINE.

—Hilda R. Heady, *West Virginia University*

Carol J. Bland et al., "Leadership Behaviors for Successful University-Community Collaborations to Change Curricula," *Academic Medicine* (November 1999); Ronald W. Richards, ed., *Building Partnerships: Educating Health Professionals for the Communities They Serve* (1996); Sally V. Rudmann, Kory M. Ward, and Sarah M. Varekojis, "University-Community Partnerships for Health: A Model Interdisciplinary Service-Learning Project," *Journal of Allied Health* (Summer 1999).

Osteopathy

In 2003 five accredited schools of osteopathic medicine were operating in the Appalachian region, out of twenty such facilities in the United States. These schools, all of which originated after 1970, have helped ease the chronic shortage of primary-care physicians in the region's rural areas. Since physicians have been historically attracted to cities, many locations in Appalachia have tended to be medically underserved.

Based on the belief that disease is the result of abnormalities of the musculoskeletal system, osteopathic medicine is patient-centered with emphases on maintenance of health, prevention of disease, and caring for the whole person, including the mental and spiritual aspects.

Osteopathic medicine was originally developed by Andrew Taylor Still (1828–1917), a native of Lee County in the Appalachian section of Virginia. The son of a Methodist minister and physician, Still learned the practice of medicine by serving as an apprentice to his father. He later served in the Civil War as a surgeon for the Union army. In the 1870s, while living in Kansas, Still developed a medical philosophy based on the ideas of Hippocrates, the Greek physician considered the father of medicine, and the concept of the unity of all body parts. Identifying the musculoskeletal system as a key element of health, he recognized the body's ability to heal itself and stressed preventive medicine and proper nutrition. Becoming increasingly critical of the use of drugs in treating patients, Still eventually separated himself from his professional counterparts and in 1892 established the American School of Osteopathy, now the Kirksville College of Osteopathic Medicine, in Kirksville, Missouri. The Andrew Taylor Still Memorial Park in Jonesville, Virginia, commemorates his birth.

The first school of osteopathy established in Appalachia was the Greenbrier College of Osteopathic Medicine, which opened in 1972 in the former Greenbrier Military School facility in Lewisburg, West Virginia. Greenbrier College accepted its first class in 1974 and two years later became the West Virginia School of Osteopathic Medicine, a unit of the West Virginia system of higher education. The mission of the school was to train primary-care physicians to serve in rural communities—particularly those of West Virginia—with an emphasis on health care for the elderly. A partner in the West Virginia Rural Health Educational Partnership, which strives to increase the retention of health sciences graduates in rural West Virginia communities, West Virginia School of Osteopathic Medicine produced graduates who were practicing medicine in forty-three of West Virginia's fifty-five counties in 2003.

To address health needs in southeastern Ohio, the Ohio legislature established the Ohio University College of Osteopathic Medicine in Athens in 1975. Named the nation's top medical school for training family physicians in 1998 by the American Medical Student Association Foundation, the college provides student training and health services through its Centers for Osteopathic Research and Education (four locations) and twelve affiliated hospitals. In 2001, 22 percent of its graduates practiced medicine in communities having fewer than ten thousand citizens, many in the rural counties of southeastern Ohio. The college has received national recognition for its Mobile Health Unit, which benefits thousands of children in rural Ohio through a childhood immunization program.

Founded by a group of osteopathic physicians at Millcreek Community Hospital in 1992, Lake Erie College of Osteopathic Medicine is located in Erie, Pennsylvania. Also producing primary-care physicians, the college is a member of Millcreek Health Systems, which operates Millcreek Community Hospital; the Millcreek Geriatric Education and Care Center, a skilled nursing care facility; and several ambulatory care clinics in Erie County, Pennsylvania. With its first class starting in 1993, the college was ranked number three on the American Medical Student Association's sixth annual Primary Care Scorecard of osteopathic medical colleges in 2000. This ranking is based on the number of graduates who continue their training as primary-care residents.

The Pikeville College School of Osteopathic Medicine in Pikeville, Kentucky, was established in 1994 as the American College of Osteopathic Medicine in Paintsville, Kentucky; that same year, the school became the Southern College of Osteopathic Medicine through the efforts of a Paintsville attorney, G. Chad Perry III, and his wife, Judy, who donated one million dollars. In 1996 the Southern College of Osteopathic Medicine merged with Pikeville College, an independent four-year liberal arts institution established in 1889 by Presbyterian missionaries from Ashland, Kentucky. Accredited by the American Osteopathic Association, the Pikeville College School of Osteopathic Medicine is dedicated to training medical students "who are committed to serving the health-care needs of communities in Eastern Kentucky and other Appalachian regions." The first class began studies in September 1997. In January 1998, the Kentucky legislature enacted the Osteopathic Scholarship Bill, which provided scholarships to state residents who agree to practice primary-care medicine in Kentucky after graduating; the scholarships are funded by Kentucky's coal severance tax. Most of the clinical training of students at the Pikeville College School of Osteopathic Medicine is completed in the Appalachian region. To provide opportunities for postgraduate training, the school established the Appalachian Osteopathic Postgraduate Training Institute Consortium, a formal association of the school with regional medical centers and other affiliated health-care institutions in Kentucky, Ohio, Virginia, and West Virginia.

Launched in 2003, the fifth osteopathic medical school established in the region is the Edward Via Virginia College of Osteopathic Medicine in Blacksburg, Virginia. Located in the Virginia Tech Corporate Research Park, the college operates under a collaborative agreement with Virginia Polytechnic Institute and State University. The Harvey W. Peters Foundation of Roanoke, Virginia, established the school with funds from the estate of the late philanthropist, Marion Bradley Via of Roanoke. Named after Via's son, the college trains primary-care physicians to serve the rural and medically underserved areas of Virginia, North Carolina, and other parts of Appalachia.

See also: UNIVERSITY OF KENTUCKY COLLEGE OF MEDICINE; UNIVERSITY OF PITTSBURGH SCHOOL OF MEDICINE; WEST VIRGINIA UNIVERSITY SCHOOL OF MEDICINE.

—Ed Speer, *Elizabethton, Tennessee*, and J. Scott Wilson and Pamela M. Zahorik, *East Tennessee State University*

Andrew Taylor Still, *Autobiography of Andrew T. Still* (1897; reprint 1972) and *The Philosophy and Mechanical Principles of Osteopathy* (1902).

Professionalization of Medicine

During the last decades of the nineteenth century, medicine in Appalachia, like medicine across the United States, was fundamentally reconstructed by a complex series of developments in education, scientific discovery, and professional institution building. Over a fifty-year period from roughly 1880 until 1930, the very definition of health-care delivery, as well as the composition of the constituency that delivered that care, underwent a major shift.

Before the transformation of medicine in Appalachia, health care was delivered by a variety of locally situated, community-based healers. Whether herb doctors whose skill was rooted in Native American tradition, domestic healers who relied upon popular medical manuals, or lay midwives, these practitioners gained their knowledge or training through practical experience, apprenticing with older, more skilled individuals or improving their abilities through trial and error.

Alongside these informally trained healers practiced physicians who had acquired their medical knowledge through brief courses at the various regional medical colleges located in urban centers on the periphery of the mountain region. In cities such as Louisville, Kentucky, Knoxville, Tennessee, Baltimore, Maryland, and Richmond, Virginia, a few ambitious mountain residents fulfilled the minimal classroom requirements and went home to serve preceptorships under the direction of established physicians who themselves possessed little or no classroom or laboratory training.

In the last quarter of the nineteenth century, reformers at leading national medical schools began to reexamine medical education. Building on the German model of laboratory and clinical training, medical educators at Harvard University, the University of Michigan, the University of Pennsylvania, and Johns Hopkins University began to reshape their curricula. They required students to master basic science requirements, to complete a series of graded courses, and to acquire significant clinical experience before becoming an M.D. These reforms ultimately redefined medical education across the nation but were slow to come to the schools that educated most Appalachian doctors.

Approximately one-half of the physicians who practiced in the central Appalachian region of Virginia, eastern Kentucky, and West Virginia at the beginning of the twentieth century were educated at either the Medical College of Virginia, the University of Louisville, or the College of Physicians and Surgeons in Baltimore. All of these schools stood above inadequately equipped proprietary institutions of the time, but they were slow to embrace innovations being introduced at Harvard and Johns Hopkins. In the 1880s, for example, the Medical College of Virginia rejected introduction of a graded curriculum and continued to require students to sit through two years of identical lectures. The University of Louisville, the largest medical school in the nation at one point during the first decade of the century, was condemned by Abraham Flexner in his 1910 American Medical Association report as "inadequate in appointment and teaching force" and "poor in respect to both quality and extent" of its clinical facilities. Flexner was impressed by the clinical instruction available at the College of Physicians and Surgeons in Baltimore, but his premonition that the independent school would be made obsolete by the growing connection between medical training and university education proved true, and the school was eventually dissolved.

Although reform was slow to come to these schools and by extension to mountain communities, medical training did begin to change by the beginning of the twentieth century. As graded curricula, laboratory and clinical requirements, and higher admission standards were implemented, the physicians who practiced in Appalachia gradually began to demonstrate greater skill and to put into practice the new scientific discoveries that were reshaping medicine across Europe and North America. With the introduction of antiseptic and aseptic practices and new advances in pathology and infectious disease control and treatment, physicians offered Appalachian residents demonstrably improved health care.

The impact of these new scientific advances was heightened by the arrival of a phalanx of doctors educated outside the region who brought with them superior skills and experiences. Possessing graduate training and enjoying the benefits of education at superior institutions, these new doctors, both native and outsider, hastened the transformation of medicine in the region. The arrival of physicians from outside the region dramatically increased the number of doctors practicing in the mountains, and their rising numbers were an indication of the growing economic importance of the region. As mountain timber and coal grew increasingly important to the national economy, physicians were attracted to the boomtowns and coal camps that sprang up across Appalachia. Whether employed as company doctors or practicing independently, these new practitioners quickly became influential actors in the communities they inhabited.

Formal medical training gave the new doctors educational legitimacy, but that alone was not always enough to convince local residents to rely upon their care rather than that of an established local healer. To eliminate competitors and to elevate the standards of medical care, physicians organized local, county, and state medical associations and looked to the government for assistance in regulating competing healers. Following the model of the American Medical Association, formally educated physicians allied in associations that excluded those who did not possess the same educational credentials or who espoused an alternative medical philosophy. By denying membership to those they identified as inferior, physicians could isolate practitioners and deny them legitimacy. Their actions eventually undermined the standing of informally trained doctors and marginalized sectarians such as chiropractors, osteopaths, and homeopaths, who established their own professional associations.

Private medical associations were aided in their efforts by the close relationships formally educated, regular physicians developed with the state. By serving as county public-health officers and controlling the licensing boards that were established in each state before the end of the nineteenth century, these doctors used the state's power to dictate what defined acceptable medical practice. Within the profession this ensured that poorly trained or alternatively trained physicians were denied the right to practice. In the larger community, this power meant that physicians could deny legal authority to whole categories of healers.

Doctors moved against herbalists, patent medicine salesmen, and faith healers, but the campaign to eliminate lay midwifery stands as the best example of the success of educated physicians in marginalizing competing caregivers. As medical historians have demonstrated, women who relied upon a physician during childbirth ultimately placed the rest of their family under the physician's care. Supplanting the midwife, however, was a sometimes difficult challenge for physicians since many mountain women relied on lay midwives for practical as well as economic reasons. In order to displace midwives, physicians argued that, while they did not offer postpartum nursing care or housekeeping services, they did provide a higher standard of care. Their crusade to displace midwives was helped by the initiation of comprehensive payment plans in some coal camps in the region. When delivery fees were included in company health plans, miners and their families accepted physicians rather than employing midwives and paying them out of their own pockets.

Women in more rural areas had fewer reasons to accept physicians' services, and doctors had less success in the countryside. Physicians across Appalachia argued that, in order to improve the quality of infant and maternal care, it was necessary to marginalize these rural midwives. By the first decades of the twentieth century, physicians, allied with state lawmakers, had initiated legislative campaigns to regulate and eventually eliminate the unlicensed lay midwife.

By denying legitimacy to physicians trained in alternative schools or systems, sectarian healers, and lay practitioners, doctors educated in the new scientific model elevated their own philosophy of practice while denigrating those held by others. Their campaign can be seen as a progressive one since they labored to introduce scientific standards of care to the region. However, one of the consequences of their success was the loss of opportunity for Appalachian residents to choose from a variety of healing philosophies and practitioners. Having introduced and elevated a new professional model in the region, physicians created a monopoly over the delivery of health care. When economic conditions in some rural parts of the region declined and fewer physicians chose to practice in the mountains, however, no other practitioners were recognized to take their place, creating a dearth of medical services that has had long-standing negative consequences for the region.

See also: FOLK MEDICINE (FOLKLORE AND FOLKLIFE); SECTION OVERVIEW.

—Sandra Barney, *Lock Haven University of Pennsylvania*

Sandra Lee Barney, *Authorized to Heal: Gender, Class, and the Transformation of Medicine in Appalachia, 1880–1930* (2000); Nancy Schrom Dye, "Mary Breckinridge, the Frontier Nursing Service and the Introduction of Nurse-Midwifery in the United States," *Bulletin of the History of Medicine* (Winter 1983); Claude A. Frazier, with F. K. Brown, *Miners and Medicine: West Virginia Memories* (1992).

Rasmussen, Donald

(1928–) Physician.

Donald L. Rasmussen, a leading medical authority on coal miners' occupational lung disease, worked as an advocate for related political causes, including recognition and prevention of black lung as well as compensation for miners disabled by the disease. The son of a veterinarian in Colorado, Rasmussen attended the University of Utah Medical School. From 1955 to 1962, he served in the U.S. Army as a physician, specializing in lung disease. He then moved to the Appalachian Regional Hospital in Beckley, West Virginia, where he remained for the rest of his professional career.

Rasmussen's treatment of and research on coal miners' respiratory disease led him to conclude that black lung becomes disabling in part because it impairs the lungs' ability to exchange oxygen with the bloodstream. This view contrasts sharply with dominant medical opinion, which holds that black lung involves the quantitative destruction of lung tissue and may be diagnosed in living miners only through X-rays.

Following the Farmington, West Virginia, mine explosion in November 1968, Rasmussen joined with two other physicians, I. E. Buff and Hawey Wells Jr., in forming the Physicians Committee for Miners' Health and Safety. At rallies throughout West Virginia, Rasmussen lent his scientific credibility to the miners' campaign to secure compensation for black lung under the state's workers' compensation program. In later years, as both federal and state black lung compensation programs adopted restrictive eligibility standards, he continued to advocate for a broader view of what constituted black lung. His life-long dedication to coal miners' occupational health earned him the respect and gratitude of miners and their families throughout the coalfields.

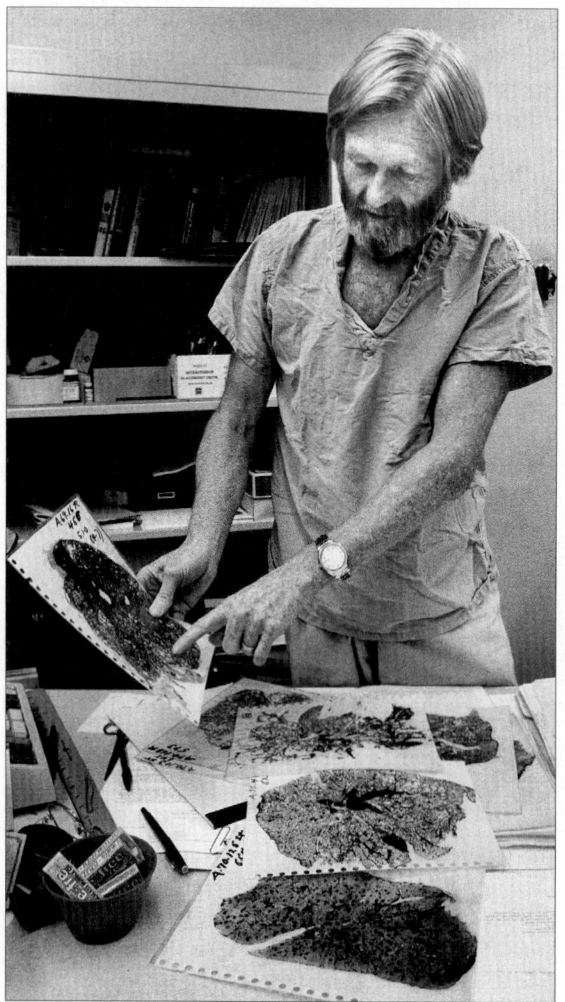

Physician Donald Rasmussen examines lung sections from deceased coal miners, Beckley, West Virginia, 1977. Rasmussen crusaded tirelessly to win recognition of black lung as a compensable work-related disease.

See also: BLACK LUNG ASSOCIATIONS; BLACK LUNG DISEASE AND THE BLACK LUNG MOVEMENT; BUFF, I. E.

—Barbara Ellen Smith, *University of Memphis*

Reproductive Cancers and Women's Health

Since the 1980s, there has been increased attention to the problem of women's reproductive cancers in Appalachia. In 1987, for example, the incidence of invasive cervical cancer for white women in eastern Kentucky was twice that of white women nationally and comparable to the rate reported for African American women. In other words, women in central Appalachia, like African American women, had a greater likelihood than women generally of dying of a disease that is treatable when detected early and for which a reliable method of diagnosis has been available since the mid-twentieth century. Moreover, despite the relatively low incidence of breast cancer, mortality from this form of cancer increased more rapidly in Appalachia than other parts of the country over the course of the 1980s.

Health authorities saw a number of possible reasons for the troubling results. Among them is the possibility that women in Appalachia are more reluctant than their counterparts elsewhere to seek diagnostic tests, whether Papanicolaou (Pap) tests or mammography. It has also been suggested that women who are mothers, caregivers, and heads of households may give preference to the health needs of other family members, especially when economic resources are limited. It is equally possible that women in the mountains face barriers to health care considered routine elsewhere. Examples of barriers include the fees associated with medical tests, distances that must be traveled to county health departments or clinics, the reluctance of providers to treat people presumed to be uninsured or underinsured, and the undervaluing of women's health both regionally and nationally. Even when cancer screening is made available for a nominal fee or no charge, restricted scheduling may undermine the accessibility of some clinics.

Only in recent years have the National Institutes of Health and the National Cancer Institute recognized that access to cancer screening may have improved with the creation of community-based programs; still, options for cancer treatment remain limited, especially for poor and working-class citizens. If community-based screening is inadequate in the nation at large, the problem is greater in places such as Appalachia, where there are fewer hospitals, smaller numbers of physicians relative to the size of the population, fewer specialized treatment facilities, and shortages of trained personnel.

The Appalachian Leadership Initiative on Cancer, organized under the auspices of the National Cancer Institute and funded from 1992 to 1999, addressed breast cancer as part of its program of community-based cancer control. In 2001 the National Institutes of Health launched an initiative to address the problem of invasive cervical cancer among specific populations of U.S. women, including women in Appalachian Kentucky. The hope is that such efforts will lead to improved availability of health care and to the recognition of women's health as a civil right as well as a public-health problem.

See also: APPALACHIA CANCER NETWORK; CANCER; MOUNTAIN SURVEILLANCE, COUNSELING, AND OUTREACH PROJECT.

—Mary K. Anglin, *University of Kentucky*

Richard A. Couto, Nancy K. Simpson, and Gale Harris, eds., *Sowing Seeds in the Mountains: Community-Based Coalitions for Cancer Prevention and Control* (1994); Gilbert H. Friedell et al., "Cervical Cancer in Kentucky," *Journal of the Kentucky Medical Association* (September 2000); Gilbert H. Friedell et al., "Community Cancer Control in a Rural, Underserved Population: The Appalachian Leadership Initiative on Cancer Project," *Journal of Health Care for the Poor and Underserved* (February 2001).

Roche, Josephine

(1886–1976) Health reformer.

Josephine Roche served as director and neutral trustee of the United Mine Workers of America Welfare and Retirement Fund from 1948 to 1971. The daughter of Colorado's largest coal operator, John J. Roche, she was educated at Vassar College and Columbia University. Roche entered public life as Juvenile Justice Officer for Denver, Colorado. In 1927 she inherited the Rocky Mountain Fuel Company and signed a contract with the United Mine Workers of America. Thus began a life-long friendship with the union's president, John L. Lewis.

With the New Deal, Roche was appointed assistant secretary of the treasury. She was a central figure in the drafting of the Social Security Act and was the New Deal's leading health reformer. As chair of the Interdepartmental Committee on Health and Welfare Activities, she led organization of a proposed national health plan in 1938 that laid the basis for the Murray-Wagner-Dingell Bill, which proposed the creation of a federally sponsored national health insurance program. Although the bill had congressional support, President Franklin D. Roosevelt did not back the measure, fearing retaliation from the American Medical Association. Angry, Roche resigned her post.

Roche's experience in health reform was invaluable to Lewis. Winning creation of the Welfare and Retirement Fund in 1946, Lewis envisioned a private welfare state offering complete health coverage for union miners and their families, as well as pensions for retirees. Roche had the knowledge to make the program work. She was also loyal to Lewis, and serving as the fund's director and neutral trustee, she ensured his control over the fund. Her influence also helped make it a leader in the area of industrial benefits and health care.

Unfortunately, the fund fell under the control of corrupt union president W. A. "Tony" Boyle after Lewis's death in 1969. Roche was inevitably tarred with the disgrace suffered by the entire union during Boyle's reign and fall from power in 1972. Ordered to resign by a federal judge, Roche lived as a near-recluse until her death in 1976.

See also: MINERS' CLINICS; UNITED MINE WORKERS OF AMERICA (LABOR); UNITED MINE WORKERS OF AMERICA HEALTH AND RETIREMENT FUNDS.

—Richard P. Mulcahy, *University of Pittsburgh at Titusville*

Socioeconomic Status and Health

See Section Overview

Tobacco and Health

Tobacco, a key agricultural product in much of Appalachia, has continued to be widely smoked and chewed in the region, notwithstanding national antismoking crusades and research establishing causal links between the use of tobacco and a wide array of health problems. Because of this extensive use, tobacco contributes to significant preventable disease in Appalachia.

Indigenous to the tropics, tobacco nevertheless has flourished as a crop in much of Appalachia and constitutes the livelihood of many farmers in the region. In 1997 Appalachian farmers produced nearly 325 million pounds of tobacco. Though only 7 percent of all Americans live in Appalachia, the region in 1997 harvested 21.2 percent of the nation's total tobacco acreage and raised 19.6 percent of its tobacco yield. More than 45 percent of the 410 Appalachian counties farm tobacco. Among the thirteen states in the region, only Appalachian New York, Mississippi, South Carolina, and Maryland do not harvest the crop. Though tobacco farming is widespread in the region, the Appalachian counties of Kentucky, Tennessee, and North Carolina produced the bulk of Appalachia's tobacco, respectively cultivating 47 percent, 19.7 percent, and 19.6 percent of all the tobacco grown in Appalachia in 1997.

Tobacco farming fosters a sense of community in the region as families join together to harvest the crop. In some areas, schools give holidays to youth from tobacco-growing families so they can assist with picking the plant. Social science studies strongly indicate that youth from tobacco-growing families are at a significantly heightened risk for tobacco use. Among the reasons for this increased risk is green tobacco sickness, an acute nicotine poisoning that follows skin contact with tobacco plants. Older harvesters often advise young ones to start smoking or use chewing tobacco or snuff to help them adapt to nicotine and thus diminish the effects of exposure.

Partly because of the crop's social and economic importance, residents of Appalachia commonly consume tobacco at higher rates than persons do outside the region. In 1993, 24.2 percent of Appalachians smoked, a significantly higher rate than the 21.9 percent of the non-Appalachian United States. This regional higher prevalence for smoking was true for both men and women. Persons in Appalachia aged eighteen to sixty-four were more likely to smoke than individuals of the same age in the rest of the country.

Inside and outside the region, lower education and income are among the socioeconomic variables strongly associated with smoking, but some evidence indicates a stronger association between these variables and smoking in Appalachia than outside the region. Though both Appalachian and non-Appalachian individuals with higher education and income reported lower rates of smoking, among persons who had dropped out of high school or those with annual incomes of less than ten thousand dollars, these rates were significantly higher in Appalachia than elsewhere.

Researchers have not examined the relative prevalence of the use of smokeless tobacco between the Appalachian and non-Appalachian portions of the nation. But in nine of the thirteen Appalachian states, males aged eighteen years and older had a greater prevalence of smokeless tobacco use during 1992–93 than such men in the rest of the country. West Virginia reported a prevalence rate among this population of 15.6 percent, the highest of any state.

The three leading causes of death in Appalachia and the nation—malignant neoplasms, ischemic heart disease, and other cardiovascular diseases—account for two-thirds of all deaths in Appalachia; the rate of mortality for each is higher in Appalachia than the United States. Medical studies have established the use of tobacco as a significant risk factor in all of these conditions.

Smoking significantly contributes to a wide range of cancers, most notably lung cancer. A smoker's probability of developing lung cancer is seven times higher than that of a nonsmoker's, and nearly 90 percent of those dying from lung cancer have been smokers. Age-adjusted lung cancer mortality rates for both men and women for 1970–94 in many counties of central Appalachia were well above the national rates. In 1993 the percentage of smokers for Appalachian Kentucky and Ohio, as well as West Virginia, was not only higher than the non-Appalachian average, but also higher than the Appalachian average. To the extent that the use of tobacco is related to lower income, the high rates of lung cancer is this area may reflect the fact that more than 75 percent of Appalachia's most distressed counties in 1997 were in these three states.

Research indicates that the close-knit structure of Appalachian families can facilitate efforts to prevent tobacco use throughout the region, whether or not tobacco is grown locally. Families are receptive to anti-tobacco messages that seek to protect children, and messages that accord respect to individuals and institutions elicit a positive response. Prevention strategies that appeal to personal experience rather than abstraction tend to be more acceptable to inhabitants of the region.

Another tobacco-related problem is that between 1992 and 1997 the number of Appalachian tobacco farms declined by 28.3 percent as small farmers abandoned the crop. As tobacco revenues have declined, threats to the physical and mental health of Appalachian tobacco communities continue to increase.

See also: CANCER; TOBACCO (AGRICULTURE); TOBACCO INDUSTRY (BUSINESS, INDUSTRY, AND TECHNOLOGY).

—Michael G. Meyer, *Toborg Associates, Inc.*

Richard A. Couto, Nancy K. Simpson, and Gale Harris, eds., *Sowing Seeds in the Mountains: Community-Based Coalitions for Cancer Prevention and Control* (1994); Melody Noland et al., "The Effectiveness of a Tobacco Prevention Program with Adolescents Living in a Tobacco-Producing Region," *American Journal of Public Health* (December 1998); Eugenia Thoenen, *Health Risks: The Appalachian Lifestyle* (1995).

United Mine Workers of America Health and Retirement Funds

More than half a century after the first one was created, the United Mine Workers of America (UMWA) Health and Retirement Funds (or "the Funds," for short) include six medical and pension benefits plans for retired coal miners and their eligible dependents. Formerly known as the UMWA Welfare and Retirement Fund, its name was changed in 1974 when it was broken into four different trusts as outlined by the Employee Retirement Income Security Act. Through the Funds, beneficiaries receive comprehensive health-care coverage, including medical services, treatment, and prescription drugs. Policy decisions to interpret provisions of the plan and invest assets are made by separate boards of trustees for each plan, variously composed of representatives from the United Mine Workers and the coal industry.

The six plans that make up the Funds are the 1950 Pension Plan, the 1974 Pension Plan, the 1992 Benefit Plan, the 1993 Benefit Plan, the Combined Benefit Fund, and the Cash Deferred Savings Plan. The 1950 and 1974 Pension Plans provide retirement benefits based on time of service. The 1992 Benefit Plan offers health benefits to eligible miners who left the coal industry before September 30, 1994. The 1993 Benefit Plan gives health benefits to certain retired and disabled miners not covered by an employer's benefit plan or by the 1950, 1974, or 1992 plans. The Combined Benefit Fund provides health and death benefits to eligible beneficiaries of the 1950 or 1974 Benefit Plans that were merged in 1993 to create the Combined Benefit Fund. The Cash Deferred Savings Plan was created under the 1988 National Bituminous Coal Wage Agreement as a 401(k) deferred compensation plan permitting as much as 15 percent of a participant's compensation to be contributed to the plan.

Taken cumulatively, exclusive of the Cash Deferred Savings Plan, these plans held assets of nearly $7.5 billion early in the new century, although dollar allotments between plans vary widely. Several collective bargaining agreements between the United Mine Workers and the Bituminous Coal Operators' Association created the 1950 and 1974 Pension Plans, the 1993 Benefit Plan, and the Cash Deferred Savings Plan. The Combined Benefit Fund and the 1992 Benefit Plan resulted from the 1992 Coal Industry Retiree Health Benefit Act.

The UMWA Welfare and Retirement Fund got its start through the efforts of union leader John L. Lewis. Beginning in 1946, Lewis led the United Mine Workers on several strikes to pressure coal operators to create a miners' health and retirement plan. President Harry Truman ordered U.S. Secretary of the Interior Julius Krug to negotiate with Lewis to fashion such a plan. On May 29, 1946, the Krug-Lewis Agreement was signed and established a health plan for miners administered jointly by the United Mine Workers and the federal government.

Krug-Lewis also called for a government survey of the medical, sanitary, housing, and other living conditions in the coal mining regions. In 1947 the government published its findings in *A Medical Survey of the Bituminous Coal Industry*, commonly referred to as the "Boone Report," after retired Rear Admiral Joel T. Boone, U.S. Navy Medical Corps, who supervised the study. The Boone Report confirmed descriptions by Lewis and others of grim circumstances prevailing in coal-mining communities.

In July 1947, the National Bituminous Coal Wage Agreement between mine operators and the United Mine Workers created the Welfare and Retirement Fund to provide health and pension benefits to miners and their beneficiaries. Conflict continued between operators and the union, and in 1950 a new wage agreement brought a more detailed structure to the Welfare and Retirement Fund. Operators would pay a five-cents-per-ton royalty on coal produced in union mines to finance the Welfare and Retirement Fund with incremental increases bringing the royalty in 1952 to forty-cents-per-ton. A trusteeship of three representatives, one labor, one industry, and one neutral chosen by mutual agreement, would administer the new plan.

One of the most important early projects of the Funds was the creation of a chain of ten hospitals in central Appalachia known as the UMWA Miners Memorial Hospitals. Dedicated in June 1956, the hospitals brought modern medical facilities and qualified personnel to the heart of the bituminous coalfields in Kentucky, Virginia, and West Virginia. The noble experiment proved too expensive, however, and the Funds sold the hospitals in 1963 to a new organization, Appalachian Regional Hospitals, a nonprofit company created by the United Presbyterian Church (USA) to keep the hospitals running. Many miners continued to use these hospitals thereafter thanks to their benefits from the Funds.

From its inception through the late 1960s, the Funds remained under the tight control of Lewis and his long-time advisor Josephine Roche, who was chosen as the neutral trustee for the fund, and later W. A. "Tony" Boyle, Lewis's successor as president of the United Mine Workers. In the late 1950s problems continued for the Funds due to a downturn in the coal industry, mechanization of mining, and the increasing cost of medical care. Some relief came with the passage of the 1965 Medicare Act and the 1969 Coal Mine Health and Safety Act. But new problems arose that would change the character of the Funds.

In 1969 a class-action suit was filed by disabled miners denied benefits, and in *Blankenship v. Boyle* the plaintiffs succeeded in proving mismanagement of the Funds by Lewis, Roche, and Boyle. Several revisions to the Funds occurred thereafter. Creation of the 1974 Pension Trust came through the 1974 National Bituminous Coal Wage Agreement, the 1974 National Coal Mine Construction Agreement, and the 1975 Western Surface Coal Wage Agreement. In 1992 the UMWA Benefit Plan was formed under provisions of the 1992 Coal Industry Retiree Health Benefit Act. The 1993 UMWA Benefit Plan came about via the 1993 National Bituminous Coal Wage Agreement. These various plans provide several types of benefits. Trusteeships on the several plans seek to reflect the shared responsibility of the union and industry to provide benefits, where suitable, for members, employees, and beneficiaries.

Headquartered in Washington, D.C., the United Mine Workers of America Health and Retirement Funds provided benefits in 2001 to approximately 110,000 beneficiaries. Funds field offices are located in the coalfield areas of Alabama, Kentucky, Indiana, Pennsylvania, Virginia, West Virginia, and Utah. The organization is a separate entity from the United Mine Workers of America and the Bituminous Coal Operators' Association.

See also: LEWIS, JOHN L. (LABOR); MINERS MEMORIAL HOSPITAL ASSOCIATION; UNITED MINE WORKERS OF AMERICA (LABOR).

—Rick Smoot, *University of Kentucky Lexington Community College*

Ivana Krajcinovic, *From Company Doctors to Managed Care: The United Mine Workers' Noble Experiment* (1997); Richard P. Mulcahy, "Serving the Union: The United Mine Workers of America Welfare and Retirement Fund, 1946–1978," Ph.D. dissertation, West Virginia University (1988).

University of Alabama School of Medicine

Dating back nearly 150 years, the University of Alabama School of Medicine, now located in Birmingham, was founded in Mobile as the Medical College of Alabama by Josiah Nott in 1859. The school was closed in 1919 and moved to the Tuscaloosa campus, where it reopened a year later as a two-year basic science program. With no other medical schools in the state at that time, graduates of the program had to transfer out of state for their clinical training. In 1945 the medical college relocated from Tuscaloosa to Birmingham, where it became known as the University of Alabama School of Medicine in 1969.

With hospitals and facilities located throughout the state, the University of Alabama School of Medicine excels in nearly all facets of medicine and at the start of the twenty-first century ranked sixteenth in the nation in funding from the National Institutes of Health. The school is a major organ-transplant center where hundreds of transplantations—of the heart, lung, kidney, liver, pancreas, small bowel, cornea, and retina—are performed each year. Ranking first in the world for the number of kidney transplants performed, the institution had completed five thousand such procedures by 2001. The school performed its five-hundredth heart transplant in early 1998.

The institution's Medical Student Enrichment Program was developed in 1995 to provide students with service and training opportunities in developing countries and underserved areas throughout the world. Similarly, programs emphasizing rural primary care have been developed in Tuscaloosa and Huntsville to serve the Appalachian population of northern Alabama and southern Tennessee. These programs satisfy third- and fourth-year clinical education requirements and offer graduates residency opportunities in family medicine.

See also: DENTISTRY.

—J. Scott Wilson, *East Tennessee State University*

University of Kentucky Center for Excellence in Rural Health

The University of Kentucky Center for Excellence in Rural Health was established in 1990 by the state's general assembly to address specific health problems in rural Kentucky. The decision to locate the center in Hazard, a town of about forty-eight hundred people in the mountainous Appalachian coalfields, reflected a commitment to issues such as chronic shortages of health professionals in rural communities, the poor health status of many rural people due to poverty and limited access to care, and the impact of health care on local rural economies. In 1999 officials decided to institutionalize the center's commitment to all rural regions across the state by establishing a campus in Morehead to serve northern and northeastern Kentucky better and one at Madison-

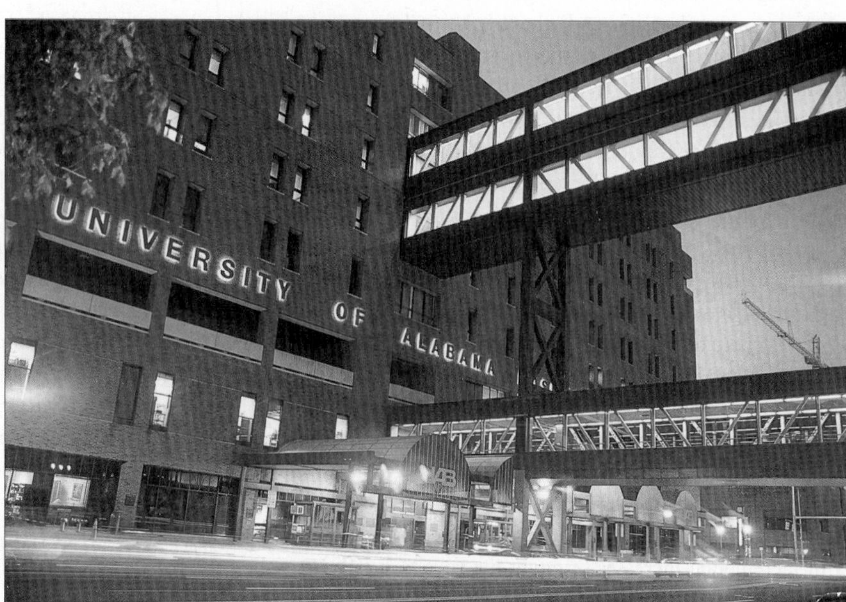

University of Alabama Hospital, Birmingham, c. 1999. The founding of the University of Alabama School of Medicine dates back to the nineteenth century. Newer medical schools in Appalachia were created to address severe shortages of primary-care physicians in the region.

ville to oversee and expand services in the western portion of the state.

The center, which is supported academically by the colleges of the University of Kentucky's Chandler Medical Center, is recognized nationally as a successful example of an academic medical center functioning in a rural area. Designed to educate health professionals in a variety of disciplines, the center had graduated 114 physical therapists, 105 nursing professionals, 66 clinical laboratory scientists, and 25 family-practice physicians by 2002. Nearly 80 percent of the center's graduates are now practicing in rural areas, primarily in Appalachian Kentucky. Other programs provide rural residents the opportunity to obtain degrees or upgrade their professional skills without traveling long distances to urban areas. The center's record led to its being named the country's Outstanding Rural Health Program by the National Rural Health Association in 2000.

Besides training health professionals, the center serves as a model for service delivery, particularly through the use of community-based lay health workers who make home visits to assess the needs of individuals and families and to link them with appropriate services. The lay health workers' role includes helping clients identify and gain access to available health-care services; assisting them in obtaining free medications; and connecting them with other agencies that can help improve their health status, including food, clothing, and home-repair services.

Other center goals are to develop and advocate, through the State Office of Rural Health, policies advantageous to rural areas. These include use and payment of nurse practitioners, state-supported loan repayment for graduates practicing in areas with shortages of health professionals, conducting applied research, elimination of income disparities, and removal of barriers to quality health care. In addition, the center collaborates with agencies and communities to provide many forms of technical support. These include assistance in identifying sources of federal grants, provision of community economic-impact data, support of rural hospitals' feasibility studies, and assistance in networking and expansion of existing services.

Aware of the economic contributions that health care makes in rural communities, the center is also a national leader in developing programs that enable communities to use health-care information for longterm community planning. One such program, Kentucky Rural Health Works, is an assessment model jointly developed by the Center for Excellence in Rural Health and the University of Kentucky College of Agriculture to gauge the impact of actual or proposed health services on local economies.

In 1997 the center received the Primary Care Achievement Award from the Pew Charitable Trusts in recognition of its contribution to the public's health and welfare and the strengthening of communities. More recently, each of the center's lay health worker programs—Kentucky Homeplace and its Southeast Kentucky Community Access Program (SKYCAP), which focuses on community creation of sustainable systems of care for the uninsured and underinsured—have gained national attention. Homeplace twice has been nominated for the Innovations in American Government Award as a state-initiated program to assist poor rural families in gaining access to health care. In 2002 the federal Health Resources and Services Administration identified SKYCAP as a national model.

See also: UNIVERSITY OF KENTUCKY COLLEGE OF MEDICINE.

—David Gross, *University of Kentucky Center for Rural Health*

Gideon Gil, "Center Hopes to Heal Rural Health-Care Woes," *Louisville Courier-Journal* (May 9, 1992); Jim Warren, "UK's Rural Health Center Receives National Award," *Lexington Herald-Leader* (September 23, 1997).

University of Kentucky College of Medicine

The Commonwealth of Kentucky and the University of Kentucky Board of Trustees established the University of Kentucky College of Medicine in Lexington in 1956 to improve the quality of health care for the state's residents. Beginning with the first class of 32 graduates in 1964, 3,391 medical students had earned the M.D. degree from the University of Kentucky College of Medicine as of 2002. The medical college is one of five (along with colleges of dentistry, health sciences, nursing and pharmacy, and the school of public health) that along with University of Kentucky Hospital comprise the University of Kentucky Chandler Medical Center. The University of Kentucky College of Medicine was ranked ninth in the *U.S. News and World Report*'s 2003 annual ranking of rural-medicine programs.

The College of Medicine has improved health care in Appalachian Kentucky through programs that bring specialty care to thousands of residents in small and remote communities. The college operates the Area Health Education Center program, which was developed to address the lack of medical personnel in rural areas. As part of the program, strategically placed Area Health Education Centers are now located in Morehead, Berea, and Hazard to promote primary-care careers and provide students and residents with opportunities to work in underserved areas.

With significant funding from the Kentucky legislature, the University of Kentucky Center for Rural Health was created in Hazard in 1990 as a major extension program of the college. The center provides educational programs in nursing, clinical laboratory sciences, and physical therapy, as well as a family practice medical residency. In 2000 the center was named the Outstanding Rural Health

Program in the United States by the National Rural Health Association.

Primary clinical teaching sites for residents and students include the University Hospital, the Lexington Veterans Affairs Medical Center, and a network of ambulatory care clinics. The college is directly affiliated with twelve medical centers, including the Kentucky Center for Excellence in Rural Health, the Davis-Mills Magnetic Resonance Imaging and Spectroscopy Center, the Markey Cancer Center, the Sanders-Brown Center on Aging, the Center on Drug and Alcohol Research, the Linda and Jack Gill Heart Institute, the Minimally Invasive Surgery Center, and the Spinal Cord and Brain Injury Center.

As of 2003, the college's Department of Physiology was ranked among the top ten nationwide among public medical schools by the National Institutes of Health, and its Center on Aging was ranked third. Major research areas include aging, cancer, neurosciences, women's health, spinal cord injuries, and drug evaluation.

See also: DENTISTRY; OSTEOPATHY.

—J. Scott Wilson and Pamela M. Zahorik, *East Tennessee State University*

University of Pittsburgh School of Medicine

The University of Pittsburgh School of Medicine is located in the Oakland district of Pittsburgh, on the university's main campus. The school originated as the Western Pennsylvania Medical College in 1886 but was made part of the University of Pittsburgh in 1908. Over the decades, the school, in partnership with the developing University of Pittsburgh Medical Center, has emerged as a major urban medical facility serving twenty-nine counties in western Pennsylvania. Gaining international prominence in the 1970s and 1980s with research related to cancer, psychiatric, neurosurgical, critical care, and transplantation medicine, the center is considered among the top ten medical facilities in the United States. At the end of the twentieth century, the University of Pittsburgh Medical Center was listed among the "best of the best" in *U.S. News and World Report*'s hospital rankings.

Though identified as an urban medical center, the University of Pittsburgh offers medical students opportunities to work in rural and underserved areas of the surrounding Appalachian region. The Western Pennsylvania Health Preceptorship Program, for example, provides students in the clinical portion of their education with opportunities to interact with community physicians in these areas.

The University of Pittsburgh Medical Center (UPMC) consists of two large tertiary hospitals (UPMC Presbyterian and UPMC Shadyside), several specialty hospitals, and nine community-based regional hospitals, as well as Children's Hospital of Pittsburgh and the Veterans Affairs Medical Center. The Starzl Transplantation Institute has developed many antirejection medications that make multiple organ transplantation possible. As of 2003, more transplantations had been performed at the center than at any other medical center in the world. Also a leader in emphysema treatment, the center is a pioneer in new treatments of lung tumors. Within the health-care system, treatments for cancer and various types of rehabilitation are provided to patients through a network of facilities located across western Pennsylvania. For example, the University of Pittsburgh Cancer Institute maintains a system of forty cancer centers for treating patients.

The largest employer in western Pennsylvania, the medical center has regional economic impact of more than $5 billion each year. It also brings the largest concentration of new construction to the area, averaging about $200 million each year.

See also: DENTISTRY; OSTEOPATHY.

—J. Scott Wilson, *East Tennessee State University*

Verghese, Abraham

(1955–) Physician and writer.

Abraham Verghese is the author of *My Own Country: A Doctor's Story of a Town and Its People in the Age of AIDS* (1994), the much-heralded memoir of a young doctor working in southern Appalachia. The book recounts Verghese's own experiences as physician-in-training at the James H. Quillen College of Medicine at East Tennessee State University in Johnson City and his first encounters with human immunodeficiency virus (HIV). A finalist for the National Book Critics Circle Awards and named by *Time* magazine as one of the five best books of 1994, *My Own Country* was widely read and received praise from both health practitioners and patients as a compassionate account about people dealing with HIV. However, *My Own Country* was not as well received by Appalachian scholars, who found the author's presentations of "rednecks" and "good ole boys" and his fascination with local traditions to be a stereotypical evocation of the culture of poverty.

My Own Country charts Verghese's passage from his childhood spent in Ethiopia as the son of southern Indian expatriate teachers to his medical studies in India, an internship and residency in Tennessee, and, finally, to the Iowa Writers' Workshop, where he learned the craft of writing and produced the text. Verghese went on to become a professor of medicine and chief of infectious diseases at Texas Tech University Health Sciences Center.

See also: EAST TENNESSEE STATE UNIVERSITY JAMES H. QUILLEN COLLEGE OF MEDICINE; HIV/AIDS.

—Mary K. Anglin, *University of Kentucky*

Veterans Affairs Medical Centers

Of the 171 major medical centers administered by the Veterans Health Administration, 16 are located in the Appalachian region. Medical centers have long been part of the federal system administered by the Department of Veterans Affairs. Prior to elevation to cabinet level status in 1989, veterans' affairs had been the responsibility of the Veterans Administration created by Congress in 1930. The Veterans Administration combined three agencies that dealt with veterans' issues: the Bureau of Pensions (established in 1833), the National Homes of Disabled Volunteer Soldiers (1866), and the Veterans Bureau (1921). The reorganization of the system throughout the twentieth century reflected the large increase in the population with veteran status and a general shift of responsibility for the well-being of veterans from local and state entities to the federal government. Health and medical programs within the Department of Veterans Affairs are the responsibility of the Veterans Health Administration, originally designated the Department of Medicine and Surgery in 1946. Large medical centers under the aegis of the Veterans Administration were created after World War I, and their numbers were boosted by large federal appropriations in the post–World War II period.

Most Veterans Affairs hospitals within the Appalachian region are located in small and medium-sized cities, although a few are in major metropolitan areas. They include medical centers in Birmingham, Tuscaloosa, and Tuskegee, Alabama; at Johnson City (Mountain Home), Tennessee; Asheville, North Carolina; Beckley, Clarksburg (Louis A. Johnson), Huntington, and Martinsburg, West Virginia; Chillicothe, Ohio; Altoona (James E. Van Zandt), Butler, Erie, Pittsburgh, and Wilkes-Barre, Pennsylvania; and Bath, New York. Additionally, Veterans Affairs medical centers with Appalachian counties in their catchment areas include Cincinnati, Ohio; Lexington, Kentucky; Salem, Virginia; Nashville, Tennessee; and Montgomery, Alabama.

Given the rural nature of much of Appalachia and the significant pockets of poverty contained within the region, Veterans Affairs medical facilities represent a significant economic and medical resource. While most of the centers have a history that precedes the establishment of the Veterans Administration, all offer a range of modern medical services. The Mountain Home facility is the oldest Veterans Affairs facility within the Appalachian region. Mountain Home, established in Johnson City in 1901, was the seventh federal facility created to care for disabled veterans, the second to be located in the South, and the first to accept both Union and Confederate veterans of the Civil War.

The centers in Appalachia vary in size and the type of services offered. All have posted Web sites that describe their missions, populations served, facilities, and range of services. Most have experienced considerable growth in the 1990s and several have added special programs for women veterans, aging veterans, and veterans with problems associated with the Vietnam and Persian Gulf conflicts. Several that served initially as national homes for disabled volunteer soldiers have campuses with domiciliaries for homeless veterans. All are sensitive to community needs and many have created community-based ambulatory clinics or collaborate with similar existing clinics.

All the centers offer primary and secondary care and treat conditions associated with veteran populations, including post-traumatic stress disorders and substance abuse, providing physical medicine and rehabilitation, physical therapy, and mental health services. The Martinsburg facility, which describes itself as a primary- and secondary-care facility providing longterm medical, surgical, and psychiatric services, is representative. However, several Veterans Affairs medical centers are major referral facilities that offer high-technology, tertiary care. The consolidated Pittsburgh center serves as a major referral center for liver transplants, geriatrics, oncology, neuropsychiatric disorders, and other specialized treatment. It serves as a backup to the Department of Defense Health Care System in time of national emergency. The Birmingham Veterans Affairs Medical Center is a primary referral center for the state of Alabama and contains one of nine Blind Rehabilitation Centers in the Veterans Affairs system.

Most Veterans Affairs medical centers in the Appalachian region are affiliated with allopathic (traditional) and/or osteopathic (a branch of medicine that emphasizes the musculoskeletal system) schools of medicine. Several serve as major training sites for medical students and residents. The Teague-Cranston legislation of 1972 created new, primary-care-oriented medical schools in medically underserved areas with universities in close proximity to major Veterans Affairs medical centers. In Appalachia this led to the establishment of the James H. Quillen College of Medicine at East Tennessee State University, which is affiliated with the Mountain Home Veterans Affairs Medical Center campus in Johnson City and Marshall University School of Medicine, affiliated with the Veterans Affairs facility in Huntington.

See also: EAST TENNESSEE STATE UNIVERSITY JAMES H. QUILLEN COLLEGE OF MEDICINE; MARSHALL UNIVERSITY JOAN C. EDWARDS SCHOOL OF MEDICINE.

—Bruce C. Bennard, *East Tennessee State University*

John Whitley Chambers II, ed., *The Oxford Companion to American Military History* (1999).

Wake Forest University School of Medicine

The Wake Forest University School of Medicine, now located in Winston-Salem, North Carolina, was founded in

1902 in the town of Wake Forest. At its creation, there were 166 medical schools operating in the United States. However, fewer than a dozen, including Wake Forest School of Medicine, required college preparation for admission. It remained a two-year program from the date of its establishment until 1941, when the school moved to Winston-Salem and the name was changed to the Bowman Gray School of Medicine. In 1997 the school was renamed for its parent university and became Wake Forest University School of Medicine on the Bowman Gray Campus.

The Wake Forest University School of Medicine is noted for its innovative medical education and for research in such areas as hypertension and vascular disease, which have a higher-than-average incidence in the Appalachian region. Cardiothoracic and heart valve surgeries are specialties as well. In 1990 Wake Forest cardiologists were the first in North Carolina to successfully open a blocked artery using a laser. Wake Forest also maintains a Women's Health Center of Excellence, which addresses such issues as breast and ovarian cancers.

The Wake Forest University Baptist Medical Center has twenty affiliate hospitals and maintains eighty-seven satellite clinics in a twenty-six county area in northwestern North Carolina and southwest Virginia. The main teaching hospital is North Carolina Baptist Hospital; other associated facilities include Forsyth Memorial Hospital and the Downtown Health Plaza of Baptist Hospital.

See also: SECTION OVERVIEW.

—J. Scott Wilson, *East Tennessee State University*

West Virginia Rural Health Education Partnerships

See Office of Rural Health at West Virginia University

West Virginia University School of Medicine

Graduating some eighty-eight students each year, the West Virginia University School of Medicine, as part of the Robert C. Byrd Health Sciences Center, trains primary-care physicians serving rural West Virginia and the surrounding Appalachian region. As of 2003, the school's more than ten thousand alumni made up about a third of the state's practicing physicians as well as two-thirds of its dentists, three-quarters of its pharmacists, and hundreds of nurses, medical and dental technologists, physical therapists, and other health professionals. The Robert C. Byrd Health Sciences Center is considered the state's primary health-care institution.

Located in Morgantown, the college of medicine originated in 1903 as a two-year affiliate of the College of Physicians and Surgeons in Baltimore. In 1912 the school became an independent two-year basic sciences program. Though serving as West Virginia's only medical training institution, it was not until 1960 that the program became a self-sufficient four-year program. Two years later, the university granted its first doctor of medicine degrees, warranting its full accreditation. The Charleston Area Medical Center became affiliated with the university in 1972, and the name was changed to the Robert C. Byrd Health Sciences Center at West Virginia University in 1993.

The center's primary teaching facility is the Ruby Memorial Hospital. In addition, West Virginia University maintains medical divisions in Charleston and Wheeling, as well as relationships with hospitals and physicians in rural areas throughout the state. Most of the school's students undergo part of their training at off-campus sites, where they learn the demands of rural health care. In addition, the school also works with the Chestnut Ridge Psychiatric Hospital, the Mountain View Regional Rehabilitation Hospital, the Mary Babb Randolph Cancer Center, the National Institute for Occupational Safety and Health, the West Virginia University Children's Hospital, and various other facilities.

See also: DENTISTRY; MARSHALL UNIVERSITY JOAN C. EDWARDS SCHOOL OF MEDICINE; OSTEOPATHY.

—J. Scott Wilson and Pamela M. Zahorik, *East Tennessee State University*

Work Disability

Although Appalachia moved steadily towards a more service-based economy in the late twentieth century, the region's continuing dependence upon manufacturing and extractive industries contributed significantly to high rates of work-related disability. A number of studies show the region to have a higher incidence of job-related injury and illness than any other part of the country. One such research project showed that in 1998 West Virginia and Kentucky ranked number one and number two among all states in the percentage of working-age individuals with disabilities limiting or preventing work. The same study, conducted for the U.S. Department of Education and the National Institute on Disability and Rehabilitation Research, showed Appalachian states as having the highest percentage of unemployed persons with work-related disabilities. West Virginia again led the nation, followed in order by Mississippi, Kentucky, Alabama, and Tennessee.

Just as local and regional economies contribute to broader health issues, so do they have an impact on worker disability and consequent needs for treatment and rehabilitation. Among the seven most common chronic conditions limiting work in America are back conditions, respiratory ailments, and distress in the lower extremities. Prevalent in

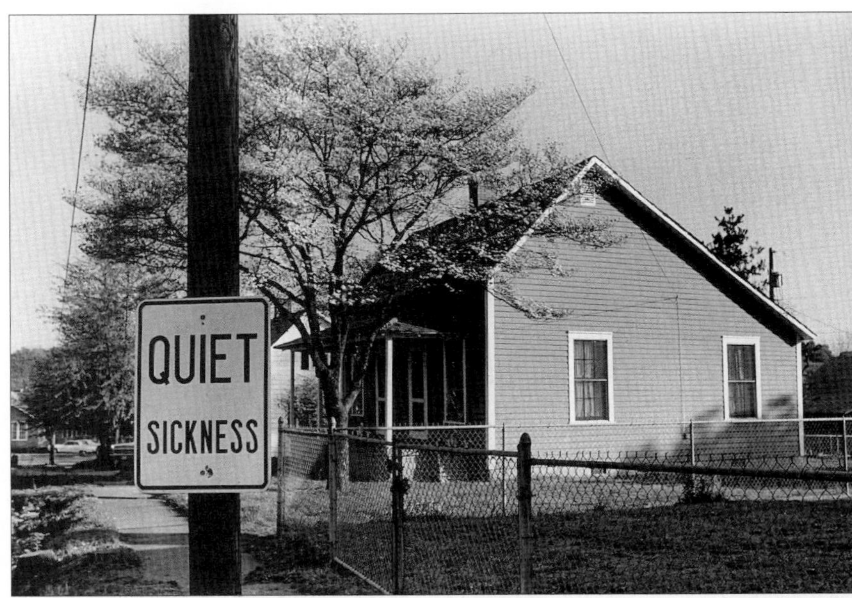

Textile mill village house, Greenville, South Carolina, 1978. The resident of this home had byssinosis, or brown lung disease, a condition caused by sustained inhalation of fine cotton and hemp particles from working in textile production. Several studies show that Appalachia has a higher incidence of job-related injury and illness than any other part of the county.

the Appalachian coalfields, such debilitating conditions are common wherever jobs involve heavy physical labor.

In the first years of the twenty-first century, the Appalachian economy still relies heavily upon physically demanding work. According to the Economic Research Service of the U.S. Department of Agriculture, some 42 percent of the region's rural counties are dependent upon either manufacturing or mining. According to the National Safety Council, mining ranked as the most dangerous industry in 2001 in terms of death rate—31.8 fatalities per 100,000 workers. Consequently, the region has fewer managers and professional people and more unskilled and lower-paid individuals in its workforce. The Appalachian workforce is exposed not only to the risk of sprains, strains, broken bones, and eventual respiratory disease from mining but also to a host of occupational hazards in timber cutting, trucking, farming, and the chemical industry.

Over the last two decades of the twentieth century, occupational injuries and illness declined across the nation, but 3.9 million American workers suffered disabling injuries while at work in 2001. In Appalachia, the number of deaths or serious injuries in the mines decreased because the workforce declined precipitously as mechanization and surface mining eliminated jobs.

As health-care costs spiraled in the late twentieth and early twenty-first centuries, the cost of disability programs rose as well. Indeed, it is difficult to calculate the total cost of disability upon the economy, nationally or regionally, for most states keep data on health costs only. Moreover, funding comes from multiple sources, including private, state, and federal workers' compensation in addition to Social Security disability and state and federal black lung programs. Federal outlays for all the various income security programs, including sums for disability, medical care, retirement, public assistance, and unemployment benefits, add up to nearly three-fourths of the federal funding to Appalachia.

Nationally, work injuries cost Americans $132.1 billion in 2001. This amounts to about $970 per worker, and the cost continues to increase. During the 1980s, the cost of unemployment insurance, medical, and hospital costs tripled. At the beginning of the new century, the cost of workers' compensation rose by 50 percent.

The sheer complexity of disability issues makes administration of the numerous programs involved extraordinarily difficult. For example, West Virginia has no fewer than ninety-two different risk classifications determining the amounts that employers pay for workers' compensation. The amounts vary from $0.53 to $42.46 for every $100.00 paid in wages, depending upon the safety records of individual companies, the risk classification, and employees' wage levels. A hardware store owner pays $1.88 for every $100.00 paid in wages, while the operator of a coal mine pays $34.44.

See also: BLACK LUNG ASSOCIATIONS; BLACK LUNG DISEASE AND THE BLACK LUNG MOVEMENT; SECTION OVERVIEW.

—Mona Counts, *Waynesburg, Pennsylvania*, and Regina Mayolo, *Fairchance, Pennsylvania*

Susan Stoddard et al., *Chart Book on Work and Disability in the United States* (1996).

Media

Section Editors: Anthony Harkins, Katherine E. Ledford, and Douglas Reichert Powell

IN THE SUMMER OF 1999, THIRTY-FIVE YEARS AFTER PRESIDENT LYNDON JOHNSON trained the spotlight of his War on Poverty on Appalachia, President Bill Clinton launched a new economic stimulus effort and sought again to focus national attention on the plight of poor Americans through the news media. Setting out on a tour of poverty-stricken communities across the nation, Clinton made central Appalachia his first stop, just as Johnson had flown to Inez, Kentucky, in 1964 and used a destitute Martin County family to call attention to poverty in America. Though Johnson's program failed to eradicate poverty, it helped to produce significant economic change across Appalachia during the years between Johnson's visit to Martin County and Clinton's national poverty tour, which began in the Tyner community of eastern Kentucky's Johnson County. Nevertheless, images of regionwide poverty, created and perpetuated by the news media, movies, television, novels, and works of nonfiction and fixed in the public mind long before Johnson's arrival, remained firmly intact when Clinton arrived. These two presidential events and the accompanying national media attention highlight the visceral place Appalachia holds in the public consciousness and serve as a window into the power of media to shape perceptions of a region and its people.

The flurry of news reports and commentaries generated by Clinton's visit emphasized not only the changes but also the similarities between the desperate conditions in Appalachia in 1964 and the poverty and economic stagnation still found in parts of the region in 1999. Indeed, the stop in Tyner was designed to do just that. In connection with the anniversary of the War on Poverty, reporters returned to some of the same places and some of the same people held up as examples of poverty in 1964. The press rediscovered Tom Fletcher, the unemployed Kentuckian whose family had become "poster people" for the original War on Poverty after they welcomed President Johnson to their front porch in 1964. Fletcher's circumstances had improved little, and the press presented him not only as an example of quintessential Appalachian poverty, but also as evidence of a failed federal policy, thereby casting doubt on the efficacy of Clinton's new program. For Appalachia's image, the result of the new focus of investigation was similar to the picture created after Johnson's visit with the Fletchers. Appalachia and its people seemed to have changed little in the intervening thirty-five years. This is not surprising. Mass media have historically

Facing page: Richard Barthelmess as David Kinemon in *Tol'able David,* 1921. A box-office and critical success from the silent era, the feud melodrama *Tol'able David* was set and filmed in the mountains of Highland County, Virginia.

relied upon stock images that hide the economic and social complexities of this diverse region, usually creating simplistic and misleading impressions of Appalachia for both national and local audiences.

The following section addresses the range of local, regional, and national media institutions, from weekly newspapers to national television programs and motion pictures, that have created persistent images and exerted a sometimes powerful impact upon the culture, community life, politics, and economy of the Appalachian region. Entries also examine changes in imagery resulting from shifting ownership and control of media sources.

Just as popular images of Appalachia have been shaped by the television and motion picture industries, so have the region's major public issues and its place in United States political and economic life been largely defined by news organizations owned and operated in distant urban centers. In Kentucky, regulation of surface mining came only after intensive coverage by the *Louisville Courier-Journal*, which won a 1967 Pulitzer Prize for its stories on the practice, photographs in *Life* magazine, and the attention of other national publications. In the late 1990s, mountaintop removal emerged as a major environmental issue after an exposé by the Washington, D.C.–based weekly magazine *U.S. News and World Report.* Coal companies had been removing tops from mountains and dumping the material in valleys and watersheds in central Appalachia for three decades before *U.S. News and World Report* published its cover story, accompanied by powerful color photographs, in October 1997. The article inspired landmark federal lawsuits, led to changes in surface-mining regulations, and ignited a firestorm of environmental controversy reaching beyond Appalachia and continuing into the new century. Not since Appalachian poverty became a subject of national news in the 1960s had the region seen such a deluge of media attention. Other national publications followed the lead of *U.S. News and World Report*, as did regional and local publishers and broadcasters. In the West Virginia state capital, the *Charleston Gazette* launched the most extensive investigation of strip mining since the 1960s. The newspaper's reporting received a number of awards, enhanced its reputation for crusading journalism, and kept the issue alive long after the interest of national news organizations had waned.

Like the region itself, Appalachia's news media have complex and contradictory histories. From their beginnings as personal instruments of politicians, publishers of official notices, and sidelines for commercial printers, newspapers have evolved with the region and its economy. A few newspapers, such as the *Mountain Eagle*, a weekly published in Whitesburg, Kentucky, have served as watchdogs, exposing inadequacies in schools, destructive effects of surface mining, and the malfeasance of officeholders. More often, however, local publications have tended to reflect the views of the local establishment and dominant economic interests. The late twentieth century saw absentee corporate owners rapidly assume control of media outlets across Appalachia—print, television, and radio alike. The impact of chain ownership was mixed, but many critics mourned the passing of local publishers and broadcasters, who had often been fixtures in civic life. Even though corporate ownership brought local outlets more economic security and the potential for editorial independence, critics and activists frequently charged absentee owners with offering bland or irrelevant stories rather than coverage of vital community issues. Except in major urban communities, the concentration of media ownership resulted in the virtual disappearance of radio news coverage in the late twentieth century, and high production costs in local television markets generally led to superficial coverage of news and public affairs. At the same time, nearby urban newspapers that once had circulated in the region came under chain ownership and increasingly concentrated on their home bases in cities such as Atlanta, Nashville, Louisville, and Cincinnati. Coverage of rural Appalachia faded. Conspicuously, the *Charleston Gazette*, which aggressively investigated not only mountaintop removal but such other major regional issues as inadequate health care, occupational disability, environmental pollution, and political corruption, remained under the control of the family that had run it for most of the twentieth century.

Newspapers, broadcast news, and documentary films have influenced both imagery and reality in the region, as coverage of the War on Poverty and mountaintop removal illustrate. Likewise, entertainment media such as motion pictures, television, and radio have created a host of entrenched stereotypes and cultural images that continue to shape popular notions about Appalachia and its people. This section also addresses the cross-fertilization between the news and the entertainment media in their creation and distribution of images of Appalachia. Because of a growing realization that the depiction of a region in popular culture can affect that region's political and economic status, media representations of Appalachia have been a source of conflict and controversy since the early 1970s. Purveyors of negative images continue to bank on the currency of the "hillbilly" image, indelibly linked in the public consciousness with Appalachia. One example of the entertainment media's penchant for trafficking in stock images, reminiscent of the news media's reliance on stereotypical views during and after the War on Poverty, was the reemergence of *The Beverly Hillbillies*, first as a movie and then as a proposed reality television show, after years in syndicated reruns.

The proposal of a television reality show and the diverse reactions it engendered are indicative of broader themes in the media's exploration and exploitation of Appalachia throughout the twentieth century. In the fall of 2002, the CBS television network announced its intention to create a "reality show" revolving around the concept that made *The Beverly Hillbillies* a hit television series in the late 1960s and early 1970s. Producers proposed to recruit an actual extended family (including grandparents, parents, and children) from the mountains of West Virginia, North Carolina, Tennessee, Kentucky, or Arkansas to relocate to a mansion in Beverly Hills for a year or more. The scenario, developed by Dub Cornett, a documentary filmmaker born in southwestern Virginia, called for the family to be given money to live a stereotypically "California" lifestyle, buying expensive cars and clothes, hiring a personal entourage of assistants and domestic help, and wining and dining at trendy restaurants and nightclubs. In keeping with the reality motif, which became a television fad at the turn of the century, a camera crew was to trail family members, capturing all of the unrehearsed clashes between rural, down-to-earth mountain people and urban sophisticates. The humor and appeal of the show would derive from this cultural friction.

Reaction to CBS's announcement of the planned show and a search for a family to star in the production was swift, negative, and revealing. The program was denounced in newspaper columns and editorials, ridiculed by members of Congress, and opposed by labor leaders such as Cecil Roberts, president of the United Mine Workers of America, who led pickets outside the annual shareholders' meeting of Viacom, CBS's parent corporation. While supporters claimed that the show would be an opportunity for a group of sympathetic, salt-of-the-earth, rural working people to show up the pretensions and posturing of Hollywood, opponents argued that it was a set-up, with the unlucky volunteers likely to become the butt of a national joke, country clods shown to be out of step with contemporary culture. As the debate gained prominence, the Center for Rural Strategies, an advocacy group based in Whitesburg,

Kentucky, created a Web site to facilitate grassroots response to CBS's plans, collected editorial responses from major media outlets, and took out large ads in the *New York Times*, *Los Angeles Times*, and other major newspapers denouncing the show as insensitive to the lives of the rural working poor. The group's strategy helped to catalyze a nationwide public discussion about the merits of the proposed show, and CBS quietly shelved the idea.

The emotional conflict over *The Real Beverly Hillbillies* exemplifies tensions between "insiders," who possess "authentic" knowledge of mountain life, and "outsiders," who co-opt or misrepresent local perspectives. Yet as Cornett's own Appalachian roots suggest, it is impossible to divorce images from the material circumstances in which they are made, distributed, and viewed. Labeling media producers as outsiders is questionable, considering that a convincing case can be made that the identity of Appalachia as a region is actually a result of media representations of it. It has been suggested that without outside media, there would be no identifiable region called Appalachia to be inside. By the same token, individuals and media outlets from Appalachia have also played an important role in the construction of both a national image and regional reality.

Historically, media interest in the Appalachian region—as in the mid-1960s, for example—has corresponded to broader political and cultural crises in the United States. Appalachia has often figured in national debates as a crucible for issues from labor rights and poverty to social programs and environmental challenges. A series of longer entries in this section examine these periods of "rediscovery" of the Appalachian region during the explosive labor conflicts of the 1910s and 1920s, the Great Depression and the New Deal, and the 1960s, especially Appalachia's central role in the election of President John F. Kennedy in 1960 and during the Great Society social welfare programs of the mid- to late 1960s.

Many important figures in Appalachian media history—Robert Mitchum, Earl Hamner Jr. (creator of *The Waltons*), and John Lair, among them—have drawn on their mountain backgrounds to create feature films, television shows, and folk music radio shows for national audiences. Moreover, the dynamics of media production, circulation, and reception frustrate easy conclusions about outside exploitation versus inside resistance. *The Beverly Hillbillies*, for example, was especially popular with rural viewers, the very group it seems to exploit. But this popularity was, ironically, the show's downfall: CBS's aversion to the "hick" reputation it was acquiring by broadcasting not only *The Beverly Hillbillies*, but also the spin-offs *Petticoat Junction* and *Green Acres*, motivated the cancellation of the program in 1971 as part of an effort to attract a younger, wealthier, and more cosmopolitan market segment.

Although media representations of Appalachia are part of the region's political and economic struggles, simple analyses of the ways images of the region are created by outsiders fail to represent adequately the complexity of this history. Whether generated from inside or outside the region, one of the persistent stereotypes about Appalachia is that it is a place devoid of modern conveniences and communication outlets where illiteracy abounds. This image is belied by the media's own rich and complex history in the region. Nevertheless, the broad notion of Appalachia as an illiterate place has been sustained by heartwarming portrayals such as the movie *Nell*, as well as in such infamous renderings as *Deliverance*. Unflattering individual portrayals that sustain ungrounded ideas are, however, only one element of the larger presence of mass-media forms and images in the history of the Appalachian Mountains and the people who live there.

An examination of broader images and issues helps to reveal the media's influence on mountain identity and mountain life. Essential to an understanding of this role is not only how Appalachian people are represented but why. Who controls access to the production of mass-media images? How do media images reflect perceptions of the peoples they portray, as well as the values of the people who make them? What alternatives do people have to the most powerful and most prevalent media forms—especially television and Hollywood motion pictures—if they wish to present their own versions of their region and the events that have shaped it? By documenting the variety of media images and forms and the people who have made them, the entries in this section are meant to address such questions about the mass media's relationship to the region.

Two central qualities of mass media are variety and constant change, and new versions of the region steadily appear. An appreciation of these qualities and knowledge of the relationship between Appalachia and the media can provide an understanding of events that might otherwise seem fleeting and unconnected. Anthropologist Allen W. Batteau *(The Invention of Appalachia)*, historian Henry D. Shapiro *(Appalachia on Our Mind)*, and film critic J. W. Williamson *(Hillbillyland)* have all argued that media texts—from the popular press of the late nineteenth century to contemporary print journalism, television, cartoons, and literature—are crucial in shaping what people believe about Appalachia. Dating back to the earliest days of cinema, feature films have explored the "mountain character," creating a tradition of depicting hillbillies as noble naturals or abject primitives. Entries in the following section explore some of these representations in film, television, and other media, as well as the people who made them. In many of these representations, mountain people are surprisingly enigmatic. The virtuous pioneer and the vice-ridden hillbilly represent a difficult paradox, not only in the regional subculture but also as a part of a larger national and global culture. Likewise, the mountains of central Appalachia tend to be presented as either a plundered and polluted sacrificial zone of the industrial economy or as an inviting landscape of extraordinary beauty and natural diversity.

Often, a single representation of the region combines features of both pioneer and hillbilly stock characters. One influential television depiction of the region, Charles Kuralt's 1963 CBS special "Christmas in Appalachia," attempted to portray both the desperate economic conditions and cultural deprivation of mountain residents as well as their strength and endurance. The program demonstrates the limitations of media efforts to present reality in a condensed form, however. Although Kuralt's intentions were widely considered to have been admirable, the show was later criticized on grounds that its subjects appeared to be powerless and defeated objects of pity. Mass-media portrayals of Appalachia seldom occur in isolation; Kuralt's came at a time when Appalachian poverty was being used to promote new governmental social welfare and economic initiatives. The acclaimed Appalshop documentary *Stranger with a Camera* subsequently put "Christmas in Appalachia" in the context of the larger outpouring of media depictions—especially documentaries—of the region during the mid-1960s. Appalshop, a grassroots cultural center sponsoring documentary film, video, radio, and the arts, was created in 1969 explicitly as an effort to gain greater control over how the region would be represented.

The dynamics of the media's role in Appalachia might best be viewed in terms of who does and who does not have access to the means to produce influential texts and images. The pioneer mythology that has been popular in the media for so long —dating back at least to the Crockett Almanacs, which invented the adventures of Davy Crockett in the early nineteenth century—is a product of a media industry that

Founder Bill Richardson with early staff at the original Appalshop building, Whitesburg, Kentucky, 1972. A community-based, nonprofit media arts center, Appalshop has earned international acclaim for its work in preserving Appalachian culture and documenting issues affecting the region.

has traditionally been based outside the region or controlled by wealthy and cosmopolitan interests whose sympathies and interests were not representative of mountain people in general. Media texts made within the region itself often give a picture quite different from the stereotypical one of a conservative, racially homogenous, and culturally static or deprived region.

Southern Appalachia, for example, was the birthplace of the *Cherokee Phoenix*, a bilingual newspaper printed both in English and in the Cherokee syllabary developed by Sequoyah. Though the paper disappeared in 1834, four years before the Cherokee removal to Oklahoma, other homegrown media outlets have represented alternative voices in United States history. Several of the nation's first abolitionist newspapers were published in east Tennessee. Though muted since the days when newspapers were undisguised political weapons, the tradition of dissent and activism survives in notable instances. Kentucky's *Mountain Eagle* is nationally known for its editorial vigor and reporting, especially for its exposés of political corruption and abuses of power by industry in the 1960s. Broadside Television represented a groundbreaking experiment in grassroots broadcasting in the 1970s. Alternative newspapers such as *The Plow* and the *Appalachian Reader* have distinguished themselves among regional publications, presenting alternative perspectives and progressive views on current events. Appalshop continues its commitment to developing a homegrown media vision of the region. All of these alternative outlets reflect a region whose politics and cultures are considerably more complicated than mainstream media generally present.

In the late twentieth century, new technology became an important factor influencing communication within Appalachia and facilitating broader national and international access to information about the region. More than any development since the arrival of television, the Internet brought the potential to alter perceptions of the region, influence the role of its mass media, and affect Appalachian cultures themselves. With dramatic speed, rural communities and individual citizens within them could access a wealth of information heretofore unavailable. This direct access to seemingly limitless sources of information had profound implications for the mass media, particularly the news media in their role as filter and interpreter of public issues and current events.

Government agencies, educational institutions, nonprofit organizations, and commercial enterprises all found Web sites particularly useful for spreading their messages. For example, the Appalachian Regional Commission's Web site quickly became the foremost repository of official data on the region and its economy. At Morehead State University in Kentucky, the Institute for Regional Analysis and Public Policy, created in 1999, built a massive Web site, the Center for Virtual Appalachia, which provided links to four thousand Appalachia-related sites by 2003. Its media portal directed users to sites for dozens of television programs and motion pictures that have influenced the region, and its news portal connected to newspapers in every county in Appalachia. Another Web site, maintained by Appalachian Focus, a nonprofit organization in Middlesboro, Kentucky, took the idea of media access a step further, experimenting from 2000 to 2002 with collecting daily newspaper articles about Appalachia and rapidly posting them to the Appalachian Focus Web site, in effect creating a massive daily regional newspaper on-line. Perhaps most importantly, the Internet provided a means to mobilize grassroots movements, such as the popular opposition to CBS's proposal to reincarnate *The Beverly Hillbillies*, and offered the prospect of more realistic perceptions of the region, with Appalachians themselves exerting a greater impact on mass-media imagery.

All this is not to suggest, however, that texts made inside the region necessarily present more positive versions of Appalachia than those originating elsewhere. Often, progressive, grassroots local media offer the most troubling and controversial accounts of mountain life. The offices of the *Mountain Eagle*, for example, have been firebombed as a result of its willingness to depict political conflict and controversy, and editors such as the *Martin (Ky.) Countian*'s Homer Marcum have been threatened. Meanwhile, outsiders have won major awards for investigative reporting in the region. In 1962 reporters Nat Caldwell and Gene Graham of the *Nashville Tennessean* were awarded the Pulitzer Prize for stories revealing collusion between John L. Lewis, president of the United Mine Workers of America, and strip-mining interests. Five years later, the *Louisville Courier-Journal* received a Pulitzer and a special citation for public service for reporting that led to new regulation of surface mining in Kentucky.

In their complexity and change, the media in Appalachia resemble the media in other places, and the history of the region's newspapers and broadcasters is part and parcel of the national history of mass media. This shared history suggests other commonalities. Issues concerning popular access to means of production are increasingly urgent throughout the United States, since consolidation portends an increase of absentee ownership of the dominant media voices in any given community. This leads to the inevitable question of whether communities can meaningfully engage with their own problems and priorities if their media voices are controlled by distant people and remote interests. Beyond issues of misrepresentation and stereotyping, Appalachian media face many of the same sensitive cultural issues that confront the media across the nation—those relating to race, nationality, class, gender, and sexuality among them. Therefore, the history of the region's media is not only about Appalachia's differences with the rest of the nation, but also about its similar challenges and perspectives.

Far from resisting literacy and modernity, Appalachia has adapted media technologies in distinctive ways. Collectively, the entries in this section detail ways the region has published, filmed, recorded, and communicated its existence to the world—and the multitude of ways its story has been analyzed and interpreted.

—Anthony Harkins, *Western Kentucky University;*
Katherine E. Ledford, *Gardner-Webb University;* and
Douglas Reichert Powell, *Columbia College Chicago*

Allen W. Batteau, *The Invention of Appalachia* (1990); Dwight B. Billings, Gurney Norman, and Katherine Ledford, eds., *Confronting Appalachian Stereotypes: Back Talk from an American Region* (1999); Anthony A. Harkins, *Hillbilly: A Cultural History of an American Icon* (2004); Bill C. Malone, *Singing Cowboys and Musical Mountaineers: Southern Culture and the Roots of Country Music* (1993); W. K. McNeil, ed., *Appalachian Images in Folk and Popular Culture* (1989); Richard A. Peterson, *Creating Country Music: Fabricating Authenticity* (1997); Henry D. Shapiro, *Appalachia on Our Mind: The Southern Mountains and Mountaineers in the American Consciousness, 1870–1920* (1978); J. W. Williamson, *Hillbillyland: What the Movies Did to the Mountains and What the Mountains Did to the Movies* (1995).

Abolitionist Newspapers

The abolitionist movement in Appalachia began with the formation of the Manumission Society of Tennessee in Greene County on February 15, 1815. East Tennessee was an important area for manumission activities, and some of the earliest and most prominent antislavery leaders got their start there. Such men as Samuel Doak, John Rankin, Charles Osborn, Benjamin Lundy, and Elihu Embree, all members of the Manumission Society of Tennessee, lived in the Appalachian region and were important in the development of abolitionist newspapers and publications.

Embree's *Manumission Intelligencer*, published in Jonesborough, Tennessee, in March 1819, was the first abolitionist newspaper in the country. Appearing every Tuesday, it not only promoted the abolitionist cause but also reported on other issues, including agriculture, foreign affairs, and culture. The weekly publication schedule soon become too much for Embree to maintain, and in April 1820 he replaced the *Intelligencer* with the *Emancipator*, a monthly limited to abolitionist topics. After only seven months, the final issue was published October 31, 1820. Embree died of a fever December 4, 1820, and prospects for resurrecting the newspaper ended.

Benjamin Lundy initially agreed to finish the *Emancipator*'s remaining issues but instead promoted his own publication, the *Genius of Universal Emancipation*. This publication was originally begun in Mount Pleasant, Ohio, in January of

THE EMANCIPATOR.

VOL. I.] JONESBOROUGH, APRIL 30, 1820. [No. 1.

EDITED AND PUBLISHED BY ELIHU EMBREE, AT $1 PER ANNUM—IN ADVANCE.

ADDRESS, *OF THE EDITOR.*

The EMANCIPATOR will be published monthly in *Jonesborough*, Ten. by *ELIHU EMBREE*, on a fine superroyal sheet of paper, in octava form, at *One Dollar* per annum, payable on receipt of the first number.

This paper is especially designed by the editor to advocate the abolition of slavery, and to be a repository of tracts on that interesting and important subject. It will contain all the necessary information that the editor can obtain of the progress of the abolition of the slavery of the descendants of Africa; together with a concise history of their introduction into slavery, collected from the best authorities.

The constitutions and proceedings of the several benevolent societies in the United States and elsewhere who have had this grand object in view, will be carefully selected and published in the Emancipator.

A correspondence between those societies, and between individuals in different parts of the nation on the subject of emancipation, will be kept up through the medium of this paper by inserting in its pages all interesting communications, letters, &c. that may come to the knowledge of the editor.

The speeches of those have been and are eminently advocating this glorious cause, either in the congress of the U. S. the state legislatures, or in the parliaments and courts of other nations, will be strictly attended to.

Biographical sketches of the lives of those who have been eminent in this cause, will also occasionally find a place in this work.

A portion of this paper is intended to be devotod as a history of the abolition of the African slave trade, in every part of the world, from its first dawn, down to the present times.

In the prosecution of this work the editor professes that he expects (like other periodical editors) to live much upon the borrow; and to make use of such materials as he may find in his way, suited to his object, without being very particular to take up much time or room in acknowledging a loan, unless he may think it necessary, willing that others should use the same freedom with him, & hoping that by offering such a fair exchange, such borrowing will be thought no robbery.

Communications on the subject, and materials for the work are solicited and will be thankfully received.both from societies and individuals friendly to the abolition of slavery. Such communications, if approved of by the editor, will find a harty welcome in the *Emancipator*.

The Manumission Society of Tenn. in particular, it is expected will afford many tracts on the subject of slavery, which the editor assures them he will feel inclined to respect; and where his judgment should not otherwise dictate, will give them an early and gratuitous insertion. They will find in the Emancipator a true chronicle of the proceedings of that benevolent society as far as the editor is enabled—And for this purpose the clerks of the conventions, and of each branch of the society are requested to forward from time to time true copies of all their minutes, which may not be really improper to publish (and it is hoped there will be none such) together with the names of their members, their places of residence, &c. all which particulars we are of opinion will not be unprofitable to the cause of abolition to be published.

Letters from one individual to another, with the names of both, we think will be often beneficial to be published. If they do nothing more they will shew that all are not asleep nor dumb to the cries of suffering humanity.

Those who have had, or may have law suits on hand for the freedom of such as are unlawfully held in bondage, are desired to forward the true history of the facts, their progress, final decision, &c. with the places of residence and names of plaintiff's and defendant's, with eve-

A.

First issue of the *Emancipator*, Jonesborough, Tennessee, 1820. East Tennessee nurtured the abolitionist movement, producing some of its earliest and most prominent leaders, including Elihu Embree, publisher of the *Manumission Intelligencer* and the *Emancipator*.

1821, under the guidance of Charles Osborn, a North Carolina native who started publishing his own antislavery newspaper, the *Philanthropist*, there in 1817. Lundy was influenced by Osborn's ideas and helped him with the *Philanthropist*. Osborn eventually sold the newspaper, and Lundy struck out on his own with the *Genius*. After Embree's death, Lundy moved his publication from Mount Pleasant to Jonesborough. There, with the help of several of Embree's family members, he built upon the success of the *Emancipator* and promoted the *Genius*, which he eventually moved to Baltimore in 1824.

Another significant publication in the Appalachian area was the *Abolition Intelligencer and Missionary Magazine* founded in Shelbyville, Kentucky, in 1822. Edited by John Finley Crow and published monthly, the magazine was solely dedicated to the antislavery cause—"to aid, so far as they may have their power, the cause of suffering humanity."

Due to the conviction and involvement of many southern mountaineers, Appalachia's abolitionist papers were an important part of the abolitionist movement not only within the southern states but in New England as well.

See also: NEWSPAPERS; SLAVERY AND ABOLITION (GOVERNMENT).

—Tracy Cannon, *East Tennessee State University*

John W. Blassingame and Mae G. Henderson, eds., *Antislavery Newspapers and Periodicals, Vol. 1: An Annotated Index of Letters in the Philanthropist Emancipator, Genius of Universal Emancipation, Abolition Intelligencer, African Observer, and the Liberator, 1817–1845* (1980); Elihu Embree, *The Emancipator* (1932; reprint 1995); Don West, *Freedom in the Mountains* (1973).

Agee Films

Founded in 1974 as the James Agee Film Project, Agee Films produces and distributes the documentary work of executive director Ross Spears, as well as documentaries by Stan Woodward, Lindsey Wilson, and Chris Farina and Reid Oechslin. The company is named for Knoxville, Tennessee–born writer James Agee.

Several of Spears's films represent important contributions to the body of Appalachian documentary films. *Agee* (1980), a biography of the east Tennessee author, draws on testimony from Agee's three wives as well as photographer Walker Evans, author Dwight Macdonald, actor/director John Huston, and former President Jimmy Carter. *To Render a Life* (1992) adapts *Let Us Now Praise Famous Men*, Agee's 1941 meditation on rural poverty in collaboration with photographer Evans. Just as Agee and Evans dwelt among sharecroppers in Alabama, Spears and writer Silvia Kersusan spent almost three years working with a poor rural Virginia family. Using Agee's words in voiceover, the film presents a complex portrayal of poverty and a meditation on the challenge of portraying the material world through words and images. *The Electric Valley* (1983), a history of the Tennessee Valley Authority (TVA) narrated by Tennessee historian and novelist Wilma Dykeman, is the film company's most important contribution to Appalachian studies. Mixing contemporary footage of the Tennessee River watershed with journalism and excerpts from the project's own propaganda films, Spears, along with writer and researcher Richard Couto, details the TVA's effects on ordinary Appalachians through its transformation from a New Deal social program to a hydroelectric and nuclear provider and a major coal customer. In 2003 Spears and Agee Films were at work on a four-part history of the region entitled *Appalachia*, spanning the period from the formation of the mountain chain through the present day.

A native of Johnson City, Tennessee, Spears frequently collaborates with fellow Johnson Citian and composer Kenneth Coe for the soundtracks to his films.

See also: AGEE, JAMES (LITERATURE); APPALSHOP; DOCUMENTARY FILMS.

—Douglas Reichert Powell, *Columbia College Chicago*

Allegheny Uprising

Directed by William A. Seiter and notable chiefly as an early vehicle for the young John Wayne, *Allegheny Uprising* (RKO Radio Pictures, 1939) is a romance of sturdy American frontiersmen poised against pompous British soldiers and unscrupulous traders in the Pennsylvania backwoods of the mid-eighteenth century. Frontiersman Jim Smith (Wayne) and his comrades discover that eastern merchants are supplying the Indians with weapons and rum. Their efforts to stop this trade are frustrated when the merchants, concerned only with profit, manage to smuggle their goods under the protection of the British army. The frontiersmen's efforts to rectify this injustice lead to conflict with both the merchants and the British.

The film's action is preposterous, serving mainly to dramatize the backwoodsmen's moral superiority. The rough frontiersmen are uncouth, quick to anger, and, as the British observe, contemptuous of authority. However, they are also honest and fair, exhibiting a punctilious respect for the law as they see it. They kill Indians heartily but, due to their wily schemes, never have to kill an English or American character to achieve their goals, despite their commitment to vigilantism. The film contrasts the true law of the backcountry, self-evident in norms of right and fair play, with the British "law of bayonets," a false law easily manipulated by the lying and cowardly merchants. In a climactic scene, Smith quiets an unruly mob of angry frontiersmen and agrees to submit to a British court. His folksy but wise sidekick tells the crowd, "In defending one law, we've come to despise all law, and if you go on like this, we'll destroy the very thing we fight for."

Modestly successful upon release, the film was, Wayne later observed, "an awful stinker."

See also: FEATURE FILMS.

—Paul V. Murphy, *Grand Valley State University*

All the Right Moves

All the Right Moves (1983), a Twentieth Century Fox film directed by Michael Chapman, depicts the efforts of young townspeople to escape a dying northern Appalachian town through success on the football field. The movie, filmed on location in Johnstown, Pennsylvania, is set in the fictitious steel town of Ampipe. Starring Tom Cruise as Stef, the son of a steelworker, Craig T. Nelson as Nickerson, the high school football coach, and Lea Thompson as Lisa, Stef's girlfriend, the film explores the tension in Appalachian life between individualism and community in the context of the decline of the region's coal and steel industries after the mid-1970s.

The plot revolves around a game between working-class, ethnic Ampipe and a wealthy rival team. At the pregame pep rally, Nickerson stresses the importance of the contest to the town as a whole: a victory will restore the pride lost as Ampipe's steel industry has languished. The players, however, view the game as a means to escape through college scholarships, and Nickerson sees it as chance to land a college-level coaching job. This tension surfaces when a group of townspeople vandalize Nickerson's home after a close loss. The conflict becomes personal when Nickerson throws Stef off the team after a locker-room dispute, leading to the latter's participation in the vandalism.

In the ensuing struggle, Stef tests his individuality against the coach's will, and he explores his willingness to recognize Lisa's need for respect. Blackballed by Nickerson, Stef turns for support to Lisa and his family, whose members pull together despite their disagreements. And though Stef triumphs by standing up for himself, he learns to appreciate Lisa's needs.

See also: FEATURE FILMS.

—Kevin D. Smith, *State University of New York at Potsdam*

Andy Griffith Show, The

This popular television series established in the national consciousness an enduring model of mid-twentieth-century small-town America and its environs. During its 249-episode run (1960–68), the series never left the Nielson top ten, generating two successful spin-offs. Broadcast by CBS, *The Andy Griffith Show* contributed to that network's reputation for "country comedies," which also included *The Beverly Hillbillies, Petticoat Junction*, and *Green Acres*.

The Andy Griffith Show was largely the brainchild of its eponymous leading man, who was born in 1926 in Mount Airy, North Carolina, and graduated from the University of North Carolina in 1949. After several television appearances in the early 1950s performing his popular "hayseed comic" routine, Griffith adapted his affable bumpkin character for the Broadway hit *No Time for Sergeants* in 1955, earning a Tony nomination. In Elia Kazan's *A Face in the Crowd* (1957), Griffith made an acclaimed film debut by turning a darkly ironic lens upon his trademark persona, but he returned to the lighter side of his yokel character the following year with the film version of *No Time for Sergeants* and the similar *Onionhead*. The development of *The Andy Griffith Show* began soon after the success of a 1960 episode of *The Danny Thomas Show* in which Griffith appeared as Andy Taylor, the affable sheriff of a small North Carolina town called Mayberry. In the series, Sheriff Taylor would become a wise, paternalistic foil for the more overtly comic citizens of Mayberry. The first episode of *The Andy Griffith Show* aired on October 3, 1960, and was an immediate hit.

Through four decades of reruns, the town of Mayberry (loosely based on Griffith's own Mount Airy) has become an emblem of mythic small-town America: slow, simple, preternaturally pure, and perched delicately between the agrarian and the commercial. Contrary to popular perception, however, Mayberry itself is not a rural town, strictly speaking, as its citizens exhibit a distinct and highly developed sense of civility that directly contrasts the manners and mores of the more overtly rural visitors from outside town. The neighbors in Mayberry are remarkably genteel, and as the town itself is situated along a figurative frontier separating the urban from the mountainous rural, it would be an oversimplification to view Mayberry as an island of unspoiled rural culture in an increasingly cosmopolitan nation. Certainly, incursion into Mayberry by urban characters is a recurrent motif of the series, and most such outsiders are censured for their exaggerated sophistication, transformed for the better by their Mayberry experiences, or returned to urban America for literal incarceration. Still, even the most unsophisticated inhabitants of the town (the Pyle cousins, for example, Gomer and Goober) are cognizant of the social parameters so carefully maintained by the show's lead characters, and those characters who are directly associated with the rural stereotype are as out of place in Mayberry as are the visiting city folk.

The Andy Griffith Show's most explicitly rural minor characters usually undergo a process of refinement intended to create the balance of rusticity and gentility that is required for Mayberry life. For example, a farm girl is introduced to cosmetics, or the unsightly home of an elderly man outside town is given an imposed redecoration. More significant still are those vividly stereotypical Appalachian characters who are beyond such reclamation. These characters are presented as romantically innocent savants (Rafe Hollister of the innately operatic voice), vaguely menacing clowns (the inimitable Ernest T. Bass), or both (the Darling family, a clan of bluegrass-picking ruffians played by Ozark musicians the Dillards, who at one point appeared in three episodes out of nine).

Sheriff Taylor, meanwhile, moves comfortably on both sides of the Mayberry frontier. Although the members of a posh gentleman's club in Raleigh seek his company, Taylor prefers playing guitar in the Darlings' mountain shack. He represents civilized law (so civilized, in fact, that he does not carry a gun), but he can deal with moonshiners and feuding families empathetically. Griffith's character embodies the model for small-town life that is implicit in the series itself: he is a link who mitigates conflict between the city and the mountains, between Appalachia and the rest of the world.

See also: *BEVERLY HILLBILLIES, THE;* TELEVISION DEPICTIONS OF THE REGION.

—John F. Keener, *Lees-McRae College*

Ken Beck and Jim Clark, *The Andy Griffith Show Book* (1985); Dan Harrison and Bill Habeeb, *Inside Mayberry: The Andy Griffith Show Handbook* (1994).

Animated Cartoons

Hollywood studio cartoons, with their reliance on humor, broad caricature, and fast-paced action synchronized to a score, have been a fertile ground for the depiction of Appalachian stereotypes. In the 1930s in particular, the Hollywood cartoon embraced the broad, stylized image of the hillbilly, reflecting the widening distribution of mountain music through radio and motion pictures and the flourishing of print cartoons featuring mountain culture. Although the setting of these cartoons is clearly the mountains, it is never specifically Appalachia.

Hugh Harman and Rudolph Ising's "I Like Mountain Music" (1933), Walter Lantz's "Hill Billys" (1935), Friz Freleng's "When I Yoo Hoo" (1936), Tex Avery's "A Feud There Was" (1938), and Bob Clampett's "Naughty Neighbors" (1939) represent early instances of the hillbilly image in the American studio cartoon. Warner Brothers cartoons incorporated hillbilly music to capitalize on its growing popularity throughout the 1930s and to boost sales of Warner's sheet music. Many of these cartoons use the feud as the basic plot device, embedding cartoon slapstick and sight gags that depict hillbilly culture: dancing, sleeping, and shooting. Some of these cartoons reflected contemporary cultural and political developments. "Naughty Neighbors" stands out for its topical use of the feud to satirize the August 1939 Nonaggression Pact between Germany and the Soviet Union.

Hillbillies continued to pop up in Hollywood cartoons, including five featuring Al Capp's Li'l Abner made at Columbia Screen Gems in 1944–45 and the "Martins and McCoys" sequence in the Disney feature film *Make Mine Music* (1946). The hillbilly image also endured in later Warner cartoons such as Robert McKimson's "Hillbilly Hare" (1950) and "Backwoods Bunny" (1959), starring Bugs Bunny as a city slicker who gets the upper hand over less savvy country bumpkins. There were a few hillbilly cartoons made in the 1960s for theatrical and television distribution. Warner Brothers' "Feud with a Dude" (1968) has Merlin the Magic Mouse meeting the Hatfields and the McCoys. For television, Paramount produced a series of Snuffy Smith cartoons for King Features, and Hanna-Barbera produced a Saturday-morning television series called *The Hillbilly Bears*.

See also: CARTOONS; COMIC STRIPS; *LI'L ABNER*.

—Michael Frierson, *University of North Carolina at Greensboro*

Appalachian Expositions of 1910 and 1911

The Appalachian Expositions staged in Knoxville, Tennessee, in the autumns of 1910 and 1911 promoted responsible development of southern Appalachian resources and showcased progress in the region's industries, agriculture, and commerce. In a broader sense, the monthlong fairs applied the New South dream of modernization, social harmony, and cultural enrichment to southern Appalachia. Although world's fairs and grand expositions were commonplace in the early twentieth century, the Appalachian Expositions were the first to focus on the region as an area of social progress and economic potential.

The various types of buildings that dotted the landscape of the fairgrounds reflected the messages of the expositions. The Minerals, Forestry, Agricultural, and Livestock Buildings lauded southern Appalachian resources and promoted the development of scientific methods. The Woman's Building endorsed the New South role of women as nurturers both in the home and community without challenging traditional female roles. Similarly, the Negro Pavilion displayed the achievements of African Americans and promoted racial harmony but did not challenge the rampant discrimination of the period.

The expositions addressed the plight and potential of Appalachian highlanders in a number of ways. On the 1910 fairgrounds, two cabins, along with their "unwholesome odor" and barefooted inhabitants, depicted the primitive side of Appalachian culture. At both fairs, however, other cabins showed the progress of the backcountry with displays of products such as baskets, wood carvings, and coverlets from settlement schools.

At both events, visiting orators echoed the expositions' themes of progress and social uplift. Former President Theodore Roosevelt lauded southern Appalachia for its "purely Native American" constituency, maintained through isolation. Renowned women's rights advocate Charlotte Perkins Gilman challenged inhabitants of the region to shed the traditions that hindered progress in order to build a better future for their children. Unlike the fairs' tame stance on race relations, some speakers exposed the limitations of the New South for minorities. Former Register of the U.S. Treasury Judson W. Lyons, for instance, spoke out against the disenfranchisement of southern African Americans.

Other features provided more whimsical entertainment. The midway at the Appalachian Expositions hosted amusements ranging from Ferari's Snake Den to the "museum of freaks." Fireworks lit up the skies with futuristic or historic themes almost nightly. During the daytime, visitors viewed dirigible balloons and aeroplanes soaring high above.

Although most visitors appear to have been from Knoxville and nearby regions, newspapers all along the East Coast printed articles on the events. The fairs generated enthusiasm for the region's betterment and led to a National Conservation Exposition in Knoxville in 1913. But their success in facilitating the growth of a New South in Appalachia hardly matched the propaganda and enthusiasm projected by the fairs' displays, events, and speakers.

See also: APPALACHIAN EXPOSITIONS (VISUAL ARTS); KNOXVILLE, TENNESSEE (TOURISM); KNOXVILLE, TENNESSEE (URBAN APPALACHIAN EXPERIENCE).

—Robert D. Lukens, *West Chester, Pennsylvania*

Robert D. Lukens, "The New South on Display: The Appalachian Expositions of 1910 and 1911," *Journal of East Tennessee History* (1997); Michael J. McDonald and William Bruce Wheeler, *Knoxville, Tennessee: Continuity and Change in an Appalachian City* (1983).

Appalachian Heritage

With the aid of a grant from the National Endowment for Humanities, regional poet Albert Stewart began the journal *Appalachian Heritage* at Alice Lloyd College in 1973. Though no longer housed at the college, it continues to provide an important venue for creative and critical writing about Appalachia.

In the first issue, Stewart stated his intention to let "the people of Southern Appalachia" present an alternative vision of their home region. Stewart published a great many interviews, poems, and short stories that emphasized the strength of the traditional rural culture in Appalachia. Unfortunately, the journal could not defray its expenses, and in 1982 Alice Lloyd College ended its sponsorship. Stewart reached an agreement with Hindman Settlement School to continue publication in 1982; this arrangement lasted through 1984. In 1985 Berea College assumed responsibility for publication and Sidney Saylor Farr, also a regional writer, was named editor. Noting that a generation of homegrown scholars had emerged in the region, Farr invited George Brosi to start a section on Appalachian books in the fall of 1985, and that feature continues to the present day. As she anticipated, Farr was able to maintain a balance of fiction, poetry, and scholarship that emphasized contributions of new writers in the region. Failing health forced Farr to retire in 1999, and in 2002 James Gage, a professor of English at Berea College, filled the position. As of 2004, the journal was housed in the Appalachian Center at Berea College with Brosi as editor.

See also: APPALACHIAN CENTERS AND INSTITUTES (CULTURAL INSTITUTIONS); *APPALACHIAN JOURNAL;* WRITING WORKSHOPS, CONFERENCES, AND FESTIVALS (LITERATURE).

—Gordon B. McKinney, *Berea College*

Appalachian Journal

Appalachian Journal: A Regional Studies Review was first published as a biannual journal in the fall of 1972 through the auspices of Appalachian State University. Within a year, it had attracted more than three hundred subscribers and had been pronounced "THE voice of Appalachian Studies" by author and educator Jesse Stuart. Featuring cross-disciplinary, peer-reviewed scholarly articles, fiction, and poetry, the journal served to fill a void left by *Mountain Life and Work*'s conversion into an advocacy publication; it lacked *Mountain Life*'s missionary spirit but added the rigors of scholarly peer review. According to its original mission statement, *Appalachian Journal* is "dedicated to a broad spectrum approach to all of Appalachia (both past and present), from New York to Alabama," and features graphic art, poetry, short fiction, and photographic essays.

Founded at the instigation of Cratis Williams and in the wake of the Foxfire project's great market success, the journal was one of three Appalachian serials introduced in 1972–73. The others were Berea College's short-lived *Appalachian Notes* and Alice Lloyd College's folksy literary magazine *Appalachian Heritage*. Edited by J. W. Williamson, *Appalachian Journal* became the standard for the fledgling field of Appalachian studies, providing a chronicle of the field's growth and diversification. In July 2000, Sandra Ballard succeeded Williamson as editor.

Under Williamson, the journal's advisory board of Appalachian State University faculty and editorial board of regional scholars and writers expanded *Appalachian Journal* into a quarterly beginning in the autumn of 1974. The publication subsequently maintained a subscriber base of four to seven hundred and a rejection rate for unsolicited manuscripts of 75 to 90 percent into the twenty-first century. Less successful columns were dropped and new ones introduced, including the popular features "Signs of the Times," beginning in 1980 as a series of extracts from the popular media, and "The Chronicle," running since 1984 and composed of chronologically sequential news items. The publication also regularly includes reviews.

Appalachian Journal has published a number of scholarly bibliographies on diverse topics; roundtable discussions of new and controversial works and ideas; and interviews with Appalachian scholars, artists, literary figures, and personalities. Many of the latter were subsequently republished in *Interviewing Appalachia: The Appalachian Journal Interviews, 1978–1992* (1994). In 1975–76 the journal serialized an abridged version of Cratis Williams's monumental dissertation, "The Southern Mountaineer in Fact and Fiction."

Beginning in 1975 with "New Perspectives on the Cherokees," *Appalachian Journal* published a series of special issues. These include "A Guide to Appalachian Studies," which became the centerpiece for the first Appalachian Studies Conference at Berea in 1978; "Process, Policy, and Context: Contemporary Perspectives on Appalachian Culture"; "Assessing Appalachian Studies"; and "Essays in Political Economy." Index issues were published in 1980, 1991, 1996, and 2001.

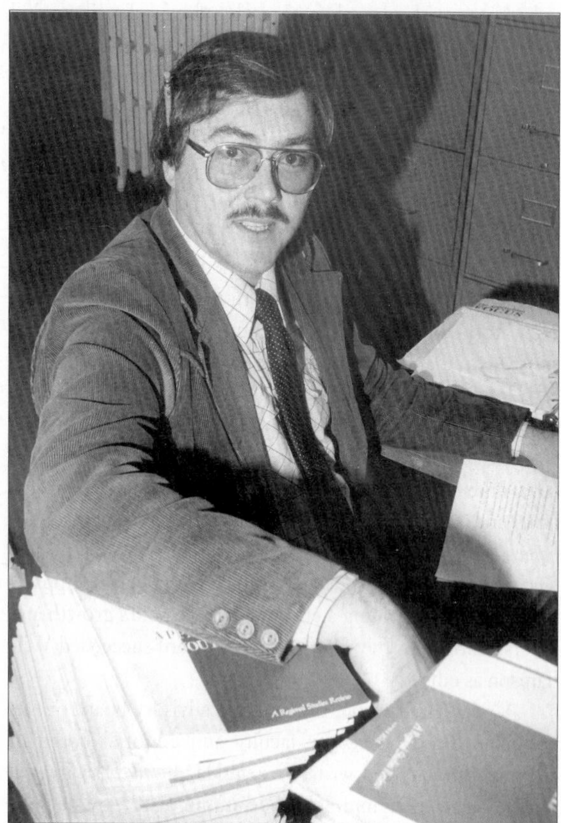

J. W. Williamson, founding editor of the *Appalachian Journal*, Boone, North Carolina, 1982. First published in 1972, the *Appalachian Journal* quickly gained recognition for its leadership in the newly developing field of Appalachian studies.

Folklorist Archie Green described *Appalachian Journal* as "America's best regional journal—the only one that makes sense of regional issues"; historian Richard B. Drake saw it as principally devoted to "the unfortunate deconstruction of writing on the region before 1965." These differing views reflect the journal's selection of materials that challenge both the boundaries and legitimacy of Appalachian studies.

See also: *APPALACHIAN HERITAGE; MOUNTAIN LIFE AND WORK;* WILLIAMS, CRATIS (LITERATURE).

—Fred J. Hay, *Appalachian State University*

Richard B. Drake, "Berea's Appalachian Commitment," *Appalachian Heritage* (Summer 1998).

Appalachian Reader

The *Appalachian Reader* is an independent not-for-profit newspaper that serves as a communication tool for organizations and individuals working for positive change and social justice. Founded in the spring of 1988 under the editorship of Kristin Layng Szakos, Jerry Hardt, and Denise Giardina, the *Reader* filled a void left by the demise of *Mountain Life and Work*, a publication with a similar vision and mission. The *Reader* provides in-depth analysis of issues related to citizens' organizations and profiles of groups and individuals working in the region. Excerpts from newsletters, Web sites, and other communication organs of individual organizations comprise the majority of articles.

In addition to news, the *Reader*'s quarterly issues include information about job openings, available resources, new publications, and activities of people in area groups. Topics cover a broad range of activist issues in the Appalachian region. Environmental concerns about mining, forestry, and pollution figure prominently, as do issues relating to labor, poverty, race, gender, sexual orientation, and politics. Activities of organizations such as Save Our Cumberland Mountains, Virginians for Justice, and the Community Farm Alliance are regularly reported. The publication's style is that of a news journal: clear, straightforward, even-handed, and nonacademic. While most pieces clearly advocate a political agenda, opinion articles are not the norm. By giving voice to issues and concerns of community organizers, combating the sense of isolation that activists often feel in rural areas, and helping grassroots organizations learn from each other's successes and failures, the *Appalachian Reader* has established itself as a valuable regional publication.

See also: GRASSROOTS ENVIRONMENTAL ACTION (ENVIRONMENT); *MOUNTAIN LIFE AND WORK;* NEWSPAPERS.

—Marie F. Jones, *East Tennessee State University*

Appalachia on Our Mind

Henry D. Shapiro's *Appalachia on Our Mind: The Southern Mountains and Mountaineers in the American Consciousness, 1870–1920* (University of North Carolina Press) was one of two books appearing in 1978 that established a new benchmark in Appalachian studies; the other is Helen Lewis's *Colonialism in Modern America: The Appalachian Case*. Shapiro's book challenges the concept of Appalachia as "a coherent region with a uniform culture and a homogeneous population" by tracing the history of this idea in American writing between 1870 and 1920 and by demonstrating that it was driven more by America's assumptions about itself than by the reality of life in the mountains. He shows how local color writers, followed by missionaries, philanthropists, and folklorists, first created the image of Appalachian "otherness" and then contrived explanations of that otherness without examining the presuppositions that underpin it.

The intellectual maneuvers Shapiro documents occasionally seem to go on in a political and economic vacuum; for example, the industrial takeover of the region during this very period is nearly invisible in his account. Moreover, Shapiro constantly implies that Appalachia's socially constructed reality contrasts poorly with some supposed actuality, which he never specifies. In spite of this, *Appalachia on Our Mind* remains an important book. When it appeared, it initiated early analytical thought related to the region that would eventually invigorate the field known as Appalachian studies. Besides its historical interest, the book's rich documentation and full references make it permanently useful.

See also: SECTION OVERVIEW (IMAGES AND ICONS); SECTION OVERVIEW (RACE, ETHNICITY, AND IDENTITY).

—Rodger Cunningham, *Alice Lloyd College*

Appalshop

Founded in fall 1969, Appalshop, a nonprofit media arts center in Whitesburg, Kentucky, produces documentary films, plays, radio programming, and educational projects aimed at preserving Appalachian culture and documenting issues affecting communities in the region. In the last three decades of the twentieth century, Appalshop produced more than one hundred films, created an internationally recognized theater company, and trained hundreds of workers in film, video, and radio production. Its several divisions include Appalshop Films, Headwaters Television, Roadside Theater, WMMT Radio, June Appal Recordings, the American Festival Project, and the Appalachian Media Institute.

Originally created as the Community Film Workshop of Appalachia, the organization was one of five film entities funded by the federal Office of Economic Opportunity. The workshop attracted local high school students, who made films about people and issues in Whitesburg and surrounding counties. When funding ran out in 1971, the filmmakers continued working, incorporating as the Appalachian Film Workshop and successfully securing grants from the Episcopal Church's youth program and the National Endowment for the Humanities. Between 1973 and 1976, the organization attracted other artists and activists, resulting in the creation of Roadside Theater, June Appal Recordings, and the now defunct *Mountain Review* magazine. Due to growth and financial pressures, the group made changes in the mid-1970s that included adopting a new name, acquiring federal tax-exempt status, and creating the nonhierarchical organizational structure that continues to guide Appalshop.

In 1982 the organization moved its operations to a renovated warehouse in Whitesburg that still serves as the Appalshop Center. With increased stability and a renewed commitment to community, Appalshop steadily grew throughout the 1980s, garnering regional, national, and international attention for its work. New filmmakers and increased interaction with Appalachian scholars broadened Appalshop's range of film topics, moving the emphasis from traditional crafts and coal mining to documentaries on West Virginia's chemical industry, mountain women working in fast-food restaurants, and problems faced by rural people living with AIDS. Appalshop's Headwaters Television division brought films to public television audiences across the country. WMMT and the Appalachian Media Institute strengthened the organization's ties within Whitesburg by providing controlled communications and media training for resident teenagers and local volunteers at the radio station. In addition, Roadside Theater went outside the region to create partnerships with community theater groups in New York City, New Orleans, and New Mexico. These partnerships form the core of Appalshop's American Festival Project, which focuses on overcoming divisions between people and cultures.

Through the years, Appalshop's presence and work have generated controversy as well as accolades. Within Whitesburg, the organization's early films on strip mining and the perception of Appalshop employees as countercultural resulted in local alienation during the 1970s. The group also drew criticism from some who felt their work perpetuated a stereotypical image of Appalachia. Although a few projects, such as the film *Strangers and Kin*, appeared to advance a single definition of the region, the organization as a whole offered diverse perspectives and promoted creative freedom within the organization.

Appalshop's presence in Appalachia represents an unusual resource in rural America—a fully staffed, equipped, and funded media arts center firmly grounded within a community and its surrounding region.

See also: DOCUMENTARY FILMS; *STRANGERS AND KIN*; *STRANGER WITH A CAMERA*.

—Stephen P. Hanna, *University of Mary Washington*

Jane Gaines, "Inventing and Preserving Appalachia: Appalshop Documentaries," *Jump Cut* (March 1989); Stephen P. Hanna, "Three Decades of Appalshop Films: Representations, Strategies, and Regional Politics," *Appalachian Journal* (Summer 1998).

Ball, Lucille

See Ball, Lucille (Humor)

Beverly Hillbillies, The

A fish-out-of-water situation comedy, *The Beverly Hillbillies* was a popular CBS television program that aired from 1962 to 1971 and long remained a mainstay of syndicated programming on cable television. The series revolves around a poor mountain widower persuaded to move to Los Angeles to provide better opportunities for his daughter after discovering oil on his property and becoming fabulously wealthy. The traditional Clampett household's reaction to their new lives among the rich, powerful, and famous provides the basis for the show's comedy. Jed Clampett (played by Buddy Ebsen), the family patriarch, retains strength, integrity, and a respect for the traditions of "back home," yet he also considers new ideas and methods without dismissing them out of hand. His daughter, Elly May (Donna Douglas), finds almost all modern social niceties restrictive and feels much more comfortable with her "critters" than with people. Jed's mother-in-law, Daisy Moses, or "Granny" (Irene Ryan), refuses to compromise traditional folkways and consistently criticizes the newfangled ways of city slickers. In sharp contrast, Jed's nephew, Jethro Bodine (Max Baer Jr.), foolishly assumes that city ways are always best, and he denigrates his traditional social heritage at every opportunity.

While the producers of *The Beverly Hillbillies* placed the original Clampett homestead in the Ozarks to allow for overlaps with the subsequent CBS rural-based series *Petticoat Junction* (1963–70) and *Green Acres* (1965–71), they tended to avoid drawing any real distinctions between the southern hill folk of the Ozarks and the Appalachians; in fact, Granny refers to folk back home in Tennessee, and the Clampetts visit old neighbors in Silver Dollar City, Missouri. This blurring of their roots perhaps expanded the program's appeal among rural audiences, but it also reflects popular media's tendency to homogenize southerners within restrictive stereotypes.

At the heart of the show's appeal is the contradictory presentation of hill people and their culture. On the one hand, audiences can laugh at the Clampetts' traditional folkways and literal interpretations of the world. Granny's reliance on folk medicine leads to trouble in a number of episodes, the Clampetts' humble food preferences (possum and greens is a favorite) sicken city people, and Granny rationalizes her love of her homemade moonshine by describing it as "rheumatis' medicine." Likewise, the Clampetts' tendency to misunderstand convoluted language and modern colloquialisms frequently makes them look ignorant. For example, when Elly May becomes engaged to a U.S. Navy frogman, Granny fears he is actually part amphibian. From the romantic entanglements Jed mistakes for genuine (if unreciprocated) love to Elly May's steadfast refusal to become a "real lady" to Jethro's boyish embrace of every new trend of the day, the Clampetts never fit into Beverly Hills society.

Yet the Clampetts' simple honesty and way of life also serve to emphasize the hollow materialism around them by satirizing the changing social mores of the 1960s. While the Clampetts may mistake a billiard table for a fancy dining table and flamingoes for weird chickens, the family has substance and a sense of identity, making them sympathetic in comparison to the parade of phonies, shysters, sycophants, trend seekers, and scoundrels who attempt to exploit them. The Clampetts are good people at heart; the few substantive people they encounter in the city admire them, and those who deride them are presented as superficial people with skewed priorities.

The Beverly Hillbillies enjoyed a great deal of popularity in heartland America; ironically, this appeal led to its cancellation as the network sought more urban-oriented young viewers for its advertisers.

See also: DEPRESSION AND THE NEW DEAL; HENNING, PAUL; TELEVISION DEPICTIONS OF THE REGION.

—Thomas Alan Holmes, *East Tennessee State University*

Boyd, Daniel

(1956–) Professor and independent filmmaker.

A professor of communications at West Virginia State University, Daniel Boyd has earned critical acclaim for his low-budget movies featuring regional settings and themes and often employing local acting talent from Boyd's own filmmaking classes.

Born in 1956 in the eastern panhandle of West Virginia in Martinsburg, Boyd earned degrees in communications from West Virginia University (1978) and in filmmaking from the University of Arkansas (1981). Starting his filmmaking career making documentaries, Boyd saw several of his short narrative films aired on regional and national television. In 1985 he joined the faculty of West Virginia State College (now University).

Boyd's first feature film, *Chillers* (1988), was a horror/fantasy anthology of five stories tied together by a bus station and stranded travelers and was cast largely with students from his filmmaking class at West Virginia State. It won the Silver Scroll Award from the Academy of Science Fiction, Fantasy and Horror Films.

In 1991 Boyd first gained the attention of a mass audience with the broadcast of his second feature film, *Strangest Dreams: Invasion of the Space Preachers*, on USA Network's *Up All Night* show with Gilbert Gottfried. *Strangest Dreams* was written and directed by Boyd as a comical spoof of some of the dominant imagery of Appalachia and was shot entirely on location in West Virginia with a local cast and crew.

After the success of his second film, Boyd wrote and directed *Paradise Park* (1992), later renamed *Heroes of the Heart* (1996), with a cast of such notables as wrestler Dusty Rhodes, silent film actress Lina Basquette, and country music stars Porter Wagoner and Johnny Paycheck, among others. The movie addresses the subject of federal poverty aid in Appalachia while retaining Boyd's signature sense of comedy. *Paradise Park* won the Gold Award at the Houston International Film Festival and the Gold Plaque Award at the Chicago International Film Festival.

In 1994 Boyd established the Paradise Film Institute at West Virginia State. The institute attempts to generate support for independent filmmaking in West Virginia by tapping various funding resources. It maintains active exchange partnerships with film schools in Russia, the Czech Republic, Venezuela, and Belize.

Recipient of a 2002 Fulbright Alumni Award, Boyd partnered with the University of Dar es Salaam in Tanzania on the pilot program Teledrum to teach filmmaking to American and African students while producing films for international aid organizations, a collaboration which resulted in the award-winning films *Duara* and *Sound the Drum*.

See also: FEATURE FILMS.

—Daniel Wayne Hampton, *Appalachian State University*

Broadcast Journalism

The first professional radio broadcast in the United States occurred in Appalachia on November 2, 1920, when KDKA in Pittsburgh aired election returns for the Cox-Harding presidential election. One year later, KDKA aired the first daily farm market reports and in 1923 hired the first full-time farm director. KDKA also was the first station to broadcast comments from a political candidate.

Radio was vital to rural America in the 1930s and 1940s, especially in small communities without a local daily newspaper. At first, listeners heard news broadcasts from larger cities in the region or from powerful stations in cities on the fringe of Appalachia such as Louisville, Cincinnati, Charlotte, and Nashville.

Few radio stations existed in small Appalachian towns until the 1940s. A typical newscast might include local crime reports, government news, farm market information, and obituaries—a necessity in towns with only a weekly newspaper. Some stations in Appalachia distinguished themselves for local broadcast journalism beginning in the 1940s, and three won the prestigious Peabody Award: WCHS in Charleston, West Virginia; WWVA in Wheeling, West Virginia; and WHLN in Harlan, Kentucky.

Originally, the Federal Communications Commission (FCC) required radio stations to ascertain the needs and interests of their communities and show how the station's programming met those needs. AM stations had to devote 8 percent of their airtime to news and public affairs programming and FM stations 6 percent. But in 1981 the FCC replaced its news and public affairs requirement with a "market-place philosophy" and radio stations were no longer mandated to air local news reports to keep their licenses.

Because producing local news is expensive and labor-intensive, many radio stations in Appalachia, especially those in small towns, eliminated much or all of their news programming. In small communities, station owners also faced financial pressures because of the loss of jobs in traditional Appalachian industries such as manufacturing, mining, steel, tobacco, and apparel and the consequent decline in advertising revenue. Technology also changed the way stations received programming. Instead of producing programming locally, many stations purchased round-the-clock, satellite-delivered, syndicated programming at little cost.

By the 1990s, the news/talk format became the fastest-growing radio format in Appalachia. Talk shows hosted by opinionated commentators such as Rush Limbaugh and Laura Schlessinger were fed to stations by satellite. The topics debated on stations throughout much of the region dealt with national rather than local issues. Public officials, civic leaders, and others have lamented the decline in local radio news, particularly in places such as eastern Kentucky, where only four daily newspapers serve fifty-one counties.

West Virginia, the only state entirely in Appalachia, provides a snapshot of broadcast journalism in the region at the beginning of the twenty-first century. West Virginia has twenty-two daily and fifty-eight weekly or semiweekly newspapers to serve more than two hundred cities and towns. Approximately 110 commercial radio stations operate in the state, but only about three dozen provide local news. Nonprofit FM stations broadcast local news in portions of the state.

Consolidation of news operations at radio and television stations owned by the same national chain has occurred in larger markets in Appalachia, but national chain ownership has not affected radio news coverage in West Virginia. Local owners or regional chains operate most of the state's radio stations. West Virginia's first television station, WSAZ-TV in Huntington, went on the air in 1949 and quickly developed a reputation for local news coverage that continues today. The state has eleven commercial television stations.

Three television stations in Appalachia have won Peabody Awards for news coverage. They are WQED-TV, a public station in Pittsburgh; KDKA-TV in Pittsburgh, the first television station in Appalachia; and WVMT-TV in Birmingham, Alabama, Appalachia's second-oldest station.

See also: RADIO BROADCASTING; TELEVISION BROADCASTING; WWVA.

—Ferrell Wellman and Elizabeth K. Hansen, *Eastern Kentucky University*

William David Sloan, James G. Stovall, and James D. Startt, *The Media in America: A History* (1989); Richard Campbell, Christopher R. Martin, and Bettina Fabos, *Media and Culture: An Introduction to Mass Communication* (2002); Alan Hedblad, ed., *Gale Directory of Publications and Broadcast Media* (137th edition, 2003); F. Leslie Smith, Milan Meeske, and John W. Wright II, *Electronic Media and Government: The Regulation of Wireless and Wired Communication in the United States* (1995).

Broadside Television

Supported by a two-year grant from the Appalachian Regional Commission, Broadside Television was founded by Ted Carpenter, a New England–educated Canadian who arrived in east Tennessee as a VISTA (Volunteers in Service to America) worker. Operations began in Johnson City, Tennessee, in November 1972. Carpenter studied mountain culture in Tennessee at Highlander Research and Education Center in New Market and small-format video at Tennessee Technological University in Cookeville. After further study in video production at New York University, he returned to Appalachia in 1971 as the coordinator of a community program in Monterey, Tennessee. There he began doing freelance video documentaries on life in east Tennessee. With his Appalachian Regional Commission grant, administered through the First Tennessee-Virginia Development District, he founded Broadside.

Because television reception was generally poor in east Tennessee, cable service was well established. Cable operators were mandated by the Federal Communication Commission to produce a certain number of hours of locally originated programming. Additional grants from the National Endowment for the Arts, the National Endowment for the Humanities, the Tennessee Arts Commission, and private sources made it possible for Carpenter and Broadside to produce programs on life in central Appalachia to fulfill this local programming requirement. Topics included coal mining, energy and environmental needs and problems, land use, traditional arts, handicrafts, music, education, storytelling, senior citizens' issues, and regional history. Carpenter's work provided opportunities for his subjects to learn about their own culture. To him, the process of interviewing the community's shopkeepers, farmers, miners, and individuals was as important as the finished documentary. Tapes were made available to schools and community groups.

In 1974 the Federal Communications Commission removed the requirement that cable owners had to provide locally originated programming, and Broadside lost a major portion of its funding. Carpenter left in 1975, and in 1978 his successors made an unsuccessful effort to operate Channel 41 as a public cable television station. Broadside was forced to file for bankruptcy in 1978. The Broadside Television tapings are now housed in the Archives of Appalachia at East Tennessee State University in Johnson City.

See also: TELEVISION BROADCASTING.

—Clara Hasbrouck, *East Tennessee State University*

Brother's Keeper

The critically acclaimed winner of five major awards, including the New York Film Critics Award and the Sundance Film Festival's Audience Award for nonfiction, *Brother's Keeper* (1992), directed by Joe Berlinger and Bruce Sinofsky, is a documentary filmed in the rural Appalachian area of western New York. Traditional Appalachian themes emerge in the story of a farming community's response when a local dairy farmer, Delbert Ward, is charged with the murder of his brother William.

Delbert and his surviving brothers are portrayed as impoverished, illiterate, isolated from contemporary society, and incompetent at negotiating the legal system. The investigation raises the specter of sexual deviance and "romance gone bad" with suggestions that William's murder may have been the result of an incestuous homosexual relationship between the brothers. The filmmakers, however, suggest that Delbert may have unwittingly waived his rights and confessed to a crime by signing papers he could not read and that the idea of deviance grew out of public misperceptions of the brothers' rural poverty.

The film's dominant theme is one of mountain people sticking together against exploitation by powerful urban interests. The local farming community perceives the case as "big city" versus "country folk." Despite their long-standing treatment of the Wards as outsiders, members of the community rise to their defense, challenging the investigators' assumption that they are ignorant and disposable people. The government investigators are depicted as out of touch with the humanity of the Wards and oblivious to the capability of the community where they live. Real estate interests and an election for the office of district attorney are implied as underlying the state's pursuit of Delbert.

See also: DOCUMENTARY FILMS.

—Tessa Kleeman, *Brooklyn, New York*

Cartoons

The genre of panel cartoons of hillbilly characters is rooted in Jacksonian-era illustrations of wild and cagey frontiersmen, from the "half-alligator, half-bear" Davy Crockett to literary characters such as Simon Suggs and Sut Lovingood. Building from this base, turn-of-the-century magazine illustrators, most notably E. W. Kemble in his depictions of John Fox Jr. moonshiners, helped establish the rifled, barefoot, and bearded hillbilly persona.

Beginning in 1934, Paul Webb's *The Mountain Boys* crystallized the iconic hillbilly. The same year Al Capp and Billy DeBeck introduced *Li'l Abner* and Snuffy Smith (in the *Barney Google* comic strip), respectively. Webb's work, which ran in *Esquire* magazine until 1954, reflected both depression-era public fears of economic collapse and social disintegration and a national fascination with rural folk in general and mountaineers in particular. As in the past, this focus on mountain people combined conceptions of the folk as impoverished, debased, and squalid with a regionalist view of them as exemplars of America's heroic past. Though they were not explicitly defined as Appalachian, many readers nonetheless associated Webb's characters with the southeastern mountains, particularly because the cartoons often appeared in *Esquire* across from articles and poems by Kentuckian James Still.

Through the words and actions of three nearly identical brothers (Luke, Willy, and Jake) and their family and neighbors, Webb presented endless variations on the standard tropes that came to define hillbillies throughout popular culture: social isolation, physical torpor and laziness, unrefined sexuality, filth and animality, comical violence, and utter ignorance of modernity. Most of Webb's gags revolve around the partially naked body and bodily functions. Dozens of the cartoons feature jokes about "Gran'pappy" in the outhouse, and male characters invariably go barefoot and laze about in long underwear. In contrast, Webb presented the women characters' lives as sheer drudgery, their nearly perpetual state of pregnancy solely another onerous chore. Despite economic deprivation and an endless series of floods, windstorms, and man-made disasters, however, Luke and his kin calmly endure all the crises they face. Contemporary audiences could thus see them as models of human endurance and a heartening symbol that the nation too could survive the current economic and social upheaval.

Webb's cartoon creations were amazingly influential, particularly in Hollywood. He so transformed and iconicized the image of the hillbilly, previously an uncertain blend of lumberjack, sharecropper, and yeoman farmer, that the terms *Esquire-style* and *Webb-like* came to evoke an instantly recognizable image of the long-bearded, gun-toting hillbilly on film and throughout popular culture.

Although no other panel cartoonist achieved the same level of influence or longevity as Webb, the hillbilly cartoon lived on after World War II in various guises, from the gentler and desexualized *Kennesaw* cartoons of Reamer Keller in *Reader's Digest* to Frank Thorne's sexually explicit *Moonshine McJuggs* (a takeoff on Capp's Daisy Mae), which appeared in *Playboy* in the 1970s and 1980s. Political cartoonists such as the *Washington Post*'s Herbert Block ("Herblock") also used hillbilly iconography in their portrayals of intransigently conservative southern members of Congress and Presidents Jimmy Carter and Bill Clinton. Although at the end of the twentieth century the image faded in light of criticism from a newly politicized cadre of activists in the southern mountains and midwestern cities, the impact of these images lived on, ready to be called upon nearly effortlessly by filmmakers, stand-up comedians, and advertisers.

See also: ANIMATED CARTOONS; COMIC STRIPS; *LI'L ABNER;* SNUFFY SMITH.

—Anthony Harkins, *Western Kentucky University*

Allen W. Batteau, *The Invention of Appalachia* (1990); Anthony A. Harkins, *Hillbilly: A Cultural History of an American Icon* (2004); J. W. Williamson, *Hillbillyland: What the Movies Did to the Mountains and What the Mountains Did to the Movies* (1995).

Charleston Gazette

West Virginia's largest and most influential newspaper, the *Charleston Gazette* established a growing reputation as a crusading publication after World War II and over the succeeding decades has won dozens of awards for investigative reporting and courageous editorials. Its probing news coverage and editorials have regularly focused attention upon central Appalachia's most pressing social and economic issues—health, education, coal-mining and trucking safety, and the environmental impacts of surface mining. For years, it was purported to be the only news organization in West Virginia employing a full-time investigative reporter.

During the late 1990s, the *Gazette* helped to make mountaintop removal an environmental issue of national as well as regional importance. For his coverage of the subject, Ken Ward, the newspaper's environmental reporter, received the ten-thousand-dollar Livingston Award for Young Journalists, made annually to journalists younger than thirty-five years of age, the Scripps Howard Public Service Award, the Thomas L. Stokes Award, the Southern Journalism Award, and other honors. Beginning in the 1980s, Paul J. Nyden, who earned a doctorate from Columbia University, won numerous national awards for his investigative reporting on subjects ranging from medical malpractice and abuses in the West Virginia workers' compensation insurance program to the environmental impacts of coal mining. Among them were the Investigative Reporters and Editors Award, the Thomas L. Stokes Award, the George Polk Award, and the Sigma Delta Chi Award. Nyden became the only reporter to twice win the Stokes Award, given by the Washington Journalism Center. James A. Haught, who also won more than a dozen news-writing awards and rose to become the *Gazette*'s editor in 1993, won the prestigious National Headliner Award and many other honors for his columns and editorials, which often dealt with the separation of church and state.

The *Gazette* traces its roots to the weekly *Kanawha Chronicle*, founded by Charles Webb in April 1873. In a column published in 1875, Webb set out his paper's central purpose, writing that it would be "devoted to news, politics and diffusions of general intelligence" and present a "liberal and progressive" political perspective. In 1877 the paper was sold to James Pemberton, later mayor of Charleston, and printer John Jarrett. By the late 1890s, it had become a fixture in a city where several papers had already come and gone. In 1907 the name was changed to the *Charleston Gazette*. Five years later, it was acquired by the family of U.S. Senator W. E. Chilton. Members of the Chilton family continued in the paper's leadership into the twenty-first century, remaining generally faithful to the purposes set forth by Webb in 1875. In 1922 W. E. Chilton Jr. became president of the newspaper's publishing organization, the Daily Gazette Company. His son, W. E. "Ned" Chilton III, who had served in various editorial and management positions, became publisher in 1961 and headed the paper until his death in 1987. During his leadership of the *Gazette*, Chilton received the Elijah Parish Lovejoy Award from Colby College, which cited him for making the paper "an indomitable instrument for truth." Chilton's widow, Elizabeth, became president of the *Gazette* in 1992 and continued to lead it more than eighty years after it was acquired by the Chilton family.

The *Gazette*'s reputation as a crusading newspaper was solidified soon after World War II with editorials sharply criticizing state government and news columns instrumental in bringing about reforms such as abolition of the sheriff's fee system and establishment of a tax on soft drinks to finance the West Virginia Medical School. Its revelations about the administration of Governor Arch Moore contributed to his conviction on corruption charges in 1990.

Adopting an economizing strategy that had become popular throughout the newspaper industry in the mid-twentieth century, the *Gazette* entered a joint operating arrangement with its competitor, the *Charleston Daily Mail*, in 1958. By sharing presses, delivery trucks, and advertising sales staffs, the two papers effected major savings while maintaining their editorial independence. On Sunday, their operating subsidiary publishes a joint edition with the work of the editorial staffs of both papers.

As the population of West Virginia and the Charleston area shrank in the 1990s, the *Gazette*'s circulation declined to about fifty thousand, but it remained the state's largest paper. The *Gazette* became accessible on the Internet in 1996, drawing as many as twenty thousand visits daily.

See also: HAUGHT, JAMES A.; NATIONAL NEWSPAPER COVERAGE; NEWSPAPERS.

—Kathleen Collins, *New York City, New York*

Stan Cohen, with Richard Andre, *Kanawha County Images: A Bicentennial History, 1788–1988* (1987).

Cherokee Phoenix

With an eighty-five-character alphabet developed by Sequoyah and adopted in 1821, the Cherokee Nation was able to create the *Cherokee Phoenix*, the first Native American newspaper. In 1826 the Cherokee Council approved the construction of a printing office in the Cherokee capital of New Echota, Georgia, and authorized the purchase of a printing press in 1827. The American Board of Commissioners for Foreign Missions, through missionary Samuel Worcester, arranged for the printing office to be built. Elias Boudinot, also known as Buck Watie, became the first editor of the *Cherokee Phoenix*, and the first issue circulated internationally on February 28, 1828. Boudinot changed the newspaper's name to the *Cherokee Phoenix and Indian Advocate* in 1829 to expand its focus to include other indigenous groups with similar interests.

Chief John Ross used the paper to inform readers of new laws and meetings and to unite the Cherokee, who were spread across many southern states. Boudinot, initially a strong supporter of Ross's nationalist movement, wrote editorials endorsing Cherokee sovereignty and opposing policies such as the Indian Removal Act of 1830, the encroachment of white settlers, and the unwillingness of courts to accept sworn testimony of Cherokee witnesses. Boudinot also supported the law that made it a crime punishable by death to give up land without the approval of the Cherokee Council.

Influenced by his uncle, Major Ridge, and cousin John Ridge, Boudinot conceded that Cherokee removal appeared inevitable and helped to create the Treaty Party in support of his newfound political beliefs. Using the *Cherokee Phoenix* as his voice, he promoted the Treaty Party's agenda in his editorials in direct opposition to Ross's policies. Ross asked him to restrict his opinions to the editorial page and finally demanded that Boudinot cease printing anything about removal. In 1832 Ross pressured Boudinot to resign from the paper and appointed his brother-in-law, Elijah Hicks, the new editor. The paper continued printing letters from Boudinot, however, until it ceased publication on May 31, 1834, when the Cherokee Nation ran out of money.

Later that year, the Georgia Guard received word that Ross intended to move the press to the old council grounds in Red Clay, Tennessee. Boudinot's brother Stand Watie joined in the raid on the newspaper that destroyed much of the soft lead type, removed the press, and set fire to the building. Boudinot became one of the signers of the 1835 Treaty of New Echota, authorizing permanent Cherokee removal. The Cherokee Constitution allowed for Boudinot's action to be considered treason, a capital offense. In 1839 Cherokee opponents took his life, as well as that of the Ridges. In 1954 Lewis Larsen, an archeologist with the Georgia Historical Commission, and Joe Caldwell, a National Park Service archeologist, excavated the original *Cherokee Phoenix* property. The men discovered seventeen hundred pieces of printing type, including six hundred Cherokee characters that are now on display in museums.

See also: NATIVE AMERICANS (RACE, ETHNICITY, AND IDENTITY); NEWSPAPERS; SEQUOYAH (RACE, ETHNICITY, AND IDENTITY).

—Ima J. Stephens, *Auburn University*

Cullen Joe Holland, *The Cherokee Indian Newspapers, 1828–1906: The Tribal Voice of a People in Transition* (1956); James Emmett Murphy and Sharon Murphy, *Let My People Know* (1981); Theda Perdue, ed., *Cherokee Editor: The Writings of Elias Boudinot* (1996).

"Christmas in Appalachia"

Aired by the CBS network on December 22, 1964, "Christmas in Appalachia" was a televised documentary that showed the bleak poverty endured at that time by many Appalachian families, contrasting it against the promise of Christmas abundance. The broadcast, with its stark black-and-white images of hungry children and their impoverished coal-miner families at Christmastime, was widely viewed and is credited by some as helping to launch the U.S. government's War on Poverty in the 1960s.

By juxtaposing religious and national symbols, the documentary's producers attempted to create a sense of moral obligation toward the people of the region. The program's narrator, correspondent Charles Kuralt, described the road that led to Pert Creek School in Letcher County, Kentucky, as typical of tens of thousands of roads winding along the creeks and hollows of Appalachia. Along these roads, he explained, were arranged the shacks of tarpaper and pine of the "permanently poor," and the broadcast ended with Kuralt making the point that "coal cars roll on through Christmas week, carrying the wealth of Appalachia away."

Following the broadcast, CBS received an immediate and large response from persons wishing to contribute food, clothing, and toys. Seventy thousand dollars of unsolicited money poured into the CBS offices, which was turned over to the American Red Cross. One viewer chartered a plane to carry food and Christmas presents to Letcher County. Public sympathies aroused by "Christmas in Appalachia" demonstrated that the region had found a place in America's moral consciousness.

The documentary, along with numerous television programs and publications such as Harry Caudill's book *Night Comes to the Cumberlands* (1963), brought attention to the region's poverty, and Presidents John F. Kennedy and Lyndon Johnson both used identification with Appalachia to great political advantage. Johnson announced the War on Poverty in his 1964 State of the Union address, and his administration established the Office of Economic Opportunity, the agency responsible for nearly all of the War on Poverty's best-known and most controversial programs. These included Head Start, Job Corps, Legal Services, and the Community Action Program, all of which benefited the Appalachian region.

See also: DEPRESSION AND THE NEW DEAL; TELEVISION DEPICTIONS OF THE REGION; WAR ON POVERTY (GOVERNMENT).

—Allen W. Batteau, *Wayne State University*

Christy

Published in 1967, Catherine Marshall's best-selling novel *Christy* tells the story of a nineteen-year-old girl from Asheville, North Carolina, who leaves a life of luxury to teach at a remote mission school in the Great Smoky Mountains. It is based on the experiences of Catherine Marshall's mother, Leonora Wood, who was a teacher in Cutter Gap, Tennessee. Noted for its vivid portrayal of mountain people in the early twentieth century, the novel explores the ways the main character, Christy Huddleston, endears herself to a mountain community that for generations trusted no one from outside the cove. The story captured the public's imagination with its initial appearance in the late 1960s and continued to do so throughout the next several decades, reappearing as a musical, a television series, and a series of three television movies.

Christy, the Musical ran for three weeks in 1992 at the Lancaster Mennonite Fine Arts Center in Lancaster, Pennsylvania. In 1993 it was performed forty-two times at the Cumberland County Playhouse in Crossville, Tennessee. With the Great Smoky Mountains National Park as a backdrop, it was performed in the summers and early falls of 1994, 1995, and 1996 at the Smoky Mountain Outdoor Amphitheater in Townsend, Tennessee. It was also produced at the Roy Acuff Theater in Nashville in the spring of 1996. The musical follows the plot of the novel closely and includes all of the principal characters. Some of the lyrics and parts of the script are derived from the novel.

The pilot for *Christy*, the CBS television series, was first broadcast on April 3, 1994, starring Kellie Martin in the title role. Filmed in Tennessee, it ran for twenty-one episodes before ending abruptly in 1995 and continuing in reruns. The television series follows the novel only generally, developing additional story lines based on its characters. During its short run, the program received awards from the Film Advisory Board, the Christian Television and Film Commission, and the Heartland Film Festival (all in 1994). The series also won the National Religious Broadcasters President's Award, the Angel Award for the best television drama series, and the Christopher Award (all in 1995). In 1996 Tyne Daly was awarded an Emmy for Outstanding Supporting Actress in a Drama Series for her role as Alice Henderson, the Quaker missionary in *Christy.*

Christy returned to television in November 2000 with the airing of *Return to Cutter Gap* (also known as *Christy: The Movie*) on the PAX television network as the pilot episode for a new series. This story opens with Christy as an elderly woman recounting to her daughter her early days in Cutter Gap. In May 2001, PAX aired a two-part miniseries titled *Christy: Choices of the Heart.* The first episode, "A Change of Seasons," takes place in 1913 as Cutter Gap is in the throes of a deadly typhoid epidemic. Christy's romantic choice between Neil MacNeill, the community's Scottish-born doctor, and the Reverend David Grantland is the focus of "A New Beginning," the second episode. The producers used Marshall's manuscript notes, which had been recently discovered, and worked closely with her heirs, so the script is faithful to the themes of the original novel. Lauren Lee Smith was cast as Christy for this series, which was filmed in British Columbia.

Marshall's work includes twenty books and countless articles drawn from personal experiences and family history. Her first two books were based on the life and ministry of her late husband, Peter Marshall, a Presbyterian minister and the chaplain of the United States Senate at the time of his death in 1949. As a young widow with a nine-year-old son, Marshall faced a bleak and uncertain future. She had kept a personal journal through the years with the hope of someday becoming a writer. She began by putting together a volume of Peter Marshall's sermons titled *Mister Jones, Meet the Master,* which became a best seller in 1949. Two years later, her book *A Man Called Peter* became a best-seller and a successful movie when produced by Twentieth Century Fox in 1955.

In 1959 Marshall married Leonard LeSourd, executive editor of *Guideposts* magazine, and continued to write for the next twenty-four years. Born in Johnson City, Tennessee, and reared in West Virginia, she won national acclaim for her work. She died in 1983 at age sixty-eight.

See also: TELEVISION DEPICTIONS OF THE REGION.

—Clara Hasbrouck, *East Tennessee State University*

Catherine Marshall, *Christy* (1967).

Coal Miner's Daughter

A movie adaptation of country singer Loretta Lynn's autobiography of the same name, *Coal Miner's Daughter* gives an insightful portrayal of not only Lynn but also the world of country music in the 1960s and 1970s. Directed by Michael Apted, it was released in 1980. The strong portrayal of an Appalachian woman as protagonist was significant in the representational history of the region in mainstream media. *Coal Miner's Daughter* was nominated for seven Academy Awards, including Best Picture and Best (Adapted) Screenplay. Sissy Spacek, who portrayed Lynn, received the Oscar for Best Actress.

The drama traces Lynn's life from her poor beginning in Butcher Hollow, Kentucky, to her rise into country music stardom. Along the way, she married, at age thirteen, Dolittle "Mooney" Lynn, portrayed by Tommy Lee Jones, and bore four children by the time she was eighteen. Lynn sang around the house until Mooney aided in her discovery by the record industry. Lynn's first single, "Honky Tonk Girl," was released in 1960 and instantly became a hit, earning her a spot on the *Grand Ole Opry.* Success brought both fame and a nervous breakdown to Lynn.

Instead of lip-synching the musical soundtrack, in the movie Spacek sings all of Lynn's songs herself. Beverly D'Angelo portrays Lynn's friend and fellow country music star Patsy Cline and does her own singing as well. Levon Helm, the former drummer for the 1960s rock group the Band, portrays Lynn's coal-miner father.

See also: ENTERTAINMENT ICONS (IMAGES AND ICONS); FEATURE FILMS; *GRAND OLE OPRY.*

—Stevan Jackson, *Radford University*

Cold Mountain

Directed by Anthony Minghella, the feature film *Cold Mountain* (2003) is an adaptation of Charles Frazier's best-selling 1997 novel of the same name. Preserving the novel's dual narrative structure, the film simultaneously recounts the journey of wounded Confederate veteran Inman (Jude Law) across the landscape of Civil War–era North Carolina to his home in the mountains and the transformation of Inman's erstwhile lover Ada (Nicole Kidman) from Charleston gentry to independent farmer after the death of her father under the tutelage of a hillbilly named Ruby (Renée Zellweger).

Inman pursues a deeply romanticized vision of his mountain home, embodied in his love for Ada, as a place that will heal both the physical and psychic wounds he carries with him from his experiences on the front lines of the Civil War. But he finds all the places on his journey to be troubling or conflicted, filled with decadence and murder and cut across by guerrilla warfare and Home Guard depreda-

First *Li'l Abner*® comic strip by Al Capp, 1934. Among the most popular cartoons ever created, *Li'l Abner* evolved into a powerful vehicle for social and political satire during its forty-plus years of publication, but it also solidified the image of the backward Appalachian hillbilly.

tions. Meanwhile, Ada and Ruby forge a complex working relationship with the mountain landscape, as Ada successfully masters the art of maintaining her family farm and discovers both personal independence and new forms of collaboration and friendship with Ruby. Inman's nostalgic view of his mountain home proves ultimately doomed, as he dies in a shootout with Confederate Home Guard troops on the verge of completing his epic journey. Ada's more grounded relationship with the land and her partnership with Ruby, we see in the film's brief epilogue, survive the tragedy and prosper, as her children and Ruby's children grow up together on the farm after the war's end.

The mountains of Romania stand in for western North Carolina in the film, which was shot on location in eastern Europe to reduce costs, despite vigorous lobbying by the North Carolina state government to bring the production to the Appalachians. Zellweger won an Academy Award for Best Supporting Actress for her performance as the earthy Ruby.

See also: FEATURE FILMS.

—Douglas Reichert Powell, *Columbia College Chicago*

Comic Strips

Throughout its hundred-year existence, the American comic strip has been largely an urban-oriented newspaper feature reflecting the values and concerns of urban and industrial society. A few comic artists, however, have been drawn to the southern Appalachian Mountains for characters and subject matter.

The first of these was Connecticut-born Al Capp, who began to draw *Li'l Abner* in 1934. Relying heavily on images of Kentucky and Ozark mountaineers in popular fiction, motion pictures, vaudeville acts, and country music, Capp (born Alfred Gerald Caplin) created a huge cast of characters led by Mammy and Pappy Yokum and their son, Li'l Abner. A handsome, muscular, honest, patriotic, and hopelessly naive young man, Abner's sole aims in life are avoiding work, fishing, and escaping the clutches of the voluptuous and persistent Daisy Mae Scragg. Although Capp initially emphasized quasi-authentic folk customs and regional characteristics based on depression-era popular fiction, the strip eventually became a vehicle for his biting social and political satire. One of the most popular of all comic strips, *Li'l Abner* developed a following of more than 60 million readers before it was retired in 1977.

The same year *Li'l Abner* began, Chicago cartoonist Billy DeBeck introduced a North Carolina mountaineer named Snuffy Smith into his already popular comic strip *Barney Google*, which had been running since 1919. DeBeck had traveled and sketched throughout the Virginia and Kentucky mountains and had read deeply in regional literature and folklore, including works by George Washington Harris, Mary Noailles Murfree, and Vance Randolph. When the squat and scruffy bootlegger Snuffy and his wife Loweezy quickly proved more popular than the titular hero, mountain lore and legendry dominated the strip until DeBeck's death in 1942. It was continued thereafter by his assistant, Fred Lasswell, until his death in 2001, when John Rose, Lasswell's assistant, took over.

Other features that have focused on Appalachian or mountain characters include Pennsylvanian Paul Webb's *The Mountain Boys* panel cartoons for *Esquire* magazine, which also began in 1934; Tennessean Ray Gotto's sports-based strips *Ozark Ike* (1945–58) and *Cotton Woods* (1955–58); and Capp's *Long Sam* (1954–62), basically a female version of *Li'l Abner*, which he produced with his brother Elliott Caplin and artist Bob Lubbers. Most comic strips based in the South, however, such as Walt Kelly's *Pogo*, Doug Marlette's *Kudzu*, and Jeff MacNelly's *Shoe*, have been set in swamps or flatland rather than in the mountains.

Some sociologists have criticized the way these artists have portrayed mountain people and have seen their work as a form of cultural imperialism meant to ridicule and demean a minority group. Others have argued that few readers in or outside Appalachia have ever taken the mountain characters in *Li'l Abner* or *Barney Google* to be anything other than fictional caricatures and that, like most satire, the humor in the strips is directed at human failure and stupidity rather than at regional characteristics. These works also belong to a rich stream of southern humor descending from William Byrd II and the early-nineteenth-century humorists of the Old Southwest down to Mark Twain, William Faulkner, William Price Fox, and Roy Blount Jr.

See also: ANIMATED CARTOONS; CARTOONS; *LI'L ABNER;* SNUFFY SMITH.

—M. Thomas Inge, *Randolph-Macon College*

Edwin T. Arnold, "Abner Unpinned," *Appalachian Journal* (Summer 1997) and "Al, Abner, and Appalachia," *Appalachian Journal* (Spring 1990); Anthony A. Harkins, *Hillbilly: A Cultural History of an American Icon* (2004); M. Thomas Inge, "Al Capp's South: Appalachian Humor in *Li'l Abner,*" *Studies in American Humor* (2001).

Crockett Almanacs

The Crockett Almanacs, published in the tradition of *Poor Richard's Almanac* and illustrated with woodcuts, contain tall tales, words of wisdom, jokes, and "receipts" (recipes) that feature Davy Crockett as the subject or author. First published for the year 1835 and continuing through 1856, the popular almanacs (which appeared under various titles) portray Crockett as a backwoods hero of mythic proportions and were a major element in creating and propagating the Crockett legend.

In agrarian nineteenth-century America, even the poorest households generally owned a Bible and an almanac. Almanacs, which provided information on sunrise, sunset, and phases of the moon and included weather predictions, were replaced each year, making them the most profitable book a printer could produce. Because the essential information provided was identical in every almanac, publishers sought ways to make their almanacs distinctive. The Crockett Almanacs are just one example of this commercial enterprise.

Although some of the Crockett Almanacs bear the notation that they are copyrighted by "Davy Crockett" and, after his 1836 death, his heirs, no evidence has surfaced to show that the real David Crockett had any connection with the almanacs. Further, the almanacs were almost certainly produced, not in Nashville as some title pages indicate, but in Boston, New York, or Philadelphia. Of the several publishers that issued Crockett Almanacs, Turner and Fisher of Boston reached the widest audience. Thus, the image of Crockett and the wilderness presented in the almanacs is one filtered through the imaginations, perceptions, and prejudices of writers and publishers in northeastern cities. The exaggerated backwoods dialect used in the tales reflects the attempts of northeastern writers to reproduce, or perhaps mock, Appalachian speech.

The Davy Crockett that emerges over two decades of almanacs is alternately heroic, coarse, funny, and boastful. In various tales, he is appointed by the president to wring the tail off a comet to save the nation from destruction, has a sexual adventure with another man's mistress, and is pursued by a bear and a wolf while swimming across the Mississippi River.

The earlier almanacs drew heavily upon two written sources: Matthew St. Clair Clarke's 1833 *Sketches and Eccentricities of Colonel David Crockett* and the 1834 *A Narrative of the Life of David Crockett of the State of Tennessee*, which Crockett wrote with Thomas Chilton. While *Narrative* can be presumed to be accurate, the Crockett of *Sketches* has more in common with the stage character Nimrod Wildfire from James Kirke Paulding's 1831 play *The Lion of the West* than with the real Crockett. Consequently, even the early Crockett Almanacs mix fable with fact, and the later ones veer more strongly away from truth into fantasy.

See also: CROCKETT, DAVID (HUMOR); CROCKETT, DAVID (SETTLEMENT AND MIGRATION); HISTORICAL HEROES (IMAGES AND ICONS).

—Claudia Milstead, *Missouri Valley College*

Michael A. Lofaro, *The Tall Tales of Davy Crockett: The Second Nashville Series of Crockett Almanacs, 1839–1841* (1987) and ed., *Davy Crockett: The Man, the Legend, the Legacy, 1786–1986* (1985); Michael A. Lofaro and Joe Cummings, eds., *Crockett at Two Hundred: New Perspectives on the Man and the Myth* (1989).

Dancing Outlaw

Dancing Outlaw is a 1991 documentary produced for the Public Broadcasting Service as part of the series *Different Drummer*. The half-hour video presents the story of Jesco White, a West Virginia resident aspiring to become a nationally known clogger. Director Jacob Young captures White clogging and interacting with his family in Boone County. The result has been labeled a "cult classic" by some and a prime example of perpetuating Appalachian stereotypes by others.

White proves himself an apt storyteller throughout, relaying his struggles with the law, his family, and substance abuse. The controlling frame of this story is White's dream to gain recognition for his clogging so that he can follow in the footsteps of his father, D. Ray White, a legendary Appalachian clogger. From the opening shots of yards filled with junked cars, rusting appliances, and dilapidated trailers to Jesco's violent threats against his wife and his extended family's rowdy mud-bog party, this documentary calls forth stereotypes of the drunken, violent hillbilly and of poor white trash. Yet Young, himself a West Virginia native, claims a fascination with backwoods Appalachian culture and believes he allows his subjects to present their own stories.

Representative of its popularity with audiences outside Appalachia, *Dancing Outlaw* gained the attention of *Roseanne* director Tom Arnold, who invited White to Hollywood for a guest appearance on the television series in 1994. Young produced a sequel documentary about that experience, *Dancing Outlaw II: Jesco Goes to Hollywood*, in 1999.

See also: DOCUMENTARY FILMS; TELEVISION DEPICTIONS OF THE REGION.

—Tina D. Parker, *Lexington, Kentucky*

Davenport, Tom

(1939–) Filmmaker.

Born in Washington, D.C., Tom Davenport settled in Delaplane, Virginia, where he makes films depicting traditional aspects of life in Appalachia. He received a bachelor of arts degree from Yale in 1961 and then studied and traveled in East Asia. Fascinated by film, Davenport went to work for the documentary team of Richard Leacock and Donn Allen Pennebaker in New York in 1967 and made his first film, *Tai Chi Ch'uan*, on a return trip to Taiwan. Afterwards, he returned to work the family farm in Appalachia and developed Davenport Films with his wife, Mimi.

Davenport's early films, *The Upperville Show, Thoughts on Fox Hunting*, and *It Ain't City Music*, were all shot close to his home in Virginia. Together with Daniel Patterson and the Curriculum in Folklore at the University of North Carolina, Davenport created the American Traditional Culture Series. These films document the lives of a medicine show performer in *Born for Hard Luck* (1976); an Appalachian storyteller in *Being a Joines* (1980); an African American gospel-singing family in *A Singing Stream* (1986); and a religious community in *The Shakers* (1970). *The Ballad of Frankie Silver* (1996) concerns the legend and mountain ballad about the first woman hanged for murder in North Carolina. The films have won numerous prizes for their filmic expertise and their accurate and captivating depictions of folk culture.

In his ongoing series *From the Brothers Grimm*, Davenport creates Appalachian versions of traditional folktales using local people as actors. Eleven films have thus far been made, including *Willa: An American Snow White*, which won the American Library Association's Carnegie Medal for Best Children's Video in 1998. Davenport's films are used in schools and libraries throughout the country.

See also: AGEE FILMS; DOCUMENTARY FILMS; SECTION OVERVIEW.

—Sharon R. Sherman, *University of Oregon*

Davy Crockett, Disney's Depiction of

The most persistent image of Davy Crockett in the public imagination is that of actor Fess Parker wearing a coonskin cap and carrying his long rifle, Old Betsy, with "Daveee, Davy Crockett, King of the Wild Frontier!" ringing in the background. This image is Walt Disney's creation, blending fact and fiction to produce a purely heroic American as an ideal role model for children. Fighting only when necessary, Davy stands up for the downtrodden, whether they are Native Americans being removed from their land or Texans fighting for their freedom. He is brave, intelligent, and kind, a common man with dignity. Davy's motto, *Be sure you're right, then go ahead*, reveals his strong sense of personal honor. Disney's Crockett is so idealized and compelling that many think of him as one of Disney's fictional characters.

The Disney version of Davy Crockett first appeared on *Disneyland*, a 1950s ABC series designed to promote Walt Disney's new amusement park in Anaheim, California. The theme of each week's show was linked to a section of the park, such as Fantasyland or Tomorrowland. Frontierland, which would feature stories about America's heroes, aired its first segment on December 15, 1954. "Davy Crockett, Indian Fighter" was an instant hit. It was followed by "Davy Crockett Goes to Congress" on January 26, 1955, and "Davy Crockett at the Alamo" on February 23, 1955. To capitalize on the success of the three episodes, Disney had them edited into a full-length movie, *Davy Crockett, King of the Wild Frontier*, released in June 1955. The movie made nearly $2.5 million, even though 90 million people had already seen the television series. Later that year, two more episodes were shown on *Disneyland:* "Davy Crockett's Keelboat Race" (November 16) and "Davy Crockett and the River Pirates" (December 14). They were edited into the movie *Davy Crockett and the River Pirates*, released in July 1956.

After the first three episodes, viewers clamored for icons of their new hero. Manufacturers responded by producing three thousand different items bearing the name or likeness of Davy Crockett, including wristwatches, lunch boxes, and children's clothing. All over America, preadolescent baby boomers were wearing coonskin caps, carrying plastic versions of Old Betsy, and singing "The Ballad of Davy Crockett." The seven-month craze (December 1954 to July 1955) brought in $300 million, and nearly ten million coonskin caps were sold.

During the 1988 television season, Disney tried to resurrect interest in Davy Crockett by presenting "Davy Crockett: Rainbow in the Thunder" and "Davy Crockett: Guardian Spirit," with Tim Dunigan in the title role, for NBC's *The Magical World of Disney*. Neither was successful, in spite of Johnny Cash's role in the first episode as an older, reminiscing Crockett. In contrast, all five of the Fess Parker episodes are frequently rerun on the Disney Channel, demonstrating the enduring appeal of the original Disney version of Davy Crockett.

See also: CROCKETT, DAVID (HUMOR); CROCKETT, DAVID (SETTLEMENT AND MIGRATION); HISTORICAL HEROES (IMAGES AND ICONS).

—Claudia Milstead, *Missouri Valley College*

Michael A. Lofaro, *Davy Crockett: The Man, the Legend, the Legacy, 1786–1986* (1985); J. G. O'Boyle, "Be Sure You're Right, Then Go Ahead," *Journal of Popular Film and Television* (Summer 1996).

Deer Hunter, The

The Deer Hunter (1978), directed by Michael Cimino, follows the lives of three men, Michael (Robert DeNiro), Steven (John Savage), and Nick (Christopher Walken), who leave their hometown of Clairton in the rural Appalachian region of Pennsylvania to fight in the Vietnam War. The film characterizes the region's people as having a strong sense of patriotism and family loyalty.

Michael, Steven, Nick, and their fellow townspeople are depicted as if belonging to one intertwined family. They work together in the town steel mill and spend their leisure time together in the Allegheny Mountains drinking beer and hunting deer. Because a wedding is a major town event attended by all residents, it also doubles in the film as a send-off for the enlisted men, illustrating the national pride and duty valued by the community.

In Vietnam, fraternal bonds between the main characters enable them to survive. In one scene, Michael lets go of a rescue helicopter, risking his own life in order to keep Steven, who has fallen off, alive. Although the men's lives are shattered by the trauma they endure, the townspeople and soldiers do not question the war. The final scene ironically depicts the enduring patriotism of the survivors, who toast their dead buddy, Nick, while tearfully singing "God Bless America." The depiction of patriotism is consistent with documentation showing that although a significant number of men who served in Vietnam came from working-class and poor backgrounds, neither they nor their families supported the antiwar movement.

The Deer Hunter was nominated for nine Academy Awards and won five, including Best Picture, Best Director, and Best Supporting Actor for both Walken and Meryl Streep (for her role as Linda).

See also: FEATURE FILMS.

—Tessa Kleeman, *Brooklyn, New York*

Deliverance

Director John Boorman's 1972 film adaptation of James Dickey's 1970 novel *Deliverance* represents a watershed event in the representation of Appalachians. Starring Ned Beatty, Burt Reynolds, Ronny Cox, and Jon Voight in what many film critics consider their definitive performances, this story of a weekend rafting trip gone hideously awry is filled with iconographic images of mountain life—the albino banjo player, demented hillbilly rapists, and a wild, menacing landscape. The film's images have profoundly influenced public perception of the Appalachian region—indeed, all exurban places—and have shaped in some way almost every Appalachian film to follow.

Ed (Voight), Lewis (Reynolds), Bobby (Beatty), and Drew (Cox) set out to test their manhood against the rapids of the Cahulawassee, a fictional north Georgia river set to become part of a hydroelectric project. All but Lewis are novice outdoorsmen, and the party encounters difficulty almost immediately, first in a strained encounter with local people at the dilapidated service station where they try to hire someone to take their truck further downriver, then when they become lost trying to find the river itself. The scene at the service station includes some of the film's most disturbing portrayals of mountain people, as it includes both the archetypal image of the albino banjo player and shots of a wizened grandmother holding a developmentally disabled child.

Once on the river, the four men initially enjoy camaraderie and natural beauty. The second day of their expedition turns nightmarish, however, as Bobby and Ed encounter two mountain men on the banks of the river who brutally rape Bobby in a scene almost unparalleled in popular film for its graphic, visceral quality. The attackers threaten to do likewise to Ed, when Lewis kills one of the attackers with bow and arrow, and the other assailant flees into the forest. The remainder of the film concerns the fallout from this incident. The men decide to bury the body of the rapist and not report the incident to the police. Their outing becomes a grueling escape from the wilderness as they travel in fear of the remaining attacker and encounter more violent rapids than they had anticipated. Drew is killed under mysterious circumstances (perhaps—but not unambiguously—by a hillside sniper), and Lewis is badly injured when a boat capsizes. It falls to Ed to climb a sheer cliff to kill a man he believes to be their mountaineer stalker. When the party reaches town at the other end of their run, they are demoralized and defeated but successfully weather interviews by police and return to their suburban lives changed but unpunished. The film ends, however, with Ed's vivid dream of the body of one of the mountaineers they have killed rising from the waters, suggesting how profoundly the experience on the river has changed who he is beneath the surface.

Though greeted with critical praise and commercial success upon its release, *Deliverance*, nominated for Best Picture of 1972, has generated controversy. Many of the north Georgia residents who worked on the location shooting around the Chattooga River felt uneasy about how the film would depict them and objected especially to the way the mentally and physically handicapped members of their community were represented. Appalachian people have lodged persistent complaints and critiques of the way the film presents life in the mountains as inherently depraved, both intellectually and morally.

These objections notwithstanding, the film stands as a major contribution to popular film art, perhaps because it generates so many unsettling questions and reactions among its viewers. Critical interpretations of the film have connected its story and images to a variety of larger cultural, political, and historical conflicts. The film can be read as a meditation on the decline of American manhood in the suburban era, as an allegory of global environmental crisis, as a commentary on the still troubled conscience of the professional classes in the New South, and even as a complex analogy to America's involvement in Vietnam. Though many Appalachian people are disparaged by its stereotypes, the film has also seemingly permanently lodged images of the backwoods in American popular culture. Even people who have never seen the film recognize allusions to "squeal like a pig" or the film's signature musical composition, "Dueling Banjos," as references to the horrific role mountain people play in the popular imagination.

See also: *DELIVERANCE* (LITERATURE); SECTION OVERVIEW (IMAGES AND ICONS); VIOLENCE AND VENGEANCE (IMAGES AND ICONS).

—Douglas Reichert Powell, *Columbia College Chicago*

Depression and the New Deal

The social, economic, and political changes of the Great Depression and the New Deal remade the image of Appalachia. As more and more Americans became subject to the hardships and deprivations following the stock market crash in 1929, the long-held idea that Appalachia was exceptionally in need of outside assistance no longer obtained. Media depictions of this era continued to promote Appalachians as the predecessors of modern Americans, caught in a backwater of time created by dense forests and deep mountain valleys. In the 1930s, however, this image was part of a broader national framework of depression, political debates over Franklin D. Roosevelt's federal recovery program, and a national interest in rediscovering a vibrant American folk tradition. National recovery, it seemed, depended as much on the cultural capital of Appalachia as it did on the mountains' natural resources. These resources, cultural and natural, defined the region's distinctiveness as well as its value to the nation, particularly in an era of regionalism and folkloric Americanism that promoted regional distinctiveness, Appalachian and otherwise, as a fundamental component of the American nation. These discussions and fascinations played out across a wide range of media formats, from novels to newsreels, movies to music, advertisements to editorials, and photographs to comic strips.

Appalachia's "hillbilly" image began to circulate widely in the mid-1920s, when record companies first marketed rural artists such as Ernest V. Stoneman and the Dixie Mountaineers, the Carter Family, Dock Boggs, and Jimmie Rodgers. The media continued to disseminate hillbilly music as the decade turned: Lily May Ledford and the Coon Creek Girls performed on a popular "barn dance" radio show into the 1930s to a potential audience of more than 12 million Americans; the Montgomery Ward catalog sold hillbilly records and magazines discussed them; and even the movie *The Singing Fool* (1928) had a trailer featuring Al Hopkins and the Hill Billies, a group from North Carolina and Virginia. The Nashville radio station WSM began to air its famous *Grand Ole Opry* nationally in 1928, and NBC started broadcasting the *National Barn Dance* in 1933. Both of these programs kept Americans listening to Appalachian music and skits such as those by the popular group Roy Acuff and the Smoky Mountain Boys. Appalachian music also included ballads and folk songs chronicling the despair and troubles of the Great Depression. As folk collectors traveled to the mountains to transcribe and record songs, songwriters from the region also gained national prominence through their role in the region's labor politics. For example, Aunt Molly Jackson and her family traveled to New York City in 1930 to play songs in support of Appalachian laborers.

These conflicts, particularly Appalachian coal-mining struggles, created some of the most dramatic incidents to circulate in the media. Coal miners and owners were embroiled in conflicts over labor policy and unionization, and the violent strikes that ensued received national attention. Leading writers of the day, including Theodore Dreiser, Sherwood Anderson, and John Dos Passos, traveled to Harlan County, Kentucky, in 1931 to report on coal strikes. Their pro-miner writings appeared in national magazines, including Dos Passos's article "Harlan: Working under the Gun" in the *New Republic* of December 2, 1931, which used Harlan to exemplify the deplorable conditions of miners throughout Appalachia, from Pittsburgh to Alabama. Coal strikes also became the subject of films, including *Black Fury* (1935), which tells the story of a simple Polish miner manipulated into leading a Pennsylvania wildcat strike.

Movie houses were a major venue for the creation and circulation of an Appalachian identity, and audiences came to know Appalachia through many of the era's animated shorts, cartoons, and films. The animated shorts "Hill Billys" (1935), "When I Yoo Hoo" (1936), "A Feud There Was" (1938), "Naughty Neighbors" (1939), and "Musical Mountaineers" (featuring Betty Boop, 1939) relied on Appalachian stereotypes, while *Kentucky Kernels* (1934) and *Kentucky Moonshine* (1938) used the same stereotypes in live-action film versions of hillbilly humor. Comic strips also disseminated a comedic Appalachian image. *Li'l Abner* first appeared in newspapers in 1934 and introduced American readers to the Yokum family. The same year, the shiftless, lazy mountaineer Snuffy Smith joined the cast of *Barney Google* and, by the late 1930s, had taken over the strip.

The movies also constructed Appalachia as a region filled with adventure and a home of true American heroes. A series of Daniel Boone movies, including RKO's 1936 *Daniel Boone* and the 1937 Republic version, *Daniel Boone, Trailblazer*, as well as the 1939 John Wayne vehicle, *Allegheny Uprising*, cast mountaineers as national folk heroes. Nor was the Hollywood mountaineer hero exclusively masculine: Katharine Hepburn, as Trigger Hicks, displayed mountain grit in *Spitfire*, set in the Ozarks (1934). The era's fascination with mountain heroes culminated in the 1941 film *Sergeant York*, a paean to the World War I hero from the Tennessee mountains, Alvin York (played by Gary Cooper). The 1936 film version of the best-selling John Fox Jr. novel *The Trail of the Lonesome Pine* departed from this vision of a heroic Appalachia, instead depicting a violent and backward "land apart." The movie dramatized the region's landscapes through its technological advances (it was the first movie shot on location to use Technicolor) while relying on standard regional stereotypes of family feuds, mountain romance, and uneducated backwoodsmen.

Although many media images exploited Appalachian stereotypes for laughs and thrills, the mountains and the people who lived there also appeared in more somber, and at times more critical, social commentaries. Muriel Earley Sheppard's *Cabins in the Laurel* (1935), illustrated with photographs by Bayard Wootten, narrated a nostalgic and celebratory view of life in the western North Carolina mountains. New York photographer Doris Ulmann made a series of photographs of the southern Appalachians between 1928 and 1934, some of which illustrated Allen H. Eaton's 1937 *Handicrafts of the Southern Highlands*, a comprehensive history and description of mountain craft traditions. In a more critical vein, the films *And So They Live* (1940) and *The Children Must Learn* (1940) established the Appalachian Mountains as an educational backwater. In 1937 Frontier Films produced *People of the Cumberland*, which promoted labor unions and federal programs as the answer to the area's poverty and problems. Novels such as Elizabeth Madox Roberts's *The Great Meadow* (1930) and Thomas Wolfe's *You Can't Go Home Again* (1940) also spread images of Appalachia through their meditations on place and home.

The surging interest in Appalachia as a center of American folklife served as material for media images of the region. In the 1930s, many festivals celebrated Appalachian folk traditions, including the White Top Folk Festival in southwest Virginia and the National Folk Festival, which was first held in St. Louis in 1934. The Southern Highland Handicraft Guild, founded in 1930, similarly disseminated information about Appalachia's rich cultural history and received the approbation of First Lady Eleanor Roosevelt and other New Dealers. Regional culture was marketed to the nation through its material products and its image, a goal that the first lady's appearance at the 1933 White Top festival aided considerably. Many critics today argue that the era's emphasis on Appalachian folk culture whitewashed the region of any ethnic or racial diversity. Dos Passos, for example, found the Harlan coal miners exemplary in part because they belonged to "old American pre-Revolutionary stock" who were not "wops and bohunks" that the "average American . . . is accustomed to see[ing] get the dirty end of the stick in labor troubles." By this reading, finding and selling America a version of its own history required a white native tradition.

The seeming ubiquity of labor troubles in Appalachia did not stop the government from investing in Appalachia's folk image. Eleanor Roosevelt's appearance at White Top signals the federal government's instrumental role in building the Appalachian identity that was spread throughout the country during the Depression and New Deal. Folklore projects under the Works Progress Administration (WPA) sent workers to the mountains to record songs and stories. The WPA's Federal Writers' Project incorporated local folklore and history in its series of state guides, which narrated the region's cultural and geographical distinctiveness through the paradigm of American national diversity. Similarly, the Resettlement and Farm Security Administrations sent photographers to chronicle rural American life, particularly scenes of despair and hardship in the region. Photographer Arthur Rothstein, for example, traveled to the Blue Ridge Mountains in 1935; Ben Shahn photographed mountain musicians around Asheville, North Carolina, in 1937; and Marion Post Wolcott documented the Kentucky mountains for the Farm Security Administration in 1940. These photographs appeared in books, exhibits, magazines, and newspapers, including the *New York Times*, *Newsweek*, *Survey Graphic*, and *Time*.

More than any other New Deal agency, the Tennessee Valley Authority (TVA) and its many projects in the region received considerable media attention and contributed to the idea of Appalachia as a land full of resources that needed only better institutional and governmental control to make use of them. It also furthered the concept of Appalachia as a distinct geographical and cultural region, a notion that enabled federal support for development of the Great Smoky Mountains and Shenandoah National Parks, both begun in the 1920s but established in 1934 and 1935, respectively. Yet the Resettlement Administration's decision to remove Appalachian families from long-held lands that would be flooded by TVA dams or become part of these parks also created a public debate over the program's potential social costs. In

1930 *National Geographic*, for example, argued that the new parks should not remove residents because the people, and not the land, would attract tourists. Although the TVA and the National Park Service ultimately decided to vacate the land of its residents, the debate exemplifies the ways in which geography and culture were central to the media's created Appalachian identity. The image of natural plenty and beauty was further developed when, in 1925, the Appalachian Trail Conference first convened. Completed in 1937, the Appalachian Trail opened the region to hikers from Maine to Georgia.

The government's creation of a unified regional identity appeared in its most instrumental and elemental form in the 1935 *Economic and Social Problems of the Southern Appalachians*, a report produced jointly by the Bureau of Agricultural Economics, the Bureau of Home Economics, and the Forest Service. This document tried to establish both the geographic and cultural parameters of the region. Despite this desire to define a single "Appalachia," the many different depictions of the region in media of the Great Depression and New Deal era prevent such a singular construct. Although Appalachia never resolved into a single image, it did maintain its regional distinctiveness. The 1930s necessarily changed what constituted this distinctiveness, however, as Appalachian identity was defined vis-à-vis a nation in need of economic and cultural growth. Governmental involvement in the region, along with the proliferation of media images, firmly anchored the region as part of and not apart from the nation.

See also: FARM SECURITY ADMINISTRATION PHOTOGRAPHY (VISUAL ARTS); FEDERAL ARTS PROJECT (VISUAL ARTS); TENNESSEE VALLEY AUTHORITY (GOVERNMENT).

—Lauren Coats, *Duke University*

Allen W. Batteau, *The Invention of Appalachia* (1990); Richard A. Peterson, *Creating Country Music: Fabricating Authenticity* (1997); David E. Whisnant, *All That Is Native and Fine: The Politics of Culture in an American Region* (1983); John Alexander Williams, *Appalachia: A History* (2002); J. W. Williamson, *Hillbillyland: What the Movies Did to the Mountains and What the Mountains Did to the Movies* (1995).

Documentary Films

Nonfiction films presenting the people, economy, and geography of Appalachia date back nearly to the dawn of American filmmaking. These films were known as actualities, educationals, travelogues, industrials, topicals, and documentaries (although the "documentary" filmmaking style did not develop until after World War I). Most of these early films no longer exist, but the titles and written descriptions indicate that they featured extraction of natural resources, resort and historical site tourism, and what was presented as a distinctive regional culture.

Industrials were some of the earliest preserved films featuring the region and promoted nascent industries in the area. *Mining Operations, Pa.* (Edison, 1904), for example, captures a scene of mining in the Pennsylvania coal region. This footage is possibly the earliest documentation of what would become known as strip mining (later labeled "surface" mining by an industry under attack in the early 1960s). *Sensational Logging* (Essanay, 1910) is set at a splash dam on Russell's Fork on the Kentucky-Virginia line. The colorful promotional description emphasized both the natural bounty and the excitement of the rough and tumble timber industry: "Up in the Cumberlands the virgin forests are falling before the axes of the sturdy Kentuckians and Virginians . . . hauling and dumping the logs and blowing up or 'splashing' . . . the dam, which releases, with a torrent of water, the many thousands of logs on their mad race down to Elkhorn."

Travelogues were another type of early documentary depicting the region. Subjects included rail trips through the Cumberland Mountains and tours of resorts, historic sites, and other places of interest, including Asheville, North Carolina, Tallulah Falls in Georgia, Chattanooga, Tennessee's Lookout Mountain, Civil War battlefields, and new dams. Another film featured the anthracite coalfields of Pennsylvania.

By the second decade of the twentieth century, the region, its people, and their ways began to be increasingly presented in the media as primitive, quaint, and lawless, and documentary films reflected these conceptual changes. *See America First, No. 65* (Gaumont, 1916), for instance, describes the "primitive beauty of the Appalachian Mountains" through "pictures of villages and mountains and cabins which give one a good idea of the life of the mountain folk." The promotional copy for *The Southern Highlands* (Pathé, 1917) stresses that the film reveals a glimpse of "people of the mountains of Tennessee and North Carolina and their primitive dwellings." *In the Moonshine Country* (Paramount, 1918) portrays mountain families in north Georgia and Kentucky through the "picturization of a quaint race" practicing a "mode of living unchanged for five generations." Similarly, *Our Southern Mountaineers* (Paramount, 1918) shows mountain folk weaving cloth, plying agriculture, and performing other duties in (according to the film) the primitive manner of their forefathers. As in films created by companies from countries with colonial empires, the Appalachian "natives" in documentaries of this era were routinely presented as quaint, exotic, mysterious, and even untamed.

In the years after World War I, the new medium of newsreels began to feature and examine personalities and popular events of the region. *Sergeant York* (Kinograms, 1919), a story of "the greatest hero of any war in the annals of history," includes pictures of the "Tennessean mountaineer" and his "mountain home." *Hope of the Hills* (Universal, 1919), best considered a "docufiction," portrays the missionary work of educator Alice Lloyd. In 1925, at a time when newsreels were projected in theaters nationwide, the Scopes trial, set in Dayton, Tennessee, captured wide attention. In both film and in print, the trial was repeatedly presented as a struggle between a regional backward fundamentalism and modernity.

In the 1930s, Appalachia became, both in reality and on the screen, a focal point of depression-era unrest and poverty and the subject of many documentary efforts. The National Film and Photo Leagues, a leading voice advocating social change, played a seminal role in spotlighting subjects that had been banned as too controversial by the newsreel industry. One of the earliest film groups to take a radical and sometimes militant stand toward social problems was Frontier Films (1937–42). Its *People of the Cumberland*, set in east Tennessee, depicts the Highlander Folk School and Myles Horton. According to the promotional copy, the film is a study of Highlander's role in stimulating "the revival of folk arts and in attacking poverty in the depressed Cumberland Plateau region by assisting in union organization." The federal government, particularly through the Resettlement Administration, also played an important role in focusing national attention on rural poverty by employing documentary filmmakers and photographers and exhibiting their works. The photographs of Doris Ullman, Ben Shahn, Walker Evans, and others included many Appalachian subjects and at least indirectly influenced the work of later documentary filmmakers.

Appalachia somewhat faded from public consciousness in the 1940s and 1950s. Documentary films covering this period are difficult to identify, and many may no longer exist. By contrast, the 1960s was a time of the intensive use of Appalachia in mass-media representations. CBS television's "Depressed Area, USA," hosted by Walter Cronkite (1964), and Charles Kuralt's "Christmas in Appalachia" (1964) portrayed poverty against a mountain backdrop and were probably viewed by more people than any other works on Appalachia up to that time. Both journalistic programs were largely inspired by John F. Kennedy's making poverty in West Virginia (where he campaigned) and America part of his 1960 presidential campaign platform. After the 1963 publication of Harry Caudill's book *Night Comes to the Cumberlands*, Appalachia became an international media subject. Caudill himself became a subject and vehicle through which British television came to uncover the region and its problems for television viewers in the United Kingdom.

During the same period, filmmaker, photographer, and folk musician John Cohen produced several important works on mountain music, including *High Lonesome Sound* (1963). Filmed mostly in Perry County, Kentucky, the film introduces its viewers to mountain music legend Roscoe Holcomb as well as Bill Monroe, the father of bluegrass music, and sacred music from a Pentecostal church service. In this and other films, Cohen portrays a far richer culture than had the CBS news specials. Unfortunately, he used very primitive early portable equipment that did not allow synchronous sound to be recorded with the picture and was far more cumbersome than newer equipment that would soon be available to others venturing into the mountains. This more portable and affordable equipment also made it possible for local people to start making films on regional topics.

The first of these locally produced films was *Holy Ghost People* (1968). Filmed primarily in a West Virginia Pentecostal church, it features candid shots of the congregation during a snake-handling service and closes on a dramatic note when a church leader is bitten by a rattlesnake. It was soon followed by the 1969 release *Appalachia: Rich Land, Poor People*, perhaps the best known of the early cinema verité documentaries to focus on Appalachia and to use the new portable equipment.

The year 1969 also marked the beginnings of the Appalachian Film Workshop (later Appalshop) and a new era of "insider" documentary approaches that would soon be recognized throughout the country. The advent of national public television and local cable access also brought new and larger audiences to the small independent films that were beginning to appear. Broadside Television in Johnson City, Tennessee, was an early local cable channel that pioneered bringing local culture to the community.

From 1970 to the present, there have been many documentaries produced about the region by both insiders and outsiders who have constructed any number of "real" Appalachias to suit a variety of purposes. In general, though, most have shifted away from being highly rhetorical to following the oral history model commonly used in the 1970s and 1980s. Perhaps the most important film of this era, with the possible exception of *Harlan County, USA* (1976), is *Stranger with a Camera* (2000), Appalshop's first major film to use first-person narration in developing the story. Director Elizabeth Barret recounts the tragic story of murdered Canadian filmmaker Hugh O'Connor as a personal story in which she, as an "insider" filmmaker, appears as a character. This movie appeared after Rory Kennedy's *American Hollow* (a portrait of the endemic poverty and dysfunction of a West Virginia mountain family) was released in 1999. These two stories, one by an "insider" and one by an "outsider," reflect the ongoing interest in Appalachia as a documentary subject and the very different approaches filmmakers can take in documenting the same culture.

See also: AGEE FILMS; APPALSHOP; DAVENPORT, TOM.

—Jack Wright, *Ohio University*

Russell Campbell, "Radical Documentary in the United States, 1930–1942," in *Show Us Life: Toward a History and Aesthetics of the Committed Documentary*, ed. Thomas Waugh (1984); Bill Nichols, "Newsreel, 1967–1972," in *Show Us Life: Toward a History and Aesthetics of the Committed Documentary*, ed. Thomas Waugh (1984); J. W. Williamson, *Southern Mountaineers in Silent Films: Plot Synopses of Movies about Moonshining, Feuding, and Other Mountain Topics, 1904–1929* (1994).

Dollmaker, The

This television adaptation of Harriette Simpson Arnow's 1954 novel tells the story of a Kentucky mountain family that migrates to Detroit during World War II and deals with difficult socioeconomic issues faced by many displaced Appalachians. Filmed on location in Sevier County, Tennessee, and in Chicago, the movie's settings juxtapose the serene beauty of the mountains with the starkness of a wartime ghetto. *The Dollmaker* chronicles the Appalachian family's culture shock as members adjust to their new environment and cope with personal tragedies.

Far from the rural, independent farm life they knew in Kentucky, family members must learn to adapt to the overcrowded government housing where protagonist Gertie Nevels struggles to raise her five children as her husband, Clovis (Levon Helm), works long shifts in a factory. Portrayed as a faithful, courageous, yet vulnerable woman, Gertie is a talented artist, helping to feed her family by selling hand-carved wooden dolls and toys. Departing from the novel's plot, the film concludes with the family's return to Kentucky.

The Dollmaker first aired on Sunday, May 13, 1984, as an ABC-TV Theatre presentation. Jane Fonda produced the film and won an Emmy for her role as Gertie. Actor Hume Cronyn and novelist Susan Cooper adapted the novel for television, as they had done with *Foxfire* three years earlier. Television veteran Daniel Petrie *(A Raisin in the Sun; My Name is Bill W.)* directed the teleplay.

See also: ARNOW, HARRIETTE SIMPSON (LITERATURE); FEATURE FILMS.

—Marianne Worthington, *Cumberland College*

Feature Films

Appalachian characters, plots, and motifs permeated popular films throughout the twentieth century and often served dual, conflicting purposes for both filmmakers and audience. In popular films, mountain culture was at times a scapegoat for negative elements in American culture such as bigotry, ignorance, violence, and xenophobia and at other times an embodiment of the nation's self-reliant pioneering heritage.

Before 1915, the year that D. W. Griffith's *The Birth of a Nation* set a new standard for commercially successful long narrative films, literally hundreds of one- and two-reel "actioners," varying in length from about eight to twenty minutes and featuring feuding mountain clans or shooting mountain moonshiners, had been produced for the nickelodeon market, a totally urban audience.

Nickelodeons in the earliest years of motion pictures depicted America as an essentially rural place with a stark moral order. The multiple upheavals that accompanied World War I changed that self-image radically, and popular culture reflected the growing importance of American cities. This change came at the time of a significant urban shift in population first revealed in the census of 1920. By the end of the twentieth century, America had become more than 75 percent urban.

The new majority of city dwellers began to tire of rural images, increasingly favoring faster-paced urban settings. City characters' pleasures, triumphs, and sins came to dominate popular culture, especially in movies. When rural characters did reappear in films, most notably as southern mountaineers or cowboys, they often came with extra emotional power by virtue of their symbolic status already well established in the urban imagination of the 1880s and 1890s as the dangerous exception to American progress. The film industry continued to foster this image of rural America as the dark side of culture but also made use of the idea of the heroic pioneer. Thus the main function of southern Appalachian characters in early feature films was either to provide a useful stand-in for depravity and dark impulses or to glorify the conquering of the frontier by white newcomers.

One successful early feature film, *Tol'able David* (1921), distilled both the heroic frontier and the bestial frontier so that an American public, somewhat exhausted by its experience of World War I in Europe, could rediscover itself in the blissfully innocent Shenandoah farm boy David Kinemon. The "evil frontier," represented by the dark Hatburn men from deepest West Virginia (stand-ins for the dreaded "Huns" of the late European war) are vanquished by "good frontier" Americanism in the person of its pure-hearted farm boy. The American moviegoing public rewarded *Tol'able David* handsomely with big profits.

The rest of the 1920s saw several attempts to imitate the *Tol'able David* formula, pitting other innocent mountain boys against mean old men (*Driven*, 1923; *The Hill Billy*, 1924; *Stark Love*, 1927; *Kentucky Courage*, 1928). Gradually, the symbolic meanness became a metaphor for sexual heat, as in Mary Pickford's 1929 Academy Award vehicle *Coquette*, which also starred Johnny Mack Brown as a crude and prideful mountaineer who ruins her reputation and is then murdered by the girl's vengeful father. The early Bette Davis feature *Cabin in the Cotton* (1932), based on the novel by Harry Harrison Kroll, likewise located a freer sexual impulse among southern "white trash." Walter Wanger's production of John Fox Jr.'s *The Trail of the Lonesome Pine* in 1936 continued the tradition of casting mountain females as symbols of unfettered sexual promise. It also happened to be the first outdoor movie shot entirely in the new Technicolor process.

Hollywood seemed particularly wedded to images of hillbillies as the antithesis of progress (*Child Bride of the Ozarks*, 1937; *Murder, He Says*, 1945; the *Ma and Pa Kettle* series, beginning in 1949). The John Ford–directed and Darryl F. Zanuck–produced *Tobacco Road*, released in 1941, proved to some people the hopeless failure of the backwoods to leave the frontier behind. Ironically, in *Sergeant York*, premiering the same year as *Tobacco Road*, the same hillbilly stereotypes used to portray the denizens of *Tobacco Road* as degenerates are used to stoke the fires of patriotism in painting the young ne'er-do-well Alvin York as an ideal foot soldier in the nation's defense.

Other than the features discussed above and a handful of others, the 1930s and 1940s saw hillbillies as mainly comic, either broadly drawn stereotypes used to menace urban comedians (*Kentucky Moonshine*, 1938, for example, with the Ritz Brothers) or country music stars essentially playing themselves in gentle depictions of a passive backcountry that was said to want no truck with urban America (*Mountain Music*, 1937; *Swing Your Lady*, 1938; *Grand Ole Opry*, 1940). This safe version of a backward yet harmless frontier was on popular display in *The Egg and I* (1947), which introduced Ma and Pa Kettle as prototypical hillbillies. The Kettles, out of the goodness of their hearts, save a pair of urban fools from total disaster.

Robert Mitchum in *Thunder Road,* 1958. Mitchum's frequent portrayal of characters from southern Appalachia, including bad-boy moonshine runner Luke Doolin in *Thunder Road,* helped to define the region's identity for a generation of American moviegoers.

Samuel Goldwyn's *Roseanna McCoy* (1949) updated the darker side of the frontier as a metaphor for old-style parenting of new-style teenagers in postwar America. The elder Hatfields and (especially) the elder McCoys are intolerant, bearing senseless grudges to their graves. *Roseanna McCoy's* teenage characters, the title character and Johnse Hatfield, become examples of open-hearted love against the implacable blood lust of the elders, and Farley Granger as Johnse is the prototypical "rebel without a cause"—six years before James Dean made that part famous in an urban California setting.

World War II plagued America's mind in subtle ways for years, with the symbolic backwoods often supplying the true grit said to have won the war. It was the rare war film in the late 1940s and the 1950s, for example, that did not include one hillbilly in every platoon. *Annie Get Your Gun* (1950) used pinup girl Betty Hutton as a kind of tribute to Rosy-the-Riveter spunk in American womanhood while insisting by the end of the story that she get out of those men's clothes and out of that man's role and go back home to housewifery. The postwar novel *No Time for Sergeants* became a starring vehicle for Andy Griffith in 1958, and while an audience was expected to laugh at the bonehead recruit from the north Georgia woods, that audience was also supposed to take some comfort that his tenacity made the American armed forces more formidable.

Thunder Road (1958) was in some ways the quintessential postwar movie (though the war referred to in the dialogue is the Korean Conflict), glorifying the lone-wolf frontiersman, the contrarian who respects neither law nor mob violence and who goes down hard. The style of Robert Mitchum's masculine persona as moonshine runner Luke Doolin captured the imaginations of a generation of small-town, semirural, and rural young men in the late 1950s who possibly related to Doolin's tragedy.

A resurgence of bad frontier arrived the same year in *A Face in the Crowd*. In the film, Andy Griffith plays Lonesome Rhodes, a vulgar but sly hillbilly opportunist who uses everyone's underestimation of his abilities as a way to climb into great fame via radio and television and then into great political power. Griffith's character successfully seduces several women through sheer animal magnetism, a whiff of the dangerous sexuality Hollywood had already depicted coming from Appalachia. The 1960s and 1970s saw this theme used often in films, from soft- and hardcore pornography (*Com-*

mon Law Wife, 1963; *Shotgun Wedding*, 1963; *Raw Love*, 1965; *Mudhoney*, 1966; *Passion in Hot Hollows*, 1969) to the movie production in 1959 of the Broadway hit musical *Li'l Abner*, essentially a raunchy burlesque revue set in a parody of the mountains. In 1964 Elvis Presley starred in *Kissin' Cousins* in a dual role. Elvis Number One is a G.I. scout sent to Tennessee to talk his hillbilly relatives into leasing their mountain lair to the government for a missile base. Elvis Number Two is a surly blonde who hates his city-reared cousin. The boys tangle, toss off songs, and attract swarms of scantily clad young beauties roaming the hills. A much more serious treatment of sexual repression came in 1970 with *I Walk the Line*, which starred Gregory Peck and Tuesday Weld, the latter as a moonshiner's daughter who tempts lawman Peck to violate his marriage vows and his oath of office. *Winter People* in 1989 likewise puts a mild-mannered urban clockmaker into the pathway of a sexually free mountain woman, with a much better outcome for the clockmaker than for Peck's sheriff.

Other feature films have washed the backwoods clean of menace, especially of sexual predators, and relocated *Tol'able David*–like virtue there. For example, *Country Music Holiday* (1958), a film popular in small-town theaters and drive-ins, exposes country music personality Ferlin Husky to the temptations of New York City but brings him safely back home to marry his sweetheart, June Carter, in Puffin Bluff, Tennessee. *Spencer's Mountain* (1963), though set in the Rocky Mountain West, was actually the first incarnation of Earl Hamner Jr.'s Walton family (of television fame), highly autobiographical characters drawn from Hamner's Blue Ridge home in Nelson County, Virginia. Henry Fonda and Maureen O'Hara preside over a large all-American passel of young'uns, led by an ambitious eldest son (James MacArthur), who goes off to college, thus proving that the get-ahead drive behind America itself grew first in the basic goodness of backwoods families. Perhaps the most sentimental treatment of the southern mountains was 1974's *Where the Lilies Bloom*, with a screenplay by Hamner. *Where the Lilies Bloom* preaches the fierce self-sufficiency of even the children of the hills, in this instance left parentless by fate.

These "good frontier" movies were poised against at least three features since the early 1970s that were essentially horror films featuring mountaineers (always male) as monsters. *Deliverance* (1972) used the same Hatburn types that had menaced young David Kinemon in *Tol'able David*. *Kalifornia* (1993) starred Brad Pitt as a hillbilly psychopath whose yuppie victim bonds with him because he sees in Pitt his darker self. Also in 1993, Martin Scorsese's remake of *Cape Fear* transformed the film's antagonist ex-con Max Cady into a demented hillbilly from a snake-handling mountain clan, forcing the adulterous lawyer played by Nick Nolte to face his own worst nature reflected in the face of a depraved cultural "other."

A separate trend in several feature films after 1960 used the political ideas of the Great Society and the War on Poverty to rouse urban guilt about the poor, especially the rural poor. In these films, able backwoods types became essentially passive victims of huge forces beyond their control. In *Wild River* (1960), a government man played by Montgomery Clift tries to save his own soul while forcing a mountain mother and her family off ancestral land for the sake of the Tennessee Valley Authority. *Medium Cool* (1969) compares the plight of West Virginia urban migrants to Chicago to the cause of black civil rights, all set against the backdrop of the rioting at the 1968 Democratic Convention. *Norma Rae* (1979) won an Academy Award for Sally Fields in the role of the real-life Crystal Lee Sutton, a textile factory worker turned union organizer. In 1984 *The River* (which starred Mel Gibson and Sissy Spacek) took a less exacting look at the role of governmental and business forces in driving farmers off their land.

The theme of social retardation in need of uplift was considerably muted in Victor Nuñez's *Ruby in Paradise* (1993) in favor of a character study of a young woman escaping the bigotry and narrowness of mountain life. The title character, Ruby Lee Gissing, played by Ashley Judd, is a put-upon Tennessee housewife who abandons her husband for the Florida coast, where she rethinks her worldview, makes big mistakes, and takes disastrous turns but somehow muddles through.

The themes of *Ruby in Paradise* show up in exaggerated forms in *Nell* (1995), a fantasy of a wild child played by Jodie Foster discovered in total isolation in the North Carolina mountains who turns out to be the font of spiritual healing. The script is adapted from a stage play set on the coast of the Pacific Northwest, but the production was moved to Appalachia for budgetary reasons and because it was believed that an educated American audience would more readily accept the idea of total isolation in the southern mountains.

Insofar as "the frontier" has been consistently imagined from the point of view of white European newcomers, the hillbilly is a version of whiteness, a projection of the best and worst traits it took to wrest North America away from its original inhabitants. The hillbilly allows a mainly white urban audience to both titillate itself when convenient and dissociate itself when necessary from its own worst historical behavior and any lingering present bad impulses. The Pathé company had the idea down pat in its "exploitation" language promoting its new feature *Forbidden Valley* in 1920: "The last stand of primitive white men in America; the last frontier of the land where men make and enforce their own laws; such is the forbidden valley in the heart of the Kentucky mountains."

See also: DEPRESSION AND THE NEW DEAL; NATIONAL POLITICS AND THE MEDIA IN THE 1960S; *TOL'ABLE DAVID*.

—J. W. Williamson, *Appalachian State University*

J. W. Williamson, *Hillbillyland: What the Movies Did to the Mountains and What the Mountains Did to the Movies* (1995) and *Southern Mountaineers in Silent Films: Plot Synopses of Movies about Moonshining, Feuding, and Other Mountain Topics, 1904–1929* (1994).

Feuds and Violence

In the late-nineteenth-century popular imagination, Appalachia was nearly synonymous with violence, social conflict, and lawlessness. Contemporaneous commentators, both scholarly and popular, applied the term *feuding* to sustained incidents of widespread violence throughout Appalachia, especially eastern Kentucky.

Fragmentary records make it impossible to determine whether this area produced unusually high levels of violence. Conflict was widespread throughout the post-Reconstruction South, the developing West, the industrial North, and the increasingly interracial environments of urban America at the same time that Appalachian feuds captured the popular imagination. Nonetheless, images of mountain strife in popular magazines, major newspapers, and academic journals did much to persuade middle-class readers throughout the rest of the United States of the strange and peculiar nature of Appalachia and its apparently "benighted" population.

One important source of public understanding of violence in nineteenth-century Appalachia was sensationalistic writing in popular magazines. Like colonialist accounts of quests into the far corners of Africa and Asia, stories by travelers into the Appalachian Mountains helped shape the image of the region as a primitive, untamed place inhabited by a primitive, untamed people. Legends of mountain feuds worked to cement this impression. In a 1902 issue of *Frank Leslie's Popular Monthly*, a local color writer described his voyage into Kentucky's mountainous region: "We swept deeper and deeper into the mountains, and traces of civilization became scarcer. Now and again we would pass a small hut. . . . Wild and poorly clad forms would appear in low doorways; faces almost expressionless would stare at us in a kind of apathetic wonder. . . . We were getting in the feudists' country, where the sun set crimson and the moon rose red."

Singling out Clay County, Kentucky, for the perceived ferocity of its populace, the writer declared it a place where "death stalks abroad at noonday like a roaring lion seeking whom he may devour." *Frank Leslie's* was far from alone in its characterization of the savagery of mountain life. A 1903 article in *Muncey's Magazine* similarly claimed that "the lust for human blood ha[d] become a malignant disease" among Kentucky mountaineers and described the Cumberland region as "a savage, primeval country, where have developed those fierce and terrible family wars, the American feuds, beside which the Italian vendetta is a childish thing, almost humane in comparison."

Newspapers from outside the mountains, another source of popular information on Appalachian conflicts, presented no less fanciful accounts of feud violence. National papers such as the *New York Times* printed exaggerated accounts of this "strange, bloody story" and offered changing explanations for what they presented as a regionally unique pattern of feuding whose "ferocity, barbarity and cruelty are appalling." Indeed, an analysis of late-nineteenth-century coverage of Appalachian feuds in the *Louisville Courier-Journal* and the *New York Times* found that while both newspapers reported numerous examples of violent community conflicts throughout Kentucky and the wider South, it was not until about 1885 that they began to denote some of these as "Appalachian" conflicts. It was even later that they began to characterize them as "feuds." Before then, violence was deplored in newspaper reports and editorials, but such conflicts were interpreted as the expression of underlying political troubles. Once certain of these episodes came to be distinguished as Appalachian, however, violence came to be seen as a cultural phenomenon rather than the result of political conflicts.

Although the audience for academic writing was much smaller than that for popular magazines and newspapers, scholars gave credence to broader media interpretations of Appalachian feuds as a manifestation of mountain people's cultural proclivity toward violence. Freighted with little evidence beyond anecdotes, vague impressions, and their own stereotypes of mountain life, turn-of-the-century social scientists depicted Appalachia as lawless and prone to violent conflict. One claimed that in the Kentucky hills "each man had been a law unto himself too long to be able to forget it immediately and look to civil law for protection." Another asserted that "isolation and poverty" had "fostered the survival of the blood-feud among the Kentucky mountaineers."

Literary, journalistic, and scholarly depictions of the Cumberland Mountains as a violent subculture shaped a discourse—a tradition of understanding—about Appalachia and its feuds. Outside writers used mountain community conflicts to help define Appalachia as a separate region, and once constructed, this idea was used to explain the forms of violence that erupted there. In various forms and language, non-local media suggested that mountain violence was the result of poverty, ignorance, and isolation and that it was triggered by trivial incidents, prolonged by primitive clan loyalties, and tolerated because of the ineffectiveness of, or hostility toward, legal institutions in mountain society. This was notwithstanding the fact that actual patterns of prolonged violence in nineteenth-century Appalachia were likely to be rooted in concrete disputes over politics, landownership, and the creation of states. Moreover, they were more apt to involve wealthy, educated, and politically powerful entrepreneurs than isolated, impoverished, and ignorant mountain dwellers.

By characterizing Appalachians as quaint yet fearsome, popular portrayals of feuding in the southern mountains paved the way for subsequent efforts to explain and justify the region's chronic poverty and suitability for resource extraction. If feuds in nineteenth-century Appalachia were seen as a result of ignorance and isolation, their eradication could be easily linked to the advance of capitalist economic development—at the very moment that corporate railroad, timber, and mineral interests were scrambling to acquire Appalachian rights and properties.

See also: FEUDS (GOVERNMENT); TRAVEL WRITING (LITERATURE); VIOLENCE AND VENGEANCE (IMAGES AND ICONS).

—Dwight B. Billings, *University of Kentucky*, and Kathleen M. Blee, *University of Pittsburgh*

Dwight B. Billings and Kathleen M. Blee, *The Road to Poverty: The Making of Wealth and Hardship in Appalachia* (2000); Henry D. Shapiro, *Appalachia on Our Mind: The Southern Mountains and Mountaineers in the American Consciousness, 1870–1920* (1978); Altina L. Waller, "Feuding in Appalachia: Evolution of a Cultural Stereotype" in *Appalachia in the Making: The Mountain South in the Nineteenth Century*, ed. Mary Beth Pudup, Dwight B. Billings, and Altina L. Waller (1995).

Gish, Tom and Pat

Gish, Tom (1926–) Newspaper editor and publisher. Gish, Pat Burnett (1927–) Newspaper editor and publisher.

Tom Gish was born on January 28, 1926, in the coal camp of Seco in Letcher County, Kentucky, the son of Ben Gish, a coal miner with a fourth-grade education who had risen to become a mine superintendent and, along the way, invented the roof bolt, a major advance in mine safety. Tom's wife, Pat, was born Patricia Burnett on January 11, 1927, in Paris, Kentucky, in the state's Bluegrass region. Together, Tom and Pat Gish edited and published the *Mountain Eagle* in Whitesburg, Kentucky, from 1957 to 2001; their son Ben has been the editor since 2001, with Tom serving as publisher. Under their stewardship, the *Mountain Eagle* has been one of the Appalachian region's most influential newspapers, and the Gishes' views have helped shape the opinions of readers, reporters, and politicians on most important issues facing the region.

Tom Gish and Pat Burnett both attended the University of Kentucky, Tom graduating in 1947 and Pat in 1949 with degrees in journalism. They married in 1948. For the first ten years of their careers, the Gishes followed conventional paths. Pat covered the courts, schools, and city government for the afternoon *Lexington Leader*, and Tom was bureau manager for the United Press International wire service in Frankfort, where the coupled lived. He principally covered the state legislature as well as events such as the Kentucky Derby.

In 1956, on a visit to his parents' home in Letcher County, Tom and Pat met with Pearl and Martha Nolan, the owners of newspapers in Whitesburg, Letcher County's seat, and Hazard, the county seat of adjacent Perry County. The Nolans offered to sell either of the papers. The Gishes scraped together forty thousand dollars and bought the *Mountain Eagle* in Whitesburg, the paper Tom had read as a boy.

The Gishes bought the paper in November 1956 and took over on January 1, 1957. They quickly turned the *Mountain Eagle* into an open forum of debate, discussion, and community news. They attended meetings of county courts, school boards, and city councils, reporting for the first time the workings of Letcher County government, often to the consternation of the people they wrote about. They also came to realize the importance of a weekly newspaper in giving voice to a wide variety of community writers. Early in their tenure, the Gishes later recalled, they "made the stupid mistake of cutting out the opinions" of local columnists, the mostly female cadre of writers who would offer the news of their communities in each week's paper. When readers rebelled, the Gishes quickly allowed their volunteer columnists editorial freedom, and through the years these writers—women such as Mabel Kiser in Millstone, Thelma Cornett in Linefork, Siller Brown and Sarah Ison in Ice, Elsie Banks in Cowen, and Gaynell Begley in Blackey—became some of the most prescient writers about twentieth-century Appalachian life.

The Gishes also published news of regional importance. Reports from Tennessee-based reporter James Branscome on the Tennessee Valley Authority exposed the agency's role in subsidizing the destruction of Appalachia in the 1970s by purchasing strip-mined coal. The *Mountain Eagle*'s persistent news reports and editorials on strip mining and mine safety abuses led to changes in federal law and enforcement. The Gishes also served as guides to the region for succeeding generations of journalists and politicians, prompting much of the news coverage from Appalachia in the early 1960s that led to both the War on Poverty and increased environmental awareness. The Gishes were instrumental in planning Senator Robert Kennedy's tour of eastern Kentucky in 1968, and with their encouragement Senator Paul Wellstone of Minnesota became an outspoken mine safety advocate before his death in an October 2002 plane crash.

The Gishes took public roles outside the *Eagle*'s offices almost from the time they moved to Whitesburg. Tom lobbied Kentucky legislators in the early 1960s to help save a chain of hospitals established by the United Mine Workers of America. In 1991 Kentucky Governor Wallace Wilkinson appointed Tom to the Kentucky State Board of Education. For eight years, he was one of the most outspoken defenders of education reform legislation passed in 1990. Pat founded and operated the Eastern Kentucky Housing Development Corporation from 1967 to 1985, using local materials and largely older, unemployed miners to build and repair homes for low-income residents.

In their years operating the paper, the Gishes survived advertising boycotts, an arson attack that nearly destroyed the paper, and the collapse of Letcher County's coal economy. The Gishes and the *Eagle* received the John Peter Zenger Award for service in support of freedom of the press from the University of Arizona in 1974; the Elijah Parish Lovejoy Award for courage in journalism from Southern Illinois University in 1977; the Hugh M. Hefner First Amendment Award for community leadership from the Playboy Foundation in 1983; the Edwards M. Templin Award for distinguished community service from the Kentucky Press Association in 1993; the Elijah Parish Lovejoy Award from Colby College in 2001; and the Helen Thomas Award from the Society of Professional Journalists in 2002. Tom and Pat Gish were inducted to the University of Kentucky Journalism Hall of Fame in 1986, and they were named "Treasures of American Journalism" by New York University's Journalism Department in 1999.

See also: *MOUNTAIN EAGLE*; NEWSPAPERS.

—Thomas N. Bethell, *Washington, D.C.*, and Bill Bishop, *Austin, Texas*

William Serrin, ed., *The Business of Journalism: Ten Leading Reporters and Editors on the Perils and Pitfalls of the Press* (2000); Studs Terkel, *American Dreams: Lost and Found* (1980).

Goldenseal

Goldenseal, a magazine subtitled *West Virginia Traditional Life*, is a quarterly publication highlighting all aspects of traditional and cultural life of West Virginia. Founded in 1975, it covers such widely varied topics as labor history, folklife and folklore, music, farming practices, religion, crafts, food, architecture, medicine, sports, industry, community celebrations, immigrant issues, and politics. Personal experiences of West Virginia citizens are paramount in the articles. *Goldenseal* is an official publication of the State of West Virginia and is produced by the Division of Culture and History. It does not carry articles pertaining to history prior to the twentieth century, nor does it publish genealogy, poetry, or fiction. Most articles are the work of freelance writers. The magazine has a circulation of twenty thousand with about 70 percent of the readership within the state. Although read by all ages and education levels, the core readership tends to be those fifty-five years of age and older who have personal experience with the rural life of West Virginia. *Goldenseal* is used in classrooms, libraries, and research facilities throughout West Virginia and other Appalachian states and has compiled many of its articles into theme books such as *The Goldenseal Book of the West Virginia Mine Wars*.

See also: SECTION OVERVIEW (FOLKLORE AND FOLKLIFE); WEST VIRGINIA PUBLIC FOLKLORE (FOLKLORE AND FOLKLIFE).

—Stevan Jackson, *Radford University*

Grand Ole Opry

When it celebrated its seventy-fifth anniversary in 2000, Nashville's *Grand Ole Opry* was the nation's oldest continuously running radio program, its premier country music institution, one of the South's leading tourist attractions, and a major cultural and economic force in the development of country music as a commercial art form. Essentially a repertory company that includes more than eighty major acts, the *Opry* has for much of its history functioned in three ways: as a live radio variety show broadcast over Nashville's powerful clear-channel station WSM; as a stage show that attracts thousands of fans each week; and as a home base for touring groups that travel throughout the eastern half of the United States. For many, it has long been synonymous with Nashville and with country music in general.

The show dates from November 28, 1925, barely two months after the National Life and Accident Insurance Company opened WSM as its flagship station. On that night, Uncle Jimmy Thompson, a seventy-eight-year-old fiddler from Laguardo, Tennessee, played an informal program of traditional fiddle tunes for the station's new manager and announcer, George D. Hay. Pleased by the huge response to the program, Hay, who had worked with the *National Barn Dance* at WLS in Chicago, was eager to produce a similar program and announced on December 26 that WSM would arrange to have an "hour or two" of "old time tunes" every Saturday night. Soon a cast of about twenty-five acts had formed, most of them composed of amateur musicians from the Nashville area. A romantic by nature, Hay sold the show, which changed its name from the *WSM Barn Dance* to the *Grand Ole Opry* in 1927, and its music to the public as "folk music" (which it originally was) and created a bucolic image with musicians dressed in overalls and adopting such colorful names as the Fruit Jar Drinkers.

Major figures during the *Opry*'s first decade included banjoist and singer Uncle Dave Macon, a vaudeville and recording artist from Readyville, Tennessee; harmonica player and string-band leader Humphrey Bate, a country doctor from Castalian Springs; Obed "Dad" Pickard, a singer and multi-instrumentalist from Ashland City who was dubbed the "One-Man Orchestra" by Hay; and DeFord Bailey, an African American harmonica player from Smith County who specialized in a novelty called "The Fox Chase."

By the 1930s, the leading stars included the Delmore Brothers (from Alabama), who brought their own original songs such as "Brown's Ferry Blues" to the show, and Fiddlin' Arthur Smith, a remarkable "long bow"–style fiddler. Although few of these early stars were actually from the Appalachians, the radio broadcasts and touring groups were heard throughout the mountains. They influenced countless musicians and helped to validate the traditional musical styles of the southern mountains and the adjoining areas.

During the following decades, a number of milestones marked the rise of the *Opry* from a regional folk-based radio show to a national country music institution. In 1933 WSM formed an Artists Service Bureau to organize tours and help attract full-time professional musicians. In 1939 a half-hour segment of the show was picked up by the NBC radio network, giving it true nationwide exposure, and in 1940 the Republic film *The Grand Ole Opry* was shown in theaters across the country.

During World War II, groups headed by *Opry* artists Pee Wee King and Minnie Pearl toured military camps around the country, spreading the music to new audiences, and in 1943 the show moved to the historic Ryman Auditorium in downtown Nashville. By the end of the war, the *Opry* was emerging as the nation's leading country radio show, and Nashville was developing a network of songwriters and recording studios to support it.

As the *Opry* became more professionalized, Hay gradually lost power to younger, more pragmatic business managers who were looking for ways to increase the show's commercial marketability. Though he continued as an announcer with the *Opry* throughout most of the 1940s, Hay was only on the show occasionally by the 1950s and eventually left Nashville disappointed by the increasingly commercial direction the *Opry* was taking. He died in 1968 and was buried in Virginia Beach, Virginia.

Although the *Opry* later attracted performers from all around the country, its two biggest stars in the 1940s were from Appalachia. Roy Acuff, from Maynardville in east Tennessee, joined in 1938 and sang songs such as "The Precious Jewel" in a high, forceful mountain style he had learned as a boy. From Berea, Kentucky, came Red Foley, who had a smooth, almost pop style miles removed from Acuff's. Other Appalachian artists who joined the show in the 1950s and 1960s included Carl Smith, a distinctive singer from the Knoxville, Tennessee, area; Wilma Lee and Stoney Cooper, West Virginians who flavored their powerful duet singing with traditional folk and gospel songs; and comedian Archie Campbell, from Bull's Gap, Tennessee.

In March 1974, the *Opry* was purchased by the Gaylord Entertainment Company and moved to the plush Grand Ole Opry House at the Opryland complex, which included a major convention hotel and theme park. In 1985 the Nashville Network began televising a weekly half-hour segment of the show.

By the end of the century, though the *Opry* featured its share of modern country singers, including Travis Tritt and Garth Brooks, it also spotlighted performers with Appalachian roots. Kentuckians Ricky Skaggs and the Osborne Brothers continued to celebrate the bluegrass tradition. Tennessean Dolly Parton often returned to the simple acoustic style of mountain folk music, and West Virginian Jimmy Dickens kept alive the vintage honky-tonk, novelty, and sentimental songs that had made him an *Opry* favorite for more than half a century. Ralph Stanley, the most celebrated among living bluegrass artists, regularly brought his Virginia traditions to the stage. Throughout its seventy-five years, the *Opry* has drawn from the complex crucible of mountain music to rejuvenate and redefine itself and country music.

See also: COUNTRY MUSIC (MUSIC); MUSIC BROADCASTING.

—Charles K. Wolfe, *Middle Tennessee State University*

Chet Hagan, *Grand Ole Opry: The Official History* (1989); Charles K. Wolfe, *A Good-Natured Riot: The Birth of the Grand Ole Opry* (1999).

Harlan County, USA

Filmmaker Barbara Kopple's documentary *Harlan County, USA* examines the personal and political tensions of a 1974 coal strike in eastern Kentucky. Released in 1976, the film won an Academy Award for feature-length documentary for its depiction of the human drama that emerged from the class struggle between management and labor as coal miners sought a union contract. During the four-year making of the film, Kopple lived for months at a time among the approximately 180 families involved in the struggle between Harlan County coal miners and the Eastover Mining Company, a subsidiary of Duke Power Company.

Harlan County, USA is considered a classic of documentary filmmaking. It dramatizes the hardships heaped on families during labor strikes, simultaneously contextualizing the events in Harlan County with the 1930s Kentucky coalfield mine wars, the area's pervasive poverty, and larger labor-management relations. Archival footage incorporated throughout the film gives historical perspective to the strike. While Kopple does not hide her animus for corporate interests, she also notes corruption within the United Mine Workers of America. The film highlights the role that women played as wives and mothers of mine workers in the struggle for unionization, higher wages, and better working conditions. Kopple captures compelling scenes of violence attendant with the strike, including the beating of workers and of the film crew and the aftermath of a murder on the picket line. Kopple also records the tensions between strikers and those who chose to cross the picket line. Traditional labor songs, sung by Nimrod Workman and Hazel Dickens, contribute to the film's emotional intensity. *Harlan County, USA* was included in the Library of Congress's National Film Registry in 1990, which secures its permanent preservation in the history of film.

See also: DOCUMENTARY FILMS; MINE WARS AND THE TWENTIETH-CENTURY MEDIA.

—Stevan Jackson, *Radford University*

Haught, James A.

(1932–) Newspaper reporter, editor, and author.

James A. Haught, reporter, columnist, and author for fifty years, is editor-in-chief of West Virginia's *Charleston Gazette* and a renowned freethinker. He was born February 20, 1932, in Reader, West Virginia, to a family that never went to church. He attended the University of Charleston and West Virginia State College, and he was an aide to Senator Robert C. Byrd in 1959.

Haught joined the *Gazette* in 1953, where he worked as a police reporter, columnist, and night city editor. He has consistently covered social issues affecting the state. When he was assigned the religion beat, he began attending a spectrum of religious services, including a national Episcopal bishop assembly, a serpent-handling worship, and faith-healing revivals. He covered the 1974 Kanawha County textbook controversy, in which church groups claimed schoolbook selections were un-Christian. Later, Haught was reassigned to investigative reporting and won fifteen national news-writing awards, among them the Gavel Citation for Justice Writing, the Hugh M. Hefner First Amendment Award for Investigative Reporting, and three National Press Club Consumer Writing Awards. In 1993 Haught became editor of the *Gazette*, and during his tenure the newspaper maintained its reputation for investigative reporting. Haught's family background and work as a religion reporter solidified his skepticism of religion and of the supernatural. Besides writing extensively about injustices resulting from religion and challenging supernatural claims, he has edited *Free Inquiry* magazine and has written five books: *Holy Horrors; Science in a Nanosecond; The Art of Lovemaking; Holy Hatred;* and *Two Thousand Years of Disbelief.*

See also: *CHARLESTON GAZETTE*; NATIONAL NEWSPAPER COVERAGE; NEWSPAPERS.

—Janet Dooley, *Marshall University*

Hee Haw

In one of its last bids to present rural programming in the late 1960s, CBS broadcast *Hee Haw* as a 1969 midsummer variety show replacement. Although *Hee Haw*'s producers essentially presented a "country" version of *Rowan and Martin's Laugh-In* (NBC, 1968–73), they made three major changes. First, the show's humor was far less controversial than that of *Laugh-In*, relying instead on old jokes and stock situations, including failures in romance, spousal disagreements, and disingenuous stupidity. Second, whereas *Laugh-In*'s characters tended to be "with it" urbanites, the citizens of *Hee Haw*'s Cornfield County were childlike in their shiftless naiveté, looking, dressing, and behaving like characters from *Li'l Abner*. Finally, unlike *Laugh-In*, *Hee Haw* presented a musical showcase. Roy Clark and Buck Owens served as the original hosts, and Clark continued with other cohosts after Owens left the show in the 1985–86 season.

Many *Grand Ole Opry* regulars, including Roy Acuff, Grandpa Jones, Stringbean, Minnie Pearl, Roni Stoneman, and Archie Campbell, were part of the "*Hee Haw* Gang," and each week the show featured leading country music artists such as George Jones and Loretta Lynn. Although CBS cancelled *Hee Haw* in 1971 as part of its purge of "rural" shows (including *The Beverly Hillbillies*, *Green Acres*, and *Petticoat Junction*), it enjoyed great success in syndication of original programming until the 1991–92 season. At that time, the producers' attempt to give the show a more contemporary feel (mainly by getting rid of older cast members in hopes of attracting younger viewers) failed. The last year of syndication, *Hee Haw Silver*, offered clips from the many past seasons but never regained *Hee Haw*'s loyal core audience.

Hee Haw depicted a culture often associated in the media with Appalachia, featuring skits that both celebrated "country" virtues and presented as comical some of the worst stereotypes of Appalachian life. The show frequently showed characters as slovenly drunks comfortable in their poverty, students delighting in their classmates' failures, and bumpkins reacting to "cornfield" one-liners. One longtime cast member, Alvin "Junior" Samples, could scarcely read and apparently could not understand some of the sketches in which he appeared. Nonetheless, the show's editors regularly highlighted his good-natured embarrassment. Costumes and sets looked as if they had been freely adapted from the Dogpatch template: all buildings were dilapidated and most costumes disheveled, with the women's garb patched strategically to emphasize sex appeal. The programs offered pure "corn," and performers knowingly subverted the stereotypes by presenting those stereotypes as the true butts of the jokes.

Yet *Hee Haw* also conveyed an innocence that appealed to many devoted fans. It was one of the few nationally syndicated programs that featured the pioneering traditionalists of country music, the cast of the *Grand Ole Opry*. Despite the revealing women's costumes, romance on the show never went beyond chaste kissing. Gospel performances became a regular feature. Producers kept a number of cast members long after they had lost their marketability to more mainstream audiences, a policy that helped preserve the show's popularity with its core audience almost until the end of its run. The program compensated for its lack of savvy with good-natured comfort, presenting characters and performers who personified a strong community grounded in faith, neighborliness, and a love of music.

See also: COUNTRY MUSIC COMEDY (HUMOR); SECTION OVERVIEW (HUMOR); TELEVISION DEPICTIONS OF THE REGION.

—Thomas Alan Holmes, *East Tennessee State University*

Henning, Paul

(1911–2005) Television writer and producer.

Successful television producer and creator of the highly popular situation comedy *The Beverly Hillbillies* (CBS, 1962–71), Paul Henning played a leading role in both exploiting and transforming the mass-media "hillbilly" stereotype.

Although many viewers associated *The Beverly Hillbillies* with Appalachia, Henning's characters were originally inspired by Ozark folk he had met in his youth in Missouri and characterizations by professional Arkansas yokel Bob Burns. Denounced by critics as embarrassingly lowbrow and by some Appalachians as a demeaning form of cultural exploitation, *The Beverly Hillbillies* was nonetheless wildly popular with audiences, becoming the highest-rated show of 1962 and 1963 and never falling from the top twenty programs until 1971, its final year. The show's enormous success stemmed largely from Henning's ability to redefine *hillbilly* from a word connoting filth and debasement to one that stood for backward yet clean and stalwart white pioneers in a constant battle with a debilitating modern "progress." Although Henning would go on to achieve great ratings success in the mid-1960s with *Petticoat Junction* (1963–70) and *Green Acres* (1965–71), two other countrified CBS sitcoms (neither based on Appalachian settings or characters), the network's 1970 decision to eliminate all rural-tinged programming marked the end of his television career (though his programs would long live on in syndication). Whether lambasted as an offensive caricaturist or praised as the upholder of traditional values in a time of social turmoil, Henning more fully captured the ambiguities inherent in the hillbilly/mountaineer stereotype than any other mass-media producer. He died March 25, 2005.

See also: *BEVERLY HILLBILLIES, THE;* NATIONAL POLITICS AND THE MEDIA IN THE 1960S; TELEVISION DEPICTIONS OF THE REGION.

—Anthony Harkins, *Western Kentucky University*

Hillbillyland

J. W. Williamson's *Hillbillyland: What the Movies Did to the Mountains and What the Mountains Did to the Movies*, published by the University of North Carolina Press in 1995, is the seminal book on hillbilly images in popular American film. Williamson surveys more than eight hundred movies to examine the pervasiveness of the hillbilly in his various guises as comic fool, frontier hero, social bandit, good old boy, monstrous deviant, and little boy-man, as well as his feminine equivalents, or what Williamson calls hillbilly gals. His research draws on films from the silent era such as *Stark Love* and *Tol'able David*, Appalachian classics such as *Thunder Road* and *Deliverance*, and films often not associated with the region such as *Medium Cool* and *Raising Arizona*. Williamson, professor emeritus at Appalachian State University in Boone, North Carolina, and founding editor of the *Appalachian Journal*, argues that the hillbilly stereotype provokes ambiguous responses in American life. These responses range from admiration for the hillbilly's flaunting of social propriety or reassurance that one's social and economic standing are far better than the hillbilly's to terror at the hillbilly's dark undercurrents of lust and violence. Extending the hillbilly metaphor, Williamson sees the hillbilly type on the rough edges of many parts of American society and points to examples from other cultures around the world. Some critics suggest Williamson claims too much reach for the hillbilly image, but there is consistent agreement that *Hillbillyland* is a provocative, well-documented work.

See also: *APPALACHIAN JOURNAL;* FEATURE FILMS; SECTION OVERVIEW.

—Jean Haskell, *East Tennessee State University*

Home and Garden Television (HGTV)

Home and Garden Television (HGTV), headquartered in Knoxville, Tennessee, offers programming about home and garden topics in five categories: gardening and landscaping; building and remodeling; crafts and hobbies; interior decorating and design; and lifestyle and special interest.

Ken Lowe, founder and first president, conceived the idea for the network in 1992 while working as a broadcast executive for Scripps Howard in Cincinnati. He chose Knoxville for the network's headquarters because he considered the city conducive to home ownership and supportive of family life, two qualities that reflected HGTV's mission.

HGTV went on the air on December 30, 1994, with 6.5 million homes in forty-four markets. In 1999 the network opened a $12-million facility, making it one of the most technically advanced cable networks. By December 2001, viewers from 80 million homes in the United States and twenty-six countries around the world could watch HGTV. Programming features tips from home builders, remodelers, decorators, interior designers, gardeners, and craft experts. Related events, such as the Tournament of Roses Parade and the Epcot International Flower and Garden Festival, are covered live. DIY (Do It Yourself) Network, which provides step-by-step instructions and demonstration tips on the air and on-line, was added in 1999.

See also: KNOXVILLE, TENNESSEE (URBAN APPALACHIAN EXPERIENCE).

—Clara Hasbrouck, *East Tennessee State University*

Invention of Appalachia, The

The Invention of Appalachia, written by cultural anthropologist Allen W. Batteau and published in 1990 by University of Arizona Press, explores myths and misconceptions relating to the southern Appalachians. An important work about the history of Appalachian images and stereotypes, the book not only attempts to debunk misconceptions but also examines the idea that politicians, journalists, and other opinion makers created and perpetrated images of Appalachia for agendas often more national than regional. Batteau claims that changes in America's view of the region had more to do with changes on the national level than with changes in Appalachia and that such a view was used for specific political purposes without regard for the needs and concerns of the residents.

Based on his field research in eastern Kentucky, Batteau's book attempts to separate authentic Appalachian life and culture from invention. He uses a Marxist analysis of socioeconomic change in presenting a theory that Appalachian image making is an archetypal and symbolic process. This process is traced from the earliest travelers' accounts of the region through local color writers, early anthropologists, and nineteenth-century apostles and critics of industrialism to the poverty warriors of the 1960s. Batteau argues that America is a "nation of Nature," with Appalachia its most natural, and therefore most American, part. This symbolic analysis intersects with an economic analysis of the destruction of nature (human and other) under capitalism.

Although *The Invention of Appalachia* has been criticized as a quasi-colonial approach to the region for not taking into account Appalachia's imagination of itself, it is regarded by many as an original perspective integrating a range of disciplines.

See also: DEPRESSION AND THE NEW DEAL; NATIONAL POLITICS AND THE MEDIA IN THE 1960S; SECTION OVERVIEW (IMAGES AND ICONS).

—Rodger Cunningham, *Alice Lloyd College*

Journal of Appalachian Studies

Issued semiannually, the *Journal of Appalachian Studies* is a refereed journal publishing academic research in the field of Appalachian studies and is an official publication of the Appalachian Studies Association. Authors appearing in the journal generally research their articles for presentation at the annual conference of the Appalachian Studies Association, although scholarship that has not been a part of the conference may also be published. Besides academic research articles, reviews of important writing pertaining to Appalachia—fiction, nonfiction, and poetry—are included in the journal. Film and video are also reviewed. The journal specializes in the humanities, including history, sociology, geography, music, literature, and cultural studies. A board of editors drawn from colleges and universities throughout the region and an international board of advisors support the journal's editor and staff.

The Appalachian Studies Association, which began in 1977, is an organization of interdisciplinary academic and nonacademic scholars, educators, activists, museum personnel, archivists, students, and others who specialize in various aspects of research for the purpose of advancing communication within the Appalachian region and between the region and the rest of the world. The *Journal of Appalachian Studies* was preceded in the organization by the publications *Proceedings* and *Journal of the Appalachian Studies Association.* The change in name indicates the growth in the field of research involving Appalachia and highlights a switch in orientation for the journal from an internal organ focused on the association to a journal participating in the larger field of regional academic studies. The *Journal of Appalachian Studies* is published by West Virginia University's Regional Research Institute with support from Marshall University in Huntington, West Virginia.

See also: APPALACHIAN CENTERS AND INSTITUTES (CULTURAL INSTITUTIONS); *APPALACHIAN HERITAGE; APPALACHIAN JOURNAL.*

—Stevan Jackson, *Radford University*

Journey of August King, The

The Journey of August King, released in 1995, is a film based on a novel of the same name by Appalachian writer John

Ehle, who also wrote the movie's screenplay. Directed by John Duigan and coproduced by Nick Wechsler and Sam Waterston, who also portrays a landowner in the movie, the film tells the story of a young man in 1815 and the trials, tribulations, and personal conflicts that build moral strength in the time of slavery. Narrated by poet Maya Angelou, the film is set in the mountains of western North Carolina.

August King, portrayed by Jason Patric, is a widower who befriends a runaway slave girl named Annalees Williamsburg, played by Thandie Newton, whom King meets while traveling home from town. She and another slave have escaped from the estate of Olaf Singletary, who is the area's richest man. Being a man of high principles, King risks great danger in helping the runaway hide from Singletary, who is played by Larry Drake. His is both a moral and a monetary decision, for five acres of land and a horse are being offered for Annalees's return. In spite of his best efforts in hiding her, word leaks out that King is indeed harboring the girl. When Singletary captures the other runaway slave, King witnesses the landowner brutally murdering him. King loses virtually all of his material possessions and nearly his life but retains his moral principles.

See also: EHLE, JOHN (LITERATURE); SLAVERY AND ABOLITION (GOVERNMENT).

—Stevan Jackson, *Radford University*

KDKA

See Radio Broadcasting

Lair, John

(1894–1985) Pioneer music broadcaster, music collector, and community historian.

John Lee Lair was an expert on Appalachian ballads and singers and an accomplished radio producer for the *National Barn Dance* on WLS Chicago during the 1930s and later his own *Renfro Valley Barn Dance*. He is credited with discovering musical talents such as Lulu Belle Wiseman, Red Foley, and Lily May Ledford, all of whom were featured in his shows.

Born and reared in Rockcastle County, Kentucky, Lair attended a one-room school before going on to finish high school in the county seat of Mount Vernon. He served in the Army Special Services Division during World War I, where he gained experience writing for the army's *Atta Boy* show produced in collaboration with the Ziegfeld Follies. During this time, his poem "If I Could Jest Go Home Once More" gained Lair national attention.

Following the war, Lair worked at several jobs, including as a schoolteacher and small-town newspaper editor. He eventually became a claims adjuster for an insurance company, which sent him to Chicago in the late 1920s, where he became interested in radio. In 1930 Lair found work with WLS as a producer, music librarian, announcer, and performer on the *National Barn Dance*. During these years, he began to research the real-life stories and events on which many old songs were based and to build a collection of sheet music. Lair also decided to create his own radio barn dance program staged in an actual barn near his Kentucky birthplace in Renfro Valley.

In 1937 Lair left Chicago and went to work for WLW in Cincinnati, where he began producing the *Renfro Valley Barn Dance*. In 1939 his country music tourist complex opened with a barnlike auditorium, the one-room schoolhouse of his childhood, and a restored water-driven gristmill. A rustic restaurant, gift shop, U.S. Post Office, and overnight cabins completed the attraction. Lair later added a pioneer museum, country store, and a monthly newspaper, the *Renfro Valley Bugle*, which featured news of his radio programs and Rockcastle County history.

The *Renfro Valley Barn Dance* ceased live national broadcasting in the 1950s due to a lack of sponsorship, though the stage shows continue to draw crowds in the twenty-first century. Sunday mornings, *The Gatherin'* is still broadcast nationwide via recorded versions. After Lair's death in 1985, his Renfro Valley holdings were sold to a group of investors who updated the facilities and in July 2000 donated them to a nonprofit group that has developed the Kentucky Music Hall of Fame and Museum in Renfro Valley.

See also: RADIO BROADCASTING; *RENFRO VALLEY BARN DANCE*.

—Sändra Henson, *East Tennessee State University*, and Kristine M. McCusker, *Middle Tennessee State University*

Last of the Mohicans, The

Since its publication in 1826, James Fenimore Cooper's novel *The Last of the Mohicans* has fascinated readers, providing inspiration for serials and television series as well as major motion pictures. One memorable film adaptation, with a screenplay by Philip Dunne, was produced in 1936 and starred actor Randolph Scott. However, a 1992 rendition (directed by Michael Mann from a screenplay by Mann and Christopher Crowe based on Dunne's 1936 version) is considered the most successful. Although Cooper's tale takes place in upstate New York, Mann shot his film almost entirely in the five-county area surrounding Asheville, North Carolina, including the Biltmore Estate and Chimney Rock Park. The cinematography of its outdoor sequences was widely acclaimed and generated a positive impact on the state's tourism and film industries. Ten years after the release of *The Last of the Mohicans*, the Asheville area continued to draw tourists who wanted to see where the film was made and couples wanting to have their marriage ceremonies on a stone bridge featured in one scene.

In the novel, Cooper explicitly pairs his two genteel European characters, Duncan Heyward and Alice Munro, and he also insinuates a then-scandalous affinity between two characters who share ancestry other than European: a Native American, Uncas, heir to the Mohican chiefdom, and Cora Munro, a white woman whose blood is adulterated by a distant connection to African slaves. Meanwhile, the noble Hawkeye is left free of interpersonal entanglement. Cooper appears to be suggesting that a close relationship to the wilderness—expressed through a combination of woodcraft and racial "purity"—precludes human relationships and the connection to civilization that those relationships entail.

Mann's 1992 film retains Cooper's interest in colonial warfare; his representation of the "dual nature" of the Native American; his manipulation of tribal politics for plot purposes; and his fascination with Yankee chivalry, rugged individualism, and romantic rusticity. However, Mann radically realigns most of Cooper's character relationships, bringing the film into line with the modern "romantic adventure" genre and, in the process, reconceptualizing Cooper's original idea of the Appalachian wilderness as it relates to colonial civilization. Mann abruptly reconciles the disparity between civilization and the wilderness by fashioning parallel relationships between characters closely associated with the wilderness and those directly linked to the civilization of the European colonies.

The noble Uncas is matched in the film with Alice Munro, the former dying in heroic battle and the latter taking her own life in an act of romantic tragedy. More interestingly, a love affair between Hawkeye and Cora Munro —whose blood is purified by Mann of any non-European elements—occupies the center of the plot and is presumably meant to extend beyond the close of the film itself. While this change was certainly made, at least in part, to combine the adventure plot with the romantic, it also serves to tame, through love, the very rusticity that had characterized Hawkeye as a romantic hero in Cooper's original sense. As a result, the wild American interior is literally domesticated in a personal, conjugal sense, as Hawkeye and Cora persevere as a couple.

See also: COOPER, JAMES FENIMORE (LITERATURE); FEATURE FILMS.

—John F. Keener, *Lees-McRae College*

Louise K. Barnett, *The Ignoble Savage: American Literary Racism, 1790–1890* (1975); Leslie Fiedler, *Love and Death in the American Novel* (1960); Stephanie Wardrop, "Last of the Red Hot Mohicans: Miscegenation in the Popular American Romance," *MELUS* (Summer 1997).

Lexington Herald-Leader

One of the major newspaper voices of central and eastern Kentucky, the *Lexington Herald-Leader* began in 1870 as the *Lexington Herald.* In 1888 the rival *Lexington Leader* was established. The national newspaper publishing company Knight Ridder bought both papers in 1973 and merged them in 1983. The *Lexington Herald-Leader* serves seventy-five counties in central and eastern Kentucky, has a daily circulation of more than 120,500 and a Sunday circulation in excess of 154,500, and employs more than 500 people, including staffers, in nine bureaus in Kentucky (Frankfort, Georgetown, Richmond, Hazard, Paintsville, Somerset, Nicholasville, and Morehead) and Washington, D.C. It has gained a national reputation for reporting excellence and was voted Newspaper of the Year by the Kentucky Press Association and the Kentucky News Photographers Association in 2000 and 2002. The *Herald-Leader* has won the Pulitzer Prize three times and been a finalist six other times since 1986.

In the mid-1980s, the newspaper dramatically expanded its coverage of the coalfields region and opened bureaus in three eastern Kentucky counties. As its reports from the mountains and features on Appalachian county governments and local school systems became more prominent, its circulation in eastern Kentucky grew and eventually surpassed that of its major competitor, the *Louisville Courier-Journal.* In addition to its consistent news coverage of the Appalachian region, the *Lexington Herald-Leader* also features a regular editorial forum in each Sunday edition called "Appalachian Voices," which offers residents opportunities to express opinions and concerns about issues of special concern in the mountains.

See also: *LOUISVILLE COURIER-JOURNAL*; NATIONAL NEWSPAPER COVERAGE; NEWSPAPERS.

—Marianne Worthington, *Cumberland College*

Li'l Abner

First published in 1934, *Li'l Abner* was a popular comic strip by Al Capp (born Alfred Gerald Caplin, 1909–1979) that during the twentieth century helped establish images of Appalachia and the hillbilly in influential ways. In the early years of the strip, Capp presented mountaineer characters as symbols of a simple yet pure alternative to the city, a place of false progress and fads where all—rich and poor, men and women, old and young—were unhappy with themselves and their world. By the postwar years, however, Capp's characters had come to solidify the popular notion that hillbillies and Appalachians were one and the same. *Li'l Abner* significantly reinforced the popular opinion that mountain people were impoverished, violent, and ignorant, but the strip also depicted the Yokum family as possessed of a native intelligence, honorable to a fault, and exhibiting a country charm.

Capp's aim was to combine the tall-tale grotesque of literary characters Sut Lovingood and Davy Crockett with the righteous indignation of political cartoonists such as

Thomas Nast. His approach was so successful that he spawned an industry. His strip ran for more than forty years and drew 60 million readers per day. It became the basis for several films and a musical performed on Broadway and in countless high school, college, and repertory theaters since 1956. It was also the inspiration for an Ozark theme park and innumerable collectables and other types of memorabilia. *Li'l Abner* graced the cover of *Life*, *Time*, and *Newsweek* magazines and launched Sadie Hawkins Day. *Li'l Abner*'s popularity easily surpassed the hillbilly drawings of Billy DeBeck's (and later Fred Lasswell's) syndicated newspaper comic strip *Barney Google and Snuffy Smith* and Paul Webb's *Esquire* cartoon, *The Mountain Boys*. Abner (depicted at age nineteen and six feet, three inches) became so American that his face even appeared as bomber nose art during World War II, as did lesser *Li'l Abner* characters such as Hairless Joe and Wolf Gal. *Li'l Abner* also helped perpetuate uncomplimentary stereotypes that equated the southeastern mountains with poverty and arrested social and mental development.

The strip included a lively and incorruptible troupe of country folks who outsmarted and out-shucked the city slicker, the booster, the shyster, and the snake-oil salesman. Capp claimed that he took his stories and situations from the daily headlines, not his imagination.

Li'l Abner, Daisy Mae, Mammy and Pappy Yokum, the Shmoos, the Kigmys, Marryin' Sam, Appasionita von Climax, Available Jones, Joe Bfstplk, Tobacco Rhoda, Evil-Eye Fleegle, Nightmare Alice, and Moonbeam McSwine paraded and circulated through a world of the highfalutin and highbrow, of snobbery and chicanery, always tolerant and good-natured but never victims, always knowing the real world around them. *Dogpatch* entered the national vocabulary alongside terms such as Damon Runyon's *monkey business* and H. L. Mencken's *boobus americanus*. Capp experimented with words and script in a new approach to cartooning, featuring outlandish drawings of everyone except Li'l Abner and Daisy Mae. Wild flourishes of dialogue embellished his language in ways that are comparable to only one other cartoon before or since—Walt Kelly's *Pogo*.

Over the years, Abner evolved from a cute country bumpkin into a backward hillbilly. Mammy Yokum came to represent all mothers—hardworking, smart, always there, possessed with goodness, and ready with a meal, while Pappy was shiftless. Both personas were heavily based on Capp's own parents. Despite the explosive growth of urban America in the mid-twentieth century, *Li'l Abner*'s newspaper circulation continued to grow, peaking at 90 million in 1970.

See also: COMIC STRIPS; *HILLBILLYLAND;* SNUFFY SMITH.

—Charles F. Moore, *East Tennessee State University*

Edwin T. Arnold, "Al, Abner, and Appalachia," *Appalachian Journal* (Spring 1990); Arthur Asa Berger, *Li'l Abner: A Study in American Satire* (1970); M. Thomas Inge, "Al Capp's South: Appalachian Humor in *Li'l Abner,*" *Studies in American Humor* (2001).

Louisville Courier-Journal

Established in 1868, the *Louisville Courier-Journal* became a powerful influence on perceptions of Appalachia in the late nineteenth and early twentieth centuries when its reportage attracted the interest of far-flung writers and publications. In 1918 the newspaper was purchased by Robert Worth Bingham, a former Louisville mayor and former Jefferson County circuit court judge. It remained in the Bingham family until 1986, when it was sold to the Gannett Company, along with the *Louisville Times* and other Bingham properties for more than $300 million. The judge's son, Barry Bingham Sr., took the reins of the *Courier-Journal* in 1937 and held various titles, including publisher, editor, president, and chairman of the board, until his death in 1988. Barry Bingham Jr. became publisher in 1971 and remained until bitter and widely publicized family discord led to the sale of all Bingham media properties.

From its early days, the *Courier-Journal* maintained a deep interest in Appalachian issues. For decades it operated two news bureaus in eastern Kentucky. Its editorial page supported environmental protection, campaigned against the broad form deed, and called for sweeping educational reform in the 1980s. The Bingham family, meanwhile, maintained close personal ties with Appalachian reformers such as lawyer-author Harry Caudill and *Mountain Eagle* publisher Tom Gish of Whitesburg. After the newspaper's sale, Mary Caperton Bingham, the widow of Barry Sr., maintained a keen philanthropic interest in Appalachia.

The Bingham family's effective monopoly of Louisville's mass media and its prominent identification with the Democratic Party made the *Courier-Journal* a subject of controversy, but the paper maintained a strong independent streak. Its editorial page occasionally endorsed candidates with whom it philosophically disagreed if it found them especially competent.

The strength of its news and editorials and its technical innovation brought the *Courier-Journal* wide professional admiration. John Gunther, in *Inside U.S.A.*, called it "one of the best newspapers in the country." *Time* magazine listed it among the ten best, and a Media Research Institute Survey of editors, publishers, and journalism professors ranked it among the top fifteen.

In 1967 the *Courier-Journal* won a Pulitzer Prize for its coverage of strip mining and its successful crusade for stronger controls of the industry in Kentucky. With the award came a medal and the Pulitzer selection committee's special citation for "meritorious public service," noting the newspaper's role in Kentucky's passage of landmark strip-mining legislation the previous year. Two years later, in 1969, *Courier-Journal* reporter John Fetterman won the prize for feature writing. His winning entry, the *Courier-Journal*'s sixth Pulitzer honor, recounted the mountain homecoming, funeral, and burial of Private First Class James Thurman "Little Duck" Gibson, a Knott County soldier killed in Vietnam.

Although the Bingham name looms largest in the *Courier-Journal*'s history, other legendary names are also part of its lore. The first of the paper's total of nine Pulitzer Prizes was awarded to the famed editor Henry Watterson in 1918 for his editorials on World War I. For a quarter of a century, Mark Ethridge, one of the country's most renowned newspaper managers, operated as a virtual partner with Bingham Sr. Arthur Krock later won four Pulitzer Prizes and served as Washington correspondent and editor of the *Courier-Journal* before beginning his long career as Washington correspondent and columnist for the *New York Times*.

See also: *LEXINGTON HERALD-LEADER;* NATIONAL NEWSPAPER COVERAGE; NEWSPAPERS.

—Rudy Abramson, *Reston, Virginia*

Arthur Krock, *Memoirs: Sixty Years on the Firing Line* (1968); Susan E. Tifft and Alex S. Jones, *The Patriarch: The Rise and Fall of the Bingham Dynasty* (1991); Joseph Frazier Wall, *Henry Watterson: Reconstructed Rebel* (1956).

Matewan

John Sayles's critically acclaimed feature film *Matewan* (1987) is loosely based on the events surrounding the May 19, 1920, gun battle at Matewan, West Virginia. The clash between union coal miners and the "gun thugs" of the Baldwin-Felts Detective Agency hired by the Stone Mountain Coal Company left ten men dead and serves as the climax of the film. Sayles learned of the mine wars as a young man while hitchhiking through the coalfields of southern West Virginia. Filmed in Thurmond, *Matewan* conveys the look and feel of 1920s-era southern West Virginia through the stunningly beautiful, Oscar-nominated work of cinematographer Haskell Wexler.

Historical inaccuracies abound in the screenplay, which condenses a year of events into a single week. Most notable of these inaccuracies is the fictional protagonist Joe Kenehan (played by Chris Cooper), a union organizer who arrives in Matewan at the film's onset and leads the locals in their struggle against the coal company. Despite this purely fictional character's central role in Sayles's narrative, the film is noteworthy for its sensitive portrayal of mountain people as multidimensional with regards to both class and ethnicity. Sympathetic to the United Mine Workers of America, the film sparked a renewed interest in the West Virginia mine wars, validated the region's labor history, and was a catalyst for the town of Matewan's recognition as a national historic landmark.

See also: MATEWAN, WEST VIRGINIA (TOURISM); MATEWAN MASSACRE (LABOR); UNITED MINE WORKERS OF AMERICA (LABOR).

—David Reynolds, *Appalshop*

Mine Wars and the Twentieth-Century Media

One of the more enduring sets of images associated with Appalachia is that of coal-mine violence, beginning with accounts of the Paint Creek and Cabin Creek strikes of 1912–13 and most recently found in Barbara Kopple's 1976 Academy Award–winning documentary *Harlan County, USA*. In all of these accounts, journalists, filmmakers, and artists grapple with discordant images of industrial machinery and conflict invading the bucolic preserve of Appalachia. Although there was industrial violence in the Pennsylvania coalfields during earlier periods, most of the journalistic accounts of the twentieth century focused on Kentucky and West Virginia.

When coal mining came to Appalachia, whether in the New River Valley in southern West Virginia, along the Kanawha River in central West Virginia, or in eastern Kentucky, a sufficient number of new jobs provided income and ensured that there were few expressions of discontent by the miners. Only as the coalfields became overexploited by the turn of the century, resulting in overproduction, cuts in wages, and increasingly severe industrial discipline, did miners begin to protest their working and living conditions.

Three major periods of mining violence mark the history of Kentucky and West Virginia in the first half of the twentieth century. Their echoes reverberated in the postwar era. The first period centered on the Paint Creek–Cabin Creek strike of 1912–13; the second climaxed with the Battle of Blair Mountain in 1921; and the third involved the battles of "Bloody Harlan" throughout the 1930s.

Three different sets of images are associated with these three periods—those of rural social problems during the Progressive era, of industrial oppression and armed revolt after World War I, and of the national disgrace of Harlan County, Kentucky, in the 1930s. The amount of press attention in New York was inversely proportional to the regional significance of the events. The Paint Creek strike in West Virginia was arguably the most momentous in that it led to the beginnings of class consciousness within the Appalachian mountain region, but the *New York Times* initially paid little attention. Only in 1913, when the U.S. Senate investigated the shooting up of a miners' camp by an armored train (the "Bull Moose Special," manned by coal-company-financed gunmen), did the *Times* begin to take notice. Progressive publications such as the *Survey* and *Literary Digest* gave the events greater coverage, although more as examples of local corruption, reflecting their agenda of local government reform.

After the First World War, with mountaineer miners increasingly aware of their national importance, labor unrest resumed. The national press responded in two ways. Progressive publications called for civic reform and the elimination of government corruption. The business press called for improved living conditions among the working class. In the industry magazine *Coal Age*, there was a monthly section entitled "Sociological Department: For the Betterment of Living Conditions in Mining Communities." Other social workers called for education to correct the "lack of ambitions and desires" among the miners.

When miners in Logan and Mingo Counties in West Virginia began an armed revolt against local authorities that culminated at Blair Mountain, urban newspapers took notice, although generally framing the events in the context of moonshining and feuding rather than as an industrial dispute. A typical *New York Times* editorial (May 24, 1921) wryly smiled at the "Highlander Ethics" behind the shooting and killing. The revolt was thus treated with amusement and disdain by mainstream publications and only received serious attention when federal troops confronted more than ten thousand miners marching on Blair Mountain. Winthrop Lane's article in the *Survey* was a rare exception that took greater cognizance of the historical issues involved.

The pattern of coal-miner resistance met by company repression was repeated again in the 1930s in Harlan County. By this time, most coal operators had reluctantly accepted the reality of unionization. Under the pressure of the New Deal, most had signed agreements with the United Mine Workers of America. The most significant holdouts were the Harlan County operators. In contrast to most other counties of Kentucky and the southern Appalachians, Harlan County saw a prolonged struggle involving pickets, evictions, tent colonies, dynamiting, and intimidation of miners by private constabularies through the decade. These events were exploited by multiple outside groups, including the Communist Party, first to score ideological points and later as a stalking horse for other industrial confrontations.

There were two major differences between the press coverage of 1921 (the year of the Blair Mountain protest) and that of 1931 (the beginnings of the Harlan County strike). First, the depression had helped discredit the business class. Second, new media (primarily radio, but also movies and newsreels) lent immediacy to what had previously seemed distant events. Escalating violence in Harlan County in 1931 led to the arrival of the Communist-affiliated National Miners Union. Although their actions resulted in little improvement in the miners' lives, they did help generate publicity in progressive New York circles. Publications focusing on the justice of the miners' cause, most notably *Harlan Miners Speak: Report on Terrorism in the Kentucky Coal Fields*, published by the National Committee for the Defense of Political Prisoners (a Communist auxiliary chaired by Theodore Dreiser) in 1932, arrayed the heroic miners against the usual corporate suspects with names such as Ford, Mellon, and Insull. These writings made Harlan County a byword for industrial oppression just at the time that industrial oppression in its rawer forms was exiting the national stage.

After the visit of the Dreiser Committee, descriptions of industrial strife and poverty in Harlan County were a staple item in major newspapers and newsmagazines, and numerous students, journalists, unionists, Quakers, and others made pilgrimages to Harlan County—the font of authentic radicalism. Despite widespread opposition, the Harlan County mine operators held out against unionization throughout the 1930s and were finally brought to heel in 1938 by the combined weight of the Senate Civil Liberties Committee, the Federal Bureau of Investigation, and the National Labor Relations Board. The Senate hearings provided the media additional opportunities to present colorful accounts of "tall, muscular, hip-swinging deputy sheriffs in broad brimmed black hats" and "scrawny miners in patches" who testified in the Senate hearing room. The stories of a union "crushed with dynamite, beatings, and bullets by 'gun thugs'" and of night rides, private constabularies, and car bombings made for great copy in ten articles in the *New York Times* from April 16 to May 7, 1937.

The national political pressure, however, was designed less to improve conditions in Harlan County than to test the instruments of federal regulatory power prior to their use on more menacing targets such as Republic Steel and Ford Motor Company. Newspaper publicity of Harlan County violence was essential to this end.

If Paint Creek marked the beginnings of class consciousness and Blair Mountain was genuine class warfare, then the events of Harlan County are best characterized as a media event. As a historical phenomenon, class warfare is threatening. As a media event, however, class warfare can be safely entertaining, particularly if the villains belong to a class that is already on its way out. If the mine owners of Harlan County, men cut from the same rough homespun as Henry Ford, found themselves beaten, then publicizing the fact could help reinforce the legitimate capitalist system.

The legacy of the images of coalfield violence, like the images themselves, has multiple layers. The most superficial layer is the establishment of eastern Kentucky and southern West Virginia as the destination of radical pilgrimages, events that were repeated by journalists, students, and filmmakers in the 1960s and 1970s. In a more significant stratum is the tangible contribution of the United Mine Workers to the national union movement in the United States. The events of Logan and Mingo Counties were amply reported in the labor press, and the leaders of the United Mine Workers played key roles in organizing both the United Automobile Workers and the Congress of Industrial Organizations.

See also: COAL IMAGES (IMAGES AND ICONS); *HARLAN COUNTY, USA*; *MOLLY MAGUIRES, THE*.

—Allen W. Batteau, *Wayne State University*

David Alan Corbin, *Life, Work, and Rebellion in the Coal Fields: The Southern West Virginia Miners, 1880–1922* (1981); John W. Hevener, *Which Side Are You On? The Harlan County Coal Miners, 1931–39* (1978); Mary Harris Jones, *The Autobiography of Mother Jones* (1925).

Mitchum, Robert

(1917–1997) Actor, writer, and producer.

Robert Mitchum appeared in more than one hundred films from 1942 until his death from lung cancer in 1997. In some of his best-remembered appearances, Mitchum played characters from a southern mountain background. Though not particularly noted for their accuracy or sensitivity of portrayal, his roles helped bring southern Appalachian identity into mainstream American consciousness. Most popular among these movies was *Thunder Road*, a low-budget film Mitchum wrote, produced, and starred in, playing a Kentucky bootlegger.

Mitchum was born August 6, 1917, in Bridgeport, Connecticut, and was reared by his mother and stepfather after he lost his biological father at age two. Rebellious and prone to wandering at an early age, he escaped from a Georgia chain gang at age fourteen after being arrested for vagrancy. Mitchum worked a number of odd jobs before beginning his acting career in 1942 at the Long Beach Theater Guild. His breakthrough came in 1945 with an Oscar nomination for best-supporting actor for *The Story of G.I. Joe*. A 1948 arrest for marijuana possession fueled his bad-boy image and seemingly did little harm to his film career.

Mitchum was cast as an eccentric southerner in three of his best-known movies. His outsider reputation and laid-back style served him well in *Cape Fear* (1962), *The Night of the Hunter* (screenplay by James Agee, 1955), and *Thunder Road* (1958). His willingness to take any part is evidenced in these three films: a mainstream horror flick, an art film, and a drive-in rock 'n' roll movie. He was also a staple of the film noir, western, and war movie genres. Mitchum's sleepy eyes and regular-guy image made him a popular film star with both men and women but divided critics, who either saw Mitchum as one of the best or worst actors of his day.

See also: *THUNDER ROAD*.

—Brandon Story, *King College*

Molly Maguires, The

The Molly Maguires is a film based on historical accounts of mine workers in Pennsylvania in 1876 and their struggle to improve working conditions. The film, directed and produced by Martin Ritt *(Norma Rae)* and written by Walter Bernstein, stars Sean Connery and Richard Harris as Irish-born immigrants. The musical score by Henry Mancini incorporates traditional Irish folk songs.

Filmed in 1968 at a coal mine in Beckley, West Virginia, and released in 1970, the film chronicles the actions of James McParlan (Harris), a real-life detective for the Pinkerton Detective Agency, who is hired by mine owners to infiltrate an illegal Irish American secret society known as the Molly Maguires and bring them to justice for the deaths of mine officials and destruction of mine property. In the mid-1800s, the Molly Maguires used classic terrorist tactics to try to win better working conditions for the oppressed miners.

McParlan befriends Molly Maguire leader Jack Kehoe (Connery). While working undercover, McParlan experiences firsthand the horrendous working conditions in the mines and the prejudiced treatment of Irish immigrants by mine owners, thus dividing his loyalty to his job and his newly found friends and countrymen. The depiction of working conditions in coal mines of the 1870s won the movie an Oscar nomination for best art and set direction. Myth and fiction are blended in this film through the depiction of the men as labor martyrs and the romanticization of terrorist tactics used by the Molly Maguires. The movie provides a view of early labor-management relations, foreshadowing the tensions of later coalfield mine wars.

See also: *HARLAN COUNTY, USA*; MOLLY MAGUIRES (LABOR).

—Stevan Jackson, *Radford University*

Mountain Eagle

Published in Whitesburg, Kentucky, since 1907, the *Mountain Eagle* achieved regional and national prominence after it was purchased by Tom and Pat Gish, who took over in 1957 and continued to manage it into the twenty-first century. Until the Gishes' arrival, the paper had been an unremarkable small-town weekly, filling its news columns with routine fare such as church and club news, official announcements, and handouts from the coal industry.

Tom Gish, a native of Letcher County and the son of a coal company superintendent, was the thirty-one-year-old Frankfort bureau chief for the United Press International wire service when he and his wife, Pat, a former reporter for the *Lexington Leader*, paid forty thousand dollars for his hometown paper and moved to Whitesburg. He became editor and publisher, and she served as his general assistant and later managing editor, as well as partner. Years later, they were joined by their sons, Ben and Ray, and a son-in-law, Freddy Oakes, in the business.

Less than a month after the Gishes took ownership, southeastern Kentucky was hit by the worst flooding of the century, and the *Mountain Eagle* demonstrated an aggressive new attitude in news coverage. Soon Tom Gish's powerful editorials became widely read and influential in Whitesburg and Letcher County affairs.

Replacing the paper's previous identity as "a friendly non-partisan weekly newspaper" by announcing "It Screams" on the masthead, the new owners crusaded against inadequate schools, political corruption, and the ravages of strip mining, taking on targets from local office holders and peace officers to coal and steel companies and the Tennessee Valley Authority. In a long October 1960 editorial citing the environmental destruction of strip mining, Gish warned that 90 percent of Letcher County's hillsides would be stripped in a decade. He called for a state law stopping all strip mining in the Kentucky mountains, arguing that an outright ban was the only logical solution.

The demand for such a ban was destined to fail, but the paper's editorials helped bring about tightened state control of surface mining. More important, the *Mountain Eagle*'s reportage and feisty editorials gained the attention of powerful regional newspapers such as the *Louisville Courier-Journal* and eventually the *New York Times* and other national news organizations. Because they helped focus the spotlight on conditions in the mountains, the Gishes, along with writer Harry Caudill, were credited with sharpening the Kennedy administration's interest in Appalachia and contributing to the eventual passage of the 1965 Appalachian Development Act, creating the Appalachian Regional Commission. But while the *Mountain Eagle* advocated federal involvement in the economy of eastern Kentucky and Appalachia, Gish took sharp issue with programs that emerged from Congress and the White House. Editorials blistered execution of the local War on Poverty, even though Pat Gish stepped aside as the *Mountain Eagle*'s managing editor and served for a time as a program official in Letcher County and the *Eagle* was among early advocates of an Appalachian agency patterned after the Tennessee Valley Authority. The Gishes also joined in promoting a plan to market electricity from publicly owned generating plants constructed at the mouth of central Appalachian coal mines. Though they championed federal involvement in economic development, they were early and persistent critics of the Appalachian Regional Commission, arguing that its structure prevented funds from reaching communities where they were most needed.

Editorial crusades for open meetings of public agencies brought the publisher and the *Mountain Eagle* numerous honors, including the John Peter Zenger Award (1974) for support of freedom of the press and the people's right to know. The wide recognition of the Gishes' work followed years of adversity—including social ostracism, advertising boycotts, death threats, and even arson.

In 1974 the offices of the *Mountain Eagle* were torched, but the Gishes continued to publish their paper from their living room. Their first edition after the incident modified the motto on its masthead, declaring, "It Still Screams." After a ten-week investigation, a former Whitesburg policeman was charged in the crime and subsequently convicted of aiding, counseling, or arranging the burning of the offices. Trial witnesses testified that the defendant had promised to pay two teenagers to set fire to newspaper's offices in retaliation for editorials criticizing the police department.

The publishers' community activism extended beyond their newspaper to membership on various boards and committees. Tom Gish served for seven years on the Kentucky School Board during a major reform movement.

In 2002 the Society of Professional Journalists presented Tom and Pat Gish with the Helen Thomas Award for lifetime achievement in recognition of their forty-five-year commitment to respecting readers and holding leaders accountable.

See also: GISH, TOM AND PAT; NEWSPAPERS.

—Rudy Abramson, *Reston, Virginia*

Michael Carlton and Steve Millburg, "Small Towns, Big News," *Southern Living* (October 1994); Dan Chapman, "Muckraking in Coal Country," *Atlanta Journal-Constitution* (February 10, 2002).

Mountain Justice

Mountain Justice, a 1937 Warner Brothers–First National motion picture, is a melodrama based on the famous case of Wise County, Virginia, schoolteacher Edith Maxwell, who became a feminist cause célèbre after her 1935 conviction for murdering her allegedly abusive father. Reflecting the widespread belief that the verdict was unjust, the film put on trial not only the Wise County court system but also Appalachia itself.

A *New York Times* reviewer called *Mountain Justice* "a hillbilly anthology" aimed at the supposed backwardness of Appalachia and the South because it alluded to the most gothic of 1920s and 1930s newspaper accounts about everything from child marriage and lynching to the Ku Klux Klan and the Scopes trial. Grafted onto this dark landscape is the story of nurse Ruth Harkins (an obvious but highly fictionalized stand-in for Maxwell), who tries to bring modern medicine to her isolated mountain community. Her romance with a New York City lawyer reprised what was, by 1937, already a cliché in film and literature: a hillbilly woman's betrayal of her kin for the love of an outsider. Ruth (Josephine Hutchinson) is portrayed as an innocent victim of Appalachian culture who is beaten by her father, eventually convicted of murdering him, and nearly lynched by a mob. Even the film's socially progressive focus on domestic violence is compromised by its dubious subtext that such brutality can only occur in a "backward" place like Appalachia.

Despite its sensational subject, *Mountain Justice* met with little critical success and became an obscure footnote in the illustrious career of its director, Michael Curtiz. Warner Brothers executives decided not to screen it in Virginia to avoid potential lawsuits stemming from its damning portrayal of mountain residents.

See also: FEATURE FILMS; GENDER AND REFORM IN THE PROGRESSIVE ERA (GOVERNMENT); MAXWELL, EDITH (GOVERNMENT).

—Sharon Hatfield, *Athens, Ohio*

Mountain Life and Work

The first issue of *Mountain Life and Work* was published in April 1925 by Berea College in Kentucky. According to Marshall Everett Vaughn, the publication's first editor, the purpose of this quarterly magazine was to alter the public image of Appalachia by changing the thinking of the outside world about the region and its people. At that time, only one-seventh of the population living in the southern mountains earned a living from industries such as coal mining, lumbering, and manufacturing. The rest of the residents were farmers or individuals who made their living by trading with farmers or selling goods to them. The magazine set out to tell the stories of farmers and their battles with nature; teachers dealing with illiteracy and poverty; miners and mine owners making a living amid the dangers of a hazardous occupation as they developed the resources of the mountains; workers in the timber and lumber industry; and unpaid ministers who preached to the people in an attempt to better their lives.

William Hutchins, president of Berea College in 1925, was listed as counselor for the publication. He regarded the magazine as a public relations tool for the college and the region. In the initial issue he expressed the desire that the publication would become an interpreter of the mountains for the region and for the country. The table of contents page noted that it was published "in the interest of fellowship and mutual understanding between the Appalachian Mountains and the rest of the nation." Three years later Hutchins called the magazine a success because he believed the articles had altered the negative image of mountaineers by emphasizing positive aspects of Appalachian life, including the people's independence, family values, traditionalism, and supposed ethnic purity.

Helen Dingman, a member of the sociology department at Berea College, was editor of the magazine when it was taken over by the Conference of Southern Mountain Workers in 1926 and remained editor, also serving as executive secretary of the Conference of Southern Mountain Workers, until 1942.

The quarterly averaged thirty-eight pages an issue and the subscription was one dollar, except for a brief period in the 1940s when it was raised to two dollars. Membership in the Conference of Southern Mountain Workers included a subscription to the magazine, and issues published at the time of meetings were conference proceedings. The magazine generally printed articles on health, agriculture, religion, and education in the region. Fiction, poetry, folktales, and plays by Appalachian writers were featured in many issues, as were book reviews, musical scores, and song lyrics. Noteworthy contributors include Jesse Stuart, James Still, Loyal Jones, and Jim Wayne Miller. The articles were "freely given" according to editorial policy.

The magazine continued to publish until the Council of the Southern Mountains disbanded in 1989. (The organization's name was changed from the Conference of Southern Mountain Workers to the Council of Southern Mountain Workers in 1944 and then finally to the Council of the Southern Mountains in 1954.) The University of Kentucky, along with Berea College and Pine Mountain Settlement School, has begun an effort to digitize this journal, which is available via Kentuckiana Digital Library.

See also: *APPALACHIAN JOURNAL*; BEREA COLLEGE (EDUCATION); SECTION OVERVIEW (IMAGES AND ICONS).

—Clara Hasbrouck, *East Tennessee State University*

Allen W. Batteau, *The Invention of Appalachia* (1990); Catherine C. Mitchell and C. Joan Schnyder, "Public Relations for Appalachia: Berea *Mountain Life and Work*," *Journalism Quarterly* (Winter 1989); Marshall E. Vaughn, "Purpose of This Magazine," *Mountain Life and Work* (April 1925).

Music Broadcasting

Early radio broadcasts helped define and develop distinctly Appalachian genres of music that continued to evolve commercially and artistically throughout most of the twentieth century. Radio provided listeners in and beyond the region relatively inexpensive access to both sacred and secular Appalachian music. Without early broadcasting, it is unlikely that modern genres such as country, bluegrass, and southern gospel would have been permanently woven into the region's cultural tapestry.

Immigrants to the United States brought with them a wealth of music heritages from their homelands. Some of the music that immigrants performed was published, but the vast majority was preserved through oral tradition. The advent of radio updated this oral tradition, distributing music among Appalachian communities. Later, broadcasting developed audiences beyond the social and geographic boundaries of Appalachia.

Radio broadcasting was wed to Appalachia from its inception. The first commercial radio signal in the United States was broadcast from Pittsburgh's KDKA in 1920, and the station's airing of Berg's String Entertainers in 1922 was the earliest broadcast of an Appalachian-style string band. The Country Music Foundation in Nashville credits WSB in Atlanta for promoting what would become early country music. WSB's 1922 broadcast of a performance by Fiddlin' John Carson is generally acknowledged to be the first documented radio performance by a solo country artist. Over the next two years, the station continued to feature many folk musicians from the Atlanta region. Smaller cities quickly followed the programming lead of WSB. For example, both Wheeling and Huntington, West Virginia, began broadcasting regional performers in 1926 on WWVA and WSAZ, respectively, and the early programming starting in 1921 at WNOX in Knoxville, Tennessee, included hillbilly variety shows.

During this period, music of Appalachia that eventually evolved into country, folk, and bluegrass was often categorized by record labels as "hillbilly" music in an attempt to develop a broadcast format that would appeal to the growing number of people in Appalachia who owned radios, and the popularity of country and folk broadcasts developed steadily. In Nashville, George D. Hay created the *WSM Barn Dance* in 1925 and renamed it the *Grand Ole Opry* in 1927. In 1932 NBC began broadcasting its *National Barn Dance* show. As the appeal of the *National Barn Dance* grew, other radio stations quickly imitated the programming format. In the Appalachian region, the *Jamboree* premiered on WWVA in Wheeling in 1933. Similar shows began on WBT in Charlotte, North Carolina; WHAS in Louisville, Kentucky; and WRVA in Richmond, Virginia. In the mid-1930s Tex Ritter was one of the early hosts of WHN's *Barndance* in New York City.

Folk and country musicians discovered that radio provided tremendous exposure and offered benefits beyond wages for radio performances. In the early 1930s, for example, the Callahan Brothers from Asheville, North Carolina, performed on WWNC for four dollars but soon realized that the geographic reach of radio helped them develop a following far beyond their hometown. Because most of their income came from personal appearances, they soon regarded radio as a promotional tool rather than as a primary income source. The Callahan Brothers' insight underscores the enormous influence of radio by the end of the decade. By 1938, 9.4 million rural families owned radios, and radio owners listened to their sets an average of five and a half hours each day. In isolated rural areas, such as large parts of Appalachia, radio was a primary source of communication and cultural transmission within and among regions.

Nonetheless, performers showcased in early music broadcasts in the Appalachian region became victims of broader economic changes. Typical radio broadcasts were quarter-hour segments of entertainment, typically sponsored by a local business. Occasional labor strikes in coal-mining communities hurt local economies, causing local radio sponsorships to be canceled. Because payment of performers was contingent on advertising revenues, many well-known local artists left the region to find cities with better opportunities. The Great Depression had a similar but more longterm effect on musicians and radio stations from 1929 until 1935.

The barn dance phenomenon continued into the 1940s (CBS Radio developed its own show in the early 1940s called the *Dixie Jamboree*, broadcast over an expansive southern regional network from WBT), but the medium also underwent changes, in part due to the development of new technologies. In the mid-1930s, radio show producers began using the carbon microphone, which was more sensitive than its predecessors. Because vocalists were no longer required to sing loud enough to be distinguished from musical instruments, singers of folk, country, gospel, and bluegrass were able to sing in a manner more true to the genre. Commercial radio stations also began producing fewer live broadcasts, relying more on "spinning" recorded performances. Two events accelerated these programming changes: a boycott of songs in the American Society of Composers, Authors, and Publishers catalog in 1941 and a strike by the American Federation of Musicians against radio stations in 1942.

Another radio format associated with central and southern Appalachia was called "airwaves of Zion," a blend of local country music, gospel music, and religious programming. This unstructured format was typically developed by a local preacher rather than a professional broadcaster. It was usually used for Sunday programming only and was supported by nonaligned church fellowships rather than larger mainline congregations.

Although religious broadcasting had been available since the inception of radio, "airwaves of Zion" programming was a unique concept that developed after World War II, when radio stations became more amenable to local preachers "renting" their airwaves. Some stations that became well known for broadcasting this format were WATA (Boone, North Carolina); WMCT (Mountain City, Tennessee); WNKY (Neon, Kentucky); WELC (Welch, West Virginia); and WNRG (Grundy, Virginia). As FM radio stations began to dominate broadcasting in the 1970s and 1980s, the AM stations that supported this form of programming struggled to remain on the air. Another factor that hurt the programming was the rise of commercial televangelism. As a result of competition from FM radio and commercial televangelism, AM-based "airwaves of Zion" programming faded after the 1980s.

The 1950s also saw the emergence of television as a new technology, and several barn dance radio shows attempted to make the transition to the new medium. One television program that preserved elements of Appalachian music plus indigenous humor was the CBS television show *Hee Haw*, which debuted in 1969 from a television studio in Nashville and continued in national syndication into the 1990s.

Although many country music shows have not survived the century, cable television continues to distribute the *Grand Ole Opry*, one of the earliest formats for music associated with Appalachia. The *Opry* is viewed nationwide on the Country Music Television network and distributed worldwide by satellite television transmissions. Broadcasting outlets from radio to television to satellite have thus played a central role in developing Appalachian music genres from regional phenomena to world art forms.

See also: *GRAND OLE OPRY*; RADIO BROADCASTING; RELIGIOUS BROADCASTING; TELEVISION BROADCASTING.

—Paul Allen and Richard Barnet, *Middle Tennessee State University*

Howard Dorgan, *The Airwaves of Zion: Radio and Religion in Appalachia* (1993); Chet Hagan, *Grand Ole Opry: The Official History* (1989); Paul Kingsbury and Alan Axelrod, eds., *Country: The Music and the Musicians* (1988); Ivan M. Tribe, *Mountaineer Jamboree: Country Music in West Virginia* (1984).

National Barn Dance

Originating from radio station WLS in Chicago, the *National Barn Dance* featured folk, hillbilly, western, and nostalgic nineteenth-century pop music, a combination that appealed to both city dwellers and listeners who either lived in Appalachia or had migrated from there to other regions of the country.

Heard on Saturday nights, the *National Barn Dance* was one of many similar radio broadcasts popular from the mid-1920s through the 1950s. The first broadcast, on April 19, 1924, featured fiddle and banjo music drawn from square dances and other musical entertainment of the rural South. The show's popularity grew steadily, and in 1933 it became a regular Saturday-night feature of the NBC radio network. An early announcer on the *National Barn Dance*, George D. Hay, later started the *Grand Ole Opry*.

Through the recruiting efforts of WLS producer and announcer John Lair, who was from Renfro Valley, Kentucky, many Appalachian singers and instrumentalists became nationally known country music artists through their performances on the *National Barn Dance*. They include singer Red Foley; all-girl string-band leader Lily May Ledford; singer Lulu Belle Wiseman of Lulu Belle and Scotty fame; folksinger Doc Hopkins; and Karl and Harty, a vocal duo who also played mandolin and guitar. Other *National Barn Dance* performers with Appalachian roots include balladeer Bradley Kincaid, comedian Pat Buttram, singers Bob Atcher and Dolph Hewitt, comedy duo Homer and Jethro, and the Prairie Ramblers string band.

In 1932 the show was moved to the Eighth Street Theatre on Wabash Avenue, where week after week fans filled the twelve-hundred-seat auditorium. When the theater changed ownership in 1957, the *National Barn Dance* was broadcast from the WLS studios and before live audiences at various tour venues. ABC bought WLS in March 1960, and the musical format shifted from country to contemporary after the *National Barn Dance* finally went off the air on April 30 of that year.

See also: COUNTRY MUSIC COMEDY (HUMOR); MUSIC BROADCASTING; RADIO BROADCASTING.

—Wayne W. Daniel, *Chamblee, Georgia*

National Newspaper Coverage

National newspapers have given prominent attention to Appalachia most often in times of natural disasters, labor violence, mine accidents, sensational trials, and political campaigns. To the extent that they have covered the region's broad social and economic issues, they have tended to perpetuate and embellish negative images and stereotypes, as have popular magazines and electronic news media.

Urban middle-class Americans were introduced to Appalachia not by newspapers but by mass-circulation magazines and popular books in the late nineteenth and early twentieth centuries. Journalists, novelists, and other writers were dispatched to the mountains by publications such as *American Century*, *Lippincott's*, *Living Age*, and *Scribner's*. Later called local color writers for their vivid imagery, these journalists generally portrayed Appalachia as an isolated and quirky place, populated by a peculiar people unlike Americans anywhere else. Because their work was generally written in sensational style and circulated to mass audiences, their periodic forays into the mountains were often presented as a "discovery" of Appalachia. Over the generations, the region has been "rediscovered" a number of times, making it an occasional subject of national interest. Images created by local color writers and their publications still survive, having been reinforced by national newspapers and magazines occasionally drawn to the region by sensational events.

For routine reporting in Appalachia, the national press for decades has relied heavily upon wire service bureaus and local journalists, or "stringers," retained to provide coverage as required. Even for reports that escalate into national news, major metropolitan papers have often depended upon wire services. Few have found it worthwhile to designate staff members to specialize in Appalachian issues. For the most part, the national press has followed the lead of the daily papers in regional centers such as Charleston, West Virginia, Knoxville, Tennessee, and Pittsburgh. Papers published within Appalachian states but outside the Appalachian region—the *Atlanta Journal-Constitution*, the *Nashville Ten-*

nessean, and the *Columbus Dispatch*, for example—exert influence from afar by alerting national organizations to important developments in Appalachia. Of regional papers published outside the mountains, the *Louisville Courier-Journal* has been one of the most influential upon the region. Historically, it has maintained two news bureaus in Appalachian Kentucky, and its reporting on major issues such as strip mining, black lung disease, and poverty has often aroused the interest of the national media.

National news coverage of Appalachia has most notably concerned sensational fare tending to confirm stereotypes of the region. The 1925 "Monkey Trial" in Dayton, Tennessee, is the best known example. Deliberately planned to test a state law banning teaching of the theory of evolution in public schools, the trial of schoolteacher John Scopes was turned into a circus with the help of big-city reporters. With eminent criminal lawyer Clarence Darrow defending Scopes and William Jennings Bryan, the former secretary of state and three-time presidential candidate, serving as a special prosecutor, the trial made headlines across the country. Nationally known journalists such as the *Baltimore Sun*'s H. L. Mencken and the *Chicago Tribune*'s Philip Kinsley vividly described the showdown, often mocking local creationists. Kinsley's stories, appearing under banner headlines, were sometimes accompanied by front-page cartoons poking fun at Bryan. The *Washington Evening Star* relied upon the Associated Press for its trial coverage, but its staff cartoonist lampooned Dayton residents with front-page drawings of a gap-toothed hillbilly.

Similarly sensational, though far darker in tone, was coverage of the rape case against the "Scottsboro Boys" in northern Alabama during the following decade. One of the longest-running national news stories of the 1930s, the trial saw eight of nine young African Americans sentenced to death for the alleged rape of two white women aboard a freight train near the town of Scottsboro. One of the accusers subsequently recanted and the youths escaped execution, but their convictions were nevertheless upheld and they were sent to prison. The trials and appeals were widely covered and denounced by European newspapers as well as the major metropolitan papers in the United States, and the cause of the Scottsboro Boys was adopted not only by the African American press but also by Communist publications such as the *New York Daily Worker* and *New Masses.*

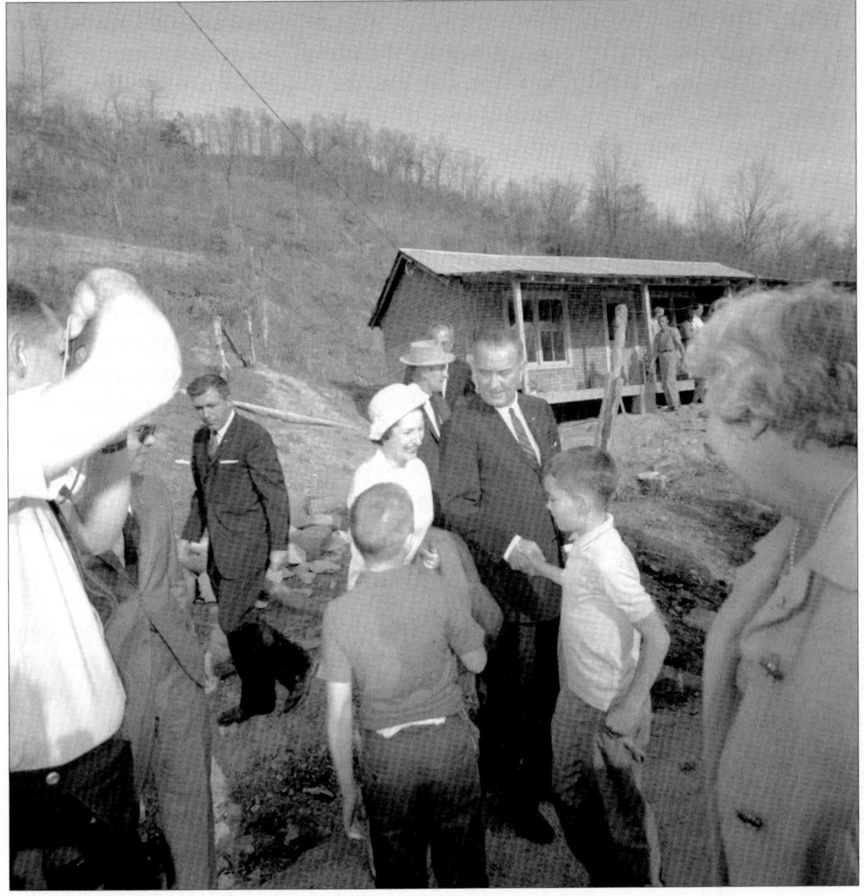

President Lyndon Johnson and First Lady Lady Bird Johnson visiting Inez, Kentucky, 1964. Economic and social problems in Appalachia became front-page news when President Johnson traveled to the region to focus attention on his War on Poverty programs. However, Appalachia disappeared from the headlines when the administration's attention, along with the media's, shifted from domestic concerns to the war in Vietnam.

In the late 1950s and early 1960s, the plight of the poor in Appalachia became front-page news in the country's major urban newspapers. As the 1960 Democratic primary campaign unfolded, West Virginia became the decisive state in a contest between Senators Hubert H. Humphrey of Minnesota and John F. Kennedy of Massachusetts. As the candidates stumped across the state, using depressed coal-mining communities and destitute families as props to dramatize their concern for the poor, they were followed by scores of journalists representing magazines, television stations, and newspapers across the nation and around the world. National media interest in Appalachia, stirred by the West Virginia campaign, continued after the election as Congress held hearings and created the Area Redevelopment Administration proposed by the Kennedy administration. *The New York Times* eventually assigned a Mid-Atlantic correspondent responsibility for covering central Appalachia. Based in the newspaper's Washington office, reporter Ben A. Franklin regularly filed stories concerning issues important in the coalfields of West Virginia and eastern Kentucky.

In October 1963, veteran *New York Times* reporter Homer Bigart, inspired by Harry Caudill's recently published *Night Comes to the Cumberlands*, traveled to eastern Kentucky and produced a stark description of poverty in the region. His reportage and a subsequent *Times* editorial prompted wide coverage elsewhere and consequently strengthened political support for a federal economic recovery program for the Appalachian region.

As President Lyndon Johnson's administration created its own agenda following the Kennedy assassination, antipoverty initiatives were placed among the nation's top domestic priorities, and Appalachia became a showcase of the needy. To dramatize his request for new federal assistance to the region, Johnson flew by helicopter to Paintsville and Inez, Kentucky, as part of a five-state poverty tour. On the porch of a cabin outside Inez he met with Tom Fletcher, a thirty-eight-year-old unemployed coal miner and sawmill worker with eight children. Reporters were allowed to watch and listen at close range, and the meeting became front-page news across the country. Fletcher became a symbol of mountain poverty. Years later, the media would return to his porch, find him still unemployed, and use him to symbolize the failure of the federal antipoverty initiative. As long as poverty remained high on the Johnson administration's agenda, the national news media covered Appalachia's economic and social problems in unprecedented depth. But as Johnson's Great Society programs were pushed into the background by the war in Vietnam, national press interest in Appalachia waned.

Faced with increasing competition from the electronic media and rising production and circulation costs, both national and regional newspapers have increasingly focused their attention on core urban areas that are home to most of their readers and subscribers. Atlanta's morning paper, the *Constitution*, and the afternoon *Journal* were combined in 2001. The *Nashville Tennessean* and the *Louisville Courier-Journal*, each owned for generations by an activist local family, became the property of the giant Gannett Company, based in MacLean, Virginia.

See also: NATIONAL POLITICS AND THE MEDIA IN THE 1960S; NEWSPAPERS; WAR ON POVERTY (GOVERNMENT).

—Rudy Abramson, *Reston, Virginia*

Allen W. Batteau, *The Invention of Appalachia* (1990); Homer Bigart, "Kentucky Miners: A Grim Winter. Poverty, Squalor, and Idleness Prevail in Mountain Area," *New York Times* (October 20, 1963); Dan T. Carter, *Scottsboro: A Tragedy of the American South* (1969); Henry D. Shapiro, *Appalachia on Our Mind: The Southern Mountains and Mountaineers in the American Consciousness, 1870–1920* (1978).

National Politics and the Media in the 1960s

In the 1960s, print and television media portrayed images of Appalachia that profoundly affected the War on Poverty in the region. The large number of television programs and journal articles on Appalachia constituted what some observers called a national "rediscovery" of the mountains. This rediscovery, the third in the twentieth century, focused on poverty and isolation, as well as the belief that people in the mountains lived in ways that differentiated them from national norms and expectations.

The rediscovery began during the 1960 presidential primaries, when Democrat John F. Kennedy made a campaign stop in the coalfields of West Virginia. Covered by scores of reporters, Kennedy's trip revealed to the nation a level of poverty that most Americans thought impossible in a postwar era of abundance. Over the next decade, reporters and filmmakers flocked to the mountains, presenting images of poverty to a national audience. Most media attention focused on the coalfields, especially in West Virginia and Kentucky. By 1965, at least six television news programs had centered on the Kentucky mountains, including CBS's "Depressed Area, USA," hosted by Walter Cronkite, and "Christmas in Appalachia," hosted by Charles Kuralt. Among the metropolitan print media, the *New York Times* published the most significant reports. Harrison E. Salisbury wrote dispatches from West Virginia during the 1960 primaries, and three years later Homer Bigart captured coal miners' distress in Letcher County, Kentucky. That same year numerous television crews visited eastern Kentucky, as did reporters from *Time*, *Look*, *Life*, *Newsweek*, the *Washington Post*, and the Communist publication *Progressive Labor*. Other parts of Appalachia also received attention. North Carolina, for example, was the subject of the documentary films *First 100* (1965) and *Beyond*

These Hills (1967), both dealing with the Office of Economic Opportunity.

For a nation that advertised its prosperity to the Third World as part of its Cold War competition with Communism, the exposure of poverty was an embarrassment. But the exposure also allowed government officials to present America (and American capitalism) as a culture that had the will and the resources to solve the problem of poverty once and for all. President Kennedy began the process with a 1963 exploratory body, the President's Appalachian Regional Commission. Lyndon Johnson continued and expanded those efforts, declaring a War on Poverty and creating the Appalachian Regional Commission as a permanent agency. To promote the federal effort against poverty, Johnson, like Kennedy, traveled to the mountains, this time paying a visit to Martin County, Kentucky, again accompanied by reporters and television crews.

The images presented in the rediscovery reinforced the political urgency of deflecting attention away from capitalist development as a cause of regional poverty. While reporters sometimes blamed poverty on the collapse of the coal industry, they more often pointed to geographic and cultural isolation as the source of the region's ills. Words and photographs depicted sad and worn people, inert and passive, living in unpainted shacks far from paved roads and good schools, cut off by mountains and governmental neglect from the progress the rest of the nation enjoyed. A photo essay in *Life* showed middle-aged men wandering aimlessly near abandoned coal tipples and adolescent girls, not in the vibrancy of youth, but downcast, solemn, and tired. They were symbols of the region as a whole: old if not wise for their age, immobile, incapable of action.

Most reporters also commented on the racial makeup of the Appalachian poor. These were, they said, white people, quintessential Americans whose ancestors migrated from the British Isles and fired the first shots of the American Revolution. The focus on whiteness and a pioneer heritage placed Appalachians in the category of the deserving poor: true, rugged, but beaten Americans whom the progress of the age had passed by. As the *McLean County (Ky.) News* put it in 1964, "Here were Kentuckians, twentieth-century product of proud Anglo-Saxon blood. No 'inferior' race, this. No 'mongrel' blood. No ignorant foreign element. Just pure, native-born Kentuckians."

Supporters of federal antipoverty programs in the 1960s drew upon and exploited the images of isolation, inertia, and whiteness spread by the media. In support of the 1965 Appalachian Regional Development Act, Senate sponsors John Sherman Cooper of Kentucky and Jennings Randolph of West Virginia wrote that the Appalachian people were "of pioneer stock" and had been "ever faithful to our needs in war, and loyal to our country through many generations." Nonetheless, "thousands of families were shown to have been passed by, partly due to the isolation and topography of the region." The solution to regional poverty, as conceived in the Appalachian Regional Development Act, was to break down isolation. The act provided mostly for new highway funds to connect the region to national markets. It also proposed to develop urban growth centers in the mountains, drawing people out of the isolated hollows and into the mainstream of American life. If successful, Cooper and Randolph asserted in *Mountain Life and Work*, "Appalachia will no longer be the Isolated Country," and "the isolation of an entire region can be finally ended."

Local reaction to the intense media attention varied widely. In Clay County, Kentucky, the *Manchester Enterprise* received about twenty letters a day reacting to the 1964 telecast of "Depressed Area, USA." Most critics contended that the program purposely showed only the worst parts of the county and ignored the rest, giving the whole region a negative image in the eyes of the nation. Business communities and chambers of commerce, anxious about their ability to attract new businesses, generally objected to the stories; officials in one county threatened to arrest members of a British news delegation if they photographed people standing in line waiting for government commodities. The most extreme form of resistance to media coverage occurred in 1967, when a Kentucky landowner shot and killed a Canadian filmmaker for filming on his property without permission.

Community activist groups were divided in their evaluation of media depictions. Some activist leaders applauded the media's efforts. Poverty, they said, was entirely genuine, and it was beyond the power and resources of local communities to solve. Only a national awakening, national resources, and a national resolve, these leaders claimed, could hope to change conditions in the mountains. Conversely, labor unions, organizations that protested strip mining, and those contesting the power of entrenched political machines argued that the media had missed the point of regional distress. These people claimed that the source of poverty in the mining regions could be found in the political and economic dominance of the coal industry, not in geographic or cultural isolation. Interpretations that ignored industrial exploitation, they said, only misled their audiences and perpetuated unfair stereotypes of mountain people.

See also: APPALACHIAN REGIONAL COMMISSION (GOVERNMENT); "CHRISTMAS IN APPALACHIA"; WAR ON POVERTY (GOVERNMENT).

—Robert S. Weise, *Eastern Kentucky University*

Allen W. Batteau, *The Invention of Appalachia* (1990); Robert F. Munn, "The Latest Rediscovery of Appalachia," *Mountain Life and Work* (Fall 1965); Laura Schuster and Sharyn McCrumb, "Appalachian Film List," *Appalachian Journal* (Summer 1984); Dan Wakefield, "In Hazard," *Commentary* (September 1963).

Nell

Though based on a stage play set in the Pacific Northwest, the feature film *Nell* (Egg Pictures, 1994) takes place during the 1990s in the Great Smoky Mountains of North Carolina. Directed by Michael Apted, who also made *Coal Miner's Daughter*, the movie was filmed on location beside the Tennessee Valley Authority's Fontana Lake. A local sheriff and a doctor (Liam Neeson) find Nell (Jodie Foster) living in a log cabin. Nell's deceased mother has never told the outside world about her child or permitted her to learn about that world. Nell's language is unique, created from southern Appalachian diction and the King James Bible's syntax, with pronunciation influenced by her mother's aphasia from strokes. Nell's independent lifestyle is threatened when her language comes to the attention of a university researcher (Natasha Richardson).

The movie explores the difficulties that outsiders have with Nell's naive, sheltered viewpoint and her problems understanding their motivations. The university researcher is portrayed as the ultimate outsider. When the researcher brings Nell to the university hospital for in-depth study, its clinical surroundings frighten Nell badly, and she hurts herself attempting to escape. In another scene, young men playing pool in a local bar encourage Nell to lift her dress and dance, depicting Nell as a sexual innocent and the townspeople as predators. The movie also depicts stereotypically positive aspects of the Appalachian character, such as honesty and unaffectedness, which bind a circle of people who become Nell's family. Throughout the movie, cinematography shapes the mountain landscape into a character that enfolds and protects Nell as her mother did, and Nell herself personifies the mountains' isolation and mystery. Though a warm-hearted depiction of the mountain region, the film also suggests mountain people as a remnant, cut off from the larger movements of American history and culture.

See also: FEATURE FILMS; SECTION OVERVIEW (IMAGES AND ICONS).

—Audra Himes, *Northern Cambria, Pennsylvania*

Newspapers

Like their city counterparts, rural and small-town Appalachian newspapers face mounting challenges. The spread of retail merchandising chains, the rise of direct-mail advertising, and the languishing of local economies have forced independent newspapers into mergers, clustered publishing operations, and transferred ownership to distant corporations and conglomerates. The omnipresence of television and the explosive growth of the Internet notwithstanding, newspapers remain the foremost purveyors of community news and continue to be prime investment properties. The quality of newspapers in Appalachia is as varied as the communities they serve, but the spread of corporate and absentee ownership has increased concern that community newspapers are fading as sources of civic vitality.

By the turn of the new century, about half of the country's approximately 8,000 weekly papers and three-fourths of its daily newspapers belonged to chains. Press ownership in Appalachia followed this national pattern. A survey in 2002 showed that 27 percent of the 308 newspapers in central Appalachia, including 35 of 56 dailies, were owned by chains with national holdings. Many of the others belonged to smaller chains or media groups made up of state or regional properties. Among the best-known absentee owners are the New York Times Company, Gannett Company, Scripps Howard Newspapers, Media General Corporation, and Advance Publications. But far more important owners of community newspapers in Appalachia are Landmark Community Newspapers, based in Shelbyville, Kentucky; Community Newspaper Holdings, of Birmingham, a property of the State of Alabama's retirement system; and Ogden Newspapers, a Wheeling, West Virginia, company founded in 1890. In 2004 these three corporations owned more than 90 weekly and small daily newspapers in Appalachia. Other owners of multiple regional properties include the Media Service Group of Greeneville, Tennessee, and Mid-South Management of Spartanburg, South Carolina.

Newspaper ownership is an issue of special community interest because the press historically has enjoyed quasi-public status. In recent decades, the trend toward local monopolies has made the issue even more compelling. Besides covering (or failing to cover) local news, the newspaper reflects a community's culture, assembles the raw material of its history, and serves as a reservoir of civic continuity. In Appalachia, as elsewhere in America, newspaper history is replete with the names of political leaders and business trailblazers whose careers began with local newspaper publishing. But by the middle of the twentieth century, observers such as Kentucky historian Thomas D. Clark were already expressing concern that these papers were losing the vitality and commitment to aggressive reporting and commentary that had characterized local journalism for decades.

The first printing presses arrived in Appalachia on the heels of early settlers. The prompt appearance of newspapers under the trying circumstances of the frontier confirmed their importance to the development of communities. Founded in 1786, the *Pittsburgh Gazette*, the first newspaper west of the Alleghenies, was printed on a small wooden press hauled across the mountains in a horse-drawn wagon. Its first issues used paper delivered by pack-horse train. Once, when paper supplies were exhausted, publishers John Scull and Joseph Hall borrowed cartridge paper from the commander of Fort Pitt. After numerous name and ownership changes, their pioneering publication's direct descendent, the *Pittsburgh Post-Gazette*, continues to be published in the twenty-first century. With a daily circulation of more than 240,000 and Sunday sales of about 425,000 copies (2002), the *Post-Gazette* is the largest newspaper published in the region.

Four years after the *Gazette* appeared in Pittsburgh, the *Potowmac Guardian*, the first paper in what would later become West Virginia, began publication in Shepherdstown. In both Kentucky and Tennessee, the first newspapers were published before the states were established. The *Kentucke Gazette*, first issued from a log cabin in the new Bluegrass community of Lexington, appeared in 1792, vigorously taking up the cause of statehood and separation from Virginia. In Tennessee, the *Knoxville Gazette* was actually published in Rogersville for its first several months because Knoxville existed only as building lot diagrams when the printing press was brought through the mountains from North Carolina in 1791. As was the case with many newspapers in the eighteenth and nineteenth centuries, the *Knoxville Gazette* was founded by a politician to disseminate his views. In this instance William Blount, a former North Carolina legislator, delegate to the Federal Constitutional Convention, an appointed governor of the Territory South of the Ohio, and later a United States senator, brought printers George Roulstone and Robert Ferguson from North Carolina to publish in Knoxville. Because of their political origins and sponsorship, early newspapers in the region frequently fostered immediate competition, and challenging economic circumstances led to the early demise of many publications.

At no time were political battle lines more stark, nor newspaper commentary more heated, than in the struggle over slavery and secession. Inevitably, the newspapers of northern Appalachia were predominantly abolitionist while those in the central and southern highlands were bitterly divided, as was public opinion. In (West) Virginia, the *Kanawha Republican*, founded in Charleston in 1842, took a staunch pro-Union stance while its competitor, the *Kanawha Valley Star*, was equally supportive of pro-slavery and secessionist views. In the hill country of northeastern South Carolina, the secession issue led to an 1832 duel in which Benjamin F. Perry, editor of the pro-Union *Greenville Mountaineer*, fatally wounded Turner Bynum, who had launched a new secessionist paper, the *Southern Sentinel*. Across the region, the political struggle over slavery led to the creation of numerous new newspapers on both sides of the issue.

While eighteenth- and nineteenth-century Appalachian papers tended to be struggling, short-lived enterprises, some nevertheless left their mark in the history of American journalism and publishing. The *Manumission Intelligencer*, founded by Elihu Embree in Jonesborough, Tennessee, in 1819, was the nation's first abolitionist newspaper. The *Cherokee Phoenix*, first printed in 1828 in the tribal capital of New Echota in northern Georgia, was the nation's first Native American newspaper. The *Pittsburgh Courier*, established in 1907 by and for African Americans, gained a national circulation of about 200,000 by the 1930s. Though its circulation declined after 1950, it continued to be published into the twenty-first century as the *New Pittsburgh Courier*.

Appalachia's main urban areas—Pittsburgh, Charleston, Knoxville, Chattanooga, and Birmingham—have historically been home to widely circulated daily papers, but major dailies in other cities such as Atlanta, Nashville, Lexington, Louisville, and Cincinnati have also considered mountain counties part of their "territory." Both the *Lexington Herald-Leader* and the *Louisville Courier-Journal* maintain bureaus in eastern Kentucky. During the late twentieth century, newspaper economics led to continuing mergers and the disappearance of once thriving urban papers, particularly those published in the afternoon. Pittsburgh, for example, was home to no fewer than seven daily newspapers after World War I. But only creation of the *Pittsburgh Tribune-Review* by Richard Mellon Scaife, a wealthy benefactor of conservative causes, kept Appalachia's largest city from becoming a town with only one daily newspaper at the century's end. As their numbers dwindled, urban papers increasingly focused their attention upon growing suburbs near their home base. After decades of publication, familiar twentieth-century dailies such as the *Knoxville Journal*, the *Louisville Times*, and the *Pittsburgh Press* ceased to exist. The *Charleston Daily Mail* and the *Birmingham Post-Herald* remained as the largest of the surviving afternoon papers in the region at the turn of the twenty-first century, operating in a joint printing arrangement with their competitors, the *Charleston Gazette* and the *Birmingham News*. The *Gazette*, established in 1873 and controlled by Charleston's Chilton family since 1912, is considered by many to have the strongest regional reportage of any daily paper published in Appalachia.

After decades of brutal competition in southeastern Tennessee, the *Chattanooga Free Press* and the *Chattanooga Times* were purchased in 1998 and 1999 by Arkansas publisher Walter E. Hussman, who combined them to create the *Chattanooga Times–Free Press*. The *Times* struggled in the increasingly competitive atmosphere of the late twentieth century, but it retained a special place in American and Appalachian newspaper history. A century and a quarter before the merger with the *Free Press*, the *Times* had been sold to a twenty-year-old former printer's devil, Adolph Ochs, for $250. Within months, Ochs turned the struggling paper into profitable business. Eighteen years later, he was able to buy the financially troubled *New York Times* and, using the same strategy he had employed in Chattanooga, began building one of the world's great newspapers.

Chattanooga's devolution into a city with one newspaper and an absentee owner was part of a pattern. In

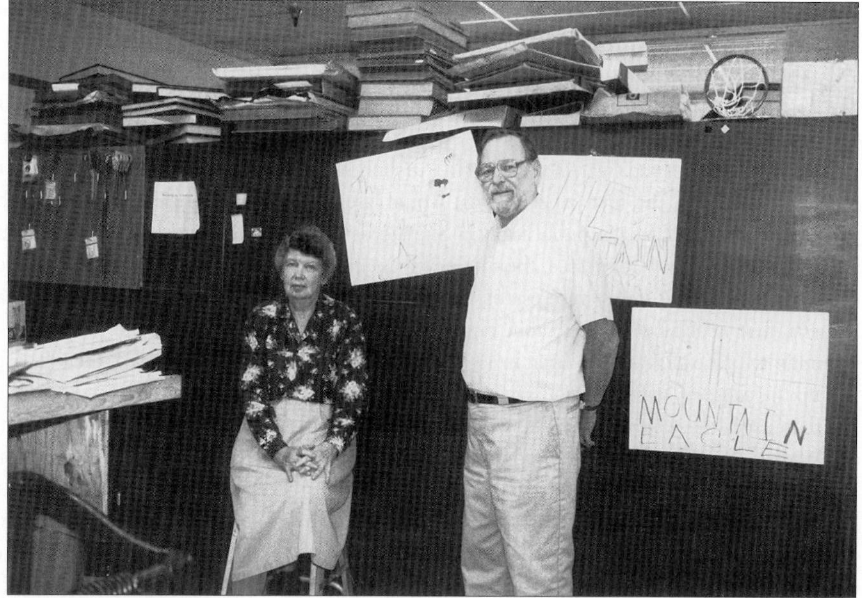

Tom and Pat Gish in the office of the *Mountain Eagle,* Whitesburg, Kentucky, 1991. Although subjected to social ostracism, advertising boycotts, death threats, and arson for their fearless tackling of controversial local issues, the Gishes, owners and editors of the *Mountain Eagle,* received some of the highest honors in American journalism.

Louisville, the *Courier-Journal* had already become the property of the Gannett Company, a giant national media conglomerate based in McLean, Virginia. In a city that had known so many newspapers, the death of the *Knoxville Journal* left Scripps-Howard's *Knoxville News-Sentinel* as the last survivor. Even Atlanta, the booming metropolis just beyond the southern Appalachians, became a one-newspaper city when Cox Newspapers merged the *Atlanta Constitution* and the *Atlanta Journal* in 2001.

Consolidation, mergers, corporate ownership, and joint operating arrangements that characterized major newspaper markets for the last several decades of the twentieth century became the norm in smaller towns and communities as well. After its founding in 1997, the Birmingham-based Community Newspaper Holdings quickly became the number one owner of Appalachian newspapers. By 2002, the company owned 49 daily, weekly, and semiweekly newspapers in the region, including 17 in eastern Kentucky.

Although a large portion of Appalachia has been served by regional and local daily newspapers since the nineteenth century, the region's numerous towns and rural communities still bestow a special importance upon the weekly publications. Arguably, weeklies retain more prominence as community institutions in Appalachia than anywhere else in the country. While some urban dailies such as the *Louisville Courier-Journal* and the *Charleston Gazette* won awards and reputations for their coverage of Appalachian issues, weeklies such as the *Mountain Eagle* in Letcher County, Kentucky, exemplified the community newspaper with its aggressive coverage of local issues such as strip mining. But while the paper's news and editorial columns won it a devoted following and national awards, publishers Tom and Pat Gish became the targets of threats and intimidation, and their offices were torched by a paid arsonist. Not far away, in Martin County, Kentucky, the *Martin Countian* investigated coal companies in the 1970s and 1980s. In retaliation, publisher Homer Marcum was threatened, arrested, sued seven times for libel, and also targeted by an arsonist.

See also: ABOLITIONIST NEWSPAPERS; *LOUISVILLE COURIER-JOURNAL;* NATIONAL NEWSPAPER COVERAGE.

—Rudy Abramson, *Reston, Virginia,* and Jenny Fuchs, *University of Edinburgh*

Jock Lauterer, *Community Journalism: The Personal Approach* (2000); George Henry Payne, *History of Journalism in the United States* (1920); Mitchell Stephens, *A History of News* (1988).

Next of Kin

Set primarily in Chicago, the 1989 action film *Next of Kin* uses social and ethnic stereotypes to create dramatic and violent conflict between rural Appalachian and urban northern groups. Directed by John Irvin, the film features Patrick Swayze at the height of his late-1980s popularity. Swayze plays Chicago policeman Truman Gates, who, along with his brother Gerald, has migrated to Chicago from eastern Kentucky. Following Gerald's murder by the Chicago Mafia, the film becomes a war of stereotypes: Appalachian hillbilly versus Mafia hood, Kentucky clan against Italian family.

Following a funeral sequence filmed near Hazard, Kentucky—featuring misty landscapes shot in muted colors, interiors of starkly desolate cabins, and a mournful song by Jean Ritchie in a cameo appearance—Truman returns to Chicago, where he struggles to reconcile his desire for vengeance with his post-migratory sense of sophistication (he is, after all, married to a concert violinist, played by future Oscar winner Helen Hunt). How well Truman may have achieved this reconciliation is never revealed, since the most primal manifestation of mountain vengeance sweeps into Chicago in the form of Truman's brother Briar Gates, depicted by Liam Neeson as a combination of wide-eyed innocent and obsessive sociopath. More troops from the mountains, including one kinsman who communes with snakes, arrive in time for the dramatic showdown. Truman, Briar, and the clan meet the enemy in a final encounter, with Truman wielding a crossbow, a lethal hybrid between the urban handgun and the rural bow and arrow. Following the battle, Italians and hillbillies lay slain, while Truman returns to his Chicago wife.

See also: FEATURE FILMS; VIOLENCE AND VENGEANCE (IMAGES AND ICONS).

—John F. Keener, *Lees-McRae College*

Now and Then

Now and Then: The Appalachian Magazine focuses on the multidisciplinary field of Appalachian studies, providing a forum for readers and writers outside of academia interested in the region's culture, politics, economics, and history. Through 2003, three issues a year of *Now and Then* were published (except for volume 16) by the Center for Appalachian Studies and Services at East Tennessee State University in Johnson City, presenting articles, interviews, essays, fiction, poetry, photography, art, music, and reviews. Statewide budget reductions, however, caused the magazine to halt publication in 2004. *Now and Then* was revived in 2005, with publication twice annually on a subscription basis.

Starting in 1984 as a three-times-a-year newsletter and eventually developing into a forty-page magazine, the publication was cofounded by folklorist and fiddler Richard Blaustein, the director of the newly formed Center for Appalachian Studies and Services at East Tennessee State University, and English professor Fred Waage. Created to interpret Appalachian culture past and present and as an avenue for publishing regional writing and art, the first issue in 1984 featured the work of writer Jo Carson and photographer Michael Smith.

Each issue deals with a specific theme related to some overlooked aspect of the region such as Appalachian blacks, Cherokees, urban life, veterans, media, or tourism. Writer Pat Arnow took over editing the journal in 1986, and folklorist Jane Harris Woodside served as editor from 1995 to 2003. Contributors over the years have included scholars specializing in Appalachia from such disciplines as folklore, sociology, anthropology, English, history, and music. Numerous writers, photographers, artists, teachers, social activists, craftspeople, musicians, farmers, and laborers publish work or are profiled in the magazine. Some of the better-known scholars and writers to have work published in *Now and Then* include Lee Smith, Wilma Dykeman, Loyal Jones, Robert J. Higgs, Jim Wayne Miller, and George Ella Lyon.

See also: APPALACHIAN CENTERS AND INSTITUTES (CULTURAL INSTITUTIONS); CENTER FOR APPALACHIAN STUDIES AND SERVICES (CULTURAL INSTITUTIONS).

—Pat Arnow, *New York City, New York*

October Sky

October Sky (1999), a movie directed by Joe Johnston and filmed in east Tennessee, is based on NASA scientist Homer Hickam's autobiography *Rocket Boys* (1998), which tells the story of seventeen-year-old Homer and his three friends who, after viewing Sputnik 1 (the world's first artificial satellite) moving across the mountain sky in October 1957, set out to build a rocket. Set in Coalwood, West Virginia, the movie is a detailed evocation of a 1950s Appalachian community and the conflicting attitudes of the time period.

Homer (Jake Gyllenhaal) leads his friends in numerous attempts and eventual success at building a rocket. With the support of the community and an inspirational teacher, the group wins the National Science Fair and obtains college scholarships—their means of escaping a life of coal mining. John, Homer's father (Chris Cooper), is a man of pragmatism rather than vision who must learn to accept his son's choices. Homer's mother, Elsie (Natalie Canerday), is a strong woman who lives a hard life in a coal company town yet never surrenders her own dream of escape. The eventual success of the "rocket boys" is portrayed as that of the entire town. Each rocket launched embodies the ways that the community's collective dreams are no longer earthbound. The film's visual contrast of the closed and cramped quarters of the coal mine with the dreams of the unlimited sky reflects the conflict of past and present ways of life represented in the film.

See also: COAL IMAGES (IMAGES AND ICONS); FEATURE FILMS.

—Debbye W. Kerns, *Walters State Community College*

On-Line Media

Beginning in the last half of the 1990s, explosive global growth of the Internet and the commensurate spread of personal computers presented the potential for an information revolution in Appalachia through rapid and uninhibited communication. For mass media, from community newspapers to television networks, the music industry, motion picture companies, and book publishing houses, the new manifestations of digital technology portended unforeseeable change in content, delivery of product, and interaction with audiences and customers. In the view of some analysts, massive and inexpensive public access to the World Wide

Web threatened the longterm existence of traditional media outlets such as local newspapers. By the end of the century, five years after the Internet passed from government management into the private sector, it was estimated more than 100 million Americans were on-line, using features such as e-mail, chat groups, and connections to Web sites of countless descriptions, purposes, and sponsorships.

As in the rest of America, virtually every facet of Appalachian commerce and civic life was swept along in a revolution that promised to equal the impact of radio, television, and other major communications advances of modern times. Early in the new century, for example, a Morehead (Kentucky) State University Web site, the Center for Virtual Appalachia, presented computer users with links to some four thousand other sites concerning Appalachia.

Like other new technologies, Internet communication took hold somewhat more slowly in Appalachia than in other parts of the country. Building the digital highway in the region proved to be difficult. The advanced Internet applications that make up the core of "new media" tools (such as audio and video applications) require broadband access through technologies such as cable modems (switching devices making it possible to transmit information in digital form) and digital subscriber lines (DSL). These systems were slow to develop outside metropolitan areas, particularly in mountainous areas of central and southern Appalachia where telephone lines were in need of modernization and wireless connection was often inhibited by the terrain.

A 2000 national survey found that only 5 percent of towns with a population of fewer than ten thousand had DSL service. Other delivery systems, such as direct satellite access and wireless broadband, were even slower to develop. A report compiled for the Appalachian Regional Commission showed Virginia and Maryland to be the leading Appalachian states in developing Internet connections while Mississippi and West Virginia lagged behind. But between 1998 and 2000, Mississippi and West Virginia rapidly increased their Internet penetration, with West Virginia's connections almost doubling from 17.6 percent to 34.3 percent of households. Nationwide, Internet service, available to 22.2 percent of the households in rural America in 1998, increased to 48.7 percent by 2001, according to statistics compiled by the U.S. Department of Commerce.

Beyond the difficulty of expanding access, Appalachian communities continued to face questions of how to best employ the new media capabilities as they became available. Unlike traditional media such as radio, television, and newspapers, computer-based media provide users the ability not only to acquire images and recordings from distant sources but also to function as independent producers and become self-publishers. Although there are examples of regionally produced media within Appalachia (such as Appalshop's films and radio production, individual university-based public radio stations, West Virginia's public radio network, and state-of-the-art digital networks in locations such as Blacksburg, Virginia), for the most part Appalachians, like other Americans, have been principally consumers of commercial media.

See also: APPALSHOP; DIGITAL ARTS (VISUAL ARTS).

—Tim Marema, *Center for Rural Strategies, Whitesburg, Kentucky*

J. S. Gonzalez, *The Twenty-First-Century Internet* (1998); Michael Oden and Sharon Strover et al., "Links to the Future: The Role of Telecommunications Technology in Appalachian Regional Development," Appalachian Regional Commission (2002).

"Our Contemporary Ancestors in the Southern Mountains"

See Frost, William Goodell and Eleanor Marsh (Education); "Our Contemporary Ancestors in the Southern Mountains" (Literature)

Parris, John

(1914–1999) Journalist and nonfiction writer.

John Parris spent his career chronicling the history and traditions of western North Carolina. Born November 23, 1914, in Sylva, North Carolina, Parris began writing for his hometown newspaper, the *Jackson County Journal*, at age thirteen. In 1934 he became a reporter for United Press International. While stationed in London during World War II, Parris received considerable acclaim for his coverage of diplomatic and military affairs.

After the war, Parris returned to the mountains of North Carolina and began writing about his native region. He became best known for "Roaming the Mountains," a column that appeared three times weekly in the *Asheville Citizen-Times* beginning in 1955. Parris's stories, written in simple, straightforward prose, described the traditions that he believed formed the basis of mountain culture. Food, folktales, daily working routines, transfer of knowledge from past generations, and traditional crafts were among his preferred subjects. His writings portrayed mountain people as having a deep reverence for the past and acknowledged the profound changes occurring as a result of the region's modernization. Collections of his work were published in six books: *The Cherokee Story* (1950); *Roaming the Mountains* (1955); *My Mountains, My People* (1957); *Mountain Bred* (1967); *These Storied Mountains* (1972); and *Mountain Cooking* (1978).

Parris wrote more than seven thousand columns before retiring in March 1997. He received numerous awards, including a doctorate of humane letters from Western Carolina University in March 1998. He died May 17, 1999, at the age of eighty-four in Sylva.

See also: NEWSPAPERS.

—Daniel J. Vivian, *National Register of Historic Places, National Park Service*

Plow, The

The Plow, an independent alternative publication for the southern Appalachians from 1975 to 1979, was directed in part toward those interested in political and social issues but was also intended to be entertaining enough to appeal to a general audience. Published in Abingdon, Virginia, the first issue was circulated in October 1975 by editor Bill Blanton and a volunteer staff of three—Steve Fisher, Larry Richman, and Janesse Trivette. In January 1976, *The Plow* began regular monthly publication; in July 1977, it changed to twice-monthly publication, which continued until the last issue in mid-August 1979. Printed in tabloid format, it ranged in size from twenty to forty pages. By design, advertising accounted for no more than 25 percent of each edition. At its peak, *The Plow* had a paid circulation of about five thousand in its primary area of Washington, Smyth, Grayson, Russell, Scott, and Wise Counties in Virginia; Sullivan and Johnson Counties in Tennessee; and Ashe, Avery, and Watauga Counties in North Carolina.

The paper offered an eclectic blend: features about people and events in the region; how-to articles on subjects ranging from cooking and gardening to holistic health and self-sufficient living; historical pieces about old ways in the mountains; reviews of music and literature; poetry and fiction; analytical articles about the issues of the times; plus some old-fashioned muckraking journalism, supporting, for example, citizens' groups opposed to a proposed pumped storage dam at Brumley Gap, Virginia.

See also: NEWSPAPERS; SECTION OVERVIEW.

—Ann Richman, *Abingdon, Virginia*

Radio Broadcasting

Since the early days of broadcasting, radio stations within the Appalachian region have contributed significantly to the growth of the broadcasting industry. The Appalachian region entered commercial radio broadcasting in November 1920 with KDKA in Pittsburgh. Owned by the Westinghouse Electric and Manufacturing Company, KDKA was the first radio station to be licensed specifically by the United States government for the purpose of operating a general broadcasting service.

The 1920s were radio's first decade as a commercial mass medium, and three radio stations dominated broadcasting in the South. In March 1922, WSB in Atlanta went on the air and became the first high-powered radio station in the southern United States. Fiddlin' John Carson was among many musicians who performed regularly at the station, not because of the widespread popularity of "hillbilly" music at the time but for reasons of practicality. Hillbilly musicians did not require complex or expensive studio arrangements, and they could play for short or for extended periods of time. Three days after WSB signed on in 1922, WBT in Charlotte, North Carolina, aired its first broadcast. During its early years, WBT promoted a variety of entertainers ranging from local dance bands and pop singers to minstrel shows and storytellers. In 1925 National Life and Accident Insurance Company entered commercial radio broadcasting at a studio on the fifth floor of its headquarters in Nashville, Tennessee. The station's call letters were an acronym for its advertising slogan, *We Shield Millions.* WSM was one of the first radio stations to receive full corporate sponsorship, an idea that had originated with Sears, Roebuck, and Company's WLS in Chicago.

Despite the popularity of large broadcasting entities, smaller radio stations prospered throughout Appalachia in the 1920s. In 1921 WNAV in Knoxville became the first radio station in Tennessee and the eighth nationwide. Built by Stuart Adcock for the People's Telephone and Telegraph Company, WNAV changed its call letters in 1925 to WNOX, when Adcock purchased the station. WNOX is known for introducing many musicians from the Knoxville area who later achieved national popularity at WSM. Another small Appalachian radio station, broadcasting from Wheeling, West Virginia, registered under the call letters WWVA. Airing its first show in 1926, WWVA provided listeners with contemporary music, informal announcements, and musical offerings from local amateur groups. WWNC Asheville went on the air in February of 1927, and Jimmie Rodgers made his first broadcast from that station on April 18, 1927; that summer Rodgers performed with his group the Tenneva Ramblers under the moniker the Jimmie Rodgers Entertainers over WWNC until his discovery at the seminal Bristol sessions in August 1927. In 1929 WOPI began transmitting from Bristol, on the Tennessee-Virginia border. It was in Bristol that Ralph Peer had first recorded Rodgers and the Carter Family in 1927. WOPI was joined by WCYB, also in Bristol, in 1946.

Appalachian culture gained national popularity in radio broadcasting during the 1920s through the barn dance format. Both large and small radio stations around the country capitalized on the hillbilly stereotype originating in the Appalachian highlands. The first of these radio barn dances began in 1923, not in the Appalachian region, but at WBAP in Fort Worth, Texas, followed by a similar show at WLS in

Tennessee Ernie Ford in the control room of WOPI, Bristol, Tennessee, late 1930s. Many small Appalachian radio stations such as WOPI provided a venue for new and established country music performers, including Ford, who began as a part-time announcer.

Chicago in 1924, which later became known as the *National Barn Dance*. WLS's show was comprised of hillbilly music, comedy sketches, and minstrel-influenced numbers. In November 1925, the *WSM Barn Dance* aired in Nashville. George D. Hay, the show's program director, formerly with WLS in Chicago, renamed the show the *Grand Ole Opry* in 1927.

Broadcasting at fifty thousand watts, WLS's *National Barn Dance* also served as a model for many hillbilly radio shows that originated in the golden age of radio, the 1930s. In 1933 WWVA first aired its *Jamboree*, which claims to be the second-oldest live radio broadcast in America. Sponsored by the Crazy Water Crystals Company, WBT began its *Crazy Water Crystals Barn Dance* in 1934 and included such stars as Bill and Charlie Monroe, J. E. Mainer and his Mountaineers, and the Briarhoppers. WNOX first aired its *Midday Merry-Go-Round* in 1935, which featured future *Opry* star Roy Acuff and his Crazy Tennesseans. In the earliest days of radio, performers were not paid for appearances on barn dances, but bands took advantage of the medium as an opportunity to advertise upcoming concert dates, sell personalized songbooks, and promote phonograph records. As a result, radio barn dances contributed greatly to the development of country music in the depression-ridden 1930s.

Radio broadcasting in the 1930s centered around three types of radio stations: network stations that originated programs and distributed them among affiliates, passive network affiliates, and unaffiliated independent stations. In efforts to solicit advertisers, networks allowed companies to sponsor whole shows of varying duration that often carried the company's name, including WSM's touring *Prince Albert Show* of the 1940s and WBT's *Crazy Water Crystals Barn Dance*. By 1938, more homes in the United States possessed radios than indoor plumbing, automobiles, or telephones.

The 1940s were a pivotal time for broadcasting. Following World War II, radio's prosperity continued until the rapid expansion of television late in the decade. In attempts to compete with the new visual medium, radio reintroduced frequency modulation (FM) to broadcasting, a technology that had been invented by Edwin Armstrong in 1930. In contrast to AM (amplitude modulation) signals, which travel through the sky, reflecting off the ionosphere, FM signals travel along the earth's surface. FM's wider bandwidth produced greater fidelity and had less static than AM transmissions.

Competition with television also forced radio to develop new approaches to programming. Independent radio stations developed formats consisting of music, news, personality disc jockeys, and station promotions appealing to local audiences. Because of their smaller size and dedication to local interests, large numbers of new stations went on the air during the postwar years. One such station was WPAQ, which first aired in 1948 from Mount Airy, North Carolina. Independently owned and operated, it broadcast regional fiddlers' conventions, readings of obituaries, and local church services in addition to weekly live music programs that included area musicians.

Advertising for many small and medium-sized radio stations of the 1930s, 1940s, and early 1950s was done in part under the "per inquiry" system. According to the practice, each station received payment by means of a commission of a specified amount on each unit of goods sold by it. Announcers known as pitchmen became crucial for their role in selling products over the air. Pitchmen were regionally famous for their individual styles and success in reading commercials. Prominent examples include Buddy Starcher at WPDX in Clarksburg, West Virginia; "Cowboy Loye" at WWVA; Charlie Monroe at WBT; and "Uncle" Joe Johnson at WPAQ. The per inquiry system slowly became extinct as television's popularity grew in the 1950s.

The second half of the twentieth century experienced many advances in radio, and recording technologies penetrated daily broadcasting operations. The invention of the transistor in the early 1950s allowed radio to become a portable medium. Phonograph records, which had been in use prior to World War II, were replaced by reusable reel-to-reel tapes and cassettes. During the 1970s automated tape and cart machines allowed radio stations to operate more economically. The recording industry moved into the age of digital audio during the 1980s with compact discs and the 1990s with minidiscs and MP3 computer audio files.

Many radio stations in the Appalachian region, such as WMMT in Whitesburg, Kentucky, can be heard globally via the World Wide Web. Such technological advances have helped keep radio broadcasting a healthy industry and have contributed to a strong movement to preserve the musical traditions of the region.

See also: MUSIC BROADCASTING; RELIGIOUS BROADCASTING; TELEVISION BROADCASTING.

—David B. Pruett, *Florida State University*

Vincent M. Ditingo, *The Remaking of Radio* (1995); Richard A. Peterson, *Creating Country Music: Fabricating Authenticity* (1997).

Real McCoys, The

Premiering on ABC on October 3, 1957, and completing its run on CBS on September 22, 1963, *The Real McCoys* was the first television program in the genre of situation comedy to take place in a rural setting. Indeed, the success of the show helped to launch a subgenre of "hillbilly" or "hayseed" sitcoms that included such 1960s hits as *The Beverly Hillbillies*, *Petticoat Junction*, and *Green Acres*.

The Real McCoys follows the misadventures of a West Virginia mountain family that has relocated to a ranch in southern California's San Fernando Valley. The center of the family and the comedic star of the show is the curmudgeonly geezer Grampa McCoy, played by longtime western actor Walter Brennan. The family includes grandson Luke (Richard Crenna), his wife, Kate (Kathleen Nolan), and Luke's younger sister and brother (Lydia Reed and Michael Winkelman). Also part of the extended family is hired hand Pepino Garcia (Tony Martinez), one of the first Hispanic characters to be featured in any weekly television show—though he most often serves as the victim of Grampa's cantankerous harangues.

Although the show's setting is California, Appalachian culture—rather, a stereotyped caricature of it—lies at the heart of *The Real McCoys*. Grampa's patriarchal leadership of the family, particularly his homespun moral idealism and stubborn refusal to accept highfalutin city ways, distinguishes the show from other family- and urban-centered situation comedies of its period. Although conflicts are invariably settled with maudlin sentimentality, the struggle of the family to reconcile themselves to urban and modern values while trying to preserve their rural pastoral traditions is a recurrent theme of the show. Numerous episodes mawkishly depict the real-world struggles of Appalachian people that were coming to light in the years the show aired.

See also: *BEVERLY HILLBILLIES, THE;* TELEVISION DEPICTIONS OF THE REGION.

—Chris J. Magoc, *Mercyhurst College*

David Marc, *Demographic Vistas: Television in American Culture* (1984).

Regional Presses

See Printing/Publishing Presses (Business, Industry, and Technology)

Religious Broadcasting

The bulk of Appalachian religious radio and television programming is produced and broadcast by small- and medium-market stations, reflecting the important role played by religion and church membership in the community life of rural and small-town Appalachia. Although nationally syndicated radio and televangelism programs dominate religious broadcast programming throughout the United States, the persistence of independently produced Sunday-morning AM radio broadcasts in Appalachia is part of the region's distinctive religious personality. Not solely a southern phenomenon, religious broadcasting is a common thread in the fabric of northern, central, and southern Appalachian life.

Most religious programs throughout the Appalachian region are broadcast by small-market commercial AM radio stations that provide a mix of local interest and public service programming, though a growing number of small UHF television stations also have begun carrying local religious shows.

To fulfill part of the public service guidelines of the Federal Communications Commission, local commercial radio and television stations offer two types of religious broadcasts. Although both seek to serve community needs, they are quite different in tone and purpose. The first type is a daily devotional program that is routinely conducted by a member of the local ministerial association and is designed to be inspirational rather than theological or evangelistic. Local stations customarily donate the airtime for these programs as a public service. Many stations also carry live remote broadcasts of larger urban denominational church services.

The second type of religious programming is the Sunday-morning show for which airtime is purchased by a local church for preaching, singing, exhortation, and ministering to the local churchgoing public and shut-ins. These programs typically feature independent local churches rather than large national and international denominations such as the Southern Baptists, Methodists, or Presbyterians. Produced by Independent, Free Will, and Missionary Baptist subgroups, highly individualistic Holiness-Pentecostal churches, or other groups, these usually evangelistic broadcasts reflect the churches' divine calling to reach out to the people in their communities. Their broadcasts are, therefore, a tool to help them achieve what they see as their God-given mission.

Because they intend these radio programs to convey the simplicity and holiness of their traditional faith and to play down the role of modern technology, traditional Appalachian preachers see no need for training in broadcast techniques and procedures. This attitude is in keeping with their general rejection of formal theological or homiletic instruction. For these broadcasts, local stations generally provide a staff studio operator to furnish needed technical support.

Beyond the prevalence of explicit religious programming, Appalachian broadcasting is also distinguished by its extensive use of religious music throughout the broadcast day. Unlike the majority of radio stations outside the region, Appalachian small-market commercial radio stations include gospel music in their daily music format. In addition to the music of traditional regional churches, they feature renowned musicians such as Doc Watson, Ricky Skaggs, and Emmylou Harris. All have recorded material from the standard *Church Hymnal* of the Church of God (Cleveland, Tennessee), which uses the shaped notation of the traditional Sacred Harp singing common in Appalachia. In most Appalachian communities, the separation between the sacred and the secular is blurred. The music mix played by many local radio stations reflects this reality and transmits the culture of the church into all areas of Appalachian society.

See also: GOSPEL MUSIC, AFRICAN AMERICAN (MUSIC); GOSPEL MUSIC, ANGLO-AMERICAN (MUSIC); RADIO BROADCASTING.

—K. Stephen Smith, *Appalachian State University*

Howard Dorgan, *The Airwaves of Zion: Radio and Religion in Appalachia* (1993); Tennessee Music Publishing and Printing Company, *Church Hymnal* (1951).

Renfro Valley Barn Dance

Renfro Valley was radio broadcaster John Lair's attempt to recreate an "old time" Appalachian community where he could stage and broadcast his weekly traditional music program, the *Renfro Valley Barn Dance*. Opened in 1939 near Mount Vernon, Kentucky, and modeled after Lair's boyhood homeplace in Rockcastle County, Renfro Valley included log cabins for guests, a one-room schoolhouse, and a replica of an early American Main Street. He envisioned his constructed community as a place where visitors could spend a weekend or longer living in the past.

After spending several years with the *National Barn Dance* in Chicago, Lair launched his own radio show, the *Renfro Valley Barn Dance,* on Cincinnati's WLW in 1937. He broadcast from there until his own complex was completed in November 1939. Ironically, despite the homespun atmosphere of the show and locale, the resort capitalized on Americans' greater access to cars, roads, and increased leisure time. It met its patrons' desire for good clean fun and featured entertainers who reflected Appalachian appreciation for hard work, good morals, and wholesome entertainment. For a time, the *Renfro Valley Barn Dance* rivaled the *National Barn Dance* and *Grand Ole Opry* in popularity. Among the show's stars were the Coon Creek Girls, Red Foley, Homer and Jethro, and A'nt Idy. The *Renfro Valley Barn Dance* radio audience dwindled in the late 1940s because of sponsor trouble, disruptive highway construction nearby, and the decline of the barn dance genre. The *Renfro Valley Barn Dance* ceased live national broadcasting in the 1950s, though the stage shows continue to draw crowds in the twenty-first century. The Sunday-morning stage show, *The Gatherin'*, is still broadcast nationwide via recorded versions.

Although no longer operated by Lair (who died in 1985), Renfro Valley remains in business. In addition to the original auditorium, one-room schoolhouse, water-driven gristmill, and log cabins, the center features a rustic restaurant, gift shop, U.S. Post Office, pioneer museum, country store, and a campground for recreation vehicles. It is located at the Mount Vernon exit of Interstate 75.

See also: GRAND OLE OPRY; LAIR, JOHN; *NATIONAL BARN DANCE.*

—Sändra Henson, *East Tennessee State University,* and Kristine M. McCusker, *Middle Tennessee State University*

Sergeant York

The Warner Brothers film *Sergeant York* opened at the Astor Theatre in New York City on July 2, 1941, and one week later President Franklin D. Roosevelt praised it as a great film about a great American after attending a special screening in Washington, D.C. Directed by Howard Hawks and starring Gary Cooper as Sergeant Alvin York of Pall Mall, Tennessee, the movie proved to be politically important, for it helped create a supportive atmosphere for America's entry into World War II.

Independent producer Jesse Lasky witnessed the ticker-tape parade in New York City when York, America's foremost hero of World War I, returned to the United States in 1919. Convinced his story would make a terrific film, Lasky pitched

Gary Cooper in *Sergeant York,* 1941. The feature film, based on Alvin York's Appalachian upbringing and heroic war experience, became a powerful tool for the political movement supporting America's entry into World War II.

the idea to York only to have the request denied. Lasky's deep interest in the story persisted, however, and he approached the mountaineer again in 1939 with the possibility of a film based on his exploits in the Argonne Forest. For a number of reasons York again refused. First, he took no pride in having killed men in battle. Second, his denomination, the Church of Christ in Christian Union, condemned movies as a sin. Third, York was averse to doing business with Jews. But Lasky was undeterred and with the help of York's friend Guy Williams and Tennessee Governor Prentice Cooper succeeded on March 24, 1940, in securing York's cooperation.

The movie that arrived in theaters in 1941 was a far cry from what York had originally sanctioned. When York signed his contract with Warner Brothers, he demanded that the film not glorify his wartime experiences; rather, it would focus on his accomplishments since the war—primarily his efforts to improve education in Tennessee. But over the course of the film's production a number of events led him to approve radical changes. As York became more acquainted with Harry Warner and Lasky, he became convinced that the movie could be used to promote American patriotism and prove that sometimes wars have righteous causes. Persuaded that the Nazi regime threatened American security, he allowed the film's focus to change.

Written by Harry Chandlee, Julien Josephson, Abem Finkel, and John Huston, the screenplay focused upon two key events in York's life—his religious conversion after years as a hell-raiser and his second conversion from conscientious objector to soldier. The script underwent four significant rewrites, eventually showing York becoming convinced that he must kill in order to save lives. Independent director Hawks guided the film through production, going over budget and making the film Warner Brothers' first production to cost more than two million dollars.

Though the film opened successfully, it soon came under attack by isolationist members of the U.S. Congress, who accused the studio and *Sergeant York* of warmongering. With a U.S. Senate subcommittee investigating propaganda, Harry and Jack Warner pulled the film from a planned August 1941 release, fearing it would become a financial liability. *Sergeant York* became one of eight films specifically charged by this committee with violating U.S. neutrality and inciting war fever in the American public. Harry Warner, president of Warner Brothers, defended the film before the subcommittee, and York himself expressed his willingness to testify. But during the subcommittee's recess, the Japanese bombed Pearl Harbor, and in January 1942 *Sergeant York* went into general release, becoming a box-office smash. The film played continuously throughout the war and copies of the print were made available to all American allies.

The finished work bore little relation to York or his life. The real York, unlike Cooper's taciturn portrayal, was a voluble man who loved to laugh. Likewise, Gary Cooper neither sounded nor looked remotely like the red-headed York, who wore a mustache his entire adult life. There are also other discrepancies. For example, the hero's religious conversion was not caused by a bolt of lightning as in the movie, and he always lived on bottomland and not in mountain backwoods. But the film created an indelible image of Sergeant York for succeeding generations, creating a beloved mythology but little understanding of the real man or what motivated him.

See also: HISTORICAL HEROES (IMAGES AND ICONS); NOBLE MOUNTAINEERS (IMAGES AND ICONS); SECTION OVERVIEW (IMAGES AND ICONS).

—Michael E. Birdwell, *Tennessee Technological University*

Michael E. Birdwell, *Celluloid Soldiers: Warner Bros.'s Campaign Against Nazism* (1999) and "'The Devil's Tool': Alvin York and the Movie *Sergeant York*," in *Hollywood's World War I: Motion Picture Images*, ed. Peter C. Rollins and John E. O'Connor (1998).

Snuffy Smith

On November 17, 1934, cartoonist William "Billy" Morgan DeBeck (1890–1942) introduced readers of his nationally syndicated newspaper comic strip *Barney Google* to a hillbilly character named Snuffy Smith. Henceforth, DeBeck set most of his stories in an imaginary Appalachian community called Hootin' Holler, and Snuffy Smith became so popular that by the end of the decade DeBeck had retitled his work *Barney Google and Snuffy Smith* and Smith's adventures took over the strip. Although his comic strip mirrored numerous other 1930s popular entertainments that cashed in on the mainstream American audience's fascination with hill country culture, DeBeck took pains to give his work an authentic foundation.

DeBeck launched *Barney Google* on June 17, 1919, and built a sizable readership over the next decade with stories about his protagonist, an urban sports fan, and his racehorse, Spark Plug. Billy Rose's 1923 smash song "Barney Google" ("with his goo-goo-googly eyes") further enhanced the strip's popularity. Throughout the 1920s, the inventive DeBeck coined numerous catch phrases that captured the public's fancy, including *heebie jeebies*, *horsefeathers*, *hotsy totsy*, and *sweet mama*. When DeBeck moved the locale of the strip from the city to the North Carolina backwoods after Barney inherited property there, he imbued his creation with colorful expressions that at times accurately reflected the argot of the hills.

Unlike other cartoonists of hillbilly imagery such as Al Capp and Paul Webb, DeBeck conversed with and sketched people in the mountains of Virginia and Kentucky and read widely about mountaineer life. He built an impressive reference library of Appalachian literature and lore that he annotated exhaustively, culling words and phrases for subsequent strips. In particular, DeBeck borrowed heavily from George Washington Harris for the dialect spellings of such words as *hyar* "here," *mought* "might," and *propitty* "property." He also concocted entirely new expressions that had the ring of Appalachian lingo including *daider'n a door-knob*, *time's a wastin'*, *a leetle tetched in the haid*, *shif'less skonk*, and *bodacious idjit*. Many of these terms, such as *balls o' fire* and *jughaid*, joined *heebie jeebies* in the popular lexicon of the day. The strip's success in the 1930s and early 1940s inspired two motion pictures and numerous animated cartoons.

Despite the general authenticity of the strip's dialect, the story lines reinforced well-established stereotypical portrayals of mountain men and women. Snuffy is always willing to "bounce a passel of rifle balls off'n punkin haids" of miscreants in his path and his wife, Loweezy, epitomizes long-suffering drudgery. Laziness, chicken thievery, feuding families, homebrewed corn whiskey, general ignorance, stubborn individuality, belief in supernatural creatures—all are frequent motifs in DeBeck's story lines. Snuffy himself is the model of the self-centered and violent but lazy mountaineer.

After DeBeck's 1942 death from cancer, his longtime assistant, Fred Lasswell, inherited the strip and continued it until his death in 2001. Lasswell over time modified the dialect in order to broaden the strip's appeal yet retained its essential folksy atmosphere.

See also: ANIMATED CARTOONS; CARTOONS; COMIC STRIPS.

—Robert C. Harvey, *Champaign, Illinois*

M. Thomas Inge, *Comics as Culture* (1990); Brian Walker, *Barney Google and Snuffy Smith: Seventy-Five Years of an American Legend* (1994).

Songcatcher

Filmed on location in Madison County, North Carolina, the independent film *Songcatcher*, which was shown in limited theater release in 2001 by Lions Gate Films, explores the early era of ballad collecting in Appalachia. Set in 1907, the story, written and directed by Maggie Greenwald, centers on musicologist Lily Penleric (played by Janet McTeer).

Angered at being repeatedly passed over for promotion in favor of male colleagues, Penleric leaves the Northeast to visit her sister, who is teaching in a rural school in the mountains of North Carolina. Penleric quickly learns that the mountains are alive with a rich tradition of ballad and folk singing and instrumental music. She begins notating the music and ultimately records it on early cylinder equipment.

Through the collecting, Penleric soon becomes entwined in the lives of the mountain people. Viney Butler (Pat Carroll), a wise and sassy mountain matriarch and singer based on well-known North Carolina ballad singer Mary Jane Queen, becomes Penleric's guide to the music and local culture. Viney's grandson, Tom Bledsoe (Aidan Quinn), is a Spanish-American War veteran who has returned to his mountain homeland more sophisticated yet more cynical of those who want to exploit mountaineers for their land or their culture. Bledsoe initially challenges Penleric's motives, but the two eventually learn respect for one another and fall in love. They decide to leave the mountains and take the music to the public through recordings. Penleric leaves her collecting and research work to a male colleague who has arrived to "assist" her.

Critical reaction to the film was mixed: some held the film in high regard, while others felt it was a stereotypical, poorly executed attempt to tell the real story of the culture that produced such remarkable music. Significantly, few reviewers referred to the collecting work of such women as Olive Dame Campbell and Maud Karpeles and their relationship with collector Cecil Sharp; echoes in the love story of Penleric and Bledsoe of local color writing and the life of writer Emma Bell Miles; or the undercurrent of exploitation by land speculators, often local elites. Much of the film's music was provided by natives of Madison County, including Sheila Kay Adams, Bobby McMillon, and Josh Goforth, rather than the film's stars, and folksingers Iris Dement and Taj Mahal contributed cameo performances. The film won the Special Jury Prize for Ensemble Performance after its premiere at the Sundance Film Festival in 2000.

See also: CAMPBELL, JOHN C. AND OLIVE DAME (EDUCATION); FEATURE FILMS; KARPELES, MAUD (FOLKLORE AND FOLKLIFE).

—Jean Haskell, *East Tennessee State University*

Stark Love

The 1927 Paramount film *Stark Love* is one of the great but obscure pieces of anti-rural propaganda in motion-picture history. On the strength of his prior outstanding work as a cameraman in Hollywood, writer and director Karl Brown obtained financing for the movie from Paramount in 1925. Brown got his idea for the production from serialized fiction by Lucy Furman published in the *Atlantic Monthly*, which confirmed Brown's preconceptions about the meanness of life in the backwoods. The quasi-documentary *Nanook of the North*, with a cast of nonindustrialized aborigines, had been a huge hit in 1922, and Brown's idea was to find some similarly atavistic mountain people and make an unsentimental movie about the despicable nature of their lives. He intended to call the film "The Log Cabin."

Brown arrived in Bryson City, North Carolina, in the winter of 1925, where he met Horace Kephart, who sent him further uphill into Graham County, where he found abandoned log cabins. By shooting the story out of sequence, he was able to induce citizens at a dollar a day to appear in his story of male tyranny and lust. The movie was brilliantly executed but appeared bizarre to the Paramount studio bosses, who shelved it. But Brown himself paid for a premiere of the film—renamed *Stark Love* by the studio in a forlorn effort to attract an audience—and it went into a brief and unremarkable national release, after which it was withdrawn and virtually disappeared.

In the late 1960s, scholar Kevin Brownlow stumbled on a foreign-release print of *Stark Love* in the Czechoslovakian national archives—the only surviving print of the movie known to exist—and became an advocate for the brilliance of Brown's work. Unfortunately, Brownlow also implicitly believed that *Stark Love* represented something approaching an anthropological documentary, though its production history suggests otherwise.

See also: FEATURE FILMS; KEPHART, HORACE (LANGUAGE).

—J. W. Williamson, *Appalachian State University*

Storytelling Magazine

The official membership publication of the National Storytelling Network, *Storytelling Magazine* was first published in 1984 as the *National Storytelling Journal*. It was the first formal magazine in the country to focus on professional storytellers and the history and practice of storytelling as an art. Initially produced quarterly through the National Association for the Preservation and Perpetuation of Storytelling (now the National Storytelling Network), the journal began as a refereed publication overseen by an editorial council whose members included children's author Jane Yolen, folklorist Ken Goldstein, and Kentucky poet Lee Pennington. During the magazine's early years, the content was provided by folklorists, librarians, scholars of oral narrative studies, and storytellers. The magazine, along with the *Yarnspinner* newsletter, also produced by the association, was significant in fueling interest in storytelling as an entertainment art form during the 1980s.

The journal was renamed *Storytelling Magazine* in 1989, when it was revamped to appeal to a wider audience. The editorial council was disbanded, and a former editor from Whittle Communications was named as editor. Sold in selected retail bookstores across the country, the magazine's circulation grew along with the nation's interest in storytelling, nearing the ten thousand mark in the early 1990s.

As other storytelling organizations emerged, however, so did publications about the storytelling art, which caused the association—renamed the National Storytelling Association in 1995—to focus more on organizational goals in the latter part of the century. When the group reorganized in 1998, its new membership branch, known as the National Storytelling Network, assumed production of the magazine. In 2001 *Storytelling Magazine* merged with *Storytelling World*, a publication of the Masters in Storytelling program at East Tennessee State University in Johnson City; it now focuses on serving the organization's membership.

See also: INTERNATIONAL STORYTELLING CENTER (PERFORMING ARTS); NATIONAL STORYTELLING NETWORK (PERFORMING ARTS); STORYTELLING IN THE TWENTIETH CENTURY, RENAISSANCE OF (PERFORMING ARTS).

—Jill Oxendine, *Johnson City, Tennessee*

Strangers and Kin

Produced by Appalshop and directed by Herb E. Smith, *Strangers and Kin* is a one-hour investigation of ways Appalachia and mountain people have been stereotyped in popular media and how these images affect the lives of the region's residents. To this end, Smith presents a montage of scenes from turn-of-the-century dime-store fiction and decades of Hollywood films and news documentaries. He then interrupts and critiques this mass-media narrative with scenes from Appalshop films and comments by Roadside Theater actors who recall how the hillbilly image has affected their lives. In addition, the same actors perform caricatures of historians, politicians, and journalists who have perpetuated the hillbilly stereotype.

Since its release in 1984, *Strangers and Kin* has provoked controversy. Tom Gish, the editor of the *Mountain Eagle* newspaper, criticized the film for its condemnation of journalistic images of Appalachia generated during the War on Poverty. He and others took issue with what they viewed as Appalshop's glorification of tradition; they feared this aspect of the film might reinforce mainstream conceptions of the region as backward. Yet the film stands with Henry D. Shapiro's *Appalachia on Our Mind* and Allen W. Batteau's *The Invention of Appalachia* as among the most comprehensive critiques of mass-media reproduction of the hillbilly stereotype. More important, the film is a successful down-to-earth presentation of how a people lose the ability to define their own identity and the impact this has on their everyday lives.

See also: APPALSHOP; ROADSIDE THEATER (PERFORMING ARTS).

—Stephen P. Hanna, *University of Mary Washington*

Stranger with a Camera

Directed, produced, and narrated by Elizabeth Barret and coproduced by Judi Jennings for Appalshop, the documentary film *Stranger with a Camera* debuted to considerable acclaim in 2000. Enthusiasm for the film at Colorado's Sundance Film Festival led to showings nationwide, and it was broadcast as part of public television's *P.O.V.* documentary series. *Stranger with a Camera* has become one of Appalshop's best-known and most respected productions.

The film explores factors that led to the 1967 shooting of Canadian documentary filmmaker Hugh O'Connor by Letcher County, Kentucky, landlord Hobart Ison. O'Connor was in the region to document Appalachian poverty as part of a larger film project entitled *US* concerning the achievements and the shortcomings of American society. Outside Whitesburg, Kentucky, his film crew passed a row of ramshackle rental houses and stopped to film coal miner Mason Eldridge sitting on a front porch with his baby. Ison, the owner of the houses, arrived on the scene, irate with the film crew over what he apparently perceived to be exploitative representations of poor mountain people and no doubt embarrassed by the prospect of houses he owned and maintained being held up as scenes of deprivation. As the film crew attempted to load its equipment and leave the scene, Ison shot O'Connor in the chest, killing him almost instantly.

Ison's case became a passionate cause for many Kentucky residents who saw him as defending the region's honor against outside agitators, especially members of the middle and upper classes who felt disparaged by images of poverty and who had a vested interest in the status quo. The trial, which attracted national media attention (including a *New Yorker* article by Calvin Trillin from which the film takes its name), was moved to neighboring Harlan County in search of an impartial jury, and Ison was convicted of manslaughter. After serving one year of a ten-year term in state prison, he returned to Letcher County, where he lived until his death in 1978.

Barret's film carefully explores not just the incident itself, but the patterns of history, politics, and culture that created the context for Ison and O'Connor's confrontation. *Stranger with a Camera* includes footage from a variety of mid-1960s documentaries about the region, which became a focal point of national anxiety, political debate, and public policy following the 1963 publication of Harry Caudill's *Night Comes to the Cumberlands* and Lyndon Johnson's Great Society legislative initiatives. Barret unpacks the ways that even the most well-meaning and sympathetic of these representations often caused ambivalence and discomfort among its subjects—reactions that sometimes reflected actual hurt feelings and other times, when the discomfort originated with local elites, represented resentment of attempts to ameliorate economic and political injustices.

Barret further contextualizes her examination of forces that converged in the confrontation of Ison and O'Connor by including elements of her own autobiography in the film. Barret recognizes that as a member of Whitesburg's upper middle class, her own relationship to the incident is more complicated than simply that of an Appalachian "insider." Not all Appalachian people, the film shows, think alike, and Barret's gender, family, and class shape her perspective on and presentation of events. On a broader scale, the film suggests that perhaps all documentaries and documentarians have vexed relationships to their subject matter and to any claim to present unambiguous truths through their media.

See also: APPALSHOP; DOCUMENTARY FILMS; NATIONAL POLITICS AND THE MEDIA IN THE 1960S.

—Douglas Reichert Powell, *Columbia College Chicago*

Television Broadcasting

Television first came to Appalachia during the 1920s, when Vladimir Zworykin, a Russian immigrant who lived in the Allegheny Mountains of western Pennsylvania, developed a way to transmit pictures electronically. Zworykin demonstrated his innovations in Pittsburgh in 1929 on a one-inch screen using an iconoscope (camera tube) and a kinescope (cathode-ray picture tube), which led to the modern television camera and receiver. The Zworykin technology was introduced at the 1939 World's Fair in New York City, and within a decade the first television stations were broadcasting in the Appalachian Mountains.

Commercial television in Appalachia began in November 1948 at WDTV in Pittsburgh, a station owned by the DuMont television network. On January 11, 1949, WDTV became the final link in a coaxial cable system reaching coast to coast. The first network broadcast in Appalachia was a remote from the Syria Mosque in Pittsburgh followed by network programming samples including some puppeteers, Arthur Godfrey, and Milton Berle.

As the only Pittsburgh VHF station in the early 1950s, WDTV captured more than 90 percent of the audience, grossing six million dollars a year, four million of which was profit, financially supporting much of the DuMont network. WDTV was the first station in the United States to broadcast a live sporting event and offer twenty-four-hour programming. In 1954 the station was sold to Westinghouse Electric, which changed the call letters to KDKA-TV, matching those of the first commercial radio station. Pittsburgh was and is the largest market in Appalachia.

In October 1949, WSAZ in Huntington, West Virginia, began broadcasting a test pattern to a small number of television set distributors and a handful of people who owned televisions, a typical development pattern in most small markets in Appalachia. A year after sign-on, only four thousand people in Huntington had television sets. In 1952 WSAZ was granted the most powerful transmitter license in the world to reach viewers in the hills and hollows of West Virginia. The transmitter was so powerful that WSAZ was received in both Cuba and Canada. With the opening of a second studio in the capital city of Charleston, WSAZ developed the nation's first two-city market, its dual city news anchors becoming a model for the Chet Huntley–David Brinkley newscast on NBC.

By the mid-1950s, dozens of stations in Appalachia were broadcasting. Eager entrepreneurs raced to get on the television bandwagon. In Johnson City, Tennessee, WJHL-TV rushed onto the air with a transmitter mounted on a telephone pole after its tower collapsed. People throughout the region gathered around sets, enchanted by a whole new world of cultural icons, including Lucille Ball, Sid Caesar, and Kukla, Fran, and Ollie.

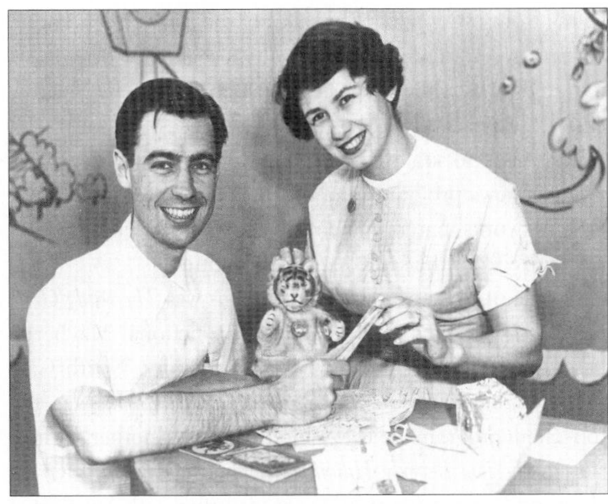

Fred Rogers (later "Mister Rogers") and Josie Carey, coproducers of *The Children's Corner* on WQED Pittsburgh, c. 1952. The nation's first community-owned television station, WQED was a pioneer in children's programming with *The Children's Corner* and its successor, *Mister Rogers' Neighborhood.* The latter became the longest-running program on public television and influenced generations of children, parents, and educators.

In 1954 WQED in Pittsburgh became the first community-owned television station in the United States. It would also become one of the most powerful forces in United States public broadcasting, winning hundreds of awards for excellence, including sixty Emmys and twelve Peabody Awards, the latter bestowed by the University of Georgia. Among the outstanding national series produced by WQED are *The Children's Corner, Mister Rogers' Neighborhood, Wonder Works, National Geographic Specials,* and *Where in the World Is Carmen Santiago?*

Along with network broadcasts, such stations as WDEF in Chattanooga, Tennessee, produced hours of local programs featuring regional celebrities, musicians, preachers, and colorful characters on shows such as *House Party, Children's Gospel Hour,* and *Mr. Chickeroonie*. In 1953 WROL-TV, the first television station in Knoxville, introduced the game show genre with a program called *TV Classroom Quiz*. In 1958 twelve-year-old Dolly Parton, from neighboring Sevier County, performed on a Knoxville television variety show. She went on to star on the *Porter Wagoner Show* and *The Dolly Parton Show,* both syndicated throughout Appalachia. Parton subsequently founded a television production company, creating specials and series for the national networks.

In 1959 politics brought a grim television image of Appalachia to the nation during the West Virginia Democratic primary campaign between Hubert H. Humphrey and John F. Kennedy. As a result, the region became a powerful symbol of rural poverty in America. News and documentary teams from every network exploited the plight of the poor, particularly in the central Appalachian coalfields. Broadcasts narrated by esteemed reporters such as Edward R. Murrow and Charles Kuralt served to raise awareness of poverty in America and to solidify traditional Appalachian stereotypes. Even as news programs and documentaries headlined poverty, networks' entertainment divisions produced comedies and satire from the same region and culture.

One of the most durable programs was *The Andy Griffith Show*, launched in 1960 and set in fictional Mayberry, based on Griffith's hometown of Mount Airy, North Carolina. Eight years later, *The Andy Griffith Show* was the top-rated program in the United States. Another ratings sensation, *The Beverly Hillbillies* (including spin-offs *Green Acres* and *Petticoat Junction*), was as identified with Appalachia as it was with the Ozark Mountains, the Clampett family's fictional home. In the 1970s, America fell in love with *The Waltons*, a highly acclaimed drama set in the Blue Ridge Mountains of Virginia during the Great Depression. "Good night, John-Boy" became part of the American lexicon.

The Appalachian Mountains presented a formidable barrier to television signals, and from the industry's earliest days cable television was employed to reach isolated rural areas while mountaintop antennas relayed signals into other small communities. The dispersion of rural homes was an economic deterrent to hard-wire cable, however. By the late 1970s, huge satellite dishes began to appear beside Appalachian homes, a technology residents used to circumvent limitations of cable and to access more programming. At the turn of the twenty-first century, small digital satellite receivers brought easier access to a multitude of channels. By then there were scores of broadcast outlets in the region, including more than a dozen broadcast markets in the top one hundred, hard-wire cable in many towns, and digital satellite service throughout the mountains.

See also: PITTSBURGH, PENNSYLVANIA (URBAN APPALACHIAN EXPERIENCE); RADIO BROADCASTING; WAR ON POVERTY (GOVERNMENT).

—Tom G. Robertson, *Brentwood, Tennessee*

Ted Bergmann and Ira Skutch, *The DuMont Television Network: What Happened?* (2002); Jeff Kisseloff, *The Box: An Oral History of Television, 1920–1961* (1997); Joseph E. Persico, *Edward R. Murrow: An American Original* (1988).

Television Depictions of the Region

Since the early days of television, images of southern mountaineers have been a staple of programming and a powerful force in shaping national conceptions of the people and the physical and social landscape of Appalachia. News accounts and documentaries emphasizing the region's poverty and isolation—from the 1964 CBS special "Christmas in Appalachia" to the 1989 CBS *48 Hours* report on Muddy Gut Hollow in Floyd County, Kentucky—have played a role in shaping public opinion. More influential, however, have been situation comedies that offered a domesticated version of the familiar hillbilly persona that had evolved over the course of the twentieth century. Although easily dismissed as simply base entertainment aimed at unsophisticated audiences, these comic portrayals also reflected, although rarely explicitly, contemporary social concerns about southern mountain people and conditions and, more generally, about the possibilities and limitations of postwar America.

The Real McCoys (ABC, 1957–63), the first rural situation comedy on network television, told the story of a West Virginia farm family seeking a better life in California's San Fernando Valley. Offering a far softer vision of southern hill migrants than that presented in many news accounts of the day, the show acknowledged American economic hardship in the midst of affluence but suggested that it was eventually surmountable solely through personal initiative. With the exception of Grampa McCoy (Walter Brennan), however, the characters' mountaineer status is generally understated; the family dresses and acts like a typical farm family and most of the plots provide humorous but didactic moral lessons on the importance of family, hard work, and integrity.

Within the next five years, two more CBS programs with Appalachian, or at least mountaineer, components joined the ranks of the most successful shows in television history: *The Andy Griffith Show* (1960–68) and *The Beverly Hillbillies* (1962–71). The former celebrated the simple pleasures of small-town life in Mayberry (based on Griffith's hometown of Mount Airy, North Carolina, on the edge of the Blue Ridge Mountains). In its first two seasons mountaineer characters—invariably presented as symbols of stubbornness, ignorance, and distrust and opposed to modern science and technology—appeared only occasionally. Beginning in March of 1963 and running through December 1964, though, the show featured recurring characters who exemplified separate but related strands of the mythic mountaineer persona. Whereas Briscoe Darling (played by Denver Pyle) and his family (in reality, the string band the Dillards from the Missouri Ozarks) represent the footloose but comfortably self-sufficient musical mountaineer, Ernest T. Bass personifies the deranged mountain man. As portrayed by Howard Morris, Bass is a half-savage with a simian gait whose trademark is throwing rocks through windows. His every encounter with civilization inevitably proves disastrous, and each episode closes with Griffith's Sheriff Taylor hastening him back to the mountains in hopes he will not return.

The timing of these "mountaineer" episodes suggests that they were shaped by the sudden reemergence in the national consciousness of the southern mountains as a distinct "problem region" in a culture of plenty. *The Andy Griffith*

Max Baer Jr., Donna Douglas (with Duke), and Buddy Ebsen in *The Beverly Hillbillies*, Hollywood, California, 1962. The extremely popular comedy poked fun at mountain people and culture typified by the "backward" Clampett family, shown here entering their Beverly Hills mansion for the first time. The program also satirized the gross materialism of the "civilized" world into which the family had moved.

Show and *The Beverly Hillbillies* each reflected the national media fascination with this "white other," an isolated population outside mainstream American society. Their upbeat portrayal of comfortable folk who were upright, self-assured, and imbued with a strong cultural tradition also lessened the sense of the American economic system's failure to prevent seemingly intractable hunger and distress. This was an attempt to redefine the "culture of poverty" said to characterize the region from a crippling cycle of degeneracy and dysfunction to a lifestyle choice of a people who valued leisure pursuits over material advancement.

The enormous popularity of *The Beverly Hillbillies* made it a focal point for a national debate about the nature of television programming. Most reviewers found the plots inane and the gags, mistaken interpretations, and corny word play embarrassing—proof of the destructive vapidity of television. But such criticisms failed to recognize that the show was successful largely because producer Paul Henning redefined the meaning and image of the hillbilly. By cleaning up and desexualizing his characters, he both upheld and challenged the "American dream." While the show reveled in the wealth and status of the Hollywood elite, it also ridiculed conspicuous consumption by portraying the world beyond the Clampett household as peopled almost exclusively by money-grubbers, snobs, and con artists. Yet the power of the show's social critique was simultaneously made possible and undermined by the impossible ignorance and childlike naiveté of the characters and the absurd story lines. Although the immediate and ongoing success of *The Beverly Hillbillies* helped reshape the look of network television, the show's more controversial cultural commentary lasted only through the mid-1960s. As its ratings leveled off and the outrage it had caused dissipated, its episodes increasingly moved away from explicit themes of cultural conflict and instead focused on Jethro's absurd ignorance or ridiculous plots featuring the shenanigans of Elly May's animals. Whereas the Clampetts once were emblematic of both rustic farce and bedrock American virtue, they now increasingly stood only for the former. Reflecting the fading national concern about Appalachia and rural poverty, CBS cancelled all its rural-based sitcoms in 1970–71, replacing them with "relevant" shows featuring young people with modern values.

The passing of the Clampetts from the primetime airwaves (both *The Beverly Hillbillies* and *The Andy Griffith Show* thrived for decades thereafter in syndication) marked the last explicitly labeled "hillbilly" characters on twentieth-century television, but it hardly signified the end of the mountaineer persona on television. *The Waltons* (CBS, 1972–81), a highly successful rural-based drama that escaped the network's purge of all things country, was based on Earl Hamner Jr.'s loosely autobiographical account of his upbringing in Schuyler, Virginia, and presented noble, hardworking Blue Ridge Mountain folk steeped in traditional rural values and protected from the worst ravages of the depression. *The Waltons* was the last great moment of national mountaineer resonance. Though some reviewers found it sappily sentimental, many Americans eagerly embraced its celebration of simple virtues and the centrality of family and place.

Highly stereotyped and romanticized portraits of Appalachia also appeared in various country music variety and comedy shows over the next three decades, from the cornpone humor of *Hee Haw* (CBS, 1969–71 and afterwards in syndication until 1992) to the "Smoky Mountain Christmas" specials of Dolly Parton to *The Dukes of Hazzard* (CBS, 1979–85), one of the highest-rated shows of the early 1980s. *The Dukes of Hazzard* drew on the name of the actual eastern Kentucky mining town of Hazard for its mythical locale of Hazzard County and featured such typical hillbilly stereotypes as scantily clad bosomy women, a grizzled but lovable old moonshiner named Uncle Jesse (played by Pyle in an updating of his Briscoe Darling role), and even an occasional outhouse joke. Nonetheless, its vaguely defined southern landscape mixed mountain stills with alligators, and the show's biggest star was a souped-up hemi-orange 1969 Dodge Charger named "the General Lee."

Appalachia-related characters and settings on network television were less prominent in the 1990s. In the short-lived fish-out-of-water series *Boston Common* (NBC, 1996–97), handyman Boyd Pritchett (Anthony Clark) follows his sister Wyleen (Hedy Burress) from the Virginia hills to a college in the Northeast. *Christy* (CBS, 1994–95), adapted from Catherine Marshall's 1967 novel of the same name, is the story of a middle-class young woman from Asheville, North Carolina, who leaves behind her comfortable life to teach in a backwoods mission school in Cutter Gap, Tennessee, in 1912. In 2003 the region was again linked to network television with CBS's attempt to recruit an actual multigenerational mountain family willing to relocate to Hollywood and star in the "reality" program *The Real Beverly Hillbillies*. Opponents feared it would ridicule poor rural folk, whereas its promoters insisted it could educate "mainstream" Americans about the tenacity and family togetherness of Appalachians. Although the program was not produced, its mere conception illustrates the continuing fascination of network television with Appalachia and its use of the region as a measuring stick of the costs and benefits of materialism and "progress."

See also: "CHRISTMAS IN APPALACHIA"; HENNING, PAUL; WAR ON POVERTY (GOVERNMENT).

—Anthony Harkins, *Western Kentucky University*

Anthony A. Harkins, *Hillbilly: A Cultural History of an American Icon* (2004); J. W. Williamson, *Hillbillyland: What the Movies Did to the Mountains and What the Mountains Did to the Movies* (1995).

That Championship Season

Written and directed by Jason Miller and based on his Pulitzer Prize–winning play, *That Championship Season* (1982) takes place in Miller's hometown of Scranton, Pennsylvania, and revolves around four of five men (played by Bruce Dern, Paul Sorvino, Stacy Keach, and Martin Sheen) who twenty years earlier had been stars of their high school's state championship basketball team. Now in their late thirties, three of the men plus their coach still reside in Scranton, while two have moved away. Each year, the remaining team members get together and reminisce. On this, the twentieth anniversary, a fourth member of the team joins the reunion to honor "Coach" (Robert Mitchum), who is recovering from stomach surgery.

The film focuses largely on the high school victory, which Coach felt gave the former mining town something to be proud of when it had nothing else. The first half hour of the film, shot on location in Scranton, emphasizes the city's economic decline since the closing of the anthracite coal mines in the early 1950s by showing deserted streets and boarded-up store windows. This backdrop supplies the implicit motivation for Coach's effort to instill in his players the drive to succeed at any cost. He largely has accomplished this goal, for the players are, in contrast to many Appalachian stereotypes, urban and successful. Yet they also share to some extent Coach's racism, anti-Semitism, misogyny, and Cold War paranoia, and they backstab each other. Coach does manage once again to reunite the men when they rally to reelect team member George Sitkowski as the city's mayor; however, in the end, it is ambiguous whether they achieve true reconciliation or merely a pathetic illusion of themselves as a team of champions.

Sorvino directed and played Coach in a 1999 remake that also starred Tony Shalhoub, Vincent D'Onofrio, Terry Kinney, and Gary Sinise.

See also: FEATURE FILMS; SCRANTON/WILKES-BARRE, PENNSYLVANIA (URBAN APPALACHIAN EXPERIENCE).

—Mary Katherine Hall, *University of Kentucky*

Thunder Road

A 1954 fatal car crash near Knoxville, Tennessee, served as the inspiration for Robert Mitchum, who wrote both the screenplay and the title song, "The Ballad of Thunder Road," for the 1958 movie *Thunder Road*, directed by Arthur Ripley. Mitchum stars as Luke Doolin, a world-weary Korean War veteran who returns to his southern Appalachian home to assume control of the family business, making and distributing moonshine. Unable to find peace and no longer interested in either city girl Francie Wymore or country girl Roxanne Ledbetter, Luke fills his days and nights running the mountain roads from Harlan County, Kentucky, to the cities of Tennessee delivering the family's homemade liquor.

The Doolin family and their mountain neighbors try to stay ahead of Agent Troy Barrett of the Bureau of Alcohol, Tobacco, and Firearms, who seeks to shut down their operation, and resist city mobster Carl Kogan, who wants to buy them out. When the Doolins refuse his buyout offer, Kogan sends his hoodlums to kill one of their drivers. Luke, concerned about his younger brothers following him in this dangerous family business, decides to make one last run before selling out. A high-speed car chase through the backwoods ends when Luke's car crashes into an electrical transformer.

Though lacking critical acclaim, *Thunder Road*, as a vehicle for Mitchum and his bad-boy image, became a classic among fans of fast cars, chase scenes, and local heroes who outsmart outsiders. Benefiting from the emerging rock 'n' roll mania of the 1950s, this drive-in favorite was among the first to feature customized automobiles with gadgetry such as was popularized in James Bond films and the *Batman* television show.

The movie was filmed on locations in east Tennessee and around Asheville, North Carolina, and many mountain communities claim that *Thunder Road* was based on their hometown and filmed in their own ancestral hollow.

See also: FEATURE FILMS; MITCHUM, ROBERT; MOONSHINE (FOOD AND COOKING).

—Brandon Story, *King College*

Tol'able David

One of the finest silent films to deal with the southern mountains, *Tol'able David* (1921) belongs to a primary genre of early Appalachian cinema—the feud melodrama. Young David Kinemon, the story's protagonist, becomes a reluctant feudist after the villainous Hatburns gun down his brother, inadvertently cause his father's death, and steal the United States mail that David carries.

Director Henry King, born near Christiansburg, shot the film on location in Highland County, Virginia, making excellent use of the mountain landscape. The camera captures log cabins, half-dovetail notching, split-rail fences, log bridges, pie safes, fly whisks, and crocks, creating a celluloid museum of Appalachian material culture. In another gesture toward realism, the film's evil Hatburns hail from Tug Fork Valley, West Virginia, which was the real-life home of the Hatfields of Hatfields-and-McCoys fame. The film's cinematography was highly advanced for its day. King was a pioneer of montage; Soviet film theorist Vsevolod Pudovkin praised the film's editing. Some prints were tinted in various pastel shades, a process that was a precursor to full-color filmmaking.

Tol'able David made a star of Richard Barthelmess, who played the title role. Also noteworthy were Ernest Torrence as Luke Hatburn and Marion Abbott as the powerful but weepy Mother Kinemon.

King's film was a box-office success. In 1930 a sound remake was issued; this version proved less successful than the original, in part because its studio shots lacked the appeal of King's on-location images.

See also: FEATURE FILMS; FEUDS (GOVERNMENT); VIOLENCE AND VENGEANCE (IMAGES AND ICONS).

—Theresa Lloyd, *East Tennessee State University*

Trail of the Lonesome Pine, The

The Trail of the Lonesome Pine is a 1936 film directed by Henry Hathaway based on John Fox Jr.'s 1908 novel of the same name. The first outdoor motion picture filmed entirely in Technicolor, the movie depicts the clash between traditional Appalachian Mountain culture and the progress of the outside world. Two earlier adaptations of the novel include legendary film director Cecil B. DeMille's 1916 silent version and Charles Maigne's 1923 sound version.

While the book makes the solitary lonesome pine and other nature motifs central to the plot, the movie treats them merely as backdrops for the action. With largely superficial and one-dimensional characterization, the film portrays the Tollivers and Falins as trigger-happy hillbillies who feud with each other and scorn anything modern. The love triangle of Dave Tolliver (Henry Fonda), June Tolliver (Sylvia Sidney), and Jack Hale (Fred MacMurray) is also stereotypical. Dave is an angry young man obsessed by his love for June and his hatred of progress. June, a fickle child-woman, tries to become civilized to please Jack. When faced with tragedy, her veneer of "civilization" strips away, exposing her as the "little savage" Jack had labeled her. Jack, an engineer responsible for building a railroad to link the coal-rich mountains with the fuel-hungry eastern factories, is a "crusader" trying to save the mountain people from their barbaric, ignorant ways without trying to understand the culture. Although the film fails to provide a careful or complex image of Appalachia, it does reveal the impact of the railroad and mining industries on a small mountain town in Virginia.

See also: FOX, JOHN, JR. (LITERATURE); OUTDOOR DRAMA (PERFORMING ARTS).

—Gloria F. Lacy and Mary Grace Meador, *East Tennessee State University*

Travel Writing

See Travel Writing (Literature)

Valley of the Tennessee

A 1944 film about the Tennessee Valley Authority (TVA), *Valley of the Tennessee* was produced by the Office of War Information, Overseas Branch, directed by Alexander Hammid, and narrated by Fredric March. One of the archetypal documentaries of the 1940s, *Valley of the Tennessee* is modeled upon films by Pare Lorentz *(The River; The Plow That Broke the Plains)* and other 1930s documentarians.

Made for overseas audiences but later distributed domestically, the film depicts mountain people as backward, suspicious of outsiders, unfamiliar with and resistant to enlightened farming practices (contour plowing, use of phosphate fertilizer, crop rotation), and befuddled by modernity in general. TVA's program of planned, technologically oriented, integrated river-basin development (flood control, power production, agricultural reform) is presented as the best of both modernity and democracy: rational, progressive, and equitable.

Approximately half of the film's sequences focus broadly upon TVA's conception and operation and feature high-level policy and planning sessions, animated maps and illustrations, working laboratory models of river systems and dams, and documentary footage of TVA projects, including the wartime construction of Fontana Dam. These scenes alternate with a dramatization of one farmer's conversion to and rehabilitation through TVA's agricultural program. In this story, a physically unattractive, poorly dressed "bad" farmer skeptically rejects the agency's invitation and fails to prosper, while an attractive, receptive, "good" farmer signs onto the proffered program, transforms his farm, harvests bumper crops, buys a new tractor, and becomes a prosperous example to his neighbors.

See also: DEPRESSION AND THE NEW DEAL; DOCUMENTARY FILMS; TENNESSEE VALLEY AUTHORITY (GOVERNMENT).

—David E. Whisnant, *Chapel Hill, North Carolina*

Waltons, The

Earl Hamner Jr. developed the long-lived television series *The Waltons* (1972–81) after his novel *Spencer's Mountain* (1961) had already been adapted into a theatrical movie of the same title in 1963. Hamner's pilot television movie, *The Homecoming* (1971), introduced the Walton family that Americans would come to know for almost a decade. Set in the Blue Ridge Mountains of rural Virginia, the film presents a family who endures Great Depression–era hardships through faith, perseverance, and love. *The Waltons* premiered in the fall of 1972, depicting traditional family values for television viewers living in a decade when Americans were attempting to reorient themselves after the social upheavals of the 1960s.

Consisting of the paternal grandparents, a wife and husband, and, at first, seven children, the Walton household contains three generations living under one roof who are kept together by a shared sense of faith, ethics, and morals. Viewers learn about the family primarily through the eyes of the oldest son, John-Boy, an aspiring writer. In spite of a chronic shortage of money, the Waltons live relatively comfortably, relying on their family sawmilling business and tempering their hardy self-reliance with genuine concern for their community and those in need. They value education, secure in the belief that, as their children better themselves in the world, they will also mature in appreciation of what they have learned at home. For the same reason, the family prizes the arts as a medium through which to develop compassion and inspiration, complementing those values they learn at church. Although familial love does not offer an instant solution to problems the Waltons face, it does provide them the endurance, dedication, and selflessness to overcome those difficulties.

The Waltons is not without its critics, who argue that the show romanticizes the past, specifically the poverty of mountain people during the Great Depression. Nonetheless, the show provides positive role models and confirmation of the importance of family. Unlike family sitcoms such as *The Brady Bunch* and *The Partridge Family*, *The Waltons* presents problems not instantly resolved by episode's end. Illnesses adversely affect how the family functions, sons go to war, daughters have unsuccessful romances, and children move far away. To be sure, the Walton's Mountain community has its share of idiosyncratic characters, but the show's refusal to present mere caricatures helped broaden its appeal to primarily rural audiences throughout the nation. Within two seasons, *The Waltons* supplanted its time-slot competitor, NBC's *The Flip Wilson Show*, as the number two show in the United States. During a time of rising inflation, redefinition of social mores, and domestic and foreign instability, *The Waltons* offered more than gentle nostalgia—it affirmed the importance of home. Its signature ending, a view of the house in twilight as all family members say "good night" to each other, became an American emblem of comfort and security.

See also: HOMEPLACE (IMAGES AND ICONS); SECTION OVERVIEW; TELEVISION DEPICTIONS OF THE REGION.

—Thomas Alan Holmes, *East Tennessee State University*

WBT

From the 1930s to the 1950s, seven days a week, radio listeners across the Carolinas tuned in Charlotte, North Carolina–based WBT to enjoy the fiddle breakdowns, gospel tunes, lively waltzes, and sweet love ballads that had become an integral part of the South's rich musical culture and a key component of the station's programming. WBT boasted a fifty-thousand-watt signal that made it the most powerful broadcast station in the Carolinas, and the popularity of live country music programs such as *Briarhopper Time*, the *Crazy Water Crystals Barn Dance*, and *Carolina Calling* gave the station a significant role in the shift of southern sounds from folk tradition to commercial industry.

The dozens of musicians who passed through the station's studios forged innovative musical forms, blending traditional styles and arrangements with new sounds and themes. Their repertoires ranged from time-honored religious tunes such as "The Old Rugged Cross" to Dorsey Dixon's thoroughly contemporary "Weave Room Blues," a depression-era tune chronicling the hardships of working in the South's booming textile industry.

WBT also served as a haven for nostalgia, particularly that of Appalachia and its culture. The station employed many pioneering Appalachian musicians, including J. E. and Wade Mainer, Zeke and Wiley Morris, and Bill and Earl Bolick (the Blue Sky Boys). But the station's primary audience lay in the rapidly industrializing Piedmont region, and its portrayal of Appalachia was colored in romantic hues, with promoters touting "the real untarnished mountain tunes" of WBT's Appalachian performers.

Although WBT remains on the air today, its role as a major outlet for Carolina country talent faded in the 1950s, when recorded music supplanted live broadcasts and rock 'n' roll became the musical rage.

See also: MUSIC BROADCASTING; OLD-TIME MUSIC (MUSIC); RADIO BROADCASTING.

—Pamela Grundy, *Charlotte, North Carolina*

West Virginia Hillbilly

A small weekly newspaper founded in 1956 by Jim Comstock and Bronson McClung and published in Richwood, West Virginia, the *West Virginia Hillbilly* quickly earned a large following of readers attracted to its folksy, homespun humor, satirical jibes, unconventional articles, and the fine feature writing of its regular column, "The Comstock Load." The paper's popularity continued to grow in the 1960s and 1970s, making it one of the most famous publications in West Virginia and the entire Appalachian region.

Despite its eventual success, the newspaper's path was often fraught with opposition, setbacks, and controversy. Initially, some individuals objected to the use of the word *hillbilly* in the title, believing it to be inappropriate and denigrating. A year later, failure to obtain sufficient advertising revenue forced the newspaper briefly to fold between 1958 and 1959. Once back in business, the paper continued to be subject to frequent criticism. An article explaining how to remove one's own appendix, for example, elicited vociferous protests. On another occasion, Comstock ran afoul of the postmaster general, who reprimanded him for the malodorous prank of mixing ramp juice (liquid from wild leeks) in with the printing ink.

Although Comstock died in 1996, the *West Virginia Hillbilly* continues. Circulation has diminished in recent years, but the newspaper still offers its readers a glimpse of life in West Virginia and a simple, unaffected perspective on the varied Appalachian experience.

See also: NEWSPAPERS.

—Larry Sean Kinder, *Western Kentucky University*

Where the Lilies Bloom

Based on a Newberry Award–winning novel by Vera and Bill Cleaver, *Where the Lilies Bloom* (Radnitz/Mattel Productions, 1974), directed by William A. Graham, tells the story of four children orphaned upon the death of their father who attempt to elude foster care and maintain their hill-country home in Watauga County, North Carolina. The family's adventures are mostly comic, as the second-eldest daughter, Mary Call (played by Julie Gholson, age fourteen and, like many of the film's actors, a nonprofessional), takes charge of the family, attempting both to hide the father's death and prevent the eldest daughter, Devola (Jan Smithers), from marrying the hated landlord Kiser Pease (Harry Dean Stanton).

The film, with an adapted screenplay by Virginian-born Earl Hamner Jr., creator of television's *The Waltons*, presents mountain people as proud and stoic, frank and resourceful, and its tone is sometimes melancholic. The maternal and feminine Devola is dismissed in the film as dreamy and impractical, but hard-driving tomboy Mary Call is the real dreamer, a would-be writer yearning for something beyond her Appalachian home, a "fair land . . . where the lilies bloom." Her writing teacher implores her to escape the Appalachian hills: "Your life should count for something." This startling message is vindicated in the film, for it becomes clear that the father was a poor and impractical farmer who had asked too much of his daughter. Mary Call realizes this by the end of the film, acknowledging, however, that she will love him even so. What is true of her father is, according to the logic of the film, implicitly true of mountain life more generally: it demands too much. At the end, Mary Call declares her intention, eventually, to leave her home.

See also: FEATURE FILMS; *WALTONS, THE.*

—Paul V. Murphy, *Grand Valley State University*

Wild River

Academy Award–winning director Elia Kazan's *Wild River* (Twentieth Century Fox, 1960), based in part on Borden Deal's *Dunbar's Cove* (1957) as well as William Bradford Huie's *Mud on the Stars* (1942), is a parable of the frontier versus civilization. Filmed on location in and around the Tennessee towns of Charleston and Cleveland, *Wild River* dramatizes the confrontation between an idealistic New Deal administrator, Chuck Glover (played by Montgomery Clift), and the aged Ella Garth (Jo Van Fleet), a widow who refuses to leave her land, which is slated to be flooded by the Tennessee Valley Authority. Garth represents stubborn backcountry individualism; Glover, cosmopolitan liberalism. When he runs afoul of the locals by employing African Americans at wages equal to whites, Glover's story ironically recapitulates Garth's, as he finds himself making his own lonely stand, in his case against a racist bully and an angry mob. Kazan identified with the character of Garth and sympathized with the country folk, making them emblems of human emotion and connection.

In a romantic subplot, Glover initiates a romance with Garth's widowed granddaughter, Carol Baldwin (Lee Remick). The rootless Glover resists emotional commitment, but Baldwin—sexually unrepressed, passionate, and ultimately stronger than Glover—coaxes him into marriage.

Glover comes to respect Garth, who leaves her land only under compulsion and then quietly passes away. "I like things running wild, like nature made them," she proclaims early in the film. The film was financially unsuccessful and received lukewarm critical reviews, but it remained one of Kazan's personal favorites.

See also: FEATURE FILMS; NATIONAL POLITICS AND THE MEDIA IN THE 1960S; TENNESSEE VALLEY AUTHORITY (GOVERNMENT).

—Paul V. Murphy, *Grand Valley State University*

Winter People

Winter People (1989), the feature film adaptation of John Ehle's 1982 novel *The Winter People*, was directed by Ted Kotcheff *(North Dallas Forty; First Blood)* and written by Carol Sobieski *(Fried Green Tomatoes; Sarah, Plain and Tall)*. The film stars Kelly McGillis as Collie Wright, an unmarried mountain woman who refuses to reveal the identity of her infant son's father. The boy's father is from a rival mountain family, a clan of brutish, barbaric trappers who guzzle moonshine and perpetuate many of the film's violent acts. Kurt Russell stars as Wayland Jackson, a young widower who with his daughter becomes stranded near Collie's property. Collie not only takes in Jackson and his daughter but convinces her father (Lloyd Bridges) to give Jackson a place in the family-owned store as a clockmaker. Only after Jackson passes a series of manly feats with Collie's three brothers and her father can he be welcomed and accepted into the community.

Ehle's carefully constructed story, drawing symbolic overtones from a western North Carolina winter during the Great Depression, generally disappears in this Columbia Pictures version. Although family allegiance, secrets, and sacrifice drive the narrative, the film draws on and reinforces broad cultural generalizations and stereotyping of mountain families by relying on stock characters and improbable events. *Winter People* was filmed on location in Avery County, North Carolina.

See also: EHLE, JOHN (LITERATURE); FEATURE FILMS.

—Marianne Worthington, *Cumberland College*

WMMT

Located in Whitesburg, Kentucky, WMMT Radio (88.7 FM) began broadcasting in November 1985 and remains a noncommercial community radio station. WMMT's programming includes rock/pop, jazz, blues, world, and Americana, but it is known primarily for its emphasis on bluegrass, old-time, and traditional folk music. One of WMMT's radio series, *Anchored in Love: The Carter Family Story*, was distributed nationally in 2000 to more than six hundred public radio stations as part of Appalshop's thirtieth-anniversary celebration. In addition to music, WMMT also broadcasts programs that focus on economic, environmental, and social issues within the Appalachian region. As a nonprofit radio station, WMMT produces most of its programming with the assistance of approximately fifty volunteers from the surrounding community. WMMT's fifteen-thousand-watt signal extends through five states in the southern Appalachians, including eastern and central Kentucky, southwestern Virginia, eastern Tennessee, southwestern West Virginia, and northwestern North Carolina. In 1986 WMMT began broadcasting live performances of regional music on its show *Bluegrass Express Live*, which has attracted artists such as Larry Sparks, Blue Highway, the Lonesome River Band, and Bill and James Monroe. The station has reached wider audiences via the World Wide Web since July 1999.

WMMT has received various awards for excellence in broadcasting. In February 1998 WMMT was named Station of the Month by the National Federation of Community Broadcasters. In 1999 WMMT received the media award from the East Kentucky Leadership Foundation for the station's outstanding public service.

See also: BLUEGRASS (MUSIC); RADIO BROADCASTING.

—David B. Pruett, *Florida State University*

WNOX

The first radio station in Knoxville, Tennessee, and eighth oldest nationwide, WNOX aired its initial broadcast in 1921. From its original programming of mountain music to its current format of talk radio, WNOX has served the southern Appalachian region and made significant contributions to the history of country music.

From 1921 to 1955, WNOX's programming included several hillbilly variety shows. The first of these, *Mac and Bob*, highlighted the musical talents of Robert A. Gardner and Lester MacFarland, who sang and accompanied themselves on mandolin and guitar, respectively. In 1935 Roy Acuff and Crazy Tennesseans began their own variety show at WNOX. When Acuff left for rival station WROL later that year, announcer and producer Lowell Blanchard expanded the show's format to include new gimmicks, more musicians, comedy material, and longer airtimes; Blanchard also changed the name to the *Midday Merry-Go-Round*, which had a weekend counterpart, the *WNOX Carnival*. The two shows featured musicians Pee Wee King, the Tennessee Ramblers, and comedian Archie Campbell.

In 1942 the *WNOX Carnival* became the *Tennessee Barn Dance*, reaching national audiences via WNOX's CBS network affiliation. The roster included artists such as Chet Atkins, Carl Story, Kitty Wells, J. E. Mainer's Mountaineers, Charlie Monroe and the Kentucky Pardners, and Mother Maybelle and the Carter Sisters. The station hoped to televise the show in 1954; however, the Federal Communications

Commission denied WNOX's request because of antitrust restrictions. After 1955 the station's popularity in country music circles gradually declined. In 1962 WNOX changed its format to rock 'n' roll.

See also: COUNTRY MUSIC COMEDY (HUMOR); FIELD RECORDING SESSIONS (MUSIC); RADIO BROADCASTING.

—David B. Pruett, *Florida State University*

WOPI

One of the earliest commercial radio stations in the Appalachian region, WOPI was founded in Bristol, Tennessee, in 1929 by W. A. Wilson, the owner of a local retail radio shop. Wilson had been conducting experimental radio broadcasts from locations in downtown Bristol and eventually obtained a license from the Federal Radio Commission to launch the station. Although ownership has changed several times since 1960, WOPI continues to operate and has kept its original call letters, which stand for "Watch Our Popularity Increase."

The station's programming in its early years consisted of drama, variety programs, live local entertainment, and news. Country music was featured prominently, and a number of commercial country music artists including Jimmie Rodgers and many musicians from east Tennessee and southwest Virginia regularly appeared. In 1935 Wilson established *Saturday Night Jamboree*, one of the first live radio barn dance programs in the area. Many famous names in the history of country music made appearances on this program, including established artists such as the Carter Family and the Tenneva Ramblers, and many who were just getting started, including Tennessee Ernie Ford, Archie Campbell, Charlie Bowman, Homer and Jethro, and Chet Atkins. Ford became a part-time announcer for WOPI while he was still in high school, departing in 1945 to become a popular recording star and later to host his own network television programs.

During the second half of the twentieth century, ownership of WOPI passed to Pioneer Broadcasting Corporation in 1960, Tri-Cities Broadcasting Company in 1965, Thomas Ray Tolar Sr. in 1972, and the United Broadcasting Company in 1978. In 1990 the station was sold to Joe Morrell, a local music store owner, who attempted to revive the station's roots by airing a heavy dose of bluegrass and old-time country music. After a year, however, Morrell joined with the WKPT radio network in nearby Kingsport, Tennessee, and began offering a broader musical format. In 1996 WOPI was acquired by the network's owner, Holston Valley Broadcasting Corporation.

See also: FORD, TENNESSEE ERNIE (MUSIC); RADIO BROADCASTING.

—Bill Mountjoy, *Elizabethton, Tennessee*, and Jill Oxendine, *Johnson City, Tennessee*

WPAQ

WPAQ Radio (740 AM) aired its first broadcast in February 1948 from Mount Airy, North Carolina, and has since maintained programming that highlights the traditional music and culture of the Appalachian region. The station is known for broadcasting live music—namely bluegrass, old-time, and gospel—and for broadcasts featuring local economic and social issues.

During the post–World War II era, WPAQ became popular through its promotion of live music from the region. Transmitting first at one thousand watts in 1948, the station increased to ten thousand watts in 1954, making it the third most powerful station in North Carolina. WPAQ's weekly live broadcast, the *Merry-Go-Round*, adopted the barn dance format of WSM's *Grand Ole Opry*. The show attracted musicians such as Lester Flatt and Earl Scruggs, J. E. and Wade Mainer, Mother Maybelle and the Carter Sisters, Tommy Jarrell, Charlie Monroe, Arthur Smith, Ralph Stanley, Carl Story, and Mac Wiseman. Airing each Saturday since 1948, the *Merry-Go-Round* is the third longest running live radio broadcast in America. WPAQ's archive comprises approximately seventy-five hundred recordings and documents more than seventy-five years of American music history.

WPAQ has received awards of excellence from the American Folklife Center, the International Bluegrass Music Association, and the National Council for the Traditional Arts. For its preservation and dissemination efforts, the station is regionally recognized as the "Voice of the Blue Ridge Mountains." This metaphor appeared in the titles of a fifteen-minute documentary film about WPAQ (Surry Arts Council, 1997) and a compact disc produced by Paul Brown and compiled by Ralph Epperson from WPAQ's recording archives (Rounder, 1999).

See also: BLUEGRASS (MUSIC); *GRAND OLE OPRY*; RADIO BROADCASTING.

—David B. Pruett, *Florida State University*

WSB

A subsidiary of the *Atlanta Journal*, WSB began broadcasting in March 1922 and is best remembered for its important role in the development of country music before World War II. Known as "The Voice of the South," WSB claimed to be the first southern radio station to broadcast old-time music (later called hillbilly music) played by local string bands, fiddlers, and Sacred Harp singers. Exposure on WSB helped launch the recording careers of many influential entertainers, including Fiddlin' John Carson, Riley Puckett, and Clayton McMichen. During the 1920s, WSB featured more than one hundred musical acts, many from southern Appalachia. The station also broadcast live studio barn dances and performers from Atlanta's annual Georgia Old-Time Fiddlers' Convention.

In 1927 WSB joined the recently organized NBC network, which drastically reduced radio appearances by local amateur talent. Instead, the station's corporate-sponsored programs throughout the 1930s relied primarily on professionals such as Dick Hartman and His Crazy Tennessee Ramblers and the Carolina Tarheels. In 1936 WSB premiered *Cross Road Follies* (1936–40), a hillbilly music variety program. That same year, the station began operating at 750 AM as a clear-channel fifty-thousand-watt station; its broadcasts could be heard throughout Appalachia and as far away as Australia.

Under new management, WSB expanded its country music offerings in 1939 with the addition of such programs as *Cracker Barrel* and *Hayride*. The following year, the station debuted *WSB Barn Dance* (1940–50), a long-running Saturday-night jamboree featuring such acts as Hank Penny and His Radio Cowboys and the Hoot Owl Hollow Girls. The station stopped airing live country music broadcasts in the mid-1950s. Today, WSB broadcasts news and talk programming, and WSB-TV, the South's first television station, operates as an ABC affiliate.

See also: COUNTRY MUSIC (MUSIC); MUSIC BROADCASTING; OLD-TIME MUSIC (MUSIC).

—Patrick Huber, *University of Missouri at Rolla*

WSM

See *Grand Ole Opry*

WWNC

See Radio Broadcasting

WWVA

For more than seventy-five years, WWVA in Wheeling, West Virginia, has been a major communications outlet in northern Appalachia. WWVA initially went on the air in mid-December 1926 as a fifty-watt radio station. On July 1, 1929, WWVA became a five-thousand-watt station and on October 8, 1942, increased to fifty thousand watts. The station's evening signal was aimed in a northwesterly direction, and as a result WWVA attracted listeners throughout rural Pennsylvania, upstate New York, "down east" New England, and adjacent portions of Canada. The station exercised its principal influence while the property of Toledo, Ohio–based Storer Broadcasting Company. George Smith, who served as station manager from 1931 until his death in 1946, saw radio as a means to "level all humanity" and disseminate the culture of the common man. Under his influence WWVA developed into an important outlet for country music, remaining so well into the mid-1950s, when the station, and others like it, could no longer afford live talent for daily programs. However, its live-audience, Saturday-night *Jamboree*, begun in 1933, has continued (under various names) until the present. During the station's early years, WWVA also provided a variety of community services and featured programs that appealed to the east European ethnic population of the upper Ohio Valley.

In recent years, WWVA has abandoned its country and western format for talk radio. Although *Jamboree USA* continues live Saturday-night country music broadcasts during the spring and fall months, it is on hiatus during January, February, and the midsummer season.

See also: COUNTRY MUSIC (MUSIC); RADIO BROADCASTING; *WWVA JAMBOREE*.

—Ivan M. Tribe, *University of Rio Grande*

WWVA Jamboree

A country music radio program originating from WWVA in Wheeling, West Virginia, the *WWVA Jamboree* (also known as *Jamboree USA*, *Original WWVA Jamboree*, and *Wheeling Jamboree*) has been a regular Saturday-night broadcast since January 7, 1933. Through most of its history—excepting the first few weeks of the production, prior to April 1, 1933, and during the period of gasoline rationing in World War II—the program has been performed before a live audience. In the early years and again after 1969, broadcasts originated in Wheeling's Capital Theater.

Several noted country music performers, including Grandpa Jones, Wilma Lee and Stoney Cooper, Hawkshaw Hawkins, and Lionel Cartwright, spent significant portions of their careers there. Others, such as the team of Doc and Chickie Williams, as well as Lee Moore and Big Slim, the Lone Cowboy (Harry C. McAuliffe), remained based at the *Jamboree* for the better part of their careers. With the passing of time and a greater concentration of the country music industry in Nashville, shows have increasingly been built around guest stars from that city, and *Jamboree* regulars have been relegated to the role of little more than opening acts. The *Jamboree* has also concentrated more on a multi-day, outdoor, midsummer festival begun in 1977 called Jamboree in the Hills, which attracts several thousand fans of contemporary country music. It has ceased operating during January and February and July and August, but continues to be broadcast on Saturday nights during the fall and spring months.

See also: COUNTRY MUSIC COMEDY (HUMOR); RADIO BROADCASTING; WWVA.

—Ivan M. Tribe, *University of Rio Grande*

Index of Contributors

I

J

K

L

M

N

O

P

R

S

T

U

V

W

Y

Z

General Index

Page numbers in **boldface** type refer to articles; page numbers in *italic* type refer to illustrations.

A

B

C

D

E

F

G

H

J

L

M

N

O

P

S

T

U

V

Y

Z

Illustration Credits

Section I • Geology

Page

2 Photograph by Robert Behling.

6 Chart by Don W. Byerly and Nancy Fischman.

8 Map by John J. Renton and Nancy Fischman.

15 Map by John J. Renton and Nancy Fischman.

31 Photograph by Paul Breeding. Courtesy of Maryland Geological Survey.

Section II • Ecology

38 Photograph by Kaylynn S. Wilster.

42 Photograph by Kaylynn S. Wilster.

46 Photograph by Craig W. Stihler.

47 Photograph by George Constantz.

57 Photograph by James N. Holmes.

63 Photograph by Kelly Bond.

66 Photograph by Katya Kaverina.

69 Photograph by Kevin & Bethany Shank/Dogwood Ridge Photography.

74 Photograph by Kaylynn S. Wilster.

82 Photograph by James N. Holmes.

83 Photograph by Kevin & Bethany Shank/Dogwood Ridge Photography.

87 Photograph by L. Yampolsky.

88 Photograph by George Constantz.

96 Photograph by James N. Holmes.

97 Photograph by Kelly Bond.

Section III • Environment

100 Photograph by Sidney V. Streator. Courtesy of Forest History Society, Durham, North Carolina.

103 Map by Nancy Fischman, adapted with permission from the AppMap, copyright Appalachian Voices, 2001.

105 Photograph by William Strode.

113 Photograph by Kenneth Murray.

120 Photograph from the *Message from the President*, Senate Document No. 84, plate LXVII. Courtesy of the Archives of Appalachia, East Tennessee State University.

122 Photograph by Richard VanDyke. Courtesy of Jean Battlo.

123 Photograph courtesy of National Archives [95G-27294A].

127 Photograph by Earl Dotter.

141 Photograph by Edward T. McMahon.

Section IV • Family and Community

148 Photograph by Kenneth Murray. Courtesy of the Archives of Appalachia, East Tennessee State University.

150 From the Blue Ridge Parkway Project collection, courtesy of the American Folklife Center, Washington, D.C. Photograph by Richard McCamant.

158 Photograph by Randy Ball.

160 Courtesy of the Southern Appalachian Archives, Berea College, Berea, Kentucky.

161 Courtesy of the Eastern Regional Coal Archives, Bluefield, West Virginia.

186 Courtesy of the West Virginia and Regional History Collection, West Virginia University Libraries, Morgantown, West Virginia.

195 Photograph by Meredith Dean. Courtesy of the Appalachian Women's Alliance.

196 Photograph by George Harvan. Courtesy of Genevieve Harvan.

Section V • Images and Icons

198 Photograph by Earl Palmer. Courtesy of Jean Haskell.

202 Photograph by Kenneth Murray. Courtesy of the Archives of Appalachia, East Tennessee State University.

208 Photograph by Pat Arnow.

211 Photograph by Pat Arnow.

211 Photograph by Peggy Calestro.

213 Photograph by Doug Yarrow. Courtesy of Candie Carawan, Highlander Center, New Market, Tennessee.

217 Courtesy of MWM Dexter, Inc.

221 Reproduced from *Tennessee: the Volunteer State, 1769–1923*, Volume 1. Courtesy of the Tennessee State Library and Archives.

224 Photograph by Peggy Calestro.

229 Courtesy of the U.S. Department of the Interior, National Park Service, Edison National Historic Site.

232 Photograph by Randy Ball.

234 Courtesy of West Virginia State Archives.

Section VI • Race, Ethnicity, and Identity

238 Photograph by Kenneth Murray. Courtesy of the Archives of Appalachia, East Tennessee State University.

240 Photograph by George Harvan. Courtesy of Genevieve Harvan.

256 Drawing by A. W. Thompson. From *Harper's Weekly*, September 28, 1867. Courtesy of John Inscoe.

259 Photograph by Carlos de Wendler-Funaro. Courtesy of the National Museum of American History, Smithsonian Institution.

267 Photograph by Coyle. Courtesy of Les and Joyce Brown and Ann Duncan.

269 Photograph by Kenneth Murray. Courtesy of the Archives of Appalachia, East Tennessee State University.

277 Photograph by Lora Gordon. Courtesy of Radford University.

280 Courtesy of John Inscoe.

Section VII • Settlement and Migration

284 George Caleb Bingham, *Daniel Boone Escorting Settlers through the Cumberland Gap* (detail), 1851–52. Oil on canvas, 36½ × 50¼″. Washington University Gallery of Art, St. Louis. Gift of Nathaniel Phillips, 1890.

288 Map by Nancy Fischman.

296 Courtesy of The Filson Historical Society, Louisville, Kentucky.

299 Courtesy of Eastern Regional Coal Archives.

315 Engraving by G. R. Hall. Courtesy of National Archives [NARA-148-GW-391].

319 Photograph by Richard E. Porter. Courtesy of David Williams.

327 Photograph by Direct-Axis. Courtesy of National Road Heritage Corridor.

333 Photograph by Charles M. Peery. From the Totten Collection, courtesy of Museum of the Middle Appalachians.

333 Painting by Greg Harlin. Courtesy of Frank H. McClung Museum, University of Tennessee.

339 Painting by Robert Lindneux. Courtesy of Woolaroc Museum, Bartlesville, Oklahoma.

Section VIII • Urban Appalachian Experience

346 Map by Nancy Fischman.

350 Photograph by Michael Melford. Courtesy of Chattanooga Area Convention & Visitors Bureau.

356 From the E. M. Ball Collection [ballp1754], courtesy of the University of North Carolina at Asheville.

360 Photograph by Stephen Shaluta. Courtesy of West Virginia Division of Tourism.

366 Photograph by Johnna L. Byers. Courtesy of Cumberland Mayor and City Council.

367 Courtesy of Scharchburg Archives, Kettering University.

370 Photograph by William B. Coxe. From the Coxe Photograph Collection. Courtesy of the Greenville County Historical Society.

377 Photograph by Norman W. Schumm.

378 Courtesy of the Portsmouth Area Convention and Visitors Bureau.

379 Courtesy of Richmond, Kentucky Tourism and Main Street Department.

386 Courtesy of University Relations, University of Alabama.

Section IX • Agriculture

394 Photograph by Kenneth Murray. Courtesy of the Archives of Appalachia, East Tennessee State University.

397 Photograph by Earl Palmer. Courtesy of Jean Haskell.

401 Photograph by Bob Nichols, USDA Natural Resources Conservation Service.

412 Photograph courtesy of the North Carolina Christmas Tree Association.

417 Photograph by Skip Thompson, North Carolina Cooperative Extension, North Carolina State University.

420 Photograph by Lyntha Scott Eiler. From Tending the Commons: Folklife and Landscape in Southern West Virginia, courtesy of the American Folklife Center, Library of Congress.

421 Photograph by David Best.

426 Photograph by Jeff Vanuga, USDA Natural Resources Conservation Service.

435 Photograph by J. L. Byrne. Courtesy of the University of Tennessee Institute of Agriculture.

438 Photograph courtesy of Cooperative Extension System Records, Special Collections and Archives, Auburn University.

Section X • Business, Industry, and Technology

440 Photograph from the Tom Franco Collection, courtesy of Rivers of Steel Archives.

442 Photograph by Kenneth Murray.

458 Photograph by Builder Levy.

469 Photograph by David R. Dodrill. Courtesy of the National Institute for Chemical Studies.

476 Photograph courtesy of the Carpet and Rug Institute.

485 Courtesy of Georgia Power Corporate Communications.

505 Photograph courtesy of National Aeronautics and Space Administration.

517 Courtesy of Oak Ridge National Laboratory, U.S. Department of Energy.

520 Courtesy of the Pennsylvania Historical and Museum Commission, Drake Well Museum, Titusville, Pennsylvania.

530 Photograph by Charles M. Peery. From the Totten Collection, courtesy of the Museum of the Middle Appalachians.

542 Photograph by Kenneth Murray.

Section XI • Labor

550 Photograph by Brian Jaudon. Courtesy of *Sojourners*.

552 Courtesy of The Chesapeake and Ohio Historical Society.

566 Photograph by Lewis W. Hine. From Photography Collections, courtesy of University of Maryland, Baltimore County.

570 From West Virginia Regional History Collection, courtesy of West Virginia University Libraries.

574 Drawing by G. A. Davis from a sketch by Charles Upham. From *Frank Leslie's Illustrated Weekly*, courtesy of Library of Congress, Prints and Photographs Division, [LC-USZ62-57205].

577 From West Virginia Regional History Collection, courtesy of West Virginia University Libraries.

581 Photograph by George Harvan.

598 From Appalachian Photographic Archives, courtesy of the Archives of Appalachia, East Tennessee State University.

601 From West Virginia Regional History Collection, courtesy of West Virginia University Libraries.

607 Photograph by Marat Moore. From Marat Moore Collection, courtesy of the Archives of Appalachia, East Tennessee State University.

Section XII • Tourism

610 Photograph by Jean E. Unglaub. Courtesy of Kentucky Department of Parks.

612 Photograph by Rhonda Howdyshell. Courtesy of the Frontier Culture Museum.

613 Courtesy of Lake County (IL) Discovery Museum, Curt Teich Postcard Archives.

621 Courtesy of Lake County (IL) Discovery Museum, Curt Teich Postcard Archives.

629 Photograph by Bill Russ. Courtesy of the North Carolina Division of Tourism, Film & Sports Development.

634 Courtesy of the New York State Historical Association and The Farmers' Museum, Inc., Cooperstown, New York.

647 Photograph by Hugh Morton.

665 Courtesy of Rivers of Steel Archives.

672 Courtesy of Pocono Mountains Vacation Bureau, Inc.

679 Photograph by John Edward Kenna. From the John E. Kenna Collection, courtesy of West Virginia State Archives.

Section XIII • Transportation

684 Courtesy of the Archives of Appalachia, East Tennessee State University.

687 Photograph by Earl Dotter.

691 Courtesy of the Appalachian Regional Commission.

694 Photograph by Earl Dotter.

697 Courtesy of the Archives of Appalachia, East Tennessee State University.

706 Photograph by Steve Shaluta, West Virginia Department of Tourism.

709 Photograph by Mona Counts.

722 Photograph by Earl Dotter.

Section XIV • Architecture

728 Photograph by Carroll Van West.

732 Photograph by David Cortner.

736 Photograph by Bess Daniels.

738 Photograph by David Cortner.

738 Photograph by David Cortner.

739 Photograph by Carroll Van West.

740 Photograph by Carroll Van West.

741 From the Ewart M. Ball Photograph Collection. Courtesy of D. H. Ramsey Library Special Collections, University of North Carolina at Asheville.

743 Photograph by David Cortner.

746 From the Ewart M. Ball Photograph Collection. Courtesy of D. H. Ramsey Library Special Collections, University of North Carolina at Asheville.

748 Photograph by Robert P. Ruschak. Courtesy of the Western Pennsylvania Conservancy.

753 Photograph by Carroll Van West.

758 Photograph by Carroll Van West.

761 Photograph by Carroll Van West.

763 Photograph by Carroll Van West.

Section XV • Crafts

769 Photograph by John Warner, Warner Photography, Asheville, North Carolina. From *Textile Art from Southern Appalachia: The Quiet Work of Women* by Kathleen Curtis Wilson, The Overmountain Press.

773 Photograph by Paul Jeanes.

779 Photograph by Kenneth Murray.

783 Photograph courtesy of William S. Rogers.

789 Courtesy of Qualla Arts and Crafts Mutual, Inc., Cherokee, North Carolina.

799 Photograph by John A. Burrison. From *Brothers in Clay: The Story of Georgia Folk Pottery* by John A. Burrison, University of Georgia Press.

809 Photograph by Doris Ulmann. Courtesy of John C. Campbell Folk School.

812 Photograph by M. Anna Fariello.

822 Photograph by Warren Brunner. Courtesy of Brunner Studios.

825 Courtesy of Tom Copenhaver.

827 Photograph by Bill and Ann Cox.

835 Photograph by Eustace Sloop. Courtesy of Crossnore Weavers & Gallery: A Working Museum.

836 Photograph by Leslie Piña.

Section XVI • Folklore and Folklife

842 Photograph by Earl Palmer. Courtesy of Jean Haskell.

847 Photograph by Ted Olson.

852 Photograph by Lyntha Scott Eiler. From Tending the Commons: Folklife and Landscape in Southern West Virginia, American Folklife Center, Library of Congress, courtesy of the Archive of Folk Culture.

856 Photograph by James K. Crissman.

878 Photograph by Lyntha Scott Eiler. From Tending the Commons: Folklife and Landscape in Southern West Virginia, American Folklife Center, Library of Congress, courtesy of the Archive of Folk Culture.

895 Courtesy of Dale W. Morrow.

895 From the Cecil Sharp Photograph Collection. Courtesy of the English Folk Dance and Song Society, London, England.

Section XVII • Food and Cooking

910 From the Earl Palmer Collection, Ms89-025, courtesy of Digital Library and Archives, University Libraries, Virginia Polytechnic Institute and State University.

922 Photograph by Linda Whittington.

926 Earl Palmer Collection, Ms89-025, Digital Library and Archives, University Libraries, Virginia Polytechnic Institute and State University.

928 Courtesy of Dixon Pentecostal Research Center, Cleveland, Tennessee.

929 Photograph by Mark Sohn.

937 Photograph courtesy of Skytop Lodge, Skytop, Pennsylvania.

941 Photograph by Annette Yurkovich Shumate. From a display at the Exhibition Coal Mine Museum in Beckley, West Virginia.

943 From the Earl Palmer Collection, Ms89-025, courtesy of Digital Library and Archives, University Libraries, Virginia Polytechnic Institute and State University.

944 Photograph by Mark Sohn.

948 Photograph by Mark Sohn.

Section XVIII • Humor

962 Courtesy of Berea College, Southern Appalachian Archives.

963 Photograph by Alan Broyles. Courtesy of University Photographic Archives, the Archives of Appalachia, East Tennessee State University.

971 Courtesy of WATE-TV and the family of Archie Campbell.

975 Courtesy of *Jamboree USA*.

977 Photograph by Theresa Lloyd.

981 Courtesy of University of North Carolina Library at Chapel Hill, Documenting the American South.

986 Courtesy of TAGSRWC Archives.

994 Courtesy of Harry Rice, Berea, Kentucky.

Section XIX • Language

998 Photograph from the FSA/OWI Collection [LC-USF33-001361-M4], courtesy of the Library of Congress.

1013 Courtesy of Prentice and Willena Robinson, Cherokee Language & Culture, Tulsa, Oklahoma.

1016 Photograph from the Joseph S. Hall Papers, the Archives of Appalachia, East Tennessee State University.

1017 Courtesy of Hunter Library, Western Carolina University.

Section XX • Literature

1034 Courtesy of Kevin E. O'Donnell.

1036 Engraving by James Smillie from a drawing by F. O. C. Darley.

1053 Illustration by Peter Catalanotto.

1061 Photograph courtesy of Harvard University, Department of Afro-American Studies.

1075 Photograph courtesy of Western Kentucky University.

1093 Photograph by Earl Palmer. Courtesy of Jean Haskell.

1097 Photograph by Tracy Hawkins. Courtesy of Tracy Hawkins Photography.

1102 Photograph from the Council on Appalachian Women Collection, the Archives of Appalachia, East Tennessee State University.

Section XXI • Music

1108 Photograph by Earl Palmer. From the Earl Palmer Collection, Ms89-025, courtesy of Digital Library and Archives, University Libraries, Virginia Polytechnic Institute and State University.

1110 Courtesy of Library and Archives Division, Historical Society of Western Pennsylvania, Pittsburgh, Pennsylvania.

1127 Courtesy of Ernestine "Parker" Rector.

1133 Photograph by Jonnie M. Clasen.

1154 Courtesy of Columbia Records.

1165 Courtesy of Dixon Pentecostal Research Center, Cleveland, Tennessee.

1167 Courtesy of Patrick County Project, Patrick County, Virginia.

1177 Photograph by Charles "Teenie" Harris. Courtesy of Carnegie Museum of Art; Purchase: Second Century Acquisition Fund and Gift of Milton and Nancy Washington.

1189 Photograph by Dick Cooper.

1193 Photograph by Scott Odell. From The J. Scott Odell Collection of Folk Music, courtesy of Archives Center, National Museum of American History, Smithsonian Institution.

1208 Courtesy of Broadman Press/LifeWay.

1216 Photograph by Edward Massery. Courtesy of the Pittsburgh Symphony.

Section XXII • Performing Arts

1224 Photograph by Tom Raymond, Fresh Air Photographics.

1227 Courtesy of the Archives of Appalachia, East Tennessee State University.

1232 Photograph by Marlin Wagner. Courtesy of Bloomsburg Theatre Ensemble.

1234 Courtesy of The Carpetbag Theatre, Inc.

1241 Photograph by Kenneth Murray.

1245 Photograph by Robert Bowman & Associates, Inc.

1250 Photograph by David Holt.

1255 Courtesy of the International Storytelling Center Archives.

1263 Courtesy of Roadside Theatre.

1264 Photograph by Arturo Patten. Courtesy of Paul Gordon.

1270 Photograph by William Wilder. Courtesy of Stone Soup Storytelling Festival.

Section XXIII • Religion

1280 Photograph by Kenneth Murray. Courtesy of the Archives of Appalachia, East Tennessee State University.

1282 Photograph by Randy Ball.

1285 Photograph by Kenneth Murray.

1287 Photograph by David Cortner.

1292 Photograph by Thomas Adler. From the Blue Ridge Parkway Folklife Project Collection. Courtesy of the American Folklife Center, Library of Congress.

1315 Photograph by Lyntha Scott Eiler. From the Blue Ridge Parkway Folklife Project Collection. Courtesy of the American Folklife Center, Library of Congress.

1318 Photograph by J. B. Collins. Courtesy of the Archives of Appalachia, East Tennessee State University.

1321 Photograph by Deb Weiner.

1324 Photograph by Howard Dorgan.

1327 Photograph courtesy of the Archives of the Mennonite Church, Goshen, Indiana.

1329 From the Methodist Collection. Courtesy of Drew University, Madison, New Jersey.

1347 Photograph courtesy of the Chautauqua Institution Archives, Chautauqua, New York.

1350 From the Sue K. Hicks Collection. Courtesy of the University of Tennessee Special Collections Library, Knoxville, Tennessee.

1352 Photograph by Kenneth Murray. Courtesy of the Archives of Appalachia, East Tennessee State University.

1357 Photograph by J. B. Collins. Courtesy of the Archives of Appalachia, East Tennessee State University.

Section XXIV • Sports and Recreation

1360 Courtesy of Special Collections, University of Tennessee Library.

1364 From the Appalachian Photographic Archive, courtesy of the Archives of Appalachia, East Tennessee State University.

1369 Photograph by Russell Lee. Courtesy of National Archives.

1371 Photograph by Nick Myers. Courtesy of University of Tennessee Photo Services.

1377 Photograph by Jim Thompson. Courtesy of Great Smoky Mountains National Park.

1384 Photograph by Ralph Sickinger, Capital Hang Gliding and Paragliding Association.

1386 Photograph by D. R. Beeson Sr. From the D. R. Beeson Sr. Papers. Courtesy of the Archives of Appalachia, East Tennessee State University.

1388 Photograph by Jeff Vanuga. Courtesy of USDA Natural Resources Conservation Service.

1395 Photograph by Steve Shaluta. Courtesy of the West Virginia Division of Tourism.

1400 Cameras in Action stock photograph. Courtesy of Bristol Motor Speedway.

1405 Photograph by Steve Shaluta. Courtesy of the West Virginia Division of Tourism.

Section XXV • Visual Arts

1406 Photograph by Jason Gibson. Courtesy of Hackley Gallery, Berea, Kentucky.

1409 Courtesy of North Carolina Museum of Art, Raleigh, North Carolina. Gift of Mr. and Mrs. George D. Finch.

1411 Courtesy of John C. Campbell Folk School.

1415 Photograph by Gary Heatherly. Courtesy of Knoxville Museum of Art. Collectors Circle Purchase, 2003.

1418 From *The Natural History of Carolina, Florida, and the Bahama Islands*, volume 1. Purchased partially from donations from friends of Colonial Williamsburg [acc.#G1984-147, 1, pl. 27]. Courtesy of the Colonial Williamsburg Foundation.

1430 Courtesy of David R. Leighton and Jack S. Blanton Museum of Art, University of Texas at Austin. Gift of the Still Water Foundation, 1987.

1431 Photograph by M. Anna Fariello. Courtesy of J. Daniel Pezzoni.

1437 Photograph by Patrick Hinely. Courtesy of Washington and Lee University.

1444 From the Reese Collection, University of Tennessee. Courtesy of James G. Buonaccorsi.

1447 Courtesy of Sue Rainey.

1453 From the Tennessee State Museum Collection [artifact #89.76]. Courtesy of Tennessee State Museum.

1455 From the North Carolina Collection. Courtesy of University of North Carolina Library at Chapel Hill.

Section XXVI • Cultural Institutions

1458 Courtesy of The Andy Warhol Museum. Copyright Andy Warhol Foundation for the Visual Arts, Inc.

1460 From the Goodman-Paxton Photographic Collection, [PA64M1 #2885], courtesy of Special Collections and Archives, University of Kentucky.

1474 Photograph by Dave Savage. Courtesy of Augusta Heritage Center.

1475 Photograph by John Nelson. Courtesy of Birmingham Civil Rights Institute.

1481 Photograph by Maggie Holtzberg. Courtesy of Alabama State Council on the Arts.

1488 From the Foxfire Archive, courtesy of The Foxfire Fund, Inc., Mountain City, Georgia.

1494 Photograph courtesy of Johnstown Heritage Association, Johnstown, Pennsylvania.

1497 Photograph courtesy of John Rice Irwin, Museum of Appalachia.

1500 Photograph by Rick Fatica, Ohio University.

1508 Photograph courtesy of Seneca-Iroquois National Museum.

1513 Photograph courtesy of U.S. Space Camp®.

Section XXVII • Education

1516 Courtesy of Highlander Archives.

1519 Photograph by Russell Lee. Courtesy of University of Kentucky Special Collections and Archives.

1526 Photograph by Corcoran Communication. Courtesy of Appalachian School of Law.

1530 Photograph courtesy of Christiansburg Institute Inc.

1538 Photograph by Candie Carawan.

1540 Courtesy of Cornell University Photography.

1543 Photograph by Earl Palmer. Courtesy of Jean Haskell.

1545 Photograph by Karen Hyder.

1551 Photograph by Mike Mullins. Courtesy of Hindman Settlement School Archives.

1553 Photograph by Elizabeth Watts. Courtesy of Hindman Settlement School Archives.

Section XXVIII • Government

1560 Photograph by William Strode.

1567 Photograph by Paul A. Moore, Tennessee Conservation Department. Courtesy of Great Smoky Mountains National Park.

1575 Courtesy of the U.S. Senate Historical Office.

1589 Courtesy of the Library of Congress, Prints and Photographs Division [LC-USZ62-67895].

1600 Photograph by Mathew B. Brady. Courtesy of the Library of Congress, Prints and Photographs Division [LC-B8184-10690].

1619 Courtesy of the Franklin D. Roosevelt Presidential Library.

1623 Courtesy of the North Carolina Office of Archives and History.

1626 From the Rose Marino Collection, courtesy of the West Virginia State Archives.

Section XXIX • Health

1630 Photograph by Earl Dotter.

1635 Photograph by Earl Dotter.

1650 Photograph by Earl Palmer. Courtesy of Jean Haskell.

1650 Photograph by Earl Palmer. Courtesy of Jean Haskell.

1660 From the West Virginia and Regional History Collection, courtesy of West Virginia University Libraries.

1662 Photograph by Earl Dotter.

1668 Photograph by Earl Dotter.

1672 Courtesy of the University of Alabama Health System.

1677 Photograph by Earl Dotter.

Section XXX • Media

1678 Courtesy of Wisconsin Center for Film and Theater Research.

1684 Courtesy of Appalshop.

1687 From the Tennessee Historical Society Collection, courtesy of the Tennessee State Library and Archives.

1692 Photograph by Thomas McGowan. Courtesy of *Appalachian Journal* and Thomas McGowan.

1701 Comic strip by Al Capp, © Capp Enterprises, Inc. All rights reserved. Courtesy of www.deniskitchen.com.

1710 Courtesy of Photofest, Inc.

1729 Photograph by Cecil Stoughton. Courtesy of the Lyndon Baines Johnson Library.

1734 Photograph by Pat Arnow.

1738 Courtesy of Holston Valley Broadcasting Corporation.

1741 Courtesy of Photofest, Inc.

1745 Courtesy of Family Communications, Inc.

1747 Courtesy of Paul Henning.